Who's Who in American Law

Who's Who in American Law®

1st edition

MARQUIS Who'sWho

Marquis Who's Who, Inc.
200 East Ohio Street
Chicago, Illinois 60611 U.S.A.

Library of Congress Catalog Card Number 77-79896
International Standard Book Number 0-8379-3501-6
Product Code Number 030202

Manufactured in the United States of America

Table of Contents

Preface

The first edition of *Who's Who in American Law* is a compilation of biographical information on approximately 18,000 lawyers, judges, and educators. Included are attorneys for federal and state agencies; United States attorneys; presidents and key committee heads of federal, state and local bar associations; general counsel to America's largest corporations; and partners and members of major law firms. Among the judicial population are federal and supreme court justices; chief judges of each federal court; Judge Advocate Generals from each branch of the armed services; and hundreds of judges from state and local courts throughout the United States. Listed also are educators—deans and professors from America's foremost law schools.

In order to compile *Who's Who in American Law,* Marquis Who's Who editors entered into a detailed process of gathering and reviewing information submitted by potential biographees. After final selection was made and sketches written, each biographee was asked to proofread and verify his or her data— thereby further assuring exact, current information. Each sketch is written in the familiar Who's Who style made famous by *Who's Who in America* (thirty-nine biennial editions in seventy-nine years). Data presented include essential facts for use in news stories, reports, speeches, and personal/professional correspondence. Such items as name, vital statistics, education, family status, career history, civic and political activities, military record, awards and special recognitions, professional/association memberships, clubs/lodges, writings, address, and office phone are provided.

Who's Who in American Law—like all other Marquis Who's Who publications— is founded on the long-standing principle of reference value based on prominence in a specific area of occupational endeavor or a significant and lasting contribution to society. It is not a "social register" of the legal profession; nor does it rate or rank the listees. Instead, it is a biographical directory of distinguished members of this important field. Prior to final commitment to this task, however, Marquis Who's Who sought the opinion of the American Bar Association Standing Committee on Ethics and Professional Responsibility on such a publishing venture. In an informal opinion, the Association reaffirmed that the publication of the biographical data contained herein does not violate rules of ethics or professional responsibility. Indeed, by publishing *Who's Who in American Law,* Marquis Who's Who has sought to meet the reference needs of researchers, librarians, lawyers, judges, students—anyone concerned with the field of law.

Standards of Admission

The fundamental means of identifying and selecting biographees for *Who's Who in American Law* is an individual's position within the American juridical structure. Therefore, the names included herein reflect the following areas of the legal profession:

Justices of the U.S. Supreme Court (active and retired)

Chief judges of U.S. Courts of Appeal

U.S. attorney general and deputy attorney general

U.S. solicitor general and deputy solicitors general

Counsel to departments and independent agencies of executive branches of the federal government

Chief justices of state and territorial supreme courts; judges of state courts of appeal; U.S. district judges

State and territorial attorneys general; chief judges of trial courts in major U.S. counties

Deans and eminent professors at leading law schools

American Bar Association officials and state bar association officials

Heads of major legal associations

General counsel for major industries

Principal counsel of prominent law firms

Other biographees of *Who's Who in American Law* are chosen because of individual achievements within the legal profession.

Key to Information in this Directory

① WATTS, Benjamin Greene, **②** b. Rockford, Ill., May 21, 1918; **③** B.S., Northwestern U., 1940; J.D., Chgo.-Kent Coll. Law, 1949. **④** Admitted to Ill. bar, 1949, U.S. Supreme Ct. bar, 1968; **⑤** mem. legal dept. Standard Publs. Corp., Chgo., 1949-57, asst. counsel, 1957-65, counsel, 1965-67; mem. firm Watts, Greene, Johnson & Miller, Oak Brook, Ill., 1967-72, partner, 1972—; **⑥** lectr. Coll. of DuPage, 1970—. **⑦** Chmn. Downers Grove (Ill.) chpt. ARC, 1965-66; mem. Elmhurst (Ill.) Dist. 407 Bd. Edn., 1970—; trustee Elmhurst Hist. Mus., 1972—. **⑧** Mem. Am., Ill., Chgo. bar assns., Am. Mgmt. Assn., Phi Delta Phi. **⑨** Author: Legal Aspects of Educational Publishing, 1965. **⑩** Home: 543 Farwell Ave Elmhurst IL 60126 **⑪** Office: Watts Greene Johnson & Miller 1428 Industrial Ct Oak Brook IL 60521 **⑫** Tel (312) 771-3320

Key

① Name
② Birthplace and date
③ Education
④ Bar admittance
⑤ Career
⑥ Career-related positions
⑦ Civic position
⑧ Professional and association memberships
⑨ Writings, awards and other special achievements
⑩ Home address
⑪ Office address
⑫ Telephone (Office)

The biographical listings in *Who's Who in American Law* are arranged in alphabetical order according to the first letter of the last name of the biographee. Each sketch is presented in a uniform order as in the sample sketch above. The abbreviations used in the sketches are explained in the Table of Abbreviations.

Table of Abbreviations

The following abbreviations and symbols are frequently used in this Directory

*Following a sketch indicates that it was researched and written by the Marquis Who's Who editorial staff and has not been verified by the biographee.

A.A. Associate in Arts
AAAL American Academy of Arts and Letters
AAAS American Association for the Advancement of Science
AAHPER American Association for Health, Physical Education and Recreation
A. and M. Agricultural and Mechanical
AAU Amateur Athletic Union
AAUP American Association of University Professors
AAUW American Association of University Women
A.B. Arts, Bachelor of
AB Alberta
ABC American Broadcasting Company
AC Air Corps
acad. academy
ACDA Arms Control and Disarmament Agency
ACLU American Civil Liberties Union
A.C.P. American College of Physicians
A.C.S. American College of Surgeons
ADA American Dental Association
a.d.c. aide-de-camp
adj. adjunct, adjutant
adj. gen. adjutant general
adm. admiral
adminstr. administrator
adminstrn. administration
adminstrv. administrative
adv. advocate
advt. advertising
A.E. Agricultural Engineer
A.E. and P., AEP Ambassador Extraordinary and Plenipotentiary
AEC Atomic Energy Commission
aero. aeronautical, aeronautic
AFB Air Force Base
AFL-CIO American Federation of Labor and Congress of Industrial Organizations
AFTRA American Federation TV and Radio Artists
agr. agriculture
agrl. agricultural
agt. agent
AGVA American Guild of Variety Artists
AIA American Institute of Architects
AID Agency for International Development
AIEE American Institute of Electrical Engineers
AIM American Institute of Management
AK Alaska
AL Alabama
ALA American Library Association
Ala. Alabama
alt. alternate
Alta. Alberta
A.M. Arts, Master of
Am. American, America
AMA American Medical Association
A.M.E. African Methodist Episcopal
Amtrak National Railroad Passenger Corporation
anat. anatomical
ann. annual
ANTA American National Theatre and Academy
anthrop. anthropological
AP Associated Press
APO Army Post Office
apptd. appointed
apt. apartment
AR Arkansas
ARC American Red Cross
archeol. archeological

archtl. architectural
Ariz. Arizona
Ark. Arkansas
Arts D. Arts, Doctor of
arty. artillery
ASCAP American Society of Composers, Authors and Publishers
ASCE American Society of Civil Engineers
ASME American Society of Mechanical Engineers
assn. association
asso. associate
asst. assistant
ASTM American Society for Testing and Materials
astron. astronomical
astrophys. astrophysical
ATSC Air Technical Service Command
AT&T American Telephone & Telegraph Company
atty. attorney
AUS Army of the United States
aux. auxiliary
Ave. Avenue
AVMA American Veterinary Medical Association
AZ Arizona

B. Bachelor
b. born
B.A. Bachelor of Arts
B. Agr. Bachelor of Agriculture
Balt. Baltimore
Bapt. Baptist
B.Arch. Bachelor of Architecture
B.A.S. Bachelor of Agricultural Science
B.B.A. Bachelor of Business Administration
BBC British Broadcasting Corporation
B.C., BC British Columbia
B.C.E. Bachelor of Civil Engineering
B.Chir. Bachelor of Surgery
B.C.L. Bachelor of Civil Law
B.C.S. Bachelor of Commercial Science
B.D. Bachelor of Divinity
bd. board
B.E. Bachelor of Education
B.E.E. Bachelor of Electrical Engineering
B.F.A. Bachelor of Fine Arts
bibl. biblical
bibliog. bibliographical
biog. biographical
biol. biological
B.J. Bachelor of Journalism
Bklyn. Brooklyn
B.L. Bachelor of Letters
bldg. building
B.L.S. Bachelor of Library Science
Blvd. Boulevard
bn. battalion
B.&O.R.R. Baltimore & Ohio Railroad
bot. botanical
B.P.E. Bachelor of Physical Education
br. branch
B.R.E. Bachelor of Religious Education
brig. gen. brigadier general
Brit. British, Britannica
Bros. Brothers
B.S. Bachelor of Science
B.S.A. Bachelor of Agricultural Science
B.S.D. Bachelor of Didactic Science
B.S.T. Bachelor of Sacred Theology
B.Th. Bachelor of Theology
bull. bulletin
bur. bureau
bus. business
B.W.I. British West Indies

CA California
CAA Civil Aeronautics Administration
CAB Civil Aeronautics Board
Calif. California
C.Am. Central America
Can. Canada
CAP Civil Air Patrol
capt. captain
CARE Cooperative American Relief Everywhere
Cath. Catholic
cav. cavalry
CBC Canadian Broadcasting Company
CBI China, Burma, India Theatre of Operations
CBS Columbia Broadcasting System
CCC Commodity Credit Corporation
CD Civil Defense
C.E. Corps of Engineers
CENTO Central Treaty Organization
CERN European Organization of Nuclear Research
ch. church
Ch.D. Doctor of Chemistry
chem. chemical
Chem. E. Chemical Engineer
Chgo. Chicago
chirurg. chirurgical
chmn. chairman
chpt. chapter
CIA Central Intelligence Agency
CIC Counter Intelligence Corps
Cin. Cincinnati
Cleve. Cleveland
climatol. climatological
clin. clinical
clk. clerk
C.L.U. Chartered Life Underwriter
C.M. Master in Surgery
C.&N.W.Ry. Chicago & Northwestern Railway
CO Colorado
Co. Company
COF Catholic Order of Foresters
C. of C. Chamber of Commerce
col. colonel
coll. college
Colo. Colorado
com. committee
comd. commanded
comdg. commanding
comdr. commander
comdt. commandant
commd. commissioned
comml. commercial
commn. commission
commr. commissioner
condr. conductor
Conf. Conference
Congl. Congregational
Conglist. Congregationalist
Conn. Connecticut
cons. consultant, consulting
consol. consolidated
constl. constitutional
constn. constitution
constrn. construction
contbd. contributed
contbg. contributing
contbr. contributor
Conv. Convention
coop., co-op. cooperative
CORDS Civil Operations and Revolutionary Development Support
CORE Congress of Racial Equality
corp. corporation
corr. correspondent, corresponding

C.&O.Ry. Chesapeake & Ohio Railway
C.P.A. Certified Public Accountant
C.P.C.U. Chartered property and casualty underwriter
C.P.H. Certificate of Public Health
cpl. corporal
C.P.Ry. Canadian Pacific Railway
C.S. Christian Science
C.S.B. Bachelor of Christian Science
CSC Civil Service Commission
C.S.D. Doctor of Christian Science
CT Connecticut
ct. court
CWS Chemical Warfare Service
C.Z. Canal Zone

d. daughter
D. Doctor
D.Agr. Doctor of Agriculture
D.A.R. Daughters of the American Revolution
dau. daughter
DAV Disabled American Veterans
D.C., DC District of Columbia
D.C.L. Doctor of Civil Law
D.C.S. Doctor of Commercial Science
D.D. Doctor of Divinity
D.D.S. Doctor of Dental Surgery
DE Delaware
dec. deceased
def. defense
Del. Delaware
del. delegate, delegation
Dem. Democrat, Democratic
D.Eng. Doctor of Engineering
denom. denomination
dep. deputy
dept. department
desc. descendant
devel. development
D.F.A. Doctor of Fine Arts
D.F.C. Distinguished Flying Cross
D.H.L. Doctor of Hebrew Literature
dir. director
dist. district
distbg. distributing
distbn. distribution
distbr. distributor
div. division, divinity, divorce
D.Litt. Doctor of Literature
D.M.D. Doctor of Medical Dentistry
D.M.S. Doctor of Medical Science
D.O. Doctor of Osteopathy
D.P.H. Diploma in Public Health
D.R. Daughters of the Revolution
Dr. Drive
D.R.E. Doctor of Religious Education
Dr.P.H. Doctor of Public Health, Doctor of Public Hygiene
D.S.C. Distinguished Service Cross
D.Sc. Doctor of Science
D.S.M. Distinguished Service Medal
D.S.T. Doctor of Sacred Theology
D.T.M. Doctor of Tropical Medicine
D.V.M. Doctor of Veterinary Medicine
D.V.S. Doctor of Veterinary Surgery

E. East
E. and P. Extraordinary and Plenipotentiary
Eccles. Ecclesiastical
ecol. ecological
ECOSOC Economic and Social Council (of the UN)
E.D. Doctor of Engineering
ed. educated

Ed.B. Bachelor of Education
Ed.D. Doctor of Education
edit. edition
Ed.M. Master of Education
edn. education
ednl. educational
EDP electronic data processing
E.E. Electrical Engineer
E.E. and M.P. Envoy Extraordinary and Minister Plenipotentiary
EEC European Economic Community
EEG electroencephalogram
EKG electrocardiogram
E.Ger. German Democratic Republic
elec. electrical
electrochem. electrochemical
electrophys. electrophysical
E.M. Engineer of Mines
ency. encyclopedia
Eng. England
engr. engineer
engring. engineering
entomol. entomological
environ. environmental
EPA Environmental Protection Agency
epidemiol. epidemiological
Episc. Episcopalian
ERDA Energy Research and Development Administration
ESSA Environmental Science Services Administration
ethnol. ethnological
ETO European Theatre of Operations
Evang. Evangelical
exam. examination, examining
exec. executive
exhbn. exhibition
expdn. expedition
expn. exposition
expt. experiment
exptl. experimental

F.A. Field Artillery
FAA Federal Aviation Administration
FAO Food and Agriculture Organization (of the UN)
FBI Federal Bureau of Investigation
FCA Farm Credit Administration
FCC Federal Communication Commission
FCDA Federal Civil Defense Administration
FDA Food and Drug Administration
FDIA Federal Deposit Insurance Administration
FDIC Federal Deposit Insurance Corporation
F.E. Forest Engineer
fed. federal
fedn. federation
fgn. foreign
FHA Federal Housing Administration
fin. financial, finance
FL Florida
Fla. Florida
FMC Federal Maritime Commission
FOA Foreign Operations Administration
found. foundation
FPC Federal Power Commission
FPO Fleet Post Office
FRS Federal Reserve System
FSA Federal Security Agency
Ft. Fort
FTC Federal Trade Commission, Federal Tariff Commission

G-1 (or other number) Division of General Staff
Ga., GA Georgia

GAO General Accounting Office
gastroent. gastroenterological
GATT General Agreement of Tariff and Trades
gen. general
geneal. genealogical
geod. geodetic
geog. geographic, geographical
geol. geological
geophys. geophysical
gerontol. gerontological
G.H.Q. General Headquarters
G.N.Ry. Great Northern Railway
gov. governor
govt. government
govtl. governmental
GPO Government Printing Office
grad. graduate
GSA General Services Administration
Gt. Great
GU Guam
gynecol. gynecological

hdqrs. headquarters
HEW Department of Health, Education and Welfare
H.H.D. Doctor of Humanities
HHFA Housing and Home Finance Agency
HI Hawaii
hist. historical, historic
H.M. Master of Humanics
homeo. homeopathic
hon. honorary, honorable
Ho. of Dels. House of Delegates
Ho. of Reps. House of Representatives
hort. horticultural
hosp. hospital
HUD Department of Housing and Urban Development
Hwy. Highway
hydrog. hydrographic

IA Iowa
IAEA International Atomic Energy Agency
IBM International Business Machines Corporation
IBRD International Bank for Reconstruction and Development
ICA International Cooperation Administration
ICC Interstate Commerce Commission
ID Idaho
IEEE Institute of Electrical and Electronics Engineers
IFC International Finance Corporation
IGY International Geophysical Year
IL Illinois
Ill. Illinois
ILO International Labor Organization
IMF International Monetary Fund
IN Indiana
Inc. Incorporated
ind. independent
Ind. Indiana
Indpls. Indianapolis
indsl. industrial
inf. infantry
info. information
ins. insurance
insp. inspector
insp. gen. inspector general
inst. institute
instl. institutional
instn. institution
instr. instructor
internat. international
intro. introduction
IRE Institute of Radio Engineers

IRS Internal Revenue Service
ITT International Telephone & Telegraph Corporation

J.B. Jurum Baccolaureus
J.C.B. Juris Canonici Bachelor
J.C.L. Juris Canonici Lector
J.D. Doctor of Jurisprudence
j.g. junior grade
jour. journal
jr. junior
J.S.D. Juris Utriusque Doctor, Doctor of Both (Canon and Civil) Laws
jud. judicial
Judge Adv. Gen. Judge Advocate General

Kans. Kansas
K.C. Knights of Columbus
K.P. Knights of Pythias
KS Kansas
K.T. Knight Templar
Ky., KY Kentucky

La., LA Louisiana
lab. laboratory
lang. language
laryngol. laryngological
LB Labrador
lectr. lecturer
legis. legislation, legislative
L.H.D. Doctor of Humane Letters
L.I. Long Island
L.I.R.R. Long Island Railroad
lit. literary, literature
Litt. B. Bachelor of Letters
Litt. D. Doctor of Letters
LL.B. Bachelor of Laws
LL.D. Doctor of Laws
LL.M. Master of Laws
Ln. Lane
L.&N.R.R. Louisville & Nashville Railroad
L.S. Library Science (in degree)
lt. lieutenant
Ltd. Limited
Luth. Lutheran

m. married
M. Master
M.A. Master of Arts
MA Massachusetts
mag. magazine
M.Agr. Master of Agriculture
maj. major
Man. Manitoba
M.Arch. Master in Architecture
Mass. Massachusetts
math. mathematical
MATS Military Air Transport Service
M.B. Bachelor of Medicine
MB Manitoba
M.B.A. Master of Business Administration
MBS Mutual Broadcasting System
M.C. Medical Corps
M.C.E. Master of Civil Engineering
mcht. merchant
M.C.S. Master of Commercial Science
M.D. Doctor of Medicine
Md., MD Maryland
M.Dip. Master in Diplomacy
mdse. merchandise
M.D.V. Doctor of Veterinary Medicine
M.E. Mechanical Engineer
ME Maine
M.E. Ch. Methodist Episcopal Church

mech. mechanical
M.Ed. Master of Education
med. medical
M.E.E. Master of Electrical Engineering
mem. member
meml. memorial
met. metropolitan
metall. metallurgical
Met. E. Metallurgical Engineer
meteorol. meteorological
Meth. Methodist
Mex. Mexico
M.F. Master of Forestry
M.F.A. Master of Fine Arts
mfg. manufacturing
mfr. manufacturer
mgmt. management
mgr. manager
M.H.A. Master of Hospital Administration
M.I. Military Intelligence
MI Michigan
Mich. Michigan
micros. microscopical
mil. military
Milw. Milwaukee
mineral. mineralogical
Minn. Minnesota
Miss. Mississippi
mktg. marketing
M.L. Master of Laws
M.L.D. Magister Legnum Diplomatic
M.Litt. Master of Literature
M.L.S. Master of Library Science
M.M.E. Master of Mechanical Engineering
MN Minnesota
mng. managing
Mo., MO Missouri
moblzn. mobilization
Mont. Montana
M.P. Member of Parliament
M.P.E. Master of Physical Education
M.P.H. Master of Public Health
M.P.L. Master of Patent Law
Mpls. Minneapolis
M.R.E. Master of Religious Education
M.S. Master of Science
MS Mississippi
M.Sc. Master of Science
M.S.F. Master of Science of Forestry
M.S.T. Master of Sacred Theology
M.S.W. Master of Social Work
MT Montana
Mt. Mount
MTO Mediterranean Theatre of Operations
mus. museum, musical
Mus.B. Bachelor of Music
Mus.D. Doctor of Music
Mus.M. Master of Music
mut. mutual

N. North
NAACP National Association for the Advancement of Colored People
NACA National Advisory Committee for Aeronautics
NAD National Academy of Design
N.Am. North America
NAM National Association of Manufacturers
NAPA National Association of Performing Artists
NARS National Archives and Record Service
NASA National Aeronautics and Space Administration
nat. national
NATO North Atlantic Treaty Organization

NATOUSA North African Theatre of Operations
nav. navigation
N.B., NB New Brunswick
NBC National Broadcasting Company
N.C., NC North Carolina
NCCJ National Conference of Christians and Jews
N.D., ND North Dakota
NDEA National Defense Education Act
NE Nebraska
N.E. Northeast
NEA National Education Association
Nebr. Nebraska
neurol. neurological
Nev. Nevada
NF Newfoundland
Nfld. Newfoundland
N.G. National Guard
N.H., NH New Hampshire
NIH National Institutes of Health
NIMH National Institute of Mental Health
N.J., NJ New Jersey
NLRB National Labor Relations Board
NM New Mexico
N.Mex. New Mexico
No. Northern
NORAD North American Air Defense
NOW National Organization for Women
N.P. Ry. Northern Pacific Railway
NRC National Research Council
N.S., NS Nova Scotia
NSC National Security Council
NSF National Science Foundation
N.T. New Testament
NT Northwest Territories
numis. numismatic
NV Nevada
NW Northwest
N.W.T. Northwest Territories
N.Y., NY New York
N.Y.C. New York City
N.Z. New Zealand

OAS Organization of American States
obs. observatory
O.D. Doctor of Optometry
OECD Organization of European Cooperation and Development
OEEC Organization of European Economic Cooperation
OEO Office of Economic Opportunity
ofcl. official
OH Ohio
OK Oklahoma
Okla. Oklahoma
ON Ontario
Ont. Ontario
ophthal. ophthalmological
ops. operations
OR Oregon
orch. orchestra
Oreg. Oregon
orgn. organization
ornithol. ornithological
OSRD Office of Scientific Research and Development
OSS Office of Strategic Services
osteo. osteopathic
otol. otological
otolaryn. otolaryngological

Pa., PA Pennsylvania
paleontol. paleontological
path. pathological
P.C. Professional Corporation

PE Prince Edward Island
P.E.I. Prince Edward Island
PEN Poets, Playwrights, Editors, Essayists and Novelists (international association)
penol. penological
P.E.O. women's organization (full name not disclosed)
pfc. private first class
PHA Public Housing Administration
pharm. Pharmaceutical
Pharm.D. Doctor of Pharmacy
Pharm.M. Master of Pharmacy
Ph.B. Bachelor of Philosophy
Ph.D. Doctor of Philosophy
Phila. Philadelphia
philol. philological
philos. philosophical
photog. photographic
phys. physical
physiol. physiological
Pitts. Pittsburgh
Pkwy. Parkway
Pl. Place
P.&L.E.R.R. Pittsburgh & Lake Erie Railroad
P.O. Post Office
P.O.B. Post Office Box
polit. political
poly. polytechnic
P.Q. Province of Quebec
P.R., PR Puerto Rico
prep. preparatory
pres. president
Presbyn. Presbyterian
presdl. presidential
prin. principal
proc. proceedings
prod. produced (play production)
prof. professor
profl. professional
prog. progressive
propr. proprietor
pros. atty. prosecuting attorney
pro tem pro tempore
psychiat. psychiatric
psychol. psychological
PTA Parent-Teachers Association
PTO Pacific Theatre of Operations
pub. publisher, publishing, public
publ. publication
pvt. private

quar. quarterly
q.m. quartermaster
Q.M.C. Quartermaster Corps
Que. Quebec

radiol. radiological
RAF Royal Air Force
RCA Radio Corporation of America
RCAF Royal Canadian Air Force
R.D. Rural Delivery
Rd. Road
REA Rural Electrification Administration
rec. recording
ref. reformed
regt. regiment
regtl. regimental
rehab. rehabilitation
rep. representative
Rep. Republican
Res. Reserve
ret. retired
rev. review, revised
RFC Reconstruction Finance Corporation

R.F.D. Rural Free Delivery
rhinol. rhinological
R.I., RI Rhode Island
R.N. Registered Nurse
roentgenol. roentgenological
ROTC Reserve Officers Training Corps
R.R. Railroad
Ry. Railway

s. son
S. South
SAC Strategic Air Command
SALT Strategic Arms Limitation Talks
S.Am. South America
san. sanitary
SAR Sons of the American Revolution
Sask. Saskatchewan
savs. savings
S.B. Bachelor of Science
SBA Small Business Administration
S.C., SC South Carolina
SCAP Supreme Command Allies Pacific
Sc.B. Bachelor of Science
S.C.D. Doctor of Commercial Science
Sc.D. Doctor of Science
sch. school
sci. science, scientific
SCLC Southern Christian Leadership Conference
SCV Sons of Confederate Veterans
S.D., SD South Dakota
SE Southeast
SEATO Southeast Asia Treaty Organization
sec. secretary
SEC Securities and Exchange Commission
sect. section
seismol. seismological
sem. seminary
sgt. sergeant
SHAEF Supreme Headquarters Allied Expeditionary Forces
SHAPE Supreme Headquarters Allied Powers in Europe
S.I. Staten Island
S.J. Society of Jesus (Jesuit)
S.J.D. Doctor Juristic Science
SK Saskatchewan
S.M. Master of Science
So. Southern
soc. society
sociol. sociological
S.P. Co. Southern Pacific Company
spl. special
splty. specialty
Sq. Square
sr. senior
S.R. Sons of the Revolution
S.S. Steamship
SSS Selective Service System
St. Saint
St. Street
sta. station
statis. statistical
S.T.B. Bachelor of Sacred Theology
stblzn. stabilization
S.T.D. Doctor of Sacred Theology
subs. subsidiary
supr. supervisor
supt. superintendent
surg. surgical
SW Southwest

TAPPI Technical Association of Pulp and Paper Industry

Tb Tuberculosis
tchr. teacher
tech. technical, technology
technol. technological
Tel.&Tel. Telephone & Telegraph
temp. temporary
Tenn. Tennessee
Ter. Territory
Terr. Terrace
Tex. Texas
Th.D. Doctor of Theology
theol. theological
Th.M. Master of Theology
TN Tennessee
tng. training
topog. topographical
trans. transaction, transferred
transl. translation, translated
transp. transportation
treas. treasurer
TV television
TVA Tennessee Valley Authority
twp. township
TX Texas
typog. typographical

U. University
UAW United Auto Workers
UDC United Daughters of the Confederacy
U.K. United Kingdom
UN United Nations
UNESCO United Nations Educational, Scientific and Cultural Organization
UNICEF United Nations International Children's Emergency Fund
univ. university
UNRRA United Nations Relief and Rehabilitation Administration
UPI United Press International
U.P.R.R. Union Pacific Railroad
urol. urological
U.S. United States
U.S.A. United States of America
USAAF United States Army Air Force
USAF United States Air Force
USAFR United States Air Force Reserve
USAR United States Army Reserve
USCG United States Coast Guard
USCGR United States Coast Guard Reserve
USES United States Employment Service
USIA United States Information Agency
USIS United States Information Service
USMC United States Marine Corps
USMCR United States Marine Corps Reserve
USN United States Navy
USNG United States National Guard
USNR United States Naval Reserve
USO United Service Organizations
USPHS United States Public Health Service
U.S.S. United States Ship
USSR Union of the Soviet Socialist Republics
USV United States Volunteers
UT Utah

VA Veterans' Administration
Va., VA Virginia
vet. veteran
VFW Veterans of Foreign Wars
V.I., VI Virgin Islands
vice pres. vice president
vis. visiting
VISTA Volunteers in Service to America
VITA Volunteers in Technical Service

vocat. vocational
vol. volunteer
v.p. vice president
vs. versus
Vt., VT Vermont

W. West
WA Washington
WAC Women's Army Corps
Wash. Washington

WAVES Women's Reserve, U.S. Naval Reserve
WCTU Women's Christian Temperance Union
W. Ger. Germany, Federal Republic of
WHO World Health Organization
WI Wisconsin
Wis. Wisconsin
WSB Wage Stabilization Board
WV West Virginia
W. Va. West Virginia
WY Wyoming
Wyo. Wyoming

YMCA Young Men's Christian Association
YMHA Young Men's Hebrew Association
YM & YWHA Young Men's and Young Women's Hebrew Association
Y.T., YT Yukon Territory
YWCA Young Women's Christian Association
yr. year

zool. zoological

Alphabetical Practices

Names are arranged alphabetically according to the surnames, and under identical surnames according to the first given name. If both surnames and first given names are identical, names are arranged alphabetically according to the second given name. Where full names are identical, they are arranged in order of age—those of the elder being put first.

Surnames beginning with De, Des, Du, etc., however capitalized or spaced, are recorded with the prefix preceding the surname and arranged alphabetically, under the letter D.

Surnames beginning with Mac are arranged alphabetically under M. This also holds for names beginning with Mc, that is, all names beginning Mc will be found in alphabetical order after those beginning Mac.

Surnames beginning with Saint or St. all appear after names that would begin Sains, and such surnames are arranged according to the second part of the name, e.g., St. Clair would come before Saint Dennis.

Surnames beginning with prefix Van are arranged alphabetically under letter V.

Surnames containing the prefix Von or von are usually arranged alphabetically under letter V; any exceptions are noted by cross reference (Von Kleinsmid, Rufus Bernhard; see Kleinsmid, Rufus Bernhard von).

Compound hyphenated surnames are arranged according to the first member of the compound.

Compound unhyphenated surnames common in Spanish are not rearranged but are treated as hyphenated names.

Since Chinese names have the family name first, they are so arranged, but without comma between family name and given name (as Lin Yutang).

Parentheses used in connection with a name indicate which part of the full name is usually deleted in common usage. Hence Abbott, W(illiam) Lewis indicates that the usual form of the given name is W. Lewis. In alphabetizing this type name, the parentheses are not considered.

Who's Who in American Law

AARON, MARCUS, II, b. Pitts., Oct. 24, 1929; A.B., Princeton U., 1950; J.D., Harvard U., 1953. Admitted to Pa. bar, 1953, D.C. bar, 1953, U.S. Supreme Ct. bar, 1969; asso. firm Glick, Berkman & Engel, Pitts., 1956-64; partner firm Berkman Ruslander Pohl Lieber & Engel, Pitts., 1965—; asst. city solicitor City of Pitts., 1957-67. Bd. dirs. Blue Cross of Western Pa., 1972—. Mem. Am., Pa., Allegheny County bar assns., Acad. Trial Lawyers Allegheny County. Home: 1925 Wightman St Pittsburgh PA 15217 Office: 20th floor Frick Bldg Pittsburgh PA 15219 Tel (412) 391-3939

AARON, SHERRY ELLEN, b. N.Y.C., Aug. 2, 1945; B.A., Queens Coll., 1965, M.S., 1967; J.D., Bklyn. Law Sch., 1971. Admitted to N.Y. bar, 1972; dist. atty. Queens County, Kew Gardens, N.Y., 1971—. Mem. bd. J.F. Kennedy Democratic Club, Jeffrey P. Cohen Found. Mem. N.Y. State, Am., Queens bar assns., A.D.A. Assn. Queens (3d v.p.), Brandeis Assn. (corr. sec.). Home: 69-45 108th St Forest Hills NY 11375 Office: 125-01 Queens Blvd Kew Gardens NY 11415 Tel (212) 520-2132

AARONS, JULIUS, b. N.Y.C., July 3, 1934; B.A., N.Y.U., 1954; LL.B., Columbia, 1958. Admitted to N.Y. State bar, 1958, Calif. bar, 1963; individual practice law, N.Y.C., 1958-62, 63-73; mem. firm Erdheim & Armstrong, N.Y.C., 1958, Paul Friedman, N.Y.C., 1958; spl. dep. atty. gen. N.Y. for Election Frauds, N.Y.C., 1958; pres., treas. firm Aarons & Aarons, Inc., Costa Mesa, Calif., 1974—; pres., treas. Aarons Law Corp., Costa Mesa, 1973—. Mem. Am., Orange County bar assns., Bar City N.Y., Calif. Bar. Office: 2790 Harbor Blvd Costa Mesa CA 92626 Tel (714) 546-6604

ABBERLEY, JOHN JOSEPH, b. Bklyn., Dec. 16, 1916; B.A., Williams Coll., 1939; LL.B., U. Va., 1942. Admitted to Va. bar, 1942, N.Y. State bar, 1946; partner firm Abberley, Kooiman, Marcellino & Clay, N.Y.C., 1952—; spl. asst. to dir. Office Econ. Affairs FOA, Paris, 1953-54. Trustee, Suffield (Conn.) Acad.; bd. dirs. Mercantile Library, N.Y.C. Mem. Am., N.Y.C. bar assns., Internat. Law Assn. (past sec.-treas.). Home: 436 Mansfield Ave Darien CT 06820 Office: 521 Fifth Ave New York City NY 10017 Tel (212) 661-5595

ABBOTT, CHARLES FAVOUR, JR., b. Sedro-Woolley, Wash., Oct. 12, 1937; A.B. in Econs., U. Wash., 1959, J.D., 1962. Admitted to Calif. bar, 1963; law clk. to Judge M. Oliver Koelsch, U.S. Ct. Appeals, Ninth Circuit, San Francisco, 1963; asso. firm Jones and Hatfield, Escondido, Calif., 1964; individual practice law, Escondido, Calif., 1964—. Mem. State Bar Calif., San Diego County Bar Assn., Am., Calif., San Diego County trial lawyers assns., Phi Delta Phi. Author: Do Your Own Legal Work, 1976; contbr. articles to legal publs. Home: 782 Chestnut St Escondido CA 92025 Office: 333 S Juniper St Escondido CA 92025 Tel (714) 745-5200

ABBOTT, CHARLES WARREN, b. Miami, Fla., Jan. 16, 1930; B.S., U. Fla., 1951, LL.B., 1953. Admitted to Fla. bar, 1953; mem. firm Maquire, Voorhis & Wells, Orlando, Fla., 1955—. Commr. Goldenrod-Dommerich Fire Control Dist. (Fla.), 1966—, chmn., 1972—; mem. Orange County (Fla.) Emergency Services Council, 1972-76. Mem. Am., Fla. bar assns., Fedn. Ins. Counsel, Internat. Assn. Ins. Counsel, Fla. Def. Lawyers Assn., Fla. Blue Key, Alpha Tau Omega, Phi Delta Phi. Office: 135 Wall St Orlando FL 32801 Tel (305) 843-4421

ABBOTT, HASKELL THOMAS, III, b. Sumter, S.C., Jan. 1, 1943; A.B., Wofford Coll., 1965; J.D., U. S.C., 1972. Admitted to S.C. bar, 1972; asso. firm H.T. Abbott, Jr., Conway, S.C., 1972-74; individual practice law, Conway, 1974—; recorder City of Conway, 1977—. Mem. com. Conway chpt. United Way, 1974-76; activities chmn. Pee Dee council Boy Scouts Am., Conway, 1975-76. Mem. Am., S.C., Horry County bar assns. Home: 907 Applewhite Ln Conway SC 29526 Office: 313 Main St Conway SC 29526 Tel (803) 248-9031

ABBOTT, JAMES A., b. 1928; B.A., U. Minn., 1954, LL.B., 1957. Labor relations rep. Gould Nat. Batteries Inc., 1958-59; with Northwest Airlines Inc., 1959—, corp. counsel, 1964-67, corp. sec., 1967, v.p. Orient region, 1967-70, v.p. law, corp. counsel, St. Paul, 1970—. Office: Northwest Airlines Inc Minneapolis-St Paul Internat Airport Saint Paul MN 55111*

ABBOTT, STEVEN LUSE, b. St. Paul, Nov. 19, 1939; B.S., U. Wis., 1961; LL.B., U. Calif., San Francisco, 1964. Admitted to Wis. bar, 1965; partner firm Rice & Abbott, Sparta and Cashton, Wis., 1965—; commr. Monroe County (Wis.) Ct., 1965—; asst. pub. adminstr. Monroe County, 1965-70; city atty. City of Sparta, 1971—. Bd. dirs. Handi-Shop Industries, Tomah, Wis. Mem. Am., Wis., Monroe County bar assns. Home: 814 W Montgomery St Sparta WI 54656 Office: 101 N Water St Sparta WI 54656 Tel (608) 269-2174

ABBOTT, WILLIAM SAUNDERS, b. Medford, Mass., June 2, 1938; A.B., Harvard U., 1960, LL.B., 1966. Admitted to Mass. bar, 1967; asso. firm Ropes & Gray, Boston, 1966; White House fellow, Washington, 1966-67; dir. agrl. programs AID, Asia, 1967-68; v.p., gen. counsel Cabot, Cabot & Forbes, Boston, 1968-77; individual practice law, Boston, 1977—. Chmn. Arlington (Mass.) Bd. Selectmen, 1970-73; Mass. commr. to Edn. Commn. of States, 1969-74; pres. Found. to Improve TV, 1969—. Mem. Mass., Boston bar assns., Phi Beta Kappa. Editor Harvard Law Rev., 1964-66. Home: Herring Way RFD 6 Plymouth MA 02360 Office: 50 Congress St Boston MA 02109 Tel (617) 523-5520

ABDELLA, G. MICHAEL, b. Parkersburg, W.Va., Apr. 21, 1941; B.S., Salem Coll., 1965; J.D., U. Toledo, 1968. Admitted to W.Va. bar, 1968; auditor W.Va. State Tax Commn., Parkersburg, 1968-69; individual practice law, Parkersburg, 1970—. Chmn. Wood County (W.Va.) Kidney Fund, 1976. Mem. Am., W.Va., Wood County (former officer) bar assns. Home: 45-B Dry Run Rd Parkersburg WV 26101 Office: 606 Market St Parkersburg WV 26101 Tel (304) 428-8279

ABDELNOUR, JOSEPH ANTHONY, b. Roanoke, Va., Mar. 4, 1936; B.A., St. Mary's Sem. and U., Balt., 1958; J.D., Coll. of William and Mary, 1972. Admitted to Va. bar, 1972; partner firm Stephens, Abdelnour & Franck, P.C., Williamsburg, Va., 1972—. Dir. United Fund, Williamsburg. Mem. Va. State Bar, Am. Bar Assn., Va. Trial Lawyers Assn. Office: 905 Richmond Rd Williamsburg VA 23185 Tel (804) 229-5510

ABDULAZIZ, SAM K., b. Baghdad, Iraq, Apr. 10, 1937; B.S. in Bus. Adminstrn., U. Calif., Los Angeles, 1962; J.D., Loyola U., Los Angeles, 1971. Admitted to Calif. bar, 1972; mgr. contracts and accounting Fairchild Space & Def. Co., El Segundo, Calif., 1964-69; asst. to pres. Gen. Corp., Chgo., 1970; adminstr. Lockheed Calif. Corp., Burbank, 1970-71; partner firm Abdulaziz & Carroll, N. Hollywood, Calif., 1972—. Mem. San Fernando Valley Bar Assn. Recipient Am. Jurisprudence award, 1968; W. Publishing Co. award, 1968. Office: 12160 Victory Blvd North Hollywood CA 91606 Tel (213) 760-2000

ABDY, GEORGE JOSEPH, b. Paterson, N.J., Sept. 21, 1948; B.A., Rutgers State U., 1970; J.D., New Eng. Sch. Law, 1973. Admitted to N.J. bar, 1973, Fla. bar, 1973, Mass. bar, 1973; asst. prosecutor Passaic County (N.J.), 1974-76; asso. firm Philip M. Saginario, Paterson, N.J., 1976—. Pres. Aleppian Charity Soc., Paterson. Mem. Am., Passaic County, Mass., Fla. bar assns., Nat. Dist. Attys. Assn. Office: care Philip M Saginario 21 Lee Pl Paterson NJ 07505 Tel (201) 881-7575

ABEE, RALPH MARVIN, b. Portland, Oreg., Feb. 15, 1934; B.A., San Jose State U., 1960; LL.B., U. Calif., Los Angeles, 1963. Admitted to Calif. bar, U.S. Dist. Ct. bar, 1963, U.S. Ct. of Appeals bar, 1973; atty., counsel Bank of Am., Los Angeles, 1963-74, asst. gen. counsel, 1974—. Mem. Town Hall, Los Angeles. Mem. Am., Los Angeles County bar assn., Comml. Law League, Am. Judicature Soc., Conf. on Personal Fin. Law, So. Calif. Fgn. Law Assn. (sec.), Am. Soc. Internat. Law. Office: 555 S Flower St Los Angeles CA 90071 Tel (213) 683-2520

ABEL, HARVEY JOSEPH, b. Phila., May 3, 1928; A.B., U. Ariz., 1950; LL.B., Stetson Coll. Law, 1959. Admitted to Fla. bar, 1959; asso. firm Rosin, Paderewski & Cramer, Sarasota, Fla., 1959-60; partner firm Rosin, Abel, Band & Rosin, Sarasota, 1960—. Office: 200 S Washington Blvd Sarasota FL 33577 Tel (813) 366-6660

ABELL, WILLIAM SHEPHERDSON, JR., b. Washington, July 8, 1943; A.B., Boston Coll., 1963; certificate U. Fribourg (Switzerland), 1964; M.P.A., Harvard, 1965; J.D., Georgetown U., 1970. Admitted to Md. bar, 1970, D.C. bar, 1975; exec. asst. to lt. gov. Md., Annapolis, 1970-73, fed. programs coordinator, 1973-74; sec. Md. Dept. Employment and Social Services, Balt., 1974-75; partner firm Furey, Doolan & Abell, Chevy Chase, Md., 1975—. Chmn., Md. Commn. on Hereditary Disorders, 1974—; mem. citizens adv. bd. Providence Hosp., Washington, 1976—. Mem. Am., Md., Montgomery County bar assns., John Carroll Soc. Home: 4309 Saul Rd Kensington MD 20795 Office: 8401 Connecticut Ave Chevy Chase MD 20015 Tel (301) 652-6880

ABELSON, ELIAS, b. N.Y.C., Nov. 17, 1932; A.B., U. Pa., 1954; J.D., Columbia U., 1959. Admitted to N.J. bar, 1960, U.S. Supreme Ct. bar, 1965; deputy atty. gen. div. law N.J. counsel div. civil rights, supr. charitable trusts and cemetery ops., 1960-63, counsel div. taxation, deputy atty. gen. in charge appellate sect., 1964-68, asst. atty. gen. in charge litigation, 1968-71, chief antitrust sect. div. criminal justice, 1971—, deputy dir. div. criminal justice, 1974-76; asso. firm Green, Robinson & Deitz, Trenton N.J., 1963-64. Staff adviser N.J. Council Against Crime, 1967; mem. jurisdictional standards-income tax com. Multistate Tax Commn., 1967; mem. N.J. Supreme Ct. Com. Applications EDP, 1968, mem. com. rules of civil and appellate procedure, 1971; mem. Princeton U. Concerts Com., 1976—; sec. Princeton Folk Music Soc., 1976—; mem. religious sch. bd. Princeton Jewish Center, 1976—. Mem. Mercer County Bar Assn. Contbr. articles to legal jours.; Walter E. Edge lectr. Princeton, 1976. Office: State House Annex Trenton NJ 08625 Tel (609) 292-8740

ABERNATHY, HARRY HOYLE, JR., b. Statesville, N.C., Mar. 28, 1925; student Mitchell Coll., Statesville, 1947; B.S., Appalachian State U., 1950; LL.B., U. S.C., 1958, J.D., 1970. Admitted to S.C. bar, 1958; individual practice law, Great Falls, S.C., 1959—; atty. City of Great Falls, 1968—. Chmn. bd. trustees Mt. Dearborn United Methodist Ch., Great Falls; pres. United Fund, Great Falls, 1974; chmn. Chester County (S.C.) Library Bd. Mem. S.C., Chester County bar assns. Home: 20 Argonne Ave Great Falls SC 29055 Office: Great Falls Bank Bldg Great Falls SC 29055 Tel (803) 482-2397

ABERNETHY, JAMES WHITFIELD, JR., b. Woodland, Miss., June 9, 1941; B.A., Miss. State U., 1965; LL.B., Miss. Coll., 1966. Admitted to Miss. bar, 1967; atty., trust officer 2d Nat. Bank, Jackson, Tenn., 1969-71; asst. to legal officer and fgn. claims officer U.S.S. Columbus, USN, 1967-68; individual practice law, Corinth, Miss., 1972—; atty. Corinth Community Devel., Inc., 1972—; atty.-advisor Corinth Urban Renewal Agy., 1976—. Vol. Boys' State, Tenn., 1958. Mem. Alcorn County, Miss. State, Am., Internat. bar assns., Sigma Delta Kappa, Nat. Beta Club. Home: 1421 Webster St Corinth MS 38834 Office: PO Box 811 Corinth MS 38834 Tel (601) 287-4134

ABERNETHY, JONES CARROLL, JR., b. Hickory, N.C., July 24, 1924; A.B., Lenoir Rhyne Coll., 1948; LL.B., Wake Forest U., 1949. Admitted to N.C. bar, 1949; practice law, Hickory; solicitor Hickory Municipal Ct. Home: PO Box 1492 Hickory NC 28601 Office: 328 4th St SW Hickory NC 28601

ABILHEIRA, LOUIS B., b. Providence, July 26, 1940; B.S., Boston Coll., 1962; certificate R.I. Coll., Providence, 1966; LL.B., Western New Eng. Coll., 1970. Admitted to R.I. bar, 1970, Fed. bar, 1975; asso. firm DeCosta & Abilheira, Warren, R.I., 1975—; probate judge Town of Bristol, 1974—; instr. Roger Williams Coll., Bristol, 1973—. Mem. Bristol Democratic Town Com. Mem. Am., R.I. bar assns., R.I. Trial Lawyers Assn. Home: 241 Chestnut St Bristol RI 02809 Office: 1052 Main St Warren RI 02885 Tel (401) 245-0700

ABKOWITZ, PAUL BERNARD, b. Revere, Mass., Mar. 8, 1916; J.D., Northeastern U., 1937. Admitted to Mass. bar, 1938, U.S. Supreme Ct. bar, 1964; individual practice law, Boston, 1938-42, Pittsfield, Mass., 1948—; atty. Bur. Yards and Docks, U.S. Dept. Navy, Washington, 1946-48. Govt. appeal agt. U.S. Draft Bd., Pittsfield, 1950-70; mem. Pittsfield Zoning Bd. Appeals, 1970—. Mem. Mass., Berkshire bar assns. Home: 58 Commonwealth Ave Pittsfield MA 01201 Office: 28 North St Pittsfield MA 01201 Office Tel (413) 443-6773

ABLARD, CHARLES DAVID, b. Enid, Okla., Oct. 25, 1930; B.B.A., U. Okla., 1952, LL.B., 1954; LL.M., George Washington U., 1959. Admitted to Okla. bar, 1954, D.C. bar, 1959, U.S. Supreme Ct. bar, 1959; asst to judge 1st Dist. Okla., Washington, 1953; judge adv. USAF, 1954-56; spl. asst. to gen. counsel Post Office Dept., Washington, 1957, jud. officer, chmn. bd. contract appeals, 1958-60; spl. counsel, spl. com. on legal services and procedure Am. Bar Assn., 1960; partner firm Ablard & Harrison, Washington, 1960-63; v.p., counsel Mag. Pubs. Assn., Inc. and Am. Soc. Mag. Editors, 1963-69; gen. counsel, congl. liaison USIA, 1969-72; asso. dep. atty. gen. Dept. Justice, 1972-74; vis. fellow Center Internat. Studies, Cambridge (Eng.) U., 1974; asso. dean Vt. Law Sch., South Royalton, 1974; gen. counsel Dept. Army, Washington, 1975-77; partner firm Obermayer Rebmann Maxwell & Hippel, Washington, 1977—; asso. mem. legal com. European Broadcasting Union, 1969-72. Chmn., Alexandria com. Washington Nat. Cathedral Fund Dr., 1967. Mem. Am. (chmn. spl. com. on revision admintrv. procedure act 1966-69, council, sect. adminstrv. law 1966-69, editor Adminstrv. Law News 1961-63), Fed. (editor Fed. Bar News 1960-62), D.C., Okla. bar assns., Am. Judicature Soc., Am. Soc. Internat. Law, Am. Arbitration Assn., Barristers Club Washington, Adminstrv. Conf. U.S. (council 1970-73), Okla. Soc. of Washington (v.p. 1972-73). Recipient Plainsman award Enid High Sch., 1973; Profl. Achievement award George Washington U. Law Assn., 1976; contbr. articles to profl. jours. Home: 229 S Pitt St Alexandria VA 22314 Office: 011 I St NW Washington DC 20006 Tel (202) 452-8833

ABLE, WALTER, JR., b. Seymour, Ind., Mar. 3, 1932; A.B., Ind. U., 1953, M.D., 1956, J.D., 1968. Admitted to Ind. bar, 1968; individual practice law, Columbus, Ind., 1968—; pres. Able Energy Co., Owensboro, Ky., 1974—. Pres. Bartholomew Sch. Bd., 1973. Mem. Am., Ind. bar assns. Home: Route 2 Columbus IN 47201 Office: 3200 Sycamore Dr Columbus IN 47201 Tel (812) 376-6626

ABLES, CLINTON E., b. O'Donnell, Tex., Jan. 26, 1940; B.S., U. Houston, 1964, J.D., 1968. Tax accountant, asst. to v.p. Hughes Tool, Co., Houston, 1963-69; admitted to Tex. bar, 1968; tax counsel Dresser Industries, Inc., Dallas, 1969-75, v.p., gen. counsel, Houston, 1975—. Mem. Am., Tex. bar assns., Tex. Soc. C.P.A.'s, Order of Barons, Phi Delta Phi. Asst. editor Houston Law Rev., 1968. Home: 5327 Green Springs Dr Houston TX 77066 Office: PO Box 6504 Houston TX 77055 Tel (713) 784-8137

ABLES, ROBERT JULIUS, b. N.Y.C., June 22, 1923; A.B. cum laude, Syracuse U., 1949; LL.B., Cornell U., 1951. Admitted to N.Y. State bar, 1952, D.C. bar, 1964; spl. counsel U.S. Senate Commerce Com., Washington, 1959-61, Presdl. R.R. Commn., 1961-62; gen. counsel Maritime Adminstrn., Washington, 1963-64; chief counsel Com. Mcht. Marine U.S. Ho. of Reps., Washington, 1969-70; arbitrator labor-mgmt. disputes, 1962—. Mem. Fed. Bar Assn., Nat. Acad. Arbitrators. Decorated D.F.C. Home: 3301 Dauphine Dr Falls Church VA 22042 Office: 1819 H St NW Washington DC 20006 Tel (202) 223-4000

ABLOFF, RICHARD LEE, b. Wichita Falls, Tex., Dec. 26, 1945; B.A. So. Ill. U., 1968; J.D., U. Mo., Kansas City, 1971, M.A. in Counseling, 1976, M.A. in Social Psychology, 1976. Admitted to Mo. bar, 1971; asso. firm Hutson, Van Horn, Schmidt & Hammett, Kansas City, 1971-73; corrections counselor Fed. Community Treatment Center, Bur. Prisons, Dept. Justice, 1975—. Mem. Mo., Kansas City bar assns., Am. Assn. Sex Educators, Counselors and Therapists, Phi Kappa Phi, Phi Alpha Delta. Contbr. articles to law jours. Home: 219 W 62d Terr Kansas City MO 64113 Office: Dept Justice Fed Community Treatment Center 404 E 10th St Kansas City MO 64113 Tel (816) 374-3946

ABRAHAM, GERALD, b. Hamburg, Germany, Oct. 18, 1930; B.A., N.Y. U., 1951, LL.B., 1953. Admitted to N.Y. State bar, 1955; teaching fellow Harvard Law Sch., 1959-61; asst. prof. law Duquesne U., 1961-62; asst. prof. Villanova U., 1962-63, asso. prof., 1963-64, prof., 1964—. Mem. Phila. Bar Assn., Soc. Am. Law Tchrs. Office: Villanova Law School Villanova PA 19085 Tel (215) 527-2100

ABRAHAM, HERBERT LEO, b. Milw., May 29, 1911; B.A., U. Wis., 1933, J.D., 1935. Admitted to Wis. bar, 1936; asso. firm Stover & Stover, Milw., 1936-39; atty. Fed. Security Agy., Washington, 1939-41; partner Adelman Laundry and Drycleaners, Milw., 1941-70; individual practice law, Milw., 1970—. Mem. Wis., Milw. bar assns., Order of Coif. Office: 161 W Wisconsin Ave Milwaukee WI 53203 Tel (414) 271-8220

ABRAHAM, JOSEPH JOHN, b. Flint, Mich., Dec. 14, 1944; B.S., Ferris State Coll., 1967; J.D., Detroit Coll. Law, 1974. Admitted to Mich. bar, 1974; individual practice law, Fenton, Mich., 1974—. Mem. Mich. State, Genesee County bar assns. Office: 110 Trealout St Fenton MI 48430 Tel (313) 629-2324

ABRAHAMSON, SHIRLEY SCHLANGER, b. N.Y.C., Dec. 17, 1933; A.B., N.Y. U., 1953; J.D., Ind. U., 1956; S.J.D. (research fellow), U. Wis., 1962. Admitted to Ind. bar, 1956, N.Y. bar, 1961, Wis. Bar, 1962; asst. dir. legis. drafting research fund Columbia, 1958-60; partner firm Lafollette, Sinykin, Anderson & Abrahamson, Madison, Wis., 1962-76; prof. law U. Wis., Madison, 1966—, mem. Wis. Bd. Bar Commrs., 1973-74, v.p., 1975-76; justice Wis. Supreme

Ct., Madison, 1976—; mem. legal activities policy bd. Tax Analysts and Advs., pub. interest tax law firm, Washington, 1975-76; mem. Wis. Supreme Ct. Com. to Study Atty. Grievance and Discipline Matters, 1975-76; mem. consumers advisory council Wis. Commr. Ins., 1975-76. Bd. dirs. Wis. Civil Liberties Union, 1967-73, chmn. Capital Area chpt., Madison, 1968-69; bd. visitors Ind. U. Sch. Law, 1972—; bd. dirs. YMCA, Madison, 1975-76, Nat. Com. Taxation with Representation, Washington, 1975-76. Mem. Am., Dane County (Wis.), Wis. bar assns. Author: Constitutions of the United States: National and State, 2 vols., 1962. Home: 2012 Waunona Way Madison WI 53713 Office: Supreme Ct Wis State Capitol Madison WI 53702 Tel (608) 266-1885

ABRAHM, MICHAEL CHARLES, b. New Orleans, July 12, 1941; B.A. in Bus., Tulane U., 1963, LL.B., 1966. Admitted to La. bar, 1966, Colo. bar, 1968; served with JAGC, U.S. Army, 1966-70; partner firm Gibson, Gerdes, Campbell & Abrahm, Colorado Springs, Colo., 1970-72; individual practice law, Colorado Springs, 1972-76, partner firm Abrahm, Frederick & Booth, Colorado Springs, 1977—; judge municipal ct., Colorado Springs, 1973—. Active Mental Retardation Commn., Colorado Springs, 1972-73; trustee Meml. Hosp., Colorado Springs, 1974—; chmn. profl. com. Colorado Springs Fine Arts Center, 1976—. Mem. La., Colo., El Paso County bar assns. Home: 808 Orion Dr Colorado Springs CO 80906 Office: 420 Holly Sugar Bldg Colorado Springs CO 80903 Tel (303) 471-1657

ABRAM, DONALD EUGENE, b. Des Moines, Feb. 8, 1935; B.S. in Bus., U. Colo., 1957, J.D., 1963. Admitted to Colo. bar, 1963; asso. firm Phelps, Fonda, Farley, Abram & Shaw and predecessor, Pueblo, Colo., 1963-68, sr. partner, 1968-74; sr. partner firm Petersen & Fonda, P.C., Pueblo, 1974-76; judge Colo. Dist. Ct., 10th Jud. Dist., 1976—; mem. Pueblo City Council, 1970-74; mayor City of Pueblo, 1973-74. Mem. Pueblo, Colo. (v.p. 1976), Am. bar assns. Named Young Man of Year Colorado Jr. C. of C., 1971. Home: 3228 Northridge Dr Pueblo CO 81008 Office: Pueblo County Jud Bldg Pueblo CO 81003 Tel (303) 542-0311

ABRAMOWITZ, GEORGE ROY, b. Paterson, N.J., Sept. 25, 1946; A.B., Colgate U., 1967; J.D., Georgetown U., 1970. Admitted to D.C. bar, 1970; asso. firm Sutherland, Asbill & Brennan, Washington, 1970-76, partner, 1976—. Mem. D.C., Am. (chmn. com. on tax accounting problems tax sect. 1976—) bar assns. Home: 13235 Query Mill Rd Gaithersburg MD 20760 Office: 1666 K St NW Washington DC 20006

ABRAMS, ALAN MICHAEL, b. Chgo., Mar. 18, 1936; B.S. in Chem. Engring., Northwestern U., 1959; J.D., DePaul U., 1963; LL.M., N.Y. U., 1968; Admitted to Ill. bar, 1963; corp. atty. Universal Oil Products, Des Plaines, Ill., 1960-67; corp. atty. Richardson Co., Des Plaines, 1967—, asst. sec., 1972-76, sec., counsel, 1976—, also sec., counsel subs., dir.; dir. Chemprene, Inc., Richardson Graphics, Richardson Chems., Richardson Export, Concal Co. Alderman, 8th Ward City of Des Plaines, 1971—; dir. Nat. Orgn. to Insure a Sound Controlled Environment, 1973; gen. counsel Elk Grove Regular Republican Orgn., 1974. Mem. Am., Ill., Chgo. Bar Assns., Chgo. Patent Law Assn., Am. Soc. Corp. Secs., Licensing Exec. Soc. Author articles on copyright law. Home: 514 Westmere Rd Des Plaines IL 60016 Office: 2400 E Devon Ave Des Plaines IL 60018 Tel (312) 297-3570

ABRAMS, FREDERICK SAUL, b. Bklyn., Apr. 23, 1928; B.S., N.Y. U., 1948, LL.B., 1951. Admitted to N.Y. bar, 1951, U.S. Supreme Ct. bar, 1956; practiced in N.Y.C., 1951—, asso. firms Tashof & Sobler, 1951-56, Maurice Edelbaum, 1956-60, partner firm Edelbaum Abrams Feitell & Edelbaum, 1956-71, individual practice law, 1971—; spl. counsel to speaker N.Y. State Assembly, Albany, 1974—. Mem. New York County Lawyers Assn., Assn. Bar City N.Y. Home: 18 Skylark Rd Masapequa Park Long Island NY 11762 Office: 250 Broadway New York City NY 10007 Tel (212) RE-2-4200

ABRAMS, GERALD HENRY, b. Bklyn., Nov. 26, 1938; B.B.A., Coll. City N.Y., 1959; LL.B., Columbia U., 1962. Admitted to N.Y. bar, 1963, Mass. bar, 1972; law clk. to chief judge Dist. Del., 1962-63; asst. U.S. atty. So. Dist. N.Y., 1963-66; prof. law Rutgers U., 1966-71; individual practice law, Newton, Mass., 1972—; cons. Fed. Commn. on Revision of Penal Laws, 1968-69, N.Y. State Commn. to Revise State Constitution, 1967-68. Mem. Mass. Bar Assn. *

ABRAMS, HAROLD EUGENE, b. Pensacola, Fla., Jan. 18, 1933; A.B., U. Mich., 1954; LL.B., Harvard, 1957. Admitted to Ga. bar, 1957; law clk. to judge U.S. Ct. Appeals, 5th Circuit, Atlanta, 1957-58; mem. firm Kilpatrick, Cody, Rogers, McClatchey & Regenstein, Atlanta, 1958-62, partner firm, 1963—; chmn. tax sec. State Bar of Ga., 1967-68; trustee So. Fed. Tax Inst., 1965—, pres., 1970, chmn. bd., 1971. Vice pres. Buckhead Little League, 1974-75; bd. dirs. Vis. Nurse Assn. of Met. Atlanta, 1967, 1st v.p., 1974. Mem. Am., Atlanta bar assns., Atlanta Lawyers Club, Atlanta Estate Planning Council. Author: The Role of the Will in the Tax Planning of an Estate, 1974; The Current Need for Estate Planning, 1976. Home: 3430 Tuxedo Rd NW Atlanta GA 30305 Office: 3100 Equitable Bldg Atlanta GA 30303 Tel (404) 522-3100

ABRAMS, JEROME LEROY, b. Long Branch, N.J., Nov. 16, 1917; B.A., Harvard, 1939, LL.B. magna cum laude, 1942. Admitted to N.Y. State bar, 1945; mem. firm Lehman, Rohrlich & Solomon, and predecessors, N.Y.C., 1945-48, 1950—; mem. firm Lans, Goldstein, Golenbach & Abrams, N.Y.C., 1948-50; lectr. Practising Law Inst. Pres., dir. Birchwood Civic Assn., Jericho, 1956-57; bd. dirs. Maurice and Marian A. Gruber Found., 1957—. Mem. N.Y. County Lawyers Assn., N.Y. State Bar Assn., Harvard Law Sch Assn., Am. Arbitration Assn. (panel), Phi Beta Kappa. Author: Arbitration Courts and Corporate Problems: A Semantic Approach, 1954. Decorated Bronze Star; recipient Felix Frankfurter award Harvard Law Sch., 1939-40; R. Emerson Stuart award N.Y. U. Sch. Law, 1954. Home: 376 W End St Long Branch NJ 07740 Office: 30 Broad St New York City NY 10004 Tel (212) 422-2255

ABRAMS, LEE NORMAN, b. Chgo., Feb. 28, 1935; A.B., U. Mich., 1951, J.D., 1957. Admitted to Ill. bar, 1957, U.S. Supreme Ct. bar, 1961, U.S. Tax Ct. bar, 1972; partner firm Mayer, Brown & Platt and predecessors, Chgo., 1966—. Mem. visitors com. U. Mich. Law Sch., 1970—; bd. assos. Nat. Coll. Edn., 1973—. Mem. Am. (council antitrust sect. 1975—, chmn. FTC com. 1972-75), Chgo. (antitrust law com. 1970—) bar assns., U.S. C. of C. (antitrust and trade regulation com. 1974—). Recipient Am. Inst. C.P.A.'s Gold medal award, 1958. Home: 6301 N Sheridan Rd Chicago IL 60660 Office: 231 S LaSalle St Chicago IL 60604 Tel (312) 782-0600

ABRAMS, ROBERT DAVID, b. Malden, Mass., May 10, 1947; B.A., Boston U., 1968, J.D., 1971. Admitted to Mass. bar, 1971; dep. asst. atty. gen. Commonwealth of Mass., Boston, 1971-73, asst. atty. gen., 1973-75; individual practice law, Framingham, Mass., 1975—. Dir., sec. Sudbury (Mass.) Nonprofit Housing Corp., 1973—; mem. Sudbury Planning Bd. Advisory Com. on Housing, 1973-75; Sudbury Democratic Town Com., 1973—. Mem. Am., Mass., Middlesex County, S. Middlesex bar assns., Sudbury Youth Hockey Assn. (dir.). Home: 143 Victoria Rd Sudbury MA 01776 Office: 116 Concord St Framingham MA 01701 Tel (617) 872-4343

ABRAMS, RUTH I., b. Boston, Dec. 26, 1930; A.B., Radcliffe Coll., 1953, LL.B., Harvard, 1956. Admitted to Mass. bar, U.S. Supreme Ct. bar, 1962; partner firm Abrams, Abrams & Abrams, Boston, 1957-61; asst. dist. atty., Cambridge, Mass., 1961-69, asst. atty.-gen., 1969-71; spl. counsel Supreme Jud. Ct., Boston, 1971-72; asso. justice Superior Ct. Commonwealth of Mass., Boston, 1972-77; asso. justice Supreme Jud. Ct. Mass., 1977—. Mem. Am. Law Inst., Am. Bar Found., Am., Mass. bar assns., Assn., Am. Trial Judges Assn., Am. Judicature Soc., Mass. Assn. Women Lawyers, Harvard Alumni Assn. (dir.). Recipient Distinguished Alumna award Radcliffe Coll., 1976. Home: 100 Memorial Dr Cambridge MA 02142 Tel (617) 523-7050

ABRAMS, SAMUEL K., b. Phila., May 31, 1913; B.A., U. Okla., 1933, LL.B., 1936; postgrad. Wharton Grad. Sch. U. Pa., 1946-47. Admitted to D.C. bar, 1949, Okla. bar, U.S. Supreme Ct. bar, 1958, U.S. Ct. Claims, 1958; asst. county atty. Logan County (Okla.), 1937-41; atty. fraud sect., claims div. U.S. Dept. Justice, Washington, 1947-49; asst. U.S. atty. D.C., 1949-50; acting asst. gen. counsel Econ. Stblzn. Agy., Washington, 1950; chief legis. and clearance sect., chief merger unit, chief mobilization unit, antitrust div. U.S. Dept. Justice, Washington, 1951-52; mem. firm Morison, Murphy, Abrams & Haddock, and predecessors, Washington, 1952—; lectr. antitrust Fed. Publs. Inc., 1972—. Mem. D.C., Okla., Pa., Am., Fed. bar assns., Order of Coif, Phi Beta Kappa. Home: 5828 Lenox Rd Bethesda MD 20034 Office: 1776 K St NW Washington DC 20006

ABRAMS, STANLEY DAVID, b. Washington, Jan. 30, 1940; B.S. in Bus. and Pub. Adminstrn., U. Md., 1962, LL.B., 1966, J.D., 1969. Dep. Clk. D.C. Superior Ct., 1964-66; admitted to Md. bar, 1966, D.C. bar, 1966; trial atty. FTC, Washington, 1966-67; sr. asst. county atty. Montgomery County (Md.), 1967-71, adminstrv. hearing examiner, 1971—; cons. in field; lectr. Montgomery-Prince George's County Continuing Legal Edn. Inst., 1975—. Mem. Citizens' Coms. to Revise Montgomery County Zoning Ordnance, 1973—. Mem. Am., Md. State, Montgomery County bar assns., Am. Judicature Soc., Urban Land Inst. Author: Guide to Maryland Zoning Decisions, 1975. Home: 15101 Emory Ln Rockville MD 20853 Office: 100 Maryland Ave Rockville MD 20850 Tel (301) 279-1314

ABRAMSON, ALAN BARRETT, b. N.Y.C., Mar. 26, 1946; B.A., Oberlin Coll., 1968; J.D., Columbia, 1972. With Abramson Bros., N.Y.C., 1972—; admitted to N.Y. bar, 1973. Mem. Am., N.Y. State, Real Estate Tax Rev. bar assns., Bar Assn. City N.Y. Office: 50 E 42d St New York City NY 10017 Tel (212) 687-2655

ABRUZZO, SALVATORE T., b. Bklyn., Sept. 9, 1906; LL.B., St. John's U., 1928. Admitted to N.Y. bar, 1929; U.S. commr. U.S. Dist. Ct., Eastern Dist. N.Y., 1957-68; judge N.Y.C. Criminal Ct., 1968—; asst. to dist. atty. King County (N.Y.), 1945. Mem. Columbian Lawyers.

ABSHIER, PHILLIP GARY, b. Owensboro, Ky., Nov. 4, 1941; B.S. in Accounting, Brescia Coll., 1964; J.D., Memphis State U., 1963. Admitted to Ky. bar, 1974; partner firm Cooper, Flaherty, Bamberger & Abshier, Owensboro, Ky., 1974—; instr. bus. law Brescia Coll., 1974—. Mem. Am., Ky., Daviess County bar assns., Owensboro Jaycees (sec. 1973). Home: 2237 N Stratford Dr Owensboro KY 42301 Office: 403 W 3d St Owensboro KY 42301 Tel (502) 926-2828

ABT, JOHN JACOB, b. Chgo., May 1, 1904; A.B., U. Chgo., 1924, J.D., 1926. Admitted to Ill. bar, 1927, U.S. Supreme Ct. bar, 1936, N.Y. State bar, 1939; asso. firm Levinson, Becker, Frank, Glenn & Barnes, Chgo., 1927-29; asso. firm Sonnenschein, Berkson, Lautmann, Levinson & Morse, Chgo., 1930-33; chief litigation Agrl. Adjustment Adminstrn., Washington, 1933-35; chief counsel Senate Subcom. on Civil Liberties, Washington, 1935-37; spl. asst. to U.S. Atty. Gen., Washington, 1937-38; gen. counsel Amalgamated Clothing Workers Am., N.Y.C., 1938-47; gen. counsel Progressive Party, N.Y.C., 1948-51; individual practice law, N.Y.C., 1951—. Mem. Nat. Lawyers Guild, N.Y. County Lawyers Assn., Am. Trial Lawyers Assn. Author: Who Has the Right to Make War, 1970. Home: 444 Central Park W New York City NY 10025 Office: 299 Broadway St New York City NY 10007 Tel (212) 267-3110

ACERS, MAURICE WILSON, b. Dallas, Aug. 27, 1907; B.A., So. Meth. U., 1929; LL.B., J.D., U. Tex., 193-; postgrad. Harvard, 1929-30, 61, 76, Met. Police Coll., London, 1938. Admitted to Tex. bar, 1934; successively personnel dir., insp., spl. agt. FBI, 1937-47; exec. sec. to Gov. Allan Shiver of Tex., 1951-55; mem. Tax Employment Commn., 1955-60; pres. Acers Investment Co., also chmn. bd., pres., gen. counsel Ebby-Halliday Realtors, Dallas, 1961—; Tex. rep., vice chmn. Interstate Oil Compact Commn., 1950-55. Chmn. bd. S.W. Research Inst., San Antonio, 1971-75; pres. Tex. United Community Services, 1969-70, chmn. bd., 1971—; dir. Austin YMCA; mem. nat. adv. council USO; nat. asso. Boys Clubs Am. Mem. Am., Tex., Dallas, Travis County, Jefferson County bar assns., Mid-Continent Oil and Gas Assn. Hon. Houstonian; Ark. Traveler; adm. Tex. Navy; hon. mayor, Hollywood, Calif.; Knight of the Neches; ambassador at large San Antonio; spl. Tex. Ranger. Office: Acers Bldg 5010 Greenville Ave Dallas TX 75206 Tel (214) 691-2728

ACH, JOSEPH, b. Milligan, Nebr., Jan. 2, 1911; A.B., U. Nebr., 1931, J.D., 1933. Admitted to Nebr. bar, 1933; city atty. Friend (Nebr.), 1937-60; atty. Saline County (Nebr.), 1939-60; judge 7th Jud. Dist. Nebr., Friend, 1960-72; individual practice law, Milligan, 1933-37, Friend, 1937-61, 72—. Home: 420 Cheery St Friend NE 68359 Office: PO Box 168 Friend NE 68359 Tel (947) 947-2121

ACKELS, LAWRENCE E., b. Dallas, Aug. 15, 1922; B.B.S., St. Edward's U., 1943; J.D., So. Methodist U., 1948. Admitted to Tex. bar, 1948, 5th U.S. Circuit Ct. Appeals bar, 1976; since practiced in Dallas; mem. firm Sessions, Sessions, Hoffman & Ackels, 1956-69, Weinberg, Sandoloski & McManus, 1973-77, Ackels, Ackels & Ackels, 1977—; corp. ct. judge City of Carrollton (Tex.), 1949-59; mem. Dallas City Council, 1972-73. Mem. Tex. (chmn. sole practitioners sect. 1976—), Dallas (mem. judiciary com., by-laws com.) bar assns. Home: 10340 Epping Ln Dallas TX 75229 Office: 1800 Republic Nat Bank Tower Dallas TX 75201 Tel (214) 748-8891

ACKER, WILLIAM M., b. Sharon, Pa., May 21, 1922; B.A., Denison U., 1951; LL.B., U. Pitts., 1949, J.D., 1968. Admitted to Pa. bar, 1951; asso firm McCrady and Nieklas, Pitts., 1959-67; individual practice law, Pitts., 1967—. Mem. Allegheny County (Pa.), Pa. bar assns. Home: 201 Thornberry Dr Pittsburgh PA 15235 Office: 304 Ross St Pittsburgh PA 15219 Tel (412) 281-9309

ACKER, WILLIAM MARSH, JR., b. Birmingham, Ala., Oct. 25, 1927; B.A., Birmingham So. Coll., 1949; LL.B., Yale U., 1952. Admitted to Ala. bar, 1952, U.S. Supreme Ct. bar, 1962, U.S. Ct. Claims bar, 1964; asso. firm Graham, Bibb, Wings & Foster, 1952-57; asso. firm Smyer & White, 1957-58; partner firm Smyer, White, Reid & Acker, 1958-71; mem. firm Dommick, Fleddier, Welding, Domnick & Acker, Birmingham, 1971—. Pres. Birmingham Met. YMCA. Mem. Am., Ala. (chmn. young lawyers sect.) bar assns., Birmingham-So. Coll. Alumni Assn. (pres.). Home: 2504 Watkins Circle Birmingham AL 35223 Office: 927 Brown-Marx Bldg Birmingham AL 35203 Tel (205) 322-0653

ACKERMAN, BRUCE ARNOLD, b. N.Y.C., Aug. 19, 1943; B.A. summa cum laude, Harvard Coll., 1964; LL.B., Yale U., 1967. Admitted to Pa. bar, 1970; law clk. to judge U.S. Ct. Appeals, 1967-68, Justice John M. Harlan, U.S. Supreme Ct., 1968-69; asst. prof. law U. Pa. Law Sch., 1969-71, asso. prof. law and pub. policy analysis, 1972-73, prof., 1973-74; vis. asst. prof. law Yale U. Law Sch., 1971-72, prof. law, 1974—. Mem. Order of Coif, Phi Beta Kappa. Author: (with others) The Uncertain Search for Environmental Quality, 1974; Private Property and the Constitution, 1977. Editor: Economic Foundations of Property Law, 1975. Office: 127 Wall St New Haven CT 06520 Tel (203) 432-4445

ACKERMAN, GEORGE OSCAR, b. Madison, Ind., Feb. 6, 1941; B.A., Marquette U., 1964; J.D., George Washington U., 1968. Admitted to D.C. bar, 1968, Md. bar, 1973; individual practice law, Washington, 1968-71; atty. Nat. Capital Housing Authority, Washington, 1971—. Mem. D.C. Bar Assn. (chmn. landlord and tenant com. young lawyers sect.). Home: 8311 Old Georgetown Rd Bethesda MD 20014 Tel (301) 656-1660

ACKERMAN, HAROLD JACK, b. Melfort, Sask., Can., Nov. 21, 1919; A.B., U. Calif., Berkeley, 1946, LL.B., 1949. Admitted to Calif. bar, 1950, U.S. Supreme Ct. bar, 1964; partner firm Drake & Ackerman, Los Angeles, 1960-65; chief dep. dist. atty. Los Angeles County, 1965-66; judge Municipal Ct., 1966-68, Superior Ct., 1969—. Mem. Criminal Cts. Bar Assn. Los Angeles County (past pres., co-founder). Recipient Jerry Geisler Meml. award, 1963. Office: Criminal Cts Bldg 210 W Temple St Los Angeles CA 90012 Tel (213) 974-5725

ACKERMAN, HAROLD THOMAS, b. Ancon, Panama Canal Zone, Aug. 20, 1921; B.C.S., U. Ala., 1954, LL.B., 1955. Admitted to Ala. bar, 1955; individual practice law, Birmingham, Ala., 1955-63; sr. partner firm Ackerman & Saltsman, Birmingham, 1963-67, Ackerman & Rice, Center Point, Ala., 1976—. Mem. Ala., Birmingham bar assns., Am., Ala. trial lawyers assns., United Comml. Travelers Am. (past state pres.), Farrah Order of Jurisprudence, Beta Gamma Sigma. Home: 2417 5th Pl NW Birmingham AL 35225 Office: 1703-B Center Point Rd Birmingham AL 35215 Tel (205) 853-6896

ACKERMAN, PHILIP CHARLES, b. Kenmore, N.Y., Feb. 14, 1944; B.S., State U. N.Y., Buffalo, 1965; LL.B., Harvard, 1968. Admitted to N.Y. bar, 1968; sec. Nat. Fuel Gas Distribution Corp., Buffalo, N.Y. Mem. planning bd. Town of Orchard Park, N.Y., chmn., 1977. Mem. Am., N.Y. bar assns., Am. Gas Assn. (chmn. ins. com. 1974-76). Home: 95 Jolls Ln Orchard Park NY 14127 Office: 10 Lafayette Sq Buffalo NY 14203 Tel (716) 854-4360

ACKERMAN, ROBERT ARTHUR, b. Buffalo, Dec. 21, 1923; B.A., Tufts U., 1946; J.D., Columbia U., 1949. Admitted to Mass. bar, 1949, D.C. bar, 1964; assignments with various U.S. Govt. agys., W.Berlin, 1953-58, Taiwan, 1959-60; trial atty. Civil Rights div. U.S. Justice Dept., Washington, 1965-68; asst. U.S. Atty., Washington, 1968-70; trial atty. Internal Security div. Justice Dept., 1970-71; pvt. practice law, Washington, 1971—. Mem. Am., Fed. bar assns., Bar Assn. D.C. Home: 606 LaSalle Bldg 1028 Connecticut Ave NW Washington DC 20036

ACKISS, PAUL WILFRED, b. Princess Anne County, Va., Aug. 17, 1901; B.A., Coll. William and Mary, 1923, B.C.L., 1925. Admitted to Va. bar, 1924; practiced in Virginia Beach, Va., 1925-66; commonwealth's atty. Princess Anne County, 1932-55; judge Va. Circuit Ct., Circuit of Virginia Beach, 1967-76, ret., 1976. Founder, bd. dirs. Virginia Beach Gen. Hosp. Home: 5207 Holly Ave Virginia Beach VA 23451 Office: POB 417 Virginia Beach VA 23458 Tel (804) 428-1204

ACKMAN, JOHN LANE, b. Williamstown, Ky., July 28, 1925; student U. Cin.; J.D., U. Ky., 1951. Admitted to Ky. bar, 1951; individual practice law, 1951—; city atty. Corinth, Ky., 1951-69, Crittenden, Ky., 1955—, Dry Ridge, Ky., 1964-70; asst. county atty. Grant County, 1970-74. Atty. pension fund Ky. Conf., United Methodist Ch., 1970—. Mem. Am., Ky., Grant, Boone County bar assns., Am. Judicature Soc., Am. Trial Lawyers Assn. Home: 121 Cynthiana St Williamstown KY 41097 Office: 200 S Main St Williamstown KY 41097 Tel (606) 824-3361

ACKMAN, MILTON ROY, b. N.Y.C., July 17, 1932; B.B.A., Coll. City N.Y., 1953; LL.B., Columbia, 1958. Admitted to N.Y. bar, 1958; partner firm Fried, Frank, Harris, Shriver & Jacobson, N.Y.C., 1959—; law sec. to judge U.S. Dist. Ct. So. N.Y. Mem. Assn. Bar City N.Y. Office: 120 Broadway New York City NY 10012 Tel (212) 964-6500

ACOMB, JAMES RICHARD, b. Athens, Ohio, Oct. 10, 1946; B.S., U. Ky., 1969; J.D., Capital U., 1973. Admitted to Ohio bar, 1973; asst. atty. gen. State of Ohio, Columbus, 1974—. Mem. Am., Ohio State bar assns. Home: Apt 174 6314 Busch Blvd Columbus OH 43229 Office: Attorney General Section 25 S Front St Columbus OH 43215 Tel (614) 885-9762

ACRET, JAMES E., b. Mpls., Dec. 19, 1930; B.A., U. Calif. at Los Angeles, 1951, LL.B., 1957. Admitted to Calif. bar, 1957; partner firm Acret & Perrochet, Los Angeles, 1959—. Author: California Construction Law Manual, 1975; California Construction Contracts and Disputes, 1976; Architects and Engineers: Their Professional Responsibilities, 1977. Home: 1033 6th St Santa Monica CA 90403 Office: Acret & Perrochet 11333 Iowa Ave Los Angeles CA 90025 Tel (213) 477-6746

ACTON, JOHN C., b. Clinton, Mass., July 24, 1921; B.A., Boston Coll., 1943, J.D., 1949. Admitted to Mass. bar, 1949; individual practice law, Framingham, Mass., 1949—. Selectman, Town of Framingham, 1949-58; mem. Framingham Redevel. Authority, 1959-67. Mem. Mass., Middlesex, South Middlesex, Boston bar assns., Boston Coll. Law Sch. Alumni Assn., Am. Trial Lawyers Assn. Co-founder Great Books of Western World, 1952. Home: 19 Mansfield St Framingham MA 01701 Office: 665 Cochituate Rd Framingham MA 01701 Tel (617) 872-6524

ACUFF, JOHN EDGAR, b. Chattanooga, July 20, 1940; B.A., David Lipscomb Coll., 1962; J.D., Vanderbilt U., 1969. Admitted to Tenn. bar, 1969, U.S. Dist. Ct. bar, 1970, U.S. Ct. Appeals bar, 1970; asso. firm Cable, McDaniel, Bowie & Bond, Balt., 1969; law clk. to Chief Judge, U.S. Ct. Appeals for 6th Circuit, 1969-70; asso. firm Crawford & Barnes, Cookeville, Tenn., 1970-71; partner Crawford Barnes & Acuff, Cookeville, 1971—. Mem. bd. Koinonia, Inc., 1970—; chmn. Putnam County Cancer Crusade, 1975; mem. advisory council Sr. Citizens Center Putnam County, 1976—. Mem. Am., Tenn., Putnam County bar assns., Tenn. Trial Assn. Lawyers, Christian Legal Soc., Alpha Kappa Psi, Phi Alpha Delta. Home: Cross Rds Farm Rt 8 Box 309A Sparta TN 38583 Office: 101 S Jefferson Ave Cookeville TN 38501 Tel (615) 526-6123

ADAIR, CHARLES ROBERT, JR., b. Narrows, Va., Sept. 29, 1914; B.S., U. Ala., 1942, LL.B., 1948, J.D., 1969. Admitted to Ala. bar, 1948, U.S. Supreme Ct. bar, 1958, ICC bar, 1961; individual practice law, Dadeville, Ala., 1948—; county solicitor Tallapossa County (Ala.), 1955-72. Bd. dirs. Horseshoe Bend Regional Library, Dadeville, 1950—, chmn., 1960-65. Mem. Am., Tallapoosa County (v.p. 1972—), Fifth Circuit bar assns., State Bar Ala., Farrah Law Soc., Newcomen Soc., U. Ala. Commerce Execs. Soc., Am. Judicature Soc., U. Ala. Law Sch. Alumni Assn. (pres. 1972-73). Home: Villa 16 Poplar Point Still Waters Dadeville AL 36853 Office: Old Bank of Dadeville Bldg Dadeville AL 36853 Tel (205) 825-9279

ADAM, ORVAL MICHAEL, b. Detroit, Apr. 25, 1930; B.B.A., Canisius Coll., 1953; LL.B., Georgetown U., 1956. Admitted to N.Y. State bar, 1956, Ill. bar, 1960; atty., advisor Chief Counsel's Office IRS, Washington, 1956-60; atty. Santa Fe Ry., Chgo., 1960-64, asst. gen. atty., 1964-67, gen. atty., 1967-71, asst. v.p. law, 1971-75, asst. v.p., tax counsel, 1976, v.p. and tax counsel, 1977—; dir. Tax Council, Washington, 1975—. Mem. fiscal bd. Infant Jesus of Prague Ch., 1973-74; bd. dirs. Heather Hill Civic Assn., 1966-71, pres., 1968-69, sec. 1969-71; trustee Village of Flossmoor (Ill.), 1973—, mem. Zoning Bd. Appeals, 1967-73, chmn. bd., 1973. Mem. Am., Fed. bar assns., Tax Execs. Inst. Recipient St. Thomas Aquinas Philosophy medal Canisius Coll., 1953; bd. editors Georgetown Law Rev., 1955-56. Office: 224 S Michigan Ave Chicago IL 60604 Tel (312) 427-4900

ADAMANY, DAVID WALTER, b. Janesville, Wis., Sept. 23, 1936; A.B., Harvard, 1958, J.D., 1961; M.S. in Polit. Sci., U. Wis., 1963, Ph.D. in Polit. Sci., 1967. Admitted to Wis. bar, 1961, U.S. Dist. Ct. bar, 1961; with Wis. Dept. Justice, Madison, 1961-63; exec. pardon counsel Wis. Gov.'s Office, Madison, 1963; commr. Wis. Pub. Service, Madison, 1963-65; instr. constl. law U. Wis., Whitewater, 1965-67; prof. polit. sci. Wesleyan U., 1967-72, dean, 1969-71; prof. constl. law U. Wis., Madison, 1972—; mem. Wis. State Elections Bd., 1974—; vice chmn., chmn. exec. com. Wis. Council on Criminal Justice, 1973-75. Mem. State Bar of Wis., Am. Polit. Sci. Assn., ACLU. Contbr. articles to profl. jours. Home: 4245 Manitou Way Madison WI 53711 Office: 410 N Hall U Wis Madison WI 53706 Tel (608) 262-2973

ADAMO, VITO, b. San Pier Niceto, Italy, June 27, 1911; B.A., U. Pitts., 1933, LL.B., 1936, J.D., 1968. Admitted to Ohio bar, 1940, Fed. bar, 1943, U.S. Supreme Ct. bar, 1961; asst. atty. gen. State of Ohio, Columbus, 1960-63. Mem. Ohio Assn. Atty. Gens. Home: 3708 Hillman St Youngstown OH 44507 Office: 1008 Metropolitan Tower Youngstown OH 44503 Tel (216) 747-1125

ADAMS, ALFRED THOMPSON, b. Nashville, Jan. 8, 1898; B.S., Vandervilt U., 1918, LL.B., 1921. Admitted to Tenn. bar, 1921; individual practice law, Nashville, 1921-56; chancellor Chancery Ct. Davidson County (Tenn.), 1957-70; of counsel firm Glasgow, Adams, Taylor & Philbin, Nashville, 1970—; prof. law Cumberland U., 1946-48, Nashville YMCA, 1947-51; mem. Tenn. Ho. of Reps., 1923-24; vice chmn. Tenn. Code Commn., 1953—. Mem. Nashville (pres. 1948-49), Tenn. (pres. 1952-53) bar assns. Office: 300 James Robertson Pkwy Nashville TN 37201 Tel (615) 244-5361

ADAMS, ARLIN MARVIN, b. Phila., Apr. 16, 1921; B.S. in Econs., Temple U., 1941; LL.B., U. Pa., 1947, M.A., 1950, D.H.L., 1964; D.Sc., Phila. Coll., 1965; LL.D., Phila. Coll. Textiles, 1966. Admitted to Pa. bar, 1947; law clk. Justice Horace Stern, Pa. Supreme Ct., 1947; asso. firm Schnader, Harrison, Segal & Lewis, Phila., 1947-50, sr. partner, 1950-63, 66-69; sec. pub. welfare Commonwealth of Pa., 1963-66; judge U.S. Ct. of Appeals, 3d Circuit, Phila., 1969—; instr. Am. Inst. Banking, Phila., 1948-50; lectr. fed. practice U. Pa. Law Sch., 1952-56, constl. law, 1972—. Hon. pres. Reform Congregation Keneseth Israel; v.p. Federated Jewish Agys., 1969-71, cabinet, exec. com., 1969—; v.p. Albert Einstein Med. Center, Phila., 1970—; chmn. bd. dirs. Moss Rehab. Hosp., Phila., Fels Inst. Govt., Phila., Sch. Social Work, Bryn Mawr (Pa.) Coll., Diagnostic and Rehab. Center, Phila.; trustee U. Pa. Law Sch., Hebrew Union Coll., Cin., Bryn Mawr Coll., Med. Coll. Pa., German Marshall Meml. Fund, Lewis H. Stevens Trust; bd. overseers Wharton Sch. Mem. Am. Law Inst., Am. Bar Found., Am. (del. 1966-67, 75—, chmn. trade assn. com.), Pa. (del. 1967-71), Phila. (chancellor 1967) bar assns., Am. Judicature Soc. (pres. 1975—), Order of Coif, Beta Gamma Sigma. Editor-in-chief U. Pa. Law Rev. Home: 3006 Foxx Ln Philadelphia PA 19144 Office: US Court House Philadelphia PA 19106 Tel (215) 597-7317

ADAMS, BILLYE LONZA, b. Strong, Ark., July 26, 1923; B.A., La. State U., 1949, LL.B., 1951. Admitted to La. bar, 1951; individual practice law, Monroe, La., 1951—. Mem. Am., 4th Jud. (v.p. 1953, 55) bar assns. Home: 2201 Mallory Pl Monroe LA 71201 Office: 2205 Justice St Monroe LA 71201 Tel (318) 388-4613

ADAMS, CARL DOUGLAS, JR., b. Washington, Dec. 23, 1925; B.A., U. Va., 1946, J.D., 1949. Admitted to Va. bar, 1949, U.S. Supreme Ct. bar, 1958; individual practice law, Annandale, Va., 1950-55; partner firm Adams & Kassabian, Annandale, 1956-74, Adams, Kassabian & Caridi, Annandale, 1974—; dir. Hamilton Bank & Trust Co. past chmn. Annandale Community Council; past bd. dirs., pres. Burgundy Farm Country Day Sch., Alexandria, Va.; past bd. dirs. Fairfax County (Va.) Human Relations Council, Va. Human Relations Council; past pres. Annandale Citizens Assn., Annandale Community Council past bd. dirs. Alexandria Hosp. Assn. Mem. Am., Va., Fairfax County (past pres.) bar assns., Fairfax County (past dir.), Annandale (dir.) Chambers Commerce. Recipient Community Service award, Health and Welfare Council of Nat. Capital Area, 1959; Outstanding Civic Accomplishments award Fairfax County Fedn. Civic Assn., 1957. Home: 5700 Gaines St Burke VA 22015 Office: 7250 Maple Pl Annandale VA 22003 Tel (703) 256-2525

ADAMS, CLAYTON JESSE, b. Denver, Oct. 23, 1945; B.A., U. Colo., 1968, J.D., 1971. Admitted to Ill. bar, 1972; asso. firms James D. Montgomery Ltd., Chgo., 1972-73, Williams, Kennon & Bryant, Chgo., 1973-74; sr. atty. in corp. legal dept. State Farm Mut. Automobile Ins. Co., Bloomington, Ill., 1974—. Pres. Blacks for Success Unltd., Bloomington, 1974-76; bd. dirs. Bloomington Day Care Center, 1975-76. Mem. Cook County, Nat., Ill. State bar assns. Asso. editor U. Colo. Law Rev., 1969-71. Home: 2614 Hall Ct Bloomington IL 61701 Office: 1 State Farm Plaza Bloomington IL 61701 Tel (309) 662-6107

ADAMS, DANIEL NELSON, b. N.Y.C., Dec. 30, 1909; B.A., Yale, 1932; LL.B. magna cum laude, Harvard, 1935. Admitted to N.Y. bar, 1937, U.S. Supreme Ct. bar, 1946; law clk. to judge U.S. Ct. Appeals, 1935-36; asso. firm Davis Polk & Wardwell, N.Y.C., 1936-49, partner, 1949—. Mem. Citizens Com. for N.Y.C., 1976. Mem. Am., N.Y. State bar assns., Assn. Bar City N.Y. (v.p. 1970-71, chmn. exec. com. 1969-70), New York County Lawyers Assn., Am. Law Inst. Decorated Legion of Merit; pres. Harvard Law Rev., 1934-35. Office: One Chase Manhattan Plaza New York City NY 10005 Tel (212) HA 2-3400

ADAMS, DAVID DUANE, b. Alto, Tex., Aug. 12, 1934; B.B.A., Stephen F. Austin State U., 1954; LL.B., Baylor U., 1961. Admitted to Tex bar, 1961, U.S. Supreme Ct. bar, 1973; partner firms Hemphill & Adams, Snyder, Tex., 1962-64, Tucker, Senff & Adams, Nacogdoches, Tex., 1966-68, Adams & Tiller, Nacogdoches, 1973—; asso. firm Rudy Rico, San Antonio, 1964-66; dist. atty. Tex. 145th Jud. Dist., 1969-76. Mem. State Bar Tex., Nacogdoches County Bar Assn. (pres. 1973-74, chmn. dist. 2B grievance com. 1974-75), Tex. Criminal Def. Attys. Assn., Tex. Bar Found. Office: 420 E Main St Nacogdoches TX 75961 Tel (713) 564-0454

ADAMS, DAVID MERRILL, b. Athens, Ga., Mar. 4, 1937; LL.B. cum laude, Massey Law Sch., 1968. Admitted to Ga. bar, 1968; partner firm Levy, Buffington & Adams, Atlanta, 1968—. Mem. Am. Bar Assn., Sigma Delta Kappa. Home: 4312 Tilly Mill Rd Doraville GA 30360 Office: 1400 First Fed Bldg Atlanta GA 30303 Tel (404) 521-2406

ADAMS, DONALD CHARLES, b. Springfield, Ill., Mar. 17, 1948; A.B., Loyola U., New Orleans, 1970; J.D., So. Meth. U., 1973. Admitted to Tex. bar, 1973; asso. frim Dennis G. Brewer Inc., Irving, Tex., 1973-76; individual practice law, Irving, 1976—. Mem. Tex. Criminal Def. Lawyers, Nat. Assn. Criminal Lawyers, Tex., Am. bar assns., Am. Trial Lawyers Assn., Dallas County Criminal Bar Assn. Home: 505 Little John Dr Irving TX 75061 Office: Suite 504 Irving Bank Tower Irving TX 75060 Tel (214) 254-4214

ADAMS, DONALD G., b. Council Bluffs, Iowa, July 10, 1931; B.S., U. Ill., 1953, LL.B., 1955. Admitted to Ill. bar; partner firm Woleyhan, Nielson & Adams, Quincy, Ill., 1966—; state's atty. Adams County (Ill.), 1960-68; chmn. Ill. Liquor Control Commn., 1968-72. Mem. Ill., Adams County bar assns., Am. Trial Lawyers Assn. Home: 29 Country Club Dr Quincy IL 62031 Office: 412 Illinois State Bank Bldg Quincy IL 62301 Tel (217) 223-3076

ADAMS, GEORGE B., JR., b. N.Y.C., Sept. 16, 1930; B.A., Yale U., 1952; LL.B., Harvard U., 1957. Admitted to N.Y. bar, 1957; asso. firm Debevoise Plimpton/Lyons & Gates, N.Y.C., 1957-66, partner, 1967—. Bd. dirs. Greater N.Y. Fund, 1972—. Mem. Bar Assn. City N.Y. (com. on internat. world rights 1973—), Am. Bar Assn., Am. Arbitration Assn. (arbitrator). Home: 1185 Park Ave New York City NY 10028 Office: 299 Park Ave New York City NY 10022 Tel (212) 752-6400

ADAMS, GEORGE E., b. Kenansville, Fla., Feb. 11, 1928; LL.B., U. Fla., 1951. Admitted to Fla. bar, 1951; individual practice law, Orlando, Fla., 1951-52; partner firm Barker & Adams, Orlando, 1952-57; judge Orange County (Fla.), 1957-65; circuit judge 9th Circuit, Orange County, 1965-72; partner firm Skolfield Gilman Cooper Nichols Tatich & Adams, Orlando, 1972, Adams Gilman & Cooper, Orlando, 1972-75, Adams Best & Sears, Orlando, 1975—; asst. county solicitor Orange County, 1953-57. Mem. Am., Orange County bar assns., Fla. Bar, Am., Fla. acads. trial lawyers. Office: 200 E Robinson St Orlando FL 32801 Tel (305) 843-4410

ADAMS, GEORGE PIUS, b. Balt., July 3, 1937; student Loyola Coll., Balt., 1958; J.D., U. Balt., 1972; LL.M., George Washington U., 1976. Admitted to Md. bar, 1972; asso. firm Israelson, Pines & Jackson, Balt., 1972-74, firm F. Wiley, Balt., 1974—; instr. bus. law Essex Community Coll., Balt., 1975—; staff judge adv. Md. N.G., Balt.; parole aid vol. Md. Dept. Parole and Probation. Vice chmn. Balt. Area council Boy Scouts Am., 1973—; bd. dirs. Tuerk House, Balt. Mem. Am., Fed., Balt. City, Md. bar assns. Home: 113 Driftwood Ct Joppa MD 21085 Office: Suite 801 201 N Charles St Baltimore MD 21201 Tel (301) 539-7210

ADAMS, GEORGE WILLIAM, b. Chattanooga, Mar. 5, 1924; student Tenn. Temple Coll.; LL.B., McKenzie Coll. Law, 1959. Admitted to Ga. bar, 1959; practiced in Rossville, 1959—; judge State Ct. of Walker County (Ga.); city atty. City of Rossville, 1968, 73. Mem. Ga. State, Lookout Mountain (past chmn.) bar assns. Recipient award for outstanding services as lawyer and judge, 1969. Home: POB 428 Rossville GA 30741 Office: 104 Bailey Ave Rossville GA 30741 Tel (404) 866-1790

ADAMS, GILBERT TIMBRELL, b. Beaumont, Tex., Oct. 21, 1905; J.D., U. Tex., 1930. Admitted to Tex. bar, 1930, U.S. Supreme Ct. bar, 1947; partner firm Adams & Browne, Beaumont, Tex.; mem. Tex. Supreme Ct. Adv. Com. on Rules of Civil Procedure, 1959—; Tex. Bar Assn. del. U.S. Jud. Conf. for 5th Circuit, 1972-75. Fellow Tex. Bar Found.; mem. Jefferson County (Tex.) Bar, State Bar Tex. (chmn. com. on liaison with fed. judiciary 1972-75) Am. Bar Assn., Tex. Trial Lawyers Assn., Assn. Trial Lawyers Am., Internat. Soc. Barristers, Internat. Acad. Trial Lawyers, Law Sci. Acad. Am. (founding mem., Gold Medal award 1967). Office: 1012-21 Goodhue Bldg Beaumont TX 77701 Tel (713) 833-5684

ADAMS, GREGORY BURKE, b. Pasadena, Calif., Sept. 28, 1948; J.D., La. State U., 1973. Admitted to La. bar, 1973; asso. firm Breazeale, Sachse & Wilson, Baton Rouge, 1973-75; asst. prof. law So. U., Baton Rouge, 1975-77; cons. La Legis. Council, 1976—. Chancellor St. Luke's Episcopal Ch., Baton Rouge, 1976—. Mem. Am., La. Baton Rouge bar assns., Assn. Henri Capitant, Order of Coif, Phi Kappa Phi. Recipient Robert Lee Tullis Moot Ct. competition award La. Supreme Ct., 1973; Jervey fellow Sch. Law Columbia, 1977—. Home: 2306 Pliny St Baton Rouge LA 70808 Office: Sch of Law Columbia U 435 W 116th St New York City NY 10027 Tel (212) 280-2671

ADAMS, HERMAN MILO, b. St. George, Utah, Jan. 5, 1927; B.S. in Bus. Adminstrn., U. So. Calif., 1949; J.D., U. Calif. at Los Angeles, 1956. Admitted to Nev. bar, 1956; individual practice law, Las Vegas, Nev., 1956—. Mem. Am. Trial Lawyers Assn., Phi Delta Phi. Office: 300 Fremont St Suite 110 Las Vegas NV 89101 Tel (702) 384-9275

ADAMS, JOHN JOSEPH, b. Marshalltown, Iowa, June 25, 1916; A.B., U. Mich., 1938, J.D., 1940. Admitted to Iowa bar, 1940, Ohio bar, 1942; law clk. to Justice Frank Murphy, Washington, 1940-41; served to capt. JAGC, U.S. Army, 1943-46; asso. firm Squire, Sanders & Dempsey, Cleve., 1941-43, 46-53, partner, 1953—. Mem. Citizens League Greater Cleve., Cleve., Ohio chambers commerce, Greater Cleve. Growth Assn., Am. (labor relations sect.), Cleve., Cuyahoga County, Ohio State bar assns., Indsl. Relations Research Assn., Order of Coif. Contbr. articles to legal publs. Home: 15404 Edgewater Dr Lakewood OH 44107 Office: 1800 Union Commerce Bldg Cleveland OH 44115 Tel (216) 696-9200

ADAMS, JOHN VICTOR, b. Pitts., Mar. 31, 1945; A.B., Westminster Coll., 1966; J.D., Duquesne U., 1969. Admitted to Pa. bar; individual practice law, Pitts., 1969—; asst. dist. atty. Allegheny County (Pa.), 1974-76. Mem. Pa., Am., Allegheny County bar assns. Home: 119 Inglewood Dr Pittsburgh PA 15228 Office: 1918 Frick Bldg Pittsburgh PA 15219 Tel (412) 391-8361

ADAMS, LEE TOWNE, b. Chatham, Ont., Can., July 12, 1922; B.A. with high distinction, U. Rochester, 1943; J.D., Yale, 1949. Admitted to N.Y. State bar, 1949, Fed. bar, 1951, individual practice law, Forestville, N.Y., 1949-72; municipal atty. Chautauqua and Cattaraugus Counties, 1952-72; judge Chautauqua County, Mayville, N.Y., 1972—. Commr. Gen. Assembly Presbyterian Ch., U.S.A., 1967. Mem. Phi Beta Kappa. Home: 21 Pearl St Forestville NY 14062 Office: Ct House Mayville NY 14735 Tel (716) 753-7111

ADAMS, LLOYD SENTER, JR., b. Humboldt, Tenn., Dec. 18, 1925; B.S., U.S. Mil. Acad., 1946; J.D., Vanderbilt U., 1952. Admitted to Tenn. bar, 1952, U.S. Supreme Ct. bar, 1973; partner firm Adams & Albright and predecessors, Humboldt, 1952-76; partner firm Adams Ryal & McLeary, Humboldt, 1976—, sr. mem., 1960—. Mem. Tenn. Law Revision Commn., 1963-67; mem. Tenn. Supreme Ct. Bar Unification Commn., 1976. Mem. Humboldt Bd. Edn., 1956-66; active 1st United Meth. Ch., Humboldt. Mem. Am., Tenn. (pres. Jr. Bar Conf. 1960-61), Gibson County (Tenn.) bar assns., Tenn. Def. Lawyers Assn., Def. Research Inst. Home: 306 Forest Dr Humboldt TN 38343 Office: Merchants State Bank Bldg Humboldt TN 38343 Tel (901) 784-2812

ADAMS, RALPH WYATT, b. Samson, Ala., June 4, 1915; A.B., Birmingham So. Coll., 1937; LL.B., U. Ala., 1940, LL.D., 1965, J.D., 1969. Admitted to Ala. bar, 1940, U.S. Supreme Ct. bar, 1950; individual practice law, Tuscaloosa, Ala., 1940-42; judge county ct., Tuscaloosa, 1946-47; mem. legal dept. U.S. Air Force, 1948-63; pres. Troy State U., 1964—. Chmn. Ala. Oil and Gas Bd., Tuscaloosa, Ala. Personnel Bd., Montgomery, Ala. Ins. Bd., Montgomery. Mem. Phi Kappa Phi, Omicron Delta Kappa, Phi Alpha Delta, Lambda Chi Alpha. Home: 110 McKinley Dr Troy AL 36081 Office: Office of President Troy State University Troy AL 36081 Tel (205) 566-3000

ADAMS, RICHARD WAYNE, b. Madisonville, Ky., Mar. 10, 1943; B.S., U. Ky., 1965, J.D., 1968. Admitted to Ky. bar, 1968; with firm Nichols, Nichols & Adams, Madisonville, Ky., 1968-76; individual practice law, Madisonville, 1976—. Mem. Am. Bar Assn., Am., Ky. trial lawyers assns. Office: POB 756 28 Court St Madisonville KY 42431 Tel (502) 825-1450

ADAMS, SEYMOURE, b. N.Y.C., May 19, 1921; B.S., St. John's U., 1943, J.D., 1948. Admitted to N.Y. bar, 1949, U.S. Supreme Ct., bar, 1961; practice law, S.I., N.Y., 1950—. Pres., Kings Oaks Co-op., N.Y.C. Mem. N.Y., Richmond Coounty bar assns. Office: 15 Beach St Staten Island NY 10304 Tel (212) 447-3742

ADAMS, URAL BEDFORD, JR., b. Memphis, Feb. 25, 1947; B.A., Howard U., 1969, J.D., Memphis State U., 1971. Admitted to Tenn. bar, 1972, U.S. Supreme Ct. bar, 1975; Earl Warren fellow NAACP Legal Def. Fund, Memphis, 1971-72; asso. firm Ratner, Sugarman & Lucas, Memphis, 1972-73; partner firm Peete & Adams, Memphis, 1973—; asst. pub. defender City of Memphis, 1973—. Trustee St. Stephens Bapt. Ch., Memphis; committeeman Chickasaw council Boy Scouts Am. Mem. Nat. Conf. Black Lawyers, Nat. (project dir. tng. project 1976), Am., Tenn., Memphis and Shelby County bar assns., Memphis Jaycees. Office: 161 Jefferson Ave 402 Tenoke Bldg Memphis TN 38109 Tel (901) 525-5771

ADAMS, VERNA A., b. Racine, Wis., Oct. 11, 1945; A.B., Wellesley Coll., 1967; J.D., Stanford U., 1970. Admitted to Calif. bar, 1971; partner firm Javitt & Adams, Inc., San Rafael, Calif., 1971—. Mem. Marin County (Calif.) Planned Parenthood Assn. (dir. 1975—). Office: 828 Mission St San Rafael CA 94901 Tel (415) 454-8980

ADAMS, WALTER LESLIE, b. Middletown, N.Y., June 8, 1931; A.B., Duke U., 1953; J.D., U. Mich., 1958. Admitted to Ill. bar, 1958; asso. firm Seyfarth, Shaw, Fairweather & Geraldson, Chgo., 1958-64, partner, 1965-74; partner firm Adams, Fox, Marcus & Adelstein, Chgo., 1974—. Mem. Am., Chgo. bar assns. Asso. editor U. Mich. Law Rev., 1957-58. Home: 695 Sheridan Rd Winnetka IL 60093 Office: 208 S Lasalle St Suite 1278 Chicago IL 60604 Tel (312) 346-7731

ADAMS, WILLIAM HESTER, III, b. Jacksonville, Fla., May 8, 1926; A.B., Duke, 1947, LL.B., with distinction, 1950. Admitted to Fla. bar, 1950; partner firm Durden & Adams, Jacksonville, Fla., 1955-57, Adams & Tjoflet, Jacksonville, Fla., 1957-60, Mahoney Hadlow & Adams, Jacksonville, Fla., 1960—; mem. Nat. Conf. Commrs. on Uniform State Laws, 1967—; vis. com. U. Miami Sch. Law, 1974—. Mem. Am., Fla., Jacksonville bar assns. Home: 5843 Point Bayou Jacksonville FL 32211 Office: 900 Barnet Bldg 100 Laura St Jacksonville FL 32201 Tel (904) 354-1100

ADAMSON, TERRENCE BURDETT, b. Calhoun, Ga., Nov. 13, 1946; B.A. in History, Emory U., 1968, J.D. with distinction, 1973. Polit. reporter Atlanta Constitution, 1969-71; admitted to Ga. bar, 1973; law clk. to judge U.S. Ct. Appeals, 5th Jud. Circuit, 1973-74; asso. firm Hansell, Post, Brandon & Dorsey, Atlanta, 1974-77; spl. asst. to atty. gen. U.S., Washington, 1977—; Henry R. Luce scholar Ishiii Law Office and Blakemore & Mitsuki, Tokyo, 1975-76. Mem. Atlanta, Am. bar assns., Atlanta Council Younger Lawyers, State Bar Ga., Order of Coif, Order of Barristers, Omicron Delta Kappa. Recipient Distinguished Service award Emory U., 1973; contbr. book revs. on law to Atlanta Jour., Atlanta Constitution; exec. editor, contbr. articles and book revs. Jour. Pub. Law (now Emory Law

Jour.), 1972-73. Office: Office of Atty Gen Dept Justice Washington DC 20530 Tel (202) 739-3991

ADANG, PETER JOSEPH, b. Syracuse, N.Y., Sept. 12, 1940; B.A., Syracuse U., 1962, J.D., 1964. Admitted to N.Y. bar, 1965, N.Mex. bar, 1967; with anti-trust div. U.S. Dept. Justice, Washington, 1964-66; trial atty. firm Modrall Sperling Roehl Harris & Sisk, Albuquerque, 1966—. Bd. dirs. Bernalillo County (N.Mex.) Planned Parenthood Assn., 1967-72, Albuquerque YMCA, 1972—. Mem. Am., Albuquerque bar assns., Albuquerque Lawyers Club. Home: 2627 Dakota NE Albuquerque NM 87110 Office: 800 Public Service Bldg PO Box 2168 Albuquerque NM 87103 Tel (505) 243-4511

ADCOCK, RAMON MAXIE, b. Cedar Hill, Tenn., Apr. 25, 1926; LL.B., Cumberland U., 1950. Admitted to Tenn. bar, 1950; since practiced in Smithville; mem. Tenn. Legislature from DeKalb Conty, 1959, 61. Mem. Tenn. Bar Assn., Tenn. Trial Lawyers Assn., Smithville C. of C. (past pres.). Home: Box 11 Smithville TN 37166 Office: 105 Walnut St Smithville TN 37166 Tel (615) 597-5575

ADDABBO, JOSEPH PATRICK, b. N.Y.C., Mar. 17, 1925; LL.B., St. John's Law Sch., 1946. Admitted to N.Y. bar, 1947; partner firm Addabbo, Desena and Desena, N.Y.C., 1961—; mem. U.S. Ho. of Reps., 1961—. Mem. N.Y. State, Queens County bar assns., Am. Judicature Soc. Office: 9611 101st Ave Ozone Park NY 11416 Tel (212) 845-4422

ADDIS, RICHARD BARTON, b. Columbus, Ohio, Apr. 9, 1929; B.A., Ohio State U., 1954, J.D., 1955. Admitted to Ohio bar, 1956, N.Mex. bar, 1966; practice law Canton, Ohio, 1956-63; individual practice law Alburquerque, 1968—; asso. firm Schall, Sceresse & Addis, Albuquerque, 1963-68. Scout master Troop 713, Boy Scouts Am., Albuquerque, 1973—. Mem. Ohio State, N.Mex. State bar assns., Am. Arbitration Assn. (arbitrator 1968—). Licensed pvt. pilot. Home: 912 Western Meadows Ct NW Albuquerque NM 87114 Office: 4008 Carlisle Blvd NE Albuquerque NM 87107 Tel (505) 881-7227

ADDISON, DAVID DUNNHAM, b. Richmond, Va., Aug. 23, 1941; B.A., Hampden-Sydney Coll., 1964; LL.B., U. Va., 1967. Admitted to Va. bar, 1967; partner firm Browder, Russell, Little, Morris & Butcher, Richmond, 1967—. Mem. Am., Va., Richmond bar assns. Home: 6004 York Rd Richmond VA 23226 Office: 1200 Ross Bldg Richmond VA 23219 Tel (804) 644-9842

ADE, JAMES LEE, b. Tampa, Fla., May 15, 1932; B.S.B.A., U. Fla., 1953, J.D., 1959. Admitted to Fla. bar, 1959, U.S. Supreme Ct. bar, 1970; asso. firm Buck, Drew & Glocker, Jacksonville, Fla., 1959-61; mem. firm Martin, Ade, Birchfield & Johnson, and predecessor, Jacksonville, 1961—. Pres., Greater Jacksonville Area Community Found. 1970-75. Mem. Am., Jacksonville (pres. 1968) bar assns., Fla. Bar (exec. council tax sec. 1960-75), Gator Bowl Assn. (pres. 1977). Office: Martin Ade Birchfield & Johnson 3000 Independent Sq Jacksonville FL 32202 Tel (904) 354-2050

ADEL, JAMES E., b. Buffalo, July 19, 1941; student Colgate U., 1963; grad. Law Sch. U. Buffalo, 1966. Admitted to N.Y. bar, 1967; practice law, Buffalo. Mem. Am., Erie County bar assns., Erie County Trial Lawyers Assn. Home: 18 Irving Pl Buffalo NY Office: 500 Ellicott Sq Bldg Buffalo NY 14203 Tel (716) 854-4920

ADELMAN, MARTIN JEROME, b. Detroit, Feb. 22, 1937; A.B., U. Mich., 1958, M.S. in Physics, 1959, J.D., 1962. Admitted to Mich. bar, 1963; law clk. U.S. Dist. Ct. Eastern Dist. Mich., 1962-63; asso. firm Honigman, Miller, Schwartz & Cohn, Detroit, 1963-64; atty. Burroughs Corp, Washington, 1964-65; asso. firm Barnard, McGlynn & Reising, Birmingham, Mich., 1965-68, partner, 1968-73; prof. law. Wayne State U., 1973—, acting dean sch. law. 1974-75; trustee spl. counsel Mich. Energy and Resource Research Assn., 1974—; bd. Antiturst Bull., 1974—. Mem. Am., Mich. Bar Assns. Contbr. articles in field to profl. jours. Home: 630 Merrick Detroit MI 48202 Office: Wayne State Univ Law Sch Detroit MI 48202 Tel (313) 577-3943

ADELMAN, STEVAN CHAZAN, b. Los Angeles, Aug. 16, 1949; B.A., Columbia, 1970; J.D., Boalt Hall Law Sch., 1973. Admitted to Calif. bar, 1973, mem. firm Berliner, Cohen & Flaherty, San Jose, Calif., 1973-76; mem. firm Lester G. Sachs, San Jose, 1976—. Mem. Am., Calif., Santa Clara County bar assns. Office: 675 N 1st St San Jose CA 95112 Tel (408) 286-5263

ADER, DAVID LINCOLN, b. Chgo., Feb. 25, 1943; B.S. in Polit. Sci., U. Ill., Champaign-Urbana, 1964; J.D., Northwestern U., 1967. Admitted to Ill. bar, 1967, U.S. Supreme Ct. bar, 1972; partner firm Ader & Ader, Chgo., 1968—; adj. prof. law Valparaiso U., 1972; lectr. air pollution EPA, 1974; hearing officer Ill. State Pollution Control Bd., 1971-75; sec., bd. dirs. Ill. Indsl. Pollution Control Financing Authority, 1973-76; bd. dirs. Programmed Acitivites for Correctional Edn., 1969—, vol. in parole, 1976—; mem. legal com. Advocates for the Handicapped, 1974—. Mem. Am., Fed., Ill. (1st prize Lincoln Essay Contest 1969), Chgo. bar assns., Chgo. Assn. Commerce and Industry, Nat. Small Bus. Assn., Chgo. Council Fgn. Relations, Internat. Visitors Center, Chgo. Hist. Soc., Landmark Preservation Council. Contbr. articles to legal jours. Home: 233 E Walton Pl Chicago IL 60611 Office: 11 S LaSalle St Chicago IL 60603 Tel (312) 726-6611

ADER, ZEAMORE ABRAHAM, b. Chgo., Nov. 18, 1910; B.A., U. Ill., 1931; J.D., Northwestern U., 1934. Admitted to Ill. bar, 1934, U.S. Ct. Claims Bar 1945, U.S. Supreme Ct. bar, 1945; individual practice law, Chgo., 1934—; spl. asst. to U.S. Atty. Gen., Chgo., 1953-56; spl. hearing officer U.S. Dept. Justice, Chgo., 1956-67; spl. asst. to Ill. Atty. Gen., 1969—; spl. counsel Ill. Dept. Bus. and Econ. Devel., 1971-72; lectr. law Northwestern U. Sch. Law, 1965-72; guest lectr. law Hebrew U., Jerusalem, 1972. Bd. dirs. Hollywood-North Park Improvement Assn., 1956—, v.p., 1971-75; vice chmn. lawyers div. ARC, 1950-52; vice chmn. Albany Park Community Council, 1948-50. Mem. Am., Fed., Ill. State, Chgo. bar assns.; fellow Am. Coll. Probate Counsel. Contbr. articles to legal jours. Home: 5645 N Central Park Chicago IL 60659 Office: 11 S LaSalle St Chicago IL 60603 Tel (312) 726-6611

ADKINS, ANDREW Z., JR., b. Gainesville, Fla., June 19, 1921; B.A., The Citadel, 1943; J.D., U. Fla., 1948. Admitted to Fla. bar, 1948; individual practice law, Gainesville, 1948—; solicitor Alachua County, 1959-72; mem. Fla. Bd. Bar Examiners, 1954-55. Mem. Fla. 8th Jud. Circuit bar assns. Named Prosectuor of Year, State of Fla, 1972. Office: POB 966 Gainesville FL 32602 Tel (904) 372-3331

ADKINS, MILTON RIDDLE, b. Moore Haven, Fla., June 14, 1928; B.S. B.A., U. Fla., 1950, LL.B., 1955, J.D., 1967. Admitted to Fla. bar, 1955, U.S. Supreme Ct. bar, 1972; asso. firm Dixon, DeJarnette, Bradford & Williams, 1955-63; individual practice law, Miami, Fla., 1963-69; partner firm Pallot, Stern, Proby & Adkins, Miami, 1969—; chmn. Fla. bar grievance com. 11th Jud. Circuit, 1958-64, mem. bd. govs., 1964-65, pres. jr. bar sect., 1965. Mem. Am., Fla., Dade County bar assns. Home: 5429 Alton Rd Miami Beach FL 33140 Office: Suite 300 627 SW 27th Ave Miami FL 33135 Tel (305) 642-5733

ADKINS, ROBERT WAYNE, b. Coalville, Utah, June 20, 1946; B.S., Weber State Coll., 1969; J.D., U. Utah, 1972. Admitted to Utah bar, 1972; dep. atty. Salt Lake County, Utah, 1972; asso. firm Roe & Fowler, Salt Lake City, 1973-75; atty. Summit County, Utah, 1975—. Mem. Utah, Salt Lake County bar assns., Rocky Mountain Mineral Law Found., Nat. Dist. Attys. Assn. Office: POB 565 Coalville UT 84017 Tel (801) 336-5931

ADKISSON, RICHARD BLANKS, b. Little Rock, Oct. 12, 1932; B.S. in Bus. Adminstrn., U. Ark., 1957, LL.B., 1959; postgrad. Nat. Coll. State Trial Judges, 1970. Admitted to Ark. bar, 1959; chief asst. atty. State of Ark., 1963-66; pros. atty. 6th Jud. Dist., Ark., 1967-70; judge 6th Jud. Circuit Ct. Dist. of Ark., Little Rock, 1971—. Mem. Am., Ark., Pulaski County bar assns., Am. Judicature Soc. Home: 2421 N Jackson St Little Rock AR 72207 Office: Suite 410 Pulaski County Ct House Little Rock AR 72201 Tel (501) 375-9855

ADLER, ABRAHAM LOUIS, b. Balt., Mar. 2, 1932; B.A., Franklin and Marshall Coll., 1952; LL.B./J.D., U. Md., 1956. Admitted to Md. bar, 1956, U.S. Supreme Ct. bar, 1974; asso. firm Sklar & Sullivan, Balt., 1956-59; asst. state's atty., Balt., 1960-62; individual practice law, Balt., 1959-77; examiner-master Balt. Supreme Ct., 1973—. Founder, 1st v.p. Retinitis Pigmentosa Found., 1972; nat. bd. dirs. young leadership div. United Jewish Appeal, 1969-70; bd. dirs. Asso. Jewish Charities and Welfare Fund Balt., 1972-73, Beth Jacob Congregation, Balt., 1958-77, pres. bd. Beth Jacob Brotherhood, 1968-69. Mem. Am., Md., Balt. bar assns., Am. Trial Lawyers Assn. Home: 3601 Anton Farms Rd Baltimore MD 21208 Office: One N Charles St Baltimore MD 21201 Tel (301) 752-7651

ADLER, ALLEN PAUL, b. Cleve., Oct. 21, 1943; B.A., Ohio U., 1967; J.D., Cleve. State U., 1971. Admitted to Ohio bar, 1971; asso. firm David Griffiths, Chagrin Falls, Ohio, 1971-72; asst. atty. gen. State of Ohio, Columbus, 1972—. Central committeeman Cuyahoga County (Ohio) Democratic Party, 1971-73, exec. committeeman, 1973-76. Mem. Ohio, Greater Cleve. bar assns. Office: State Office Tower Columbus OH 43215 Tel (614) 466-5414

ADLER, ERWIN ELLERY, b. Flint, Mich., July 22, 1941; B.A., U. Mich., 1963, LL.M., 1967; J.D., Harvard, 1966. Admitted to Mich. bar, 1966, Calif. bar, 1967; asso. firm Pillsbury, Madison & Sutro, San Francisco, 1967-73; asso. Lawler, Felix & Hall, Los Angeles, 1973-77, partner, 1977—. Bd. dirs. Hollywood Civic Opera Assn., 1975-76. Mem. Am., Calif. bar assns., Phi Beta Kappa, Phi Kappa Phi. Office: 700 S Flower St 30th Floor Los Angeles CA 90017 Tel (213) 620-0060

ADLER, FREDERICK JOHN, b. Yonkers, N.Y., Oct. 14, 1925; LL.B., J.D., U. Ill., 1951. Admitted to N.Y. State bar, 1951, U.S. Supreme Ct. bar, 1959; city mgr. Yonkers, 1965-68, corp. counsel, 1964-65, justice of peace, 1960-64; counsel Lt. Gov. State of N.Y., 1958-60; individual practice law, Yonkers, 1960—. Chmn. bd. govs. Jewish Community Center, Yonkers, 1972-74; chmn. Heart Fund, Yonkers, 1966. Mem. Yonkers Bar Assn. Office: 20 S Broadway Yonkers NY 10701 Tel (914) 963-9300

ADLER, NORMAN PAUL, b. San Francisco, May 20, 1929; B.A., U. San Francisco, 1951, LL.B., 1959. Admitted to Calif. bar, 1959; asst. sec. Di Giorgio Corp., San Francisco, 1958-60, sec., 1960-74, v.p., 1974—. Mem. Am. Soc. Corp. Sec. Office: 1 Maritime Plaza San Francisco CA 94111 Tel (415) 362-8972

ADLER, SAMUEL M., b. N.Y.C., Feb. 16, 1902; LL.B., N.Y. U., 1924. Admitted to N.J. bar, 1925; sr. partner firm Adler Mezey & Pressler, New Brunswick, N.J.; individual practice law, Edison, N.J., 1967—. Past pres. Urban League of Greater New Brunswick, Jewish Fedn. of Raritan Valley (N.J.), 1966. Mem. New Brunswick (past pres.), Middlesex County (past chmn. resolutions com.) bar assns., VFW (past judge adv.), Trial Lawyers Assn. Middlesex County. Address: 25 Perry Rd Edison NJ 08817 Tel (201) 572-2439

ADLER, SYDNEY, b. Longbranch, N.J., Apr. 21, 1926; B.A., U. Miami (Fla.), 1948, LL.B., 1953, J.D., 1967. Admitted to Fla. bar, 1953; individual practice law, Bradenton, Fla., 1954—; developer mobile home parks, various locations, 1954—; cons. cemetary industry; cons. com. on aging U.S. Ho. of Reps., 1961-62; com. on vets affairs, US Senate, 1974; chmn. Mobile Home Financing Seminars Practicing Law Inst., 1973, 75. Mem. Pre-Internment Assn. Am., Fla. Mobile Home Assn., Nat. Assn. Cemeteries, Am. Bar Assn. Office: 6016-D 14th St W Bradenton FL 33507 Tel (813) 758-7748

ADUJA, PETER AQUINO, b. Vigan, Philippines, Oct. 19, 1920; B.A., U. Hawaii, 1944; J.D., Boston U., 1951. Admitted to Hawaii bar, 1953, U.S. Ct. Appeals bar, 1972; dep. atty. gen. State of Hawaii, 1957-60; judge Honolulu Dist. Ct. of Hawaii, 1960-62; individual practice law, Honolulu, 1962—. Mem. Hawaii State Legislature, 1954-56, 64-74; del. State Constl. Conv., 1968; pres. Oahu Health Council, 1965-67; active Boy Scouts Am., 1960—; bd. dirs. Salvation Army Men's Center; bd. govs. Goodwill Industries Hawaii; pres. U.S.-Philippines Vets. Assn., 1966—. Mem. Hawaii Bar Assn., Hawaii Assn. Realtors. Office: 1136 Union Mall Suite 204 Honolulu HI 96813 Tel (808) 536-2503

ADVOCATE, MICHAEL, b. Bklyn., Mar. 3, 1941; student U. Okla., 1958; B.S., N.Y. U., 1962; LL.B., Bklyn. Law Sch., 1966, J.D., 1966. Admitted to N.Y. bar, 1966, U.S. Supreme Ct. bar, 1971; clk. firm Corwin & Beck, N.Y.C., 1965-66, asso., 1966-67; individual practice law, Bedford Hills, N.Y., 1968-76; partner firm Advocate & Matlin, Mt. Kisco, N.Y., 1976—; instr. Westchester County (N.Y.) Bd. Realtors Real Estate Sch. at Pace U., 1971—. Fire commr. City of Bedford Hills (N.Y.), 1976—. Mem. N.Y. State, Westchester County, No. Westchester bar assns., Bedford Hills C. of C. (pres. 1975-76), No. Westchester Jaycees (pres. 1971-72). Home: 74 Cottage Terr Bedford Hills NY 10507 Office: 153 Main St Mount Kisco NY 10549 Tel (914) 241-0606

AFFATATO, PETER THOMAS, b. N.Y.C., Feb. 11, 1924; student St. John's U.; LL.B., St. John's Law Sch. Admitted to N.Y. State bar, 1949; individual practice law, Hicksville, N.Y. Mem. Island Trees Sch. Bd., N.Y. Mem. Am., N.Y. State, Nassau County bar assns., Nassau-Suffolk Trial Lawyers Assn. (chmn.). Office: 57 N Broadway Hicksville NY 11802 Tel (516) 681-4030

AGATSTON, WARREN STUART, b. Bronxville, N.Y., Aug. 19, 1937; B.A., Syracuse U., 1959, LL.B., 1961, J.D., 1968. Admitted to N.Y. State bar, 1962; asso. firm Rappaport Bros., Esq., N.Y.C., 1963, Kobock & Chase, White Plains, N.Y., 1964-65; partner firm Rubin & Rubin, 1966-69, Rubin, Bobrow & Agatston, New Rochelle, N.Y., 1970—. Scoutmaster Boy Scouts Am., Rye, N.Y., 1961-62, cubmaster, 1974-75; pres. New Rochelle Jaycees, 1969-70; pres. Temple Israel Brotherhood, New Rochelle, 1973-74. Mem. N.Y. State, New Rochelle bar assns., Legal Aid Commn. of Westchester County. Recipient Brotherhood Outstanding award, New Rochelle, 1975. Home: 15 Paddock Rd Rye Town NY 10573 Office: 271 North Ave New Rochelle NY 10801 Tel (914) 632-5050

AGEL, GEORGE LYNWOOD, b. Boston, Dec. 2, 1898; LL.B., Boston U., 1919. Admitted to Vt. bar, 1920; probation officer Chittenden County, Vt., 1920-21; city prosecutor Burlington, Vt., 1921; Democratic chmn. Chittenden County, 1951-52; practice law, Burlington. Del., Nat. Democratic Conv., 1952; police, fire and airport commr. Burlington, 1940-52. Mem. Vt., Chittendon County bar assns. Home: Manor Woods Apt 21 Kennedy Dr Burlington VT 05401 Office: 109 S Winuoski Ave Burlington VT 05401 Tel (802) 864-5135

AGER, WILLIAM F., JR., b. Detroit, Sept. 29, 1921; ed. U. Mich., 1943, LL.B., 1949. Admitted to Mich. bar, 1949; pros. atty. Washtenaw County (Mich.), Ann Arbor, 1959-63; circuit judge Washtenaw County, Ann Arbor, 1963—. Dir., Ann Arbor Area Found., Boy Scouts Am. Mem. Am., Mich., Washtenaw County bar assns., Mich. Judges Assn. (past pres.), Nat. Coll. State Trial Judges, Am. Judicature Soc. Contbr. articles in field to legal jours. Office: 222 Washtenaw County Bldg Ann Arbor MI 48108 Tel (313) 944-2551

AGGER, CAROLYN EUGENIA, b. N.Y.C., May 27, 1909; B.A., Barnard Coll., 1931; M.A., U. Wis., 1932; LL.B., Yale U., 1938. Admitted to D.C. bar, 1938, U.S. Tax Ct., 1943, U.S. Supreme Ct., 1950; economist, legal div. U.S. Agrl. Adjustment Adminstrn., Washington, 1934-35; asst. atty. U.S. Farm Security Adminstrn., Washington, 1935-36; legal staff U.S. Senate Subcom. Edn., Labor, Washington, 1936; spl. tax expert U.S. Dept. Treasury, Washington, 1937; atty. NLRB, Washington, 1938-39; prin. atty. tax div. U.S. Dept. Justice, Washington, 1939-43; asso. firm Lord Day & Lord, N.Y.C., 1943-46; asso. firm Paul Weiss Rifkind Wharton & Garrison, N.Y.C., 1946-48, partner, 1949-60; sr. partner firm Arnold & Porter, Washington, 1960—. Trustee Found. Preservation Historic Georgetown Inc., Washington, 1967—. Mem. Am., D.C., Fed. bar assns. Home: 3210 R St NW Washington DC 20007 Office: 1229 19th St NW Washington DC 20036

AGNEW, RAYMOND GREER, b. Chester, Pa., Aug. 14, 1941; B.A., Dickinson Coll., Carlisle, Pa., 1964; J.D., Am. U., 1967. Admitted to Pa. bar, 1967, Calif. bar, 1971; clk. Senator Hugh Scott, 1964-65, Congressman Olin E. Teague, 1966-67; liaison officer Sec. of Army, The Pentagon, Washington, 1967-69. individual practice law, Berkeley, Calif., 1971-72; staff counsel Workers Compensation Appeal Bd., San Francisco, 1972—. Mem. Pa., Calif., San Francisco bar assns., Nat. Lawyers Guild. Recipient Am. Jurisprudence award Am. U., 1965. Home: 190 Stonewall Rd Berkeley CA 94705 Office: 455 Golden Gate Ave San Francisco CA 94102 Tel (415) 557-2250

AGUIAR, ANTONE SOUZA, JR., b. Fall River, Mass., Jan. 2, 1930; B.A., Yale, 1952; LL.B., Georgetown U., 1955. Admitted to Mass. bar, 1956; partner firm Aguiar & Camara, Fall River, 1956—; selectman City of Swansea (Mass.), 1961-70; mem. Mass. Ho. of Reps., 1964—. Mem. Fall River, Bristol County (Mass.), Boston bar assns. Home: 22 Hetherington Dr Swansea MA 02777 Office: 60 Columbia St Fall River MA 02721 Tel (617) 674-7236

AGUILAR, ROBERT PETER, b. Madera, Calif., Apr. 15, 1931; B.A., U. Calif., Berkeley, 1954, J.D., Hastings Coll. of Law, San Francisco, 1958. Admitted to Calif. bar, 1960, U.S. Supreme Ct. bar, 1966; partner firm Aguilar & Edwards, San Jose, Calif., 1960—; mem. Regional Criminal Justice Planning Bd., 1974—; chmn. Santa Clara County (Calif.) Juvenile Justice Commn., 1975. Mem. Santa Clara County Drug Abuse Task Force, 1974. Mem. Calif. Trial Lawyers Assn., Santa Clara County Criminal Trial Lawyers Assn., Am., Calif. State, Santa Clara County (pres. 1972) bar assns. Office: 28 N 1st St San Jose CA 95113 Tel (408) 287-6193

AHDERS, WILLIAM BRAY, b. Butte, Mont., Mar. 3, 1916; B.B.A., U. Mont., 1938, LL.B., 1941. Admitted to Mont. bar, 1941, Tex. bar, 1969; agt. FBI, 1942-68; judge municipal ct., Midland, Tex., 1968—. Mem. Alcoholism Council of Tex., Midland Council on Alcoholism; bs. dirs. Clover House, Odessa, Tex. Mem. Am. Judges Assn., Tex. Bar Assn. (mem. municipal ct. sect. bd. dirs., com. cts. of ltd. jurisdiction), Am. Judicature Soc., Nat. Conf. Spl. Ct. Judges (com. on standards of jud. conduct). Home: 1410 Lanham St Midland TX 79701 Office: POB 1152 404 E Texas St Midland TX 79701 Tel (915) 683-4281

AHERN, PAUL LEE, b. Edina, Mo., Dec. 11, 1919; B.S. in Chemistry, U. Denver, 1941; J.D., DePaul U., 1949. Chemist E.I. duPont Co., Wilmington, Del., 1941-46; admitted to Ill. bar, 1950; lawyer, Spencer, Marzall, Johnston & Cook, Chgo., 1950-52, Abbott Labs, North Chicago, Ill., 1952-61; instr. John Marshall Law Sch., Chgo., 1959—; mem. firm Leydig, Voit, Osann, Mayer & Holt, Chgo., 1964—; alderman City of Lake Forest (Ill.), 1960-66. Pres. Lake Forest Open Lands Assn., 1970—. Mem. Am., Chgo. bar assns., Am., Chgo. patent law assns. Home: 1350 N Green Bay Rd Lake Forest IL 60045 Office: Suite 4600 One IBM Plaza Chicago IL 60611 Tel (312) 822-9666

AHLGRIMM, JOHN C., b. Racine, Wis., June 3, 1925; B.A., U. Wis., 1946, LL.D., 1949; grad. (Univ. fellow) Nat. Coll. Juvenile Ct. Judges U. Colo., 1968; grad. Nat. Coll. Juvenile Justice U. Nev., 1973. Admitted to Wis. bar, 1949; partner firm Ahlgrimm & Ahlgrimm, Racine, 1949-62; judge br. Racine County (Wis.) Ct., 1962—; chmn. children's code revision com. Wis. State Bd. Juvenile Ct. Judges, 1974-75. Bd. dirs. Learning Disability Council Greater Racine; pres. Big Bros., Greater Racine; trustee St. Luke's Hosp., Racine; chmn. nominations Racine County Planning Council, chmn. Racine County Children Devel. Study. Mem. Racine County, Wis. State (chmn. com. family ct.), Am. bar assns., Am. Judicature Soc., Nat. Council Juvenile Ct. Judges (del. World Youth Magistrate Conf. of UN, Geneva, 1970, Oxford, Eng., 1974), World Assn. Judges. Home: 2500 N Main St Racine WI 53403 Office: Courthouse Racine WI 53403 Tel (414) 636-3141

AHLMANN, GEORGE JOHN, b. Milw., Apr. 5, 1941; B.S., Carroll Coll., Waukesha, Wis., 1966; J.D., U. N.Mex., 1970. Admitted to N.Mex. bar, 1970; asso. gen. counsel The Navajo Tribe, Window Rock, Ariz., 1970-72, chief tech. assistance div. Office of Program Devel., 1972-73; partner firm Schuelke, Wolf & Ahlmann, Gallup, N.Mex., 1973-76; individual practice law, Navajo, N.Mex., 1976—. Mem. Am., McKinley County bar assns. Home and Office: PO Box 1279 Navajo NM 87328 Tel (505) 777-2498

AHRENSFELD, THOMAS FREDERICK, b. Bklyn., June 30, 1923; A.B., Bklyn. Coll., 1948; LL.B., Columbia, 1948. Admitted to N.Y. bar, 1948; asso. firm Conboy, Hewitt, O'Brien & Boardman, N.Y.C., 1948-57, partner, 1957-59; sec., asso. gen. counsel Philip Morris Inc., N.Y.C., 1959-70, v.p., gen. counsel, 1970-76, sr. v.p., gen. counsel, dir., 1976—; dir. Mission Viejo (Calif.) Co., 1970—. Trustee Trinity Episcopal Schs. Corp., 1976—. Mem. Assn. Bar City N.Y. Am. Bar Assn. Home: 85 Nannahagen Rd Pleasantville NY 10570 Office: 100 Park Ave New York City NY 10017 Tel (212) 679-1800

AIBEL, HOWARD JAMES, b. N.Y.C., Mar. 24, 1929; A.B. magna cum laude, Harvard, 1950, LL.B. cum laude, 1951. Admitted to N.Y. bar, 1952; asso. firm White & Case, N.Y.C., 1952-57; with Gen. Electric Co., 1957-64, litigation counsel, 1960-64; with ITT, 1964—, sr. v.p., gen. counsel; dir. ITT World communications, ITT Continental Baking Co., Internat. Standard Electric Co. Home: 21 Berkely Rd Westport CT 06880 Office: 320 Park Ave New York City NY 10022*

AIDINOFF, M(ERTON) BERNARD, b. Newport, R.I., Feb. 2, 1929; B.A., U. Mich., 1950; LL.B., Harvard, 1953. Admitted to N.Y. bar, 1954, D.C. bar, 1953; served to 1st lt. JAGC, U.S. Army, 1953-55; law clk. Judge Learned Hand, U.S. Ct. Appeals 2d Circuit, N.Y.C., 1955-56; mem. firm Sullivan & Cromwell, N.Y.C., 1956-63, partner, 1963—; dir. Gibbs & Cox, Inc., N.Y.C.; lectr. in field. Trustee Spence Sch., N.Y.C., 1971—. Mem. Internat., Am. (vice chmn. sect. on taxation 1974-77), N.Y. bar assns., Assn. Bar City N.Y., Am. Law Inst. Editor in chief: Tax Lawyer, 1974-77. Home: 1120 Fifth Ave New York City NY 10028 Office: 48 Wall St New York City NY 10005 Tel (212) 952-8084

AIELLO, JAMES ANDREW, b. Phoenix, Mar. 5, 1940; B.A., U. Ariz., 1962; J.D., U. San Francisco, 1965. Admitted to Calif. bar, 1966, U.S. Supreme Ct. bar, 1971; dep. atty. gen. State of Calif., 1965-70; dep. dist. atty. County of San Mateo (Calif.), 1970-73, asst. dist. atty., 1973—. Mem. Calif., San Mateo County bar assns., World Peace through Law Center, Lawyers-Pilots Bar Assn. Office: Hall of Justice and Records Redwood City CA 94063 Tel (415) 364-5600

AIKEN, WILLIAM JAMES, JR., b. Braddock, Pa., Dec. 4, 1920; A.B., Allegheny Coll., 1942; LL.B., U. Pitts., 1948. Admitted to Pa. bar, 1949, U.S. Supreme Ct. bar, 1966; individual practice law, Pitts., 1949—; spl. asst. atty. gen. Commonwealth Pa., 1963-71; justice peace Borough Edgewood, Allegheny County, Pa., 1950-68. Mem. Allegheny County Bar Assn., Delta Sigma Rho, Phi Delta Phi. Home: 206 Maple Ave Pittsburgh PA 15218 Office: 1010 Grant Bldg Pittsburgh PA 15219 Tel (412) 261-6400

AIKMAN, JOHN EDGAR, b. Brockway, Pa., Jan. 1, 1919; B.S. in Mech. Engring., Pa. State U., 1940; J.D., U. Pitts., 1948. Admitted to Pa. bar, 1949; partner firm Sykes & Aikman, Brookville, Pa., 1949-59; individual practice law, Brookville, 1959-68; sec. Brockway Glass Co., Inc., 1968-70, v.p., gen. counsel, 1970—; dir. Brockway Citizens Bank. Bd. dirs., pres. YMCA, Brookville, 1961-65; trustee Clarion (Pa.) State Coll., 1967-73. Mem. Pa., Jefferson County bar assns. Registered profl. engr., Pa. Home: Northview Dr Brookville PA 15825 Office: McCullough Ave Brockway PA 15824 Tel (814) 261-6270

AINSWORTH, MARILYN VIRGINIA, b. Bowling Green, Ky., Aug. 31, 1945; B.A., Va. State Coll., 1966; J.D., U. Calif., Los Angeles, 1973. Admitted to Calif. bar, 1973; dir. Los Angeles Center for Dispute Settlement div. Am. Arbitration Assn., 1973-75; exec. dir. Black Law Jour. U. Calif., Los Angeles, 1974-75; teaching fellow Boston Coll. Law Sch., Newton, Mass., 1975-76; asso. prof. law U. Kans., Lawrence, 1976—. Home: 27 Ketch St #1 Marina Del Rey CA 90291 Office: Sch Law U Kans Lawrence KS 66045 Tel (913) 864-4550

AISO, JOHN FUJIO, b. Burbank, Calif., Dec. 14, 1909; A.B. cum laude, Brown U., 1931, A.M. (hon.), 1950; J.D., Harvard, 1934; postgrad Chuo U., Tokyo, 1936-37; certificate in Taxation, U. So. Calif., 1951; LL.D. (hon.), Chapman Coll., 1960. Admitted to N.Y. State bar, 1935, Calif. bar, 1941, U.S. Supreme Ct. bar, 1960; clerk, asso. firm Patterson, Eagle, Greenough & Day, N.Y.C., 1934-37; house counsel Manchurian & Kwantung Leased Terr. subs. of Britich-American Tobacco Co., Ltd., Mukden, Manchoukuo, 1937-40; partner firm Maeno & Aiso, Los Angeles, 1947-48; individual practice law, Los Angeles, 1949-50; partner firm Aiso, Chuman & McKibbin, Los Angeles, 1950-52; commr. Superior Ct. Los Angeles County, 1952-53; judge Municipal Ct. Los Angeles Judicial Dist., 1953-57; judge Superior Ct., Los Angeles County, 1957-67; asso. justice Calif. Ct. Appeals, Los Angeles, 1967-72, pro tem, 1967-68; spl. counsel firm O'Melveny & Myers, Los Angeles, 1973—; lectr. law U. So. Calif., 1960-61. Bd. trustees Los Angeles Law Library, 1965-68. Mem. Am., Los Angeles County bar assns., Am. Inst. Internat. Law, Judge Advocates Assn., Phi Alpha Delta. Office: 611 W 6th St Los Angeles CA 90017 Tel (213) 620-1120

AITKEN, JOHN RICHARD, b. Rockford, Ill., June 24, 1947; B.A., U. Ill., 1969; J.D., U. Iowa, 1972. Admitted to bar; asso. firm Cax H. Christie, Davenport, Iowa, 1972—; asst. atty. City of Bettendorf, Iowa, 1973—. Mem. Am., Iowa, Scott County bar assns. Home: 1515 W Columbia St Davenport IA 52804 Office: 606 1st National Bldg Davenport IA 52801 Tel (319) 322-1020

AITKEN, WYLIE ARTHUR, b. Detroit, Jan. 4, 1942; J.D., Marquette U., 1965. Admitted to Calif. bar, 1966; asso. firm Hunt, Liljestrom & Wentworth, Santa Ana, Calif., 1966-69; partner firm Aitken, Bradshaw & Andres, Santa Ana, 1969—; Mem. Orange County (Calif.) Bicentennial Com. Mem. Orange County, Calif., Am. bar assns., Orange County (pres. 1970), Calif. (pres. 1976—), Am. trial lawyers assns. Home: 1341 Valencia St Placentia CA 92670 Office: 611 Civic Center Dr W 301 Santa Ana CA 92701 Tel (714) 834-1424

AJELLO, CARL RICHARD, JR., b. Ansonia, Conn., Aug. 22, 1932; B.S., U. Conn., 1953; LL.B., N.Y. U., 1956, J.D.S., 1962. Admitted to Conn. bar, 1956; served from 1st lt. to capt. JAGC, U.S. Army, 1957-60; justice of peace City of Ansonia, 1960-62, corp. counsel, 1965-68; mem. Conn. Gen. Assembly, 1963-74, asst. majority leader, 1967, majority leader, 1969, 71-72, minority leader, 1973-74; atty. gen. State of Conn., 1975—. Mem. Ansonia Charter Revision Commn., 1975-76, Gov.'s Adv. Commn. on Adult Edn., 1973-76; Conn. mem. N.E. Regional Forest Fire Protective Compact, 1972-76; bd. dirs. Julia Day Nursery, Inc.; corporator Savs. Bank of Ansonia, Griffin Hosp., Derby, Conn. Mem. Nat. Legis. Conf. (com. on fed. and intergovtl. relations), Am., Conn., Naugatuck Valley (pres. 1970-71) bar assns., Am. Trial Lawyers Assn., Am. Judicature Soc., Nat. Assn. Attys. Gen., Lower Naugatuck Valley Mental Health Planning Council. Recipient Distinguished Service award Ansonia Jr. C. of C., 1965; named Outstanding Young Man Am., 1965-66. Home: Pulaski Hwy Ansonia CT 06401 Office: 30 Trinity St Hartford CT 06115 Tel (203) 566-2026

AKERMAN, ALEX, JR., b. Macon, Ga., Jan. 12, 1910. Student Mercer U., 1927-30; LL.B., U. Fla., 1933; postgrad. Naval Sch. Mil. Govt. and Adminstrn. Columbia, 1943, Sch. Naval Justice, Newport, R.I., 1950. Admitted to Fla. bar, 1933, U.S. Suprme Ct. bar, 1950; practiced in Tampa and Orlando, Fla., 1933-42, Orlando, 1945-50; with JAGC U.S. Navy, 1950-53; trial atty. Civil div. Dept. Justice, Washington, 1953; sec., dir. bur. adminstrn. FTC, 1953-54, exec. dir., Washington, 1954-58; mem. firm Shipley, Smoak, Akerman, Stein & Kaps, Washington, 1958-69; U.S. commr. U.S. Dist. Ct., Eastern Dist. Va., 1965-69, U.S. magistrate, 1969—; judge Orlando Municipal Ct., 1942, 45-46; mem. Fla. Ho. of Reps., 1946-48. Active Episcopal Ch. Mem. Am. Bar Assn., Phi Delta Phi, Omicron Delta Kappa. Home: POB 694 Alexandria VA 22313 Office: 206 N Washington St POB 909 Alexandria VA 22313 Tel (703) 549-0200

AKIN, BARRY NOEL, b. Copperhill, Tenn., Jan. 6, 1939; B.S. in Bus. Mgmt., Tenn. Tech. U., 1962; LL.B., U. Tenn., 1963. Admitted to Ariz. bar, 1964; mem. firm Miller, Pitt & Feldman, Tucson, 1968—. Mem. Ariz., Puma County bar assns., Am., Ariz. (pres. 1976) trial lawyers assns. Home: 3325 N Bentley St Tucson AZ 85716 Office: 111 S Church St Tucson AZ 85701 Tel (602) 792-3826

AKIN, HENRY DAVID, b. Graham, Tex., Jan. 24, 1900; A.B magna cum laude, Southwestern U., Georgetown, Tex., 1922; J.D., U. Tex., Austin, 1925. Admitted to Tex. bar, 1925, U.S. Ct. Appeals 5th Dist. bar, 1942, U.S. Suprme Ct. bar, 1971, U.S. Dist. Ct. D.C., 1971; asso. firm Kay, Akin & Smedley, Wichita Falls, Tex., 1925-26; partner firm Monning & Akin, Amarillo, Tex., 1926-38, Saunders, Akin & Williams, Dallas, 1938-41, Leachman, Gardere, Akin, Porter & DeHay, Dallas, 1942-66, Akin, Gump, Strauss, Hauer & Feld, Dallas, 1966—; adj. prof. So. Meth. U., 1942-74. Mem. Am., Tex., Dallas bar assns., Am. Judicature Soc., Tex. Bar Found., Am. Coll. Probate Counsel, Am. Arbitration Assn. Contbr. articles to profl. jours. Home: 7164 Elmridge Dr Dallas TX 75240 Office: 2800 Republic National Bank Bldg Dallas TX 75201 Tel (214) 655-2704

AKIN, TED MARTIN, b. Pasadena, Calif., Jan. 5, 1932; B.A., So. Meth. U., 1953, J.D., 1955. Admitted to Tex. bar, 1955; with JAGC, USAF, 1955-57; individual practice law, Dallas, 1957-63, 69-73; judge Dallas County (Tex.) Ct. at Law 4, 1963-69, Tex. Dist. Ct., 95th Jud. Dist., 1973-75; asso. justice Ct. Civil Appeals 5th Supreme Jud. Dist. of Tex. at Dallas, 1975—. Mem. Am. Judicature Soc., Am., Dallas bar assns., Newcomen Soc. N.Am., Tex. Kennel Club, Sigma Alpha Epsilon (alumni pres. 1972), Phi Alpha Delta. Home: 5323 N Dentwood Dr Dallas TX 75225 Office: Dallas County Courthouse 600 Commerce St Dallas TX 75202 Tel (214) 749-8381

AKOLT, JOHN PATRICK, JR., b. Denver, May 16, 1918; B.S., U. Denver, 1940, LL.B., 1946. Admitted to Colo. bar, 1946, U.S. Dist. Ct. for Dist. Colo. bar, 1946, U.S. 10th Circuit Ct. Appeals bar, 1946, U.S. Supreme Ct. bar, 1966; asso. firm Akolt, Dick & Akolt and predecessors, Denver, 1946-52, partner, 1953—. Bd. dirs. Colo. Tb Assn., 1958-61. Mem. Denver, Colo. bar assns., Nat. Assn. Coll. and Univ. Attys. (dir. 1968-69). Home: 630 Glencoe St Denver CO 80220 Office: 1510 Lincoln Center Bldg Denver CO 80264 Tel (303) 861-2480

ALAND, LINDA BESS, b. Dallas, Oct. 13, 1947; student Wellesley Coll., 1965-67, So. Meth. U., Dallas, 1967-68; B.S., U. Ala., Tuscaloosa, 1969; J.D., So. Meth. U., 1972. Admitted to Tex. bar, 1972, U.S. Tax Ct. bar, 1973; individual practice law, Dallas, 1972-73; asso. firm Strother, Davis, Stanton & Levy, Dallas, 1973—; instr. Moot Ct., So. Meth. U., 1972. Mem. Am., Tex., Dallas bar assns., Kappa Beta Pi. Home: 9120 Coral Cove St Dallas TX 75231 Office: 20002 Bryan Tower Suite 3838 Dallas TX 75201 Tel (214) 651-1888

ALBAN, BENNETT MICHAEL, b. Chgo., Apr. 16, 1945; B.S.C., U. Ill. Champaign, 1967; J.D., DePaul U., Chgo., 1970, M.S. in Taxation, 1974. Admitted to Ill. bar, 1970; tax mgr. Lester Witte & Co., C.P.A.'s, Chgo., 1968-74; individual practice law, Chgo., 1974—; seminar leader; has appeared on Sta. WGLO, also Kennedy and Co. TV. Mem. Fed., Ill., Chgo. bar assns., Am. Inst. C.P.A.'s, Ill. Soc. C.P.A.'s, Beta Alpha Psi. Home: 100 E Bellevue #22E Chicago IL 60657 Office: 111 E Wacker Dr 3024 Chicago IL 60601 Tel (312) 644-0450

ALBEA, EMMETTE HARVEY, b. Scotts Station, Ala., Jan. 28, 1920; LL.B., Atlanta Law Sch., 1947, LL.M., 1948; A.B., Oglethorpe Coll., 1949; M.A., Peabody U., 1951; J.D., Mercer U., 1963. Admitted to Ga. bar, 1947; practiced in Atlanta, 1947-50, 52-57, 63-64; judge Calhoun County (Ala.) Juvenile and Domestic Relations Ct., 1957-60, 67-77; registrar, prof. U. System of Ga., 1964-67; prof. law Gadsden State Jr. Coll., 1971—; cons. on youth legislation; mem. Citizens Com. on Reorganizing Ala. Cts. Chmn. bd. Coosa Valley (Ala.) Regional Juvenile Center, Mem. Am., Ga. State, Ala. State bar assns., Nat. Council Juvenile Ct. Judges, Ala. Juvenile Ct. Judges' Assn. (pres. 1972-73), Ala. Intermediate Ct. Judges' Assn., NEA (life), Calhoun County Bar Assn., Am. Council Marriage Enrichment. Named Outstanding Citizen K.C., 1969. Home: 613 Inglewood Dr Anniston AL 36201 Office: Juvenile and Domestic Relations Ct of Calhoun County Courthouse Annex 2 Anniston AL 36201 Tel (205) 236-3418

ALBERG, MARK DUANE, b. Tomahawk, Wis., Nov. 15, 1948; B.B.A., U. Wis., 1971; J.D., Memphis State U., 1974. Admitted to Wis. bar, 1974, Fed. Eastern Dist. Wis., 1974, Western Dist. Wis., 1974; asso. firm James T. Rogers, Merrill, Wis., 1974—. Mem. State Bar Wis. (mem. young lawyers div. com. on law office adminstrn., com. lawyer relationships), Wis. (Lincoln County chmn. law day, 1976), Lincoln County bar assns. Home: 223 E Lincoln Ave Tomahawk WI 54487 Office: 120 S Mill St Merrill WI 54452 Tel (715) 536-5501

ALBERI, DANTE JAMES, b. Mount Vernon, N.Y., Nov. 12, 1942; B.S., Fordham Coll., 1964; J.D., Fordham U., 1967. Admitted to N.Y. bar, 1968; partner firm Alberi, Periconi & Alberi, Mount Vernon, 1968—; gen. counsel, dir. Die Mesh Corp. gen. counsel N.Y. chpt. Inst. Scrap Iron and Steel. Mem. N.Y., Westchester County, Mount Vernon (pres. 1977-78) bar assns.; N.Y. Kiwanis Club (dir.). Office: 100 Stevens Ave Mount Vernon NY 10550 Tel (914) 668-5020

ALBERT, BURTON LEE, b. Sioux City, Iowa, Sept. 25, 1941; A.B., Darmouth Coll., 1963; J.D., Duke U., 1966. Admitted to Va. bar, 1968; atty. Lawyers Title Ins. Corp., Richmond, Va., 1967-68, NLRB, Los Angeles, 1968-69; asso. firm Morton Honeyman, Roanoke, Va., 1969-71; individual practice law, Roanoke, 1971—; pres. Arnold Schlossberg & Assos., Inc., Roanoke, 1973-74. Mem. Am., Roanoke bar assns. Ann. contbr. Developing Labor Law. Office: 4502 Starkey Rd Roanoke VA 24014 Tel (703) 989-0903

ALBERT, ELAINE HEARST, b. Kingston, Pa., Nov. 15, 1942; B.A., U. Calif., 1964, LL.B., 1968. Admitted to Calif. bar, 1968; partner firm Albert & Albert, Century City, 1968-74, firm Albert & Oliker, Century City, 1974—. Pres. United Circle Young Democrats, Los Angeles. Mem. Calif. State Bar Assn. Recipient Bankroft Whitney Legal Research and Writing award, 1966. Office: 1801 Century Park E Los Angeles CA 90067 Tel (213) 277-5800

ALBERT, STANLEY NORTON, b. N.Y.C., Apr. 20, 1929; B.S. in Pharmacy, Fordham U., 1952; LL.B., N.Y. Law Sch., 1961. Admitted to N.Y. bar, 1962, U.S. Dist. Ct. (Eastern and Southern dists.), 1963, U.S. Supreme Ct. bar, 1966; asst. counsel to Majority Leader N.Y. State Senate, 1965; law sec. to Judge Arnold L. Fein, Civil Ct., N.Y. County, 1965-67; trial counsel Leahey & Johnson, N.Y.C., 1968; counsel State Wide Ins. Co., N.Y.C., 1969; individual practice law N.Y.C., 1970—. Mem. East Midtown Democratic Club (v.p., 1970-72), Civil Ct. Law Secs. Assn., (pres., 1966-67). Mem. N.Y. State Bar Assn. Home: 50 E 89th St New York City NY 10028 Office: 360 Lexington Ave New York City NY 10017 Tel (212) 490-2706

ALBERT, STEVEN WILLIAM, b. Toledo, Dec. 13, 1946; A.B. in Polit. Sci., Am. U., 1968; J.D., U. Toledo, 1971. Admitted to Ohio bar, 1971; asso. firm Kitchen, Messner & Deery, Cleve., 1972—. Mem. Cleve., Ohio, Am. bar assns., Ohio, Cleve. def. assns. Recipient Am. Jurisprudence award in antitrust, 1971. Home: 14499 E Carroll St University Heights OH 44118 Office: 1305 The Superior Bldg Cleveland OH 44114 Tel (216) 241-5614

ALBERT, WARREN G., b. Columbus, Nebr., Nov. 19, 1904; LL.B., U. Nebr. Admitted to Nebr. bar, 1933; practice law, Columbus. Mem. Platte County, Am., Nebr. bar assns. Office: 1465 27th Ave Columbus NE 68601 Tel (402) 564-3274

ALBERTS, HAROLD, b. San Antonio, Apr. 3, 1920; LL.B., U. Tex., 1942. Admitted to Tex. bar, 1943, U.S. Supreme Ct. bar, 1958, Ct. Mil. Appeals bar, 1959; individual practice law, Corpus Christi, Tex., 1946—; tchr. U. Tex., 1942; legal officer Chase Field, 1944. Pres. Southwest Regional Anti-Defamation League, Tex. and Okla., 1953, chmn., 1969-72; chmn. Nueces County (Tex.) Red Cross, 1959-61; v.p. Little Theater, Corpus Christi, 1964; chmn. Corpus Christi chpt. NCCJ, 1967-69, nat. dir., 1974-76; chmn. Coastal Bend Council on Alcoholism, Corpus Christi, 1975; pres. Combined Jewish Appeal, Corpus Christi, 1974-76. Mem. Am., Tex., Nueces County bar assns. Office: 702 Wilson Tower Corpus Christi TX 78401 Tel (512) 882-8816

ALBERTSON, JOSEPH LESTER, b. Bklyn., Jan. 1, 1903; B.S., Hamilton Coll., 1924; J.D., N.Y. Law Sch., 1927. Admitted to N.Y. bar, 1927; clk. firm Shearman & Sterling, N.Y.C., 1924-28; asso. firm Seacord, Richie & Young, New Rochelle, N.Y., 1928; founder, sr. partner firm Albertson, Simmons & Butler and predecessors, N.Y.C., 1929-70, New Rochelle, 1929—; asst. dist. atty. Westchester County (N.Y.), 1929-32; govt. appeal agt. Local Bd. 9 Selective Service System, New Rochelle, 1941-70; vice chmn. Arnold Bakers, Inc., Greenwich, Conn.; dir., sec. Alvord and Swift Co., N.Y.C.; dir. Ward Pavements, Inc., Haverstraw, N.Y., Westchester Colprovia Corp., Katonah, N.Y., Watson Bldg. Corp., Eastchester, N.Y. Councilman, City of New Rochelle, 1939-43; bd. govs. New Rochelle Hosp. Med. Center. Mem. Am., N.Y., Westchester County, New Rochelle bar assns., Am. Arbitration Assn. (nat. panel arbitrators). Home: 93 Wilmot Rd New Rochelle NY 10804 Office: 271 North Ave New Rochelle NY 10801 Tel (914) 636-4400

ALBERTSON, THOMAS BENEDICT, b. New Rochelle, N.Y., Feb. 3, 1937; B.A., Williams Coll., 1959; LL.D., Cornell U., 1962. Admitted to N.Y. bar, 1962; asso. firm Cadwalader, Wickersham & Taft, N.Y.C., 1962-65, Albertson, Simmons & Butler, New Rochelle, N.Y., 1965-67, partner, 1967—; v.p., dir. N-Con Systems Co., Inc., New Rochelle, 1973—; sec., dir. Daniel F. MacNamee & Co., Inc., Katonah, N.Y., 1975—. Bd. dirs. New Rochelle Humane Soc., 1969-73, Family Service of Westchester, White Plains, N.Y., 1973-75; bd. dirs., trustee New Rochelle Boys Club, 1971—; mem. planning bd. Town of Somers (N.Y.), 1973—; trustee Somers Library Assn., 1974—. Mem. New Rochelle, Westchester County (surrogates ct. com. 1976—) bar assns. Office: 271 N Ave New Rochelle NY 10801 Tel (914) 636-4400

ALBIN, BARRY GALE, b. Wichita, Kans., Oct. 6, 1948; B.A. in History and Polit. Sci., U. Kans., 1970, J.D., 1973. Admitted to Kans. bar, 1973, Fed. Dist. Kans. bar, 1973; partner Albin & Agazarian, Kansas City, 1973-74; staff counsel Wyandotte County Legal Aid, Kansas City, 1974-76; individual practice law, Kansas City, 1976—. Mem. Bd. Econ. Opportunity Found., Inc.; sec., legal counsel Western Wyandotte Action Group, Inc. Mem. Am., Kans., Wyandotte County bar assns. Office: 907 N 7th St Suite 1014 Kansas City KS 66101 Tel (913) 371-0102

ALBRECHT, NIKOLAUS, b. Tirol, Austria, Apr. 10, 1944; B.A., Willamette U., 1965, J.D., 1968. Admitted to Oreg. bar, 1968; individual practice law, Portland. Home: 5565 SW 88th St Portland OR Office: 1123 SW Yamhill St Portland OR 97205 Tel (503) 223-3303

ALBRECHT, RICHARD RAYMOND, b. Storm Lake, Iowa, Aug. 29, 1932; B.A., U. Iowa, 1958, J.D., 1961. Admitted to Wash. bar, 1961, U.S. Supreme Ct. bar, 1976; asso. firm Perkins, Coie, Stone, Olsen & Williams, Seattle, 1961-67, partner, 1968-74; gen. counsel Dept. Treasury, Washington, 1974-76; v.p., counsel, sec. The Boeing Co., Seattle, 1976—. Mem. Wash. State Council Higher Edn., 1970-74, chmn., 1973-74; chmn. Wash. State Higher Edn. Assistance Authority, 1973-74, King County (Wash.) Bd. Freeholders, 1967-68; trustee Shoreline Pub. Library, 1966-69, pres., 1967-68. Mem. Am., Fed., Wash. State, Seattle-King County bar assns., Am. Judicature Soc. Recipient Outstanding Citizen of Year award Seattle-King County Municipal League, 1968-69. Home: 1940 Shenandoah Dr E Seattle WA 98112 Office: Boeing Co POB 3707 Seattle WA 98124 Tel (206) 655-5578

ALBRIGHT, R(OBERT) MAYNE, b. Raleigh, N.C., Apr. 5, 1910; A.B., U. N.C., 1931, M.A., 1933, J.D., 1936. Admitted to N.C. bar, 1936; individual practice law, Raleigh, 1948-56, 69—; partner firm Albright, Parker & Sink, and predecessors, Raleigh, 1956-69; state dir.

U.S. Employment Service, 1937-41. Mem. AIA (hon.), N.C., Wake County (past pres.) bar assns. Co-editor: Handbook of N.C. Bldg. Laws, 1966, 2d edit., 1975. Home: 3078 Granville Dr Raleigh NC 27609 Office: Branch Bank Bldg PO Box 1206 Raleigh NC 27602 Tel (919) 833-1118

ALCARESE, JOSEPH PATRICK, b. Balt., Apr. 1, 1922; Ph.B., Loyola Coll. Balt., 1949; J.D., U. Md., 1972. Admitted to Md. bar, 1952, U.S. Dist. Ct. Md., 1952, U.S. Supreme Ct. bar, 1960; atty. U.S. Govt. DOD, Washington, 1952-58; div. counsel Martin Marietta Corp., Balt., 1958-76; counsel Chesapeake Park, Inc., Balt., 1971-76; instr. Drexel U., 1960—. Mem. Fed. Bar Assn. Home: 225 Meadowvale Rd Lutherville MD 21093 Office: 103 Chesapeake Pk Plaza Baltimore MD 21220 Tel (301) 687-3800

ALCORN, HUGH MEADE, JR., b. Suffield, Conn., Oct. 20, 1907; A.B., Darmouth, 1930; LL.B., Yale, 1933; LL.D. (hon.), U. Hartford, 1974. Admitted to Conn. bar, 1933, U.S. Supreme Ct. bar, 1959; asst. state's atty. Conn., 1935-42, state's atty., 1942-48; asso. firm Alcorn, Bakewell & Smith, Hartford, Conn., 1933—; mem. Conn. Gen. Assembly, 1937-41, speaker, 1941; gen. counsel Republican Nat. Com., 1959-61, chmn., 1957-59; mem., floor leader Conn. Constl. Conv., 1965. Mem. Am., Conn. (pres. 1950-51), Hartford County bar assns., Am. Bar Found., Am. Coll. Trail Lawyers, Am. Judicature Soc., Phi Beta Kappa. Home: 49 Russell Ave Suffield CT 06078 Office: One American Row Hartford CT 06103 Tel (203) 522-1216

ALCORN, WENDELL BERTRAM, JR., b. Wharton, Tex., Dec. 19, 1939; J.D. magna cum laude, U. Houston, 1969. Admitted to Tex. bar, 1969, N.Y. State bar, 1970, S.C. bar, 1974, Ga. bar 1975; asso. firm Cadwalader, Wickersham & Taft, N.Y.C., 1969-73, 75-77, partner, 1977—; asso. firm Hull, Towill, Norman, Barrett & Johnson, Augusta, Ga., 1973-75; dir. Houston Law Review, Inc., 1971-75; contbr. Carter-Mondale Policy Planning Group 1976; prof. Adelphi U. Grad. Sch. Bus., 1976-77. Mem. Tex., N.Y. State, S.C., Ga., Am. bar assns., Fed. Bar Council. Recipient Houston Law Review Alumni award, 1976. Contbr. articles to legal jours. Home: 14 Homestead Rd Darien CT 06820 Office: 1 Wall St New York City NY 10005 Tel (212) 785-1000

ALCORNS, CARL AUGUST, b. Pitts., Aug. 3, 1938; A.A., St. Petersburg Jr. Coll., 1961; B.A., Fla. State U., 1963; J.D., Stetson Law Sch., 1968. Admitted to Fla. bar, 1968, Calif. bar, 1970; asst. trust officer 1st Gulf Beach Bank & Trust, St. Petersburg, Fla., 1968-69; asst. trust officer Crocker Nat. Bank, San Francisco, 1969-71, trust officer, Los Angeles, 1971—. Mem. Am., Fla., Hollywood bar assns. Home: 10394 Rochester Ave 8 Los Angeles CA 90024 Office: 10110 Santa Monica Blvd Los Angeles CA 90067 Tel (213) 550-2964

ALDEN, CHARLES FRANKLIN, III, b. Little Rock, May 6, 1947; B.A. in Polit. Sci., Okla. State U., 1969; J.D., Oklahoma City U., 1973. Admitted to Okla. bar, 1973; asst. city atty. Oklahoma City, 1973; asst. dist. atty. Okla. County, 1974-75; asso. firm Rhodes, Hieronymus, Holloway & Wilson, Oklahoma City, 1976—; legal intern atty. gen. of Okla., 1972-73; bailiff Dist. Ct. Okla. County, 1971-72. Mem. Okla., Okla. County bar assns., Phi Delta Phi (grad. of year 1973). Recipient Am. Jurisprudence award in Civil Procedure. Home: 2609 Carlton Way Oklahoma City OK 73120 Office: suite 1100 101 Park Ave Oklahoma City OK 73102 Tel (405) 235-8503

ALDEN, JOHN, b. Upper Darby, Pa., Dec. 15, 1942; B.A., Villanova U., 1966, J.D., 1969. Admitted to Pa. bar, 1970; U.S. Supreme Ct. bar, 1975; asso. firm Mulroy, Ryan & Semeraro, Media, Pa., 1969-70, firm Pillegi, Desmond & Sachs, Chester, Pa., 1970-71; partner firm Groover & Alden, Wayne, Pa., 1971-76; individual practice law, Wayne, 1976—; asst. pub. defender Deleware County (Pa.), 1970-71; instr. real estate law Main Line Paralegal Inst., Wayne, 1975—. Mem. Radnor Twp. Bd. Commrs., 1972—, v.p., 1974-75, pres., 1975—; dir. Wayne, Inc., 1973—; advisor Boy Scouts Am., Wayne, 1973-75. Mem. Am., Pa. bar assns., Am., Pa. trial lawyers assns. Home: 102 Walnut Ave Wayne PA 19087 Office: 121 N Wayne Ave Wayne PA 19087 Tel (215) 687-4110

ALDEN, ROBERT F., b. Terre Haute, Ind., Dec. 30, 1946; B.A., DePauw U., 1968; J.D., cum laude, Ind. U., 1972. Admitted to Ind. bar, 1972; asso. firm Klineman, Rose & Wolf, Indpls., 1972-74; individual practice law, Indpls., 1974—; dep. prosecutor Marion County (Ind.), Indpls., 1972-74; dep. atty. gen. State of Ind., 1975; dep. prosecutor City of Indpls., 1975-76. Mem. Ind., Indpls. bar assns. Home: 6038 N Olney St Indianapolis IN 46220 Office: 110 N Delaware St Indianapolis IN 46204 Tel (317) 634-9800

ALDERSON, FRANK RAYMOND, b. Trenton, Mo., Nov. 18, 1925; B.S., U. Oreg., 1950, LL.B., 1951. Admitted to Oreg. bar, 1951; title examiner Rogue River Title Co., Grants Pass, Oreg., 1951; dep. dist. atty. Klamath County (Oreg.), 1952, dist. atty., 1952-55; dep. dist. atty. Lane County (Oreg.), 1955-61; judge Lane County Dist. Ct., Eugene, 1961—. Chmn. Five Nations Dist. Oreg. Trail Council Boy Scouts Am., 1965-68. Mem. Oreg. State, Lane County bar assns. Recipient Key Man award Eugene Jaycees, 1960, Jaycee of Month award, 1960, 61, Presdl. award, 1962. Home: 2120 Rocky Ln Eugene OR 97401 Office: Dist Ct Lane County Courthouse Eugene OR 97401 Tel (503) 687-4225

ALDOCK, JOHN DOUGLAS, b. Silver Spring, Md., Jan. 20, 1942; B.S. with honors, Northwestern U., 1964; LL.B. cum laude, U. Pa., 1967. Admitted to D.C. bar, 1968, U.S. Supreme Ct. bar, 1972, Md. bar, 1973; law clk. to Judge Luther W. Youngdahl, U.S. Dist. Ct. for D.C., 1967-68; asst. U.S. atty. D.C., 1968-71; asso. firm Shea & Gardner, Washington, 1971-75, partner, 1975—. Mem. Am., Md., D.C. bar assns., Jud. Conf. D.C. Circuit, Assn. U.S. Attys. (pres. 1975). Editor: U. Pa. Law Rev., 1965-67. Home: 6427 Dahlonega Rd Mohican Hills MD 20016 Office: 734 15th St NW Washington DC 20005 Tel (202) 737-1255

ALDRICH, RUPERT FREMONT, b. South Paris, Maine, Apr. 1, 1908; student Bates Coll., 1926-28, Peabody Law Sch., 1928-31. Admitted to Maine bar, 1936; clk. Oxford County (Maine) Superior Ct., 1930-68; individual practice law, South Paris, 1936—; owner, operator Norway Flying Service, Aldrich Motor Co., Aldrich Realty Co. Del., Republican Nat. Conv., 1948, 52. Mem. Am., Maine, Oxford County bar assns., Oxford Hills C. of C. Home: 69 Pleasant St Norway ME 04268 Office: 207 Main St South Paris ME 04281 Tel (207) 743-6308

ALDRIDGE, JOHN EUGENE, JR., b. Raleigh, N.C., Dec. 6, 1943; A.B., U. N.C., 1966, J.D., 1969. Admitted to N.C. bar, 1969; asso. firm Dupree, Weaver, Horton, Cockman & Alvis, 1969-71, Cockman, Alvis & Aldridge, 1971-75, Cockman, Akins & Aldridge, 1975-76; partner Cockman, Aldridge & Davis, Raleigh, 1976—. Mem. Am., N.C., Wake County bar assns. Office: PO 17623 Raleigh NC 27609 Tel (919) 782-1211

ALDRIDGE, VICTOR E., JR., b. Martin County, Ind., Jan. 31, 1919; A.B., Ind. U., 1941, J.D. with distinction, 1943. Served with Judge Adv. Gen. Corps USAR, 1943-46; admitted to Ind. bar, 1943, U.S. Ct. Mil. Appeals bar, 1956, U.S. Tax Ct. bar, 1970; individual practice law, Terre Haute, Ind., 1946—. Mem. Terre Haute (pres. 1959-60), Ind. State Western Ind. (pres. 1955-56) bar assns., Order of Coif, Phi Delta Phi. Home: 524 Deming St Terre Haute IN 47807 Office: 1200 Sycamore Bldg Terre Haute IN 47807 Tel (812) 232-8175

ALESIA, JAMES HENRY, b. Chgo., July 16, 1934; B.S., Loyola U., Chgo., 1956; J.D., Chgo-Kent Coll. Law Ill. Inst. Tech., 1960; grad. Nat. Coll. State Judiciary U. Nev., 1976. Officer, Chgo. Police Dept., 1957-60; admitted to Ill. Supreme Ct. bar, 1960, Minn. Supreme Ct. bar, 1970, U.S. Supreme Ct. bar, 1971; asso. Anthony Scariano, Chicago Heights, Ill., 1960-61; asso. firm Pretzel, Stouffer, Nolan & Rooney, Chgo., 1961-63, Rerat, Crill, Foley & Boursier, Mpls., 1970-71; asst. gen. counsel Chgo. & North Western Railway Co., 1963-70; dep. chief civil div. U.S. Atty's. Office, No. Dist. Ill., 1971-73; trial counsel Chessie System, Chgo., 1973; U.S. adminstrv. law judge, Chgo.; 1973—. Mem. Am., Fed. bar assns., Justinian Legal Soc., Assn. Adminstrv. Law Judges (gov.), Blue Key, Phi Alpha Delta. Home: 1025 S Lincoln Ave Park Ridge IL 60068 Office: 2645 Kluczynski Fed Bldg 230 S Dearborn St Chicago IL 60604

ALESSANDRONI, VENAN JOSEPH, b. N.Y.C., Mar. 1, 1915; A.B., Columbia, 1937, J.D., 1939; Admitted to N.Y. bar, 1941, Korean Supreme Ct. bar, 1946; announcer CBS Artists Service, Inc., 1940; U.S. atty. Bd. Econ. Warfare, 1942; mem. U.S. Fgn. Econ. Adminstrn. Mission, Belgian Congo, 1943; with firm Wormser, Kisly, Alessandroni & McCann, and predecessors, N.Y.C., 1946—, sr. partner, 1959—; dir. Am. Lurgi Corp., legal officer Mil. Govt. Korea, 1945-46; legal adv. to provincial govt. Kyunggi-Do, Korea, 1946; chief provost judge City of Seoul, 1946; adj. prof. U. Miami Law Sch., 1974—; lectr. in field. Mem. Assn. Bar City N.Y. Author: The Executor, 1963; Applied Estate Planning, 1963; contbr. articles to legal jours.; departmental editor Jour. Taxation, 1955-56. Home: Eggleston Ln Old Greenwich CT 06870 Office: 100 Park Ave New York City NY 10017 Tel (212) 889-8480

ALESSI, ROBERT HAROLD, b. Jamestown, N.Y., Sept. 23, 1933; B.A., Syracuse U., 1959; J.D., State U., N.Y., Buffalo, 1963. Admitted to N.Y. bar, 1963; partner firm Alessi & Alessi, Jamestown, 1963—; instr. Jamestown Community Coll., 1964-67; atty. Jamestown Dept. Social Services, 1968-69; corp. counsel City of Jamestown, 1970-74; estate tax atty., appraiser State of N.Y., 1975—. Chmn., Jamestown Zoning Bd. Appeals, 1975—. Mem. Jamestown, N.Y. State bar assns. Home: 17 Valleyview Ave Jamestown NY 14701 Office: Fenton Bldg Jamestown NY 14701 Tel (716) 664-4315

ALEXANDER, ABNER, b. Winston-Salem, N.C., May 20, 1929; A.B., Guilford Coll., 1952; LL.B., Wake Forest U., 1957. Admitted to N.C. bar, 1957; asst. dist. atty. Middle Dist. of N.C. Ct., 1960; partner firm Alexander & Sharpe, Winston-Salem, 1960-68; chief judge N.C. 21st Jud. Ct., 1968—. Mem. Exchange Club (pres.). Office: Forsyth County Hall of Justice Main St Winston-Salem NC 27100 Tel (919) 761-2478

ALEXANDER, ARVIN JOHN, b. Lethbridge, Alta., Can., May 10, 1909; LL.B., Ohio State U., 1936, J.D., 1970. Admitted to Ohio bar, 1938; partner firm Alexander, Ebinger, Holschuh, Fisher & McAlister, Columbus, Ohio, 1946—. Mem. Columbus City Council, 1939-43, pres., 1943; mem. Met. Airport Com., 1956-63; chmn. trustees Columbus Better Bus. Bur. Central Ohio, 1958-61; mem. Downtown Area Commn. Bd., 1965-73; trustee, chmn. exec. com. Mut. Investing Found., Columbus, 1968—; trustee Columbus Sinking Fund., 1954-57, pres. 1957-58; trustee Citizens Research, Inc., 1962—; pres., 1962-64, chmn., 1964-66, life bd. dirs., 1976—. Mem. Am., Ohio State, Columbus bar assns., Navy League (judge advocate 1963), Am. Judicature Soc. Home: 3725 Olentangy Blvd Columbus OH 43214 Office: 17 S High St Columbus OH 43215 Tel (614) 221-6345

ALEXANDER, CRUZAN, b. Port Arthur, Tex., June 28, 1918; B.S. in Chem. Engring., U. Mich., 1940, M.S. in Chem. Engring., 1941, J.D., 1943, postgrad., 1943-44. Admitted to Mich. bar, 1943, Okla. bar, 1945, N.Y. State bar, 1950, Minn. bar, 1958; patent atty. Philips Petroleum Co., Bartlesville, Okla., 1944-46; patent atty., asst. gen. patent counsel M.W. Kellogg Co., N.Y.C., 1946-57; patent atty., counsel Alexander, Sell, Steldt & DeLaHunt, St. Paul, 1957-76; patent atty., chief patent counsel 3MCo., St. Paul, 1976—. Mem. Minn. Bar Assn. (chmn. CLE planning com. 1975—), Minn. Patent Law Assn. (pres.-elect 1976-77), Am., Mich., Okla. bar assns., Licensing Exec. Soc., Am. Inst. Chem. Engrs., Am. Chem. Soc., Assn. of Corporate Patent Counsel, Am. Arbitration Assn., Intellectual Property Owners (mem. operating com.), Sigma Xi, Phi Lamda Upsilon, Theta Xi. Home: 20 Hay Camp Rd North Oaks St Paul MN 55110 Office: 3M Co 3M Center St Paul MN 55101 Tel (612) 733-1511

ALEXANDER, CYRUS ANDREW, b. Chgo., Apr. 22, 1928; B.A., U. Ill., 1953; M.A., U. Pa., 1954, J.D., Chgo.-Kent Coll. Law, 1972. Internat. rep. Hotel and Restaurant Internat. Union, Cin., 1957-59; v.p., gen. mgt. Top Transp. Co., Inc., Phila., 1966-68; admitted to Ill. bar, 1974; atty. NLRB, Chgo., 1974, chief counsel, dir. Ill. Office Collective Bargaining, Springfield, Chgo., 1975-77, asso. prof. U. Ill., Chgo. Circle Center, fall 1977. Mem. Am., Ill., Chgo. bar assns., Assn. Trial Lawyers Am., Soc. Profls. in Dispute Resolution, Am. Arbitration Assn. Home: 5813 N Maplewood St Chicago IL 60659 Tel (312) 372-8587

ALEXANDER, DAVE ALMON, b. Decatur, Ala., Dec. 28, 1915; B.A., Vanderbilt U., 1939, J.D., 1942. Admitted to Tenn. bar, 1942; with firm Eggleston, Campbell & Alexander, 1950-52; individual practice law, 1952-74; sr. partner firm Alexander, Hartzog, Harris & Silva, Franklin, Tenn., 1974—; spl. counsel to Gov. Gordon Browning, Tenn., 1951; mem. Gov.'s Select Com. on Bank Taxation, 1975-76. Mem. council City of Franklin, 1950. Mem. Am., Tenn. (chmn. grievance com. 1955-60, v.p. 1960-61), Williamson County (pres. 1976-77) bar assns. Home: Route 6 Brentwood TN 37027 Office: Alexander Bldg Court Sq Franklin TN 37064 Tel (615) 794-6601

ALEXANDER, GABRIEL N., b. Detroit, Mar. 1, 1910; B.A., U. Mich., 1930, J.D., 1933. Admitted to Mich. bar, 1933; asso. firm Alexander & Alexander, Detroit, 1933-47; individual practice law, arbitrator, Oak Park, Mich., 1947—; adj. prof. law Wayne State U., 1955—; hearing officer Detroit War Labor Bd., 1944-46; pub. mem. Detroit Regional Wage Stblzn. Bd., 1952-54. Mem. Mich. Bar Assn., Nat. Acad. Arbitrators, Indsl. Relations Research Assn. Office: 21910 Greenfield Rd Oak Park MI 48237 Tel (313) 968-5010

ALEXANDER, GARY ROSS, b. Washington, Nov. 16, 1942; B.A., U. Va., 1964; LL.B., George Washington U., 1967. Admitted to Md. bar, Va., D.C. bars, 1967; individual practice law, Washington, 1967-70; partner firm Giordano Alexander Haas Mahoney & Bush, Oxon Hill, Md., 1970—; state people's counsel Md. Pub. Service Commn., 1974-76. Mem. So. Md. Health Systems Agy., 1976—, Spl. Md. Legis. Task Force on Utility Regulation, 1976; chmn. Prince George's County (Md.) Drug Adv. Council, 1974-76; mem. state regulatory adv. com. Fed. Energy Adminstrn., 1975-77. Mem. Am. (chmn. automobile law com. 1974-77), Md., D.C., Va. bar assns., Am. Trial Lawyers Assn., Phi Delta Phi. Author: State Consumer Advocates, 1975. Office: 9401 Indian Head Hwy Oxon Hill MD 20022 Tel (301) 248-6500

ALEXANDER, GEORGE JONATHAN, b. Berlin, Mar. 8, 1931 (parents Am. citizens); B.A. with major honors, U. Pa., 1953, J.D. cum laude, 1959; LL.M., Yale, 1964, J.S.D., 1969. Admitted to Ill. bar, 1960, N.Y. bar, 1961, U.S. Supreme Ct. bar, 1964, Calif. bar, 1974; instr. law (Bigelow teaching fellow) U. Chgo., 1959-60; instr. Naval Reserve Officers Sch., Park Forest, Ill., 1959-60; prof. law. Syracuse U., 1960-70, asso. dean Sch. Law., 1967-69; prof. law. U. Santa Clara, 1970—, dean Law Sch., 1970—; vis. asst. prof. law. U. So. Calif., summer 1963. Cons. White House Conf. on Aging, 1972. Mem. Internat. Inst. Space Law of the Internat. Fedn. Aero. and Astronautics (life mem.; dir. mem. exec. com. 1968—), Internat. Commn. on Human Rights (London), Am. Assn. Abolition Involuntary Hospitalization (co-founder, dir 1970—; chmn. 1975—), ACLU (dir. central N.Y. chpt. 1965-70; chmn. 1965-67; dir. mental commitment com., 1967-70; vice-chmn. 1969-70), Am. (vice chmn. legal problems aging com.), Calif. bar assns., Soc. Am. Law Tchrs. (bd. govs. 1974—; exec. com. 1975—), Order of the Coif, Justinian Honor Soc., Phi Alpha Delta. Author: Cases and Materials for Legislation and Legislative Drafting, 1960; Cases and Materials for Legal Method, 1962; Civil Rights, U.S.A., Public Schools, Cities in the North and West, 1963; Jury Instructions on Medical Issues, 1966; Cases for Antitrust, 1966; Honesty and Competition, False Advertising Law and Policy Under FTC Adminstration, 1967; Commercial Torts, 1973; Cases and Materials on Aerospace Law, 1971; (with Lewin) The Aged and the Need for Surrogate Management, 1972; contbr. articles to law reviews. Office: Univ Santa Clara School Law Santa Clara CA 95053 Tel (408) 984-4361

ALEXANDER, JANE MARIETTA, b. Williamsport, Pa., Nov. 10, 1929; B.S., Dickinson Coll., Carlisle, Pa., 1951, LL.B., 1954, LL.D., 1973. Admitted to Pa. bar; partner firm Alexander, Alexander & Tucker, York, Pa., 1954—, also Dillsburg; dep. sec. of agr. Pa. Dept. Agr., Harrisburg, 1972—; mem. Pa. Ho. of Reps.; dir. Pa. Bur. Foods and Chemistry; mem. Dep. Secs. Ad Hoc Com.; hon. chmn. Pa. Farm/City Week, 1975; mem. Pa. Farm Products Show Commn. Chmn. Pa. Heart Sunday, 1973-74; mem. state adv. council Pa. comprehensive Health Planning; 1st v.p., mem. exec. com., dir. Pa. Lung Assn.; parliamentarian Pa. Fedn. Democratic Women. Mem. York County, Pa., Am. bar assns., Dickinson Sch. Law Alumni Assn. (pres.), Phi Delta Delta (province dir.), Delta Kappa Gamma (hon. mem. Beta Delta chpt.). Recipient Outstanding Alumni award Gen. Alumni Assn. Dickinson Coll., 1974. Home: 148 S Baltimore St Dillsburg PA 17019 Office: 2301 N Cameron St Harrisburg PA 17120 Tel (717) 787-3419

ALEXANDER, JOHN HEALD, b. Denver, Nov. 15, 1904; A.B., Yale U., 1926, LL.B., 1928. Admitted to N.Y. state bar, 1929, N.J. bar, 1943, D.C. bar, 1966; sr. partner firm Mudge, Rose, Guthrie & Alexander, N.Y.C., 1946—; dir. Stone & Webster, Inc., Straight Enterprises, Inc. Chmn. Pres.'s Task Force on Bus. Tax, 1969-70. Mem. Am., N.Y. State bar assns., Assn. Bar City N.Y., Am. Law Inst. Home: 1 Beekman Pl New York City NY 10022 Office: 20 Broad St New York City NY 10005 Tel (212) 422-6767

ALEXANDER, LAWRENCE ALAN, b. Ft. Worth, Sept. 23, 1943; B.A., Williams Coll., 1965; LL.B., Yale, 1968. Admitted to Calif. bar, 1969; research atty. Calif. Ct. Appeals, Los Angeles, 1968-70; prof. law U. San Diego, 1970—. Mem. Am., Calif. State, San Diego County bar assns. Contbr. articles to profl. jours. Home: 6410 Chandler Dr San Diego CA 92117 Office: Alcala Park San Diego CA 92110 Tel (714) 291-6480

ALEXANDER, LEOTA HEIL, b. Riverton, Wyo., June 7, 1941; B.A. with honors, U. Wyo., 1963; J.D. with honors, Tex. Tech. U., 1970. Admitted to Tex. bar, 1970; asst. atty. Lubbock County (Tex.) Atty's. Office, 1970-71; asso. firm Splawn Law Offices, Inc., Lubbock, 1972-73; individual practice law, Lubbock, 1974—; treas. Lubbock County Bar, 1972-73, chmn. legal aid com., 1976; sec. State Tex. Bar, 1975-77. Bd. dirs. Lubbock United Way Agy., 1972-76, So. Plains Info. and Referral Service, 1976. Mem. Tex. Trial Lawyers Assn., Phi Beta Kappa. Office: 1107 Main St Lubbock TX 79401 Tel (806) 763-5231

ALEXANDER, MILES JORDAN, b. Reading, Pa., Nov. 20, 1931; B.A., Emory U., 1952; LL.B., Harvard, 1955. Admitted to Ga. bar, 1955; served with JAGC, USAF, 1955-57; teaching fellow Law Sch. Harvard, Cambridge, Mass., 1957-58; asso. firm Kilpatrick, Cody, Rogers, McClatchey & Regenstein, Atlanta, 1958-63, partner, 1963—. Chmn. Atlanta License Rev. Bd., 1976—; chmn. Am. Jewish Com., Atlanta, 1975—, nat. exec. com., 1976—; S.E. adv. bd. Anti-Defamation League, Atlanta, 1965—; mem. community relations council Jewish Welfare Fedn., 1971—. Mem. Lawyers Club Am., Am., Ga., Atlanta bar assns., ACLU, Harvard Law Sch. Assn. Ga. (pres.), Phi Beta Kappa, Omicron Delta Kappa. Editoral bd. Trademark Reporter, 1971—. Home: 1127 Judith Way Atlanta GA 30324 Office: 3100 Equitable Bldg 100 Peachtree St Atlanta GA 30303 Tel (404) 522-3100

ALEXANDER, RALPH LAWRENCE, b. Edinburg, Tex., Sept. 9, 1928; B.A., U. Tex., 1950, J.D., 1953. Admitted to Tex. bar, 1952, U.S. Supreme Ct. bar, 1973; partner firm Kelley, Looney & Alexander, Edinburg, Tex., since 1953, now mng. partner; atty. City of Donna (Tex.). Bd. regents Pan Am. Coll., 1965-70; mem. Hidalgo County (Tex.) Democratic Exec. Com., 1968; bd. dirs., v.p. Edinburg (Tex.) Indsl. Found., pres., 1969-73; chmn. Edinburg Econ. Devel. Bd., 1969; bd. dirs. Tip of Tex. council Girl Scouts U.S.A., 1970-71; mem. Edinburg Capital Improvement Bd. and Model Cities Planning Council, 1970—; bd. dirs., pres. Community Coordinated Child Care, Inc., 1972—; sec. Greater Edinburg Council, 1972-73; pres. Edinburg United Way, 1974-75; mem. Edinburg Sch. Parent Adv. Council, 1975-76. Mem. San Antonio Trial Lawyers Assn., Tex. Criminal Def. Lawyers, Inter-Am. Bar Assn., Edinburg C. of C. (pres. 1968-69). Recipient Pub. Service award SBA, 1962, Community Leader of Am. award, 1969. Home: 731 Patricia St San Antonio TX 78216 Office: 424 E Nueva by La Villita San Antonio TX 78205 Tel (512) 224-5811

ALEXANDER, TERRY KEITH, b. Spartanburg, S.C., June 25, 1945; B.S., Clemson U., 1968; J.D., U. S.C., 1973. Admitted to S.C. bar, 1973, asso. firm Rentz, Anders & Deberry, Columbia, S.C., 1973-75;

asst. solicitor 5th Jud. Circuit, Columbia, 1975; partner firm Busbee, Hickey & Alexander, Aiken, 1975—; prosecutor City of Aiken, 1976—. Mem. bd. dirs. United Way, Aiken, 1977—. Mem. Am., S.C., Aiken County bar assns., Am. Judicature Soc., Am., S.C. trial lawyers assns. Home: 347 Hillcrest Dr SW Aiken SC 29801 Office: 147 Newberry St NW Aiken SC 29801 Tel (803) 648-3255

ALEXANDER, WILLIAM HENRY, b. Macon, Ga., Dec. 10, 1930; B.S., Ft. Valley State Coll., 1951; J.D., U. Mich., 1956; LL.M., Georgetown U., 1961. Admitted to Ga. bar, 1957, Mich. bar, 1957, U.S. Supreme Ct. bar, 1969; practiced in Atlanta, 1963-75; judge Atlanta City Ct., 1975-76, Fulton County (Ga.) Criminal Ct., 1976-77, State Ct. Fulton County, 1977—; mem. Ga. Ho. of Reps., 1966-75. Mem. State Bar Ga., Atlanta, Am., Gate City bar assns., Practising Law Inst., Lawyers Club Atlanta, Am. Judicature Soc., Am. Judges Assns., Assn. Trial Lawyers Am., Atlanta Legal Aid Soc. (pres. 1973), ACLU (pres. Ga. 1968-69). Home: 3725 Dover Blvd SW Atlanta GA 30331 Office: 160 Pryor St SW Atlanta GA 30303 Tel (404) 572-2737

ALFANO, CHARLES JOSEPH, b. Paterson, N.J., Feb. 23, 1907; B.A., N.Y. U., 1928, J.D., 1931. Admitted to N.J. bar, 1933; individual practice law, Paterson, 1933—; atty. City of Paterson, 1951; judge Paterson Municipal Ct., 1958-66. Mem. N.J., Passaic County bar assns. Home: 17 River St Paterson NJ 07505 Office: 5 Colt St Paterson NJ 07505 Tel (201) 742-5010

ALFANO, CHARLES THOMAS, b. Suffield, Conn., June 21, 1920; B.A. cum laude, U. Conn., 1943; LL.B., U. Mich., 1948. Admitted to Conn. bar, 1948, since practiced in Hartford; judge town ct. Suffield, Conn., 1949-51, 55-59; mem. Conn. Senate, 1959-77, asst. majority leader, 1966, pres. pro tem, 1967-72, minority leader, 1972-75, dep. pres. pro tem, 1975-77; dir. Suffield Savs. Bank, Trustee Conn. Pub. Television, 1972—. Mem. Am., Conn., Hartford County bar assns., Am. Trail Lawyers Assn. Home: 50 Marbern Dr Suffield CT 06078 Office: 100 Constitution Plaza Hartford CT 06103 Tel (203) 527-3225

ALFORD, STEVE A., JR., b. Orange, Tex., Aug. 12, 1920; B.A., U. Southwestern La., 1942; LL.B., La. State U., 1948; grad. Nat. Coll. State Judiciary, 1974. Admitted to La. bar, 1948; individual practice law, 1948—; judge La. Dist. Ct., 19th Jud. Dist., 1971—; atty. La. Dept. Pub. Safety, 1961-69. Gov. La.-Miss.-West Tenn. Dist. Kiwanis Internat., 1962, trustee internat., 1965-70, v.p., 1970. Mem. Am., La. State bar assns., Phi Delta Phi. Home: 750 Marquette St Baton Rouge LA 70806 Office: 1101 Florida St Baton Rouge LA 70802 Tel (504) 343-4861

ALFORD, WILLIAM VAN METER, b. Hartford, Ala., Jan. 27, 1916; B.S., Hampden-Sydney Coll., 1936; LL.B., U. Va., 1947. Admitted to Ky. bar, 1948; with firm McDonald, Alford & Roszell, and predecessors, Lexington, Ky., 1948—, partner, 1956—. Bd. dirs. Lexington YMCA, 195S-60; mem. adv. bd. Salvation Army, Lexington, 1960—; chmn. bd. trustees Lee Jr. Coll., Jackson, Ky., 1967-70; chmn. bd. trustees Transylvania Presbytery, Presbyterian Ch., Lexington, 1969-76. Mem. Am., Ky., Fayette County (chmn. unauthorized practice of law com. 1950-60, pres. 1961-62) bar assns. Home: 2092 Waters Edge St Lexington KY 40502 Office: 156 Market St Lexington KY 40507 Tel (606) 252-8981

ALHADEFF, ELLIOTT RICHARD, b. Montgomery, Ala., Dec. 17, 1943; B.S., U. Ala., 1965, LL.B., 1967; LL.M., U. Miami, 1973. Admitted to Ala. bar, 1967, Fla. bar, 1967, U.S. Supreme Ct. bar, 1971; served with JAGC, U.S. Army, Vietnam, 1969; mem. firm Abbott, Frumkes & Alhadeff, Miami Beach, Fla., 1970—; asso. judge Town of Surfside (Fla.), 1976. Chmn. planning bd. City of Miami Beach. Mem. Am., Fla., Miami Beach (sec., dir.) bar assns., Miami Beach Taxpayers Assn. (pres. 1974), Pres. Council Miami Beach (pres.). Book rev. editor Ala. Law Rev., 1966-67. Office: 420 Lincoln Rd Suite 441 Miami Beach FL 33139 Tel (305) 538-0494

ALHOLM, ANTHONY JOSEPH, b. Chgo., Apr. 19, 1949; B.B.A., U. Notre Dame, 1969, J.D., 1973; postgrad. Faculty of Laws Univ. Coll. U. London, 1971. Admitted to Ill. bar, 1973; asso. firm Graham & Graham, Springfield, Ill., 1973—. Pres. Notre Dame Club of Central Ill. Mem. Sangamon County, Ill. State bar assns. Home: 2154 S Glenwood St Springfield IL 62704 Office: 1201 S 8th St Springfield IL 62703 Tel (207) 523-4569

ALIDOR, GARY PAUL, b. Mobile, Ala., Nov. 5, 1943; A.B., Spring Hill Coll., 1965; J.D., U. Ala., 1968. Admitted to Ala. bar, 1968, U.S. Supreme Ct. bar, 1972; asso. firm Marr & Friedlander, Mobile, 1968-72; individual practice law, Mobile, 1973—. Mem. Am., Fed., Mobile bar assns., Comml. Law League Am., Assn. Trial Lawyers Am. Office: 4367 Downtowner Loop POB 16564 Mobile AL 36616 Tel (205) 342-4762

ALIX, JAMES EDMOND, b. Worcester, Mass., Oct. 27. 1933; B.S. in Chemistry, Holy Cross Coll., Worcester, 1955, M.S. in Chemistry (Univ. fellow), 1956; LL.B., Georgetown U., 1962. Chemist, Union Carbide Corp., Cleve., 1956-59; examiner U.S. Patent Office, Washington, 1959-61; law clk. Chief Judge Worley U.S. Ct. Customs and Patent Appeals, Washington, 1961-62; admitted to Va. bar, 1962, Conn. bar, 1964; asso. firm Prutzman, Hayes, Kalb & Chilton, Hartford, Conn., 1962-66, partner, 1967—. Mem. Hartford County, Conn., Am. bar assns., Am. Conn. (pres. 1974-75) Patent law assns., Am. Chem. Soc. Home: 74 Bainbridge Rd West Hartford CT 06119 Office: 799 Main St Hartford CT 06103 Tel (203) 527-9211

ALLAN, DANIEL W., b. Tulsa, Sept. 11, 1941; B.A., U. Tulsa, 1964, J.D., 1967. Admitted to Okla. bar, 1967; mem. firm Logan, Lowry, Castor & Allan, Vinita, Okla., 1969—. Mem. Okla. Bar Assn., Okla. Trial Lawyers Assn., Am. Judicature Soc. Office: 101 SW Wilson St Vinita OK 74301 Tel (918) 256-7511

ALLAN, HOLLIS PAUL, b. Delphos, Ohio, June 16, 1921; B.A., U. Akron, 1946; J.D., U. Mich., 1949. Admitted to Ohio bar, 1949; asst. law dir. City of Akron, 1949-52; mem. firm Burroughs, Gillen & Allan, Akron, 1952-56; individual practice of law, Akron, 1956-62; asso. prof. law Akron U., 1972—; lawyer Ohio Edison Co., 1962-65, mgr. personnel and indsl. relations, 1965-72. Mem. Am., Ohio State, Akron bar assns., Am. Judicature Soc., Assn. Am. Law Sch. Profs. Home: 1611 Grant Ave Cuyahoga Falls OH 44223 Office: Univ Akron Akron OH 44325 Tel (216) 375-7331

ALLAN, RICHARD, b. N.Y.C., Apr. 15, 1931; B.A., N.Y. U., 1953, LL.B., 1962. Admitted to N.Y. bar, 1962; asst. dist. atty. New York County (N.Y.), 1962-65; partner firm Jesse Moss, Attys. at Law, N.Y.C., 1965-69; asso. firm Kelley, Drye & Warren, N.Y.C., 1969-73; asst. prof. law Bklyn. Law Sch., 1973-75, asso. prof., 1975-77, prof., 1977—; lectr. Inst. Internat. and Comparative Law, Paris, summer 1975. Mem. Bar Assn. City N.Y. Home: 534 LaGuardia Pl New York City NY 10012 Office: 250 Joraleman St Brooklyn NY 11201

ALLAN, RICHMOND FREDERICK, b. Billings, Mont., Apr. 22, 1930; B.A., U. Mont., 1955, J.D., 1957; postgrad. U. London, 1957-58. Admitted to Mont. bar, 1957, D.C. bar, 1965; law clk. to chief judge U.S. Ct. Appeals 9th Circuit, 1958-59; partner firm Kurth, Conner, Jones & Allan, Billings, 1959-61; asst. U.S. atty., Mont., 1961-64; trial atty. Dept. Justice, Washington, 1965; asso. solicitor Dept. Interior, Washington, 1966-67, dep. solicitor, 1968; partner firm Weissbrodt & Weissbrodt, Washington, 1969-76, Casey, Lane & Mittendorf, Washington, 1977—. Mem. Fed. Bar Assn. (pres. Mont. chpt. 1964). Home: 9120 Wooden Bridge Rd Potomac MD 20854 Office: 815 Connecticut Ave NW Washington DC 20006 Tel (202) 285-4949

ALLARD, JEAN, b. Trenton, Mo., Dec. 16, 1924; A.B., Culver-Stockton Coll., 1945; M.A., Washington U., 1947; J.D., U. Chgo., 1953. Admitted to Ill. bar, 1953, Ohio bar, 1959; counselor psychology dept. U. Chgo., 1948-51, v.p. bus. and fin., 1972-75; research asso. U. Chgo. Law Sch., 1953-58, asst. dean, 1956-68; asso. firm Fuller, Harrington, Seney & Henry, Toledo, 1958-59, Lord, Bissell & Brook, Chgo., 1959-62; sec., gen. counsel Maremont Corp., Chgo., 1962-72; partner firm Sonnenschein Carlin Nath & Rosenthal, Chgo., 1976—; dir. Commonwealth Edison Co., Chgo., LaSalle Nat. Bank Chgo., Marshall Field & Co., Chgo., Maremont Corp., Chgo. Trustee Culver-Stockton Coll., 1976—. Mem. Am., Ill., Chgo. bar assns., Am. Soc. Corporate Secs. Home: 5844 Stony Island Ave Chicago IL 60637 Office: 8000 Sears Tower Chicago IL 60606 Tel (312) 876-8057

ALLBRITTON, OWEN SAMPSON, b. Clearwater, Fla., July 25, 1926; J.D., U. Fla., 1951. Admitted to Fla. bar, 1951, U.S. Supreme Ct. bar, 1956; partner firm Allbritton and Barber, Clearwater, Fla., 1966—; asst. city atty., Clearwater, 1956-60; municipal judge, Clearwater, 1960-66; city atty., Indian Rocks Beach, Fla., 1957-72; gen. master 6th Judicial Circuit, 1972—; pres. Fla. Municipal Judges Assn., 1964. Gen. chmn. Clearwater Fun'n Sun Festival, 1958-59. Mem. Am., Fla., Clearwater bar assns., Fla. Trial Lawyers Assn. Home: 305 Jasmine Way Clearwater FL 33516 Office: 425 S Garden Ave Clearwater FL 33517 Tel (813) 446-0528

ALLDREDGE, JOHN BROOKS, b. Cullman, Ala., Dec. 6, 1921; B.A., U. Calif., Berkeley, 1947; J.D., U. Calif., Hastings, 1950. Admitted to Tex. bar, 1952; gen. purchasing agent Gen. Dynamics Corp., Ft. Worth, 1950-63; chief shuttle engring. and equipment procurement br. NASA, Johnson Space Center, Houston, 1963—. Mem. Tex. Bar Assn., Nat. Contract Mgmt. Assn. Address: 1101 W Shoreacres La Porte TX 77571 Tel (713) 471-2523

ALLDREDGE, JOHN CROMER, b. Anderson, Ind., Mar. 6, 1902; student Manchester Coll., 1922-24; B.A., J.D., Ind. U., 1928. Admitted to Ind. bar, 1926, U.S. Supreme Ct. bar, 1969; pros. atty. Madison County (Ind.), 1929-31; pub. defender, 1939-43; dep. atty. gen. State of Ind., 1944-64; individual practice law, Anderson, 1964—. Bd. dirs. Wilson's Boys Club, 1969-74; active Boy Scouts Am., diamond badge for distinguished service, 1968; mem. Madison County Election Bd., 1971-76. Mem. Phi Delta Phi. Home: 609 Hendricks St Anderson IN 46016 Office: 357 Citizens Bank Bldg Anderson IN 46016 Tel (317) 644-5242

ALLEN, A. JACKSON, b. Kellerton, Iowa, May 19, 1930; B.A., State U. Iowa, 1952, J.S., 1957. Admitted to Iowa bar, 1957; partner firm Riehm & Allen, Garner, Iowa, 1957-61; state counsel, asst. atty. gen. State of Iowa, Des Moines, 1961-65, dep. indsl. commr., 1965; asso. firm Hoersch & Werner, Davenport, Iowa, 1965-68; individual practice law, Davenport, 1968-70; sr. asso. Allen Fagan & Van Driel, Davenport, 1970—. Mem. nat. legal com. VFW, 1962-64. Tel (319) 322-5911

ALLEN, ARNON REMINGTON, b. Mauston, Wis., Sept. 10, 1930; B.A., U. Wis., 1952, LL.B., 1957. Admitted to Wis. bar, 1957; asso. McAndrews & Allen and predecessor firms, Madison, Wis., 1957-58, partner, 1958-60; asst. prof. law U. Wis., 1960-61; asst. prof. agrl. law U. Ill., 1961-63; prof. law, agrl. economics U. Wis., 1963—, asso. dean continuing edn. and outreach, U. Wis. Law Sch., 1977—. Home: 109 Island Dr Madison WI 53705 Office: 905 University Av U Wis Madison WI 53706

ALLEN, DAVID GRAY, b. Memphis, Dec. 31, 1932; B.B.A., U. Miami, 1955, J.D., 1963. Admitted to Fla. bar, 1963; asso. firm Copeland, Therrel, Baisden & Peterson, Miami Beach, Fla., 1963-68; asso. firm Snyder, Young, & Stern, North Miami Beach, 1968-70; mem. firm Russo, Van Doren & Allen, Coral Gables, Fla., 1971—. Mem. Fla. Bar Assn. Home: 6460 S W 73rd St South Miami FL 33143 Office: 4685 Ponce de Leon Blvd Coral Gables FL 33146 Tel (305) 665-0414

ALLEN, DAVID JAMES, b. East Chicago, Ind., May 3, 1935; B.S., Ind. U., 1957, A.M.T., 1959, J.D., 1965. Admitted to Ind. bar, 1965; U.S. Supreme Ct. bar, 1968, U.S. Tax Ct., 1967, U.S. Ct. Mil. Appeals, 1968; individual practice law, Terre Haute, Ind., 1969-70, Munster, Ind., 1970-74; partner firm Hagemier, Allen & Smith, Indpls., 1974—; adj. prof. Ind. U., 1977; adminstrv. asst. to Ind. Govs., 1961-69; adminstr. Ind. Traffic Safety Agy., 1966-68; mem. spl. commn. exec. reorgn. State Ind., 1967-69; mem. Ind. Law Enforcement Tng. Bd. and Adv. Council, 1968—; counsel bd. trustees Ind. State U., 1969-70; mem. Pub. Service Commn. State Ind., 1970-75; counsel majority party Ho. Reps. State Ind., 1975-76, spl. counsel majority party Senate State Ind., 1977—. Mem. Ind. State, Am. bar assns. Office: 819 Circle Tower Bldg Indianapolis IN 46204 Tel (317) 632-6661

ALLEN, DAVID LAWRENCE, b. Visalia, Calif., Jan. 20, 1930; B.A., Fresno State U., 1952; LL.B., Hastings Coll. Law, 1955. Admitted to Calif. bar, 1955; counsel Tulare County (Calif.), 1956-58, dept dist. atty., 1958; practiced in Visalia, 1958-72; judge Municipal Ct., Visalia, 1972—; mem. Visalia City Council, 1967-72. Mem. Calif. Trial Lawyer's Assn., Conf. Calif. Judges. Home: 3339 Harvard St Visalia CA 93277 Office: 210 N Church St Visalia CA 93277 Tel (209) 732-3426

ALLEN, E(RNEST) LEE, JR., b. Nashville, Feb. 17, 1936; B.S.B.A., U. Tenn., Knoxville, 1960, LL.B., 1960, J.D., 1966. Admitted to Tenn. bar 1961; asst. cashier Hamilton Nat. Bank, Knoxville, 1962-63; spl. agt. FBI, Cleve. and N.Y.C., 1963-65; asst. met. atty. Met. Govt. of Nashville and Davison County, 1965-67; spl. counsel Davidson County Pub. Defender's Office, 1967-69; mem. firms Gracey, Buck, Maddin and Cowan, 1965-67, Murphy, Gordon and Allen, 1967-68, Wallace, Steele, Allen and Kyle, 1968-76 (all Nashville); staff atty. Tenn. Dept. Employment Security, Nashville, 1976—. Mem. Nashville, Tenn. bar assns. Home: 519 Crieve Rd Nashville TN 37201 Office: 18th Floor 1st American Center Union St Nashville TN 37238 Tel (615) 242-5090

ALLEN, FRANCIS ALFRED, b. Kansas City, Kans., Oct. 25, 1919; A.B., Cornell Coll., 1941; LL.B., Northwestern U., 1946. Admitted to Ill. bar, 1950, Mich. bar, 1968; mem. faculty Northwestern U., 1948-53, Harvard, 1953-56, U. Chgo., 1956-62, 63-66; mem. faculty U. Mich., 1962—, dean Law Sch., 1966-71, Edson R. Sunderland prof. law, 1971—. Chmn. Atty. Gen.'s Com. on Poverty and Fed. Criminal Justice, 1961-63; drafting chmn. Ill. Criminal Code, 1956-62. Fellow Am. Acad. Arts and Scis.; mem. Am. Law Inst. (council 1969-75), Assn. Am. Law Schs. (pres. 1975-76), Am. Bar Assn., Ill. Acad. Criminology (pres. 1961-62), Am. Correctional Assn., Order of Coif, Phi Beta Kappa. Guggenheim fellow, 1971-72; author: The Borderland of Criminal Justice, 1964; The Crimes of Politics, 1974; editor: Standards of American Legislation (Freund), 1965; contbr. articles to law jours. Home: 414 Huntigton Pl Ann Arbor MI 48104 Office: Legal Research Bldg U Mich Ann Arbor MI 48109 Tel (313) 763-4374

ALLEN, FRANKLIN GLENN, b. Athens, Ohio, Sept. 12, 1925; B.A. in Physics, Ohio State U., 1950, J.D., 1952; LL.M. in Antitrust and Securities Law, N.Y. U., 1959; M.B.A. in Finance, U. Chgo., 1963. Admitted to Ill. bar, 1952, Ohio bar, 1952, N.Y. State bar, 1956; asso. firm Vedder Price Kaufman & Kammholz, Chgo., 1952-53, Hume, Clement, Brinks, Willian & Olds, Chgo., 1953-54, David Polk & Wardwell, N.Y.C., 1954-57; asst. sec. Dyson Kissner Corp., N.Y.C., 1957-64; v.p., gen. counsel, sec. The Marmon Group, Inc., Chgo., 1964-69; corp. partner firm Sachnoff Schrager Jones & Weaver, Chgo., 1969—. Mem. Am., Ill., Chgo. bar assns. Home: 1321 W Berwyn Ave Chicago IL 60640 Office: One IBM Plaza Suite 4700 Chicago IL 60611 Tel (312) 644-2400

ALLEN, GEORGE VENABLE, JR., b. Athens, Greece, Dec. 10, 1935; B.A., Princeton, 1958; LL.B., U. Va., 1962. Admitted to Va. bar, 1962, D.C. bar, 1963; asso. firm Covington & Burling, Washington, 1962-68; mem. bd. mine safety appeals Dept. of Interior, Washington, 1969; dep. asst. adminstr. for enforcement EPA, Washington, 1970-73; partner firm Shaw, Pittman, Potts & Trowbridge, Washington, 1973—; gen. counsel Planned Parenthood of Washington, 1966-69. Mem. D.C., Va. bar assns. Home: 3100 Foxhall Rd NW Washington DC 20016 Office: 1800 M St NW Washington DC 20016 Tel (202) 331-4100

ALLEN, GRANT ROBERT, b. Marshall County, Ind., July 31, 1905; A.B., U. Notre Dame, 1928, J.D., 1930. Admitted to Ind. bar, 1930, U.S. Supreme Ct. bar, 1940; dep. pros. atty. St. Joseph County (Ind.), 1935-36; mem. 76th-80th Congresses from 3rd Ind. Dist.; judge U.S. Dist. Ct., No. Dist. Ind., 1957-61, chief judge, 1961-72, sr. judge, 1972—; appointee Temporary Emergency Ct. Appeals U.S., 1976—. Chmn. bd. trustees St. Josephs Hosp., S. Bend, Ind.; trustee Ind. Central U. Mem. Am., Ind., St. Joseph County bar assns. Home: 98 Schellinger Sq Mishawaka IN 46544 Office: US Dist Ct Fed Bldg South Bend IN 46601 Tel (219) 232-4236

ALLEN, HARRY BERKLEY, b. Portland, Oreg., Aug. 4, 1916; A.B., U. Calif., Los Angeles, 1939, M.A., 1941; Ph.D., Calif. Inst. Tech., 1949; LL.B., George Washington U., 1966, J.D., 1968. Admitted to D.C. bar, 1967, Md. bar, 1967; U.S. Supreme Ct. bar, 1970; partner firm McDonough & Allen, Oxon Hill, Md., 1967-68; asso. firm Giordano Alexander & Haas & Mahoney, Oxon Hill, 1970-72; sr. partner firm Allen & Marzetti, Oxon Hill, 1972—. Bd. dirs. Am. Cancer Soc., 1972—. Mem. Am., Md., Prince George County bar assns., Am. Trial Lawyers Assn. Home: 4605 Sharon St Temple Hills MD 20031 Office: 6188 Oxon Hill Rd Oxon Hill MD 20021 Tel (301) 839-3600

ALLEN, HENRY WILLIAM, b. Nevada, Mo., Apr. 7, 1944; B.A., Southwestern at Memphis, 1966; J.D., Washington U., St. Louis, 1969; postgrad. Northwestern U. Law Sch., 1969-70. Admitted to Ark., Mo., Ill. bar, 1969; asst. U.S. atty. Dept. Justice, Chgo., 1969-70; spl. asst. to pres. Am. Bar Assn., Chgo., 1970-71; mem. firm Wright, Lindsey & Jennings, Little Rock, 1971—. Bd. dirs. Little Rock Presbyn. Urban Council, 1974-75; deacon 2d Presbyn. Ch., Little Rock, 1973-76. Mem. Am. (bd. govs.), Ark., Mo., Ill. bar assns. Home: 5708 N Country Club Rd Little Rock AR 72207 Office: 2200 Worthen Bank Bldg Little Rock AR 72201 Tel (501) 371-0808

ALLEN, JAMES TRUEMAN, b. El Paso, Tex., Jan. 16, 1943; B.A., U. Tex., 1965, J.D., 1968. Admitted to Tex. bar, 1968, U.S. Supreme Ct. bar, 1976; mem. firm Yetter, Johnson & Allen, El Paso, 1968-72, firm Johnson, Allen & Aycock, El Paso, 1972—. Mem. Am., Tex., El Paso, Fed. bar assns., El Paso Trial Lawyers Assn. Home: 2008 Solano St El Paso TX 79935 Office: 5959 Gateway W Suite 542 El Paso TX 79925 Tel (915) 779-3571

ALLEN, JOHN BAKER, JR., b. Columbia, S.C., Oct. 31, 1940; A.B., U. S.C., 1963, J.D., 1972. Admitted to S.C. bar, 1972, U.S. Supreme Ct. bar, 1976; claims adjuster S.C. Gen. Adjustment Bur., Columbia and Charleston, 1963-65; claims rep. So. Farm Bur. Ins. Co., Orangeburg, S.C., 1965-67; sr. claims rep. So. Farm Bur. Casualty Ins. Co., Columbia, 1967-69, subrogation examiner, 1969-72, dist. claims mgr., 1972-73; individual practice law, 1973-76; sr. partner firm Allen & Cox, Columbia, 1976—. Mem. Richland County, S.C., Am. bar assns., Am., S.C. trial lawyers assns. Office: PO Box 9507 Columbia SC 29290 Tel (803) 776-8380

ALLEN, JOHN CHARLES, b. Los Angeles, June 30, 1916; B.B.A., U. Calif., Los Angeles, 1938; J.D. (Archbald Mayo scholar), U. So. Calif., 1941. Admitted to Calif. bar, 1941; law sec. to justice Calif. State Supreme Ct., San Francisco, 1942; mem. firm Highsmith & Allen, Los Angeles, 1949-55; individual practice law, Los Angeles, 1955-61; served with JAGC, Korea, 1950-52; pres. Nettleship Co., ins. brokerage, Los Angeles, 1961—. Mem. Los Angeles Bar Assn., State Bar Calif., Med-Legal Soc. Editorial bd. U. So. Calif. Law Rev., 1941. Home: 1800 Cielito Dr Glendale CA 91207 Office: 1200 Wilshire Dr Los Angeles CA 90017 Tel (213) 482-4610

ALLEN, JOHN EDWARD, b. Jacksonville, Fla., May 30, 1948; B.B.A., U. Ga., 1970, J.D., 1973. Admitted to Ga. bar, 1973; asso. firm Fortson, Bentley & Griffin, Athens, Ga., 1973—. Mem. Western Circuit, Athens (sec. 1976—) bar assns., Ga. Trial Lawyers Assn. Home: 480 Highland Ave Athens GA 30601 Office: PO Box 1744 Athens GA 30601 Tel (404) 548-1151

ALLEN, JULIAN BERNARD, b. Jacksonville, Fla., Mar. 4, 1931; A.B., U. Mich., 1953; J.D., Cleve. State U., 1963. Admitted to Ohio bar, 1963, Ind. bar, 1963; since practiced in Gary; partner firm Shropshire & Allen and predecessors, 1964—; bd. dirs. Lake County Economic Opportunity Council, 1965-68; bd. dirs., legal counsel Planned Parenthood NW Ind., Inc., 1964-75; bd. dirs., pres. Legal Aid

Soc. NW Ind., 1966-67; bd. dirs. Mental Health NW Ind., 1966-68; bd. dirs. Planned Parenthood Fedn. Am., 1968-74, regional rep., 1970-72, chmn. exec. com., 1972-74; bd. dirs. Ind. Family Planning and Health Council, Inc., 1976. Mem. Nat., Ind., Gary, Lake County (sec.-treas. 1968-69, pres. 1970-71), Hoosier State bar assns., Nat. Conf. Black Lawyers, Thurgood Marshall Law Assn. (pres. 1976—). Home: 237 McKinley Gary IN 46404 Office: 2009 Broadway Gary IN 46407 Tel (219) 886-3666

ALLEN, LAURENCE CAME, b. Sanford, Maine, Aug. 5, 1899; B.A., Bowdoin Coll., 1923; student Harvard Law Sch., 1923-24. Admitted to Maine bar, 1926; individual practice law, Sanford, 1926—; clk., atty. Capitol Realty Corp., 1931-68; owner, operator, profl. counsel Allen's Motel & Chateau, Sanford, 1931—. Mem. Harvard Law Sch. Assn., Am. Judicature Soc., Am., Maine, York County bar assns. Home and office: 279 Main St Sanford ME 04073 Tel (207) 324-2160

ALLEN, LAYMAN EDWARD, b. Turtle Creek, Pa., June 9, 1927; student Washington and Jefferson Coll., 1946-47; A.B., Princeton, 1951; M.P.A., Harvard, 1952; LL.B., Yale, 1956. Admitted to Conn. bar, 1956; faculty Yale Law Sch., 1957-65; prof. law U. Mich., 1966—; mem. adv. com. on personal data systems HEW, 1971-73. Trustee Center for Responsive Law, 1967—. Mem. Am. Bar Assn. (council sect. sci. and tech.), Assn. for Symbolic Logic, AAAS, Nat. Council Tchrs. Math., N.Am. Simulation and Gaming Assn. Fellow Center for Advanced Study in the Behavioral Scis.; mem. Law Sch. Admissions Council Test Research and Devel. Com.; mem. Shepard's Editorial Adv. Bd.; author: Communications Science and Law, 1963; Wif 'n Proof, 1961; Equations, 1964; contbr. articles to profl. jours. Home: 1407 Brooklyn Ave Ann Arbor MI 48104 Office: Law Sch U Mich Ann Arbor MI 48109 Tel (313) 764-9339

ALLEN, LEON ARTHUR, JR., b. Springfield, Mass., July 15, 1933; B.E.E., Cornell U., 1955; postgrad. U. Denver, 1957-58; LL.B., N.Y. U., 1964. Engr., Phila. Elec. Co., 1955-56; tech. editor McGraw-Hill Pub. Co., N.Y.C., 1958-62; cons. engr. Gilbert Assos., Inc., N.Y.C., 1962-64; admitted to N.Y. bar, 1964; asso. firm LeBoeuf, Lamb, Leiby & MacRae, N.Y.C., 1964-71, partner, 1971—. Mem. Am., Fed. Power bar assns., Assn. Bar City N.Y. (chmn. adminstrv. law com. 1972-74). Home: 530 E 86th St New York City NY 10028 Office: 140 Broadway New York City NY 10005 Tel (212) 269-1100

ALLEN, MARTIN, b. Chgo., Dec. 9, 1943; student U. Ill., 1962, B.S., 1966; J.D., Ind. U., 1971. Admitted to Ill. bar, 1971; tax accountant Sinclair Refining Co., Chgo., 1967-68; jr. partner firm Morton, Jaffe, Levy & Katfes, Chgo., 1971-74; mgr. Halsted Auto Wreckers, Chgo., 1973—. Mem. Am., Ill., Chgo. bar assns. Home: 3037 Barclay St Wilmette IL 60091 Office: 660 Halsted St Chicago IL 60622 Tel (312) SE8-0286

ALLEN, MERLE MAESER, JR., b. Prescott, Ariz., June 6, 1932; B.S. in Mktg., Brigham Young U., 1954; J.D., U. Ariz., 1960. Admitted to Ariz. bar, 1960; asso. firm Moore, Romley, Kaplan, Robbins & Green, Phoenix, 1966-73; partner firm Moore & Romley, Phoenix, 1966-73; partner firm Udall, Shumway, Blackhurst, Allen, Bentley & Lyons, Mesa, Ariz., 1973—. Bd. dirs. Mesa YMCA, 1974—; active Boy Scouts Am., 1966—. Mem. State Bar Ariz., Fedn. Ins. Counsel. Recipient spl. award ASCAP, 1960. Home: 904 N Heritage St Mesa AZ 85201 Office: 30 W 1st St Mesa AZ 85201 Tel (602) 834-7200

ALLEN, MICHAEL CHARLES, b. Denver, July 14, 1945; B.S. in Bus., W.Va. U., 1967, J.D., 1971. Admitted to W.Va. bar, 1971; asso. firm Jackson Kelly Holt and O'Farrell, Charleston, W.Va., 1971-73; individual practice law, Charleston, 1973—; adminstrv. hearings examiner Workman's Compensation Commn., 1974. Mem. Charleston Human Rights Commn., 1974—. Office: Suite 513 240 Capitol St Charleston WV 25314 Tel (304) 344-8345

ALLEN, PHILLIP ELWOOD, b. Joplin, Mo., Jan. 18, 1931; B.S. in Bus. Adminstrn., U. Ark., 1959; J.D., 1962. Admitted to Ark. bar, 1962, Ky. bar, 1971; asso. firm Rose, Meek, House, Barron, Nash & Williamson, Little Rock, 1962-64, partner, 1965-67; individual practice law, Little Rock, 1968; partner firm Allen, Dahlen & Young, Little Rock, 1969-71; individual practice law, Louisville, 1971—. Mem. Am., Ark., Ky., Louisville bar assns., Am. Judicature Soc. Editor in chief Ark. Law Rev., 1961-62. Home: 703 Circle Hill Rd Louisville KY 40207 Office: Suite 307 400 Sherburn Ln Louisville KY 40207 Tel (502) 897-6479

ALLEN, RICHARD BLOSE, b. Aledo, Ill., May 10, 1919; B.S., U. Ill., 1941, J.D., 1947. Admitted to Ill., bar, 1947, U.S. Supreme Ct. bar, 1967; asst. editor Am. Bar Assn. Jour., Chgo., 1947-48, 63-67, exec. editor, 1967-70, editor, 1970—; partner firm Allen & Allen, Aledo, Ill., 1949-57; gen. counsel Ill. State Bar Assn., Springfield, 1957-63. Mem. Am., Ill. Chgo. bar assns., Am. Judicature Soc., Selden Soc., Scribes, Sigma Delta Chi, Phi Delta Phi. Home: 702 Illinois Rd Wilmette IL 60091 Office: 775 Wacker Dr Chicago IL 60606 Tel (312) 947-4150

ALLEN, RICHARD CHESTER, b. Swampscott, Mass., Jan. 24, 1926; A.B., Washington U., 1948, J.D., 1950; LL.M., U. Mich., 1963. Admitted to Mo. bar, 1950, Kans. bar, 1956, Minn. bar, 1976; asso. firm Thompson, Mitchell, Thompson & Douglas, St. Louis, 1950; atty. gen. legal dept. Southwestern Bell Telephone Co., St. Louis, 1952-56, area counsel Topeka, 1956-59; partner firm Gray & Allen, Topeka, 1956-59; joint faculty Washburn U. and Menninger Sch. Psychiatry, Topeka, 1959-63; asso. prof. law. George Washington U., 1963-65, prof. law, dir. inst. law, psychiatry and criminology, 1965-76, chmn. dept. forensic scis., 1973-76; dean Hamline U. Sch. Law, St. Paul, 1976—; mem. Nat. Adv. Council on Correctional Manpower and Tng., Washington, 1967-70; cons. Pres.'s. Com. on Mental Retardation, Washington, 1963-73; editor-in-chief MH Jour., Nat. Assn. Mental Health, 1972-76. Trustee Forensic Scis. Found., 1974—. Fellow Am. Acad. Forensic Sciences; mem. Am., Mo., Kans., Minn. (bd. govs.) bar assns., Nat. Council on Crime and Delinquency, Internat. Assn. Penal Law, Am. Trial Lawyers Assn., ACLU (chmn. nat. right to privacy com. 1969-72), Mental Health Assn. Minn. (dir.), Minn. Civil Liberties Union (dir.). Author: Readings in Law and Psychiatry, 1963, 2d edit., 1975; Mental Impairment and Legal Incompetency, 1968; Legal Rights of the Disabled and Disadvantaged, 1969; contbr. articles to legal jours. Home: apt 815 2835 Rice St Roseville MN 55113 Office: Hamline Univ Sch Law Saint Paul MN 55104 Tel (612) 641-2342

ALLEN, RICHARD FRANKLIN, b. Oakland, Calif., Aug. 23, 1933; B.A., Yale, 1955; LL.B., Georgetown U., 1961. Admitted to Wash. State Supreme Ct. bar, 1961, U.S. Dist. Ct. bar for Western Dist. Wash., 1961, U.S. Ct. Appeals bar, 9th Circuit, 1965, U.S. Customs Ct. bar, 1967; partner firm Lane, Powell, Moss & Miller, Seattle, 1961—; served with JAGC, USNR. Mem. Puget Sound Navigator Safety Commn., 1974. Mem. Am., Wash. State, Seattle-King County bar assns., Maritime Law Assn., Fedn. Ins. Counsel, Lawyer-Pilots Bar Assn. Home: 103 96th St NE Bellevue WA 98004 Office: 1700 Washington Bldg Seattle WA 98101 Tel (206) 223-7000

ALLEN, RICHARD H., b. Wilmington, Del., May 16, 1932; A.B., Bowdoin Coll., 1954; J.D., U. Chgo., 1959. Admitted to Del. bar, 1959, Pa. bar, 1969; asso. firm Morris, Nichols, Arsht & Tunnell, Wilmington, 1959-63; atty. Atlas Chem. Industries, Inc., Wilmington, 1963-66; asst. gen. counsel Rockwell Internat. Corp., Pitts., 1966-76; gen. counsel, sec. Incom Internat, Inc., Pitts., 1976—; counsel Del. Human Relations Council, 1964-66; trustee Pa. Bar Ins. Fund, 1972-75. Pres. bd. trustees Fox Chapel Country Day Sch., Pitts., 1973-74. Mem. Am., Pa. Allegheny County (Pa.) bar assns. Home: 8202 Brittany Pl Pittsburgh PA 15237 Office: 415 Holiday Dr Pittsburgh PA 15220 Tel (412) 928-3237

ALLEN, RICHARD MCNIEL, b. Moorhead, Miss., Dec. 10, 1925; student Sunflower Jr. Coll., Millsaps Coll.; LL.B., U. Miss., 1950, J.D., 1950. Admitted to Miss. bar, 1950; partner firm Allen & Allen, 1950-60; partner firm Cooper and Allen, Indianola, Miss., 1960—. Chmn. Sunflower County Democratic Exec. com.; trustee Sunflower County Library. Mem. Am., Miss., Sunflower County bar assns. Office: 115 Main St PO Box 688 Indianola MS 38751 Tel (601) 887-2878

ALLEN, ROBERT FRANK, b. Jackson Twp., Ohio, Jan. 6, 1906; student Ohio No. U., 1926-29. Admitted to Ohio bar, 1930; practiced in Richwood, Ohio, 1930-60; judge probate and juvenile divs. Union County (Ohio) Ct. Common Pleas, 1960—; solicitor City of Richwood, 1931-55. Pres. Lions Club, Richwood, 1935-36. Mem. Union County (pres. 1940-41), Ohio State bar assns., Ohio Assn. Common Pleas Judges, Nat. Council Juvenile Ct. Judges, Delta Theta Phi. Recipient award A Rugged Man's Life, 1968. Office: Probate and Juvenile Ct Courthouse Marysville OH 43040 Tel (513) 642-7085

ALLEN, ROBERT TALCOTT, b. Oct. 30, 1914; B.A., U. Calif., Berkeley, 1936, J.D., 1939. Admitted to Calif. bar, 1936; mem. legal dept. Pacific Gas & Electric. Co., 1937; individual practice law, Oakland, Calif., 1937-41, Berkeley, 1947—; prof. law Lincoln U., also pres. Univ.; prof. law Armstrong Coll., 1969—. Pres. Berkeley council Camp Fire Girls; bd. dirs. Armstrong Coll., 1970—. Mem. Calif., Alameda County, Berkeley-Albany bar assns. Home: 131 La Salle Ave Piedmont CA 94610 Office: 2140 Shattuck Ave Berkeley CA 94704 Tel (415) 848-6697

ALLEN, ROBERT WILSON, b. Los Angeles, Sept. 13, 1919; A.B., U. Calif., Los Angeles, 1942; A.M., So. Meth. U., 1947; Docteur, U. Paris, 1952; LL.B., John Marshall U., 1961, J.D., 1962. Admitted to Ga. bar, 1963; individual practice law, Oxford, Ga., 1963—, Covington, Ga., 1968—; mem. faculty Emory U., Oxford, 1953-68; justice 1525th Dist. Ga. Militia, 1965—; judge Recorder's Ct., City of Oxford, 1974—, City of Porterdale (Ga.), 1975—. Mem. Ga., Alcovy Jud. Circuit bar assns., Lambda Phi Alpha. Home: 309 W Stone St Oxford GA 30267 Office: 8 Starr Bldg 1112 Monticello St SW Covington GA 30209 Tel (404) 786-3027

ALLEN, ROLAND HAROLD, b. Waco, Tex., Apr. 16, 1921; J.D., Baylor U., 1951. Admitted to Tex. bar, 1951, U.S. Supreme Ct. bar, 1973; law clk., liaison for mil. and vets. affairs U.S. Congressman W.R. Poage, Washington, 1951-52; partner firm Gassaway & Allen and predecessors, Borger, Tex., 1953-68; asst. atty. gen. State of Tex., Austin, 1969—. Precinct chmn. Democratic Party, Borger, 1960-62; mem. Borger Tax Equalization Bd., 1965-67, chmn., 1967; bd. dirs. Hutchinson County (Tex.) Child Welfare, 1967-69. Mem. State Bar Tex., Am., Travis County (Tex.) bar assns., Am. Judicature Soc., Supreme Ct. Hist. Soc. Home: 2903 Clarice Ct Austin TX 78731 Office: B-424 Supreme Ct Bldg Austin TX 78701 Tel (512) 475-3131

ALLEN, THOMAS DRAPER, b. Detroit, June 25, 1926; B.S., Northwestern U., 1949; J.D., U. Mich., 1952. Admitted to Ill. bar, 1952; asso. firm Kirkland & Ellis, Chgo., 1952-60, partner, 1961-67; partner firm Wildman Harrold Allen & Dixon, Chgo., 1967—. Mem. Hinsdale (Ill.) Bd. Edn., 1965-71, pres., 1971; v.p. W. Suburban Council Boy Scouts Am., 1972—, chmn. nat. scout advancement subcom., 1976—; chmn. Hinsdale Community Caucus, 1960-61. Fellow Am. Coll. Trial Lawyers; mem. Am., Ill., Chgo. (past chmn. civil practice com., vice-chmn. legis. com. 1975—), DuPage County bar assns., Law Club Chgo., Legal Club Chgo., Soc. Trial Lawyers. Home: 940 Taft Rd Hinsdale IL 60521 Office: Wildman Harrold Allen & Dixon One IBM Plaza Suite 3000 Chicago IL 60611 Tel (312) 222-0400

ALLEN, THOMAS ERNEST, b. Salt Lake City, Sept. 30, 1939; A.B., Dartmouth Coll., 1961; J.D., U. Mich., 1967. Admitted to Minn. bar, 1967, Mo. bar, 1976; partner firm Peterson, Peterson & Allen, Albert Lea, Minn., 1967-76; asso. firm Biggs, Curtis, Casserly and Barnes, St. Louis, 1976-77; partner firm Curtis, Crossen, Hensley, Allen & Curtis, Clayton, Mo., 1977—. Chmn. Freeborn County (Minn.) Republican party, 1970-72; mem. Overall Econ. Devel. Com. Freeborn County, 1975-76. Mem. Am., Minn., Mo., Freeborn County (pres. 1974) bar assns., Bar Assn. Met. St. Louis. Home: Miriam St Kirkwood MO 63122 Office: 7912 Bonhomme St Room 304 Clayton MO 63105 Tel (314) 725-8788

ALLEN, T(HOMAS) EUGENE, III, b. Columbia, S.C., Aug. 29, 1944; B.A., U. S.C., 1966, J.D., 1969. Admitted to S.C. bar, 1969; partner firm Nexsen, Pruet, Jacobs & Pollard, Columbia, 1969—. Chmn. Columbia group Sierra Club. Mem. Am., S.C., Richland County (S.C.) bar assns., S.C. Def. Attys., Columbia Young Lawyers Club, Phi Alpha Delta, Wig and Robe Soc. Author: The Building Permit and Reliance Thereon, 1969. Home: 917 Rolling View Ln Columbia SC 29210 Office: First Nat Bank Bldg Columbia SC 29201 Tel (803) 771-8900

ALLEN, THOMAS FREDERICK, b. Boston, Nov. 11, 1907; LL.B., Suffolk Law Sch., 1930; postgrad. Harvard, 1936, 38. Admitted to Mass. bar, 1932; with firm Schneider, Reilly & McArdle, Boston, 1954-60, Schneider & Reilly, Boston, 1960-70, Robert L. Schneider, Randolph, Mass., 1970. Asst. registrar voters City of Boston, 1956-60. Mem. Mass. Bar Assn., Assn. Trial Lawyers Am., Credit Union League. Home: 293 W Squantum St N Quincy MA 02171 Tel (617) 328-3191

ALLEN, TOM MORRIS, b. Columbus, Ga., July 31, 1926; J.D., U. Ga., 1953. Admitted to Ga. bar, 1953; individual practice law, Decatur, 1954-56; asso. firm Allen, Smith & Tomlinson and predecessor firms, 1956-72; judge Superior Ct., Stone Mountain Jud. Circuit, 1972-76; practice law, Atlanta, 1977—; mem. adv. com. Atlanta Restitution Shelter; mem. adv. com. on ct. structure to Juvenile Justice Masterplan Steering Com. Scoutmaster, neighborhood commr., instl. rep., Explorer rep. Boy Socuts Am., 1954-70; past pres. Decatur Civitan Club; chmn. bd. DeKalb Police Athletic League, 1973-57. Mem. Am. (chmn. subcom. of family law sect.), Ga. bar assns. Author foreward to 2d edit. Georgia Juvenile Law (Paul S. Liston), 1975; Ga.'s on-line selection juries by computer legislation, model family ct. and law proposals; lectr. in field. Office: 53 6th St Atlanta GA 30308 Tel (404) 881-1573

ALLEN, VIRGINIA LEE, b. Montrose, Colo., May 26, 1919; LL.B. with distinction, Pacific Coast U., 1948. Admitted to Calif. bar, 1949; individual practice law, Huntington Park and Downey, Calif., 1952—; dep. city atty. City of Maywood (Calif.), 1973-75. Mem. S.E. Dist. (pres. 1968), Los Angeles County bar assns. Tel (213) 923-3244

ALLEN, WALTER DICKEY, b. Worcester, Mass., Mar. 15, 1896; LL.B. magna cum laude, Boston U., 1917. Admitted to Mass. bar, 1917, U.S. Supreme Ct. bar; mem. Common Council, Worcester, 1921-22; mem. Mass. Legislature, 1923-26; asst. city Solicitor, Worcester, 1926-32, city solicitor, 1932-47; justice Central Dist. Ct. Worcester County, 1947-73, 1st justice, 1963-73; ltd. practice law, Harwich, 1973—; mem. administrv. com. Mass. Dist. Ct., 1963-73, appellate div. Mass. Dist. Cts., 1962-73. Mem. Worcester County, Mass. bar assns., Phi Delta Phi. Address: 56 Oak St PO Box 677 Harwich MA 02645 Tel (617) 432-1618

ALLEN, WILLIAM GARRISON, b. Dixon Springs, Tenn., Oct. 15, 1919; B.S., U. Ala., 1941; LL.B., Cumberland Law Sch., 1947. Admitted to Tenn. bar, 1947, D.C. bar, 1971, Ky. bar, 1974; partner firm MacFarland and Allen, Columbia, Tenn., 1947-52, Ortman, Welch and Allen, D.C., 1971-73; gen. counsel Island Creek Coal Co., Lexington, Ky., 1973—; adminstrv. asst. U.S. Senator Albert Gore, 1953-71. Mem. Ky., D.C. bar assns. Home: 3337 Overbrook Dr Lexington KY 40502 Office: 2355 Harrodsburg Rd PO Box 11430 Lexington KY 40511 Tel (506) 276-1525

ALLEN, WILLIAM HAYES, b. Palo Alto, Calif., Oct. 19, 1926; student Deep Springs Coll., 1942-44; B.A., Stanford U., 1948, LL.B., 1956. Admitted to D.C. bar, 1958; law clk. U.S. Supreme Ct., 1956-57; asso. firm Covington & Burling, Washington, 1957-64, partner, 1964—; chmn. jud. rev. com. Adminstrv. Conf. U.S., 1972—. Mem. Fair Housing Bd. Arlington County (Va.), 1974—. Mem. Am. (council adminstrv. law sect. 1969-72), D.C. bar assns., D.C. Bar (legal ethics com. 1974—, chmn. 1976—), Am. Law Inst., Order of Coif. Contbr. articles to legal jours. Home: 3036 N Pollard St Arlington VA 22207 Office: 888 16th St NW Washington DC 20006 Tel (202) 452-6192

ALLEN, WILLIAM HOWARD, b. Spokane, Wash., Jan. 3, 1917; B.A., Minot (N.D.) State Coll., 1938; LL.B., U. Colo., 1948. Admitted to Colo. bar, 1948; partner firm, Ft. Collins, Colo., 1948-51; sr. partner firm Allen, Stover and Mitchell, Ft. Collins, 1951-67; sr. partner firm Allen, Mitchell, Rogers and Metcalf, Ft. Collins, 1967—. Pres. Larimer County (Colo.) Red Cross, 1950; mayor City of Ft. Collins, 1955-58; pres. Poudre R-1 Sch. Dist., Larimer County, 1960-64. Mem. Am., Colo., Larimer County (pres. 1960) bar assns., Ft. Collins Area C. of C. (pres. 1973). Home: 2408 N County Rd 9 Fort Collins CO 80521 Office: 300 W Oak St Fort Collins CO 80521 Tel (303) 482-5058

ALLEN, WILLIAM LEROY, III, b. Louisville, Aug. 10, 1943; B.A., Pepperdine U., 1965; J.D., U. Louisville, 1968. Admitted to Ind. bar, 1968; partner firm Hanger, Allen & Engebretson, and predecessor, Clarksville, Ind., 1968—; judge Jeffersonville (Ind.) City Ct., 1968-74. Mem. Am., Ind. trial lawyers assns., Ind. State, Am., Clark County bar assns. Named Outstanding Grad. Pepperdine U., 1965, recipient Alumni award, 1965; Founder's award Pepperdine U. Alumni Assn., 1976. Home: 304 Whippoorwill Heights New Albany IN 47150 Office: 321 E Brooks Ave Clarksville IN 47130 Tel (812) 283-7928

ALLEN, WILLIE GEORGE, b. Sanford, Fla., Mar. 3, 1936; B.A., Fla. A. and M. U., 1958; J.D., U. Fla., 1962. Admitted to Fla. bar, 1963; mem. firm Allen & Brown, Ft. Lauderdale, Fla., 1963—. Mem. Nat. (pres. 1975-76), Am. (bd. govs. 1976-77), Fla. bar assns. Recipient Meritorious award Fla. A. and M. U., 1974; NAACP award, 1962. Home: 2161 NW 30th Ave Fort Lauderdale FL 33311 Office: 116 S E 6th Ct Fort Lauderdale FL 33301 Tel (305) 463-6681

ALLEY, GRANVILLE MASON, JR., b. El Dorado, Ark., Jan. 8, 1929; B.A., John B. Stetson U., 1950; J.D., U. Ala., 1952; LL.M. in Labor Law, Columbia, 1953. Admitted to Ala. bar, 1951, Fla. bar, 1952; partner firm Fowler, White, Gillen, Humkey & Trenam, Tampa, Fla., 1953-68; sr. partner firm Alley & Alley, Tampa, and Miami, Fla., 1968—; chmn. Coll. of Law labor relations forums John B. Stetson U., 1955—, vis. prof. labor law, 1955—. Bd. dirs. Nat. right to work Com., 1959-65; mem. nat. panel Am. Arbitration Assn. Mem. Dade County (Fla.), Hillsborough Tampa, Orange County (Fla.), Am., Fed. bar assns., Fla. Bar (past chmn. com. labor relations). Contbr. articles to profl. publs. Office: 205 Brush Ave POB 1427 Tampa FL 33601 Tel (305) 856-2810 also 2412 S Dixie Hwy POB 450547 Miami FL Tel (813) 229-6481

ALLEY, JOHN-EDWARD, b. El Dorado, Ark., 1940; B.S. in Econs. and Accounting, U. Fla., 1962, J.D., 1965; LL.M., N.Y.U., 1968. Admitted to Fla. bar, 1966; asso. firm Clayton, Arnow, Duncan, Johnston, Clayton & Quincey, Gainesville, Fla., 1966-67; asso. firm Paul & Thomson, Miami, Fla., 1969-71, partner, 1971-74; partner firm Alley and Alley, Tampa and Miami, 1974-75, mng. partner, 1975—; adj. prof. labor relations law Stetson U. Coll. Law, 1975—; asst. prof. social scis. U. Fla., 1965-67, adj. prof. Coll. Bus. Adminstrn., 1974—. Mem. Am., Dade, Hillsborough-Tampa and Orange Counties bar assns., The Fla. Bar. Contbr. articles to profl. jours. Office: 205 Brush Ave Tampa FL 33602 Tel (813) 229-6481 also 2412 S Dixie Hwy Miami FL 33145 Tel (305) 856-2810

ALLISON, DANIEL BOONE, II, b. Seattle, Nov. 9, 1939; B.A., Yale, 1961; J.D., Stanford, 1964. Admitted to Wash., Calif. bars, 1965, N.Y. bar, 1966; prin. Allison & Allison, Seattle. Mem. Am. (sect. on real property, probate and trust law, also tax law), Wash. State (sect. on corp. bus. and banking law, sect. on real property, probate and trust law, sect. on tax law), Seattle-King County (sect. on adminstrv. law, sect. on internat. and comparative law, sect. on municipal law, sect. on real property, probate and trust law, sect. on tax law) bar assns. Office: Suite 910 Bank of California Center Seattle WA 98164 Tel (206) 682-1780

ALLISON, MARSHALL LORETZ, b. Lavonia, Ga., Mar. 3, 1897; A.A., Young Harris Coll., 1915. Admitted to Ga. bar, 1926, U.S. Supreme Ct. bar, 1936; city atty. Lavonia, 1927-36; asst. atty. gen. Ga., Atlanta, 1937-38, 38-41, 43-45; judge Superior Ct. No. Jud. Circuit Ga., Lavonia, 1938; law asst. Supreme Ct. Ga., Atlanta, 1942-43; individual practice law, Atlanta, 1945-53, Lavonia, 1953—.

Trustee Young Harris Coll., 1942—. Mem. Am., Ga., No. Circuit bar assns. Home and Office: 55 Bowman St Lavonia GA 30553 Tel (404) 356-8207

ALLISON, PAUL JUDSON, b. Tacoma, Wash., Nov. 5, 1926; B.A., Wash. State U., 1948; J.D., U. Chgo., 1951. Admitted to Wash. bar, 1952; teaching fellow law Stanford U., 1951-52; asso. firm Randall & Danskin, Spokane, Wash., 1952-59, partner, 1959—. Pres. Spokane United Cerebral Palsy, 1954, Greek Orthodox Ch. of Holy Trinity, Spokane, 1968. Mem. Am., Wash., Spokane County bar assns., Phi Beta Kappa (past pres. local chpt.), Order Coif. Home: E 13408 22d Ave Spokane WA 99216 Office: 600 Lincoln Bldg Spokane WA 99201 Tel (509) 747-2052

ALLISON, RICHARD CLARK, b. N.Y.C., July 10, 1924; B.A., U. Va., 1944, LL.B., 1948. Admitted to N.Y. bar, 1948, U.S. Supreme Ct. bar, 1966; asso. firm Satterlee, Warfield & Stephens, N.Y.C., 1948-52, 1954-55; asso firm Reid & Priest, N.Y.C., 1955-60, partner, 1961—. Chmn. planning bd. Village Roslyn (N.Y.) 1957-60; mem. adv. bd. Southwestern Legal Found. Internat. and Comparative Law Center; trustee Buckley Country Day Sch., North Hills, N.Y., 1966-73. Mem. Am. (chmn. internat. law sect., Inter-Am., N.Y.C. bar assns., Am. Fgn. Law Assn., Am. Soc. Internat. Law, Council on Fgn. Relations, Pan Am. Soc., Center Inter-Am. Relations, N.Y. C. of C. (world trade com.), Am. Arbitration Assn. (nat. panel), Phi Beta Kappa, Omicron Delta Kappa, Phi Delta Phi. Contbr. articles to legal publs. Home: 224 Circle Dr Plandome Manor NY 11030 Office: 40 Wall St New York City NY 10005 Tel (212) 344-2233

ALLISON, STANTON WILLETTS, b. New Orleans, Dec. 14, 1896; A.B., Columbia U., 1917, J.D., 1924. Admitted to Oreg. bar, 1924; asst. sec., trust officer Commonwealth Trust and Title Co., Portland, Oreg., 1930-36; v.p. and chief counsel Commonwealth Inc. (later Oreg. Title Ins. Co.), 1936-61; pres., Title Ins. and Trust Co. Alaska, Anchorage, 1953, v.p., chief counsel, 1953-61; exec. sec., treas. Oreg. Land Title Assn., 1962-73. Exec. sec. Jud. Council Oreg., 1971. Mem. Multnomah Bar Assn., City Club of Portland (research editor), Oreg. Roadside Council (treas.). Drafter 1969 Oreg. Probate Code; author: The Clerks of the Courts, a manual, 1974, chpts. in Oreg. State bar pub.; editor, co-editor: Oreg. State Bar pubs., 1964, 70, 75, 76; recipient Award of Merit, Oreg. State bar, 1970, City Club award, 1972, Sr. Phi Alpha Delta award, 1972. Home: 2444 S W Broadway Dr Portland OR 97201 Tel (503) 223-4739

ALLMAN, ROBERT G., b. Atlantic City, July 23, 1918; B.A., U. Pa., 1939; J.D., 1942. Admitted to Pa. bar, 1942; individual practice law, Phila., 1938—. Mem. Phi Beta Kappa. Home: 6338 Sherwood Rd Philadelphia PA 19151 Office: 2116 Two Girard Plaza Philadelphia PA 19102 Tel (215) LO4-0745

ALLPORT, WILLIAM WILKENS, b. Cleve., May 31, 1944; A.B., Gettysburg Coll., 1966; J.D., Case Western Res. U., 1969. Admitted to Ohio bar, 1969, U.S. Supreme Ct. bar, 1973; practiced in Cleve., 1969—; asso. firm Baker, Hostetler & Patterson, 1969-75; chief labor counsel Leaseway Transp. Corp., 1975—. Ward chmn. Republican Party; explorer advisor Boy Scouts Am.; active Citizens League Greater Cleve. Mem. Am., Ohio, Cleve. bar assns., Internat. Law Soc., Pi Lambda Sigma, Phi Delta Phi, Theta Chi. Mem. editorial staff Case Western Res. U. Law Rev. Home: 3337 Thomson Circle Rocky River OH 44116 Office: 21111 Chagrin Blvd Cleveland OH 44122 Tel (216) 991-8800

ALLRED, JOEL MELVIN, b. Salt Lake City, Mar. 7, 1936; B.A., Brigham Young U., 1957; J.D., U. Utah, 1964. Admitted to Utah bar, 1964; law clk. Utah Supreme Ct., 1963-64; dep. atty. Salt Lake County, 1964-67; individual practice law, Salt Lake City, 1967—. Mem. Utah (chmn. young lawyers sect. 1972), Salt Lake County bar assns., Assn. Trial Lawyers Am., Utah Trial Lawyers Assn. (bd. govs. 1969-70), Am. Bar Assn. (exec. council young lawyers sect. 1972-73), Am. Judicature Soc. Home: 2853 Oakhurst Dr Salt Lake City UT 84108 Office: 345 S State St Salt Lake City UT 84111 Tel (801) 322-3508

ALLRED, MICHAEL SYLVESTER, b. Natchez, Miss., July 10, 1945; B.A. in Polit. Sci., Miss. State U., 1968; J.D., U. Miss., 1970. Admitted to Miss. bar, 1970; law clk. Miss. Supreme Ct., 1970-71; asso. firm Satterfield, Allred & Colbert, and predecessors, Jackson, Miss., 1971-75, partner, 1976—; instr. Jackson (Miss.) Sch. Law, 1971-75. Mem. state exec. com. Miss. Republican Party, 1972-76, gen. counsel, 1976—. Mem. Miss. Def. Lawyers Assn., Def. Research Inst., Hinds County, Miss., Am. bar assns. Casenote and articles editor Miss. Law Jour., 1970. Home: 1160 Woodfield Dr Jackson MS 39211 Office: PO Box 847 1000 Bankers Trust Plaza Jackson MS 39205 Tel (601) 354-2540

ALLRED, STEVEN WESLEY, b. Ogden, Utah, Sept. 4, 1947; B.S. in Polit. Sci., U. Utah, 1969, J.D., 1971. Admitted to Utah bar, 1971; asso. firm Roe, Fowler, Jerman & Dart, Salt Lake City, 1971-72; individual practice law, Salt Lake City, 1972—; atty. Office Legislative Gen. Counsel, Utah State Legislature, 1974—. Mem. Am. Bar Assn., Salt Lake City-County C. of C. (chmn. judicial revision subcom. 1976—). Office: 211 E 3d S Salt Lake City UT 84111 Tel (801) 533-0701

ALMON, WILLIAM FREDERICK, b. Stockton, Calif., Aug. 24, 1943; B.A., Seattle U., 1966; J.D., U. Wash., 1969. Admitted to Wash. bar, 1969, U.S. Ct. of Appeals 9th Circuit Ct. bar, 1975; partner firm Halverson, Applegate & McDonald, Yakima, Wash., 1969—. Mem. Am., Wash. State, Yakima County bar assns., Lawyer-Pilots Bar Assn. Home: 1104 S 48th Ave Yakima WA 98908 Office: 415 N 3d St Yakima WA 98907 Tel (509) 575-6611

ALOIA, FRANK JOHN, b. Cranford, N.J., July 24, 1936; A.B., Fla. So. Coll., 1959; J.D., Stetson U. Coll. Law, 1966. Admitted to Fla. bar, 1966; mem. firm Walter O. Sheppard, Ft. Myers, Fla., 1966-70, Adderly, Aloia & Dudley, Cape Coral, Fla., 1970—; judge Cape Coral Municipal Ct., 1970-76. Active United Fund. Mem. Fla., Am., Lee County bar assns., Lawyers Title Guaranty Fund. Recipient Cape Coral City Council award for Outstanding Ability and Distinguished Service as Municipal Judge, 1977. Home: 1247 Burtwood Dr Fort Myers FL 33901 Office: 1714 Cape Coral Pkwy Cape Coral FL 33904 Tel (813) 542-4733

ALPER, HARVEY MARTIN, b. Bklyn., Nov. 19, 1946; B.S. in Journalism with honors, U. Fla., 1968, J.D., 1971. Admitted to Fla. Bar, 1971, D.C. bar, 1971, U.S. Supreme Ct. bar, 1975; asst. gen. counsel, City of Jacksonville, Fla., 1971-72; partner firm Alper & Wack, Altamonte Springs, Fla., 1972—. Bd. dirs. United Appeal, Seminole County, Fla., 1973—. Mem. Fla., D.C., Seminole County bar assns., Fla. Blue Key, Altamonte-Casselberry C. of C., Omicron Delta Kappa. Home: 111 Cashew Ct Longwood FL 32750 Office: 165 Whooping Loop Altamonte Springs FL 32701 Tel (305) 831-4339

ALPER, IRWIN, b. N.Y.C., Feb. 8, 1902; M.D., Downstate N.Y. Med. Sch., 1925, LL.B., 1947; admitted to N.Y. bar, 1947; individual practice law, Utica, N.Y.; practice medicine and medico-legal jurisprudence; med. dir. Dept. Social Services, Utica, N.Y. Mem. Oneida County Bar Assn., Oneida County Med. Assn. Address: 1026 Park Ave Utica NY 13501 Tel (315) 733-4566

ALPERIN, HOWARD JAY, b. Haverhill, Mass., Mar. 31, 1941; B.A., U. Mass., Amherst, 1962; J.D., Boston Coll., 1965. Admitted to Mass. bar, 1966; trial atty. Mass. Defenders Com., Boston, 1966-67; legal writer Lawyers Coop. Pub. Co., Rochester, N.Y., 1968-70; individual practice law, Boston, 1970—. Mem. Mass. Bar Assn. Author: (with Simpson) Summary of Basic Law, 1974, 2d edit.; contbr. annotations to legal jours. Home: 2302 Broughton Dr Beverly MA 01915 Office: 6 Beacon St Boston MA 02108 Tel (617) 523-5321

ALPERN, DAVID, b. N.Y.C., Nov. 8, 1914; B.S. in Social Scis., Coll. City N.Y., 1936; LL.B., N.Y.U., 1939. Admitted to N.Y. bar, 1940; individual practice law, N.Y.C., 1946—; master New York County Civil Ct., 1966-68; mem. med. malpractice panel New York County Supreme Ct., 1976. Mem. New York County Lawyers Assn., Am. Bar Assn. (vice chmn. com. trial practice 1975-76), N.Y. State Trial Lawyers Assn. (chmn. com. on bldg. 1966). Office: 15 Park Row New York City NY 10038 Tel (212) 222-8296

ALPERT, LEE KANON, b. Detroit, Oct. 19, 1946; B.S., U. So. Calif., 1971; J.D., Loyola U., Los Angeles, 1972. Admitted to Calif. bar, 1972, U.S. Fed. Ct. bar, 1972; law clk. Newson & Wolfberg, Beverly Hills, 1970-72, asso. firm, 1972-73; asso. firm Ruderman, Levin, Ballin, Plotkin & Graf, North Hollywood, 1973-74; individual practice law, Encino, Calif., 1974-76; partner firm Mink and Alpert, Encino, staff mem. Community Legal Assistance Center, Los Angeles, 1970-71; judge pro tempore Los Angeles Municipal Cts., 1974—. Mem. Am., San Fernando Valley, Los Angeles County bar assns., Lawyers Club Los Angeles, Am. Arbitration Assn. (comml. arbitrator), St. Thomas More Soc., Phi Delta Phi, Tau Epsilon Phi (Extra-Curricular Activities award), Alpha Kappa Delta, Omicron Delta Kappa. Office: Encino Law Center 15915 Ventura Blvd Encino CA 91436 Tel (213) 995-1400

ALSCHULER, LEON SAMUEL, b. Chgo., June 20, 1910; A.B., Antioch Coll., 1932; J.D., Northwestern U., 1938. Admitted to Ill. bar, 1938, Calif. bar, 1946; atty. SEC, Washington, 1938-41, Los Angeles, 1941-43; mem. firm Loeb & Loeb, Los Angeles, 1946-51; partner firm Schwartz & Alschuler, Los Angeles, 1959-74, Schwartz, Alschuler & Grossman, Los Angeles, 1974—; sec. Am. Med. Internat., Inc. Trustee, Antioch Coll., 1966-68; mem. exec. com. Los Angeles chpt. Am. Jewish Com., 1947—, hon. chpt. vice chmn., 1969—, nat. exec. com., 1964—, nat. bd. trustees, 1970—. Mem. Am. (com. on fed. regulation securities 1964), Los Angeles County, Beverly Hills bar assns. Home: 818 N Doheny Dr Los Angeles CA 90069 Office: 1880 Century Park E Los Angeles CA 90067 Tel (213) 277-1226

ALSUP, DANIEL ARTHUR, b. Ogden, Utah, Nov. 11, 1917; student Weber Coll., Ogden, 1937; J.D., U. Utah, 1942. Admitted to Utah bar, 1942; individual practice law, Ogden, 1946-49, 52—; asst. gen. atty. Union Pacific R.R., Salt Lake City, 1949-52; U.S. magistrate State of Utah, 1970—. Trustee ARC, Ogden, 1955-58, Ogden Children's Aid Soc., 1959-61, St. Benedict's Hosp., Ogden, 1973—. Mem. Am. Coll. Trial Lawyers, Nat. Conf. U.S. Magistrates, Utah State Bar Assn., Am. Bar Assn. Home: 3315 Baker Dr Ogden UT 84403 Office: 1007 First Security Bank Bldg 2404 Washington Blvd Ogden UT 84401

ALSUP, RICHARD CLAYBOURNE, b. Hobbs, N.Mex., Apr. 29, 1940; B.B.A., U. Tex., El Paso, 1962; LL.B., U. Houston, 1968. Admitted to Tex. bar, 1968; individual practice law, 1968-69; v.p., gen. counsel Houston Natural Gas Corp., 1969—. Mem. Am., Tex., Houston bar assns., Am. Soc. Internat. Law. Office: 1200 Travis St Houston TX 77002 Tel (713) 654-6614

ALSUP, WILLIAM DEWITT, b. Ft. Worth, Sept. 20, 1925; B.A., U. Tex., 1960, J.D., 1962. Admitted to Tex. bar, 1962, U.S. Dist. Ct. for So. Tex. bar, 1964, U.S. 5th Circuit Ct. Appeals bar, 1972; partner firm Alsup & Alsup, 1962—; asst. dist. atty., 105th Jud. Dist., 1962-69; asst. county atty., Nueces County, Tex., 1972—; prof. law Tex. A & I U., 1974-76. Mem. Nueces County Trial Lawyers Assn. (pres. 1971-72), Nueces County Bar Assn., Am. Hosp. Attys. Assn., Nat. Health Lawyers Assn. Home: 202 Leaming St Corpus Christi TX 78401 Office: 3210 S Alameda St Corpus Christi TX 78404 Tel (512) 884-6321

ALTAFFER, DABNEY ROCHER, b. Tucson, Jan. 20, 1928; B.A., Swarthmore Coll., 1951; J.D., U. Ariz., 1956. Admitted to Ariz. bar, 1956, U.S. Supreme Ct. bar, 1973; individual practice law, Tucson, 1956-75; partner firm Strickland and Altaffer, Tucson, 1976—. Pres. bd. Ariz. chpt. Am. Heart Assn., 1966-68; pres. bd. Green Fields Sch., Tucson, 1975—; treas. Planned Parenthood Tucson, 1975—. Mem. Am., Pima County, Ariz. bar assns., Am. Judicature Soc. Home: 19 E Sierra Vista Dr Tucson AZ 85719 Office: 177 N Church St Tucson AZ 85701 Tel (602) 622-3661

ALTER, PETER MICHAEL, b. Flushing, N.Y., Nov. 15, 1947; B.A. magna cum laude, Brandeis U., 1969; J.D., Columbia U., 1972. Admitted to Mich. bar, 1972; asso. firm Honigman, Miller, Schwartz & Cohn, Detroit, 1972-76, partner, 1977—. Vice chmn., bd. dirs. Anti-Defamation League of B'nai B'rith, Mich., also mem. nat. law com.; mem. exec. com. Jewish Welfare Fedn., Detroit Met. Jewish Community Council. Mem. Am. Civil Liberties Union of Mich. (dir.), State Bar Mich. (chmn. com. on constitutional law 1976—), Am., Detroit (chmn. young lawyers com. on arbitration of consumer disputes 1975—) bar assns., Phi Beta Kappa. Contbr. article to law rev. Office: 2290 1st National Bldg Detroit MI 48226 Tel (313) 962-6700

ALTIN, MORTIMER, b. Bklyn., Apr. 9, 1922; B.A., Bklyn. Coll., 1942; J.D., N.Y.U., 1952. Admitted to N.Y. State bar, 1952; chief trademark counsel Am. Home Products Corp., N.Y.C., 1950—. Mem. Am. Bar assn., Am. Patent Law Assn., Internat. Patent and Trademark Assn. (exec. com. 1972—), U.S. Trademark Assn. (past v.p.). Home: 183 Green Ave Freeport NY 11520 Office: 685 3d Ave New York City NY 10017 Tel (212) 986-1000

ALTMAIER, MARTIN DAVID, b. Delaware, Ohio, Oct. 13, 1942; A.B., Duke, 1964; J.D., Ohio State U., 1967. Admitted to Ohio bar, 1967; with firm Morrow, Gordon & Byrd, Newark, Ohio, 1967—, partner, 1973—; tchr. Central Ohio Tech. Coll., Newark, 1976—. Treas., Legal Aid Soc. Mem. Am., Licking County bar assns. Home: 61 Granville St Newark OH 43055 Office: 33 W Main St Newark OH 43055 Tel (614) 345-9764

ALTMAN, ALAN WESTREICH, b. Bklyn., June 8, 1945; B.A., U. Pitts., 1967; J.D., Bklyn. Law Sch., 1970. Admitted to N.Y. bar, 1971; partner firm Altman & Altman, N.Y.C., 1971-76, firm Brecher, Moskowitz & Altman, N.Y.C., 1976—. Office: 230 Park Ave New York City NY 10017 Tel (212) 689-3600

ALTMAN, DONALD ARTHUR, b. N.Y.C., July 23, 1931; B.S., Bklyn. Coll., 1953; M.A., N.Y. U., 1957, J.D., 1963. Admitted to N.Y. bar, 1963; U.S. Supreme Ct., 1967; asso. firm Otto F. Fusco, Esq., Bronx, N.Y., 1963-65; individual pracitce law, Bronx and Haverstraw, N.Y., 1965—; acting justice Village Haverstraw, 1971-74; mem. permanent lecturing faculty Nat. Coll. Criminal Defense Lawyers & Pub. Defenders, Houston. Mem. N.Y., Bronx County Criminal Cts., Rockland County bar assns., N.Y. State Magistrates' Assn. Office: 4A Main St Haverstraw NY 10927 Tel (914) 429-3444

ALTMAN, STEVEN DALE, b. Newark, June 25, 1944; B.A., U. Bridgeport, 1966; J.D., Suffolk U., 1969. Admitted to N.J. bar, 1969; dep. atty. gen. N.J., 1970; asst. prosecutor Middlesex City (N.J.), 1970-75; partner firm Mulligan & Altman, New Brunswick, N.J., 1975—. Mem. Am., N.J., Middlesex County bar assns., Middlesex City Trial Lawyers Assn., Nat. Dist. Attys. Assn. Home: 1050 George St New Brunswick NJ 08901 Office: 178 Livingston Ave New Brunswick NJ 08903 Tel (201) 249-5311

ALVAREZ, ISMAEL, b. Las Cruces, N. Mex., Feb. 20, 1938; B.A. in Govt., N. Mex. State U., 1970; J.D., U. Notre Dame, 1973. Admitted to N. Mex. bar, 1973, Ind. bar, 1973; atty. migrant farmworker program Amos, Inc., South Bend, Ind., 1973-76, Equal Employment Opportunity Commn., Chgo., 1976—. Mem. Am. Bar Assn., Assn. Immigration and Nationality Lawyers. Office: 55 E Jackson Blvd Chicago IL 60604 Tel (312) 353-8086

ALVAREZ, RAMON ROBLES, b. Deming, N.M., Jan. 31, 1934; B.A. in History and Political Science, U. Ariz., 1956; J.D., 1958. Admitted to Ariz. bar, 1958, U.S. Dist. (Ariz) Ct. bar, 1962, U.S. 9th Circuit Ct. Appeals Bar, 1972, U.S. Supreme Ct. bar, 1974; individual practice law, Douglas, Ariz., 1958—; dep. atty. Cochise County, Ariz., 1958-60; city atty. Douglas, Ariz., 1965—. Mem. Ariz., Cochise County Bar Assn., Am., Ariz. Trial Lawyers Assn. Home: 2805 Ninth St Douglas AZ 85607 Office: 541 Tenth St Douglas AZ 85607 Tel (602) 364-3466

ALVERSON, LUTHER AARON, b. Atlanta, Aug. 13, 1907; LL.B., Atlanta Law Sch., Emory U., 1941. Admitted to Ga. bar, 1941; practiced in Atlanta, 1941-52; mem. firms Hooper, Hooper & Miller, 1941-43, Woodruff, Alveron & O'Neal, 1946-48; mem. Ga. Ho. of Reps., 1948-52; judge Fulton County Criminal Ct., Atlanta, 1952-56; judge Atlanta Jud. Circuit Superior Ct., 1957—. Bd. dirs. YMCA, Atlanta, chmn., 1956-57; bd. dirs. Community Council, Ga. Assn. Mental Health; bd. dirs. Nat. Assn. Mental Health, chmn., pres., 1957-59; bd. regents Internat. Acad. Trial Judges, 1974—. Fellow Internat. Acad. Trial Judges (sec.-treas. 1977); mem. Ga. Council Superior Ct. Judges (pres. 1965-66), Am., Ga., Atlanta bar assns., Atlanta Lawyers Club, Delta Theta Phi. Recipient Outstanding Trial Ct. Judge in U.S. award Am. Trial Lawyers Assn., 1974. Home: 3635 Rembrandt Rd NW Atlanta GA 30327 Office: Fulton County Courthouse Atlanta GA 30303 Tel (404) 572-2414

ALVEY, THOMAS WILLIAM, JR., b. Lincoln, Ill., Sept. 2, 1939; A.B., Va. Mil. Inst., 1961; J.D., Washington U., 1966. Admitted to Ill. bar, 1966; asso. firm Pope & Driemeyer, Bellville, Ill., 1966-70, partner, 1970—. Mem. Ill., St. Clair, E. St. Louis, Am. Bar Assns. *

ALYEA, ETHAN DAVIDSON, b. Clifton, N.J., Feb. 2, 1896; A.B., Princeton, 1916, M.A., 1917; LL.B., Harvard, 1922. Admitted to N.Y. bar, 1923; partner firm Dewey, Ballantine, Bushby, Palmer & Wood, N.Y.C. 1931—; dir. The Fairbanks Co., 1947—, Royal Bank of Can. Trust Co., 1951—, Punta Alegre Sugar Corp., 1956-61, Grand Central Art Galleries, 1961-69. Bd. dirs. Cintas Found., Inc., N.Y.C., 1957—, sec., 1957-68, pres., 1968—; trustee Montclair (N.J.) Pub. Library, 1947-57; trustee Montclair Community Chest, 1954-57, also chmn. budget com.; trustee Montclair Art Mus., 1953-67, Adult Sch. Montclair, 1946-65, pres., 1946-48; pres. Council Social Agencies Montclair, 1948-50. Mem. Am. (chmn. com. internat. trade and investment, 1955-56), N.Y.C. bar assns., N.Y. County Lawyers Assn., Internat. Law Assn. Home: 77 Highland Ave Montclair NJ 07042 Office: 140 Broadway New York City NY 10005 Tel (212) 344-8000

AMANDES, RICHARD BRUCE, b. Berkeley, Calif., Mar. 29, 1927; A.B., U. Calif., Berkeley, 1950; J.D., U. Calif., San Francisco, 1953; LL.M., N.Y.U., 1956. Admitted to Calif. bar, 1954, Wash. bar, 1959, Tex. bar, 1967; instr. U. Wash., 1954-55; teaching fellow N.Y.U., 1955-56; vis. asst. prof. U. Wash., 1956-57; asst. prof. U. Wyo., 1957-58; asst. prof. Asst. dean. U. Wash., 1958-60, asso. prof., 1960-64; asso. dean, Robert W. Harrison prof. law, U. Calif. Hastings Coll. Law, 1964-66; dean, prof. Law. Tex. Tech. U., 1966—. Tex. Commr. Nat. Conf. Commrs. on Uniform State Laws, 1972-74; chmn. Bar Exam. Revision Com., 1969—; adminstr. Continuing Legal Edn., State Wash., 1959-64; mem. exec. com. Law Schl. Admission Council, 1962-64, prelaw com., 1969-71, finance com., 1971-72; mem. accreditation com. Assn. Am. Law Schs., 1972-75. Mem. bd. Equalization, City Lubbock (Tex.), 1972—, chmn. 1974. Mem. Am., Calif., Tex., Wash. bar assns., Nat. Assn. Juvenile Ct. Judges (asso.), Order of the Coif, Phi Kappa Phi, Edward S. Thurston Honor Soc. Contbr. articles in field to legal periodicals; named Man of the Year, Tex. Tech. U., 1971. Home: 3306 39th Lubbock TX 79413 Office: Tex Tech Univ Schl Law Lubbock TX 79409 Tel (806) 742-3791

AMARI, JOHN EMANUAL, b. Birmingham, Ala., Aug. 7, 1948; B.S. cum laude, U. Montevallo, 1970; J.D., Cumberland Sch. Law, 1974. Admitted to Ala. bar, 1974; law clk. to judge Circuit Ct. 10th Jud. Circuit Ala., 1972-74; individual practice law, Birmingham, 1974—. Pres. Roebuck Neighborhood, Birmingham community devel. plan, 1975-76. Mem. Birmingham, Ala. bar assns. Asso. editor Cumberland-Samford Law Rev., 1972-73. Home: 816 Shelton St Birmingham AL 35215 Office: suite 1726 2121 Bldg Birmingham AL 35215 Tel (205) 252-2441

AMATUCCI, RICHARD D., b. Tulsa, May 8, 1939; B.A., Tulsa U., 1962, J.D., 1965. Admitted to Okla. bar, 1965; with 1st Nat. Bank & Trust Co., Tulsa, 1965-71, The Williams Cos., Tulsa, 1971-75. Mem. Okla., Tulsa County bar assns. Home: 4017 S 26th St Tulsa OK 74114 Office: 2251 E Skelly Dr Tulsa OK 74105 Tel (918) 747-3459

AMBLER, LARRY LEONARD, b. Mishawaka, Ind., Mar. 25, 1946; B.B.A., U. Dayton, 1968; J.D., U. Notre Dame, 1971. Admitted to Ind. bar, 1971; asso. firm Patrick Brennan and Assos., South Bend,

Ind., 1970-76; individual practice law, South Bend, 1976—. Mem. Ind., St. Joseph County bar assns. Editorial asso. Notre Dame Lawyer, 1970-71. Office: 313 Chamber of Commerce Bldg South Bend IN 46601 Tel (219) 232-3349

AMBLER, READ, b. Hinsdale, Ill., July 23, 1939; B.A., Dartmouth Coll., 1961; LL.B., Stanford U., 1968. Admitted to Calif. bar, 1969; asso. firm Morgan, Beauzay & Hammer, San Jose, 1969-70; dep. pub. defender Santa Clara County Pub. Defenders Office, San Jose, 1970-73; shareholder firm MacLeod, Fuller, Muir & Godwin, Los Altos, 1973-75; partner firm Nichols & Ambler, Palo Alto, 1975—. Chmn. Western region Nat. Law Exploring Com., 1974-75; bd. dirs. Community Legal Services; trustee Good Samaritan Hosp.; bd. visitors Stanford U. Law Sch., 1968-71. Mem. Am. (certificate of performance young lawyers sect. 1973), Calif., Santa Clara County (certificate of merit 1968, Hon. Service award 1975, pres. 1977), Palo Alto Area bar assns., Calif. Attys. for Criminal Justice, Calif. Trial Lawyers Assn., Santa Clara County Barristers Club (pres. 1973). Recipient certificate of appreciation for outstanding vol. service Vol. Action Center of Santa Clara County, Jr. League San Jose, 1975. Office: 505 Hamilton Ave Suite 210 Palo Alto CA 94301 Tel (415) 327-3253

AMBLER, ROBERT STERLING, b. Cleve., Aug. 1, 1931; B.C.E., U. Colo., 1954; LL.B., U. Denver, 1961. Admitted to Colo. bar, 1962; partner firm Weller, Friedrich, Hickisch & Hazlitt, Denver, 1962—. Trustee, Nat. Hemophilia Found., 1968-75. Mem. Am., Colo., Denver bar assns., Denver Law Club. Home: 654 Vine St Denver CO 80206 Office: 900 Capitol Life Center Denver CO 80203 Tel (303) 861-8000

AMBROSE, ARLEN STANLEY, b. Pueblo, Colo., Sept. 29, 1937; B.A. In Bus., U. Colo., 1959; J.D., Georgetown U., 1961. Clk. U.S. Senator John A. Carroll, Washington, 1959-63; admitted to Colo. bar, 1963; law clk. U.S. Dist. Judge William E. Doyle, Denver, 1963-64; asso. firm McNichols, Wallace Nigro & Johnson, Denver, 1964-69, Hays & Thompson, Denver, 1969-73; individual practice law, Denver, 1973-75; partner firm Hays, Patterson & Ambrose, Denver, 1975—; ad. bd. U.S. Housing and Home Finance Agy., Washington, 1960-61. Co-founder, trustee, officer Temple Sinai, Denver, 1967—; treas. Babi Yar Park Found., Denver, 1970—; treas., v.p. Synagogue Council of Greater Denver, 1976—; co-founder, trustee Cook Park Homeowners Assn., Denver, 1970—. Mem. Denver, Colo., Am. bar assns., Phi Alpha Delta. Home: 6535 E Colorado Dr Denver CO 80224 Office: Suite 909 1660 S Albion St Denver CO 80222 Tel (303) 758-4535

AMBROSE, JOSEPH MARK, b. Arlington, Mass., May 10, 1921; A.B. cum laude in Govt., Harvard, 1942, LL.B., 1948. Admitted to Mass. bar, 1948; individual practice law, Boston, 1948-53; atty. Mass. Dept. Youth Service, Boston, 1953-64; maj. gen. Mass. N.G., adj. gen. Mass., Boston, 1964-69; exec. sec. Mass. Council on Juvenile Behavior, Boston, 1970-73; U.S. property and fiscal officer for Mass., temporary col. U.S. Army, Natick, 1973—. Mem. Danvers (Mass.) Town Meeting, 1946-54, mem. fin. com.; mem. N. Shore Vocat. High Sch. Planning Com., 1970-72. Mem. Salem, Essex bar assns., numerous mil. and vets. groups. Decorated Legion of Merit; named Man of Year, Internat. Halfway Houses Assn., 1976. Home: 114 Howe St Framingham MA 01701 Office: US Property and Fiscal Office 143 Speen St Natick MA 01760 Tel (617) 235-8440

AMDURSKY, ROBERT SIDNEY, b. Syracuse, N.Y., July 7, 1937; B.A. with honors, Cornell U., 1959; J.D. cum laude, Harvard, 1962. Admitted to N.Y. bar, 1962, U.S. Supreme Ct. bar, 1974, D.C. bar, 1975; confdl. law clk. N.Y. State Appellate Div., 1962-63; partner firm L.H. & R.S. Amdursky, Oswego, N.Y., 1964-70; partner firm Willkie, Farr & Gallagher, N.Y.C., 1970—; counsel N.Y. State Joint Legis. Com. on Housing and Urban Devel., 1966-70; asst. counsel to Minority com. on health, housing and social services N.Y. State Constl. Conv., 1967; asso. counsel Majority Leader N.Y. State Senate, 1970, spl. counsel, 1971-72; dep. chmn., counsel State of N.Y. Mortgage Agy.; 1970-74; lectr. U. Buffalo Law Sch., 1963-64, Syracuse U. Law Sch., 1965-66. Mem. Am., N.Y. (sec. com. on state constitution 1972—) bar assns., Am. Arbitration Assn. (panel). Contbr. articles to legal jours. Home: 6 Glen Dr Harrison NY 10528 Office: 120 Broadway New York City NY 10005 Tel (212) 248-1000

AMELKIN, STANLEY PHILIP, b. Far Rockaway, N.Y., Sept. 30, 1936; B.S., U. Pa., 1958; LL.B., N.Y. Law Sch., 1961. Admitted to N.Y. State Bar, 1962, U.S. Supreme Ct. bar, 1966, Ct. Military Appeals, 1966, Eastern Dist. and So. Dist. bars, 1968. Vice chmn. Zoning Bd. Appeals, Huntington, N.Y. Mem. N.Y., Nassau County, Suffolk County bar assns., Nassau Lawyers Assn. of L.I. (corr. sec., treas.). Office: 380 N Broadway Jericho NY 11753 Tel (516) 433-2424

AMEMIYA, RONALD YOSHIHIKO, b. Wahiawa, Hawaii, Feb. 14, 1940; B.B.A., U. Hawaii, 1962; J.D., Hastings Coll. Law, 1967. Admitted to Hawaii bar, 1967; dep. atty. gen. Hawaii, 1967-69, 70-72; dir. State Office Consumer Protection, 1972-74; commr. State Motor Vehicle Ins. Div., 1974; atty. gen. Hawaii, 1974—. Mem. Am., Hawaii bar assns. Office: State Capitol Honolulu HI 96813 Tel (808) 548-4740

AMER, PATRICK JOSEPH, b. Sandusky, Ohio, Aug. 21, 1937; A.B., St. Louis U., 1960; LL.B., N.Y. U., 1963. Admitted to Ohio bar, 1963; since practiced in Cleve., asso. firm Jones, Day, Reavis & Pogue, 1963-71, partner, 1972-73; partner firm Spieth, Bell, McCurdy & Newell, 1973—; chmn. Cleve. Tax Inst. Mem. Am., Ohio State, Greater Cleve. bar assns. Home: 2777 Edgehill Rd Cleveland Heights OH 44106 Office: 1190 Union Commerce Bldg Cleveland OH 44115 Tel (216) 696-4700

AMERINE, LARRY FRANK, b. Harlingen, Tex., May 13, 1942; B.A. magna cum laude, Baylor U., 1964; LL.B. cum laude, U. Tex., 1967. Admitted to Tex. bar, 1967; partner firm Biggers Lloyd Biggers Beasley & Amerine, Dallas, 1967—. Mem. State Bar Tex., Dallas Bar Assn. Office: 2909 Republic Nat Bank Dallas TX 75201

AMES, EDWARD ALMER, JR., b. Onley, Va., Jan. 22, 1903; student Randolph Macon Coll., 1919-21; B.A., Washington and Lee U., 1924, LL.B., 1925. Admitted to Va. bar, 1924; partner firm Ames & Ames, Onancock, Va., 1925—; atty. Accomack County, Va., 1943-55; mem. Va. State Senate, 1956-68. Mem. Am., Va., Va. State, Accomack County bar assns., Phi Beta Kappa, Phi Delta Phi. Home: Seven Gables Accomack VA 23301 Office: Ames Bldg Onancock VA 23417 Tel (804) 787-3535

AMES, GERALD BENSION, b. Bklyn., Mar. 31, 1937; B.A., U. Calif., Los Angeles, 1958; J.D., Stanford, 1961. Admitted to Calif. bar, 1962; since practiced in San Jose, Calif.; partner firm Bean, Ames, Ames & Bean, 1963-69; individual practice law, 1970-72; partner firm Rushing, Ames, Norman & Perryman, 1972—; instr. West Valley Jr. Coll., 1976. Mem. Am., Calif., Santa Clara County bar assns., Santa Clara County Estate Planning Council, Santa Clara County Assn. Fin. Planners. Home: 19311 Vineyard Ln Saratoga CA 95070 Office: 111 W St John St San Jose CA 95113 Tel (408) 288-9100

AMES, HARRY CLIFTON, JR., b. Washington, Mar. 27, 1913; A.B., George Washington U., 1936, LL.B., 1938. Admitted to D.C. bar, 1938, U.S. Ct. Appeals D.C. bar, 1938, U.S. Supreme Ct. bar, 1955; partner firm Ames, Hill & Ames, Washington, 1939-73, pres., 1973—. Mem. Am. Bar Assn., Motor Carrier Lawyers Assn., Assn. ICC Practitioners. Home: 5304 Duval Dr Washington DC 20016 Office: Suite 805 666 11th St NW Washington DC 20001 Tel (202) 628-9243

AMES, MARC LESTER, b. Bklyn., Mar. 14, 1943; LL.B., J.D., Bklyn. Law Sch., 1967; LL.M., N.Y.U., 1968. Admitted to N.Y. bar, 1967; individual practice law, N.Y.C., 1967—; instr. L.I.U., N.Y.C. Community Coll.; apptd. arbitrator Am. Arbitration Assn. Mem. N.Y. State Bar Assn., N.Y.C. Lawyers' Assn., Assn. Immigration and Nationality Lawyers. Office: 11 Park Pl New York City NY 10007 Tel (212) 962-2390

AMES, ROBERT F., b. San Diego, July 16, 1930; B.A., Pomona Coll., 1953; M.B.A., Stanford U., 1957, J.D., 1960; Admitted to Calif. bar, 1961; partner Gray, Cary, Ames & Frye, San Diego, 1961—. Mem. State Bar Calif., Am. Bar Assn. Home: 3766 Garden Ln San Diego CA 92106 Office: 2100 Union Bank Bldg San Diego CA 92101 Tel (714) 236-1661

AMES, WALTER DONALD, b. N.Y.C., Aug. 18, 1925; B.S., Pa. State U., 1945; LL.B., George Washington U., 1954. Admitted to N.Y. bar, 1955, U.S. Supreme Ct. bar, 1965, D.C. bar, 1966; asso. firm Pollard, Johnston, Smythe & Robertson, N.Y.C., 1956-60 atty. Gen. Foods Corp., White Plains, N.Y., 1960-65; Watson, Cole, Grindle & Watson, Washington, 1965-68, partner, 1968—. Mem. Am. Patent Law Assn., Order of Coif. Home: 6718 Wemberly Way McLean VA 22101 Office: 1909 K St NW Washington DC 20006 Tel (202) 628-0088

AMGOTT, ALLEN EDWIN, b. N.Y.C., Sept. 28, 1925; B.E.E., U. Okla., 1948; LL.B., Bklyn. Law Sch., 1951, J.D., 1967. Admitted to N.Y. State bar, 1951, Okla. bar, 1963, Pa. bar, 1966; asst. head patent operation Office of Naval Research, N.Y.C., 1952-58; patent atty. Gen. Electric LMED, Utica, N.Y., 1958-60; dept. patent counsel Gen. Electric Def. Systems, Syracuse, N.Y., 1960-63, mil. systems dept., Oklahoma City, 1963-65, patent counsel space div., Phila., 1965—; electronics engr. N.Y. Naval Shipyard, Bklyn., 1948-52. Mem. Am., Pa., Okla. bar assns., Am., Phila. patent law assns., Eta Kappa Nu. Home: 315 Earle's Ln Newtown Square PA 19073 Office: PO Box 8555 Philadelphia PA 19101

AMICK, JOHN MORGAN, b. Oklahoma City, Jan. 31, 1923; J.D., Okla. U., 1949. Admitted to Okla. bar, 1948; county atty. Grant County (Okla.), 1949-54; individual practice law, Medford, Okla., 1955-59; asst. U.S. Atty. Western Dist. Okla., 1959-61; asst. county atty. Oklahoma County, 1961-65; partner firm Love, Camp & Amick, Oklahoma City, 1965-68; county judge Oklahoma County, asso. dist. judge Oklahome County, 1969-73; asso. prof. law Oklahoma City U., 1973-76; gen. counsel Okla. Bar Assn., 1976—. Bd. dirs. Okla. Counseling and Guidance Center, pres., 1972. Mem. Okla. Jud. Conf. (v.p. 1973), Okla. County Bar Assn. (pres. 1976-77), Phi Delta Phi. Named Delta Theta Phi Prof. of Year Okla. City U. Law Sch., 1974. Home: 7112 N Grand Dr Oklahoma City OK 73116 Office: 1901 N Lincoln St Oklahoma City OK 73105 Tel (405) 524-2365

AMIDON, EDWIN HENRY, JR., b. Syracuse, N.Y., Dec. 8, 1934; A.B., Williams Coll., 1956; LL.B. cum laude, Harvard, 1963. Admitted to Mass. bar, 1963, Vt. bar, 1969; asso. firm Foley, Hoag & Eliot, Boston, 1963-69; asst. Atty. Gen. State of Vt., 1969-70; asso. firm Coffrin & Pierson Burlington, Vt., 1970-71; partner firm Pierson, Affolter & Amidon, Burlington, 1972-76; judge Vt. Superior Ct., 1976—. Mem. Am., Vt. bar assns. Home: Hill's Point Rd Charlotte VT 05445 Office: care Court Administrator Montpelier VT Tel (802) 828-3281

AMIS, ROBERT WRIGHT, b. Dallas, Apr. 10, 1936; B.S. in Geology, U. Okla., 1958; LL.B., U. Tex., 1962; Admitted to Tex. bar, 1962, Okla. bar, 1967; asst. dist. atty. Denton County (Tex.), 1962-64; individual practice law, Lewisville, Tex., 1964-66; municipal ct. judge City of Lewisville, 1964-66; partner firm Reynolds & Ridings, Oklahoma City, 1966-69, firm Garrett, Pool, Amis & Coldiron, Oklahoma City, 1969-76; individual practice law, Oklahoma City, 1976—; asst. prof. law Oklahoma City U., 1968-69. Mem. State Bar Tex., Okla., Oklahoma County bar assns. Home: 2726 S Berry Rd Norman OK 73069 Office: 1001 Midland Center Oklahoma City OK 73102 Tel (405) 235-8339

AMRAM, PHILIP W., b. Phila., Mar. 14, 1900; A.B., U. Pa., 1920; B.S. in Agronomy; Pa. State U., 1922, LL.B., 1927. Admitted to Pa. bar, 1927, D.C. bar, 1945; mem. firm Wolf, Block, Schorr & Solis-Cohen, Phila., 1927-45, Guggenheimer, Untermyer, Goodrich & Amram, Washington, 1945-57, Amram, Hahn & Sundlun and successors, Washington, 1957-76; counsel Washington office Wolf, Block, Schorr & Solis-Cohen, 1976—; tchr. U. Pa. Law Sch., 1929-42; asst. gen. counsel Bd. Econ. Warfare, 1942, chief rep. S. Pacific area, 1943; spl. asst. U.S. atty. gen. charge Standard Oil litigation, 1943-45; mem. civil procedural rules com. Supreme Ct. Pa., 1937—, vice chmn., 1942-58, chmn., 1958—; spl. advisor to alien property custodian U.S., 1943-45; chmn. adv. com. U.S. Commn. on Internat. Rules Civil Procedure, 1959-66; mem. U.S. dels. Hague Conf. Pvt. Internat. Law, 1956-76, chmn., 1972; mem. adv. com. pvt. internat. law U.S. Dept. State, 1964-76, vice chmn., 1971-76. Pres., United Community Services of Washington, 1956-58, La Fondation del'Ecole Francaise Internationale de Washington, 1966-76. Mem. Am., Fed., Internat., Pa., D.C. bar assns., Am. Law Inst., Order of Coif, Phi Kappa Phi. Author: Amram's Pennsylvania Common Pleas Practice, 7th edit., 1970; Goodrich-Amram Procedural Rules Service, 1940—; editor-in-chief U. Pa. Law Rev., 1926-27; decorated officer Legion d'Honneur, comdr. Ordre des Palmes Academiques (France). Tel (202) 783-3344

AMSDELL, ROBERT JAMES, b. Oil City, Pa., July 21, 1940; B.A. (George Wright scholar), Westminister Coll., 1962; postgrad. (Fed. Govt. Research grantee) Am. U., 1960-61; J.D. (John Rufus Ranney scholar) Case Western Res. U., 1965. Admitted to Ohio bar, 1965; asso. firm Squire, Sanders & Dempsey, Cleve., 1965-70; partner firm Calfre, Halter & Griswold, Cleve., 1970-76, firm Amsdell & Slivka, Cleve., 1976—. Active United Appeal, Citizens League. Mem. Cleve., Cuyahoga, Am. (chmn. midwest com. condemnation, zoning and land use 1976) bar assns. Home: 21725 Aberdeen Rd Rocky River OH 44116 Office: 1539 Leader Bldg Cleveland OH 44114 Tel (216) 781-5252

AMSTERDAM, ANTHONY GUY, b. Phila., Sept. 12, 1935; A.B., Haverford Coll., 1957; LL.B., U. Pa., 1960. Law clk. to U.S. Supreme Ct. Justice Felix Frankfurter, 1960-61; admitted to D.C. bar, 1960; asst. U.S. atty., 1961-62; prof. law U. Pa. Law Sch., 1962-69, Stanford Law Sch., 1969—; cons. litigating atty. numerous civil rights groups; cons. govt. commns. Mem. Commn. to Study Disturbances at Columbia, 1968. Trustee Center Law and Social Policy, ACLU No. Calif., Lawyers Constl. Def. Com., So. Poverty Law Center. Named Outstanding Young Man of Year, Phila. and Pa. Jaycees, 1967; recipient First Distinguished Service award U. Pa. Law Sch., 1968, Haverford award, Haverford Coll., 1970; Arthur V. Briesen award Nat. Legal Aid and Defender Assn., 1972; named Lawyer of Year, Calif. Trial Lawyers Assn., 1973. Author: The Defensive Transfer of Civil Rights Litigation From State to Federal Courts, 1964; (with B. Segal and M. Miller) Trial Manual for the Defense of Criminal Cases, 3d edit., 1974; also numerous articles. Editor-in-chief U. Pa. Law Rev. 1959-60. Home: 1104 Laureles Dr Los Altos CA 94022 Mailing Address: Stanford U Law Sch Stanford CA 94305*

ANAGNOST, CATHERINE COOK, b. Greece, Feb. 10, 1919; student Loyola U., Chgo., 1942; diploma in commerce Northwestern U., 1942; student U. Ill., 1943, U Chgo., 1944. Admitted to Ill. bar, 1948, U.S. Supreme Ct. bar, 1960; intern firm of Themis Anagnost, Chgo., 1944-48; partner firm Anagnost & Anagnost, Chgo., 1948—; mem. nat. panel arbitrators Am. Arbitration Assn. Bd. dirs. v.p. Beverly Farm Found., Godfrey, Ill., 1963-73; alt. del. Republican Nat. Conv., 1964; bd. dirs. adv. council N.Y. World's Fair, 1964-65. Mem. Am. (ho. of dels. 1965-67), Ill., Chgo., West Suburban (pres. 1958-59), Hellenic (pres. 1955) bar assns., Internat., Nat. (pres. 1963-64) assns. women lawyers, Women's Bar Assn. Ill., Am. Assn. Atty.-C.P.A.'s. Recipient Phi Gamma Nu Scholarship key Northwestern U. Sch. Commerce, 1942, Merit award, 1964. Home: 2345 N Oak Park Ave Chicago IL 60635 Office: 11 S LaSalle St Chicago IL 60603 Tel (312) 263-0770

ANAGNOST, TIMOTHY GEORGE, b. Chgo., May 18, 1943; B.A., U. Miami, 1965, J.D., 1968. Admitted to Fla. bar, 1968; asso. firm Preddy, Haddad, Kutner and Kardy, Miami, 1968-73, partner firm, 1973—. Bd. dirs. Southwest Boys Club, Miami, 1974—. Mem. Fla. Bar, Am., Dade County bar assns., Assn. Trial Lawyers Am. Home: 420 Vittorio Ave Coral Gables FL 33146 Office: Concord Bldg Miami FL 33130 Tel (305) 358-6200

ANAST, NICHOLAS JAMES, b. Gary, Ind., Apr. 20, 1947; A.B., Ind. U., 1969, J.D., 1972. Admitted to Ind. bar, 1972, U.S. Supreme Ct. bar, 1976; asso. firm Pappas, Tokarski & Anast, Gary, 1972-74; partner Tokarski & Anast, Gary, 1974—; dep. pros. atty. Lake County, Ind., 1972-75; pauper atty. Lake County Superior Ct. Juv. div., 1975—; counsel to Gary Fire Civil Service Commn., 1974. Bd. dirs. Glen Park Youth, 1973-74. Mem. Am., Ind. State, Lake County bar assns., Am. Judicature Soc., Am. Arbitration Assn. Home: 8462 Pine Island Dr Crown Point IN 46307 Office: 4981 Broadway Gary IN 46409 Tel (219) 884-1196

ANASTASIO, EUGENE JOSEPH, b. Scranton, Pa., Feb. 19, 1935; B.S. in Econs., U. Pa., 1956; LL.B., Dickinson Law Sch., 1960; LL.M. in Taxation, N.Y. U., 1961. Admitted to Pa. bar, 1961, U.S. Supreme Ct. bar, 1967; mem. firm Warren, Hill, Henkelman & McMenamin, Scranton, 1961—; dep. atty. gen. Dept. Justice, Harrisburg, Pa., 1963—; dir. First Nat. Bank, Peckville, Pa., 1964—. Mem. Am., Lackawanna County, Pa. bar assns. Home: 811 Conodoguinet Dr Camp Hill PA 17011 Office: 405 Finance Bldg Harrisburg PA 17120 Tel (717) 787-7193

ANAYA, TONEY, b. Moriarty, N.Mex., Apr. 29, 1941; student N.Mex. Highlands U., 1959; B.S. in Fgn. Service, Georgetown U., 1964; J.D., Am. U., 1968. Admitted to N.Mex. bar, 1968, D.C. bar, 1968, U.S. Supreme Ct. bar, 1973; with U.S. Dept. Labor, Washington, 1959-66; exec. asst. to asst. sec. State, Washington, 1966; legis. counsel to U.S. Senator Montoya, 1966-69; partner firm Franklin & Anaya, Albuquerque, 1970; adminstrv. asst., legal adv. to Gov. Bruce King of N.Mex., 1970-72; asst. dist. atty. Santa Fe County (N.Mex.), 1973-74; individual practice law, Santa Fe, 1973-74; atty. gen. N.Mex., Santa Fe, 1975—. Mem. N.Mex., Am. bar assns. Home: 826 Gonzales Rd Santa Fe NM 87501 Office: PO Drawer 1508 Santa Fe NM 87501 Tel (505) 988-8851

ANDERMAN, MARVIN, b. N.Y.C., Feb. 10, 1936; B.A., Bklyn. Coll., 1956; LL.B., Columbia, 1959. Admitted to N.Y. bar, 1960; asso. firm Silverman & Goldstein, N.Y.C., 1960-62; partner firm Silverman, Goldstein & Anderman, N.Y.C., 1963-70; partner firm Goldstein & Anderman, N.Y.C., 1970—; officer JAGC, USAR, 1966—. Mem. N.Y. County Lawyers Assn., N.Y. Trial Lawyers Assn. Office: Goldstein & Anderman 225 Broadway New York City NY 10007 Tel (212) 962-2510

ANDERMAN, ROBERT PHILLIP, b. Phila., Apr. 30, 1938; student West Chester (Pa.) State Coll.; J.D., Temple U., 1965. Admitted to Pa. bar, 1965, U.S. Supreme Ct. bar, 1969; with firm Anderman, Hughey & Flick, Media, Pa., now sr. partner. Vice pres. Thornbury Hist. Soc. Mem. Am., Pa., Delaware County bar assns. Editor Delaware County Legal Jour. Home: 16 Timber Ln Thornton PA 19373 Office: 117 N Monroe St Media PA 19063 Tel (215) 565-4670

ANDERSEN, DANIEL JOHANNES, b. Jamestown, N.Y., Nov. 3, 1909; A.B., George Washington U., Washington, 1937, LL.B., 1940; J.D., Army War Coll., 1965. Admitted to D.C. bar, 1939, U.S. Dist. Ct. D.C. bar, 1940, U.S. Ct. Appeals bar, 1939, U.S. Supreme Ct. bar, 1947, U.S. Ct. Mil. Appeals bar, 1953, U.S.Army Ct. Mil. Rev. bar, 1950, U.S. Ct. Claims and U.S. Treasury Dept. bars, 1953, U.S. Tax Ct. bar, 1953; procedural analyst USES, 1937-40; judge adv. Mil. Dist. Washington, 1941-42; staff judge adv. U.S. Forces in Eastern Can. and Atlantic div. Air Transport Command, 1942-46; res. judge adv. Air Force Systems Command, Washington, 1955-63; individual practice law, Washington 1946—. Mem. Fed., D.C. bar assns., Judge Advs. Assn. (past pres.). Office: 613 Woodward Bldg Washington DC 20005 Tel (202) 737-2153

ANDERSON, ADOLPH NATHANIEL, JR., b. Providence, May 8, 1926; B.A., Brown U., 1950; LL.B., Boston Coll., 1953. Admitted to R.I. bar, 1953, U.S. Dist. Ct. for Dist. R.I. bar, 1958, U.S. Supreme Ct. bar, 1958, U.S. Ct. Mil. Appeals bar, 1958, U.S. 1st Circuit Ct. Appeals bar, 1965; legal officer USAF, 1954-56; individual practice law, Providence; spl. counsel Gov. R.I., 1960; chief Temporary Disability Ins. for R.I., 1960-61. Bd. dirs. Am. Lung Assn., R.I. Lung Assn., Scandinavian Home for Aged, Cranston, R.I. Mem. Am., R.I. (chmn. com. liaison with banks and trust coms. 1975-76) bar assns., Am. Trial Lawyers Assn. Named Man of Year, Cranston Jaycees, 1960. Office: Suite 711 Union Trust Bldg 170 Westminster St Providence RI 02903 Tel (401) 421-2117

ANDERSON, ALAN GARFIELD, b. Xenia, Ohio, Aug. 24, 1948; B.S., Wright State U., 1970; J.D., Ohio State U., 1973. Admitted to Ohio bar; asso. firm Clagg & Ford, Columbus, Ohio, 1973—; individual practice law, Xenia; dir. Total Fitness Inst., North Fork, Calif., Wilderness Survival Sch. Mem. Am., Ohio State, Franklin County bar assns., ACLU. Home: 67 Crestview Rd Columbus OH 43202 Office: 941 Chatham Ln Columbus OH 43221 Tel (614) 451-2722

ANDERSON, ALBERT EDWIN, b. Denver, July 7, 1937; B.A., U. Colo., 1963, J.D., 1966. Admitted to Colo. bar, 1966; individual practice law, Wheat Ridge, Colo., 1966—; municipal judge Town of Mountain View (Colo.), 1967-69. Mayor city Wheat Ridge, 1969-74. Mem. 1st Jud. Dist., Colo. bar assns. Named Man of Year, Wheat Ridge Sentinel Newspaper, 1969; recipient Community Service award Wheat Ridge C. of C., 1974. Home: 4098 Field Dr Wheat Ridge CO 80033 Office: 3798 Marshall St Suite 4 Wheat Ridge CO 80033 Tel (303) 423-3410

ANDERSON, ARNOLD STUART, b. N.Y.C., June 4, 1934; B.A., Coll City N.Y., 1956; J.D., Columbia, 1959. Admitted to N.Y. bar, 1959, U.S. Supreme Ct. bar, 1971; gen. atty., office gen. counsel FAA, Washington, 1960-61; asso. firm Fly, Shunebruck, Blume & Gaguine, N.Y.C., 1962-63; asst. counsel N.Y. Moreland Commn. on Alcoholic Beverage Control Law, N.Y.C., 1963-64; asso. firm Winthrop, Stimson, Putnam & Roberts, N.Y.C., 1964—; Suprem Ct. appellate div. 2d dept. asst. counsel Investigation into Jud. Conduct, 1970. Mem. Am., N.Y., N.Y.C. bar assns. Author: (with R.S. Taft) N.Y. Practice Series, Personal Taxation, Vol. I, 1975; contbr. articles to legal jours. Home: 40 Schenck Ave Great Neck NY 11021 Office: 40 Wall St New York City NY 10005 Tel (212) 943-0700

ANDERSON, ARTHUR ALLAN, b. Grand Rapids, Mich., Apr. 16, 1939; A.B. in History, B.S. in Chemistry, Brown U., 1962; LL.B., Yale, 1965. Admitted to N.Y. bar, 1966; asso. firm Fish & Neave, N.Y.C., 1965-69; founder, pres. Source Securities Corp., N.Y.C., 1970-71; gen. counsel, asst. sec. Teleprompter Corp., N.Y.C., 1972-73; partner firm Anderson & Goldman, N.Y.C., 1974—. Mem. Assn. Bar City N.Y. (sec. com. on copyright and lit. property 1974—), Am., Fed. Communications bar assns., Phi Delta Phi. Editor: (with Jay E. Ricks) New Communications Services: The Era of Competition, 1975. Home: 136 W 24th St New York City NY 10011 Office: 295 Madison Ave New York City NY 10011 Tel (212) 679-2400

ANDERSON, CHARLES AUSTIN, b. Waynesville, Ohio, Mar. 14, 1920; B.A., Ohio State U., 1941, J.D., 1944. Admitted to Ohio bar, 1944, U.S. Supreme Ct. bar, 1950; mem. firm Cowden Pfarrer Crew & Becker, Dayton, Ohio, 1944-62; judge U.S. Bankruptcy Ct., Dayton, 1962—; city atty. City of Moraine (Ohio), 1958-60; chief asst. pros. atty. Montgomery County (Ohio), 1960-62; U.S. 6th Circuit del. Nat. Conf. Spl. Ct. Judges, 1970—, mem. exec. com., 1972—; writer and lectr. in field. Mem. Centerville (Ohio) Bd., Edn., 1958-62. Mem. Am., Dayton bar assns., Am. Judicature Soc., Lawyers Club, Chancery Club, Am. Acad. Polit., Social Sci., Acad. Polit. Sci., Nat. Conf. Bankruptcy Judges. Office: 809 Fed Bldg 200 W Second St Dayton OH 45402 Tel (513) 223-3149

ANDERSON, CHARLES DAVID, b. Balt., Aug. 4, 1943; B.A., Yale, 1964; J.D. cum laude, U. Chgo., 1967. Admitted to Wis. bar, 1967, D.C. bar, 1970, Calif. bar, 1972; asso. Air Force Gen. Counsel's Office, Washington, 1967-70; Caplin & Drysdale, Washington, 1970-72; Tuttle & Taylor, Los Angeles, 1972-75, partner, 1975—; staff mem. Cabinet Task Force, Wash., D.C., 1969-70; lectr. U. So. Calif., Los Angeles, 1976—. Mem. Los Angeles County, Calif., D.C., bar assns., Order of Coif. Contbr. articles to Yale Law Jours., Univ. Chgo. Law Review Office: 609 S Grand Ave Los Angeles CA 90017 Tel (213) 683-0600

ANDERSON, CHARLES HILL, b. Chattanooga, June 16, 1930; J.D., U. Tenn., 1953. Admitted to Tenn. bar, 1953, U.S. Dist. Ct. bar, 1953, U.S. Ct. Appeals bar, 1956, U.S. Supreme Ct. bar, 1956, U.S. Ct. Mil. Appeals, 1964; asso. firm Chambliss, Brown & Hodge, Chattanooga, 1953-58; individual practice law, Chattanooga, 1958-60; asso. gen. counsel Life & Casualty Ins. Co. Tenn., Nashville, 1960-69; U.S. atty. Middle Dist. Tenn., Nashville, 1969—; lt. col. staff Judge Adv., Tenn. N.G., 1973—; mem. adv. com. U.S. atty. gen., 1973—. Del., Tenn. Constl. Conv., 1965-66; chmn. Republican Party 5th Dist., 1965-66, vice chmn. research and policy com., 1967-69, legis. counsel, 1966-68; trustee Brentwood (Tenn.) Acad., 1973-75. Mem. Am., Fed. (pres. Nashville 1972), Tenn., Nashville bar assns., Assn. Life Ins. Counsel, Barristers Club, Phi Delta Phi, Phi Kappa Phi. Editor: Tenn. Law Rev., 1950-53. Home: 4704 Granny White Pike Nashville TN 37220 Office: 879 US Courthouse Nashville TN 37203 Tel (615) 251-5151

ANDERSON, CHARLES HOBERT, b. Crab Orchard, Ky., Nov. 28, 1924; student Roosevelt U., 1953; LL.B., Lincoln U., 1956. Admitted to Ky. bar, 1958; staff supr. Domestic Ins. Co., Louisville, 1958-60; referee Ky. Workmen's Compensation Bd., Frankfort, 1960-68; staff atty. Legal Aid Soc., Louisville, 1967-69; judge 3rd magisterial dist. ct. Jefferson, Ky., 1969-75; judge Circuit Ct 3rd div. chancery, Jefferson County Ky., 1975—. Vice pres., bd. dirs. Travelers Aid Soc., Louisville, 1972— v.p. bd. dirs. Family & Childrens Agency, Louisville, 1971. Mem. Ky., Louisville bar assns., Am. Judicature Soc. Recipient Recognition award, Religious edn., 1972. Office: Jefferson County Hall Justice 600 W Jefferson St Louisville KY 40202 Tel (502) 581-6010

ANDERSON, CROMWELL A., b. Palatka, Fla., Feb. 26, 1926; A.B., U. Rochester, 1948; LL.B., U. Fla., 1950, J.D., 1967. Admitted to Fla. bar, 1950; spl. agt. FBI, 1951-54; asso. firm Smathers and Thompson, Miami, Fla., 1954-59, partner, 1959—. Mem. Dade County, Fed., Am. (chmn. maritime ins. law com., sect. ins. negligance and compensation 1973-75) bar assns., Maritime Law Assn. U.S., Internat. Assn. Ins. Counsel. Home: 1021 Manati Ave Coral Gables FL 33146 Office: 1301 Alfred I DuPont Bldg Miami FL 33131 Tel (305) 379-6523

ANDERSON, DANIEL PHILIP, b. Plymouth, Wis., Jan. 1, 1945; B.S., U. Wis., 1967, J.D. cum laude, 1973. Admitted to Wis. bar, 1974; mem. firm Anderson, Damp & Anderson, Plymouth, 1974—; cons. legal edn. Lakeshore Tech. Inst., Cleveland, Wis., 1975—; instr. agrl. law Lakeshore Tech. div. adult edn., 1975—. Trustee Plymouth Pub. Library, 1974—; gen. campaign chmn. United Fund of Plymouth, Inc., 1974, dir., 1975; chmn. Sheboygan County (Wis.) Democratic Party, 1975-76. Mem. Sheboygan County, Wis., Am. bar assns. Recipient Am. Jurisprudence Award in Adminstrv. Law, 1973. Home: 953 Dooley Rd Plymouth WI 53073 Office: 623 E Mill St Plymouth WI 53073 Tel (414) 893-8421

ANDERSON, DAVID BRIGHAM, b. Springfield, Mass., Sept. 20, 1940; B.S. in Bus. and Adminstrn., Am. Internat. Coll., Springfield, 1963, M.A. in Human Relations and Community Devel., 1971; J.D., Boston U., 1966. Admitted to Mass. bar, 1967, U.S. Supreme Ct. bar, 1970; individual practice law, Springfield, 1967—; counsel Monarch Life Ins. Co., Springfield, 1967—; dir. Home and Sitter Services, Inc., Bond Cons. Servies, Inc., Qualified Plan Ins. Brokerage Corp., Profl. Leasing Corp., Springfield Ednl. Consts. (all Springfield); dir., treas. Whitney Anderson Paper Co., Inc., Springfield; mng. parnter Wilder Ponds, Springfield; asst. clk. Casey Chevrolet, Inc., Chicopee, Mass. Vice pres., clk. Drug Abuse Found. of Pioneer Valley, Inc., Springfield; corporator Western Mass. Med. Center; chmn. devel. and resources com. Laughing Brook, Inc., Audubon Soc. Mass. Mem. Health Ins. Assn. Am., Life Ins. Assn. Am., Hampden County (Mass.) Estate Planning Council, Mass., Am., Hampden County bar assns., Am. Assn. C.L.U.'s., Assn. Life Ins. Council, Am. Life Ins. Assn. Named Outstanding Jaycee Springfield, 1970; C.L.U. Office: 1250 State St Springfield MA 01101 Tel (413) 785-5811

ANDERSON, DONALD KEITH, b. Kansas City, Mo., Mar. 11, 1940; B.A., Washburn U., Topeka, 1964; J.D., 1967. Admitted to Kans. bar, 1967; partner firm Kaplan, McMillan & Anderson, Wichita, 1967-73, Anderson & Foster, Valley Center, Kans., 1974-76; individual practice law, Valley Center, 1973-74, 76-77; judge Derby (Kans.) Municipal Ct., 1973-74; asso. dist. judge 18th Jud. Dist., Sedgwick County, Kans., 1977—. Pres. Valley Center C. of C., 1975-76. Mem. Kans., Wichita (sec.-treas. 1974, gov. 1976—) bar assns. Home: 200 S Dexter St Valley Center KS 67147 Office: 210 W Main St Valley Center KS 67147 Tel (316) 755-1273

ANDERSON, DONALD T., b. Kalamazoo, Mich., Nov. 18, 1911; A.B., Kalamazoo Coll., 1933; J.D., U. Mich., 1936. Admitted to Mich. bar, 1936; individual practice law, Kalamazoo, 1936-49; judge Kalamazoo County Probate Ct., also Juvenile Ct., Kalamazoo, 1949-61; edn. dir. Children's Charter of Cts. Mich., 1961-70; judge Mich. 9th Circuit Ct., Kalamazoo, 1971—. Mem. Am., Mich., Kalamazoo County bar assns., Am. Judicature Soc. Recipient Meritorious Service award, Nat. Council Juvenile Ct. Judges, 1967. Home: 2844 Fairfield Ave Kalamazoo MI 49004 Office: Court C County Bldg Kalamazoo MI 49006 Tel (616) 383-8916

ANDERSON, DORIS ELAINE, b. Elkhart, Ind., Nov. 6, 1934; Mus.B., U. Mich., 1956; postgrad. Northwestern U., 1958; J.D., U. Calif., 1964. Admitted to Calif. bar, 1968; tchr. music Niles (Mich.) Jr. High Sch., 1956-59; adminstrv. asst. to Corp. sec. Fibreboard Corp., San Francisco, 1965-68, atty. asst. to v.p., corp. sec., 1968—. Mem. Am. Bar Assn., State Bar Calif. Home: 1079 Cragmont Ave Berkeley CA 94708 Office: 55 Francisco St San Francisco CA 94133

ANDERSON, EARLE KARL, b. Huntington, W.Va., Mar. 30, 1931; B.B.A., So. Methodist U., 1953, LL.B., 1960. Admitted to Tex. bar, 1960, U.S. Supreme Ct. bar, 1971; dist. claims mgr. Allstate Ins. Co., Dallas, 1958-63; individual practice law, Dallas, 1963—. Mem. Am. Bar Assn., Dallas Assn. Trial Lawyers (dir. 1964-65, 74-75) Trial Lawyers Assn. Am., Tex. Trial Lawyers Assn., Delta Theta Phi, Sigma Iota Epsilon. Home: 4549 Belclaire St Dallas TX 75205 Office: 2612 Mercantile Bank Bldg Dallas TX 75201 Tel (214) 742-3941

ANDERSON, EDWARD CLIVE, b. Madras, India, Mar. 24, 1947; B.A. in Law, Worcester Coll., Oxford U., 1967, B.Civil Law, 1968. Called as barrister to bar of Eng. and Wales, 1970, admitted to Pa. bar, 1972; instr. legal methods U. Pa. Law Sch., Phila., 1968-70; asso. firm Morgan, Lewis & Bockuns, Phila., 1969—. Mem. Am., Pa., Phila. bar assns. Home: 430 5th St Philadelphia PA 19147 Office: 2100 Fidelity Bldg Philadelphia PA 19109 Tel (215) 491-9219

ANDERSON, EUGENE CARROLL, b. Anacortes, Wash., Oct. 4, 1929; B.S., U. Wash., 1952, J.D. with honors, 1957. Admitted to Wash. bar, 1957; individual practice law, Anacortes, Wash., 1957—; sr. mem. firm Anderson & Mansfield, Anacortes, 1969-72, firm Anderson & Anderson, Anacortes, 1974—; dist. ct. judge., 1959—, municipal judge, Anacortes, 1969—; mem. Wash. State Law Examiners, 1967—. Founding pres., Skagit group Ranch Homes, 1969, bd. dirs., 1969—, pres., 1976—; pres. Anacortes United Good Neighbors, 1958; bd. dirs. Anacortes Sch. Bd., 1963-70. Mem. Wash. State Bar, Wash. State Magistrates Assn., Am. Judicature Soc., Order of Coif. Recipient Anacortes Jaycees Distinguished Service award, 1964. Home: 2910 I St Anacortes WA 98221 Office: 1011 8th St Anacortes WA 98221 Tel (206) 293-5783

ANDERSON, GEORGE ROSS, JR., b. Anderson, S.C., Feb. 29, 1929; B.C.S., Southeastern U., 1949; student George Washington U., 1949-52; postgrad. U. S.C., 1954. Admitted to S.C. bar, 1954; partner firm Anderson Kenyon & Epps, Anderson, S.C., 1954—; mem. S.C. Ho. of Reps., 1954-56; adminstrv. asst. to S.C. Senator Olin Johnston, 1947-51; del. Chief Justice's Conf., Charleston, S.C., 1972; permanent mem. 4th Circuit Jud. Conf. Bd. dirs. Anderson YMCA, 1968-74, Salvation Army; mem. fin. bd. Anderson Coll., 1st Baptist Ch. Anderson. Fellow Internat. Acad. Trial Lawyers; mem. Am., S.C. (past circuit v.p.), Anderson County (pres. 1960) bar assns., Assn. Trial Lawyers Am. (bd. govs. 1969-71), Ga., S.C. (dir. 1958—, pres. 1971-72) trial lawyers assns., Am. Judicature Soc., Am. Assn. Forensic Scientists, Wig and Robe, Omicron Delta Kappa. Asst. editor U. S.C. Law Rev., 1953-54. Home: 105 Postelle Dr Anderson SC 29621 Office: 230 W Whitner St Anderson SC 29621 Tel (803) 224-2111

ANDERSON, HAROLD JANWAY, b. Holdrege, Nebr., Sept. 9, 1909; LL.B., William Mitchell Coll., 1935. Admitted to Minn. bar, 1936; spl. agent FBI, Tenn, La., Alaska and Okla., 1942-46; mem. Minn. House of Rep., 1951-73; individual practice law, 1936—. Mem. Minn. Bar Assn., Mpls. C. of C. (dir. 1954-55). Home: 4919 Colfax Ave S Minneapolis MN 55409 Office: 654 Midland Bank Blvd Minneapolis MN 55401 Tel (612) 339-2731

ANDERSON, HAROLD L., b. Bismarck, N.D., Feb. 15, 1927; student Bismarck Jr. Coll.; J.D., U. N.D., 1952. Admitted to N.D. bar, 1952; now mem. firm Pearce, Anderson, Thames and Durick, Bismarck; state's atty. Burleigh County (N.D.), 1955-63. Bd. dirs. N.D. Luth. Welfare Soc., 1960-63; pres. Bismarck Sch. Bd., 1968-69. Mem. Am., Burleigh County (pres. 1968) bar assns., State Bar Assn. N.D. (pres. 1977-78), Am. Judicature Soc., Soc. Hosp. Attys., Assn. Ins. Attys. (N.D. chmn. 1974—), Phi Alpha Delta. Office: 314 E Thayer Ave Suite 300 PO Box 400 Bismarck ND 58501 Tel (701) 223-2890*

ANDERSON, HENRY BRACKENRIDGE, b. Wilkinsburg, Pa., May 30, 1918; B.A., Wesleyan U., Conn., 1940, M.A., 1948; LL.B. cum laude, U. Conn., 1948. Admitted to Conn. bar, 1948; trial justice Town of Sherman (Conn.), 1948-50, town counsel, 1948-76; partner firm Cramer & Anderson, and predecessors, New Milford, Conn., 1951—;. judge probate dist. Sherman, 1951-58; corporator New Milford Savs. Bank, 1961—; mem. exec. com. Conn. Probate Assembly, 1955-58; dir. deSherbinin Products Inc., Conn. Attys. Title Guaranty Fund. Trustee U. Conn. Law Sch. Found., 1974—, New Milford Hosp., 1964—; chmn. Sherman Bd. Edn., 1967-70. Mem. Nat. Conf. Bar Examiners, Am., Conn. (exec. com. real properties sect. 1965), Litchfield County (pres. 1963-65) bar assns. Decorated Silver Star, Bronze Star. Home: Holiday Point Sherman CT 06784 Office: 51 Main St New Milford CT 06776 Tel (203) 354-3987

ANDERSON, J. BLAINE, b. Trenton, Utah, Jan. 19, 1922; student U. Idaho So. Br., 1940-41, U. Wash., 1945-46; LL.B., U. Idaho, 1949, J.D., 1970. Admitted to Idaho bar, 1949, U.S. Dist. Ct. Idaho, 1949, U.S. Supreme Ct., 1960, U.S. Ct. of Appeals, 9th Circuit, 1970, U.S. Tax Ct., 1955; individual practice law, Blackfoot, Idaho, 1949-55; asso. firm Furchner, Anderson & Martsch and predecessor firms, Blackfoot, 1955-71; judge U.S. Dist. Ct. Idaho, Boise, 1971-76; circuit judge U.S. Ct. Appeals, 1976—; city atty., Arco, Idaho, 1951-53, Blackfoot, 1964-68; Sch. Dist. atty., Blackfoot and Bingham County, 1962-71. Chmn., Blackfoot Zoning Commn., 1950-52; chmn. Idaho Air Pollution Control Commn., 1958-60; mem. personnel security rev. bd. U.S. AEC, Idaho Ops. Office, Idaho Falls, 1964-71; pres., bd. dirs. Airport Park Recreation Assn., 1953-58; v.p., bd. dirs. Blackfoot Kiwanis Club, 1954-62. Fellow Am. Coll. Probate Counsel, Am. Coll. Trail Lawyers; mem. Am. (del. 1964-71, bd. govs. 1971-74), Idaho (pres. 1960-61, bd. commrs. 1958-61), SE Idaho Dist. (pres. 1957) bar assns., Am. Judicature Soc. (dir. 1961-66). Recipient award for services Idaho Bar Commn., 1965, Faculty award of legal merit U. Idaho Coll. Law, 1974; mem. adv. bd. Am. Bar Jour., 1970-73. Home: Route 1 Brookside Ln Boise ID 83702 Office: US Court Bldg 550 W Fort St Boise ID 83724 Tel (208) 384-1612

ANDERSON, JAMES A., b. Auburn, Wash., Sept. 21, 1924; B.A., U. Wash., 1949, J.D., 1952. Admitted to Wash. bar; dep. pros. atty. King County (Wash.), 1953-57; asso. firm Lycette, Diamond & Sylvester, 1957-61; partner firm Clinton, Andersen, Fleck & Glein, Seattle, 1961-74; judge Wash. Ct. Appeals, 1975—; mem. Wash. State Ho. of Reps., 1959-67, Wash. State Senate, 1967-72, minority leader; mem. Wash. State Jud. Council. Mem. Wash. State (hon.), Seattle-King County (hon.), Am. bar assns., Delta Theta Phi. Recipient Distinguished Service award Jr. C. of C., 1956. Home: 3008-98th St NE Bellevue WA 98004 Office: Wash Ct Appeals Div 1 11th floor Pacific Bldg Seattle WA 98104

ANDERSON, JEROME, b. St. Paul, Apr. 13, 1921; B.A., Mont. State U., 1948, J.D., 1948. Admitted to Mt. bar, 1948; partner firm Anderson, Symmes, Forbes, Peete & Brown, and predecessors, Billings, Mont., 1953—; chief dep. county atty. Yellowstone County (Mont.), 1949-52; asst. city atty. Billings, 1952-53; mem. Mont. Ho. of Reps., 1955-62, majority floor leader, 1961-63. Mem. Yellowstone County Republican exec. com., 1954-68, mem. Mont. state exec. com., 1953-56, vice chmn. central com., 1955-56, state chmn. Goldwater for Pres. Com., 1963-64; chmn. March Dimes, 1961-62; mem. Mont. Territorial Centennial Commn., 1963-64. Mem. Motor Carriers Lawyers Assn., ICC Practitioners, Yellowstone County, Mont., Am. bar assns. Home: 1315 Yellowstone Ave Billings MT 59102 Office: 100 Transwestern Bldg 404 N 31st St Billings MT 59101 Tel (406) 248-2611

ANDERSON, JOHN BAYARD, b. Rockford, Ill., Feb. 15, 1922; B.A., U. Ill., 1942, J.D., 1946; LL.M., Harvard, 1949; Admitted to Ill. bar, 1946; individual practice law, Rockford, 1946-48, 50-52, 55-56; instr. Northeastern U., 1948-49; mem. career diplomatic service Dept. State, 1952-55; Winnebago County (Ill.) state's atty., 1956-60; mem. 87th to 95th Congresses from 16th Dist. Ill. Bd. dirs. Trinity Coll., Deerfield, Ill., Youth for Christ Internat. Mem. Winnebago County Bar Assn. Named outstanding layman of year Nat. Assn. Evangelicals, 1964; author: Between Two Worlds: a Congressman's Choice, 1970; Vision and Betrayal in America, 1976; editor: Worlds: Congress and Conscience, 1970. Office: 1101 Longworth House Office Bldg Washington DC 20515 Tel (202) 225-5676

ANDERSON, JOHN EDWARD, b. Mpls., Sept. 12, 1917; B.S., U. Calif., Los Angeles, 1940; M.B.A., Harvard, 1942; J.D., Loyola U., 1950. Admitted to Calif. bar, 1950; asso. firm Hill, Farrer & Burrill, Los Angeles, 1950-53; partner firm Kindel & Anderson, Los Angeles, 1953—; dir. Applied Magnetics Corp., Bourns, Inc., Nat. Accommodations, Inc., Toyomenka (Am.), Inc., Pinehurst Corp., Data Services, Inc., Diamond Perforated Metals, Digitek Timeshare, Inc., Sloan Tech. Corp., Topa Topa Ranch. Bd. dirs. St. John's Hosp. and Health Center Found., YMCA; trustee Claremont Men's Coll.; bd. advisors Applied Fin. Econs. Center; bd. ednl. advisors AMR Internat., Inc. Mem. Am. Bar Assn. (com. on corporate stockholder relationships), Assn. Tax Counsel. Home: 10445 Bellagio Rd Los Angeles CA 90024 Office: 555 S Flower St 26th Floor Los Angeles CA 90071 Tel (213) 680-2222

ANDERSON, JOHN MILTON, b. San Francisco, Sept. 19, 1936; B.A., Pomona Coll., 1958; J.D., U. Calif., Berkeley, 1961. Admitted to Caif. bar, 1962, U.S. Supreme Ct. bar, 1968; asso. firm Landels, Ripley & Diamond, San Francisco, 1967-69, partner, 1969—; asso. prof. law Golden Gate U., 1971-72. Mem. Am., San Francisco bar assns., NAACP (dir. legal def. fund). Contbr. articles to newspapers. Office: 450 Pacific Ave San Francisco CA 94133 Tel (415) 788-5000

ANDERSON, JON M., b. Rio Grande, Ohio, Jan. 10, 1937; A.B., Ohio U., 1958; J.D., Harvard, 1961. Admitted to Ohio bar, 1961; law clk. to justice Ohio Supreme Ct., 1961-62; asso. firm Wright, Harlor, Morris & Arnold, Columbus, Ohio, 1962-68, partner, 1968-77; partner firm Porter, Wright, Morris & Arthur, Columbus, 1977—; mem. Bd. Bar Examiners State of Ohio, 1970-75, chmn., 1974-75; adj. prof. law Ohio State U., 1975—. Moderator First Congregational Ch., Columbus, 1976—; trustee Berea (Ky.) Coll., 1976—. Mem. Am., Ohio, Columbus bar assns. Home: 2545 Sherwood Rd Bexley OH 43209 Office: 37 W Broad St Columbus OH 43215 Tel (614) 224-4125

ANDERSON, KEITH, b. Phoenix, June 21, 1917; A.B., Dartmouth, 1939; LL.B., Harvard, 1942. Admitted to N.Y. bar, 1942, Ariz. bar, 1946, Colo. bar, 1950; asso. firm Carter, Ledyard & Milburn, N.Y.C., 1946-50; counsel Boettcher Cos., Denver, 1950-52; individual practice law, Denver, 1952-54; partner firm Holme, Roberts & Owen, Denver, 1954-70; individual practice law, 1972—; chmn. Republic Nat. Bank Englewood (Colo.), 1963-76; pres. Mountain Banks Ltd., 1970-72; pres., chmn. Mine and Smelter Corp., 1976—. Pres., Denver Mental Health Assn., 1958-59; pres. Graland School, Denver, 1961-62; mem. Denver Planning Bd., 1962-63. Mem. Colo., Denver bar assns. Office: 780 Denver Club Bldg 518 17th St Denver CO 80202 Tel (303) 534-3137

ANDERSON, LAVERNE ERIC, b. Rockford, Ill., Feb. 24, 1922; LL.B., U. Ill., 1944; J.D., U. Ill. Coll. Law, 1946. Admitted to Ill. bar, 1947, admitted to practice U.S. Treasury Dept., Fed. Ct.; individual practice law, Rockford, 1947-64; partner firm Nordquist and

Anderson, 1965—; city atty., Rockford, 1947-53, corp. counsel 1953-57. Mem. Ill., Winnebago County bar assns., Broadway Bus. Assn., Phi Eta Sigma, Phi Beta Kappa, Phi Kappa Phi, Masons, Shriners (rep. Imperial Council, dir. El Hajj Caravanserai No. 4, potentate Tebala Shrine Temple, 1977). Office: 724 Broadway Rockford IL 61108 Tel (815) 968-8808

ANDERSON, LEE BERGER, b. Holden, W.Va., Feb. 22, 1912; LL.B., Nat. U., Washington, 1939, LL.M., 1941; J.D., George Washington U., 1968. Admitted to D.C. bar, 1939, Idaho bar, 1949, Md. bar, 1973, U.S. Supreme Ct. bar, 1947, U.S. Ct. of Claims, 1947; legal clk.-sec. Fed. Savs. & Loan Ins. Corp., Washington, 1933-42; atty. Office of Solicitor, Dept. Labor, Washington, 1942-43, criminal div. Dept. Justice, Washington, 1943-48; partner firm Anderson & Anderson, Caldwell, Idaho, 1948-53; trial atty. Office Alien Property, Dept. Justice, Washington, 1953-60, appellate atty., internal security div., 1960-72; individual practice law, North Chevy Chase, Md., 1972—; lectr. YWCA Sch. Adult Edn., Washington, 1965-71; mem. Nat. Conf. on Causes Popular Dissatisfaction with Adminstrn. Justice, Jud. Conf. U.S. Ct. of Appeals for D.C. Circuit, Jud. Conf. D.C. Ct. of Appeals and Superior Ct. Pres., Caldwell LWV, 1948-53; sec.-treas. Idaho LWV, 1948-53; chmn. legal sub-com. D.C. Commn. on Status of Women, 1967-69; arbitrator Office Consumer Affairs, Montgomery County, Md.; active Equal Rights Amendment Ratification Council, U.S. Com. Cooperation with Inter-Am. Commn. Women. Mem. Am., Fed., Internat., Md., D.C., Montgomery County bar assns., Am. Arbitration Assn. (panel), Nat. Assn. Women Lawyers (pres. 1976—, editor Women Lawyers Jour. 1972-73, del. to Internat. Bar, 1976—), Womens Bar Assn. D.C. (pres. 1969-70), Phi Delta Delta, Phi Alpha Delta. Recipient certificate of award Dept. Justice, 1962, 69. Home and office: 3809 Montrose Driveway North Chevy Chase MD 20015 Tel (301) 656-1272

ANDERSON, LEVY, b. Phila., Apr. 7, 1910; J.D., Temple U., 1937. Admitted to Pa. Supreme Ct. bar, 1938, U.S. Supreme Ct. bar, 1948; practiced in Phila., 1938-71; judge Phila. Ct. of Common Pleas, 1972—; dep. City of Phila., 1952-56, 1st dep., 1956-70, city solicitor, 1970-71. Pres. Congregation Ner Zedek-Ezrath Israel, Phila., 1973-75; bd. dirs. Theodore F. Jenkins Law Library, Phila. Mem. Am., Pa., Phila. (gov. 1970-71) bar assns., Lawyers Club of Phila., Am. Judicature Soc., Temple U. Law Alumni (exec. com.). Office: 192 City Hall Philadelphia PA 19107 Tel (215) MU 6-7316

ANDERSON, LEWIS RAYMOND, b. Meeker, Colo., June 4, 1943; B.A., Western State Coll., 1965; J.D., St. Louis U., 1972. Admitted to Colo. bar, 1972; asso. firm James M. Pughe, Craig, Colo., 1972-73; individual practice law, 1974-76; partner firm Anderson and Osborne, P.C., Craig, 1976—. Mem. N.W. Colo., Colo., Am. bar assns. Home: 794 Steele St Craig CO 81625 Office: PO Box 876 Craig CO 81625 Tel (303) 824-3254

ANDERSON, MARK BURTON, b. Storm Lake, Iowa, Jan. 11, 1948; B.A., St. Olaf Coll., 1970; J.D., Vanderbilt U., 1973. Admitted to Iowa bar, 1973; asso. firm C.J. Anderson, Cresco, Iowa, 1973-75; partner firm Anderson, Story and Anderson, Cresco, 1975—; county atty. Howard County (Iowa), 1975—. Mem. Am., Iowa, Howard County bar assns. Home: 408 3d St E Cresco IA 52136 Office: PO Box 280 112 N Elm St Cresco IA 52136 Tel (319) 547-4534

ANDERSON, MARTIN, b. Los Angeles, Nov. 16, 1923; A.B., U. Calif., Berkeley, 1943; B.A., Stanford, 1948, LL.B., 1949. Admitted to Calif. bar, 1950, Hawaii bar, 1951; partner firm Goodsill, Anderson & Quinn, Honolulu, 1951—, McCutchen, Doyle, Brown & Emersen, San Francisco, 1974—. Mem. Am., Calif., Hawaii bar assns. Home: 1170 Sacramento St San Francisco CA 94108 Office: 601 California St San Francisco CA 94108 Tel (415) 981-3400

ANDERSON, MASON HOMER, b. Shallotte, N.C., Feb. 7, 1935; B.S., Clemson U., 1957; J.D., U. N.C., 1967. Admitted to Brunswick County bar, 1967; individual practice law, Shallotte. Mem. Am. Bar Assn., Am., N.C. trial lawyers assns., C. of C. (chmn.). Office: 1 Pine St Shallotte NC 28459

ANDERSON, OVERTON SUTFIELD, II, b. England, Ark., Jan. 21, 1943; B.B.A., So. Meth. U., 1965, J.D., 1968. Admitted to Tex. bar, 1968, Ark. bar, 1973; with JAGC, USNR, 1968-72; asso. firm Smith, Williams, Friday, Eldredge & Clark, Little Rock, 1972—. Mem. Ark., Tex., Am. bar assns. Asso. editor Southwestern Law Jour., 1968. Home: 1918 N Monroe St Little Rock AR 72207 Office: 1st Nat Bldg 20th floor Little Rock AR 72201 Tel (501) 376-2011

ANDERSON, PAUL BENJAMIN, JR., b. Selma, Ala., Oct. 27, 1947; A.A., Marion Mil. Inst., 1968; B.A., Samford U., 1969; J.D., Cumberland Sch. Law, 1972. Admitted to Ala. Supreme Ct., 1973, U.S. Ct. Mil. Appeals, 1974; asso. law firm Richard S. Manley, Atty.-At-Law, Demopolis, Ala., 1973-74; chief, mil. justice div. Office of Staff Judge Advocate, U.S. Army Infantry Center, Fort Benning, Ga., 1974—. Mem. adminstrv. bd. Marion United Meth. Ch., Marion, Ala., 1972-74, St. Mary's Road United Meth. Ch., Columbus, Ga., 1976—. Mem. Am., Ala. bar assns., Nat. Dist. Atty.'s Assn., Am. Trial Lawyers Assn., Phi Alpha Delta. Home: 643 Gibson Dr Fort Benning GA 31905 Office: Office of Staff Judge Advocate US Army Infantry Center Fort Benning GA 31905

ANDERSON, PAUL EDWARD, b. Iron River, Mich., Mar. 5, 1925; A.B., U. Mich., 1948, J.D., 1950. Admitted to Calif. bar, 1951; instr. Stanford Law Sch., 1950-51; spl. asst. to chief counsel IRS, San Francisco, 1951-52; partner firm Kent, Brookes and Anderson, San Francisco, 1952-60; individual practice law, San Francisco, 1969—; prof. law Hastings Coll. Law, San Francisco, 1958-75. Mayor, City San Mateo, Calif., 1957-59; chmn. taxation com. State Bar of Calif., 1966-67. Mem. Am., Internat. bar assns. Author: Tax Factors in Real Estate Operations, 1976; Tax Planning of Real Estate, 1976; editor Jour. of Taxation, 1962-75. Home: 1730 Kearny St San Francisco CA 94133 Office: 235 Montgomery St 1301 San Francisco CA 94104 Tel (415) 434-0943

ANDERSON, PHILIP SIDNEY, b. Little Rock, May 9, 1935; B.A., Univ. Ark., 1959, LL.B., 1959. Admitted to Ark. bar, 1960, U.S. Supreme Ct. bar, 1966; partner firm Wright, Lindsey & Jennings, Little Rock, 1960—; mem. Supreme Ct. Com. Jury Instructions, Ark. Supreme Ct., 1962—. Trustee Donaghey Found.; bd. dirs. Little Rock Unlimited Progress, Inc. Mem. Am., Ark., Pulaski County bar assns., fellow Ark. Bar Found., mem. Am. Law Inst., Am. Jud. Soc. Recipient Meritorious Service award Ark Bar Assn., 1966. Home: 4716 Crestwood Little Rock AR 72207 Office: 2200 Worthen Bank Building Little Rock AR 72201 Tel (501) 375-6481

ANDERSON, RALPH MILTON, b. Tekamah, Nebr., Apr. 14, 1899; LL.B., U. Nebr., 1923. Admitted to Nebr. bar, 1923; individual practice law, Tekamah, 1923-65; partner firm Anderson & Anderson, Tekamah, 1965—; county atty. Burt County (Nebr.), 1926-35. Mem. Am., Nebr. bar assns., Tekamah C. of C. (sec. 1925-50). Home: 216 N 15th St Tekamah NE 68061 Office: 234 S 13th St Tekamah NE 68061 Tel (402) 374-1476

ANDERSON, RAYMOND PETER, b. Norfolk, Va., Aug. 11, 1943; B.A., Oberlin Coll., 1965; LL.B., Yale, 1969. Admitted to Mass. bar, 1969; staff atty. Boston Legal Assistance Project, 1969-71; instr. law Northeastern Law Sch., Boston, 1975—; staff atty. Mass. Law Reform Inst., Boston, 1971—; mem. med. care adv. bd. Mass. Dept. Pub. Welfare, 1976—. Exec. bd. William Monroe Trotter Sch. Parents Assn., Roxbury, Mass. Recipient Beverly Pub. Service award Greater Mass. Chpt. Nat. Assn. Social Workers, 1975. Home: 2 Lawnwood Pl Charlestown MA 02129 Office: 2 Park Sq Boston MA 02116 Tel (617) 482-0890

ANDERSON, RICHARD LEE, b. Gary, Ind., Mar. 20, 1945; B.S., Ind. U., 1967, J.D., 1970. Admitted to Ind. bar, 1970, U.S. Dist. Ct. bars for So. Dist. Ind., 1970, No. Dist. Ind., 1971; practiced in No. Ind., 1970—; judge Portage (Ind.) City Ct., 1974—; dep. pros. atty. Porter County (Ind.), 1970-74; atty. Portage Met. Police Commn., 1972-74; atty. bd. trustees Chesterton Police Pension Fund. Bd. dirs. YMCA, Portage C. of C., Rotary Club, Portage. Mem. Am., Porter County bar assns., Am. Judges Assn. Home: 1953 Hamilton St Portage IN 46368 Office: 5927 Central Ave Portage IN 46368 Tel (219) 762-7711

ANDERSON, ROBERT CARL, b. San Francisco, June 18, 1922; J.D., U. Pacific, 1962. Admitted to Calif. bar, 1963, U.S. Supreme Ct. bar, 1970; individual practice law, Sacramento, 1963-71, br. office, San Francisco, 1970-75, Aptos, Calif., 1971—; licensed real estate broker, Calif., 1947-63. Mem. Santa Cruz County Bar Assn. Home: 509 Vista Del Mar Aptos CA 95003 Office: 8048 Soquel Dr Aptos CA 95003 Tel (408) 688-1424

ANDERSON, ROBERT JOHN, b. Chgo., July 29, 1920; A.A., N. Park Coll., 1940; J.D., Kent Coll. Law, 1963. Admitted to Ill. bar, 1963; individual practice law, Long Grove, Ill., 1963—; pres. R. J. Anderson, Inc. Mem. Park Ridge (Ill.) Zoning Bd. Appeals, 1959-64; mem. Prairie View (Ill.) Bd. Edn., 1966-75, sec., 1969-72, pres., 1972-75. Mem. Am., Ill., Chgo., Lake County bar assns. Contbr. articles in field to legal jours. Office: POB 456 Palatine IL 60067 Tel (312) 438-2321

ANDERSON, ROBERT LANIER, b. Macon, Ga., Aug. 3, 1899; s. A.B., U. Ga., 1920, LL.B., 1922. Admitted to Ga. bar, 1922; since practiced in Macon, partner firm Anderson Walker & Reichert, and predecessors, 1922—. Mem. State Bar Ga. (sec. 1943-48), Macon Circuit Bar Assn. (past pres.), Am. Judicature Soc., Internat. Assn. Ins. Counsel. Home: 475 Vista Circle Macon GA 31204 Office: 404 First Nat Bank Bldg Macon GA 31201 Tel (912) 743-8651

ANDERSON, ROBERT LEONARD, b. Middleboro, Mass., Oct. 19, 1923; B.S., Mass. Maritime Acad., 1951; J.D. with honors, Boston U., 1950. Admitted to Mass. bar, 1950, U.S. Ct. of Mil. Appeals bar, 1953, U.S. Tax Ct. bar, 1954, U.S. Dist. Ct. bar, 1955, U.S. Supreme Ct. bar, 1971; legal officer U.S. Navy, 1951-52; instr. Naval Justice Sch., Newport, R.I., 1952-53; individual practice law, Middleboro, Mass., 1954-57; asst. dist. atty. Plymouth County (Mass.), 1957-69, dist. atty., 1969-73; presiding judge 4th Dist. Ct. of Plymouth, 1973—; mem. Gov.'s Proposal Rev. Bd., 1969-71, Gov.'s Com. on Law Enforcement and Adminstrn. of Justice, 1969-73. Mem. Am., Mass., Plymouth County bar assns. Home: 126 North St Middleboro MA 02346 Office: Marion Rd Wareham MA 02571 Tel (617) 295-1515

ANDERSON, ROBERT MONTE, b. Logan, Utah, Feb. 19, 1938; A.B., Columbia, 1960; LL.B., U. Utah, 1963. Admitted to Utah bar, 1963; mem. firm Van Cott, Bagley, Cornwall & McCarthy, Salt Lake City, 1963—. Bd. dirs. Children's Center, 1972-75, Salt Lake Tng. Center for Retarded Adults, 1966-69. Mem. Utah State, Salt Lake County (exec. com. 1966-74, pres. 1973-74), Am. bar assns. Home: 2066 Walker Ln Salt Lake City UT 84117 Office: 141 E First South St Salt Lake City UT 84111 Tel (801) 532-3333

ANDERSON, RODERICK BRUCE, b. Hammer, S.D., Mar. 14, 1934; B.E.E., S.D. State U., 1957; J.D., Seton Hall U., 1961. Admitted to D.C. bar, 1962, N.J. bar, 1964; tchr. elementary schs., Sisseton, S.D., 1954-55; patent examiner U.S. Patent Office, Washington, 1957-58; mem. patent staff Bell Labs., Murray Hill, N.J., 1958-61, patent atty., 1961-63, 1964-75; asso. firm Hughes, Hartlaub & Dotten, Summit, N.J., 1963-64; patent atty. Western Electric, N.Y.C., 1975-76, internat. patent atty. Princeton, N.J., 1976—. Mayor Berkeley Heights (N.J.), 1972-73; mem. Union County (N.J.) Democratic Com., 1969-70, Berkeley Heights N.J. Twp. Com., 1970-74. Mem. Am., N.J. (pres. 1973-74) patent law assns., Am. Bar Assn. Contbr. articles to legal jours. Home: 48 Ethan Dr Murray Hill NJ 07974 Office: PO Box 901 Princeton NJ 08540 Tel (609) 639-2325

ANDERSON, RONALD ABERDEEN, b. Chgo., Dec. 11, 1911; A.B., U. Pa., 1933, J.D., 1936. Gowan research fellow U. Pa. Law Sch., 1937; research asst. procedural rules com Pa. Supreme Ct., 1937-50; law clk. Estates Ct., Phila., 1940-65; practiced law, Phila., 1937-66; prof. law and govt. Drexel U., Phila., 1946—; tchr. law, econs. and polit. sci. Charles Morris Price Sch. Advt., Phila., 1946-53. Vol., Central br. YMCA, Phila., bd. dirs., 1947-52; founder, bd. dirs. Save Am. Manpower, Social Security Citizens Found.; bd. dirs. Chapel of Four Chaplains. Mem. Am., Pa., Phila. bar assns., Am. Bus. Law Assn., Am. Hotel Law Inst. (dir.). Author: Anderson on the Uniform Commercial Code, 6 vols.; Couch Cyclopedia on Insurance, 2d edit., 24 vols.; Anderson's Pennsylvania Civil Practice, 17 vols.; Purdon's Pennsylvania Forms, 15 vols.; Social Forces and the Law; Government Regulation of Business; Hotelman's Basic Law; Insurer's Tort Law; Running a Professional Corporation; sr. author Principles of Business; Business Law Principles and Cases; cons. editor Pennsylvania Law Ency., 45 vols. Office: 252 S Van Pelt St Philadelphia PA 19103 Tel (215) 546-3285

ANDERSON, RONALD PAUL, b. Denver, Aug. 12, 1939; B.S., U. Oreg., 1962, LL.B., 1965. Admitted to Oreg. bar, 1965; asso. firm Veatch, Lovett & Stiner, Portland, Oreg., 1965-67; v.p. Music Craft, Inc., San Francisco, 1967-68; individual practice law, Portland, 1968-70; partner, pres. firm Anderson, Hall, Lowthian, Gross & Grebe, Portland, 1970—. Chmn. Portland Mayor's Fin. Com., 1976. Mem. Am., Oreg. State, Multnomah County (Oreg.) bar asssns., Assn. Trial Lawyers Am. Home: 5545 SW Sweetbriar St Portland OR 97221 Office: 1530 SW Taylor St Portland OR 97205 Tel (503) 228-9381

ANDERSON, SIGURD, b. Arendal, Norway, Jan. 22, 1904; A.B., U. S.D., 1931, LL.B., 1937; LL.D., Yankton (S.D.) Coll., Gettysburg (Pa.) Coll. Admitted to S.D. bar, 1937, U.S. Supreme Ct. bar, 1956; practiced in Webster, S.D., 1937-41, 64-67; Commr. Fed. Trade Commn., 1955-64; judge S.D. Circuit Ct., 5th Circuit, 1967-75; state's atty. Day County (S.D.), 1938-41; atty. gen. State of S.D., 1947-50, gov., 1951-55; lectr. in field. Mem. State Bar S.D., Am., Fed. bar assns., Am. Judicature Soc., Phi Beta Kappa, Delta Theta Phi. Contbr. numerous articles to legal publs. Home: 313 W 7th Ave Webster SD 57274 Tel (605) 345-3950

ANDERSON, SUSAN LOU, b. D.C., July 14, 1947; A.B. in Chemistry, Eastern Coll., 1969; J.D., Villanova U., 1972. Admitted to Pa. bar, 1972; v.p., asst. counsel, asst. sec. Fidelcor, Inc., Phila., 1972—; sec., treas. Pa. State Bd. Law Examiners, Phila., 1976—. Mem. Am., Pa., Phila. bar assns. Home: 3644 Darby Rd Bryn Mawr PA 19010 Office: The Fidelity Bldg Broad and Walnut Sts Philadelphia PA 19109 Tel (215) 985-8922

ANDERSON, THOMAS TENNYSON, b. Seattle, July 9, 1928; B.B.A., U. Oreg., 1949; B.S., Willamette U., 1954; LL.B., U. Calif., 1955. Admitted to Calif. bar, 1955; prin. Thomas T. Anderson, Indio, Calif., 1955—. Trustee Palm Springs (Calif.) Boy's Club, 1973-76, Palm Valley Sch., 1964—. Mem. Calif. (pres. 1970-71, gov. 1963-66), Western (gov. 1965-70) trial lawyers assns., Desert (pres. 1963-65), Calif. bar assns., Assn. Trial Lawyers Am. (gov. 1971—, asso. editor 1965—, chmn. membership com. 1971, mem. exec. com. 1974-75). Co-author: Anatomy of a Personal Injury Lawsuit, a Handbook of Basic Trial Advocacy, 1968; contbr. articles to legal jours. Home: 1184 Camino Mirasol Palm Springs CA 92262 Office: 45-926 Oasis St Indio CA 92201 Tel (714) 347-3364

ANDERSON, TRACY EUGENE, b. Rock Rapids, Iowa, May 18, 1938; B.A., U. No. Iowa, 1960; M.A. in History, U. Iowa, 1961, J.D., 1972. Admitted to Iowa bar, 1972; partner firm Griffiths, Anderson & Buffer, 1975; atty. Washington County, Washington, Iowa, 1972-74; city atty., Kalona, 1976. Mem. Am., Iowa State bar assns., Assn. Trial Lawyers Iowa. Office: Box 848 Kalona IA 52247 Tel (319) 656-2227

ANDERSON, WALTER MARK, III, b. Montgomery, Ala., Mar. 19, 1937; B.S., U. Ala., 1960, J.D., 1962. Admitted to Ala. bar, 1962, U.S. Supreme Ct. bar, 1967; law clk. Supreme Ct. Ala., 1962-63; asst. atty. gen. State of Ala., 1963-65, spl. asst. atty. gen., 1967-71; partner firm Gallion, Hare & Anderson, Montgomery, 1966, firm Hare & Anderson, Montgomery, 1967-70; individual practice law, Montgomery, 1971—; spl. judge Probate Ct. Montgomery County, 1971, county atty., 1972-76. Mem. Ala. State, Montgomery County bar assns., Montgomery Area C. of C., Montgomery Jaycees (dir. 1962-73), Phi Alpha Delta. Home: 1546 Gilmer Ave Montgomery AL 36104 Office: 428 S Perry St Suite A Montgomery AL 36104 Tel (205) 262-6694

ANDERSON, WARREN MATTICE, b. Bainbridge, N.Y., Oct. 16, 1915; A.B., Colgate U., 1937; LL.B., Albany Law Sch., 1940. Admitted to N.Y. bar, 1940; asst. county atty. Broome County, N.Y., 1940-42; asso. firms Riley H. Heath, Binghamton, N.Y., Palmer & Hankin, Binghamton; mem. firm Hinman, Howard & Kattell, Binghamton, 1951—; with JAGC, U.S. Army, 1944; mem. N.Y. State Senate, 1952—, pres. pro tem, majority leader, 1973—. Mem. Broome County, N.Y. State, Am. bar assns. Office: Hinman Howard & Kattell Security Mut Bldg Binghamton NY 13901 Tel (607) 723-5341

ANDERSON, WENDELL R., b. St. Paul, Feb. 1, 1933; B.A., U. Minn., 1954, LL.B., 1960. Admitted to Minn. bar, 1960, U.S. Supreme Ct. bar, 1976; asso. firm Thuet, Todd & Anderson, now partner; mem. Minn. Ho. of Reps., 1959-62, Minn. Senate, 1963-70, gov., 1971—; mem. exec. com. Dem. Nat. Com.; chmn. Dem. Gov.'s Caucus, 1974-75; mem. exec. com. Nat. Gov.'s Conf., 1971-72; chmn. platform com. Dem. Nat. Conv., 1976; leader del. to People's Republic of China, 1975. Mem. Dem. Adv. Council of Elected Ofcls. Named one of leaders of tomorrow, Time Mag., 1974; named Outstanding Minn. Legislator, Eagleton Inst. Politics, Rutgers U.; named Swedish-Am. of Year, Swedish-Am. Vasa Soc., 1975. Home: 1006 Summit Ave Saint Paul MN Office: 130 State Capitol Bldg Saint Paul MN 55155 Tel (612) 296-3391

ANDERSON, WILLIAM EARL, b. Tyler, Tex., Jan. 28, 1947; A.B., U. Ga., 1969, J.D., 1972. Admitted to Ga. bar, 1972; mem. firm Glover & Davis, Newnan, Ga., 1972—. Area chmn. joint Tech.-Ga. Devel. Fund, 1975. Mem. Newnan-Coweta Bar Assn. (dist. rep. Younger Lawyers Sect., exec. council, 1976). Contbr. articles to legal jours. Home: 30 Wesley St Newnan GA 30263 Office: 16 E Broad St Newnan GA 30263 Tel (404) 253-4330

ANDERSON, WILLIAM EUGENE, b. Moscow, Idaho, June 19, 1936; B.S. in Bus., U. Idaho, 1959, J.D., 1967. Admitted to Idaho bar, 1967; savs. officer 1st Fed. Savs. & Loan Assn. of Lewiston, Moscow; judge police ct., Moscow, 1964-65; justice of peace, Latah County, Idaho, 1965-66, judge probate ct., 1967, dep. pros. atty., 1967-68, pros. atty., 1969-73. Bd. dirs. Ballet Folk, U. Idaho Scholarship Com., U. Idaho Alumni Exec. Bd.; Moscow Central Bus. Dist. Com.; chmn. Moscow Traffic Commn., People Awareness Council, Talisman. Mem. Idaho, Clearwater, Latah County bar assns., U. Idaho Alumni Assn. (v.p.). Home: 907 E 7th St Moscow ID 83843 Office: 114 E 3rd St Moscow ID 83843 Tel (208) 882-4536

ANDERSON, WILLIAM HARLAN, b. Citronelle, Ala., Dec. 17, 1927; LL.B., U. Fla., 1949. Admitted to Fla. bar, 1949; practiced in Pensacola, Fla., 1954-73; judge Escambia County (Fla.) Ct., 1973—; asst. county solicitor Escambia County, 1955-56; judge Escambia County Small Claims Ct., 1956-61. Chmn. bd. dirs. East Hill Christian Sch., Pensacola, 1975-76. Mem. Escambia-Santa Rosa Bar Soc., Fla. Bar, Soc. Bar 1st Jud. Circuit. Home: 116 Mango St Pensacola FL 32503 Office: County Courthouse 402 Jefferson St Pensacola FL 32501 Tel (904) 432-3344

ANDERSON, WILSON, b. Welch, W.Va., Aug. 25, 1906; A.B., Ohio Wesleyan U., 1927; LL.B., W.Va. U., 1930. Admitted to W.Va. bar, 1930, Va. bar, 1939; pros. atty. McDowell County (W.Va.), 1930-37; partner firm Steptoe & Johnson, Charleston, W.Va., 1943—; mem. W.Va. Senate, 1956-60, W.Va. Banking Commn., 1969—. Mem. Kanowha County (pres. 1953), W.Va. (pres. 1966-67), Am., Va. bar assns., Internat. Assn. Ins. Counsel, Am. Coll. Trial Lawyers, Am. Judicature Soc. (dir. 1973—), Fedn. Ins. Counsel, 4th Circuit Jud. Conf. (permanent mem.). Home: 1600 Loudon Heights Rd Charleston WV 25314 Office: POB 1588 Charleston WV 25326 Tel (304) 342-2191

ANDRE, PETER RICHARD, b. San Luis Obispo, Calif., Jan. 3, 1918; B.S., U. Santa Clara, 1940; LL.B., U. So. Calif., 1948. Admitted to Calif. bar, 1948, U.S. Supreme Ct. bar, 1969; individual practice law, San Luis Obispo, 1948; dep. city atty. San Luis Obispo, 1952-55; legal counsel Calif. Fine Wire Co., 1961—, San Luis Obispo County Hist. Assn., 1952—, Tar Springs Oil Co., 1960—, Harmony Valley Creamery Assn., 1957-72, S. County San. Service, Inc., 1963—, San

Luis Obisopo County Farm Supply Co., 1960—, San Luis Garbage Co., 1949—, Cold Canyon Land Fill, Inc., 1967—; mem. adv. bd. Bank Am. Nat. Trust and Savs. Assn. Vice chmn. San Luis Obispo Young Republicans, 1950; San Luis Obispo county chmn. Richard Nixon senatorial campaign, 1950, Eisenhower and Nixon presl. election campaign, 1952, 56, Nixon for pres. campaign, 1968; chmn. San Luis Obispo County Air Pollution Hearing Bd., 1970—. Mem. Calif. Cattlemens Assn., Farm Bur. (4-H leader 1963-74), San Luis Obispo C. of C. (dir. 1949-51), Caballeros de San Luis Obispo (pres. 1952, sec. 1954—), Am. Legion Native Sons Golden West, San Luis Obispo County Bar Assn. (pres. 1969-71). Home: 1801 Woodland Dr San Luis Obispo CA 93401 Office: 1150 Osos St San Luis Obispo CA 93401

ANDREEN, PHILIP NORRIS, b. San Diego, Jan. 31, 1940; B.A., Pomona Coll., 1961; LL.B., U. Calif., Los Angeles, 1964. Admitted to Calif. bar, 1965; served to lt. JAGC, U.S. Navy, 1965-68; staff atty. Defenders, Inc., 1968-70; individual practice law, San Diego, 1970—; judge pro tem Municipal Ct.; dir. Defenders, Inc., Appellate Defenders, Fed. Defenders; prof. law Cabrillo Pacific Law Sch., 1974-76. Mem. Coronado (Calif.) Sch. Bd., 1970-76, pres., 1974-75; candidate 79th Assembly Dist. of Calif., 1976; chmn. bar assn. campaign United Way, 1973-74. Mem. San Diego Bar Assn. Named San Diego Trial Lawyer of Month, Mar. 1977. Office: Suite 1200 1200 3d Ave San Diego CA 92101 Tel (714) 239-3357

ANDRES, EUGEN CHARLES, b. Boston, July 15, 1939; B.S. in Econs., U. Calif. at Los Angeles, 1961; LL.B., Hastings Coll. Law, 1968. Admitted to Calif. bar, 1969; dep dist. atty. Orange County, Calif., 1969-71; individual practice law, Santa Ana, Calif., 1971-72; partner firm Aitken, Bradshaw & Andres, Santa Ana, 1972—. Mem. bd. dirs. Bowers Mus. Found., Santa Ana, 1976, chmn. auction com., 1976. Mem. Am. Bar Assn., Calif. Trial Lawyers Assn. (chmn. criminal law sect.), Orange County Trial Lawyers Assn. (dir. 1976), Calif. State Bar (mem. criminal justice com.), Orange County Bar Assn. (dir. 1976). Home: 1912 Greenleaf St Santa Ana CA 92706 Office: 611 Civic Center Dr W Santa Ana CA 92701 Tel (714) 834

ANDREW, THOMAS JOHNSTON, b. Syracuse, N.Y., Sept. 5, 1938; A.B., Dartmouth Coll., 1960; J.D., Duke, 1964. Admitted to N.Y. State bar, 1966, Mass. bar, 1967; legal advisor to Ethiopian Govt., Peace Crops, 1964-66; asso. firm Hale and Dorr, Boston, 1966-70; asst. prof. law U. N.C., 1970-75, asso. prof., 1975—; mem. N.C. Legis. Sutdy Commn. on Sexual Assaults. Mem. Am. Assn. Law Schs. (chairperson sect. on criminal law 1977). Contbr. articles in field to profl. jours. Office: School of Law Univ N C Chapel Hill NC 27514 Tel (919) 933-5106

ANDREWS, EDWARD REED, b. Providence, Mar. 1, 1934; A.B., Brown U., 1956; LL.B., New Eg. Sch. Law, 1965. Admitted to Mass. bar, 1965, R.I. bar, 1966; individual practice law, Providence, 1965—. Mem. Am. Arbitration Assn., Am. Judicature Soc., Am., R.I., Mass., Boston bar assns., Am. Trial Lawyers Assn. Recipient Philo Sherman Bennett prize Brown U., 1955. Home: 14 Anstis St Cranston RI 02905 Office: 906 Old Colony Bank Bldg Providence RI 02903 Tel (401) 272-5010

ANDREWS, ERNEST EDWARD, b. Tocca, Ga., Nov. 28, 1897; LL.B., U. Ga., 1921. Admitted to Ga. bar, 1921; mem. State Senate of Ga., 1925-26; asst. solicitor gen., Ga., 1936-44, solicitor gen., 1945-47; mem. faculty Atlanta Law Sch., 1925-44; judge Superior Ct. of Fulton County Atlanta Jud. Circuit, 1947-61, emeritus judge, 1971—, Pres., dir. Atlanta Times, 1971. Mem. Lawyers Club of Atlanta, Atlanta Bar Assn., Council of Superior Ct. Judges of Ga. Home: 44 Blackland Rd NW Atlanta GA 30342 Office: 609 County Ct House Atlanta GA 30303 Tel (404) 572-2831

ANDREWS, H. RAYMOND, JR., A.B., U. W.Va., 1952, LL.B., 1956. Admitted to W.Va. bar, 1956; asso. firm Oliver D. Kessel, Ripley, W.Va., 1956; individual practice law, Ripley, 1956-57; partner firm Andrews & Adams, Ripley, 1957-58; atty. legal dept. United Fuel Gas Co., Charleston, W.Va., 1958-73; sr. atty. law dept. Columbia Gas Transmission Corp., Charleston, 1973—. Pres., bd. dirs. Charleston Symphony Orch.; v.p. W.Va. Kidney Found. Mem. W.Va. State Bar (chmn. young lawyers sect. 1966), Am., W.Va. bar assns., Ky. Oil Natural Gas Assn. (chmn. legal com.). Office: PO Box 1273 Charleston WV 25325 Tel (304) 346-0951

ANDREWS, HORACE ALLAN, b. Plant City, Fla., Oct. 2, 1932; B.B.A., U. Fla., 1954; J.D., Stetson Coll. Law, 1970. Admitted to Fla. bar, 1970, U.S. Supreme Ct. bar, 1976; partner firm Harris, Harris & Andrews, St. Petersburg, Fla., 1970—. Mem. Am., St. Petersburg (exec. com. 1972-75, treas. 1974) bar assns., Am. Judicature Soc. Office: 602 Florida National Bank Bldg St Petersburg FL 33701 Tel (813) 896-3674

ANDREWS, J. DAVID, b. Decatur, Ill., July 5, 1933; B.A. in Polit. Sci., U. Ill., 1955, J.D., 1960. Admitted to Wash. bar, 1960, U.S. Supreme Ct. bar, 1972; mem. firm Perkins, Coie, Stone, Olsen & Williams, Seattle, 1960—. Bd. dirs. Cornish Inst., 1973—, exec. com. and v.p., 1976—; bd. dirs. Fund for Pub. Edn., AEF Pension Fund; bd. visitors U. Puget Sound Law Sch., 1975—. Fellow Am. Bar Found. (dir.); mem. Am. (treas. 1975—, bd. govs.), Wash., Seattle-King County bar assns., Am. Judicature Soc., Am. Bar Retirement Assn. (dir.). Mem. bd. Am. Bar Jour., 1975. Home: 10320 Bedford Ct NW Seattle WA 98177 Office: 1900 Washington Bldg Seattle WA 98101 Tel (206) 682-8770

ANDREWS, JOHN EDWARD, b. Des Moines, Apr. 17, 1917; LL.B., 1950, J.D., 1968. Admitted to Iowa bar; spl. agt. U.S. Office Price Adminstrn., 1950-53; individual practice law, Des Moines, 1950—; justice peace Bloomfield Twp., 1950; state rep. Polk County, Iowa, 1956-60; mem. Iowa State Bd. Parole, 1965-71. Mem. Polk County Zoning Commn., 1962-73, Central Iowa Regional Planning Commn., 1965—. Mem. Polk County, Iowa, bar assns. Office: 210 Euclid Ave Des Moines IA 50313 Tel (515) 288-6805

ANDREWS, JOHN FONTAINE, b. Montgomery, Ala., Jan. 6, 1938; B.S., Auburn U., 1959; J.D., Tulane U., 1962. Admitted to Ala. bar, 1962; mem. firm Capell, Howard, Knabe & Cobbs, P.A., Montgomery, 1963-67, partner, 1967—. Mem. Am., Ala. State, Montgomery County bar assns., Order of Coif. Editorial bd. Tulane Law Rev., 1960-62. Home: 1945 Graham St Montgomery AL 36106 Office: 57 Adams Ave Montgomery AL 36103 Tel (205) 262-1671

ANDREWS, KENNETH LEE, b. Albany, Ky., June 23, 1942; A.B. in Polit. Sci., Ind. U., 1965, J.D., 1968. Admitted to Ind. bar, 1968; tax accountant Am. Fletcher Nat. Bank, Indpls., 1967-69; asso. firm Bolinger, Van Dorn & Andrews, Kokomo, Ind., 1969-70; individual practice law, Kokomo, 1970-71; partner firm Andrews, Dechert and Ferries, Kokomo, 1971—; atty. City Kokomo, 1972-75. Vol. worker United Way, Kokomo, 1970-72, 1976; mem. com. first, second and third class cities Ann. Assn. Cities and Towns Meeting, Evansville, Ind., 1973. Mem. Ind., Howard County, Am. bar assns., Kokomo C. of C. (chmn. com. polit. edn. 1974). Home: 2004 S Main St Kokomo IN 46901 Office: 300 N Main St Kokomo IN 46901 Tel (317) 452-0011

ANDREWS, MILTON DARRELL, b. Enid, Okla., July 15, 1937; B.S., Phillips U., 1959; J.D., U. Okla., 1963, LL.M., 1966; postgrad. George Washington U., 1966-67, U. Paris. Admitted to Okla. bar, 1963, N.Y. bar, 1967, D.C. bar, 1967, U.S. Supreme Ct. bar, 1967; atty. U.S. Dept. Justice, 1963-66; asso. firm Busby, Aiukin, Sherman, Levy and Rehm, N.Y.C., Washington, 1967-71, partner, 1972—; legal entries editor Librairie La Rousse, Paris, 1966-67. Mem. Am., D.C., Okla. bar assns., Bar Assn. D.C. Ford Found. fellow, 1963; contbr. articles in field to legal jours. Home: 5355 Macarthur Blvd NW Washington DC 20016 Office: 900 17th St NW Washington DC 20006 Tel (202) 347-6007

ANDREWS, ROGER CLINTON, b. Chariton, Iowa, Aug. 6, 1917; B.S.C., Creighton U., 1940, LL.B., 1942. Admitted to Nebr. bar, 1942, Fed. bar, 1955; individual practice law, Omaha, 1942-48; legal dept. World Ins. Co., Omaha, 1948—, asst. gen. counsel, 1955—. Mem. Am., Nebr., Omaha bar assns. Home: 150 N 31st St Omaha NE 68131 Office: World Ins Co 203 S 18th St Omaha NE 68102 Tel (402) 342-1402

ANDRIN, ALBERT ANTAL, b. Chgo., Dec. 2, 1928; B.A., Roosevelt U., 1952; LL.B., Chgo. Kent Coll. Law, 1956. Admitted to Ill. bar, 1956; asso. firm Axelrod, Goodman & Steiner, Chgo., 1956-61; partner firm Levy, Andrin & Stillerman, Chgo., 1961-75; partner firm Burke, Kerwin & Towle, Chgo., 1975—. Mem. Ill., Chgo. bar assns., Motor Carrier Lawyers Assn. Home: 9016 S Lemont Rd Downers Grove IL 60515 Office: 180 N LaSalle St Chicago IL 60601 Tel (312) 332-5106

ANDROUS, MELVIN D., b. Marigold, Calif., Mar. 24, 1925; A.A., Yuba Coll., 1948; J.D., U. San Francisco, 1951. Admitted to Calif. bar, 1970; atty., adv. bd. Calif. Cling Peach Bd., Yuba City, 1952-60; in-charge field ops. Androus Ins. and Realty, Yuba City, 1960-70; individual practice law, Yuba City, 1970—; mgr. Calif. Rice Research Bd., 1969—. Chmn. hearing bd. Air Pollution Control, Yuba City, 1972—; mem. Calif. State Republican Central com., Yuba City, 1973—; chmn. Sutter County (Calif.) Rep. Central com., Yuba City, 1973—. Mem. Calif., Am., Yuba-Sutter bar assns., Comml. Law League. Office: 335 Teegarden St Yuba City CA 95991 Tel (916) 673-8223

ANDRUS, VANCE ROBERT, b. Opelousas, La., Oct. 26, 1947; B.A., U. Southwestern La., 1969; J.D., La. State U., 1972. Admitted to La. bar, 1972; mem. firm Fontenot, Gautreaux & Andrus, Lafayette, La., 1976—; law clk. to Hon. Albert Tate, La. Supreme Ct., 1972. Mem. La. Democratic State Central Com., 1976; chmn. 7th Congl. Dist. Dem. Exec. Com., 1976. Mem. Am. Bar Assn., Phi Kappa Phi, Omicron Delta Kappa. Contbr. articles to legal jours. Office: PO Drawer HH Lafayette LA 70502 Tel (318) 233-5390

ANGE, GRACE MARIE, b. Rochester, N.Y., Jan. 11, 1932; student U. Rochester, 1954; grad. U. Buffalo Law Sch., 1957, J.D., 1968. Admitted to N.Y. bar, 1957; partner firm Klocke & Ange, and predecessor, Buffalo, 1957—; lectr. in field. Mem. Am. Acad. Matrimonial Lawyers, Am., N.Y., Erie County bar assns., Am. Arbitration Assn., Assn. Women Attys., Indsl. Relations and Research Assn., Bus. and Profl. Women's Assn. of Buffalo, Kappa Beta Pi. Office: 314 Statler Office Bldg Buffalo NY 14202 Tel (716) 847-0700

ANGEL, MARINA, b. N.Y.C., July 21, 1944; B.A., Barnard Coll., 1965, J.D. magna cum laude, Columbia, 1969. Admitted to N.Y. bar, 1969, Pa. bar, 1971, U.S. Supreme Ct. bar, 1974; chief appeals div. Juvenile Defender Office, Phila. Voluntary Defender Assn., 1969-71; lectr. Rutgers U. Law Sch., Camden, N.J., 1970; asso. prof. law Hofstra U., Hempstead, N.Y., 1971—. Mem. Am., Phila. bar assns., Assn. Bar City N.Y. Home: 120 Cabrini Blvd New York City NY 10033 Office: School of Law Hofstra U Hempstead NY 11550 Tel (516) 560-3607

ANGEL, PAUL FREDERICK, b. Racine, Wis., Oct. 21, 1942; B.B.A., Milton Coll., 1967; J.D., U. S.D., 1970; LL.M., U. Mo., Kansas City, 1973. Admitted to Iowa bar, 1970, Wis. bar, 1970; with JAGC, U.S. Army, 1971-72; partner firm Morrow, Pope & Angel, Dodgeville, Wis., 1973—. Mem. Dodgeville C. of C. (pres. 1975), Iowa County (pres. 1974—), Wis., Iowa bar assns. Home: 304 Virginia Ct Dodgeville WI 53533 Office: 103 W Merrimac St Dodgeville WI 53533 Tel (608) 935-3346

ANGELL, GEORGE B., b. Cortland, N.Y., Jan. 11, 1934; B.S. in Bus. Adminstrn., Lafayette Coll., 1958; LL.B., Temple U., 1961. Admitted to Pa. bar, 1962; individual practice law, Port Allegheny, Pa., 1963—. Home and office: Box 333 Port Allegheny PA 16743 Tel (814) 642-7761

ANGELO, HOMER GLENN, b. Alameda, Calif., June 8, 1916; A.B., U. Calif., Berkeley, 1938, J.D., 1941; LL.M., Columbia, 1947; Admitted to Calif. bar, 1941; individual practice law, San Francisco, Geneva, Brussels and London, 1947—; prof. law Stanford U., 1954-58, U. Calif., Davis, 1968—, Institut d'Etudes Europeenees, U. Brussels, 1968—. Mem. Am. Bar Assn. (chmn. sect. on internat. and comparative law, 1957-59). Home: Sage House Genoa NV 89701 Office: Sch of Law U Calif Davis CA 95616 also 30 Pall Mall London SW1 England Tel (916) 752-2890

ANGELOFF, CARL, b. Detroit, Apr. 29, 1930; student Columbia U., 1949; B.A. cum laude, U. Rochester, 1953; LL.B. magna cum laude, Harvard, 1959. Admitted to N.Y. bar, 1959, U.S. Supreme Ct. bar, 1964, Fla. bar, 1973; asso. firm Nixon, Hargrave, Devans & Doyle, Rochester, N.Y., 1959-60; partner firm Robinson, Williams & Angeloff, Rochester, 1960—; confdl. legal asst. to justice N.Y. Supreme Ct., 1960-70. Mem. Monroe County, N.Y. State, Am. bar assns., Am. Arbitration Assn. (nat. panel arbitrators 1965—). Editor Harvard Law Rev., 1958-59. Home: 49 Mill Rd Fairport NY 14450 Office: 1600 1st Fed Plaza Rochester NY 14614

ANGERMUELLER, HANS H., b. 1924; B.A., Harvard U., 1946, M.S., Sch. Engring., 1947, LL.B., 1950. Partner firm Shearman & Sterling, 1950-72; sr. v.p., gen. counsel Citicorp, N.Y.C., 1973—. Office: 399 Park Ave New York City NY 10022*

ANGEVINE, GEORGE BRAUD, b. Newark, June 26, 1918; B.A., Rutgers U., 1940; LL.B., U. Pitts., 1948. Admitted to Pa. bar, 1948; mgr. labor relations West Penn Power Co., Pitts., 1948-56, partner firm Thorp, Reed & Armstrong, Pitts., 1956-63; v.p., gen. counsel, sec. Nat. Steel Corp., Pitts., 1963—. Bd. dirs. Allegheny Trails council Boy Scouts Am., Pitts., Health and Welfare Assn. Allegheny County, Pitts.; trustee Chatham Coll., Pitts. Decorated D.F.C., Air medal. Mem. Am. Iron and Steel Inst., Am., Pa., Mich., Allegheny County bar assns. Home: 502 Linden Pl Apts Sewickley PA 15143 Office: 2800 Grant Bldg Pittsburgh PA 15219*

ANGLE, ROBERT OREN, b. Ford City, Pa., Oct. 26, 1931; A.B., Harvard, 1953; J.D., Stanford, 1959. Admitted to Calif. bar, 1960; law clk. justice Calif. Ct. Appeal 1st Dist., 1959-60; asso. firm Hoge, Fenton, Jones & Appel, Monterey, Calif., 1960-62, firm Cavalleto, Webster, Mullen & McCaughey, Santa Barbara, Calif., 1962-66, mem. firm Hollister, Brace, & Angle, Santa Barbara, 1966-74; individual practice law, Santa Barbara, 1974—. Mem. City of San Santa Barbara Airport Commn., 1969. Mem. Santa Barbara County, Am. bar assns., Calif. Trial Lawyers Assn., Order of Coif. Author: Handbook of Probate Law, 1976. Home: 612 Mission Ridge Rd Santa Barbara CA 93103 Office: 30 W Sola St suite 6 Santa Barbara CA 93101 Tel (805) 963-7858

ANGLIN, WILLIAM ENGLISH, b. Burnsville, N.C., Oct. 24, 1907; B.S., U. N.C., Chapel Hill, 1934, LL.B., 1934, J.D., 1969. Admitted to N.C. bar, 1934, U.S. Dist. Ct. bar for Western Dist. N.C., 1934; practiced in Burnsville, 1934-42, 46-65; judge N.C. Superior Ct., 1965-74, emergency judge, 1975—. Mem. 24th Jud. Dist., N.C. bar assns., N.C. State Bar. Home: Burnsville NC 28714 Office: POB 217 Burnsville NC 28714 Tel (704) 682-2459

ANNAKIN, JOSEPH WOODY, b. Terre Haute, Ind., Apr. 29, 1939; student Kent State U., 1960; B.A., Ind. State U., 1961, J.D., 1965. Admitted to Ind. bar, 1965, U.S. Dist. Ct. So. Dist. Ind. bar 1965, U.S. 7th Circuit Ct. Appeals bar, 1965, U.S. Supreme Ct. bar, 1976; U.S. atty. U.S. Dept. Justice, Indpls., 1965-67; asso. firm Fine, Hatfield, Sparrenberger & Fine, Evansville, Ind., 1967-70; partner firm Lacey, Terrell, Annakin, Held & Baugh, Evansville, 1970-76; U.S. magistrate So. Dist. Ind., 1971-76; mem. Ind. Criminal Law Study Commn., 1973—. Mem. Am., Ind. State, Evansville bar assns., Assn. Trial Lawyers Am., Nat. Council U.S. Magistrates. Office: 5011 Washington Ave Evansville IN 47715 Tel (812) 477-6159

ANNAS, GEORGE J., b. St. Cloud, Minn., July 13, 1945; A.B. magna cum laude, Harvard U., 1967, J.D., 1970, M.P.H., 1972. Admitted to Minn. bar 1970, Mass. bar, 1970; law clk. to justice Mass. Supreme Judicial Ct., Boston, 1970-71; vis. prof. Boston Coll. Law Sch., Brighton, Mass., 1972-73; asst. prof. Boston U. Sch. of Medicine, 1975—; dir. Center for Law and Health Scis., Boston U., 1973—; partner firm Annas, Glantz & Rollins, Boston, 1976—. Chmn., Mass. Health Facilities Appeals Bd., 1973-76; vice chmn. Mass. Bd. of Registration and Discipline in Medicine, 1976—. Author: (with B. Katz and L. Glantz) Informed Consent to Human Experimentation: The Subject's Dilemma, 1977; The Rights of Hospital Patients, 1975. Editor: (with Aubrey Milunsky) Genetics and the Law, 1976; Medicolegal News, 1973—. Columnist, Hastings Center Report, 1976—, Orthopaedic Review, 1975—, Centerscope, 1975—. Office: Center for Law and Health Science 209 Bay State Rd Boston MA 02215 Tel (617) 353-2910 also (617) 227-0040

ANNESS, MILFORD EDWIN, b. Metamora, Ind., Feb. 14, 1918; LL.B., Ind. U., Indpls., 1954, B.A., 1940. Admitted to Ind. bar, 1954; judge Fayette Circuit Ct., Connersville, Ind., 1955-62; individual practice law, Columbus, Ind., 1962-65; partner Anness & Holland, Columbus, 1965—; mem. Ind. Jud. Council, 1960-64. Mem. Ind., Bartholomew County bar assns. Author: Song of Metamoris, 1962; Forever the Song, 1964; Stars Above America, 1968. Home and Office: Box 623 Columbus IN 47201 Tel (812) 376-3091

ANSARY, CYRUS A., b. Shiraz, Iran, Nov. 20, 1933; B.S., Am. U., 1955; LL.B., Columbia U., 1958. Admitted to Md. bar, 1959, D.C. bar, 1960, Va. bar, 1961, U.S. Supreme Ct. bar, 1964; practiced law, Washington, 1959-72; sr. partner firm Ansary, Kirkpatrick and Rosse, 1964-72; dir. Fired. Krupp GmbH, Essen, Fed. Republic of Germany, 1974—; fin. advisor Govt. Iran, 1974—; lectr. bus. adminstrn. Am. U., 1967-70; dir. numerous corps. Trustee Am. U., 1968—, trustee Inst. Internat. and Fgn. Trade Law Georgetown U., 1977—. Mem. D.C. Bar, Va. State Bar. Contbr. articles to profl. jours. Home: 5425 Falmouth Rd Bethesda MD 20016 Office: 1000 Connecticut Ave 302 Washington DC 20036 Tel (202) 452-1140

ANSBACHER, LEWIS, b. Jacksonville, Fla., Nov. 23, 1928; B.S. in Bus. Adminstrn., U. Fla., 1948, J.D., 1951; LL.M., George Washington U., 1955. Admitted to Fla. bar, 1951; served to 1st lt. JAGC, U.S. Army, 1952-55; asso. firm Philip Selber, Jacksonville, 1955-62; partner firm Selber & Ansbacher, Jacksonville, 1963-73; individual practice law, Jacksonville, 1973—. Vice pres. Jewish Family and Children's Service, Jacksonville, 1962-65, pres., 1965-68; v.p. Jacksonville Jewish Center, 1967-70; mem. planning bd. United Fund, 1965. Mem. Duval County Legal Aid Assn. (pres. 1964-65), Am. Arbitration Assn. Mem. Hall Fame U. Fla. Author chpt. Fla. Real Property Practice, Vol. II, 1975. Home: 2247 Segovia Ave Jacksonville FL 32217 Office: 2218 Gulf Life Tower Jacksonville FL 32207 Tel (904) 398-8352

ANSEL, JAMES EARL, b. Springfield, W.Va., Nov. 3, 1915; A.B., Shepherd Coll., 1940; J.D., W.Va. U., 1948. Admitted to W.Va. bar, 1948; individual practice law, Moorefield, W.Va., 1948—; served to comdr. JAGC, USN. Mem., pres. W.Va. Bd. Edn., 1955-60; deacon Moorefield Presbyn. Ch., 1968-72, elder, 1972-76. Mem. South Branch Valley, W.Va., Am. bar assns., Judge Advs. Assn. Home: Old Fields WV 26845 Office: 129 N Main St Moorefield WV 26836

ANSEL, WILLIAM HENRY, JR., b. Springfield, W. Va., Jan. 23, 1914; student Shepherd Coll., Potomac State Coll., W. Va. U. Admitted to W. Va. bar, 1948; mem. W. Va. Legislature, 1942-48; asst. atty. gen. State W. Va., 1949, treas., 1950-57; dir. Bank of Romney (W. Va.). Mem. Am., W. Va. bar assns. Home: Box 107 Springfield WV 26763 Office: 44 E Main St Romney WV 26757 Tel (304) 822-3028

ANSELL, EDWARD ORIN, b. Superior, Wis., Mar. 29, 1926; B.S. in Elec. Engring., U. Wis., 1948; J.D., George Washington U., 1955. Admitted to D.C. bar, 1955, U.S. Patent Office bar, 1956, Calif. bar, 1960; patent atty. RCA Labs., Princeton, N.J., 1955-57; gen. mgr. Aero Chem. Research Labs, Inc., Princeton, 1957-58; patent atty. Aerojet-Gen Corp., El Monte, Calif., 1958-63, corp. patent counsel, 1963—, asst. sec., 1970—; adj. prof. LaVerne Coll. Law Sch., 1972—. Spl. adviser Commn. Govt. Procurement, 1971. Mem. Pomona Valley, Am., Fed. bar assns., Patent Law Assn. Los Angeles, Calif. Patent Law Assn., Phi Alpha Delta. Contbr. articles to legal jours.

Home: 142 W 11th St Claremont CA 91711 Office: 9100 E Flair Dr El Monte CA 91734 Tel (213) 572-6156

ANSELMO, SCOTT ROBIN, b. Meadville, Pa., Sept. 28, 1940; B.A., U. Fla., 1962, J.D., 1965. Admitted to Fla. bar, 1965, U.S. Supreme Ct. bar, 1971; mem. firm Fleming O'Bryan & Fleming, Fort Lauderdale, Fla., 1965-69, partner, 1969—. Mem. Am., Broward County, Fla. bar assns., Fla. Defense Lawyers Assn., Internat. Assn. Ins. Counsel, Phi Beta Kappa, Phi Kappa Phi, Phi Delta Phi, Phi Eta Sigma. Home: 545 S Atlantic Blvd Fort Lauderdale FL 33316 Office: PO Drawer 7028 Fort Lauderdale FL 33338 Tel (305) 764-3000

ANSLEY, SHEPARD BRYAN, b. Atlanta, July 31, 1939; B.A., U. Ga., 1961; LL.B., U. Va., 1964. Admitted to Ga., bar, 1967; asso. firm Carter, Ansley, Smith & McLendon, Atlanta, 1967-73, partner, 1973—. Mem. Vestry St. Luke's Episcopal Ch., Atlanta, Ga., 1971-74; treas., mem. bd. sponsers Alliance Theatre Co., Atlanta, Ga., 1974—; bd. trustee Atlanta Music Festival Assn., 1975—. Mem. Am., Ga., Atlanta bar assns., Atlanta Lawyers Club, Am. Coll Mortgage Attys., Phi Delta Phi. Bd. dirs. Jour. Pub. Law, Emory U., 1961-62. Home: 2505 Rivers Rd NW Atlanta GA 30305 Office: 1810 1st Nat Bank Tower Atlanta GA 30303 Tel (404) 658-9220

ANTER, SAMUEL SIMON, b. Central Falls, R.I., Feb. 18, 1927; B.A., R.I. State Coll., 1949; LL.B., Boston U., 1952. Admitted to R.I. bar, 1952, Nev. bar, 1964; individual practice law, Pawtucket, R.I., 1952-63, Las Vegas, Nev., 1964—. Mem. Central Falls City Council, 1953-59. Mem. Am., R.I., Nev., Clark County bar assns. Home: 3779 Monument St Las Vegas NV 89121 Office: 2217 Paradise Rd Las Vegas NV 89105 Tel (702) 734-2984

ANTHIS, JOE M., b. Batesville, Ark., Mar. 23, 1942; B.S. in Bus. Adminstrn., U. Tulsa, 1964, J.D., 1966. Admitted to Okla. bar, 1966; individual practice law, Tulsa, 1966—. Mem. Tulsa County Bar Assn. (named outstanding jr. mem. 1973), Comml. Law League Am. Home: 3718 E 82d St Tulsa OK 74135 Office: 5272 S Lewis Ave Tulsa OK 79105 Tel (918) 743-8845

ANTHOINE, ROBERT, b. Portland, Maine, June 5, 1921; A.B., Duke, 1942; J.D., Columbia, 1949. Admitted to N.Y. bar, 1949; research asso. Am. Law Inst., N.Y.C., 1949-50; asso. firm Cleary, Gottlieb, Friendly & Cox, N.Y.C., 1950-52; asso. prof. law Columbia, 1952-56, prof., 1956-64, adj. prof., 1964—; partner firm Winthrop, Stimson, Putnam & Roberts, N.Y.C., 1963—; partner-in-charge firm Winthrop, Stimson, London, 1972-76. Mem. Am. Law Inst., Am., Internat. bar assns., Assn. Bar City N.Y., Internat. Fiscal Assn. Contbr. articles to legal jours. Home: 1065 Lexington Ave New York City NY 10021 Office: 40 Wall St New York City NY 10005 Tel (212) 943-0700

ANTHONY, JOHN ROBERT, b. Longview, Tex., June 12, 1889; diploma N. Tex. State Normal U. at Denton, 1909; B.A., U. Tex. at Austin, 1916, LL.B., 1921, M.A., 1928. Admitted to Tex. bar, 1921; asst. prof. English, Tex. Christian U., Ft. Worth, 1916-18; atty.-counselor Humble Oil & Refining Co., Houston, 1929-54; prof. law S. Tex. Coll. Law, Houston, 1955-57; atty. Gen. Land Office Tex., Austin, 1961; now in partial retirement. Mem. State Bar Tex. (past vice chmn., chmn. com. on real estate, probate and trust law), Pi Sigma Alpha (author original initiation ritual). Recipient Tex. State Bar award; prin. co-author and draftsman Tex. Probate Code; contbr. articles to legal jours. including Stayton's Texas Legal Forms, So. Tex. Law Jour. (The Story of Tex. Probate Code, 1955); author Missing First Chapter History Texas Law Review. Address: POB 3536 Bryan TX 77801 Tel (713) 846-3414

ANTHONY, JOHN WOOD, b. New Orleans, May 16, 1920; B.A., Tulane U., 1940, J.D., 1942. Admitted to La. bar, 1942; mem. Talley Anthony Hughes & Knight, Bogalusa, La., 1946—; individual practice law, Bogalusa, 1945—. Mem. Washington Parish (La.) (pres. 1957), La. State, Am. bar assns., Order of Coif. Editorial bd. Tulane Law Rev., 1940-42, civil law editor, 1941-42. Home: Route 3 POB 287 Bogalusa LA 70427 Office: 322 Columbai St Bogalusa LA 70427 Tel (504) 732-7151

ANTHONY, JOSEPH JAMES, b. Holyoke, Mass., Oct. 3, 1919; M.A., John Marshall, then LL.B., 1954. Admitted to bar, 1969; ind. ins. claims adjuster, 1954-69; individual practice law, Franklin, Ga., 1969—. Mem. Am., Ga. bar assns. Home: Route 1 Box 452 Roopville GA 30170 Office: 1777 W Washington Ave East Point GA 30364 Tel (404) 767-6336

ANTON, RONALD DAVID, b. Phila., Nov. 9, 1933; J.D., U. Buffalo, 1958; LL.M., U. Pa., 1959; Yale, 1960. Admitted to N.Y. bar, 1959; partner firm Boniello, Anton, Conti & Boniello, Niagara Falls, N.Y., 1960—; lectr. Law Sch. U. Buffalo, 1961-65, Niagara County (N.Y.) Police Tng. Sch., 1961-63, Niagara County Community Coll., 1962-66; cons. N.Y. State Legislature, 1961-64; research counsel Greater Buffalo Devel. Found., 1961. Pres., Niagara County Legal Aid Soc., 1976—; past pres. Community Missions of Niagara County, Niagara Republican Club. Mem. Am. Trial Lawyers Assn., Niagara County, Niagara Falls (pres. 1974-75) bar assns. Author: Urban Renewal in New York, 1963; moderator TV series The Law for You; host TV series Christ for Contemporaries, Niagara Falls. Home: 5079 Woodland Dr Lewiston NY 14092 Office: 770 Main St Niagara Falls NY 14302 Tel (716) 285-3525

ANVARIPOUR, MARK ABOLFAZL, b. Tehran, Iran, Jan. 23, 1935; B.S., U. San Francisco, 1959; LL.B., Tehran U., 1956; student U. Calif. Hastings Coll. Law; J.D., Chgo.-Kent Sch. Law, 1973. Admitted to Iranian bar, 1956, Ill. bar, 1973, U.S. Supreme Ct. Bar, 1976; legal adviser Iran Ministry of Agr., Tehran, 1956-57; dir. Am. Friends of the Middle East, Inc., Tehran, 1962-66; dean internat. edn. services Ill. Inst. Tech., 1966—; individual practice law, Tehran, 1956-57, 62-66, Chgo., 1973—; legal adviser Consulate Gen. Iran, Chgo., 1973—; aux. lawyer N.A.A.C.P., Chgo., 1973-74. Ill. chmn. Nat. Assn. Fgn. Student Affairs, 1968-69; pres. Ill. Inst. Tech. Armour Faculty Club, 1977. Mem. Am., Chgo., Ill., Iran-Am. (sec. gen. 1962-66) bar assns., Nat. Assn. Immigration Lawyers (sec.-treas. Chgo. chpt. 1976—), Assn. Immigration and Nationality Lawyers. Home: 990 Lake Shore Dr Chicago IL 60611 Office: 30 N Michigan Ave Chicago IL 60602 Tel (312) 567-3308

APICELLA, JOSEPH AUGUST, b. Jersey City, Nov. 14, 1946; B.S. in Econs., St. Peter's Coll., 1969; J.D., Bklyn. Law Sch., 1972. Admitted to N.J. bar, 1972; dep. atty. gen. Div. Criminal Justice, Trenton, N.J., 1972-73; asst. prosecutor Essex County (N.J.), Newark, 1973-77; house counsel Washington Savs. Bank, Hoboken, N.J., 1977—. Mem. Am., Essex County bar assns. Home: 54 Bonn Pl Weehawken NJ 07087 Office: 101 Washington St Hoboken NJ 07030 Tel (201) 659-0013

APKER, BURTON MARCELLUS, b. Chetek, Wis., Aug. 26, 1924; J.D. magna cum laude, U. Notre Dame, 1948. Admitted to Wis. bar, 1949, Ariz. bar, 1961; individual practice law, Chetek, 1949-59; atty. City of Chetek, 1950-52; asso. counsel Phoenix Title & Trust Co. (now Transam. Title Ins. Co.), Tucson and Phoenix, 1959-61; mem. firm Evans, Kitchel & Jenckes, Phoenix, 1961—; instr. Phoenix Coll., Maricopa Tech. Coll., Am. Inst. Banking, Am. Savs. and Loan Inst., 1961-75. Mem. City of Phoenix Adjustment Bd., 1964-67, chmn., 1967; sec. Barron County (Wis.) Community Council, 1952-53. Mem. Am. Bar Assn. Note editor: Notre Dame Lawyer, 1948. Office: 363 N 1st Ave Phoenix AZ 85003 Tel (602) 262-8800

APODACA, RUDY SAMUEL, b. LasCruces, N.M., Aug. 8, 1939; B.S., N.Mex. State U., 1961; J.D., Georgetown U., 1964. Admitted to N.Mex. bar, 1964, U.S. Dist. Ct. for N.Mex. bar, 1965, U.S. 10th Circuit Ct. Appeals bar, 1965, U.S. Supreme Ct. bar, 1971; individual practice law, Las Cruces, 1966—; dir., counsel Citizens Bank Las Cruces, 1976—. Mem. Gov.'s Coordinating Council for Higher Edn., Santa Fe., 1975—; advisor to registrants, SSS, Dona Ana County, N.Mex., 1971—; pres. bd. regents N.Mex. State U., 1975—. Mem. Am., N.Mex. bar assns., Assn. Trial Lawyers Am., Am. Inst. Banking, Nat. Legal Aid and Defender Assn., Mus. N.Mex. Found., La Raza Nat. Lawyers Assn., Rio Grande Writers Assn., Phi Kappa Phi. Author: The Waxen Image (Novel). Home: 3300 West Las Cruces NM 88001 Office: PO Box 1626 Las Cruces NM 88001 Tel (505) 523-4542

APOTHAKER, LOUIS DAVID, b. Phila., Dec. 6, 1931; B.S., U. Pa., 1953, LL.B., 1956. Admitted to D.C. bar, 1956, Pa. bar, 1957, Republic of Korea bar, 1958; mem. firm Blank, Rudenko, Klaus & Rome, Phila., 1959—; tchr., Korea, 1958. Chmn. United Fund, Center City, Pa., 1962; Republican candidate Pa. Legislature, 1961; officer Rep. Lawyers Com.; Phila. bar del. Pa. House of Delegates, 1965-69; chmn. Pa. Commn. to Regulate Charities, 1967—. Mem. Am., Fed., Republic of Korea, D.C., Pa., Phila. (mem. speakers bur. 1967—) bar assns., Del. Valley Council C. of C. Author: (with Marvin Comisky) Criminal Procedure in the U.S. District and Military Courts, 1963. Home: 1907 Panama St Philadelphia PA 19103 Office: 4 Penn Center Plaza Philadelphia PA 19103

APPEL, ALFRED, b. N.Y.C., May 8, 1906; A.B., Cornell U., 1926, J.D. with honors, 1928. Admitted to N.Y. bar, 1928; asso. firm Proskauer Rose Goetz & Mendelsoh, N.Y.C., 1928-40, partner, 1940—, now sr. partner; dir. McGregor-Doniger, Inc., C. H. O. Enterprises, Inc. Mem. adv. council Cornell U. Law Sch., 1967—; bd. dirs. S. L. Hoffman Found., N.Y.C. Mem. Assn. Bar City N.Y., N.Y. County Lawyers Assn., N.Y. State, Am., Internat. bar assns., Order of Coif, Phi Kappa Phi. Editor, bus. mgr. Cornell Law Rev., 1927-28. Home: 200 E 57th St New York City NY 10022 Office: 300 Park Ave New York City NY 10022 Tel (212) 593-9208

APPELBAUM, ALEXANDER, b. N.Y.C., July 30, 1915; J.D., St. John's U., 1938. Admitted to N.Y. State bar, 1940; individual practice law, N.Y.C., 1940-41, Florida, N.Y., 1951-70; partner firm Salm & Appelbaum, N.Y.C., 1945-51; partner Appelbaum & Kunert, Florida, 1971-74, pres., 1974—; village atty. Florida, 1956-74, police justice, 1956-65; atty. Florida Fire Dist., 1956—, Florida Union Free Sch. Dist., 1956—, Town of Warwick, 1970-74. Former pres. Young Republican Club of Florida; hon. mem., atty. Florida Vol. Fire Co. and Ambulance Service. Mem. Orange County Bar Assn. (v.p.), Fla. C. of C. (past pres.). Office: Profl Bldg Florida NY 10921 Tel (914) 651-4028

APPERT, RICHARD H., b. Allendale, N.J., Jan. 15, 1913; A.B. summa cum laude, Fordham Coll., 1934, J.D. cum laude, 1938. Admitted to N.Y. bar, 1938, D.C. bar, 1976, U.S. Supreme Ct. bar, 1959; asso. firm White & Case, N.Y.C. and Washington, 1938-44, 45-54, partner, 1954—; atty. U.S. Steel Corp. Del., Pitts., 1944-45. Mem. Am. (chmn. sect. taxation 1974-75), N.Y. State (chmn. tax sect. 1972) bar assns., Assn. Bar City N.Y. (sec. com. taxation 1955-58), N.Y. County Lawyers Assn., Lawyers Club, Fordham Coll. (pres., achievement award in law), Fordham Law Sch. alumni assns. Contbr. articles to profl. jours. Office: 1747 Pennsylvania Ave NW Washington DC 20006 Tel (202) 872-0013

APPERT, ROBERT JOHN, b. Duluth, Minn., June 12, 1946; B.A., Coll. St. Thomas, 1969; J.D., William Mitchell Coll. Law, 1973. Admitted to Minn. bar, 1973; asso. firm Robins, Meshbesher, Singer & Spence, Mpls., 1973-76; partner firm Appert, Grossman, Brady & Pyle, Mpls., 1977—; prof. Antioch Coll., 1974—. Mem. Am. Judicature Soc., Am., Minn. bar assns., Am., Minn. trial lawyers assns., Nat. Coll. Criminal Def. Lawyers, Minn. Pub. Defenders Assn., Phi Alpha Delta. Home: 312 Summit Ave Saint Paul MN 55103 Office: Suite 500 E 100 N 6th St Minneapolis MN 55404

APPLBAUM, EDWARD ALAN, b. Pitts., Feb. 15, 1943; B.S., U. Calif., Los Angeles, 1965; J.D., Calif. Western U., 1968. Admitted to Calif. bar, 1969; staff atty. Defenders Inc. of San Diego, 1969-70; partner firm Douglas & Applbaum, and predecessor, San Diego, 1970—; lectr. Calif. Western U. Law Sch., 1972—. Mem. Criminal Def. Lawyers Club of San Diego, San Diego County Bar Assn., Am. Judicature Soc., Barristers Club. Editorial bd. Calif. Western Law Rev., 1967-68. Home: 1529 Garrison Pl San Diego CA 92106 Office: 303 A St San Diego CA 92101 Tel (714) 235-6405

APPLE, MARVIN JAY, b. Kittanning, Pa., Aug. 27, 1926; B.S., U. Pitts., 1948. Admitted to U.S. Supreme Ct. bar, 1965; asso. firm Grossman & Foreman, Pitts., 1952-57; individual practice law, Pitts., 1957-67; partner firm Apple & Bernstein, Pitts., 1968—, pres., 1977—. Mem. Am., Pa., Allegheny County bar assns., Comml. Law League Am. Home: 5454 Kipling Rd Pittsburgh PA 15217 Office: 1000 Manor Bldg 564 Forbes Ave Pittsburgh PA 15219 Tel (412) 471-1466

APPLEBAUM, HARVEY MILTON, b. Birmingham, Ala., Mar. 1, 1937; B.A., Yale U., 1959; LL.B., Harvard U., 1962. Admitted to Ala. bar, 1962, D.C. bar, 1964; asso. firm Covington & Burling, Washington, 1963-71, partner, 1971—; adj. prof. law Georgetown U., 1971-75; instr. antitrust practice seminar Va. Law, Charlottesville, 1969—. Mem. D.C. Dem. Central Com., 1966-68. Mem. Am. Bar Assn. Contbr. articles to profl. jours. Home: 2912 Albemarle St NW Washington DC 20008 Office: 888 16th St NW Washington DC 20006 Tel (202) 452-6338

APPLEBERRY, MILES HARTMAN, b. Washington, Feb. 23, 1943; San Antonio Coll., 1963; B.A., U. Tex. at Austin, 1965, LL.B., 1967. Admitted to Tex. bar, 1967, Fed. bar, 1971, U.S. Ct. Mil. Appeals bar, 1968, U.S. Ct. Claims, 1968, U.S. Supreme Ct. bar, 1972; served with JAGC, U.S. Army, 1967-71; mem. staff Bexar County Legal Aid Assn., San Antonio, 1971-73; partner firm Appleberry, Deyeso & Haase, San Antonio, 1973—; lectr. San Antonio Coll., 1975—. Mem. San Antonio, San Antonio Jr. bar assns., State Bar Tex., Phi Alpha Delta. Home: 10711 Edgefield St San Antonio TX 78233 Office: 901 NE Loop 410 Suite 618 San Antonio TX 78209 Tel (512) 828-0703

APPLEGATE, JOHN STIRLEN, b. Walla Walla, Wash., Oct. 22, 1909; B.A., Whitman Coll., 1932; J.D., U. Wash. 1941. Admitted to Wash. bar, 1941; phys. edn. dir. Yakima YMCA, 1932-38; individual practice law Yakima, Wash., 1940—; partner firm Halverson, Applegate, & McDonald, Yakima, 1946—. Mem. Yakima Bd. Adjustment, 1947-50; mem. Yakima Met. Park Commn., 1950-72, chmn., 1970-72; dir. Yakima YMCA, 1946-72, pres., 1962-69; bd. overseers Whitman Coll., 1956—. Mem. Yakima County (pres. 1953), Wash. (gov. 1962-65), Am. bar assns., Am. Judicature Soc. Contbr. articles to profl. jours. Home: 606 S 32d Ave Yakima WA 98902 Office: 415 N 3d St Yakima WA 98901

APPLETON, BYRON YATES, b. Evanston, Ill., Feb. 25, 1931; A.B., U. So. Calif., 1951; J.D., Southwestern U., 1961. Admitted to Calif. bar, 1965, U.S. Supreme Ct. bar, 1972; asso. firms Thomas Moore & Assos., Los Angeles, 1966-71, Owen A. Silverman, Inc., Torrance, Calif., 1971—; arbitrator Am. Arbitration Assn., 1970—; panel of arbitrators Los Angeles County Superior Ct., 1976—; notary pub. County of Los Angeles, 1972—. Mem. Los Angeles Trial Lawyer Assn., Am., Los Angeles County bar assns., Calif. State Bar, Gen. Alumni Assn. U.So. Calif. Office: 23224 Crenshaw Blvd Torrance CA 90505 Tel (213) 530-3990

APPLETON, PETER MADSEN, b. Santa Monica, Calif., Aug. 5, 1942; A.B., U. Calif., Los Angeles, 1964, J.D., 1967. Admitted to Calif. bar, 1967; asso. firm Tyre & Kamins, Los Angeles, 1967-72, partner, 1973—. Mem. Beverly Hills (Calif.) (gov. 1973—, asso. editor jour. 1973-74, mng. editor jour. 1974-75 sr. editor 1975-76), Los Angeles County, Am. bar assns., Order of Coif. Sr. editor U. Calif. at Los Angeles Law Rev., 1966-67. Office: Suite 1000 1800 Century Park E Los Angeles CA 90067 Tel (213) 553-6822

APPOLONIA, FELIX ANTONIO, b. W. Warwick, R.I., Nov. 9, 1925; LL.B., Northeastern U., 1952. Admitted to R.I. bar, 1952; mem. R.I. Gen. Assembly, 1958-64; solicitor W. Warwick, 1964-68; sec., chmn. W. Warwick Democratic Town Com., 1958—; dir. Colonial Plumbing & Heating Co., Coventry, R.I., Central Heat & Air Conditioning Co., Coventry, Columbus Door Co., Warwick, Kingstown Motor Co., N. Kingstown, R.I. Bd. incorporation Kent County Meml. Hosp., Warwick, 1963—; mem. R.I. Constl. Commn., 1961; del. R.I. Constl. Conv., 1964. Mem. R.I., Kent County bar assns., Northeastern Law Alumni Assn. Recipient Am. Legion Post No. 2 Merit Award, 1963. Home: 16 Alden Dr West Warwick RI 02893 Office: 312 Cowesett Ave West Warwick RI 02893 Tel (401) 821-3830

ARABIAN, ARMAND, b. N.Y.C., Dec. 12, 1934; B.S. in Bus. Adminstrn., Boston U., 1956, J.D., 1961; LL.M., U. Calif., 1970. Admitted to Calif. bar, 1962, U.S. Supreme Ct. bar, 1966; dep. dist. atty., Los Angeles County, Calif., 1962-63; individual practice law, Van Nuys, Calif., 1963-72; judge municipal ct., Los Angeles, 1972-73, Los Angeles County Superior Ct., Van Nuys, 1973—. Mem. Am. Bar Assn., San Fernando Valley Criminal Cts. Bar Assn., Calif. Judges Assn., Internat. Footprint Assn., Sigma Phi Epsilon (dist. gov. 1968-69). Office: 6230 Sylmar Ave Van Nuys CA 91401 Tel (213) 787-3350

ARANOW, EDWARD ROSS, b. N.Y.C., Apr. 30, 1909; A.B., Columbia, 1929, J.D., 1932. Admitted to N.Y. State bar, 1933, U.S. Supreme Ct. bar, 1945; sr. partner Aranow, Brodsky, Bohlinger, Benetar & Einhorn, N.Y.C., 1946—. Mem. Am., Fed., N.Y. State, N.Y. County bar assns., Bar Assn. City of N.Y., Columbia Law Sch. Alumni Assn. (pres. 1965-67). Author: (with Herbert A. Einhorn) Proxy Contests for Corporate Control, revised edit., 1968; Tender Offers for Corporate Control, 1973; decorated Royal Order of Vasa (Sweden); recipient Distinguished Alumni medal Columbia. Home: 47 Colby Ln Scarsdale NY 10583 Office: 469 Fifth Ave New York City NY 10017 Tel (212) 889-1470

ARATA, DON MICHAEL, b. New Orleans, May 21, 1938; B.B.A., Loyola U., New Orleans, J.D. Admitted to La. bar, 1962; mem. firm Richardson & Arata, Bogalusa, La., 1964-73; individual practice law, Bogalusa, 1973—. Mem. Washington Parish Bar Assn. (pres. 1975-76). Home: 1634 Piney Branch Rd Bogalusa LA 70427 Office: 216 Austin St Bogalusa LA 70427 Tel (504) 735-1368

ARCH, JOHN GEORGE, b. Pitts., Nov. 24, 1939; B.A., St. Vincent Coll., Latrobe, Pa., 1961; J.D., U. Pitts., 1964. Admitted to Pa. bar, 1964; asso. firm Bolte & McKay, Pitts., 1968-70; partner firm McKay, Arch & Stele, Pitts., 1970-72; individual practice law, Pitts., 1972—; served with JAGC, U.S. Navy, 1964-68, lt. comdr. Res., 1968—; asst. county solicitor Allegheny County, 1972—. Mem. bd. mgrs. Allegheny County Workhouse; solicitor, dir. Allegheny County Employees Fed. Credit Union; mem. profl. advisory bd. People Concerned for the Unborn Child. Mem. Pa., Allegheny County bar assns., Am., Pa. assns. trial lawyers. Home: 311 Kittanning Pike Pittsburgh PA 15215 Office: 315 Frick Bldg Pittsburgh PA 15219 Tel (412) 391-5330

ARCHAMBEAULT, GERALD THOMAS, b. Ft. Peck, Mont., Feb. 1, 1942; B.B.A., U. Mont., 1964, J.D., 1967. Admitted to Mont. bar, 1967; partner firm Gallagher & Archambeault, Glasgow, Mont., 1965—. Dir. Valley County (Mont.) Red Cross, 1968—, First Evangelical Lutheran Ch., 1972—; chmn. Valley County Drug Abuse, 1970-72. Mem. Mont. Bar Assn., Am. Judicature Soc., Am. Trial Lawyers Assn., Comml. Law League Am., Phi Delta Phi. Home: 632 4th Ave N Glasgow MT 59230 Office: 605 3d Ave S Glasgow MT 59230 Tel (496) 228-9331

ARCHER, DAVID R., b. Huntsville, Ala., Nov. 20, 1917; A.B., U. Ala., 1949, LL.B., 1951, J.D., 1969. Admitted to Ala. bar, 1951, U.S. Supreme Ct. bar, 1961; legal officer USN, 1951-52; individual practice law, Huntsville, 1953-61; mem. Ala. Senate, 1958-61; judge 23d Jud. Circuit Ct. Ala., Huntsville, 1961—; spl. hearing officer U.S. Dept. Justice, 1951-52. State rep. So. Regional Edn. Bd., 1958-61, mem., 1962—; mem. Ala. Ethics Commn. Bd., 1971—; presdl. elector, 1960; former bd. dirs. dist. council Boy Scouts Am. Mem. Am., Fed., Ala., Huntsville bar assns., Am. Judicature Soc., Ala. Circuit Judges Assn., World Peace Through Law, Am. Judges Assn. Author: Criminal Charges, 1974; Civil Forms of Action, 1976. Home: 3002 Barcody Rd Huntsville AL 35802 Office: Courthouse Huntsville AL 35801 Tel (205) 536-5911

ARCHER, DENNIS WAYNE, b. Detroit, Jan. 1, 1942; J.D., Detroit Coll., 1970. Admitted to Mich. bar, 1970, D.C. bar, 1972, U.S. Supreme Ct. bar, 1974; mem. firm Gragg & Gardner, Detroit, 1970-71, Hall, Stone, Allen, Archer & Glenn, Detroit, 1971-73,

Charfoos & Charfoos, Detroit, 1973—; asso. prof. Detroit Coll. Law, 1972—; TV host on Issue WXYZ, Southfield, Mich., 1974-76. Mem. Taxi Cab Commn., Detroit, 1976-77, Mich. State Bar Commn. Mem. Am. Bar Assn. (jud. qualifications com., planning com., spl. chmn. com. to certify trial advs., mem. rep. assembly). Contbr. articles to legal jours. Office: 4000 City Nat Bank Bldg Detroit MI 48226 Tel (313) 963-8080

ARCHER, EVAN CHANDLEE, JR., b. Camden, N.J., Aug. 2, 1939; A.B., Williams Coll., 1961; LL.B., U. Pa., 1966. Admitted to Vt. bar, 1966; asso. firm Wick Dinse & Allen, Burlington, Vt., 1966-68, Yandell & Page, Burlington, 1969-70; partner firm Yandell Archer & Foley, and predecessors, Burlington, 1971—. Treas., Burlington YMCA, 1975—; bd. dirs. Howard Mental Health Services, 1969-75, pres., 1973-74. Mem. Am., Vt., Chittenden County bar assns. Office: 156 College St PO Box 336 Burlington VT 05401 Tel (802) 862-6451

ARCHIBALD, WILLIAM KENNETH, b. Helena, Mont., Aug. 12, 1934; A.B., U. Wyo., 1956, J.D., 1958. Admitted to Wyo. bar, 1958, U.S. Supreme Ct. bar, 1961; mem. firm Holstedt & Archibald, Sheridan, Wyo., 1968—; asst. county atty., 1964; city judge, 1968; justice of peace, 1975. Mem. County Sch. Dist. Reorgn. Com., 1972, Mental Health Center. Mem. Sheridan County, Wyo., Am. bar assns., Council Sch. Bd. Attys. Home: 638 S Thurmond St Sheridan WY 82801 Office: 113 W Brundage St Sheridan WY 82801 Tel (307) 674-7479

ARCHIBOLD, JOHN EWING, b. Denver, Mar. 15, 1933; A.B., Princeton U., 1955; LL.B., U. Denver, 1959; LL.M., Georgetown U., 1965. Admitted to Colo. bar, 1960, D.C. bar, 1964, U.S. Supreme Ct. bar, 1965; spl. liaison asst. Dept. State, Washington, 1960; trial atty. Dept. Justice, Washington, 1960-66; trial atty. firm Grant, Shafroth, Toll & McHendrie, Denver, 1966-68; partner firm Casey, Klene, Horan & Archibold, Denver, 1968-69; asst. atty. gen. State of Colo., Denver, 1970-72; counsel Colo. Pub. Utilities Commn., Denver, 1974—. Chmn. Citizenship Day Com., Denver, 1967; vice chmn. Law Day Com., 1968-69. Mem. Am., Colo., Denver bar assns., Christian Legal Soc., Order of St. Ives. Home: 700 Lafayette Denver CO 80218 Office: 1525 Sherman St Denver CO 80203 Tel (303) 892-3188

ARDIFF, WILLIAM BIRRELL, b. Beverly, Mass., Feb. 20, 1937; A.B., Dartmouth, 1959; J.D., Cornell U., 1962; LL.M., Boston U., 1963. Admitted to Mass. bar, 1962; founding partner Ardiff, Ardiff & Morse, and predecessors, Danvers, Mass., 1963—. Mem. Danvers Sch. Com., 1963-66. Mem. Salem Bar Assn. (v.p.), Danvers Hist. Soc. (past pres.). Home: 40 Conant St Danvers MA 01923 Office: 32 Maple St Danvers MA 01923 Tel (617) 774-7121

AREN, EDWARD ABRAHAM, b. Chgo., Nov. 26, 1920; A.A., Central YMCA Coll., 1942; LL.B., J.D., Chgo. Kent Coll. Law, 1944; Ph.B., Northwestern U., 1951; postgrad. Roosevelt U. Grad Sch., 1964. Admitted to Ill. bar, 1945; individual practice law, Chgo., 1945-75, Oak Park, Ill., 1976—. Mem. Chgo., Ill. State, Am. bar assns., Am. Judicature Soc. Home and office: 732 S Humphrey Ave Oak Park IL 60304 Tel (312) 386-1899

ARENT, ALBERT EZRA, b. Rochester, N.Y., Aug. 25, 1911; A.B., Cornell U., 1932, LL.B., 1935. Admitted to N.Y. bar, 1935, U.S. Supreme Ct. bar, 1940, U.S. Tax Ct. bar, 1944, D.C. bar, 1945; atty. Office Chief Counsel Bur. Internal Revenue, Washington, 1935-39; spl. asst. to atty. gen. U.S. Dept. Justice, Washington, 1939-44; partner firm Arent, Fox, Kintner, Plotkin & Kahn and predecessors, Washington, D.C., 1944—; adj. prof. taxation Geogetown U. Law Center, 1951-73. Pres. Jewish Community Council Greater Washington, 1957-61; chmn. Nat. Jewish Community Relations Adv. Council, 1970-73; chmn. Commn. Social Action Reform Judaism, 1973-77; steering com. Nat. Urban Coalition, 1972—. Mem. Am., Fed., D.C. bar assns., Am. Law Inst., Am. Judicature Soc., Nat. Lawyers Club. Recipient Stephen S. Wise Medallion award Nat. Capital Chpt. Am. Jewish Congress for community service, 1965; Vicennial medal, Georgetown U. Law Center, 1971; Nat. Humanitarian award, B'nai B'rith, 1975. Contbr. articles on taxation to legal jours. Home: 2510 Virginia Ave NW Washington DC 20037 Office: 1815 H St NW Washington DC 20006 Tel (202) 857-6185

ARENWALD, WALTER PHILLIPS, b. N.Y.C., Mar. 28, 1919; A.B. magna cum laude, Harvard, 1938; A.M. in Econs., U. Chgo., 1940; J.D., Harvard, 1948. Admitted to N.Y. bar, 1948; asso. firm Gainsburg, Gottlieb, Levitan & Cole, N.Y.C., 1948-57, partner, 1957—. Mem. Am. Bar Assn., Assn. Bar City N.Y., Estate Planning Council N.Y.C. Home: 350 Cedar Dr Briarcliff Manor NY 10510 Office: 122 E 42d St New York City NY 10017 Tel (212) OX7-3440

AREY, GARY CLIFTON, b. Dallas, Oct. 11, 1947; B.A., N. Tex. State U., 1970; J.D., So. Meth. U., 1973. Admitted to Tex. bar, 1973; individual practice law, Dallas County, Tex., 1973-74; asst. dist. atty. Dallas County, 1974—. Mem. Tex., Dallas bar assns., Delta Theta Phi. Office: Dallas County Courthouse Commerce St Dallas TX 75202 Tel (214) 749-8511

ARGO, GEORGE ERNEST, b. Dalton, Ga., Feb. 6, 1940; LL.B., Atlanta Law Sch., 1966, LL.M., 1967. Admitted to Ga. bar, 1973; asst. dist. atty. Atlantic Jud. Circuit, 1973-74; asso. firm W. L. Salter, Jr., Vidalia, Ga., 1974-75; individual practice law, Vidalia, 1975—. Mem. Am., Ga., Middle Jud. Circuit, Toombs County bar assns. Home: 17 Clydette Blvd Vidalia GA 30474 Office: PO Box 960 Meadows St Vidalia GA 30474 Tel (812) 537-9265

ARGUE, JOHN CLIFFORD, b. Glendale, Calif., Jan. 25, 1932; A.B., Occidental Coll., 1953; LL.B., U. So. Calif., 1956. Admitted to Calif. bar, 1957; partner firm Argue & Argue, Los Angeles, 1958-60, Flint & MacKay, Los Angeles, 1960-72, Argue, Freston & Myers, Los Angeles, 1972—. Pres. So. Calif. Com. for Olympic Games, 1972—; sec. Calif. State Club Assn., 1974—; bd. dirs. Los Angeles affiliate Am. Heart Assn.; bd. dirs. So. Calif. Golf Assn., 1971—, treas., 1977; trustee Verdugo Hills Hosp., 1975—, vice chmn., 1977. Mem. Am., Calif., Los Angeles bar assns. Home: 1314 Descanso Dr La Canada CA 91011 Office: 626 Wilshire Blvd Suite 1000 Los Angeles CA 90017 Tel (213) 628-1291

ARKIN, GEORGE O., b. N.Y.C., Aug. 29, 1901; student Stevens Inst. Tech., 1918-19; LL.B., N.Y. U., 1922. Admitted to N.Y. State bar, 1923, U.S. Supreme Ct. bar, 1968; individual practice law, N.Y.C., 1934-41, 57-64; mem. firm Gerdes & Montgomery, N.Y.C., 1941-51; v.p., counsel Lawyers Mortgage & Title Co., 1948-57; sr. title officer Security Title & Guaranty Co., v.p., counsel, 1964-75, v.p., gen. counsel, 1976—; vets. relief commr. N.Y. State, 1924-27; asst. corp. counsel City of N.Y., 1927-34. Mem. Am., N.Y. State, N.Y.C., N.Y. County bar assns., N.Y. State Land Title Assn., N.Y. U. Moot Ct. Justices Assn. (chmn.). Recipient N.Y. U. Meritorious Service award, 1939, Louis D. Brandeis Distinguished Service Gold medal, 1956; author: The Vexed Mineral Rights of the Philipses in Putnam County, 1971; editor N.Y. U. Law Ann. and Rev., 1922. Home: 215 E 68th St New York City NY 10021 Office: Security Title & Guaranty Co 630 Fifth Ave New York City NY 10020 Tel (212) 765-7110

ARKIN, L. JULES, b. N.Y.C., Mar. 19, 1929; student Emory U., 1946-48; J.D., U. Miami, 1952. Admitted to Fla. bar, 1952; partner firm Meyer, Weiss, Rose, Arkin, Sheppard & Shockett, Miami Beach, Fla., 1954—. Vice pres. Greater Miami Jewish Fedn., 1970—; v.p., trustee Mt. Sinai Med. Center, Miami Beach, 1972—. Mem. Am., Dade County (Fla.), Miami Beach bar assns. Recipient Young Leadership award Greater Miami Jewish Fedn., 1969; named Civic Leader of Year, Miami Beach Civic League, 1971. Office: 407 Lincoln Rd Miami Beach FL 33139 Tel (305) 538-2531

ARKIN, MICHAEL BARRY, b. Washington, Jan. 11, 1941; A.A., George Washington U., 1961; B.A., U. Okla., 1962, J.D., 1965. Admitted to U.S. Ct. Claims bar, 1966, U.S. Ct. Appeals bar, 1970, Calif. bar, 1970, Okla. bar, 1965, U.S. Supreme Ct. bar, 1968, U.S. Tax Ct., 1970; trial atty. Tax Div., U.S. Dept. Justice, Washington, 1965-68, appellate atty. Tax Div., 1968-69; asso. firm Surr & Hellyer, San Bernardino, Calif., 1969-72, partner, 1973—; consul County Council Community Services Drug Abuse Program, 1970-72. Consul, San Bernardino Area Mental Health Assn., 1970-72, Agape House, 1970-72, Reach Out Rialto, 1972-73, AMA Drug Abuse Com., 1970-72; chmn. legal div. Arrowhead United Fund, 1973-74; chmn. legal div. Am. Cancer Soc. campaign, 1973-74; bd. dirs. San Bernardino Legal Aid Soc., 1970-73, pres., 1973. Mem. Am., Calif. (resolutions com.), San Bernardino County (dir. 1973-75, sec.-treas. 1973-75), Okla. bar assns. Editor San Bernardino County Bar Bull., 1972-73; contbr. New Voices in American Poetry, 1976. Office: PO Box 6086 599 N Arrowhead Ave San Bernardino CA 92412 Tel (714) 884-4704

ARLAN, CHLOE, b. Chgo., Sept. 16, 1942; J.D., DePaul U., 1969, B.A., 1970. Admitted to Ill. bar, 1969; with Chgo. Title & Trust Co., 1962-74, trust officer, 1970-74; trust officer Albany Bank & Trust Co. N.A., Chgo., 1974—. Mem. Women's Bar Assn. Ill., Chgo., Ill., Am. bar assns. Home: 2040 N Sheffield St Chicago IL 60614

ARMANI, FRANK HENRY, b. Syracuse, N.Y., Sept. 12, 1927; B.A., Syracuse U., 1950, J.D., 1956. Admitted to N.Y. bar, 1956, U.S. Supreme Ct. bar, 1964; individual practice law, Syracuse, 1956—; legal aid counsel Onondaga County (N.Y.), 1956—, asst. dist. atty., 1961-69; spl. Am. counsel Fabrique Reolon, Grenoble, France, 1975—; adv. counsel Nationwide Ins. Co., Syracuse, 1960-62; lectr. Albany Sch. Law, Ill. Bar Assn. Forum. Mem. Am., N.Y. State, Onondaga County bar assns., Am. Trial Lawyers Assn., N.Y. State Assn. Plaintiffs Trial Lawyers, Upstate Trial Attys. Assn. (dir. 1960—). Home: 121 Munro Dr Camillus NY 13031 Office: 4300 W Genesee St Syracuse NY 13219 Tel (315) 487-2551

ARMBRECHT, CONRAD PATERSON, II, b. Mobile, Ala., Aug. 10, 1945; B.A., U. of the South, 1967; J.D., U. Ala., 1971. Admitted to Ala. bar, 1972. U.S. Supreme Ct. bar, 1976; asso. firm Armbrecht, Jackson, De Mouy, Crowe, Holmes & Reeves, Mobile, 1972-75, partner, 1975—. Chmn. bd. trustees Wilmer Hall, Episc. children's home, Mobile, 1977—. Mem. Ala., Mobile (sec. 1973), Am. bar assns., Mid-Continent Oil and Gas Assn., Phi Delta Phi. Home: 171 S Georgia Ave Mobile AL 36604 Office: POB 290 Mobile AL 36601 Tel (205) 432-6751

ARMEL, LARRY DANIEL, b. Iola, Kans., Feb. 12, 1942; B.A., Kans. U., 1965, J.D., 1968. Admitted to Kans. bar, 1968, Mo. bar, 1968; asso. firm Stinson, Mag, Thomson, McEvers & Fizzell, 1968-72; asso. counsel Security Benefit Life Ins. Co., Topeka, 1972—. Active fund raising YMCA, Topeka United Way, YWCA, Stormont-Vail Hosp. Fellow Life Office Mgmt. Assn.; mem. Am., Kans., Topkea bar assns., Topeka C. of C. Registered prin. Nat. Assn. Security Dealers, 1973. Home: 3200 W 33d Ct Topeka KS 66614 Office: 700 Harrison St Topeka KS 66636 Tel (913) 295-3000

ARMENTROUT, WALTER SCOTT, b. Martinsburg, W.Va., Nov. 9, 1941; A.B., Brown U., 1963; LL.B., Washington and Lee U., 1966. Admitted to Va. bar, 1966, W.Va. bar, 1967, Md. bar, 1967; atty. Balt. & Ohio R.R. Co., Balt., 1966-73; counsel Nat. R.R. Passenger Corp. (AMTRAK), Washington, 1973-74, asst. to pres. AMTRAK, asst. sec., 1974-76, N.E. Corridor, counsel, asst. sec., Phila. and Washington, 1976—; dir. Washington Terminal Co. Home: 209 Upnor Rd Baltimore MD 21212 Office: 1617 J F Kennedy Blvd Room 534 Philadelphia PA 19103 also 955 L'Enfant Plaza SW Washington DC 20024

ARMIJO, DAVID LUIS, b. Las Vegas, N.Mex., Aug. 19, 1922; B.A., N.Mex. Highlands U., 1949; J.D., Vanderbilt U., 1949. Admitted to N.Mex. bar, 1949; individual practice law, Las Vegas, 1949-67, 69—; judge N.Mex. Ct. Appeals, Santa Fe, 1967-68. Mem. N.Mex. State Hwy Commn., 1969-75. Office: PO Box 1626 Las Vegas NM 87701 Tel (505) 425-3503

ARMIJO, JOSEPH L., JR.; B.S. in Law, U. So. Calif., 1962; J.D., Boalt Hall U. Calif., 1964. Admitted to bar; asso. firm Smithers, Good, Potter, Wildman & Gregory, 1964-65; individual practice law, Carson, Calif., 1965-73; judge Municipal Ct., Compton (Calif.) Judicial Dist., 1973—; mem. Atty. Gen's. Citizen Com. on Crime of Calif. Bd. advisers Calif. State Coll., Dominguez Hills; bd. dirs. Legion Lex; trustee Trojan Barristers, U. So. Calif. law alumni support group. Mem. Mexican Am. Lawyers Club (pres.), Calif. Trial Lawyers Assn., Am. Judicature Soc., Am., Long Beach (Calif.), South Bay, South Central, S.E. bar assns., Phi Delta Phi. Office: Municipal Ct Compton Jud Dist 212 S Acacia St Compton CA 90220

ARMIJO, M.L., JR., b. Las Vegas, N.Mex., Apr. 22, 1927; B.A., U. Wis., 1949, J.D., 1950. Admitted to Wis. bar, 1950, N.Mex. bar, 1953, U.S. Supreme Ct. bar, 1955, U.S. Ct. Appeals bar, 1963; law examiner Office of Atty. Gen. of Wis., Madison, 1950-52; asst. dist. atty. 4th Jud. Dist. N.Mex., Las Vegas, 1953-56; individual practice law, Las Vegas, 1957-67, 69—; atty.-adviser Office of Solicitor, U.S. Dept. Interior, Washington, 1967-69; designated atty. FHA, N.Mex., 1961-67; lectr. N.Mex. State Police Sch., Santa Fe, 1960-61. Mem. Delta Theta Phi. Home: 2820 Old National Rd Las Vegas NM 87701 Office: 504 Douglas Ave Las Vegas NM 87701 Tel (505) 425-9587

ARMKNECHT, PHILIP CROSBY, b. Council Bluffs, Iowa, Oct. 26, 1932; B.A., Monmouth (Ill.) Coll., 1954; J.D., Drake U., 1960. Admitted to Iowa bar, 1960; asso. firm Gordon K. Darling, Winterset, Iowa, 1960-62; partner firm Feese & Armknecht, Red Oak, Iowa, 1962—; atty. Montgomery County, 1964-68; atty. City of Red Oak, 1969—. Mem. Iowa, Montgomery County (past pres.) bar assns. Office: 510 4th St Red Oak IA 51566 Tel (712) 623-4510

ARMS, BREWSTER LEE, b. Pasadena, Calif., Dec. 18, 1925; B.A., Stanford, 1948, LL.B., 1951. Admitted to Calif. bar, 1952; with Bankline Oil Co., 1952-59, atty., corp. sec., 1955-59; atty. The Signal Companies, Inc. (formerly Signal Oil and Gas Co.), Los Angeles, 1959-63, atty., corp. sec., 1963-70, v.p., gen. counsel, 1970—, also dir. Mem. Am., Calif., Los Angeles bar assns., Am. Soc. Corps. Secs. Office: 9665 Wilshire Blvd Beverly Hills CA 90212*

ARMSTRONG, DANIEL LEWIS, b. Houston, July 16, 1938; B.A., U. Tex., 1961, J.D., 1966. Admitted to Tex. bar, 1966; asst. to county atty. El Paso County (Tex.), 1967-69; partner firm Guevara, Rebe, & Armstrong, El Paso, 1969-75, firm Armstrong Sergent & Hardie, El Paso, 1977—; individual practice law, El Paso, 1975-76. Mem. El Paso Trial Lawyers Assn. (dir. 1975—), El Paso Jr. Bar Assn. (dir. 1970). Home: 6776 Fiesta St El Paso TX 79912 Office: Suite 16A El Paso Nat Bank El Paso TX 79901 Tel (915) 544-5222

ARMSTRONG, FREDERICK PERLEY, JR., b. Buffalo, Dec. 15, 1907; B.A., Dartmouth, 1929; LL.B., Fordham U., 1933. Admitted to N.Y. State bar, 1934, Maine bar, 1940, U.S. Dist. Ct. for Maine bar, 1940, U.S. Dist. Ct. for Eastern Dist. N.Y. bar, 1936, U.S. Dist. Ct. for So. Dist. N.Y. bar, 1938; asso. firm Porter and Taylor, N.Y.C., 1935-37; claim mgr. Great Am. Ins. Co., Portland, Maine, 1944-72; individual practice law, Portland, 1940—. Mem. bd. selectmen Town of Cape Elizabeth (Maine), 1964-67, chmn. 1967; mem. Town council, Cape Elizabeth, 1967-70. Home and office: 13 Lawson Rd Cape Elizabeth ME 04107 Tel (207) 799-2977

ARMSTRONG, GENE LYNDON, b. Waterloo, Iowa, Dec. 29, 1940; B.S., U. Wis., 1963, M.S. in Econs., 1964; J.D., Stanford, 1967. Admitted to Ill. bar, 1967; asso. firm Isham, Lincoln & Beale, Chgo., 1967-74; partner firm Roan & Grossman, Chgo., 1974—; atty. Park Dist. of Oak Park (Ill.), 1970—. Mem. Am., Chgo. bar assns. Office: 120 S LaSalle St Chicago IL 60603 Tel (312) 263-3600

ARMSTRONG, GORDON HUTCHINSON, b. Glendale, Calif., May 31, 1927; B.S., Wash. State U., 1951; J.D., U. Pacific, 1961. Admitted to Calif. bar, 1962; asst. chief pub. defender, San Francisco, 1969—. Mem. Calif. (mem. legal services sect.), San Francisco (dir.) bar assns., Nat. Coll. Criminal Def. Lawyers. Office: Room 205 Hall of Justice 850 Bryant St San Francisco CA 94103 Tel (415) 553-1671

ARMSTRONG, GRANT, b. Raymond, Wash., Sept. 30, 1907; LL.B., U. Wash., 1929. Admitted to Wash. bar, 1930, U.S. Dist. Ct. bar, Western Dist. Wash., 1938; partner firm Armstrong, Vander Stoep & Remund and predecessors, Chehalis, 1930—. Bd. regents U. Wash., 1950-57. Fellow Am. Bar Found., Am. Coll. Probate Counsel, Am. Coll. Trial Lawyers; mem. Am. (del. 1965-74, bd. govs. 1974—), Wash. (bd. govs. 1957-60, pres. 1964-65) bar assns., Am. Judicature Soc., Order of Coif, Phi Delta Phi. Home: 215 NE Glen Rd Chehalis WA 98532 Office: 345 NW Pacific Ave Chehalis WA 98532 Tel (206) 748-4401

ARMSTRONG, HAZEN ROBERT, b. Saginaw, Mich., Aug. 12, 1910; A.B., Denison U., 1933; J.D., U. Cin., 1936. Admitted to Ohio bar, 1936, Mich. bar, 1936. asso. firm Crane & Crane, Saginaw, Mich., 1937-43; asst. prosecutor Saginaw County, 1945-47, chief asst. prosecutor, 1947-55, pros. atty., 1955-56; judge Municipal Ct., Saginaw, 1956-66, Mich. 10th Jud. Circuit. Ct., 1967—. Bd. dirs. Child-Family Service, Saginaw, 1959—; pres. Adult Mental Health, Saginaw, 1967. Mem. Am. Bar Assn., State Bar Mich., Mich. Judges Assn. Office: Courthouse Saginaw MI 48602 Tel (517) 793-9100

ARMSTRONG, HENRY BOLDEN, III, b. New Haven, Dec. 12, 1919; B.A., with honors, Yale, 1941, LL.B., 1943. Admitted to N.Y. bar, 1946, Conn. bar, 1947; with Sullivan & Cromwell, N.Y.C., 1946-47; with Travelers Ins. Cos., Hartford, Conn., 1947—, counsel, 1963-66, asso. gen. counsel, 1966-69, gen. counsel, 1969—; dir. Caribbean Atlantic Life Ins. Co. Chmn. Farmington (Conn.) Republican Town Com., 1966-67. Mem. Am., Conn., Hartford bar assns. Home: 290 Mountain Spring Rd Farmington CT 06032 Office: 1 Tower Sq Hartford CT 06115*

ARMSTRONG, JAMES ELWOOD, III, b. Balt., Sept. 26, 1929; B.S. in Chem. Engring., Mich. State U., 1951; postgrad. Denver U., 1951; J.D., U. Md., 1957. Admitted to Md. bar, 1957, D.C. bar, 1970; chem. engr. W.R. Grace & Co., 1953-55, patent agt., 1955-57; patent atty. Koppers, 1957-70; partner firm Armstrong, Nikaido & Marmelstein, and predecessors, Washington, 1970—; v.p. Schmitz & Assos.; dir. Japan Engring. Devel. Co. Trustee Boys' Clubs Am., Shady Side, Pitts., 1969-70. Mem. D.C. Bar, Am. Bar Assn., Am. Patent Law Assn., Md. Bar Assn. Patentee. Home: 2205 Solmar Dr Silver Spring MD 20904 Office: 1725 K St NW Suite 912 Washington DC 20006 Tel (202) 659-2930

ARMSTRONG, JAMES GAYLORD, b. Nacogdoches, Tex., Aug. 3, 1939; student Harvard, 1960; B.A., Baylor U., 1961; LL.B., U. Tex., 1968. Admitted to Tex. bar, 1968; asso. firm McGinnis, Lochridge & Kilgore, Austin, Tex., 1968-73, partner, 1973—; staff asst. to Congressman W.R. Poage of Tex., 1962-64; adminstrv. asst. to Congressman Ray Roberts of Tex., 1964-65. Chmn. United Way, Austin, 1975-76; chmn. Austin Drug Control, 1970-71. Mem. State Bar Tex., Tex. Bar Found. Home: 2604 Jarratt Ave Austin TX 78703 Office: 900 Congress Ave Austin TX 78701 Tel (512) 476-6982

ARMSTRONG, JAMES L., III, b. Miami, Fla., Jan. 7, 1932; B.A., Yale U., 1955, LL.B., 1958. Admitted to Fla. bar, 1958; partner firm Smathers and Thompson, Miami, 1958—. Alumni rep. Phillips Exeter Acad., 1960-68; pres. Orange Bowl Com., 1975; bd. dirs. Am. Cancer Soc. Mem. Dade County (pres. 1971-72), Am. bar assns., Am. Judicature Soc. Home: 4911 Alhambra Circle Coral Gables FL 33146 Office: 1301 Alfred I DuPont Bldg Miami FL 33131 Tel (305) 379-6523

ARMSTRONG, RICHARD DAVID, JR., b. Chelsea, Mass., Apr. 2, 1946; A.B., Boston Coll., 1968, J.D., 1972; LL.M., Georgetown U., 1975. Admitted to Mass. bar, 1972; counsel to chmn. NLRB, Washington, 1972-76; asso. firm Snyder, Tepper & Berlin, Boston, 1976—. Town meeting mem., Milton, Mass., 1972-75. Mem. Am., Mass. bar assn., Common Cause, John Carroll Soc., ACLU. Home: 11 Bradford Rd Milton MA 02186 Office: 73 Tremont St Boston MA 02108 Tel (617) 277-8420

ARMSTRONG, THOMAS WAYNE, b. Chgo., Apr. 27, 1940; B.B.A., So. Methodist U., 1960, LL.B., 1966. Admitted to Tex. bar, 1967, D.C. bar, 1970; trial atty. SEC, Washington, 1967-69; partner firm Sullivan & Worcester, Washington, 1969—. Mem. Fed. Bar Assn. Home: 621 Bennington Ln Silver Spring MD 20910 Office: 1025 Connecticut Ave Washington DC 20036 Tel (202) 293-6170

ARMSTRONG, TIMOTHY JOSEPH, b. Atlanta, June 17, 1945; B.A., Dartmouth Coll., 1967; J.D., U. Ga., 1970. Admitted to Ga. bar, 1970, Fla. bar, 1971; law clk. to Hon. David W. Dyer, U.S. Ct. of Appeals, Fifth Circuit, Miami, Fla., 1970-71; asso. firm Batchelor, Brodnax, Guthrie & Kindred, Miami, 1971-75; partner firm Batchelor, Brodnax, Guthrie & Primm, Miami, 1975—. Mem. Am., Fed., Fla., Ga. Dade County bar assns., Maritime Law Assn. of the U.S., Am. Judicature Soc. Contbr. articles to legal jours. Office: 2550 First Federal Bldg 1 SE 3d Ave Miami FL 33133 Tel (305) 358-4962

ARMSTRONG, WILLIAM GRANT, b. Seattle, June 12, 1921; A.B. Washington U., St. Louis, 1943, LL.B., 1946. Admitted to Mo. bar, 1953; spl. asst. personnel Mo. Pacific R.R. Co., St. Louis, 1951-74, asst. dir. labor relations, 1975—. Home: 7229 Kingsbury St Louis MO 63130 Office: 210 N 13th St St Louis MO 63103 Tel (314) 622-2041

ARNABOLDI, LEO PETER, JR., b. Paterson, N.J., Dec. 28, 1924; B.A., Amherst Coll., 1947; J.D., Yale, 1950. Admitted to N.Y. State bar, 1951; asso. firm Willkie, Farr & Gallagher, N.Y.C., 1950-52; asso. firm Olwine, Connelly, Chase, O'Donnell & Weyher, N.Y.C., 1952-59, partner, 1960-68, sr. partner 1969—. Mem. Am., N.Y. State, N.Y.C. bar assns. Home: 26 Cedarwood Dr Greenwich CT 06832 Office: 299 Park Ave New York City NY 10017 Tel (212) 688-0400

ARNASS, JOHN P., b. Yankton, S.D., Feb. 8, 1927; A.B., Harvard U., 1949; J.D., Georgetown U., 1951. Admitted to D.C. bar, 1952, Md. bar, 1958, U.S. Supreme Ct. bar, 1965; clk. to Chief Judge of U.S. Ct. Appeals, Washington, 1951-52; now mem. firm Hogan & Hartson, Washington; lectr. in law Cath. U. Am., 1969-71. Fellow Am. Coll. Trial Lawyers, Internat. Acad. Trial Lawyers; mem. Bar Assn. D.C. (pres. 1977—), Am., Md., Montgomery County bar assns., Am. Judicature Soc., Def. Research Inst., Inc., Fedn. Ins. Counsel, Internat. Assn. Ins. Counsel, Phi Delta Phi. Office: 815 Connecticut Ave NW Washington DC 20006 Tel (202) 331-4553*

ARNE, COURTLAND DONALD, b. Davenport, Iowa, Apr. 14, 1929; B.A., U. Calif., Berkeley, 1951; J.D., 1954. Admitted to Calif. bar, 1955; asso. firm Sanford & Jackson, Oakland, Calif., 1956-59; partner firm Naphan & Arne, Oakland, 1959-71; judge Municipal Ct., Oakland-Piedmont Jud. Dist., Oakland, 1971—; mem. City of Oakland Civil Service Commn., 1970-71. Mem. Calif. Judges Assn. Office: 600 Washington St Oakland CA 94601 Tel (415) 874-6381

ARNESON, JOHN FINCH, b. Mpls., Apr. 14, 1920; B.A., Macalester Coll., 1941; student Harvard, 1944; LL.B., J.D., U. Minn., 1948. Admitted to Minn. bar, 1948, N.Y. State bar, 1961; partner Elliot & Arneson firm, Mpls., 1948-56; individual practice law, Mpls., 1956-59, Syracuse, N.Y., 1960—. Mem. Internat. Polit. Sci. Assn. Contbr. articles to legal jours. Home: 216 Hampton Rd Syracuse NY 13203 Office: 2827 James St Syracuse NY 13206 Tel (315) 463-9730

ARNETT, RUSSELL EUGENE, b. Oak Park, Ill., July 28, 1927; student Central Coll., Fayette, Mo., 1946-48; LL.B., Northwestern U., 1951. Admitted to Alaska bar, 1955; U.S. Commr., Nome, Alaska, 1952; asso. firm E.L. Arnell, Anchorage, 1955-56; individual practice law, Anchorage, 1956—; partner firm Opland, Johnston and Arnett, Anchorage, 1976—; city atty. Kodiak, Nome and Whittier (Alaska); spl. master U.S. Dist. Ct., Superior Ct., Alaska; mem. com. jud. discipline removal Alaska Jud. Council, 1967-68; Alaska v.p. Nat. Assn. Claimants Compensation Attys., 1959. Mem. Alaska (bd. govs. 1968-71), Anchorage (pres. 1966-67) bar assns. Office: 510 "L" St Anchorage AK 99501 Tel (907) 272-4624

ARNEY, REX ODELL, b. Ashland, Ky., Jan. 11, 1940; B.A., U. Wyo., 1962, M.A., 1963; J.D., U. Ill. 1968. Admitted to Wyo. bar, 1968; partner firm Redle, Yonkee & Arney, Sheridan, Wyo., 1968—; mem. Wyo. Ho. of Reps., 1973-76, Wyo. Senate, 1977—. Bd. dirs. Community Concert Assn., Day Care Center, Salvation Army (all Sheridan). Mem. Am., Wyo., Sheridan County bar assns., Am. Trial Lawyers Assn., Am. Judicature Soc. Recipient Distinguished Service award Sheridan Jaycees, 1971. Office: Box 6288 Sheridan WY 82801 Tel (307) 674-7454

ARNIM, EDWARD ALEXANDER, b. Flatonia, Tex., Aug. 21, 1902; B.A., U. Tex., 1923, postgrad. Law Sch., 1926. Admitted to Tex. bar, 1926, U.S. Supreme Ct. bar, 1957; individual practice law, Flatonia, 1924-35, 43—; county judge Fayette County (Tex.), 1935-43. Mem. Am., Tex. bar assns. Home: 221 9th St Flatonia TX 78941 Office: Old Bank Bldge Flatonia TX 78941

ARNING, JOHN FREDRICK, b. Lansing, Mich., May 4, 1925; LL.B. magna cum laude, Harvard, 1949. Admitted to N.Y. bar, 1949; asso. firm Sullivan & Cromwell, N.Y.C., 1949-57, partner, 1957—. Mem. Am. Bar Assn., Assn. Bar City N.Y., Union Internationale des Avocats. Home: 201 E 28th St New York City NY 10016 Office: Sullivan & Cromwell 48 Wall St New York City NY 10005 Tel (212) 952-8034

ARNOFF, HARVEY ALBERT, b. Canaan, Conn., Nov. 18, 1942; B.A., U. Conn., 1964; J.D., Bklyn. Law Sch., 1967. Admitted to N.Y. bar, 1968; atty. Suffolk County (N.Y.) Legal Aid Soc., 1969-70; asst. dist. atty. Suffolk County, 1970-71; asso. firm Gatz and Arnoff, Riverhead, N.Y., 1971-73, partner, 1973-76, owner, 1976—; dir. Suffolk County Legal Services Corp. Mem. N.Y., Suffolk County bar assns., Suffolk County Criminal Bar Assn. Office: 16 W Main St Riverhead NY 11901 Tel (516) 727-4160

ARNOLD, BENJAMIN FELKER, b. Little Rock, Jan. 8, 1943; B.A. with honors, Hendrix Coll., 1965; LL.B., U. Ark., 1968. Admitted to Ark. bar, 1968; asso. firm Moses, McClellan, Arnold, Own & McDermott, Little Rock, 1969-71, partner, 1971—; dir. Union Nat. Bank of Little Rock, 1976. Mem. Am., Ark., Pulaski County bar assns., Am. Judicature Soc. Home: 23 Queenspark Rd Little Rock AR 72207 Office: 212 Center St Little Rock AR 72201 Tel (501) 374-3774

ARNOLD, CHARLES LEONARD, b. N.Y.C., Oct. 28, 1946; J.D., U. Ariz., 1970. Admitted to Ariz. bar, 1970; asso. firm Randolph, Kelly & Corbin, Phoenix, 1970-73; partner firm Arnold, Schneider, Moore & Demaree, and predecessor, Phoenix, 1973—. Pres., dir. Terros, Inc., Phoenix. Mem. Ariz., Am., Maricopa County bar assns. Home: 220 E Winter Dr Phoenix AZ 85020 Office: 8650 N 35th Ave Suite 100 Phoenix AZ 85021 Tel (602) 249-9000

ARNOLD, CHARLES WILLIAM, b. Howell, Mich., July 12, 1945; B.A. in Chemistry, U. Ky., 1967, J.D., 1970. Admitted to Ky. bar, 1971; city atty., Lexington, Ky., partner firm Arnold & Willmott. Mem. Men's Com. for Lexington Philharmonic. Mem. Mich., Mo., Ky., Fed. bar assns. Home: 3 Mentelle Park Lexington KY 40502 Office: 1502 1st Nat Bldg Lexington KY 40507 Tel (606) 252-6765

ARNOLD, DAVID, b. Rochester, N.Y., Apr. 29, 1941; B.A., Ohio State U., 1963, LL.B., 1966, J.D., 1966. Admitted to Ohio bar, 1966; asso. firm Disbro and Ellerin, Cleve., 1966-69; partner firm Pilloff & Arnold, Cleve., 1969-72, Selker, Einbund, Rubenstein & Mosher, Cleve., 1972—. Mem. Cuyahoga County Bar Assn. (3d v.p.). Home: 24375 Hilltop Dr Beachwood OH 44122 Office: 3000 Terminal Tower Cleveland OH 44113 Tel (216) 696-6010

ARNOLD, FRED ENGLISH, b. Mexico, Mo., May 10, 1938; A.B., Harvard, 1960, LL.B., 1963. Admitted to Mo. bar, 1963; asso. firm Thompson & Mitchell, St. Louis, 1964-70, partner, 1971—. Mem. Am., Mo., Met. St. Louis bar assns. Home: 6369 Wydown Blvd Clayton MO 63105 Office: One Mercantile Center Saint Louis MO 63101 Tel (314) 231-7676

ARNOLD, GEORGE JOHN, b. Fort Benning, Ga., Sept. 9, 1942; B.S. in Bus. Adminstrn., Ohio State U., 1964; J.D., Capital U., 1970. Admitted to Ohio bar, 1970, Fla. bar, 1970; chief real estate atty. City of Columbus (Ohio), 1972-74, spl. projects coordinator, 1975-77; asso. firm Moritz, McClure, Hughes and Hadley, Columbus, 1977—. Mem. Am., Ohio State, Fla. State bar assns., Franklin County (Ohio) Trial Lawyers, Columbus Bd. Realtors, Soc. Real Estate Appraisers (asso.), Aquinas High Sch. Alumni Assn. (pres.), Phi Alpha Delta Alumni (justice 1975—). Contbr. articles to legal jours. Home: 675 S Kellner Rd Columbus OH 43209 Office: 155 E Broad St Columbus OH 43215 Tel (614) 224-0888

ARNOLD, JOHN FOX, b. St. Louis, Sept. 17, 1937; student U. Colo., 1955-56; A.B., U. Mo., 1959, LL.B., 1961. Admitted to Mo. bar, 1961, U.S. Supreme Ct. bar, 1971; partner firm Green, Hennings, Henry & Arnold and predecessors, St. Louis, 1963-70, Lashly, Caruthers, Thies, Rava & Hamel and predecessors, St. Louis, 1970—. Vice pres. Legal Aid Soc. St. Louis and St. Louis County, 1970-71; mem. St. Louis County Charter Revision Commn., 1967. Mem. Am., Mo. bar assns., Bar Assn. Met. St. Louis (pres. 1975-76), Nat. Conf. Commrs. Uniform State Laws (Mo. rep. 1973—). Recipient distinguished service award Mo. Jr. C. of C., 1968. Home: 210 Rosemont St St Louis MO 63119 Office: 818 Olive St St Louis MO 63101 Tel (314) 621-2939

ARNOLD, MORRIS SHEPPARD, b. Texarkana, Tex., Oct. 8, 1941; grad. Phillips Exeter Acad., 1959; student Yale, 1959-61; B.S. in Elec. Engring., U. Ark., 1965, LL.B., 1968; LL.M., Harvard, 1969, S.J.D., 1971. Admitted to Ark. bar, 1968, Ind. bar, 1976; asso. firm Arnold & Arnold, Texarkana, Ark., 1968, of counsel, 1974—; teaching fellow in law Harvard, 1969-70; Frank L. Knox Meml. fellow U. London, 1970-71; asst. prof. law Ind. U., 1971-74, asso. prof., 1974-76, prof., 1976—; vis. prof. U. Pa. Law Sch., spring 1977. Mem. Selden Soc., Medieval Acad. Am., Am. Soc. Legal History (editor Studies in Legal History series 1975—). Author: The Year Book of 2 Richard II, 1378-79, 1975; contbr. articles to profl. jours. Home: 2911 Fawkes Way N Bloomington IN 47401 Office: Ind U Law Sch Bloomington IN 47401 Tel (812) 337-3844

ARNOLD, SAM WILLIAM, III, b. Cynthiana, Ky., Mar. 8, 1947; B.A., Ky. Wesleyan Coll., 1969; J.D., U. Ky., 1972. Admitted to Ky. bar, 1972; individual practice law, Cynthiana, 1972—; asst. atty. Harrison County (Ky.), 1975—. Deacon Cynthiana Christian Ch., 1968. Mem. Am., Ky., Harrison County bar assns., Harrison County Realtors Assn. Home: 516 E Bridge St Cynthiana KY 41031 Office: 16 E Pike St Cynthiana KY 41031 Tel (606) 234-6439

ARNOLD, TIMOTHY ROSS, b. Toledo, July 8, 1943; A.B., Ohio U., 1965; J.D., Case Western Res. U., 1968. Admitted to Ohio bar, 1968, Colo. bar, 1972, U.S. Supreme Ct. bar, 1975; staff atty. Cleve. Legal Aid Soc., 1969-71; asst. solicitor gen. Colo. State Dept. Law, Denver, 1972—; instr. bus. law Denver Community Coll., 1972; spl. legal advisor State Affirmative Action com. Colo. State Personnel Bd., 1976. Mem. Am. Bar Assn. Office: 1525 Sherman St Denver CO 80203 Tel (303) 892-3611

ARNOLD, TOM, b. Houston, Nov. 20, 1923; B.S.E.E., U. Tex., 1944, J.D., 1949. Admitted to Tex. bar, 1949; staff atty. U.S. Dept. Justice, Washington, 1949-51; asso. and partner firm Hutcheson, Taliaferro & Hutcheson, Houston, 1951-56; founder, sr. partner firm Arnold, White & Durkee, and predecessors, Houston, 1956—; mem. adv. com. Tex. Legis. Council, 1966-67; mem. Dept. Commerce Patent Adv. Com., 1968-73; mem. Tex. Bd. Legal Specialization, 1976—. Fellow Tex. Bar Found.; mem. Tex. Conf. Bar Pres.'s, State Bar Tex. (chmn. patent, trademark and copyright sect. 1955-56), Am. (past chmn. patent sect.), Houston (pres. 1977-78) bar assns., Nat. Council Patent Law Assns. (past chmn.), Am. Patent Law Assn. (pres. elect 1977-78), Licensing Execs. Soc. (sec. 1973—), Order of Coif. Asst. editor Tex. Law Rev., 1948-49; contbr. articles to profl. publs.; recipient Jefferson medal, 1974. Office: 2100 Transco Tower Houston TX 77056 Tel (713) 621-9100

ARNOLD, WILLIAM JOHN, b. Beallsville, Ohio, Apr. 9, 1913; J.D., Ohio No. U., 1940. Admitted to Ohio bar, 1940, N.J. bar, 1948; individual practice law, Hackensack, N.J., 1946-54; asst. prosecutor Bergen County (N.J.), 1954-60; pres. judge Bergen County Dist. Ct., 1960-67; judge County Ct., Hackensack, 1967—. Mem. Am., N.J., Bergen County bar assns. Home: 21 W Ivy Ln Englewood NJ 07631 Office: Bergen County Court House Hackensack NJ 07601

ARNOLD, WILLIAM LINDSAY, b. Chgo., Oct. 17, 1924; student Northwestern U., 1946-49; LL.B., DePaul Coll., 1951. Admitted to Ill. bar, 1951, U.S. Supreme Ct. bar, 1962; partner firm Morris, Liss, Arnold & Hennessy, Chgo., 1953-71; sr. partner firm Arnold, Hennessy, Liss & Reda, Chgo., 1971—; gen. counsel Internat. Food Service Mfrs. Assn., 1953—; approved counsel Underwriters at LLoyd's, London, 1955—. Mem. Am., Ill., Chgo. bar assns., Internat. Assn. Ins. Counsel, Fedn. Ins. Counsel, Assn. Ins. Attys., Soc. Trial Lawyers. Home: 505 N Lake Shore Dr Chicago IL 60611 Office: 32 W Randolph St Chicago IL 60601 Tel (312) 427-7676

ARNOLD, WILLIAM STRANG, b. Yonkers, N.Y., Feb. 5, 1921; A.B., U. Ark., 1942, J.D., 1947; LL.M., Columbia, 1948. Admitted to Ark. bar, 1947; sr. partner firm Arnold, Hamilton & Streetman, Crossett, Ark., 1948—; atty. City of Crossett, 1961-68; commr. uniform law State of Ark., 1969—. Fellow Am. Coll. Trial Lawyers, Am. Coll. Probate Counsel, Am. Bar Found.; mem. Am., Ark. bar assns., Am. Judicature Soc., Internat. Assn. Ins. Counsel. Home: 904 Hickory St Crossett AR 71635 Office: PO Drawer A 302 Main St Crossett AR 71635 Tel (501) 364-2213

ARNOW, WINSTON EUGENE, b. Micanopy, fla., Mar. 13, 1911; B.S. in Bus. Adminstrn., U. Fla., 1932, J.D., 1933. Research clk. Supreme Ct. of Fla., 1932; admitted to Fla. bar, 1933; individual practice law, Gainesville, 1935-42; mem. firm Clayton, Arnow, Duncan, Johnston, Clayton & Quincey, Gainesville, 1946-67; judge U.S. Dist. Ct., No. Dist. Fla., Pensacola, 1968—, chief judge, 1969—; chmn. steering com. Fla. Civil Practice Before Trial. Fellow Am. Coll. Probate Counsel; mem. Am., Fla. (certificates of service as mem. bd. govs. 1956-58), Escambia-Santa Rosa bar assns., Am. Law Inst., Am. Judicature Soc., Order of Coif (hon.), Scabbard and Blade, Fla. Blue Key, Sigma Phi Epsilon, Phi Delta Phi, Tau Kappa Alpha, Phi Delta Epsilon. Recipient certificate of merit U.S. Jr. C. of C., 1954, Distinguished Alumnus award U. Fla., 1972; author: Florida Practice Rules Annotated, 1937; contbr. articles to profl. jours. Office: POB 12347 Pensacola FL 32581 Tel (904) 434-2631

ARNTZ, WILLIAM CHARLES, b. Seattle, Apr. 24, 1942; B.A., U. San Francisco, 1964, J.D., 1967. Admitted to Ill. bar, 1970; law clk. firm Bohnert, Flowers & McCarthy, San Francisco, 1966-67; served to capt. Adj. Gen. Corps, U.S. Army, 1967-69; law clk., atty. law dept. Libby, McNeill & Libby, Chgo., 1969-70; atty. Wash. Nat. Ins. Co., Evanston, 1970-72, asst. counsel, 1972-76, asst. gen. counsel, 1976-; sec., counsel Wash. Nat. Trust Co., 1977—. Mem. Glenayre Property Owners Assn., 1972-77, chmn. zoning com., 1972-74. Mem. Am., Ill. State, Chgo. (sect. chmn. corp. law com.) bar assns., Phi Alpha Delta. Office: 1630 Chicago Ave Evanston IL 60201 Tel (312) 866-3075

ARONOW, CEDOR BORIS, b. Odessa, Russia, Sept. 2, 1910; A.B., U. Wash., 1931, LL.B., 1933. Admitted to Mont. bar, 1933; partner firm Aronow, Anderson, Beatty & Lee, and predecessors, Shelby, Mont., 1933—; ind. oil and gas producer, 1949—; city atty. Shelby, 1959-61; county atty. Toole County, 1937-43; Toole County rep. Mont. Legislature, 1949-52; del. Mont. State Constl. Conv., 1972; del. Nat. Democratic Conv., 1956; pres. Nat. Com. Young Dems. of Mont., 1936-38. Mem. Mont. (dist. v.p. 1939-41), Am. (vice-chmn. com. on Indian law 1958-62) bar assns., Mont. Trial Lawyers Assn. (dir. 1968, v.p. 1970-71), Rocky Mountain Oil and Gas Assn. (dir.), Mont. Broadcasters Assn. (pres. 1950-51). Office: Aronow Anderson Beatty & Lee Drawer D Shelby MT 59474

ARONOWITZ, GARY DAVID, b. Bronx, N.Y., Aug. 4, 1948; B.B.A., City U. N.Y., 1970; J.D., Northeastern U., 1973; postgrad N.Y. U. Admitted to N.J. bar, 1974; atty. Mut. Benefit Life Ins. Co., Newark, 1973-75, asst. dir. advanced underwriting services, 1975—. Mem. Am. Bar Assn., NW N.J. Estate Planning Council. Home: Gerie Ave White Meadow Lake Rockaway NJ 07866 Tel (201) 481-8775

ARONS, JOHN LESTER, b. N.Y.C., Aug. 7, 1943; B.A., Colgate U., 1965; LL.B., Boston U., 1968. Admitted to N.Y. State bar, 1969; individual practice law, 1969-76; partner firm Goodhue, Lange & Arons, Mount Kisco, N.Y., 1976—; dep. town atty. Town of Caramel, N.Y., 1975, town atty., 1976. Chmn. zoning bd. of appeals Town of Carmel, 1970-74. Mem. Am., N.Y. State, Westchester, Putnam, No. Westchester bar assns. Home: Cherry Hill Rd Carmel NY 10512 Office: 61 Smith Ave Mount Kisco NY 10549 Tel (914) 666-8033

ARONS, STEPHEN, b. San Diego, Calif., Sept. 19, 1943; A.B., U. Pa., 1965; J.D., Harvard, 1969. Admitted to Mass. bar, 1969; sr. atty. Harvard Center for Law and Edn., 1969-71; research fellow Center for Study of Pub. Policy, Cambridge, Mass., 1971-72; practiced in Cambridge, 1971; asst. prof. legal studies U. Mass., Amherst, 1972—, dir. mental patients advocacy project, 1976—; dir. Mass. Pub. Interest Law Firm, Boston, 1975—. Chmn. bd. dirs. Group Sch. Inc., Cambridge, 1970-72; bd. selectmen Town of Shutesbury (Mass.), 1973-74. Mem. Phi Beta Kappa. Author: Before the Law, 1974; Doing Your Own School, 1972; contbr. articles to legal jours. Home: 365 Amherst RD 2 Amherst MA 01002 Office: Legal Studies Program U of Mass Amherst MA 01003 Tel (413) 545-2000

ARONWALD, GEORGE M., b. Douglas, Ariz., May 23, 1908; LL.B., St. John's U., Bklyn., 1929. Admitted to N.Y. State bar, 1931, U.S. Supreme Ct. bar, 1943; arbitrator N.Y.C. Small Claims Ct., 1951—; hearing officer U.S. Dept. Justice, N.Y.C., 1966—. Mem. Queens County Bar Assn. Recipient Silver Beaver award Boy Scouts Am., 1948. Office: 253 Broadway New York City NY 10007 Tel (212) 962-4140

ARONWALD, WILLIAM I., b. Bklyn., Nov. 11, 1940; B.A., Hofstra U., 1962; J.D., Bklyn. Law Sch., 1965. Admitted to N.Y. bar, 1966; asst. dist. atty. N.Y. County, 1967-71; spl. atty. organized crime and racketeering sect. U.S. Dept. Justice, 1971-72; asst. atty. in charge Organized Crime Strike Force, So. Dist. N.Y., 1972-75, atty. in charge, 1975-76, chief atty., criminal div. Eastern Dist. N.Y., Thiells, 1976-77; individual practice law, N.Y.C., 1977—; cons. in field; mem. faculty Nat. Coll. Dist. Attys., 1975—. Mem. Queens County (N.Y.) Bar Assn. Recipient Spl. Commendation award U.S. Dept. Justice, 1973. Home: 27 Riverglen Dr Thiells NY 10984 Office: 600 Madison Ave New York City NY 10022 Tel (212) 330-7022

AROSTEGUI, ALBERT J., b. Stockton, Calif., Feb. 17, 1927; J.D., U. San Francisco, 1951. Admitted to Calif. bar, 1952, U.S. Supreme Ct. bar, 1958; partner firms Steel & Arostegui, 1954-76, Arostegui, Islip, Cooke, Marquez, Epley & Gengler, Marysville, Calif., 1976—; sec. Yuba River Lumber Co., Inc., 1955-76, Brunswick Timber Products Corp., 1965-76; mem. nat. panel arbitrators Am. Arbitration Assn. Mem. Calif. State, Yuba-Sutter, Am. bar assns., Calif. Trial Lawyers Assn. Home: 2235 Buchanan St Marysville CA 95901 Office: 225 Sixth St Marysville CA 95901 Tel (916) 742-3223

ARRINGTON, JOHN LESLIE, JR., b. Pawhuska, Okla., Oct. 15, 1931; A.B., Princeton U., 1953; LL.B., Harvard, 1956, LL.M., 1957. Admitted to Okla. bar, 1956, U.S. Supreme Ct. bar, 1960; asso. firm Huffman, Arrington, Scheurich & Kihle and predecessors, Tulsa, 1957-61, partner, 1961—; dir. Computing and Info. Scis. Corp., Tulsa, 1969—, Woodland Bank, Tulsa, 1976—. Trustee Holland Hall Sch., Tulsa, 1967—; bd. dirs. Tulsa County Legal Aid Soc., 1965-70, pres., 1967-70; bd. dirs. Tulsa Family and Children's Service, 1966—, pres., 1974; bd. dirs. Tulsa Charity Horse Show, 1973—. Mem. Tulsa County (Jr. award 1962, pres. 1970), Okla., Am., bar assns., Fed. Power Bar Assn., Am. Soc. Internat. Law, Harvard Law Sch. Assn. of Okla. (pres. 1961). Named Outstanding Young Man Tulsa Jaycees, 1963. Home: 4217 S Wheeling Ave Tulsa OK 74105 Office: 5th Floor Okla Natural Bldg Tulsa OK 74119 Tel (918) 585-8141

ARROLL, MARK EDWARD, b. N.Y.C., Nov. 27, 1935; B.A., Ill. Coll., 1956; LL.B., J.D., Cornell U., 1959; postgrad. N.Y. U. Admitted to N.Y. State bar, 1960; partner firm Martin & Arroll, N.Y.C., 1960-63; asso. firm Reilly, Curry & Gibbons, N.Y.C., 1963-64; individual practice law, N.Y.C., 1964—; dep. asst. corp. counsel N.Y.C., 1966-69; prof. Para Legal Inst., N.Y.C., 1972—; instr. Law Bds. Inst., 1970-71. Mem. CAP, N.Y.C., 1967; trustee John W. Lindsay Reform Club, 1966-68; mem. Friends of Library, founders club Ill. Coll. Mem. N.Y. County Lawyers Assn. (fed. criminal justice panel), N.Y. Trial Lawyers Assn. (def. panel), Phi Beta Kappa. Recipient State Championship award in Debate. Home: 250 W Beech St Long Beach NY 11561 Office: 261 Broadway New York City NY 10007 Tel (212) 732-3375

ARTHUR, ROBERT HENRY, b. West, Tex., Jan. 20, 1935; B.A., Tex. Tech. Coll., 1959; J.D. U. Tex., Austin, 1962. Admitted to Tex. bar, 1962; individual practice law, Dallas, 1962-64; atty. Halliburton Co., Dallas, 1964-66; atty. Halliburton Profit Sharing and Savs. Plan, Duncan, Okla., 1966—, sec., 1976—; asst. sec. Life Ins. Co. of S.W., Dallas, 1964-66. Trustee Halliburton Employees' Benefit Fund, Duncan, 1970-76. Bd. dirs. Stephens County Assn. Mental Health, 1973—, Duncan Community Residence, Inc., 1975; mem. Duncan Sch. Bd., 1976. Mem. Tex. Bar Assn. Home: 1205 Avalon St Duncan OK 73553 Office: PO Drawer 1431 Duncan OK 73533 Tel (405) 251-3261

ARTHUR, ROBERT JAMES, b. Scranton, Pa., Feb. 28, 1932; B.A., U. Scranton, 1953; J.D., Georgetown U., 1958. Examiner Govt. Employees Ins. Co., Washington, 1956-58; admitted to Va. bar, 1958; partner firm Varoutsos, Koutoulakos, Arthur, and Dolan, Arlington, Va., 1963-76; partner firm Robert J. Arthur, 1977—; mem. tort com. Va. State Bar, 1969. Chmn. Boy Scouts Am., Arlington County, Va., 1960-66. Mem. Am., No. Va. (pres. 1975), Arlington County (pres. 1974-75) bar assns., No. Va. Lawyers Assn. (dir. 1974—), Am. Judicature Soc., Am. Trial Lawyers Assn. Home: 3812 N Woodrow St Arlington VA 22207 Office: 1400 N Uhle St Suite 702 Arlington VA 22201 Tel (703) 243-5100

ARTHUR, ROY WILLIAM, b. Lousia County, Va., May 16, 1917; A.B., Coll. William and Mary, 1938, J.D., 1940. Admitted to Va. bar, 1939; individual practice law, Wytheville, Va., 1940-48; partner firm Parsons and Arthur, Wytheville, Va.; 1948-69; judge Va. Circuit Ct., 27th Circuit, Wytheville, 1969—; mayor City Wytheville, 1946-52. Bd. vistors Coll. William and Mary, Williamsburg, Va., 1954-62, 1966-69; mem. Va. Commission Higher Edn., 1964-65; chmn. bd. Wytheville Community Coll., 1963-69. Mem. Va., Am. bar assns., Va. Municipal League (pres. 1963-64), Omicron Delta Kappa. Home: 385 E Washington St Wytheville VA 24382 Office: Box 380 Wytheville VA 24382 Tel (703) 228-2155

ARTUSO, LOUIS HARRY, b. Pitts., Feb. 8, 1907; A.B., Grove City Coll., 1930; LL.B., U. Pitts., 1933. Admitted to Pa. bar, 1933, U.S. Supreme Ct. bar, 1969; solicitor McKees Rocks Borough (Pa.), 1936-37; sheriff Allegheny County (Pa.), 1942-43; asst. staff JAG, 6th Army Hdqrs., 1946; post judge adv. Camp Hahn, Calif., 1945; atty. Pa. Turnpike Commn., 1950-56; solicitor Verona Borough (Pa.), 1951-52; vice-chmn. Allegheny County Bd. of Property Assessments, Appeals and Rev. Pitts., 1958—. Bd. dirs. Boys' Clubs of W. Pa. Mem. Allegheny County Bar Assn. (past pres.), Pa. Bar Assn. (bd. govs.). Home: 286 Oriole Dr Pittsburgh PA 15220 Office: 421 Frick Bldg Pittsburgh PA 15219 Tel (412) 261-1816

ARTZ, WILLIAM EDWARD, b. Cambridge, Mass., June 21, 1943; B.S., Ohio Wesleyan U., 1965; J.D., Am. U., 1969. Admitted to Va. bar, 1969, U.S. Supreme Ct. bar, 1972; asso. firm Harrigan & Morris, Arlington, Va., 1969-72; partner firm Harrigan Morris & Artz, Arlington, 1972-75, Harrigan & Artz, Arlington, 1975—. Mem. Am., Arlington County (exec. com. 1972-75, 75—), Va. bar assns., No. Va. Young Lawyers Assn. (past sec., past pres.), Va. Trial Lawyers Assn., Am. Judicature Soc. Home: 7621 Provincial Dr McLean VA 22101 Office: 2060 N 14th St Arlington VA 22201 Tel (703) 522-9200

ARVIDSON, FRED BIRK, b. Rockford, Ill., Feb. 7, 1949; B.A., DePauw U., 1970; J.D., U. Chgo., 1973. Admitted to Alaska bar, 1973; partner firm Hughes, Thorsness, Gantz & Brundin, Anchorage, 1975—; lectr. U. Alaska, 1976—. Mem. Am., Alaska, Anchorage bar assns., Lawyer Pilots Assn., Phi Beta Kappa, Omicron Delta Epsilon. Office: 509 W 3d Ave Anchorage AK 99501 Tel (907) 274-7522

ARVIDSON, PHILIP RUSSEL, b. St. Louis, Apr. 1, 1938; B.S. in Mech. Engring., Okla. State U., 1961; J.D., George Washington U., 1965. Patent examiner U.S. Patent Office, Washington, 1961-65; patent agt., then patent atty. Allied Chem. Corp., 1965-67, div. patent counsel, Morris Twp., N.J., 1968; admitted to N.J. bar, 1967, U.S. Patent Office bar, 1967; div. patent counsel Allied Chem. Corp., Morris Twp., patent atty. Inmont Corp., Clifton, N.J., 1968-73, atty., asst. sec., 1973—, dir. govtl. and environ. affairs, 1975—. Councilman, Borough of Mendham (N.J.), 1970-75, pres., 1975; mem. West Morris (N.J.) Regional High Sch. Bd. Edn., 1968-70. Mem. N.J. State, Am. bar assns., Delta Theta Phi. Home: 15 Gunther St Mendham NJ 07945 Office: 1255 Broad St Clifton NJ 07015 Tel (201) 773-8200

ARYE, LEONARD A., b. N.Y.C., Jan. 16, 1925; LL.D., N.Y. U., 1950. Admitted to N.Y. State bar, 1950; asso. firm Julien & Zale, N.Y.C., 1950-53; partner firm Arye & Moser, N.Y.C., 1953-66; partner firm Arye & Kors, N.Y.C., 1966—; dir. L.I.V.E., 1974—. Mem. N.Y. State Trial Lawyers Assn., N.Y.C. Lawyers Assn. Office: 20 Vesey St New York City NY 10007 Tel (212) RE2-4992

ASBELL, MAX B., b. Cochran, Ga., Sept. 8, 1931; A.B., Mercer U., 1958, LL.B., 1960, J.D., 1970. Admitted to Ga. bar, 1959; asst. claims supr. Coca-Cola Bottlers Assn., Atlanta, 1960-61; legal asst. to fed. judge, Atlanta, 1961-62; partner firm Burke & Asbell, Warner Robins, Ga., 1962-64; individual practice law, Warner Robins, 1964—; judge Recorders Ct. of Warner Robins, 1964-74. Trustee Green Acres Baptist Ch. Bldg. Fund, 1975-76; mem. mayor's advisory com., Warner Robins, 1968-72. Mem. Ga., Houston County (v.p. 1968, pres. 1973-74) bar assns., Ga. Sheriffs Assn., Warner Robins Realtors Assn. Home: 206 Gilchrist Dr Warner Robins GA 31093 Office: 1612 Watson Blvd PO Drawer 1040 Warner Robins GA 31093 Tel (912) 923-7125

ASBILL, MAC, JR., b. Atlanta, Mar. 15, 1922; B.A., Princeton U., 1942; LL.B. magna cum laude, Harvard U., 1948. Admitted to D.C. bar, 1948, Ga. bar, 1957; clk. to asso. justice U.S. Supreme Ct., Washington, 1948-49; asso. firm Sutherland, Tuttle & Brennan, Washington, 1949-53, partner, 1953—; atty. office of dep. counsel Dept. U.S. Army, 1950-51; mem. Commr. of Internal Revenue's Adv. Group, 1975. Mem. Fed. City Council, 1973—, mem. exec. com., 1975-76; pres. D.C. Municipal Research Bur., 1977—. Mem. Am. (chmn. sect. taxation 1971-72), D.C. bar assns., Am. Law Inst.; fellow Am. Bar Assn. Contbr. articles to profl. jours. Home: 9717 Corral Dr Potomac MD 20854 Office: 1666 K St NW Washington DC 20006 Tel (202) 872-7813

ASBILL, RICHARD JAMES, b. Los Angeles, Apr. 18, 1932; A.A., Modesto Jr. Coll., 1952; A.B., U. Calif., Berkeley, 1957, J.D., 1960. Admitted to Calif. bar, 1961; asso. firm Daniel S. Carlton, Redding, Calif., 1960-64; partner firm Carr, Kennedy & Asbill, Redding, 1964-65, firm Carlton and Asbill, Redding, 1965-68; individual practice law, Redding, 1968—. Mem. traffic and parking commn. City of Redding, 1961-68. Mem. Shasta-Trinity Counties Bar Assn. (pres. 1974), Am. Arbitration Assn. (arbitrator 1966—). Home: 3665 Altura St Redding CA 96001 Office: 1626 Court St Redding CA 96001 Tel (916) 241-9300

ASBILL, RICHARD MCKENRIE, b. Wilmington, Del., Nov. 9, 1943; A.B., Princeton, 1965; J.D., U. N.C., 1968. Admitted to Ga. bar, 1968, U.S. Supreme Ct. bar, 1971; since practiced in Atlanta; asso. firm Jones, Bird & Howell, 1968-73; partner firm Smith, Harman, Asbill, Roach & Nellis, 1973—; adj. prof. Emory U. Sch. Law, 1973—. Mem. Am. (vice chmn. com. on significant current trends, sect. real property, probate and trust law), Atlanta bar assns., State Bar Ga. Home: 255 Pineland Rd NW Atlanta GA 30342 Office: Suite 555 Day Bldg 2751 Buford Hwy NE Atlanta GA 30324 Tel (404) 325-5555

ASCHE, RICHARD MILTON, b. N.Y.C., Oct. 26, 1943; A.B. magna cum laude, Princeton, 1964; LL.B. cum laude, Harvard, 1967. Admitted to N.Y. State bar, 1967; clk. to U.S. Dist. Judge Milton Pollack, N.Y.C., 1967-68; asso. firm Pollack & Singer, N.Y.C., 1968-69, 70-74; staff atty. S. Bklyn. Legal Services, Bklyn., 1969-70; partner firm Pollack & Kaminsky, N.Y.C., 1975—; dir. Sta. WBAI-FM, 1977—; counsel Day Care Legal Action Coalition, 1976—. Bd. dirs. and sec. Boys Harbor, Inc., 1973—, Consumer Commn. on the Accreditation of Health Services Inc., 1973—; mem. Democratic County Com., Manhattan, 1975—. Mem. N.Y. County Lawyers Assn. Home: 350 Central Park W New York City NY 10025 Office: 61 Broadway New York City NY 10006 Tel (212) 952-0330

ASCHEMEYER, F(RANK) NEIL, b. St. Louis, June 18, 1929; A.B., Princeton, 1951; LL.B., U. Mich., 1954. Admitted to Mo. bar, 1954, Wis. bar, 1974; law clk. to Judge Roy W. Harper, U.S. Dist. Ct. for Eastern Jud. Dist. Mo., 1956-57; practiced in St. Louis 1957-74, asso. firms Shepley, Kroeger, Fisse, Shepley, St. Louis, 1957-62, Stolar Heitzmann & Eder, St. Louis, 1962-67, partner firm Rebman & Aschemeyer, 1967-74; v.p., gen. counsel Gateway Transp. Co., Inc., La Crosse, Wis., 1974—; mem. Mo. Ho. of Reps., 1959-62. Mem. Wis., Mo. bars, Am. Bar Assn., Motor Carrier Lawyers Assn., Bar Assn. Met. St. Louis, Assn. ICC Practitioners. Home: 3731 Cliffside Dr La Crosse WI 54601 Office: 455 Park Plaza Dr La Crosse WI 54601 Tel (608) 784-6470

ASCHENBRENER, DANIEL FRANK, b. Shawano, Wis., Mar. 20, 1941; B.S. in Polit. Sci., U. Wis. at Madison, 1963, LL.B., 1965. Admitted to Wis. bar, 1965; asso. firm Holden & Halvorsen, Sheboygan, Wis., 1965-66; partner firm Aschenbrener, Shawano, 1966-68, Aschenbrener & Koenig, 1973-75; asso. Aschenbrener & Koenig, S.C., 1975—; dist. atty. Shawano, Menominee Counties, 1967-72. Mem. Shawano County (past sec.-treas., pres.), Wis. State bar assns. Home: 208 E Center Shawano WI 54166 Office: 208 W Green Bay St Shawano WI 54166 Tel (715) 526-3191

ASFOOR, WAYNE LOUIS, b. LaCrosse, Wis., Mar. 1, 1947; B.A. cum laude, St. Mary's Coll.; LL.B., Marquette U. Admitted to Wis. bar, 1972; asso. firm Patrick R. Doyle, LaCrosse, 1972-73; individual practice law, LaCrosse, 1973—. Home: 103 N 23rd St LaCrosse WI 54601 Office: Suite 416 Rivoli Bldg LaCrosse WI 56401 Tel (608) 782-2377

ASH, RUSSELL KEITH, b. Kansas City, Kans., Mar. 29, 1946; B.A., Wichita State U., 1969; B.A. in History, Washburn U., 1972. Admitted to Kans. bar, U.S. Dist. Ct. bar, 1973; dep. dir. cts. Kans. Gov.'s Com. on Criminal Adminstrn., 1972-74; staff atty. Kans. Dept. Transp., 1974—. Dir., Shawnee County Democratic Headquarters, 1970; precinct committeeman, Topeka, 1970-72. Mem. Am., Kans. bar, assns. Home: 2517 Burnett Rd Topeka KS 66614 Office: 7th Floor State Office Bldg Topeka KS 66612 Tel (913) 296-3831

ASHBY, ROBERT SAMUEL, b. Crawfordsville, Ind., July 9, 1916; A.B., Ind. U., 1938, LL.B., Harvard U., 1941. Admitted to Ind. bar, 1941, N.Y. State bar, 1942; asso. firm Carter, Ledyard & Milburn, N.Y.C., 1941-42; served from ensign to lt. comdr. USNR, 1942-46; partner firm Barnes, Hickam, Pantzer & Boyd, Indpls., 1946-. Pres. Indpls. Mus. Art, 1954-56, trustee, 1951—. Mem. Am., Ind. State, Indpls., 7th Circuit bar assns., English-Speaking Union (pres. Indpls. br. 1974—). Contbr. articles to legal jours. Home: 7248 N Pennsylvania St Indianapolis IN 46240 Office: 1313 Merchants Bank Bldg Indianapolis IN 46204 Tel (317) 638-1313

ASHCROFT, JOHN DAVID, b. Chgo., May 9, 1942; A.B. cum laude, Yale U., 1964; J.D., U. Chgo., 1967. Asst prof. law S.W. Mo. State U., 1967-71, coordinator for jud. affairs, 1969-73, asso. prof., 1971-73; state auditor State of Mo., 1973-77, atty. gen., 1977—. Mem. exec. bd. Greene County (Mo.) unit ARC, Springfield; bd. dirs. Sunshine Children's Home. Mem. Am., Greene County bar assns., Phi Delta Phi, Phi Sigma Epsilon. Co-author: College Law for Business, 1971. Home: Route 2 Willard MO 65781 Office: Office of Atty Gen Supreme Ct Bldg Jefferson City MO 65101*

ASHDOWN, GERALD GRANT, b. Iowa City, Sept. 20, 1947; B.B.A., U. Iowa., 1969, J.D., 1972. Admitted to Iowa Bar, 1973; instr. law U. Iowa, 1972-73; asst. prof. law. U. Ky., 1973-77, asso. prof., 1977—. Mem. Order of the Coif. Home: Route 10 Lexington KY 40511 Office: Univ Ky Coll Law Lexington KY 40506 Tel (606) 257-3780

ASHE, BERNARD FLEMMING, b. Balt., Mar. 8, 1936; B.A., Howard U., 1956, J.D., 1961. Tchr., Balt. pub. schs., 1956-57; admitted to Va. bar, 1961, D.C. bar, 1963, Mich. bar, 1964, N.Y. bar, 1971; atty. NLRB, Washington, 1961-63; asst. gen. counsel Internat. Union UAW, Detroit, 1963-71; gen. counsel N.Y. State United Tchrs., Albany, 1971—; mem. panel Am. Arbitration Assn., 1972—. Bd. dirs. Pub. Employment Relations Research Inst., Washington, 1973—. Mem. N.Y., Va. state bars, State Bar Mich., Bar Assn. D.C., Assn. Bar City N.Y., Fed., Am. (council sect. labor relations law 1974—) bar assns., Nat. Lawyers Club. Office: 80 Wolf Rd Albany NY 12205 Tel (518) 459-5400

ASHE, DAVID I(RVING), b. Bklyn., Nov. 13, 1910; B.S., Coll. City N.Y., 1929; J.D., Columbia, 1932. Admitted to N.Y. bar, 1933, U.S. Supreme Ct. bar, 1955; since practiced in N.Y.C., sr. partner firm Ashe & Rifkin, 1940—; gen. counsel United Parents Assn., N.Y.C., 1950—; Workmen's Circle Circle, 1964—, Jewish Daily Forward, 1969—; cons. ACLU. Mem. N.Y.C. Bd. Higher Edn., 1966-73, Gov.'s Task Force on State Aid to Edn., 1975-76; v.p. research found. City U. N.Y., 1969-77, pres., 1977—; pres. United Parents Assns. N.Y.C., 1949-50; chmn. N.Y., Jewish Labor Com., 1966—; dir. N.Y.C. Council on Econ. Edn., 1975—. Mem. Assn. Bar City N.Y., N.Y. County Lawyers Assn. Contbr. articles in field to legal jours. Home: 1020 Park Ave New York City NY 10028 Office: 225 Broadway New York City NY 10007 Tel (212) 962-5550

ASHER, ALLAN FRANKLIN, b. Portland, Oreg., Feb. 23, 1922; A.B., U. Denver, 1946, LL.B., J.D., 1947. Admitted to Colo. bar, 1948; prin. firm Allan F. Asher, Colorado Springs, Colo., 1948—; municipal judge, Colorado Springs, 1960-65; city atty. Manitou Springs (Colo.), 1969—; county atty. Park County (Colo.), 1975—. Mem. Plumbing Bd. Colorado Springs, 1960-66. Mem. Colo., El Paso County bar assns., Am. Arbitration Assn., Phi Alpha Delta. Office: Suite 303 Finance Center 430 N Tejon St Colorado Springs CO 80903 Tel (303) 473-3737

ASHFORD, CLINTON RUTLEDGE, b. Honolulu, Mar. 23, 1925; A.B., U. Calif., 1945, J.D., U. Mich., 1950. Admitted to Hawaii bar, 1950, U.S. Supreme Ct. bar, 1967; asso. Peter A. Lee, 1950-53; dep. atty. gen. Hawaii, 1953-55; partner firm Ashford & Wriston, Honolulu, 1955—; mem. Hawaii Commn. on Uniform State Laws, 1953-63; dir. Legal Aid Soc. Hawaii, 1958-60. Bd. dirs. Hawaii Child and Family Service, 1967-73, pres., 1970; dir. Aloha United Way, 1974—; bd. trustees Hawaii Loa Coll., 1969-74. Fellow Am. Coll. Probate Counsel; mem. Internat. Acad. Estate and Trust Law, Am. (ho. dels. 1972, 74-76), Hawaii (past bd. dirs., past pres.) bar assns., Order of Coif. Home: 45-628 Halekou Pl Kaneohe HI 96744 Office: 235 Queen St Honolulu HI 96813 Tel (808) 524-4787

ASHKINS, ROBERT JOSEPH, b. Bridgeport, Conn., Aug. 3, 1928; B.A., U. Bridgeport, 1951; J.D., Yale U., 1958. Admitted to Conn. bar, 1958; asso. firm Cohen & Wolf, Bridgeport, 1958-61, partner 1961—. Pres., chmn. bd. Park City Hosp., 1972-75; v.p. United Jewish Council of Bridgeport, 1974-76; chmn. Council Pres.'s 1971-73; mem. exec. com. Nat. Jewish Community Relations Advisory Council; trustee New Eng. region nat. exec. bd. Am. Jewish Com.; bd. dirs. Greater Bridgeport YMCA, Intergroup Council, Congregation Rodeph Sholom. Mem. Am., Conn., Bridgeport bar assns. Named young man year, United Jewish Council, 1968. Home: 93 Richard Place Fairfield CT 06430 Office: 1600 State Nat Tower Bridgeport CT 06604 Tel (203) 368-0211

ASHMORE, ROBERT THOMAS, b. Greenville County, S.C., Feb. 22, 1904; LL.B., Furman U., 1927, J.D., 1972; grad. JAG Sch. U. Mich., 1943; LL.D., Bob Jones U., 1968. Admitted to S.C. bar, 1928; individual practice law, S.C., 1928—; solicitor Greenville County (S.C.) Ct., 1931-34, 13th Jud. Circuit S.C., 1937-53; mem. 83d-90th Congresses from 4th Dist. S.C., former chmn. judiciary com. subcoms. Pres. S.C. Appalachian Council of Govts., 1970-72, mem. exec. com., 1973—. Recipient Algernon Sidney Sullivan Distinguished Service award Furman U., 1970. Home: Route 9 Manly Dr Greenville SC 29609 Office: POB 10164 Greenville SC 29603 Tel (803) 232-3344

ASHMORE, ROBERT WALTER, IV, b. Tallahassee, Mar. 18, 1940; A.B. cum laude, Harvard, 1962; LL.B., U. Va., 1969. Admitted to Va. bar, 1969, Ga. bar, 1970; asso. firm Fisher & Phillips, Atlanta, 1969-74, partner, 1975—. Mem. Am. (subcom. on freedom of info. act labor law sect.), Atlanta bar assns. Contbr. article to Mercer Law Rev., 1977. Home: 90 Palisades Rd NE Atlanta GA 30309 Office: 3500 1st National Bank Tower Atlanta GA 30303 Tel (404) 658-9200

ASHMORE, WILLIAM THOMAS, JR., b. Batesburg, S.C., Feb. 14, 1912; A.B., Mercer U., 1935, LL.B. Admitted to Ga. bar, 1937; clk., trust dept. 1st Nat. Bank & Trust Co., Macon, Ga., 1937-41; adminstrv. asst. quartermaster purchasing War Dept., Augusta, Ga., 1941-44; v.p., sec. Fine Products Co., Inc., Augusta, 1944-45; sec.-treas., dir. Richmond Bonded Warehouse Corp., 1967—. Mem. Augusta City Council, 1959-63, 68-73; trustee Mercer U., 1974—; bd. dirs. Augusta chpt. A.R.C., 1965-67, Easter Seal Soc., 1963-69; pres. bd. dirs. Augusta-Richmond County Pub. Library, 1966-68. Mem. Ga. Bar Assn. Home: 2429 McDowell St Augusta GA 30904 Office: 833 Telfair St Augusta GA 30903 Tel (404) 724-5481

ASHWORTH, DON WILSON, b. Pioche, Nev., Sept. 18, 1937; B.S., Brigham Young U., 1962, M.Accountancy, 1963; J.D., U. Utah, 1966. Admitted to Utah bar, 1966, Nev. bar, 1969; asst. dir. trust and estate planning Brigham Young U., Provo, Utah, 1966-68; pres. firm Ashworth & Cox, Las Vegas, Nev., 1969—; mem. Western Bar Liason Coms. with IRS, 1975—; pres. So. Nev. Estate Planning Council, 1975. Mem. exec. com., exec. bd. Boulder Dam Area council Boy Scouts Am., 1970—. Mem. Nev. (chmn. tax sec. 1972-75), Utah, Clark County, Am. bar assns. Editorial bd. Community Property Jour., 1975—. Office: 228 S 4th St #300 Las Vegas NV 89101 Tel (702) 384-5451

ASKEW, ANTHONY BARTHOLOMEW, b. Atlanta, May 13, 1940; B.A. in Chemistry, Vanderbilt U., 1962; LL.B., Emory U., 1965. Admitted to Ga. bar, 1965, D.C. bar, 1969, U.S. Patent bar; asso. firm Newton, Hopkins, Jones & Ormsby, Atlanta, 1965-67; atty. Eastman Kodak Co., Kingsport, Tenn., 1967-68; asso. firm Jones, Thomas & Askew, and predecessors, 1968-70, partner, 1970—. Mem. Am., D.C., Ga. bar assns., Am. Patent Law Assn. Home: 65 W Wesley Rd NW Atlanta GA 30305 Office: 1620 Gas Light Tower Atlanta GA 30303 Tel (404) 688-7944

ASKIN, STEVEN MORRIS, b. Washington, Apr. 4, 1948; B.S. in Social Sci., Lockhaven State Coll., 1970; J.D., W.Va. U., 1973. Admitted to W. Va. bar, 1973; partner firm Radosh & Askin, Martinsburg, W.Va., 1973—. Mem. W.Va. Bar Assn. Home: Tuaf Trailer Ct Charleston WV 25414 Office: Berkeley Plaza Martinsburg WV 25401 Tel (304) 263-3361

ASKINS, JEROME PILKINGTON, JR., b. Hartsville, S.C., Oct. 18, 1923; grad. U. S.C., 1946; LL.B., Stetson U., 1950; Admitted to S.C. bar, 1950; practice law, Hemingway, S.C., 1951—; mem. S.C. Ho. of Reps., 1955-56. Pres., Hemingway Indsl. Corp. Home: Richardson and Lafayette Sts Hemingway SC 29554 Office: Askins Bldg Hemingway SC 29554 Tel (803) 558-3234

ASKINS, KNOX WINFRED, b. Houston, July 19, 1937; student Blinn Jr. Coll., 1955-56; B.F.A., U. Houston, 1958, J.D. (W. St. John Garwood scholar), 1962. Admitted to Tex. bar, 1962, U.S. Supreme Ct. bar, 1970; asso. firm Kiibler & Kiibler, LaPorte, Tex., 1962-65; individual practice law, LaPorte, 1965—; atty. City LaPorte, 1965—; gen. counsel, dir. Bayshore Nat. Bank LaPorte, 1966—; govt. appeal agt. SSS, LaPorte, 1970-72; mem. bd. Houston Area Rapid Transit Authority, 1974. Vol. counsel Bay Area Fine Arts Assn., LaPorte, 1970—. Mem. Am., Tex., Houston bar assns., Am. Judicature Soc., Tex. City Attys. Assn., Nat. Inst. Municipal Legal Officers, LaPorte C. of C. (pres. 1973-74), Order of Barons, Delta Theta Phi. Home: 1010 S Country Club Dr LaPorte TX 77571 Office: 122 S Broadway LaPorte TX 77571 Tel (713) 471-1886

ASPEN, MARVIN EDWARD, b. Chgo., July 11, 1934; B.S., Northwestern U., 1956, J.D., 1958. Admitted to Ill. bar, 1958; practiced in Chgo., 1958-60, asst. State atty. Cook County, 1960-63; head appellate div. Chgo. Law Dept., 1963-71; judge Cook County (Ill.) Circuit Ct., 1971—; lectr. Northwestern U. Sch. Law, 1969—; chmn. advisory bd. Chgo.-Kent Sch. Law Inst. for Criminal Justice Ill. Inst. Tech., 1971—. Mem. Cook County Bd. Corrections, 1971-75, Ill. Law Enforcement Com., 1972-73. Mem. Chgo., Ill. State, Am. bar assns. Author: Criminal Law For The Police, 1971; Evidence Law For the Police, 1972. Office: 1605 Chicago Civic Center Chicago IL 60602 Tel (312) 443-8292

ASPERGER, PAUL, b. Tucson, Apr. 26, 1928; A.B., U. Calif., Berkeley, 1949, J.D., 1952. Admitted to Calif. bar, 1953, U.S. Supreme Ct. bar, 1971; partner firm Thomas, Snell, Jamison, Russell, Williamson & Asperger, Fresno, Calif., 1956—. Mem. Calif. State Bar, Fresno, Kern County (Calif.), Am. bar assns. Home: 5655 N Thorne Ave Fresno CA 93711 Office: 10th Floor Fresno's Townehouse Fresno CA 93721 Tel (209) 442-0600

ASPINWALL, CHARLES SPENCER, b. Springfield, Ill., Sept. 19, 1939; B.S., U. Wyo., 1963, J.D., 1967. Admitted to Wyo. bar, 1967; partner firms Whitaker & Aspinwall, Casper, Wyo., 1968-69, Leimback, Aspinwall & Hofer and predecessor, Casper, Wyo., 1969-76, Aspinwall & Duncan, Casper, Wyo., 1976—; mayor City of Casper, 1973-74; mem. faculty Nat. Coll. Criminal Def. Lawyers; Indian affairs cons. Law Enforcement Assistance Adminstrn. Bd. dirs. YMCA, Casper, 1972-73, Nat. Conf. Mayors, 1973-74. Nat. League Cities, 1973-74. Mem. Am., Wyo., Mont., bar assns., Am. Trial Lawyers Assn., Nat. Assn. Criminal Def. Lawyers. Recipient Scholastic award Wyo. Bar Assn., 1967; editor U. Wyo. Law Rev., 1967. Office: 110 Western Resources Bldg Casper WY 82601 Tel (307) 265-0934

ASPINWALL, JAMES HAMILTON, III, b. Bridgeport, Ct., Mar. 10, 1930; A.B., Fairfield U., 1952; J.D., U. Conn., 1955. Admitted Conn. bar, 1955; mem. firm Paul V. McNamara, 1959-61; individual practice law, Stratford, Conn., 1961—; asst. town atty., Stratford, 1965-67; chmn. Conn. State Claims Comm., 1959-71. Councilman, Town of Stratford, 1961-63; Stratford Democratic chmn., 1966-69. Mem. Bridgeport, Conn. bar assns. Home: 222 Meadowmere Rd Stratford CT 06497 Office: 3200 Main St Stratford CT 06497 Tel (203) 377-7348

ASPLEN, PHILIP LEROY, JR., b. Balt., Aug. 15, 1938; B.S., Johns Hopkins, 1960; J.D., U. Md., 1969; M.B.A., Loyola Coll., 1973. Admitted to Md. bar, 1969; with Bendix Corp., Balt., 1961-64, Martin-Marietta Corp., Balt., 1964-67, Westinghouse Corp., Balt., 1967-74; mem. firm Acquisto, Asplen & Morstein, Ellicott City, Md., 1969—. Mem. Am., Md., Howard County bar assns. Home: 917 Litchfield Rd Baltimore MD 21239 Office: 8361 Court Ave Ellicott City MD 21043 Tel (301) 465-3919

ASTLE, DAVID L., b. Anaconda, Mont., Sept. 15, 1944; B.A., Carroll Coll., Helena, Mont., 1966; J.D., U. Mont., 1970. Admitted to Mont. bar, 1970; law clk. Mont. Supreme Ct., 1970-71; legal counsel Mont. Pub. Service Commn., 1971; partner firm Vadala, Springer & Astle, 1971-73; partner firm Astle & Astle, Kalispell, Mont., 1973—. Mem. Am., Mont. bar assns. Home: 696 Liesure Dr Kalispell MT 57901 Office: 705 Main St Kalispell MT 57901 Tel (406) 755-5393

ASTLE, WILLIAM EDGAR, b. Anaconda, Mont., June 19, 1941; B.A. in Polit. Sci., Carroll Coll., 1963; J.D., Am. U., 1967. Admitted to Va. bar, 1968, Mont. bar, 1974; trial atty. ICC, Washington, 1967-68; atty. Fairfax County (Va.) Atty.'s Office, Fairfax, 1968-71; mem. firm Fitzgerald & Smith, Fairfax, 1971-73; individual practice law, Kalispell, Mont., 1974—. Mem. Am., Mont., NW Mont. bar assns. Home: 753 1st Ave E-N Kalispell MT 59901 Office: 705 Main St Kalispell MT 59901 Tel (406) 755-5393

ATEN, WILBER STREMMEL, b. Ragan, Nebr., May 19, 1903; LL.B., U. Nebr., 1924. Admitted to Nebr. bar, 1924; asso. firm Clarence A. Davis, Hodredge, Nebr., 1924-42, Norris Chadderdon, Holdrege, 1942-52; sr. mem. firm Aten, Noble & Ide, Holdrege, 1960—; mem. exam. bd. Nebr. Bar Commn., 1947-75. Mem. Am., Nebr. (pres.) bar assns. Office: 417 West Ave Holdrege NE 68949 Tel (308) 995-8624

ATHAS, GUS JAMES, b. Chgo., Aug. 6, 1936; B.S., U. Ill., 1958; J.D. cum laude, Loyola U., Chgo., 1965. Admitted to Ill. bar, 1965; asso. firm Isham, Lincoln & Beale, Chgo., 1965-69; asso. regional counsel ITT Midwest Legal Office, Chgo., 1969—. Asst. counsel Chgo. Riot Study Com., 1968. Mem. Am. (spl. com. atomic energy law), Ill., Chgo. bar assns. Home: 1240 Hawthorne Ln Downers Grove IL 60515 Office: 100 S Wacker Dr Suite 1530 Chicago IL 60606 Tel (312) 346-4700

ATHERHOLT, JOHN ERIC, b. Phila., Aug. 3, 1947; B.A., Dickinson Coll., Carlisle, Pa., 1969; J.D., Dickinson Sch. Law, 1972. Admitted to Pa. bar, 1972; asso. firm Pratt, Clark, Gathright & Price, Doylestown, Pa., 1972—. Exec. sec. Doylestown Athletic Assn., 1973-76. Mem. Pa., Bucks County (Pa.) (chmn. com. young lawyers 1976) bar assns. Home: 4699 Woodfield Circle Doylestown PA 18901 Office: 68 E Court St Doylestown PA 18901 Tel (205) 345-1600

ATHERTON, ROBERT ASHLEY, b. Wichita, Kans., Oct. 4, 1937; A.B., Washburn U., 1962, LL.B., 1962, J.D., 1970. Admitted to Kans. bar, 1962, Okla. bar, 1972; estate and gift tax examiner IRS, Wichita, 1962-64; partner firm Munroe & Atherton, Augusta, Kans., 1964-67; asso. firm Glenn, Cornish and Leuenberger, Topeka, 1967-70, Colmery, McClure, Funk & Hannah, Topeka, 1970-71; counsel Halliburton Services, Duncan, Okla., 1971—; municipal judge City of Augusta, 1966-67. Mem. adv. com. New Sunrise Ministries, Duncan, 1975-76; trustee 1st United Meth. Ch. of Duncan. Mem. Kans., Okla., Stephens County bar assns. Home: 1312 Spruce St Duncan OK 73533 Office: Halliburton Services POB 1431 Duncan OK 73533 Tel (405) 251-3409

ATKINS, BENJAMIN SLOAN, b. Waynesville, N.C., Apr. 12, 1914; student Rutherford Jr. Coll., 1929-30, Wofford Coll., 1930-31, U. N.C., 1931-36; LL.B., Atlanta Law Sch., 1948, LL.M., 1949. Personnel dir. U.S. Engring. Dept., S.C., 1940-43; supr. corr. VA, Atlanta, 1945-49; admitted to Ga. bar, 1949, U.S. Supreme Ct. bar, 1963; individual practice law, Atlanta, 1949-59; partner firm Atkins & Atkins, Atlanta, 1959—. A founder, gov. Atlanta City Coll. Mem. Atlanta, Ga., Am. bar assns. Home: 4069 State Wood Rd NE Atlanta GA 30342 Office: 1221 1st Nat Bank Tower Atlanta GA 30303 Tel (404) 658-9477

ATKINS, DOROTHY DUBOIS, b. Charleston, S.C., Nov. 3, 1922; certificate in bus. adminstrn. Perry Bus. Coll., 1948; LL.B., Atlanta Law Sch., 1948, LL.M., 1949. Admitted to Ga. bar, 1949; with U.S. Govt., 1942-59; Regional Counsel's Office, IRS, 1947-59; partner firm Atkins & Atkins, Atlanta, 1959—. Mem. Ga. Bar Assn. Home: 4069 Statewood Rd NE Atlanta GA 30303 Office: 1221 First National Bank Tower Atlanta GA 30303 Tel (404) 658-9477

ATKINS, EDWARD J., b. Miami, Fla., July 16, 1926; A.B., U. Fla., 1949; LL.B., U. Miami, 1951. Admitted to Fla. bar, 1951; now partner firm Walton, Lantaff, Schroeder & Carson, Miami. Mem. Fed., Am., Dade County (pres. 1965-66) bar assns., Fla. Bar (pres. 1976-77), Internat. Assn. Ins. Counsel, Judge Advs. Assn., Phi Alpha Delta. Office: 900 Alfred I DuPont Bldg Miami FL 33131 Tel (305) 379-6411*

ATKINS, HENRY SAMUEL, JR., b. Augusta, Ga., Aug. 1, 1944; B.A., U. Ga., 1966, J.D., 1969. Admitted to Ga. bar, 1969, Fla. bar, 1969; asso. firm Sanders, Hester & Holly, Augusta, 1970; partner firm Cooney and Atkins, Augusta, 1971-72; individual practice law, Augusta, 1972—; atty. City of Hephzibah, Ga., 1972-75; instr. bus. law, polit. sci. Augusta Coll. Bd. dirs. Lynndale Sch., Augusta, 1972-75. Mem. Am., Ga., Fla., Augusta bar assns. Home: 1712 Goshen Rd Augusta GA 30906 Office: 2320 Lumpkin Rd Augusta GA 30906 Tel (404) 798-9816

ATKINS, RALPH L., b. Springfield, Mass., Oct. 3, 1942; A.B., St. Anselm's Coll., 1964; J.D., U. Conn., 1967. Admitted to Conn. bar, 1967, Mass. bar, 1968; exec. asst. to mayor City of Springfield, 1967; atty. Mass. Pub. Defenders Office, Springfield, 1968-70; individual practice law, Chicopee, Mass., 1971-77; asso. city solicitor Chicopee, 1976—. Mem. Mass., Conn., Hampden County bar assns. Home: 74 Bayne St Longmeadow MA 01028 Office: 31 Elm St Springfield MA 01101 Tel (413) 733-2116

ATKINS, RONALD RAYMOND, b. Kingston, N.Y., Mar. 8, 1933; B.S. in Econs., Wharton Sch. Finance and Commerce U. Pa., 1954; J.D., Columbia, 1959. Admitted to N.Y. State bar, 1959; asso. firm Pell, Butler, Curtis & LeViness, N.Y.C., 1959-61, partner, 1962-67; partner firm Bisset & Atkins, N.Y.C., 1967—. Mem. Assn. Bar City N.Y., N.Y. State, Am. bar assns. Home: Hobby Hill Farm Bedford NY 10506 Office: 299 Park Ave New York City NY 10017 Tel (212) 421-2900

ATKINS, THOMAS IRVING, b. Elkhart, Ind., Mar. 2, 1939; B.A., Ind. U., 1961; M.A., Harvard, 1963, J.D., 1969; Ph.D. (hon.), Northeastern U., 1970. Admitted to Mass. bar, 1970; mem. Boston City Council, 1968-71; sec. for community devel. Mass. Gov's. Cabinet, Boston, 1971-75; individual practice law, Boston, 1975—; chmn. FCC Advisory Sub-Com. on Fed.-State-Local Cable TV Relations; lectr. in urban politics Wellesley U. Pres. Boston NAACP; chmn. Boston Model Cities Community Conf.; bd. dirs. Boston Urban League, Boston Sci. Museum, Ford Hall Forum, Boston Anti-Poverty Agy., Mass. Center for Polit. Studies, Harvard-Mass. Inst. Tech. Joint Center for Polit. Studies, Nat. Council Equal Bus. Opportunity, Pub. Broadcasting Service; mem. Harvard Bd. Overseers. Mem. Boston, Mass., Nat. bar assns. Named 1 of 10 Outstanding Young Men U.S. Jr. C. of C., 1970. Home: 54 Townsend St Boston MA 02119 Office: 451 Massachusetts Ave Boston MA 02118 Tel (617) 267-1058

ATKINSON, TYRUS RUDOLPH, JR., b. Atlanta, Nov. 15, 1935; B.A. in Journalism, 1957, LL.B., 1965. Admitted to Ga. bar, 1964; asst. U.S. atty. Macon, Ga., 1965-69; asst. dist. atty. Atlanta, 1970-72; individual practice law, Atlanta, 1972—; asst. v.p. counsel Columbia Nitrogen Corp, Augusta, Ga., 1969-70. Mem. Am., Atlanta, Ga. Bar Assns. Home: 27 Spruell Springs Rd Atlanta GA 30342 Office: 2900 Nat Bank Ga Bldg Atlanta GA 30303 Tel (404) 688-2100

ATKINSON, WILLIAM WILDER, b. Little Rock, May 18, 1910; B.A., U. N.Mex., 1936; J.D., U. Colo., 1948. Admitted to N.Mex. bar, 1948, U.S. Supreme Ct. bar, 1975; asst. office mgr. Charles Ilfeld Co., Albuquerque, 1923-44; partner firm Atkinson and Kelsey, Albuquerque, 1974—. Mem. Albuquerque City Commn., 1955-63, vice chmn., 1962-63; del. N.Mex. State Constl. Conv., 1969; pres. N.Mex. Municipal League, 1962-63; pres. Albuquerque Community Council, 1964-65; pres. Albuquerque-Bernalillo County Economic Opportunity Bd., 1967-68; chmn. personnel bd. City Albuquerque, 1964-65; mem. Human Rights Commn., 1974—; pres. Goodwill Industries N.Mex., 1973-76; bd. dirs. N.Mex. chpt. NCCJ, 1974—; mem. exec. com. Presbyn. Hosp. Found., Albuquerque, 1976—; trustee Bernalillo County Mental Health and Mental Retardation Center, 1968-73; mem. U. N.Mex. Governance Advisory Com., 1970; mem. Gov.'s Task Force Municipal Finances, 1976. Mem. Albuquerque (pres. 1970-71), Am., N.Mex. bar assns., Albuquerque Lawyers Club (pres., 1954), U. N.Mex. Alumni Assn. (bd. dirs. 1960-66), Order of Coif, Phi Kappa Phi, Phi Delta Phi. Home: 1637 Kit Carson Ave SW Albuquerque NM 87104 Office: 1300 Bank of New Mexico Bldg Albuquerque NM 87103 Tel (505) 842-6111

ATLAS, MORRIS, b. Houston, Dec. 25, 1926; B.B.A., U. Tex., 1948, LL.B., 1950. Admitted to Tex. bar, 1950; since practiced in McAllen, Tex., individual practice law, 1950-53; sr. partner firm Atlas, Hall, Schwarz Mills, Gurwitz & Bland, 1953—; mem. Fed. Ct. Systems Study Com., 1973-75, chmn., 1974-75; mem. Gulf Coast Adv. Council on Water Resources, 1974, 1sts for Tex. Senate Com.; adv. bd. New Century Fund; chmn. 1st Nat. Bank McAllen. Chmn. Cancer Dr., McAllen, 1960; chmn. fund dr. McAllen Internat. Mus. 1975; trustee McAllen Gen. Hosp., 1974—; mem. bd. regents Pan Am. U., 1965-76, chmn., 1972-73. Fellow Tex. Bar Found., Am. Coll. Trial Lawyers; mem. Am., Hidalgo County bar assns., State Bar Tex., Tex. Assn. Def. Council, Assn. Ins. Attys., Phi Delta Phi. Home: 1600 Iris McAllen TX 78501 Office: PO Drawer 3725 McAllen TX 78501 Tel (502) 682-5501

ATTERBURY, LEE RICHARD, b. Newark, Aug. 25, 1948; B.A. cum laude, Lawrence U., Appleton, Wis., 1970; J.D., U. Wis., 1974. Admitted to Wis. bar, 1974; asso. firm Callahan, Arnold & Stoltz, Columbus, Wis., 1974—; asst. pub. Dodge County (Wis.) Ind. News, Juneau, 1969. Mem. Wis., Columbia County, Dane County, Dodge County bar assns. Notes and comment editor Wis. Law Rev., 1974. Home: 712 S Dickinson St Madison WI 53703 Office: 159 S Ludington St Columbus WI 53925 Tel (414) 623-2330

ATTIAS, JACK PHILIP, b. Bklyn., July 26, 1942; B.S., U. Miami (Fla.), 1965, J.D., 1969. Admitted to Fla. bar, 1969; individual practice law, Miami, 1969—. Mem. Am., Fla., Dade County bar assns. Office: 7200 Bird Rd Miami FL 33155 Tel (305) 361-3339

ATWELL, ANTHONY, b. Dallas, May 10, 1936; B.A., Williams Coll., 1957; J.D., Harvard, 1960. Admitted to Tex. bar, 1960; clk. to judge U.S. Dist. Ct., No. Dist. Tex., Dallas, 1960-61; partner firms Atwell, Grayson & Atwell, Dallas, 1961-68, Atwell, Maloof & Musslewhite, Dallas, 1968-73, Atwell, Cain and Davenport, Dallas, 1973—. Mem. Am., Tex., Dallas bar assns., Assn. Life Ins. Counsel. Home: 3303 Princeton St Dallas TX 75205 Office: 2605 Republic National Bank Tower Dallas TX 75201 Tel (214) 741-5061

ATWOOD, ROY F., b. Springfield, Mass., Nov. 27, 1926; B.A., Wash. State U., 1949, J.D., U. Wash., 1951. Admitted to Wash. bar, 1952; asso. firm Pemberton & Orloff, Bellingham, Wash., 1953-62; partner firm Asmundson, Rhea & Atwood, Bellingham, 1967—; councilman City Bellingham, 1957-63, pres. city council, 1961-62; mem. Wash. Senate, 1963-75, minority floor leader, chmn. Rep. Caucus, 1967-75, vice chmn. legis. budget com., 1967-69, 1973, 1975; spl. atty. gen. Utilities & Transp. Commn., Olympia, 1975—. Active United Good Neighbors Budget Com., Bellingham, 1975—; sec. St. Luke's Hosp., Bellingham, 1975—; active Alcoholism Adminstrv. Bd. Whatcom County (Wash.), 1975—; state committeeman Whatcom County Republican Party. Mem. Am., Wash., Whatcom County bar assns., Home: 317 Park Ridge St Bellingham WA 98225 Office: 805 Dupont St Suite 5 Bellingham WA 98225 Tel (733-3370

AUBERT, RONALD DAVID, b. Niagara Falls, N.Y., Mar. 28, 1936; B.A., U. Calif., Berkeley, 1959; J.D., U. Calif., San Francisco, 1966. Admitted to Calif. bar, 1966; dep. county counsel; trial div. Los Angeles County, 1966-69; asst. counsel Pacific Mut. Life Ins. Co., Los Angeles, 1969-70; asso. counsel Larwin Group, Inc., Beverly Hills, Calif., 1970-72; v.p., gen. counsel Levitt-West, Inc., also Levitt Multihousing Corp., Los Angeles, 1972-75; individual practice law, Los Angeles, 1975—; lectr. EPA, 1967-72. Mem. Calif., Los Angeles County, Century City (Calif.) bar assns. Home: 22630 Flamingo St Woodland Hills CA 91364 Office: 1888 Century Park E Suite 910 Los Angeles CA 90067 Tel (213) 556-1561

AUBUCHON, DANIEL COLLINS, b. St. Louis, Nov. 5, 1947; B.A., Spring Hill Coll., 1969; J.D., U. Mo., 1972. Admitted to Mo. bar, 1973; asso. firm Aubuchon & Lavin, St. Louis, 1973-74; partner firm Aubuchon & Aubuchon, St. Louis, 1975—. Mem. Am., Mo., Met. St. Louis bar assns., Am. Trial Lawyers Assn., Lawyers Assn. St. Louis. Home: 27 Sappington Acres Saint Louis MO 63127 Office: 705 Olive St Suite 1314 Saint Louis MO 63101 Tel (314) 621-1575

AUBUCHON, JOSEPH RAMEY, b. St. Louis, Oct. 7, 1944; B.A., Washington U., St. Louis, 1966; J.D., U. Mo., 1969. Admitted to Mo. bar, 1969; asst. pub. defender St. Louis County, 1971-74; asso. Wilburn Duncan, Clayton, Mo., 1975; 1st asst. pros. atty. Franklin County (Mo.), 1975—. Mem. Am. Bar Assn., Am. Judicature Soc. Office: POB 229 414 E Main St Union MO 63084 Tel (314) 583-2100

AUCHINCLOSS, LOUIS STANTON, b. N.Y.C., Sept. 27, 1917; B.S., Yale, 1939; LL.B., U. Va., 1941; Litt.D., N.Y. U., 1974. Admitted to N.Y. State bar, 1941; asso. firm Sullivan & Cromwell, N.Y.C., 1941-51; asso. firm Hawkins, Delafield & Wood, N.Y.C., 1954-57, partner, 1957—. Pres., Mus. City of N.Y., 1966—; mem. adminstrv. com. Dumbarton Oaks Research Library, Washington, 1969—; trustee Josiah Macy, Jr., Found., 1968—. Mem. Am., N.Y. State bar assns., Assn. Bar City N.Y. (exec. com. 1975—), Nat. Inst. Arts and Letters. Author: The House of Five Talents, 1960; Powers of Attorney, 1963; The Rector of Justin, 1964; The Embezzler, 1966; The Partners, 1974; The Winthrop Covenant, 1976; The Dark Lady, 1977; others. Home: 1111 Park Ave New York City NY 10028 Office: 67 Wall St New York City NY 10005 Tel (212) 952-4851

AUER, DOUGLASS BRADFORD, b. Malden, Mass., Sept. 11, 1938; A.B., Norwich U., 1960; LL.B., Boston U., 1963. Admitted to Mass. bar, 1963, Colo. bar, 1970; partner firm Auer & Manzanares, Denver, 1971-73, firm Pacheco Auer & Manzanares, Denver, 1973-74, firm Pacheco & Auer, Denver, 1974-77; individual practice, 1977—. Bd. dirs. Spalding Rehab. Center, Denver, 1971—. Mem. Am., Colo., Denver, Mass. bar assns. Office: 777 Capitol Life Center Denver CO 80203 Tel (303) 892-5700

AUERBACH, CARL ABRAHAM, b. N.Y.C., Oct. 2, 1915; A.B., L.I.U., 1935; LL.B., Harvard, 1938. Admitted to N.Y. bar, 1938, Wis. bar, 1956, Minn. bar, 1973; atty. U.S. Dept. Labor, Washington, 1938-40; asst. gen. counsel Office of Price Adminstrn., Washington, 1940-43, gen. counsel, 1946-47; asso. gen. counsel Office Econ. Stablzn., Washington, 1946-47; prof. law U. Wis., 1947-61; prof. law U. Minn., 1961—, dean Law Sch., 1972—. Mem. Am., Minn. bar assns., Am. Acad. Arts and Scis., Am. Law Inst. Recipient Fulbright and Advanced Research award, London Sch. Econs. and Polit. Sci., 1953-54; co-author: The Legal Process, 1961; The Federal Regulation of Transportation, 1953. Home: 3230 Kyle Ave N Golden Valley MN 55422 Office: U Minn Law Sch Minneapolis MN 55455 Tel (612) 373-2717

AUERBACH, MARSHALL JAY, b. Chgo., Sept. 5, 1932; student U. Ill., 1952; J.D., John Marshall Law Sch., 1955. Admitted to Ill. bar, 1955; individual practice law, Evanston, Ill., 1955-72; partner firm Jenner & Block, Chgo., 1972—; mem. faculty Ill. Inst. Continuing Legal Edn., 1967. Dir. United Community Services Evanston, 1970-74. Fellow Am. Acad. Matrimonial Lawyers; mem. Am. (vice chmn. family law sect. com. liaison with sect. on taxation 1974—), Ill. State (chmn. family law sect. 1971-72, mem. assembly 1972—). Contbr. articles to legal jours. Home: 2314 Orrington Ave Evanston IL 60201 Office: One IBM Plaza Suite 4400 Chicago IL 60611 Tel (312) 222-9350

AUERBACH, ROGER STEPHEN, b. Albany, N.Y., Feb. 7, 1943; B.A., Mich. State U., 1965; J.D., U. Mich., 1968. Admitted to Ariz. bar, 1971, U.S. Supreme Ct. bar, 1977; audit staff Coopers & Lybrand, N.Y.C., 1968; tax staff Touche, Ross & Co., Los Angeles, 1970; staff atty. Pub. Defender's Office Pima County (Ariz.), Tucson, 1971-73; partner firm Auerbach & Freeman, Tucson, 1973—. Office: 806 Transamerica Bldg Tucson AZ 85701 Tel (602) 882-9960

AUFDENSPRING, MICHAEL CHARLES, b. St. Louis, July 26, 1946; A.B., St. Louis U., 1968, J.D., 1971. Admitted to Ill. bar, 1971, Mo. bar, 1971, U.S. Ct. Appeals 8th Circuit, 1971, 7th Circuit, 1975; asso. firm Ruppert & Schleuter, Clayton, Mo., 1971-77, Barnard and Baer, St. Louis, 1977—. Mem. Am., Ill., Mo., Met. St. Louis bar assns. Office: 818 Olive St Suite 1400 St Louis MO 63101 Tel (314) 241-5500

AUFORTH, FREDERIC CORTLANDT, b. Pasadena, Calif., June 17, 1927; B.A., Stanford, 1950; LL.B., U. Tex., 1954. Admitted to Tex. bar, 1954; partner firms Park Harphilla Auforth, Snyder, Tex., 1954-59, Auforth, Kens, McCrury & Kenilmor, Corpus Christi, Tex., 1976—; asst. dist. atty. Nuecas County (Tex.), 1961-63. Mem. Neucas County, Tex. bar assns. Home: 345 Palmetto St Corpus Christi TX 78412 Office: 3318 S Alameda St Corpus Christi TX 78411 Tel (512) 854-0171

AUFRECHT, MICHAEL D., b. Chgo., Oct. 4, 1940; J.D., Northwestern U., 1965. Admitted to Ill. bar, 1965; asso. firm Taylor, Miller, Magner, Sprowl & Hutchings, Chgo., 1965—. Mem. Chgo., Ill. bar assns. Home: 6619 N Monticello St Lincolnwood IL 60645 Office: 120 S LaSalle St Chicago IL 60603 Tel (312) 782-6070

AUGENBRAUN, BARRY S., b. N.Y.C., May 26, 1939; B.A., Columbia, 1960; B.A., Cambridge (Eng.) U., 1962, M.A., 1966; LL.B., Harvard, 1965. Admitted to N.Y. State bar, 1965, Pa. bar, 1975; asso. firm Simpson, Thacher & Bartlett, N.Y.C., 1965-67, Bressler, Meislin, Tauber & Bressler, N.Y.C., 1967-69, partner, 1969-73; asso. firm Wachtell, Lipton, Rosen & Katz, N.Y.C., 1973-75; gen. counsel firm Laventhol & Horwath, Phila., 1975—; adj. asso. prof. law N.Y. Law Sch., 1975—. Mem. Am., N.Y. State, N.Y.C., Phila. (com. on securities regulation) bar assns. Contbr. articles in field to profl. jours. Home: 908 Carroll Rd Philadelphia PA 19151 Office: 1845 Walnut St Philadelphia PA 19103 Tel (215) 491-1600

AUGUST, ANN, b. Cleve., Mar. 17, 1934; B.A., U. Dayton, 1955; J.D., U. Cin., 1958. Admitted to Ohio bar, 1958, Calif. bar, 1966, U.S. Supreme Ct. bar, 1973; asso. with Paul N. McCloskey, Jr., Palo Alto, Calif., 1965-66; asso. firm McCloskey, Wilson, Mosher & Martin, Palo Alto, 1965-66; individual practice law, Palo Alto, 1966—; asst. city atty. City of Sunnyvale (Calif.), 1964-65; lectr. Mem. State Bar Calif., State Bar Ohio, Palo Alto Area, San Mateo County, Santa Clara County bar assns., Calif. Trial Lawyers Assn. Contbr. articles to legal jours. Office: 332 Santa Barbara Savs Bldg 550 Hamilton Ave Palo Alto CA 94301 Tel (415) 326-2525 also 12092 Woodside Ave Lakeside CA 92040 Tel (714) 561-5222

AUGUST, SOL LOUIS, b. Chgo., Nov. 13, 1905; LL.B. cum laude, Chgo. Law Sch., 1925. Admitted to Ill. bar, 1927; mem. firm August, Malkes & Best, Chgo., 1927-29; individual practice law, Chgo., 1929—. Home: 1230 Western Ave Lake Forest IL 60045 Office: 188 W Randolph St Chicago IL 60601 Tel (312) 236-5160

AUGUST, STUART IVES, b. Newark, N.J., Apr. 16, 1947; A.B., Boston U., 1969, J.D., Suffolk U., 1972. Admitted to Mass. bar, 1972; asso. firm T.F. Broderick, Boston, 1972-75, firm Nathan Hillman, Boston, 1975—; guest lectr. civil rights, constl. law, North Community Coll., Beverly, Mass., 1973—; lectr. legal writing, drafting, research, Suffolk U. Law Sch., Boston, 1974-75. Mem. Mass., Boston, Norfolk County bar assns. Recipient Am. Jurisprudence Assn. award outstanding scholarship in labor law, 1972. Staff Suffolk U. Law Rev., 1970-72, notes editor, 1971-72. Home: 25 Lyndon Rd Sharon MA 02067 Office: 89 State St Boston MA 02109

AULISI, ARTHUR CAVOUR, b. Laviano, Italy, Nov. 4, 1907; student Union Coll., 1926-27; LL.B., Albany Law Sch., 1930. Admitted to N.Y. bar, 1931; gen. practice law, 1931-66; judge Gloversville (N.Y.) City Ct., 1938-42; asst. dist. atty. Fulton County, N.Y., 1943-46, dist. atty., 1947-48; judge Fulton County Ct., 1949-68; justice N.Y. State Supreme Ct., Gloversville, 1969—; dir. Fulton County Nat. Bank and Trust Co. Gloversville. Mem. exec. bd., v.p. Sir William Johnson council Boy Scouts Am., recipient Silver Beaver award, 1951; bd. dirs. Gloversville YMCA, ARC; chmn. Gloversville Community Chest; trustee Our Lady Mt. Carmel Ch., Gloversville. Mem. N.Y., Fulton County (pres.), Montgomery County bar assns., County Judges Assn. Office: 40 N Main St Gloversville NY 12078 Tel (518) 725-7149

AULT, DAVID ALLEN, b. Rochester, Ind., Jan. 27, 1948; B.A., Wabash Coll., 1970; J.D., Ind. U., 1973. Admitted to Ind. bar, 1973, U.S. Dist. Ct. bar, 1973; clerk Allen Superior Ct., Fort Wayne, Ind., 1973-74; asso. firm Wernle, Ristine & Ayers, Crawfordsville, Ind., 1974—. Mem. Montgomery County Bar Assn. (v.p. 1976). Home: 1002 W Wabash St Crawfordsville IN 47933 Office: 416 Ben Hur Bldg Crawfordsville IN 47933

AUMER, ROBERT THEODORE, b. Pitts., Dec. 10, 1946; B.A., U. Dayton, 1968; J.D., U. Toledo, 1971. Admitted to Pa. bar, 1972, Ohio bar, 1971; with Moore, Leonard and Lynch, Pitts., 1971—; now asst. v.p. for underwriting municipal bond issues. Office: 315 Dixon St Pittsburgh PA 15216

AURELL, JOHN KARL, b. Tulsa, Sept. 26, 1935; B.A., Washington and Lee U., 1956; LL.B., Yale, 1964. Admitted to Fla. bar, 1964, D.C. bar, 1971; mem. firm Mahoney, Hadlow & Adams, Miami, 1975—; chmn. grievance com. "C", Fla. Bar, 1967-72. Pres. Fla. Internat. U. Found., 1971-73; mem. exec. com. Yale Law Sch. Assn., 1975—. Mem. Dade County, Am. bar assn., Fla. Bar, Am. Judicature Soc. Home: 1030 Hardee Ave Coral Gables FL 33146 Office: 1401 1st Fed Bldg One S E 3d Ave Miami FL 33131 Tel (305) 358-5550

AUSTENSEN, PHILLIP BRUCE, b. Washington, D.C., Sept. 16, 1935; B.A., U. Md., 1957; J.D., Am. U., 1960. Admitted to Md. bar, 1960; atty. Rouse Co., Columbia, Md., 1967-69; Washington regional counsel ITT, 1969-73; individual practice law, 1973—. Home: 15790 Old Frederick Rd Woodbine MD 21797 Office: Riesterstown & Delight Rds Riesterstown MD 21136 Tel (301) 833-2250

AUSTERN, HERMAN THOMAS, b. N.Y.C., Sept. 19, 1905; B.S., N.Y. U., 1926; LL.B. magna cum laude (Langdell fellow), Harvard, 1929. Admitted to N.Y. bar, 1931, D.C. bar, 1933; legal sec. U.S. Circuit Judge Julian W. Mack, 1929, Justice Louis D. Brandeis, U.S. Supreme Ct., 1930; lectr. bus. law N.Y. U., 1948, adj. prof. law, 1957—; lectr. Harvard Law Sch., 1968; practice law, Washington, 1931-36; partner firm Covington & Burling, Washington, 1936—; chief counsel Nat. Canners Assn., 1942—; dir. Ludlow Corp., Boston; mem. patent adv. panel AEC, 1949-56; adv. council Food Law Inst., 1949—. Mem. Am. (adv. bd. antitrust and trade regulation report 1970—, chmn. com. food standards, banking and comml. law sect.), N.Y. State (chmn. FTC com., antitrust law sect.), D.C. bar assns., Nat. Lawyers Club, AAAS, Phi Beta Kappa, Alpha Lambda Phi, Delta Kappa Delta. Pres. Harvard Law Rev., 1929; editorial adv. bd. Food Drug Cosmetic Law Jour.; mem. adv. bd. Jour. of Reprints for Antitrust Law and Econs.; contbr. articles to legal jours. Home: 4200 Massachusetts Ave NW Washington DC 20016 Office: 888 16th St NW Washington DC 20006 Tel (202) 452-6130

AUSTIN, C. WILSON, b. Lyndon, Ky., May 20, 1908; A.B., U. Pa., 1930, LL.B., 1933. Admitted to Pa. bar, 1933; mem. firm Speicher & Austin, Reading, Pa., 1934-62, Austin, Speicher, Boland, Connor & Giorgi, Reading, 1964—; asst. dist. atty. Berks County (Pa.), 1937-48; city solicitor City of Reading, 1948-62; judge Ct. Common Pleas, Berks County, 1962-64, county solicitor, 1975—. Adv. bd. Salvation Army, Reading. Mem. Am., Pa., Berks County bar assns. Office: 38-44 N 6th St Reading PA 19601 Tel (215) 374-8211

AUSTIN, HARRY GREGORY, JR., b. N.Y.C., Mar. 18, 1936; B.M.E., Yale, 1957, postgrad., 1958; J.D., U. Mich., 1961. Admitted to Colo. bar, 1962, U.S. Supreme Ct. bar, 1974; asso. firm Holland & Hart, Denver, 1962-68, partner, 1968-73, 77—; gen. counsel U.S. SBA, Washington, 1973-75; solicitor Dept. Interior, Washington, 1975-77. Mem. Colo. Treas. Adv. Commn., 1968-72. Mem. Am., Fed., Colo., Denver bar assns., Adminstrv. Conf. U.S. Office: 500 Equitable Bldg 730 17th St Denver CO 80202 Tel (303) 292-9200

AUSTIN, JOHN ANTHONY, b. Oklahoma City, Nov. 1, 1946; B.A., Johns Hopkins, 1968; J.D., George Washington U., 1972. Admitted to Md. bar, 1972; law clk. to judge Circuit Ct., Balt. County, Towson, Md., 1972-73; asso. firm Arnold Fleischmann, Towson, 1973-76; individual practice law, Towson, 1977—; asst. state's atty. Balt. County, Towson, 1973-75; atty. gen. State of Md., Balt., 1975-76; office of law, Balt. County, Towson, 1976—. Mem. Md. State, Balt. County, Balt. City, Am. bar assns. Home: 1222 Deanwood Rd Baltimore MD 21234 Office: 102 W Pennsylvania Ave Towson MD 21204 Tel (301) 296-1434

AUSTIN, JOHN DELONG, b. Cambridge, N.Y., May 31, 1935; A.B., Dartmouth, 1957; J.D., Albany Law Sch., 1969. Admitted to N.Y. bar, 1970; editorial dir. Glens Falls (N.Y.) Times, 1960-66; individual practice law, Glens Falls, 1970—; law asst. Warren County (N.Y.) Judge and Surrogate, 1975—. Councilman Town of Queensbury (N.Y.), 1969-71, supr., 1972-74; budget officer Warren County, 1974. Mem. Am., N.Y., Warren County bar assns. Editor: New England Hist. and General Geneal. Register, 1970-73. Contbr. numerous hist. and geneal. articles to periodicals. Home: E Sunnyside RD RFD 1 Glens Falls NY 12801 Office: 21 Bay St Glens Falls NY 12801 Tel (518) 792-7355

AUSTIN, JOSEPH R(ILEY), b. Davenport, Iowa, Mar. 25, 1939; A.B., Coe Coll., 1961; LL.B., Harvard, 1964. Admitted to Calif. bar, 1965, U.S. Supreme Ct. bar, 1970; asso. firm McCutchen Black Verleger & Shea, Los Angeles, 1966-71; partner firm Tuttle & Taylor, Los Angeles, 1971—; lectr. U. Nigeria, Nsukka, 1965-66; mem. statewide steering com. Vols. in Parole, 1971-76. Trustee Coe Coll., 1976—; mem. Los Angeles World Affairs Council, 1966—, Los Angeles Town Hall, 1966—. Mem. Am. Judicature Soc., Los Angeles County Bar Assn. (past trustee). Office: 609 S Grand Ave Los Angeles CA 90071 Tel (213) 683-0600

AUSTIN, WILLIAM WINTER, b. Effingham, Ill., June 18, 1945; B.S. in Fin., U. Ill., 1967, J.D., 1970. Admitted to Ill. bar, 1970; asst. atty. gen. State of Ill., 1971, spl. asst. atty. gen., 1971—; partner firm Parker, Brummer, Siemer & Austin, Effingham, 1973—; dir. Crossrds. Bank of Effingham, 1975—; capt. JAGC, 1975—. Bd. dirs. Effingham County Assn. for Mentally Retarded, 1973-76, Effingham County 708, 1976—. Mem. Effingham County, Ill., Am. bar assns. Office: 307 N 3d St Effingham IL 62401 Tel (217) 342-9291

AUTEN, DAVID CHARLES, b. Phila., Apr. 4, 1938; A.B., U. Pa., 1960, J.D., 1963. Admitted to Pa. bar, 1963; asso. firm Elliott & Munson, Phila., 1963-68, partner, 1969—, chmn., 1977—. Vice chmn. annual giving U. Pa., 1975—; pres. Soc. of Alumni of Coll., 1975—. Mem. Am., Pa. (chmn. com. on real estate financing, 1974—), Phila. bar assns., Juristic Soc. (pres. 1974—). Speaker, panelist at confs.; contbr. articles to legal publs. Home: 120 Delancey St Philadelphia PA 19106 Office: 1600 Western Savings Bank Bldg Philadelphia PA 19107 Tel (215) KI 5-3700

AUTORINO, RALPH J., b. Montclair, N.J., June 1, 1910; LL.B., Rutgers U., 1933. Admitted to N.J. bar, 1935; asso. firm Parsonnet, W Weitzman & Oransky, Newark, 1945-65, Giannone & Capone, E. Orange, N.J., 1965— Mem. Lawyers Club of Union (N.J.). Home and office: 221 Lincoln Ave Union NJ 07083 Tel (201) 688-4107

AUTY, JON JOSEPH, b. Middletown, N.J., Apr. 2, 1944; B.S. cum laude, Farleigh Dickinson U., 1969; J.D. cum laude, Seton Hall U., 1972. Admitted to N.J. bar, 1972; asso. firm Breslin & Breslin, Hackensack, N.J., 1970—. Mem. Am., Bergen County bar assns., Am. Trial Lawyers Assn., Omicron Delta Epsilon, Phi Omega Epsilon. Staff writer Seton Hall Law Rev. 1971-72. Home: 78 Sycamore Ave HoHoKus NJ 07423 Office: 41 Main St Hackensack NJ 07601 Tel (201) 342-4014

AVANCE, JAMES DREW, b. Hoxie, Ark., Nov. 7, 1909; B.A., Henderson State Coll., 1932; postgrad. Yale, 1932-33; LL.B., Ark. Law Sch., 1939; M.A., Ark. State U., 1958. Admitted to Ark. bar, 1939; individual practice law, Little Rock, 1939-40, 57-58, 59-65, 73—; atty. Little Rock Va., 1946-57; instr. Ark. Law Sch., 1948-69; atty. Pulaski County (Ark.) Legal Aid. Bur., Little Rock, 1969-70. Bd. dirs. State Central Credit Union of Ark., Fed. Credit Union, Ark. Credit Union League. Home: 200 Cherokee Circle Little Rock AR 72205 Tel (501) 225-3387

AVE, PAUL EDWARD, b. Clinton, Ind., June 2, 1933; B.S. in Bus. Adminstrn., Ind. U., 1954, J.D., 1959. Admitted to Ind. bar, 1959, Tex. bar, 1960; asso. firm Turner, White, Atwood, McLaine & Francis, Dallas, 1959-62; asst. legal counsel LTV Corp. (Vought Aeros.), Dallas, 1962-65, asso. gen. counsel, 1965-68; v.p., gen. counsel, sec. Altec Corp., Dallas, 1968-73, v.p. corp. affairs and dir., 1973—; dir. Tamar Corp., 1970-73, Staco Corp., 1968-70. Mem. Am., Tex. bar assns., Am. Soc. Corp. Secs. Home: 10807 Pinocchio St Dallas TX 75229 Office: Box 30385 Dallas TX 75230 Tel (214) 231-7111

AVERBOOK, DANIEL ZACHARY, b. Austin, Minn., Feb. 26, 1941; B.S.B., U. Minn., 1963; J.D., U. Miami (Fla.), 1969. Admitted to Fla. bar, 1969; staff accountant Peat, Marwick, Mitchell & Co., Mpls., 1963-66, tax supr., Miami, 1969-73; tax supr. Laventhol & Horwath, Miami, 1973-76; individual practice law, Miami, 1976—. Treas. Zool. Soc. Fla. 1975—; bd. dirs. Men's Club, Miami Philharmonic, 1976—. Mem. Am., Fla., Dade county bar assns., Am. Assn. Attys. and C.P.A.'s, Am. Inst. C.P.A.'s, Fla. Inst. C.P.A.'s, Nat. Assn. Accountants (dir. 1975-76), Minn. Soc. C.P.A.'s. C.P.A., Minn., Home: 1408 S E Bayshore Dr #1009 Miami FL 33131 Office: Suite 2770 One Biscayne Tower Miami FL 33131 Tel (305) 374-4184

AVERILL, LAWRENCE HERMAN, JR., b. Pitts., Oct. 7, 1940; A.B., Ind. U., 1962; J.D., Am. U., 1964; LL.M., George Washington U., 1965. Admitted to Md. bar, 1964, D.C. bar, 1965, Wyo. bar, 1970; asst. prof. law, 1973—; teaching fellow in law, George Washington U., 1964-65, vis. prof. law, 1973; vis. prof. law, U. S.D., 1975. Chmn. United Fund Univ. Drive, 1973-74. Mem. Am., D.C. bar assns., Wyo. State Bar, Omicron Delta Kappa Named Outstanding Young Man Am., 1976; contbr. articles to jours. Home: 2620 Park Ave Laramie WY 82070 Office: Univ Sta Box 3035 Laramie WY 82071 Tel (307) 766-2182

AVERY, CAMERON SCOTT, b. Evanston, Ill., May 9, 1938; B.S.E., Princeton, 1960, J.D., Harvard, 1963. Admitted to Ill. bar, 1963; asso. firm Bell Boyd Lloyd Haddad & Burns, Chgo., 1963-70, partner, 1971—. Pres. Opportunity Centers; trustee Cartwright Found. Mem. Am. (past vice-chmn. subcom. on charitable trusts), Chgo., Ill. bar assns., Princeton Engring. Assn., Christian Laymen of Chgo., Ravinia Festival Assn. Home: Winnetka IL 60093 Office: 135 S LaSalle St Chicago IL 60603 Tel (312) 372-1121

AVERY, ISAAC THOMAS, JR., b. Morganton, N.C., Mar. 11, 1916; A.B., U. N.C., 1938, J.D., 1940. Admitted to N.C. bar, 1940. Chmn. exec. com. Iredell County Democratic Party, 1974—. Mem. N.C. Bar Assn. (pres. 1962-63, recipient Meritorious Service award 1976). Recipient award merit Selective service System, 1976. Home: 307 Oakhurst St Statesville NC 28677 Office: 212-A E Broad St Statesville NC 28677 Tel (704) 873-7233

AVERY, JOHN PHILLIP, b. Terre Haute, Ind., Sept. 6, 1945; B.S., Butler U., 1970; J.D. cum laude, Ind. U., 1973. Admitted to Ind. bar, 1973; partner firm Farlow, Perry & Avery, Paoli, Ind., 1974-76; dep. prosecutor Orange County (Ind.), 1975-76; dep. atty. gen. State of Ind., Indpls., 1976; mem. firm Davis, Neel & Headlee, Indpls., 1976—. Sec., Orange County Mental Health Assn., 1975-76, now bd. dirs. Mem. Am., Ind., Indpls. bar assns. Author: Habitual Offender, 1973. Office: 21 N Pennsylvania St Indianapolis IN 46204 Tel (317) 634-4530

AVERY, ROBERT WILSON, b. Bridgeport, Conn., July 10, 1927; B.S., U. Bridgeport, 1950; J.D., Syracuse U., 1954. Admitted to N.Y. bar, 1954, Conn. bar, 1954; individual practice law, Trumbull, Conn., 1965-70, Hamden, Conn., 1970—; claims mgr. Allstate Ins. Co., Hartford, Conn., 1954-65. Mem. Conn., New Haven County, Bridgeport bar assns. Home: 182 Lake Ave Trumbull CT 06611 Office: 261 Skiff St Hamden CT 06517 Tel (203) 248-8563

AVGERIS, GEORGE NICHOLAS, b. Chgo., Apr. 18, 1939; B.A., N. Central Coll., 1961; LL.B., U. Ill., 1964. Admitted to Ill. bar, 1964; asso. firm John R. Collis, Hinsdale, Ill., 1965-67, Sweeney & Riman, Chgo., 1967-69; individual practice law, Hinsdale, Ill., 1969—. Active Hinsdale Area Legal Aid Program, 1973-74. Mem. Ill., Du Page County (chmn. med.-legal com. 1975—) bar assns., Am., Ill. trial lawyers assns. Home: 320 E Hickory St Hinsdale IL 60521 Office: 29 E 1st St Hinsdale IL 60521 Tel (312) 654-4161

AVINS, ALFRED, b. N.Y.C., June 29, 1934; B.A., Hunter Coll., 1954; LL.B., Columbia, 1956; LL.M., N.Y. U., 1957; M.L., U. Chgo., 1961, J.S.D., 1962; Ph.D., Cambridge (Eng.) U., 1965. Admitted to Fla. bar, 1956, D.C. bar, 1956, N.Y. bar, 1956, U.S. Supreme Ct. bar, 1959, Ill. bar, 1962, Del. bar, 1971; research asst. Am. Law Inst., 1955-62; law asst. U.S. atty's. Office, Eastern Dist. N.Y., 1956; spl. dep. atty. gen. State of N.Y., 1957; instr. Rutgers U. Law Sch., Newark, 1957-58; atty. FPC, Washington, 1958, NLRB, Washington, 1959-60; asst. prof. law John Marshall Law Sch., 1960-61; asso. prof., faculty adviser law rev. Chgo.-Kent Coll. Law, 1961-63; spl. counsel Va. Commn. on Constl. Govt., Richmond, 1964; prof. Memphis State U., 1965-67; staff counsel U.S. Senate Judiciary Com., 1967; asst. dist atty. N.Y.C., 1967-68; spl. counsel Del. Bd. Edn., 1971; founder, dean Del. Law Sch., Wilmington, 1971-74, dean emeritus, 1974—. Mem. Phi Beta Kappa. Author: The Law of AWOL, 1957; Open Occupancy vs. Forced Housing, 1963; The Reconstruction Amendments Debates, 1967; contbr. articles to legal jours. Office: Delaware Law Sch 2001 Washington St Wilmington DE 19802 Tel (302) 658-8531

AVRACH, STEPHEN J., b. Phila., Aug. 5, 1935; B.B.A., U. Miami, 1957, J.D., 1965. Admitted to Fla. bar, 1965; asst. city atty. City of Miami Beach (Fla.), 1967-68; partner firm Frankel & Avrach, Miami Beach, 1968-74; individual practice law, Miami Beach, 1975—. Mem. Am. Bar Assn. Home: 1701 NE 115th St Miami FL 33781 Office: 420 Lincoln Rd Miami Beach FL 33139 Tel (305) 531-8334

AVRAM, GERALD WAYNE, b. Pontiac, Mich., Dec. 16, 1945; A.B., U. Colo., 1968; J.D., U. Denver, 1972. Admitted to Colo. bar, 1973; individual practice law, Arvada, Colo., 1973—. Mem. Am., Colo., Denver (vol. atty. 1973—) bar assns. Home: 11929 W 58th Ave Arvada CO 80002 Office: 7855 Ralston Rd Arvada CO 80002 Tel (303) 423-7034

AX, TONI SUE, b. Evansville, Ind., Oct. 1, 1940; A.B. cum laude, Butler U., 1962, Ed.S., 1966; M.A.T., Harvard, 1963; J.D. magna cum laude, Ind. U., 1970. Admitted to Ind. bar, 1970, U.S. Fed. Dist. Ct. So. Dist. Ind., 1970, U.S. Tax Ct., 1971, U.S. Ct. Appeals, 1972; asso. firm Barnes, Hickam, Pantzer and Boyd, Indpls., 1970-76, partner, 1977-; chief contract adminstrn. br. Naval Avionics Facility, Indpls., 1967-70. Chmn. atty.'s div. United Way Greater Indpls., 1976; dir. Central Ind. council Campfire Girls, 1975—. Mem. Ind. (co-chmn. written publs. com., chmn. draft com., ho. of dels., pub. relations, Law Day U.S.A. coms), Am. (taxation sect.), Indpls. (chmn. membership com., United Way com.) bar assns., Bar Assn. 7th Fed. Circuit, Estate Planning Council Indpls., Ind. U. Sch. Law-Indpls. Alumni Assn. (dir. 1973-76, treas. 1974, v.p. 1975, pres. 1976). Recipient nat. leadership award Delta Delta Delta, 1962. Home: 3705 Cheviot Pl Indianapolis IN 46205 Office: 1313 Merchants Bank Bldg Indianapolis IN 46204 Tel (317) 638-1313

AXELRAD, PETER FREDERICK, b. Montreal, Que., Can., Nov. 21, 1940; student McGill U., 1957-59; A.B., Duke, 1961; LL.B., U. Pa., 1964. Admitted to Md. bar, 1964; clk. Judge Prendergast, Balt., 1964-65; asso. firm Frank Bernstein, Conaway & Goldman, Balt., 1965-70, partner, 1970—. Mem. Am., Balt., Md. bar assns., Am. Judicature Soc., Assn. Def. Trial Counsel. Home: 1 Susan Ct Owings Mills MD 21117 Office: 1300 Mercantile Bank Bldg 2 Hopkins Pl Baltimore MD 21201 Tel (301) 547-0500

AXELROD, CARL F(ABER), b. N.Y.C., Nov. 5, 1906; A.B., Columbia, 1927, J.D., 1929. Admitted to N.Y. bar, 1930; partner firm Netter, Dowd, Ness, Alfieri & Stern, N.Y.C., 1950—. Vice pres., sec., mem. bd. exec. com. Muscular Dystrophy Assn., Inc., N.Y.C., 1950—. Mem. Am. Bar Assn. Home: 175 Victory Blvd New Rochelle NY 10804 Office: 660 Madison Ave New York City NY 10021 Tel (212) 486-8626

AXENFELD, GARY MAX, b. Syracuse, N.Y., July 27, 1935; A.B., Syracuse U., 1957, LL.B., 1959. Admitted to N.Y. State bar, 1959; asst. Atty. Gen. State of N.Y., 1959-61; partner firm Axenfeld, Webb, Marshall, Bersani & Scolaro, Syracuse, 1961—; spl. counsel N.Y. State Thruway Authority, 1961-64; counsel N.Y. Senate Com. on Codes, 1961-64, N.Y. State Senate Com. on Judiciary, 1965-72; minority counsel to Com. on Judiciary, N.Y. State Constl. Conv., 1967; partner firm Fisher, Axenfeld & Bersani, Bklyn., 1973—, Axenfeld, Marshall & Bersani, Albany, N.Y., 1973—; adj. prof. law Syracuse U. Coll. of Law, 1975-77; mem. subcom. no. 4, U.S. Nat. Com. on tunneling and tech., Nat. Acad. Scis. and Nat. Acad. of Engring. Mem. Am., N.Y. State, Onondaga County bar assns. Home: 6851 Knollwood Rd Fayetteville NY 13066 Office: 500 S Salina St Syracuse NY 13202 Tel (315) 422-9201

AXLEY, FREDERICK WILLIAM, b. Chgo., June 23, 1941; B.A., Holy Cross Coll., 1963; M.A., U. Wis., 1966; J.D., U. Chgo., 1969. Admitted to Ill. bar, 1969; asso. firm McDermott, Will & Emery, Chgo., 1969-74, partner, 1974—. Mem. Am., Ill., Chgo. bar assns.,

Chgo. Council Lawyers. Office: 111 W Monroe St Chicago IL 60603 Tel (312) 372-2000

AXSON, WILLIAM ALAN, b. Orangeburg, S.C., Oct. 27, 1946; B.S., Clemson U., 1968; J.D., Tulane U., 1972; M.D., Med. U. S.C., 1976. Admitted to bar; extern Charing Cross Hosp. Med. Sch., London, 1975; intern Charity Hosp., Tulane U. Div., New Orleans, 1976—. Fellow Am. Coll. Legal Medicine; mem. S.C., Am. bar assns. Home: 4323 S Carrollton St Apt 7 New Orleans LA 70119 Office: Charity Hosp Tulane Ave New Orleans LA

AXTELL, CLAYTON MORGAN, JR., b. Deposit, N.Y., 1916; A.B., Cornell U., 1937, LL.B., 1940. Admitted to N.Y. bar, 1940; partner firm Hinman, Howard & Kattell, Binghamton, N.Y., 1948—. Pres., Valley Devel. Found., Conrad and Virginia Klee Found., Binghamton; sec. 6th Jud. Dist. N.Y. Republican Jud. Com. Mem. Am., N.Y. State, Broome County (pres. 1967-68) bar assns., Cornell Law Assn. Home: 1338 Chenango St Binghamton NY 13901 Office: 724 Security Mutual Bldg Binghamton NY 13901 Tel (607) 723-5341

AYABE, SIDNEY KUNIYOSHI, b. Honolulu, June 15, 1945; B.A., Lawrence U., 1967; J.D., U. Iowa, 1970. Admitted to Hawaii bar, 1970; dep. atty. gen. State Atty. Gen's. Office, Honolulu, 1970-72; partner firm Libkuman, Ventura, Moon & Ayabe, Honolulu, 1972—; mem. Honolulu Bd. Realtors. Mem. Am., Hawaii bar assns. Home: 2600 Pualani Way Honolulu HI 96815 Office: Suite 412 700 Bishop St Honolulu HI 96813 Tel (808) 537-6119

AYCOCK, JOSEPH BRUCE, b. Alexandria, La., Mar. 18, 1921; B.A., St. Mary's U., 1952, LL.B., 1951, J.D., 1970. Admitted to Tex. bar, 1952; asst. criminal dist. atty. Bexar County (Tex.), 1952-55; individual practice law, 1955-59; partner firm Aycock & Steinle, 1959-64; asst. city atty. San Antonio, 1964-70, city atty., 1970-75; city atty. Corpus Christi (Tex.), 1976—; instr. St. Mary's U. Sch. Law, 1953-55. Chmn., Baden Powell dist. Boy Scouts Am., 1975; mem. parish council St. Joseph's Parish, Amarillo, 1975. Mem. Tex. State Bar, Nueces County Bar Assn., Tex. City Attys. Assn. (pres.), Nat. Inst. Municipal Law Officers (chmn. airports com.). Home: 1314 Casa Verde Corpus Christi TX 78411 Office: PO Box 9277 Corpus Christi TX 78408 Tel (512) 884-3011

AYCOCK, KEITH BYRON, b. Lawton, Okla., July 5, 1947; A.A., Cameron U., 1967; B.B.A., U. Okla., 1969, J.D., 1972. Admitted to Okla. bar, 1973; asso. firm Newcombe & Redman, Inc., Lawton, 1973-76; spl. dist. judge Comanche County (Okla.), Lawton, 1976—. Mem. Am., Okla., Comanche County bar assns. Home: 128 SW 49th St Lawton OK 73501 Office: Comanche County Court House Lawton OK 73501 Tel (405) 355-6128

AYER, GORDON CURTIS, b. Portland, Maine, Dec. 9, 1946; B.A., Nasson Coll., 1969; J.D., U. Maine, 1972. Admitted to Maine bar, 1972; partner firm Reagan, Ayer & Adams, Kennebunk, Maine, 1970—; counsel Town of Kennebunkport. Mem. Maine, York County bar assns., Maine Trial Lawyers Assn. Office: 11 Main St Kennebunk ME 04043 Tel (207) 985-7181

AYERS, EDWARD KENT, b. Canton, Ill., Mar. 7, 1942; A.B., Wabash Coll., Ind., 1964; J.D., U. N.D., 1968. Admitted to Ill. bar, 1969; midwestern rep. Council of State Govts., Chgo., 1968-69; asst. to dir. Ill. Dept. Mental Health, Chgo., 1969-71; partner firm Murphy, Timm, Lennon, Spesia & Ayers, Joliet, Ill., 1971—; asst. states atty. Will County (Ill.), 1974-75. Vice pres. bd. dirs. Ill. Assn. Mental Health, Springfield, 1973-74; regional dir. ARC, Joliet, 1973-76; dir. Crisis Line of Will County, Joliet, 1976. Mem. Ill., Will County bar assns., Am. Arbitration Assn. Office: 5 E Van Buren St Joliet IL 60435 Tel (815) 726-4311

AYLWARD, RONALD LEE, b. St. Louis, May 30, 1930; A.B., Washington U., St. Louis, 1952, J.D., 1954; postgrad. U. Va., 1955. Admitted to Mo. bar, 1954, Ill. bar, 1961, U.S. Supreme Ct. bar, 1968; with Judge Adv. Gen. Corps U.S. Army, 1955-58; asso. firm Heneghen, Roberts & Cole, St. Louis, 1958-59; asst. counsel Olin Corp., East Alton, Ill., 1960-64; asst. gen. counsel Interco Inc., St. Louis, 1964-66, asso. gen. counsel, mgr. dept. law, 1966-69, asst. sec., 1966-74; gen. counsel, 1969—, mem. operating bd., 1970—, v.p., 1971—, exec. com., dir., 1975—; mem. Dept. Commerce Dist. Export Council, 1974—. Bd. dirs Linda Vista Montessori Sch., St. Louis; bd. dirs. St. Louis-St. Louis County chpt. Nat. Found. March of Dimes, 1974—, sec., 1976—; bd. dirs. Cardinal Ritter Inst., St. Louis, 1975—, St. Louis Bi-State chpt. ARC, 1977—. Mem. Am., Mo. bar assns., Bar Assn. Metroplitan St. Louis (chmn. sect. bus. law, 1970-72), Am. Judicature Soc., Am. Footwear Industries Assn. (chmn. nat. affairs 1971-75), Nat. Assn. Mfrs., Asso. Industries of Mo. (dir. 1973—, chmn. com. membership 1973—, 2d v.p. 1974-76, pres. 1976—), Am. Soc. Corp. Secs. (pres. St. Louis Regional Group 1972-73), Delta Theta Phi (pres. St. Louis Alumni chpt. 1963, Mo. dist. chancellor 1970—). Home: 55 Muirfield St Louis MO 63141 Office: 10 Broadway Saint Louis MO 63102 Tel (314) 231-1100

AZULAY, JACOB DANIEL, b. Tel Aviv, Dec. 3, 1944; A.A., Liberal Arts Coll., Skokie, Ill., 1965; B.A., Roosevelt U., 1965; J.D. with honors, Ill. Inst. Tech.-Chgo.-Kent Coll. Law, 1973. Admitted to Ill. bar, 1973, Fla. bar, 1975; nat. title examiner Chgo. Title & Trust Co., 1973-75; real estate and corporate atty. Abbott Labs., N. Chgo., 1975-76; individual practice law, Chgo., 1973—; asst. prof. Roosevelt U., Chgo., 1973—; asst. states atty. civil div. Cook County (Ill.); nat. hearing officer Am. Arbitration Assn., Ill. Dept. Edn. Mem. Am., Ill., Chgo., Fla. bar assns., Am. Soc. Internat. Law, Am. Judicature Soc. Contbr. articles to legal jours. Home: 2909 W Jarvis Ave Chicago IL 60645 Office: 134 N LaSalle St Suite 806 Chicago IL 60602 Tel (312) 726-7111

BAAB, GEORGE WILLIAM, b. Greeley, Colo., July 23, 1942; B.A., Carleton Coll., 1964; J.D., U. Tex., Austin, 1967. Admitted to Tex. bar, 1967, U.S. Supreme Ct. bar, 1976; atty.-advisor NLRB, Washington, 1967-69; mem. firm Mullinax, Wells, Mauzy & Baab and predecessor, Dallas, 1969—; adj. prof. So. Meth. U. Sch. Law, 1976—; panel speaker SW Legal Found. Labor Law Seminar, 1974, Practicing Law Inst., Dallas, 1975. Reginald Heber Smith fellow, 1968-69. Office: Mullinax Wells Mauzy & Baab Suite 200 8204 Elmbrook Dr Dallas TX 75247 Tel (214) 630-3672

BABB, FRANK EDWARD, b. Maryville, Mo., Dec. 22, 1932; B.S., N.W. Mo. U., 1954; LL.B., Harvard, 1959. Admitted to Ill. bar, 1959; partner firm McDermott, Will & Emery, Chgo., 1959—. Mem. Am., Ill., Chgo. bar assns. Home: 123 Melrose Ave Kenilworth IL 60043 Office: 111 W Monroe St Room 1900 Chicago IL 60603 Tel (312) 372-2000

BABBITT, BRUCE B., b. June 27, 1938; B.A. magna cum laude, U. Notre Dame; M.A., U. Newcastle (Eng.), 1963; LL.B., Harvard U., 1965. Practiced law in Phoenix; former spl. asst. to dir. VISTA, Washington; now atty. gen. State of Ariz.; chmn. manpower tng. com. Phoenix LEAP Commn. Trustee Verde Valley Sch., Dougherty Found. Mem. Nat. Assn. Attys. Gen. Office: Atty Gen of Ariz State Capitol 1700 W Washington St Phoenix AZ 85007*

BABCOCK, BARBARA ALLEN, b. Washington, July 6, 1938; A.B., U. Pa., 1960; LL.B., Yale U., 1963. Admitted to D.C., Md. bars, 1963; law clk. to judge U.S. Ct. Appeals for D.C., 1963; asso. firm Edward Bennett Williams, Washington, 1964-66; staff atty. D.C. Legal Aid Agy., 1966-68; dir. pub. defender service of D.C., 1968-72; asso. prof. Stanford Law Sch., 1972-77; asst. U.S. atty. gen. civil div. Dept. Justice, Washington, 1977—; chairperson bd. dirs. Equal Rights Advocates, Inc., 1971—; mem. planning bd. Nat. Conf. Women and the Law, Center for Research on Women, 1975—; dir. Women's Law Project, Phila., 1974—; mem. com. on evaluation of sound spectrographs Nat. Acad. Scis. Mem. Nat. Legal Aid and Defender Assn. (dir., exec. com. 1970—), Am. Bar Assn. (past mem. criminal justice council), Nat. Coll. Criminal Def. Lawyers and Pub. Defenders (past mem. bd. regents), Soc. Am. Law Tchrs. (exec. bd.). Author: (with Freedman, Norton & Ross) Sex Discrimination and the Law: Causes and Remedies, 1975; (with Carrington) Civil Procedure: Cases and Comments on the Process of Adjudication, 1976; also articles. Home: 2111 Franklin St San Francisco CA 94109 Office: Dept Justice Constitution Ave and 10th St NW Washington DC 20530*

BABCOCK, WILLIAM HORACE, b. Bklyn., May 13, 1918; student The Citadel, 1938-39, John Marshal Law Sch., 1945-46, legal offices, Wis., Maine, 1946-49. Admitted to Maine bar, 1949, U.S. Supreme Ct. bar, 1961, Alaska bar, 1966; individual practice law, Maine, 1949-52, Sitka, Alaska, 1966—; served as judge adv. USAF, 1952-62; dist. magistrate, Sitka, 1962-65. Alaska state comdr. Am. Legion, 1970-71. Mem. Alaska, Am. bar assns., Am. Trial Lawyers Assn. Home and Office: 407 Etolin Way Box A Sitka AK 99835 Tel (907) 747-3261

BABER, WILLIAM HUGH, III, b. San Francisco, Oct 27, 1946; B.A. in Polit. Sci., U. Santa Clara, 1968, J.D., 1971, Admitted to Calif. bar, 1972; asso. firm Minasian, Minasian & Minasian, Oroville, Calif., 1972-74; partner firm Minasian, Minasian, Minasian, Spruance & Baber, Oroville, 1974—; law clk. firm Stubbeman, McRae, Sealy, Laughlin & Browder, Midland, Tex., summer 1970. Mem. Calif., Butte County bar assns., Butte County Barristers assn. (sec.-treas.), Oroville Area C. of C. (dir. 1975). Mng. editor Santa Clara Lawyer, 1970-71. Home: 1533 Manchester Rd Chico CA 95926 Office: 1681 Bird at Oak St Oroville CA 95926 Tel (916) 533-2885

BABINGTON, BRIAN ALEXANDER, b. El Paso, Sept. 8, 1945; B.A. in Econs., U. N.Mex., 1968, J.D., 1971. Admitted to N.Mex. bar, 1971; asst. dist. atty. N.Mex. 2d Jud. Dist. for Bernalillo County, 1972—. Home: 10600 Central St SE Space 49 Albuquerque NM 87123 Office: Room 215 Bernalillo County Courthouse 415 Tijeras St NW Albuquerque NM 87102 Tel (505) 766-4322

BABITT, ROY, b. N.Y.C., Sept. 28, 1926; B.A., N.Y.U., 1948, LL.B., 1951. Admitted to N.Y. bar, 1951; atty. U.S. Immigration and Naturalization Service, N.Y.C., 1954-64; spl. asst. U.S. Atty.-So. Dist. N.Y., 1955-64; judge U.S. Bankruptcy Ct., 1964—; mem. nat. faculty for bankruptcy judges Fed. Jud. Center. Home: 275 Kneeland Ave Yonkers NY 10705 Office: US Courthouse Foley Square New York City NY 10007 Tel (212) 791-0145

BABLER, WAYNE E., b. Orangeville, Ill., Dec. 8, 1915; B.A., Ind. Central Coll., 1936, LL.D., 1966; J.D., U. Mich., 1938. Admitted to Mich. bar, 1938, N.Y. bar, 1949, Mo. bar, 1955, Wis. bar, 1963, U.S Supreme Ct. bar, 1956; asso. firm Bishop & Bishop, Detroit, 1938-42; chief price atty. OPA, 1942-44; atty. Fisher Body div. Gen. Motors Corp., 1944-45; partner firm Bishop & Babler, Detroit, 1945-48; atty. AT&T, N.Y.C., 1948-55; gen. solicitor Southwestern Bell Telephone Co., St. Louis, 1955-63, v.p. and gen. counsel, 1965-76, v.p., gen. counsel and sec., 1976—; v.p., gen. counsel Wis. Telephone Co., Milw., 1963-65; part-time prof. Detroit Coll. Law, 1938-44. Bd. dirs. St. Louis Symphony Soc., 1976; chmn., dir. St. Louis Soc. Crippled Children, 1953-76. Mem. Am., FCC, Wis., Milw., Mo., St. Louis bar assns. Office: 1010 Pine St St Louis MO 63101 Tel (314) 247-4492

BACA, JOSEPH FRANCIS, b. Albuquerque, Oct. 1, 1936; B.A. in Edn., U. N.Mex., 1960; J.D., George Washington U., 1964; grad. Nat. Coll. State Judiciary, 1973. Admitted to N.Mex. Supreme Ct. bar, 1965, U.S. Dist. Ct. for Dist. N.Mex. bar, 1965, U.S. 10th Circuit Ct. Appeals bar, 1966; asst. dist. atty. City of Santa Fe, 1965-66; asso. firm Hartley, Olson & Baca and predecessor, Albuquerque, 1966-68, partner, 1968-71; asso. firm Ortega & Snead, Albuquerque, 1971-72; judge N.Mex. Dist. Ct., for 2d Jud. Dist., 1972—; spl. asst. atty. gen. Albuquerque, 1966-72. Del. N.Mex. Constl. Conv., 1969; bd. dirs. Family Counseling Service, Albuquerque, 1969-76, Legal Aid Soc., Albuquerque, 1972—, U. N.Mex. Alumni Assn., 1976—; mem. Met. Criminal Justice Coordinating Council, Albuquerque. Mem. N.Mex. Bar Assn., Am. Judicature Soc., Am. Judges Assn., Nat. Council Juvenile Ct. Judges, Nat. Juvenile Ct. Services Assn., Phi Alpha Delta. Home: 7428 Gila St NE Albuquerque NM 87109 Office: POB 488 Albuquerque NM 87103 Tel (505) 881-8956

BACCUS, STEVE ARNOLD, b. Haleyville, Ala., Nov. 12, 1946; B.S. in Bus. Adminstrn., U. Ala., 1970, J.D., 1973. Admitted to Ala. bar, 1973; law clk. U.S. Dist. judge, Birmingham, Ala., 1973; mem. firm Almon McAlister & Ashe, Sheffield, Ala., 1974—. Mem. Am., Ala., Birmingham bar assns., Ala. Def. Lawyers Assn. Home: 212 Village Dr Sheffield AL 35660 Office: PO Drawer N Sheffield AL 35660 Tel (205) 383-6357

BACH, EDWIN JAMES, b. Milw., Mar. 21, 1928; B.S. in Econs., U. Wis., 1951; LL.B., Marquette U., 1958. Admitted to Wis. bar, 1958; individual practice law, Milw., 1955-60; mem. firm Rowan, Hagen & Bach, and predecessors, Milw., 1960-70, Huiras, Farrell & Engelking, Port Washington, Wis., 1970—; ct. commr. Ozaukee County, Wis., 1974—; mem. panel arbitrators Am. Arbitration Assn., 1973—. Mem. planning commn. Town of Belgium, Ozaukee County. Mem. Wis., Ozaukee County bar assns. Home: RTE 1 Belgium WI 53004 Office: 116 W Grand Ave Port Washington WI 53074 Tel (414) 284-2664

BACH, ROBERT E., b. Highland, Ind., Oct. 7, 1933; B.S., Ind. U., 1956; J.D., John Marshall Law Sch., Atlanta, 1966. Admitted to Ga. bar, 1966, U.S. Supreme Ct. bar, 1973; mem. firm Gary, Bach, Kerr, Norman, Mableton, Ga., 1967—. Co-founder original Girls Little League Sports, Mableton, 1966—. Mem. Am., Cobb County, Atlanta bar assns., Internat. Platform Assn., Am. Judicature Soc., Ga., Am. trial lawyers assns. Office: 511 Bankhead Hwy Mableton GA 30059 Tel (404) 941-8890

BACH, STEVE CRAWFORD, b. Jackson, Ky., Jan. 31, 1921; A.B., Ind. U., 1943, J.D., 1948; postgrad. U. Mich., 1944, U. Nev., 1966, U. Minn., 1967. Admitted to Ky. bar, 1948, Ind. bar, 1948; asso. firm Bach & Bach, Jackson, 1948-51; investigator U.S. Civil Service Commn., Indpls., 1951-54; individual practice law, Mt. Vernon, Ind., 1954-65; judge 11th Jud. Circuit, Mt. Vernon, 1965—; bd. dirs. 8th Region, Ind. Criminal Justice Planning Agy., 1969—; del. Internat. Youth Conf., Geneva, Switzerland, 1970, Oxford, Eng., 1974; mem. juvenile justice div. Ind. Jud. Study Commn., Indpls., 1975—; mem. Ind. Gov.'s Juvenile Justice Delinquency Prevention Adv. Bd., 1976—. Pres. Greater Mt. Vernon Assn., 1958-59; bd. dirs. Regional Mental Health Planning Com., Evansville, Ind.; trustee Ind. Jr. Hist. Soc. Mem. Ind. (del.), Posey County bar assns., Ind. Judges Assn. (bd. mgrs. 1966-71), Ind. Council Juvenile Ct. Judges (v.p. 1976). Home: 512 Walnut St Mount Vernon IN 47620 Office: POB 190 Mount Vernon IN 47620 Tel (812) 838-4897

BACH, THOMAS HANDFORD, b. Vineland, N.J., Dec. 25, 1928; A.B., Rutgers U., 1950; LL.B., Harvard, 1956. Admitted to N.Y. State bar, 1957; asso. firm Hawkins, Delafield & Wood, N.Y.C., 1956-61, firm Reed, Hoyt, Washburn & McCarthy, N.Y.C., 1961-62; sr. partner firm Bach & Condren, N.Y.C., 1963-71, firm Bach & McAuliffe, N.Y.C., 1971—; mem. N.Y. State Commn. Constl. Tax Limitations, 1974-75; chmn. N.Y. Municipal Analysts Group, 1973-74; asst. counsel N.Y. State Senate Housing and Urban Renewal Com., 1971; fiscal cons. N.Y.C. Fin. Adminstrn., 1967-70; asst. counsel N.Y. State Fin. Com. N.Y. State Constl. Conv., 1967. Mem. Am., N.Y. State, N.Y. County bar assns., Municipal Fin. Officers Assn. U.S. and Can., Municipal Fin. Officers N.J., N.Y. Municipal Analysts Group, N.Y. Municipal Forum. Contbr. articles to legal jours. Home: 4 E 89th St New York City NY 10028 Office: 80 Wall St New York City NY 10005 Tel (212) 269-3932

BACHARACH, BERNARD RALF, b. N.Y.C., Feb. 10, 1939; B.S., Hunter Coll., 1960, J.D., Bklyn. Law Sch., 1963, LL.M., 1967. Admitted to N.Y. State bar, 1963, U.S. Supreme Ct. bar, 1970; sr. partner firm Bacharach, Green & Bass, White Plains, N.Y. N.Y., 1966—; Pres. bd. edn. Union Free Sch. Dist. #9, Elmsford, N.Y., 1970-73; 1st v.p. Union Child Daycare Center, White Plains, 1975—; trustee Elmsford/Greenburgh Community Action Program, White Plains, 1973-75. Mem. Criminal Cts. Bar Assn. (treas. 1976-77, trustee 1971—), Westchester County, White Plains (trustee 1976) bar assns. Home: 67 Durham Rd White Plains NY 10607 Office: 200 Mamaroneck Ave White Plains NY 10601

BACHARACH, CLIFFORD GORDON, b. N.Y.C., July 23, 1926; B.S., Coll. City N.Y., 1947; M.A., Columbia, 1950; LL.B., N.Y. U., 1956, LL.M., 1959. Admitted to N.Y. State bar, 1956, U.S. Supreme Ct. bar, 1961; law clk. to judge U.S. Dist. Ct. for Eastern Dist. N.Y., 1956-57; instr. N.Y. U. Law Sch., 1957-60; individual practice law, N.Y.C., 1958—. Mem. Queens County (N.Y.) Bar Assn. Editorial bd. N.Y. U. Law Rev. Home: 162-41 Powells Cove Blvd Beechhurst Queens NY 11357 Office: 250 W 57th St New York City NY 10019 Tel (212) 617-5660

BACHELDER, JOSEPH ELMER, III, b. Fulton, Mo., Nov. 13, 1932; B.A., Yale, 1955; LL.B., Harvard, 1958. Admitted to N.Y. State bar, 1959; asso. firm Mudge Rose Guthrie & Alexander, N.Y.C., 1959-67, McKinsey & Co., N.Y.C., 1967-69; partner firm Satterlee & Stephens, N.Y.C., 1969-73, firm LeBoeuf, Lamb, Leiby & MacRae, N.Y.C., 1973—; chmn. Nat. Pension Inst., 1974-76; lectr. in field. Mem. Am., N.Y. State, N.Y.C. (com. on taxation 1963-66) bar assns., Beta Theta Pi. Contbr. articles to legal jours. Home: 226 Constitution Dr Princeton NJ 08540 Office: 140 Broadway New York City NY 10005 Tel (212) 269-1100

BACHMAN, CARL OTTO, b. Watertown, N.Y., Jan. 4, 1916; A.B., Syracuse U., 1937; J.D., Columbia, 1940. Admitted to N.Y. State bar, 1941; with Utica Mut. Ins. Co., 1940-41; investigator U.S. CSC, 1941-43; asso. firm Tripp & Dunk, Watertown, 1946-52, Dunk, Conboy, McKay & Bachman, Watertown, 1952-66, Conboy, McKay, Bachman & Kendall, Watertown, 1966—; active Hudson River-Black River Regulating Dist., 1964-76, pres., 1970-76; mem. com. on character and fitness 5th Jud. Dist., N.Y. Supreme Ct., 1966—, grievance and ethics com. 5th Jud. Dist., 1974—. Mem. Watertown Bd. Edn., 1955-61, pres., 1958; trustee Jefferson Community Coll., 1961—, pres., 1967-70; trustee Watertown YWCA, 1965-67; bd. dirs. Watertown United Fund, 1952-59, pres., 1958; dir. Syracuse U. Alumni Assn., 1974-78. Fellow Am. Coll. Trial Lawyers; mem. Am., N.Y. State (ho. of dels. 1976—, mem. endowment fund 1976—), Jefferson County (pres. 1964) bar assns., Am. Judicature Soc., Def. Research Inst., Phi Delta Phi. Decorated Bronze Star. Home: 451 Paddock St Watertown NY 13601 Office: 407 Sherman St Watertown NY 13601 Tel (315) 788-5100

BACHMAN, KENNETH LEROY, JR., b. Washington, Aug. 24, 1943; A.B. summa cum laude, Ohio U., 1965; J.D. cum laude, Harvard, 1968. Admitted to D.C. bar, 1968; law clk. U.S. Dist. Ct., So. Dist. N.Y., 1968-70; asso. firm Cleary, Gottlieb, Steen & Hamilton, Washington, 1970-76, partner, 1976—; mem. faculty Am. Law Inst. seminar, 1974; mem. faculty Practising Law Inst., seminar 1977. Mem. Am. Bar Assn., Phi Beta Kappa, Omicron Delta Kappa. Home: 5412 Duvall Dr Bethesda MD 20016 Office: 1250 Connecticut Ave NW Washington DC 20036

BACHMAN, ROBERT, b. Detroit, July 4, 1941; B.S., in Bus. Adminstrn., Wayne State U., 1963, J.D., 1966. Admitted to Mich. bar, 1966; with Touche Ross & Co., Detroit, 1966-70; mgr. Elmer Fox, Westheimer & Co., Detroit, 1970-76; individual practice accounting, Southfield, Mich., 1976—. Mem. Mich. Bar assn., Mich. Assn. C.P.A.'s, Am. Inst. C.P.A.'s, Am. Assn. Atty.-C.P.A.'s. Home: 31110 Hunters Whip Ln Farmington Hills MI 48018 Office: 17117 W Nine Mile Rd suite 1740 Southfield MI 48075 Tel (313) 559-8870

BACHSTEIN, HARRY SAMUEL, JR., b. Oakland, Calif., Aug. 6, 1943; B.S. in Bus. Adminstrn., No. Ariz. U., 1966; J.D. (Univ. honors 1966-67), U. Ariz., 1969. Admitted to Ariz. bar, 1969, U.S. Supreme Ct. bar, 1973; asso. firm Richard E. Bailey, Tucson, 1969-71; individual practice law, Tucson, 1971-73; sr. partner firm Bachstein & Coffey, Tucson, 1973—; spl. investigator ethics com. Pinal County Bar, 1971; juvenile ct. referee Ariz. Superior Ct., 1972—. Mem. Devel. Authority for Tucson's Expansion, 1970—. Mem. State Bar Ariz. (sec. exec. council young lawyers' sect. 1972-73), Am. (Ariz. rep. com. on div. law and procedures 1976—), Pima County bar assns., Assn. Trial Lawyers Am., Am. Judicature Soc., Nat. Council Juvenile Ct. Judges. Editor: Ariz. Law Rev., 1967-69. Office: 316 Transamerica Bldg Tucson AZ 85701 Tel (602) 792-9462

BACINE, DANIEL EDWARD, b. Bklyn., May 27, 1946; B.S., Temple U., 1967; J.D., Villanova U., 1971. Admitted to Pa. bar, 1971, D.C. bar, 1972; atty.-adviser HUD, Washington, 1971-72; asso. firm David Berger, Phila., 1972-75, Harry Norman Ball, Phila., 1975—.

Bd. dirs. Germantown Jewish Centre. Mem. Am., Pa., Phila. bar assns. (mem. exec. com. young lawyers' sect. local assn.), Am. Judicature Soc., Order of the Coif. Recipient Law & Bus. award Temple U., 1967; Mich. Legis. fellow, 1967-68; editor Villanova Law Rev., 1970-71. Home: 219 Pelham Rd Philadelphia PA 19119 Office: Suite 1900 Three Penn Center Plaza Philadelphia PA 19102 Tel (215) 561-4700

BACINE, NATHAN, b. Bklyn., Apr. 26, 1925; LL.B., Bklyn. Law Sch., 1951. Admitted to Appellate Div. 2d Dept. bar, 1952; individual practice law, Bklyn., 1952-61, 64-69; asso. Michael Wollin, Bklyn., 1961-64; partner firm Bacine & Erlitz, Bklyn., 1968—; asst. minority counsel, N.Y. State Legislature, 1963-69. Mem. law com. Regular Democratic Orgn. of 42d Assembly Dist., N.Y., 1971-76. Mem. Bklyn. Bar Assn. Office: 407 Utica Ave Brooklyn NY 11213 Tel (212) 772-2351

BACKMAN, ROSA SARAH, b. Russia, May 15, 1900; LL.B. magna cum laude, New Eng. Law Sch., 1926, LL.M., 1946. Admitted to Mass. bar, 1926, U.S. Supreme Ct. bar 1965; individual practice law, Lynn, Mass., 1929—. Asso. mem. Lynn Zoning Bd. Appeals; bd. dirs. Jr. Achievement, N. Shore Community Center. Mem. Mass. Bar Assn., Mass., Nat. assns. women lawyers, Mass. Assn. Trial Lawyers, Bus. and Profl. Women's Club (hon. pres. 1935—). Home: 317 Lynn Shore Dr Lynn MA 01902 Office: 31 Exchange St Lynn MA 01901 Tel (617) 592-2345

BACKSTROM, JAMES WALTON, b. Mobile, Ala., Aug. 29, 1942; B.B.A., U. Miss., 1965, J.D., 1967. Admitted to Miss. bar, 1967; landman Humble Oil & Refining Co., New Orleans, 1967; asso. firm Sumrall, Aultman & Pope, Hattiesburg, Miss., 1968-70; individual practice law, Lucedale, Miss., 1970-73; partner firm Bryan, Nelson, Allen & Schroeder, Pascagoula, Miss., 1973—. Chmn. ARC, Lucedale, Miss., 1970-73. Mem. Am., Miss. State bar assns., Miss. Def. Lawyers Assn., Comml. Law League Am., George County Jaycees (v.p. 1971), Phi Delta Phi. Home: 8621 Bayou Castelle Gautier MS 39553 Office: 1103 Jackson Ave Pascagoula MS 39567 Tel (601) 762-6631

BACON, BRETT KERMIT, b. Perry, Iowa, Aug. 8, 1947; B.A. cum laude, U. Dubuque, 1969; J.D., Northwestern U., 1972. Admitted to Ohio bar, 1972; mem. firm Thompson, Hine and Flory, Cleve., 1972—. Bd. dirs. Cleve. Jaycees; pres. No. Ohio Northwestern U. Alumni chpt.; bd. dirs. Cleve. Totlot Found.; active Citizens League, City Club. Mem. Am., Ohio State bar assns., Bar Assn. Greater Cleve. Recipient Jaycee Award of Merit, 1976. Office: 1100 National City Bank Bldg Cleveland OH 44114 Tel (216) 241-1880

BACON, SYLVIA, b. Watertown, S.D., July 9, 1931; A.B., Vassar Coll., 1952; certificate Lincoln Sch. Economics, 1953; LL.B., Harvard; LL.M., Georgetown U., 1959. Admitted to U.S. Dist. Ct. bar, 1956; law clk. to Judge Barnita Shelton Matthews, 1956-57; asst. U.S. Atty, Washington, 1957-65; asso. dir. Pres.'s Commn. Crime in D.C., 1965-66; trial atty. Dept. Justice, 1967-69; exec. asst. U.S. atty. for D.C., 1969-70; asso. judge D.C. Superior Ct., 1970—; adj. prof. Georgetown U. Law Center, 1965-70; faculty Nat. Coll. State Judiciary, 1975—. Bd. dirs. Nat. Center State Cts., 1975—. Mem. Am. Bar Assn. (council criminal justice sect., chmn. sect. com. women and criminal justice), UN Congress Prevention Crime and Treatment of Offenders. Office: 613 G St NW Washington DC 20003 Tel (202) 727-1444

BACON, WILLIAM ARTHUR, b. Durant, Miss., Feb. 8, 1912; LL.B., U. Miss., 1935, J.D., 1968. Admitted to Miss. bar, 1935; city atty. Durant (Miss.), 1935-40; asst. U.S. dist. atty. for So. Dist. Miss., 1940-42, 46; state bond atty. Miss., 1951—; city atty. Pearl (Miss.), 1973—; individual practice law, Jackson and Pearl, Miss. Mem. Miss. Ho. of Reps., 1936-40. Mem. Am. Judicature Soc., Am., Miss. (past pres.), Hinds County (past pres.) bar assns. Home: 3909 Pinewood Dr Jackson MS 39211 Office: POB 15 Jackson MS 39205 Tel (601) 355-3451

BADER, ALBERT XAVIER, JR., b. Bklyn., Oct. 19, 1932; B.S. magna cum laude, Georgetown U., 1953; LL.B., Columbia U., 1956. Admitted to N.Y. bar, 1956, U.S. Supreme Ct. bar, 1965; asso. firm Simpson, Thacher & Bartlett, N.Y.C., 1965-68, partner, 1969—. Mem. Am., N.Y. State bar assns., Assn. Bar City N.Y. (chmn. bankruptcy com. 1970-73), N.Y. County Lawyers. Office: 1 Battery Park Pl New York City NY 10004 Tel (212) 483-9000

BADER, IZAAK WALTON, b. June 20, 1922; A.B. in Chemistry, N.Y. U., 1942, J.D., 1948. Admitted to N.Y. bar, 1948, D.C. bar, 1952; asso. firm Duell & Kane, N.Y.C., 1948-49; atty. FTC, N.Y.C., 1950-51; investigator Hart Com. on Edn., N.Y.C., 1947; sec. Trade Mark Service Corp., N.Y.C., 1950-65; patent counsel Yeshiva U., N.Y.C., 1955—; counsel Ind. Investor Protective League, 1970—; patent counsel Swingline, Inc., 1955-72; partner firm Bader & Bader, N.Y.C., 1952—. Mem. Nat. Dem. Club, 1964—. Mem. Am., N.Y., Bklyn., Westchester County bar assns., N.Y. Patent Law Assn. Home: Beech Tree Rd Brookfield Center CT 06805 Office: 65 Court St White Plains NY 10601 Tel (212) 532-6860 also 270 Madison Ave New York City NY

BADER, JOHN MERWIN, b. Wilmington, Del., June 29, 1919; A.B., Villanova U., 1941; LL.B., U. Pa., 1948. Admitted to Del. bar, 1948, U.S. Supreme Ct. bar, 1956; mem. firm Balick & Bader, Wilmington, 1956-61, firm Bader & Biggs, Wilmington, 1961-66, firm Bader Dorsey & Kreshtool, Wilmington, 1970—; atty. Town of Elsmere (Del.), 1950-53. Pres. People's Settlement Assn., Wilmington, 1957-60; pres. Boys' Home of Del., Wilmington, 1965-66, Geriatric Services of Del., Wilmington, 1975—. Mem. Del. State Bar Assn., Del. Trial Lawyers Assn. (pres. 1956-57, 76—), Assn. Trial Lawyers Am. (bd. govs. 1969-72, 75—). Home: 1107 Nottingham Rd Wilmington DE 19805 Office: 1102 West St Box 2202 Wilmington DE 19899 Tel (302) 656-9850

BADER, MICHAEL HALEY, b. Tacoma, Aug. 28, 1929; A.A., George Washington U., 1949, LL.B., 1952. Admitted to D.C. bar, 1954, U.S. Supreme Ct. bar, 1957; asso. firm Haley, Bader & Potts, and predecessors, Washington, 1954-57, partner, 1957—; dir. MCI Communications Corp., Washington, 1968—, Missiles-Jets & Automation Fund, Inc., Washington, 1957-60; asst. sec. Axe Sci. Fund, 1960-64. Gen. counsel Theodore Karman Found., Washington, 1966—. Mem. Am., D.C., Fed. Communications (exec. com. 1969-72) bar assns. Contbr. to books. Home: 5211 Wehawken Rd Bethesda MD 20016 Office: 1730 M St NW Washington DC 20036 Tel (202) 331-0606

BADER, W. REECE, b. Portland, Oreg., Oct. 31, 1941; B.A., Williams Coll., 1963; LL.B., Duke, 1966. Admitted to D.C. bar, 1967, Calif. bar, 1969; law clk. to Hon. Warren E. Burger, U.S. Ct. Appeals, D.C. Circuit, 1966-68; asso. firm Orrick, Herrington, Roweky & Sutcliffe, San Francisco, 1968-73, partner, 1974—; mem. ad hoc com. on ct. facilities and design U.S. Jud. Conf., 1971-74. Mem. Am., Calif., San Francisco bar assns., D.C. Bar, Calif. Trial Lawyers Assn., Lawyers Club San Francisco, Am. Judicature Soc., Supreme Ct. Hist. Soc. Editorial bd. Duke Law Jour., 1964-66. Office: 600 Montgomery St 12th Floor San Francisco CA 94111 Tel (415) 392-1122

BADOLATO, RICHARD J., b. Newark, Aug. 20, 1940; B.B.A., Fairfield U., 1962; LL.B., Rutgers U., 1965. Admitted to N.J. bar, 1965; now mem. firm Morgan, Melhuish, Monaghan & Spielvogel, Livingston, N.J. Mem. N.J. State, Essex County (pres. 1977-78) bar assns. Office: 301 S Livingston Ave Livingston NJ 07039 Tel (201) 944-2500*

BAECHLE, JAMES J., b. 1932; B.S.B.A., Ohio State U., 1954; LL.B., Harvard U., 1957. Asso. firm White & Case, 1959-67; v.p., sec., gen. counsel Brown Co., 1967-71; v.p., gen. counsel Bankers Trust N.Y. Corp., N.Y.C., 1971-75, sr. v.p., gen. counsel, 1975—; dir. Bankers Trust of Suffolk NA & BT Credit Co. Inc.; sr. v.p., gen. counsel Bankers Trust. Co. Office: 280 Park Ave New York City NY 10017*

BAECHTOLD, GEORGE HOWARD, b. Granite City, Ill., Aug. 19, 1928; B.S., Elmhurst Coll., 1950; J.D., U. So. Calif., 1959. Admitted to Calif. bar, 1960; partner firm Baechtold and Bedrosian, Van Nuys, Calif., 1960-62, firm Walleck, Shane and Baechtold, Van Nuys, 1962-68; individual practice law, Van Nuys, 1968—; asso. prof. bus. law Calif. State U., Northridge, 1969—. Mem. State Bar Calif., Am., Los Angeles County, San Fernando Valley bar assns., AAUP, Pacific S.W. Bus. Law Assn., Phi Alpha Delta. Home: PO Box 429 Northridge CA 91324 Office: Suite 228 9010 Reseda Blvd Northridge CA 91324 Tel (213) 993-9888

BAECHTOLD, ROBERT LOUIS, b. Jersey City, Dec. 18, 1937; B.S., Rutgers U., 1958; J.D. summa cum laude, Seton Hall U., 1966. Admitted to N.Y. State bar, 1967, N.J. bar, 1970; research chemist Am. Cyanamid, Bound Brook, N.J., 1958-62; patent agt. M & T Chems., Rahway N.J., 1962-65; since practiced in N.Y.C., asso. firm Ward, McElhannon, Brooks & Fitzpatrick, 1965-68, partner firm, 1968-69, partner firm Fitzpatrick, Cella, Harper & Scinto, 1969—. Mem. Cranford (N.J.) Bd. Edn., 1971-74; residential chmn. Cranford United Way, 1970-71, trustee, counsel, 1975—; mem. adv. com. on sex edn., Cranford, 1969-71. Mem. Am., N.Y. patent law assns., N.Y. State Bar Assn., N.J. Patent Law Assn. (treas. 1974-75, sec. 1975-76, 2d v.p. 1976-77, 1st v.p. 1977—). Leopold Schepp Found. grantee, 19754-58; Nat. Starch Products scholar, 1954-58. Home: 11 Woods Hole Rd Cranford NJ 07016 Office: 277 Park Ave New York City NY 10017 Tel (212) 758-2400

BAER, DAVID, JR., b. Belleville, Ill., Sept. 24, 1905; J.D., Washington U., St. Louis, 1928. Admitted to Mo. bar, 1928, Ill. bar, 1928; asso. firm Carter, Jones & Turney, and successors, St. Louis, 1928-50, partner, 1950-73; partner firm Barnard, Baer, Lee, Timm & McDaniel (now Barnard & Baer), St. Louis, 1973—; dir. Lindell Trust Co., St. Louis. Mem. endowment fund com. St. Louis Council Boy Scouts Am. Mem. Am., Mo., Met. St. Louis (chmn. group ins. spl. com. 1966, mem. prepaid legal ins. com. 1970) bar assns., Assn. Def. Counsel, Washington U. Law Alumni Assn. Home: 725 S Skinker Blvd Saint Louis MO 63105 Office: 818 Olive St Suite 1400 Saint Louis MO 63101 Tel (314) 241-5500

BAER, ISADORE BENJAMIN, b. Memphis, Dec. 23, 1915; B.S., Tenn. State Tchrs. Coll., 1938; J.D., Northwestern U., 1941. Admitted to Ill. bar, 1941, Tenn. bar, 1942; practice law, Memphis. Mem. Am., Memphis and Shelby County bar assns., Am., Tenn. trial lawyers assns. Contbr. articles to legal jours. Home: 70 E Cherry Dr Memphis TN 38117 Office: Suite 504 46 N 3d St Memphis TN 38103 Tel (901) 525-7316

BAER, THOMAS J., b. N.Y.C., May 11, 1927; B.S., Columbia, 1955, LL.B., 1957. Admitted to N.Y. State bar, 1958, U.S. Supreme Ct. bar, 1960; partner firm Hawkins, Delafield & Wood, N.Y.C., 1967—. Mem. Am., N.Y. State bar assns., Municipal Forum N.Y., Municipal Fin. Officers Assn. (asso.), Internat. Bridge, Tunnel and Turnpike Assn. Home: 22 Westcott St Old Tappan NJ 07675 Office: 67 Wall St New York City NY 10005 Tel (212) 952-4758

BAETY, EDWARD LUNDY, b. Jacksonville, Fla., Mar. 13, 1944; B.A., Morris Brown Coll., 1965; J.D., Howard U., 1968. Admitted to Ga. bar, 1969; mem. firm Hill, Jones & Farrington, Savannah, Ga., 1972-76; asso. judge City Ct. of Atlanta, 1976—. Mem. Atlanta, Gate City bar assns. *

BAGBY, GLEN STOVALL, b. Memphis, Sept. 1, 1944; A.B., Transylvania U., 1966; J.D., U. Ky., 1969. Admitted to Ky. bar, 1969, U.S. Supreme Ct. bar, 1972, U.S. Tax Ct. bar, 1972, U.S. Ct. Claims bar, 1975; asso. firm Brock, Brock & Bagby and predecessor, Lexington, Ky., 1969-71, partner, 1972—; pub. defender, Lexington, 1969-70; asst. commonwealth's atty., Lexington, 1970-72. Mem. Lexington Housing Bd. Appeals, 1971—; chmn. Julius Marks Home for Elderly, Lexington, 1975—. Mem. Am., Ky. State, Fayette County (Ky.) bar assns. Home: 321 Lakeshore Dr Lexington KY 40502 Office: Suite 7-C Citizens Bank Square Lexington KY 40507 Tel (606) 255-7795

BAGDASARIAN, JOHN DER, b. Phila., Dec. 18, 1932; B.S., Harvard, 1955; J.D., U. Conn., 1961. Admitted to Conn. bar, 1961, U.S. Supreme Ct. bar, 1969; asso. firm Diloreto, Karaian & McQueen, New Britain, Conn., 1961-64; law clk. Ct. of Common Pleas, New Britain, 1963-67; individual practice law, 1964—; corp. counsel City of New Britain, 1974—. Trustee St. Stephens Ch., New Britain, 1965-70. Mem. Am., Conn., Hartford County, New Britain bar assns. Home: 78 Varmor Dr New Britain CT 06051 Office: 233 Main St New Britain CT 06051 Tel (203) 225-6344

BAGILEO, JOHN R., b. Jersey City, Jan. 16, 1941; B.S., Georgetown U., 1962; LL.B., Boston Coll., 1966. Admitted to Mass. bar, 1966, D.C. bar, 1969; atty. ICC, 1966-68; now mem. firm Rea, Cross & Auchincloss, Washington. Mem. D.C. Bar, Fed., Am. bar assns. Office: World Center Bldg Suite 700 918 16th St NW Washington DC 20006 Tel (202) 785-3700*

BAGWELL, DAVID ASHLEY, b. Winston-Salem, N.C., Nov. 12, 1945; B.A. in History, Vanderbilt U., 1968; J.D., U. Ala., 1973. Admitted to Ala. bar, 1974; Law clk. to chief judge U.S. Dist. Ct. for Middle Dist. Ala., 1973-74; partner firm McRight, Sims, Rowe & Bagwell, Mobile, Ala., 1974—. Mem. Am., Ala., Mobile bar assns., Maritime Law Assn. U.S., Southeastern Admiralty Law Inst., Order of Coif, Omicron Delta Kappa, Sigma Alpha Epsilon (pres. local chpt. 1968). Corning Travelling fellow, 1969; contbr. articles to Ala. Law Rev., 1972—. Office: Commerce Bldg 5th floor Mobile AL 36601 Tel (205) 434-6961

BAHAKEL, IZAS, b. Birmingham, Ala., Sept. 21, 1931; A.B., Birmingham-So. Coll., 1955; LL.B., U. Ala., 1957, J.D., 1969. Admitted to Ala. bar, 1957; practice law, Birmingham, 1957—. Mem. Ala., Birmingham, FCC bar assns., Am., Ala. trial lawyers assns. Office: Legal Arts Bldg 2131 12th Ave N Birmingham AL 35234 Tel (205) 328-9796

BAIAMONTE, PHILLIP D., b. Hot Springs, New Mex., Oct. 1, 1931; B.A., U. N.Mex., 1953; J.D., U. Colo., 1956. Admitted to Colo. bar, 1956, N.Mex. bar, 1959, U.S. Ct. Mil. Appeals bar, 1960, U.S. 10th Circuit Ct. Appeals bar, 1962, U.S. Supreme Ct. bar, 1973; served with JAGC, U.S. Army, 1956-59; practiced in Albuquerque, 1959-74; judge N. Mex. Dist. Ct., 1974—. Mem. Albuquerque Bar Assn. (pres. 1974), Am. Trial Lawyers Assn. Home: 1815 Newton Pl NE Albuquerque NM 87106 Office: PO Box 488 Albuquerque NM 87103 Tel (505) 842-3483

BAIER, ALAN LEIGH, b. White Plains, N.Y., July 1, 1941; B.A. in Polit. Economy, Williams Coll., 1963; LL.B., Duke U., 1966. Admitted to Ga. bar, 1967; asso. firm Hansell, Post, Brandon & Dorsey, Atlanta, 1966-69; pres., prin. The Baier Corp., Atlanta, 1970—. Bd. sponsors Atlanta Symphony Orch.; mem. men's adv. com. Atlanta Music Club. Named Hon. French consul State of Ga., 1974—. Home: 1632 Ponce de Leon Ave NE Atlanta GA 30307 Office: POB 1827 Decatur GA 30031 Tel (404) 378-4226

BAILEY, EDWARD EVANS, b. Alhambra, Calif., Nov. 4, 1937; B.S. in B.A., U. Ark., Fayetteville, 1961; J.D., U. Mo., Kansas City, 1970. Admitted to Mo. bar, 1971, U.S. Dist. Ct. Western Dist. Mo. bar, 1971; partner firm Bailey, Dowell, McNearney & Desselle, Independence, Mo., 1971-75, Bailey & Williamson, Independence, 1975—. Pres. Independence C. of C., 1976; former pres. Neighborhood Council 15, Independence, 1975. Mem. Am., Kansas City, Eastern Jackson County bar assns., Am. Judicature Soc., Delta Theta Phi. Home: 810 W Waldo St Independence MO 64050 Office: 115 W Lexington St PO Box 1078 Independence MO 64051 Tel (816) 836-3900

BAILEY, FRANCIS LEE, b. Waltham, Mass., June 10, 1933; student Harvard; LL.B., Boston U. Admitted to Mass. bar, 1960; partner firm Bailey, Alch & Gillis, Boston; pub. Gallery mag., 1972—; pres. Enstrom Helicopter Corp., 1972—. Mem. Am. Bar Assn. Author: (with Harvey Aronson) The Defense Never Rests, 1972. Address: 1 Center Plaza Boston MA 02108*

BAILEY, GARRETT DIXON, b. Burnsville, N.C., June 23, 1927; A.B., Berea Coll., 1947; J.D., Wake Forest Coll., 1951; student JAG Sch., U. Va., 1952. Admitted to N.C. bar, 1951; asso. firm W.E. Anglin, Burnsville, N.C., 1951-52, 54-59; partner firm Anglin & Bailey, Burnsville, 1959-65; individual practice law, Burnsville, 1965—; county atty. Yancey County (N.C.), Burnsville, 1958-60. Mem. Yancey County Planning Bd., 1967—; pres. Burnsville PTA, 1965-66. Mem. N.C., Yancey County (pres. 1975—) bar assns., Am. Judicature Soc., Yancey County C. of C. (chmn. com. edn. and govt. 1968-69, dir. 1964-75), Phi Alpha Delta. Home: PO Box 43 Burnsville NC 28714 Office: PO Box 217 Burnsville NC 28714 Tel (704) 682-2183

BAILEY, GEORGE GILBERT, b. Wheeling, W.Va., Dec. 1, 1913; A.B., W.Va. U., 1935, LL.B., 1937. Admitted to W.Va. bar, 1937, since practiced in Wheeling; partner firm Bailey, Byrum & Vieweg, 1976—; city solicitor, Wheeling, 1955-72. Sec.-treas. Sandscrest Found., 1954—; pres. Oglebay Inst., 1958-60. Fellow Am. Bar Found.; mem. Am. (del. 1964—, bd. govs. 1974—), W.Va. (pres. 1963-64), Ohio County (pres. 1962-63) bar assns., Am. Coll. Trial Lawyers, Am. Judicature Soc. Home: Dement Rd RD 2-Triadelphia WV 26059 Office: Central Union Bldg Wheeling WV 26003 Tel (304) 232-6675

BAILEY, GLENN BOYETTE, b. Wilson, N.C., July 31, 1929; student Oak Ridge Mil. Inst., 1946-48; A.B., U. N.C., 1950, LL.B., 1953. Admitted to N.C. bar, 1963; atty. State Farm Mut. Auto Ins. Co., Charlottesville, Va., 1956-72; mem. firm Hamilton Bailey & Boshamer, Morehead City, N.C., 1972—. Mem. N.C., Carteret County, Third Dist. bar assns. Office: PO Drawer 188 Morehead City NC 28557 Tel (919) 726-6134

BAILEY, HENRY JOHN, III, b. Pitts., Apr. 4, 1916; B.A., Pa. State U., 1939; J.D., Yale, 1947. Admitted to N.Y. bar, 1948, Mass. bar, 1963, Oreg. bar, 1974; atty. Fed. Res. Bank of N.Y., N.Y.C., 1947-55; asst. v.p. Empire Trust Co., N.Y.C., 1955-56; atty. legal dept. Am. Bankers Assn., N.Y.C., 1956-62; editor Banking Law Jour., Boston, 1962-65; asso. prof. Willamette U. Coll. Law, Salem, Oreg., 1965-69, prof., 1969—; lectr. Banking Sch. of South, Baton Rouge, La., 1972, 73, 75. Mem. Am. (past chmn. subcom. on comml. paper), Oreg., Marion County bar assns., Am. Law Inst. (editorial bd. The Practical Lawyer 1976—). Author: The Law of Bank Checks, 1960, 4th edit., 1969; Modern Uniform Commercial Code Forms, 1963; (with Clarke and Young) Bank Deposits and Collections, 4th edit., 1972; (with R.D. Hursh) The American Law of Products Liability, 2d edit., 1976; (with W.D. Hawkland) The Sum and Substance of Commercial Paper, 1976; Secured Transactions in a Nutshell, 1976; also articles. Home: 4156 Riverdale Rd S Salem OR 97302 Office: Coll Law Willamette U Salem OR 97301 Tel (503) 370-6382

BAILEY, HERMAN TRACY, b. Winfield, Iowa, Mar. 25, 1922; B.S., Iowa State U., 1947; J.D., State U. Iowa, 1949. Admitted to Iowa bar, 1949; with law dept. Bankers Life Co., Des Moines, 1955—, now sr. v.p., gen. counsel; asst. county atty. Wapello County, Iowa, 1952-53. Mem. Assn. Life Ins. Counsel, Am. Counsel Life Ins., Am., Iowa, Polk County bar assns., Order Coif. Contbr. aticles to profl. jours.

BAILEY, JASON SAMUEL, b. Portland, Oreg., Jan. 3, 1915; B.S., U. Oreg., 1937, J.D., 1940. Admitted to Oreg. bar, 1940, Calif. bar, 1946. Asso. firm Platt, Henderson, Warner & Cram, Portland, Oreg., 1940; atty. U.S. Dept. Justice, Washington and Juneau, Alaska, 1941-43, San Francisco and Seattle, 1946-48; asst. JAG, U.S. Army, CBI, 1945-46; atty. Office of Dist. Atty. Multnomah County, Portland, Oreg., 1948-50; various assignments CIA, 1950-70; judge pro-tem Dist. Ct., Portland, Oreg., 1971—. Pub. mem. Columbia-Willamette Air Pollution Authority, Portland, 1971-72. Mem. Oreg., Calif. bar assns., Phi Alpha Delta. Home and office: 9520 SE 14th St Vancouver WA 98664 Tel (206) 892-8737

BAILEY, JOE DEMPSEY, b. Mexico, Mo., Mar. 28, 1943; A.B., Harvard, 1965, LL.B., 1968. Admitted to Oreg. bar, 1968; clk. Oreg. Supreme Ct., Salem, 1968—; mem. firm Schwenn, Bradley &

Batchelor, Hillsboro, Oreg., 1969—. Office: 139 E Lincoln St Hillsboro OR 97123 Tel (503) 648-6677

BAILEY, LANCE RICHARDSON, b. Memphis, Dec. 13, 1940; B.S., West Tex. State U., 1966; J.D., Samford U., 1969. Admitted to N.Mex. bar, 1969; individual practice law, Albuquerque, 1969-70; asst. dist. atty. N.Mex. 7th Jud. Dist., Estancia, 1970-73; asso. firm Chavez, Cowper & Bailey, Socorro, N.Mex., 1973, sr. partner, 1973—; city atty. City of Estancia, City of Mountainair (N.Mex.); spl. prosecutor N.Mex. 7th Jud. Dist.; atty. Socorro Electric Coop. Mem. Am., N.Mex. bar assns., Delta Theta Phi. Tel (505) 835-2511

BAILEY, ROBERT SHORT, b. Bklyn., Oct. 17, 1931; A.B., Wesleyan U., Middletown, Conn., 1953; J.D., U. Chgo., 1956. Admitted to U.S. Dist. Ct. for D.C., 1956, U.S. Supreme Ct. bar, 1960, U.S. Ct. Appeals 7th Circuit bar, 1960, Supreme Ct. Ill. bar, 1965, U.S. Ct. Appeals 9th Circuit bar, 1965; asst. U.S. Dept. Justice, 1956-61; asst. U.S. atty., No. Dist. Ill., 1961-65; partner firm LeFevour & Bailey, Oak Park, Ill., 1965-68; individual practice law, Chgo., 1968—; mem. faculty Nat. Coll. Criminal Def. Lawyers, 1975-76. Mem. Nat. Assn. Criminal Def. Lawyers (legis. chmn. 1976-77). Home: 17 Timber Trail St Streamwood IL 60103 Office: 53 W Jackson Blvd Suite 1220 Chicago IL 60604 Tel (312) 427-6050

BAILEY, SAMUEL, JR., b. Cin., May 13, 1940; A.B., Trinity Coll., Hartford, Conn., 1962; J.D., U. Conn., 1969. Admitted to Conn. bar, 1969; asso. firm Robinson, Robinson & Cole, Hartford, 1969-75, partner, 1975—. Mem. Farmington (Conn.) Town Council, 1971—, chmn., 1975—. Mem. Am., Conn., Harford County bar assns. Editor-in-chief Conn. Law Review, 1968-69. Home: 211 Mountain Spring Rd Farmington CT 06032 Office: 799 Main St Hartford CT 06103 Tel (203) 278-0700

BAILEY, WILLIAM DONALD, JR., b. Newburgh, N.Y., Dec. 12, 1935; A.B., U. Notre Dame, 1956, J.D., 1959. Admitted to Del. bar, 1960; partner firm Bayard, Brill & Handelman, Wilmington, Del., 1960—; parlimentarian, House of Reps., State of Del., 1965-66; rate counsel, Pub. Service Commn., State of Del., 1973—. Mem. Assn. Bar City N.Y., Am., Del. bar assns., N.Y. State Trial Lawyers Assn. Office: PO Box 1271 Wilmington DE 19899 Tel (302) 575-0130

BAILEY, WILLIAM MELVILLE, b. Columbus, Ohio, May 13, 1932; B.S. in Commerce, Washington and Lee U., 1953, J.D., 1955; Admitted to Va. bar, 1955, Ohio bar, 1955, N.Y. State bar, 1961; asso. firm Mudge, Rose, Guthrie & Alexander, N.Y.C., 1959-65; sr. fin. counsel Western Union Corp., N.Y.C., 1966-70; individual practice law, Wilmington, Ohio, 1970—; instr. So. State Coll., Wilmington; sponsor, trustee Pub. Defender Program, Greene and Clinton Counties, 1974—. Chmn. Clinton County Cancer Fund Drive, 1958. Mem. Ohio, Clinton County bar assns., Wilmington C. of C. (pres. 1958). Asso. editor Washington and Lee Law Rev., 1954-55. Home: 1594 Wayne Rd Wilmington OH 45177 Office: 62 E Sugartree St Wilmington OH 45177 Tel (513) 382-4312

BAILEY, WILLIAM RUFUS, b. N.Y.C., Nov. 16, 1916; A.B., Yale, 1939; LL.B., U. Va., 1947. Admitted to N.Y. bar, 1949, Ohio bar, 1951; asso. firm Breed, Abbott & Morgan, N.Y.C., 1948-51; asst. counsel, counsel Armco Steel Corp., Middletown, Ohio, 1951-68, v.p. law, sec., 1968—. Mem. Am., Ohio bar assns. Office: 703 Curtis St Middleton OH 45042 Tel (513) 425-2267

BAILYS, CARL, b. Owatonna, Minn., June 4, 1908; B.Chem.Engring., U. Detroit, 1931; LL.B., Detroit Coll. Law, 1941, J.D., 1968. Admitted to Mich. bar, 1941, U.S. Dist. Ct. for Eastern Dist. Mich. bar, 1941, U.S. Patent bar, 1943, U.S. Ct. Appeals bar for 6th Circuit, 1960; corp. resident counsel, Detroit, 1941-52; individual practice law, Detroit, 1952—. Mem. State Bar Mich., Detroit Bar Assn., Sigma Nu Phi. Office: 19672 Yonka St Detroit MI 48234

BAIN, CECIL WILLIAM, b. San Antonio, June 22, 1943; B.B.A., U. Tex., 1965; J.D., U. Tex., 1968. Admitted to Tex. bar, 1968, U.S. Supreme Ct. bar, 1971, U.S. Ct. Appeals, 5th Circuit bar, 1973; partner firm Cobb, Thurmond Bain & Clark, Bain, Inc., San Antonio, 1974—; instr. San Antonio Jr. Coll., 1974-77. Chmn., bd. dirs. Drug Abuse Central of San Antonio, 1974—. Mem. San Antonio Young Lawyers Assn. (pres. 1974-75), State Bar Tex., San Antonio Bus. and Econ. Soc. (pres. 1973-74), Alamo Area Council of Govts., Commercial Law League, Am. Judicature Soc., Assn. Trial Lawyers Am., Am., San Antonio (sec. treas. 1976—), Fed. bar assns., Tex. Criminal Def. Lawyers Assn., San Antonio Trial Lawyers (dir. 1976-77), Tex. Trial Lawyers Assn., Nat. Assn. Criminal Def. Lawyers. Certified criminal law specialist Tex. Bd. Legal Specialization. Home: 5419 Billington St San Antonio TX 78230 Office: 1665 Frost Bank Tower San Antonio TX 78205 Tel (512) 226-0311

BAIRD, BOYD, C., b. Argo, Ill., Aug. 12, 1926; J.D., Wayne State U., 1949. Admitted to Mich. bar, 1949; individual practice law, Gaylord, Mich., 1950; city atty., Gaylord, 1950; judge Probate and Juvenile Ct. Otsego County (Mich.), Gaylord, 1955—; cons., instr. juvenile ct. seminars of Mich. Mem. Am. Judicature Soc., Am. Bar Assn. Nat. Council Juvenile Ct. Judges, Mich. Probate Judges Assn. (past pres.). Home: Box 397 Gaylord MI 49735 Office: Room 213 City-County Bldg Gaylord MI 49735 Tel (517) 732-5250

BAIRD, JAMES KENNETH, b. Tanta, Egypt, Jan. 10, 1917; A.B., Monmouth Coll., 1937; M.B.A., Northwestern U., 1938, J.D., 1941. Admitted to Ill. bar, 1941, Wis. bar, 1968, Fla. bar, 1975, U.S. Supreme Ct. bar, 1949; atty. solicitor's office U.S. Dept. Labor, Washington, 1941-42; asst. to judge Tax Ct. U.S., Washington, 1941-43; practice law, Chgo., 1946-51; house counsel Turtle Wax Auto Polish, Chgo., 1953-58; mem. firm Baird & Lundquist, Zion, Ill., 1958-67; sr. v.p., gen. counsel, dir. Universal Telephone Inc., Milw., 1967—. Mem. sch. bd., Zion, 1963-64. Mem. Ill., Chgo., Wis., Milw., Fla., Am. bar assns. Article editor Northwestern U. Law Rev. Home: 4617 N Wilshire Rd Milwaukee WI 53211 Office: 231 W Wisconsin Ave Milwaukee WI 53203 Tel (414) 278-7000

BAIRD, JOHN PIERSON, b. St. Louis, Nov. 1, 1925; student U. Ill., 1946-49; LL.B., St. Louis U., 1952. Admitted to Mo. bar, 1952; asso. firm Fordyce, Mayne, Hartman, Renard & Stribling, St. Louis, 1952-57, partner, 1956-57; dir. labor relations and prodn. personnel Ralston Purina Co., St. Louis, 1957-61, sec., 1961-65, sec., gen. counsel, 1965-67, v.p., sec., gen. counsel, 1967—; dir. Asso. Industries Mo., 1965; mem. adv. bd. Southwestern Legal Found.'s Internat. and Comparative Law Center, 1967. Bd. dirs. Family and Children's Service, 1972, Downtown St. Louis, Inc., 1976. Mem. Am., Inter-Am., Mo., St. Louis bar assns., Am. Soc. Corporate Secs., Mo. C. of C. (dir.-at-large 1975). Home: 11 Bellerive Country Club Grounds Saint Louis MO 63141 Office: 835 S 8th St Saint Louis MO 63188 Tel (314) 982-2211

BAIRD, ROBERT SAMUEL, b. Trimble, Ala., May 5, 1896; A.B., U. Ala., 1924; J.D., U. Chgo., 1929. Admitted to Mich. bar, 1937; city atty. City of Cheboygan (Mich.), 1943-45; judge Cheboygan County Probate Ct., 1945-65; individual practice law, Cheboygan, 1965—. Mem. Mich. Bar Assn. Home: 808 W Lincoln Ave Cheboygan MI 49721 Office: 234 S Main St Cheboygan MI 49721 Tel (616) 627-2410

BAIRD, VICTOR MCEVER, b. Athens, Ga., Dec. 22, 1943; B.S., U. Ga., 1965, J.D., 1974. Admitted to Ga. bar, 1974; asso. firm Fulcher, Hagler, Harper & Reed, Augusta, Ga., 1974-76; asst. atty. gen. State of Ga., 1976—. Mem. Am. Bar Assn. Office: 835 B Mentelle Dr NE Atlanta GA 30308

BAIRSTOW, RICHARD RAYMOND, b. Waukegan, Ill., Sept. 26, 1917; A.B., U. Ill., 1939, J.D., 1947; student Nat. U. Mex., 1937, George Washington U. Law Sch., 1939-41. Admitted to Ill. bar, 1947, U.S. Supreme Ct. bar, 1963; U.S. Ct. Mil. Appeals bar, 1963, U.S. Dist. Ct. bar, 1964; asso. firm Hall, Meyer & Carey, Waukegan, Ill., 1947-49; asst. states atty. Lake County, Ill., 1949-53; partner firm McClory & Bairstow, Waukegan, 1953-60, McClory, Bairstow, Lonchar & Nordigian, Waukegan, 1960-66, Richard R. Bairstow, and Assos., Waukegan, 1966—; hearing referee State Ill. Dept. Revenue, 1953—; dist. atty. Foxlake Fire Protection Dist., 1948—. Mem., pres. adv. bd. Salvation Army of Waukegan and Lake County, Ill., 1954-66; bd. dirs. ARC of Waukegan and Lake County, Ill., 1947-63. Mem. Lake County, Ill., Am. bar assns., Phi Alpha Delta. Home: 2122 Ash St Waukegan IL 60085 Office: 33 N County St Waukegan IL 60085 Tel (312) 623-0112

BAISDEN, TYSON EDWARD, JR., b. Columbus, Ga., Nov. 9, 1927; student aero. engring., Auburn U., 1944-46; student engring. Duke, 1945-46; LL.B., Emory U., 1949. Admitted to Ga. bar, 1949, U.S. Dist. Ct. Middle Dist. Ga. bar, 1949, No. Dist. Ga. bar, 1961; individual practice law, Columbus, Ga., 1949-51, also Atlanta, Decatur, Ga.; zone dep. collector IRS, 1951; practice ins. claims adjusting; judge pro tem City of College Park (Ga.), 1974—. Vol. parole officer Stone Mountain Correctional Inst. Mem. Atlanta Bar Assn., Ga. Trial Lawyers Assn. (v.p.). Home: 4055 Hilltop Dr College Park GA 30337 Office: 1711 Candler Rd Decatur GA 30032 Tel (404) 284-6624

BAKER, BARTON, b. Webster, N.Y., Jan. 9, 1901; LL.B., Cornell U., 1922, D.C.L. cum laude, 1926; Ph.D., Chgo. Law Sch., 1928. Admitted to N.Y. bar, 1923, U.S. Dist. Ct. bar, 1925, U.S. Supreme Ct. bar, 1926; asst. Legal Aid Soc., Rochester, N.Y., 1921; asso. MacFarlane & Harris, Rochester, 1922-26; partner firm Baker & Carver, Rochester, 1929—. Former council chief, lone scout div. Boy Scouts Am., N.Y., N.J.; dir. Internat. Bell Orch., 1952—; former pres. Allied Forces, Inc., also Drug and Alcohol Council; past chmn. Truth for Youth, Inc.; founder Barton Baker Youth Edn. Center, 1973. Recipient award of achievement Internat. Assn. Fairs and Expositions, 1977. Author: Constitutional Law: Legislative Tendencies in Modern Divorce Law; columnist Damascus News. Home: 100 Brookwood Rd Rochester NY 14610 Office: 1030 Times Square Bldg Rochester NY 14614

BAKER, CHARLES WAYNE, b. Boonville, Mo., Nov. 29, 1940; B.A. U. Mo., Columbia, 1962, J.D., 1965. Admitted to Mo. bar, 1965, Ark. bar, 1968; asso. firm Rogers, Field & Gentry, Kansas City, Mo., 1965-67; partner firm Moses, McClellan, Arnold, Owen & McDermott, Little Rock, 1968-72; prin. firm Baker & Probst, Little Rock, 1973—; bankruptcy judge Eastern, Western Dist. Ark., Little Rock, 1973—. Mem. Am., Ark., Pulaski County bar assns., Am., Ark. trial lawyers' assn., Nat. Conf. Bankruptcy Judges. Contbr. articles to legal jours. Home: 49 Sherrill Heights Little Rock AR 72202 Office: 115 E Capitol Ave Little Rock AR 72201 Tel (501) 375-2388

BAKER, DAVID LLOYD, b. Louisville, Nov. 23, 1940; B.A., U. Louisville, 1964, J.D., 1969. Admitted to Ky. bar, 1970; legal affairs officer U. Louisville, 1972-73, dir. pub. relations, 1973-76, univ. counsel, 1976—. Bd. dirs. Louisville Sch. Art, 1974-75. Mem. Nat. Assn. Coll. and Univ. Attys., Louisville, Ky., Am. bar assns., Council for Advancement and Support Edn., AAUP. Home: 1837 Lauderdale Rd Louisville KY 40205 Office: 2301 S 3rd St Louisville KY 40208 Tel (502) 588-5417

BAKER, DONALD IRWIN, b. Englewood, N.J., June 4, 1934; B.A., Woodrow Wilson Sch. Pub. and Internat. Affairs, Princeton, 1957; B.A. in Law, U. Cambridge (Eng.), 1959; LL.B., Harvard, 1961. Admitted to Mass. bar, 1963, D.C. bar, 1964; asso. firm Slaughter and May, London, 1961-62, firm Nutter, McClennen & Fish, Boston, 1963-66; trial atty., sect. chief, dir. policy planning Dept. of Justice, Washington, 1966-75, asst. atty. gen. antitrust div., 1976-77; vis. prof. law Cornell U., 1975-76, prof. law on leave, 1976-77, prof. law, 1977—; spl. counsel firm Cadwalader, Wickersham & Taft, N.Y.C., Washington and London, 1975-76; counsel firm Jones Day Reavis & Pogue, Cleve., Washington and Los Angeles, 1977—. Mem. Fed., Am. bar assns. Recipient Distinguished Service award U.S. Atty. Gen., 1972; contbr. articles to legal jours. Home: Wilkins Rd RD 3 Ithaca NY 14850 Office: Cornell Law Sch Ithaca NY 14850 Tel (607) 256-3469

BAKER, DONALD PAUL, b. Los Angeles, Oct. 27, 1947; B.A., U. Redlands, 1970; J.D., U. Calif., Los Angeles, 1973. Admitted to Calif. bar, 1973; asso. firm Latham & Watkins, Los Angeles, 1973—. Mem. Los Angeles County Bar Assn. (sec.-treas. barristers sect.), Order of Coif. Asso. editor U. Calif. Los Angeles Law Rev. Office: 555 S Flower St Los Angeles CA 90071 Tel (213) 485-1234

BAKER, EMILY VAUGHN, b. New Orleans, Aug. 16, 1930; student Tulane U., U. So. Miss.; LL.B. cum laude, Jackson Sch. Law, 1969, J.D. cum laude, 1970; grad. Nat. Coll. Juvenile Ct. Judges U. Nev. 1975, Nat. Coll. State Judiciary, 1975. Admitted to Miss. bar, 1969, Fed. Ct. bar, 1970; practiced in Jackson, Hinds County and Pascagoula, Miss., 1969-74; pub. defender Jackson County, Pascagoula, 1973-74; judge Jackson County Youth Ct., 1975—; tchr. Miss. Bar Rev., Jackson, 1973-74; mem. Miss. Criminal Justice Standards Commn.; mem. judges adv. com. Miss. Dept. Pub. Welfare; mem. regional four council Law Enforcement Assistance Div.; mem. adv. com. for Juvenile Delinquency and Prevention Act, 1975—. Pres. Colmer Jr. High PTA, Pascagoula, 1972-73; mem. Pascagoula City Council, 1972-73; mem. adv. bd. Miss. Lung Assn., 1972-75. Fellow Miss. Bar Found.; mem. Jackson County, Miss., Am. bar assns., Nat. Council Juvenile Ct. Judges, Nat. Juvenile Ct. Services Assn., Am. Judicature Soc., Miss. Trial Lawyers, Nat. Assn. Trial Lawyers, Nat. Assn. Women Lawyers, Miss. Conf. Judges (sec., chmn. county ct. judges), Miss. Council Juvenile Judges (pres.), Tulane U., Miss. Coll. alumni assns., League of Women Voters. Named Woman of Achievement, Riverside Bus. and Profl. Women's Club of Jackson, 1972, Pascagoula Bus. and Profl. Women's Club, 1973, Miss. Fedn. of Bus. and Profl. Womens Club, 1974; hon. staff col. to Miss. Gov. Office: POB 1734 Pascagoula MS 39567 Tel (601) 762-7370

BAKER, FRANK EDMOND, b. Olympia, Wash., Feb. 28, 1921; B.S. in Polit. Sci. and Gov., U. Oreg., 1943; LL.B., U. Wash., 1948; grad. Nat. Coll. State Trial Judges. Admitted to Wash. bar, 1948; partner firm Parr & Baker, Olympia, 1948-69; judge Thurston County, (Wash.) Superior Ct., 1969—. Mem. Thurston-Mason County (pres. 1958-59), Wash. State, Am. bar assns., Am. Judges Assn., Wash. State Superior Ct. Judges Assn. Author: Our Jury System: A Bastion Against Prejudice, Or A Whirlpool Toward Oblivion?, 1975. Office: Superior Ct Thurston County Courthouse Olympia WA 98501 Tel (206) 753-8150

BAKER, GARY HUGH, b. Broken Arrow, Okla., Nov. 18, 1947; B.A., U. Okla., 1970; J.D., U. Chgo., 1973. Admitted to Okla. bar, 1973; asso. firm Conner, Winters, Ballaine, Barry & McGowen, Tulsa, 1973—. Mem. Okla., Tulsa County, Am. bar assns., Phi Beta Kappa, Omicron Delta Kappa. Home: 2409 S Saint Louis St Tulsa OK 74114 Office: 2400 1st Nat Tower Tulsa OK 74103 Tel (918) 586-5689

BAKER, GEORGE WILLIAM, b. Balt., Jan. 15, 1922; A.B., Loyola Coll., 1943; J.D. cum laude, U. Md., 1949. Admitted to Md. bar, 1948; practiced law, Balt., 1948—; partner firm Allen, Burch and Baker, 1963-74; sr. partner firm Baker and Baker, 1974—; judge Orphans (Probate) Ct., City of Balt., 1961-62, dep. city solicitor, 1962-63, spl. tax trial counsel, Balt., 1963-65. Dir. numerous corps.; lectr. Am. Inst. Banking, 1954-61. Mem. Balt. Washington Internat. Airport Bd., 1960-66, Balt. Anne Arendel County Airport Zoning Bd., 1961-65; pres. Golfers' Charitable Assn., 1976—. Mem. Bar Assn. Balt. City, Am., Md. bar assns., Am. Judicature Soc., Delta Theta Phi. Home: 5600 N Charles St Baltimore MD 21210 Office: 10 Charles Plaza Suite 202 Baltimore MD 21201 Tel (301) 539-2840

BAKER, H(ARRY) PAUL, b. Bristol, Pa., June 27, 1927; J.D., U. Miami, Coral Gables, Fla., 1952; postgrad Northwestern U., 1958. Admitted to Fla. bar, 1952; individual practice law, Miami, Fla., 1952-56; asst. state atty. 11th Jud. Circuit Fla., 1957-67; judge Dade County (Fla.) Criminal Ct. of Record, 1967-73, Fla. 11th Jud. Circuit Ct., 1973—. Mem. Am. Bar Assn., Fla. Bar, Am. Judicature Soc., Phi Alpha Delta. Home: 7725 SW 171 Terr Miami FL 33157 Office: 1351 NW 12th St Miami FL 33125 Tel (305) 547-7696

BAKER, JOHN WILLIAM, b. San Francisco, Oct. 13, 1914; student, U. Calif., Los Angeles, 1931-33; LL.B., U. So. Calif., 1936, J.D., 1939. Admitted to Calif. bar, 1940, since practiced in Los Angeles. Mem. Internat. Assn. Ins. Def. Counsel, Am. Bd. Trial Advs. Home: 10450 Bainbridge Ave Los Angeles CA 90024 Office: 700 S Flower St suite 902 Los Angeles CA 90017 Tel (213) 626-2676

BAKER, KENNETH LEE, b. Mt. Pleasant, Pa., Jan. 21, 1947; B.A., Washington and Jefferson Coll., 1968; J.D., U. Pitts., 1971. Admitted to Pa. bar, 1971; asso. firm Peacock, Keller, Yohe, Day & Ecker, Washington, Pa., 1971-72, 75—; served with JAGC, U.S. Army, 1972-75. Bd. dirs. Family Service of Washington (Pa.), 1975—; round table commr. Boy Scouts Am., 1976—; chmn. registration dr. Washington County Republican Com., 1976—. Mem. Am., Pa., Washington County bar assns. Home: 215 N Wade Ave Washington PA 15301 Office: 68-70 E Beau St Washington PA 15301 Tel (412) 222-4520

BAKER, LESTER G., b. Dearborn County, Ind., July 11, 1914; LL.B., Ind. U., 1937. Admitted to Ind. bar, 1937; pros. atty. 7th Jud. Circuit Ind., 1941-43, 47-49, judge, 1949—. Mem. Ind. Bar Assn., Ind. Judges Assn. (pres. 1972-74). Home: Outer Dr Aurora IN 47001 Office: Court House Lawrenceburg IN 47025 Tel (812) 537-0686

BAKER, LLOYD HARVEY, b. Bklyn., Sept. 17, 1927; student Colgate U.; LL.B., N.Y. U., 1951. Admitted to N.Y. State bar, 1951; asso. firm Milligan, Reilly, Lake & Schneider, Babylon, N.Y., 1952-53; staff Fgn. Claims Commn., Washington, 1954; spl. atty. Windfall investigation FHA, Washington, 1955; asst. U.S. atty. for Eastern Dist. N.Y., 1955-59; individual practice law, Bayshore and Islip, N.Y., 1959-67; atty. Suffolk County (N.Y.) Legal Aid Soc., 1967-69; dep. chief civil div. U.S. Atty.'s Office for Eastern Dist. N.Y., 1969-74; asst. counsel met. region Penn Central R.R. and Conrail, N.Y.C., 1975—. Mem. Suffolk County Republican Com., 1963-71. Mem. Suffolk County Bar Assn. (chmn. fed. ct. com.). Home: 5 Mulberry Rd Islip NY 11751 Office: Consol Rail Corp 466 Lexington Ave New York City NY 10017 Tel (212) 340-3015

BAKER, M. DAVID, b. N.Y.C., May 29, 1936; B.A., Columbia, 1957; LL.B., N.Y.U., 1960, LL.M. in Criminal Law, 1965. Admitted to N.Y. bar, 1961, U.S. Supreme Ct. bar, 1967, Pa. bar, 1974; individual practice law, Bklyn., 1961—; arbitrator Civil Ct. City N.Y., 1977—. Vice pres. Hemlock Farms Community Assn., Hawley, Pa., 1972-75. Mem. N.Y. State Bar Assn., Immigration and Nationality Bar Assn. (v.p. N.Y. chpt. 1969-70), Kings County (N.Y.) Criminal Bar Assn. (dir. 1963-67). Home: 10 Cardinal Dr East Hills NY 11576 Office: 66 Court St Brooklyn NY 11201 Tel (212) 624-7956

BAKER, RICHARD CLAIRE, b. Holdrege, Nebr., Oct. 11, 1930; B.B.A., U. Tex., 1957; LL.D., U. Tex., 1958. Admitted to Tex. bar, 1957; asso. counsel Tex. Gas Corp., Houston, 1958-59; partner firm Johnson & Baker, 1959-67, Brown, Maroney, Rose, Baker & Barber, Austin, Tex., 1967—; dir. N. Austin State Bank, 1970—, Farmers State Bank, Round Rock, Tex., 1970—, Austin Industries, Inc., 1974—. Mem. Travis County (Tex.) Bar Assn. Office: Brown Maroney Rose Baker Barber 1300 American Bank Tower Austin TX 78701 Tel (512) 472-5456

BAKER, RICHARD SOUTHWORTH, b. Lansing, Mich., Dec. 18, 1929; student DePauw U., 1947-49; A.B. cum laude, Harvard U., 1951; J.D., U. Mich., 1954. Admitted to Ohio bar, 1957, Fed. bar, 1958, U.S. Supreme Ct. bar, 1971, U.S. Tax Ct. bar, 1960; mem. firm Fuller, Henry, Hodge & Snyder, Toledo, 1956-61, partner, 1961—. Mem. Nat. Com. Mich. Law Sch. Fund, 1967—; bd. dirs. Assn. Harvard Alumni, 1970-73. Mem. Am., Ohio, Toledo bar assns., Phi Delta Phi. Mem. code and rule revision task force Indsl. Commn. Ohio, and Bur. Workmen's Compensation, 1975-76. Home: 2819 Falmouth Rd Toledo OH 43615 Office: 300 Madison Ave Toledo OH 43604 Tel (419) 255-8220

BAKER, ROBERT CLIFFORD, b. Madison, S.D., May 21, 1924; B.A., U. Minn., 1948; J.D., George Washington U., 1952. Admitted to D.C. bar, 1952, Minn. bar, 1955; atty. div. army patents JAGC, Pentagon, 1952-53; asso. firm Carpenter, Abbott, Coulter & Kinney, St. Paul, 1954-64, partner, 1965-67; individual practice law, St. Paul, 1967—. Mem. St. Paul Mental Health Study Com., 1967-68; del. Minn. Republican Conv., 1972. Mem. Am., Minn. bar assns., Am., Minn. patent law assns., St. Paul C. of C., Delta Theta Phi. Home: 80 Birnamwood Dr Burnsville MN 55337 Office: 1395 Northwestern Nat Bank Bldg St Paul MN 55101 Tel (612) 224-5796

BAKER, ROBERT FLOWERS, b. Durham, N.C., Dec. 15, 1935; B.A., Davidson Coll., 1958; J.D., Duke, 1961. Admitted to N.C. bar, 1961; asso. firm Spears, Spears & Barnes, Durham, 1963-66; partner firm Spears, Barnes, Baker & Boles, Durham, 1967—. Div. chmn. Durham United Fund, 1965. Mem. Durham C. of C. (chmn. crime control task force 1976—), Am., N.C. (chmn. young lawyers sect. 1971-72, chmn. com. on practical tng. 1972—, gov. 1974—), Durham County bar assns. Home: 3112 Cornwall Rd Durham NC 27707 Office: 433 W Main St Durham NC 27702 Tel (919) 682-5721

BAKER, ROBERT J., b. N.Y.C., Aug. 26, 1930; B.B.A., Coll. City N.Y., 1955; LL.B., Bklyn. Law Sch., 1959. Admitted to D.C. bar, 1970, Nebr. bar, 1970, N.J. bar, 1971; atty. Merck & Co., Inc., Rahway, N.J., 1970-73. sr. atty., 1973-74, dir. labor relations, 1974—. Mem. Am., N.J. bar assns. Office: Merck & Co Inc PO Box 2000 Rahway NJ 07065 Tel (201) 574-6431

BAKER, ROBERT LISLE, b. Louisville, Aug., 2, 1942; A.B., Williams Coll., 1964; LL.B., Harvard, 1968. Admitted to Mass. bar, 1968; asso. firm Hill and Barlow, Boston, 1968-73; asso. prof. law Suffolk U. Law Sch., 1973—; Mem. Am., Mass., Boston (chmn. environment com. 1975—) bar assns. Home: 137 Suffolk Rd Chestnut Hill MA 02167 Office: 41 Temple St Boston MA 02167 Tel (617) 723-4700

BAKER, ROBERT LYN, b. Murfreesboro, Tenn., Sept. 11, 1944; B.S. cum laude, David Lipscomb Coll., 1965; J.D., Vanderbilt U., 1968. Admitted to Tenn. bar, 1968; asso. firm Gracey, Buck, Maddin & Cowan, Nashville, 1968-73; partner firm Buck, Baker & Baker, Nashville, 1973—. Mem. Tenn., Nashville bar assns., Motor Carrier Lawyers Assn. Office: United American Bank Bldg Nashville TN 37219 Tel (615) 255-6576

BAKER, SHELDON S., b. St. Paul, Dec. 4, 1936; B.A., Rutgers U., 1958; J.D., Stanford, 1961. Admitted to Calif. bar, 1962, U.S. Dist. Ct. Bar, 1962, U.S. Supreme Ct. bar 1971; individual practice law, Los Angeles 1962-65; partner firm Halstead & Baker, 1965—. Mem. West Glendale (Calif.) Kiwanis Club (pres. 1969-70), also dir., Glendale Speech & Hearing Found., 1964-68; mem. exec. bd. Verdugo Hills council Boy Scouts Am., 1965—; mem. Glendale Bd. Edn., (pres. 1967-68, 72-73); del. assembly, dir. Calif. Sch. Bd. Assn., 1969—; trustee, dir. Los Angeles County Sch. Trustees Assn., 1972—, pres., 1976—; dir. Glendale Regional Arts Council, 1974-75; mem. Brand Park Property Owners Assn. (chmn. 1971), Glendale Community Coll. Bd. Edn. (pres. 1967-68, 71-72, 75-76), Rutgers Univ. Alumni Club So. Calif. (pres. 1969-71). Mem. Am., Calif., Los Angeles County, Glendale bar assns., Order of Coif, Phi Beta Kappa, Delta Upsilon. Named One of 5 Outstanding Young Men of Calif., Calif. Jaycees, 1964; recipient Silver Beaver award Boy Scouts Am., 1972; certified specialist in taxation law. Contbr. articles in field to law jours. Office: 640 W Sixth St Los Angeles CA 90017 Tel (213) 628-7341

BAKER, WADE FRANKLIN, b. Carbondale, Ill., Dec. 30, 1919; B.E., So. Ill. U., Carbondale, 1941; LL.B., Lincoln Coll. Law, Springfield, Ill., 1950. Admitted to Ill. bar, 1950, Mo. bar, 1957; asst. sec., counsel Ill. State Bar, Assn., Springfield, 1946-57; exec. dir. Mo. Bar, Jefferson City, 1957—. Trustee Meml. Hosp., Jefferson City, 1970, pres., 1971-72. Mem. Am., Cole County (Mo.) bar assns., Mo. Bar (Spl. Bicentennial award 1976), Am. Judicature Soc., Phi Alpha Delta (William H. Pitman Hon. award U. Mo. Lawson chpt. 1972). Recipient Non-Alumni award U. Mo., 1975. Home: 2505 Orchard Ln Jefferson City MO 65101 Office: 326 Monroe St Jefferson City MO 65101 Tel (314) 635-4128

BAKER, WALLACE RUSSELL, b. Chgo., June 11, 1927; A.B., Harvard U., 1948, LL.B., 1952; J.D., U. Libre de Brussels, 1962; Licencie, U. Paris Law Sch., 1972. Admitted to Ill. bar, 1952; partner firm Baker & McKenzie, Chgo., 1953-59, Brussels, 1959-63, Paris, 1963—. Contbr. articles to legal jours. Office: 94 rue du Faubourg Saint Honore Paris France 75008 Tel 265-20-14

BAKER, WILLIAM DUNLAP, b. St. Louis, June 17, 1932; A.B., Colgate U., 1954; J.D., U. Calif., Berkeley, 1960. Admitted to Calif. bar, 1961, Ariz. bar, 1961, U.S. Supreme Ct. bar, 1969; clk. firm Stokes & Moring, Coolidge, Ariz., 1960; spl. investigator Office of Pinal County Atty., Florence, Ariz., 1960-61; dep. county atty., 1961-63; partner firm McBryde, Vincent, Brumage & Baker, Florence, 1961-63; asso. firm Rawlins, Ellis, Burrus & Kiewit, Phoenix, 1963-65, partner, 1965—. Mem. Ariz. Environmental Planning Commn., 1974-75; chmn. Maricopa County (Ariz.) Republican Com., 1969-72, legal counsel Rep. State Com., Phoenix, 1964-69; trustee St. Lukes Hosp. Med. Center, 1976—; bd. dirs. Maricopa County chpt. Nat. Found. March Dimes, 1970-75. Mem. Am., Calif., Ariz., Maricopa County bar assns. Home: 5309 N 34th St Phoenix AZ 85018 Office: 2300 Valley Bank Center 201 N Central St Phoenix AZ 85073 Tel (602) 257-5700

BAKER, WILLIAM PARR, b. Balt., Sept. 5, 1946; B.A., St. Francis Coll., Pa., 1968; J.D., U. Md., 1971. Admitted to Md. bar, 1972; partner firm Baker & Baker, and predecessors, Balt., 1972—; law clk. to asso. judge Md. Ct. Appeals, 1971-72. Mem. Am., Md. bar assns., Bar Assn. Balt. City. Home: 110 W 39th St Apt 1611 Baltimore MD 21210 Office: 10 Charles Plaza Suite 202 Baltimore MD 21201 Tel (301) 539-2840

BAKES, ROBERT ELDON, b. Boise, Idaho, Jan. 11, 1932; B.A., U. Idaho, 1954, LL.B., 1956. Admitted to Idaho bar, 1956, U.S. Circuit Ct. of Appeals bar, 1963; instr. law U. Ill., Champaign, 1956-57; legal counsel Idaho State Tax Collector, Boise, 1959-61; asst. U.S. atty., Boise, 1961-66; sr. partner firm Bakes, Ward & Bates, Boise, 1969-71; justice Idaho Supreme Ct., Boise 1971—; dir. continuing legal edn. program Idaho State Bar; chmn. rules com., chmn. jud. edn. com. Idaho Supreme Ct.; mem. faculty appellate judges seminars N.Y.U. Sch. Law. Mem. Am. Bar Assn. (exec. bd. appellate judges conf., faculty appellate judges seminars). Office: 451 W State St Boise ID 83720 Tel (208) 384-3288

BALABAN, HENRY L., b. Syracuse, N.Y., Nov. 8, 1902; J.D., De Paul U., 1920. Admitted to Ill. bar, 1923, Fla. bar, 1951; asst. U.S. Atty., Chgo., 1928-31; judge Municipal Ct., Miami, Fla., 1955-57; commr., vice mayor of Miami, 1955-57; judge Circuit Ct. Dade County (Fla.), 1962—. Mem. Ill., Fla. bar assns. Home: 1237 N Venetian Way Miami FL 33139 Office: 73 W Flagler St Miami FL 33130 Tel (305) 579-5421

BALANOFF, GILBERT LANCE, lawyer; b. Arlington, Mass., Jan. 4, 1947; B.A., Ithaca Coll., 1968; J.D., State U. N.Y., Buffalo, 1972. Admitted to N.Y. bar, 1973, Fed. Bar N.Y., 1975. Trial atty., investigator organized crime activities Nassau County (N.Y.) Dist. Atty.'s Office, 1972-76, asst. dist. atty., 1973-76; partner firm Roth & Balanoff, Mineola, N.Y., 1976—. Mem. Lawrence-Cedarhurst Republican Club, 1972—. Mem. N.Y. State, Nassau County bar assns., Former Asst. Dist. Atty's. Assn. Nassau County. Home: 106 Alhambra Dr Oceanside NY 11572 Office: 194 Old Country Rd Mineola NY 11501

BALBACH, STANLEY BYRON, b. Normal, Ill., Dec. 26, 1919; B.S., U. Ill., 1940, LL.B., 1942. Admitted to Ill. bar, 1942, U.S. Supreme Ct. bar, 1950; practiced law, Hoopeston, Ill., 1945-48, Urbana, Ill., 1948—; mem. firm Webber, Balbach & Thies, Urbana, 1948—; pres., chmn. bd. Attys.' Title Guaranty Fund, Inc. of Ill., 1964-72, now dir.; pres. Nat. Attys.' Title Assurance Fund, Inc., 1971—. Chancellor, Central Ill. Conf., United Methodist Ch. Fellow Am. Coll. Probate Counsel (Ill. chmn.), Am. Bar Found.; mem. Am. (chmn. jr. bar conf. 1955, mem. spl. com. membership 1955, mem. ho. dels. 1955, 61, mem. spl. com. lawyers' title guaranty funds 1961, chmn. com. 1962-69, mem. council legal econs. sect., chmn. conveyancing com. real property, probate and trust law sect., vice chmn. com. gen. practice sect.), Ill. (chmn. younger mems. sect. 1946, mem. bar econs. com. 1962), Champaign County, Chgo. bar assns., 7th Fed. Circuit Bar Assn., Am. Judicature Soc. (dir., exec. com. 1961-63), Phi Delta Phi. Contbr. articles to legal jours. Home: 1005 S Douglas St Urbana IL 61801 Office: Box 189 Urbana IL 61801 Tel (217) 367-1126

BALD, LEROY, b. Balt., Nov. 8, 1918; B.A., Colgate U., 1942; LL.B., U. Md., 1949, J.D., 1949. Admitted to Md. bar, 1949; asso. firm Levy, Byrnes & Gordon, Balt., 1948-52; partner firms Childs and Bald, Annapolis, Md., 1952-65, Bald, Smith & Lucke, Annapolis, 1965-76, Bald & Hale, Annapolis, 1976—. Vestryman St. Martin's-in-the-Field Episcopal Ch., Severna Park, Md., 1970-74; mem. com. of mgmt. YMCA, Annapolis, 1966-68. Mem. Am., Md. State, Anne Arundel County (Md.) (pres. 1965-66) bar assns., alumni assns. Colgate U., U. Md. Decorated Bronze Star. Home: 1137 Asquith Dr Arnold MD 21012 Office: POB 947 Annapolis MD 21404 Tel (301) 267-9300

BALDINGER, MILTON IRVING, b. Olyphant, Pa., June 29, 1911; B.A. with 1st honors, Pa. State U., 1933; LL.B., U. Pitts., 1936; LL.M., Georgetown U., 1939, S.J.D., 1941. Admitted to Pa. bar, 1936, D.C. bar, 1937, U.S. Supreme Ct. bar, 1940; atty. Fed. Home Loan Bank Bd., Washington, 1937-38; asst. counsel REA, Washington, 1938-40; prof. law Nat. U. (later merged with George Washington U.), 1940-51; individual practice law, Washington, 1940—; adviser nat. hdqrs. SSS, 1943; lectr. JAG Sch., U.S. Army, 1943-45. Chmn. Met. Washington chpt. Nat. Found., 1966-70. Mem. Am. Law Inst., Am., D.C. bar assns., Am. Judicature Soc., Order of Coif, Tau Epsilon Rho, Delta Sigma Rho, Phi Kappa Phi. Author: The General Welfare Clause, 1939; Constitutionality and Other Phases of Selective Service, 1941; Cases and Materials On Federal Income Taxation, 1947; author Tax Chats column Washington Law Reporter, 1961—; editor in chief U. Pitts. Law Rev., 1935-36, D.C. Bar Jour, 1959-66. Home: 4536 Linnean Ave NW Washington DC 20008 Office: 608 13th St NW Washington DC 20005 Tel (202) 347-9463

BALDRIDGE, GEORGE CROCKER, b. Webb City, Mo., Apr. 20, 1929; B.S. in Bus. Administrn., Kent State U., 1950; LL.B., U. Okla., 1957. Admitted to Okla. bar, 1957, Mo. bar, 1957, U.S. Supreme Ct. bar, 1964; individual practice law, Joplin, Mo., 1957—; pros. atty. Jasper County (Mo.), 1965-66; city atty. Carterville (Mo.), 1958-62; judge magistrate ct. Jasper County, 1962; city atty. Joplin, 1970—. Mem. Jasper County, Mo. (sec., treas. 1962), Okla. bar assns., Mo. Bar. Home: 1300 E 15th St Joplin MO 64801 Office: 1300 E 15th St Box 426 Joplin MO 64801 Tel (417) 623-4533

BALDRIDGE, WILLIAM KARNES, b. Barltett, Tex., Aug. 13, 1908; student N. Tex. State U., 1933-36; LL.B., So. Meth. U., 1942. Admitted to Tex. bar, 1940; asst. county atty. Denton County (Tex.), 1941-45, county atty., 1945-51; dist. atty. Denton County Ct., 1945-51; judge Denton County Ct., 1957-69, Denton County Ct. at Law, 1969-71; partner firm Coleman, Baldridge & Whitlock, Denton, 1971—; lectr. police sci. Cooke County Coll., 1971-75. Chmn. bd. 1st Christian Ch., Denton, 1958-61, 69-72, tchr. Sunday sch., 1942—, elder, 1942—. Mem. Tex., Denton County (pres. 1944) bar assns., ARC (hon. life), 4-H Clubs (hon life). Named Outstanding Ch. Mem. 1st Christian Ch., 1959; recipient Outstanding County Judge award Denton County Bar Assn., 1970. Home: 2015 Locksley Ln Denton TX 76201 Office: 326 McKinney St Denton TX 76201 Tel (817) 387-7411

BALDWIN, EDWIN STEEDMAN, b. St. Louis, May 5, 1932; A.B., Princeton, 1954; LL.B., Harvard, 1957. Admitted to Mo. bar, 1957; asso. firm Armstrong, Teasdale, Kramer & Vaughan, St. Louis, 1957—. Mem. Am., Mo., St. Louis bar assns. Home: 1 Dromara Rd St Louis MO 63124 Office: 611 Olive St St Louis MO 63101 Tel (314) 621-5070

BALDWIN, JOHN ARTHUR, b. Seattle, Dec. 22, 1943; B.S. in Fin., Fla. State U., 1966; J.D., Cumberland Sch. Law, Birmingham, Ala., 1969. Admitted to Fla. bar, 1969; mem. firm Baldwin & Dikeou, Fern Park, Fla., 1969-71; individual practice law, Fern Park, 1971—; asst. county solicitor Brevard County (Fla.). Mem. Seminole County (Fla.) Bar Assn. (pres. 1976). Office: 500 Hwy 17-92 Fern Park FL 32730 Tel (305) 834-1424

BALDWIN, RAY DOUGLAS, b. Laurel, Miss., Dec. 1, 1937; B.A. in Polit. Sci., U. Miss., 1959, LL.B., 1962, J.D., 1962, LL.M., 1970. Admitted to Miss. bar, 1962, Ky. bar, 1973; spl. agt. FBI, 1962-63; coll. prof., 1968-73; individual practice law, Miss., 1963-68, Ky., 1973—. Mem. Miss., Ky. bars, Am. Bar Assn. Home: 303 N 3d St Williamsburg KY 40769 Office: 102 53d St Williamsburg KY 40769 Tel (606) 549-0333

BALES, JERALD KEITH, b. Newton, Iowa, July 13, 1926; A.B., U. Kans., 1950, LL.B., 1951. Admitted to Mo. bar, 1951, Kans. bar, 1951; practiced in Kansas City, Mo., 1951-55; trust officer Union Nat. Bank, Kansas City, Mo., 1955-60; atty. Bus. Men's Assurance Co., Kansas City, 1960-63, counsel, 1963-66, asso. gen. counsel, 1966-67, v.p., asso. gen. counsel, 1967-71, v.p., gen. counsel, 1972-76, exec. v.p. and gen. counsel, 1977—, dir., 1970—, mem. exec. com., 1972-77; police judge City of Mission (Kans.), 1958-61. Mem. Mission City Council, 1955-58; bd. dirs. Greater Kansas City YMCA, Village Presbyterian Ch., Shawnee Mission. Mem. Am., Mo. bar assns., Lawyers Assn. Kansas City, Assn. Life Ins. Counsel, Am. Council Life Ins. (Mo. v.p. 1965-67, 76-77, sec. legal sect. 1975-76, chmn. 1976-77), Mo. C. of C., Phi Delta Phi, Delta Upsilon. C.L.U. Home: 5328 Falmouth St Shawnee Mission KS 66205 Office: 1464 BMA Tower 700 Karnes Blvd Kansas City MO 64108 Tel (816) 753-8000

BALES, SARA JOAN, b. Sioux Falls, S.D., Jan. 23, 1945; A.B. summa cum laude, Marquette U., 1967; J.D., U. Chgo., 1970. Admitted to Wis. bar, 1970, since practiced in Milw.; staff atty. Freedom Through Equality, Inc., 1970-71; partner firm Greenberg, Karp, Heitzman & Edhlund, 1971-72, Edhlund & Bales, 1972—; instr. modernization processes concentration, U. Wis. Green Bay, 1976, enrichment program Alverno Coll., 1973—. Mem. State Bar Wis., Am., Milw. Jr. bar assns., Lawyers Assn. for Women (Milw.), Wis. Civil Liberties Union, ACLU, NOW, YWCA, Women's Equity Action League, Delta Sigma Rho, Tau Kappa Alpha, Pi Gamma Mu, Phi Alpha Theta. Office: 536 W Wisconsin Ave Milwaukee WI 53203 Tel (414) 273-1040

BALEY, JAMES MAJOR, JR., b. Greensboro, N.C., Jan. 23, 1912; A.B., U. N.C., 1932, LL.B., 1933. Admitted to N.C. bar, 1933; mem. firm Roberts & Baley, Marshall, N.C., 1933-42, 1946-53; mem. firm Parker, McGuire & Baley, Asheville, N.C., 1961-68; mem. firm McGuire, Baley & Wood, Asheville, 1968-73; U.S. Atty., Western Dist. N.C., 1953-61; judge N.C. Ct. Appeals, 1973-74; spl. judge Superior Ct. of N.C., Raleigh, 1975—. Mem. Daniel Boone council Boy Scouts Am. Mem. Buscombe County, N.C., Am. bar assns. Recipient Silver Beaver award Boy Scouts Am., 1974; Alumnus of Year award Mars Hill Coll., 1959. Home: 81 Edgemont Rd Asheville NC 28801 Office: POB 7424 Asheville NC 28807 Tel (704) 255-5158

BALICK, HELEN SHAFFER, b. Bloomsburg, Pa., Oct. 2, 1935; J.D., Dickinson Sch. Law, 1966. Admitted to Pa. bar, 1967, Del. bar, 1969; probate adminstr. Girard Trust Bank, Phila., 1966-68; staff atty. Legal Aid Soc. Del., Wilmington, 1968-71; master Family Ct. State Del., Wilmington, 1971-74; bankruptcy judge, Fed. Magistrate, Wilmington, Del., pres. bd. trustees Community Legal Aid. Soc., Del., 1972-74. Mem. Wilmington Bd. Edn., 1974; bd. dirs. Jewish Family Service Del. 1974-77; mem. Citizens Adv. Com., Wilmington, 1973-74. Mem. Del. Bar Assn., Del. Council Crime and Justice, Nat. Council U.S. Magistrates, Nat. Conf. Bankruptcy Judges, Nat. Assn. Women Lawyers, Phi Alpha Delta. Office: 844 King St Lockbox 38 U S Court House Wilmington DE 19801 Tel (302) 571-6174

BALKIND, BENJAMIN HART, b. N.Y.C., Apr. 22, 1931; A.B., Harvard, 1953; LL.B., Yale, 1957. Caribbean rep. Richard Nathan Corp., N.Y.C., 1952-53; admitted to N.Y. bar, 1957; law clk. to judge Dist. Ct., So. Dist. N.Y., 1957-58; asso. firm Curtis, Mallet-Prevost, Colt & Mosle, N.Y.C., 1958-68, partner, 1968—; dir. and sec. Liberia Mining Co., Ltd., African Affairs Soc. Am., Ltd., 1963-66; acting justice Village of Laurel Hollow (N.Y.), 1968-76, mem. planning bd., 1970—, chmn. planning bd., 1972-76. Mem. Am., N.Y. State, N.Y.C., Inter-Am. bar assns., African-Am. C. of C., Fed. Bar Council. Office: Curtis Mallet-Prevost Colt & Mosle 100 Wall St 15th Floor New York City NY 10005 Tel (212) 248-8111

BALL, CHESTER GEORGE, b. Alliance, Ohio, Aug. 1, 1930; B.A., Mt. Union Coll., 1952; LL.B., So. Meth. U., 1955; Admitted to Ohio bar, 1975, Tex. bar, 1955; partner firm Harris & Ball, Arlington, Tex., 1957-69, firm Harris, Ball, Graham & Hill, Arlington, 1969-72, firm Blumensteil & Ball, Alliance, 1974-76; owner firm Ball & Landrith, Arlington, 1976—. Mem. Am., Tarrant County, Arlington bar assns., State Bar Tex., State Bar Ohio. Office: 601 W Abram St Arlington TX 76010 Tel (817) 261-3114

BALL, DWIGHT NICHOLAS, b. Gulfport, Miss., May 26, 1944; B.A., U. Miss., 1966, J.D., 1969, LL.M., 1976. Admitted to Miss. bar, 1969, Fed. Cts. bar, 1969; spl. agt. FBI, Seattle, 1969-71; instr. U. Miss., Oxford, 1971—; city prosecutor Oxford, 1974—; individual practice law, Oxford, 1973—. Mem. Lafayette County (pres.), Miss. bar assns., Nat. Dist. Attys. Assn., Miss. Prosecutors Assn. (dir.). Home: The Square Oxford MS 38655 Office: 1123 Jackson Ave Oxford MS 38655 Tel (601) 234-7777

BALL, DWIGHT RICHARD, b. Kingston, N.Y., Apr. 28, 1935; B.A., Union Coll., 1957; LL.B., Cornell U., 1960. Admitted to N.Y. bar, 1960; asso., partner firm Gerhart & Kuhnen, Binghamton, N.Y., 1960-72; partner firm Night, Keller, O'Connor, Ball & McDonough, Binghamton, 1972—. Pres., Broome County YMCA, 1974-75; bd. dirs. Home Start Program, 1974. Mem. Am., N.Y. State, Broome County bar assns. Home: 3 Crestmont Rd Binghamton NY 13095 Office: 316 Security Mutual Bldg Binghamton NY 13901 Tel (607) 724-4328

BALL, E. J., b. Monette, Ark., Jan 21, 1917; B.S.B.A. in Accounting, U. Ark., Fayetteville, 1948, LL.B., 1950, M.B.A. in Banking Fin. 1953. Admitted to Ark. bar, 1950; mem. firm Ball & Mourton, and predecessors, Fayetteville, 1950—; prof. taxation and bus. law U. Ark., 1950-72. Mem. Ark., Washington County (Ark.) bar assns. Office: Ball & Mourton POB 567 Fayetteville AR 72701

BALL, ERVIN LINCOLN, JR., b. Asheville, N.C., Mar. 9, 1945; B.S., U. Tenn., 1967, J.D., 1970. Admitted to N.C. bar, 1970, U.S. 4th Circuit Ct. Appeals bar, 1973, U.S. Supreme Ct. bar, 1975; asso. firm Uzzell & Du Mont, Asheville, 1970-72; partner firm Lentz & Ball, Profl. Assn., Asheville, 1972—. Mem. N.C. Acad. Trial Lawyers, N.C. Bar, N.C. State, Buncombe County (N.C.) bars, Trial Lawyers Am. Office: 17 N Market St Asheville NC 28807 Tel (704) 259-4385

BALL, GERALD TODD, b. DeKalb, Ill., Mar. 2, 1939; B.S. Northwestern U., 1961, M.B.A., 1968; J.D., U. Mich., 1964. Admitted to Ill. bar, 1964; partner Arthur Anderson & Co., Washington 1975—. Mem. Am., Ill. bar assns., Am. Inst. C.P.A.'s. Co-Author: The Indirect Credit, 1975. Home: 8506 Sparger St McLean VA 22101 Office: 1666 K St NW Washington DC 20006 Tel (202) 785-9510

BALL, LLOYD RICHARD, b. Hawarden, Iowa, Feb. 12, 1931; B.A., U. Iowa, 1953; LL.B., U. Nebr., 1956. Admitted to Iowa bar, 1956, U.S. Dist. Ct. for No. Dist. Iowa bar, 1965; served with Judge Adv. Gen. Dept., USAF, 1956-58; individual practice law, Hawarden, 1958—; mayor City of Hawaden, 1960-62, city atty., 1968-70. Mem. Am., Iowa State, Sioux County, Am. bar assns., Am. Judicature Soc., Internat. Platform Assn., Delta Tau Delta, Delta Theta Phi. Home: 1025 Ave M Hawarden IA 51023 Office: 817 Central Ave Hawarden IA 51023 Tel (712) 552-1661

BALL, RAYFORD LEVE, b. Graham, Tex., Mar. 24, 1911; B.S., N.Tex. State U., 1937; J.D., So. Methodist U., 1944. Admitted to Tex. bar, 1944; practice law, Lubbock. Mem. Lubbock County, Am. bar assns., State Bar Tex. Home: 2520 24th Lubbock TX 79410 Office: 208 Myrick Bldg Lubbock TX 79401 Tel (806) 763-9632

BALL, RICHARD ARLEDGE, JR., b. Montgomery, Ala., June 24, 1938; A.B., U. Ala., 1960, J.D., 1962. Admitted to Ala. bar, 1962; served as capt. JAGC, U.S. Army, Heidelberg, Germany, 1962-64; partner firm Ball, Ball, Duke & Matthews, Montgomery, 1964—; dir. Alaga Whitfield Foods, Inc. Bd. dirs. Montgomery Community Action Com., 1974-76; dir. Montgomery chpt. ARC, 1968. Mem. Am. Judicature Soc., Internat. Assn. Ins. Counsel, Phi Delta Phi. Home: 2411 E Cloverdale Pk Montgomery AL 36111 Office: One Court Sq Montgomery AL 36014 Tel (205) 834-7680

BALL, ROBERT SPENCER, b. Red Lodge, Mont., May 19, 1941; B.A., Whitman Coll., 1964; J.D., U. Calif. at Berkeley, 1967. Admitted to Oreg. bar, 1967; asso. firm Morrison & Bailey, Portland, Oreg., 1967-69; partner firm Smith Todd & Ball, Portland, 1969—. Mem. Tigard (Oreg) Planning Commn., 1972-75; mem. Portland Met. Area Local Govt. Boundary Commn., 1975—, vice chmn., 1976—. Mem. Am. Bar Assn., Am. Judicature Soc., Common Cause, Oreg. Environ. Council, ACLU. Author: (with others) Easements, 1975; (with W.P. Hutchison, Jr.) Representing a Neighborhood Group in a Landuse Case, 1976. Home: 12765 S W Bull Mountain Rd Tigard OR 97223 Office: Smith Todd & Ball 400 Oregon National Bldg Portland OR 97205 Tel (503) 228-6375

BALL, ROYCE EUGENE, b. McKinney, Tex., May 17, 1924; A.A. in Sociology, Hillsboro (Tex.) Jr. Coll., 1946, LL.B., Baylor U., 1949, J.D., 1969. Admitted to Tex. bar, 1950; asst. city atty. City of Lubbock (Tex.), 1952-54; investigator VA, Lubbock, 1954-55; city atty. City of Floydada (Tex.), 1955; asso. firm Richard Stovall, Floydada, 1955, firm Burton & Brown, Lubbock, 1955-66; individual practice law, Lubbock, 1966—. Sec. Little League Baseball, Lubbock, 1957-58. Mem. Tex. Criminal Law Assn., Am. Criminal Bar Assn. Home and Office: 4411 32d St Lubbock TX 79410 Tel (806) 799-0484

BALL, THOMAS ARMOUR, b. San Antonio, Oct. 3, 1927; B.A., Tex. U., 1949, LL.B., 1950. Admitted to Tex. bar, 1950; judge Bexar County (Tex.) Ct. at Law, San Antonio, 1963—. Mem. San Antonio, Am., Tex. bar assns. Home: 218 Canterbury Hill San Antonio TX 78209 Office: Bexar County Courthouse San Antonio TX 78205 Tel (512) 220-2678

BALL, WILLIAM KENNETH, b. DeQueen, Ark., Jan 15, 1927; J.D., U. Ark., 1953; Admitted to Ark. bar, 1953, U.S. Supreme Ct. bar, 1971; law clk. Ark. Supreme Ct., 1953-54; partner firm Williamson, Ball & Bird, Monticello, Ark., 1954—; spl. justice Ark. Supreme Ct., 1975; mem. Ark. Bd. Law Examiners, 1975—; city atty. Monticello, 1961—. Mem. Monticello Sch. Bd., 1957-58. Mem. Am., Ark., Southeast Ark. (pres. 1957-58) bar assns., Am. Coll. Probate Counsel, Delta Theta Phi. Contbr. article to law rev. Home: 104 Westwood Ln Monticello AR 71655 Office: Main St at Oakland Monticello AR 71655 Tel (501) 367-6288

BALLANTINE, THOMAS AUSTIN, JR., b. Louisville, Sept. 22, 1926; A.B., U. Ky., 1948; J.D., U. Louisville, 1954. Admitted to Ky. bar, 1954; asso. firm McElwain, Dinning, Clarke & Winstead, Louisville, 1954-64; dep. commr. Jefferson County (Ky.) Circuit Ct., Louisville, 1958-62, judge, 1964—; commr. Jefferson County Fiscal Ct., 1962-64; instr. law U. Louisville, 1969-76. Mem. Ky., Louisville bar assns. Home: 48 Hill Rd Louisville KY 40204 Office: Jefferson Hall of Justice Louisville KY 40202 Tel (502) 581-6018

BALLANTYNE, JAY RAINEY, b. Lincoln County, Wyo., May 4, 1926; A.A., Occidental Coll., 1945; B.S., U. So. Calif., 1948; LL.B., Southwestern U., 1951. Admitted to Calif. bar, 1952; U.S. Dist. Ct. bar, 1952; partner firm McKinney & Ballantyne, Visalia, Calif., 1953-58; dist. atty. Tulare County (Calif.), Visalia, 1958-66; judge Superior Ct. Tulare County, Visalia, 1966—. Mem. Am. Bar Assn., Am. Judicature Soc., Calif. Judges' Assn. Office: Superior Cts Court House Visalia CA 93277 Tel (209) 733-6561

BALLARD, EDGAR DOZIER, JR., b. Berwyn, Ill., Sept. 29, 1928; B.S., Ind. U., 1950; J.D., Northwestern U., 1955. Admitted to Ill. bar, 1955; clk. Judge Walter C. Lindley, U.S. Ct. Appeals, Chgo., 1958-60; partner firm Schuyler, Ballard & Cowen, Chgo. Chmn. local draft bd., 1962-72; trustee Village of Riverside, Ill., 1973—. Mem. Am., Ill. Chgo. bar assns. Bd. editors Northwestern Law Rev., 1955. Home: 208 Lawton Rd Riverside IL 60546 Office: 100 W Monroe St Chicago IL 60603

BALLER, MARGARET LEBAIR, b. Phila., Oct. 14, 1922; LL.B., Rutgers U., 1951. Admitted to N.J. bar, 1951, U.S. Dist. Ct. N.J. bar, 1951; U.S. Supreme Ct. Bar, 1961; individual practice law, Trenton, N.J., 1951-66; Somerset, N.J., 1966—; tchr. bus. law and law for layman Franklin Twp. Adult Edn. Program, 1976—. Gen. counsel Franklin Just Useage of Nature through Conservation, Pine Grove (N.J.) PTA; volunteer parole officer Franklin Twp., N.J., 1975—. Active Girl Scouts U.S.A. Mem. N.J., Mercer County bar assns. Home and office: 226 Blake Ave Somerset NJ 08873 Tel (201) 246-1666

BALLINGER, JULIUS OWEN, b. Elk City, Kans., Feb. 23, 1925; B.S., Kans. State U., 1950; J.S.D., Washburn Law Sch., 1952. Admitted to Kans. bar, 1952, U.S. Supreme Ct. bar, 1966; individual practice law, Wichita, 1953-56; dept. dist. atty. Sedgwick County, Kans., 1956-71; judge Sedgwick County Ct. Common Pleas, Wichita, 1971-76; judge 18th Judicial Dist. Kans., 1977—. Mem. Kans., Wichita bar assns. Home: 528 W 27th St St Wichita KS 67217 Office: 525 N Main St Wichita KS 67203 Tel (317) 268-7191

BALLMAN, BENEDICT GEORGE, b. N.Y.C., Feb. 7, 1931; A.A., B.S., Am. U., 1955, J.D., 1957; LL.M., Georgetown U., 1961. Admitted to D.C. bar, 1957, Md. bar, 1958; sr. partner firm Bellman & McDonald, Wheaton, Md., 1960-65; individual practice law, 1965-69; sr. partner firm Staley, Prescott & Ballman, Kensington, Md., 1969—. Dir., treas. Bethesda Chevy Chase Rescue Squad, 1948-50; dir. Montgomery County Young Democrats, 1960-61. Mem. Montgomery County (treas. 1960), Md., Am. bar assns., Am. Trial Lawyers Assn. Home: 12002 River Rd Potomac MD 20854 Office: 5th Floor Citizens Savings Bldg Kensington MD 20795 Tel (301) 933-1234

BALLMAN, ROBERT ELLIOTT, b. San Diego, Sept. 29, 1932; B.A., Wash. U., 1953, J.D., 1955. Admitted to Mo. bar, 1958, Fec. bar, 1958; partner firm Farrell & Ballman, St. Louis, 1963—. Mem. St. Louis, Am. bar assns., Lawyers Assn. of St. Louis, Am., Mo. trial lawyers assns., Am. Judicature Soc. Contbr. articles to legal jours. Home: 10114 Ingleside Dr St Louis MO 63124 Office: 818 Olive St Suite 743 St Louis MO 63101 Tel (314) 231-5055

BALLOU, RICHARD DONALD, b. Honesdale, Pa., Sept. 16, 1937; B.S., U. Scranton, 1968; J.D., Duquesne U., 1971. Admitted to Pa. bar, 1971, to U.S. Fed. Ct. bar, 1972; individual practice law, Honesdale, 1971—; chief pub. defender Wayne County, Pa., 1971-74; tchr. Lackawanna Jr. Coll.; solicitor 6 twps., Wayne County Indsl. Devel. Authority, Wayne County Sheriff, Wayne County Auditors. Dir. WIDCO, Tre-hab, Inc.; exec. mem. Wayne County Republican Party. Mem. Pa., Wayne County bar assns. Home: RD 1 Box 8B Honesdale PA 18431 Office: 105 9th St Honesdale PA 18431 Tel (717) 253-4112

BALOG, JAMES TIMOTHY, b. Watertown, S.D., May 12, 1932; B.B.A., U. Mich., 1954; J.D., John Marshall Law Sch., 1970. Dep. clk. U.S. Ct., Chgo., 1962-67; admitted to Ill. bar, 1970, U.S. Supreme Ct. bar, 1973; U.S. Commr., Chgo., 1967-71; U.S. Magistrate, Chgo., 1971—. Mem. Fed. Bar Assn., Phi Alpha Delta. Home: 1555 N Dearborn Pkwy Chicago IL 60610 Office: 219 S Dearborn St Chicago IL 60604 Tel (312) 435-5636

BALOTTI, RICHARD FRANKLIN, b. Louisville, Apr. 19, 1942; B.A., Hamilton Coll., 1964; LL.B., Cronell U., 1967. Admitted to Del. bar, 1967; asso. firm Richards, Layton & Finger, Wilmington, Del., 1967-70, partner, 1971—; mem. Del. Long Range Cts. Planning Com., adv. com. on rules Del. Supreme Ct., 1974—; counsel Republican State Com., 1974-75. Mem. Am., Del. (sec. 1974-75, exec. com.) bar assns., Order of Coif, Phi Kappa Phi. Home: 1106 Hopeton Rd Wilmington DE 19807 Office: DuPont Bldg Wilmington DE 19801 Tel (302) 658-6541

BALSLEY, STEPHEN G., b. Beloit, Wis., Jan. 14, 1947; B.S. with honors, U. Wis., 1969; J.D. with honors, U. Ill., 1972. Admitted to Ill. bar, 1972; now mem. firm Barrick, Jackson, Switzer, Long & Balsley, Rockford, Ill. Mem. Am., Ill., Winnebago County bar assns., Order of Coif. Editor Note and Comment, 1971-72. Office: 611 Illinois Nat Bank 228 N Main St Rockford IL 61101 Tel (815) 962-6611*

BAM, FOSTER, b. Bridgeport, Conn., Jan. 11, 1927; B.A., Yale, 1950, LL.B., 1953, J.D., 1953. Admitted to N.Y. bar, 1954, Conn. bar, 1967; atty. firm Spence & Hutchkiss, N.Y.C., 1953-55; asst. U.A. atty. So. Dist. N.Y., 1955-57; partner firm Feldman, Kramer, Bam & Nessen, N.Y.C., 1957-67; partner firm Cummings & Lockwood, Stamford, Conn., 1967—; dir. Cities Service Co., DPF Inc., State Nat. Bank. Trustee Oceanic Soc. Mem. Am., Conn., N.Y., Greenwich bar assns. Office: 2 Greenwich Plaza Greenwich CT 06830 Tel (203) 327-1700

BAMBACUS, JOSEPH S., b. Richmond, Va., Jan. 26, 1923; student Va. Poly. Inst.; LL.B., U. Richmond, 1950, J.D., 1950. Admitted to Va. bar, 1950, U.S. Ct. Appeals 4th Circuit bar, 1955, U.S. Supreme Ct. bar, 1960; U.S. atty. Eastern Dist. Va., 1958-61; spl. asst. Atty. Gen. U.S., Washington, 1961; partner firm Herberle and Bambacus, 1961-72; chmn. Bambacus and Assos., Richmond. Mem. Am., Va., Fed., Richmond bar assns., Am. Judicature Soc., Va. State Bar. Office: 418 Mutual Bldg 9th St and Main St Richmond VA 23219 Tel (804) 648-4434

BAMBERGER, EDWARD CLINTON, JR., b. Balt., July 2, 1926; B.S., Loyola Coll., Balt., 1949; J.D., Georgetown U., 1951. Admitted to Md. bar, 1951, D.C. bar, 1971, U.S. Supreme Ct. bar, 1962; law clk. to judge Md. Ct. Appeals, 1951-52; asso. firm Piper & Marbury, Balt., 1952-60, partner, 1960-69; asst. atty. gen. State of Md., 1958-59; dir. Legal Services Program OEO, Balt., 1965-66; dean law sch. Catholic U. Am., Washington, 1969-75; vis. prof. law Stanford, 1974-75; exec. v.p. Legal Services Corp., Washington, 1975—. Del. Md. Constl. Conv., 1967; pres. bd. trustees Md. Hosp. Services, Inc., 1963-65; chmn. Balt. City Hosps. Commn., 1967-69. Fellow Am. Bar Found.; mem. Am. Law Inst., D.C. Bar, Am. (chmn. sect. on legal edn. and bar admissions 1975-76), Nat., Md. bar assns., Soc. Am. Law Tchrs. Contbr. articles to legal jours. Home: 3515 Shepherd St Chevy Chase MD 20015 Office: 733 15th St NW Washington DC 20005

BAMBERGER, GERALD JULIAN, b. Chgo., Oct. 12, 1936; A.B., Washington U., St. Louis, 1959, LL.B., 1960. Admitted to Mo. bar, 1960; asst. county counselor St. Louis County, 1961-64; mem. firms Schwartz Schwartz & Gilden, 1964-65, Herman M. Katcher, 1966-67; individual practice law, St. Charles, Mo., 1970—; gen. counsel Am. Inst. Mktg. Systems, Inc., St. Louis, 1972-73. Treas., v.p. Hillel Found., Washington U., 1967-71; chmn. Old Newsboys Dr., St. Charles County, Mo., 1973-76. Mem. Mo. Bar Assn. of St. Louis County, St. Charles County Bar Assn. (pres. 1974). Office: 114 N Main St Saint Charles MO 63301 Tel (314) 946-6500

BAMBERGER, RONALD JOSEPH, b. Detroit, July 15, 1942; B.A., Bresica Coll., Owensboro, Ky., 1965; J.D., U. Ky., Lexington, 1968. Admitted to Ky. bar, 1968; asso. firm Bratcher, Cooper & Flaherty, 1968-71, Cooper, Flaherty & Bamberger, 1971-75, Cooper, Flaherty, Bamberger & Abshier, Owensboro, 1975—. Bd. dirs. Ownesboro Area Mus., 1974-75; asso. prof. Brescia Coll., 1969—. Mem. Am., Ky., Daviess County (sec.) bar assns. Home: 4045 Kensington Pl Owensboro KY 42301 Office: 403 W 3d St Owensboro KY 42301 Tel (502) 926-2828

BAMFORD, BARBARA (MRS. ROBERT M. LYNYAK), b. Cleve., Sept. 22, 1943; A.B. in Math., Wellesley Coll., 1965; J.D., Catholic U. Am., 1970. Admitted to Calif. bar, 1971, N.Y. bar, 1974; asso. firm Loeb & Loeb, Los Angeles, 1970-73, Shearman & Sterling, N.Y.C., 1970, 73—; Mem. Am. Bar Assn. Contbr. articles to law publs. Home: 309 Summit Ave Summit NJ 07901 Office: 53 Wall St New York City NY 10005 Tel (212) 483-1000

BANAHAN, JAMES ECKLUND, b. Lexington, Ky., Oct. 26, 1925; J.D., U. Ky., 1948. Admitted to Ky. bar, 1948; individual practice law, Lexington, 1948, 56, 62—; partner firm Potter & Co., CPA's, Lexington, 1962—; agent IRS, Lexington, 1956-61. Sec. Pub. Service Commn. Ky., Frankfort, 1953-56. Mem. Ky., Fayette County bar assns., Ky. Soc. CPA's, Am. Inst. CPA'S, Am. Assn. Attys. CPA's. Office: 2228 Young Dr Lexington KY 40505 Tel (606) 266-2186

BANCROFT, MARK WILLIAM, b. Marcus, Iowa, Oct. 29, 1905; student Morningside Coll., 1923-24, Creighton U., 1924-26; LL.B., U. Minn., 1930. Admitted to Iowa bar, 1930, Minn. bar, 1930; individual practice law, Marcus, 1931—; served with JAG, U.S. Army, 1943-46. Mem. Am., Iowa bar assns. Home: 118 S Elm St Marcus IA 51035 Office: 320 N Main St Marcus IA 51035 Tel (712) 376-2414

BANDER, EDWARD JULIUS, b. Boston, Aug. 10, 1923; B.A., Boston U., 1949, LL.B., 1951; M.S. in Library Sci., Simmons Coll., 1955. Admitted to Mass. bar, 1951; asso. Cohen & Kantrowicz, Boston, 1951-52; with Cuyahoga County (Ohio) Juvenile Ct., 1952-53; asst. ref. librarian Law Sch., Harvard, Cambridge, Mass., 1954-55; librarian U.S. Ct. Appeals, Boston, 1955-60; asso. prof. law N.Y. U., 1960—, asso. law librarian, 1960—. Mem. Assn. Am. Law Schs., Am. Assn. Law Librarians, New Eng. Law Librarians (pres.), Law Library Assn. N.Y. (pres.). Editor: Mr. Dooley on the Choice of Law, 1963, Justice Holmes Ex Cathedra, 1967, Corporation in a Democratic Society, 1976; editor Law Library Jour. Home: 5601 Riverdale Ave New York City NY 10471 Office: 40 Washington Square New York City NY 10012 Tel (212) 598-3040

BANDY, JACK DONALD, b. Galesburg, Ill., June 19, 1932; A.B., Knox Coll., 1954; LL.B., U. San Fernando Valley, 1967. Safety engr. Indsl. Indemnity Co., Los Angeles, 1960-65, sr. safety engr., 1965-69, resident engr., 1969-72; admitted to Calif. bar, 1972; atty. Employers Ins. of Wausau, Los Angeles, 1972—. Youth leader YMCA, Mission Hills, Calif., 1965-72; active Los Angeles PTA, 1963—, San Fernando Little League, 1972-73; precinct worker, 1967-72. Mem. Calif. State Bar, San Fernando Valley Bar Assn., Am. Soc. Safety Engrs. (certified profl. Los Angeles chpt.). Home: 16411 Calahan St Sepulveda CA 91343 Office: 3130 Wilshire Blvd Los Angeles CA 90010 Tel (213) 381-6611

BANGEL, STANLEY JEROME, b. Norfolk, Va., July 16, 1925; J.D., U. Va., 1947. Admitted to Va. bar, 1947; partner firm Bangel & Bangel, Portsmouth, Va., 1947-49; partner firm Bangel, Bangel & Bangel, Portsmouth, 1949-. Permanent mem. Jud. Conf. U.S. Ct. Appeals for 4th Circuit. Fellow Internat. Acad. Trial Lawyers; mem. Am., Va., Portsmouth (pres. 1967), Norfolk-Portsmouth bar assns., Tidewater Trial Lawyers Assn. (bd. govs. 1958-70), Law Sci. Acad. Am., Va. Trial Lawyers Assn. (pres. 1967-68), Am. Judicature Soc., N.Y. State Assn. Trial Lawyers, Nat. Assn. Criminal Def. Lawyers, Assn. Trial Lawyers Am. (v.p. 1953-57, bd. govs. 1957-59). Home: 204 Park Rd Portsmouth VA 23707 Office: 505 Court St PO Box 760 Portsmouth VA 23705 Tel (804) 397-3471

BANKERT, ROBERT ANTHONY, b. Utica, N.Y., Aug. 15, 1921; A.B., Hamilton Coll., 1943; J.D., Cornell U., 1950. Admitted to N.Y. bar, 1950, U.S. Supreme Ct. bar, 1961; asso. firm Ferris, Hughes, Dorrance & Groben, Utica, 1950-53; partner firm Evans, Severn, Bankert & Peet, Utica, 1953—; trustee Savs. Bank of Utica, 1976—. Pres., Mohawk Valley Assn. for Progress, 1976—; mem. New Hartford (N.Y.) Sch. Bd., 1963—; commr. City of Utica Water Bd., 1976—. Mem. Am., N.Y. State, Oneida County (sec. 1955-64) bar assns. Home: 6 Tanglewood Rd New Hartford NY 13413 Office: 301 Mayro Bldg Bank Pl Utica NY 13501 Tel (315) 724-4151

BANKS, PATRICIA, b. Marianna, Ark., Feb. 6, 1949; B.A., U. Ill., Chgo., 1969; J.D., U. Wis., 1972. Admitted to Wis. bar, 1972, Ill. bar, 1973; atty. regional solicitor's office Dept. Labor, Chgo., 1972-73, Leadership Council for Met. Open Communities, Chgo., 1973-74, Sears Roebuck & Co., Chgo., 1974—. Bd. dirs. Home Investment Fund, League of Black Women, Chgo., 1973—, NAACP, 1974—. Mem. Cook County (Ill.) (Young Lawyer of Year award 1975, v.p. 1975—), Chgo., Am., Wis., Ill., Fed. bar assns. Home: 4800 Chicago Beach Dr apt 1611N Chicago IL 60615 Office: Sears Towers 69th floor Chicago IL 60684 Tel (312) 875-9240

BANKS, ROBERT SHERWOOD, b. Newark, Mar. 28, 1934; A.B., Cornell U., 1955, LL.B., 1958. Admitted to N.Y. bar, 1969, N.J. bar, 1959; individual practice law, Newark, 1959-61; atty. E.I. DuPont Co., Wilmington, Del., 1961-67; atty. Xerox Corp., Stamford, Conn., 1967-75, v.p., gen. counsel, 1976—. Mem. Am., Conn. bar assns., Cornell Law Assn. Adv. bd. Columbia U. Center for Law and Econ. Studies. Office: Xerox Corp Stamford CT 06904 Tel (203) 329-8711

BANKS, WILLIAM FRANCIS, b. Bklyn., Feb. 12, 1925; A.B. in History, Fordham U., 1948; J.D., Cornell U., 1951. Admitted to N.Y. bar, 1952, U.S. Supreme Ct. bar, 1964; jr. asst. to county atty. Westchester County (N.Y.), White Plains, 1951-53; asso. firm Smith, Ranscht, Mitchell & Croake, White Plains, 1953; partner firm Banks & Bray, Bedford, N.Y., 1953-55; individual practice law, Bedford, 1955-63; partner firm Anderson, Banks Moore & Hollis, Mt. Kisco, N.Y., 1963—; judge Town of Bedford, 1960—. Bd. dirs., treas. Boy's Club Mt. Kisco, 1964-74; sec. Bedford Zoning and Planning bds., 1954-59. Mem. Am., N.Y. State, Westchester County, No. Westchester bar assns., Bedford Hist. Soc. (dir., sec. 1963—). Home: Cantitoe St Bedford NY 10506 Office: 61 Smith Ave Mount Kisco NY 10549 Tel (914) 666-2161

BANKSON, JOHN PALMER, JR., b. Cleve., Mar. 2, 1931; B.A., Yale U., 1952; LL.B., Harvard U., 1955. Admitted to Pa. bar, 1956, D.C. bar, 1958, U.S. Supreme Ct. bar, 1963; asso. firm Miller, Schroeder & Bankson and predecessor, Washington, 1957-60, partner, 1960-73; partner Hamel, Park, McCabe & Saunders, Washington, 1973—. Vice chmn. Montgomery County, Md. Republican State Central Com., 1970-74; lay reader St. Philip's Chapel (Aquasco, Md.). Mem. Fed. Communications (pres. 1976—), Am., D.C. bar assns. Home: 4308 Rosemary St Chevy Chase MD 20015 Office: 1776 F St NW Washington DC 20006 Tel (202) 785-1234

BANKSTON, RUSSELL, b. Baton Rouge, May 30, 1928; B.S., La. State U., 1948, LL.B., 1958, J.D., 1968. Admitted to La. bar, 1958; partner firm Parker & Bankston, Zachary, La., 1958-71; partner firm Bankston & Lord, Zachary, 1972—; city atty. Zachary, 1960-73, city judge, 1974—; atty., dir. Bank of Zachary. Edler Zachary Presbyn. Ch. Mem. Am. Judicature Soc., La. City Judges Assn. Home: 3757 Nelson St Zachary LA 70791 Office: 4863A Main St Zachary LA 70791 Tel (504) 654-8291

BANNER, DONALD WITTE, b. Chgo., Feb. 23, 1924; B.S. in Elec. Engring., Purdue U., 1948; J.D., U. Detroit, 1952; M.P.L., John Marshall Law Sch., 1958. Admitted to Mich. bar, 1953, Ill. bar, 1953, U.S. Ct. Customs and Patent Appeals and U.S. Patent Office bars, 1953, U.S. Supreme Ct. bar, 1962; gen. patent counsel Borg-Warner Corp., Chgo., 1964—; adj. prof. law John Marshall Law Sch., dir. grad. sch. intellectual property law; mem. U.S. del. Washington Diplomatic Conf. Patent Cooperation Treaty; Am. Bar Assn. del. Vienna Diplomatic Conf. Trademark Registration Treaty; U.S. del. internat. exec. com. Assn. Internationale pour la Protection de la Propriété Industrielle. Trustee John Marshall Law Sch., 1965—. Mem. Am., Ill. State (chmn., council mem. Am., Ill. sects. patent trademark, copyright law), 7th Circuit, Chgo., Kane County bar assns., Am. Patent Law Assn. (pres.), Patent Law Assn. Chgo. (v.p.), Internat. Patent and Trademark Assn. (v.p.), Assn. Corporate Patent Counsel (former pres.), Licensing Execs. Soc. (past trustee), Tau Beta Pi, Eta Kappa Nu. Home: 268 Carriage Hill Dr Aurora IL 60506 Office: 200 S Michigan Ave Chicago IL 60604 Tel (312) 663-2152

BANNO, CARL CHARLES, b. San Cataldo, Sicily, Italy, May 25, 1915; B.S. cum laude in Econs., St. John's U., 1935, J.D., 1936; J.S.D., St. Lawrence U., 1939. Admitted to N.Y. State bar, 1937, U.S. Supreme Ct. bar, 1947; individual practice law, N.Y.C., 1937-42, 1946-49; partner firm Yellon, Banno & Lombardo, N.Y.C., Mineola, N.Y., 1949-65; individual practice law, Mineola, 1965-75; partner firm Banno, Pajion, Jewell & Livoti, Mineola, 1975—; served to col. USAF, chief legal officer, chief judge Superior and Gen. Cts. of Occupation in Italy, 1943-45; dir. 1st Nat. Bank E.Islip, N.Y., 1974-76. Mem. Am., Fed., N.Y. State, Nassau County (chmn. aero. com., grievance com., med. jurisprudence com., matrimonial law com.), bar assns., Am. Judicature Soc., Am., N.Y. State trial lawyers assns., Columbian Lawyers Assn., Judge Adv. Assn., Catholic Lawyers Guild (past pres.). Home: 105 Oakdale Ln Roslyn Heights NY 11577 Office: 146 Old Country Rd Mineola NY 11501 Tel (516) 742-0372

BANTA, DON ARTHUR, b. Chgo., Mar. 10, 1926; B.S., Northwestern U., 1948, LL.B., 1950. Admitted to Ill. bar, 1950, U.S. Supreme Ct. bar, 1967; partner firm Naphin, Banta & Cox, Chgo., 1953—. Mem. bd. edn. Wilmot Sch. Dist., Deerfield, Ill., 1964-70 (pres. 1968-69). Mem. Am., Ill., Chgo. bar assns., Phi Delta Phi. Home: 836 Northwoods Dr Deerfield IL 60015 Office: 105 W Adams St Chicago IL 60603 Tel (312) 236-0177

BANTA, JAMES CLINTON, b. Spokane, Wash., Feb. 4, 1914; LL.B., Gonzaga U., 1949, J.D., 1967. Admitted to Wash. State bar, 1950; judge Dist. Ct., Spokane, Wash., 1961—, Municipal Ct. Millwood (Wash.), 1962—, Municipal Ct. Rockford (Wash.), 1974—. Active, Spokane Valley council Boy Scouts Am., 1960—. Home: E 8611 Riverway St Spokane WA 99206 Office: N 2709 Argonne St Spokane WA 99206 Tel (509) 926-5478

BANTON, STEPHEN CHANDLER, b. St. Louis, Feb. 19, 1947; B.A., Bowdoin Coll., 1969; J.D., Washington U., St. Louis, 1972, M.B.A., 1974. Admitted to Mo. bar, 1973; asst. pros. atty. St. Louis County, 1972-75; individual practice law, Clayton, Mo., 1975—; lectr. bus. law Washington U., 1974—. Bd. dirs. St. Louis County League of Chambers; pres. Ozark Area council Am. Youth Hostels. Mem. Mo. Bar, Am. Bar Assn., Bar Assn. Met. St. Louis, Am. Trial Lawyers Assn., Nat. Dist. Attys. Assn., ACLU. Author: The Brief Case, St. Louis Bar Jour. column. Home: 172 Forest Brook St Saint Louis MO 63141 Office: 225 S Meramec St Clayton MO 63105 Tel (314) 725-1616

BANYAS, ANDREW JOHN, III, b. Homestead, Pa., Apr. 8, 1934; B.S. in Bus. Adminstrn., Duquesne U., 1965; J.D., 1968. Admitted to Pa. bar, 1968, law clk. to judge Ct. Common Pleas of Allegheny County (Pa.), Pitts., 1968-69; asso firm Meyer, Darragh, Buckler, Bebenek & Eck, Pitts., 1969-72, jr. partner, 1972-74, sr. partner, 1974—; solicitor Borough of Munhall (Pa.) Zoning Hearing Bd., 1973—. Mem. Munhall Vol. Fire Dept., 1960—; sec. Munhall Civil Service Commn., 1970—. Mem. Am., Pa., Allegheny County bar assns. Office: 2500 Grant Bldg Pittsburgh PA 15219 Tel (412) 261-6600

BARADEL, RONALD ARTHUR, b. St. Louis, May 29, 1943; B.S., Mt. St. Mary's Coll., 1964; J.D., Georgetown U., 1967. Admitted to D.C. bar, 1969, Md. bar, 1971; spl. agt. FBI, Ind., N.Y.C., 1967-70; law clk. judge Thomas B. Finan Ct. Appeals Md., Annapolis, 1970-71; asso. firm Hartman & Crain, Annapolis, Md., 1971-75, partner, 1975—. Mem. Am., Md., Anne Arundel County (exec. com. 1975) bar assns. Office: Box 1989 Annapolis MD 21404 Tel (301) 267-8166

BARAKAT, GEORGE M., b. Camden, Maine, Mar. 16, 1904; B.A., Bowdoin Coll., 1926; LL.B., J.D., Harvard, 1937. Admitted to Maine bar, 1937, Mass. bar, 1937; advisor dels. San Francisco Conf., 1945, Am. Law Inst. Bill of Human Rights, 1945; asst. dir. Near East Coll. Assn., 1946-47; dir. Am. Middle East Relief, Inc., N.Y.C., 1948-62; individual practice law, Boston, 1963—. Pres. Syrian and Lebanese Am. Fedn. of Middle Eastern States, Boston, 1942-46; pres. Nat. Assn. Fedn. Syrian and Lebanese Am. Club, 1954-55. Recipient citation Am. Friends of Middle East; gold medal of merit Govt. of Lebanon, 1952; medal of merit Govt. of Syria, 1955. Home: 2221 NE 68th St Apt 912 Fort Lauderdale FL 33308 also George Barakat 5 Chequaquet Way Centerville MA 02632 Office: 120 Boylston St Boston MA 02116 Tel (305) 491-0047 also (617) 775-6294

BARAM, MICHAEL SAMPSON, b. Woonsocket, R.I., Sept. 7, 1935; B.S., Tufts U., 1957; LL.B., Columbia, 1960. Admitted to Mass. bar, 1962; mem. spl. faculty Boston U. Sch. Law, 1970-76; environ. law Mass. Inst. Tech., Cambridge, 1970—; prof. Franklin Pierce Law Center 1976—; mem. firm Bracken, Selig & Baram, Boston, 1974—, partner, 1976—; mem. coms. radiation standards and environ. manpower Nat. Acad. Scis. Mem. Am. Bar Assn. (vice chmn. environ. law com. gen. practice sec.; chmn. tech. assessment com. sci., tech. and law sect.). Author: Environmental Law and the Siting of Facilities, 1976; Artificial Islands for Energy Facilities, 1976; contbr. articles to sci. and legal jours. Office: 33 Mt Vernon St Boston MA 02110 Tel (617) 742-4950

BARASCH, CLARENCE SYLVAN, b. N.Y.C., May 20, 1912; A.B., Columbia, 1933, J.D., 1935. Admitted to N.Y. bar, 1936; asso. firm Sidney Hoffman, N.Y.C., 1935-36, Edelman & Edelman, N.Y.C., 1936-39, Pfeiffer & Crames, N.Y.C., 1939-55; individual practice law, N.Y.C., 1955—. Mem. adv. bd. to religious counselor Columbia, 1950-70, chmn., 1970. mem. coll. alumni religious affairs com., 1962—, chmn. Law Sch. Class of 1935 Ann. Fund, 1965—, mem. exec. com. Law Sch. Fund, 1967—; pres. Jewish Campus Life Fund, 1971—. Mem. Am., N.Y. State bar assns., N.Y. County Lawyers Assn. (legis. com.), Real Estate Bd. N.Y. (legis. com.). Author: (with Elliott L. Biskind) The Law of Real Estate Brokers, 1969; contbr. articles to legal jours. Home: 1016 Fifth Ave New York City NY 10028 Office: 540 Madison Ave New York City NY 10022 Tel (212) 838-6670

BARATTA, JOHN BAPTIST, b. Phila., Jan. 26, 1895; student Princeton U., 1913-14; LL.B., Dickinson Sch. Law, 1925. Admitted to N.J. bar, 1927, U.S. Supreme Ct. bar, 1938; individual practice law, Atlantic City, 1927—; asst. city solicitor Atlantic City, 1941-44, municipal pros. atty., 1964-72; apptd. commr. N.J. Supreme Ct., 1940; spl. master-in-chancery N.J. Ct. Chancery, 1944; del. N.J. Jud. Conf., 1954-56. Co-founder, chmn. bd. Columbus Scholarship Found. Atlantic County, 1938-42. Mem. N.J., Atlantic County, Am. bar assns. Recipient citation for distinguished accomplishment Dickinson Sch. Law, 1959. Home: A 5 Hartford Ct Atlantic City NJ 08401 Office: 525 Guarantee Trust Bldg Atlantic City NJ 08401 Tel (609) 345-0655

BARBALUNGA, ALFRED ANTHONY, b. Pittsfield, Mass., Jan. 10, 1942; student U. Notre Dame, 1960-62; B.S. in Bus. Adminstrn., U. Akron, 1964; LL.B., Suffolk U., 1967. Admitted to Mass. bar, 1967; since practiced in Pittsfield, 1968—; spl. asst. atty. gen. State of Mass., 1975—. Mem. Lawyers Solicitations United Way Campaign Fund Dr., Berkshire County, Mass., 1969-71; bus. and industry chmn. Pittsfield div. Am. Cancer Soc. Crusade, 1969-72; bd. dirs. Campfire Girls of Pittsfield, Inc., 1974—, pro bono legal council, 1974—; mem. Berkshire County solicitations bldg. fund campaign Cranwell Preparatory Sch., 1969, mem. alumni council, 1974. Mem. Am., Mass. (fee arbitration bd.), Berkshire bar assns., Am. Arbitration Assn. Contbr. articles to legal jours. Home: 1 Eagle's Nest Rd Pittsfield MA 01201 Office: 78 Bartlett Ave Pittsfield MA 01201 Tel (413) 499-1650

BARBEE, LLOYD AUGUSTUS, b. Memphis, Aug. 17, 1925; B.A. in Social Sci., LeMoyne Coll., Memphis, 1949; law certificate U. Wis., Madison, 1955, J.D., 1956. Admitted to Wis. bar, 1956, U.S. Supreme Ct. bar, 1965; individual practice law, Madison Wis., 1956-57; law examiner Indsl. Comm. Wis., Unemployment Compensation Dept., Madison, 1957-62; mem. firm Barbee & Jacobson, Milw., 1962-68, Barbee & Goldberg, Milw., 1976—; mem. Wis. Assembly, 1965—; lectr. U. Wis. Law Sch., 1969, 70, 72, 73; mem. Milw. Legal Services, 1973-76. Chmn. Madison Mayor's Commn. on Human Rights, 1957-62; vice chmn. Wis. Citizens for Fair Housing, 1962; bd. dirs. E.B. Phillips Day Care Center, Milw., 1964-68; mem. Wis. Gov.'s Commn. for UN, 1963—; del. Democratic Nat. Conv., 1968, 72; bd. dirs. Interfaith Housing Found. Wis. and Upper Mich., Inc., 1970. Mem. NAACP (chmn. Wis. chpt. 1958-61, region III 1963-64), Milw. Citizens for Equal Opportunity, Negro Am. Labor Council, Milw. Parents Tchrs. Orgn. Milw. PTA, Nat. Black Elected Officials, Freedom Through Equality (pres. 1969-73), Wis. Civil Liberties Union, United Black Artists, Abortion Reform Assn. (asso.), Black Legislators Assn. (dir.), Nat. Black Assembly, Wis. Black Polit. Caucus (chmn. 1972), Wis. Black Elected and Appointed Ofcls. (chmn. 1971), Wis. Black Lawyers Assn. (chmn. 1973), Zero Population Growth (recipient Humanitarian award 1973). Recipient Legis. award Milw. Courier, 1970; Excellence award Black Press Wis., 1972; Achievements award Milw. Star Times, 1972; Outstanding Service award Nat. Assn. Black Vets., 1974. Home: 321 E Meinecke Ave Milwaukee WI 53212 Office: 152 W Wisconsin Ave Milwaukee WI 53202 Tel (414) 273-5755

BARBER, AZRO LUCIEN, b. Syracuse, N.Y., May 5, 1885; A.B., Syracuse U., 1907; LL.B., George Washington U., 1912. Admitted to D.C. bar, 1912, Ark. bar, 1914, U.S. Supreme Ct. bar, 1920; partner firm Barber, Henry & Thurman and predecessors, Little Rock, Ark., 1918-70, firm Barber, McCaskill & Amsler, Little Rock, 1970-76. Mem. Am., Ark. bar assns., Am. Coll. Trial Lawyers, Comml. Law League Am. Home: 412 Midland Ave Little Rock AR 72205 Office: 1500 Union National Bank Bldg Little Rock AR 72201 Tel (501) 372-6175

BARBER, DONALD WILLIAM, b. Monterey Park, Calif., Apr. 4, 1941; A.A., Fullerton Jr. Coll., 1962; B.A., Orange State Coll., 1964; J.D., Southwestern U., 1971. Admitted to Calif. bar, 1972; individual practice law, Los Angeles, 1972—. Mem. Am., Calif., Los Angeles County, Whittier bar assns. Office: 1540 Wilshire Blvd Los Angeles CA 90017 Tel (213) 483-7491

BARBER, HENRY PARKE CUSTIS WILSON, b. Evanston, Ill., May 28, 1907; B.A., Princeton 1928; J.D., Northwestern U., 1931. Admitted to Ill. bar, 1931; asso. firm Peterson, Ross, Rall, Barber & Seidel, and predecessors, Chgo., 1931-44, partner, 1944—. Alderman City of Evanston, 1945-53, chmn. zoning amendment com., 1964-71; trustee Nat. Coll. Edn., Evanston, 1974—. Mem. Chgo., Am. Ill. bar assns. Home: 1519 Hinman Ave Evanston IL 60201 Office: 135 S LaSalle St Chicago IL 60603 Tel (312) 263-7300

BARBER, MONTY CLYDE, b. Rockdale, Tex., Jan. 12, 1931; B.B.A., U. Tex., 1953, LL.B., 1955, J.D., 1955. Admitted to Tex. bar, 1955; since practiced in Dallas; partner firm Biggers, Baker, Lloyd & Carver, 1957-67; v.p. gen. counsel Liquid Paper Corp., 1967-68; v.p., sec., gen. counsel Mary Kay Cosmetics, Inc., 1968—, also dir.; dir. Mary Kay Found., 1968—. Mem. Literacy Instruction for Texas, 1965—, Tex. Council on Economic Edn., 1972—. Mem. Am., Tex., Dallas bar assns., Direct Selling Assn. (dir. 1968—), Am. Soc. Corp. Secs., Phi Delta Phi, Alpha Tau Omega. Contbr. articles to law reviews. Home: 3508 Crescent Dallas TX 75205 Office: 8900 Carpenter Freeway Dallas TX 75247 Tel (214) 631-3942

BARBERO, GEORGE J., b. Port Chester, N.Y., Oct. 20, 1923; A.B. cum laude, Cath. U. Am., 1950; M.A. (O'Hara fellow), U. Notre Dame, 1952; J.D., N.Y. Law Sch., 1957. Admitted to N.Y. bar, 1958; teaching fellow U. Notre Dame, 1952-53; practiced in N.Y.C., 1958-60, New Rochelle, N.Y., 1966-73; litigation appeals atty. Spl. Funds Conservation Com., N.Y.C., 1960-65; instr. bus. law Iona Coll., 1966-68, asst. prof., 1968-72, asso. prof., 1972—. Mem. N.Y. State Bar Assn., Am. Bus. Law Assn., Nat. Assn. Bus. Law Tchrs. Home: 14 Myrtle Blvd Larchmont NY 10538 Office: Dept of Bus Law Iona Coll 715 North Ave New Rochelle NY 10801

BARBIERI, JOSEPH NICHOLAS, b. Bklyn., Sept. 14, 1942; student Coll. of William and Mary; B.A., Ky. Wesleyan Coll., 1970. Admitted to Ky. bar, 1973; partner firm Bush, Barbieri and Bachmeyer, and predecessor, Lexington, 1973—; pub. defender Fayette County, Ky., 1976—; atty. Dept. Labor, State of Ky., 1974-75. Mem. Am. Bar Assn. Recipient Green River Steel award, 1969, 70. Home: 1318 Centre Pkwy Lexington KY 40502 Office: 512 Security Trust Bldg Lexington KY 40507 Tel (606) 253-1658

BARBOUR, JOHN BAXTER, b. Pitts., June 9, 1929; B.A., Franklin Marshall Coll., 1952; LL.B., U. Pitts., 1955. Admitted to Pa. bar, 1955, Ohio bar, 1976; trust officer Fidelity Trust Co., Pitts., 1955-60, Pitts. Nat. Bank, 1960-64; partner firm McVey and Barbour, New Kensington, Pa., 1965—. Chmn. Ind. Twp. Zoning Hearing Bd. Mem. Pa., Am. trial lawyers assns., Allegheny County, Westmoreland County bar assns. Home: 150 Rawlins Run Rd Pittsburgh PA 15238 Office: 201 Pittsburgh Nat Bank Bldg New Kensington PA 15068 Tel (412) 781-8828

BARCO, CARROLL SMITH, b. Orlando, Fla., Aug. 10, 1925; LL.B., U. Fla., 1950. Admitted to Fla. bar, 1950, U.S. Tax Ct. bar, 1973; corporate sec. Robert F. Coleman of Fla., Inc., Orlando, 1952-67; individual practice law, Orlando, 1967—; claims examiner Res. Life Ins. Co., Dallas, 1950-52. Mem. Am., Orange County, Fla. bar assns., Am. Judicature Soc., Ins. Soc. N.Y., Am. Trial Lawyers Assn., Def. Research Inst., Delta Theta Phi, Pi Kappa Alpha. Office: 6900 S Orange Blossom Trail Orlando FL 32809 Tel (305) 851-9320

BARD, DEAN FLOYD, b. Williams, Minn., July 29, 1933; student Bemidji (Minn.) State Coll., 1951-53, 63-64; Ph.B., U. N.D., Grand Forks, 1967, J.D., 1968. Admitted to N.D. bar, 1968, Fed. Dist. Ct. bar N.D., 1970, 8th Circuit Ct. Appeals bar, 1976; bursar U. N.D., 1965-68; com. counsel N.D. Legislative Council, Bismarck, 1968-69, asst. dir., 1969-71; exec. dir. N.D. Constnl. Conv., Bismarck, 1971-72; individual practice law, Bismarck, 1972—; exec. dir. N.D. Sch. Bds. Assn.; exec. sec. N.D. Funeral Dirs. Assn.; spl. asst. atty. gen. N.D. Real Estate Commn. Mem. exec. bd. Council Econ. Edn., 1974—, N.D. Alliance for Arts Commn., 1974—, N.D. High Sch. Activities Assn., 1974—; chmn. Lewis and Clark dist., mem. Mo. Valley council exec. bd. Boy Scouts Am., 1970—. Mem. N.D., Burleigh County bar assns. Recipient Allen Smith award Allen Smith Pub. Co., 1968, Ins. Counsel Jour. award Internat. Assn. Ins. Counsel, 1968, Am. Jurisprudence award Bancroft-Whitney Co., 1968, Dist. Award of Merit Boy Scouts Am.; contbr. articles to profl. jours. and books; columnist Real Estate News and Views. Home: 229 Nova St Bismarck ND 58501 Office: 233 1/2 W Broadway Bismarck ND 58501 Tel (701) 258-7330

BARDEN, JAMES JOSEPH, b. Stevens Point, Wis., May 2, 1939; B.S., B.A., Marquette U., 1961, J.D., 1963. Admitted to Wis. bar, 1963, U.S. Supreme Ct., 1967; atty. R.F. Newman, Inc., Milw., 1963-65; gen. counsel, sec. Mortgage Assos. Inc., Milw., 1965-73; partner firm Gray & Barden, Milw., 1973-77; instr. law Bay Path Jr. Coll., Longmeadow, Mass., 1977—. Mem. Am., Wis., Milw. bar assns., Mortgage Bankers Assos. Home: 186 Converse St Longmeadow MA 01106 Office: 528 Longmeadow St Longmeadow MA 01106 Tel (413) 567-0621

BARDENWERPER, FRED LOUIS, b. Milw., June 12, 1929; B.A., Valparaiso U., 1953, J.D., 1955. Admitted to Wis. bar, 1958; asst. research dir., lawyer, writer Def. Research Inst., Milw., 1969—. Mem. State Bar Wis., Phi Alpha Delta. Contbr. articles to profl. jours.; editorial rev. bd. Quality Progress, 1974—. Office: 1100 W Wells St suite 702 Milwaukee WI 53233 Tel (414) 272-5995

BARDWIL, RICHARD BRIAN, b. Salt Lake City, Oct. 24, 1922; student U. Calif., Los Angeles, 1940-42, Stanford, 1943; LL.B., Pacific Coast U., 1951; B.S. U. So. Calif., 1950. Admitted to Calif. bar, 1952, U.S. Supreme Ct. bar, 1960; individual practice law, Encino, Calif., 1952—; judge pro tem, Los Angeles Municipal Ct., Van Nuys, Calif.; arbitrator, Am. Arbitration Assn., 1963-76. Mem. Am., Calif., Los Angeles County (mem. speakers bur.), W. Hollywood (pres. 1960-61), San Fernando Valley bar assns. Home: 5265 Genesta Ave Encino CA 91316 Office: 15760 Ventura Blvd Ninth Floor Encino CA 91436 Tel (213) 986-8484

BARENGO, ROBERT ROSMINO, b. Reno, Aug. 28, 1941; B.S., Calif. State U., Hayward, 1966; J.D., U. Santa Clara, 1969; postgrad. Nat. Coll. Dist. Attys. Career Prosecutor course, 1971. Admitted to Nev. bar, 1970. law clk to T.O. Craven, 1969; dep. dist. atty. Washoe County, Nev., 1970-73; partner firm Legarza, Lee, Barengo and Doyle, Reno, 1973—; mem. Nev. State Assembly, 1972—, chmn. Nev. State Assembly Jud. Com., 1974—; dir. Nev. Indian Legal Services, Commr. Nat. Conf. Commrs. on Uniform State Laws, 1975-76. Mem. State of Nev., Washoe County, Am. bar assns., Nat. Dist. Attys. Assn. Home: 1431 N Virginia St Reno NV 89504 Office: 241 Ridge St Reno NV 89505 Tel (702) 786-5317

BARENS, ARTHUR HUGO, b. Los Angeles, June 2, 1944; A.B., U. Calif., Los Angeles, 1965; J.D., U. So. Calif., 1968. Admitted to Calif. bar, 1968; partner firm with Marvin Mitchelson, 1968-70; partner firm Flier, Ross and Barens, Los Angeles, 1970—; dir. Hong Kong Bank, 1972; sec. to Gov. Brown. Mem. nat. bd. trustees City of Hope. Mem. Calif., Los Angeles County, Beverly Hills bar assns. Recipient Polit. Sci. award Pi Sigma Alpha, 1965. Office: 9255 Sunset Blvd Suite 727 Los Angeles CA 90069 Tel (213) 273-4811 also 878-4810

BARGFREDE, JAMES ALLEN, b. Seguin, Tex., Sept. 10, 1928; B.S., Tex. A. and M. U., 1950; J.D., St. Mary's U., 1957. Admitted to Tex. bar, 1957, U.S. Patent Office bar, 1961; engr. San Antonio Gen. Depot, 1950-52, San Antonio Pub. Service Bd., 1953-57; patent counsel Hubbard & Co., Chgo., 1958-59; practiced in Chgo., 1959-60, Houston, 1960—; mem. firm Butler, Binion, Rice, Cook & Knapp, 1960-68; individual practice law, 1968-74, 75-77; patent corporate counsel Hydrotech Internat., Inc., Houston, 1977—; mem. firm Bargfrede & Thompson, 1974-75. Mem. Am., Houston bar assns., State Bar Tex., Houston, Am. patent law Aassns. Home: 5649 Piping Rock Houston TX 77056 Office: 4800 W 34th St Houston TX 77092 Tel (713) 688-1491

BARHAM, MACK ELWIN, b. Bastrop, La., June 18, 1924; LL.B., U. Colo.; J.D., La. State U., 1946. Admitted to La. bar, 1946; judge Bastrop City Ct., 1948-61, La. Dist. Ct., 4th Jud. Dist., 1961-68, U.S. Ct. Appeals, 2d Circuit, 1968; asso. justice La. Supreme Ct., 1968-75; prof. law Tulane U., 1975—, La. State U., 1973-74; counsel firm Lemle, Kelleher, Kohlmeyer & Matthews, New Orleans, 1975—; mem. faculty Am. Acad. Jud. Edn., U. Ala. Mem. La. Juvenile Ct. Judges Assn. (past pres.), Am. (trust and probate sect.), New Orleans, La. (gov.) bar assns., La. State Law Inst. (council), Am. Judicature Soc., Internat. Acad. Estate and trust Law, Scribes, Order of Coif, Blue Key, Phi Alpha Delta, Lambda Chi Alpha, Omicron Delta Kappa, Phi Delta Phi. Contbr. articles to legal jours.; recipient Valley Forge Freedoms Found. award, 1969. Home: 5837 Bellaire Dr New Orleans LA 70124 Office: 1800 1st Nat Bank of Commerce Bldg New Orleans LA 70112 Tel (504) 586-1241

BARISH, GEORGE, b. Outwood, Ky., Aug. 11, 1938; B.B.A., U. Miami, 1960, J.D., 1963. Admitted to Fla. bar, 1963; asso. firm John V. Christie, Miami, Fla., 1963-65; individual practice law, Miami, 1965—. Mem. Fla. Bar, Dade County (Fla.) bar assns., U. Miami Band Alumni (pres. 1964-65). Recipient Distinguished Service award S.W. Miami Jaycees, 1966; senator Jr. Chamber Internat., 1971. Home: 1101 SW 99th Pl Miami FL 33174 Office: 9526 Bird Rd Miami FL 33165 Tel (305) 223-0311

BARKDULL, THOMAS HENDRY, JR., b. Miami, Fla., Aug. 15, 1925; LL.B., U. Fla., 1949. Admitted to Fla. bar, 1949; mem. firm Sibley, Grusmark, Barkdull & King, Miami Beach, 1949-61; judge 3d Dist. Ct. Appeal, State of Fla., Miami, 1961—, chief judge, 1963-65, 72-76; mem. adv. com. on rules Supreme Ct. Fla.; of counsel Bd. County Commrs. of Dade County, 1957, Rules and Calendar Com., Fla. Ho. of Reps., 1961; mem. Fla. Jud. Qualifications Commn. Mem. Am. Law Inst., Inst. Jud. Adminstrn. Recipient Good Govt. award Fla. Jr. C. of C., 1964. Outstanding Service awards Miami Beach Bar Assn., 1964, 76. Home: 7500 Old Cutler Rd Coral Gables FL 33143 Office: 2001 SW 117th Ave PO Box 650307 Miami FL 33165 Tel (305) 552-2900

BARKER, DON W., b. Milton, Iowa, Jan. 15, 1912; B.A., U. No. Iowa, 1935; J.D., U. Iowa, 1941. Admitted to Iowa bar, 1941, U.S. Supreme Ct. bar, 1960; atty. County of Hardin, Iowa, 1947-50; sr. mem. firm Barker & McNeal, Iowa Falls, Iowa. Mem. Am., Iowa bar assns. Home: 400 Jason Ave Iowa Falls IA 50126 Office: Barker Bldg Iowa Falls IA 50126 Tel (515) 648-4261

BARKER, FRANK EDWARD, b. Chattanooga, Sept. 7, 1938; B.A. in English, U. Chattanooga, 1961; J.D., U. Cin., 1964. Admitted to Tenn. bar, 1964, Tex. bar, 1967; asso. firm Chambliss, Chambliss & Hodge, Chattanooga, 1964-65; served to capt. JAGC, U.S. Army, 1965-68; asso. firm McCampbell & McCampbell, Corpus Christi, Tex., 1968-72; partner firm Harris, Cook, Browning & Barker, Corpus Christi, 1972—; pres., dir. The Hearth, Corpus Christi, 1971—. Bd. dirs. Multiple Sclerosis Soc., Corpus Christi, 1973-74. Mem. Am., Tenn., Tex., Nueces County bar assns. Recipient Outstanding Young Lawyer award Nueces County, Tex., 1973. Office: 1717 Bank & Trust Tower Corpus Christi TX 78403 Tel (512) 883-1946

BARKER, FRANK PENDLETON, JR., b. Kansas City, Mo., Aug. 29, 1919; A.B., Davidson Coll., 1941; LL.B., Georgetown U., 1950. Admitted to D.C., Mo. bars, 1950; partner firm Jackson, Barker & Sherman, Kansas City, Mo., 1955-69; judge U.S. Bankruptcy Ct., 1969—, chief judge, 1973—. Chmn. Jackson County, Mo., Merit System, 1965-67. Mem. Am., Mo. bar assns., Lawyers Assn. Author: Missouri Creditor's Remedies, 1967. Home: 1009 W 63d Kansas City MO 64113 Office: 919 U S Court House Kansas City MO 64106 Tel (816) 374-5121

BARKER, J(OHN) EMERY, b. Phoenix, Jan. 28, 1936; B.A., U. Ariz., 1957, J.D., 1960. Admitted to Ariz. bar, 1960, U.S. Supreme Ct. bar, 1971; asso. firm Merchant, Parkman, Miller & Pitt, Tucson, 1960-63; individual practice law, Tucson, 1963-65, 70—; partner firm Odgers and Barker, Tucson, 1965-70; pres. Pima County (Ariz.) Legal Aid Soc., Tucson, 1969-71; mem. Ariz. Legal Services Adv. Council; mem. panel of arbitrators Am. Arbitration Assn. Mem. council Dove of Peace Lutheran Ch., Tucson, 1975—; sec. St. Luke's In The Desert, Inc., Tucson, 1976—; v.p. Met. YMCA's of Tucson. Mem. State Bar Ariz., Am., Pima County (pres. 1975-76) bar assns., Ariz. Trial Lawyers Assn. Home: 6241 N Camino Santa Valera Tucson AZ 85718 Office: Suite 501 31 N Stone St Tucson AZ 85701 Tel (602) 624-8367

BARKER, ROBERT ALAN, b. Syracuse, N.Y., Oct. 17, 1931; A.B., Syracuse U., 1953, LL.B., 1958. Admitted to N.Y. State bar, 1958; atty. U.S. Dept. Justice, 1958; research head Appellate Div. 3d Dept., Albany, N.Y., 1959-67; prof. law Union U., Albany Law Sch., 1967—; exec. dir. N.Y. State Law Revision Commn., 1974—; panel reporter N.Y. Judicial Conf. Judge's Seminar, 1969—. Trustee, elder Delmar (N.Y.) Presbyterian Ch. Mem. Am., N.Y. State bar assns. Contbr. articles in field to profl. jours. Home: 53 Jordan Blvd Delmar NY 12054 Office: 488 Broadway St Albany NY 12207 Tel (518) 474-1181

BARKER, SAMUEL HENRY, b. Ogden, Utah, Aug. 1 1911; B.S., U. Utah, 1933, LL.B., 1935, J.D., 1967. Admitted to Utah bar, 1935, U.S. Supreme Ct. bar, 1957; asst. atty. City of Ogden, 1940-41, 44-47; atty. City of Roy (Utah), 1948-52, City of Riverdale (Utah), 1949-70, City of N. Ogden (Utah), 1950—, Town of Huntsville (Utah), 1956—, City of Harrisville (Utah), 1962-72, City of Plain City (Utah), 1965—. Commr. Ogden City Civil Service, 1948-51, 52—. Mem. Utah, Weber County bar assns. Home: 547 13th St Ogden UT 84404 Office: 621 Eccles Bldg 385 24th St Ogden UT 84401 Tel (801) 393-5376

BARKET, GEORGE E., b. Jacksonville, Fla., Mar. 29, 1925; LL.B., U. Miami, 1960. Admitted to Fla. bar, 1960, U.S. Supreme Ct. bar, 1967; individual practice law, Miami, Fla., 1960—; mem. Miami Com. to Appoint City Atty. Mem. Am. Trial Lawyers Assn., Am., Fla., Dade County bar assns. Home: 2001 SW 4th Ave Miami FL 33129 Office: 2935 SW 3d Ave Miami FL 33129 Tel (305) 854-3505

BARKMAN, EDWIN CLAIRE, b. Sept. 24, 1885; LL.B., Syracuse Coll. Law, 1909. Admitted to N.Y. bar, 1910; individual practice law, Watkins Glen, N.Y., 1910-75, ret., 1975; dist. atty. Schuyler County (N.Y.), 1915-20, 1933-37; judge Schuyler County Ct., 1943-54. Mem. Schuyler County Bar Assn. Home: 300 N Decatur St Watkins Glen NY 14891

BARKMAN, FRANCIS ELWOOD, b. Cumberland, Md., Aug. 8, 1916; B.A. magna cum laude with honors in Econs., St. John's Coll., Annapolis, Md., 1938; J.D., Duke U., 1941; Ford Found. fellow Harvard Law Sch., 1959-60; LL.M., N.Y. U., 1967. Admitted to Md. bar, 1941, N.Y. State bar, 1947, Ohio bar, 1958, U.S. Supreme Ct. bar, 1947; asso. firm Sullivan & Cromwell, N.Y.C., 1946-56; faculty U. Toledo, 1956-59, 60—, prof. law, 1962—; vis. prof. law Gonzaga U., Spokane, Wash., 1975-76; cons. Ohio Jud. Conf., 1967-68. Mem. Assn. Am. Law Schs. (accreditation com. 1972-75), League Ohio Law Schs. (sec.-treas. 1971-72), Am., Toledo bar assns., AAUP (pres. local chpt.). Home: 6248 Valley Stream Rd Toledo OH 43615 Office: Coll Law U Toledo Toledo OH 43606 Tel (419) 536-4116

BARKOFF, RUPERT MITCHELL, b. New Orleans, May 7 1948; B.A. with high distinction, U. Mich., 1970, J.D. magna cum laude, 1973. Admitted to Ga. bar, 1974; asso. firm Kilpatrick, Cody, Rogers, McClatchey & Regenstein, Atlanta, 1973—. Mem. Ga., Am. bar assns. Home: 450 Valley Green Dr NE Atlanta GA 30342 Office: 3100 Equitable Bldg 100 Peachtree St Atlanta GA 30303 Tel (404) 522-3100

BARKSDALE, JOHN ROBERTSON, b. Elkhorn, W.Va., Apr 13, 1904; A.B., Va. Mil. Inst., 1924; LL.B., U. Va., 1927. Admitted to Va. bar, 1927, Del. bar, 1968; mem. editorial staff Edward Thompson Law Pub. Co., Northport, L.I., N.Y., 1927-29; asso. firm M.J. Fulton, Richmond, Va., 1930-33; atty. legal dept. E.I. duPont de Nemours & Co., Wilmington, Del., 1933-69; dep. atty. gen. Del. Dept. Justice, 1969-73; individual practice law, Wilmington, 1973—. Mem. Am., Del. bar assns. Contbr. articles to legal publs. Office: 824 Market Tower Wilmington DE 19801 Tel (302) 655-5545

BARKSDALE, RHESA HAWKINS, b. Jackson, Miss., Aug. 8, 1944; B.S., U.S. Mil. Acad., 1966; J.D., U. Miss., 1972. Admitted to Miss. bar, 1972; law clk. Justice Byron R. White, U.S. Supreme Ct., 1972-73; partner firm Butler, Snow, O'Mara, Stevens & Cannada, Jackson, 1973—; instr. U. Miss. Sch. Law, 1975-76, Miss. Coll. Law Sch., 1976—. Mem. exec. com. Miss. Arthritis Found., mem. steering com. for Jimmy Carter Hinds County (Miss.); mem. vestry St. James Ch., Jackson. Mem. Miss. Bar, Am. Bar Assn., Phi Delta Phi. Named Outstanding Grad. U. Miss. Law Sch., 1972, Outstanding Mem. in Nation Phi Delta Phi, 1972. Office: PO Box 22567 Jackson MS 39205 Tel (601) 948-5711

BARLAND, THOMAS HOWARD, b. San Francisco, Mar. 3, 1930; B.A., U. Wis., 1951, LL.B., 1956. Admitted to Wis. bar, 1956; since practiced in Eau Claire; asso. firm Ramsdell, King, Carroll & Barland, and predecessor, 1956-57, partner, 1957-67; judge Eau Claire County Ct., 1967-75, 23d Jud. Circuit Ct., 1976—; mem. Wis. Legislature, 1961-67. Mem. Am. Bar Assn., Am. Judicature Soc., Wis. State Hist. Soc. (pres. 1967-70, bd. curators, 1963—), Order of the Coif. Home: 1617 Drummond St Eau Claire WI 54701 Office: Court House Eau Claire WI 54701 Tel (715) 839-4809

BARLOW, ADELBERT WILLIAM, b. Passaic, N.J., Oct. 19, 1906; student Law Sch. Fordham U., 1926-31; LL.B., St. John's Law Sch., N.Y.U., 1932. Admitted to N.J. bar, 1934, Md. bar, 1946, Hawaii bar, 1947, U.S. Supreme Ct. bar, 1951; practiced in Paterson, N.J., 1934-41; atty. 9th region CAA, Honolulu, 1946-52; U.S. dist. atty. for Dist. Hawaii, 1952-54; mem. firm Barlow & O'Connor, Honolulu, 1954—; mem. standing com. on discipline U.S. Dist. Ct. for Hawaii, 1965, chmn., 1966—. Mem. Am., Fed., Inter-Am. bar assns., Hawaii Bar (chmn. ethics com. 1958-60) Am. Soc. Internat. Law, UN League Lawyers, Internat. Acad. Trial Lawyers, Nat. Assn. Def. Lawyers in Criminal Cases, Am. Judicature Soc., Internat. Acad. Law, Sci., Am., Calif. trial lawyers assn. Home: 3000 Makalei Pl Honolulu HI 96815 Office: Suite 1010 Amfac Bldg 700 Bishop St Honolulu HI 96813 Tel (808) 537-5381

BARLOW, JAMES E., b. Winters, Tex., July 27, 1928; B.S. in Bus. Adminstrn., Trinity U., 1951; J.D., St. Mary's U., 1953. Admitted to Tex. bar, U.S. Dist. Ct. bar, U.S. Supreme Ct. bar; asso. firm Adrian A. Spears, San Antonio, until 1960; mem. Tex. House of Reps., 1960-61; dist. atty., San Antonio, 1961-69; judge 186th Dist. Ct., San Antonio, 1969—; instr. law St. Mary's U., 1966—. Mem. Am., Tex., San Antonio bar assns. Office: Court House San Antonio TX 78204 Tel (512) 220-2505

BARLOW, JAMES RUSSELL, II, b. Concord, N.C., Nov. 1, 1941; A.B., U. N.C., 1963; J.D., Wake Forest U., 1970. Admitted to N.C. bar, 1970, S.C. bar, 1974; clk. to chief judge Ct. Appeals N.C., Raleigh, 1970; asso. firm Hoyle, Hoyle & Boone, Greensboro, N.C., 1971-72; gen. counsel, corp. sec. C. Douglas Wilson & Co., Greenville, S.C., 1973-76; asso. firm Davenport & Fisher, Nashville, N.C., 1976—. Mem. Am., N.C., S.C. bar assns. Home: 301 E Washington St Nashville NC 27856 Office: 207 W Washington St Nashville NC 27856 Tel (919) 459-2124

BARLOW, JOHN SMITH, JR., b. Bardstown, Ky., Nov. 5, 1905; LL.B., Vanderbilt U., 1929. Admitted to Ky. bar, 1929; partner firm Barlow & Barlow, Bardstown, 1970—; atty. Nelson County, Ky., 1942-50; city atty., Bardstown, 1950-65; referee Ky. Workmen's Compensation Bd., 1950-56; spl. circuit judge 11th Jud. Dist. Ky., 1966; dir. Farmers Bank & Trust Co., Maker's Mark Distillery, Inc. Mem. Nelson County, Ky., Am. bar assns., Bardstown C. of C. Home: 112 Hillcrest Dr Bardstown KY 40004 Office: 101-03 Oakley Bldg Bardstown KY 40004 Tel (502) 348-8527

BARLOW, WILLIAM LONNIE, b. Cochran, Ga., May 31, 1942; B.A., Tulane U., 1964; J.D., Mercer U., 1967. Admitted to Ga. bar, 1971; asso. firm A. Newell NeSmith, Cochran, 1971-74; atty., sec.-treas. W.C. Lawson Cotton Co. Ga., Cochran, 1974—. Deacon 1st Baptist Ch. Cochran. Mem. Am., Cochran, Oconee Jud. Circuit bar assns., Delta Theta Phi. Home: 201 6th St Cochran GA 31014 Office: 112 2d St PO Box 618 Cochran GA 31014 Tel (912) 934-7837

BARNA, NICHOLAS ANDREW, b. Waymart, Pa., May 21, 1946; B.A., Wilkes Coll., 1968; J.D., U. N.D., 1971. Admitted to Pa. bar, 1971; asst. dist. atty. Wayne County (Pa.), 1971-76, dist. atty., 1976—; partner firm Conway, Barna & Spall, Honesdale, Pa., 1971—. Mem. Am., Pa. bar assns., Am., Pa. trial lawyers assns. Home: 421 Ridge St Honesdale PA 18431 Office: Box 510 214 Ninth St Honesdale PA 18431 Tel (717) 253-4921

BARNAKO, FRANK RICHARDSON, b. Easton, Pa., Aug. 2, 1912; B.A., Lafayette Coll., 1933; J.D., U. Mich., 1936. Admitted to Pa. bar, 1937; law clk. firm Coffin & Coffin, Easton, 1936-37; practiced law, Easton, 1937-42; asst. to mgr. safety and workmen's compensation div., indsl. relations dept. Bethlehem Steel Corp. (Pa.), 1942-47, asst. mgr., 1947-50, mgr., 1951-75; chmn. Occupational Safety and Health Rev. Commn., Washington, 1976—. Bd. dirs. Nat. Safety Council, v.p. fin. mem. nat. adv. com. occupation safety and health, 1971-75; bd. dirs. Lehigh Valley (Pa.) Safety Council, 1952—. Mem. Am. Iron and Steel Inst. (emeritus mem., past chmn. safety com.), Am. Soc. Safety Engrs., Am., Pa., Northampton County bar assns. Recipient Silver Beaver award Boy Scouts Am., 1965, Distinguished Service to Safety citation Nat. Safety Council, 1969. Home: 2445 Main St Bethlehem PA 18017 Office: 1825 K St NW Washington DC 20006 Tel (202) 634-7970

BARNARD, JOHN, JR., b. Cleve., Aug. 13, 1917; B.A., Harvard U., 1939, LL.B., 1947. Admitted to Mass. bar, 1947; asso. firm Gaston, Snow, Motley & Holt, and predecessors, Boston, 1947-51, partner, 1951-63; gen. counsel Mass. Investors Trust, Boston, 1963-69, mng. trustee, 1969—; gen. counsel Mass. Investors Growth Stock Fund, Boston, 1963-69, v.p., dir., 1969-77; dir., sr. v.p. Mass. Fin. Services, Inc., 1969-77, mng. partner, 1977—; v.p., dir. Mass. Income Devel. Fund, Boston, 1971-77; dir. Mass. Capital Devel. Fund, Boston, 1971-77, Mass. Fin. Devel. Fund, Boston, 1975-77; Mass. Fin. Bond Fund, Boston, 1975-77; trustee Mass. Cash Mgmt. Fund, Boston, 1967-77, MFS Managed Municipal Bond Trust, Boston, 1976-77; Suffolk Franklin Savs. Bank. Mem. investment com. New Eng. Deaconess Hosp., Bsoton, 1975—, mem. audit com., 1976-77, trustee, 1969—. Mem. Nat. Assn. Securities Dealers (investment cos. com. 1977—), Greater Boston C. of C. (dir. 1976—), Investment Co. Inst. (chmn. investment advisor div. 1975—, bd. govs., 1970—, chmn. bd. govs., 1970-72). Office: 200 Berkeley St Boston MA 02116 Tel (617) 423-3500

BARNARD, ROBERT C., b. Portland, Oreg., Oct. 31, 1913; B.A., Reed Coll., 1935; Dean's Spl. scholar, Columbia Law Sch., 1935-36; B.A., Oxford U., 1938, B.C.L. (Rhodes scholar), 1939; M.A., 1951. Admitted to Wash. bar, 1940, D.C. bar, 1947, U.S. Supreme Ct. bar, 1943; chief appelate sect. Antitrust div., chief legal adviser Office Asst. Solicitor Gen., Dept. Justice, 1939-47; mem. firm Cleary, Gottlieb, Steen & Hamilton, 1947—, charge Paris office, 1949-52, Washington office, 1952-61, sr. partner, 1961—. Mem. com. apptd. by D.C. Jud. Conf. to report on adminstrn. justice under emergency conditions in D.C. Mem. Am., Fed., D.C., Wash. bar assns. Contbr. articles to legal jours. Home: 5409 Dorset Ave Chevy Chase MD 20015 Office: 1250 Connecticut Ave NW Washington DC 20036 Tel (202) 223-2151

BARNELL, THOMAS MICHAEL, b. Syracuse, N.Y., Aug. 18, 1935; B.B.S., LeMoyne Coll., 1956; LL.B., Syracuse U., 1959. Admitted to N.Y. bar, 1960; asso. firm Gale, Farrell, Crowley & Martin, Baldwinsville, N.Y., 1958-60; partner firm Farrell, Martin & Barnell, Baldwinsville, 1961—; mem. Onondaga County Legislature, 1971-75, chmn. edn. and libraries com., 1974-75; justice, Town of Van Buren, N.Y., 1963-71; acting police justice Village of Baldwinsville, 1965. Mem. Am., N.Y. State, Onondaga County (chmn. real property com. 1976) bar assns., Onondaga County Title Assn. Recipient Distinguished Service award Baldwinsville Jaycees, 1969. Home: 2503 Country Ln Baldwinsville NY 13027 Office: 42 Oswego St Baldwinsville NY 13027 Tel (315) 635-3959

BARNES, ALEXANDER HALL, b. Murfreesboro, N.C., Apr. 4, 1931; B.A., U. N.C., 1954, J.D. with honors, 1956. Admitted to N.C. bar, 1956, U.S. Ct. Mil. Appeals bar, 1959; asso. firm Spears, Barnes, Baker & Boles, Durham, N.C., 1959-62, partner, 1962—. Mem. adv. bd. Durham Salvation Army, 1970—. Mem. Am., N.C., Durham County bar assns., Am. Arbitration Assn., Am. Judicature Soc., Order of Coif. Home: 6300 Garrett Rd Durham NC 27707 Office: Spears Barnes Baker & Boles 433 W Main St Durham NC 27702 Tel (919) 682-5721

BARNES, CLARKE CORDNER, b. Fort Dodge, Iowa, Oct. 3, 1942; B.A. in Sociology, U. Iowa, 1964, J.D., 1967. Admitted to Iowa bar, 1967, Ill. bar, 1972; judge adv. USMC, 1967-72; with office of states atty. Rock Island County (Ill.), 1972-74; partner firm McNeal & Barnes, Moline, Ill., 1974-77; asso. circuit judge 14th Ill. Jud. Circuit, Rock Island County, 1977—; pub. defender Rock Island County, 1974-77. Mem. adminstrv. bd. First United Meth. Ch. of Rock Island, 1973—. Mem. Ill., Am. bar assns., Nat. Dist. Attys. Assn., Ill. Pub. Defenders Assn., Am. Judicature Soc. Home: 2530 30th St Rock Island IL 61201 Office: Rock Island County Courthouse Rock Island IL 61201

BARNES, F. WAINWRIGHT, b. N.Y.C., Oct. 28, 1940; A.B., Duke U., 1962; LL.B., Washington and Lee U., 1965. Admitted to D.C. bar, 1965, Md. bar, 1966; asso. firm Brault, Graham, Scott and Brault, Washington, 1966-71, partner, 1971—. Mem. Md., D.C., Am. bar assns., D.C. Defense Lawyers (sec. 1971-72). Home: 304 St Lawrence Dr Silver Spring MD 20901 Office: 1314 19th St NW Washington DC 20036 Tel (202) 785-1200

BARNES, HARRIS HASTINGS, III, b. Clarksdale, Miss., Sept. 17, 1946; B.S., Miss. State U., 1968; J.D., U. Miss., 1972. Admitted to Miss. bar, 1972; asso. firm Cunningham, Booneville, Miss., 1972-73, firm Mize, Thompson, and Blass, Gulfport, Miss., 1973-75; individual practice law, Gulfport 1975—. Active United Way; adv. bd. Salvation Army. Mem. Am., Harrison County, Miss. bar assn. Home: 1513 19th Ave Gulfport MS 39501 Office: 1317 22d Ave Gulfport MS 39501 Tel (601) 868-2720

BARNES, HERSCHIEL SEVIER, b. Cookeville Tenn., Dec. 19, 1919; student Tenn. Tech. 1936-39; B.A., George Peabody Coll., 1940; J.D., Vanderbilt U., 1948. Admitted to Tenn. bar, 1947; mem. firm Crawford, Barnes & Acuff, Cookeville, 1948—; referee in bankruptcy Northeastern div. U.S Dist. Ct. Middle Dist. Tenn., 1955-59; dir. Crest Lawn Cemetery, Citizens Bank, Cookeville. Bd. dirs. Cookeville Gen. Hosp., 1961-72, chmn., 1968-72; treas. Putnam County chpt. ARC; trustee Putnam County Library. Mem. Am., Tenn. (chmn. com. on uniform laws, 1976—), Putnam County bar assns., Putnam County C. of C. Editor in chief Vanderbilt Law Rev., 1947-48. Home: 957 Sunset Dr Cookeville TN 38501 Office: 101 S Jefferson St Cookeville TN 38501 Tel (615) 526-6123

BARNES, J. REYNOLDS, b. Sacramento, Sept. 15, 1942; B.A., Lewis and Clark Coll., 1965, J.D., 1970. Admitted to Oreg. bar, 1970, since practiced in Portland; mem. firm Barnes, Laman & Barnes, now sr. partner. Home: 14124 SW Goodall Rd Lake Oswego OR 97034 Office: 621 SW Morrison St Portland OR 97205 Tel (503) 222-9111

BARNES, ROBERT DEAN, b. Flandraeu, S.D., July 9, 1922; B.S., S.D. State U., 1947; J.D., Northwestern U., 1950. Admitted to Ill. bar, 1950, S.D. bar, 1950; spl. agt. FBI, Conn. and N.Y.C., 1950-53; asso. firm McBride & Baker, Chgo., 1953-60; partner firm McBride, Baker, Wienke & Schlosser, Chgo., 1960—; dir. The W.W. Rice Co., 1976. Mem. Am., Ill., S.D. State, Chgo., DuPage County bar assns., Maritime Law Assn. U.S., Soc. Former Spl. Agts. FBI. Home: 320 S Garfield St Hinsdale IL 60521 Office: 110 N Wacker Dr Chicago IL 60606 Tel (312) 346-6191

BARNES, WALLACE RAY, b. Easton, Pa., Nov. 7, 1928; A.B., Duke, 1950; LL.B., Harvard, 1957. Admitted to Pa. bar, 1958, Ohio bar, 1973, Fed. Power bar, 1973; atty. Allegheny Ludlum Steel Co., Pitts., 1957-62, Columbia Gas of Md., Columbia Gas of Pa. and Columbia Gas of N.Y., Pitts., 1962-73; sec. sec., gen. counsel Columbia Gas of Ky., Md., N.Y., Pa., Ohio, W.Va., and Va., Columbus, Ohio, 1973—; dir. Columbia Gas of Ohio and N.Y. Dir. Pitts. Better Bus. Bur., 1972-74. Mem. Am., Fed. Power, Ohio, Columbus bar assns., Phi Beta Kappa. Office: 99 N Front St Columbus OH 43215 Tel (614) 460-2549

BARNETT, ELIOTT B., b. Jersey City, N.J., June 30, 1935; B.A., Lehigh U., 1954; J.D., Columbia U., 1957. Admitted to N.Y. bar, 1957, Fla. bar, 1959, U.S. Supreme Ct. bar, 1970; sr. partner Ruben, Barnett, McClosky, Schuster and Schmerer, Ft. Lauderdale, Fla., 1959—; gen. counsel Downtown Devel. Authority, City of Ft. Lauderdale, 1975—; lectr. U. Miami Law Sch., Real Estate Inst. N.Y.U. Pres., Ft. Lauderdale Mus. Art; bd. dirs. Ft. Lauderdale Symphony; bd. govs. Nova U. Law Sch. Mem. Am., Fla. bar assns., N.Y. County Lawyers Assn. Office: 900 NE 26th Ave Fort Lauderdale FL 33304 Tel (305) 565-9362

BARNETT, HARVEY JOEL, b. Chgo., May 22, 1943; B.A., U. Ill., 1964; J.D. Northwestern U., 1967. Admitted to Ill. bar, 1967, U.S. Supreme Ct. bar, 1971; since practiced in Chgo., asso. firm Arnstein, Gluck, Weitzenfeld & Minow, 1967-69; asso. firm Rosenthal and Schanfield, 1969-72, partner, 1972—. Mem. Sch. Dist. #107 Bd. Edn., Highland Park, Ill., 1975—. Mem. Ill., Chgo. bar assns., Ill. Trial Lawyers Assn. Home: 1863 Cloverdale Highland Park IL 60035 Office: 105 W Adams St Chicago IL 60603 Tel (312) CE6-5622

BARNETT, HOLLIS HERMAN, b. Seattle, May 27, 1939; B.B.A., Seattle U., 1961; J.D., Gonzaga U., 1969. Admitted to Wash. bar, 1969; clk. atty. gen's. office State of Wash., Spokane, 1968-69; dep. pros. atty. Peirce County (Wash.), 1969-71; asso. firm Campbell, Dille, Barnett & McCarthy, and predecessors, Puyallup, Wash., 1971, partner, 1971—; atty. Town Orting (Wash.), 1971-77, Town Eatonville (Wash.), 1976-77; judge Puyallup Municipal Ct., 1976—. Chmn., Puyallup Valley United Way Dr., 1975. Mem. Am., Wash., Peirce County bar assns., Wash. Trial Lawyers Assn. Contbr. articles Gonzaga Law Rev. Home: 13529 118th St E Puyallup WA 98371 Office: 319 S Meridian St Puyallup WA 98371 Tel (206) 848-3513

BARNETT, JOHN H., b. Natchez, Miss., Oct. 19, 1942; B.B.A., U. Miss., 1965, J.D., 1968. Admitted to Miss. bar, 1968, U.S. Dist. Ct. bar, 1968, U.S. Supreme Ct. bar, 1972; judge municipal ct., Gulfport, Miss., 1969-75; partner firm Breland & Barnett, Gulfport, 1971—. Mem. Am., Miss. bar assns. Home: 17 Keyser Ln Gulfport MS 39501 Office: 1206 31st Ave Gulfport MS 39501 Tel (601) 863-2217

BARNETT, ROBERT EARL, b. New Orleans, Nov. 24, 1943; B.A. with honors, Occidental Coll., 1965; J.D., U. Calif. at Berkeley, 1968. Admitted to Calif. bar, 1969; dep. pub. defender, Solano County, Calif., 1969-71; asso. firm McPherson & Harris, Fairfield, Calif., 1971-73; partner firm McPherson & Barnett, Fairfield, 1973—; chmn. bd. dirs. Solano County Legal Assistance, 1973-75. Pres. Am. Cancer Assn., Fairfield, 1975-77. Mem. Solano County Bar Assn., Am., Calif. (v.p. Solano County) trial lawyers assns. Home: 3677 Rockville Rd Suisun CA 94585 Office: 712 Empire St Fairfield CA 94533 Tel (707) 425-0671

BARNETT, STEPHEN, b. Chattanooga, Apr. 18, 1931; A.B., Stanford, 1952, J.D., 1954. Admitted to Calif. bar, 1955; partner firm Stammer, McKnight, Barnum, Bailey & Barnett, Fresno, Calif., 1956-71, firm McCormick, Barstow, Sheppard, Coyle & Wayte, Fresno, 1971—. Pres. Family Service Center of Fresno, 1969. Mem. Am., Fresno County (pres. 1974) bar assns., State Bar Calif. Home: 4386 N Wishon St Fresno CA 93704 Office: 400 Guarantee Savings Bldg Fresno CA 93721 Tel (209) 442-1150

BARNETT, STEPHEN GARY, b. Tulsa, Jan. 26, 1947; B.B.A., So. Meth. U., 1969, J.D., 1972, LL.M., 1976. Admitted to Tex. bar, 1972, U.S. Supreme Ct. bar, 1976; corporate atty. Dresser Industries, Inc., Dallas, 1972—. Bd. mgmt. Camp Grady Spruce Br. YMCA, Dallas, 1972—. Mem. Am., Tex., Dallas bar assns. Home: 2912 Westminster Ave Dallas TX 75205 Office: 1505 Elm St Dallas TX 75201 Tel (214) 745-8879

BARNETT, WILLIAM A., b. Chgo., Oct. 13, 1916; LL.B., Loyola U., Chgo., 1941. Admitted to Ill. bar, 1941; with Chief Counsel's office IRS, Chgo., 1948-55; chief tax atty. U.S. Atty.'s Office, Chgo., 1955-60; individual practice law, Chgo., 1960—. Mem. Am., Fed., Chgo., 7th Circuit (gov.) bar assns. Office: 135 S LaSalle St Chicago IL 60603 Tel (312) RA 6-4480

BARNETTE, CURTIS HANDLEY, b. St. Albans, W.Va., Jan. 9, 1935; A.B. with high honors, W.Va. U., 1956; diploma in Internat. Law (Fulbright scholar) U. Manchester, 1957; J.D., Yale, 1962; postgrad. Harvard Bus. Sch., 1974-75. Admitted to Conn. bar, 1962, Pa. bar, 1968, U.S. Supreme Ct. bar, 1966; atty. firm Wiggin & Dana, New Haven, 1962-67; atty. Bethlehem Steel Corp. (Pa.), 1967-70, gen. atty., 1970-72, asst. sec., 1972-76, asst. gen. counsel, 1972-77, asst. to v.p., 1974-76, sec., 1976—, asst. v.p., 1976-77, v.p., gen. counsel, 1977—; lectr. U. Md., 1958-59. Mem. Am., Pa., Conn., Fed., Northampton County bar assns., Am. Iron and Steel Inst., Phi Beta Kappa, Beta Theta Pi, Phi Alpha Theta, Phi Delta Phi. Home: 1112 Prospect Ave Bethlehem PA 18018 Office: Bethlehem Steel Corp Martin Tower Bethlehem PA 18016 Tel (215) 694-6137

BARNETTE, HENRY VANCE, JR., b. Raleigh, N.C., June 6, 1939; A.B., Duke, 1961; J.D., Wake Forest U., 1964. Admitted to N.C. bar, 1964; asso. firm Bunn, Hatch, Little, Bunn and Jones, Raleigh, 1964; asst. city solicitor City of Raleigh, 1964-65, city solicitor, 1965-68; judge N.C. Dist. Ct., 10th Jud. Dist., 1968—. Mem. Am., N.C., Wake County bar assns., Am. Judicature Soc., Am. Judge Assn., N.C. Conf. Dist. Ct. Judges. Home: 312 Hillandale Dr Raleigh NC 27607 Office: Wake County Courthouse Raleigh NC 27601 Tel (919) 733-2477

BARNEY, ALBERT WILKINS, b. St. Johnsbury, Vt., Oct. 23, 1920; A.B., Yale U., 1942; LL.B., Harvard U., 1948. Admitted to Vt. bar, 1949; asso. firm Starry R. Waterman, 1948-49, Richardson & Caldbeck, 1949-50; mem. Vt. Legislature, Montpelier, 1951-52; judge Caledonia Municipal Ct., 1951-52; superior judge Vt. Supreme Ct., 1952-58, chief superior judge, 1958-59, asso. justice, 1959-74, chief justice, 1974—. Trustee St. Johnsbury (Vt.) Acad., 1974—. Mem. Am., Vt. bar assns., Am. Judicature Soc. Home: 72 Summer St St Johnsbury VT 05819 Office: 111 State St Montpelier VT 05602 Tel (802) 828-3277

BARNEY, THOMAS MCNAMEE, b. Indpls., Mar. 14, 1938; A.B., Cornell U., 1960; J.D., cum laude, Ind. U., 1966; LL.M., N.Y.U., 1967. Admitted to Ind. bar, 1966, N.Y. bar, 1967; clk. firm Barney & Hughes, Indpls., 1963-66; asso. firm Dewey, Ballantine et. al., N.Y.C., 1967-69; asso. firm Phillips, Lytle, Hitchcock, Blaine & Huber, Buffalo, 1969-74, partner, 1975—; lectr. State U.N.Y., Buffalo, 1969—, U. Buffalo Tax Inst., 1971-75; N.Y. State Bankers Assn. Tax Sch., 1974-75; N.Y. State Bankers Asso. Trust Adminstrn. Sch., 1974, 76. Mem. Am. (tax sec.), Ind., N.Y. State (tax and estates and trusts sects.), Erie County bar assns. Contbr. articles to profl. jours. Office: 3400 Marine Midland Center Buffalo NY 14203 Tel (716) 847-8480

BARNHILL, EARL STANTON, b. Junction City, Kans., Apr. 3, 1932; B.S., Kans. State U., 1956; J.D., Washburn U., 1959. Admitted to Kans. bar, 1959; asso. firm Weary, Weary & Sangster, Junction City, Kans., 1959-62; partner Weary, Weary &Barnhill, 1962-64; individual practice law, Junction City, 1964-66; dir. dept. law enforcement Central Mo. State U., Warrensburg, 1966-69; dir. security Mid-Am. Bankcard, Omaha, Nebr., 1969-71; asso. prof. criminal justice U. Nebr., Omaha, 1971-73, U. Nev., Reno, 1973—; city prosecutor Junction City, 1959-64; mem. Kans. House of Reps., 1964-66; asst. county atty. Geary County, Kans., 1965; city atty. Junction City, 1966. Mem. Am., Kans. bar assns., Nat. Dist. Attys. Assn., Internat. Assn. Chiefs of Police. Contbr. articles in field to profl. jours. Home: 12950 S Hills Dr Reno NV 89511 Office: Dept Criminal Justice U Nev Reno NV 89557 Tel (702) 784-6164

BARNHOUSE, ROBERT BOLON, b. Marietta, Ohio, July 18, 1937; B.A., Ohio Wesleyan U., 1959; LL.B. (Root-Tilden scholar), N.Y. U., 1962. Admitted to Md. bar, 1962, U.S. Supreme Ct. bar, 1970; mem. firm Piper & Marbury, Balt., 1970—; instr. continuing legal edn. U. Md., 1974—. Counsel Md. div. Am. Cancer Soc., 1970—, bd. dirs., 1970—, chmn. budget and fin. com., 1974—. Mem. Balt., Md. bar assns., Assn. Def. Trial Counsel (pres. 1972). Home: 1050 Cedar Ridge Ct Annapolis MD 21403 Office: 2000 First Maryland Bldg 25 S Charles St Baltimore MD 21201 Tel (301) 539-2530

BARNTHOUSE, WILLIAM JOSEPH, b. Jefferson City, Mo., Nov. 25, 1948; A.B. in English and Philosophy, Rockhurst Coll., 1970; J.D., U. Mo. at Kansas City, 1973, LL.M., 1976. Admitted to Mo. bar, 1973, Colo. bar, 1976, U.S. Supreme Ct. bar, 1977; law clk. to judge 16th Circuit Ct. Mo., Kansas City, 1972-73; asst. pros. atty. Jackson County, Mo., 1973; research atty. Mo. Ct. Appeals, Kansas City, 1974; teaching fellow, instr. U. Mo. at Kansas City Sch. Law, 1974-75; lectr. Avila Coll., Kansas City, 1974-75; lectr. Rockhurst Coll., Kansas City, 1974; lectr. Jackson County Regional Center Criminal Justice, Kansas City, 1973; atty. Gulf Oil Corp., Denver 1975—; judge adv. gen. Colo. N.G., 1975—. Mem. Am., Mo. Kansas City, Jackson County, Cole County, Colo., Denver bar assns., Am. Judicature Soc. Author: Excess Liability: Insurance and Negligence Cases, 1971; Multinational Corporations and International Law, 1973. Nat. Inst. Trial Advocacy scholar. Home: 2795 E Jamison Pl Littleton CO 80122 Office: 1720 S Bellaire St Denver CO 80222 Tel (303) 758-1700

BARON, CHARLES HILLEL, b. Phila., Aug. 18, 1936; A.B., U. Pa., 1958, Ph.D., 1972; LL.B., Harvard, 1961. Admitted to Pa. bar, 1967, U.S. Supreme Ct. bar, 1970, Mass. bar, 1972; asst. prof. law U. Pa., 1965-66; asso. firm Blank, Rome, Klaus & Comisky, Phila., 1966-68; consumers advocate, chief law reform Community Legal Services, Phila., 1968-70; asso. prof. law Boston Coll., 1970-73, asso. dean, 1972-74, prof. law, 1973—, faculty advisor, Legal Assistance Bur. and Environ. Affairs; mem. Mass. Health Facilities Appeals Bd., 1974-75; chmn. Com. on Transplants from Child Donors, Spl. Mass. Legis. Commn. on Human Experimentation and Exptl. Therapy; exec. dir. Resource Center for Consumers of Legal Services, Washington, 1975—. co-dir. Boston Coll.-Tufts U. Joint Center for the Study of Law, Medicine and the Life Scis., 1969—; bd. dirs. Boston U. Center for Law and Health Scis. Mem. Prepaid Legal Services Com., Mass. Bar Assn. (prepaid legal services com.), Hastings Inst. of Society, Ethics and the Life Scis., Soc. for Philosophy and Pub. Affairs. Home: 6823 Barr Rd Bethesda MD 20016 Office: 1302 18th St NW Washington DC 20036 Tel (202) 659-8514

BARON, GAIL CUMINS, b. N.Y.C., June 6, 1939; A.B. cum laude, U. Mich., 1960; J.D., Harvard, 1963. Admitted to N.Y. bar, 1963, U.S. Dist. Ct. for So. and Eastern N.Y. bars, 1970; asso. firm Sharretts, Paley, Carter & Blauvelt, N.Y.C., 1964-68, partner, 1968—; sec., treas. Internat. Apparel Importers Assn.; legal adviser Fashion Accessories Assn., Am. Importers Assn., 1971—. Mem. Customs, N.Y. State bar assns., Am. Soc. Internat. Law, Phi Sigma Alpha. Home: 1050 Fifth Ave New York City NY 10028 Office: 80 Broad St New York City NY 10004 Tel (212) 425-0055

BARON, JOSEPH M., b. Chgo., July 16, 1912; B.A., U. Chgo., 1931, J.D., 1934. Admitted to Ill. bar, 1934; asso. firm McChesney, Whiteford & Wells, Chgo., 1934-35, Smietanka, Wilson & Conlon, Chgo., 1935-42, Posanski, Johansen & Krohn, Chgo., 1942-50, 71—; v.p. loan dept., lawyer Mfrs. Nat. Bank, Chgo., 1950-71. Mem. Ill., Chgo. bar assns., Advocates Soc. Home: 6700 N Nokomis Ave Lincolnwood IL 60646 Office: 11 S LaSalle St Chicago IL 60603 Tel (312) 782-6795

BARON, MARTIN LEWIS, b. N.Y.C., Mar. 14, 1924; B.B.A., Coll. City N.Y., 1946; LL.B., N.Y. Law Sch., 1952, J.D., 1968. Admitted to N.Y. state bar, 1954; asst. atty. gen. N.Y. State, N.Y.C., 1956-69; atty. firm White & Case, N.Y.C., 1969—. Chmn. New Rochelle (N.Y.) Narcotics Guidance Council, 1969-70; pres. Bayberry-New Rochelle Assn. Property Owners, 1970. C.P.A. Mem. Am. Inst. CPAs, N.Y. Law Sch. Alumni Assn. (pres. 1971-72). Office: 14 Wall St New York City NY 10005 Tel (212) 732-1040

BARON, STEVEN J., b. N.Y.C., June 4, 1943; B.A. in Chemistry, U. Cin., 1965; J.D., N.Y. Law Sch., 1968. Admitted to N.Y. bar, 1969, U.S. Patent Office bar, 1970; atty. Colgate-Palmolive Co., N.Y.C., 1973—; legal intern N.Y. Legal Aid Soc., 1966-68. Mem. Am. Bar Assn., N.Y. Patent Lawyers Assn., Am. Patent Law Assn. Home: 24 Stanton Circle New Rochelle NY 10804 Office: 685 3d Ave New York City NY 10017 Tel (212) 986-1000

BARR, ALBERT STEPHEN, III, b. Pitts., Aug. 18, 1940; A.B., Princeton, 1962; LL.B., Rutgers U., 1965. Admitted to Md. bar, 1965, U.S. Supreme Ct. bar, 1970; law clk. to judge U.S. Dist. Ct. for Dist. Md., 1965-66; partner firm Piper & Marbury, Balt., 1972—. Mem. Md. State (chmn. sect. taxation 1976-77, chmn. sect. estate and trust law 1977—), Am. bar assns. Contbr. articles to Md. Bar Jour. Office: 2000 First Md Bldg 25 S Charles St Baltimore MD 21201 Tel (301) 539-2530

BARR, CULVER KENT, b. Rochester, N.Y., Jan. 27, 1936; A.B., Syracuse U., 1957; LL.B., Albany Law Sch., 1960, J.D., 1968. Admitted to N.Y. bar, 1961; practiced in Rochester, 1960-67; judge Rochester City Ct., 1968-72, Monroe County (N.Y.) Ct., 1972—. Home: 11 Landing Rd N Rochester NY 14625 Office: 218 Hall of Justice Rochester NY 14614 Tel (716) 428-5276

BARR, DON ALBERT, b. Glendale, W.Va., Sept. 10, 1926; A.B., W.Va. U., 1947, J.D., 1950. Admitted to W.Va. bar, 1950, U.S. Supreme Ct. bar, 1970; individual practice law, Moundsville, W.Va., 1950—; city atty. Moundsville, 1953-56; commr. circuit ct. Marshall County, W.Va., 1957—. Mem. Marshall County (pres. 1975-76), W.Va. bar assns., Phi Beta Kappa. Home: 306 Lee St Glendale WV 26038 Office: 703 5th St Moundsville WV 26041 Tel (304) 845-8373

BARR, EARL LEO, b. Milw., June 27, 1912; B.S., U.S. Mil. Acad., 1935; J.D., U. Okla., 1955. Admitted to Olka. bar, 1955, U.S. Patent Office bar, 1957; patent atty. Halliburton Services, Inc., Duncan, Okla., 1955-61; individual practice law, Marlow, Okla., 1961—; municipal judge City of Marlow, 1973—. Treas., Assumption Ch., Duncan, 1975-76. Mem. Am. Arbitration Assn. Home: 1509 N 13th St Duncan OK 73533 Office: 103 N 2d St Marlow OK 73055 Tel (405) 658-2390

BARR, FORREST N., b. Berkeley, Calif., June 24, 1929; student U. Ariz., 1947-49; A.B., Stanford, 1951, LL.B., 1953. Admitted to Ariz. bar, 1953; practiced law, Tucson, 1953-54; asst. dir. ins. State of Ariz., Phoenix, 1954-63; legal counsel Blue Cross and Blue Shield of Ariz., Phoenix, 1963—. Bd. dirs., mem. speaker's bur. Planned Parenthood Assn. Phoenix, 1965—. Mem. Ariz. (adminstrv. law com.), Maricopa County bar assns., Ariz. Hosp. Assn. (council on govtl. affairs). Home: 2053 W Pierson St Phoenix AZ 85015 Office: 321 W Indian School Rd Phoenix AZ 85013 Tel (602) 279-5341

BARR, GLENN FLEMING, b. Manchester, Iowa, Nov. 28, 1904; B.A. U. Iowa, 1926, J.D., 1928; postgrad. Harvard, 1926-27. Admitted to Iowa bar, 1928, U.S. Dist. Ct. bar, 1934; with Comml. Nat. Bank, Waterloo, Iowa, 1928-30, Harris Trust & Savings Bank, Chgo., 1930-32; individual practice law, Manchester, Iowa, 1932-72, Cedar Rapids, Iowa, 1972—; owner, mgr. Barr Lumber Co., Manchester, 1953-72; magistrate Linn County, Iowa, 1973-74. Mem. SCORE, 1973—. Home: 4357 Eaglemere Ct SE Cedar Rapids IA 52403 Office: 309 S First St Manchester IA 52057 Tel (319) 927-4652

BARR, HARVEY STEPHEN, b. Bklyn., June 4, 1941; student Fairleigh Dickinson U., 1958, Rutgers U., 1958-61; LL.B., N.Y. Law Sch., 1964. Admitted to N.Y. bar, 1964, U.S. Supreme Ct. bar, 1968; individual practice law, Spring Valley, N.Y., 1965—; village atty. Village of Spring Valley, 1965-67, Village of Sloatsburg, 1969-74, Village of Suffern, 1975—; first asst. county atty. Rockland County (N.Y.), 1970-74. Counsel, assemblyman 96th dist. N.Y. State Assembly, 1969-70; chmn. Town of Ramapo Republican Com., 1974—. Mem. Rockland County, N.Y. State, Am. bar assns., Comml. Law League, Phi Delta Phi (magister 1963-64). Office: 664 S Main St Spring Valley NY 10977 Tel (914) 352-4080

BARR, JAMES THOMAS, b. Milw., Mar. 4, 1921; Ph.B., Carroll Coll., 1947; J.D., Marquette U., 1950. Admitted to Wis. bar, 1950, Ohio bar, 1966; gen. counsel Mall Tool Co. (now part Remington Admiral Corp.), Chgo., 1956-57, chief counsel, 1958-62; chief counsel Eltra Corp. (Autolite), Toledo, 1962-65; individual practice of law, Ohio, 1965-71, Hancock, Wis., 1972—. Mem. Wis., Waushara-Marquette bar assns. Home: Rural Route # 3 Wautoma WI 54982 Office: Box 153 Main St Hancock WI 54943

BARR, JOHN DOUGLAS, b. Yreka, Calif., Apr. 3, 1942; B.A., Reed Coll., 1964; U. Chgo., 1967. Admitted to Calif. bar, 1967; asso. firm Coshow & Barr, Redding, Calif., 1967-73; individual practice, Redding, 1973-75; asso. firm Barr & Minoletti, Redding, 1975—. Mem. Shasta-Trinity Counties Bar Assn. (pres. 1976), Calif. State Bar, Assn. Def. Counsel No. Calif., Calif. Trial Lawyers Assn. Office: 1824 Court St PO Box 4417 Redding CA 96001 Tel (916) 243-8008

BARR, ROY RASSMANN, b. Chgo., Sept. 28, 1901; Ph.B., U. Chgo., 1923; J.D. John Marshall Law Sch., 1924. Admitted to Ill. bar, 1924, U.S. Dist. Ct. No. Dist. Ill. bar, 1928, U.S. Ct. Appeals 7th Circuit bar, 1929; partner firm Barr & Barr, 1924-27, Barr, Barr & Corcoran, Chgo., 1927-73; individual practice law, Chgo., 1973—. Mem. Am., Ill., Chgo., West Suburban bar assns., Am. Judicature Soc. Home: 423 Lenox St Oak Park IL 60302 Office: 10 S LaSalle St Chicago IL 60603 Tel (312) FR2-4876

BARRATTA, JOSEPH PETER, b. N.Y.C., Oct. 1, 1938; B.S., Fordham U., 1960, LL.B., 1963. Admitted to N.Y. bar, 1963; asso. firm Lauritano & Schcacter, N.Y.C., 1963-65; asso. firm Baratta & Goldstein and predecessors, N.Y.C., 1965-69, partner, 1969—. Mem. N.Y. State Bar Assn. Recipient Title award Fordham U. Law Sch. Lawyers. Office: 1250 Broadway New York City NY 10001 Tel (212) 736-8088

BARRELL, NATHANIEL ADSIT, b. Buffalo, June 28, 1914; A.B., Williams Coll., 1936; J.D., U. Buffalo, 1950. Admitted to N.Y. State bar, 1940, U.S. Dist. Ct. bar, 1946; partner firm Wilcox and Van Allen, Buffalo, 1940-60, firm Cox, Barrell & Walsh, Buffalo, 1960—; chief atty. OPA, 1942-44; prosecutor War Crimes Trials, Tokyo, 1945-46; exec. atty. Legal Aid Bur., Buffalo, 1962—. Founder, chmn. Buffalo-Kanazawa, Japan Sister City Com., 1962—; vice-chmn. Buffalo Redevel. Bd., 1961-63; mem. Erie County Landmark Commn., 1970—. Mem. Am., N.Y. State, Erie County bar assns., Nat. Legal Aid and Defender Assn., Phi Delta Phi. Home: 1230 Delaware Ave Buffalo NY 14209 Office: 1000 Rand Bldg Buffalo NY 14203 Tel (716) 856-0153

BARRETT, DAVID I., b. N.Y.C., Nov. 4, 1939; LL.B., J.D., N.Y. U., 1964; LL.M., Bklyn. Law Sch., 1966. Admitted to N.Y. State bar, 1965, U.S. Supreme Ct. bar, 1972; law sec. to judge N.Y. Civil Ct., N.Y.C.; mem. firm Beldock and Kushnick, N.Y.C.; individual practice law, N.Y.C.; arbitrator Am. Arbitration Assn.; hearing officer N.Y.C. Parking Violations Bur.; arbitrator N.Y. Small Claims Ct. Dir. World Fellowship of Religions. Mem. N.Y. County Lawyers Assn., Bronx County Bar Assn., Voluntary Lawyers for the Arts, Copyright Soc., Panel for Indigent Defendants. Office: 430 W 24th St New York City NY 10011 Tel (212) 243-0620

BARRETT, EDWARD LOUIS, JR., b. Wellington, Kans., Aug. 11, 1917; B.S., Utah State U., 1938; J.D., U. Calif. at Berkeley, 1941. Admitted to Calif. bar, 1941, U.S. Supreme Ct. bar, 1954; legal research asst. Calif. Jud. Council, San Francisco, 1941-42; asso. prof. law U. Calif. at Berkeley, 1948-50, prof., 1950-52, prof. law and criminology, 1962-64; dean Coll. Law, prof. U. Calif. at Davis, 1964-71, prof., 1971—; spl. asst. atty. gen. U.S., Washington, 1957; mem. adv. com. on criminal rules Jud. Conf. U.S., 1966-71. Fellow Am. Bar Found.; mem. Am. Bar Assn., Am. Judicature Soc. Guggenheim fellow, 1964. Author: The Tenney Committee, 1951; Constitutional Law: Cases and Materials, 5th edit., 1977; also articles. Home: 518 Antioch Dr Davis CA 95616 Office: Sch Law U Calif Davis CA 95616 Tel (916) 752-2754

BARRETT, JANE HAYES, b. Dayton, Ohio, Dec. 13, 1947; B.A., Calif. State U., Long Beach, 1969; J.D., U. So. Calif., 1972. Admitted to Calif. bar, 1972; asso. firm Lawler, Felix & Hall, Los Angeles, 1972—; lectr. bus. fin. Calif. State U., Long Beach, 1972-74. Mem. Am. (dir. young lawyers sect.), Calif., Los Angeles County bar assns., Women Lawyers Los Angeles (treas.). Office: 700 S Flower St Los Angeles CA 90017 Tel (213) 629-9300

BARRETT, MALCOLM MCLEOD, b. San Francisco, Dec. 11, 1924; B.A. in Econs., Stanford, 1948, J.D., 1950. Admitted to Calif. bar, 1951; research atty. to asso. justice Supreme Ct. of Calif., 1951-52; asso. gen. counsel San Francisco Bay Area Rapid Transit Dist., 1958-69; asso. firm Pillsbury, Madison & Sutro, San Francisco, 1952-69; gen. counsel San Francisco Bay Area Transit Dist., Oakland, Calif., 1969—. Mem. Am., Calif., San Francisco bar assns. Home: 1221 Greenwich St Apt 6 San Francisco CA 94109 Office: 800 Madison St Oakland CA 94607 Tel (415) 465-4100

BARRETT, PHILLIP HESTON, b. Detroit, May 7, 1943; B.S., Ohio State U., 1965, J.D., 1968. Admitted to Ohio bar, 1968; partner firm Porter, Stanley, Platt & Arthur, Columbus, Ohio, 1970—. Trustee, Columbus Hearing and Speech Center. Mem. Am Am., Ohio, Columbus bar assns. Office: 37 W Broad St Columbus OH 43215 Tel (614) 228-1511

BARRETT, ROGER WATSON, b. Chgo., June 26, 1915; A.B., Princeton, 1937; J.D., Northwestern U., 1940. Admitted to Ill. bar, 1940; mem. firm Poppenhusen, Johnson, Thompson & Raymond, Chgo., 1940-43, 1945-50; regional counsel Econ. Stblzn. Agy., Chgo., 1951-52; partner firm Mayer, Brown & Platt, Chgo., 1952—; in charge documentary evidence Nuremberg Trial, 1944-45. Vice-pres. Mus. Contemporary Art, Chgo., 1972—. Mem. Am., Ill. State, Chgo. bar assns. Co-editor U.S. Govt. vols. on Nuremberg trials. Home: 84 Indian Hill Rd Winnetka IL 60093 Office: 231 S LaSalle St Chicago IL 60604 Tel (312) 782-0600

BARRETT, THOMAS JAMES, b. Bridgeport, Conn., Nov. 9, 1921; student U. Conn., 1948; J.D., Boston Coll., 1951. Admitted to Conn. bar, 1951, U.S. Supreme Ct. bar, 1963; individual practice law, Bridgeport, 1951—; pub. defender Fairfield County (Conn.), 1953; judge City Ct. of Bridgeport, 1959-60; chief prosecutor Circuit Ct. # 2, Conn., 1961-62; dir. labor relations City of Bridgeport, 1965-71, City of Stamford (Conn.), 1971—. Pres. Bridgeport Bd. Fire Commrs., 1957-60; mem. Bridgeport CSC, 1958-73; mem. Gov's. Commn. on Municipal Collective Bargaining, 1966-70. Mem. Conn., Bridgeport bar assns. Home: 100 Nancy Dr Bridgeport CT 06606 Office: 285 Congress St Bridgeport CT 06604 Tel (203) 366-7517

BARRICK, HAROLD WILLIAM, b. Sedalia, Mo., June 21, 1922; B.S., Central Mo. State U., 1947; J.D., U. Mich. 1950. Admitted to Mo. bar, 1950; individual practice law, Sedalia, 1950-62, New London, Mo., 1963-72; gen. chmn. Mo. Bar Adminstrn. Bar Coms., Sedalia, 1972—; pros. atty. Pettis County (Mo.), 1953-60, Ralls County (Mo.), 1965-72. Pres. United Cerebral Palsy Assn. Mo., 1961-63. Mem. Am., Pettis County, Mo. bar assns., Bar Assn. Met. St. Louis. Recipient Distinguished Service award Sedalia Jaycees, 1955; named Outstanding Young Man of Sedalia, Jaycees, 1955.

Home: Route 6 Box 104 Sedalia MO 65301 Office: Box 349 Sedalia MO 65301 Tel (816) 826-7890

BARRICK, WILLIAM HENRY, b. Byron, Ill., May 10, 1916; A.B., U. Ill., 1936, LL.B., 1938, J.D., 1968; postgrad. Judge Adv. Sch., U. Mich., 1945. Admitted to Ill. bar, 1938, U.S. Supreme Ct. bar, 1945, Fla. bar, 1969; partner firm Barrick, Jackson, Switzer, Long & Balsley, Rockford, Ill., 1938—; sr. sec. Ill. Supreme Ct. Justice Fulton, 1942-51; asst. exec. Office Judge Adv. Gen. U.S. Army, D.C., 1945-46; city atty., Rockford, 1941. Fellow Am. Coll. Probate Counsel; mem. Winnebago County (Ill.) (pres. 1966-67), Fed., Am. Fed. Communications bar assns., Bar Assn. of 7th Fed. Circuit, Am. Judicature Soc., Am. Bar Found. Decorated Legion of Merit; editor Synopsis of Ill. Laws, Rand McNally & Co., Bankers Directory, 1950-70. Home: 2849 Ware Rd Rockford IL 61111 Office: 228 S Main St Rockford IL 61101 Tel (815) 962-6611

BARRICKMAN, UHEL OVERTON, b. Bedford, Ky., Sept. 4, 1920; A.B., U. Ky., 1941, J.D., 1947. Admitted to Ky. bar, 1942; sr. partner firm Richardson, Barrickman & Dickinson, Glasgow, Ky., 1947—; U.S. Magistrate, Mammoth Cave Nat. Park, 1956—. Mem. Glasgow City Council, 1954-56. Mem. Am., Ky., Barren County bar assns., Internat. Soc. Barristers, Am. Coll. Trial Lawyers. Recipient Paul Harris Fellow award Rotary Internat., 1975. Home: 412 Garmon Ave Glasgow KY 42141 Office: 118 E Public Sq Glasgow KY 42141 Tel (502) 651-2116

BARRINGER, THOMAS LAWSON, b. Kannapolis, N.C., Nov. 8, 1940; B.S. in Indsl. Engring., N.C. State U., 1963; J.D., Vanderbilt U., 1968. Admitted to N.C. bar, 1968; law clk. N.C. Ct. Appeals, 1968-69; asso. firm Hollowell & Ragsdale, Raleigh, N.C., 1969-71; individual practice law, Raleigh, 1971-73; partner firm Barringer & Howard, Raleigh, 1973—. Mem. Raleigh CSC, 1975—, Raleigh Community Relations Commn., 1973-75, Wade Ave. Community Adv. Task Force, Raleigh, 1974—. Mem. Am., N.C., Wake County bar assns. Office: 1st Federal Bldg Raleigh NC 27601

BARRINGTON, JOHN CHARLES, b. Wooster, Ohio, Mar. 15, 1942; B.A., Coll. Wooster, 1965; J.D., Ohio State U., 1968. Admitted to Ohio bar, 1968; solicitor City of Wooster, 1969-71; asso. firm Logee Lehman & Reynolds, Wooster, 1968-73, partner, 1973-75; individual practice law, Wooster, 1975-76; solicitor cities Apple Creek and Smithville (Ohio), 1972—. Mem. Am., Ohio, Wayne County bar assns., Order of Coif. Office: 567 N Market St Wooster OH 44691 Tel (216) 264-8679

BARRON, HAROLD SHELDON, b. Detroit, July 4, 1936; A.B., U. Mich., 1958, J.D., 1961. Admitted to N.Y. bar, 1963, Mich. bar, 1961; practice in N.Y.C., 1962-68, Southfield, Mich., 1968—; atty. Hughes Hubbard & Reed, 1962-68; corp. counsel Bendix Corp., 1968-69, sec., asso. gen. counsel, 1969-72, sec., gen. counsel, 1972—, v.p., 1974—. Mem. nat. adv. council and faculty Practising Law Inst., N.Y.C. Mem. Am. (com. on corporate law depts.), Mich., N.Y. bar assns., Assn. Bar City N.Y., Am. Arbitration Assn. Home: 32288 Robinhood Dr Birmingham MI 48010 Office: Bendix Center Southfield MI 48076*

BARRON, JEROME AURE, b. Tewksbury, Mass., Sept. 25, 1933; A.B., Tufts Coll., 1955; LL.B., Yale, 1958; LL.M., George Washington U., 1960. Admitted to Mass. bar, 1959, D.C. bar, 1960; law clk. to Hon. Marvin Jones, chief judge U.S. Ct. Claims, Washington, 1960-61; asso. firm and individual practice law, Washington, 1961-62; asst. prof. U. N.D., Grand Forks, 1962-64; vis. asso. prof. U. N.Mex., Albuquerque, 1964-65; asso. prof. George Washington U., Washington, 1965-68, prof., 1968-72, 73—; dean Syracuse U. Coll. Law, 1972-73; spl. cons. Sen. spl. com. presdl. campaign activities (Watergate), 1973-74. Mem. D.C., Am. (mem. com. on free press-fair trial, 1973, legal advisory com. on free-press-fair trial, 1973-74) bar assns., Bar Assn. of D.C., Am. Assn. Law Schs. (chmn. Supreme Ct. Decisional Com., 1967-68), Phi Beta Kappa. Author: (with Donald Gillmor) Cases and Comment on Mass Communication Law, 1974; Freedom of the Press for Whom? The Right of Access to the Mass Media, 1973; (with C. Thomas Dienes) Constitutional Law: Principles and Policy, Cases and Materials, 1975; contbr. articles to legal jours. Home: 2530 Trophy Ln Reston VA 22091 Office: Nat Law Center George Washington Univ Washington DC 20052 Tel (202) 676-6837

BARRON, RUSSELL R., b. Lockhart, Tex., Oct. 17, 1941; B.B.A., U. Tex., 1965, LL.B., 1966. Admitted to Tex. bar, 1966; spl. agt. FBI, Washington, 1967-70; partner firm Judin, Ellis, Gonzales & Barron, McAllen, Tex., 1970—. Pres. Jackson Sch. PTA, McAllen, 1975-76. Mem. Assn. Trial Lawyers Am., Am., Tex., Hidalgo County (dir. 1974-75, sec. 1972-73) bar assns., Tex. Trial Lawyers Assn. (dir. Austin). Home: 124 W Iris St McAllen TX 78501 Office: 920 N Main St McAllen TX 78501 Tel (512) 682-0111

BARRON, THOMAS WILLIS, b. Newnan, Ga., Apr. 9, 1949; B.A., Emory U., 1971; J.D., Mercer U., 1974. Admitted to Ga. bar, 1974, U.S. Dist. Ct. No. Dist. Ga., 1974, U.S. Ct. Appeals, 1974; asso. firm Sanders, Mottola, Haugen, Wood and Goodson, 1974—. Adviser, Explorer Post 55, Boy Scouts Am., 1974—; trustee United Way, Newnan, 1974—, Central Health Council, 1975—; deacon First Bapt. Ch.; Newnan, 1975—. Mem. Am., Newnan-Coweta, Coweta Circuit bar assns., Am. Trial Lawyers Am., Phi Alpha Delta, Omicron Delta Kappa, Sigma Chi. Home: 15 Lakeview Dr Newnan GA 30263 Office: 11 Perry St Newnan GA 30263 Tel (404) 253-3880

BARROS, A. RICHARD, b. Phila., July 13, 1938; B.A., U. Del., 1961; J.D., Dickinson Sch. Law, 1964. Admitted to Del. bar, 1965, U.S. Supreme Ct. bar, 1971; asso. firm Herman C. Brown, Dover, Del., 1965-69; partner firm Brown, Shiels & Barros, Dover, 1970—; comptroller Kent County (Del.), 1969-72; instr. Wesley Jr. Coll., 1968; mem. Gov.'s Child Care Com., 1969-72. Bd. dirs., pres. Congregation Beth Sholom, Dover, 1965—; bd. dirs., v.p. Modern Maturity Center, sr. citizens orgn., Dover, 1972—; trustee Del. State Coll., 1977—. Mem. Am., Del., Kent County bar assns., Am. Del. trial lawyers assns. Home: 7 McBry Ct Dover DE 19901 Office: WSFS Bldg State and Reed Sts Dover DE 19901 Tel (302) 734-4766

BARROW, ALLEN EDWARD, b. Okemah, Okla., Jan. 22, 1914; student Okla. A. and M. Coll. 1935-36; B.A., U. Okla., 1936; postgrad. U. Tulsa; LL.B., Southeastern State Coll., 1942. With FBI, 1940-42; admitted to Okla. bar, 1942, also Supreme Ct. U.S.; pvt. practice, Tulsa, 1946-50, 54-62; counsel Southwestern Power Adminstrn., Dept. Interior, Tulsa, 1950-54; chief judge U.S. Dist. Ct. No. Dist. Okla., 1962—. Adv. bd. Tulsa Salvation Army, 1956—; bd. dirs. ARC. Mem. Am., Okla. (Outstanding Service award 1959) bar assns., S.A.R. (pres. Okla. 1954), Delta Theta Phi, Phi Eta Sigma, Sigma Chi (pres. alumni assn. 1950, Significant Sig award). Home: 2142 E 25th Pl Tulsa OK 74114 Office: US Courthouse Tulsa OK 74103*

BARROW, CHARLES KIMBRO, b. Houston, June 26, 1945; B.A., Rice U., 1967; J.D., U. Tex., 1970. Admitted to Tex. bar, 1970; trial atty. FPC, Washington, 1970-72; mem. firm Naman, Howell, Smith, Lee & Muldrow, Waco, Tex., 1972—; dir. Waco-Mclennan County Lawyer Referral Service com., 1975-76, Waco Jr. Bar, 1976—. Mem. State Bar Tex., Waco-Mclennan County bar, Am. Bar Assn., U. Tex. Alumni Assn. of Waco (dir. 1976—). Home: 313 Randle St Waco TX 76710 Office: POB 1470 Waco TX 76703 Tel (817) 754-1421

BARRY, DAVID F., b. Marblehead, Mass., Aug. 3, 1940; B.S., Salem State Coll., 1963; J.D., Suffolk U., 1967. Admitted to Mass. bar, 1968; asso. firm Samuel E. Zoll., Salem Mass., 1967-70; atty. VA, Boston, 1970-73; individual practice law, Marblehead, 1973—; instr. Salem State Coll., 1974—; mem. youth adv. com. VA. Active Marblehead Hist. Soc. Mem. Mass., Essex County (Mass.) bar assns., Mass. Trial Lawyers Assn. Home and office: 11 Robert Rd Marblehead MA 01945 Tel (617) 631-0077

BARRY, DAVID JOHN, b. Medford, Mass., Dec. 12, 1946; A.B. cum laude, Boston Coll., 1968, J.D., 1971. Admitted to Mass. bar, 1971; mem. firm Bishop & Ahern, Medford, 1971—. Mem. Mass., Middlesex County, 1st Dist. Ct. E. Middlesex bar assns. Home: 57 Washington St Medford MA 02155 Office: 11 Riverside Ave Medford MA 02155 Tel (617) 396-0055

BARRY, JAMES THOMAS, JR., b. New Rochelle, N.Y., June 12, 1945; B.B.A., U. Notre Dame, 1967; J.D. cum laude, St. Louis U., 1970. Admitted to Mo. bar, 1970; tax cons. Touche Ross & Co., St. Louis, 1970-72; mem. firm Lashly, Caruthers, Thies, Rava & Hamel, St. Louis, 1972—. Bd. dirs. Notre Dame Club of St. Louis. Mem. Am., Met. St. Louis, St. Louis County bar assns., Phi Delta Phi, Alpha Sigma Nu. Contbr. articles to legal jours. Office: 818 Olive St Suite 1300 Saint Louis MO 63101 Tel (314) 621-2939

BARRY, WILLIAM HENRY, JR., b. Nashua, N.H., Feb. 3, 1930; B.S., Holy Cross Coll., 1956; LL.B., Suffolk U., 1960. Admitted to N.H. bar, 1960; with Liberty Mut. Ins. Co., Worcester, Mass., 1956-60; asso. firm Harkway Barry Gall, Nashua, 1961-65; with SBA, Concord, N.H., 1965-66; asst. U.S. Atty., Concord, 1966-69; clk.-magistrate U.S. Dist. Ct., Concord, 1969—; part-time instr. Rivier Coll., 1973—. Mem. Nashua Zoning Bd., 1962-66; trustee N.H. Indsl. Sch., 1965-66. Mem. Nashua, N.H., Am. bar assns. Home: 2 Denise St Nashua NH 03060 Office: U S Dist Ct 55 Pleasant St Concord NH 03101 Tel (617) 228-0506

BARSAMIAN, ARMON, b. San Francisco, Mar. 4, 1936; A.B., San Francisco State U., 1961; J.D., Golden Gate U., 1967. Admitted to Calif. bar, 1967; labor relations asso. Pacific Maritime Assn., San Francisco, 1962-68; atty. San Francisco region, NLRB, 1968-70; individual practice law, San Francisco, 1970-71; labor arbitrator, San Rafael, Calif., 1971—; permanent arbitrator No. Calif. for Internat. Longshoremen's and Warehousemen's Union, Pacific Maritime Assn., 1971—. Mem. City of San Rafael Bd. Rev., 1974—. Mem. Soc. for Profls. in Dispute Resolution. Home: 16 Esmeyer Dr San Rafael CA 94903 Office: 16 Esmeyer Dr San Rafael CA 94903 Tel (415) 472-1825

BART, EDWARD HENRY, b. Elizabeth, N.J., Mar. 9, 1920; B.S. in Econs., U. Pa., 1940; J.D., Fordham U., 1949. Admitted to N.Y. State bar, 1949; with legal dept. U.S. Guarantee Co., 1945-50; v.p., gen. counsel Motor Haulage Co., N.Y.C., 1950-52; spl. rep. Great West Life Assurance Co., Chgo., 1956-61; pres. E.H. Bart & Assos., Inc., Chgo., 1959—; mem. firm Heckmann, Dunn, Bart Ltd., Northfield, Ill., 1975—. Mem. Chgo. Estate Planning Council, Am. Soc. Pension Actuaries, Am. Bar Assn., Assn. Advanced Life Underwriters. Contbr. articles in field to profl. jours. Home: 6 Henneberry Ln Golf IL 60029 Office: 550 Frontage Rd Northfield IL 60093 Tel (312) 446-7200

BARTA, JAMES JOSEPH, b. St. Louis, Nov. 5, 1940; B.A., St. Mary's U., 1963; J.D., St. Louis U., 1966. Admitted to Mo. bar, 1966; spl. agt. FBI, Washington, Cleve., N.Y.C., 1966-70; chief trial atty. St. Louis Circuit Atty., 1970-76; asso. firm Guilfoil, Symington & Petzall, St. Louis, 1976—; asst. U.S. atty. Eastern Dist. Mo., 1977—; lectr. Greater St. Louis Police Acad., 1970-76; spl. asst. atty. gen. Mo., St. Louis, 1974-75; spl. ast. atty. (circuit), St. Louis, 1976—; mem. tech. adv. com. St. Louis Council on Criminal Justice, 1972-74; dir. Organized Crime Task Force, St. Louis, 1972-74; project dir. St. Louis Crime Commn., 1975—. Mem. Am., Mo. bar assns., Am. Judicature Soc., Former Spl. Agts. FBI, Nat. Dist. Atty. Assn., Mo. Pros. Attys. Assn., Nat. Conf. on Organized Crime (prosecution rep. St. Louis). Home: 9542 General Lee Dr St Louis MO 63126 Office: 1114 Market St St Louis MO 63103 Tel (314) 425-4200

BARTA, RONALD DEAN, b. Kansas City, Mo., Mar. 20, 1937; B.B.A., Kans. U., 1959, LL.B., 1962, J.D., 1968. Admitted to Kans. bar, 1962, U.S. Supreme Ct. bar, 1973; asst. city atty. Salina (Kans.), 1962—, also partner firm Barta & Barta, Salina, 1962—; U.S. magistrate U.S. Dist. Ct. Dist. Kans., 1972—. Mem. Am., Kans. bar assns., Assn. Trial Lawyers Am., Kans. Trial Lawyers Assn. Home: 901 S Front St Salina KS 67401 Office: 611 E Iron St Salina KS 67401 Tel (913) 825-5413

BARTELS, ANTHONY WILLIAM, b. Appleton City, Mo., Feb. 10, 1941; A.B., Rockhurst Coll., 1963; LL.B., Ark. Law Sch., 1967. Admitted to Ark. bar, 1968, U.S. Supreme Ct. bar, 1974; individual practice law, Jonesboro, Ark., 1968—; co-counsel Abilities Unltd., Jonesboro, 1972—. Pres. Civitan Club, Jonesboro, 1974, Concerned Citizens of Jonesboro, 1974. Mem. Am., Ark., Craighead County bar assns. Home: 805 Southwest Dr Jonesboro AR 72401 Office: 316 S Church St Jonesboro AR 72401 Tel (501) 972-5000

BARTELS, MILLARD, b. Syracuse, N.Y., Feb. 24, 1905; A.B., Cornell, 1927, LL.B., 1929. Admitted to Conn. bar, 1930, Fed. bar, 1931; gen. counsel Travelers Ins. Co., Hartford, Conn., 1945-69, chmn. exec. com., 1955-70; of counsel firm Alcorn Bakewell & Smith, Hartford. Pres. West Hartford Town Council, 1943-45; mem. parole bd. Conn. State Prison, 1953-55. Mem. Am., Conn., Hartford County bar assns., Assn. Life Ins. Counsel (pres. 1957-58). Home: 29 Westwood Rd West Hartford CT 06117 Office: 1 American Row Hartford CT 06103 Tel (203) 522-1216

BARTH, STUART IRWEN, b. Chgo., Mar. 6, 1938; B.A., U. Minn., 1959; J.D., U. Ariz., 1962. Admitted to Ariz. bar, 1962, Calif. bar, 1963; partner firm Goldflam and Barth, Los Angeles, 1965—; prof. law Calif. Coll., Los Angeles, 1965—. Mem. Am., Calif., Ariz. bar assns., Am. Arbitration Assn., Calif. Applicants Counsel, Calif. Trial Lawyers Assn. Office: 1325 Wilshire Blvd Los Angeles CA 90017 Tel (213) 483-6182

BARTHOLOMEW, PHILLIP RAYMOND, b. New Castle, Pa., Oct. 12, 1942; B.A., Westminster Coll., 1964; J.D., Vanderbilt U., 1967. Admitted to Pa. bar, 1968, U.S. Dist. Ct. for Western Dist. Pa. bar, 1969, U.S. 3d Circuit Ct. Appeals bar, 1976; law clk. Ct. Common Pleas Mercer County, Pa., 1967; asso. firm Cusick, Madden, Joyce and McKay, Sharon, Pa., 1968—; atty., Shenango Valley Osteopathic Hosp., Farrell, Pa., 1969—; solicitor W. Middlesex Area Sch. Dist., Pa., 1971—. Pres. Pa. Christian Endeavor Union, 1972-76; v.p. Internat. Christian Endeavor, 1975—; elder Unity United Presbyn. Ch., Mercer, Pa., 1976—. Mem. Am., Pa., Mercer County bar assns., Christian Legal Soc., Order Coif, Omicron Delta Kappa. Recipient Vanderbilt Law Review Medal, 1967; contbr. article to law review. Home: 90 Wick Ave Sharon PA 16146 Office: 1st Fed Bldg Sharon PA 16146 Tel (412) 981-2000

BARTILSON, WILLIAM ROBERT, SR., b. Braddock, Pa., Jan. 24, 1937; B.S. in Chemistry, Ohio State U., 1965; J.D., U. Akron, 1972. Lab. Technician Ohio Dept. Health, 1960-62; chemist Goodyear Tire and Rubber Co., 1965—; admitted to Ohio bar, 1972; partner firm Bartilson, Horton & Smith, Akron, Ohio, 1972—. Mem. Akron, Ohio State, Am. bar assns. Office: 1650 W Market St Akron OH 44313 Tel (216) 867-9224

BARTKE, RICHARD H., b. Oakland, Calif., June 30, 1936; B.A., U. Calif., Berkeley, 1958; J.D., U. San Francisco, 1966. Admitted to Calif. bar, 1967; since practiced in Richmond, legal counsel Calif. Jaycees, 1969-70; councilman City of El Cerrito (Calif.), 1970—, mayor pro tem, 1971-72, 76-77, mayor, 1972-73, 77-78. Exec. bd. Assn. Bay Area Govts., 1970—, chmn. citizens services com., 1975—; chmn. bylaws and policy com. Contra Costa Mayors Conf., 1972—; commn. mem. Golden Gate Nat. Recreation Area, 1974—. Mem. Richmond Bar Assn. Office: 207 37th St Richmond CA 94805 Tel (415) 234-4212

BARTL, RICHARD ALLEN, b. Lafayette, Ind., May 6, 1935; B.S., Purdue U., 1957; J.D. with honors, George Washington U., 1962. Admitted to D.C. bar, 1962, Va. bar, 1968; law clk. U.S. Ct. Claims, Washington, 1962-63; asso. firm Kelly and Nicolaides, Washington, 1963-67; counsel, Export Import Bank, Washington, 1967-68; partner firm Burkhardt and Bartl, Alexandria, Va., 1968—; mem. panel of arbitrators, Am. Arbitration Assn. Mem. Va. State Bar, D.C., Alexandria bar assns. Office: 803 Prince St Alexandria VA 22314 Tel (703) 549-5000

BARTLER, JOHN CHARLES, b. Chgo., July 22, 1931; B.S., Northwestern U., 1953, J.D., 1956. Admitted to Ill. bar, 1956, U.S. Ct. Mil. Appeals bar, 1957, U.S. Supreme Ct. bar, 1964, U.S. Ct. Appeals, 1973; atty. JAGC, U.S. Army, Germany, 1958-61, dir. res. affairs 5th U.S. Army, Chgo., 1961-62, maj. USAR, 1965-67; asso. firm McKenna, Storer, Rowe, White & Farrug, Wheaton, Ill., 1962-67, partner, 1967—; lectr. Ill. Inst. Continuing Legal Edn. Mem. Am., Ill. (chmn. Ins. Law Council 1971-72, editor The Policy, 1968-69, vice-chmn. interprofl. coop. com. 1976—), DuPage County (co-chmn. com. pub. relations 1975—) bar assns., Ill. Def. Counsel, Theta Chi, Phi Delta Phi. Office: 333 S Cross St Wheaton IL 60187 Tel (312) 653-2616

BARTLETT, GEORGE ALEXANDER, b. Warrensburg, Mo., Aug. 7, 1937; B.A., Central Mo. State U., 1959, LL.B., U. Mo., 1961. Admitted to Mo. bar, 1962; asso. firm Hendren & Andrae, Jefferson City, Mo., 1965-71, partner, 1972—; lectr. law U. Mo. Law Sch., Columbia, 1965-66. Bd. dirs. Capitol area chpt. ARC, 1972. Mem. Mo. (chmn. young lawyers sec. 1972-73), Cole County bar assns., Order of Coif, Phi Alpha Delta, Sigma Tau Gamma. Bd. editors Mo. Law Rev., 1960-61, Fed. Bar Jour., 1964-65; recipient Mo. Bar Assn. Pres.'s award, 1976; Mo. bar Found. Smithson award for contbns. to jud. improvement, 1976. Home: 818 Boonville Rd Jefferson City MO 65101 Office: Central Trust Bldg Jefferson City MO 65101 Tel (314) 636-8135

BARTLETT, GEORGE ROBERT, JR., b. Walden, N.Y., Sept. 5, 1927; LL.B., Colgate U., 1951. Admitted to N.Y. bar, 1951, U.S. Supreme Ct. bar, 1958, D.C. bar, 1974; partner firm Bartlett & Bartlett, Walden, N.Y., 1951—; trustee, acting mayor, Village of Walden, 1958-60; mem. Orange County Legislature, 1970—. Mem. D.C., Am., N.Y. State, Orange County (pres. 1967-68) bar assns., Assn. Bar City N.Y. Home: 62 Riverview St Walden NY 12586 Office: 11 Orchard St Walden NY 12586 Tel (914) 778-5621

BARTLETT, JEFFERY WARNER, b. Chgo., Dec. 8, 1943; A.B., Beloit Coll., 1965; J.D., George Washington U., 1968. Admitted to Ill. bar, 1968; v.p., gen. counsel Searle World Wide Pharms., G.D. Searle & Co., Chgo., 1969—. Mem. Internat., Am. Chgo., (Writing Contest winner, 1972) bar assns. Office: POB 5110 Chicago IL 60690 Tel (312) 982-7870

BARTLETT, JOHN LAURENCE, b. Los Angeles, June 9, 1942; A.B., U. Calif., Los Angeles, 1963; LL.B., Stanford, 1967. Admitted to D.C. bar 1967, U.S. Supreme Ct. bar, 1976; asso. firm Kirkland, Ellis & Rowe, Washington, 1967—, partner, 1972—. Mem. Am., FCC bar assns., Computer Law Assn., Order of Coif, Phi Alpha Delta. Office: 1776 K St NW Washington DC 20006 Tel (202) 857-5000

BARTLETT, JOSEPH WARREN, b. Boston, June 14, 1933; A.B., Harvard U., 1955; LL.B., Stanford U., 1960. Admitted to Mass. bar; law clk. to Earl Warren, Chief Justice U.S., 1960-61; partner firm Gaston, Snow & Ely Bartlett, Boston; spl. asst. atty. gen. Mass.; counsel, commr. adminstrn. Mass., 1964-65; gen. counsel Dept. Commerce, 1967-68; acting dir. Office Fgn. Direct Investments, 1968; under sec. commerce, 1968-69; spl. counsel Boston Redevel. Authority, 1969-70; instr. law Boston U. Bd. visitors Fletcher Sch. Law and Diplomacy, Harvard Grad. Sch. Edn.; mem. exec. com., bd. visitors Stanford Law Sch.; bd. dirs. A Better Chance, Inc.; mem. trustee council U. Mass. Mem. Boston Bar Assn. (pres., past chmn. com. on ethics). Order of Coif. Home: 143 West St Beverly Farms MA 01915 Office: 225 Franklin St Boston MA 02110

BARTLEY, ROBERT W., b. Pueblo, Colo., Oct. 17, 1915; B.A. in Bus., Centenary Coll., 1939; LL.B., U. Colo., 1950; LL.D. (hon.) U. So. Colo., 1969. Admitted to Colo. bar, 1959; U.S. Dist. Ct. for Colo. bar, 1952, U.S. Supreme Ct. bar, 1963; partner firm Bartley & Glover and predecessors, Pueblo, 1950—. Trustee State Colls. Colo., 1961-74, v.p. bd. trustees, 1968-69, pres. bd. trustees, 1970, trustee emeritus 1976; mem. alumni exec. bd. U. Colo., 1956-50. Mem. Am., Colo. (mem. bus. and banking council 1960-66, law com., 1956-60), Pueblo County (pres. 1969-70) bar assns., Am. Arbitration Assn., Phi Alpha Delta. Recipient Colo. U. Alumni Recognition award, 1961, Rotary Community Service award, 1976. Home: 220 Argyle Pueblo CO 81004 Office: 701 Thatcher Bldg Pueblo CO 81003 Tel (303) 544-7534

BARTLO, SAM D., b. Cleve., Oct. 5, 1919; B.B.A., Western Res. U., 1941; J.D., Cleve.-Marshall Law Sch., 1950. Admitted to Ohio bar, 1950, U.S. Tax Ct. bar, 1952, U.S. Supreme Ct. bar, 1958; now mem. firm Buckingham, Doolittle & Burroughs, Akron, Ohio. Fellow Am. Bar Found.; mem. Akron (pres. 1967-68, exec. com. 1968-70), Ohio State (council dels. 1970—), Am. bar assns., Am. Judicature Soc., Nat. Conf. Bar Presidents. Office: 15th Floor One Cascade Plaza Akron OH 44308 Tel (216) 376-5300*

BARTOLINI, DANIEL JOHN, b. Trenton, N.J., Aug. 7, 1935; A.B. in Philosophy, Villanova U., 1957; J.D., U. Md., 1969. With Social Security Adminstrn., Balt., 1959—, sr. research analyst. 1968-71, supplemental security income planning specialist, 1971—; asso. firm Francomano, Clements and Park, Balt., 1975—. Pres., chmn. bd. Birthright of Md., Inc.; pres. Holy Family Home-Sch. Assn., Balt., 1973-75, chmn. Centennial Com., 1975-76. Mem. Am., Md. bar assns. Recipient citation Under-Sec. HEW, 1971. Home: 3600 Kings Point Rd Randallstown MD 21133 Office: 116 W Mulberry St Baltimore MD 21201 Tel (301) 837-1100

BARTON, CURTIS STANLEY, b. Oklahoma City, Feb. 16, 1913; J.D., U. Ark., 1939. Admitted to Ark. bar, 1939, Mo. bar, 1952; individual practice law, Logan County, Ark., 1939-42; spl. agt. IRS, Denver, 1943-47; individual practice law, Little Rock, 1947-49; claims mgr. St. Paul Fire & Marine Ins., Kansas City Mo., 1952-63, atty., 1963-77; asso. firm Hines & Magee, Kansas City, 1977—. Mem. Mo., Ark., Kansas City (Mo.), bar assns. Home: 9637 Mohawk Dr Leawood KS 66206 Office: 1130 Westport Rd Kansas City MO 64105 Tel (816) 753-7171

BARTON, DAVID JOSEPH, b. St. Louis, Jan. 5, 1943; B.S. in Commerce, St. Louis U., 1967, J.D., 1970. Admitted to Mo. bar, 1970; individual practice law, St. Louis, Jefferson County, Mo., 1971—; of counsel firm Slonim & Ross, St. Louis, 1975; atty. Village of Hillsdale (Mo.), 1974-75. Mem. Am., Met. St. Louis bar assns. Home: 25 Brookwood Dr Fenton MO 63026 Office: Box 337 Arnold MO 63010 Tel (314) 296-8383

BARTON, JAMES MILLER, b. White Plains, N.Y., Apr. 13, 1942; B.A., Yale, 1964; LL.B., U. Va., 1967. Admitted to Conn. bar, 1967; asso. firm Cummings & Lockwood, Stamford, Conn., 1967-75, partner, 1975—; lectr. Inst. Securities Laws and Regulations Sch. Continuing Edn. N.Y. U. Mem. Am., Conn., Greenwich bar assns. Staff mem. U. Va. Law Rev., 1966-67. Office: 2 Greenwich Plaza Greenwich CT 06830 Tel (203) 327-1700

BARTON, JAMES RUSSELL, b. Ottawa, Ill., Dec. 27, 1936; B.A., Miami U., 1958; J.D., Ohio State U., 1961. Admitted to Ohio bar, 1961; counsel Ohio State Life Ins. Co., 1963-65; 2d v.p., counsel Columbus Mut. Life Ins. Co. (Ohio), 1966—. Pres. bd. edn. Canal Winchester Local Sch. Dist., 1975, mem., 1972—; chmn. bd. mgmt. Suburban East YMCA, Columbus; trustee Faith United Methodist Ch., 1971-74. Mem. Am., Ohio, Columbus bar assns. Home: 355 Cherokee Dr Canal Winchester OH 43110 Office: 303 E Broad St Columbus OH 43215 Tel (614) 221-5875

BARTON, JOSEPH CHARLES, b. Jersey City, Mar. 24, 1936; B.A., Ohio State U., 1957; J.D., U. San Francisco, 1966. Admitted to Calif. bar, 1966, Fed., Ct. bar, 1966, U.S. Supreme Ct. bar, 1972; habeas corpus writ clk. U.S. Dist. Ct., San Francisco, 1965-66, law clk. to chief judge, 1966-67; partner firm Feeney, Sparks & Barton, San Francisco, 1967-74; partner firm Barton & Stretch, San Francisco, 1974—. Bd. dirs. Florence Crittenton Services, San Francisco, 1970—. Mem. Am., San Francisco bar assns. Home: Box 1141 Ross CA 94957 Office: Suite 1001 433 California St San Francisco CA 94104 Tel (415) 986-1630

BARTON, KENNETH WAYNE, b. Jackson, Miss., Dec. 24, 1946; B.A., Millsaps Coll., 1970; J.D. with honors, U. Miss., 1972. Admitted to Miss. bar, 1972, U.S. Supreme Ct. bar, 1976; mem. firm Butler, Snow, O'Mara, Stevens & Cannada, Jackson, 1973—; reporter 1973 Miss. Citizens Conf. on Adminstrn. Justice. Mem. Am., Miss. State, Hinds County (Miss.) bar assns., Jackson Young Lawyers Assn. Editor-in-chief Miss. Law Jour., 1972. Home: 4854 N State St Jackson MS 39206 Office: POB 22567 1700 Deposit Guaranty Plaza Jackson MS 39205 Tel (601) 948-5711

BARTON, THOMAS PERKINS, b. El Dorado, Ark., Oct. 5, 1935; B.A., U. Ark., 1957; LL.B., Columbia, 1964. Admitted to N.Y. bar, 1964, Tex. bar, 1968; asso. firm Milbank, Tweed, Hadley & McCloy, N.Y.C., 1964-67; asso. firm Wynne & Jaffe, Dallas, 1967-70, partner, 1970—. Mem. Am., Dallas bar assns., State Bar Tex. Home: 3821 Maplewood St Dallas TX 75205 Office: 1000 LTV Tower Dallas TX 75201 Tel (214) 748-7211

BARTON, WALTER ELBERT, b. Wadesville, Ind., Nov. 7, 1886; LL.B., George Washington U., 1914. Admitted to D.C. bar, 1920, U.S. Supreme Ct. bar, 1924; individual practice law, Washington, 1920—. Mem. D.C. Bar Assn. Home: 2500 Q St Washington DC 20007 Office: 1511 K St Washington DC 20005 Tel (202) 628-9358

BARTOSIC, FLORIAN, b. Danville, Pa., Sept. 15, 1926; B.A., Pontifical Coll., 1948; B.C.L., Coll. William and Mary, 1956; LL.M., Yale U., 1957. Admitted to Va. bar, 1956, U.S. Supreme Ct. bar, 1959; asst. instr. Yale U., 1956-57; asso. prof. law Villanova (Pa.) U., 1957-59; atty. NLRB, Washington, 1956, 57, 59; counsel Internat. Brotherhood of Teamsters, Washington, 1959-71; prof. law Wayne State U., Detroit, 1971—; adj. prof. law George Washington U., Washington, 1966-71, Cath. U., 1969-71; mem. panel arbitrators Fed. Mediation and Conciliation Service, Nat. Mediation Bd., 1972—; hearing officer Mich. Civil Rights Commn., 1974—, Mich. Employment Relations Commn., 1972—. Bd. dirs. Mich. Legal Services Corp., 1973—, Inst. Labor and Indsl. Relations, U. Mich., Wayne State U., 1976—. Mem. Am. Law Inst., Soc. Profls. in Dispute Resolution, Indsl. Relations Research Assn., Internat. Soc. Labor Law and Social Legis., Internat. Indsl. Relations Assn., Am. Arbitration Assn. (panel), Am. Bar Assn. (sec. labor relations law sect. 1974-75), ACLU (dir. Detroit chpt. 1976—). Contbr. articles to legal jours. Home: Apt 401 603 Merrick St Detroit MI 48221 Office: Wayne State U Law Sch Detroit MI 48202 Tel (313) 577-3960

BARTUNEK, JOSEPH WENCESLAUS, b. Cleve., Feb. 16, 1924; B.S., Case Western Reserve U., 1948; LL.B., Cleve. State U., 1955; grad. Nat. Coll. for State Trial Lawyers U. Nev., 1969. Admitted to Ohio bar, 1955; individual practice law, Cleve., 1955-64; probate judge Cuyahoga County, Cleve., 1964-70; of counsel firm Guren, Merritt, Sogg & Cohen, Cleve., 1970-75; partner firm Bartunek, Bennett & Garofoli, Cleve., 1975—; law dir. City of Solon (Ohio), 1975—. Mem. Ohio State Senate, 1949-58, 61-64; bd. trustees St. Luke's Hosp., Cleve., 1951—; bd. trustees Cleve. State U., 1964—; bd. trustees Greater Cleve. Hosp. Assn., 1970-76; chmn. Cuyahoga County Bd. Elections, Cleve., 1971-72. Mem. Am. Judicature Soc., Bar Assn. Greater Cleve., Am., Ohio State, Cuyahoga County bar assns., Assn. Trial Lawyers Am., Law Dirs. Assn. Cuyahoga County. Recipient Samuel Eells award, 1969; Outstanding Alumnus award, Cleve.-Marshall Coll. Law of Cleve. State U., 1971; Alumni Distinguished Service award, Cleve. State U. Alumni Assn., 1973; Cleve. State U. Viking award, 1974. Office: 1003 Bond Ct Bldg 1300 E 9th St Cleveland OH 44114 Tel (216) 623-1400

BARUTH, MAURICE W., b. Pitts., Jan. 24, 1924; B.A., Dartmouth, 1947; J.D., Columbia, 1950. Admitted to Pa. bar, 1951; since practiced in Pitts., asso. firm Kaplan, Finkel & Roth, 1951-54, spl. asst. atty. gen. Commonwealth of Pa., 1955-63; mem. firm Tolochko & Baruth, 1963-73, individual practice law, 1973—; judge adv. Fedn. War Soc. Allegheny County, 1965—, counsel Squirrel Hill Elderly Service Assn., 1973—. Dept. comdr. AMVETS, 1958-59; pres. Squirrel Hill Bd. Trade, 1970-72; mem. Pa. Vets. Commn., 1958-59. Mem. Am., Pa., Allegheny County bar assns., Acad. Polit. Sci. Recipient Distinguished Service award AMVETS. Home: 308 S Lang Ave Pittsburgh PA 15208 Office: 418 Frick Bldg Pittsburgh PA 15219 Tel (412) 281-8195

BARZ, DIANE GAY, b. Bozeman, Mont., Aug. 18, 1944; student U. Heidelberg (Germany), 1963-64; A.B., Whitworth Coll., 1965; postgrad. Law Sch. U. Mont., 1968. Admitted to Mont. bar, 1968; law clk. Mont. Supreme Ct., 1968-70; dep. county atty. Yellowstone County, 1970-74; partner firm Poppler & Barz, Billings, Mont., 1973—; atty. City-County Planning Bd., 1975; mem. organizational com. Unified Bar in Mont., 1974-75; elected pub. adminstr. Yellowstone County, 1975-79. Mem. bd. dirs. Yellowstone Exhbn. and Metra, 1975-77; mem. advisory bd. S. Central Mental Health Center, 1974-77. Mem. Mont., Yellowstone County bar assns., Bus. and Profl. Women's Club (dir.), Jr. League. Named Outstanding Young Career Woman Mont., 1971. Home: 3425 Laredo Pl Billings MT 59102 Office: 229 Stapleton Bldg Billings MT 59101 Tel (406) 248-7833

BASBAS, MONTE GEORGE, b. Manchester, N.H., May 6, 1921; A.B. in Govt., Dartmouth Coll., 1946; J.D., Boston U., 1949. Admitted to N.H. bar, 1949, Mass. bar, 1949, U.S. Supreme Ct. bar, 1969; partner firm Basbas, Johnson & George, Boston, 1949-55; individual practice law, Manchester, N.H., 1949-65, Newton, Mass., 1955-72; city clk. City of Newton, Mass., 1953-65, workmen's compensation agent, 1953-65, chmn. election commn., 1960-65, mayor, 1966-71; judge Newton Dist. Ct., 1972-76, 1st justice, 1976—; mem. Gov.'s Commn. on Law Enforcement and Adminstrn. of Criminal Justice, 1967-71; chmn. Gov.'s Advisory Com. on Community Affairs, 1970-71. Pres. Mass. Mayor's Assn., 1969-70; mem. fin. com. Town of Sudbury, Mass., 1974-76; mem. advisory bd. for pub. adminstrn. Bently Coll., 1969-72; bd. dirs. Parker Hill Med. Center, 1969-76; Norumbega council Boy Scouts Am., 1968—; bd. visitors bus. adminstrn. Boston U., 1968-72; bd. trustees Nichols Coll., Dudley, Mass., 1968-76. Mem. Boston, Waltham-Watertown-Weston-Newton bar assns., Am. Judicature Soc. Named Man of Year, Newton C. of C., 1966, Temple Reyim, Newton, 1975; recipient numerous citations. Office: 1309 Washington St West Newton MA 02165 Tel (617) 244-3600

BASFORD, RONALD, b. Winnipeg, Man., Can., Apr. 22, 1932; B.A., U. B.C. (Can.), 1955, LL.B., 1956. Practiced law in Vancouver, B.C., until 1963; mem. Ho. of Commons of Can. from Vancouver Centre, 1963—, minister of consumer and corp. affairs, 1968-72, minister of urban affairs, 1972-74, minister of nat. revenue, 1974-75, now minister of justice and atty. gen. of Can.; parliamentary observer 18th session UN Gen. Assembly, 1963; spl. adviser to govt. delegation 49th Conf. Internat. Labour Orgn., Geneva, 1965; leader Canadian Del., 11th Commonwealth Parliamentary Assn. Conf., Wellington, N.Z., 1965, del. 12th Conf., Ottawa, 1966; co-chmn. Spl. Joint Com. of Senate and Ho. of Commons on Consumer Credit and Cost of Living, 1967. Mem. John Howard Soc., Canadian Bar Assn., Law Soc. B.C., Canadian NATO Parliamentary Assn., Interparliamentary Union. Home: 31 Holborn St Ottawa ON Canada Office: Ho of Commons Ottawa ON K1A OA6 Canada also Dept of Justice Ottawa ON K1A OH8 Canada*

BASHIAN, GARY EDWARD, b. N.Y.C., Nov. 7, 1942; A.B., Gettysburg Coll., 1964; J.D., Boston U., 1967; LL.M. in Taxation, N.Y. U., 1971. Admitted to N.Y. State bar, 1968, U.S. Supreme Ct. bar, 1973, U.S. Tax Ct. bar, 1975; served with JAGC, U.S. Army, 1968-69; asso. firm Clark, Gagilardi & Miller, White Plains, N.Y., 1971-76; McCarthy, Fingar, Donovan & Glatthaar, White Plains, 1976—; instr. Jacksonville (Ala.) State U., 1968-69. Mem. Am., N.Y., Westchester County (chmn. tax sect. 1977—) bar assns., Estate Planning Council Westchester, Inc. Contbr. article to Duke U. Law Jour., 1972. Home: 588 The Parkway Mamaroneck NY 10543 Office: 175 Main St White Plains NY 10601 Tel (914) 946-3700

BASHWINER, STEVEN LACELLE, b. Cin., Aug. 3, 1941; A.B., Coll. of the Holy Cross, 1963; J.D., U. Chgo., 1966; Admitted to Ill. bar, 1966, No. Dist. Ill. bar, 1966, 7th Circuit bar, 1968, U.S. Supreme Ct. bar, 1970; asso. firm Kirkland & Ellis, Chgo., 1966-71, partner, 1972-75; partner firm Friedman & Koven, Chgo., 1976—; lectr. Columbia, 1968-69. Mem. jr. governing bd. Chgo. Symphony Orch., 1972-75. Mem. Chgo. Bar Assn., Chgo. Council Lawyers, U. Chgo. Alumni Assn. (dir.). Office: 208 S LaSalle St Chicago IL 60604 Tel (312) 346-8500

BASILE, PAUL LOUIS, JR., b. Oakland, Calif., Dec. 27, 1945; B.A., Occidental Coll., 1968; J.D., U. Calif., Los Angeles, 1971. Admitted to Calif. bar, 1972; asso. firm Parker, Milliken, Kohlmeier, Clark & O'Hara, Los Angeles, 1971-72; corporate counsel TFI Cos., Inc., Los Angeles, 1972-73; individual practice law, Culver City, Calif., 1973—. Trustee exec. com. Free Pub. Theatre Found., Los Angeles, 1974-75; trustee, sec., exec. com. Nat. Repertory Theatre Found., Los Angeles, 1975—; trustee, sec., mem. exec. com. Hippovideo; trustee The Found. for Multi-Media and the Arts, Los Angeles, 1975-76; trustee, v.p., sec. exec. com. Acad. Stage and Cinema Arts, Los Angeles, 1976—. Mem. Los Angeles Jr. C. of C. (dir. 1975—, v.p. 1977—, Best New Project award, 1972-73, named Mem. of Month, 1973), Am., Los Angeles County bar assns., Phi Alpha Delta. Home and Office: 9037-1/2 Lucerne Ave Culver City CA 90230 Tel (213) 559-5861

BASILE, SALVATORE, b. Casablanca, Morocco, Aug. 27, 1935; came to U.S., 1939, naturalized, 1945; A.B.A., San Jose State U., 1959; B.A., Internat. Acad., B.C., Can., 1969; J.D., Lincoln U., 1973. Admitted to Calif. bar, 1973; mgr. escrow dept. Wells Fargo Bank, Santa Cruz, Monterey and San Benito Counties (Calif.), 1969-75; individual practice law, Santa Cruz, Calif., 1975—. Mem. citizens' com. City of Santa Cruz, 1968-71; chmn. collective bargaining com. Santa Cruz County Bd. Edn. Mem. Calif., Santa Cruz bar assns. Contbr. article to legal jour. Home: 330 Cabrillo Ave Santa Cruz CA 95060 Office: 74 River St suite 201 Santa Cruz CA 95061 Tel (408) 427-2500

BASKERVILLE, LANETA ILENE, b. Eastland, Tex., May 25, 1927; B.B.A., Howard Payne Coll., 1948. Admitted to Tex. bar, 1960; U.S. Dist. Ct. for No. Dist. Tex. bar, 1965; since practiced in Fort Worth, asso. firm John W. Herrick, 1961-63; asst. dist. atty. for Tarrant County, 1963-64; asso. firm Spurlock & Schattman, 1964-69; ofcl. ct. reporter 96th dist. ct., 1969—. Active 1st United Meth. Ch., Fort Worth, 1963—. Mem. Fort Worth-Tarrant County, Tex. bar assns., Tarrant County Ct. Reporters Assn. (sec. 1976—), Fort Worth Legal Secs. Assn. Home: 1382 E Seminary Dr Fort Worth TX 76115 Office: 96th Dist Ct Civil Cts Bldg Fort Worth TX 76102 Tel (817) 334-1451

BASKETTE, ROGER DUVAL, b. Nashville, Dec. 12, 1924; LL.B., Cumberland U., 1947. Admitted to Tenn. bar, 1948; individual practice law, Nashville. Mem. Nashville-Davidson County-Met. County Council, 1971-75; trustee, deacon Bellevue Ch. of Christ, 1967-76. Mem. Tenn., Nashville bar assns., Comml. Law League Am. Office: 706 Stahlman Bldg Nashville TN 37201 Tel (615) 255-2725

BASKIN, JOHN ROLAND, b. Cleve., Dec. 23, 1916; A.B., Case Western Res. U., 1938, LL.B., 1940. Admitted to Ohio bar, 1940, FCC bar, 1949, U.S. Supreme Ct. bar, 1955; asso. firm Baker, Hostetler & Patterson, Cleve., 1941-54, partner, 1954—. Mem. Cleve., Ohio, Am. bar assns., Order of Coif, Phi Beta Kappa. Home: 2679 Ashley Rd Shaker Heights OH 44122 Office: 1956 Union Commerce Bldg Cleveland OH 44115 Tel (216) 621-0200

BASKIN, PETER JAY, b. N.Y.C., Feb. 11, 1944; B.A., Hofstra U., 1965; J.D., Bklyn. Law Sch., 1968. Admitted to N.Y. State bar, 1968; trial atty. Dept. Justice, N.Y.C., 1968-71; asso. firm Rode & Qualey, N.Y.C., 1971-77, firm Sharretts, Paley, Carter & Blauvelt, P.C., N.Y.C., 1977—. Pres. Carriage Hill Civic Assn., 1974-75. Mem. Customs Bar Assn. (mem. com. 1974-75), Hofstra Alumni Assn. (bd. dirs. 1965—). Recipient Meritorious Service Award Bklyn. Law Sch. Law Review, 1968. Home: Wellington Rd Locust Valley NY 11560 Office: 80 Broad St New York City NY 10004 Tel (212) 425-0055

BASS, KENNETH CARRINGTON, III, b. Richmond, Va., Feb. 11, 1944; A.B. summa cum laude, Duke U., 1965; LL.B., Yale, 1969. Admitted to Va. bar, 1970, D.C. bar, 1971; asso. firm Paul, Weiss, Rifkind, Wharton & Garrison, D.C., 1970-74; asso. firm Reasoner, Davis & Vinson, D.C., 1974—; law clerk Justice Hugo L. Black, U.S. Supreme Ct., 1969-70; legis. asst. Congressman E.Q. Daddario, 1970. Pres. Hillcrest Cluster Assn., Reston, Va., 1972, Lank Pre-Sch., Reston, 1976-77; mem. Fairfax County (Va.) Task Force on Multipurpose Tax Dists. Mem. Va. State Bar, D.C. Bar. Contbr. articles to profl. jours. Home: 11160 Saffold Way Reston VA 22090 Office: 800 17th St NW Washington DC 20006 Tel (202) 298-8100

BASS, MARY ALICE, b. Niagara Falls, N.Y., Dec. 1, 1927; A.A., Phoenix Coll., 1965; A.B., Ariz. State U., 1967, J.D., 1970; grad. Nat. Coll. Juvenile Justice U. Nev., 1975. Admitted to Ariz. bar, 1971; makeup artist, Metro-Goldwyn-Mayer, Phoenix, 1959; TV actress, Buffalo, 1956, Phoenix, 1960-61; dept. atty. Maricopa County, Ariz., 1971; referee Maricopa County Juvenile Ct., Phoenix, 1973—, chief referee, 1976—. Mem. Ariz. Women's Commn., 1975—. Mem. Am., Maricopa County bar assns., State Bar Ariz., Am. Trial Lawyers Assn., Nat. Dist. Attys. Assn., Ariz. Probation, Parole and Corrections Assn. Home: 102 W Maryland Ave Phoenix AZ 85013 Office: 3125 W Durango St Phoenix AZ 85009 Tel (602) 269-4254

BASS, SAM HOWARD, b. Rosebud, Tex., Aug. 9, 1926; LL.B., Baylor U., 1954. Admitted to Tex. bar, 1954; partner firm Bass & Farmer, Freeport, Tex., 1971—; mem. Tex. Legis., 1956-59. Office: 304 W Park Ave Freeport TX 77541 Tel (713) 233-5241

BASS, STANLEY ALLAN, b. N.Y.C., May 30, 1939; B.S., Coll. City N.Y., 1960; J.D., U. Chgo., 1963. Admitted to Ill. bar, 1963, U.S. Supreme Ct. bar, 1968, N.Y. State bar, 1974; law clk. to U.S. Dist. Ct. for No. Dist. Ill., 1964-65; dir.-counsel Civil Legal Aid Service Cook County (Ill.) Jail, Chgo., 1966-68; dir. litigation Community Legal Counsel, Chgo., 1968-70; staff atty. NAACP Legal Def. and Ednl. Fund, Inc., N.Y.C., 1970—. Mem. Council N.Y. Law Assos. Office: 10 Columbus Circle Room 2030 New York City NY 10019 Tel (212) 586-8397

BASSECHES, ROBERT TREINIS, b. N.Y.C., Jan. 24, 1934; B.A., Amherst Coll., 1955; LL.B., Yale, 1958. Admitted to N.Y. State bar, 1959, D.C. bar, 1962; asso. firm Shea & Gardner, Washington, 1960-63, partner, 1963—; law clk. to Judge David L. Bazelom, U.S. Ct. Appeals for D.C., 1958-59, to Justice Hugo L. Black, U.S. Supreme Ct., 1959. Pres., Chevy Chase (Md.) Village Citizens Assn., 1976; trustee Green Acres Sch., 1971—, pres., chmn. bd., 1973-75. Mem. Maritime Adminstrv. (past sec. 1967-69, pres. 1969-71), Am. (chmn. maritime transp. com. 1969-71) bar assns., Order of Coif, Phi Beta Kappa, Phi Alpha Delta. Office: Shea & Gardner 734 15th St NW Washington DC 20005 Tel (202) 737-1255

BASSETT, JOHN EDWARD, b. Weymouth, Mass., Dec. 27, 1921; LL.B., Boston U., 1951. Admitted to Mass. bar, 1951, Fla. bar, 1958, U.S. Tax Ct. bar, 1973; city atty. Hialeah Gardens (Fla.) City, 1961-68; judge Medley (Fla.) Municipal Ct., 1962. Chmn. N. Miami (Fla.) Mayors Advisory Com., 1972; mem. Biscayne Park (Fla.) Bicentennial Com., 1976. Mem. North Dade (county, Fla.), Fla. bars, Am. Arbitration Assn. Recipient certificate of appreciation City of North Miami (Fla.). Office: 12402 W Dixie Hwy North Miami FL 33161 Tel (307) 893-6460

BASSETT, JOHN WALDEN, JR., b. Roswell, N.Mex., Mar. 21, 1938; A.B. in Econs., Stanford, 1960; LL.B. with honors, U. Tex., 1964, J.D. Admitted to Tex. bar, 1964, N.Mex. bar, 1964; asso. firm Atwood & Malone, Roswell, N.Mex., 1964-66; White House fellow, spl. asst. to U.S. Atty. Gen., Washington, 1966-67; partner firm Atwood, Malone, Mann & Cooter, and predecessors, Roswell, 1966—; dir. Security Nat. Bank Roswell. Chmn. United Way campaign, Chaves County, 1972, pres., 1973; bd. dirs. St. Mary's Hosp., Roswell, 1976; mem. Roswell Planning and Zoning Commn., 1977. Mem. Am., Tex., N.Mex., Chaves County bar assns., White House Fellows Assn., Order of Coif. Asso. editor: Tex. Law Rev., 1962-64. Home: 600 Rosemary Ln Roswell NM 88201 Office: PO Drawer 700 Roswell NM 88201 Tel (505) 622-6221

BASSETT, RANDALL CRAIG, b. Los Angeles, Jan. 22, 1945; B.A., U. Calif., Berkeley, 1966; J.D. cum laude, Harvard, 1969. Admitted to Calif. bar, 1970; asso. firm Latham & Watkins, Los Angeles, 1969-77, mem., 1977—. Mem. State Bar Calif., Los Angeles County, Am. bar assns., Fin. Lawyers Conf. Office: 555 S Flower St Los Angeles CA 90071 Tel (213) 485-1234

BASSETT, WILLIAM RANDALL, b. Montgomery, Ala., May 23, 1937; B.C.E., Auburn U., 1959; J.D., Emory U., 1967. Admitted to Ga. bar, 1968; asso. firm Wiggins & Smith, Atlanta, 1968-71; individual practice law, Atlanta, 1972—; gen. counsel Atlanta Regional Commn., 1972—; collaboraton Zoning Law of Ga. Pres. Exec. Park Kiwanis Club, 1972-73; trustee Smith Found. Birth Defective Infants, Atlanta, 1971—. Mem. Am. Judicature Soc., Am., Ga., Atlanta bar assns. Home: 1157 Hampton Hall Dr NE Atlanta GA 30319 Office: 57 Executive Park South NE suite 310 Atlanta GA 30329 Tel (404) 325-8196

BASSETT, WOODSON WILLIAM, JR., b. Okmulgee, Okla., Nov. 7, 1926; J.D., U. Ark., 1949. Admitted to Ark. bar, 1949, U.S. Supreme Ct. bar, 1976; v.p. and claims atty. Preferred Risk Ins. Co., Fayetteville, Ark., 1955-62; partner firm Putman, Davis & Bassett, Fayetteville, 1962—. Chmn. bd. dirs. Fayetteville Pub. Library. Mem. Am., Ark., Washington County (pres. 1974-75) bar assns., Ark. Trial Lawyers Assn., Assn. Am. Trial Lawyers. Home: 2210 Manor Dr Fayetteville AR 72701 Office: 19 E Mountain St Fayetteville AR 72701 Tel (501) 521-7600

BASSFORD, RITA IRENE, b. Pitts., July 22, 1921; LL.B., LaVerne (Calif.) Coll., 1972. Admitted to Calif. bar, 1972; legal sec., Calif., 1939-72; asso. firm Hayton & Peach, San Bernardino, Calif., 1972-73; research atty. Calif. State Ct. Appeals, San Bernardino, 1973-74, sr. staff atty., 1974—. Mem. Calif. Women Lawyers Assn., Calif. State Bar Assn., San Bernardino County Bar Assn. Contbr. to Legal Secs. Handbook, 1971. Office: Room 640 State Bldg 303 W 3d St San Bernardino CA 92401

BASSICK, EDGAR WEBB, b. Bridgeport, Conn., Sept. 26, 1927; B.A., Yale, 1950; J.D., Harvard, 1955. Admitted to Conn. bar, 1955; asso. firm Pullman, Conley, Bradley & Reeves, 1955-60, partner, 1960—. Ringmaster Barnum Festival, Bridgeport, 1966. Fellow Am. Acad. Matrimonial Lawyers, mem. Am., Conn., Bridgeport bar assns., Am. Judicature Soc., Am. Arbitration Assn. Home: 510 Barlow Rd Fairfield CT 06430 Office: 855 Main St Bridgeport CT 06604 Tel (203) 334-0122

BASSIOUNI, M. CHERIF, b. Cairo, Egypt, Dec. 9, 1937; A.B., Coll. Holy Family, Cairo, 1955; postgrad. Dijon U., France, 1955-57, U. Geneva, Switzerland, 1957; LL.B., U. Cairo, 1961; J.D., Ind. U., 1964; LL.M., John Marshall Lawyers Inst., 1966; S.J.D., George Washington U., 1973. Admitted to Ill. bar, 1967, D.C. bar, 1967; individual practice law, Chgo., 1967—; prof. law DePaul U., Chgo., 1964—; Fulbright-Hays vis. prof. internat. criminal law U. Freiburg, Germany, 1970; vis. prof. law N.Y. U., 1971; guest scholar Woodrow Wilson Internat. Center for Scholars, Washington, 1972; chmn. adv. bd. law in Am. soc. project, 1972—. Bd. dirs., dean Internat. Inst. Advanced Criminal Scis., Italy. Recipient Outstanding Citizen of Yr. award Citizenship Council Met. Chgo., 1967. Mem. World Peace Through Law, Am. Soc. Internat. Law, Assn. Internat. de Droit Penal (sec.-gen.), Am. (chmn. com. internat. legal edn.), Ill. (chmn. sect. internat. law 1972-74), Chgo. (chmn. com. criminal legis. 1967-69) bar assns., Ill. Commn. on Law and Justice Edn., Phi Alpha Delta. Author: Criminal Law and Its Processes, 1969; The Law of Dissent and Riots, 1971; (with V.P. Nanda) Internat. Criminal Law, 2 vols., 1973; (with Eugene Fisher) Storm Over the Arab World, 1972; Internat. Terrorism and Political Crimes, 1975; Internat. Extradition and World Public Order, 1974; Issues in the Mediterranean, 1976; Citizen's Arrest, 1977; Substantive Criminal Law, 1977; also numerous articles; editor-in-chief Revue Internat. de Droit Penal, 1973—; editor The Globe, 1970—, Am. Jour. Comparative Law, 1972—. Home: 1130 N Lake Shore Dr Chicago IL 60611 Office: 25 E Jackson St Chicago IL 60604 Tel (312) 321-7748

BASSLER, HARRY WARREN, b. Nashville, Mar. 7, 1948; B.A., Emory U., 1970, J.D., 1973. Admitted to Ga. bar, 1974, U.S. Supreme Ct. bar, 1977; asso. firm Horton & Crim, 1974-76, firm Hopkins & Gresham, Atlanta, 91976—. Mem. Am., Ga., Atlanta bar assns., Am. Judicature Soc. Office: 101 Marietta Tower Suite 1902 Atlanta GA 30303

BASTEMEYER, NORMAN GLENN, b. Rock Valley, Iowa, Oct. 7, 1931; A.B., U. No. Colo., 1953; J.D. summa cum laude, U. S.D., 1960. Admitted to Iowa bar, 1960, S.D. bar, 1960; law clk. to chief judge U.S. Dist. Ct. State of S.D., 1960-61; partner firm Klay, Bastemeyer & Veldhuizen, Orange City, Iowa, 1962—; prof. bus. law Northwestern Coll., Orange City, 1973-74. Pres. Orange City Devel. Corp., 1972-75; chmn. Orange City Housing Authority, 1970—; gen. chmn. Orange City Tulip Festival, 1964-65. Mem. Am., Iowa, Sioux County (pres.) bar assns., Iowa Conf. Bar Assn. Presidents (gov.), Phi Delta Phi. Home: 104 Jefferson Ave SE Orange City IA 51041 Office: 121 Albany Ave NE Orange City IA 51041 Tel (712) 737-4851

BASTIAN, JAMES HAROLD, b. Hannibal, Mo., Nov. 26, 1927; B.S. in Bus. Adminstrn., U. Mo., 1950; J.D. with honors, George Washington U., 1956. Admitted to D.C. bar, 1956, Va. bar, 1957, Md. bar, 1976; asso. firm Adair, Ulmer, Murchison, Kent & Ashby, Washington, 1956-62; partner firm Howard, Poe & Bastian, Washington, 1965—; v.p., sec. Pacific Corp., 1961-74; sec. Air America Inc., 1961-74; v.p., sec., dir. So. Air Transport, 1974—; sec., dir. Permawick Co., 1974—. Mem. Am., D.C., Va., Md. bar assns., Order of Coif. Home: 9000 Congressional Ct Potomac MD 20854 Office: 1701 Pennsylvania Ave NW Washington DC 20006 Tel (202) 298-8333

BASYE, PAUL EDMOND, b. Nappanee, Ind., Oct. 1, 1901; A.B., U. Mo., 1923; J.D., U. Chgo., 1926; LL.M., U. Mich., 1943, S.J.D., 1946. Admitted to Mo. bar, 1926, Calif. bar, 1945; individual practice law, Kansas City, Mo., 1926-42, San Francisco, 1944-48; mem. firm Basye, Prior & Kavanaugh, Burlingame, Calif., 1948—; prof. law U. Mo., Kansas City, 1938-42, U. Calif. Hastings Coll. Law, San Francisco, 1948—. Mem. Am. (chmn. sect. real property, probate and trust law 1965-66), Calif. bar assns. Author: (with Lewis M. Simes) Problems in Probate Law, Including a Model Probate Code, 1946; Clearing Land Titles, 2d edit., 1970; contbr. numerous articles in field to legal jours. Home: 1427 Floribunda Ave Burlingame CA 94010 Office: 330 Primrose Rd Burlingame CA 94010 Tel (415) 348-5660

BATCH, NICHOLAS CHARLES, b. Hastings, Mich., July 15, 1944; A.B., U. Mich., 1965; M.B.A., Western Mich. U., 1971; J.D., Wayne State U., 1969. Admitted to Mich. bar, 1969; legal instr. Q.M. Sch. U.S. Army, 1969-70; asst. pros. atty. Calhoun County (Mich.), 1971-74; asst. prof. bus. Western Mich. U., Kalamazoo, 1972—. Chmn., Calhoun County Republican Party, 1976—; mem. Mich. Rep. Com., 1977—. Mem. Am. Bar Assn., Am. Bus. Law Assn., Civil Affairs Assn., Am. Judicature Soc., Phi Alpha Delta. Tel (616) 963-0530

BATE, CHARLES THOMAS, b. Muncie, Ind., Nov. 14, 1932; B.A., Butler U., 1955; J.D., Ind. U., 1962. Mem. claims dept. Statesman Ins. Group, Indpls., 1956-62; admitted to Ind. bar, 1962, U.S. Supreme Ct. bar, 1967; atty., Statesman Ins. Group, 1962-63; mem. firm Smith & Yarling, Indpls., 1963-67; v.p. and gen. counsel Disc. Life Ins. Co., Indpls., 1965-68; partner firm Soshnick & Bate, Shelbyville, Ind., 1967—. Sec. nat. bylaws com. Ch. of God, 1971-75, bd. pensions, 1972-76; trustee Warner Pacific Coll., Portland, Oreg., 1977—. Mem. Am., Ind. State, Shelby County (treas. 1977—), Indpls. bar assns., Am., Ind. trial lawyers assns., Am. Arbitration Assn. (arbitrator 1970—). Recipient Certificate of Merit award, Ind. Jud. Council, 1962. Home: PO Box 26 Shelbyville IN 46176 Office: 24 W Broadway st Shelbyville IN 46176 Tel (317) 392-2597

BATEMAN, FRED WILLOM, b. Roper, N.C., Sept. 18, 1916; A.B., Wake Forest U., 1939; LL.B., U. N.C., 1942. Admitted to Ill. bar, 1947, Va. bar, 1950; individual practice law, Newport News, Va., 1951—; sr. mem. firm Bateman Downing Redding & Conway, Newport News, 1977—; mem. Va. Senate, 1960-68, Va. Jud. Inquiry and Rev. Com., 1971—, Va. State Bd. Corrections, 1976—. Mem. Newport News (pres. 1964), Va. State (pres. 1964-65), Am. (ho. of dels. 1973—) bar assns. Home: 23 Cedar Ln Newport News VA 23601 Office: 11048 Warwick Blvd Newport News VA 23601 Tel (804) 596-7627

BATEMAN, WILLIAM CAREY, JR., b. Memphis, May 6, 1938; J.D., Memphis State U., 1965. Admitted to Tenn. bar, 1965, Fed. bar, 1965; asso. firm Chandler Manire Johnson & Harris, Memphis, 1966-71; partner firm Warlick & Bateman, Memphis, 1971-73; individual practice, Memphis, 1973—; asst. city atty. Memphis, 1972—, counsel to City Council, 1975—; lt. comdr. JAGC, USNR, 1970. Bd. dirs. Vis. Nurses Assn.; bd. dirs., pres. Family Services Memphis. Mem. Am. Judicature Soc., Am., Tenn., Memphis-Shelby County bar assns. Home: 5419 Southwood St Memphis TN 38117 Office: 3001 100 N Main St Memphis TN 38103 Tel (901) 526-0412

BATES, BEVERLY BAILEY, b. Atlanta, Jan. 23, 1938; A.B., Mercer U., 1959, LL.B., 1961. Admitted to Ga. bar, 1961, D.C. bar, 1966, U.S. Supreme Ct. bar, 1966; appellate counsel U.S. Army Judiciary, Washington, 1962-66; asst. U.S. atty. No. Dist. Ga., 1966-74; partner firm Bates, Baum and Landey, Atlanta, 1974—. Pres. Mercer U. Law Sch. Alumni Assn., 1976—. Mem. Am., Fed. (pres. Atlanta chpt. 1971-72), Atlanta bar assns. Lawyers Club Atlanta, Nat. Lawyers Club. Recipient Younger Fed. Lawyer award Atlanta chpt. Fed. Bar Assn., 1972. Office: Suite 2301 101 Marietta Tower Atlanta GA 30303 Tel (404) 681-2200

BATES, DOUGLAS THOMPSON, III, b. Nashville, June 4, 1947; B.A., Vanderbilt U., 1969; J.D., U. Tenn., 1973. Admitted to Tenn. bar, 1974; individual practice law, Centerville, Tenn., 1974—; asst. dist. atty. 17th Jud. Circuit. Mem. Indsl. Bd., Am., Tenn. bar assns. Decorated Bronze Star with oak leaf cluster, Vietnamese Cross of Gallantry with Palm. Office: 120 Perry St Centerville TN 37033 Tel (615) 729-4085

BATES, G(EORGE) WALLACE, b. Battle Lake, Minn., May 17, 1908; A.B., U. Minn., 1928, LL.B., 1930; LL.M., Columbia, 1931, Admitted to Minn. bar, 1930; U.S. Supreme Ct. bar, 1935, N.Y. bar, 1936, Mo. bar, 1950; with Root, Clark, Buckner & Ballantine, N.Y.C., 1931-43; atty. AT&T, N.Y.C., 1943-50, gen. atty., 1953-57; gen. counsel Southwestern Bell Telephone Co., St. Louis, 1950-53; v.p., gen. counsel, dir. N.Y. Telephone Co. and Empire City Subway Co., Ltd., N.Y.C., 1958-73; pres. Bus. Roundtable, N.Y.C., 1973—. Bd. dirs. Police Athletic League, N.Y., 1959, N.Y. State Traffic Safety Council, 1963. Mem. Am. (ho. of dels. 1973-75), N.Y. State (v.p. 1974-75, ho. of dels. 1972-75, exec. com. 1969-72) bar assns., N.Y. C. of C. (pres. 1970-71, chmn. exec. com. 1968-70). Home: 67 Glenville Rd Greenwich CT 06830 Office: 405 Lexington Ave New York City NY 10017 Tel (212) 682-6370

BATES, RICHARD WARDEN, b. Petoskey, Mich., Apr. 24, 1929; B.A., Stetson U., 1951, LL.B., 1953. Admitted to Fla. bar, 1953; with JAGC, U.S. Army, 1953-56; practiced in Orlando, Fla., since 1956, asso. firm Gurney, McDonald & Handley, 1956-60, partner firms McCarty & Bates, 1960-62, Maguire Voorhis & Wells, 1969-73, individual practice law, 1962-69, 73—. Trustee Holiday Hosp., Orlando; mem. phys. fitness council YMCA, Orlando. Mem. Assn. Trial Lawyers Am., Fla. Acad. Trial Lawyers, Am., Fla. bar assns. Home: 2354 Lake Shore Dr Orlando FL 32803 Office: suite 1599 CNA Tower 255 S Orange Ave Orlando FL 32801 Tel (305) 841-7026

BATES, WILLIAM JONES, b. Moncks Corner, S.C., Mar. 28, 1944; A.B., Wofford Coll., 1966; J.D., Duke, 1969. Admitted to S.C. bar, 1969; asso. firm Young, Clement & Rivers, Charleston, S.C., 1969-72, partner, 1972—. Mem. Am., S.C., Charleston County bar assns., Phi Beta Kappa. Office: PO Box 993 28 Broad St Charleston SC 29402 Tel (803) 577-4000

BATOR, PETER ANTHONY, b. Budapest, Hungary, July 2, 1929; A.B., Harvard, 1951, LL.B. magna cum laude (Sheldon fellow), 1954. Admitted to N.Y. bar, 1955; asso. firm Davis Polk & Wardwell, N.Y.C., 1955-61, partner, 1961—; dir. ICI Americas Inc., and predecessors, N.Y.C., 1969—, Kreutoll Realization Corp., N.Y.C., 1969—. Vice-chmn., chmn. exec. com. Beekman Downtown Hosp., N.Y.C., 1972—; mem. alumni standing com. Groton (Mass.) Sch., 1975—. Mem. Harvard Law Sch. Assn. N.Y.C. (trustee), Am., N.Y. State bar assns., Bar Assn. City N.Y., Am. Law Inst., Am. Inst. Internat. Law, Internat. Law Soc., Phi Beta Kappa. Editor Harvard Law Rev. Home: 1185 Park Ave New York City NY 10028 Office: Davis Polk & Wardwell 1 Chase Manhattan Plaza New York City NY 10005 Tel (212) 826-6954

BATSON, ARTHUR GLYNN, b. Dallas, May 21, 1945; B.A. in Polit. Sci., Grove City Coll., 1967; J.D., U. Pitts., 1972. Admitted to Pa. bar, 1972; atty. VA, Pitts., 1972-73; asso. firm Koegler & Tomlinson, Pitts., 1973-75; chief counsel Midland of Pa., Inc., title co., Pitts., 1975—; asso. broker Robert Young Realty Co., Pitts.; ins. agt. Pioneer Nat. Title Co., Norristown, Pa. Mem. Allegheny County, Pa., Am. bar assns. Home: 608 National Dr Pittsburgh PA 15235 Office: Suite 102 Grant Bldg Grant St Pittsburgh PA 15219 Tel (412) 391-3911

BATSON, RICHARD NEAL, b. Nashville, May 1, 1941; B.A., Vanderbilt U., 1963, J.D., 1966. Admitted to Ga. bar, 1967; law clk. U.S. Ct. Appeals 5th Circuit, Atlanta, 1966-67; asso. firm Alston, Miller and Gains, Atlanta, 1967-71, partner, 1971—; adj. prof. Emory U. Sch. Law, 1973-74. Mem. Am., Ga., Atlanta bar assns., Lawyers Club Atlanta, Order of Coif. Contbr. articles to law jours. Office: 1220 C & S Nat Bank Bldg Atlanta GA 30303 Tel (404) 588-0300

BATT, RAYMOND WARREN, b. Jamaica, N.Y., July 5, 1933; B.A., St. John's U., 1955, LL.B., 1958. Admitted to N.Y. State bar, 1959, U.S. Supreme Ct. bar, 1964; individual practice law, Shirley, N.Y., 1960-75; partner firm Batt, Messinetti, Shirley, 1975—. Mem. Suffolk County (chmn. community relations com. 1975—), N.Y. State bar assns., Am. Trial Lawyers Assn., Mastics C. of C. (pres. 1968-70). Named Man of Year, Shirley, 1966; asso. editor St. Johns Law Rev., 1954-55. Home: 13 Palmetto Dr Shirley NY 11967 Office: 210 William Floyd Pkwy Shirley NY 11967

BATTAGLIA, ANTHONY SYLVESTER, b. Binghamton, N.Y., Aug. 21, 1927; B.A. with honors, U. Fla., 1949, LL.B., 1953, J.D., 1953. Admitted to Fla. bar, 1953, U.S. Supreme Ct. bar, 1966; asst. to U.S. dist. atty. for So. Dist. Fla., Justice Dept., 1953-56; partner firm Battaglia, Ross, Stolba and Forlizzo and predecessors, St. Petersburg, Fla., 1956—; mem. Fla. Pub. Service Commn., 1971—. Fla. Republican nat. committeeman, 1956-64; Mem. Acad. Fla. Trial Lawyers, Am., Fed., Fla., St. Petersburg, Internat. bar assns., Assn. Trial Lawyers Am., Am. Judicature Soc. Elected to U. Fla. Hall of Fame, 1951. Office: 980 Tyrone Blvd N St Petersburg FL 33743 Tel (813) 381-2300

BATTAGLIA, JOSEPH CHARLES, b. Buffalo, Feb. 8, 1941; B.A., U. So. Calif., 1962; J.D., Loyola U., 1965. Admitted to Calif. bar, 1966; asso. firm Abeles & DeBro, Beverly Hills, 1966-67; individual practice law, Westwood, 1967-68, Century City, 1973-76; partner firm Lasky & Battaglia, Century City, 1968-73; instr. Mid-Valley Coll. Law, Encino, Calif., 1972-73. Active Italo-Americans Calif. Civic Orgn., 1970—; mem. United Democratic Fin. Com., 1975-76; bd. commrs. Los Angeles Conv. Center, 1976-77. Mem. Calif., Los Angeles trail lawyers assns., Calif., Century City (past pres.) bar assns. Office: 215 S La Cienega Blvd Suite 201 Beverly Hills CA 90211 Tel (213) 653-8365

BATTERSON, JAMES ROBERT, b. Tiffin, Mo., May 14, 1937; B.S., Mo. U., Columbia, 1959; J.D., Mo. U., Kansas City, 1965. Admitted to Mo. bar, 1965; asso. firm Ernest Hubbell, Kansas City, Mo., 1965-67; 2d v.p. Employers Reins. Corp., Kansas City, 1967—. Mem. Kansas City, Am. bar assns., Lawyers Assn., Kansas City Claims Assn. (pres.). Home: Route 1 Box 70 Platte City MO 64079 Office: 21 W 10th St Kansas City MO 64105 Tel (816) 283-5000

BATTIN, JAMES FRANKLIN, b. Wichita, Kans., Feb. 13, 1925; certificate Eastern Mont. Coll., 1948; J.D., George Washington U., 1951. Admitted to D.C. bar, 1951, Mont. bar, 1953, U.S. Supreme Ct. bar, 1968; practiced in Washington, 1951-52, Billings, Mont., 1953-59; dep. county atty. Yellowstone County (Mont.), 1953-55; asst. city atty. City of Billings, 1955-57, city atty., 1957-59; mem. Mont. Ho. of Reps., 1958-59; mem. 87th-91st Congresses from 2d Dist. Mont.; judge. U.S. Dist., Ct., Dist. of Mont., 1969—. Sec.-counsel City-County Planning Bd., Billings, 1955; Mont. del. to Republican Nat. Conv., 1964, 68; mem. exec. com. Rep. Congl. Campaign Com., 1968. Mem. Am., Mont., Yellowstone County bar assns., Am. Judicature Soc. Recipient Distinguished Service award U.S. Jaycees, 1954, Billings C. of C., 1969; named to DeMolay Legion of Honor. Office: POB 1476 Billings MT 59103 Tel (406) 657-6503

BATTISTI, FRANK J., b. Youngstown, Ohio, Oct. 4, 1922; A.B., Ohio U., 1947; J.D., Harvard, 1950. Admitted to Ohio bar, 1950; asst. atty. gen. Ohio, 1950; atty. adviser C.E., Dept. Army, Washington, 1951-52; instr. law Youngstown U., 1952-54; first asst. dir. law City of Youngstown, 1954-58; judge Ct. of Common Pleas, 1958; judge U.S. Dist. Ct., No. Dist. Ohio, Cleve., 1961-69, chief judge, 1969—. Mem. Fed. Dist. Judges Assn. (pres. 6th Circuit). Decorated comdr. Order of Merit, Republic of Italy; named Outstanding Trial Judge, Assn. Trial Lawyers Am., 1976. Office: US Courthouse Public Sq Cleveland OH 44114 Tel (216) 522-4250

BATTISTI, JAMES J., JR., b. Catskill, N.Y., Aug. 7, 1925; B.S., St. Lawrence U., 1950; LL.B., Albany Law Sch., 1954. Admitted to N.Y. State bar, 1955; judge Greene County Ct., Catskill, 1974—; asst. county atty. Greene County, 1964-74, social services atty., 1964-74. Mem. N.Y. State, Greene County bar assns. Home: 48 Wildwing St Catskill NY 12414 Office: Greene County Court House Catskill NY 12414 Tel (518) 943-2171

BATTLES, HAYDEN RANDALL, b. Cullman, Ala., Aug. 11, 1946; B.A., U. Ala., 1969, J.D., 1974. Admitted to Ala. bar, 1974; individual practice law, Cullman, 1974—. Mem. Cullman Bd. Adjustment; municipal recorder Cities of Hanceville and Garden City (Ala.). Mem. Am., Ala. (assembly del. to. young lawyers sect.) bar assns., Ala. Criminal Def. Lawyers Assn., Ala. Trial Lawyers Assn. Home: 440 Oak Manor Apts Cullman AL 35055 Office: 207 Downtown Plaza Cullman AL 35055 Tel (205) 734-6330

BATZ, CARL CASPER, b. Argos, Ind., Sept. 7, 1906; B.E.E., Purdue U., 1929, E.E., 1933; J.D., U. Chgo., 1935. Admitted to Ill. bar, 1935, U.S. Patent Office bar, 1937, U.S. Ct. Customs and Patent Appeals bar, 1943; asso. firm Dyrenforth Lee Chritton & Wiles, Chgo., 1935-37; patent counsel Bendix Corp., Chgo., 1937, Armour and Co., Chgo., 1938-71; partner firm Fidler Patnaude & Batz, Oak Brook, Ill., 1971—; dir. Kemlite Corp Joliet, Ill., Speer Filler Strip Co., Western Springs, Ill. Bd. dirs. Community Center Found., Palos Park, Ill., 1975—. Mem. Internat., Am., Chgo. patent law assns., Ill. State Bar Assn., Assn. Internat. for Protection of Indsl. Property, Assn. Corp. Patent Counsel. Author: Trademarks, 1973. Home: 5011 Grand Ave Western Springs IL 60558 Office: 1211 W 22d St Oak Brook IL 60521 Tel (312) 986-1030

BAUDE, PATRICK LOUIS, b. Independence, Kans., Apr. 7, 1943; A.B., U. Kans., 1964; J.D., 1966; LL.M., Harvard, 1968. Admitted to Wis. bar, 1966, U.S. Supreme Ct. bar, 1972; asso. firm Foley & Lardner, Milw., 1966-67; asst. prof. law Ind. U., 1968-71, asso. prof., 1971-74, prof., 1974—. Mem. AAUP (pres. Ind. U. chpt. 1974-75), Soc. Am. Law Tchrs., Wis. Bar Assn., Bar Assn. 7th Fed. Circuit. Contbr. articles to law jours. Office: 311 Law Bldg Ind Univ Bloomington IN 47401 Tel (812) 337-5927

BAUDUIT, HAROLD STEPHEN, b. New Orleans, Aug. 27, 1930; B.S., U.S. Naval Acad., 1956; M.A., M.S., U. Colo., 1967, J.D., 1972. Admitted to Colo. bar, 1972, U.S. Dist. Ct. Colo. bar, 1972; asst. prof. U. Colo., 1972—. Mem. Sigma Iota Epsilon. Martin Luther King Jr. fellow, Wood Wilson Nat. Fellowship Found. fellow, 1969-71. Home and Office: 2760 Iliff St Boulder CO 80303 Tel (303) 494-7254

BAUER, EDWARD GREB, JR., b. Jeannette, Pa., Aug. 10, 1928; B.S., Princeton U., 1951; LL.B., Harvard U., 1957. Admitted to Pa. bar, 1958; asso. firm Ballard, Spahr, Andrews, & Ingersoll, Phila., 1957-62; exec. asst. to mayor city Phila., 1962-63, city solicitor Phila., 1963-70; v.p., gen. counsel, Phila. Elec. Co., 1970—; dir. Susquehanna Power Co., Susquehanna Elec. Co., Phila. Elec. Power Co., Adwin

Realty Co., Adwin Equipment Co., Eastern Pa. Devel. Co. Bd. dirs. Citizens Crime Commn. Phila.; bd. govs. Am. Heart Assn.; dir. Defender Assn. Phila. Mem. Am., Pa., Phila. bar assns., Pa. C. of C. (dir. Pa. 1971). Home: 1799 E Willow Grove Ave Philadelphia PA 19118 Office: 2301 Market St Philadelphia PA 19101 Tel (215) 841-4250

BAUER, KEITH JAY, b. Portland, Oreg., Sept. 24, 1947; B.A., Willamette U., Salem, Oreg., 1969, J.D., 1973. Admitted to Oreg. bar, 1973; asso. firm Rhoten, Rhoten & Speerstra, Salem, 1973—. Bd. dirs. Benedictine Nursing Center (Mt. Angel, Oreg.), Salem Vol. Bur. Mem. Am., Oreg., Marion County bar assns., Oreg. Trial Lawyers Assn., Oreg. Assn. Def. Counsel. Home: 1775 Fairmount Ave S Salem OR 97302 Office: Pioneer Trust Bldg Salem OR 97301 Tel (503) 364-6733

BAUER, WILLIAM RUDOLPH, b. Los Angeles, Nov. 5, 1943; B.S., U. S.C., 1968, J.D., 1973. Admitted to S.C. bar, 1973; title atty. Lawyer Title Ins. Co., Columbia, S.C., 1973-74; asso. firm Haskell & Haskell, Columbia, 1974—. Mem. Phi Alpha Delta. Home: 118 Fifeshire Dr Columbia SC 29210 Office: 1223 Washington St Columbia SC 29201 Tel (803) 799-9369

BAUERNSCHMIDT, GEORGE WILLIAM, JR., b. Long Beach, Calif., Apr. 18, 1924; A.B., George Washington U., 1949; M.B.A., N.Y. U., 1957; J.D., U. Md., 1965. Admitted to Md. bar, 1965; with RCA, Indpls., 1950-51, Newark, 1951-52; ops. officer States Marine Corp., N.Y.C., 1952-57; gen. mgr. N.Y. Paper Co., Balt., 1957-60; program analyst Md. Nat. Bank, Balt., 1960-67; trust officer Union Trust Co. Md., Balt., 1967-75; individual practice law, Severna Park, Md., 1975—; v.p. N.Y. Maritime Assn., N.Y.C., 1953-57. Chmn. Oak Hill Sch. Citizens' Adv. Com., 1970-72; pres. Wroxeter Patrons Club, Arnold, Md., 1967-69. Contbr. to States Marine Lines Safety Bull., 1953-54. Home: 686 Hendler Rd Severna Park MD 21146 Office: 686 Hendler Rd Severna Park MD 21146 Tel (301) 647-3830

BAUGH, GARY TODD, b. Sweetwater, Tex., Oct. 12, 1941; B.A., Rice U., 1964; LL.B., U. Tex., 1967. Admitted to Mont., Tex., Colo. bars, 1967; since practiced in Billings, Mont.; individual practice law, 1968; partner firm Scott, Scott & Baugh, 1969-71; asso. firm Kurth, Davidson & Calton, 1972-74; partner firm Davidson, Veeder, Baugh & Broeder, 1975—; asst. atty. Yellowstone County, Mont., 1970-72; U.S. magistrate Dist. Mont., 1972—. Bd. dirs. Housing Authority of Billings. Mem. Am., Mont., Tex., Colo. bar assns. Office: 805 Midland Nat Bank Bldg Billings MT 59101 Tel (406) 248-9156

BAUM, ROBERT MELVIN, b. Bklyn., June 29, 1930; A.B., Centre Coll. Ky., 1952; LL.B., Columbia, 1955. Admitted to N.Y. bar, 1956, U.S. Supreme Ct. bar, 1963; partner firm Baum, Skigen, Lefkowitz, Sak & Purcell, Smithtown, N.Y., 1972—; justice Nissequogue, N.Y., 1974—. Mem. N.Y. State, Suffolk County bar assns., Suffolk County, N.Y. State magistrates assns. Home: Box 188 River Rd St James NY 11780 Office: 278 E Main St Smithtown NY 11787 Tel (516) 265-7777

BAUM, STANLEY MARTIN, b. Bronx, N.Y., Mar. 6, 1944; B.S., in Commerce, Rider Coll., 1966; J.D., John Marshall Law Sch., Atlanta, 1969. Law clk. U.S. Atty., No. Dist. Ga., Atlanta, 1969; admitted to Ga. bar, 1970; legal aide Ga. Gen. Assembly, Atlanta, 1970, 71; asst. U.S. atty. No. Dist. Ga., Atlanta, 1971-74; partner firm Bates & Baum, Atlanta, 1974-76; partner firm Bates, Baum & Landey, Atlanta, 1976—. Pres. Congregation Shearith Israel, Atlanta, 1976—. Mem. Am., Ga., Fed. (pres. chpt. 1976-77, nat. council 1974-77), Decatur-Dekalb bar assns., Am. Judicature Soc., Nat. Dist. Attys. Assn., Nat. Lawyers Club. Home: 1340 Bramble Rd NE Atlanta GA 30329 Office: Suite 2301 101 Marietta Tower Atlanta GA 30303

BAUM, VICTOR JOSEPH, b. Detroit, July 2, 1923; A.B., U. Mich., 1946; J.D., Harvard, 1950. Admitted to Mich. bar, 1951; staff atty. Ford Motor Co., Detroit, 1950-52; asso. firm Marx, Levi, Thill & Wiseman, Detroit, 1952-57; judge Mich. Circuit Ct., 3d Jud. Dist., 1957—; faculty adviser Nat. Coll. State Trial Judges, Reno, Nev., 1969. Mem. Detroit, Am. bar assns., Mich. State Bar, Nat. Assn. Family Conciliation Cts. Services (pres. 1970). Author: Mich. Ct. Marriage Counseling Services Act, 1964. Office: 1701 City-County Bldg Detroit MI 48226 Tel (313) 224-5173

BAUMAN, BERT, b. Bklyn., Apr. 28, 1932; B.A., Bklyn. Coll., 1953; LL.B., N.Y.U., 1955. Admitted to N.Y. bar, 1958; practiced in N.Y.C., 1958—; asso. firm Pillinger, Raiskin & Weiser, 1958, Phillip Smith, 1958, George Popkin, 1959; asso. firm Spatt & Bauman and predecessor, 1959-65, partner, 1965—; arbitrator Small Claims Ct., N.Y.C., 1968—; arbitrator Am. Arbitration Assn., 1975—, Civil Ct., 1972—. Dist. leader 81st Assembly Dist. Democratic Party, 1964-68; del. Dem. Nat. Conv., 1976; chmn. Bronx County Planning Bd. No. 11, 1969-72; chmn. community bd. BMHS Hosp., 1972; mem. Comprehensive Health Planning Bd., 1971-72. Mem. Bronx Bar Assn., N.Y. State Trial Lawyers Assn. Recipient Bronx Borough Pres.'s award, 1975; co-editor of N.Y. State Trial Lawyers News, 1976; columnist Parkway News, 1974-75. Home: 19 Mirrielees Circle Great Neck NY 11021 Office: 225 W 34th St New York City NY 10001 Tel (212) 564-3555

BAUMAN, CARL J.D., b. Pendleton, Oreg., Aug. 2, 1947; B.A., U. Oreg., 1970, J.D., 1973. Admitted to Alaska bar, 1973; asso. firm Hughes, Thorsness, Lowe, Gantz & Clark, Anchorage, 1973-75; partner firm Hughes, Thorsness, Gantz, Powell & Brundin, Anchorage, 1975—. Mem. Am., Alaska, Anchorage bar assns. Exec. editor Oregon Law Rev., 1972-73. Home: 2911 Lexington Ave Anchorage AK 99502 Office: 509 W Third St Anchorage AK 99501 Tel (907) 274-7522

BAUMAN, JEROME ALAN, b. N.Y.C., July 7, 1931; B.S., Queens Coll., 1953; LL.B. cum laude, Harvard, 1958. Admitted to N.Y. bar, 1959; Fla. bar, 1971; asso. firm Levin, Rosmarin & Schwartz, N.Y.C., 1958-62; firm Sperry, Wineberg & Cutler, N.Y.C., 1962-64; gen. counsel Inland Credit Corp., N.Y.C., 1964-66; asso. Golenbock and Barell, N.Y.C., 1966-68; asso. counsel GAC Corp. and subs., Allentown, Pa. and Miami, Fla., 1968-70; gen. counsel GAC Properties, Inc., Miami, 1970-72; v.p. gen. counsel Gulfstream Land & Devel. Corp., Plantation, Fla., 1972—; dir. Barnett Bank of Plantation. Pres. Plantation Jewish Congregation, 1975—. Home: 1081 W Tropical Way Plantation FL 33317 Office: 8751 W Broward Blvd Plantation FL 33324 Tel (305) 472-4200

BAUMAN, LEEDS CLIFFORD, b. Mpls., Apr. 1, 1924; B.S., U. Minn., 1947; B.B.A., U. Minn., 1948, LL.B., 1950. Admitted to Minn. bar, 1950, Calif. bar, 1963; asso. firm Nunam, Qualey & Colwell, Mpls., 1952-54; asso. firm Mandel & Bauman, Mpls., 1958-62; individual practice law, Santa Barbara, Calif., 1965—; contracts mgr. U.S. Industries, Goleta, Calif., 1962-63, E. G. & G., Inc., Goleta, 1963-65. Mem. Minn. Merit System Council, 1959-61. Mem. Assn. Goleta Attys. Home: 6860 Sabado Tarde St Goleta CA 93017 Office: suite 2L 5276 Hollister Ave Santa Barbara CA 93111 Tel (805) 964-4747

BAUMAN, PAUL, b. N.Y.C., Apr. 17, 1922; B.A., N.Y. U., 1947; J.D., Harvard U., 1950. Admitted to N.Y. State bar, 1950, U.S. Supreme Ct. bar, 1967; asso. firm Herman Goldman, N.Y.C., 1951-65; partner firm Brauner Baron Rosenzweig Kligler & Sparber, N.Y.C., 1965—; dir. S. African Marine Corp., 1965—, Circuit Tech. Inc., 1968—, Superior Cable Corp., 1976—. Pres. Audubon Woods Civic Assn., Huntington, N.Y., 1958; pres. N. Shore Community Arts Center, Great Neck, N.Y., 1974; bd. dirs. Herman Goldman Found., 1977—. Mem. N.Y. State, N.Y.C., Am. bar assns. Author: (with Rufus King) A Critical Analysis of the Gambling Laws, 1952. Home: 21 Shadow Ln Great Neck NY 11021 Office: 120 Broadway New York City NY 10005 Tel (212) 732-5535

BAUMAN, RICHARD GEORGE, b. Youngstown, Ohio, Sept. 12, 1917; student Youngstown U., U. Ala.; J.D., Ohio State U., 1941. Admitted to Ohio bar, 1941, Fed. Dist. Ct. Cleve. bar, 1942, U.S. Supreme Ct. bar, 1960; adjudicator, authority officer rating bd., claims div. VA, Pitts., 1942-49; individual practice law, Youngstown, 1949-52, Warren, Ohio, 1969—; title examiner, agent Louisville Title Ins. Co., Youngstown, 1952-59; asst. v.p., reviewer Land Title Ins. Co., Youngstown, 1959-61, title officer, reviewer, 1968-69; 1st asst. law dir. City of Youngstown, 1962-63; title reviewer, agent Commonwealth Land Title Ins. Co., Youngstown, 1963-65, agent, atty., Warren, 1969—; asst. prosecuting atty. Mahoning County, Youngstown, 1965-69. Mem. Am., Ohio (real property sect.), Trumbull County, Mahoning County bar assns., Ohio Land Title Assn. Home: 32 Norwick Dr Youngstown OH 44505 Office: 905 2d National Tower Warren OH 44481 Tel (216) 394-1522 or 545-1282

BAUMANN, RICHARD GORDON, b. Chgo., Apr. 7, 1938; B.S., U. Wis., 1960, J.D., 1964. Admitted to Wis. bar, 1964, Calif. bar, 1970, U.S. Supreme Ct. bar, 1973; asso. firm Kohner, Mann & Kailas, Milw., 1964-69; asso. firm Sulmeyer, Kupetz, Baumann & Rothman and predecessors, Los Angeles, 1969-71, partner, 1971—. Mem. Wis., Calif., Los Angeles County bar assns., Comml. Law League Am. Office: 615 S Flower St Los Angeles CA 90017 Tel (213) 626-2311

BAUMANN, RIECKE, b. Lake Charles, La., Sept. 1, 1947; B.A., McNeese State U., 1970; J.D., La. State U., 1973. Admitted to La., Tex. bars, 1974; asso. firm Maley, House & Bobbitt, Houston, 1974; individual practice law, Houston, 1975—; of counsel firm Taylor and Rea, Baton Rouge, 1975—. Mem. Am., Houston bar assns. Home: 1604 Hawthorne St Houston TX 77006 Office: 1602 Hawthorne St Houston TX 77006 Tel (713) 529-4161

BAUMANN, WILLIAM MCCONNELL, b. Fremont, Ohio, May 12, 1909; B.A., Amherst Coll., 1930; LL.B., Harvard, 1933. Admitted to Ohio bar, 1933, U.S. Supreme Ct. bar, 1948; individual practice law, Fremont, 1933-43, Lakewood, Ohio, 1953-60, 73—; regional atty. Rent Control, Cleve., 1943-53; gen. atty. Immigration and Naturalization Service, Dept. Justice, Cleve., 1960-73; conciliation commr. in bankruptcy Sandusky County (Ohio), 1934-43. Chmn. Pres.'s Birthday Ball Com., Sandusky County, 1938; chmn. war price and rationing bd. Sandusky County, 1942. Mem. Ohio State Bar Assn., Harvard Law Sch. Assn., Am. Philatelic Soc., Beta Theta Pi. Recipient U.S. Treasury Dept. award U.S. Savs. Bond Program, 1968; Spl. Achievement award Immigration and Naturalization Service, 1970-71. Home: 15432 Edgewater Dr Lakewood OH 44107 Office: 15432 Edgewater Dr Lakewood OH 44107 Tel (216) 226-0669

BAUMBUSCH, PETER LAWRENCE, b. Lakewood, Ohio, Aug. 5, 1944; A.B., Dartmouth, 1965; postgrad. Magdalen Coll., Oxford, 1966; J.D., Harvard, 1972. Admitted to Calif. bar, 1973; asso. firm Gibson, Dunn & Crutcher, Los Angeles, 1972—. Mem. bd. dirs. Californians for Campaign Reform, 1972-73; elder Brentwood Presbyn. Ch., 1976-77. Mem. Am., Calif., Los Angeles County (chmn. spl. com. fair polit. practices commn., mem. exec. com., treas. human rights sect., sec. tax sect. com. on interstate taxation) bar assns. Author: Campaign & Lobbying Law Handbook. Office: 515 S Flower St Los Angeles CA 90017 Tel (213) 488-7456

BAUMER, THOMAS MAXWELL, b. Jacksonville, Fla., Apr. 16, 1939; A.B., U. Notre Dame, 1961; LL.B., U. Fla., 1964. Admitted to Fla. bar, 1964, U.S. Supreme Ct. bar, 1971; asst. U.S. atty. Middle dist. Fla., Dept. Justice, 1965-67; asso. firm Mahoney Hadlow & Adams, Jacksonville, 1967-70, partner, 1970—. Mem. Jacksonville U. Council, 1976—. Mem. Jacksonville (pres. sect. young lawyers 1971), Am. bar assns., Am. Judicature Soc., Fla. Bar (instr., author continuing edn. courses). Home: 3758 Cathedral Oaks Pl N Jacksonville FL 32217 Office: 100 Laura St Jacksonville FL 32202 Tel (904) 354-1100

BAUMIL, RAYMOND SCOTT, b. Charleston, S.C., July 26, 1949; B.A., Coll. Charleston, 1970; J.D., U. S.C., 1973. Admitted to S.C. bar, 1973; law clk. to justice S.C. Supreme Ct., Charleston, 1973-74; asso. firm Solomon, Kahn, Roberts & Smith, Charleston, 1974—. Mem. Am., S.C. bar assns., Am., S.C. trial lawyers assns. Home: 1718 McLeod Ave Charleston SC 29412 Office: 39 Broad St PO Box 486 Charleston SC 29402 Tel (803) 577-7182

BAUTISTA, DAVID FRANCIS, b. Elizabethton, Tenn., July 24, 1939; B.S., East Tenn. State U., 1961; J.D., U. Tenn., 1963. Admitted to Tenn. bar, 1963, U.S. Dist. Ct. for Eastern Dist. Tenn. bar, 1968; individual practice law, Elizabethton, 1966-68; asso. firm Street, Banks, Merryman, Bautista & Banks, Elizabethton, 1968-69, partner, 1969—; mem. Tenn. Supreme Ct. Commn., 1972-73; mem. U.S. Dist. Ct. Admissions and Examining Com. for N.E. Dist. Tenn., 1975—; instr. mil. law ROTC East Tenn. State U., 1975—. Mem. Carter County (Tenn.) Election Commn., 1971—, vice chmn., 1971-73, sec., 1973-74; pres. bd. trustees, legal advisor Carter County Emergency and Rescue Squad Inc., 1974—; col. aide de camp Gov. of Tenn., 1973—; mem. Carter County Bi-Centennial Com., 1976. Mem. Carter County (pres. 1970), Tenn. (v.p. East Tenn. chpt. 1970, gov. 1st congressional dist. 1971—), Am. bar assns., Tenn. Trial Lawyers Assn., Assn. Trial Lawyers Am., Am. Judicature Soc., Nat. Lawyers Club, Tenn. Local Bar Conf. (v.p. East Tenn. region 1972). Named Outstanding Young Man of Year, Carter County Jaycees, 1973; Ky. Col. Home: 625 Crescent Dr Elizabethton TN 37643 Office: Riverview Bldg Elk Ave Elizabethton TN 37643 Tel (615) 543-3100

BAVOSO, WILLIAM DAVID, b. Passaic, N.J., Nov. 3, 1946; B.J., U. Fla., 1968; J.D., St. Johns U., 1971. Admitted to N.Y. bar, 1972, Fla. bar, 1974. Partner firm Cohen, Levy, Bavoso & Weinstein, and predecessors, Port Jervis, N.Y., 1971—; trustee, atty. Neversink Valley Area Mus., Cuddebackville, N.Y., 1974—. Mem. N.Y. (standing com. village, town and city cts. 1972—), Orange County (N.Y.), Port Jervis bar assns. Office: 24 Front St Port Jervis NY 12771 Tel (914) 856-4444

BAX, JOE G., b. Houston, Aug. 30, 1948; B.A., U. Houston, 1970, J.D., 1972. Admitted to Tex. bar, 1973; partner firm Hoover, Cox & Miller, Houston, 1973—. Mem. Am., Tex., Houston bar assns. Office: 2200 S Post Oak Rd Suite 301 Houston TX 77056 Tel (713) 623-4440

BAXLEY, WADE HAMPTON, b. Dothan, Ala., Nov. 1, 1943; B.S., U. Ala., 1965, J.D., 1968. Admitted to Ala. bar, 1968; partner firm Ramsey & Baxley, Dothan, 1969—; asst. atty. City of Dothan, 1969-73, atty., 1973—. Mem. Am., Ala., Houston County bar assns., Dothan Houston County C. of C. (dir.). Home: 408 Gwaltney Dr Dothan AL 36301 Office: POB 1464 Dothan AL 36301 Tel (205) 792-2694

BAXLEY, WILLIAM JOSEPH, b. Dothan, Ala., June 27, 1941; B.S., U. Ala., 1962, LL.B., 1964. Admitted to Ala. bar, 1964; law clk. Ala. Supreme Ct., 1964-65; mem. firm Lee & McInish, Dothan, 1966; dist. atty. 20th Jud. Circuit Ala., 1966-71, atty. gen. Ala., 1971—. Bd. dirs. Dothan Boys Club. Mem. Houston County Bar Assn. (pres. 1969), United Comml. Travelers, Kappa Sigma, Alpha Kappa Psi, Phi Alpha Delta. Home: Woodley Sq Apts Montgomery AL 36111 Office: State Capitol Bldg Montgomery AL 36104*

BAXTER, FRED JOHAN, b. Juneau, Alaska, Mar. 17, 1944; B.A., Pacific Luth. U., 1966; M.P.A., U. Wash., 1968; J.D., U. Colo., 1971. Admitted to Alaska bar, 1972, U.S. Dist. Ct. for Alaska bar, 1972, U.S. Ct. Appeals bar, 1972; dep. borough atty. Greater Anchorage Area Borough, 1972-73; partner firm Gregg, Fraties, Petersen, Page & Baxter, Juneau, 1973-77; individual practice as Fred J. Baxter, Juneau, 1977—; adminstrv. asst. to city mgr. City of Bellevue, Wash., 1967-68; asst. to undersec. Dept. Transp., Washington, 1968, asst. to asst. sec., 1969, 70. Chmn. parks and recreation com. City and Borough Juneau, 1975—; bd. dirs. Boy Scouts Am. of Southeast Alaska, 1975—. Mem. Am., Alaska, Juneau (pres. 1977-78) bar assns., Am. Trial Lawyers Assn., Alaska Pioneers. Home: PO Box 762 Juneau AK 99802 Office: 9099 Glacier Hwy Box 2819 Juneau AK 99803 Tel (907) 789-2140

BAXTER, GLENN NELSON, b. Columbus, Ga., Jan. 28, 1946; B.A., U. Ala., 1968, J.D., 1971. Admitted to Ala. bar, 1971; since practiced in Tuscaloosa, Ala.; city prosecutor, 1971-75, asst. city atty., 1971-76; partner firm Baxter & Wilson, 1977—. Mem. bd. deacons 1st Presbyterian Ch.; bd. dirs. Regional Alcoholism Council of Bibb, Pickens & Tuscaloosa Counties, 1973—, Phoenix House, Inc., 1972—; pres. YMCA Men's Club. Mem. Tuscaloosa County, Ala. State, Am. bar assns., Pi Sigma Alpha. Home: 45 Woodland Hills Tuscaloosa AL 35401 Office: 2604 7th St Tuscaloosa AL 35401 Tel (205) 349-1830

BAXTER, HARRY STEVENS, b. Ashburn, Ga., Aug. 25, 1915; A.B., U. Ga., 1936, LL.B., 1939. Admitted to Ga. bar, 1941, U.S. Supreme Ct. bar, 1957; instr. law U. Ga., Athens, 1941; asso. firm Kilpatrick, Cody, Rogers, McClatchey & Regenstein, Atlanta, 1941-51, partner, 1951—; chmn. Ga. Bd. Bar Examiners, 1961-66. Pres., Met. Atlanta Community Services, 1963; co-chmn. Joint Tech.-Ga. Devel. Fund, 1967-68; chmn. U. Ga. Found., 1973-76. Fellow Am. Bar Found.; mem. Ga. (chmn. younger lawyers sect. 1947-48), Atlanta, Am. bar assns., Lawyers Club Atlanta (pres. 1958-59), Am. Law Inst., Am. Judicature Soc. Recipient Distinguished Alumnus award U. Ga. Law Sch., 1967. Home: 3197 Chatham Rd NW Atlanta GA 30305 Office: 3100 Equitable Bldg 100 Peachtree St Atlanta GA 30303 Tel (404) 522-3100

BAXTER, HOWARD HENRY, b. Cleve., July 31, 1931; B.S. in Indsl. Econs., Iowa State Coll., 1953; LL.B., J.D., Franklin Thomas Backus Sch. Law, Western Res. U., 1956. Admitted to Ohio bar, 1956; asso. firm McNeal and Schick, Cleve., 1956-60; atty., group counsel, Harris Corp., Cleve., 1960-76; v.p., gen. counsel Langston div., sec. Molins Machine Co., Cherry Hill, N.J., 1976—. Exec. v.p. and counsel Gt. Lakes Hist. Soc., 1972-76, trustee, 1970—. Mem. Cleve., Ohio, Am., Inter-Am. bar assns., Am. Soc. Internat. Law, Am. Judicature Soc., Am., Ohio assns. trial lawyers.

BAXTER, JAMES THOMAS, III, b. Columbus, Miss., Nov. 23, 1947; B.S. in Bus. Adminstrn., Auburn U., 1970; J.D. cum laude, Samford U., 1973. Admitted to Ala. bar, 1973; asso. firm Cloud, Berry, Ables, Blanton & Tatum, Huntsville, Ala., 1973-75, partner, 1975—. Mem. Citizen's Adv. Bd. on Recreation and Tourism, Intergovtl. Cooperation Commn. of Ala., 1972. Mem. Am., Huntsville-Madison County bar assns., Ala. State Bar, Ala. Trial Lawyers Assn., Assn. Trial Lawyers Am. Home: 1208 Owens Dr SE Huntsville AL 35801 Office: 315 Franklin St SE Huntsville AL 35801 Tel (205) 533-3740

BAXTER, THOMAS ALLEN, b. Decatur, Ind., Aug. 30, 1946; B.A., Purdue U., 1968; J.D. with honors, George Washington U., 1971, LL.M., 1977. Admitted to D.C. bar, 1971; spl. asst. for litigation Price Commn. and Cost of Living Council, Washington, 1972-73; asso. firm Shaw, Pittman, Potts & Trowbridge, Washington, 1973—. Mem. Am., D.C. bar assns. Recipient Meritorious Service award Price Commn., Office of Pres., 1973. Office: 1800 M Street NW Washington DC 20036 Tel (202) 331-4100

BAXTER, WILLIAM FRANCIS, b. N.Y.C., July 13, 1929; A.B., Stanford 1951, J.D., 1956. Admitted to Calif. bar, 1956, U.S. Supreme Ct. bar, 1960; asst. prof. law Stanford, 1956-58, prof., 1960—; antitrust counsel Marcor, 1971—; counsel Citicorp, 1975—; mem. Pres.'s Task Force on Antitrust Policy, 1968; cons., project dir. FAA Study on Legal and Econ. Aspects of Aircraft Noise, 1966-68; cons. Fed. Res. Bd., 1969-73, Brookings Instn., 1968-72, Pres.'s Task Force on Communications Policy, 1968; vis. prof. law Yale 1964-65; asso. firm Covington & Burling, Washington, 1958-60. Mem. Calif. Bar Assn.; Fellow Center Advanced Study in Behavioral Scis., 1973-74; co-author: Retail Banking in the Electronic Age: The Law and Economics of EFTS, 1977; contbr. articles to legal jours. Office: Stanford Law Sch Sanford CA 94305 Tel (415) 497-2470

BAYARD, ALEXIS IRENEE DUPONT, b. Wilmington, Del., Feb. 11, 1918; B.A., Princeton U., 1940; LL.B., U. Va., 1947. Admitted to Del. bar, 1948, U.S. Supreme Ct. bar, 1965; asso. firm Richards, Layton & Finger, Wilmington, 1948-52; individual practice law, Wilmington, 1952-61; partner firm Herrmann, Bayard, Brill & Gallagher, Wilmington, 1961-65, Bayard, Brill & Handelman, Wilmington, 1965-76, pres., 1976—; lt. gov. State of Del., 1949-53; mem. Nat. Commn. Uniform Laws, 1961-71; mem. censor com. Del. Supreme Ct., 1966-72. Campaign chmn. Democratic Com., 1954, state chmn., 1967-69; mem. fin. com. Nat. Dem. Com., 1970, mem. exec. com. 1975—; bd. dirs. Del. Project Hope, 1962, Blood Bank Del., 1955-70; state chmn. Nat. Found. March Dimes, 1965—; pres. Del. State Bd. Pardons, 1949-53; vice chmn. Del. River and Bay Authority, 1965-66, chmn., 1967-69. Mem. Assn. Bar City N.Y., Del.,

Am. bar assns., Am. Judicature Soc. Home: 9 Red Oak Rd Wilmington DE 19806 Office: 300 Market Tower Wilmington DE 19801 Tel (302) 575-0130

BAYER, FRANK JOSEPH, b. Akron, Ohio, Sept. 6, 1928; B.A., Kent State U., 1951; LL.B., Western Res. U., 1954. Admitted to Ohio bar, 1954; partner firm Bailey, Bayer and Bayer, Akron, 1960-69; judge Municipal Ct., Cuyahoga Falls, Ohio, 1969-77, Summit County Common Pleas Ct., 1977—. Mem. Akron,, Ohio State, Am. bar assns., Am. Judicature Soc., Am. Judges Assn. Recipient Excellent Jud. Service award Ohio Supreme Ct., 1975, Superior Jud. Service award, 1975. Home: 1515 Clairhaven Dr Hudson OH 44236 Office: Summit County Court House Akron OH 44308 Tel (216) 379-5140

BAZELON, DAVID LIONEL, b. Superior, Wis., Sept. 3, 1909; B.S.L., Northwestern U., 1931, LL.D. (hon.), 1974; LL.D. (hon.), Colby Coll., 1966, Boston U., 1969, Albert Einstein Coll. Medicine, Yeshiva U., 1972, U. So. Calif., 1977. Admitted to Ill. bar, 1932; asst. U.S. atty. No. Dist. Ill., 1935-40; sr. mem. firm Gottlieb & Schwartz, Chgo., 1940-46; asst. atty. gen. U.S., 1946-49; judge U.S. Ct. Appeals for D.C. Circuit, 1949—, chief 1962—; lectr. law and psychiatry U. Pa., 1957-59; Sloan vis. prof. Menninger Found., Topeka, 1960-61; lectr. psychiatry Johns Hopkins U., 1964—; Niles Meml. lectr. Hebrew U., 1966; clin. prof. psychiatry George Washington U., 1966-75; chmn. Task Force on Law, Pres.'s Panel on Mental Retardation, 1961-62; mem. U.S. Mission on Mental Health to USSR, 1967; spl. cons. Guidelines for Sterilization of Minors and Legally Imcompetent Individuals, HEW, 1973; cons. Inst. Corrections, Am. Found., 1970, Children Today, 1973, Judge Baker Guidance Center, Children's Hosp. Med. Center and Harvard Med. Sch., 1974. Bd. dirs. Citizens Bd. Inquiry into Health Services for Americans, 1969-71, Center for Psychosocial Studies, Chgo., 1973, Human Services Inst. for Children and Families, 1974-75, Nat. Com. for Prevention Child Abuse, 1975, Nat. Council on Crime and Delinquency, 1974, Washington Sch. Psychiatry; bd. dirs. Coop. Health Info. Center Vt., 1971-75, adv. council, 1975; trustee William Alanson White Found., 1958, Salk Inst. for Biol. Studies, 1961; chmn. adv. bd. Boston U. Center for Law and Life Scis., 1970; chmn. adv. com. Model Sch. div. D.C. Pub. Schs., 1964-66; mem. adv. bd. Center for Advanced Study in Behavioral Scis., 1971-75; mem. nat. adv. com. John F. Kennedy Center for Research on Edn. and Human Devel., 1968; mem. adv. com. on child devel. NRC-Nat. Acad. Scis., 1971; bd. visitors City Coll. N.Y., 1973; bd. overseers Center for Study of Violence, Brandeis U., 1966-70. Hon. fellow Am. Psychiat. Assn. (Isaac Ray award 1962, Distinguished Service award 1975), Am. Coll. Legal Medicine; fellow Am. Acad. Arts and Scis.; mem. Am. Bar Assn., Am. Psychol. Assn., Am. Bar Found., Am. Orthopsychiat. Assn. (dir. 1965-72, pres. 1969-70). Editorial adv. bd. Criminology Jour., 1973-75; cons. Children Today, 1973—. Home: 2700 Virginia Ave NW Washington DC 20037 Office: US Courthouse Washington DC 20001 Tel (202) 426-7118

BAZELON, RICHARD LEE, b. Chgo., Mar. 11, 1943; B.A., Haverford Coll., 1965; LL.D., U. Pa., 1968. Admitted to Pa. bar, 1968; law clk. Ct. of Common Pleas Phila. County, 1968-69; asso. firm Dilworth, Paxson, Kalish & Levy, Phila., 1969—, partner, 1974—; clin. asst. prof. Hahnemann Med. Coll., 1976—. Mem. U. Pa. Law Alumni Soc. (bd. mgrs. 1976—). Home: 3009 Foxx Ln Philadelphia PA 19144 Office: 123 S Broad St Philadelphia PA 19109 Tel (215) 546-3000

BEACH, ROBERT EDWARD, b. Hollywood, Calif., July 26, 1930; B.A., U. Tampa, 1955; LL.B., Stetson U., 1958; grad. Nat. Coll. State Trial Judges, 1969, 71, 73, Nat. Coll. Juvenile Justice, 1974, 76. Admitted to Fla. bar, 1958; asso. firm Paul H. Roney, St. Petersburg, Fla., 1959-62, partner, 1962-68; judge Ill. Circuit Ct., 6th Jud. Circuit for Pinellas County, 1968—; instr., mem. bd. overseers Stetson Coll. Law; lectr. in field; pres. Interprofessional Family Council, Inc., 1971-72. Asst. campaign chmn. Pinellas County Republican Party, 1960, 66, campaign chmn., 1964; bd. dirs. Nat. Found. Infantile Paralysis, Futures Untld., workshop for retarded; mem. com. fund raising Museum Fine Arts, St. Petersburg; pres. South Side Jr. High Sch. PTA, St. Petersburg, 1971-72. Mem. Fla. Bar (chmn. pub. relations com. 1975—), Am., St. Petersburg (Liberty Bell award 1965—) bar assns., Pinellas Trial Lawyers Assn. (pres. 1966), Stetson Lawyers Assn. (pres. 1968), U. Tampa Alumni Assn. (pres. 1973), Sigma Phi Epsilon, Phi Alpha Delta (Outstanding Alumnus 1970). Home: 545 1st Ave N Saint Petersburg FL 33701 Office: Courthouse Saint Petersburg FL 33701

BEACHLER, EDWIN HARRY, III, b. Pitts., Nov. 21, 1940; B.A., Georgetown U., 1962; LL.B., U. Pitts., 1965. Admitted to Pa. bar, 1966; mem. firm McArdle, Henderson, Caroselli, Spagnolli & Beachler, Pitts., 1972—; hearing examiner Pa. Labor Relations Bd., 1972-73. Treas., St. Thomas Moore Soc., 1976. Mem. Am., Pa., Allegheny County (treas. 1975, sec. 1976) bar assns., Assn. Trial Lawyers Am., Neighborhood Legal Services Assn. (asst. sec.-treas. 1975-76). Home: 5660 Darlington Rd Pittsburgh PA 15217 Office: 1100 Law and Finance Bldg Pittsburgh PA 15219 Tel (412) 391-9860

BEAGAN, THOMAS JAMES, JR., b. Flushing, N.Y., Nov. 1, 1931; B.A., Allegheny Coll., 1953; J.D., Dickinson Sch. Law, 1956. Admitted to Pa. bar, 1959, U.S. Supreme Ct. bar, 1975; asso. firm John J. McDevitt, III, Phila., 1961-64; mem. firm Liebert, Harvey, Herting and Short, Phila., 1964-69; individual practice of law, Media, Pa., 1969-76; mem. firm Beagan, Gannon and Barnard, Media, 1976—; legal assistance advisor U.S. Army, Frankfurt, W. Ger., 1957-59; spl. agt. FBI, Washington and Atlanta, 1959-61; solicitor Middletown Twp., Delaware County, Pa., 1973—. Elected mem. bd. suprs. Middletown Twp., 1970-72. Mem. Am., Pa., Del. County bar assns., Soc. Former Spl. Agents FBI. Home: 922 Winding Ln Media PA 19063 Office: 218 W Front St Media PA 19063 Tel (215) 566-2870

BEAKLEY, ROBERT PAUL, b. Millville, N.J., Sept. 29, 1946; B.A., W.Va. Wesleyan Coll., 1969; J.D., Washington and Lee U., 1972. Admitted to N.J. bar, 1972; asso. firm Albert M. Ash, Ocean City, N.J., 1972-73; mgmt. trainee Coastal State Bank, Ocean City, 1973-74; staff atty. Cape Atlantic Legal Services, Atlantic City, 1974—; instr. Am. Inst. Banking. Dir. Cape Atlantic Jr. Achievement; advisor Young Episcopal Churchmen, Ocean City. Mem. Ocean City Jaycees, Atlantic County Bar Assn., Phi Delta Phi. Home: 244 Seaspray Rd Ocean City NJ 08226 Office: 1516 Atlantic Ave Atlantic City NJ 08401 Tel (609) 348-4208

BEAL, ROBERT LEE, b. Chgo., Oct. 27, 1944; B.S., U. Ariz., 1966, J.D., 1969. Admitted to Ariz. bar, 1969, U.S. Supreme Ct. bar, 1976; partner firm Healy and Beal, Tucson, 1969—; mem. ins. com. State Bar Ariz.; 1975-76. Football ofcl. Ariz. High Sch., Western Athletic Conf. Mem. Ariz., Am. bar assns., Am. Arbitration Assn., Am. Trial Lawyers Assn. Office: 32 N Stone Ave Tucson AZ 85701 Tel (602) 624-5555

BEALL, KIRKE MONROE, b. Pensacola, Fla., Sept. 26, 1920; J.D., U. Fla., 1948. Admitted to Fla. bar, 1948; asst. county solicitor Escambia County, Fla., 1948-50; judge Ct. of Record of Escambia County, 1953-72, 1st Jud. Circuit Ct. of Fla., Pensacola, 1973—. Mem. Fla. Bar Assn. Office: Room 309 County Ct House Pensacola FL 32501 Tel (904) 433-4394

BEALS, JOHN DAVID, b. N.Y.C., Jan. 19, 1896; A.B., Columbia, 1917, LL.B., 1921. Admitted to N.Y. bar, 1921; partner firms Beals & Nicholson, N.Y.C., 1921-53, Townsend & Lewis, N.Y.C., 1958-73; of counsel firm Thacher, Proffitt & Wood, N.Y.C., 1973—; asso. govt. appeal agt. SSS, N.Y.C., 1944. Bd. mgrs. Am. Soc. Prevention of Cruelty to Animals, N.Y.C., 1938-76, pres., 1948-52. Mem. Bar Assn. City N.Y., Am., N.Y. State bar assns., New York County Lawyers Assn., Soc. Colonial Wars, Soc. War 1812, Soc. Mayflower Descs. (past gov.), Sigma Alpha Epsilon, Phi Alpha Delta. Home: 1220 Park Ave New York City NY 10028 Office: 40 Wall St New York City NY 10005 Tel (212) 483-5984

BEALS, RONALD WAYNE, b. San Francisco, Aug. 28, 1947; A.A., Coll. San Mateo, 1967; A.B., U. Calif., Santa Barbara, 1969; J.D. (John Woodward Ayer fellow), U. Calif., Berkeley, 1972. Admitted to Calif. bar, 1972, U.S. Supreme Ct. bar, 1976; intern Citizens Communications Center, Washington, 1970; staff counsel Legal Aid Soc. San Mateo, Redwood City, Calif., 1972-73; legal counsel Calif. Dept. Transp., Sacramento, 1973—; instr. social sci. Sierra Coll., 1976—. Mem. Calif. Bar Assn., State Trial Lawyers Assn., Phi Beta Kappa. Office: 1120 N St Sacramento CA 95814 Tel (916) 445-8836

BEAM, BYRON JONATHAN, b. Los Angeles, Jan. 18, 1939; B.S. cum laude, U. So. Calif., 1961; J.D., U. Calif. at Berkeley, 1964. Admitted to Calif. bar, 1965; asso. firm Parker, Stanbury, McGee & Babcock, Santa Ana, Calif., 1965-71; partner firm Beam, Ure, Barbaro & Brobeck, and predecessors, Santa Ana, 1971—; panel of arbitrators Orange County (Calif.) Superior Ct., 1976—; adj. prof. law Pepperdine U., Anaheim, Calif., 1976—; panelist Calif. Continuing Edn. of Bar, 1977. Mem. Orange County Bar Assn. (dir. 1975—), Assn. So. Calif. Def. Counsel (dir. 1975—), Am. Bd. Trial Advs. (asso.), Am. Arbitration Assn. (panel), State Bar Calif., Am. Bar Assn., Phi Delta Phi. Home: 57 Lagunita Laguna Beach CA 92651 Office: 888 N Main St suite 700 Santa Ana CA 92701 Tel (714) 558-3944

BEAMAN, DOROTHY MAY, b. Winchester, Ky., Sept. 15, 1921; B.S. with honors, Johns Hopkins, 1965; J.D. summa cum laude, U. Balt., 1968. Personnel mgr. Catalyst Research Corp., Balt., 1955-68, safety and security officer, 1960-68, legal counsel, 1969-71; admitted to Md. bar, 1968; asso. firm Hooper Kiefer and Cornell, Balt., 1971-73, partner, 1974—. Bd. dirs. Catonsville Concert Assn., Baltimore County, Catonsville Hist. Soc. Mem. Am., Md. State, Balt. City bar assns., Women's Bar Assn. Md. Office: 343 N Charles St Baltimore MD 21201 Tel (301) 727-4700

BEAMAN, NATHANIEL, III, b. Norfolk, Va., Apr. 29, 1925; student Va. Mil. Inst., 1942-43; A.B., Duke, 1945, J.D., 1949. Admitted to Va. bar, 1949; asso. firm Breeden & Hoffman, Norfolk, 1949-50; asso. trust officer 1st Citizens Bank & Trust Co., Raleigh, N.C., 1952-54; v.p., trust officer So. Bank of Norfolk, 1955-62; partner firm Davis, Boyd & Beaman, also individual practice law, Norfolk, 1962-66; v.p., trust officer, regional dir. 1st & Mchts. Nat. Bank, Norfolk, 1966—. Bd. dirs. Tidewater Heart Assn., 1960-64; mem. trustees com. Eastern Va. Med. Sch., 1974—; vice chmn. Norfolk City Employees Retirement Trust, 1970-74; mem. trustees com. Norfolk Found., 1967—, Portsmouth Community Trust, 1973—; bd. dirs. Navy League, Tidewater, 1972—; treas. DePaul Hosp. Bldg. Fund, Norfolk, 1968—. Mem. Va., Norfolk-Portsmouth bar assns. Home: 5220 Edgewater Dr Norfolk VA 23508 Office: One Bank St Norfolk VA 23510 Tel (804) 857-0631

BEAMON, ARTHUR LEON, b. Stantonsburg, N.C., Aug. 21, 1942; B.S., U.S. Air Force Acad., 1965; M.A., George Washington U., 1970; J.D., U. Chgo., 1972. Admitted to D.C. bar, 1973, Md. bar, 1973; atty. FDIC, Washington, 1972—. Mem. Md., D.C., Nat. bar assns. Home: 2707 Weller Rd Silver Spring MD 20906 Office: 550 17th St NW Washington DC 20429 Tel (202) 389-4637

BEAN, LORENZO LEE, JR., b. Ft. Meade, Fla., Mar. 10, 1916; student Hampden-Sydney Coll., 1934-35, 37-38; LL.B., U. Va., 1941, S.J.D., 1970. Admitted to Va. bar, 1940, U.S. Supreme Ct. bar, 1947; atty. REA, USDA, 1941-47; individual practice law, Arlington, Va., 1947—; legal advisor Methodist Bd. Missions, 1951—, Nat. Hosp., 1964-72; adv. bd. Washington-Lee Savs. & Loan Assn. Mem. Arlingoton Bd. Zoning Appeals, 1954-57, Arlington Sch. Bd., 1958-61; bd. visitors Radford Coll., 1968-74. Mem. Am., Va., Arlington County (pres. 1961-62) bar assns., Am., Va. (pres. 1966-67) trial lawyers assns. Co-author: Sources of Proof, 1964, 76. Home: 3820 N 37th St Arlington VA 22207 Office: 2045 N 15th St Arlington VA 22201 Tel (703) 524-4044

BEANE, DARRELL MATHEWS, b. Dayton, Ohio, Jan. 5, 1933; B.A., Earlham Coll., 1955; J.D., U. Cin., 1972. Dir. admissions Earlham Coll., 1958-64, asst. to pres., 1964-66, 67-69; asst. to pres., Albion Coll., 1966-67; admitted to Ind. bar, 1972; atty. firm Reller, Mendenhall, Kleinknecht & Milligan, Richmond, Ind., 1973—; judge City Ct. of Richmond (Ind.), 1976—; mem. bd. dirs. Social Services Planning, Richmond, 1976—, Reid Meml. Hosp. Found., 1976—, Wayne County chpt. Am. Cancer Soc., 1976—, Wayne County Mental Health Assn., 1976—. Mem. Wayne County, Am. bar assns. Address: 3701 Pinehurst Dr Richmond IN 47374 Tel (317) 962-1541

BEAR, HYMEN, b. Superior, Wis., Mar. 28, 1929; B.S., Wis. State Coll., 1952; J.D., U. Wis., 1959. Admitted to Wis. bar, 1959, Ill. bar, 1968; atty. NLRB, Chgo., 1958-67; sr. labor atty. Sears, Roebuck & Co., Chgo., 1967—; mem. employee rations coms. Nat. Retail Mchts. Assn. and Am. Retail Fedn., 1975—. Mem. Wis., Ill., Chgo., Am. bar assns. Home: 750 Sumac Rd Highland Park IL 60035 Office: Sears Tower Suite 6900 Chicago IL 60684 Tel (312) 875-9204

BEAR, JOSEPH, b. Bklyn., Oct. 14, 1900; B.C.S., Northeastern U., 1923, J.D., 1935. Admitted to Mass. bar, 1936, U.S. Dist. Ct., U.S. Ct. Appeals bars, 1937, Va. bar, 1976; atty. Boston Legal Aid Soc., 1936-50; guest lectr. Boston Coll., Harvard; cons. survey legal profession Am. Bar Assn. cons. in field. Past trustee Parker Hill Med. Center. Mem. Am., Mass., Va., Boston bar assns., Assn. Trial Lawyers Am. (gov. 1966-67). Contbr. articles in field to profl. jours. Home: 221 E York Dr Emporia VA 23847 Office: 300 S Main St Emporia VA 23847 Tel (804) 634-6111

BEARD, CHARLES RICHARD, b. St. Louis, July 30, 1929; B.A., Washington U., 1950, J.D., 1955. Admitted to Mo. bar, 1955, U.S. Supreme Ct. bar, 1963; individual practice law, St. Louis, 1955-68; asst. gen. counsel, asst. sec. May Dept. Stores Co., St. Louis, 1968—; col. JAGC, U.S. Army Res., 1975—. Mem. Clayton (Mo.) Parks and Recreation Commn., 1968-71, chmn., 1970-71. Mem. Am., Mo., Met. St. Louis bar assns., Am. Retail Fedn. (consumer credit com.), Nat. Retail Mchts. Assn. (lawyers com. 1969—, legis. steering com. 1973—). Mchts. Research Council, Phi Delta Phi. Home: 440 Edgewood Dr Clayton MO 63105 Office: 611 Olive St Saint Louis MO 63101 Tel (314) 436-3300

BEARD, JOSEPH JAMES, b. Winthrop, Mass., Aug. 27, 1933; B.S. in Elec. Engring., Tufts U., 1956; J.D. cum laude, Suffolk U., 1969; M.B.A. with highest distinction, Babson Coll., 1971; LL.M., Boston U., 1974. Admitted to Mass. bar, 1970; engr. Boeing Corp., Seattle, 1962, N.Am. Aviation Co., Los Angeles, 1963-65, Honeywell Corp., Waltham, Mass., 1965-67; engr. project Intrex, Mass. Inst. Tech., 1967-69; prof. law New England Sch. Law, 1970—; rep. to Joint Task Force to Computerize Law in Mass., 1973—; cons. Nat. Commn. New Technol. Uses Copyrighted Works. Mem. Am., Boston bar assns., Comml. Law League Am., Tau Beta Pi. Author: (with Maleson and Callahan) Cases and Materials in Contemporary Commercial Law; contbr. articles to law jours.; registered profl. engr., Mass. Home: 3 Laverdure Circle Framingham MA 01701 Office: 126 Newbury St Boston MA 02116 Tel (617) 267-9655

BEARDEN, JAMES CALEB, b. Hollis, Okla., Apr. 30, 1920; J.D., U. Tex., 1948. Admitted to Tex. bar, 1948; sr. field atty. VA, Waco, Tex., 1967—; instr. bus. law Lubbock Christian Coll., 1966-69; treas. Fed. Employees Credit Union. Vice chmn. bd. devel. Lubbock Christian Coll., 1970. Mem. VA Employees Assn. (pres. 1964). Home: 4015 30th St Lubbock TX 79410 Office: Room 122B Fed Bldg 1205 Texas Ave Lubbock TX 79401 Tel (806) 762-7415

BEARMAN, MORTON ROBERT, b. St. Louis, June 11, 1922; B.B.A., Washington U., St. Louis, 1943, J.D., 1947. Admitted to Mo. bar, 1947; counsel firm Susman, Stern, Agatstein & Heifetz, St. Louis, 1971—. Commr. Mo.-Ill. Bi-State Devel. Agy., 1955-60, vice chmn., 1965-72. Mem. Mo., St. Louis bar assns. Home: 801 Barnes Rd Saint Louis MO 63124 Office: 7733 Forsyth Blvd Saint Louis MO 63105 Tel (314) 862-0900

BEARSE, EDWARD WALTER, b. Williamston, Mich., Dec. 12, 1941; B.A. with honors in Econs., Mich. State U., 1967; J.D., U. Minn., 1970. Admitted to Minn. bar, 1970, Ind. bar, 1971; staff atty. Fort Wayne (Ind.) Legal Services, 1970-71, Legal Assistance of Ramsey County, St. Paul, 1971-72; staff criminal div. Anoka County (Minn.) County Atty.'s Office, 1972-74, chief prosecutor, 1974-75; partner firm Steffen, Munstenteiger, Bearse & Parta, and Predecessors, Anoka, 1975—; asst. pub. defender Minn. Dist. Ct., Anoka, 1975—. Mem. Minn., Anoka County bar assns., Minn. Trial Lawyers Assn., Minn. Pub. Defenders Assn. Contbg. author: Minnesota County Attorneys Associaton Handbook, 1976. Home: 813 40th Ln Anoka MN 55303 Office: 403 Jackson St Anoka MN 55303 Tel (612) 427-6300

BEART, ROBERT WOODWARD, b. Chgo., Nov. 13, 1917; advanced mgmt. program Harvard, 1933; B.A., Augustana Coll., Rock Island, Ill., 1939; J.D., Chgo. Kent Coll., 1947; M.Patent Law, John Marshall Law Sch., 1950; grad. Advanced Mgmt. Program, Harvard U., 1957. Admitted to Ill. bar, 1947, U.S. Patent Office bar, 1952; jr. partner firm Olson, Trexler, Wolters & Bushnell, Chgo., 1946-48, also dir.; sr. v.p. Ill. Tool Works Inc., Chgo., 1948—, gen. and patent counsel, 1948-74, gen. patent counsel, 1974—, also dir.; dir. Lutheran Mut. Life Ins. Co. Trustee Ill. Inst. Tech., 1975—, Inst. Gas Tech., 1976—. Mem. Chgo. Bar Assn., Chgo., Am. patent law assns., Nat., Ill. assns. mfrs. Home: 20680 W Exeter Rd Kildeer IL 60047 Office: 8501 W Higgins Rd Chicago IL 60631 Tel (312) 693-3040

BEASLEY, ALBERT FERRELL, b. Birmingham, Ala., Mar. 19, 1907; student Samford U., 1928; J.D., George Washington U., 1932. Admitted to Ala. bar, 1931, D.C. bar, 1931, U.S. Supreme Ct. bar, 1935; asso. firm Brashears & Townsend, 1931-35; mem. firm Brashears, Townsend, O'Brien & Beasley, Washington, 1935-42, Brashears, Beall & Beasley, Washington, 1942-51; individual practice law, Washington, 1951—; mem. Jud. Conf. D.C. Circuit, 1959-61, 63, 65-68, 70, 72-74. Fellow Am. Coll. Trial Lawyers (D.C. chmn. 1962-64); mem. Am. Bar Assn., Bar Assn. D.C., D.C. Integrated Bar, Am. Judicature Soc. Home: 6001 Corewood Ln Bethesda MD 20016 Office: Investment Bldg 1511 K St NW Washington DC 20005 Tel (202) 628-3800

BEASLEY, DOROTHY TOTH, b. Garfield, N.J., Oct. 5, 1937; A.B., St. Lawrence U., 1959; LL.B. (Daish scholar), Am. U., 1964. Admitted to D.C. bar, 1964, Va. bar, 1965, Ga. bar, 1969, U.S. Supreme Ct. bar, 1971; law clk. Circuit Ct. Arlington County (Va.), 1964-66; asso. firm Shadyac, Berg & Nolen, Arlington, Va., 1966-67, firm Fisher & Phillips, Atlanta, 1967-69; asst. atty. gen. Ga., Atlanta, 1969-73; asst. U.S. atty., No. Dist. Ga., Atlanta, 1973-77; judge State Ct. of Fulton County (Ga.), Atlanta, 1977—. Bd. dirs. Luth. Towers sr. citizens' home, 1975—; active Leadership Atlanta, 1974-75, study group leader, 1975-76, v.p., 1977—. Mem. State Bar Ga. (com. on correctional facilities and services 1975—), Ga. Assn. Women Lawyers (pres. 1975-76), Am. Law Inst. Grantee-participant Nat. Endowment for Humanities seminar for lawyers on founding documents of our nation, 1976. Office: 160 Pryor St SW Atlanta GA 30303

BEASLEY, JERE LOCKE, b. Tyler, Tex., Dec. 12, 1935; B.S. in Econs., Auburn U., 1959; LL.B., U. Ala., 1962. Admitted to Ala. bar, 1962; asso. firm Zeanah & Donald, Tuscaloosa, Ala., 1962-64; partner firm Beasley, Williams & Robertson, Clayton and Eufaula, Ala., 1964-70; lt. gov. State of Ala., 1971—. Mem. Am., Ala. bar assns. Office: Room 201 State Capitol Montgomery AL 36104 Tel (205) 262-7339

BEASLEY, OSCAR HOMER, b. Denver, Sept. 30, 1925; B.A., U. Omaha, 1949; J.D., U. Iowa, 1950. Admitted to Iowa bar, 1949, N. Mex. bar, 1952, Calif. bar, 1964; asso. firm Joseph L. Smith, Albuquerque, 1955-59; partner firms Ertz & Beasley, Albuquerque, 1959-62, Beasley & Colberg, Albuquerque, 1962-64; atty. 1st Am. Title Ins. Co., Santa Ana, Calif., 1964-70, chief title counsel, 1970—; mem. N. Mex. Ho. of Reps., 1958-62; dir. Title Guaranty of Wyo.; instr. Western State U. Coll. Law, Fullerton, Calif., 1970—. Mem. Am., Calif., Orange County, Los Angeles County, N.Mex., Iowa bar assns. Office: 421 N Main St Santa Ana CA 92701 Tel (714) 558-3211

BEASLEY, ROBERT POWER, b. Nashville, Feb. 26, 1914; student Duke, 1932-33; A.B., Vanderbilt U., 1935, M.B.A., 1937; LL.B., Akron U., 1954. Admitted to Ohio bar, 1954; exec. v.p., dir. Firestone Tire & Rubber Co., Akron, 1968-76, vice chmn., 1976—. Mem. Ohio, Am. bar assns. Home: 2253 Tinkham Rd Akron OH 44313 Office: 3200 W Market St Akron OH 44313 Tel (216) 867-4220

BEASLEY, WILLIAM REX., b. Tulsa, Aug. 29, 1934; B.S., U. Tulsa, 1959, J.D., 1967. Admitted to Okla. bar, 1968, U.S. Dist. Ct. bar for No. Dist. Okla., 1968; asst. dist. atty. City of Tulsa, 1968-71; chief asst. dist. atty. Pittsburgh County (Okla.), 1971-73; asso. judge Tulsa County Dist. Ct., 1973—. Active Boy Scouts Am., 1968-72; coach Little League, Tulsa, 1968-75; co-chmn. Court Fund Bd., Tulsa County, 1975—. Mem. Okla., Am., Tulsa County bar assns., Okla. Jud. Conf. Home: 8519 E 32d St Tulsa OK 74145 Office: Courthouse Tulsa OK 74103 Tel (918) 627-2907

BEASLEY, WILLIAM ROBERT, b. Highland Park, Mich., Jan. 7, 1919; A.B., U. Mich., 1940, LL.B., 1942. Admitted to Mich. bar, 1943, U.S. Supreme Ct. bar, 1957; partner firm Forsythe & Beasley, Ferndale, Mich., 1947-67; judge Oakland County (Mich.) Circuit Ct., 1966-76; judge Mich. Ct. Appeals, Detroit, 1976—; city atty. Ferndale, 1961-62, Huntington Woods, 1963-66; atty. Ferndale Sch. Bd., 1956-66, Birmingham Sch. Bd., 1963-66; adj. prof. legal advocacy Cooley Law Sch., 1974-76. Commr. city Ferndale, 1951-53; mem. S. Oakland Hosp. Auth., 1954-66; mem. Ferndale Library Bd., 1949-51, 54-60. Mem. Oakland County Legal Aid Soc. (pres. 1961-63), Mich. State, Am., Oakland County (pres. 1957-58, dir. 1956-59), South Oakland bar assns. Contbr. articles to legal jours. Office: 900 1st Fed Bldg Detroit MI 48226 Tel (313) 256-2603

BEATIE, RUSSEL HARRISON, JR., b. Lawrence, Kans., Jan. 20, 1938; A.B., Princeton, 1959; LL.B. cum laude, Columbia, 1964. Admitted to N.Y. bar, 1964, U.S. Supreme Ct. bar, 1969; asso. firm Dewey, Ballantine, Bushby, Palmer & Wood, N.Y.C., 1964-66, 68-72, mem., 1972—; asso. firm Royall, Koegel & Rogers, N.Y.C., 1966-68. Mem. Assn. Bar City N.Y. Editorial adv. bd. Pofl. Liability Reporter. Home: Grey House Ardsley on Hudson NY 10503 Office: 140 Broadway New York City NY 10005 Tel (212) 344-8000

BEATTY, GEORGE WOOD, b. Princeton, N.J., Oct. 30, 1932; A.B. summa cum laude, Princeton U., 1954; LL.B. cum laude, Harvard U., 1957. Admitted to Mich. bar, 1957, D.C. bar, 1959; atty., appellate sect., tax div. Dept. Justice, Washington, 1957-59; mem. firm Lee, Toomey & Kent, Washington, 1959-65, partner, 1965—; lectr. tax insts. N.Y. U., Tulane U., Tax Execs. Inst., Fed. Bar Assn., Am. Mgmt. Assn., World Trade Inst. Mem. Am. Bar Assn. (past chmn. com. on corporate stockholder relationships, tax sect.). Contbr. articles to legal jours. Home: 3438 34th Pl NW Washington DC 20016 Office: 1200 18th St NW Washington DC 20036 Tel (202) 457-8528

BEATTY, JOHN CABEEN, JR., b. Washington, Apr. 13, 1919; A.B., Princeton, 1941; J.D., Columbia, 1948. Admitted to Oreg. bar, 1948; practiced in Portland, Oreg., 1948-70, partner firm Dusenbery, Martin, Beatty, Bischoff & Templeton, 1956-70; judge 4th dist. Oreg. Circuit Ct., Portland, 1970—; mem. Oreg. Bd. Bar Examiners, 1953-54. Mem. Oreg. CSC, 1962-64; mem. legis. com. Nat. Sch. Bd. Assn., 1966-68; chmn. council large city sch. bd., 1967-68; mem. Oreg. Law Enforcement Council, 1974, Gov.'s Task Force on Corrections, 1975-77; chmn. legis. com. Oreg. Jud. Conf., 1976-77; counsel Oreg. Democratic Party, 1956-58; co-chmn. Oreg. for Kennedy Com., 1968; bd. dirs. Portland Pub. Schs., 1964-70. Mem. Am., Oreg., Multnomah County bar assns., Oreg. Hist. Soc. (dir. 1973—), Am. Judicature Soc. Recipient City Club of Portland Award, 1967. Home: 2958 SW Doesch Rd Portland OR 97201 Office: 572 Multnomah County Courthouse Portland OR 97204

BEATTY, JOHN FRANCIS, b. Miami Beach, Fla., July 5, 1946; A.B., Harvard, 1969, J.D., 1972. Admitted to Mass. bar, 1972, Fla. bar, 1973, N.Y. State bar, 1974; asso. firm Debevoise, Plimpton, Lyons & Gates, N.Y.C., 1973—; summer asst. U.S. Atty. for So. Dist. N.Y., 1971; lectr. pub. adminstrn. Harvard 1972-73; sec. com. energy policy Nat. Acad. Engring., 1972. Mem. Am., Fla. bar assns., Assn. Bar City N.Y., Fed. Bar Council. Home: 209 W 78th St New York City NY 10024 Office: 299 Park Ave New York City NY 10017 Tel (212) 752-6400

BEATTY, PAUL STEPHEN, b. Long Branch, N.J., Sept. 29, 1941; B.A., U. Md., 1963, J.D., 1966. Admitted to Md. bar, 1967; partner firm Hecht & Beatty, Balt., 1973-77; practice law, Laurel, Md., 1977—. Mem. Bar Assn. Balt. City, Md. State, Am. bar assns., Tau Kappa Alpha, Pi Sigma Alpha. Home: 9639 Whiteacre Rd A 1 Columbia MD 21045 Office: PO Box M Laurel MD 20810 Tel (301) 490-6900 also (301) 792-0525

BEATTY, WILLIAM C., b. Phila., May 31, 1931; B.A., Dickinson Coll.; LL.B., J.D., Temple U. Admitted to Pa. bar, U.S. Supreme Ct. bar, 1960, Fed. bar; mem. firm Butler Beatty Greer & Johnson, Media, Pa., 1960—. Bd. dirs. Delaware Valley Hemophilia Found., Family Service of Delaware County, Media. Mem. Am., Pa., Delaware County (dir.) bar assns., Am. Judicature Soc., Pa. Trial Lawyers Assn., Pa. Def. Inst. Home: 914 Truepenny Rd Media PA 19063 Office: 17 South Ave PO Box 140 Media PA 19063 Tel (215) LO 6-8200

BEATTY, WILLIAM CLEMENS, b. Ironton, Ohio, Sept. 14, 1925; B.A. summa cum laude, Morris Harvey Coll., 1948; M.A., U. Cin., 1949; LL.B. summa cum laude, Washington and Lee U., 1952. Admitted to Va. bar, 1952, W.Va. bar, 1952; asso. firm Huddleston, Bolen, Beatty, Porter & Copen, and predecessors, Huntington, W.Va., 1952-68, partner, 1968—. Fellow Am. Coll. Trial Lawyers; mem. W.Va. (pres. 1975-76), Am. bar assn., Jud. Council W.Va., Va., W.Va. (pres. 1966, certificate of merit 1960) State bars, Am. Judicature Soc., Internat. Assn. Ins. Counsel, Nat. Assn. Ry. Trial Counsel, Order of Coif, Phi Beta Kappa, Phi Delta Phi. Home: 5942 Wilson Dr Huntington WV 25705 Office: POB 2185 Huntington WV 25722 Tel (304) 529-6181

BEAUCHAMP, GEORGE ANTHEME, b. Superior, Wis., May 4, 1899; LL.B., Detroit Coll. Law, 1926, J.D., 1968. Admitted to Mich. bar, 1927; partner firm Beauchamp, Gillis, Cavanagh, Nelson and Gallagher, Detroit, 1945-60; justice of peace, Grosse Pointe Twp., Mich., 1965-69; supr. Grosse Pointe Twp., 1972-76; ret., 1976. Home: 11 Vernier Rd Grosse Pointe Shores MI 48236

BEAUCHAMP, WOODROW OTTIS, JR., b. Chiefland, Fla., May 25, 1940; B.S. in Arts and Scis., Fla. State U., 1962; J.D., Cumberland Law Sch. Samford U., 1966; grad. Nat. Coll. State Judiciary, 1976. Admitted to Fla. bar, 1966; asst. atty. gen. State of Fla., 1966-70; individual practice law, Tallahassee, 1969-73; judge Levy County (Fla.) Ct., 1973—; pros. atty. Leon County (Fla.) Juvenile Ct., 1971-72; staff atty. Fla. Ho. of Reps. Com. on Cummunity Affairs, 1972. Mem. Fla. Conf. County Ct. Judges (dir. 1975-76), Levy County C. of C. (pres. 1975-76), Phi Delta Phi (charter mem. Cumberland Sch. Law chpt.). Home: POB 917 Chiefland FL 32626 Office: POB 327 Bronson FL 32621 Tel (904) 486-2074

BEAUDRY, G. WARD, b. Boston, May 23, 1942; B.A. in Econs. and Govt., Austin Coll., 1963; J.D., U. Tex., 1965. Admitted to Tex. bar, 1965; served as staff judge adv., spl. ct. marshall judge U.S. Marine Corps., 1965-69; partner firm Lane, Savage, Counts & Winn, Dallas, 1969—. Elder, First Presbyterian Ch., Dallas, 1974—. Mem. Am., Tex., Dallas bar assns. Office: 3330 Republic National Bank Bldg Dallas TX 75201 Tel (214) 741-3633

BEAUREGARD, HENRY GEORGE, b. Worcester, Mass., June 17, 1915; A.B., Boston Coll., 1936; LL.B., Harvard, 1939. Admitted to N.Y. State bar, 1940, Mass. bar, 1942, D.C. bar, 1950; asst. counsel Bur. Aeros. Dept. Navy, D.C., 1946-47, counsel for fiscal dir., 1947, spl. legal asst. to Sec. Navy, 1947-49, asst. gen. counsel, 1949-50; mem. firm Sullivan, Beauregard, Clarkson, Moss & Brown, and predecessors, D.C., 1950—. Mem. D.C., Am., Fed., Mass. bar assns. Contbr. articles to profl. jours.; mem. editorial bd. Harvard Law Review, 1937-39. Home: 4701 Willard Ave Chevy Chase MD 20015 Office: Suite 925 N Lobby 1800 M St NW Washington DC 20036 Tel (202) 785-8000

BEAVERS, ADDISON MORTON, b. nr. Mt. Summit, Ind., May 29, 1910; A.B., Butler U., 1935; J.D., Ind. U., 1934. Admitted to Ind. bar, 1934; dual practice law, Boonville, 1934-51; judge Warrick County (Ind.) Circuit Ct., 1951—; county atty. Warrick County, 1934-36, 39-41; pros. atty. Warrick County, 1937-39; dept. atty. gen. Ind., 1941-43; chmn. Ind. Civil Code Study Commn. Past pres. Ind. Soc. Crippled Children and Adults; 1st chmn, Regional Mental Health Planning Commn. S.W. Ind., 1963-66; mem. Regional Health Planning Commn., 1967-73. Mem. Am., Ind. (past chmn. ho. of dels.) bar assns., Am. Judicature Soc. (recipient Herbert Hartley award 1974), Ind. Judges' Assn. (pres. 1956-57), Nat., Ind. councils juvenile ct. judges, Ind. Conf. Social Workers, Ind. Corrections Assn., Nat. Council Crime and Delinquency. Recipient Gresham award Evansville (Ind.) Bar Assn., 1968; Outstanding Pub. Servant award Boonville Jaycees, 1974. Home: 121 Hargrave St Boonville IN 47601 Office: Ct House Boonville IN 47601 Tel (812) 897-3480

BEAZLEY, HERBERT MALCOLM, b. Houston, Sept. 16, 1932; B.S. in Pub. Adminstrn., U. Ariz., 1954; postgrad. in Spl. Studies U. London, 1957; J.D., U. Tex., 1959. Admitted to Tex. bar, 1959; asst. city atty. City of Houston, 1959-67; individual practice law, Houston, 1967—. Mem. State Bar Tex., Phi Delta Phi. Office: 912 River Oaks Bank & Trust Tower Houston TX 77005 Tel (713) 523-6430

BEC, PETER EDWARD, b. Buenos Aires, Argentina, Nov. 6, 1942; B.S., Alliance Coll., 1965; J.D., Detroit Coll. Law, 1970. Admitted to Mich. bar, 1970; assn. firm Spector & McCarron, Detroit, 1971; mem. staff legal dept. Mfrs. Nat. Bank, Detroit, 1971-72; atty. legal dept. Frank Murphy Hall of Justice, Wayne County Prosecutor's Office, 1972-74; individual practice law, Southgate, Mich., 1974—; judge Municipal Ct., Southgate, 1974—. Mem. Am., Downriver bar assns., Advocate Club, Polish-Am. Congress. Office: 13247 Toledo Rd Southgate MI 48195 Tel (313) 283-2341

BECHT, ARNO CUMMING, b. East Peoria, Ill., Feb. 17, 1910; B.A., Colgate U., 1931; J.D., U. Chgo., 1936; LL.M., Columbia, 1938, S.J.D., 1951. Admitted to N.Y. bar, 1939, Mo. bar, 1942; asso. firm Miller, Owen, Otis & Bailey, N.Y.C., 1937-39; asso. prof. law U. Ga., Athens, 1939-40; asst. prof. law Washington U., St. Louis, 1940-45, asso. prof., 1945-50, prof., 1950—, Madill prof., 1962—; asso. firm Igoe, Carroll, Keefe & Coburn, St. Louis, 1942. Mem. Phi Beta Kappa, Order of Coif. Recipient Washington U. Alumni award, 1975; author: (with Frank W Miller) The Test of Factual Causation in Negligence and Strict Liability Cases, 1961; contbr. articles to legal jours. Home: 7950 Delmar Blvd University City MO 63130 Office: Washington U Sch Law Lindell & Skinker Sts St Louis MO 63130 Tel (314) 863-0100

BECHTEL, ROBERT WARREN, b. Slaton, Tex., July 29, 1933; B.S. in Petroleum Engring., Okla., U., 1957, LL.B., 1961. Admitted to Tex. bar, 1962; engr. Halliburton Co., Midland, Tex., 1957-58; title analyst Shell Oil Co., Midland, 1961-62; trust officer 1st Nat. Bank Midland, 1962-68, planning officer, pres. computing subs. 1969-73, legal counsel, 1974—. Bd. dirs. Potts & Sibley Found., 1965—; bd. dirs., sec. treas. Beal Found., 1964—. Mem. Tex., Midland County bar assns., Tex. Assn. Bank Counsel (dir. 1976—). Author: Uniform Commercial Code in Texas, 1966, 74; Lending Officers Guide to the UCC, 1974; Negotiable Instruments in Texas Banks, 1976. Office: 1st Nat Bank Midland TX 79701 Tel (915) 683-4231

BECK, DENNIS MICHAEL, b. Kings County, N.Y., June 8, 1944; B.S., N.Y. U., 1966; J.D., John Marshall Law Sch., 1969. Admitted to N.Y. bar, 1970; asso. firm Friedmann & Fischman, 1969-71; individual practice law, 1971-76; partner firm Sparrow, Sparrow & Singer, Kew Gardens, Queens, N.Y., 1976—. Mem. Queens County (N.Y.) Bar Assn., N.Y. State, Am. trial lawyers assns. Author: Practice Before the Family Court, 1975. Office: 125-10 Queens Blvd Kew Gardens Queens NY 11415 Tel (212) 261-4040

BECK, GEORGE ARTHUR, b. Kingston, N.Y., June 22, 1931; B.S., Siena Coll., 1952; J.D., Albany Law Sch. Union U., 1955. Admitted to N.Y. bar, 1955, U.S. Supreme Ct. bar, 1961; with JAGC, U.S. Army, Frankfort, Germany, 1956-57; partner firm Ewig & Beck, Kingston, 1958-67; individual practice law, Kingston, 1967—; spl. judge Kingston City Ct., 1961—; atty. Kingston Urban Renewal Agy., 1967-72, Kingston Water Dept., 1976—. Chmn. Kingston Zoning Bd. Appeals, 1958-65. Mem. Ulster County (pres. 1966), N.Y. State bar assns. Home: 81 Merilina Ave Kingston NY 12401 Office: 42 Main St Kingston NY 12401 Tel (914) 338-0700

BECK, JAMES HAYES, b. Canton, Ohio, Aug. 29, 1935; A.B., Wittenberg U., 1956; LL.B., U. Va., 1959, J.D., 1970. Admitted to Ohio bar, 1959, U.S. Dist. Ct. bar for No. Dist. Ohio, 1960, U.S. Supreme Ct. bar, 1971; individual practice law, Cleve., 1959-63; asso. firm Leanza, Longano, Farina & Mendelson, Cleve., 1964-66, firm Nadler & Nadler, Youngstown, 1966-73; individual practice law, Canfield, Ohio, 1973—; instr. real estate law Youngstown State U., 1972. Precinct committeeman, Canfield, 1976; pres. Canfield Civic Assn., 1972-73, SMR Residents' Council, Inc., 1976-77. Mem. Am., Ohio, Mahoning County bar assns., Am. Arbitration Assn., Phi Alpha Theta, Tau Kappa Alpha, Pi Sigma Alpha. Home: 265 Saw Mill Run Rd Canfield OH 44406 Office: 558 E Main St Canfield OH 44406 Tel (216) 533-9811

BECK, LAURENCE DAVID, b. Arlington, Va., Dec. 21, 1945; B.A., Duke U., 1967; J.D., U. Va., 1972. Admitted to Md. bar, 1972, D.C. bar, 1972; research asst. Center Study Responsive Law, Washington, 1970; counsel U.S. Senate Labor Subcom., Washington, D.C., 1971-72; litigation atty. U.S. Equal Employment Opportunity Commn., Washington, D.C., 1972-74; asst. states atty. Montgomery County, Rockville, Md., 1974—; legal intern FTC, Washington, 1971; legal asst. Va. Constitutional Commn., Charlottesville, 1968-70. Mem. Md., Montgomery County bar assns. Author: (with Stuart Rawlings) Coal: The Captive Giant, 1971; editorial asst. Va. Lawyer, 1968-70; editor Charlottesville Consumer Comment, 1970-71. Office: 50 Monroe St Rockville MD 20850 Tel (301) 279-8211

BECK, WILLIAM HAROLD, b. Frankfort, Ky., Jan. 15, 1917; LL.B., J.D., U. Louisville, 1942. Admitted to Ky. bar, 1942; individual practice law, Lexington, 1945—; judge Fayette Fiscal Ct., Lexington, 1957—. Mem. Am., Ky., Fayette County bar assns. Author: Tax Ideas for the Throughbred Industry, 1958; contbr. articles in field to profl. jours. Home: 1115 Slashes Rd Lexington KY 40502 Office: 404 Lexington Bldg 201 W Short St Lexington KY 40507 Tel (606) 252-4338

BECKEMEIER, GILBERT NEWTON, JR., b. St. Louis, June 11, 1942; A.B., St. Louis U., 1965, J.D., 1972. Admitted to Mo. bar, 1972, U.S. Supreme Ct. bar, 1976; asso. firm Holtkamp & Amelung, St. Louis, 1972; partner firm Holtkamp, Beckemeier & Liese and predecessors, St. Louis, 1973—. Mem. Am., St. Louis County bar assns., Bar Assn. Met. St. Louis, Assn. Def. Council, Lawyers Assn. St. Louis. Home: 729 Lexington Ave St Louis MO 63122 Office: 818 Olive St St Louis MO 63101 Tel (314) 621-7773

BECKER, BENTON LEE, b. Washington, Feb. 22, 1938; B.A., U. Md., 1960; J.D., Am. U., 1966. Admitted to D.C. bar, 1966, Md. bar, 1966, U.S. Supreme Ct. bar, 1971; trial atty. criminal div., fraud sect., Dept. Justice, 1966-68; asst. U.S. atty. Washington, 1968-70; individual practice law, Kensington, Md. and Washington, 1970; partner firm Cramer, Haber & Becker, Washington, 1970—; counsel Republican Nat. Com., 1975-; counsel to Pres. Ford during confirmation procs. and presdl. transition, 1974; vis. prof. U. Miami Law Sch., 1977. Nat. bd. dirs. Anti-Defamation League, 1976—. Mem. Md., D.C., Fed. bar assns. Home: 11507 Karen Dr Potomac MD 20854 Office: Cramer Haber & Becker 475 L'Enfant Plaza SW Washington DC 20024 Tel (202) 554-1100

BECKER, BRUCE, b. N.Y.C.; B.A., Bklyn. Coll., 1947; LL.B., N.Y. U., 1961. Producer play: Tonight in Samarkand, on Broadway; operator Tappan Zee Playhouse, Nyack, N.Y.; producer film: Three, United Artists; individual practice law, N.Y.C. Mem. Delta Sigma Rho. Author: Backgammon For Blood. Office: 160 E 48th St New York City NY 10017 Tel (212) 753-6230

BECKER, DAVID MANDEL, b. Chgo., Dec. 31, 1935; A.B., Harvard, 1957; J.D., U. Chgo., 1960. Admitted to Ill. bar, 1960; asso. firm Becker & Savin, Chgo., 1960-62; instr. law, U. Mich., Ann Arbor, 1962-63; asst. prof. law Washington U., St. Louis, 1963-66, asso. prof. law, 1966-69, prof. law, 1969—; instr. Council Legal Edn. Opportunity Midwest Summer Inst., St. Louis, 1971. Author: (with Benjamin M. Becker, Ronald N. Mora) Simplified Estate Planning—A Guide for Estate Planners, 1965; (with Benjamin M. Becker, Bernard Savin) Legal Checklists, 1976; Legal Checklists—Specially Selected Forms, 1977; contbr. numerous articles in field to profl. jours.; recipient Founders Day award Washington U., 1973. Home: 843 Woodmoor Dr Olivette MO 63132 Office: Washington University School of Law St Louis MO 63130 Tel (314) 863-0100

BECKER, EDWARD FREDERICK, b. Elizabeth, N.J., Apr. 19, 1906; A.B., Univ. Mont., 1930; M.B.A., Harvard, 1932; LL.B., Yale, 1946, J.D., 1971. Admitted to Conn. bar, 1946, U.S. Supreme Ct. bar, 1950; individual practice law, New Haven, and Killingworth, Conn., 1946—; spl. counsel to New Haven, West Haven, E. Haven, Hamden, 1973. Pres. Community Free Pub. Library, Hamden, Conn., 1946. Contbr. articles in field to profl. jours. Address: Elward Forest RFD 2 Killingworth CT 06417 Tel (203) 663-1363

BECKER, FRANCIS H., b. Dubuque, Iowa, Oct. 15, 1915; student St. Louis U., 1934-36; J.D., Washington U., St. Louis, 1939. Admitted to Iowa bar, 1939; asst. county atty. Dubuque County, 1941-42, 45-46, county atty., 1947-51; justice Iowa Supreme Ct., 1965-72; partner firm Patterson, Lorentzen, Duffield, Timmons, Irish & Becker, Des Moines, 1972—. Mem. Am., Iowa, Polk County bar assns. Office: 729 Insurance Exchange Bldg Des Moines IA 50309 Tel (515) 283-2147

BECKER, IRVING LEONARD, b. Balt., Jan. 27, 1931; B.A., U. Md., 1953, LL.B., 1962. Admitted to Md. bar, 1962, U.S. Supreme Ct. bar, 1969; individual practice law, Balt., 1962—; labor relations officer Social Security Adminstrn., Balt., 1969—, dir. labor relations, 1969—; labor arbitrator Am. Arbitration Assn. Parent rep. City of Balt., 1975—. Mem. Fed. Bar Assn. Home: 5703 Rusk Ave Baltimore MD 21215 Office: G-2608 W Social Security Bldg Baltimore MD 21235 Tel (301) 594-2563

BECKER, JOHN F., b. Pitts., Nov. 17, 1943; A.B., U. Notre Dame, 1965; J.D., St. John's U., N.Y.C., 1968. Admitted to N.Y. State bar, 1969, Pa. bar, 1971; asso. firm Benjamin Purvin, N.Y.C., 1969; asst. dist. atty., 1970-73; asso. firm Sikov & Love, Pitts., 1973—. Mem. parish council ednl. com. St. Margaret's Roman Cath. Ch., Green Tree, Pitts. Mem. Am., Pa., Allegheny County bar assns., Am. Trial Lawyers Assn., Western Pa. Trial Lawyers (bd. govs.). Office: 600 Plaza Bldg Pittsburgh PA 15220 Tel (412) 261-4202

BECKER, JOSEPH ALFRED, b. Cleve., May 8, 1931; A.B., Ohio U., 1955; LL.B., Cleve. Marshall Law Sch., 1961; J.D., Cleve. State U., 1969. Admitted to Ohio bar, 1961, Mass. bar, 1967; individual practice law, Cleve., 1961-65, Boston, 1969-75; dep. chief counsel NASA, Cambridge, Mass., 1965-68; adminstrv. judge Bd. Contract Appeals, GSA, Washington, 1975—. Office: 572 Washington St Wellesley MA 02181 Tel (617) 235-6666

BECKER, JOSEPH DUFFNER, b. La Crosse, Wis., June 27, 1928; B.A. in Econs., U. Notre Dame, 1950; LL.B., U. Wis., 1954, LL.D., 1966. Admitted to Wis. bar, 1954, U.S. Supreme Ct. bar, 1960; mem. firms Hale, Skemp, Hanson, Schnurrer & Skemp, La Crosse, 1954-72, Edwards, Becker, Lynch, Parke & Heim, Ltd., La Crosse, 1973—. Chmn. La Crosse Housing Authority. Mem. Am., Wis., La Crosse County bar assns., Am. Judicature Soc., Am. Arbitration Assn. Home: 1402 King St La Crosse WI 54601 Office: 502 Hoeschler Exchange Bldg La Crosse WI 54601 Tel (608) 784-1605

BECKER, RALPH ELIHU, b. N.Y.C., Jan. 29, 1907; LL.B., St. John's U., 1928. Admitted to N.Y. bar, 1929, U.S. Supreme Ct. bar, 1940, D.C. bar, 1949; practice in Westchester County, N.Y., 1929-56, Washington, 1948-76, 77—; U.S. ambassador to Honduras, 1976-77; gen. counsel Am. Thrift Assembly, 1937-76; gen. counsel, sec. Albert Schweitzer Fund, 1953; gen. counsel Met. Washington Bd. Trade, 1964-72, dir., 1964-76, hon. dir., 1976—; gen. counsel Wolf Trap Found., 1964-76, dir., 1964—; gen. counsel Nat. Capitol Area Found., 1964-62; gen. counsel, trustee John F. Kennedy Center for Performing

Arts, 1968-76; gen. counsel Voice Found., 1970-76, dir., 1970—; gen. counsel, trustee Belford Towers Found., Inc.; mem. advisory com. Wolf Trap Farm Park for Performing Arts, Vienna, Va.; minority counsel privileges and election com. U.S. Senate, 1951; dir. emeritus Nat. Bank Washington; participant workshops legal problems atomic energy U. Mich., 1956; del., mem. drafting com. World Sugar Conf., Geneva, 1958; rep. of Pres. L.B. Johnsom with rank spl. ambassador Independence Ceremonies, Swaziland, 1968; U.S. Chmn. 2500th Anniversary of Founding of Persian Empire by Cyrus the Great, 1971-72. Treas., D.C. chpt. Am. Nat. Theater Acad.; mem. Arctic Expdn. for polar bears Washington Zoo, 1962, Antarctic-S. Pole Operation Deepfreeze, 1963; chmn. arrangements com. Lincoln Inaugural Centennial Com., 1961, 65; chmn. Nat. Cherry Blossom Festival, Washington, 1971-72; mem. advisory council George Washington U. Nat. chmn. Young Republicans, 1946-49; mem. Rep. Nat. Exec. Com., 1948—; mem. exec. com. Rep. Nat. Com., 1958-59; mem. Pres.'s Inaugural Com., 1953, 57, 69, 73; mem. Vice Pres. Rockefeller Inaugural Medal Com. Mem. advisory com. Friends of Nat. Zoo; bd. dirs. Inst. Contemporary Arts. Donor collection polit. American to Smithsonian Inst., 1960, Dartmouth Coll., St. Albans Sch., L.B.J. Library-U. Tex., Austin. Fellow Corcoran Gallery Art, Aspen Inst. Humanistic Studies; mem. Am., D.C., N.Y. State, Internat., Fed. (nat. council), Inter-Am. bar assns., Fed. Ins. Counsel (v.p., sec.-treas. 1956-60) Fed. Bar Found. (advisory), Am. Law Inst., Fgn. Law Assn., Judge Adv. Gen. Assn., Soc. Internat. Law, Am. Judicature Soc., Am. Legion, Jud. Conf. D.C., Am. Soc. French Legion of Honor, Am. Polit. Items Collectors Assn., Nat. Trust Historic Preservation, Co. Mil Historians, Am. Inst. Aeros. and Astronautics, 30th Inf. Div. Assn. (pres. 1958), Smithsonian Assos., Brazilian-Am. Cultural Inst., Japan-Am. Soc., U.S. Capitol Hist. Soc. (dir.), N.Y. State Soc. (pres. 1963-64), Iran-Am. Soc. (pres. 1964-76), Soc. More Beautiful Capitol (dir.), Am. Historic and Cultural Soc. (dir.), Arctic Polar Inst. (hon.), Supreme Ct. Hist. Soc. (founding dir., trustee), Fedn. Musicians (hon.), Choral Arts Soc. (hon.). Decorated Bronze Star medal (U.S.); chevalier Legion of Honor, Croix de Guerre with palm (France): Belgian Fourragere; chevalier, officer So. Cross of Brazil; Order Homayoun, Order of Taj (Iran); Knight's Cross, Order of Dannebrog (Denmark); Gt. Cross for Meritorious Services to Austrian Republic; Royal Order de Vasa (Sweden); Order Rising Sun (Japan); recipient Smithsonian Instn. Benefactor medal; Antarctic Service medal; honored by OAS, 1968; author numerous booklets, articles. Office: 1819 H St NW Suite 950 Washington DC 20006

BECKER, RICHARD OTTO, b. Chgo., Aug. 14, 1939; B.S. in Fin., U. Colo. at Boulder, 1961; J.D., Northwestern U., 1964. Admitted to Ill. bar, 1964, U.S. Ct. Mil. Appeals bar, 1965; corporate group counsel Bell and Howell Co., Chgo., 1973—; asso. firm Popejoy, Nelson, Lucas & Speer, Wheaton, Ill., 1968-70, 64-65; U.S. Navy Judge Adv., Great Lakes, Ill., Pensacola, Fla.; individual practice law, Glenview, Ill., 1970—. Asst. scoutmaster Boy Scouts Am. Glen Ellyn, Ill., 1968-70; precinct capt., 1970-72. Mem. Am., Chgo., DuPage County, Ill. bar assns. Home: 2232 Dewes St Glenview IL 60025 Office: Bell and Howell 6800 McCormick Rd Lincolnwood IL 60645 Tel (312) 675-7603

BECKER, RICHARD SANFORD, b. Washington, June 29, 1942; B.A., Miami U., 1964; J.D., U. Mich., 1967; LL.M., George Washington U., 1970. Admitted to U.S. Ct. Appeals for D.C. bar, 1968, U.S. Supreme Ct. bar, 1972; asso. firm Scharfeld, Bechhoefer & Baron, Washington, 1967-68; asso. firm Smith & Pepper, Washington, 1968-72; partner firm Powell & Becker, Washington, 1972-73; individual practice law, Washington, 1973-76; pres. firm Becker, Gurman & Lukas, Washington, 1976—. Mem. Am., D.C., Fed. Communications bar assns. Home: 2737 Devonshire Pl NW Washington DC 20008 Office: 1156 15th St NW Suite 516 Washington DC 20005 Tel (202) 872-0190

BECKER, ROBERT HOWARD, b. N.Y.C., Mar. 12, 1930; B.S., City Coll. N.Y.; J.D., Yale. Admitted to N.Y. State bar, 1954, D.C. bar, 1969, U.S. Ct. of Appeals bar, 1964; trial atty. FDA, Washington, 1954-60; house counsel Norwich (N.Y.) Pharmacal Co., 1960-69; partner firm Kleinfeld, Kaplan & Becker, Washington, 1969—; lectr. George Washington U., 1972—. Democratic committeeman, Fairfax County, Va., 1970-73. Mem. Am., N.Y. State, D.C., Fed. bar assns. Home: 2117 Post Rd Vienna VA 22180 Office: 1200 17th St NW Washington DC 20036 Tel (202) 659-2155

BECKER, STEVEN ALLEN, b. San Bernardino, Calif., Sept. 23, 1944; B.A., U. Calif., 1965, J.D., 1968. Admitted to Calif. bar, 1970; dep. pub. defender Monterey County (Calif.), 1970-73; partner firm Novack and Becker, San Bernardino, 1973-75; individual practice law, San Bernardino, 1975—; judge pro tem juvenile ct. San Bernardino Superior Ct., 1974-76. Dir. Congregation Emanu El, San Bernardino, 1974-76; co-chmn. San Bernardino United Jewish Welfare Fund Dr., 1975; bd. dir. Home of Neighborly Service, San Bernardino, 1976. Mem. Calif. State Bar, San Bernardino Criminal Defense Attys. Assn., San Bernardino County Bar Assn., Calif. Attys. for Criminal Justice. Office: Suite 420 330 N D St San Bernardino CA 92401 Tel (714) 888-2211

BECKER, WILLIAM HENRY, b. Brookhaven, Miss., Aug. 26, 1909; student La. State U., 1927-28; LL.B., U. Mo., 1932. Admitted to Miss. bar, 1930, Mo. bar, 1932, U.S. Supreme Ct. bar, 1937; asso. firm Clark & Becker, Columbia, Mo., 1932-36, mem. firm, 1936-44, 46-61; spl. asst. to dir. Econ. Stblzn. Commn., Washington, 1945-46; judge U.S. Dist. Ct., Western Dist. Mo., Kansas City, 1965, chief judge, 1965—; spl. counsel Mo. Ins. Dept., 1936-44; counsel to Gov. Lloyd Stark in Kansas City criminal investigation, 1938-39; spl. commr. Supreme Ct. Mo., 1954-58; chmn. Mo. Supreme Ct. Com. to Draft Mo. Rules of Civil Procedure, 1952-59; mem. U.S. Jud. Conf. Coordinating Com. on Multiple Litigation, 1962-68, vice chmn., 1967-68; mem. U.S. Jud. Panel on Multidist. Litigation, 1968-77, faculty Fed. Judicial Center seminars for new U.S. dist. judges, 1968—. Fellow Am. Bar Found., Am. Coll. Trial Lawyers, Am. Coll. Probate Counsel; mem. Am. Judicature Soc., Am., Fed., Mo., Kansas City bar assns., Lawyers' Assn. Kansas City, Order of Coif. Mem. bd. editors Manual for Complex Litigation, 1968—. Office: 654 US Court House 811 Grand Ave Kansas City MO 64106 Tel (816) 842-8258

BECKER, WILLIAM WATTERS, b. New Orleans, Apr. 1, 1943; B.A., Dartmouth, 1964, M.B.A., 1965; LL.B., Harvard, 1968. Admitted to Mass. bar, 1968, D.C. bar, 1970; atty. community legal assistance office, Cambridge, Mass., 1968-69; partner firm Becker & Feldman, Washington, 1969-76, sr. partner, 1976—; asso. gen. counsel JFK Center for the Performing Arts, Washington, 1977—; gen. counsel Kennedy Center Productions, Inc., Washington, 1972—. Mem. Model Cities Commn., Washington, 1972-73; dir., gen. counsel The Voice Found., Washington, 1976—; Belford Tower Found., 1976—. Mem. Am. Bar Assn., Assn. ICC Practitioners, Phi Beta Kappa. Home: 3053 Porter St NW Washington DC 20008 Office: 1819 H St NW Washington DC 20006 Tel (202) 293-1919

BECKETT, RILEY MICHAEL, b. Oakland, Calif., Dec. 19, 1945; B.S. in Bus. Adminstrn., U. Nev., 1968; J.D., U. San Francisco, 1971. Admitted to Calif. bar, 1971, Nev. bar, 1971; counsel Dept. Hwys. Atty. Gen. State of Nev., 1972-75; gen. counsel Nev. Indsl. Commn., 1975-77; partner firm Eck & Harkins, Ltd., Carson City, Nev., 1977—. Mem. Calif., Am., Nev. trial lawyers assns., state bars Nev., Calif., Phi Alph Delta. Home: 1116 Potomac Pl Carson City NV 89701 Office: 310 N Stewart St Carson City NV 89701 Tel (702) 883-1890

BECKETT, WILLIAM ARTHUR, b. Pelston, Mich., Feb. 15, 1928; B.A., U. Mich., 1950, LL.B., 1953. Admitted to Mich. bar, 1953, Oreg. bar, 1955; research analyst U. Mich., 1953-54; asst. prof., research atty. U. Oreg. Bur. Municipal Research and League of Oreg. Cities, 1954-57; judge Dist. Ct., Lane County, Oreg., 1957-75, Circuit Ct., Lane County, 1975—. Moderator 1st Congregational Ch., Eugene, Oreg., 1974-76; pres. bd. dirs. YMCA, Eugene, 1975-76. Mem. Oreg., Mich., Lane County (Oreg.) bar assns., Circuit Judges Assn., Am. Judicature Soc. Contbr. articles to legal jours. Home: 2199 Fairmount St Eugene OR 97403 Office: Lane County Courthouse Eugene OR 97401 Tel (503) 687-4240

BECKETT, WILLIAM WADE, b. Charleston, S.C., Feb. 2, 1928; B.S. in Civil Engring., The Citadel, 1948; J.D. with highest honors, George Washington U., 1956. Admitted to D.C. bar, 1956; asso. firm Burns, Doane, Benedict & Irons, D.C., 1956-60; partner firm Schuyler, Birch, Swindler, McKie & Beckett, D.C., 1960—; engr. Am. Bridge Co., Ambridge, Pa., 1948. Trustee Internat. Students Inc., 1962-65; area com. Young Life, 1965-72; elder Fourth Presbyterian Ch., Bethesda, Md., 1972—. Mem. D.C. (council patent, trademark and copyright sects.), Am. bar assns., Wash. Patent Lawyers Club (pres. 1966-67), Am. Patent Law Assn. Home: 9300 Renshaw Dr Bethesda MD 20034 Office: 1000 Connecticut Ave Washington DC 20036 Tel (202) 296-5500

BECKLEY, JAMES EMMETT, b. St. Joseph, Mo., Aug. 30, 1941; A.B., Rockhurst Coll., 1964; J.D., Northwestern U., 1967. Admitted to Ill. bar, 1968; asso. firm Kirkland & Ellis, Chgo., 1967-69; asso. firm Franklin J. Lunding, Jr., Chgo., 1969-71; asso. firm Roan & Grossman, 1972-73, partner, 1973—. Mem. Am. (mem. sects. on antitrust and gen. litigation), Ill. (mem. sects. antitrust, gen. litigation, trial practice; chmn. consumer law subcom. 1970), Chgo. bar assns., Assn. Trial Lawyers Am., Assn. for Computing Machinery. Home: 824 N Howard St Wheaton IL 60187 Office: 120 S LaSalle St Chicago IL 60603 Tel (312) 263-3600

BECKLEY, WILLIAM BRUCE, b. Las Vegas, Mar. 22, 1915; B.S., Calif. Inst. Tech., 1936; J.D., Stanford, 1939. Admitted to Calif. bar, 1939, U.S. Supreme Ct. bar, 1944, Nev. bar, 1954; partner firm Boyken, Mohler & Beckley, San Francisco, 1939-54; individual practice law, Las Vegas, 1954-69; mem. firm Beckley, Singleton, DeLanoy, Jemison & Reid, Las Vegas, 1969—; gen. atty. Union Pacific R.R. Co., Las Vegas, 1968—; spl. dep. atty. gen. Nev. Dept. Commerce, 1962-66; dir. Nev. Savs. & Loan Assn., 1970—; instr. San Francisco Law Sch., 1941-54; mem. Nev. Bd. Bar Examiners, 1961-66. Trustee, Nev. Devel. Authority, 1959—, pres., 1971-74. Mem. Am., Clark County bar assns., State Bar Nev. Home: 2409 Plaza Del Grande Las Vegas NV 89102 Office: Beckley Singleton DeLanoy Jemison & Reid 302 E Carson Ave Las Vegas NV 89101 Tel (702) 385-3373

BECKMAN, GAIL MCKNIGHT, b. N.Y.C., Apr. 8, 1938; B.A., Bryn Mawr Coll., 1959; M.A. in Legal History, U. Pa., 1966; J.D., Yale, 1967; postgrad. (Fulbright scholar) U. Tubingen (Germany) Law Faculty, 1959-60, Hague (Netherlands) Acad. Internat. Law, 1975. Admitted to Pa. bar, 1964, D.C. bar, 1964, U.S. Supreme Ct. bar, 1968, Ga. bar, 1971; counsellor Legal Aid Soc. of Phila., summer 1961; research asso. O. W. Holmes Devise for a History of U.S. Supreme Ct., Phila., summer 1963; asso. firm Morgan, Lewis & Bockius, Phila., 1963-66; lectr. in law U. Glasgow (Scotland), 1967-71; asso. prof. law Ga. State U., 1971-76, prof., 1976—; research asso. Am. Philos. Soc., 1966-70. Founder St. Andrews Soc. of Atlanta, 1971. Mem. State Bar Ga., Am. (chmn. internat. estates), Atlanta bar assns., Ga. Assn. Women Lawyers, Juristic Soc., Yale Law Assn. of Ga. (vice chmn. 1975-77), Internat. Acad. Probate and Trust Lawyers, Gamma Iota Sigma, Beta Gamma Sigma. Author: The Statues at Large of Pennsylvania, 1680-1700, 1976; Law for Business and Management, 1975; author videotape scripts; contb. articles and book revs. to legal jours. Home: 3200 Lenox Rd Atlanta GA 30324 Office: Georgia State U Atlanta GA 30303 Tel (404) 658-3840

BECKMAN, HENRY PATRICK, b. Chgo., Dec. 29, 1934; J.D., John Marshall Law Sch., 1966. Admitted to Ill. bar, 1966; partner firm Burgeson, Laughlin, Cunningham & Smith, Chgo., 1975—; v.p. Safety & Claims Service, Inc., Chgo., 1969-73. Mem. Oak Forest (Ill.) Bd. Zoning Appeals, 1968-71. Mem. Ill. Bar Assn. Home: Route 5 Box 251 Lockport IL 60441 Office: 221 N LaSalle St Chicago IL 60601 Tel (312) 263-0093

BECKNER, JAMES EDWARD, b. Appalachia, Va., May 30, 1939; grad. cum laude, Carson-Newman Coll., 1963; LL.B., U. Tenn., 1965. Admitted to Tenn. bar, 1966; practice law; now judge Criminal Ct. 20th Jud. Circuit Tenn., Morristown. Bd. dirs. Morristown Boys Club, Morristown Theatre Guild. Mem. Tenn., Am. trial lawyers assns., Tenn., Hamblen County bar assns., Am. Jud. Conf. Named outstanding Young Man of Year, Hamblen County, 1970. Home: RTE 2 Box 354C Morristown TN 37814 Office: Hamblen County Courthouse Morristown NJ 37814 Tel (615) 586-8640

BECKWITH, DAVID MORGAN, b. Lorain, Ohio, Dec. 26, 1938; B.A., DePauw U., 1961; J.D., Western Res. U., 1964. Admitted to Ohio bar, 1964, W.Va. bar, 1966, Pa. bar, 1972; clk. U.S. 6th Circuit Ct. Appeals, Akron, Ohio, 1964-65; atty. Wheeling Steel Corp. (W.Va.), 1964-69, Leaseway Corp., Cleve., 1969-70; Bethlemen Steel Corp. (Pa.), 1970—. Mem. Am., Pa., Ohio bar assns., Pa. Def. Inst. Office: Room 2071 Martin Tower Bethlehem PA 18016 Tel (215) 694-2963

BECKWITH, FRANK LOUIS, b. Ft. Collins, Colo., Aug. 24, 1928; B.S. in Bus., U. Colo., 1959, LL.B., 1962. Admitted to Colo. bar, 1962, U.S. Dist. for Colo. bar, 1962, 10th Circuit Ct. Appeals bar, 1963; field claims rep. State Farm Ins. Co., Denver, 1962; asso. firm James D. Doyle, Denver, 1963; individual practice law, Lakewood, Colo., 1964; atty. Colo. Dept. Revenue, Denver, 1965-73, chief taxation, 1973—; chmn. sales and use tax com. Multi-State Tax Commn., 1975—. Bd. dirs. Denver Metro Village, Inc., 1967—; mem. Lakewood (Colo.) Incorporation Com., 1968; vice chmn. Lakewood Planning Commn., 1968-70. Mem. Am. Bar Assn., Western States Assn. Tax Adminstrs. (dir. 1974-75). Home: 2440 S Garland Ct Lakewood CO 80227 Office: 1375 Sherman St Denver CO 80203 Tel (303) 892-3048

BECKWITH, RAYMOND WARNER, b. Bridgeport, Conn., Feb. 11, 1927; B.A., Yale, 1947; LL.B., Harvard, 1953. Admitted to Conn. bar, 1953; asso. firm Marsh, Day & Calhoun, Bridgeport, 1953-58, partner, 1958—; mem. Conn. Bar exam. com., 1970—. Mem. Am., Conn., Greater Bridgeport (v.p. 1976—) bar assns., Am. Judicature Soc. Home: 6 Red Fox Ln Trumbull CT 06611 Office: 955 Main St Bridgeport CT 06604 Tel (203) 368-4221

BECNEL, PHILIP ALFRED, III, b. Schenectady, Nov. 27, 1942; B.S., U. S. Naval Acad., 1964; postgrad. Georgetown U., 1968-69; J.D., U. San Francisco, 1969-72. Admitted to Calif. bar, 1972; sr. nuclear engr. Bechtel Corp., San Francisco, 1969-72, counsel, 1973—. Mem. Am., Calif., San Francisco bar assns. Home: 8 Dias Way San Rafael CA 94903 Office: 50 Beale St San Francisco CA 94105 Tel (415) 768-4574

BEDDOW, THOMAS JOHN, b. Frackville, Pa., Oct. 30, 1914; A.B., Ursinus Coll., 1936, LL.D., 1973; LL.B., U. Pa., 1939. Admitted to Pa. bar, 1939, N.J. bar, 1941, D.C. bar, 1941, Md. bar, 1950. Asso. firm Gardner, Morrison, Sheriff & Beddow, Washington, 1941, 42, 46, partner, 1947—; asso. firm Arthur T. Vanderbilt, Newark, 1939-40. Mem. Bar Assn. D.C., Md., N.J., D.C. bar assns. Contbr. articles to legal jours. Home: 5015 Wyandot Ct Bethesda MD 20016 Office: 1126 Woodward Bldg 733 15th St Washington DC 20005 Tel (202) 783-6800

BEDELL, SUSANNA ESZENYI, b. Budapest, Hungary, Dec. 22, 1918; A.B., Vassar Coll., 1940; J.D., Columbia, 1944. Admitted to N.Y. bar, 1948, U.S. Supreme Ct. bar, 1952; asso. firms Sherman & Sterling & Wright, N.Y.C., 1944-51, Wilmer & Bround, Washington, 1953-54; individual practice law, 1968-70; of counsel firm Van De Water and Van De Water, Poughkeepsie, N.Y., 1970—; atty. Hoover Commn., 1948; chmn. bd. trustees Joseph F. Barnard Meml. Library, Dutchess County (N.Y.) Supreme Ct. Library, Poughkeepsie, 1968—; bd. dirs. Mid-Hudson Valley Legal Services Project, Poughkeepsie, 1974-77; bd. dirs., pres. pro tem. Mid-Hudson Legal Services, Inc., 1977—. Bd. dirs. Dutchess County Mental Health Soc., 1962—; v.p. bd. dirs. Astor Child Guidance Clinic, Poughkeepsie, 1966—. Mem. Assn. Bar City N.Y., N.Y. State, Dutchess County (chmn. com. continuing legal edn. 1975—), Am. bar assns. Home: 20 Sunrise Ln Poughkeepsie NY 12603 Office: 54 Market St Poughkeepsie NY 12602 Tel (914) 452-5900

BEDFORD, WILLIAM WHYTE, b. Corinth, Miss., Jan. 1, 1923; B.S., Auburn U., 1948; J.D., Samford U., 1966. Admitted to Ala. bar, 1966; partner firm Bedford & Bedford, Russellville, Ala., 1966—. Home: City Lake Dr Russellville AL 35653 Office: PO Box 669 316 Coffee Ave Russellville AL 35653 Tel (205) 332-2880

BEDRICK, LEON IRVING, b. N.Y.C., Dec. 31, 1913; B.A., U.N.C., 1934; LL.B., Bklyn. Law Sch., 1937, J.D., 1961. Admitted to N.Y. State bar, 1937; chmn. bd. Bedrick-Kaitz Agency, Inc. (gen. ins.), N.Y.C., 1973—. Mem. Phi Beta Kappa. Home: 5 Manor Ln Woodmere NY 11598 Office: 1 Penn Plaza New York City NY 10001 Tel (212) 563-5800

BEDROSSIAN, PETER STEPHEN, b. Hoboken, N.J., Sept. 15, 1926; B.B.A., St. John's U., 1949, LL.B., 1954. Admitted to N.Y. State bar, 1954, Calif. bar, 1972, U.S. Supreme Ct. bar, 1962; dir. taxes Stauffer Chem. Co., N.Y.C., 1948-70, San Francisco, 1971-75; asso. firm Dobbs, Doyle & Nielsen, San Francisco, 1976—. Mem. Am., N.Y. State, Calif. bar assns., Internat. Assn. Assessing Officers, San Francisco Lawyers Club, Internat. Fiscal Assn. Office: Alcoa Bldg 1 Maritime Plaza Suite 2500 San Francisco CA 94111 Tel (415) 362-1940

BEDWELL, EDWARD ELISHA, b. Fort Smith, Ark., Jan. 21, 1921; B.A., U. Okla., 1942; J.D., U. Ark., 1948. Admitted to Ark. bar, 1948, U.S. Supreme Ct. bar, 1969; individual practice law, Ft. Smith, 1948-50; dep. pros. atty. City of Ft. Smith, 1950-51; mem. firm Bedwell and Bedwell, Ft. Smith, 1951-58, Green and Bedwell, Ft. Smith, 1958-63, Shaw and Bedwell, Ft. Smith, 1963-70; individual practice law, Ft. Smith, 1970—; dir. City Nat. Bank, Ft. Smith, 1955—. Chmn. Ft. Smith Hist. Dist. Commn., 1973; legal advisor Ft. Smith Heritage Found.; mem. Ft. Smith Downtown Improvement Dist.; trustee First Prebyterian Ch. Mem. Sebastian County Bar Assn. (pres. 1955), Ark. Bar Assn. Home: 2200 S 46th St Fort Smith AR 72903 Office: 24 N 7th St Fort Smith AR 72901 Tel (501) 783-0476

BEEBE, MIKE D., b. Amagon, Ark., Dec. 28, 1946; B.A., Ark. State U., 1968; J.D., U. Ark., 1972. Admitted to Ark. bar, 1972; partner firm Lightle, Tedder, Hannah & Beebe, Searcy, Ark., 1972—; judge Judsonia Municipal Ct., 1973—. Chmn. bd. trustees Ark. State U., Jonesboro, 1974—. Mem. Am., Ark., White County (pres.) bar assns., Searcy C. of C. Contbr. article to Ark. Law Review, editor-in-chief, 1971—. Home: 900 N Sunnyhill St Searcy AR 72143 Office: 310 N Spring St Searcy AR 72143

BEEBE, RAYMOND MARK, b. Council Bluffs, Iowa, May 14, 1942; B.S., Iowa State U., 1964; J.D. cum laude, U. Iowa, 1967. Admitted to Iowa bar, 1967; asso. firm Jones, Cambridge & Carl, Atlantic, Iowa, 1967-68; asst. atty. gen. Des Moines, 1968-69; partner firm Cooper, Sinnard & Beebe, Forest City, Iowa, 1969—; sec., gen. counsel Winnebago Industries, Inc., 1974—. Pres. Forest City United Fund, 1974-75. Mem. Am., Iowa, Winnebago County (pres. 1970-75) bar assns., Forest City C. of C. (v.p. 1974-75). Mem. editorial bd. Iowa Law Review, 1966-67. Home: Rural Route 3 Box 79B Forest City IA 50436 Office: 145 S Clark St Forest City IA 50436 Tel (515) 582-2712

BEEBE, WALTER HENRY, b. N.Y.C., May 24, 1940; B.A. cum laude, Harvard, 1962; LL.B., Stanford, 1965. Asso. firm Olwine, Connelly, Chase, O'Donnell & Weyher, N.Y.C., 1965-75; admitted to N.Y. bar, 1966, U.S. Dist. Cts. for So. and Eastern Dists. N.Y. bars, 1967, U.S. 2d Circuit Ct. Appeals bar, 1967, U.S. Supreme Ct. bar, 1976; asso. firm Davis & Cox, N.Y.C., 1975, partner, 1976—. Trustee, Bank St. Coll. Edn., 1976—; cons., bd. dirs. N.Y. Citizens Union, East Harlem Vol. Legal Services. Mem. Assn. Bar City N.Y., Am. Judicature Soc. Home: 6 W 77th St New York City NY 10024 Office: One State St Plaza New York City NY 10004 Tel (212) 425-0500

BEEBE, WILLIAM BOVELL, b. Weber, Iowa, May 1, 1919; A.B., George Washington U., 1946, LL.B., 1950. Admitted to D.C. bar, 1950, Md. bar, 1957; since practiced in Washington, mem. firm Glassie, Pewett, Beebe & Shanks and predecessors, 1951—. Founder Bethesda (Md.) Boys' Club, 1969, pres., 1970-73, gen. counsel, 1973—. Mem. D.C. Bar Assn., Am. Judicature Soc. Home: 5713 Marengo Rd Bethesda MD 20016 Office: 1737 H St NW Washington DC 20006 Tel (202) 466-4310

BEEKS, WILLIAM TRULOCK, b. El Reno, Okla., May 5, 1906; LL.B., U. Wash., 1932. Admitted to Wash. bar, 1932; asso. firm Bogle, Bogle & Gates, Seattle, 1932-42; partner firm Evans, McLaren, Lane, Powell & Beeks, Seattle, 1946-61; judge U.S. Dist. Ct., 1961-71, chief judge, 1971-73, sr. judge, 1973—. Mem. Am., Wash. Seattle-King County bar assns., Maritime Law Assn. U.S., Order of Coif. Office: 502 U S Court House Seattle WA 98104 Tel (206) 442-4414

BEELER, VIRGIL L., b. Indpls., June 6, 1931; A.B., Ind. U., 1953, J.D., 1959. Admitted to Ind. bar, 1959, U.S. Supreme Ct. bar, 1972; asso. firm Baker and Daniels, Indpls., 1959-65, partner, 1966—. Mem. Indpls., Ind., Am. bar assns., Bar Assn. Seventh Fed. Circuit, Order of Coif, Phi Beta Kappa. Office: 810 Fletcher Trust Bldg Indianapolis IN 46204 Tel (317) 636-4535

BEEM, JACK DARREL, b. Chgo., Nov. 17, 1931; A.B., U. Chgo., 1952, J.D., 1955. Admitted to Ill. bar, 1955; asso. firm Wilson & McIlvaine, Chgo., 1958-63; partner firm Baker & McKenzie, Chgo., 1963—. Mem. Am., Chgo. bar assns. Home: 175 E Delaware Pl apt 8104 Chicago IL 60611 Office: Baker & McKenzie 2900 Prudential Plaza Chicago IL 60601 Tel (312) 565-0025

BEEMER, JOHN BARRY, b. Scranton, Pa., Sept. 4, 1941; B.S., U. Scranton, 1963; LL.B., George Washington U., 1966. Admitted to Pa. bar, 1966; law clk. trial div. U.S. Ct. Claims, Washington, 1966-67, U.S. Dist. Judge William J. Nealon, judge Middle Dist. Pa., 1967-68; asso. firm Warren, Hill, Henkleman, McMenamin, Scranton, Pa., 1968-72; partner firm Beemer, Brier, Rinaldi & Fendrick, Scranton, 1972—. Co.-chmn. U. Scranton Nat. Alumni Fund, 1971-72, chmn. com. on redrafting constrn. Lackawanna County (Pa.) United Fund, 1972. Mem. Am., Pa., Lackawanna County bar assns., Pa. Trial Lawyers Assn., Assn. Trial Lawyers Am. Office: 200 Scranton Life Bldg Washington and Adams Sts Scranton PA 18503 Tel (717) 346-7441

BEERS, JOHN ROGER, b. Trenton, Mo., Feb. 13, 1943; B.A., Baylor U., 1968; LL.B., Harvard U., 1968. Admitted to Calif. bar, 1970; asso. firms Dewey, Ballantine, Bushby Palmer & Wood, N.Y.C., 1968-69, Heller, Ehrman, White, & McAuliffe, San Francisco, 1969-73; staff atty. Natural Resources Def. Council, Palo Alto, Calif., 1973—; mem. adv. com. Calif. Regulatory Commn. Fed. Energy Adminstrn. Mem. Calif., San Francisco, Am. bar assns. Author: (with others) Who's Minding the Shore, 1976. Home: 468 Channing St Palo Alto CA 94302 Office: 2345 Yale St Palo Alto CA 94306 Tel (415) 327-1080

BEERS, THOMAS JOSEPH, b. Missoula, Mont., Apr. 14, 1948; B.S. in Bus. Adminstrn., U. Mont., 1970, J.D., 1973. Admitted to Mont. bar, 1973; dep. atty. gen. State of Mont., Helena, 1973-74, chief dep. criminal div., 1974-75, prosecutor workmen's compensation investigation, 1975-76; spl. prosecutor W. Mont. Spl. Prosecution Unit, Missoula, 1976—; mem. Mont. Bd. Crime Control, 1973-75. Mem. Am., Mont. bar assns. Office: Missoula County Courthouse Missoula MT 59801 Tel (406) 728-9594

BEESON, DAVID GLENN, b. Columbia, Mo., Nov. 1, 1946; B.S. in Edn., SE Mo. State U., 1968; postgrad. Mo. U., 1970-71; J.D., Memphis State U., 1973. Admitted to Mo. bar, 1974; asso. firm Buerkle, Buerkle & Lowes, Jackson, Mo., 1974—. Mem. Am. Bar Assn., Am. Trial Lawyers Assn. Home: 306 Connie St Jackson MO 63755 Office: 709 E Main St Jackson MO 63755 Tel (314) 243-3541

BEETZ, JEAN, b. Montreal, Que., Can., Mar. 27, 1927; student St. Laurent Coll., Montreal, 1939-47; B.A., U. Montreal, 1947, L.L.L., 1950; postgrad. Pembroke Coll., Oxford, Eng., 1951-53; B.A., honour sch. jurisprudence, Oxford, Eng., 1953, M.A., Oxford, 1958. Called to Que. bar, 1950; individual practice law, Montreal, Que., 1950-51; asst. prof. civil law, Faculty of Law U. Montreal, 1953-59, asso. prof., 1959-66, dean of law, 1968-70, prof., 1966-73; asst. sec. to cabinet, Ottawa, 1966-68; spl. counsel to prime minister Can. on constnl. matters, Ottawa, 1968-71; judge Quebec Ct. Appeal, Montreal, 1973-74, Supreme Ct. Can., 1974—. Fellow Royal Soc. Can., Pembroke Coll. (hon.). Home: 400 Stewart # 2405 Ottawa ON KIN 6L2 Canada Office: Supreme Ct Canada Wellington St Ottawa ON K1A 0J1 Canada Tel (613) 996-5350

BEGAM, ROBERT GEORGE, b. N.Y.C., Apr. 5, 1928; B.A., Yale, 1949, LL.B., 1952. Admitted to N.Y. State bar, 1952, Ariz. bar, 1956; mem. firm Cravath, Swaine & Moore, N.Y.C., 1952-54; served as 1st lt. JAG, USAF, 1954-56; gen. counsel Ariz. Securities Div., 1956-57; spl. counsel State of Ariz., 1957-59; partner firm Langerman, Begam, Lewis, Leonard & Marks, Phoenix, 1958—; counsel Ariz. State Democratic Party, 1972—. Dir. Phoenix Civic Theater; pres. Ariz. Repertory Theater, 1963-66. Fellow Internat. Soc. Barristers; mem. Am., Fed. bar assns., Assn. Trial Lawyers of Am. (pres. 1976-77), Western Trial Lawyers Assn. (past pres.), Am. Judicature Soc., World Assn. of Lawyers. Home: 77 E Missouri St #12 Phoenix AZ 85012 Office: 1400 Ariz Title Bldg Phoenix AZ 85003 Tel (602) 254-6071

BEGAN, WILLIAM DENTON, b. Colon, Panama, Nov. 25, 1929; A.A., U. Calif., Berkeley, 1949, J.D., Hastings Coll. Law, 1952; postgrad. Advanced Profl. Program U. So. Calif. Law Center, 1972. Admitted to Calif. bar, 1953, U.S. Supreme Ct. bar, 1971, U.S. Ct. Mil. Appeals bar, 1973; gunnery and legal officer USN, 1953-56; chief atty. Legal Aid Found., Long Beach, Calif., 1956; pub. defender City of Long Beach, 1956-58; partner firm Baker, Began & Auw, Long Beach, 1958—; v.p. State Bar Calif. Conf. of Barristers, 1960. Bd. dirs. Sightman Meml. Goodwill Industries, Long Beach, 1960-76; mem. Southland Water Com. for So. Calif., 1970-76; bd. visitors Hastings Coll. Law U. Calif., 1973-74; trustee Hastings 1066 Found., 1975-76. Fellow Am. Acad. Law, Sci.; mem. Assn. Trial Lawyers Am., Calif., Los Angeles County, Long Beach bar assns., Am. Judicature Soc., Supreme Ct. Hist. Soc., Judge Advs. Assn., Assn. So. Calif. Def. Counsel. Home: 6234 Monita St Long Beach CA 90803 Office: PO Box 7566 3610 Long Beach Blvd Long Beach CA 90807 Tel (213) 426-7155

BEGLEY, LOUIS, b. Stryj, Poland, Oct. 6, 1933; A.B., Harvard, 1954, LL.B., 1959. Admitted to N.Y. State bar, 1961, U.S. Ct. Appeals for D.C. bar, 1975; asso. firm Debevoise, Plimpton, Lyons & Gates, N.Y.C., 1959-68, partner, 1968—. Mem. Assn. Bar City N.Y. Home: 925 Park Ave New York City NY 10028 Office: 299 Park Ave New York City NY 10017 Tel (212) 752-6400

BEHBEHANI, ZOHREH SAEED, b. Tehran, Iran, Feb. 24, 1936; naturalized, 1972; LL.B., U. Tehran, 1958; LL.M., U. Mo., Kansas City, 1968. Admitted to Kans. bar, 1975; asso. firm Matney & Roth, Overland Park, Kans., 1975—; instr. in field Johnson County Community Coll., Shawnee Mission, Kans. Founder, Internat. Cooperative Playschool, coordinator, 1969-70; co-founder Mini-Mundo, orgn. internat. women. Mem. Internat. Fedn. Women Lawyers, Am., Kans., Johnson County bar assns., UN Assn. Greater Kansas City (dir.). Home: 3812 W 51st St Shawnee Mission KS 66205 Office: 7373 W 107th St Overland Park KS 66212 Tel (913) 341-4242

BEHNKE, HENRY, b. Marinette, Wis., Mar. 22, 1909; B.A., U. Wis., 1931, LL.B., 1933, J.D., 1956. Admitted to Wis. bar, 1933; first dist. atty. Dane County, Wis., 1936-39; exec. v.p. Mautz Paint Co., Madison, Wis., 1945-60, pres., gen. counsel, 1960—. Mem. Dane County, Wis. bar assns. Home: 29 Harbort Dr Madison WI 53704 Office: 939 E Washington Ave Madison WI 53701 Tel (608) 255-1661

BEHR, BARBARA ELLEN, b. Jersey City, July 9, 1934; B.A., Cornell U., 1956; J.D., Rutgers U., 1958; M.A., Hunter Coll., 1971. Admitted to N.Y. State bar, 1958; legal editor The Corp. Trust Co., N.Y.C., 1958-61; asso. firm Mark D. Trachtenberg, N.Y.C., 1965-67; individual practice law, N.Y.C., 1967-70; adj. lectr., coll. asso. Hunter Coll., 1970-72, asst. prof. econs., 1972-77, dept. adviser, 1974-77; asso. prof. Sch. Bus., Bloomsburg (Pa.) State Coll., 1977—. Mem. N.Y. State Bar Assn., Cornell Law Assn., Nat., Northeastern bus. law assns., Omicron Delta Epsilon. Author: Economic Consequences of Patents and Copyrights, 1971; Commercial Banking Practices and the Antitrust Law; Women, Law and Economics. Office: Bloomsburg State College Bloomsburg PA 17815 Tel (717) 389-3806

BEHR, LEON ERNST, b. Jersey City, Apr. 20, 1904; A.B., Cornell U., 1925; J.D., Rutgers U., 1929. Admitted to N.J. bar, 1929; partner firm Behr & Behr, Jersey City, 1929-50, individual practice law, Jersey City, 1950—. Mem. Hudson County Bar Assn. Office: 26 Journal Sq Jersey City NJ 07306 Tel (201) 653-5678

BEHRINGER, JOHN WILLIAM, b. Leetonia, Ohio, Jan. 29, 1938; B.S. in Chemistry, U. Dayton, 1959; J.D. George Washington U., 1968. Admitted to D.C. bar, 1968; asso. firm McLean, Morton & Boustead, Washington, 1968-69, partner, 1970; partner firm Morton, Bernard, Brown, Roberts & Sutherland, Washington, 1970—; examiner U.S. Patent Office, 1962-64. Mem. D.C., Am. bar assns., Am. Patent Law Assn., Internat. Patent and Trademark Law Assn., Licensing Execs. Soc. Home: 8524 Etta Dr Springfield VA 22152 Office: 1700 K St NW Washington DC 20006 Tel (202) 457-4600

BEIER, SAMUEL K., b. N.Y.C., Sept. 22, 1900; A.B., Coll. City N.Y., 1921; LL.B., N.Y.U., 1921. Admitted N.Y. bar, 1922, U.S. Supreme Ct. bar, 1938; individual practice law, N.Y.C., 1922—; spl. dep. atty. gen., 1926-38. Republican candidate for U.S. Congress; mem. Condemnation and Appraisal Commn. Mem. N.Y. County, Bar Assn., N.Y. County Lawyers Assn. Home: 334 W 86th St New York City NY 10024 Office: 250 Broadway New York City NY 10007 Tel (212) WO4-2660

BEIGHIE, DONALD J., b. Deer Lodge, Mont., Dec. 30, 1933; B.S., Mont. State Coll., 1958; LL.B., U. Mont., 1961. Admitted to Mont. bar, 1961, Alaska bar, 1970; legal asst. to chief justice Mont. Supreme Ct., Helena, 1961-62; partner firm McElwain & Beighle, Deer Lodge, 1962-66; also county atty. Powell County (Mont.), 1962-66; atty. SEC, Seattle, 1966-70; asst. atty. gen. State of Alaska, Juneau, 1970-73; counsel Sealaska Corp., Juneau, 1973—. Mem. Am., Mont., Alaska bar assns. Home: Rural Route 4 Box 4308 Juneau AK 99803 Office: 811 W 12th St Juneau AK 99801 Tel (907) 586-1512

BEIGHLE, DOUGLAS PAUL, b. Deer Lodge, Mont., June 18, 1932; B.S., U. Mont., 1954, J.D. with honors, 1958; LL.M., Harvard, 1960. Admitted to Mont. bar, 1958, Wash. State bar, 1959, U.S. Supreme Ct. bar, 1970; practiced in Seattle, 1960—; asso. firm Perkins, Coie, Stone, Olsen & Williams, 1960-67, partner, 1967—; chief legal counsel Puget Sound Power and Light Co., Bellevue, 1970—. Mem. adv. council Nathan Hale Area Citizens, 1972-74, Municipal League Seattle, 1960—. Mem., Am., Mont. State, Wash. State, Seattle-King County bar assns., Am. Judicature Soc. Contbr. articles to profl. jours. Home: 4011 NE 98th Seattle WA 98115 Office: 1900 Washington Bldg Seattle WA 98101 Tel (206) 682-8770

BEIK, STEPHEN WRIGHT, b. Darby, Pa., Feb. 1, 1947; A.B., Wesleyan U., 1968; J.D., Vanderbilt U., 1971. Admitted to Pa. bar, 1972; spl. planner on cts. Pa. Gov's. Justice Commn., 1971-72; law clk. R. Paul Campbell, Centre County, Pa., 1971-72; partner firm Miller, Kistler, Campbell, Mitinger & Beik, State College, Pa., 1972—. Mem. devel. com. State College C. of C., 1974—; v.p. Nittany Sunrise Kiwanis. Mem. Centre County, Pa., Am. bar assns., Pa. Soc., Phi Alpha Delta. Named Outstanding Young Man Am., 1975. Office: 1500 S Atherton St State College PA 16801 Tel (814) 238-0554

BEILENSON, NORTON YALE, b. St. Louis, June 29, 1937; B.S.B.A., Washington U., St. Louis, 1959, J.D., 1962. Admitted to Mo. bar, 1962; gen. partner firm Dolgin & Beilenson, St. Louis, 1962—; mem. nat. law commn. Anti-Defamation League. Mem. Am. Trial Lawyers Assn., Am., Mo., St. Louis County, Met. St. Louis bar assns. Office: 7777 Bonhomme Ave suite 1910 Clayton MO 63105 Tel (314) 725-5150

BEIMFOHR, EDWARD GEORGE, b. Marissa, Ill., Dec. 31, 1932; A.B., Washington U., 1953, LL.B., 1956. Admitted to Mo. bar, N.Y. bar, N.J. bar; asso. firm Thompson, Mitchell, Thompson & Douglas, St. Louis, 1956-57; asso. firm Sullivan & Cromwell, N.Y.C., 1957-65; partner firm Casey, Lane, & Mittendorf, N.Y.C., 1965—; lectr. in field. Mem. Am., N.Y. State, N.Y.C. bar assns. Office: 26 Broadway New York City NY 10004 Tel (212) 943-3000

BEIN, RICHARD HUGO, b. Chgo., Oct. 5, 1932; Ph.B., Ill. Wesleyan U., 1954; J.D., U. Calif., Los Angeles, 1961. Admitted to Calif. bar, 1961; law clk. to judge U.S. 9th Circuit Ct. Appeals, 1961-66; dep. dist. atty. County of San Diego (Calif.), 1962-71, in charge of appellate and tng. div., 1967-71; judge County of San Diego Municipal Ct., El Cajon Jud. Dist., 1971—, presiding judge, 1974—. Mem. Calif. Conf. Judges, San Diego County Municipal Ct. Judges Assn. (pres. 1975). Office: 110 E Lexington St El Cajon CA 92020 Tel (714) 579-4121

BEINS, HUGH JOSEPH, b. Bronx, N.Y., Mar. 5, 1932; B.S.S., Georgetown U., 1953, LL.B., 1956. Admitted to D.C. bar, 1957, U.S. Supreme Ct. bar, 1960. Trial atty. NLRB, 1957-60; gen. counsel Eastern Conf. Teamsters, Bethesda, Md., 1960—; spl. counsel Internat. Brotherhood of Teamsters, Washington, 1969-74; adj. prof. law Georgetown U., 1961—; lectr in field. Mem. Am., D.C. bar assns. Contbg. editor The Developing Labor Law, 1971. Home: 3812 Kanawha St NW Washington DC 20015 Office: 4641 Montgomery Ave Bethesda MD 20014 Tel (301) 656-6006

BEIZER, DAVID BENJAMIN, b. Hartford, Conn., May 24, 1938; B.A., Harvard, 1960; LL.B., Columbia, 1963. Admitted to Ct. bar, 1964; atty. FCC, Wash., D.C., 1964-65; asst. atty. gen. State of Conn., 1965-70; exec. dir. Ct. Action Now, New Haven, 1970-71; exec. sec. Conn. Bankers Assn., Hartford, 1971—; instr. Sch. Law Univ. Ct., 1972-76. Mem. Bd. Edn. Town Avon, Conn., 1975—. Russell Sage Found. research fellow Columbia, 1963-64. Home: 100 Paper Chase Trail Avon CT 06001 Office: 100 Constitution Plaza Suite 956 Hartford CT 06103 Tel (203) 522-7236

BEKEMEYER, DENNIS LEE, b. Harrisburg, Ill., Oct. 4, 1943; A.B., Dartmouth, 1965; J.D., U. Ill., 1969; postgrad. U. Freiburg (Germany), 1970. Admitted to Wash. bar, 1970; asso. firm Perkins, Cole, Stone, Olsen & Williams, Seattle, 1970-77, partner, 1977—. Mem. Am., Wash., Seattle-King County bar assns. Volkswagen Found. fellow, 1969-70. Office: 1900 Washington Bldg Seattle WA 98101 Tel (206) 682-8770

BEKMAN, PAUL DAVID, b. Washington, Mar. 31, 1946; B.A., U. Md., 1968, J.D., 1971. Admitted to Md. bar, 1972, U.S. Supreme Ct. bar; asso. firm Kaplan, Heyman, Greenberg, Engelman & Belgrad, Balt., 1971—. Mem. Bar Assn. Balt. City (exec. council young lawyers sect.), Md. Bar Assn., Md. Trial Lawyers Assn., Maritime Law Assn. U.S. Office: 10th Floor Sun Life Bldg Baltimore MD 21201 Tel (301) 539-6967

BELCHER, ALLISON VERNON, b. Eufla, Ala., Jan. 10, 1915; LL.B., Cumberland U.; J.D., Sanford U., Birmingham, Ala. Admitted to Tenn. bar, 1941, Ga. bar, 1941; practiced in LaGrange, Ga., 1949-65, Greenville, Ga., 1965-72; judge Ga. State Ct. in Troup County, 1972—. Mem. Ga., Am. bar assns. Home: PO Box 281 Upper Big Springs La Grange GA 30240 Office: Ct Square Greenville GA 30222 Tel (404) 882-6931

BELCHER, NATHANIEL LEE, b. Plymouth, N.C., Aug. 17, 1929; A.B., N.C. Central U., 1952, LL.B., 1958, J.D., 1970. Admitted to N.C. bar, 1958; asso. firm C.J. Gates, 1958-61, Bumpass & Belcher, Durham, N.C., 1961-67; partner firm Bumpass, Belcher & Avant, Durham, 1967—. Trustee White Rock Bapt. Ch. Mem. Am., Nat., N.C., George White bar assn. Home: 1015 Red Oak Ave Durham NC 27707 Tel (919) 688-1705

BELDING, BRUCE WALTER, b. San Francisco, Feb. 27, 1936; A.B., U. Calif., Berkeley, 1958; J.D., U. Calif., San Francisco, 1963. Admitted to Calif. bar, 1964, U.S. Supreme Ct. bar, 1975; asso. firm Gray Cary Ames & Frye, San Diego, 1963-67; asso. firm Dinkelspiel & Dinkelspiel, San Francisco, 1967-69, partner, 1969—; lectr. U. Calif. Continuing Edn. of the Bar, 1972—. Bd. dirs. Convent of Good Shepherd, San Francisco, 1973—; mem. pub. affairs com. Aid to Retarded Citizens, San Francisco, 1974—; bd. dirs. Travelers Aid Soc. San Diego, 1966-69, 1st v.p., 1968-69. Mem. State Bar Calif., Am., San Francisco (chmn. com. bus. litigation 1975-76) bar assns., San Francisco Lawyers Club, Am. Judicature Soc., Hastings Alumni Assn. (bd. govs. 1972—), Am. Counsel Assn. (sec.-treas. 1974—), Order of Coif, Thurston Honor Soc., Phi Delta Phi, Phi Kappa Sigma (nat. exec. bd. 1971—). Editorial bd. Hastings Law Jour., 1962-63. Home: 77 San Jacinto Way San Francisco CA 94127 Office: Steuart St Tower One Market Plaza San Francisco CA 94105 Tel (415) 777-4700

BELIN, GASPARD D'ANDELOT, b. Scranton, Pa., May 30, 1918; B.A., Yale U., 1939, LL.B., 1946. Admitted to Mass. bar, 1947, U.S. Dist. Ct. bar, 1947; asso. firm Choate, Hall & Stewart, Boston, Mass., 1947-55, partner, 1955-62, 65—; gen. counsel U.S. Treas. Dept., 1962-65. City councillor, Cambridge, Mass., 1962; dir. New England Mchts. Nat. Bank, New England Mchts. Co.; v.p., Peter Bent Brigham Hosp.; trustee, Affiliated Hosps. Center, Museum of Science, Boston Athenaeum; mem. Council Com. on Med. Affairs, Yale U.; trustee Athenaeum; mem. Council Comm. on Med. Affairs, Yale U.; v.p. Yale Devel. Bd.; mem. Cambridge Indsl. Devel. Finance Bd.; mem. New England Com. NAACP Legal Defense Fund. Fellow Am. Acad. of Arts and Scis.; mem. Am., Mass., Boston bar assns. Home: 4 Willard St Cambridge MA 02138 Office: 28 State St Boston MA 02109 Tel (617) 5020

BELL, ALBERT LEO, b. Columbus, Ohio, May 22, 1930; B.J., Ohio State U., 1956, J.D., 1958. Admitted to Ohio bar, 1959, U.S. Supreme Ct. bar, 1975; individual practice law, Columbus, 1959-64, 65-71; referee Franklin County Probate Ct., 1964-65; counsel Ohio Bar Assn., Columbus, 1971—. Active, U.S. Power Squadron, Forest Park Civic Assn., YMCA Indian Guides. Mem. Nat. Orgn. Bar Counsel (pres. 1975—), Am., Ohio, Columbus bar assns., Ohio State U. (life), St. Charles Borromeo (pres. 1963) alumni assns., Sigma Delta Chi, Phi Delta Phi. Home: 1743 Sandalwood Pl Columbus OH 43229 Office: 33 W 11th Ave Columbus OH 43201 Tel (614) 421-2121

BELL, ALEXANDER WAYNE, b. Lubbock, Tex., Jan. 20, 1944; B.A., Duke, 1966; J.D., U. Tex., 1969. Admitted to Tex. bar, 1969, Va. bar, 1974; law clk. to U.S. Dist. Judge Jack Roberts, Austin, Tex., 1969-70; asst. prof. law U. Va., Charlottesville, 1970-73, asso. prof., 1973-75, vis. asso. prof., 1975-76; partner firm Bell, Coward, Morrison & Spies, Lynchburg, Va., 1976—; cons. to Adminstrv. Conf. U.S., 1972-75. Mem. Am., Va., Lynchburg bar assns. Contbr. articles to profl. jours. Office: 715 Court St POB 739 Lynchburg VA 24505 Tel (804) 528-0411

BELL, CHARLES THOMAS, b. Carthage, Ill., Dec. 20, 1915; B.A., Carthage Coll., 1937; postgrad Coll. Law, U. Ill., 1937-38; pvt. studies law, 1938-40. Admitted to Ill. bar, 1941, U.S. Supreme Ct. bar, 1970; partner firm Scofield & Bell, Carthage, 1941-65; individual practice law, Carthage, 1965—; asst. atty. gen. State of Ill., 1957-61. Bd. dirs. Coll. Ednl. Found., 1964-67; trustee, treas. Robert Morris Coll., 1965-68. Mem. Am., Ill. bar assns. Recipient Pres. citation for Selective Service work, 1951. Office: 416 Main St Carthage IL 62321 Tel (217) 357-2118

BELL, CLARENCE DESHONG, b. Upland, Pa., Feb. 4, 1914; B.A., Swarthmore Coll., 1935; J.D., Harvard U., 1938; grad. U.S. Army Command and Gen. Staff Coll., 1942. Admitted to Pa. bar, 1939; individual practice law, Chester, Pa., 1946-58; mem. firm Bell Harvey Pugh & Sinclair, Media, Pa., 1958-75, firm Bell & Bell, Media, 1975—; mem. Pa. State Senate, 1960—, chmn. judiciary com., 1966-70, minority chmn., 1971-75; mem. Pa. Ho. of Reps., 1954-60. Mem. Am., Pa., Delaware County bar assns. Decorated Legion of Merit; Pa. Distinguished Service medal, 1972, 74. Home: 400 W 24th St Upland PA 19013 Office: 40-50 W Front St Media PA 19063 Tel (215) 566-3100

BELL, DENNIS ARTHUR, b. Chgo., July 5, 1934; B.S. in Accounting, U. Ill., 1955; J.D., DePaul U., 1961. Admitted to Ill. bar, 1961; U.S. Supreme Ct. bar, 1964; auditor Peat, Marwick, Mitchell, Chgo., 1957-62; staff accountant, atty. SEC, D.C., 1962-65; group controller Nat. Student Mktg. Corp., Chgo., 1970-72; fin. advisor U.S. AID Mission to Turkey and Vietnam, 1965-68; counsel, dir. corporate fin. Rothschild Securities Corp., Chgo., 1973-75; corporate sec., asso.

gen. counsel MW Stock Exchange, MW Clearing Corp., MW Securities Trust Co., MW Stock Exchange Service Corp., Chgo., 1975—. Spl. event fundraiser Am. Cancer Soc., 1975, 76; fundraiser DePaul U. Law Sch., 1973. Mem. Ill. C.P.A. Soc., Am. Inst. C.P.A.'s, Chgo., Fed., Am. bar assns. Home: 1825 N Lincoln Plaza Chicago IL 60614 Office: 120 S LaSalle St Chicago IL 60603 Tel (312) 368-2569

BELL, GLEN HUGH, b. Sac City, Iowa, Aug. 1, 1902; B.A., U. Wis., 1925, LL.B., 1927, J.D., 1927. Admitted to Wis. bar, 1927, U.S. Supreme Ct. bar, 1940; partner firm Bell, Blake & Metzner, and predecessors, Madison, 1927—; lectr. law U. Wis., 1939-52; dir. Wis. So. Gas Co., NW Telephone Co. Bd. dirs. Dane County (Wis.) United Way, 1951, Univ. YMCA, 1949-58. Mem. Am., Wis. (pres. 1939), Fed. Power bar assns., Am. Coll. Trial Lawyers, Phi Beta Kappa, Order of Coif, Phi Alpha Delta, Delta Sigma Rho. Home: 3906 Cherokee Dr Madison WI 53711 Office: 222 W Washington Ave PO Box 1807 Madison WI 53701 Tel (608) 257-3764

BELL, GRIFFIN BOYETTE, b. Americus, Ga., Oct. 31, 1918; student Ga. Southwestern Coll.; LL.B. cum laude, Mercer U., 1948, LL.D., 1967. Admitted to Ga. bar, 1947; asso. firm Lawton & Cunningham, Savannah, 1948-52; partner firm Maddox & Bell, Rome, 1952-53; partner firm King & Spalding, Atlanta, 1953-59, mng. partner, 1959-61, partner, 1976; U.S. judge 5th Circuit, 1961-76; atty. gen. U.S., 1977—; hon. chief of staff Ga. Gov. Ernest Vandiver, 1959-61; chmn. Atlanta Commn. on Crime and Juvenile Delinquency, 1965-66; mem. com. on innovation and devel. Fed. Jud. Center, 1968-70, bd. dirs., 1973-76. Bd. deacons Second-Ponce de Leon Baptist Ch.; trustee Mercer U., Inst. for Continuing Legal Edn. in Ga., 1974—; mem. vis. com. Vanderbilt U. Law Sch. Mem. Am. Bar Assn. (commn. on standards of jud. adminstrn. 1971—), Am. Law Inst. Home: 3100 Habersham Rd NW Atlanta GA 30305 Office: Dept Justice Washington DC 20530 Tel (202) 739-2001

BELL, H. CLARK, b. Washington, Nov. 18, 1933; B.S., Georgetown U., 1957; George Washington U., 1961. Admitted to N.Y., Bar, 1962, U.S. Supreme Ct. bar, 1967; mem. staff Congressman J. Earnest Wharton, Catskill Mountains, N.Y., 1953-54, Senator Herbert H. Lehman, N.Y.C., 1954-57, Evening Star Newspaper, Washington, 1958; staff mem. CIA, 1958-61; research counsel N.Y. State Joint Legis. Com. on Study of Alcoholic Beverage Control Law, 1962-64; asso. counsel N.Y. State Select Bi-Partisan Com. on Off-Track Betting, 1964; counsel N.Y. Senate Com. on Affairs of City N.Y. sub-com. on N.Y. Waterfront Commn., 1965; partner firm St. John, Ronder and Bell, Kingston, N.Y., 1964—; mem. N.Y. State Assembly, 1968-74, chmn. com. spl. assembly personnel practices, 1971, chmn. select com. on laws affecting local govt., 1973-75; vice chmn. Temporary State Commn. on Water Supply Needs of Southeastern N.Y., 1970-75; dir. Colonial Coop. Ins. Co., 1974—. Mem. Republican 101st Assemlby Dist. State Com., 1969—; trustee State U. N.Y., New Paltz, 1974-76, Coll. at New Paltz Found., Inc., 1976—; mem. exec. com. Rip Van Winkle council Boy Scouts Am., 1974—; alt. del. Rep. Nat. Conv., 1976. Mem. N.Y. State, Ulster County (N.Y.), Am. bar assns., N.Y., Am. trial lawyers assns. Home: POB 734 Chimney Rd Woodstock NY 12498 Office: 280 Wall St Kingston NY 12401 Tel (914) 338-4500

BELL, JAMES FINLEY, b. London, Ohio, Jan. 12, 1915; A.B. DePauw U., 1936; LL.B., Ohio State U., 1939, J.D., 1959. Admitted to Ohio bar, 1939, Fla. bar, 1968; individual practice law, London, Ohio, 1939-42; spl. agent FBI, New Haven, N.Y.C., Louisville, 1942-46; judge Ct. Common Pleas, Madison County, Ohio, 1947-54; judge Supreme Ct. Ohio, Columbus, 1955-62; partner firm Power, Griffith, Jones & Bell, Columbus, 1962-70; v.p., gen. counsel Gen. Telephone Co. of Fla., Tampa, 1971—. Bd. edn. London (Ohio) schs., 1940-42. Mem. Ohio, Fla., Am. bar assns., Phi Delta Phi, Sigma Chi. Contbr. articles in field to mag. Home: 4215 Fairway Run Tampa FL 33624 Office: POB 110 Tampa FL 33601 Tel (813) 224-4001

BELL, JAMES FREDERICK, b. New Orleans, Aug. 5, 1922; A.B. cum laude, Princeton, 1943; LL.B., Harvard, 1948. Admitted to D.C. bar, 1949, U.S. Supreme Ct. bar, 1960, U.S. Ct. Appeals 7th Circuit bar, 1976; asso. firm Pogue & Neal, Washington, 1948-53; partner firm Jones, Day, Reavis & Pogue, Washington, 1953—. Mem. Fed., Am., D.C. bar assns., Bar Assn. D.C. Contbr. articles in field to profl. jours. Home: 5307 Elliott Rd NW Washington DC 20016 Office: 1100 Connecticut Ave NW Washington DC 20036 Tel (202) 452-5829

BELL, JOHN EDWARD, b. Paterson, N.J., Oct. 20, 1945; B.S., Xavier U., Cin., 1968; J.D., St. Louis U., 1971. Admitted to Mo. bar, 1971, U.S. Supreme Ct. bar, 1974; asst. pub. defender City of St. Louis, 1971-74; asso. firm Suelthaus, Krueger, Cunningham & Yates, P.C., and predecessor, Clayton, Mo., 1974—. Mem. Am. (criminal law and litigation sects.), Mo. bar assns. Asso. editor St. Louis U. Law Jour., 1970-71, contbr. article, 1969. Office: 7711 Carondelet Ave Suite 500 Clayton MO 63105 Tel (314) 727-7676

BELL, LEE JOHN, b. Little Falls, N.Y., Dec. 22, 1947; B.S., State U. N.Y., 1969; J.D., Ind. U., 1973. Admitted to Ohio bar, 1973; asso. firm Carson, Vogelesang, Sheehan and Howes, Canton, Ohio, 1973—; legal counsel Canton Jaycees, 1976—. Mem. Am., Ohio State, Stark County (social chmn.) bar assns., Am., Ohio State trial lawyers assns. Home: 125 17th St NW Canton OH 44703 Office: 424 Citizens Savings Bldg Canton OH 44703 Tel (216) 456-3483

BELL, MILDRED BAILEY, b. Sanford, Fla., June 28, 1928; A.B., U. Ga., 1950, J.D. cum laude, 1969; postgrad. N.Y.U., 1976. Admitted to Ga. bar, 1969; law clk. for Judge Newell Edenfield, U.S. Dist. Ct. No. Dist. Ga., Atlanta, 1969-70; asst. prof. law Mercer U. Law Sch., Macon, Ga., 1970-74, asso. prof., 1974-76, prof., 1977—. Mem. Am., Western Jud. Bar Assns., State Bar Ga., Phi Beta Kappa, Phi Kappa Phi. Mem. bd. editors Ga. State Bar Jour., 1974-76; contbr. articles to legal publs. Home: 240 Tanglewood Dr Athens GA 30601 Office: Mercer Univ Law Sch Macon GA 31207 Tel (912) 745-6811

BELL, PAUL BUCKNER, b. Charlotte, N.C., July 29, 1922; B.S., Wake Forest U., 1947, J.D., 1948. Admitted to N.C. bar, 1948, U.S. Patent Office bar, 1949, U.S. Supreme Ct. bar, 1971; pres. firm Bell, Seltzer, Park & Gibson, and predecessors, Charlotte, 1948—; guest lectr. patent law Wake Forest U. Sch. Law, 1974-77; lectr. Practising Law Inst., 1974. Pres. bd. trustees Alezander Children's Center; trustee Presbyn. Home Charlotte, Mountain Retreat Assn. Mem. Am., N.C., 26th Jud. bar assns., Am. Patent Law Assn., Licensing Execs. Soc., Sigma Phi Epsilon, Phi Alpha Delta. Office: 1211 E Morehead St Charlotte NC 28237

BELL, RICHARD CLIFTON, b. Albuquerque, Oct. 29, 1945; B.S., Clemson U., 1967; J.D., U.S.C., 1973; M.A. in Teaching, The Citadel, 1976. Admitted to S.C. bar, 1974; asso. firm Lourie, Draine, & Curlee, Columbia, S.C., 1974-76; individual practice law, Mt. Pleasant, S.C., 1976—; asst. solicitor Ninth Jud. Circuit, 1977. Mem. Am. Judicature Soc., Am., S.C. trial lawyers assns., Am. Bar Assn. Address: PO Box 985 Mt Pleasant SC 29464 Tel (803) 884-5103

BELL, RICHARD GORDON, b. Bedford, Ohio, Jan. 31, 1928; A.B., U. Ky., 1949; J.D., Case Western Reserve U., 1951, LL.M., 1961. Admitted to Ohio bar, 1951, N.C. bar, 1967; partner firm Ralph W. & Richard G. Bell, Bedford, 1951-65; asso. prof. law Wake Forest U., Winston-Salem, N.C., 1965-67, prof. law, 1967—. Mem. N.C., Ohio, Forsyth County bar assns. Contbr. articles in field to profl. jours. Home: 104 Belle Vista Court Winston-Salem NC 27106 Office: Box 7206 Winston-Salem NC 27109 Tel (919) 761-5430

BELL, ROBERT SAMUEL, b. Milw., May 29, 1915; A.B., U. Calif., Los Angeles, 1937; J.D., Harvard, 1940, D.Sc. (hon.), Heald Coll. Engring., 1957. Admitted to Calif. bar, 1940; asso. firm Gibson, Dunn & Crutcher, Los Angeles, 1939-41; served with JAGC, USAAF, Japan, 1943-46; spl. asst. U.S. Supreme Ct. Justice T.C. Clark, 1941-43; owner, mgr. Burnham Mfg. Co., Los Angeles, 1947; asst. to pres. Packard Bell Electronics, Los Angeles, 1947-48, v.p., 1949, exec. v.p., gen. mgr., 1950-54, pres., chief exec. officer, 1955-60, chmn. bd., pres., 1961-64, chmn., chief exec. officer, 1964-67; v.p. Teledyne, Los Angeles, 1968—; dir. Gen. Telephone Co. Calif. Bd. dirs. Kennedy Child Care Center, Studio Watts Workshop, Calif. Mus. Found.; bd. regents St. John's Hosp., Santa Monica, 1953—; trustee City of Hope, Duarte, Calif., 1956—; chmn. bequest and deferred giving com. Los Angeles County Heart Assn., 1970, heart attack intervention systems com., 1974, dir. 1970—; mem. research com. Am. Heart Assn., 1975-76; v.p. Great Western council Boy Scouts Am., 1953; bd. dirs. Orthopaedic Hosp. Los Angeles, 1976—, Los Angeles Mus. Sci. and Industry, 1976—. Mem. Judge Advs. Assn., Air Force Hist. Assn., Newcomen Soc. N.Am., Radio Pioneers So. Calif., DeForest Pioneers, Navy League, Def. Orientation Conf. Assn., Beverly Hills Wine and Food Soc., Confrerie des Chevaliers du Tastevin, Commanderie de Bordeaux, Confrerie de la Chaine des Rotissiers, Phi Kappa Sigma, Beta Gamma Sigma. Office: 1901 Ave of the Stars Los Angeles CA 90067 Tel (213) 277-3311

BELL, ROSALYN BLAKE, b. Trenton, N.J., Apr. 22, 1923; B.S., Simmons Coll., Boston, 1944; J.D., Nat. U., 1951. Admitted to D.C. bar, 1951, Md. bar, 1965; individual practice law, Washington, 1951-67; partner firm Raysor, Ortman, Barbour Welch & Bell, Washington, 1967-71, firm Raysor, Barbour & Bell, Chevy Chase, Md., 1971-75; partner/pres. firm Bell, Bell, & Bell, Silver Spring, Md., 1975—. Trustee Tokoma Park-Silver Springs Community Found., 1973—. Mem. Mont. Bar Assn., Md. State Bar (gov. 1976—), Women's Bar Md., Women's Bar D.C. (Lawyer of Year 1975). Home: 16301 Dustin Ct Burtonsville MD 20730 Office: 8630 Fenton St Silver Spring MD 20910 Tel (301) 585-6272

BELL, STEWART LYNN, b. Los Angeles, Feb. 6, 1945; B.S. in Bus. Adminstrn., U. Nev., Las Vegas, 1967; J.D., U. Calif., Los Angeles, 1970. Admitted to Caif. bar, 1971, Nev. bar, 1971; law clk to judge Nev. Dist. Ct., Las Vegas, 1970-71; dept. pub. defender Clark County (Nev.), 1971-72; asso. counsel firm Bell & LeBaron, Las Vegas, 1972-73; sr. partner Bell, Leavitt & Green, Las Vegas, 1974—. Mem. Nev., Calif., Clark County bar assns., Phi Kappa Phi. Office: 601 E Bridger Ave Las Vegas NV 89101 Tel (702) 382-5111

BELL, THEODORE MICHAEL, b. Shanghai, China, Jan. 11, 1941; came to U.S., 1957; A.B., U. Calif., Berkeley, 1961, J.D., 1964. Admitted to Calif. bar, 1967; partner firm Dubrow and Bell, Beverly Hills, Calif., 1961-70; partner firm Scheinman and Bell, Los Angeles, 1971—. Mem. Am., Los Angeles County, Beverly Hills bar assns., State Bar Calif. Contbr. articles to legal jours. Office: 1888 Century Park E Suite 1112 Los Angeles CA 90067 Tel (213) 553-5572

BELL, THOMAS ALVIN, b. Grenada, Miss., Jan. 1, 1922; B.A., U. Miss., 1949, LL.B., 1949, J.D., 1968. Admitted to Miss. bar, 1949, U.S. Supreme Ct. bar, 1972; pros. atty. Grenada County (Miss.), 1950-51; individual practice law, Grenada, 1953-62; sr. partner firm Daniel, Coker, Horton, Bell & Dukes, Jackson, Miss., 1962—; city judge Grenada, 1956-62; prof. Jackson Sch. Law, 1963-75, Miss. Coll. Law Sch., 1975-76. Mem. Internat. Assn. Ins. Counsel, Miss. Def. Lawyers Assn., Fed. Bar Assn., Am. Judicature Soc., Phi Alpha Delta. Home: 4120 Northeast Dr Jackson MS 39211 Office: 405 Tombigbee St Jackson MS 39205 Tel (601) 352-7600

BELL, THOMAS DYE, b. Boonville, Mo., Jan. 2, 1946; B.A., Williams Coll., 1968; J.D., U. Wis., 1971. Admitted to Wis. bar, 1971, Minn. bar, 1972; law clk. to Earl R. Larson, U.S. Dist. Ct. judge, Minn., 1971-72; partner firm Doar, Drill, Norman, Bakke, Bell & Skow, New Richmond, Wis., 1972—; counsel to com. on judiciary of U.S. Ho. of Reps. 93d Congress, 1974. Mem. Am., Wis., St. Croix County bar assns., Am. Trial Lawyers Assn., Ins. Trial Counsel Wis., Order of the Coif. Contbr. articles in field to profl. jours.; mem. editorial bd. Wis. Law Rev., 1970-71. Home: RFD 2 New Richmond WI 54017 Office: 103 N Knowles Ave New Richmond WI 54017 Tel (715) 246-2211

BELL, WILLIAM HENRY, b. Yenangyaung, Burma, Dec. 15, 1926; B.A., Duke, 1947; B.B.A., Tex. Agrl. and Indsl. U., 1950; J.D., U. Tulsa, 1954; L.H.D., Okla. Christian Coll., 1973. Admitted to Okla. bar, 1954; partner firm Rogers and Bell, Tulsa, 1954—; atty. Chapman-McFarlin-Barnard Interests; mem. Okla. State Hwy. Commn., 1969-74. Trustee U. Tulsa, Trinity U., John Brown U., Phillips U., Southwestern Legal Found., Hillcrest Med. Center, Tulsa, Tulsa Edn. Found.; bd. dirs. Okla. Med. Research Found., Bank of Okla., Okla. Heritage Assn. Fellow Am. Bar Found., Am. Coll. Probate Counsel, Southwestern Legal Found.; mem. Tulsa County (past pres.), Okla. (pres. elect), Am. (chmn. com. youth edn. for citizenship) bar assns., Fed. Power Bar Assn. Recipient Distinguished Service award U.S. Jr. C. of C., 1961, Boys' Club medallion Boys' Clubs Am., 1962; named Man of Year Downtown Tulsa Unltd., 1973; named to Okla. Hall of Fame, 1974. Office: 320 S Boston St suite 801 Tulsa OK 74103 Tel (918) 582-5201

BELLACOSA, JOSEPH WILLIAM, b. Bklyn., Sept. 1, 1937; B.A., St. John's U., 1959; LL.B., 1961, J.D., 1965. Admitted to N.Y. State bar, 1961; staff gen. counsel's office N.Y. Life Ins. Co., N.Y.C., 1961-63; law sec. to appellate div. N.Y. Supreme Ct., Bklyn., 1963-70; prof. law, asst. dean St. John's U., Hillcrest, N.Y., 1970-75; chief clk. N.Y. State Ct. Appeals, Albany, 1975—. Mem. Am., N.Y. State, Nassau County bar assns., Am. Law Inst. Home: 8 Leda Ln Guilderland NY 12084 Office: Ct of Appeals Hall Eagle St Albany NY 12207 Tel (518) 474-3211

BELLAMY, GIL WORTHINGTON, b. Oregon City, Oreg., July 14, 1943; B.S. (Univ. scholar), U. So. Calif., 1965; J.D., Willamette U., 1969. Admitted to Oreg. bar, 1970; law clk. Oreg. Legis. Counsel's Office, Salem, 1967-69; judge pro tem McMinnville Municipal Ct., 1976; guest lectr. Willamette U. Coll. Law, Salem; adminstr. Oreg. Traffic Safety Commn., Salem, 1969—; mem. transp. research bd. Nat. Acad. Scis. Exec. dir. Oreg. Trauma Soc., 1976—. Mem. Oreg. State, Am. bar assns. Named Jr. 1st Citizen of Salem, Salem Jr. C. of C., 1977. Home: 2945 Island View Dr Salem OR 97303 Office: 895 Summer St NE Salem OR 97310 Tel (503) 378-3669

BELLAMY, HOWELL VAUGHT, JR., b. Conway, S.C., Oct. 2, 1936; A.B., Davidson Coll., 1959; LL.B., U. S.C., 1959. Admitted to S.C. bar, 1962; partner firm Bellamy, Rutenberg, Copeland, Epps, Gravely & Bowers, Myrtle Beach, S.C., 1962—. Mem. Am., Horry County bar assns. Home: 5706 Long Leaf Dr Myrtle Beach SC 29577 Office: suite 303 Myrtle Offices 16th Ave N and Oak St Myrtle Beach SC 29577 Tel (803) 448-2406

BELLI, MELVIN MOURON, b. Sonora, Calif., July 29, 1907; A.B., U. Calif. at Berkeley, 1929, LL.B., 1933; J.D. (hon.), New Eng. Sch. Law. Admitted to Calif. bar, 1933; sr. partner firm Belli & Choulos, and predecessors, San Francisco, 1940—, Los Angeles, 1968—; condr. Belli Seminars in Law, 1953—; pres. Belli Found. Lectrs., 1960—. Mem. Calif. Bldg. Standards Commn.; bd. dirs. Disability and Casualty Inter-Ins. Exchange, N.W. Affairs Council. Fellow Internat. Acad. Trial Lawyers (dir., past dean); mem. Authors Guild, Am. Acad. Forensic Scis., Tuolumne County Hist. Soc., Inter-Am., Am., Calif., San Francisco, Fed., Internat. (patron) bar assns., Internat. Legal Aid Assn., San Diego, Hollywood, Beverly Hills bar assns., Am. Trial Lawyers Assn. (past pres., chmn. torts sect. 1959, asso. editor Law Jour. 1950—), Barristers Club San Francisco (past dir.), Lawyers Club San Francisco, La Asociacion Nacional de Abogados Mexico (hon.), Société Droit (pres.), Phi Delta Phi, Delta Tau Delta. Named dean emeritus Coll. Law, Riverside U.; decorated grand ofcl. St. Brigidian Order; author: Modern Trials and Modern Damages, 6 vols., 1954, abridged edit., 1962; Ready for the Plaintiff, 1956; Trial and Tort Trends, 14 vols., 1954-62; The Adequate Award, 1953; Demonstrative Evidence and the Adequate Award, 1955; Malpractice, 1955; Modern Trials (student edit.); (with Danny Jones) Life and Law in Russia; Life and Law in Japan; (with Maurice Carroll) Dallas Justice, 1964; The Law Revolt, 2 vols., 1968; Melvin Belli: My Life on Trial, 1976; adv. editor Negligence and Compensation Service, 1955—; legal adv. bd. Traumatic Medicine and Surgery for the Atty., 1958—; contbr. articles to legal jours., also syndicated column So That's The Law. Home: San Francisco CA Office: Belli Bldg 722 Montgomery St San Francisco CA 94133 also 6300 Wilshire Blvd Los Angeles CA 90048 Tel (415) 981-1849

BELLINGER, EDGAR THOMSON, b. N.Y.C., Sept. 3, 1929; B.A., Haverford Coll., 1951; J.D., George Washington U., 195S. Admitted to D.C. bar, 1955, Md. bar, 1955; law clk. U.S. Dist. Ct. for D.C., 1955-57; asst. U.S. atty. for D.C., 1957-59; partner firm Pope, Ballard & Loos, Washington, 1959—; chmn. com. unauthorized practice of law D.C. Ct. Appeals, 1972—, also mem. organizational com. for D.C. bar, mem. Jud. Conf. D.C., Jud. Conf. D.C. Circuit. Bd. dirs. D.C. chpt. ARC; mem. corp. bd. Children's Hosp. D.C. Mem. Am., D.C., Md., Montgomery County bar assns., D.C. Bar (orgnl. com. 1971), Am. Judicature Soc. Office: 888 17th St NW Washington DC 20006 Tel (202) 298-8600 also 22 W Jefferson St Rockville MD 20850 Tel (301) 424-5420

BELLONI, ROBERT CLINTON, b. Riverton, Oreg., Apr. 4, 1919; B.A., U. Oreg., 1941, LL.B., 1951. Admitted to Oreg. bar, 1951; individual practice law, Coquille, 1951-52; partner firm Belloni, Engelgau & Jones, Coquille, 1952-57; judge Oreg. Circuit Ct. for Coos and Curry Counties, 1957-67; judge U.S. Dist. Ct., 1967—, chief judge, 1971—; councilman City of Myrtle Point (Oreg.), 1953-55, mayor, 1955-57; mem. planning com., faculty continuing edn. for experienced judges Fed. Jud. Center; mem. liaison com. 9th Circuit Dist. and Circui Judges; mem. Fed. Jud. Center Com. to Study Prisoner Petition Cases, 1973—. Mem. Am., Oreg. bar assns., 9th Circuit Judges Assn. (sec.-treas. 1975-76). Robert C. Belloni Boys' Ranch named by Coos County Bd. Commrs., 1968. Office: 612 US Courthouse Portland OR 97205 Tel (503) 221-2242

BELLOTTI, FRANCIS XAVIER, b. Dorchester, Mass., May 3, 1923; A.B., Tufts Coll., 1947; LL.B., Boston Coll., 1952. Admitted to Mass. bar, 1952, U.S. Supreme Ct. bar, 1965; individual practice law, Quincy, 1952-74; lt. gov. Mass., 1963-64; atty. gen. Mass., 1975—; chmn. Criminal History System Bd., Com. on Criminal Justice, Organized Crime Control Council, Com. on Privacy and Consumer Rights. Fellow Am. Coll. Trial Lawyers; mem. Nat. Assn. Def. Lawyers in Criminal Cases, Am. Trial Lawyers Assn. (dir. Mass. chpt.), New Eng. Law Inst., Am. Judicature Soc., Justinian Law Soc. Office: One Ashburton Pl Boston MA 02108 Tel (617) 727-2200

BELLOWS, CAROLE KAMIN, b. Chgo., May 24, 1935; B.A., U. Ill., 1957; J.D., Northwestern U., 1960. Admitted to Ill. bar, 1960; law clk. Chief Justice Ill. Ct. of Claims, Chgo., 1962-72; partner Bellows & Bellows, Chgo., 1970—. Recipient Maurice Weigle award for outstanding service to organized bar, 1970, U. Ill. Mothers Assn. medallion of honor, 1975. Fellow Am. Bar Found.; mem. Am. (sec. 1967-73, chmn. sect. individual rights and responsibilities 1975—, mem. ho. of dels., 1975—), Ill. (chmn. Bill of Rights com. 1965-67, bd. govs. 1969—, 2d v.p. 1975-76, pres. 1977-78), Chgo. (chmn. constl. revision com. 1973-74) bar assns., Am. Law Inst., League Women Voters of Ill., Womens Bar Assn. Ill., Decalogue Soc. Editor: Your Bill of Rights, 1967, 69. Home: 725 LaPorte St Wilmette IL 60091 Office: 1 IBM Plaza Chicago IL 60611 Tel (312) 467-1750*

BELLWOOD, SHERMAN J(EAN), b. Sugar City, Idaho, June 13, 1917; B.A., U. Idaho, 1938; J.D., U. Mich., 1941; grad. Nat. Coll. State Judiciary U. Nev., Reno, 1969, 75. Admitted to Idaho bar, 1942; practiced in Hailey, Ketchum and Sun Valley, Idaho, 1942-47; served detached duty Judge Adv. Gen. Corps, U.S. Army, San Francisco, 1943-44, Philippines, 1945-46; partner firms Baker & Bellwood, Rupert, Idaho, 1947-48, Bellwood & Goodman, Rupert, 1954-57, 60-66; individual practice law, Rupert, 1948-54; judge Dist. Ct., 5th Jud. Dist. of Idaho, 1957-60, 60—; city atty. City of Rupert, 1947-57, 60-66; pros. atty. Minidoka County (Idaho), 1951-57. Mem. Idaho State Bar (commr. and pres. 1957-60), Am. Bar Assn. (ho. of dels. 1958-59, 61-66), Am. Judicature Soc., Nat. Conf. State Trial Judges, Nat. Conf. Conciliation Cts., Am. Judges Assn. Named Distinguished Citizen, Idaho Statesman, Boise, 1970; recipient Annual Chase Clark Meml. award Idaho VFW, 1971. Office: Courthouse Ruper ID 83350 Tel (208) 436-9041

BELLY, ARMANDO TROCONIS, b. Trenton, N.J., Nov. 27, 1946; B.A., U. Pitts., 1968; J.D., N.Y. U., 1972. Admitted to N.Y. bar, 1973; asso. firm Willkie Farr & Gallagher, N.Y.C., 1972—. Mem. N.Y., N.Y.C. bar assns. Office: Willkie Farr & Gallagher 1 Chase Manhattan Plaza New York City NY 10003 Tel (212) 248-1000

BELMAR, WARREN, b. N.Y.C., May 1, 1942; B.A. cum laude, Bklyn. Coll., 1963; LL.B. cum laude, Columbia U., 1966. Admitted to N.Y. State bar, 1967, D.C. bar, 1968; law clk. U.S. Ct. Appeals for the Dist. of Columbia Circuit, 1966-67; atty. Office of Legal Counsel U.S.

Dept. Justice, 1967-69; asso. Dickstein, Shapiro & Galligan, Washington, 1969-72; asso. firm Arent, Fox, Kintner, Plotkin & Kahn, Washington, 1972-76, partner, 1977; partner firm Fulbright & Jaworski, Washington, 1977—. Mem. Am., (chmn. emergency econ. controls com. sect. of adminstrv. law 1974), D.C., Fed. bar assns. Office: 1150 Connecticut Ave NW Washington DC 20036 Tel (202) 452-6800

BELSER, TOWNSEND MIKELL, JR., b. Columbia, S.C., Apr. 30, 1937; B.Chem.Engring., Ga. Inst. Tech., 1958; LL.B., George Washington U., 1965. Nuclear propulsion engr. naval reactors br. AEC, Washington, 1958-62; patent asst. firm Cushman, Darby & Cushman, Washington, 1962-65; admitted to S.C. bar, 1965, U.S. Patent Office bar, 1966, U.S. Supreme Ct. bar, 1969, D.C. bar, 1974; asso. firm Belser, Baker, Belser, Barwick & Toal and predecessor, Columbia, 1965-67, partner, 1968—; with JAGC, USNR, 1967—; instr. in law U. S.C., 1973; real estate broker, Columbia, 1973—. Chmn. kindergarten com. Temple Bapt. Ch., Columbia, 1976—. Mem. Richland County (S.C.), Am. bar assns., S.C. Bar, D.C. Bar, Am. Patent Law Assn., Am. Judicature Soc., Supreme Ct. Hist. Soc., Delta Theta Phi. Home: 407 Prince Wales Dr Columbia SC 29209 Office: 1213 Lady St POB 11848 Columbia SC 29211 Tel (803) 799-9091

BELSON, JAMES ANTHONY, b. Milw., Sept. 23, 1931; A.B., Georgetown U., 1953, J.D., 1956, LL.M., 1962. Admitted to D.C. bar, 1956, Md. bar, 1962, U.S. Supreme Ct. bar, 1967; law clk. to Judge D.C. Circuit U.S. Ct. of Appeals, 1956-57; officer JAGC U.S. Army, 1957-60; asso. firm Hogan & Hartson, Washington, 1960-66, partner, 1967-68; judge D.C. Superior Ct. (formerly D.C. Ct. Gen. Sessions), 1968—; faculty Nat. Coll. State Judiciary, 1973, 75, 77. Mem. Am., D.C. (chmn. jr. bar sect. 1965-66, dir. 1966-67, chmn. legal aid com. 1967-68, nat. award for chmn. jr. bar sect. 1966) bar assns., Fed. Jud. Conf. D.C. (com. civil legal aid 1967-73, com. implementation of standards for criminal justice 1972-73), Am. Judicature Soc., World Peace Through Law Center. Home: 2220 46th St Washington DC 20007 Office: 451 Indiana Ave NW Washington DC 20001 Tel (202) 727-1700

BELSTNER, RAYMOND EDWARD, b. Chgo., May 29, 1941; J.D., U. Ill., 1966. Admitted to Ill. bar, 1967, U.S. Supreme Ct. bar, 1973; labor relations asst. Ill. Central Gulf R.R., Chgo., 1966-68, atty., 1968-74, gen. atty., 1974—. Mem. Am., Ill., Chgo. bar assns., Am. Trial Lawyers Assn., Nat. Assn. R.R. Trial Counsel, Am. Arbitration Assn. Home: 900 Dewitt St Chicago IL 60611 Office: 233 N Michigan Ave Chicago IL 60601 Tel (312) 565-1600

BELSTOCK, LEE JAY, b. Denver, May 17, 1941; B.A., U. Colo., Boulder, 1963, J.D., 1966. Admitted to Colo. bar, 1966, U.S. Dist. Ct. Colo. bar, 1966, U.S. Supreme Ct. bar, 1974; law clk. U.S. Dist. Ct. Colo., Denver, 1968-69; asso. firm Edison and Berman, Denver, 1969-70; asso. firm Towney and Smith, Westminster, Colo., 1970-71; chief appellate dep. pub. defender State of Colo., Denver, 1974—; vol. U.S. Peace Corps., 1966-68; participant Des Moines Project coordinating community corrections Nat. Inst. Law Enforcement and Criminal Justice, Casper, Wyo., 1975. Mem. Denver East Central Civic Assn. Mem. Colo. Trial Lawyers Assn., Nat. Legal Aid and Defender Assn., Colo. Bar Assn., Phi Alpha Delta. Contbr. articles to law jours. Home: 650 Adams Denver CO 80206 Office: 1575 Sherman Suite 719 Denver CO 80203 Tel (303) 892-2665

BELT, WILLIAM ALVIN, b. Kenton, Ohio, July 13, 1903; A.B., Ohio Wesleyan U., 1924; J.D., U. Mich., 1927. Admitted to Ohio bar, 1928; partner firm Marshall Melborn Black & Belt, Toledo, 1933-76; counsel Marshall Melborn Cole Hummer & Spitzer, 1977—; dir. emeritus Toledo Trust Co., Champion Spark Plug Co. Mem. Ohio, Toledo, Am. bar assns., Am. Assn. Trial Lawyers. Home: 5602 Ryan Rd Toledo OH 43614 Office: 1434 Nat Bank Bldg Toledo OH 43604 Tel (419) 243-4200

BELTRAMO, MARIO LOUIS, JR., b. San Francisco, Feb. 4, 1947; B.A., U. San Francisco, 1969; J.D. with honors, U. Notre Dame, 1972. Admitted to Calif. bar, 1972; partner firm McCormick, Barstow, Sheppard, Coyle & Wayte, Fresno, Calif., 1972—. Bd. dirs. Notre Dame Law Sch., 1973—. Mem. Am., Calif., Fresno County bar assns., Assn. No. Calif. Def. Counsel, Fresno County Barristers (sec.-treas. 1975-76). Office: 1171 Fulton Mall Fresno CA 93721 Tel (209) 442-1150

BELUE, CLARENCE THOMAS, b. Cheyenne, Wyo., Mar. 16, 1942; B.S., Brigham Young U., 1966; J.D., U. Mont., 1969. Admitted to Mont. bar, 1969, U.S. Supreme Ct. bar, 1975; individual practice law, Hardin, Mont., 1969—; dep. atty. Big Horn County, Mont., 1970-74; U.S. Magistrate, Hardin, 1972—. Commr., Hardin Govt. Study, 1975—. Mem. Am., Mont. bar assns. Home: 502 W 2d St Hardin MT 59034 Office: 201 W 4th St Hardin MT 59034 Tel (406) 665-1161

BELZ, BOB, b. Chgo., Mar. 6, 1936; A.A., Lamar Jr. Coll., 1960; B.A., U. Okla., 1963; J.D., Humphreys Coll., 1972. Admitted to Calif. bar, 1973, U.S. Dist. Ct. for Eastern Dist. Calif. bar, 1973; individual practice law, Stockton, Calif., 1973—. Chmn. finance campaign 49er Council Boy Scouts Am., Manteca, Calif. Mem. Am. Bar Assn., Calif. (state dir. 1976-77, chpt. pres. 1976-77), Am. trial lawyers assns., Nu Beta Epsilon (pres. Baker chpt. 1971-72). Home: 455 Curtwood Ct Manteca CA 95336 Office: 211 E Weber St Stockton CA 95202 Tel (209) 465-3478

BELZER, JEFFREY A., b. Mpls., Sept. 8, 1941; B.A., St. Cloud State Coll., 1963; J.D., Drake U., 1968. Admitted to Minn. bar, 1968; asso. firm Henretta, Muirhead & McGinty, Ltd., Mpls., 1968-71; pres., sr. mem. Belzer & Brenner, Ltd., and predecessor, Mpls., 1971—; pres. Walesch Devel. Co., Mpls., 1969—, pres. Walesch Estates, Inc., 1971—. Mem. Am., Minn., Hennepin County (Minn.) bar assns. Staff, Drake Law Rev., 1967-68. Office: 7200 France Ave S Suite 337 Minneapolis MN 55435 Tel (612) 927-5664

BENAKIS, GUS NICK, b. Chgo., July 3, 1934; B.S., U. Wis., 1956; LL.B., Harvard, 1959. Admitted to Minn. bar, 1959; asso. firm Fredrickson, Byron, Calborn and Hanson, 1959-62; exec. v.p. firm Mathieu & Benakis, Inc., Mpls., 1962—. Home: 7004 Sally Ln Edina MN 55435 Office: 4930 W 77th St Minneapolis MN 55435 Tel (612) 835-5090

BENASSI, JAMES PATRICK, b. Frankfort, Ky., Aug. 13, 1947; B.B.A., U. Ky., 1969; J.D., U. Louisville, 1973. Admitted to Ky. bar, 1973; individual practice law, Frankfort, 1973—. Mem. Ky., Franklin County bar assns., Home: 215 Capital Ave Frankfort KY 40601 Office: 508 McClure Bldg Frankfort KY 40601 Tel (502) 223-3935

BENBOW, TERENCE HOWARD, b. Wyandotte, Mich., June 4, 1929; B.A. with honors, U. Mich., 1951; postgrad. Horace Rackham Grad. Sch., 1951-53; postgrad. (Fulbright scholar) U. Brussels, 1951-53; LL.B., Yale U., 1956. Admitted to N.Y. bar, 1957, U.S. Supreme Ct. bar, 1963; asso. firm Winthrop, Stimson, Putnam & Roberts, N.Y.C., 1956-67, partner, 1967—; instr. bus. law and econs. Bernard Baruch Sch. Bus. Adminstrn., Coll. City N.Y., Pace Coll., S.I. Community Coll. Bd. dirs. N.Y. Landmarks Conservancy, Inc.; vice chmn. Landmarks Preservation Commn. City N.Y. Mem. Assn. Bar City N.Y., Am., N.Y., N.Y. County bar assns. Book reviewer Banking Law Jour., 1976; contbr. articles in field to legal jours. Home: 245 Benedict Rd Staten Island NY 10304 Office: 40 Wall St New York City NY 10005 Tel (212) 943-0700

BENCH, LAWRENCE THOMAS, b. Wareham, Mass., Jan. 6, 1945; A.B., Boston Coll., 1966, J.D., 1969. Admitted to Mass. bar, 1969, U.S. Supreme Ct. bar, 1975; law clk. to asso. justice Supreme Jud. Ct. Mass., Boston, 1969-70; asst. atty. gen. Commonwealth of Mass., Boston, 1971-74; asso. counsel U. Mass., Boston, 1974—. Home: 2 Upland Rd W Arlington MA 02174 Tel (617) 723-7820

BENCKENSTEIN, JOHN HENRY, b. Detroit, Nov. 28, 1903; LL.B., U. Va., 1928, J.D., 1970. Admitted to Tex. bar, 1928, La. bar, 1948, U.S. Ct. Appeals, 1931, U.S. Dist. Ct. Western Dist. La., 1948, U.S. Supreme Ct. bar, 1952, others. Partner firm Benckenstein & Norvell, Beaumont, Tex., 1963—. Fellow Tex. Bar Found., Trial Attys. Am.; mem. Am., Tex. bar assns., State Bar Tex., Tex. Def. Counsel, Federation Ins. Counsel, Motor Carrier Counsel, Phi Delta Phi. Home: 2625 Gladys St Beaumont TX 77702 Office: 1305 Petroleum Bldg Beaumont TX 77701 Tel (713) 833-4300

BENDALIN, SHERMAN RAY, b. Phoenix, Mar. 1, 1941; B.A., Dartmouth, 1963; J.D., U. Ariz., 1969. Admitted to Ariz. bar, 1969, 9th Circuit Ct. of Appeals bar, 1972; asso. firm Gorey & Ely, Phoenix, 1969-70; individual practice law, Phoenix, 1971—. Active Valley Big Bros., Tucson and Phoenix, 1969—; bd. dirs. Phoenix South Community Mental Health Center, 1972—, pres., 1974—; bd. dirs. Ariz. Lung Assn., 1972—; mem. South Phoenix Planning Com., Phoenix Planning Commn. Mem. Am., Maricopa County (Ariz.) bar assns., State Bar Ariz., Assn. Trial Lawyers Am. Office: 114 W Adams St 707 Phoenix AZ 85003 Tel (602) 252-6033

BENDER, ANN WILLIAMS, b. Tulsa, Feb. 2, 1941; B.A., U. Tulsa, 1966; J.D., Stanford, 1970. Admitted to Calif. bar, 1970; individual practice law, Menlo Park, Calif., 1972-74; asso. firm Donegan, Logan & Bender, Palo Alto, Calif., 1975—. Mem. Santa Clara County Commn. Status Women, 1975-76, asst. chairperson, 1976; Mem. Calif., Palo Alto Area, Santa Clara County bar assns., Calif. Women Lawyers, Jr. League Palo Alto (dir. 1975-76), Palo Alto NOW (dir. 1975-76). Office: 801 Welch Rd Suite 101 Palo Alto CA 94304 Tel (415) 326-4262

BENDER, DAVID, b. Providence, Oct. 26, 1939; B.S., Brown U., 1961; postgrad. Cornell U., 1961-63; LL.B., U. Pa., 1968; LL.M., George Washington U., 1969, S.J.D., 1975. Admitted to D.C. bar, 1969, N.Y. State bar, 1971; engr. Ford Motor Co., 1963-65; mathematician Hughes Aircraft Co., 1965-66; research fellow Computers in Law Inst., George Washington U., 1968-70; asso. firm Malcolm A. Hoffmann, N.Y.C., 1970-75; atty. dept. patent litigations Western Electric Co., Inc., N.Y.C., 1975—. Mem. Am., N.Y. State bar assns., Am. Patent Law Assn. Home: 19 Hillside Ave Croton on Hudson NY 10520 Office: 222 Broadway New York City NY 10038 Tel (212) 571-2529

BENDER, HAROLD JOHNSON, b. Winston-Salem, N.C., Sept. 16, 1942; A.B., Greensboro Coll., 1966; J.D., U. N.C., 1969. Admitted to N.C. bar, 1969; since practiced in Statesville; asso. firm Collier, Harris & Homesley, 1969-70, partner firm McMillan & Bender, 1970-72, Pope, McMillan & Bender, 1972—; solicitor Iredell County Recorders Ct., 1970; city atty. City of Statesville, 1975—. Mem. Am., N.C. bar assns., Comml. Law League, Jaycees (pres. statesville 1973-74, legal counsel N.C. 1974-75). Home: 1108 Forest Park Dr Statesville NC 28677 Office: 309 Davie Ave Statesville NC 28677 Tel (704) 873-2131

BENDER, PAUL, b. Bklyn., May 31, 1933; A.B., Harvard, 1954, LL.B., 1957. Asso. firm Paul, Weiss, Rifkind, Wharton and Garrison, N.Y.C., 1957; admitted to D.C. bar, 1958, U.S. Supreme Ct. bar, 1966; law clk. judge Learned Hand U.S. Ct. Appeals 2d Circuit, N.Y.C., 1958-59, Justice Felix Frankfurter, U.S. Supreme Ct., 1959-60; prof. law U. Pa., 1960—; asst. to U.S. Solicitor-Gen., Washington, 1965-66; gen. counsel U.S. Commn. on Obscenity and Pornography, Washington, 1969-70; spl. counsel Fed. Election Commn., Washington, 1975—. Recipient certificate of merit Am. Bar Assn., 1972; author: (with N. Dorsen and B. Neuborne) Political and Civil Rights In The United States, 2 vols., 1976; contbr. articles on law to Harper's Mag., 1972—. Office: 3400 Chestnut St Philadelphia PA 19174 Tel (215) 243-7417

BENDER, RONALD ANDREW, b. Butte, Mont., Sept. 29, 1946; B.A. in Bus. Adminstrn. with honors, Carroll Coll., 1968; J.D. with honors, U. Mont., 1971. Admitted to Mont. bar, 1971; law clk. to chief judge U.S. Dist Ct. Dist. Mont., 1971-73; asso. firm Worden, Thane & Haines, Missoula, Mont., 1973—. Mem. Am., Mont., Western Mont. bar assns., Mont. Trial Lawyers (award 1970), Missoula Young Lawyers (pres. 1974), Phi Delta Phi. Contbr. articles to legal jours. Home: 408 Ben Hogan Dr Missoula MT 59801 Office: Savings Center Missoula MT 57801 Tel (406) 543-8251

BENDHEIM, ALICE LOEB, b. Ashland, Wis., Aug. 9, 1930; A.B., Miami (Ohio) U., 1952, M.A., State U. N.Y., Buffalo, 1957; J.D., Ariz. State U., 1973. Admitted to Ariz. bar, 1973; partner firm Bendheim & Mote, and predecessors, Phoenix, 1973—; mem. bd. dirs. Ariz. Center for Law in the Pub. Interest, 1974—; spl. commr. domestic relation Maricopa County Superior Ct. Mem. Am., Ariz., Maricopa County bar assns., Ariz. Civil Liberties Union (v.p. Ariz. chpt. 1972—). Contbr. articles to legal jour. Home: 11613 N 32nd Dr Phoenix AZ 84029 Office: 17 E Thomas Rd Phoenix AZ 85012 Tel (602) 274-3693

BENDURE, RANDALL SCOTT, b. Middletown, Ohio, Mar. 3, 1948; B.A., Ohio No. U., 1970, J.D., 1973. Admitted to Ohio bar, 1973; asso. firms Wilmer and Wilmer, Middletown, 1973, Arthur F. Graham, Tiffin, Ohio, 1974; individual practice law, Tiffin, 1975—. Pres. Tiffin Jaycees, 1975-76. Mem. Seneca Bar Assn. Office: 89 E Perry St Tiffin OH 44883 Tel (419) 448-8755

BENEDICT, RONALD LOUIS, b. Cin., Feb. 22, 1942; A.B. in Polit. Sci., U. Cin., 1964; J.D., Salmon P. Chase Coll. Law, 1968. Admitted to Ohio bar, 1968; asst. gen. counsel Ohio Nat. Life Ins. Co., Cin., 1969—; sec., compliance dir. O.N. Equity Sales Co., 1973—; sec. O. N. Investment Mgmt. Co., 1971—; sec. O. N. Fund, Inc., 1975—; mem. SEC rules com. Investment Co. Inst., 1976—; arbitrator for ct. of common pleas, Hamilton County, Ohio, 1976—. Certified Adult Christian Edn. Found., 1977; mem. tri-state Billy Graham Crusade Com., 1974—. Fellow Life Mgmt. Inst.; mem. Am., Ohio State, Cin. bar assns., Cin. Law Library Assn., Assn. Life Ins. Counsel. Home: 5874 Jessup Rd Cincinnati OH 45239 Office: 237 William H Taft Rd Cincinnati OH 45219 Tel (513) 861-3600

BENEFIEL, PHILIP B., b. Lawrenceville, Ill., June 25, 1923; J.D., U. Ill., 1949. Admitted to Ill. bar, 1949; state's atty. Lawrence County, Ill., 1949-52; city atty., Lawrenceville, 1961-65; mem. Ill. Senate, 1964-66; asso. judge 2d Jud. Circuit Ct. of Ill., Lawrenceville, 1968-71, circuit judge, 1971—, chief judge, 1975-77. Mem. Am., Ill., Lawrence County bar assns., Ill. Judges Assn. (pres. 1975). Recipient Best Legislators award Ind. Voters of Ill., 1965. Home: 333 Lincoln Dr Lawrenceville IL 62539 Office: Ct House Lawrenceville IL 62439 Tel (618) 943-5000

BENETAR, DAVID L., b. N.Y.C., Nov. 19, 1906; student N.Y. U., 1923-25; LL.B., Bklyn., Law Sch., 1928; postgrad. N.Y. U., 1928-29. Admitted to N.Y. bar, 1929, U.S. Supreme Ct. bar, 1963; since practiced in N.Y.C., partner firm Nordlinger, Riegelman, Benetar & Charney, 1933-70, Aranow, Brodsky, Bohlinger, Benetar & Einhorn, 1971—; prin. mediation officer, dir. disputes div., pub. panel mem. War Labor Bd. 1942-45; mem. Gov.'s Labor-Mgmt. Adv. Panel, N.Y. State Mediation Bd. 1969—. Bd. dirs. Econ. Devel. Council N.Y.C., 1968—; mem. labor relations com. U.S. C. of C., 1965-69. Recipient Edward Corsi Labor-Mgmt. Relations Inst. ann. award, 1976. Mem. Assn. Bar City N.Y. (chmn. com. on labor and social security legislation 1950-53, exec. com. 1957-60, vice chmn. grievance com. 1961-64, co-chmn. labor law sect. com. on post admission legal edn. 1969-73), N.Y. State (chmn. com. labor law 1959-63), Am. (labor law sect. 1965—), Fed. (chmn. labor com. Empire State chpt. 1971—) bar assns. Contbr. articles to legal jours. Home: 35 Sutton Pl New York City NY 10022 Office: 469 5th Ave New York City NY 10017 Tel (212) 889-1470

BENHAM, PAUL BURRUS, III, b. Memphis, Oct. 9, 1946; B.A., Vanderbilt U., 1968; J.D., U. Ark., 1971. Admitted to Ark. bar, 1971; law clk. to chief justice Ark. Supreme Ct., 1971-72; asso. firm Friday, Eldredge & Clark, Little Rock, 1972—. Mem. Am., Ark., Pulaski County bar assns. Home: 13815 Edgemond St Little Rock AR 72212 Office: First National Bldg 20th floor Little Rock AR 72201 Tel (501) 376-2011

BENJAMIN, WILLIAM MORRIS, b. Los Angeles, Feb. 7, 1947; B.A., U.S. Internat. Univ., 1969; J.D., Calif. Western U., 1973. Admitted to Calif. bar, 1976; individual practice law, San Diego, 1976—. Chmn. Common Cause, San Diego, 1975—. Mem. Am., Calif., San Diego County bar assns. Home: 2624 Worden St San Diego CA 92110 Office: 1200 3d Ave Suite 400 San Diego CA 92101 Tel (714) 235-6161

BENKARD, JAMES WILLARD BARTLETT, b. N.Y.C., Apr. 10, 1937; B.A., Harvard, 1959; LL.B., Columbia, 1963. Admitted to N.Y. State bar, 1963; asso. firm Davis Polk & Wardell, N.Y.C., 1963-66, 68-73, partner, 1973—; law sec. to Justice Charles D. Breitel, N.Y. Supreme Ct. Appellate Div., 1st Dept., 1966; law clk. to Judge Brietel, asso. judge N.Y. State Ct. Appeals, 1967. Mem. Bar Assn. City N.Y., Am. Bar Assn. Home: 1192 Park Ave New York City NY 10028 Office: 1 Chase Manhattan Plaza New York City NY 10005 Tel (212) HA 2-3400

BENNETT, CASLON KENT, b. Marshall, Ill., Dec. 27, 1911; B.S., U. Ill., 1933, LL.B., 1936. Admitted to Ill. bar, 1936; atty. City Marshall, 1936-42, 48-64; partner firm Bennett & Bennett, Marshall, 1938-68; asso. judge Ill. Circuit Ct., 5th Circuit, Marshall, 1968-70; judge, 1970—. Mem. Ill., Clark County bar assns. Home: RR 3 Box 310 Marshall IL 62441 Office: Court House Marshall IL 62441 Tel (217) 826-8713

BENNETT, EARL WARREN, b. Columbus, Ohio, Sept. 6, 1945; B.A., Otterbein Coll., 1967; J.D., U. Mich., 1969. Admitted to Mich. bar, 1970, Ohio bar, 1975; asst. pros. atty. City of Bay City (Mich.), 1970-72; pros. atty. City of Coldwater (Mich.), 1972; probate judge, 1972-75, dist. judge, Coldwater, 1975—. Office: Branch County Courthouse Coldwater MI 49036 Tel (517) 279-8411

BENNETT, ERNEST RAY, b. Gwinnett County, Ga., July 2, 1928; student in Bus. Adminstrn., Ga. State Coll., 1954; LL.B., John Marshall Law Sch., 1957. Admitted to Ga. bar, 1959, U.S. Dist. Ct. bar, 1976; supr., mgr., gen. mgr. computer services ops. Delta Air Lines, Inc., Atlanta, 1945-76. Deacon, tchr. Sunday sch. Corinth Baptist Ch., 1976—; comdr. Am. Legion Post 232, 1954. Mem. State Bar of Ga., Gwinnett County Bar Assn. Tel (404) 346-6246

BENNETT, HERBERT H., b. Cambridge, Mass., Dec. 18, 1928; A.B., Bowdoin Coll., 1950; LL.B., Boston U., 1953. Admitted to Maine, Mass. bars, 1954, U.S. Supreme Ct. bar, 1965; partner firm Bennett, Kelly & Zimmerman, Portland, Maine; dir. Casco Bank & Trust Co. Mem. Am., Maine, Cumberland County bar assns., Assn. Trial Lawyers Am. (assoc. editor 1963-65, chmn. home office and budget com. 1964—, chmn. com. on nat. awards 1967-68, chmn. labor law com. 1968, recipient citation of exceptional merit 1968), Roscoe Pound Am. Trial Lawyers Found. (trustee 1969, 1st v.p. 1971, pres. 1972-75, award for leadership, 1976), Am. Soc. Law and Medicine (dir.); New England Law Inst. Office: 482 Congress St Portland ME 04111 Tel (207) 773-4775

BENNETT, JACQUELINE DIANNE, b. LaGrange, Ga., Mar. 22, 1946; B.A., Clark Coll., 1967; J.D., Emory U., 1971. Admitted to Ga. bar, 1973; dir. community edn., staff atty. Atlanta Legal Aid Soc., 1971-73; regional gen. counsel OEO, 1973-74; dir. community edn., staff atty. Atlanta Legal Aid Soc., 1974-75, dir. paralegal unit, 1975—; cons. lay legal advocacy VISTA Tng. Center, Gen. Learning Corp., Atlanta, 1972-73. Bd. dirs. Ga. Vol. Lawyers for the Arts; mem. Mayor's Adv. Council on Employment and Tng.; mem. citizens recommending com. Atlanta Turnkey III Program, 1976. Mem. Am., Nat., Ga., Gate City, Fed. bar assns., Ga. Conf. Black Lawyers, Phi Alpha Delta. Recipient Incentive award for Outstanding Performance, OEO, 1974. Home: 1401 Bankhead Hwy NW Atlanta GA 30318 Office: 11 Pryor St SW Atlanta GA 30303 Tel (404) 524-5311

BENNETT, LYMAN H., b. Butte, Mont., Mar. 20, 1947; B.S. in Math., Mont. State U., 1969; J.D., U. Mont., 1972. Admitted to Mont. bar, 1972; partner firm Bennett & Bennett, Bozeman, Mont., 1972—; town atty. Town of Belgrade (Mont.), 1972—. Vestryman St. James Episcopal Ch., 1972-76. Mem. Mont., Gallatin County bar assns., Def. Research Inst. Recipient commendation Internat. Acad. Trial

Lawyers. Home: 318 N 17th Ave Bozeman MT 59715 Office: PO Box 460 24 W Main St Bozeman MT 59715 Tel (406) 587-4503

BENNETT, OLGA, b. Viroqua, Wis., May 5, 1908; B.A., U. Wis., 1928, LL.B., 1935. Admitted to Wis. bar, 1935; law clk. Supreme Ct. of Wis., Madison, 1936-41; individual practice law, Viroqua, 1941-70; judge Vernon County Ct., 1970-76; individual practice law, Viroqua, 1976—; city atty., Viroqua, 1944-46. Mem. Wis. (sec.-treas.), Vernon County bar assns., Am. Judicature Soc., The Benchers, Law Alumni Assn. Home: 322 N Dunlap Ave Viroqua WI 54665 Office: 210 N Main St Viroqua WI 54665 Tel (608) 637-3300

BENNETT, RAY CRAWFORD, b. Yuma, Ariz., June 5, 1930; B.A., Stanford, 1954; J.D., U. Calif., Los Angeles, 1959. Admitted to Calif. bar, 1960; partner firm Bennett & Alcaraz, and predecessor, Los Angeles, 1960-75; individual practice law, Los Angeles, 1976; prof. Mid-Valley Sch. Law, 1973—. Home: 3433 Green Vista Dr Encino CA 91436 Office: 624 S Grand Ave #2620 Los Angeles CA 90017 Tel (213) 624-4651

BENNETT, RICHARD ALLAN, b. Richmond, Va., Apr. 1, 1946; B.A., Golden Gate U., 1969; J.D., U. Calif., San Francisco, 1973. Admitted to Calif. bar, 1973; partner firm Jones & Bennett, Calistoga, Calif., 1973—; asst. city atty. City of Calistoga, 1976. Bd. dirs. Napa County (Calif.) chpt. Am. Cancer Soc., Napa County Legal Assistance Found. Mem. Calif. Trial Lawyers Assn., Criminal Cts., Lawyer-Pilots bar assns., Calif. Attys. Criminal Justice. Office: 1424 1/2 Lincoln Ave Calistoga CA 94515 Tel (707) 942-6212

BENNETT, ROBERT THOMAS, b. Columbus, Ohio, Feb. 8, 1939; B.S., Ohio State U., 1960; J.D., Cleve. Marshall Law Sch., 1967. Accountant, Ernst & Ernst, Cleve., 1960-63; admitted to Ohio bar, 1967; asst. chief dep. Cuyahoga County (Ohio) Auditor's Office, 1965-70; individual practice law, Cleve., 1970-72; exec. vice chmn. Cuyahoga County Republican Orgn., Cleve., 1972—; partner firm Bartunek, Bennett, Garofoli & Hill, Cleve., 1975—. Mem. Am., Ohio, Cleve., Cuyahoga County bar assns., Am. Inst. C.P.A.'s, Ohio, Cleve. socs. C.P.A.'s, Am. Soc. Atty.-C.P.A.'s, Home: 4800 Mastick Rd Fairview Park OH 44126 Office: 1300 E 9th St 1003 Bond Ct Bldg Cleveland OH 44114 Tel (216) 623-1400

BENNETT, ROBERT WILLIAM, b. Chgo., Mar. 30, 1941; B.A., Harvard, 1962, LL.B., 1965. Admitted to Ill. bar, 1965, U.S. Dist. Ct. for No. Dist. Ill. bar, 1965, U.S. 7th Circuit Ct. Appeals bar, 1965; legal asst. Hon. Nicholas Johnson FCC, Washington, 1966-67; OEO Reginald Heber Smith fellow Chgo. Legal Aid Bur., 1967-68; asso. firm Mayer, Brown & Platt, Chgo., 1968-69; asst. prof. law Northwestern U., 1969-71, asso. prof., 1971-74, prof., 1974—. Pres. Fund for Justice, Chgo., 1976—. Mem. Chgo. Council Lawyers (pres. 1971-72), Am. Bar Assn., Nat. Legal Aid and Defenders Assn. Author: (with others) Hornbook On Law of the Poor, 1973; Representing the Audience in Broadcast Proceedings, 1974; contbr. articles to legal jours. Office: 357 E Chicago Ave Chicago IL 60611 Tel (312) 649-8430

BENNETT, ROBERTS OSBORNE, b. Jacksonville, Fla., May 30, 1947; A.B., Harvard, 1969; J.D., Duke, 1972. Admitted to Fla. bar, 1972, Ga. bar, 1972, U.S. Dist. Ct. No. Dist. Ga. bar, 1972, U.S. Ct. Appeals 5th Circuit bar, 1973; since practiced in Atlanta; asso. firm Fisher & Phillips, 1972; dep. asst. atty. gen. State Ga., 1972-73; individual practice law, 1973-75; partner firm Bennett & Johnson, 1976—. Mem. Am., Ga., Fla. bar assns., Am. Judicature Soc. Supreme Ct. Hist. Soc. Home: 82 Montgomery Ferry Dr NE Atlanta GA 30309 Office: 1400 Rhodes-Haverty Bldg Atlanta GA 30303 Tel (404) 688-9100

BENNETT, RUSSELL JAY, b. Edgewood Arsenal, Md., Oct. 5, 1943; B.S., U. Md., 1964, J.D., 1967. Admitted to Md. bar, 1967, U.S. Supreme Ct. bar, 1972; since practiced in Balt.; clk. firm Allen, Burch & Baker, 1965-66; mem. firm Bernard J. Sevel, 1967-76; partner firm Bennett & Rubenstein, 1976—; Bd. dirs. Jewish Big Brother League 1971—. Mem. Md. State, Am. bar assns., Phi Alpha Delta. Recipient ARC Service to Humanity award, Leadership award Student Bar Assn., Service award Legal Aid Bureau. Home: 2309 Sugarcone Rd Baltimore MD 21209 Office: 603 Vermont Federal Bldg 25 W Fayette St Baltimore MD 21201 Tel (301) 837-5767

BENNETT, WENDELL ELLERY, b. Ogden, Utah, May 31, 1937; B.S. in Sociology, U. Utah, 1962, J.D., 1964; Admitted to Uah bar, 1964; partner firm Strong & Hanni, Salt Lake City, 1965-75; individual practice law, 1975—; asst. dist. atty. 2d Jud. Dist., Utah, 1968-69; spl. agt. FBI, 1964-65; pro tem judge Bountiful (Utah) City Ct., 1972—; mem. authorship com. Utah auto ins. and domestic relations laws. Mem. bd. SSS, 1974-76. Office: Wendell E Bennett 370 E 500 St S Suite 100 Salt Lake City UT 84111 Tel (801) 532-7846

BENNETT, WILLIAM PERRY, b. Inglewood, Calif., Aug. 28, 1938; A.B., Calif. State U., Long Beach, 1961; J.D., U. So. Calif., 1964. Admitted to Calif. bar, 1965; asso. firm Powars & Tretheway, Compton, Calif., 1964-66; partner firm Powars, Tretheway & Bennett, Long Beach, Calif., 1966-72, law shareholder, 1972; asso. prof. bus. law Calif. State U., Long Beach. Mem. Los Angeles County, Long Beach (bd. govs. 1970-71, 73-74, 75-76) bar assns., Long Beach Barristers Club (pres. 1971), Long Beach Legal Aid Found. (dir., v.p. 1973), Am. Arbitration Assn. (nat. panel arbitrators). Contbr. articles to legal publs. including So. Calif. Law Rev., Ins. Law Jour., Jour. Am. R.R. Counsel, Jour. Forensic Medicine, Lawyers Med. Cyclopedia. Home: 1600 Catalina Ave Seal Beach CA 90740 Office: 3907 Atlantic Ave Long Beach CA 90807 Tel (213) 426-9446

BENNINGTON, RONALD KENT, b. Hillsboro, Ohio, July 16, 1936; B.A. magna cum laude, Kenyon Coll., 1958; J.D. summa cum laude, Ohio State U., 1961. Admitted to Ohio bar, 1961; asso. Black, McCuskey, Souers & Arbaugh, Canton, Ohio, 1964-69, partner, 1969—; sec. Hoover Worldwide Corp., N.Y.C., 1976—. Chmn. Canton ARC, 1975; bd. dirs. Canton United Way, 1976—; trustee Christ United Presbyn. Ch., Canton. Mem. Am., Stark County bar assns. Named Outstanding Man of Year Canton C. of C., 1969. Home: 3528 Darlington NW Canton OH 44708 Office: 1200 Harter Bank Bldg Canton OH 44711 Tel (216) 456-8341

BENNISON, WILLIAM HAROLD, b. College Point, N.Y., Aug. 25, 1918; LL.B., Albany Law Sch., 1942. Admitted to N.Y. State bar, 1942, Tex. bar, 1969, U.S. Supreme Ct. bar, 1953; served to lt. col. JAG USMC, 1942-69; chief prosecutor Dallas, 1969-72; judge Municipal Ct., Dallas, 1972—. Home: 3848 Port Royal Dr Dallas TX 75234 Office: Municipal Ct Dallas TX 75201 Tel (214) 748-9711

BENSON, CLARENCE JULIUS, b. Verona, Pa., Nov. 21, 1911; A.B., W.Va. U., 1934, LL.B., 1937, J.D., 1937. Admitted to W.Va. bar, 1937; asso. firms Richardson & Brown, Charleston, W.Va., 1937-38, F. B. Shannon, Charleston, 1938-41; individual practice law, Charleston, 1941-73; partner firm Benson & Riggs, Charleston, 1973—. Mem. Charleston Human Rights Commn., 1969-72; lay witness coordinator W.Va. Conf. United Meth. Ch., 1969—, pres. bd. trustees, 1972—; trustee Found. of Evangelism United Meth. Ch., 1972—. Mem. Kanawha County (W.Va.) (pres. 1957), W.Va., W.Va. State, Am. bar assns., Am. Judicature Soc., Phi Alpha Delta. Home: 272-A Oakwood Rd Charleston WV 25314 Office: PO Box 906 Charleston WV 25323 Tel (304) 342-1196

BENSON, CRAIG THOMAS, b. Angola, Ind., Nov. 5, 1947; B.A. cum laude, Tulane U., 1969; J.D., U. Tex., 1972. Admitted to Ind. bar, 1972, U.S. Dist. Ct. No. Dist. Ind. bar, 1972; asso. firm Van Horne & Van Horne, Auburn, Ind., 1972—; pros. atty. 85th Judicial Circuit Ct., 1975—. Mem. Am., Steuben County, DeKalb County bar assns. Home: POB 51 Angola IN 46703 Office: POB 51 Angola IN 46703 Tel (219) 665-6111

BENSON, DONALD LEE, b. Cherokee, Okla., July 12, 1933; B.B.A., U. Okla., 1959, J.D., 1961. Admitted to Okla. bar, 1961, U.S. Dist. Ct. Western Dist. Okla. bar, 1962, U.S. Supreme Ct. bar, 1964, 10th Circuit U.S. Ct. Appeals bar, 1970; asso. firm John B. Doolin, Alva, Okla., 1961-63; partner firm Morford, Benson & Gruber and predecessor, Alva, 1963—. Mem. Am., Okla. (coninuing legal edn. com. 1965—), woods county bar assns., Okla. U. Coll. Law Assn. (past pres.). Home: 518 14th St Alva OK 73717 Office: POB 488 Alva OK 73717 Tel (405) 327-1197

BENSON, DORIS, b. Phila., Mar. 22, 1936; B.A., U. Pa., 1957, J.D., 1972. Admitted to Pa. Supreme Ct. bar, 1972, U.S. Dist. Ct. bar for Eastern Dist. Pa., 1973; asso. firm Pepper, Hamilton & Scheetz, Phila. Mem. Am. Bar Assn. Editorial bd. U. Pa. Law Rev., 1971-72. Home: 1564 Buck Hill Dr Huntingdon Valley PA 19006 Office: 20th floor 123 S Broad St Philadelphia PA 19109 Tel (205) 545-1234

BENSON, HENRY NATHANIEL, b. St. Peter, Minn., June 4, 1916; B.A., Gustavus Adolphus Coll., 1937; LL.B., U. Minn., 1940. Admitted to Minn. bar, 1940; individual practice law, St. Peter, 1945-62; city atty. City of St. Peter, 1947-60; judge probate and juvenile divs. Probate Ct. of Nicollet County (Minn.), 1961-72, Nicollet County Ct., 1972—. Bd. dirs. Gustavus Adolphus Coll., 1947-56. Mem. Am. Bar Assn., Minn. Bar. Home: 736 Valley View Rd Saint Peter MN 56082 Office: Courthouse Saint Peter MN 56082 Tel (507) 931-2540

BENSON, J.D., b. Silver Creek, Miss., Oct. 11, 1937; B.A. magna cum laude, U. So. Miss., 1959; J.D. magna cum laude, Mercer U., 1972. Admitted to Ga. bar, 1972; asso. firm Hansell, Post, Brandon & Dorsey, Atlanta, 1972—. Mem. bd. visitors W.F. George Sch. Law, Mercer U., 1972—. Mem. Am., Ga., Cobb bar assns. Home: 3265 Brookview Dr Marietta GA 30067 Office: 3300 1st Nat Bank Tower Atlanta GA 30303 Tel (404) 422-4800

BENSON, MORRIS, b. Bklyn., Jan. 8, 1913; student U. Md.; LL.B., Nat. U., 1937; J.D., George Washington U., 1968; spl. courses Columbia. Admitted to D.C. bar, 1938; mem. firm Benson, Stien & Braunstein, Washington, 1938—; pres. Benson Investment Co., Washington. Mem. Am., D.C. bar assns., Am. Trial Lawyers Assn. (chmn. com. admissions to U.S. Supreme Ct.), Assn. Plaintiff's Trial Lawyers D.C. Office: 653 Washington Bldg Washington DC 20005 Tel (202) 393-8500

BENSON, PAUL, b. Verona, N.D., June 1, 1918; B.S.C., U. N.D., 1942; LL.B., George Washington U., 1949. Admitted to N.D. bar; adminstrv. asst. to Senator Milton R. Young, 1946-49; asso. firm H.B. Spiller and Cavalier, 1949-50; mem. firm Shaft, Benson, Shaft and McConn, 1950-71; atty. gen. State of N.D., 1954-55; now chief judge U.S. Dist. Ct., Dist. N.D., Fargo. Tchr. U. N.D. Chmn. Grand Forks County chpt. A.R.C., 1954-55. Mem. Am. Bar Assn., Am. Judicature Soc., State Bar Assn. N.D., Am. Legion, V.F.W. Home: 619 21st Ave South Fargo ND 58102 Office: 340 Federal Bldg US Courthouse Fargo ND 58102*

BENSON, ROBERT RAYMOND, b. Owatonna, Minn., Aug. 2, 1945; B.A., Augsburg Coll., 1967; J.D., William Mitchell Coll. Law, 1971. Rating bd. specialist VA, St. Paul, 1967-72; admitted to Minn. bar, 1971, U.S. Dist. Ct. bar for Minn., 1971; partner firm Joerg & Benson, Ltd., Preston, Minn., 1972—; county atty. Fillmore County, Minn., 1974—. Mem. Minn., Am., Fillmore County (pres. 1976) bar assns., Minn. Trial Lawyers Assn., Nat. Dist. Attys. Assn. Home: PO Box 26 Preston MN 55965 Office: PO Box 257 Preston MN 55965 Tel (507) 765-3862

BENTLEY, PETER, b. Jersey City, Sept. 1, 1915; A.B., Princeton, 1938; LL.B., Yale, 1941. Admitted to N.Y. State bar, 1942, Conn. bar, 1952, asso. firm Simpson, Thacher & Bartlett, N.Y.C., 1941-52, firm Maguire & Cole, Stamford, Conn., 1952-56; partner firm Maguire, Cole, Bentley & Babson, Stamford, 1956—. Mem. Am., Conn., Stamford bar assns. Home: 176 Shore Rd Old Greenwich CT 06870 Office: 1 Atlantic St POB 1356 Stamford CT 06904

BENTON, LEE FREDERIC, b. Springfield, Ohio, Feb. 18, 1944; A.B., Oberlin Coll., 1966; J.D., U. Chgo., 1969. Admitted to Calif. bar, 1970; teaching fellow Stanford Law Sch., 1969-70; asso. firm Cooley, Godward, Castro, Huddleson & Tatum, San Francisco, 1970-75, partner, 1975—. Trustee San Francisco Neighborhood Legal Assistance Found., 1971-75, Marinview Community Assn., Mill Valley, Calif., 1975-77. Mem. Am., San Francisco bar assns., Order of Coif, Phi Beta Kappa. Exec. editor U. Chgo. Law Rev., 1968-69. Office: One Maritime Plaza 20th Floor San Francisco CA 94111 Tel (415) 981-5252

BENTZEN, MICHAEL PORTER, b. Evansville, Ind., Apr. 1, 1939; B.A., DePauw U., Greencastle, Ind., 1960; postgrad. De Paul U. Law Sch., 1961-62; J.D., George Washington U., 1964. Admitted to D.C. bar, 1965, U.S. Ct. Claims, 1965, U.S. Supreme Ct. bar, 1969; asso. firm Covington & Burling, Washington, 1964-67; partner firm Jacobs and Speiller, Washington, 1967-71, firm Reasoner, Davis & Vinson, Washington, 1971—. Sec. House of Mercy, Washington; trustee Popluation Reference Bur., Washington, Barker Found., Washington, John Edward Fowler Meml. Found. Mem. D.C. Bar, Am., Md. State bar assns., Bar Assn. D.C., The Barristers. Home: 11141 Hurdle Hill Dr Potomac MD 20854 Office: 800 17th St NW Washington DC 20006 Tel (202) 298-8100

BERALL, FRANK STEWART, b. N.Y.C., Feb. 10, 1929; B.S., Yale U., 1950, J.D., 1955; LL.M. in Taxation, N.Y. U., 1959. Admitted to N.Y. bar, 1955, Conn. bar, 1960, U.S. Supreme Ct. bar, 1961; asso. firm Mudge, Stern, Baldwin & Todd, N.Y.C., 1955-57, Townley, Updike, Carter & Rodgers, N.Y.C., 1957-60; atty. Conn. Gen. Life Ins. Co., Bloomfield, 1960-65; atty. trust dept. Hartford Nat. Bank and Trust Co. (Conn.), 1965-67; asso. firm Cooney & Scully, Hartford, 1968-70; partner firm Neiman, Schor & Berall, Hartford, 1970-71, Schor & Berall, Hartford, 1971-72, Copp, Brenneman, Tighe, Koletsky & Berall, Hartford, 1973—; v.p., sec., gen. counsel, dir. John M. Blewer Inc., Essex, Conn., 1969—; adj. asst. prof. tax U. Hartford Grad. Tax Program, 1974-75; lectr. U. Conn. Law Sch., 1972-73; instr. Am. Coll. Life Underwriters, 1968-69; mem. Conn. State Tax Commr.'s Commn., 1972-75; mem., also counsel tax com. Conn. Gov.'s Strike Force for Full Employment, 1971-72; cons. Gov.'s Commn. on Tax Reform, 1972-73; lectr. in field. Mem. adv. council U. Hartford Tax Inst., 1970—. Mem. Internat. Acad. Estate and Trust Law, Am. Coll. Probate Counsel (chmn. Conn. chpt. 1975-, chmn. estate and gift tax reform com. 1976—, regent 1977—), Hartford Tax Club (pres. 1975-76), Hartford County (chmn. liaison com. IRS 1972-74), Conn. (chmn. tax sect. 1969-72), Am. (vice chmn. com. significant current lit. 1974—, chmn. membership com. 1977-, real property, probate and trust sect., tax sect.) bar assns. Editorial adv. bd. Estate Planning, 1973—; editorial bd. Am. Coll. Probate Counsel, 1975—; sr. editor Conn. Bar Jour., 1970—; contbr. articles to legal jours. Home: 9 Penwood Rd Bloomfield CT 06002 Office: 60 Washington St Hartford CT 06106 Tel (203) 249-5261

BERARDINO, SABINO J., b. N.Y.C., May 11, 1923; B.B.A., Fordham U., 1948; LL.B., Georgetown U., 1951. Admitted to N.Y. bar 1952, D.C. bar 1951; partner Garbarini, Scher, DeCicco & Berardino, N.Y.C., 1962-75; individual practice law, N.Y.C., 1975—; co-counsel Judiciary com., N.Y. State Assembly, 1962. Mem. parish council St. Thomas More Roman Catholic Ch., N.Y.C. Mem. N.Y. State Bar Assn., N.Y. County, Columbia (pres. 1974, chmn. bd. 1972) lawyers assns. Home: 40 E 88th St New York City NY 10028 Office: 110 E 42d St New York City NY 10017 Tel (212) 697-0700

BERCH, PAUL SENDER, b. Washington, June 8, 1946; B.A., George Washington U., 1967; J.D., U. Chgo., 1970. Admitted to Vt. bar, 1970, U.S. Supreme Ct. bar, 1976; asso. Langrock & Sperry, Middlebury, Vt., 1970-72; partner Brown & Berch, Woodstock, Vt., 1972; individual practice law, Reading, Vt., 1972-75; pub. defender Windham County (Vt.), Brattleboro, 1975—. Vice-pres. Vt. Civil Liberties Union, 1972—. Mem. Vt., Windham County bar assns., Nat. Lawyers Guild. Home: Route 1 Box 88 Newfaine VT 05345 Office: 40 High St Brattleboro VT 05301 Tel (802) 254-2351

BERDO, ROBERT HENRY, b. Washington, Iowa, Jan. 28, 1930; B.S. in Chemistry, U. Iowa, 1956; J.D., George Washington U., 1960. Admitted to D.C. bar, 1960, U.S. Supreme Ct. bar, 1965; patent examiner U.S. Patent Office, Washington, 1956-59; mem. patent dept. Union Carbide Corp., Washington, 1959-60; mem. firm Beale & Jones, Washington, 1960-68, partner, 1963-68; partner firm Roylance, Abrams, Berdo & Kaul, Washington, 1968—. Mem. Bar Assn. D.C., Am. Bar Assn., Am. Patent Law Assn., Am. Chem. Soc. Home: 7306 Brookcrest Pl Annandale VA 22003 Office: 1225 Connecticut Ave NW Washington DC 20036 Tel (202) 659-9076

BERENA, JOHN PAUL, JR., b. Cleve., July 13, 1942; B.A., Baldwin-Wallace Coll., 1964; J.D., Case-Western Res. U., 1967. Admitted to Ohio bar, 1967, Hawaii bar, 1974, U.S. Supreme Ct. bar, 1971; mem. legal dept. Hanna Mining Co., Cleve., 1967-70; asst. county prosecutor Cuyahoga County (Ohio), Cleve., 1970-72; individual practice law, Cleve., 1967-72; asst. U.S. atty. No. Dist. Ohio, Cleve., 1972-76; pvt. practice law, Cleve., 1977—. Active Boy Scouts Am., YMCA. Mem. Cleve., Cuyahoga County, Ohio State bar assns. Home: 28 Parkview Dr Berea OH 44017 Office: 1108 Illuminating Bldg 55 Public Sq Cleveland OH 44113 Tel (216) 621-1206

BEREND, ROBERT WILLIAM, b. Miami Beach, Fla., Dec. 31, 1931; B.A., N.Y.U., 1952; LL.B., Yale, 1955. Admitted to N.Y. bar, 1955; U.S. Dist. Ct. for So. and Eastern Dist. N.Y., 1959; asst. gen. atty., trustee Hudson & Manhattan Ry. Co., N.Y.C., 1958-61; asso. firm Delson & Gordon, N.Y.C., 1961-64, partner, 1965-76; sr. v.p., gen. counsel Mgmt. Assistance Inc., N.Y.C., 1976—, sec. dir., 1970—. Mem. Am., N.Y. State bar assns., Bar Assn. City N.Y. Home: 132 E 35th St New York City NY 10016 Office: 300 E 44th St New York City NY 10017 Tel (212) 557-8453

BERESFORD, ROBERT, b. Buenos Aires, Argentina, Nov. 20, 1912; (parents Am. citizens); B.A., Yale, 1934, LL.B., 1937. Admitted to N.Y. bar, 1938, Calif. bar, 1946; asso. firm Donovan, Leisure, Newton & Lumbard, N.Y.C., 1937-41; individual practice law, San Jose, Calif., 1946-63; judge Calif. Municipal Ct., San Jose, 1963—. Pres. Visiting Nurse Assn., San Jose, 1958, World Affairs Council, 1959, advisory council Friends Outside, 1974—. Mem. Nat. Conf. Spl. Ct. Judges (chmn., 1970-71), Nat. Coll. State Judiciary, Calif. Coll. Trial Judges, Am. (council jud. adminstrn. div. 1974—), Santa Clara County (awards 1976) bar assns., Nat. Center State Cts. (advisory council, 1971-76), Calif. Judges Assn. (chmn. municipal cts. com., 1970), Criminal Justice Standard Com. (chmn., 1974-75), Penal Code Revision Com., 1969-75, Am. Judicature Soc., Am. Judges Assn., World Assn. Judges. Contbr. articles to profl. jours. Jud. innovator: pretrial release without bail, 1964, driver edn. in lieu of fines, 1965, jud. edn., 1968, unification trial cts., 1971, criminal justice standards, 1972, neighborhood small claims project, 1976. Home: 2004 Adele Pl San Jose CA 95125 Office: 200 W Hedding St San Jose CA 95110 Tel (408) 299-2268

BERESTECKI, PHILIP PETER, b. Boston, Mar. 23, 1944; B.S. cum laude in Chemistry, Boston Coll., 1965, J.D., 1969. Admitted to Mass. bar, 1969, U.S. Ct Customs and Patent Appeals, U.S. Patent Office bar. With E.I. DuPont de Nemours, Wilmington, Del., 1969-72, CIBA-Geigy Corp., Ardsley, N.Y., 1972, Foster Grant Co., Inc., Leominster, Mass., 1972—. Mem. Licensing Exec. Soc., Boston Patent Law Assn., Am., Mass. bar assns. Home: 1702 Stearns Hill Waltham MA 02154 Office: 289 N Main St Leominster MA 02154 Tel (617) 534-6511

BERFIELD, MORTON LANG, b. Blytheville, Ark., Dec. 12, 1933; B.A., DePauw U., 1955; J.D., U. Mich., 1958. Admitted to Ill. bar, 1958, D.C. bar, 1964; staff atty. FCC, Washington, 1959-64; partner firm Cohen & Berfield, Washington, 1964—. Mem. Fed. Communications Bar Assn., Phi Alpha Delta. Home: 7211 Selkirk Dr Bethesda MD 20034 Office: 1129 20th St NW Washington DC 20036 Tel (202) 466-8565

BERG, JOHN GORDON, b. Phila., Aug. 26, 1941; B.S. in Econs., Drexel U., 1964; J.D., U. Pa., 1967. Admitted to Pa. bar, 1967, U.S. Supreme Ct. bar, 1977; prin. firm Berg & Daniels, Plymouth Meeting, Pa., 1973-75; pres., dir. Fidelity Am. Mortgage Co., Plymouth Meeting, 1975-77; instr. real estate law and fin. Pa. State U. Extension Sch., King of Prussia, 1973—; solicitor Whitpain Twp. Zoning Bd., 1972-73. Dist. dir. The Conservative Caucus, 1976. Mem. Pa., Montgomery County bar assns. Office: 100 Plymouth Plaza Plymouth Meeting PA 19462 Tel (215) 825-4900

BERGDOLL, JOHN GEORGE, b. York, Pa., Feb. 22, 1944; A.B., U. Pa., 1966; J.D., Duquesne U., 1969. Admitted to Pa. bar, 1970; individual practice law, York, 1970—. Home and Office: 300 W Market St York PA 17401 Tel (717) 845-5131

BERGEN, THOMAS JOSEPH, b. Prairie du Chien, Wis., Feb. 7, 1913; J.D., Marquette U., 1937. Admitted to Wis. Supreme Ct. bar, 1937, Wis. bar, 1937, U.S. Supreme Ct. bar, 1972; practiced in Milw., 1937—; individual practice law, Milw., 1937—; gen. counsel Wis. Assn. Nursing Homes, Inc., 1957-71, Am. Coll. Nursing Home Adminstrns., 1967-68, Nat. Geriatrics Soc., 1971—. Pres. Wis. Justice Found., Inc., 1971—. Mem. Milw., Wis., Am. bar assns., Nat. Geriatrics Soc. (award for outstanding leadership 1976), Real Estate Profls. Assn., Wis. Assn. Health Care Facilities. Recipient ward of merit Wis. Assn. Nursing Homes, Inc., 1962; contbr. articles to profl. jours. Home: 10324 W Vienna Ave Wauwatosa WI 53222 Office: 212 W Wisconsin Ave Milwaukee WI 53202 Tel (414) 276-0575

BERGER, AUGUST FRED, b. Davenport, Iowa, Mar. 26, 1934; B.A., U. Iowa, 1955, J.D., 1957. Admitted to Iowa bar, 1957; asso. firm Filseth & Berger and predecessor, Davenport, 1958—; asso. Scott County (Iowa) Courthouse, Davenport, 1961-64; individual practice law, Davenport, 1965-73; asst. county atty. Scott County, 1961-64, 1st asst. county atty., 1968—; U.S. commr. So. Dist. Iowa, Davenport div., 1965-67. Pres. Home Ownership Made Easy, Inc., Davenport; pres. Quad-City Arts Council, Rock Island, Ill.; mem. Quad-City Urban Design Council; chmn. Com. City Planners, Rock Island; cubmaster Pack 129 Illowa Council Boy Scouts Am.; mem. Republican Precinct Com. Mem. Assn. Trial Lawyers Iowa (founding, dir.), Am. Trial Lawyers Assn., Am., Iowa, Scott County bar assns., Iowa Acad. Trial Lawyers (dir.). Home: POB 59 Pleasant Valley IA 52767 Office: 609 Kahl Bldg Davenport IA 52801 Tel (319) 326-3596

BERGER, DANIEL M., b. Pitts., May 6, 1933; B.A., U. Pitts., 1953; LL.B., Yale, 1956. Admitted to Pa. bar, 1956, U.S. Supreme Ct. bar, 1974; partner firm Berger, Kapetan & Malakoff, and predecessors, Pitts., 1956—; lectr. Pa. Bar Inst., 1975—. Pres., Western Pa. chpt. Ams. for Democratic Action, 1972—; past counsel, v.p., bd. dirs. Greater Pitts. chpt. ACLU. Mem. Pa. (past dir.), Western Pa. (past pres.) trial lawyers assns. Office: Berger Kapetan & Malakoff 508 Law Finance Bldg Pittsburgh PA 15219 Tel (412) 281-4200

BERGER, EDWARD, b. Bronx, N.Y., Feb. 22, 1929; B.A., U. Ariz., 1952, M.A., 1952; J.D. cum laude, N.Y. U., 1959. Admitted to N.Y. bar, 1959, U.S. Supreme Ct. bar, 1964, Ariz. bar, 1960, D.C. bar, 1971; jr. high sch. tchr., Tucson, 1952-56, 60; asst. to v.p. Simpson Coal & Chem. Co., N.Y.C., 1958-59; acting dir. Pima County Legal Aid, Tucson, 1960; dep. county atty. Pima County (Ariz.), 1961-62; mem. firm Whitehill, Berger, Karp & West, Tucson, 1960—, pres., 1970—; chief magistrate Town of South Tucson, 1965-75; pres. Pima County Legal Aid Soc., 1967-69, dir., 1967-71. Bd. dirs. Ariz. State Sch. for Deaf and Blind, 1966-67, 76—, pres., 1976—; mem. Devel. Authority for Tucson's Economy, 1967-70; trustee Palo Verde Found. for Mental Health, 1966-69, Ret. Citizens Sr. Vol. Program, 1976-77. Mem. Ariz., Pima County, Fed. (Indian law com. 1976—), Am. bar assns., Nat. Legal Aid and Defender Assn. (dir. 1968-71), Rocky Mountain Mineral Law Found., Nat. Council Am. Indians, State Bar Ariz. (antitrust sect. 1977—), Am. Soc. Hosp. Attys., N.Am. Judges Assn. Office: 259 N Meyer Ave Tucson AZ 85701 Tel (602) 623-6354

BERGER, HAROLD, b. Archbald, Pa., Jun 10, 1925; B.E.E., U. Pa., 1948, J.D., 1951. Admitted to Pa. bar, 1951, since practiced in Phila; judge Ct. Common Pleas, Philadelphia County, 1971-72; chmn., moderator Internat. Aeorspace Meetings, Princeton, 1965-66; chmn. Western Hemisphere Internat. Law Conf., San Jose, Costa Rica, 1967; permanent mem. Jud. Conf. 3d Circuit Ct. Appeals; mem. County Bd. Law Examiners, Philadelphia County, 1961-71; chmn. World Conf. Internat. and Aerospace Law, Caracas, Venezuela, 1969; mem. Nat. and State confs. trial judges, Nat. Conf. Juvenile Ct. Judges; chmn. Pa. Com. Ind. Judiciary, 1973—; chmn. Internat. Conf. Environ. and Internat. Law, U. Pa., 1974, Internat. Conf. Global Interdependence, Princeton, 1975. Fellow Brit. Interplanetary Soc.; mem. Inter-Am. (chmn. aerospace law com.), Fed. (nat. chmn. aerospace law com, pres. Phila. chpt., nat. exec. council, recipient Presdl. award 1970), Am. (vice chmn. space law com., Spl. Presdl. Program medal 1975) bar assns., Assn. U.S. Mems. Internat. Inst. Space Law, Internat. Astronautical Fedn (v.p.), Internat. Acad. Astronautics, Am. Inst. Aero. Astronautics. Mem. editorial adv. bd. Jour. Space Law, U. Miss. Sch. Law, 1973; contbr. articles to profl. jours. Office: 1622 Locust St Philadelphia PA 19103 Tel (215) 732-8000

BERGER, HOWARD J., b. N.Y.C., Aug. 25, 1928; B.S., N.Y.U., 1955, J.D., 1957. Admitted to N.Y. bar, 1957; individual practice law, N.Y.C., 1957-59, 62-69; asst. prof. law Fresno (Calif.) State Coll., 1959-60, Hofstra Coll., Hempstead, N.Y., 1960-62; asso. prof. law Bernard M. Baruch Coll., City U.N.Y., N.Y.C., 1969—. Mem. Am. Bar Assn., N.Y. County Lawyers' Assn., Am. Bus. Law Assn., Am. Arbitration Assn. Author: (with Leonard Lakin) A Guide to Secured Transactions, 1970, CPA Law Examination Review, 1972; contbr. articles to profl. jours. Office: 17 Lexington Ave New York City NY 10010 Tel (212) 725-3346

BERGER, LAWRENCE, b. Newark, May 21, 1928; B.S. in Econs., U. Pa., 1949; J.D., Rutgers U., 1952. Admitted to D.C. bar, 1953, N.J. bar, 1953, Nebr. bar, 1973; individual practice law, N.J., 1956-59; asst. prof. law U. Nebr., 1960-62, asso. prof., 1962-64, prof., 1964—; vis. prof. U. Minn., 1969-70, U. Calif., Los Angeles, 1974-75. Mem. Am., Nebr. bar assns. Mem. advisory com. Jour. Legal Edn., 1971-74. Home: 7300 Old Post Rd Apt 6 Lincoln NE 68520 Office: U of Nebr Coll of Law Lincoln NE 68503 Tel (402) 472-1240

BERGER, M., b. Bklyn., July 24, 1908; B.S., Washington Sq. Coll. N.Y. U., 1928, LL.B., Sch. Law, 1929. Admitted to N.Y. bar, 1930, U.S. Supreme Ct. bar, 1961; practiced in N.Y.C., 1930-37; house counsel N.Y. Post, N.Y.C., 1937-41, bus. mgr., 1955-63, gen. counsel, sec., 1949-63; asso. pub. N.Y. Law Jour., 1963-70, v.p., 1964-68, pres., 1968-70; judge N.Y.C. Criminal Ct., 1970—; mem. N.Y. State Jud. Conf., 1974—. Mem. Assn. Judges Criminal Ct. City N.Y. (pres. 1973—), New York County Lawyers Assn. (chmn. com. pub. relations 1958-60), Am. (com. on communications 1968-70), N.Y. State (chmn. com. pub. relations jud. sect.), Queens County (N.Y.) bar assns., Assn. Bar City N.Y., N.Y. Law Inst., Inst. Jud. Adminstrs., Am. Judicature Soc., Am. Judges Assn, Legal Aid Soc. Contbr. articles to Judicature, N.Y. State Bar Jour.; bd. editors N.Y. State Bar Jour., 1974—. Office: Criminal City NYC 100 Centre St New York City NY 10013 Tel (212) 643-7216

BERGER, MELVIN GERALD, b. Bklyn., June 13, 1943; B.S., Coll. City N.Y., 1965; M.S., N.Y. U., 1967; J.D., George Washington U., 1971, LL.M., 1975. Admitted to Md. bar, 1972; patent examiner U.S. Patent Office, Washington, 1967-69; patent adviser Dept. Navy, Washington, 1969-72, patent atty., 1972-73; law clk. U.S. Ct. Claims, Washington, 1973-74; atty. antitrust div. U.S. Dept. Justice, Washington, 1974—. Mem. Am. Bar Assn., Order of Coif, Phi Beta Kappa. Recipient Spl. Achievement award U.S. Dept. Justice, 1976; Superior Performance award U.S. Dept. Navy, 1973. Home: 6147 New Leaf Ct Columbia MD 21045 Office: 10th and Constitution Aves NW Washington DC 20530 Tel (202) 739-3252

BERGER, MORRIS MILTON, b. Montreal, Que., Can., Oct. 10, 1904; B.A., U. Pitts., 1925, M.A., 1927, J.D., 1928. Admitted to Pa. bar, U.S. Supreme Ct. bar, 1974; sr. mem. firm Berger, Kapetan & Malakoff, Pitts. Mem. Alleghany County Bar Assn., Am. Trial Lawyers Assn. Home: 15K Gateway Towers P Pittsburgh PA 15222 Office: 508 Law & Finance Bldg Pittsburgh PA 15219 Tel (412) 281-4200

BERGER, ROBERT MICHAEL, b. Chgo., Jan. 29, 1942; A.B., U. Mich., 1963; J.D., U. Chgo., 1966. Admitted to Ill. bar, 1966, U.S. Supreme Ct. bar, 1975; law clk. to circuit judge U.S. Ct. Appeals, 2d Circuit, N.Y.C., 1966-67; atty. Chgo. Legal Aid Bur. Law Reform Unit, 1967-68; mem. firm Mayer, Brown & Platt, Chgo., 1968-72, partner, 1972—; lectr. Northwestern U. Law Sch., 1973; summer inst. faculty Nat. Inst. Law-Focused Edn., Chgo., 1969-74; mem. hearing bd. Ill. Supreme Ct. Atty. Disciplinary System, 1973—; mem. spl. tax adv. commn. to Ill. Dept. Ins., 1972; mem. bd. dirs., legal counsel Consumer Fedn. Ill., 1967-71; mem. consumer adv. council FTC, 1969; bd. dirs., chmn. program com. Legal Assistance Found. Chgo., 1975—. Mem. Am. Law Inst., Am., Chgo. (bd. mgrs. 1970-72) bar assns., Chgo. Council Lawyers (bd. govs. 1969-71), Order of Coif, Phi Beta Kappa, Phi Kappa Phi. Comment editor U. Chgo. Law Rev., 1965-66; author: Law and the Consumer, 1969, 74; contbr. articles to legal jours. Office: 231 S LaSalle St Suite 1955 Chicago IL 60604 Tel (312) 782-0600

BERGER, SANFORD JASON, b. Cleve., June 29, 1926; A.B., Western Res. U., 1950, LL.B., J.D., 1952. Admitted to Ohio bar, 1952; individual practice law, Cleve., 1952—; licensed securities dealer, real estate broker, Ohio, 1961—. Mem. Cuyahoga County Bar Assn. Home: 25515 Bryden Rd Beachwood OH 44122 Office: 1836 Euclid Ave Room 305 Cleveland OH 44115 Tel (216) 781-5950

BERGER, SAUL, b. Passaic, N.J., Mar. 12, 1907; B.A., Coll. City N.Y., 1927; LL.B., Fordham U., 1930. Admitted to N.Y. bar, 1932; individual practice law, N.Y.C. Mem. New York County Lawyers Assn., Am. Bar Assn. Tel (212) 673-4040

BERGER, VINCENT GEORGE, JR., b. N.Y.C., Nov. 19, 1937; B.A., St. John's U., 1959, LL.B., 1962. Admitted to N.Y. bar, 1963, U.S. Supreme Ct. bar, 1970; individual practice law, Commack, N.Y., 1963—; counsel to pub. adminstr. Suffolk County (N.Y.), law sec. to judge County Ct. Suffolk County, Riverhead, 1970. Mem. Suffolk County, N.Y. bar assns., N.Y. Trial Lawyers Assn., Columbian Lawyers Assn. (pres. 1971-72). Office: 6351 Jericho Turnpike Commack NY 11725 Tel (516) 864-6443

BERGERMAN, GEORGE MELBOURNE, b. N.Y.C., Aug. 19, 1934; B.A., Trinity Coll., Hartford, Conn., 1956; LL.B., N.Y. U., 1959, J.D., 1968. Admitted to N.Y. bar, 1961; tribunal adminstr. Am. Arbitration Assn., N.Y.C., 1960-61; asso. firm Granik, Garson, Silverman & Nowicki, New City, N.Y., 1961-66; asso. firm Wexler, Bergerman and Crucet, and predecessor, Pearl River, N.Y., 1966-67, partner, 1968—; dep. town atty. Town of Orangetown (N.Y.), 1970-74, town justice, 1976—. Bd. dirs. United Way of Rockland County, 1971-75. Mem. N.Y. State, Rockland County magistrates assns., Am., N.Y. State, Rockland County bar assns., Assn. Bar City N.Y., Tax and Estate Planning Council of Rockland County. Home: 2 Rockland Pl Nyack NY 10960 Office: 117 N Middletown Rd Pearl River NY 10965 Tel (914) 735-4076

BERGERON, ALLEN JOSEPH, JR., b. New Orleans, July 5, 1935; B.A., La. State U., 1959, J.D., 1968. Admitted to La. bar, 1968; asso. firm Burton, Roberts & Ward, Baton Rouge, 1968-74; individual practice law, Baton Rouge, 1974-75; partner firm Burton & Bergeron, Baton Rouge, 1975—; asso. atty. La. Dept. Revenue, 1974—. Mem. La., Baton Rouge bar assns. Office: Suite 410 251 Florida St Baton Rouge LA 70801 Tel (504) 383-3236

BERGHOFF, JOHN C., JR., b. Chgo., July 1, 1941; B.A. with honors, Northwestern U., 1963, J.D., 1966. Admitted to Ill. bar, 1966, U.S. Supreme Ct. bar, 1974; partner firm Chadwell, Kayser, Ruggles, McGee & Hastings, Chgo., 1966—. Mem. jr. governing bd. Chgo. Symphony Orch., 1971—; pres. Northwestern Club Chgo., 1976-77. Mem. Am., Ill., Chgo. bar assns. Recipient Wigmore Key Northwestern Sch. Law, 1966; antitrust law editor Law Notes, 1970-72. Office: 135 S LaSalle St Chicago IL 60603 Tel (312) 726-2545

BERGMAN, ALAN M., b. Bayonne, N.J., Jan. 5, 1941; A.B., Rutgers U., 1962; LL.B., Seton Hall U., 1965, J.D., 1967. Admitted to N.J. bar, 1965, Calif. bar, 1975; asst. gen. counsel, asst. sec. Diana Stores Corp., North Bergen, N.J., 1966-70; asst. gen. counsel, asst. sec. Daylin, Inc., Beverly Hills, Calif., 1970-75; v.p., gen. counsel First Charter Fin. Corp., Beverly Hills, 1975—. Mem. Am., Los Angeles, Beverly Hills bar assns., Calif. Savs. and Loan League (attys. com.). Office: 9465 Wilshire Blvd Beverly Hills CA 90212 Tel (213) 273-3300

BERGMAN, PAUL B., b. Bklyn., May 15, 1943; B.A., City Coll. N.Y., 1964; LL.B., Bklyn. Law Sch., 1967. Admitted to N.Y. bar, 1968, U.S. Supreme Ct. bar, 1971; law clk. to judge N.Y. State Supreme Ct., 1968-70; asso. firm Mudge, Rose, Guthrie & Alexander, N.Y.C., 1970-72; asst. U.S. atty., 1972-76, chief appeals div. U.S. Atty.'s Office Eastern Dist. N.Y., 1974-76; partner firm Ford, Marrin, Esposito, Witmeyer & Bergman, N.Y.C., 1976—. Mem. Fed., Nassau County bar assns. Recipient award Better Bklyn. Com. 1967. Office: 25 Broadway New York City NY 10004 Tel (212) 269-4900

BERGMAN, RONALD BRUCE, b. Wilmington, Del., Mar. 18, 1948; B.S., U. Del., 1970; J.D., George Washington U., 1973. Admitted to Md. bar, 1973; asso. firm Pickett, Houlon & Berman, Hyattsville, Md., 1973—. Mem. Am. Trial Lawyers Assn., Am., Prince George's County bar assns., Am. Judicature Soc., Assn. Trial Lawyers Am. Home: 5814 Lone Oak Dr Bethesda MD 20014 Office: 7515 Annapolis Rd Hyattsville MD 20784 Tel (301) 577-8200

BERGNER, WALTER BERNARD, b. N.Y.C., May 26, 1927; B.S. in Elec. Engring., U. Mich., 1948; J.D., Harvard, 1951. Admitted to N.Y. bar, 1952, U.S. Dist. Ct. for Eastern and So. Dist. N.Y. bars, 1957, U.S. Supreme Ct. bar, 1964; partner firm Bergner & Bergner, N.Y.C., 1952—; atty. Village of E. Rockaway, N.Y., 1967-68, justice, 1968-76. Mem. Am., N.Y. State, Nassau County bar assns., N.Y. County Lawyers Assn., Nassau County Magistrates Assn., N.Y. State Assn. Magistrates. Office: 11 Park Pl New York City NY 10007 Tel (212) 227-8280

BERGSMARK, EDWIN MARTIN, b. Cin., July 14, 1941; B.B.A., U. Cin., 1964; J.D., U. Toledo, 1972. Admitted to Ohio bar, 1972, U.S. Supreme Ct., 1976, U.S. Tax Ct., 1973, U.S. Ct. Customs and Patent Appeals, 1974; sr. v.p., gen. counsel The Toledo Trust Co., 1972—; gen. counsel N.W. Ohio Bancshares, Inc., Toledo, 1972—. Chmn., United Appeal Campaign, 1974-; bd. dirs., vice-chmn. Consumer Protection Bd. Toledo; bd. dirs. Kidney Found. N.W. Ohio, Toledo Opera Assn., 1976—. Mem. Toledo, Ohio, Am., Fed. bar assns., Ohio, Am. bankers assns. Office: Toledo Trust Co 245 Summit St Toledo OH 43603

BERGSTEIN, ALAN ARTHUR, b. Bklyn., Dec. 17, 1937; A.B., Moravian Coll., Bethlehem, Pa., 1959; LL.B., N.Y. Law Sch., 1962. Admitted to N.Y. bar, 1962, Fla. bar, 1975; asso. firm Siwek, Zimmerman & Silberkleit, White Plains, N.Y., 1963-64; mem. firm U. Lawrence Bergstein, 1964-69; asso. firm Blum & Ross, 1969-72; partner firm Blum, Ross, Weisler, Bergstein & Golden and predecessor, Lawrence, N.Y., 1973—; dep. village counsel-prosecutor Village of Cedarhurst, 1976—. Mem. Village of Cedarhurst Bd. Zoning Appeals, 1974-76; fin. sec., mgr. Cedarhurst Central Little League, 1973—. Mem. N.Y. County Lawyers Assn., Nassau County Bar Assn. Home: 414 Oak Ave Cedarhurst NY 11516 Office: 389 Central Ave Lawrence NY 11559 Tel (516) 569-3900

BERHENKE, FREDERICK THOMAS, b. Bay City, Mich., July 14, 1943; A.B. in Actuarial Math., U. Mich., 1965, J.D., 1968. Admitted to Mich. bar, Colo. bar, U.S. Dist. Ct. bar, 1969; since practiced in Denver; asso. firm Grant, Shafroth, Toll & McHendrie, 1969-71; partner firm Barnes & Jensen, 1972; claims atty. King Resources Co. Reorgn., 1972-74; asst. atty. gen. State of Colo.; adminstr. Colo. Consumer Credit Code, 1975—; cons. to Office of Saver and Consumer Affairs, Fed. Res. Bd., Washington, 1976. Mem. Am., Colo., Denver bar assns. Home: 1634 Locust St Denver CO 80220 Office: 1525 Sherman St 3d Floor Denver CO 80203 Tel (303) 892-3611

BERINGER, WILLIAM ERNST, b. Madison, Wis., Oct. 24, 1928; B.A. summa cum laude, Lawrence Coll., 1950; J.D. with distinction, U. Mich., 1953. Admitted to Mich. bar, Wis. bar; asso. firm Vedder, Price, Kaufman & Kammholz, Chgo., 1953-56; law dept. Swift & Co., Chgo., 1956-71; dir. gen. law dept. Allis-Chalmers Corp., Milw., 1971—. Bd. dirs. Du Page County (Ill.) Girl Scouts, 1969-71, Clarendon Hills (Ill.) Community Chest, 1968-70, Hinsdale (Ill.) Community Concert Assn., 1966-71; vice-chmn. Clarendon Hills Human Relations Commn., 1968-70. Mem. Am., Wis., Milw. bar assns., U. S. C. of C. (antitrust and trade regulation com.). Contbr. articles to legal jours. Home: 9429 N Regent Ct Bayside WI 53217 Office: Allis-Chalmers Corp 1205 S 70th St West Allis WI 53214 Tel (414) 475-3231

BERK, GERALD ALAN, b. Cleve., Apr. 8, 1943; B.S., Ohio State U., 1966; J.D., Cleve. State U., 1970. Admitted to Ohio bar, 1970; revenue agent IRS, Cleve., 1968-72; asso. firm Steuer, Escouar & Berk, Cleve., 1972—. Mem. sch. bd. Richmond Heights, Ohio, 1976—. Mem. Am., Ohio, Cleve., Cuyahoga County bar assns. Office: 800 Superior Ave Cleveland OH 44143 Tel (216) 771-8121

BERK, HAROLD ROBERT, b. Chgo., Mar. 1, 1947; B.A., U. Ill., 1968; J.D., U. Minn., 1971. Admitted to Ind. bar, 1971, U.S. Supreme Ct. bar, 1974, Pa. bar, 1975; staff atty. Legal Services Orgn. of Indpls., 1971-75, Community Legal Services, Phila., 1975—; mem. bd. Pub. Action in Correctional Effort, Indpls., 1974-75. Mem. Amnesty Internat. (legal com.), Indpls. Council Lawyers (chmn. 1974-75). Home: 405 S 12th St Philadelphia PA 19147 Office: Community Legal Services Sylvania House Juniper and Locust Sts Philadelphia PA 19107 Tel (215) 893-5306

BERKA, JERRY GEORGE, b. Bay Shore, N.Y., May 7, 1942; B.A. cum laude, Wesleyan U., Middletown, Conn., 1963; J.D., Cornell, 1966. Admitted to N.Y. bar, 1967, D.C. bar, 1967; served with Judge Adv. Gen. Corps U.S. Navy, 1966-69; partner firm Donner, Fagelson, Hariton & Berka, P.C., Bay Shore, 1969—. Pres. Bay Shore Bd. Edn., 1971-73; chmn. Bay Shore Student Aid Fund. Mem. N.Y., Am., Suffolk County bar assns. Mem. Cornell U. Law Rev., 1966. Home: 90 Bay Way Ave Brightwaters NY 11718 Office: 2115 Union Blvd Bay Shore NY 11706 Tel (516) 666-7400

BERKEMEYER, JOHN B., b. Mt. Sterling, Mo., Mar. 17, 1944; student St. Louis Coll. Pharmacy, 1962-75; B.S. in Chemistry, U. Mo., 1967, J.D., 1971; postgrad. George Washington U., 1970-71. Admitted to Mo. bar, 1972; individual practice law, Union, Mo., 1971-73, Hermann, Mo., 1973—; pros. atty. Gasconade County (Mo.), 1973—. Bd. dirs. Gasconade Area Counseling Center, 1975—. Mem. Am., 20th Jud. bar assns., Mo. Bar, Phi Alpha Delta, Kappa Psi. Home: 208 E 8th St Hermann MO 65041 Office: 303 Schiller St PO Box 150 Hermann MO 65041 Tel (314) 486-3124

BERKETT, MARIAN MAYER, b. Baton Rouge, Mar. 29, 1913; B.A., La. State U., 1933, M.A., 1935; postgrad. Geneva Sch. Internat. Studies; LL.B., Tulane U., 1937. Admitted to La. bar, 1937, U.S. Supreme Ct. bar, 1965; partner firm Deutsch, Kerrigan & Stiles, New Orleans; commr. La. State CSC, 1963-75. Mem. commn. Jefferson Parish (La.), 1963; bd. dirs. Family Service Soc., Community Chest New Orleans, New Orleans Lawyer Referral Service; chmn. La. Civil Service League (hon.). Mem. New Orleans, La. State, Am., Fed., Internat. bar assns., Am. Judicature Soc., Notarial Assn. New Orleans. Author: Workmen's Compensation Law in Louisiana, 1937; contbr. articles to legal jours. Home: 332 Iona St Metairie LA 70005 Office: 4700 One Shell Sq New Orleans LA 70139 Tel (504) 581-5141

BERKMAN, ANDREW STEPHEN, b. N.Y.C., Apr. 7, 1944; B.A., Yale U., 1966; J.D., N.Y. U., 1971. Admitted to N.Y. bar, 1971; asso. firm Robinson, Silverman, Pearce, Aronsohn, Sand & Berman, N.Y.C., 1971—. Mem. N.Y. State Bar Assn., Assn. Bar City N.Y. Cozo Found. fellow, 1966-67. Home: 27 W 96th St New York City NY 10025 Office: Robinson Silverman Pearce et al 230 Park Ave New York City NY 10017 Tel (212) 689-7766

BERKOWITZ, EDWARD C., b. Perth Amboy, N.J., Apr. 9, 1935; B.A., Cornell U., 1956; LL.B., Harvard U., 1959. Admitted to N.J. bar, 1960, D.C. bar, 1964, U.S. Supreme Ct. bar, 1964; asso. firm Garretson & Levine, Perth Amboy, N.J., 1960-64; atty., advisor NLRB, 1964-66; gen. atty. Communications Satellite Corp., Washington, D.C., 1966-70; v.p. Lane & Edson, P.C., Washington, 1970—; lectr. Practicing Law Inst., Inst. for Profl. Edn. Devel. Mem. Am., D.C. (chmn. real estate com.) bar assns. Contbr. articles to profl. jours. Home: 3339 Legation St NW Washington DC 20015 Office: 1800 M St NW Washington DC 20036 Tel (202) 457-6800

BERKOWITZ, NORMAN RAPHAEL, b. N.Y.C., Nov. 15, 1936; B.S. in Accounting, N.Y. U., 1957; J.D., Bklyn Law Sch., 1961; M.B.A. in Taxation, City U. N.Y., 1964. Admitted to N.Y. State bar, 1962, U.S. Tax Ct. bar, 1962, U.S. Supreme Ct. bar, 1966; partner firm Berkowitz & Ross, N.Y.C., 1968—; lectr. taxation Pace U., N.Y.C., 1968—. Mem. N.Y. State, Am. bar assns. Cons. tax editor Washington Publ., 1966—, Trusts and Estates mag., 1971—; contbr. articles to legal jours. Home: 39 Gramercy Park New York City NY 10010 Office: 666 Fifth Ave New York City NY 10019 Tel (212) 582-0620

BERKSTRESSER, JERRY WILLIAM, b. Omaha, Sept. 7, 1934; B.S. in Chemistry, Allegheny Coll., 1957; J.D., Dickinson Sch. Law., 1963. Admitted to Pa. bar, 1964; mgmt. trainee Youngstown (Ohio) Sheet & Tube Co., 1956-56; research chemist Callery Chem. Co., 1957-60; asso. firm Paul and Paul, Phila., 1963-65; atty. Eastman Kodak Co., Rochester, N.Y., 1965-70; patent counsel Dentsply Internat. Inc., York, Pa., 1970-76; gen. counsel Davol, Inc., Cranston, R.I., 1976—. Mem. coms. York Area C. of C., 1970-73. Mem. Phila., Am. patent law assns. Home: 80 Jefferson Dr East Greenwich RI 02818 Office: 100 Sockanosset Crossroad Cranston RI 02920

BERLIN, STANTON HENRY, b. Chgo., May 24, 1934; B.B.A., U. Mich., 1955, M.B.A, 1956, J.D., 1959. Admitted to Ill. bar, 1959, Mich. bar, 1959; asso. firm Bell, Boyd, Lloyd, Haddad & Burns, Chgo., 1959-67, partner, 1968—. Mem. Am., Ill., Chgo. bar assns., Legal Club Chgo., Law Club Chgo., Chgo. Mortgage Attys. Assn. Home: 750 Willow Rd Winnetka IL 60093 Office: Suite 3500 135 S LaSalle St Chicago IL 60603 Tel (312) 372-1121

BERLINER, EPHRAIM, b. N.Y.C., Jan. 21, 1891; A.B., Coll. City N.Y., 1910; M.A., Columbia U., 1912, J.D., 1913. Admitted to N.Y. bar, 1913, U.S. Supreme Ct. bar, 1931; partner firm Zeiger & Berliner, N.Y.C., 1919-42, Schlesinger & Berliner, N.Y.C., 1942—. Mem. N.Y.C. Bar Assn., Phi Beta Kappa. Home: 365 West End Ave New York City NY 10024 Office: 200 Park Ave New York City NY 10017 Tel (212) 687-1334

BERLINER, HENRY ADLER, b. Washington, Feb. 9, 1934; B.A., U. Mich., 1956; J.D. with honors, George Washington U., 1964. Admitted to D.C. bar, 1965, U.S. Supreme Ct. bar, 1968; asso. firm Craighill, Aiello, Gasch & Craighill, Washington, 1965-66; asst. U.S. atty. for D.C., 1966-67; partner firm Berliner, Maloney, Gimer & Jaffe, Washington, 1967—; cons. USIA, 1970; mem. threshold rev. bd. U.S. Dept. State, 1971-72; mem. Dept. Commerce Regional Export Expansion Council, 1970-73. Mem. D.C. Pub. Welfare Adv. Com. 1969-70; mem. D.C. Commn. Judicial Disabilities and Tensure, 1971—, chmn., 1975—. Mem. Bar, Bar Assn. D.C. (chmn. young law lawyers sect. 1968-69), Am. Bar Assn., Phi Delta Phi (pres. 1975—). Home: 2870 Upton St Washington DC 20008 Office: 1100 Connecticut Ave NW Washington DC 20036 Tel (202) 293-1414

BERLINER, SELMA MUNTER LOBSENZ, b. N.Y.C., June 12, 1898; A.B., Hunter Coll., 1920, J.D., N.Y.U., 1923. Admitted to N.Y. bar, 1924; researcher in law Johns Hopkins Inst. for Study Law, Balt., 1928-32, N.Y. State Constl. Conv., 1938; partner firm Schlesinger & Berliner, N.Y.C., 1947—. Mem. N.Y. State Advisory Council on Employment and Unemployment Ins., 1944-58. Mem. Assn. Bar City N.Y. Republican nominee N.Y. State Supreme Ct., 1956; elected to Hunter Coll. Hall of Fame, 1974; author: Hearings Under N.Y. State Workmen's Compensation Law, 1934; contbr. articles in field to law jours. Home: 365 W End Ave New York City NY 10024 Office: 200 Park Ave New York City NY 10017 Tel (212) 687-1334

BERMACK, EUGENE, b. N.Y.C., June 16, 1929; B.A., N.Y.U., 1951; J.D., Rutgers U., 1954. Admitted to N.Y. bar, 1956, U.S. Dist. Ct. bar for So. and Eastern Dists. N.Y., 1974; partner firm Bermack and Bermack, Great Neck, N.Y., 1957—. Mem. New York County Lawyers Assn., C.W. Post Tax Inst. Tel (516) 487-5668

BERMAN, BENNETT, b. Chgo., Oct. 29, 1918; B.S., U. Ill., 1940; LL.B., Harvard, 1943. Admitted to Ill. bar, 1947, gen. counsel real estate Nat. Tea Co., Rosemont, Ill., 1966-74, chief counsel, sec., 1974—. Mem. Chgo. (chmn. landlord and tenant subcom. 1974-75), Ill. bar assns. Contbr. articles to legal jours. Home: 1640 E 50th St Chicago IL 60615 Office: 9701 W Higgins Rd Rosemont IL 60018 Tel (312) 693-5100

BERMAN, BERNARD MAYER, b. Phila., May 9, 1940; A.B., Swarthmore Coll., 1962; LL.B., Columbia, 1965, J.D., 1969. Admitted to Pa. bar, 1965, U.S. 3d Circuit Ct. Appeals, U.S. Dist. Ct. Eastern Dist. Pa. bars, 1965, U.S. Supreme Ct. bar, 1969; individual practice law, Phila., 1965; partner firm Scallan, March, Berman, Del Fra, & Wochok and predecessors, Media, Pa., 1966—; law clk. Phila. Ct. Common Pleas, 1965, Delaware County Ct. Common Pleas, 1967-74; pub. defender trial atty. Delaware County, 1966; mem. Delaware County Spl. Com. to Revise Rules Civil Procedure, 1974-75. Mem. Young men's com. Phila. Fedn. Jewish Agencies, 1965, sec. 1966; dir. Ohev Shalom Synagogue, Wallingford, Pa., 1974—, chmn. publicity, editor newspaper 1974-76, chmn. membership participation, 1976—; chmn. com. on orgn. Jewish Community Council of Lower Delaware County, 1976, pres., 1977—. Mem. Pa., Delaware County bar assns., B'nai B'rith (fin. sec. Simon Wolf Lodge, 1975-76, v.p. 1976), Phi Assn. Phi Sigma Kappa (dir. 1966—, pres. 1969-75; recipient Founders award, 1976). Home: 28 Furness Ln Wallingford PA 19086 Office: 20 W 3d St Media PA 19063 Tel (215) 565-3950

BERMAN, DANIEL LEWIS, b. Washington, Dec. 14, 1934; B.A. cum laude, Williams Coll., 1956; LL.B., Columbia, 1959. Admitted to N.Y. bar, 1960, Utah bar, 1962, U.S. Supreme Ct. bar, 1972; asso. firm Chadbourne, Parker, Whiteside & Wolfe, 1959-60; asst. prof. law U. Utah, 1960-62; individual practice law, Salt Lake City, 1962—. Mem. Coordinating Council Higher Edn., 1965-68; gov. Salt Lake Area C. of C. Mem. Salt Lake County Bar Assn. Office: Kearns Bldg Salt Lake City UT 84101 Tel (801) 533-8383

BERMAN, DAVID TOBACK, b. N.Y.C., Oct. 11, 1919; student N.Y. U. Sch. Commerce, 1936-37, City Coll. N.Y. Sch. Commerce, 1937-44; LL.B., St. Johns U., N.Y.C., 1946. Admitted to N.Y. bar, 1946, U.S. Supreme Ct. bar, 1952; individual practice law, Bklyn., 1946-70, Selden, N.Y., 1969—; spl. asst. dep. atty. gen. State of N.Y., 1946-47; arbitrator N.Y.C. Civil Ct., 1959-64; counsel Temple Beth Judah, Bklyn., 1952-56, True Urban Renewal, Bklyn., 1964-68. Mem. N.Y., Suffolk and Kings Counties (N.Y.) bar assns. Home: 16 College Dr Stony Brook NY 11790 Office: 1064 Middle Country Rd Selden NY 11784 Tel (516) 698-0222

BERMAN, EUGENE BRUCE, b. Holyoke, Mass., June 1, 1928; B.A., U. Nebr., 1951; J.D., Boston U., 1952. Admitted to Mass. bar, 1952, U.S. Supreme Ct. bar, 1960; sr. mng. partner, pres. firm Kamberg, Berman & Hendel, and predecessor, Springfield, 1953—. Pres., Mattoon St. Hist. Preservation Com.; adv. com. on paralegal tng. U. Mass.; bd. dirs., past v.p. Pioneer Valley Credit Counseling Assn., Inc., Dunbar Community Center, Inc., Springfield Jewish Home for Aged, Hampden County chpt. ACLU, World Affairs Council of Conn. Valley, Inc., Legal Aid Soc. Springfield; incorporator Springfield Day Nursery, Inc., Pioneer Valley United Way, Inc., Jewish Social Service Bur.; trustee Williston-Northampton Sch. Fellow Comml. Law Found.; mem. Am., Mass., Hampden County bar assns., Comml. Law League Am. (chmn. Mass. mems. New Eng. dist. 1972-76, bd. govs. 1976—), Assn. Comml. Fin. Attys., Am. Judicature Soc., Conf. on Personal Fin. Law, Nat. Found. for Consumer Credit, Inc., Internat. Platform Assn., Mass. Bar Found. Author: How to Collect a Debt, 1966 (ann. revisions); Representing a Bankrupt, 1974; contbr. articles to legal jours. Home: 169 Lynnwood Dr Longmeadow MA 01106 Office: 31 Elm St Springfield MA 01103 Tel (413) 781-1300

BERMAN, FREDERIC SANFORD, b. N.Y.C., Mar. 7, 1927; A.B., Columbia, 1949; LL.B., N.Y. Law Sch., 1951. Admitted to N.Y. State bar, 1952, U.S. Supreme Ct. bar, 1961; practiced in N.Y.C., 1952-61, 69-70; adj. prof. law N.Y. Law Sch., 1958—; gen. counsel N.Y.C. Dept. Real Estate, 1962-64; mem. N.Y. State Senate, 1964-65; counsel Burlingham, Underwood, N.Y.C., 1965; commr. N.Y.C. Rent and Housing Dept., 1966-69; lectr. New Sch. For Social Research Center for N.Y.C. Affairs, 1971—; judge N.Y.C. Criminal Ct., 1973—; acting justice N.Y. State Supreme Ct., 1976—; mil. judge USAR, 1974—; mem. faculty Nat. Coll. State Judiciary, Reno, Nev., 1975—. Mem. Am., N.Y. State bar assns., Assn. Bar City N.Y., Assn. Judges City N.Y. Criminal Ct. (sec. 1975—). Office: NYC Criminal Ct 100 Centre St New York City NY 10013 Tel (212) 374-6216

BERMAN, HARRY STANFORD, b. Easton, Pa., July 17, 1934; A.B., U. Calif., 1956, J.D., 1959. Admitted to Calif. bar, 1960; asst. counsel div. inheritance and gift tax State of Calif., Los Angeles, 1960-67; program atty. Calif. Continuing Edn. of Bar U. Calif. Extension, Berkeley, 1967-68; individual practice law, Canoga Park, Calif., 1968; asso. trust counsel Security Pacific Nat. Bank, Los Angeles, 1968—. Mem. State Bar Calif., Los Angeles County (chmn. com. on continuing edn. of bar 1964-67), Am. bar assns., Estates Planning Council of Hollywood (Calif.), Inc. Office: 333 S Hope St 43d floor Los Angeles CA 90071 Tel (213) 613-7093

BERMAN, HERBERT ELI, b. Bklyn., Oct. 8, 1933; student L.I. U., 1956; LL.B. cum laude, N.Y. U., 1959. Admitted to N.Y. bar, 1959; individual practice law, Bklyn., 1959-67, 71—; partner firm Greenspun, Berman & Fink, Bklyn., 1967-69, firm Spector, Meissner, Greenspun, Berman & Fink, Bklyn., 1969-71. Mem. N.Y.C. Council, 1975—. Mem. Criminal, Bklyn. bar assns. Office: 16 Court St Brooklyn NY 11241 Tel (212) 624-2580

BERMAN, JOHN ARTHUR, b. Hartford, Conn., Feb. 29, 1932; A.B., Wheaton Coll., 1954; LL.B., U. Conn., 1957. Admitted to Conn. bar, 1957; mem. firm Berman & Berman, Hartford, 1958-70; mem. firm Berman & Bourns, Hartford, 1970—; mem. Conn. Ho. of Reps., 1977—; asst. corp. counsel, West Hartford, Conn., 1960-62. Pres. Conn. Half Way House, Inc., 1966-70; chmn. Parks and Recreation Adv. Bd., West Hartford, 1974—. Mem. Am., (family law sec.),Conn., Hartford County bar assns., Am. Trial Lawyers Assn. Home: 37 Glenwood Rd West Hartford CT 06107 Office: 242 Trumbull St Hartford CT 06103 Tel (203) 278-1302

BERMAN, MARTIN SAMUEL, b. Boston, May 30, 1933; B.S. in Bus. Adminstrn., Boston U., 1956; LL.B., Portia Law Sch., 1965. Admitted to Mass. bar, 1965; partner firm Berman & Shuman, Boston, 1965—; pres. Berman & Sons, Inc., 1960—; lectr. in field. Mem. Mayor's Com. for Minority Group Housing, Boston, 1960-61; community chmn. Mass. Bay United Fund. Boston, 1967-68; vice-chmn., dir. Boston chpt. ARC, 1976—; dir. Jewish Big Brother Assn., Boston, 1976—. Mem. Am., Mass., Boston bar assns., Greater Boston Real Estate Bd. (past v.p.), Rental Housing Assn. (past pres.). Office: 89 State St Boston MA 02109 Tel (617) 523-1307

BERMAN, NAOMI EILEEN-COHEN, b. Bklyn., May 30, 1947; B.A. in Social Work, Pa. State U., 1969; J.D., Temple U., 1972. Admitted to Ohio bar, 1972, Fed. bar, 1972; prof. law and psychology Ohio Inst. Tech., 1973—; instr. criminal justice Columbus Tech. Inst., 1973—; individual practice law, Columbus, 1974—; atty. Ohio State Legal Services. Mem. Am., Ohio State bar assns. Home and office: 1460 Lillian Ln Columbus OH 43227 Tel (614) 861-8547

BERMAN, SAMUEL, b. New Haven, Dec. 15, 1923; B.S. in Bus. Adminstrn., U. Denver, 1948, LL.B., 1951. Admitted to Colo. bar, 1952; individual practice law, Denver, 1952—. Mem. Denver, Colo. bar assns., Am. Trial Lawyers. Home: 703 S Ivy St Denver CO 80222 Office: 710 Capitol Life Center Denver CO 80203 Tel (303) 861-0505

BERMAN, SANFORD Z., b. Balt., Aug. 8, 1942; B.A., U. Md., 1964; J.D., Am. U., 1967. Admitted to Md. bar, 1967, D.C. bar, 1968; pub. defender D.C., 1967-69; partner firm Pickett, Houlon & Berman, Hyattsville, Md., 1969—. Mem. D.C. Mayor's Com. Crime and Delinquency, 1968-69; v.p., bd. dirs. Hebrew Home of Greater Washington, 1973-77. Mem. Am. (del. young lawyers sect. 1976-77), D.C. (treas. young lawyers sect. 1975-76, exec. bd. 1973-74), Md. bar assns., Nat. Assn. Criminal Def. Lawyers., Assn. Plaintiff's Trial Attys. Home: 16013 Wallingford Rd Silver Spring MD 20906 Office: 7515 Annapolis Rd Hyattsville MD 20784 Tel (301) 577-8200

BERMAN, STANLEY, b. Elizabeth, N.J., Oct. 14, 1923; B.S. in Econs., U. Pa., 1943; LL.B., Cornell U., 1948. Admitted to N.Y. bar, 1949, D.C. bar, 1954; chief counsel FHA, Washington, 1954-57, asso. dep. commr. for operations, 1963-64; individual practice law, N.Y.C., 1960-63; exec. dir. FHA dept., firm Pearce, Mayer & Greer, N.Y.C., 1964-65; sr. partner Robinson, Silverman, Pearce, Aronsohn, Sand & Berman, N.Y.C., 1965—; lectr. Practicing Law Inst., N.Y. Law Jour.; mem. Industry Task Force Reviewing FHA Multi-family Processing; mem. N.J. Housing Fin. Agy. Task Force Reviewing Mortgage Forms. Trustee Jewish Assn. for Services for Aged, N.Y.C., 1972—, Citizens Housing and Planning Council, N.Y.C., 1974—, Community Service Soc., N.Y.C., 1974—; mem. N.Y.C. Mayor's Task Force on Mitchell-Lama Program. Mem. D.C., N.Y. State, Am. bar assns., Am. Arbitration Assn. Home: 370 E 76th St New York City NY 10021 Office: 230 Park Ave New York City NY 10017 Tel (212) 698-7766

BERMANT, GEORGE WILSON, b. Los Angeles, July 2, 1926; B.A. magna cum laude, U. So. Calif., 1950; LL.B. cum laude, Yale, 1953. Admitted to Calif. bar, 1953; asso. firm Gibson, Dunn & Crutcher, Los Angeles, 1953-61, partner, 1961—. Pres. Hathaway Home for Children, Los Angeles, 1962. Mem. Am., Los Angeles (bd. govs. sect. comml. law and bankruptcy 1976—) bar assns., Fin. Lawyers Conf. (pres. Los Angeles chpt. 1967-68). Contbr. articles to continuing edn. programs. Home: 1511 N Ogden Dr Los Angeles CA 90046 Office: 515 S Flower St Los Angeles CA 90071 Tel (213) 488-7474

BERMAS, STEPHEN, b. N.Y.C., Apr. 27, 1925; B.S., Cornell U., 1949, LL.B., 1950; LL.M., N.Y. U., 1957. Admitted to N.Y. State bar, 1950; instr. law Queen's Coll., N.Y.C., 1964-68; law sec. to chief judge U.S. Dist. Ct., So. Dist. N.Y., N.Y.C., 1951-55; asso. firm Wagner, Quillinan, Wagner & Tennant, N.Y.C., 1950-51; partner firm Feltman & Bermas, N.Y.C., 1964-66, firm Medine & Bermas, N.Y.C., 1959-63; asso. firm Gordon, Brady, Caffrey & Keller, N.Y.C., 1955-59; sr. atty. Columbia Gas System Corp., N.Y.C., 1966-69; sr. atty. Continental Group Inc., N.Y.C., 1969-71, group counsel, 1971-76, asst. gen. counsel, 1976—. Mem. N.Y. State, Am., Nassau County bar assns. Home: 4 Reed Ct Great Neck NY 11024 Office: Continental Group Inc 633 3d Ave New York City NY 10017 Tel (212) 551-7306

BERNACCHI, RICHARD LLOYD, b. Los Angeles, Dec. 15, 1938; B.C.S., U. Santa Clara, 1961; LL.B., U. So. Calif., 1964. Admitted to Calif. bar, 1965; asso. firm Irell & Manella, Los Angeles, 1964-70, partner, 1970—; chmn. Preconf. Symposium on Law and Computers, Tokyo, 1974—; co-chmn. Regional Transp. Com., Los Angeles, 1970-72. Mem. Am., Los Angeles County, Beverly Hills bar assns., Computer Law Assn., Am. Fedn. Info. Processing Socs., Order of Coif, Phi Delta Phi, Beta Gamma Sigma, Alpha Sigma Nu. Co-author: Data Processing Contracts and the Law, 1974; contbr. article to legal jour. Office: 1800 Ave of the Stars Los Angeles CA 90067 Tel (213) 277-1010

BERNARD, HUGH Y(ANCEY), JR., b. Athens, Ga., July 17, 1919; A.B., U. Ga., 1941; B.S. in L.S., Columbia, 1947; J.D., George Washington U., 1961. Tchr. pub. high sch., Moultrie, Ga., 1941; clk. VA, Atlanta, 1946; librarian Library of Congress Copyright Office, 1947-59, sr. cataloger manuscripts project, 1959-60; law librarian George Washington U., 1960—, asst. prof. law, 1966-68, asso. prof., 1968-70, prof., 1970—; admitted to D.C. bar, 1961, U.S. D.C. Circuit Ct. Appeals bar, 1962, U.S. Supreme Ct. bar, 1969; cons. in field. Trustee Luther Rice Coll., 1972—. Mem. Am. Bar Assn., D.C. Bar, Am. Assn. Law Libraries, Law Librarian Soc. Washington, Nat. Lawyers' Club, Order of Coif (faculty mem.), Phi Beta Kappa, Phi Alpha Delta. Author: The Law of Death and Disposal of the Dead, 1966; Public Officials, Elected and Appointed, 1968; (with P.J.T. Callahan) Your Complete Guide to Estate Planning, 1971; contbr. articles to legal jours. Home: 1911 Paul Spring Pkwy Alexandria VA 22308 Office: George Washington U Nat Law Center Library Washington DC 20052 Tel (202) 676-7337

BERNARD, WILLIAM NEIL, b. Hastings, Minn., Nov. 18, 1928; B.S., B.Aero. Engring., U. Minn., 1955, J.D., William Mitchell Coll. Law, 1963. Admitted to Minn. bar, Fed. bar, 1964; engr. Mpls. Honeywell Co., 1955-59; engr., atty. Univac div. Sperry Rand Corp., 1959-64; asso. firm Davis & Strauman, Willmar, Minn., 1964-66; individual practice law, Willmar, 1966—; instr.-lectr. U.S. Air Force Inst., 1957-58. Mem. Am., Minn. Kandiyohi County bar assns. Home: 1415 Willmar Ave Willmar MN 56201 Office: 520 W Litchfield Ave Willmar MN 56201 Tel (612) 235-2522

BERNARD, WILLIAM ROBERT, b. Washington, June 2, 1942; B.A., U. Va., 1965; LL.B., Tulane U., 1968. Admitted to D.C. bar, 1969; partner firm Cross, Murphy & Smith, Washington, 1971-76, firm Hogue, Crothers & Bernard, Washington, 1977—; mng. dir. Reynolds Bank & Trust Co., Ltd., 1973-76; chmn. bd. British W. Indies Guaranty Trust Co., Ltd., 1976—; mng. dir. British W. Indies Ins., Ltd., 1976—. Mem. Am., D.C. bar assns., Bar Assn. D.C. Office: 1128 16th St NW Washington DC 20036 Tel (202) 857-0123

BERNHARD, BERL, b. N.Y.C., Sept. 7, 1929; B.A. in Govt. magna cum laude (Rufus Choate scholar), Dartmouth, 1951; LL.B., Yale, 1954; LL.D., Central Ohio State Coll., 1963. Admitted to D.C. bar, 1954, U.S. Supreme Ct. bar, 1957; law clk. firm Davis, Polk, Wardwell, Sunderland & Kiendl, N.Y.C., 1953; law clk. U.S. Dist. Judge Luther W. Youngdahl, Washington, 1954-56; individual practice law, Washington, 1956-58; partner firm Verner, Liipfert, Bernhard & McPherson, and predecessors, Washington, 1959—; partner firm Hughes, Hubbard, & Reed, Washington, 1972-75; gen. counsel Democratic Senatorial Campaign Com., 1966-71, Evening Star Newspaper Co., Washington, 1974—, also dir.; gen. counsel Evening Star Broadcasting Co., 1976—; adj. prof. law Georgetown U. Law Center. Mem. Bar Assn. D.C., Am. Bar Assn., Assn. Interstate Practitioners, Am. Arbitration Assn. (mem. panel of arbitrators 1963—), Phi Beta Kappa, Sigma Nu, Phi Delta Phi. Recipient Arthur S. Flemming award, D.C. Jr. C. of C., 1960, Outstanding Young Man award U.S. Jr. C. of C., 1962. Home: 5405 Blackistone Rd Bethesda MD 20016 Office: 1660 L St NW Washington DC 20036 Tel (202) 452-7424

BERNHARD, GEORGE GREGORY, b. N.Y.C., May 1, 1928; B.B.A., Manhattan Coll., 1950; LL.B., cum laude N.Y. Law Sch., 1959. Admitted to N.Y. State bar, 1959, U.S. Dist. Ct. bar, 1969, U.S. Supreme Ct. bar, 1971; individual practice law, Pawling, Poughkeepsie, N.Y., 1959-72; village atty. Village of Pawling, 1966, justice of the peace, 1966-68, town justice, 1968-72; judge Family Ct. Dutchess County (N.Y.), 1972—; cons. in field. Active Dutchess County Cancer Fund; bd. dirs. Heart Fund; adv. com. on criminal justice Dutchess Community Coll., 1973-76. Mem. N.Y. State, Dutchess County bar assns., N.Y. State, Dutchess County (pres.) magistrates assns. N.Y. State Assn. Family Court Judges. Office: care Family Court 28 Market St Poughkeepsie NY 12601 Tel (914) 485-9783

BERNHARD, HERBERT ASHLEY, b. Jersey City, Sept. 24, 1927; student Mexico City Coll., 1948; B.S., N.J. Inst. Tech., 1949; M.A., Columbia, 1950; J.D. cum laude, U. Mich., 1957. Research engr. Curtiss-Wright Co., Caldwell, N.J., 1950-52; research engr. Boeing Aircraft Co., Cape Canaveral, Fla., 1952-55; admitted to Calif. bar, 1958; asso. firm O'Melveny & Myers, Los Angeles, 1957-62; partner firm Greenberg, Bernhard, Weiss & Karma, Inc., Los Angeles, 1962—; instr. math. U. Fla., 1952-55; instr. elec. engring. U. Mich., 1955-57. Vice pres. So. Calif. div. Am. Jewish Congress; chmn. adv. com. Skirball Mus.; mem. bd. overseers Hebrew Union Coll., Am., Calif., Los Angeles bar assns., IEEE, Math. Assn. Am., Order of Coif, Tau Beta Pi, Omicron Delta Kappa. Recipient Henry M. Bates award Mich. Law Rev., 1957. Home: 1105 Tower Rd Beverly Hills CA 90210 Office: 1880 Century Pk E Los Angeles CA 90067 Tel (213) 553-6111

BERNHARDT, ROGER HARRIS, b. Cleve., May 27, 1934; B.A., U. Chgo., 1955, M.A., 1957, J.D., 1960. Admitted to Calif. bar, 1961; prof. law Golden Gate U. Law Sch., 1961-64, 69—; individual practice law, San Francisco, 1964-69. Mem. Am., San Francisco bar assns. Author: Real Property in a Nutshell, 1975; contbr. articles to legal jours. Home: 662 9th Ave San Francisco CA 94118 Office: 536 Mission St San Francisco CA 94105 Tel (415) 391-7800

BERNHEIM, JACOB LEONHARD, b. Buchau, Ger., Dec. 7, 1919; B.A., U. Wis. at Madison, 1948, LL.B., 1949. Admitted to Wis. bar, 1949, U.S. Supreme Ct. bar, 1956; research asst. U. Wis. at Madison Law Sch., 1948-49, research asso., 1958-59; atty. office solicitor U.S. Dept. Agr., Washington, 1949-51; atty., exec. asst. to chmn. Wage Stblzn. Bd. Region VII, Chgo., 1951-53; asso. firm Lamfrom & Peck, Milw., 1953-63, partner, 1964-66; partner firm Michael, Best & Friedrich, Milw., 1966—. Mem. adv. bd. Saint Lawrence Seaway Devel. Corp., Washington, 1969—. Mem. State Bar Wis., Am., Fed., Milw. bar assns., Indsl. Relations Research Assn. Bd. editors Wis. Law Rev., 1948-49. Home: 1705 E Olive St Shorewood WI 53211 Office: 250 E Wisconsin Ave Suite 2000 Milwaukee WI 53202 Tel (414) 271-6560

BERNIGER, MICHAEL AUGUSTINE, b. Las Vegas, N. Mex., July 18, 1941; B.A., U. Colo., 1963; LL.B., U. Tex., 1966. Admitted to Tex. bar, 1966, Colo. bar, 1968; asso. firm Smith & Duncan, Colorado Springs, Colo., 1970-71; partner firm Smith, Duncan, Berniger & Nuss, Colorado Springs, 1971-73; individual practice law, Colorado Springs, 1973—. Bd. dirs. Civic Theatre, Colorado Springs, 1974-76. Mem. Am., Tex., Colo., El Paso County bar assns., U. Colo. Alumni Assn. (pres. 1971-74). Office: suite 430 105 E Vermijo St Colorado Springs CO 80903 Tel (303) 473-7700

BERNS, SHELDON, b. Cleve., Dec. 13, 1932; B.S. summa cum laude, Ohio State U., 1958; LL.B., Case Western Res. U., 1960. Admitted to Ohio bar, 1960, U.S. Supreme Ct. bar, 1970; asso. firm Kahn, Kleinman, Yanowitz & Arnson, Cleve., 1960-69, partner, 1969—. Councilman, City of Beachwood (Ohio), 1971—; mem. Cuyahoga County Republican Exec. Com., 1968—. Mem. Ohio State, Cuyahoga County, Greater Cleve. bar assns., Assn. Trial Lawyers Am., Order of Coif, Beta Gamma Sigma. Home: 24711 Beechmont Ct Beechmont OH 44122 Office: 1300 Bond Court Bldg Cleveland OH 44114 Tel (216) 696-3311

BERNSON, HAROLD B., b. Denver, Nov. 7, 1914; LL.B./J.D., U. So. Calif., 1938. Admitted to Calif. bar; partner firm Gilford & Bernson, Hollywood, Calif., 1940-42, Leslie & Bernson, Beverly Hills, Calif., 1955-63, Goldstein & Bernson, Beverly Hills and Century City, Calif., 1963-66; practice law, Los Angeles; legal officer U.S. Air Force, 1944-45. Mem. Am. Bar Assn., State Bar of Calif., Am. Arbitration Assn. Office: 11110 W Ohio Ave Suite 105 Los Angeles CA 90025 Tel (213) 479-3728

BERNSTEIN, ALBERT, b. Memphis, Nov. 27, 1907; LL.B., U. Tenn., Knoxville, 1932. Admitted to Tenn. bar, 1932; individual practice law, Memphis. Home: 830 Bartlett Rd Apt 15 Memphis TN 38122 Office: 828 Dermon Bldg 46 N 3rd St Memphis TN 38103 Tel (901) 525-1761

BERNSTEIN, BERNARD, b. N.Y.C., Nov. 30, 1908; A.B., Columbia U., 1928, J.D. (Kent scholar), 1930. Admitted to N.Y. bar, 1931, U.S. Supreme Ct. bar, 1936, D.C. bar, 1947; asso. firm Mitchell, Taylor, Capron & Marsh, N.Y.C., 1930-33; atty. Dept. Treasury, 1933-42, asst. gen. counsel, 1938-42; U.S. adviser Inter-Am. Conf. on Systems Econ. and Fin. Control, 1942; col. Gen. Staff and fin. adviser to Gen. Eisenhower, 1942-45; legal adviser Am. Jewish Conf., 1946-48; chmn. working com. Jewish orgns. for treaties with enemy countries, 1946-47; cons. on behalf Coordinating Bd. Jewish orgns. to ECOSOC, 1949-53; individual practice law, N.Y.C., 1946—. Chmn. Kings Point (N.Y.) Bd. Appeals, 1971-75. Mem. N.Y. County Lawyers Assn. (chmn. com. fgn. and internat. law 1964-69), Am. Soc. Internat. Law, Mil. Govt. Assn., Am., N.Y. State bar assns., Bar Assn. City N.Y., Am. Fgn. Law Assn., Am. Soc. French Legion of Honor, Tau Delta Phi. Editor Columbia Law Rev., 1928-30. Home: 34 Elm Ridge Rd Kings Point NY 11024 Office: 745 Fifth Ave New York City NY 10022 Tel (212) 753-4895

BERNSTEIN, DANIEL LEWIS, b. Durham, N.C., Aug. 19, 1937; A.B., Amherst Coll., 1959; LL.B., Harvard, 1962. Admitted to N.Y. bar, 1964, D.C. bar, 1976; since practiced in N.Y.C., asso. firm Abraham L. Bienstock, 1964-66; asso. firm Hale Russell Gray Seaman & Birkett and predecessors, 1966-69, partner, 1969—. Mem. Am. Bar Assn., Assn. Bar City N.Y. Home: 1 Essex Pl Bronxville NY 10708 Office: 122 E 42d St New York City NY 10017 Tel (212) 697-1850

BERNSTEIN, JOEL MICHAEL, b. San Francisco, July 31, 1945; B.A., U. Mich., 1966; J.D., U. Chgo., 1969. Admitted to Ill. bar, 1970, Calif. bar, 1971; asso. firm Nossaman, Waters, Krueger & Marsh, Los Angeles, 1970-75; mem. firm Stern, Hanessian, Clarke & Stambul, Los Angeles, 1975—. Bd. dirs. U. Chgo. Law Sch. Alumni, 1971—, U. Mich. Alumni Assn. of Los Angeles, 1974—, U. Chgo. Law Sch. Alumni So. Calif. chpt., 1975—. Mem. Am., Calif. State, Los Angeles County bar assns., Phi Beta Kappa. Office: 11661 San Vicente Blvd Los Angeles CA 90049 Tel (213) 476-7311

BERNSTEIN, MERTON CLAY, b. N.Y.C., Mar. 26, 1923; B.A., Oberlin Coll., 1943; LL.B., Columbia, 1948. Admitted to N.Y. bar, 1948; asso. firm Schlesinger and Schlesinger, N.Y.C., 1948; atty. NLRB, Washington, 1948-51; counsel Nat. Enforcement Commn., Washington, 1951, U.S. Senate subcom. on Labor, 1952; legis. asst. Senator Wayne Morse, Washington, 1953-56; spl. counsel U.S. Senate Com. on Labor and Public Welfare, Washington, 1957-58; asso. prof. law U. Nebr., 1958-59; lectr. Yale, 1960-65; prof. law Ohio State U., 1965-75; vis. prof. Columbia, 1967-68; Fulbright vis. prof. law Leiden U. (Netherlands), 1975-76; Walter D. Coles prof. law Washington U., 1975—; chmn. adv. com. on research U.S. Social Security Adminstrn., Washington, 1967-70; mem. Ohio Retirement Study Commn., Columbus, 1972-75. Mem. Planning and Zoning Commn. Bethany, 1963-65. Mem. Am. Bar Assn. (sec. sect. on labor law 1968-69, co-chmn. com. on pensions and related benefits 1964-67), Nat. Acad. Arbitrators, Indsl. Soc. for Labor Law and Social Legislation, Indsl. Relations Research Assn. Author: Private Dispute Settlement, Cases and Materials on Arbitration, 1969; The Future of Private Pensions, 1964; contbr. articles to legal jours.; recipient Elizur Wright award, 1965. Office: Sch Law Washington U Saint Louis MO 63130 Tel (314) 863-0100 X 4847

BERNSTEIN, MICHAEL IRWIN, b. Bklyn., Mar. 31, 1938; B.A. in Econs., U. Mich., 1959; LL.B., Columbia, 1962. Admitted to N.Y. bar, 1963; U.S. Dist. Ct. for So. and Eastern Dist. N.Y. bar, 1970, U.S. 2d Circuit Ct. Appeals bar, 1970, U.S. Supreme Ct. bar, 1974; since practiced in N.Y.C.; atty. NLRB, 1962-65; asso. firm Nordlinger, Riegelman, Benetar & Charney, 1965-70; partner firm Aranow, Brodsky, Bohlinger, Benetar & Einhorn, 1971—; ad hoc trial examiner N.Y. State Pub. Employment Relations Bd., 1967-69. Vice pres. Lakeridge Civic Assn., Matawan, N.J., 1967-68. Mem. Assn. Bar City N.Y. (chmn. com. on labor and social security legis.), Am. (com. on fed. labor standards, labor law sect.), N.Y. State (sec. com. on labor law) bar assns. Contbr. articles to law reviews. Home: 15 Indiancreek Rd Matawan NJ 07747 Office: 469 Fifth Ave New York City NY 10017 Tel (212) 889-1470

BERNSTEIN, NEIL NORLIN, b. Cheyenne, Wyo., b. May 18, 1932; B.A., U. Mich., 1954; LL.B., Yale U., 1957. Admitted to Wyo. bar, 1957, D.C. bar, 1957, N.Y. State bar, 1962, Mo. bar, 1973; motions clk. U.S. Ct. Appeals, Washington, 1957-58; asso. firm Fisher, Willis & Panzer, Washington, 1958-60; vis. asst. prof. law Washington U., St. Louis, 1960-61, asso. prof., 1967-71, prof., 1971—; atty. AT&T, N.Y.C., 1961-67; gen. counsel Mo. Div. Ins., 1973-74; mem. staff Atty. Gen. of Mo., 1974-75; arbitrator Fed. Mediation and Conciliation Service, Iowa Pub. Employment Relations Bd., Am. Arbitration Assn., 1968—. Vice pres. University City Bd. Edn., 1970-72. Mem. Am., Mo., Met. St. Louis bar assns., Nat. Acad. Arbitrators, Am. Arbitration Assn., AAUP, Order of Coif, Phi Beta Kappa. Contbr. articles to legal revs. Home: 42 Hillvale Dr Saint Louis MO 63105 Office: Sch Law Washington U Saint Louis MO 63130 Tel (314) 863-0100 x 4500

BERNSTEIN, RALPH LEONARD, b. N.Y.C., July 27, 1914; student Coll. City N.Y., 1931-35; LL.B., Fordham U., 1938. Admitted to N.Y. bar, 1939, Fla. bar, 1963, D.C. bar, 1963, Calif. bar, 1966, U.S. Supreme Ct. bar, 1957; individual practice law, N.Y.C., 1939-45, 47-51; asso. firm Bernstein, Weiss and Tomson, 1945-47; partner firms Bernstein Margolin and Balin and predecessor, New Hyde Park, N.Y., 1950-61, Bernstein Sherr Hodges Lancer and Brand, Sarasota, Fla., 1963—; of counsel firm Joel J. Bernstein, Torrance, Calif., 1976—. Mem. Fla. Sarasota, Calif., Am. bar assns. Contbr. articles to profl. publs. Office: 523 S Washington Blvd Sarasota FL 33577 Tel (813) 958-8888 also 1876 W Torrance Blvd Torrance CA 90501 Tel (213) 328-8116

BERNSTEIN, SAUL JASON, b. Hilliards, Pa., Nov. 6, 1918; B.S., Washington and Jefferson Coll., 1940; J.D., U. Pitts., 1948. Admitted to Pa. bar, 1949; mng. partner firm Bernstein and Campbell, Butler, Pa., 1949—. Chmn. United Way of Butler County, 1973-75. Mem. Am. Judicature Soc., Butler County Bar Assn. (pres. 1963). Recipient Jr. C. of C. Distinguished Service award, 1974. Home: 516 N McKean St Butler PA 16001 Office: 2 Reiber Bldg Butler PA 16001 Tel (412) 287-5176

BERNSTEIN, SIMON, b. Hartford, Conn., Jan. 17, 1913; B.A., Trinity Coll., Hartford, 1933; LL.B., Harvard, 1936. Admitted to Conn. bar, 1936; individual practice law, Hartford, 1936-70; clk. Hartford City and Hartford Police Ct., 1946; judge Bloomfield (Conn.) Town Ct., 1955-60, Conn. Circuit Ct., 1970-75, Conn. Ct. Common Pleas, 1975—; law clk. Conn. State Legis. Judiciary Comm., 1949-50; dep. sec. of state State of Conn., 1961-62. Mem. Hartford Bd. Aldermen, 1945-48; mem. Bloomfield Bd. Edn., 1951-55; del. Conn. Constitutional Conv., 1965. Mem. Conn. Bar Assn., Am. Judicature Soc., Am. Judges Assn. Home: 35 Gabb Rd Bloomfield CT 06002 Tel (203) 242-1986

BERNSTEIN, STEPHEN RICHARD, b. Detroit, July 14, 1947; J.D., Detroit Coll. Law, 1973. Admitted to Mich. bar, 1973; staff atty. Am. Title Ins. Co., Oak Park, Mich., 1973-74; supervising atty. Oakland County Legal Aid Soc., Pontiac, Mich., 1974-75; mem. firm Bernstein & Rabinovitz, Southfield, Mich., 1975—; dir. Oakland U. Legal Assistance Program, 1975; judge moot ct. competition Detroit Coll. Law, 1976; lectr. Am. Soc. Sedation in Dentistry, Madison Heights, Mich., 1976—. Vol. atty. Oakland County Legal Aid Soc., Pontiac, 1975—. Mem. Am., Oakland County Bar Assns., State Bar Mich. Recipient Am. Jurisprudence awards, 1971; contbr. articles to legal publs. Office: 21751 W Eleven Mile Rd Suite 201 Southfield MI 48076 Tel (313) 353-5151

BEROLZHEIMER, KARL, b. Chgo., Mar. 31, 1932; B.A. with highest honors, U. Ill., 1953; J.D. cum laude, Harvard, 1958. Admitted to Ill. bar, 1958, U.S. Supreme Ct. bar, 1976; asso. firm Ross, Hardies, O'Keefe, Babcock & Parsons, Chgo., 1958-66, partner, 1966-76; v.p. Central Telephone & Utilities Corp., Chgo., 1976—, gen. counsel, 1977—; arbitrator Am. Arbitration Assn., 1966—; dir. Will County Water Co., 1967-77, Armor Metal Products, Inc., 1972-76, Milton Industries Inc., 1973—; sec. Consol. Water Co., 1967-72. Mem. troop 16 com. N.E. Ill. council Boy Scouts Am., 1972-75; mem. Evanston (Ill.) Mental Health Bd., 1975—, vice chmn., 1976. Mem. Am., Ill. State, Chgo. (chmn. com. on devel. of law 1971-73) bar assns., Chgo. Council Lawyers, Phi Beta Kappa. Home: 414 Ashland St Evanston IL 60202 Office: 5725 East River Rd Chicago IL 60631 Tel (312) 399-2725

BERREY, ROBERT WILSON, III, b. Kansas City, Mo., Dec. 6, 1929; A.B., William Jewell Coll., 1950; M.A., U. S.D. 1952; J.D., Kansas City U., 1955; LL.M., U. Mo., Kansas City, 1972; grad. Nat. Coll. State Judiciary U. Nev., 1972-75, Ariz. State U., 1974, 76, 77. Admitted to Kans. bar, 1955, Mo. bar, 1955; practiced in Kansas City, Mo., 1955-62; judge Jackson County (Mo.) 4th Dist. Magistrate Ct., 1962—, presiding judge, 1975—; mem. Mo. Jud. Planning Commn., instr. numerous search and seizure seminars Kansas City (Mo.) Police Dept., 1969—; lectr. Mo. Trial Judges Coll., 1974, Mo. Small Claims Act, 1976. Mem. exec. com. Urban League, Kansas City, Mo.; bd. dirs. Kansas City Retarded Children, Sober House, Kansas City, Kansas City Council Alcoholism, Pre-Trial Trial Diversion Services, Inc.; mem. Midwest regional advisory com. Nat. Park Service, 1973-76, 76—, chmn., 1973—; pres. Naturalization Council Kansas City, 1973-74; vol. legal cons. Psychiat. Receiving Center, 1961; rep. Pres.'s Nat. Conf. Crime Control, 1967; del. at large White House Conf. Aging, 1972; trustee Kansas City Mus., 1972-73; active Boy Scouts Am. Mem. Mo. (certificate of appreciation 1973), Kansas City bar assns., Delta Theta Phi (life), Pi Gamma Mu, Tau Kappa Epsilon. Office: 415 E 12th St 705 Jackson County Courthouse Kansas City MO 64106 Tel (816) 881-3731

BERRY, BURT, b. Killeen, Tex., Sept. 17, 1926; B.B.A., LL.B., So. Methodist U. Admitted to Tex. bar; practice law, Dallas. Mem. Dallas, Tex., Am. bar assns., Am., Tex. Trial Lawyers. Home: 2913 Fondren St Dallas TX 75205 Office: 601 Mercantile Securities Bldg Dallas TX 75201 Tel (214) 742-2551

BERRY, CHARLENE, b. Borger, Tex., Oct. 21, 1932; A.A., Odessa Coll., 1951; B.A., U. Tex. at Austin, 1953, LL.B., 1959. Admitted to Tex. bar, 1959; asso. with John Watts, Odessa, Tex., 1959; exec. dir. legal aid clinic, Ft. Worth, 1959-62; individual practice law, Ft. Worth, 1962-69; atty. adv. HUD, Region VI, Dallas, 1969—. Mem. bd. dirs. Ft. Worth YWCA, 1965-69. Mem. Tex. Fedn. Bus. and Profl. Women's Clubs, Inc. (pres. 1976-77), Ft. Worth-Tarrant County Bar Assn. Home: 8016 Llano Fort Worth TX 76116 Tel (214) 749-7431

BERRY, DEAN L., b. Chgo., Jan. 20, 1935; B.A., DePauw U., Greencastle, Ind., J.D., U. Mich., Ann Arbor. Admitted to Ohio bar, 1961; asso. firm Squire, Sanders & Dempsey, Cleve., 1960-70, partner, 1970—. Councilman, City of Rocky River (Ohio), 1967-71. Author: Local Government in Michigan, 1960; contbr. chpts. to legal books. Office: 1800 Union Commerce Bldg Cleveland OH 44115 Tel (216) 696-9200

BERRY, HENRY NEWHALL, III, b. Boston, Sept. 25, 1930; B.A., U. Maine, 1955, LL.B. with honors, 1964. Admitted to Maine bar, 1964, U.S. Supreme Ct. bar, 1967; law clk. U.S. Dist. Ct. Bankruptcy Ct., Dist. Maine, 1965-66; pvt. practice law, Portland, Maine, 1964-72; county atty. Cumberland County (Maine), 1973-74, dist. atty., 1975—; mem. Cape Elizabeth (Maine) Town Council, 1967-71. Home: Two Lights Rd Cape Elizabeth ME 04107 Office: 142 Federal St Portland ME 04111 Tel (207) 772-2838

BERRY, JAMES WILLIAM, b. Rock Island, Ill., June 14, 1947; B.S., U. Iowa, 1969, J.D. with distinction, 1973. Admitted to Iowa bar, 1973, Ill. bar, 1975; asso. firm Dircks & Saylor, Davenport, Iowa, 1973-75; individual practice law, Davenport, 1975—. Mem. Am., Iowa State, Ill. State, Scott County (Iowa) bar assns. Home: 4843 Gaines St Davenport IA 52806 Office: suite 12 1414 W Locust St Davenport IA 52804 Tel (319) 322-6253

BERRY, JIMMY DODD, b. Marietta, Ga., May 16, 1943; B.S., Fla. So. Coll., 1966; J.D., John Marshall Law Sch. Admitted to Ga. bar, 1971; asso. firm John Schindelar, 1971-72, Allen & Berry, 1972-76; partner firm Friedewald & Berry, Marietta, 1976—; registrar Piedmont Life Ins. Co., Atlanta, 1971. Bd. dirs. Ballet Guild. Mem. Cobb County Bar Assn., Ga. Trial Lawyers Assn., Young Lawyers Assn., Nu Beta Epsilon. Recipient Am. Jurisprudence awards, Corpus Juris Secundum award. Home: 107 Francis Ave Marietta GA 30060 Office: 260 Washington Ave Marietta GA 30060 Tel (404) 424-7600

BERRY, MAX NATHAN, b. Cushing, Okla., Dec. 29, 1935; B.A., U. Okla., 1958, LL.B., 1960; LL.M., Georgetown U., 1963. Admitted to Okla. bar, 1960, U.S. Ct. Mil. Appeals, 1964, D.C. bar, 1967, U.S. Supreme Ct. bar, 1967; served to capt. JAGC, U.S. Army, 1960-63; atty. office gen. counsel Dept. Treasury, 1963-67, office chief counsel Bur. Customs, 1963-67; partner firm Berry, Epstein, Sandstrom & Blatchford, Washington, 1967—; mem. Law Revision Commn. D.C., 1975—. Chmn. Com. for Congressman Walter Fauntroy, 1972-76; mem. D.C. Democratic Central Com., 1972—; bd. dirs. Close Up Found., 1972—, United Jewish Appeal Greater Washington, 1974—, Washington Hebrew Congregation, 1976—. Mem. East-West Trade Council (dir., founder 1972—), Am., Fed., D.C., Okla., Inter-Am. bar assns., D.C. Bar, Am. Soc. Internat. Law. Home: 2716 Chesapeake St NW Washington DC 20008 Office: 1700 Pennsylvania Ave NW Washington DC 20006

BERRY, RICHARD SANDER, b. N.Y.C., June 20, 1945; A.B., U. Pa., 1967; J.D., N.Y. U., 1970. Admitted to N.Y. bar, 1970; since practiced in N.Y.C., asso. firm Lord, Day & Lord, 1970-74; partner, gen. counsel Zuberry Assos., 1974—. Mem. Bar Assn. City N.Y. Home: 123 E 75th St New York City NY 10021 Office: 305 E 47th St New York City NY 10017 Tel (212) 838-5020

BERRY, THORNTON GRANVILLE, JR., b. Sutton, W.Va., Dec. 13, 1904; A.B., Va. Mil. Inst., 1928; LL.B., Washington and Lee U., 1934. Admitted to W.Va. bar, 1934, U.S. Supreme Ct. bar, 1939; asso. firm Strother and Curd, Welch, W.Va., 1934-36; mem. firm Strother, Curd and Berry, Welch, 1936-37, firm Strother, Herndon and Berry, 1937-42; asst. U.S. atty. So. Dist. W.Va., 1939-40; pros. atty. McDowell County (W.Va.), 1940-42; judge 8th Jud. Circuit W.Va., 1952-58; justice Supreme Ct. Appeals W.Va., Charleston, 1959-72, chief justice, 1972-76; of counsel firm Kelly Holt & O'Ferrall, Charleston, 1977—. Fellow Am. Bar Found.; mem. Am., W.Va. bar assns., Am. Law Inst., W.Va. Jud. Assn., Order of Coif, Phi Delta Phi. Home: 1575 Kanawka Blvd E Charleston WV 25311 Office: One Valley Sq Charleston WV 25322 Tel (304) 345-2000

BERRYHILL, JOHN ARTHUR, b. San Francisco, Mar. 3, 1943; A.B., U. Calif. at Santa Barbara, 1965; J.D., U. Calif. at San Francisco, 1968; LL.M., Georgetown U., 1971. Admitted to Calif. bar, 1969; asst. city atty. City of Santa Barbara, 1969-70; partner firm Hatch & Parent, Santa Barbara, 1971—; instr. probate procedures, state and fed. death taxes U. Calif., Santa Barbara. Mem. State Bar Calif. (taxation sect.), Santa Barbara County Bar Assn. (past co-chmn., now chmn. probate sect.). Office: 21 E Carrillo St Santa Barbara CA 93101 Tel (805) 963-1971

BERRYHILL, WENDELL WADE, b. Jonesboro, Ark., Sept. 2, 1946; B.S., Ark. State U., 1967, J.D., U. Ark., 1972; LL.M., Columbia, 1976. Admitted to Ark. bar, 1972; partner firm Moore, Logan & Berryhill, Harrison, Ark., 1972-76; asst. prof. law U. Richmond, 1976—. Mem. Am., Ark. bar assns. Office: T C Williams Sch Law Univ Richmond Richmond VA 23173 Tel (703) 285-6230

BERSCH, ROBERT SHERRILL, b. Lynchburg, Va., Aug. 29, 1935; B.S.C. with distinction, U. Va., 1957, LL.B., 1960; LL.M. in Law and Taxation, Coll. William and Mary, 1961. Admitted to Va. bar, 1960, U.S. Supreme Ct. bar, 1965, U.S. Ct. Claims bar, 1965, D.C. bar, 1965, U.S. Tax Ct. bar, 1961; tax. atty., Office of chief counsel IRS, Washington, 1961-65; asso. firm Haynes & Miller, Washington, 1965-70; partner firm Eggleston & Glenn, Roanoke, Va., 1970—; tchr. Am. Coll. C.L.U.'s, Roanoke, 1973—, adult div. Roanoke City and County Schs., 1971—; officer Roanoke Estate Planning Council, 1975—; lectr. joint com. on continuing legal edn. Va. Bar, 1976. Mem. Am., Va., D.C. Fed., Roanoke bar assns., Va. State Bar (bd. govs. tax sect. 1971-76), Internat. Platform Assn., Raven Soc., Beta Gamma Sigma, Phi Eta Sigma. Home: 2360 Cantle Ln SW Roanoke VA 24018 Office: 315 Shenandoah Bldg POB 2887 Roanoke VA 24011 Tel (703) 342-1851

BERSCHLER, ARNOLD ISAAC, b. Phila., May 7, 1946; B.A., Pa. State U., 1969; J.D., Temple U., 1973. Admitted to Calif. bar, 1973; exec. counsel Calif. office firm Pechner, Dorfman, Wolffe & Rounick, Phila., 1974-75; individual practice law, San Francisco, 1975—. Mem. San Francisco Bar Assn. (mem. admiralty com., bar reform com., ethics com.). Office: 690 Market St Suite 500 San Francisco CA 94104 Tel (415) 398-1040

BERSHAD, JACK R., b. Phila., May 20, 1930; B.S., Temple U., 1951; LL.B., Harvard, 1954. Admitted to D.C. bar, 1954, Pa. bar, 1955; law clk, U.S. Ct. Appeals 3rd Circuit, Phila., 1956-57; staff counsel SBA, Phila., 1957-58; partner firm Blank, Rome, Klaus & Comisky, Phila., 1958—; dir. Indsl. Valley Title Ins. Co. Bd. dirs. Phila. Coll. Performing Arts. trustee Phila. Prisons, 1964-67; mem. Phila. Fair Housing Commn., 1967. Mem. Am., Pa., Phila. (chmn. sect. corp. banking and bus. law 1977) bar assns. Home: 311 Clwyd Rd Bala-Cynwyd PA 19004 Office: 4 Penn Center Plaza Philadelphia PA 19103 Tel (215) 569-3700

BERSON, MARK IRA, b. Boston, May 13, 1943; B.A., U. Vt., 1965; LL.B., Suffolk U., 1968; LL.M., N.Y. U., 1969. Admitted to Mass. bar, 1968, U.S. Supreme Ct. bar, 1972; mem. firm Levy, Winer & Hodos, Greenfield, Mass., 1972—; asst. atty. gen. Commonwealth of Mass., Boston, 1970-73. Pres. Family Planning Council of Western Mass.

Inc., Northampton, 1973—, Temple Israel, Greenfield, 1976—. Mem. Am., Mass., Franklin County (Mass.) bar assns., Nat. Assn. Health Lawyers. Office: 277 Main St Greenfield MA 01301 Tel (413) 774-3741

BERSON, NORMAN SCOTT, b. N.Y.C., Nov. 19, 1926; A.B., Temple U., 1950; LL.B., U. Pa., 1953. Admitted to D.C. bar, 1953, Pa. bar, 1954; asso. firm Folz Bard Kamsler Goodis & Greenfield, Phila., 1954-60; partner firm Freedman Berson & O'Donnell, Phila., 1960—. Democratic committeeman, Philadelphia County, 1970-76; mem. Pa. Ho. of Reps., 1966-76; chmn. Ho. Judiciary Com., 1975-76. Mem. Phila. Bar Assn. Home: 2421 Spruce St Philadelphia PA 19103 Office: 300 Three Penn Center Plaza Philadelphia PA 19102 Tel (215) LO3-8254

BERTA, ROBERT JOSEPH, b. Derby, Conn., July 20, 1939; B.A., Holy Cross Coll., 1961; LL.B., U. Va., 1964. Admitted to Conn. bar, 1964, U.S. Dist. Ct. Conn., bar, 1964, 2d Circuit U.S. Ct. Appeals, bar, 1966; partner firm Marsh, Day & Calhoun, Bridgeport, Conn., 1964—; counsel town Easton, Conn., 1975—. Bd. dirs. Rehab. Center Bridgeport, 1974—. Mem. Am., Conn., Bridgeport bar assns., Am. Arbitration Assn. (arbitrator). Home: Norton Rd Easton CT 06680 Office: 955 Main St Bridgeport CT 06604 Tel (203) 368-4221

BERTAGNOLLI, JAMES SHERIDAN, b. Colorado Springs, Colo., Feb. 12, 1943; diploma U. N.M., 1965; J.D., Creighton U., 1968. Admitted to Nebr. bar, 1968, Colo. bar, 1969; since practiced in Colorado Springs, Colo., legal editor Shepard Citations, 1968-69; dep. state public defender, 1970-71; asso. firm Darrell D. Thomas, 1971-74; partner firm Bertagnolli and Tegtmeier, 1974-75; individual practice law, 1975—; municipal judge, 1973-76; instr. El Paso Community Coll., 1975-76. Mem. Nebr., Colo., Am., El Paso County bar assns., Am., Colo. El Paso County trial lawyers assns. Diplomate Court Practice Inst., 1975. Home: 1627 W Cheyenne Blvd Colorado Springs CO 80906 Office: POB 1481 Colorado Springs CO 80901 Tel (303) 471-1657

BERTAIN, G(EORGE) JOSEPH, JR., b. Scotia, Calif., Mar. 9, 1929; A.B., St. Mary's Coll. of Calif., 1951; grad. Catholic U. Am. Columbus Sch. Law, 1955. Admitted to Calif. bar, 1957; trial asst. to Joseph L. Alioto, San Francisco, 1955-57, 59-65; asst. U.S. atty. No. Dist. Calif., 1957-59; pvt. practice law, San Francisco, 1966—; spl. confidential advisor on jud. selection to Gov. Reagan, 1967-74. Mem. Am., Fed., Calif. bar assn., Assn. Former U.S. and Asst. U.S. Attys. for No. Calif. (past pres.). Office: Suite 955 50 California St San Francisco CA 94111 Tel (415) 981-4938

BERTHELSEN, GILBERT JOHN, b. Racine, Wis., Sept. 6, 1942; B.S. in English, U. Wis., 1964, J.D., 1967. Admitted to Wis. bar, 1967; asso. firm Foley & Capwell, Racine, 1967—. Mem. Bd. Edn. Racine, 1972-75, v.p., 1973-74, pres., 1974-75; mem. Commn. Equal Opportunities in Housing, Racine, 1968-70; mem. Human Rights Commn. Racine, 1970-71. Mem. Am., Wis., Racine County (chmn. legal aid com.) bar assns. Home: 5914 Crown Chase Dr Racine WI 53402 Office: 835 Wisconsin Ave Racine WI 53403 Tel (414) 637-1266

BERTIN, EMANUEL ALAN, b. Bklyn., Nov. 10, 1944; B.A., Moravian Coll., 1966; J.D., U. Richmond, 1969. Admitted to Va. bar 1969, Pa. bar, 1969; atty. adv. U.S. Def. Dept., Phila., 1969-70; asso. firm Moss, Rounick & Hurowitz, Norristown, Pa., 1970-74; partner firm Pechner, Dorfman, Wolffe, & Rounice, Norristown, 1974—. Mem. Am., Pa. bar assns., Am. Arbitration Assn. (panelist). Recipient Am. Jurisprudence award adminstrv. law, 1969, in estate planning, 1969. Home: 546 White Oak Rd Blue Bell PA 19422 Office: 68 E Penn St Norristown PA 19401 Tel (215) 272-6666

BERTINETTI, MICHAEL JOHN, b. San Francisco, Dec. 12, 1948; B.S. in History, U. San Francisco, 1970; J.D., U. Calif., Berkeley, 1973. Admitted to Calif. bar, 1973; law clk. Hon. John W. Kerrigan, Asso. Justice Calif. State Ct. Appeals, 4th Dist., 1973-74; asso. firm John M. Thorpe, Hayward, Calif., 1975; asso. firm Severson, Werson, Berke, & Melchior, San Francisco, 1976—. Mem. State Bar Calif. Asso. editor: Calif. Law Review, 1972-73. Tel (415) 398-3344 398-3344

BERTINI, CHARLES LOUIS, b. Union City, N.J., Apr. 9, 1911; LL.B., Rutgers, 1934; LL.B., Bloomfield Coll., 1970. Admitted to N.J. bar, 1936; dir. Woodridge (N.J.) Nat. Bank, 1954—, Central Guarantee Mortgage & Title Co., 1950-70; municipal atty. Borough of Wood-Ridge, 1948-52, 56-57, 60-62, Borough of Westwood, 1958-61; spl. counsel Borough of Moonachie, 1959-62. Pres. Wood Ridge Bd. Edn., 1942-44; mem. Motor Vehicle Study Commn., Trenton, 1965, N.J. Commn. Investigation, Trenton, 1969-76; del. N.J. Constl. Conv., Trenton, 1966. Mem. Am., Bergen County (pres. 1959-60), N.J. State (pres. 1969-70) bar assns., Am. Judicature Soc. Recipient Outstanding Achievement award Wood-Ridge Jaycees, 1969; Achievement award Wood-Ridge Lions, 1969-70. Home: 345 Columbia Blvd Wood-Ridge NJ 07075 Office: 255 Hackensack St Wood-Ridge NJ 07075 Tel (201) 939-8800

BERTOLET, JOHN HERBINE, b. Reading, Pa., May 8, 1906; B.A., Franklin and Marshall Coll., 1927; LL.B., U. Pa., 1931. Admitted to Pa. bar, 1931; asso. firm Stevens & Lee, Reading, 1931-54, partner, 1954-72, pres., 1973—; dir. Reading Eagle Co. Bd. dirs. Vis. Nurse Assn. Reading and Berks County, 1960—. Mem. Berks County, Pa., Am. bar assns., Order of Coif, Phi Delta Phi. Home: 500 Friedensburg Rd Reading PA 19606 Office: 607 Washington St Reading PA 19601 Tel (215) 376-9781

BERWICK, ERNA HOFMANN, b. N.Y.C., Nov. 2, 1912; B.A., Wellesley U., 1934; LL.B., St. John's Coll. of Law, 1938, J.D., 1968. Admitted to N.Y. State bar 1938; asst. dist. atty. Onondaga County, Syracuse, N.Y., 1942-48; asso. firm Bond, Schoeneck & King, Syracuse, 1939-42; mem. firm Murphy, Mawhinney & Young, Syracuse, 1942-50; individual practice law, Syracuse, N.Y., 1939—; lectr. Syracuse U., 1950-52. Mem. Syracuse Bd. of Edn., 1952-60, pres., 1954-57. Mem. Am., N.Y. State Bar assns., Am. Assn. of Women Lawyers, Beta Sigma Phi. Contbr. articles to trade jours. Home and office: 709 Scott Ave Syracuse NY 13224

BERZ, MICHAEL RICHARD, b. Chgo., Aug. 16, 1937; B.A., U. Ill., 1959, postgrad. in Sociology, 1961-63; J.D., Drake U., 1966. Admitted to Iowa bar, 1966, Ill. bar, 1966, U.S. Supreme Ct. bar, 1969; mem. firm Walker, Gende, Hatcher, Berx & Giamanco, Kankakee, Ill., 1966—; asst. state's atty., chief felony prosecutor Kankakee County (Ill.), 1966-67, asst. pub. defender, 1969-71; law clk. 3d Appellate Dist. Ill., Kankakee, 1971-72; chmn. Ill. Liquor Control Commn., 1973-77; chmn. Central States, Nat. Conf. State Liquor Adminstrs., 1976-77; atty. Village of Bourbonnais (Ill.), 1973—. Bd. dirs. Kankakeeland Legal Aid Soc., 1970-75, pres. 1974-75; bd. dirs. Martin Luther King Adult Edn. Center, Kankakee, 1975—. Mem. Am., Ill. trial lawyers assns., Nat. Legal Aid and Defenders Assn., Ill., Iowa, Am., Kankakee County bar assns., Phi Alpha Delta. Office: 175 N Dearborn Ave Kankakee IL 60901 Tel (815) 939-7111

BESHAR, CHRISTINE VON WEDEMEYER, b. Paetzig, Germany, Nov. 6, 1929; student U. Hamburg (Germany), 1950-52, U. Tuebingen (Germany), 1952; B.A., Smith Coll., 1953; came to U.S., 1952, naturalized, 1957. Admitted to N.Y. bar, 1960, U.S. Supreme Ct. bar, 1971; asso. firm Casey, Lane & Mittendorf, N.Y.C., 1960-63, Cravath, Swaine & Moore, N.Y.C., 1964-70, partner, 1971—; mem. nat. adv. council Practicing Law Inst., N.Y.C. Fellow Am. Coll. Probate Counsel; mem. Am. Aribtration Assn. (comml. panel), Am., Internat., N.Y. (ho. of dels. 1972—), N.Y. County, N.Y.C. bar assns., UN Assn. U.S.A. (dir.), Catalyst (dir.). Recipient Distinguished Alumnae medal Smith Coll., 1974. Home: 120 East End Ave New York City NY 10028 Office: One Chase Manhattan Plaza New York City NY 10005 Tel (212) 422-3000

BESS, LEON DAVID, b. Flint, Mich., Sept. 11, 1937; B.S., U. Detroit, 1960; J.D., Detroit Coll. Law, 1963. Admitted to Mich. bar, 1963, Fla. bar, 1970, Ariz. bar, 1970, U.S. Supreme Ct. bar, 1970; assoc. firm Butzel, Long, Gust, Klein & Van Zile, Detroit, 1963-66; mem. legal dept. Ford Motor Co., Dearborn, Mich., 1966-67; individual practice law, Detroit, 1968-70; partner firm Evans Kitchel & Jenckes, Phoenix, 1970—. Mem. Am., Mich., Fla., Ariz. bar assns., Ariz. Assn. Def. Counsel. Home: 6028 N Quail Run Rd Paradise Valley AZ 85253 Office: 363 N 1st Ave Phoenix AZ 85003 Tel (602) 262-8821

BESSE, RALPH MOORE, b. Shadyside, Ohio, Nov. 23, 1905; A.B. magna cum laude, Heidelberg Coll., 1926, L.H.D., 1957; J.D., U. Mich., 1929; LL.D., Baldwin-Wallace Coll., 1957, Oberlin Coll., 1962, Case Inst. Tech., 1962, Western Res. U. 1963, Cleve.-Marshall Law Sch., 1959; L.H.D., Wilberforce Coll., 1963, Ursuline Coll., 1970. Admitted to Ohio bar, 1930; asso. firm Squire, Sanders & Dempsey, Cleve., 1929-40, partner, 1940-48, 70—; v.p. Cleve. Electric Illuminating Co., 1948-53, exec. v.p., 1953-60, pres, 1960-67, chmn. bd., chief exec. officer, 1967-70, also dir.; dir. Tremco Mfg. Co., 1961—, Nat. Machinery Co., 1962—. Acme-Cleve. Corp., 1969—, 1st Union Comml. Properties Expansion Co., 1974—; speaker profl. and civic meetings. Trustee Heidelberg Coll., 1949—, Ursuline Coll., 1963—, John Huntington Art and Poly. Trust, John Huntington Fund for Edn., Cleve., 1966—. Mem. Ct. of Nisi Prius, Garfield Soc. Recipient Cleve. medal for Pub. Service, Cleve. C. of C., 1960, Distinguished Service award United Appeal, 1963, Ursula Laurus award Ursuline Coll., 1964, Bus. Statesmanship award Harvard Bus. Sch. Club of Cleve., 1964, Human Relations award NCCJ, 1967, Sr. Citizen of Year award Cuyahoga Sr. Citizen's Council, 1973, Univ. medal Case Western Res. U., 1976; contbr. articles to profl. and civic publs. Home: 2701 Ashley Rd Shaker Heights OH 44122 Office: 1800 Union Commerce Bldg Cleveland OH 44115 Tel (216) 696-9200

BESSEY, KENNETH PRINCE, b. Zanesville, Ohio, Nov. 18, 1911; B.S. in Bus. Adminstrn., Ohio State U., 1933; LL.B., Franklin U., 1942; J.D., Capital U., 1966. Admitted to Ohio bar, 1942; since practiced in Columbus, partner firm Bessey, Frasch & Lawson, 1976—. Trustee Franklin U., Columbus, 1944—. Mem. Am., Ohio, Columbus bar assns. Home: 362 Pittsfield Dr Worthington OH 43085 Office: 330 S High St Columbus OH 43215 Tel (614) 224-2241

BEST, CHARLES READ, b. San Francisco, Mar. 19, 1930; A.A., Coll. Marin, 1951; A.B., U. Calif., Berkeley, 1954, LL.B., Hastings Coll. Law, San Francisco, 1960, J.D., 1960. Admitted to Calif. bar, 1961, U.S. Tax Ct. bar, 1961, U.S. Supreme Ct. bar, 1965; faculty asst. Hastings Coll. Law, 1960; practiced in San Francisco, 1961-69, San Rafael, Calif., 1969-72; judge Calif. Superior Ct., 1973—. Pres. San Francisco chpt. Muscular Dystrophy Assn. Am., 1969-70; chmn. San Rafael campaign March of Dimes, 1969, 70, 71; bd. dirs. Colls. of Marin Found., 1973—; trustee Marin County Community Coll. Dist., 1971-72, Marin County Law Library, 1973—. Mem. Calif. Conf. Judges. Recipient citation of merit Muscular Dystrophy Assns. Am., 1970. Office: Hall of Justice Civic Center San Rafael CA 94903 Tel (415) 479-1100

BEST, EUGENE, b. Riverside, Calif., July 20, 1893; B.A., Stanford, 1916. Admitted to Calif. bar, 1918; practice law, Riverside. Fellow Am. Bar Found.; mem. Am. Coll. Probate Counsel, Riverside, Calif. State (bd. 1945-48, v.p. 1948) bar assns. Home: 4041 Glenwood Riverside CA 92501 Office: 4200 Orange St Riverside CA 92501 Tel (714) 686-1450

BEST, HOLLIS GARBER, b. Curry County, N.Mex., July 10, 1926; A.B., Fresno State Coll., 1948; J.D., Stanford, 1951. Admitted to Calif. bar, 1951; trial dep. Fresno County (Calif.) Dist. Atty.'s Office, 1951-53; partner firm Dubsick, Helon, Manfredo, Best & Forbes and predecessor, Fresno, 1953-63, McCormick, Barstow, Sheppard, Coyle & Best, Fresno, 1963-72; judge Fresno County Superior Ct., 1973—, presiding judge, 1974—; instr. San Joaquin Coll. Law, 1973—. Mem. Fresno County Bar Assn. (pres. 1963), Conf. Calif. State Bar (exec. com. 1970-72). Named Outstanding Instr. San Joaquin Coll. Law, 1970-74. Office: 1100 Van Ness Ave Fresno CA 93721 Tel (209) 488-3586

BETHARD, HENRY WILLIAM, III, b. Coushatta, La., Dec. 9, 1924; student La. State U., 1941-43, Calif. Poly. Inst., 1943-44; J.D., La. State U., 1948. Admitted to La. bar, 1948; partner firm Bethard & Bethard, Coushatta, 1948-75; partner firm Bethard & Davis, Coushatta, 1975—; city atty. Coushatta, 1948—, village Hall Summit, Edgefield & Martin, 1961—; chmn. bd. dirs. Bank Coushatta, 1974—; pres. Advance Devel. Corp., Better Finance Co., Inc., Value Finance Corp., Red River Realty, Inc., Edgerton Agy. Inc. Chmn. Red River Parish Devel. Com., 1953—; mem. N.W. Regional Devel. Bd. La., 1957—; bd. stewards Shreveport Dist. Methodist Conf., 1958-62. Mem. Natchitoches-Red River, La. State, Am. bar assns. Recipient conservation award U.S. Soil Conservation Service, 1975; La. Forestry award La. Forestry Commn., 1974. Home: 101 Twitchell St Coushatta LA 71019 Office: Bethard Bldg Ringgold Ave Coushatta LA 71019 Tel (318) 932-4071

BETHUNE, EDWIN RUTHVIN, JR., b. Pocahontas, Ark., Dec. 19, 1935; student U. Ark, 1953, Little Rock Jr. Coll., 1957-58; B.B.A., U. Ark., Fayetteville, 1959, J.D., 1963. Admitted to Ark. bar, 1963, U.S. Supreme Ct. bar, 1972; spl. agt. FBI, 1964-68; asso. firm Herbert McAdams, Jonesboro, Ark., 1963; individual practice law, Pocahontas, 1963-64; dep. pros. atty. Randolph County (Ark.), 1963-64; pros. atty. 1st Jud. Dist., 1970-71; partner firm Pollard, Bethune, Cavaneau, Searcy, Ark., 1968-72; individual practice law, Searcy, 1972—; chmn. Fed. Home Loan Bank Bd., 9th Dist., 1973-77; chmn. procedural com. Criminal Code Revision Commn. State Ark., 1971—. Past chmn. bd. First United Meth. Ch. Mem. Am., Ark., White County bar assns. Recipient Jr. C. of C. Distinguished Service award, 1971; named Outstanding Young Man of Searcy, 1971. Contbr. articles in field to profl. jours.; panelist, speaker various seminars. Home: Country Club Circle Searcy AR 72143 Office: 210 Vine Searcy AR 72143 Tel (501) 268-8661

BETKE, JAMES EARL, b. Kalamazoo, Mar. 20, 1940; B.A., Hope Coll., 1961; M.A., U. Chgo., 1963, J.D., 1966. Admitted to Ill. bar, U.S. Dist. Ct. bar, 1966; asso. firm McDermott, Will & Emery, Chgo., 1966-72, partner, 1972—. Mem. Chgo. Bar Assn., Chgo. Council Lawyers. Office: 111 W Monroe St Chicago IL 60603 Tel (312) 372-2000

BETLEY, JOSEPH JOHN, b. Manchester, N.H., Oct. 19, 1910; LL.B., Cath. U. Am., Washington, 1934. Admitted to D.C. bar, 1934, N.H. bar, 1936; individual practice law, Manchester, 1936—; U.S. Bankruptcy Ct. judge Dist. N.H., 1945—; city solicitor Manchester, 1942-47; mem. N.H. Ho. of Reps., 1939, 41; Democratic nominee for U.S. Senate, 1944. Mem. Nat. Confs. U.S. Bankruptcy Judges, N.H., Manchester bar assns. Home: 722 Chestnut St Manchester NH 01131 Office: 944 Elm St Manchester NJ 03101 Tel (603) 623-3543

BETTS, DAVID EDWARD, b. Atlanta, Sept. 23, 1947; B.A., St. Andrews Coll., 1969; J.D., U. Ga., 1974. Admitted to Ga. bar, 1974; asso. firm Webb, Young, Daniel & Murphy, Atlanta, 1973—; dep. asst. county atty. Fulton County (Ga.), 1975—. Mem. Am., Ga., Atlanta bar assns., Phi Delta Phi. Contbr. articles to legal jours. Home: 998 Northcliffe Dr Atlanta GA 30318 Office: 1901 Cain Tower Peachtree Center Atlanta GA 30303 Tel (404) 522-8841

BETTS, ROBERT IAN, b. Aberdeen, Wash., Oct. 3, 1943; B.A. in Polit. Sci., U. Wash., 1965, J.D., 1968. Admitted to Wash. bar, 1968, U.S. Ct. of Appeals bar, 1970; law clk. Wash. State Supreme Ct., Olympia, 1968-69; asso. firm Williams, Lanza, Kastner & Gibbs, Seattle, 1969-74, partner, 1975—. Mem. exec. bd. S. Snohomish County Homeowners Assn., 1976—; bd. dirs. Shoreline Univac Youth Activities Club, 1973-74. Mem. Am., Wash. State, Seattle-King County bar assns., Estate Planning Council of Seattle, Order of Coif. Home: 3216 218th St SE Bothell WA 98011 Office: 1440 Washington Bldg 1325 4th Ave Seattle WA 98101 Tel (206) 628-6600

BETZ, FRANK EDWARD, b. Eau Claire, Wis., Dec. 7, 1917; B.S., U. Wis., 1938, J.D., 1941. Admitted to Wis. bar, 1941; partner firm Betz, LeBarron & Poquette, Eau Claire, 1960—. Mem. VFW (state comdr. Wis. 1954-55), Wis., Eau Claire, Am. bar assns. Home: 321 W MacArthur Ave Eau Claire WI 54701 Office: 300 First Wis Nat Bank Bldg Eau Claire WI 54701 Tel (715) 834-2996

BEUMLER, HENRY WEBER, b. Douglas, Ariz., May 27, 1913; B.A., U. Ariz., 1934, J.D., 1936. Admitted to Ariz. bar, 1936; partner firm Beumler & Beumler, Douglas, 1936-58; individual practice law, Douglas, 1958-76, Portal, Ariz., 1976—; city atty., Douglas, 1939-42; dep. county atty., Cochise County (Ariz.), 1940-42; mayor, Douglas, 1950-60; U.S. Commr., Douglas, 1948-68. Mem. Ariz. Devel. Bd., 1955-59, Ariz. Civil Rights Commn., 1956-57. Mem. Am., Ariz., Cochise County bar assns. Address: POB 166 Portal AZ 85632 Tel (602) 558-2211

BEVAN, KENNETH VAN, b. Jacksonville, Fla., Dec. 20, 1941; A.A., St. Petersburg Jr. Coll., 1962; B.A., U. Fla., 1963; J.D., Cumberland Sch. Law, 1966. Admitted to Fla. bar, 1966; mem. firm Swape and Stabs, Miami Shores, Fla., 1970—; instr. Miami-Dade Community Coll., 1966—. Home: 5431 N 36 Ct Hollywood FL 33021 Office: 9519 NE Second Ave Miami Shores FL 33138 Tel (305) 751-8556

BEVERIDGE, BRENT EDWARD, b. Fairmont, W.Va., July 21, 1946; A.B. in Edn., Fairmont State Coll., 1968; J.D., W.Va. U., 1973. Admitted to W.Va. bar, 1973; individual practice law, Fairmont, W.Va., 1973—; asso. prof. bus. law and criminal law Fairmont State Coll., 1976-77. Chmn. Marion County Human Rights Commn., 1974-76; bd. dirs. Marion County Humane Soc., 1975-77. Mem. Marion County Bar Assn., W.Va. Trial Lawyers Assn. Home: 219 Fairmont Ave Fairmont WV 26554 Office: 219 Fairmont Ave Fairmont WV 26554 Tel (304) 363-1907

BEVERIDGE, NORWOOD PIERSON, JR., b. Boston, Nov. 5, 1936; A.B., Harvard, 1958, LL.B., 1962. Admitted to N.Y. State bar, 1963; since practiced in N.Y.C.; asso. firm Kramer, Marx, Greenlee & Backus, 1962-68, partner, 1969-71; asst. gen. counsel, asst. sec. Amerace Corp., 1971-73, corp. counsel, sec., 1973—. Mem. Am. Soc. Corp. Secs., Am., N.Y. State bar assns., Assn. Bar City N.Y. Home: 59 Old Briarcliff Rd Briarcliff Manor NY 10510 Office: Amerace Corp 245 Park Ave New York City NY 10017 Tel (212) 986-8282

BEVILACQUA, JOSEPH A., b. Providence, Dec. 1, 1918; B.A., Providence Coll., 1940; LL.B., Georgetown U., 1948. Practice law; asst. adminstr. charitable trusts Dept. R.I. Atty. Gen., 1950-54; mem. R.I. Ho. of Reps., Providence, dep. majority leader, 1965, speaker of house; now chief justice R.I. Supreme Ct. Mem. Democratic state com. R.I., 1950-54; del. Dem. Nat. Conv., 1968. Home: 125 Pocasset Ave Providence RI 02903 Office: Providence County Courthouse Providence RI 02903*

BEVINS, RONALD HAROLD, b. Van Horne, Iowa, Nov. 26, 1933; student Loyola U., Los Angeles, 1951-54, J.D., 1957. Admitted to Calif. bar, 1958, U.S. Supreme Ct. bar, 1965; law clk. U.S. Dist. Ct. for So. Calif., 1957-58; dep. city atty. Santa Ana (Calif.), 1958-59; city atty. Buena Park (Calif.), 1959—; partner firm Holden & Bevins, Anaheim, Calif., 1971—. Mem. Am., Calif., Orange County bar assns., Nat. Inst. Municipal Law Officers, Calif. League Cities, Orange County City Attys. Assn. (past pres.). Contbr. articles to legal jours. Home: 1237 Gordon Pl Anaheim CA 92801 Office: 300 S Harbor Blvd Suite 910 Anaheim CA 92805 Tel (714) 553-7070

BEX, RICHARD ELMER, b. Portland, Oreg., July 27, 1921; student Kalamazoo Coll., 1944; A.A., Am. U., 1946; J.D., John Marshall Law Sch., 1953. Admitted to Ill. bar, 1953; asst. gen. counsel Continental Assurance Co., Chgo., 1953-75; sr. counsel Fireman's Fund Am. Life Ins. Co., San Rafael, Calif., 1976—. Mem. Am. (vice chmn. Life Ins. Law Com.), Ill. State bar assns., Am. Council of Life Ins. (legal sect.), Assn. of Life Ins. Counsel. Contbr. article to legal jours. Office: 1600 Los Gamos Dr San Rafael CA 94911 Tel (415) 485-5214

BEYER, EUGENE EDWARD, JR., b. New Brunswick, N.J., Aug. 31, 1920; B.A. magna cum laude, Williams Coll., 1941; LL.B., Yale, 1943. Admitted to D.C. bar, 1944, Calif. bar, 1946, N.Y. bar, 1950; law clk. to Justice Douglas, 1943-44; spl. asst. to atty. gen. tax div. Dept. Justice, 1944-46; asso. firm Brobeck, Phleger & Harrison, San Francisco, 1946-47; with RCA, N.Y.C., 1947—, staff v.p., gen. atty., 1962-73, v.p., gen. atty., 1973—. Mem. Am. Bar Assn., Assn. Bar City N.Y., Order of Coif, Phi Beta Kappa, Phi Delta Phi, Delta Upsilon.

Home: 27 W 71st St New York City NY 10023 Office: 30 Rockefeller Plaza New York City NY 10020 Tel (212) 598-4475

BEYER, STEPHEN LUCIAN, b. New London, Wis., Feb. 13, 1940; student U. Wis., 1958-61; LL.B., Marquette U., 1964; admitted to Wis. bar, 1964; partner firm Winter & Beyer, Shawano, Wis., 1964-65; partner firm Werner, Beyer & Lindgren, New London, 1965—; chmn. bd. Curtis Corp.; dir. Sylvan Devel. Corp. Bd. dirs. St. Joseph Residence, Inc., New London, 1965—; pres., bd. dirs. New London Community Hosps., 1973—. Mem. Am., Waupaca County bar assns., State Bar Wis. Asso. editor Marquette Law Rev., 1963-64. Contbr. articles to legal jours. Home: 1909 Mayflower Ct New London WI 54961 Office: 308 Saint John's Pl New London WI 54961 Tel (414) 982-5711

BEYTAGH, FRANCIS XAVIER, b. Savannah, Ga., July 11, 1935; B.A. magna cum laude, U. Notre Dame, 1956; J.D., U. Mich., 1963. Admitted to Ohio bar, 1964, Ind. bar, 1972, U.S. Supreme Ct. bar, 1967; clk. firm Fuller, Seney, Henry & Hodge, Toledo, 1961; sr. law clk. Chief Justice Earl Warren, U.S. Supreme Ct., Washington, 1963-64; asso. firm Jomes, Day, Cockley and Reavis, Cleve., 1964-66; asst. to Solicitor Gen. U.S., Dept. Justice, Washington, 1966-70; prof. law Notre Dame U., 1970-74, 75-76; vis. prof. law U. Va., Charlottesville, 1974-75, prof., dean Toledo Coll. Law, 1976—. Mem. Am., Ohio, Toledo bar assns., Order of Coif. Editor in chief Mich. Law Rev., 1962-63; contbr. articles in field to profl. jours. Home: 3033 Westchester Rd Ottawa Hills OH 43615 Office: 2801 W Bancroft St Toledo OH 43606 Tel (419) 537-2379

BEZANSON, RANDALL PETER, b. Cedar Rapids, Iowa, Nov. 17, 1946; B.S. in Bus. Administrn., Northwestern U., 1968; J.D. summa cum laude, U. Iowa, 1971. Admitted to Iowa bar, 1971; law clk. to Hon. Roger Robb, U.S. Ct. Appeals, Washington, 1971-72, Justice Harry Blackmun, U.S. Supreme Ct., Washington, 1972-73; asst. prof. Coll. Law U. Iowa, Iowa City, 1973-76, asso. prof., 1976—, spl. asst. to pres., 1976-77. Trustee Iowa City Pub. Library, 1976-77. Mem. Iowa Bar Assn., Iowa Supreme Ct. Advisory Council, Order of the Coif. Contbr. articles in field to profl. jours. Office: U Iowa Coll Law Iowa City IA 52240 Tel (319) 353-6984

BIAGGI, MARIO, b. N.Y.C., Oct. 26, 1917; LL.B., N.Y. Sch. of Law, 1963. Admitted to N.Y. State bar, 1966; sr. parnter firm Biaggi, Ehrlich & Lang, N.Y.C., 1966—; mem. Congress from 10th N.Y. Dist. Mem. Am., Bronx County bar assns., Am. Trial Lawyers Assn., Columbian Lawyers Assn., Guild Cath. Lawyers, N.Y. Law Sch. Alumni Assn., Trial Lawyers Assn. Home: 100 E Mosholu Pkwy South Bronx NY 10458 Office: 299 Broadway New York City NY 10007 Tel (212) 233-1177

BIAGINI, BRUCE JOHN, b. Chgo., July 12, 1946; B.A., St. John's U., 1968; J.D., U. Ill., 1971. Admitted to Ill. bar, 1971; asst. state's atty., McDonough County (Ill.), 1971-73; city atty. City of Macomb (Ill.), 1974—; partner firm Hunt, Biagni, Holland & McMillan, Bushnell, Ill., 1974—. Pres., Lamoine Valley Assn. Mem. Am., McDonough County, Ill. State bar assns., Nat. Inst. Municipal Law Officers. Recipient Distinguished Service award Jaycees, 1974. Home: 629 S Randolph St Macomb IL 61455 Office: 232 E Jackson St Macomb IL 61455 Tel (309) 772-3178

BIALCZAK, JEANETTE ELAINE, b. Oak Hill, W.Va., May 11, 1948; B.A. summa cum laude in History, Ohio State U., 1970, J.D. cum laude, 1973. Admitted to Ohio bar, 1973; staff atty., regional counsel IRS, 1973-74; adminstrv. asst. Ohio State U. Ombudsman, 1974; asst. atty. gen. State of Ohio, Columbus, 1974—. Bd. dirs. St. John the Evangelist Ch. Fair Housing Corp., Inc., 1975—. Mem. Ohio Bar Assn., U.S. Figure Skating Assn., Phi Beta Kappa. Home: 3077 Melva Ave Columbus OH 43224 Office: 30 E Broad St Columbus OH 43215 Tel (614) 466-5967

BIALKIN, KENNETH J., b. N.Y.C., Sept. 9, 1929; A.B., U. Mich., 1950; LL.B., Harvard, 1953. Admitted to N.Y. State bar, 1953, U.S. Supreme Ct. bar, 1963; partner firm Willkie, Farr & Gallagher, N.Y.C., 1961—; adj. prof. law N.Y. U., 1968—; mem. advisory com. SEC, 1975-76. Mem. Am. (chmn. fed. regulation of securities com. 1973—, mem. council sect. of corp. banking and bus. law 1972—), N.Y. State bar assns., N.Y. County Lawyers Assn. (chmn. com. on securities and exchanges 1973), Assn. Bar City N.Y. Contbr. articles to legal jours. Home: 211 Central Park W New York City NY 10024 Office: 1 Chase Manhattan Plaza New York City NY 10005 Tel (212) 248-1000

BIANCHI, LOUIS ANTHONY, b. Chgo., June 7, 1943; B.S. in Accounting, St. Joseph's Coll., 1965; J.D., U. Notre Dame, 1968. Admitted to Ill. bar, 1968; state's atty. Cook County (Ill.), 1968-73, McHenry County (Ill.), 1973-75; partner firm Boback & Bianchi, Crystal Lake, Ill., 1975—. Mem. Ill. State, Chgo., McHenry County bar assns., Downtown Retail Businessmen's Assn., Crystal Lake. Office: 31 E Crystal Lake Ave Crystal Lake IL 60014 Tel (815) 459-9155

BIANCHI, MARTHA HILDA, b. Campana, Province Buenos Aires, Argentine, Mar. 17, 1938; elementary edn. degree Escuela Normal E. Costa, Campana; D. Law and Social Scis., U. Buenos Aires, 1964; postgrad. New Sch. Social Research, 1965-66. Admitted to Argentine Bar, 1964, N.J. bar, 1969; law clk. firm Krowen, D'Amico & Cherin, East Orange, N.J., 1967-69; asso firm Robert J. Jerome, Newark, N.J., 1969-71; individual practice law, Dover, N.J., 1971—; trustee Legal Aid Soc. Morris County, 1976—. Mem. bd. edn. Campana, 1962-64. Home: Delwood Rd Chester NJ 07930 Office: 7 W Blackwell St Dover NJ 07801 Tel (201) 366-7200

BIBB, ALLEN, b. Birmingham, Ala., Dec. 25, 1921; student Birmingham So. Coll.; B.S., Auburn U., 1948; LL.B., U. Ala., 1950. Admitted to Ala. bar, 1950; now partner firm London, Yancey, Clark & Allen, Birmingham. Fellow Am. Coll. Trial Lawyers; mem. Am., Birmingham (exec. com. 1960-64, pres. 1964-65) bar assns., Ala. State Bar (pres. 1976-77), Internat. Assn. Ins. Counsel, Fedn. Ins. Counsel, Internat. Acad. Trial Lawyers (diplomate), Ala. Def. Lawyers Assn. (pres. 1970-71), Phi Delta Phi, Omicron Delta Kappa. Office: 2100 First Nat-So Natural Bldg Birmingham AL 35203 Tel (205) 323-7291*

BIBLE, JOHN B., b. Tulsa, July 10, 1940; student U. Tex.; grad. S. Tex. Coll. of Law. Admitted to Tex. bar, 1966; mem. firm Thomas E. Lucas, Ungerman, Hill, Ungerman & Angrist, after 1966; now prin. firm John B. Bible & Assos., Inc., Houston. Mem. Dallas, Houston bar assns. Home: 7406 Marinette St Houston TX 77075 Office: 1770 St James Pl Suite 506 Houston TX 77056 Tel (713) 627-3900

BICHLER, ROBERT HERMAN, b. Cedar Grove, Wis., Aug. 16, 1934; A.B., St. Felix Coll., 1958; J.D., Marquette U., 1964. Admitted to Wis. bar, 1964; law clk. to chief justice Wis. Supreme Ct., Madison, 1964-65; since practiced in Racine, Wis., partner firm Heft, Coates, Heft, Henzl & Bichler, 1965-74, Thompson & Coates, 1975—; counsel to Bd. Wis. Bar Commrs., 1970—. Mem. Am., Racine County bar assns. Home: 3000 Chatham St Racine WI 53402 Office: 840 Lake Ave Racine WI 53403 Tel (414) 632-7541

BICKEL, DWIGHT FRANKLIN, b. Trilla, Ill., Feb. 1, 1931; B.S., U. Ill., 1955, J.D., 1957. Admitted to Ill. bar, 1957, Idaho bar, 1958; individual practice law, Boise, Idaho, 1957-58, 62-63, 67-69, 71—; asst. atty. gen. State Idaho, Boise, 1958-61; exec. v.p. Idaho Investment Corp., Twin Falls, 1963-64; v.p., sec. Mich. Chem. Corp., Chgo., 1964-67; pres. I.U.C., Inc., Seattle, Santa Ana, Calif., 1969-71; lectr. Boise State U. Mem. Am., Ill. bar assns., Idaho Trial Lawyers Assn. Home: 8976 Craydon Pl Boise ID 83704 Office: Bickel Suiter and Anderson 2309 Mountain View Dr Boise ID 83707 Tel (208) 376-1022

BICKEL, JOHN HAROLD, b. Evansville, Ind., Sept. 24, 1931; A.B., Stanford U., 1952, LL.B., 1960. Admitted to Calif. bar, 1961; partner Landels, Ripley & Diamond, San Francisco, 1960—. Bd. dirs. San Francisco Boys Club, 1970—, San Francisco Symphony Found., 1970—. Mem. Am., Calif., San Francisco bar assns. Home: 3220 Jackson St San Francisco CA 94118 Office: 450 Pacific Ave San Francisco CA 94133 Tel (415) 788-5000

BICKFORD, PETER HOLDEN, b. Elmira, N.Y., Jan. 26, 1940; B.A., U. Buffalo, 1961; LL.B., State U. N.Y., Buffalo, 1964; LL.M., N.Y. U., 1968. Admitted to N.Y. bar, 1964; asst. gen. counsel U.S. Life Ins. Co., N.Y.C., 1964-66, sec. parent co., 1967-69; asso. firm Eaton, Van Winkle, Greenspoon & Grutman, and predecessor, N.Y.C., 1969-76, partner, 1977—. Mem. N.Y. State Bar Assn. Contbr. articles to legal jours. Home: 50 Park Ave New York City NY 10016 Office: Eaton Van Winkle et al 600 3d Ave New York City NY 10016 Tel (212) 867-0606

BICKLEY, NATHAN ALEXANDER, b. Abilene, Tex., Mar. 7, 1918; student McMurry Coll., Abilene, 1935-38; J.D., U. Tex., 1941. Admitted to Tex. bar; asso. firm Smith, Bickley & Pope, and predecessor, Abilene, 1946-58; city atty. City of Abilene, 1955-58; 1st asst. to city atty. City of Dallas, 1958-65, city Atty., 1965-76; exec. v.p. Dallas Citizens Council, 1976—; prof. oil gas legis. McMurry Coll., 1956-57; chmn. Inst. Eminent Domain, Southwestern Legal Found., 1964-76, prof. Law Acad. Am. and Internat. Law, 1965-75, trustee, 1974-76. Mem. Am., Tex., Dallas bar assns., Nat. Inst. Municipal Law Officer (pres. 1974-75), Tex. City Attys. Assn. (pres. 1965-66). Named Outstanding Young Man Abilene, 1947; contbr. articles to legal jours. Office: suite 815 1505 Elm St Dallas TX 75201 Tel (214) 747-7113

BICKS, DAVID PETER, b. N.Y.C., Mar. 16, 1933; A.B. cum laude, Harvard, 1955; LL.B., Yale, 1958. Admitted to N.Y. State bar, 1959; asst. U.S. atty. So. Dist. N.Y., 1959-61; spl. counsel SEC, N.Y. regional office, 1961-66; asso. firm LeBoeuf, Lamb, Leiby & MacRae, N.Y.C., 1966-68, partner, 1969—; lectr. Practicing Law Inst. Mem. Am. Bar Assn. Bd. editors Yale Law Jour., 1956-58. Home: 21 E 87th St New York City NY 10028 Office: 140 Broadway New York City NY 10005 Tel (212) 269-1100

BIDDICK, WILLIAM, JR., b. Stockton, Calif., June 29, 1920; A.B., U. Pacific, 1941; LL.B., Stanford U., 1948. Admitted to Calif. bar, 1948, U.S. Supreme Ct. bar, 1955; individual practice law, Stockton, 1948-50, 1957-60; dep. dist. atty. San Joaquin County, Calif., 1950-52; atty. City Stockton, 1952-56; mem. Calif. Assembly, 1957-60; judge San Joaquin County Superior Ct., 1960—; mem. Calif. Jud. Qualifications Commn., 1964-72. Home: 104 W Mariposa Ave Stockton CA 95204 Office: County Courthouse Stockton CA 95202

BIDDISON, JAMES ALBERT, JR., b. Balt., Mar. 22, 1919; LL.B., U. Balt., 1939, LL.M., 1942. Admitted to Md. bar, 1940, U.S. Dist. Ct. bar, 1943, U.S. Supreme Ct. bar, 1968; since practiced in Balt.; partner firm Bartlett, Poe & Claggett, 1935-50; atty. Balt. Gas and Electric Co., 1950—, gen. counsel 1967—. Mem. Am., Md. State, Balt. City bar assns. Office: 17th Floor Gas & Electric Bldg Baltimore MD 21201 Tel (301) 234-5601

BIDDLE, TIMOTHY MAURICE, b. San Jose, Calif., Dec. 1, 1940; A.B. in History and Philosophy, Georgetown U., 1962; J.D., Cath. U., Washington, 1971. Admitted to Va. bar, 1971, D.C. bar, 1972; auditor IRS, Bailey's Crossroads, Va., 1967-68; law clk. D.C. Superior Ct., 1968-70; asst. to gen. counsel Am. Gas Assn., Rosslyn, Va., 1970-71; asso. firm Jones, Day, Reavis & Pogue, Washington, 1971-76, partner, 1977—. Mem. Am., Va., D.C. bar assns. Office: 1100 Connecticut Ave NW Washington DC 20036 Tel (202) 452-5800

BIDWELL, SETH ROLAND, b. Girard, Mich., May 6, 1900; J.D., U. Mich., 1924. Admitted to Mich. bar, 1924; partner firm Bidwell, Schmidt & Martin, Grand Rapids, Mich., 1924-51; asst. pros. atty. Kent County (Mich.), 1924-26; mem. city com. E. Grand Rapids, Mich.; dir. Hasselbring Co., Niles Chem. Paint Co., Bijou Theatrical Enterprise Co., Butterfield Mich. Theatres Co., Blodgett Uncrated Furniture Co., Bradfield & Bidwell, Inc., Ann Arbor, Mich., Lansing Bd. Mich. Nat. Bank. Trustee W.S. Butterfield Estate, Grand Rapids Youth Commonwealth; pres. Ingham County unit Am. Cancer Soc.; chmn. Ingham County chpt. ARC, 1952-53. Mem. Am. Bar Assn., State Bar Mich., Grand Rapids Bar Assn. (sec.), Nat. Stationers Assn., SAR (pres. Kent County 1960), Barristers Soc., Phi Alpha Delta. Home: Box 111 72d St Baldwin MI 49304 Tel (616) 745-4035

BIE, EUGENE FREDERICK, b. Lake Worth, Fla., Aug. 16, 1932; B.S. in Journalism, U. Fla., 1954, J.D., 1956. Admitted to Fla. bar, 1957; partner firm Blakeslee, Herring and Bie, West Palm Beach, Fla., 1957-62; individual practice law, North Palm Beach, Fla., 1962—; judge Municipal Ct., Lake Park, Fla., 1962-74, North Palm Beach, 1962-68, Palm Beach Gardens, Fla., 1963-76. Mem. Phi Delta Phi. Office: Lakeview Bldg North Palm Beach FL 33403 Tel (305) 848-1463

BIEBERSTEIN, ADOLPH JOSEPH, b. Phillips, Wis., Dec. 17, 1902; B.A., LL.B., U. Wis., 1926. Admitted to Wis. bar, 1927, U.S. Supreme Ct. bar, 1935; partner firm Bull, Biart & Bieberstein, Madison, Wis., 1927-49, Bieberstein, Cooper, Bruemmer, Gartzke & Hanson and predecessors, Madison, 1949—. Mem. Am., Wis., Dane County bar assns., Motor Carrier Lawyers Assn. Office: 121 W Doty St Madison WI 53703 Tel (608) 256-0606

BIELINSKI, THOMAS CHARLES, b. Chgo., Mar. 2, 1941; B.S.C. in Accountancy, De Paul U., 1966; J.D., John Marshall Law Sch., 1969. Admitted to Ill. bar, 1969; asso. firms Tim J. Harrington, Chgo., 1969-72, Morrill, Koutsky, Chuhak & Upton, Chgo., 1972-76, Sheldon O. Zisouk Ltd., 1976—; instr. trial practice Loyola U. Law Sch., Chgo., 1975—, Ct. Practice Inst., Chgo., 1975—. Mem. Ill. (gen. assembly), Chgo., North Suburban, N.W. Suburban bar assns., Advocate Soc., Ill. Trial Lawyers Assn. Office: 100 N LaSalle St Chicago IL 60602 Tel (312) 332-7933

BIERMAN, HERBERT BERNARD, b. Newark, Apr. 25, 1925; B.S. in Mech. Engring., Pa. State U.; J.D., Rutgers U. Admitted to N.J. bar, 1953; individual practice law, to 1974; partner firm Bierman & Haber, Parlin, N.J., 1974—; judge, Sayreville Municipal Ct., 1971—, Union Beach Municipal Ct., 1971—. Bd. dirs., YMCA, Parlin; chmn. March of Dimes. Mem. Am., N.J., Middlesex County bar assns., Am. Jud. Assn., Am. Trial Lawyers Assn. Home: Water Tower Ln Sayreville NJ 08872 Office: 777 Washington Rd Parlin NJ 08859 Tel (201) 254-8500

BIERMAN, JAMES NORMAN, b. St. Louis, Nov. 23, 1945; A.B. magna cum laude, Washington U., 1967; J.D., Harvard U., 1970. Admitted to D.C. bar, 1970, U.S. Supreme Ct. bar, 1974; asso. firm Hogan & Hartson, Washington, 1970-72; asst. dean Harvard Law Sch., 1973-75; asso. firm Foley, Lardner, Hollabaugh & Jacobs, Washington, 1975—. Mem. D.C. Bar, Fed. Bar Assn., Phi Beta Kappa, Omicron Delta Kappa, Pi Sigma Alpha, Phi Eta Sigma. Managing editor Harvard Jour. on Legis., 1969-70. Home: 906 Peacock Station Rd McLean VA 22101 Office: 1775 Pennsylvania Ave Washington DC 20006 Tel (202) 862-5300

BIERMAN, NORMAN, b. St. Louis, July 1, 1907; B.A., Washington U., St. Louis, 1929, LL.B. (Hitchcock thesis prize), 1929, J.D., 1929. Admitted to Mo. bar, 1929; asso. firm Anderson, Gilbert, Wolfort, Allen & Bierman, St. Louis, 1929-36, partner, 1936—. Mem. Mo. Council Nat. Civil Service League, 1940—; chmn. Mo. Fedn. for Merit System, 1938-43, CSC, University City, Mo., 1969-70; pres. Jewish Med. Social Service Bur., 1947-51, St. Louis div. Mo. Assn. for Social Welfare, 1948; v.p. Jewish Child Welfare Assn., 1950, Jewish Orthodox Old Folks Home, 1954-55; vice chmn. St. Louis Child Welfare Adv. Com., 1952-55, Health and Welfare Council Met. St. Louis, 1952-55; bd. govs. Community Chest of Greater St. Louis, 1950-52; sec. Jewish Hosp., St. Louis, 1954—; life mem. bd. dirs.; life bd. dirs. Vocat. Counselling Service, 1957—; chmn. University City (Mo.) Plan Commn., 1971—. Mem. Am., Mo., St. Louis bar assns., Am. Judicature Soc., Judge Advs. Assn., Am. Soc. Internat. Law, Pi Lambda Phi. Contbr. articles to legal jours. Home: 7117 Cornell Ave St Louis MO 63130 Office: 705 Olive St St Louis MO 63101

BIESTEK, JOHN PAUL, b. Chgo., May 28, 1935; B.S., Loyola U., Chgo., 1957, J.D., 1964. Admitted to Ill. bar, 1964; partner firm Biestek & Facchini, Chgo. and Arlington Heights, Ill., 1964-74; individual practice law, Arlington Heights, 1974—. Mem. N.W. Suburban (exec. v.p., pres.-elect 1976—), Chgo., Ill., Am. bar assns., Am., Ill. trial lawyers assns. Office: 10 E Campbell St Arlington Heights IL 60005 Tel (312) 255-6667

BIGELOW, ROBERT P., b. N.Y.C., Jan. 17, 1927; A.B. cum laude, Harvard, 1950, J.D., 1953. Admitted to Mass. bar, 1953, U.S. Supreme Ct. bar, 1973; law clk. Supreme Jud. Ct. Mass., 1953-54; counsel Hennessy & Kilburn, Boston, 1973—; individual practice law, Boston, 1966—; lectr. in field Supreme Ct. N.J., 2d and 3d Nat. Confs. on Law Office Econs. and Mgmt., Am. Inst. C.P.A.'s, Am. Mgmt. Assn., Practicing Law Inst., Harvard and other univs. Fellow Brit. Computer Soc.; mem. Am. (editor Computers and the Law 1966, Jurimetrics Jour. 1971-74), Mass. (chmn. econs. com. 1969-73), Boston (com. chmn.), Fed. Communications bar assns., Computer Law Assn. (sec.-treas. 1972-75, pres. 1977—), Assn. Computing Machinery (nat. lectr. 1969-70, group chmn. 1969-71), Data Processing Mgmt. Assn., Computer Soc. IEEE, Assn. Legal Adminstrs., Canadian Info. Processing Soc., Am. Assn. Law Libraries. Author: (with Susan Nycum) Your Computer and the Law, 1975; editor Law Office Economics and Management, 1969—, Computer Law Service, 1973—, Computer Law and Tax Report, 1974—; contbr. articles to profl. jours. Office: 28 State St Boston MA 02109 Tel (617) 742-8300

BIGGAR, EDWARD SAMUEL, b. Kansas City, Mo., Nov. 19, 1917; A.B., U. Mich., 1938, J.D. with distinction, 1940. Admitted to Mo. bar, 1940; asso. firm Stinson, Mag, Thomason, McEvers & Fizzell, 1948-50, partner, 1950—. Chmn. Citizens Assn. of Kansas City, 1959-60, Transp. Planning Commn. of Kansas City, 1965; pres. Kansas City chpt. Am. Cancer Soc., 1958-59; bd. dirs. Met. YMCA Kansas City, 1962-68, 70—, v.p., 1970—; trustee Sunset Hill Sch., Kansas City, 1971—; mem. Met. Planning Commn., Kansas City, 1970-72. Mem. Am., Mo., Kansas City bar assns., Lawyers Assn. Kansas City (pres. 1966-67), Am. Judicature Soc., Order of Coif, Phi Beta Kappa. Home: 1221 Stratford Rd Kansas City MO 64113 Office: 2100 Ten Main Center Kansas City MO 64105

BIGLER, GLADE S., b. Brigham City, Utah, Apr. 21, 1928; B.S., U. Utah, 1950, J.D., 1956. Admitted to Utah bar, 1956, U.S. Supreme Ct. bar, 1970; ins. adjuster Travelers Ins. Co., Salt Lake City, 1956-58; atty. Fed. Govt., Salt Lake City, 1958-68, gen. loan guaranty atty., 1968-74, dist. counsel, 1974—. Asst. dist. commr. Boy Scouts Am., 1964-68. Mem. Fed. Bar Assn. (pres. Utah chpt. 1964-65), Fed. Execs. Assn., Res. Officers Assn., Nat. Fedn. Fed. Employees (pres. Utah chpt. 1961-62), Recipient Pub. Service awards VA, 1971, 73. Home: 3003 Kenwood St Salt Lake City UT 84106 Office: 125 S State St Salt Lake City UT 84138 Tel (801) 524-5950

BIGLER, ROSS LOWELL, b. Helena, Mont., Feb. 21, 1923; student U. Mont., 1940-42, 48; J.D., San Francisco Law Sch., 1953. Admitted to Calif. bar, 1954; asso. Chas. Lederer, Alturas, Calif., 1956-60; partner firm Hurley & Bigler, and predecessors, Yreka, Calif., 1960-64; individual practice law, Yreka, 1964-76; judge Shasta Valley Jud. Dist., 1977—; magistrate U.S. Dist. Ct., Yreka, 1971—; referee Siskiyou County Juvenile Ct., 1972—. Chmn. Siskiyou County Republican Com., 1961-65, State Central Com., 1962-65; chmn. Siskiyou County Air Pollution Hearing Bd., 1972—, Siskiyou County Assessment Appeals Bd., 1973—. Mem. Yreka C. of C. (pres. 1963-64), Am., Siskiyou County (pres. 1972) bar assns., Am., Calif. trial lawyers assns., No. Calif. Def. Counsel Assn. Am. Judicature Soc., Am. Judges Assn. Home: 326 Herzog Blvd Yreka CA 96097 Office: 400 4th St Yreka CA 96097 Tel (916) 842-4488

BIGMAN, ANTON W., b. Braddock, Pa., Apr. 6, 1929; A.B. cum laude, U. Pitts., 1951; LL.B., Harvard U., 1954. Admitted to Pa. Supreme Ct. bar, 1955, U.S. Supreme Ct. bar, 1965; individual practice law, 1955—; solicitor Braddock (Pa.) Sch. Dist., 1956-71, No. Braddock Sch. Dist., 1957-69, No. Braddock Sch. Bldg. Authority, 1960-69, Gen. Braddock Area Sch. Dist., 1971-72. Mem. Am., Pa., Allegheny County bar assns., Am. Trial Lawyers Assn. Home: 485 Bigelow Apts Pittsburgh PA 15219 Office: 708 Plaza Bldg Pittsburgh PA 15219 Tel (412) 471-2644

BIKOFSKY, AARON KATZ, b. Cambridge, Mass., Dec. 9, 1936; A.B., Tufts U., 1958; LL.B., Boston Coll., 1961. Admitted to Mass. bar, 1961; partner firm Bikofsky, Walker & Tuttle, Framingham, Mass., 1961—; asst. dist. atty. Middlesex County (Mass.), 1961-68; asst. atty. gen. Commonwealth of Mass., 1969; town counsel Town of Framingham, 1971—; instr. Coll. Criminal Justice, Northeastern U., 1971-75. Mem. Am., Mass., Middlesex County bar assns., City Solicitors and Town Counsel Assn. (exec. com.). Office: 281 Pleasant St Framingham Centre MA 01701 Tel (617) 879-5000

BILBRO, WALTER, JR., b. Jacksonville, Fla., May 24, 1941; B.S. in English and History, U. S.C., 1963, M.S. in English, 1964, J.D., 1966. Admitted to S.C. bar, 1966; pres. Bilbro & Sink, Charleston, S.C., 1973—. Pres., St. Andrews Council of Civic Clubs, 1972, Northbridge Civic Club, 1969-76. Mem. Am., S.C. trial lawyers assns. Office: PO Box 643 Charleston SC 29402 Tel (803) 722-7776

BILBY, RICHARD MANSFIELD, b. Tucson, May 29, 1931; B.S., U. Ariz., 1955; LL.B., U. Mich., 1958. Admitted to Ariz. bar, 1959; law clk. to judge 9th Circuit Ct. Appeals, Tucson, 1958-59; asso. firm Bilby, Shoenhair, Warnock & Dolph, Tucson, 1959-66, partner, 1966—; conscientious objection hearing officer U.S. Dept. Justice, 1959-62; instr. trial practices U. Ariz. Law Sch., 1975-77; mem. Pima County Med.-Legal Panel, 1963-75, chmn., 1968-70; chmn. com. regulation contingent fee contracts State Bar Ariz. Trustee St. Joseph's Hosp., 1970—, chmn., 1972-75; mem. Region 8 adv. bd. Am. Hosp. Assn., 1973-; mem. Ariz. Town Hall, 1965—, bd. dirs., 1976—. Mem. Am., Ariz., Pima County bar assns., Am. Bd. Trial Advs. Home: 4717 Brisa Del Sur Tucson AZ 85718 Office: 9th Floor Valley Nat Bank Bldg Tucson AZ 85701 Tel (602) 792-4800

BILD, BRIAN ALAN, b. St. Louis, Feb. 4, 1946; B.A., U. Mo., 1967; J.D., U. Mich., 1972; M.B.A., U. Calif., Los Angeles, 1973. Admitted to Mo. bar, 1972, Mich. bar, 1973, D.C. bar, 1973; research analyst adminstrs. office Mo. Supreme Ct., Jefferson City, 1974; partner firm Bild & Patton, St. Louis, 1974—; instr. St. Louis Community Coll., Lindbergh Sch. Dist., 1975—. Mem. Am., Mo., Mich., D.C. bar assns., Beta Gamma Sigma. Contbr. articles to legal jours. Office: 11648 Gravois Rd Saint Louis MO 63126 Tel (314) 843-7133

BILDER, LAWRENCE, b. Newark, Aug. 2, 1923; B.S. with credit U.S. Naval Acad., 1946; LL.B. cum laude, Harvard, 1954. Admitted to N.J. bar, 1954; partner firm Bilder, Bilder & Freeman, Newark, 1954-55, 56-62; teaching fellow Harvard Law Sch., Cambridge, Mass., 1955-56; sec., counsel Gov. Richard J. Hughes of N.J., 1962-68; Superior Ct. of N.J., 1968—. Mem. Am. Judicature Soc., N.J. Bar Assn. Office: Hudson County Courthouse Administration Bldg Jersey City NJ 07306 Tel (201) 792-3737

BILGRE, SEYMOUR, b. N.Y.C., Dec. 5, 1929; LL.B., Bklyn. Law Sch., 1953. Admitted to N.Y. bar, 1953, U.S. Supreme Ct. bar, 1971; law sec. to state supreme ct. justice, Westchester, N.Y., 1962-69; regional counsel HUD, N.Y.C., 1969-72; acquisition counsel Arlen Realty & Devel. Corp., N.Y.C., 1972-73; v.p. law Gale Orgn., White Plains, N.Y., 1973-74; v.p., FHA/Closing counsel Sonneblick-Goldman Corp., N.Y.C., 1975-76; practice law, N.Y.C., 1976—. Mem. White Plains, Fed. bar assn. Home: 14 Soundview Circle White Plains NY 10606 Office: 1345 Ave of Americas Suite 3125 New York City NY 10019 Tel (212) 765-1717

BILL, ALBERT SEYMOUR, SR., b. Hartford, Conn., Nov. 30, 1895; B.A., Yale, 1918, LL.B., 1922. Admitted to Conn. bar, 1922, U.S. Ct. Appeals bar, 1950; since practiced in Hartford; clk. Conn. Ho. Reps. and State Senate, 1923-37; judge, West Hartford, Conn., 1929-37; corp. counsel City of West Hartford, 1946-55; state's atty. Hartford County, Conn., 1949-59; mem. Hartford County Bar Grievance Com., 1946-49, 1970—. Home: 18 Pelham Rd West Hartford CT 06107 Office: 50 State St Hartford CT 06103 Tel (203) 522-6207

BILLINGS, DONALD RAY, b. Wilkesboro, N.C., Aug. 13, 1934; A.B., Duke U., 1956, J.D., 1963. Admitted to N.C. bar, 1963; mem. firm Billings and Billings, Winston-Salem, 1963—; standing trustee Wage Earner Plans for Fed. Bankruptcy Ct., 1968—; adj. prof. Wake Forest U. Sch. Law, Winston-Salem, 1976—; mem. N.C. Gen. Statues Commn., 1973—. Mem. Forsyth County, N.C., Am. bar assns. Home: Route 1 Williams Rd Lewisville NC 27023 Office: Suite A Lower Plaza NCNB Bldg Winston-Salem NC 27101 Tel (919) 722-8195

BILLINGS, FRANKLIN SWIFT, JR., b Woodstock, Vt., June 5, 1922; B.S., Harvard, 1944; J.D., U. Va., 1947; postgrad. Yale, 1945, U. Nev., 1967, N.Y. U., 1975. Admitted to Vt. bar, 1948, U.S. Supreme Ct. bar, 1958; partner firm Billings & Sherburne, Woodstock, 1948-66; judge superior Ct., 1961-75; asso. justice Vt. Supreme Ct., Woodstock, 1975—; municipal judge, Hartford, Vt., 1955-63. Sec., Vt. Senate, Montpelier, 1953; mem., speaker Vt. Ho. of Reps., 1961-66. Mem. Am., Vt. bar assns., Inst. Jud. Adminstrn. Home: Quaker House Woodstock VT 05091 Office: Courthouse Woodstock VT 05091 Tel 457-2121

BILLINGS, JARED MALONE, b. Nashville, Aug. 31, 1931; B.B.A., U. Miami, 1953, LL.B., 1957. Admitted to Fla. bar, 1957; partner firm Dean, Adams, Fisher & Gautier, Miami, Fla., 1959-62, Nichols, Gautier, Beckham, Colson & Spence, Orlando, Fla., 1962-65, Billings, Frederick, Wooten & Honeywell, Orlando, 1966—. Fellow Am. Coll. Trial Lawyers; mem. Fla. State Bar (past mem. bd. govs.), Acad. Fla. Trial Lawyers, Am. Trial Lawyers Assn., Am. Judicature Soc., Phi Alpha Delta, Central Fla. C. of C. (coms.). Home: 1421 Tusca Trail Casselberry FL 32707 Office: 236 S Lucerne Circle Orlando FL 32801 Tel (305) 843-7060

BILLINGS, RHODA BRYAN, b. Wilkesboro, N.C., Sept. 30, 1937; A.B., Berea Coll., 1959; J.D., Wake Forest U., 1966. Admitted to N.C. bar, 1966; partner firm Billings & Billings, Winston-Salem, N.C., 1966-68; judge N.C. 21st Jud. Dist., 1968-72; asst. prof. law Wake Forest U., 1973-74, asso. prof. law, 1974—; standing trustee Bankruptcy Ct., Winston-Salem div., Middle Dist. N.C., 1967-68; cons. N.C. Criminal Code Commn., 1975—; counsel Billings & Billings, 1973—. Bd. dirs. Child Guidance Clinic, Forsyth County, N.C., 1973—, Forsyth County Day Sch., 1974—. Mem. N.C., Forsyth County bar assns. Project dir. Comparative Analysis, Am. Bar Assn. Standards for Criminal Justice-N.C. Pretrial Criminal Procedure Act, 1975. Home: Route 1 Williams Rd Lewisville NC 27023 Office: Wake Forest U Sch Law Winston-Salem NC 27109 Tel (919) 761-9711

BILLINGS, RICHARD WILLIAM, b. Rome, N.Y., Nov. 3, 1927; A.B., U. Mich., 1949, J.D. with distinction, 1952. Admitted to R.I. bar, 1953; asso. firm Mudge, Stern, Williams and Tucker, N.Y.C., summer 1951; asso. firm Hinckley, Allen, Salisbury & Parsons, Providence, 1952-60, partner, 1960—; dir., officer various local corps. Moderator, clk. 1st Bapt. Ch. in Am., Providence, 1955—; bd. dirs. Children's Friend and Services, Providence, 1962-71, v.p., 1968-70; pres. R.I. Philharmonic Orch., Providence, 1965-68; trustee Wheeler Sch., Providence, 1970-76. Mem. R.I. (ho. of dels. 1971-75), Am. bar assns. Asst editor U. Mich. Law Rev., 1951-52. Office: 2200 Indsl Bank Bldg Providence RI 02903 Tel (401) 274-2000

BILLINGSLEY, LANCE WILLIAM, b. Buffalo, Apr. 18, 1940; B.A., U. Md., 1961; J.D., U. Buffalo, 1964. Admitted to Md. bar, 1964. D.C. bar, 1965; partner firm Nylen & Gilmore, Hyattsville, Md., 1964-75, Meyers, Billingsley & Chapin, Riverdale, Md., 1975, Meyers & Billingsley, 1976—; asst. atty. gen. Md., 1967-68; atty. City of College Park, Md., 1966-67. Chmn. Democratic Party of Prince George's County, Md., 1974—. Mem. Am., Md. State (gov. 1970-72) bar assns., Am. Judicature Soc., World Peace Through Law Center. Mem. Editorial bd. Barrister Mag., 1973-75. Home: 2717 Curry Dr Adelphi MD 20783 Office: 6801 Kenilworth Ave Riverdale MD 20840 Tel (301) 699-5800

BILLMAN, DONALD LYNN, b. Columbus, Ohio, Nov. 24, 1940; B.S., Wittenberg U., Springfield, Ohio, 1966; J.D., U. Toledo, 1971. Admitted to Ohio bar, 1972, U.S. Supreme Ct. bar, 1976; asst. atty. gen. State of Ohio, Columbus, 1973-76; hearing officer Ohio Dept. Rehab. and Correction, Adult Parole Authority, Columbus, 1976; individual practice law, Columbus, 1976—. Mem. Am. Judicature Soc., Assn. Trial Lawyers Am., Ohio, Columbus bar assns. Contbr. articles to legal jours. Home: 651 D'Lyn St Columbus OH 43228 Office: 915 S High St Columbus OH 43206 Tel (614) 443-0506

BILLS, CHARLES WILFRED, b. Evanston, Ill., Feb. 23, 1937; B.A., U. Ill., 1959; J.D., Georgetown U., 1963. Admitted to D.C. bar, 1964 Md. bar, 1973; partner firm Cross, Murphy & Smith, Washington, 1971—. Home: 7207 Brennon Lane Chevy Chase MD 20015 Office: 1128 16th St N W Washington DC 20036 Tel (202) 393-8668

BILLYARD, ROGER ERNEST, b. Dunnville, Ont., Can., Nov. 26, 1942; B.A., State U. N.Y., Buffalo, 1969, J.D., 1970. Admitted to N.Y. State bar, 1971; trial lawyer Legal Aid Bur. of Buffalo, Inc., 1971-72; sr. atty. N.Y. State Div. for Youth; mem. firm Billyard, Hughes, Lazroe & King, Buffalo and Corfu, N.Y., 1972—. Mem. Erie County (N.Y.), Livingston County (N.Y.), Genesee County (N.Y.) bar assns., N.Y. State Trial Lawyers Assn., Am. Arbitration Assn. Recipient certificate of excellence Am. Trial Lawyers Assn. of Erie County, 1970. Home: 25 Massachusetts St Nunda NY 14517 Office: 1093 Smith St Buffalo NY 14212 Tel (716) 853-7732 also M & T Bank Bldg Allegheny St Entrance Corfu NY 14036 Tel (716) 599-3300

BILYEU, BYRON LEE, b. Ozark, Mo., Dec. 13, 1936; B.A. in Polit. Sci., U. Nev., Reno, 1968; J.D., U. So. Calif., 1971. Admitted to Nev. bar, 1971, Calif. bar, 1972; dep. dist. atty. Elko County, Nev., 1971-72; partner firm Evans and Bilyeu, Elko, Nev., 1972—; dep. dist. atty. Eureka County, Nev., 1971-75; mem. Nev. Bd. Bar Examiners, 1975—. Bd. dirs. Elko County Retarded Children's Assn., Nev. Home Health Services; mem. Elko Aviation Com.; chmn. Elko County Republican Party; mem. exec. com. Nev. Rep. Party. Mem. Am. Trial Lawyers Assn. Office: 575 Court St Elko NV 89801 Tel (702) 738-3171

BIN, ENRIQUE PEDRO, b. Guines, Havana, Cuba, Apr. 27, 1937; B.A., Inst. Guines, Havana, 1955; D.Civil Law cum laude, U. Havana, 1960; J.D., Southwestern U., Los Angeles, 1970. Admitted to Calif. bar, 1971; head docket dept. firm Gibson, Dunn & Crutcher, Los Angeles, 1963-70; pres. firm Enrique P. Bin, P.C., Los Angeles, 1971—. Founder, sec. Circulo Guinero of Los Angeles, 1965-70. Mem. Nat. Notary Assn., State Bar Calif., Cuban Nat., Los Angeles County, Am. bar assns., Am. Trial Lawyers Assn. Recipient Meritorious Service award Cuban Bar Assn., 1974; Meritorious Service award, Cuban Am. Tchrs. Assn., 1976. Office: 2500 Wilshire Blvd Penthouse Los Angeles CA 90057 Tel (213) 388-2377

BINDELGLASS, HOWARD, b. Passaic, N.J., Nov. 2, 1929; B.S., Union Coll., Schenectady, 1951; LL.B., N.Y. U., 1954. Admitted to N.Y. bar, 1955; law asst. surrogate's ct. Queens County (N.Y.), 1957-59; asso. firm Marshall, Bratter, Greene, Allison & Tucker, N.Y.C., 1959-64, partner, 1964—; adj. prof. law N.Y. U. Mem. Am. Bar Assn., Assn. Bar City N.Y. Office: 430 Park Ave New York City NY 10022 Tel (212) 421-7200

BINDER, BOB, b. Paris, Tex., Nov. 17, 1944; B.B.A., U. Tex. at Austin, 1967; J.D., 1972. Admitted to Tex. bar, 1972, Calif. bar, 1975; individual practice law, Austin, 1972-73, 76—; partner firm Binder, Chapman & Hargadon, Austin, 1973-75; of counsel firm Harvey Lerer, Inc., Los Angeles, 1975-76. City councilman, Austin, 1973-75. Mem. Calif., Tex., Am. trial lawyers assns, Tex., Calif., Travis County bar assns., Mensa, Phi Alpha Delta. Office: 1405 Rio Grande Austin TX 78701 Tel (512) 474-1515

BINDER, DAVID FRANKLIN, b. Beaver Falls, Pa., Aug. 1, 1935; A.B., Geneva Coll., 1956; J.D., Harvard, 1959. Law clk. to Chief Justice Charles Alvin Jones of Pa. Supreme Ct., 1959-61; admitted to Pa. bar, 1960, U.S. Supreme Ct. bar, 1967; counsel Fidelity Mut. Life Ins. Co., Phila., 1964-66; partner firm Bennett, Bricklin & Saltzburg, Phila., 1967-68; mem. firm Richter, Syken, Ross & Binder, Phila., 1969-72; partner firm Raynes, McCarty & Binder, Phila., 1972—; lectr. Pa. Bar Inst., Phila. Bar Assn. Mem. Am., Pa., Phila. bar assns., Am., Pa., Phila. trial lawyers assns. Author: The Hearsay Handbook, 1975. Home: 1412 Flat Rock Rd Penn Valley PA 19072 Office: 1845 Walnut St Suite 2000 Philadelphia PA 19103 Tel (215) 568-6190

BINELLI, RUDOLPH RONALD, JR., b. N.Y.C., Feb. 24, 1943; B.S., St. Peter's Coll., Jersey City, 1964; LL.B., N.Y. Law Sch., 1967. Admitted to N.J. bar, 1970; asso. counsel, asst. v.p. Pioneer Nat. Title Ins. Co., Hackensack, N.J., 1970—. Mem. Bergen County Bar Assn. Home: 25 Addicks Rd Westwood NJ 07675 Office: 1 Essex St Hackensack NJ 07601 Tel (201) 487-4300

BINES, HARVEY ERNEST, b. Winthrop, Mass., Nov. 25, 1941; B.S., Mass. Inst. Tech., 1963; J.D., U. Va., 1970. Admitted to Va., Mass. bars, 1971; law clk. U.S. Ct. Appeals 4th Circuit, 1970-71; asst. prof. law U. Va., 1971-74, asso. prof., 1974-76; asso. firm Sullivan & Worcester, Boston, 1976—; summer vis. prof. SEC, 1974. Mem. Va. State Bar, Mass. Bar Assn. Contbr. articles to legal jours. Office: 100 Federal St Boston MA 02110 Tel (617) 338-2828

BING, ROBERT KENDREW, b. Colchester, Vt., July 8, 1930; B.A., U. Vt., 1953; LL.B., Yale, 1956 Admitted to Vt. bar, 1956; law clk. firm Latham & Peisch, Burlingt Vt., 1955-56; law clk. to U.S. dist. judge, Vt., 1956-57; asso. ana partner firm Gravel & Bing, and successor, Burlington, Vt., 1963-69; individual practice law, Burlington, 1969-70; partner firm Bing & Reed, Williston, Vt., 1971-75, firm Bing Bauer & Cain, Burlington, 1975—; mayor City of Burlington, 1961-63; exec. dir. Gov. Vt. Commn. Crime Control and Prevention, 1969-70. Mem. Vt. (pres. 1969-70), Chittenden County bar assns., Am. Trial Lawyers Assn. (state committeeman 1965-71). Office: Bing Bauer & Cain 350 Main St Burlington UT 05401 Tel (802) 863-5538

BINGAMAN, ANNE KOVACOVICH, b. Jerome, Ariz., July 3, 1943; B.A., Stanford, 1965, LL.B., 1965; gen. course certificate with honors London Sch. Econs. and Polit. Sci., 1965. Admitted to Calif. bar, 1969, Ariz. bar, 1969, N. Mex. bar, 1969; clk. firm Brown & Bain, Profl. Assn., Phoenix, 1968-69; atty. N. Mex. Bur. Revenue, Santa Fe, 1969; asso. firm Modrall, Sperling, Roehl, Harris & Sisk, Albuquerque, 1970; asst. atty. gen. N. Mex. Atty. Gen's. Office, Santa Fe, 1971; asst. prof. law U. N.Mex., 1972-74, asso. prof., 1974-76; individual practice, Santa Fe, 1976—; cons. Fed. Res. Bd., 1975; atty. N. Mex. Planned Parenthood, 1972—. Mem. state bars Calif., Ariz., N.Mex., Am. Bar Assn. (vice chmn. marital property div. sect. real property probate and trust). Author: A Commentary on the Effect of the Equal Rights Amendment on State Laws and Institutions, 1975; contbr. articles to legal jours. Home: 222 Camino Del Norte Santa Fe NM 87501 Office: 3 Jefferson Pl POB 2208 Santa Fe NM 87501 Tel (505) 982-8868

BINGHAM, LOYD EDWARD, JR., b. San Antonio, Oct. 8, 1942; A.A., San Antonio Coll., 1962; B.B.A., St. Mary's U., Tex., 1965, J.D., 1967. Admitted to Tex. bar, 1967; partner firm House, Mercer, House, Brock & Wilson, San Antonio, 1976—. Mem. Am., Tex., San Antonio bar assns., Bexar County Legal Aid Assn. (dir. 1973), Tex. Def. Counsel, San Antonio Young Lawyers Assn., Delta Theta Phi. Home: 4419 Newport Woods St San Antonio TX 78249 Office: 1007 Nat Bank Commerce Bldg San Antonio TX 78205 Tel (512) 226-9211

BINGHAM, ROBERT EVAN, b. Cleve., Apr. 26, 1918; A.B., Amherst Coll., 1940; J.D., Harvard U., 1947. Admitted to Ohio bar, 1947; asso. firm Thompson, Hine & Flory, Cleve., 1947-58, partner, 1958-77; officer-dir. firm Spieth, Bell, McCurdy & Newell, Cleve., 1977—. Councilman, Shaker Heights, Ohio, 1955-59; pres. Greater Cleve. chpt. ARC, 1956-57; pres. Cleve. Ch. Fedn., 1953-59, Cleve. Health Edn. Museum, 1976—, Cleve. Mental Health Assn., 1954-56; trustee United Appeal, St. Luke's Hosp., Boy Scouts Am., Univ. Circle Found., Shaker Heights Pub. Library, Urban League, Hiram House, Golden Age Centers. Mem. Am. Judicature Soc., Am. (chmn. com. significant decisions in real property law), Ohio, Cuyahoga County, Cleve. (chmn. juvenile ct. com.) bar assns. Home: 2027 Lyndway Rd Lyndhurst OH 44121 Office: 1190 Union Commerce Bldg Cleveland OH 44115 Tel (216) 696-4700

BINKOWSKI, DON, b. Detroit, Oct. 26, 1929; B.A., U. Mich., 1951; evening student U. Detroit, 1951-53; J.D., Wayne State U., 1956. Field rep. Social Security Adminstrn., Detroit, 1951-53, 55; admitted to Mich. bar, 1957; asst. atty. gen. State of Mich., 1957-59; state dept. officer Mich. Dept. of State, 1959-60; atty. Wayne County, 1960-61; del. Mich. Constl. Conv., Lansing, 1961-62; mem. Mich. Labor Mediation Bd., 1962-63; individual practice law, Warren, 1961-69; judge 37th Dist. Ct., 1969—; councilman City of Warren, 1965-68. Chmn., Warren Hist. Commn., 1962-63; sec. Polish-Am. Found. Mich., 1961-62. Mem. Am., Mich., Advocates bar assns., Am. Judges Assn., Nat. Council on Crime and Delinquency, Mich. Corrections Assn., Am. Acad. Polit. and Social Sci., Macomb County Hist. Soc., Am. Youth Hostel, VFW, Polish Legion of Am. Vets. Home: 29107 Dover St Warren MI 48093 Office: 8300 Common Rd Warren MI 48093

BINNS, JOHN HOWARD, b. Shelton, Wash., June 22, 1895; B.A., Wash. State U., 1916; M.A., Oxford U., 1921, B.C.L., 1921. Admitted to Wash. bar, 1922, U.S. Ct. Appeals 9th Circuit bar, 1951; individual practice law, Tacoma, 1923-24, 27-35; dept. pros. atty., Tacoma, 1924-27; partner firm Binns & Cunningham, Tacoma, 1935-42, Williamson, Binns & Cunningham, Tacoma, 1942-50, Binns, Cunningham & Fletcher, Tacoma, 1950-56, Binns, Petrich, Hester & Robson, Tacoma, 1974—; judge Tacoma Superior Ct., 1946; dir. enforcement office of Price Stablzn., Western Wash., 1950-52; gen. counsel Port of Tacoma, 1956-67. Bd. dirs. Tacoma Sch. Dist. 10, 1931-35; adminstr. Wash. Nat. Youth Adminstrn., Tacoma, 1935-41; chmn. Pierce County (Wash.) chpt. The Nat. Found., 1938-58; chmn. Democratic party Pierce County, 1942-46; regent Wash. State U., 1945-49; trustee Tacoma Community Coll., 1967-71. Mem. Am., Wash. State, Tacoma-Pierce County bar assns., Am. Legion (post comdr. 1926-27, state vice comdr. 1927-28). Home: 7410 E Side Dr NE Tacoma WA 98422 Office: 1008 S Yakima Ave Tacoma WA 98405 Tel (206) 272-2157

BINZ, BARRY, b. Chgo., Oct. 13, 1919; A.A., U. Fla., 1941, B.A., 1950, LL.B., 1950, J.D., 1967. Admitted to Fla. bar, 1950, U.S. Dist. Ct. bar So. Dist. Fla., 1950, U.S. Bd. Immigration Appeals bar, 1950; individual practice law, Sarasota, Fla., 1950—. Lt. gov. Fla. dist. Optimist Internat., 1970-71; pres. Indian Beach Assn. Sarasota County, 1951-54, Gulf Gate Community Assn., 1963-66; chmn. Gulf Gate Lighting Dist. of Sarasota County, 1965-70; Democratic County committeeman, 1950-52, 57-58. Mem. Am., Fla., Sarasota County bar assns. Am. Judicature Soc. Home: 2704 Seaspray St Sarasota FL 33581 Office: 2136 Gulf Gate Dr Sarasota FL 33581 Tel (813) 924-0935

BIONDI, OTTAVIO FRANCIS, b. Wilmington, Del., Jan. 1, 1933; B.A. magna cum laude, LaSalle Coll., 1954; M.A. in Econs., Boston Coll., 1955; LL.B., U. Pa., 1958. Admitted to Del. bar, 1958, U.S. Supreme Ct. bar, 1965; law clk. to city solicitor City of Wilmington (Del.), 1959-61, 1st asst. solicitor, 1961-63, solicitor, 1963-69; dep. atty. gen. State of Del., 1961-69; individual practice law, 1967; sr. partner firm Biondi & Babiarz, Wilmington, 1968-73, pres., 1973—; dir. 1st Nat. Bank, Wilmington, 1966—; chmn. Del. Crime Reduction Task Force, 1973-74, Del. Gov.'s Investigative Strike Force, 1973-74; vice-chmn. Del. Agy. to Reduce Crime, 1973-74. Chmn. Del. Corp. Franchise Tax Com., 1974, Del. Tomorrow Commn., 1975—; mem. Del. Council on Banking, 1971—. Mem. Del., Am. bar assns. Am. Judicature Soc. Home: 406 Irving Dr Wilmington DE 19802 Office: 1300 King St Wilmington DE 19801 Tel (302) 655-3395

BIRBROWER, LEONARD JAY, b. Bronx, N.Y., Jan. 21, 1935; B.A., Mich. State U., 1957; J.D., N.Y. Law Sch., 1963. Admitted to N.Y. bar, 1963, U.S. Ct. Appeals 2d Circuit bar, U.S. Supreme Ct. bar, 1972; supr. Aetna Casualty & Surety Co., N.Y.C., 1958-64; asso. firm Levine & Broder, N.Y.C., 1964-65; atty. Zurich Ins. Co., N.Y.C., 1965-69; partner firm Hirshfield, Birbrower, Montalbano & Condon, P.C., New City, N.Y., 1972—. Chmn. bd. Rockland County (N.Y.) Center for Physically Handicapped, 1977. Mem. Am., N.Y., Rockland County bar assns., Assn. Trial Lawyers Am., N.Y. State Trial Lawyers Assn., Commercial Law League of Am., Am. Arbitration Assn. Home: 84 Lyncrest Ave New City NY 10956 Office: 20 Squadron Blvd New City NY 10956 Tel (914) 634-7010

BIRCH, RONALD GILBERT, b. N.Y.C., Nov. 2, 1941; B.A., Colgate U., 1962; J.D., Columbia, 1965. Admitted to Alaska bar, 1966, D.C. bar, 1972, U.S. Supreme Ct. bar, 1969; law clk. Alaska Supreme Ct., 1965-66; dist. atty. City of Juneau (Alaska), 1967; staff atty. to Senator E.L. Bartlett, Alaska, 1968; adminstrv. asst. to U.S. Senator Ted Stevens of Alaska, 1968-70; sr. partner firm Birch, Jermain, Horton & Bittner, Anchorage, 1971—; instr. in bus. law and polit. sci. U. Alaska, 1966-68. Mem. Am., Alaska, D.C. bar assns. Tel (202) 244-4250

BIRCH, STANLEY FRANCIS, JR., b. Langley Field, Va., Aug. 29, 1945; B.A., U. Va., 1967; J.D., Emory U., 1970, LL.M. in Taxation, 1976. Admitted to Ga. bar, 1970; law clk. to chief judge Sidney O. Smith, Jr., U.S. Dist. Ct., No. Dist. of Ga., 1972-74; asso. firm Greer, Sartain & Carey, Gainesville, Ga., 1974-75; partner firm Greer, Deal, Orr & Jarrard, Gainesville, 1976—. Dir., Kiwanis Club of Met. Gainesville, 1974-76. Mem. Am. (com. civil and criminal tax penalties), Gainesville-Northeastern bar assns., State Bar Ga. (dir., exec. council young lawyers sect.). Office: 212 Green St Gainesville GA 30501 Tel (404) 532-9978

BIRCH, TERRELL CALHOUN, b. Washington, D.C., Mar. 23, 1935; B.Elec. Engring., George Washington U., 1959, J.D., 1963. Admitted to D.C. bar, 1963, Md. bar, 1972; searcher patent dept. Bendix Aviation, Washington, 1954-55; law clk. firm Beale and Jones, Washington, 1955-59; mem. firm Birch & Birch, and predecessor, Washington, 1959-63, partner, 1963-75; partner firm Birch, Stewart, Kolasch & Birch, Falls Church, Va., 1975—. Mem. Bar Assn. D.C., Am. Bar Assn., Am. Patent Law Assn., Patent Lawyers Club D.C. (pres. 1973), Am. Arbitration Assn. (arbitrator). Office: PO Box 209 301 N Washington St Falls Church VA 22046

BIRCH, WILLIS DANIEL, b. Chgo., Feb. 13, 1925; B.S. in Commerce and Law, U. Ill., 1949; LL.B., Cornell U., 1951, J.D., 1969. Admitted to N.Y. bar, 1952; asso. firm Deyo, Turnbull, Turner & Normile, Binghamton, N.Y., 1951-53, firm Chernin & Gold, Binghamton, 1953-56; partner firm Night, Keller & Birch, Binghamton, 1957-63; individual practice law, Binghamton, 1963—; justice Town of Fenton (N.Y.), 1953-70. Mem. N.Y. State, Broome County bar assns., N.Y. State Assn. Trial Lawyers. Office: PO Box 891 19 Chenango St Binghamton NY 13901 Tel (607) 724-2444

BIRD, FRANCIS MARION, b. Comer, Ga., Sept. 4, 1902; A.B., U. Ga., 1922, LL.B., 1924; LL.M., George Washington U., 1925. Admitted to Ga. bar, 1924, D.C. bar, 1925; asso. Hoke Smith, Washington and Atlanta, 1925-30; individual practice law, Atlanta, 1930-45; partner firm Jones, Bird & Howell; and predecessor, Atlanta 1945—; part-time U.S. referee in bankruptcy, 1945-54; spl. asst. to U.S. Atty. Gen.; mem. Ga. Supreme Ct. Permanent Rules Com.; chmn. Ga. Bd. Bar Examiners, 1954-61; chmn. Met. Altanta Commn. Crime and Juvenile Delinquency, 1969-70. Mem. Com. for Preparation Plan of Govt. City of Atlanta and County Area; trustee Young Harris Coll., U. Ga. Found., Emory U., Atlanta Lawyers Found. Fellow Am. Bar Found. (life); mem. Am. Judicature Soc. Am. Law Inst. (life mem. council, chmn. membership com. 1960—), Am., Ga. (pres. 1951-52), Atlanta (pres. 1941-42, Distinguished Service award 1977) bar assns., Assn. Bar City N.Y. (permanent editorial bd. Uniform Comml. Code), Fed. Jud. Conf. for 5th Circuit, U. Ga. (certificate of Merit award 1952, pres. 1948-49), George Washington U. (Achievement award 1965) alumni assns., Laywers Club Atlanta (pres. 1938-39), Atlanta C. of C. (pres. 1957), Phi Delta Phi, Phi Kappa Phi, Sigma Chi. Recipient Altanta Civic Service award Atlanta C. of C., 1957, Distinguished Service citation U. Ga. Law Sch., 1963; named Hon. Alumnus Emory U. Bd. Trustees, 1965. Home: 89 Brighton Rd NE Atlanta GA 30309 Office: Haas-Howell Bldg 75 Poplar St Atlanta GA 30303 Tel (404) 522-2508

BIRD, FRANCIS MARION, JR., b. Atlanta, Apr. 14, 1938; A.B., Princeton U., 1959; LL.B., Emory U., 1964; LL.M., Harvard U., 1966. Admitted to Ga. bar, 1964; asso. firm Jones, Bird & Howell, Atlanta, 1964-69, partner, 1970—; chmn. Ga. Health Laws Study Com., 1975. Mem. State Bar Ga. (chmn. publs. com. 1977—), Atlanta (vice chmn. sect. bankruptcy law 1975-76), Am. bar assns., Southeastern Bankruptcy Law Inst. (dir. 1975-76), Ga. Soc. Hosp. Attys. (pres. 1976-77). Office: Haas-Howell Bldg Atlanta GA 30303 Tel (404) 522-2508

BIRD, FRANK BABINGTON, b. Athens, Tenn., Mar. 12, 1917; J.D., U. Tenn., 1941. Admitted to Tenn. bar, 1941, U.S. Supreme Ct. bar, 1946; atty. TVA, Knoxville, 1942, Office Price Adminstrn., Washington, 1942, 46; partner firm Bird, Navratil & Bird, Maryville, Tenn., 1946—. Mem. World Assn. Lawyers, Am., Tenn., Blount County (pres. 1951, 72) bar assns., Blount County C. of C. (former pres.). Contbr. articles Bus. Lawyer, Practical Lawyer; case note editor Tenn. Law Rev., 1940-41. Office: 100 N Court St Maryville TN 37801 Tel (615) 982-1800

BIRD, JOHN COMMONS, b. Chgo., Nov. 16, 1922; A.B., Dartmouth Coll., 1943; LL.B., U. Cin., 1948. Admitted to Ohio bar, 1948, Pa. bar, 1950, Ky. bar, 1956; atty. U.S. Steel Corp., Pitts., 1948-52, 58-66, asst. sec., 1952—, atty. homes div., New Albany, Ind., 1952-58, gen. atty., Fairfield, Ala., 1966-75, sr. gen. atty., 1975—; sec. Birmingham Forest Products, Cordova, Ala., 1970-74; mem. planning com. Southeastern Corp. Law Inst., 1966—. Mem. Am., Ala. (asso.), Birmingham (asso.) bar assns., Asso. Industries Ala., Birmingham C. of C., Warrior and Tombigbee Devel. Assn., Phi Delta Phi. Home: 3125 Guilford Rd Mountain Brook AL 35223 Office: POB 599 Fairfield AL 35064 Tel (205) 783-2351

BIRD, ROSE ELIZABETH, b. Tucson, Nov. 2, 1936; A.B. magna cum laude, L.I. U., 1958; J.D., U. Calif. at Berkeley, 1965. Admitted to Calif. bar, 1965, U.S. Supreme Ct. bar; clk. to chief justice Nev. Supreme Ct., 1965-66; dep. pub. defender, sr. trial dep. and chief appellate div. Santa Clara County (Calif.), 1966-74; cabinet sec. Calif. Agr. and Services Agy., 1975-77; chief justice Supreme Ct. Calif., San Francisco, 1977—; legis. asst. Calif. State Assembly, 1960, spl. cons. com. on govtl. orgn., 1961; tchr. Stanford Law Sch., 1972-74; mem. com. on appellate cts. Calif. State Bar, 1972—, vice chairperson com. on resolution 4-4, 1973-74. Mem. Western regional selection panel Pres.'s Commn. on White House Fellowships; bd. dirs. Santa Clara County chpt. Law in a Free Soc., 1972-73; bd. councilors U. So. Calif. Law Center; pres. bd. dirs. Hastings Coll. Law. Mem. Commn. Jud. Appointments, Am. Law Inst., Nat. Conf. Chief Justices, Santa Clara County Bar Assn. (trustee 1969-74), Calif. Pub. Defenders Assn. (trustee 1968-74), Calif. Acad. Appellate Lawyers. Ford Found. fellowship grantee, 1960. Office: 350 McAllister St San Francisco CA 94102 Tel (415) 557-2367

BIRD, SAMUEL NORTON, b. Eldorado, Ark., Jan. 19, 1940; B.S., Fla. State U., 1962; J.D., U. Ark., 1970. Admitted to Ark. bar, 1970; mem. firm Williamson Ball & Bird, Monticello, Ark., 1970—; pres. S.E. Ark. Legal Inst., 1975-76. Mem. Am., Ark. bar assns. Tel (501) 367-6288

BIRENBAUM, DAVID E(LIAS), b. Waterbury, Conn., Nov. 30, 1937; A.B., Brown U., 1959; LL.B., Harvard, 1962. Admitted to Conn. bar, 1962, D.C. bar, 1964; asst. gen. counsel Nat. Advisory Commn. on Civil Disorders, Washington, 1967-68; partner firm Fried, Frank, Harris, Shriver & Kampelman, Washington, 1971—; resident partner Fried, Frank, Harris, Shriver & Jacobson, London office, 1971-73. Domestic policy coordinator Humphrey for Pres. campaign, 1968; issues dir., gen. counsel Shriver for Pres. Com., 1975-76; mem. Md. Democratic State Central Com., 1970. Mem. Am. Bar Assn., Bar D.C. Home: 6106 Tilden Ln Rockville MD Office: 600 New Hampshire Ave NW Washington DC 20037

BIRENBAUM, HERBERT ABRAHAM, b. Phila., Nov. 30, 1937; B.S. in Chem. Engring., U. Pa., 1959; J.D., Temple U., 1963. Admitted to Pa. bar, 1964, Ill. bar, 1970, Calif. bar, 1973, D.C. bar, 1965; chem. process engr. Day & Zimmermann, Inc., Phila., 1959-64; patent examiner U.S. Patent Office, Washington, 1965-66; atty. Atlantic Richfield Co., Phila., 1966-69, 71-72, Chgo., 1969-71, Los Angeles, 1972—, trademark counsel, Los Angeles, 1972—. Mem. Am., Pa., Phila., Ill., Chgo., Calif. bar assns. Home: 11801 Thunderbird Ave Northridge CA 91324 Office: 515 S Flower St Los Angeles CA 90071 Tel (213) 486-1529

BIRNHOLZ, STANDFORD PETER, b. Newark, Apr. 19, 1937; B.B.A. in Accounting, U. Miami, 1959, J.D., 1964. Admitted to Fla. bar, 1964; agt. IRS, Miami, Fla., 1959-68; individual practice law, Miami, 1968-71; prin. Standford P. Birnholz, Miami, 1971—. Mem. Fla. Bar, Beta Alpha Psi. C.P.A., N.J. Home: 7605 SW 108th Terr Miami FL 33156 Office: Biscayne Bldg Suite 720 19 W Flagler St Miami FL 33130

BIRRELL, GEORGE ANDREW, b. Warren, Ohio, Apr. 25, 1921; B.A., Yale, 1942, LL.B., 1947. Admitted to N.Y. bar, 1948; asso. firm Donovan, Leisure, Newton & Irvine, N.Y.C., 1947-55, partner, 1956-58; with Mobil Oil Corp., N.Y.C., 1959—, gen. counsel, 1970—, sec., 1972-75, v.p., gen. counsel, 1975—, dir., 1976—; v.p., gen. counsel Mobil Corp., 1976—; mem. adv. bd. Internat. and Comparative Law Center, Internat. Oil and Gas Ednl. Center, S.W. Legal Found.; mem. adv. com. Law of Sea, Dept. State. Mem. Planning Commn., Rye, N.Y., 1957-60, Bd. Zoning Appeals, 1962-67; mem. City Council, Rye, 1968-72, acting mayor, 1970-72. Fellow Am. Bar Found.; mem. Am. Bar Assn., Assn. Bar City N.Y., Assn. Gen. Counsel. Home: Pecksland Rd Greenwich CT 06830 Office: 150 E 42d St New York City NY 10017 Tel (212) 883-2297

BISCONE, JOHN JOSEPH, b. Ravena, N.Y., Apr. 18, 1914; LL.B., Albany Law Sch., 1937. Admitted to N.Y. State bar, 1938, U.S. Supreme Ct. bar, 1960; individual practice law, Albany and Ravena, N.Y., 1938—; mem. firms Biscone & Biscone, 1971—; atty. Village of Ravena, 1948—, Town of Coeymans (N.Y.), 1950—; asst. county atty. County of Albany (N.Y.), 1946—. Mem. N.Y. State, Am., Albany County bar assns., Hudson-Mohawk Assn. Village Officers (pres. 1971-73). Home: 12 Hillcrest Dr Ravena NY 12143 Office: 75 State St Albany NY 12207 Tel (518) 465-2239

BISHIN, WILLIAM ROBERT, b. Queens, N.Y., Sept. 1, 1939; A.B. cum laude, Columbia, 1960; LL.B. magna cum laude, Harvard, 1963. Admitted to N.Y. State bar, 1964, Calif. bar, 1965; asso. firm Paul, Weiss, Rifkind, Wharton & Garrison, N.Y.C., 1962; faculty U. So. Calif., 1963—, prof. law, 1968—; partner firm Edwards & Bishin, Los Angeles, 1973-75. Am. Council Learned Socs. Study fellow, 1968; recipient Justin Dart award for Innovative Teaching, 1969. Co-author: (with C.D. Stone) Law, Language and Ethics, 1965; contbr. articles in field to profl. jours. and periodicals. Office: Univ So Calif Law Center Univ Park Los Angeles CA 90007 Tel (213) 746-2183

BISHOP, ALFRED LEWIS, b. Laurel, Mont., Feb. 19, 1925; student Great Falls (Mont.) Coll. Edn., 1948-49; LL.B., U. Mont., Missoula, 1952, J.D., 1970. Admitted to Mont. bar, 1952; asso. firm Cline, Hendrickson & Bishop, Billings, Mont., 1952-66; partner firm Hendrickson & Bishop, Billings, 1966—. Mem. Mont. Bar Assn. Home: 2713 Downer Ln Billings MT 59102 Office: Hart Albin Bldg Billings MT 59101 Tel (406) 245-6238

BISHOP, BRYAN EDWARDS, b. Providence, Nov. 29, 1945; B.S., U. Tex. at Arlington, 1968; J.D., Harvard, 1972. Admitted to Tex. bar, 1972; asso. firm Rain Harrell Emery Young and Doke, Dallas, 1972—. Mem. Am., Dallas bar assns., State Bar Tex. Office: 4200 Republic Nat Bank Tower Dallas TX 75201 Tel (214) 742-1021

BISHOP, DAVID EVAN, b. Lancaster, Pa., Feb. 15, 1945; B.A., DePauw U., Greencastle, Ind., 1967; J.D., Coll. William and Mary, Williamsburg, Va., 1974. Admitted to Ohio bar, 1974, U.S. Customs Ct. bar, 1975; asso. firm Calfee, Halter & Griswold, Cleve., 1974—. Mem. Am., Ohio, Cleve. bar assns. Home: 18314 Scottsdale Blvd Shaker Heights OH 44122 Office: 1800 Central Nat Bank Bldg Cleveland OH 44114 Tel (216) 781-2166

BISHOP, DAVID JAMES, b. Tremonton, Utah, Sept. 20, 1942; B.A., San Jose State Coll., 1968; J.D., U. Santa Clara, 1971. Admitted to Calif. bar, 1972; asso. firm Sedgwick, Detert, Moran & Arnold, San Francisco, 1972—. Mem. Calif., San Francisco bar assns. Articles editor Santa Clara Lawyer, 1970-71; contbr. articles to legal jours. Home: 2615 Monte Cresta Dr Belmont CA 94002 Office: 111 Pine St San Francisco CA 94111 Tel (415) 982-0303

BISHOP, DOUGLAS, b. Skiatook, Okla., July 16, 1931; LL.B., U. Tulsa, 1961. Admitted to Okla. bar, 1961; judge advocate USAF, 1962-64; county atty. County of Logan (Okla.), 1964-65. Office: 2431 E 51st St Tulsa OK 74105 Tel (918) 743-4484

BISHOP, JOSEPH WARREN, JR., b. N.Y.C., Apr. 15, 1915; B.A., Dartmouth, 1936; LL.B., Harvard, 1940; M.A. (hon.), Yale, 1959. Admitted to D.C. bar, 1941, N.Y. State bar, 1954, Conn. bar, 1963; spl. asst. to Undersec. of War, Washington, 1940-43; with Judge Adv. Gen. Corps AUS, 1943-46; spl. asst. to atty. gen. Office Solicitor Gen., Washington, 1947-50; asst. gen. counsel U.S. High Commn. in Occupied Germany, 1950-52; dep. gen. counsel Dept of Army, Washington, 1952-53, acting gen. counsel 1953; asso. prof. law Yale, 1957-59, prof., 1959—, Richard Ely prof. law, 1967—. Author: (with George T. Washington) Indemnifying the Corporate Executive, 1963; Obiter Dicta, 1971; Justice Under Fire: A Study of Military Law, 1974; contbr. articles and revs. to legal jours. and popular mags. Home: 83 E Rock Rd New Haven Ct 06511 Office: Yale Law Sch New Haven CT 06520 Tel (203) 432-4696

BISHOP, RICHARD SHERWIN, b. Hazletown, Pa., Aug. 18, 1946; B.A., Pa. State U., 1968; J.D., Temple U., 1971. Admitted to Pa. bar, 1971; asso. firm Gelb & Myers, Scranton, Pa., 1971—. Trustee, Louis Wolf Found., 1973—; bd. dirs. Scranton Mental Health/Mental Retardation Center, Inc., 1975—. Mem. Am., Pa., Lackawana County bar assns. Recipient Distinguished Service award, Temple Univ. br. Legal Aid Soc., 1971. Home: 7 Pen-y-bryn Dr Scranton PA 18505 Office: 700 Scranton Life Bldg Scranton PA 18503 Tel (717) 342-8316

BISHOP, RODNEY LAMAR, b. Salt Lake City, July 23, 1937; B.S. in Accounting, U. Utah, 1964, J.D., 1968. Admitted to Ohio bar, 1970, Ill. bar, 1972; controller H.K. Ferguson Co., Cleve., 1967-71; accountant Goettsche, Tranen & Co., Chgo., 1972-73; individual practice law Chgo., 1973—. Active Mental Health Assn. Chgo., 1974—. Mem. Am., Ill., Chgo. bar assns., Ill. Soc. C.P.A.'s, Am. Inst. C.P.A.'s. C.P.A., Ill., Utah. Office: 11 S LaSalle St Chicago IL 60603 Tel (312) 263-1948

BISHOP, THOMAS BRAD, b. Roanoke, Ala., Jan. 7, 1940; B.A., Samford U., 1961, J.D., 1971; M.A., U. Ala., 1962. Tchr., Fairfield (Ala.) High Sch., 1962-63; instr. Miss. State U., 1963-67; asso. prof. Samford U., 1967-71; admitted to Ala. bar, 1971; prof. Cumberland Sch. Law, Samford U., 1971—; asso. dean, 1975—; labor arbitrator, 1972—. Mem. Am., Ala., Birmingham bar assns., Am. Forensic Assn., Assn. Am. Law Schs. Contbr. articles to legal jours; recipient Outstanding Law Prof. award Samford U., 1973-74, Outstanding Alumnus award, 1973-74. Home: Route 1 Box 331 Helena AL 35080 Office: POB 2202 Samford U Birmingham AL 35209 Tel (205) 870-2701

BISHOP, WILLIAM WARNER, JR., b. Princeton, N.J., June 10, 1906; A.B., U. Mich., 1928, J.D., 1931; postgrad. Columbia, 1938-39. Admitted to Mich. bar, 1931, U.S. Supreme Ct. bar, 1941; research and teaching asst. U. Mich., 1931-35; asso. firm Root, Clark, Buckner & Ballantine, N.Y.C., 1935-36; lectr. politics Princeton, 1936-38; asst. legal adviser U.S. Dept. State, Washington, 1939-47; prof. law U. Mich., 1948—; vis. prof. law U. Pa., 1947-48; vis. prof. internat. law Columbia, 1948; legal adviser, U.S. del. Council of Fgn. Ministers, Paris Peace Conf., 1946. Mem. Am. Soc. Internat. Law (hon. v.p.), Am., Mich. bar assns., Internat. Law Assn. Editor-in-chief: Am. Journal Internat. Law, 1953-55, 62-70; author: Internat. Law Cases and Materials, 1949, 1951, 1961, 1971; contbr. articles to law jours. Home: 1612 Morton Ave Ann Arbor MI 48104 Office: U Mich Law Sch Ann Arbor MI 48109 Tel (313) 764-9347

BISSEL, CUSHMAN BREWER, b. St. Marys, Ohio, July 20, 1900; A.B., U. Ill., 1923; J.D., Harvard, 1926; LL.D. (hon.), Loyola U., Chgo., 1965. Admitted to Ill. bar, 1926, U.S. Supreme Ct. bar, 1933, D.C. bar, 1960; partner firm Lord, Bissell & Kadyk, Chgo., 1931-54; partner firm Lord, Bissell & Brook, Chgo., 1954—, now sr. partner; chmn. bd. Northwest Nat. Bank 1942-63, chmn. exec. com., 1963—. Bd. dirs. Cath. Charities Chgo., 1946—, pres., 1949-53; v.p. Community Fund Chgo., 1949-53; chmn. bd. Joyce Found, 1975—; pres. Chgo. Charitable Found.; bd. dirs. USO, 1951-53, United Def. Fund, 1951-53; trustee Art Inst. Chgo., 1952—, Loyola U., Chgo., 1959—, U. Ill., 1952-59, Chgo. Ednl. TV Assn., 1953-60; council mem. Harvard Law Sch., 1956-60. Mem. Am. (chmn. law lists com. 1942-45), Ill., Chgo. (pres. 1951-52) bar assns., Harvard Law Soc. Ill. (pres. 1952-53), Pi Kappa Alpha (Outstanding Alumnae 1976). Recipient citation of merit John Marshall Law Sch., 1966; named One of 100 Outstanding Citizens of Chgo., Loyola U., 1957. Home: 1530 N State Pkwy Chicago IL 60611 Office: 115 S La Salle St Chicago IL 60603 Tel (312) 443-0252

BISSELL, JEAN GALLOWAY (MRS. GREGG CLAUDE BISSELL), b. Due West, S.C., June 9, 1936; student Erskine Coll., 1952-54; B.S., U. S.C., 1956, LL.B., 1958; LL.D., Converse Coll., 1976. Admitted to S.C. bar, 1958; asso. firm Haynsworth, Perry, Bryant, Marion & Johnstone, Greenville, S.C., 1958-65, partner, 1965-71; partner firm McKay, Sherrill, Walker, Townsend & Wilkins, Columbia, 1971-76; sr. v.p., gen. counsel S.C. Nat. Bank, S.C. Nat. Corp., Columbia, 1976—; lectr. law U. S.C., 1971—. Mem. adv. council S.C. State Library, Columbia, 1971-76, Furman U., 1972—, Columbia Coll., 1974—; trustee Erskine Coll., 1971—, Greenville County Pub. Library, 1961-71, Daniel Found., 1968—, Richland County (S.C.) Pub. Library, 1973—. Mem. Am., S.C., Richland County bar assns., S.C. State Bar, S.C. Library Assn. (chmn. trustee sect. 1966-67, award for distinguished service 1973, Friend of Libraries award 1976), Am. Library Trustee Assn. (v.p., regional dir. 1965-66), S.C. C. of C. (dir. 1977—), Phi Beta Kappa. Home: 3102 Keenan Dr Columbia SC 29201 Office: SCN Center POB 168 Columbia SC 29202 Tel (803) 765-3294

BISSELL, NICHOLAS LOUIS, b. Bloomfield, N.J., Jan. 14, 1947; B.S., Wagner Coll., 1968; J.D., Am. U., 1971. Admitted to N.J. bar, 1971, U.S. Dist. Ct. for N.J. bar, 1971; asso. firm Borrus, Goldin & Foley, New Brunswick, N.J., 1971-73; asst. dep. pub. defender, Somerville, N.J., 1972-73; asst. prosecutor, Somerset County, N.J., 1973-76, spl. dep. atty. gen., 1976; partner firm Ross and Bissell, Sommerville, N.J., 1976—; judge municipal ct., Franklin Twp. and Millstone Borough, N.J., 1976—; adj. prof. law Somerset County Coll., 1976—. Mem. N.J. State, Somerset County bar assns., Nat. Dist. Attys. Assn., Am. Judges Assn., Am. Trial Lawyers Assn., Am. Arbitration Assn. Home: 770 Old Farm Rd Bridgewater NJ 08807 Office: 21 N Bridge St Somerville NJ 08876 Tel (201) 526-2433

BISSELL, PELHAM ST. GEORGE, III, b. N.Y.C., Oct. 20, 1912; B.A., Rutgers U., 1936; LL.B., N.Y. U., 1939. Admitted to N.Y. bar, 1941; asso. firm Barnes, Richardson & Colburn, N.Y.C., 1939-41, 45-51; law sec. Ct. Gen. Sessions, N.Y. County, N.Y.C., 1945-51; justice municipal ct., N.Y.C., 1952-62, judge civil ct., 1962—. Mem. Am., N.Y. State bar assns., Bar Assn. City N.Y., N.Y. County Lawyers Assn., Judge Advs. Assn., Am. Judges Assn. Home: 22 E 36th St New York City NY 10016 Office: 111 Centre St New York City NY 10013 Tel (212) 374-8470

BITNER, GEORGE EDWARD, b. Fort Harrison, Ind., Sept. 16, 1939; A.B., Ohio Wesleyan U., 1961; J.D., George Washington U., 1964. Admitted to Va. bar, 1964, D.C. bar, 1965; asso. firm Kinney, Smith & Bitner, Arlington, Va., 1964-67, partner, 1967-76; individual practice law, Falls Church, Va., 1976—. Deacon Falls Church Presbyn Ch., 1970-73; bd. dirs. Arlington YMCA, 1973-74. Mem. Am., Va., Fairfax County bar assns., Va. Jaycees (pres. Falls Church chpt. 1968-69). Home: 10421 Adel Rd Oakton VA 22124 Office: 6521 Arlington Blvd PO Box 2303 Falls Church VA 22042 Tel (703) 241-2600

BITTEL, JORDAN, b. N.Y.C., Apr. 15, 1929; B.A., U. Fla., 1949; J.D., Harvard, 1952; LL.M., Miami Law Sch., 1972. Admitted to Fla. bar, 1952; partner firm Bittel, Langer & Blass, and predecessors, Miami, Fla., 1957—; partner firm Shutts & Bowen, Miami, 1975—;

adj. prof. law U. Miami, 1977—. Mem. Dade County (Fla.), Fla., Am., Internat. bar assns., Internat. Fiscal Assn. Office: 2250 1st Fed Bldg 1 SE 3d Ave Miami FL 33131 Tel (305) 377-9351

BITTEL, TIMOTHY M., b. Cleve., Sept. 10, 1945; B.S. cum laude, Case Inst. Tech., 1967; J.D. magna cum laude, Cleve. State U., 1971. With B.F. Goodrich Chem. Co., 1967-71; admitted to Ohio bar, 1971, Fla. bar, 1974; asso. firm Sweeney, Mahon & Vlad, Cleve., 1971—. Mem. Ohio, Fla., Greater Cleve. bar assns. Home: 550 Glen Park Dr Bay Village OH 44140 Office: 1205 Bond Ct Cleveland OH 44114 Tel (216) 696-0606

BITTER, JOSEPH JAMES, b. Dubuque, Iowa, Nov. 9, 1937; B.S., Loras Coll., 1960; J.D., Iowa U., 1964. Admitted to Iowa bar, 1964, Ill. bar, 1964; individual practice law, Dubuque, 1964—; mem. Dubuque City Council, 1970-73, mayor, 1973. Mem. Iowa, Ill. bar assns. Home: 2615 Hillcrest Rd Dubuque IA 52001 Office: 770 Fischer Bldg Dubuque IA 52001 Tel (319) 588-4608

BITTING, WILLIAM MCCLURE, b. Santa Monica, Calif., Apr. 17, 1939; A.B., U. Calif., Los Angeles, 1961, J.D., 1965. Admitted to Calif. bar, 1966, U.S. Dist. Ct. bar, 1966; partner firm Hill, Farrer & Burrill, Los Angeles, 1972—; spl. counsel to bd. dirs. Fed. Home Loan Bank, Washington, 1970-71. Mem. Am., Los Angeles County bar assns. Office: 445 S Figueroa St 34th Los Angeles CA 90071 Tel (213) 620-0460

BITZEGAIO, HAROLD JAMES, b. Coalmont, Ind., Jan. 29, 1921; B.S., Ind. State U., 1948; J.D., Ind. U., 1953. Admitted to Ind. bar, 1953; individual practice law, Terre Haute, 1953-58; judge Superior Ct., 1959—; mem. Ind. adv. com. U.S. Commn. on Civil Rights, 1961-70. Bd. dirs. Wabash Valley Council Boy Scouts Am., 1960—; chmn. Mayor's Commn. Human Relations, 1967-68. Mem. Am., Ind., Terre Haute bar assns., Ind. Judges' Assn. pres. 1977—, Am. Judicature Soc., Ind. U. Law Alumni Assn. (pres. 1973-74), Nat. Rifle Assn. Recipient Distinguished Service award City of Terre Haute, 1964; contbr. articles to profl. jours. Home: 1710 Ohio St Terre Haute IN 47807 Office: Rm 38 Court House Terre Haute IN 47807 Tel (812) 232-3301

BIVENS, CULL, b. Tulsa, June 21, 1930; student U. Okla., 1954-56; LL.B., U. Tulsa, 1961. With dept. credit Sun Ray Oil Co., Tulsa, 1956-58; credit mgr. Nat. Trailer Convoy (now Pepsico), Tulsa, 1958-61; owner Poteau Abstract Co. (Okla.), 1961-63; admitted to Okla. bar, 1961; county atty. LeFlore County, Okla., 1963-65; asst. county atty. Tulsa County, 1965-66, asst. dist. atty., 1966-68; asso. firm VanCleave Gresham Liebler, Dalton & Bivens, Tulsa, after 1968, partner, to 1973; partner firm Gresham & Bivens, Tulsa, 1973-75; individual practice law, Tulsa, 1975—. Mem. Am., Okla. (Outstanding Service award Com. Adminstrn. of Justice), Tulsa County bar assns., Okla. Trial Lawyers Assn., U. Okla., U. Tulsa alumni assns., Delta Theta Phi. Office: 905 Mayo Bldg Tulsa OK 74103 Tel (918) 582-5277

BIXBY, R. BURDELL, b Schenectady, Oct. 11, 1914; A.B., Colgate U., 1936; LL.B., Albany Law Sch., 1940, J.D., 1968. Admitted to N.Y. State bar, 1940; partner firm Best, Kline & Bixby, Hudson, N.Y., 1946-48; partner firm Dewey, Ballantine, Bushby, Palmer, & Wood, N.Y.C., 1955—; asst. sec. Gov. State N.Y., 1948-50, exec. asst., 1950-52, sec., 1952-54; sec. treas. N.Y. State Thruway Auth., 1950-60, chmn., 1960-74. Trustee Albany (N.Y.) Law Sch., 1959—; trustee Hudson (N.Y.) City Savs. Inst., 1970—. Mem. Assn. Bar City N.Y., Am., N.Y. State, Columbia County bar assns., N.Y. County Lawyers Assn., Am. Judicature Soc. Home: 7 Joslen Pl Hudson NY 12534 Office: 140 Broadway New York City NY 10005 Tel (212) 344-8000

BIXLER, JOHN MOURER, b. Washington, Oct. 14, 1927; B.S., U. Pa., 1949; LL.B., Harvard U., 1954. Admitted to D.C. bar, 1954, U.S. Supreme Ct. bar, 1964, Md. bar, 1960; staff mem. Charles S. Rockey & Co., C.P.A.'s, Phila., 1949-51; asso. firm Miller & Chevalier, Washington, 1954-61, partner, 1962—; trustee D.C. Legal Aid Soc., 1975—; dir. Rubicon Devel. Co., 1975—; lectr. in field. Trustee U. Pa., 1975—; dir., sec.-treas. The Rockport Fund, Inc.; trustee Concord-St. Andrew's United Methodist Ch., 1975—. Mem. Am. (chmn. nat. office and joint com. procedures com., tax sect. 1977—), Fed., D.C., Md. bar assns., Am. Coll. Probate Counsel, Am. Judicature Soc., D.C. Estate Planning Council, Am. Inst. C.P.A.'s. Editorial bd. Estate Planning Jour., 1975—; contbr. articles to legal jours. Home: 5304 Moorland Ln Bethesda MD 20014 Office: Suite 800 1700 Pennsylvania Ave NW Washington DC 20006 Tel (202) 393-5660

BJERKE, JACK ALLEN, b. Buffalo, July 23, 1945; B.S. in Bus. Adminstrn., Wittenberg U., 1967; J.D., Case Western Res. U., 1970. Admitted to Ohio bar, 1970; mem. firm Tingley, Hurd & Emens, Columbus, Ohio, 1970—. Mem. Am., Ohio, Columbus bar assns. Home: 2542 Chester Rd Columbus OH 43221 Office: 250 E Broad St Columbus OH 43215 Tel (614) 221-6527

BJERTNESS, DONALD ELTON, b. Hatton, N.D., Nov. 25, 1930; B.A., U. N.D., 1955, J.D., 1957. Admitted to N.D. bar, 1957, Mont. bar, with land dept. Humble Oil Co., 1957-65; dep. county atty. Yellowstone County, Mont., 1965-66; asso. firm Luedke & Packwood, Billings, Mont., 1966; partner firm Packwood & Bjertness, Billings, 1967-69; individual practice law, Billings, 1969—; judge Billings City Ct., 1966—; vice chmn. Mont. Bd. Crime Control, 1969—; mem. Mont. Justice Project. Bd. dirs. Rimrock Guidance Found., Billings, 1976—. Mem. Yellowstone County, Mont. bar assns., Am. Judges Assn. Home: 1912 Howard Ave Billings MT 59102 Office: 221 Hedden-Empire Bldg Billings MT 59103 Tel (406) 259-7489

BJORK, WALTER MONSON, b. Madison, Wis., Dec. 5, 1914; B.A., U. Wis., 1935, LL.B., 1937. Admitted to Wis. bar, 1938, U.S. Supreme Ct. bar, 1960; dep. dist. atty. Dane County (Wis.), Madison, 1938-42; partner firm Roberts, Boardman, Sohr, Bjork & Curry, Madison, 1942-60; gen. counsel Dairyland Ins. Co., Scottsdale, Ariz., 1960—; lectr. in field. Pres. Madison Police and Fire Commn., 1957; bd. dirs. Wis. Council Safety, Madison. Mem. Dane County (pres. 1948), Wis., Am. bar assns., Am. Coll. Trial Lawyers, Fed. Ins. Council (dir.), Internat. Assn. Ins. Counsel, Wis. Jud. Council. Contbr. articles to legal jours. Home: 6800 Caballo Dr Scottsdale AZ 85253 Office: 9501 E Shea Blvd Scottsdale AZ 85260 Tel (602) 994-7002

BLACK, CHARLES LUND, JR., b. Austin, Tex., Sept. 22, 1915; B.A., U. Tex., 1935, M.A., 1938; LL.B., Yale, 1943; LL.D., Boston U., 1975. Admitted to N.Y. State bar, 1946, U.S. Supreme Ct. bar, 1960; asso. firm Davis, Polk, N.Y.C., 1946-47; prof. law Columbia, 1947-56; Henry R. Luce prof. jurisprudence Yale U. Law Sch., 1956-75, Sterling prof. law, 1975—; mem. adv. com. on admiralty rules U.S. Supreme Ct., 1960-70; legal cons. NAACP Def. and Edn. Fund. Mem. Maritime Law Assn., Order of Coif, Phi Delta Phi. Recipient Distinguished Alumnus award U. Tex., 1975; author 9 books; contbr. articles to profl. jours. Office: Yale U Law Sch New Haven CT 06520 Tel (203) 432-4306

BLACK, DEWITT TALMADGE, b. Morrilton, Ark., Oct. 31, 1945; B.S., U. Ark., 1967; J.D., Memphis State U., 1973. Admitted to Ark. bar, 1974; asso. firm McKay, Chandler and Choate, Magnolia, Ark., 1974—. Mem. Am., Ark., Columbia County (sec. treas. 1975, v.p. 1976) bar assns., Ark. Trial Lawyers Assn. Home: 509 N Jefferson St Magnolia AR 71753 Office: 201 S Jackson St Magnolia AR 71753 Tel (501) 234-1036

BLACK, FRANK THOMAS, b. Mansfield, Ohio, July 8, 1933; A.B., Princeton U., 1955; M.A., Northwestern U., 1958; J.D. summa cum laude, Ohio State U., 1968. Tchr., Mansfield Sr. High Sch., 1956-63; v.p., gen. mgr. Resorts Inc., Butler, Ohio, 1963-65; tchr. Westerville (Ohio) High Sch., 1965-66; admitted to Ohio bar, 1969; asso. firm Baker, Hostetler & Patterson, Cleve., 1968-73, partner, 1974—. Mem. Cleve., Ohio State, Am. bar assns., Order of Coif. Editor-in-chief Ohio State Law Jour., 1968. Office: 1956 Union Commerce Bldg Cleveland OH 44115 Tel (216) 621-0200

BLACK, GERALD JOSEPH, b Cin., Dec 5, 1946; B.A., Loyola U., Chgo., 1968; J.D., Northwestern U., 1971. Admitted to Ill. bar, 1972; asst. atty. gen. State of Ill., Springfield, 1971-73; asst. counsel Prudential Ins. Co. Am., Chgo., 1973. Mem. Ill. Chgo. bar assns. Home: 2306 Brookway Dr Geneva IL 60134 Office: 500 N Prudential Plaza Chicago IL 60601 Tel (312) 822-3570

BLACK, HENRY FRANKLIN, b. Newport, Vt., Mar. 27, 1906; B.S., Norwich U., 1928, LL.D., 1974; J.D., George Washington U., 1933. Admitted to Vt. bar, 1934, U.S. Supreme Ct. bar, 1973; state's atty. Windsor County, Vt., 1937-41; judge Vt. Superior Ct., 1941-50; sr. partner firm Black & Plante, White River Junction, Vt., 1950—; dir. Vt. Mut. Ins. Co., No. Security Ins. Co., Dartmouth Nat. Bank of Hanover (Vt.). Moderator, Town of Hartford (Vt.), 1967—; trustee Norwich U., 1972—. Fellow Am. Bar Found., Am. Coll. Trial Lawyers; mem. Windsor County (pres. 1937-38), Vt. (pres. 1956-57), Am. (gov. 1975—) bar assns., Am. Judicature Soc., Fedn. Ins. Counsel, Assn. Ins. Attys. Recipient Distinguished Alumni award Norwich U., 1975. Office: 24 N Main St White River Junction VT 05001 Tel (802) 295-3151

BLACK, HUGH LAWRANCE, b. Cleve., Mar. 8, 1942; B.A., Coll. Wooster, 1964; J.D., Case-Western Res. U., 1967. Admitted to Ohio, Fla. bars, 1968, D.C. bar, 1969; asst. trust officer Cleve. Trust Co., 1968-70; trust officer, asst. v.p. Coconut Grove Bank, Miami, Fla., 1970-72; asst. city atty. and city prosecutor City N. Miami, 1972-73; mem. firm Kahn & Clein, 1972-73; individual practice law, Miami and Palm Beach, Fla., 1973-76; mktg. specialist Wells Fargo Bank, Beverly Hills, Calif., 1976—. Dir., Coconut Grove (Fla.) Community Devel. Corp., 1970-73; chmn. steering com. Common Cause, Miami, 1971-73; counsel, dir. Coconut Grove Cares for Youth, Inc., 1973-76; chmn. Coconut Grove Art Festival, 1972-76. Mem. Am., Ohio, Fla., D.C., Palm Beach County bar assns. Office: 9600 Santa Monica Blvd Beverly Hills CA 90210 Tel (213) 550-2191

BLACK, HUGO LAFAYETTE, JR., b. Birmingham, Ala., Apr. 29, 1922; A.B., U. Ala., 1946; LL.B., Yale, 1949. Admitted to Ala. bar, 1949, Fla. bar, 1962, U.S. Supreme Ct. bar, 1950; partner firm Kelly, Black, Black & Kenny, Miami, Fla., 1962—. Mem. Am., Fed., Dade County bar assns. Author: My Father, A Remembrance, 1976. Home: 12305 SW 73 Ave Miami FL 33156 Office: 1400 A I duPont Bldg Miami FL 33131 Tel (305) 358-5700

BLACK, IRYNE CODON, b. Los Angeles, Sept. 3, 1928; A.B. cum laude, Stanford, 1950, J.D., 1958. Admitted to Calif. bar, 1959, D.C. bar, 1969, U.S. Supreme Ct. bar, 1964; dept. atty. gen. State of Calif., 1958-59, 1959-61; atty. solicitor's office Dept. Labor, Washington, 1961-62; atty. NLRB, Washington, 1962, Office of Gen. Counsel, Peace Corps., Washington, 1967-69; asst. gen. counsel Smithsonian Instn., Washington, 1962-64; dep. county counsel Orange County (Calif.), Santa Ana, 1970—; cons. HEW, Washington, 1968-69. Mem. Orange County Bar Assn. (chairperson individual and women's rights sect. 1976-77), Calif. Elected Women's Assn. for Edn. and Research dir., Calif. State Bar Conv. (del. 1976), Calif. Women Lawyers, D.C. Calif. bar assns. Bd. editors Stanford Law Rev. 1957-58. Home: 1646 Irvine Ave Newport Beach CA 92660 Office: POB 1379 Santa Ana CA 92702 Tel (714) 834-3300

BLACK, JAN MATTHEW STEPHEN, b. Camden, N.J., Aug. 16, 1945; B.S. in Indsl. Engring., Lehigh U., 1967; J.D., Georgetown U., 1971. Admitted to D.C. bar, 1971, Del. bar, 1972; clk. Del. Ct. Chancery, 1971-72; asso. firm Prickett, Ward, Burt & Sanders, Wilmington, Del., 1972-77; with legal dept. E.I. duPont de Nemours & Co., Wilmington, 1977—. Mem. New Castle County Bd. Contract Rev. 1975-76. Mem. Am., Del. (sec.) bar assns. Office: Room 7052 DuPont Bldg Wilmington DE 19898 Tel (302) 774-5443

BLACK, LAWRENCE DEAN, b. Des Moines, Mar. 21, 1939; B.S., Drake U., 1962, M.S., 1964; J.D., Creighton U., 1966. Admitted to Iowa bar, 1966, Nebr. bar, 1966, Fla. bar, 1967, U.S. Supreme Ct. bar, 1973; individual practice law, Largo, Fla., 1973—; exec. dir. Pinellas County (Fla.) Classroom Tchrs. Assn., 1966-73; mem. Belleair Beach (Fla.) City Council, 1973-76. Mem. Am., Fla., Iowa, Nebr. bar assns., Am. Judicature Soc. Recipient Bancroft Whitney award for excellence in writing Creighton U. Sch. Law, 1966. Home: 119 13th St Belleair Beach FL 33535 Office: 152 Eighth Ave SW Largo FL 33540 Tel (813) 585-2031

BLACK, LEON DAVID, JR., b. Saluda, S.C., Nov. 11, 1926; A.B., Miami U., 1948; LL.B., Yale U., 1952. Admitted to Fla. bar, 1952; asso. firm E.F. P. Brigham, Miami, Fla., 1952-55; partner firm Birgham, Black, Niles & Wright, Miami, 1956-58, Kelly, Black, Black & Kenny, and predecessors, Miami, 1958—. Chmn. bd. Am. Heart Assn. Greater Miami, 1976—. Fellow Am. Coll. Trial Lawyers; mem. Am., Fla. (mem. steering com. 1971—, chmn. eminent domain com. 1974-75), Dade County bar assns. Contbg. author Florida Eminent Domain Practice and Procedure Manual, 2d edit., 1971, 3d edit., 1977. Home: 3840 Alhambra Ct Coral Gables FL 33134 Office: 1400 Alfred I duPont Bldg Miami FL 33131 Tel (305) 358-5700

BLACK, LEWIS STANLEY, JR., b. Wilmington, Del., June 29, 1938; A.B., Princeton, 1960; LL.B., Yale, 1963. Admitted to N.Y. bar, 1963, Del. bar, 1964, D.C. bar, 1965; asso. firm Milbank, Tweed Hadley & McCloy, N.Y.C., 1965-68, firm Morris, Nichols, Arsht & Tunnell, Wilmington, 1968-70, partner, 1970—. Mem. Am., Del., N.Y. bar assns. Contbr. articles to legal jours. Home: 1502 Gilpin Ave Wilmington DE 19806 Office: 12th and Market Sts Wilmington DE 19899 Tel (302) 658-9200

BLACK, MELVIN SIDNEY, b. Miami, Fla., Mar. 21, 1944; B.A., U. Fla., 1966; J.D., U. Miami, Coral Gables, Fla., 1969. Admitted to Fla. bar, 1969, U.S. Supreme Ct. bar, 1973; atty. VISTA, 1969-70; asst. dir law reform unit Legal Services of Greater Miami Model Cities Law Center, 1970-72; exec. asst. pub. defender Dade County (Fla.), 1973-76; partner firm Buchbinder & Black, Miami, 1976—; lectr. in field; arbitrator Am. Arbitration Assn. Mem. Met. Dade County Youth Relations Bd. Mem. Fla. Criminal Def. Attys. Assn., ACLU, Fla. Bar. Asso. editor Barrister Mag. Home: 1852 SW 24th St Miami Fl 33145 Office: 2721 S Bayshore Dr Miami FL 33133 Tel (305) 442-1700

BLACK, MILTON, b. N.Y.C., July 4, 1911; A.B., Columbia, 1932, LL.B., 1934. Admitted to N.Y. bar, 1934; U.S. Supreme Ct. bar, 1958; asso. firm Mudge, Stern, Williams & Tucker, N.Y.C., 1934-47, partner, 1948-64; partner firm Mudge, Rose, Guthrie & Alexander, N.Y.C., 1964—; labor relations rep. Matam Corp., N.Y.C., 1944-45. Pres., trustee Conservative Synagogue of Fifth Ave, N.Y.C., 1960—. Mem. Am., N.Y. State, N.Y. County (past mem. labor relations com.), D.C. bar assns., Phi Beta Kappa. Editor: Columbia Law Rev., 1932-34; Pulitzer scholar, 1929-33; Stone scholar, 1933-34. Home: 40 E 9th St New York City NY 10003 Office: Mudge Rose Guthrie & Alexander 20 Broad St New York City NY 10005 Tel (212) 422-6767

BLACK, OWEN, b. Kansas City, Mo., Feb. 16, 1897; student Okla. U., 1914-17; LL.B., George Washington U., 1920, B.A., 1922; postgrad. U. Va., Northwestern U., 1945. Admitted to Okla. bar, 1918, Philippines bar, 1946; asst. clk. pub. lands com. U.S. Ho. of Reps., Washington, 1917-18; law clk. to justice Okla. Supreme Ct., Oklahoma City, 1918; served to sgt. maj. JAGC, U.S. Army, 1918-19; partner firm Black & Black, Lawton, Okla., 1922-32; atty. City Lawton, 1922-28; atty. VA, Oklahoma City, 1932-38, chief atty., Muskogee, Okla., 1938-40, 48-57, Manila, Philippines, 1945-48; individual practice law, Muskogee, 1957—; mem. Okla. Ho. of Reps., 1930-32. City councilman Muskogee, Oklahoma City, 1962-68. Mem. Okla., Muskogee County bar assns., Phi Delta Phi. Home and Office: 1000 N 40th St Muskogee OK 74401 Tel (918) 687-7662

BLACK, ROBERT LOUNSBURY, JR., b. Cin., Dec. 11, 1917; A.B., Yale, 1939; LL.B., Harvard, 1942. Admitted to Ohio bar, 1946; asso. firm Robert L. Black, Sr., Cin., 1946-53; partner firm Gradon, Head & Ritchey, Cin., 1953-72; judge Hamilton County (Ohio) Ct. of Common Pleas, 1973-77; judge First Appellate Dist. Ohio Ct. Appeals, 1977—; mayor City of Indian Hill (Ohio), 1959-65; mem. com. on jury instructions Ohio Jud. Conf., 1973—. Chmn. Cin. Human Relations Com., 1967-70. Mem. Cin., Ohio, Am. bar assns., Nat. Conf. State Trial Judges, Phi Beta Kappa. Decorated Bronze Star medal. Home: 5900 Drake Rd Cincinnati OH 45243 Office: Hamilton County Courthouse 1000 Main St Cincinnati OH 45202 Tel (513) 632-8338

BLACK, STEPHEN LOUNSBURY, b. Cin., Dec. 3, 1948; A.B., Harvard, 1971, J.D., 1974. Admitted to Ohio bar, 1974; law clk. U.S. Ct. Appeals 6th Circuit, Cin., 1974-75; asso. firm Graydon, Head & Ritchey, Cin., 1975—. Mem. Am., Ohio, Cin. bar assns., Am. Judicature Soc. Home: 937 Paradrome St Cincinnati OH 45202 Office: 1900 Fifth Third Center 511 Walnut St Cincinnati OH 45202 Tel (513) 621-6464

BLACK, THOMAS BOWMAN, b. Austin, Tex., Aug. 1, 1928; B.A., U. Tex., 1949, LL.B., 1952. Admitted to Tex. Bar, 1952; individual practice law, Austin, 1955-73; spl. asst. atty. gen. Tex., 1973-74; prof. law St. Mary's U., 1974—; reporter Speedy Trial Planning Group So. and Western Dists. Tex., 1975—. Chmn. Human Relations Com., Austin, 1967-69. Mem. San Antonio Bar Assn. Contbr. articles to law revs. Home: 2525 W Gramercy San Antonio TX 78228 Office: One Camino Santa Maria San Antonio TX 78289 Tel (512) 436-3424

BLACKBURN, CHARLES FRANKLIN, b. Cleveland, Tenn., Apr. 30, 1925; student Davidson Coll., 1942-43, U. N.C., 1945-46; J.D., Washington and Lee U., 1949. Admitted to N.C. bar, 1949, U.S. Supreme Ct. bar, 1975; since practiced in Henderson, N.C., partner firm Blackburn & Blackburn, 1949-63, firm Perry, Kittrell, Blackburn & Blackburn, 1963—; pros. atty. Vance County (N.C.) Recorders Ct., 1950-54; city atty. City of Henderson, 1967-73; mem. N.C. Senate, 1959-61; lt. col. JAGC, USNG, 1956. Chmn. Kerr Reservoir Devel. Commn., 1962-67; chmn. bd. trustees Vance-Granville Community Coll., 1967—; mem. Commn. to Study Pub. Sch. Edn. of Exceptionally Talented Children, 1959-61; pres. Henderson-Vance County C. of C., 1977. Mem. N.C., N.C. State bar assns., Nat. Assn. Trial Lawyers. Home: 645 Lakeview Dr Henderson NC 27536 Office: 109 Young St Henderson NC 27536 Tel (919) 438-8131

BLACKBURN, JOHN GILMER, b. Opelika, Ala., Oct. 21, 1927; B.S., Auburn U., 1950; LL.B., U. Ala., 1954; LL.M., N.Y. U., 1956. Admitted to Ala. bar, 1954; individual practice law, Decatur, Ala., 1954—; mayor Decatur, 1962-68. Vice chmn. Auburn U. Found., 1964. Mem. Auburn U. Alumni Assn. (pres. 1967-68), Ala. Bar Assn. (chmn. tax sect. 1964).

BLACKBURN, MILFORD GENE, b. Grand Junction, Iowa, July 27, 1922; B.A., Drake U., 1953, J.D., 1955. Admitted to Iowa bar, 1955; asso. firm Prince & Guthrie, Webster City, Iowa, 1955-56; partner firm Guthrie & Blackburn, Webster City, 1956-65, Mitchell, Murray & Blackburn, Fort Dodge, Iowa, 1975—; faculty Drake U., Des Moines, 1965—; county atty. Hamilton County, Iowa, 1958-59; city atty. Webster City, 1961-65. Bd. trustees, sec. Polk County Legal Aid Soc., 1968-70. Mem. Am., Iowa, Webster County bar assns., Nat. Order of Barristers, Order of Coif, Phi Beta Kappa, Delta Theta Phi. Editor Drake Law Rev., 1955. Contbr. articles to legal jours. Home: 1342 N 13th St Fort Dodge IA 50501 Office: 142 N 9th St Fort Dodge IA 50501 Tel (515) 576-2171

BLACKBURN, PHILIP HOUSTON, b. Hillsboro, Ill., Feb. 4, 1943; A.B., Westminster Coll., 1965; J.D., Vanderbilt U., 1970. Admitted to Fla. bar, 1970, U.S. Dist. Ct., 1970; partner firm Billings, Frederick, Wooten & Honeywell, Orlando, Fla., 1970-; consul to Honduras; mem. specialization com. Fla. bar, 1974-76. Mem. Orlando Human Relations Rev. Bd., 1973-76; advisor youth group First Presbyterian Ch. Mem. Orange County, Am. bar assns., Am. Trial Lawyers Assn., Acad. Fla. Trial Lawyers. Founder Vanderbilt Advocacy Inst., 1976. Office: 236 S Lucerne Circle Orlando FL 32801 Tel (305) 843-7060

BLACKBURN, WILLIAM KEATON, b. Ft. Worth, Jan. 11, 1947; B.B.A., St. Mary's U., San Antonio, 1969, J.D., 1971. Admitted to Tex. bar, 1972; partner Blackburn Law Offices, Junction, Tex., 1972—. Pres. adminstrv. bd. 1st United Methodist Ch.; chmn. Kimble County (Tex.) Democratic Com. Mem. Am., Tex., Hill County bar assns., Home and office: POB 446 Junction TX 76849 Tel (915) 446-3336

BLACKBURN, WILLIAM THOMAS, b. Little Rock, Aug. 26, 1933; B.A., Hendrix Coll., 1955; LL.B., So. Meth. U., 1958. Admitted to Tex. bar, 1958, U.S. Supreme Ct. bar, 1974; asso. firm Warwick & Jenkins, Waxahachie, Tex., 1958; asst. atty. gen. State of Tex., 1959-61; asst. city atty. City of Houston, 1961-63; mem. legal dept. Coastal States Gas Prodn. Co., 1963-73; individual practice law, Corpus Christi, Tex., 1973—. Regional v.p. Tex. Assn. Retarded Citizens, 1971-75; mem. Corpus Christi State Sch. Pub. Responsibility Com., 1976. Mem. Am. Judicature Soc., Assn. Trial Lawyers Am., Tex. Trial Lawyers Assn., Am., Tex., Nueces County bar assns. Editorial bd. Southwestern Law Jour., 1957-58, named outstanding mem. bd., 1958. Home: 801 Crestview St Corpus Christi TX 78412 Office: Suite 1200 The 600 Bldg Corpus Christi TX 78401 Tel (512) 883-1993

BLACKFORD, JASON COLLIER, b. Findlay, Ohio, Oct. 30, 1938; B.A., magna cum laude, Denison U., 1960; LL.B., Yale, 1963. Admitted to Ohio bar, 1964, U.S. Supreme Ct. bar, 1972; asso. firm Weston, Hord, Fallon, Paisley & Howley, Cleve., 1963-70, partner, 1970—; lectr.-at-law Cleve. State U., 1974-75. Mem. Bar Assn. Greater Cleve., Am., Ohio bar assns. Author: Ohio Corporation Law and Practice, 2 vols., 1972; contbr. articles to legal jours. Home: 3207 Somerset Dr Shaker Heights OH 44122 Office: 2500 Terminal Tower Cleveland OH 44113 Tel (216) 241-6602

BLACKMAN, JOHN CALHOUN, b. Monroe, La., Dec. 13, 1944; B.A., La. State U., 1966, J.D., 1969. Admitted to La. bar, 1969; partner firm Hudson, Potts & Bernstein, Monroe, 1969—; pres. Estate Planning Council N.E. La., 1975-76. Mem. Am., La. (chmn. tax sect. 1976—), 4th Jud. Dist. (pres. 1976-77) bar assns., Order of Coif, Phi Kappa Phi, Phi Delta Phi, Omicron Delta Kappa. Asso. editor La. Law Rev., 1968-69; contbr. articles in field to legal jours. Home: 1500 Emerson St Monroe LA 71201 Office: 1000 Ouachita National Bank Bldg PO Box 3008 Monroe LA 71201 Tel (318) 388-4400

BLACKMAN, ROBERT IRWIN, b. N.Y.C., May 16, 1928; B.S., Rutgers U., 1948; J.D., N.Y. Law Sch., 1950. Admitted to N.Y. bar, 1951; partner firm Blackman, Lefrak, Galgay, Myerson & Feld, N.Y.C., 1951-73, of counsel, 1973-76; exec. v.p. Trust Mortgage Corp., N.Y.C., 1973-76; dir. Emmons Industries, Inc., York, Pa., 1971-76; trustee, sr. v.p. TMC Mortgage Investors, Boston, 1973-76; v.p. mortgage loan dept. Mass. Mut. Life Ins. Co., Springfield, 1976—. Mem. Ardsley (N.Y.) Bd. Edn., 1966-69. Mem. N.Y. State Assn. Atty.-C.P.A.'s, (dir.), Am. Inst. C.P.A.'s., Am., N.Y. State bar assns., Beta Gamma Sigma. Home: 145 Primrose Dr Longmeadow MA 01106 Office: 1295 State St Springfield MA 01111 Tel (413) 788-8411

BLACKMAR, CHARLES BLAKEY, b. Kansas City, Mo., Apr. 19, 1922; A.B., Princeton, 1942, J.D., U. Mich., 1948. Admitted to Mo. bar, 1948, U.S. Supreme Ct. bar, 1952; partner firm Swanson, Midgley, Jones, Blackmar and Eager, Kansas City, Mo., 1948-66; prof. law St. Louis U., 1966—; asst. atty. gen. State of Mo., 1969—. Mem. Human Rights Commn., Kansas City, Mo. 1964-66; chmn. Fair Pub. Accommdations Com., Kansas City, Mo., 1963-66. Mem. Mo. Bar Assn., Am. Law Inst., Nat. Acad. Arbitrators, Soc. Am. Law Tchrs. Author: (with Devitt) Federal Jury Practice and Instructions, 2nd. edit., 1970. Home: 7305 Maryland St Louis MO 63130 Office: St Louis Law Sch 3642 Lindell St Louis MO 63108 Tel (314) 725-8143

BLACKMON, EDWARD BARTON, b. Orangeburg, S.C., Oct. 24, 1921; A.B., Wofford Coll., 1942; LL.B., U. S.C., 1950. Admitted to S.C. bar, 1950; legal asst. to dist. dir. IRS, Columbia, S.C., 1952-59; atty. Office of regional counsel IRS, Atlanta, 1954; individual practice law, Orangeburg, 1963—; judge adv. post 2779 VFW, Orangeburg, 1960—. Mem. bd. stewards Trenholm Rd. Meth. Ch., Columbia, 1959-63; trustee St. Paul's Meth. Ch., Orangeburg, 1975—. Mem. S.C. State, Orangeburg County bar assns. Home: 1151 Ruple Dr Orangeburg SC 29115 Office: 1145 Blvd NE Orangeburg SC 29115 Tel (803) 536-4001

BLACKMON, JACK RUSSELL, b. Leesville, La., Feb. 5, 1918; A.A., Wesley Coll., 1936; LL.B., So. Meth. U., 1939; LL.D., U. Corpus Christi, 1975. Admitted to Tex. bar, 1939; partner firms Berger, Swearingen & Blackmon, Corpus Christi, Tex., 1946-49, North Blackmon & White and predecessor, Corpus Christi, 1949-72; judge Tex. Dist. Ct., 117th Dist., 1973—; commr. City of Corpus Christi, 1963-65, mayor pro tem, 1965-67, mayor, 1967-71; capt. Judge Adv. Gen.'s Corps USNR. Chmn. bd. trustees U. Corpus Christi, 1971—; mem. advisory bd. Tex. A. and I. U., Corpus Christi, 1973—. Mem. State Bar of Tex., Nueces County (Tex.) Bar Assn. (pres. 1953-54), Corpus Christi Jr. C. of C. (life), Corpus Christi Civitan Club (charter, life, gov. Tex. Dist. 1968-69, v.p. Civitan Internat. 1973-75). Recipient Tex. Citizenship Builder award Tex. Dist. Civitan Internat., 1971, Honor Key Civitan Internat., 1975; named Outstanding Citizen of Corpus Christi Corpus Christi Bd. Realtors, 1973. Home: 101 Alta Plaza Corpus Christi TX 78411 Office: 117 Dist Ct Courthouse Corpus Christi TX 78401 Tel (512) 884-9357

BLACKMUN, HARRY ANDREW, b. Nashville, Ill., Nov. 12, 1908; B.A. summa cum laude, Harvard, 1929, LL.B., 1932. Admitted to Minn. bar, 1932; law clk. for John B. Sanborn, judge 8th circuit, U.S. Ct. of Appeals, St. Paul, 1932-33; asso. Dorsey, Owen, Barker, Scott & Barber, Mpls., 1934-38, jr. partner, 1939-42, gen. partner, 1943-50; instr. St. Paul Coll. Law, 1935-41, U. Minn. Law Sch., 1945-47; resident counsel Mayo Clinic, Mayo Assn., Rochester, 1950-59, mem. sect. adminstrn., 1950-59; judge 8th Circuit, U.S. Ct. of Appeals, 1959-70; asso. justice U.S. Supreme Ct., 1970—. Mem. bd. members Mayo Assn. Rochester, 1953-60; bd. dirs., mem. exec. com. Rochester Meth. Hosp., 1954-70; trustee Hamline Univ., St. Paul, 1964-70, William Mitchell Coll. Law, St. Paul, 1959-74. Mem. Am., Minn., Olmsted County, 3d Jud. Dist. bar assns., Phi Beta Kappa, Contbr. profl. articles legal, med. jours. Office: Supreme Ct US Washington DC 20543*

BLACKSHEAR, AUGUSTUS TROY, b. Attoyac, Tex., July 24, 1903; LL.B., Baylor U. Admitted to Tex. bar, 1926, Fed. bar, 1951; county atty. Jasper County, Tex., 1928-30; individual practice law Jasper, Tex., 1930-34; atty. HOLC, Dallas, 1934-44; atty. Disability Rating Bd. VA, Dallas, 1944-51; sr. atty. Fedn. Nat. Mortgage Corp., Dallas, 1951-53, asst. agy. counsel, 1953-64, agy. counsel, 1964-68, ret., 1968. Mem. Tex. State Bar, Fed. Bar Assn. Home: 5012 Lilac Ln Dallas TX 75209

BLACKSHER, JAMES URIAH, b. Mobile, Ala., Oct. 4, 1940; B.S. in Physics, U. Utah, 1962; J.D., U. Ala., 1971. Admitted to Ala. bar, 1971; law clk to U.S. dist. judge No. Dist. Ala., 1971; partner firm Crawford, Blacksher, Figures & Brown and predecessors, Mobile, 1972—. Mem. Social Justice Commn. of Mobile Catholic Diocese, 1972—; bd. govs. Cath. Social Services; mem. human rights com. Searcy Hosp. Mem. Ala., Mobile County, Fed. bar assns., Am. Judicature Soc. Home: 304 S Monterey St Mobile AL 36604 Office: 1407 Davis Ave Mobile AL 36603 Tel (205) 432-1691

BLACKSTOCK, JERRY BYRON, b. Monticello, Ga., Mar. 9, 1945; B.A., Davidson Coll., 1966; J.D., U. Ga., 1969. Admitted to Ga. bar, 1969; partner firm Powell, Goldstein, Frazer, & Murphy, Atlanta, Ga., 1969—; adj. prof. law Emory U., Atlanta, 1974—. Mem. adminstrv. bd. United Methodist Ch., Atlanta, 1976—. Mem. Am., Atlanta bar assns., Lawyers Club Atlanta, State Bar Ga., Am. Assn. Trial Lawyers. Contbg. author: Georgia Lawyers Basic Practice Handbook, 2d edition, 1976. Home: 3364 Chatham Rd NW Atlanta GA 30305 Office: 1100 C & S National Bank Bldg Atlanta GA 30303 Tel (404) 521-1900

BLACKSTOCK, LEROY, b. El Reno, Okla., Apr. 19, 1914; grad. Draughon's Bus. Inst., Tulsa, 1933; LL.B., U. Tulsa, 1938. Admitted to Okla. bar, 1938; with Phillips Petroleum Co., Tulsa, 1933-41, asst. credit mgr., 1939-41; practiced in Tulsa, 1941—; sr. partner firm Blackstock Joyce Pollard Blackstock & Montgomery; chmn. Okla. Supreme Ct. Bar Orgn. Com., 1966; pres. Jud. Reform, Inc., 1966—; mem. nat. adv. com. Practicing Law Inst., 1969—; lectr. in field Coll. Law, U. Tulsa, 1970—; chmn. Okla. State Council on Jud. Complaints, 1974—; dir. 4th Nat. Bank, Tulsa, 1969-76, Owasso (Okla.) 1st State Bank, 1967-70; pres. Skelly Stadium Corp., Tulsa, 1964—; pres., trustee Great Western Investment Trust, 1966—; chmn. Tulsa U. Law Schs. Commn., 1960-74. Chmn. citizens adv. com. Tulsa County Commrs., 1963-66; mem. Govt.'s Acad. for State Govt., 1966-68; pres. Tulsa Sci. Center, 1968—; pres. Tulsa Camp Fire Council, 1971-72, Tulsa Baptist Laymen's Corp., 1962-66; bd. dirs. Tulsa County Legal Aid Soc., 1958-66, pres., 1961-62; bd. dirs. Tulsa County Mental Health Assn., 1963-70, Tulsa Psychiat. Found., 1964-67, Tulsa Downtown YMCA, 1976—; trustee Okla. Ind. Coll. Found., Inc., 1975—; founding mem. Tulsa County Hist. Soc. Fellow Am. Coll. Probate Counsel; mem. Am. (ho. of dels. 1965-67, standing com. econs. and law office mgmt. 1962-71, spl. com. nat. coordination disciplinary enforcement 1969-72, standing com. profl. discipline 1973—), Okla. (bd. govs. 1965-67, pres. 1966), Tulsa County (pres. 1962, Outstanding Atty. award 1961), World Assn. Lawyers (founding mem., mem. judiciary com. 1976—), Okla. (trustee 1966, patron), Tulsa County (pres., dir. 1962-66) bar founds., Phi Alpha Delta. Recipient Distinguished Citizens award Okla. Psychol. Assn., 1963; Distinguished Alumni award U. Tulsa, 1969; author: Paper Dolls; Laywers Fees. Home: 3740 Terwillegar Tulsa OK 74105 Office: 300 Petroleum Club Bldg Tulsa OK 74119 Tel (918) 585-2751

BLACKSTOCK, VINCENT CRAIG, b. Tulsa, Dec. 30, 1942; B.A., Washington and Lee U., 1964; J.D., U. Tulsa, 1966. Admitted to Okla. bar, 1967; partner firm Blackstock, Joyce, Pollard, Blackstock & Montgomery, Tulsa, 1969—. Mem. Am., Okla., Tulsa County (exec. com. 1975, chmn. com. on econs. 1975) bar assns. Home: 2210 E 34th St Tulsa OK 74105 Office: 300 Petroleum Club Bldg Tulsa OK 74119 Tel (918) 585-2751

BLACKWELL, JOSEPH HENRY, b. Centralia, Ill., Jan. 14, 1928; B.S., U. Ill., 1951; J.D., Cleve. State U., 1963. Admitted to Ohio bar, 1963; asso. firm Benesch, Friedlander, Mendelson & Coplan, 1968-69; partner firm Willis, Whitehead, Adrine, Childs & Blackwell, Cleve., 1973—; lectr. tax and accounting Case Western Res. U.; lectr. tax and bus. law Cleve. State U. Mem. Am., Nat., Cleve. bar assns. Home: 3650 Winchell Rd Shaker Heights OH 44122 Office: 1212 Bond Court Bldg Cleveland OH 44114 Tel (216) 523-1100

BLACKWOOD, JOHN FEELY, b. Havre, Mont., Oct. 27, 1933; B.S., U. Mont., 1955, J.D., 1958. Admitted to Mont. bar, 1958; asst. U.S. atty. Dist. Mont., Billings, 1958-61; asso. to partner firm Jardine, Stephenson, Blewett & Weaver, Great Falls, Mont., 1961-72; partner firm McDonald & Blackwood, Livingston, Mont., 1972—; mem. Mont. Supreme Ct. Commn. Rules of Evidence, 1974—. Mem. Citizens Com. for New City-County Bldg., Livingston, 1973-74; pres. Friends of Livingston Pub. Library, 1976—. Mem. Am., Mont., Park-Sweetgrass bar assns., Am. Judicature Soc. Recipient Student Achievement award Wall St. Jour., 1955. Home: 925 W Lewis St Livingston MT 59047 Office: 116 W Callender St Livingston MT 59047 Tel (406) 222-2941

BLADE, THOMAS ARTHUR, b. Moline, Ill., Aug. 4, 1943; B.A., Augustana Coll., Rock Island, Ill., 1965; M.A., U. Ill., 1966; J.D., U. Chgo., 1969. Admitted to Ill. bar, 1969; asso. firm Lloyd A. Schwiebert, Moline, 1970-71; individual practice law, Moline, 1971-76; partner firm Schwiebert, Blade & Schwiebert, Moline, 1977—. Vice pres. Marriage and Family Counseling Service, Inc., Rock Island, Ill., 1972-73, pres., 1973—; v.p. Legal Aid Services of Rock Island County, 1975—. Mem. Rock Island County, Ill. State, Am. bar assns., Am. Assn. Trial Lawyers. Office: Room 304 Reliance Bldg 1518 5th Ave Moline IL 61265 Tel (309) 762-9369

BLAINE, JAMES WILLIAM, b. Boise, Idaho, July 15, 1909; LL.B., George Washington U., 1938. Admitted to Idaho bar, 1939, U.S. Supreme Ct. bar, 1972; pros. atty. Ada County (Idaho), 1940-50; partner firm Blaine and Ambrose, Boise, 1946-54; spl. asst. atty. gen. State of Idaho, Boise, 1950-58, dept. atty. gen., 1969—; pros. atty. Owyhee County (Idaho), 1959-69. Mem. Idaho State Bar, Am. Assn. Motor Vehicle Adminstrs. Home: 480 Cotterell Dr Boise ID 83705 Office: 914 W Jefferson St Statehouse Boise ID 83720 Tel (208) 384-2223

BLAINE, WILLIAM EMERSON, JR., b. Columbus, Ohio, Jan. 2, 1924; B.A., Bowdoin Coll., 1948; J.D., Ohio State U., 1952, M.B.A., 1975. Admitted to Ohio bar, 1952; partner firm Willcox, Horst, Park & Hoffman, Columbus, 1952-59; atty. lumber co., Worthington, Ohio, pres., 1959—. Mem. Am., Ohio, Columbus bar assns., Ohio Lumber and Bldg Material Dealers Assn. Author: House Explosion, 1965. Home: 2390 Onandaga Dr Columbus OH 43221 Office: 5479 Linworth Rd Worthington OH 43085 Tel (614) 885-4421

BLAIR, C(HARLES) STANLEY, b. Kingsville, Md., Dec. 20, 1927; B.S. in Bus. and Pub. Administrn., U. Md., 1951, LL.B., 1953. Admitted to Md. bar, 1953; asso. firm Frank, Bernstein, Gutberle & Conaway, Balt., 1956-57; asso. firm Cameron, Close, Reed & Blair, Bel Air, Md., 1957-61, partner, 1961-69; mem. Ho. Dels. Md. Gen. Assembly, 1963-67; sec. of state State of Md., 1967-69; chief of staff Vice Pres. U.S., 1969-70; judge U.S. Dist. Ct., Dist. Md., 1971—. Mem. Am. Bar Assn., Md. State Bar. Editor U. Md. Law Rev., 1952-53. Office: US Dist Ct US Courthouse Baltimore MD 21202 Tel (301) 962-2722

BLAIR, FORBES WESLEY, b. Chester, W.Va., Dec. 17, 1926; A.B., W.Va. U., 1950, J.D., 1952. Admitted to W.Va. bar, 1950, D.C. bar, 1953, Md. bar, 1959; clk. Office of U.S. Atty., Washington, 1952-54, asst., 1955-57; asso. firm Welch & Morgan, Washington, 1957-66, partner, 1966-69; partner firm Bilger & Blair, Washington, 1970—; clk. Adminstrv. Office U.S. Cts., Washington, 1952. Pres., Paint Branch Farms Civic Assn., Silver Spring, Md., 1962; v.p. Greater Colesville Civic Assn., Silver Spring, 1975-76; bd. govs. W.Va. Soc. Washington, 1970-77, pres., 1977—. Mem. Fed., Am., D.C. bar assns., Am. Judicature Soc., FCC Bar Assn. Editor Civitan Bull., 1962-69; contbr. F.C. Bar Jour. Home: 13826 Overton Ln Silver Spring MD 20904 Office: 1730 M St NW Washington DC 20036 Tel (202) 659-4230

BLAIR, HOMER ORRIN, b. Tacoma, Apr. 11, 1925; B.S. in Chemistry, U. Wash., 1948, B.S. in Physics, 1951, J.D., 1953. Admitted to Wash. bar, 1954, Mass. bar, 1967, U.S. Supreme Ct. bar, 1957; atty. Westinghouse Electric Co., East Pittsburgh, Pa., 1954-58, Boeing Co., Seattle, 1958-61, Kaiser Aluminum & Chem. Corp., Oakland, Calif., 1961-62; chief atty chem. unit Celanese Corp., N.Y.C., 1962-66; dir. patents and licensing ITEK Corp., Lexington, Mass., 1966-71, v.p. patents and licensing, 1971—; del. US/USSR Exchange on Patent Mgmt. and Patent Licensing, 1971, UN Conf. on Trade and Devel.-Patent System and Tech. Transfer, Geneva, 1975, 77; mem. Internat. Indsl. Property Adv. Panel, U.S. Dept. State, 1976—; speaker in field. Mem. Am. Bar Assn., Licensing Execs. Soc. (sec. 1968-72, v.p. 1972-73, pres. 1974-75), Am., Boston patent law assns., Assn. Corp. Patent Counsel, U.S. Trademark Assn., PTC Found. (editorial adv. bd. Idea), World Peace through Law Center, Intellectual Property Owners, Internat. Patent and Trademark Assn., Assn. Advancement of Invention and Innovation. Contbr. articles to legal jours. Office: Itek Corp 10 Maguire Rd Lexington MA 01741 Tel (617) 276-2470

BLAIR, RICHARD BRYSON, b. Athens, Ohio, Oct. 1, 1945; B.A., Franklin and Marshall Coll., 1967; J.D., Ohio No. U., 1970. Admitted to Ohio bar, 1970; asso. firm Roth & Stephens, Youngstown, Ohio, 1970-74, partner firm, 1975—. Bd. dirs. Mahoning County Council of Campfire Girls 1973—, Mahoning County Council on Alcoholism, 1974—, Hungarian Resettlement Home, 1975—. Mem. Am., Ohio, Mahoning County bar assns., Ohio Def. Assn., Am. Arbitration Assn. Home: 180 Ewing Rd Youngstown OH 44512 Office: 1000 Union Nat Bank Bldg Youngstown OH 44503 Tel (216) 744-5211

BLAIR, TERRY BERNARD, b. Balt., Jan. 23, 1947; A.B. M.L., Loyola Coll., Balt., 1968; J.D., Catholic U. Am., Washington, 1971. Admitted to Md. bar, 1972; law clk. asso. judge Ct. Appeals Md., 1971-72; asso. firm Sybert, Sybert & Nippard, Ellicott City, Md., 1972-75, partner, 1975—. Mem. Am., Md., Howard County bar assns. Office: 3701 Court House Dr Ellicott City MD 21043 Tel (301) 465-5300

BLAKE, ARTHUR JOHN, b. Jersey City, Feb. 23, 1942; B.S. in History, Coll. Holy Cross, Worcester, Mass.; LL.B., Seton Hall U. Admitted to N.J. bar, 1966; asso. firm Ryan, Saws, Davis & Stone, Elizabeth, N.J., 1967-69, Lum, Buino & Tompkins, Newark, 1969-70, Siver, Dentsman & Norman, Newark, 1970-71; asst. prosecutor Essex County (N.J.), 1971-73; dep. atty. gen. criminal justice, Trenton, N.J., 1974-76; mem. firm Joseph DiRienzo, Westfield, N.J., 1976—. Office: 555 Westfield Ave Westfield NJ 07090 Tel (201) 233-6700

BLAKE, EDWARD JOSEPH, b. Phila., May 18, 1926; B.S. in Polit. Sci., St. Joseph Coll., 1950; J.D., U. Pa., 1954. Admitted to Pa. bar, 1955, U.S. Supreme Ct. bar, 1955; individual practice law, Phila., 1955-61; chief law clk. Ct. Common Pleas, Phila., 1954-62; partner firm McSorley & McSorley, Phila., 1961-64; chief dep. ct. adminstr. Ct. Common Pleas and Quarter Sessions Phila. County, 1962-64, ct. adminstr., 1964-72; judge Common Pleas Ct. 1st Jud. Dist. Commonwealth Pa., Phila., 1971—. Mem. Phila., Pa. bar assns., Lawyers Club Phila. County, Am. Judicature Soc., Am. Acad. Polit. and Social Sci., Nat. Assn. Trial Ct. Adminstrs. (dir. 1972—), Pa. Conf. State Trial Judges, Brehon Law Soc., The Irish Soc. Author (with L.P. Polansky) Computer Streamlines Caseload at Philadelphia Common Pleas Court, 1969; contbg. editor Wolffe on Zoning. Office: Room 692 City Hall Philadelphia PA 19107 Tel (215) 686-2610

BLAKE, JOHN FRANCIS, b. Dayton, Ohio, Mar. 9, 1937; B.A., U. Dayton, 1967; J.D., Ohio No. U., 1970. Admitted to Ohio bar, 1970, U.S. Supreme Ct. bar, 1974; asso. firm Turner & Badger, Mt. Vernon, Ohio, 1970-72; individual practice law, Dayton, 1972—; 1st asst. pros. atty. Knox County (Ohio), 1970-72; pros. atty. City of Kettering (Ohio), 1972—; counsel Kettering Bd. Community Relations, 1972—. Mem. Ohio, Dayton bar assns., U.S. Naval Inst. Recipient Distinguished Achievement Arts and Science of Advocacy award Internat. Acad. Trial Lawyers, 1970. Home: 1251 Fernshire Dr Centerville OH 45459 Office: 3600 Shroyer Rd Kettering OH 45429 Tel (513) 296-2400

BLAKE, ROGER JOHN, b. Chgo., Mar. 21, 1918; B.S., Northwestern U., 1939; LL.B., J.D., U. Mich., 1942. Admitted to Mich. bar, 1946, Ill. bar, 1947, Ariz. bar, 1948; served to lt. col. JAG, USAF, 1948-71; staff judge advocate 51st Fighter Interceptor Wing, Korea; acting staff judge advocate March and Anderson AFB's, ret., 1971; individual practice law, Phoenix, 1971—. Mem. Am. Trial Lawyers Assn. Home: 4819 N 56th Dr Phoenix AZ 85003 Office: 609 Luhrs Bldg Phoenix AZ 85003 Tel (602) 254-6731

BLAKE, WESLEY CLARENCE, b. Hinsdale, Ill., June 26, 1914; B.S., LL.B., St. Paul Coll. Law, 1950. Admitted to Minn. bar, 1950, U.S. Supreme Ct. bar, 1954, Calif. bar, 1965; served to maj. JAGC, USMC, 1950-64; individual practice law, San Diego, 1965—. Mem. Am., San Diego County bar assns. Office: 4425 Cass St San Diego CA 92109 Tel (714) 273-2460

BLAKELY, JOHN TRELEAVEN, b. Beloit, Wis., May 26, 1944; B.A. with distinction, Duke, 1966; J.D. cum laude, U. Mich., 1969. Admitted to Wis. bar, 1969, Fla. bar, 1970; instr. U. Wis. Law Sch., 1969-70; asso. firm Carlton, Fields, Ward, Emmanuel, Smith & Cutler, Tampa, Fla., 1970-73; partner firm Johnson, Blakely & Pope, Clearwater, Fla., 1973—; municipal judge, Belleair Beach, Fla., 1974-76, Belleair, Fla., 1974-75. Mem. Am., Wis., Fla. bar assns., Am. Assn. Trial Lawyers, Acad. Fla. Trial Lawyers. Editor Hillsborough County (Fla.) Bar Bull., 1972-73. Home: 416 Lotus Path Clearwater FL 33516 Office: PO Box 1368 Clearwater FL 33517 Tel (813) 441-2440

BLAKELY, NEWELL HILLIS, b. Prescott, Ark., July 23, 1919; B.A., Ouachita Coll., 1943, Ph.M., U. Wis., 1944, LL.B., U. Tex., 1947, LL.M., U. Mich., 1954. Admitted to Tex. bar, 1947, U.S. Dist. Ct. So. Dist. Tex. bar, 1948, U.S. Supreme Ct. bar, 1960; partner firm Blakely & Sloan, Harlingen, Tex., 1947-49; asst. prof. law U. Houston, 1949-52, asso. prof., 1952-55, asst. dean, 1951-56, acting dean, 1956-57, dean, 1957-65, prof., 1955—. Mem. Am., Tex., Houston bar assns. Author: (with Hippard) Cases and Materials on Criminal Law, 1974. Home: 19 W Broad Oaks Houston TX 77056 Office: Coll Law U Houston 3801 Cullen Houston TX 77004 Tel (713) 749-3151

BLAKESLEE, EDWARD EATON, b. N.Y.C., July 23, 1921; LL.B. cum laude, N.Y. U., 1947, LL.M. in Taxation, 1957; postgrad. Columbia Exec. Program in Bus. Adminstrn., 1966. Admitted to N.Y. bar, 1947; with Mut. Life Ins. Co. of N.Y., N.Y.C., 1947—, gen. solicitor, 1970-73, 2d v.p., 1970-72, v.p., gen. counsel, 1974—. Mem. Am. Bar Assn., Assn. Bar City N.Y., Am. Council Life Ins., N.Y. U. Alumni Assn., Vanderbilt Assos. Home: 15 Sleepy Hollow Dr Ho-Ho-Kus NJ 07423 Office: 1740 Broadway New York City NY 10019 Tel (212) 586-4000

BLAKEY, RICHARD WATSON, b. Janesville, Wis., Oct. 17, 1911; B.A., Beloit Coll., 1933; LL.B., U. Wis., 1936. Admitted to Wis. bar, 1936, Nev. bar, 1945, U.S. Supreme Ct., bar, 1950; individual practice law, Beloit, 1936-42, Reno, 1946-47; asst. atty. City of Reno, 1947-51; partner firm McCarran, Wedge, Blakey & Gabrielli, Reno, 1951-55, firm Woodburn, Wedge, Blakey, Folsom & Hug, Reno, 1955—; mem. Bd. Bar Examiners, 1949-63, chmn., 1956-63. Trustee Nev. Children's Found., Reno, 1946-73, 76. Mem. Am. Law Inst., Am. Coll. Trial Lawyers, Am. Bd. Trial Advs., Nat. Assn. R.R. Trial Counsel, State Bar Nev. (pres. 1971-72). Home: 2225 Lindley Way Reno NV 89509 Office: 1 E First St Reno NV 89501 Tel (702) 329-6131

BLAKEY, WALKER JAMESON, b. Beattyville, Ky., July 3, 1940; A.B., Harvard, 1963; J.D. summa cum laude, Ohio State U., 1967. Admitted to Ohio bar, 1967; practiced in Columbus, 1967-71; faculty asst. Harvard, 1969-71; asst. prof. law U. N.C., Chapel Hill, 1971—; reporter Com. on Pattern Jury Instrns., N.C. Conf. Superior Ct. Judges. Mem. Am., Ohio, Columbus bar assns., Order of Coif, Soc. Barristers. Author: (with Howe) Assignments in Trial Practice, 1975. Home: 10-G Sharon Heights Chapel Hill NC 27514 Office: Sch Law U N C Chapel Hill NC 27514 Tel (919) 933-5106

BLAN, OLLIE LIONEL, JR., b. Ft. Smith, Ark., May 22, 1931; A.A., Ft. Smith Jr. Coll., 1951; LL.B., U. Ark., 1954. Admitted to Ark. bar, 1954, Ala. bar, 1959; research analyst Ark. Legislative Council, 1954-55; law clk. U.S. Dist. Ct. No. Dist. Ala., 1959-60; asso. firm Spain, Gillon, Riley Tate & Etheredge and predecessors, Birmingham, Ala., 1960-64, partner, 1965—; tchr. Am. Inst. Banking, 1965-68. Mem. Jefferson County (Ala.) Rep. Exec. Com., 1973-76; dir. sec. World Wide Jewish Missions, 1975—; treas. Jefferson County Hist. Commn., 1972—. Mem. Am., Ark., Ala., Birmingham bar assns., Ala. Def. Lawyers Assn., Am. Life Ins. Assn., Mountain Brook Jaycees (pres. 1964-65), Phi Alpha Delta. Contbr. articles to law jours. Home: 2100 22d Ave S Birmingham AL 35223 Office: 800 John A Hand Bldg Birmingham AL 35203 Tel (205) 328-4100

BLANC, ROBERT SMITH, III, b. N.Y.C., Sept. 22, 1943; B.A., Yale U., 1965; LL.B., Columbia U., 1968. Admitted to N.Y. bar, 1969, U.S. Tax Ct. bar, 1971; asso. firm Shearman & Sterling, N.Y.C., 1969—; legal adviser Garden City (N.Y.) Nursery Sch., 1975—. Dist. capt. Garden City Community Fund, 1974—; mem. alumni schs. com. Yale U., 1976. Mem. Assn. Bar City N.Y. Office: 53 Wall St New York City NY 10005 Tel (212) 483-1000

BLANCHARD, H. J., b. Denison, Tex., Dec. 21, 1923; B.A., Tex. Tech. U., 1951; J.D., So. Meth. U., 1951. Admitted to Tex. bar, 1951; partner firm Blanchard, Clifford, Sims & Kidd, and predecessors, Lubbock, Tex., 1953-74; individual practice law, Austin, Tex., 1974—; v.p. pub. and govtl. affairs Mitchell Engring. & Devel. Corp., Houston, 1974-75; mem. Tex. Ho. of Reps., 1957-61, Tex. Senate, 1963-75. Mem. Am. Bar Assn., Motor Carrier Lawyers Assn. Home: 2504 Galewood Pl Austin TX 78703 Office: 1910 American Bank Tower Austin TX 78701 Tel (512) 477-9467

BLANCK, RICHARD LABRUM, b. Murray, Utah, July 25, 1940; B.S., Utah State U., 1962; J.D., U. Utah, 1965. Admitted to Utah bar, 1965, U.S. Supreme Ct. bar, 1968; served as judge adv. USAF, 1965-69; asso. firm Owen, Ward & Geldzahler, Salt Lake City, 1969-72; asso. firm Prince, Yeates, Ward & Geldzahler and predecessors, Salt Lake City, 1972-73, partner, 1973—. Mem. Am., Utah, Salt Lake County bar assns. Office: 455 S 3d E Salt Lake City UT 84111 Tel (801) 521-3760

BLANCO, DAVID BENNETT, b. Peoria, Ill., Mar. 23, 1941; B.A., Duke, 1963, LL.B., 1966. Admitted to N.C. bar, 1966; law clk. to Eugene A. Gordon, Chief Judge U.S. Dist. Ct. Middlee Dist. N.C., 1966-68; staff trust dept. Wachovia Bank and Trust Co. (N.C.), 1968-71; asst. v.p. Wachovia Mortgage Co/Wachovia Realty Investments, Winston-Salem, N.C., 1971-73; partner firm House and Blanco, Winston-Salem, 1973—. Chmn. Environ. Affairs Bd. Forsyth County, N.C., 1976—. Mem. Am. (reporter N.C., mem. sub com. significant decisions sect. real property, probate and trust law), N.C., N.C. State, Forsyth County bar assns., Phi Delta Phi. Office: Stratford Exec Park 265 Olson St Winston-Salem NC 27103 Tel (919)768-4330

BLAND, RONALD J., b. Mount Vernon, N.Y., Apr. 7, 1935; A.B., Yale, 1957, LL.B., 1960. Admitted to Wash. bar, 1961; partner firm Levinson, Friedman, Vhugen, Duggan Bland & Horowitz, Seattle. Mem. Am., Wash., King County bar assns., Am., Wash. State (bd. govs. 1974—) trial lawyers assns. Home: 9418 SE 33d St Mercer Island WA 98040 Office: 1600 Seattle Tower Seattle WA 98101 Tel (206) 624-8844

BLANDFORD, JOHN LLOYD, b. Greenville, S.C., Nov. 4, 1937; B.S., The Citadel, 1959; postgrad. Atlanta Law Sch., 1965-66; J.D., John Marshall Sch. Law, 1968. Admitted to Ga. bar, 1968; asst. solicitor gen. Fulton County (Ga.) Criminal Ct., 1969-70; partner firm Cobb Blandford & Werbin, Chamblee, Ga., 1970—; judge Chamblee Recorders Ct., 1970—; martial officer Ga. N.G. Cts. Mem. Am., Ga., Decatur DeKalb bar assns., Ga. Assn. Criminal Def. Lawyers. Office: 3508 Broad St Chamblee GA 30341 Tel (404) 458-0186

BLANK, ANDREW RUSSELL, b. Bklyn., June 13, 1945; A.B., U. Fla., 1966; J.D., U. Miami (Fla.), 1970. Admitted to Fla. bar, 1970, Ga. bar, 1971, U.S. Supreme Ct. bar, 1976; since practiced in Atlanta, law clk. U.S. Dist. Ct., 1970-72; partner firm Ross & Finch, 1977—; lectr. Continuing Legal Edn., Savannah and Albany, Ga., 1976. Mem. Com. Devel. Advisory Council to Atlanta Regional Commn., 1974; chmn. City-County Legislative Reorganization Com. Atlanta Jr. C. of C., 1973. Mem. Am., Ga., Fla., Atlanta bar assns., Am. Judicature Soc., Ga. Trial Lawyers Assn., Phi Delta Phi, Phi Kappa Phi. Home: 4569 Amberly Ct S Doraville GA 30360 Office: 3417 First Nat Bank Tower Atlanta GA 30303 Tel (404) 658-9070

BLANK, PHILIP BERNARDINI, b. Bronx, N.Y., May 22, 1934; B.S., Fordham Coll., 1956, LL.B., 1959. Admitted to N.Y. bar, 1960; mem. legal dept. Allstate Ins. Co., 1960-62; asso. firm Stewart W. Rowe, White Plains, N.Y., 1962-66; mem. legal dept. County Trust Co., White Plains, 1966-68; law asst. Surrogate's Ct. West County (N.Y.), White Plains, 1968—; mem. faculty N.Y. State Bar Assn. of Continuing Legal Edn., Manhattanville Coll., N.Y. U. Sch. Continuing Legal Edn., Practising Law Inst., N.Y.C. Mem. White Plains, Westchester County bar assns. Home: 2 Colonial Ln Valhalla NY 10595 Office: 111 Grove St White Plains NY 10601 Tel (914) 682-2796

BLANKE, MEL HAROLD, b Plymouth, Wis., Apr. 24, 1949; A.B., cum laude, Harvard, 1971; J.D., Boston U., 1974. Admitted to Wis. bar, 1974; research asst. Harvard Bus. Sch., 1969-72; intern U.S. Attys. Office, Boston, 1972-74; intern Mass. Defenders Office, Boston, 1973-74; individual practice law, Plymouth, 1974—; dir. United Savs. & Loan, Plymouth; instr. Lakeshore Tech. Inst., 1976—. Chmn. United Fund Campaign, Plymouth, 1975, bd. dirs., 1976—. Mem. Am., Wis., Sheboygan County bar assns., Plymouth Assn. Commerce (pres. 1977), Plymouth Jaycees (treas. 1975, dir. 1976—). Home: 343 Stafford St Plymouth WI 53073 Office: 408 E Mill St Plymouth WI 53073 Tel (414) 892-4451

BLANKENSHIP, GEORGE THOMAS, b. Indpls., Aug. 13, 1946; B.S., Ind. U., 1968, J.D., 1971. Admitted to Ind. bar, 1971; partner firm Blankenship & Caudill, Indpls., 1971—; inheritance tax adminstr. State of Ind., 1969-71. Mem. Indpls. Bar Assn. Office: 7050 Madison Ave Indianapolis IN 46227 Tel (317) 783-3167

BLANKENSHIP, GERALD, JR., b. Glendale, Calif., Feb. 13, 1938; A.B., U. So. Cal., 1960, J.D., 1963. Admitted to Calif. bar, 1965; dep. dist. atty. Kings County, Calif., 1965-67; asso. prof. bus. law Calif. State U., Fresno, 1967-73; dep. county counsel, Riverside County, Calif., 1973—. Mem. State Bar of Calif., Riverside County, Am. bar assns. Office: 3535 10th St Riverside CA 92501

BLANKFEIN, RICHARD STEPHEN, b. N.Y.C., June 5, 1935; B.A., U. Vt., 1957; LL.B., N.Y. Law Sch., 1963. Admitted to N.Y. State bar, 1964; individual practice law, Queens, N.Y., 1964-69, Carle Place, N.Y., 1971-73; estate tax atty. IRS, 1970-71; partner firm Blankfein & Giddings, Carle Place, 1973—. Mem. Town of Oyster Bay Youth Bd., 1976-77. Mem. Am., Nassau County, N.Y. State bar assns. Home: 11 Lincoln Ave Glen Head NY 11545 Office: One Old Country Rd Carle Place NY 11514 Tel (516) 742-0883

BLANKINGSHIP, A. HUGO, JR., b. Norfolk, Va., Aug. 9, 1930; B.A., U. Va., 1952, LL.B., 1957. Admitted to Va. bar, 1957; now mem. firm Boothe, Prichard & Dudley, Fairfax; city atty. City of Fairfax, 1964-68. Trustee Protestant Episcopal Theol. Sem. of Va., 1976. Mem. Am., Va. (exec. com. 1972—, pres. 1977-78), Fairfax (pres. 1974—) bar assns., Va. State Bar, Omicron Delta Kappa, Phi Alpha Delta. Office: 4085 University Dr PO Box 338 Fairfax VA 22030 Tel (703) 273-4600*

BLANTON, FRED, b. Muscle Shoals, Ala., July 2, 1919; A.B. cum laude, Birmingham-So. Coll., 1939; LL.B., U. Va., 1942, J.D., 1970; postgrad. U. Ala., 1946; Cook fellow, U. Mich., 1951. Admitted to Ala. bar, 1946, U.S. Supreme Ct. bar, 1963; individual practice law, Birmingham, 1946-48, 54—; instr. Law Birmingham-So. Coll., 1947-48; prof. law Dickinson Sch. Law, 1948-49; asst. prof. law. U. Va., 1949-51; asso. firm Martin & Blakey, Birmingham, 1951-54. Mem. Ala. Bar Assn., Am. Soc. EEG Techs. Contbr. articles to legal jours. Home: 1912 KC DeMent Ave Fultondale AL 35068 Office: 3716 5th Ave S Birmingham AL 35222 Tel (205) 251-6821

BLANTON, JAMES CHARLES, b. American Falls, Idaho, Feb. 6, 1926; LL.B., U. Idaho., 1951. Admitted to Idaho bar, 1951, U.S. Tax Ct., 1958, U.S. Supreme Ct., 1962; dep. pros. atty. Ada County, Idaho, 1952-55; partner firm Wallis & Blanton, Boise, Idaho, 1956-62, Moffatt, Thomas, Barrett & Blanton, Boise, 1962—. Chancellor Episcopal Diocese of Idaho, 1960-71; bd. dirs. Idaho Elks Rehab. Hosp., 1970. Mem. Am., Boise (past pres.) bar assns., Am. Coll. Probate Counsel, Internat. Acad. Estate and Trust Law, Nat. Assn. Coll. and Univ. Attys., Fedn. Ins. Counsel, Defense Research Inst., Idaho State Bar (editor The Advocate 1957-60), Boise Estate Planning Council (past pres.), Greater Boise C. of C. Home: 3602 Hillcrest Dr Boise ID 83705 Office: 300 1st Security Bldg Boise ID 83701 Tel (208) 345-2334

BLANTON, LEWIS MICHAEL, b. Cape Girardeau, Mo., Mar. 5, 1934; A.B., St. Louis U., 1958, M.A., 1962; J.D. (Guy A. Thompson scholar), U. Mo., 1965. Admitted to Mo. bar, 1965; asso. firm Thompson, Walther & Shewmaker, St. Louis, Mo., 1965-69, Blanton, Blanton, Rice & Sickal, Sikeston, Mo., 1969-71; partner firm Robison & Blanton, Sikeston, 1971—; city atty. Chaffee, Mo., 1973-75. Bd. dirs. Sikeston United Fund, 1971-76; vice chmn. bd. dirs. Sikeston Child Devel. Center, 1973—, Tri-County Counseling Center, Sikeston, 1975-76; advisory bd. mem. Group Home #IV Mo. Div. of Youth Services, 1974-76. Mem. Am., Mo., Scott County bar assns., Bar Assn. Met. St. Louis, Phi Delta Phi. Mem. bd. student editors Mo. Law Rev. 1963-65, revising editor, 1964-65; contbr. articles to law jours. Home: 304 Powers St Sikeston MO 63801 Office: 300 W North St Sikeston MO 63801 Tel (314) 471-5583

BLASDELL, DANIEL ALLEN, b. New Castle, Pa., July 12, 1944; B.A., Muskingum Coll., 1967; J.D., Ohio No. U., 1972. Admitted to Ohio bar, 1973, Fed. Ct. bar, 1974; atty. Village New Waterford (Ohio), 1973—; asst. pros. atty. Columbiana County (Ohio), 1974-76; partner firm Allison and Blasdell, East Palestine, Ohio, 1975—; municipal atty. Village of Columbiana (Ohio), 1976—. Bd. dirs. Columbiana County Bd. Mental Retardation, 1976—. Mem. Am., Ohio State, Columbiana County bar assns. Home: 576 E Taggart St East Palestine OH 44413 Office: 25 E Rebecca St East Palestine OH 44413 Tel (216) 426-9391

BLAU, EDWARD, b. N.Y.C., Aug. 3, 1922; B.B.A., Coll. City N.Y., 1948; LL.B., Harvard, 1951. Admitted to N.Y. bar, 1951, Calif. bar, 1954; mem. firm Sargoy & Stein, N.Y.C., 1951-52; atty. MCA TV Ltd., N.Y.C., 1952-54; mem. firm Pacht, Ross, Warne, Bernhard & Sears, Los Angeles, 1954—. Mem. Los Angeles Copyright Soc., Beverly Hills, Los Angeles County bar assns. Office: 1800 Ave of Stars Suite 500 Los Angeles CA 90067 Tel (213) 277-1000

BLAU, HARVEY RONALD, b. N.Y.C., Nov. 14, 1935; A.B., N.Y.U., 1957, LL.M., 1965; LL.B., Columbia, 1961. Admitted to N.Y. bar, 1961; law sec. U.S. Dist. Ct. So. Dist. N.Y., 1962-63; asst. U.S. Atty., N.Y., 1963-66; individual practice law, N.Y.C., Jericho, N.Y., 1966-74; sr. partner firm Blau and Kramer, Jericho, 1975—; served to capt. JAGC, 1958-66; sec., dir. Instrument Systems Corp., Huntington, N.Y., 1966-74. Mem. Fed. Bar Council, Bar Assn. City N.Y., N.Y. State, Nassau County bar assns. Home: 125 Wheatley Rd Old Westbury NY 11568 Office: 410 Jericho Turnpike Jericho NY 11753 Tel (516) 822-4820

BLAUGRUND, DANIEL JOHN, b. N.Y.C., Feb. 26, 1914; A.B., Cornell U., 1935, J.D., 1937. Admitted to N.Y. bar, 1937; practiced in Utica, N.Y., 1937-39, Herkimer, 1939—; judge Herkimer County (N.Y.) Family Ct., 1954—. Chmn. Herkimer (N.Y.) Planning Bd., 1954-68, Herkimer chpt. ARC, 1947-48. Mem. Herkimer County (pres. 1963-65), N.Y. State, Am. bar assns., Assn. Judges of Family Ct. State of N.Y. (1st v.p.). Mng. editor Cornell Law Rev., 1936-37. Home: 510 W German St Herkimer NY 13350 Office: County Office Bldg Herkimer NY 13350 Tel (315) 866-1840

BLAUSTEIN, ALBERT PAUL, b. N.Y.C., Oct. 12, 1921; A.B., U. Mich., 1941; J.D., Columbia, 1948. Admitted to N.Y. State bar, 1948, N.J. bar, 1962; mem. firm Blaustein & Blaustein, N.Y.C., 1948-50, 1952-55; counsel Nierenberg, Zeif & Weinstein, N.Y.C., 1971—; law faculty Rutgers U., Camden, N.J., 1955—, prof. law, 1959—. Mem. Assn. Bar City N.Y., U.S. Trademark Assn., Copyright Soc. U.S.A., Internat. Soc. Mil. Law and Laws of War. Author: Constitutions of the Countries of the World, 1971—; Constitutions of Dependencies and Special Sovereignties, 1975—; others; co-editor Legal Malpractice Reporter, 1976—; mem. World Policy Com. for World Habeas Corpus and Commn. for Internat. Due Process of Law; contbr. articles to legal jours. Home: 415 Barby Ln Cherry Hill NJ 08003 Office: Fifth and Penn Sts Camden NJ 08102 Tel (609) 757-6182

BLAUVELT, JAMES NELSON, b. Rockville Centre, N.Y., Nov. 4, 1933; B.S., Antioch Coll., 1956; M.B.A., Columbia U., 1959; J.D., Fordham Law Sch., 1967. Admitted to N.J. bar, 1967, U.S. Patent Office, 1964; patent engr. Singer, Stern & Carlberg, N.Y.C., 1961-63; patent atty. Mobil Oil Corp., N.Y.C., 1963-66; sr. patent atty. Exxon Research & Engring. Co., Linden, N.J., 1966-69, E. R. Squibb & Sons, Princeton, N.J., 1969-70; individual practice law, resident U.S. counsel Marks & Clerk, London, 1970-73; sr. patent atty. GAF Corp., Wayne, N.J., 1974—. Mem. Am., N.J. State bar assns., Brit. Chartered Inst. Patent Agts., Sigma Alpha. Home: 60 Fells Rd Verona NJ 07044

BLAYLOCK, CHARLES RICHARD BRADLEY, b. Houston, Feb. 24, 1943; B.A., N.E. La. State U., 1965; J.D., La. State U., 1969. Admitted to La. bar, 1969; individual practice law, Monroe, La., 1969—. Coordinator, Miss Ouachita Parish (La.) Pageant, 1971-72. Mem. Am., La., 4th Dist. bar assns., Am. Judicature Assn. Home: 215 Breard St Monroe LA 71201 Office: 401 N Third St Monroe LA 71201 Tel (318) 323-8388

BLAZEK, DORIS DEFIBAUGH, b. Easton, Md., Nov. 17, 1943; B.A., Goucher Coll., 1965; J.D., Georgetown U., 1968. Admitted to Virgin Islands bar, 1969, D.C. bar, 1969; asso. firm Young & Isherwood, St. Croix, U.S. Virgin Islands, 1969-70; asso. firm Covington & Burling, Washington, 1970-76, partner, 1976—. Mem. Am., D.C. bar assns. Contbr. articles to legal jours. Home: 4213 Thornapple St Chevy Chase MD 20015 Office: 888 16th St Washington DC 20006 Tel (202) 452-6110

BLECHER, JACK MARTIN, b. Bklyn., July 21, 1931; B.A., Bklyn. Coll., 1951; LL.B., Columbia, 1954, J.D., 1969. Admitted to N.Y. bar, 1955; partner firm Blecher & Blecher, N.Y.C. and Spring Valley, N.Y., 1956—; asst. county atty. Rockland County (N.Y.), 1965-70, 74—; Pub. Employment Relations Commn. of N.J., 1970-74. Mem. Rockland County Bar Assn., Am. Arbitration Assn. Home: 28 Bruck Ct Spring Valley NY 10977 Office: 10 Chestnut St POB 31 Spring Valley NY 10977 Tel (914) 352-2100

BLECKWENN, ALFRED THEODORE, b. Madison, Wis., Aug. 17, 1929; B.S., U. Wis., 1951, LL.B., 1954, J.D., 1976. Admitted to Wis. bar, 1954, U.S. Supreme Ct. bar, 1975; sec.-treas. N.W. Adjustors, Inc., Madison, 1954-59; partner firm Brimmer & Bleckwenn, Madison, 1959—. Pres., Village of Shorewood Hills (Wis.), 1963-65; sec.-treas. Met. Madison Refuse Dist., 1965—; sec. Ind. Housing Assn., 1967-69; 1st v.p. Dane County Cancer Soc., 1976. Mem. Wis., Dane County bar assns., Phi Delta Phi. Recipient award Am Cancer Soc., 1974. Home: 3441 Crestwood Dr Madison WI 53705 Office: 411 W Main St Madison WI 53703 Tel (608) 255-5323

BLEDSOE, CARTER, b. Washington, Mar. 25, 1930; B.A., Haverford Coll., 1952; LL.B., George Washington U., 1955. Admitted to D.C. bar, 1955, Pa. bar, 1960; atty. Congl. Joint Com. on Internal Revenue Taxation, Washington, 1955-58, appellate sect. Dept. Justice Tax Div., Washington, 1958-60; asso. firm Pepper, Hamilton & Scheetz, Phila., 1960-65; partner firm Squire, Sanders, & Dempsey, Cleve., 1965—. Home: 3372 Glencairn Rd Shaker Heights OH 44122 Office: 1800 Union Commerce Bldg Cleveland OH 44115 Tel (216) 696-9200

BLEDSOE, JAMES ALEXANDER, JR., b. Jacksonville, Fla., Oct. 4, 1947; A.B., Princeton; 1969; J.D., U. Va., 1972. Admitted to Fla. bar, 1972; mem. firm Mahoney Madlow & Adams, Jacksonville, 1972—. Mem. Jacksonville, Fla., Am. bar assns., Princeton Alumni Assn. No. Fla. (sec.-treas. 1974—). Home: P O Box 361 Atlantic Beach FL 32233 Office: 100 Laura St Jacksonville FL 32202 Tel (904) 354-1100

BLEDSOE, ROBERT C., b. Marfa, Tex., Aug. 23, 1930; student N.Mex. Mil. Inst., Roswell, 1947-49; B.B.A., U. Tex., 1951, J.D., 1955. Admitted to Tex. bar, 1955, N.Mex. bar, 1958; asso. firm Baker, Botts, Andrews & Shepherd, Houston, 1955-57, Hervey, Dow & Hinkle, Roswell, 1957-59; asso., then partner firm Stubbeman, McRae, Sealy, Laughlin & Browder, Midland, Tex., 1959-74; partner firm Cotton, Bledsoe, Tighe, Morrow & Dawson, Midland, 1974—. Bd. dirs., chmn. Salvation Army, Midland, 1970—; bd. dirs. Cerebral Palsy Center, Midland; mem. Com. for Young Life, Midland. Mem. Am., Tex. (dist. grievance com. 1972-76), Midland County (pres. 1975-76), N.Mex. bar assns. Author: Joint Creditor Problems, 1972. Home: 1601 Gulf Ave Midland TX 79701 Office: 1930 Wilco Bldg Midland TX 79701 Tel (915) 684-5782

BLEICHER, SAMUEL ABRAM, b. Omaha, June 21, 1942; B.A., Northwestern U., 1963; J.D., Harvard, 1966. Admitted to Nebr. bar, 1966, Ohio bar, 1972, U.S. Supreme Ct. bar, 1976; asst. prof. law U. Toledo, 1966-69, asso prof. law, 1970-73, prof. law, 1975—; vis. asst. prof. law U. Mo., 1969-70; dep. dir. for regulation and enforcement Ohio Environ. Protection Agy; 1972-75. Bd. dirs. Northwestern Ohio Lung Assn., 1976—; bd. govs. U. Toledo Environ. Scis. Inst., 1970-71; mem. Work Group on Utility Rate Structure, Gov.'s Energy Task Force, 1974; del. candidate for Morris K. Udall for Pres., 9th Congress. Mem., Am., Toledo bar assns., Am. Soc. Internat. Law, World Peace Through Law. Contbr. articles in field to profl. jours. Home: 2671 Cheltenham Rd Toledo OH 43606 Office: Univ Toledo Coll Law Toledo OH 43606 Tel (419) 537-2949

BLEIWEISS, LORRY ROBERT, b. Cleve., Nov. 26, 1924; B.S. in Econs., U. Pa., 1947; J.D., Case Western Res. U., 1949. Admitted to Ohio bar, 1949; mem. firm Payer, Bleiweiss and Crow, Cleve., 1949—; substitute judge Willoughby Municipal Ct., 1972—. Trustee Lakeland Community Coll., 1974—, chmn., 1976; chmn. Wickliffe Civil Service Commn., 1971-76. Mem. Cleve. Bar Assn., Fraternal Order Police Assos. (v.p. 1975). Home: 9341 Hilo Farm Dr Kirtland Hills OH 44060 Office: 2025 Superior Bldg Cleveland OH 44114 Tel (216) 621-7110

BLEND, STANLEY LOUIS, b. Dallas, June 28, 1942; B.A., Tulane U., 1964; J.D., cum laude, U. Houston Bates Coll. Law, 1967; LL.M. in Taxation, Georgetown U., 1971. Admitted to Tex. bar, 1967, U.S. Tax Ct. bar, 1967, U.S. Supreme Ct. bar, 1970, U.S. Ct. Claims bar, 1968; teaching fellow Bates Coll. Law U. Houston, 1967; with chief counsel's office IRS, Washington, 1967-71, asst. br. chief, 1971-72; asso. firm Oppenheimer, Rosenberg, Kelleher & Wheatley, Inc., San Antonio, 1972-75, mem. firm, 1975—; lectr. in fed. taxation. Bd. dirs. San Antonio Jewish Social Service Fedn., 1975—, San Antonio Jewish Community Center, 1976—. Mem. Fed. (treas. San Antonio chpt. 1974-75, sec. 1975-76, dir. 1976—), Am., Tex., San Antonio bar assns. Recipient Bancroft Whitney award, 1966; bd. editors Houston Law Rev., 1966-67. Home: 5411 Lancashire San Antonio TX 78230 Office: Suite 620 711 Navarro San Antonio TX 78205 Tel (512) 224-7581

BLEUEL, BARTLEY STEINER, b. Sacramento, June 7, 1941; A.B., St. Mary's Coll., 1963; LL.B., J.D., U. Calif., San Francisco, 1966. Admitted to Calif. bar, 1966; research asst. League of Calif. Cities, 1967; legal officer USN, 1967-69; dep. dist. atty. Sacramento County (Calif.), 1969-73; partner firm Kelly & Bleuel, Ventura, Calif., 1973—. Mem. Criminal Def. Family Law, Estate Planning-Probate bar assns. Certified specialist in criminal law Calif. Bd. Legal Specialization. Home: 9409 Santa Maria St Ventura CA 93003 Office: 455 E Main St Suite 7 and 8 Ventura CA 93001 Tel (805) 643-2251

BLEVEANS, JOHN, b. Danville, Ill., Mar. 29, 1938; B.A., Trinity U., 1960; LL.B., U. Tex., 1965. Admitted to Tex. bar, 1965, D.C. bar, 1967, Ill. bar, 1971, U.S. Supreme Ct. bar, 1969; mem. gen. counsel's office Acacia Mut. Life Ins. Co., Washington, 1967-68; trial and appellate atty., civil rights div. U.S. Dept. Justice, Washington, 1966-67, 68-70; exec. dir. Washington Lawyer's Com. Civil Rights Under Law, 1970-71; chief counsel Lawyer's Com. Civil Rights Under Law, Cairo, Ill., 1971-72; asso. firm Mayer, Brown & Platt, Chgo., 1972-74, partner, 1974—. Mem. Am., Tex., D.C. bar assns. Office: 231 S LaSalle St Chicago IL 60604 Tel (312) 782-0600

BLEVINS, GARY LEE, b. Wayne, Okla., Mar. 12, 1945; B.A., U. Okla., 1967, J.D., 1973. Admitted to Okla. bar, 1973; individual practice law, Purcell, Okla., 1973; asso. dist. judge McClain County (Okla.), Purcell, 1973—. Mem. Am. Bar Assn., Am. Judicature Soc., Am. Coll. State Judiciary, Phi Alpha Delta. Home: 705 N 3rd St Purcell OK 73080 Office: Box 648 Purcell OK 73080 Tel (405) 527-6651

BLEY, J(OSEPH) RUSSELL, JR., b. St. Louis, Mar. 23, 1939; B.A., St. Louis, 1961; J.D., U. Notre Dame, 1964. Admitted to Mo. bar, 1964; law clk. U.S. Ct. Appeals, Chgo., 1964-65; atty. Monsanto Co., St. Louis, 1965—, asst. corporate counsel, 1975—; participant Nat. Endowment for Humanities charter legal seminar program. Past pres. St. Louis U. Sch. Arts and Scis. alumni bd.; chmn. St. Louis U. Alumni Council; trustee Tealwood subdiv., St. Louis; past pres. Tealwood Men's Assn. Mem. Am., Mo. bar assns., Bar Assn. Met. St. Louis, Contbr. article to Nat. Indsl. Conf. Bd. publ. Home: 51 Tealwood Dr Creve Coeur MO 63141 Office: 800 N Lindbergh Blvd Creve Coeur MO 63166 Tel (314) 694-2868

BLICK, CLAYTON LEWIS, b. Waterbury, Conn., Aug. 7, 1917; A.B., N.Y. U., 1938, J.D., 1941. Admitted to Conn. bar, 1941; asso. firm A. Herny Weisman, Waterbury, Conn., 1941-42; asso. firm David Cramer, Litchfield, Conn., 1945-48; partner firm Hubbard & Cramer, Litchfield, 1948-56; partner firm Cramer, Blick & FitzGerald, Litchfield 1956-58; partner firm Cramer, Blick, FitzGerald & Hume, Litchfield, 1958-62; partner firm Cramer & Anderson, Litchfield, 1962—; dir. First Nat. Bank of Litchfield. Mem. Town of Litchfield Bd. Edn., 1958-70. Mem. Am., Conn. bar assns. Home: Deer Island Morris CT 06763 Office: South Litchfield CT 06759 Tel (203) 567-8717

BLINDER, ALBERT ALLAN, b. N.Y.C., Nov. 27, 1925; A.B., N.Y.U., 1944; J.D., Harvard, 1948. Admitted to N.Y. bar, 1949; asst. U.S. atty. N.Y.C., 1950-53; asst. dist. atty. Bronx, N.Y., 1954-60; partner firm Saxe, Bacon & O'Shea, N.Y.C., 1960-64; partner firm Blinder, Steinhaus & Hochhauser, N.Y.C., 1965-73; judge N.Y. State Ct. Claims, 1973—; asst. counsel N.Y.C. Bd. High Edn., 1953-54; counsel various N.Y. State Commns., 1965-73. Mem. Am., Internat., N.Y. State bar assns., Assn. Bar City N.Y., N.Y. County Lawyers Assn. Office: NY State Ct Claims Chambers 2 World Trade Center New York City NY 10047 Tel (212) 775-0100

BLINN, KEITH WAYNE, b. Hutchinson, Kan., July 28, 1917; A.B., Washington and Lee U., 1940; LL.B. (Sterling fellow), Yale, 1951. Admitted to Wis. bar, 1941, Tex. bar, 1953, N.Y. bar, 1966; atty. TVA, 1942, NLRB, 1942-46; prof. law U. N.D., 1946-52; vis. prof. law U. Ida., 1952; sr. v.p. gen. counsel Continental Oil Co., N.Y.C., 1962—; lectr., seminar participant, 1964—; arbitrator Am. Arbitrator Assn., 1961—. Atty. adviser OPA, 1951; chmn. regional enforcement commn. WSB, Mpls., 1952. Mem. bd. zoning appels, Bellaire, Tex., 1957, mem. city council, 1959. Mem. Am. Bar Assn., Assn. Bar City N.Y., Order of Coif, Phi Delta Phi. Home: Valley Rd New Canaan CT 06840 Office: Continental Oil Co High Ridge Park Stamford CT 06904*

BLISS, CHARLES FRED, JR., b. Muskogee, Okla., Dec. 7, 1908; student Northeastern Okla. State U., 1927-29, student U.S. Naval Acad., 1928. Admitted to Okla. bar, 1934; mem. firm Bliss & Bliss, Tahlequah, Okla., 1934-37, 40-52, 55-58; individual pracitce law, Tahlequah, 1952-55; county atty. Cherokee County (Okla.), 1937-40; city atty. City of Tahlequah, 1941-56; judge Dist. Ct., 15th Jud. Dist. Okla., 1958-72, Ct. Criminal Appeals of State of Okla., 1972—; mem. Okla. Jud. Conf. Mem. Okla. Bar Assn. Home: 711 Shawnee St Tahlequah OK 74464 Office: State Capitol Bldg Oklahoma City OK 73105 Tel (405) 521-2158

BLISS, FRANCIS WALTER, b. Gilboa, N.Y., Apr. 27, 1892; A.B., Cornell U., 1913; LL.B., Albany Law Sch., 1915, J.D., 1968; LL.D., Central Coll., Pella, Iowa, 1939. Admitted to N.Y. bar, 1915; individual practice law, Middleburgh, N.Y., 1916-30, Schoharie, N.Y., 1963—; partner firm Bliss & Bouck, Albany, N.Y. and Schoharie, 1945-62; county atty. Schoharie County (N.Y.), 1922-26; justice N.Y. Supreme Ct., Albany, 1930-44, N.Y. 3d Dept. Appellate Div., Albany, 1933-44; pres. Howe Caverns, Howes Cave, N.Y.; pres. First Nat. Bank Middleburgh, 1936-39, 43-54. Mem. Am., N.Y. State, Schoharie County bar assns. Recipient Gold medal Albany Law Sch., 1975. Home: 4595 Clauverwie Rd Middleburgh NY 12122 Office: 316 Main St Schoharie NY 12157 Tel (518) 295-8118

BLISS, JAMES IRELAND, b. Milw., June 10, 1944; B.S., U. Ill., 1965, J.D., 1967. Admitted to Ill. bar, 1967, U.S. Ct. Appeals bar, 1968, Mo. bar, 1970; asso. firm Keck, Cushman, Mahin & Cate, Chgo., 1967-69; atty. Monsanto Co., St. Louis, 1969-71; pres. Bliss Group Cos., Bloomington, Ill., 1971—; mem. firm Bane, Allison & Saint, Bloomington, 1972—; sec., dir. Thomas Jefferson Indemnity Co., Champaign, Ill., 1973-75. Mem. Am. (vice-chmn. com. on use of modern tech.), Ill. State, Mo., Ind. State, Inter-Am., McLean County bar assns., Order of Coif. Author ins. chpt. Ill. Municipal Law Handbook, 1965; bd. editors U. Ill. Law Forum. Home: 3 Golf Ct Bloomington IL 61701 Office: 210 E Washington St Bloomington IL 61701 Tel (309) 829-7086

BLISS, JOHN E., b. Wausau, Wis., Aug. 30, 1924; B.S., Marquette U., 1949, J.D., 1957. Admitted to Wis. bar, 1957; claims mgr. Employers Mutual Casualty Ins. Co., Milw., 1951-57; mem. firm Tinkham, Smith, Bliss, Patterson & Richards, and predecessors, Wausau, Wis., 1957—. Fellow Am. Coll. Trial Lawyers; mem. Am., Wis. Bar Assns., Internat. Assn. Ins. Counsel. Home: 3112 N 13th St Wausau WI 54401 Office: 640 4th St Wausau WI 54401 Tel (715) 845-1151

BLISS, WALTER ERNEST, b. Greeley, Colo., May 3, 1918; B.A., U. Colo., 1942. Admitted to Colo. bar, 1943, Hawaii bar, 1946; spl. agt. FBI, 1942-44; individual practice Honolulu, 1946-57; partner firm Goodsill, Anderson & Jenks and predecessors, Honolulu, 1957—. Mem. Legal Aid Soc. Hawaii (pres. 1960), Bar Assn. Hawaii (exec. com. 1966, chmn. ethics com. 1968, pres. 1970). Am. Bar Assn., Beta Theta Pi, Phi Delta Phi. Home: 44-023 Kaimalu Place Kaneohe HI 96744 Office: Castle and Cooke Bldg Honolulu HI 96813 Tel (808) 531-5066

BLISSARD, LOUIS BATEMAN, b. Port Norris, N.J., July 15, 1913; A.B., Princeton, 1935; J.D., U. Va., 1938. Admitted to Ariz. bar, 1947, Hawaii bar, 1949, U.S. Supreme Ct. bar, 1954; atty. Phoenix VA, 1946-48, Honolulu, 1949-51; labor relations advisor Coal Mines Adminstrn., Washington, 1947; enforcement dir. Office of Price Stblzn. Hawaii, 1951-53; U.S. atty., Hawaii, 1954-61; individual practice law, Honolulu, 1961—; mng. dir. Seven Seas Travel Agy., Honolulu, 1968-73; developer Hotel Moorea Lagoon, French Polynesia, 1969-72; dir. Sociètè d'Exploitation de L'Hotel Moorea Plage, Lincoln Fin. Corp., Hawaii. Trustee Pacific Prep. Acad., 1965-75. Mem. Am., Hawaii bar assns., Am. Law Inst., Phi Delta Phi. Brig. gen. USMCR. Home: 700 Richards St Honolulu HI 96813 Office: 1855 Pacific Trade Center Honolulu HI 96813 Tel (808) 537-5942

BLITZ, WILLIAM JULES, b. Napoleon, Ohio, July 29, 1942; B.S. in Edn., Ohio U., 1965; J.D., Cleve. State U., 1972; With Allstate Ins. Col.. Hudson, Ohio, 1968-73; admitted to Ohio bar, 1973; asso. firm Sindell, Sindell, Stern & Guidubaldi, Cleve., 1973-74; asso. firm McGrath & Riemenschneider, Berea, Ohio, 1974—; mem. inst. adv. council Cleve. Psychiat. Inst., 1976—; trustee Far West Counseling and Info. Center, 1976—; mem. Task Force on Legislation, Fedn. for Community Planning, 1975—; mem. jud. selection com. Citizens League, 1974-75. Mem. Am., Ohio, Greater Cleve., Cuyahoga County bar assns., Legal Aid Soc. Cleve. Contbr. articles to law review. Office: 300 Comml Bank Bldg Berea OH 44017 Tel (216) 243-1222

BLITZER, SIDNEY MILTON, JR., b. Baton Rouge, May 25, 1944; A.B. in Econs., Duke, 1966; J.D., La. State U., 1969. Admitted to La. bar, 1969; asso. firm Kantrow, Spaht, Weaver & Walter, Baton Rouge, 1969-72, partner, 1972—; spl. advisor continuous revision trust com. La. Law Inst., 1975-76; instr. security devices La. State U. Law Sch., 1975-76. Bd. dirs. Baton Rouge Assn. Retarded Citizens, La., Baton Rouge Easter Seal socs. Mem. Am., La., Baton Rouge bar assns., Baton Rouge Estate and Bus. Planning Council. Contbr. articles to profl. publs. Office: POB 2997 Baton Rouge LA 70821 Tel (504) 383-4703

BLOCH, DONALD MARTIN, b. Lynn, Mass., May 16, 1939; B.A., Bowdoin Coll., 1960; LL.B., Harvard, 1963. Admitted to Mass. bar, 1963; asso. firm Nathanson & Rudofsky, Boston, 1966-71, partner, 1972—. Mem. Framingham (Mass.) Town Govt. Com., 1968—. Mem. Boston Bar Assn., Phi Beta Kappa. Home: 668 Salem End Rd Framingham MA 01701 Office: 201 Devonshire St Boston MA 02110 Tel (617) 357-5200

BLOCH, GERALD JOSEPH, b. New London, Wis., Apr. 26, 1939; B.A. Lawrence U., 1961; LL.B., U. Wis., 1964. Admitted to Wis. bar, 1964; asso. firm Aberg, Bell, Blake & Metzner, Madison, Wis., 1964-66; partner firm Phillips, Hoffman & Bloch, Milw., 1966—. Mem. Am. Wis., bar assn., Am., Wis. (pres. 1972-74) acads. trial lawyers. Contbr. articles to law jours. Home: 929 N Astor St Milwaukee WI 53202 Office: 161 W Wisconsin Ave Milwaukee WI 53203 Tel (414) 271-4262

BLOCH, RICHARD, b. Balt., May 2, 1946; A.B., George Washington U., 1968; J.D., U. Md., 1972. Admitted to Md. bar, 1972; law clk. to sr. dist. judge R. Dorsey Watkins, U.S. Dist. Ct. for Dist. Md., 1972; asso. firm Anderson, Coe & King, Balt., 1972-77, partner, 1977—. Mem. Am., Md., Balt. bar assns. Home: 7427 Kathydale Rd Pikesville MD 21208 Office: 800 Fidelity Bldg Baltimore MD 21201 Tel (301) 752-1630

BLOCK, ALAN DAVID, b. Boston, Sept. 19, 1930; A.B., Harvard U., 1952, J.D., 1955. Admitted to Mass. bar, 1955, Calif. bar, 1964; agt. IRS, Los Angeles, 1961-63; practice law, Palos Verdes Peninsula, Calif., 1964-66; partner firm Block & Osofsky, Torrance, Calif., 1966—. Mng. dir. Legal Aid Found., Torrance, 1967-69. Mem. Am., Los Angeles County, S.Bay bar assns. Home: 2048 Via Visalia St Palos Verdes Estates CA 90274 Office: 2520 Torrance Blvd Torrance CA 90503 Tel (213) 320-7700

BLOCK, ELI, b. Iron Mountain, Mich., Oct. 25, 1910; student U. Wis., 1928-31, J.D., 1934. Admitted to Wis. bar, 1934; partner firm Geffs, Geffs, Block & Geffs, Janesville, Wis., 1935-68; individual practice law, Janesville, 1968—. Mem. Rock County (pres.), State of Wis. bar assns., Am., Wis. trial lawyers assns. Office: 100 W Court St Janesville WI 53545 Tel (608) 754-8111

BLOCK, EMIL HAROLD, b. Long Island City, N.Y., Dec. 14, 1908; LL.B./J.D., Rutgers U., 1929; LL.M., Mercer Beaseley Sch. Law, Newark, 1935. Admitted to N.J. bar, 1930; individual practice law, Newark and Maplewood, N.J., 1930—; pres. Mayfair Corp., Newark, 1948, Audubon Raceway, Inc., Henderson, Ky., 1963-71. Pres., Career and Counseling Services of No. N.J., B'nai B'rith, 1954-74; mem. nat. adv. bd. youth services B'nai B'rith, 1954—; active Boy Scouts Am. Mem. N.J., Fed. bar assns. Home: 206 Wyoming Ave Maplewood NJ 07040 Office: 7 Highland Pl Maplewood NJ 07040

BLOCK, FREDRIC MARTIN, b. Phila.; B.A., Gettysburg Coll., 1963; J.D., Rutgers U., 1968. Admitted to N.J. bar, 1968, U.S. Ct. Appeals for 3d Circuit bar, 1972, U.S. Supreme Ct. bar, 1972; atty. Camden Regional Legal Services OEO, 1968-70; asst. county prosecutor Camden County (N.J.), 1970-72; individual practice law, Willingboro, N.J., 1968-70, Marlton, N.J., 1970—. Co-founder, solicitor, bd. dirs. Marlton (N.J.) Bus. Assn., 1972. Mem. Am., N.J., Burlington County (N.J.) bar assns. Home and office: 55 Overington Ave Marlton NJ 08053 Tel (609) 983-2177

BLOCK, HAROLD MARTIN, b. Thibodaux, La., July 24, 1945; B.A., U. Va., 1968; J.D., Tulane U., 1971. Admitted to La. bar, 1971, U.S. Supreme Ct. bar, 1975; partner firm Block, Block & Parro, Thibodaux, 1971—. Chmn. Thibodaux chpt. Am. Cancer Soc., 1971—; mem. La. Ednl. TV Authority, 1974—, treas., 1975-76, vice chmn., 1977—; mem. planned gifts com. Tulane U., 1976—. Mem. Lafourche Parish (La.) (pres. 1976), La. State, Am. bar assns. Home: 411 Bermuda Pl Thibodaux LA 70301 Office: 312 Saint Louis St Thibodaux LA 70301 Tel (504) 446-0418

BLOCK, JULIUS, b. N.Y.C., Feb. 3, 1907; student Coll. City N.Y., 1925-37; LL.B., St. Lawrence U., 1929; LL.M., Bklyn. Law Sch., 1941. Admitted to N.Y. bar, 1930, U.S. Dist. Ct. for Eastern Dist. N.Y. bar, 1931, for So. Dist. N.Y. bar, 1934, U.S. Supreme Ct. bar, 1955; individual practice law, Holliswood, N.Y., 1930—; sr. atty. exec. dept. N.Y. State Div. Human Rights, N.Y.C., 1976—; atty., treas. Victor Metal Products Corp., Newport, Ark., Victor Slug Div., Inc., Newport, 1948-57. Office: 190-25 Mc Laughlin Ave Holliswood NY 11423 Tel (212) SP6-6034

BLOCK, MELVIN, b. Bklyn., Oct. 26, 1927; LL.B., Bklyn. Law Sch., 1950, LL.M., 1954. Admitted to N.Y. bar, 1950; individual practice law, Bklyn.; mem. impartial jud. screening com. 2d Jud. Dept., State of N.Y., 1974—; police judge, Massapequa Park, N.Y.; pros. atty. Massapequa Park, atty. Zoning Bd.; lectr. various univs., med. socs., engrng. socs., service clubs and orgns.; founder Legal Advocacy Intern Program, Bklyn. Law Sch. Bd. dirs. Paralegal Inst., L.I. U.; mem. adv. com. on products liability Dept. Commerce; active Roscoe Pound Found. Mem. Am., N.Y. State, Bklyn., Nassau bar assns., Am. (nat. sec., chmn. communications dept., mem. exec. com.), N.Y. State (dir., pres. 1972-74, editor-in-chief Trial Lawyers Quar. 1966-72), Met. trial lawyers assns., Nassau County Lawyers Assn., Nat. Legal Aid and Defender Assn., Am. Judicature Soc., Nat. Assn. Def. Counsel in Criminal Cases, Scribes, Inner Circle Advs. Recipient Presdl. pen and citation White House, 1966; editor The Art of Summation; Medical Malpractice. Home: 229 Grant St Massapequa Park NY 11762 Office: 16 Court St Brooklyn NY 11241 Tel (212) 875-8703

BLOCK, ROBERT BENJAMIN, b. N.Y.C., Apr. 3, 1912; B.A., Columbia, 1933, LL.B., 1935. Admitted to N.Y. State bar, 1935, U.S. Dist. Ct. So. Dist. N.Y. bar, 1946, U.S. Ct. Appeals 2d Circuit bar, 1949, U.S. Dist. Ct. Eastern Dist. N.Y. bar, 1958, U.S. Supreme Ct. bar, 1970, U.S. Ct. Appeals 6th Circuit bar, 1973; practiced in N.Y.C., 1935—; asso. firm Geller & Saslow and predecessor 1935-52, partner firm Saslow, Block & Sonenschein, 1952-53, firm Heffner, Block & Block, 1953-63, firm Pomerantz, Levy, Haudek & Block, 1963—. Mem. Assn. Bar City N.Y., Am., N.Y. State bar assns., N.Y. County Lawyers' Assn. Home: 20 E 35th St New York City NY 10016 Office: 295 Madison Ave New York City NY 10017 Tel (212) 532-4800

BLOMQUIST, BARRY LOUIS, b. Onamia, Minn., Sept. 27, 1932; B.A., U. Minn., 1967, J.D., 1970. Admitted to Minn. bar, 1971; individual practice law, North Branch, Minn., 1971—; judge Municipal Ct., North Branch, 1971-72; asst. county atty. Chisago County (Minn.), 1972-76, county atty., 1976—; region 7E commr. Minn. Regional Devel. Act, chmn. econ. devel. subsom., 1976—. Mem. Minn., Am. bar assns., Minn. Assn. County Attys. Home and office: 762 Elm St North Branch MN 55056 Tel (612) 674-4818

BLOODWORTH, ALBERT WILLIAM FRANKLIN, b. Atlanta, Sept. 23, 1935; A.B. in History and French, Davidson Coll., 1957; J.D. magna cum laude, U. Ga., 1963. Admitted to Ga. bar, 1962, U.S. Supreme Ct. bar, 1971; asst. dir. alumni and pub. relations Davidson Coll., 1959-60; asso. firm Hansell, Post, Brandon & Dorsey, Atlanta, 1963-68, partner, 1969—; counsel Met. Atlanta Commn. on Crime and Juvenile Delinquency, 1965-67. Asst. sec., counsel Met. Found. Atlanta, 1968-76; bd. dirs. Atlanta Presbytery, Inc., 1974—. Mem. Am. (chmn. significant current legis. com, real property, probate and trust sect.), Atlanta (chmn. elections com. 1972-73) bar assns., State Bar Ga., Lawyers Club Atlanta, Atlanta Estate Planning Council, Phi Beta Kappa, Phi Kappa Phi, Omicron Delta Kappa, Phi Delta Phi (recipient grad. of year for SE award 1963), Alpha Tau Omega. Home: 4110 Peachtree Dunwoody Rd NE Atlanta GA 30342 Office: 3300 1st Nat Bank Tower Atlanta GA 30303 Tel (404) 581-8000

BLOODWORTH, JAMES NELSON, b. Decatur, Ala., Jan. 21, 1921; B.S., U. Ala., 1942, LL.B., 1947. Admitted to Ala. bar, 1947; partner firm Calvin & Bloodworth, Decatur, Ala., 1947-59; judge 8th Ala. Circuit Ct., 1959-68; justice Ala. Supreme Ct., 1968—; judge Decatur Recorder's Ct., 1948-51; county solicitor Morgan County (Ala.), 1951; mem. Ala. Bd. Pardons and Paroles, 1951-52; pres. Morgan County Jury Commn., 1962-68; faculty adviser, lectr. Nat. Coll. State Judiciary; mem. faculty Am. Acad. Jud. Edn.; lectr., seminar leader in field. Mem. Ala., Morgan County, Montgomery County bar assns. Author: (with George Huddleston) Index Alabama Constitutional Convention, 1901, 1948; contbr. articles to profl. jours. Home: 3221 Bankhead Ave Montgomery AL 36106 Office: POB 218 Montgomery AL 36101 Tel (205) 832-6430

BLOODWORTH, RALPH R., b. Corning, Ark., Apr. 24, 1916; A.B., U. Mo., 1938, LL.B., 1940. Admitted to Mo. bar, 1940; pros. atty., Butler County, Mo., 1943, 47-50, War Crime Trials, Manila, 1945-46; individual practice law. Mem. Am. (asso. editor tort law jour. 1958—), Mo. (past pres.) trial lawyers assns., Butler County Bar Assn., Mo. Assn. Claimants' Attys. (past editor bull.). Home: Rural Route 7 Box 431 Poplar Bluff MO 63901 Office: Hwy 60 E and B St Poplar Bluff MO 63901 Tel (314) 785-6425

BLOOM, ARNOLD SANFORD, b. Syracuse, N.Y., Sept. 3, 1942; B.S., Syracuse U., 1964, M.B.A., 1967, J.D., 1967; LL.M., N.Y. U., 1968. Admitted N.Y. State bar, 1967; asso. firm Marshall, Bratter, Greene, Allison & Tucker, N.Y.C., 1968-74; sr. atty. Kane-Miller Corp., Tarrytown, N.Y., 1974-76, asst. gen. counsel, 1976—. Mem. Am., N.Y., N.Y.C. bar assns., Westchester-Fairfield Corp. Counsel

Assn. Office: 555 White Plains Rd Tarrytown NY 10591 Tel (914) 631-6900

BLOOM, ARTHUR LOUIS, b. Jeannette, Pa., Nov. 19, 1937; B.B.A., U. Pitts., 1959; J.D., U. WVa., 1962. Admitted to WVa. bar, 1962, Pa. bar, 1963; partner firm Feldstein, Bloom, Grinberg, Stein & McKee, Pitts., 1967—. Mem. Am., Pa., W.Va., Allegheny County bar assns., Pi Lambda Phi. Home: 5600 Munhall Rd Pittsburgh PA 15217 Office: 1401 Law and Finance Bldg Pittsburgh PA 15219 Tel (412) 765-1495

BLOOM, CHARLES JOSEPH, b. Pitts., July 7, 1946; A.B., Princeton, 1967; J.D. magna cum laude, U. Pa., 1971. Admitted to Pa. bar, 1971; asso. firm Pepper, Hamilton & Scheetz, Phila., 1972—. Mem. govt. relations com. United Way of Phila., 1973-76; dir. Franklin Inst. Firsts, Phila. Mem. Am., Pa., Phila. bar assns., Am. Judicature Soc., Phila. Lawyers Club. Home: 2125 Delaney Pl Philadelphia PA 19103 Office: 123 S Broad St Philadelphia PA 19109 Tel (215) 545-1234

BLOOM, LACKLAND HOWARD, b. St. Louis, Aug. 20, 1914; A.B., Washington U., St. Louis, 1939, J.D., 1939; postgrad. Nat. Coll. State Trial Judges, 1966. Admitted to Mo. bar, 1939, U.S. Dist. Ct. bar, 1940, U.S. Supreme Ct. bar, 1963; with legal dept. Office Circuit Clk., St. Louis, 1939-40; partner firm Neuhoff & Millar, St. Louis 1940-42; with U.S. Air Corps, 1943-44; with legal dept. Curtiss-Wright Corp., St. Louis, Buffalo, 1945-46; partner firms Murphy & Bloom, 1947-54, Bloom & Herzog, 1966; individual practice law, St. Louis, 1954-65; judge Circuit Ct. of St. Louis, 1965—; instr. Mo. law Washington U., 1939-40. Trustee Deaconess Hosp., St. Louis. Mem. Am., Mo., St. Louis (v.p. 1949-50, exec. com.) bar assns., Am. Judicature Soc., Nat. (dir.), Mo. (pres.) pilots assns., Lawyers-Pilots Bar Assn. (v.p. 1965), Order of Coif, Phi Delta Phi, Sigma Alpha Epsilon. Co-editor: Mo. Bar Jour., 1940-41. Home: 6787 Westway Rd St Louis MO 63109 Office: Civil Courts Bldg St Louis MO 63101 Tel (314) 453-4321

BLOOM, LAURENCE JAMES, b. Cambridge, Mass., Feb. 6, 1942; A.B., Boston Coll., 1963; J.D., Harvard, 1966. Admitted to Mass. bar, 1966; partner firm Ficksman & Conley, Boston, 1966-72; solicitor City of Somerville (Mass.), 1973-75; partner firm Bloom & Buell, Somerville, 1974—; lectr. Northeastern U., Boston, 1969—. Mem. Somerville Rent Control Bd., 1971-72. Mem. Mass. Bar Assn. Home: 15 Evergreen Ave Somerville MA 02145 Office: 99 Highland Ave Somerville MA 02143 Tel (617) 628-4910

BLOOM, LEONARD, b. Wilmerding, Pa., Mar. 2, 1929; B.E., Johns Hopkins U., 1951; LL.B., U. Md., 1957. Admitted to Md. bar, 1957; patent engr. Westinghouse Electric Corp., 1953-58; patent atty., now dir. patents and licenses Black and Decker Mfg. Co., Towson, Md., 1958—. Mem. C. of C. Met. Balt., IEEE, Am., Fed. bar assns., Am. Patent Law Assn., Am. Mgmt. Assn., Licensing Execs. Soc. Office: 701 E Joppa Rd Towson MD 21204 Tel (301) 828-3240

BLOOM, MARTIN, b. Phila., Nov. 13, 1907; LL.B., Dickinson Sch. Law, Carlisle, Pa., 1929. Admitted to N.J. bar, 1930, U.S. Supreme Ct. bar, 1943; indiviudal practice law, Atlantic City, 1930-76; of counsel firm Horn, Weinstein, Kaplan & Goldberg, Atlantic City, 1976—; mayor, Margate City, N.J., 1959-75. Mem. Margate Sch. Bd. Edn., 1951-59; pres. Atlantic County (N.J.) League Municipalities, 1965; v.p. Atlantic County Mayor's Conf., 1973-74. Mem. Am., N.J. Atlantic County (pres. 1960) bar assns., N.J. Trial Attys. Assn., Am. Arbitration Assn. Recipient citation of merit N.J. Conf. Mayors, 1972. Home: Apt 1602 9100 Atlantic Ave Margate City NJ 08402 Office: 1301 Atlantic Ave Atlantic City NJ 08401 Tel (609) 348-4515

BLOOM, MARTIN FRANKLIN, b. Newark, N.J., Dec. 25, 1936; B.A., Antioch Coll., 1959; J.D., U. Chgo., 1962. Admitted to Calif. bar, 1963; asso. firm Smith, Prante & Biggins, San Diego, Calif., 1963-66; individual practice law, San Diego, 1966—. Bd. dirs. Planned Parenthood Assn. San Diego County, 1975—; founding dir. Citizens United for Racial Equality, San Diego, 1968-70. Mem. Calif., San Diego County (chmn. arbitration com. 1976-77) bar assns. Home: 5935 Waverly Ave LaJolla CA 92037 Office: Suite 1200 Security Pacific Plaza 1200 3d Ave San Diego CA 92101 Tel (714) 231-1531

BLOOMER, HAROLD FRANKLIN, JR., b. N.Y.C., Nov. 4, 1933; A.B., Amherst Coll., 1956; LL.B. cum laude (James Kent scholar), Columbia. Admitted to Conn. bar, 1967, N.Y. State bar, 1968; asso. firm Debevoise, Plimpton, Lyons & Gates. N.Y.C., 1967—. Trustee Sanitary Products Trust, 1965-74; mem. Representative Town Meeting, Greenwich, Conn, 1962-74, chmn. pub. works. com. 1969-74; mem. Republican Town Com., Greenwich, 1972-74. Mem. N.Y.C. Bar Assn. Editor: Columbia Law Rev., 1966-67. Office: 299 Park Ave New York City NY 10017 Tel (212) 752-6400

BLOOMFIELD, DAVID SOLOMON, b. Cleve., Dec. 13, 1944; B.Sc., Ohio State U., Columbus, 1966, J.D., 1969. Admitted to Ohio bar, 1969, U.S. Tax Ct. bar, 1970, U.S. Supreme Ct. bar, 1972, U.S. Ct. Appeals for 6th Circuit bar, 1977; mem. staff Lybrand Ross Bros. & Montgomery, N.Y.C., 1969-70; chief tax sect. Office of Ohio Atty. Gen., Columbus, 1970-71; partner firm Fontana Ward Kaps & Perry, Columbus, 1971—; instr. Ohio Paralegal Inst., 1972-73, Capital U., 1973—; chief hearing officer Ohio State U., 1973—; spl. counsel to Ohio Atty. Gen., 1971-74. Pres. Franklin County Democratic Lawyers Club, 1976. Mem. Am., Ohio, Columbus bar assns., Ohio Trial Lawyers Assn., Am. Judicature Soc. Recipient award of merit Ohio Legal Center, 1975. Home: 306 E Sycamore St Columbus OH 43206 Office: 50 W Broad St Columbus OH 43215 Tel (614) 224-9224

BLOOMFIELD, ROGER EARL, b. Lakewood, Ohio, Dec. 31, 1945; B.S. in Bus. Adminstrn., Wittenberg U., 1967; J.D., Case Western Res. U., 1974. Admitted to Ohio bar, 1974, U.S. Tax Ct. Bar, 1977; asso. firm Calfee, Halter & Griswold, Cleve., 1974-76; dir. deferred giving and univ. counsel Wittenberg U., Springfield, Ohio, 1976—; served with JAG, USAF, 1969-73. Mem. Am., Ohio State, Greater Cleve. bar assns., Springfield Bar and Law Library Assn., Nat. Assn. Coll. and Univ. Attys., Council for Advancement and Support of Edn., Omicron Delta Kappa. Contbr. articles to legal jours. Home: 1504 N Plum St Springfield OH 45504 Office: Alumni House Wittenberg U Springfield OH 45501 Tel (513) 327-7414

BLOOMFIELD, SALLY WARD, b. Columbus, Ohio, July 20, 1943; student Ohio Wesleyan U., 1961-63; B.A., St. Louis U., 1965; J.D., Ohio State U., 1969, postgrad., 1974—; postgrad. N.Y. U., 1971. Admitted to Ohio bar, 1969, N.Y. State bar, 1970, U.S. Tax Ct. bar, 1970; mem. staff tax dept. Price Waterhouse & Co., N.Y.C., 1969-76; atty. examiner Pub. Utilities Commn. of Ohio, Columbus, 1970, counsel, 1971, asst. to commn., 1971-73, commr., 1973-77; asso. firm Bricker Evatt Barton & Eckler, 1977—; asst. atty. gen. State Ohio, 1971; 1st program dir. Tech. Edn. Conf., Pub. Utilities Commn., 1976; mem. FPC Nat. Gas Survey Curtailment Strategies-Tech. Advisory Com. Task Force, mem. U.S. Atty. Gen's. Task Force Implementation Equal Rights Amendment; mem. nat. council Ohio State U. Coll. Law. Trustee Columbus Area Leadership Lab., Inc., CALL; mem. adv. councils Ohio State U. Sch. Home Econs., Bowling Green State U. Sch. Speech Communications. Mem. Nat. Assn. Regulatory Utility Commrs., Am., Ohio State, Columbus bar assns. Recipient 10 Outstanding Citizens of Columbus award Columbus Jaycees and Jaycee Women, 1975. Home: 306 E Sycamore St Columbus OH 43206 Office: 100 E Broad St Columbus OH 43215 Tel (614) 221-6651

BLOOMINGDALE, ARTHUR LEE, JR., b. Omaha, Sept. 20, 1930; B.S. Commerce, Creighton U., 1954, J.D., 1954; LL.M., U. Mich., 1955. Admitted to Nebr. bar, 1954, U.S. Supreme Ct. bar, 1961; Cook research fellow U. Mich., 1954-55; asso. firm Boland, Mullin and Walsh, OMaha, 1955-60; with Mut. Protective Ins. Co. and Medico Life Ins. Co., Omaha, 1961—, gen. counsel, 1961—, sec., 1969—, exec. v.p., 1969—, also dir.; asst. prof. law Creighton U., 1955-59, asso. prof., 1959-62, prof., 1962-71; com. counsel Omaha Charter Revision Commn., 1973. Mem. Nebr.; Omaha bar assns., Nebr., Am. assns. trial lawyers, Am. Arbitration Assn. Home: 2044 S 86th Ave Omaha NE 68124 Office: 4625 Farnam St Omaha NE 68132 Tel (402) 346-7987

BLOSSER, JAMES JOSEPH, b. Ft. Wayne, Ind., Mar. 27, 1938; B.B.A., U. Miami, 1960, postgrad., 1961, J.D., 1965. Admitted to Fla. bar, 1965; mem. firm English, McCaughan & O'Bryan, Ft. Lauderdale, Fla., 1965—; mem. Legal Aid Services, Broward County (Fla.). Pres. Children's Rehab. Services, Ft. Lauderdale, 1973; mem. Cath. Service Bur. Broward County; mem. U. Miami Citizens Adv. Bd. Mem. Fla. (bd. govs. young lawyers sect. 1969-73), Broward County (exec. com.) bar assns., Am. Trial Lawyers Assn. Office: English McCaughan & O'Bryan 301 E Las Olsa Blvd Fort Lauderdale FL 33301 Tel (305) 462-3301

BLOSSOM, DAVID ROBINSON, b. Quogue, N.Y., Aug. 13, 1910; B.A., Princeton, 1932; J.D., N.Y. U., 1936, J.S.D., 1941. Admitted to N.Y. bar, 1937; asso. firm Alexander & Green, N.Y.C., 1936-63; individual practice law, Bklyn., 1964-72, Jamestown, N.Y., 1972—; town justice Town of Kiantone (N.Y.), 1974—. Mem. Am., N.Y. State, Jamestown bar assns., New York County Lawyers Assn., Nat. Legal Aid and Defender Assn. Home and Office: RD 5 PO Box 243 545 Kiantone Rd Jamestown NY 14701 Tel (716) 569-5754

BLOTNER, J. JOSEPH, b. New Orleans, Oct. 7, 1932; LL.B., Tulane U., 1956. Admitted to La. bar, 1956; individual practice law, Gretna, La., 1956—. Mem. La., Jefferson New Orleans Bar Assns. Home: 7331 Jade St New Orleans LA 70124 Office: 614 2d St Gretna LA 70053 Tel (504) 366-3551

BLOW, GEORGE, b. Chgo., Oct. 4, 1928; A.B. cum laude, Harvard U., 1950; LL.B., U. Va., 1953. Admitted to Va. bar, 1953, D.C. bar, 1954; asso. firm Covington & Burling, Washington, 1953-63; partner firm Patton, Boggs & Blow, Washington, 1963—. Mem. Washington Inst. Fgn. Affairs (treas., dir. 1976—), Soc. Cin., Order of Coif, Phi Delta Phi. Home: 2424 Kalorama Rd NW Washington DC 20008 Office: 1200 17th St NW Washington DC 20036 Tel (202) 223-4040

BLUE, JAMES MONROE, b. St. Petersburg, Fla., Oct. 5, 1941; A.B., Fla. State U., 1963; J.D. cum laude, Stetson U., 1967. Admitted to Fla. bar, 1967; asso. firm Carlton Fields Ward Emmanuel Smith & Cutler, Tampa, Fla., 1967-69; mem. firm Alley Alley & Blue, Tampa and Miami, Fla., 1969-75; mem. firm Smith Young & Blue, Naples and Tallahassee, 1975—. Active Dade County United Way, 1974-76, Jr. C. of C. Mem. Dade and Leon County, Fla. (labor law com.), Am. bar assns., Tallahassee C. of C., Phi Delta Phi. Contbr. articles to legal jours.; editorial bd. Profl. Corp. Digest. Home: 1524 Argonne Rd Tallahassee FL 33303 Office: Barnett Bank Bldg Suite 740 Tallahassee FL 32302 Tel (904) 222-7206

BLUER, HERBERT AARON, b. Oakland, Calif., Dec. 1, 1929; B.A., Calif. U., 1952, LL.B., 1955. Admitted to Calif. bar, 1955; asso. firm Harold L. Strom, Oakland, 1955-56; partner firm Strom, Bluer & Weiser, Oakland and Walnut Creek, Calif., 1956-75; individual practice law, Walnut Creek, 1975—. Mem. Mt. Diablo Bar Assn. Editorial bd. Calif. Law Rev., 1954-55; chmn., Calif. State Bar Adminstrn. Com. Home: 238 Northcreek Circle Walnut Creek CA 94598 Office: 1211 Newell Ave Walnut Creek CA 94596 Tel (415) 933-8150

BLUESTEIN, LOUIS ALLEN, b. Chgo., June 20, 1944; B.A., U. Calif., Berkeley, 1966; J.D., U. Colo., Boulder, 1969. Admitted to Colo. bar, U.S. Dist. Ct. bar, 1969; asst. to exec. v.p., lectr. dept. polit. sci. State U. N.Y., Stony Brook, 1969-71; asso. firm Ott, Caskins, Castillo & Rhodes, Denver, 1971; dept. state pub. defender, Denver, 1972-74; individual practice law, Denver, 1974—; partner firm Bluestein & Simon, 1976—. Bd. dirs. Mountain State Hillel Council, Denver, 1973—; bd. dirs. City Coalition Inc., 1975-76; Democrat precinct, committeeman, Arapahoe County, Colo., 1968; del. Colo. Dem. Assembly, 1974, 76. Mem. Colo., Denver bar assns., ACLU, Phi Delta Phi, Alpha Phi Omega. Editor, U. Colo. Law Review, 1968-69. Home: 1120 Forest St Denver CO 80220 Office: 770 Grant St Suite 244 Denver CO 80203 (303) 837-1411

BLUM, STEPHEN ALFRED, b. Bklyn., Mar. 7, 1932; B.A., U. Miami, 1953, D.L., 1955. Admitted to Fla. bar, 1955, N.Y. bar, 1956; atty., investigator Contract Rev. Agy., U.S. Army, assisting McLellan Senate Com., Phila., 1957-58; individual practice law, N.Y.C., 1958—; chief counsel Flatbush Consumer Aid Bur., Concerned Citizens of Flatbush, Flatbush Tenants Assn., 1971-74. Mem. N.Y. State, Fla. bar assns. Home: 27 Pond Ln Rock Hill NY 12775 Office: 39 Broadway New York City NY 12775

BLUM, WALTER J., b. Chgo., Aug. 17, 1918; A.B., U. Chgo., 1939, J.D., 1941. Admitted to Ill. bar, 1941, D.C. bar, 1941; prof. law U. Chgo. Law Sch., 1953—, mem. faculty 1946—; legal counsel Bull. Atomic Scientists, 1948—. Mem. Chgo., Am. bar assns., Am. Law Inst., Chgo. Fed. Tax Forum, Law Club Chgo. Author: (with Harry Kalven, Jr.) The Uneasy Case for Progressive Taxation, 1953; (with Stanley A. Kaplan) Corporate Readjustments and Reorganizations, 1976. Office: 1111 E 60th St Chicago IL 60637 Tel (312) 753-2459

BLUMBERG, AARON DAVID, b. N.Y.C., Mar. 9, 1938; B.S. in Econs., U. Pa., 1960, LL.B. cum laude, 1963. Admitted to Pa. bar, 1964; law clk. to judge Fed. Dist. Ct., 1963-65; asso. firm Pepper, Hamilton and Scheetz, Phila., 1966-72; asso. firm S. Gerald Litvin, 1972-75; partner firm Litvin, Blumberg, Matusow & Young, Phila., 1976—; lectr. bus. law Wharton Sch. Bus., U. Pa., 1964-68; instr. Temple U. Law Sch., 1970-71; speaker Phila. Naval Hosp.; lectr. Phila. Sch. Optometry, 1974, 75. Fellow Acad. Advocacy; mem. Am., Phila. (med. legal com. and civil procedure com.) bar assns., Am. Assn. Trial Lawyers, Order of Coif. Home: 406 D S Croskey Mews Philadelphia PA 19146 Office: 117 S 17th St 22nd floor Architects Bldg Philadelphia PA 19103 Tel (215) 665-0400

BLUMBERG, GUNAR JOHN, b. Riga, Latvia, May 21, 1937; A.B., Harvard U., 1959; J.D., Rutgers U., 1964. Admitted to Ill. bar, 1964; sr. patent atty. Standard Oil Co., Chgo., 1964—. Mem. Am., Chgo. patent law assns., Am. Bar Assn. Home: 1016 N Delphi Ave Park Ridge IL 60068 Office: 200 E Randolph Dr Chicago IL 60605 Tel (212) 856-5967

BLUMBERG, MALCOLM MARK, b. Phila., June 12, 1941; A.B., U. Pa., 1962, J.D., 1965. Admitted to Pa. bar, 1965; partner firm Isenberg, Goldin & Blumberg, Phila., 1969—. Mem. Am., Pa., Phila. bar assns. Home: 3239 Bridlepath Ln Dresher PA 19025 Office: Suite 623 Four Penn Center Plaza Philadelphia PA 19103 Tel (215) 567-7760

BLUMBERG, PHILLIP IRVIN, b. Balt., Sept. 6, 1919; A.B. magna cum laude, Harvard U., 1939, J.D. magna cum laude, 1942. Admitted to N.Y. bar, 1942, Mass. bar, 1970; asso. firm Willkie, Owen, Otis, Farr & Gallagher, N.Y.C., 1942-43; asso. firm Szold, Brandwen Meyers & Blumberg, and predecessors, N.Y.C., 1946-49, partner, 1949-66; pres. Federated Devel. Co., and predecessors, N.Y.C., 1962-68; prof. law Boston U. Sch. Law, 1968-74; dean U. Conn., 1974—; chmn. Conn. Com. to Rev. Law of Corps., 1976-77; mem. Conn. Gov.'s Com. to Rev. Jud. Nominations, 1975—; mem. adv. com. transnat. enterprises Dept. State. Mem. Am. Law Inst., Am., Conn. bar assns., Phi Beta Kappa. Author: Corporate Responsibility in a Changing Society, 1972; The Megacorporation in American Society, 1975; contbr. articles to legal jours.; treas. Harvard Law Rev., 1941-42. Home: 791 Prospect Ave West Hartford CT 06105 Office: 1800 Asylum Ave West Hartford CT 06117

BLUME, FRED, b. Phila., Mar. 14, 1941; B.S., Temple U., 1963; J.D., U. Pa., 1966. Admitted to Pa. bar, 1966, Fla. bar, 1975; clk. to judge Phila. Cts. Common Please, 1966-67; asso. firm Blank, Rome, Klaus & Comisky, Phila., 1967-72, partner, 1972—. Pres. bd. alumni mgrs. bus. sch. Temple U., Phila., 1975-76; vice chmn. trade and industry Am. Cancer Soc., Phila., 1975-76. Mem. Am., Pa., Phila., Fla. bar assns., Order of Coif, Beta Gamma Sigma. Office: 4 Penn Center Plaza Philadelphia PA 19103 Tel Tel (215) 569-3700

BLUMENFELD, ELI, b. N.Y.C., May 17, 1933; B.S. with honors, U. Calif., Los Angeles, 1959, LL.B., J.D., 1963. Admitted to Calif. bar, 1964, U.S. Tax Ct. bar, U.S. Supreme Ct. bar, 1976; trial lawyer for regional counsel IRS, Los Angeles, 1964-69; individual practice law, Los Angeles, 1969—. Vice pres. B'nai B'rith, 1955—; v.p. Am. Friends of Hebrew U.; advisory counsel to Los Angeles Schs., 1970-71. Mem. Los Angeles County, Beverly Hills bar assns., Am. Judicature Soc. Certified tax specialist, C.P.A. Home: 9636 Heather Rd Beverly Hills CA 90210 Office: 1900 Ave of the Stars Suite 2440 Los Angeles CA 90067 Tel (213) 553-6668

BLUMENFELD, JACK ROSS, b. Chgo., June 23, 1942; B.A., U. Ala., 1965; J.D., U. Miami, 1967. Admitted to Fla. bar, 1967, U.S. Ct. Appeals 5th Circuit bar, 1969, U.S. Supreme Ct. bar, 1971; law clk. to U.S. Dist. Judge, Miami, Fla., 1967-69; asst. state atty. Dade County (Fla.), Miami, 1969-74; partner firm Kogan & Blumenfeld, Miami, 1974-77, law offices Jack R. Blumenfeld, 1977—; spl. counsel U.S. House Select Com. Crime, 1972. Mem. Am., Dade County bar assns., Fla. Criminal Def. Attys. Assn., Nat. Assn. Criminal Def. Lawyers. Office: 619 NW 12th Ave Miami FL 33136 Tel (305) 324-5040

BLUMENTHAL, MAX ELLIOT, b. Hartford, Conn., June 4, 1940; B.A., Lehigh U., 1961; LL.B., U. Pa., 1964. Admitted to Md. bar, 1964; counsel Gov's. Commn. Rev. Criminal Sentences, Balt., 1964-65; asso. firm Frank, Bernstein, Conaway & Goldman, Balt., 1967-71, partner, 1971—. Bd. dirs. Jewish Community Center, Balt. Mem. Am., Md., Balt. City bar assns., Balt. Assn. Tax Counsel. Editor article Md. Bar Jour. Office: 1300 Mercantile Bank and Trust Bldg Baltimore MD 21201 Tel (301) 547-0500

BLUMER, MARK EDWARD, b. Detroit, Sept. 19, 1949; B.A., Mich. State Univ., 1971; J.D., U. Detroit, 1974. Admitted to Mich. bar, 1974; hearing examiner Mich. Dept. State, 1975-76; asst. atty. gen., Lansing, Mich., 1976—. Mem. Am., Mich. bar assns. Home: 3891 New Salem Okemos MI 48864 Office: 7th Floor Law Building Lansing MI 48913 Tel (517) 373-8060

BLUMING, SIDNEY DAVID, b. Bklyn., Aug. 8, 1944; B.A. in Accounting, Queens Coll., 1965; J.D., Bklyn., 1968. Admitted to N.Y. State bar, 1968; asso. firm Guggenheimer & Untermyer, N.Y.C., 1968-71; asso. firm Phillips, Nizer, Benjamin, Krim & Ballon, N.Y.C., 1971—. Mem. Am. Bar Assn. Contbr. articles in field to profl. jours. Home: 2 Madison Pl Jericho NY 11753 Office: 40 W 57th St New York City NY 10019 Tel (212) 977-9700

BLUMSACK, RICHARD EARL, b. Boston, Oct. 31, 1938; B.A., Harvard, 1960, LL.B., 1963. Admitted to Mass. bar, 1964; partner firm Joseph Blumsack and Richard E. Blumsack, Somerville, Mass., 1964—; master Middlesex County (Mass.) Probate and Superior Cts., 1973—. Mem. Middlesex, Somerville, Mass., Boston bar assns., Mass. Trial Lawyers Assn. Home: 11 Rutledge Rd Belmont MA 02178 Office: 319 Broadway Somerville MA 02145 Tel (617) 625-2132

BLUMSTEIN, JAMES FRANKLIN, b. N.Y.C., Apr. 24, 1945; B.A., Yale, 1966, M.A. in Econs., 1970, LL.B., 1970. Admitted to Tenn. bar, 1970, U.S. Supreme Ct. bar, 1974; asst. prof. law Vanderbilt U., 1970-73, asso. prof. law, 1973-76, prof. law, 1976—, acting dir. Urban and Regional Devel. Center, 1972-74; vis. asso. prof. law and policy scis. Duke, 1974-75; law clk. FCC, Washington, 1967, Mobilization for Youth Legal Services, 1968; asso. firm Cahill, Gordon, Sonnett, Reindel & Ohl, N.Y.C., 1969; cons. in field; mem. Adv. Com. on Family Planning, State of Tenn., 1973, 74. Mem. AAUP, Soc. Am. Law Tchrs., Common Cause, Soc. for Health and Human Values, Alan Guttmacher Inst., Planned Parenthood Fedn. Am., Assn. Am. Law Schs., Tenn. Civil Liberties Union (dir. 1971-76, chmn. legal com. 1971-74). Author: (with Eddie J. Martin) The Urban Scene in the Seventies, 1974; (with Benjamin Walter) Growing Metropolis, Aspects of Development in Nashville, 1975; contbr. articles to legal and health policy jours. Home: 200 Cantrell Ave Nashville TN 37205 Office: Vanderbilt Law Sch Nashville TN 37240 Tel (615) 322-2613

BLUTH, WILLIAM HAROLD, b. N.Y.C., Oct. 31, 1945; B.A., City Coll. of City U.N.Y., 1966; J.D., Boston Coll., 1969. Admitted to N.Y. bar, 1969, Ohio bar, 1970, U.S. Dist. Ct. bar, 1972; law clk. to U.S. Dist. Judge Orrin G. Judd, N.Y.C., 1969-70; prof. law, dir. clin.

programs Capital U. Law Sch., Columbus, Ohio, 1970—; bd. trustees Legal Aid and Defender Soc., 1975—; bd. dirs. ACLU Central Ohio, 1972-74. Mem. Am., Ohio, Columbus (chmn. criminal law and constitutional rights com. 1974-76), bar assns. Am. Judicature Soc., Order of the Coif. Contbr. articles in field to profl. jours.; mem. editorial staff Boston Coll. Indsl. and Comml. Law Rev. Office: 793 S Pleasant Ridge Ave Columbus OH 43209 Tel (614) 236-7171

BLYTHE, JAMES DAVID, II, b. Indpls., Oct. 20, 1940; B.S., Butler U., 1962; LL.B., J.D., Ind. U., 1966. Admitted to Ind. bar, 1966; individual practice law, Indpls., 1966—; U.S. Congressional staff asst., 1965-69; majority atty. Ind. Ho. of Reps., 1967-69; dep. prosecutor Marion County, 1966-68; travel agt. Skyline Travel, Inc., 1972-75; legal advisor Ind. Subcontractors Assn., 1970-72, 76-77; legis. atty. Police League of Ind., 1970-73; legal counselor, advisor Indpls. Jaycees, 1967—. Bd. dirs. Marion County chpt. Am. Cancer Soc., 1971-76, exec. com., 1973-76, chmn. crusades, 1971, 72, 74, 75, v.p., 1973-75, pres., 1975-76; active Ind. div. Am. Cancer Soc., 1974-76; bd. dirs. Crossroads of Am. council Boy Scouts Am., 1971—, exec. bd., 1971, 72, 73, 75, 76, 77, chmn. coms., 1971-77; state chmn. W. Indies Ambassador Exchange, Ind. State Jaycees, 1972-73, state chmn. W. Indies Nat. Jaycees Conv., 1972-74, 74-75; ambassador of goodwill to W. Indies, 1971; active fund raising com. Indpls. Mus. Art, 1973-74; co-chmn. membership Friends of Channel 20, 1975-77; bd. dirs. Salvation Army, 1977; asso. mem. Five Hundred Festival, 1977. Diplomate Ct. Practice Inst., 1974. Mem. Indpls. (active coms. 1969—), Ind. (drug abuse com.), Am. bar assns., Trial Lawyers Assn. Ind., Phi Delta Phi, Kappa Sigma. Apptd. mem. com. on character and fitness Ind. Supreme Ct., 1974—; recipient Richard E. Rowland award Indpls. Jaycees, 1971-72, Outstanding Service award, 1972-73, Distinguished Service award, 1976; Scroll of Friendship award Country of Jamaica, 1971; named Man of Year, Marion County, Am. Cancer Soc., 1974, certificates, awards, 1971, 74, 75. Home: 11028 Lake Shore Dr E Carmel IN 46032 Office: 156 E Market St Room 500 Indianapolis IN 46204 Tel (317) 639-2525

BOAGNI, KENNETH, JR., b. Opelousas, La., Aug. 24, 1936; B.A., U. Southwestern La., 1957; LL.B., Tulane U., 1961. Admitted to La. bar, 1961; practiced in Opelousas, 1961—; city atty. City of Opelousas, 1970-73; judge Opelousas City Ct., 1973—. Bd. dirs. Queens of Angels Cath. Ch., Opelousas. Mem. La., St. Landry. bar assns., La. State Juvenile Judges Assn. (v.p. 1976-77). Recipient Mankind of Year award Sertoma, 1974. Home: 922 Edward Ave Opelousas LA 70570 Office: 142 W Bellevue St Opelousas LA 70570 Tel (318) 942-4445

BOAL, ARTHUR MCCLURE, b. Cherry Tree, Pa., Feb. 14, 1889; A.B., Harvard, 1914, LL.B., 1916. Admitted to Mass. bar, 1917, N.Y. bar, 1930; since practiced in N.Y.C.; admiralty counsel U.S. Shipping Bd., 1925-29; asso. firm Chapman, Snyder, Duke & Boal, 1930-32; partner firm Boal, McQuade, & Fitzpatrick and predecessor firms, 1932-72; partner firm Boal, Doti & Larson, 1972—; v.p. Internat. Maritime Com., 1969—. Mayor, Village of Pelham, N.Y., 1949-53, mem. sch. bd., 1960-70, pres., 1965-67. Mem. Am., N.Y. State bar assns., Assn. Bar City N.Y., Maritime Law Assn. U.S. (pres. 1958-60). Home: 246 Corona Ave Pelham NY 10803 Office: 225 Broadway New York City NY 10007 Tel (212) 233-2500

BOAND, CHARLES WILBUR, b. Bates County, Mo., Aug. 19, 1908; A.A., Jr. Coll. Kansas City, 1927; LL.B. cum laude, U. Chgo., 1933, M.B.A., 1957. Admitted to Mo. bar, 1931, D.C. bar, 1936, U.S. Supreme Ct. bar, 1936, Ill. bar, 1937, also U.S. Cts. Appeal; asso. firm Moore & Fitch, St. Louis, 1933; atty. Office of Gen. Counsel to Sec. Treasury, Washington, 1933-36; partner, chmn. exec. com. firm Wilson & McIlvaine, Chgo., 1945—. Trustee Muskingum Coll., 1965—. Mem. Am. (mem. Nat. Conf. Lawyers and C.P.A.s 1976—), Ill. (chmn. sect. on corp and securities law 1954-56), Chgo. (chmn. corp. law com. 1970), Fed. bar assns., Law Club Chgo., Legal Club Chgo., U. Chgo. Alumni Assn. (pers. 1975—), Order of Coif, Beta Gamma Sigma. Editor: U. Chgo. Law Rev., 1933. Home: Route 1 Cuba Rd Barrington IL 60010 Office: 135 S LaSalle St Chicago IL 60603 Tel (312) 263-1212

BOARMAN, ANTHEA MARY, b. London, Nov. 26, 1944; A.B., Tulane U., 1964; J.D., U. Ky., 1967. Admitted to Ky. bar, 1968; partner firm Gilliam, Bush & Boarman, 1968-70; judge Fayette County (Ky.) Juvenile Ct., 1970; dir. Ky. Child Advocacy Council, 1970-73; asst. pub. defender Commonwealth of Ky., 1973; asst. to dir. children's unit Spindletop Research Orgn., Lexington, Ky., 1974; mem. Affirmative Action Adv. Com., 1975—; bd. dirs. Fayette County Day Treatment Center, 1972-73; v.p. Ky. Legal Aid and Defender Assn., 1973—; mem. adv. bd. Lexington Children's Bur., 1972-73; exec. dir. Lexington-Fayette Human Rights Commn., 1975—. Mem. Nat. Assn. Human Rights Workers, Internat. Assn. Ofcl. Human Rights Agys., Nat. Council Juvenile Ct. Judges, Ky., Fayette County bar assns. Home: 194 Castlewood Dr Lexington KY 40505 Office: 207 N Upper St Lexington KY 40505

BOATRIGHT, DAVID RUSSELL, b. Van Buren, Ark., May 7, 1914; LL.B., 1936, J.D., 1970. Admitted to Ark. bar, 1935, U.S. Supreme Ct. bar, 1942; asst. U.S. atty. Western Dist. Ark., 1946-50, 53-54; asst. city atty. City of Ft. Smith (Ark.), 1946-48, 62-63. Alderman City of Van Buren, 1937-38. Mem. Ark. Bar Assn. Home: 201 N 39th St Apt 15 Fort Smith AR 72903 Office: 503 Merchant Bldg Fort Smith AR 72901 Tel (501) 782-9785

BOBBITT, ARCHIE NEWTON, b. Eckerty, Ind., Sept. 3, 1895; ed. Central Norman Coll., 1916-19; LL.B., Benjamin Harrison Law Sch., 1927, Ind. U., 1936. Admitted to Ind. bar, 1925, Fed. Dist. Ct. bar, 1962, U.S. Supreme Ct. bar, 1965; prin. Alton (Ind.) High Sch., 1917-18, Marengo (Ind.) High Sch., 1919-20; auditor Crawford County, Ind., 1921-25; gasoline tax collector, Ind., 1925-29; auditor State of Ind. Indpls., 1929-31; asso. Clyde Hoffman, 1931-33; mem. firm Hoffman, Bobbitt & Pike, Indpls., 1930-43, Bobbitt, Martz & Beattey, Indpls., 1944-51; Ruckelshaus, Bobbitt & O'Connor and predecessors, Indpls., 1963—; pres. N.Am. Gasoline Tax. conf., 1932, exec. sec., 1933-39; chmn., gen. counsel Great Fidelity Life Ins. Co. of Ind., 1963-68; atty. City of Indpls., 1943-44; corp. counsel City of Indpls., 1944-49; judge Supreme Ct., Ind., 1951-63, chief justice, 1951, 56, 61; past mem. Judges Advisory com. Ind. chpt. Nat. Council Crime and Delinquency; mem. character and fitness com. Supreme Ct. Ind., 1974—; chmn. Judges Retirement Bd. Ind., 1954-63. Bd. visitors Ind. U.-Indpls. Law Sch., 1971—. Mem. Indpls. Bar Found. (dir. 1969—), Indpls., Ind. (bd. mgrs. 1967, 68, chmn. ho. dels. 1967-69), Am. bar assns., Sigma Delta Kappa. Recipient meritorious service award Am. Legion, 1961. Author: Indiana Appellate Practice and Procedure with Forms, 2 vols.; Bobbitt's Revision Work's Indiana Practice, 6 vols. Contbr. publs. to law jours. Home: 3635 Totem Ln Indianapolis IN 46208 Office: 120 E Market St #410 Indianapolis IN 46204

BOBRICK, EDWARD ALLEN, b. Chgo., June 30, 1935; B.S., U. Ill., 1958; J.D., DePaul U., 1964. Admitted to Ill. bar, 1964, U.S. Ct. Appeals, 1964, U.S. Supreme Ct. bar, 1972; trial atty. Office of Solicitor Dept. Labor, Region V, Chgo., 1966-74, counsel for Occupational Safety and Health, 1974—; speaker in field of occupational safety and health litigation to Am. Bar Assn. Mem. Ill., Fed., Lawyer-Pilots bar assns., Decalogue Soc. of Lawyers. Home: 88 W Schiller St Chicago IL 60610 Office: 230 S Dearborn Chicago IL 60604 Tel (312) 353-6973

BOBROFF, HAROLD, b. Bronx, N.Y., Apr. 29, 1920; B.B.A., City U. N.Y., 1947; J.D., N.Y. Law Sch., 1951. Admitted to N.Y. bar, 1952; partner firm Bobroff, Olonoff & Scharf, and predecessor, N.Y.C., 1953—; chief dep. county atty. County of Nassau (N.Y.), 1962-63; chief counsel com. on intergovtl. relations N.Y. State Constl. Conv., 1967; counsel to legis. coms. N.Y. State Assembly. Pres. Temple Sinai of L.I., Laurence, 1971-75; trustee Nassau Community Coll., 1959—, acting chmn., 1976—. Mem. New York County Lawyers Assn., Nassau County Bar Assn. Home: 795 Hampton Rd Woodmere NY 11598 Office: 122 E 42d St New York City NY 10017 Tel (212) 697-9180

BOBROW, WALTER ARNOLD, b. N.Y.C., Nov. 8, 1925; student U. Paris, 1946; B.S., N.Y.U., 1948; J.D., Harvard, 1951. Admitted to N.Y. State bar, 1951, U.S. Dist. Ct. for So. N.Y., bar, 1953, U.S. Dist. Ct. for Eastern N.Y. bar, 1954, U.S. 2d Circuit Ct. Appeals bar, 1959, U.S. Supreme Ct. bar, 1959, U.S. Dist. Ct. for Western Okla. bar, 1969; asso. firm Singer, Corwin & Bobrow and predecessors, N.Y.C., 1951-62, partner, 1962-70; partner firm Rubin, Bobrow & Agatston, New Rochelle, N.Y., 1970—; arbitrator Small Claims Ct., N.Y.C., 1961-70, New Rochelle, 1971—; instr. N.Y.U., 1974-76, Manhattanville Coll., 1976—. Mem. Advisory com. on Urban Renewal and Community Improvement, City Council, New Rochelle, 1972-75. Mem. Am., N.Y. State, New Rochelle bar assns., Am. Arbitration Assn. Office: 271 North Ave New Rochelle NY 10801 Tel (914) 632-5050

BOBULSKI, EDWARD, b. Peoria, Ill., Apr. 7, 1939; B.S., U. Ill., Champaign-Urbana, 1959, LL.B., 1961, J.D., 1975. Admitted to Ill. bar, 1961, U.S. Supreme Ct. bar, 1968; mem. legal dept. Tintux Corp., Chgo., 1961-65, counsel 1965-69; individual practice law, Chgo., 1969—; instr. Triton Coll., 1968-74. Democratic precinct capt., 1970—; bd. dirs. D.A. Smythe Found., 1970—. Mem. Am., Ill., Chgo. bar assns., Sigma Chi. Author: Significant Litigations in Environmental Boundary Disputes, 1974. Office: 6121 N Sheridan Rd Chicago IL 60660

BODDICKER, JOE LAWRENCE, b. Independence, Iowa, Sept. 13, 1939; B.A., Loras Coll., 1961; J.D., U. Iowa, 1964. Admitted to Iowa bar, 1964; mem. firm Reimer, Boddicker & Vipond, Denison, Iowa, 1964-69; individual practice law, Denison and Charter Oak, Iowa, 1969—; city atty. Charter Oak, 1964-73; county atty. Crawford County (Iowa), Denison, 1967-69; jud. magistrate Crawford County, Denison, 1975—. Mem. Am., Iowa, Crawford County (past pres.) bar assns. Home and office: 39 Pleasant St Denison IA 51442 Office: 50 Main St Charter Oak IA 51439 Tel (712) 263-2209 also 687-3597

BODE, WILLIAM H., b. El Paso, Tex., Apr. 18, 1942; B.S., U.S. Air Force Acad., 1964; M.S., Stanford U., 1966; J.D., George Washington U., 1971. Admitted to Va. bar, 1972, D.C. bar, 1972; asso. firm Batzell & Nunn, Washington, 1971-72, partner, 1973-75; propr. Batzell, Nunn, & Bode, Washington, 1975-75, partner, 1976—. Mem. D.C., Va., Am. (adminstrv. law sect., energy com., natural resources law sect.). Home: 2525 N 10th St Arlington VA 22201 Office: 1523 L St NW Washington DC 20005

BODEN, ROBERT FRANCIS, b. Milw., June 4, 1928; Ph.B., Marquette U., 1950; J.D., 1952; LL.D., Carthage Coll., 1975. Admitted to Wis. bar, 1952; asso. firm Quarles, Spence & Quarles, Milw., 1952-56; individual practice law, Milw., 1956-63; lectr. law Marquette U., 1959-63, asst. prof. law, 1963-65, acting dean, asso. prof. law, 1965-66, dean, asso. prof., 1966-71, dean, prof., 1971—; mem. Wis. Jud. Council, 1961-72, chmn. 1963-65; chmn. Wis. Supreme Ct. Chief Judge Study Com., 1974-75; chmn. Wis. Supreme Ct. Attys. Discipline Com., 1975-76; mem. Gov.'s Task Force on Ct. Reorgn. 1971-73. Fellow Am. Bar Found.; mem. Am. Law Inst., Am. (council sect. on legal edn. 1970-76), Wis., Milw. bar assn., Woolsack Soc., Alpha Sigma Nu., Delta Theta Phi. Author: Bankruptcy Practice in Wis., 1966; Wis. Creditor-Debtor Law, 1971; Basic Bankruptcy Law, 1973; contbr. articles to profl. jours. Home: 1404 Lynne Dr Waukesha WI 53186 Office: 1103 W Wisconsin Ave Milwaukee WI 53233 Tel (414) 224-7090

BODENHEIMER, EDGAR, b. Berlin, Mar. 14, 1908; J.D., U. Heidelberg, 1933; LL.B., U. Wash., 1937. Admitted to Wash. bar, 1940; asso. firm Rosenberg Goldbark & Colin, N.Y.C., 1933-35; atty. U.S. Dept. Labor, Washington, 1940-42; atty. Office Alien Property Custodian, Washington, 1942-46; asso. prof. law U. Utah, 1946-51, prof. law, 1951-66; prof. law U. Calif. Davis, 1966-75, prof. emeritus, 1975—. Mem. Wash. State Bar Assn., Am. Soc. for Political and Legal Philosophy. Author: Treatise on Justice, 1967; Power, Law, and Society, 1973; Jurisprudence, rev. edit., 1974; contbr. articles to law reviews; recipient Fulbright awards, 1953, 1959, 1973; research award Nat. Endowment for the Humanities. Home: 542 Miller Dr Davis CA 95616 Office: Sch Law Univ Calif Davis CA 95616 Tel (916) 752-2750

BODENHEIMER, G. M., b. Corsicana, Tex., Aug. 15, 1917; LL.B., La. State U., 1938. Admitted to La. bar, 1938, U.S. Supreme Ct. bar, 1971; practice law, Shreveport, La., 1938—; mem. firm Bodenheimer, Jones, Klotz & Simmons. Mem. Shreveport, La., Am. bar assns. Office: 705 Lane Bldg Shreveport LA 71101 Tel (318) 221-1507

BODGER, RICHARD ALAN, b. Mpls., Sept. 23, 1925; B.S.L., U. Minn., 1950, J.D., 1951. Admitted to Minn. bar, 1951; individual practice law, Benson, Minn., 1952-60; partner firm Bennett & Bodger, Benson, 1960-68; judge Juvenile and Probate Ct., Swift County, 1968-72; judge Swift County (Minn.) Ct., 1972—; city atty. City of Benson (Minn.), 1958-68; atty. Benson Housing and Redevel. Authority, 1965-68. Lectr. Minn. State Trooper Sch., 1976—. Vice pres. Benson Lions Club, 1976. Mem. Am. Judicature Soc., 12th Jud. Dist., Am. bar assns., Minn. State Bar, Am., Minnesota County (dir. family ct. div.) judges assns. Home: 301 Sanford Rd Benson MN 56215 Office: Courthouse Benson MN 56215 Tel (612) 843-2744

BODIN, HARRY SABBATH, b. Oct. 11, 1899; A.B., Columbia, 1921, J.D., 1923. Admitted to N.Y. bar, 1924; counsel to Hofheimer Gartlir Gottlieb & Gross, N.Y.C., 1966—; lectr. in law Columbia U. Sch. Law, 1954-55; lectr. Practising Law Inst. 1935-70, chmn. trial technique courses, 1948-68. Mem. Practising Law Inst., Assn. Bar City N.Y., N.Y. State, Am. (asso. editor Law Notes, 1964—) bar assns., Am. Judicature Soc. Editor, co-author: Trial Technique Library, 1946-75; Civil Litigation and Trial Techniques, 1976. Home: 25 Sutton Pl S New York City NY 10022 Office: 100 Park Ave New York City NY 10017 Tel (212) 725-0400

BODNE, MICHAEL DOUGLAS, b. Charleston, S.C., Sept. 18, 1937; B.S., B.A. in Accounting, U. Fla., 1959, J.D., 1962; LL.M. in Taxation, N.Y.U., 1963. Admitted to Fla. bar, 1962; asso. firm Culverhouse, Tomlinson, Taylor & DeCarion, Miami, Fla., 1963-64, firm Byron L. Sparber, Miami Beach, Fla., 1964-65; partner firm Forest, Friedman & Bodne, Miami, 1965-67, firm Sager, Silverman & Bodne, Miami, 1967-70, firm Greenberg, Bodne & Kuperstein, Miami, 1970-76, firm Male, Bloom, Bodne, Kuperstein & Eisenberg, Miami, 1976—. Mem. Am., Fla., Dade County bar assns., Greater Miami Tax Inst. Home: 2081 N E 205th St North Miami Beach FL 33179 Office: 1401 Brickell Ave Suite 1101 Miami FL 33131 Tel (305) 358-4300

BODNER, HOWARD JOEL, b. N.Y.C., June 21, 1946; B.A., Yeshiva Coll., 1968, J.D., Columbia, 1971. Admitted to N.Y. bar, 1972, U.S. Supreme Ct. bar, 1976; asso. firm Marlow & Marlow, Great Neck, N.Y., 1971-73; partner firm Hollenberg, Levin, Marlow & Bloom, Mineola, N.Y., 1974—. Pres. Lido Beach (N.Y.) Jewish Center, 1975-76; bd. dirs. Hebrew Acad. of Long Beach (N.Y.), 1975-76. Mem. N.Y., Nassau County bar assns. Home: Lido Beach NY Office: 170 Old Country Rd Mineola NY 11501 Tel (516) 747-4700

BODOFF, LIPPMAN, b. Bklyn., May 28, 1930; B.S.S., Coll. City N.Y., 1950; J.D., Yale, 1953. Admitted to N.Y. bar, 1953, U.S. Dist. Ct. for So. Dist. N.Y. bar, 1955; U.S. Ct. Appeals, 1965; atty. Cooper, Ostrin & DeVarco, N.Y.C., 1953-56; atty. Western Electric Co., N.Y.C., 1956-75, dir. regulatory matters, 1975-76, gen. mgr. regulatory matters, 1976—. Mem. Am. (mem. antitrust and public utility law sects.), N.Y. State bar assns., Phi Beta Kappa. Contbr. articles and papers to profl. jours. and confs. Office: 222 Broadway New York City NY 10007 Tel (212) 571-5601

BODURTHA, CHARLES ECKLEY, b. Delaware, Ohio, July 14, 1902; A.B., Ohio Wesleyan U., 1924; postgrad. Harvard Sch. Bus., 1924-25; J.D., Harvard, 1928. Admitted to Ohio bar, 1928; partner firm Jones, Day, Reavis & Pogue, Cleve., 1942—. Trustee Ohio Wesleyan U., 1957-72, Karamu House, Cleve. Council on World Affairs; pres. Cleve. Inst. Music, 1974—; former trustee Cleve. Center on Alcoholism; former pres. Ohio Wesleyan Alumni Assn. Mem. Am., Cleve., Ohio State bar assns. Home: 24255 Community Dr Cleveland OH 44122 Office: 1700 Union Commerce Bldg Cleveland OH 44115 Tel (216) 696-3939

BOE, NILS ANDREAS, b. Baltic, S.D., Sept. 10, 1913; A.B., U. Wis., 1935, LL.B., 1937; LL.D., Huron Coll., 1972. Admitted to Wis. bar, 1937, S.D. bar, 1938, D.C. bar, 1970; spl. investigator State's Atty's Office Minnehaha County (S.D.), 1937-40, dep. state's atty., 1941-42; partner firm Stordahl, May & Boe, Sioux Falls, S.D., 1946-65; chief judge U.S. Customs Ct., N.Y.C., 1971—; mem. S.D. Ho. of Reps., 1951-53, 53-55, speaker of house, 1955-57, 57-59; lt. gov. State of S.D., 1963-65, gov., 1965-67, 67-69; dir. Office Intergovtl. Relations, Exec. Office of Pres., 1969-71. Mem. Am. Bar Assn., VFW, Am. Legion, Phi Alpha Delta. Home: 71 Island Dr N Manursing Island Rye NY 10580 Office: One Fed Plaza New York City NY 10007 Tel (212) 264-2800

BOEHM, DAVID O., b. Phila., May 3, 1922; grad. St. Joseph's Coll., Phila., 1943; J.D., Temple U., 1946. Admitted to N.Y. bar, 1947, U.S. Supreme Ct. bar, 1947; mem. firm Stone, Hoffenberg, Maas & Boehm, Rochester, N.Y., 1947-58, Cucci, Welch & Boehm, Rochester, 1959-68; adminstrv. judge Monroe County (N.Y.) Ct., 1972-75, judge, 1969-75; justice N.Y. Supreme Ct. 7th Jud. Dist., Rochester, 1975—; instr. legal rights of women U. Rochester, Monroe Community Coll. Police Tng. Center. Bd. dirs. Arts Council of Rochester, Inc., Jewish Home and Infirmary, Inc., Rochester; trustee Boys' Clubs Am. Mem. Am., N.Y. State (exec. com. sect. criminal justice), Monroe County (pres. 1967) bar assns., Practicing Law Inst. (instr.). Recipient Outstanding Com. Service award Monroe County Bd. Suprs., 1965, Man of Year award Alliance Ind. Unions, 1970. Home: 418 Oakdale Dr Rochester NY 14618 Office: 433 Hall of Justice Rochester NY 14614 Tel (716) 428-5137

BOETTGER, THOMAS EDWARD, b. Phila., Oct. 2, 1938; B.A., St. Vincent Coll., 1960; LL.B., Dickinson U., 1964. Admitted to Pa. bar, 1966; partner firm Rose, Schmidt & Dikon, Pitts., 1964-70; v.p., gen. counsel, sec. Eastern Asso. Coal Corp., Pitts., 1970—. Mem. Am., Allegheny County bar assns. Home: 3325 Ponoka Rd Pittsburgh PA 15241 Office: Koppers Bldg Pittsburgh PA 15219 Tel (412) 288-8223

BOETTNER, JOHN LEWIS, JR., b. Frostburg, Md., June 18, 1943; A.B., W.Va. U., J.D. Admitted to W.Va. bar, 1968; staff atty. Legal Aid Soc. Charleston, W.Va., 1968-71; atty. Appalachian Research and Def. Fund, Inc., 1971-73; sr. partner Boettner and Campbell, Charleston, 1973—; mem. W.Va. Ho. Dels., 1974-76. Mem. Am., W.Va. State bar assns., W.Va. Trial Lawyers, Sierra Club (pres. Appalachian Group 1973—). Home: 847 Edgewood Dr Charleston WV 25301 Office: 1532 Charleston Nat Plaza Charleston WV 75501 Tel (304) 342-4191

BOETTO, DOMINIC FRANCIS, b. Joliet, Ill., Aug. 16, 1922; B.A., Notre Dame U., 1943; J.D., DePaul U., 1949. Admitted to Ill. bar, 1949, Fed. bar, 1953; individual practice law, Joliet; owner mgr. Boetto & Boetto Ins. Agency. Chmn. Joliet Diocese Obscene Literature Com., 1976—. Mem. Ill. State, Will County bar assns., Ill., Joliet independent ins. agents. Named Notre Dame U. Man of the Year, 1972. Home: 956 Western Ave Joliet IL 60435 Office: 423 Chalstrom Bldg Joliet IL 60431 Tel (815) 726-7308

BOEYE, JOHN F., b. Webster City, Iowa, Nov. 22, 1921; B.S.C., LL.B., U. Iowa. Admitted to Iowa bar, 1950; partner firm Swanson, Boeye & Bloom, Red Oak, Iowa, 1950—. Mem. Am., Iowa, S.W. Iowa bar assns., Red Oak C. of C. (pres. 1954), Iowa County Attys. Assn. (pres. 1962). Home: 700 8th St Red Oak IA 51566 Office: 209 Coolbaugh St Red Oak IA 51566 Tel (712) 623-2554

BOGARD, DONALD PAUL, b. Winchester, Ind., Sept. 10, 1941; B.S., Ball State U., Muncie, Ind., 1967, postgrad., 1975; J.D., Ind. U., Indpls., 1971. Admitted to Ind. bar, 1971, U.S. Supreme Ct. bar, 1974; adminstrv. asst. City of Indpls., 1971; dep. atty. gen. State of Ind., Indpls., 1971-73, asst. atty. gen., 1973-75, exec. asst. atty. gen., 1975-77, chief counsel, 1977—; instr. Ind. U., Indpls., 1976-77. Mem. Ind., Indpls. bar assns. Home: 7434 Pawtucket Ct Indianapolis IN 46250 Office: 3300 Tower Suite 1 Indiana Sq Indianapolis IN 46204 Tel (317) 637-1877

BOGARDUS, FRANK EDWARD, b. Cooperstown, N.Y., Nov. 8, 1946; B.A., State U. N.Y., Albany, 1969; J.D., Albany Law Sch., 1972. Admitted to N.Y. State bar, 1973; asst. counsel Bur. Legis., Office of Legal Affairs, Dept. Social Services State of N.Y., Albany, 1972—. Mem. N.Y. State Bar Assn., Am. Pub. Welfare Assn. Home: 28 Thornton St Albany NY 12206 Office: 40 N Pearl St Albany NY 12243 Tel (518) 474-9493

BOGART, EDWARD J., b. Buffalo, Jan. 24, 1930; B.S., Fordham U., 1951; LL.B., Seton Hall U., 1954. Admitted to N.J. bar, 1955; individual practice law, Jersey City, 1955—; atty. Statewide Savs. & Loan Assn. Mem. Hudson County, N.J., Am. bar assns. Home: 44 Great Oak Dr Short Hills NJ 07078 Office: 70 Sip Ave Jersey City NJ 07306 Tel (212) 653-0272

BOGENSCHUTZ, STEPHEN ANDREW, b. Covinton, Ky., Sept. 24, 1947; B.A. in History, U. N.C., Chapel Hill, 1969; J.D., Ohio State U., 1973. Admitted to Ohio bar, 1973; asso. firm Neatherton, Peterson & Hammond, Xenia, Ohio, 1973—. Sec. Spirit of '74 Com., Xenia, 1976-77. Mem. Greene County (Ohio) Bar Assn. Home: 920 N Detroit St apt 9 Xenia OH 45385 Office: 18 Allen Bldg Xenia OH 45385 Tel (513) 372-3584

BOGERT, GEORGE T., b. Ithaca, N.Y., Sept. 20, 1920; A.B., Cornell U., 1941; LL.B., Harvard U., 1948. Admitted to Ill. bar, 1949; mem. firm Hopkins, Sutter, Halls, DeWolfe & Owen, Ill., 1948-51; gen. counsel to pres. Guardian Electric Mfg. Co., Ill., 1951-54; mem. firm Crowell & Leibman, and predecessors, Chgo., 1954-60, partner, 1960-66; partner firm Mayer, Brown & Platt, Chgo., 1966—. Vice chmn., sec. Chgo. Nursery and Half Orphan Asylum, Chgo. Mem. Chgo., Ill. State, Am. bar assns., Am. Law Inst., Chgo. Estate Planning Council, Am. Coll. Probate Counsel. Co-author, editor: Trust and Trustees. Home: 2440 N Lakeview Ave Chicago IL 60614 Office: 231 S LaSalle St Chicago IL 60604 Tel (312) 782-0600

BOGGS, DANNY JULIAN, b. Havana, Cuba, Oct. 23, 1944; A.B. cum laude, Harvard, 1965; J.D., U. Chgo., 1968. Admitted to Ill. bar, 1969, Ky. bar, 1969, U.S. Supreme Ct. bar, 1973; instr. U. Chgo., 1968-69; dep. commr. Ky. Dept. Econ. Security, 1969-70; adminstrv. asst., legal counsel Ky. Gov., 1970-71; minority counsel Ky. Gen. Assembly, 1972; asst. to solicitor gen. U.S., 1973-75; individual practice law, Bowling Green, Ky., 1975—; asst. to chmn. FPC, 1976—. Del. Republican nat. conv., 1972. Mem. Am., Ky., Warren County bar assns., Am. Judicature Soc., Mont Pelerin Soc., Order of Coif, Phi Delta Phi. Home: 357 Marylan Dr Bowling Green KY 42101 Office: 825 N Capitol NE Room 9000 Washington DC 20426 Tel (202) 275-4192

BOGGS, RALPH STUART, b. Toledo, June 6, 1917; A.B., Denison U., 1939; LL.B., U. Mich., 1947. Admitted to Ohio bar, 1942, U.S. Supreme Ct. bar, 1961; partner firm Boggs, Boggs & Boggs, & Guthrie, Profl. Assn., and predecessor firms, Toledo, 1946-72, v.p., dir., 1972—; spl. agent FBI, 1942-45. Mem. sch. bd. Maumee Bd. Edn., 1959-69, past pres. Mem. Am., Ohio, Lucas County, Toledo bar assns., Am. Judicature Soc.

BOGUE, EVERETT ALAN, b. Centerville, S.D., Mar. 21, 1901; B.A., U. Wis., 1924, B. Laws, 1927. Admitted to S.D. bar, 1927; mem. firm Bogue, Weeks & Rusch, and predecessors, Vermillion, S.D., 1940-51; individual practice law, Parker, S.D., 1927-40, Vermillion, 1940—; state's atty. Turner County (S.D.), 1933-37; city atty. City of Vermillion, 1941-51. Mem. Am., S.D. bar assns. Home: 322 Canby St Vermillion SD 57069 Office: 1 E Main St Vermillion SD 57069 Tel (605) 624-2619

BOHANON, LUTHER LEE, b. Ft. Smith, Ark., Aug. 9, 1902; LL.B., U. Okla., 1927. Admitted to Okla. Supreme Ct. bar, 1927, U.S. Supreme Ct. bar, 1937; asst. county atty. Seminole County (Okla.), 1927-28; partner firms Murrah & Bohanon, Oklahoma City, 1928-37, Bohanon & Adams, Oklahoma City, 1937-54, Bohanon & Barefoot, Oklahoma City, 1937-61; served with JAGC USAAF, Denver, 1943-44, Ft. Worth, 1944-45; judge, Oklahoma City, 1961—. Mem. Oklahoma County, Okla., Fed. bar assns., Phi Alpha Delta. Co-author: Otoes and Missourias. Home: 1617 Bedford Dr Oklahoma City OK 73116 Office: 3301 Fed Courthouse Oklahoma City OK 73102 Tel (405) 239-2681

BOHLING, WILLIAM BRINTON, b. Salt Lake City, Oct. 22, 1941; B.S.E.E., U. Utah, 1965; J.D., 1968. Admitted to Utah bar, 1968; atty. Antitrust div. Honors program U.S. Dept. Justice, Washington, 1968-71; asso. firm Jones, Waldo, Holbrook & McDonough, Salt Lake City, 1971-73; asst. prof. law Tex. Tech. U., 1973-75, asso. prof. 1975—. Mem. Am. Bar Assn., Order of the Coif, Phi Delta Phi. Contbr. articles in field to profl. jours. Office: Tex Tech Univ Sch Law Lubbock TX 79409 Tel (806) 742-3785

BOHNER, ROBERT JOSEPH, b. Bklyn., Nov. 11, 1934; B.A., St. John's U., 1956, LL.B., 1958, J.D., 1968. Admitted to N.Y. bar, 1959, U.S. Supreme Ct. bar; partner firm Bohner & Bohner, P.C., Rego Park, N.Y., 1960—. Pres. bd. Sacred Heart Sch., Merrick, N.Y., 1975—. Mem. Queens County, N.Y. State (exec. com. trial lawyers sect.), Nassau County bar assns., Assn. Trial Lawyers Am., N.Y. Trial Lawyers Assn., Am. Arbitration Assn. (arbitrator), Blackstone Lawyers Club (v.p.). Office: 62-55 Woodhaven Blvd Rego Park NY 11374 Tel (212) DE 5-8373

BOICE, JOHN EDGAR, JR., b. San Francisco, Aug. 12, 1918; B.S., U. Md., 1941; LL.B., N.Y. U., 1948. Admitted to N.Y. bar, 1949, D.C. bar, 1951; with tax dept. Cities Service Co., N.Y.C., 1945-50; sr. accountant tax dept. Arthur Andersen and Co., N.Y.C., 1950-51; partner firm Reasoner, Davis and Vinson, Washington, 1951—. Mem. D.C., Am. bar assns., Phi Alpha Delta. Home: 7910 Glendale Rd Chevy Chase MD 20015 Office: 800 17th St NW 11th floor Washington DC 20006 Tel (202) 298-8100

BOIES, WILBER H., b. Bloomington, Ill., Mar. 15, 1944; A.B., Brown U., 1965; J.D., U. Chgo., 1968. Admitted to Ill. Supreme Ct. bar, 1968, U.S. Dist. Ct. bars for No. Dist. Ill., 1968, Eastern Dist. Wis., 1973, U.S. Ct. Appeals, 7th Circuit bar, 1974, 5th Circuit bar, 1975; asso. firm Altheimer & Gray, Chgo., 1968-71; asso. firm McDermott, Will & Emery, Chgo., 1971-75, partner, 1975—. Mem. Am., Chgo. bar assns., Chgo. Counsel of Lawyers. Office: 111 W Monroe St Chicago IL 60603 Tel (312) 372-2000

BOIKESS, OLGA SHNIPER, b. N.Y.C., Dec. 25, 1938; B.A., Barnard Coll., 1960; J.D., U. Calif. at Los Angeles, 1964. Admitted to Calif. bar, 1964, D.C. bar, 1969; law clk. U.S. Dist. Ct. So. Dist., Los Angeles, 1964-65; atty. Gen. Counsel's Office, OEO, Exec. Office of Pres., Washington, 1965-68; asso. firm Gallard, Klarasch, Calkins & Brown, Washington, 1968-74; partner firm Cailand, Kharasch, Calkins & Short, Washington, 1975—; cons. in field. Office: 1054 31st St NW Washington DC 20007 Tel (202) 333-2200

BOIRE, HAROLD ARTHUR, b. Mooers, N.Y., May 21, 1914; B.S., Am. U., 1950; LL.M., Nat. U., 1949; J.D., Stetson U., 1940. Admitted to Fla. bar, 1940, U.S. Supreme Ct. bar, 1944; atty. NLRB, Washington, 1948-56, asst. gen. counsel, 1956-57, regional dir., Tampa, Fla., 1957—; exec. sec. to Congressman Joe Hendricks of Fla., Washington, 1942-46. Mem. Phi Alpha Delta. Home: 3905 Pearl Ave Tampa FL 33611 Office: 706 Fed Office Bldg 500 Zack St Tampa FL 33602 Tel (813) 228-2646

BOISAUBIN, ALFRED LOUIS, b. St. Louis, June 24, 1921; A.B., St. Louis U., 1941; LL.B., Washington U., St. Louis, 1947, also J.D. Admitted to Mo. bar, 1947; partner firm Chopin & Boisaubin, 1949-73; practice law, Clayton, Mo., 1973—; judge Warson Woods (Mo.) Municipal Ct., 1965-66; mayor City of Warson Woods, 1964-65. Mem. Mo., St. Louis bar assns. Home: 9 Upper Ladue Rd Ladue MO 63124 Office: 230 S Bemiston Ave Clayton MO 63105 Tel (314) 862-8621

BOISFONTAINE, CURTIS RICH, b. New Orleans, June 30, 1929; B.A., Tulane U., 1951, LL.B., 1952. Admitted to La. bar, 1952, U.S. Supreme Ct. bar, 1955; asso. firm Porteous & Johnson, New Orleans, 1955-61; partner firm Sessions, Fishman, Rosenson, Snellings & Boisfontaine, New Orleans, 1961—. Fellow Am. Coll. Trial Lawyers, Am. Bar Found.; mem. Internat. Soc. Barristers, Internat. Assn. Ins. Counsel, Fedn. Ins. Counsel, Trial Attys. Am., La. Assn. Def. Counsel (dir. 1966-67, pres. 1971-72), Am. (ho. of dels. 1977), La. (ho. of dels. 1964-66, bd. govs. 1967-70, chmn. pub. relations com. 1971-73, pres. 1976—), New Orleans (exec. com. 1968-70, chmn. legis. com. 1971-72, chmn. nominating com. 1972) bar assns., Am. Judicature Soc., New Orleans Def. Lawyers Assn. Office: 1010 Common St New Orleans LA 70112 Tel (504) 581-5055

BOISSELLE, ARMAND PAUL, SR., b. Haverhill, Mass., Dec. 16, 1931; B.S. in Edn., Bridgewater State Coll., 1953; M.S. in Chemistry, Boston Coll., 1957; Ph.D. in Chemistry, U. Notre Dame, 1961; J.D., Case Western Res. U., 1965. Admitted to Ohio bar, 1965, S.C. bar, 1967, U.S. Patent Office, 1965; research chemist Lubrizol Corp., Cleve., 1960-61, patent agt., 1961-66; patent atty. Deering Millikan Research Corp., Spartanburg, S.C., 1966-71; asso. firm Donnelly, Maky, Renner and Otto, Cleve., 1971-73, partner, 1973—. Councilman Village of Timberlake, Ohio, 1964-65. Mem. Am. Bar Assn., Cleve. Patent Law Assn., Am. Chem. Soc. Patentee in field of chemistry; contbr. tech. articles to chem. jour. Home: 33450 Shaker Blvd Pepper Pike OH 44124 Office: 601 Rockwell Ave Cleveland OH 44114 Tel (216) 621-1113

BOITEL, HENRY JOHN, b. Bklyn., Sept. 23, 1939; B.A., St. John's U., 1961; LL.B., U. Notre Dame, 1965. Admitted to N.Y. bar, 1965, U.S. Supreme Ct. bar, 1970; asso. firm Sabbatino & Todarelli, N.Y.C., 1966-69; individual practice law, N.Y.C., 1969—; spl. asst. atty. gen. N.Y. State, 1975-77. Mem. Am., Bklyn. bar assns., N.Y. County Lawyers Assn., Columbian, Catholic lawyers assns., U.S. Supreme Ct. Hist. Soc. (founding mem.). Office: 233 Broadway New York City NY 10007 Tel (212) RE2-8104

BOKOR, BRUCE HOWARD, b. Tampa, Fla., Sept. 18, 1947; B.S. in Bus. Adminstrn. with honors, U. Fla., 1969; J.D. with honors, 1972; LL.M. in Taxation N.Y.U., 1973. Admitted to Fla. bar, 1972; asso. firm Greenberg, Traurig, Hoffman, Lipoff, Quentel & Wright, Miami Fla., 1973-76; partner firm Johnson, Blakely, Pope & Bokor, profl. corp., Clearwater, Fla., 1977—; Mem. exec. council Fla. Bar Tax sect., 1973—. Mem. Am., Dade County Clearwater bar assns. Editor-in-chief U. Fla. Law Rev. 1971-72. Contbr. articles to profl. jours. Home: 1706 Belleair Forest Dr Belleair FL 33516 Office: 20 N Ft Harrison Ave Clearwater FL 33517 Tel (813) 441-2440

BOLAN, THOMAS ANTHONY, b. Lynn, Mass., May 30, 1924; LL.B. summa cum laude, St. Johns U., 1950, B.A. summa cum laude, 1952. Admitted to N.Y. bar, 1951; sec.-clk. Burroughs & Brown, N.Y.C., 1942-43, 45-50, asso. firm, 1951-53; asst. U.S. atty. Dept. Justice, 1953-57; asso. Roy M. Cohn, Esq., 1957-59; mem. firm Saxe, Bacon & Bolan, N.Y.C., 1960-71, counsel, 1972—; pres., chmn. bd. Fifth Ave. Coach Lines, Inc., Championship Sports, Inc., N.Y.C.; chmn. bd. Mercantile Nat. Bank, Gateway Nat. Bank, Chgo.; instr. law St. Johns U., 1957-61. Pres., Parish Council, Cambria Heights, N.Y., 1968-70; judge adv. Cath. War Vets., Queens County, N.Y., 1965—, Patriotic Service award, 1968, Distinguished Service medal, 1977; chmn. East Side Conservative Club, N.Y.C., 1973—; founder Conservative Party N.Y. State, 1962, mem. exec. com., 1974—; pres., bd. dirs. Pro Ecclesia Found., 1972-73; v.p., bd. dirs. Heiser Found., Inc., N.Y.C., 1955-73; sec., bd. dirs. Am. African Affairs Assn., N.Y.C., 1975—; treas. Ednl. Reviewer, Inc., 1960—; trustee Community Boys Club Assn., Cambria Heights, 1968-72; regent St. Francis Coll., Bklyn. Mem. Fed. Bar Council, Am., N.Y. State, New York County bar assns., Nat. Assn. Coll. and Univ. Attys. Office: 39 E 68th St New York City NY 10021 Tel (212) 472-1400

BOLAND, ROBERT WILLIAM, JR., b. Boulder, Colo., June 12, 1947; B.S.B.A. in Accounting, Rockhurst Coll., 1971; J.D., U. Mo., Kansas City, 1973, LL.M. candidate in Taxation, 1977. Admitted to Mo. bar, 1974, U.S. Dist. Ct. for Mo. bar, 1974, U.S. Tax Ct. bar, 1976; mem. firm Boland & McQuain; instr. paralegal program Rockhurst Coll. Mem. Am. (sect. on taxation), Mo., Eastern Jackson County (Mo.), Kansas City (Mo.) bar assns. Office: 403 Seville Sq Country Club Plaza 500 Nichols Rd Kansas City MO 64112 Tel (816) 531-0509

BOLDEN, RAYMOND ALAN, b. Chgo., Dec. 17, 1933; student Joliet Jr. Coll., 1953; B.S., U. Ill., 1961, LL.B., 1961. Admitted to Ill. bar, 1962; partner firm Montgomery, Holt & Bolden, 1964; asst. states atty., 1964-68; individual practice law, 1968-76; partner firm Murer & Bolden, Joliet, Ill., 1976—. Bd. dirs. Joliet-Will County CAA, Stanish Center, Joliet. Mem. NAACP (pres. 1964-68), Will County, Nat. bar assns., Nat. Black Lawyers Conf. Office: 54 N Ottawa Joliet IL 60431 Tel (815) 727-4766

BOLDING, EDWARD PORTER, b. San Angelo, Tex., Jan. 30, 1936; B.B.A., U. Tex., 1959, J.D., 1960. Admitted to Tex. bar, 1960, Ariz. bar, 1970, U.S. Supreme Ct. bar, 1974; city atty. San Angelo, Tex., 1961-63; asst. atty. gen. Tex., Austin, 1963-64; partner firm Garrison & Bolding, Gilmer, Tex., 1964-65; city judge, San Angelo, 1965; partner firm Webb, Stokes & Bolding, San Angelo, 1965-69; pub. defender Pima County, Ariz., Tucson, 1970-74; partner firm Bolding, Oseran & Zavala, Tucson, 1974—; mem. Ariz. State Legislature Criminal Code Revision Commn., 1973-75. Mem. Assn. Trial Lawyers Am., Ariz. Trial Lawyers Assn. (dir. 1974—, v.p. 1976, pres. elect 1977), Am. Bar Assn. Office: 402 Toluca Bldg La Placita Village Tucson AZ 85702 Tel (602) 884-7100

BOLDT, GEORGE H(UGO), b. Chgo., Dec. 28, 1903; B.A., (Straughn Scheuch scholar), U. Mont., 1925, LL.B., 1926; LL.D., Coll. Puget Sound, 1954. Admitted to Mont. bar, 1926, Wash. bar. 1928; asso. firm W. D. Rankin, Helena, Mont., 1926-27; partner firms Ballinger, Hutson & Boldt, Seattle, 1927-45, Metzger, Blair, Gardner & Boldt, Tacoma, Wash., 1945-53; judge U.S. Dist. Ct., Western Dist. Wash., 1953—, chief judge, 1971, sr. judge, 1971—; chmn. pay bd. Econ. Stblzn. Program, Washington, 1971-73. Chmn. bd. visitors U. Puget Sound Law Sch., 1972—; trustee U. Mont. Found., 1973—, pres., 1975-76; trustee U. Puget Sound, 1975—. Mem. Am., Wash. State, Fed., Pierce County, King County (Wash.) bar assns., Inst. Jud. Adminstrn., Internat. Inst. Juridical Studies, Am. Judicature Soc., Am. Law Inst., Phi Delta Phi, Sigma Chi (grand trustee). Author (with others), editor: Manual for Complex and Multidistrict Litigation, 1970. Home: 110 Country Club Dr SW Tacoma WA 98498 Office: US Courthouse Room 338 Tacoma WA 98401 Tel (206) 593-6526

BOLES, ROBERT LEWIS, b. San Diego, Sept. 15, 1945; B.A., San Diego State Coll. 1967; J.D., Calif. Western U., 1970. Admitted to Calif. bar, 1971, U.S. Supreme Ct. bar, 1974; trial atty. Fed. Defenders of San Diego, Inc., 1971-76; partner firm Hagerstrom, Geller and Boles, San Diego, 1976; dep. dist. atty. San Diego County, 1976—. Mem. Calif., San Diego bar assns., San Diego County, Calif. dist. attys. assns., Phi Delta Phi. Office: 220 W Broadway San Diego CA 92101 Tel (714) 236-3951

BOLIN, JANE MATILDA, b. Poughkeepsie, N.Y., 1908; A.B., Wellesley Coll., 1928; LL.B., Yale, 1931; LL.D., Morgan State Coll., Tuskegee Inst., Hampton Coll., Western Coll. For Women. Admitted to N.Y. State bar, 1932; practiced in N.Y.C., 1932-37; asst. corp. counsel City of N.Y., 1937-39; justice N.Y.C. Domestic Relations Ct., 1939-62, N.Y. State Family Ct., 1962—. Mem. Harlem Lawyers' Assn., Assn. Bar City N.Y., Nat. Bar Assn., N.Y. State, N.Y.C. assns. family ct. judges Office: Family Court of State of NY 135 E 22d St New York City NY 10010 Tel (212) 460-8810

BOLIN, MICHAEL FRANKLIN, b. Birmingham, Ala., Oct. 1, 1948; B.S. Samford U., 1970; J.D., Cumberland Sch. Law., 1973. Admitted to Ala. bar, 1973; asso. firm Hanes, Hanes and Bolin, Birmingham, 1973—. Mem. Am., Ala. Bar assns., Ala., Birmingham trial lawyers assns. Home: 2284 Larkspur Dr Birmingham AL 35226 Office: 933 Frank Nelson Bldg Birmingham AL 35203 Tel (205) 324-9536

BOLKOVATZ, WALTER HENRY, b. Anaconda, Mont., May 27, 1909; B.S. in Fgn. Service, Georgetown U., 1931, J.D., 1934. Admitted to D.C. bar, 1935, Mont. bar, 1935; asst. atty. gen. State of Mont., 1935-37; individual practice law, Anaconda, Mont., 1935-42; with JAGC, U.S. Army, 1942-46, mem. firm Bolkovatz Romine & Bell, Helena, Mont., 1946—; vice chmn. Mont. Hwy. Commn., 1945-49. Mem. Mont. Bar Assn. Home: 300 S Montana St Helena MT 59601 Office: 320 E 6th St POB 1691 Helena MT 59601 Tel (406) 442-2220

BOLLER, STEPHEN WINSHIP, b. Los Angeles, Nov. 14, 1927; B.A. in Econs. E. Wash. State Coll., 1959; LL.B., U. Idaho, 1963. Admitted to Idaho bar, 1963; asst. atty. gen. State of Idaho, 1963-65; partner firm Murphy & Boller, Shoshone, Idaho, 1965-69; partner Jeppesen & Boller, Hailey, Idaho, 1970-71; individual practice law, Hailey, 1971—; dep. pros. atty. Blaine County (Idaho), 1970-71, pros. atty., 1971-74; city atty. Hailey, 1969—. Adv. bds. Shoshone Dist. and State Bur. Land Mgmt. for Recreation, 1975—. Mem. Idaho, Fifth Dist. bar assns. Home: S Bellevue ID 83313 Office: Box 908 101 N Main St Hailey ID 83333 Tel (208) 788-4551

BOLLIGER, RALPH WENDELL, b. Portland, Oreg., Sept. 22, 1931; B.A., Willamette U., 1953, J.D., 1955. Admitted to Oreg. bar, 1955, U.S. Dist. Ct. bar for Dist. Oreg., 1959, U.S. Ct. Appeals bar, 9th Circuit, 1971, U.S. Supreme Ct. bar, 1972; asso. firms Peterson, Pozzi & Lent, Portland, 1959, Reiter, Day & Anderson, Portland, 1959-63; partner firm Bolliger, Hampton & Tarlow, Beaverton, Oreg., 1963—. Chmn. Washington County (Oreg.) Intermediate Edn. Dist., 1966—. Mem. Washington County, Am., Oreg. State bar assns. Home: 1885 SW Warwick Ave Portland OR 97225 Office: 4240 SW Cedar Hills Blvd Beaverton OR 97005 Tel (503) 641-7171

BOLTE, FRANK RICHARD, b. Marianna, Pa., Jan. 13, 1913; B.A. in Edn., U. Pitts., 1934; postgrad. U. Mich., 1935; J.D., Duquesne U., 1938. Admitted to Pa. bar, 1939, U.S. Supreme Ct. bar, 1958; individual practice law, Pitts., 1939-70; judge Ct. of Common Pleas, Allegheny County, 1970-72; mem. firm Baskin, Boreman, Wilner, Sachs, Gondelman & Craig, Pitts., 1972—; judge adv. gen. 75th Inf. Div. and 89th Inf. Div., World War II; bond counsel for Allegheny County and Commonwealth Pa.; labor arbitrator Fed. Mediation and Conciliation Service, 1972—. Sec., Upper St. Clair Twp. Sch. Authority, 1958-74; bd. dirs. St. Francis Gen. Hosp., Civic Light Opera Assn. Pitts. Mem. Am., Pa., Allegheny County (past chmn. jud. com.) bar assns., World Peace Through Law Soc., Am. Hosp. Attys. Assn., Soc. Hosp. Attys. Am., Soc. Hosp. Attys. Western Pa., Am. Arbitration Assn. (panel). Home: 101 Amesbury Dr Pittsburgh PA 15241 Office: 10th Floor Frick Bldg Pittsburgh PA 15219 Tel (412) 562-8651

BOLTON, ARTHUR K., b. Griffin, Ga., May 14, 1922; student N.Ga. Coll., 1939-41; LL.B., U. Ga., 1943, postgrad., 1947; postgrad. U. Ala., 1946. Admitted to Ga. bar, 1943; individual practice law, Griffin, 1947-65; mem. Ga. Gen. Assembly, 1949-65, chmn. spl. jud. com., 1961-62, vice chmn. rules com., floor leader, 1963-65; county adminstr. Spalding County, 1952-65; judge Recorders Ct., Criminal Ct. of Griffin, 1965-65; atty. gen. Ga., Atlanta, 1965—. Chmn. adv. bd. Griffin Assn. Retarded Citizens, 1969—; past pres. La Grange Coll. Parents Assn.; past trustee La Grange Coll. Mem. Am., Ga. (gov. 1958-59, 62-63, chmn. legis. com. 1962-63), Griffin Circuit (pres. 1976—) bar assns., Ga. Law Sch. Alumni Assn. (pres. 1969-70), Nat. Assn. Attys. Gen. (exec. com.), Am. Judicature Soc., Phi Delta Phi. Recipient Pub. Service award Ga. Mcpl. Assn., 1965, Key Citizenship award, 1970, Mental Health award Griffin Jaycettes, 1972, Statesmanship award Active Voters Ga., 1961-62, Distinguished Service scroll U. Ga. Law Sch. Alumni, 1975; named Man of Year, Griffin, 1962, Outstanding Alumnus N.Ga. Coll., 1970-71; inducted in Officers Candidate Sch. Hall of Fame, Ft. Benning, Ga., 1973. Office: 132 State Judicial Bldg Atlanta GA 30334 Tel (404) 656-4585

BOLTON, MICHELE BREMER, b. Brownsville, Tex., June 6, 1949; B.A. in English, U. Tex., 1970, M.A. in Am. Civilization, 1971, J.D., 1974. Admitted to Tex. bar, 1973; partner firm Bolton & Bolton, Cedar Park, Tex., 1973-76; atty. United Gas Pipe Line Co., Houston, 1976—; planner Urban Research Group, Austin, 1971-72. Mem. Tex., Fed. Power bar assns. Home: 4633 Wild Indigo # 543 Houston TX 77027 Office: 700 Millam Box 1478 Houston TX 77001 Tel (713) 237-5438

BOMAN, JOHN HARRIS, JR., b. Anniston, Ala., Mar. 8, 1910; A.B., Marquette U., 1930; J.D., U. Mich., 1933. Admitted to Ga. Bar, 1933; asso. firm Grenshaw & Hansel (now Hansell, Post, Brandon & Dorsey), Atlanta, 1933-39, sr. mem., 1939—; sec., dir. Jackson Packing Co. (Miss.) 1946—. Gen. counsel Atlanta Area council Boy Scouts Am.; pres. Atlanta Legal Aid Soc., 1956; sec. Met. Found. Atlanta; trustee Atlanta Lawyers Found. Fellow Am. Bar Found.; mem. Am., Atlanta bar assns., State Bar Ga., Lawyers Club Atlanta (pres. 1950), Am. Law Inst. Home: 3497 Paces Valley Rd NW Atlanta GA 30327 Office: 3300 First National Bank Tower Atlanta GA 30303 Tel (404) 581-8056

BOMES, STEPHEN D., b. Providence, Jan. 15, 1948; B.S. in Bus. Adminstrn., Boston U., 1968; J.D., U. Calif., 1971; LL.M., N.Y.U., 1975. Admitted to Calif bar, 1972, D.C. bar, 1975, Fla. bar, 1975, N.Y. bar, 1976; instr. law U. Calif., 1971-73, N.Y.U., 1973-75; asso. firm Milbank, Tweed, Hadley & McCloy, N.Y.C., 1975—; adj. asst. prof. econs. City U.N.Y., 1973-74. Mem. Am., Calif., N.Y. State, Fla., D.C. bar assns., Bar Assn. City N.Y. Author: (with W. F. Johnson) Real Estate Transfer Development and Finance 1975; The Dead Hand, A Last Grasp, 1976. Office: 1 Chase Manhattan Plaza New York City NY 10005 Tel (212) 422-2660

BOMMER, TIMOTHY J, b. Columbus, Ohio, Dec. 9, 1940; B.A., U. Wyo., 1963, J.D., 1970. Admitted to Wyo. bar, 1970, Colo. bar, 1970; partner firm Ranck & Bommer, Jackson, Wyo., 1970—; dep. pros. atty. Teton County (Wyo.), 1970-74; U.S. magistrate, 1976—. Mem. Colo., Wyo. State, Am. bar assns., Assn. Trial Lawyers Am. Home: POB 1728 575 Aspen Dr Jackson WY 83001 Office: POB 1728 20 E Simpson St Jackson WY 83001 Tel (307) 733-3515

BOMZE, JAY IRA, b. Phila., Jan. 4, 1947; B.A., George Washington U., 1968, J.D., 1972. Admitted to Pa. bar, 1972; law clk. to judge Common Pleas Ct., Phila., 1972; asst. city solicitor City of Phila., 1973-75; asso. firm Zarwin, Baum, Arangio & Somerson, Phila., 1975—; adminstrv. asst. Senator Robert F. Kennedy, 1967-68; researcher NBC's Meet the Press, 1969-72. Mem. Am., Pa., Phila. bar assns., Pa. Trial Lawyers Assn., Am. Judicature Soc., Am. Arbitration Assn. Home: 843 Meadowbrook Dr Huntingdon Valley PA 19006 Office: 715 Widener Bldg Philadelphia PA 19107 Tel (215) LO 9-2800

BONAGUIDI, STEVEN COLLINS, b. Chgo., Aug. 24, 1944; B.S., Loyola U., Chgo., 1966; J.D., Chgo. Kent Coll. Law, 1972. Admitted to Ill. bar, 1972, Wis. bar, 1972, Fed. bar, 1972; contract officer Santa Fe Ry. Co., 1970-72; asst. atty. gen. State of Ill., 1972-73; individual practice law, Des Plaines, Ill., 1973—. chmn. profl. sect. Community Chest Dr., Des Plaines, 1974; mem. bd. edn. St. Emily's, Mt. Prospect, Ill., 1976—. Mem. Ill., Chgo. (aviation com.), N.W. Suburban, Lawyer Pilots bar assns. Asso. editor Chgo. Kent Law Review, 1969-71. Home: 379 Cornell Ave Des Plaines IL 60016 Office: 464 Northwest Hwy Des Plaines IL 60016 Tel (312) 827-1818

BOND, DONALD WARNER, b. Memphis, Tenn., Dec. 30, 1943; B.S., Miss. State U., 1966, J.D., 1969. Admitted to Miss. bar, 1969; individual practice law, Winona, Miss., 1969—; pres. N. Central Savings & Loan 1972—. Scout leader Boy Scouts Am. 1974—. Mem. Montgomery County, Miss., Am. bar assns., Miss. Trial Lawyers Assn. Montgomery County C. of C. (pres. 1975). Home: 414 Little John Rd Winona MS 38967 Office: Ouitman St Winona MS 38967 Tel (601) 283-1351

BOND, GEORGE CLINE, b. Abingdon, Ill., May 30, 1920; A.B., Swarthmore Coll., 1942; J.D., Stanford, 1949. Admitted to Calif. bar, 1949, D.C. bar, 1956; asso. counsel Union Title Ins. & Trust Co., 1949-51; asst. sec., atty. Consol. Vultee Aircraft Corp., San Diego, 1951-53; sec., gen. counsel Pacific Airmotive Corp., Burbank Calif., 1953-55; atty. Union Oil Co. Calif., Los Angeles, 1955-60, asst. to chmn. bd., 1960-62, asst. to sr. v.p. fin., 1962-63, asst. counsel, 1963-69, asso. gen. counsel, 1969-73, v.p., gen. counsel, 1973—; mem. Fair Employment Practices Comm. State Calif., 1968-69. Pres., Pasadena (Calif.) Beautiful Found., 1970. Mem. Am., Los Angeles County bar assns. Home: 1419 Wellington Ave Pasadena CA 91103 Office: 461 S Boylston St Los Angeles CA 90017 Tel (213) 486-6121

BOND, GILBERT ALONZO, b. N.Y.C., Mar. 14, 1929; B.A., Coll. City N.Y., 1952; LL.B., N.Y. U., 1958, LL.M., 1960. Admitted to N.Y. bar, 1959, Calif. bar, 1973; individual practice law, N.Y.C., 1959-61; asst. U.S. atty. Eastern Dist. N.Y., 1961-64; adminstr. N.Y.C., Rent Control, 1965-69; asst. prof. comml. law Pace Coll., 1965-69; sr. corporate atty. Atlantic Richfield Co., Los Angeles, 1969—. Past mem. adv. and devel. com. Angel Guardian Home, N.Y.C. Mem. Am., Calif., Bklyn. (past mem. grievance com.) bar assns. Home: 4411 Los Feliz Blvd apt 1206 Los Angeles CA 90027 Office: 515 S Flower St suite 3017 Los Angeles CA 90071 Tel (213) 486-1468

BONDOC, ROMMEL, b. Pomona, Calif., June 23, 1938; B.A., Stanford U., 1959, J.D., 1963. Admitted to Calif. bar, 1964, U.S. Supreme Ct. bar, 1969; asso. firm Belli, Ashe & Gerry, San Francisco, 1964-66; asso. firm Vincent Hellinan, San Francisco, 1966-69; individual practice law, San Francisco, 1969—. Mem. No. Calif. Criminal Trial Laywers Assn. (dir. 1972—, 1st v.p. 1976-77), Calif. Attys. for Criminal Justice (bd. govs. 1975—). Home: 509 Canyon Rd Novate CA 94941 Office: 708 Montgomery St San Francisco CA 94111 Tel (415) 391-4223

BONDURANT, WALTON GIBSON, JR., b. Norfolk, Va., Nov. 12, 1944; B.A., U. Va., 1967; J.D., U. Richmond, 1970. Admitted to Va. bar, 1970; asso. firm Moody, McMurran & Miller, Portsmouth, Va., 1970-73, partner, 1973—. Bd. dirs. Chesapeake (Va.) Mental Health and Mental Retardation Bd., 1976—, Cath. Family and Childrens Service, Portsmouth, 1975-77. Mem. Va. State Bar, Norfolk and Portsmouth Bar Assn., Assn. Trial Lawyers Am., Va. Trial Lawyers. Home: 4009 San Salvador Dr Chesapeake VA 23321 Office: 201 Central Bldg Portsmouth VA 23704 Tel (804) 393-4093

BONER, MARIAN OLDFATHER, b. Cleburne, Tex., June 25, 1909; B.A., U. Tex., 1930, M.A., 1931, LL.B., 1955. Admitted to Tex. bar, 1955; research asso. U. Tex., 1956-60, reference librarian, 1960-65, asso. librarian, 1965-72, asst. prof. law, 1965-69, asso. prof., 1969-72; dir. State Law Library of Tex., 1972—. Mem. Austin Pub. Library Commn., 1969-76. Mem. Am. (pres. 1974-75), Southwestern (pres. 1969-70) assns. law libraries, Order of Coif, Phi Beta Kappa, Kappa Beta Pi. Author: Reference Guide to Texas Law and Legal History, 1976. Contbr. articles in field to profl. jours. Home: 1508 Hardouin Ave Austin TX 78703 Office: Supreme Court Bldg Austin TX 78711 Tel (512) 475-3807

BONESIO, WOODROW MICHAEL, b. Hereford, Tex., Dec. 27, 1943; B.A., Austin Coll., 1966; J.D., U. Houston Bates Coll. Law, 1971. Admitted to Tex. bar, 1971, U.S. Dist. Ct. bars for Western Dist. Tex., 1972, for No. Dist. Tex., 1973, U.S. Ct. Appeals bar, 5th Circuit, 1973; law clk. to D. W. Suttle, U.S. Dist. Ct. Judge, Western Dist. Tex., 1971-73; asso. firm Akin, Gump, Strauss, Hauer & Feld, Dallas, 1973—. Mem. Tex., Fed., Am., Dallas bar assns., Am. Judicature Soc., Order of Barons (pres. U. Houston chpt. 1971), Phi Alpha Delta. Articles editor: Houston Law Rev., 1970-71. Home: 8518 Bacardi St Dallas TX 75238 Office: 2800 Republic Bank Bldg Dallas TX 75201 Tel (214) 655-2706

BONESTEEL, RICHARD DAVID, b. Seattle, May 26, 1931; B.A. in Bus. Adminstrn., U. Wash., 1953, J.D., 1956; certificate Sch. Mortgage Banking Northwestern U., 1966. Admitted to Wash. bar, 1956; asso. firm Evans, McLaren, Lane, Powell & Beeks, Seattle, 1956-61; sec.-treas., v.p., counsel, dir. Seafirst Mortgage Corp., Seattle, 1961—. Mem. Am. (real property div. real estate financing com. 1976-77), Wash. (continuing legal edn. seminar panel 1976), Seattle-King County bar assns., Wash. (pres. 1973-74), Seattle (gov. 1975-76) mortgage bankers assns., Am. Land Title Assn. (chmn. lender counsel group 1976), Phi Delta Phi. Revisions editor Wash. Law Rev., 1955-56. Home: 2203 W Viewmont Way W Seattle WA 98199 Office: Seafirst Mortgage Corp Securities Bldg Seattle WA 98101 Tel (206) 583-7078

BONEZZI, WILLIAM DAVID, b. Cambridge, Eng., Nov. 25, 1945; B.S. in Edn., Bowling Green State U., 1970; LL.B., Cleve. State U., 1973. Admitted to Ohio bar, 1973; asso. firm York, Bonezzi & Thomas, Cleve., 1973—. Mem. Ohio, Cleve. bar assns. Home: 8600 Evergreen Dr Parma OH 44129 Office: 1501 Euclid Ave Cleveland OH 44115 Tel (216) 861-2388

BONFIELD, ARTHUR EARL, b. N.Y.C., May 12, 1936; B.A., Bklyn. Coll., 1956; J.D., Yale, 1960, LL.M., 1961, postgrad. (sr. fellow), 1961-62. Admitted to Conn. bar, 1961, Iowa bar, 1966; asst. prof. law U. Iowa, 1962-65, asso. prof., 1965-66, prof., 1966-69, Law Sch. Found. prof. 1969-72, John Murray prof., 1972—; cons. Adminstrv. Conf. U.S., 1968—; mem. spl. com. state adminstrv. procedure act Iowa Gen. Assembly, 1974-75; exec. br. State of Iowa, 1975. mem. com. constl. law Multi-State Bar Exam., 1975—. Mem. Am. Law Inst., Am. (chmn. div. state adminstrv. law sect. adminstrv. law 1976—, chmn. com. adminstrv. law 1971—, Iowa State bar assns. Recipient Outstanding Service to Civil Liberties award Iowa Civil Liberties Union, 1974—; prin. draftsman Iowa Civil Rights Act, 1965, Iowa Fair Housing Act, 1967, Iowa Adminstrv. Procedure Act, 1975; contbr. numerous articles to legal jours. Home: 615 Holt Ave Iowa City IA 52240 Office: U Iowa Law Sch Iowa City IA 52242 Tel (319) 353-4566

BONGIOVANNI, JOSEPH NATHANIEL, JR., b. Phila., 1920; A.B. cum laude, Villanova U., 1940; J.D., U. Pa., 1943; postgrad. U. Colo., 1944. Admitted to Pa. bar, 1942, U.S. Supreme Ct. bar, 1960; since practiced in Phila., partner firm Speese, Bongiovanni & Copeland, 1970—; substitute prof. pharm. law Temple U., 1945, lectr., 1976; asst. counsel Nat. Conv. Corp. Am. Legion, 1949; appointed to Gov.'s Commn. on Sexual Minorities, 1976. Mem. exec. com. Big Bros. Phila., 1949. Mem. ACLU, Am., Pa., Phila. (chancellor 1973, chmn. subcom. on unauthorized practice com. 1965, chmn. internat. law com. 1976-77, bd. govs. 1969—, ho. of dels. 1970—, chmn. criminal law sect. 1971-72) bar assns., Lawyers Club, Brandeis Soc., Am. Legion (3rd dist. comdr. 1955-57), Venetian Social Club (past pres.), Justinian Soc., Fed. Bar Assn., Tau Epsilon Rho. Contbr. articles to law rev.; Recipient Outstanding Service award Big Bros., 1949. Office: 617 4 Penn Center Plaza Philadelphia PA 19103 Tel (215) 568-3410

BONHAM, WILLIAM DONALD, b. Iola, Tex., Dec. 27, 1930; B.A., U. Tex., 1952. LL.B., 1954. Admitted to Tex. bar, 1954; prof. law Provost Marshall Gen. Sch., Ft. Gordon, Ga., 1954-55; asso. firm W.D. Bonham, Houston, 1955-70; partner firm Bonham, Carrington & Fox, Houston, 1970-76. Mem. Am., Tex., Houston bar assns., Phi Delta Phi, Delta Tau Delta. Author: Substance Over Form, 1969. Home: 2704 Mid Ln Houston TX 77027 Office: 1200 S Post Oak Rd Houston TX 77056 Tel (713) 627-0123

BONIELLO, RALPH A., b. Bklyn., Feb. 26, 1914; LL.B., Niagara U., LL.D., 1976; postgrad. U. Buffalo Law Sch. Admitted to bar, 1938; sr. mem. firm Boniello, Anton, Conti & Boniello, Niagara Falls, N.Y.; dep. corp. counsel City of Niagara Falls; atty. Niagara Falls Bd. Edn.; mem. advisory bd. Marine Midland Bank; trustee, counsel, sec. Niagara U.; gen. counsel Niagara County Home Builders, Niagara Falls Area Bd. Realtors. Mem. Niagara County, N.Y. State, Niagara Falls bar assns. Home: 715 4th St Niagara Falls NY 14303 Office: 770 Main St Niagara Falls NY 14301 Tel (716) 285-3525

BONILLA, TONY, b. Calvert, Tex., Mar. 2, 1936; grad. Del Mar Coll., 1955; B.A. in Edn., Baylor U., 1958; LL.B., U. Houston, 1960. Admitted to Tex. bar, 1960; mem. firm Bonilla, Read, Nutto & Bonilla, Inc., Corpus Christi, Tex., 1960—; rep. Tex. State Legislature, 1964-66; mem. Tex. Constl. Revision Commn., 1973. Bd. dirs. League United Latin Am. Citizens, 1972-75; mem. coordinating bd. Tex. Coll. and Univ. System, 1973-79. Mem. Am. Bar Assn., Tex. Trial Lawyers Assn., Corpus Christi C. of C. (dir. 1973-78). Appeared on Today Show to discuss problems of Hispanic citizens, 1974. Home: 327 Baycliff St Corups Christi TX 78412 Office: 2590 Morgan Ave Corpus Christi TX 78405 Tel (512) 882-8284

BONINA, JOHN ANTHONY, b. Bklyn., Aug. 26, 1937; B.S. in Social Studies, Villanova U., 1959; LL.B., Bklyn Law Sch., 1961. Admitted to N.Y. bar, 1962, U.S. Supreme Ct. bar, 1967; claims mgr. State Farm Ins. Co., Bklyn., 1961-63; individual practice law Bklyn., 1962—. Mem. N.Y. State, Bklyn. bar assns., Bay Ridge, Columbian lawyers assns., Kings County Defenders Assn., Lawyers Interested in Victim's Equality, Catholic Lawyers Guild. Contbr. articles to profl. jours. Home: 225 83d St Brooklyn NY 11209 Office: 16 Court St Brooklyn NY 11241 Tel (212) 522-1786

BONNER, JOSEPH W., b. Chgo., Feb. 15, 1924; B.S., DePaul U., 1947, J.D., 1953. Admitted to Ill. bar, 1953; with firm Wolfe, Klein & Bonner, Chgo., 1958—. Mem. Skokie (Ill.) Water Pollution Commn., 1971-72; chmn. Skokie Environ. Control Commn., 1973. Mem. Ill., Chgo. bar assns., Decologue Soc. Office: 221 N LaSalle St Suite 2200 Chicago IL 60601 Tel (312) 372-5100

BONNER, LEONARD JOHN, b. Wilmington Del., May 23, 1938; B.A., LaSalle Coll., Phila., 1960; LL.B., U. Md., 1965. Admitted to U.S. Dist. Ct. bar for D.C., 1968, U.S. Ct. Appeals bar for D.C., 1968, U.S. Supreme Ct. Bar, 1971, U.S. Ct. Mil. Appeals bar, 1973, Md. Ct. Appeals bar, 1973; U.S. Dist. Ct. bar of Dist. Md., 1975; claims atty. Nationwide Mut. Ins. Co., Annapolis, Md., 1968, asso. firm Macleay, Lynch, Bernhard & Gregg, Washington, 1969-70; trial atty. firm Giordano, Alexander, Haas, Mahoney & Bush, Oxon Hill, Md., 1972-76; asst. gen. counsel D.C. Transit System Inc., Washington, 1970-72; legal counsel Prince George's Delegation to Md. Ho. of Dels., 1976-77. Lectr. St. Ignatius Ch., Oxon Hill, 1974—. Mem. Am., Prince George's County (Md.), Md. State bar assns., Bar Assn. D.C., Bar D.C., Assn. Trial Lawyers Am., LaSalle Coll. Alumni Assn. Home: 1570 Potomac Heights Dr Oxon Hill MD 20022 Office: 10905 Fort Washington Rd Oxon Hill MD 20022 Tel (301) 292-5900

BONNER, WALTER JOSEPH, b. N.Y.C., Nov. 18, 1925; A.B. cum laude, Cath. U. Am., 1951; J.D., Georgetown U., 1955. Admitted to D.C. bar, 1955, Va. bar, 1960, U.S. Supreme Ct. bar, 1967; law clk. to judge D.C. Ct. Appeals, 1954-55, U.S. Dist. Ct., 1955-56; asst. U.S. atty. D.C., 1956-60; individual practice law, Washington, 1960—; adj. prof. law Georgetown U., 1957-58, 67—, chmn. bd. advisors legal intern program, 1965—; del. D.C., Jud. Conf., 1976, 77. Fellow Am. Coll. Trial Lawyers; mem. Am., Fed. bar assns., Bar Assn. D.C., Va. Trial Lawyers Assn., Naval Res. Lawyers Assn., Res. Officers Assn., Naval Res. Assn. Home: 9628 Parkwood Dr Bethesda MD 20014 Office: 900 17th St Washington DC 20016 Tel (202) 659-4660

BONNER, WILLIAM NEELY, JR., b. Wichita Falls, Tex., June 12, 1923; student Rice U., 1940-42; J.D., U. Tex., 1948. Admitted to Tex. bar, 1948, U.S. Supreme Ct. bar, 1958, Fed. Power bar, 1954; staff atty. Houston div. Phillips Petroleum Co., 1948-52; gen. counsel, sec. Tex. Gas Corp. and New Ulm Corp., Houston, 1952-55; sr. corporate atty. Transcontinental Gas Pipe Line Corp., Houston, 1955—. Mem. Am., Tex., Houston bar assns., Interstate Natural Gas Assn. Am., Phi Delta Phi. Home: 1015 Briarmead Dr Houston TX 77057 Office: Transco Tower 2700 S Post Oak Rd POB 1396 Houston TX 77056 Tel (713) 626-8100

BONTEMPO, RALPH ANTHONY, b. Bklyn., Mar. 11, 1936; B.S., Niagara U., 1957; LL.B., St. John's U., Bklyn., 1962. Admitted to N.Y. bar, 1962; bailiff, law asst. Judge Matthew Abruzzo, U.S. Dist. Ct. for Eastern Dist. N.Y., 1962-65; asst. U.S. Atty. U.S. Dist. Ct., Eastern Dist. N.Y., 1965-70; atty. N.Y. Telephone Co., N.Y.C., 1970—. Mem. sch. bd. St. Aidens Sch., Williston Park, N.Y., 1975—. Mem. N.Y. State, Am., Nassau County bar assns., Nassau-Suffolk Trial Lawyers. Office: 1095 Ave of the Americas New York City NY 10036 Tel (212) 395-0086

BOOCHEVER, ROBERT, b. N.Y.C., Oct. 2, 1917; A.B., Cornell U., 1939, LL.B., 1941. Admitted to N.Y. bar, 1944, Alaska bar, 1947; asst. U.S. atty., Juneau, 1946-47; partner firm Faulkner, Banfield, Boochever & Doogan, Juneau, 1947-72; asso. justice Alaska Supreme Ct., 1972—; chmn. Alaska Jud. Conf., 1975—; mem. Conf. Chief Justices, 1975—; dir. First Nat. Bank, Juneau, 1955-61; mem. adv. bd. Nat. Bank of Alaska. Chmn. Juneau chpt. ARC, 1949-51, Juneau Planning Commn., 1956-61; mem. Alaska Devel. Bd., 1949-52, Alaska Jud. Qualification Commn., 1972-75; adv. bd. Juneau-Douglas Community Coll. Fellow Am. Coll. Trial Attys.; mem. Am. Law Inst., Am., Alaska (pres. 1961-62), Juneau (pres. 1971-72) bar assns., Am. Judicature Soc. (dir. 1970-74), Juneau C. of C. (pres. 1952, 55), Alaskans United (chmn. 1962). Named Juneau Man of Year, 1974. Home: 500 Douglas Hwy Juneau AK 99801 Office: Pouch U Court and Office Bldg Juneau AK 99801 Tel (907) 465-3410

BOOKER, DONALD WARNER, b. Wilmington, Del., Dec. 1, 1921; A.B., Colgate U., 1942; J.D., U. Va., 1948. Admitted to Del. bar, 1949; individual practice law, Wilmington, 1949—. Mem. Del. State, Am. bar assns., Am. Judicature Soc. Home: Center Mill Rd Wilmington DE 19807 Office: 905 Market Tower Wilmington DE 19801 Tel (302) 658-9301

BOOKOUT, JOHN GARBER, b. Birmingham, Ala., Oct. 17, 1935; B.S. in Law, U. Ala., 1958, LL.B., 1959, J.D., 1969. postgrad. Am. Acad. Jud. Edn., Ariz. State U., 1975, Nat. Coll. State Judiciary, U. Nev., 1976. Admitted to Ala. bar, 1959, U.S. Supreme Ct. bar, 1965; asst. atty. gen. Ala., Montgomery, 1959-67, chief asst. and dep. atty. gen. Ala., 1967-71; commr. ins. Ala., Montgomery, 1971-75; judge Ct. Criminal Appeals, Montgomery, 1975—, mem. Jud. Planning Com. Ala., 1977—. Co-founder, dir. Lurleen B. Wallace Cancer Hosp. Fund, U. Ala. Med. Center, Birmingham, 1968—; state chmn. Leukemia Soc. Am., 1974-75; pres. Montgomery Area council Boy Scouts Am., 1974-78. Mem. Am., Ala. bar assns., Ala. Law Inst. Council. Recipient Ala. Commendation medal, 1971, distinguished service award, Montgomery Jaycees, 1969. Home: 2633 McGehee Rd Montgomery AL 36111 Office: Ala Ct Criminal Appeals State Judicial Bldg Montgomery AL 36130 Tel (205) 832-3509

BOOKWALTER, THOMAS EDWARD, b. Dayton, Ohio, June 29, 1946; B.A., U. Dayton, 1967; J.D., U. Cin., 1970. Admitted to Ohio bar, 1970; legal officer U.S. Army, 1970-72; asso. firm Tracy & Tracy, West Carrollton, Ohio, 1972—; city prosecutor Miamisburg (Ohio), 1973—. Mem. Am., Ohio, Dayton bar assns. Office: 31 E Central Ave West Carrollton OH 45449 Tel (513) 859-3628

BOONE, EDWIN EUGENE, JR., b. Greensboro, N.C., Sept. 28, 1921; B.S. in Commerce, U. N.C., 1944; LL.B., Duke, 1949. Admitted to N.C. bar, 1949; partner firm Hoyle & Hoyle, Greensboro, 1949-63, Hoyle, Boone, Dees & Johnson, Greensboro, 1963-69; sr. partner Hoyle, Hoyle & Boone, Greensboro, 1969—. Mem. N.C., Greensboro bar assns., Greensboro Bd. Realtors (affiliate), N.C. Home Builders Assn. (asso.). Home: 3007 Round Hill Rd Greensboro NC 27408 Office: 440 W Market St Greensboro NC 27402 Tel (919) 273-2535

BOONE, HENRY SHAFFER, b. Wedowee, Ala., Dec. 30, 1908; B.S. in Bus., U. Ala., 1931, LL.B., 1934, J.D., 1934. Admitted to Ala. bar, 1934; individual practice law, Tuscaloosa, Ala., 1934-35, Montgomery, Ala., 1968-74, 75—; spl. agt. FBI, 1935-41; claims specialist VA, Montgomery, 1946-68; atty. fin. dept. State of Ala., Montgomery, 1974-75. Mem. Ala. Bar Assn. Patentee engines and pumps. Home and Office: 2342 Midfield Dr Montgomery AL 36111 Tel (205) 263-4724

BOONE, RICHARD WINSTON, b. Washington, July 19, 1941; B.A. with honors, U. Ala., 1963; J.D., Georgetown U., 1970. Admitted to Va. D.C. bars, 1970, U.S. Supreme Ct. bar, 1974; asso. firm Carr, Bonner, O'Connell & Thompson, Washington, 1974-75; partner firm Carr, Jordan, Coyne & Savits, Washington, 1975—. Mem. Am., D.C., Fed. bar assns., Am., Va. trial lawyers assns., D.C. Def. Lawyers Assn. Nat. Champion Nat. Moot Ct. Competition, 1968. Home: 1949 Hopewood Dr Falls Church VA 22043 Office: 900 17th St NW Washington DC 20006 Tel (202) 659-4660

BOONIN, LAWRENCE ISRAEL, b. Phila., Aug. 22, 1922; B.S. in Econs., U. Pa. Wharton Sch., 194'; J.D., Harvard, 1948. Admitted to Pa. bar, 1949, U.S. Dist. Ct. bar for Eastern Dist. Pa., 1949; individual practice law, Phila., 1949-57, 76—; asso firm Blank, Rudenko, Klaus, & Rome, Phila., 1957-61, partner, 1961-65; v.p., gen. counsel Auerbach Assos., Inc., Phila., 1965-76; mem. legal staff Cantor/Franklin/Grodinsky, P.C., Phila., 1977—; lectr. law Temple U., Phila., 1977—. Mem. Am., Pa., Phila. bar assns., IEEE (asso.),

Computer Law Assn., Soc. History of Tech. Contbr. articles to profl. jours. Office: 1845 Walnut St Philadelphia PA 19103 Tel (215) LO3-6060

BOORSTYN, NEIL, b. N.Y.C., Oct. 11, 1931; student Coll. City N.Y., 1948-52; LL.B., Bklyn. Law Sch., 1954. Admitted to N.Y. State bar, 1955; Calif. bar, 1972; partner firm Steger & Boorstyn, N.Y.C., 1963-68; partner firm Hofer & Boorstyn, N.Y.C., 1968-70; individual practice, N.Y.C., 1958-63, San Francisco, 1972—; adj. prof. Hastings Coll. Law, San Francisco, 1976—. Mem. Bar Assn. San Francisco. Office: 655 Redwood Hwy Mill Valley CA 94941 Tel (415) 383-9090

BOOTH, CHARLES HARLEY, b. N.Y.C., Sept. 25, 1931; B.A., U. Chgo., 1959, J.D., 1962. Admitted to Calif. bar, 1964; contract adviser Gen. Dynamics Astronautics, San Diego, 1962-64; dep. city atty. City of San Diego, 1964-65; partner firm Morrow, Young, Hargrove & Booth, San Diego, 1965-67; gen. counsel Stromberg Datagrapix, Inc., San Diego, 1967-70; group counsel Xerox Corp., El Segundo, Calif., 1970—. Mem. Am., Fed., Los Angeles County bar assns., State Bar Calif., Assn. Bus. Trial Lawyers. Home: 20 Shady Vista Rd Rolling Hills Estates CA 90274 Office: Xerox Corp 701 S Aviation Blvd El Segundo CA 90245 Tel (213) 679-4511 x 2122

BOOTH, FRANK RUSSELL, b. Austin, Tex., Sept. 20, 1930; A.B., U. Tex., Austin, 1952, S.J.D., 1958. Admitted to Tex. bar, 1957, U.S. Supreme Ct. bar, 1975, U.S. Ct. Claims bar, 1976; gen. counsel Tex. Water Rights Commn., Austin, 1958-60, exec. dir., 1965-69; gen. counsel U.S. Study Commn., Tex., 1960-63; asst. atty. gen. Tex., 1963-65; dep. chief Tex. Natural Resources Div., Austin, 1964-65; individual practice law, Austin, 1969-75; partner firm Booth Lloyd & Simmons, Austin, 1975—. Mem. State Bar Tex., Travis County, Am. bar assns., Tex., Am. trial lawyers assns. Home: 3000 Willowood Circle Austin TX 78703 Office: 302 San Jacinto Bldg Austin TX 78701 Tel (512) 478-9506

BOOTH, GORDON DEAN, JR., b. Columbus, Ga., June 25, 1939; B.A., Emory U., 1961, J.D., 1964, LL.M., 1973. Admitted to Ga. bar, 1963, Supreme Ct. bar, 1973; asso. firm. Hansell, Post, Brandon & Dorsey, Atlanta, 1964-66; atty. Delta Air Lines, Inc., Atlanta, 1966-68; partner firm Troutman, Sanders, Lockerman & Ashmore, Atlanta, 1968—; v.p., dir. Stallion Music, Inc., Nashville, 1966—. Trustee Met. Atlanta Crime Commn., 1977—. Mem. Am., Internat. (chmn. aero. law com., mem. council sect. on bus. law), Ga. bar assns., Am. Judicature Soc., Am. Soc. Internat. Law, Pub. Utility Law Assn. (aviation com.), Assn. Bar City N.Y., Lawyers Club Atlanta. Contbr. articles, editroial notes and revs. to profl. publs. Home: 580 Old Harbor Dr Atlanta GA 30328 Office: 1400 Candler Bldg Atlanta GA 30303 Tel (404) 658-8008

BOOTH, JOHN MARSHALL, b. Providence, Oct. 3, 1907; LL.B., Northeastern U., 1931. Admitted to R.I. bar, 1931, U.S. Dist. Ct. bar, 1933; asso. firm Booth & Brodsky, Providence, 1961—; asso. judge R.I. Juvenile Ct., 1947-60. Town solicitor, Smithfield, R.I., 1946-47. Home: 24 Highland Ave N Providence RI 02911 Office: 155 Westminster St Providence RI 02903 Tel (407) 751-3400

BOOTH, SAMUEL MASLON, b. Burlington, N.C., Jan. 27, 1936; B.S. in Bus. Adminstrn., U. N.C., 1959, LL.B., 1961. Admitted to N.C. bar, 1962; spl. agt. FBI, Washington, Indpls. and Pitts., 1961-63; staff atty. Atty. Gens. Office, Raleigh, N.C., 1963-64; partner firm Roberts, Frye & Booth, Winston-Salem, N.C., 1965-75, Frye, Booth & Porter, Winston-Salem, 1976—. Mem. N.C., Forsyth County bar assns. Home: 156 Mayfield Rd Winston Salem NC 27104 Office: 203 Northwestern Bank Bldg Winston Salem NC 27101 Tel (919) 725-9333

BOOTHMAN, CLAUD OTHO, b. Denison, Tex., Jan. 8, 1910; B.A., So. Meth. U., 1932, J.D., 1933. Admitted to Tex. bar, 1933, U.S. Supreme Ct. bar, 1960; individual practice law, Sherman, Tex., 1933-36; asst. dist. atty. Grayson County (Tex.), 1936-38; asst. atty. gen. State of Tex., Austin, 1939-42, 46; partner firm Gibson, Gibson & Boothman, Austin, 1947-48, Dumas, Huguenin, Boothman and Morrow, Dallas, 1948—. Life fellow Tex. Bar Assn.; mem. Am. (chmn., local govt. law sect. 1968-69, ho. dels. 1970-72), Dallas, Grayson County (past pres.), Internat. bar assns., Am. Judicature Soc., Wold Assn. Lawyers, Phi Alpha Delta. Home: 6539 Northport Dallas TX 75230 Office: Suite 1212 United Nat Bank Bldg 1509 Main St Dallas TX 75201 Tel (214) 741-3458

BOOTLE, WILLIAM AUGUSTUS, b. Colleton County, S.C., Aug. 19, 1902; A.B., Mercer U., 1924; LL.B., 1925. Admitted to Ga. bar, 1925; practiced in Macon, Ga., 1925-28, 33-54; asst. U.S. atty. Middle Dist. Ga., 1928-29, U.S. dist. atty., 1929-33; judge U.S. Dist. Ct., Middle Dist. Ga., 1954—, sr. judge, 1972—; prof. law Mercer U. Law Sch., 1926-37, acting dean, 1933-37, trustee, 1933-38, 40-46, 48-52, 54-58, 60-64, 66-70, 71-75, chmn. exec. com. bd., 1940-52; trustee Walter F. George Sch. Law Found., Macon, 1961—, v.p., 1962-64, pres., 1964-66. Mem. Phi Delta Theta, Phi Alpha Delta. Recipient Distinguished Alumnus award Mercer U., 1971. Home: 365 Old Club Rd Macon GA 31204 Office: PO Box 26 Macon GA 31202 Tel (912) 746-1338

BOOZER, ROBERT CHARLES, b. Birmingham, Ala., June 18, 1930; A.B., Emory U., 1952; J.D., Harvard U., 1955; postgrad. (Fulbright scholar) Netherlands Inst. Econs., 1955-56. Admitted to Ga. bar, 1954; asso. firm Alston, Miller & Gaines, and predecessors, Atlanta, 1956-61, partner, 1961-65; partner firm Troutman, Sanders, Lockerman & Ashmore, and predecessors, Atlanta, 1965—. Bd. dirs. Eighth Ward Civic Assn., 1971—; panelist Am. Arbitration Assn., 1960—. Mem. Am., Ga. State, Atlanta bar assns., Lawyers Club Atlanta. Home: 899 W Wesley Rd NW Atlanta GA 30327 Office: 1400 Candler Bldg 127 Peachtree St NE Atlanta GA 30303 Tel (404) 658-8010

BORASKI, WILLIAM, b. Pittsfield, Mass., Dec. 12, 1929; student Worcester Poly. Inst., 1948-50; LL.B., Northeastern U., 1953. Admitted to Mass. bar, 1953; individual practice law, Pittsfield, 1953—. Mem. Berkshire, Mass., Am. bar assns. Home: 105 Partridge Rd Pittsfield MA 01201 Office: 28 North St Pittsfield MA 01201 Tel (413) 445-4584

BORDELON, JOHN STEPHEN, b. Opelousas, La., Dec. 4, 1947; J.D., La. State U., 1972; LL.M. in Taxation, So. Meth. U., 1973. Admitted to La. bar, 1972, U.S. Tax Ct. bar, 1973; partner firm Guillory, McGee & Mayeaux, Eunice, La., 1973-74; since practiced in Lafayette, La., pres., prin. John Bordelon, Profl. Law Corp., 1974-75; partner firm Breaux & Bordelon, 1976—. Mem. Am., La., Lafayette Parish bar assns., Greater Lafayette C. of C., Lafayette-Met. La. State U. Alumni Fedn. (pres. 1975-77). Office: PO Box DD 305 W Main St Lafayette LA 70502 Tel (318) 233-1678

BORDEN, KENNETH PARKER, b. Providence, July 16, 1936; A.B., Brown U., 1958; LL.B., Columbia, 1961. Admitted to R.I. bar, 1962; partner firm Higgins, Cavanagh & Cooney, Providence, 1962—. Bd. dirs. Am. Cancer Soc., Scituate, R.I., 1967—, pres., 1969-72; bd. trustees Rotary Charities Found., 1976—, sec., 1976—. Mem. Am., R.I. (mem. house of dels. 1975—) bar assns., R.I. Defense Counsel Assn. (sec. 1974—). Home: Wilkinson Rd North Scituate RI 02857 Office: 600 Turks Head Bldg Providence RI 02903 Tel (401) 272-3500

BORDWELL, RICHARD STEWART, b. Washington, Iowa, Jan. 29, 1946; B.S., Iowa State U., 1969; J.D., U. Iowa, 1972. Admitted to Iowa bar, 1972; atty. Washington County, Iowa, 1975—; individual practice law, Washington, Iowa, 1976—. Mem. Iowa County Attys. Assn., Nat. Dist. Attys. Assn., Am. Iowa, Washington County bar assns., Assn. Trial Lawyers Iowa, Washington County Peace Officers Assn. Office: 103 1/2 N Marion St Washington IA 52353 Tel (319) 636-3021

BORGERDING, EDWARD FRANCES, b. Balt., June 18, 1923; LL.B., U. Balt., 1950, J.D., 1968, LL.M., 1953. Admitted to Md. bar, 1951, U.S. Supreme Ct. bar, 1961; practiced in Balt., 1951-73; asst. state's atty. City of Balt., 1954-57, 1st asst. state's atty., 1957-59; asst. atty. gen., 1st asst. to chief criminal div. State of Md., 1965-73; asso. judge Md. Dist. Ct., Balt., 1973-74, adminstrv. judge, 1974—; instr. U. Md., U. Balt., Mt. Vernon Sch. Law, Essex Community Coll.; cons. Conf. Circuit Adminstrv. Judges; mem. Legis. Ad Hoc Com. to Study State Prosecution Function. Exec. asst. Mayor City of Balt., 1959-62; mem. Balt. Bd. Municipal and Zoning Appeals, 1962-65; chmn. Md. Boy Scout Week; mem. activities bd. Balt. council Boy Scouts Am.; mem. Balt. Mayor's Coordinating Council on Criminal Justice. Mem. Md. Jud. Conf. (chmn. exec. com., chmn. on liaison with bar assns.), Am., Md. State bar assns., Bar Assn. Balt. City. Home: 8 W Lake Ave Baltimore MD 21210 Office: 211 E Madison St Baltimore MD 21202 Tel (301) 837-9740

BORK, ROBERT HERON, b. Pitts., Mar. 1, 1927; B.A., U. Chgo., 1948, J.D., 1953. Admitted to Ill. bar, 1953; asso. firm Willkie, Owen, Farr, Gallagher & Walton, N.Y.C., 1954-55; asso., partner firm Kirkland, Ellis, Hodson, Chaffetz & Masters, Chgo., 1955-62; asso. prof. law Yale U., 1962-65, prof., 1965-75, Chancellor Kent prof. law and legal history, 1977—; solicitor gen. U.S. Dept. Justice, 1973-77; resident scholar Am. Enterprise Inst., Washington, 1977; mem. Presdl. Task Force on Antitrust, 1968; spl. master to reapportion Ct. Gen. Assembly, 1972; cons. U.S. Cabinet Com. on Edn., 1972. Trustee Woodrow Wilson Internat. Center for Scholars. Home: 142 Huntington St New Haven CT 06511 Office: Yale U Law Sch New Haven CT 06520

BORKIN, JOSEPH, b. N.Y.C., Nov. 12, 1911; B.S., N.Y.U., 1933, M.A., 1937; student Nat. Law Sch., Washington, 1942-44. Admitted to Va. bar, 1945, D.C. bar, 1969, U.S. Supreme Ct. bar, 1952; security markets survey staff 20th Century Fund, 1933-34; investigator U.S. Senate, 1934-35, FCC, 1935-36; spl. asst. to atty. gen., antitrust div. Dept. Justice, 1938-46; individual practice law, Washington, 1946—; lectr. Cath. U., 1974—. Mem. Am., Fed. bar assns. Author: Corrupt Judge, 1962. Home 4701 Willard Ave Chevy Chase MD 20015 Office: 1156 15th St Washington DC 20005 Tel (202) 293-2240

BORLAND, DAVID G., b. Arlington, Va., Mar. 22, 1948; B.A., Case Western Reserve U., 1970, J.D., 1973. Admitted to Ohio bar, 1973; asst. county prosecutor criminal div. Cuyahoga County (Ohio), 1974—. Mem. Ohio, Cuyahoga County bar assns. Office: Courts Tower Bldg Justice Center 1 Ontario St Cleveland OH 44123 Tel (216) 623-7832

BORMAN, EDWARD HENRY, b. Webster Groves, Mo., Sept. 26, 1926; B.S., Washington U., St. Louis, 1950; J.D., St. Louis U., 1965. With Equitable Life Assurance Soc. U.S., St. Louis, 1950-57; with Gen. Am. Life Ins. Co., St. Louis, 1957-70, dir. health ins. claims, 1966-70; admitted to Mo. bar, 1965; exec. dir. Mo. Osteo. Assn., Jefferson City, 1970—; pres. Mo. Health Council, 1972; chmn. adv. com. Mo. Center for Health Statistics, 1975—. Bd. dirs. Still Hosp. Mem. Mo. Soc. Assn. Execs. Home: 1610 Greenberry Rd Jefferson City MO 65101 Office: 325 E McCarty St Jefferson City MO 65101 Tel (314) 634-3415

BORNHEIMER, ALLEN MILLARD, b. Brewer, Maine, June 10, 1942; B.A., Harvard, 1965, LL.B., 1968. Admitted to Mich. bar, 1968, Mass. bar, 1971; asso. firm Dickinson, Wright, McKeon & Cudlip, Detroit, 1968-70; asso. firm Choate, Hall & Stewart, Boston, 1970-76, partner, 1976—. Mem. fin. com. Town of Duxbury (Mass.), 1973-76, chmn., 1975-76, capital budget com., 1976—; dir., corporator Jordan Hosp., Plymouth, Mass., 1974—; trustee N. Yarmouth (Maine) Acad., 1976—. Mem. Am. Bar Assn. Office: 28 State St Boston MA 02109 Tel (617) 227-5020

BOROUGHS, P. THOMAS, b. Conway, S.C., June 13, 1939; A.B., U. S.C., 1961; J.D., Duke, 1968. Admitted to Fla. bar, 1968; asso. firms Akerman, Senterfitt, Edison & Wharton, Orlando, Fla., 1968-69, Rush, Marshall, Bergstrom & Robison, Orlando, 1969-71; partner firm Mairs, Wood, Muller & Boroughs, Winter Park, Fla., 1971-75; individual practice law, Winter Park, 1975—; trustee Legal Aid Soc. of Orange County (Fla.), Inc. Mem. Am. Bar Assn., Fla. (exec. council sect. real property, probate and trust law, chmn. com. fed. regulation of land use), Orange County (exec. council) bars. Home: 474 Lakewood Dr Winter Park FL 32789 Office: 200 W Welbourne Ave Winter Park FL 32789 Tel (305) 628-4440

BOROVSKY, HERBERT LAWRENCE, b. Chgo., Jan. 14, 1931; A.B., Dartmouth Coll., 1953; J.D., Northwestern U., 1956. Admitted to Ill. bar, 1956, U.S. Supreme Ct. bar, 1975, D.C. bar, 1975; atty.-adviser NLRB, Washington and Chgo., 1956-60; asso. firm Murphy Pearson & O'Connor, Chgo., 1960-64; sr. partner Borovsky, Smetana, Ehrlich & Kronenberg, Chgo., 1964-; chmn. attys. com. Internat. Found. Employee Benefit Plans, Inc., Chgo., 1966-67, dir., 1968-71, mem. industry relations com., 1974-76. Mem. Am., Ill. State, Chgo., D.C. bar assns. Contbr. chpts. to texts, articles to legal jours. Home: 685 Country Ln Glencoe IL 60022 Office: 120 S LaSalle St Suite 1280 Chicago IL 60603 Tel (312) 368-8500

BOROWIECKI, LAWRENCE R., b. Chgo., Nov. 12, 1946; B.A., St. Mary's Coll. (Minn.), 1968; J.D., U. Notre Dame, 1971. Admitted to Ill. bar, 1971; law clk. to justice Ill. Appellate Ct., 1971-73; atty. regional counsel div. Fed. Nat. Mortgage Assn., Chgo., 1973—. Mem. Ill. Bar Assn. Home: 955 Darius Ln Naperville IL 60540 Office: 150 S Wacker Dr Chicago IL 60606 Tel (312) 641-0740

BORRADAILE, EARL EDWARD, b. Liberty, Ind., Jan. 12, 1930; A.B., Miami U., Ohio, 1952; LL.B., U. Mich., 1955. Admitted to Mich. bar, 1956; partner firm Karr, Wumkes & Borradaile, Flint and Davison, Mich., 1958-70; circuit judge Genesee County, Mich., Flint, 1970-71, probate judge, 1971—. Mem. Bd. of Edn. Davison Community Schs., 1967-70. Mem. Am., Mich., Genesee County bar assns., Am. Judges Assn. Home: 601 Maxine Dr Davison MI 48423 Office: Room 513 County Courthouse Flint MI 48502 Tel (313) 766-8712

BORRELLO, ROGER FRANK, b. Bklyn., May 27, 1938; B.S. in Psychology, Fordham Coll., 1960; J.D., Georgetown U., 1964. Admitted to Va. bar, 1964, Mass. bar, 1964, D.C. bar, 1965, Fla. bar, 1968; asso. firm Sharrillo, Fortunato & Tempone, Medford, Mass., 1964-67; individual practice, law, Lexington, Mass., 1967-68; asst. county solicitor Broward County, Fla., 1968-69; asst. pub. defender, Broward County, 1968-69; individual practice law, Plantation, Fla., 1972—. Chmn. United Fund, Bedford, Mass., 1967-68. Mem. Am. Trial Lawyers Assn., Broward County Bar Assn. Home: 5200 SW 9th St Plantation FL 33317 Office: 5309 W Broward Blvd Plantation FL 33317 Tel (305) 584-1005

BORROR, CAYWOOD JOSEPH, b. Chgo., June 16, 1930; B.S. in Bus. Adminstrn., Ohio State U., 1951, J.D., 1953. Admitted to Ohio bar, 1953, Calif. bar, 1957, U.S. Supreme Ct. bar, 1971; with JAGC, USAR, 1953-57; dep. dist. atty. San Bernardino County (Calif.), 1957-59; asso. firm Wilson, Borror & Dunn, and predecessors, San Bernardino, 1959—, partner, 1962—. Bd. dirs. Family Services Agy., San Bernardino, 1970-73, Children's Home Soc., Riverside, Calif., 1968-70. Mem. San Bernardino County (pres. 1971-72), Am. bar assns., State Bar Calif., Assn. So. Calif. Def. Counsel (pres. 1974-75), Def. Research Inst., Calif. Trial Lawyers Assn., Am. Judicature Soc. Home: 5761 Sycamore Ave Rialto CA 92376 Office: 255 N D St Suite 307 PO Box 540 San Bernardino CA 92401 Tel (714) 884-8855

BOSCO, ANTHONY J., b. Chgo., Feb. 24, 1928; A.B., Roosevelt U., 1953; J.D. DePaul U., 1956. Admitted to Ill. bar, 1956; individual practice law, Chgo., 1956-72; asso. judge Cook County Circuit Ct., 4th Municipal Dist., Oak Park, Ill., 1972—. Mem. Ill., Chgo., West Suburban bar assns., Justinian Soc. of Lawyers, Delta Theta Phi. Office: 1500 Maybrook Dr Maywood IL 60153 Tel (312) 865-6060

BOSCO, JOHN I., b. N.Y.C., Apr. 10, 1933; B.S., Fordham U., 1954, LL.B., 1959. Admitted to N.Y. bar, 1959; law clk. Hon. John W. Clancy, U.S. Dist. Judge, So. Dist. N.Y., 1959-60; asso. firm Arthur, Dry & Dole, N.Y.C., 1960-64; partner firm Farelli, Moore, Bosco, Penzel & McMillan, New Rochelle, N.Y., 1964—. Mem. Citizen's Budget Task Force, New Rochelle, 1976—. Mem. New Rochelle C. of C. (pres.) Home: 27 Flint Ave Larchmont NY 10538 Office: 271 North Ave New Rochelle NY 10801 Tel (914) 632-4700

BOSCO, JOSEPH A., b. Boston, Mar. 25, 1938; A.B. cum laude, Harvard U., 1960, LL.B., 1965. Admitted to Mass. bar, 1966, D.C. bar, 1973; law clk. to chief justice and asso. justices Mass. Superior Ct., 1965-67; asst. legal counsel to Gov. Mass., 1967-68; spl. asst. to sec. U.S. Dept. Transp., 1969-73; partner firm vom Baur, Coburn, Simmons, and Turtle, Washington, 1973—. Chmn. Citizens Adv. Group on Light Rail Transp. in D.C., 1973. Mem. Am., Fed., D.C., Mass., Boston bar assns., Harvard Law Sch. Assn., Energy Commn., Am. Pub. Transit Assn., Pub. Transit Commn. (chmn. 1973). Named by presdl. appointment to Nat. Highway Safety Adv. Com., U.S. Dept. Transp., 1973-76. Home: 3121 Newark St Washington DC 20008 Office: 1700 K St NW Washington DC 20006 Tel (202) 833-1420

BOSS, FREDERICK L., JR., b. Muskogee, Okla., Oct. 15, 1936; B.S. in Bus. Adminstrn., U. Ark., 1959; J.D., Tulsa U., 1970. Admitted to Okla. bar, 1970; individual practice law, Tulsa, 1970—. Adviser, Parents without Partners, Inc., 1970—. Mem. Am., Okla., Tulsa County bar assns., Okla. Trial Lawyers Assn. Home: 2994 E 78th St Tulsa OK 74136 Office: 4401 S Harvard St Tulsa OK 74135 Tel (918) 747-8031

BOSSARD, STERLING REYNOLD, b. Denver, Dec. 10, 1911; J.D., U. Utah, 1936. Admitted to Utah bar, 1936; judge 4th Dist. Juvenile Ct. State of Utah, Cedar City, 1944-50, 62—; as asso. firm Gustin, Richards & Mattsson, Richfield, Utah, 1950-54; dist atty. 6th Jud. Dsit. Utah, Richfield, 1954-57; commr. Utah State Bar, 1961-71, pres., 1969-70. Mem. adv. bd. Upward Bound Program, 1970-75. Mem. Am., So. Utah (pres. 1959-60) bar assns., Am. Judicature Soc., Utah Bd. Juvenile Ct. Judges (presiding judge 1971-72), Soc. Bar and Gavel. Contbr. articles to legal jours. Home: 1874 E 5150 S Salt Lake City UT 84117 Office: 369 S 6th E Salt Lake City UT 84111 Tel (801) 586-9832

BOSSELMAN, FRED PAUL, b. Oak Park Ill., June 14, 1934; B.A., U. Colo., 1956; J.D., Harvard, 1959. Admitted to Ill. bar, 1959; asso. firm Ross, Hardies, O'Keefe, Babcock & Parsons, Chgo., 1959-67, partner, 1967—; asso. reporter Am. Law Inst., 1969-75; dir. Met. Housing and Planning Council Chgo., 1971—; commr. Housing Authority Cook County (Ill.), 1973—. Mem. Am. (chmn. environ. law com., sect. on real property, probate and trust law, 1974—), Chgo. bar assns., Am. Soc. Planning Ofcls. (dir. 1977—). Author: (with David Callies) The Quiet Revolution in Land Use Control, 1971; (with David Callies and John Banta) The Taking Issue, 1973; (with Richard Babcock) Exclusionary Zoning, 1974. Home: 2715 Woodbine Ave Evanston IL 60201 Office: Suite 3100 One IBM Plaza Chicago IL 60611 Tel (312) 467-9300

BOSSES, STEVAN JOEL, b. Bronx, N.Y., July 29, 1937; B.M.E., Cornell U., 1960; LL.B. (Harlan Fisk Stone scholar), Columbia, 1963. Admitted to N.Y. State bar, 1963, U.S. Dist. Ct. for So. dist. N.Y. bar, 1964, U.S. Dist. Ct. for Eastern dist. N.Y., 1964, U.S. Patent Office bar, 1964, U.S. 2d Circuit Ct. Appeals bar, 1970, U.S. Ct. Customs and Patent Appeals, 1973; asso. firm Watson, Leavenworth, Kelton & Taggart, N.Y.C., 1963-71, partner, 1972—. Mem. Am. (patent and antitrust sects.), N.Y. State, Weschester County bar assns., Am., N.Y. patent law assns., ASME. Home: 309 W Hartsdale Ave Hartsdale NY 10530 Office: 100 Park Ave New York City NY 10017 Tel (212) 683-4220

BOST, THOMAS GLEN, b. Oklahoma City, July 13, 1942; B.S. summa cum laude, Abilene Christian Coll., 1964; LL.B., Vanderbilt U., 1967. Admitted to Tenn. bar, 1967, Calif. bar, 1969; asst. prof. law Vanderbilt U., 1967-68; asso. firm Latham & Watkins, Los Angeles, 1968-75, partner; 1975—; lectr. in taxation field. Bd. regents, sec. and mem. exec. com. Pepperdine U., 1974—. Mem. Am., Los Angeles County (exec. com., chmn. com. income tax sect. taxation) bar assns., State Bar Calif., Order of Coif. Recipient Founder's medal Vanderbilt U. Sch. Law, 1967. Office: 555 S Flower St Los Angeles CA 90071 Tel (213) 485-1234

BOSTER, STANFORD RODNEY, b. July 3, 1929; B.A., U. Cin., 1951, J.D., 1953. Admitted to Ohio bar, 1953, Ky. bar, 1974; individual practice law, Cin. and Augusta, Ky.; exec. v.p., dir. Eagle Savings Assn., Cin., 1967-70, Wabash Consol. Corp., Cin., 1967-71;

sec., dir. gen. counsel Farmers Liberty Bank, Augusta, 1974—; city atty. City of Augusta, 1974—. Mem. Ky., Ohio State, Cin. bar assns., Cin. Law Library Assn. Contbr. articles to Cin. Law Rev. Home: 180 Ridgeview St Cincinnati OH 45215 Office: 8250 Winton Rd Cincinnati OH 45231 Tel (513) 522-8100 also 101 Frankfort St Augusta KY 41002 Tel (606) 756-2526

BOSTETTER, MARTIN VAN BUREN, JR., b. Balt., Mar. 11, 1926; B.A., U. Va., 1950, LL.B., 1952. Admitted to Va. bar, 1952, Md. bar, 1953, D.C. bar, 1962; spl. asst. city atty. City of Alexandria (Va.), 1952-57; asso. judge Municipal Ct., Alexandria, 1957-59; judge U.S. Bankruptcy Ct., U.S. Dist. Ct. for Eastern Dist. Va., 1959—. Mem. Alexandria (pres. 1962-63), Va., Am. bar assns., Va. bar. Office: 200 N Fairfax St Alexandria VA 22314 Tel (703) 683-0032

BOSTICK, CHARLES DENT, b. Gainesville, Ga., Dec. 28, 1931; A.B., Mercer U., 1952, J.D., 1958. Admitted to Ga. bar, 1957, also Tenn. bar; practice law, Gainesville, Ga., 1957-66; partner firm Telford, Wayne & Greer, 1966-68; asst. prof. law U. Fla., 1966-68, asso. prof., 1968; asso. prof. Vanderbilt U., 1968-71, prof., 1971—, asso. dean Law Sch., 1975—. Mem. State Bar Ga., Tenn. Bar Assn. Contbr. articles to legal jours. Home: Route 5 Jordan Rd Franklin TN 37064 Office: Sch of Law Vanderbilt U Nashville TN 37240 Tel (615) 322-2615

BOSTWICK, DONALD WARREN, b. Wichita, Kans., Aug. 25, 1943; B.S. in Bus., U. Kans., 1965, J.D., 1968. Admitted to Kans. bar, 1968, U.S. Supreme Ct. bar, 1975; asso. . firm Adams, Jones, Robinson & Malone, Wichita, 1968—. Mem. Wichita, Kans., Am. bar assns., Am., Kans. trial lawyers assns., Order of Coif. Bd. editors Kan. Law Rev., 1967, mng. editor, 1968. Home: 6520 Oneida St Wichita KS 67206 Office: Suite 301 201 N Main St Wichita KS 67201 Tel (316) 265-8591

BOSTWICK, RICHARD RAYMOND, b. Billings, Mont., Mar. 17, 1918; student U. Colo., 1937-38; B.A., U. Wyo., 1943, J.D., 1947. Admitted to Wyo. bar, 1947; partner firm Murane, Bostwick, McDaniel, Scott, Greenlee & Owens, Casper, Wyo., 1948—. Pres., Blue Envelope Health Fund, 1970-71; chmn. Selective Service Bd., Casper, 1952-70. Mem. Internat. Assn. Ins. Counsel, Fedn. Ins. Counsel, Internat. Soc. Barristers (pres. 1975), Am. Judicature Soc. (sec. 1975—), Am., Wyo. (pres. 1964-65), Natrona County (pres. 1956) bar assns., Am. Coll. Trial Lawyers, Assn. Ins. Counsel, Casper C. of C. (v.p. 1955-57). Contbr. articles to legal jours. Home: 1137 Granda St Casper WY 82601 Office: 504 Wyoming Bldg Casper WY 82601 Tel (307) 234-9345

BOSWELL, DON RAY, b. Elba, Ala., Apr. 17, 1946; B.S., U. Ala., 1967, M.B.A., 1968; J.D., U. Va., 1972. Admitted to Fla. bar, 1972; asst. U.S. atty. So. Dist. Fla., Miami, 1973—. Mem. Am., Fed., Palm Beach County bar assns., Am. Soc. Internat. Law, Fla. Bar. Home: PO Box 010344 Miami FL 33101 Office: 300 Ainsley Bldg 14 NE 1st Ave Miami FL 33132 Tel (305) 350-4471

BOSWELL, JAMES HAROLD, b. Marion, Ky., Jan. 24, 1922; student Lambuth Coll., 1940-42; J.D., Vanderbilt U., 1949. Admitted to Tenn. bar, 1950; individual practice law, Jackson Tenn., 1950—; rep. Tenn. Gen. Assembly, 1955-58; U.S. Commr., Jackson, 1959-71; U.S. Magistrate, Jackson, 1971—. Elder 1st Christian Ch. Jackson, 1960—. Mem. Am., Tenn. (bd. govs.), Jackson-Madison County (past pres.) bar assns., Phi Alpha Delta. Home: 23 Fairfield Pl Jackson TN 38301 Office: 202 Pythian Bldg Jackson TN 38301 Tel (901) 427-2621

BOTT, FREDERICK REYNOLDS, b. New Orleans, Feb. 21, 1933; B.B.A., Tulane U., 1955, LL.B., 1960. Admitted to La. bar, 1960; asso. firm Detusch, Kerrigan & Stiles, New Orleans, 1960-66, partner, 1966—. Bd. dirs. Kingsley House, 1973—; bd. govs. La. Civil Service League, 1976—. Mem. Am., La., New Orleans bar assns., La., New Orleans assns. def. counsel, Internat. Assn. Ins. Counsel. Home: 5236 Pitt St New Orleans LA 70115 Office: One Shell Sq 47th floor New Orleans LA 70139 Tel (504) 581-5141

BOTTARO, SALVATORE A., b. Buffalo, N.Y., June 17, 1938; LL.B., U. Buffalo, 1965, J.D., 1967. Admitted to N.Y. State bar, 1966, Fla. bar, 1975; individual practice law, Buffalo, 1967—. Mem. Erie County Bar Assn., N.Y., Erie County trial lawyers assn. Office: 736 Brisbane Blvd Buffalo NY 14203 Tel (716) 847-1777

BOTTI, ALDO EZRA, b. Bklyn., Dec. 27, 1936; A.B., Rockhurst Coll., 1962; J.D., St. Louis U., 1965. Admitted to Ill., Mo. bars, 1966; asso. firm William J. O'Brien, Chgo., 1966-69; asst. state's atty. DuPage County (Ill.), Wheaton, 1969-70, pub. defender, 1970-71; partner firm Teschner, Botti & Fawell, Wheaton, 1972-74, firm Teschner & Botti, 1974-75; prin. firm A.E. Botti, Wheaton, 1975—; atty. Village of Villa Park (Ill.), 1976—; mem. DuPage County Law Enforcement Commn. Bd. dirs. Hinsdale (Ill.) Community Service, 1973-76, chmn., 1975-76. Mem. Am., Ill., Chgo., DuPage County bar assns., Am., Ill. trial lawyers assns., Am. Judicature Soc., Ill. Municipal League, Nat. Dist. Attys. Assn., Nat. Criminal Def. Lawyers Assn. Office: 330 Naperville Rd Wheaton IL 60187 Tel (312) 653-2100

BOTTLER, EDGAR O., b. Bartlesville, Okla., Nov. 6, 1923; B.S. Chem. Engring., Rice U., 1944; LL.B., U. Tex., 1949. Spl. asst. to U.S. atty. gen., 1954; asst. U.S. atty. So. Dist. Tex., 1955-58, 1st asst. U.S. atty., 1957-58; atty. Gulf Interstate Gas Co., 1958-59; sec., counsel Columbia Gulf Transmission Co., 1959-63; sr. atty. Columbia Gas System Service Corp., 1963-67; sec., legal counsel Continental Can Co., N.Y.C., 1967—, v.p., 1973—. Mem. council Rice U. Fund, 1971-72; sec. Keep Am. Beautiful, 1973—. Bd. dirs. Greenwich Philharmonia, v.p., 1973—, bd. dirs. N.Y. State 4-H Found. Mem. Am., Fed. Power, Tex. bar assns., Rice U. Alumni Assn. (exec. bd. 1971-74), Theodore Gordon Flyfishers (pres. 1974-75), Defenders of Wildlife, Order of Coif, Phi Delta Phi, Phi Gamma Delta. Home: 132 Beachside Ave Greens Farms CT 06436 Office: 633 3d Ave New York City NY 10017*

BOTTOMS, DAVID NEWTON, JR., b. Auburn, Ala., Mar. 30, 1939; B.A., Coll. William and Mary, 1961; LL.B., U. Va., 1964. Admitted to N.Y. bar, 1967; partner firm Lord, Day & Lord, N.Y.C., 1967—; spl. asst. dist. atty. Westchester County, 1971-73; vis. lectr. U. Va., 1977. Sec., Rec. for Blind, 1972—; pres. bd. trustees Huguenot Meml. Ch., 1976-77; councilman Town of Pelham, N.Y., 1976—. Mem. N.Y. State Bar Assn., Assn. Bar City N.Y. Home: 475 Monterey Ave Pelham NY 10803 Office: 25 Broadway New York City NY 10004 Tel (212) 344-8480

BOTTONI, JAMES ANDREW, JR., b. Milw., Aug. 25, 1942; B.S., U. Wis. at Milw., 1965; J.D., Marquette U., 1970. Admitted to Wis. bar, 1970; contract negotiator, budget analyst Milw. Model Cities program, 1970-71; legal counsel Childrens Ct., Milw. County Dept. Social Services, 1971-73; corp. counsel Washington County (Wis.), West Bend, 1973-77; asst. pub. defender State of Wis., 1977—. Founder and first pres. Kettle Moraine Chess Club; exec. com. Washington County Dem. Party, now vice chmn. Mem. Am. (state membership chmn.), Wis. (v.p. young lawyers sect.) bar assns. Home: 554 Highland View Dr West Bend WI 53095 Office: 819 N 6th St State Office Bldg Milwaukee WI Tel (414) 224-4794

BOTULA, JON CHARLES, b. Pitts., Oct. 21, 1941; B.B.A., U. Pitts., 1963; J.D., Duquesne U., 1967. Admitted to Pa. bar, 1967, Fla. bar, 1975; practice law, Pitts. Mem. Pa., Fla., County bar assns. Home:

BOTWINIK, DAVID ARTHUR, b. Union City, N.J., Aug. 17, 1930; A.B., Cornell U., 1951; J.D., Yale, 1954; B.S. in Accounting, Hofstra Coll., 1956. Admitted to N.Y. bar, 1954, U.S. Supreme Ct. bar, 1962; with Judge Adv. Gen. Corps USAF, 1954-56; asso. firm Pavia & Harcourt, N.Y.C., 1957-64, partner, 1965—; sec., dir. Consol. Royalty Oil Co., Casper, Wyo., 1960-69; dir. De Jur Amsco Corp., N.Y.C., 1972-73; mem. nat. panel arbitrators Am. Arbitration Assn., 1968—. Active Jewish Big Bros. of Jewish Bd. Guardians, N.Y.C., 1959—, chmn., 1970-72; sec., dir. Harry de Jur Found., N.Y.C., 1962—; bd. dirs. Phoenix Sch., N.Y.C., 1973—; v.p., dir. Hebrew Free Loan Soc., N.Y.C., 1973—. Mem. Am., N.Y. State bar assns., New York County Lawyers Assn., Am. Fgn. Law Assn., Consular Law Soc., Am. Judicature Soc. Contbr. articles to Internat. Lawyer. Office: 63 Wall St New York City NY 10005 Tel (212) 248-5500

BOTZ, JAMES PETER, b. Glendale, Calif., Aug. 11, 1936; A.B., U. Calif., Berkeley, 1959, J.D., 1964. Admitted to Calif. bar, 1965; dep. county counsel San Joaquin County (Calif.), 1965-66; dep. county counsel Sonoma County (Calif.), 1966-72, county counsel, 1972—. Mem. County Counsels Assn. Calif., Am. Bar Assn. Home: 1633 Austin Way Santa Rosa CA 94504 Office: 2555 Mendocino Ave Santa Rosa CA 95401 Tel (707) 527-2421

BOUBLITZ, JOHN LOUIS, b. Balt., May 21, 1913; LL.B., U. Balt., 1936. Admitted to Md. bar, 1936; mem. firm Curry & Boublitz, Balt., 1936-41; mem. firm Weinberg & Green, Balt., 1941-52; mem. firm Ready, Boublitz & Broadwater, Hagerstown, Md., 1952-67; mem. firm Boublitz, Colton & Broadwater, Hagerstown, 1967-71; judge Dist. Ct. of Md., Hagerstown, 1971—; Hagerstown city atty., 1966-70. Mem., chmn. Washington County Planning and Zoning Commn., 1970—. Mem. Md. State Bar Assn. (dir. 1964-65, mem. grievance com., chmn. coms. 1969-70), Am. Judicature Soc., Am. Judges Soc., Washington County, Am. bar assns., Jud. Conf. (exec. com. 1975-76, ethics com. 1971-75). Home: Milestone Garden Apts-6G Williamsport MD 21795 Office: 35 W Washington St Hagerstown MD 21740 Tel (301) 797-0210

BOUDIN, LEONARD B., b. N.Y.C., July 20, 1912; B.S.S., City Coll. N.Y., 1933; LL.B., St. John's U., 1935. Admitted to N.Y. bar, 1935, U.S. Supreme Ct. bar, 1949; with Mortgage Commn., State of N.Y., 1936-37; asso. firm Boudin, Cohn & Glickstein, Esqs., N.Y.C., 1936-43, 43-47; partner firm Rabinowitz, Boudin & Standard, Esqs., N.Y.C., 1947—; vis. prof. Harvard Law Sch., 1970-71; lectr. Yale Law Sch., 1974; Distinguished vis. prof. U. Calif., Berkeley, 1975; hon. fellow U. Pa. Law Sch., 1974; exec. asst. to labor mems. Nat. War Labor Bd., 1943-44. Pres. Downtown Community Sch., 1944-50; gen. counsel Nat. Emergency Civil Liberties Com., 1951—. Mem. Am. Soc. Internat. Law., Assn. Bar City of N.Y., Am. Fgn. Law Assn., Nat. Lawyers Guild. Contbr. articles to legal jours.

BOUDREAUX, CHARLES JEROME, b. Scott, La., Oct. 20, 1923; A.B., U. SW La., 1943; J.D., Tulane U., 1949. Admitted to La. bar, 1949; partner firm Pugh & Boudreaux, Lafayette, La., 1950—; U.S. commr. Western Dist. La., 1959-72, U.S. magistrate, 1972-75. Mem. Am., La. State (ho. of dels.), Lafayette bar assns., Order of Coif, Am. Legion, Phi Delta Phi. Student bd. editors Tulane Law Rev. Office: POB 3118 112 W Vermilion St Lafayette LA 70502 Tel (318) 235-7508

BOUDREAUX, DONALD L., b. Beaumont, Tex., Mar. 6, 1942; B.B.A., Lamar U., 1964; LL.B., J.D., U. Tex., 1967. Admitted to Tex. bar, 1967; with Jefferson County (Tex.) Dist. Attys. Office, Beaumont, 1967-68; asso. firm M.H. Oldham, Beaumont, 1968-69, R. Leon Pettis, Beaumont, 1969—. Mem. Tex. Bar Assn., Criminal Law Assn. Home: 533 Yorktown Rd Beaumont TX 77706 Office: Goodhue Bldg Beaumont TX 77701 Tel (713) 832-7080

BOUGHEY, JAMES DENNIS, b. Chgo., Nov. 20, 1943; A.B., U. Mich., 1966; J.D., U. Ill., 1969. Admitted to Calif. bar, 1970; partner firm Dorr, Cooper & Hays, San Francisco, 1969—. Mem. State Bar Calif., Am. Bar Assn., Maritime Law Assn. U.S. Office: 260 California St San Francisco CA 94111 Tel (415) 398-2800

BOUKIS, KENNETH, b. Cleve., Aug. 28, 1940; B.B.A., Cleve. State U., 1963, LL.M., 1976; J.D., Case-Western Res. U., 1966. Admitted to Ohio bar, 1966; partner firm Strangward, Marshman, Lloyd & Malaga, Cleve., 1966-69, Schaaf, Chalko & Boukis, Cleve., 1970-71, Chalko, Hohmann, Boukis & Boukis, Cleve., 1971—. Mem. Cleve., Ohio bar assns. Home: 8230 W Ridge Dr Broadview Heights OH 44147 Office: 1000 Standard Bldg Cleveland OH 44113 Tel (216) 696-1076

BOUKUS, CHARLES PAUL, JR., b. New Britain, Conn., Feb. 22, 1942; B.S. magna cum laude, Brown U., 1964; J.D., Georgetown U., 1968. Admitted to Va. bar, 1969, D.C. bar, 1970; asso. with Western Electric Co., Washington, 1964-68; clk. to judges U.S. Ct. Claims, Washington, 1968-69; asso. firm Finnegan, Henderson, Farabow & Garrett, Washington, 1969-75; individual practice law, Arlington, Va., 1976—. Bd. dirs. No. Va. Assn. for Retarded Citizens, Annandale, 1970—, treas., 1975-76; bd. dirs., treas. Arlington Community Residences, Inc., 1975—. Mem. Am., D.C. bar assns., Am. Patent Law Assn., Patent Lawyers Club Washington. Co-author Ct. Claims Practice Manual for D.C. Bar Assn., 1976. Home: 3928 N Woodstock St Arlington VA 22207 Office: suite 209 2001 Jefferson Davis Hwy Arlington VA 22202 Tel (703) 920-6120

BOULT, REBER FIELDING, JR., b. Nashville, Nov. 17, 1936; B.E., Vanderbilt U., 1968, LL.B., 1964. Admitted to Tenn. bar, 1964, Ga. bar, 1971, U.S. Supreme Ct. bar, 1969; asso. firm Boult, Hunt, Cummings & Conners, Nashville, 1964-67; staff counsel ACLU, Atlanta, 1968-71; counsel Nat. Lawyers Guild Mil. Law, Iwakuni, Japan, 1972-73; individual practice law, Atlanta, 1973-75; partner firm Law Project of R. Boult et al., Atlanta, 1975—; staff Inst. for So. Studies, 1971-72. Mem. Am., Ga. bar assns., Nat. Lawyers Guild, Ga. Assn. Criminal Def. Lawyers, Tau Beta Pi, Order of Coif. Contbr. articles to law jours. Office: 834 15 Peachtree St Atlanta GA 30303 Tel (404) 523-4611

BOUMA, JOHN JACOB, b. Fort Dodge, Iowa, Jan. 13, 1937; B.A., U. Iowa, 1958, J.D., 1960. Admitted to Iowa bar, 1960, Wis. bar, 1960, Ariz. bar, 1962, U.S. Supreme Ct. bar, 1975; asso. firm Foley, Sammond & Lardner, Milw., 1960; asso. firm Snell & Wilmer, Phoenix, 1962-66, partner, 1966—; served from 1st lt. to capt. JAGC, U.S. Army, Ft. Huachuca, Ariz., 1960-62. Chmn., Phoenix Human Relations Commn., 1973-75; mem. Phoenix Commn. on LEAP, 1971-72; bd. dirs. Phoenix Legal Aid Soc., 1970-76. Mem. Maricopa County (pres.-elect.), Ariz., Am. bar assns., Phoenix Assn. Def. Counsel (pres. 1972), Order of Coif, Phi Beta Kappa. Home: 800 E Circle Rd Phoenix AZ 85020 Office: 3000 Valley Center Phoenix AZ 85073 Tel (602) 257-7216

BOURCIER, JOHN PAUL, b. Providence, Mar. 27, 1927; A.B., Brown U., 1950; J.D., Vanderbilt U., 1953. Admitted to R.I. bar, 1953; individual practice law, Providence, 1953-56; partner firm Bourcier & Bordieri, Providence, 1956-74; judge R.I. Superior Ct., 1974—; judge Johnston (R.I.) Probate Ct., 1960-62; town solicitor Town of Johnston, 1962-70. Mem. R.I. Bar Assn., R.I. Plaintiff's Trial Lawyers Assn. (pres. 1972-73). Contbr. articles to Vanderbilt Law Rev., R.I. Bar Jour.; asst. mng. editor Vanderbilt Law Rev., 1952-53. Home: 20 Burnett St Johnston RI 02919 Office: RI Superior Ct 250 Benefit St Providence RI 02903 Tel (401) 277-3210

BOURDEAU, J. FRED, b. Great Falls, Mont., June 17, 1923; LL.B., U. Mont., 1952, J.D., 1971. Admitted to Mont. bar, 1952; adjustor United Pacific Ins. Co., 1952-54, Howard Connor Adjustors, 1954-56; individual practice law, Great Falls, 1956-75; dep. atty. Cascade County (Mont.), 1959-61, chief dep. atty., 1961-70, county atty., 1970—. Mem. Mont. State Bar Assn. Home: 24 Prospect Dr Great Falls MT 59405 Office: Cascade County Courthouse Great Falls MT 59401 Tel (406) 761-6700

BOURGEOIS, ADAM, b. Chgo., May 12, 1929; student Xavier U., 1946-48; LL.B., Loyola U., Chgo., 1951. Admitted to Ill. bar, 1951; asso. firm Brown, Brown, Cyrus & Greene, Chgo., 1951-62; adminstr. JOBS, Chgo., 1962-65; mem. cabinet Mayor A.J. Cervantes, St. Louis, 1966-68; exec. dir. Office Human Resources and mem. Gov.'s Cabinet, State of Ill., 1968-69; prof. edn. Ohio State U., 1969-72; asso. firm Howard, Taylor & Mann, Chgo., 1972-73; individual practice law, Chgo., 1973—. Mem. Ill. Bar Assn., Chgo. Council Lawyers. Home: 175 E Delaware Pl Chicago IL 60611 Office: 188 W Randolph St Chicago IL 60601 Tel (312) 332-1413

BOURNE, JUDITH LOUISE, b. N.Y.C., July 2, 1945; A.B., Cornell U., 1966; J.D., N.Y. U., 1972, LL.M. in Internat. Law, 1974. Admitted to N.Y. bar, 1972, S.C. bar, 1974, U.S. Supreme Ct. bar, 1977; asso. firm Bernard R. Fielding, Charleston, S.C., 1973-74; individual practice law, Charleston, 1974—. Chmn. rights and responsibilities Trident Forum for Handicapped, Charleston, 1975—; bd. dirs. Cannon St. YMCA, 1975-76, Charleston Vol. Action Center, 1975—. Mem. Nat. Conf. Black Lawyers (nat. co-chmn.), S.C. Black Lawyers Assn. (treas.), Am. Trial Lawyers Assn. Office: Suite 120 205 King St PO Box 2522 Charleston SC 29403 Tel (803) 722-3376

BOUTHILET, KIRBY OTTESON, b. Madison, Wis., Nov. 2, 1948; B.A. in German with honors, U. Wis., 1971, J.D., 1973. Admitted to Wis. bar, 1973; staff atty. Fort Howard Paper Co., Green Bay, Wis., 1973—, corp. sec., 1974—. Mem. Wis. State, Brown County (Wis.), Am. bar assns. Office: 1919 S Broadway Green Bay WI 54303 Tel (414) 435-8821

BOUVIER, JOHN ANDRÉ, JR., b. Marion County, Fla., May 16, 1903; A.B., U. Fla., 1928, LL.B., 1929, J.D., 1964; M.B.A., Northwestern U., 1930. Admitted to Fla. bar, 1929, U.S. Supreme Ct. bar, 1940; asso. firm Gautier, Worley & Bouvier, Miami, Fla., 1931-34, Bouvier & Green, Miami, 1934-38, Bouvier, Haskins & Goldberg, Miami, 1938-46, Bouvier, Hilliwell & McCaul, Miami, 1946-54; gen. counsel Patterson, Maloney & Frazier, Ft. Lauderdale, Fla., 1964-70; individual practice law, Ft. Lauderdale and Miami, 1970—. Chmn., Malecon Com., Miami, 1930-35; mem., sec. Dade County Zoning Bd., Miami, 1948-56, Dade County Planning Bd., 1949-56. Mem. Am., Fla., Broward County, Dade County bar assns., Am. Judicature Soc., Am. Acad. Polit. Sci. Author: Legal Aspects of Municipal Ownership, 1930. Home: 2756 NE 17th St Fort Lauderdale FL 33305 Office: 6886 NW 7th Ave Miami FL 33150 also Box 11297 Fort Lauderdale FL 33339 Tel (305) 836-1390

BOVE, JANUAR D., JR., b. Wilmington, Del., Aug. 17, 1920; B.A. with honors, U. Del., 1941; J.D., Harvard, 1948. Admitted to Del. bar, 1949, U.S. Supreme Ct. bar, 1959; partner firm Connolly, Bove & Lodge, Wilmington, 1953—; asst. city solicitor, Wilmington, 1949-50, city solicitor, 1953-57; dep. atty. gen. State of Del., 1950-53, atty. gen., 1959-62; dir. Del. Citizens' Crime Commn., 1963-70. Chmn., Del. Crusade for Freedom, 1958. Mem. Am., Del. bar assns., Del. C. of C. (past dir.). Recipient Good Govt. award Com. of '39, 1962, Wyman award Nat. Assn. Attys. Gen., 1962. Home: 714 Princeton Rd Westover Hills Wilmington DE 19807 Office: Connolly Bove & Lodge Farmers Bank Bldg Wilmington DE 19899 Tel (302) 658-9141

BOVEIA, GARY J., b. Waverly, Iowa, Sept. 18, 1942; B.A., Wartburg Coll.; J.D., U. Iowa, 1968. Admitted to Iowa bar, 1968; law clk. Iowa Supreme Ct., 1968-70; asso. firm Mosier, Thomas, Beatty, Dutton & Braun, Waverly, 1970-73; asst. atty. Black Hawk County, Iowa, 1970-73; partner firm Engelbrecht, Ackerman & Boveia, Waverly, 1974-75; individual practice law, Waverly, 1976—. Mem. Am., Iowa State bar assns. Home: 1811 Second Ave NW Waverly IA 50677 Office: 93 E Bremmer Ave Waverly IA 50677 Tel (319) 352-5900

BOWE, WILLIAM J., b. Long Branch, N.J., June 7, 1906; A.B., Fordham Coll., 1929; LL.B., Harvard, 1933. Admitted to N.Y. State bar, 1933, Mass. bar, 1946, Tenn. bar, 1949, Colo. bar, 1957; partner firm Leslie, Holt, Halstead and Frost, N.Y.C., 1933-41; asst. sec., lectr. Harvard Law Sch., 1946-48; prof. law Vanderbilt U., Nashville, 1948-56; prof. law U. Colo., Boulder, 1956—; counsel State Farm Life Ins. Co., Bloomington, Ill., 1954—. Mem. Assn. Life Ins. Counsel. Author: Tax Planning for Estates, 1949; Life Insurance and Estate Tax Planning, 1951; Estate Planning and Taxation, 1956. Home: 1401 Bluebell St Boulder CO 80302 Office: U Colo Boulder CO 80302 Tel (303) 492-6151

BOWE, WILLIAM JOHN, b. Chgo., June 23, 1942; B.A., Yale, 1964; J.D., U. Chgo., 1967. Admitted to Ill. bar, 1967; asso. firm Ross, Hardies, O'Keefe, Babcock, McDugald & Parsons, Chgo., 1967-68; with Office of Asst. Chief of Staff for Intelligence Dept. of Army, Washington, 1968-71; partner firm Roan & Grossman, Chgo., 1972—. Gen. counsel Gov.'s Task Force on Sch. Fins. State of Ill., 1975. Pres., Clarence Darrow Community Center, Chgo., 1976. Mem. Ill., Chgo. bar assns., Chgo. Council of Lawyers. Contbr. articles in field to legal jours. Office: 120 S LaSalle St Chicago IL 60603 Tel (312) 263-3600

BOWEN, CLARENCE STEELE, b. Pickens, S.C., Nov. 3, 1898; LL.B., U. S.C., 1924. Admitted to S.C. bar, 1924, U.S. Supreme Ct. bar, 1956; individual practice law, Greenville, S.C., 1924-; legal counsel Bob Jones U., Greenville, 1963-67. Mem. S.C., Greenville County bar assns. Home: 31 Riverside Dr Greenville SC 29605 Office: 708 Insurance Bldg Greenville SC 29601 Tel (803) 232-6801

BOWEN, E. HOWLAND, b. Fall River, Mass., Mar. 19, 1931; A.B., Brown U., 1952, LL.B., 1955. Admitted to R.I. bar, 1956; partner firm Hanson, Curran, Bowen & Parks, Providence, 1965-76; judge Probate Ct., Little Compton, R.I., 1972—; ins. and corporate legis. counsel R.I. Gen. Assembly, 1956—. Vice pres., counsel Little Compton (R.I.), 1975-76; vice chmn. Little Compton Conservation Commn. Mem. R.I., Am. bar assns., Am. Judicature Soc., Nat. Coll. Probate Judges, Estate Council R.I., Def. Counsel Assn. R.I., Phi Delta Phi. Home: Warren's Point Rd Little Compton RI 02837 Office: 702 Old Colony Bank Bldg Providence RI 02903 Tel (401) 272-1702

BOWEN, GLENN WILLIAM, b. Mpls., Nov. 6, 1931; A.L.A., U. Minn., 1954; B.E.E., Ill. Inst. Tech., 1960; J.D., William Mitchell Coll. Law, 1964. Admitted to Minn. bar, 1964, Ill. bar, 1971; computer design engr. Univac div. Sperry-Rand Corp., St. Paul, 1960-64; patent lawyer Nat. Cash Register Co., Dayton, Ohio, 1965-69, Sunbeam Corp., Chgo., 1970-73, Ill. Tool Works, Chgo., 1973—; instr. patent law Chase Coll. Law, Cin., 1968. Mem. Am., Chgo. bar assns., Am. Patent Law Assn. Office: 8501 W Higgins Rd Chicago IL 60631 Tel (312) 693-3040

BOWEN, ROBERT ENOCHS, b. Mpls., Feb. 28, 1924; B.A., U. Minn., 1946. J.D., 1948. Admitted to Minn. bar, 1949, U.S. Dist. Ct. bar for Dist. Minn., 1949, U.S. 8th Circuit Ct. Appeals bar, 1958, U.S. 7th Circuit Ct. Appeals bar, 1968; individual practice law, Mpls., 1949-59; partner firm Bowen, Preus, Farrell & Adams, Mpls., 1959-66, firm Gray, Plant, Mooty & Anderson, Mpls., 1966-73; judge Hennepin County (Minn.) Municipal Ct., 1973—; mem. Jud. Council Minn., 1974—; mem. Minn. Jud. Planning Commn., 1976—. Chmn. Minnetonka (Minn.) Charter Commn., 1968. Mem. Hennepin County, Minn., Am. bar assns., Am. Judges Assn., Am. Judicature Soc., Nat. Conf. Spl. Ct. Judges, Order of Coif, Phi Beta Kappa. Home: 2600 Newton Ave S Minneapolis MN 55405 Office: C-639 Government Center Minneapolis MN 55487 Tel (612) 348-4445

BOWEN, WILLARD GENE, b. Union City, Ind., Oct. 31, 1921; B.S. in Bus. Adminstrn., Ohio State U., 1947; J.D., U. Mich., 1949. Admitted to Ind. bar, 1949, asso. firm Bowen & Duning, Richmond, Ind., 1949-55, firm Bowen & O'Maley, Richmond, 1955-66; asso. and pres. firm Bowen, Cecere, O'Maley & Tripp, and predecessors, Richmond, 1967—; mem. Ind. Gen. Assembly, 1955-57. Mem. Wayne County, Ind. State, Am. bar assns. Home: 174 Minneman Rd Richmond IN 47374 Office: 101 S 10th St Richmond IN 47374 Tel (317) 966-5521

BOWENS, JOHN MICHAEL, b. Jersey City, Jan. 21, 1949; A.B., U. Notre Dame, 1970; J.D., Georgetown U., 1973. Admitted to N.J. bar, 1974; law clk. U.S. Dist. Ct. for N.J.; asst. U.S. atty., Newark, 1974—; aide to U.S. Rep. D. U. Daniels, 1972. Home: 130 New Rd Apt D-15 Parsippany NJ 07054 Office: 970 Broad St Suite 500 Newark NJ 07102 Tel (201) 645-2395

BOWER, MORRIS LEWIS, b. Auksta Dvaris, Lithuania, Jan. 31, 1896; A.B., Harvard U., 1918, LL.B., 1921. Admitted to N.Y. bar, 1922; asso. firm Pitkin, Rosensohn & Henderson, N.Y.C., 1922-26; individual practice law, N.Y.C., 1926—. Mem. N.Y. County Lawyers Assn. Office: 10 Columbus Circle New York City NY 10019 Tel (212) 765-0624

BOWER, PAUL GEORGE, b. Chgo., Apr. 21, 1933; B.A., Rice U., 1955; postgrad. Calif. Inst. Tech., 1959; LL.B., Stanford, 1963. Admitted to Calif. bar, 1964, U.S. Supreme Ct. bar, 1969; asso. firm Gibson, Dunn & Crutcher, Los Angeles, 1963-67, partner, 1969—; asso. dir. Nat. Advisory Commn. on Civil Disorders, Washington, 1967-68; spl. asst. to dep. atty. gen. Dept. Justice, Washington, 1968; consumer counsel, 1969; speaker profl. seminars. Bd. dirs. Legal Aid Found. of Los Angeles, 1975—. Mem. State Bar Calif., Los Angeles County, Am. (Commn. to Study Fed. Trade Commn.) bar assns., Order of Coif. Contbr. articles to profl. jours. Office: 515 S Flower St Los Angeles CA 90071 Tel (213) 488-7538

BOWER, TERRY LEE, b. Akron, Ohio, Oct. 18, 1942; B.S. in Accounting, U. Akron, 1967, J.D., 1971. Admitted to Ohio bar, 1971; mgr. accounting Babcock & Wilcox, Barberton, Ohio, 1970-71; atty. div. contracts, Canton, Ohio, 1971-73, mgr. div. contracts, N. Canton, 1973-76, gen. counsel, Barberton, 1976—. Small bus. solicitor United Fund, Akron, 1967-70; mgr. Little League, 1968-69. Mem. Akron, Ohio bar assns. Home: 446 Yager Rd Clinton OH 44216 Office: 20 S Van Buren St Barberton OH 44203 Tel (216) 753-4511

BOWERMAN, DONALD BRADLEY, b. Portland, Oreg., Aug. 15, 1934; student Oreg. State U., 1953, Portland State U., 1955, Lewis & Clark Coll., 1959; J.D., Northwestern Sch. Law, 1959. Admitted to Oreg. bar, 1959, U.S. Supreme Ct. bar, 1971, U.S. Dist. Ct. Dist. Oreg., 1959; dist. atty. Clackamas County, Oreg., 1960; individual practice law, Portland, 1963-67, Oregon City, Oreg., 1967—; partner firm Hibbard, Caldwell, Canning, Bowerman & Schultz; gov. Oreg. State Bar. Chmn. bd. West Linn (Oreg.) Sch. Dist., 1965-76. Mem. Clackamas County (pres. 1968), Am., Oreg., Lawyer Pilots bar assns., Assn. Trial Lawyers Am., Oreg. Council Sch. Attys., Oreg. Trial Lawyers Assn. Home: 1285 S Marylhurst Dr West Linn OR 97068 Office: 710 Center St Oregon City OR 97045 Tel (503) 656-5207

BOWERS, CHARLES HOWARD, III, b. Washington, Feb. 6, 1943; B.S., Auburn U., 1965; J.D. with honors, Emory U., 1968. Admitted to Ga. bar, 1968, Fla. bar, 1969; asso. firm Jones, Paine and Foster, W. Palm Beach, Fla., 1968-70; sr. atty. Sears, Roebuck Co., Atlanta, 1970—; judge adv. officer JAGC, USAR, 1972-75; counsel Child Service Family Counselling Center, Atlanta, 1974—. Office: Sears Roebuck Co 675 Ponce de Leon Ave NE Annex 95 Atlanta GA 30395 Tel (404) 885-3873

BOWERS, QUINTON R., b. Samson, Ala., Mar. 20, 1921; B.S., U. Ala., 1949; LL.B., Birmingham Sch. Law, 1955, J.D., 1968. Admitted to Ala. bar, 1956; individual practice law, Birmingham, Ala., 1957—; mem. Ho. of Reps. from Jefferson County, Ala., 1963-75. Home: 1528 Shades Crest Rd Birmingham AL 35226 Office: 426 Woodward Bldg Birmingham AL 35203 Tel (205) 323-2445

BOWERS, WILLIAM MARVIN, JR., b. Albuquerque, Feb. 23, 1926; B.B.A., U. Ga., 1948; J.D., Woodrow Wilson Coll., 1968, LL.M., 1969. Admitted to Ga. bar, 1969; partner firm Beasley, Bowers & Burke, P.C., Atlanta. Mem. Broad River Dist. Bar Assn. Recipient Silver Beaver award Boy Scouts Am. Home: 2358 Parkview Circle College Park GA 20337 Office: 830 W Peachtree St Suite 205 Atlanta GA 30308 Tel (404) 881-8761

BOWIE, PETER WENTWORTH, b. Alexandria, Va., Sept. 27, 1942; B.A., Wake Forest Coll., 1964; J.D., U. San Diego, 1971. Admitted to Calif. bar, 1972, D.C. bar, 1972; trial atty. Dept. Justice, Washington, 1971-74; asst. U.S. Atty. So. Dist. Calif., San Diego, 1974—; lectr., instr. Atty. Gen.'s Advocacy Inst. Mem. Calif., D.C., Am., Fed., San Diego (cons. Fed. Ct. Civil Com. 1975, chmn. 1976-77) bar assns. Office: 940 Front St Room 5-N 19 San Diego CA 92189 Tel (714) 293-5658

BOWIE, WILLIAM BEALL, b. Largo, Md., Aug. 8, 1913; A.B., U. Md., 1936; LL.B., Georgetown U., 1939; grad. Nat. Coll. State Trail Judges, Boulder, Colo., 1964; postgrad. in criminal law and sentencing Nat. Coll. State Judiciary, Reno, 1973. Admitted to D.C. bar, 1940, Md. bar, 1946; atty. investigator Dept. Agr., Phila. and N.Y.C., 1941-42; adjudicator VA, Washington, 1945-46; practiced in Upper Marlboro, Md., 1946-61; asso. judge Md. 7th Jud. Circuit, 1961—; examiner in chancery Circuit Ct. Prince George County, Md., 1949-61; mem. Bd. Property Rev., Prince George County, 1958-61; chmn. Md. Jud. Conf., 1967—. Mem. Prince George's County Bd. Trade, 1959-63. Mem. Prince George's County, Md. State, Am. bar assns., Nat. Conf. State Trial Judges, Am. Judicature Soc., Supreme Ct. Hist. Soc., Am. Legion, Prince George's County C. of C., Vansville Farmers Club (pres. 1976). Recipient Distinguished Service award Georgetown U. Law Center, 1973. Home: 1705 Largo Rd Upper Marlboro MD 20870 Office: Courthouse Main St Upper Marlboro MD 20870 Tel (301) 952-3766

BOWLER, CLARA ANN, b. Green Bay, Wis., Dec. 4, 1941; B.A., U. Chgo., 1963, M.A.T., 1965; J.D., DePaul U., 1969. Admitted to Ill. bar, 1969; staff atty. OEO Legal Aid, Chgo., 1969-72; research asst. U. Chgo Law Sch., 1972—. Mem. Am., Ill. bar assns. Co-editor U. Chgo. lit. mag., 1975—; author The Henry C. Simon Papers, 1973; contbr. articles profl. journs. Home: 1700 E 56th St Apt 507 Chicago IL 60637

BOWLES, GORDON GRIFFITH, b. Pitts., July 25, 1947; B.A., William Penn Coll., 1969; J.D., Drake U., 1972. Admitted to Iowa bar, 1972; asst. atty. gen. State of Iowa, 1972-73; asso. firm Rogers & Phillips, Des Moines, 1973-74; partner firm Denman, Albers, Judkins & Bowles, Des Moines, 1974—. Lt. gov. Kiwanis Internat., 1976—; trustee William Penn Coll. Mem. Am., Iowa, Polk County bar assns., Phi Alpha Delta, Alpha Chi. Office: Suite 330 Key Bldg Des Moines IA 50309 Tel (515) 288-2161

BOWLES, JAMES GORDON, b. Oakland, Calif., Dec. 16, 1934; B.S., U. Calif., Berkeley, 1957, J.D., Hastings Coll. Law, San Francisco, 1961. Admitted to Calif. bar, 1962; dep. dist. atty. Kern County (Calif.), 1962-63; partner firm Gill & Bowles, Bakersfield, Calif., 1963-69; individual practice law, Bakersfield, 1969-74; sr. partner firm Bowles & Etcheverry, Bakersfield, 1974—. Pres. Boys' Club of Bakersfield, 1969. Mem. State Bar Calif., Kern County Bar Assn. (1st v.p.), Am. Trial Lawyers Assn. Office: 1415 18th St suite 706 Bakersfield CA 93301 Tel (805) 327-7376

BOWLES, RICHARD BAKER, b. Chgo., Sept. 25, 1946; B.A., DePauw U., 1968; J.D., Northwestern U., 1971. Admitted to Ohio bar, 1972; asso. firm Squire, Sanders & Dempsey, Cleve., 1971—. Mem. Greater Cleve., Ohio, Am. bar assns. Home: 3551 Lytle Rd Shaker Heights OH 44122 Office: 1800 Union Commerce Bldg Cleveland OH 44115 Tel (216) 696-9200

BOWLING, W. KERBY, b. Memphis, May 2, 1927; J.D., U. Miss. Admitted to Miss. bar, 1950, Tenn. bar, 1953; indsl. relations coordinator Ford Motor Co., Memphis, 1959; with Kullman & Lang, New Orleans, 1960-63; partner firm Bowling & Jackson, Memphis, 1963—. Mem. Am. Arbitration Assn. (arbitrator), Phi Alpha Delta. Recipient Freed Found. award, 1961. Home: 343 Clove Dr Memphis TN 38137 Office: Clark Tower Suite 1212 5100 Poplar Ave Memphis TN 38137 Tel (901) 682-7631

BOWMAN, KEN, b. Chgo., Dec. 15, 1942; B.S., U. Wis., J.D. Admitted to Wis. bar, 1971; v.p., negotiator Nat. Football League Players Assn., 1970-72; asso. firms Morris, Vanden, Heuvel and Basten, De Pere, Wis., 1971-72, Winner, McCallum and Hendee, Madison, Wis., 1973-74; partner firm Bowman, Lingl & Matyas, De Pere, 1975—. Wis. chmn. Mentally Retarded, 1972; candidate for Wis. Senate, 1976. Home: Rural Route 3 De Pere WI 54115 Office: 366 Main Ave De Pere WI 54115 Tel (414) 336-3437

BOWMAN, PEYTON GRAHAM, III, b. Richmond, Va., Feb. 3, 1929; B.A., U. Va., 1952, LL.B., 1953. Admitted to Va. bar, 1952, D.C. bar, 1958, U.S. Supreme Ct. bar, 1966; served as 1st lt. JAGC, U.S. Army, 1953-56; asso. firm Reid & Priest, Washington, now partner. Mem. Fed. Power Bar (treas. 1963-65), Am. Bar Assn. Home: 4940 Hillbrook Ln NW Washington DC 20016 Office: 1701 K St NW Washington DC 20006

BOWMER, JIM DEWITT, b. Temple, Tex., May 4, 1919; A.A., Temple Jr. Coll., 1938; B.A. cum laude, Baylor U., 1940, LL.B. cum laude, 1942. Admitted to Tex. bar, 1942, U.S. Supreme Ct. bar, 1966; mem. firm Bowmer, Courtney, Burleson & Pemberton, Temple; lectr. Baylor U. Law Sch., 1949-50, 56-57; county atty. Bell County, 1946-47. Mem. Battleship Tex. Commn., 1963-70; pres. Tex. chpt. Nature Conservancy, Inc., 1971-72; past chmn. bd. Pythian Children's Home, Weatherford, Tex.; bd. dirs. Nat. Park Found., 1968-69, Tex. Hist. Found., 1968-74; trustee Mary Hardin Baylor Coll.; past regent, v.p. bd. regents Temple Jr. Coll.; founder, 1st pres. Evang. Found.; founder, sec. Temple Indsl. Found. Fellow Tex. Bar Found.; mem. Am., Tex. (chmn. bd. dirs. 1970-71, pres. 1972-73), Bell-Lampasas-Mills Counties (pres. 1954-55) bar assns., Am. Law Inst., Am. Judicature Soc., Tex. Assn. Def. Counsel, Baylor Law Alumni Assn. (pres. 1962-63), Baylor Ex-Students Assn. (dir. 1962-63), Temple C. of C. (past pres.), Phi Alpha Delta. Contbr. articles to profl. jours. Home: Box 120 Rural Route 2 Killeen TX 76541 Office: First Fed Savs Bldg PO Box 844 Temple TX 76501 Tel (817) 778-1355

BOWNES, HUGH HENRY, b. N.Y.C., Mar. 10, 1920; B.A., Columbia, 1941, LL.B., 1948. Admitted to N.H. bar, 1948, since practiced in Laconia; partner firm Nighswander, Lord & Bownes, 1951-66; asso. justice N.H. Superior Ct., 1966-68; U.S. dist. ct. judge, Concord, N.H., 1968—. Mem. Laconia City Council, 1953-57; chmn. Laconia Democratic Com., 1954-57; mayor, Laconia, 1963-65; mem. Dem. Nat. Com. from N.H., 1963-66. Chmn., Laconia chpt. A.R.C., 1951-52; pres. bd. Laconia Hosp. Assn., 1963-64. Decorated Silver Star. Mem. Am., N.H., Belknap County (pres. 1965—) bar assns., Laconia C. of C. (past pres.). Home: 4 Poor Richard's Dr Concord NH 03301 Office: Fed Courthouse Concord NH 03301*

BOWSER, CHARLES JOSEPH, b. Cambridge, Mass., Aug. 2, 1945; A.B., Boston Coll., 1967, J.D., 1970. Admitted to Mass. bar, 1970, U.S. Dist. Ct. bar Dist. Mass., 1970, U.S. Ct. Appeals bar 1st Circuit, 1973; asso. firm Warner & Stackpole, Boston, 1970-76; partner firm Atwood & Wright, Boston, 1976—. Mem. Am., Mass. bar assns. Home: 210 Concord Rd Sudbury MA 01776 Office: Mason House 211 Commonwealth Ave Boston MA 02116 Tel (617) 267-9600

BOWYTZ, ROBERT BERNARD, b. Pitts., Apr. 21, 1938; B.S., Pa. State U., 1959; J.D., U. Pitts., 1962; LL.M., George Washington U., 1969. Admitted to Pa. bar, 1962, U.S. Supreme Ct. bar, 1967, D.C. bar, 1968, Md. bar, 1976; served with JAGC, U.S. Army, 1963-66; atty., advisor Office of Counsel, Naval Air Systems Command, 1967-69; individual practice law, Washington, 1969, now partner firm Ebert & Bowytz, Washington; legis. cons. Model Procurement Code for State and Local Govts., Washington, 1975—; gen. counsel Am. Assn. Small Research Cos., 1975—. Mem. Am., Fed., Pa., D.C., Md. bar assns., Nat. Contract Mgmt. Assn., D.C. Bar, Judge Adv. Gens. Assn. Asso. editor Comml. Law Jour., 1973-75. Office: 2000 L St NW Washington DC 20036 Tel (202) 659-3408

BOX, DAVID ALLEN, b. Muskogee, Okla., Apr. 30, 1945; A.A., Bacone Coll., 1966; B.A., Tulsa U., 1968, J.D., 1972. Admitted to Okla. bar, 1973; atty. Tulsa County Legal Aid Soc., 1973; asso. firm Eversele & Settle, Muskogee, Okla., 1974-76; asst. dist. atty., Muskogee County, 1975; municipal judge, Town of Haskell, Okla., 1974-76, Town of Ft. Gibson, Okla., 1976; individual practice law, Muskogee, 1976—. Mem. Am., Okla. bar assns. Home: POB G104 Haskell OK 74436 Office: 440 Court St Muskogee OK 74401 Tel (918) 683-6561

BOX, DWAIN DURWOOD, b. Stuart, Okla., Sept. 15, 1916; LL.B., Cumberland U., 1940. Admitted to Okla. bar, 1940; individual practice law, Oklahoma City, 1940-56; judge Ct. of Common Pleas Okla. County, Oklahoma City, 1956-69; asso. judge Dist. Ct. Okla. County, Div. 2, Oklahoma City, 1969-71; judge Okla. Ct. of Appeals, Div. 1, Oklahoma City, 1971—; mem. Okla. Ho. of Reps., 1947-49. Sec., Okla. County Election Bd., 1953-56. Mem. Okla. County Bar Assn., Okla. Jud. Conf., Oklahoma City C. of C. Home: 4805 N Linn St Oklahoma City OK 73107 Office: Rm 210-A State Capitol Bldg Oklahoma City OK 73105 Tel (405) 521-3751

BOXELL, EARL FRANCIS, b. Marion, Ind., Dec. 3, 1894; B.A., U. Mich., 1921, J.D., 1923. Admitted to Ind. bar, 1921, Ohio bar, 1923; mem. firm Tracy, Chapman & Welles, and successors, Toledo, 1923-43; mem. firm Boxell, Bebout, Torbet & Potter, and predecessors, Toledo, 1943-74. Mem. Maumee (Ohio) City Council, 1948-58, pres., 1954-58. Mem. Am., Ohio, Toledo (pres. 1961) bar assns., Am., Ohio bar founds., Phi Alpha Delta, Delta Sigma Rho, Am. Legion (post comdr. 1940). Home: 1718 N Cove Blvd Toledo OH 43606 Office: 245 N Summit St Toledo Trust Bldg Toledo OH 43604

BOXER, DANIEL ELLIS, b. Newburyport, Mass., Sept. 13, 1945; B.A., Bowdoin Coll., 1967; J.D., Cornell U., 1970. Admitted to Maine bar, 1970; asso. firm Pierce, Atwood, Scribner, Allen & McKusici, Portland, Maine, 1970-76, partner, 1976—. Mem. fin. com. Maine State Democratic Com., 1976—; mem. Cumberland County Dem. Com., 1976—; active United Fund; mem. exec. com. Pine Tree council Boy Scouts Am. Mem. Am., Maine bar assns., Am. Arbitration Assn. (panel). Contbr. articles to legal jours. Home: 19 Hunts Point Rd Cape Elizabeth ME 04107 Office: One Monument Sq Portland ME 04111 Tel (207) 773-6411

BOYAZIS, JAMES, b. Warren, Ohio, Aug. 13, 1936; B.E. in Indsl. Engring., Youngstown State U., 1958; J.D., U. Akron, 1966. Admitted to Ohio bar, 1967; indsl. engr. Republic Steel Corp., Warren, 1959-62; indsl. engr. Goodyear Aerospace Corp., Akron, 1962-65, systems analyst Goodyear Tire & Rubber Co., Akron, 1965-68, indsl. engr. Goodyear Internat. Corp., Salonika, Greece, 1969-71; mgr. adminstrn. sec.'s office Goodyear Tire & Rubber Co., Akron, 1971—. Advisory com. E. Akron YMCA, 1973—; v.p., trustee Annunciation Ch., Akron, 1975—; mem. Akron U. Small Bus. Advisory Commn., 1974-75; Northeastern Ohio Med. Sch. Consortium Com., Akron, 1975. Mem. Akron Bar Assn. Home: 3753 Chesterfield Dr Akron OH 44319 Office: 1144 E Market St Akron OH 44316 Tel (216) 794-2906

BOYCE, LEROY CLIFFORD, b. Tacoma, Oct. 9, 1942; A.B. in Polit. Sic., U. Wash., Seattle, 1965, J.D., 1968. Admitted to Wash. bar, 1969; law clk. Judge Warren Chan, King County Superior Ct., Seattle, 1968; asst. city atty. Tacoma, 1969-70; mem. firm Estes, Damis & Boyce, Tacoma, 1971-74; chief civil dep. pros. atty. Pierce County, Tacoma, 1975—. Democratic state committeeman Pierce County, 1975-76; pres. Tacoma-Pierce County chpt. ACLU, 1973, v.p., 1972, 74; mem. state bd. ACLU of Wash., 1971-72. Mem. Wash. State, Tacoma-Pierce County (mem. bd. trustees 1975, chmn. pub. relations sect. 1974, pres. Young Lawyers Sect. 1975, v.p. 1976), Am. bar assns., Am., Wash. State trial lawyers assns., Wash. State Assn. Municipal Attys. Home: 12761 Gravelly Lake Dr SW Tacoma WA 98499 Office: 946 County City Bldg Tacoma WA 98402 Tel (206) 593-4224

BOYCE, RONALD NELSON, b. Salt Lake City, Sept. 5, 1933; B.S.L., U. Utah, 1955; J.D., 1957. Admitted to Utah bar, 1956; served with JAG Gen.'s Dept., USAF, 1957-60; asst. deputy chief asst., Utah Arry. Gen's Office, 1960-66; asso. firm Clyde, Mecham & Pratt, Salt Lake City, 1960-66; spl. dep. Balt. Lake County Atty's Office, 1971—; prof. of law U. Utah, 1966—. Mem. Utah Commn. on Indian Affairs, 1960-66; personal counsel Gov. George Dewey Clyde, 1961; U.S. Commr. Dist. of Utah, 1966-69; mem. state counsel Criminal Justice Adminstrn., 1961-64. Mem. Order of Coif, Selden Soc., Am., Utah bar assns. Author: Utah Prosecutor Handbook, 1973; Utah Prosecutor Handbook Revised Edition, 1975; numerous law review articles. Office: College of Law University of Utah Salt Lake City UT 84112 Tel (801) 581-7358

BOYD, ALAN WILSON, b. Indpls., Mar. 11, 1897; A.B., U. Mich., 1918, J.D., 1921. Admitted to Ind. bar, 1921, U.S. Supreme Ct. bar, 1934; partner firm Noel, Hickam & Boyd, Indpls., 1923-26, firm Noel, Hickam, Boyd & Armstrong, Indpls., 1926-40, firm Barnes, Hickam, Pantzer & Boyd, Indpls., 1940—; mem., sec. Ind. State Bd. Bar Examiners, 1937-42. Mem. Indpls. Sch. Bd., 1935-39, pres., 1938. Mem. Am. Law Inst. (life), Am., 7th Circuit, Ind., Indpls. (pres. 1948) bar assns., Order of Coif. Home: 4000 N Meridian St Indianapolis IN 46208 Office: 1313 Merchants Bank Bldg Indianapolis IN 46204 Tel (317) 638-1313

BOYD, ARTHUR ELLIOTT, b. Plainview, Tex., Sept. 15, 1921; A.A., Glendale Coll., 1940; A.B. magna cum laude, U. So. Calif., 1942; LL.B., U. So. Calif., 1947. Admitted to Calif. bar, 1947; individual practice law, Mill Valley, Calif., 1961—; mng. editor Calif.

Points and Authorities, Calif. Forms Pleading and Practice, Matthew Bender Co., San Francisco, 1962-68; mng. editor Calif. Supreme Ct. and Calif. Cts. Appeal Ofcl. Reports, Bancroft-Whitney Co., San Francisco, 1970—. Mem. Calif. State Bar, Phi Beta Kappa, Phi Kappa Phi. Home: 908 Vernal Way Mill Valley CA 94941 Office: Bancroft-Whitney Law Pub Co 301 Brannan St San Francisco CA 94107 also 908 Vernal Way Mill Valley CA 94941 Tel (415) 986-4410 also (415) 388-2092

BOYD, FLETCHER EMERSON, b. Indpls., Dec. 28, 1914; A.B., Franklin Coll. of Ind., 1936; J.D., U. Mich., 1939. Admitted to Ind. bar, 1939; partner firm Locke, Reynolds, Boyd & Weisell, Indpls., 1939—. Fellow Am. Coll. Trial Lawyers; mem. Internat. Assn. Ins. Counsel, Am. (ho. of dels. 1976-77), Ind. State, Indpls. (pres. 1977) bar assns. Home: 1403 W 52d St Indianapolis IN 46208 Office: One Indiana Sq Suite 2120 Indianapolis IN 46204 Tel (317) 639-5534

BOYD, JOHN THOMAS, b. Plainview, Tex., Aug. 28, 1927; student Va. Mil. Inst., 1944-45; B.A., Baylor U., J.D., 1950. Admitted to Tex. bar, 1950; partner firm Morehead, Sharp & Boyd, 1957-69; judge Dist. Ct., 64th Jud. Dist. Tex., 1969—; mem. legis. com. Tex. Jud. Conf.; lectr. Tex. Def. Lawyers, 1976. Pres. Plainview (Tex.) Ind. Bd. Trustees, 1968-69. Mem. State Bar Tex., Plainview (pres.), 64th Jud. Dist. (pres.) bar assns. Home: 1411 W 11th St Plainview TX 79072 Office: County Courthouse Plainview TX 79072 Tel (806) 296-5810

BOYD, LON VERNON, b. Kingsport, Tenn., Aug. 15, 1928; B.S., East Tenn. State U., 1951; LL.B., U. Tenn., 1957, J.D., 1957. Admitted to Tenn. bar, 1957; individual practice law, Kingsport, 1957-61; partner firm Boyd, Lauderback & Snodgrass and predecessor, Kingsport, 1961—; judge Sullivan County (Tenn.) Ct., 1966—. Chmn. Tri-County Indsl. Park of Sullivan County, 1976—; pres., chmn. bd. Kingsport City Mission, 1976—; mem. exec. com. 1st Tenn.-Va. Devel. Dist. Mem. Kingsport, Tenn. bar assns., Tenn. Trial Lawyers Assn. Named Outstanding Young Man of Year Kingsport Jaycees, 1964. Home: 3352 Fort Henry Dr Kingsport TN 37664 Office: 434 Shelby St Kingsport TN 37660 Tel (615) 246-2101

BOYD, RALPH CYRIL, b. Balt., Jan. 21, 1927; J.D., U. Balt., 1955. Admitted to Md. bar, 1955, U.S. Supreme Ct. bar, 1960; trial judge dist. ct. level Anne Arundel County (Md.), 1959-63; individual practice law, Glen Burnie, Md., 1955—; atty. Anne Arundel County Election Bd., 1968-70. Mem. Am. Trial Lawyers Assn., Md., Anne Arundel County bar assns. Home:

BOYD, RANDALL, b. Whittier, Calif., July 7, 1900. Admitted to Calif. bar, 1925; with Security Pacific Nat. Bank, Los Angeles, 1916-65, gen. counsel, 1940-65, v.p., 1940-65, sec., 1929-65, ret., 1965; dir. So. Realty Co. Bd. dirs. Lung Assn. Orange County (Calif.), 1972, Mental Health Assn. Orange County, 1972; bd. dirs., sec. Saddleback Community Hosp., Laguna Hills, Calif., 1974, Info. and Referral Service, Los Angeles County. Mem. Calif. State Bar, Los Angeles County Bar Assn., Am. Soc. Corp. Secs. (nat. pres. 1963-64). Contbr. articles to Bankers Monthly, Nat. Auditgram, Calif. Banker. Home: 326-A Avenida Carmel Laguna Hills CA 92653 Tel (714) 837-3055

BOYD, ROBERT KENNETH, b. Elkton, Md., Aug. 10, 1934; A.B., Washington Coll., Chestertown, Md., 1956; LL.B., U. Balt., 1965. Admitted to Md. bar, 1966; individual practice law, Elkton, 1966—; trial magistrate Town of North East (Md.), 1971-72. Bd. dirs. Cecil County (Md.) YMCA; senator Jr. Chamber Internat. Mem. Cecil County (sec. 1966—), Md. bar assns., Greater Elkton Jaycees (Best Com. Chmn. 1970, 71), Am. Judicature Soc., North East C. of C. (pres. 1968-69). Named Outstanding Young Man of Year Cecil County Jaycees, 1970. Home: Shady Beach Farm RD 2 PO Box 196 North East MD 21901 Office: 140 1/2 E Main St Elkton MD 21921 Tel (301) 398-0606

BOYD, SCOTT MACKINNON, b. Lakewood, Ohio, June 26, 1948; B.A., U. Wis., 1970, J.D., 1973. Admitted to Wis. bar, 1973, Ill. bar, 1974; asst. dist. atty., Sheboygan, Wis., 1973-76; asso. firm Barrick, Jackson, Switzer, Long & Balsley, Rockford, Ill., 1976—; chief law clk. div. criminal investigation Wis. Dept. Justice, Madison, 1971-73. Mem. State Bar Wis., Ill., Winnebago County bar assns., Wis. Dist. Attys. Assn. Home: 913 N Main St Rockford IL 61103 Office: 228 S Main St Rockford IL 61101 Tel (815) 962-6611

BOYENS, BRUCE, b. Los Angeles, May 7, 1945; B.A., Western Mich. U., 1970; J.D., U. Ky., 1972. Admitted to W.Va. bar, 1973; counsel United Mine Workers Am. Dist. 17, Charleston, W.Va., 1973-76; head gate man longwall mining system Armco Steel number 7 Mine, Montcoal, W.Va., 1975—. Address: Box 41 Sharon WV 25182 Tel (304) 595-5909

BOYER, BENJAMIN FRANKLIN, b. St. Joseph, Mo., Sept. 17, 1904; student U. Va., 1922-24; A.B., U. Mo., 1926, J.D., 1928; LL.M., Columbia, 1941; LL.D., Waynesburg Coll., 1952, Dickinson Coll., 1959. Admitted to Mo. bar, 1928, Pa. bar, 1950; asst. atty. Mo. State Hys. Commn., 1928-33; mem. firm Otto & Boyer, Washington, Mo., 1933-37; asso. prof. law U. Kansas City, 1937-41, prof., 1941-47; dean U. Kansas City Sch. Law, 1940-47; prof. law Temple U., 1947-69. 1947-69, dean, 1947-65; prof. law Hastings Coll., U. Calif., 1969—. Chmn. Kansas City Personnel Bd., 1946-47; pres. Legal Aid Soc. Phila., 1960-69; mem. Mayor's Com. on Labor Relations, Phila.; mem. Pa. Gov. Commn. on Labor Relations, Harrisburg. Mem. Am., Phila., San Francisco bar assns., Nat. Acad. Arbitrators, Phi Beta Kappa, Phi Delta Phi, Order of Coif. Recipient Arthur V. Briesen medal Nat. Legal Aid and Defder Assn., 1968. Editor: (with others) Selected Readings on Legal Profession, 1962. Home: 2030 Vallejo St San Francisco CA 94123 Office: 198 Mc Allister St San Francisco CA 94120 Tel (415) 557-3204

BOYER, ROBERT MALCOLM, b. Omaha, Dec. 23, 1918; B.A., U. Chgo., 1940, J.D., 1948. Admitted to Ill. bar, 1948; atty. Fed. Trade Commn., Chgo., 1948-53, Leo Burnett Co., Inc., Chgo., 1953—. Mem. Chgo. Bar Assn. Home: 1163 Tower Rd Winnetka IL 60093 Office: Prudential Plaza Chicago IL 60601 Tel (312) 236-5959

BOYER, SPENCER HARRY, b. West Chester, Pa., Sept. 23, 1938; B.S.E.E., Howard U., 1960; LL.B., George Washington U., 1965; LL.M., Harvard U., 1966. Asso. engr. IBM, Endicott, N.Y., 1960-63, 63; patent examiner Patent Office, U.S. Dept. Commerce, Washington, 1964-65; prof. law Howard U., 1966—; admitted to D.C. bar, 1967; vis. prof. U. Fla., 1968, U. Iowa, 1977; distinguished lectr. U. Buffalo Sch. Law, 1970; nat. chmn. Caucus Black Law Tchrs., 1969-70; reporter Law Revision Commn. D.C., 1977. Mem. Am. Council on Edn. (permanent mem. com. taxation), Nat. Acad. Sci.-NRC, Nat., D.C. bar assns., Am. Trial Lawyers Assn., Assn. Am. Law Schs. Contbr. articles to profl. publs. Home: 8305 Oakford Pl Silver Spring MD 20910 Office: Howard U Sch Law 2935 Upton St NW Washington DC 20008 Tel (202) 686-6422

BOYERS, MARTIN ROGER, b. Jersey City, Apr. 28, 1944; B.A. (Henry Rutgers scholar), Rutgers U., 1966; J.D., Calif. Western U., 1969. Admitted to Nev. bar, 1971; law clk. firm Cromer & Barker, Las Vegas, 1971; asso. firm Lionel, Sawyer, Collins & Wartman, 1971-73; staff Clark County (Nev.) Pub. Defender's Office, 1973-75; individual practice law, Las Vegas, 1975—; counsel Clark County Community Corrections, Inc., Las Vegas, 1975—. Mem. Nev. Bar Assn. Winner Bronze medal U.S. Masters Nat. AAU swimming championships, 1974. Office: 401 S 3d St Las Vegas NV 89101 Tel (702) 382-6711

BOYKIN, HAMILTON HAIGHT, b. N.Y.C., Feb. 3, 1939; A.B., Trinity Coll., Hartford, Conn., 1961; LL.M., Georgetown U., 1964. Admitted to Va. bar, 1964, D.C. bar, 1965; asso. firm Colton & Boykin, Washington, 1964-70, partner, 1970—; speaker in field. Mem. D.C. Bar Assn. Contbr. articles to profl. jours. Home: 15112 Redgate Dr Silver Spring MD 20904 Office: 1133 15th St NW Washington DC 20005 Tel (202) 872-8240

BOYKIN, LYKES MULLER, b. Lamar, S.C., Dec. 6, 1919; B.S. in Commerce, Presbyn. Coll., Clinton, S.C., 1940; LL.B., Georgetown U., 1948. Admitted to D.C., S.C. bars, 1948; asso. firm Cleary, Gottlieb, Friendly & Cox, Washington, 1949-51; asso. counsel Fed. CD Adminstrn., Washington, 1951-53; partner firm Boykin & De Francis, Washington, 1953-73, firm Colton & Boykin, Washington, 1974-76; chmn. bd. Boykin Corp., Washington, 1973—; pres. Panorama Real Estate, Inc., McLean, Va., 1975—. Mem. Am., D.C. bar assns., Kappa Alpha, Delta Theta Phi. Office: 600 New Hampshire Ave Washington DC 20037 Tel (202) 338-4860

BOYLAN, ALFRED GEORGE, b. Plattsburgh, N.Y., July 26, 1917; A.B., Georgetown U., 1939; J.D., Harvard, 1942. Admitted to N.Y. bar, 1942; asso. law firm Nixon, Hargrave, Middleton & Devans, Rochester, N.Y., 1946-51; pvt. practice law, Rochester, N.Y., 1951-66; partner law firm Middleton-Wilson (and predecessor firms), Rochester, N.Y., 1966—. Mem. Monroe County (mem. real estate com. 1971-72), N.Y. State, Am. bar assns., Am. Arbitration Assn. Home: 350 Ambassador Dr Rochester NY 14610 Office: 900 Midtown Tower Rochester NY 14604

BOYLE, GEORGE ARTHUR, b. Meadow, Utah, Feb. 16, 1930; B.S., Los Angeles City Coll., 1959; LL.M., Van Norman U., 1965. Admitted to Calif. bar, U.S. Supreme Ct. bar, 1970, U.S. Dist. Ct. bar, U.S. Ct. of Appeals bar; Counsel Comml. Trade Bur. Calif., Bakersfield, Video Telephonics, Sivad Corp., Learning Inst. for Fibrotic/Metabolic Disease Edn., 1970—, also Am. Thermal Resources, Chgo.; asso. counsel Calvary Bible Church Corp.; regional counsel Am. Nat. Ins. Co. Fellow Roscoe Pound Found.; mem. Am., Los Angeles County, Kern County (dir.) bar assns., Calif. Applicant Attys. Assn., Calif., Los Angeles trial lawyers' assns., Calif. Attys. Criminal Justice, Am. Arbitration Assn. (arbitrator), Assn. Trial Lawyers Am., Am. Judicature Soc., Themis Soc. Contbr. articles in field to profl. jours. Office: POB 2366 Bakersfield CA 93303 Tel (805) 327-2531

BOYLE, JAMES BARRETT, b. Ogden, Utah, Jan. 16, 1904; A.B., U. Mich., 1925, J.D., 1927. Admitted to Calif. bar, 1928; asso. firm Cruikshank, Brooke & Evans, Pasadena, Calif., 1927-37, partner, 1937-41; partner firm Evans & Boyle, Pasadena, 1941-45; partner firm Boyle, Holmes & Garrett, Pasadena, 1945-50; partner firm Boyle, Atwill & Robinson and predecessor, Los Angeles and Pasadena, 1950—. Fellow Am. Bar Found.; mem. Pasadena (pres. 1950), Los Angeles County, Am., Internat. bar assns., State Bar Calif. (bd. govs. 1957-60, v.p. 1960). Home: 570 B Orange Grove Circle Pasadena CA 91105 Office: 170 S Euclid Ave Pasadena CA 91101 Tel (213) 796-7181

BOYLE, JOHN FRANCIS, b. Newton, Mass., Sept. 4, 1933; B.S. cum laude, Boston Coll., 1956; J.D., Suffolk U., 1968; LL.M., Boston U., 1974. Admitted to Mass. bar, 1968; with Sentry Ins. Co., Boston, 1956-70; partner firm Fleming and Boyle, Wellesley, Mass., 1968-73; asst. legal counsel Lottery Commn., State of Mass., 1973-76, chief legal counsel, 1976—; staff com. on rules Mass. State Senate, 1971-73; spl. asst. atty. gen. State of Mass., 1976. Mem. exec. bd. Newton City Democratic Com., 1967-72, ward 3 Dem. com., 1964-76. Mem. Mass. Bar Assn. Home: 15 Taft Ave West Newton MA 02165 Office: 15 Rockdale St Braintree MA 02184 Tel (617) 848-7755

BOYLE, JOHN STEPHEN, b. Chgo., July 17, 1901; LL.B., DePaul U., 1926, also J.D. Admitted to Ill. Supreme Ct. bar, 1926, U.S. Supreme Ct. bar, 1949; individual practice law, 1926-31, 52-60; asst. corp. counsel City of Chgo., 1931-33, 16th Ward alderman, 1939-43; asst. state's atty. of Cook County (Ill.), 1933-39, state's atty., 1948-52; judge Ill. Superior Ct. of Cook County, 1960; judge Criminal Ct. of Cook County, 1960-62, chief justice, 1962-63; chief judge U.S. Ct. Appeals, Circuit Ct. Cook County, 1964—; mem. Cook County Jud. Advisory Council, Cook County Ad Hoc Com. on Criminal Justice, Chgo.-Cook County Criminal Justice Commn. Mem. Chgo., Ill. State, Am. bar assns., Am. Judicature Soc., Cletic Legal Soc. (dir.), Cath. Lawyers Guild (v.p.), Nat. Conf. Metropolitan Cts. (pres., exec. com.), Law Club, Chief Judges Assn. Ill. (chmn.). Recipient Chgo. Alumni award Phi Alpha Delta, 1949, Spl. commendation Chgo. Crime Commn., 1963, Order of Lincoln 1st citation for Distinguished Service in Category of Law State of Ill. Lincoln Acad. of Ill., 1965, award of Merit Celtic Legal Soc., 1965, Pub. Service award for Distinguished Achievement De Paul U., 1968, Lex Legio award, 1973, Tom C. Clark award Nat. Conf. Met. Cts., 1974; editorial bds. Bklyn. Law Rev., DePaul Law Rev. Home: 1100 N Euclid Ave Oak Park IL 60302 Office: 2600 Chicago Civic Center Chicago IL 60602 Tel (312) 443-8000

BOYNTON, FREDERICK CHARLES, b. South Bend, Ind., Feb. 5, 1948; B.B.A., U. Dayton, 1970; J.D., Valparaiso U., 1973. Admitted to Ind. bar, 1973; asso. firm Doran, Manion, Boynton & Jamm, South Bend, 1974—. Bd. dirs. Goodwill Industries of Michiana, 1976—, sec., 1977—. Mem. Am., Ind., St. Joseph County bar assns., Estate Planning Counsel Michiana. Home: 1715 Cedar St South Bend IN 46601 Office: Doran Manion Boynton & Kamm 725 Saint Joseph Bank Bldg South Bend IN 46601 Tel (219) 233-6117

BOYNTON, STEPHEN SLATER, b. Schenectady, June 13, 1937; B.A., Ohio State U., 1959; LL.B., U.S.C., 1965. Admitted to S.C. bar, 1965, U.S. Supreme Ct. bar, 1970, D.C. bar, 1966; asso. Hogan & Hartson, Washington, 1965-69; legis. asst. to U.S. Senator Ernest F. Hollings, Washington, 1969-71; partner firm McIntosh & Boynton, Washington, 1971-75, Boynton & Maloney, Washington, 1975-76, Boynton & Toppelberg, Washington, 1976—; mem. D.C. Law Revision Com., 1975—. Mem. Am. (del. young lawyers sect. conv. 1972, named Young Lawyer of Year young lawyers sect. D.C. 1972-73), S.C., D.C., Fed. bar assns., Bar Assn. D.C. (exec. council young lawyers sect. 1967-71, vice chmn. young lawyers sect. 1971-72). Moderator Law and the Lawyer Sta. WRC-TV, Washington, 1974; editor S.C. Law Rev. Home: 1711 Massachusetts Ave NW Washington DC 20036 Office: 1050 17th St NW Suite 560 Washington DC 20036 Tel (202) 466-2360

BOYNTON, WYMAN PENDER, b. Portsmouth, N.H., Oct. 8, 1908; S.B., Mass. Inst. Tech., 1931; LL.B., U. Mich., 1936. Admitted to N.H. bar, 1936; asso. firm Jeremy R. Waldron, Portsmouth, 1936-40; partner firm Boynton, Waldron, Dill & Aeschliman and predecessors, Portsmouth, 1940—; mem. N.H. Ho. of Reps., 1933-34, Portsmouth City Council, 1937-38; county atty. Rockingham County (N.H.), 1947-50; trustee Portsmouth Co-op. Bank, 1946—, v.p., 1973—. Mem. Portsmouth City Mgr. Charter Commn., 1947-49, Portsmouth Sch. Bd., 1954-58, 62-70, Portsmouth Spl. Water Adv. Com., 1958-62; del. Republican Nat. Conv., 1952, N.H. Constl. Conv., 1975; trustee Portsmouth Hist. Soc., 1940—, v.p., 1946—; trustee Chase Home for Children, 1946—, pres., 1950—; trustee Mark H. Wentworth Home for Chronic Invalids, 1948—, pres., 1950—; trustee Portsmouth YWCA, 1949-70; trustee Portsmouth Athenaeum, pres., 1977—; trustee Portsmouth Pub. Library, 1955-72; trustee N.H. Indsl. Sch., Manchester, 1956-66, chmn., 1958-66; exec. bd. Daniel Webster council Boy Scouts Am., 1951-58, commr., 1953-54, pres., 1954-55. Mem. Am., N.H., Rockingham County bar assns., Nat., N.H. socs. profl. engrs., Soc. Am. Mil. Engrs. Recipient Silver Beaver award Boy Scouts Am., 1955; registered profl. engr., N.H. Home: 668 Middle St Portsmouth NH 03801 Office: 70 Court St Portsmouth NH 03801 Tel (603) 436-4010

BOZARTH, BENNETT EARL, b. Riverside, N.J., Sept. 22, 1946; A.B., Johns Hopkins, 1968; J.D., Columbia, 1971, M.B.A., 1972. Admitted to N.Y. bar, 1972, N.J. bar, 1972, Pa. bar, 1974; individual practice law, Delran, N.J., 1974—; dir. Mt. Holly State Bank (N.J.); solicitor Evesham Planning Bd., Marlton, N.J., 1976; asst. county solicitor Burlington County (N.J.), 1976; chmn. Burlington County chpt. N.J. Employers Legis. Council, 1976—; pros. atty. Town of Medford (N.J.), 1977—; adj. faculty Burlington County Coll., 1973. Mem. N.J., Burlington County bar assns. Home: 117 Creek Rd Delran NJ 08075 Office: 1611 Fairview St Delran NJ 08075 Tel (609) 764-1900

BOZORTH, SQUIRE NEWLAND, b. Portland, Oreg. Oct. 25, 1935; B.S., U. Oreg., 1958; LL.B., N.Y. U., 1961. Admitted to N.Y. State bar, 1961; asso. firm Milbank, Tweed, Hadley & McCloy, N.Y.C., 1961-70, partner, 1970—; asso. counsel Rockfeller U., 1973—. Bd. dirs., mem. exec. com., sec. Fedn. Protestant Welfare Agys. Mem. Am., N.Y. State bar assns., Assn. Bar City N.Y. Home: 38 Olmsted Rd Scarsdale NY 10583 Office: 1 Chase Manhattan Plaza New York City NY 10015 Tel (212) 422-2660

BRACH, RICHARD STEPHEN, b. Mexico City, July 3, 1948; A.B., Princeton, 1969; J.D., Columbia, 1972; certificate Hague Acad. Internat. Law, 1972. Admitted to N.Y. bar, 1973; asso. firm Milbank, Tweed, Hadley & McCloy, N.Y.C., 1972—. Mem. Am., N.Y. (legis. rep. 1973-74, state legis. com. 1975—) bar assns., Assn. Bar City N.Y. Home: 60 Sutton Pl S New York City NY 10022 Office: 1 Chase Manhattan Plaza New York City NY 10005 Tel (212) 422-2660

BRACHER, JOHN ALLEN, b. Honolulu, Sept. 26, 1939; A.B., Dartmouth Coll., 1961; J.D., Dickinson Coll., 1966. Admitted to Pa. bar, 1967, U.S. Ct. Mil. Appeals bar, 1970; chief trial counsel USMC, 1969; asso. firm Victor Dell'Alba, Esquire, York, Pa., 1970-71; individual practice law, York, 1971—. Solicitor, York Adams Mental Health Mental Retardation Program, 1972—; solicitor York Opportunities Industrialization Center, Inc., 1971—. Mem. Am., Pa., York County bar assns. Recipient Presdl. award York Jaycees, 1975. Home: 532 Greendale Rd York PA 17403 Office: 135 E Market St York PA 17401 Tel (717) 843-8921

BRACHMAN, JAMES MARVIN, b. Milw., Feb. 10, 1933; A.B., Princeton, 1955; LL.B., Harvard, 1958; Docteur en Droit (Fulbright fellow), U. Liege (Belgium), 1959. Admitted to Wis. bar, 1958, N.Y. bar, 1960; asso. firm Kaye, Scholer, Fierman, Hays & Handler, N.Y.C., 1960-62; asst. U.S. atty. Dept. Justice, N.Y.C., 1962-65; asst. corp. counsel, chief div. penalties, N.Y.C. Law Dept., 1966-70; partner firm Freeman, Meade, Wasserman & Sharfman, N.Y.C., 1970-75; spl. counsel firm Greenbaum, Wolff & Ernst, N.Y.C., 1975—; chmn. clemency com. N.Y. Com. to Abolish Capital Punishment, 1960-62; mem. law com. Fedn. Jewish Philanthropies of N.Y., N.Y.C., 1970—. Mem. Am., N.Y. State bar assns., State Bar Wis., Assn. Bar City N.Y., Fed. Bar Council. Home: 8 Terrace Dr Great Neck NY 11021 Office: 437 Madison Ave New York City NY 10022 Tel (212) 758-4010

BRACKEN, JOHN PAUL, b. Carnegie, Pa., June 10, 1912; A.B., U. Pitts., 1934; postgrad. George Washington U., 1934-35; J.D., U. Pa., 1939; postgrad. Armed Forces Staff Coll., 1950-51. Admitted to Pa. bar, 1940, D.C. bar, 1940, U.S. Supreme Ct. bar, 1950; asso. firm Morgan, Lewis & Bockius, Phila., 1939-55, partner, 1955—, mng. partner, 1960-71, sr. partner, 1971—; pres. Am. Bar Endowment, 1973. Vice chmn. Phila. Tax Study Commn., 1970; chmn. Phila. Bicentennial Corp., 1972. Mem. Phila., Pa., Am. (chmn. ho. of dels. 1974-76), Inter-Am., Internat. (sec.-gen. 1976—) bar assns., World Peace Through Law, Lawyers Club Phila. Decorated Legion of Merit (U.S.); Order of Orange-Nassau (Netherlands); recipient Distinguished Civilian award Dept. Army, 1956, William Penn award for Distinguished Civic Leadership, Greater Phila. C. of C., 1972; named Hon. Belgian Consul in Phila., 1971. Tel (205) 491-9305

BRACKEN, WILLIAM EARL, JR., b. Phila., Jan. 25, 1934; B.B.A., Baylor U., 1956, LL.B., 1958. Admitted to Tex. bar, 1958, U.S. Supreme Ct. bar, 1966; served with JAG, USAF, 1958-61; asso. firm Bryan, Wilson & Olson, Waco, Tex., 1961-63; asst. city atty. Waco, 1963-67, city atty., 1967—; lt. col. JAG, USAFR. Vice chmn. com. on nominations Instl. Bd., Baptist Gen. Conv. Tex., 1967-68; deacon First Bapt. Ch., 1976—; pres., dir. Lake Air Little League, 1964-68; bd. dirs. Evangelia Settlement, 1974-77, Baylor Waco Found., Baylor U. Devel. Council. Mem. Tex. City Attys. Assn. (pres. 1969-71), Waco-Mclennan County Bar Assn. (treas., dir., pres. jr. bar assn. 1969-73), Jaycees (dir. Waco 1965-68, recipient Outstanding Dir. award 1966-67, Distinguished Service award 1970). Home: 5000 Ridgeview Dr Waco TX 76710 Office: PO Box 1370 City Hall Waco TX 76703 Tel (817) 756-6161

BRACKHAHN, RICHARD ALLEN, b. Muskogee, Okla., Dec. 20, 1939; B.S., Memphis State U., 1962, J.D., 1965; postgrad. U. Okla. Admitted to Tenn. bar, 1965, U.S. Supreme Ct. bar, 1974; partner firm Fowler, Brackhahn, Young & Perl, Memphis, 1965-70, Bowling, Brackhahn & Jackson, Memphis, 1970-75; sr. partner law offices Richard A. Brackhahn, Memphis, 1975—; participant Fed. Meidation and Conciliation Service, Southwestern U., 1971, U. Miss., 1972, Memphis State U., 1973; spl. judge State of Tenn. Mem. Am., Tenn.,

Memphis and Shelby County bar assns. Office: 813 Ridge Lake Blvd Suite 300 Memphis TN 38138 Tel (901) 767-6376

BRADBURY, MICHAEL DON, b. Los Angeles, Feb. 16, 1942; B.S., U. Oreg., 1964; J.D., U. Calif., 1967; grad. Nat. Dist. Attys. Coll., U. Houston, 1972. Admitted to Calif. bar, 1967; chief asst. dist. atty. Ventura County (Calif.), 1973—; instr. law and history Calif. Community Colls.; lectr. Ventura Coll. Law; cons. Law Enforcement Assistance Adminstrn. Bd. dirs. Rape Crisis Center, Ventura, 1974-78. Mem. Ventura County Bar Assn. (exec. com. 1974-76). Author: Sexual Assault: Rape and Molestation. Tel (805) 648-6131

BRADEN, BERWYN BARTOW, b. Pana, Ill., Jan. 10, 1928; student Carthage Coll., 1946-48, U. Wis., 1948-49; J.D., U. Wis., 1959. Admitted to Wis. bar, 1959, U.S. Supreme Ct. bar, 1965; partner firm Genoar & Braden, Lake Geneva, Wis., 1959-63, Braden & English, 1968-72, Braden & Olson, 1974—; individual practice law Lake Geneva, 1963-68, 72-74; city atty., Lake Geneva, 1962-64; dir. Citizens Nat. Bank, Lake Geneva, Bd. dirs. Lake Geneva YMCA 1961-62. Mem. Wis. Acad. Trial Lawyers (sec. 1975, treas. 1976, dir. 1977), Am. Assn. Trial Lawyers Am., Walworth County (pres. 1962-63), Chgo. bar assns. Home: 851A Lake Shore Dr Lake Geneva WI 53147 Office: POB 512 Lake Geneva WI 53147 Tel (414) 248-6636

BRADFIELD, MARK MAURICE, b. Borger, Tex., Oct. 2, 1941; B.A., U. Fla., 1963, J.D., 1965. Admitted to Fla. bar, 1965; served with JAG, USNR, 1965-68; asso. firm Saunders, Curtis, Ginestra & Gore, Ft. Lauderdale, Fla., 1968-69; asst. county solicitor, Palm Beach County, Fla., 1969-73; partner firm Staab & Bradfield, West Palm Beach, Fla., 1973—; 1st asst. County Solicitor 1971-73. Mem. Fla., Palm Beach County bar assns. Home: 807 Easterly Rd North Palm Beach FL 33408 Office: 329 3d St West Palm Beach FL 33401 Tel (305) 832-3658

BRADFORD, ADDISON MORTON, JR., b. Lee County, Ark., Jan. 2, 1918; B.A., Ark. State U., 1939; postgrad. So. Meth. U., 1940-41, J.D., 1948. Admitted to Tex. bar, 1948, U.S. Supreme Ct. bar; practiced in Dallas, 1948—; partner firm Bradford & Pritchard, 1953-68, Anderson, Henley, Shields, Bradford & Pritchard, 1968-77, firm Bradford & Pritchard, 1977—; dir. Central Bank & Trust Co., R.B. Wilber C. Co.; v.p., dir. Town & Country Vending Service, Inc., Mahard Pullet Farms, Inc., Mahard Egg Farm, Inc., Mahard Egg Co., Mahard Feed Mill, Inc., S.L. Ewing Co., Inc.; sec., dir. O.E.M. Industries, Inc., Tex. Sign Supply Co., Tex. Screen Process, Inc. Mem. Am., Dallas bar assns., State Bar Tex., Am. Judicature Soc., Delta Theta Phi. Home: 3511 Golfing Green Dallas TX 75234 Office: Heritage Sq 4835 LBJ Freeway Dallas TX 75234 Tel (214) 233-9394

BRADFORD, CARL O., b. Dallas, Nov. 16, 1932; student U. Detroit; J.D., U. Maine, 1962. Admitted to Maine bar, 1963, U.S. Dist. Ct. for Dist. Maine bar, 1963, U.S. Ct. Appeals bar, 1st Circuit, 1963; asst. atty. gen. State of Maine, 1963-64; now mem. firm Powers & Bradford, Freeport, Maine; mem. Commn. on Uniform State Laws, 1972—, Spl. Com. on Uniform Exemptions Act, 1974—. Mem. Cumberland County, Maine State (pres. 1977—), Am. bar assns., Maine Trial Lawyers Assn. (gov. 1971—), Assn. Trial Lawyers Am., Am. Judicature Soc., Am. Soc. Hosp. Attys. Office: Powers & Bradford Brunswick Savs Bldg Freeport ME 04032 Tel (207) 865-3135*

BRADFORD, CARTER ALLAN, b. Orlando, Fla., May 18, 1937; B.A., U. Fla., 1959, LL.B., 1962, J.D., 1967. Admitted to Fla. bar, 1962, U.S. Supreme Ct. bar, 1968; asso. firm Sidney Ward, Orlando, 1962-63; partner firm Ward & Bradford, Orlando, 1963-64, Ward, Bradford & Oswald, Orlando, 1964-71; partner firm Bradford, Oswald, Tharp & Fletcher, Orlando, 1971-76, firm Bradford Tharp & Fletcher, Orlando, 1976—. atty. Orange County (Fla.), 1969-72. Mem. Am., Orange County bar assns. Home: 880 Bonita Dr Winter Park FL 32789 Office: 90 E Livingston St PO Box 875 Orlando FL 32802 Tel (305) 841-7131

BRADFORD, JAMES WILLIAM, b. Greenwood, S.C., Apr. 9, 1914; student The Citadel, 1931-33; J.D., Georgetown U., 1939. Admitted to D.C. bar, 1938, S.C. bar, 1939, U.S. Supreme Ct. bar, 1975; practice law, Greenwood, 1945—; mem. firm Burns, McDonald, Bradford, Erwin & Patrick, 1957—; mem. S.C. State Senate, 1959-60, S.C. Ednl. TV Commn., 1960-76. Bd. dirs. Lander Found., 1967—, chmn., 1971-73. Mem. S.C., Am., Greenwood County bar assns., Am. Judicature Soc., Delta Theta Phi. Home: 308 Hunting Rd Greenwood SC 29646 Office: PO Box 1207 Greenwood SC 29646 Tel (803) 229-2511

BRADFORD, LEWIS ADDISON, b. St. Joseph, Mo., Dec. 25, 1944; B.A., Grinnell Coll., 1967; M.B.A., Washington U., St. Louis, 1969; J.D., Loyola U., 1973. Admitted to Ill. bar, 1973; investment mgr. Boatmen's Bank, St. Louis, 1969-71; trust investment officer Chgo. Title and Trust Co., 1971—. Treas. Sojourner Truth Day Care Center, 1974—; sec. Coordinating Conf. Landmark Preservation, 1976—. Mem. Chgo. Bar Assn., Investment Analysts Soc. Chgo. Home: 5132 S Woodlawn St Chicago IL 60615 Office: 111 W Washington St Chicago IL 60615 Tel (312) 630-2933

BRADFORD, WILLIAM HOLLIS, JR., b. St. Petersburg, Fla., Feb. 11, 1937; A.B., Duke U., 1959, J.D., 1962; LL.M., George Washington U., 1964. Admitted to D.C. bar, 1962, Md. bar, 1972; asso. firm Hamel, Park, McCabe and Saunders, Washington, 1962-67, partner, 1967—. Vice pres. Young Democrats of Md., 1966-67, Montgomery County Dem. Central Com., 1974—; pres. Hillmead Citizens Assn., Bethesda, Md., 1966-67; bd. govs. Washington Figure Skating Club, 1974-77, v.p., 1975-76. Mem. Am., D.C., Md. State, Fed. Bar Assns., Bar Assn. D.C. Editor Am. Bar Assn. sect. of Taxation Annual Report, 1972-73; co-editor Report on Md. Gen. Assembly, 1967. Home: 1202 Azalea Dr Rockville MD 20850 Office: 1776 F St NW Washington DC 20006 Tel (202) 785-1234

BRADIE, MICHAEL, b. N.Y.C., Feb. 18, 1932; B.S., N.Y. U., 1954, LL.B., 1957. Admitted to N.Y. bar, 1957; mem. firm Lapp & Schacher, Cedarhurst, N.Y., 1960-68; partner firm Lapp, Schacher & Bradie, Cedarhurst, 1968—; served to lt. JAG, 1958—, Res., 1974—; acting village judge Village of Malverne (N.Y.), 1975—. Mem. Bar Assn. Nassau County, Far Rockaway Lawyers Club. Office: 123 Grove Ave Cedarhurst NY 11516 Tel (516) 295-3344

BRADLEY, CHARLES HARVEY, JR., b. Indpls., July 17, 1923; B.A., Yale U., 1945, LL.B., 1949. Admitted to Ind. bar, 1949; asso. firm Smith, Morgan & Ryan, Indpls., 1949-50, partner, 1950-60; with Eli Lilly & Co., Indpls., 1960—, sec., gen. counsel, 1964—, dir., 1973—; mem. mgmt. mem. com. character and fitness Ind. Supreme Ct.; dir. Indpls. Water Co., Crown Hill Cemetery Mausoleum; Elanco Products Co. Vice pres. Yale Law Sch. Assn. Mem. Am., Ind., Indpls. (chmn. corporate and instl. counsel com.) bar assns., Lawyers Club, Am. Soc. Corporate Secs., Assn. Gen. Counsel. Home: Rural Route 1 Box 186 Zionsville IN 46077 Office: 307 E McCarty St Indianapolis IN 46206 Tel (317) 261-2703

BRADLEY, DAVID HAMMOND, b. Keene, N.H., May 8, 1936; A.B., Dartmouth, 1958; J.D., Harvard, 1965. Admitted to N.H. bar, 1965; asso. firm Stebbins & Bradley, and predecessors, Hanover, N.H., 1965-68, partner, 1968—; mem. N.H. Ho. of Reps., 1971-72; mem. N.H. Senate, 1973—, chmn. judiciary com., 1973—. Mem. Hanover Sch. Bd., 1967-70, chmn., 1968-70. Mem. Am., N.H., Grafton County (N.H.) bar assns., Am. Trial Lawyers Assn., Nat. Assn. Coll. and Univ. Attys. Office: 41 S Park St Hanover NH 03755 Tel (603) 643-3737

BRADLEY, F. JAMES, b. Bancroft, Iowa, 1927; student Loras Coll.; B.A., U. Iowa, 1948, J.D., 1950. Admitted to Iowa bar, 1950; now partner firm Simmons, Perrine, Albright & Elwood, Cedar Rapids, Iowa. Mem. Dist. Ct. Jud. Nominating Com., 1964-71, Iowa Supreme Ct. Jud. Nominating Commn., 1965-71, Iowa Supreme Ct. Advisory Council, 1975-76. Mem. Linn County (pres. 1967-68, gov. 1968-70), Iowa State (pres. 1976-77), Am. bar assns., Delta Theta Phi. Office: 1200 Merchants Nat Bank Bldg Cedar Rapids IA 52401 Tel (319) 366-7641*

BRADLEY, FRANCIS MACLEOD, b. Town Creek, Ala., Apr. 29, 1921; B.S. in Bus. Adminstrn., U. Fla., 1942; LL.B./J.D., Albany Law Sch., 1947; grad. Sch. Savs. and Loan, Ind. U., 1963. Admitted to N.Y. bar, 1947; mem. firm Bown & Bradley, Rochester, N.Y., 1947-56, Bown, Jefferson & Bradley, Rochester, 1956-58; individual practice law, East Rochester, N.Y., 1958—; pres., exec. officer Home Fed. Savs. and Loan Assn., East Rochester, 1958—. Pres. Rochester Neighbors, Inc.; past v.p. Better Rochester, Inc.; chmn. Penfield (N.Y.) Recreation Commn., 1956-61, 72; pres. Penfield Community Chest; founder Penfield Little League, Fresh Air Program; dist. 32 Democratic County committeeman, Perinton; trustee Episcopal Diocese of Rochester, 1973-76; bd. dirs. Rochester Area Council Chs., 1964-71, Rochester Theol. Inst. Mem. Am., N.Y., Monroe County (past chmn. religion and law com.) bar assns., U.S., N.Y. (dir. consumer affairs com.) savs. and loan leagues, Am. Savs. and Loan Inst. Home: 2 Dunbridge Heights Fairport NY 14450 Office: 401 Main St East Rochester NY 14445 Tel (716) 586-0220

BRADLEY, JOHN CURTIS, b. Idaho Falls, Idaho, Aug. 12, 1920; A.A., George Washington U., 1942, J.D., 1948. Admitted to D.C. bar, 1948, Va. bar, 1976; asso. firm Rice, Carpenter and Carraway, Washington and Arlington, Va., 1954-58, partner, 1958—. Pres., McLean (Va.) Citizens Assn, Langley Forest (Va.) Citizen's Assn, 1958. Mem. D.C. bar, Va. State Bar, Motor Carrier Lawyers Assn. Home: 828 Mackall Ave McLean VA 22101 Office: Suite 1301 1600 Wilson Blvd Arlington VA 22209 Tel (703) 522-0900

BRADLEY, JOHN DANIEL, III, b. Atlanta, May 26, 1946; B.A., The Citadel, 1968; J.D., U. S.C., 1971. Admitted to S.C. bar, 1971; individual practice law, Charleston, S.C., 1972-73; mem. firm Bradley & Worley, Mt. Pleasant, S.C., 1973-76, firm Bradley, Worley & Levya, Mt. Pleasant, 1975—; mem. S.C. Ho. of Reps., 1974—. Deacon 1st Bapt. Ch. of Charleston, 1975—. Mem. Am., S.C., Charleston County bar assns., Charleston Lawyers Club, Washington Light Inf., S.C.V. Home: 308 Swift Ave Charleston SC 29407 Office: PO Box 157 Mount Pleasant SC 29464 Tel (803) 884-2833

BRADLEY, JOHN FRANCIS, b. Phila., July 9, 1946; A.B., Georgetown U., 1968; J.D. magna cum laude, Villanova (Pa.) U., 1973. Admitted to Pa. bar, 1973, U.S. Supreme Ct. bar, 1977; asso. firm Berkman, Ruslander, Pohl, Lieber & Engel, Pitts., 1973-74; individual practice law, Pitts., 1975-76; partner firm Horton, D'Arrigo & Bradley, Pitts., 1977—. Trustee Civic Club Allegheny County, 1974—; Republican candidate for Congress 14th Dist. Pa., 1976. Mem. Am., Pa., Allegheny County bar assns., Order of Coif. Recipient Silver Key award Am. Bar Assn., 1973. Home: Apt 703 7 Allegheny Center Pittsburgh PA 15212 Office: 915 Frick Bldg Pittsburgh PA 15219 Tel (412) 288-9587

BRADLEY, MICHAEL ROBERT, b. Bryn Mawr, Pa., Aug. 9, 1938; B.S., St. Joseph's Coll., 1960; LL.B., Villanova U., 1963, J.D., 1970. Admitted to Pa. bar, 1963; partner firm Brooks, Bradley and Kenney, Media, Pa., 1963—; instr. St. Joseph's Coll., 1963-71. Mem. Am., Pa., Delaware County (dir.) bar assns. Office: 2d and Plum St Media PA 19063 Tel (215) 565-4800

BRADLEY, REBECCA LOUISE, b. Los Angeles, Mar. 28, 1941; B.S. in Math cum laude, U. Denver, 1963, J.D., 1966. Admitted to Colo. bar, 1966, U.S. Dist. Ct. bar for Colo., 1966, U.S. 10th Circuit Ct. Appeals bar, 1967, U.S. Supreme Ct. bar, 1969; partner firm Carroll & Bradley, Denver, 1966—. Mem. Am., Colo., Adams County, Denver, Boulder bar assns., Am., Colo. (mem. bd. govs. 1973-75, dir.; 1975-76) trial lawyers assns., Nat. Assn. Women Lawyers. Office: 61 W 84th Ave Denver CO 80221 Tel (303) 427-2454 also 595 Canyon Blvd Boulder CO 80302 Tel (303) 443-3874

BRADLEY, ROBERT DONALD, b. Clinton, Ill., Apr. 26, 1941; B.A., Monmath Coll., 1963; J.D., U. Denver, 1966. Admitted to bar; individual practice law, Denver, 1971—. Trustee First Unitarian Ch. Mem. Colo. Trial Lawyers Assn. Home: 1760 Bellaire Denver CO 80220 Office: 760 Sherman Denver CO 80203 Tel (303) 831-8307

BRADLEY, SARAH MCCOY, b. Norfolk County, Va., July 9, 1946; B.A., U. N.Mex., 1968, J.D., 1972. Admitted to N.Mex. bar, 1972; law clk. Hon. Edwin L. Mechem U.S. Dist. Ct. of N.Mex., 1972-74; asso. firm LeRoi Farlow P.A., Albuquerque, 1974—; U.N.Mex. mem. Nat. Moot Ct. Team, 1971-72. Mem. Albuquerque, N. Mex. (dir. sect. young lawyers), Am. bar assns. Mng. editor N. Mex. Law Rev., 1971-72, Natural Resources Jour., 1971-72. Office: 1720 1st Nat Bank Bldg E Albuquerque NM 87108 Tel (505) 265-7749

BRADLEY, WAYNE BERNARD, b. Decatur, Ga., Oct. 11, 1944; student Young Harris Jr. Coll., 1964; A.B. in Economics U. Ga., 1966; J.D., John Marshall U., 1972. Admitted to Ga. bar, 1972, U.S. Supreme Ct. bar, 1975; asst. dist. atty. Ocmulgee Judicial Circuit, Ga., 1972-74; partner firm Peugh & Bradley, Milledgeville, Ga., 1975—. Mem. Big Brothers Milledgeville, Ga., 1977. Mem. Ga., Am., Balamin Co. bar assns., Ocmulgee Bar. Home: 15 Nature Creek Milledgeville GA 31061 Office: Sanford Bldg Milledgeville GA 31061 Tel (912) 452-3587

BRADLEY, WILLIAM BRUCE, b. Memphis, Apr. 16, 1933; B.B.A., So. Meth. U., 1955; J.D., YMCA Night Law Sch., Nashville, 1969. Admitted to Tenn. bar, 1969; individual practice law, Brentwood, Tenn., 1969-74; partner firm Elledge & Bradley, Brentwood, 1974—; chmn., pres. Hermitage Life Ins. Co., Brentwood, 1961—; organizer, sec. Liberty Bank Brentwood, 1974—. Pres., founder Brentwood Exchange Club, 1972-73. Mem. Nashville, Tenn., Williamson County bar assns., Tenn., Nashville trial lawyers assns. Home: 1825 Cromwell Dr Nashville TN 37215 Office: Box 217 Moores Ln at I-65 Brentwood TN 37027 Tel (615) 790-1237

BRADSHAW, DELBERT CHANNING, b. Gilmer, Tex., Nov. 15, 1941; B.A., Brigham Young U., 1966; J.D., U. Houston, 1969. Admitted to Tex. bar, 1969; individual practice law, 1969-70; partner firm Borup and Bradshaw, 1970-74; partner firm Bradshaw and Cass, Pasadena, Tex., 1974—. Mem. Pasadena Bar Assn. (v.p. 1974-75). Home: 10827 Sageberry St Houston TX 77089 Office: 3376 S Shaver St Pasadena TX 77504 Tel (713) 946-2182

BRADSTREET, ROBERT EDWARD, b. Shields, Kans., Apr. 4, 1931; A.B., U. Kans., 1953, LL.B., 1955, J.D., 1968. Admitted to Kans. bar, 1955, Calif. bar, 1963; mem. JAGC, USAF, 1955-62; atty. Dist. Atty.'s Office, Merced County (Calif.), 1963-64; asso. firm Frederick Jacobus, Visalia, Calif., 1964-65; individual practice, Visalia, 1965-75; judge Visalia Municipal Ct., 1975—. Mem. Am., Calif. bar assns., Calif. Conf. Judges. Office: 210 N Church St Visalia CA 93277 Tel (209) 732-3428

BRADY, H. HOWELL, JR., b. Mayfield, Ky., June 15, 1944; B.A., U. Ky., 1966, J.D., 1969. Admitted to Ky. bar, 1971; dir. forensics U. Ky., 1969-71; pvt. bus., Louisville, 1971-73; gen. counsel Ky. Dept. Mental Health, 1973; exec. dir. Ky. Jud. Conf. and council, 1973-75; gen. counsel Ky. Sec. State Office, 1976—; counsel Ky. State Bd. Election, 1976—; individual practice law, Georgetown, Ky., 1975—. Mem. Ky., Louisville, Scott County bar assns., U. Ky. Alumni Assn., Delta Theta Phi. Office: 100 S Broadway Georgetown KY 40324 Tel (502) 863-5400

BRADY, JOHN AUGUSTINE, b. San Diego, July 22, 1928; student St. Mary's Coll., 1948-50; B.A., U. So. Calif., 1951, J.D., 1954. Admitted to Calif. bar, 1955, U.S. Supreme Ct. bar, 1966; dep. dist. atty. San Diego County (Calif.), 1955-57; asso. firm Holt, Macomber & Graham, San Diego, 1957-58; partner firm Ashley, Brady & Cerniglia, San Diego, 1958—. Bd. dir. Legal Aid Soc., San Diego, 1965; bd. archtl. control City San Diego, 1966. Mem. San Diego County Bar Assn. (sec., 1966, pres., 1967). Contbr. article to Dicta. Home: 4156 Eastridge Dr LaMesa CA 92041 Office: Suite 914 530 Broadway St San Diego CA 92101 Tel (714) 232-7521

BRADY, JULIO ANTHONY, b. St. Thomas, V.I., Aug. 23, 1942; B.A., Cath. U. P.R., 1964; J.D., N.Y. Law Sch., 1969. Admitted to N.Y. bar, 1969, V.I. bar, 1973; atty. Legal Aid Soc., N.Y.C., 1969-71; asst. U.S. atty., St. Croix, V.I., 1971-73, U.S. atty., 1973—; mem. Speedy Trial Planning Group for V.I., 1976, Lawyers Adv. Com. to U.S. Ct. of Appeals, 3d Circuit. Active, Law Enforcement Orgn. V.I., Law Enforcement Planning Commn., V.I. council Boy Scouts Am. Mem. V.I. Bar Assn. (pres. elect 1976). Recipient Sigma Tau Delta award Cath. U. P.R., 1964, Am. Jur prize New York Law Sch., 1967. Home: 2B Snegle Gade Saint Thomas VI 00801 Office: PO Box 1441 Dist Ct Annex Saint Thomas VI 00801 Tel (809) 774-1431

BRADY, MICHAEL JEFF, b. Midland, Tex., Sept. 15, 1941; B.A. in History, Stanford U., 1964; LL.B., Harvard, 1967. Admitted to Calif. bar, 1967; mem. firm Ropers, Majeski, Kohn, Bentley & Wagner, Redwood City, Calif., 1967—. Mem. San Mateo County Bar Assn., Calif. Assn. Defense Counsel, Calif. Acad. Appellate Lawyers. Home: 40 Campo Bello Ct Menlo Park CA 94025 Office: 1125 Marshall St Redwood City CA 94063 Tel (415) 364-8200

BRADY, WALLACE A., b. Almond, Wis., Oct. 20, 1921; B.A., U. Wis., 1943, LL.B., 1947. Admitted to Wis. bar, 1947; since practiced in Elroy, Wis.; city atty. City of Elroy, 1948—; mem. North Central Wis. Planning Commn., 1973—. Mem. Am., Wis., Juneau County (Wis.) bar assns. Decorated Navy Cross. Office: PO Box 26 Elroy WI 53929 Tel (608) 462-8271

BRAFFORD, WILLIAM CHARLES, b. Pike County, Ky., Aug. 7, 1932; J.D., U. Ky., 1957; LL.M., U. Ill., 1958. Admitted to Ky. bar, 1957, Ga. bar, 1965, Ohio bar, 1966, Pa. bar, 1973; trial atty. NLRB, 1958-60; atty. Louisville & Nashville R.R. Co., 1960-62, So. Bell Tel. & Tel. Co., 1962-65; asst. gen. counsel NCR Corp., 1965-72; sec., gen. counsel Betz Labs., Inc., Trevose, Pa., 1972—; dir. Betz Internat., Inc., Betz Entec, Inc., Kay-Ray, Inc., internat. fgn. subsidiaries Betz Internat., Inc. Mem. Am., Ky., Ga., Ohio, Pa. bar assns. Comments editor, contbr. to Ky. Law Jour. Home: 10 Fairfield Ln Doylestown PA 18901 Office: 4636 Somerton Rd Trevose PA 19047 Tel (215) 355-3300

BRAIMAN, MYER, b. Rochester, N.Y., June 25, 1907; student U. Rochester, 1925-28; J.D., Columbia U. Admitted to N.Y. bar; referee Workmen's Compensation Ct., 1941-42; individual practice law, Rochester; clin. asso. forensic medicine dept. surgery U. Rochester Med. Sch., until 1972. Bd. visitors Gowanda State Hosp. Home: 2500 E Ave Rochester NY 14610 Office: 45 Exchange St Rochester NY 14614 Tel (716) 454-7718

BRAKE, ROBERT MERLE, b. Detroit, Sept. 30, 1926; student Wayne State U., 1945-47, U. Chgo., 1947-48; LL.B., U. Mich., 1950. Admitted to Mich. bar, 1951, Fla. bar, 1951; asso. firm Turner, Hendrick, Fascell & Brake, and predecessors, Coral Gables, Fla., 1952-55, partner, 1956-59; individual practice law, Coral Gables, 1960—; municipal judge City of Coral Gables, 1958; city atty. City of Sweetwater (Fla.), 1966; spl. city atty. City of Miami Springs (Fla.), 1972; hearing examiner Met. Dade County Personnel Appeals System, 1975—. City commr. Coral Gables, 1971—; v.p. Dade County League of Cities, 1975—; mem. Fla. Ho. of Reps., 1966-67; commr. Met. Dade County, 1962-64; mem. U.S. Cath. Bishops' Adv. Council, 1973-76, vice chmn., 1975-76; co-chmn. Archbishops' Charities Dr., Archdiocese of Miami, 1976; sec. Save Our Children, Inc., 1977; founder, pres. Dade County Council on Adoptable Children, 1970; bd. dirs. Right to Life Crusade, Inc., 1971—; trustee Lourdes Acad., 1970-71. Mem. Am., Dade County, Coral Gables (past pres.) bar assns., Coral Gables C. of C. (dir. 1968-72), Greater Miami United Chambers of Commerce (past pres.), Delta Theta Phi. Columnist Greater Miami Jour., 1965-74. Home: 1300 Coral Way Coral Gables FL 33134 Office: 1830 Ponce de Leon Blvd Coral Gables FL 33134 Tel (305) 444-1694

BRAMAN, JOHN CHARLES, b. Spokane, Wash., June 14, 1921; B.S. in Law, U. Wash., 1943, LL.B., 1947, J.D., 1947. Admitted to Wash. bar, 1947, Calif. bar, 1969; clk. Supreme Ct. Wash., 1947-48; asso. firm Emory, Howe, Davis & Riese, Seattle, 1948-50; counsel Office Price Stablzn., Seattle, 1951-52; credit mgr. and adminstr., Pacific Car and Foundry, Renton, Wash., 1952-57; contract adminstr. Boeing Corp., Seattle, 1958-63; counsel Bechtel Corp., San Francisco,

1963—. Mem. State Bar Calif. Office: Legal Dept Bechtel Corp 50 Beale St San Francisco CA 94106 Tel (415) 768-9410

BRAMAN, LEONARD, b. Phila., Aug. 21, 1925; B.S., Temple U., 1949; LL.B., U. Va., 1952. Admitted to D.C. bar, 1952; law clk. to judge U.S. Ct. Appeals, Circuit D.C., 1952-53; asst. U.S. atty. for D.C., 1953-54; Bigelow teaching fellow U. Chgo. Law Sch., 1954-55; asso. firm Newmyer & Bress, Washington, 1955-61; partner firms Bress, Braman & Hilmer, Washington, 1961-65, Surrey, Karasik, Greene & Hill, Washington, 1965-70; asso. judge D.C. Superior Ct., 1970—. Mem. State Trial Judges Assn., Am. Judicature Soc., Am., D.C. bar assns. Home: 12600 Springloch Ct Silver Spring MD 20904 Office: 440 G St NW 202 Washington DC 20001 Tel (202) 727-1717

BRAME, FRANK AYERS, III, b. Greenville, Tex., July 17, 1932; B.S., U.S. Naval Acad., 1954; J.D., U. Colo., 1967, M.B.A., 1976; LL.M. in Taxation, N.Y. U., 1970. Admitted to Colo. bar, 1967, U.S. Tax Ct. bar, 1969; atty. AEC, Albuquerque, 1967-69; asso. firm Seawell & Cohen, profl. corp., Denver, 1970-73, officer, dir., 1974—; lectr. continuing legal edn. taxation program, 1974-76. Leader Centennial council Cub Scouts, 1975—. Mem. Am. (profl. corps. com. of tax sect.), Colo. (taxation sect. exec. council, liaison rep. to SW region IRS), Denver bar assns., Greater Denver Tax Counsels Assn., Rocky Mountain Estate Planning Council, Phi Eta Sigma, Beta Gamma Sigma, Phi Delta Phi. Author: Annual Survey of Colorado Law: Taxation, 1975, 76. Editorial bd. U. Colo. Law Rev., 1965-67. Home: 5329 Morning Glory Ln Littleton CO 80123 Office: 1660 Lincoln St Suite 1518 Denver CO 80264 Tel (303) 892-6330

BRAMLETT, PAUL KENT, b. Tupelo, Miss., May 31, 1944; A.A., Itawamba Jr. Coll., 1964; B.A., David Lipscomb Coll., 1966; J.D., U. Miss., 1969. Admitted to Miss. bar, 1969, U.S. Dist. Ct. for Western Dist. Tenn. bar, 1976, U.S. Supreme Ct. bar, 1974, U.S. Ct. Appeals for 5th Circuit bar, 1974; individual practice law, Tupelo, Miss., 1969-71; mem. firm Bramlett, Mounce & Soper and predecessor, Tupelo, 1975—. Mem. Am., Miss., Lee County (Miss.), bar assns., Am., Miss. (gov. 1976) trial lawyers assns. Office: Bramlett Mounce & Soper 301 N Broadway Tupelo MS 38801 Tel (601) 842-3723

BRAMMER, JAMES WILLIAM, b. Des Moines, Mar. 13, 1916; B.A., U. Iowa, 1938; J.D, U. Mich., 1941. Admitted to Iowa bar, 1941; jr. partner firm Brammer, Brody, Charlton, Parker & Roberts, Des Moines, 1946-49; partner firm Brammer & Davis, Des Moines, 1950-62, firm Williams & Brammer, Des Moines, 1963; individual practice law, Des Moines, 1964-69; asso. firm Dreher, Wilson, Adams & Jensen, Des Moines, 1970—. Mem. Des Moines Bd. Edn., 1957-63. Mem. Am., Iowa, Polk County bar assns. Home: 2017 74th St Des Moines IA 50322 Office: Stephens Bldg Des Moines IA 50309 Tel (515) 288-0247

BRANCH, BARRINGTON (BARRY) HEATH, b. Atlanta, May 9, 1940; B.A., Davidson Coll., 1962; J.D., Duke, 1966. Admitted to Ga. bar, 1966; asso. firm Hansell, Post, Brandon & Dorsey, Atlanta, 1966-71; exec. v.p., gen. counsel Portman Properties, Atlanta, 1971—; counsel, mem. organized crime com. Met. Atlanta Commn. on Crime and Juvenile Delinquency, 1967-68; gen. partner The Peachtree Hotel Co., The Peachtree Harris Co., Terminus Internat.; ltd. partner The Los Angeles Portman Co.; sec., dir. The Midnight Sun, Inc., The Atlanta Mdse. Mart Corp. Bd. dirs. Sheltering Arms Day Care Centers, Atlanta, 1967-74. Mem. Am. Bar Assn., State Bar Ga. (exec. com. young lawyers sect. 1970-71), Duke U. Atlanta (v.p. 1971—), Davidson Coll. Atlanta (pres. 1975—), Westminster (pres. 1969-70) alumni assns. Office: 225 Peachtree St NE suite 1900 Atlanta GA 30303 Tel (404) 688-7541

BRANCH, THOMAS BROUGHTON, III, b. Atlanta, June 5, 1936; B.A. cum laude, Washington and Lee U., 1958, J.D., 1960. Admitted to Ga. bar, 1960; asso. firm Kilpatrick, Cody, Rogers, McClatchey & Regenstein, Atlanta, 1960-64; individual practice law, Atlanta, 1964-65; asso. firm Greene, Buckley, DeRieux, & Jones, Atlanta, 1965-69, partner, 1969—; staff asso. for devel. Washington and Lee U., 1975. Clk. session First Presbyterian Ch., Atlanta, 1975—. Mem. Am., Atlanta bar assns., State Bar Ga., Am. Judicature Soc., Washington and Lee U. Alumni Assn. (pres. 1976—), Lawyers Club Atlanta (pres. 1976-77). Office: Suite 1515 Peachtree Center South 225 Peachtree St NE Atlanta GA 30303 Tel (404) 522-3541

BRANCO, RICHARD FREDERICK, b. Holstein, Iowa, June 11, 1926; B.S., U. Notre Dame (Ind.), 1948, J.D., 1950. Admitted to Iowa bar, 1950; partner firm Leonard and Branco, Holstein, 1950-65; individual practice law, Holstein, 1965-72; partner firm Branco and Boerner, Holstein, Ida Grove and Odebolt, Iowa, 1972—; atty. Ida County (Iowa), 1957—. Mem. Am., Iowa State bar assns., Iowa County Attys. Assn. (pres. 1977), Nat. Dist. Attys. Assn., Iowa Acad. Trial Lawyers, Assn. Trial Lawyers Am. Home: 407 S Hamburg St Holstein IA 51025 Office: 117 E 2nd St Holstein IA 51025 Tel (712) 368-2127

BRAND, FRANZ WALTER, b. Monroe, Wis., Dec. 17, 1926; B.A., Beloit Coll., 1948; J.D., U. Wis., 1951. Admitted to Wis. bar, 1951, U.S. Dist. Ct. bar, 1951; partner firm Kittelsen, Brand, & Barry, Monroe, Wis., 1951-74; judge Green County (Wis.), 1974—; dist. atty. Green County, 1955-61. Home: 532 22d Ave Monroe WI 53566 Office: Court House Monroe WI 53566 Tel (608) 325-9145

BRAND, JOSEPH LYON, b. Urbana, Ohio, Aug. 11, 1936; A.B., U. Mich., 1958; M.A., Ohio State U., 1959; J.D. with honors, George Washington U., 1963. Admitted to Ohio and D.C. bars, 1963; partner firm Brand, Wagner & Dodd, Washington 1963-65; asso. firm Barco, Cook, Patton & Blow, Washington, 1965-67; partner firm Patton, Boggs & Blow and predecessor, Washington, 1967—; v.p. Internat. Investment Co., 1963-65. Mem. Am., D.C. bar assns., Am. Soc. Internat. Law, George Washington Law Assn. (past v.p.), Washington Fgn. Law Soc., Washington Inst. Fgn. Affairs, Middle East Inst., Order of Coif. Home: 1701 Putter Ln Reston VA 22090 Office: Patton Boggs & Blow 1200 17th St NW Washington DC 20036 Tel (202) 223-4040

BRAND, MALCOLM LEIGH, b. Inglewood, Calif., Mar. 5, 1935; B.A. in Econs., Willamette U., 1957, J.D., 1964. Admitted to Oreg. bar; atty. Salem Title Co. (Oreg.), 1964-68; asst. city atty. City of Salem, 1968-69; partner firm Rhoten, Rhoten & Speerstra, Salem, 1969—. Mem. Marien County (Oreg.) Bar Assn. (pres.). Home: 720 McGilchrist St SE Salem OR 97302 Office: 300 Pioneer Trust Bldg Salem OR 97301 Tel (503) 364-6733

BRAND, STUART HARVEY, b. Chgo., May 14, 1940; B.S. in Mech. Engring., U. Ill., 1961; M.S. in Engring., U. Calif., Los Angeles, 1965; J.D., U. So. Calif., 1967. Admitted to Calif. bar, 1968; individual practice law, Sherman Oaks, Calif., 1968-70; partner firm Brand & MacMiller, Sherman Oaks, 1970—. Mem. adv. council San Fernando Valley Elementary Schs., 1971-73, San Fernando Valley Jr. High Schs., 1973-75; active Little League, Park League, YMCA. Mem. State Bar Calif., San Fernando Valley Bar Assn. Home: 16447 Stare St Sepulveda CA 91343 Office: 15233 Ventura Blvd Suite 312 Sherman Oaks CA 91403 Tel (213) 783-4311

BRANDENBURG, JAMES MICHAEL, b. Taos, N.Mex., Dec. 10, 1942; B.A., U. N.Mex., 1966, J.D., 1969. Admitted to N.Mex. bar, 1969; asst. dist. atty. N.Mex. 8th Jud. Dist., Taos, 1969-76; partner firm Bradenburg & Brandenburg, Taos, 1971—; town atty. Town of Taos, 1976—. Dist. chmn. Sangre de Christo council Boy Scouts Am., 1975-76; mem. Taos Vol. Fire Dept., 1969—. Mem. N.Mex. Bar Assn., Nat., N.Mex. dist. attys. assns., N.Mex. Municipal Attys. Assn., Nat. Inst. Municipal Law Officers, U. N.Mex. Alumni Assn. (dir.). Home: POB 1237 Taos NM 87571 Office: POB 617 Taos NM 87571 Tel (505) 758-4261

BRANDENBURG, ROBERT FAIRCHILD, JR., b. Oklahoma City, Mar. 6, 1938; B.A., U. Okla., 1961, J.D., 1966. Admitted to Okla. bar, 1966; individual practice law, Norman, 1968-75; partner firm Floyd, Brandenburg & Rogers and predecessor, Norman, 1975—; pres., dir. Brandenburg Enterprises, Inc., 1970—; co-trustee John B. Brandenburg Trust, 1971—; pres., dir. Cumberland Heights, Inc., 1973—. Sec., fin. chmn., dir. Norman Alcohol Info. Center, Inc., 1972—; vice chmn., trustee Lueto Found. to Aid the Chemically Dependent, Norman, 1975—; vestryman St. Michael's Episcopal Ch., Norman, 1976—. Mem. Okla., Am., Cleve. County bar assns., Phi Alpha Delta. Home: 430 Macy St Norman OK 73069 Office: 116 E Main St Norman OK 73069 Tel (405) 321-3632

BRANDENBURG, ROBERT HOWARD, b. Wasito, Ky., Nov. 10, 1914; B.S., Washington U., St. Louis, 1940, B.A., 1940, J.D., 1940. Admitted to Mo. bar, 1940, N.Mex. bar, 1940; individual practice law, Taos, N.Mex., 1940—; dir. First State Bank of Taos; mem. jud. standard commn. State of N.Mex. Bd. dirs. Taos Animal Shelter, Taos Fiesta Bd., Harwood Found., Taos, Sierra Vista Cemetary Assn., Taos; leader Kit Carson council Boy Scouts Am., Taos. Mem. Am., N.Mex., Taos County (past pres.) bar assns., Am. Coll. Probate Counsel. Home: POB 1958 Taos NM 87571 Office: POB 617 Taos NM 87571 Tel (505) 758-4261

BRANDER, JOHN MORRAN, b. San Francisco, Jan. 26, 1932; B.Sc., Univ. Coll., Cardiff, Wales, 1954; B.A. with honors, Rand U., 1967, LL.B., 1967; LL.M., Univ. Coll., London, Eng., 1968; LL.M., Georgetown U., 1971. Admitted to D.C. bar, 1971, Md. bar, 1972, Calif. bar, 1974; asso., counsel firm McDaniel, Burton, Daniels and Brady, Washington, 1972-74; atty. Dept. Agr., Washington, 1974-76; atty. Pres.'s Clemency Bd., 1975, staff counsel Calif. Dept. Savs. and Loan, Los Angeles, 1976—; legis. asst. State Mental Health Program Dirs., Washington, 1972-73. Mem. Calif. State Bar, D.C., Md. bar assns., Am. Soc. Internat. Law. Contbr. articles to profl. jours. Home: 1749 N Las Palmas Ave Apt 205 Los Angeles CA 90028 Office: Calif Dept Savs and Loan 600 S Commonwealth Ave Los Angeles CA 90005 Tel (213) 736-2801

BRANDT, FRED WILLIAM, b. Chgo., Apr. 11, 1933; student Pomona Coll., 1951; A.B. in Econs., Stanford, 1955, postgrad., 1958-59; LL.B., Southwestern U., 1964; postgrad. U. So. Calif., 1969. Admitted to Calif. bar, 1964; dep. county counsel Los Angeles County, 1964-66; asso. firm Jarrett & Woodhead, Los Angeles, 1966-73; partner firm Jarrett & Brandt, Los Angeles, 1973—. Mgr. Pasadena SW Little League; running commr. Los Angeles Athletic Club. Mem. Los Angeles County, Am. bar assns., State Bar Calif., Am. Bd. Trial Advs., Assn. So. Calif. Def. Counsel. Home: 770 Oak Knoll Circle Pasadena CA 91105 Office: 315 W Ninth St suite 515 Los Angeles CA 90015 Tel (213) 627-5711

BRANDT, PETER H., b. N.Y.C., Feb. 6, 1896; B.S., Case Western Res. U., 1919, M.E., 1924; LL.B., Fordham Law Sch., 1927. Admitted to N.Y. bar, 1928; dir. engring. and counsel United Real Estate Owners Assn., N.Y.C., 1928-32; partner firm Peter H. & Hubert J. Brandt, N.Y.C. Chmn. N.Y.C. Selective Service Bd.; mem. N.Y.C. Tax Exemption-Tax Inequalities Service Adv. Com. Mem. Bronx County, Real Property Assessment Tax Rev. bar assns. Home: 3701 Henry Hudson Pkwy Riverdale NY 10463 Office: Empire State Bldg New York City NY 10001 Tel (212) 563-2200

BRANDT, ROBERT SANDFORD, b. Norris, Tenn., May 25, 1941; A.B., Centre Coll. Ky., 1963; J.D., Vanderbilt U., 1966. Admitted to Tenn. bar, 1966; asst. dist. atty. Nashville, 1966-70; asso. firm Schulman, McCarley, Hollins & Pride, Nashville, 1970-73; partner firm Barrett, Brandt & Barrett, Nashville, 1974-76; judge chancery ct. Davidson County (Tenn.), Nashville, 1976—. Chmn. Tenn. Conservation Commn., 1975-76, Tenn. chpt. Sierra Club, 1973-75; vestryman Christ Episcopal Ch., 1975—; del. Tenn. Constl. Conv., 1971. Mem. Tenn., Am., Nashville bar assns. Named Conservationist of the Year, Tenn. Scenic Rivers Assn., 1974. Home: 700 Woodleigh Dr Nashville TN 37215 Office: Metropolitan Courthouse Nashville TN 37219 Tel (615) 259-6155

BRANDT, SUSAN MASCETTE, b. Syracuse, N.Y., Feb. 12, 1947; A.B., Cornell U., 1968; J.D. cum laude, N.Y.U., 1971. Admitted to N.Y. bar, 1972; asso. firm Paul, Weiss, Rifkind, Wharton & Garrison, N.Y.C., 1971-73; asst. prof. Bklyn. Law Sch., 1973-76, asso. prof., 1976—. Mem. Am., N.Y. Women's bar assns. Note and comment editor N.Y.U. Law Rev., 1970-71. Office: 250 Joralemon St Brooklyn NY 11201 Tel (212) 625-2200

BRANHAM, CHARLES THORNWELL, JR., b. Memphis, Sept. 21, 1925; A.A., Tenn. Wesleyan Coll., 1948; LL.B., U. Tenn., 1952. Admitted to Tenn. bar, 1952, Fla. bar, 1954; individual practice law, Coral Gables, Fla., 1955-64; asso. firm Blackwell, Walker & Gray, Miami, Fla., 1964; judge Ct. Indsl. Claims, Coral Gables, 1965—, sr. judge Miami office, 1972—. Ruling elder Palmetto (Fla.) Presbyn. Ch., 1964-66, 73-75, deacon, 1960-62, 70-72; dist. chmn. hurricane dist. South Fla. council Boy Scouts Am., 1971-72; charter mem., 1st chmn. Coral Gables Youth Adv. Com., 1965-69; asst. state dir. Khoury League of Fla., 1969-70. Mem. Fla., Dade County, Coral Gables (pres. 1965) bar assns., Phi Delta Phi. Home: 6505 SW 93d Ave Miami FL 33173 Office: Dept of Commerce Bur of Workmen's Compensation 2801 Ponce de Leon Blvd Coral Gables FL 33173 Tel (305) 445-9371

BRANIGIN, ROGER DOUGLAS, JR., b. Louisville, Mar. 1, 1931; A.B., Dartmouth, 1952; LL.B., Harvard, 1955. Admitted to Ind. bar, 1955; asso. firm Stuart, Branigin, Ricks & Schilling, Lafayette, Ind., 1957-62, partner, 1962—; dir. Lafayette Nat. Bank, Duncan Electric Co. Trustee Lafayette Sch. Corp., 1963-64, 65-69, pres., 1969; pres. United Community Service, 1966-67, Lafayette Boys' Club, 1976—. Mem. Am., Ind., Tippecanoe County bar assns. Office: 801 Life Bldg PO Box 1010 Lafayette IN 47902 Tel (317) 423-1561

BRANNICK, GEORGE JOSEPH, b. Jackson, Mich., Mar. 18, 1928; B.A., U. Mich., 1951; J.D., U. Detroit, 1954. Admitted to Mich. bar, 1954, U.S. Supreme ct. bar, 1959; individual practice law, 1954-59, Jackson, Mich., 1967—; trial lawyer NLRB, 1959-62; chief labor lawyer U.S. Air Force, 1962-67; instr. Jackson Community Coll., 1972—. Mem. Mich. Bar., Jackson C. of C. (dir.), Delta Theta Phi. Office: 605 W Michigan Ave Jackson MI 49210 Tel (517) 787-1303

BRANNIGAN, EUGENE J., b. Bklyn., June 26, 1926; student Darmouth Coll., Fordham U.; LL.B., N.Y. Law Sch., 1950. Admitted to N.Y. bar, 1953; U.S. Supreme Ct. bar, 1966; counsel State Farm Ins. Co. Mem. N.Y. State Bar Assn. Home: 89 Wallace St Freeport NY 11520 Office: 1539 Franklin Ave Mineola NY 11501 Tel (516) PI6-6611

BRANSKY, PHILIP LEE, b. Chgo., June 14, 1935; B.S., Northwestern U., 1957; J.D., U. Chgo., 1961. Admitted to Ill. bar, 1961; with Legal Aid Bur., Chgo., 1962-63; asso. firm Morgan, Halligan, Lanoff & Cook, Chgo., 1963-67, firm Gordon, Reicin & West, Chgo., 1968-72; partner firm Wilczynski, Wilczynski, Ciambrone, Karwoski & Bransky, Chicago Heights, Ill., 1972—. Chmn. Homewood Ethics Commn., 1975—; mem. Homewood Zoning Bd. Appeals, 1971—; mem. Ill. Gov's. Commn. for Revision of Mental Health Code, 1975—; bd. dirs. Handicamp Assn. for Handicapped Children, 1967—, S. Suburban Council for Mentally Disabled Citizens, 1974—. Mem. Am., Ill. State (standing com. on mental disabilities 1976—), Chgo. (vice chmn. probate com. 1967-68, land trust com. 1969-72, real property com. 1971-72), bar assns. Office: 1515 Halsted St Chicago Heights IL 60411 Tel (312) 755-9133

BRANT, CHARLES ENSIGN, b. Dayton, Ohio, Mar. 6, 1930; B.A., U. Dayton, 1952; J.D., Ohio State U., 1959; LL.M., Northwestern U., 1960. Admitted to Ohio bar, 1959, U.S. Supreme Ct. bar, 1973; partner firm Wright, Harlor, Morris, Arnold & Glander, Columbus, Ohio, 1960-71, Glander, Brant, Ledman & Newman, Columbus, 1971—; lectr. law Ohio State U., Columbus, 1962; col., staff judge adv. USAR, 1968-76, commr. 9th Mil. Law Center, Columbus, 1976—. Pres. Central Ohio Planned Parenthood Assn., 1971-72. Mem. Am., Fed., Ohio (chmn. negligence law com. 1977), Columbus bar assns. Home: 2251 Oxford Rd Upper Arlington OH 43221 Office: 250 E Broad St Columbus OH 43215 Tel (614) 221-2121

BRASCH, ROBERT ERNEST, b. Lewiston, Idaho, Aug. 5, 1937; B.S., U. Oreg., 1960, J.D., 1966. Admitted to Oreg. bar, 1966, U.S. Dist. Ct. Oreg. bar, 1968, U.S. Ct. Appeals 9th Circuit bar, 1968, So. Ct. U.S. bar, 1971; asst. dist. atty. Coos County, Oreg., 1966-67, dist. atty., 1968—; faculty Bd. on Police Studies and Tng., 1972—, Summer Inst. for Prosecutors, 1973—. Mem. Nat., Oreg. dist. attys. assns., Oreg. Bar Assn., U. Oreg. Alumni Assn., U. Oreg. Devel. Fund. Office: Courthouse Coquille OR 97423 Tel (503) 396-3121

BRASHER, REX LANDRETH, JR., b. Memphis, Mar. 23, 1943; B.A., Memphis State U., 1965, J.D. with honors (Memphis Bar Assn. scholar), 1967. Admitted to Tenn. bar, 1968; asso. firm Larkey, Dudley & Blanchard, Memphis, 1968-72; partner firms Rickey, Shankman, Blanchard, Agee, Harpster & Klein, Memphis, 1972-76, Brown, Smith, Trotter, Brasher, Memphis, 1976—. Bd. dirs., legal counsel Memphis YWCA; election insp. Shelby County (Tenn.). Mem. Tenn., Memphis-Shelby County, Am bar assns., Am., Tenn. trial lawyers assns., Omicron Delta Kappa. Mem. editorial staff Memphis State U. Law Rev., 1966-67, asso. editor, 1968. Home: 5554 Fannin St Memphis TN 38118 Office: 2515-51 Poplar Ave Memphis TN 38137 Tel (901) 761-1010

BRASLOW, DEAN GERALD, b. Mt. Vernon, N.Y., Mar. 10, 1934; B.A., Yale U., 1955; J.D., Columbia U., 1961. Admitted to N.Y. bar, 1961; dep. asst. atty. gen. State N.Y., 1961-63, asst. atty. gen., 1963; opinion clk., legal asst. Surrogate's Ct. Westchester County, White Plains, N.Y., 1963-66; asso. firm Parker, Duryee, Zunino, Malone & Carter, and predecessor, N.Y.C., 1966-68, partner, 1969—; lectr. in field. Active United Way; legis. chmn. North St. Sch. PTA, White Plains, 1975—; Mem. Am., N.Y. State (exec. com. trusts and estates, 1968-72), Westchester County, White Plains bar assns., Assn. Bar City N.Y. Author: (with Cox, Arenson and Medina) N.Y. Civil Practice, 1970. Editor Report on the Uniform Probate Code, 1976. Home: 10 Antony Rd White Plains NY 10605 Office: 1 E 44th St New York City NY 10017 Tel (212) 573-9358

BRASSARD, RAYMOND MAURICE, b. Manchester, N.H., May 29, 1947; B.A., also B.B.A., U. Tex., 1969, J.D., 1972. Admitted to Tex. bar, 1973; mem. firm Adams & Browne, Beaumont, Tex., 1973—. Mem. Am. Bar Assn., Beaumont Estate Planning Council, S.E. Tex. C.P.A.'s, Tex. Soc. C.P.A.'s. Home: 820 Chatwood St Beaumont TX 77706 Office: 1012 Goodhue Bldg Beaumont TX 77701 Tel (713) 833-5684

BRASWELL, EDWIN MAURICE, b. Rocky Mount, N.C., Dec. 16, 1922; LL.B., U.N.C., Chapel Hill, 1950. Admitted to N.C. Bar, 1950; individual practice law, Fayetteville, N.C., 1950-59; partner firm Clark, Braswell & Hill, Fayetteville, 1959-62; sr. resident judge Superior Ct., Fayetteville, 1962—; dist. atty., Fayetteville, 1955-62. Mem. Am., N.C. (v.p. 1974-75), Cumberland County bar assns., Am. Judicature Soc., N.C. Conf. Superior Ct. Judges (pres. 1974-75), N.C. Criminal Justice Edn., Tng. System Council (chmn.). Home: 333 DeVane St Fayetteville NC 28305 Office: Cumberland County Court House Gillespie St Fayetteville NC 28301 Tel (919) 483-9071

BRATCHER, RHODES. Admitted to Ky. bar; asst. U.S. atty. Western Ky. Dist., 1953-55; now judge U.S. Dist. Ct., Western Dist. Ky. Address: Owensboro KY 42301*

BRATTEN, THOMAS ARNOLD, b. Dayton, Ohio, Sept. 11, 1934; M.E., U. Cin., 1957; J.D., Chase Coll., Cin., 1968. Admitted to Ohio bar, 1968, Fla. bar, 1968, U.S. Supreme Ct. bar, 1972; engr. in tng. Gen. Motors, 1953-57, test engr., 1957-59, project engr., 1963-68, sr. project engr., 1968; design engr. Pratt & Witney Aircraft, 1959-61; gen. mgr. Auto Technia, Inc., 1961-63; partner firm Campbell, Colbath, Kapner & Bratten, W. Palm Beach, Fla., 1969-72, firm Bratten and Harris, W. Palm Beach, 1973—. Mem. exec. com. Palm Beach County (Fla.) Republican Party, 1971—. Mem. The Fla. Bar, Acad. Fla. Trial Lawyers, Assn. Trial Lawyers Am., Palm Beach County Bar Assn., Pi Tau Sigma. Office: 319 Clematis St suite 500 Comeau Bldg West Palm Beach FL 33401 Tel (305) 659-2400

BRATTON, JAMES HENRY, JR., b. Pulaski, Tenn., Oct. 9, 1931; B.A., (Optime Merens), U. of South, 1952; B.A., Oxford (Eng.) U., 1954; LL.B., Yale, 1956. Admitted to Tenn. bar, 1956, Ga. bar, 1957; asso. firm Gambrell, Harlan, Russell, Moye & Richardson and successors, Atlanta, 1956-63, partner, 1964—; summer intern U.S. Dept. Justice, 1955; vis. lectr. U. Ga., 1967. Bd. dirs. Protestant Welfare & Social Services, Atlanta, 1960-67, Christian Council Met.

Atlanta, Inc., 1968—; Chs. Home for Bus. Girls, 1970—. Mem. Am. Law Inst., Am. (mem. standing com. aero. law, chmn. 1977—), Ga. (founding chmn. sect. environ. law), Atlanta bar assns., Atlanta Lawyers Club. Home: 63 N Muscogee Ave NW Atlanta GA 30305 Office: 4000 1 Nat Bank Tower Atlanta GA 30303 Tel (404) 658-1620

BRAUER, ROBERT EMIL, b. Staunton, Ill., Apr. 7, 1923; B.A., Washington U., St. Louis, 1949, LL.B., 1951. Admitted to Ill. bar, Mo. bar, 1951; asso. firm Mattingly, Boas & Richards, St. Louis, 1951-53; asst. U.S. atty., St. Louis, 1953-59; mem. firm Rassieur, Long & Yawitz, St. Louis, 1960-61; bankruptcy judge Eastern and Western Dists. of Mo., 1961—. Mem. Mo., St. Louis bar assns., Am. Judicature Soc., Nat. Conf. Bankruptcy Judges, Comml. Law League, Order of Coif. Home: 4279 Mansard St St Louis MO 63125 Office: U S Court House Rm 730 1114 Market St St Louis MO 63101 Tel (314) 425-4222

BRAUN, FREDERICK BICKNELL, b. Cin., Aug. 4, 1942; A.B., U. Cin., 1967; M.S. in Social Adminstrn., Case Western Res. U., 1969, J.D., 1973. Admitted to Ohio bar, 1973; asso. firm Beckman, Lavercombe, Fox and Weil, Cin., 1973—; chmn. Ohio Title XX Social Services Adv. Bd., 1976—. Mem. Cin., Ohio, Am. bar assns. Office: 1714 1st Nat Bank Bldg Cincinnati OH 45202 Tel (513) 621-2100

BRAUN, GEORGE, b. Budapest, Hungary, May 17, 1923; B.A. in English, Case Western Reserve U., 1946, M.A. in English, 1947, LL.B., 1949. Admitted to Ohio bar, 1949; Admitted to Ohio bar, 1949; practice law, Cleve., 1949—; gen. counsel, dir. Ohio Paralegal Inst.; sec., dir. Marshallan Mfg. Co., sec. Bedel Holding Co.; judge Cleve. Area Law Sch. Moot Ct. Competitions. Chmn. sch. bd., trustee Taylor Rd. Synagogue, 1960-72; trustee Adelbert Coll., Case Western Res. U., Case Western Reserve U. Law alumni assns.; mem. Cleve. Mayer's Adv. Bd. Mem. Cleve., Cuyahoga County, Ohio bar assns., Cleve. Legal Aid Soc., Omicron Delta Kappa. Contbr. articles Cleve. State Law Jour. Home: 20001 S Park Blvd Shaker Hts OH 44122 Office: 1420 Investment Plaza Cleveland OH 44114 Tel (216) 771-3500

BRAUN, ROBERT WILLIAM, b. Wichita Falls, Tex., Aug. 30, 1938; B.B.A., U. Iowa, 1960, J.D., 1963. Admitted to Iowa bar, 1963; partner firm Mosier, Thomas, Beatty, Dulton & Braun, Waterloo, Iowa, 1970—; asst. atty. Black Hawk County (Iowa), 1970-75; atty. City of LaPorte, Iowa, 1974—; exec. com. young lawyers sect. Iowa State Bar, 1971-75. Vestryman, sr. warden Trinity Episc. Ch., Waterloo, 1974—. Mem. Am., Iowa, Black Hawk County bar assns. Home: 165 Woodlawn St Waterloo IA 50701 Office: 3151 Brockway Rd Waterloo IA 50701 Tel (319) 234-4471

BRAY, ABSALOM FRANCIS, JR., b. San Francisco, Nov. 24, 1918; A.B., Stanford U., 1940; J.D., U. So. Calif., 1949. Admitted to Calif. bar, 1949, U.S. Supreme Ct. bar, 1960; sr. partner firm Bray, Baldwin, Egan, Breitwieser & Starr, Martinez and Dublin, Calif., 1949—. Chmn. Martinez Recreation Commn., 1949-54; chmn. nat. bd. dirs. Camp Fire Girls, 1959-61, 69-71; pres. Contra Costa County (Calif.) Devel. Assn., 1959-60. Mem. State Bar Calif. (chmn. adoption com. 1955-56), Contra Costa County Bar Assn. (pres. 1964), Delta Theta Phi. Home: 1031 Ulfinian Way Martinez CA 94553 Office: Ward and Ferry Sts Martinez CA 94553 Tel (415) 228-2550

BRAY, ALLAN DODD, b. East Orange, N.J., Apr. 17, 1938; B.A., Marietta Coll., 1960; LL.B., Duke U., 1963. Admitted to Nev. bar, 1970, U.S. Supreme Ct. bar, 1976; spl. agt. FBI, Dallas, 1963-65, Los Angeles, 1965-67, night supr., Los Angeles, 1967; chief criminal dep., City atty's office, Las Vegas, 1971-73; individual practice law, Las Vegas, 1973—. Mem. Nev. State, Clark County bar assns., East Charleston Optimist Club (pres. 1973-74, v.p. 1976—), Omicron Delta Kappa, Tau Pi Phi, Pi Gamma Mu, Pi Kappa Delta. Recipient Outstanding Man of Year award Las Vegas Jaycees, 1973. Home: 3115 Camelback Dr Las Vegas NV 89109 Office: 302 E Carson Suite 920 Las Vegas NV 89101 Tel (702) 384-1111

BRAY, HOMER ALLEN, b. Morristown, Tenn., Aug. 11, 1944; B.S., U. Tenn., 1967, J.D., 1973. Admitted to Tenn. bar, 1973; partner firm Fox and Bray, Alcoa, Tenn., 1973—; municipal judge Municipal Ct. City Alcoa, 1975—. Mem. Blount County Bar Assn. (sec.-treas. 1975-76). Recipient Wm. Brownville Meml. award Jaycees, 1975. Home: 304 Hudson St Maryville TN 37801 Office: 356 Sanderson St Alcoa TN 37701 Tel (615) 983-7710

BRAYTON, ANTHONY, b. Fall River, Mass., July 11, 1902; A.B., Williams Coll., 1924; B.Law, Harvard, 1927, J.D., 1968. Admitted to Mass. bar, 1927, Hawaii bar, 1969; mem. firm Hale & Dorr, Boston, 1927-67; legal cons. Bishop Trust Co., Honolulu, 1967—. Office: PO Box 2390 Honolulu HI 96813 Tel (808) 536-3771

BRAZIER, GEOFFREY LANGFORD, b. Helena, Mont., Nov. 8, 1929; B.S. in Mining Engring., Mont. Sch. Mines, 1951; LL.B., Mont. State U. (now to U. Mont.), 1957, J.D., 1970. Admitted to Mont. bar, 1957; asso. firm Skedd, Harris, & Massman, Helena, 1957; individual practice law, Helena, 1958-64; partner firm Brazier, Dowling & Erickson, and predecessor, Helena, 1964-73; Mont. Consumer Counsel, Helena, 1973—; dep. county atty. Lewis and Clark County (Mont.), 1971; atty. Mont. Milk Control Bd., 1957-73, exec. sec., 1964-71; mem. Mont. Constl. Conv., 1972. Trustee Lewis and Clark County (Mont.) Sch. Dist. 1, 1969-71. Mem. 1st Dist. Bar Assn. of Mont. (past pres.), Mont. Bar., Assn. ICC Practitioners. Home: 516 Harrison Ave Helena MT 59601 Office: 34 W 6th Ave Helena MT 59601 Tel (406) 449-2771

BRAZIL, DAN MCCALL, b. Lufkin, Tex., Oct. 5, 1927; B.A., Baylor U., 1947, LL.B., 1951. Admitted to Tex. bar, 1952; city atty. City of Lufkin, 1959-60; county atty. County of Angelina, 1961-68; dist. atty. Angelina County, 1969-72; individual practice law, Lufkin, 1972—. Pres. Lufkin Community Playhouse; bd. dirs. Lufkin Community Concerts Assn. Mem. Am., Tex., Angelina County bar assns. Home: 325 Sunset St Lufkin TX 75901 Office: 208 Lufkin Ave Lufkin TX 75901 Tel (713) 632-5417

BREAULT, THEODORE EDWARD, b. N.Y.C., Mar. 7, 1938; B.S., Manhattan Coll., 1960; J.D., Cath. U. Am., 1963. Admitted to D.C. bar, 1964, Va. bar, 1964, Pa. bar, 1970; asso. firm Seltzer & Suskind, Washington, 1964-69; individual practice law, Fairfax, Va., 1964-69; asso. firm Egler & Reinstadtler, Pitts., 1969-77; individual practice law, Pitts., 1977—. Pres. Sewickley (Pa.) Symphony Orch., 1974, 75. Mem. D.C., Va. State, Pa., Allegheny County bar assns., Allegheny County Med.-Legal Com., Pa. Workmen's Compensation Survey Com., Am. Soc. Law and Medicine, Am. Arbitration Assn. (panel). Home: 108 Claridge Dr Coraopolis PA 15108 Office: 428 Forbes Ave Pittsburgh PA 15219 Tel (412) 391-8230 also 890 Beaver Grade Rd Coraopolis PA 15108 Tel (412) 264-1414

BREAZEALE, HOPKINS PAYNE, JR., b. Baton Rouge, Apr. 1, 1920; B.A., La. State U., 1941, J.D., 1948. Admitted to La. bar, 1948, U.S. Supreme Ct. bar, 1959; with firm Breazeale, Sachse & Wilson, Baton Rouge, 1948—, now sr. partner; officer, dir. Moran Industries, TJM Corp., Wolf Baking Co., Inc. (La.), E.J. Spangler Co., Phila., Gulf Internat. Cinema Corp.; dir. Fidelity Nat. Bank, Baton Rouge. Trustee U. South, 1967-73; pres. La. State U. Found., 1972-74. Mem. Am. (com. mem.), Fed. (com. mem.) bar assns., Am. Judicature Soc., La. Law Inst., Internat. Soc. Labor Law (Am. nat. com.), La. State U. Alumni Fedn. (pres. 1968-69), Baton Rouge C. of C. (pres. 1966-67). Home: 4152 Claycut Rd Baton Rouge LA 70806 Office: 7th Floor Fidelity Nat Bank Bldg PO Box 3197 Baton Rouge LA 70821 Tel (504) 387-4000

BREBBIA, JOHN HENRY, b. Boston, Feb. 16, 1932; A.B., Stonehill Coll., 1953; LL.B., Boston Coll., 1956. Admitted to Mass. bar, 1957, D.C. bar, 1965; asso. firm Davies, Richberg, Tydings, Landa & Duff, Washington, 1965-67; mng. partner Washington office Alston, Miller & Gaines, Washington and Atlanta, 1967—; trial atty. FTC, Bur. Restraint of Trade, 1961-64; mem. Atomic Safety and Licensing Bd. Panel, U.S. Nuclear Regulatory Commn., 1972—. Mem. Am., Fed., D.C. (chmn. antitrust law com. 1972-74) bar assns. Recipient FTC Meritorious Service award, 1964, Superior Service award, 1966; contbr. articles to legal jours. Home: 3232 Klingle Rd NW Washington DC 20008 Office: 1800 M St NW Washington DC 20036 Tel (202) 223-1300

BRECHER, ARMIN GEORGIE, b. Prague, Czechoslavakia, July 7, 1942; B.A. summa cum laude, Emory U., 1966; LL.B., U. Va., 1969. Admitted to Ga. bar, 1970; asso. firm Powell, Goldstein, Frazer & Murphy, Atlanta, 1969-75, partner, 1975—. Mem. Am., Atlanta bar assns. Home: 1100 Old Woodbine Rd Atlanta GA 30319 Office: 1100 C & S Nat Bank Bldg 35 Broad St Atlanta GA 30303 Tel (404) 521-1900

BRECK, LAWRENCE DAVID, b. Pitts., Jan. 29, 1942; B.A., U. Pitts., 1963, LL.B., 1966; M.B.A., Harvard, 1973. Admitted to U.S. Supreme Ct. bar, 1970, Pa. Supreme Ct. bar, 1967, Fed. Dist. Ct. bar, 1967; staff asst. Westinghouse Electric Corp., Pitts., 1966-68; asst. legal counsel Blue Cross of Western Pa., Pitts., 1968-71; corporate sec., legal counsel Kobacker Stores, Inc., Brilliant, Ohio, 1975—. Mem. Am., Pa., Allegheny County bar assns., Am. Soc. Corporate Sec., Harvard Bus. Sch. Assn. of Pitts. Home: 415 Devonshire St Pittsburgh PA 15213 Office: 198 Penn St Brilliant OH 43913 Tel (412) 687-0835

BRECKENRIDGE, PAUL GEORGE, b. Los Angeles, June 12, 1927; A.B., Stanford U., 1950, LL.B., 1952. Admitted to Calif. bar, 1953; jr. counsel State Compensation Ins. Fund, Los Angeles, 1953; pub. defender Los Angeles County, 1953-68, chief trial dep., 1965-66, chief dept., 1967-68; judge Superior Ct. of Calif., Los Angeles, 1968—. Mem. Calif. Judges Assn. Office: 111 N Hill St Los Angeles CA 90012 Tel (213) 974-1234

BREDELL, HAROLD HOLMES, b. Indpls., June 18, 1907; A.B., Butler U., 1929; LL.B., Harvard U., 1932. Admitted to Ind. bar, 1932, U.S. Supreme Ct. bar, 1939; lectr. Ind. Law Sch., Indpls., 1938-40; dir. 1st Nat. Bank N. Vernon (Ind.), 1969—; chmn., pres. Vernon Fin. Corp., 1969—; chmn. bd. dirs. Vernon Fire & Casualty Ins. Co. and Vernon Gen. Ins. Co., 1947—; mem. firm Bredell, Martin, McTuran & Meyer, Indpls., 1947—. Mem. Indpls., Am. (treas. bd. govs. 1949-59, ho. of dels. 1939—), Ind. State bar assns., Am. Bar Endowment (pres. 1971-73, dir. 1959-75), Ind. Soc. Chgo., Harvard Law Assn. Home: 5524 Roxbury Terr Apt B Indianapolis IN 46226 Office: 2430 Indiana Nat Bank Tower Indianapolis IN 46204 Tel (317) 639-4294

BREDENBECK, ARTHUR HURST, b. Los Angeles, Dec. 20, 1939; A.B., Stanford, 1961, J.D., 1963. Admitted to Calif. bar, 1963; asso. firm Carr, McClellan, Ingersoll, Thompson & Horn, Burlingame, Calif., 1963-69, partner, 1969—. Pres., Bay Area Assn. Suicide Prevention Center, 1968-71, Suicide Prevention Center San Mateo County, 1972; pres. San Mateo County council Boy Scouts Am., 1974-76, trustee Golden Gate Scouting; chmn. Calif. adv. council Episcopal Ch. Found. Mem. Am., Calif., San Mateo County bar assns., Peninsula Estate Planning Council (officer 1969), Western Pension Conf. Tel (415) 342-7461

BREED, JOHN CARROLL, b. Houston, Apr. 16, 1933; B.A., Rice U., 1955; J.D., S. Tex. Coll., 1962. Admitted to Tex. bar, 1962, U.S. Supreme Ct. bar, 1966; atty. Tenneco, Inc., Houston, 1960-72; individual practice law, Houston, 1972—; dir. Town & Country Bank. Trustee Boy's Country, Houston; deacon Tallowood Baptist Ch., Houston; mem. pres.'s council Houston Bapt. U. Mem. Houston Natural Gas Men's Assn. Home: 306 Hickory Post Houston TX 77079 Office: 2000 W Loop Suite 1455 Houston TX 77027 Tel (713) 960-9111

BREEN, FRANCIS RICHMOND, b. Reno, Dec. 1915; B.A., U. Nev., 1939; J.D., Stanford, 1947. Admitted to Nev. bar, 1946, Calif. bar, 1947, U.S. Supreme Ct. bar, 1957; sr. mem. firm Breen, Young, Whitehead & Hoy, Chartered, Reno, 1965-68, pres., 1969-73, chmn. bd., 1974—; asst. sgt. at arms U.S. Senate, 1941-42; v.p. Squaw Valley Devel. Co., 1960—, Squaw Valley Ski Corp., 1974—. Trustee Ducks Unltd., 1966-75, trustee emeritus, 1975—, chmn. Nev. chpt., 1975. Mem. Washoe County (Nev.), Nev., Am., Inter-Am. bar assns. Office: 232 Court St Reno NV 89501 Tel (702) 786-7600

BREEN, PETER INGRAM, b. Reno, Nov. 8, 1939; B.A., U. Nev., 1960; LL.B., U. Santa Clara, 1963. Admitted to Nev. bar, 1963; individual practice law, Reno, 1963-66; partner firms McCune & Breen, Reno, 1966-67, Dickerson, Welsh & Breen, Carson City, Nev., 1971, Wilson & Breen, Reno, 1971-73; dep. atty. gen. Nev. Atty. Gen's Office, Carson City, 1967-70; judge 2d Jud. Dist. Ct., 1973—. Bd. dirs. No. Area Substance Abuse Council of Nev., 1974—. Mem. Nev., Am., Washoe County (Nev.) bar assns., Nev. Dist. Judges Assn. Office: PO Box 1125 87504 Washoe County Courthouse Reno NV 89504 Tel (702) 785-4269

BREEZE, DEAN, b. Los Angeles, Mar. 15, 1921; J.D., U. Chgo., 1950. Admitted to Nev. bar, 1953, U.S. Ct. Mil. Appeals, 1956; partner firm Breeze & Breeze, Las Vegas, Nev., 1953-67; individual practice law, Las Vegas, 1968—; municipal judge City N. Las Vegas, 1963-67; bd. dirs. Clark County Legal Service Program, 1965. Mem. Am. Bar Assn., Am. Judicature Soc. Home: 4465 Denia Circle Las Vegas NV 89101 Office: 106 S 3d St Las Vegas NV 89101 Tel (702) 384-2465

BREINER, RICHARD HARRY, b. Milw., Feb. 28, 1935; A.B., U. Mo., 1957, J.D., 1961. Admitted to Mo. bar, 1961, Calif. bar, 1962; atty. Dept. Labor, San Francisco, 1961-62; asso. firm Gladstein, Leonard & Sibbett, San Francisco, 1962-65; partner firm Conn, Breiner, Birkie & Ragghianti, San Rafael, Calif., 1965-77; judge Marin County (Calif.) Superior Ct., San Rafael, 1977—; city atty. City of Belvedere (Calif.), 1976-77; dep. city atty. City of Tiburon (Calif.), 1965-77. Mem. Am., Marin County (pres. 1977) bar assns., State Bar Calif., Phi Beta Kappa. Home: 43 St Francis Ln San Rafael CA 94901 Office: Hall of Justice San Rafael CA 94903 Tel (415) 479-1100

BREITEL, CHARLES DAVID, b. N.Y.C., Dec. 12, 1908; A.B., U. Mich., 1929; LL.B., Columbia, 1932. Admitted to N.Y. bar, 1933; asst. dist. atty., 1935-41; counsel to Gov. Dewey, 1943-49; justice N.Y. Supreme Ct., 1950-52, N.Y. Appellate Div., 1952-66; judge Ct. of Appeals, N.Y.C., 1967-73, chief judge, 1974—. Hon. fellow Am. Bar Found.; mem. Assn. Bar City N.Y., Am., N.Y. State bar assns., New York County Lawyers Assn., Am. Acad. Arts and Scis., Columbia Law Sch. Alumni Assn. (medal for excellence). Home: 146 Central Park W New York City NY 10023 Office: 74 Trinity Pl New York City NY 10006 Tel (212) 269-4676

BREITENBERG, JOHN FRANCIS, b. Chgo., May 17, 1948; B.A., U. Md., 1970; J.D., Georgetown U., 1973. Admitted to Md. bar, 1973, D.C. bar, 1975; served with JAGC, USAF, 1973; adminstrv. asst. to majority leader Md. Senate, 1974; law clk. to judge Md. Ct. Spl. Appeals, 1974-75; legis. asst. to congressman, Washington, 1975; counsel Post Office and Civil Service Com., 94th to 95th Congresses, Washington, 1975—. Mem. Am., D.C., Md. bar assns. Home: 13123 Foxhall Dr Wheaton MD 20906 Office: Committee on Post Office and Civil Service House of Representatives Cannon House Office Bldg Washington DC 20515 Tel (202) 225-9370

BREITHAUPT, HARRY JAMES, JR., b. Salem, Va., June 25, 1916; A.B., Roanoke Coll., 1935; M.A., Washington and Lee U., 1936; J.D., George Washington U., 1941. Admitted to Va. bar, 1941, D.C. bar, 1942, U.S. Supreme Ct. bar, 1959; practiced in Washington, 1947-50; with law dept. Assn. Am. R.R.'s., Washington, 1950—, v.p., 1975—, gen. counsel, 1971—; professorial lectr. in law Washington Coll. Law Am. U., 1947-54. Mem. Bar Assn. D.C., D.C. Bar Assn., Va. State Bar, Am. Bar Assn., Assn. ICC Practitioners, Barristers, Order of Coif, Phi Delta Phi. Home: 1026 16th St NW Washington DC 20036 Office: 1920 L St NW Washington DC 20036 Tel (202) 293-4096

BREMAN, JOSEPH ELIOT, b. New Kensington, Pa., Feb. 10, 1945; B.S. in Econs., U. Pa., 1967; J.D., Duquesne U., 1972. Admitted to Pa. bar, 1972, U.S. Supreme Ct. bar, 1976; asso. firm Heilman & McClister, Kittaning, Pa., 1972-73; individual practice law, Kittanning, 1973—; asso. firm Goldberg and Wedner Pitts., 1973—. Bd. dirs. Armstrong County United Fund, 1975—. Mem. Allegheny County, Armstrong County (pres. 1976) Pa., Am. bar assns., Pa. Trial Lawyers. Home: 1410 Barnsdale St Pittsburgh PA 15217 Office: 1317 Frick Bldg Pittsburgh PA 15219 also 342 Market St Kittanning PA 16201 Tel (412) 281-9484

BRENAN, FRANCIS WILLIAM, b. Newark, Nov. 18, 1919; A.B., Princeton, 1940; LL.B., Harvard, 1943, J.D., 1947. Admitted to N.J. bar, 1947, Calif. bar, 1973; asso. firm Pitney, Hardin & Ward, Newark, 1947-53; gen. counsel Calif. Oil Co., Perth Amboy, N.J., 1953-54; v.p., sec., gen. counsel P. Ballantine & Sons, Newark, 1954-71, Rheingold Breweries, Inc., Bklyn., 1971-72; v.p., gen. counsel E & J Gallo Winery, Modesto, Calif., 1972—. Mem. State Bar Calif., Stanislaus County (Calif.), Essex County (N.J.) bar assns. Office: 600 Yosemite Blvd Modesto CA 95353 Tel (209) 521-3716

BRENDEMUHL, WILLIAM JOHN, JR., b. Elgin, Ill., Aug. 30, 1946; B.B.A., Ohio U., 1968; J.D., Valparaiso U., 1971. Admitted to Ill. bar, 1971; asso. firm Marion Tiernan, Flossmoor, Ill., 1971-75; individual practice law, Park Forest, Ill., 1976—; asst. dir. Valparaiso (Ind.) U. Sch. Law Legal Aid Program, 1970-71. Mem. council Trinity Lutheran Ch. of Park Forest, 1972-74; mem. Park Forest Recreation and Park Bd., 1976-; bd. dirs. S. Suburban Chgo. chpt. Amigos de las Americas. Mem. Am., Ill., Chgo., S. Suburban bar assns., Park Forest Jaycees (named Outstanding Dir. 1976, dir. 1975—, legal counsel 1976-77), Park Forest C. of C. (chmn. legis. com.). Home: 513 Lakewood St Park Forest IL 60466 Office: 24 Plaza Park Forest IL 60466 Tel (312) 748-5770

BRENEMAN, KENNETH DALE, b. Pattonsburg, Mo., June 7, 1929; B.S. in Physics, Kans. State Coll., 1955; J.D., Denver U., 1964. Admitted to Colo. bar, 1965; individual practice law, Ft. Morgan, Colo., 1965—; judge Ft. Morgan Municipal Ct., 1972—. Mem. Morgan County (Colo.), Am. bar assns., Colo. Trial Lawyers. Office: 231 Main St Fort Morgan CO 80701 Tel (303) 867-9424

BRENNAN, DANIEL THOMAS, b. Riverside, Calif., Oct. 27, 1916; B.A., U. Calif., Los Angeles, 1939; LL.B., U. So. Calif., 1942. Admitted to Calif. bar, 1942; partner firm Overton, Lyman & Prince, Los Angeles, 1946—; mem. com. fed. cts. Calif. Bd. Bar Govs., 1967-70; lawyer del. 9th Circuit Jud. Conf., 1967-76; chmn. admiralty com. 9th Jud. Circuit, 1970—. Mem. Am., Calif., Los Angeles bar assns., Maritime Law Assn. U.S. Author: Pleading and Practice, California Pleasure Boating Law, 1963. Office: Overton Lyman & Prince 550 S Flower St Los Angeles CA 90071 Tel (213) 683-1100

BRENNAN, FRANCIS WILLIAM, b. Newark, Nov. 18, 1919; A.B., Princeton, 1940; LL.B., Harvard, 1943, J.D., 1947. Admitted to N.J. bar, 1947, Calif. bar, 1973; asso. firm Pitney, Hardin & Ward, Newark, 1947-53; gen. counsel Calif. Oil Co., Perth Amboy, N.J., 1953-54; v.p., sec., gen. counsel P. Ballantine & Sons, Newark, 1954-71, Rheingold Breweries, Inc., Bklyn., 1971-72; v.p., gen. counsel E & J Gallo Winery, Modesto, Calif., 1972—. Mem. State Bar Calif., Stanislaus County (Calif.), Essex County (N.J.) bar assns. Office: 600 Yosemite Blvd Modesto CA 95353 Tel (209) 521-3716

BRENNAN, JOSEPH EDWARD, b. Portland, Maine, Nov. 2, 1934; B.S., Boston Coll., 1958; LL.B., U. Maine, 1963. Admitted to Maine bar, 1963, U.S. Supreme Ct. bar, 1975; practiced in Portland, 1963-71, 73-74; county atty. Cumberland County (Maine), 1971-72; atty. gen. State of Maine, Augusta, 1975—; mem. Maine Ho. of Reps., 1965-71, asst. minority leader, 1967-70; mem. Maine Senate, minority leader, 1973-74; chmn. Maine Trial Ct. Revision Commn.; ex officio mem. Maine Jud. Council, Maine Law Enforcement Planning and Assistance Agy. Mem. Baxter State Park Authority. Mem. Nat. Assn. Attys. Gen. Home: 92 Craigie St Portland ME 04102 Office: State House Dept Atty Gen Augusta ME 04333 Tel (207) 289-3661

BRENNAN, MARY MURPHY, b. Boston, Dec. 13, 1919; B.A., Regis Coll., 1942; M.Ed., Harvard, 1943; certificate in Personnel Adminstrn., Radcliffe Coll., 1943; LL.B., Boston Coll., 1950. Admitted to Mass. bar, 1950, US- Ct. Mil. Appeals bar, 1970; individual practice law, Boston, 1950-60; asst. U.S. atty., Boston, 1967—. Mem. Boston, Mass., Fed. bar assns. Home: 117 Rutherford

Ave Boston MA 02129 Office: 1107 J W McCormack Post Office Bldg Boston MA 02109 Tel (617) 223-6393

BRENNAN, VAUGHN CARPENTER, b. Berlin, N.H., June 5, 1933; B.A., U. Ill., 1968; J.D., U. Balt., 1972; certificate of Mandarin Chinese, Yale U. Inst. Fgn. Langs., 1953. Admitted to Fla. bar, 1972, U.S. Supreme Ct. bar, 1975; individual practice law, Lakeland, Fla., 1972—; dist. mgr. Fla.-Caloric Corp., Topton, Pa.; nat. sales mgr. GFN Copying Products, Tuckahoe, N.Y.; southeastern regional sales mgr. Nashua Corp., N.Y.C.; in mktg. Burroughs Corp., Chgo., Atlanta, Chattanooga, Greenville, S.C. Dir. Am. Red Cross, Lakeland, Fla. Mem. Polk County Criminal Defense Lawyers Assn., Am., 10th Judicial Circuit, Lakeland bar assns., Am., Fla. acads. trial lawyers, Polk County Trial Lawyers Assn., Phi Delta Phi. Home: 5218 Charnes Pl Lakeland FL 33803 Office: 2005 Bartow Rd Lakeland FL 33801 Tel (813) 682-2139

BRENNAN, WILLIAM CHRISTOPHER, b. New York County, N.Y., Oct. 11, 1918; LL.B., N.Y. U., 1948. Patrolman, N.Y.C. Transit, 1941-45; ct. officer, asst. ct. clk. Magistrates Ct., 1945-49; admitted to N.Y. bar, 1949; individual practice law, N.Y.C., 1949-64, 66-69; mem. N.Y. State Assembly, 1955-64; judge Criminal Ct., N.Y.C., 1964-65; mem. N.Y. Senate, 1966-69; judge Civil Ct., N.Y.C., 1969; justice Supreme Ct. N.Y., Jamaica, 1970—. Mem. Queens County, Criminal Cts. bar assns., Queens C. of C., Blackstone Lawyers Club, Am. Legion, DAV, Cath. War Vets. Home: 55-27 84th St Elmhurst NY 11373 Office: 8811 Sutphin Blvd Jamaica NY 11435 Tel (212) 520-3500

BRENNAN, WILLIAM JOSEPH, JR., b. Newark, Apr. 25, 1906; B.S., U. Pa., 1928; LL.B., Harvard, 1931, also LL.D.; LL.D., U. Notre Dame, 1968. Admitted to N.J. bar, 1931, practiced Newark, 1931-49, mem. firm Pitney, Hardin, Ward & Brennan; superior ct. judge, 1949-50; appellate div. judge, 1950-52; justice Supreme Ct. N.J., 1952-56; asso. justice U.S. Supreme Ct., 1956—. Decorated Legion of Merit. Address: Supreme Ct US Washington DC 20543*

BRENNEMAN, FREDERICA SHOENFIELD, b. Ann Arbor, Mich., July 10, 1926; A.B., Radcliffe Coll., 1947; LL.B., Harvard U., 1953. Admitted to D.C. bar, 1953, Mass. bar, 1954, Conn. bar, 1956; atty. Antitrust div. U.S. Dept. Justice, Washington, 1955-56; asso. firm Greene & Cook, Torrington, Conn., 1956-61, firm Copp, Brenneman & Tighe, New London and Essex, Conn., 1961-67; law clk. Judiciary Com., Conn. Gen. Assembly, 1967; judge Juvenile Ct. State of Conn., Hartford, 1967—. Bd. dirs. Conn. Child Abuse Com. Mem. Am., Conn. bar assns., Nat. Council Juvenile Ct. Judges, Nat. Council on Crime and Delinquency. Home: 244 Carriage Dr Glastonbury CT 06033 Office: 322 Washington St Hartford CT 06106 Tel (203) 522-5253

BRENNEN, JOSEPH E., b. Portland, Maine, Nov. 2, 1934; B.S., Boston Coll., 1958; LL.B., U. Maine, 1963. Practiced law, 1963-71, 73-74; mem. Maine Ho. of Reps., 1965-71, asst. minority leader, 1967-70; county atty. Cumberland County (Maine), 1971-72; mem. Maine Senate, 1973-74, minority leader; atty. gen. State of Maine, 1975—; chmn. Maine Trial Ct. Revision Commn. Past mem. bd. visitors Gov. Baxter State Sch. for Deaf. Mem. Maine Bar Assn. (past mem. exec. bd.), Nat. Assn. Attys. Gen. Office: Atty Gen of Maine State House Augusta ME 04330*

BRENNER, DONALD RICHARD, b. Wellington, Ohio, June 8, 1924; J.D., Ohio State U., 1948, Sc.B., 1956. Admitted to Ohio bar, 1949, D.C. bar, 1951, Md. bar, 1956; adminstrv. asst. to Congressman Stephen M. Young of Ohio, 1949-51; individual practice law, Washington and Md., 1951—; asso. prof. bus. law, real estate law Am. U., Washington, 1971—, dir. div. real estate-bus. law, 1976-77. Mem. Am. Bar Assn., Am. Bus. Law Assn., Am. Judicature Soc., AAUP, Lambda Alpha. Co-author: Sexual Behavior, Psycho-Legal Aspects, 1961; columnist Washington Post, Realtor mag.; contbr. numerous articles in field to profl. jours. Home: 5802 Deal Pl Chevy Chase MD 20015 Office: 918 16th St NW Washington DC 20006 Tel (202) 737-7075

BRENNER, ROBERT MICHAEL, b. Mapleton, Iowa, Oct. 18, 1948; B.S. in Bus. Adminstrn., Creighton U., 1971, J.D., 1972. Admitted to Nebr. bar, 1973, U.S. Tax Ct., 1976; law clk. firm White, Lipp, Simon and Powers, Omaha, 1972-73; asso. firm Holtorf, Hansen, Kovarik and Nuttleman, Profl. Corp., Gering, Nebr., 1973-75; individual practice law, Gering, 1975—; city atty. Cities of Gering, Lyman and Minatare (Nebr.), 1973-75; sec. Central Irrigation Dist., Gering, 1974-75; v.p. bd. dirs. Panhandle Legal Services, Scottsbluff, Nebr., 1974—. Bd. dirs. Alcoholism Council Inc., Scottsbluff, 1974—, Homestead Halfway House, Scottsbluff, 1974—; trustee Christ the King Ch., Gering, 1976—; pres. Gering Jr. C. of C., 1976-77. Mem. Am., Nebr., Scottsbluff bar assns., Am. Nebr. assns. trial attys., Scottsbluff-Gering C. of C., Creighton U. Law Alumni, Delta Theta Phi. Named Outstanding Dir. of Year, Gering Jaycees, 1975-76, Outstanding Com. Chmn. for Year, 1975-76, Outstanding Jaycee of Year, 1976. Home: 1820 S St Gering NE 69341 Office: 1545 11th St Gering NE 69341 Tel (308) 436-3424

BRENT, JASON G., b. N.Y.C., Apr. 9, 1936; B.S. in Indsl. Engring., Lehigh U., 1956; M.S. in Bus. Adminstrn., Columbia, 1957, LL.B., 1960. Admitted to N.Y. State bar, 1960, Calif. bar, 1971; mgmt. cons. Touche Ross & Co., N.Y.C., 1960-62; asst. to sr. v.p. REA Express, N.Y.C., 1962-66; controller Rugoff Theatres, N.Y.C., 1966-67, feature div. Paramount Pictures, Los Angeles, 1967-70; mem. firm Donnenfeld & Brent, Los Angeles; prin. Brent, Silverman and Berkowitz, C.P.A.'s, 1970—. Mem. Calif., N.Y. socs. C.P.A.'s, San Fernando Valley Bar Assn., Am. Mensa Soc. Office: 1888 Century Park E Los Angeles CA 90067 Tel (213) 553-8171

BRENT, PHILIP DAVID, b. N.Y.C., Mar. 24, 1928; B.B.A., Coll. City N.Y., 1949; J.D., N.Y. U., 1952. Admitted to N.Y. bar, 1952, U.S. Supreme Ct. bar, 1964; accountant firm Eisner & Lubin, N.Y.C., 1948-49, firm Gedzelman & Co., C.P.A.'s, N.Y.C., 1949-54; sr. partner B. Waltzer & Co., N.Y.C., 1955-65; individual practice law, N.Y.C., 1952-64; partner firm Brent, Phillips, Auerbach & Dranoff, N.Y.C., 1965-70; pres. firm Brent, Phillips, Dranoff & Davis, Nanuet, N.Y., 1970—; lectr. taxation Coll. City N.Y., Bernard Baruch Sch. Bus. Adminstrn., 1956-60, So. Meth. U., 1976; dir. Robert Cea & Co., investment bankers, N.Y.C., 1969-70. Founder, bd. dirs. Dellwood Park Civic Assn., 1969-71; tech. legal adv. econs. N.Y. Joint Legis. Com. Consumer Protection, 1971; bd. dirs. Rockland Center Performing Arts, 1972-73. Mem. Am. (pres. 1965-66, dir. 1966—), N.Y. (pres. 1962-64) assns. atty.'s-C.P.A.'s, Am., N.Y., Rockland County bar assns., Nat. Assn. Security Dealers, Am. Arbitration Assn. (nat. panel 1968—), Am. Inst. Accountants. Contbr. articles to profl. jours. Home: 31 Windgate Dr New City NY 10956 Office: 20 Old Turnpike Rd Nanuet NY 10954 Tel (914) 623-2800

BRESNAHAN, ROBERT JAMES, b. Meridian, Miss., Aug. 6, 1948; B.A., Tulane U., 1970; J.D., U. Miss., 1973. Admitted to Miss. bar, 1973; individual practice law, Meridian, 1973—. Mem. Miss., Lauderdale (Miss.) bar assns., Miss. Trial Lawyers Assn. Home: 1614 23d Ave Meridian MS 39301 Office: 407 Greater Miss Life Bldg Meridian MS 39301 Tel (601) 693-6386

BRESSLER, DAVID NADLER, b. Phila., Oct. 6, 1925; A.B., U. Pa., 1948, LL.B., 1952. Admitted to N.Y. bar, 1960, U.S. Tax. Ct. bar, 1968, U.S. Supreme Ct. bar, 1968, Pa. bar, 1975; asso. firm Shapiro, Rosenfield, Stalberg and Cook, Phila., 1952-55, partner, 1961-67; partner firm Robinson, Greenberg and Lipman, Phila., 1955-57; atty. office of gen. counsel AEC, Washington, 1957-58; counsel Office of Atomic Devel., State of N.Y., Albany, 1959-61; partner firm Dilworth, Paxon, Kalish, Cohn and Levy, Phila., 1967-69, firm Shapiro and Bressler, Phila., 1969—; instr. Rutgers U., 1950-57, 65-66, U. Pa., 1955-56; law mem. Phila. Com. on Radiation, 1961-65, Phila. Com. on Hazards of Asbestos, 1969-71. Mem. Bar Assn. City Phila., Order of Coif. Home: 320 Brookway Rd Merion PA 19066 Office: 21 S 12th St Philadelphia PA 19107 Tel (215) 665-9191

BRETT, JAY ELLIOT, b. Somerville, N.J., June 4, 1931; B.S., Cornell U., 1953; LL.B., Harvard, 1958. Admitted to N.Y. bar, 1958; mem. firm Cohen Swados Wright Hanifin Bradford & Brett, and predecessors, Niagara Falls, N.Y., 1958—. Del., Republican Nat. Conv., 1976. Mem. N.Y. State, Erie County, Niagara Falls bar assns. Home: 20 Colonial Dr Amherst NY 14226 Office: 256 Third St Niagara Falls NY 14303 Tel (716) 693-8000

BRETT, THOMAS EDMUND, b. Bklyn., Jan. 15, 1932; B.A., St. John's Coll., 1953, LL.B., 1957. Admitted to N.Y. bar, 1958; trial atty. Legal Aid Soc., N.Y.C., 1959-65; mem. firm Brett & Finkin, Forest Hills, N.Y., 1965—. Mem. Queens County Bar Assn., Criminal Cts. Bar Assn. Queens County. Office: 118-21 Queens Blvd Forest Hills NY 11375 Tel (212) 261-0090

BRETTSCHNEIDER, RITA ROBERTA FISCHMAN, b. N.Y.C., Nov. 12, 1931; B.A. in Biology, Bklyn. Coll., 1953; LL.B., Bklyn. Law Sch., 1956, J.D., 1967; postgrad. N.Y. U., 1968-69; grad. Nat. Inst. Trial Advocacy Program, 1976. Admitted to N.Y. State bar, 1961, U.S. Dist. Ct. bar, 1971; individual practice law, Huntington, N.Y., 1970—; spl. asso. prof. law New Coll., Hofstra U.; mem. faculty N.Y. Law Jour. Symposium on Matrimonial Law, 1976. Chmn. matrimonial com. L. I. chpt. NOW, 1971-72; alt. arbitrator Suffolk County (N.Y.) Med. Malpractice Arbitration Com., 1974-76; bd. dirs. Planning Parenthood of North Suffolk, L.I., 1974—, Consumer Protection Bd., Huntington, 1975—. Mem. N.Y. State, Nassau County (N.Y.) (chmn. subcom. pub. relations matrimonial com.), Suffolk bar assns., Nassau-Suffolk Trial Lawyers Assn., Nassau-Suffolk Women's Bar Assn. (dir.). Home: 2 Crosby Pl Huntington NY 11743 Office: 43 Prospect St Huntington NY 11743 Tel (516) 367-3111

BREUER, ALEXANDER, b. Wiener Neustadt, Austria, May 6, 1926; B.A. in Accounting, George Washington U., 1949; J.D., Am. U., 1957. Mgmt. audit staff GAO, Washington, 1955-61; admitted to D.C. bar, 1957, Md. bar, 1963; staff atty. com. U.S. Congress, 1961-62; asst. insp. gen. Dept. Agr., Washington, 1963-68; individual practice law, Marlow Heights, Md., 1968—. Mem. exec. com. Prince George's County (Md.) chpt. NCCJ. Mem. Am., Md., Prince George's County, Fed. bar assns., Am. Judicature Soc., World Peace Through Law Soc., Am. Inst. C.P.A.'s, Prince George's County C. of C. (chmn. com. criminal justice). Home: 2008 Kirklin Dr Oxon Hill MD 20021 Office: 4235 28th Ave Marlow Heights MD 20031 Tel (301) 899-6350

BREUER, FRANK G., b. 1916; B.S., U. Oreg., 1937; LL.B., Yale U., 1940. House counsel M & M Woodworking Co., 1951-56; with Georgia-Pacific Corp., 1956—, gen. counsel, asst. sec., Portland, Oreg., 1962—, v.p., 1972—. Office: 900 SW 5th Ave Portland OR 97204*

BREWER, ALBERT PRESTON, b. Bethel Springs, Tenn., Oct. 26, 1928; A.B., U. Ala., 1952, LL.B., 1952; LL.D., Samford U., 1968; LL.D. (hon.) Jacksonville State U., 1968. Admitted to Ala. bar, 1952, U.S. Supreme Ct. bar, 1971; individual practice law, Decatur, Ala., 1952-57; sr. partner firm Brewer and Lentz, Decatur, 1957-68; sr. partner firm Robison, Belser, Brewer & Mancuso, Montgomery, Ala., 1971—; mem. Ala. Ho. of Reps., 1954-66, speaker, 1963-67; lt. gov. Ala., 1967-68, gov., 1968-71; chmn. Decatur City Planning Commn., 1956-63. Mem. Am., Ala. State bar assns., Am. Trial Lawyers Assn., Ala. Acad. Honor. Office: PO Drawer 1470 Montgomery AL 36102 Tel (205) 834-7000

BREWER, CHARLES MOULTON, b. Washington, June 9, 1931; B.S., U. Md., 1953; J.D., George Washington U., 1957. Admitted to Ariz. bar, 1959; law clk. Ariz. Supreme Ct., 1958-59; individual practice law, Phoenix, 1959—. Mem. Am., Ariz., Maricopa County bar assns., Am. Judicature Soc., Am. Bd. Trial Advocates, Am., Calif. trial lawyers assns. Contbr. articles to legal jours. Office: 1400 1st Nat Bank Plaza Phoenix AZ 85003 Tel (602) 252-8787

BREWER, JAMES MALONE, b. Oklahoma City, Oct. 3, 1940; B.S., Oklahoma City U., 1965, J.D., 1972; postgrad. in Mktg., La. State U., 1967-68. Admitted to Okla. bar, 1972, U.S. Dist. Ct. for Western Dist. Okla. bar; intern John C. Moran, Oklahoma City, 1972-73; partner firm Bewer Brill Grace & Hucklebery, Oklahoma City, 1973; legal counsel to youthful offenders, 1973; asst. pub. defender Oklahoma County, 1973-75, asst. dist. atty., 1975-76; partner firm Palmer & Brewer, Oklahoma City, 1976—; mfg. supr. Western Electric, Inc., Shreveport, La., 1965-70. Mem. Okla. Trial Lawyers Assn., Okla., Am. criminal def. assns., Am., Okla. State, Oklahoma County bar assns., Okla. Dist. Attys. Assn., Fin. Club Am., Nat. Coll. Criminal Def. Lawyers and Pub. Defenders, Phi Alpha Delta. Named Outstanding Mem., NW Tips Club, 1972, Honorable Okie, 1973. Home: 11200 Folkstone St Yukon OK 73099 Office: 2000 Classen Blvd suite 214-A Oklahoma City OK 73106 Tel (405) 521-0882

BREYER, CHARLES ROBERTS, b. San Francisco, Nov. 3, 1941; A.B. cum laude, Harvard, 1963; J.D., U. Calif., Berkeley, 1966. Admitted to Calif. bar, 1966, U.S. Supreme Ct. bar, 1974; law clk. U.S. Dist. Ct. for No. Dist. Calif., 1966-67; asst. dist. atty. San Francisco, 1967-73; asst. spl. prosecutor Watergate Spl. Prosecution Force, 1973-74; partner firm Jacobs, Sills & Coblentz, San Francisco, 1974—. Mem. civil grand jury, San Francisco, 1975-76. Mem. San Francisco Bar Assn. Office: 555 California St Suite 3100 San Francisco CA 94104 Tel (415) 391-4800

BREZINA, JOHN CHARLES, b. Chgo., Jan. 22, 1930; B.A., U. Iowa, 1951; LL.B., Chgo.-Kent Coll. Law, 1953, J.D., 1969; M.P.L., John Marshall Law Sch., 1963. Admitted to Ill. bar, 1953, U.S. Supreme Ct. bar, 1957; partner firms Brezina & Buckingham, Chgo., 1953-64, Brezina & Lund, and predecessor, Chgo., 1964—. Mem. Am., Ill., Chgo., West Suburban bar assns., Bohemian Lawyers Assn., Lawyers-Pilots Assn. Home: 8733 Rockefeller Ave Brookfield IL 60513 Office: 29 S La Salle St Chicago IL 60603 Tel (312) 726-2718

BREZINA, JOHN F., b. Czechoslovakia, Dec. 19, 1902; LL.B. cum laude. Admitted to Ill. bar, 1929; partner firm Brezina & Buckingham, Chgo. and Brookfield, Ill., 1929—; mem. Midas Trade Mark Bureau, Chgo., 1926-29. Mem. Ill., West Suburban bar assns., Am. Czechoslovak Engrs. Soc. Contbr. articles in field to law jours. Home, 1506 Robinhood Ln LaGrange Pk IL Office: 3747 Grand Blvd Brookfield IL 60513 Tel (312) 485-1025

BRIAN, ALEXIS MORGAN, JR., b. New Orleans, Oct. 4, 1928; B.A., La. State U., 1949, J.D., 1956; M.S., Trinity U., 1954. Admitted to La. bar, 1956, Supreme Ct. bar, 1971; asso. firm Deutsch, Kerrigan & Stiles, New Orleans, 1956-60, partner, 1961—; lectr. Inst. Continuing Legal Edn., La. State U. Law Center, 1972—. Mem. La. State U. Found., 1975—, La. Civil Service League, 1975—, sponsor club Sta. WYES-TV, 1974—, Internat. House, New Orleans, 1972—; mem. steering com. United Fund, New Orleans, 1964; asst. scoutmaster New Orleans Area council Boy Scouts Am., 1963-70; bd. dirs. New Orleans Goodwill Industries, 1968—, mem. exec. com., v.p., 1975—; bd. dirs. Inter-Varsity Christian Fellowship, New Orleans, 1974—; mem. bd. trustees New Orleans Bapt. Theol. Sem., 1961-74, pres., 1968-74, mem. bd. devel., 1961-63; bd. dirs. New Orleans Bapt. Theol. Sem. Found., 1972—. Mem. Am., La. State (asst. examiner admissions com. 1968—), New Orleans (lectr. continuing legal edn. programs 1968—) bar assns., Internat. Assn. Ins. Counsel, La. Assn. Def. Counsel, Def. Research Inst., Am. Arbitration Assn. (panel arbitrators), Phi Delta Phi. Recipient Boss of Year award New Orleans Legal Secs. Assn., 1966; contbr. articles to legal jours. Home: 1738 S Carrollton Ave New Orleans LA 70118 Office: 4700 One Shell Sq New Orleans LA 70139 Tel (504) 581-5141

BRICKER, HARRY LEROY, JR., b. Harrisburg, Pa., July 27, 1928; B.S., Lebanon Valley Coll., 1950; J.D., Dickinson Coll., 1957. Admitted to Pa. bar, 1958, U.S. Tax Ct. bar, 1960, U.S. Supreme Ct. bar, 1969; law clk. to presiding judge Orphans Ct. of Dauphin County (Pa.), Harrisburg, 1957-58; asso. firm Compton, Zeigler & Hepford, Harrisburg, 1958-60; individual practice law, Harrisburg, 1960—; instr. in field. Mem. adv. com. Dauphin County Child Care Service, 1963-69; chmn. bd. dirs. Dauphin County Parks and Recreation Dept., 1972—. Mem. Am., Pa., Dauphin County (dir., chmn. pub. service com. 1970—) bar assns., Pa., Am. trial lawyers assns., Central Pa. Legal Services Assn. (dir.), Lebanon Valley Coll. Alumni Assn. (pres. 1968-72). Home: 921 Bradford Rd Harrisburg PA 17112 Office: 407 N Front St Harrisburg PA 17101 Tel (717) 236-9318

BRICKER, WILLIAM TECUMSEH SHERMAN, b. Balt., Oct. 10, 1929; A.A., Balt. Jr. Coll., 1951; LL.B., U. Balt., 1957, J.D., 1957. Admitted to Md. bar, 1958; individual practice law, Balt., 1958—; asst. mgr. Md. Unsatisfied Claim and Judgement Fund, 1958-62, chmn. bd. dirs., 1965-66; asst. states atty. City of Balt., 1962-66; spl. counsel Md. Legis. Council, 1964; spl. atty. State of Md. Roads Commn., 1965-66; asst. atty. gen. Dept. Motor Vehicles, 1966-70; dep. motor vehicle adminstr., 1970—; lectr. in field. Mem. Am. (cons.), Md. State (cons.) bar assns., Bar Assn. Balt. City, Md. State Attys. Assn., Nat. Dist. Attys. Assn., Sigma Delta Kappa. Home: 907 Lenton Ave Baltimore MD 21212 Office: 6601 Ritchie Hwy NE Glen Burnie MD 21062 Tel (301) 768-7276

BRICKLE, THOMAS CHARLES, b. Fond du Lac, Wis., Sept. 6, 1934; B.S., U. Wis., 1956, J.D., 1961. Admitted to Wis. bar, 1961, D.C. bar, 1967, Va. bar, 1969; with U.S. Dept. Justice, Washington, 1962-64; asso. firm Whitlock Markey and Tait, 1967-69, Reed Smith Shaw and McClay, 1969-70, Treese Ruffner and Brickle, 1970-72 (all Washington); legis. counsel Ind. Bankers Assn. Am., Washington, 1973-75; mem. firm Cervera Brickle and Fabricant, Washington, 1975—. Mem. Wis., D.C., Va. bar assns. Office: S-1100 1000 Connecticut Ave NW Washington DC 20036 Tel (202) 296-3477

BRICKLEY, JAMES MORTON, b. Mt. Sterling, Ky., July 12, 1940; B.A. with honors, Transylvania U., 1963; J.D., Stetson U., 1966. Admitted to Fla. bar, 1966; individual practice law, St. Petersburg, Fla., 1966-73; partner firm Brickley & Martin, St. Petersburg, 1973—. Regional dir. Young Life, 1973-77. Mem. Am., Fla., St. Petersburg bar assns. Home: 2434 Woodlawn Circle E Saint Petersburg FL 33705 Office: 2100 34th St S Saint Petersburg FL 33711

BRICKMAN, KENNETH ALAN, b. Hannibal, Mo., Sept. 10, 1940; B.B.A., Culver Stockton Coll., 1963; J.D., U. Mo., 1970. Admitted to Mo. bar, 1970, Ill. bar, 1970, U.S. Supreme Ct. bar, 1975; asso. firm Scholz Staff & Brickman, Quincy, Ill., 1970-72, partner, 1972—. Admissions officer W.Central Ill., U.S. Air Force Acad., 1972—; vice-chmn. adv. bd. Quincy Demolay, 1971—. Mem. Am., Mo., Ill., Adams County (chmn. indigent services com.) bar assns., Phi Alpha Delta. Home: 3 Chatten Dr Quincy IL 62301 Office: 625 Vermont St Quincy IL 62301 Tel (217) 223-3444

BRICKNER, PAUL, b. N.Y.C., Aug. 7, 1940; B.A., U. Richmond, 1962; J.D., Case Western Reserve U., 1966; grad. Judge Adv. Gen.'s Sch., 1977. Admitted to Ohio bar, 1966, Va. bar, 1967, Fed. bar, 1968, U.S. Ct. Appeals, 1972; atty.-adv. NASA Lewis Research Center, Cleve., 1966; served with Judge Adv. Gen.'s Corps, 1966-68; asst. U.S. Atty., Columbus, Ohio, 1968-69; atty. inspector Ohio Div. Securities, Columbus, 1969-70; asst. prosecutor City of Cleve., 1970-71; prosecutor City of Cleveland Heights, 1971-72; asst. U.S. Atty., Cleve., 1972-76; dir. Cleve. Dist. Office, Ohio Indsl. Commn., Cleve., 1976—; instr. Lakeland Community Coll., Mentor, Ohio, 1977. Mem. Fed., Ohio State, Va., Lake County bar assns. Received commendation FBI. Home: Pine Ridge Valley 2250 Par Lane Suite 1120 Willoughby Hills OH 44094 Office: 740 Superior Ave W Cleveland OH 44113 Tel (216) 579-2891

BRICTSON, DAVID NEIL, b. Chgo., Mar. 1, 1937; B.A., U. Colo., 1958, LL.B., 1961. Admitted to Wash. bar, 1961, Colo. bar, 1963; corporate sec., asso. gen. counsel Frontier Airline, Denver, 1967—. Mem. Colo., Wash., Denver bar assns. Office: 8250 Smith Rd Denver CO 80207

BRIDGES, DOUGLAS, b. Indpls., Feb. 12, 1935; B.S.M.E., Purdue U., 1957; J.D., Ind. U., 1966. Admitted to Ind. bar, 1966, U.S. 7th Circuit Ct. Appeals bar, 1966, U.S. Dist. Ct. bar for So. Dist. Ind., 1966; partner firm Ferguson, Berry, Ferguson & Bridges, Bloomington, Ind., 1966-71; judge Monroe County (Ind.) Superior Ct., 1972—; dep. prosecutor Ind. 10th Jud. Circuit, 1966-71; majority atty. Ind. Ho. of Reps., 1971; adj. prof. law Ind. U., fall 1974, 75; mem.

Ind. Lawyer's Commn., Ind. Organized Crime Control Commn.; lectr. in field. Bd. dirs. Boys' Club, Bloomington, Big Bros./Big Sisters, Bloomington. Mem. Ind., Monroe County bar assns., Am. Judicature Soc., Okla. Soc. Profl. Engrs. Registered profl. engr., Okla. Home: 2301 Montclair Ct Bloomington IN 47401 Office: Superior Ct 2 Courthouse Bloomington IN 47401 Tel (812) 339-1625

BRIDGEWATER, ERLE HENRY, b. Chauncey, Ohio, Mar. 27, 1919; B.S., Ohio U., 1940; J.D., Ohio State U., 1946. Admitted to Ohio bar, 1946; since practiced in Athens, Ohio, partner Bridgewater & Robe, and predecessors, mem. Bd. Commrs. Grievances and Discipline Ohio Supreme Ct., 1968-74. Mem. Athens City Sch. Bd., 1958-62. Fellow Am., Ohio bar founds., Am. Coll. Probate Counsel; mem. Am., Ohio (past pres.), Athens County bar assns., Am. Ohio trial lawyers assns., Am. Law Inst., Am. Judicature Soc., Order of Coif. Office: 14 W Washington St Athens OH 45701 Tel (614) 593-5576

BRIEN, JAMES BUTLER, JR., b. Mayfield, Ky., Aug. 4, 1942; B.S., Murray State U., 1965; J.D., U. Ky., 1969. Admitted to Ky. bar, 1969; partner firm Neely & Brien, Mayfield, 1971—; asst. commonwealth's atty. 52d Jud. Dist., 1975. Chmn. drive United Way Graves County, 1971; bd. dirs. Mayfield-Graves County (Ky.) chpt. ARC. Mem. Am., Ky. bar assns., Mayfield C. of C. Home: 804 Weda St Mayfield KY 42066 Office: 238 N 7th St Mayfield KY 42066 Tel (502) 247-4422

BRIGGS, FLORENCE ANNE BURCHETT, b. Ashland, Ky., Feb. 23, 1934; A.B., Randolph-Macon Woman's Coll., 1955; LL.B., U. Ky., 1958. Admitted to Ind., Ky. bars, 1958; partner firm Briggs & Briggs, Flora, Ind., 1958—; dep. pros. atty. Carroll County (Ind.), 1963-70. Home: 515 E Main St Flora IN 46929 Office: PO Box 2 Flora IN 46929 Tel (219) 967-3631

BRIGGS, GEORGE SCOTT, b. Amesbury, Mass., Jan. 10, 1944; A.B., Brown U., 1966; J.D., Vanderbilt U., 1969. Admitted to Colo. bar, 1971, U.S. Supreme Ct. bar, 1975; asso. firm Evans, Peterson, Torbet & Briggs, Colorado Springs, 1971, partner, 1972-74; partner firm Evans & Briggs, Colorado Springs, 1975—. Mem. Am., Colo., El Paso County bar assns., Colo. Trial Lawyers Assn., El Paso County Contractors Assn. (sec. 1974—). Home: 1415 N Nevada Ave Colorado Springs CO 80907 Office: suite 222 Mining Exchange Bldg 8 S Nevada Ave Colorado Springs CO 80903 Tel (303) 473-4660

BRIGGS, STAIRS KENNETH, b. Salt Lake City, May 6, 1911; J.D., Drake U., 1934. Admitted to Iowa bar, 1934, Wyo. bar, 1934; individual practice law, Rawlins, Wyo., 1934—; atty. Wyo. Ho. of Reps., 1939; county atty. Carbon County, Wyo., 1943-47, pros. atty., 1943-47, dep. county and pros. atty., 1963-67; atty. Wyo. Senate, 1953, 55, 57, 61. Mem. Wyo., Am. bar assns., Phi Alpha Delta. Office: 318 5th St PO Box 978 Rawlins WY 82301 Tel (307) 324-5031

BRIGGS, STEVEN ERNEST, b. San Diego, Aug. 18, 1942; B.A., U. San Diego, 1964, J.D. magna cum laude, 1970. Admitted to Calif. bar, 1971; partner firm Christensen, Fazio, McDonnell, Briggs, Ward & DeSales, La Habra, Calif., 1971—. Mem. Orange County Bar Assn. (lectr.), Orange County Trial Lawyers Assn. Contbr. articles to legal jours. Home: 1219 E Melody Ln Fullerton CA 92632 Office: 440 E La Habra Blvd Law Habra CA 90631 Tel (714) 870-9972

BRIGHTMIRE, PAUL WILLIAM, b. Washington, Mo., June 12. 1924; B.A., U. Tulsa, 1949, J.D., 1951. Admitted to Okla. bar, 1951, U.S. Supreme Ct. bar, 1973; partner firms Rogers & Brightmire, Tulsa, 1954-57, Brightmire & Assos., Tulsa, 1957-70; judge Okla. Ct. of Appeals, div. 2, 1971—, presiding judge, 1971—; vis. prof. jurisprudence Okla. Coll. Osteo. Medicine and Surgery, 1975—. Fellow Internat. Acad. Law and Sci.; mem. Okla. (Outstanding Service award 1969), Tulsa County (Outstanding Service award 1965) bar assns., Tulsa (pres. 1966), Okla. (pres. 1967) trial lawyers assns. Founding editor Tulsa Lawyer, 1962-64; editor-in-chief The Advocate, 1967-70. Home: 4041 S Birmingham St Tulsa OK 74105 Office: 601 State Office Bldg 4th and Houston Sts Tulsa OK 74127 Tel (918) 581-2711

BRILL, JOHN FENN, b. Wilmington, Del., May 8, 1937; A.B., Princeton, 1958; LL.B., U. Va., 1961. Admitted to R.I. bar, 1962, U.S. Dist. Ct. for R.I. bar, 1963; asso. firm Edwards & Angell, Providence, 1961-69, partner, 1969—. Mem. R.I. Bar Assn., Estate Planning Council R.I. Home: 25 George St Providence RI 02906 Office: 2700 Hosp Trust Tower Providence RI 02903 Tel (401) 274-9200

BRILL, MAURICE, b. N.Y.C., Dec. 20, 1926; B.S., Columbia, 1949, LL.B., 1952. Admitted to N.Y. bar, 1953, U.S. Supreme Ct. bar, 1968; with Bur. of Ships, U.S. Dept. Navy Legal Aid Soc., 1954-62; partner firm Brill & Hochhauser, N.Y.C., 1962-73; partner Brill & Nashman, N.Y.C., 1973—. Mem. Fed. Bar Council, Bklyn. bar assns., Kings County Criminal bar assn. Office: 291 Broadway New York City NY 10007 Tel (212) BA7-6680

BRIMMER, CLARENCE ADDISON, b. Rawlins, Wyo., July 11, 1922; B.A., U. Mich., 1944, J.D., 1947. Admitted to Wyo. bar, 1948, practice in Rawlins, 1948-71; municipal judge, Rawlins, 1948-54; U.S. commr., magistrate, 1963-71; atty. gen. Wyo., Cheyenne, 1971-74; U.S. atty., 1974-75; chief judge U.S. Dist. Ct., Cheyenne, 1975—; dir. Nat. Bank of Rawlins. Sec. Rawlins Bd. Pub. Utilities, 1954-66. Sec. Gov.'s Com. on Wyo. Water, 1963-65. Republican County chmn., 1948-56; Rep. state committeeman, 1961-62, 64-67; del. Rep. Nat. Conv., 1956; chmn. Wyo. Rep. Platform Com., 1966; sec. Wyo. Rep. Com., 1966, chmn., 1967-71; Rep. gubernatorial candidate, 1974. Trustee Rocky Mountain Mineral Law Found. Episcopalian (lay reader 1948—). Home: 1420 W 6th Ave Cheyenne WY 82001 Office: PO Box 985 Cheyenne WY 82001*

BRIND, DAVID HUTCHISON, b. Albany, N.Y., Feb. 4, 1930; A.B., Union Coll., 1951; LL.B., Albany Law Sch., 1954; J.D., Union U., 1968; L.H.D., N.Y. State Inst. Tech., 1971. Admitted to N.Y. State bar, 1954, U.S. Supreme Ct. bar, 1970; library asst. N.Y. State Law Library, 1949-54; with law div. N.Y. State Dept. Edn., Albany, 1954-55; partner firm Chacchia and Brind, Geneva, N.Y., 1957-64; individual practice law, Geneva, 1964—; judge Geneva City Ct., 1974—; real estate counsel N.Y. State Dormitory Authority, 1960—; gen. counsel Geneva Gen. Hosp., 1966—. Bd. dirs. Geneva Community Chest, 1965—, campaign chmn., 1968-69, pres., 1969-71; bd. dirs. United Way of Greater Rochester, 1976—; trustee Geneva Hist. Soc., 1963—, pres., 1970-73; chmn. Geneva Historic Commn., 1969—; exec. bd. Finger Lakes council Boy Scouts Am., 1968—; dir. Seven Lakes council Girl Scouts U.S.A., 1966-73; trustee Geneva Gen. Hosp., 1962-73, pres., 1969-71; bd. dirs., pres. Geneva Gen. Hosp. Nursing Home Co., Inc., 1969-71; v.p. Geneva Bd. Edn., 1962-67; mem. pres.'s council Eisenhower Coll., 1972—, Hobart and William Smith colls., 1967—. Mem. N.Y. State Sch. Bds. Assn. (law revisions com. and constl. conv. com. 1964-68), Monroe County (judiciary com. 1976—), Ontario County, N.Y. State bar assns., N.Y. State Land Title Assn., Am. Arbitration Assn., Am. Hosp. Assn., Soc. Hosp. Attys. Recipient Geneva Community Service citation Community Chest-ARC, 1969; named Man of Year, C. of C., 1971. Home: 43 DeLancey Dr Geneva NY 14456 Office: 17 Seneca St Geneva NY 14456 Tel (315) 789-1751

BRINITZER, MICHAEL, b. Oppeln, Germany, Aug. 22, 1932; A.B., Columbia, 1954, J.D., 1957. Admitted to N.Y. bar, 1958; counsel to N.Y. State Assembly minority leader, 1958-59; house counsel The Dime Savs. Bank, Bklyn., 1959-63; asso. firm Cullen & Dykman, N.Y.C., 1963-66, 72-76; staff atty. Equitable Life Assurance Soc. U.S., N.Y.C., 1966-72; house counsel Lincoln Savs. Bank, 1976; mem. adv. bd. First Am. Title Ins. Co.; panel Am. Arbitration Assn.; judge N.Y.C. Small Claims Ct. Office: 177 Montague St Brooklyn NY 11201 Tel (212) 855-9000

BRINK, DAVID RYRIE, b. Mpls., July 28, 1919; B.A., U. Minn., 1940, B.S.L., 1941, J.D. with honors, 1947. Admitted to Minn. bar, 1948; asso. firm Dorsey, Windhorst, Hannaford, Whitney & Halladay, Mpls., 1947—. Fellow Am. Bar Found.; mem. Am. (del. 1968—), Minn. (exec. com. 1974—, sec. 1974—, gov. 1968-72, 74—), Hennepin County (pres. 1967-68) bar assns., Am. Bar Retirement Assn. (pres., dir.), Am. Coll. Probate Counsel, Am. Judicature Soc., Nat. Conf. Bar Presidents, Hennepin County Bar Found., Lawyers' Com. Civil Rights Under Law (trustee). Contbr. articles to legal jours. Home: 1901 Humboldt Ave S Minneapolis MN 55403 Office: 2300 First Nat Bank Bldg Minneapolis MN 55402 Tel (612) 340-2704

BRINSON, EDWARD, b. Kissimmee, Fla., Apr. 10, 1925; B.A., Rollins Coll., 1949; LL.B., Emory U., 1952, J.D., 1970. Admitted to Fla. bar, 1953; asso. firm Brinson & Smith, Kissimmee, 1962—; city atty. Kissimmee, 1962-72, 74-77. Mem. Am. Bar Assn., Am. Trial Lawyers Assn., Acad. Fla. Trial Lawyers. Home: Lakeview Dr Kissimmee FL 32741 Office: 815 W Emmett St Kissimmee FL 32741 Tel (305) 847-5127

BRINTON, BRADFORD HICKMAN, b. Queens, N.Y., Jan. 26, 1935; B.A., Union Coll., 1958; LL.B., Albany Law Sch., 1961, J.D., 1968. Admitted to N.Y. State bar, 1961, U.S. Supreme Ct. bar, 1967; individual practice law, Keeseville, N.Y., 1961—; town atty. Town of Chesterfield (N.Y.), 1973—; atty. Ausable Valley Central Sch., Keeseville, 1968—; village atty. Village of Keeseville, 1969—; tax atty. County of Essex (N.Y.) 1975—; local counsel Am. Title Ins. Co., 1967—; asso. prof. bus. Clinton Community Coll., Plattsburgh, N.Y.C., 1971-75. Mem. Keeseville Youth Commn., 1970—; pres. Essex County Com. for Econ. Improvement, 1966-68, Keeseville Library Assn., 1970—; sec. Keeseville Youth Hockey Assn., 1971—. Mem. N.Y. State, Essex County bar assns. Home: Brinton Rd Keeseville NY 12944 Office: 12-A Front St Keeseville NY 12944 Tel (518) 834-7900

BRIOLA, PETER, b. Ambridge, Pa., Apr. 15, 1904; A.B., Pa. State U., 1927; LL.B., Georgetown U., 1929, J.D., 1929. Admitted to Ky. bar, 1929, Tex. bar, 1932, Maine bar, 1933, U.S. Supreme Ct. bar, 1936; exam. atty. Dept. Interior, Acadia Nat. Park, Bar Harbor, Maine, 1936-38; city atty. Ellsworth (Maine), 1938-40; disclosure commr. Hancock County (Maine), 1940-47; asst. dist. atty. Bexar County (Tex.), San Antonio, 1948-49; chief pros. atty. City of San Antonio, 1949-54; judge Lincoln (Maine) Municipal Ct., 1959-63; town atty. Lincoln, 1967-70; dir. N.E. Bank, Lincoln. Mem. exec. bd. Katahdin Area council Boy Scouts Am., Bangor. Mem. Am., Maine, Tex., Ky., Penobscot County bar assns., Sigma Nu Phi. Home and Office: 43 W Broadway Lincoln ME 04457 Tel (207) 794-2461

BRISACH, EDGAR GEORGE, b. N.Y.C., June 28, 1914; A.B., Princeton, 1935; J.D., Columbia, 1939. Admitted to N.Y. bar, 1939, U.S. Supreme Ct. bar, 1955; individual practice law, N.Y.C., 1940-41; maj. JAGD, U.S. Army, 1941-46; asst. engring. dept. Williamsburgh Savings Bank, Bklyn., 1946-50; partner firm Kelly, Finn & Brisach, N.Y.C., 1951-53, Mineola, N.Y., 1956-59; asst. U.S. atty. U.S. Dist. Ct. for Eastern Dist. N.Y., 1953-55; asso. firm Corner, Weisbrod, Froeb & Charles, Garden City, N.Y., 1959-62; individual practice law, Hempstead, N.Y., 1962-65; partner firm Brisach & Sullivan, Mineola, 1965-72, Brisach, Sullivan & Sperendi, Mineola, 1973—; U.S. magistrate Eastern Dist. N.Y., 1971-75. Mem. Am., Fed., N.Y. State, Nassau County bar assns., Protestant Lawyers Assn. Home: 1 Linden St Garden City NY 11530 Office: 1539 Franklin Ave Mineola NY 11501 Tel (516) 746-1141

BRISCOE, HATTIE ELAM, b. Shreveport, La., Nov. 13, 1916; B.A., Wiley Coll., 1937; M.S., Prairie View A. and M. Coll., 1951; LL.B., St. Marys Coll., 1956, J.D., 1970. Tchr., Booker Washington Sch., Wichita Falls, Tex., 1937-41; beauty operator Briscoes Beauty Salon, San Antonio, Tex., 1941-45; cosmetology instr. Wheatley High Sch., San Antonio, 1945-51; clk.-typist Kelly Air Force Base, Tex., 1952-56; admitted to Tex. bar, 1956; individual practice law, San Antonio, 1956—. Mem. Am., Nat. bar assns., Nat. Assn. Def. Lawyers in Criminal Cases, Nat. Assn. Black Women Attys. Recipient Hist. Achievement award, Smart Set Social Club, 1962; Model Community award, Miss Black San Antonio Bd., 1974; Superior Achievements award, Delta Sigma Theta Sorority, 1973. Home: 820 S Pine St San Antonio TX 78210 Office: 1416 E Commerce St San Antonio TX 78205 Tel (512) 224-5101

BRISCOE, JACK CLAYTON, b. Bradford, Pa., July 23, 1920; B.S. in Econs., U. Pa., 1943; LL.B., Harvard U., 1948. Admitted to Pa. bar, 1950; since practiced in Phila., asso. Robert C. Duffy, 1950-66, partner firm Briscoe and Haggerty, 1966—; instr. U. Pa., 1950-56; dir. Pocono Airlines, Country Store Products, Inc., Cardo Automotive Products, Inc. Bd. dirs. Phila. Flag Day Assn., 1970—, Pop Warner Little Scholars, 1974—; chmn. Community Christian Fellowship Center, Phila., 1968—; mem. corp. Lancaster Bible Coll., 1974—; dir. Radio Bible Hour, Inc., 1962—; elder United Presbyn. Ch. Manoa, Pa., 1965—; sec. World Evang. Found., 1968—; fellow Harry S. Truman Library Inst. Mem. Am., Phila., Pa. bar assns., Am. Arbitration Assn. (panel), Pa. Soc., Lawyers Club Phila., Pa. Bible Soc. (dir.), Beta Gamma Sigma, Pi Gamma Mu. Home: 1132 Belfield Ave Drexel Hill PA 19026 Office: 1404 Phila Nat Bank Bldg Philadelphia PA 19107 Tel (215) LO8-4965

BRISCOE, JOSEPH RANDOLPH, JR., b. St. Louis, Jan. 31, 1937; B.S., St. Louis U., 1958, J.D., 1972. Admitted to Mo. bar, 1972; engaged in newspaper and radio advt., St. Charles, Mo., 1959-64, life ins. sales, 1964-69; advt. mgr. Gen. Am. Life Ins. Co., St. Louis, 1969-74, asst. counsel, 1974—; lectr. Lindenwood Coll., 1975—; mem. City Council St. Charles, 1962-72, municipal judge, 1973—. Mem. Mo., St. Charles County, Met. St. Louis bar assns. Home: 1102 Tompkins St Saint Charles MO 63301 Office: 700 Market St Saint Louis MO 63166 Tel (314) 231-1700

BRISKMAN, DONALD MAYER, b. Phila., May 1, 1942; B.S., U. Ala., 1964, LL.B., 1967. Admitted to Ala. bar, 1967; partner firm Perloff Reid & Briskman, Mobile, Ala., 1967—. Mem. Am., Ala., Mobile bar assns., Ala. Trial Lawyers Assn. Home: 202 Rapier Ave Mobile AL 36604 Office: 257 Saint Anthony St Mobile AL 36604 Tel (205) 433-5412

BRISTOW, WALTER JAMES, JR., b. Columbia, S.C., Oct. 14, 1924; A.B., U. N.C., 1947; LL.B. cum laude, U. S.C., 1949; LL.M., Harvard, 1950. Admitted to S.C. bar, 1950; mem. firm Marchant, Bristow and Bates, Columbia, 1953-76; resident judge 5th Jud. Circuit, 1976—; mem. S.C. Ho. of Reps., 1956-58, S.C. Senate, 1958-76. Active, Nat. Assn. Boys Clubs of Am., 1958-76; past council comdr. central S.C. council Boy Scouts Am.; past pres. Carolina Carillon; former trustee Elvira Wright Fund for Crippled Children; deacon First Presbyterian Ch. Mem. Am., S.C., Richland County bar assns., Fedn. Ins. Counsel, Am. Trial Lawyers Assn., Conf. Ins. Legislators (nat. pres. 1974-75), Wig and Robe, Alpha Tau Omega, Pi Gamma Mu. Home: 4149 E Buchanan Dr Columbia SC 29206 Office: 2020 Hampton St Columbia SC 29201 Tel (803) 256-8001

BRITT, HENRY MIDDLETON, b. Olmsted, Ill., June 9, 1919; A.B., U. Ill., 1941, J.D., 1947. Admitted to Ill. bar, 1947, U.S. Supreme Ct. bar, 1954, Ark. bar, 1948; individual practice law, Hot Springs, Ark., 1948-53, 1958-66; asst. U.S. Atty. Western dist. Ark., Ft. Smith, 1953-58; judge 18th Jud. Circuit Ct. of Ark., Hot Springs, 1967—; mem. exec. com. Ark. Jud. Council, 1973; mem. Ark.-Fed. Jud. Council, 1973—; faculty adviser Nat. Coll. State Judiciary, 1973; mem. Midwestern Tng. Conf. Organized Crime and Law Enforcement at U. Notre Dame, 1972; mem. exec. com. Ark. Commn. Crime and Law Enforcement, 1968-71; mem. central planning council Ark. Crime Commn.; Served to capt. JAGC, AUS, 1941-46. Republican candiate for Gov. Ark., 1960; gen. counsel Ark. Rep. party, 1962-64; permanent mem. Ark. Rep. Com.; mem. Garland County Bd. Election, 1962-64. Mem. Am., Ark., Ill. State, Garland County bar assns., Am. Judges Assn., Am. Judicature Soc., Nat. Coll. State Trial Judges, Phi Alpha Delta. Jaycees (v.p. Ark. 1950). Home: 126 Trivista St Hot Springs AR 71901 Office: 301 County Ct House Hot Springs AR 71901 Tel (501) 321-2211

BRITT, MICHAEL ALTON, b. New Orleans, Nov. 18, 1944; B.A., Tulane U., 1966, J.D., 1969. Admitted to La. bar, 1969; U.S. Supreme Ct. bar, 1973; asso. firm Normann & Normann, New Orleans, 1969-71; asso. firm Leach, Paysse & Baldwin, New Orleans, 1971—. Mem. La. State, Am., New Orleans bar assns., La. Assn. Def. Counsel. Office: Suite 1540 One Shell Square New Orleans LA 70139 Tel (504) 581-6211

BRITT, PERCY GRANVILLE, b. Jersey City, N.J., Feb. 26, 1893; LL.B., Rutgers U., 1915. Admitted to N.J. bar, 1916; since practiced in Jersey City; asso. firm McDermott & Enright, 1917-22; partner firm Warren, Britt & Stanton, 1922-24; individual practice law, 1924—. Alt. del. Republican Nat. Conv., 1924. Mem. Hudson County Bar Assn. (life) North Hudson Lawyers Club. Contbr. articles in field to profl. jours. Home and office: 140 78th St North Bergen NJ 07047 Tel (201) 869-6750

BRITTAIN, JACK OLIVER, b. Greenwood, La., Sept. 24, 1928; B.A., La. Poly. Inst., 1949; J.D., La. State U., 1957. Admitted to La. bar, 1957; asso. firm Watson & Williams (now Brittain & Williams), Natchitoches, La., 1957-59, partner, 1959—. Bd. dirs. Natchitoches Youth Assn., Inc.; orgn. pres. Natchitoches Parish Com. Drug Abuse, 1972-74; del. Democratic Nat. Conv., Chgo., 1968, N.Y.C., 1976; mem. Dem. nat. fin., com. Mem. La. Municipal Attys. Assn. (pres. 1971), Natchitoches and Red River Parish, La., Am. bar assns., La. Trial Lawyers Assn., Def. Research Inst., Natchitoches Parish C. of C. (pres. 1961), U.S. Jr. C. of C. (dir. 1962, Distinguished Service award 1958). Named Outstanding Young Man, Natchitoches Parish, 1959. Home: 919 Parkway Dr Natchitoches LA 71457 Office: Box 2662 Natchitoches LA 71457

BRITTIN, W. DON, JR., b. Springfield, Ill., Oct. 29, 1941; B.S. in Bus. Adminstrn., Northwestern U., 1963; J.D., U. Iowa, 1966. Admitted to Iowa bar, 1966; law clk. to U.S. Dist. Judge So. Dist. Iowa, 1966-68; partner firm Nyemaster, Goode, McLaughlin, Emery & O'Brien, Des Moines, 1968—; chmn. Iowa Supreme Ct. Commn. on Continuing Legal Edn., 1975—. Mem. Am., Iowa (pres. young lawyers sect. 1975-76, recipient sect. award of merit 1976, bd. govs. 1975-76), Polk County bar assns., Assn. Trial Lawyers Iowa, Order of Coif. Editorial bd. Iowa Law Rev., 1965-66. Office: Hubbell Bldg Des Moines IA 50309 Tel (515) 284-1940

BRITZ, HARLAND MARSHALL, b. Toledo, Ohio, July 2, 1931; B.A., U. Mich., 1953, M.A. in English, 1956, LL.B., 1956. Admitted to Ohio bar, 1956, U.S. Ct. of Appeals bar, 1957; asst. U.S. atty. No. Dist. Ohio, 1961-63; partner firm Fuhrman, Gertner, Britz & Barkan, Toledo, Ohio, 1964-73, Britz & Zemmelman, Toledo, 1973—. Active ACLU, 1965—; v.p. Interfaith Housing, Inc., 1968—; bd. mem. Toledo Symphony Orch., 1974—. Mem. Am., Fed., Ohio, Toledo bar assns. Home: 4128 Terrace View N Toledo OH 43607 Office: 340 Spitzer Bldg Toledo OH 43604 Tel (419) 242-7415

BRITZ, STEPHEN JOSEPH, b. N.Y.C., July 25, 1941; B.A. in Econs., Marietta Coll., 1964; J.D., Georgetown U., 1967. Admitted to D.C. bar, 1968, Md. bar, 1972; atty., advisor Superior Ct. D.C., 1968-72; asso. firm Goodman & Bloom, Annapolis, Md., 1972-76, partner, 1976—; master in chancery Anne Arundel County (Md.) Circuit Ct., 1976—. Mem. Md. Commn. on Human Relations, 1973—. Mem. Am., Md. State, Anne Arundel County bar assns. Home: 3128 Anchorage Dr Annapolis MD 21403 Office: PO Box 909 Annapolis MD 21404 Tel (301) 268-4500

BRIZZOLARA, CHARLES ANTHONY, b. Chgo., Nov. 20, 1929; B.A., Lake Forest Coll., 1951; J.D., Ill. Inst. Tech., 1957. Admitted to Ill. bar, 1959; individual practice law, Chgo., 1959-67; with Walter E. Heller & Co., and Walter E. Heller Internat. Corp., Chgo., 1967—, v.p., sec., gen. counsel, 1974—; v.p. Chgo. Bears Football Club, 1975—. Mem. Am., Ill. State bar assns., World Assn. Lawyers. Home: 70 E Walton Pl Chicago IL 60611 Office: 105 W Adams St Chicago IL 60690 Tel (312) 346-2300

BROADBEAR, MICHAEL WEBSTER, b. Birmingham, Ala., Nov. 26, 1941; B.A., Vanderbilt U.; J.D., Emory U. Admitted to Ga. bar, 1966; since practiced in Atlanta, asso. firm Huie & Harland, 1966-67; asso. firm E. D. Brookins, 1969-70; asso. firm Barwick, Bentley & Binford, 1970—; chmn. Municipal Traffic Ct. Com., 1976—. Mem. Am., Ga., San Francisco, Atlanta (vice-chmn. family law sect. 1974-75, chmn. 1975-76) bar assns., Ga. Trial Lawyers Assn. Contbr. articles to law reviews. Home: 865 N Island Dr Atlanta GA 30307 Office: 301 1 Piedmont Center 3665 Piedmont Rd Atlanta GA 30305 Tel (404) 261-2333

BROADFOOT, FREDERICK M., b. 1920; A.B. in Econs., Lafayette Coll., 1941; J.D., Dickinson U., 1948. Asso. firm Ward & McGinnis, 1948-49; with Pub. Service Electric and Gas Co., 1949—, gen. atty., 1968-73, v.p. law, Newark, 1973—; dir. Energy Devel. Corp. Office: 80 Park Pl Newark NJ 07101*

BROADWATER, DOUGLAS DWIGHT, b. Preston, Minn., May 31, 1944; A.B. cum laude, Harvard, 1966; J.D. cum laude, Columbia, 1969. Admitted to N.Y. bar, 1969, U.S. Supreme Ct. bar, 1975; atty. Nat. Employment Law Project, N.Y.C., 1969-71; asso. firm Cravath, Swaine Moore, N.Y.C., 1971—; spl. counsel to chmn. N.Y. State Advisory Com. to U.S. Civil Rights Commn., 1971. Mem. Am. Bar Assn. Office: One Chase Manhatten Plaza New York City NY 10005 Tel (212) 422-3000

BROADY, EARL CLIFFORD, b. Los Angeles, Dec. 24, 1904; B.A., U. So. Calif., 1934; LL.B., Los Angeles, Coll. Law, 1937; LL.D., Bishop Coll., 1976. Admitted to Calif. bar, 1944; individual practice law, 1944-64; chief dep. dist. atty. Los Angeles County, 1965; judge Superior Ct. Los Angeles County, 1965—; mem. McCone Commn. on Watts Riots, 1965. Mem. Am. Bar Assn., Am. Judicature Soc., Los Angeles Criminal Ct. Bar Assn. (pres. 1963-64). Named Man of Year, So. Calif. chpt. Howard U. Alumni Assn., 1965. Office: 210 W Temple St Los Angeles CA 90012 Tel (213) 974-5771

BROCARD, JAMES S., b. W. Orange, N.J., Mar. 15, 1920; B.S., Georgetown U., 1949, J.D., 1952. Admitted to D.C. bar, 1952, Md. bar, 1962; individual practice law, Washington. Home: 12112 Whipporwill Ln Rockville MD 20852 Office: 717 Nat Press Bldg Washington DC 20045 Tel (202) 347-2353

BROCK, DANIEL NATHAN, b. Lexington, Ky., May 23, 1920; student U. Richmond, 1939-41; LL.B., U. Ky., 1949. Admitted to Ky. bar, 1949; mem. firm Brock, Brock & Bagby, Lexington, 1952—. Mem. Am., Ky. bar assns. Home: 3337 Braemer Dr Lexington KY 40603 Office: Citizens Bank Square Lexington KY 40507 Tel (606) 255-7795

BROCK, DELBERT, b. Grandfield, Okla., Dec. 27, 1931; B.A. in Edn., Southeastern State U. Okla., 1956; LL.B., U. Tulsa, 1964. With IRS, Tulsa, 1961-64; individual practice law, Tulsa, 1964—. Dir., mem. budget com. Okla. League for the Blind, Oklahoma City, 1975. Mem. Am. Blind Lawyers Assn. (dir.), Am. Legion, VFW. Home: Office: Univ Club Tower Tulsa OK 74119 Tel (918) 584-5115

BROCK, GLEN PORTER, JR., b. Mobile, Ala., Nov. 13, 1937; B.S., Auburn U., 1959; J.D., U. Ala., 1963; LL.M. in Taxation, N.Y. U., 1964. Admitted to Ala. bar, 1963; asso. firm Hand, Arendall, Bedsole, Greaves & Johnston, Mobile, Ala., 1964-68, partner, 1969—. Mem. Am., Ala. (past chmn. tax sect.), Mobile bar assns. Chmn. U. Ala. Fed. Tax Clinic, 1977. Home: 737 Westmoreland Dr W Mobile AL 36609 Office: 30th Floor First Nat Bank Bldg Mobile AL 36602 Tel (205) 432-5511

BROCK, JAMES SIDNEY, b. Newbury, Vt., Sept. 2, 1913; B.S., Middlebury Coll., 1935; J.D., Bklyn. Law Sch., 1942. Admitted to N.Y. bar, 1942, Vt. bar, 1947; asso. firm LeBoeuf, Lamb & Leiby, N.Y.C., 1942-47; individual practice law, Montpelier, Vt., 1947-50; with Nat. Life Ins. Co., Montpelier, 1950—, sr. v.p., 1968-70, exec. v.p.-corporate relations, 1970-73, exec. v.p., 1973—, dir., 1975—; judge Vt. Municipal Ct., Montpelier, 1948-50; pres. Vt. Legal Aid, Inc., 1972-74, bd. dirs., 1972—. Mem. Montpelier Zoning Bd., 1954-62. Mem. Am., New Eng. (dir.), Vt. (sec. 1949-51, bd. mgrs. 1964-77, pres. 1975-76) bar assns., Assn. Life Ins. Counsel. Home: 9 Jordan St Montpelier VT 05602 Office: Nat Life Dr Montpelier VT 05602 Tel (802) 223-3431

BROCK, WALTER EDGAR, b. Wadesboro, N.C., Mar. 21, 1916; B.S., U. N.C., 1941, J.D., 1947. Admitted to N.C. bar, 1948; partner firm Brock & McLendon and predecessors, Wadesboro, N.C., 1948-62; judge Anson County (N.C.) Criminal Ct., 1952-54, N.C. Superior Cts., 1963-67; judge N.C. Ct. Appeals, 1967-73, chief judge, 1973—. Bd. dirs. Piedmont Area Devel. Assn., 1957-67; chmn. Anson County Democratic Exec. Com., 1957-63. Mem. N.C., Am. bar assns., Am. Judicature Soc. Office: 1 W Morgan St Raleigh NC 27601 Tel (919) 829-4225

BROCK, WARREN RICHARD, b. Buffalo, Mar. 30, 1919; B.A., U. Mich., 1940; J.D., U. Ariz., 1952. Admitted to Ariz., N.Y. bars, 1952; individual practice law, Tucson, 1952—; spl. ct. commr., Tucson, 1975; chmn. law sch. brief contest Univ. Ariz., 1966. Mem. Tucson Zoning Commn., 1955; del. Democratic Presdl. Nominating Conv., 1976, local precinct committeeman, 1952-56; mem. character guidance com. Tucson YMCA; judge Tucson High Schs. Am. Democracy Essay Contest, 1954. Mem. Am. Arbitration Assn. (panel arbitrators 1972-76), So. Ariz. Claimants Compensation Attys. Assn. (co-founder, treas. 1959-63), Nat. Assn. Claimant's Counsel Assn. (former treas. local chpt.), Am., Ariz., N.Y. bar assns., Am. (sustaining), Ariz., Calif., Pima County trial lawyers assns., Am. Judicature Soc., Phi Alpha Delta. Named Tucson Community Leader, Tucson Sun newspaper, 1954; editor Pleasure Mag., 1946-48; contbr. weekly sports column Green Valley News. Home: 5242 N Genematas St Tucson AZ 85704 Office: 244 W Drachman St Tucson AZ 85705 Tel (602) 624-2411

BROCKMAN, EUGENE EARL, b. Mills, N.Mex., Apr. 7, 1931; J.D., U. N.Mex., 1960. Admitted to N.Mex. bar, 1960; partner firm Hart & Brockman, Tucumcari, N.Mex., 1961-64; individual practice law, Tucumcari, 1964-74; partner firm Brockman & Villani, Tucumcari, 1974—. Chmn. Quay County (N.Mex.) Republican Party, 1966-69; bd. regents Eastern N.Mex. U., 1962-70. Mem. Tucumcarci-Quay County C. of C. (dir.), State Bar N.Mex., Am., Plains bar assns. Home: 2101 S 10th St Tucamcari NM 88401 Office: 201 S 2d St POB 984 Tucumcari NM 88401 Tel (505) 661-0797

BROCKWAY, BRIAN GEORGE, b. Grand Rapids, Mich., Aug. 31, 1933; B.S., Northwestern U., 1957; J.D., Georgetown U., 1961, LL.M., 1963. Admitted to Va. bar, 1961; tax law specialist IRS, Washington, 1961-63; asso. prof. bus. law, chmn. dept. mgmt., fin., mktg. and law Lehigh U., Bethlehem, Pa., 1963-67, dean Coll. Bus. and Econs., 1971—; dean U. Detroit Sch. Law, 1969-71. Mem. Am. Assembly Collegiate Schs. Bus. (chmn. Faculty Fellows Program). Recipient Linback award for outstanding teaching, 1967, 76; contbr. articles to profl. jours. Office: Coll Bus and Economics Lehigh U Bethlehem PA 18015 Tel (215) 691-7000

BROD, E. DENNIS, b. Jersey City, Oct. 27, 1939; B.A. in Govt., Pa. State U., 1960; J.D., Rutgers U., 1963. Admitted to N.J. bar, 1964, D.C. bar, 1964, U.S. Supreme Ct. bar, 1970, Fla. bar, 1972; partner firm Rose, Poley & Brod, Hackensack, N.J., 1967-71; individual practice law, Miami, Fla.; mem. Washington (N.J.) City Council, 1968-71, pres., 1971; pub. defender City of Hialeah (Fla.), 1973. Office: 1320 S Dixie Hwy Coral Gables FL 33160

BRODE, MARVIN JAY, b. Memphis, Aug. 26, 1931; B.A., Vanderbilt U., 1953, LL.B., 1954; postgrad. U. Chgo. Law Sch., 1954, Harvard Law Sch., 1962. Admitted to Tenn. bar, 1955; asso. firm Brode & Sugg, Memphis, 1970—; asst. city atty. City of Memphis, 1965-67; mem. Tenn. Ho. of Reps., 1962-66. Mem. Pres's. Com. on Traffic Safety, 1965-67; mem. Tenn. Art Commn., 1972; past bd. dirs. West Tenn. chpt. Arthritis and Rheumatism Found. Mem. Am., Tenn., Memphis, Shelby County bar assns. Home: 4841 Walnut Grove Rd Memphis TN 38117 Office: 100 N Main Bldg Memphis TN 38101 Tel (901) 527-0763

BRODEK, RICHARD CORNELIUS, b. Chgo., July 28, 1932; B.S., U. Wis., 1957, LL.B., 1959. Admitted to Wis. bar, 1959; individual practice law, Racine, Wis., 1963-66; v.p. M & I Am. Bank & Trust Co., Racine, 1966-73; partner firm DeMark, Kolbe & Brodek, Racine, 1973—; lectr. U. Wis. Mem. Caledonia Police and Fire Commn.; active Boy Scouts Am.; bd. dirs. Wis. Cancer Soc., Rosehart Montessori Sch.; bd. dirs., treas., Franksville Businessmen's Assn. Mem. Am., Wis., Beloit, Racine County (bd. govs.) bar assns. Home: 7411 W River Rd Caledonia WI 53108 Office: 212 5th St Racine WI 53403 Tel (414) 633-2406

BRODER, JOSEPH ARNOLD, b. Hartford, Conn., Jan. 19, 1939; A.B., Trinity Coll., Hartford, 1960; J.D., Harvard, 1963. Admitted to Conn. bar, 1963, N.Y. bar, 1964, U.S. Supreme Ct. bar, 1976; asso. firm Dammann & Hemming, N.Y.C., 1964-65; individual practice law, Colchester, Conn., 1965—; corp. counsel Town and Borough of Colchester, 1965—; served to lt. comdr. JAGC, USNR. Chmn. Colchester YMCA, 1968-73; dir. Colchester Synagogue, 1968—; mem. Town Indsl. Devel. Commn., 1973—. Mem. Am., Lawyers Pilots, Conn., New London bar assns., Am. Trial Lawyers Assn., Naval Res. Lawyers Assn. (sec. 1975—). Home: Lynn Ln Colchester CT 06415 Office: 12 Amston Rd Colchester CT 06415 Tel (203) 537-2443

BRODERICK, DANIEL THOMAS, III, b. Duluth, Minn., Nov. 22, 1944; B.S., U. Notre Dame, 1966; M.D., Cornell U., 1970; J.D., Harvard, 1973. Admitted to Calif. bar, 1973; asso. firm Gray, Cary, Ames & Frye, San Diego, 1973—; lectr. Nat. U., San Diego. Fellow Am. Coll. Legal Medicine; mem. Am., Calif., San Diego bar assns., AMA. Home: 5555 Coral Reef Ave La Jolla CA 92037 Office: 2100 Union Bank Bldg 525 B St San Diego CA 92101 Tel (714) 236-1661

BRODERICK, JAMES VINCENT, b. Brighton, Mass., Sept. 11, 1924; LL.B., New Eng. Law Sch., 1950. Admitted to N.H. bar, 1951, also Fed. bar; since practiced in Manchester, N.H., mem. firm Broderick & Broderick, 1951-58, Broderick & Loughlin, 1958-63, Broderick, Craig, Bourque & Costakis, 1953-71, individual practice law; spl. judge Manchester Dist. Ct., 1964—. Bd. dirs. Am. Cancer Soc., 1968. Mem. Manchester (pres. 1965), Am., N.H. bar assns., Am. Judges Assn., Nat. Council Juvenile Ct. Judges. Home: 55 Bay St Manchester NH 03104 Office: 53 Bay St Manchester NH 03104 Tel (603) 625-6401

BRODERICK, RAYMOND JOSEPH, b. Phila., May 29, 1914; A.B. magna cum laude, U. Notre Dame, 1935; J.D., U. Pa., 1938. Admitted to D.C. bar, 1939, Pa. bar, 1945; since practiced in Phila., sr. partner, mem. firm Broderick, Schubert & Fitzpatrick, 1938-41, 45-71; lt. gov. Pa., 1967-71; judge U.S. Dist. Ct. Eastern Dist. Pa., 1971—; pres. Senate of Pa., 1967-71; pres. Pa. Constl. Conv., 1967-68. Mem. exec. com. Republican State Com., 1967-69; bd. dirs. USO, Phila., 1971-72. Mem. Am., Pa., Phila. bar assns., Notre Dame Law Assn. Home: 6408 Church Rd Philadelphia PA 19151 Office: 10613 U S Court House 601 Market St Philadelphia PA 19151 Tel (215) 597-7500

BRODIE, RALPH GRAY, b. Marshall, Ark., Mar. 24, 1940; B.S. in Indsl. Engring., U. Ark., 1963, J.D., 1966; LL.M. in Taxation, N.Y. U., 1973. Admitted to Ark. bar, 1966; law clk. to chief justice Ark. Supreme Ct., 1966-67; asst. atty. gen. State of Ark., Little Rock, 1967-69; house counsel Diversified Fin. Services Internat., Little Rock, 1969-72; individual practice law, Little Rock, 1973—; exec. dir. Ark. Tax Revision Commn., 1976—. Mem. Ark. (vice chmn. tax sect.), Am. bar assns., Pulaski Tax Counsel (pres. 1976-77), Little Rock Jaycees (v.p. 1968). Home: 1023 Kavanaugh Blvd Little Rock AR 72205 Office: 1133 Worthen Bank Bldg Little Rock AR 72201 Tel (501) 376-2327

BRODLEY, JOSEPH FRANKLIN, b. Washington, Sept. 22, 1926; B.A., U. Calif., Los Angeles, 1949; LL.B., Yale, 1952; LL.M., Harvard, 1953. Admitted to Calif. bar, 1953, N.Y. bar, 1956; asso. firm Dewey, Ballantine, Bushby, Palmer & Wood, N.Y.C., 1956-61; partner firm Richards, Watson, Dreyfuss & Gershon, Los Angeles, 1961-68; prof. law Ind. U., 1968—. Mem. Am. Bar Assn. (adv. bd. Antitrust Bull. 1968, Jour. Reprints for Antitrust Law and Econs. 1964). Contbr. articles to profl. jours. Home: 2300 Browncliff St Bloomington IN 47401 Office: Ind U Law Sch Bloomington IN 47401 Tel (812) 337-4846

BRODSKY, CHARLES IRA, b. Bklyn., July 15, 1938; B.E.E., City U. N.Y., 1960, M.B.A., 1966; LL.B., N.Y. U., 1966. Admitted to N.Y. bar, 1966, N.J. bar, 1971, U.S. Supreme Ct. bar, 1973. Counsel, Hazeltine Corp., Little Neck, N.J., 1960-65; sr. counsel RCA Corp., Princeton, N.J., 1964-69, 70-74; atty. firm Ostrolenk, Faber, Gerb & Soffen, N.Y.C., 1969-70; individual practice law, Marlboro, N.J., 1973—; pros. atty. Marlboro, 1972-73; atty. Marlboro Twp. Utilities Authority, 1974; municipal judge, Marlboro, 1975—. Pres. Whittier Oaks Homeowners Assn., Marlboro, 1969-70; trustee Marlboro Jewish Center, 1971—. Mem. Am., N.J., N.Y., Monmouth County bar assns. Recipient Am. Law Reports award, 1964, 66. Home: 15 Fletcher Dr Morganville NJ 07751 Office: 9 S Main St Marlboro NJ 07746 Tel (201) 431-1333

BRODSTEIN, ELLIS, b. Phila., Jan. 4, 1896; A.B., Lehigh U., 1916; J.D., U. Pa., 1920. Admitted to Pa. bar, 1920; individual practice law, Reading Pa., 1920—. Pres. Reading lodge B'nai B'rith, 1934. Mem. Berks County (pres. 1952), Pa. bar assns., Endlich Law Club (pres. 1940). Author: The Trustee's Role in Bankruptcy, 1957; Forestry Laws of the United States, 1921. Home: 2607 Cumberland Ave Mount Penn Reading PA 19606 Office: #418 Berks Title Bldg 607 Washington St Reading PA 19601 Tel (215) 376-5171

BRODY, DAVID ALLAN, b. Bklyn., June 24, 1916; B.S.S., Coll. City N.Y., 1936; LL.B., Columbia, 1940; Admitted to N.Y. bar 1940, D.C. bar, 1951, U.S. Supreme Ct. bar 1969; atty. Office of the Solicitor, U.S. Dept. of Agriculture, Washington, 1940-42, 46-49; legal assistance officer USNR, 1944-46; Washington counsel, Anti-Defamation League B'nai B'rith, Washington, 1949—; individual practice law, Washington, 1953—. Mem. Am., Fed., D.C. Bar assns., Bar Assn. of D.C. (chmn. Com. on Trademarks 1975-76), Phi Beta Kappa. Legis. editor Columbia Law Review, 1939-40. Home: 2805 Washington Ave Chevy Chase MD 20015 Office: 818 18th St NW Washington DC 20006 Tel (202) 347-7352

BRODY, ROBERT SAMUEL, b. Chgo., Apr. 5, 1928; student Roosevelt U., 1946-48, U. Ill., 1948-49; J.D., Chgo.-Kent Coll. Law, 1953. Admitted to Ill. bar, 1953; individual practice law, Chgo., 1956—; tech. adviser to Auditor of Pub. Accounts, State of Ill., 1970-72, to Comptroller, State of Ill., 1973; tech. adviser, hearing officer to Sec. of State, State of Ill., 1973—; mem. inquiry bd. atty. regulation and disciplinary commn. Ill. Supreme Ct. Mem. regional bd. trustees Bellefaire Residential Treatment and Child Care Center of Cleve. Mem. Am., Ill., Chgo. bar assns. Home: 9522 Keystone Ave Skokie IL 60076 Office: 33 N Dearborn St Chicago IL 60602 Tel (312) 372-0144

BRODY, STUART ALAN, b. Chgo., Nov. 29, 1933; A.B., U. Calif., Los Angeles, 1955; M.A., U. So. Calif., 1958, Ph.D., 1962; J.D., U. Pacific, 1968. Asso. human factors scientist System Devel. Corp., Santa Monica, Calif., 1958-62; research social scientist Calif. Dept. Mental Hygiene, Sacramento, 1962-65; spl. cons. Calif. State Dept. Edn., Sacramento, 1965-67; exec. sec. Calif. Bd. Edn., 1967-69; admitted to Calif. bar, 1969; asso. prof. law U. Pacific, Sacramento, 1969—, asst. dean, 1969-73, dir. research McGeorge Sch. of Law, 1973—; staff judge advocate Calif. Air N.G., Sacramento, 1975—; mem. faculty Nat. Coll. for State Judiciary, Reno, 1976; mem. adv. com. paralegal program Am. River Coll., Sacramento, 1975—; legal counsel Calif. Assn. Human Services Technologists, 1970—. Mem. Am., Sacramento bar assns., Law and Psychology Assn. Author: (with Walter Bromberg) Contemporary Issues in Psychiatry and Law, 1973; recipient Corpus Juris Secundum award McGeorge Sch. Law, 1965. Home: 6601 Willowbrae Way Sacramento CA 95831 Office: 3200 5th Ave Sacramento CA 95817 Tel (916) 452-6051

BROEKER, JOHN MILTON, b. Berwyn, Ill., May 27, 1940; B.A. in Econs., Grinnell (Iowa) Coll., 1962; LL.B. cum laude, U. Minn., 1965. Admitted to Minn. bar, 1965, U.S. Tax Ct. bar, 1969; law clk. to Hon. Charles J. Vogel, U.S. Ct. of Appeals, 8th Circuit, 1965-66; partner firm Haverstock, Gray, Plant, Mooty and Anderson, Mpls., 1966-71, Broeker, Hartfeldt, Hedges & Grant, 1971—; instr. law U. Minn., 1967-72; lectr. numerous health law courses; bd. dirs. Legal Advice Clinic, 1968-69. Bd. dirs. Minn. Environ. Sci. Found., Inc., Golden Valley, 1971-74; chmn. Midwest regional conservation com. Sierra Club, 1972-74, regional v.p., 1973-74, bd. dirs., 1974-76. Mem. Nat. Health Lawyers Assn., Am. Health Care Assn. (legal coordinating com.), Am., Minn. (chmn. environ. law com. 1970-72), Hennepin County (chmn. environ. law com., chmn. legis. com. 1972-76) bar assns., Grinnell Coll. Alumni Assn. (dir. 1968-71). Recipient Hall of Fame award Heritage Rembrandt Corp., 1972; Outstanding Alumnus award Grinnell Coll., 1973; Spl. Achievement award Sierra Club, 1974. Home: 4233 23d Ave S Minneapolis MN 55407 Office: 2850 Metro Dr Suite 504 Minneapolis MN 55420 Tel (612) 854-5263

BROGAN, WILLIAM ROBERT, b. Balt., Feb. 8, 1910; LL.B., John Marshall Coll. Law, 1939. Admitted to N.J. bar, 1942, U.S. Supreme Ct. bar, 1962; individual practice law, Clifton, N.J., 1946—; trustee Legal Aid Soc., Passaic County. Activie, Clifton Fed. Veterans' Housing Assn., 1948; mem. Clifton Planning Bd., 1950; councilman City of Clifton, 1951, 52, 54. 58. Home: 10 Thanksgiving Ln Clifton NJ 07013 Office: 1300 Van Houten Ave Clifton NJ 07013 Tel (201) 773-0011

BROMBERG, JACOB, b. N.Y.C., Dec. 28, 1907; LL.B., St. John's U., Bklyn., 1929. Admitted to New York State bar, 1931, U.S. Supreme Ct. bar, 1947; individual practice law, N.Y.C., 1931—; mem. Kings County panel legal service to indigent defendants. Mem. N.Y. County Lawyers Assn. Home: 140 Cadman Plaza W Brooklyn NY 11201 Office: 30 Vesey St New York City NY 10007 Tel (212) 227-8240

BROMBERG, JOHN EDWARD, b. Dallas, May 9, 1946; B.A., Columbia, 1968; J.D., U. Tex., 1972. Admitted to Tex. bar, 1972; asso. firm Johnson, Bromberg, Leeds & Riggs, Dallas, 1972—. Home: 6146 Park Ln Dallas TX 75225 Office: 211 N Ervay St suite 1500 Dallas TX 75201 Tel (214) 748-8811

BROMFIELD, HAROLD ARTHUR (TED), b. Portsmouth, N.H., Nov. 11, 1945; A.B., Colby Coll., 1968; J.D., Calif. Western U., 1971. Admitted to Calif. bar, 1972, Maine bar, 1973, U.S. Supreme Ct. bar, 1976; dep. city atty., San Diego, 1972—. Mem. atty. gen.'s com. on obscenity; mem. Young Democrats Assn. Mem. Calif. Bar Assn., Calif. Trial Lawyers Assn. Contbr. articles to legal publs. Home: 4341 Piedmont Dr San Diego CA 92107 Office: 202 C St San Diego CA 92101 Tel (714) 236-6220

BROMLEY, J(AMES) ROBERT, b. Stamford, Conn., Apr. 9, 1936; B.A., Yale, 1958, LL.B., 1962; postgrad. Sorbonne U. Paris, 1963. Admitted to Conn. bar, 1962; asso. firm Durey and Pierson, Stamford, 1963-68; partner firm Pierson, Duel, Holland and Bromley, Darien, Conn., 1968-70; individual practice law, Stamford, 1970-72; corp. counsel City of Stamford, 1971-74; partner firm Mead and Bromley, Stamford 1972—. Mem. Stamford Bd. Reps., 1965-70, asst. maj. leader and chmn. legis. and rules com. 1965-70. Mem. Stamford, Conn. bar assns. Author: Abraham Davenport, 1715-1789, 1976. Home: 55 Cedar Heights Rd Stamford CT 06905 Office: PO Box 160 Stamford CT 06901 Tel (203) 325-4477

BROMLEY, MICHAEL RUPERT, b. London, Oct. 13, 1944; A.B., Dartmouth, 1966; certificate (Rotary Internat. fellow), U. Geneva, 1967; J.D. (Carnegie fellow), U. Va., 1970. Asso. firm Thatcher, Proffitt, Prizer, Crawley & Wood, N.Y.C., 1970-71; admitted to N.Y. bar, 1971, Colo. bar, 1972, U.S. Supreme Ct. bar, 1975; asso. firm Cole, Hecox, Tolley, Edwards & Keene, P.C., Colorado Springs, Colo., 1971-75, dir., 1976—. Mem. exec. bd., treas. Pikes Peak Legal Services, Colorado Springs, 1975—; mem. exec. bd. Pikes Peak Council Boy Scouts Am., Colorado Springs, 1976—. Mem. Colo., El Paso County (Colo.), Am. bar assns. Office: 3 S Tejon St Colorado Springs CO 80902 Tel (303) 473-4444

BRONAUGH, JOHN REEDER, b. Washington, Aug. 3, 1924; B.M.E., Va. Poly. Inst., 1947; J.D., George Washington U., 1951, LL.M., 1953; M.B.A., U. Pitts., 1974. Patent liaison agt. IBM, Endicott, N.Y., 1947-48; patent examiner U.S. Patent Office, Washington, 1948-50; admitted to U.S. Supreme Ct. bar, 1952, D.C. bar, 1952, Mich. bar, 1967, Pa. bar, 1967; patent agt. firm Straugh Nolan, Neale, Neis & Bronaugh, and predecessors, Washington, 1950-52, partner, 1952-54, 55-66; trial atty., antitrust div. Dept. Justice, Washington, 1954-55; dir. patents RockWell-Standard Corp., Troy, Mich., 1966-67; corp. patent counsel N.Am. Rockwell Corp. and Rockwell Internat. Corp., both Pitts., 1967—, asst. gen. counsel,

1977—. Mem. Am., Fed., Pa., Allegheny County (Pa.) bar assns., Am. Patent Law Assn. Office: 600 Grant St room 5304 Pittsburgh PA 15219 Tel (412) 565-2907

BRONCHICK, FRANK, b. Bklyn., Nov. 9, 1928; B.S., L.I. U., 1950; LL.B., Bklyn. Law Sch., 1962. Admitted to N.Y. bar, 1963, U.S. Dist. Ct. bar for So. Dist. N.Y., 1975, U.S. Ct. Appeals bar, 2d Dist., 1976; individual practice law, N.Y.C., 1963-71; partner firm Tilles/Bronchick, Huntington Station, N.Y., 1971—. Mem. Huntington Consumer Protection Bd., 1972—. Mem. Suffolk County (N.Y.) Bar Assn., Huntington C. of C., 49ers Credit Assn. Office: One Huntington Quadrangle Huntington Station NY 11746 Tel (516) 420-8313

BRONNER, WILLIAM ROCHE, b. N.Y.C., Mar. 13, 1946; B.A., Dartmouth, 1967; J.D., Columbia, 1970. Admitted to N.Y. State bar, 1971; law clk. to judge U.S. Dist. Ct., N.Y.C., 1970-72; asst. U.S. Atty., 1972-76; asso. firm Burns, Jackson, Miller, Summit & Jacoby, N.Y.C., 1976—. Mem. Fed. Bar Assn., Assn. Bar City N.Y. Home: 7 E 9th St New York City NY 10003 Office: 445 Park Ave New York City NY 10022 Tel (212) 980-3200

BRONSON, KENNETH, b. Detroit, Feb. 3, 1934; A.B., U. Mich., 1958, LL.M., 1959; J.D., Wayne State U., 1957. Admitted to Mich. bar, 1957; asso. firm Bonisteel & Bonisteel, Ann Arbor, Mich., 1957-59; city atty., Ypsilanti, Mich., 1959-65; judge Municipal Ct., Saline, 1965-68; sr. partner firm Bronson, Egnor & Hamilton, Ypsilanti, 1969-74; judge Mich. Dist. Ct., Ann Arbor, 1975—; spl. asst. prosecutor Washtenaw County, 1959-65; city atty. Ypsilanti, 1965-74; fed. trial counsel Eastern Mich. U., 1969-74; mem. Gov.'s Spl. Com. Traffic Safety, 1964-68. Mem. Mich. Council B'nai B'rith, 1966-67; pres. Washtenaw County Jewish Community Council, 1969-71. Mem. Am. Mich. (chmn. spl. com. State Bar Jour.), Washtenaw County, Ypsilanti bar assns., Am. Judicature Soc. Sr. editor Wayne State U. Law Rev., 1956-57. Home: 3520 E Huron River Dr Ann Arbor MI 48104 Office: 4133 Washtenaw Ave Ann Arbor MI 48104 Tel (313) 971-6050

BRONSTEIN, AARON JACOB, b. Balt., May 6, 1905; A.B., Harvard, 1925, LL.B., 1928. Admitted to Mass. bar, 1928, U.S. Supreme Ct. bar, 1957; practice law, Boston, 1928—; partner firm Schneider, Bronstein, Wolbarsht & Deutsch, 1944-69, Brown, Rudnick, Freed & Gesmer, 1969—; sec., dir. Bennett Importing Co., Inc. (Lynn, Mass.), Am. Biltrite, Inc. (Cambridge, Mass.). Pres. New Eng. div. Am. Jewish Congress, 1955-59, Jewish Community Fedn. Greater Lynn, 1962-67, Jewish Community Council Boston, 1959-61, New Eng. Zionist Region, 1949-51, Hillel Acad. North Shore, 1973; trustee Am. Biltrite Rubber Charitable Trust. Mem. Am., Mass., Essex County, Boston bar assns. Home: 28 Atlantic Ave Swampscott MA 01907 Office: 85 Devonshire St Boston MA 02109 Tel (617) 726-7800

BRONSTEIN, DANIEL A., b. Balt., Dec. 12, 1942; A.B., Johns Hopkins U., 1963; LL.B., U. Md., 1966; LL.M., U. Mich., 1971, S.J.D., 1972. Admitted to Md. bar, 1966, Mich. bar, 1973; asso. firm Paul Berman, Balt., 1966-68; individual practice law, Balt., 1968-71; research asso. U. Md. Law Sch., 1968-70; research scholar U. Mich. Law Sch., 1971-72, asst. prof., 1972-77; asso. prof. Mich. State U., 1977—; legal advisor Balt. Community Relations Commn., 1966-68, sec., 1968-69. Sec., Balt. Small Bus. Devel. Corp. Mem. Am. (chmn. com. environ. law 1975—, co-chmn. subcom. racial discrimination 1973-75, 76—), Mich. bar assns., Am. Psychology-Law Soc. Contbr. articles to legal jours. Home: 1650 Sylvan Glen Rd Okemos MI 48864 Office: Dept Resource Devel Mich State U East Lansing MI 48824

BROOK, HERBERT CECIL, b. Stronghurst, Ill., Feb. 11, 1910; A.B., Northwestern U., 1932; J.D., U. Chgo., 1936. Admitted to Ill. bar, 1936, U.S. Supreme Ct. bar, 1943, D.C. bar, 1966; asso. firm Lord, Bissell & Brook, Chgo., 1936-48, partner, 1948—; instr. Northwestern Law Sch., 1952-57; Ill. atty.-in-fact Lloyds of London, 1961-75. Pres., Hinsdale (Ill.) Retirement Homes, Inc.; chmn. Chgo. Goodwill Industries, 1976; pres. Village of Hinsdale, 1969-73. Mem. Am., Ill., Chgo. bar assns. Contbr. articles to profl. jours. Home: 135 Park St Hinsdale IL 60521 Office: 115 S La Salle St Chicago IL 60603 Tel (312) 443-0700

BROOKE, CHARLES PATRICK, b. Three Forks, Mont., Sept. 8, 1914; B.S., Carroll Coll., 1937; M.D., St. Louis U., 1941; J.D., U. Mont., 1964. Intern, St. Anthony Hosp., St. Louis, 1941, Sacred Heart Hosp., Spokane, 1941-42; resident Regional Hosp., Camp Swift, Tex., Camp White Sta. Hosp., Medford, Oreg., 1944-46; gen. practice medicine, Missoula, Mont., 1946—; admitted to Mont. bar, 1964; individual practice law, Missoula, 1964—; mem. staffs St. Patrick, Missoula Gen. and Missoula Community hosps.; mem. Mont. Bd. Med. Examiners, 1966-76, pres., 1970; lectr. forensic medicine U. Mont. Law Sch., 1968—. Recipient Judge Pray award U. Mont. Law Sch.; named Citizen of Year Missoula, Western Broadcasting Co., 1969. Office: 5th and Orange Sts Missoula MT 59801 Tel (406) 549-6411

BROOKE, CHARLES WINSTON, b. Savannah, Ga., Feb. 1, 1943; B.A., U. Wis., 1965; J.D., U. Iowa, 1968. Admitted to Iowa bar, 1968; mem. firm Lane & Waterman, Davenport, Iowa, 1968—. Bd. dirs. Tri City Symphony. Mem. Am., Iowa Scott County bar assns., Davenport C. of C. (dir.). Office: 700 Davenport Bank Bldg Davenport IA 52801 Tel (319) 324-3246

BROOKE, JAMES ROYAL, b. Sacramento, Oct. 1, 1930; B.A., U. Nev., 1954; J.D., U. San Francisco, 1957. Admitted to Nev. bar, 1957; law clk. Nev. Supreme Ct., 1957-58; city atty. City of Sparks (Nev.), 1959-71; legis. bill drafter Nev. State Legislature, 1958-61; legis. analyst Nev. State Bar, 1973, 75; individual practice law, Reno, 1957—. Sec. Washoe County United Fund, 1962-64, dir., 1959-64; pres. Sparks YMCA, 1961-65, Sparks Young Republicans, 1958-60. Mem. Am., Nev., Washoe County bar assns., Am. Arbitration Assn. (nat. panel), Phi Alpha Theta, Phi Alpha Delta, Sigma Nu. Recipient U.S. Law Week award, 1957, Distinguished Service award U.S. Jr. C. of C., 1961, Superior Club Leadership award Sertoma Internat., 1961, Spl. Recognition award Sparks YMCA, 1971. Office: 1 E 1st St Suite 1100 Reno NV 89501 Tel (702) 322-6931

BROOKE, JOHN ALLAN, b. Balt., Sept. 29, 1936; LL.B., Mt. Vernon Coll., 1963; J.D., U. Balt., 1970. Admitted to Md. bar, 1964, U.S. Supreme Ct. bar, 1972; partner firm Brooke and Ripperger, Balt. Mem. Am., Md., Balt. City, Fed. bar assns. Office: 1719 Gough St Baltimore MD 21231 Tel (301) 327-2333

BROOKMAN, MARC D., b. Phila., Dec. 10, 1942; B.S., Temple U., 1964, J.D., 1968. Admitted to Pa. bar, 1968; eastern counsel Nat. Automatic Merchandising Assn., Phila., 1968-70; asso. firm Pechner, Dorfman, Wolffe, Rounick & Cabot, Phila., 1968-74, partner, 1975—. Officer and dir. Golden Slipper Club, Phila., 1975-77. Mem. Am., Phila. bar assns. Contbr. articles to legal jours. Office: 1845 Walnut St Suite 1300 Philadelphia PA 19103 Tel (215) 561-7100

BROOKS, CHARLES EDWARD, b. Balt., July 2, 1938; B.S. Towson U., 1961; J.D., U. Balt., 1964. Admitted to Md. bar, 1965; asso. firm W. Lee Harrison, Towson, Md., 1965-71; sr. partner firm Brooks & Turnbull, Towson, 1971—; legal counsel Towson Jr. C. of C. Mem. Md., Balt. County (chmn. jud. selection com. 1972-75) bar assns. Office: 610 Bosley Ave Towson MD 21204 Tel (301) 296-2600

BROOKS, CODY HAMILTON, b. Scranton, Pa., Jan. 12, 1934; A.B., Dickinson Coll., 1955, LL.B., 1958. Admitted to Pa. bar, 1959, U.S. Supreme Ct. bar, 1973; asso. firm Henkelman, McMenamin, Kreder & O'Connell, Scranton, 1959-63, partner, 1963—; asst. dist. atty. Lackawanna County, Pa., 1970-73. Active Boy Scouts Am., Scranton; bd. dirs. Bellvue Community Center, Scranton, 1960-65; trustee Waverly (Pa.) Community House, 1972-75. Mem. Am., Pa. bar assns. Home: RD 4 Miller Rd Clarks Summit PA 18411 Office: Northeastern Bank Bldg PO Box 956 Scranton PA 18501 Tel (717) 346-7922

BROOKS, DON GARY, b. Terre Haute, Ind., Apr. 2, 1941; B.S., Ind. State U., 1962; LL.B., Ind. U., Bloomington, 1965. Admitted to Ind. bar, 1965, Idaho bar, 1972; law clk. to Chief Justice Idaho Supreme Ct., 1965-66; dep. pros. atty. Vigo County, Ind., 1966-71; mem. firm Moffatt, Thomas Barrett & Blanton, Chartered, Boise, Idaho, 1971—. Mem. Am. Bar Assn., Idaho Def. Attys. Office: PO Box 829 Boise ID 83701 Tel (208) 345-2334

BROOKS, HUBERT STANWOOD, b. St. Johnsbury, Vt., Jan. 17, 1903. Admitted to Vt. bar, 1924; treas., mgr. C.H. Goss Co., 1941-68; state's atty. Caledonia County (Vt.), 1934-40; dir., chmn. adv. bd. Howard Bank, 1948-76; individual practice law and accounting, St. Johnsbury, 1924-41; dir. Vt. Asso. Industries; mem. Vt. Bd. Accountancy, 1934-38. Chmn. Vt. Council of New Eng. C.P.A., Vt. Mem. Vt. Bar Assn., Vt. Soc. C.P.A.'s, St. Johnsbury C. of C. (Man of Year 1971, pres.). Home: 22 Mount Pleasant St Saint Johnsbury VT 05819 Office: 22 Mount Pleasant St Saint Johnsbury VT 05819 Tel (802) 748-3216

BROOKS, JOHN, JR., b. N.Y.C., Oct. 24, 1926; B.A., Yale U., 1949; LL.B., Denver U., 1955. Admitted to Colo. bar, 1955; asso. firm Hodges Silverstein Hodger and Harrington, 1955-60; individual practice law, 1961-62; judge Municipal Ct., Denver, 1961-62, Denver County Ct., 1962-66, Colo. Dist. Ct., 1966—. Bd. dirs. Mt. Airy Psychiat. Found. Hosp., 1966—. Mem. Denver, Colo. bars. Home: 155 Gilpin St Denver CO 80218 Office: City-County Bldg Denver CO 80202 Tel (303) 297-2797

BROOKS, JOHN WHITE, JR., b. Long Beach, Calif., Sept. 3, 1936; A.B. with honors (Alfred P. Sloan scholar), Stanford 1958, LL.B. (Rocky Mountain Mineral Law Found. research scholar), 1966. Admitted to Calif. bar, 1966; asso. firm Luce, Forward, Hamilton & Scripps, San Diego, 1966-71, partner, 1971—. Mem. Am. Bar Assn., Am. Arbitration Assn., Corp. Fin. Council San Diego. Contbr. article Nat. Resources Jour. Office: 110 W A St San Diego CA 92101 Tel (714) 236-1414

BROOKS, RICHARD OLIVER, b. Lake Forest, Ill., Oct. 11, 1934; B.A., U. Chgo., 1956, M.A., 1958; LL.B., Yale, 1962; Ph.D., Brandeis U., 1974. Admitted to Conn. bar, 1962; assoc. firm Barker, Badger & Fisher, Greenwich, Conn., 1962-63; counsel Community Progress, Inc., New Haven, 1963-65; exec. dir. Thames Valley Council, 1965-68; asso. prof. law and planning U. R.I., 1970—. Mem. Conn., New Haven County bar assns., NAACP, ACLU, Planned Parenthood League, Conservation Law Found., R.I. Ecology Action. Author: New Towns and Communal Values, 1974; The Law of New Town Development, 1975; contbr. articles in field to profl. jours. Home: 9 Northwood Rd Quaker Hill CT 06375 Office: Dept Law Univ RI Kingston RI 02881 Tel (401) 792-2248

BROOKS, ROBERT NORMAN, b. Carthage, Miss., May 9, 1944; B.S., Miss. Coll., 1966; J.D., U. Miss., 1969. Admitted to Miss. bar, 1969; partner firm Barnett & Brooks, Carthage, 1969—; dist. atty. for 8th Jud. Dist., 1977—. Pres., Leake County (Miss.) Indsl. Assn., Carthage, 1975-76. Mem. Leake County, Miss., Am. bar assns., Phi Alpha Delta. Home: 907 Pine Hill Circle Carthage MS 39051 Office: 211 N Pearl St Carthage MS 39051 Tel (601) 267-2781

BROOKS, ROY HOWARD, JR., b. Columbus, Ga., Feb. 10, 1923; J.D., U. Miami, 1954. Admitted to Fla. bar, 1954, U.S. Supreme Ct. bar, 1960; partner firm Kelly and Brooks, Coral Gables, Fla., 1955—; commr. Fla. Dept. Vet. Affairs, 1962-70, chmn. commn., 1964—, mem. Gov.'s adv. council Fla. Div. Vet. Affairs, 1970—; mem. Coral Gables Personnel Trial Bd., 1975—. Vice pres. Dade County Hearing and Speech Center, 1975—; mem. bd. First Methodist Ch., Coral Gables. Mem. Fla. Bar (com. aid to servicemen), Fla. Soc. So. Families (v.p.), SAR, VFW (recipient distinguished service award 1955, outstanding citizen award 1955), Am. Legion. Recipient medal of honor DAR, 1977. Home: 930 NW 41st Ave Miami FL 33126 Office: 2625 Ponce De Leon Blvd Coral Gables FL 33134 Tel (305) 445-2424

BROOM, DAVID LAURENCE, b. Spokane, Wash., July 16, 1938; B.A., U. Wash., 1960, J.D., 1963. Admitted to Wash. bar, 1966; legal officer procurement U.S. Army Ordnance Corps, 1964-66; asso. firm Randell & Danskin, Spokane, 1966-69; devel. officer U. Wash., 1969-72; mem. firm Hamblen, Gilbert & Brooks, Spokane, 1972—. Pres. Spokane Art Sch., 1975; mem. exec. com. Wampum; trustee U. Wash. Ann. Fund, 1972-76. Mem. Am., Fed., Wash. bar assns., Wash. Trial Lawyers Assn. Mem. editorial adv. bd. Wash. State Bar News. Home: S 1807 Rockwood Blvd Spokane WA 99203 Office: 601 Main Ave Spokane WA 99201 Tel (509) 624-3303

BROOMFIELD, ARLINE ABBY, b. Providence, May 4, 1936; A.B., Hunter Coll., 1968; J.D., St. John's U., 1970. Admitted to N.Y. bar, 1970; atty. Prentice Hall Pub. Co., Englewood, N.J., 1970; atty. juvenile rights div. Legal Aid Soc., N.Y.C., 1970-73, criminal def. div., 1973—. Mem. N.Y. Bar Assn. Home: 10 Park Ave New York City NY 10016 Office: 80 Lafayette St New York City NY 10013 Tel (212) 577-3650

BROOMFIELD, ROBERT CAMERON, b. Detroit, June 18, 1933; B.S., Pa. State U., 1955; LL.B., U. Ariz., 1961. Admitted to Ariz. bar, 1961; partner firm Carson Messinger Elliott Laughlin & Ragan, 1962-70; judge Superior Ct., 1971—, presiding judge, 1974—; asst. juvenile Ct., 1971-74, presiding judge, 1972-74; mem. Phoenix Jud. Selection Adv. Bd., 1975—, Ariz. Criminal Justice Group, 1975—. Mem. Paradise Valley Sch. Bd., 1965-70, pres., 1969-70; mem. adv. bd. Theodore Roosevelt council Boy Scouts Am., 1968—, Cactus Pine council Girls Scouts U.S.A., 1971—. Mem. Am., Maricopa County (Ariz.) bar assns., State Bar Ariz. Home: 41 N Barbados Pl Phoenix AZ 85021 Office: 101 W Jefferson St Phoenix AZ 85003 Tel (602) 262-3916

BROTMAN, JEFFREY HART, b. Tacoma, Sept. 27, 1942; A.B., U. Wash., 1964, J.D., 1967. Admitted to Wash. bar, 1967; sr. v.p. and chief adminstrv. officer ENI Corp., Seattle, 1975—; partner firm Lasher, Brotman & Sweet, Seattle, 1970-75; asst. atty. gen. State of Wash., 1967-70; instr. bus. Seattle Community Coll., 1968-73. Mem. Am., Wash. State bar assns. Home: 2360 43rd St E Seattle WA 98112 Office: 1401 Bank of California Blvd Seattle WA 98164 Tel (206) 223-4306

BROUGH, MICHAEL BANNON, b. Syracuse, N.Y., May 1, 1947; B.A., Georgetown U., 1969; M. Pub. Adminstrn., Syracuse U., 1973; J.D., U. Mich., 1973. Admitted N.C. bar, 1974; asst. prof. pub. law and govt. Inst. of Govt., U. N.C., Chapel Hill, 1974-76; partner firm Young & Brough, Chapel Hill, 1976—. Pres. Devonshire Manor Civic Assn., 1975-76. Mem. N.C. State Bar, N.C. Internat. Personnel Mgmt. Assn. Contbr. articles to legal jours. Home: 5319 Beaumont Dr Durham NC 27707 Office: 121 S Estes Dr Chapel Hill NC 27514 Tel (919) 929-0348

BROUGHTON, LEN GASTON, JR., b. Knoxville, Tenn., Apr. 23, 1919; J.D., U. Tenn., 1942. Admitted to Tenn. bar, 1942; practiced in Knoxville, 1942-66; asst. dist. states atty. gen., 1942, 46, 48; trial atty. City of Knoxville, 1951-52; chancellor 11th Chancery div. Knox County Chancery Ct., Knoxville, 1966—; chmn. com. on ct. modernization Tenn. Jud. Conf., 1969-73, sec., 1969-70, mem. exec. com., 1972-73, pres., 1974-75; mem. Citizens for Ct. Modernization, 1968-74. Elder, deacon Presbyterian Ch.; v.p. Knoxville Civitan Club, 1949. Mem. Am., Tenn. (bd. govs. 1974-75), Knoxville bar assns., Am. Judicature Soc., Sigma Alpha Epsilon. Office: Court House Knoxville TN 37902 Tel (615) 524-0769

BROUSSARD, MARCUS ANSON, JR., b. Abbeville, La., Feb. 14, 1929; B.A., U. Southwestern La., 1952; J.D., Loyola U., New Orleans, 1955. Admitted to La. bar, 1955; partner firm Broussard, Broussard and Moresi and predecessor, Abbeville, 1955-73, Broussard, Broussard and Moresi, Ltd., Abbeville, 1973—; judge Abbeville City Ct., 1968—. Chmn. Vermilion Parish (La.) Democratic Exec. Com., 1966-76. Mem. Am. Judicature Soc., N.Am. Judges Assn., Juvenile Judges Assn., City Judges Assn. La. Recipient Outstanding Citizen award Abbeville Am. Legion, 1963, Outstanding Kiwanian award Abbeville Kiwanians, 1963, 64. Home: PO Box 7 Abbeville LA 70510 Office: 105 Tivoli St Abbeville LA 70510 Tel (318) 893-3423

BROWDER, OLIN LORRAINE, JR., b. Urbana, Ill., Dec. 19, 1913; A.B., U. Ill., 1935, LL.B., 1937; S.J.D., U. Mich., 1941. Admitted to Ill. bar, 1939; asso. firm Nicholson Snyder, Chadwell & Fagerburg, Chgo., 1938-39; atty. TVA, Knoxville, Tenn., 1942-43; asst. prof. U. Tenn., Knoxville, 1941-42; prof. law U. Okla., 1946-53, U. Mich., Ann Arbor, 1953—. Mem. Am. Bar Assn., AAUP, Order of Coif, Phi Beta Kappa, Beta Theta Pi. Author: (with others) American Law of Property, 1952; (with R.A. Cunningham and J.R. Julin) Basic Property Law, 1973; (with L.W. Waggoner and R.V. Wellman) Family Property Settlements, 2d edit., 1973. Home: 1520 Edinborough St Ann Arbor MI 48104 Office: Hutchins Hall Ann Arbor MI 48109 Tel (313) 764-0547

BROWN, AARON CLIFTON, JR., b. Paris, Tenn., Apr. 12, 1940; student, U. Ariz., 1958-61, Sorbonne U., (Paris), 1960; J.D., U. Tenn., 1964. Admitted to Tenn. bar, 1965; individual practice law, Paris, Tenn., 1965-71; U.S. Magistrate, Memphis, 1971—. Home: 937 Rustling Oaks Memphis TN 38117 Office: 930 Federal Bldg Memphis TN 38103 Tel (901) 521-3995

BROWN, ARNOLD EDWARD, b. Englewood, N.J., Apr. 21, 1932; A.B., Bowling Green State U., 1954; J.D., Rutgers U., 1957. Admitted to N.J. bar, 1957, U.S. Supreme Ct. bar, 1969; individ individual practice law, Englewood; mem. N.J. Gen. Assembly, 1966-67. Mem. Am., N.J., Bergen County, Garden State, Nat. bar assns. Office: 106 W Palisade Ave Englewood NJ 07631 Tel (201) 567-3611

BROWN, ARTHUR WILLIAM, JR., b. Chgo., July 11, 1939; B.B.A., U. Mich., 1964; J.D. magna cum laude, NorthwesternU., 1964. Admitted to Ill. bar, 1964; asso. firm Altheimer & Gray, Chgo., 1964-71, partner, 1971—. Bd. dirs. Jewish Fedn. Met. Chgo., 1971—; mem. young leadership cabinet United Jewish Appeal, N.Y.C., 1971—. Mem. Am., Ill., Chgo. bar assns., Am. Coll. Probate Counsel. Home: 1620 Linden Ave Highland Park IL 60035 Office: 1 IBM Plaza Suite 3700 Chicago IL 60611 Tel (312) 467-9600

BROWN, BAILEY, b. Memphis, June 16, 1917; A.B., U. Mich., 1939; LL.B., Harvard U., 1942. Admitted to Tenn. bar, 1941; mem. firm Burch, Porter, Johnson & Brown, Memphis, 1946-61; judge U.S. Dist. Ct., Western Dist. Tenn., Memphis, 1961-65, chief judge, 1966—; mem. Jud. Conf. com. on ct. adminstrn., 1969—. Vice chmn. Memphis Urban League, 1956-57; mem. chpt. St. Mary's Episcopal Cathedral, 1976—; pres. Memphis Orchestral League, 1958-60. Mem. Phi Alpha Delta; recipient Liberty Bell award Memphis and Shelby County Bar Assn., 1971. Home: 115 Morningside Park Memphis TN 38104 Office: 1157 Federal Bldg Memphis TN 38103 Tel (901) 534-3201

BROWN, BARRY SPENCER, b. Fort Worth, Jan. 25, 1945; B.A., Ind. State U., 1967; J.D., Ind. U., 1971. Admitted to Ind. bar, 1971; legal advisor Monroe County Police, Bloomington, Ind., 1971-74; pros. atty. Monroe County, Bloomington, 1975—. Mem. Monroe County Bar Assn., Ind. Pros. Attys. Assn. Home: 2908 Fawkes Way N Bloomington IN 47401 Office: Monroe County Courthouse Bloomington IN 47401 Tel (812) 332-1111

BROWN, BENJAMIN LEONARD, b. Balt., Sept. 19, 1929; B.A. in Polit. Sci., Lincoln U., Oxford, Pa., 1951; LL.D., U. Md., 1959. Admitted to Md. Ct. Appeals bar, 1959, U.S. Dist. Ct. bar for Dist. Md., 1963, U.S. Ct. Appeals bar, 4th Circuit, 1964; practiced in Balt., 1960-68; mng. partner firm Howard, Brown & Williams, Balt., 1968-71; dep. state's atty. City of Balt., 1971-73; asso. judge 1st Md. Dist. Ct., 1973-74; city solicitor City of Balt., 1974—; gen. counsel Municipal Employees Credit Union, Inc., 1974—, Md. State Credit Union Ins. Corp., 1975—; spl. lectr. in law enforcement and adminstrn. of justice Coppin State Coll., 1975-76. Chmn. bd. dirs. Echo House Found., Balt., 1969—; mem. exec. bd. SE region Boy Scouts Am., 1973—. Mem. NAACP, Urban League, Nat., Md. State, Balt. City, Monumental City bar assn., Nat. Assn. Municipal Law Officers (dir.). Office: 508 Tower Bldg Baltimore MD 20202 Tel (301) 396-3304

BROWN, BERNARD CLIFTON, b. Genoa, Ill., Oct. 4, 1906; B.S., Mont. State U., 1930; J.D., U. Utah, 1939. Admitted to Utah bar, 1940, D.C. bar, 1946, U.S. Supreme Ct. bar, 1946, Ga. bar, 1950, Ky. bar, 1966; spl. agt. in charge FBI, Newark, N.Y.C., Detroit, Pitts., Louisville, 1940-65; asst. prof. Eastern Ky. U., 1967-69; asst. prof. U. Louisville, 1969-71, asso. prof., 1971-73, prof., 1974—, chmn. degree programs div., 1972—. Mem. Am., Louisville, Ky. bar assns., AAUP. Home: 6904 Wythe Hill Circle Prospect KY 40059 Office: Univ Louisville Louisville KY 40208 Tel (502) 588-6567

BROWN, BOWMAN, b. N.Y.C., May 3, 1941; B.A., Coll. Wooster, 1964; M.B.A., Cornell U., 1968, J.D., 1968. Admitted to Fla. bar, 1968; asso. firm Shutts & Bowen, Miami, Fla., 1968-71, partner, 1971—. Bd. dirs. Greater Miami Salvation Army; v.p., gen. counsel, dir. Jr. Achievement of Greater Miami. Mem. Am., Fla., Dade County (Fla.) bar assns Contbr. articles to legal publs. Home: 4100 Monserrate St Coral Gables FL 33146 Office: 10th Floor 1st Nat Bank Bldg Miami FL 33131 Tel (305) 358-6300

BROWN, BOYCE REID, JR., b. Shelby, N.C., Sept. 27, 1942; B.A. in Internat. Studies, U. N.C., Chapel Hill, 1966; J.D., Harvard, 1969. Admitted to Hawaii bar, 1970; asso. firm Moore, Torkildson & Schulze, Honolulu, 1969-72; partner firm Mattoch, Kemper & Brown, Honolulu, 1972-75, firm Brown & Bettencourt, Honolulu, 1975—; lectr. U. Hawaii, 1971—, also Law Sch., 1976—, Kapiolani Community Coll., 1975—. Bd. dirs. Am. Lung Assn. of Hawaii, 1974—. Mem. Am., Hawaii bar assns., Phi Beta Kappa. Home: 2324 Makanani Dr Honolulu HI 96817 Office: Suite 1100 130 Merchant St Honolulu HI 96813 Tel (808) 524-3491

BROWN, CARL CECIL, JR., b. Augusta, Ga., Oct. 24, 1948; A.B., Mercer U., 1970, also J.D. Admitted to Ga. bar, 1973; partner firm Ruffin & Brown, Augusta, Ga., 1973—. Vice-pres. Augusta Conf. Black Lawyers and Assos. Mem. Phi Delta Phi, Omega Psi Phi. Home: Route 7 Box 424 Augusta GA 30906 Office: 1101 11th St Augusta GA 30901 Tel (404) 724-8891

BROWN, CECIL HOWARD, b. Darlington, Fla., Mar. 11, 1923; B.S., Fla. State U., 1951; LL.B., U. Fla., 1952. Admitted to Fla. bar, 1952; practiced in Williston, 1952, Orlando, 1953-73; judge Fla. Circuit Ct. for 9th Jud. Circuit, 1973—; atty. Orlando (Fla.) Civil Service Bd., 1957-73. Mem. Navy League. Home: 530 Mandalay Rd Orlando FL 32809 Office: 14 Osceola County Courthouse Kissimmee FL 32741 Tel (305) 846-6348

BROWN, CHARLES EARL, b. Columbus, Ohio, June 6, 1919; A.B., Ohio Wesleyan U., 1941; J.D., U. Mich., 1949. Admitted to Ohio bar, 1949; since practiced in Toledo; individual practice law, 1949-50; asso. firm Zachman, Boxell, Bedbout & Torbet, 1950-53; partner firm Brown, Baker, Schlageter & Craig, and predecessors, 1953—; pres., dir. Maumee Fabrics Co.; sec., dir. Herman Bros., Inc. County chmn. policy com. Republican Party, 1968-74, mem. exec. com., 1968-74. Fellow Am. Bar Found., Ohio State Bar Found., Am. Coll. Probate Counsel; mem. Ohio (gov. real property sect., council of dels.), Am., Toledo (exec. com.) bar assns., Toledo Area C. of C. (past trustee), Res. Officers Assn., Assn. U.S. Army, Automotive Service Industry Assn. (past chmn. steering and exec. coms. auto trim wholesalers sect.), Phi Beta Kappa. Home: 3758 Brookside Rd Toledo OH 43606 Office: Toledo Trust Bldg Toledo OH 43604 Tel (419) 243-6281

BROWN, CHARLES FREEMAN, b. Boston, Mar. 7, 1914; A.B., Harvard, 1936, LL.B., 1941. Admitted to Mass. bar, 1941; asso. firm Sherburns, Powers & Needham, Boston, 1941-43; asst. gen. counsel, gen. counsel OSRD, Washington, 1943-47; counsel Research and Devel. Bd. and mil. liaison com., mem. Govt. Patents Bd., Office Sec. Def., counsel Def. Prodn. NATO, dept. asst. sec. gen. for prodn. and logistics NATO detailed from Office Sec. Def., Washington, London, Paris, 1947-53; asst. to pres. Hydrofoil Corp., Annapolis, Md., 1953-54; asso. gen. counsel CIA, Washington, 1954-60; v.p., treas. Sci. Engring. Inst., Waltham, Mass., 1960-66; dep. gen. counsel NSF, Washington, 1966-73, gen. counsel, 1973-76, chmn. interim compliance panel, 1970-71. Trustee, Belmont (Mass.) Day Sch., 1963-66. Mem. Fed. Bar Assn., Nat. Lawyers Club. Home and office: 3500 Macomb St NW Washington DC 20016 Tel (202) 362-6978

BROWN, CHARLES STUART, b. Freedom, Wyo., June 30, 1918; B.S., Utah State U., 1943; J.D., U. Utah, 1950. Admitted to Wyo. bar, 1950, Utah bar, 1950; practiced in Kemmerer, 1950-65; judge 3d Jud. Dist., 1965—; pros. atty., Kemmerer, 1959-65; asso. solicitor Dept. Interior, 1961-62. Mem. Am. Bar Assn., Am. Judicature Soc., Internat. Acad. Trial Judges. Author: Wyoming Ranch and Farm Law, 1959. Home: 903 Cedar St Kemmerer WY 83101 Office: PO Box 1 Kemmerer WY 83101 Tel (307) 877-6606

BROWN, CHARLES WARD, b. Bklyn., June 21, 1904; LL.B., Union U. Albany Law Sch., 1927. Admitted to N.Y. State bar, 1928, U.S. Supreme Ct. bar, 1956; mem. law dept. Gen. Electric Co., Schenectady, N.Y., 1927-29; asso. firm Richmond D. Moot, Esquire, Schenectady, 1929-36; individual practice law, Schenectady, 1936—; counsel to Oswald D. Heck, Speaker of N.Y. State Assembly, 1937-39, spl. counsel, 1939-52; corp. counsel City of Schenectady, 1952-62. Mem. Schenectady County Bar Assn., Inc. (pres. 1961-62). Recipient Distinguished Pub. Service award Nat. Inst. Municipal Law Officers, Denver, 1960. Home and office: 2000 McClellan St Schenectady NY 12309 Tel (518) 374-4658

BROWN, CLAUDE HILDING, b. Des Moines, Iowa, July 18, 1905; A.B., Drake U., 1927, LL.B., 1928; J.S.D., Yale, 1929. Admitted to Iowa bar, 1928, Ariz. bar, 1944; partner firm McNett, Kuhns & Brown, Ottumwa, Iowa, 1929-34; asst. prof. law U. Oreg., 1934-36, asso. prof., 1936-38; prof. Stetson U., 1938-41, U. Ariz., 1941-46, 47—, U. Cin., 1946-47. Mem. State Bar Ariz., Order of Coif, Phi Beta Kappa, Phi Kappa Phi. Author: (with Vestal and Ladd) Cases on Pleading and Procedure, 1953, supplement, 1960; (with others) Cases on Procedure Before Trial, 1968; contbr. numerous articles to legal jours. Home: 5320 Camino Real Tucson AZ 85718 Office: U of Ariz Coll of Law Tucson AZ 85721 Tel (602) 884-1166

BROWN, CLYDE, b. Hanna, La., June 16, 1913; A.B., Northwestern State U., 1935; J.D., S. Tex. Coll. Law, 1961. Admitted to Tex. bar, 1972, La. bar, 1964; tchr. St. Landry Parish, La., 1935-37; with Continental Oil Co., Houston, 1937—, dir. conservation, 1967—. Mem. Soc. Petroleum Engrs. (dir. Delta sect. 1964), La. State Bar Assn., State Bar Tex., Clean Atlantic Assos. (chmn. legal subcom. 1976—), Am. Petroleum Inst. (mem. legal adv. group of offshore com. 1976—, com. on coastal zone mgmt. 1976—), Offshore Operators Com. (legal subcom., exec. subcom. 1967—), Alaska Subarctic Offshore Com. (drilling and prodn. com.), N.Mex. (legal, regulatory practices, environ. affairs coms. 1970—]), Mid-Continent (legal, legislative coms.) oil and gas assns. Home: 2006 Elmgate St Houston TX 77080 Office: PO Box 2197 Houston TX 77001 (713) 965-1382

BROWN, DANIEL LUCIUS, b. Norwich, Conn., June 23, 1891; A.B., Brown U., 1912, LL.D., 1952; LL.B., Harvard, 1919. Admitted to Conn. bar, 1919, Mass. bar, 1919; mem. firm Hale and Dorr, Boston, 1919—. Mem. Am., Mass. bar assns. Office: 28 State St Boston MA 02109

BROWN, DANIEL PUTNAM, JR., b. Evanston, Ill., Apr. 21, 1943; B.A., Williams Coll., 1965; LL.B., Yale, 1968. Admitted to Conn. bar, 1968; asso. firm Shipman & Goodwin, Hartford, Conn., 1968-75, partner, 1975—. Trustee Hartford Conservatory, 1969-74; bd. dirs. Granby (Conn.) Land Trust, Inc., 1969—; bd. dirs. Farmington River (Conn.) Watershed Assn., 1971-74, Talcott Mountain (Conn.) Forest Protective Assn., Inc., 1972—; mem. Planning & Zoning Com., Granby, Conn., 1973—; mem. bd. selectmen, Granby, 1969-73. Mem. Phi Beta Kappa. Office: 799 Main St Hartford CT 06103 Tel (203) 549-4770

BROWN, DAVID SHELDON, b. Detroit, Jan. 27, 1932; B.A., U. Mich., 1953; postgrad. (Fulbright scholar) U. Vienna (Austria), 1953-54; LL.B., Harvard, 1957. Admitted to Mich. bar, 1957, N.Y. bar, 1959, D.C. bar, 1967, U.S. Supreme Ct. bar, 1967. Partner firm Galland, Kharasch, Calkins & Brown, N.Y.C., 1966-77, firm Austrian, Lance & Stewart, N.Y.C., 1977—. Bd. advisors Lower E. Side Service Center, N.Y.C., 1975—. Mem. Am., N.Y. State bar assns., Maritime Law Assn., State Bar Mich. Office: 630 Fifth Ave New York City NY 10020 Tel (212) 489-9500

BROWN, DAVID ST. JOHN, b. Hartford, Conn., May 15, 1939; B.A., Williams Coll., 1961; LL.B., U. Conn., 1964; LL.M., Georgetown U., 1965. Admitted to Conn. bar, 1964, D.C. bar, 1973, U.S. Supreme Ct. bar, 1968; law clk. judge U.S. Ct. Appeals, D.C. Circuit, 1965-66; atty. U.S. Dept. Justice, Antitrust div. Appellate Sect., Washington, 1966-68; legis. and adminstrv. asst. to U.S. Congressman from Calif., Washington, 1968-73; asso. firm Nicholson & Carter, Washington, 1973-77; dir. govt. affairs Monsanto Co., Washington, 1977—. Mem. Am., Conn., Hartford County bar assns., Am. Judicature Soc. Office: 1101 17th St NW Washington DC 20036 Tel (202) 452-8880

BROWN, DICK TERRELL, b. Houston, Feb. 6, 1944; B.S. in Mech. Engring., U. Tex. at Austin, 1966; J.D., St. Mary's U., 1972. Admitted to Tex. bar, 1973; with firm Matthews, Nowlin, MacFarlane & Barrett, San Antonio, 1973-77, firm Soules & McCamish, San Antonio, 1977—; engr. Naval Air Systems, Washington, 1966-69, Air Force Logistics Command, Kelly AFB, Tex., 1969-71. Mem. Am. Bar Assn. (sec. natural resources, litigation and pub. utility), State Bar Tex., San Antonio Bar Assn. Home: 308 Grandview Pl San Antonio TX 78209 Office: 800 Milam Bldg San Antonio TX 78205 Tel (512) 225-5500

BROWN, DONALD RAMSEY, b. Monroe, La., Mar. 6, 1937; B.S., La. State U., 1959, J.D., 191. Admitted to La. bar, 1961; asso. firm McKeithen, Mouser & McKinley, 1962-67; partner firm McKinley, Dimos & Brown, 1967-74, firm Dimos, Brown & Erskine, Monroe, 1974—. Mem. La., 4th Dist. bar assns., Am., La. (state bd. 1973, 74), N.E. La. (v.p.) trial lawyers assns. Office: 1216 Stubbs St Monroe LA 71207 Tel (318) 388-4303

BROWN, EDWARD RANDOLPH, b. Cleve., Sept. 17, 1933; A.B., Harvard, 1955; LL.B., Case Western Res. U., 1962. Admitted to Ohio bar, 1962, U.S. Supreme Ct. bar, 1968; asso. firm Squire, Sanders & Dempsey, Cleve., 1962-63; staff atty. Cleve. Legal Aid Defenders Office, 1963-67; partner firm Arter & Hadden, Cleve., 1967—; pres. Legal Aid Soc. of Cleve., Inc., 1976—. Mem. Am. Law Inst., Am., Ohio, Cleve. bar assns. Home: 15901 Chadbourne St Shaker Heights OH 44120 Office: 1144 Union Commerce Bldg Cleveland OH 44115 Tel (216) 696-1144

BROWN, EDWIN C., JR., b. Washington, Sept. 20, 1935; B.A., Howard U., 1957, LL.B., 1960. Admitted to D.C. bar, 1960; staff atty. Legal Aid Agy., 1960; trial atty. Dept. Justice, 1961-64; asst. U.S. atty. U.S. Atty.'s Office, Washington, 1964-65; staff atty. Pres's. Commn. on Crime, Washington, 1966-67; partner firm Brown and Brown, Washington, 1967—. Mem. Nat., D.C. bar assns. Home: 6313 32d St Washington DC 20015 Office: 1100 6th St Washington DC 20001 Tel (202) 667-7305

BROWN, EDWIN LEWIS, JR., b. Parker, S.D., Mar. 15, 1903; J.D., U. Nebr., 1926. Admitted to Nebr. bar, 1926, Ill. bar, 1933; individual practice law, Omaha, 1926-32, Chgo., 1933-52; partner firm Brown, Stine, Cook & Hanson, Chgo., 1952—. Mem. Am. Ill. (sr. counsellor 1976), Chgo. bar assns., Am. Judicature Soc., Comml. Law League (pres. 1963-64), Phi Alpha Delta. Home: 2617 Hurd Ave Evanston IL 60201 Office: 135 S LaSalle St Chicago IL 60603 Tel (312) 782-0244

BROWN, EDWIN TRACY, JR., b. South Pasadena, Ind., May 4, 1927; LL.B., Valparaiso U., 1951, J.D., 1972. Admitted to Ind. bar, 1952; partner firm Brown & Brown, Gary, Ind., 1952—. Mem. Ind., Gary bar assns. Home: 3400 E 70th St Merrillville IN 46410 Office: 5201 Broadway Gary IN 46409 Tel (219) 884-7778

BROWN, ERNEST WESLEY, b. Baraga, Mich., Oct. 19, 1908; A.B., Albion Coll., 1931; LL.B., U. Mich., 1933. Admitted to Mich. bar, 1933; city atty. Iron Mountain (Mich.), 1934-38; pros. atty. Dickinson County (Mich.), 1938-44; city atty. City of Kingsford (Mich.), 1945-47; judge 41st Jud. Circuit Ct., Iron Mountain, 1955—. Mem. Dickinson County Bar Assn. Home: 601 East F St Iron Mountain MI 49801 Office: Court House Iron Mountain MI 49801 Tel (906) 774-2266

BROWN, FLORENCERUTH JONES, b. Chgo., Nov. 23, 1929; B.A. in Econs., U. N.Mex., 1950, J.D., 1953. Admitted to N.Mex. bar, 1953; individual practice, Santa Fe, 1954-76; asst. atty. gen. for child support enforcement N.Mex. Health and Social Services Dept., Santa Fe, 1975—. Del. to Internat. Women's Year, Mexico City, 1975; active Girl Scouts U.S.A., 1967-75. Mem. 1st Jud. Dist. Bar Assn. Home: Route 2 Box 312 Santa Fe NM 87501 Office: PO Box 2348 Santa Fe NM 87503 Tel (505) 827-5355

BROWN, FRANCIS ALMON, b. Baileyville, Maine, Feb. 13, 1922; B.S. in Chem. Engring., U. Maine, 1943; postgrad. in Electronics, Harvard-Mass. Inst. Tech. Army Advanced Electronics Tng. Center, 1944; J.D., Boston U., 1950. Admitted to Maine bar, 1950; individual practice law, Calais, Maine, 1950-71; partner firm Brown & Tibbetts, Calais, 1971—; county atty. Washington County (Maine), 1962-66; mem. Maine Bd. Bar Examiners, 1970—; mem., chmn. criminal rules adv. com. Maine Supreme Jud. Ct., 1963-75. Past pres. and dir. Calais Regional Hosp., Calais Free Library; trustee U. Maine, 1973—; dist. chmn. Rotary Found. com., 1970—. Mem. Am., Maine, Washington County (past pres. and sec.) bar assns., Am. Judicature Soc., Nat. Inst. Municipal Legal Officers, Tau Beta Pi. Recipient Paul Harris fellowship award Rotary, 1975. Home: 271 Main St Calais ME 04619 Office: 143 Main St Calais ME 04619 Tel (207) 454-7543

BROWN, FRANCIS CABELL, JR., b. Washington, Jan. 6, 1936; B.A., Princeton U., 1958; LL.B., Harvard, 1961. Admitted to N.Y. State bar, 1962, D.C. bar, 1964; asso. firm White & Case, N.Y.C., Paris, and Brussels, Belgium, 1961-67; spl. asst. to asst. atty. gen. Div. Antitrust, Dept. Justice, Washington, 1968; individual practice law, N.Y.C., 1969—. Bd. regents Georgetown U., Washington, 1970-76; bd. dirs. N.Y. Eye and Ear Infirmary, 1974—; trustee Convent of the Sacred Heart, 1976—. Mem. Am., N.Y. State, Internat. bar assns., Assn. of Bar of City N.Y. Home: 520 E 86th St New York City NY 10028 Office: 200 Park Ave Suite 1402 New York City NY 10017 Tel (212) 986-5155

BROWN, FRANK JOSEPH, b. N.Y.C., Feb. 15, 1934; B.S., U. Conn., 1958; LL.B., Boston U., 1960. Admitted to Conn. bar, 1960; individual practice law, Hartford, Conn., 1960—; hearing examiner Commn. on Human Rights and Opportunities, Hartford, 1973-78; justice of the peace, 1968-73, 74—. Bd. dirs. United Cerebral Palsy Assn. Hartford County, 1976-80. Mem. Hartford County Bar Assn. Home: 104 Gilman St Hartford CT 06114 Office: 57 Pratt St Hartford CT 06103 Tel (203) 247-6454

BROWN, FRANK RAY, b. Berwyn, Okla., Dec. 22, 1921; certificate in Law, Southwestern U., 1956. Policeman, Los Angeles Police Dept., 1947-58; admitted to Calif. bar, 1956; mem. firm Lindholm, Piser & Brown, Van Nuys, Calif., 1958-60; individual practice law, Van Nuys, 1960—. Mem. Am., Los Angeles County, San Fernando Valley bar assns. Office: 6259 Van Nuys Blvd Van Nuys CA 91404 Tel (213) 786-0813

BROWN, GARY ELSON, b. Auburn, Ind., July 26, 1948; B.A., Western Mich. U., 1970; J.D., Ind. U., 1973. Admitted to Ind. bar, 1973, Ohio bar, 1973, U.S. Supreme Ct. bar, 1976; asst. atty. gen. State of Ohio, Columbus, 1973—. Mem. Am., Ohio, Ind., Columbus bar assns. Author: The Right to Inspect Public Records in Ohio, 1976. Home: 656 Thurber Dr W Columbus OH 43215 Office: 30 E Broad St Columbus OH 43215 Tel (614) 466-8600

BROWN, GARY RANDALL, b. Schenectady, Oct. 9, 1944; B.S., Syracuse U., 1966; J.D., Union U., 1969. Admitted to Vt. bar, 1970; asso. firm Williams, Witten, Carter & Dollard, Bennington, Vt., 1969-70; partner firm O'Donnell & Brown, Woodstock, Vt., 1970-72; individual practice law, Woodstock, 1972—. Chmn. Woodstock Village Zoning Bd., 1974—; trustee Village of Woodstock, 1974—. Mem. Am., Vt., Windsor County bar assns., Am. Trial Lawyers Assn. Office: 14 Central St Woodstock VT 05091

BROWN, GEORGE WILLIAM, JR., b. LaFayette, Ga., Oct. 24, 1941; B.S., U. Ga., 1965; LL.B., Walter F. George Sch. Law Mercer U., 1968. Admitted to Ga. bar, 1969; asso. firm Schuder & Brown and predecessors, Gainesville, Ga., 1969-71, partner, 1971-76; partner firm Lawson & Brown, Gainesville, 1976—; judge Hall County (Ga.) Juvenile Ct., 1974—; sec. Ga. Council Juvenile Ct. Judges, 1977; also mem. exec. council. Bd. dirs. Gainesville Jaycees Vocat. Rehab. Center, 1973—, vice chmn. bd., 1975-76, chmn. bd., 1976—; bd. dirs. Gainesville-Hall County Boys' Club, 1974—; mem. advisory bds. NE Ga. Mental Health, 1975—, Hall County Tng. Center, 1975—; tchr. Sunday sch. 1st Bapt. Ch. Gainesville. Mem. State Bar Ga., Gainesville-Northeastern, Am. bar assns., Ga. Trial Lawyers Assn., Assn. Trial Lawyers Am., Phi Delta Phi, Alpha Tau Omega. Home: 158 Piedmont Ave Gainesville GA 30501 Office: 454 Green St Lanier Bldg Gainesville GA 30501 Tel (404) 536-2304

BROWN, H. TEMPLETON, b. St. Joseph, Mo., Feb. 5, 1902; A.B., Yale U., 1923; LL.B., Harvard U., 1926. Admitted to Mo. bar, 1926, Ill. bar, 1943, U.S. Supreme Ct. bar; partner firm Brown, Douglas & Brown, St. Joseph, 1926-42; partner firm Mayer, Brown & Platt and predecessors, Chgo., 1942—; dir. emeritus UAL, Inc., United Air Lines, Inc.; dir. Scott, Foresman & Co., South-Western Pub. Co., A.M. Castle & Co. Chmn. pres.'s council Nat. Coll. Edn.; mem. Northwestern U. Assos., Chgo. Zool. Soc.; dir. emeritus Northwestern Meml. Hosp., Chgo. Mem. Am., Ill., Chgo. bar assns., Am. Bar Found., Am. Judicature Soc., Am. Soc. Internat. Law, Am. Coll. Trial Lawyers, Bar Assn. 7th Fed. Circuit, Beta Theta Pi. Home: 1010 Hubbard Ln Winnetka IL 60093 Office: 231 S LaSalle St Chicago IL 60604 Tel (312) 782-0600

BROWN, HAROLD, b. St. Louis, Sept. 15, 1915; A.B., Yale, 1936; LL.B., Harvard, 1939, LL.M., 1940. Admitted to Mass. bar, 1939, U.S. Supreme Ct. bar, 1944; staff atty. Dept. Labor, Washington, 1941-42, Nat. War Labor Bd., Washington, 1942-44; sr. partner firm Brown, Prifti, Leighton, & Cohen, Boston, 1945—. Mem. Am., Mass., Boston bar assns. Lectr., author books on franchising; contbr. numerous articles to profl. jours. Office: 66 Long Wharf Boston MA 02110 Tel (617) 227-9265

BROWN, HARRY LEWIS, b. Warsaw, N.Y., Dec. 27, 1924; A.B., Rutgers U., 1945; J.D., U. Buffalo, 1947. Admitted to N.Y. State bar, 1949, U.S. Supreme Ct. bar, 1970; partner firm Brown & Brown, Warsaw, 1949—; commr. elections Wyoming County (N.Y.), 1958—; chmn. adv. com. N.Y. State Bd. Elections, N.Y. State Legis. Election Law. Pres. Warsaw Central Sch. Bd. Edn., 1945-50. Mem. N.Y., Wyoming County bar assns., N.Y. State Election Commn. Assn. (pres. 1972-74). Home: 89 Genesee St Warsaw NY 14569 Office: 5 W Buffalo St Warsaw NY 14569 Tel (716) 796-3168

BROWN, HERBERT RUSSELL, b. Columbus, Ohio, Sept. 27, 1931; A.B., Denison U., 1953; J.D., U. Mich., 1956. Admitted to Ohio bar, 1956, U.S. Supreme Ct. bar, 1959; served in office JAG, U.S. Army, 1956-59; with firm Vorys, Sater, Seymour & Pease, Columbus, 1960—; examiner Ohio State Bar, 1967-72; multistate bar examiner, 1971-76; fed. dist. ct. land commr., 1966-67; treas., dir. Sunday Creek Coal Co., 1973—. Mem. governing bd. 1st Community Ch., 1975—; bd. dirs. Central Community House, 1968-74. Mem. Am., Ohio State, Columbus bar assns., Am. Assn. Ins. Attys., Def. Research Inst. Asst. editor Mich. Law Rev., 1955-56. Home: 1466 Teeway St Columbus OH 43220 Office: 52 E Gay St Columbus OH 43215 Tel (614) 464-6400

BROWN, HERBERT SHANKLIN, b. Trenton, Mo., Oct. 3, 1915; A.A., Trenton (Mo.) Jr. Coll., 1935; LL.B., U. Mo., 1938. Admitted to Mo. bar, 1938; pros. atty. Grundy County, Mo., 1939-40, 47-50; spl. agent FBI, various locations, 1941-43; individual practice law, Trenton, 1950-74; judge probate and magistrate cts. Grundy County, 1974—. Mem. Elks, Masons. Shriners, Am. Legion, Am. Judicature Soc., Am., Mo., Grundy County bar assns. Home: 600 Town and Country Ln Trenton MO 64683 Office: Courthouse Trenton MO 64683 Tel (816) 359-6909

BROWN, JAMES B., JR., b. Utica, N.Y., June 25, 1939; A.B., Hamilton Coll., 1961; LL.B., Cornell U., 1964. Admitted to N.J. bar, 1965, U.S. Supreme Ct. bar, 1968; clk. Daniel L. Golden, S. River, N.J., 1964, asso., 1964-68; individual practice law, Old Bridge and East Brunswick, N.J., 1968—; bd. adjustment atty. Borough of Jamesburg (N.J.), 1966-67. Mem. Middlesex County (jud. com. domestic relations and matrimonial practice 1977—), N.J., Am. bar assns., Middlesex County Trial Lawyers Assn. Office: 522 State Hwy 18 PO Box L East Brunswick NJ 08816 Tel (201) 257-9797

BROWN, JAMES EDWARD, b. Everret, N.C., May 26, 1938; B.S., Va. State Coll., 1966; J.D., Howard U., 1969. Admitted to Commonwealth Va. bar, 1969, D.C. bar, 1970, U.S. Supreme Court, 1973; law clerk Dept. Commerce, Washington, 1968; fin. analyst Gen. Foods Corp., White Plains, N.Y., 1969-70; public defender, trial atty., Washington, 1970-73; prof. law Antioch Sch. Law, Washington, 1973-74; dir. criminal justice act program, Washington, 1974-76; administrv. law judge D.C. Bd. Edn., 1976—; individual practice law, Washington, 1976—. Chmn. Citizens for Progress, Washington, 1977—. Mem. Phi Alpha Delta. Home: 8038 16th St NW Washington DC 20012 Office: 1028 Connecticut Ave NW Washington DC 20036 Tel (203) 296-8980

BROWN, JAMES ENOCH, b. Grand Forks, N.D., Nov. 23, 1940; LL.B., U. Calif., San Francisco, 1966. Admitted to Calif. bar, 1966; dep. dist. atty. Kern County (Calif.), 1968-70; mem. firm Clifford, Jenkins & Brown, Bakersfield, Calif., 1970—. Mem. Calif., Kern County bar assns. Office: 1605 G Bakersfield CA 93301 Tel (805) 322-6023

BROWN, JAMES JOSEPH, b. Terre Haute, Ind., Feb. 27, 1941; B.A., U. Nev. at Reno, 1965; J.D., U. Utah, 1968. Admitted to Nev. bar, 1968; asso. firm Harry E. Claiborne, Las Vegas, 1968—; v.p. bd. dirs. Clark County Legal Services Program, 1970—. Named Bancroft-Whitney Outstanding Student Family Law, U. Utah, 1968. Home: 1904 Loch Lomand Las Vegas NV 89102 Office: 108 S 3d St Las Vegas NV 89101 Tel (702) 384-3553

BROWN, JAMES KNIGHT, b. Rainelle, W.Va., Sept. 25, 1929; B.S., W.Va. U., 1951, LL.B., 1956. Admitted to W.Va. bar, 1956; asso. firm Jackson, Kelly, Holt & O'Farrell, Charleston, W.Va., 1956-61, partner, 1961—. Mem. Kanawka County (W.Va.) (pres. 1970-71), W.Va. State (pres. 1975-76, chmn. bd. 1976—) bars, Am. Bar Assn. (ho. of dels. 1975—), Order of Coif, Phi Beta Kappa. Tel (304) 345-2000

BROWN, JAMES MICHAEL, b. Hinton, W.Va., July 31, 1945; B.A., W.Va. U., 1967, J.D., 1970. Admitted to W.Va. bar, 1970; law clk. to judge U.S. Dist. Ct. So. Dist. W.Va., 1970-71; asso. firm Bowers, File, Hodson & Payne, Beckley, W.Va., 1971-73; partner firm File, Payne, Scherer & Brown, Beckley, 1971—; dir. W.Va. Legal Services, Inc., 1976. Bd. dirs. St. Stephens Episcopal Day Sch., Beckley, 1973-74, Raleigh County (W.Va.) Scholarship Fund., 1974—. Mem. Am., W.Va., Raleigh County (sec. treas. 1971-72) bar assns., W.Va. Trial Lawyers Assn. Editor W.Va. Law Rev. Office: 130 Main St Beckley WV 25801 Tel (304) 253-3358

BROWN, JAMES MITCHELL, b. Cleve., Mar. 16, 1946; B.S. in Journalism, Ohio U., 1968; J.D., Cleve. State U., 1973. Admitted to Ohio bar, 1973; atty. Shapiro & Kendis Co., Cleve., 1973—. Trustee Shaker 100, Inc., Charlton Coll.; instr. Shaker Heights Bd. Edn. Mem. Am., Ohio, Cleve., Cuyahoga County bar assns., Assn. Trial Lawyers Am., Ohio Trial Lawyers Assn. Office: 33 Public Sq Cleveland OH 44113 Tel (214) 621-2030

BROWN, JAMES NELSON, III, b. Lodi, Ohio, Mar. 17, 1942; A.B., Kenyon Coll., 1963; J.D., Western Res. U., 1966. Admitted to Ohio bar, 1966; sr. v.p., trust officer, Old Phoenix Nat. Bank, Medina, Ohio, 1966—; dir. Medina County Travel Service, Inc. Budget and admissions dir. United Fund, Medina, 1966-71. Mem. Ohio Bar Assn. Contbr. note to legal publ. Office: Box 160 Medina OH 44256 Tel (216) 722-5555

BROWN, JAMES SYLVESTER, JR., b. Bklyn., May 7, 1932; B.S., Georgetown U., 1954; LL.B., St. John's U., 1959. Admitted to N.Y. bar, 1959; asso. firm Willkie Farr & Gallagher, N.Y.C., 1959-67, partner, 1968—. Fellow Am. Coll. Probate Counsel; mem. Am. (com. drafting wills and trusts, probate div.), N.Y. State (vice-chmn. com. on legislation, trusts and estates law sect.) bar assns., Phi Delta Phi. Home: 18 Hadden Rd Scarsdale NY 10583 Office: Willkie Farr & Gallagher One Chase Manhattan Plaza New York City NY 10005 Tel (212) 248-1000

BROWN, JAMES WILLIAM, b. Des Moines, June 23, 1930; B.A., Grinnell Coll., 1952; J.D., Drake U., 1959. Admitted to Iowa bar, 1959; claim rep. Allied Mut. Ins. Co., Des Moines, 1959-62; asst. atty. City of Des Moines, 1962-65; partner firm Reynoldson, Brown & Van Werden, Osceola, Iowa, 1966-75, Brown & Ramsey, Osceola, 1975—. Mem. Osceola Planning and Zoning Commn., 1970—; bd. dirs. Osceola Airport, 1971—. Mem. Am., Iowa, Clarke County (pres. 1967-74) bar assn., Assn. Trial Lawyers Iowa (bd. dirs. 1972—). Home: 229 W Cass St Osceola IA 50213 Office: 231 S Main St Osceola IA 50213 Tel (515) 342-6216

BROWN, JOE ALBERT, b. Virdin, Ill., Oct. 27, 1896; LL.B., Okla. U., 1920, J.D., 1970. Admitted to Okla. bar, 1920, U.S. Supreme Ct. bar, 1949; area rent atty. Office Price Adminstrn., McAlester, Okla., 1942-43, rent atty., dir. McAlester and Muskogee, Okla., 1943, dist. rent. atty. Tulsa, 1944, rent atty. Region V., Dallas, 1944-45, regional compliance officer, Dallas, 1945-46, chief field ops., Dallas, 1948, dep. regional housing expeditor for vet. affairs, 1948; relief adminstr. Pittsburg County, 1935-36, Okla. Emergency Relief Administr., McAlester; project supt. WPA, McAlester, Norman, and Lexington, Okla., 1936-42. Mayor Hartshorne (Okla.), 1929-35. Mem. Okla., Pittsburgh County bar assns., Phi Delta Phi. Home: 1020 Kali Inla Hartshorne OK 74547 Office: 838 1/2 Penn Ave Hartshorne OK 74547 Tel (918) 297-2916

BROWN, JOHN DAVID, b. Shreveport, La., Aug. 13, 1930; B.B.A., U. Cin., 1953, LL.B., 1955, J.D., 1968. Admitted to Ohio bar, 1955, since practiced in Cin.; asso. firm Ralph E. Pott, 1955; partner firm Pott & Brown, 1956, Rich, Pott, Wetherell & Brown, 1957-67, Brown & Kerr, 1974—; individual practice law, 1967-74; dir. Lebanon Citizens Nat. Bank (Ohio); sec., dir. Cin. Sprinkler Co., Daysco, Inc.; asst. sec., dir. Fin. Discounting, Inc.; dir. Drs. Brunsman and Elliott, Inc., Gladstone Labs., Inc. Chmn. ofcl. bd. Westwood United Methodist Ch., Cin., 1965-66, trustee, 1964—; trustee A.B. Kaufman Scholarship Fund, Lebanon, 1966—. Mem. Ohio, Cin. bar assns., Lawyer's Club Cin. Mem. bd. editors Cin. Law Rev., 1954-55. Office: 4025 Glenway Ave Cincinnati OH 45205 Tel (513) 921-2700

BROWN, JOHN POLK, JR., b. Nashville, Jan. 6, 1942; B.S.Ph., U. Tenn., 1964; J.D., YMCA Law Sch., Nashville, 1969. Admitted to Tenn. bar, 1969; individual practice law, Nashville, 1969—. Mem. Am., Tenn., Nashville bar assns., Am. Trial Lawyers Assn., Am. Judicature Soc. Office: 3716 Hillsboro Rd Nashville TN 37215 Tel (615) 383-6536

BROWN, JOHN ROBERT, b. Funk, Nebr., Dec. 10, 1909; A.B., U. Nebr., 1930, LL.D., 1965; J.D., U. Mich., 1932, LL.D., 1959. Admitted to Tex. bar, 1932, practiced in Houston and Galveston, mem. Royston & Rayzor, 1932-55; judge 5th Circuit, U.S. Ct. Appeals, 1955—, serving as chief judge, 1967—. Chmn. Harris County Republican Com., 1953-55. Mem. Am., Tex., Houston bar assns., Am. Judicature Soc., Am. Law Inst., Maritime Law Assn. U.S., Assn. ICC Practitioners, Order of Coif, Phi Delta Phi, Sigma Chi. Home: 3209 Ela Lee Ln Houston TX 77019 Office: US Courthouse Houston TX 77002*

BROWN, JOHN SEAWARD, b. Weatherford, Okla., May 14, 1903; grad. Southwestern Okla. State Normal Sch., 1921; LL.B., U. Okla., 1925. Admitted to Okla. bar, 1925, Hawaii bar, 1926; individual practice law, Wailuku, Hawaii, 1926—. Mem. Hawaii, Maui County bar assns., Maui C. of C. (pres. 1947—), Am. Coll. Probate Counsel. Home: 2260 Kihei Rd Kehei HI 96753 Office: 6 Central Ave Wailuku HI Tel (808) 244-4895

BROWN, JOHN STANLEY, b. Lubbock, Tex., Dec. 28, 1943; B.A., U. Tex. at Austin, 1966, J.D., 1969. Admitted to Tex. bar, 1969; staff atty. Tex. Legis. Council, Austin, 1969-71; asso. Jack Wilingham, Atty., Hamlin, Tex., 1971-72; individual practice law, Abilene, Tex., 1972—. Mem. Abilene C. of C. (aviation com.), Tex. Criminal Def. Lawyers Assn., Abilene Trial Lawyers Assn., Abilene Bar Assn. (past sec.-treas.). Office: PO Box 3122 Abilene TX 79604 Tel (915) 677-1851

BROWN, JUDITH OLANS, b. Boston, May 29, 1941; A.B., Mt. Holyoke Coll., 1962; LL.B., Boston Coll., 1965. Admitted to Mass. bar, 1965; law clk. Supreme Jud. Ct., 1965-66; asso. firm Foley, Hoag & Eliot, Boston, 1966-69; chief counsel Mass. Dept. Community Affairs, 1969-70; atty. advisor Office of Regional Counsel, HUD, 1970-71, asst. regional counsel, 1971, asso. regional counsel, 1971-72; asso. prof. Northeastern U., 1972-76, prof., 1976—; mem. steering com. Boston Lawyers Com. for Civil Rights Under Law, 1974—; corporator Arlington 5 Cents Savs. Bank. Mem. Order of Coif, Phi Beta Kappa. Loeb fellow Harvard Grad. Sch. Design, 1972-73. Home: 336 North Ave Weston MA 02193 Office: 400 Huntington Ave Boston MA 02115 Tel (617) 437-3335

BROWN, KENNETH LLOYD, b. N.Y.C., Sept. 28, 1927; B.A., N.Y. U., 1951; LL.B., St. John's U., 1954. Admitted to N.Y. State bar, 1955; asst. corp. counsel City of N.Y., 1963—; individual practice law, N.Y.C., 1955—. Past pres. F.D.R. Lodge B'nai B'rith; pres. Continental Regular Democratic Club; del. N.Y. State Constl. Conv. Mem. Queens County Bar Assn., Jewish War Vets. U.S.A. (past county comdr.). Home: 10106 67 Dr Forest Hills NY 11375 Office: 108 03 Queens Blvd Forest Hills NY 11375 Tel (212) BO1-5157

BROWN, LARRY ALAN, b. Glendale, Calif., Sept. 29, 1942; B.B.A., U. Oreg., 1965, J.D., 1968. Admitted to Oreg. bar, 1968; dep. dist. atty. Lane County, Oreg., 1968-72; partner firm Flinn, Lake & Brown, Eugene, Oreg., 1972—. Mem. Oreg., Lane County bar assns. Home: 1063 Leigh St Eugene OR 97401 Office: 777 High St Eugene OR 97401 Tel (503) 686-1883

BROWN, LAWRENCE, b. N.Y.C., July 30, 1945; J.D., U. Pacific, 1971. Admitted to Calif. bar, 1971; sr. partner firm Chern & Brown, Sherman Oaks, Caif., 1974—; prof. law Mid-Valley Coll. Law, Van Nuys, Calif., 1974—. Mem. Am., Calif., Los Angeles County, San Fernando Valley, San Fernando Valley Criminal bar assn. Office: 15233 Ventura Blvd Sherman Oaks CA 91403 Tel (213) 990-0900

BROWN, LAWRENCE I., b. Bklyn., Apr. 18, 1931; B.A., N.Y.U., 1953; J.D., U. Mich., 1955. Admitted to Mich. bar, 1956, N.Y. bar, 1956; asso. firm Lewis, Rassner & Bermas, Bklyn., 1955-57; partner firm Hefler & Brown, N.Y.C., 1958-61; partner firm Hirsh, Newman, Cohen & Brown, N.Y.C., 1962—. Mem. Am., N.Y. State, Westchester County bar assns., Maritime Law Assn., Am. Acad. Matrimonial Lawyers, Lawyers Pilots Bar Assn. Home: 45 Popham Rd Scarsdale NY 10583 Office: 489 Fifth Ave New York City NY 10017 Tel (212) 687-6110

BROWN, LAWRENCE ROBERT, b. Maitland, Mo., Feb. 28, 1912; B.S., Maryville State Coll., 1932; LL.B., U. Mo., 1936. Admitted to Mo. bar, 1936, U.S. Supreme Ct. bar, 1936; asso., then partner firm Sturson, Mag, Thomson, McEvers & Fizzell, Kansas City, Mo., after 1936. Mem. Am., Mo., Kansas City bar assns., Kansas City Lawyers Assn., Order of the Coif. Home: 631 Greenway Terr Kansas City MO 64113 Office: 2000 Main Center Bldg Kansas City MO 64105 Tel (816) 842-8600

BROWN, LEO, b. Glen Lyon, Pa., Dec. 13, 1904; B.S. in Social Sci., Coll. City N.Y., 1925; J.D., N.Y. U., 1928. Admitted to bar, 1928; practice law, 1928-37, 46-54, 59-62; asst. corp. counsel City of N.Y., 1938-46, then acting corp. counsel; asst. counsel to Gov. N.Y. State, 1955; counsel N.Y. State Bldg. Code Commn., 1956-59; commr. N.Y.C. Dept. Marine and Aviation, 1962-66; dep. transp. adminstr. City N.Y., 1966-68; justice N.Y. Supreme Ct., Queens County, 1969—; mem. Interdepartmental Com. on Adminstrn. Justice, mem. subcom. on relation of pub. and private agys. with cts. Bd. dirs. Jamaica (L.I.) Jewish Center, also v.p.; v.p. L.I. region Zionist Orgn. Am., chmn. L.I. adminstrv. council, pres. Jamaica dist.; chmn. exec. com. Greater N.Y.C. Histadrut Council. Mem. Assn. Bar City N.Y., Queens County Bar Assn., Assn. Supreme Ct. Justices (chmn. subcom. on evidence of bench book com.). Home: 172-70 Highland Ave Jamaica NY 11432 Office: 8811 Sutphin Blvd Jamaica NY 11435

BROWN, LOUIS M., b. Los Angeles, Sept. 5, 1909; A.B. cum laude, U. So. Calif., 1930; J.D., Harvard, 1933; LL.D., Manhattan Coll., 1977. Admitted to Calif. bar, 1933, U.S. Supreme Ct. bar, 1944; individual practice law, Los Angeles, 1933-35; with Emil Brown & Co., Dura Steel Products Co., Los Angeles, 1936-41; counsel RFC, Washington, 1942-44; partner firm Pacht, Warne, Ross and Bernhard, Los Angeles and Beverly Hills, Calif., 1944-47; partner firm Irell & Manella, Los Angeles, 1947-69, counsel, 1969-72; lectr. in law Southwestern U. Law Sch., Los Angeles, 1939-41, U. Calif., Los Angeles, 1944-46, U. So. Calif., 1950-51, lectr., adj. prof. law, 1960-73; prof., 1973—, acad. dir. program for legal para-profls., 1970—, mem. planning com. Tax Inst., 1948-69; mem. nat. panel arbitrators Am. Arbitration Assn., 1956-63; vis. prof. law Loyola U., Los Angeles, 1977. Mem. com. Jewish Personnel Relations Bur., Community Relations Com., 1950-60; founder, adminstr. Emil Brown Fund Preventive Law Prize Awards, 1963—; pres. Friends of Beverly Hills Pub. Library, 1960; bd. visitors U. Oreg. Sch. Law, 1974—. Fellow Am. Bar Found.; mem. Am. (chmn. standing com. legal assistance for servicemen, 1969-72, chmn. com. client Counseling Competition), Beverly Hills (pres. 1961), Los Angeles County (chmn. prepaid legal services com., 1970—), San Francisco Bar Assns., State Bar Calif., Am. Judicature Soc., Am. Bus. Law Assn., Town Hall Los Angeles, Order of Coif. Author: Preventive Law, 1950; How to Negotiate a Successful Contract, 1955; contbr. articles to profl. jours.; editor of Major Tax Problems, 3 vols., 1948-51; issue of Calif. Law Rev. pub. in his honor, 1975. Home: 606 N Palm Dr Beverly Hills CA 90210 Office: U So Calif Sch Law Los Angeles CA 90007 Tel (213) 746-7887

BROWN, MATTHEW, b. N.Y.C., Mar. 26, 1905; B.S., N.Y. U., 1925; LL.B., Harvard U., 1928. Admitted to Mass. bar, 1928, U.S. Supreme Ct. bar, 1935; sr. partner firm Brown, Rudnick, Freed & Gesmer, Boston, 1940—; spl. justice Boston Municipal Ct., 1962-72. Selectman Town of Brookline, 1953-63, chmn., 1962, 63; mem. Town Meeting Brookline, 1948-71; chmn. bd. Boston Broadcasters, Inc. Mem. Mass., Boston, Norfolk County, Am. bar assns. Home: 180 Beacon St Boston MA 02116 Office: 85 Devonshire St Boston MA 02109 Tel (617) 726-7800

BROWN, MEREDITH MASON, b. N.Y.C., Oct. 18, 1946; A.B. summa cum laude, Harvard, 1961, J.D. magna cum laude, 1965. Admitted to N.Y. bar, 1965; clk. to judge U.S. Ct. Appeals 2d Circuit, N.Y.C., 1965-66; asso. firm Debevoise Plimpton Lyons & Gates, N.Y.C., 1966-72, partner, 1973—. Mem. Am., N.Y.C. (chmn. com. profl. ethics) bar assns. Home: 271 Central Park W New York City NY 10024 Office: Debevoise Plimpton Lyons & Gates 299 Park Ave New York City NY 10017 Tel (212) 752-6400

BROWN, MERWYN HAROLD, b. Winnemucca, Nev., Aug. 23, 1901; A.B., Stanford, 1923. Admitted to Nev. bar, 1925, Calif. bar, 1928, U.S. Supreme Ct. bar, 1945; dist. atty. Humboldt County (Nev.), 1928-46; dist. judge 6th Jud. Dist. Ct., Humboldt and Pershing Counties (Nev.), 1946-66. Mem. Am., Calif., Nev. (pres. 1945-46) bar assns. Recipient Distinguished Nevadan award U. Nev., 1960. Home: 10 E 4th St Winnemucca NV 89445 Office: 407 Bridge St PO Box 72 Winnemucca NV 89445 Tel (702) 623-2572

BROWN, MICHAEL JOHN, b. Racine, Wis., Sept. 28, 1933; B.A., U. Notre Dame, 1955; LL.B./J.D., U. Ariz., 1959. Admitted to Ariz. bar, 1959, U.S. Supreme Ct. Bar, 1974; law clk. firm Chandler, Tullar, Udall & Richmond, Tucson, Ariz., 1959; asso. W. Edward Morgan, Tucson, Ariz., 1959-60; chief city prosecutor City of Tucson, 1960-63; partner firm Brown, Finn & Rosenberg, Tucson, 1962-64, Brown & Finn, Tucson, 1964-73; individual practice law, Tucson, 1973—. Bd. govs. Pima Community Coll., 1967-71, pres., 1971; agt. SSS, Tucson, 1967-71; active Los Ayudantes, Inc., 20-30 Internat. Mem. Am. Judicature Soc., Am. Trial Lawyers Assn., State Bar Ariz., Pima County Bar Assn. Recipient Presdl. certificate of Appreciation, 1971. Home: 2825 W Ironwood Hills Dr Tucson AZ 85705 Office: 222 N Court Ave Tucson AZ 85701 Tel (602) 623-5458

BROWN, MORRIS YALE, b. New Haven, Aug. 28, 1910; B.A., Clark U., 1931; LL.B., Boston U., 1935. Admitted to Conn. bar, 1935; individual practice law, Shelton, Conn., 1935—; pros. atty. City Ct. Shelton, 1941-42, 45-46, asst. prosecutor, 1952-53; mem. Conn. Legislature, 1953-54; corp. counsel, 1957-58; justice of peace, 1957-58. Mem. Conn., Valley bar assns. Home: 494 Long Hill Ave Shelton CT 06484 Office: PO Box 93 Shelton CT 06484 Tel (203) 735-0448

BROWN, PATRICIA IRENE, b. Boston; A.B., Suffolk U., 1955, J.D., 1965, M.B.A., 1970; M.T.S., Gordon-Conwell Theol. Sem., S. Hamilton, Mass., 1977. Admitted to Mass. bar, 1965; asst. law librarian Suffolk U. Law Sch., 1965—. Bd. dirs. Children's Haven, Inc., E. Douglas, Mass.; dir. Sr. Citizen Referral Center, Boston, 1977—. Mem. Mass., Boston bar assns., Am. Judicature Soc., Assn. Am. Law Libraries. Office: 41 Temple St Boston MA 02114 Tel (617) 723-4700

BROWN, PAUL EDMONDSON, b. Troy, Iowa, Dec. 24, 1915; B.A., U. Iowa, 1938, J.D., 1941. Admitted to Iowa bar, 1941, U.S. Supreme Ct. bar, 1968; county atty. Boone County (Iowa), 1948-52; mem. firm Mahoney, Brown & Mahoney, Boone, 1946-52; v.p., counsel Bankers Life Co., Des Moines, 1952—. Mem. Am., Iowa, Fed. bar assns., Iowa Life Ins. Assn. (pres.), Am. Council Life Ins. (state v.p.), Health Ins. Assn. Am. (state chmn.). Named Outstanding Young Man, Iowa Jaycees, 1948; contbr. articles to legal jours. Home: 5804 Harwood Dr Des Moines IA 50312 Office: 711 High St Des Moines IA 50307 Tel (515) 247-5878

BROWN, PAUL VARINA, JR., b. Portsmouth, N.H., Dec. 30, 1932; B.S. in Bus. Adminstrn., Boston U., 1954, J.D., 1956. Admitted to N.H. bar, 1957; asso. firm Shaines & Brown, Portsmouth, 1957-65; individual practice law, Portsmouth, 1965-70; partner firm Brown & Fitzpatrick, Portsmouth, 1970—. Pres. Portsmouth YMCA, 1962-66, dir., 1960-74, 76—, trustee, 1974—; mem. exec. bd. N.H. YMCA, 1968—, chmn. exec. bd., 1974-77. Mem. Am., N.H., Rockingham, Portsmouth (sec.-treas. 1965—) bar assns. Office: 224 State St Portsmouth NH 03801 Tel (603) 436-3730

BROWN, PEYTON EARLE, b. Goodnight, Tex., Apr. 19, 1888; student Central State Normal Sch., Edmond, Okla., 1908-09, Okla. U., 1910-12. Admitted to Okla. bar, 1913; U.S. Supreme Ct. bar, 1925; individual practice law, Blackwell, Okla.; city atty. Blackwell, 1948-51. Mem. Phi Delta Phi, Sigma Alpha Epsilon. Office: 124 S Main St Blackwell OK 74631 Tel (405) 363-2330

BROWN, RALPH HEADEN, b. Petersburg, Va., Dec. 13, 1919; student St. Augustine Coll., 1942; LL.B., Franklin U., 1962; J.D., Capital U., 1966. Admitted to Ohio bar, 1962, U.S. Supreme Ct. bar, 1971; atty. examiner Ohio Pub. Utilities Commn., 1962-71; judge U.S. adminstrv. law, Columbus, Ohio, 1971—. Trustee Neighborhood House, Columbus. Mem. Am. Trial Lawyers Assn., Am. Bar Assn. Home: 4968 Wintersong Ln Westerville OH 43081 Office: 50 W Broad St Room 1006 Columbus OH 43215 Tel (614) 469-7404

BROWN, RANDOLPH THOMAS, b. St. Louis, Sept. 4, 1943; B.A., U. Notre Dame, South Bend, Ind., 1965; J.D., U. Minn., Mpls., 1970. Admitted to Mo. bar, 1970, Minn. bar, 1971; atty. Northwestern Nat. Life Ins. Co., Mpls., 1971-72; mem. firm Brown & Saetre, Long Prairie, Minn., 1972—; asst. county atty. Todd County (Minn.), 1972-74, county atty., 1975—; asst. prof. Gen. Coll., U. Minn., Morris, 1972-75. Mem. Am., Mo., Minn. bar assns. Home: 808 1st Ave SE Long Prairie MN 56347 Office: 314 Central Ave Long Prairie MN 56347 Tel (612) 732-6112

BROWN, REGINALD CLARENCE, b. Sumter, S.C., Feb. 16, 1940; A.B., U. S.C., 1962, J.D., 1965; LL.M., Yale, 1966. Admitted to S.C. bar, 1965; partner firm Hyman, Morgan & Brown, Florence, S.C., 1966—; prosecutor Florence City Court. Mem. Am. Bar Assn., S.C. Trial Lawyers Assn. Home: 1310 Madison Ave Florence SC 29501 Office: PO Box 1770 170 Courthouse Sq Florence SC 29503 Tel (803) 662-6321

BROWN, REMBERT THOMAS, b. Lemon Grove, Calif., May 24, 1926; A.B., San Diego State U., 1949; M.A., U. Mich., 1950; J.D., U. Calif. at Los Angeles, 1954; postgrad. in law U. So. Calif., 1955-59. Admitted to Calif. bar, 1955, U.S. Supreme Ct. bar, 1974; asst. U.S. atty. So. dist. Calif., Los Angeles, 1955-58; dep. pub. defender Los Angeles County, Calif., 1959-60; individual practice law, La Mesa, Calif., 1961—. Mem. Calif. Trial Lawyers Assn., Am. Judicature Soc., State Bar Calif. Office: 4965 Glen St La Mesa CA 92041 also 4154 30th St San Diego CA 92104 Tel (714) 466-5590

BROWN, RICHARD CHARLES, b. Milw., July 20, 1935; B.A., Princeton, 1957; LL.B., Harvard, 1961; J.D., Tulane U., 1962. Admitted to La. bar, 1962; asso. firm Phelps, Dunbar, Marks, Claverie & Sims, New Orleans, 1962-72; asso. prof. law Oklahoma City U., 1973—. Mem. AAUP (pres. Oklahoma City U. chpt.). Recipient Oklahoma City U. Iota Tau Tau Prof. of Year award, 1976. Home: 2622 N Meridean St Apt 208 Oklahoma City OK 73107 Office: Oklahoma City Univ School of Law Oklahoma City OK 73106 Tel (405) 525-5411

BROWN, RICHARD JOHNSTON, b. Camden, N.J., Jan. 2, 1935; A.B., Johns Hopkins U., 1956; M.D., Hahnemann Med. Coll., 1960; J.D., Seton Hall U., 1973. Intern, West Jersey Hosp., Camden, N.J., 1960-61; resident in pediatrics Hahnemann Hosp., Phila., 1961-63; practice medicine specializing in pediatrics, 1963—; dir. med. research planning Hoffmann-La Roches, Inc., Nutley, N.J., 1969—; admitted to N.J. bar, 1973, U.S. dist. Ct. for Dist. N.J. bar, 1973, U.S. Ct. Appeals for 3d Circuit bar, 1974. Mem. Matawan (N.J.) Bd. Edn., 1975—. Diplomate Am. Bd. Pediatrics. Mem. Am. Bar Assn., AMA, Am. Coll. Legal Medicine, Am. Acad. Pediatrics. Home: 3 Inwood Pl Matawan NJ 07747 Tel (201) 235-3926

BROWN, RICHARD PEABODY, b. Kansas City, Mo., Apr. 11, 1927; A.B., U. Mo., 1949, LL.B., 1952. Admitted to Mo. bar, 1952; individual practice law, Kansas City, Mo., 1952-54, 72—; atty. Bendix Corp., 1954-72. Mem. Mo. Bar Assn., Lawyers Assn. Kansas City. Home: Office: 6314 Brookside Plaza Kansas City MO 64113 Tel (816) 523-4700

BROWN, RICHARD RALPH, b. Tiffin, Ohio, Aug. 22, 1941; B.A., Heidelberg Coll., 1962; M.Ed., Bowling Green State U., 1964; J.D., Cleve.-Marshall Law Sch., 1968; postgrad. Case Western Res. U., 1967-68. Admitted to Ohio bar, 1968; individual practice law, Elyria, Ohio, 1968-75, Ada and Findlay, Ohio, 1976—; atty. Cleve. Trust Co., 1969-72; sr. real estate atty. and analyst Firestone Tire & Rubber Co., Akron, Ohio, 1972-75; v.p., trust officer BancOhio Western Security Bank, Sandusky, Ohio, 1975-76; asso. prof. law Ohio No. U., Ada, 1976—. Active YMCA, Boy Scouts Am. Mem. Am., Ohio, Hancock County bar assns. Home: 432 West Chester Dr Findlay OH 45840 Office: Coll Law Ohio No U Ada OH 45810 Tel (419) 634-9921

BROWN, ROBERT ALEXANDER, b. St. Joseph, Mo., May 9, 1899; B.A., Yale, 1922, LL.B., 1924. Admitted to Mo. bar, 1924, U.S. Supreme Ct. bar, 1949; partner firm Brown, Douglas and Brown, and predecessors, St. Joseph, 1924—. Chmn. St. Joseph Community Chest, Conservation Fedn. Mo., Jefferson City, 1954—; pres. St. Joseph Museum; mem. Mo. Conservation Commn., 1945-51. Fellow Am. Coll. Trial Lawyers, Am. Coll. Probate Counsel; mem. Mo., Am. bar assns., Am. Judicature Soc. Named Distinguished Citizen Mo., 1968, Master Conservationist Mo., Mo. Dept. Conservation, 1968. Home: 1307 Ashland St Saint Joseph MO 64506 Office: 510/A Francis St Saint Joseph MO 64501 Tel (816) 232-7748

BROWN, ROBERT CLARENCE, JR., b. Evanston, Ill., Sept. 7, 1906; B.S., Northwestern U., 1926, M.S., 1928, J.D., 1928. Admitted to Ill. bar, 1929; since practiced in Chgo., mem. firm Gillson Mann & Cox, 1929-38, Mann & Brown, 1938-50, Mann, Brown & Hansmann, 1950-54; sr. partner firm Mann, Brown and McWilliams, 1954-76; of counsel firm Mason, Kolehmainen, Rathburn & Wyss, 1976—. Mem. Chgo. Patent Law Assn. (pres. 1960), Am. Bar Assn. Office: Suite 3200 20 N Wacker Dr Chicago IL 60606 Tel (312) 346-1677

BROWN, ROBERT EUGENE, b. Winnemucca, Nev., Apr. 1, 1908; B.A., U. Idaho, 1930, LL.B., 1932. Admitted to Idaho bar, 1932; individual practice law, Kellogg, Idaho, 1934-48; partner firm Brown, Peacock, Keane & Boyd, and predecessors, Kellogg, 1948—; pros. atty. Shoshone County, Idaho, 1937-39; city atty. Kellogg, 1941-50; dir. Bunker Hill Co., 1962—, Gulf Resources & Chem. Corp., 1968—. Mem. Western Govs. Mining Adv. Council, 1955-70; mem. Idaho State Air Pollution Control Commn., 1959-67. Fellow Am. Bar Found., Am. Coll. Probate Counsel; mem. Am., Idaho (pres. 1953) bar assns., Rocky Mountain Mineral Law Found. (trustee), Phi Alpha Delta. Office: 311 Main St POB 659 Kellogg ID 83837 Tel (208) 784-1105

BROWN, ROBERT WAYNE, b. Allentown, Pa., July 6, 1942; A.B., Franklin and Marshall Coll., 1964; J.D., Connell, 1967. Admitted to Ill. bar, 1969, Pa. bar, 1971; VISTA atty. Community Legal Services, Detroit, 1967-68; asst. prof. law U. Ill., Campaign, 1968-70; law clk., adminstr. Hon. Kenneth H. Koch Lehigh County Ct. Common Pleas, Allentown, Pa., 1971-72; partner firm Gross & Brown, Allentown, 1972-76; individual practice law, Allentown, 1976—; asst. pub. defender Lehigh County, 1973-74. Bd. dirs. Lehigh Valley Legal Services, Easton, Pa., treas., 1973—. Mem. Am., Pa., Lehigh County bar assns., Order of the Coif. Home: 225 Parkview Ave Allentown PA 18104 Office: 513 Linden St POB 789 Allentown PA 18105 Tel (215) 433-6771

BROWN, (ROBERT) WENDELL, b. Mpls., Feb. 26, 1902; A.B., U. Hawaii, 1924; LL.B., U. Mich., 1926. Admitted to Mich. bar, 1926, U.S. Supreme Ct. bar, 1934, also U.S. Dist. Ct. Eastern and Western Mich., U.S. Tax Ct. bar, 1973; practiced in Detroit, 1926—, asso. firm Nichols & Fildew, and predecessors, 1926-28, Frank C. Sibley, 1928-29, Ferguson & Ferguson, 1929-31; asst. atty. gen. State of Mich., 1931-32; mem. legal staff Union Guardian Trust Co., 1933-34; individual practice law, 1934—; legal adviser graft grand jury Wayne County (Mich.), 1939-40, asst. pros. atty. civil div., 1940; spl. asst. atty. Highland Park (Mich.), 1950-51. Trustee Farmington Sch. Bd., 1950-56, pres., 1952-56; trustee Farmington Twp., 1957-61. Mem. Detroit Bar Assn. (dir. 1939-49, treas. 1942-44, sec. 1944-46, 2d v.p. 1946-47, 1st v.p. 1947-48, pres. 1948-49), State Bar Mich. (chmn. civil liberties com. 1946-48, mem. com. on Am. citizenship 1953-59, chmn. 1956-58; mem. com. on profl. and jud. ethics 1950-60, com. on ct. adminstrn. 1958-72, com. on civil procedures 1970-72), Friends of Detroit Library (original corporator), Farmington Hist. Soc. (hon.), St. Anthony's Guild (hon.). Home: 29921 Ardmore Farmington Hills MI 48018 Office: 1722 Ford Bldg Detroit MI 48226 Tel (313) 961-4772

BROWN, RODERICK EARL, b. Bedford, Que., Can., Apr. 14, 1924; B.Comm., Sir George Williams Coll., 1959; M.S. in Edn., U. So. Calif., 1960; M.I., U. Toronto, 1955; J.D., Loyola U., Los Angeles, 1965. Admitted to Calif. bar, 1965, U.S. Dist. So. Calif. Ct. bar, 1966; partner firm Brown and Brown, Ventura, Calif., 1966—; instr. law Ventura Community Coll., 1968—; Mem. Calif., Ventura County bar assns. Home: 72 Estates Ave Ventura CA 93003 Office: 2781 Loma Vista Rd Ventura CA 93003 Tel (805) 648-4144

BROWN, ROGER ALLEN, b. Hawthorne, Calif., July 30, 1946; B.A. in Polit. Sci., Calif. State U., Fullerton, 1968; J.D., U. Calif., 1972. Admitted to Calif. bar, 1972; supervising dep. dist. atty. Yolo County (Calif.), Woodland, 1973—. Mem. Yolo County Sexual Assault Center Advisory Bd., 1977, Yolo County Safety Commn., 1976. Mem. Calif. Dist. Attys. Assn., Yolo County, Calif. bar assns., Yolo County Attys. Assn. (pres.), Consumer Protection Council, Family Support Council. Office: PO Box 446 204 F St Davis CA 95616 Tel (916) 758-4840

BROWN, ROGER EARL, b. Dayton, Ohio, Jan. 2, 1939; B.A., U. Cin., 1962; J.D., Salmon P. Chase Coll., 1966. Admitted to Ohio bar, 1966; with Union Central Life Ins. Co., Cin., 1962—, elected officer, 1973, 2d v.p., 1975—. Pres. Pleasant Run Farms Civic Assn., Cin. Mem. Northeast Pensions Dirs., Upper Midwest Pension Assn. CLU, Ohio. Tel (513) 825-1880

BROWN, RONALD LAMING, b. Springfield, Mass., Aug. 26, 1944; student in Bus. and Econs., Chapman Coll., 1968-70; J.D., Creighton U., 1972. Admitted to Nebr. bar, 1973, Wyo. bar, 1974; 2d v.p. Omaha Nat. Bank, 1973-74; individual practice law, Casper, Wyo., 1974-76; asso. firm Brown, Drew, Apostolos, Barton and Massey, Casper, 1976—; asst. pub. defender City of Casper, 1974; dep. county and pros. atty. Natrona County (Wyo.), 1975-76; guest lectr. Casper Coll., 1974-75, SBA, 1974-75. Bd. dirs. Montessori Meadlowlark Sch., Casper, 1975-76. Mem. Am., Wyo., Nebr. State bar assns., Wyo. Trial Lawyers, Nat. Assn. Dist. Attys., Gray Key Honor Soc. Home: 1022 S Wolcott St Casper WY 82601 Office: 512 Petroleum Bldg Casper WY 82601 Tel (307) 265-9210

BROWN, ROSS EATON, JR., b. Oswego, N.Y., Sept. 11, 1905; A.B., Williams Coll., 1929; grad. Bklyn. Law Sch., 1935. Admitted to N.Y. bar, 1935; individual practice law, Morristown, N.Y., 1935—. Mem. N.Y. State Bar Assn. Home and Office: Main St Morristown NY 13664 Tel (315) 375-8836

BROWN, ROWINE HAYES, b. Harvey, Ill., Feb. 15, 1913; B.S., U. Ill., 1938, M.D., 1938; J.D., Chgo. Kent Coll., 1961. Admitted to Ill. bar, 1963; intern Ill. Research and Ednl. Hosp., 1938-39; resident Children's Meml. Hosp., 1940-42, 43, Municipal Contagious Disease Hosp., 1942; asst. med. supr., children's div. Cook County Hosp., Chgo., 1950-73, med. dir., 1973—; clin. prof. pediatrics U. Ill.; adj. prof. law Chgo. Kent Coll. Bd. dirs. Women's Share Pub. Service, Chgo., 1972-74; sec. bd. trustees Chgo. Foundling Home; bd. dirs. YWCA Met. Chgo., 1973—. Mem. Women's Bar Assn. Ill. (pres. 1975-76), Am., Ill. State, Chgo. bar assns., AMA, Chgo. Med. Soc. Recipient Kent Student Bar Assn. Distinguished Alumnae award, 1974. Contbr. articles in field to profl. jours. Home: 1700 E 56th St Chicago IL 60637 Office: 1825 W Harrison St Chicago IL 60612 Tel (312) 633-7445

BROWN, ROY EDWARD, b. Big Spring, Tex., Sept. 27, 1939; B.B.A., N. Tex. State U., 1962; J.D., S. Tex. Coll. Law, 1970. Admitted to Tex. bar, 1970; partner firm Wellborn, Britt & Brown, Alvin, Tex., 1970—. Mem. Tex., Brazoria County bar assns., Am., Tex. trial lawyers assns., Order of Lytae. Home: 1309 S Hill St Alvin TX 77511 Office: Alvin State Bank Bldg Alvin TX 77511 Tel (713) 331-4441

BROWN, STANLEY MELVIN, b. Derry, N.H., May 29, 1916; A.B. (Coll. fellow), Dartmouth Coll., 1939; J.D., Cornell U., 1942. Admitted to N.Y. bar, 1942, N.H. bar, 1945; partner firm McLane, Graf, Greene & Brown, Manchester, N.H., 1950-74; pres. firm Brown and Nixon, Manchester, 1975—; mem. N.H. Senate, 1951-53. Mem. Bradford (N.H.) Town Planning Bd., 1950-60, chmn., 1959-60. Fellow Am. Bar Found.; mem. Am. Coll. Trial Lawyers, Am. Law Inst., Internat. Soc. Barristers, N.H. (pres. 1969-70), Am. (assembly del. 1974-76, chmn. ho. of dels. 1976—, bd. govs. 1969-72) bar assns., Order of Coif, Phi Beta Kappa. Recipient Churchill award Dartmouth Coll., 1936; bus. mgr. Cornell Law Quar., 1940-41. Office: 672 Central St Manchester NH 03101 Tel (603) 668-5860

BROWN, STEPHEN ALLEN, b. Dallas, Feb. 17, 1938; B.A., Yale U., 1959, LL.B., 1962. Admitted to Va. bar, 1962, D.C. bar, 1965; law clk. to judge U.S. Circuit Ct., Alexandria, Va., 1962-63; asso. firm Kuykendall & Whiting, Winchester, Va., 1963-64; asso. firm Kirkland Ellis & Rowe, Washington, 1965-69, partner, 1970-76; v.p. law Grocery Mfrs. Am., Washington, 1977—. Mem. Econ. Opportunities Commn., Alexandria, 1970-75, chmn., 1973-75, com. Regulation, Growth and Devel., Alexandria, 1974-76. Mem. Am., Fed. bar assns. Home: 205 Yoakum Pkwy Alexandria VA 22304 Office: 1425 K St NW Washington DC 20005

BROWN, STEPHEN MICHAEL, b. Yakima, Wash., Aug. 9, 1943; B.A., U. Wash., 1965; J.D., Stetson U. Coll. Law, 1973. Admitted to Wash. bar, 1973; asso. firm Velikanje, Moor & Shore, 1973-74, Yakima, partner, 1975—; adjunct prof. real estate law Yakima Valley Coll., 1974. Vice pres., Yakima Valley Synagogue, 1975, pres., 1976; mem. Greater Yakima Valley C. of C., 1974—. chmn. mil. affairs com. Mem. Am., Washington State (trustee Young Lawyers' Sect., 1975-78, chmn. civil rights com. 1977-78), Yakima Valley bar assns., Wash. State Trial Lawyers Assn., Am. Trial Lawyers Assn. Recipient Clint Green Award, Stetson U. Coll. Law, 1973. Home: 723 S 32d Ave Yakima WA 98902 Office: 303 East D St Yakima WA 98901 Tel (509) 248-6030

BROWN, STEWART HARMAN, b. Balt., May 24, 1926; A.B., Princeton, 1950; LL.B., U. Va., 1964. Admitted to Colo. bar, 1965; individual practice law, Vail, Colo., 1965—. Home: Unit 308 Lionshead Arcade Bldg Vail CO 81657 Office: Box 101 Vail CO 81657 Tel (303) 476-5475

BROWN, STUART ELLETT, JR., b. Richmond, Va., Apr. 25, 1916; B.S., U. Va., 1938, LL.B., 1940. Admitted to Va. bar, 1939, Md. bar, 1940; partner firm Niles, Barton, Morrow & Yost, Balt., 1940-41, 46-50; individual practice law, Berryville, Va., 1951—. Author: Annals of Blackwater and the Land of Canaan; The Guns of Harpers Ferry; The Horses of Arlington; Virginia Baron; The Story of Thomas 6th Lord Fairfax; contbr. articles to various mags. and publs. Home: Poulshot Millwood VA 22646 Office: Berryville VA 22611 Tel (703) 955-1428

BROWN, THOMAS CONROY, b. Orange, N.J., June 21, 1938; B.A., St. Francis Coll., 1961; LL.B., Rutgers U., 1964. Admitted to N.J. bar, 1966; mem. legal service program, Montclair, N.J., 1966-67; asst. pros. atty. Essex County (N.J.), 1967-72; individual practice law, E. Orange, N.J., 1972—; atty. W. Orange Planning Bd., 1972-75. Mem. Am., N.J., Essex County bar assns. Home: 2 Cobane Terr W Orange NJ 07052 Office: 725 Park Ave E Orange NJ 07017 Tel (201) 673-4060

BROWN, THOMAS PHILIP, III, b. Washington, Dec. 18, 1931; B.S., Georgetown U., 1953, LL.B., 1956.1956. Admitted to D.C. bar, 1956, Md. bar, 1961, U.S. Supreme Ct. bar, 1961; mem. firm Rhyne & Rhyne, Washington, 1958-65; individual practice law, Washington, 1965—. Pres. Cath. Youth Orgn. Washington, 1972. Mem. Am., Montgomery County bar assns., D.C. Bar, Bar Assn. D.C. (sec., dir. 1975—). Contbr. articles in field to legal jours. Home: 5430 Wickford Dr Rockville MD 20852 Office: 5530 Wisconsin Ave Washington DC 20015 Tel (301) 652-3111

BROWN, TOM WATSON, b. Washington, Jan. 28, 1933; A.B., Princeton, 1954; LL.B., Harvard, 1959. Admitted to Ga. bar, 1958; law clk. U.S. Dist. Ct. No. Dist. Ga., 1959-60; asso. firm Smith, Swift, Currie, McGhee & Hancock, Atlanta, 1960-64; partner firm Huie, Brown & Ide, 1967-75; partner firm Huie, Ware, Sterne, Brown & Ide, Atlanta, 1976—. Pres. Atlanta Legal Aid Soc., 1975-76; trustee, sec. Atlanta Hist. Soc., 1967—. Mem. Am., Ga. (chmn. banking and corp. law sect. 1974-75), Atlanta bar assns., Lawyers Club Atlanta (pres. 1975-76). Home: 2631 W Wesley Rd NW Atlanta GA 30327 Office: 1200 Standard Fed Bldg Atlanta GA 30303 Tel (404) 522-8700

BROWN, UDELL CALVIN, b. Memphis, May 2, 1927; B.S. in Bus. Adminstrn., Washington U., 1949, J.D., 1949. Admitted to Mo. bar, 1949, Tex. bar, 1957, Ill. bar, 1969; asso. firm Blackinton, Reid & Clarke, St. Louis, 1949-50; title atty., asst. tax commr. St. Louis Southwestern Ry. Lines, St. Louis, 1950-54; tax commr. Tyler (Tex.), 1954-67; gen. mgr. property taxes Chgo., Rock Island & Pacific R.R. Co., Chgo., 1967—. Mem. bd. edn. Chgo. Christian High Sch., 1968-71. Mem. Ill., Mo., Tex. bar assns., Nat. Tax Assn. (dir.), Nat. Assn. Ry. Tax Commrs. (pres. 1968), Nat. Com. R.R. and Pub. Utility Tax Reps. (chmn. 1972-73), Phi Delta Phi. Home: 9010 W 121st St Palos Park IL 60464 Office: 745 S La Salle St Chicago IL 60605 Tel (312) 435-7529

BROWN, WADE EDWARD, b. Blowing Rock, N.C., Nov. 5, 1907; student Mars Hill Coll., 1928; J.D., Wake Forest Coll., 1931. Admitted to N.C. bar, 1930; individual practice law, Boone, N.C., 1931-67, 1973—; served with JAGC, USN, 1944-46; chmn. N.C. Bd. Paroles, Raleigh, 1967-72; cons. atty. gen. N.C. Dept. Justice, Raleigh, 1973; mem. N.C. Senate, 1947-49, N.C. Ho. of Reps., 1951-53; mayor Town of Boone, 1961-67. Tel (704) 264-8234

BROWN, WALTER EARL, III, b. Rochester, Minn., Mar. 27, 1942; B.A., Colo. U., 1964; diploma Def. Lang. Inst., 1966; J.D., U. Tulsa, 1971. Admitted to Colo. bar, 1972, Okla. bar, 1972; dep. dist. atty. Golden (Colo.), 1972-76; chief trial dep. 9th Jud. Dist. Colo., 1976-77; spl. prosecutor Dist. Atty's Office, Denver, 1976—; lectr. Rape Prevention Program, Arvada City, Colo., 1976; vol. probation officer, Golden, 1972-76. Mem. Okla. Bar Assn. Office: Bank of Glenwood Bldg PO Box 983 905 Grand Ave Glenwood Springs CO 81601 Tel (303) 945-8582

BROWN, WALTER HAROLD, b. Johnson City, Tenn., May 20, 1910; LL.B., Columbia, 1934. Admitted to N.Y. bar, 1935, since practiced in N.Y.C.; partner firm Willkie, Farr & Gallagher and predecessors, 1943—; dir. Metminco, Inc.; gen. counsel Seaboard Coast Line R.R. Co., 1965-70; reorgn. mgr. Mo. Pacific R.R. Co., 1956. Trustee Finch Jr. Coll., 1943-53. Fellow Am. Bar Found.; mem. Am., N.Y. State bar assns. Home: 100 Ivy Way Port Washington NY 11050 Office: 1 Chase Manhattan Plaza New York City NY 10005 Tel (212) 248-1000

BROWN, WESLEY ERNEST, b. Hutchinson, Kans., June 22, 1907; LL.B., U. Mo. at Kansas City, 1933. Admitted to Kans. bar, 1933, Mo. bar, 1933, Fed. bar, 1938, U.S. Supreme Ct. bar, 1944; partner firm Martindell, Carey, Brown & Brabets, Hutchinson, 1933-58; county atty. Reno County, Kans., 1934-39; referee in Bankruptcy, Fed. Cts., 1958-62; judge U.S. Dist. Co., Wichita, Kans., 1962—, chief judge, 1971—; mem. Judicial Conf. U.S., 1976—, com. on bankruptcy adminstrn., 1963-70. Mem. Am., Kans. (mem. exec. council 1950-64, pres. 1964-65), Wichita, S.W. bar assns., Delta Theta Phi. Home: 1401 W River Blvd Wichita KS 67203 Office: PO Box 28 Wichita KS 67201 Tel (316) 267-6311 extension 497

BROWN, WILLIAM ALFRED, b. Chelsea, Mass., May 26, 1942; B.E.E., Northeastern U., 1964, M.E.E., 1966; J.D., Suffolk Law Sch., 1969. Admitted to Mass. bar, 1969; law clk. to judge U.S. Dist. Ct., Boston, 1969-70; asso. firm Wolf, Greenfield & Sacks, Boston, 1970-71; asst. U.S. atty., Boston, 1971—, U.S. atty. chief civil div., 1973—; asst. prof. Suffolk Law Sch., Boston, 1970—. Mem. Am., Mass. bar assns. Recipient Outstanding Performance award Dept. Justice, 1974; contbr. articles Suffolk Law Rev. Office: Room 1107 US PO and Courthouse Boston MA 02109 Tel (617) 223-3258

BROWN, WILLIAM ARMISTEAD, b. Jackson, Tenn., Nov. 19, 1931; B.S., U. Idaho, 1953, LL.B., 1955, J.D., 1969. Admitted to Ill. bar, 1955; partner Schlagenhauf & Brown, Quincy, Ill., 1955-65; individual practice law Quincy, 1965-69, 76—; partner firm Deege & Brown, Quincy, 1969-75; asst. state's atty. Adams County, Ill., 1956—. Bd. dirs. Quincy Symphony Orch., 1962-70, sec., 1964-68; bd. dirs. Quincy Family Service Agency, 1957-68, pres., 1960-62; bd. dirs. Woodland Home, 1967—, Chaddock Boys Sch., Quincy, 1964-68. Mem. Am., Ill. Adams County (past pres., sec. 1974—) bar assns., Ill. State's Attys. Assn., Ill. Bar Officers Conf., Phi Alpha Delta. Home: 2009 Hampshire St Quincy IL 62301 Office: 428 N 6th St Quincy IL 62301 Tel (217) 222-3914

BROWN, WILLIAM DOUGLAS, b. Newark, Feb. 16, 1946; B.A. in History, Lafayette Coll., 1968; J.D., U. Va., 1971. Admitted to Pa. bar, 1972; law clk. firm Shanley & Fisher, Newark, 1970; asso. firm McNees, Wallace & Nurick, Harrisburg, Pa., 1971-75; atty. legal dept. Air Products & Chems. Inc., Trexlertown, Pa., 1975—. Sec., Harrisburg Tb Soc. Mem. Pa., Am. bar assns., Licensing Execs. Soc., Lafayette Alumni Soc. (pres. local chpt.). Home: 623 Alden Dr Emmaus PA 18049 Office: Air Products & Chems Inc Trexlertown PA 18105 Tel (215) 398-7795

BROWN, WILLIAM HENRY CHARLES, b. Mpls., Apr. 21, 1939; B.A. cum laude, U. N.D., 1961, J.D. cum laude, 1963. Admitted to N.D. bar, 1963, Colo. bar, 1967, U.S. Supreme Ct. bar, 1971; judge adv. U.S. Air Force, McClellan AFB, Sacramento, 1964-67; partner firm Fischer, Brown, Huddleson and Gunn, Ft. Collins, Colo., 1972—. Active Ft. Collins C. of C., 1969—, legis. com., 1972; active Designing Tomorrow Today, 1972-73. Mem. Am., Colo., Larimer County bar assns., Am. Arbitration Assn., Phi Beta Kappa, Order of Coif, Phi Delta Phi. Office: First Nat Tower Bldg 11th Floor PO Drawer J Fort Collins CO 80522 Tel (303) 482-1056

BROWN, WILLIAM JOSEPH, b. Youngstown, Ohio, July 12, 1940; B.A., Duquesne U., 1963; J.D., Ohio No. U., 1967. Admitted to Ohio bar, 1967; practice law, 1967—; atty. gen. State of Ohio, 1971—. Mem. Am., Ohio, Mahoning County bar assns. Home: 833 Mission Hills Lane Worthington OH 43085 Office: State Office Tower Columbus OH 43215*

BROWN, WILLIAM ROGER, b. Sault Ste. Marie, Mich., Apr. 16, 1929; B.A., U. Mich., 1952, J.D. cum laude, 1953. Admitted to Mich. bar, 1953; partner firm Murchie Calcutt & Brown, Traverse City, Mich., 1955-73; judge Mich. Circuit Ct., 13th Jud. Circuit, 1973—. Mem. Traverse City Civil Service Commn., 1965-72. Mem. Am. Judicature Soc., Mich. Judges Assn. Home: 411 N Elmwood St Traverse City MI 49684 Office: Grand Traverse County Courthouse Traverse City MI 49684 Tel (616) 947-0330

BROWN, WILLIAM VINCENT, JR., b. Texarkana, Tex., Dec. 29, 1919; B.B.A., U. Tex., 1941; J.D., George Washington U., 1944; grad. Tex. Coll. of Judiciary, 1974, Nat. Coll. of State Judiciary, Reno, Nev., 1976. Admitted to Tex. bar, 1944; partner firm Brown & Brown, Texarkana, Tex., 1948-74; judge Tex. Dist. Ct., 102 Jud. Dist., 1975—; city atty. City of Texarkana, 1953-60; judge Texarkana City Ct., 1964-65. Mem. State Bar Tex., N.E. Tex. (pres. 1969), Texarkana, Am. bar assns. Office: County Bldg 4th and Texas Blvd Texarkana TX 75501 Tel (214) 793-3611

BROWNE, ELIZABETH (BETTY), b. Mpls., Apr. 4, 1926; B.A. in Polit. Sci. and Econs., U. Minn., 1948; M.A. in Internat. Studies, U. Chgo., 1951; J.D., U. Oreg., 1966. Admitted to Oreg. bar, 1966; mem. Oreg. Ho. of Reps., 1969-70, Oreg. Senate, 1971-77; tchr. Dade County, Fla.; individual practice law, Eugene, Oreg.; prof. U. Oreg. Law Sch., Eugene, 1975—; instr. Lane Community Coll., 1969; referee Lane County Circuit Ct., 1967-68. Mem. Lane County Auditorium Assn.; bd. dirs. Sch. Dist. #76 (chmn.); adv. bd. to Law Enforcement Assistance Adminstrn. Mem. Am. Bar Assn. (jt. com. on juvenile justice), Nat. Assn. Legal Aid and Defendants, Am. Judicature Soc., Nat. Conf. Juvenile Ct. Judges, Nat. Conf. State Legislators, Western Conf. State Govts., Council State Govts., Oreg. Bar Assn. (com. on family and juvenile law), Lane County Bar Assn. (past chmn. med. legal com., juvenile law com., legis. liaison com.). Author: A Right to Treatment for Civilly Committed Persons, 1975; contbr. articles to legal jours.; past editor Juvenile Ct. Digest, Child Neglect and Dependency, Family Law News Jour. of Family Law Newsletter, Continuing Legal Edn. Handbook on Juvenile Law. Home: 1715 McLean Blvd Eugene OR 97405 Tel (503) 344-3557

BROWNE, FRANCIS CEDRIC, b. Cleve., Jan. 22, 1915; A.B., U. Akron, 1936; J.D., Cleve.-Marshall Sch. Law, 1942. Admitted to D.C. bar, 1945, Md. bar, 1954; partner firm Browne, Beveridge, DeGrandi & Kline and predecessors, Washington, 1948-75; trial judge U.S. Ct. Claims, Washington, 1975—. Mem. Am., Fed. bar assns. Home: 4601 N Park Ave Apt 319 Chevy Chase MD 20015 Office: 717 Madison Pl NW Washington DC 20005 Tel (202) 382-2522

BROWNE, JOHN PATRICK, b. E. Cleve., Dec. 17, 1935; B.S., John Carroll U., 1957; J.D., U. Detroit, 1960; M.L.S., Case Western Res. U., 1965. Admitted to Ohio bar, 1960, Mich. bar, 1960; asso. firm Gallagher, Sharp, Fulton, Norman & Mollison, Cleve., 1965-69; prof. law Cleve. State U., 1969—. Mem. Am., Ohio, bar assns., State Bar Mich., Bar Assn. Greater Cleve., Def. Research Inst., Scribes, Am. Assn. Law Libraries, Ohio Regional Law Libraries, AAUP. Contbr. articles in field to profl. jours. Home: 1801 E 12th St apt 820 Cleveland OH 44114 Office: Cleveland Marshall College Law Cleveland State Univ Cleveland OH 44115 Tel (216) 687-2330

BROWNE, PERCY NEWBY, b. Lake Providence, La., May 18, 1884; student La. State U., Columbia. Admitted to La. bar, 1910, since practiced in Shreveport; mem. firm E.W. and P.N. Browne, 1920-47; sr. mem. firm Browne & Lafargue, 1959-65; individual practice law, 1965—. Mem. counsel La. Hwy. Dept., 1940-48; city editor Monroe (La.) Evening News, 1906. Mem. Shreveport Council Civilian Def., SSS, Govt. Appeal Agy., World War II; life mem. bd. adminstrs. First Meth. Ch., Shreveport; del. Democratic Nat. Conv., Balt., 1912. Mem. Am. (life), La. (life), Shreveport (life) bar assns., Assn. Ins. Attys. (exec. council 1963-65), Nat. Assn. Ins. Counsel (exec. council), Caddo-Bossier Rental Assn. (past pres.), Am. Legion (charter, past comdr. post). Home: 250 Kings Hwy Shreveport LA 71104 Office: Suite 513 Lane Bldg Shreveport LA 71101 Tel (318) 222-4220

BROWNELL, HERBERT, b. Peru, Nebr., Feb. 20, 1904; B.A., U. Nebr., 1924; LL.B., Yale U., 1927. Admitted to N.Y. bar, 1928, U.S. Supreme Ct. bar, 1953; asso. firm Root, Clark, Buckner & Ballantine, N.Y.C., 1927-29; asso. firm Lord, Day & Lord, N.Y.C., 1929-32, partner, 1932-52, 58-76, of counsel, 1976—; atty. gen. U.S., 1953-57; dir. James S. Kemper & Co.; assemblyman State of N.Y., 1932-37. Bd. dirs. Ludwig Inst. for Cancer Research. Mem. Am., N.Y., N.Y.C. bar assns., Order of Coif, Phi Beta Kappa, Sigma Delta Chi, Delta Upsilon. Contbr. articles to legal jours. Office: Lord Day & Lord 25 Broadway New York City NY 10004 Tel (212) 344-8480

BROWNELL, JONATHAN NOBLE, b. Greenwich, Conn., Feb. 4, 1936; B.A., Yale, 1957, LL.B., 1960. Admitted to N.Y. bar, 1961, Vt. bar, 1966; asso. firm Lord, Day & Lord, N.Y.C., 1960-65; gen. counsel Vt. Dept. Taxes, 1965-66; asst. atty. gen. State Vt., 1966-67; dep. atty. gen., 1967-68; partner firm Paterson, Gibson, Noble & Brownell, Montpelier, Vt., 1968—; spl. counsel on Land Use Legislation to Vt. Gen. Assembly, 1971-74; to Adirondack Park Agency, 1973-74; Com. on Edn. to Vt. Ho. Reps., 1975-76; adj. prof. environ. studies, Dartmouth, 1968—; mem. environ. studies bd. Nat. Acad. Scis., 1973—; cons. div. advanced environ. research and tech. NSF, 1975—; dir. Nat. Audubon Soc., 1973—; chmn. Nat. Affairs Com. Nat. Wildlife Fedn., 1971-75; chmn. Vt. Nat. Resources Council, 1973-75; dir. ACLU Vt., 1975—. Dir. Pub. Affairs Center, Dartmouth, 1976—. Mem. Am., Vt., Washing County Assns., Bar Assn. State N.Y., Assn. Bar City N.Y. Contbr. articles in field to profl. jours. Home: Calais VT 05648 Office: POB 159 Montpelier VT 05602 Tel (802) 229-9106

BROWNELL, THOMAS FORTUNE, b. Boston, Mar. 25, 1940; B.S. cum laude, Suffolk U., 1963, J.D., 1967; grad. Law Sch. Taxation, Boston U., 1972; postgrad. Harvard, 1976. Admitted to Mass. bar, 1967, Fed. bar, 1970, U.S. Supreme Ct. bar, 1975; asst. atty. gen. Commonwealth Mass., 1970-71; individual practice law, Quincy, Mass., 1967-76; mem. firm Brownell, Delahunt, Fleming & Langlois, 1974-75; mem. Mass. Ho. of Reps., 1971—; lectr. Suffolk Law Sch., 1974-76, Suffolk U., 1969—. Mem. Mass., Quincy, Norfolk County bar assns. Home: 15 Moreland Rd Quincy MA 02169 Office: 1359 Hancock St Quincy MA 02169 Tel (617) 773-0066

BROWNER, JULIUS HARVEY, b. N.Y.C., June 14, 1930; B.A., Bklyn. Coll., 1952; LL.B., Columbia U., 1957. Admitted to N.Y. bar, 1959, Fla. bar, 1973; individual practice law, Bklyn., 1959—, Margate, Fla., 1973—. Chmn. Community Dist. Planning Bd., Bklyn. 1972-74. Mem. Bklyn., Fla. bar assns., Assn. of Arbitrators (v.p. small claims div. 1976). Home and office: 841 SW 49th Way Margate FL 33068 Tel (305) 971-8686

BROWNFIELD, LYMAN, b. Uniontown, Pa., June 6, 1913; B.A., Mt. Union Coll., 1934; LL.B., Duke, 1937. Admitted to Ohio bar, 1937, U.S. Supreme Ct. bar, 1955, D.C. bar, 1961; asso. firm Vorys, Sater, Seymore & Pease, Columbus, Ohio, 1937-42; capt. JAGC, U.S. Army, 1942-46; partner firm Brownfield & Malone, and predecessors, Columbus, 1946-59, Brownfield, Rosen & Malone, Washington, 1961-62, Brownfield, Kosydar, Bowen, Bally & Sturtz, Columbus, 1961—; gen. counsel HHFA, Washington, 1961-62. Vice-chmn. Columbus Urban Renewal Commn., 1961-66. Mem. Am., Fed., Ohio, Columbus bar assns., Nat. Lawyers Club. Office: 140 E Town St Columbus OH 43215 Tel (614) 221-5834

BROWNING, CHAUNCEY HOYT, b. Logan, W.Va., May 15, 1903; A.B., W.Va. U., 1924, LL.B., 1927. Admitted to W.Va. bar, 1927; asst. pros. atty. Logan Co., W.Va., 1927-28, pros. atty., 1944-52; atty. City of Logan, W.Va., 1930-32; sec. W.Va. Workmen's Compensation Commn., 1933-44; atty. gen. W.Va., 1952—, judge Supreme Ct. Appeals, 1952-72. Mem. W.Va. Bar Assn., Kappa Sigma. Home: 3901 Kanawha Av SE Charleston WV 25304 Office: State Capitol Charleston WV 25305*

BROWNING, JAMES LOUIS, JR., b. Globe, Ariz., Dec. 8, 1932; B.A., Fresno State U., 1954; LL.B., U. Calif., San Francisco, 1959. Admitted to Calif. bar, 1960; sr. tax editor Commerce Clearing House, Inc., San Francisco, 1959-61; chief trial dep. and supr. superior ct. div. Office of Dist. Atty. County of San Mateo (Calif.), Redwood City, 1961-70; U.S. atty. No. Dist. Calif., 1970—; with JAGC, USAFR, 1960-72; mem. U.S. Attys'. Adv. Com. to Atty. Gen., 1973-76. Vice pres. Calif. Young Republicans, 1954; mem. exec. com., dir. Golden Gate chpt. ARC. Mem. State Bar Calif., Fed. Bar Assn. (chmn. council on law observance and adminstrn. of justice). Office: 450 Golden Gate Ave San Francisco CA 94102 Tel (415) 556-2308

BROWNING, JAMES ROBERT, b. Great Falls, Mont., Oct. 1, 1918; LL.B., U. Mont., 1941. Admitted to Mont. bar, 1941, D.C. bar, 1952; atty. antitrust div. U.S. Dept. Justice, Washington, 1951-52, 1st asst. civil div., 1951-52, exec. asst. atty. gen. U.S., Washington, 1952-53, chief Exec. Office for U.S. Attys., 1953; partner firm Perlman, Baldridge, Lyons & Browning, Washington, 1953-58; clk. U.S. Supreme Ct., Washington, 1958-61; circuit judge U.S. Ct. of Appeals, San Francisco, 1961—, chief judge, 1976—. Mem. Am., Fed. bar assns., Am. Law Inst., Am. Judicature Soc. (dir.), Am. Soc. Legal History. Home: 438 Magee Ave Mill Valley CA 94941 Office: PO Box 547 San Francisco CA 94101 Tel (415) 556-4388

BROWNING, ROBERT ROSS, b. Greenville, N.C., Apr. 12, 1936; A.B., Duke U., 1957; J.D., U. N.C., 1966. Admitted to N.C. bar, 1966; individual practice law, 1966-71; partner law firm Owens, Browning & Haigwood, 1971-73; spl. judge N.C. Superior Ct., Greenville, N.C., 1973—. Mem. N.C. Bd. Transp., 1973; mem. N.C. Commn. on Correctional Programs, 1975—; mem. Greenville Parking Authority, sec., 1966-67. Mem. N.C., Am., Pitt County, 3d Jud. Dist. bar assns. Home: 113 Cheshire Dr Greenville NC 27834 Office: Pitt County Courthouse Greenville NC 27834 Tel (919) 756-6751

BROWNSTEIN, CHARLES SIDNEY, b. N.Y.C., May 11, 1921; student pre-law Columbia, 1952; LL.B., Bklyn. Law Sch., 1956. Admitted to N.Y. bar, 1957, U.S. Dist. Ct. for So. Dist., 1958, Eastern Dist., 1975, U.S. Supreme Ct. bar, 1960, U.S. Ct. Mil. Appeals, 1964, U.S. Ct. of Claims bar, 1964; contracting officer Dept. Def., N.Y.C., 1957-74; law asst. N.Y. Supreme Ct. in Queens County, 1975-76; atty. litigation bur. N.Y. State Div. Housing and Community Renewal, N.Y.C., 1976—. Mem. Am., N.Y. State, Queens County bar assns., New York County Lawyer's Assn. Home: 69-36 174th St Flushing NY 11365 Office: Div Housing and Community Renewal 2 World Trade Center New York City NY 10047 Tel (212) 488-7098

BROWNSTEIN, DANIEL JACOB, b. N.Y.C., June 10, 1935; LL.B., Cornell U., 1959; B.A., Alfred U., 1956. Admitted to N.Y. bar, 1960, U.S. Supreme Ct., 1964; partner firm Black, Brownstein & Friedman, Great Neck, N.Y., 1970—. Mem. N.Y. State, Queens County, Nassau County bar assns. Office: 98 Cutter Mill Rd Suite 338 Great Neck NY 11021 Tel (516) 466-3033

BROWNSTEIN, HOWARD BROD, b. Dec. 29, 1950; B.S. in Econs., U. Pa., 1971, B.A., 1971; J.D., M.B.A., Harvard U., 1975. Admitted to Mass. bar, 1975, Pa. bar, 1976, Fla. bar, 1977; pres., founder Cambridge (Mass.) Legal Research, Inc., 1973—; with Del. Steel Co., Inc., Phila., 1977—. Mem. Am., Pa., Mass., Fla. bar assns., Am. Soc. Internat. Law, Am. Judicature Soc., MENSA, Boston Aid to the Blind, Alpha Kappa Psi. Contbr. articles to legal jours. Office: 100 Presidential Blvd N Bala Cynwyd PA 19004 Tel (215) 839-1200

BROWNSTEIN, NORMAN, b. Denver, May 23, 1943; B.S., U. Colo., 1965, J.D., 1968. Admitted to Colo. bar 1968; partner firm Brownstein, Hyatt, Farber & Madden and predecessor, Denver, 1968—. Co-chmn. Keeping Denver a Great City, 1976; trustee Nat. Jewish Hosp. at Denver, 1976. Mem. Am., Colo., Denver bar assns., U. Colo. Alumni Assn. (pres. 1973), U. Colo. Asso. Alumni (dir.). Author: (with Steven Farber) King Colorado Practice Methods, 1976; bd. editors Colo. Real Estate Manual, 1976. Office: 1700 Lincoln Center 1660 Lincoln St Denver CO 80264 Tel (303) 534-6335

BROWNSTEIN, PAUL GARY, b. Trenton, N.J., July 7, 1942; B.S. in Nonwestern Studies, Pa. State U., 1964; J.D., Temple U., 1967. Admitted to Pa. bar, 1970; house counsel USF & G Ins. Co., Phila., 1970; asst. gen. counsel ARA Services, Inc., Phila., 1971-76, dir. equal employment opportunity, 1974-76; pres. Symposia Cons., Phila., 1977—; mem. faculty U. Mich. at Ann Arbor, 1975-77, Practising Law Inst., 1973—. Mem. Phila., Pa., Am. bar assns. Contbr. articles to legal jours. Home: 3229 Ethan Allen Ct Cornwalls Heights PA 19020 Office: PO Box 868 Philadelphia PA 19105 Tel (215) 752-7744

BROWNSTEIN, PHILIP NATHAN, b. Ober, Ind., Feb. 14, 1917; student George Washington U., 1935-37; LL.B., Columbus U., 1940, LL.M., 1941. Admitted to D.C. bar, 1940; chief benefits dir. VA, Washington, 1961-63; asst. sec. for mortgage credit HUD, Washington, 1966-69; commr. FHA, Washington, 1963-69; partner firm Brownstein Zeidman Schomer & Chase, Washington, 1969—; dir. Loan Guaranty Service, Va., 1958-61, Fed. Nat. Mortgage Assn., 1963-72; dir. Nat. Commn. Against Discrimination in Housing, 1970—; vice chmn. Nat. Housing Conf., 1969—. Mem. Am., D.C., Fed. bar assns. Recipient VA Exceptional Service award, 1960, House and Home Top Performance in Housing, 1964, Career Service award Nat. Civil Service League, 1967. Home: 550 N St SW Washington DC 20024 Office: 1025 Connecticut Ave Washington DC 20036 Tel (202) 457-6516

BROWNTON, WESLEY FREDERICK, b. Canyon City, Oreg., July 6, 1908; A.B., U. Wash., 1933; J.D., Willamette U., 1935; grad. Nat. Coll. Trial Judges, 1968. Admitted to Oreg. bar, 1935, U.S. Supreme Ct. bar, 1942; practiced in La Grande, Oreg., 1935-57; judge Oreg. Circuit Ct., 10th Jud. Dist., 1957-75, sr. circuit judge of Oreg., 1975—; atty. Oreg. State Indsl. Accident Com., 1940; served with field judiciary Judge Adv. Gen. Corps USAR, 1960-61, ret. lt. col. Mem. Oreg. Bd. Bar Examiners, 1947-49. Mem. Oreg. State Bar. Home: 1200 B Ave La Grande OR 97850 Office: Courthouse La Grande OR 97850 Tel (503) 963-3041

BROYLES, JOHN LARRY, b. Brawley, Calif., Mar. 19, 1938; A.B., U. S.C., 1959, LL.B., 1962. Admitted to S.C. bar, 1962, Ga. bar, 1967; atty. Office Regional Counsel IRS, Atlanta, 1962-67; partner firm Hull, Towill, Norman, Barrett & Johnson, Augusta, Ga., 1967—. Bd. trustees Augusta County Day Sch., Augusta Prep. Sch. Mem. Am., S.C., Augusta bar assns., State Bar Ga. (chmn. sect. taxation 1975-76), Order of Wig and Robe. Asst. editor: S.C. Law Rev. Office: First National Bank Bldg Broad St Augusta GA 30902 Tel (404) 722-4481

BROZ, FRANK P., b. N.Y.C., Oct. 6, 1914; student Coll. City N.Y., 1931-34; LL.B., St. John's U., 1936; B.S., N.Y. U., 1950. Admitted to N.Y. bar, 1937, D.C. bar, 1968, Ariz. bar, 1976, U.S. Supreme Ct. bar, 1961; asso. firm Holtzmann, Wise & Shepard, and predecessors, N.Y.C., 1937-54, partner, 1954-75, of counsel, 1975—; acting police justice Village of Mt. Kisco (N.Y.), 1957-58. Chmn. Mt. Kisco Zoning Bd. Appeals, 1956-58, 70-75. Mem. Am., N.Y. State, Maricopa County bar assns., N.Y. County Lawyers Assn., Sun City Lawyers Club. Home: 108 05 Manzanita Dr Sun City AZ 85351 Office: 30 Broad St New York City NY 10004

BROZINSKY, EDWARD, b. Bklyn., Feb. 20, 1943; B.S., N.Y. U., 1964; J.D., Bklyn. Law Sch., 1968. Admitted to N.Y. bar, 1969; pvt. practice, 1969—; asst. adj. prof. Nassau Community Coll., Garden City, N.Y., 1970—. Home and Office: 15 Meredith Dr Greenlawn NY 11740 Tel (516) 757-0949

BRUCE, CHARLES MOORE, b. Washington, Aug. 1, 1945; B.A., Washington and Lee U., 1967; J.D., George Washington U., 1971. Admitted to D.C. bar, 1972; atty., adviser U.S. Tax Ct., 1971-73; asso. firm Hamel, Park, McCabe & Saunders, Washington, 1973—; adj. prof. law Georgetown U., 1977—. Mem. Am., D.C. bar assns., Internat. Fiscal Assn. Office: 1776 F St NW Washington DC 20006 Tel (202) 785-1234

BRUCE, JOHN THOMAS, b. Colorado Springs, Colo., Feb. 15, 1945; B.A. in Polit. Sci., Colo. Coll., 1967; J.D., U. Colo., 1972. Admitted to Colo. bar, 1972; since practiced in Colorado Springs; dep. city atty. City of Colorado Springs, 1972-74; partner firm Lake & Bruce, 1974—; municipal judge, Green Mountain Falls, Colo., 1975—. Mem. Colo., El Paso County bar assns. Home: Box 2061 Woodland Park CO 80863 Office: 12 E Pikes Peak Colorado Springs CO 80903 Tel (303) 471-4157

BRUCE, NORMAN MACDONALD, b. N.Y.C., Jan. 9, 1941; A.B., Duke, 1961; J.D., So. Meth. U., 1967. Admitted to Tex. bar, 1967; v.p. state relations and group ins. Transport Life Ins. Co., Ft. Worth, 1968—. Office: 714 Main St Fort Worth TX 76102 Tel (817) 335-9521

BRUCE, ROBERT DENTON, b. Houston, Jan. 29, 1943; A.A., Tyler Jr. Coll., 1964; B.B.A., U. Tex., Austin, 1966; J.D., St. Mary's U., San Antonio, 1972. Partner, Bruce & Bruce Oil Properties Co., Mineola, Tex., 1968-69; admitted to Tex. bar, 1972; individual practice law, Mineola, 1972—; mgr. Wood County Title Co., Mineola, 1972—. Bd. dirs. Mineola Indsl. Found., 1972—, Mineola Civic Center, 1972—; mem. adminstrv. bd. 1st United Meth. Ch. Mineola, 1972—, chmn. bd., 1977—; mem. Mineola Sch. Bd., 1976—. Mem. N.E., Tex., Wood County bar assns., Phi Delta Phi (pres. local chpt. 1971-72). Recipient Am. Jurisprudence award Lawyers Coop. Pub. Co., 1972, Planning Com. award City of Mineola, 1974. Home: 545 Peachtree Dr Mineola TX 75773 Office: 228 W Broad St POB 266 Mineola TX 75773 Tel (214) 569-3864

BRUCE, WILLIAM ROLAND, b. Portsmouth, Va., July 13, 1935; B.A., U. Va., 1956, LL.B., 1959. Admitted to Va. bar, 1959, Tenn. bar, 1960, U.S. Supreme Ct. bar, 1964; practiced in Memphis, 1959-, asso. firm Martin, Tate & Morrow, 1959-62; individual practice law, 1963-65; mem. firm Bruce & Southern, and predecessor, 1965—, pres., 1973—; mem. Tenn. Ho. of Reps., 1966-68; mem. Tenn. Senate, 1968-72, majority leader, 1969-70, chmn. com. calendar and rules, 1971-72; mem. faculty Practising Law Inst., 1971-72; lectr. Vanderbilt U. Sch. Law, 1972—. Del. White House Conf. on Children, 1970; chmn. Health Systems Mgmt., Inc., 1972-76. Mem. Memphis and Shelby County (Sam A. Myar Meml. award), Tenn., Va., Am. bar assns., Am. Judicature Soc. Named Outstanding Young Man in Tenn., Tenn. Jaycees, 1968. Home: 2921 Tishomingo Ln Memphis TN 38111 Office: 100 N Main Bldg Suite 3201 Memphis TN 38103 Tel (901) 523-7111

BRUCH, CAROL SOPHIE, b. Rockford, Ill., June 11, 1941; A.B., Shimer Coll., 1960; J.D., U. Calif., Berkeley, 1972. Admitted to Calif. bar, 1973; law clk. to justice U.S. Supreme Ct., 1972-73; acting prof. law U. Calif. Davis, 1973—. Bd. dirs. Jewish Fellowship Davis Religious Sch., 1974-75. Mem. Am., Calif. bar assns., ACLU, Calif. Women Lawyers, Order of Coif. Contbr. articles to profl. jours. Home: 1013 Stanford Dr Davis CA 95616 Office: Martin Luther King Sch Law U Calif Davis CA 95616 Tel (916) 752-2535

BRUCKER, ANDREW GERALD, b. Bklyn., Apr. 22, 1943; A.B. with honors, U. Rochester, 1964; LL.B., Yale, 1967. Admitted to Conn. bar, 1967, Am. Samoa bar, 1968; asst. atty. gen. Am. Samoa, 1967-69, atty. gen., 1969; asso. firm Weinstein, Shields, Schaffer, Hirsch & Lev, Norwalk, Conn., 1970-74, partner, 1974—; counsel Greater Norwalk Day Care, 1974. Sec., bd. dirs. South Norwalk Community Center, 1970—; chmn. Norwalk/Wilton chpt. ARC,

1974—; sec. Conn. Blood Program, 1976; treas. Wilton Democratic Town Com., 1976—. Mem. Conn., Am., Norwalk/Wilton bar assns. Home: 288 Rivergate Dr Wilton CT 06897 Office: 94 East Ave Norwalk CT 06852 Tel (203) 853-1234

BRUCKNER, ARNOLD DAVID, b. Phila., June 10, 1940; B.B.A., George Washington U., 1964, J.D., 1970. Admitted to D.C. bar, 1971, Md. bar, 1972; asso. firm A.D. Bruckner, Bowie, Md., 1973-74, Bryan & Bury, Hyattsville, Md., 1974, Joseph M. Bryan, Hyattsville, 1974-75; partner firm Bruckner & Olshonsky, Riverdale, Md., 1975-76; individual practice law, Riverdale, 1976—. Pres., mem. bd. Belair Town II Townshouse Assn., Bowie, 1971-74. Mem. Am., D.C., Md., Prince George's County (exec. com.) bar assns., Phi Alpha Delta, Alpha Kappa Psi. Patentee corrugated fiberboard container system with stacking tray for letter mail. Office: 6411 Baltimore Ave Riverdale MD 20840 Tel (301) 779-6700

BRUCKNER, DANIEL WILLIAM, b. Milw., Dec. 12, 1946; B.S., Marquette U., 1969, J.D., 1972. Admitted to Wis. bar, 1972; individual practice law, Milw., 1972—. Mem. Wis., Milw. bar assns., Phi Alpha Delta. Recipient Am. Jurisprudence award; service award Legal Aid Soc. of U. Wis. Home: 201 E Holt Ave Milwaukee WI 53207 Office: 3408 S Burrell St Milwaukee WI 53207 Tel (414) 475-1113 also (414) 483-3350

BRUCKNER, LAWRENCE LLOYD, b. Savanna, Ill., Apr. 15, 1950; B.A., Trinity Coll., 1971, M.A., 1971; J.D., Coll. William and Mary, 1973. Admitted to Va. bar, 1973, Ill. bar, 1974; asso. firm George F. Nichols, Dixon, Ill., 1974—; counsel Lee County Council on Aging, 1975-77. Mem. Am., Ill. Lee County bar assns., Am. Trial Lawyers Assn., N.W. Council Elected Govt. Ofcls. (v.p. 1976-77). Office: 109 Galena Ave Dixon IL 61021 Tel (815) 284-2232

BRUCKNER, WILLIAM JOSEPH, b. Atlanta, Mar. 28, 1945; B.S., The Citadel, 1966; J.D., U. Ga., 1969. Admitted to Ga. bar, 1970; tax atty. Arthur Anderson & Co., Atlanta, 1969-71; asst. solicitor gen. Fulton County Solicitor's Office, Atlanta, 1971-73; atty. So. Bell Tel. & Tel. Co., Atlanta, 1973—. Mem. Am., Ga., Atlanta bar assns., Atlanta Council of Younger Lawyers. Home: 1069 Meadow Lane Rd Atlanta GA 30338 Office: 1245 Hurt Bldg Atlanta GA 30303 Tel (494) 529-6361

BRUERE, JOHN TWEEDIE, b. St. Charles, Mo., Mar. 2, 1942; J.D., U. Mo., 1968. Admitted to Mo. bar, 1968; asst. pros. atty. St. Charles County, 1968-70; spl. counsel City of O'Fallon (Mo.), 1968-71; atty. City of St. Charles, 1971-75; sr. partner firm Bruere & Rollings, St. Charles, 1971—; city atty. Lake St. Louis (Mo.), 1976—. Mem. Am., Mo., St. Charles County bar assns., St. Louis Met. Bar Assn. Contbr. articles to legal jours. Home: 98 Crest Ct Lake Saint Louis MO 63367 Office: 2209 First Capitol Dr Saint Charles MO 63301 Tel (314) 946-6086

BRUGGEMAN, DAN ROBERT, b. Lucas County, Ohio, July 26, 1938; B.A. in Econs., Mich. State U., 1960; LL.B., U. Mich., 1963. Admitted to Mich. bar, 1963, U.S. Supreme Ct. bar, 1967; legal officer USN, 1964-67; prin. firm Dan. R. Bruggeman, profl. corp., Adrian, Mich., 1968—; asst. pros. atty. Lenawee County (Mich.), 1968—. Bd. dirs. Environ. Council Lenawee, 1971—, pres., 1974, sec.-treas., 1975—. Mem. Lenawee County Bar Assn. (pres. 1974). Office: 112 E Front St Adrian MI 49221 Tel (517) 263-7897

BRUGGER, GEORGE ALBERT, b. Erie, Pa., Jan. 19, 1941; B.A., Gannon Coll., 1963; J.D., Georgetown U., 1967. Admitted to Md. bar, 1968, U.S. Supreme Ct. bar, 1974; law clk. Asst. Atty. Gen. of U.S. criminal div. Dept. Justice, Washington, 1963-66; legis. rep. Air Transport Assn. of Am., Washington, 1966-68; asso. firm Beatty & McNamee, Hyattsville, Md., 1968-71, partner, 1971-75; partner firm Fossett & Brugger, Seabrook, Md., 1975—. Dir. Ardmore Developmental Center, 1975—. Mem. Am., Md., Prince George's County (dir.) bar assns. Office: 10210 Greenbelt Rd Suite 720 Seabrook MD 20801 Tel (301) 794-6900

BRUGMAN, LAWRENCE WILLIAM, b. Chgo., June 2, 1908; B.S. in M.E., U. Ill., 1930, LL.B., George Washington U., 1934. Admitted to D.C. bar, 1934, Ill. bar, 1952, U.S. Supreme Ct. bar, 1966; partner firm Rasmussen & Brugman, Chgo., 1936-40; asso. firm Sheridan, Davis and Cargill, Chgo., 1940-54; partner firm McCaleb, Lucas & Brugman, and predecessors, Chgo., 1954—. Mem. Chgo. Bar Assn., Patent Law Assn. Chgo. Home: 6235 N Tripp Ave Chicago IL 60646 Office: 230 W Monroe St Chicago IL 60606 Tel (312) 236-4711

BRUHN, SOREN FREDERICK, b. Enumclaw, Wash., May 24, 1928; B.A., U. Wash., 1952; J.D., 1959. Admitted to Wash. bar, 1959; asst. atty. gen. State of Wash., Olympia, 1959-61, chief dep. ins. commr., 1961-67; asso. gen. counsel Safeco Corp., Seattle, 1972-74, gen. counsel, 1974—. Mem. Am., Wash., Seattle-King County bar assns. Asso. editor Wash. Law Rev., 1958-59. Home: 1508 9th Ave W Seattle WA 98119 Office: Safeco Plaza Seattle WA 98185 Tel (206) 545-5664

BRUMBAUGH, JOHN MAYNARD, b. Annapolis, Md., Feb. 9, 1927; B.A., Swarthmore Coll., 1948; J.D., Harvard, 1951. Admitted to D.C. bar, 1951; law clk. firm Haight, Deming, Gardner, Poor & Havens, N.Y.C., 1951, 53-55; teaching fellow Harvard, 1955-56; asst. prof. law U. Md., 1956-59, asso. prof., 1959-63, prof., 1963—; asst. prof. legal medicine, 1976—. Mem. Am. Law Inst., Am., Md. bar assns., AAUP, Soc. Am. Law Tchrs. Contbr. articles in field Office: 500 W Baltimore St Baltimore MD 21201 Tel (301) 528-7188

BRUMFIELD, CHARLES E., b. Oceanside, Calif., June 9, 1948; B.S. in Bus. Adminstrn. and Econs., magna cum laude, U. San Diego, 1970, J.D., 1973. Admitted to Calif. bar, 1974; with Leach Industries, San Diego, 1971—. Bd. dirs. Internat. Racquetball Assn., 1973-76. Office: 5567 Kearney Villa Rd San Diego CA 92123 Tel (714) 279-1000

BRUMMER, BENNETT HOWARD, b. N.Y.C., Apr. 16, 1941; A.B., U. Miami, Coral Gables, Fla., 1962, J.D., 1965. Admitted to Fla. bar, 1965, N.Y. State bar, 1966, U.S. Supreme Ct. bar, 1970; staff atty. Legal Services of Greater Miami, 1968-71, sr. atty., 1969-71; asst. pub. defender 11th Judicial Circuit, Dade County, Fla., 1971-76; chief appellate div. office pub. defender, 1973-76, pub. defender, 1977—; adj. prof. law U. Miami 1974—. Mem. Fla. Pub. Defenders Assn. (treas. 1976—), Fla. Criminal Defense Attys. Assn. (dir. 1974—) ACLU Legal Panel. Home: 1200 Andora Ave Coral Gables FL 33146 Office: 800 Metropolitan Justice Bldg Miami FL 33125 Tel (305) 547-4922

BRUNDIN, BRIAN JON, b. St. Paul, Oct. 11, 1939; B.B.A. cum laude, U. Alaska, 1961; J.D., Harvard, 1964. Admitted to Alaska bar, 1966; prin. partner firm Hughes, Thorsness, Gantz, Powell & Brundin, and predecessors, Anchorage, 1966—; instr. law and accounting U. Alaska, 1965-69. Bd. regents U. Alaska, 1969—, chmn. fin. com., 1970-75, v.p., 1974-75, pres., 1975—; pres. U. Alaska Found., 1974-77. Mem. Am., Alaska, Anchorage bar assns., Alaska Soc. C.P.A.'s, Am. Inst. C.P.A.'s, Am. Trial Lawyers Assn. Home: 1430 Crescent St Anchorage AK 99504 Office: 509 3d Ave Anchorage AK 99501 Tel (907) 274-7522

BRUNER, PHILIP LANE, b. Chgo., Sept. 26, 1939; A.B., Princeton U., 1961; J.D., U. Mich., 1964; M.B.A., U. Syracuse, 1967. Admitted to Wis. bar, 1964, Minn. bar, 1968; since practiced in St. Paul; mem. firm Briggs and Morgan, 1967—; instr. William Mitchell Coll. Law, St. Paul, 1970—; lectr. in field. Mem. Am., Fed., Wis., Minn., Ramsay County bar assns. Author: Inspection and Acceptance Under Fixed Price Supply Contracts, 1971; Inspection, Acceptance and Warranties, 1977; mem. bd. contributors Developments in Government Contract Law, 1976—. Named Outstanding Young Citizen St. Paul, St. Paul Jaycees, 1974; One of Ten Outstanding Young Minnesotans, Minn. Jaycees, 1975. Office: 2200 1st Nat Bank Bldg St Paul MN 55101 Tel (612) 291-1215

BRUNING, RICHARD CARL, b. Ft. Scott, Kans., Jan. 26, 1943; B.B.A., U. Iowa, 1965, J.D., 1968. Admitted to Iowa bar, 1968, U.S. Ct. Mil. Appeals bar, 1968, U.S. Ct. Mil. Review bar, 1971, U.S. Supreme Ct. bar, 1971, U.S. Ct. Claims, 1972; atty. U.S. Army, 1968-70, mil. judge, 1970-71; prof. Law JAG Sch., Charlottesville, Va., 1972-76, trial atty. 1976—. Author: (with Clifford Brooks) How to Seek Recovery for Govt. Breach of Contract (in text) Basic Techniques of Public Contracts Practice, 1975; contbr. articles in field to law jours. Home: 5500 Kempton Dr Springfield VA 22151 Office: Dept Army 5600 Columbia Pike Falls Church VA 22041 Tel (202) 756-2170

BRUNN, GEORGE, b. Vienna, Austria, June 28, 1924; A.B., Stanford, 1947, J.D., 1950. Admitted to Calif. bar, 1951; practiced in San Francisco, 1951-66; judge Berkeley (Calif.) Municipal Ct., 1966—; mem. faculties Calif. Coll. Trial Judges, 1967, Nat. Coll. State Judiciary, 1974, 75, Conf. on Ct. Modernization, San Francisco, 1975; vice chmn. Judicial Coordinating Com. on Pretrial Services, 1975-76, chmn., 1976-77; mem. Calif. Com. Economic Litigation, 1977. Bd. dirs. Consumers Union, Mt. Vernon, N.Y., 1966—; mem. Calif. Atty. Gen's. Consumer Protection Task Force, 1972—. Mem. Conf. Calif. Judges, Alameda County (Calif.), Berkeley-Albany bar assns., Alameda County Municipal Ct. Judges Assn. Contbr. articles oto profl. publs. Office: 2120 Grove St Berkeley CA 94704 Tel (415) 644-6975

BRUNNER, THOMAS JOHN, JR., b. Chgo., Mar. 7, 1941; A.B., U. Notre Dame, 1963, LL.B., 1966, M.A., 1967. Admitted to Ind. bar, 1966; staff atty. NLRB, Washington, 1968; legis. asst. to Senator Vance Hartke, Washington, 1969-72; v.p. Assos. Corps. of N.Am., South Bend, Ind., 1972-74; mem. firm Chapleau, Roper, McInerny, Minczeski & Farabaugh, South Bend, 1974—; instr. polit. sci. St. Francis Coll., Loretto, Pa., 1967-68; instr. labor law U. South Bend, 1974—; city atty. City of South Bend, 1976—. Bd. dirs. Legal Aid Soc. of St. Joseph County (Ind.), Inc., Art Center, Inc., South Bend. Mem. Ind. State, St. Joseph County, Am. bar assns. Home: 1132 Bronson St South Bend IN 46615 Office: 316 1st Bank Bldg South Bend IN 46601 Tel (219) 233-5173

BRUNO, DAVID JAMES, b. Denver, Oct. 30, 1947; B.A. with distinction, Colo. State U., 1969; J.D., U. Colo., 1973. Admitted to Colo. bar, 1973; partner firm Bruno, Bruno and Bruno, Denver, 1974—. Pres. Colo. Alliance for the Achievement of Children's Potential, Lakewood, 1975-76. Mem. Am., Colo. bar assns., Order of Coif. Office: 1175 Captiol Life Center 225 E 16th St Denver CO 80203 Tel (303) 861-8397

BRUNO, LOUIS BYRON, b. Denver, June 26, 1944; B.A., U. Colo., 1965, J.D., 1968. Admitted to Colo. bar, 1968, U.S. Ct. Appeals bar, 10th Circuit, 1971, U.S. Dist. Ct. for Dist. Colo. bar, 1968; partner firm Bruno, Bruno & Bruno, Denver, 1969—; atty. Policeman's Protective Assn., Denver Police Dept. Vice pres., dir. Jefferson County (Colo.) Community Center for Retarded; bd. dirs. Jefferson County Assn. for Retarded. Office: 1175 Capitol Life Center Denver CO 80203 Tel (303) 861-8397

BRUNS, ERNEST EVERETT, b. Madison, Wis., Nov. 16, 1918; B.A. in Commerce, U. Wis., 1939, J.D., 1942. Admitted to Wis. bar, 1942; claims rep. Hartford Accident & Indemnity Co., Milw., 1946-48; mgr. br. claims Iowa Nat. Mut. Ins. Co., Madison, 1948-73; mem. firm Winner, McCallum and Hendee, Madison, 1974—. Mem. Am., Wis. State, Dane County bar assns. Home: 3702 Council Crest St Madison WI 53711 Office: 111 S Fairchild St Madison WI 53701 Tel (608) 257-0257

BRUNSVOLD, BRIAN GARRETT, b. Mason City, Iowa, Apr. 10, 1938; B.S. in Chem. Engring., Iowa State U., 1960; J.D. with honors, George Washington U., 1967. Admitted to Va. bar, 1967, D.C. bar, 1967; law clk. U.S. Ct. Claims, Washington, 1966-67; asso. firm Finnegan, Henderson, Farabow & Garrett, Washington, 1968-71, partner, 1972—; asso. profl. lectr. George Washington U. Law Sch., 1973—. Bd. dirs. Lake Barcroft Community Assn., 1970-72; treas. Faith Lutheran Ch., Arlington, Va., 1974-76. Mem. Bar Assn. D.C., Am. Bar Assn., Am. Patent Law Assn., Licensing Execs. Soc. Contbr. articles to legal jours. Home: 6346 Crosswoods Dr Falls Church VA 22044 Office: Finnegan Henderson et al 1775 K St NW Washington DC 20006 Tel (202) 293-6850

BRUNWASSER, ALLEN NORMAN, b. Pitts., Dec. 5, 1921; B.A., U. Pitts., 1943; LL.B., Harvard, 1948. Admitted to Pa. bar, 1950, U.S. Supreme Ct. bar, 1971; individual practice law, Pitts., 1950—. Mem. Allegheny County Bar Assn. Home: Gateway Towers Pittsburgh PA 15222 Office: 903 B Grant Bldg Grant St Pittsburgh PA 15219 Tel (412) 391-0728

BRUSS, ROBERT JACQUES, b. Mpls., May 2, 1940; B.S. in Bus. Adminstrn., Northwestern U., 1962; J.D., Hastings Coll. Law, U. Calif., 1967. Admitted to Calif. bar, 1967; individual practice law, Menlo Park, Calif., 1967-71; investment mgr. Grubb & Ellis Co., San Francisco, 1971-74; lectr. real estate law Coll. San Mateo, 1976—; syndicated columnist Real Estate Mailbag, San Francisco, 1974—. Mem. Am., Calif. State bar assns. Office: 2652 Baker St San Francisco CA 94123 Tel (415) 368-6704

BRYAN, DAVID BARCLAY, b. Los Angeles, Aug. 30, 1933; B.A., Duke U., 1955; J.D., U. Calif., Berkeley, 1958. Admitted to Hawaii bar, 1964, U.S. Supreme Ct. bar, 1969; dep. pros. atty. City and County Honolulu, 1965-68; partner firm Kai, Dodge & Evensen, Honolulu, 1968—; labor relations mgr. Hawaiian Airlines, Honolulu, 1960-61; personnel dir. Labon Civil Air Transport, Taipei, Taiwan, 1961-63. Pres., Hawaii Tng. Assn., Honolulu, 1964-65; mem. exec. com. Muscular Dystrophy Assn., Honolulu, 1974—. Mem. Am., Hawaii bar assn., Am. Trial Lawyers Assn. Recipient Scholastic Improvement award, Buf. Nat. Affairs, 1958. Home: 70 Wailupe Circle Honolulu HI 96821 Office: 1808 Financial Plaza of Pacific Honolulu HI 96813 Office: Tel (808) 536-7744

BRYAN, J. SHEPARD, JR., b. 1922; B.S., U.S. Naval Acad.; LL.B., Harvard U. Admitted to Fla. bar, 1950; practiced law, 1950-54; with Winn-Dixie Stores, Inc., Jacksonville, Fla., 1954—, sec., 1961—, gen. counsel, 1963—, v.p., 1966—. Office: Winn-Dixie Stores Inc 5050 Edgewood Ct Jacksonville FL 32203*

BRYAN, JAMES PERRY, JR., b. Houston, Jan. 17, 1940; B.A., U. Tex., 1962, LL.B., 1965; grad. Am. Grad. Sch. Internat. Mgmt., 1966. Admitted to Tex. bar, 1966; asst. treas. Morgan Guaranty Trust Co., N.Y.C., 1966-69; v.p., exec. com. Dominick & Dominick, N.Y.C. and Houston, 1969-74; pres. MortgageBanque, Inc. (formerly Universal Capital Mortgage Co.), Houston, 1974—; chmn. bd. Criterion Mgmt. Co.; dir. Mich. Gas Utilities Co., S. Main Center Assn., R.C. Memhard Co., Greenwich, Conn. Chmn. fin. River Oaks Baptist Sch. Mem. Tex. Bar Assn., Houston Mortgage Bankers Assn., Houston Bd. Realtors. Home: 3 Shadowlawn Houston TX 77005 Office: 6900 Fannin St Houston TX 77030 Tel (713) 797-9899

BRYAN, MILDRED GOTT, b. Washington, Oct. 20; student Mt. Holyoke Coll., 1924-26; A.B. magna cum laude, Trinity Coll., 1928; J.D. cum laude, George Washington U., 1932. Admitted to D.C. bar, 1932; atty. real estate div. War Dept., U.S. Dept. Def., Washington, 1942-46; individual practice law, Washington, 1952—; pres. Eastland Gardens, Inc. Sec. Westmoreland Hills Citizens Assn. Md., 1949. Mem. Am., Inter-Am., Internat., D.C. bar assns., Nat. Assn. Women Lawyers, World Peace Thru Law. Home: 4840 Quebec St NW Washington DC 20016 Office: 1028 Connecticut Ave NW Washington DC 20036 Tel (202) 659-4455

BRYAN, PAUL JACKSON, b. Newberry, Fla., June 8, 1923; B.A., U. Fla., 1948; LL.B., Harvard U., 1951. Admitted to Fla. bar, 1951, U.S. Supreme Ct. bar, 1956; adminstrv. asst. to Congressman Mathews, 1952-59; exec. dir. Fla. Petroleum Council, 1959-64; individual practice law, Palatka, Fla.; atty. Palatka Natural Gas Authority, dist. bd. trustees St. Johns River Jr. Coll. Sec. Greater Palatka Improvement Com.; chmn. leadership and tng. dist. com. Boy Scouts Am.; bd. dirs. local chpt. ARC, United Fund. Mem. Putnam County (Fla.), Am. (vice chmn. com. on taxation gen. practice sect.) bar assns., Palatka C. of C. (dir.), Palatka Jaycees (sec., dir.). Office: PO Drawer C 119 N 2d St Palatka FL 32077 Tel (904) 325-3000

BRYAN, ROBERT J., b. Bremerton, Wash., Oct. 29, 1934; B.A., U. Wash., 1956; J.D., 1958; grad. Nat. Coll. of State Judiciary, 1967. Admitted to Wash. bar, 1959, U.S. Dist. Ct. bar, 1959; Tax Ct. U.S., 1967; partner firm Bryan & Bryan, Bremerton, 1959-67; judge Superior Ct., 1967—. Mem. Am., Wash., Kitsap County bar assns., Superior Ct. Judges Assn., Wash. Correctional Assn., Phi Delta Phi. Home: 2137 Madrona Point Dr Bremerton WA 98310 Office: 614 Division St Kitsap County Courthouse Port Orchard WA 98366 Tel (206) 876-7140

BRYAN, THOMAS HARTZ, b. Evansville, Ind., Sept. 14, 1944; B.M.E., Purdue U., 1966; J.D., Ind. U., 1969. Admitted to Ind. bar, 1969, Ill. bar, 1971; staff atty. Employers Ins. Co. of Wausau (Wis.), 1971-73; asso. firm John A. Doyle, Ltd., Chgo., 1973-77; mem. firm Fine Hatfield Sparrenburger & Fine, Evansville, Ind., 1977—. Office: Fine Hatfield et al Old Nat Bank Bldg Evansville IN 47708 Tel (812) 425-3592

BRYAN, THOMAS LYNN, b. Wichita, Kans., June 10, 1935; B.A., U. Kan., 1957; LL.B., Columbia, 1960. Admitted to N.Y. bar, 1960, U.S. Supreme Ct. bar, 1966, U.S. Dist. Ct. bar for So. Dist. N.Y., 1975; asso. firm Willkie Farr & Gallagher, N.Y.C., 1960-66, partner, 1967—. Mem. Am., N.Y. State bar assns., Assn. Bar City N.Y. Home: 342 Hillcrest Rd Ridgwood NJ 07450 Office: 1 Chase Manhattan Plaza New York City NY 10005 Tel (212) 248-1000

BRYANT, FREDERICK BOYCE, b. Malone, N.Y., Dec. 5, 1911; A.B., Middlebury Coll., 1933; LL.B., Columbia U., 1936. Admitted to N.Y. bar, 1936; asso. firm Breed, Abbott & Morgan, N.Y.C., 1936-38; asst. dist. atty. N.Y. County (N.Y.), 1938-39; individual practice law, Malone, N.Y., 1939-41; asso. gen. counsel Coop. G.L.F. Exchange, Ithaca, N.Y., 1942-46; asso. firm Cobb, Cobb & Simpson, Ithaca, 1946-60; dist. atty. Tompkins County (N.Y.), 1947-56; partner Bryant, Mazza & Williamson, Ithaca, 1960-68; justice N.Y. State Supreme Ct., 1968—. Chmn. Tompkins County Republican Party, 1956-68. Mem. N.Y., Tompkins County bar assns., N.Y. State Supreme Ct. Justice Assn. Home: 107 Northway Rd Ithaca NY 14850 Office: County Courthouse Ithaca NY 14850 Tel (606) 274-5429

BRYANT, GEORGE HERBERT, b. Hartwell, Ga., Oct. 3, 1928; LL.B., Woodrow Wilson Coll. Law, 1964. Rep., Delta Loan Corp., Atlanta, 1952-55; asst. mgr. Comml. Loan Corp., Atlanta, 1955-57; asst. credit mgr. Standard Oil Co. of Calif., Atlanta, 1957-71; admitted to Ga. bar, 1966; individual practice law, Danielsville, Ga. Mem. State Bar Ga., No. Bar Assn. (v.p. 1975-76). Home: Route 1 Danielsville GA 30633 Office: PO Box 265 Danielsville GA 30633 Tel (404) 795-2133

BRYANT, JACKSON COLEMAN, b. Seattle, Jan. 18, 1918; A.A., Santa Monica Jr. Coll.; B.A., U. Calif., Los Angeles; LL.B., J.D., U. So. Calif. Admitted to Calif. bar, 1950; partner firm Nichols & Bryant, Los Angeles, then Pomona, Calif.; individual practice law, Pomona; counsel Preston Printing, Inc., Teletronics, Inc. Chmn. Pomona Planning Commn.; active Crippled Children's Hosp., Los Angeles. Mem. Pomona C. of C., Phi Delta Phi. Office: 592 N Park Ave Pomona CA 91767 Tel (714) 629-5512

BRYANT, MICHAEL LEE, b. Woodbury, N.J., Jan. 8, 1944; A.B., Duke, 1966; J.D., U. Fla., 1969. Admitted to Fla. bar, 1969; individual practice law, Gainesville, Fla., 1969-74; partner firm Birr, Bryant & Saba, and predecessor, Gainesville, 1974—; asst. prof. bus. law U. Fla., Gainesville, 1969-70, faculty mem. coll. law, 1970-73. Mem. exec. council Episcopal Diocese Fla., 1976-77; pres. Reentry Gainesville, Inc., 1974-77. Mem. Fla., Bar, Am., 8th Jud. Circuit bar assns., Storefront Legal Aid, Phi Delta Phi. Home: 901 N W 20th Terr Gainesville FL 32603 Office: PO Box 658 Gainesville FL 32602 Tel (904) 373-3539

BRYANT, THOMAS EARLE, JR., b. Lebanon, Tenn., Aug. 10, 1934; B.S., U. Ala., 1956, LL.B., 1963. Admitted to Ala. bar, 1963; asso. firm McDermott & Slepian, Mobile, Ala., 1965-69; partner firm Gaston, Bryant & Gaston, Mobile, 1969—. Chmn. Mobile Municipal Auditorium Bd., 1976—; mem. Mobile Emergency Med. Services, 1973. Mem. Ala., Mobile (sec. 1974-75) bar assns. Home: 5221 S Maudelayne Dr Mobile AL 36609 Office: PO Drawer 1465 Mobile AL 36601 Tel (205) 432-4671

BRYANT, TRAVIS HILTON, b. Collins, Miss., May 11, 1938; B.A., U. So. Miss., 1965; J.D., Jackson Sch. Law, 1970. Admitted to Miss. bar, 1971; instr. Copiah-Lincoln Jr. Coll., Wesson, Miss., 1965; field claims rep. State Farm Ins. Co., Brookhaven, Miss., 1966-68; individual practice law, Mendenhall, Miss., 1970—. Active Boy Scouts Am., Magee, Miss., 1969. Mem. Miss., Am. trial lawyers assns., Am. Judicature Soc., Miss. State, Fed., Four County, Simpson County bar assns. Home: Route 1 Box 47A Magee MS 39111 Office: 145 Maud Mendenhall MS 39114 Tel (601) 847-1262

BRYDGES, LOUIS WORTHINGTON, b. Fox Lake, Ill., June 24, 1932; student Beloit (Wis.) Coll., 1950-54; J.D., Washington U., St. Louis, 1958. Admitted to Ill. bar, 1958, Mo. bar, 1958, U.S. Supreme Ct. bar, 1963; practice law, Waukegan, Ill.; dir. Trans-Air Corp. Bd. dirs. Lake County YMCA, 1972—. Mem. Am., Fed., Mo., Ill., Lake County (gov. 1960—, chmn. ethics com. 1976-77), Lawyers-Pilots bar assns., Soc. Trial Lawyers, Internat. Assn. Ins. Counsel, Assn. Ins. Attys., Ill. Def. Counsel, Def. Research Inst., Lake County Trial Lawyers Assn. (dir. 1975—). Home: 262 Harding Ave Waukegan IL 60085 Office: 111 N County St Waukegan IL 60085 Tel (312) 662-8611

BRYER, STANLEY, b. N.Y.C., Apr. 23, 1925; B.M.E., Cornell U., 1947; LL.D., N.Y. Law Sch., 1954. Admitted to N.Y. bar, 1955; individual practice law, N.Y.C., 1960—. Bd. dirs. Theodore Gordon Flyfishers, Inc. Mem. N.Y. State, N.Y. County bar assns., Am. Trial Lawyers Assn. Office: 200 E 42d St New York City NY 10017 Tel (212) MU 2-0790

BRYSON, DEAN FREDRICK, b. Portland, Oreg., Sept. 27, 1910; LL.B., Northwestern Coll. Law, 1934; LL.D., Pacific U., 1975. Admitted to Oreg. bar, 1934; partner firm Bryson & Deich, Portland, 1953-61; judge Multnomah County (Oreg.) Circuit Ct., 1961-70; justice Oreg. Supreme Ct., 1970—; mem. exec. com. Oreg. Jud. Conf., 1976; dir. Oreg. Physicians' Service, 1961—. Mem. Oreg. State Bar (pres. 1960-61). Office: Supreme Ct Salem OR 97310 Tel (503) 378-6026

BRYSON, WILLIAM HAMILTON, b. Richmond, Va., July 29, 1941; B.A., Hampden-Sydney Coll., 1963; LL.B., Harvard, 1967; LL.M., U. Va., 1968; Ph.D. (William Senior scholar), Cambridge U., 1972. Admitted to Va. bar, 1967; fellow Max Planck Inst., Frankfurt am Main, Germany, 1972-73; asst. prof. law U. Richmond (Va.), 1973-76, asso. prof., 1976—. Mem. Va. Bar Assn., Royal, Va. hist. socs., Am. Soc. Legal History, Medieval Acad. Am., Selden Soc. (corr. for Va.), Phi Beta Kappa. Recipient Yorke prize, 1973; Fulbright grantee, 1963-64; author: Interrogatories and Depositions in Virginia, 1969; Equity Side of the Exchequer, 1975; Dictionary of Sigla, 1975. Home: 5406 Grove Ave Richmond VA 23226 Office: Sch Law U Richmond Richmond VA 23173 Tel (804) 285-6387

BRZECZEK, RICHARD JOSEPH, b. Chgo., Oct. 8, 1942; B.S., Loyola U., Chgo., 1965; M.Pub. Adminstrn., Ill. Inst. Tech., 1968; J.D., John Marshall Law Sch., 1972. Admitted to Ill. bar, 1972; since practiced in Chgo.; exec. asst. to supt. Chgo. Police Dept., 1973—; instr. John Marshall Law Sch., 1973-74. Mem. Am. (Silver Key award 1971), Ill., Chgo. (chmn. police-lawyer relations com.) bar assns., Internat. Assn. Chiefs Police, Advocates Soc., Chgo. Assn. Commerce and Industry (crime prevention com. 1974—), Phi Alpha Delta. Home: 6301 N Legett Ave Chicago IL 60646 Office: 1121 S State St Room 400 Chicago IL 60605 Tel (312) 744-5501

BSCHORR, PAUL JOSEPH, b. N.Y.C., Jan. 3, 1941; B.A., Yale, 1962; LL.B., U. Pa., 1965. Admitted to N.Y. bar, 1965, D.C. bar, 1975, U.S. Supreme Ct. bar, 1974; asso. firm White & Case, N.Y.C., 1965-72, partner, 1972—. Mem. Am., N.Y. State, D.C. bar assns., Assn. Bar City N.Y. Office: White and Case 14 Wall St New York City NY 10005 Tel (212) 732-1040

BUA, NICHOLAS JOHN, b. Chgo., Feb. 9, 1925; J.D., DePaul U., 1950; postgrad. U. Nev., 1966. Admitted to Ill. bar, 1953; house counsel U.S. Fidelity & Guaranty Co., Chgo., 1953-54; individual practice law, Chgo., 1954-56; partner firm M.A. Garretson, Esq., Chgo., 1956-63; judge Village Ct. of Melrose Park (Ill.), 1963-64; asso. judge Circuit Ct. of Cook County (Ill.), 1964-71, judge, 1971-76; justice Ill. Appellate Ct., 1st Dist., Cook County, 1976—; vice chmn. exec. com. Jud. Conf., State of Ill., 1975; mem. Supreme Ct. Rules Com., 1972. Charter mem. Chgo. Council on Am.-Italian Relations; judge Triton Coll. Student Achievement Recognition Program. Mem. Am. Justinian Soc. Jurists (1st v.p.), Am., Ill. State, Chgo., West Suburban bar assns., Justinian Soc. Lawyers. Contbr. articles to legal jours. Home: 520 Rose Dr Melrose Park IL 60160 Office: 2800 Chicago Civic Center Chicago IL 60602 Tel (312) 443-8088

BUBANY, CHARLES PHILLIP, b. Kirksville, Mo., Dec. 20, 1940; B.A., St. Ambrose Coll., 1962; J.D., Washington U., St. Louis, 1965. Admitted to Mo. bar, 1966; asst. prof. law U. W.Va., Morgantown, 1966-67; legal specialist JAG, U.S. Navy, 1967-70; asso. firm Goldstein & Price, St. Louis, 1970-71; prof. Tex. Tech. U. Sch. Law, 1971—. Mem. Tex. Criminal Def. Lawyers Assn. (affiliate). Contbr. articles in field to legal jours. Home: 3519 78th Dr Lubbock TX 79423 Office: Tex Tech U Sch Law Lubbock TX 79409 Tel (806) 742-3785

BUCCI, EARL MICHAEL, b. Schenectady, Nov. 15, 1926; A.B., Brown U., 1948; J.D. N.Y. U., 1954. Admitted to N.Y. bar, 1954, U.S. Supreme Ct. bar, 1962; individual practice law, Schenectady, 1954—; asso. counsel, pres. pro tem N.Y. State Senate, 1965. Pres. bd. dirs. Schenectady Symphony Orch. Assn., 1965-68, Schenectady Sr. Citizens Center, 1966-68; pres. Schenectady Torch Internat., 1974-76. Mem. Estate Planning Council Eastern N.Y. (exec. com. 1976—), Am. (chmn. real property, probate and trust sect. com. administrn. and distribution decedents' estates 1970-75) N.Y. State (exec. com. sect. trusts and estates 1975—) bar assns., Brown Club of Northeastern N.Y. (pres. 1967-69), Phi Delta Phi. Contbr. articles to legal jours. Office: 311 State St Schenectady NY 12305 Tel (518) 372-6414

BUCHANAN, JOSEPH MARION, b. Carrollton, Miss., July 30, 1932; B.S., U. So. Miss., 1958; LL.B., Jackson Sch. Law, 1965. Admitted to Miss. bar, 1966; mem. firm Buchanan, Haltom & Saucier, Indianola, Miss., 1966—, sr. partner, 1969—. Commr., Little League Baseball, 1968-75; bd. dirs. Sunflower County Progress, 1969-74. Mem. Miss., Sunflower County (past sec.-treas.) bar assns., Miss. Trial Lawyers Assn. Home: 21 Morningside Dr Indianola MS 38751 Office: 210 2d St Indianola MS 38751 Tel (601) 887-4222

BUCHANAN, MARVIN CHARLES, b. Wenatchee, Wash., Dec. 27, 1914; B.A., U. Wash., 1939, J.D., 1942. Admitted to Wash. bar, 1944, U.S. Dist. Ct. bar, 1973; spl. agent FBI, 1942-66; individual practice law, Oak Harbor, Wash., 1972—; judge U.S. Dist. Ct. Island County (Wash.), Oak Harbor, 1974—, Municipal Ct. City of Oak Harbor, 1974—; mem. Regional Law and Justice Planning Com. Mem. Wash., Island County bar assns., Wash. Trial Lawyers Assn., Magistrates Assn. Wash., Am. Judicature Soc., Soc. Former Spl. Agents FBI. Home: 6451 60th St NW #53 Oak Harbor WA 98277 Office: 4086 400th Ave W Oak Harbor WA 98277 Tel (206) 675-6686

BUCHANAN, VICTOR WAYNE, b. Albany, Ga., Mar. 13, 1942; A.B., U. N.C. at Chapel Hill, 1964, J.D., 1968. Admitted to N.C. bar, 1968; law clk. N.C. Ct. Appeals, Raleigh, 1968-69; asso. firm Uzzell & Dumont, Asheville, N.C., 1969-71; mem. firm Patla, Straus, Robinson & Moore, Asheville, 1971—. Mem. Buncombe County, N.C., Am. bar assns. Office: PO Box 7625 Asheville NC 28807 Tel (704) 255-7641

BUCHBINDER, MARK, b. Bklyn., June 10, 1943; B.A., U. Miami, 1964, M.S. in Urban & Regional Planning, 1976; LL.B., Columbia U., 1967. Admitted to Fla. bar, 1967; vol. Vista, Broward County, Fla., 1967-68; atty. Fla. Rural Legal Services, Broward County, 1968-69; individual practice law, Miami, 1969—. Pres. Greater Miami Epilepsy Found.; pres. Fla. Epilepsy Found., 1976-77. Mem. Am. Bar Assn., Fla. Bar, Am. Inst. Planners. Home: 8600 SW 118th St Miami FL 33156 Office: Suite 201 9300 S Dadeland Blvd Miami FL 33156 Tel (305) 667-4821

BUCHHEIT, MARK DOMINIC, b. Festina, Iowa, Apr. 27, 1923; A.B., U. Iowa, 1950, LL.B., 1950; J.D., Cath. U. Am., 1953. Admitted to Iowa bar, 1950, U.S. Supreme Ct. bar, 1959; spl. investigator Employers Mut. of Wausau, Wis., 1950-51; mem. firm Miller, Pearson and Buchheit, Decorah, Iowa, 1951-53, individual practice law, W. Union, Iowa, 1953—; Fayette County atty., 1955-60; lobbyist for Iowa Coin Laundry Assn., 1974—. Judge adv. N.E. Iowa 40 & 8, 1963, Iowa VFW, 1965-67; adv. W. Union Council K.C., 1956; internat. counselor Lions Internat., 1963, dist. gov., 1962-63; Fayette County comdr. Am. Legion, 1953-54; pub. relations chmn. C. of C., 1956-57; Iowa comdr. VFW, 1969-70; v.p. Cath. Lawyers Guild Archdiocese Dubuque, 1957-58. Mem. Fayette County, Iowa Bar Assns., Iowa Defense Counsel Assn., Def. Research Inst. Recipient certificate appreciation, Lions Club, 1962; contbr. articles to publs. Home and Office: 113 1/2 N Vine St West Union IA 52175 Tel (319) 422-5174

BUCHOLTZ, ALAN HOWARD, b. Bklyn., Aug. 1, 1937; A.B., Utica Coll. of Syracuse U., 1959; J.D., U. Denver, 1965. Admitted to Colo. bar, 1965; with Harry L. Arkin, Esq., Denver, 1965-66; individual practice law, Denver, 1966-68; partner firm Quiat, Bucholtz and Bull, Denver, 1969—; adj. prof. law. U. Denver, 1966—. Pres. Virginia Vale Improvement Assn., 1967-68. Mem. Am., Colo., Denver bar assns., Colo. Trial Lawyers Assn. (pres.-elect), Assn. Trail Lawyers Am. Contbr. articles to legal jours. Office: 1776 First Nat Bank Bldg Denver CO 80202 Tel (303) 623-1776

BUCK, ROBERT EWING, b. Gallipolis, Ohio, Mar. 15, 1946; B.B.A., Ohio U., 1968; J.D., Ohio State U., 1971. Admitted to Ohio bar, 1972; asso. firm Bernard V. Fultz, Pomeroy, Ohio, 1972-74; individual practice law, Pomeroy, 1974—; judge Meigs County (Ohio) Ct., 1975—. Vice pres. Gallia, Jackson, Meigs Counties (Ohio) Community Mental Health Center; bd. dirs. S.E. Ohio Regional Council on Alcoholism, Council on Aging, Pomeroy, Ret. Sr. Vol. Program, Pomeroy; fund chmn. Meigs County council Boy Scouts Am., Easter Seals, Meigs County. Mem. Ohio Bar Assn. Recipient Superior Jud. Service award Ohio Supreme Ct., 1975, 76. Home: 129 Mulberry Ave Pomeroy OH 45769 Office: 104 Mulberry Ave Pomeroy OH 45769 Tel (614) 992-5847

BUCKLE, WILLIAM THOMAS, b. Houston, Apr. 8, 1945; B.A., Rice U.; J.D., U. Tex. Admitted to Tex. bar, 1970; staff Travis County (Tex.) Legal Aid & Defender Soc., 1970-73, Tex. Air Control Bd., 1973-75; Tex. Atty. Gen's. Office, Austin, 1975—. Bd. dir. Travis County Legal Aid Soc., 1974—. Mem. Travis County Bar Assn. (dir. 1973-74). Tel (512) 475-4143

BUCKLES, EARL C., JR., b. Omaha, Sept. 11, 1942; B.A., U. Omaha, 1967; J.D., U. Nebr., 1970. Admitted to Nebr. bar, 1970, Mo. bar, 1970, Kans. bar, 1972; asso. firm Smith, Schwegler, Swartzman & Winger, Kansas City, Mo., 1970-76; atty. Gen. Electric Credit Corp., Kansas City, 1976—; municipal judge, Shawnee, Kans., 1972-74; instr. Rockhurst Coll., Kansas City, 1975-76. Home: 6121 Ballentine Ave Shawnee KS 66203 Office: 9233 Ward Pkwy Kansas City MO Tel (816) 363-4431

BUCKLEY, COLLEEN RUTH, b. LeMars, Iowa, June 22, 1930; B.A., Briar Cliff Coll., 1952; J.D., Creighton U., 1962; H.L.D., Coll. St. Mary, Omaha, 1976. Tchr. pub. jr. high sch., Atlantic, Iowa, 1952-54, pub. schs., Sterling, Ill., 1955-59, Omaha Dist. 66, 1958-59; social worker Good Shepard Home for Cath. Charities, Sioux City, Iowa, 1954-55; admitted to Iowa bar, 1962, Nebr. bar, 1962; atty., dir. Legal Aid Soc. of Omaha, 1963-68; dep. county atty. Douglas County (Nebr.), 1968-72; judge Douglas County Separate Juvenile Ct., 1973—. Bd. dirs. Omaha Downtown Br. YMCA, Christ Child Soc., Omaha, Woodson Center, Omaha; bd. govs. Boys Clubs of Omaha. Mem. Nebr. Bar Assn., Iowa Bar, Nat. Council Juvenile Ct. Judges. Office: 600 Courthouse Omaha NE 68102 Tel (402) 444-7888

BUCKLEY, EMMETT BRUCE, b. Miami, Fla., Feb. 1, 1945; B.S., Fla. State U., 1967; J.D. (coll. scholar), 1970. Admitted to Fla. bar, 1970; spl. agt., research specialist Fla. Dept. Criminal Law Enforcement, Tallahassee, 1970, 72-74; atty. Fla. Dept. Law Enforcement, Tallahassee, 1971; cts. planner Fla. Bur. Criminal Justice Planning, Tallahassee, 1974—; mem. com. automated legal research Project SEARCH, 1976. Mem. Am. Bar Assn., Am. Judicature Soc., Nat. Dist. Atty's Assn., Fla. Bar (reporter com. on statewide prosecution function 1976). Home: 4924 Lester Rd Tallahassee FL 32301 Office: 620 S Meridian St Tallahassee FL 32304 Tel (904) 878-2585

BUCKLEY, HELEN ANN, b. San Francisco, June 12, 1926; A.B., U. Calif., Berkeley, 1951, LL.B., 1954. Admitted to Calif. bar, 1955, D.C. bar, 1956, U.S. Supreme Ct. bar, 1958; asso. in law U. Calif., Berkeley, 1954-55; trial atty. tax div. appellate sec. U.S. Dept. Justice, Washington, 1955-60; tax counsel Hunt Foods & Industries Inc., (name changed to Norton Simon Inc.), Fullerton, Calif., 1961-63; partner firm Pacht, Ross, Warne, Bernhard, Los Angeles, 1963-71; counsel Norton Simon Inc., Los Angeles, 1971-74; instr. Coll. Law, U. So. Calif., Los Angeles, 1973; prof. law U. Iowa, Iowa City, 1974—; vis. prof. law Hasting Coll. of Law, U. Calif., San Francisco, summer 1976. Mem. Am., D.C., Calif. bar assns., ACLU, NOW. Mem. editorial rev. bd. U. Iowa Press, 1975—. Home: 725 N Linn St Iowa City IA 52240 Office: Coll Law Univ Iowa Iowa City IA 52242 Tel (319) 353-3433

BUCKLEY, RICHARD ROBERT, b. Charleston, W.Va., Dec. 21, 1932; student Duke U., 1951-52; B.S., U. Ga., 1958, J.D., 1960. Admitted to Ga. bar, 1960; law clk. to judge Fulton County (Ga.) Superior Ct., 1960; individual practice law, Tifton, Ga., 1961—; judge Recorders Ct., City of Tifton, 1969—. Chmn., Tifton-Tifton County Zoning Bd., 1966—. Mem. Tifton County, Ga. bar assns., Ga. Trial Lawyers Assn., Jaycees (dist. v.p. 1962-63). Home: 408 W 18th St Tifton GA 31794 Office: 409 Love Ave Tifton GA 31794

BUCKLIN, DONALD THOMAS, b. Providence, July 11, 1938; B.S., Providence Coll., 1960; J.D. cum laude, Am. U., 1967. Admitted to D.C. bar, 1968, Va. bar, 1968, U.S. Supreme Ct. bar, 1971; law clk. to judge U.S. Dist. Ct., Washington, 1967-68; asst. U.S. atty. Dept. Justice, Washington, 1968-71; partner firm Rowley & Scott, Washington, 1971-74, Truitt, Fabrikant, Bucklin & Lenzner, Washington, 1974-76, Wald, Harkrader & Ross, Washington, 1977—. Mem. Am., D.C., Va. bar assns. Named Young Lawyer of Year D.C. Bar Assn., 1975. Office: 1320 19th St NW Washington DC 20036 Tel (202) 296-2121

BUCKLIN, LEONARD HERBERT, b. Mpls., Apr. 17, 1933; B.S. in Law, U. Minn., 1955, J.D., 1957. Admitted to Minn. bar, 1957, N.D. bar, 1960; law clk. Minn. Supreme Ct., 1957; partner firm Larson, Loevinger, Lindquist, Freeman & Fraser, Mpls., 1957-60, Zuger & Bucklin, Bismarck, N.D., 1960—. Bd. dirs. United Fund of Bismarck, 1969-70; deacon First Presbyterian Ch., 1967-70, elder, 1974—. Mem. Burleigh County (pres. 1973), 4th Jud. Dist., N.D. (chmn. civil procedure com. 1965-75, chmn. specialization com. 1976—), Am. bar assns., Am. Trial Lawyers Assn., Internat. Acad. Trial Lawyers, Internat. Soc. Barristers, Order of Coif, Phi Delta Phi, Delta Sigma Rho. Author: Civil Practice of North Dakota, 1976. Home: 1021 Crescent Ln Bismarck ND 58501 Office: PO Box 1695 Bismarck ND 58501 Tel (701) 223-2711

BUCKMAN, JAMES EDWARD, b. N.Y.C., Oct. 2, 1944; A.B., Fordham Coll., 1966; J.D., Yale, 1969. Admitted to N.Y. bar, 1969, Ga. bar, 1974; asso. firm Dewey, Ballantine, Bushby, Palmer & Wood, N.Y.C., 1969-72; asst. gen. counsel Gable Industries, Inc., Atlanta, 1972-74; asso., then partner firm Troutman, Sanders, Lockerman & Ashmore, Atlanta, 1974—. Mem. Am., N.Y. State, Ga. State, Atlanta bar assns. Office: 1400 Chandler Bldg Atlanta GA 30303 Tel (404) 658-8000

BUCKMAN, MELVIN JOSEPH, b. Phila., Aug. 24, 1930; B.S. in Econs., U. Pa., 1951; LL.B. cum laude, Harvard, 1954. Admitted to Pa. bar, 1955, D.C. bar, 1954; law clk. City of Phila., 1954; legal assistance clk. Ft. Chaffee, Ark., 1956; atty. adviser U.S. Small Bus. Adminstrn., Phila., 1957-59; gen. lawyer Gen. Electric Co., Phila. and Valley Forge, Pa., 1959-64, Office of Gen. Counsel, Trade Regulation Legal Service, N.Y.C., 1964-65; asso. firm Mesirov, Gelman, Jaffe & Cramer, Phila., 1965-67, partner, 1967—. Dir. Temple Beth Hillel, Wynnewood, Pa.; chmn., legal counsel, dir. Developmental Center for Autistic Children, Phila.; vice chmn. United Way, Phila. Mem. Am., Pa., Phila. bar assns., Harvard Law Sch. Assn. Office: 15th Floor The Fidelity Bldg Philadelphia PA 19109 Tel (215) 893-5034

BUCZKOWSKI, ARTHUR WALTER, b. Lathrup Village, Mich., Oct. 27, 1930; LL.B., J.D., U. Detroit, 1956. Admitted to Mich. bar, 1957, U.S. Supreme Ct. bar, 1969; asso. firm Bernstein & Bernstein, Detroit, 1959; with Ford Motor Co., Dearborn, Mich., 1955—; individual practice law, Lathrup Village, 1968—. Mem. Mich., Am. bar assns., Comml. Law League Am. Office: 18485 Dolores Ave Lathrup Village MI 48076 Tel (313) 559-4275

BUDA, JAMES BERNARD, b. South Bend, Ind., Mar. 9, 1947; B.A. in Polit. Sci., magna cum laude, Ball State U., 1969; J.D., U. Notre Dame, 1973. Admitted to Ind. bar, 1973; gen. counsel Morgan Drive-Away, Inc., Elkhart, Ind., 1973—. Mem. Am. (adminstrv. law and anti-trust sects.), Ind. (adminstrv. law, young lawyers and corporate counsel sects.) bar assns., Jaycees, Motor Carrier Lawyers Assn., ICC Practitioners Assn., Delta Nu Alpha. Home: 26891 County Rd 4 W Elkhart IN 46514 Office: 28651 US 20 W Elkhart IN 46514 Tel (219) 295-2200

BUDD, RUTH RAHN, b. Furth, Germany, June 15, 1936; B.A., Smith Coll., 1958; student U. Geneva, 1956-57; M.A. in Teaching, Harvard, 1959; LL.B., Boston Coll., 1968. Admitted to Mass. bar, 1968; with Mass. Atty. Gen.'s Office, 1968-69; asso. firm Michaels, Adler & Wilcon, Boston, 1969-71, Frank & Shubow, Boston, 1972-73, Choate, Hall & Stewart, Boston, 1973—. Counsel New Eng. Region com. law and social action Am. Jewish Congress, 1971-73; mem. Lexington (Mass.) Town Meeting, 1970-73. Fellow Am. Acad. Matrimonial Lawyers (bd. mgrs. Mass. chpt.); mem. Am., Boston (council) bar assns., Mass. Assn. Women Lawyers, Phi Beta Kappa, Order of Coif. Home: 24 Percy Rd Lexington MA 02173 Office: 28 State St Boston MA 02109 Tel (617) 227-5020

BUDE, GEORGE JAMES, b. St. Louis, Apr. 15, 1937; A.B., Washington U., 1958, J.D., 1963. Admitted to Mo. bar, 1963; asso. firm Ziercher, Hocker, Tzinberg, Human & Michenfelder and predecessors, St. Louis, 1963-69, partner, 1969—. Solicitor, Old News Boys; trustee St. Louis chpt. Cystic Fibrosis Research Found., 1967-72; solicitor, capt. and chmn. Legal sect. St. Louis County United Fund. Mem. Am., Mo. (chmn. sch. law com.), St. Louis County (pres. 1973) bar assns. Named Outstanding Young Lawyer of St. Louis County, St. Louis County Bar Assn., 1971; recipient Distinguished Alumnus award Hancock Place Sch. Dist., 1973. Home: 7399 Norwood St St Louis MO 63130 Office: 130S Bemiston St Suite 405 St Louis MO 63105 Tel (314) 727-5822

BUDER, GUSTAVUS A., JR., b. St. Louis, Mar. 14, 1901; LL.B., Washington U., St. Louis, 1922. Admitted to Mo. bar, 1922, U.S. Supreme Ct. bar, 1927; asso. firm Buder & Buder, St. Louis, 1922-46; individual practice law, St. Louis, 1946—. Mem. adv. bd. Salvation Army, 1938—. Mem. Am., Mo., St. Louis bar assns., St. Louis Law Library Assn. (past pres., dir.). Recipient William Booth award Salvation Army, 1967, Torch of Freedom award Mo. Young Ams. for Freedom, 1975. Home: 29 Upper Ladue Rd St Louis MO 63124 Office: 7 N 7th St St Louis MO 63101 Tel (314) 621-2808

BUDIC, ROBERT MARK, b. W. Allis, Wis., Nov. 28, 1942; B.S., U. Wis., 1971; J.D., Marquette U., 1972. Admitted to Wis. bar, 1972, U.S. Tax Ct. bar, 1973, U.S. Supreme Ct. bar, 1975, U.S. Ct. Appeals, 1977; partner firm Rausch & Budic, West Allis, Wis., 1972-73;

individual practice law, West Allis, 1973—. Bd. mgrs. S.W. Suburban YMCA, West Allis. Mem. Wis., Am., Milwaukee County, Waukesha, Ozaukee County bar assns., U. Wis. Alumni Assn., Marquette Alumni Assn., Phi Alpha Delta. Home: 13928 N Birchwood Ln Mequon WI 53092 Office: 7231 W Greenfield Ave Suite 208 West Allis WI 53214 Tel (414) 475-1900

BUE, CARL OLAF, JR., b. Chgo., Mar. 27, 1922; A.A., U. Chgo., 1942; student U. Rome, 1945; Ph.B., Northwestern U., 1951; LL.B., U. Tex., 1954. Admitted to Tex. bar, 1954; asso. firm Royston, Rayzor & Cook, Houston, 1954-58, partner, 1958-70; judge U.S. Dist. Ct., So. Dist. Tex., Houston Div., 1970—; lectr. in field. Mem. Houston, Fed., Am. bar assns., State Bar Tex., Maritime Law Assn. U.S., Am. Judicature Soc., English Speaking Union, Houston Philos. Soc., Alpha Delta Phi, Phi Alpha Delta. Contbr. articles to legal jours. Home: 338 Knipp Rd Houston TX 77024 Office: 9535 Fed Bldg 515 Rusk Ave Houston TX 77002 Tel (713) 226-5471

BUELL, EUGENE FRANKLIN, b. Elrama, Pa., Dec. 3, 1916; B.S., St. Vincent's Coll., 1938; postgrad. Carnegie Inst. Tech., 1938-40, U. Pitts., 1941, Johns Hopkins U., 1942; J.D., Duquesne U., 1944. Admitted to D.C. bar, 1949, U.S. Patent Office bar, 1948, Canadian Patent Office bar, 1949, U.S. Supreme Ct. bar, 1953; asso. firm Stebbins, Blenko & Webb, Pitts., 1945-48; partner firm Blenko, Leonard & Buell, and predecessors, Pitts., 1949-73; pres. firm Blenko, Buell, Ziesenheim & Beck, Pitts., 1973—; pres. Tartan Industries, Inc., Duncansville, Pa., 1964—; chmn. bd. dirs. Schuyler Devel. Co., Reading, Pa., 1967—; sec. Porta-Drill, Inc., Pitts., 1965—; dir. Metaltronics, Inc., Pitts.; instr. patent law U. Pitts., 1954-59, adj. prof. law, 1959—. Pres., Richland Com. for Better Govt., 1950-54; bd. dirs. Babcock Sch. Dist., Allegheny County, Pa., 1961-67; treas. Richland Township Sch. Authority 1974—. Mem. Am., Pa., Allegheny County bar assns., Assn. Bar City N.Y. (asso.), Engrs. Soc. Western Pa., Am., Pitts. patent law assns., Inter-Am. bar Assn., Am. Arbitration Assn., U.S. Trademark Assn., Chartered Inst. Patent Agents, Licensing Exec. Socs., Order of Coif. Founder, editor The Richlander Newspaper, 1950-64. Home: Box 418 RD 2 Gibsonia PA 15044 Office: 301 5th Ave Pittsburgh PA 15222 Tel (412) 471-1590

BUELOW, HENRY DEAN, b. Los Angeles, Sept. 11, 1932; B.S., Mcalester Coll., 1956; LL.B., William Mitchell Coll. Law, 1962, J.D., 1969. Admitted to Minn. bar, 1962, Mont. bar, 1974; individual practice law, Mpls., 1962-74; Miles City, Mont., 1974—. Mem. Am., Minn., Mont. trial lawyers assns., Am. Arbitration Assn., VFW. Home: 413 1/2 Main St Miles City MT 59301 Office: 501 Main St Miles City MT 59301 Tel (406) 232-5865

BUENZLI, WILLIAM LEWIS, b. Madison, Wis., Sept. 2, 1912; Ph.B., U. Wis., 1934, LL.B., 1936. Admitted to Wis. bar, 1936, U.S. Dist. Ct. Wis. bar, 1936; practiced in Madison, 1936-61; acting judge Wis. Superior Ct., 1940-61; commr. Dane County (Wis.) Ct., 1951-61; judge Dane County Criminal and Traffic Ct., 1962—; founder, dir. Traffic Safety Sch. of Dane County; co-founder, dir. Group Dynamics Traffic Safety Sch. Mem. Dane County Bar Assn., State Bar Wis., County Judges of Dane County (chmn.). Recipient awards for conducting spl. safety sch. in Dane County Govs. Wis., 1964, 72. Home: 4924 Whitcomb Dr Madison WI 53711 Office: 210 Monona Ave Madison WI 53703 Tel (608) 271-0044

BUERGENTHAL, THOMAS, b. Lubochna, Czechoslovakia, May 11, 1934; B.A., Bethany (W.Va.) Coll., 1957; J.D., N.Y.U., 1960; LL.M., Harvard, 1961, S.J.D., 1968. Admitted to N.Y. bar, 1961; instr. in legal method U. Pa., Phila., 1961-62; prof. law State U.N.Y., Buffalo, 1962-75; prof. internat. law U. Tex., Austin, 1975—; chmn. U.S. Govt. delegation to UNESCO meeting of experts on internat. edn., 1974; mem. exec. com. U.S. Nat. Commn. for UNESCO, 1976—. Mem. Am. Soc. Internat. Law, Am. Fgn. Law Assn. Author: Law-Making in the International Civil Aviation Organization, 1969; (with L.B. Sohn) International Protection of Human Rights, 1973; (with J.V. Torney) International Human Rights and International Education, 1976; editor Am. Jour. Internat. Law., contbr. artilces legal jours. Home: 6103 Highland Hills Dr Austin TX 78731 Office: Sch Law U Tex 2500 Red River St Austin TX 78705 Tel (512) 471-5151

BUESSER, ANTHONY CARPENTER, b. Detroit, Oct. 15, 1929; B.A. in English with honors, U. Mich., 1952, J.D., 1960. Admitted to Mich. bar, 1961; asso. firm Chase, Goodenough & Buesser, Detroit, 1961-66; partner firm Buesser, Buesser, Snyder & Blank, Detroit, also Bloomfield Hills, 1966—. Trustee, sec. Detroit Country Day Sch., Birmingham, Mich., 1970—. Recipient Avery Hopwood award Major Fiction U. Mich., 1953. Mem. Am., Mich., Detroit (sec. 1972-73, pres. 1976-77), Oakland County bar assns., Am. Judicature Soc., Am. Arbitration Assn. (arbitrator), Alpha Delta Phi, Phi Delta Phi. Home: 2204 1300 E Lafayette St Detroit MI 48207 Office: 4100 Penobscot Bldg Detroit MI 48226 Tel (313) 962-4370*

BUETENS, MELVIN WILLIAM, b. N.Y.C., Mar. 16, 1927; student Queens Coll., Pa. State U.; LL.B., Syracuse U., 1950. Admitted to N.Y. bar, 1950, Fla. bar, 1975; practice law, Rochester, N.Y. Mem. N.Y., Fla., Monroe County bar assns. Office: 505 Reynolds Arcade Bldg Rochester NY 14614 Tel (716) 325-2418

BUFALINO, CHARLES J., JR., b. Pittston, Pa., Apr. 17, 1931; B.S., Villanova Coll., 1952; LL.B., U. Pa., 1955. Admitted to Pa. bar, 1956, U.S. Supreme Ct. bar, 1964; law clk. Luzerne County (Pa.) Common Pleas Ct., 1956-61; spl. asst. atty. gen. State of Pa., Wilkes-Barre, 1961-69; mem. firm Charles J. Bufalino, Sr., 1969-70; recorder of deeds Luzerne County; referee Pa. State Workmen's Compensation; dir. West Side Bank, West Pittston. Solicitor Vis. Nurse Assn. Pittston; bd. dirs. Wyoming Valley San. Authority, Luzerne County Bd. Mental Health and Mental Retardation. Mem. Am., Pa., Luzerne County (exec. com.) bar assns., Columbus League. Office: 341 Wyoming Ave Pittston PA 18643

BUFFA, BETTE MEYER, b. St. Louis, Feb. 6, 1927; J.D., Washington U., St. Louis, 1947. Admitted to Mo. bar, 1947, U.S. Supreme Ct. bar, 1976; asso. firm Neulfoff, Millar, Tremayne & Schaeffer, St. Louis, 1947-49; corp. atty. Am. Investment Co., St. Louis, 1949-53, Monsanto Co. St. Louis, 1966—. Mem. Am., Mo., Met. St. Louis Women's (pres.) bar assns., Order of Coif. Recipient Breckenridge prize, 1947. Home: 143 Fiesta Circle Creve Coeur MO 63141 Office: 800 N Lindbergh Blvd Saint Louis MO 63166 Tel (314) 694-4306

BUFFINGTON, HERBERT LUTHER, JR., b. Nelson, Ga., Jan. 29, 1922; diploma Reinhardt Coll., 1941; A.B., U. Ga., 1946, LL.B., Atlanta Law Sch., 1945. Admitted to Ga. bar, 1942; partner law firm Vandiviere and Buffington, Canton, Ga., 1945-68; pvt. practice law, Canton, Ga., 1968-75; partner law firm Buffington and Gober, Canton, Ga., 1976—. Mem. Canton, Blue Ridge Circuit, Am. bar assns., State Bar of Ga., Am. Judicature Soc., Am. Trial Lawyers Assn., Moose Lodge, Burns Club of Atlanta, Ga. Lions Club. Home: 140 Muriel St Canton GA 30114 Office: Exec Bldg Suite 2 Main St Canton GA 30114

BUFFON, CHARLES EDWARD, b. Topeka, Kans., Sept. 8, 1939; A.B. magna cum laude, Dartmouth Coll., 1961; LL.B. cum laude, Harvard U., 1964. Admitted to D.C. bar, 1964, U.S. Supreme Ct. bar, 1971; asso. firm Covington & Burling, Washington, D.C., 1964-73, partner, 1973—; instr. seminar antitrust litigation, U. Va. Law Sch., 1968-77. Mem. Am. Bar Assn., D.C. Bar, Phi Beta Kappa. Home: 8 Oxford St Chevy Chase MD 20015 Office: 888 16th St NW Washington DC 20006 Tel (202) 452-6350

BUGBEE, (LUCIAN) WILLIS, JR., b. Southbridge, Mass., Nov. 12, 1899; student Mass. Inst. Tech., 1917-18; B.A. with honors in Physics, Oxford (Eng.) U., 1921, M.A., 1925; M.S., Purdue U., 1922; LL.B., Ind. U., 1928. Admitted to Ind. bar, 1928, Mich. bar, 1940, U.S. Supreme Ct. bar, 1940; dir. research Continental Optical Co., Indpls., 1922-30; mem. sci. bur. Bausch & Laumb Optical Co., Rochester, N.Y., 1930-32; individual practice law, Dayton, Ohio, 1932-39; partner firm Barthel & Bugbee, Detroit, 1939—; instr. Naval Res. Officers Sch., Detroit, 1954-64. Mem. funds allocation com. United Community Services, Detroit, 1966-72; treas. Meth. Children's Home Soc., Detroit, 1965-72. Mem. Am. Bar Assn., Am. Patent Law Assn., State Bar Mich., Engring. Soc. Detroit, AAAS, U.S. Naval Inst., Nat. Naval Affairs Com., Res. Officers Assn. U.S. Patentee; contbr. articles to optical and legal jours. Home: 1329 Joliet Pl Detroit MI 48207 Office: care Barthel & Bugbee 409 Griswold St Suite 603 Detroit MI 48226 Tel (313) 961-4115

BUGG, JOHN EUGENE, b. Durham, N.C., Aug. 27, 1944; A.B. in Econs., Duke, 1966; J.D., U. N.C., 1970. Admitted to N.C. bar, 1970; partner firm Nye, Mitchell & Bugg, Durham, 1970—. Mem. Durham City Council, 1970-75. Mem. N.C., 14th Jud. Dist. bar assns., Order of Coif. Home: 3220 Banbury Way Durham NC 27707 Office: Suite 209 Northwestern Bank Bldg Durham NC 27701 Tel (919) 688-2351

BUGLIONE, VICTOR ANTHONY, b. N.Y.C., May 22, 1932; LL.B., Bklyn. Coll. Law, 1957. Admitted to N.Y. bar, 1957; individual practice law, Bklyn., 1958-75, 76—; partner firm Cowin, Kilcommons & Buglione, Bklyn., 1975-76; counsel, dir. D'Agostino Yerow & Assos. Registered Security Analyst, 1965-71; sec., counsel Computer Circuts Corp., 1968-75; pres. Comprehensive Coverages Corp., 1972—. Home: 106-16 75th St Jamaica NY 11417 Office: 26 Court St Brooklyn NY 11242 Tel (212) MA 4-1222

BUHL, HERBERT EDWARD, III, b. Rahway, N.J., Jan. 21, 1945; B.A., U. S.C., 1967, J.D., 1970. Admitted to S.C. bar, 1970, W.Va. bar, 1970, D.C. bar, 1971; Reginald Heber Smith Community lawyer Legal Aid Soc., Charleston, W.Va., 1970-71; Reginald Heber Smith community lawyer Legal Aid Service Agency, Columbia, S.C., 1971-72, staff atty., 1972-73; partner firm Buhl, Primus & Babgy, Columbia, 1973—; staff atty. ACLU, of S.C., Columbia, 1973—; atty. Am. Friends Service Com., Columbia, 1973—. Mem. S.C. Bar, Nat. Legal Aid and Defender Assn. Home: 525 Harden St Columbia SC 29205 Office: 2016 1/2 Green St Columbia SC 29205 Tel (803) 799-3767

BUHLER, WILLIAM IVES, b. St. Paul, Jan. 31, 1930; B.S., U. Minn., 1952; J.D., U. N.Mex., 1956. Admitted to N.Mex. bar, 1957; sr. partner firm Buhler, Smith, Fitch & Stout, Truth or Consequences, N.Mex., 1972—; chmn. bd. 1st State Bank Sierra County, Truth or Consequences, 1973—. Commr., City of Truth or Consequences, 1961-65. Mem. Am. Bar Assn., Truth or Consequences-Sierra County C. of C. (pres. 1958-59), Sierra County Hist. Soc. (pres. 1969—). Home: 1800 Riverside Dr Truth or Consequences NM 87901 Office: 418 Main St Truth or Consequences NM 87901 Tel (505) 894-3031

BUIE, GEORGE ARCHIE, JR., b. Lake City, Fla., Mar. 8, 1907; LL.B., U. Fla., 1929, J.D., 1967. Admitted to Fla. bar, 1929; county atty. Columbia County (Fla.), 1930-36, county judge, 1941-69; city atty. Lake City, 1937-40, city judge, 1969-73; dir. 1st Fed. Savs. Loan Assn., Lake City, 1934—, atty., 1967—; dir. Columbia County Bank, 1960—, v.p., 1964—. Mem. Am., Fla. (bd. govs. 1947) bar assns. Office: PO Box 490 Lake City FL 32055 Tel (904) 752-5023

BUIKEMA, RONALD, b. Chgo., Aug. 2, 1939; A.B., Calvin Coll., 1961; J.D., Valparaiso U., 1964. Admitted to Ill. bar, 1964, U.S. Supreme Ct. bar, 1970; sr. partner firm Buikema & Malak, South Holland, Ill., 1966-72; partner, office mgr. firm Jacobs, Buikema & Malak, South Holland, 1972—; village atty., prosecutor Village of South Holland, 1974—. Bd. dirs. Harvey (Ill.) YMCA; active South Holland Community Chest; elder, chmn. com. bldg. and fin. Peace Christian Reformed Ch., South Holland. Mem. Am., Chgo. bar assns., Nat. Inst. Municipal Law Officers, Am. Judicature Soc., Calvin Coll. Alumni Assn. (pres. Chgo. chpt. 1971-72, nat. dir. 1972-74). Recipient Outstanding Young Man award South Holland Jaycees, 1975. Home: 1150 E 173d Pl South Holland IL 60473 Office: 16231 Wausau Ave South Holland IL 60473 Tel (312) 333-1234

BULAN, HAROLD PAUL, b. N.Y.C., July 28, 1938; B.S. in Econs., U. Pa., 1960; M.B.A., U. Mich., 1961; J.D., State U.N.Y., 1965. Admitted to N.Y. State bar, 1965; partner firm Goldstein, Navagh, Bulan & Chiari, Buffalo, 1965—. Mem. Erie County Bar Assn., Comml. Law League Am. Home: 18 Barberry Ln Williamsville NY 14221 Office: 10 Lafayette Sq Buffalo NY 14203 Tel (716) 854-1332

BULGRIN, LEILA FRANCES, b. Riverside, Calif., Nov. 16, 1924; student U. So. Calif., LL.B., 1947. Admitted to Calif. bar, 1947; asst. U.S. atty., Los Angeles, 1947-60; judge Los Angeles Municipal Ct., 1960—; practiced in Los Angeles, 1947-51. Pres. Valley Center Boys Club, Van Nuys, Calif., 1968-75. Mem. Los Angeles, San Fernando bar assns., Women Lawyers Assn., San Fernando Criminal Bar Assn., Phi Alpha Delta. Office: 6230 Sylmar St Van Nuys CA 91401 Tel (213) 787-3350

BULLARD, JAMES CLIFTON, b. Oxford, Miss., Sept. 25, 1935; B.S., U. Miss., 1956, LL.B., 1958. Admitted to Miss. bar, 1958, Mo. bar, 1958; mem. firm Dalton, Treasure & Bullard, Kennett, Mo., 1958-75; individual practice law, Kennett, 1975—; asst. atty. gen. State of Mo., 1964. Mem. Dunklin County, Mo., Am. bar assns. Home: 1601 N Lincoln St Kennett MO 63857 Office: 115 St Francis St Kennett MO 63857 Tel (314) 888-4636

BULLARD, ROBERT OLIVER, JR., b. Glens Falls, N.Y., Aug. 5, 1943; A.B., Union Coll., 1965; LL.B., Boston U., 1968. Admitted to Mass. bar, 1968; trust officer Newton Waltham Bank and Trust Co. (Mass.), 1968-70; asso. firm Gaston, Snow, Ely & Bartlett, Boston, 1971—. Mem. Boston, Mass., Am. bar assns. Home: 41 Hubbard Rd Weston MA 02193 Office: 1 Federal St Boston MA 02110

BULLARD, WILLIAM THURMAN, JR., b. Boulder, Colo., Dec. 1, 1942; B.A., U. Colo., 1964; M.J., Northwestern U., 1965; J.D., U. Colo., 1968. Admitted to Colo. bar, 1968, Calif. bar, 1972; partner firm Robinson, Sullivan & Bullard, Boulder, 1970-72; dep. county counsel Fairfield County (Calif.), 1972-74; asst. city atty. Santa Rosa (Calif.), 1974—; law editor Clearing House, 1971. Mem. League Calif. Cities (conflicts of interest com.). Home: 427 Scenic Ave San Anselmo CA 94960 Office: 100 Santa Rose Ave Santa Rosa CA 95403 Tel (707) 528-5261

BULLION, BRUCE THOMAS, JR., b. Little Rock, Feb. 13, 1914; student Little Rock Jr. Coll., 1931-32, Washington and Lee U., 1935; J.D., U. Ark., 1938. Admitted to Ark. bar, 1938, U.S. Supreme Ct. bar, 1952. asso. Bruce T. Bullion, Sr., Little Rock, 1938-42; chief atty. Ark. Revenue Dept., Little Rock, 1946-48; mem. firm Bailey, Warren & Bullion, Little Rock, 1948-58, Warren & Bullion, 1958—; chancellor 1st Circuit Chancery Ct., State of Ark., 1976—. Bd. dirs. Vis. Nurses Assn., Little Rock chpt. NCCJ; bd. advisors Little Rock Jr. League. Mem. Am., Ark. (pres. 1964-65), Pulaski County bar assns. Mem. Ark. Law Rev., 1936-38. Home: 5411 Edgewood Rd Little Rock AR 72207 Office: Pulaski County Courthouse Little Rock AR 72201 Tel (501) 374-0254

BULLOCK, BRUCE STANLEY, b. Kissimee, Fla., Oct. 29, 1933; B.A., U. Fla., 1955, J.D., 1962. Admitted to Fla. bar, 1962; asso. firm Marks, Gray, Conroy & Gibbs and predecessor, Jacksonville, Fla., 1962-66, partner, 1967-73; partner firm Bullock & Alexander, Profl. Assn., Jacksonville, 1973-74; pres. firm Bullock, Sharp & Childs, Profl. Assn., Jacksonville, 1974—. Pres. South Ponte Vedra Assn., South Ponte Vedra Beach, Fla., 1974-75. Mem. Fla. Bar, Jacksonville Am. bar assns. Home: 10740 Scott Mill Rd Jacksonville FL 32217 Office: Suite 105 4077 Woodcock Dr Jacksonville FL 32207 Tel (904) 396-7722

BULMAN, LEONARD ZINNAMON, b. Washington, Dec. 3, 1933; B.A., U. Md., 1956; J.D., George Washington U., 1960. Admitted to D.C. bar, 1960, Md. bar, 1961; individual practice law, Washington, 1961-72, Annapolis, Md., 1972—. Mem. Am., Md., Anne Arundel County, D.C. bar assns. Office: 155 Duke of Gloucester St Annapolis MD 21401 Tel (301) 268-4887

BUMPASS, RONALD EUGENE, b. Lubbock, Tex., Jan. 6, 1948; B.S. in Pub. Adminstrn., U. Ark., 1970, J.D., 1974. Admitted to Ark. bar, 1974; individual practice law, Fayetteville, Ark., 1974—; lectr. dept. polit. sci. U. Ark., Fayetteville, 1976. Mem. Bd. Housing Appeals, City of Fayetteville, 1975—. Mem. Am., Ark., Washington County bar assns., Nat. Assn. Criminal Def. Lawyers, Fayetteville C. of C. (legis. action com.). Home: 790 Longview Acres St Fayetteville AR 72701 Office: Suite 212 17 E Center St Fayetteville AR 72701 Tel (501) 521-3172

BUMSTEAD, JACOB FRANKLIN, b. Trinity, Tex., May 5, 1936; B.A. cum laude, U. Houston, 1958, J.D. cum laude, 1960. Admitted to Tex. bar, 1960, U.S. Supreme Ct. bar, 1963, U.S. Tax Ct. bar, 1966; trial staff, criminal div. U.S. Dept. Justice, Washington, 1960-64, tax div, 1964-66; asst. U.S. atty. for Eastern Tex., Beaumont, 1966-69; dir. compliance sect., comptroller currency, U.S. Treasury Dept., Washington, 1969-71; individual practice law, Houston, 1971-74, Livingston, Tex., 1974—. Mem. Fed., Houston, Jefferson County bar assns., Delta Theta Phi, Order of Barons. Home: Box 4050 Route 8 Livingston TX 77351 Office: Rebel Plaza PO Box 597 Livingston TX 77351 Tel (713) 967-4969

BUNDLIE, ORDNER THORWALD, JR., b. Duluth, Minn., Oct. 24, 1919; B.S., U. Minn., 1940, LL.B., 1947. Admitted to Minn. bar, 1948; partner firm Bundlie and Bundlie, Pipestone, Minn., 1948-56, 60-70; asst. atty. gen. State of Minn., St. Paul, 1956-60; partner firm Bundlie & Trygstad, Pipestone, 1971-76; county judge Pipestone County, 1976—; pub. defender 5th Jud. Dist. Minn., 1967-76. Chmn. Pipestone County ARC, 1950-56; sec. Pipestone YMCA, 1962—; pres. 1st Lutheran Ch. Pipestone, 1965-66, sec., 1970-76, deacon, 1966-68, trustee, 1968-70. Mem. Minn., 13th Dist. (past pres., v.p., sec.) bar assns. Home: 23 Skyway Pk Pipestone MN 56164 Office: Courthouse Pipestone MN 56164 Tel (507) 825-4603

BUNDY, SUSAN LOUISE, b. Lebanon, Va., Oct. 16, 1944; B.A., Lynchburg Coll., 1967; J.D., Coll. William and Mary, 1971. Admitted to Va. bar, 1971; individual practice law, Tazewell, Va., 1971-74, Lebanon, Va., 1974-76; judge juvenile and domestic relations 29th Judicial Dist., Russell, Dickenson and Bachanan counties, Va., 1976—. Home: Rosedale VA 24266 Office: Dist Ct Clk's Officer Lebanon VA 24266 Tel (703) 889-1811

BUNKS, ABE, b. Mt. Vernon, N.Y., Sept. 27, 1933; B.S., N.Y.U., 1955, LL.B., 1958. Admitted to N.Y. State bar, 1958; Partner firm Danzig, Bunks, & Silk, N.Y.C. Mem. Representative Town Meeting, Westport, Conn., 1968-75. Mem. N.Y. State Bar. Assn., N.Y. County Lawyers Assn., Am., N.Y. State trial lawyers assns. Office: 401 Broadway New York City NY 10013 Tel (212) 966-1545

BUNN, EDWARD DEVERE, b. Miami, Fla., July 26, 1936; LL.B., Stetson Coll., 1965; LL.M., George Washington U., 1970. Admitted to Fla. bar, 1964, D.C. bar, 1965, Va. bar, 1975; spl. asst. to atty. gen. Fla., Tallahassee, 1965; legis. advisor U.S. Dept. Justice, Washington, 1965-68; practice law, Arlington and Bailey's Crossroads, Va. Author: Presidential War Powers, 1972. Tel (703) 820-3300 or 525-7555

BUNN, ROBERT BURGESS, b. Boise, Idaho, May 31, 1933; A.B. cum laude, Harvard, 1955, LL.B., 1961. Admitted to Hawaii bar, 1961; partner firm Cades, Schutte, Fleming & Wright, and predecessors, Honolulu, 1961—. Mem. Am., Hawaii bar assns. Home: 2493 Makiki Heights Dr Honolulu HI 96822 Office: POB 939 17th FL 165 S King St Honolulu HI 96808 Tel (808) 531-7232

BUNN, ROBERT PHILLIP, b. Washington, Jan. 4, 1946; B.A., Morgan State Coll., 1967; M.P.A., Harvard U., 1971, J.D., 1971. Admitted to Mass. bar, 1971, Md. bar, 1972, D.C. bar, 1972; law clk. to U.S. Circuit judge, Balt., 1971-72; since practiced in Washington, asso. firm Arent, Fox, Kintner, Plotkin & Kahn, 1972-76, Danzansky, Dickey, Tydings, Quint & Gordon, 1976—. Mem. Am. (depreciation com.), Mass., Fed. bar assns., D.C. Unified Bar (lectr.). Home: 10904 Citreon Ct Gaithersburg MD 20760 Office: 1120 Connecticut Ave NW Washington DC 20036 Tel (202) 857-4080

BUNNAGE, MILFORD ALAN, b. Los Angeles, Jan. 23, 1936; A.A., U. Calif., Los Angeles, 1956, B.A., 1957, LL.B., 1960. Admitted to Calif. bar, 1961; dist. atty. Los Angeles County, 1960; mem. firm Freshman, Marantz & Comsky, Beverly Hills, Calif., 1963-64; individual practice law, Beverly Hills, 1964—. Mem. Am., Beverly Hills, W. Hollywood, Los Angeles County bar assns., Assn. Bus. Trial Lawyers, Los Angeles Trial Lawyers Assn., Beverly Hills Jr. C. of C.

(pres. 1967-68, Phi Alpha Delta. Office: 8383 Wilshire Blvd #552 Beverly Hills CA 90211 Tel (213) 655-3450

BURBY, WILLIAM E., b. Niles, Mich., Dec. 25, 1893; A.B., U. Mich., 1917, J.D., 1934; LL.D., Calif. Western U., 1976. Admitted to Mich. bar, 1924, Calif. bar, 1927, U.S. Supreme Ct. bar, 1939; prof. law Notre Dame U., 1922-24; prof. U. N.D. Sch. of Law, 1924-26; prof. law U. So. Calif., Los Angeles, 1926-64; prof. law Calif. Western U., 1964—. Home: 5771 Rutgers Rd La Jolla CA 92037 Tel (714) 454-1356

BURCH, FRANCIS BOUCHER, b. Balt., Nov. 26, 1918; Ph.B. summa cum laude, Loyola Coll., Balt., 1941; LL.B., Yale U., 1943; LL.D., U. Balt., 1976. Admitted to Md. bar, 1943, U.S. Supreme Ct. bar, 1948; instr. bus. law Loyola Coll. Evening Sch., 1945-47; counsel, v.p., chmn. exec. com. Balt. Jr. Assn. Commerce, 1950-54; city solicitor, Balt., 1961-63; atty. gen. Md., 1966—. Chmn. Md. Cath. Lawyers Retreat, 1957-59; mem. Mayor's Com. on Conflict of Interest, 1960; chmn. Mayor's Com. on Mass Transit, 1961; mem. Balt. Pension Study Com., 1961; mem. Standard Salary Bd. Md., 1960-61; pres. Civil Service Commn. Balt., 1960-61; chmn. Mayor's Com. on Scholarship Program, 1961; pres. St. Thomas More Soc. Md., 1961-63, Balt. Safety Council, 1963-65; mem. Bd. Estimates Balt., 1961-63; lay chmn. papal vols. com. for Latin Am., Archdiocese Balt., 1962-65; chmn. Constl. Prayer Found., Inc., 1963-66; commr. Md. State Ins., 1965-66; chmn. Cancer Crusade Md., 1967-68, Loyola Coll. Devel. Program, 1972; mem. Md. Code Revision Commn., 1972—, Md. Correctional Tng. Commn., 1975—; bd. dirs. Legal Aid Bur., 1954, Goodwill Industries, Inc., 1959-65, NCCJ, 1967-69, Balt. Credit Union, 1961-63; trustee Camp Fire Girls, Inc., 1960-70, Loyola-Notre Dame Library Campaign, 1971, Loyola Coll., 1974-75. Fellow, Md. Bar Found.; mem. Am. (del. 1970), Md., Balt. bar assns., Am. Judicature Soc., Am. Arbitration Assn., Nat. Assn. Attys. Gen. (chmn. consumer protection com. 1970-73, past pres., mem. exec. com. 1970—), Council State Govts. (exec. com. 1972—). Recipient Spiritum award Cardinal Gibbons High Sch., 1966, Man of Year award Hibernian Soc. Md., 1967, Pub. Servant award Md. Cath. War Vets., 1967, Humanitarian award Nu Beta Epsilon, 1968, Nat. Jewish Hosp. award, 1969, Alumnus of Year award, 1970, Andrew White medal, 1973 both from Loyola Coll., Wyman award Nat. Assn. Attys. Gen., 1975; author: On Calling a Constitutional Convention, 1950. Home: 207 Chancery Rd Baltimore MD 21218 Office: 1 S Calvert St Baltimore MD 21202 Tel (301) 383-3720

BURCH, ROBERT EUGENE, b. Memphis, Mar. 11, 1947; A.B., The Citadel, 1969; J.D., Vanderbilt U., 1972. Admitted to Tenn. bar, 1972; partner firm White, Regen, Burch & Beasley, Dickson, Tenn., 1976—; referee Dickson County Juvenile Ct., 1975—. Chmn., Dickson County Heart Assn., 1974, 75, 76; chaplain Dickson Jaycees, 1974; county devel. com. Middle Tenn. Heart Assn. Mem. Tenn. Assn. Criminal Def. Lawyers (dir. 1976—), Am., Tenn., Dickson County bar assns., Tenn. Trial Lawyers Assn. Licensed flight instr., jumpmaster, expert parachutist, airline transport pilot; recipient Jaycees Presdl. award of honor, 1973. Home: Route 4 Box 26 Dickson TN 37055 Office: 110 N Mathis Dr Dickson TN 37055 Tel (615) 446-2882

BURCHETT, DALE, b. Pike County, Ky., Aug. 2, 1936; A.B., U. Ky., 1958, J.D., 1960. Admitted to Ky. bar, 1960; corp. counsel City of Cave City (Ky.), 1962-69; judge Barren County (Ky.) Ct., Glasgow, 1970—. Mem. Barren County Bar Assn. (pres. 1970-71). Home: 210 Morningside Dr Glasgow KY 42141 Office: Courthouse Glasgow KY 42141 Tel (502) 651-3131

BURCHFIELD, JAMES RALPH, b. Vincennes, Ind., Feb. 6, 1924; B.A., Ohio State U., 1947, J.D., 1949. Admitted to Ohio bar, 1949, U.S. Supreme Ct. bar, 1960; practiced in Columbus, Ohio, 1949—; mem. firm Burchfield, Smith & Nelson, Columbus, 1954—. Mem. Mayor's Spl. Com. on Transit, Columbus, 1955-58; trustee Columbus Goodwill; active Boy Scouts Am., fund-raising drives United Appeal, Hosp. Fedn.; exec. dir. Franklin County (Ohio) Eisenhower Orgn., 1952; trustee Sertoma Found., 1970—, internat. pres., 1967. Mem. Am., Ohio (com. on individual rights 1973—), Columbus (co-chmn. state conv. com.) bar assns., Am., Ohio, Franklin County trial lawyers assns., Am. Judicature Soc., Nat. Consumer Fin. Assn., E. Side Bus. Assn. (pres. 1955), United Bus. Men's Assn. (pres. 1958), Ohio State U. Alumni Assn. (life), Am., Ohio State (life) hist. assns., Phi Alpha Theta. Named Outstanding Young Man of Year, Columbus Jr. C. of C., 1956. Home: 42 Park Dr Columbus OH 43209 Office: 1313 E Broad St Columbus OH 43205 Tel (614) 252-1131

BURDEN, JAMES EWERS, b. Sacramento, Oct. 24, 1939; B.S., U. Calif. at Berkeley, 1961; J.D., U. Calif. at San Francisco, 1964; postgrad. U. So. Calif., 1964-65. Admitted to Calif. bar, 1965, U.S. Supreme Ct. bar, 1970; asso. firm Elliott & Aune, Santa Ana, Calif., 1964-65, firm White, Harbor, Fort & Schei, Sacramento, 1965-67; asso. firm Miller, Starr & Regalia, Oakland, Calif., 1967-68, partner, 1969-73; individual practice law, San Francisco, 1973-74; partner firm Burden, Reis & Krinsky, San Francisco, 1974, firm Burden, Reis & Aiken, and predecessors, San Francisco, 1975—; lectr. law U. Calif. Extension, 1970-73. Mem. Bar Assn. San Francisco, Alameda County, Am. bar assns., State Bar Calif., Am. Judicature Soc. Contbr. articles to legal jours. Office: 451 Jackson St 2d Floor San Francisco CA 94111 Tel (415) 421-0404

BURDETT, THOMAS LEE, b. Blanco, Tex., Oct. 12, 1942; B.B.A., U. Tex., 1965, J.D., 1967. Admitted to Tex. bar, 1967; asso. firm Witherspoon, Aikin, Thomas & Langley, Hereford, Tex., 1967-72; partner firm Thomas & Burdett, Hereford, 1972—; asst. atty. Deaf Smith County (Tex.), 1967-69. Bd. dir. United Way, Hereford, 1968-70; chmn. Hereford Day Care Center, 1971-72. Mem. Am., Tex., Hereford, 69th Jud. Dist. (sec. 1968-72) bar assns., Deaf Smith County C. of C. (dir. 1971-74). Home: 312 Douglas St Hereford TX 79045 Office: 116 S 25 Mile Ave Hereford TX 79045 Tel (806) 364-5700

BURDITT, GEORGE MILLER, b. Chgo., Sep. 21, 1922; B.A., Harvard, 1944, LL.B., 1948. Admitted to Ill. bar, 1949, U.S. Supreme Ct. bar, 1974; with Swift & Co., Chgo., 1948-54; partner firm Chadwell, Kayser, Ruggles, McGee & Hastings and predecessor firms, Chgo., 1954-69; partner firm Burditt & Calkins, Chgo., 1969—; instr. law Northwestern U., 1968—; gen. counsel Food and Drug Law Inst.; mem. Ill. Ho. Reps., 1965-72. Rep. candidate U.S. Senate, 1974. Mem. Am., Ill., N.Y., Chgo. bar assns., Law Club Chgo., Legal Club Chgo. Contbr. articles to law jours. Home: 179 Lake Shore Dr Chicago IL 60611 Office: 135 S LaSalle St Chicago IL 60603 Tel (312) 641-2121

BUREK, ANTHONY SIMON, b. Chgo., July 18, 1929; Ph.B., De Paul U., 1955, J.D., 1958. Admitted to Ill. bar, 1958, U.S. Supreme Ct. bar; title officer, Chgo. Title Ins. Co., 1966-73, office counsel, 1974, asst. gen. counsel, 1975—; lectr. Ill. Inst. Continuing Legal Edn., 1974—; instr. Inst. Fin. Edn., 1968—. Mem. Am., Ill., Chgo. bar assns., Delta Theta Phi. Office: 111 W Washington Chicago IL 60602 Tel (312) 630-2900

BURFORD, REX LAYFIELD, b. Charleston, W.Va., Sept. 20, 1939; B.A., Duke, 1961; LL.B., W.Va. U., 1964. Admitted to W.Va. bar, 1964; asso. firm Peters, Merricks, Leslie, Kenna & Mohler, Charleston, 1964-66; treas. W.Va. Engine & Transmission Co. Inc., S. Charleston, 1969—; sec.-treas. W.Va. Oil and Natural Gas Assn., Charleston, 1976—; dir. Gov's. Hwy. Safety Bur., Charleston, 1967-68. Mem. W.Va. State Bar Assn. Tel (304) 344-1442

BURFORD, ROBERT HAROLD, b. Huntington, W.Va., Jan. 9, 1926; B.S., Marshall U., 1949; J.D., U. Mich., 1952. Admitted to W.Va. bar, 1952; partner firm Beckett, Burford & James, and predecessors, Huntington, 1952—; commr. accounts Cabell County (W.Va.), 1958-74; municipal judge, Huntington, 1955-56. Chmn. Cabell County Democratic Exec. Com., 1956-61. Mem. W.Va. State Bar, W.Va., Cabell County (pres. 1971-72) bar assns. Home: 1503 Ritter Blvd Huntington WV 25701 Office: 418 8th St Huntington WV 25701 Tel (304) 697-4100

BURGE, DAVID ALAN, b. Anderson, Ind., July 22, 1943; B.S. with highest honors in Gen. Engring., U. Ill., 1966; postgrad. Georgetown U., 1966-68; J.D., U. Louisville, 1970. Admitted to Ky. bar, 1970, Ohio bar, 1971; patent counsel Gen. Electric Co., Louisville, 1970; asso. firm Watts, Hoffmann, Fisher & Heinke, Cleve., 1971-75; individual practice law, Cleve., 1975—. Mem. Am. Patent Law Assn., Am., Cleve. (chmn. small practices task force young lawyers sect. 1976-, mem. sect. exec. council 1977—), Cuyahoga, Ohio bar assns. Office: 240 Tower East 20600 Chagrin Blvd Cleveland OH 44122 Tel (216) 295-1300

BURGE, FRANK OTIS, JR., b. Birmingham, Ala., Jan. 21, 1927; B.S. in Zoology, Tulane U., New Orleans, 1947, LL.B., 1951. Admitted to Ala. bar, 1953; asso. firm Jackson, Rives, Pettus & Peterson, partner successor firms, Birmingham, 1953-76; individual practice law, Birmingham, 1975—; speaker on trial tactics profl. assns. Chmn. bd. Spastic Aid of Ala., 1969, United Cerebral Palsy of Greater Birmingham, 1973; dir. Vis. Nursing Assn. Ala., Jefferson County Legal Aid Soc.; ruling elder Shades Valley Presbyterian Ch. Mem. Am., Ala., Birmingham bar assns., Am., Ala. trial lawyers assns., Am. Judicature Soc. Home: 4113 Old Leeds Ln Birmingham AL 35213 Office: First Alabama Bank Bldg Birmingham AL 35203 Te! (205) 251-9729

BURGER, JOHN EDWARD, b. Phoenix, Oct. 26, 1944; B.S., U.S. Mil. Acad., 1966; J.D. cum laude, Ariz. State U., 1973. Admitted to Ariz. bar, 1973; asso. firm Jennings, Strauss & Salmon, Phoenix, 1973—. Mem. Maricopa County (Ariz.), Ariz., Am. bar assns. Author: The NBA's Four Year Rule: A Technical Foul?, 1972; Law and the Social Order, 1972. Office: 111 W Monroe St Phoenix AZ 85003 Tel (602) 262-5824

BURGER, WARREN EARL, b. St. Paul, Sept. 17, 1907; student U. Minn., 1925-27; LL.B. magna cum laude, St. Paul Coll. Law (now Mitchell Coll. Law), 1931. Admitted to Minn. bar, 1931; partner firm Faricy, Burger, Moore & Costello (and predecessor firms), 1935-53; faculty Mitchell Coll. Law, 1931-48; asst. atty. gen. U.S., 1953-56; judge U.S. Ct. Appeals, Washington, 1956-69; Chief Justice U.S., 1969—. Hon. master bench Middle Temple, 1969; pres. Bentham Club, U. Coll. London, 1972-73; hon. chmn. Inst. Jud. Adminstrn., criminal justice project Am. Bar Assn. Chancellor, bd. regents Smithsonian Instn.; chmn. bd. trustees Nat. Gallery Art, Washington; trustee emeritus Macalester Coll., St. Paul, Mayo Found., Rochester, Minn. Office: Supreme Ct Bldg Washington DC 20543*

BURGESS, BENJAMIN LOUIS, JR., b. Salina, Kans., July 20, 1943; B.A., Kans. Wesleyan U., 1966; J.D., Washburn U., 1971. Admitted to Kans. bar, 1972; asst. county atty. Reno County (Kans.), 1972; asst. U.S. Atty. Dist. Kans., Wichita, 1973—. Mem. Am., Kans., Wichita bar assns. Home: 2510 Halstead St Wichita KS 67204 Office: PO Box 2098 Wichita KS 67201 Tel (316) 267-6311 ext 481

BURGESS, DOUGLAS ROBERT, b. Rochester, N.Y., Feb. 2, 1948; A.B., U. Rochester, 1969; J.D., State U. N.Y. at Buffalo, 1972. Admitted to N.Y. bar, 1973; asso. firm Houghton & Pappas, Rochester, 1973-74; individual practice law, Rochester, 1974—. Mem. Am., N.Y. State, Monroe County bar assns. Home: 39 Scotch Ln Rochester NY 14617 Office: 2691 Dewey Ave Rochester NY 14616 Tel (716) 663-1820

BURGWEGER, FRANCIS JOSEPH, JR., b. Evanston, Ill., July 5, 1942; B.A., Yale, 1964; J.D., U. Pa., 1970. Admitted to Calif. bar, 1971; law clk. to judge U.S. Ct. Appeals 9th Circuit Bar, Los Angeles, 1970-71; asso. firm O'Melveny & Myers, Los Angeles, 1971—. Mem. Am., Calif. State bar assns. Tel (213) 620-1120

BURGWIN, GEORGE COLLINSON, III, b. Pitts., Aug. 24, 1921; B.A., Yale, 1943; LL.B., U. Pitts., 1949. Admitted to Pa. bar, 1950; partner firms Burgwin, Ruffin, Perry, Pohl & Springer, Pitts., 1951-68, Berkman Ruslander Pohl Lieber & Engel, Pitts. 1968—; mem. Pa. Appellate Ct. Nominating Commn., 1973—. Pres., trustee St. Barnabas Free Home, Gibsonia, Pa.; chmn. com. on canons Protestant Episcopal Diocese of Pitts. Mem. Am., Pa., Allegheny County (Pa.) bar assns. Editorial bd. U. Pitts. Law Rev., 1948-49. Home: 5700 Fair Oaks St Pittsburgh PA 15217 Office: 20th floor Frick Bldg Pittsburgh PA 15219 Tel (412) 391-3939

BURK, JOHN, b. Binghamton, N.Y., May 5, 1927; B.S., U. Wyo., 1950; J.D., U. Denver, 1965. Admitted to Wyo. bar, 1965, U.S. Supreme Ct. bar, 1972; pros. atty. Watrona County (Wyo.), Casper, 1970-74; partner firm Burk & Painter, Casper, 1975—; dir. Central Savs. & Loan. Mem. Am. Bar Assn., Am., Wyo. trial lawyers assns. Home: 2727 S Poplar St Casper WY 82601 Office: Suite A Wyoming Bldg Casper WY 82601 Tel (307) 265-6500

BURKE, CARROLL A., b. Bowling Green, Ky., Jan. 1, 1928; LL.B., Stetson Law Sch., 1956. Admitted to Fla. bar, 1957; asso. firm Mack N. Cleveland, Jr., Sanford, Fla., 1957-64; individual practice law, Sanford, 1964—. Mem. Seminole County (Fla.) (pres. 1962), Fla. bars. Office: 612 Atlantic Nat Bank Bldg Sanford FL 32771 Tel (305) 322-7680

BURKE, CHERYL CRANDALL, b. New Orleans, Nov. 17, 1947; B.A., Oberlin (Ohio) Coll., 1969; J.D., Northeastern U., 1973. Admitted to D.C. bar, 1975, Md. bar, 1973; asso. firm Alper, Schoene, Horkan & Mann, and predecessor, Washington, 1973-77, partner, 1977—. Mem. Women's Nat. Democratic Club, ACLU, NOW. Mem. Am., Md., D.C. bar assns., Assn. Trial Lawyers Am. Home: 1802 Lamont St NW Washington DC 20010 Office: 818 18th St NW Suite 1020 Washington DC 20006 Tel (202) 298-9191

BURKE, COLEMAN, b. Summit, N.J., Feb. 1, 1914; A.B., Hamilton Coll., 1934; J.D., Harvard, 1938; LL.D., Rikkyo U., Tokyo, 1958. Admitted to N.Y. bar, 1938, N.J. bar, 1943; asso. firm Burke & Burke, N.Y.C., 1937-42, partner, 1942—; partner firm Burke & Peer, and predecessors, Summit, 1943—; dir. Keuffel & Esser Co., LFE Corp., Summit and Elizabeth Trust Co. Chmn. bd. dirs. Hamilton Coll., Humane Soc. U.S., Washington, Christian Herald Mag., Chappaqua, N.Y., Bowery Mission, N.Y.C., Children's Home, Chappaqua; v.p. Am. Bible Soc., N.Y.C. Mem. Am., N.Y., N.J. bar assns., Assn. Bar City N.Y., Phi Beta Kappa, Chi Psi. Home: 45 Stewart Rd Short Hills NJ 07078 Office: 30 Rockefeller Plaza New York City NY 10020 Tel (212) 489-0400

BURKE, DANIEL BARLOW, b. Phila., Oct. 12, 1902; B.S. in Econs., U. Pa., 1925, M.B.A., 1928; J.D., N.Y.U., 1930; Admitted to D.C. bar, 1929, Pa. bar, 1930, U.S. Supreme Ct. bar, 1941; individual practice law, Phila., 1930—; prof. law and govt. Drexel U., Phila., 1930-40; mem. polit. sci. faculty U., Pa., Phila., 1931-38, 41-42; asst. dist. atty City of Phila., 1938-42, 1945-46; lectr. Sch. Law, Temple Phila., 1948-65; dep. prothonotary Phila. Ct. Common Pleas, 1946-55, prothonotary, 1955-70; referee Workman's Compensation, Phila., 1970-71; asso. mem. Conf. Adminstrv. Law Judges. Bd. dirs. Phila. chpt. ARC; pres. Presbyterian Social Union Phila., 1969-70. Mem. Am., Pa., Phila. (dir.) bar assns., Lawyers Club Phila. (dir.), SAR (former pres. local chpt., former chancellor). Recipient Outstanding Pub. Service award Com. of Seventy, Phila., 1964; contbr. articles to legal jours. Home: 200 N Wynnewood Rd Wynnewood PA 19096 Office: 423 City Hall Annex Philadelphia PA 19107 Tel (215) MU6-5687

BURKE, DANIEL MARTIN, b. Casper, Wyo., Sept. 9, 1946; B.A., U. Wyo., 1968, J.D., 1970. Admitted to Wyo. bar, 1970; law clk. to judge U.S. 10th Circuit Ct. Appeals, Wyo., 1970; asst. atty. gen. State of Wyo., 1970-71; asst. city atty. Casper, 1971-74; partner firm Burke & Burke, Casper, 1972-74, firm Burke, Horn & Lewis, Casper, 1975—; pros. atty. Natrona County (Wyo.), 1975—; instr. bus. law, criminal law and evidence Casper Coll., 1971-74. Mem. Wyo. State Bar (sec.-treas. 1973-75), Natrona County, Am. bar assns., Nat. Dist. Attys. Assn., Am. Judicature Soc. Home: 1008 S Wolcott St Casper WY 82601 Office: Suite 200 City Center Bldg Casper WY 82601 Tel (307) 265-6375

BURKE, EDMOND WAYNE, b. Ukiah, Calif., Sept. 7, 1935; B.A., Humboldt State Coll., 1957, M.A., 1958; J.D., Hastings Coll. Law, 1964. Admitted to Calif. bar, 1965, Alaska bar, 1968; law clk. firm Stanley Pugh, Red Bluff, Calif., 1964, asso., 1965; asso. firm Fitzgerald, Rattigan and Von der Mehden, Santa Rosa, Calif., 1965-66; asst. atty. gen. and dist. atty. Alaska Dept. Law, Juneau and Anchorage, 1967-68; partner firm Hendrickson, Burke & Rowland, Anchorage, 1968-69; judge Alaska Superior Ct., 3d Jud. Dist., 1970-75; justice Alaska Supreme Ct., 1975—. Mem. Alaska, Calif. bars. Office: 303 K St Anchorage AK 99501 Tel (907) 274-8611

BURKE, EDMUND, b. Bozeman, Mont., Sept. 22, 1934; B.S., U.S. Naval Acad., 1956; LL.B., U. Calif. at Berkeley, 1963. Admitted to Calif. bar, 1964, Hawaii bar, 1966. Asso. firm Barnes, Benton, Orr, Duval and Buckingham, Ventura, Calif., 1963-66; partner firm Hamilton, Gibson, Nickelsen, Rush & Moore, Honolulu, 1966—. Mem. State Bar Calif., Hawaii, Am. bar assns., Hawaii Young Lawyers Bd. Home: 17 Kailuana Pl Kailua HI Office: suite 2000 745 Fort St Honolulu HI 96813 Tel (808) 521-2611

BURKE, HENRY PATRICK, b. Scranton, Pa., May 12, 1942; B.S. in History, U. Scranton, 1964; J.D., Villanova U., 1967. Admitted to Pa. bar, 1968, Commonwealth Ct. of Pa. bar, 1970; law clk. Ct. of Common Pleas Lackawanna County, Pa., 1968-69; asso. firm Haggerty & McDonnell, Scranton, 1969-75; asso. in practice law with Donald G. Douglass, Scranton, 1975—; lectr. bus. law U. Scranton, 1968-69; spl. asst. atty. gen. of Pa., 1972—. Bd. govs. U. Scranton Alumni, 1969—, Scranton Prep. Sch., 1968-71; active Am. Heart Assn., chmn. annual fund, 1972, asst. treas. Keystone chpt., Pa. exec. com., 1973-74. Mem. Am., Pa., Lackawanna bar assns. Chmn. economic com. Dem. Nat. Platform Com., 1972. Home: 319 Church St Dunmore PA 18512 Office: 410 Scranton Electric Bldg Scranton PA 18503 Tel (717) 961-3666

BURKE, JOHN EDWARD, b. Oak Park, Ill., Jan. 14, 1939; A.B., Holy Cross Coll., 1960; J.D., U. Mich., 1963. Admitted to Ill. bar, 1964; trial atty. U.S. Dept. Justice, Antitrust Div., 1963-69; partner firm Ross, Hardies, O'Keefe, Babcock & Parsons, Chgo., 1969—. Mem. Am., Ill., Chgo. bar assns. Office: Suite 3100 One IBM Plaza Chicago IL 60611 Tel (312) 467-9300

BURKE, JOHN F., b. Langdon, N.D., Dec. 1, 1938; B.S. in Bus. Adminstrn., U. N.D., 1960, LL.B., 1967, also J.D. Admitted to N.D. bar, 1967; partner firm Burke, Hodny & Burke, Grafton, N.D.; judge Grafton Municipal Ct., 1972-74; state's atty. Walsh County, N.D., 1975—. Chmn. Walsh County Red Cross, 1970-76. Mem. Walsh County (pres. 1971-72), Am. bar assns., Nat. Dist. Attys. Assn., N.D. States' Attys. Assn., N.D. Peace Officers Assn. Office: 607 Hill Ave Grafton ND 58237 Tel (701) 352-2810

BURKE, JOHN FRANCIS, b. Washington, June 3, 1929; B.S. in Econs., Georgetown U., 1951, J.D., 1958. Admitted to D.C. bar, 1959, Md. bar, 1969; law clk. to judge U.S. Dist. Ct. for D.C., 1958-59; asso. firm Keogh, Carey, & Costello, Washington, 1960-69; asso. firm Bulman, Goldstein, Feld & Dunie, Bethesda, Md., 1969-74, partner, 1974—. Pres., Coquelin Run Citizens Assn., 1965-66. Mem. Am., D.C., Md. bar assns., Montgomery County Bar. Office: 7427 Arlington Rd Bethesda MD 20014 Tel (301) 656-1177

BURKE, JOHN JAMES, b. Butte, Mont., July 25, 1928; B.S. in Bus., U. Mont., 1950, B.S. in Law, 1950, J.D., 1952. Admitted to Mont. bar, 1952, U.S. Supreme Ct. bar, 1957; partner firm Weir, Gough, Booth and Burke, Helena, Mont., 1954-59; with legal dept. Mont. Power Co., Butte, 1960-67, v.p., 1967—. Mem. U. Mont. Council of 50. Mem. Silver Bow County (Mont.), Am. bar assns., State Bar Mont. Inc., U. Mont. Alumni Assn. (dir.), Butte C. of C., Phi Delta Phi. Office: 40 E Broadway St Butte MT 59701 Tel (406) 723-5421

BURKE, JOSEPH, b. Claremorris, Ireland, Mar. 2, 1888; B.A., DePaul U., 1908, LL.B., 1909, LL.M., 1910, J.D., 1970. Admitted to Ill. bar, 1909; practiced in Chgo., 1909-1917, 1919-28; judge Municipal Ct., Chgo., 1922-30, Cook County (Ill.) Circuit Ct., 1930-38, Ill. Appellate Ct., Ill. 1st Dist., 1938-76; judge adv. gen. Mil. Order of World Wars, 1954-65. Pres. Cancer Research Found., Chgo. Mem. Am., Ill. State, Chgo. bar assns., Ill. Judges Assn., Lex Legio.

Home: 6736 N Hermitage Ave Chicago IL 60626 Office: 77 W Washington St Chicago IL 60602 Tel (312) FR2-2477

BURKE, JULIAN, b. Harvey, Ill., July 8, 1927; B.S., Northwestern U., 1951; LL.B., Georgetown U., 1954. Admitted to D.C. bar, 1954, Calif. bar, 1958; law clk. U.S. Ct. Appeals, Washington, 1954-55; law clk. to judge U.S. Supreme Ct., 1955-56; asso. firm Dow, Lohnes & Albertson, Washington, 1956-57, O'Melveny & Myers, Los Angeles, 1957-62; partner firm Tuttle & Taylor, Los Angeles, 1963—. Bd. dirs. So. Calif. Rapid Transit Dist., 1974. Mem. Am., Calif., Los Angeles, D.C. bar assns. Note editor: Georgetown Law Rev., 1953-54. Office: 609 S Grand Ave Los Angeles CA 90017 Tel (213) 683-0600

BURKE, LILLIAN WALKER, b. Thomaston, Ga., Aug. 2, 1917; B.S., Ohio State U., 1947; LL.B., Cleve. State U., 1951, postgrad., 1964-66. Admitted to Ohio bar, 1951; practiced in Cleve., 1952-63; asst. atty. gen. State of Ohio, 1963-66; mem., vice chmn. Ohio Indsl. Commn., Columbus, 1966-69; judge Cleve. Municipal Ct., 1969—; lectr. women in politics Heidelberg (Ohio) Coll., John Carroll U. Vice-pres.-at-large Greater Cleve. Safety Council, 1970—; mem. advisory com. on accreditation and instl. eligibility Bur. Higher Edn. HEW, 1972—; mem. Cuyahoga County (Ohio) Republican Central Com., 1957-69; bd. dirs. Greater Cleve. Neighborhood Assn., Cath. Youth Counselling Services, Cleve.; trustee Consumers League of Ohio; bd. dirs. Greater Cleve. Neighborhood Assn., Cath. Youth Counselling Services, Cleve.; trustee Consumers League of Ohio; bd. dirs., v.p. Downtown Restoration Soc., Cleve. Mem. AAUW (exec. bd.), Nat. Council Negro Women (pres. Cleve. chpt. 1954-57), Women Lawyers Assn. (hon. adviser), Am., Nat. (Black jud. council), Ohio, Cuyahoga County, Cleve. bar assns., Greater Cleve. Municipal Judges Assn. (pres. 1975), Greater Cleve. Judges Assn. (pres. 1976). NAACP (life), Am. Judicature Soc., Alpha Kappa Alpha. Recipient Martin Luther King Jr. award Musical Soc. Pitts., 1970; achievement award Parkwood Colored Meth. Episcopal Ch., 1966, Bus. League Cleve., 1970; Woman of Year award Inter Club Council of Cleve., 1973; Merit award Ohio Supreme Ct., 1975, 76. Home: 829 East Blvd Cleveland OH 44108 Office: 1300 Lakeside Justice Center Cleveland OH 44114

BURKE, MARLIN WILLIAM, b. Sioux Falls, S.D., Jan. 9, 1944; B.A., U. S.D., 1966; J.D., U. Denver, 1971; Admitted to Colo. bar, 1971, Fed. Dist. Ct. bar, 1971; dep. city atty. in charge prosecution City of Lakewood, Colo., 1971-75; individual practice law, Lakewood, 1975—. Mem. Child Abuse Rev. Bd., Lakewood, 1976—. Mem. Am., Colo., 1st Jud. bar assns., Am., Colo. trial lawyers assns., Nat. Dist. Attys. Assn. Home: 1587 S Garrison St Lakewood CO 80226 Office: 5945 W Mississippi Ave Lakewood CO 80226 Tel (303) 922-6389

BURKE, RICHARD WILLIAM, b. Chgo., Oct. 3, 1933; A.B. cum laude, U. Notre Dame, 1955; J.D., U. Chgo., 1958. Admitted to Ill. bar, 1959; asso. William T. Kirby, Chgo., 1958-68; partner firm Hubachek, Kelly, Rauch & Kirby, Chgo., 1968—. Mem. Chgo. Bicentennial Commn., 1976; bd. dirs. Irish Fellowship Club. Mem. Chgo., Ill., Am. bar assns. Home: 922 William St River Forest IL 60305 Office: 3100 Prudential Plaza Chicago IL 60601 Tel (312) 944-2400

BURKE, STEPHEN RUSSELL, b. Shreveport, La., Dec. 19, 1945; student La. Tech. Coll.; J.D., La. State U., 1970. Admitted to La. bar, 1970; asso. firm Theus, Grisham, Davis & Leigh, Monroe, La., 1971, firm Henry G. Hobbs, Minden, La., 1971-75; individual practice law, Minden, 1975—. Mem. Am., La., Webster Parish bar assns. Office: 111 Pearl St Minden LA 71055 Tel (318) 377-6972

BURKE, TERENCE JOSEPH, b. Scranton, Pa., Mar. 29, 1939; B.S. in Physics, U. Scranton, 1960; M.S. in Physics, Union Coll., 1968; J.D., Albany Law Sch., 1971. Nuclear physicist Knolls Atomic Power Lab., Schenectady, 1962-68; admitted to N.Y. bar, 1972; asso. firm Nolan & Heller, Albany, N.Y., 1971-74; partner firm Burke & Cavalier, Albany, 1974—; legis. counsel to State Sen. John Dunne, Albany, 1974—; adj. prof. Rensselaer Poly. Inst., 1975, State U. N.Y. at Albany, 1976. Mem. N.Y. State, Albany County bar assns., Assn. Legis. Counsel. Home: 124 Fleetwood Ave Albany NY 12209 Office: 41 State St Albany NY 12207 Tel (518) 463-1117

BURKE, THOMAS MICHAEL, b. Whatcomb County, Wash., Mar. 15, 1922; student Eastern Ill. State Coll., 1949; J.D., U. Ill., 1952. Admitted to Ill. bar, 1952; state's atty. Coles County (Ill.), Charleston, 1956-60; police magistrate, Charleston, 1961-64; pub. defender Coles County, Charleston, 1965-66; judge 5th Circuit Ct., Charleston, 1966—. Mem. Ill., Coles County bar asssns. Home: 1224 Montgomery Dr Charleston IL 61920 Office: POB 458 Charleston IL 61920 Tel (217) 345-5322

BURKE, WILLIAM LOWE, JR., b. Dallas, Dec. 16, 1940; B.B.A., McMurry Coll., 1963; J.D., U. Tex., Austin, 1966. Admitted to Tex. bar, 1966, U.S. Supreme Ct. bar, 1974; asst. city atty. City of Abilene (Tex.), 1966-67; individual practice law, Abilene, 1967—; tchr. McMurry Coll., 1967-68. Mem. Abilene Planning and Zoning Commn., 1975—; bd. dirs. Abilene YMCA, 1974—. Mem. Tex. Bar Assn., Tex., Abilene trial lawyers assns. Home: 890 Meander St Abilene TX 79605 Office: 302 Chestnut St PO Box 769 Abilene TX 79604 Tel (915) 673-3792

BURKETT, CHARLES WATSON, b. San Francisco, Dec. 22, 1913; A.B., Stanford, 1936, J.D., 1939. Admitted to Calif. bar, 1939, Interstate Commerce Commn., 1944, U.S. Supreme Ct. bar, 1945; individual practice law, San Francisco and Oakland, Calif., 1940-44, 63—; with law dept. So. Pacific R.R., 1944—; dir. San Francisco Law Sch., 1942—, pres., 1967-76. Mem. Am., San Francisco Bar Assns., Calif. State Bar, Assn. ICC Practitioners. Home: 97 Leon Way Atherton CA 94025 Office: 1 Market Plaza San Francisco CA 94105 Tel (415) 362-1212 Ext 22181

BURKEY, LEE MELVILLE, b. Beach, N.D., Mar. 21, 1914; B.A., U. Ill., 1936, A.M., 1938; J.D. with honors, John Marshall Law Sch., 1943. Admitted to Ill. bar, 1944; atty. Office of the Solicitor, U.S. Dept. Labor, 1944-51; partner firm Asher, Gubbins and Segall, 1951-65, Asher, Greenfield, Gubbins and Segall, 1965-75; v.p. Asher, Greenfield, Goodstein, Pavalon and Segall, Ltd., Chgo., 1975—. Trustee Village of LaGrange (Ill.), 1962-68, mayor, 1968-73, village atty., 1973—; mem. Northeastern Ill. Planning Commn., 1969-73, pres., 1971. Mem. Am., Ill. State, Fed., Chgo. bar assns. Asso. editor: John Marshall Law Quar., 1942-43. Home: 926 S Catherine Ave LaGrange IL 60525 Office: 228 N LaSalle St Chicago IL 60601 Tel (312) 263-1500

BURKHALTER, HARRY HULBERT, b. Reidsville, Ga., Nov. 29, 1924; A.B., Mercer U., 1948, LL.B., 1950, J.D., 1967; M.S., Air Force Inst. Tech., 1967. Admitted to Ga. bar, 1949, U.S. Supreme Ct. bar, 1971, U.S. Ct. Mil. Appeals bar, 1959; served to col. JAGC, USAFR, 1958—; individual practice law, Macon, Ga., 1949-50, 76-77, Forsyth, Ga., 1970-71. Deacon, Baptist Ch., 1954—, chmn. bd., 1970-72. Mem. Res. Officers Assn., Ret. Officers Assn., Am. Legion, VFW, DAV, Nat. Chaplains Assn., Am. Assn. Ret. Persons, Mensa, Delta Theta Phi. Home: 4005 N Napier Ave Macon GA 31204

BURKHEAD, HARLAN DAVID, b. Concordia, Kans., Feb. 1, 1943; B.A., U. Kans., 1965, J.D., 1968. Admitted to Kans. bar, 1968, Mo. bar, 1969; asso. firm Lathrop, Koontz, Righter, Clagett, Parker & Norquist, Kansas City, Mo., 1969-74, partner, 1975—; atty., City of Westwood Hills (Kans.), 1970-72, judge municipal ct., 1973—; judge municipal ct. City of Mission Woods (Kans.), 1973—. Mem. Am., Mo., Kansas City bar assns., Lawyers Assn. Kansas City. Home: 2013 W 48th Terr Westwood Hills KS 66205 Office: 1500 Ten Main Center Kansas City MO 64105 Tel (816) 842-0820

BURKITT, WILLIAM ROBERT, b. Santa Monica, Calif., Aug. 14, 1941; B.S., U. So. Calif., 1963, J.D., 1966. Admitted to Calif. bar, 1966; law clk. U.S. Dist. Ct. Judge, Central Dist. Calif., 1966-67; asso. firm Brydolf, Gray & Whyte, Pasadena, Calif., 1967-69; partner firm Gray, Whyte & Burkitt, Pasadena, 1969—. Mem. Los Angeles County, Calif., Pasadena (sec. 1970-71) bar assns. Office: 301 E Colorado Blvd Pasadena CA 91101 Tel (213) 681-0665

BURKLEY, WALTER RODNEY, JR., b. Wildwood, N.J., June 22, 1935; B.A. cum laude, Dartmouth, 1958; LL.B., Harvard, 1964. Admitted to Calif. bar, 1965; dep. county counsel Los Angeles County, 1964-66; partner firm Moore & Lindelof, Los Angeles, 1966-69, Burkley & Moore, Torrance, Calif., 1969-76, Barrett Stearns Collins Gleason & Kinney, 1976—; dir. Eden Nat. Steel Corp., Winona Pacific Inc., Polymers-West, Inc. Mem. Am., Calif. (conv. del.), Los Angeles, South Bay (dir.) bar assns. Home: 3405 La Selva Pl Palos Verdes Estates CA 90274 Office: 1150 Union Bank Tower Torrance CA 90503 Tel (213) 540-2020

BURKS, LAWYER LEE, JR., b. Chgo., May 19, 1939; B.S., U. Wis., 1963; J.D., Ill. Inst. Tech., 1968. Admitted to Ill. bar, 1970, U.S. Dist. Ct. bar for No. Ill., 1970, U.S. Ct. Appeals bar, 1972; real estate rep. Standard Oil Co. Ind., Chgo., 1968-70; labor relations rep. Employers Assn. Greater Chgo., 1970-71; individual practice law, Park Forest, Ill., 1972—; commr. human relations commn., Park Forest, 1973-76; dir. Leadership Resources, Harvey, Ill., 1976. Commr. U.S. Bicentennial Commn., Park Forest, 1975-76; dir. U. Without Walls Gov. State U., Park Forest South, Ill., 1976—. Mem. Am., Ill., Chgo. bar assns., Am. Judicature Soc. Recipient Letters of appreciation, Park Forest, 1976. Home: 332 Waverly Park Forest IL 60466 Office: 24 Plaza Park Forest IL 60466 Tel (312) 747-0187

BURLANT, PAUL, b. Uscilug, Poland, Jan. 1, 1924; LL.B., Bklyn. Law Sch., 1950. Admitted to N.Y. bar, 1950, U.S. Dist. Ct. for So. and Eastern dists. N.Y. bars, 1954, U.S. Supreme Ct. bar, 1956; partner firm Burlant & Lehrer, Huntington Station, N.Y. Mem. Nassau County bar assns., N.Y. State Assn. Trial Lawyers, Am. Arbitration Assn. Office: 1 Huntington Quadrangle Huntington Station NY 11746 Tel (516) 420-9100

BURLEIGH, WILLIAM BARRETT, b. Alexandria, Va., Dec. 2, 1934; B.A. cum laude, U. Colo., 1960; J.D., U. Calif. at Berkeley, 1963. Admitted to Calif. bar, 1964; individual practice law, Carmel, Calif., 1965-73; city atty. Carmel, 1965-73; judge municipal ct., Monterey, Calif., 1973—. Vice chmn. Republican Central Com., Monterey County, Calif., 1971-73; active Legal Aid Soc., 1965-69. Contbr. articles to legal jours. Named City Atty. of Year, Calif., 1970. Home: Box 4278 Carmel CA 93921 Office: Box 751 Monterey CA 93940 Tel (408) 372-5826

BURLESON, PHILIP LOUIS, b. Harrison, Ohio, Nov. 16, 1933; B.A., U. Tex., Arlington; J.D., S.Tex. Law Sch., Houston, 1958. Admitted to Tex. bar, 1959, U.S. Supreme Ct. bar, 1970; briefing atty. Ct. of Criminal Appeals, Tex., 1958-59; asst. dist. atty., Dallas County, 1959-62; partner firm Burleson, Bondies, Baldwin & Pate, Dallas, 1962—; chmn. Criminal Def. Lawyers Project, 1972—; mem. adv. bd. Southwestern Legal Found., 1973—; chmn. Bd. Legal Specialization, 1976—. Mem. State Democratic Exec. Com., 23d Dist., 1966-68. Mem. Tex. (Pres.'s award 1976), 6th Dist. (chmn. grievance com. 1970-74), Dallas (chmn. criminal law sect. 1966-68, dir. 1966-68, vice chmn. bd. 1968-69, pres. 1977—) bar assns., Delta Theta Phi. Office: Suite 1717 2001 Bryan Tower Dallas TX 75201 Tel (214) 744-0755

BURLESON, WILLIAM ANDERSON, b. Bakersville, N.C., Apr. 25, 1929; student Mars Hill Jr. Coll., Western Carolina Coll., Denver U.; B.A., U. N.C., 1956; J.D., Am. U., 1960. Admitted to D.C. bar, 1960, U.S. Supreme Ct. bar, 1976; clk. Superior Ct. D.C., 1956-60, dir. legal aid agy., 1961; practice law, Washington, 1961—; commr. human rights, Washington, 1971-74; lectr. in field. Founder, trustee Jeter C. and Alta R. Burleson Meml. Recreational Park and Town Center, Bakersville, N.C. Mem. Am., D.C. bar assns., Nat. Found. for Consumer Credit, Supreme Ct. Hist. Soc. Office: 1000 Pennsylvania Ave SE Washington DC 20003 Tel (202) 544-4111

BURMAN, SHELDON VICTOR, b. Bklyn., Aug. 24, 1933; B.B.A., Coll. City N.Y., 1954; J.D., N.Y. U., 1960. Admitted to N.Y. State bar, 1960, U.S. Supreme Ct. bar, 1972; asso. firm Walsh, Aarons, Salonger & Fleishaker, N.Y.C., 1961-62, Livingston, Livingston & Harris, N.Y.C., 1963-65; individual practice law, N.Y.C., 1965—; adj. prof. consumer rights law City U. N.Y., 1974-75; spl. counsel N.Y. State Gov.'s Temporary Commn. on Living Costs and Economy, 1973-74. Mem. Assn. Bar City N.Y., N.Y. Women's Bar Assn., N.Y. State Trial Lawyers Assn. (chmn. consumer protection sect. 1974—). Recipient award for distinguished service in field of consumer protection FTC, 1976; contbr. articles to legal jours.; class action editor Trial Lawyers Quar. Office: 21 E 40th St New York City NY 10016

BURMASTER, M. R., b. Milw., May 2, 1934; B.B.A., U. Wis., 1956, LL.B., 1959. Admitted to Wis. bar, 1959, Ohio bar, 1960; atty. Clark Oil & Refining Corp., Milw., 1961-70, asst. sec., 1970-73, sec., 1973-75, v.p., gen. counsel, 1975—. Mem. Milw. Art Center. Mem. Am., Wis., Ohio, Milw. bar assns. Office: 8530 W National Ave Milwaukee WI 53201 Tel (414) 321-5100

BURN, STEVEN A., b. N.Y.C., Dec. 5, 1934; B.B.A., N.Y. U., 1955, LL.B., 1959, LL.M., 1969. Admitted to N.Y. bar, U.S. Supreme Ct. bar; partner Rosenblum, Rubin Burn & Taau, C.P.A.'s, 1956-72; sec., treas., dir. Royary Controls Corp., 1969—; chmn. bd., pres. Royal Gen. Corps., 1972—. Mem. N.Y. State, Am. bar assns. Office: 10 Columbus Circle New York City NY 10019

BURNAM, JACK LEONARD, b. St. Joseph, Mo., Sept. 29, 1924; B.A., U. Calif., also LL.D. Admitted to Calif. bar, 1953; individual practice law, San Francisco, 1953—, Novato, Calif., 1968—. Pres. Parent Faculty group San Marin High Sch. Mem. Am., San Francisco, Marin County bar assns., Trial Lawyers Assn. Office: Suite 802 703 Market St San Francisco CA 94103 Tel (415) 781-6372 also 97 San Marin Dr Novato CA 94947

BURNET, WILLIAM TERRY, b. St. Louis, Apr. 16, 1946; B.A., Washington U., 1968; J.D., U. Mo., 1973. Admitted to Mo. bar, 1974, Fed. bar, 1974; asso. firm McDonald, Wright & Bryan, St. Louis, 1973-76; asst. pub. defender 21st Judicial Circuit Ct., St. Louis, 1976—. Mem. Met. Bar Assn. St. Louis, Phi Delta Phi. Office: 1320 Market St Saint Louis MO 63101 Tel (314) 453-4241

BURNETT, GROSVENOR TURRILL, b. Boston, June 29, 1946; B.A. in English Lit. cum laude with honors, Brown U., 1968; J.D., U. N.C., Chapel Hill, 1971. Admitted to N.Mex. bar, 1972; staff counsel Rio Grande chpt. Sierra Club and N.Mex. Citizens for Clear Air & Water, Inc., Santa Fe, 1972-74; individual practice law, Santa Fe, 1974-76; partner firm Ginsburg Burnett & Rothstein, Santa Fe, 1976—. Home: Route 1 PO Box 8A Glorieta NM 87535 Office: 136 Grant Ave Santa Fe NM 87501 Tel (505) 988-8004

BURNETT, HAROLD W., b. 1923; attended Dakota Wesleyan U.; LL.B., U. S.D. Now chief justice High Ct. of Mariana Islands, U.S. Trust Terr. of Pacific Islands. Office: High Ct Saipan Mariana Islands 96943*

BURNETT, JACK WADDELL, b. Dickenson, N.D., June 10, 1921; B.S. in Accounting, U. Wyo., 1947; LL.B., U. Mont., 1950. LL.M., N.Y. U., 1951. Admitted to Mont. bar, 1950, N.Y. State bar, 1953; tax atty. Shell Oil Co., N.Y.C., 1951-52, firm Cleary, Gottlieb, Friendly & Hamilton, N.Y.C., 1952-54; individual practice law, Billings, Mont., 1954—; lectr. tax insts. U. Mont., U. Wyo. Mem. Am., Mont., Yellowstone County (Mont.) bar assns., Phi Delta Phi, Alpha Kappa Psi. Contbr. articles to legal jours. Home: 2210 11th St W Billings MT 59102 Office: 612 Midland Bank Bldg Billings MT 59101 Tel (406) 252-4910

BURNETT, PERRY PIATT, b. Bloomington, Ill., Mar. 31, 1919; B.A., Ill. Wesleyan U., 1941; J.D., U. Chgo., 1948. Admitted to Ill. bar, 1949, Colo. bar, 1951, Nev. bar, 1964. Tax editor Commerce Clearing House, Chgo., 1949-50; editor, supr. Shepards Citations, Colorado Springs, 1950-53; engaged in ins. bus., Colorado Springs and Reno, 1953-63; asst. dist. atty. Washoe County (Nev.), Reno, 1965-68; staff atty. Nev. Legis. Counsel Bur., Carson City, 1963-65, 68-74; legis. counsel Nev. Legislature, Carson City, 1974-75; legal counsel Colorado Counties, Inc., Denver, 1975—. Mem. Commn. on Uniform State Laws, 1974-75. Mem. Am., Colo., Denver bar assns. Home: 3319 S Verbena Ct Denver CO 80231 Office: 1500 Grant St Suite 301 Denver CO 80203 Tel (303) 534-6326

BURNEY, BILLY CARPENTER, b. Ala., Feb. 14, 1936; B.S., U. North Ala., 1960; J.D., Cumberland Sch. Law, Samford U., 1966. Admitted to Ala. Supreme Ct. bar, 1966; dist. atty. Ala. 36th Jud. Circuit, 1966-69; judge Ala. Circuit Ct., 36th Jud. Circuit, 1969—; adv. com. on criminal procedure Ala. Supreme Ct. Chmn. Lawrence County (Ala.) Christmas Seal Campaign, 1975-76; pres. Ala. Lung Assn.; mem. Ala. Democratic Exec. Com. Mem. Am., Ala., Lawrence County bar assns., Ala. Assn. Circuit Judges. Recipient Orchid award Ala. Lung Assn., 1975-76. Home: 104 Cedar Ln Moulton AL 35650 Office: Courthouse POB 395 Moulton AL 35650 Tel (205) 974-0618

BURNLEY, JAMES HORACE, IV, b. High Point, N.C., July 30, 1948; B.A. magna cum laude, Yale, 1970; J.D., Harvard, 1973. Admitted to N.C. bar, 1973; asso. firm Brooks, Pierce, McLendon, Humphrey & Leonard, Greensboro, N.C., 1973-75; asso. firm Turner, Enochs, Foster & Burnley, and predecessors, Greensboro, 1975-76, partner, 1976—. Chmn. Greensboro Young Lawyers Com. Child Abuse, 1976; chmn. Guilford County Rep. party, 1976; gen. counsel N.C. Fedn. Young Reps., 1975—, named Man of Yr., 1977; mem. N.C. Zool. Park Council, 1975—. Mem. Am., N.C., Greensboro (dir. 1977—) bar assns.

BURNS, CHARLES FOSTER, b. Springfield, Mo., Sept. 22, 1904; A.B., U. Tulsa, 1928, LL.B., 1940; A.M., Washington U., St. Louis, 1931. Admitted to Okla. bar, 1940; individual practice law, Tulsa and Miami, Okla., 1949-42; atty. loyalty and investigation div. U.S. Civil Service Commn., San Francisco, and Washington, 1942-46; U.S. Commr., U.S. Dist. Ct. for No. Dist. Okla., 1947-49, 1947-71, U.S. magistrate, 1971—. Fin. chmn. Tulsa chpt. ARC, 1949-51; county chmn. (Okla.) Boy Scouts Am., 1953-54; elder Presbyn. Ch., Miami, Okla. Mem. Am., Ottawa County (past pres.) bar assns., Am. Judicature Soc., Delta Theta Phi. Author: Auguste and Pierre Chouteau, 1934. Home: 813 G St NW Miami OK 74354 Office: PO Box 551 Miami OK 74354 Tel (918) 542-3009

BURNS, CLAUDE MITCHELL, JR., b. Gadsden, Ala., May 6, 1943; B.S., U. Ala., 1965, J.D., 1968. Admitted to Ala. bar, 1968; asso. firm Burns and Burns, Tuscaloosa, Ala., 1968-70, partner, 1970-73; individual practice law, Tuscaloosa, 1974—. Mem. Tuscaloosa County Bd. Edn., 1974—, pres., 1976—. Mem. Comml. Law League Am., Am., Ala. trial lawyers assns., Ala., Tuscaloosa bar assns. Office: PO Box 337 Tuscaloosa AL 35401 Tel (205) 349-2737

BURNS, DONALD EDWARD, b. Teaneck, N.J., Nov. 3, 1938; A.B., Georgetown U., 1961; LL.B., Yale, 1964. Admitted D.C. bar, 1965, Calif. bar, 1975; law clk. to judge Calif. Supreme Ct., San Francisco, 1965-66; asst. gen. counsel Fed. Home Loan Bank Bd., Washington, 1968-70; spl. asst. to gen. counsel Fed. Home Loan Mortgage Corp., 1970-71; partner firm Gailor, Burns & Elias and predecessors, Washington, 1971-74; sec. Calif. Bus. Transp. Agy., Sacramento, 1975-76; of counsel firm Landels, Ripley & Diamond, San Francisco, 1977—. Mem. Fed., Am. bar assns., D.C. Bar, State Bar Calif. Author: (with F.R. Gailor) Savings and Loan Conversions: An Overview, 1973. Home: 1181 Chestnut St San Francisco CA 94109 Office: 450 Pacific Ave San Francisco CA 94133 Tel (415) 788-5000

BURNS, EDWARD JONES, b. Carthage, N.C., July 12, 1904; A.B., Duke, 1927, LL.B., 1930. Admitted to N.C. bar, 1930; atty. Carthage (N.C.) United Meth. Ch., 1930—; town atty. Carthage, 1935-40, mayor, 1945-47; town atty. Whispering Pines (N.C.), 1959-64. Home and Office: Monroe St Carthage NC 28327 Tel (919) 947-2282

BURNS, GEORGE ALOYSIUS, b. Milw., July 21, 1929; B.A., Marquette U., 1951, LL.B., 1953. Admitted to Wis. bar, 1953; law clk. Chief Justice Wis. Supreme Ct., 1952-53; served with JAGC, U.S. Army, 1953-56; practiced in Milw., 1957-70; commr. 2d Wis. Jud. Circuit Ct., 1965-70, judge, 1973—; judge Milw. Circuit Ct., 1970-73; presiding judge 19th Ct. Jury and Equity Div., 1976—; lectr. in field. Mem. State Bar Wis. Home: 6440 N Elm Tree Rd Glendale WI 53217 Office: 901 N 9th St Milwaukee WI 53233 Tel (414) 278-4525

BURNS, LYTLE DEWITT, b. Atlanta, Mar. 26, 1914; student U. Va., Woodrow Wilson Law Sch.; LL.B., 1941. Admitted to Ga. bar, 1941; asso. firm Powell, Goldstein, Frazer & Murphy, Atlanta, 1941-45; atty. rent control U.S. Govt., 1945-48; with firm James Dorsey & Phillip Etheridge, 1948-50, then with firms Reynold, Cox, Brown, Arnold & Burns, and Tyler, Burns & Tyler, Atlanta. Deacon Presbyn. Ch. Mem. Ga., Atlanta bar assns., Atlanta Lawyers Club. Home: 2341 Montview Dr NW Atlanta GA 30305 Office: Suite 1747 Equitable Bldg 100 Peachtree St Atlanta GA 30303 Tel (404) 523-6254

BURNS, ROBERT HOWARD, b. Bklyn., July 10, 1931; B.A. in Philosophy, U. Miami, 1960, J.D., 1964. Admitted to Fla. bar, 1964; asso. firm J.Y. Swidler, Miami Beach, Fla., 1964-65; individual practice law, Miami Beach, 1965-74; partner firm Burns & Arnovitz, and predecessor, Miami Beach, 1974—; mem. personnel bd. City of Miami Beach, 1964, charter rev. bd., 1972-74. Mem. Am. Arbitration Assn. (arbitrator 1967, 76). Named Outstanding Young Man, Voters Inc. Miami Beach, 1973. Office: 420 Lincoln Rd Miami Beach FL 33139 Tel (305) 538-4421

BURNS, ROBERT MICHAEL, b. Oak Park, Ill., July 31, 1934; B.S. in Commerce, Loyola U., 1956, J.D., 1961. Field audit agt. IRS, Chgo., 1956-57, spl. agt. intelligence div., 1957-63, trial atty. office of chief counsel, Omaha, 1963, Milw., 1963-72; admitted to Ill. bar, 1962, Wis. bar, 1971, U.S. Supreme Ct. bar, 1971; adminstrv. law judge HEW and Social Security Adminstrn., Milw., 1972—. Mem. Ill., Wis. bar assns., Assn. Adminstrv. Law Judges HEW. Recipient Am. Jurisprudence award Bancroft-Whitney Pub. Co., 1959, commendation letter Chief Counsel IRS, 1966. Home: 321 E Wynbrook Dr Oak Creek WI 53154 Office: 735 W Wisconsin Ave Milwaukee WI 53233 Tel (414) 224-3141

BURNS, THOMAS MOORE, b. Huron County, Mich., May 1, 1914; A.A., Bay City Jr. Coll., 1935; LL.B., Detroit Coll. Law, 1939. Admitted to Mich. bar, 1939; individual practice law, Saginaw, Mich., 1939-42, 67-68; 1947-56; chmn. Pub. Service Commn., Lansing, Mich., 1957-62; legal adviser Mich. Consol. Gas, 1963-66; judge Mich. Ct. Appeals, 1969—; mem. Mich. Ho. of Reps., 1953-56; asst. prosecutor Saginaw County (Mich.), 1947-52. Mem. Mich. Bar Assn. Am. Trial Lawyers Assn. Home: 4411 Seidel St Saginaw MI 48603 Office: 5090 State St Saginaw MI 48603 Tel (517) 799-8982

BURNS, WILLIAM CASEY, b. Hartford City, Ind., Apr. 13, 1933; B.S., Ind. U., 1955, LL.B., 1957, J.D., 1957. Admitted to Ind. bar, 1957, Fed. Dist. Ct. bar, 1958; practice law, Lafayette, Ind., 1958—; partner firm Schultze, Ewan & Burns. Mem. Am., Ind. bar assns. Home: 440 Southern Dr Lafayette IN 47905 Office: Lafayette Bank and Trust Bldg POB 1493 Lafayette IN 47901 Tel (317) 742-8464

BURNS, WILLIAM GRADY, b. Ashdown, Ark., Apr. 16, 1907; Ph.B., U. Chgo., 1929, J.D., 1931. Admitted to Ill. bar, 1931, since practiced in Chgo.; mem. firm Bell, Boyd, Lloyd, Haddad & Burns, 1943—, chmn. exec. com. 1971-75. Chmn., reviewing coms. Community Fund Chgo., 1968-70; mem. Joseph Sears Bd. Edn., Kenilworth, Ill., 1956-62, pres. 1960; trustee Village of Kenilworth, 1965-69; mem. citizens bd. and nat. devel. council U. Chgo.. Mem. Am., Ill., Chgo. bar assns., Law Club Chgo., Legal Club Chgo., U. Chgo. Law Sch. Alumni Assn. (pres., dir. 1970-72), Phi Beta Kappa, Order of the Coif. Home: 320 Cumberland Ave Kenilworth IL 60043 Office: 135 S LaSalle St Chicago IL 60603 Tel (312) 372-1121

BURNSIDE, THOMAS REUBEN, JR., b. Augusta, Ga., Apr. 7, 1938; B.B.A., U. Ga., 1960, LL.B., 1962. Admitted to Ga. bar, 1961; mem. firm Burnside, Dye, Miller & Bowen, Augusta, 1971—. Bd. dirs. State YMCA of Ga., 1966—; mem. adv. bd. Gracewood State Sch. and Hosp., Augusta, 1975—; chmn. bd. trustees Westminster Day Sch., Augusta, 1976—. Mem. Am., Ga., Augusta bar assns., Am., Ga., Augusta trial lawyers assns. Office: 453 Greene St PO Box 2426 Augusta GA 30903 Tel (404) 722-0771

BURRELL, DONALD EUGENE, b. Springfield, Mo., June 19, 1928; A.B., S.W. Mo. State U., 1951; LL.D., U.Mo., 1954; postgrad. Northwestern U. Sch. Law, 1959. Radio newsman Radio Sta., KGBX, Springfield, 1949; asst. prosecuting atty. City of Springfield, 1953; admitted to Mo. bar, 1953; practiced in Springfield, 1953-66; pros. atty. Greene County (Mo.), 1958-66; judge Greene County Probate Ct., 1966—; mem. Mo. Ho. of Reps., 1954-58; instr. in bus. law U. Mo., 1952-53, in sociology S.W. Mo. State U., 1953-54; mem. Mo. Jud. Reorgn. Commn., Mo. Press Bar Commn. Deacon Nat. Ave. Christian Ch., Springfield; bd. dirs. Greene County Guidance Clinic, Greene County Mental Health Assn., Law Enforcement Assistance Council, region 2; commr. Mo. Dept. Mental Health, 1974—; mem. Div. Mental Health Task Force on Availability and Effectiveness of Mental Health Services in Mo. Mem. Mo. Prosecuting Atty's. Assn. (pres.), Mo. Assn. Probate, Magistrate Judges (pres.), S.W. Mo. State U. Alumni Assn., Mo. Bar Assn. (lectr. continuing legal edn.), Am. Judicature Soc., Phi Alpha Delta. editorial bd. Mo. U. Law Rev. Office: Courthouse Springfield MO 65802 Tel (417) 869-3581

BURRIS, DONALD JEVNE, b. Mpls., July 6, 1941; B.A., Dartmouth Coll., 1963; LL.B., U. Minn., 1966. Admitted to Minn. bar, 1967, Colo. bar, 1976; asso. firm Larkin, Hoffman, Daly & Lindgren Ltd., Mpls., 1970-75; partner firm Grassby, Holloran and Burris, Steamboat Springs, Colo., 1976—. Mem. Am., Colo., Minn. bar assns. Author: (with Robert Stein) Stein on Probate, 1976. Home and office: PO Box 9069 Steamboat Springs CO 80477 Tel (303) 879-2410

BURRIS, JOSEPH JENNINGS, b. Aberdeen, S.D., Dec. 29, 1913; A.B., Stanford, 1936, J.D., 1940. Admitted to Calif. bar, 1942; sr. partner Burris, Lagerlof, Swift & Senecal, Los Angeles, 1960—; dir. Stauffer Chem. Co., Raffles, Inc. Asst. sec. Orthopedic Hosp., 1947—, Los Angeles Orthopedic Found., 1947—, Los Angeles Orthopedic Med. Center, 1947—, Crippled Childrens Hosp., 1947—; mem. Los Angeles World Affairs Council, 1972—; mem. exec. com. of bd. trustees Republican Assos., pres., 1976; pres., bd. dirs. Stanford Club Los Angeles, 1948-50; emeritus dir. Stanford Buck Club, chmn., 1955-57; emeritus mem. Stanford Athletic Bd., chmn., 1961-65; pres. Stanford Alumni Assn., 1952-53, Stanford Law Soc. So. Calif., 1957-58; bd. govs. Stanford Assos., 1954-60; sec., bd. dirs. Louis McDonald Pollution Abatement Found., 1969—; bd. overseers Hoover Instn. on War, Revolution and Peace, Stanford, 1971—, vice chmn. bd., 1976—; bd. govs. Town Hall of Calif., 1973—, v.p., 1975—; trustee Pacific Legal Found., 1973—, chmn. legal rev. com., 1975—, vice chmn. bd., 1976—; trustee Eisenhower Med. Center, Ind. Colls. So. Calif.; bd. govs. Pasadena-Foothill Tennis Patrons Los Angeles. Mem. Am., Calif., Los Angeles County (exec. com. law office mgmt. sect. 1974—), Wilshire bar assns., Phi Delta Theta. Home: 827 W Inverness St Pasadena CA 91103 Office: 3435 Wilshire Blvd #2500 Los Angeles CA 90010 Tel (213) 385-4345

BURRIS, ROLAND WALLACE, b. Centralia, Ill., Aug. 3, 1937; B.A. in Polit. Sci., So. Ill. U., 1959; postgrad. in Internat. Law, U. Hamburg (Ger.), 1959-60; J.D., Howard U., 1963. Admitted to Ill. bar, 1964; comptroller currency Nat. Bank, 1963-64; 2d v.p., comml. banking officer, tax cons. Continental Ill. Nat. Bank and Trust Co., Chgo., 1964-73; dir. Ill. Dept. Gen. Services, Chgo., 1973-77; nat. exec. dir. Operation PUSH, Chgo., 1977—. Trustee St. John Baptist Ch. Mem. Am. Inst. Banking, Ill., Chgo., Am., Cook County bar assns., Cosmopolitan C. of C., NAACP, Nat. Bus. League. Recipient Pub. Service award Cook County Bar Assn., 1975; Operation Push Community Service award, 1975. Home: 8358 S Indiana Ave Chicago IL 60619 Office: 930 E 50th St Chicago IL 60615 Tel (312) 373-3366

BURROUGHS, JOHN DAVID, b. Savannah, Ga., Dec. 7, 1947; Asso. degree Oxford Coll. of Emory U., 1968; B.A. in History, Emory U., 1970; J.D., U. Ga., 1974. Admitted to Ga. bar, 1974, Fla. bar, 1974; govtl. research analyst Inst. Govt., U. Ga., 1974-75; asso. firm John Ray Nicholson, Athens, Ga., 1975-76; gen. counsel Ga. Mountains Planning and Devel. Commn., Gainesville, 1976—. Mem. Am., Ga., Fla. bar assns. Mem. editorial bd. Ga. Jour. Internat. and Comparative Law, U. Ga. Sch. Law, 1973-74. Office: 1010 Ridge Rd PO Box 1720 Gainesville GA 30501 Tel (404) 536-3431

BURROUGHS, RICHARD RAY, b. Baytown, Tex., Aug. 13, 1946; Asso. B.A., Lee Coll., Baytown, 1966; B.A., Baylor U., 1968, J.D., 1973. Admitted to Tex. bar, 1973; partner firm Joe L. Price, Trinity, Tex., 1972-73; asso. firm Wayne Carter, Cleveland, Tex., 1973; individual practice law, Cleveland, 1974—; city atty. City of Trinity, 1972. Mem. New Caney (Tex.) Ind. Sch. Dist. Sch. Bd., 1973-74. Home: 306 Magnolia Bend New Caney TX 77357 Office: 112 S Bonham Ave PO Drawer 1676 Cleveland TX 77327 Tel (713) 592-5234

BURROUGHS, ROBERT CHARLES, b. Greeley, Colo., Nov. 27, 1936; B.A., U. Colo., 1959, J.D., 1961. Admitted to Colo. bar, 1961; individual practice law, Ault, Colo., 1966—. Mem. Am., Colo. trial lawyers assns., Am., Colo., Weld County (Colo.) bar assns. (pres. 1975-76). Office: 115 2nd Ave Ault CO 80610 Tel (303) 834-1333

BURROWS, CECIL JACKSON, b. Schuyler County, Ill., Mar. 21, 1922; B.S., Western Mich. U., 1944; J.D., Northwestern U., 1952. Admitted to Ill. bar, 1952; practiced in Pittsfield, Ill., to 1970; judge Circuit Ct., 8th Jud. Circuit Ill., 1970—; city atty. City of Pittsfield, 1957-64; state's atty., Pike County (Ill.), 1964-70; atty. municipalities. Mem. Am., Ill. State, Pike County bar assns. Home: 437 W Washington St Pittsfield IL 62363 Office: Pike County Courthouse Pittsfield IL 62363 Tel (217) 285-2025

BURROWS, KENNETH DAVID, b. N.Y.C., Mar. 26, 1941; B.A., Brown U., 1962; J.D., Fordham U., 1970. Admitted to N.Y. bar, 1971, U.S. Supreme Ct. bar, 1973; asso. firm Phillips, Nizer, Benjamin, Krim & Ballon, N.Y.C., 1970—; small claims ct. arbitrator Civil Ct. City N.Y., 1975—. Trustee Jewish Family Service, 1973—; mem. com. law and social policy Fedn. Jewish Philanthropies, 1975—. Mem. Assn. Bar City N.Y. (civil ct. com. 1972-75, com. state cts. superior jurisdiction 1975—), Am. Arbitration Assn. (vol. arbitrator 1972—). Office: 40 W 57th St New York City NY 10019 Tel (212) 977-9700

BURRUS, OTIS CLAYTON, b. Wheatfield, Ind., July 10, 1924; B.A., Valparaiso U., 1948, LL.B., 1952, J.D., 1970. Admitted to Ind. bar, 1952; individual practice law, Zionsville, Ind., 1953—; town atty. Zionsville, 1960—; mem. Ind. State Ho. of Reps., 1958-59. Mem. Indpls., Boone County (pres. 1959-60) bar assns. Office: 15 E Oak St Zionsville IN 46077 Tel (317) 873-2150

BURRUS, ROBERT LEWIS, JR., b. Orange County, Va., Sept. 16, 1934; B.A., U. Richmond, 1955; LL.B., Duke U., 1958. Admitted to Va. bar, 1958; asso. firm McGuire, Woods & Battle, and predecessors, 1958-63, partner 1963—; dir. Best Products Co., Inc., 1970—; Heilig-Meyers Co., 1973—; sec., ben. counsel Va. Real Estate Investment Trust, 1970—; lectr. in field. Pres. St. Christopher's Sch. Found., 1975-77. Mem. Va. State Bar (chmn. bd. govs. bus. law sect. 1976—), Am., Richmond bar assns. Home: 220 Ampthill Rd Richmond VA 23226 Office: 1400 Ross Bldg Richmond VA 23219 Tel (804) 644-4131

BURSTEIN, MERWYN JEROME, b. Springfield, Mass., Apr. 6, 1938; B.A. in Psychology, Am. Internat. Coll., 1959; LL.B., Boston Coll. 1960; J.D., New Eng. Sch. Law, 1963. Admitted to Mass. bar, 1963; practiced in Springfield, 1963—; partner firm Michelman & Burstein, Assn., 1963-70, Burstein & Dupont, 1973—; individual practice law, 1970-73; pres., treas. Springfield Investment Assos., 1963—, Exec. Growth Fund, 1964-72. Class chmn. alumni fund raising dr. Am. Internat. Coll., 1969-76; vice chmn. Longmeadow Democratic Town Com. Mem. Hampden County, Mass. bar assns., Comml. Law League Am. (author pamphlet You and The Law, 1963). Recipient Gold Key award Am. Internat. Coll., 1958, McGowan Trophy, 1959. Home: 29 Willett Dr Longmeadow MA 01106 Office: 1331 E Columbus Ave Springfield MA 01105 Tel (413) 734-6421

BURT, CHARLES DUANE, b. Willaminia, Oreg., Mar. 19, 1928; B.A., Willamette U., 1950, LL.D., 1953. Admitted to Oreg. bar, 1953; mem. firm Day & Burt, Salem, Oreg., 1954-58, Burt & Ertsgaard, Salem, 1958-64, Brown, Burt & Swanson, Salem, 1964—; prof. Williamette U. Coll. Law, 1973-76; atty. Oreg. Air Pollution Authority, 1953-56; adj. prof. Willamette U. Coll. Law, 1974-77. Mem. Am., Marion County (dir.), Oreg. State bar assns., Oreg. (sec.-treas. 1976, v.p.), Am. trial lawyers assns., Am. Judicature Soc., Marian County Bar Assn. (dir.). Editor Willamette Legal Handbook, 1952-53. Home: 3951 Croison Creek Rd S Salem OR 97301 Office: 1005 Capital Tower Salem OR 97301 Tel (503) 581-2421

BURTCH, JACK WILLARD, JR., b. Youngstown, Ohio, Dec. 11, 1946; B.A., Wesleyan U., 1969; J.D., Vanderbilt U., 1972. Admitted to Ohio bar, 1972, Va. bar, 1973; asso. firm Hunton & Williams, Richmond, Va., 1973—. Bd. dirs. Children's Home Soc. Va., Richmond, 1976—; vestryman Ch. of the Holy Comforter, Richmond, 1976—. Mem. Am., Va. bar assns. Home: 3504 Moss Side Ave Richmond VA 23222 Office: PO Box 1535 Richmond VA 23212 Tel (804) 788-8520

BURTELL, JOSEPH JAMES, b. Detroit, July 3, 1931; B.A., Wayne State U., 1954, J.D., 1956. Admitted to Mich. bar, 1956, U.S. Supreme Ct. bar; village atty., Flat Rock, 1959-60; asso. firm Gazley & Tuchow, Detroit, 1959; asst. dist. counsel U.S. Army C.E., 1960-61; asst. city atty., Dearborn, 1962-66, dep. city atty., 1966-69, city atty., 1969-74; judge Dist. Ct., Dearborn, 1975—; instr. criminal justice Henry Ford Community Coll., 1968-69; vis. judge Circuit Ct., 1976; chmn. Dearborn Law Day, 1963-64. Sec., bd. dirs. Am.-Polish Action Council; bd. dirs. Polish Advocates Club Detroit, 1969, Dearborn Assn. for Retarded Children, 1974—; bd. dirs. Civitan Club, 1972-73, pres., 1974-75, state judge adv., 1974—. Mem. Mich., Wayne County dist. judges assns., Nat. Inst. Municipal Law Officers (com. chmn. 1972-73), Mich. (dir. 1973-75), Detroit, Dearborn (pres. 1968) bar assns., Am. Arbitration Assn., Delta Theta Phi, Pi Kappa Alpha. Author: (with others) Michigan Employment Relations Manual, 1974. Office: 16077 Michigan Ave Dearborn MI 48126 Tel (313) 584-1200

BURTON, BERNARD OTTWAY, b. Pittsylvania, Va., Mar. 12, 1916; B.S. U. N.C., Chapel Hill, 1941, J.D., 1945; postgrad. Harvard Sch. Bus. Adminstrn., 1943. Admitted to N.C. bar, 1945; individual practice law, Asheboro, N.C., 1945—; spl. right of way counsel City of Asheboro, 1948-49; counsel Randolph County (N.C.) Airport Commn., 1948-50; spl. right of way counsel N.C. Right of Way Commn., 1965-68. Mem. Randolph County (pres. 1958-59), N.C. State, Am. bar assns., N.C. State Bar, Am. Trial Lawyers Assn., N.C. Acad. Trial Lawyers. Office: 115 N Fayetteville Law Bldg Asheboro Inc Asheboro NC 27203 Tel (919) 625-4338

BURTON, BRUCE WILLIAM, b. Mpls., Mar. 6, 1939; B.S. cum laude, Mankato State U., 1961; J.D. magna cum laude, U. Minn., 1968. Admitted to Minn. bar, 1968; asso. firm Dorsey, Marquart, Windhorst, West & Halladay, Mpls., 1968-72; gen. counsel Cedar Riverside Assos., Inc., Mpls., 1972-73; asst. prof. William Mitchell Coll. Law, 1973-74, asso. prof., acting dean, 1975-76, dean, prof., 1976—. Mem. Minn. State (mem. real property sect.; bd. govs.; housing and urban devel. com.), Am. bar assns., Minn. Civil Liberties Union, Phi Delta Phi, Order of Coif. Recipient spl. awards Minn. Continuing Legal Edn. 1973-76. Office: William Mitchell Coll Law 875 Summit Ave St Paul MN 55105 Tel (612) 698-3885

BURTON, EDWARD GOULD, b. Providence, July 20, 1940; A.B. cum laude, Princeton, 1962; LL.B., Harvard, 1965. Admitted to Alaska bar, 1966, U.S. Dist. Ct. bar for Dist. Alaska, 1966, U.S. Ct. Appeals bar, 9th Circuit, 1966; asso. firm Burr, Pease & Kurtz, Inc. and predecessor, Anchorage, 1965-69, partner, 1969—; lectr. Anchorage Community Coll. U. Alaska, 1968. Bd. dirs. Prospect Heights Assn., Inc., Anchorage, 1970—; sec., dir. Hillside Rd. Maintenance, Inc., Anchorage, 1972—; vestryman, jr. warden St. Mary's Episcopal Ch., Anchorage, 1975—. Mem. Am., Alaska, Anchorage bar assns., Am. Judicature Soc. Alaskan editor Liens & Claims. Office: 825 W Eighth Ave Anchorage AK 99501 Tel (901) 279-2411

BURTON, JAMES AUGUSTUS, b. New Orleans, Oct. 3, 1947; B.A., Tulane U., 1969, J.D., 1972. Admitted to La. bar, 1972, U.S. Ct. Appeals 5th Circuit bar, 1975; asso. firm Deutsch, Kerrigan & Stiles, New Orleans, 1972-75, partner, 1976—. Mem. Am., La., New Orleans bar assns., Order of the Coif, Phi Beta Kappa. Asst. editor: Tulane Law Review, 1971-72. Home: 543 Octavia St New Orleans LA 70115 Office: 4700 1 Shell Square New Orleans LA 70139 Tel (504) 581-5141

BURTON, RILEY PAUL, b. Franklin, Nebr., Jan. 6, 1921; A.B., U. Wash., Seattle, 1948, J.D., 1950, B.A. in Law Librarianship, 1951. Admitted to Wash. bar, 1950; asst. prof., librarian, U. Utah, Salt Lake City, 1952-53; asst. prof., librarian, U. So. Calif., Los Angeles, 1953-56, asso. prof., librarian, 1956-59, prof., librarian, 1959-72, prof., curator Law Library, 1972—. Mem. Am. So. Calif. assns. law libraries, Am. Judicature Soc., Law and Soc. Assn. Home: 5935 Flores Ave Los Angeles CA 90056 Office: U Southern Calif University Park Los Angeles CA 90007 Tel (213) 746-2843

BURTON, WILFORD MOYLE, b. Salt Lake City, Feb. 5, 1910; B.A., U. Utah, 1931, LL.B., 1933, J.D., 1965. Admitted to Utah bar, 1933; partner firms Armonstrong & Burton, Salt Lake City, 1933-37, McKay, Burton, McMurray & Thurman, and predecessors, Salt Lake City, 1943—; judge Salt Lake City Ct., 1937-43; mem. Utah State Bar Commn.; dir., mem. exec. com. U and I Inc.; pres. Indsl. Western, Inc. Bd. dirs. Salt Lake City Library; bd. regents U. Utah. Mem. Utah State, Salt Lake County, Am. bar assns., Utah Restaurant Assn. (exec. sec.). Home: 668-17th Ave Salt Lake City UT 84103 Office: 500 Kennecott Bldg Salt Lake City UT 84133 Tel (801) 521-4135

BURTON, WILLARD CHANDLER, b. Rigby, Idaho, Apr. 19, 1910; LL.B., U. Idaho, 1941. Admitted to Idaho bar, 1943; individual practice law, St. Anthony, Idaho, 1945-57; pros. atty. Fremont County (Idaho), 1950-53; city atty. City of St. Anthony, 1953-57; atty. Idaho State Legislature, 1957; judge Idaho 12th Jud. Dist. Ct. 1957-67, 7th Jud. Dist. Ct., 1967—, adminstrv. judge, 1969-70. Chmn. Madison County (Idaho) Community Chest. Mem. Idaho State, Am. bar assns., Am. Judicature Soc., State Trial Judges Assn. (pres. 1969-70, nat. del. 1970). Decorated Bronze Star; recipient award of Merit for work with SSS, Pres. U.S., 1957. Home: 464 Linden Ave Rexburg ID 83340 Office: Courthouse Rexburg ID 83440 Tel (208) 356-6880

BURTT, DOUGLAS ALLEN, b. Lawrence, Mass., Dec. 15, 1946; A.B. in History, Ohio No. U., 1965, J.D., 1973. Admitted to Ohio bar, 1973, U.S. Dist. Ct., No. Dist. Ohio bar, 1974; since practiced in Tiffin, Ohio, asso. firm McMahon & Burtt, 1973; individual practice law, 1974—; asst. dir. Senaca County (Ohio) Pub. Defenders, 1975—. Bd. dirs. Sandusk Valley Substance Abuse, 1975—. Mem. Am., Ohio, Senaca County bar assns., Acad. Trial Attys. Recipient Wall St. Jour. award. Home: 423 Circular St Tiffin OH 44883 Office: 36 Madison St Tiffin OH 44803 Tel (419) 447-6242

BUSACCA, PAUL GORDON, b. Fresno, Calif., July 6, 1935; B.S., U. Santa Clara, 1957; LL.D., U. San Francisco, 1960. Admitted to Calif. bar, 1961; asso. firm Halley & Cornell, San Francisco, 1961-63, firm Walch, Griswold, Braden, Dittmar & Busacca, Fresno, 1963-66, firm Hanna & Brophy, Fresno, 1966-70, firm Chain, Younger, Jameson, Lemucchi, Busacca & Williams, Bakersfield, Calif., 1970—; lectr. in field. Mem. Am., Calif. State, Kern County bar assns., Calif. Trial Lawyers Assn., Calif. Applicants Attys. Assn., Assn. Calif. Tchr. Attys. Office: 1128 Truxtun Ave Bakersfield CA 93301 Tel (805) 324-6501

BUSBY, DAVID, b. Ada, Okla., Jan. 29, 1926; B.A., Yale, 1948; LL.B., Okla. 1951. Admitted to Okla. bar, 1950, N.Y. State bar, U.S. Supreme Ct. bars, 1959; asso. firm Busby, Harrell & Trice, Ada, 1951-53; partner firm Busby, Standfield, Busby & Deaton, Ada, 1953-55; counsel U.S. Senate Subcom. Automobile Mktg. Practices, Subcom. Fgn. Commerce, Interstate and Fgn. Commerce Com., 1955-58; partner firm Hays, Busby & Rivkin, N.Y.C., 1958-62, firm Busby, Rivkin, Sherman, Levy & Rehm, Washington, 1962—; city judge, Ada, 1952-53. Bd. dirs. Legal Aid Soc. of D.C., 1974—; East-West Trade Council, 1973—; mem. Nat. Motor Vehicle Safety Advisory Council, 1966-68; mem. bldg. com. Washington Cathedral. Mem. Am., (chmn. standing com. customs law 1973-76), D.C., Customs bar assns., Phi Delta Phi. Office: 900 17th St NW Washington DC 20006 Tel (202) 347-6007

BUSBY, DONALD LEE, b. Meridian, Tex., Aug. 16, 1940; B.B.A., North Tex. State U.; LL.B., U. Tex., Austin. Admitted to Tex. bar, 1965; practiced in Cleburne, Tex.; past asst. dist. atty.; city atty. City of Killeen (Tex.); judge Bell County (Tex.) Ct., to 1971; state judge, 1971—; lectr. in field. Co-chmn. Temple (Tex.) Art Fair, 1976; bd. dirs. Youth Services Bur. Mem. Tex., Johnson County (pres. 1968), Bell, Lampasas and Mills Counties (pres.-elect) bar assns. Home: 2625 Daniels Dr Temple TX 76501 Office: PO Box 324 Belton TX 76513 Tel (817) 939-3521

BUSBY, JAMES G., b. Tucson, Ariz., May 4, 1944; B.S. in Bus., U. Ariz., 1968, J.D., 1972. Admitted to Ariz. bar, 1972; partner firm Johnson, Hayes & Dowdall, Tucson, 1972—. Mem. Ariz., Pima City, Am. bar assns., Am. Trial Lawyers Assn. Home: 5122 Via Condesia St Tucson AZ 85718 Office: 250 N Church St Tucson AZ 85702 Tel (602) 624-8741

BUSBY, RICHARD GIRARD, b. Memphis, Aug. 18, 1927; LL.B., U. Memphis, 1952, Memphis State U., 1963. Admitted to Tenn. bar, 1953; mem. firm Busby and Blount, Memphis, 1953—. Mem. Memphis-Shelby County Bar Assn. Home: 2097 Meadowview Ln Memphis TN 38116 Office: 824 Dermon Building Memphis TN 38103 Tel (901) 525-5386

BUSCAGLIA, WILLIAM KENNETH, b. Buffalo, May 5, 1907; grad. Canisius Coll., 1926; LL.B., U. Buffalo, 1929. Admitted to N.Y. bar, 1930; individual practice law, Buffalo, 1930—; asst. atty. gen. State of N.Y., 1942-45; commr. N.Y. Liquor Authority, 1945-54; dir. sales tax Erie County (N.Y.), 1963-68, tax dir., 1968-70, commr. fin., 1970-73. Mem. N.Y., Erie County bar assns., Thomas More Legal Soc. Address: 120 Huntley Rd Buffalo NY 14215 Tel (716) 834-5115

BUSCH, BENJAMIN, b. N.Y.C., June 12, 1912; student Coll. City N.Y., 1928-30; LL.B., St. Lawrence U., 1933. Admitted to N.Y. bar, 1934; partner firm Katz & Somerich, N.Y.C., 1946-76; counsel firm Hamburger, Weinschenk, Molnar & Busch, N.Y.C., 1976—; adj. prof. internat. and comparative law N.Y. Law Sch., 1973—. Active Boy Scouts Am. Mem. Am. (chmn. sect. internat. law 1972-73, observer to UN 1973—), N.Y.C. (internat. law com., 1973-76), N.Y. State bar assns., Am. Judicature Soc., Am. Fgn. Law Assn. (pres. 1969-70), Consular Law Soc. (dir.) Am. Soc. Internat. Law. Author: (with Otto C. Sommerich) Foreign Law - A Guide to Pleading and Proof, 1959; contbr. articles to legal jours. Office: 630 Fifth Ave New York City NY 10020 Tel (212) 267-1900

BUSCH, CLEMENS RAYMOND, b. Rugby, N.D., May 30, 1921; B.A., St. Paul Seminary, 1945; postgrad. in Pub. Adminstrn., U. N.D., 1977—. High sch. tchr., 1948-49; exec. officer S.W. Dept. Health dist. health dept., 1949-54; in clothing bus., 1954-63; admitted to N.D. bar, 1969; asst. dir. div. health facilities N.D. Dept. Health, Bismarck, 1963—. Mem. N.D. State Bar. Home: 2007 N 2d St Bismarck ND 58501 Office: ND State Dept Health State Capital Bismarck ND 58505 Tel (701) 224-2352

BUSCH, ROBERT GENE, b. Ft. Collins, Colo., Dec. 22, 1942; A.B., Dartmouth Coll., J.D., U. Denver. Admitted to Colo. bar; mem. firm Alperstein, Plaut and Busch, Lakewood, Colo. Pres. Colo. Council to Abolish Capital Punishment; mem. Rocky Flats Permanent Monitoring Com. Mem. Am., Denver, Colo., First Jud. bar assns., Colo. Trial Lawyers Assn. Home: 2140 Routt St Lakewood CO 80215 Office: 7000 W 14th Ave Lakewood CO 80215 Tel (303) 232-5151

BUSCHMAN, HOWARD CHARLES, III, b. Red Bank, N.J., July 25, 1944; B.A., William Coll., 1966; LL.B., U. Va., 1969. Admitted to N.Y. bar, 1969; asso. firm Willkie Farr & Gallagher, N.Y.C., 1969-75, partner, 1976—. Mem. Bar Assn. City of N.Y. Office: Willkie Farr & Gallagher One Chase Manhattan Plaza New York City NY 10005 Tel (212) 248-1000

BUSH, F. M., III, b. Washington, Feb. 26, 1945; B.A., Brown U., 1967; J.D., U. Miss., 1969; LL.M., Harvard U., 1972. Admitted to Miss. bar, 1969; partner firm Mitchell, McNutt, Bush, Lagrone & Sams, Tupelo, Miss., 1969—. Mem. Miss. State Bar (pres. sect. young lawyers 1976—). Home: 1009 Fawn Dr Tupelo MS 38801 Office: 316 Court St Tupelo MS 38801 Tel (611) 842-3871

BUSH, JAMES M., b. Tucson, Sept. 30, 1922; B.A., U. Ariz., 1948, LL.B., 1950. Admitted to Ariz. bar, 1950; now mem. firm Evans, Kitchel & Jenckes, P.C., Phoenix; mem. Ariz. Commn. on Uniform State Laws, 1961—; chmn. exec. com. Nat. Conf. Commrs. on Uniform State Laws, 1973-75, pres., 1975—. Mem. State Bar Ariz., Am., Maricopa County bar assns., Phi Delta Phi. Bd. editors Ariz. Bar Jour., 1969-74. Office: 363 N 1st Ave Phoenix AZ 85003 Tel (602) 262-8894*

BUSH, JULIAN SEYMOUR, b. N.Y.C., Aug. 26, 1915; A.B., Columbia Coll., 1934; J.D., 1936. Admitted to N.Y. State bar, 1937; asso. Leon R. Jillson, N.Y.C., 1936-45; asso. T. Roland Berner, N.Y.C., 1946-60; partner firm Leventritt, Bush, Lewittes & Bender, N.Y.C., 1960-68; partner firm Bush & Schlesinger, N.Y.C., 1968-72; partner Roberts & Holland, N.Y.C., 1972-75, of counsel, 1975—; adj. prof. Law Sch. Columbia, 1958—. Pres. Gt. Neck Edn. Assn., 1953-54; dir. Gt. Neck Coop. Sch., 1947-53. Mem. Am., N.Y. State Bar Assns., N.Y. County Lawyers Assn., Estate Planning Council of N.Y.C., (pres. 1976-77), Internat. Acad. Estate and Trust Law (v.p. 1976-78), Am. Coll. Probate Counsel. Author: (with E. Schlesinger), The Best of Trusts and Estates, 1965; contbr. articles to profl. jours.; mem. editorial bd. Columbia Law Review; hon. col. staff of Gov. of Ky. Home: 24 Beverly Rd Great Neck NY 11021 Office: 1301 Ave of the Americas New York City NY 10019 Tel (212) 586-5200

BUSH, PETER J., b. Niagara Falls, N.Y., June 16, 1944; A.B., Dartmouth, 1965; M.A., Yale, 1967; J.D., State U. N.Y., Buffalo, 1971. Admitted to N.Y. bar, 1972; asso. firm Nixon, Hargrave, Devans & Doyle, Rochester, N.Y., 1972-74; regional atty. N.Y. State Dept. Environ. Conservation, Avon, N.Y., 1974—. Mem. Am., Monroe County bar assns. Office: PO Box 57 Avon NY 14414 Tel (716) 226-2466

BUSH, ROBERT ALAN, b. Oak Park, Ill., Dec. 4, 1942; B.A., Beloit Coll., 1964; J.D., Chgo. Kent Coll., 1967. Admitted to Ill. bar, 1967; asso. firm McLennon, McLennon & Nelson, Park Ridge, Ill., 1967-68; partner firm Bush & Bush, Mt. Prospect, Ill., 1969—. Bd. dirs. Blind Skiing Found., 1973—. Mem. Am., Chgo., Ill., N.W. Suburban (sec. 1970-71, 2d v.p. 1971-72, 1st v.p. 1974-75, pres. 1975-76) bar assns., Mt. Prospect C. of C. Home: 405 N Willie St Mount Prospect IL 60056 Office: 119 S Emerson St Mount Prospect IL 60056 Tel (312) 259-4140

BUSHEL, GLENN EPHRAIM, b. Albany, N.Y., Jan. 15, 1949; B.A., U. Maine, 1970; J.D., Syracuse U., 1973. Admitted to Md. bar, 1973, D.C. bar, 1974; law clk. to asso. judge Ct. Appeals of Md., Balt., 1973-74; asst. atty. gen. Md. Dept. Transp., Balt., 1974-76; asst. atty. gen. Office of Atty. Gen., Balt., 1976—. Mem. Md. State, D.C. bar assns. Home: 1 Velvet Ridge Dr Owings Mills MD 21117 Office: 1 S Calvert St Baltimore MD 21202 Tel (301) 383-3750

BUSHNELL, GEORGE EDWARD, JR., b. Detroit, Nov. 15, 1924; B.A., Amherst Coll., 1948; LL.B., U. Mich., 1951. Admitted to Mich. bar, 1951, U.S. Supreme Ct. bar; asso. firm Miller, Canfield, Paddock & Stone, Detroit, 1953-60, partner, 1961-76; partner firm Bushell, Gage & Reizen, Detroit, 1977—; mem. Mich. Jud. Tenure Commn., 1969—; chmn. Detroit Adv. Council, 1970—. Com. on Code of Ethics for Comml. Arbitrators, 1973—; commr. State Bar Mich., 1970-76, rep. Assembly, 1976—. Mem. Gov.'s Adv. Commn. on Electric Power Alternatives, 1975—; bd. dirs. New Detroit, Inc., chmn. bd., 1974-75; bd. dirs. Econ. Growth Council of Detroit, 1976—. Fellow Am. Bar Found.; mem. Am. (del. 1976—), Fed., Mich. (pres. 1975—), Detroit (pres. 1964-65) bar assns., Am. Arbitration Assn. (dir. 1970—), Am. Coll. Trial Lawyers, Internat. Soc. Barristers, U.S. 6th Circuit Jud. Conf., Def. Research Inst., Phi Delta Phi. Office: Suite 2380 400 Renaissance Center Detroit MI 48243 Tel (313) 444-4848

BUSHNELL, RALPH WILLIAM, b. Athens, Ga., Apr. 28, 1938; LL.B., U. Wis., 1962. Admitted to Wis. Supreme Ct. bar, 1962, U.S. Supreme Ct. bar, 1973; partner firm Stafford, Rosenbaum, Rieser & Hansen, Madison, Wis.; spl. counsel U. Wis., 1970. Mem. Am., Wis., Dane County bar assns. Home: 4921 Woodburn Dr Madison WI 53711 Office: 131 W Wilson St Madison WI 53701 Tel (608) 256-0226

BUSICK, LARRY LEE, b. Decatur, Ind., July 19, 1941; A.B., Valparaiso U., J.D. Admitted to Ind. bar, 1966, U.S. Supreme Ct. bar, 1972; practice law, Columbia City, Ind., 1966—; judge Decatur City Ct., 1968-72; bd. dirs. Ind. Criminal Justice Planning Agy. for N.E. Ind., 1968-71. Pres., Zion Luth. Ch., Columbia City, 1975—. Mem. Allen County, Ind. bar assns. Home: Rural Route 4 Columbia City IN 46725 Office: 1015 Anthony Wayne Bank Bldg Fort Wayne IN 46802 Tel (219) 422-0923

BUSSEWITZ, ROY JON, b. Hartford, Wis., Mar. 19, 1944; B.S., U. Wis., 1967; J.D., Valparaiso U., 1973. Admitted to Wis. bar, 1973; asst. to dean of scis. U. Wis. at Milw., 1973-74, asst. to dir. allied health studies, 1974-75, asst. to dean Sch. Allied Health Professions, 1975-76, asst. prof., 1976—. Mem. Wis. Bar Assn. Home: 9707 W National Ave Apt 10 West Allis WI 53227 Office: U Wis 110 Pearse Hall Milwaukee WI 53201

BUSSEY, REUBEN THOMAS, JR., b. Atlanta, Mar. 7, 1943; B.A., Morris Brown Coll., 1965; J.D., Tex. So. U., 1969. Admitted to Tex. bar, 1969, Ga. bar, 1971; mem. staff Legal Aid Soc., Inc., Atlanta, 1969; atty. FTC, Boston, 1969-71; partner firm Kennedy, Bussey & Sampson, P.C., Atlanta, 1971-76; mem. Atlanta Jud. Commn. Co-gen. counsel A.M.E. Ch. Mem. Nat. Bar Assn., State Bar Ga., State Bar Tex. Home: 2600 Camp Creek Pkwy 19-G College Park GA 30337 Office: PO Box 92361 Atlanta GA 30314 Tel (404) 752-7472

BUSSIERE, EMILE ROLAND, b. Manchester, N.H., May 16, 1932; student St. Anselm's Coll.; LL.B., Boston Coll., 1954. Admitted to N.H. bar, 1954; individual practice law, Manchester, 1956—; U.S. Commr., State of N.H., 1960-63; atty. Hillsborough County, N.H., 1963-68. Mem. N.H. Bar Assn. Home: 55 Carpenter St Manchester NH 03104 Office: 15 North St Manchester NH 03104 Tel (603) 622-1002

BUSSMAN, DONALD H., b. Lakewood, Ohio, July 15, 1925; Ph.B., U. Chgo., 1947, J.D., 1951. Admitted to Ill. bar, 1951; mgr. personnel and transp. law div. Swift & Co., Chgo., 1960—. Mem. Am., Chgo. bar assns. Home: 860 N Dewitt Pl Chicago IL 60611 Office: 115 W Jackson Blvd Chicago IL 60604 Tel (312) 431-2636

BUTCHER, JAMES ROBERT, b. Detroit, Mar. 9, 1933; B.A., Wittenberg U., 1955; LL.B., Valparaiso U., 1958. Admitted to Ind. bar, 1958, Ill. bar, 1962, U.S. Supreme Ct. bar, 1966; asso. firm Bolinger, Butcher & Van Dorn, 1964-67; owner firm Butcher & Ball, Kokomo, Ind., 1968—; atty. Howard County Planning Commn., Kokomo Urban Renewal Commn. Pres., founder, dir. Kokomo Area Youth for Christ, 1965—; pres., founder Kokomo Christian Bus. Men's Assn.; founder Kokomo Connie Mack Baseball League, 1969; mem. exec. com. Christian Bus. Men's Commn.; bd. dirs. Kokomo Rescue Mission; chmn. bd. deacons Bible Bapt. Ch., Kokomo. Recipient Distinguished Parent of Year award Taylor U., 1976. Home: 213 Branded Ct Kokomo IN 46901 Office: 201 N Buckeye St Kokomo IN 46901 Tel (317) 457-1126

BUTERA, ROBERT JAMES, b. Norristown, Pa., Jan. 21, 1935; B.S., U. Pa., 1956; LL.B., Dickinson Sch. Law, 1959. Admitted to Pa. bar, 1960; partner Butera & Butera, Norristown, 1960-62, Butera & Detwiler, 1962-64, Butera & Dewiler, and predecessors, Norristown, 1964-73, King of Prussia, Pa., 1973—; mem. Pa. Gen. Assembly, 1963—, majority whip, 1967-68, minority whip, 1969-72, majority leader, 1973-74, minority leader, 1975—. Mem. Montgomery County, Pa. bar assns. Home: 1926 Brandon Rd Norristown PA 19401 Office: 700 Valley Forge Plaza King of Prussia PA 19406 Tel (215) 265-0800

BUTLER, A. BATES, b. Wheeling, W.Va., May 23, 1908; A.B., W.Va. U., 1931, LL.B., 1932. Admitted to W.Va. bar, 1932; spl. agt. FBI, Washington, Pitts. and Tenn., 1942-63; mgr. Pima County Atty. Office, Tucson, 1965-69; justice of peace, Tucson, 1969—. Home: 4041 Calle Chica St Tucson AZ 85711 Office: 115 N Church St Tucson AZ 85701 Tel (602) 792-8134

BUTLER, ALBERT ELWIN, b. Savannah, Ga., Apr. 24, 1919; A.B., Presbyterian Coll., 1942; grad. John B. Stetson Coll. Law; LL.B., Woodrow Wilson Coll. Law, 1950. Admitted to Ga. bar, 1950, U.S. Supreme Ct. bar; aide to adj. gen. State of Ga., 1950-51; tax examiner, 1951-56; individual practice law, Savannah and Jesup, Ga., 1956—; free-lance writer. Mem. Internat. Platform Assn., Nat. Writers Club, Ga. Bar, Assn., Oceanic Soc., U.S. Naval Inst., Am. Security Counsel, Inst. Strategic Services. Home: 779 S 4th St Jesup GA 31545 Office: 105 SE Broad St Jesup GA 31545 Tel (912) 427-6603

BUTLER, CAROLE, b. Lansing, Mich., May 30, 1943; B.S., Mich. State U., 1967; J.D., Ohio State U., 1970. Admitted to Ohio bar, 1970, Mich. bar, 1971; asso. firm Hildebrandt, King & Smith, Lansing, Mich., 1970-71; instr. law Capital U., 1972--, asst. prof. law, 1974—. Mem. Am., Ohio, Columbus bar assns., Pitts. Inst. Legal Medicine. Home: 3877 Rushmore Dr Columbus OH 43220 Office: 2199 E Main St Columbus OH 43209 Tel (614) 236-6395

BUTLER, CECIL VICTOR, JR., b. Quincy, Fla., Dec. 24, 1942; B.S., Auburn U., 1967; J.D., U. Fla., 1969. Admitted to Fla. bar, 1970; asso. firm Gurney & Skolfield, Fla., 1969-72, firm Adams, Gilman & Cooper, 1972-74, firm Butler Kirkland & Englehardt, Orlando, 1974—. Mem. Fla., Orange County, Am. bar assns., Fla., Am. trial lawyers assns. Home: 1923 E Washington St Orlando FL 32802 Office: 1113 E Robinson St Orlando FL 32801 Tel (305) 422-6600

BUTLER, DENNIS FRANCIS, b. Cleve., Jan. 11, 1940; B.A., U. Notre Dame, 1962; J.D., Cleve.-Marshall Law Sch., 1969. Admitted to Ohio bar, 1970; partner firm Butler, Butler & Clarke, Cleve., 1974—; asst. city prosecutor Olmsted Falls (Ohio), 1971; asst. atty. gen. State of Ohio, 1971-74; sr. trial atty. Pub. Defenders Office, 1974-76; co-founder, gen. counsel Pretrial Supervised Release Program, Cuyahoga County Cts., 1974-76. Mem. Big Bros. Assn., 1963-68, Cath. Commn. for Community Action, 1973; vice chmn. Cuyahoga County Democratic Party. Mem. Nat. Assn. Criminal Def. Attys. and Pub. Defenders, Cuyahoga County Bar Assn., Bar Assn. Greater Cleve. Office: 1600 Williamson Bldg 215 Euclid Ave Cleveland OH 44114 Tel (216) 621-3980

BUTLER, DUGE, JR., b. Indpls., Jan. 7, 1928; LL.B., Ind. U., 1954. Admitted to Ind. bar, 1955; sr. partner Butler, Brown, Hahn and Little, Indpls., 1955—; city atty., Beech Grove, Ind., 1956-67. Mem. Ind., Indpls. bar assns., Ind. Trial Lawyers Assn., Phi Alpha Delta. Office: 156 E Market St 4th Floor Indianapolis IN 46204 Tel (317) 632-9411

BUTLER, EDWARD FRANKLYN, b. Memphis, July 1, 1937; B.A. in Polit. Sci., U. Miss., 1958; J.D., Vanderbilt U., 1961; postgrad. Memphis State U., 1963-64. Admitted to Tenn. bar, 1961, Tex. bar, 1973; asso. dir. Vanderbilt U. Devel. Found., 1961; Asso. firm Nelson, Wilson & Thomason, Memphis, 1961-63; asso. firm Erie S. Henrich, Memphis, 1963; partner firm Cobb & Butler, Memphis, 1963-67; partner firm Butler & McDowell, Memphis, 1967-72; gen. counsel Hibbard, O'Connor & Weeks, Inc. and affiliates, Memphis, N.Y.C., Houston, 1972-74; individual practice law, Houston, Memphis, 1974—; gen. counsel, sec. Safety First Fire Control Co., Memphis, 1963—; gen. counsel Tenn. Jr. C. of C., 1964-65; lectr. Memphis State U., 1963-64; moderator TV program Issues in Action, 1964-66; spl. judge Memphis & Shelby County Juvenile Ct., 1966—, Shelby County General Sessions Ct., 1966—, Memphis City and Traffic Cts., 1966—. Mem. Memphis & Shelby County Safety Counsel, 1963-68; dir. Memphis Navy League, 1967-69; state chmn. govt. affairs Tenn. Jr. C. of C., 1963—; mem. Memphis C. of C. (mem. mil. affairs com. 1976); Houston C. of C. (mil. affairs com., 1974—). Mem. Am., Tenn., Tex., Memphis, Shelby County bar assns. Recipient Key to the City of Memphis, 1973; appointed Ky. Colonel, 1971; Tenn. Colonel, 1968. Home: 59 N White Stone Rd Memphis TN 38117 Office: 202 Adams Ave Memphis TN 38103 Tel (901) 523-8888

BUTLER, GEORGE HARRISON, b. Jackson, Miss., Mar. 9, 1917; B.A., U. Miss., 1938, LL.B. with distinction, 1940. Admitted to Miss. bar, 1940; mem. firm Butler, Snow, O'Mara, Stevens & Cannada, Jackson, 1940—. Mem. Am., Miss. bar assns., Phi Delta Phi, Omicron Delta Kappa. Home: 4005 Old Canton Ln Jackson MS 39206 Office: 1700 Deposit Guaranty Plaza Jackson MS 39205 Tel (601) 948-5711

BUTLER, JOHN PATRICK, b. Cleve., May 13, 1905; A.B., U. Notre Dame, 1927; LL.B., Western Res. U., 1929. Admitted to Ohio bar, 1930, U.S. Supreme Ct. bar, 1961; asst. police prosecutor Cleve., 1932, sec. to mayor, 1933; asst. county prosecutor, Ohio, 1936-42; enforcement atty. regional office OPA, Cleve., 1942-43; asst. regional atty. War Products Bd., Cleve., 1943; mem. firm Squire, Sanders & Dempsey, Cleve., 1944-45, Carney & Carney, Cleve., 1945-47; exec. asst. to mayor Cleve., 1947-50; sec. to County Charter Commn., Cleve., 1950; mem. firm Carney & Carney, 1951; regional atty. Office Price Stblzn. for Ohio, Mich., Ky., 1951; individual practice law, Cleve., 1951—; asst. atty. gen. criminal div., Ohio, 1958-60; lectr. John Marshall Law Sch., Cleve. State U., 1975; criminal law tchr. Cleve. Para-Legal Inst.; instr. criminal evidence Cleve. Police Acad., 1936-39. Mem. Cleve., Cuyahoga County bar assns., Delta Phi. Home: 19331 Beachcliff Blvd Rocky River OH 44116 Office: 1600 Williamson Bldg Cleveland OH 44114 Tel (216) 621-3870

BUTLER, KENNETH CLIFFORD, b. London, Mar. 12, 1917; LL.B., Wayne State U., 1943, J.D., 1943. Admitted to Mich. bar, 1943; individual practice law, Detroit; atty. dept. judge adv. Amvets of Mich., 1955-56, legis. dir., 1961-65. Mem. Mich., Macomb County (Mich.) bar assns., Comml. Law League. Office: 24487 Gratiot Ave East Detroit MI 48021 Tel (313) 777-0770

BUTLER, MICHAEL FRANCIS, b. Pitts., Aug. 17, 1935; B.A. magna cum laude, Harvard U., 1957; LL.B., Yale U., 1960. Admitted to Pa. bar, 1960; asso. firm Kirkpatrick, Lockhart, Johnson & Hutchison, Pitts., 1960-69; asst. gen. counsel, later dep. gen. counsel Dept. Commerce, Washington, 1969-73; v.p., gen. counsel Overseas Pvt. Investment Corp., Washington, 1973-75; gen. counsel Fed. Energy Adminstrn., Washington, 1975-77; partner firm Andrews, Kurth, Campbell & Jones, Houston and Washington, 1977—. Mem. Am., Pa., Allegheny County bar assns., Am. Soc. Internat. Law, Am. Judicature Soc., Adminstrv. Conf. U.S. Home: 3412 O St NW Washington DC 20007

BUTLER, MORRIS R., b. Metcalfe County, Ky., Dec. 20, 1923; J.D., U. Louisville, 1952. Admitted to Ky. bar, 1954; practiced since in Greensburg, Ky. Mem. Ky. Bar Assn. Home and Office: 202 Court St Greensburg KY 42743 Tel (502) 932-4821

BUTLER, SAMUEL COLES, b. Logansport, Ind., Mar. 10, 1930; A.B. magna cum laude, Harvard, 1951, LL.B. magna cum laude, 1954; LL.M., N.Y.U., 1959. Admitted to Dist. Columbia bar, 1954, Ind. bar, 1954, N.Y. State bar, 1957, U.S. Supreme Ct. bar, 1966; asso. firm Barnes, Hickam, Pantzer & Boyd, Indpls., 1954; law clk. to U.S. Supreme Ct. Justice Minton 1954; asso. firm Cravath, Swaine & Moore, N.Y.C., 1956-60, partner, 1960—. Mem. N.Y. State, Am. bar assns., Assn. Bar City N.Y. Contbr. articles to legal jours. Home: 1220 Park Ave New York City NY 10028 Office: One Chase Manhattan Plaza New York City NY 10005 Tel (212) 422-3000

BUTLER, THOMAS JOSEPH, JR., b. Herington, Kans., Jan. 17, 1912; LL.B., Drake U., 1934, J.D., 1968. Admitted to Iowa bar, 1934, Kans. bar, 1939; asso. firm Ostrus, Hansen & Butler, Des Moines, 1934-39; individual practice law, Herington, 1939—; atty. City of Herington, 1945-53, 63—. Mem. Kans., Dickinson County bar assns., City Attys. Assn. Kans. Home: 608 N Broadway Herington KS 67449 Office: 12 S Broadway Herington KS 67449 Tel (913) 258-2267

BUTLER, WALLACE WEBB, b. Sibley, Iowa, Apr. 6, 1920; B.S. in Elec. Engring., State U. Iowa, 1942, J.D., 1948. Admitted to Iowa bar, 1948; partner firm Clark & Butler, Waterloo, Iowa. Mem. Am., Iowa bar assns. Home: Winter Ridge Rd Cedar Falls IA 50613 Office: Box 596 Waterloo IA 50704 Tel (319) 234-5701

BUTOWSKY, DAVID MARTIN, b. Phila., Aug. 14, 1936; A.B., Temple U., 1958; LL.B., George Washington U., 1962. Admitted to Md. bar, 1962, U.S. Supreme Ct. bar, 1970, N.Y. State bar, 1971; chief enforcement atty. div. corp. regulation SEC, Washington, 1962-70; asso. firm Breed, Abbott & Morgan, N.Y.C., 1970-71; partner firms Butowsky, Schwenke & Devine, N.Y.C., 1971-75, Gordon Hurwitz Butowsky Baker Wietzen & Shalov, N.Y.C., 1975—; dir. Oppenheimer Centennial Capitol Funds; guest lectr. Bklyn. Law Sch.; lectr. Practicing Law Inst. Mem. Am., N.Y. County, Fed., City bar assns. Contbr. articles to legal jours. Home: 73 Highridge Rd Mount Kisco NY 10549 Office: 299 Park Ave New York City NY 10017 Tel (212) 486-1550

BUTT, THOMAS FRANKLIN, b. Eureka Springs, Ark., Mar. 26, 1917; LL.B., U. Ark., 1938, J.D., 1969. Admitted to Ark. bar, U.S. Dist. Ct. bar, 1938, U.S. Supreme Ct. bar, 1955, U.S. Ct. Mil. Appeals bar, 1968; individual practice law, Eureka Springs and Fayetteville, Ark., 1938-40, 46-50; judge Chancery and Probate Cts., Fayetteville, 1950—; instr. law. U. Ark., 1939-40; atty. U.S. Office Price Adminstrn., 1946-50. Active West Ark. council Boy Scouts Am., 1955-65. Mem. Ark. (exec. council ho. of dels. state assn. 1971—), Washington County bar assns., Ark. Jud. Council (pres. 1957-58), U.S. Army Mil. Govt. Assn., Judge Advocate Gens. Sch. Alumni Assn. Home: 1004 Rebecca St Fayetteville AR 72701 Office: Ct House Fayetteville AR 72701 Tel (501) 521-8400

BUTTARO, PETER JOSEPH, b. Syracuse, N.Y., May 20, 1930; A.B., Syracuse U., 1952; M.S. in Hosp. Adminstrn., Northwestern U., 1957; J.D., Suffolk U., 1968. Admitted to S.D. bar, 1968; adminstr. St. Lukes Hosp., Aberdeen, S.D., 1967-69; pres. Health Care Facility Cons., Aberdeen, 1969—; states atty. Brown County, S.D., 1974-76. Pres., Aberdeen Sr. Center, 1969-71, Northeastern Mental Health Center, Aberdeen, 1973. Mem. S.D. Trial Lawyers Assn., Am., S.D. bar assns. Author adminstrn. nursing homes and legal home study course, legal manual for nursing homes. Home: 1505 N Jay St Aberdeen SD 57401 Office: 122 S Lincoln St Aberdeen SD 57401 Tel (605) 225-2795

BUTTERFIELD, CHARLES ROBERT, b. Ruston, La., Jan. 22, 1943; B.A., U. Miss., 1965; J.D., 1968. Admitted to Miss. bar, 1968, Tex. bar, 1969; law clk. to judge U.S. Ct. of Appeals, 5th Circuit, Montgomery, Ala., 1968; asso. firm Wynne & Jaffe, Dallas, 1968-75, partner, 1975—. Mem. Am., Dallas bar assns., State Bar Tex. (mem. securities and investment banking com. 1974—), The 500 Inc., Phi Delta Phi, Omicron Delta Kappa. Mem. editorial bd. Miss. Law Jour. 1967-68. Home: 4754 Alta Vista Circle Dallas TX 75229 Office: 1000 LTV Tower Dallas TX 75201 Tel (214) 748-7211

BUTTERFIELD, FRANKLIN HERMAN, b. Riverton, Utah, Apr. 19, 1926; B.A. and S. with honors, U. Utah, 1949; LL.B., George Washington U., 1956. Admitted to Utah bar, 1956; individual practice law, Orem, Utah, 1956—; dep. atty. Utah County (Utah), Provo, 1968-72; city atty. City of Orem, 1970-76. Home: 409 E 1200 N St Orem UT 84057 Office: 056 N State St Orem UT 84057 Tel (801) 225-4170

BUTTERWORTH, JAMES NEWBY, b. Marietta, Ga., Feb. 3, 1943; B.S., North Ga. Coll., 1965; J.D., Walter F. George Sch. Law, Mercer U., 1968. Admitted to Ga. bar, 1969; partner firm Melton, McKenna and House, Macon, Ga., 1968-74, Griggs and Butterworth, Cornelia, Ga., 1974—; spl. adviser to com. criminal law study Middle Ga. Area Planning Commn., Macon, 1969-70. Pres., bd. dirs. United Cerebral Palsy of Macon and Middle Ga., 1969-72; adviser Legal Explorer/Post Middle Ga. council Boy Scouts Am., 1972-73, troop and pack adviser NE Ga. Council, 1975-76. Mem. Am., Mountain Jud. bar assns., Am., Ga. Trial lawyers assns., Habersham County (Ga.) C. of C. (dir., v.p. 1976—). Home: Safford Springs Demorest GA 30535 Office: 309 Clarkesville St Cornelia GA 30531 Tel (404) 778-2134

BUTTNER, JOSEPH ROBERT, b. Boston, Dec. 18, 1923; B.A., Tufts Coll., 1945; LL.B., Boston Coll., 1950. Admitted to Mass. bar, 1951; mem. firm Schair and Duquet, Braintree, Mass., 1965; mem. Bernard Cohen, Inc., Brockton, Mass., 1966—; with Travelers Ins. Co., Boston, 1950-62; chief sec. to Lt. Gov. Mass., 1963-64; recodification counsel State of Mass., 1966-70; counsel of speaker Mass. Ho. of Reps., 1970-75. Mem. Democratic Town Com. Scituate (Mass.), 1960-65, Dem. City Com., Brockton, 1966-76; mem. Brockton Civic Action Com., 1966-72. Mem. Mass., Plymouth County (workmen's compensation legis. com., legis. com. Mass.) bar assns. Home: 261 Keith Ave Brockton MA 04201 Office: 288 N Main St Brockton MA 04201 Tel (617) 586-5353

BUTTON, ROBERT YOUNG, b. Culpeper, Va., Nov. 2, 1899; LL.B., U. Va., 1922. Admitted to Va. bar, 1922; asso. firm Button, Slaughter, Yeaman & Morton; and predecessors, Culpeper, 1922-24, partner, 1924-58, sr. partner, 1958—; atty. gen. State Va., 1962-70; mem. Va. Senate, 1946-61. Mem. Va. Bd. Edn., 1945-60, Potomac River Commn., 1958, Va. Commn. Pub. Edn., 1954. Fellow Am. Coll. Trial Lawyers; mem. Am., Va., Richmond, Culpeper bar assns. Home and Office: 139 W Davis St Culpeper VA 22701 Tel (703) 825-0766

BUTTREY, DONALD WAYNE, b. Terre Haute, Ind., Feb. 6, 1935; B.S., Ind. State U., 1956; J.D., Ind. U., 1961. Admitted to Ind. bar, 1961, U.S. Supreme Ct. bar, 1972; law clk. U.S. Dist. Ct., So. Dist. Ind., Indpls., 1961-63; mem. firm McHale, Cook & Welch, Indpls., 1963-67, partner, 1967—; dir. So. Ind. R.R., 1969-76. Dir., Tabernacle Recreation Program, Indpls., 1972-74; mem. Greater Indpls. Democratic Fin. Com., 1972, 76—. Mem. Am., Ind., Indpls., 7th Circuit bar assns., Phi Delta Phi. Editor Ind. Law Jour., 1960-61. Home: 38 E 52d St Indianapolis IN 46205 Office: 906 C of C Bldg 320 N Meridian St Indianapolis IN 46204 Tel (317) 634-7588

BUTZBAUGH, ELDEN W., JR., b. Benton Harbor, Mich., Dec. 2, 1937; B.A., Western Mich. U., 1961, M.B.A., 1964; J.D., U. Mich., 1968. Admitted to Mich. bar, 1968; individual practice law, St. Joseph, Mich., 1968—; mem. jury service and selection com. for U.S. Fed. Ct., standing com. for para-legal service State Bar Mich. Bd. dirs., crusade chmn., v.p. Am. Cancer Soc., Mich. div., Berrien County, 1969-73; bd. dirs. Vols. in Probation, 1973—, Y-Uncles for Berrien County, 1968-71; del. state Republican. Conv., 1972; chmn. nat. com. U. Mich. Law Sch. Fund. Mem. Berrien County Bar Assn. (indigent defendant def. com., library chair), Am., Mich. trial lawyers assns., Twin Cities C. of C. (ambassador), Western Mich. U. Mgmt. Alumni Assn., Phi Alpha Delta. Home: 218 S Sunnybank St Saint Joseph MI 49085 Office: Courthouse Sq 715 Ship St Saint Joseph MI 49085 Tel (616) 983-0121

BUTZNER, JOHN DECKER, JR., b. Scranton, Pa., Oct. 2, 1917; B.A., U. Scranton, 1938; LL.B., U. Va., 1941. Admitted to Va. bar, 1940; individual practice law, Fredericksburg, Va., 1941-42, 1946-58; asso. judge 15th Jud. Circuit Ct. of Va., 1958-60; judge 39th Jud. Circuit Ct. of Va., 1960-62; judge U.S. Dist. Ct. Eastern Dist. of Va., 1962-67; circuit judge U.S. Ct. Appeals 4th Circuit, Richmond, Va., 1967—. Home: 5507 Dorchester Rd Richmond VA 23225 Office: U S Ct House 10th and Main Sts Richmond VA 23219 Tel (804) 648-7732

BUXBAUM, RICHARD MANFRED, b. Friedberg, Germany, Apr. 16, 1930; A.B., Cornell U., 1950, LL.B., 1952; LL.M., U. Calif., Berkeley, 1953. Admitted to N.Y., Calif. bars, 1953; individual practice law, Canandaigua, N.Y., 1953; served with JAGC, U.S. Army, 1954-57; asso. firms Sutherland, Linowitz & Williams, Rochester, N.Y., 1957, Harris, Beach, Keating, Wilcox, Dale & Linowitz, Rochester, 1958-61; prof. Sch. Law U. Calif., Berkeley, 1961—, dir. Earl Warren Legal Inst., 1970-74. Pres. Univ. YMCA, Berkeley; bd. dirs. Internat. House, Berkeley, Equal Rights Advocates, San Francisco; trustee Center Law in Pub. Interest, Los Angeles. Mem. Am. Bar Assn. Author: (with Lattin and Jennings) Corporations—Cases and Materials, 4th edit., 1968; contbr. articles to legal jours. Office: 478 Boalt Hall U Calif Berkeley CA 94720 Tel (415) 642-1771

BUXBAUM, STEVEN ANDREW, b. Jamaica, N.Y., Aug. 23, 1948; B.A. cum laude, Dartmouth, 1970; J.D. with honors, U. Tex., 1973. Admitted to Tex. bar, 1973; atty. Justice J. Curtiss Brown Ct. Civil Appeals 14th Supreme Jud., Houston, 1973-74; asso. firm Childs, Fortenbach, Beck & Guyton, Houston, 1974—. Mem. State Bar Tex., Am., Houston, Houston Jr. bar assns., Order of Coif, Phi Delta Phi. Home: 8803 Haverstock St Houston TX 77031 Office: 402 Pierce Ave PO Box 391 Houston TX 77001 Tel (713) 659-6681

BUYCK, MARK WILSON, JR., b. Columbia, S.C., Dec. 25, 1934; A.B. in Journalism, U. S.C., 1956, J.D., 1959. Admitted to S.C. bar, 1959; staff judge adv. USAF, 1959-62; partner firm Willcox, Hardee, Palmer, O'Farrell, McLeod & Buyck, Florence, S.C., 1962-75, 77—; U.S. atty. Dist. of S.C., Columbia, 1975-77; vis. prof. U. S.C., Florence, 1963-69. Pres., Florence Little Theatre, 1963-64; chmn. Carolina Scholars Selection Com., 12th Jud. Circuit, 1968—, S.C. Alliance Arts in Edn. Com., 1973—; v.p. S.C. unit Am. Cancer Soc., 1973-74; mem. adv. bd. John F. Kennedy Center, Washington, 1969—; mem. state bd. Cancer and Heart Assns., 1965-75; mem. bd. visitors Winthrop Coll., 1975—. Mem. Am., S.C. (v.p. 1970-74), Florence County bar assns., Am. Judicature Soc., Am. Assn. R.R. Trial Council, S.C. Def. Attys. Assn. (sec.-treas. 1976, pres.-elect 1977), Fedn. Ins. Counsel. Home: Bonnie Shade 1439 Cherokee Rd Florence SC 29501 Office: POB 1909 248 W Evans St Florence SC 29503 Tel (803) 662-3258

BUZANE, DAVIS PETER, b. Kosmas, Greece, May 25, 1903; student U. Chgo.; LL.B., DePaul U., Chgo., 1927; B.S. in Law, Northwestern U., J.D., 1928. Admitted to Ill. bar, 1927; practice law. With War Dept. AAF Material Services, Mid-Western Dist., 1943-45; registrants advisor, govt. appeal agt. Selective Service Bd., 1942-69; supreme legal counselor Greek Am. Progressive Assn., 1943-49; trustee St. Demetrios Greek Orthodox Ch., Ft. Lauderdale, Fla., 1972-75. Mem. Chgo Bar Assn. Recipient certificate of commendation for services to Selective Service Act.

BUZZELL, ARTHUR LEE, b. Emmetsburg, Iowa, June 29, 1947; B.B.A., Drake U., 1969, J.D., 1971. Admitted to Iowa bar, 1971; partner firm Newport, Buzzell & Liebbe, and predecessors, Davenport, Iowa, 1947—. Mem. Am., Iowa State bar assns., Am., Iowa trial lawyers assns., Order of Coif. Home: 245 Hillcrest Ave Davenport IA 52803 Office: 306 Citizens Federal Bldg Davenport IA 52801 Tel (319) 323-9963

BYAM, CLARK RUTHERFORD, b. Westfield, N.J., Dec. 28, 1943; grad. Wesleyan U., 1966; law degree Hastings Coll., 1972. Admitted to Calif. bar, 1972; partner firm Hahn & Hahn, Pasadena, Calif., 1972—. Mem. Calif., Los Angeles County, Am. bar assns. Recipient Am. Jurisprudence award Constitutional Law; contbr. articles to legal jours. Home: 2020 Woodlyn Rd Pasadena CA 91109 Office: 301 E Colorado Blvd Suite 900 Pasadena CA 91101 Tel (213) 790-9123

BYBEE, SHANNON LARMER, JR., b. Tropic, Utah, Aug. 29, 1938; B.A., U. Nev., 1966; J.D., U. Utah. Admitted to Nev. bar, 1969; law clk. Nev. Supreme Ct., 1969-70; asso. firm Lionel, Sawyer & Wartman, Las Vegas, 1970; mem. State Gaming Control Bd., Nev., 1971-75; partner firm Hilbrecht, Jones, Schreck & Bybee, Las Vegas, 1975—; instr. hotel law Clark County Community Coll., 1974-75, mem. adv. com., 1976—. Vice-pres. Boulder Dam Area council Boy Scouts Am., 1975—. Mem. Nev., Clark County bar assns., Order of Coif, Phi Kappa Phi. Contbr. articles to legal jours. Office: 600 E Charleston St Las Vegas NV 89104 Tel (702) 382-2101

BYE, JAMES E., b. Thief River Falls, Minn., May 2, 1930; B.B.A. with distinction, U. Minn., 1951; LL.B. cum laude, Harvard U. Admitted to Colo. bar, 1957; partner firm Holme, Roberts & Owen, Denver, 1960—; adj. prof. law U. Denver. Mem. Am., Colo., Denver bar assns., Denver Estate Planning Council. Home: 5236 E Princeton Ave Englewood CO 80110 Office: Suite 1010 1700 Broadway Denver CO 80202 Tel (303) 573-8000

BYERS, JAMES WALSH, b. Green Bay, Wis., Aug. 16, 1926; B.S., U. Wis., 1951, J.D., 1956. Admitted to Wis. bar, 1956; mem. firm Strehlow, Cranston, Byers & Brown, Green Bay, 1956-61; judge Brown County Ct. Br. II, Green Bay, 1962—; mem. faculty Nat. Coll. Juvenile Justice, Reno, 1973-74; mem. bd. fellows Juvenile Justice Research Inst., U. Pitts., 1977—; ad hoc instr. law U. Wis., 1972-75. Mem. Nat. Council Juvenile Ct. Judges (pres. 1977—). Home: 440 Roselawn Blvd Green Bay WI 54301 Office: 125 S Adams St Green Bay WI 54301 Tel (414) 497-3377

BYERS, JOHN KAYE, b. Knoxville, Tenn., Sept. 7, 1930; LL.D., U. Tenn., 1959. Admitted to Tenn. bar, 1959; mem. firm West & Fuller, Kingsport, Tenn., 1959-62, Byers & Kirkpatrick, 1962-65; county atty. Sullivan County (Tenn.), 1966; judge 26th Jud. Circuit of Tenn., 1966-76, Ct. Criminal Appeals, 1976—. Pres. Kingsport Council of Churches, 1962-63. Mem. Kingsport Bar Assn. (pres. 1963-64). HOme: 900 Broadwood Dr Kingsport TN 37660 Office: 317 Shelby St Kingsport TN 37660 Tel 247-3551

BYERS, MAURICE, b. Louisville, Oct. 11, 1924; J.D., U. Louisville, 1950; B.D., Lexington Theol. Sem., 1958. Admitted to Ky. bar, 1950, Ga. bar, 1963; ordained to ministry Christian Ch., 1959; pastor 1st Christian Ch., Dixon, Ill., 1959-61, Dublin, Ga., 1961-63; individual practice law; judge Laurens County (Ga.) Juvenile Ct., 1970—. Mem. Dublin, Ga. bar assns. Home: POB 952 Dublin GA 31021 Office: Carroll Bldg Dublin GA 31021 Tel (912) 272-6972

BYERS, MICHAEL WILLIAM, b. Los Angeles, Mar. 13, 1943; B.A. in Psychology, U. Hawaii, 1965; J.D., Southwestern U. Admitted to Calif. bar, 1971; city atty. City of Los Angeles, 1971-73; asso. firm Gilbert, Kelly, Crowley & Jennett, Los Angeles, 1973—. Mem. Am. Bar Assn. Office: 1541 Wilshire Blvd Los Angeles CA 90017 Tel (213) 484-2330

BYINGTON, JOHN HOWARD, JR., b. Brookline, Mass., May 24, 1932; A.B., Holy Cross Coll., Worcester, Mass., 1953; LL.B., St. John's U., 1962. Admitted to N.Y. bar, 1963; asso. firm Winthrop, Stimson, Putnam & Roberts, N.Y.C., 1962-74, partner, 1974—. Mem. Assn. of Bar City N.Y. Office: 40 Wall St New York City NY 10005 Tel (212) 943-0700

BYNUM, FREDERICK WILLIAMSON, JR., b. Aberdeen, N.C., Nov. 7, 1921; A.B., Duke, 1943; LL.B., Harvard U., 1948. Admitted to N.C. bar, 1948; partner firms Bynum & Bynum, Rockingham, N.C., 1948-51, 54-63, Preyer & Bynum, Greensboro, N.C., 1951-54, Leath, Bynum, Kitchin & Neal, Rockingham, 1963-. Mem. Internat. Assn. Ins. Counsel, Am. Coll. Trial Lawyers, N.C. Bar Assn. (gov. 1970-73). Home: Laurel Ledge Rockingham NC 28379 Office: 111 Washington Sq Rockingham NC 28379 Tel (919) 997-2206

BYRD, CLARENCE CARTER, b. Florence, S.C., Dec. 1, 1917; LL.B., U. S.C., J.D., 1956. Admitted to S.C. bar, 1956; individual practice law, Florence, 1956—. Office: 716 Florence Trust Bldg PO Box 787 Florence SC 29503 Tel (803) 669-8515

BYRD, RICHARD DUNCAN, b. Balt., Dec. 27, 1928; B.S., U. Md., 1950; J.D., U. Balt., 1962. Admitted to Md. bar, 1962, U.S. Supreme Ct. bar, 1966; mem. firm Ritchey, McCurdy & Byrd, Towson, Md., 1962-68; dep. state's atty. Balt. County (Md.), 1963-67, spl. asst. county solicitor, 1967-76; mem. firm Walker & McCadden, Balt., 1976—; counsel Balt. County Police and Fire Depts., 1967-76. Mem. City Council, Balt., 1955-59; treas. Md. Democratic Party, 1958; campaign aide Pres. Kennedy, 1960. Mem. Balt. County Bar Assn., Md. Trial Lawyers Assn. Recipient Emmy nomination for writing, producing, directing TV documentary on constn. A Framework for Living, 1968. Home: 3438 University Pl Baltimore MD 21218 Office: 306 Court Sq Bldg Baltimore MD 21202 Tel (301) 727-3710

BYRD, STANLEY RICHARD, b. Rapid City, S.D., Sept. 13, 1939; B.A. in Polit. Sci., Idaho State U., 1964; J.D., U. Wash., 1966. Admitted to Wash. bar, 1967; asso. firm Clinton, Fleck, Glein & Brown, Seattle, 1970—; instr. real estate law Shoreline Community Coll., 1976—. Precinct chmn. Republican party, Seattle, 1967-76. Mem. Am., Seattle-King County (chmn. young lawyer family law sect.) bar assns. Editor U. Wash. Law Sch. newspaper, 1965-66. Home: 421 NW 181st St Seattle WA 98177 Office: 500 Third & Lenora Bldg Seattle WA 98121 Tel (206) 624-6831

BYRNE, EUGENE JOSEPH, b. N.Y.C., Sept. 24, 1938; B.S., Mt. St. Mary's Coll., Emmitsburg, Md., 1960; LL.B., Villanova U., 1963; grad. Nat. Coll. State Judiciary, Reno, 1976. Admitted to N.J. bar, 1963; clk. to John E. Hughes, Upper Montclair, N.J., 1962, 63-64; asso. John W. McGeehan, Jr., Newark, 1964-71; individual practice law, Upper Montclair, 1971—; atty. hearing examiner N.J. Dept. Pub. Utilities, Newark, 1971—. Pres. Montclair Property Owners Assn., 1973-75; N.J. State pres. Ancient Order Hibernians, 1968-70; co-chmn. N.J. chpt. Am. Irish Nat. Immigration Com., 1968—. Mem. Montclair-W.Essex, Essex County (Bon Ton Repertory Co.), N.J., Am. bar assns., Trial Attys. N.J., Assn. Trial Lawyers Am., Assn. Immigration and Nationality Lawyers (sec. N.J. chpt.). Named Young Man of Year, Friendly Sons of St. Patrick of the Oranges, 1967, Essex County Citizen of 1967, Essex County Am. Legion, For Country Award, Cath. War Vets., Essex County Chpt., 1968. Home: 142 Gordonhurst Ave Upper Montclair NJ 07043 Office: Dept Pub Utilities 1100 Raymond Blvd Newark NJ 07102 Tel (201) 648-2574

BYRNE, JAMES JAY, b. Great Neck, N.Y., Apr. 14, 1930; A.B., Harvard, 1952; LL.B., St. John's U., 1958. Admitted to N.Y. State bar, 1959; asso. firm Hogan & Kelleher, N.Y.C., 1958-61; asst. dist. atty. Nassau County, N.Y., 1961-64; partner firm Root & Mack, Northport, N.Y., 1964-72; mem. firm Root, Roberts & Byrne, Huntington, N.Y., 1972—; village atty., Lloyd Harbor, N.Y., 1973-75. Mem. N.Y. State, Suffolk bar assns., Estate Planning Council of Suffolk County, Assn. Former Asst. Dist. Attys. of Nassau County, Huntington Lawyers Club. Home: 70 Woodhull Pl Northport NY 11768 Office: 234 Main St Huntington NY 11743 Tel (516) 421-5353

BYRNE, JEROME CAMILLUS, b. Grand Rapids, Mich., Oct. 3, 1925; A.B., Aquinas Coll., 1948; LL.B., Harvard U., 1951. Admitted to Calif. bar, 1952; asso. firm Gibson, Dunn & Crutcher, Los Angeles, 1952-60, partner, 1960—; spl. counsel Regents of U. Calif., 1965. Mem. State Bar Calif., Am., Los Angeles County, Beverly Hills, Internat. bar assns., Indsl. Relations Research Assn. Office: 9601 Wilshire Blvd Beverly Hills CA 90210 Tel (213) 273-6990

BYRNE, KENNETH VINCENT, b. Kansas City, Mo., June 3, 1940; LL.B., St. Louis U., 1964, J.D., 1967. Admitted to Mo. bar, 1964, U.S. Dist. Ct. bar, 1966, Circuit Ct. of Appeals bar, 1975; individual practice law, St. Louis, 1964—. Mem. Mo., St. Louis bar assns. Home: 3 Ferrand Woods St Louis MO 63124 Office: 411 N 7th St Suite 1401 St Louis MO 63101 Tel (314) 421-0390

BYRNE, LOUIS PAUL, b. Richmond, Va., Jan. 15, 1920; J.D., U. Richmond, 1950. Admitted to Va. bar, 1949, U.S. Supreme Ct. bar, 1972; practiced in Richmond, Va., 1949—; asso. firm Rooke & Merhige, 1949-52; partner firm Byrne, Spinnella & Thomas, 1953-58, Bremner, Merhige, Byrne, Montgomer & Baber, 1958-67, Bremner, Byrne, Baber & Janus, 1967—; asst. commonwealth's atty. County of Henrico Va., 1952-54. Chmn., bd. dirs., gen. counsel Old Diminion Eye Bank & Research, Inc., Richmond; bd. dirs., gen. counsel Eye Bank Assn. Am., Winston Salem, N.C. Mem. Va., Am. bar assns., Va. Trial Lawyers Assn., Am. Judicature Soc. Home: 7313 Durwood Crescent Richmond VA 23229 Office: Suite 1500 701 E Franklin St PO Box 826 Richmond VA 23207 Tel (804) 644-0721

BYRNE, WILLIAM EDWARD, b. Berkeley, Calif, Sept. 14, 1928; A.B., U. Calif., Berkeley, 1950; LL.B., Hastings Coll. Law, 1957; grad. Nat. Coll. Judges U. Nev., 1966. Admitted to Calif. bar, 1958; partner firms Milham & Bryne, Placerville, Calif., 1948-61, Byrne & Hamilton, Placerville, 1961-64; judge Dorado County (Calif.) Superior Ct., 1964—; mem. faculty Calif. Coll. Judges, 1967. Active El Dorado C. of C. Mem. Am. Bar Assn., Calif. Conf. Judges. Office: 495 Main St Placerville CA 95667 Tel (916) 626-2431

BYRNES, FRANK ALBERT, b. Bklyn., Feb. 17, 1905; A.B., N.Y. U., 1925; LL.B., Fordham U., 1931. Admitted to N.Y. bar, 1931; mem. legal staff N.Y. Life Ins. Co., N.Y.C., 1951—, counsel, 1951-54, asst. gen. counsel, 1954-57, asso. gen. counsel, 1957-65, v.p., gen. counsel, 1965-70. Fellow Am. Bar Found.; mem. Am., N.Y. State bar assns., Assn. Bar City N.Y., Am. Land Title Assn., N.Y. State Title Assn., N.Y. Law Inst., Am. Judicature Soc., Assn. Life Ins. Counsel. Home: 43 Ridge Rd New Rochelle NY 10804

BYRNES, JOHN JOSEPH, b. Milw., Oct. 19, 1913; LL.B., Georgetown U., 1938. Admitted to D.C. bar, 1937, Wis. bar, 1947; examiner ICC, Washington, 1938-41; practiced in Elkhorn, Wis., 1947-74; judge Walworth County (Wis.) Ct., 1974—; mem. Wis. Bd. County Judges, 1974—; U.S. commr. Wis., 1958-66. Page, U.S. Ho. of Reps., 1930-31. Mem. Am., Wis. State, Walworth County (pres. 1953-54, 70-71) bar assns. Office: Courthouse Elkhorn WI 53121 Tel (414) 723-4900

BYRON, BARRY MICHAEL, b. Cleve., July 20, 1931; B.S. in Social Sci., Georgetown U., 1954; J.D., Case Western Res. U., 1956; postgrad. Stanford, 1957-58. Admitted to Ohio bar, 1956, U.S. Supreme Ct. bar, 1962; law clk. U.S. Dist. Ct., Cleve., 1958-60; asst. dir. law, Eastlake, Ohio, 1960; first asst. pros. atty. Lake County (Ohio), 1961-66; partner firm Baker, Byron and Hackenburg, Painesville, Ohio, 1966—; asst. dir. law, Willoughby Hills, Ohio, 1964-67, dir. law, 1968-77; dir. law, Willowwick, Ohio, 1973-77; gen. counsel Lake Met. Housing Authority, Painesville, 1966-77; gen. counsel Lake County Charter Commn., 1971; acting judge Willoughby (Ohio) Municipal Ct., 1971-72; spl. counsel Lake County, Madison, Ohio, Grand River, Ohio, 1967-75. Treas. Lake County Dem. Exec. and Central Coms., 1970-77. Mem. Am., Fed., Lake County, Ohio bar assns., Nat. Dist. Attys. Assn. Contbr. articles to law jours. Home: 38033 Dodd's Hill Dr Willoughby Hills OH 44094 Office: 420 Lakeshore Trust Bldg Painesville OH 44077 Tel (216) 354-4364

BYRON, DANIEL PIERCE, b. Indpls., Apr. 2, 1937; A.B. in Polit. Sci., Ind. U., 1959, J.D., 1962. Admitted to Ind. bar, 1962; asst. U.S. Atty., Indpls., 1967; first asst. U.S. atty., 1968-69; asso. firm McHale, Cook and Welch, Indpls., 1969—, partner, 1972—; served to capt., JAGC, U.S. Army, 1962-67. Bd. dirs. Christamore House, Inc., 1975-76, pres., 1977—. Mem. Seventh Circuit, Am., Indpls. bar assns. Home: 8640 Emerald Ln Indianapolis IN 46260 Office: 906 Chamber of Commerce Bldg Indianapolis IN 46204 Tel (317) 634-7588

BYRON, GOODLOE EDGAR, b. Williamsport, Md., June 22, 1929; B.A., U. Va., 1951; J.D., George Washington U., 1953. Admitted to Md. bar, 1953; individual practice law, Frederick County (Md.), 1958—; mem. Md. Ho. of Dels., 1962-66, Md. Senate, 1966-70, U.S. Ho. of Reps., 1970—. Bd. visitors Md. Sch. for Deaf, U.S. Naval Acad., Hood Coll. Marathon runner Boston 26 mile marathon 5 times, J.F.K. 50 mile race 2 times. Home: 306 Grove Blvd Frederick MD 21701 Office: US Ho of Reps DC 20515 Tel (202) 225-2721

BYRON, STUART DAVID, b. N.Y.C., Dec. 13, 1933; B.A., Yale, 1955; J.D., Columbia, 1958; Admitted to N.Y. State bar, 1959; asso. firm Sheldon & Olshan, N.Y.C., 1959; asst. house counsel Uris Bldgs. Corp., N.Y.C., 1960-64; partner firm Fink, Weinberger, Fredman & Charney, N.Y.C., 1965—; research asso. Comr. of Investigation N.Y. State, 1956. Mem. Am. Arbitration Assn., Assn. Bar City N.Y., Queens County Bar Assn., Columbia Law Sch. Alumni Assn. (class com. N.Y.C., 1962—, past chmn. local chpt.), Alumni Schs. Com. Yale, St. Elmo Soc. Yale (bd. govs. 1961—), Phi Delta Phi. Contbg. author: Purchase of a Medical Practice, 1975. Home: 324 E 41st St New York City NY 10017 Office: 551 5th Ave New York City NY 10017 Tel (212) MU2-0546

BYSE, CLARK MILTON, b. Oshkosh, Wis., Aug. 23, 1912; B.E., State Tchrs. Coll. Oshkosh, 1935; LL.B., U. Wis., 1938; LL.M., Columbia, 1939, J.S.D., 1952; M.A. (hon.), Harvard, 1958. Admitted to Wis. bar, 1938, Pa. bar, 1953; with firm Thompson, Gruenwald & Frye, Oshkosh, 1938; instr. law U. Ia., 1939-40, asst. prof., 1940-41; staff office gen. counsel SEC, 1941, legal asst. commrs., 1941-42, staff office solicitor, 1945-46; office gen. counsel Bd. Econ. Warfare, 1942, spl. rep. bd. Econ. Warfare and Def. Supplies Corp., Colombia, S.Am., 1942-43; counsel office war areas trade Dept. Commerce, 1946; asst. prof. law U. Pa., 1946-47, asso. prof., 1947-48, prof., 1948-58; prof. law Harvard, 1958-70, Bussey prof., 1970—. Vis. prof. law Stanford, summer 1947, U. Wis., 1955, Harvard, 1957-58, U. Tex. 1962, U. Minn., 1969-70; Salzburg Seminar in Am. Studies, 1958, 65. Mem. Mass. adv. com. U.S. Com. Civil Rights, 1962—. Mem. Adminstrv. Conf. U.S., ACLU (Mass. dir.), AAUP (counsel 1962-64, pres. 1966-68), Phi Beta Sigma, Phi Kappa Delta, Kappa Delta Pi, Pi Gamma Mu, Order of Coif. Author: Administrative Law Cases and Comments (with W. Gellhorn), 1970; (with Louis Joughn) Tenure in American Higher Education, 1959. Editorial bd. law book dept. Little, Brown & Co., 1956—, James Madison Constl. Law Inst., 1968—. Contbr. articles to Ency. Brit., legal publs. Home: Leverett House Towers Cambridge MA 02138 Office: Langdell Hall Harvard Cambridge MA 02138*

BYSSHE, FREDERICK HERBERT, JR., b. Long Beach, Calif., Sept. 16, 1937; B.A., U. Redlands, 1959; J.D., U. Calif., 1962. Admitted to Calif. bar, 1963; dep. dist. atty. Riverside (Calif.) County Dist. Atty.'s Office, 1963-66, chief trial dep., 1966-68, chief dep., 1968-70; partner firm Lucking, Bertelsen, Bysshe, Kuttler & Smiley, Ventura, Calif., 1971—; lectr. U. Calif., 1968-69. Pres., Riverside County Peace Officers Assn., 1968; trustee, v.p. Ventura County Law Library, 1974—; bd. dirs. Ventura Girls' Clubs, Ventura County YMCA, 1972—. Mem. Am., Ventura County (exec. com. 1973-74) bar assns., Calif., Ventura County (pres.-elect 1977) trial lawyers assns. Asso. editor Hastings Law Rev., 1961-62. Office: 10 S California St Ventura CA 93001 Tel (805) 648-3224

CABALLERO, RAYMOND CESAR, b. El Paso, Tex., Feb. 6, 1942; B.B.A., U. Tex., El Paso, 1963; LL.B., U. Tex., 1967; LL.M., George Washington U., 1972. Admitted to Tex. bar, 1966, U.S. Supreme Ct. bar, 1971, Calif. bar, 1972; asst. U.S. atty. Dept. Justice, El Paso, 1967-69, trial atty. tax div., Washington, 1969-73; individual practice law, El Paso, 1973—. Democratic chmn. El Paso County, 1974-76. Mem. Am., El Paso (sec., 1976-77), Tex., Calif., Fed. bar assns., Tex. (dir. 1977—), El Paso (v.p. 1977) trial lawyers assns., Tex. Criminal Def. Lawyers Assn. (asso. dir. 1977). Contbr. articles to legal publs. Home: 4520 Cumberland Circle El Paso TX 79903 Office: 1610 State National Plaza El Paso TX 79901 Tel (915) 544-2114

CABANISS, CHARLEY ELLIS, b. Clinton, Okla., Jan. 10, 1947; B.S., Southwestern State Coll., Weatherford, Okla., 1969; J.D., U. Okla., 1972. Admitted to Okla. bar, 1973; partner firm Graft, Rodolph & Cabaniss, Clinton, 1976—. Legal counsel Clinton Jaycees. Mem. Am., Okla., Custer County bar assns., Order of Coif. Recipient Am. Jurisprudence awards. Home: 308 S 24th St Clinton OK 73601 Office: 525 N 6th St Clinton OK 73601 Tel (405) 323-1516

CABE, ROBERT DUDLEY, b. Little Rock, June 25, 1942; B.A., Hendrix Coll., 1963; LL.B., Duke, 1966. Admitted to Ark. bar, 1966; asso. firm Wright, Lindsey & Jennings, Little Rock, 1966-69, partner, 1970—. Trustee Hendrix Coll., 1971—; bd. dirs. Kidney Found. of Ark., 1975—. Mem. Am., Ark., Pulaski County bar assns., Ark. Personnel Assn. Home: 415 Colonial Ct Little Rock AR 72205 Office: 2200 Worthen Bank Bldg Little Rock AR 72201 Tel (501) 371-0808

CABIBI, PHILLIP JOSEPH, b. Pueblo, Colo., Nov. 1, 1926; A.A., Pueblo Jr. Coll., 1948; LL.B., U. Colo., 1952. Admitted to Colo. bar, 1952, U.S. Dist. Ct. bar, 1954; individual practice, Pueblo, 1952-65; county judge, Pueblo, 1965-74; judge Dist. Ct., Pueblo, 1974—. Mem. Colo., Pueblo County bar assns. Home: 129 Cornell Circle Pueblo CO 81005 Office: Judicial Bldg Pueblo CO 81003 Tel (303) 542-0311

CABLE, PAUL ANDREW, b. N.Y.C., Apr. 13, 1939; B.A., Wesleyan U., 1961; M.A., U. Manchester (Eng.), 1963; LL.B., Harvard, 1966. Admitted to D.C. bar, 1967, N.Y. bar, 1970, Calif. bar, 1976; clk. Anderson, Mori & Rabinowitz, Tokyo, 1966-69; asso. firm Anderson & Martin, N.Y.C., 1969-70; partner firm Anderson, Martin & Cable, 1970-72; partner firm Whitman & Ransom, N.Y.C., 1972-76, Los Angeles, 1976—. Mem. Assn. Bar City N.Y. (com. on profl. responsibility 1973-76), D.C. Bar, State Bar Calif. Contbg. author: East-West Business Transactions, 1974. Home: 14001 Palawan Way Marina del Rey CA 90291 Office: 555 S Flower St Los Angeles CA 91311

CABOT, STEPHEN JAY, b. Phila., Nov. 21, 1942; B.S., Villanova U., 1964; J.D., U. Pa., 1967. Admitted to Pa. bar, 1967; asso. firm Obermayer, Rebmann Maxwell & Hippel, Phila., 1969-73; partner firm Pechner, Dorfman, Wolffe Rounick & Cabot, Phila., 1973—; mem. NLRB, Pitts., 1967-69; mem. labor panel Am. Arbitration Assn., 1972—. Mem. Phila., Pa., Am., Fed. bar assns. Author: Your First Organizational Campaign; contbr. numerous articles to profl. publs. Home: 57 Meadows Ln Haverford PA 19041 Office: 1845 Walnut St Suite 1300 Philadelphia PA 19103 Tel (215) 561-7100

CACCIATORE, SAMMY S., JR., b. Tampa, Fla., Aug. 2, 1942; A.A., Orlando Jr. Coll., 1962; A.B., Stetson U., 1966, J.D., 1966. Admitted to Fla. bar, 1966, U.S. Supreme Ct. bar, 1971; asst. pub. defender 9th Circuit Ct. Fla., 1966; asso. firm Billing, Frederick & Rumberger, Orlando, Fla., 1966, James Nance, Melbourne, Fla., 1967-71; mem. firm Nance & Cacciatore, Melbourne, 1971—. Trustee A. Max Brewer Meml. Law Library, 1973—, chmn. 1973-75. Mem. Fla. Bar (mem. exec. council trial lawyers sect., lectr. continuing legal edn.), Am., Brevard County (dir. 1969-72, 74, 76—) bar assns., Acad. Fla. Trial Lawyers (dir. 1969-76), Assn. Trial Lawyers Am. Home: 8 Yacht Club Ln Indian Harbour Beach FL 32937 Office: 525 N Harbor City Blvd Melbourne FL 32935 Tel (305) 254-8416

CACHERIS, PLATO, b. Pitts., May 22, 1929; B.S., Georgetown U., 1951, J.D., 1956. Admitted to D.C. bar, 1956, Va. bar, 1956; trial atty., U.S. Dept. Justice, Wash. D.C., 1956-60; 1st asst. U.S. Atty., Eastern Dist. Va., 1960-65; individual practice law, Alexandria, Va., 1965-71; partner firm Hundley & Cacheris, Wash. D.C., 1971—; chmn. Alexandria Crime Commn., 1969. Mem. Alexandria, Am. (criminal justice sect.) bar assns., Bar Assn. of D.C., Nat. Assn. Criminal Defense Lawyers.; fellow Am. Coll. Trial Lawyers. Home: 1319 Bishop Ln Alexandria VA 22312 Office: 1709 NY Ave NW Suite 205 Washington DC 20006 Tel (202) 833-3583

CADDIS, CHARLES OWINGS, b. Anniston, Ala., Oct. 2, 1943; A.B., U. Ala., 1965, LL.B., 1967. Admitted to Ala. bar, 1967; partner firm Kracke, Caddis, Gwin, Bashinsky & Woodward, Birmingham. Mem. Am., Ala., Birmingham bar assns., Phi Gamma Delta, Phi Delta Phi. Home: 37 Fairway Dr Birmingham AL 35213 Office: 2220 Highland Ave Birmingham AL 35205 Tel (205) 933-2756

CADICK, JEREMIAH L., b. Grand View, Ind., Jan. 17, 1902; A.B., Ind. U., 1922; LL.B., Yale, 1925. Admitted to Ind. bar, 1926; asso. firm John G. Rauch, Indpls., 1926-35; individual practice law, Indpls., 1935-46; mem. firm, Cadick & Burns and predecessors, 1946—. Pres. United Fund of Indpls. Mem. Am., Ind., Indpls. (pres. 1945) bar assns., Indpls. Legal Aid Soc. (pres. 1940-43), Am. Law Inst., Am. Bar Found. Home: 5632 Walden Ln Indianapolis IN 46208 Office: 45 N Pennsylvania St Indianapolis IN 46204 Tel (317) 639-1571

CADIGAN, PATRICK JOSEPH, b. Springfield, Ill., Nov. 1, 1936; B.A., Washington U., St. Louis, 1958; J.D., U. Ill., 1961. Admitted to Ill. bar, 1961, U.S. Supreme Ct. bar, 1971; asso. firm Roberts & Kepner, Springfield, 1961-65; magistrate Circuit Ct. Sangamon County (Ill.), 1965-67; partner firm Gillespie, Cadigan & Gillespie, Springfield, 1967—; parliamentarian Ill. State Senate, Springfield, 1965, 67, 75—; asst. to Gov. Ill., 1968; chmn. bd. Ill. Project, Law in Am. Soc., 1974—. Pres., Springfield Park Dist., 1975—. Mem. Am., Ill. (chmn. younger mems. conf. 1972-73, bd. govs. 1973-75), Sangamon County bar assns. Home: 2117 Willemoore St Springfield IL 62704 Office: 217 S 7th St Springfield IL 62701 Tel (217) 528-7375

CADY, ELWYN LOOMIS, JR., b. Ames, Iowa, Feb. 21, 1926; student Washington U., 1943-44, 46-48, U. Kansas City, 1949-50; J.D., Tulane U., 1951; B.S. in Medicine, U. Mo., 1955. Admitted to Mo. bar, 1951, U.S. Supreme Ct. bar, 1965; dir. Law-Medicine Program, U. Kansas City (Mo.), 1951-56; asst. dir. Law-Sci. Inst., asso. prof. law U. Tex., Austin/Galveston, 1956-57; sec. Law-Sci. Acad. Am., 1956-57; counsel firm Koenig Dietz, Herrmann & Abels, St. Louis, 1959-74; gen. counsel., sec., treas. Elliott Oil, Inc., Independence, Mo., 1966—. Mem. com. on mgmt. Eastern Jackson County Planned Parenthood Clinics, 1970-75; post comdr. Kansas City Am. Legion, 1966-67, Mo. chmn. Blood Donor Program, 1968-69. Mem. Am. Acad. Forensic Scis., AAAS, Am., Eastern Jackson County bar assns., Mo. Bar, Bar Assn. Met. St. Louis, Internat. Platform Assn., Scribes, Mo. Writers' Guild. Author: Law and Contemporary Nursing, 1963; contbr. medicolegal publs.; recipient gold medal Law-Science Acad. Am., 1968. Home and Office: 1919 Drumm Ave Independence MO 64055 Tel (816) 252-2219 also 252-3324

CADY, FRANCIS COWLES, b. Hartford, Conn., Jan. 8, 1916; B.A., Yale U., 1938; LL.B., Harvard U., 1941. Admitted to Conn. bar, 1946; asso. firm Davis, Lee, Howard & Wright, Hartford, 1946-47; individual practice law, Kent, Conn., 1947-63; prof. law U. Conn., West Hartford, 1963—, acting dean Sch. Law, 1972-74; mem. Conn. Gen. Assembly, 1953-59; mem. Conn. State Senate, 1959-63, asst. minority leader, 1961-63; mem. Conn. Commn. on Medicolegal Investigations, 1972—, Conn. Child Abuse Com., 1974—; chmn. Conn. Law Revision Commn., 1974—. Mem. Conn. Bar Assn. (past chmn. com. on profl. ethics, mem. spl. com. adminstrn. disciplinary procedures 1971—). Home: 24 Main St Farmington CT 06032 Office: 1800 Asylum Ave West Hartford CT 06117 Tel (203) 523-4841

CAEMMERER, JOHN DAVID, b. Bklyn., Jan. 19, 1928; B.S.C., U. Notre Dame, 1949; J.D., St. John's U., 1957. Admitted to N.Y. bar, 1957; asso. firm Kirlin, Campbell & Keating, N.Y.C., 1957-60; dep. atty. Nassau County (N.Y.), 1960-62, Town of N. Hempstead (N.Y.), 1963-65; partner firm McKnight & Caemmerer, Mineola, N.Y., 1965-66, firm Farrell, Fritz, Caemmerer & Cleary, and predecessors, Williston Park, N.Y., 1967—; atty. Village of Williston Park, 1959-66; mem. N.Y. State Senate, 1966—. Mem. Am., N.Y., Nassau County bar assns., Maritime Law Assn., Cath. Lawyers Assn., Nassau County Lawyers Assn. Home: 11 Post Ave East Williston NY 11596 Office: 374 Hillside Ave Williston Park NY 11596 Tel (516) 741-1111

CAFARELLA, JOAN MARIE COURSOLLE, b. Mpls., May 25, 1926; B.S. in Law, U. Minn., 1947, LL.B., 1949. Admitted to Minn. bar, 1949; asso. firm Coursolle, Preus & Maag, Mpls., 1949-56; individual practice law, Wayzata, Minn., 1956-59, Excelsior, Minn., 1959-77, Wayzata, Minn., 1977—; gen. counsel Ben Franklin Fed. Savs. and Loan Assn., 1955-65; exam. atty. Midwest Fed. Savs. and Loan Assn., 1965—. Mem. Minn., Hennepin County bar assns. Home: 5155 Weeks Rd Excelsior MN 55331 Office: 1421 E Wayzata Blvd Wayzata MN 55391 Tel (612) 473-0632

CAFFREY, ANDREW AUGUSTINE, b. Lawrence, Mass., Oct. 2, 1920; A.B. cum laude, Holy Cross Coll., 1941; LL.B. cum laude, Boston Coll., 1948; LL.M., Harvard U., 1948. Admitted to Mass. bar, 1948, U.S. Supreme Ct. bar, 1958; asso. prof. law Boston Coll., 1948-55; asst. U.S. atty., chief civil div., Boston, 1955-59, 1st asst. U.S. atty. Dist. Mass., 1959-60; judge U.S. Dist. Ct., Boston, 1960-72, chief judge, 1972—; mem. jud. panel on multidist. litigation, 1975—. Mem. Am., Fed., Boston bar assns., Am. Law Inst., Harvard Law Sch. Alumni Assn., Jud. Conf. U.S. Home: 47 Woodland Rd Andover MA 01810 Office: 1629 Post Office and Court House Bldg Boston MA 02109 Tel (617) 223-2929

CAGEN, PHILIP M., b. Chgo., Feb. 5, 1918; LL.B., Chgo. Kent Coll. Law, 1946. Admitted to Ill. bar, 1942, U.S. Dist. Ct. No. Dist. Ill. bar, 1946, Ind. bar, 1953, U.S. Dist. Ct. No. Dist/Ind. bar, 1957, U.S. Ct. Appeals (7th circuit), 1958; asso. firm Mayer, Mayer, Austrian & Platt (now Mayer, Brown & Platt), Chgo., 1942-53; individual practice law, Valparaiso, Ind., 1953—; served with JAGC, 1951-53. Mem. Am., Ind., Porter County bar assns., Am. Trial Lawyers Assn., Am. Judicature Soc. Home: 1705 Lafayette Valparaiso IN 46383 Office: 9 Lincolnway Valparaiso IN 46383 Tel (219) 462-4154

CAGLE, JOE NEAL, b. Lexington, Tenn., Jan. 10, 1939; B.A., Olivet (Mich.) Coll., 1961; J.D., Wake Forest U., 1964; M.A., Goddard Coll., Plainfield, Vt., 1975; B.S., State U. N.Y., 1976. Admitted to N.C. bar, 1964, U.S. Supreme Ct. bar, 1970; research asst. to justice N.C. Supreme Ct., 1964-65; partner firm Cagle and Houck, Hickory, N.C., 1965—. Bd. dirs. Viewmont Fire Dept.; adj. faculty Am. Christian Bible Coll., 1976—; adv. bd. Berean Christian Coll., 1975—. Mem. Hickory Jaycees, N.C. State Bar, Am., Catawba County, 25th Jud. Dist. bar assns. Office: PO Box 2050 Hickory NC 28601 Tel (704) 322-2207

CAHAN, MELVIN SAUL, b. Chgo., Oct. 23, 1941; student Cornell U.; B.A., Ripon Coll., 1964; M.A., Northwestern U., 1964; J.D., DePaul U., 1967. Admitted to Ill. bar, 1967; U.S. Dist. Ct. for No. Dist. Ill., 1967; U.S. 7th Circuit Ct. Appeals bar, 1971; law clk. Ill. Appellate Ct., Chgo., 1967-68; atty. Atchison, Topeka & Santa Fe Ry., Chgo., 1968-73; partner firm Lurie & Cahan, Ltd., Chgo., 1973—; instr. DePaul U., 1972-74; lectr. Ill. Continuing Legal Edn., 1970-74. Mem. Am., Ill., Chgo. bar assns. Winner 1st place Ill. State Bar Assn. Writing award, 1969; contbr. articles to legal jours. Home: 1686 N McCraren Highland Park IL 60035 Office: 105 W Adams St Suite 2200 Chicago IL 60603 Tel (312) 782-9101

CAHILL, RICHARD MICHAEL, b. N.Y.C., Feb. 3, 1939; B.S., U. Md., 1961; LL.B., George Washington U., 1964. Admitted to D.C. bar, 1964, Md. bar, 1965, Fla. bar, 1967, N.Y. bar, 1969; law clk. U.S. Dist. Ct., Washington, 1964-66; instr. bus. law U. Md., 1965-68; asst. U.S. atty. Dept. Justice, Washington, 1966-68; lawyer Texaco Inc., N.Y.C., 1968-69; gen. counsel Gen. Telephone Co. of Upstate N.Y., Johnstown, 1969-73; sr. atty. GTE Service Corp., Stamford, Conn., 1973-76; asst. gen. counsel, 1976—. Mem. Bar Assn. D.C., Md., Fla., N.Y., Am. bar assns. Office: 1 Stamford Forum Stamford CT 06904

CAHILL, THOMAS JAMES, b. Louisville, June 25, 1944; B.A., U. Iowa, 1966, J.D., 1969. Admitted to Iowa bar, 1969; partner firm Nelson Vasey & Cahill, Nevada, Iowa, 1969—. Mem. Am., Iowa, Story County (Iowa) (v.p. 1975-76) bar assns., Iowa Def. Counsel, Nevada C. of C. (pres. 1976). Home: Route 1 Nevada IA 50201 Office: 1015 5th St Nevada IA 50201 Tel (515) 382-6571

CAHN, HERMAN, b. W.Ger., Nov. 4, 1932; B.A., Coll. City N.Y., 1953; LL.B., Harvard, 1956. Admitted to N.Y. bar, 1956, U.S. Supreme Ct. bar, 1964; asso. firm Grossman & Grossman, N.Y.C., 1956-63; partner firms Cahn & Rype, N.Y.C., 1963-74, Cahn & Levinson, N.Y.C., 1975—; individual practice law, N.Y.C., 1975; judge N.Y.C. Civil Ct., 1977—. Pres. Jewish Community Council of Washington Heights, N.Y., and Inwood, N.Y. Mem. N.Y. State Bar Assn., New York County Lawyers Assn. Office: 111 Centre St New York City NY 10013

CAHN, RICHARD CALEB, b. Bklyn., June 11, 1932; A.B., Dartmouth Coll., 1953; LL.B., Yale, 1956. Admitted to N.Y. bar, 1956, Fla. bar, 1966, U.S. Supreme Ct. bar, 1960; student asst. to U.S. atty. So. Dist. N.Y., N.Y.C., 1955; atty. U.S. Dept. Justice, Washington, 1956-57; prin. asst. dist. atty. Suffolk County, N.Y., 1965-66; dep. atty. Town Huntington, N.Y., 1966-68; spl. counsel towns Smithtown, Brookhaven, Babylon, N.Y., 1967-68, Islip, N.Y., 1976—; hearing officer N.Y. State Edn. Dept., Nassau and Suffolk counties, 1971—; spl. dist. atty. Suffolk County, 1972; participant World Peace Through Law Conf., 1967, Malpractice Mediation Panel, 2d dept., 1974—, Gov.'s Jud. Nominating Com. 2d Dept., 1975—; mem. screening com. bankruptcy judges U.S. Dist. Ct., Eastern Dist. N.Y., 1976—, mem. screening com. U.S. magistrates, 1977—; regional counsel State U. N.Y., Stony Brook, 1972—. Bd. dirs. Stony Brook Found., 1974—. Mem. Am., N.Y. (fed. ct. com.), Suffolk County (chmn. coms., dir. 1968-71), Fed. bar assns., Am. Judicature Soc., Fed. Bar Council, Huntington Lawyers Club. Contbr. articles to legal jours.; bd. editors Yale Law Jour., 1954. Office: 196 E Main St Huntington NY 11743 Tel (516) 427-3050

CAHN, ROBERT ALLEN, b. Kansas City, Mo., Sept. 27, 1946; B.S. in Pub. Adminstrn., U. Mo., 1968, J.D., 1969. Admitted to Mo. bar, 1972; legal advisor in govt. affairs U. Mo., 1972-73; adminstrv. atty. Jud. Panel on Multidistrict Litigation, Washington, 1973-75, exec.

atty., 1975—; mem. faculty seminars for U.S. dist. judges Fed. Jud. Center, 1976-77; cons. Edwin A. Robson Found., 1975-76. Mem. holocaust com. Jewish Community Council of Greater Washington, 1976—. Mem. Am., Fed., Mo. bar assns., Independent Legal Services Assn. Exec. editor Manual for Complex Litigation, 1975—; contbr. articles in field to profl. jours. Office: 1030 15th St NW 320 Executive Bldg Washington DC 20005 Tel (202) 653-6090

CAIFANO, RICHARD BRUCE, b. Chgo., Apr. 9, 1940; B.S. in Bus. Adminstrn., Marquette U., 1962; J.D., Chgo.-Kent Coll. Law, 1965. Admitted to Ill. bar, 1965, U.S. Dist. Ct. for No. Dist. Ill. bar, 1965, U.S. 7th Circuit Ct. Appeals bar, 1971, U.S. Supreme Ct. bar, 1973; individual practice law, Chgo., 1965—; instr. bus. law Walton Sch. Commerce, Chgo., 1966-71, trial practice and procedure John Marshall Law Sch., 1973-74; panel atty. Fed. Defender Program, Chgo., 1972—. Mem. Ill. State, Chgo. bar assns., Justinian Soc. Lawyers, Nat. Assn. Criminal Def. Attys. Office: 7 S Dearborn Chicago IL 60603 Tel (312) 346-0570

CAILLOUET, CLYDE CHARLES, b. Thibodaux, La., July 24, 1917; LL.B., Loyola U., New Orleans, 1941, J.D., 1968. Admitted to La. bar, 1941; individual practice law, Thibodaux, 1946-52, 74-77; partner firm Caillouet & Falgout, Thibodaux, 1952-56, Caillouet & Wise, 1956-74; city atty. City of Thibodaux, 1975; mem. La. Senate, 1952-56. Mem. Am., La. bar assns., Am. Judicature Soc. Home: 1102 Menard St Thibodaux LA 70301 Office: 102 W 2d St Thibodaux LA 70301 Tel (504) 447-2631

CAIN, ALAN FRANCIS, b. Missoula, Mont., Apr. 22, 1939; B.A., U. Colo., 1961; J.D. with honors, U. Mont., 1969. Admitted to Mont. bar, 1969; law clk. Hon. Russell E. Smith, Missoula, 1969-70; asso. firm Hughes & Bennett, Helena, Mont., 1970-73, partner, 1973—. Trustee Lewis and Clark Library, Helena; mem. Helena Police and Civil Service Commn., 1973—. Mem. State Bar Mont. (co-chmn. legal affairs com. 1975—), Am., Mont. (dir. young lawyers sect. 1973-74), 1st Jud. Dist. (pres. 1975-76) bar assns. Contbr. article to law rev. Office: 406 Fuller Ave Helena MT 59601 Tel (406) 442-3690

CAIN, DONALD EZELL, b. San Marcos, Tex., Oct. 8, 1921; A.S., North Tex. Agrl. Coll., 1941; B.B.A., U. Tex., Austin, 1943, LL.B., 1948; grad. Nat. Coll. of State Judiciary U. Nev., Reno, 1974. Admitted to Tex. bar, 1948; with dept. contracts Convair Co., Ft. Worth, 1948-50; def. atty. USN, Korea and Japan, 1950-51; practiced in Pampa, Tex., 1951-76; county atty. Gray County (Tex.), 1955-68, county judge, 1971-77, dist. judge, 1977—. Bd. dirs. United Fund, Pampa, 1956-60; pres. Adobe Walls council Boy Scouts Am., 1957-59. Mem. Gray County (pres. 1968), Am. bar assns., State Bar Tex., Am. Judicature Soc. Recipient Silver Beaver award Boy Scouts Am., 1958. Home: 1826 Williston St Pampa TX 79065 Office: Courthouse POB 2160 Pampa TX 79065 Tel (806) 665-6062

CAIN, LOUIS THOMAS, b. Atlanta, Nov. 30, 1948; B.A., Presbyn. Coll., Clinton, S.C., 1970; J.D., Mercer U., 1973. Admitted to Ga. bar, 1974; individual practice law, Lawrenceville, Ga., 1974—. Home: 209 King Arthur Dr Lawrenceville GA 30245 Office: 1300 Plaza Dr suite 3 Lawrenceville GA 30245 Tel (404) 963-0289

CAIN, WILLIAM ALLEN, b. Chgo., Nov. 9, 1924; J.D., DePaul U., 1946. Admitted to Ill. bar, 1947, U.S. Supreme Ct. bar, 1960; partner firm Cain & Cernek, Chgo., 1947—; host Pantomime Party, Sta. WBKB-TV, Chgo., 1952-53; disc jockey Sta. WAIT, Chgo., 1953; profl. lectr., hypnotist. Pres., Ind. Democrats Niles Township, Ill., 1955, SE Highland Park Homeowners Assn., 1972; commr. Ill. Sheriff's Commn. on Narcotics and Drug Abuse, 1972-73; mem. lay bd. DePaul U. Mem. Am. (speaker's bur. 1947-77), Ill. Chgo. (chmn. com. def. indigent prisoners 1947, chmn. narcotics and drug abuse com. 1975) bar assns., Am. Judicature Soc., Am. Trial Lawyers Assn., Nat. Assn. Criminal Def. Lawyers (Ill. chmn. strike force 1976-77), AGVA (chmn. Chgo. br. 1968), DePaul Alumni Assn. Office: 221 N La Salle St Suite 3316 Chicago IL 60601 Tel (312) 346-4756

CAINE, CECIL BOYD, JR., b. Birmingham, Ala., Nov. 16, 1942; B.S., Florence State U., 1966; J.D., U. Ala., 1970. Admitted to Ala. bar, 1970, U.S. Dist. Ct. bar for Middle Dist. Ala., 1970, for No. Dist. Ala., 1973; clk. Ala. Ct. Criminal Appeals, Montgomery, 1970-71; asso. dir. Am. Acad. Jud. Edn., Tuscaloosa, Ala., 1971; individual practice law, Moulton, Ala., 1972—; judge Lawrence County (Ala.) Intermediate Ct., 1972-77. Bd. dirs. Arrowhead Regional council Boy Scouts Am., 1975—; v.p. Lawrence County Mental Health Assn., 1975-76; mem. Moulton Park and Recreation Bd., 1975—; chmn. Lawrence County chpt. Ala. Lung Assn., 1977—. Mem. Lawrence County (pres. 1976), Ala., Am. bar assns. Home: 17 Woodland Terr Moulton AL 35650 Office: 226 Walnut St PO Box 667 Moulton AL 35650 Tel (205) 974-1126

CALABRESE, DOMINIC JOHN, b. N.Y.C., June 21, 1932; B.S., Fordham U., 1954, LL.B., 1959. Admitted to N.Y. bar, 1959, U.S. Supreme Ct. bar, 1965; asso. firm Kirlin, Campbell & Keating, N.Y.C., 1960-62; partner firm Vallone & Calabrese, Astoria, N.Y., 1962—. Vol. counsel Astoria Civic Assn., 1976—. Mem. Am., Queens County bar assns. Office: 22-55 31st St Astoria NY 11105 Tel (212) 274-0909

CALABRESI, GUIDO, b. Milan, Italy, Oct. 18, 1932; came to U.S., 1939, naturalized, 1948; B.S. in Analytical Econs., Yale, 1953, LL.B., 1958, M.A. (hon.), 1962; B.A. in Politics, Philosophy and Econs., Magdalen Coll., Oxford (Eng.) U., 1955, M.A., 1959. Admitted to Conn. bar, 1958; law clk. to Supreme Ct. Justice Hugo L. Black, 1958-59; mem. faculty Yale, 1959—, prof. law, 1962—, John Thomas Smith prof. law, 1970, fellow Timothy Dwight Coll., 1960—. Dir. Crosby Co., Mpls., First New Haven Nat. Bank. Mem. bd. edn., Woodbridge, Conn., 1967-69; selectman, Woodbridge, 1970; mem. Woodbridge Democratic Town Com., 1968—. Bd. dirs. St. Thomas More Chapel (Yale); trustee Conn. Coll., Lehrman Inst., Russell Sage Found.; trustee, pres. Hopkins Grammar Sch. Rhodes scholar, 1953. Named One of Outstanding Young Men in Am., U.S. Jr. C. of C., 1962. Fellow Am. Acad. Arts and Scis.; mem. Conn. Bar Assn., Inst. Medicine (council), Nat. Acad. Sci., Assembly Behavioral and Social Scis., NRC, Phi Beta Kappa. Home: Amity Rd Woodbridge CT 06525 Office: 127 Wall St New Haven CT 06520*

CALDECOTT, WILLIAM ARTHUR, b. Pennsboro, W.Va., Aug. 11, 1917; A.B., U. Calif., Los Angeles, 1938; LL.B., U. So. Calif., 1941. Admitted to Calif. bar, 1941, U.S. 9th Circuit Ct. Appeals bar, 1949, U.S. Supreme Ct. bar, 1970; asso. firm Walker, Wright, Tyler & Ward and predecessors, Los Angeles, 1946-52, partner, 1952-70; judge Calif. Superior Ct., Los Angeles, 1971—. Mem. Los Angeles, Am. bar assns. Office: Courthouse of Los Angeles 111 N Hill St Los Angeles CA 90012 Tel (213) 974-1234

CALDWELL, JOHN TODD, b. Talladega, Ala., Aug. 10, 1946; B. of Textile Mgmt., Auburn U., 1968; J.D., Samford, 1971. Admitted to Ala. bar, 1971; partner firm Love, Love & Caldwell, Talladega, 1971-73; partner firm Stewart, Colvin & Caldwell, Anniston, Ala., 1973-75; individual practice law, Anniston, 1975—; house counsel Colonial Refrigerated Transp. Co., Birmingham, Ala., 1973, Colonial Fast Freights, Inc., Birmingham, 1973. Mem. Calhoun County Bar Assn., Anniston Jaycees, Phi Alpha Delta. Home: 1912 Valley Creek Rd Anniston AL 36201 Office: 407 First Nat Bank Bldg Anniston AL 36201 Tel (205) 237-6671

CALDWELL, MILLARD FILLMORE, b. Knoxville, Tenn., Feb. 6, 1897; student Carson and Newman Coll., 1914-15, U. Miss., 1917-18, U. Va., 1919-22. Admitted to Tenn. bar, 1922, Fla. bar, 1925; individual practice law, Milton, Fla., 1925-33; mem. 73d to 76th Congresses, 1933-41; partner firm Caldwell, Parker, Foster & Wigginton, Tallahassee, 1941-45; gov. State of Fla., 1945-49; partner firm Caldwell, Parker, Foster & Madigan, Tallahassee, 1949-61; justice Fla. Supreme Ct., 1962-69; of counsel firm Madigan, Parker, Gatlin, Truett & Swedmark, Tallahassee, 1969—; mem. Fla. Legislature, 1928-32; chmn. Nat. Gov.'s Conf., 1946-47; pres. Council State Govts., 1946-48. Adminstr., Fed. Civil Def., 1950-52; chmn. bd. control So. Regional Edn., 1947-50, Fla. Commn. Constl. Govt., 1957-66. Mem. Am., Fla., Tallaha ssee bar assns. Home: 3502 Old Bainbridge Rd Tallahassee FL 32303 Office: 318 N Monroe St Tallahassee FL 32302 Tel (904) 222-3730

CALDWELL, WILLIAM WEBSTER, JR., b. N.Y.C., Oct. 3, 1938; B.S. in Econs., U. Pa., 1960; J.D., U. Fla., 1964. Admitted to Fla. bar, 1964; asso. firm Fleming, O'Bryan & Fleming, Ft. Lauderdale, Fla., 1964-67; partner firm Gustafson, Calowell, Stephens & Ferris, Ft. Lauderdale, 1967—; atty. City of Lighthouse Point (Fla.), 1967-73, City of Ft. Lauderdale, 1973—. Mem. Fla., Broward County bar assns. Office: 1415 E Sunrise Blvd Fort Lauderdale FL 33304 Tel (305) 763-9330

CALDWELL, WYLIE HASKELL, JR., b. Florence, S.C., Aug. 29, 1942; A.B., U. S.C., 1964, J.D., 1967. Admitted to S.C. bar, 1967; asso. W.H. Caldwell, Florence, 1967-69; individual practice law, Florence, 1969—; county prosecutor Florence County (S.C.), 1968-69; city prosecutor Florence, 1969-72, city atty., 1976; asst. solicitor 12th Jud. Circuit S.C., 1973-75. Pres. Palmetto Civitan Club, 1969; chmn. city Democratic Party, Florence, 1970-72; mem. adv. bd. Salvation Army, 1974—; mem. Pee Dee Speech and Hearing Bd., 1972—; lay chmn. ch. council St. Luke Lutheran Ch. Mem. S.C. Trial Lawyers Assn., S.C., Florence County, Am. bar assns., Am. Judicature Soc. (vice chmn. Florence County council 1977). Home: 1151 Brunwood Dr Florence SC 29501 Office: 226 S Irby St Florence SC 29501 Tel (803) 662-4331

CALECHMAN, JACK HENRY, b. New Haven, Mar. 13, 1927; A.B., Yale, 1948; LL.B., U. Mich., 1951. Admitted to Conn. bar, 1951, Mass. bar, 1956; with regional counsel's office IRS, N.Y.C. and Boston, 1952-56; asso. firm Lourie & Cutler, Boston, 1956-59, firm Brown, Rudnick, Freed & Gesmer, Boston, 1959—. Home: 340 Commonwealth Ave Chestnut Hill MA 02167 Office: 85 Devonshire St Boston MA 02109 Tel (617) 726-7800

CALFAS, JOHN A., b. Hartford, Conn., Nov. 29, 1926; B.S. in Accounting, U. Calif., Los Angeles, 1951, LL.B., 1956. Admitted to Calif. bar, 1957; partner firm Calfas & Williams, Santa Monica, Calif., 1957—; sec. Genisco Tech. Corp., 1951—; dir. The Hawaii Corp., 1969-75; dir. Nat. Environment Corp., 1968-70. Mem. Bd. Pension Commrs., City of Los Angeles, 1975—. Tel (213) 828-5545

CALFEE, JOHN BEVERLY, b. Cleve., May 2, 1913; B.A., Yale, 1935; LL.B., Western Res. U., 1938. Admitted to Ohio bar, 1939; sr. partner Calfee, Halter & Griswold, Cleve., 1975—. Mem. Am., Ohio, Cleve. bar assns., Ohio Bar Found. Home: 4897 Clubside Rd Lyndhurst OH 44124 Office: 1800 Central Nat Bank Bldg Cleveland OH 44114 Tel (216) 781-2166

CALHOUN, DONALD EUGENE, JR., b. Columbus, Ohio, May 15, 1926; B.A., Ohio State U., 1948, J.D., 1951. Admitted to Ohio bar, 1951; asso. firm Lurie & Gifford, Columbus, 1951-53, Irish & Southwick, Columbus, 1953-58; individual practice law, Columbus, 1958-68; partner firm Folkerth, Calhoun, Webster, Maurer & O'Brien, Columbus, 1968—; mem. labor panel Am. Arbitration Assn. Vice pres. Columbus Jaycees, 1957, named one of 10 outstanding young men, 1957, recipient Keyman award, 1958; mem. Columbus Bd. Edn., 1963-71, pres., 1967, 70. Mem. Am., Ohio, Columbus (Community Service award 1972, pres. 1967-68, dir. 1961-69) bar assns. Home: 216 W Beechwold Blvd Columbus OH 43214 Office: 230 E Town St Columbus OH 43215 Tel (614) 228-2945

CALHOUN, J. GONTHWIN, b. Gordo, Ala., Dec. 19, 1926; B.S., Tuskeegie Inst., 1948, LL.B., 1950; postgrad. La Salle Law Course. Admitted to Ala. bar, 1954; practice law, Tougaloo, Miss.; atty. NAACP, ACLU, Freedom Riders of Am., Calhoun Ltd., Tougaloo, Miss.; adviser South African Liberation Com. Pres. Afro Club of Am., 1972-73. Mem. Ala. Bar Assn. Author: Civil Rights in Modern Times. Tel (601) 956-1231

CALHOUN, JAMES PHILLIP, b. Clarendon, Ark., Sept. 10, 1916; J.D. magna cum laude, U. Miami (Fla.), 1953. Admitted to Fla. bar, 1953; individual practice law, Tampa, Fla., 1953-54; mem. firm Calhoun, Killian, Miller & Sloane, Tampa, 1955-56; mem. firm Calhoun, Yado, Keel & Nelson, Tampa, 1957-61; judge Municipal Ct., Tampa, 1962-68; judge Juvenile & Domestic Relations Ct. Hillsborough County, Fla., 1969-72; judge Circuit Ct. of Fla., Tampa, 1973—. Mem. Tampa, Hillsborough County bar assns. Home: Rt 7 Box 456M Tampa FL 33615 Office: Courthouse Annex Tampa FL 33602 Tel (813) 272-5775

CALHOUN, PAUL WENDELL, JR., b. Vidalia, Ga., Mar. 25, 1937; A.B., LL.B., U. Ga., 1963. Admitted to Ga. bar, 1964, Fed. bar, 1967, Ga. Appellate Ct., 1964; partner firm Calhoun & Bryant, Vidalia. Mem. Ga. Bar Assn., Phi Delta Phi, Kappa Alpha. Home: 200 Kissingbower St Vidalia GA 30474 Office: 800 E 1st St Vidalia GA 30474

CALIENDO, ANTHONY, b. Cervinara, Italy, Oct. 27, 1919; J.D., DePaul U., 1944. Admitted to Ill. bar, 1944; individual practice law, Melrose Park, Ill., 1944-46, 48—; adjudicator U.S. VA, Chgo., 1946-48. Bd. dirs. Christian Bus. Men's Com., Chgo., 1962. Mem. Ill., Chgo., W. Suburban bar assns., Justinian Soc. Lawyers, Am. Judicature Soc., Am. Arbitration Assn. Home: 1540 N Lee Ave Melrose Park IL 60160 Office: 154 Broadway St Melrose Park IL 60161 Tel (312) FI4-2000

CALIFANO, JOSEPH ANTHONY, JR., b. Bklyn., May 15, 1931; A.B., Holy Cross Coll., 1952; LL.B., Harvard, 1955. Admitted to N.Y. State bar, 1955; with firm Dewey, Ballatine, Bushby, Palmer & Wood, N.Y.C., 1958-61; spl. asst. to gen. counsel Dept. Def., 1961-62; spl. asst. to sec. army, 1962-63; gen. counsel Dept. Army, 1963-64; spl. asst. to sec. and dep. sec. def., 1964-65; spl. asst. to Pres., 1965-69; mem. firm Arnold & Porter, Washington, 1969-71; partner firm Williams, Connolly & Califano, Washington, 1971-77; sec. HEW, 1977—; gen. counsel Democratic Nat. Com., 1970-72. Bd. overseers law sch. vis. com. Harvard; bd. dirs. Child Welfare League, Children's Hosp., Washington; trustee Mater Dei Sch. Recipient Distinguished Civilian Service award Dept. of Army, 1964; Man of Year award Justinian Soc. Lawyers, 1966; One of Ten Outstanding Young Men of America, 1966; Distinguished Service medal Dept. Def., 1967. Mem. Am., Fed., D.C. bar assns., Am. Judicature Soc. Author: The Student Revolution: A Global Confrontation, 1969; A Presidential Nation, 1975. Home: 3551 Springland Lane NW Washington DC 20008 Office: HEW 200 Independence Ave SW Washington DC 20201*

CALIFF, JUNIUS PAUL, b. Carthage, Ill., Mar. 4, 1910; B.S., U. Ill., 1932, LL.B., 1933. Admitted to Ill. bar, 1933; county judge Rock Island County (Ill.) Ct., 1938-46; asst. atty. gen. State of Ill., 1948-52; partner firm Califf Harper Fox Dailey, Moline, Ill., 1946—. Mem. Rock Island (Ill.) Sch. Dist. 41 Sch. Bd., 1947-62, pres., 1952-61; pres. Ill. State Sch. Bd. Assn., 1960-61. Mem. Ill. State, Rock Island County bar assns., Rock Island C. of C. (pres. 1966), Phi Delta Phi. Home: 3408 20th St Ct Rock Island IL 61201 Office: 506 15th St Moline IL 61265 Tel (309) 764-8361

CALKINS, HUGH, b. Newton, Mass., Feb. 20, 1924; A.B., Harvard, 1945, LL.B., 1949. Admitted to D.C. bar, 1950, Ohio bar, 1951; law clk. to judge U.S. Ct. Appeals 2d Circuit, N.Y.C., 1949-50; law clk. Justice Felix Frankfurter, U.S. Supreme Ct., 1950-51; asso. firm Jones, Day, Reavis & Pogue, Cleve., 1951-57, partner, 1958—; dep. dir. Pres.'s Commn. on Nat. Goals, 1959; dir. Premier Indsl. Corp., Jeffrey Co., Brown & Sharpe Mfg. Co. Mem. Cleve. Bd. Edn., 1965-69; chmn. Nat. Adv. Council Vocat. Edn., 1969-71; fellow Harvard Coll., 1968—. Mem. Am. Bar Assn. (council tax sect.) Am. Law Inst. (council), Council Fgn. Relations. Contbr. articles to legal jours. Home: 2477 Guilford Rd Cleveland Heights OH 44118 Office: 1700 Union Commerce Bldg Cleveland OH 44115 Tel (216) 696-3939

CALKINS, RICHARD M., b. Washington, Oct. 1, 1931; B.A., Dartmouth, 1953; J.D., Northwestern U., 1959. Admitted to Ill. bar, 1959; partner firm Burdett & Calkins, Chgo., 1969—; prof. law John Marshall Law Sch., Chgo., 1964—. Mem. Am., Fed., Ill., Chgo. bar assns. Contbr. articles to legal jours. Home: 1725 Central Ave Wilmette IL 60097 Office: 135 S La Salle St Chicago IL 60603 Tel (312) 641-2121

CALL, DAVID HARLOW, b. Longview, Wash., Jan. 25, 1938; A.B., Harvard, 1960; postgrad. Trinity Coll., Oxford, Eng., 1960-61; J.D., Stanford, 1964. Admitted to Calif. bar, 1965, Alaska bar, 1966; clk. firm Ely, Guess, Rudd & Havelock, Anchorage, 1964-65; asst. U.S. atty., Fairbanks, Alaska, 1965-66; partner firm Yeager & Call, Fairbanks, 1966-67, Call, Haycraft & Fenton, Fairbanks, 1968—. Mem. Calif., Alaska (gov. 1969-72, v.p. 1971-72), Tanana Valley (pres. 1976) bar assns. Office: 1919 Lathrop St Fairbanks AK 99701 Tel (907) 452-2296

CALLAGHAN, THOMAS ANTHONY, b. Troy, N.Y., July 8, 1941; A.B., Boston Coll., 1963; J.D., Union U., 1966. Admitted to N.Y. bar, 1966, U.S. Supreme Ct. bar, 1974; asso. firm Cooper, Erving & Savage, Albany, N.Y., 1969-73, partner, 1973—; arbitrator Albany Small Claims Ct., 1974—; instr. Colonie Adult Edn., 1970-73. Mem. Albany County Legislature, 1975—; coach Schenectady Youth Hockey Assn., 1975—. Mem. Am., N.Y. State (chmn. young lawyers sect.), Albany County bar assns., Capital Dist. Trial Lawyers Assn. (charter). Home: 3291 Marilyn St Schenectady NY 12303 Office: Cooper Erving & Savage 35 State St Albany NY 12207 Tel (518) 434-8131

CALLAHAN, CARROLL BERNARD, b. Montello, Wis., June 14, 1908; LL.B., U. Wis., 1931. Admitted to Wis. bar, 1931; sr. partner firm Callahan, Arnold & Stoltz, Columbus, Wis., 1931—; pres. 1st Nat. Bank, Columbus, 1960—; sec., dir. Rio Fall River (Wis.) Union Bank, 1939—. Fellow Am. Coll. Trial Lawyers; mem. Am. Bar Assn., Am. Legion, State Bar Wis. (past pres.), Phi Alpha Delta. Home: 856 S Charles St Columbus WI 53925 Office: 150 S Ludington St Columbus WI 53925 Tel (414) 623-2330

CALLAHAN, DENNIS WILLIAM, b. San Francisco, Oct. 29, 1947; A.A., Merced Coll., 1967; B.S., Fresno State Coll., 1969; J.D., U. of the Pacific, 1972. Admitted to Calif. bar, 1973; individual practice law, Atwater, Calif., 1973—. Mem. Am., Merced County bar assns., Calif. State Bar, Atwater C. of C., Assn. Trial Lawyers Am., Commercial Law League Am. Home: 2792 Glen Ave Merced CA 95340 Office: 800 Bellevue Rd Atwater CA 95301 Tel (209) 358-6481

CALLAHAN, JAMES CARROLL, b. Longview, Tex., June 7, 1923; established acad. equivalency U. Mont., 1962; LL.B., LaSalle U., 1963; LL.B., Blackstone Sch. Law, Chgo., 1964, J.D., 1970. Admitted to Mont. bar, 1963, U.S. Supreme Ct. bar, 1969, Tex. bar, 1975; individual practice law, Helena, Mont., 1963—, Longview, Tex., 1975—; gen. counsel Carolane Investment Co., Helena and Longview, 1963—. Chmn. bd. elders Founders Christian Ch., 1975-76. Mem. Am. Bar Assn., Am. Judicature Soc., State Bar Tex., Gregg County (Tex.) Bar Assn., State Bar Mont. Named Paul Harris fellow Rotary Internat., 1975. Address: PO Box 1428 Callahan Rd Longview TX 75601 also PO Box 795 Helena MT 59601 Tel (214) 758-2242

CALLAHAN, JOHN OTIS, b. Powell, Wyo., Mar. 8, 1922; J.D., U. Wyo., 1950. Admitted to Wyo. bar, individual practice law, Lovell, Wyo., 1950-57, Basin Wyo., 1957-66; partner firm Sigler & Callahan, Torrington, Wyo., 1967-72; mem., chmn. Wyo. Pub. Service Commn., Cheyenne, Wyo., 1972-75; judge Wyo. Dist. Ct., 2d Jud. Dist., 1975—; mem. Wyo. Senate, 1964—, chief clk., 1965; county atty. Big Horn County, Wyo., 1957-63, Goshen County, Wyo., 1969-70. Mem. Wyo. State Bar, Wyo. Jud. Conf. Home: 120 W Pine St Rawlins WY 82301 Office: POB 1410 Rawlins WY 82301 Tel (307) 324-4381

CALLEN, MICHAEL EDWARD, b. Denver, July 31, 1944; B.A., U. Kans., 1966, J.D., 1969. Admitted to Kans. bar, 1970, Mo. bar, 1971; asso. firm Melvin L. Kodas, Kansas City, Mo., 1969-72; individual practice law, Kansas City, 1972—. Mem. Am., Kans., Mo., Wyandotte County bar assns., Assn. Trial Lawyers Am., Kans. Trial Lawyers Assn. (bd. govs.). Home: 8742 Foster St Overland Park KS 66212 Office: 816 N 9th St Kansas City KS 66101 Tel (913) 342-2016

CALLEN, RALPH IRVING, b. Los Angeles, Apr. 25, 1931; student Compton Coll., 1948-49, U. Calif. at Berkeley, 1949-50; B.A., U. So. Calif., 1954, LL.B., 1957, J.D., 1967. Admitted to Calif. bar, 1958, U.S. Supreme Ct. bar, 1969; individual practice law, Los Angeles, 1958-59; partner firm Cornell & Callen, Compton, Calif., 1959-60; asso. firm English & Horton, Orange County, Calif., 1960-61; individual practice law, Anaheim, Calif., 1961; partner firm Behm & Callen, and predecessors, Anaheim, 1961-73; individual practice law, Anaheim, 1973—. Bd. dirs. Anaheim City Library, 1975-76. Mem. Orange County Trial Lawyers Assn. (pres. 1962), Am., Orange County, Calif., Orange County Criminal Cts. bar assns. Office: 2141-C W LaPalma Ave Anaheim CA 92801 Tel (714) 772-5222

CALLI, WILLIAM S., b. Utica, N.Y., Dec. 27, 1923; grad. Dartmouth Coll., 1947; LL.B., Albany Law Sch. Union U., 1949. Admitted to N.Y. bar, 1949; partner firm Calli, Calli & Monescalchi and predecessors, Utica, mem. N.Y. State Assembly, 1951-64, N.Y. State Senate, 1965. Active Mohawk Valley Assn. for Progress. Mem. Oneida County (N.Y.) (dir.), N.Y. State, Am. bar assns. Home: 215 Bigby Rd Utica NY 13501 Office: 506 Bleecker St Utica NY 13501 Tel (315) 733-0455

CALLIES, DAVID LEE, b. Chgo., Apr. 21, 1943; A.B. cum laude, DePauw U., 1965; J.D., U. Mich., 1968; LL.M., U. Nottingham (Eng.), 1969. Admitted to Ill. bar, 1969; asst. state's atty. McHenry County (Ill.), 1969-70; asso. firm Ross, Hardies, O'Keefe, Babcock & Parsons, Chgo., 1970-74, partner, 1975—; adj. asso. prof. dept. urban planning U. Wis.-Milw., 1975—; adj. asso. prof. Coll. Urban Scis., U. Ill., Chgo. Circle, 1975. Mem. Downtown Devel. Commn., Clarendon Hills, Ill., 1974-75. Mem. Am., Ill., Chgo. bar assns., Am. Soc. Planning Ofcls., Community Planning Assn. (Can.), Nat. Trust (Eng.). Mng. editor Mich. Jour. Law Reform, 1967-68; co-author: The Quiet Revolution in Land Use Controls, 1972; The Taking Issue, 1974; contbr. articles to profl. jours. Office: Suite 3100 One IBM Plaza Chicago IL 60611 Tel (312) 467-9300

CALLISON, PRESTON HARVEY, b. Lexington, S.C., Jan. 22, 1923; A.B., U. S.C., 1942, LL.B., J.D., 1947. Admitted to S.C. bar, 1947; practice in Columbia, S.C., 1947—; asso. firm Fulmer & Barnes, 1947-49; partner Callison & Lind, 1950-56; individual practice law, 1956-72; partner firm Callison, Tighe, Nauful & Rush, 1972—. Pres. S.C. Bapt. Conv., 1969; exec. com. So. Bapt. Conv., 1971—; mem. S.C. Legislature, 1965-66, 69-70. Mem. Am., S.C., Richland, Lexington bar assns., Am. Judicature Soc., Am. Soc. Hosp. Attys. Home: 1520 Alpine Dr West Columbia SC 29169 Office: 1400 Pickens St Columbia SC 29201 Tel (803) 252-9790

CALLOW, KEITH MCLEAN, b. Seattle, Jan. 11, 1925; student Alfred U., 1943, Coll. City N.Y., 1944, Biarritz (France) Am. U., 1945; B.A., U. Wash., 1949, J.D., 1952; grad. Nat. Coll. State Trial Judges U. Nev., 1970. Admitted to Wash. bar, 1952, U.S. Supreme Ct. bar, 1968; asst. atty. gen. State of Wash., 1952; law clk. to justice Wash. Supreme Ct., 1953; dep. pros. atty. King County (Wash.), 1954-56; partner firm Little, LeSourd, Palmer, Scott & Slemmons, Seattle, 1956-64; partner firm Barker, Day, Fleming, Callow & Taylor, Seattle, 1964-69; judge pro tem Municipal Ct., Seattle, 1960-64; judge King County Superior Ct., 1969-71, Wash. State Ct. Appeals, 1972—; mem. Wash. State Pattern Jury Instructions Com. Pres. Young Men's Republican Club of King County, 1957; bd. dirs. Evergreen Safety Council, Seattle. Mem. Am., D.C., Wash., Seattle-King County bar assns., Seattle Estate Planning Council, Psi Upsilon, Phi Delta Phi. Mem. editorial bd. Wash. Law Rev., 1950-52. Home: 4560 52d Ave NE Seattle WA 98105 Office: 1000 Pacific Bldg Seattle WA 98104 Tel (206) 464-7655

CALLOW, WILLIAM GRANT, b. Waukesha, Wis., Apr. 9, 1921; Ph.B., U. Wis., 1943, J.D., 1948. Admitted to Wis. bar, 1948; partner firm Hippenmeyer and Callow, Waukesha, 1948-52; city atty. City of Waukesha, 1952-60; judge Waukesha County Ct., 1961—; Wis. commr., mem. exec. com. Nat. Conf. Commrs. on Uniform State Laws; mem. faculty Wis. Jud. Coll., 1968-75; asst. prof. law U. Minn., 1951-52; speaker on teenage marriage, misconduct and the law to numerous Wis. high schs. Bd. dirs. Jr. Achievement, Waukesha. Mem. Wis. Bar Assn. (dir. sect. family law, initiator TV series on responsibilities under the law), N.Am. Judges Assn. (chmn. sect. parents and juvenile offenders). Recipient Distinguished Service award Waukesha Jr. C. of C., 1956, Dale Carnegie Good Human Relations award, 1969, Lawyers Wives of Wis. Assn., 1974; Outstanding Alumnus award U. Wis., 1973; contbr. articles to Am. Bar Assn. Jour., S.D. Law Rev.; initiator Vols. in Probation for Waukesha County, 1971, Victim Offender Confrontation program for Waukesha County, 1973. Home: 421 Tenny Ave Waukesha WI 53186 Office: 515 Moreland Blvd Waukesha WI 53186 Tel (414) 544-8200

CALLOWAY, CURTIS ALONZO, b. Fairfield, Ala., Dec. 9, 1939; B.A., Miles Coll., 1962; J.D., So. U., Baton Rouge, 1965. Admitted to La. bar, 1969; staff atty. Legal Aid Soc., Baton Rouge, 1969-71; mem. firm Lacour & Calloway, Baton Rouge, 1972—. Mem. Am., Nat. bar assns., Am. Judicature Soc., Louis A. Martinet Legal Soc. Home: POB 73805 Baton Rouge LA 70807 Office: POB 73588 8050 Scenic Hwy Baton Rouge LA 70807 Tel (504) 775-6297

CALTON, JIMMY SPURLOCK, b. Eufaula, Ala., May 12, 1944; B.A., Birmingham So. Coll., 1965; J.D., Vanderbilt U., 1968. Admitted to Ala. bar, 1968; partner firm Corretti, Newsom, Rodgers, May & Calton, Birmingham, 1971-73; individual practice law, Eufaula, 1973—. Chmn., treas. United Way Fund Drive, Eufaula, 1976. Mem. Am., Ala., Birmingham, Barbour County bar assns., Ala. Trial Lawyers Assn. Home: 43 Anderson Rd Eufaula AL 36027 Office: POB 449 Eufaula AL 36027 Tel (205) 687-3563

CALVARUSO, EDMUND ANTHONY, b. Rochester, N.Y., Apr. 17, 1944; B.A., St. John Fisher Coll., 1966; J.D., St. John's U., 1969. Admitted to N.Y. bar, 1970, U.S. Dist. Ct. bar for western Dist. N.Y., 1970; city clk., City of Rochester, 1970-73; asst. pub. defender, Monroe County, N.Y., 1973-75; individual practice law, Rochester, 1975—; atty., Assigned Counsel Program, Monroe County, 1975—; arbitrator Compulsory Arbitration Program, 1975—; sec., mem. Monroe County-Rochester Port Authority, 1973-74; alternate del. 7th Jud. Conv., Monroe County, 1974-76. Mem. N.Y. State, Monroe County bar assns. Named Outstanding Young Man of Am., Monroe County Jr. C. of C., 1970. Home: 92 Cheltenham Rd Rochester NY 14612 Office: 25 E Main St Rochester NY 14614 Tel (716) 325-4110

CALVERT, DAVID PETER, b. Winfield, Kans., Nov. 29, 1941; B.S.B., Kans. State Coll., 1963; J.D., Washburn U., 1967. Admitted to Kans. bar, 1967; dept. county atty. Sedgwick County, Wichita, Kans., 1967-72; judge div. 9 18th Jud. Dist. of Kans., Wichita, 1973—. Mem. Am., Kans. bar assns., Kans. Dist. Judges Assn. Author: Help Yourself! A Handbook on Consumer Fraud, 1970; Help Yourself, Mr. Businessman! 1971. Home: 6032 Legion St Wichita KS 67204 Office: 525 N Main St Wichita KS 67203 Tel (316) 268-7471

CALVERT, GERRY LYNN, b. Decatur, Ill., Sept. 19, 1935; B.A., U. Ky., 1958, M.A., 1959; LL.B., J.D., U. Louisville, 1965. Admitted to Ky. bar, 1965; individual practice law, Lexington, Ky., 1965—. Pro-tem judge, Fayette County, Ky., 1966-68. Mem. Am., Ky., Fayette County Bar Assns., Am. Trial Lawyers Assn. Office: 309 Security Trust Bldg Lexington KY 40507 Tel (606) 233-4277

CALVERT, GORDON RODNEY, b. Washington, Sept. 18, 1947; B.A. with honors, U. Va., 1969; J.D., Harvard, 1972. Admitted to Md. bar, 1972; asso. firm Piper & Marbury, Balt., 1972—. Mem. Am., Md., Balt. City bar assns. Tel (301) 539-2530

CALVERT, JAY HAMILTON, JR., b. Charleston, S.C., Mar. 19, 1945; B.A., Amherst Coll., 1967; J.D., U. Va., 1970. Admitted to Pa. bar, 1970, Fed. Ct. bar, 1970; asso. firm Morgan, Lewis & Bockius, Phila., 1970-71, 72—; staff atty. Community Legal Services, Phila., 1971-72. Vice chmn. law firm div. United Fund Touch Dr., Phila., 1976. Mem. Am., Pa., Phila. bar assns., Fed. Criminal Def. Panel, Nat. Assn. R.R. Trial Counsel. Mem. editorial bd. Va. Law Rev., 1968-70. Office: 123 S Broad St Philadelphia PA 19109 Tel (215) 491-9462

CALVERT, ROBERT WILBURN, b. Lawrence County, Tenn., Feb. 22, 1905; LL.B., U. Tex., 1931. Admitted to Tex. bar, 1931; asso. firm Collins & Martin, Hillsboro, Tex., 1931-34; partner firm Morrow & Calvert, Hillsboro, 1934-43, 47-50; asso. justice Tex. Supreme Ct., 1950-61, chief justice, 1961-72; of counsel firm McGinnis, Lochridge & Kilgore, Austin, Tex., 1972—; mem. Tex. Ho. of Reps., 1933-39, speaker, 1937-39; chmn. Nat. Conf. State Chief Justices, 1970-71. Chmn. Tex. Constl. Revision Com., 1973-75. Mem. Travis County Bar Assn., State Bar Tex., Am. Judicature Soc. (Herbert Lincoln Harley award 1973). Recipient Outstanding Alumnus award U. Tex. Sch. Law, 1972, Texan of Year award Greater New Braunfels C. of C., 1973, Hatton B. Sumners award Southwestern Legal Found., 1974; contbr. numerous articles to legal jours. Home: 1411 W 29th St Austin TX 78703 Office: 900 Congress Ave Austin TX 78701 Tel (512) 476-6982

CALVIN, WILLIAM CARROL, b. Mattoon, Ill., May 21, 1923; student Ill. State Normal U., 1941-43, U. N.D., 1943; B.S., U. Ill., 1947, LL.B., 1948, J.D., 1968. Admitted to Ill. bar, 1949; partner firm Mitchell & Calvin, Havana, Ill., 1949-51; individual practice law, Clinton, Ill., 1951-62; judge DeWitt County (Ill.) Ct., 1954-64; acting judge Platt County (Ill.) Ct., 1957-58, 60-62, Macon County (Ill.) Ct., 1960-62; asso. judge Circuit Ct. of 6th Jud. Circuit of Ill., 1965-71, judge, 1971—; mem. Ill. and Chgo. Bar Assns. Joint Com. for Implementation of Jud. Article, 1963-65; mem. exec. com. Ill. Jud. Conf., 1976—. Mem. ofcl. bd. Clinton Meth. Ch., 1952—, chmn., 1966-68; bd. dirs. Fine Arts Center, Clinton, 1960—; mem. exec. bd. Corn Belt and W.D. Boyce councils Boy Scouts Am., 1960—, chmn. Prairie Trails Dist. council, 1972-73; chmn. DeWitt County unit Am. Cancer Soc., 1963-65, bd. dirs., 1954—. Mem. Am., Ill., DeWitt County (pres. 1966-67) bar assns., Ill. Judges Assn., Am. Judicature Soc., Phi Delta Phi. Home: 819 W Adams St Clinton IL 61727 Office: Courthouse Clinton IL 61727 Tel (217) 935-2584

CALVIRD, CHARLES AUGUSTUS, b. Clinton, Mo., Oct. 28, 1884; LL.B., Mo. U., 1912; city atty. Clinton, 1914-21; judge 29th Jud. Circuit Mo., 1935-41; individual practice law, Clinton. Pres. bd. regents Central Mo. State Coll., 1935-39; mem. Clinton Housing Authority, 1965-70. Mem. Mo., Henry County bar assns. Named hon. Mo. Col., 1949. Address: 404 N 2d St Clinton MO 64735

CAMBRICE, ROBERT LOUIS, b. Houston, Nov. 23, 1947; B.A. cum laude, Tex. So. U., 1969; J.D., U. Tex., 1972. Admitted to Tex. bar, 1973; asst. city atty., Houston, 1974-76; individual practice law, Houston, 1976—. Mem. Am., Nat. bar assns., Houston Lawyers Assn., NAACP, Smithsonian Assos., U. Tex., Tex. So. U. alumni assns., Alpha Kappa Mu. Office: 1609 Blodgett St Houston TX 77004 Tel (713) 526-8317

CAMENISCH, ROBERT LINCOLN, b. La Salle, Ill., Feb. 12, 1921; J.D., Northwestern U., 1948. Admitted to Ill. bar, 1949; atty. FTC, Chgo., 1951-67, regional dir., 1967-74; adminstrv. law judge HEW, Milw., 1974—. Mem. Am., Chgo. (chmn. antitrust com. 1973-74), Ill. State, Fed. bar assns., Bar Assn. 7th Fed. Circuit. Home: 494 Atwood Ct Elmhurst IL 60126 Office: Room 800 735 W Wisconsin Ave Milwaukee WI 53233 Tel (414) 224-3141

CAMERA, PAUL GEORGE, b. San Francisco, Nov. 3, 1935; B.A., Stanford, 1957; J.D., Hastings Coll., San Francisco, 1960. Admitted to Calif. bar, 1961; asso. firm Field, DeGoff & Rieman, San Francisco, 1961-66, partner, 1965-66; individual practice law, San Francisco, 1966—, San Rafael, Calif., 1966—; mem. faculty San Francisco Law Sch., 1965-66, Lincoln Law Sch., 1966-67; Hastings Coll. Law, 1967-72; lectr. Calif. Continuing Edn. of the Bar, 1972. Mem. Calif. State Bar Assn., Lawyers Club San Francisco. Office: 55 Professional Center Pkwy San Rafael CA 94903 Tel (415) 472-5700

CAMERON, DUNCAN HUME, b. Brandon, Man., Can., May 26, 1934; B.A. cum laude, Harvard, 1956; LL.B., Columbia, 1959, Ph.D., 1965. Admitted to N.Y. bar, 1959, D.C. bar, 1967, U.S. Supreme Ct. bar, 1970; asso. firm Paul, Weiss, Rifkind, Wharton & Garrison, N.Y.C., 1959-62; dep. asst. gen. counsel AID, 1963-67; partner firm Appleton, Rice & Perrin, Washington, 1967-71, Cameron, Hornbostel & Adelman, Washington, 1972—; adj. prof. law Georgetown U., 1970—, instr. Sch. Fgn. Service, 1974—. Mem. Am., Inter-Am., Fed., D.C. bar assns. Home: 3616 Davenport St NW Washington DC 20008 Office: 1707 H St NW Washington DC 20006 Tel (202) 965-4690

CAMERON, E. COLBY, b. Hanover, N.H., Aug. 19, 1941; A.B., Brown U., 1963; J.D., U. Denver, 1968. Admitted to R.I. bar, 1969, Colo. bar, 1974; asso. firm Edwards & Angell, Denver, 1968-74, sec., gen. counsel Am. Television & Communications Corp., Denver, 1974-75, partner firm Edwards & Angell, Providence, 1975—. Vice chmn. bd. Providence Central YMCA. Mem. R.I., Am. bar assns. Office: 125 Carlton Ave Warwick RI 02889 Office: 2700 Hospital Trust Tower Providence RI 02903 Tel (401) 274-9200

CAMERON, JAMES DUKE, b. Richmond, Calif., Mar. 25, 1925; B.A., U. Calif., Berkeley, 1950; J.D., U. Ariz., 1954. Admitted to Ariz. bar, 1954; practiced in Yuma, 1955-65; judge Yuma County (Ariz.) Superior Ct., 1960, Ariz. Ct. Appeals, 1965-70; justice Ariz. Supreme Ct., 1971-75, chief justice, 1974—. First vice chmn. Conf. Justices U.S., 1976; mem. Ariz. Bd. Pub. Welfare, 1960-64, chmn., 1963-64; trustee Yuma City-County Library, 1956-67, chmn., 1962-63. Mem. Am. (pres.-elect and dir. Appellate Judges' Conf.), Ariz., Yuma County (pres. 1959-60) bar assns., Inst. Jud. Adminstrn., Am. Law Inst., Am. Judicatures Soc. (Herbert Lincoln Harley award 1976). Author: Arizona Appellate Forms and Procedures, 1967; contbr. articles to legal jours. Office: State Capitol Bldg Phoenix AZ 85007 Tel (602) 271-4535

CAMERON, JAMES NOEL, b. Bronx, N.Y., Dec. 25, 1940; B.B.A., St. Francis Coll., 1962; J.D., St. Johns U., 1965. Admitted to N.Y. State bar; asso. firm David T. Walsh, 1965-67, firm Gill & Sheehan, 1967-69, firm Amann, Zachary & Marchi, 1969-75; individual practice law, S.I., N.Y., 1974—. Mem. N.Y. Def. Lawyers Assn. (asso. zone leader), N.Y. State, Richmond County bar assns., S.I. Trial Lawyers, Catholic Lawyers Guild. Home: 81 Woodvale Ave Staten Island NY 10309 Office: 171 Broad St Staten Island NY 10304 Tel (212) 442-5544

CAMERON, PHILLIP D., b. Shenendoah, Pa., Feb. 10, 1942; B.S. in Indsl. Engring., Ohio State U., 1964; J.D., U. Detroit, 1969. Admitted to Ohio bar, 1969; individual practice law, Worthington, Ohio, 1969—. Home: 8382 Kirkaldy Ct Dublin OH 43017 Office: 6649 N High St Worthington OH 43085 Tel (614) 846-2946

CAMERON, WILLIAM W., b. Internat. Falls, Minn., June 5, 1941; B.A. in Polit. Sci., U. Minn., Duluth, 1963, J.D., 1969. Admitted to Minn. bar, 1971; partner firm Cameron & Lundell, Mpls., 1971—. Mem. Am., Minn., Hennepin County bar assns., Bar Assn. Air Carrier Pilots (pres.). Tel (612) 824-0773

CAMILLETTI, PAUL CARMEN, b. Wheeling, W.Va., Oct. 25, 1932; B.A., Mt. St. Mary's Coll., Emmitsburg, Md., 1954; J.D., U. W.Va., 1957. Admitted to W.Va. bar, 1957; partner firm Camilletti and Camilletti, Wheeling, 1957-69, 73—; U.S. atty. No. Dist. W.Va., Wheeling, 1969-73; tchr. Am. Inst. Banking, 1958-68; lectr. Wheeling Coll., 1966-69. Mem. Am., W.Va. bar assns., W.Va. Trial Lawyers Assn. (pres. 1975-76). Home: 1325 National Rd Wheeling WV 26003 Office: Peoples Federal Bldg Wheeling WV 26003 Tel (304) 233-2541

CAMINEZ, JON DAVID, b. N.Y.C., Sept. 22, 1941; B.A., U. N.C., 1964, J.D., 1967. Admitted to N.Y. bar, 1968, Fla. bar, 1970; atty. Dept. Justice, Washington, 1968-70; individual practice law, Tallahassee, 1970—; state hearing examiner for Baker Act, State of Fla. Chmn. Jefferson County (Fla.) Republican Party. Mem. Am., Fla. bar assns., N.Y. State Bar. Recipient Distinguished Service citation Fla. Psychologist Assn.; named Pub. Citizen of Year N.W. Fla. chpt. Nat. Assn. Social Workers, 1974. Office: 1030 E Lafayette St Tallahassee FL 32303 Tel (904) 877-6159

CAMP, BILL ADKINS, b. Ft. Worth, Aug. 28, 1948; B.A., U. Tex., 1970, J.D., 1972. Admitted to Tex. bar, 1972; asst. dist. atty. Harris County (Tex.) Dist. Attys. Office, Houston, 1973—. Mem. Am., Houston, Houston Jr., San Antonio bar assns., Tex. Dist. and County Attys. Assn., Nat. Dist. Attys. Assn. Home: 4010 Linkwood St #1062 Houston TX 77025 Office: 500 Harris County Court House Houston TX 77002 Tel (713) 221-5800

CAMP, DANIEL PARKS, b. Rome, Ga., Sept. 20, 1946; A.B., Mercer U., 1968, J.D., 1970. Admitted to Ga. bar, 1970, Fla. bar, 1970; partner firm Wiggins & Camp, Carrollton, Ga., 1970—. Elder, trustee Carrollton Presbyn Ch. Home: Route 10 Box 199 Carrollton GA 30117 Office: 203 Tanner St Carrollton GA 30117 Tel (404) 832-2482

CAMP, JAMES DAVID, JR., b. Ft. Lauderdale, Fla., Feb. 3, 1928; B.A., U. Fla., 1949, LL.B., 1951, J.D., 1967. Admitted to Fla. bar, 1951; mem. firm McCune, Hiaasen, Crum, Ferris & Gardner, Ft. Lauderdale, 1951—; chmn. bd. Century Nat. Bank of Broward, Century Banks, Inc.; dir. Century Nat. Bank of Ft. Lauderdale, Lauderdale Lakes Nat. Bank, Century Nat. Bank of Coral Ridge. Past chmn. bd. Broward County Heart Assn. Mem. Am., Broward County bar assns., Fla. Bar, Am. Judicature Soc., Phi Delta Phi, Ft. Lauderdale C. of C. (past pres.). Recipient Distinguished Service award Broward Community Coll. Office: Suite 600 Century Bank Bldg 25 S Andrews Ave Fort Lauderdale FL 33301 Tel (305) 462-2000

CAMP, JAMES HARRY, b. Sparta, Tenn., Oct. 30, 1936; B.S., Tenn. Tech. U., 1958; J.D., Vanderbilt U., 1967. Admitted to Tenn. bar, 1967; asso. firm Manier, White, Herod, Hollabaugh & Smith, Nashville, 1967-69, partner, 1970; partner firm Camp & Camp, Sparta, 1971—; spl. commr. Tenn. Supreme Ct., 1973-75; dir. Sparta Monumental Works, Sparta Limestone Corp. Mem. Sparta Mayor's Advisory Com., 1975—. Mem. Am., Tenn., White County bar assns., Tenn. Def. Lawyers Assn. Office: POB 467 Rhea St Sparta TN 38583 Tel (615) 836-3291

CAMP, JOHN CLAYTON, b. Arab, Ala., Sept. 23, 1923; student Birmingham So. Coll., 1940-42, U. Ala., 1943, Auburn U., 1944; LL.B., La. State U., 1948. Admitted to La. bar, 1948, D.C. bar, 1973; asso. firm Thompson Lawes & Cavanaugh, Lake Charles, La., 1948-55; partner firm Camp, Carmouche, Palmer, Carwile & Barsh, Lake Charles, 1955—; asst. atty. gen. La. Dept. Justice, 1972—; dir., v.p. Land & Royalty Owners La.; dir. Calcasieu Marine Nat. Bank Lake Charles; spl. counsel, legal adviser on energy matters Gov. La., 1974. Chmn. Calcasieu Indsl. Devel. Bd., 1963-64; committeeman La. Bd. Edn.; adv. com. La. Law Inst.; mem. La. Pub. Affairs Research and Council for Better La. Assns.; adv. bd. La. div. SBA, 1969-70. Fellow Internat. Acad. Law and Sci.; mem. Am., Fed., La., Fed. Power, D.C. bar assns., Fgn. Relations Assn. New Orleans, Houston Estate and Fin. Forum, Am. Mgmt. Assn., La. Service League (dir. 1970—), Miss. Valley World Trade Council, La.-Miss. Export Expansion Council, La. Intercoastal Seaway Assn. (dir. 1970—), U.S. (internat. com. 1972), La. (dir. 1971), Greater Lake Charles (pres. 1971, dir.) chambers commerce. Home: 224 W Spring St Lake Charles LA 70605 Office: PO Drawer 2001 Lake Charles LA 70602

CAMP, THOMAS LEE, b. Fairburn, Ga., Mar. 9, 1905; A.B., Oglethorpe U., 1925, LL.D., 1975; LL.B., J.D. George Washington U., 1931; student Mercer U., 1922-23, Atlanta Law Sch., 1926-27, Emory U. Law Sch., 1928; Tchr. pub. schs., Atlanta, 1925-27; sec. Congressman Leslie J. Steele, also Congressman Robert Ramspeck, also clk. civil service com. U.S. Ho. of Reps., 1927-44; partner firm Camp & Camp, Atlanta, 1944-57; judge Fulton County (Ga.) Civil Ct. (now State Ct. of Fulton County), 1957—, chief judge, 1966—; commr. Fulton County, 1947-57. Chmn. bd. adminstrn. St. Mark United Methodist Ch., Atlanta, 1957-58, trustee, 1972—; trustee Oglethorpe U., 1962-75, emeritus, 1975—. Mem. Atlanta, Ga., Am. bar assns., Lawyers Club Atlanta, Old War Horse Lawyers Club (pres. 1973-74). Home: 169 Robin Hood Rd NE Atlanta GA 30309 Office: 216 State Ct Bldg Atlanta GA 30303 Tel (404) 572-2641

CAMPAGNA, RICHARD S., b. Scranton, Pa., Oct. 1, 1924; B.S., U. Scranton, 1950; postgrad. Pa. State U., 1950-51; LL.B., Temple U., 1953. Admitted to Lackawanna County bar, 1954, Pa. Superior Ct. bar, 1954, Pa. Supreme Ct. bar, 1954, U.S. Dist. Ct. No. Dist. Pa. bar, 1954, U.S. Ct. Appeals 3rd Circuit bar, 1967, U.S. Supreme Ct. bar, 1968; asst. solicitor City of Scranton, 1962-65; solicitor Scranton-Lackawanna Health and Welfare Authority, 1962—; hearing examiner Pa. Sales Tax Bd. Appeals, 1966-70. Mem.

Lackawanna, Pa. bar assns., Pa. Trial Lawyers Assn., Assn. Trial Lawyers Am. Home: 203 Mary Ln Scranton PA 18505 Office: 803 Connell Bldg Scranton PA 18503 Tel (717) 342-8194

CAMPANELLA, MARTIN JAMES, b. Chgo., June 14, 1946; B.S. with high honors, U. Ill., 1968; J.D., Harvard U., 1971. Admitted to Ill. bar, 1971; asso. firm Defrees & Fiske, Chgo., 1971—; lectr. Roosevelt U. Paralegal Inst., 1974-76. Mem. Am. (co-chmn. meetings com. young lawyers sect. 1976-77), Chgo (chmn. architecture and law com. of young lawyers sect. 1975-76, sec. sect. 1976-77, editorial bd. Young Lawyers Jour. 1976—), bar assns., Harvard Law Sch. Assn., Phi Kappa Phi, Beta Gamma Sigma, Beta Alpha Psi. Home: 439 B Grant Pl Chicago IL 60614 Office: 72 W Adams Suite 1500 Chicago IL 60603 Tel (312) 372-4000

CAMPBELL, ALEXANDER BRADSHAW, b. Summerside, P.E.I., Can., Dec. 1, 1933; B.A., Dalhousie U., 1958, LL.B., 1959; LL.D., McGill U., 1967. Called to P.E.I. bar, 1959, created Queen's counsel, 1966; practice in Summerside, 1959-66; mem. P.E.I. Legislature, 1965, leader Liberal Party, 1965, premier, 1966—, atty.-gen., minister justice, 1966-69, 74—, minister devel., 1969-72, minister agr., 1972-74. Mem. Privy Council Can., 1967; past sec. Summerside Bd. Trade. Past v.p. Young Liberal Assn. Home: 330 Beaver St Summerside PE Canada Office: Provincial Adminstrv Bldg PO Box 2000 Charlottetown PE C1A 7N8 Canada

CAMPBELL, ARTHUR WALDRON, b. Bklyn., Mar. 29, 1944; A.B., Harvard U., 1966; J.D., W.Va. U., 1971; LL.M., Georgetown U., 1974. Admitted to W.Va., D.C. bars, 1971, Calif. bar, 1974, U.S. Supreme Ct. bar, 1975; spl. asst. U.S. atty., Washington, 1972-73; chief civil div. D.C. Law Students In Ct. Program, 1973, chief criminal div., 1975, dep. dir., 1976; asst. prof. law Calif. Western Sch., 1976—; advisor W.Va. Legis. Com. to Rewrite Criminal and Juvenile Law, 1971-72. Scoutmaster, Monongalia council Boy Scouts Am., Morgantown, W.Va., 1970-71. Mem. Am. Bar Assn., Nat. Legal Aid and Defenders Assn., Nat. Assn. Criminal Def. Lawyers (chmn. Va. strike force 1976-77), Assn. Am. Law Schs. Prettyman fellow, 1971-73. Home: 5694 Sweetwater Rd Bonita CA 92002 Office: 350 W Cedar St San Diego CA 92102 Tel (714) 239-0391

CAMPBELL, CHARLES FRANKLIN, JR., b. Ft. Lauderdale, Fla., Apr. 28, 1944; B.A. in Polit. Sci., U. Tex., Arlington, 1966; J.D., So. Meth. U., 1969. Admitted to Tex. bar, 1969; asst. dist. atty., Houston, 1969-71; county atty., Hill County, Tex., 1972-76, dist. atty., 1976—; dir. Cause, Inc., 1972-74. Mem. Am., Tex. bar assns., Tex. Trial Lawyers Assn., Nat. Dist. Atty.'s Assn. Home: 105 N 8th St Hubbard TX 76648 Office: PO Box 400 Hillsboro TX 76645 Tel (817) 582-3453

CAMPBELL, C(HARLES) PHILIP, JR., b. Boulder, Colo., Feb. 18, 1948; student Notre Dame Internat. Sch., 1964-66; A.B., Rutgers, The State U., 1970; J.D., Stetson Coll., 1973. Admitted to Fla. bar, 1973; asso. firm Bradham, Lyle, Skipper & Cramer, St. Petersburg, Fla., 1973-74; asso. firm Jacobs, Robbins & Gaynor, St. Petersburg, 1974—. Bd. dirs. John Knox Housing, St. Petersburg, 1977; bd. dirs. Leadership St. Petersburg, 1977; mem. Pinellas County Sch. Bd. Task Force, 1977. Mem. Am., Fla., St. Petersburg bar assns., Pinellas County Trial Lawyers, Acad. Fla. Trial Lawyers. Office: 445 31st St N Saint Petersburg FL 33713 Tel (813) 895-1971

CAMPBELL, DOUGLAS GREGORY, b. Harlan, Ky., June 7, 1941; B.S., Washington and Lee U., 1964, LL.B., 1964. Admitted to Va. bar, 1967; asso. firm Harman & Harman, Tazewell, Va., 1969-70; partner firms Harman & Campbell, Tazewell, 1970-75, Campbell & Newlon, Tazewell, 1975—. Deacon Tazewell Presbyn. Ch. Mem. Va. State, Tazewell County (pres. 1971-72) bars. Office: PO Box 838 Tazewell VA 24651 Tel (703) 988-6554

CAMPBELL, DOUGLAS NEIL, b. Lockport, N.Y., Aug. 15, 1937; B.S., U.S. Mil. Acad., 1959; B.Mus., U. Cin., 1969; J.D., Emory U., 1973. Asso. firm Gambrell, Russell, Killorin & Forbes, Atlanta, 1973—; admitted to Ga. bar, 1974. Mem. Am., Atlanta bar assns., Ga. State Bar. Home: 648 Channing Dr NW Atlanta GA 30318 Office: 4000 First Nat Bank Tower Atlanta GA 30318 Tel (404) 658-1620

CAMPBELL, F. LEE, b. Tacoma, Aug. 24, 1923; B.A., U. Wash., 1947, J.D., 1950. Admitted to Wash. bar, 1950; now mem. firm Karr, Tuttle, Koch, Campbell, Mawer & Morrow, Seattle; town atty. Town of Clyde Hill (Wash.), 1953-74, councilman, 1953-54. Fellow Am. Coll. Trial Lawyers; mem. Seattle-King County (pres. 1976-77), Wash. State (chmn. sect. trial practice 1974-75), Am. bar assns., Internat. Assn. Ins. Counsel, Wash. Assn. Def. Counsel (pres. 1965-66), Phi Delta Phi. Office: 2600 Seattle First Bldg 1001 Fourth Ave Seattle WA 98154 Tel (206) 223-1313*

CAMPBELL, GEORGE EMERSON, b. Piggott, Ark., Sept. 23, 1932; J.D., U. Ark., Fayetteville, 1955. Admitted to Ark. bar, 1955, U.S. Supreme Ct. bar, 1971; law clk. to justice Ark. Supreme Ct., 1959-60; asso. firm Kirsch, Cathey & Brown, Paragould, Ark., 1955; mem. firm Rose, Nash, Williamson, Carroll, Clay & Giroir, Little Rock, 1960—. Del. 7th Ark. Constl. Conv., 1969-70; regional v.p. Nat. Municipal League, 1974—. Mem. Am., Ark., Pulaski County bar assns., Am. Law Inst., Am. Judicature Soc., Ark. Automobile Club (pres. 1977—). Office: 720 W 3d St Little Rock AR 72201 Tel (501) 375-9131

CAMPBELL, HUGH BROWN, b. Waynesville, N.C., Mar. 14, 1907; A.B., Amherst Coll., 1929; J.D., U. N.C., 1932. Admitted to N.C. bar, 1931; mem. firm. J. Faison Thomson, Goldsboro, N.C., 1932-34; mem. firm Tillett, Tillett & Kennedy, Charlotte, N.C., 1934-37, Tillett, Campbell & Boyle, Charlotte, 1937-40, Tillett & Campbell, Charlotte, 1940-45, Tillett, Campbell, Craighill & Rendleman, Charlotte, 1945-52, Campbell, Craighill, Rendleman & Kennedy, Charlotte, 1952-55; judge Superior Ct. of N.C., 1955-67; judge Ct. of Appeals of N.C., Raleigh, 1967—. Mem. Am., N.C., Internat. bar assns., Am. Judicature Soc. Home: 1626 Queens Rd Charlotte NC 28207 Office: 1 W Morgan St Raleigh NC 27602 Tel (704) 332-5725

CAMPBELL, JAMES SARGENT, b. Chgo., Sept. 19, 1938; B.A., Yale U., 1960; LL.B., Stanford U., 1964. Admitted to D.C. bar, 1966; law clk. to Justice William O. Douglas, U.S. Supreme Ct., 1964-65; spl. asst. Antitrust div. Dept. Justice, 1967-68; gen. counsel Nat. Commn. Causes and Prevention of Violence, 1968-69; asso. firm Wilmer, Cutler & Pickering, Washington, 1965-67, 70-71, partner, 1972—; cons. Office of Sec. HUD, 1977. Counsel credentials com. Democratic Nat. Conv., 1972; dir. Nat. Council to Control Handguns, 1975-76, Center Study and Prevention of Handgun Violence, 1977. Mem. Am., D.C. bar assns. Author: (with J. Sahid and D. Stang) Law and Order Reconsidered, 1970; contbr. articles to legal jours. Office: 1666 K St NW Washington DC 20006 Tel (202) 872-6336

CAMPBELL, JAMES WALLACE, b. McLeansboro, Ill., Mar. 29, 1920; B.S., U. Ill., 1940, LL.B., St. Louis U., 1948. Admitted to Ill. bar, 1948, Colo. bar 1962; spl. agt. FBI, 1942-44, 46-47; individual practice law, E. St. Louis, Ill., 1948-52; atty. Texaco Inc., Chgo., 1952-58, N.Y.C., 1958-61, Denver, 1961-69, gen. atty., 1969—. Mem. Am. Bar Assn. Office: PO Box 2100 Denver CO 80201 Tel (303) 573-7571

CAMPBELL, JEFFREY LYNN, b. Omaha, Dec. 16, 1941; B.A. in Polit. Sci., U. Nebr., 1963, J.D., 1966; grad. Calif. Coll. Mortuary Sci., Los Angeles, 1967. Admitted to Nebr. bar, 1966; asso. firm Hascall, Campbell & Reagan, Bellevue, Nebr., 1968-70; dep. county atty. Sarpy County (Nebr.), 1968-72; judge Nebr. Dist. County Ct., Dist. 2, 1973—. Mem. Nat. Dist. Attys. Assn., Nebr. State, Am. bar assns., Nebr. County Judges Assn., Conf. Funeral Service Examining Bds. (registered). Licensed funeral dir., embalmer, Nebr. Home: 1201 Skyview Dr Bellevue NE 68005 Office: Courthouse Hall of Justice Papillion NE 68046 Tel (402) 339-2277

CAMPBELL, JOE BILL, b. Bowling Green, Ky., Jan. 28, 1943; B.A., Western Ky. U., 1965; J.D., U. Ky., 1968. Admitted to Ky. bar, 1968, U.S. Supreme Ct. bar, 1971; partner firm Campbell & Crandall, Bowling Green, 1968—; instr. law Western Ky. U., 1969-72. Pres. Bowling Green Boys' Club, 1973; bd. dirs. United Givers Fund, 1972-74. Mem. Am., Ky. bar assns., Def. Research Inst., Order of Coif. Asso. editor Ky. Law Jour., 1967-68. Home: 1704 Singletree Ln Bowling Green KY 42101 Office: 1010 College St Bowling Green KY 42101 Tel (502) 842-4293

CAMPBELL, JOHN FLOYD, b. McLean, Tex., Mar. 16, 1927; B.S. in Chem. Engring., Okla. U., 1949; J.D., U. Tex., 1961. Admitted to Tex. bar, 1961; partner firm Campbell & Davidson, Austin, Tex., 1972—. Mem. Tex., Am. bar assns., Pampa Jr. C. of C. Tel (512) 476-6036

CAMPBELL, PAUL BARTON, b. Owosso, Mich., Feb. 24, 1930; B.B.A. with distinction, U. Mich., 1951; M.B.A. with distinction, J.D., 1954. Admitted to Mich. bar, 1954, Ohio bar, 1955; asso. firm Squire, Sanders & Dempsey, Cleve., 1954-66, partner, 1966—; sec. Ferro Corp., Cleve., 1970—; dir. Union Commerce Bank, Cleve., 1975—. Mem. Am., Ohio, Cleve. bar assns. Home: 13610 Shaker Blvd apt 203 Cleveland OH 44120 Office: 1800 Union Commerce Bldg Cleveland OH 44115 Tel (216) 696-9200

CAMPBELL, ROBERT BLAIR, b. New Enterprise, Pa., Oct. 3, 1919; A.B., Franklin and Marshall Coll., 1941; LL.B., U. Pa., 1948. Admitted to Pa. bar, 1949; law clk. Supreme Ct. Pa., 1948-50; partner firm Nelson, Campbell & Levine, Altoona, Pa., 1950-75; judge Ct. Common Pleas Blair County (Pa.), Hollidaysburg, 1975—; mem. hearing com. Pa. Supreme Ct. Disciplinary Bd., 1972-75. Mem. Blair County, Pa., Am. bar assns., Pa. Trial Judges Assn. Home: 36 Sylvan Heights Dr Hollidaysburg PA 16648 Office: Blair County Court House Hollidaysburg PA 16648 Tel (814) 695-5541

CAMPBELL, ROBERT BRENT, b. San Diego, Dec. 29, 1945; B.A. in Polit. Sci., San Diego State Coll., 1968; J.D., Calif. Western Sch. Law, 1970. Admitted to Calif. bar, 1971; practice law, San Diego. Mem. San Diego County Bar Assn. Home: 11211 Posthill Rd Lakeside CA 92103 Tel (714) 239-9051

CAMPBELL, ROBERT JAMES, b. Sidney, Mont., Dec. 21, 1940; B.S., U. Mont., 1963, J.D., 1967. Admitted to Mont. bar, 1967; individual practice law, Missoula, Mont., 1967—; del. Mont. Constl. Conv., 1972; chmn. correctional facilities and services com. State Bar Mont., 1974-76. Mem. Am., Western Mont. bar assns., Am. Judicature Soc. Named Outstanding Young Man Am., 1972. Home: Route 5 Miller Creek Rd Missoula MT 59801 Office: 501 Western Bank Bldg Missoula MT 59801 Tel (406) 543-3005

CAMPBELL, ROBERT LEE, b. St. Louis, Jan. 13, 1930; A.B., Washington U., St. Louis, 1953, J.D., 1953. Admitted to Mo. bar, 1953; individual practice law, Clayton, Mo., 1953-66; judge St. Louis County Circuit Ct., Clayton, 1967—. Alderman, City of Frontenac, 1951-56; chmn. bd. dirs. Humane Soc. of Mo., 1970—. Home: 417 Summit St Webster Groves MO 63119 Office: 7900 Carondelet St Clayton MO 63105 Tel (314) 889-2678

CAMPBELL, ROBERT SANDERS, JR., b. Boise, Idaho, Sept. 8, 1933; B.A., U. Idaho, 1955; J.D., U. Colo., 1958. Admitted to Utah bar, 1959, Idaho bar, 1958, U.S. Supreme Ct. bar, 1964; asst. atty. gen. State of Idaho, 1958-59; asst. atty. gen., chief trial lawyer litigation div. State of Utah, 1959-63, spl. asst. atty. gen. air matters, 1969-74, chmn. adv. com. rules of procedure to Supreme Ct., 1964—; bar examiner, 1971-73; partner firm Parsons, Behle & Latimer, Salt Lake City, 1964-69; prin. partner firm Watkiss & Campbell, Salt Lake City, 1969—; vis. and seminar lectr., trial and appellate practice Coll. Law U. Utah, 1973-76; bd. trustees Utah Legal Services, Inc., 1964-67. Mem. Am. Bd. Trial Advs., Am. Bar Assn. (select com. on fed. rules of civil procedure 1963-75). Contbr. articles to legal jours. Office: 310 S Main St 12th floor Salt Lake City UT 84101 Tel (801) 363-3300

CAMPBELL, ROY TIMOTHY, JR., b. Newport, Tenn., Aug. 8, 1927; LL.B., U. Tenn., 1950, J.D., 1950. Admitted to Tenn. Supreme Ct. bar, 1951, U.S. Dist. Ct. bar for Eastern Dist. Tenn., 1953, U.S. Ct. Appeals bar, 6th Circuit, 1962; practiced in Newport, 1951—, individual practice law, 1951-64; mem. firm Campbell & Hooper, 1964—, sr. partner, 1965—; city atty. Town of Newport, 1968-76; dir. Mchts. and Planters Bank, Newport. Sec. Republican Exec. Com. of Cocke County, Tenn., 1960-76; chmn. Cocke County Election Commn., 1975—; trustee Union Cemetery, 1976—, 1st United Methodist Ch., 1976—; bd. dirs. Cocke County Indsl. Devel. Bd., 1965-76. Mem. Newport C. of C. (pres. 1955-56), Tenn., Cocke County (pres. 1972-74) bar assns., U. Tenn. Alumni Assn., Sigma Alpha Epsilon. Home: 712 College St Newport TN 37821 Office: 406 E Main St Newport TN 37821 Tel (615) 623-3082

CAMPBELL, RUTH BENEDICT, b. Butler, Pa., Dec. 10, 1916; B.A., Wellesley Coll., 1938; B.S., Carnegie Inst. Tech., 1940; LL.B., U. Pitts., 1947. Admitted to Pa. bar, 1948; individual practice law, Butler, 1948-54; partner firm Bernstein & Campbell, Butler, 1954—; tchr. bus. law Butler Bus. Coll., 1951-54. Mem., v.p. Butler Area Sch. Bd., 1954-56; mem., pres. Butler County Sch. Bd., 1966. Mem. Butler County, Pa. bar assns. Home: 516 N McKean St Butler PA 16001 Office: 2 Reiber Bldg Butler PA 16001 Tel (412) 287-5176

CAMPBELL, TIMOTHY FISHER, b. Alton, Ill., Mar. 19, 1947; B.A. (Rector scholar), De Pauw U., 1969; J.D., U. Ill., 1972. Admitted to Ill. bar, 1972, U.S. Dist. Ct. for So. Dist. Ill. bar, 1972; asso. firm Chapman & Chapman, Granite City, Ill., 1972-75; individual practice law, Bethalto, Ill. and Hardin, Ill., 1975-76; counsel Village of South Roxana (Ill.). Mem. Am., Ill. State, Madison County (Ill.), Southwestern, Alton-Wood River bar assns., Am. Ill. trial lawyers assns. Named Distinguished Mil. Grad. U. Ill., 1971. Office: 3017 Godfrey Rd Godfrey IL 62035 Tel (618) 466-8034 310 S County Rd Hardin IL 60247

CAMPBELL, WILLARD DONALD, b. New Philadelphia, O., June 6, 1901; A.B., Muskingum Coll., 1922; M.A., U. Pitts., 1923; postgrad Cornell U., 1924, Western Theol. Sem., 1922-23; LL.B. (fellow), Yale U., 1925. Admitted to Ohio bar, 1925, Fla. bar, 1926; city solicitor City of Cambridge, O., 1928-30; prosecuting atty. County of Guernsey (Ohio), 1930-34, judge Common Pleas Ct., 1938-39; mem. Ohio State Senate, Columbus, 1935-36; mem. staff Office Price Adminstrn., Columbus, Ohio, 1941-46; dir. Bur. Code Revision, Columbus, 1946-53; mem. nat. exec. com. Council State Govt., Chgo., 1952-53; spl. counsel Ohio Sch. Survey Com., Columbus, 1955; exec. dir. Ohio Commn. Uniform Laws, Columbus, 1957-58; spl. asst. atty. gen. State of Ohio, Columbus, 1957-59; chmn. Bd. of Review, Bur. of Employment Services, State of Ohio, Columbus, 1963—. Mem. Ohio, Columbus, Fla. bar assns., Columbus Torch Club, Ohio Commadores, Navy Club, Athletic Club, Masons, Shriners. Author: Ohio Revised Code, 1953; prepared Accumulated Index to Ohio Atty. Gen.'s Opinions, 1910-1958. Home: 3249 Tremont Rd Columbus OH 43221 Office: 145 S Front St Columbus OH 43215 Tel (614) 466-3027

CAMPBELL, WILLIAM AUBREY, b. Springfield, Mo., Mar. 30, 1940; B.A. with distinction, Southwestern at Memphis, 1962; LL.B., Vanderbilt U., 1965. Admitted to Mo. bar, 1965, N.C. bar, 1976; instr. law U. N.C., 1965-66, asso. prof., 1969-74, prof., 1974—; served with JAGC, USNR, 1966-69; counsel Commn. for Study of Local and Ad Valorem Tax Structure of N.C., 1970, Environ. studies Com. N.C. Legislature, 1972. Mem. Order of Coif. Author: Property Tax Collection in N.C., 1974; Home: 301 Colony Woods Dr Chapel Hill NC 27514 Office: Inst of Govt Chapel Hill NC 27514 Tel (919) 966-5381

CAMPBELL, WILLIAM F., JR., b. N.Y.C., Sept. 12, 1914; LL.B., N.Y. Law Sch., 1941; admitted to N.Y. bar, 1942, U.S. Supreme Ct. bar, 1946; asso. firm Wait Wilson & Newton, N.Y.C., 1941, 46-50, partner, 1950-54; asso. firm Marshall Rooney, Pearl River, N.Y., 1955; atty. adviser to gen. counsel FHA, Washington and N.Y.C., 1956; asst. sec. Thiokol Chem. Corp., Denville, N.J., 1959-62; acting police judge, South Nyack County Village, N.Y., 1954-55; asso. firm Gasser & Hayes, N.Y.C., 1976; mem. Am., N.Y. State, Fed. bar assns. Home: 7 Michigan Ave Wharton NJ 07885 Office: 30 Rockefeller Plaza New York City NY 07885 Tel (212) 247-6800

CAMPBELL, WILLIAM JOHN, b. Grand Junction, Colo., Feb. 10, 1945; B.A. cum laude in Econs., Colo. Coll., 1967; Rotary Found. grad. fellow in econs. U. Newcastle, N.S.W., Australia, 1969; J.D., U. Colo., 1971. Admitted to Colo. bar, 1971; mem. firm Bradley Campbell & Carney, Golden, Colo., 1971—; mem. bd. dirs. Jefferson County (Colo.) Legal Aid, Inc., 1974-76. Mem. nat. alumni council Colo. Coll., 1972-76. Mem. Am., Colo., 1st Jud. Dist. (Colo.) (trustee 1974—) bar assns., Phi Beta Kappa. Articles editor U. Colo. Law Rev., 1970-71. Office: 1717 Washington Ave Golden CO 80401 Tel (303) 278-3300

CAMPBELLE, ROY BARTLEY JAMES, JR., b. Union City, Tenn., Jan. 1, 1923; B.S., Tenn. State U., 1945, also M.S.; J.D., U. Tenn., 1956. Admitted to Tenn. bar, 1956; dean men Sam Houston Coll., 1945-47; chmn. dept. commerce Ala. State Coll., 1947-53; individual practice law and accounting, 1956-73; asst. prof. dept. criminal justice adminstrn. Middle Tenn. State U., 1973—; juvenile defender Metro Juvenile Ct., Nashville, 1972-73. Mem. Mayors Citizens Com., Nashville, 1971-73; chmn. project Area Com. Urban Renewal for So. Nashville, 1971-73. Mem. Tenn. Bar Assn., Phi Delta Phi. Office: Dept Criminal Justice Middle Tenn State Univ Murfreesboro TN 37130 Tel (615) 898-2630

CAMPION, EILEEN, b. Great River, L.I., N.Y.; J.D., U. Miami, 1961. Admitted to Fla. bar, 1962, U.S. Supreme Ct. bar, 1967; individual practice law, Miami, Fla., 1962-64; law editor Lawyers Coop. Pub. Co., Rochester, N.Y., 1964-65; tax atty. Dept. Treasury, Miami, 1965—; city rep. Bd. Legal Services, Greater Miami, 1974-75. Mem. Metro Dade County Water and Sewer Bd., 1974-75. Mem. Fed. Bar Assn. (recipient outstanding service award 1968, 69), Am. Arbitration Assn. (panel), Women's Com. of 100 (founder 1970-73), AAUW. Recipient highest award for best legal article in internat. competition Phi Delta Delta, 1963. Mem. Fla. Bar (penal reform com. 1976-77). Home: 453 Brickell Ave Miami FL 33131 Office: 51 SW 1st Ave Miami FL 33130 Tel (305) 350-4146

CAMPITI, VINCENT PETER, b. Elkhart, Ind., Mar. 5, 1940; A.B., Ind. U., 1962, J.D., 1964. Admitted to Ind. bar, 1964; law clk. to judge U.S. Dist. Ct. for No. Ind., 1964-67; mem. firm Crumpacker, May, Searer, Oberfell & Helling, S. Bend, Ind., 1967-71, partner, 1971—. Mem. Am., Ind., St. Joseph County bar assns., Order of Coif, Phi Beta Kappa, Delta Theta Phi. Home: 52314 Tammy Dr Granger IN 46530 Office: 224 W Jefferson Blvd South Bend IN 46601 Tel (219) 232-2031

CANADAY, ARTHUR CARY, b. N.Y.C., Nov. 27, 1932; A.B., Princeton, 1954; LL.B., U. Fla., 1959; LL.M., Yale, 1961. Admitted to Fla. bar, 1959; chief asst. Congressman Charles E. Bennett, Washington, 1960-63; asso. firm Hector, Faircloth & Davis, Miami, 1963-66; Frates, Foy, Floyd & Pearson, Miami, 1966; asst. atty. gen. State of Fla., Tallahassee, 1967-73; gen. counsel to gov. of Fla., Tallahassee, 1973-76; mem. Indsl. Relations Commn. Fla., 1976—. Recipient Lopez award U. Fla. Law Sch., 1959; exec. editor U. Fla. Law Rev., 1958-59. Home: 2301 Old Bainbridge Rd Tallahassee FL 32303 Office: 1321 Executive Center Dr Tallahassee FL 32304 Tel (904) 488-4082

CANAVAN, CHARLES DURANT, b. Lowell, Mass., Feb. 15, 1918; B.A., Am. Internat. Coll., 1940; J.D., Duke, 1943. Admitted to Mass. bar, 1946; spl. agent FBI, Washington, 1946-53; individual practice law, Springfield, Mass., 1953—; counsel Richard Salter Storrs Library, Longmeadow, Mass. Incorporator, Carew Hill Girls' Club, Springfield, bd. corporators Mt. St. Vincent Home, Holyoke, Mass. Mem. Mass., Hampden County bar assns., Estate Planning Council. Home: 65 York Dr Longmeadow MA 01106 Office: 1383 Main St Springfield MA 01103 Tel (413) 781-2230

CANAVESI, KARL JOSEPH, b. Rockford, Ill., Nov. 27, 1931; B.A., Rockford Coll., 1959; J.D., U. Wis., 1962. Admitted to Wis. bar, 1962, Ill. bar, 1965; U.S. Supreme Ct. bar, 1972; law asst. Gerald F. Tuite, Rockford, 1962-64; asso. firm Theodore D. Woolsey, Beloit, Wis., 1964-65; individual practice law, Rockford, 1965—; asst. atty. City of Rockford, 1965-70. Mem. Am. Judicature Soc., Ill., Winnebago County, Wis., Rock County bar assns. Home: 750 Halsted Rd Rockford IL 61103 Office: 125 N Church St Rockford IL 61101 Tel (815) 964-2323

CANBY, WILLIAM CAMERON, JR., b. St. Paul, May 22, 1931; A.B., Yale, 1953; LL.B., U. Minn., 1956. Admitted to Minn. Supreme Ct. bar, 1956, Ariz. Supreme Ct. bar, 1972, U.S. Supreme Ct. bar, 1967; asst. staff judge adv. USAF, 1956-58; law clk. to Justice Charles E. Whittaker of U.S. Supreme Ct., 1958-59; asso. firm Oppenheimer, Hodgson, Brown, Baer & Wolff, St. Paul, 1959-62; prof. law Ariz. State U., Tempe, 1967—; asso., dep. dir. Peace Corps, Ethiopia, 1962-64; dir., Uganda, 1964-66; asst. to Sen. Walter Mondale, D.C., 1966. Bd. dirs. Maricopa County Legal Aid Soc., 1973—, Ariz. Center for Law in Public Interest, 1974—; mem. Ariz. Legal Services Advisory Council, 1976—. Mem. Minn. Bar Assn., AAUP. Named Fulbright prof. law Makerere Univ., Kampala, Uganda, 1970-71; contbr. articles in field to profl. jours. Home: 413 E Loyola Dr Tempe AZ 85282 Office: College of Law Arizona State University Tempe AZ 85281 Tel (602) 965-6463

CANDLER, JOHN SLAUGHTER, II, b. Atlanta, Nov. 30, 1908; A.B. magna cum laude, U. Ga., 1929; J.D., Emory U., 1931. Admitted to Ga. bar, 1931, U.S. Supreme Ct. bar, 1948; partner firm Candler, Cox, Andrews & Hansen, and predecessors, Atlanta, 1931—; dep. asst. atty. gen. State of Ga., 1951-68. Sr. warden Cathedral St. Philip, Atlanta, 1955, lay reader, 1971—; pres. Atlanta USO, 1974-75. Fellow Internat. Acad. Law and Sci., Am. Coll. Probate Counsel (regent 1968-74); mem. Am. Judicature Soc., Atlanta Estate Planning Council (pres. 1963-64), Nat. Tax Assn.-Tax Inst. Am. (mem. adv. council 1969-72), Am., Atlanta bar assns., Lawyers Club Atlanta, State Bar Ga. (chmn. fiduciary law sect. 1964-65), Phi Delta Phi. Office: 2400 Gas Light Tower Atlanta GA 30303 Tel (404) 577-9400

CANE, MYLES ADRIAN, b. Union City, N.J., Dec. 30, 1930; student Rutgers U., 1949-53; LL.B. (Dupont fellow), U. Va., 1955. Admitted to N.J. bar, 1955, N.Y. bar, 1956, Va. bar, 1956; asso. firm Stein, Stein & Engel, Jersey City, 1956-60; individual practice law, N.Y.C., 1961-68; partner firm Baer, Marks & Upham, N.Y.C., 1968—; dir. various orgns., corps. Mem. Am., N.J. bar assns., N.Y. County Lawyers Assn., Order of Coif, Phi Delta Phi. Editorial bd. Va. Law Rev., 1953-55. Office: 70 Pine St New York City NY 10005 Tel (212) 344-1700

CANE, R. THOMAS, b. Ontonagon, Mich., Mar. 28, 1939; B.B.A., U. Mich., 1961; J.D., Marquette U., 1964. Admitted to Wis. bar, 1964; served with JAGC, USAF, Okinawa, 1964-67; asso. firm McCarty, Swetz & Curry, Kaukauna, Wis., 1967-69; dep. dist. atty. Outagamie County (Wis.), 1969-72; judge Outagamie County Ct., br. 3, Appleton, 1972—. Bd. dirs. Fox Valley Region Big Bros., 1973—, Appleton YMCA, 1975—; judge adv. Appleton VFW, 1974—. Mem. Wis., Outagamie bar assns., Wis. County Judges (dir.), Nat. Juvenile Ct. Judges Assn. Named Wis's. Outstanding Young Man, Jaycees, 1975. Home: 5725 W Spencer St Appleton WI 54911 Tel (414) 739-5583

CANFIELD, AUSTIN FRANCIS, JR., b. Washington, Feb. 8, 1930; A.B., Georgetown U., 1952, J.D., 1955. Admitted to D.C. bar, 1956, Md. bar, 1970; trial atty. Caliher, Clarke, Martell & Donnelly, and predecessors, Washington, 1955-73, jr. partner, 1963-73; trial atty. Gorman & Canfield and predecessors, Washington, 1973-75, partner, 1975—. Mem. Bar Assn. D.C. (past pres., past pres. research found.), D.C. Profl. Council (pres. 1977—), Am. (del. from D.C. 1973-76), Inter-Am. bar assns., World Assn. Lawyers, D.C. Defense Lawyers Assn., Am. Judicature Soc., Md. State Bar, Am. Arbitration Assn. (arbitrator). Home: 10910 Chandler Rd Potomac MD 20854 Tel (202) 244-5695

CANFIELD, EDWARD FRANCIS, b. Phila., Apr. 7, 1922; B.A., St. Joseph's Coll., 1943; LL.B., U. Pa., 1949. Admitted to Pa. bar, 1949, D.C. bar, 1972; asso. firm McCarthy, Mullaney & Quinn, Phila., 1949-51; legal and contract mgmt. exec. RCA, 1953-60; corporate dir. contracts, v.p. govtl. relations Philco Ford Corp., 1960-69; pres. Leisure Times Industries, Inc., 1970; partner firm Casey, Scott & Canfield, Washington, 1971—; served with JAGC, USNR, 1943-46, 51-53; ret. lt. comdr. Res.; dir. Woodlawn Nat. Bank. Mem. Am., Fed., Phila., D.C. bar assns., IEEE. Office: 517 Ring Bldg 1200 18th St NW Washington DC 20036 Tel (202) 223-5750

CANN, WILLIAM FRANCIS, b. Sommerville, Mass., Oct. 10, 1922; student Tufts U., 1940-42; LL.B., Boston U., 1948; grad. Nat. Coll. State Judiciary, Reno, 1972. Admitted to Mass. bar, 1948, N.H. bar, 1959, U.S. Supreme Ct. bar, 1970; sr. claim examiner Am. Mut. Ins. Cos., Wakefield, Mass., 1948-60; law asst. N.H. Office Atty. Gen., Concord, 1960-61, asst. atty. gen., 1961-67, dep. atty. gen., 1967-71; asso. justice N.H. Superior Ct., 1971—, alt. mem. sentence rev. bd., 1976—, chmn. incarcerating facilities com., mem. profl. bondsman, rules and marital masters coms.; mem. adv. bd. N.H. Prison Community Corrections Center, Concord, 1973—, Franklin Pierce Law Center Civic Intern Program, 1976—. Mem. Am., N.H., Merrimack County (N.H.) bar assns., Am. Judicature Soc. Home: 36 Roger Ave Concord NH 03301 Tel (603) 225-3236

CANNON, JOHN JAMES, b. Phila., Jan. 10, 1938; A.B., Villanova U., 1959, J.D., 1962; postgrad. Georgetown U., 1963-64. Admitted to D.C. bar, 1962, Pa. bar, 1966; with antitrust div. U.S. Dept. Justice, Washington, D.C., 1962; with Judge Adv. Gen.'s Corp., 1963-65; asso. firm Pepper, Hamilton & Scheetz, Phila., 1965-68; asso. firm Kania & Ganbarino, Bala Cynwyd, Pa., 1968-71; prof. law Villanova U. Sch. Law, Villanova, Pa., 1971—; instr. bus. law U. Md., 1965; instr. Bar Review Center Am., Inc., 1976—. Mem. Am., Pa., Phila. bar assns. Office: Villanova U Sch Law Villanova U Villanova PA 19085 Tel (215) 527-2100 ext 710

CANNON, KIM DECKER, b. Salt Lake City, Oct. 15, 1948; A.B. cum laude, Dartmouth Coll., 1970; J.D., U. Colo., 1974. Admitted to Wyo. bar, 1974; asso. firm Burgess & Davis, Sheridan, Wyo., 1974—. Mem. Am., Wyo., Sheridan County bar assns. Home: PO Box 16 Wyarno WY 82845 Office: 101 W Brundage St Sheridan WY 82801 Tel (307) 672-2173

CANNON, ROSS WARREN, b. Butte, Mont., May 1, 1929; B.A. in Bus. Adminstrn., U. Mont., 1952, LL.B., 1957; LL.M., George Washington U., 1959. Admitted to Mont. bar, 1957; partner firm Cannon & Gillespie, and predecessors, Helena, Mont., 1959—; atty. advisor ICC, Washington, 1957-59. Mem. Mont. Commn. Planning Econ. Devel., 1968-71. Office: 1721 11th Ave Helena MT 59601 Tel (406) 442-9930

CANNON, RUSSELL ANDERSON, b. Salt Lake City, June 25, 1928; B.A., U. Calif., Los Angeles, 1951; J.D., U. So. Calif., 1954. Admitted to Calif. bar, 1955; law clk. to Presiding Justice Clement L. Shinn, Calif. Dist. Ct. Appeal, 1955-56; dep. city atty. City of Burbank (Calif.), 1956-58; asso. firm Blaise and Cannon, Burbank, 1958-59; individual practice law, 1960-74; asso. firm Cannon & Checketts, 1974-75, Cannon & Stress, 1975-76; individual practice law, Vista, Calif., 1976—; city atty. City of Vista, 1966-68. Pres. Republican Club of Vista, 1965; mem. sch. bd. Vista Unified Sch. Dist., 1965-66. Mem. Am., Calif. State, San Diego County, North San Diego County bar assns. Home: 1006 Bonnie Brae Pl Vista CA 92083 Office: 761 E Vista Way Vista CA 92083 Tel (714) 724-7131

CANNON, T(HOMAS) QUENTIN, b. Salt Lake City, Apr. 29, 1906; A.B., U. Utah, 1931; LL.B., George Washington U., 1935; J.D., Georgetown U., 1938, LL.M. with distinction, 1972. Admitted to D.C. bar, 1935, Utah bar, 1938; with Reconstrn. Fin. Corp., 1935-39; individual practice law, 1939-54; mem. firm Cannon & Duffin, Salt Lake City, 1954—; chief dep. atty. gen. State of Utah, 1962-64; dep. atty. Salt Lake County, 1964-70; spl. asst. U.S. Atty., Utah, 1945-47; law clk. to chief justice Utah Supreme Ct., 1939-41; atty. RFC, Washington, 1935-39; enforcement atty. Office Price Adminstrn., Salt Lake City, 1941-47; mem. Utah Ho. of Reps., 1968—; mem. Nat. Hwy. Safety Commn. (chmn. Fed.-State Relations Com.); chmn. Utah Jud. Qualification Commn. Pres. Salt Lake City Bd. Edn., Salt Lake County Recreation Bd.; v.p. Salt Lake Area Vocat. Sch. Bd. Mem. Am., Fed. bar assns., Am. Trial Lawyers Assn. Home: 5340 Cottonwood Ln Salt Lake City UT 84117 Office: 510 Ten Broadway Bldg Salt Lake City UT 84101 Tel (801) 521-3600

CANNON, THOMAS RICHARD, b. Milw., Aug. 21, 1946; B.A., Marquette U., 1967; J.D., U. Wis., 1971. Admitted to Wis. bar, 1971, U.S. Supreme Ct. bar, 1975; staff atty. Legal Aid Soc., Milw., 1971-74, chief atty., 1974—. Mem. ACLU, Environ. Def. Fund, Nat. Lawyers Guild, Nat. Legal Aid and Def. Assn. Office: 1204 W Wisconsin Ave Milwaukee WI 53233 Tel (414) 765-0600

CANONI, JOHN DAVID, b. Newton, Mass., May 11, 1939; B.A., Amherst Coll., 1960; LL.B., Yale, 1963. Admitted to N.Y. State bar, 1964; asso. firm Townley & Updike, N.Y.C., 1963-72, partner, 1972—. Mem. Am., N.Y. State, N.Y.C. bar assns., Fed. Bar Council, Am. Judicature Assn. Home: 172 Ellison Ave Bronxville NY 10708 Office: 220 E 42nd St New York City NY 10017 Tel (212) 682-4567

CANTOR, ANDREW BERT, b. Phila., June 25, 1939; B.A., Trinity Coll., 1961; grad. U. Pa. Law Sch., 1964. Admitted to Pa. bar, 1965; law clk. Judge Robert W. Honeyman, 1965-66; asso. firm Wisler, Pearlstone, Talone, Craig & Garrity, Norristown, Pa., 1965-72, partner, 1972—. Mem. Montgomery County Legal Aid Assn. (dir. 1970-76, treas. 1973-75), Am., Pa., Montgomery County (dir. 1975—) bar assns., Montgomery County Trial Lawyers Assn. (sec. 1971-75, v.p. 1976—). Office: 515 Swede St Norristown PA 19401 Tel (215) 272-8400

CANTOR, ROBERT ALAN, b. Phila., July 27, 1946; A.B., Princeton, 1968; J.D., Yale, 1971. Admitted to D.C. bar, 1971; asso. firm Mudge Rose Guthrie and Alexander, Washington, 1971-75, 76—; asso. firm Covington and Burling, Washington, 1975-76. Mem. Phi Beta Kappa. Home: 3747 Kanawha St NW Washington DC 20015 Office: 1701 Pennsylvania Ave NW Washington DC 20006 Tel (202) 298-5970

CANTRELLE, NELSON JOSEPH, JR., Marrero, La., Feb. 23, 1941; J.D., May 27, 1971. Admitted to La. bar, 1971, U.S. Supreme Ct. bar, 1975; individual practice law, Gretna, La., 1971-75; pres., sec., treas. Nelson J. Cantrelle, Jr., P.C., Gretna, 1975—; asst. parish atty. Parish of Jefferson. Mem. Am., Jefferson bar assns., Am., La. trial lawyers assns., Acad. New Orleans Trial Lawyers, La., Comml. Law League Am. Home: 3108 6th St Harvey LA 70058 Office: 300 Huey P Long Ave Gretna LA 70053 Tel (504) 368-5195

CANTWELL, ROBERT, b. Buffalo, Sept. 12, 1931; A.B., Cornell U., 1953, LL.B., 1956; LL.M., N.Y. U., 1959. Admitted to N.Y. bar, 1956; asso. firm Jaeckle, Fleischmann & Mugel, and predecessor, Buffalo, 1956-62; mem. legal dept. Colgate-Palmalive Co., N.Y.C. and London, 1962-68, dep. gen. counsel, N.Y.C., 1972-73, v.p., gen. counsel, 1973—, sec., 1974—; v.p., sec., gen. counsel Roblin Industries, Inc., Buffalo, 1968-72. Mem. Am., N.Y. State, Erie County bar assns., Assn. Bar City N.Y., Am. Soc. Corp. Secs., Brit. Inst. Internat. and Comparative Law. Office: 300 Park Ave New York City NY 10022 Tel (212) 751-1200

CANU, PIERRE HENRY, b. Neuilly-sur-Seine, France, Feb. 16, 1943; A.B. in Polit. Sci., Yale, 1964; J.D., U. Va., 1971. Admitted to Ala. bar, 1971, Mich. bar, 1976. Asso. firm Cabaniss, Johnson, Gardner, Dumas & O'Neal, Birmingham, Ala., 1971-76; atty. Ford Motor Co., Dearborn, Mich., 1976—. Mem. Am., Birmingham bar assns., Am. Judicature Soc. Home: 1024 Buckingham Rd Grosse Pointe Park MI 48230 Office: Office General Counsel Ford Motor Co Room 1066 American Rd Dearborn MI 48121 Tel (313) 337-6429

CAPISTRAN, ARMAND, b. Manchester, N.H., Nov. 19, 1925; A.B., St. Anselm Coll., 1948; A.M., l'Universite Laval, Quebec, Que., Can., 1952; LL.B., Boston U., 1957. Admitted to N.H. bar, 1957; mem. firm Lemelin & Capistran, Manchester, 1957-70; justice Manchester Dist. Ct. (N.H.), 1970—; mem. Ho. of Reps. Gen. Ct. N.H., 1963-70. Mem. Manchester, N.H. bar assns., Am. Judicature Soc., Am., N.H. judges assns. Home: 26 Congress St Manchester NH 03102 Office: 27 Market St Manchester NH 03101 Tel (603) 624-4068

CAPIZZI, MICHAEL ROBERT, b. Detroit, Oct. 19, 1939; B.S. in Bus. Adminstrn., Eastern Mich. U., 1961; J.D., U. Mich., 1964. Admitted to Calif. bar, 1965, U.S. Supreme Ct. bar, 1971; dep. dist. atty. Orange County (Calif.), 1965-68, head writs, appeals and spl. assignments sect., 1968-71, asst. dist. atty., dir. spl. ops., 1971—; legal counsel, mem. exec. bd. Interstate Organized Crime Index, 1971—, Law Enforcement Intelligence Unit, 1971—; instr. criminal justice Santa Ana Coll., 1967-76, Calif. State U., 1976—. Commr. city Planning Commn. Fountain Valley, Calif., 1971—, vice chmn., 1972-73, chmn., 1973-75. Mem. Calif., Orange County (chmn. cts. com. 1977—) bar assns., Nat., Calif. dist. attys. assns. Home: 9626 Ringde Circle Fountain Valley CA 92708 Office: 700 Civic Center Dr W Santa Ana CA 92702 Tel (714) 834-2554

CAPLAN, BARRY PAUL, b. Portland, Oreg., Dec. 4, 1940; B.A., U. Wash., 1962; LL.B., U. Calif., 1965. Admitted to Oreg. bar, 1965; dep. dist. atty. Multnomah County (Oreg.), 1965-68; asso. firm Sussman, Shank, Wapnick & Caplan, and predecessor, Portland, 1968-72, partner, 1972—. Mem. Oreg. State (spl. counsel 1975), Am., Multnomah County bar assns., Comml. Law League Am. Home: 7895 S W Broadmoor Terr Portland OR 97225 Office: 621 S W Morrison St # 1111 Portland OR 97205 Tel (503) 227-1111

CAPLIN, MORTIMER MAXWELL, b. N.Y.C., July 11, 1916; B.S., U. Va., 1937, LL.B., 1940; J.S.D., N.Y. U., 1953; LL.D., St. Michael's Coll., 1964. Admitted to Va. bar, 1941, N.Y. bar, 1942, D.C. bar, 1964; law clk. to judge U.S. Ct. Appeals, 4th Circuit, 1940-41; asso. firm Paul, Weiss, Wharton & Garrison, N.Y.C., 1941-50; prof. law U. Va., 1950-61, vis. prof. law, 1964—; commr. IRS, Washington, 1961-64; sr. partner firm Caplin & Drysdale, Washington, 1964—; counsel firm Perkins, Battle & Minor, Charlottesville, Va., 1952-61; dir. Prentice-Hall, Inc., 1964—, Norton Simon Inc., 1972—, Webb Resources, Inc., 1974—. Trustee Coll. V.I., St. Thomas, 1963—, George Washington U., 1965—; trustee Nat. Civil Service League, 1965—, chmn., 1976—; bd. dirs. Internat. Student House, Washington, 1972—; chmn. Am. Council on Internat. Sports, 1975—; chmn. nat. citizens adv. com. Assn. Am. Med. Colls., Washington, 1976—. Mem. Bar Assn. D.C., Va., Fed., Am. bar assns., Am. Law Inst., Order of Coif, Phi Beta Kappa, Omicron Delta Kappa. Recipient Alexander Hamilton award Treasury Dept., 1964; Achievement award Tax Soc. N.Y. U., 1962; Judge Learned Hand Human Relations award Am. Jewish Com., 1963; Distinguished Service award Tax Execs. Inst., 1964; author: Proxies, Annual Meetings and Corporate Democracy, 1953; Doing Business in Other States, 1959; contbr. articles to legal jours.; editor-in-chief Va. Law Rev., 1939-40. Home: 4536 29th St NW Washington DC 20008 Office: 1101 17th St NW Washington DC 20036 Tel (202) 862-5050

CAPOZZI, ANTHONY PATRICK, b. Buffalo, June 28, 1945; B.A., U. Buffalo, 1967; J.D., U. Toledo, 1970. Admitted to Ohio bar, 1971, Ill. bar, 1972, Calif. bar, 1976; law clk. to U.S. Dist. judge for So. Ill., 1970-73; asst. U.S. atty. for Eastern Calif., 1973—; adj. prof. law San Joaquin Law Sch., Fresno, Calif. Mem. campaign staff Ill. Senator Charles Percy, 1972; chmn. combined fed. campaign United Way, 1976. Mem. Am., Calif. bar assns. Office: 1130 O St Fresno CA 93721 Tel (209) 487-5172

CAPOZZOLA, CARL ANTHONY, b. Pueblo, Colo., Dec. 27, 1938; B.A., U. Colo., 1963; postgrad. U. Calif., Los Angeles, 1965; J.D., U. W. Los Angeles, 1969. Admitted to Calif. bar, 1969; dep. dist. atty. Los Angeles County, 1969-73; partner firm Moore & Capozzola, Torrance, Calif., 1973—, now v.p. Bd. dirs. W. Los Angeles Sch. Law. Mem. Calif., Los Angeles County, Criminal Cts., S. Bay bar assns., W. Los Angeles Law Sch. Alumni Assn. Author, editor: California Looseleaf Search and Seizure Handbook, 1972. Office: 21515 Hawthorne Blvd 1140 Torrance CA 90503 Tel (213) 327-1515

CAPOZZOLI, LOUIS JOSEPH, b. Cosenza, Italy, Mar. 6, 1901; LL.B., Fordham U., 1922. Admitted to N.Y. State bar, 1923; asst. dist. atty. N.Y. County, 1930-37; N.Y. State assemblyman, 1939-40; mem. 77th and 78th congresses from N.Y.; justice City Ct., N.Y.C., 1947-50; judge Ct. of Gen. Sessions, N.Y.C., 1951-57; justice Supreme Ct. N.Y. County, 1957-66; asso. justice appellate div. Supreme Ct., N.Y.C., 1966—. Mem. Am., N.Y. State, N.Y.C. bar assns., N.Y. County Columbian lawyers' assns., Fordham Law Alumni Assn. Home: 2 Fifth Ave Apt 11-G New York City NY 10011 Office: 27 Madison Ave New York City NY 10010 Tel (212) 532-1000

CAPPELLO, HENRY JULIUS, b. San Francisco, Apr. 28, 1920; A.B., U. Calif. at Berkeley, 1941; J.D., Cath. U. Am., 1952. Admitted to Va. bar, 1952, Calif. bar, 1952, D.C. bar, 1962, U.S. Supreme Ct., 1964; commd. ensign U.S. Navy, 1941, advanced through grades to capt., 1959, dir. Legis. div. Navy Office of Legis. Affairs, Washington, 1959-62; ret., 1962; partner firm Gosnell, Durkin & Cappello, Washington, 1964-69, firm Durkin & Cappello, Washington, 1969-71, firm Rothwell, Cappello & Berndtson, Washington, 1971—; gen. counsel Nat. Small Bus. Assn., Washington, 1969—; adj. prof. Internat. Sch. Law, Washington, 1974-76. Mem. Fed., Am. bar assns. Editor Cath. U. Law Rev., 1951-52. Home: 301 N Washington St Alexandria VA 22314 Office: 1730 K St NW Washington DC 20006

CAPRON, ALEXANDER MORGAN, b. Hartford, Conn., Aug. 16, 1944; B.A., Swarthmore Coll., 1966; LL.B., Yale, 1969. Admitted to D.C. bar, 1970; law clk. U.S. Ct. Appeals, D.C., 1969-70; lectr., research asso. Yale, 1970-72; asst. prof. law U. Pa., 1972-75, asso. prof. 1975—, vice-dean, 1976; cons. NIH, Office Tech. Assessment. Vice-chmn. bd. dirs. Washington Sq. West Project Area Com., Phila., 1975-77. Fellow Inst. Society, Ethics and the Life Scis. (dir.); mem. Soc. Am. Law Tchrs., AAUP (mem. exec. com. Pa. chpt.), Swarthmore Coll. Alumni Soc. (v.p. 1974-77). Author: (with Katz) Catastrophic Diseases, Who Decides What?, 1976; contbr. articles to profl. jours. Home: 2213 Delancey Pl Philadelphia PA 19103 Office: U Pa Law Sch 3400 Chestnut St Philadelphia PA 19104 Tel (215) 243-7852

CAPRON, JOHN MURRAY, b. Mt. Vernon, Ohio, Apr. 14, 1942; A.B., Kenyon Coll., 1964; LL.B., U. Pa., 1967. Admitted to Pa. bar, 1968, Ga. bar, 1971; asso. firm Morgan, Bewis & Bockius, Phila., 1967-70; asso. firm Fisher & Phillips, 1970-74, partner, 1975—. Mem. Am., Ga. bar assns. Home: 3048 Rhodenhaven Dr Atlanta GA 30327 Office: 3500 First Nat Bank Tower Atlanta GA 30303 Tel (404) 658-9200

CAPURRO, WAYNE NOLAN, b. Reno, Aug. 21, 1940; B.A., Northwestern U., Evanston, Ill., 1962; J.D., Willamette U., Salem, Oreg., 1965. Admitted to Nev. bar, 1965, U.S. Tax Ct. bar, 1976; asso. firm Leslie B. Gray, 1965-68, Swanson & Swanson, Reno, 1968-71; partner firm Swanson, Swanson & Capurro, Reno, 1971—. Mem. nat. adv. bd. Bur. Land Mgmt.; past pres., dir. Nev. Wildlife Fedn.; past pres., trustee Nev. 4-H Club Found. Mem. Am., Nev., Washoe County bar assns. Home: 5334 Valley Vista Dr Sparks NV 89431 Office: PO Box 2417 Reno NV 89505 Tel (702) 329-8686

CAPUTO, A. RICHARD, b. Port Chester, N.Y., May 22, 1938; A.B., Brown U., 1960; LL.B., U. Pa., 1963. Admitted to Pa. bar, 1963; served with JAGC, USAF, 1964-67; mem. firm Shea, Shea & Caputo, Wilkes-Barre, Pa., 1967—. Mem. 3d Circuit Jud. Conf., Wilkes-Barre Law and Library Assn., Pa. (pub. contract law com.), Am. bar assns. Home: 41 Druid Hills Shavertown PA 18612 Office: 626 First Eastern Bldg Wilkes-Barre PA 18701 Tel (717) 823-2151

CARADONNA, PAUL P., b. Malden, Mass., Nov. 10, 1931; A.B., Boston U., 1959; J.D., New Eng. Sch. Law, 1965. Admitted to Mass. bar, 1966; individual practice law, Everett, Mass. Sec., Greater Boston Football League, 1974-76. Mem. Am. Trial Lawyers Assn., Middlesex, Mass., 1st Dist. Eastern Middlesex (pres.) bar assns., Am. Judicature Soc. Home: 590 Broadway Everett MA 02149 Office: 459 Broadway Everett MA 02149 Tel (617) 387-2241

CARAWAY, NATIE PRIESTLY, b. Oak Grove, La., May 7, 1933; B.A., U. Miss., 1955, LL.B., 1958. Admitted to Miss. bar, 1958; clk. to Judge Ben Cameron, U.S. Ct. Appeals, 5th Circuit, 1958-59; partner firm Wise Carter Child Steen & Caraway, and predecessor, Jackson, Miss., 1966—; mem. Miss. Ho. of Reps. 1960-63; chmn. Miss. Gov.'s Study Com. on Workmen's Compensation, 1973. Mem. Hinds County (Miss.) (chmn. coms. 1972-73), Miss. State (chmn. com. on workmen's compensation, 1973), Am. bar assns., Miss. Def. Lawyers Assn., Hinds County Ole Miss Alumni Assn. (pres. 1976—), Fedn. Ins. Counsel, Am. Judicature Soc., Phi Alpha Delta. Home:

5325 Red Fox Rd Jackson MS 39211 Office: PO Box 651 925 Electric Bldg Jackson MS 39205 Tel (601) 354-2385

CARBERRY, EDMUND JOSEPH, b. Providence, Apr. 14, 1914; Ph.B., Providence Coll., 1936; J.D., Georgetown U., 1940. Admitted to D.C. bar, 1939, R.I. bar, 1941; individual practice law, Providence, 1941—. Mem. Am., R.I. bar assns. Home: 3 Ann Dr Barrington RI 02806 Office: 1231 Industrial Bank Bldg Providence RI 02903 Tel (401) 421-1283

CARBONE, ADOLPH VINCENT, b. Newark, Apr. 29, 1925; L.L.S., Seton Hall Coll., 1955, J.D., 1971. Admitted to N.J. bar, 1971; individual practice law, Toms River, N.J., 1971; parole officer Vols. in Parole Program, Trenton N.J. Mem. Am., N.J., Ocean County, bar assns., Disabled Am. Vets. Home and Office: 30 Cedar Grove Rd Toms River NJ 08753 Tel (201) 244-1895

CARDEN, EDWIN DOYLE, b. Hot Springs, Ark., Apr. 14, 1931; LL.B., U. Tulsa, 1964; grad. Nat. Coll. State Judiciary U. Nev., 1973. Admitted to Okla. bar, 1964, U.S. Dist. Ct. bar for Northeastern Dist. Okla., 1965; practiced in Claremore, Okla., 1964-67; asst. dist. atty. Rogers County (Okla.), 1967-72; asso. dist. judge Okla. Dist. Ct., 12th Jud. Dist., 1975—. Chmn. Rogers County March of Dimes Dr., 1967. Mem. Rogers County Bar, Am. Bar Assn. Office: POB 1047 Claremore OK 74017 Tel (918) 341-5656

CARDILE, JULIUS JOSEPH, b. Old Forge, Pa., Jan. 24, 1918; LL.B., Fordham U., 1943; LL.M., N.Y. U., 1949. Admitted to N.Y. bar, 1946, U.S. Supreme Ct. bar, 1955; individual practice in Bklyn., 1946—; referee in incompetency N.Y. Supreme Ct., 1976. Home: 283 Burns St Forest Hills NY 11375 Office: 16 Court St Brooklyn NY 11241 Tel (212) TR 5-1626

CARDILLO, JOSEPH, JR., b. N.Y.C., Oct. 12; B.A., Coll. William and Mary, 1934; postgrad. in Internat. Law (Inst. scholar) U. Florence (Italy), 1934-35; LL.B., N.Y. Law Sch., 1938. Admitted to N.Y. bar, 1939, U.S. Supreme Ct. bar, 1958; practiced in N.Y.C., 1939—; clk. firm Kuzmier, Cotter, Milan & O'Rourke, 1937-39, asso., 1939; asso. firm Charles A. Loretto, 1940-41, firm Harold Francis Berg, 1942, firm Bigham Englar Jones & Houston, 1943-53, individual practice law, 1953-54, partner firm Cardillo & Smith, 1954-63, sr. partner firm Cardillo & Corbett, 1969—; arbitrator Internat. Congress Maritime Arbitrators; lectr. admiralty symposium. Trustee Village of Flower Hill (N.Y.), 1955-60. Mem. Maritime Law Assn. of U.S., Marshall-Wythe Hon. Law Soc., Marshall-Wythe Law Soc., Pi Delta Epsilon (hon.). Office: 29 Broadway New York City NY 10006 Tel (212) 344-0464

CARDIN, MAURICE, b. Balt., July 19, 1909; LL.B., 1929. Admitted to Md. bar, 1930; practice law, 1930-66; magistrate, 1947-50; commr., Workmen's Compensation Commn., State of Md., 1966—; state legislator, 1951-66. Vice pres. Met. Civic Assn., Balt., 1960; pres. Safety First Club, 1965. Mem. Md. State, Balt. City bar assns. Recipient Humanitarian award Save-a-Heart Found, Jewish Nat. Fund award, 1969. Tel (301) 383-4730

CARDIN, MEYER MELVIN, b. Balt., July 14, 1907; LL.B., U. Md., 1929. Admitted to Md. bar, 1929; mem. Md. Ho. of Dels., 1935-39; chief police magistrate Balt. City, 1955-57; chief judge Balt. Traffic Ct., 1957-58; asso. judge Balt. City Supreme Bench, 1961—; chmn. Workmen's Compensation Commn., 1958-61; mem. Md. Gov's. Permanent Commn. for Full-time Magistrates, 1959-61; chmn. Injured Workers' Rehab. Com., 1960-61. Chmn. bd. Beth Tfiloh Congregation, Balt. 1954-60, pres., 1976—; bd. dirs. Talmudical Acad., Balt. Mem. Trial Magistrates Assn. Md. (certificate of merit and appreciation 1962). Recipient State of Israel award, 1957-58; Distinguished Service award Safety 1st Club, 1958; Forest in Israel award Jewish Nat. Fund, 1969; Humanitarian award Save A Heart, 1975, others. Home: 6210 Park Hts Ave Baltimore MD 21215 Office: Courthouse Baltimore MD 21202 Tel (301) 396-5100

CARDOSE, CHRISTOPHER VICTOR, b. Canton, Ill., Oct. 8, 1898; B.A., U. Ill., 1921, LL.B., 1923. Admitted to Ill. bar, 1923, since practiced in Springfield; supr. Sangamon County, 1955-65; spl. asst. atty. gen. Ill., 1963. Judge advocate Am. Legion, 1962, Navy Club, 1970; pres. Roman Cultural Soc., 1965. Mem. Ill., Sangamon County bar assns., Am. Legion (jr. comdr. post 1932-33), Forth and Eight (chef de gare 1932, grand cheminot Ill. 1932). Home: 125 Pebble Beach Dr Springfield IL 62704 Office: 216 Reisch Bldg Springfield IL 62701 Tel (217) 522-8875

CARELLI, EDWARD EUGENE, b. Denver, Apr. 23, 1925; B.A., Denver U., 1955, B.S. in Law, also LL.B. 1955. Admitted to Colo. bar, 1955; since practiced in Denver, dep. dist. atty., 1960-65; asso. firm Burnete, Watson & Horan, 1965-72; hearing officer Dept. of Excise & License, 1972-74; county judge, 1974—; vol. lawyer Denver C. of C. Defender Program, 1970-72. Committeeman, dist. capt. Democratic Party, 1955-73. Mem. Am., Colo., Denver bar assns., Am. Judicature Soc., Am. Judges' Assn., Assn. County Judges Colo. Home: 2741 W 38th Ave Denver CO 80211 Office: Room 124D C & C Bldg Denver CO 80211 Tel (303) 5104

CAREY, ARCHIBALD JAMES, JR., b. Chgo., Feb. 29, 1908; B.S., Lewis Inst., 1929; B.D., Garrett Theol. Sem., 1932; J.D. (Edmund W. Burke scholar), Chgo.-Kent Coll. Law, 1935; D.D., Wilberforce U., 1943; LL.D., John Marshall Law Sch., 1954; H.H.D., Paul Quinn Coll., 1955; grad. Nat. Coll. State Trial Judges, 1970. Ordained to ministry A.M.E. Ch.; minister Woodlawn (Ill.) A.M.E. Ch., 1930-49; minister Quinn Chapel, 1949-67, minister-emeritus, 1967—; admitted to Ill. bar, 1936, U.S. Supreme Ct. bar, 1956; practice law, 1936-66; judge Ill. Circuit Ct. of Cook County, 1966—; alderman Chgo. 3d Ward, 1947-55; U.S. del. UN 8th Gen. Assembly, 1953; chmn. Pres's Com. on Govt. Employment Policy, 1957-61, vice chmn., 1955-57; v.p., then dir. Ill. Fed. Savings & Loan Assn., 1936-66, pres., 1957-66; treas. Cook County Jud. Advisory Council; asst. gen. counsel N.C. Mut. Life Ins. Co., 1961-66; instr. John Marshall Law Sch., 1962-63. Bd. dirs. Community Fund of Chgo., 1966-76; founding trustee Garrett-Evangel. Theol. Sem.; trustee Central Ch. of Chgo.; speaker Republican Nat. Conv., 1952. Mem. Chgo., Cook County (Expression of Esteem 1967) bar assns., Ill. Judges Assn. Recipient 1st oratorical prize Chgo. Daily News, 1924, Useful Citizen award U. Chgo., 1954, Service to Mankind award Sertoma Club, 1956; named knight comdr. Liberian Humane Order, 1955; contbr. articles to The Pulpit Speaks of Race, The Negro Speaks. Home: 4934 S Michigan Ave Chicago IL 60615 Office: 2002 Richard J Daley Center Chicago IL 60602 Tel (312) 443-8356

CAREY, BERNARD, b. 1934; A.B., U. Miami; J.D., DePaul U. Admitted to Ill. bar, 1958; state's atty. Cook County (Ill.), 1973—. Office: 500 Civic Center 50 W Washington St Chicago IL 60602 Tel (312) 443-5500*

CAREY, CHARLES GEORGE, b. Pitts., July 15, 1931; B.A., St. Vincent Coll., 1953; J.D., U. San Deigo, 1963. Admitted to Calif. bar, 1965, U.S. Dist. Ct. bar for So. Dist. Calif., 1965; trial dep. atty. San Diego Dist. Atty's Office, 1963-68; asso. firm Loperdo & Hefner, Escondido, Calif., 1968-70; mem. firm Dowd & Carey, P.C., Escondido, 1970-75; individual practice law, Escondido, 1976—; judge pro - tempore North County (Calif.) Superior Ct., 1975—; legal adviser Escondido Youth Encounter, 1972—, chmn., 1974. Chmn. Citizen's Advisory Com. Escondido Union Sch. Dist., 1971-72; vice chmn. Classified Personnel Commn., 1971-75. Mem. San Diego County, North County (chmn. law day 1975) bar assns., Calif. Trial Lawyers Assn., Phi Delta Phi. Recipient Am. Jurisprudence Achievement award, 1962. Home: 6309 Avenida Cresta La Jolla CA 93037 Office: 651 E Grand Ave Escondido CA 92025 Tel (714) 745-6342

CAREY, HARVEY LOCKE, b. Parkin, Ark., Jan. 19, 1915; B.A., U. Ark., 1935; M.A., La. Poly. Inst., 1936; J.D., Tulane U., 1939. Admitted to La. bar, 1940, U.S. Dist. Ct. bar, 1940, U.S. Supreme Ct. bar, 1943, U.S. Circuit Ct. bar, 1950, U.S. Ct. of Claims bar, 1952, ICC bar, 1954; atty. War Dept., 1939-42; partner firm Barret & Carey, Shreveport, La., 1946-48; sr. partner firm Carey, Ferris & Achee, Shreveport, 1946-50; asst. atty. gen. La., Baton Rouge and Shreveport, 1948-50; U.S. atty. Western Dist. La., 1950-52; atty. Vets.' Commn. La., Shreveport and Baton Rouge, 1956-60; sr. mem., prin. firm Harvey L. Carey, Attys., Jamestown, La., 1956—; acting judge Shreveport City Ct., 1968-71; atty. Caddo Levee Bd. Mem. Democratic Exec. Com., Shreveport, La., 1948-56, State Central Com., 1948-64. Mem. Am., La. bar assns., Am. Judicature Soc., ICC Bar Assn., Phi Delta Phi. Tel (318) 544-2521

CAREY, JOHN, b. Phila., June 11, 1924; B.A., Yale, 1947; LL.B., Harvard, 1949; LL.M., N.Y. U., 1965; asso. firms Morgan Lewis & Bockius, Phila., 1949-51, Pepper Bodine Frick Sheetz & Hamilton, Phila., 1954-55; asst. dist. atty. Philadelphia County, 1952-54; cons. Assn. Bar City N.Y., 1955-56; asso. firm Coudert Bros., N.Y.C., 1956-61, partner, 1961—; councilman City of Rye (N.Y.), 1963-67, 71-73, mayor, 1973—; adj. asst. prof. N.Y. U. Law Sch., 1967-72. Alt. U.S. mem. UN Subcommn. on Discrimination and Minorities, 1966—; alt. U.S. rep. UN Human Rights Commn., 1968. Mem. Am., N.Y. State, N.Y.C., Phila. bar assns., Internat. Law Assn., Am. Soc. Internat. Law. Author: (with Thomas M. Franck) The Role Of The United Nations In The Congo, 1963; UN Protection Of Civil and Political Rights, 1970; editor UN Law Reports, 1966—; The Dominican Republican Crisis 1965, 1967; Race, Peace, Law And Southern Africa, 1968; Law and Policy Making For Trade Among Have' and Have-not' Nations, 1968; International Protection of Human Rights, 1968; contbr. articles to profl. publs. Home: 860 Forest Ave Rye NY 10580 Office: 200 Park Ave New York City NY 10017 Tel (212) 973-4752

CAREY, KENNETH STOUT, b. Provo, Utah, Sept. 17, 1922; B.A., Stanford U., 1948, LL.B., 1950. Admitted to Calif. bar, 1950, Ct. Appeals 9th Circuit bar, 1950, Calif. U.S. Dist. Ct. bar, 1950, U.S. Supreme Ct bar, 1961; mem. firm Everett S. Layman, San Francisco, 1951-65; partner firm Harzstein, Maier & Carey, San Francisco, 1965-70; individual practice law, Redwood City, Calif., 1970—; dir. San Francisco Bay Title Co., Western Med. Enterprises, Inc. Bd. dirs., pres. Community Assn., Ladera, Calif. Mem. State Bar Calif., Am., San Mateo County, San Francisco bar assns. Office: 626 Jefferson Ave Redwood City CA 94063 Tel (415) 364-0274

CAREY, ROBERT GEORGE, b. Oil City, Pa., Sept. 22, 1934; B.A., Gannon Coll., 1961; J.D., Temple U., 1967. Admitted to Del. bar, 1967; asso. firm Prickett, Ward, Burt & Sanders, Wilmington, Del., 1967-70, partner, 1970—; counsel Gov. of Del., 1973-74; chmn. Gov.'s Crime Reduction Task Force, Wilmington, 1975—; chmn. Del. Agy. to Reduce Crime, Wilmington, 1975—; chmn. Juvenile Justice Adv. Group, Wilmington, 1976—. Mem. Am., Del. (jud. appointments com. 1975—, ins. com. 1970—) bar assns., Am. Judicature Soc. Home: 3A Harlan Circle Woodshade Newark DE 19711 Office: 1310 King St Wilmington DE 19899 Tel (302) 658-5102

CAREY, RONALD CARTER, b. Waynesville, Ohio, Jan. 21, 1938; A.B., Wilmington Coll., 1959; J.D., Chase Coll. Law, 1964. Admitted to Ohio bar, 1964; asso. firm Dennis & Cartwright, Wilmington, Ohio, 1968-72; asso. firm Watson & Burreson, Batavia, Ohio, 1972-73; individual practice law, Wilmington, 1973-76; partner firm Carey & Peelle, Wilmington, 1976—; asst. pros. atty. Clinton County, Ohio, 1969-72, pros. atty., 1972—. Pres. Clinton County unit Am. Cancer Soc., 1974-76; trustee Clinton County United Way, 1976—. Mem. Am., Ohio Clinton County bar assns., Ohio Pros. Attys. Assn., Nat. Dist. Attys. Assn. Office: 20 W Birdsall St Wilmington OH 45177 Tel (512) 382-0995

CARGILL, ROBERT MASON, b. Atlanta, Nov. 15, 1948; B.S. in Physics, Ga. Inst. Tech., 1970; J.D. magna cum laude, Harvard U., 1973. Admitted to Ga. bar, 1973, D.C. bar, 1975; comptroller office asst. sec. defense, Washington, D.C., 1973-74; mem. staff Commn. on CIA Activities Within the U.S., 1975; mem. staff Office Counsel to the Pres., Washington, D.C., 1976-76; mem. firm Hansell, Post, Brandon & Dorsey, Atlanta, 1976—. Home: 6430 Scott Valley Rd NW Atlanta GA 30328 Office: 33d Floor 1st Nat Bank Tower Atlanta GA 30303 Tel (404) 581-8318

CARGO, DAVID FRANCIS, b. Dowagiac, Mich., Jan. 13, 1929; A.B., U. Mich., 1951, M.S. in Pub. Adminstrn., 1953, J.D., 1957. Admitted to Mich., N.Mex. bars, 1957, Oreg. bar, 1974; gov. State of N.Mex., 1966-71; mem. N.Mex. Ho. of Reps., 1962-66; practice law, Portland, Oreg. Home: 750 Briercliff Ln Lake Oswego OR 97034 Office: 621 SW Morrison St Portland OR 97205 Tel (503) 248-9751

CARL, BEVERLY MAY, b. Richmond, Va., Nov. 13, 1932; B.S.L., U. So. Calif., 1955, J.D., 1956; LL.M., Yale, 1957; postgrad. (Fulbright scholar) U. Chile Law Sch., 1958-59. Admitted to Va. bar, 1961, Tex. bar, 1971; instr. Quinnipiac Coll., Hamden, Conn., 1960; atty. Office Internat. Fin., U.S. Dept. Treasury, Washington, 1960-61; spl. asst. to dep. asst. sec. U.S. Dept. Commerce, 1961-63; spl. asst. to asst. adminstr. for pvt. enterprise AID, Washington, 1963-64, investment guaranty officer, 1964-65, chief pvt. investment div., U.S. embassy, Rio de Janeiro, Brazil, 1965-67, asst. chief Nigeria-Biafra Relief Program, 1968-70; prof. law So. Methodist U., 1970—; mem. U.S. delegation to Orgn. of Am. States Conf. on Pvt. Internat. Law, Panama, 1974; hearing officer City of Dallas. Mem. Am. Bar Assn., State Bar Tex., Dallas Internat. Law Assn. (past pres.), Am. Soc. Internat. Law, Inter-Am. Assn. Profs. Pvt. Internat. Law, Am. Assn. Law Schs. Mem. editorial bd. So. Calif. Law Review, 1955-56, Internat. Lawyer, 1974—. Author: Guide to Incentives for Investing in Brazil, 1972. Contbr. articles in field to profl. jours. Home: 7510 W Northwest Hwy Apt 2 Dallas TX 75275 Office: Law School Southern Methodist University Dallas TX 75222 Tel (214) 692-2574

CARL, COLIN JOSEPH, b. Houston, Nov. 18, 1943; A.B. magna cum laude, Harvard, 1965; J.D., U. Tex., 1970. Admitted to Tex. bar, 1970; law clk. to judge U.S. Dist. Ct. Eastern Dist. Tex., Tyler, 1970-72; with election div. Office of Sec. of State, Austin, 1972; asst. atty. gen., office of atty. gen. Tex., Austin, 1973—. State Democratic exec. committeeman, 14th senatorial dist., 1972-76. Mem. State (exec. com. 1975—), Jr. bars Tex., Travis County, Am., Austin Jr. bar assns. Home: 5908 Highland Hills Dr Austin TX 78731 Office: Box 12548 Austin TX 78711 Tel (512) 475-4369

CARL, JACK DABNEY, b. Nashville, Mar. 24, 1938; A.B., Vanderbilt U., 1962, J.D., 1965. Admitted to Ala. bar, 1965; asso. firm Martin, Balch, Bingham, Hawthorne & Williams, Birmingham, Ala., 1965-67; with legal dept., atty. and asst. sec. Vulcan Materials Co., Birmingham, 1967—. Mem. bd. mgmt. Downtown Br. YMCA, 1975—; mem. dist. com. Birmingham Area council Boy Scouts Am.; bd. dirs., mem. planning com. The Fresh Air Farm, 1974-76; bd. deacons Ind. Presbyterian Ch., 1974-76. Mem. Ala., Am. bar assns. Home: 5 Clarendon Rd Birmingham AL 35213 Office: One Metroplex Dr Birmingham AL 35216 Tel (205) 877-3204

CARLBERG, CHARLES WALTER, b. Cherokee, Iowa, Dec. 25, 1945; B.S., Morningside Coll., 1969; J.D., Drake U., 1972. Admitted to Iowa bar, 1972; asso. firm Don Carlos & Don Carlos, Greenfield, Iowa, 1972-74, partner firm Don Carlos, Don Carlos & Carlberg, Greenfield, 1974—; asst. county atty. Adair County (Iowa), 1972; city atty. Greenfield, 1973—, Orient (Iowa), 1975—; city prosecutor Fontanelle (Iowa), 1975—, Adair, 1976—. Bd. dirs. Adair County Health Planning Council, 1973-76, pres., 1974-76; vice chmn. Adair County Republican Central Com., 1974—; v.p. Area XIV Health Planning Council, 1975. Mem. Am., Iowa State, 5th Jud. Dist., Adair County (treas. 1974—), bar assns. Home: RFD Greenfield IA 50849 Office: 113 W Iowa St Greenfield IA 50849 Tel (515) 243-6195

CARLEN, LEON C., b. N.Y.C., Oct. 22, 1915; B.A., Bklyn. Coll., 1936, LL.B., 1939. Admitted to N.Y. State bar, 1940, U.S. Supreme Ct. bar, 1960; partner firm Jaffe & Carlen, Mineola, N.Y., 1970—. Trustee Bethpage Pub. Library. Mem. Nassau County, N.Y. State bar assns., Am. Arbitration Assn. (arbitrator). Home: 2 Caffrey Ave Bethpage NY 11714 Office: 100 E Old Country Rd Mineola NY 11501 Tel (516) 742-7090

CARLEY, STEPHEN FRANKLIN, b. Atlanta, Feb. 4, 1941; B.S., U. Notre Dame, 1963; J.D., Georgetown U., 1970. Admitted to Ga. bar, 1970; actuary, 1963-70; asso. firm Stack & O'Brien, Atlanta, 1970-75; partner firm Tarver, Stowers, Roane & Carley, Atlanta, 1976—. Mem. Am., Ga. Atlanta bar assns., Lawyers Club Atlanta, Washington (dir. 1968-69), Atlanta (asso. dir. 1967) jr. chambers commerce. Office: 2400 Cain Tower 229 Peachtree St Atlanta GA 30303 Tel (404) 588-0500

CARLILE, ROBERT TOY, b. Phila., July 27, 1926; B.B.A., U. Miami, 1949; J.D., U. Fla., 1958. Admitted to Fla. bar, 1958; asso. firm Grimditch & Smith, Deerfield Beach, Fla., 1958-60; individual practice law, Deerfield Beach, 1960-65, 73—; sr. partner Carlile & Pulskamp, Deerfield Beach, 1965-69, Carlile, Pulskamp & Fletcher, Deerfield Beach, 1969-72, Carlile & Fletcher, 1972-73; individual practice, 1973—; city atty. City of Deerfield Beach, 1963-68, municipal judge, 1971-77. Mem. Fla., North Broward County (pres. 1966), Broward County bar assns., Phi Alpha Delta. Office: 1215 E Hillsboro Blvd Deerfield Beach FL 33441 Tel (305) 427-0933

CARLIN, ANGELA GENOVESE, b. Cleve., Mar. 8, 1930; B.A., Bowling Green State U., 1952; J.D. (fellow), Case-Western U., 1955. Admitted to Ohio bar, 1955; partner firm Rippner, Schwartz & Carlin, Cleve., 1962—. Mem. steering com. for parish council St. Bernadette Ch., Westlake, Ohio, 1971-72; pres. St. Bernadette Sch. Bd., 1972-75; trustee Ursuline Coll., 1977-78, Cath. Charities Corp. Mem. Cath. Lawyers Guild (pres. 1974-75), Altrusa Internat., Cleve. Women Lawyers Assn., Erieview Bus. and Profl. Women's Orgn., Am. Ohio State, Cuyahoga County, Cleve. (trustee 1976-79) bar assns., Case-Western Res. U. Law Alumni Assn. (trustee 1977-78), Ohio Legal Center Inst. Recipient Merit award Ohio Legal Center Inst., 1974. Asso. editor Baldwin's Rev. Code, Annotated, 1958, 64; coordinating editor Merrick-Reppner Ohio Probate Law, Practice and Forms, 1960-77. Home: 2820 Gibson Dr Rocky River OH 44116 Office: 960 Illuminating Bldg Cleveland OH 44113 Tel (216) 696-8121

CARLIN, CHARLES WILLIAM, b. St. Cloud, Minn., Sept. 1, 1906; student St. Cloud Coll., 1923-24, 27-28, B.S., Creighton U., 1925; B.S., U. Minn., 1933; LL.B., U. Notre Dame, 1952, J.D., 1969. Admitted to N.Y. bar, 1953, Mich. bar, 1956, Tex. bar, 1971; atty. Uniroyal, Mishawaka, Ind. and N.Y.C., 1945-55; atty. Dow Chem. Co., Midland, Mich. and Freeport, Tex., 1945-71; individual practice law, Midland, 1956-70, Clute, Tex., 1971-75; instr. Brazosport Coll., Lake Jackson, Tex., 1972-75, Clark County Community Coll., N. Las Vegas, Nev., 1976-77. Mem. MENSA, Am. Chem. Soc., Phi Delta Kappa. Address: Fort Davis TX 79734

CARLIN, DENNIS JAY, b. Chgo., Aug. 23, 1941; B.B.A., U. Wis., 1963; J.D., DePaul U., 1967; LL.M., Georgetown U., 1971. Admitted to Ill. bar, 1967, U.S. Supreme Ct. bar, 1970; asso. atty. Tax Ct. Litigation Div. Tech. Br., Office Chief Counsel, IRS, Washington, D.C., 1967-71; asso. firm Frankel, McKay, Orlikoff, Denten & Kostner, Chgo., 1971-74, partner, 1974-77; partner firm Horwood, Carlin & Hindin, 1977—; lectr. in field; asso. firm Checkers, Simon & Rosner CPA's, Chgo., 1963-67. Pres. Centre Park W. Condominium Assn., 1975-77. Mem. Am., Ill. State, Chgo. bar assns., Common Cause. Author: Partnership versus Corporation, Non-Tax Shelter Enterprise. Editor in chief DePaul Law Rev., 1967. Home: 2112 F St Johns Ave Highland Park IL 60035 Office: 10 S LaSalle St Suite 1642 Chicago IL 60603 Tel (312) 263-7350

CARLIN, DONALD WALTER, b. Gary, Ind., Aug. 27, 1934; B.S. in Engring., U. Notre Dame, 1956; LL.B., U. Mich., 1959. Admitted to Ind. bar, 1959, Ill. bar, 1960; asso. firm Anderson, Luedeka, Even & Tabin, Chgo., 1960-65; mem. firm Fitch, Even, Tabin, Luedeka, Chgo., 1965-72; sr. atty. Kraft, Inc., Glenview, Ill., 1972-73, asst. v.p., asst. gen. counsel, 1973-74, v.p., asst. gen. counsel, 1974—. Mem. Am., Chgo. bar assns., Patent Law Assn. Chgo., Am. Patent Law Assn., Licensing Execs. Soc., Assn. Corp. Patent Counsel. Home: 3020 Normandy Pl Evanston IL 60201 Office: Kraft Ct Glenview IL 60025 Tel (312) 998-2488

CARLIN, JOHN JOSEPH, b. Anamosa, Iowa, Aug. 12, 1932; B.A., St. Ambrose Coll., 1954; J.D., Iowa U., 1959. Admitted to Iowa bar, 1959, U.S. Dist. Ct. bar for Dist. Iowa, 1959; asso. firm McCracken and Carlin and predecessors, Davenport, Iowa, 1959-61, partner, 1961-74; partner firm Carlin and Darbyshire, Davenport, 1974—; instr. criminal law St. Ambrose Coll., 1974-75; mem. Iowa Bd. Bar Examiners, 1976. Mem. Scott County (Iowa) Zoning Bd. and Scott

County Zoning Bd. Adjustment, 1965-67; mem. CSC, 1975-76. Mem. Scott County, Iowa State bars, Am. Bar Assn., Am. Trial Lawyers Assn., Def. Research Inst., Iowa Acad. Trial Lawyers, Nat. Assn. Criminal Def. Lawyers, Finkbine Honor Soc. Office: 700 Union Arcade Bldg Davenport IA 52801 Tel (319) 326-5321

CARLINS, JOEL MILES, b. Chgo., Dec. 31, 1935; B.S. in Journalism, U. Ill., 1957; J.D., DePaul U., 1960. Admitted to Ill. bar, 1960; sr. partner firm Carlins & Kamensky, Chgo., 1960—; dir. Bank Of Hillside (Ill.). Mem. Am., Ill. Chgo. bar assns., Ill. Trial Lawyers Assn. Office: 120 S LaSalle St Chicago IL 60603 Tel (312) 368-1666

CARLON, JOHN A., b. Danville, Ill., Dec. 27, 1929; B.S. in Edn., Ill. State U., 1958; LL.B., U. Ill., 1964. Admitted to Ill. bar, 1964; asst. state's atty. McLean County (Ill.), Bloomington, 1964-65; partner firm Carlon & Carlon, Normal, Ill., 1965—. Curator, Funk Mus., Ill. State U., Normal. Mem. McLean County Bar Assn. Home: 1110 E Emerson St Bloomington IL 61701 Office: 4 Citizens Sq Normal IL 61761 Tel (309) 452-9405

CARLSMITH, CURTIS WADE, b. Hilo, Hawaii, Aug. 25, 1940; B.A., Stanford, 1962; LL.B., Harvard, 1965. Admitted to Hawaii bar, 1965; asso. firm Carlsmith, Carlsmith, Wichman & Case, 1965-70; individual practice law, Honolulu, 1970—; pres. Carlsmith Corp., Honolulu, 1970—; pres. 2121 Ala Wai Devel. Corp., Honolulu, 1974—. Mem. Am., Hawaii bar assns. Home: Ala Wai Yacht Harbor Honolulu HI 96815 Office: 841 Bishop St Suite 2102 Honolulu HI 96808 Tel (808) 524-7200

CARLSMITH, DONN WENDELL, b. Hilo, Hawaii, Mar. 17, 1929; A.B., Stanford, 1950; J.D., Harvard, 1953. Admitted to D.C. bar, 1953, Hawaii bar, 1954; with firm Carlsmith, Carlsmith, Wichman & Case and predecessor, Honolulu and Hilo, asso., 1953-59, partner, 1959-; mng. dir. Dillingham Investment Corp., Captain Cook Investment Co., Inc.; dir. Hawaii Planning Mill, Ltd., Magoon Bros., Ltd., Magoon Estate, Ltd. Bd. govs. Hawaii Prep. Acad., Kamuela, Hawaii; trustee Pacific Tropical Bot. Garden; trustee Lyman House Meml. Museum. Mem. Am., Hawaii bar assns. Home: Onomea Bay HI 96783 Office: 121 Waianuenue Ave Hilo HI 96720 Tel (808) 935-6644

CARLSON, CLAIRE FERGUSON, b. Des Moines, Feb. 6, 1927; B.A., State U. Iowa, 1949, J.D., 1950. Admitted to Iowa bar, 1950; research asst. State U. Iowa, 1945-50; mem. firm Bastian, Beisser & Carlson, Ft. Dodge, Iowa, 1964-72; mem. firm Kersten, Opheim, Carlson & Estes, Ft. Dodge, 1972—; mem. ethics com. Iowa Legislature. Mem. Ft. Dodge City Planning Commn., 1956-58; sec. Webster County (Iowa) Republican Central Com., 1950-52; mem. Iowa Workers' Compensation Adv. Com. Mem. Webster County (v.p., mem. grievance com. 1976—), Iowa (chmn. workmen's compensation and casualty ins. law com. 1974—), Am. bar assns., Iowa Def. Counsel, Fedn. Ins. Counsel, Order of Coif. Home: 1210 10th Ave N Fort Dodge IA 50501 Office: Snell Bldg Fort Dodge IA 50501 Tel (515) 576-4127

CARLSON, DAVID BRET, b. Jamestown, N.Y., Aug. 16, 1918; A.B., Brown U., 1940; LL.B., Harvard, 1947. Admitted to N.Y. bar, 1947, U.S. Supreme Ct. bar, 1972; asso. firm Debevoise, Plimpton, Lyons & Gates, N.Y.C., 1947-53, partner, 1953—. Mem. Am., N.Y. State bar assns., Bar Assn. City N.Y., Am. Law Inst., Tax Forum, Soc. Mining Engrs. of AIME. Contbr. articles to profl. publs. Home: 2700 Redding Rd Fairfield CT 06430 Office: 299 Park Ave New York City NY 10017 Tel (212) 752-6400

CARLSON, JON GORDON, b. Wakefield, Mich., June 25, 1943; A.B., U. Ill., 1965, J.D., 1967. Admitted to Ill. bar, 1967; partner firm O'Malley & Carlson, E. St. Louis, Ill., 1967-68; asso. firm Kassly, Weihl & Bone, Belleville, Ill., 1968-70; partner firm Kassly, Weihl, Bone, Becker & Carlson, Belleville, 1970—; speaker various continuing edn. seminars. Mem. Ill., St. Clair County, E. St. Louis bar assns., Ill. Trial Lawyers Assn., Assn. Trial Lawyers Am. Home: 25 Berkshire Belleville IL 62223 Office: 7705 W Main Belleville IL 62223 Tel (618) 397-2700

CARLSON, RICHARD HENRY, b. Los Angeles, June 27, 1941; student Harvard, 1959; A.B. in History, U. Calif., 1963; LL.B., Hastings Coll., 1966. Admitted to Calif. bar, 1967; law clerk to Jesse W. Curtis U.S. Dist. Judge, Los Angeles, 1966-67; mem. firm Hoberg, Finger, Brown, Carlson, Cox & Molligan, San Francisco, 1967-; lectr. Continuing Edn. of Bar; mem. Calif. State Bar Commn. on Adminstrn. of Justice; asso. Am. Bd. Trial Advocates. Mem. State Bar Calif., Calif. Trial Lawyers Assn., San Francisco Bar Assn. Office: 703 Market St San Francisco CA 94103 Tel (415) 543-9464

CARLSON, ROBERT FREDRICK, b. Sacramento, Jan. 28, 1928; A.B., St. Marys Coll., Calif., 1949; LL.B., U. Calif. Hastings Coll. Law, 1952, J.D., 1952. Admitted to Calif. bar, 1953, U.S. Supreme Ct. bar, 1966; asst. chief counsel Calif. Dept. Transp., Sacramento, 1952—; adj. prof. law U. of the Pacific McGeorge Coll. Law, Sacramento, 1975—. Pres. Calif. State Employees' Assn., Sacramento, 1968-70; pres. Associated Calif. Employees, Sacramento, 1970-72; mem. bd. adminstrn. Calif. Pub. Employees Retirement System, Sacramento, 1971—, pres. of bd., 1976—. Mem. Am., Sacramento County bar assns., Calif. State Trial Attys. Assn., Assembly Govtl. Employees (Washington) (pres. 1975—). Contbr. articles to legal jours. Home: 2120 Lambeth Way Carmichael CA 95608 Office: 1120 N St Sacramento CA 95807 Tel (916) 445-2404

CARLSON, THEODORE LEE, b. Wakefield, Nebr., July 23, 1938; B.A., Omaha U., 1960; LL.B. (Univ. scholar), Creighton U., 1963, J.D., 1968. Admitted to Nebr. bar, 1963; asso. firm Miller Moldenhauer & Vardenack, Omaha, 1964-66; prosecutor City of Omaha, 1966-71; judge Municipal Ct., Omaha, 1971—; instr. U. Nebr., Omaha, 1972—. Mem. Omaha, Nebr., Am. bar assns., Am. Judicature Soc. Office: Omaha Douglas Civic Center 1819 Farnham St Omaha NE 68102 Tel (402) 444-5434

CARLTON, CHARLES T., b. Fort Pierce, Fla., Nov. 7, 1935; B.A., U. Fla., 1957; J.D., Stetson Coll. Law, 1963. Admitted to Fla. bar, 1963; partner firm Carlton, Brennan & McAliley, Ft. Pierce, 1963-67; state atty. Fla. 19th Jud. Circuit, 1967-70; judge Fla. Circuit Ct., 20th Jud. Circuit, 1970—, dep. chief judge, 1972-75, chief judge, 1977—. Pres. U. Fla. Alumni Assn., 1965; 1st v.p. United Fund, 1966. Mem. Am. Bar Assn., Fla. Bar, Circuit Judges Conf. Recipient Distinguished Service award Fla. Jaycees, 1969. Home: 193 Eugenia Dr Naples FL 33940 Office: Collier County Courthouse Naples FL Tel (813) 774-7066

CARLTON, LOUIS CORNELIUS, b. Denver, May 2, 1901; B.A., U. Richmond, 1923, LL.B., 1932. Admitted to Va. bar, 1930; tchr. McGuires U. Sch., Richmond, Va., 1923; tax accountant State-Planters Bank & Trust Co., Richmond, 1924-30; individual practice law, Richmond, 1930-33, 66—; asst. gen. counsel law dept. Life Inst. Co. Va., Richmond, 1933-66; retirement counselor, City of Richmond, 1966-70. Mem. Urban Design Com., Richmond, 1970-76. Mem. Va., Richmond bar assns., Sigma Nu Phi. Contbr. articles to profl. jours. Home and office: 3213 Seminary Ave Richmond VA 23227 Tel (804) 355-4152

CARLTON, RICHARD EDWIN, b. Concord, Mass., Sept. 6, 1939; B.A., Harvard, 1961, LL.B., 1965. Admitted to N.Y. bar, 1967; partner firm Sullivan & Cromwell, N.Y.C., 1973—. Mem. Am., N.Y. bar assns., Bar Assn. City N.Y. Home: Old Aspetong Rd Katonah NY 10536 Office: 48 Wall St New York City NY 10005 Tel (212) 952-8100

CARLUCCI, JOSEPH PAUL, b. Port Chester, N.Y., Aug. 21, 1942; B.A., Georgetown U., 1964; J.D., Fordham U., 1967. Admitted to N.Y. bar, 1969; chief legis. counsel Senator J. Pisani, N.Y. State Legis., 1971-74, spl. counsel, 1974-75; chief counsel N.Y. State Select Com. State's Economy, 1974-75; counsel Sound Shore Hotline, Westchester County, N.Y. Trustee, Village of Port Chester, 1974—; chmn. Port Chester Indsl. Devel. Agy., 1974—; mem. Narcotics Guidance Council Port Chester, 1970-72, Village Port Chester Pub. Employees Relations Bd., 1971-74, Port Chester Village Govt. Study Comm., 1972-73, Westchester County (N.Y.) Econ. Devel. Council, 1976—; Salvation Army Adv. Bd., United Fund; bd. dirs. Port Chester YMCA, 1970—, sec., 1972-75. Mem. Am., N.Y., Westchester County, Port Chester-Rye (sec. 1970-74, v.p. 1974-75, pres. 1976—) bar assns. Recipient Golden "R" award The Renaissance Project, Inc., 1972; contbr. article N.E. Indsl. World Mag. Home: 37 Tower Hill Dr Port Chester NY 10573 Office: 5 Blind Brook Ln Rye NY 10580 Tel (914) 939-3300

CARLYLE, JOHN ALBERT, b. Kansas City, Mo., Jan. 18, 1909; LL.B., Washington U., 1932; B.A., Elmhurst Coll., 1967. Admitted to Mo. bar, 1932, Ill. bar, 1934; with Allstate Ins. Co., Skokie, Ill., 1936-66, zone claim mgr. 1949-62; instr. Coll. DuPage, 1968-75; asst. prof. law Lewis U., 1975—. Mem. Mo., Ill. State bar assns., Am. Judicature Soc., Am. Bus. Law Assn. Home: 733 Highview Ave Glen Ellyn IL 60137 Office: Lewis U Coll Law Ill 53 at Roosevelt Rd Glen Ellyn IL 60137 Tel (312) 858-7200

CARMAN, ERNEST DAY, b. Mpls.; B.A., U. So. Calif.; M.A., Stanford; Dr. és Sci. Pol., U. Geneva; J.D., U. San Francisco. Admitted to Calif. bar, 1957, U.S. 9th Circuit Ct. Appeals bar, 1957, U.S. Dist. Ct. No. Calif., U.S. 1957, Dist. Nev., 1967; U.S. Ct. Appeals D.C., 1971; U.S. Supreme Ct. bar, 1973; U.S. Dist. Ct. Central Calif., 1975; since practiced in San Jose, Calif.; partner firm Bean, Diel, Carman & Diller, 1958-60, Adams, Ball, & Carman, 1960-61, Carman & Mansfield, 1962-65, Adams, Carman, Mansfield, Ball & Wenzel, 1965-69, Carman & Mansfield, 1969—; judge pro tempore superior ct. Santa Clara County, Calif. Chmn. Santa Clara County Democratic Central Com., 1967-71; candidate for U.S. Ho. of Reps., 1964. Mem. State Bar Calif., Am., Santa Clara (chmn. judicial selection com. 1971-72), Orange County bar assns., Trial Lawyers Assn. Author: Soviet Imperialism, 1950; contbr. articles to profl. jours. Office: 2445 E Coast Hwy Corona Del Mar CA 92625 Tel (714) 675-0200 also 111 West St John St San Jose CA 95113 Tel (408) 295-1411

CARMICHAEL, CHARLES ELMORE, JR., b. Tuscumbia, Ala., Sept. 1, 1923; student U. North Ala.; LL.B., U. Ala., 1949. Admitted to Ala. bar, 1949; since practiced in Tuscumbia. Mem. Ala. State Bd. Correction; mem. Ala. State Bd. Edn., 1975—; mem. Tuscumbia City Bd. Edn. Mem. Colbert County, Am., Ala. bar assns., Phi Gamma Delta. Home: 100 N East St Tuscumbia AL 35674 Office: 301 S Dickson St Tuscumbia AL 35674 Tel (205) 383-5565

CARMICHAEL, DAVID H., b. Torrington, Wyo., Nov. 18, 1939; A.B. in Mathematics, U. Wyo., 1964, J.D., 1967. Admitted to Wyo. bar, 1967, U.S. Supreme Ct. bar, 1972; asso. firm Kline & Tilker, Cheyenne, Wyo., 1967-68, firm Hanes, Carmichael, Johnson, Gage & Speight, Cheyenne, 1970-76; individual practice law, Cheyenne, 1976-77; mem. firm Carmichael & Statkus, 1977—; mem. permanent rules com. Wyo. Supreme Ct., 1975—. Mem. Cheyenne Police Civil Service Commn., 1974—, Wyo. Fair Employment Practices Commn., 1970-75; mem. Rocky Mountain region Nat. Parks Adv. Bd.; sec. Wyo. Republican Central Com., 1974—; asst. city atty., Cheyenne, 1969-72. Mem. Am., Wyo. (dir. 1971-74) trial lawyers assns., Wyo. State Bar Assn. Sr. editor Wyoming Land and Water Rev., 1966-67. Home: 921 Evergreen St Cheyenne WY 82001 Office: 3001 Henderson St Cheyenne WY 82001 Tel (307) 635-4111

CARMICHAEL, DONALD MONROE, b. Lynchburg, Va., Feb. 7, 1937; A.B., Davidson; Coll., 1958; LL.B., U. Louisville, 1963; LL.M., U. Wis., 1964. Admitted to Ky. bar, 1963, Wis. bar, 1964; fellow in law U. Wis., Madison, 1964, Ford Found fellow in law, 1967-68; asso. firm Ross, Stevens & Pick, Madison, 1964-67; asso. prof. law U. Colo., Boulder, 1968—, dir. Ford Found. Environ. Legal Intern Program, 1970-73; bd. dirs. legal defense fund Sierra Club, 1971—; mem., legal cons. City of Boulder Growth Study Commn. Mem. Wis. Bar Assn., Internat. Council Environ. Law. Contbr. articles in field to legal jours. Home: Salina Star Route Sunshine Canyon Boulder CO 80302 Office: Fleming Law Bldg U Colo Boulder CO 80302 Tel (303) 492-8081

CARMICHAEL, LARRIE ARTHUR, b. Hope, N.D., Dec. 7, 1934; B.S. in Law, U. Utah, 1961, J.D., 1963. Admitted to Utah bar, 1963; individual practice law, Roy, Utah, 1963—. Home: 2363 W 5650 S Roy UT 84067 Office: 2035 W 5600 S POB 163 Roy UT 84067 Tel (801) 825-9129

CARMICHAEL, PARKS M., b. Monticello, Fla., Apr. 2, 1909; LL.B., U. Fla., 1931, also J.D. Admitted to Fla. bar, 1931; mem. firm Scruggs and Carmichael, Gainesville, Fla., 1944— (now Scruggs, Carmichael, Long, Tomlinson, Roscow, Pridgeon, Helpling & Young). Mem. Fla. Bar (past chmn. real property sect., past mem. bd. govs.), 8th Jud. Circuit, Am. bar assns., Fla. Bd. Bar Examiners (vice chmn., 1975-76, chmn., 1976-77). Home: 501 NE 8th Ave Gainesville FL 32601 Office: 3 SE 1st Ave Gainesville FL 32601 Tel (904) 376-5242

CARMODY, DONALD RAYMOND, b. St. Louis, July 23, 1942; B.S., Spring Hill Coll., 1964; J.D., U. Mo., 1967. Admitted to Mo. bar, 1967; asst. city counselor City of St. Louis, 1968-69; with firm Sumner, Hanlon, Sumner, MacDonald & Nouss, 1969—, sr. mem., 1976—; lectr. bus. law St. Louis U. Sch. Commerce and Fin., 1970-76. Mem. Mo., St. Louis County, Met. St. Louis bar assns., Am. Trial Lawyers Assn. Home: 9 Picardy Ln Ladue MO 63105 Office: 7733 Forsyth Blvd Saint Louis MO 63105 Tel (314) 862-0200

CARMODY, THOMAS HENRY, b. Palo Alto, Calif., Aug. 4, 1946; B.A., Stanford, 1968; J.D., U. Calif., 1971. Admitted to Calif. bar, 1972, U.S. Supreme Ct. bar, 1975; dep. dist. atty. Santa Clara County (Calif.), 1972-75; partner firm Blacker Carmody & Thompson, San Jose, Calif., 1975—; mem. Santa Clara County Supvs. Jail Task Force Com., 1976. Mem. Santa Clara County Bar Assn. (chmn. criminal law sect., 1976, exec. bd., legal services, editor Rap Sheet Newsletter, chmn. pub. relations 1977). Home: 945 Harriet St Palo Alto CA 94301 Office: 151 W St James St San Jose CA 95110 Tel (408) 286-4300

CARMODY, WILLIAM FRANKLIN, b. Chgo., June 9, 1943; B.A., U. Houston, 1965; J.D., Chgo.-Kent Coll. Law, 1969. Admitted to Ill. bar, 1970; asst. states atty. Cook County (Ill.), 1971-72; asso. firm Ross & East, Chgo., 1972-74; partner firm Ross, Scott & Carmody, 1974—. Mem. Ill., Chgo., S. Chgo. (treas. 1976-77) bar assns., Chgo. Trial Lawyers Assn. Home: 3443 S Wallace St Chicago IL 60616 Office: 39 S LaSalle St Chicago IL 60603 Tel (312) 782-8474

CARMOUCHE, EDWARD MOSS, b. Lake Charles, La., June 21, 1921; B.S., La. State U., 1943; J.D., U. Va., 1948; M. in Civil Law, Tulane U., 1949. Admitted to La. bar, 1949, D.C. bar, 1975; partner firm Camp, Carmouche, Palmer, Carwile & Barsh, Lake Charles, 1962—; asst. atty. gen. State of La., 1956—; pres. Lutcher & Moore Cypress Lumber Co., River Parishes Co., Inc.; v.p. Magdelena Oil Co., Magnet Gas Co., San Andreas Oil Co.; dir. M-Heart, Inc., M.G.S. Lake Charles, Inc., Matilda Geddings Gray Found., Mecom, Ltd., Cron & Gracey, Lake Charles Dredging & Towing Co. Mem. La. State U. Found., 1970—; trustee Southwestern at Memphis, 1971—; mem. pres.'s council Tulane U., 1976—. Mem. Am., D.C., La. bar assns., Phi Delta Phi. Office: PO Box 2001 Louisiana Savings Bldg Lake Charles LA 70601 Tel (318) 433-0355

CARNAHAN, ROBERT NARVELL, b. Littlefield, Tex., Nov. 22, 1928; B.A. in English, Tex. Tech. U., 1950; LL.B., U. Tex.. 1957. Admitted to Tex. bar, 1956; asst. county atty. Potter County (Tex.), 1957; partner firm Stokes, Carnahan & Fields, Amarillo, Tex., 1967—. Mem. Am. Judicature Soc., Am., Amarillo Jr. (pres. 1962) bar assns., Tex. Assn. Def. Counsel, Tex. Criminal Def. Lawyers Assn. Contbr. article to legal jour. Home: 105 Palomino St Amarillo TX 79106 Office: 1002 Amarillo Nat Bank Bldg Amarillo TX 79101 Tel (806) 374-5317

CARNER, RONALD STEPHAN, b. Bklyn., May 19, 1939; B.A., Brandeis U., 1962; J.D., Loyola U., Chgo., 1966. Admitted to N.Y. bar, 1967; partner firm Belli, Sarisohn, Creditor, Carner, Thierman & Steindler, Commack, N.Y., 1974—. Mem. Assn. Trial Lawyers Am., N.Y. State Trial Lawyers Assn., Suffolk County Bar Assn. Home: 2 Coconut Dr Commack NY 11725 Office: 1020 E Jericho Turnpike Commack NY 11725 Tel (516) 543-7667

CARNES, JAMES ALLEN, b. Toledo, Sept. 23, 1937; B.A., So. U., Baton Rouge, 1969, J.D., 1970. Admitted to La. bar, 1972; staff atty. Legal Services Orgn. of Indpls., 1970-71, Legal Aid Soc. of Baton Rouge, 1972-73; asst. to gen. counsel La. Dept. Hwys., Baton Rouge, 1973-74; with JAGC, U.S. Army, 1974-76; mem. firm Walkins & Carnes, Baton Rouge, 1972-74, firm Wilkins Carnes & Jackson, Baton Rouge, 1976—; coordinator atty's panel on legal edn. Indpls. Sch. Dist., 1970-71. Founding father Y's Men's Club Internat. YMCA Alpha chpt., Baton Rouge, 1969, 1st pres., 1969-70. Mem. Am., Nat., La. State, Baton Rouge bar assns., Louis A. Martinet Legal Soc. Inc., Am. Lawyers Assn. Home: PO Box 1186 Baton Rouge LA 70821 Office: 8538 Scenic Hwy Baton Rouge LA 70807 Tel (504) 775-9851

CARNES, LAMAR, b. Beaumont, Tex., Aug. 19, 1923; B.A., Cornell U., 1941, M.B.A., 1942; J.D., So. Meth. U., 1948. Admitted to Tex. bar, 1948, U.S. Supreme Ct. bar, 1954; individual practice law, Houston, 1948-68, Dallas, 1969—; v.p., gen counsel ADA Oil Co., Houston, 1953-58. Mem. Am., Tex., Dallas bar assns. Home: 6211 W Northwest Hwy Dallas TX 75225 Office: 2401 Adolphus Tower 1412 Main St Dallas TX 75202 Tel (214) 744-1171

CARNES, MICHAEL PHLEMON, b. San Antonio, Feb. 16, 1944; B.B.A., U. Tex., 1967, J.D., 1969. Admitted to Tex. bar, 1969, U.S. Supreme Ct. bar, 1976; atty. organized crime sect. Dept. Justice, Washington, 1969-70; trial atty. Organized Crime Strike Force, New Orleans, 1970-72; asst. U.S. atty. No. Dist. Tex., Ft. Worth, 1972-76, U.S. atty., 1976—; dept. chief criminal div. U.S. Atty.'s Office, Ft. Worth, 1975, chief, 1976. Recipient Atty. Gen.'s Spl. Achievement award, 1971; rated Outstanding Asst. U.S. Atty., 1973, 74, 75. Home: 717 Sandlin St Bedford TX 76021 Office: 310 US Courthouse Fort Worth TX 76102 Tel (817) 334-3291

CARNEY, EDWARD HARRISON, b. Erie, Pa., June 26, 1913; A.B., Allegheny Coll., 1936; LL.B., U. Pitts., 1939. Admitted to Pa. bar, 1940; served with FBI, 1942-46; individual practice law, 1946-64; dist. atty. Erie County (Pa.), 1964-65; judge Ct. of Common Pleas, Erie, 1966-67, pres. judge, 1967—; mem. Pa. Jud. Inquiry & Rev. Bd. Office: Erie County Court House Erie PA 16501 Tel (814) 455-9136

CARNEY, GEORGE VERNON, b. Medford, Oreg., Sept. 16, 1934; B.S., Lewis and Clark Coll., 1956; LL.B., Northwestern Coll. Law, Portland, Oreg., 1963, J.D., 1969. Admitted to Oreg. bar, 1964; dist. conferee IRS, Portland, Oreg., 1971—; instr. Portland State U., 1974—. Office: 1220 SW 3d St Portland OR 97205 Tel (503) 292-8305

CARNEY, HOWARD AUGUSTUS, b. Atlanta, Tex., Jan. 20, 1904; LL.B., Cumberland U., Lebanon, Tenn., 1926. Admitted to Tex. bar, 1926; partner firm Carney, Mays & Carney, and predecessors, Atlanta, Tex., 1926—; mem. Tex. Senate, 1944-52; sec. of state State of Tex., 1953-54; mem. Tex. Game and Fish Commn., 1955-62. Trustee Atlanta (Tex.) Ind. Sch. Dist., 1930-36, 1st Bapt. Ch., Atlanta, 1918. Mem. Am., Tex., N.E. Tex., Cass County (Tex.) bar assns. Home: 609 E Hirma St Atlanta TX 75551 Office: 103 W Hirma St Atlanta TX 75551 Tel (214) 796-2801

CARNEY, JAMES ANTHONY, b. Cleve., Jan. 24, 1946; B.S. in Hotel Adminstrn., Cornell U., 1968; J.D., Case Western Res. U., 1972. Admitted to Ohio bar, 1973; asst. pros. atty. Cuyahoga County Prosecutors Office, Cleve., 1973-76; individual practice law, Cleve., also asst. atty. gen. State of Ohio, 1976—; prof. hotel law Cuyahoga Community Coll., Cleve. Mem. Cleve. Democratic Exec. Com., 1976. Mem. Cornell Soc. Hotelmen, Citizens League Cleve. Home: 20670 Morewood Pkwy Rocky River OH 44116 Office: 1509 Investment Plaza Cleveland OH 44114 Tel (216) 579-0888

CARNEY, JOSEPH B., b. Greensburg, Ind., July 8, 1928; A.B., DePauw U., 1950; LL.B., Harvard U., 1953. Admitted to D.C. bar, 1953, Ind. bar, 1953, U.S. Supreme Ct. bar, 1957; asso. firm Hogg, Peters & Lenord, Ft. Wayne, Ind., 1953-54; served with JAGC, U.S. Army, 1954-57; asso. firm Baker & Daniels, Indpls., 1957-62, partner, 1962—. Mem. Am. (mem. environ. law com.), Ind., Indpls. bar assns., Bar Assn. Seventh Fed. Circuit (bd. govs.), Am. Judicature Soc. Home: 5306 N Pennsylvania St Indianapolis IN 46220 Office: 810 Fletcher Trust Bldg 108 N Pennsylvania St Indianapolis IN 46204 Tel (317) 636-3545

CARNEY, WILLIAM JOHN, JR., b. Chgo., May 10, 1937; B.A., Yale, 1959, LL.B., 1962. Admitted to Colo. bar, 1962, Wyo. bar, 1975; U.S. Supreme Ct. bar, 1973; asso. firm. Hart & Holland, Denver, 1962-68, partner, 1968-70; partner firm Shellman, Carney & Edwards, Aspen, Colo., 1971; individual practice law, Aspen, Colo., 1972-73; asso. prof. law U. Wyo., 1973-76, prof. law, 1976—. Mem. Univ. Faculty Assn. (pres. 1976—). Contbr. articles to law reviews. Home: 1829 Rainbow Laramie WY 82070 Office: POB 3035 Univ Station Laramie WY 82070 Tel (307) 766-2274

CARNEY, WILLIAM RAY, b. Chgo., Nov. 3, 1940; student Cornell U., 1958-59; A.B., Northwestern U., 1962; J.D., Loyola U., Chgo., 1967. Admitted to Ill. bar, 1967; since practiced in Chgo., partner firm Bell, Boyd, Lloyd, Haddad & Burns, 1967—; dir. subject team, Chgo. team to Nat. Commn. on Causes and Prevention Violence, 1968. Mem. bd. edn. Sch. dist. 28, Ill., 1971-73. Mem. Am., Ill., Chgo. bar assns., Alpha Sigma Nu. Home: 2135 Illinois Rd Northbrook IL 60062 Office: 135 S LaSalle St Chicago IL 60603 Tel (312) 372-1121

CAROLAN, ROBERT FRANCIS, b. Decorah, Iowa, Mar. 27, 1945; B.A., St. Mary's Coll., Winona, Minn., 1967; J.D., U. Iowa, 1970. Admitted to Iowa bar, 1970, Minn. bar, 1970, U.S. Supreme Ct. bar, 1973; sp. asst. atty. gen. State of Minn., St. Paul, 1970-74; asst. atty. County of Dakota, Hastings, Minn., 1974—. Mem. Minn. Bar Assn., Nat. Dist. Attys. Assn. Contbg. author: Minnesota Prosecutors Manual, 1976. Home: 6004 Lower 131st St Ct Apple Valley MN 55124 Office: 1560 W Hwy #55 Hastings MN 55033 Tel (612) 437-3191

CAROSELLI, WILLIAM RUDY, b. Braddock, Pa., Dec. 14, 1941; B.A., Brown U., 1963; J.D., Dickinson U., 1966. Admitted to Pa. bar, 1966, U.S. Supreme Ct. bar, 1966; partner firm McArdle, Henderson, Caroselli, Spagnolli & Beachler, Pitts., 1972—; asst. solicitor Alleghany County (Pa.), 1972-75. Mem. Am., Pa., Alleghany County bar assns., Am., Pa. trial lawyers assns., Am. Judicature Soc. Home: 100 Dewey St Pittsburgh PA 15218 Office: 1100 Law and Finance Bldg Pittsburgh PA 15219 Tel (412) 391-9860

CARP, ELIZABETH DOROTHY, b. El Paso, Tex., Dec. 9, 1916; LL.B., So. Meth. U., 1940. Admitted to Tex. bar, 1941; U.S. Supreme Ct. bar, 1950; individual practice law, Dallas, 1941-72; partner firm Carp & Eddleman, Dallas, 1972—. Mem. Am., Tex., Dallas (sec.-treas., dir. 1956-57) bar assns., Am., Tex., Dallas trial lawyers assns., Am. Judicature Soc., Southwestern Legal Found., Dallas Criminal Bar Assn., D.A.R., Kappa Beta Pi. Home: 7149 Northaven Dallas TX 75230

CARPENETI, RICHARD WALTER, b. San Francisco, May 16, 1942; B.A., U. Santa Clara, 1964; J.D., U. Calif. Hastings Coll. Law, 1969. Admitted to Calif. bar, 1970. U.S. Supreme Ct. bar, 1973; asso. firm Nathan Cohn, San Francisco, 1970-73; partner firm Carpeneti & Carpeneti, San Francisco, 1973-74, firm Carpeneti, Carpeneti & Carpeneti, San Francisco, 1974—; arbitrator Am. Arbitration Assn. Mem. Calif., San Francisco (gov.) trial lawyers assns., Criminal Trial Lawyers Assn. No. Calif., San Francisco Bar Assn. (speakers bur.), Calif. Attys. for Criminal Justice, San Francisco Barristers' Club. Home: 350 Texas St San Francisco CA 94107 Office: 1255 Post St Suite 1025 San Francisco CA 94109 Tel (415) 441-8000

CARPENETI, WALTER ISIDORE, b. San Francisco, Aug. 3, 1909; A.B., U. Calif., Berkeley, 1931, J.D., 1934. Admitted to Calif. bar, 1934; partner firm Lawrence, Tuttle & Harper and predecessor, San Francisco, 1934-53; judge San Francisco Municipal Ct., 1953-56; judge Calif. Superior Ct., 1956-74, mem. appellate dept., 1962-72; of counsel firm Carpeneti, Carpeneti & Carpeneti, San Francisco, 1974—; editor Calif. Cts. Commentary, 1976—. Pres. Calif. Horse Racing Assn. Charitable Found. Mem. Am. Justinian Soc. (pres. elect), Am., San Francisco bar assns., Calif. State Bar, Am. Judicature Soc., U. Calif. Law Sch. Assn. (pres. 1962-63), Phi Beta Kappa. Decorated cavalliere Order of Merit, Star of Solidarity (Italy); recipient certificate of appreciation Pres. of U.S., 1953, resolution of appreciation City of San Francisco, 1956; contbr. articles to Calif. Law Rev., The Brief Case. Office: 1255 Post St Suite 1025 San Francisco CA 94109 Tel (415) 441-8000

CARPENTER, DONALD ALFRED, b. Greeley, Colo., Jan. 2, 1907; J.D., George Washington U., 1931. Admitted to Tex. bar, 1931, Colo. bar, 1949; individual practice law, El Paso, Tex., 1931-34; dir. Colo. Use Tax Div., Denver, 1938-40; adminstrv. asst. to Hon. William S. Hill, mem. U.S. Congress, Washington, 1940-43; judge Weld County (Colo.) Ct., 1946-52, Colo. Dist. Ct., 8th Jud. Dist., 1952-64; chief judge 19th Jud. Dist., 1964—; adminstrv. judge No. Colo. Water Conservancy Dist., 1965—; adminstrv. judge Central Colo. Water Conservancy Dist., 1965—; water judge South Platte River System, 1969—; master for Colo. Supreme Ct., 1960-61; mem. Gov.'s Jud. Conf. Colo., 1957, 58; mem. Colo. Jud. Council, 1958, chmn. com. on appellate practice, 1958; mem. jud. council Chief Justice Colo. Supreme Ct., 1973—. Mem. Am., Colo., Tex., Weld County bar assns., Colo. Dist. Judges Assn., Nat. Coll. Probate Judges, Am. Judicature Soc., Nat. Conf. State Trial Judges, World Assn. Judges, Am. Acad. Polit., Social Scis. Home: 14953 Weld County Rd 70 Greeley CO 80631 Office: Courthouse Greeley CO 80631 Tel (303) 353-8050

CARPENTER, EDMUND NELSON, II, b. Phila., Jan. 27, 1921; A.B., Princeton, 1943; LL.B., Harvard, 1948. Admitted to Del. bar, 1949, U.S. Supreme Ct. bar, 1957; asso. firm Richards, Layton & Finger, Wilmington, Del., 1949-53, partner, 1953—; dep. atty. gen. State of Del., 1953-54, spl. dep. atty., 1960-62; chmn. Superior Ct. Jury Study Com., 1963-66; mem. Del. Gov.'s Commn. Law Enforcement and Adminstrn. Justice, 1969-69, chmn. Del. Agy. to Reduce Crime, 1970-71; chmn. Del. Supreme Ct. Adv. Com. on Profl. Fin. Accountability, 1974-75, long range cts. planning com., 1976—; dir. Bank Del., 1971—. Trustee U. Del., 1971—, Princeton U., 1974—, Wilmington Med. Center, 1965—; chmn. Lawyers Adv. Com. U.S. Ct. Appeals 3d Circuit, 1975—; mem. Del. Health Care Injury Ins. Study Commn., 1976—. Mem. Am., Del. State bar assns., Am. Judicature Soc. (dir. 1974—), Am. Acad. Trial Lawyers, Am. Trial Lawyers Assn.; fellow Am. Coll. Trial Lawyers, Am. Bar Found. Home: Office: 4072 DuPont Bldg Wilmington DE 19899 Tel (302) 658-6541

CARPENTER, GORDON AMBLER, b. Providence, Apr. 10, 1941; B.A., Amherst Coll., 1963; LL.B., U. Va., 1966. Admitted to Mass bar, 1966; asso. firm Ropes & Gray, Boston, 1966-73; v.p., gen. counsel Taylor Rental Corp., Springfield, Mass., 1973—. Bd. dirs. Tribune WGBY-TV, pub. TV, Springfield, 1974—. Mem. Am., Mass. bar assns. Home: 25 Pleasant View Rd Wilbraham MA 01095 Office: 570 Cottage St Springfield MA 01101 Tel (413) 781-7730

CARPENTER, JAMES WILLARD, b. Columbus, Ohio, Feb. 28, 1935; B.A., Ohio State U., 1961, J.D., 1964, J.D. summa cum laude, 1967. Admitted to Calif. bar, 1965, Ohio bar, 1966; asso. firm McCutchen, Black, Verleger & Shea, Los Angeles, 1964-65; prof. law, dir. legal clinic Ohio State U., Columbus, 1965-71; counsel The Western & So. Life Ins. Co., Cin., 1971—; adj. prof. law No. Ky. State Coll., Ft. Thomas, 1973—; partner firm Sullivan & Carpenter, Cin., 1975—. Mem. Am., Calif., Ohio, Cin. bar assns., Order of Coif, Cin. C. of C. Contbr. articles to Ohio State Law Jour., Tex. Law Review, Cornell Law Review. Office: 8006 Beechment Ave Cincinnati OH 45230 Tel (513) 232-2230

CARPENTER, RICHARD NORRIS, b. Cortland, N.Y., Feb. 14, 1937; B.A. magna cum laude, Syracuse U., 1958; LL.B., Yale, 1962. Admitted to N.Y. bar, 1962, N.Mex. bar, 1963, U.S. Supreme Ct. bar, 1973; asso. firm Breed, Abbott & Morgan, N.Y.C., 1962, Bigbee & Byrd, Santa Fe, 1963-67; partner firm Bigbee, Stephenson, Carpenter & Crout, Santa Fe, 1967—; spl. asst. atty. gen. N.Mex., 1963-74. Bd. dirs., v.p. Santa Fe Community Council; bd. dirs., pres. Santa Fe YMCA; trustee, pres. 1st Presbyterian Ch., Santa Fe. Mem. N.Y. State, 1st Jud. Dist. bar assns., State Bar N.Mex. Rotary Found. fellow for internat. understanding U. Panjab, Lahore, Pakistan, 1959-60. Home: 1048 Bishop's Lodge Rd Santa Fe NM 87501 Office: PO Box 669 Santa Fe NM 87501 Tel (505) 982-4611

CARPENTER, STACY ROY, b. McAllen, Tex., Feb. 6, 1937; B.S.B.A., U. Denver, 1961, J.D., 1967. Admitted to Colo. bar, 1967; claims atty. Imperial Casualty Ins. Co., Omaha, 1967-68; partner firm Elder, Phillips & Carpenter, Grand Junction, Colo., 1968—. Bd. dirs. Mesa County chpt. March of Dimes, 1968-75. Mem. Colo., Mesa County (Colo.) bar assns. Home: 3154 Lakeside Dr Apt 206 Grand Junction CO 81501 Office: 562 White Ave Grand Junction CO 81501 Tel (303) 243-0946

CARR, DWAINE ALFRED, b. Ft. Wayne, Ind., Oct. 20, 1938; B.S., Miami U., Oxford, Ohio, 1963; J.D., Stetson U., 1966. Admitted to Fla. bar, 1966, Ga. bar, 1970; atty., regional counsel IRS, Atlanta, 1966-71; mem. firm Hoffman, Hendry, Parker & Smith, Orlando, Fla., 1971—. Mem. Am., Fla., Ga. bar assns. Office: 1500 Hartford Bldg 200 E Robinson St Orlando FL 32801 Tel (305) 843-5880

CARR, LAURENCE WILLIAM, b. Redding, Calif., June 12, 1912; Ph.B., Santa Clara U., 1933; LL.B., Georgetown U., 1937. Admitted to D.C. bar, 1936, Calif. bar, 1937; dist. atty. Shasta County (Calif.), 1939-43; legis. sec. to Hon. Earl Warren, Gov. Calif., 1943; partner firm Carr, Kennedy, Peterson & Frost, and predecessor, Redding, 1946—. Mem. Calif. Vets. Bd., 1946-53, chmn., 1953; trustee Shasta Union High Sch. Dist., 1963-75. Mem. Shasta/Trinity, Calif. State, D.C. bar assns. Home: Route 1 PO Box 2100 Anderson CA 96007 Office: 1640 West St PO Box 2007 Redding CA 96001 Tel (916) 241-2432

CARR, LAWRENCE EDWARD, JR., b. Colorado Springs, Colo., Aug. 10, 1923; B.S., U. Notre Dame, 1948, LL.B., 1949; LL.M., George Washington U., 1954. Admitted to Colo. bar, 1949, D.C. bar, 1950, Md. bar, 1961; individual practice law, Washington, 1952-60; mem. firm Carr, Jordan, Coyne and Savits and predecessors, Washington, 1960—. Pres. Groome Child Guidance Center, Washington. Mem. Bar Assn. of D.C. (pres., 1974-75), Am. (ho. of dels., 1974-76), D.C., Md. bar assns., Internat. Assn. Ins. Counsel, D.C. Defense Lawyers, Defense Research Inst. Home: 12001 Piney Glen Ln Potomac MD 20854 Office: 900 17th St NW Washington DC 20006 Tel (202) 659-4660

CARR, MICHAEL LEGRAND, b. Erie, Pa., Nov. 19, 1940; B.A., Yale, 1962, LL.B./J.D., 1965; postgrad. U.S. Naval Justice Sch., 1966, 77. Admitted to Pa. bar, 1965; asso. firm MacDonald, Illig, Jones & Britton, Erie, 1969-70; gen. counsel Pa. Gas Co. (now NFG), Erie, 1970-74; individual practice law, Erie, 1974-76; partner firm Carr & Blackwood, Erie, 1976—; served with JAGC, U.S. Navy, 1966-69, now lt. comdr. Res. Bd. dirs. Arts Council, Art Center, Florence Crittenton Home, Childbirth Edn. Assn., WQLN-TV/FM, Erie. Mem. Am., Pa., Erie County bar assns., Navy Lawyers Assn., Judge Advs. Assn. (life). Editor Erie County Legal Jour., 1973-76. Office: 218 Marine Bank Bldg Erie PA 16501 Tel (814) 459-4559

CARR, WILLARD ZELLER, b. Richmond, Ind., Dec. 18, 1927; B.S., Purdue U., 1948; LL.B., Ind. U., 1950. Admitted to U.S. Supreme Ct. bar, 1963, Calif. bar, 1951; partner firm Gibson, Dunn & Crutcher, Los Angeles, 1952—; mem. nat. panel arbitrators Am. Arbitration Assn. Chmn. men's adv. com. Los Angeles County-U. So. Calif. Med. Center Aux. for Recruitment, Edn. and Service; mem. Calif. Republican Central Com.; trustee Pacific Legal Found., Sacramento, 1973, vice-chmn., 1976—; bd. dirs. Los Angeles Police Meml. Found. Mem. Calif. State Bar, Los Angeles County, Am. (chmn. com. econ. and resources controls, sect. corp. banking and bus. law, vice chmn. membership com., sect. adminstrv. law), Internat. (chmn. com. labor law, sect. bus. law) bar assns., Nat. Def. Exec. Res., Los Angeles World Affairs Council, Los Angeles Area C. of C. (v.p. domestic trade and human relations div. 1977). Home: 123 N McCadden Pl Los Angeles CA 90004 Office: 515 S Flower St Los Angeles CA 90071 Tel (203) 488-7238

CARR, WILLIAM PITTS, b. Thomasville, Ga., June 21, 1947; B.B.A., U. Ga., 1969; J.D., Duke, 1972. Admitted to Ga. bar, 1972; mem. firm Neely, Freeman & Hawkins, Atlanta, 1971-73; partner firm Carr, Wadsworth, Abney & Tabb, Atlanta, 1973—; spl. counsel to Gov. State of Ga., 1975-76. Vice chmn. Ga. State Democratic Party, 1974—; trustee St. Jude's House, Atlanta, 1974-77; vestryman All Saints Episcopal Ch., Atlanta. Mem. Am., Ga. bar assns., Am. Trial Lawyers Assn., Ga. Def. Lawyers Assn., Atlanta Lawyers Club. Office: 2620 Equitable Bldg 100 Peachtree St NW Atlanta GA 30303 Tel (404) 688-7993

CARRATT, HARRY GUS, b. Macon, Ga., Sept. 12, 1930; B.A., U. Fla., 1952, J.D., 1957. Admitted to Fla. bar, 1957, U.S. Ct. Appeals 5th Circuit bar, 1958, U.S. Supreme Ct. bar, 1967; asso. firm Anderson, Gundlach and Hull, Ft. Lauderdale, Fla., 1956-58; partner firm Carratt and O'Conor, Ft. Lauderdale, 1958-60; partner firm Morgan, Carratt and O'Conor, Ft. Lauderdale, 1960—. Dist. gov. State of Fla. Am. Hellenic Ednl. Progressive Assn., 1963-64. Mem. Fla. Bar (chmn. grievance com. 1974-76), Am., Broward County (mem. exec. com. 1975-77, chmn. continuing legal edn. com. 1976-77) bar assns., Broward County Fla. Trial Lawyers Assn., Order of Coif, Phi Kappa Phi. Editor in Chief: U. Fla. Law Review, 1956. Home: 4322 NE 22d Ave Fort Lauderdale FL 33308 Office: Suite 605 Kenann Bldg 3101 N Federal Hwy Fort Lauderdale FL 33306 Tel (305) 566-1521

CARRELL, DANIEL ALLAN, b. Louisville, Ky., Jan. 2, 1941; A.B., Davidson Coll., 1963; B.A. (Rhodes scholar), Oxford U., 1965, M.A., 1968; J.D., Stanford U., 1968. Admitted to Va. bar, 1972; asso. firm Hunton & Williams, Richmond, Va., 1971—; asst. prof. social scis. U.S. Mil. Acad., West Point, N.Y., 1968-71. Counsel pro bono Conservation Council Va., 1975—. Mem. Richmond (sec. young lawyers sect. 1976-77), Va. (co-chmn. com. law related edn. young lawyers sect., 1976—), Am. bar assns., Va. State Bar, Christian Legal Soc. Home: 3537 Grandview Dr Richmond VA 23225 Office: PO Box 1535 707 E Main St Richmond VA 23212 Tel (804) 788-8297

CARREN, JEFFREY PAUL, b. Chgo., Oct. 8, 1946; A.B., U. Ill., 1968; J.D., Northwestern U., 1972. Admitted to Ill. bar, 1973; asso. firm Chadwell, Kayser, Ruggles, McGee & Hastings, Chgo., 1972—. Mem. Am., Ill., Chgo. bar assns. Office: 233 S Wacker Dr Chicago IL 60606 Tel (312) 876-2147

CARRERE, CHARLES SCOTT, b. Dublin, Ga., Sept. 26, 1937; B.A., U. Ga., 1959; LL.B., Stetson U., 1961. Admitted to Ga. bar, 1960, Fla. bar, 1961, U.S. Supreme Ct. bar, 1965; law clk. to U.S. Dist. Judge, 1962-63; asst. U.S. atty., Middle Dist. Fla., 1963-66, 68-69, spl. asst. to U.S. Atty., 1966-67, chief trial atty. for U.S. Middle Dist. Fla., 1965-66, 68-69; partner firm Harrison, Greene, Mann, Rowe & Stanton, St. Petersburg, Fla., 1970—. Mem. Am. Bar Assn., Ga. Trial Lawyers Assn., Phi Beta Kappa. Home: 115 17th Ave NE St Petersburg FL 33704 Office: 1000 Florida Federal Bldg St Petersburg FL 33701 Tel (813) 896-7171

CARRETTA, ALBERT ALOYSIUS, b. N.Y.C., Dec. 23, 1907; B.S. in Govt., Coll. City N.Y., 1930; J.D., Georgetown U., 1940. Admitted to D.C. bar, 1940, Va. bar, 1941; individual practice law, Arlington, Va., 1947-52, Washington, 1947-52, 54—; commr. FTC, Washington, 1952-54; lectr. law Cath. U. Am., Washington, 1942-54. Mem. Am., Fed. bar assns., Bar Assn. D.C., D.C. Bar, Va. State Bar. Contbr. articles to legal jours. Home: 1823 N Glebe Rd Arlington VA 22207 Office: 1819 H St NW Washington DC 20006 Tel (202) 659-2811

CARRIER, JACK RYDEN, b. Kingsport, Tenn., Sept. 28, 1943; B.A., Wake Forest U., 1965; J.D., U. Tenn., 1968. Admitted to Tenn. bar, 1968; asso. firm Herrin & Sherwood, Johnson City, Tenn., 1971; asst. dist. atty. 1st Jud. Dist. Tenn., 1971-73; asso. firm Weller & Miller, Johnson City, 1973—. Mem. Am., Tenn., Washington County bar assns., Am. Judicature Soc. Office: 2101 N Roan St Johnson City TN 37601 Tel (615) 928-6142

CARRO, JOHN PLACID, b. N.Y.C., Jan. 14, 1920; LL.B., St. John's U. Admitted to N.Y. bar, 1949; claims mgr. Allstate Ins. Co., Bklyn., 1951-57; individual practice law, N.Y.C., 1957—. Active Boy Scouts Am. Mem. N.Y. State Assn. Trial Lawyers, Am. Trial Lawyers Assn., Columbian Lawyers Assn. Kings County. Home: 29 Liso Dr Mount Sinai NY 11766 Office: 299 Broadway New York City NY 10007 Tel (212) 964-6410

CARROLL, FREDERICK ARNOLD, b. Hobart, N.Y., Apr. 11, 1911; J.D., Syracuse U., 1934. Admitted to N.Y. State bar, 1935, Calif. bar, 1963; v.p., gen. counsel-dir. Transamerica Ins. Co., Los Angeles, 1963-76; mem. firms Robert E. Brimberry, Inc., Newport Beach, Calif., 1976—. Mem. Internat. Assn. Ins. Counsel (v.p. 1974-76), Am., Los Angeles, Orange County bar assns., Phi Delta Phi. Contbr. articles to legal jours. Home: 3747 Vista Campana So Oceanside CA 92054 Office: 900 Wilshire Blvd Los Angeles CA 90017 Tel (213) 642-6201

CARROLL, JOHN EDWARD, b. Covington, Ky., May 10, 1912; LL.B., Ind. U., 1932. Admitted to Ind. bar, 1933; law editor Bobbs-Merrill Co., Inc. (became Bobbs-Merrill Co. div. ITT Pub. Co. 1966), Indpls., 1936-62, exec. editor, 1962—. Mem. Indpls., Ind. State bar assns. Home: 1806 E 12th St Indianapolis IN 46201 Office: 4300 W 62d St Indianapolis IN 46268 Tel (317) 291-3100

CARROLL, JOSEPH J., b. N.Y.C., Sept. 18, 1936; B.S., Manhattan Coll., 1958; LL.B., St. John's U., 1963; LL.M., N.Y. U., 1968. Admitted to N.Y. State bar, 1964, Supreme Ct. bar, 1968; partner firm Mudge Rose Guthrie & Alexander, N.Y.C., 1967—; adminstrv. asst. to exec. dir. N.Y. State Housing Fin. Agy., 1964-67. Mem. Am., N.Y. bar assns., Phi Alpha Delta. Office: 20 Broad St New York City NY 10005 Tel (212) 422-6767

CARROLL, KENNETH, b. Pitts., Jan. 8, 1944; B.A. in History and Polit. Sci., U. Calif., Los Angeles, 1968; J.D., Loyola U., Los Angeles, 1971. Asso. firm Gray & Jeppson, Beverly Hills, Calif., 1971-72; admitted to Calif. bar, 1972; pub. defender City of San Francisco, 1973-74; asso. firm Kinkle, Rodiger, Dewberry & Spriggs, Ventura, Calif., 1974—. Home: 22328 Pacific Coast Hwy Malibu CA 90265 Office: 584 Poli St Ventura CA 93001 Tel (805) 643-2141

CARROLL, MARY JOE, b. Wichita Falls, Tex., June 25, 1914; B.A., U. Tex., 1934, M.A., 1935, LL.B., 1955. Admitted to Tex. bar, 1955, U.S. Supreme Ct. bar, 1971; research asst. U. Tex. Law Sch., 1932-55; asso., then partner firm Clark, Thomas, Winters & Shapiro, Austin, 1955—. County chmn. Tex. State Hist. Survey Com., Travis County; parliamentarian Tex. senate, 1961, 66. Mem. Am., Tex., Travis County bar assns., Am. Judicature Soc., Philos. Soc. Tex., Order of Coif, Zeta Tau Alpha, Kappa Beta Pi. Home: 3203 A Pecos St Austin TX 78703 Office: Capital National Bank Bldg Austin TX 78701 Tel (512) 472-8442

CARROLL, SEAVY ALEXANDER, b. Lumberton, N.C., Feb. 4, 1918; B.A., Wake Forest U., 1940, LL.B., 1956, J.D. 1970; postgrad. St. Andrews Coll., Eng., 1959, Ind. U., 1965, Nat. Coll. State Judiciary, 1973. Adviser Duke Legal Aid Clinic, 1946-47; admitted to N.C. bar, 1947; individual practice law, Fayetteville, N.C., 1947-58; partner firm Carroll & Herring, Fayetteville, 1958-59; missionary United Meth. Ch., Rhodesia, Africa, 1959-70; supt. schs. Nyadiri, Rhodesia, 1960; dir. Publicity and Promotion, Salisbury, Rhodesia, 1961-69; judge 12th Dist. Ct., Fayetteville, 1970-74; mem. N.C. State Senate, 1957-59; judge Cumberland County Recorder's Ct., 1952-56; individual practice law, Fayetteville, 1974—. Chmn. United Fund, 1949. Mem. Am. (com. on standards of jud. conduct), N.C. State, N.C. 12 Jud. Dist., Cumberland County bar assns. Contbr. articles to religious jours. Home: 2404 Morgantown Rd Fayetteville NC 28303 Office: 101 Gillespie St Fayetteville NC 28301 Tel (919) 483-9202

CARROW, ROBERT DUANE, b. Marshall, Minn., Feb. 5, 1934; B.A., U. Minn., 1956; J.D., Stanford, 1958. Admitted to Calif. bar, 1958; partner firm Carrow & Forest, San Francisco and Novato, Calif.; councilman City of Novato, 1963-64, mayor, 1964-66. Mem. Marin County (Calif.), Calif. bar assns., Am., Calif. trial lawyers assns., Calif. Attys. for Criminal Justice. Office: 1450 Grant Ave Novato CA 94947 Tel (415) 897-2101

CARRUTH, LOWELL THORSON, b. Oakland, Calif., Apr. 11, 1938; A.B., Stanford U., 1959; LL.B., U. Calif., Berkeley, 1962. Admitted to Calif. bar, 1963; asso. firm Kimble, Hamlin & MacMichael, Fresno, Calif., 1963-64; dep. dist. atty. Fresno County (Calif.), 1964-66; asso. firm McCormick, Barstow, Sheppard, Coyle & Wayte, Fresno, 1966-69, partner, 1969—. Mem. Am., Calif., Fresno County (past sec.) bar assns., Am. Bd. Trial Advs. (pres. Fresno chpt. 1973-74), Assn. Def. Counsel (dir. 1975—). Home: 1493 W Twain St Fresno CA 93711 Office: 1171 Fulton Mall Fresno CA 93721 Tel (209) 442-1150

CARRUTH, ROBERT LOUIS, b. Kentwood, La., Dec. 10, 1925; LL.B., J.D., La. State U., 1954. Admitted to La. bar, 1954; practiced in New Orleans, 1954—; asso. firm Beard, Blue & Schmitt, 1954-60; partner firm Collins & Carruth, 1960-65; asst. atty. gen. State of La. Home: 5037 Bissonet Dr Metairie LA 70003 Office: Suite 1001 333 Saint Charles Ave New Orleans LA 70130 Tel (504) 525-2121

CARSON, DAVID WILLIAM, b. Kansas City, Kans., Aug. 2, 1916; A.B., U. Kans., 1936; LL.B., U. Mich., 1939. Admitted to Kans. bar, 1939; individual practice law, Kansas City, Kans., 1939—. Mem. Kans. Bar Assn., Am. Trial Lawyers Assn. Home: 1400 N 69th St Kansas City KS 66102 Office: 302 Brotherhood Bldg Kansas City KS 66101 Tel (913) 371-2314 also 281-0422

CARSON, JAMES BERKLEY, b. Lexington, N.C., Aug. 7, 1932; A.B. in Am. Studies, U. Md., 1954, M.A. in Am. Studies, 1955, LL.B., J.D., 1962. Admitted to Md. bar, 1962, U.S. Supreme Ct. bar, 1971; asso. firm Berman & Berman, Balt., 1963-64; partner firm Felluca & Carson, Balt., 1964—; adj. prof. bus. law, head dept. Essex Community Coll., Balt., 1969—. Mem. SSS, 1974—. Mem. Am., Md. bar assns., AAUP, Am. Judicature Soc., Am. Acad. Polit. and Social Scis., Res. Officers Assn. U.S. (nat. judge adv. 1971-72, Md. state pres. 1972, state judge adv. 1972—). Home: 70 Milburn Circle Pasadena MD 21122 Office: 3617 E Lombard St Baltimore MD 21224 Tel (301) 732-8034

CARSON, LORTON RONALD, b. What Cheer, Iowa, Aug. 26, 1907; B.A., U. Iowa, 1930, J.D., 1932. Admitted to Iowa bar, 1932, U.S. Dist. Ct. bar, 1932, U.S. Supreme Ct. bar, 1960; county atty. Mahaska County (Iowa), 1940; city atty. City of Oskaloosa (Iowa), 1939; judge U.S. Dist. Ct., Oskaloosa, 1958—. Mem. Am., Iowa bar assns. Home: 210 N 8th St Oskaloosa IA 52577 Office: Mahaska County Court House Oskaloosa IA 52577 Tel (515) 673-4810

CARSON, MARION THOMAS, b. St. Louis, Aug. 18, 1937; student San Antonio Coll., 1960-61; B.A., St. Mary's U., San Antonio, 1964, J.D., 1967. Admitted to U.S. Dist. Ct. bar for Western Dist. Tex., 1971, for So. Dist. Tex., 1972, U.S. Ct. Appeals bar, 5th Circuit, 1976, Tex. Supreme Ct. bar, 1967; asso. firm Lieck & Lieck, San Antonio, 1967-68; individual practice law, San Antonio, 1968—; counsel Sr. Citizen's Bldg. Fund, Sr. Citizen's Council, Nat. Fiddlers Assn. Mem. San Antonio Bar Assn., San Antonio Trial Lawyers Assn., Tex. Criminal Def. Lawyers Assn., San Antonio Jr. C. of C. Home: Star Route PO Box 161 Poteet TX 78065 Office: 505 Petroleum Commerce Bldg 201 N Saint Mary's St San Antonio TX 78205 Tel (512) 222-9572

CARSON, MICHAEL JAY, b. Denver, Mar. 29, 1944; B.A., U. Colo., 1966, J.D., 1969. Admitted to Colo. bar, 1969, Okla. bar, 1973; gen. atty. FCC, Washington, 1969-70; trial atty. FTC, Washington, 1970-73; asso. firm Rosenstein, Fist & Ringold, Tulsa, 1973-75; judge Municipal Criminal Ct., Tulsa, 1975—. Mem. Tulsa Alcoholism Adv. Com., 1976. Mem. Okla., Am. bar assns. Recipient Meritorious Service award FTC, 1972. Office: 600 Civic Center Tulsa OK 74013 Tel (918) 581-5381

CARSON, ROBERT CARY, b. Ft. Worth, Nov. 16, 1901; grad. Sch. Law, Baylor U., 1925, J.D. (hon.), 1969. Admitted to Tex. bar, 1925; mem. firm Hyer & Christian, Ft. Worth, 1925-30; individual practice law, Ft. Worth, 1930-40, 60—; atty., legal counsel Wholesale & Mfrs. Bur., 1940-60; pres. Am. Collectors Assn., Inc., 1925—. Dist. commr. Boy Scouts Am., 1955-69, Silver Beaver award, 1944. Mem. Tarrant County Bar Assn., Am. Collectors Assn. (exec. bd. 1959-64, editor Monthly mag. 1962-63), Nat. Assn. Wholesale Credit Men, Nat. Retail Mchts. Assn., Ft. Worth C. of C. (dir. 1959-63). Home: 6386 Greenway Rd Fort Worth TX 76116 Office: 100 N University Dr PO Box 9258 Fort Worth TX 76107 Tel (817) 332-9342

CARSON, WILLIAM HARRISON, JR., b. Chgo., Apr. 12, 1940; B.S. in Economics, U. Ill., 1966; J.D., U. Calif., Berkeley, 1969. Admitted to Calif. bar, 1970; dep. dist. atty., chief trial dep. Humboldt County (Calif.), 1970-73; partner firm Huber, Goodwin, Murray, Cissna, Prior & Carson, Eureka, Calif., 1974—; tchr. Coll. Redwoods, Eureka, 1972-74. Pres., Humboldt County Easter Seal Soc., 1972, bd. dirs., 1973-75. Mem. Calif. Trial Lawyers Assn. Office: Box 23 Eureka CA 95501 Tel (707) 443-4573

CARSTEDT, WILLIAM DOUGLAS, b. Chgo., Mar. 9, 1938; B.S.Law, Northwestern U., 1959, J.D., 1960. Admitted to Ill. bar, 1960; asso. firm. Shaheen, Lundberg & Callahan, Chgo., 1960-68; partner firm Springer, Carstedt & Kurlander, Chgo., 1968—. Mem. Am., Ill., Chgo. bar assns., Chgo. Estate Planning Council. Home: 773 Prospect Ave Winnetka IL 60093 Office: 39 S LaSalle St Chicago IL 60603 Tel (312) 236-6200

CARTANO, JOHN DANIEL, b. Seattle, Apr. 4, 1909; A.B., U. Wash., 1930; J.D., Harvard, 1934. Admitted to Wash. bar, 1934; with firm Cartano, Botzer & Chapman, Seattle, 1934—, sr. partner, 1958—. Pres., Pacific Northwest Trade Assn., 1964; pres. Seattle C. of C., 1961-62, trustee, 1975—. Mem. Am., Wash. State, Seattle-King County bar assns. Home: 10519 SE 32nd St Bellevue WA 98004 Office: 1300 IBM Bldg Seattle WA 98101 Tel (206) 623-6700

CARTER, CAREY CADE, JR., b. Hartwell, Ga., Dec. 11, 1919; J.D., U. Ga., 1949. Admitted to Ga. bar, 1949, U.S. Dist. Ct. No. Dist. Ga. bar, 1949, U.S. Ct. of Appeals, 5th Circuit, 1962; pres., chmn. bd. Amelia by the Sea, Inc., Fernandina Beach, Fla., 1976—; chief dep. sheriff, Hart County, Ga., 1946-48. Mem. Am., No. Jud. Circuit bar assns., State Bar Ga., Ga. Trial Lawyers Assn., Ga. Criminal Def. Lawyers Assn., Lawyers-Pilots Bar Assn., Aircraft Owners and Pilots Assn. Office: POB 728 Hartwell GA 30643 Tel (404) 376-7111

CARTER, CHARLES LOVEBERRY, JR., b. Stamford, Tex., Sept. 16, 1920; B.A. with honors, Lake Forest (Ill.) Coll., 1954; J.D. summa cum laude, U. Balt., 1959. Admitted to Md. bar, 1959, Tex. bar, 1969; asso. firm O'Connor & Preston, Balt., 1959-64, mng. partner, 1964-69; individual practice law, Crockett, Tex., 1969-71; sr. partner firm Carter Gordon & von Doenhoff, Crockett, 1972—; justice of the peace, Houston County, Tex., 1971-74. Pres., Houston County Easter Seal Soc., 1970—. Mem. Am. Bar Assn., Tex. Trial Lawyers Assn., State Bar Tex. (grievance com. 1975—). Home: Dellwood Ranch POB 1146 Crockett TX 75835 Office: 509 E Goliad PO Box 1146 Crockett TX 75835 Tel (713) 544-2091

CARTER, GENE, b. Milbridge, Maine, Nov. 1, 1935; B.A., U. Maine at Orono, 1958; LL.B., N.Y. U., 1961. Admitted to Maine bar, 1962; partner firm Rudman, Rudman & Carter, Bangor, Maine, 1965—; chmn. adv. com. to Supreme Jud. Ct. on rules of civil procedure, 1976—. Chmn. Bangor Housing Authority. Mem. Am. Trial Lawyers Assn., Internat. Soc. Barristers. Office: 84 Harlow St Bangor ME 04401 Tel (297) 947-4501

CARTER, HAROLD MARTIN, b. McDowell, W.Va., Aug. 21, 1920; B.S., Roanoke Coll., 1942; J.D. with Honors, George Washington U., 1949. Admitted to Va. bar, 1950, U.S. Supreme Ct. bar, 1953; atty. regulatory div. Office of Gen. Counsel USDA, Washington, 1950-63, dep. dir. 1963-68, dir. 1968-75; asst. gen. counsel, 1975—. Active Nat. Capital Area Council Boy Scouts Am., 1963—; vice chmn. adminstrv. bd., trustee Annandale United Meth. Ch.; mem. legal adminstrn. com. U.S. Dept. Agr. Grad. Sch. Mem. Va., Fed. bar assns. Recipient Certificate Merit USDA, 1960, 1970; USDA Superior Service Award, 1971. Home: 3911 Bruce Ln Annandale VA 22003 Office: 14th St and Independence Ave Washington DC 20250 Tel (202) 447-7219

CARTER, HELEN STRICKLER, b. Hobart, Okla., June 20, 1926; student Stephens Coll., 1943-44, U. Okla., 1944-45, Kiowa County Jr. Coll., 1945; B.A., U. N.Mex., 1947; postgrad. George Washington U., 1948; LL.B., U. Utah, 1951, J.D., 1968. Admitted to D.C. bar, 1951, N.Mex. bar, 1954; atty. representing Sen. Clinton P. Anderson, U.S. Senate Subcom. on Indian Affairs, 1951-52; partner firm Carter & Carter, Albuquerque, 1953-65; asso. in law, lectr. III in law librarianship, legal research librarian U. N.Mex. Sch. Law Library, Albuquerque, 1965—; legal cons. City of Albuquerque, 1970-71, ACLU, 1967—. Sponsor, YMCA Tri-Hi-Y, 1969-71; asst. City of Albuquerque Legal Staff. Mem. Am., N.Mex. bar assns., Am. Assn. Law Libraries, N.Mex. Library Assn., U. N.Mex., U. Utah alumni assns. Home: 2913 Cutler Ave NE Albuquerque NM 87106 Office: 1117 Stanford St NE Albuquerque NM 87131 Tel (505) 277-5131

CARTER, JAMES EDWARD, b. Phoenix, Apr. 9, 1935; B.S., Grand Canyon Coll., 1957; M.Ed., Ariz. State U., 1960; LL.B., U. Ariz., 1964. Admitted to Ariz. bar, 1964; asso. firm Cox & Hedberg, Phoenix, 1964-65. Asst. city prosecutor, Phoenix, 1965-72, city prosecutor, 1972-74; asst. city atty., Phoenix, 1974—; instr. law Grand Canyon Coll., Phoenix, 1975-77. Mem. com. phys. edn. YMCA, Phoenix, 1968-73; bd. trustees Phoenix Baptist Hosp., 1965—. Mem. Am. Bar Assn., State Bar Ariz., Phi Delta Phi. Home: 2301 E Orangewood St Phoenix AZ 85020 Office: 251 W Washington St Phoenix AZ 85003 Tel (602) 262-6761

CARTER, KEITH MELVIN, b. San Francisco, Jan. 25, 1940; B.A. in Polit. Sci., U. Calif., 1961, J.D., 1968. Admitted to Calif. bar, 1969; dep. dist. atty. Ventura County (Calif.), 1969-72; individual practice law, Oxnard, Calif., 1972-73, Ventura, Calif., 1973—. Mem. Calif. Trial Lawyers Assn., Calif. Attys. for Criminal Justice, Ventura County Criminal Def. Assn. (dir.). Office: 5808 E Telephone Rd Ventura CA 93003 Tel (805) 647-9267

CARTER, ROBERT EDWIN, b. Oakland, Calif., May 18, 1931; A.B., U. So. Calif., 1953, J.D., 1959. Admitted to Calif. bar, 1960; partner firm Hahn & Hahn, Pasadena, Calif., 1960—. Pres. Legal Aid Soc., Pasadena, 1968; mem. San Marino (Calif) Planning Commn. Mem. Am., Calif., Los Angeles County (exec. com.) bar assns., Order of Coif. Home: 1090 St Albans Rd San Marino CA 91108 Office: 301 E Colorado Blvd Suite 900 Pasadena CA 91101 Tel (213) 796-9123

CARTER, ROBERT LEE, b. Caryville, Fla., Mar. 11, 1917; A.B., Lincoln U. of Pa., 1937, D.C.L., 1966; LL.B., Howard U., 1940; LL.M., Columbia, 1942. Admitted to N.Y. State bar, 1945; asst. counsel NAACP, N.Y.C., 1945-56, gen. counsel, 1956-68; dir. vets. affairs Am. Vets. Com., Washington, 1946-47; spl. asst. U.S. atty. So. Dist. N.Y., 1962; fellow Columbia Urban Center, 1968-69; sr. partner firm Poletti Freidin Prashker Feldman & Gartner, N.Y.C., 1969-72; judge U.S. Dist. Ct. So. Dist. N.Y., N.Y.C., 1972—; mem. N.Y.C. Mayor's Com. on Judiciary, 1966-72; mem. Departmental Com. on Ct. Adminstrn. of 1st and 2d Jud. Depts., 1968-69, mem. N.Y. State Temp. Commn. on State Ct. System, 1971-72. Pres. Nat. Com. Against Discrimination on Housing, 1966-72; mem. N.Y. State Spl. Commn. on Attica, 1971-72; bd. dirs. ACLU, 1968-72; trustee Pub. Edn. Assn., 1969-72. Contbr. articles to profl. jours.; editorial bd. N.Y. Law Jour., 1969-73. Home: 65 Central Park W New York City NY 10023 Office: 2903 US Courthouse Foley Square New York City NY 10007 Tel (212) 791-0959

CARTER, ROBERT MICHAEL, b. Buffalo, June 15, 1950; A.B., Dartmouth Coll., 1971; J.D., Harvard U., 1974. Admitted to Ohio bar, 1974; asso. law firm Thompson, Hine & Flory, Cleve., 1974—. Vice chmn., mem. exec. com. Progressive Action Council, Inc., Cleve.; bd. dirs. Cleve. Com. for UNICEF. Mem. Cleve. Bar Assn. Office: Nat City Bank Bldg Cleveland OH 44114 Tel (216) 241-1880

CARTER, WILLIAM G., b. Berkeley, Calif., Oct. 5, 1940; B.S., U. Oreg., 1962, LL.B., 1965. Admitted to Oreg. bar, 1965; dep. dist. atty. Douglas County (Oreg.), 1965-68; individual practice law, Medford, Oreg., 1969—; judge Medford Municipal Ct., 1969—; atty. City of Central Point (Oreg.) and City of Gold Hill (Oreg.), 1975—. Office: 221 W Main St Medford OR 97501 Tel (503) 773-8471

CARTON, LAURENCE ALFRED, b. Chgo., Oct. 11, 1918; A.B., Princeton, 1940; J.D., U. Chgo., 1947. Admitted to Ill. bar, 1947; asso. firm Gardner, Carton & Douglas, Chgo., 1947-52, partner 1952—. Mem. Am., Ill., Lake County bar assns. Home: 285 W Laurel Ave Lake Forest IL 60045 Office: 1 1st Nat Plaza Chicago IL 60603 Tel (312) 726-2452

CARTON, THOMAS WILLIAM, JR., b. Coshocton, Ohio, Sept. 25, 1948; B.A., Bowling Green U., 1970; J.D., Ohio State U., 1973. Admitted to Ohio bar, 1973; asso. firm Gingher & Christensen, Columbus, Ohio, 1973-76, firm Moritz, McClure, Hughes & Hadley, Columbus, 1976—; city prosecutor Worthington (Ohio), 1973-76. Mem. Am., Ohio State, Columbus bar assns. Home: 1091 B Fountain Ln Columbus OH 43213 Office: 155 E Broad St Columbus OH 43215 Tel (614) 224-0888

CARTOON, STUART FORREST, b. N.Y.C., Jan. 1, 1935; B.A., Columbia, 1956, J.D., 1959. Admitted to N.Y. bar, 1960; U.S. Dist. Ct. So. and Eastern Dists. N.Y. bar, 1962, U.S. Supreme Ct. bar, 1964, U.S. Ct. Appeals 2d Circuit bar, 1974; asso. firm Gainsburg, Gottlieb, Levitan & Cole, N.Y.C., 1960-65; mem. firm Lynton, Klein, Opton & Saslow, N.Y.C., 1965-76; asso. firm Rubin Baum Levin Constant & Friedman, N.Y.C., 1976—. Mem. Assn. Bar City N.Y., Am., N.Y. State bar assns., Fed. Bar Council. Home: 33 McKeel Ave Tarrytown NY 10591 Tel (212) 759-2700

CARTWRIGHT, CHARLES LORN, b. Hereford, Tex., Feb. 2, 1904; B.A., Trinity U., 1924; LL.B., Jefferson Sch. Law, 1932; postgrad. U. Houston, 1952. Admitted to Tex. bar, 1932; asst. tax commr. Pure Oil Co., 1926-34; atty. Amoco Prodn. Co., Ft. Worth, 1935-43, Houston, 1943-69; cons., individual practice law, Bellaire, Tex., 1969—. Chmn. zoning and planning commn. City of West University Place, 1945-47, chmn. bd. adjustment, 1947-49, chmn. design and constrn. municipal swimming pool, 1946; troop committeeman, neighborhood commr., dist. commr., mem. dist. camping com. Boy Scouts Am., 1945-55. Mem. Tex., Houston bar assns. Recipient Outstanding Civic Service award West University Place Civic Club, 1948. Home and office: 4512 Teas St Bellaire TX 77401

CARUSO, FELIX WILLIS, b. Chgo., Apr. 26, 1933; B.A., Northwestern U., 1955, J.D., 1961. Admitted to Ill. bar, 1962, U.S. Supreme Ct. Bar, 1974; asso. firm Sidley and Austin, Chgo. and Washington, 1961-69; gen. counsel Leadership Council for Met. Open Communities, Chgo., 1969—. Asso. bd. dirs. LaGrange Community Meml. Hosp. (Ill.), LaGrange YMCA, Helping Hand Sch., LaGrange. Mem. Am., Fed., Ill., Chgo., DuPage County bar assns. Author: Guide to Practice Open Housing Law, 1975. Office: 407 S Dearborn St Chicago IL 60606 Tel (312) 341-9345

CARY, CHARLES, b. Buffalo, Oct. 24, 1916; B.S., Harvard, 1939; J.D., U. Va., 1942. Admitted to N.Y. State bar, 1947; mem. firm Hodgson, Russ, Andrews, Woods & Goodyear, Buffalo, 1947-53; mem. firm Diebold & Millonzi, Buffalo, 1953-67; individual practice law, Buffalo, 1967—. Bd. dirs., v.p. Buffalo and Erie County Hist. Soc., 1948-66, Albright Knox Art Gallery, 1950-74. Mem. N.Y. State, Erie County bar assns., Harvard U. Alumni Assn. (nat. dir. 1966-69), Phi Delta Phi. Home: 1271 Sweet Rd East Aurora NY 14502 Office: 721 Marine Trust Bldg Buffalo NY 14202 Tel (716) 853-4886

CARY, JOHN BARRY, JR., b. Richmond, Va., Sept. 10, 1938; B.A. in English, Va. Mil. Inst., Lexington, 1960; J.D., U. Va., Charlottesville, 1971; postgrad. in behavioral scis. Cath. U., Washington, 1976—. Admitted to Va. bar, 1971, D.C. bar, 1972, U.S. Supreme Ct. bar, 1975; law clk. to Superior Ct. D.C., 1971-72; atty. adviser Office of Opinions and Review, FCC, Washington, 1972-75; atty. adviser Renewal Br. Broadcast Bur., FCC, Washington, 1975-76, sr. atty. adviser, 1976—. Trustee The Old Mansion, Bowling Green, Va., 1970—. Mem. Am., Fed. bar assns., U. Va. Law Sch. D.C. Alumni, VMI Alumni Assn., Soc. Cincinnati, Kappa Alpha, Phi Delta Phi. Home: 503 Roosevelt Blvd A602 Falls Church VA 22044 Office: 1919 M St NW Washington DC 20554 Tel (202) 632-7542

CARY, WILLIAM LUCIUS, b. Columbus, Ohio, Nov. 27, 1910; A.B., Yale, 1931; J.D., 1934; M.B.A., Harvard, 1938; LL.D., Amherst Coll., 1965. Admitted to Ohio bar, 1934, D.C. bar, 1947, Mass. bar, 1947, Ill. bar, 1949, N.Y. State bar, 1957; atty. SEC, Washington, 1938-42; lectr. Harvard, 1946-47; prof. Northwestern U., 1947-55; dep. counselor Dept. Army, Washington, 1951-52; prof. Columbia, 1955-61; chmn. SEC, Washington, 1961-64; Dwight prof. law Columbia, 1964—; counsel firm Patterson, Belknap & Webb & Tyler, N.Y.C., 1964—; mem. pub. rev. bd. Arthur Andersen & Co., 1974—; dir. Newark Telephone Co. (Ohio); vis. prof. Yale, 1957-58, 72, Stanford, summer 1954, U. Calif. at Berkeley, 1950; U. Paris I (France), spring 1976. Bd. dirs. N.Y. State Urban Devel. Corp., 1975; trustee Robert Coll., Istanbul, Turkey, 1966-74. Mem. Am., N.Y. bar assns., Am. Law Inst., Am. Acad. Arts and Scis., Council on Fgn. Relations, Phi Beta Kappa. Co-author: Effects of Taxation on Corporate Mergers, 1951; Cases & Materials on Corporations, 1969; The Law and the Lore of Endowment Funds, 1969; author: Politics and the Regulatory Agencies, 1969; Cases and Materials on Corporations, 1970. Office: Columbia Univ Schl Law New York City NY 10027 Tel (212) 280-2644

CASAD, ROBERT CLAIR, b. Council Grove, Kans., Dec. 8, 1929; A.B., U. Kans., 1950, M.A., 1952; J.D. with honors, U. Mich., 1957. Admitted to Kans. bar, 1957, Minn. bar, 1958; instr. in law U. Mich., 1957-58; asso. firm Streater & Murphy, Winona, Minn., 1958-59; asst. prof. law U. Kans., 1959-62, asso. prof., 1962-64, prof., 1964—; fellow in law teaching Harvard Law Sch., 1965-66; vis. prof. U. Calif., Los Angeles, 1969-70, U. Ill., 1973-74. Mem. Kans., Am. bar assns., Order of Coif. Recipient Coblentz prize for law rev. writing U. Mich. Law Sch., 1957; author: Expropriation Procedures In Central America and Panama, 1975; Res Judicata In A Nutshell, 1976; contbr. numerous articles to legal jours. Home: 1130 Emery Rd Lawrence KS 66044 Office: U of Kans Sch of Law Lawrence KS 66045 Tel (913) 864-4194

CASALE, MICHAEL JOSEPH, b. Williamsport, Pa., Mar. 19, 1922; B.S., Mansfield State Tchrs. Coll.; LL.B., John B. Stetson Sch. Law. Admitted to Pa. bar; asso. with Michael J. Maggio, 1952-56; partner firm Hess, Wise, and Casale, 1956-64; individual practice law, 1964-72; asso. with John R. Bonner, Williamsport, Pa., 1972—; county solicitor Lycoming County (Pa.), 1963-68; city solicitor Williamsport, 1974—. Mem. Lycoming Law Assn. (sec. 1975). Home: 1716 Walnut St Williamsport PA 17701 Office: 329 Market St Williamsport PA 17701 Tel (717) 323-3731

CASALEGGIO, GILES WAYNE, b. Paterson, N.J., Oct. 28, 1947; B.S. in Bus. Adminstrn., Fairleigh Dickinson U., 1969; student in law U. Tenn., 1969-70; J.D., St. John's U., 1972. Admitted to N.J. bar, 1972; student legal asst. U.S. Atty.'s Office for So. Dist. N.Y., 1971-72; asso. firm Belmont & Belmont, Butler, N.J., 1972; legal asst. Bergen County Atty's Office, Hackensack, N.J., 1973; asst. county prosecutor Union County, Elizabeth, N.J., 1973-75, Passaic County Paterson, 1975—. Mem. Nat. Dist. Attys. Assn., Am. N.J., Passaic County bar assns., N.J. County Prosecutors Assn., Phi Alpha Delta. Contbr. articles to profl. publs. Home: 13 East St Wanaque NJ 07455 Office: Prosecutors Office Passaic County Court House Paterson NJ Tel (201) 525-5000

CASAR, JOHN ROBERT, b. Canton, Ohio, Oct. 14, 1933; B.S., B.A., Ohio State U., 1958, J.D., 1960; M.L., Case Western Res. U., 1972. Admitted to Ohio bar, 1964; with Harter Bank and Trust Co. Trust Dept., Canton, 1960—, sr. v.p., trust officer, 1974—. Bd. dirs. Great Trail council Girl Scouts U.S.A., 1975—, chmn. fin. com., 1973—. Mem. Stark County, Ohio State, Am. bar assns., Ohio, Am. bankers assns. Office: Harter Bank and Trust Co PO Box 500 Canton OH 44701 Tel (216) 453-7081

CASCIO, JOSEPH DOMINIC, JR., b. Monroe, La., Feb. 16, 1936; B.A., N.E. La. State Coll., 1959; J.D., Tulane U., 1964. Admitted to La. Supreme Ct. bar, 1964, U.S. Supreme Ct. bar, 1974; individual practice, 1964; partner firm Hayes, Harkey, Smith & Cascio, Monroe, 1970—. Bd. dirs. La. Heart Assn., 1971-73, YMCA, Monroe—West Monroe, Inc., 1976—, Ouachita Valley council Boy Scouts Am.,

1976. Mem. La. State, Am. bar assns., Am. Trial Lawyers Assn., La. Def. Lawyers Assn. Home: 2017 Valencia St Monroe LA 71201 Office: 1504 Stubbs St Monroe LA 71201 Tel (318) 387-2422

CASCIO, PAUL KEITH, b. Ft. Knox, Ky., Sept. 5, 1947; B.A., The Citadel, 1969; J.D., Boston Coll., 1972; M.S. in Systems Mgmt., U. So. Calif., 1975. Admitted to Mass. bar, 1972, Fed. Dist. Ct., 1976, U.S. Ct. Mil. Appeals bar, 1976; asso. firm Lee & Pollard, Westfield, Mass., 1972-73, 75-76; commd. 1st lt. U.S. Army, 1973, capt. JAGC, 1976; fed. prosecutor U.S. Magistrate Ct., 1977. Mem. Boston, Mass., Am., Westfield bar assns., Am. Judicature Soc.

CASE, BRACE KAE, b. Clare, Mich.; B.S. in Bus. Adminstrn., Central Mich. U., 1960; J.D., Detroit Coll. Law, 1974. Admitted to Mich. bar, 1974; mgr. capital planning dept. Manley, Bennett, McDonald, Detroit, 1975—; mem. Anchor Annuity Adv. Bd. Mem. Mich., Macomb County bar assns., Sales Mktg. Execs. Detroit, Internat. Assn. Fin. Planners, SE Mich. Fin. Planners Assn. (steering com.), Jaycees (past v.p. Fraser (Mich.) chpt., past pres. Utica (Mich.) chpt., past v.p. Detroit chpt., recipient Presdl. award 1972). Home: 36743 Harwick Ct Fraser MI 48026 Office: 1100 Buhl Bldg Detroit MI 48226 Tel (313) 225-5585

CASE, JAMES HEBARD, b. Lihue, Hawaii, Apr. 10, 1920; A.B., Williams Coll., 1941; J.D., Harvard, 1949. Admitted to Hawaii bar, 1949; asso. firm Pratt, Tavares & Cassidy, Honolulu, 1949-51, Carlsmith & Carlsmith, Hilo, Hawaii, 1951-59, partner firm Carlsmith, Carlsmith, Wichman & Case, Honolulu, 1959—. Pres., dir. Central Union Ch., Honolulu, 1973, Hawaii Assn. Retarded Children, Honolulu. 1965-74; bd. dirs. Hanahauoli Sch., Honolulu, Hawaii, 1967. Mem. Am., Hawaii bar assns. Home: 3757 Round Top Dr Honolulu HI 96822 Office: Box 656 Honolulu HI 96809 Tel (808) 524-5112

CASE, RICHARD WERBER, b. Washington, Mar. 21, 1918; A.B., U. Md., 1939, LL.B., 1942. Admitted to Md. bar, 1942; practiced in Balt., 1942—, asso. firm Marshall, Carey & Doub, 1942-46, partner firms Semmes, Bowen & Semmes, 1946-55, Smith Somerville & Case, 1955—; asst. atty. gen. State of Md., 1946-49. Trustee Peabody Inst. of City of Balt., 1953—, vice chmn., 1971—; trustee Md. Sch. for Blind, Balt., 1956—, Balt. Museum of Art, 1971—, Johns Hopkins U., 1975—; chmn. task force on financing community health services and facilities Nat. Commn. on Community Health Services, 1964-67. Fellow Am., Md. bar founds.; mem. Md. State, Balt. City, Am. bar assns., Am. Law Inst. Contbr. articles to profl. jours. Home: 15600 Chilcoat Rd Sparks MD 21152 Office: 6th Floor 100 Light St Baltimore MD 21202 Tel (301) 727-1164

CASEY, ARTHUR FREDERIC, b. Albany, N.Y., Aug. 7, 1930; B.S. in Psychology, Union Coll., 1952; grad. G.E. Fin. Mgmt. Training Program, 1957; J.D., Albany Law Sch., 1969. Admitted to N.Y. bar, 1969, U.S. Dist. Ct. bar, 1969, U.S. Tax Ct. bar, 1970; fin. analyst Gen. Electric Co., Schenectady, and Hendersonville, N.C., 1954-66; asso. firm Wemple & Daly, Schenectady, 1969-71; partner firm Wemple, Daly, Casey & Hayes and predecessors, Schenectady, 1971—. Mem. Am., New York State, Schenectady County bar assns. Prize winner, estate planning competition, Albany Law Sch., 1969; contbg. editor: How to Live (and die) with N.Y. Probate, 1975. Office: 508 Union St Schenectady NY 12305 Tel (518) 374-9125

CASEY, DAVID STODDER, b. St. Louis, Sept. 18, 1915; LL.B., St. Louis U., 1937. Admitted to Mo. bar, 1937, Calif. bar, 1947; individual practice law, San Diego, 1947—. Fellow Internat. Acad. Trial Lawyers; mem. Calif. Bar Assn. (pres. 1975-76), State Bar Calif. (gov. 1974-76), Am. Bd. Trial Advs. (diplomate). Home: 1550 El Paso Reul La Jolla CA 92101 Office: 110 Laurel St San Diego CA 92101 Tel (714) 238-1811

CASEY, EDWARD M., b. 1923; A.B., Harvard U., 1943; LL.B., Boston U., 1949. Admitted to Mass. bar, 1949; now mem. firm Bingham, Dana & Gould, Boston. Mem. Am., Boston (pres. 1976-77) bar assns. Office: 35th Floor 100 Federal St Boston MA 02110 Tel (617) 357-9300*

CASEY, FRANCIS LAWTON, JR., b. Ithaca, N.Y., Feb. 2, 1927; B.S., Georgetown U., 1950, J.D., 1952. Admitted to D.C. Bar, 1953, U.S. Supreme Ct. bar, 1968; clk. firm Hogan & Hartson, Washington, 1951-53, asso., 1953-64, partner, 1964—; gen. counsel The Georgetown Shop, 1963-74; mem. com. on grievances U.S. Ct. for the D.C., 1972—; chmn. counsel, dir. Pro Found.; dir. Sursum Corda, Inc. Bd. trustees Gonzaga Coll. High Sch., Washington, 1971—, vice chmn., 1974—; presidential counsellors Georgetown U.; mem. presidents council Trinity Coll.; Mem. Am., D.C. (chmn. judicial appointment com. 1976—) bar assns., Internat. Assn. Ins. Counsel, Am. Coll. Trial Lawyers, Am. Judicature Soc., D.C. Defense Lawyers Assn., Phi Delta Phi. Recipient John Carroll Medal of Merit, 1974. Home: 5910 Cedar Pkwy Chevy Chase MD 20015 Office: Suite 600 815 Connecticut Ave NW Washington DC 20006 Tel (202) 331-4563

CASEY, FREDERICK JOSEPH, b. Brainerd, Minn., Apr. 20, 1942; B.A., Concordia Coll., Moorhead, Minn., 1964; J.D., U. Minn., 1967. Admitted to Minn. bar, 1967; asso. firm Erickson & Casey, Brainerd, Minn., 1967—; asst. atty. Crow Wing County (Minn.), 1967-74. Mem. Am., Minn. State, Crow Wing County, Aitkin County bar assns., Brainerd Area C. of C. (dir. 1974-76, pres. 1976). Home: 2104 Graydon Ave Brainerd MN 56401 Office: 319 S 6th St Brainerd MN 56401 Tel (218) 829-9226

CASEY, JAMES DAVID, b. Brookline, Mass., May 10, 1917; A.B., Boston Coll., 1934; LL.B., Harvard, 1941. Admitted to Mass. bar, 1942, Calif. bar, 1949, Ct. Mil. Appeals; spl. agt. FBI, 1941-44; individual practice law, Boston, 1949—; with O.P.A., 1946-48. Mem. Boston Bar Assn. (asso.), Am., Mass. bar assns., Am. Coll. Trial Lawyers. Home: 32 Squantam St Milton MA 02186 Office: 378 Stuart St Boston MA 02117 Tel (617) 357-9500

CASEY, JOSEPH EDWARD, b. Clinton, Mass., Dec. 27, 1898; LL.B., Boston U., 1920. Admitted to Mass. bar, 1920, U.S. Supreme Ct. bar, 1944, D.C. bar, 1945; individual practice law, Washington. Town moderator, Clinton, Mass., 1921-31, sch. committeeman, 1926-34; U.S. Congressman, 1934-42. Mem. Mass., Am., Worcester County (Mass.) bar assns., Am. Trial Lawyers Assn. Home: 4763 Indian Ln Washington DC 20016 Office: 1200 18th St NW Washington DC 20036 Tel (202) 223-5750

CASEY, JOSEPH JAMES, b. Albany, N.Y., July 18, 1904; LL.B., Union U., 1925. Admitted to N.Y. bar, 1926, U.S. Dist. Ct. No. Dist. N.Y. bar, 1962; practiced in Albany, 1927—; partner firm Thacher & Casey, 1940-45, Thacher, Casey & Honikel, 1945-49, Casey, Honikel & Wisely, 1949-60, Dugan Casey, Burke & Lyons, 1960-69, Casey, Yanas and Mitchell, 1969—; asst. dist. atty. Albany County (N.Y.), 1932-35; corp. counsel City of Albany, 1935-40; counsel Albany Port Dist. Commn., 1940-43. Mem. Am., N.Y. State, Albany County bar assns. Home: 225 Euclid Ave Albany NY 12208 Office: 100 State St Albany NY 12207 Tel (518) 463-3267

CASEY, LOIS PATRICIA, b. Topeka, Apr. 29, 1943; B.A., Washburn U., 1965, B.M., 1965, J.D., 1970. Admitted to Kans. bar, 1971; atty. Kans. Labor Dept., Topeka, 1971—; individual practice law, Topeka, 1972—. Trustee 1st Methodist Ch., Topeka, 1974—. Mem. Am., Kans. bar assns., Tau Delta Pi, Kappa Alpha Phi, Mu Alpha Pi. Office: 500 Topeka Ave Topeka KS 66603 Tel (913) 357-5281

CASEY, RALPH EDWARD, b. Boston, May 25, 1911; A.B., Harvard, 1932, LL.B., 1935; LL.M., Georgetown U., 1941. Admitted to Mass. bar, 1935, D.C. bar, 1972; individual practice law, Boston, 1935-39; with GAO, Washington, 1939-55, asso. gen. counsel, 1948-55; chief counsel Mcht. Marine and Fisheries Com., 1955-56; pres. Am. Mcht. Marine Inst., Inc., 1956-68; chmn. bd. Gray Mfg. Co., 1958-62; exec. v.p. Am. Inst. Mcht. Shipping, 1969-70; spl. counsel Mcht. Marine and Fisheries Com., 1970-71, chief counsel, 1971-72; partner firm Haight, Garner, Poor & Havens, Washington, 1972—; counsel Hardy Commn. on U.S. Govt. Ops., 1950-52; v.p. Internat. Shipping Fedn., London, 1965-68; vice chmn. bd., chmn. exec. com. Nat. Com. Internat. Trade Documentation, 1967-70. Mem. Fed. Bar Assn. Home: Box 331 Mobile AL 36564 Office: 1819 H St NW Washington DC 20006 Tel (202) 737-7847

CASH, WILBUR FRANKLIN, b. Reberie, Tenn., Sept. 24, 1917; B.S., Memphis State Coll., 1938; J.D., Vanderbilt U., 1949. Admitted to Tenn. bar, 1948; individual practice law, Covington, Tenn., 1948—; city atty. Covington, 1963—, city judge, 1965-75, atty. Covington Regional Planning Commission 1963—. Pres. Covington Lions Club, chmn. Boy Scouts Troup Com., chmn. bd. 1st United Methodist Church 1968-69. Mem. Am. Bar Assn. Home: 1515 Walters Covington TN 38019 Office: 105 Abernathy Bldg Covington TN 38019 Tel (901) 476-9530

CASHDAN, DAVID ROBERT, b. Detroit, Oct. 13, 1939; B.A. in Govt., Oberlin Coll., 1961; LL.M., U. Mich., 1964. Admitted to D.C. bar, 1967, U.S. Supreme Ct. bar, 1970; atty. office gen. counsel FPC, Washington, 1964-65; chief dist. ct. sect., office gen. counsel Equal Employment Opportunity Commn., Washington, 1965-71; partner firm Roisman, Kessler & Cashdan, Washington, 1971—; adj. prof. law U. Denver, 1972-75. Mem. Am. Bar Assn. (liaison com. with Equal Employment Opportunity Commn.), D.C. Bar (steering com.). Named Outstanding Younger Atty., Fed. Bar Assn., 1969. Office: 1025 15th St NW Washington DC 20005 Tel (202) 833-9070

CASHEN, HENRY CHRISTOPHER, II, b. Detroit, June 25, 1939; A.B. in Classics with honors, Brown U., 1961; LL.B., U. Mich., 1963. Admitted to Mich. bar, 1964, D.C. bar, 1973, U.S. Supreme Ct. bar, 1969; asso. firm Dickinson, Wright, McKean and Cudlip, Detroit, 1964-69; dep. asst. to Pres., Washington, 1969-73; mem. firm Dickstein, Shapiro and Morin and predecessor, Washington, 1973—. Mem. Barristers Soc., Psi Upsilon, Phi Delta Phi. Home: 3037 O St NW Washington DC 20006 Office: 2101 L St NW Washington DC 20037 Tel (202) 785-9700

CASHILL, WILLIAM PATTERSON, b. Reno, Aug. 22, 1944; B.A., U. Notre Dame, 1966; J.D., U. Colo., 1969. Admitted to Nev., Colo. bars, 1969; asso. firm Laxalt, Berry & Allison, Carson City, Nev., 1969; asst. U.S. atty. Dist. Nev., U.S. Dept. Justice, Las Vegas, 1970-71; spl. atty. St. Louis Strike Force, 1971-73; asso. firm Laxalt, Berry & Allison, Carson City, 1973-76; individual practice law, Reno, 1976—; instr. bus. law U. Nev. Mem. State Bar Nev., Washoe County, Colo. bar assns. Home: 1300 Feather Way Reno NV 89501 Office: 241 Ridge St Reno NV 89501

CASHIN, HARRY LEO, JR., b. Augusta, Ga., July 16, 1933; B.B.A., U. Ga., 1955, LL.B., 1959. Admitted to Ga. bar, 1960; individual practice law, Atlanta, 1960; asso. firm Huie, Ethridge & Harland, Atlanta, 1960-64, partner, 1964-67; partner firm Harland, Cashin, Chambers, Davis & Doster and predecessor, Atlanta, 1967—. Chmn. fin. com. Ch. of the Holy Spirit; pres. Roxbory Valley Civic Assn.; v.p., sec. Hibernian Soc. Atlanta; trustee Elaine Clark Center for Exceptional Children; active Archdiocese of Atlanta Property Commn. Mem. Am., Ga., Atlanta (exec. com. 1970—, pres. 1975—) bar assns., Lawyers Club Atlanta (pres. 1971-72, chmn. exec. com. 1972-73), Old War Horse Lawyers Club Atlanta, Atlanta Lawyers Found. (chmn. bd. trustees 1975—), Am., Ga. (v.p. 1972—, chmn. ann. seminar 1971, 74, 76) trial lawyers assns., Pi Kappa Alpha. Home: 4730 Paran Valley NW Atlanta GA 30327 Office: 1045 Hurt Bldg Atlanta GA 30303 Tel (404) 522-7360

CASKEY, WAYNE F., b. Washington, Apr. 8, 1937; B.A. in Econs. cum laude, Harvard U., 1958; LL.B., Yale U., 1961. Admitted to Mo. bar, 1962; asso. firms Barker, Fallon, Jones & Parker, Kansas City, Mo., 1961-63, Smith, Schwegler, Swartzman & Winter, Kansas City, 1963-68; mgr. labor relations Interstate Brands Corp., Kansas City, Mo., 1968-73, dir. indsl. relations, 1973-76, chief adminstrv. officer, v.p., corp. sec., 1976—. Mem. Mo. Democratic Com., 1970-72; trustee Bapt. Meml. Hosp., 1971—; chmn. personnel appeals bd. City of Kansas City, 1975—. Mem. Mo., Am. bar assns. Tel (816) 561-6600

CASLIN, JOHN J., JR., b. N.Y.C., Oct. 22, 1939; B.A., Fordham U., 1961, LL.B., 1965. Admitted to N.Y. State bar, 1965; asso. firm Chadbourne O'Neil & Thomson, N.Y.C., 1965-68; mem. firm Kane, Dalsimer, Kan, Sullivan & Kurucz, N.Y.C., 1968-76; trademark counsel GAF Corp., Wayne, N.J., 1976—. Mem. Am. Bar Assn., Am. Soc. Internat. Law, Am., N.Y. patent law assns. Office: GAF Corp 1361 Alps Rd Wayne NJ 07470 Tel (201) 628-3538

CASNER, A(NDREW) JAMES, b. Chgo., Feb. 7, 1907; A.B., U. Ill., 1930, LL.B., 1929; J.S.D., Columbia, 1941; A.M. (hon.), Harvard, 1942, LL.D. (hon.), 1969; S.J.D. (hon.), Suffolk U., 1970. Admitted to Ill. bar, 1929, Md. bar, 1934, Mass. bar, 1940, U.S. Supreme Ct. bar, 1937; instr. law U. Ill., 1929-30, prof., 1936-38; prof. law U. Md., 1930-35; prof. law Harvard, Cambridge, Mass., 1938—, asso. dean Law Sch., 1961-67, acting dean, 1967-68; mem. firm Ropes, Gray, Best, Coolidge & Rugg, Boston, 1945-58; dir. Old Colony Trust Co., 1947-70; mem. trust bd. First Nat. Bank of Boston, 1970; chmn. editorial bd. Little Brown & Co. Mem. Am., Mass., Boston bar assns., Am. Law Inst. (chief reporter for Restatement of Property), Practicing Law Inst. (trustee), Assn. Am. Law Schs. (com. and sect. chmn. 1973-74), Order of Coif, Sigma Chi, Phi Delta Phi, Delta Sigma Rho. Recipient Ann. research award Am. Bar Found., 1971, Harrison Tweed award Assn. Continuing Legal Edn. Adminstrs., 1972; author: Estate Planning, 2 vols. with ann. supplement, 1961; (with W.B. Leach) Cases and Text on Property, 1969 with supplement, 1976; editor-in-chief American Law of Property, 8 vols. treatise, 1952 with supplement, 1976. Home: 19 Chauncy St Cambridge MA 02138 Office: Harvard Law Sch Langdell W 323 Cambridge MA 02138 Tel (617) 491-3252

CASO, RALPH GEORGE, b. Manhattan, N.Y., Nov. 26, 1917; student St. Lawrence U., 1935-36, Hofstra U., 1936-37; B.S., N.Y. U., 1939, J.D., 1948. Admitted to N.Y. bar, 1949; individual practice law, N.Y., 1948-65; councilman Town of Hempstead (N.Y.), 1953-61, supr., 1961-65, presiding supr., 1965-70; Nassau County Exec., Mineola, N.Y., 1971—; chmn. Met. Regional Council, 1973. Hon. chmn. bd. United Cerebral Palsy Assn.; hon. mem. bd. dirs. Assn. for Help of Retarded Children; mem. Merrick Republican Club. Mem. Nassau County Bar Assn., Nassau Lawyers Assn., Nat. Assn. Counties (chmn. welfare steering com. 1973-74, pub. transp. com. 1975-76), N.Y. State County Execs. Assn. (pres. 1972-74), Sons of Italy, Am. Legion, K.C. Recipient Torch of Liberty award B'nai B'rith Anti-Defamation League; Man of Year award Assn. for Help of Retarded Children; Americanism award N.Y. State VFW; citation for meritorious service Pres's. Com. on Employment of Handicapped. Home: 2045 Baldwin Ct Merrick NY 11566 Office: 1 West St Mineola NY 11501 Tel (516) 535-3131

CASON, GEORGE MARSHALL, JR., b. Eagle Lake, Tex., Aug. 3, 1933; B.S., Tex. A. and M. U., 1955, M.S., 1961; J.D., South Tex. Coll. Law, 1965. Admitted to Tex. bar, 1965; individual practice law, League City, Tex., 1965—; gen. counsel Nat. Assn. Conservation Dists., Washington, 1974—; city atty. City of Kemah (Tex.), 1974—; dir. 1st Nat. Bank of League City. Mem. Galveston County (Tex.) Planning Commn., 1976—. Mem. Galveston County (v.p. 1976—), Mainland, Tex. Aggie (charter), Am. bar assns., Order of Lytae, Phi Alpha Delta. Office: 1424 E Main St League City TX 77573 Tel (713) 332-2444

CASPER, EDGAR RONALD, b. Berlin, Germany, Sept. 1, 1927; LL.B., U. London, 1947, LL.M., 1948; LL.M., Harvard, 1954. Admitted to Pa. Supreme Ct. bar, 1961, U.S. Supreme Ct. bar, 1965, U.S. Ct. Appeals 3d Circuit bar, 1975; asso. Sidney G. Handler, Harrisburg, Pa., 1958-61; dep. atty. gen. Commonwealth of Pa., 1961-72; chief counsel Pa. Dept. Community Affairs, 1972-73; partner firm Krank, Gross, & Casper, Harrisburg and Lancaster, Pa., 1973—; cons. Pa. Developmental Disabilities Council, Harrisburg, 1973-76. Mem. Dauphin County Bar Assn. Contbr. articles in field to profl. jours. Home: 19 Center Dr Camp Hill PA 17011 Office: Suite H 1801 N Front St Harrisburg PA 17102 Tel (717) 234-4931

CASS, MYRON C., b. Havana, Cuba, June 3, 1922; B.S., U. Ill., 1946; J.D., DePaul U., 1949. Admitted to Ill. bar, 1949, U.S. Patent and Trademark Office bar, 1953; individual practice law, Chgo., 1949; partner firm Silverman & Cass, and predecessors, Chgo., 1956—. Mem. Ill., Chgo., Am. bar assns., Am., Chgo. patent law assns., Inter-Am. Arbitration Assn., Internat. Assn. Jewish Lawyers and Jurists. Home: 3933 Estes St Lincolnwood IL 60645 Office: 105 W Adams St Chicago IL 60603 Tel (312) 726-6006

CASS, WILLARD WARN, JR., b. Jamestown, N.Y., Nov. 3, 1930; B.S., Mich. State U., 1952; LL.B., Albany Law Sch., 1957, J.D., 1968. Admitted to N.Y. bar, 1957, U.S. Supreme Ct. bar, 1963; individual practice law, Jamestown, 1957-71; judge Surrogate Ct., Mayville, N.Y., 1972—; estate tax atty. N.Y. State, 1959-71; justice of the peace Town of Carroll (N.Y.), 1960-71. Mem. Am., N.Y. State, Jamestown bar assns., N.Y. State Surrogates' Assn., Am. Coll. Probate Judges. Home: 72 Pearl St Frewsburg NY 14738 Office: County Office Bldg Mayville NY 14757 Tel (716) 753-4337

CASSADY, RALPH, b. Mpls., Sept. 10, 1932; A.B., Stanford, 1955; LL.B., U. Calif., Los Angeles, 1961. Admitted to Calif. bar, 1962; asso. firm Hahn Cazier Hoegh & Leff and predecessors, Los Angeles, 1962-68, partner, 1969—. Mem. Los Angeles County Bar Assn., Bus. Trial Lawyers Assn., U. Calif., Los Angeles Law Sch., Stanford U. alumni assns. Co-author monograph. Office: 611 W Sixth St Los Angeles CA 90017 Tel (213) 485-9001

CASSAVECHIA, GARY, b. Norwalk, Conn., Feb. 24, 1946; B.A., Duquesne U., Pitts., 1968, J.D., 1971. Admitted to N.H. bar, 1971; asso. firm Michael & Wallace, Rochester, N.H., 1971-75; partner firm Mullaney, Richardson & Cassavechia, Rochester, 1975-77; individual practice law, Rochester, 1977—. Dir. Greater Rochester Red Cross, 1971—, Dollars for Scholars, Rochester, 1974—; adv. bd. Rochester Alternative Sch., 1976—. Mem. Am., N.H., Strafford County bar assns. Home: 106 Old Dover Rd Rochester NH 03867 Office: 3 Wakefield St Rochester NH 03867 Tel (603) 332-8216

CASSCELLS, KERMIT JOSHUA, b. Charlottesville, Va., Mar. 20, 1920; LL.B., St. John's U., 1946. Admitted to N.Y. bar, 1946, U.S. Supreme Ct. bar, 1975; asst. dist. atty. Richmond County (N.Y.), 1952-55; dep. pres. Borough of S.I. (N.Y.), 1966-73; arbitrator Civil Ct. City of N.Y., 1976—. Chmn. bd. Salvation Army, S.I., 1964-74; bd. dirs. S.I. Council Boy Scouts Am. Mem. N.Y., Richmond County bar assns. Home: 218 Hart Blvd Staten Island NY 10301 Office: 350 Saint Marks Pl Staten Island NY 10301 Tel (212) 981-3030

CASSEB, PAUL ERNEST, b. San Antonio, May 14, 1919; B.A., St. Mary's U., San Antonio, 1941, LL.B., 1941, J.D., 1970. Admitted to Tex. bar, 1941; individual practice law, San Antonio and Mexico City, 1941—; prof. constl. law, adminstrv. law and bus. orgn. law St. Mary's U., 1947-57; mem. Terrell Hills (Tex.) City Council and mayor pro tempore City of Terrell Hills, 1961-65. Mem. San Antonio, Am. bar assns., Tex. State Bar, Am. Judicature Soc. Named Distinguished Law Alumnus St. Mary's U. Sch. Law, 1976. Home: 651 Terrell Rd San Antonio TX 78209 Office: suite 1400 Frost Bank Tower San Antonio TX 78205 Tel (512) 223-9443

CASSEL, LEO JOSEPH, b. Lindenwood, Ill., Oct. 7, 1918; A.B., Creighton U., 1942; J.D., U. Mich., 1949. Admitted to Mich., Iowa bar, 1949; gen. partner firm McMahon & Cassel, Algona, Iowa. Mem. Algona C. of C., Am., Iowa, Kossuth County (pres.) bar assns., Assn. Trial Lawyers. Home: 621 E Call St Algona IA 50511 Office: 120 N Thorington St Algona IA 50511 Tel (515) 295-3532

CASSELL, MARTIN LEROY, b. Evanston, Ill., May 30, 1944; B.A., Wabash Coll., 1966; J.D., U. Ill., 1969. Admitted to Ill. bar, 1970; asso. firm Goldsmith, Dyer, Thelin, Schiller and Dickson, Aurora, Ill., 1970—. Mem., legal counsel Aurora Festival Assn., 1975—; bd. dirs. Shoestring Gallery. Mem. Kane County, Ill. bar assns. Home: 601 Redwood St Aurora IL 60506 Office: 104 E Downer Pl Aurora IL 60504

CASSELL, MARTIN LEROY, JR., b. Vincennes, Ind., Oct. 3, 1910; A.B., U. Ill., 1933, LL.B., 1935. Admitted to Ill. bar, 1935; asso. firm Hamilton, Black & Klatt, Peoria, Ill., 1935-40; asst. gen. atty. Chgo., RocIsland and Pacific R.R. Co., Chgo., 1940-44, gen. atty., 1944-57, gen. solicitor, 1957-74, gen. counsel, 1974—. Pres., High Sch. Bd.

Edn., Barrington, Ill., 1958-62; exec. com. Tri-County Div. Ill. Assn. Sch. Bds., 1960, chmn., 1961-63; dir. Ill. Sch. Bd. Assn., pres., 1965-67; v.p., dir. Contemporary Concerts, Inc., Chgo.; pres. Barrington Hills Planning Commn., 1974—. Mem. Am., Ill., Chgo. bar assns., ICC Practitioners Assn. (pres. 1962-63), Western R.R. Club, Union League Club, Chgo. Traffic Club. Recipient Silver Freight Car award R.R. Progress Inst., 1961. Home: Rural Route 2 Box 331 Sutton Rd Barrington IL 60010 Office: Room 1025 La Salle St Station 139 W Van Buren St Chicago IL 60605 Tel (312) 435-7426

CASSELMAN, JAMES KIRK, b. Kansas City, Mo., Dec. 24, 1945; B.A., Yale, 1968; J.D., Columbia, 1971. Admitted to Pa. bar, 1971; asso. firm Morgan, Lewis & Bockius, Phila., 1971—. Mem. Am., Pa., Phila. bar assns. Home: PO Box 453 Chester Springs PA 19425 Office: 123 S Broad St Philadelphia PA 19109 Tel (215) 491-9435

CASSITY, DONN EDWARD, b. Tooele, Utah, May 31, 1926; B.A., George Washington U., 1950, J.D., 1953. Admitted to Utah bar, 1953; asso. firm Romney, Nelson & Cassity, Salt Lake City, 1953-71, partner firm, 1972—; asst. atty. gen. State of Utah, 1954-56; atty. CSC, Salt Lake City, 1956-59; judge pro tem Salt Lake City, 1958. Chmn. bd. govs. Salt Lake Repertory Orch.; bd. dirs., mem. exec. com. Days of '47, Inc. Mem. U.S. Supreme Ct., Am., Utah, Salt Lake County bar assns., Am. Trial Lawyers Assn., Phi Delta Phi. Editor in Chief Americus Curiae, George Washington U., 1951-53. Home: 1448 Devonshire Dr Salt Lake City UT 84108 Office: 136 S Main St Salt Lake City UT 84101 Tel (801) 328-3261

CASSON, RICHARD FREDERICK, b. Boston, Apr. 11, 1939; A.B., Colby Coll., Waterville, Maine, 1960; J.D., U. Chgo., 1963. Admitted to Ill. bar, 1963, Mass. bar, 1964; with U.S. Army JAGC 1964-67, chief of mil. justice 1st Air Cavalry div., 1965-66; partner firm Casson & Casson, Boston, 1967-68; asst. gen. counsel, sec. Bankers Leasing Corp. and Subs., Boston, 1968-76; asso. gen. counsel, asst. sec. PruLease, Inc., Boston, 1976—, PruLease Mgmt., Inc., Boston, 1976—. Bd. dirs. Children's Speech and Hearing Found., Boston, 1968—. Home: 182 Beacon St Boston MA 02116 Office: 1255 Boylston St Boston MA 02215 Tel (617) 266-4950

CASTAGNA, JOHN ANTHONY, b. New Haven, Nov. 13, 1916; LL.B., U. Balt., 1941. Admitted to Md. bar, 1941, D.C. bar, 1950; asso. firm Watson E. Sherwood, Balt. 1942; counsel Md. Office of Price Adminstrn., Balt., 1946-48; town atty. Capitol Heights (Md.), 1966—; individual practice law, Glenn Dale, Md., 1948—; legal officer, Ft. Myer, Va., 1949-50, internat. prosecution staff, Tokyo, 1945, 46. Office: POB 302 Glenn Dale MD 20769 Tel (301) 390-6766

CASTELLANI, ROBERT JOSEPH, b. Syracuse, N.Y., July 4, 1941; B.A., Hobart Coll., 1963; J.D., Emory U., 1966. Admitted to Ga. bar, 1965, Fla. bar, 1970, U.S. Supreme Ct. bar, 1969; asso. firm Lipshutz, Zusmann & Sikes, Atlanta, 1966-67; asst. atty. gen. State of Ga., Atlanta, 1967-73; partner firm Brent, Castellani & Palmer, Atlanta, 1973—; mem. steering com. Ga. Juvenile Justice Masterplan, 1975-76; gen. counsel Nat. Govs.'s Conf. Task Force on Medicaid Reform, 1976—; gen. counsel Ga. Pub. Service Commn., 1972—. Coach YMCA Youth Soccer League, Atlanta, 1975—; trustee, treas. Paideia Sch., Atlanta, 1974—. Mem. Am., Ga. (chmn. adminstrv. law sect. 1975-76), Fla., Atlanta, Decatur-Dekalb bar assns., Mensa, Am. Judicature Soc., Ga. Soccer Assn. Home: 832 Springdale Rd NE Atlanta GA 30306 Office: 808 Candler Bldg Atlanta GA 30303 Tel (404) 681-3770

CASTELLO, LUIGI JOSEPH, b. Candida, Italy, Nov. 7, 1913; B.A., U. N.H., 1935; LL.B., Boston U., 1938. Admitted to N.H. bar, 1938; practiced in Woodsville, N.H., 1938—; justice Municipal Ct., Haverhill, N.H., 1951—, N.H. Dist. Ct., Dist. of Haverhill, 1964—. Home: RFD 2 Woodsville NH 03785 Office: 37 Court St Woodsville NH 03785 Tel (603) 747-3394

CASTELLUCCIO, PATRICK ERNEST, b. Greenvale, N.Y., June 6, 1928; B.A., St. John's Coll., 1950, J.D., 1952. Admitted to N.Y. State bar, 1952; chief law asst. Surrogate's Ct. Nassau County, Mineola, N.Y., 1966—. Mem. Nassau County Bar Assn. (vice chmn. com. on estates and trusts), N.Y. State Bar Assn., Delta Theta Phi. Contbr. articles to legal jours. Home: 217 Roslyn Rd Roslyn Heights NY 11527 Office: 262 Old Country Rd Mineola NY 11501 Tel (516) 535-2042

CASTERLINE, CECIL W., b. Rockport, Tex., Dec. 31, 1938; B.A. in English, Baylor U., 1961, LL.B., 1966. Admitted to Tex. Supreme Ct. bar, 1967, U.S. Ct. Appeals 5th Circuit bar, 1974, U.S. Supreme Ct. bar, 1977; asso. firm Kleberg, Mobley, Lockett & Weil, Corpus Christi, Tex., 1967-69; partner firm Lee, Douglass, Dletcher & Casterline, Dallas, 1969-75; partner firm Shank, Irwin, Conant, Williamson & Grevelle, Dallas, 1975—. Pres. Baylor Bear Club, named outstanding mem. Dallas chpt., 1974-75. Mem. Trial Lawyers of Am., Tex. Assn. Dept. Counsel, Tex., Am. bar assns., Tex. Assn. Defense Counsel. Editor in chief: Baylor Law Review; Recipient Am. Jurisprudence award. Contbr. articles in field to profl. jours. Home: 7223 Holyoke Dallas TX 75248 Office: 1st National Bank Bldg Dallas TX 75202 Tel (214) 748-9696

CASTLEBERRY, JAMES NEWTON, JR., b. Chatom, Ala., Dec. 28, 1921; J.D. magna cum laude, St. Mary's U., 1952. Admitted to Tex. bar, 1952; asst. atty. gen. State of Tex., 1953-55; asso. dean, prof. law St. Mary's U., 1955—. Mem. Am., Tex. bar assns., Phi Delta Phi (internat. v.p. 1975-77). Co-author: Waters & Water Rights, 1970; contbr. articles to law jours. Home: 7727 Woodridge San Antonio TX 78209 Office: 1 Camino Santa Maria San Antonio TX 78284 Tel (512) 436-3424

CASTLES, JOHN WESLEY, III, b. N.Y.C., June 13, 1921; B.A., Yale, 1943; LL.B., Columbia, 1948. Admitted to N.Y. bar, 1949, U.S. Supreme Ct. bar, 1969; asso. firm Lord, Day & Lord, N.Y.C., 1949-54, partner firm, 1954—. Pres., Rec. for Blind, 1969-76, bd. dirs., 1965—; mem. bd. tax review, Darien, Conn., 1958-60; chmn. Darien United Fund, 1962-63. Mem. Assn. Bar N.Y.C. (chmn. admissions com., 1964-65, exec. com. 1966-69, grievance com. 1975—), N.Y. State, Am. bar assns., Maritime Law Assn. (chmn. com. on revision Supreme Ct. Admiralty Rules 1961-64), Am., N.Y. State bar founds., Am. Judicature Soc., Am. Coll. Trial Lawyers, Am. Law Inst., Fgn. Policy Assn. (dir. 1967-76). Contbr. articles to legal jours. Home: 468 Oenoke Rd New Canaan CT 06840 Office: 25 Broadway New York City NY 10004 Tel (212) 344-8480

CASTNER, LYNN S., b. Mpls., Apr. 11, 1934; B.A., U. Minn., 1960, J.D., 1963. Admitted to Minn. bar, 1963, U.S. Supreme Ct. bar, 1967; individual practice law, Mpls., 1963-64, 70—; exec. dir., legal counsel Minn. Civil Liberties Union, 1964-70, pres., 1974—, also bd. dirs.; bd. dirs. ACLU, 1974—; instr. Wm. Mitchell Coll. Law, 1976—; asst. dir. Minn. Gov.'s Human Rights Commn., 1963; research dir. St. Paul Fair Employment Practices Commn., 1961-62; mem. Minn. Gov.'s Commn. on Law Enforcement and Adminstrn. Justice, 1964-65. Mem. Minn. State, Hennepin County bar assns. Author: Police Review Boards, 1965; Adminstration of Justice and the American Indian, 1967. Home: 5537 E Bavarian Pass Fridley MN Office: 812 Midland Bank Bldg Minneapolis MN 55401 Tel (612) 339-0080

CASTO, DON MONROE, III, b. Cin., Jan. 28, 1945; B.A., Stanford U., 1966, J.D., 1969; LL.M., George Washington U., 1970. Admitted to Calif. bar, 1970, Ohio bar, 1972; counsel, dir. leasing Don M. Casto Orgn., Columbus, 1972—; dir. Huntington Nat. Bank. Mem. Am., Columbus, San Francisco bar assns., Urban Land Inst., Internat. Council Shopping Centers. Contbr. articles to legal jours. Office: 42 S 4th St Columbus OH 43215 Tel (614) 228-5331

CATALINOTTO, MICHAEL ELIO, b. N.Y.C., Sept. 29, 1933; B.S. in Accounting, N.Y. U., 1955; LL.D., Columbia, 1961. Admitted to N.Y. State bar, 1961; asso. firm Maynard, O'Connor & Smith, Albany, 1961-67, partner, 1967—; acting police justice Village of Saugerties (N.Y.), 1963-67, town justice, 1968-75, town atty., 1976—. Mem. Ulster County Republican Com., 1966-69; chmn. Saugerties (N.Y.) Rep. Com., 1975—. Mem. Am., N.Y. State, Albany County, Ulster County bar assns., Am. Judicature Soc., N.Y. State Assn. Magistrates. Home: 4559 Rt 9 W Saugerties NY 12477 Office: 90 State St Albany NY 12207 Tel (518) 465-3553

CATANIA, MATTHEW JOSEPH, b. Passaic, N.J., Feb. 17, 1948; B.A., Fairleigh Dickinson U., 1970; J.D., Rutgers U., 1973. Admitted to N.J. bar, U.S. Dist. Ct. N.J. bar, 1974; law sec. Essex County Ct., 1973-74; asst. dep. pub. defender N.J. Dept. Pub. Advocate, Office Public Defender, Hackensack, N.J., 1974—. Mem. Bergen County Adv. Bd. on Youth, 1976-77. Mem. Am., N.J., Bergen County bar assns., Assn. Trial Lawyers Am., Phi Alpha Theta, Phi Omega Epsilon. Bd. editors Rutgers Law Record, 1972-73. Office: 47 Essex St Hackensack NJ 07602 Tel (201) 489-3107

CATCHINGS, PATRICIA ANN, b. Jackson, Miss., Apr. 4, 1949; B.A., Jackson State Coll., 1970; J.D., Tex. So. U., 1972. Admitted to Miss. bar, 1973; asso. firm Tucker & Smith, Jackson, 1974; mem. firm Tucker & Catchings, Jackson, 1974—. Mem. Am., Miss., Hinds County, Magnolia bar assns., Nat. Conf. Black Lawyers. Recipient Am. Jurisprudence award in Negotiable Instruments, 1972. Home: 1244 Aberdeen St Jackson MS 39209 Office: PO Box 2169 Jackson MS 39205 Tel (601) 353-6293

CATE, BYRON LEE, b. Norman, Okla., Jan. 18, 1942; J.D., U. Okla., 1972. Admitted to Okla. bar, 1972; mem. Okla. Ho. of Reps., 1966-73; partner firm Lucas and Cate, Norman, 1972—; mem. Okla. Senate, 1973—. Mem. Okla., Cleveland County bar assns., Okla. Trial Lawyers Assn., Norman C. of C. (past dir.). Home: 2712 Aspen Circle Norman OK 73069 Office: 231 S Peters St Norman OK 73069 Tel (405) 329-5731

CATE, JEROME JOSEPH, b. Baker, Mont., Sept. 19, 1939; B.A. in Bus. Adminstrn. and Econs., Carroll Coll., 1961; postgrad. in law Georgetown U., 1961-63; LL.B., U. Mont., 1966, J.D., 1966; admitted to Mont. bar, 1966, U.S. 9th Circuit Ct. Appeals bar, 1967, U.S. Supreme Ct. bar, 1967; partner firms Sandall, Moses & Cayan, Billings, Mont., 1966-71, Cate, Lynaugh, Fitzgerald & Huss, Billings, 1971—; chmn. legis. com. Mont. Criminal Justice Project. Del. Mont. Constl. Conv., 1971-72; mem. Billings Local Govt. Rev. Commn., 1975—. Mem. Am., Mont. bar assns., Am. Trial Lawyers Assn., Am. Judicature Soc., Yellowstone Ct. Barristers (pres. 1973-74). Home: 229 Clark St Billings MT 59102 Office: Suite 500 Midland Bank Bldg Billings MT 59101 Tel (406) 252-3461

CATER, RICHARD HAROLD, b. Fort Lee, Va., Dec. 28, 1945; B.S., U. N.Ala., 1967; J.D., Cumberland Sch. Law, Samford U., 1972. Admitted to Ala. bar, 1972, Fla. bar, 1972; partner firm Merrill, Merrill & Vardaman, Anniston, Ala., 1972—. Bd. dirs. Calhoun County chpt. ARC, 1976—, Children's Services of Calhoun County, 1976—. Mem. Am. (Ala. co-chmn. subcom. on comml. litigation 1976-77), Fla., Ala. (exec. com. young lawyers sect. 1976-77), Calhoun County (sec.-treas. 1974-76, pres. young lawyers sect. 1975-76, chmn. law day com. 1973-74, chmn. legal aid com. 1976-77) bar assns., Ala. Trial Lawyers Assn., Anniston C. of C. (v.p. 1976). Office: POB 1498 10th Floor Commercial National Bank Bldg Anniston AL 36202 Tel (205) 237-1601

CATLETT, GEORGE MACKLIN, b. Louisville, Aug. 6, 1924; LL.B., U. Ky., 1949, J.D., 1970. Admitted to Ky. bar, 1949; law clk. Ky. Ct. Appeals, 1949-50; asst. for code revision Ky. Civil Code Com., Frankfort, 1950-52; gen. counsel Ky. Dept. Motor Transp., Frankfort, 1952-56; individual practice law, Frankfort, 1956—. Mem. Ky., Franklin County bar assns., Motor Carrier Lawyers Assn., Assn. ICC Practitioners. Home: 100 Crittenden Rd Frankfort KY 40601 Office: 708 McClure Bldg Frankfort KY 40601 Tel (502) 227-7384

CATLETT, RICHARD H., JR., b. Boston, May 1, 1921; B.S., Va. Mil. Inst., 1943; LL.B., U. Richmond, 1952. Admitted to Va. bar, 1952; asso. firm Christian, Barton, Epps, Brent & Chappell, Richmond, 1952-57, partner, 1957-76; partner firm McGuire, Woods & Battle, Richmond, 1976—; instr. commercial law Am. Inst. Banking, Richmond, 1952-57; dir., gen. counsel James River Corp. of Va., So. Bankshares, Inc. Chmn. personnel bd. City of Richmond, 1952—; vestry St. James Episcopal Ch., Richmond. Mem. Va. State Bar (chmn. bus. law sect. 1971-72), Am., Va. (chmn. corporate law sect. 1972-73), Richmond bar assns. Tel (804) 644-4131

CATLETT, STANLEY BOULWARE, b. Sidell, Ill., June 23, 1899; student U. Chgo., 1920; LL.B., U. Okla., 1921, J.D., 1970. Admitted to Okla. bar, 1921, U.S. Supreme Ct. bar, 1945; individual practice law, Weleetka, Okla., 1922-25, Okemah, Okla., 1925-32; mem. firm Catlett & Kerr, Oklahoma City, 1934-45, Kerr, Catlett, Lambert & Conn, 1945-51; v.p., dir. Denver Producing & Refining Co., 1948-49; pres. Catlett Minerals Corp., Oklahoma City, 1967—; individual practice law, 1951—. Trustee Robert Glenn Rapp Found., 1951—. Mem. Am., Okla., Okla. County bar assns. Office: 1140 NW 63d St Oklahoma City OK 73116 Tel (405) 840-3289

CAUDILL, MICHAEL EDWARD, b. Louisville, May 24, 1948; B.A., Western Ky. U., 1970; J.D., U. Louisville, 1973. Admitted to Ky. bar, 1973; law clk. to justice Ky. Supreme Ct., 1974-75; asst. commonwealth atty. Ky. 8th Jud. Dist., 1975—. Mem. Am., Ky. bar assns., Ky. Commonwealth Attys. Assn., Ky. Hist. Soc., Jr. C. of C. Office: 416 E 10th St Bowling Green KY 42101 Tel (502) 842-4301

CAULDWELL, ROBERT WATSON, b. Trenton, N.J., July 22, 1907; A.B., Columbia, 1929; J.D., N.Y. U., 1931, LL.M., 1948. Admitted to N.Y. bar, 1932, U.S. Supreme Ct. bar, 1945; partner firm McDermott, Turner, Hart & Hart, N.Y.C., 1941-61, sr. partner, 1961—; atty. Village of E. Williston (N.Y.) Bd. Edn., 1963-71; apptd. by ct. as mem. com. on character and fitness of applicants for admission to bar for 2d, 10th and 11th jud. dists., 1952-66. Chmn. zoning bd. appeals Village of E. Williston, 1973-76.; pres. bd. trustees Berkeley Inst., Bklyn.; trustee Bklyn. Hosp., Samaritan Hosp., Bklyn., pres. 1964-66; dir. Good Will Industries, N.Y.C.; trustee Indsl. Home for Blind, Bklyn., 1973-77. Mem. Bklyn. Bar Assn. (pres. 1968-69). Home: 179 Hillside Ave Williston Park NY 11596 Office: 111 Broadway New York City NY 10006 Tel (212) 267-8260

CAUMMISAR, ROBERT LEE, b. Louisville, Mar. 5, 1939; B.A., Bellarmine Coll., 1964; J.D., U. Ky., 1967. Admitted to Ky. bar, 1967, U.S. Dist. Ct. for Eastern Dist. Ky. bar, 1968; staff atty. N.E. Ky. Legal Services, Inc., Grayson, 1967-70, exec. dir., 1972-75; exec. dir. Citizens Commn. on Consumer Protection, Frankfort, Ky., 1970-71; individual practice law, Grayson, 1975—; city atty. City of Grayson, 1975—; pub. defender Carter County (Ky.), 1975—. Vice pres. Consumers Assn. Ky.; chmn. Carter County Pub. Library Dist., 1976—. Mem. Carter County, Ky., Am. bar assns., Nat. Legal Aide and Defenders Assn. Named hon. Ky. col. Home: 303 Horton St Grayson KY 41143 Office: 119 S Hord St Grayson KY 41143 Tel (606) 474-9522

CAVACOS, THEODORE ANDREW, b. Balt., Mar. 6, 1942; A.A., George Washington U., 1964; B.S., Med. Coll. Va., 1967; J.D., U. Balt., 1971. Admitted to Md. bar, 1972; individual practice law, Balt., 1972—. Mem. Am., Balt. City, Md. State bar assns., Nat. Assn. Retail Druggists, Am. Hellenic Ednl. and Progressive Assn., Young Lawyers Assn. (lectr. pub. relations sect.). Home: 1001 W 36th St Baltimore MD 21211 Office: 929 W 36th St Baltimore MD 21211 Tel (301) 467-6883

CAVALLI, RALPH LOUIS, b. San Marco in Lamis, Foggia, Italy, Aug. 23, 1920; B.S., Fordham Coll., 1942; postgrad. Law Sch. Columbia, 1942-43, 46-47, Harvard, 1947-48; J.D., U. Denver, 1971. Admitted to Colo. bar, 1973, U.S. Dist. Ct. bar, 1973, U.S. Ct. Appeals 10th Circuit, 1976, U.S. Supreme Ct. bar, 1976; commd. 2d lt. USAF, 1943, advanced through grades to lt. col., ret., 1968; individual practice law, Lakewood, Colo., 1973—. Home: 400 S Kline St Lakewood CO 80226 Office: Westland Bank Bldg Suite 760 10403 W Colfax Ave Lakewood CO 80215 Tel (303) 232-9551

CAVALLO, ROBERT MICHAEL, b. N.Y.C., Dec. 8, 1932; B.S., Manhattan Coll., 1954; LL.B., St. John's U., 1957. Admitted to N.Y. State bar, 1958; asso. Thomas J. Flood, N.Y.C., 1958-61, James I. Lysaght, N.Y.C., 1961-62; individual practice law, N.Y.C., 1962—; faculty N.Y. U., N.Y.C., 1974—. Mem. N.Y. State Bar Assn., Fed. Bar Council, Columbian Lawyers Assn. Author: Photography: What's the Law?, 1976; also articles. Address: 1065 Park Ave New York City NY 10028 Tel (212) 860-4662

CAVANAGH, JOHN EDWARD, b. Winnipeg, Man., Can., Nov. 15, 1918; came to U.S., 1920, naturalized, 1942; A.B., U. Oreg., 1942; J.D., George Washington U., 1949, LL.M., 1952. Admitted to D.C. bar, 1949, Cal. bar, 1957; grad. asst. social sci. U. Ore., 1941-42; hwy. economist U.S. Bur. Pub. Rds., 1946-49; chief congl. investigations br. Q.M.C., counsel to dep. quartermaster gen. for operations Dept. Army, 1950-56; asst. counsel Lockheed Aircraft Corp., 1956-58; asst. counsel Lockheed Missiles & Space Co., 1958-62, counsel, 1962-68; chief counsel, asst. sec. Lockheed Aircraft Corp., Burbank, Cal., 1968-71, v.p., gen. counsel, 1971—; lectr. U. Santa Clara Law Sch., 1960-68; mem. adv. bd. fed. contracts report Bur. Nat. Affairs, 1968—. Pres. Santa Clara County Taxpayers Assn., 1964-67. Bd. dirs. Chaminade Prep. Sch., 1973—. Mem. Am., Fed. bar assns., Nat. Contract Mgmt. Assn., Mfrs. Aircraft Assn. (dir. 1973—), Order of Coif, Delta Theta Phi. Home: 17341 Gresham St Northridge CA 91324 Office: PO Box 551 Burbank CA 91503*

CAVITCH, ZOLMAN, b. Traverse City, Mich., Nov. 17, 1925; A.B., U. Mich., 1948, J.D., 1950. Admitted to Ohio bar, 1951; asso. firm Grossman, Schlesinger & Carter, Cleve., 1950-56, partner, 1956-64; partner firm Stotter, Familo, Cavitch, Elden & Durkin, Cleve., 1964—; lectr. law Case Western Res. U. Sch. Law, 1955-74; pres. Ohio Legal Center Inst., Columbus, 1975—. Pres. Suburban Temple, Cleve., 1971-73. Mem. Bar Assn. Greater Cleve., Ohio State Bar Assn. Author: Ohio Corporation Law with Federal Tax Analysis, 1961; Business Organizations, 10 vols., 1963; Tax Planning for Corporations and Shareholders, 1974. Home: 3120 Morley Rd Shaker Heights OH 44122 Office: 1401 E Ohio Bldg Cleveland OH 44114

CAVNESS, JACK CHARLEBOIS, b. Los Angeles, July 30, 1920; J.D. with distinction, U. Ariz., 1943. Admitted to Ariz. bar, 1944, U.S. Supreme Ct. bar, 1972; spl. asst. atty. gen. State of Ariz., 1952; individual practice law, Phoenix, 1946—. Mem. Ariz., Am. bar assns. Recipient Nathan Burkan Meml. award U. Ariz., 1943. Home: 2022 Encanto Dr SE Phoenix AZ 85007 Office: 810 Luhrs Bldg Phoenix AZ 85003 Tel (602) 257-9600

CAWOOD, STEPHEN CARL, b. Pineville, Ky., Oct. 14, 1943; B.A., Eastern Ky. U., 1965; J.D., U. Ky., 1968. Admitted to Ky. bar, 1970; field rep. United Presbyn. Bd. Nat. Missions, Atlanta, 1968-70; Ky. dir. Appalachian Research and Def. Fund, Barbourville, 1970-71; individual practice law, Pineville, 1971—. Bd. dirs. Salvation Army, 1975-76. Mem. Am. (natural resources com. 1974—), Ky. (Bell judicial commn.), Bell County (pres. 1975-76) bar assns., Am. Trial Lawyers Assn. Home: 344 Tennessee Ave Pineville KY 40977 Office: Courthouse Sq Pineville KY 40977 Tel (606) 337-6104

CAZZELL, RICHARD LEE, b. Amarillo, Tex., Jan. 28, 1922; B.Sci. and Law, U. Denver, 1949, J.D., 1950. Admitted to Colo. bar, 1951, Tex. bar, 1952; judge Corp. Ct., Amarillo, 1951-53; asso. firm Culton, Morgan, Britain & White, Amarillo, 1953-57, partner, 1957—. Chmn., Amarillo Planning and Zoning Commn., 1960-65. Mem. Tex., Amarillo (pres. 1969-70) bar assns. Office: 1600 American Nat Bank Bldg PO Box 189 Amarillo TX 79105 Tel (806) 374-1671

CECHMAN, JOHN BURNS, b. Sunbury, Pa., Nov. 10, 1944; B.A. in Math., Indiana (Pa.) U., 1967; J.D., Fla. State U., 1972. Admitted to Fla. ba,r 1972; mem. firm Goldberg, Rubinstein & Buckley, Fort Myers, Fla., 1972—. Mem. Am., Fla., Fed. bar assns., Am. Trial Lawyers Assn., Acad. Fla. Trial Lawyers. Office: POB 2366 Fort Myers FL 33902 Tel (813) 334-1146

CECIL, LESTER LE FEVRE, b. Miami County, Ohio, Nov. 21, 1893; LL.B., U. Mich., 1917; LL.D., Ohio No. U., 1956. Admitted to Ohio bar, 1917; asso. firm E. H. & W. B. Turner, Dayton, Ohio, 1917-22; pros. atty. Dayton, 1922-26; judge Municipal Ct., Dayton, 1926-29; judge Common Pleas Ct. of Montgomery County (Ohio), 1929-53; judge U.S. Dist. Ct., So. Dist. Ohio, 1953-59; judge U.S. Ct. Appeals 6th Circuit, Dayton, 1959-65, sr. judge, 1965—. Mem. Am., Ohio State, Montgomery County bar assns. Home: 531 Belmonte

Park N Dayton OH 45405 Office: PO Box 758 Mid City Station Dayton OH 45402 Tel (513) 228-6062

CELAREK, FRANK JOHN, b. Ft. Wayne, Ind., Nov. 15, 1919; B.S., Butler U., 1943; J.D., Ind. U., 1946. Admitted to Ind. bar, 1947; individual practice law, Ft. Wayne, 1950-64; judge Allen County Superior Ct., Ft. Wayne, 1965—. Mem. Am., Allen County bar assns., Nat. Coll. Probate Judges, Nat. Coll. Juvenile Judges, Nat. Coll. State Judiciary. Home: 5630 Chester Blvd Fort Wayne IN 46819 Office: Allen County Superior Ct Allen County Ct House Fort Wayne IN 46802 Tel (219) 423-7249

CELEBREZZE, ANTHONY JOSEPH, b. Anzi, Italy, Sept. 4, 1910; ed. John Carroll U.; LL.B., Ohio No. U., also LL.D.; D.Humanities, Wilberforce U.; LL.D., Fenn Coll., Boston Coll., LaSalle Coll., Cleve. State U.; Ph.D. (hon.), R.I. Coll.; D.Pub. Service (hon.), Bowling Green State U.; L.H.D., Miami U., Oxford Ohio. Admitted to Ohio bar, 1938; atty. Ohio Bur. Unemployment Compensation; partner firm Celebrezze & Celebrezze, Cleve., 1939-53; mem. Ohio Senate, 1950-53; mayor City of Cleve., 1953-62; sec. HEW, 1962-65; judge U.S. Ct. Appeals, 6th Circuit, 1965—; mem. Advisory Commn. on Intergovernmental Relations, Washington, 1960-65. Pres. Am. Municipal Assn. (name now Am. League of Cities), 1958, U.S. Conf. Mayors, 1962. Mem. Cuyahoga County (Ohio), Fed., Am., Cleve. bar assns., Delta Theta Phi (hon. life). Decorated Order of Merit (Italy); recipient numerous awards. Home: 25043 Westwood Rd Westlake OH 44145 Office: 312 US Courthouse Cleveland OH 44114 Tel (216) 522-4270

CELEBREZZE, ANTHONY JOSEPH, JR., b. Cleve., Sept. 8, 1941; B.S., U.S. Naval Acad., 1963; M.S., George Washington U., 1966; J.D., Cleve. State U., 1973. Admitted to Ohio bar, 1973; partner firm Celebrezze & Marco, Cleve., 1973—; v.p. Lake Erie Regional Transp. Authority, Cleve., 1972-74; mem. Ohio State Senate, 1974—. Bd. mgrs. Central Cleve. YMCA, 1971-75. Mem. Ohio State, Cuyahoga County bar assns., Bar Assn. Greater Cleve., LWV, Citizens League Greater Cleve. Home: 16401 Marquis Ave Cleveland OH 44111 Office: 4168 Rocky River Dr Cleveland OH 44135 Tel (216) 476-9030

CERCHIARA, VINCENT FRANCIS, b. Bronx, N.Y., Nov. 1, 1925; B.S. in Bus. Adminstrn., LaSalle Coll., Phila., 1949; LL.B., N.Y. Law Sch., 1951; postgrad. Pohs Inst Ins., N.Y.C., 1952, U.S. Treasury Enforcement Sch., 1955, N.Y.C. Police Dept. Tng. Sch., 1957. Admitted to N.Y. State bar, 1952; partner firm Cerchiara and Cerchiara, Mt. Vernon, N.Y., 1952—; criminal investigator U.S. Treasury Dept., Washington, 1954-55; spl. investigator Waterfront Commn. N.Y. Harbor, N.Y.C., 1955-57; spl. counsel, investigator jud. inquiry Supreme Ct. Kings County, Bklyn., 1957-61; atty. Legal Aid Soc., Westchester County, N.Y., 1967—; arbitrator various small claims cts., 1962—; atty. N.Y. State Recreation and Park Soc., Inc., Peekskill, N.Y., 1972-76. Mem. Recreation Commn. Greenburgh (N.Y.), 1964-74; 1st. v.p., sec.-treas. N.Y. State Recreation and Parks Soc. Commn., 1970-75; mem. Citizens Com. for Selection of Low Income Housing Sites, Greenburgh, 1965-67; mem. Dist. #7 Bd. Edn., Hartsdale, N.Y., 1967-68; mem. parish council Sacred Heart Roman Catholic Ch., Hartsdale, 1972—. Mem. Bronx. County Bar Assn., Hartsdale Italian-Am. Civic Assn. Home: 23 Maple St Hartsdale NY 10530 Office: 145 Mount Vernon Ave Mount Vernon NY 10550 Tel (914) 699-0100

CERCONE, WILLIAM F., b. Stowe Twp., Allegheny County, Pa., Aug. 13, 1912; B.A., U. Pitts., 1936; LL.B., Duquesne U., 1941. Admitted to Pa. bar, 1941; asst. dist. atty. Allegheny County Office Dist. Atty., 1948-51; asst. U.S. atty. Justice Dept., 1952; judge Ct. of Common Pleas of Allegheny County, 1956-68, Superior Ct. of Pa., 1969—. Mem. Allegheny County, Pa. bar assns. Recipient Allegheny County Trial Lawyer's award, 1963. Office: 810 City-County Bldg Pittsburgh PA 15219 Tel (412) 261-1639

CERTILMAN, MORTON LAWRENCE, b. N.Y.C., Jan. 26, 1932; LL.B. cum laude, Bklyn. Law Sch., 1956. Admitted to N.Y. State bar, 1956; asst. atty. gen. N.Y. State, 1956-59; partner firm Rutenberg & Certilman, N.Y.C., 1959-62, firm Wofsey, Certilman, Haft & Lebow, N.Y.C. and Valley Stream, N.Y., 1965—; individual practice law, N.Y.C., 1962-65; lectr. in field. Mem. N.Y. State, Am. bar assns. Contbr. articles to legal jours. Office: 55 Broad St New York City NY 10004 Tel (212) 425-4320

CERVANTES, LEONARD PAUL, b. Moline, Ill., July 6, 1948; B.A., St. Ambrose Coll., 1970; J.D., St. Louis U., 1973. Admitted to Iowa bar, 1973, Mo. bar, 1973; asso. firm Igoe & Igoe, St. Louis, 1973-76, partner, 1976—. Active Park Forest Neighborhood Assn., 1975—, Mexican-Am. Cultural Commn., 1975—. Mem. Iowa State, Mo., Am. bar assns., Bar Assn. Met. St. Louis (trial demonstration com.), Mexican-Am. Legal Def. and Edn. Fund, St. Louis Lawyers Assn. Home: 4530 Laclede Ave Saint Louis MO 63108 Office: 722 Chestnut St Suite 800 Saint Louis MO 63101 Tel (314) 231-8177

CERVERA, NICHOLAS JOSEPH, b. N.Y.C., Sept. 25, 1940; B.S., Troy State U., 1963; J.D., Samford U., 1966. Admitted to Ala. bar, 1966; partner firm Cervera & Folmar, Troy, Ala., 1967—; prof. law Troy State U., 1966—; judge Pike County (Ala.) Inferior Ct., 1973—. Am., Fed. bar assns. Home: 106 Lakeview Circle Troy AL 36081 Office: 914 S Brundidge St Troy AL 36081 Tel (205) 566-0116

CERZA, ALPHONSE, b. Italy, Nov. 13, 1905; B.S.L., Northwestern U., 1929; J.D., Loyola U., Chgo., 1931. Admitted to Ill. bar, 1932; asst. corp. counsel City of Chgo., 1935-42; instr. law John Marshall Law Sch., 1953-74; mem. firm Giachini, Cerza, Ley & Cross, Chgo., 1944-53; individual practice law, Chgo., 1953—. Author: Fundamentals of Illinois Civil Procedure, 1961; Illinois Civil Procedure Cases, 1962. Home and office: 237 Millbridge Rd Riverside IL 60546 Tel (312) 447-5895

CETRULO, ROBERT CAMILLUS, b. Covington, Ky., Feb. 13, 1935; Xavier U., Cin., 19S2-55; J.D., U. Ky., 1958. Admitted to Ky. bar, 1958, U.S. Supreme Ct. bar, 1961; individual practice law, Covington, 1958-61 mem. firm O'Hara, Ruberg, Cetrulo & Osborne, Covington, 1961—; lectr. polit. sci., constl. law U. Ky. No. Community Coll., 1958-67; U.S. magistrate for Eastern Jud. Dist. Ky., 1960-75. Pres. North Ky. Legal Aid Soc., 1967-68; bd. dirs. No. Ky. Community Action Commn., 1968-71, No. Ky. Assn. Retarded, 1972-73. Mem. Ky. (chmn. com. continuing legal edn. 1971-72), Am., Kenton County (pres. 1968) bar assns., Am. Trial Lawyers Assn., Nat. Council U.S. Magistrates (v.p. 1974). Editorial bd., contbr. articles to Ky. Law Jour., 1956-57. Home: 1716 Mount Vernon Dr Fort Wright KY 41011 Office: 600 Greenup St Covington KY 41011 Tel (606) 581-3222

CHADEAYNE, WILLIAM RASHLEIGH, b. Newburgh, N.Y., May 30, 1929; A.B., Kenyon Coll., 1950; postgrad. (Fulbright scholar) U. Manchester (Eng.), 1950-51; J.D., Harvard, 1954. Admitted to Ohio bar, 1954; served with U.S. Army, 1954-56; asso. firm Bricker, Evatt, Barton & Eckler, Columbus, 1957-61, partner, 1962—; gen. counsel Ohio Air Quality Devel. Authority, 1970—; spl. counsel to atty. gen. State of Ohio, 1975—. Sec., Kenyon Coll., 1968—, trustee, 1970—. Mem. Ohio, Columbus bar assns., Phi Beta Kappa. Asso. editor: Crowley's Ohio Municipal Law, Banks-Baldwin Ohio School Law, Banks-Baldwin Ohio Township Law. Office: 100 E Broad St Columbus OH 43215 Tel (614) 221-6651

CHAFFEE, DAVID ROBERT, b. Long Beach, Calif., Mar. 6, 1948; B.A., Calif. State U., Long Beach, 1969; J.D., Loyola U., Los Angeles, 1973. Admitted to Calif. bar, 1973; dep. atty. gen. Calif. Dept. Justice, Los Angeles, 1974—. Mem. Am., Los Angeles County bar assns. Contbr. article to law rev. Office: 3580 Wilshire Blvd Los Angeles CA 90010 Tel (213) 736-2123

CHAFFIN, DAVID E., b. Bennington, Vt.; B.S. in Accounting, Seton Hall U., 1968; J.D., Seton Hall Sch. Law, Newark, 1972. Admitted to N.J. bar, 1972; legal investigator Law Office of Henry O. Habick, East Orange, N.J., 1969-72; asso. firm Robert J. Casulli, Cranford, N.J., 1972-75, Bergamino & DeGonge, P.A., Bloomfield, N.J., 1975—. Office: 230 Montgomery St Bloomfield NJ 07003 Tel (201) 748-7400

CHAIKIN, DONALD JOEL, b. Jersey City, Aug. 12, 1933; B.A., U. Md., 1961; LL.B., Am. U., 1964. Admitted to Md. bar, 1964, D.C. bar, 1964; mem. firm Chaikin, Kaep, & Greenberg, Washington, 1969—; arbitrator Am. Arbitration Assn; panelist M.D. Malpractice Arbitration Com. Pres., Silver Spring Jewish Day Inst.; pres. Bet Shalom Potomac Syangogue, Potomac, Md. Mem. Am. Bar Assn, Bar Assn, D.C. Home: 19300 Holly Hill Pl Potomac MD 20036 Office: 1225 Connecticut Ave NW Washington DC 20036 Tel (202) 659-8383

CHALFIN, PAUL M., b. Phila., June 8, 1917; B.S.C., Temple U., 1938; LL.B., U. Tenn., 1941. Admitted to Pa. bar, 1946; asst. dist. atty. City Phila., 1952-59, 1st asst. dist. atty., 1959-61, acting dist. atty., 1961; partner firm Lipschitz & Chalfin, Phila., 1962-69; judge State Ct. Common Pleas, Phila., 1969—. Office: 692 City Hall Philadelphia PA 19107 Tel (215) MU6-2634

CHALK, JOHN ALLEN, b. Lexington, Tenn., Jan. 16, 1937; A.A., Freed-Hardeman Coll., Henderson, Tenn., 1956; B.S., Tenn. Tech. U., 1962, M.A., 1967; J.D., U. Tex., 1973. Admitted to Tex. bar, 1973; ordained to ministry Ch. of Christ, 1956; pastor chs., Dayton, Ohio, 1956-60, Cookeville, Tenn., 1960-66, Abilene, Tex., 1966-71; asso. firm Rhodes and Seamster, Abilene, 1973-74, firm Rhodes and Doscher, Abilene, 1974; partner firm Rhodes, Doscher, Chalk and Heatherly, Abilene, 1975—. Trustee Abilene Regional Mental Health Mental Retardation Center; chmn. Abileen Bicentennial Com., 1975-76; nat. adv. council Ams. United for Separation of Ch. and State; nat. devel. council Abilene Christian U. Mem. Am., Tex., Abilene bar assns., Tex. Criminal Def. Lawyers Assn., Am., Tex. trial lawyers assns. Author: The Praying Christ, 1964; Three American Revolutions, 1970; Jesus' Church, 1970; The Christian Family, 1973; Great Biblical Doctrines, 1973; contbr. articles to religious jours. Home: 618 Gill St Abilene TX 79601 Office: Suite 104 Citizens Nat Bank Bldg Abilene TX 79601 Tel (915) 677-2493

CHAMBERLAIN, WILLIAM EDWARD, b. Balt., Sept. 20, 1927; grad. U. Balt., 1947; J.D., U. Md., 1951. Admitted to Md. bar, 1951; individual practice law, Balt., 1955—. Mem. Am., Md., Balt. County bar assns., Am. Trial Lawyers Assn. Office: 1760 Eastern Blvd Baltimore MD 21221 Tel (301) 686-9493

CHAMBERS, LOUIS, b. Lebanon, Tenn., Mar. 22, 1890; A.B., Lipscomb Coll., 1910; LL.B., Cumberland U., 1912, postgrad. Vanderbilt U., 1912. Admitted to Tenn. bar, 1912; individual practice law, Nashville, 1912-13, Lebanon, Tenn., 1913—; mem. Tenn. Senate, 1927-29, 35-37, 39-41. Mem. Tenn. State Constl. Convs., 1959, 65. Mem. Tenn. Bar Assn. Contbr. articles to law jours. Home and office: 133 Public Sq Lebanon TN 37087 Tel (615) 444-1201

CHAMBLIN, JAMES HAMMERLY, b. Leesburg, Va., Sept. 9, 1946; B.A., Hampden-Sydney Coll., 1968; J.D., U. Richmond, 1971. Admitted to Va. bar, 1971; since practiced law in Leesburg, individual practice law, 1971; partner firm Phillips & Chamblin, 1972-73, firm Ottinger, Nalls & Chamblin, 1973—. Mem. Leesburg Town Council, 1975-76, Leesburg Airport Commn., 1973-75. Mem. Loudoun County (treas. 1972), Am., Va. bar assns., Va. Trial Lawyers Assn., Phi Beta Kappa, Omicron Delta Kappa. Editor U. Richmond Law Rev., 1969-71, exec. editor, 1970-71. Office: PO Box 741 32 E Market St Leesburg VA 22075 Tel (703) 777-4000

CHAMPLIN, MALCOLM MCGREGOR, b. San Francisco, Apr. 13, 1911; B.S., U.S. Naval Acad., 1934; D.J., U. Calif., 1939; postgrad. U.S. Naval War Coll., 1944. Admitted to Calif. bar, 1940; spl. agt. FBI, Balt., 1940-41; asso. firm Fitzgerald, Abbott & Beardsky, Oakland, Calif., 1940-41, 45-47; founding partner firm Stark & Champlin, Oakland, 1947-67; judge Oakland Municipal Ct., Piedmont Jud. Dist. 1967—, presiding judge, 1973-74; mem. presiding judges com. conf. Calif. Judges, 1974-75. Bd. dirs. 1st agrl. dist. Alameda County, Calif., 1956-60. Mem. Alameda County Bar Assn., Am. Judicature Soc. Decorated Navy Cross, Army Silver Star; recipient George Washington Honor medal Freedom's Found., 1965. Office: 600 Washington St Oakland CA 94604 Tel (415) 874-6781

CHAMSON, ALLAN, b. N.Y.C., Sept. 11, 1933; J.D., Bklyn. Coll. Admitted to N.Y. bar, 1959; individual practice law, N.Y.C. Office: 276 5th Ave New York City NY 10001 Tel (212) 679-9288

CHAN, CHARLES MAURICE, JR., b. Balt., Md., May 9, 1921; A.B. summa cum laude, Dartmouth Coll., 1943; J.D. cum laude, Harvard U., 1950. Admitted to Md. bar, 1950; with firm Blades & Rosenfeld, Balt., 1951—, sr. mem. Pres. Jewish Family and Children's Service, Balt.; bd. dirs. Levindale Geriatric Hosp., Asso. Jewish Charities and Welfare Fund, Helath and Welfare Council Central Md., Jewish Community Center. Mem. Balt., Md., Am. bar assns., Md. Assn. Mental Health, Phi Beta Kappa. Home: 3317 Woodvalley Dr Baltimore MD 21208 Office: 1200 One Charles Center Baltimore MD 21201 Tel (303) 539-7558

CHAN, SAU-UNG LOO, b. Honolulu; student U. So. Calif., 1923; B.A., U. Hawaii, 1926; J.D., Yale, 1928; postgrad. in Psychology, U. Hong Kong, 1932-34. Head pub. relations Sang Hop Constrn. Co., Hong Kong, 1933-40; asst. legal counsel William Hunt & Co., Hong Kong, 1937-40; spl. investigator Immigration and Naturalization Service, Dept. Justice, Washington and N.Y.C., 1940-41; admitted to Hawaii bar, 1943; estate and guardianship atty. 1st Circuit Ct. Hawaii, Honolulu, 1944-76, ret., 1976; individual practice law, Honolulu, 1976—; legal adviser Chinese Cultural Found. Hawaii. Bd. dirs. Internat. Inst. Hawaii, Honolulu, 1955-61. Mem. Am., Fed., Hawaii bar assns., Estate Planning Council Hawaii (exec. bd. 1966-68), Legal Aid Soc., Kappa Beta Pi. Home: 2730 Terrace Dr Honolulu HI 96822 Office: PO Box 3315 Honolulu HI 96801 Tel (808) 988-4246

CHANAK, NICHOLAS S., b. Hibbing, Minn., May 12, 1912; B.Sc. in Law, U. Minn., 1937, LL.B., 1939. Admitted to Minn. Supreme Ct. bar, 1939; asso. firm Johnson & Hultstrand, 1939-42; judge Municipal Ct., Hibbing, 1947-64, dist. judge, 1965—; asso. justice Minn. Supreme Ct., 1975. Pres. Minn. Yugoslav Assn., Serb Orthodox Ch.; mem. supreme trial bd. Serb Nat. Fedn. Mem. Am. Bar Assn., Minn. State, Range (pres.) bars, Minn. Municipal Judges Assn. (state pres.). Home: 2425 10th Ave E Hibbing MN 55746 Office: County Courthouse Hibbing MN 55746 Tel (218) 262-2565

CHANCE, CHESTER BURT, b. Mineola, N.Y., Oct. 3, 1940; B.S., U. Fla., 1962, J.D., 1964. Admitted to Fla. bar, 1965, U.S. Dist. Ct. bar, Middle Dist. Fla., 1965, No. Dist. Fla., 1966, U.S. Supreme Ct. bar, 1973; asso. firm Albritton, Gordon, Sessums & Ryder, Tampa, 1965; partner firm Wershow, Burwell, Chance & Wright, Gainesville, 1965-73; judge Alachua County Ct., 1973—; asst. pub. defender, 1966-68; exec. dir. Alachua County Housing Authority; 8th Jud. Circuit chmn. Supreme Ct. Bicentennial Com.; instr. bus. law U. Fla.; instr. law enforcement Santa Fe Community Coll. Chmn. Alachua County Citizens for Tax Reform, Citizens Adv. Com., City of Gainesville; past chmn. Alachua County Democratic Exec. Com.; bd. dirs. Alachua County Dem. Club; bd. dirs. Gator City Kiwanis Club, Gainesville Neighborhood Devel., Inc., Gainesville Boys Club. Mem. Am., Fla., 8th Jud. Circuit bar assns., Nat. Conf. Spl. Ct. Judges (chmn. manuals com., recognized by resolution for contbn. to improvement adminstrn. of justice 1975), Fla. Conf. County Ct. Judges (dir., co-chmn. edn. com.), Gainesville Area C. of C. (chmn. state govt. com.). Author: (with Gerald Bennett) Bench Book Guide to the Implementation of American Bar Association Standards of Criminal Jusitice, 1975; contbr. sect. to Florida Trial Judges Bench Book, 1976. Home: 6915 NW 65th Ave Gainesville FL 32601 Office: Alachua County Courthouse Gainesville FL 32601 Tel (904) 373-5181

CHANDLER, EDWARD GROVER, b. Santa Cruz, Calif., Sept. 26, 1905; A.B., U. Calif., 1926; J.D., Harvard, 1929. Admitted to Calif. bar, 1930, U.S. Supreme Ct. bar, 1944; partner firm Athearn, Chandler & Hoffman, San Francisco, 1930—. Mem. Calif. State Bar, Am., San Francisco bar assns., Am. Law Inst. Home: 2611 Etna St Berkeley CA 94704 Office: 111 Sutter St San Francisco CA 94104 Tel (415) 421-5484

CHANDLER, GEORGE EDMOND, b. Moscow, Tex., Jan. 28, 1939; B.A., Baylor U., 1960, LL.B., 1963. Admitted to Tex. bar, 1963; individual practice law, Lufkin, Tex. Chmn. Diboll Cancer Crusade, Lufkin Multiple Sclerosis Dr.; bd. dirs. Wilson-McKewen Treatment Center, 1st v.p., pres.; trustee St. Cyprian's Day Sch. Mem. Am., Angelina County, Angelina County Jr. (sec-treas.), Neuces County Jr. (v.p.) bar assns., Tex. (state committeeman), Am. trial lawyers assns. Office: 522 E Shepherd Lufkin TX 75901 Tel (713) 632-7778

CHANDLER, LOUIS, b. Portland, Maine, Apr. 25, 1911; J.D., Boston U., 1934. Admitted to Maine, Mass. bars, 1934, U.S. Supreme Ct. bar, 1971; partner firm Stoneman, Chandler & Miller, Boston, 1945—; former dir. disputes div. War Labor Bd.; vis. lectr. Harvard Bus. Sch., Holy Cross Labor Inst. Mem. Am., Boston bar assns. Home: 105 Baldpate Hill Newton Center MA 02159 Office: 99 High St Boston MA 02109 Tel (617) 542-6789

CHANDLER, MALCOLM ARTHUR, b. Louisville, May 14, 1923; A.B. cum laude, Harvard, 1947, LL.B., S.D. cum laude, 1949. Admitted to Mass. bar, 1949, Ill. bar, 1950, U.S. Supreme Ct. bar, 1974; asso. firm Bell, Boyd, Marshall & Lloyd, Chgo., 1949-57; individual practice law, Chgo., 1958—. Mem. Am., Ill. State, Chgo. bar assns., Legal Club of Chgo., Law Club of Chgo. Home: 172 W Laurel Ave Lake Forest IL 60045 Office: 135 S LaSalle St Chicago IL 60603 Tel (312) 641-2121

CHANDLER, STEPHEN SANDERS, b. Blount County, Tenn., Sept. 13, 1899; LL.B., U. Kans., 1922, J.D., 1968. Admitted to Okla. bar, 1922, U.S. Supreme Ct. bar, 1927; individual practice law, Oklahoma City, 1922-43; judge U.S. Dist. Western Dist. of Okla., Oklahoma City, 1943—, chief judge, 1956-69; faculty Oklahoma City Univ. Sch. Law, 1957-60. Mem. Am., Internat., Inter-Am. bar assns. Recipient Hatton Sumners Award, 1961; author: Discovery and Pre-Trial Procedure in Federal Courts, 1959; The Role of the Trial Judge in the Anglo-American Legal System, 1964. Home: Oklahoma City OK 73101 Office: US Ct House NW 4th St POB 895 Oklahoma City OK 73101 Tel (405) 239-2621

CHANDLESS, HARRY HUTMAN, JR., b. Hackensack, N.J., Apr. 23, 1930; LL.B., Columbia U., 1952, J.D., 1954. Admitted to N.J. bar, 1954, U.S. Dist. Ct. bar, 1955; partner firm Chandless, Weller & Kramer, Hackensack, N.J., 1954-64; pvt. practice law, Hasbrouck Heights, N.J., 1964—; municipal judge Borough of Hasbrouck Heights, N.J., 1966—, prosecutor, 1958-66; pres. Bergen County Young Republican Club, 1965. Mem. Bergen County Bar Assn., Bergen County Mcpl. Judges Assn., Am. Judges Assn., Am. Judicature Soc., Save Ocean Soc. (dir. 1971-74). Harlan Fiske Stone scholar, 1954. Home: 291 Terrace Ave Hasbrouck Heights NJ 07604 Office: 230 Boulevard St Hasbrouck Heights NJ 07604

CHANEY, VINCENT VERLANDO, b. Elkins, W.Va., June 12, 1913; A.B., W.Va. U., 1936, J.D., 1938. Admitted to W.Va. bar, 1938; asso. firm Kay, Casto & Chaney, and predecessor, Charleston, W.Va., 1938-49, partner, 1949—. Trustee Charleston Area Med. Center, 1966—, sec., 1972-73, vice chmn., 1973-74, chmn., 1974—. Mem. Am., W.Va., Kanawha County (W.Va.) bar assns., Am. Judicature Soc. (gov. 1970-73), Am. Bar Found., Am. Law Inst., W.Va. State Bar (pres. 1961-62). Home: 1209 Williamsburg Way Charleston WV 25314 Office: PO Box 2031 Charleston WV 25327 Tel (204) 343-4831

CHANEY, WILLIAM EDWARD, b. Barnesville, Ohio, Nov. 3, 1927; B.A., Ohio Wesleyan U., 1950; J.D., Ohio State U., 1953. Admitted to Ohio bar, 1953; individual practice law, Barnesville, 1953—; dir. 1st Nat. Bank Barnesville, 1963—. Mem. Barnesville Bd. Edn., 1966—. Mem. Am., Ohio, Belmont County (pres. 1965) bar assns. Home: RD 2 Barnesville OH 43713 Office: 111 E Main St Barnesville OH 43713 Tel (614) 425-1211

CHANG, KENNETH BYUNG CHO, b. Seoul, Korea, July 8, 1929; B.A., Earlham Coll., 1954; LL.B., U. Santa Clara, 1960. Admitted to Calif. bar, 1963, Korean bar (hon.), 1967; practice law, 1963; dep. dist. atty. Santa Clara County, Calif., 1964-67; chief criminal jurisdiction div. JAG Office, U.S. Army, Seoul, 1967-71; practice law, Los Angeles, 1971—; partner firm Caldwell & Toms, Los Angeles, 1975—. Bd. dirs. Korean Philharmonic Assn., 1975—. Mem. State Bar Calif. Home: 720 Cloyden Rd Palos Verdes Estates CA 90274 Office: 611 W 6th St Los Angeles CA 90017 Tel (213) 628-1300

CHAPEL, CHARLES SIDNEY, b. Delight, Ark., Feb. 17, 1941; B.S. with honors, San Diego State U., 1966; Tulsa U., 1968. Admitted to Okla. bar, 1969, U.S. Supreme Ct. bar, 1971; partner firm Blackstock, Joyce & Pollard, Tulas, firm Chapel, Wilkinson, Riggs & Abney, Tulsa, 1972—. Mem. Am., Okla., Tulsa County bar assns. Office: 1640 S Boston St Tulsa OK 74119 Tel (918) 587-3161

CHAPIN, HUGH ARTHUR, b. Whitesville, N.Y., Sept. 3, 1925; B.C.E., Cornell U., 1948; LL.B., Harvard U., 1951. Admitted to N.Y. State bar, 1951; partner firm Kenyon & Kenyon, Reilly, Carr & Chapin, N.Y.C., 1957—; prof. patent law New York Law Sch., 1957-59. Mem. Madison (N.J.) Planning Bd., 1975—. Mem. Am. (com. chmn. 1972-77), N.Y. (pres. 1968-69) patent law assns., N.Y. State Bar Assn., Assn. Bar City N.Y., Tau Beta Pi. Home: 165 Woodland Rd Madison NJ 07940 Office: 59 Maiden Ln New York City NY 10038 Tel (212) 425-7200

CHAPIN, JAMES CHRIS, b. Washington, Oct. 24, 1940; B.A., Furman U., 1962; J.D. Georgetown U., 1965. Admitted to D.C. bar, 1965, Md. bar, 1966, U.S. Supreme Ct. bar, 1974; partner firm Nylen & Gilmore, Hyattsville, Md., 1965-75; atty. City Laurel, Md., 1968-75; partner firm Meyers, Billingsley & Chapin, Riverdale, Md., 1975; atty. Prince George's County, Md., 1975—; lectr. Univ. Md., College Park, 1976, Prince George's Coll., Largo, Md., 1976. Mem. Am., D.C., Md., Prince George's County (dir.) bar assns., Am. Judicature Soc., Am. Trial Lawyers Assn., Md. Municipal League (dir. 1973-75), Md. Municipal Attys. Assn. (v.p. 1974, pres. 1975), Greater Laurel C. of C. Home: 9300 St Andrews Pl College Park MD 20740 Office: Courthouse Upper Marlboro MD 20870 Tel (301) 627-3000

CHAPIN, MELVILLE, b. Boston, Dec. 14, 1918; grad. Phillips Acad., Andover, Mass., 1936; B.A., Yale, 1940; J.D., Harvard, 1943. Admitted to Mass. bar, 1943; with firm Warner & Stackpole, Boston, 1946—, partner, 1954—; dir. New Eng. Mchts. Nat. Bank, Boston Envelope Co., Grand Rapids Gypsum Co., H.B. Smith Co., Inc., Weymouth Art Leather Co.; sec., trustee William Underwood Co.; chmn., trustee Security Mortgage Investors. Chmn. Mass. Eye and Ear Infirmary, Boston; trustee Phillips Acad., Frederick J. Kennedy Meml. Found.; bd. dirs. Chewonki Found., Wiscasset, Maine, United Community Planning Corp., Boston, United Way, Boston. Mem. Internat., Am., Mass., Boston bar assns. Home: 15 Traill St Cambridge MA 02138 Office: 28 State St Boston MA 02109

CHAPIN, ROBERT DECOURCY, b. Boston, Oct. 13, 1938; A.B., Brown U., 1961; LL.B., U. Va., 1964. Admitted to Fla. bar, 1964, Ohio bar, 1964; asso. firm Weston, Hurd, Fallon, Paisley & Howley, Cleve., 1964-67, Burke, Haber & Berick, Cleve., 1967-70; partner firm Gezelschap & Chapin, Delray Beach, Fla., 1970—; spl. counsel City of Cleve., 1967-68; City of Delray Beach, 1971-75. Chmn. Beach Restoration Com., Delray Beach, 1972-74; vice-chmn. Delray Beach City Charter Com., 1974-76; mem. Delray Beach City Council, 1977—; pres. S. Palm Beach County Planned Parenthood chpt., 1975-77. Mem. Am., Fla., South Palm Beach County (pres. 1975-76) bar assns., Am. Judicature Soc. Home: 2012 NW 3d Ave Delray Beach FL 33444 Office: 1045 E Atlantic Ave PO Box 2350 Delray Beach FL 33444 Tel (305) 278-2833

CHAPLIN, CHARLES KALIS, b. Coatesville, Pa., Oct. 2, 1919; LL.B., George Washington U., 1941, LL.M., 1947, M.P.A., 1967. Admitted to D.C. bar, 1942; with U.S. Govt., 1938—; chief judge Occupational Safety and Health Rev. Commn., Washington, 1974—. Mem. Am., Fed. bar assns., Res. Officers Assn., Conf. Adminstrv. Law Judges. Office: 1825 K St NW Washington DC 20006 Tel (202) 634-7980

CHAPLOWE, M. LEWIS, b. New Haven, Dec. 22, 1934; B.A., Bates Coll., 1956; J.D., Columbia, 1959. Admitted to Conn. bar, 1959; partner firm Chaplowe and Chaplowe, Stratford, Conn., 1960—. Chmn. Stratford Citizens Adv. Com., 1974-75; chmn. Stratford chpt. ARC, 1974—; bd. dirs., exec. bd. Greater Bridgeport (Conn.) Regional Emergency Med. Service Council, 1975—; bd. dirs. Friends of Stratford Library, 1975—. Mem. Am., Conn., Bridgeport bar assns., Assn. Trial Lawyers Am., Am. Judicature Soc., Comml.-Law League. Recipient Stratford Civitan Club Man of Yr. award, 1975; Stratford Jaycees Outstanding Man of the Yr. award, 1975. Home: 120 Lantern Rd Stratford CT 06497 Office: 2420 Main St Stratford CT 06497 Tel (203) 377-7200

CHAPMAN, CARLYLE HORATIO, JR., b. Baton Rouge, Oct. 17, 1948; A.B. with honors, Ind. U., 1970; J.D., U. Mich., 1973. Admitted to Tex. bar, 1973; asso. firm Mullinax, Well, Mauzy & Baab, Inc., Dallas, 1973—; research asst. Louisville-Jefferson County Crime Commn., 1970; law clk. LeBeouf, Lamb, Lieby & McCrea, N.Y.C., summer 1971; Goodman, Eden, Millander, Goodman & Bedrosion, Detroit, summer 1972. Bd. dirs. Pub. Communication Found. for N. Tex., 1975—, Greater Dallas Housing Opportunity Council, 1976—; advisory council U. Tex., Dallas, 1976. Mem. Am., Dallas bar assns., Am., Tex. trial lawyers assn., J.L. Turner Legal Soc. Home: 11047 Wallbrook Dr Dallas TX 75238 Office: 8204 Elmbrook Dr Suite 200 Dallas TX 75247 Tel (214) 630-3672

CHAPMAN, HOWARD STUART, b. Chgo., Oct. 16, 1941; B.S. with honors, U. Ill., 1963, J.D. with honors, 1967. Admitted to Ill. bar, 1968, U.S. Supreme Ct. bar, 1971; asso. firm John J. Kennelly, Chgo., 1967-69; asso. firm Altheimer & Gray, Chgo., 1969-71; mem. faculty Ill. Inst. Tech., Chgo.-Kent Coll. Law, 1971—, prof. law, 1976—, asso. dean, 1973—; lectr. DePaul U., 1975—; vol. arbitrator Better Bus. Bur. Chgo., 1975—. Treas., Glenbrook Countryside Assn., 1974—. Mem. Am., Ill., Chgo. bar assns., Decalogue Soc. Lawyers, Order of Coif. C.P.A., Ill. Home: 245 Elm Ct Northbrook IL 60062 Office: 77 S Wacker Dr Chicago IL 60606 Tel (312) 567-5008

CHAPMAN, JAMES WINSTON, b. Houston, Feb. 7, 1947; B.A., U. Tex., 1969, J.D., 1973. Admitted to Tex. bar, 1973; partner firm Levbarg, Weeks and Chapman, Austin, Tex., 1973—. Mem. Tex. County Bar Assn., Tex. Trial Lawyers Assn. Office: 807 Rio Grande St Austin TX 78701 Tel (512) 476-6096

CHAPMAN, ROBERT FOSTER, b. Inman, S.C., Apr. 24, 1926; B.S., U.S.C., 1945, LL.B., 1949. Admitted to S.C. bar, 1949; asso. firm Osborne, Butler & Moore, Spartanburg, S.C., 1949-51; partner firm Butler & Chapman, Spartanburg, 1953-65; partner firm Butler, Chapman, Parler & Morgan, Spartanburg, 1965-71; judge U.S. Dist. of S.C., Florence, 1971—. Chmn. S.C. Republican Party, 1961-63. Fellow Am. Coll. Trial Lawyers; mem. Am., S.C. bar assns. Home: 1822 Fair St Camden SC 29020 Office: Fed Ct House Florence SC 29501 Tel (803) 662-7611

CHAPMAN, STEVEN FRANKLIN, b. Waxahachie, Tex., May 8, 1940; B.B.A., So. Meth. U., 1962, LL.B., 1965. Admitted to Tex. bar, 1965; partner firm Chapman, Chapman & Ellyson, Waxahachie, 1965—; city atty. City of Waxahachie, 1969—, City of Midlothian (Tex.), 1971-74. Pres. Community Chest, Waxahachie, 1968-69, United Fund, 1968-69, Ellis County (Tex.) Mus., 1972-73; pres. bd. trustees Central Presbyn. Ch., Waxahachie, 1972-73. Mem. Tex. Bar, Am., Ellis County (pres. 1970-71), Central Tex. bar assns. Home: 419 Bird Ln Waxahachie TX 75165 Office: Citizens Nat Bank Bldg PO Box 641 Waxahachie TX 75165 Tel (214) 937-2720

CHAPON, ROBERT JOSEPH, b. Sewickley, Pa., Nov. 4, 1933; B.B.A., Ohio U., 1963; J.D., Ohio No. U., 1966. Admitted to Ohio bar, 1966; mem. firm Hendershott, Huffman & Peckinpaugh, Cleve., 1967-73; individual practice law, Cleve., 1973—. Mem. Bar Assn. Greater Cleve., Cuyahoga County Bar Assn. Home: 2072 Lewis Dr Lakewood OH 44107 Office: 1866 W 25th St Cleveland OH 44113 Tel (216) 696-2299

CHAPPELL, PAUL MILTON, b. Fall River, Mass., Mar. 28, 1928; student U. of R.I.; LL.B., Boston U. Admitted to R.I. Supreme Ct. bar, 1951; partner firm Dolbashian, Chappell & Chace, Portsmouth, R.I., 1951—. Sec. Portsmouth Planning Bd. Mem. Newport County (past pres.), R.I., Am. bar assns., Am. Judicature Soc. Tel (401) 683-1400

CHAPPELL, ROBERT HARVEY, JR., b. Clarksville, Va., Nov. 28, 1926; B.A., Coll. William and Mary, 1948, B.C.L., 1950. Admitted to Va. bar; partner firm Christian, Barton, Epps, Brent & Chappell, Richmond, Va., 1950—; dir., gen. counsel Thalhimer Bros., Inc.; pres. Va. State Bar. Mem. Richmond Independence Bicentennial Commn., community facilities adv. bd. City of Richmond; mem. bd. visitors Coll. William and Mary; former pres. and mem. exec. com. Crippled Children's Hosp.; bd. dirs. Richmond Eye Hosp. Fellow Am. Bar Found., Am. Coll. Trial Lawyers; mem. Am., Va. (exec. com.), Richmond (past pres.) bar assns., State Bar Va. (pres.), Internat. Assn. Ins. Counsel (past exec. com.), Phi Beta Kappa, Omicron Delta Kappa. Editor Ins. Counsel Jour., 1963-72. Home: 4607 Menokin Rd Richmond VA 23225 Office: Mutual Bldg Richmond VA 23219 Tel (804) 644-7851

CHAPPLE, JOHN LOUIS, b. Daytona Beach, Fla., July 23, 1943; B.A., Stanford U., 1965, M.B.A., 1969, J.D., 1970. Admitted to Calif. bar, 1971; profl. football player San Francisco Forty Niners, 1964-66; counsel Ampex Corp., Redwood City, Calif., 1970-72; counsel Itel Corp, San Francisco, 1972-74, v.p., gen. counsel, 1974—, gen. counsel Data Products Group; v.p. Itel Data Products Corp.; treas. Itel Field Services Corp. Mem. Am., San Francisco, San Mateo bar assns. Mem. Stanford Law Rev., 1968-69. Office: 1 Embarcadero Center San Francisco CA 94111 Tel (415) 983-0390

CHAR, VERNON FOOK LEONG, b. Honolulu, Dec. 15, 1934; B.A., U. Hawaii, 1956; LL.B., Harvard, 1959. Admitted to Hawaii bar, 1959; dep. atty. gen. State of Hawaii, Honolulu, 1959-60, 62-65; partner firm Damon, Shigekane, Key & Char, Honolulu, 1965—. Mem. State ethics comm. State of Hawaii, Honolulu, 1968-75. Mem. Am. Bar Assn. Office: 810 Richards St Honolulu HI 96821 Tel (808) 531-8031

CHARACTER, CARL JULIUS, b. Cleve., Dec. 29, 1929; B.B.S., Ohio State U., 1951; J.D., U. Mich., 1954; LL.M., Cleve. Marshall Law Sch., 1961. Admitted to Ohio bar, 1954; asso. with Theodore M. Williams, Cleve., 1956-59; investigator dept. domestic relations Cuyahoga County Common Pleas Ct., Cleve., 1957-59; partner firm Gillespie, Terry and Character, Cleve., 1959-62; individual practice law, Cleve., 1962—. Mem. Ohio, Am., Nat. (pres. 1976-77), Cuyahoga County, Cleve. bar assns., Am. Trial Lawyers Assn., John Harlan Law Club, Tau Epsilon Rho. Office: 33 Public Sq Suite 801 Cleveland OH 44113 Tel (216) 579-0500

CHARITY, RUTH HARVEY, b. Danville, Va., Apr. 18; A.B., Howard U., also J.D. Admitted to Va. bar; individual practice law, Danville, Va., 1953—; spl. rep. for First State Bank, Danville; spl. counsel Harvey's Funeral Home, Inc., SCLC, NAACP; trustee Va. Sem. and Coll., Lynchburg, Palmer Meml. Inst., Sedalia, N.C., Howard U. Mem. Danville City Council, 1970-74; apptd. Va. State advisory com. to U.S. Civil Rights Commn., Va. Commn. on Status of Women; mem. exec. com. Dem. Nat. Com.; Nat. Committeewoman Dem. Party from Va.; mem. Va. Dem. Party Steering, Central Coms.; mem. sr. choir High St. Baptist Ch., Danville; former nat. officer Nat. Council Negro Women; mem. League Women Voters, YWCA, NOW, AAUW. Mem. Old Dominion (pres.), Nat. (mem. bd. dirs., organizer women's sect.) bar assns., Internat. Fedn. Women Lawyers, Nat. Assn. Black Women Attys. (officer). Recipient awards from service and polit. orgns. Home: 514 S Main St Danville VA 24541 Office: 453 S Main St Danville VA 24541 Tel (804) 793-5751 also 793-8912

CHARLES, ALFRED W., b. N.Y.C., Aug. 25, 1931; B.A., N.Y.U., 1952, J.D., 1955. Admitted to N.Y. bar, 1955, U.S. Supreme Ct. bar, 1961; partner firm Feinberg & Charles, N.Y.C., 1965—. Treas. com. sch. bd. #3, N.Y.C., 1973—. Mem. Am. Bar Assn., Assn. Bar City N.Y. Home: 425 Central Park W New York City NY 10025 Office: 415 Madison Ave New York City NY 10017 Tel (212) 688-6400

CHARLES, EDWIN BARRETT, b. Hawkins County, Tenn., Mar. 22, 1943; B.S., E. Tenn. State U., 1966; J.D., U. Tenn., 1967. Admitted to Tenn. bar, 1968; individual practice law, Johnson City, Tenn., 1968—. Mem. Tenn., Washington County bar assns., Johnson City Jaycees (1st v.p. 1975-76), Am., Tenn. trial lawyers assns. Named Outstanding Young Man of Johnson City, 1974. Home: 1017 Grace Dr Johnson City TN 37601 Office: 100 Spring St Johnson City TN 37601 Tel (615) 928-1651

CHARLES, GEORGE JAMES, b. Toronto, Ont., Can., Mar. 21, 1918; B.A. with honors, U. Pa., 1950; J.D. with honors, George Washington U., 1952. Admitted to D.C. bar, 1953, Md. bar, 1958, U.S. Supreme Ct. bar, 1960; practice law, Washington, 1953—. Mem. Am., D.C. bar assns., Nat. Lawyers Club, Phi Delta Phi. Home: 7604 Carter Ct Bethesda MD 20034 Office: 1250 Connecticut Ave Washington DC 20036 Tel (202) 223-4686

CHARLEY, FRANCES WOERNER, b. Atlantic City, June 18, 1946; B.A., Pa. State U., 1968; J.D., Temple U., 1971. Admitted to Pa. bar, 1971; asso. firm Morgan Lewis & Bockius, Phila., 1971—. Mem. Am. Bar Assn. Office: 2100 Fidelity Bldg Philadelphia PA 19109 Tel (215) 491-9423

CHARLTON, CLARENCE DEAN, b. Chgo., Nov. 14, 1903; LL.B., J.D., U. Ill., 1926. Admitted to Ill. bar, 1926; atty. Western Clock Co., LaSalle, Ill., 1926-27; individual practice law, LaSalle, 1928-29, 1974; pres., trust officer LaSalle Nat. Bank, LaSalle, 1929-74. Trustee, sec., bus. mgr. Hygienic Inst. for LaSalle-Peru-Oglesby, Ill., Oak Wood Cemetery Assn.; treas., exec. com. Starved Rock Area council Boy Scouts Am.; bd. dirs. dir. Tri City Tuberculosis Assn.; mem. finance com. St. Mary's Hosp., LaSalle. Mem. Ill. (sr. counselor), Am., LaSalle County, Tri-City, bar assns., Ill. Bankers Assn. (pres. trust div.), Gamma Eta Gamma. Home: 1427 Argyle Rd LaSalle IL 61301 Office: 10-11 LaSalle Nat Bank Bldg 105 Marquette St LaSalle IL 61301 Tel (815) 223-3635

CHARLTON, RICHARD EDMUND, III, b. Akron, Ohio, Jan. 6, 1943; B.S., Auburn U., 1964; J.D., U. Ala., 1969. Admitted to Ala. bar, 1969, Tenn. bar, 1970; partner firm Winchester, Walsh, Marshall, Huggins, Charlton & Leake, Memphis. Mem. Am., Ala., Tenn., Memphis and Shelby County (dir. young lawyers sect. 1975) bar assns. Home: 1975 Vinton Ave Memphis TN 38104 Office: Suite 3200 100 N Main Bldg Memphis TN 38103 Tel (901) 526-7374

CHARMASSON, HENRI JOSEPH AUGUSTE, b. Nimes, France, Sept. 7, 1938; baccalaureat U. Montpellier (France), 1958; student U. Grenoble (France), 1959-60; J.D., Western State U., Calif., 1973. Admitted to Calif. bar, 1973, U.S. Patent Office bar, 1974; tech. agt. French Atomic Energy Commn., France, 1959-61; design engr. Electro Instrument, Inc., San Diego, 1962-65; sr. engr. Honeywell, Inc., San Diego, 1966-71, Doric Sci. Corp., San Diego, 1972; partner law firm Isbell, Charmasson, Kinsella & Kinsella, San Diego, 1973-75, Isbell & Charmasson, San Diego, 1975—. Mem. State Bar Calif., Am., San Diego County bar assns., San Diego Patent Law Assn. Office: 1818 First Ave San Diego CA 92101 Tel (714) 239-0388

CHARNEY, LEON HARRIS, b. Bayonne, N.J., July 23, 1938; B.A., Yeshiva U., 1960, B. Hebrew Letters, 1961; J.D., Bklyn. Law Sch., 1964. Admitted to N.Y. State bar, 1965, U.S. Supreme Ct. bar, 1973; asso. firm Colton & Pinkham, N.Y.C., 1964-65; individual practice law, N.Y.C., 1965-70; partner firm Charney & White, N.Y.C., 1970-75; partner firm Charney, White & Weinberg, N.Y.C., 1975—. Mem. N.Y. Bar Assn. Office: 140 Broadway New York City NY 10005 Tel (212) 422-7550

CHARNEY, NORMAN MURRY, b. N.Y.C., July 19, 1931; B.A., Bklyn. Coll., 1953; D.O., Phila. Coll. Osteo. Medicine, 1957; M.D., Calif. Coll. Medicine, 1962; J.D., Western State U., Calif., 1971. Admitted to Calif. bar, 1971; mem. firm Hara-Mordkin Inc. & Norman M. Charney, Fullerton, Calif., 1975—; instr. law and medicine, Western State U. Coll. Law, Fullerton. Fellow Am. Coll. Legal Medicine; mem. Am., Orange County bar assns., Calif., Orange County trial lawyers assns. Office: 2555 E Chapman Ave Fullerton CA 92631 Tel (714) 526-4638

CHARNOFF, GERALD, b. N.Y.C., Apr. 18, 1930; B.A., Bklyn. Coll., 1951; M.S., Columbia U., 1952; LL.B., N.Y.U., 1957. Admitted to N.Y. State bar, 1957, U.S. Supreme Ct. bar, 1962, D.C. bar, 1966; with office Gen. Counsel SEC, Washington, 1957-62; staff counsel Atomic Indsl. Forum, Washington, 1960-66; partner firm Shaw, Pittman, Potts & Trowbridge, D.C., 1966—. Mem. D.C., Am. bar assns. Contbr. articles to profl. jours. Home: 805 Lamberton Dr Silver Spring MD 20902 Office: 1800 M St NW Washington DC 20036 Tel (202) 331-4100

CHARTRAND, PHILIP EDWARD, b. Moulmein, Burma, Oct. 20, 1936; A.B., Harvard U., 1959, M.Pub.Adminstrn., 1962, LL.B., 1963; Ph.D., Syracuse U., 1974. Admitted to D.C. bar, 1964; lectr. law and pub. adminstrn. U. Malawi, Blantyre, 1963-64; lectr. polit. sci. Syracuse (N.Y.) U., 1964-66; asst. prof. politics and law Cath. U. Am., Washington, 1971-77; asst. prof. law Potomac Sch. Law, Washington, 1977—. Mem. Am. Soc. Internat. Law, Am. Polit. Sci. Assn., Japanese Am. Soc. for Legal Studies. Recipient Outstanding Tchr. award Cath. U., 1975-76; author: (with L.W. Holborn and Rita Chartrand) Refugees—A Problem of Our Time: The Work of the U.N. High Commissioner for Refugees, 1951-72, 2 vols., 1975. Home: Route 1 Box 346 Harpers Ferry WV 25425 Office: Potomac Sch Law Washington DC 20012

CHASAN, ROSLYN PEARL, b. Wilkes Barre, Pa., Sept. 22, 1932; A.A., Los Angeles City Coll., 1952; J.D., Southwestern U., 1967. Admitted to Calif. bar, 1968; individual practice law, Torrance, Calif., 1968—. Mem. S.W. Jewish Council Torrance. Mem. Calif. State Bar, Los Angeles County (legal-med. relations com.), South Bay bar assns., Calif., Los Angeles (bd. govs., chmn. law student liasion) trial lawyers assns., Women Lawyers Assn. Los Angeles. Office: 670 Union Bank Tower 21515 Hawthorne Blvd Torrance CA 90503 Tel (213) 370-3633

CHASANOW, HOWARD STUART, b. D.C., Apr. 3, 1937; B.A., U. Md., 1959, J.D., 1961; LL.M., Harvard, 1962. Admitted to Md. bar, 1961, U.S. Supreme Ct. bar, 1965; asst. state's atty. Prince George's County Md., 1963-64; dep. state's atty., 1964-68; substitute judge People's Ct., Md., 1970-71; judge Dist. Ct. of Md., Upper Marlboro, 1971-77; judge 7th Jud. Circuit, 1977—; lectr. U. Md. Sch. Law, 1973—; cons. Ct. of Appeals rules com. 1974-75. Founder Prince George's County Drinking Driver Sch.; judge advocate Am. Legion, Dept. Md., 1970-71. Mem. Md. State (chmn. criminal law sect. 1974-75), Prince George's (chmn. profl. ethics com.) bar assns. Home: 6905 96th Ave Seabrook MD 20801 Office: Ct House Main St Upper Marlboro MD 20870 Tel (301) 952-4173

CHASE, ARNOLD, b. Hackensack, N.J., Aug. 30, 1939; B.A. magna cum laude, Columbia, 1961, J.D. summa cum laude, 1964. Admitted to N.Y. bar, 1964; asso. firm Botein, Hays, Sklar & Herzberg, N.Y.C., 1964-72, partner, 1973—. Trustee Ednl. Alliance, Inc., 1976—. Mem. N.Y. State, N.Y.C. bar assns. Home: 47 Duke Dr Paramus NJ 07652 Office: 200 Park Ave New York City NY 10017 Tel (212) 867-5500

CHASE, GEORGE HILTON, b. Cambridge, Mass., Apr. 26, 1904; A.B., Bates Coll., 1926; LL.B., Boston U., 1930. Admitted to Mass. bar, 1930; partner firm H.M. & G.H. Chase, Boston, 1930-47; individual practice law, Oak Bluffs, Mass., 1947—; treas. Wesley House, Inc., Oak Bluffs, 1945—, Winemack Homes, Inc., Oak Bluffs, 1945—; gen. counsel Mass. Hotel Assn., 1931-45. Mem. Oak Bluffs Water Bd., 1958—. Mem. Mass., Dukes County bar assns. Home and office: Commonwealth Square Oak Bluffs MA 02557 Tel (617) 693-0135

CHASE, JONATHAN SCOTT, b. Houston, Mar. 14, 1946; B.A. in Polit. Sci., U. Houston, 1968, J.D., 1971. Admitted to Tex. bar, 1973; legal officer 1st Field Army Support Command, Ft. Lee, Va., 1971-72; gen. counsel U.S. Army Troop Support Agy., Ft. Lee, 1972-73; asso. counsel Campbell Taggart, Inc., Dallas, 1973-76; staff atty. Dr. Pepper

Co., Dallas, 1976—, asst. sec., 1977—; lectr. Am. Mgmt. Assn., Tex. Safety Assn. Vice-pres. Ft. Lee Ecology Club, 1972-73. Mem. Am. (past mem. environ. quality com., young lawyers sect.), Dallas (civic affairs com. 1974—) bar assns., State Bar Tex., Phi Alpha Delta. Office: PO Box 5086 Dallas TX 75222 Tel (214) 824-0331

CHASE, LUCIUS PETER, b. Rochester, N.Y., Jan. 1, 1902; B.A., U. Wis., 1923, J.D., 1925; LL.D., Lakeland Coll., 1972. Admitted to Wis. bar, 1925, U.S. Supreme Ct. bar, 1932; spl. asst. to atty. gen. U.S., Washington, 1925-26; v.p. Kohler Co. (Wis.), 1960-68, sr. v.p., 1968-71, dir., 1937—; partner firm Chase, Olson, Kloet & Gunderson, Sheboygan, 1971—; dir. emeritus Citizens Bank Sheboygan, 1971—. Mem. Am., Wis., Sheboygan County bar assns., Am. Legion, VFW, Mil. Order Purple Heart, Order Coif, Scabbard and Blade, Alpha Sigma Phi, Gamma Eta Gamma. Contbr. articles to legal jours. Home: 624 School St Kohler WI 53044 Office: 602 N 6th St Sheboygan WI 53081

CHASE, NICHOLAS JOSEPH, b. Windsor, Conn., Jan. 9, 1913; A.B., Catholic U. Am., 1933, A.M., 1934; LL.B., Georgetown U., 1940. Admitted to D.C. bar, 1939, Md. bar, 1943, U.S. Supreme Ct. bar, 1943; mem. firm Leahy & Hughes, Washington, 1940-48, Chase & Williams, Washington, 1949-52, Chase & McChesney, Washington, 1953-63, Chase & Colton, Washington, 1964—; prof. law Cath. U. Am., 1943-45, Georgetown U., 1946-66; gen. counsel Village of Chevy Chase (Md.), 1943-49. Mem. Washington Law Enforcement Council, 1951-54, Washington Jud. Conf., 1952-62. Mem. Am. Arbitration Assn., Bar Assn. D.C. Author: Real Estate Taxation in the District of Columbia, 1934; Judicial Proof of the Death of John Wilkes Booth, 1946; Learned Hand and the Trial of a Law Suit, 1954; Thomas More: Sir and Saint, 1957; editor D.C. Bar Jour., 1944-54. Home: 5205 Oakland Rd Chevy Chase MD 20015 Office: 777 14th St Washington DC 20015 Tel (202) ST3-1776

CHASE, OSCAR GOTTFRIED, b. N.Y.C., Apr. 5, 1940; B.A. with honors, N.Y. U., 1960; J.D., Yale, 1963. Admitted to N.Y. bar, 1966, U.S. Supreme Ct. bar, 1972; counsel Lower West Side Community Corp., N.Y.C., 1966-67; asst. gen. counsel and dir. law reform Community Action for Legal Services, Inc., N.Y.C., 1968-72; asso. prof. law Bklyn. Law Sch., 1972—; cons. ACLU, summer 1974; dir. Nat. Employment Law Project, Inc., N.Y.C., 1974—; dir. Untapped Resources, Inc., N.Y.C., 1975—. Mem. Assn. Bar City N.Y., Council N.Y. Law Assos. Contbr. articles to legal jours.; revision author N.Y. Civil Practice, 1975-77. Office: 250 Joralemon St Brooklyn NY 11201 Tel (212) 625-2200

CHASE, THEODORE, b. Boston, Jan. 23, 1912; A.B., Harvard, 1934, LL.B., 1937. Admitted to Mass. bar, 1937, U.S. Supreme Ct. bar, 1944; asso. firm Palmer & Dodge, Boston, 1937-42, partner, 1942, 46—; counsel fin. div. Office of Procurement, U.S. Navy, Washington, 1943-46; dir. State St. Boston Fin. Corp., State St. Bank and Trust Co. Selectman, Town of Dover (Mass.), 1951-57, chmn., 1954-57; mem. Mass. Bd. Regional Community Colls., 1959-75, chmn., 1967-75; gen. chmn. Greater Boston Red Feather Campaign, 1955; pres. United Community Services of Boston, 1961-63; trustee Northfield Mt. Hermon Sch., 1951—, chmn., 1959-67; trustee Groton Sch., 1957-75; chmn. Harvard Fund Council, 1961; chief marshall Harvard 25th reunion, 1959. Mem. Am., Mass., Boston (past pres.) bar assns., Mass. Hist. Soc. (standing com. trustees of reservations 1969-75, chmn. 1976—, council 1970—). Recipient Charles M. Rogerson award United Community Services, 1968. Home: 74 Farm St Dover MA 02030 Office: Palmer & Dodge One Beacon St Boston MA 02108 Tel (617) 227-4400

CHASEN, HAROLD ALFRED, b. Norwich, Conn., May 30, 1929; B.A., U. Conn., 1950; J.D., Boston U., 1952. Admitted to Conn. bar, 1952, Tex. bar, 1959; individual practice law, Houston, 1959—. Home: 5531 Spellman St Houston TX 77096 Office: 11505 Chimney Rock Houston TX 77035 Tel (713) 729-1737

CHASSEN, CHARLES IAN, b. Long Beach, N.Y., Dec. 2, 1936; B.A., Colgate U., 1958; LL.B., Bklyn. Law Sch., 1961, LL.M., 1966. Admitted to N.Y. bar, 1961, Fla. bar, 1973; dep. county atty. Nassau County, N.Y., 1964-65; individual practice law, Atlantic Beach, N.Y., 1965—; hearing examiner N.Y.C. Parking Violations Bur., 1971—. Lt. Atlantic Beach (N.Y.) Aux. Police. Mem. Fla. Bar, Nassau County Bar Assn., Long Beach (N.Y.) Lawyers Assn. Office: 2015 Park St Atlantic Beach NY 11509 Tel (516) 371-4243

CHATZ, JAMES ALAN, b. Chgo., July 30, 1935; B.S., Northwestern U., 1956, J.D., 1958. Admitted to Ill. bar, 1958; partner firm with Robert B. Chatz, Chgo., 1958-75, with Mordecai J. Sugarman and Leonard O. Abrams, 1962; prin. partner firm James A. Chatz, Mordecai J. Sugarman, Leonard O. Abrams, Joel A. Haber and Melvyn A. Abrams, Chgo., 1976—. Apptd. chmn. Fair Housing Review Bd., Evanston, Ill., 1968; chmn. Hosp. Reimbursement Review Bd., State of Ill., 1975. Mem. Chgo. (chmn. bankruptcy com. 1975-76), Am. bar assns., Comml. Law League Am. (ednl. com. 1975). Columnist for Chgo. Daily Law Bull.; contbr. articles to publs. Home: 1430 Ridge St Evanston IL 60201 Office: 105 W Adams St Chicago IL 60603 Tel (312) 346-7500

CHAUNCEY, CARL ODLIN, b. Melrose, Mass., Apr. 13, 1898; LL.B., Northeastern U., 1925. Admitted to Mass. bar, 1933; legal dept. Farm Credit Banks of Springfield (Mass.), 1934-63, gen. counsel, 1962-63. Mem. Mass., Hampden County bar assns.

CHAVEZ, FRANK NORMAN, b. Socorro, N.Mex., Feb. 9, 1941; B.S., N.Mex. State Coll., 1962; J.D., U. N.Mex., 1969. Admitted to N.Mex. bar, 1969; asso. Les Houston, Albuquerque, 1969; asst. atty. gen. State of N.Mex., Santa Fe, 1970-73; asst. city atty. Las Cruces (N.Mex.), 1973-75, city atty., 1975—. Mem. Nat. Inst. Municipal Law Officers (N.Mex. state chmn.). Office: Box 1316 Las Cruces NM 88001 Tel (505) 526-0432

CHAZEN, BERNARD, b. N.Y.C., Sept. 14, 1923; student John Marshall Coll., 1941-42, Middlebury Coll., 1943-44; LL.B., J.D., Columbia, 1948; LL.M., Rutgers U., 1951. Admitted to N.J. bar, 1949, U.S. Ct. Mil. Appeals bar, 1950, U.S. Supreme Ct. bar, 1956; partner firms Wood & Chazen, Westfield, N.J., 1948-50, Baker, Garber & Chazen, Hoboken, N.J., 1950-70, Canter & Chazen, Jersey City, 1970-71; individual practice law, Englewood, N.J., 1971—. Mem. Englewood Bd. Edn., 1965-69. Mem. Naval Res. Lawyers Assn., Am., N.J., Bergen County (N.J.), Hudson County (N.J.) bar assns., Am. Trial Lawyers Assn., Am. Judicature Soc. (trustee 1971-75), Internat. Law Assn. Asso. editor N.J. Law Jour., 1967—. Home: 331 Starling Rd Englewood NJ 07631 Office: PO Box 470 10 Grand Ave Englewood NJ 07631 Tel (201) 567-5500

CHAZEN, HARTLEY JAMES, b. N.Y.C., Feb. 14, 1932; A.B., Coll. City N.Y., 1953; LL.B., Harvard, 1958; LL.M. (Univ. fellow), N.Y.U., 1959. Admitted to N.Y. bar, 1959; mem. firms Hays, St. John, Abramson & Heilbron, 1959-65, Shea, Gallop, Climenko & Gould, 1965-68, Rosenman, Colin, Kay, Petschek & Emil, 1968-70, N.Y.C.; partner firm Monasch Chazen Stream & Feinberg, N.Y.C., 1970—; lectr. in field. Mem. Am., N.Y., N.Y.C. bar assns. Home: 75 Perkins Rd Greenwich CT 08530 Office: 777 3d Ave New York City NY 10017 Tel (212) 759-7220

CHAZKEL, MICHAEL FREDRIC, b. Bklyn., Jan. 20, 1940; B.S., Bklyn. Coll., 1965; M.S., L.I. U., 1967; J.D., Bklyn. Law Sch., 1971. Admitted to N.J. bar, 1971; Internat. dir. real estate Gen. Adjustment Bur. Inc., N.Y.C., 1968-69; dir. real estate and ins. Consol. Edison Co., N.Y.C., 1969-71; prosecutor, New Brunswick, N.J., 1975-76; exec. dir., Public Adjusters Assn. N.J., 1974—. Mem. Am., N.J., New Brunswick, Middlesex County bar assns., Am., Middlesex County trial lawyers assns. Home: 1050 George St New Brunswick NJ 08901 Office: 87 Bayard St New Brunswick NJ 08903 Tel (201) 828-7117

CHEATHAM, FRANK SELLARS, JR., b. Savannah, Ga., Jan. 11, 1924; A.A., Armstrong Jr. Coll., 1944; A.B., U. Ga., 1946, LL.B., 1948. Admitted to Ga. bar, 1948; asso. firm Douglas, McWhorter & Adams, Savannah, 1948-53; partner firm Cheatham, Beckmann & Exley, Savannah, 1953-55, Cheatham, Bergen & Sparkman, Savannah, 1959-60; individual practice law, Savannah, 1960-72; judge Chatham County Superior Ct., Eastern Circuit, Savannah, 1972—; mem. State Ga. Disciplinary Bd., 1967-70, Jud. Council Ga., 1975—; mem. Ga. Ho. of Reps., 1953-60, chmn. appropriations com., 1957-60. Trustee Cardler Gen. Hosp., Savannah; bd. curators Ga. Hist. soc., Savannah; bd. dirs. Savannah YMCA, 1951—, pres., 1963-67. Mem. Am., Savannah (pres. 1969) bar assns., Am. Judicature Soc., Phi Delta Phi. Home: 1 E 67th St Apt 3 Savannah GA 31405 Office: County Courthouse Room 214 Savannah GA 31401 Tel (912) 232-1214

CHEATHAM, RICHARD REED, b. Pulaski, Tenn., July 14, 1943; B.S., U. Va., 1965; LL.B., Harvard, 1968. Admitted to Ga. bar, 1969; instr. bus. law and taxation U. Ga., 1968-69; asso. firm Kilpatrick, Cody, Rogers, McClatchey & Regenstein, Atlanta, 1969-75, partner, 1975—. Mem. Am. Bar Assn. Office: 3100 Equitable Bldg Atlanta GA 30303 Tel (404) 522-3100

CHEELEY, JOSEPH E., JR., b. Buford, Ga., Nov. 4, 1928; J.D., U. Ga., 1950; postgrad. Nat. Coll. State Judiciary, Nev., 1975. Admitted to Ga. bar, 1950; partner firm Cheeley & Chandler, Buford, 1950—; pros. atty. Gwinnett County (Ga.), 1955-58; judge State Ct. Gwinnett County, 1958—; bd. govs. Ga. State Bar, 1977—; mem. State Disciplinary Bd., 1977—. Chmn. Lake Lanier Islands Authority, 1975—; lt. gov. Kiwanis Internat., 1957; pres. Upper Chattahoochee Devel. Authority, 1974—. Mem. Gwinnett, Ga., Am. bar assns., Lawyers Club Atlanta, Am. Judges Assn., Am. Judicature Soc., Nat. Criminal Justice Standards Assn. (chmn.). Named One of Five Outstanding Young Men of Ga., Ga. C. of C., 1963; Outstanding Young Man of Am., Jaycees, 1964. Home: 5936 Shadburn Ferry Rd Buford GA 30518 Office: PO Drawer 380 Buford GA 30518 Tel (404) 945-7646

CHEEVER, LYLE EUGENE, b. Brookings, S.D., Nov. 14, 1910; student S.D. State U., Brookings, 1928-31; LL.B., U. Minn., 1934. Admitted to S.D. bar, 1934; practiced in Brookings, 1934-54; asst. U.S. Atty. for Justice Dept., 1954-60; judge S.D. Dist. Ct., 7th Dist., 1969-75; judge 3d County Circuit Ct., 1975—; city commr. City of Brookings, 1950-52, mayor, 1952-54; pres. Dist. Judges Assn., 1973. Home: 925 5th St Brookings SD 57006 Office: Brookings County Courthouse Brookings SD 57006 Tel (605) 692-7328

CHEMA, THOMAS VINCENT, b. East Liverpool, Ohio, Oct. 31, 1946; A.B., U. Notre Dame, 1968; J.D., Harvard, 1971. Admitted to Ohio bar, 1971; asso. firm Arter & Hadden, Cleve., 1971-76. Trustee Hough Area Devel. Corp., Cleve., 1976—; dir., officer Shaker Heights Youth Center, Inc., 1973—; dir. Citizens League Greater Cleve., 1971—; campaign mgr. Metzenbaum for Sen. com. 1976. Mem. Ohio State Bar Assn., Bar Assn. Greater Cleve., Am. Arbitration Assn. Home: 3670 Gridley Rd Shaker Heights OH 44122 Office: 1144 Union Commerce Bldg Cleveland OH 44115 Tel (216) 696-1144

CHENEY, JOHN NELSON, b. Juneau, Alaska, Jan. 9, 1915; B.A., U. Wash., 1937, J.D., 1939. Admitted to Wash. bar, 1940; individual practice law, Anacortes, Wash., 1946—; justice peace Anacortes Precinct, 1946-58. Mem. Wash., Skagit County bar assns., N.W. Wash. Estate Planning Council. Home: 1104 Marine Dr Anacortes WA 98221 Office: Box 437 Anacortes WA 98221 Tel (206) 293-2641

CHENEY, THOMAS FRITTS, b. Omaha, Apr. 15, 1938; B.S., Colo. State U., 1960; J.D., U. Colo., 1966. Admitted to Colo., D.C. bars, 1966; partner firm Cashen, Cheney, Johnston & Adamson, Montrose, Colo., 1966—; dep. dist. atty. Montrose and Ouray Counties, Colo., 1968-69; U.S. magistrate for Dist. Colo., 1971-75. Mem. Permanent Jud. Conf. of the Synod of the Rocky Mountains United Presbyn. Chs., 1972—. Mem. Am., Colo. bar assns. Home and office: POB 387 Montrose CO 81401 Tel (303) 249-6611

CHENEY, VAN, b. Macon, Ga., Mar. 18, 1946; A.B., U. Ga., 1967, J.D., 1970. Admitted to Ga. bar, 1971; asso. firm Burt, Burt & Rentz, Albany, Ga., 1970-72; individual practice law, Reidsville, Ga., 1973—; councilman, mayor pro-tem, Reidsville, 1974—. Mem. Am., Ga., Atlantic Circuit bar assns., Am. Judicature Soc. Home and Office: PO Box 500 Reidsville GA 30453 Tel (912) 557-4768

CHERNE, LEO, b. N.Y.C., Sept. 8, 1912; grad. N.Y. U., 1931; LL.B., N.Y. Law Sch., 1934; LL.D., Pace Coll., 1967, N.Y. Law Sch., 1967. Admitted N.Y. bar, 1934; exec. dir. the Research Inst. Am., Inc. Hon. mem. faculty, mem. bd. advisers Indsl. Coll. of Armed Forces; lectr. New Sch. for Social Research, 1946-52; chmn. bd. dirs. Internat. Rescue Com., 1953—; adviser on taxation and fiscal policy to Gen. MacArthur, 1946; chmn. bd. Lawyers Co-op. Pub. Co. Dir. Viacom. Internat. Inc. Bd. dirs. Willkie Meml.; bd. dirs., chmn. exec. com. Freedom House, 1946—; mem. select commn. Western Hemisphere Immigration, 1967-68; mem. U.S. Adv. Commn. on Internat. Ednl. and Cultural Affairs; mem. Pres.'s Fgn. Intelligence Adv. Bd., 1973—; mem. Commn. on Critical Choices for Ams.; mem. Panel on Internat. Information, Edn. and Cultural Relations, 1974-75. Decorated Comdr.'s Cross of Order of Merit (Fed. Republic of Germany); Kim Khanh Medal (Vietnam); Nat. Order Legion Honor (French Republic). Mem. Hudson Inst. Author: Adjusting Your Business to War, 1939; M-Day and What it Means to You, 1940; The Rest of Your Life, 1944. Sculptor: Bronze of John F. Kennedy, Berlin Germany, bronze portrait Lyndon B. Johnson at Lyndon Baines Johnson Library, bronze of Abraham Lincoln, White House; bronze portrait of Boris Pasternak, Am. Acad. Arts and Letters; represented at the Smithsonian Instn., Phoenix Art Mus., Sibelius Mus., Helsinki, U. Cal. at Los Angeles, U. Bahia (Brazil), Lincoln Mus., Washington, Presdl. Palaces, New Delhi, India, Mexico City, U.S. Pavilion, N.Y. World's Fair, 1964-65, Winston Churchill Meml., Fulton, Mo. Mem. Nat. Sculpture Soc. (adviser). Office: 589 Fifth Ave New York City NY 10017*

CHERNER, MARVIN, b. Bessemer, Ala., Oct. 21, 1924; B.S. in Chem. Engring., Northwestern U., 1947; LL.B., Harvard, 1951. Admitted to Ala. bar, 1951; individual practice law, Birmingham, Ala., 1953-77; circuit judge 10th Jud. Circuit Ala., 1977—. Mem. Am. Law Inst., Am., Ala. (vice chmn. unauthorized practice of law com. 1976), Birmingham (co-chmn. profl. ethics com. 1970-71, chmn. unauthorized practice of law, 1966) bar assns. Office: Jefferson County Courthouse Birmingham AL 35203 Tel (205) 325-5280

CHERNICK, RICHARD, b. Los Angeles, May 22, 1945; A.B., U. Calif., Los Angeles, 1967; J.D., U. So. Calif., 1970. Admitted to Calif. bar, 1971, U.S. Supreme Ct. bar, 1974; law clk. to Chief Justice Donald R. Wright, Calif. Supreme Ct., 1970-71; individual practice law, Beverly Hills, Calif.; instr. Sch. Pub. Adminstrn. U. So. Calif., 1972, 74—. Mem. Los Angeles County, Am. bar assns., Calif. State Bar, Order of Coif. Articles editor: U. So. Calif. Law Rev., 1968-70. Office: 9601 Wilshire Blvd Beverly Hills CA 90210 Tel (203) 273-6990

CHERNOF, STEPHEN LAWRENCE, b. Chgo., Feb. 28, 1944; B.S., U. Wis., 1965; J.D. cum laude, 1968. Admitted to Wis. bar, 1968; law clk. to judge U.S. Dist. Ct., Milw., 1968-69; partner firm Levin, Blumenthal, Herz & Levin, Milw., 1969—. Chmn. bus. div. Milw. Jewish Fedn. Campaign, 1976. Mem. Am., Wis., Milw. bar assns., Order of Coif, Tau Epsilon Rho. Articles editor Univ. Wis. Law Review, 1968. Office: 777 E Wisconsin Ave Milwaukee WI 53202 Tel (414) 273-4333

CHERNOFF, ARNOLD HOWARD, b. Mt. Vernon, N.Y., Dec. 26, 1940; B.A., Mich. State U., 1962; J.D., N.Y. U., 1965. Admitted to N.Y. bar, 1966; mem. firm Carb, Luria, Glassner, Cook & Kufeld, N.Y.C., 1966—. Pres., mem. exec. com. Congregation B'nai Israel, Fairlawn, N.J. Mem. Assn. Bar City N.Y. (mem. spl. com. eminent domain), Real Estate Tax Rev. Bar Assn. Home: 0-69 Pine Ave Fair Lawn NJ 07410 Office: 529 Fifth Ave New York City NY 10017 Tel (212) 986-3131

CHERNOFF, DANIEL PAREGOL, b. Washington, Jan. 24, 1935; B.E.E. with distinction, Cornell U., 1957, LL.B., 1959. Admitted to N.Y. State bar, 1959, D.C. bar, 1959, U.S. Patent and Trademark Office bar, 1960, Oreg. bar, 1967; asso. firm Fish & Neave, N.Y.C., 1961-67, Davies, Biggs, Strayer, Stoel & Boley, Portland, Oreg., 1967-70; partner firm Chernoff & Vilhauer, Portland, 1970—. Home: 710 N W Winchester Terr Portland OR 97210 Office: 400 Oregon Nat Bldg 610 SW Alder St Portland OR 97205 Tel (503) 227-5631

CHERNOFF, JOEL SHANE, b. Chgo., Nov. 30, 1942; B.S. in Accounting, Russian, Northwestern U., 1964, J.D., 1967. Admitted to Ill. bar, 1970, U.S. Dist. Ct. bar, 1970; tchr. Chgo. Bd. Edn., 1967-69; mem. firm John Klepak, Chgo., 1970; partner firm Asher & Chernoff, Chgo., 1970-73; partner firm Beaubien, Asher & Chernoff, Palatine, Ill., 1973-76; individual practice law, Hoffman Estates, Ill., 1976—. Mem. Am., Ill. State, Chgo., North Suburban, Northwest Suburban, DuPage County, Lake County, McHenry County bar assns. Office: 2308 W Higgins Rd Hoffman Estates IL 60195 Tel (312) 884-0048

CHEROS, JOHN GEORGE, b. Greenville, S.C., Feb. 10, 1939; B.A., Furman U., 1962; LL.B., U. S.C., 1964. Admitted to S.C. bar, 1964; asso. firm Love, Thornton & Thompson, Greenville, 1964-70, partner, 1970-72; partner firm Cheros & Patterson, Greenville, 1972-76; individual practice law, Greenville, 1976—; issuing agt. title ins. cos. Bd. dirs. St. George Greek Orthodox Ch., Greenville, 1965-69, Mitchell Rd. Christian Ministries Retirement Center, 1976—; active United Fund, 1966-67. Mem. S.C., Greenville County, Am. bar assns., Wig and Robe Honor Soc., Phi Beta Kappa., Phi Delta Phi. Recipient Lawyers Title award in real property law U. S.C., 1964, Am. Jurisprudence award in wills, 1964, in trust, 1964; Claude N. Sapp award, 1964; contbr. articles to S.C. Law Rev., Recent Decisions, Editor S.C. Law Rev., 1964. Home: Route 2 POB 523 Raven Rd Greenville SC 29607 Office: POB 10025 611 N Academy St Greenville SC 29603 Tel (803) 233-7401

CHERRY, DAVID EARL, b. Fort Worth, Sept. 10, 1944; B.B.A., Tex. Christian U., 1967; J.D., Baylor U., 1968. Admitted to Tex. bar, 1968; asso. firm Pakis & Sanders, Waco, Tex., 1969, William R. Pakis, Waco, 1969-70; partner firm Pakis & Cherry, and predecessors, Waco, 1971—. Bd. dirs. Waco-McLennan County Legal Aid Soc., 1971-73, Waco YMCA, 1976—, Waco Lighthouse for the Blind, 1971-74; mem. bd. council, trustee Woodway (Tex.) First United Methodist Ch., 1976—; bd. devel. Tex. Baptist Children's Home, 1975—; mem. Woodway Planning and Zoning Commn., 1973—, chmn., 1975-76; mem. nat. exploring com. Boy Scouts Am.; mem. Woodway Charter Commn., 1973-74. Mem. Am., Tex., Tex. Jr., Waco-McLennan County Jr. (past dir., pres. 1974-75) bar assns., Am. Judicature Soc. Office: 800 First Nat Bldg Waco TX 76701 Tel (817) 753-4511

CHERRY, DONALD GORDON, b. Rochester, N.Y., Nov. 4, 1942; A.B. with distinction, U. Rochester, 1964; LL.D., Cornell U., 1967. Admitted to N.Y. State bar, 1967, Fla. bar, 1970, Md. bar, 1972, Ky. bar, 1973, U.S. Supreme Ct. bar, 1971, U.S. Ct. Mil. Appeals, 1970; atty. IBM, Armonk, N.Y., 1967-68, atty., staff atty. Fed. Systems Div., IBM, Gaithersburg, Md., 1971-72, area counsel Office Products Div., Lexington, Ky., 1971-75, sr. atty. IBM Europe, Paris, France, 1975—; served with JAC, U.S. Navy, 1968-71, now lt. comdr. JAGC, USNR. Mem. Fla., Ky., Am. bar assns., Cornell Law Assn., Phi Alpha Delta. Mem. editorial bd. Cornell Law Review, 1966-67. Home: care 36 Clover Park Dr Rochester NY 14618 Office: 8-10 Cité du Retiro 75008 Paris France 266-33-11

CHERRY, JOHN ROBERT, b. Iowa City, Jan. 5, 1945; B.A., Coe Coll., 1967; J.D., Fla. State U., 1970. Admitted to Fla. bar, 1970, Iowa bar, 1971; asso. firm Pappas & Dunn, Mason City, Iowa, 1970, firm Bryant & Cherry, Mason City, 1970—; magistrate Cerro Gordo County (Iowa), 1975—. Mem. Iowa, Am., Cerro Gordo County bar assns. Home: Route 1 Dodges Point Beach Clear Lake IA 50428 Office: 322 Brick and Tile Bldg Mason City IA 50401 Tel (515) 424-2921

CHERRY, PATRICK FRANK, b. Lansing, Mich., Jan. 3, 1946; B.A., U. Mich., 1966; J.D., Wayne State U., 1969. Admitted to Mich. bar, 1969; law clk. to judge in Ingham County (Mich.), 1969-70; asst. prosecutor Ingham County, pros. atty., 1970-75, chief criminal div., 1974-75; judge Dist. Ct. 54-A, Lansing, 1975—. Mem. Am., Ingham County bar assns., Am. Judicature Soc., Nat. Conf. Spl. Ct. Judges. Office: 6th Floor City Hall Lansing MI 48933 Tel (517) 487-1350

CHERRY, ROBERT BRUCE, b. Phila., Sept. 9, 1933; B.Indsl. Engring., Ga. Inst. Tech., 1956; J.D., Seton Hall U., 1967. Admitted to N.J. bar, 1967; asso. firm Gelman & Gelman, Paterson, N.J., 1967-68; individual practice law, Paterson, 1968-75; partner firm Cherry & Petrie, Paterson, 1975-77, Cherry, Petrie & Vallario, Paterson, 1977—; lectr. in field. Mem. Am., N.J., Passaic County bar assns., N.J. Assn. Health Care Facilities. Home: 21 Petrie Ln Wayne NJ 07470 Office: 251 Union Blvd Totowa Boro NJ 07512 Tel (201) 523-9797

CHESLEY, GEORGE LONGLEY, b. Rochester, Minn., Feb. 24, 1947; A.B., U. Mich., An Arbor, 1969; J.D., U. Ill., 1972. Admitted to Ill. bar, 1972; mem. firm DePew, Grimes, and Chesley, Bloomington, Ill., 1972—; asst. pub. defender McLean County (Ill.), 1974-76. Mem. Am., Ill. State, McLean County bar assns., McLean County Trial Lawyers Assn. Home: 2704 Hall Ct Bloomington IL 61701 Office: 317 N Main St Bloomington IL 61701 Tel (309) 829-7002

CHESTER, JOHN JONAS, b. Columbus, Ohio, July 13, 1920; B.A. cum laude, Amherst Coll., 1942; J.D., Yale, 1948. Admitted to Ohio bar, 1948; partner firms Chester & Chester, Columbus, 1948-57, Chester & Rose, Columbus, 1958-70, Chester, Hoffman, Park, Willcox & Rose, Columbus, 1971—; mem. Ohio Ho. of Reps., 1953-58; spl. counsel to Pres. U.S., 1974. Trustee Columbus Acad. Mem. Am., Ohio State Columbus bar assns., Am. Judicature Soc., Am. Trial Lawyers Assn., Ohio Hist. Soc. (trustee). Home: 4906 Riverside Dr Columbus OH 43220 Office: 16 E Broad St Columbus OH 43215 Tel (614) 221-4000

CHESTER, SAMUEL, b. N.Y.C., Dec. 17, 1917; B.A., City Coll. N.Y., 1936; LL.B., Columbia U., 1939. Admitted to N.Y. State bar, 1939, U.S. Fed. Cts. bar, 1939; individual practice law, N.Y.C., 1940—; arbitrator Trade Bd. N.Y. Smoked Fish Industry. Mem. N.Y. State Trial Lawyers Assn., Am. Arbitration Assn. (arbitrator). Home: 33 Huntington Dr Yonkers NY 10704 Office: 25 W 43d St New York City NY 10036 Tel (212) 354-2828

CHEW, HON, b. Oakland, Calif., Dec. 2, 1929; B.S., U. Calif., Berkeley, 1952, LL.B., 1955, J.D., 1955. Admitted to Calif. bar, 1955, U.S. Dist. Ct. bar, 1955, U.S. Supreme Ct. bar, 1968; individual practice law, Oakland, 1956—. Chmn. Oakland Relocation Appeals Bd., 1974—; mem. Alameda Regional Criminal Justice Planning Bd., 1970—. Mem. Alameda County Bar Assn., State Bar Calif., Lawyers Club Alameda County. Office: 919 Harrison St Oakland CA 94607 Tel (415) 444-1646

CHICLANA, JOSE ANTONIO, b. Santa Clara, Cuba, Apr. 2, 1930; J.D., Havana U., 1960; J.D. Seton Hall U., 1973. Admitted to N.J. bar, 1973; individual practice law, Union City, N.J., 1973—. Mem. Am., N.J., Hudson County bar assns., North Hudson Lawyers Club. Home: 380 Mountain Rd Union City NJ 07087 Office: 3600 Bergenline Ave Union City NY 07087 Tel (201) 864-0034

CHIDIAC, NORMAN JERRY, b. Paterson, N.J., May 19, 1938; B.S. in Secondary Edn., Seton Hall U., 1961; J.D., U. Louisville, 1969. Admitted to N.J. bar, 1970; individual practice law, Paterson, 1970—. Mem. Passaic County Bar Assn., Am. Trial Lawyers Assn. Home: 360 Grove St Clifton NJ 07513 Office: 140 Market St Paterson NJ 07505 Tel (201) 742-7799

CHIDNESE, PATRICK N., b. Neptune, N.J., May 26, 1940; A.B., U. Miami, 1964, J.D., 1968. Admitted to Fla. bar, 1968; asso. firm Sinclair, Louis & Huttoe, Miami, Fla., 1968-69, firm Stephens, Demos, Magill & Thornton, Miami, 1969-70, firm Howell, Kirby, Montgomery, D'Aiuto, Dean & Hallowes, Ft. Lauderdale, Fla., 1970-71; individual practice law, Ft. Lauderdale, 1971—; ct. atty. Broward County Juvenile Ct., 1971-72. Mem. Fla. Bar (vice chmn. no-fault ins. com. 1974-76, lectr. convs. 1975, 76), Broward County Bar Assn., Acad. Fla. Trial Lawyers, Broward County Trial Lawyers Assn. (bd. dirs. 1974—). Office: 200 SE 6th St Suite 600 Fort Lauderdale FL 33301 Tel (305) 462-8484

CHIEFFO, DOMINIC JAMES, b. Youngstown, Ohio, Jan. 14, 1942; B.B.A., Ohio U., 1963; J.D., Ohio State U., 1966. Admitted to Ohio bar, 1966; partner firm Jones and Chieffo, Columbus, Ohio, 1969-75; partner firm Plymale and Chieffo, Columbus, 1976—. Pres. Franklin County (Ohio) Juvenile Probation Council, 1974-75; dir. One to One, Columbus, 1975—. Mem. Assn. Trial lawyers Am., Ohio Acad. Trial Lawyers, Franklin County Trial Lawyers Assn., Am., Ohio, Columbus bar assns. Office: 529 S 3d St Columbus OH 43215 Tel (614) 221-1166

CHIESA, ROBERT LOUIS, b. Denver, Mar. 31, 1931; A.B., Dartmouth Coll., 1953; LL.B., Boston U., 1960. Admitted to N.H. bar, 1960, U.S. Supreme Ct. bar, 1971; asso. firm Wadleigh, Starr, Peters, Dunn & Kohls, Manchester, N.H., 1960-67, partner, 1967—. Trustee St. Paul Methodist Ch., Elliot Hosp.; mem. adv. bd. Salvation Army. Mem. Def. Research Inst., Internat. Assn. Ins. Counsel, No. New Eng. Def. Counsel, N.H. (bd. govs. 1971-73, pres. 1977—), Manchester (pres. 1973-74), Am. bar assns. Home: 364 Ray St Manchester NH 03104 Office: 95 Market St Manchester NH 03101 Tel (603) 669-4140

CHILCOTE, LEE ALFRED, b. Cleve., May 5, 1942; B.A., Dartmouth Coll., 1964; B.S., Thayer Sch. of Engring., 1965; J.D., U. Calif., 1972. Admitted to Ohio bar, 1972; mem. firm Thompson, Hine and Flory, Cleve., 1972—. Mem. fin. institutions advisory com., Cleveland Heights, Ohio; planning commr. City of Cleveland Heights, also mem city council; trustee Hough Housing Corp., Elder Lot, Inc. Mem. Am., Ohio State bar assns., Order of the Coif, Thurston Soc. Contbr. articles to legal jours. Home: 2322 Delamere Dr Cleveland OH 44106 Office: 1100 National City Bank Bldg Cleveland OH 44114 Tel (216) 241-1880

CHILD, RAMON MORLEY, b. Salt Lake City, July 9, 1923; B.S., U. Utah, 1950, J.D., 1952. Admitted to Utah bar, 1952, U.S. Supreme Ct. bar, 1962; partner firm Child, Spafford & Young, Salt Lake City, 1954-60, Ray, Quinney & Nebeker, Salt Lake City, 1962-74; asst. dist. atty. 3d Dist. Utah, 1956-58; U.S. atty. for Dist. Utah, Salt Lake City, 1975—. Diplomate Am. Bd. Trial Advocates. Fellow Am. Coll. Trial Lawyers. Home: 3644 S 860 E Salt Lake City UT 84117 Office: 200 US Court House 350 S Main St Salt Lake City UT 84101 Tel (801) 524-5687

CHILDERS, J. RICHARD, b. Metropolis, Ill., Apr. 18, 1939; B.A., So. Ill. U., 1962; J.D., U. Ill., 1967. Admitted to Ill. bar, 1967; asso. firm Reno, O'Byrne & Kepley, Champaign, Ill., 1967-69; asso. firm Peterson, Ross, Schloerb & Seidel, Chgo., 1969-75, partner, 1975—. Mem. Am., Ill. State bar assns., Ill. Def. Counsel, Chgo. Council Lawyers. Office: 200 E Randolph Dr Suite 7300 Chicago IL 60601 Tel (312) 861-1400

CHILDERS, JESSE LEE, b. LaGrange, Mo., Dec. 25, 1911; B.A., Culver Stockton Coll., Canton, Mo., 1931; J.D., U. Mo., Kansas City, 1935. Admitted to Mo. bar, 1934, U.S. Supreme Ct. bar, 1971; asso. firm Brewster, Brewster & Brewster, 1935, firm Lathrop, Crane, Reynolds, Sawyer & Mersereau, 1936; mem. law dept. Standard Oil Co. of Ind., 1936-60; regional atty. firm Madden & Burke, Kansas City, Mo., 1960-64; asso. firm Hillix, Hall, Childers, Brown & Hoffaus, Kansas City, 1964-69; of counsel firm Dietrich, Davis, Dicus, Burrell & Rowlands, Kansas City, 1969—. Mem. Am., Mo., Kansas City bar assns., Lawyers Assn. Kansas City, Delta Theta Phi (Distinguished Alumni award 1963). Recipient Distinguished Alumni Recognition award Culver Stockton Coll., 1958; Recognition award, Law Found., U. Mo. at Kansas City, 1965. Home: 1204 W 69th St Kansas City MO 64113 Office: 1001 Dwight Bldg 1004 Baltimore St Kansas City MO 64105 Tel (816) 221-3420

CHILDRESS, RICHARD JEFFERSON, b. Erlanger, Ky., Jan. 31, 1922; B.S., St. Louis U., 1947; J.D., U. Cin., 1949; postgrad. Harvard U., 1959-60. Admitted to Mo. bar, 1958; instr. law St. Louis U., 1949-50, asst. prof., 1950-56, asso. prof., 1956-59, prof., 1959—, dean Sch. Law, 1969—, also faculty advisor, founder St. Louis U. Law Jour.; spl. asst. circuit atty. City St. Louis, 1958. Exec. com. bd. dirs. Urban League St. Louis, 1967—, recipient Contbr. to Human Rights award, 1974; chmn. commn. human rights Archdiocese St. Louis, 1967-71, campaign human devel., 1975; bd. dirs. Legal Aid Soc. St. Louis, 1969-70, Tower Village Retirement Home, St. Louis, 1976—. Mem. Am., Met. St. Louis bar assns., Am. Law Inst., St. Louis Lawyers Assn., Am. Trial Lawyers Assn. Editor U. Cin. Law Rev., 1948. Home: 4711 Prague Ave Saint Louis MO 63109 Office: 3642 Lindell Blvd Saint Louis MO 63108 Tel (314) 535-3300

CHILDS, LOUANNE SCHAFER, b. Phila., Nov. 20, 1934; B.A., Swarthmore Coll., 1956; J.D., U. Pa., 1959. Admitted to Ohio bar, 1959; asso. firm Beard & Childs, Van Wert, Ohio, 1960-75; partner firm Childs & Childs, Van Wert, 1975—; juvenile officer Van Wert County, 1961-75, juvenile ct. referee, 1975—. Mem. Van Wert City Sch. Bd., 1964-75; trustee Van Wert YMCA, 1976—. Mem. Am., Ohio, Northwestern Ohio, Van Wert County bar assns. Home: 315 N Jefferson St Van Wert OH 45891 Office: 215 N Market St Van Wert OH 45891 Tel (419) 238-S307

CHILDS, MARJORIE MAY VICTORIA, b. N.Y.C., July 13, 1918; B.A., U. Calif., Berkeley, 1948; J.D., U. San Francisco, 1956; LL.D., Iowa Wesleyan Coll., 1973. Admitted to Calif. bar, 1957, U.S. Supreme Ct. bar, 1969; law clk. Regional Counsel's Office, Dept. Navy, Ft. Mason, San Francisco, 1957-60; asst. county counsel Office of Humboldt County (Calif.) Counsel, 1960-62; individual practice law, Eureka, Calif., 1960-62; partner firm Berry, Childs & Berry, San Francisco, 1962-64; referee Juvenile Ct., San Francisco, 1964—; commr. Superior Ct. assigned to Juvenile Ct., San Francisco, 1971—. Founding mem. San Francisco Mayor's Com. on Status of Women, 1971-74; bd. dirs. United Cerebral Palsy Assn. San Francisco, 1974—, United Cerebral Palsy Assn. Calif., 1976—. Fellow Am. Bar Found.; mem. State Bar Calif., Am., Internat., Feb. bar assns., Nat. Assn. Women Lawyers, Queen's Bench, Calif. Women Lawyers. Recipient James A. Harlan award Iowa Wesleyan Coll., 1969, certificate of merit San Francisco Bd. Suprs., 1969, Outstanding Achievement award San Francisco sect. Nat. Council Jewish Women, 1974, Woman of Achievement award Pacifica of San Francisco Bus. and Profl. Women's Club, 1974, 75; contbr. articles to Women Lawyers Jour., Am. Bar Jour. Home: 64 Turquoise Way San Francisco CA 94131 Office: 375 Woodside Ave San Francisco CA 94127 Tel (415) 731-5740

CHILDS, OZRO WILLIAM, b. Los Angeles, Feb. 21, 1945; B.A., Stanford, 1966, J.D., 1969. Admitted to Calif. bar, 1970; VISTA vol., 1969-70; individual practice law, San Francisco, 1970—. Mem. Calif. Attys. for Criminal Justice. Editorial bd. Stanford Law Rev., 1967-69. Office: 3025 Fillmore St San Francisco CA 94123 Tel (415) 563-7545

CHILES, JOHN HOUSER, b. Waxahachie, Tex., Oct. 4, 1928; B.B.A., Baylor U., 1950, J.D., 1952. Admitted to Tex. bar, 1952, U.S. Supreme Ct. bar, 1970; with JAGC, USAFR, 1952-55; atty. law dept. Exxon Co. U.S.A., Houston, 1956-64, region atty., 1964-66, chief mktg. atty., 1966-72, sr. counsel, 1972—. Fellow Tex. Bar Found.; mem. Am., Fed. bar assns., Am. Judicature Soc. Home: 5616 Green Tree St Houston TX 77056 Office: PO Box 2180 Houston TX 77001 Tel (713) 656-3366

CHILES, JOHN PARHAM, b. Kingsport, Tenn., Mar. 12, 1943; B.A., U. Va., 1965; J.D., U. Tenn., 1970. Admitted to Tenn. bar, 1971, U.S. Supreme Ct. bar, 1974; asso. atty. firm Roberts, Weill, Ellis, Weems & Copeland, Chattanooga, Tenn., 1971-73; asso. atty. firm Hunter, Smith, Davis, Norris & Treadway, Kingsport, Tenn., 1973-75; individual practice law, Kingsport, 1975—. Bd. dirs. 1st Baptist Ch., Kingsport, 1975-77; pres.-elect Kingsport Kiwanis Club. Mem. Kingsport, Tenn., Am. bar assns., Am. Trial Lawyers Assn., Phi Alpha Delta, Sigma Phi Epsilon. Home: 4541 Glenbrook Dr Kingsport TN 37664 Office: 205 Broad St Kingsport TN 37660 Tel (615) 246-4500

CHILIMIGRAS, JAMES COSTADINOS, b. Naphlion, Greece, Sept. 26, 1943; B.B.A. in Mktg., Western Mich. U., 1968, B.Edn., U. Detroit, J.D., 1971. Admitted to Mich. bar, 1972; partner firm Chilimigras, Powers & Conlon, Kalamazoo, 1972—. Office: 115 E Michigan Kalamazoo MI 49007 Tel (616) 381-1611

CHILSON, JOHN HATFIELD, b. Loveland, Colo., Jan. 28, 1937; B.A., Dartmouth, 1959; J.D., U. Colo., 1966. Admitted to U.S. Dist. Ct. bar, 1966; asso. firm Lynn A. Hammond, Loveland, 1966-68; partner firm Hammond & Chilson, 1968-76; partner firm Cogswell, Chilson, Dominick & Whitelaw, Denver, 1976—, asst. city atty., Loveland, 1970-76; spl. counsel water matters Town of Morrison, Colo., asst. town atty., Estes Park, Colo., 1975—. Bd. dirs. United Fund, 1968-73, Cloverleaf Charities, 1974—. Mem. Colo., Larimer County, Denver bar assns., Am. Trial Lawyers Assn., Rocky Mountain Mineral Law Inst. Home: 629 S County Rd 23E Loveland CO 80537 Office: Lincoln Center Bldg Suite 2510 1660 Lincoln Denver CO 80203

CHILSON, OLIN HATFIELD, b. Pueblo, Colo., Nov. 22, 1903; LL.B., U. Colo., 1927. Admitted to Colo. bar, 1927, U.S. Supreme Ct. bar, 1954; individual practice law, La Jara, Greeley, Loveland, Colo., 1927-56; dist. atty. 8th Jud. Dist. Colo., 1940-48; asst. sec. and under-sec. Dept. Interior, Washington, 1956-58; mem. firm Grant, Shafroth, Toll, Chilson & McHendrie, Denver, 1958-60; judge U.S. Dist. Ct., Denver, 1960—. Mem. Colo. (pres. 1951), Denver, Am. bar assns. Home: 1200 Humboldt St Apt 1101 Denver CO 80218 Office: Room 571 1929 Stout St Denver CO 80202 Tel (303) 893-1856

CHING, DONALD H., b. Honolulu, Jan. 13, 1926; B.A., U. Hawaii, 1950; LL.B., George Wash. U., 1953. Admitted to Hawaii bar, 1954; v.p. Bank Hawaii, Honolulu, 1963—; mem. Hawaii Ho. of Reps., 1958-66, Hawaii Senate, 1966—. Mem. Am., Hawaii bar assns. Home: 2005 Aamanu St Pearl City HI 96786 Office: Box 2900 Honolulu HI 96846 Tel (808) 537-8111

CHING, PHILIP HOO, b. Honolulu, Jan. 11, 1931; B.A., Colgate Univ., 1952; LL.B., Univ. Calif., Berkeley, 1955. Admitted to Hawaii bar, 1958; asst. v.p. Cooke Trust Co., Honolulu, 1957-66, v.p., 1964-66; v.p., trust officer First Hawaiian Bank, Honolulu, 1966-72, v.p., 1972—. Trustee Chaminade Coll. Edn. Found., Honolulu. Mem. Am., Hawaii bar assns., Hawaii Soc. Corporate Planners. Home: 1700 Palaau St Honolulu HI 96821 Office: 165 S King St Honolulu HI 96847 Tel (808) 525-8119

CHINNERY, CARL LLOYD, b. Kansas City, Kans., Oct. 28, 1941; B.A., Beloit Coll., 1964; J.D., U. Mo., Kansas City, 1967. Admitted to Mo. bar, 1967; asst. counsel Kans. City Life Ins. Co., 1971-73, asst. v.p., 1971-73, v.p., dir. customer service, 1973—. Mem. diocesan Council and steering com., Diocese W. Mo.; bd. dirs. Optimist Club (Kansas City), Lee's Summit Sertoma, C. of C. (Lee's Summit) Jr. C. of C. (Kansas City), Harry S. Truman Children's Neurol. Center, St. Paul's Episcopal Ch. Mem. Am., Kansas City, Mo. Bar assns., Lawyers Assn. Home: 401 Wildplum Ct Lees Summit MO 64063 Office: 16 E 3d St Lee's Summit MO 64063 Tel (816) 524-3535

CHIPMAN, JOHN MCLELLAND, b. San Francisco, Oct. 4, 1945; B.S., Utah State U., 1967; J.D., U. Utah, 1970. Admitted to Utah bar, 1970, Va. bar, 1972; asso. E. Eugene Gunter, Winchester, Va., 1972-75, firm Hanson, Wadsworth & Russon, Salt Lake City, 1975—; residential dir. Grafton Sch. Children Learning Disabilities, Berryville, Va., 1971-72. Mem. Am., Salt Lake County, Winchester-Frederick County (treas. 1972-73) bar assns. Home: 1553 E Park Pl N Salt Lake City UT 84121 Office: 702 Kearns Bldg Salt Lake City UT 84101 Tel (801) 359-7611

CHITTUM, ROGER DEAN, b. Millersburg, Ohio, Mar. 21, 1939; A.B., Coll. of Wooster, Ohio, 1962; LL.B., Stanford, 1966. Admitted to D.C. bar, 1967, Calif. bar, 1973; asso. firm Cleary, Gottlieb, Steen & Hamilton, Washington, 1966-71; asst. to pres. Tosco Corp., N.Y.C. and Los Angeles, 1972-73, v.p., 1973—. Mem. Am. Bar Assn., Licensing Execs. Soc. Office: 10100 Santa Monica Blvd Los Angeles CA 90067 Tel (213) 552-7077

CHITWOOD, MARTIN DILLARD, b. Dalton, Ga., Jan. 28, 1944; A.B., U. Ga., 1966, J.D., 1973, M.A., 1976. Admitted to Ga. bar, 1973; mem. firms Dennis & Fain, 1973-74, Carroll, Chitwood, Greenfield & Poole, 1974-75; individual practice law, 1976—. Mem. Atlanta, Ga., Am. bar assns. Author: The Effects of the English Common Law on the Development of Commonwealth West African Legal Systems, 1976. Home: 229 Colonial Homes Circle Atlanta GA 30309 Office: Suite 411 Candler Bldg 127 Peachtree St Atlanta GA 30303 Tel (404) 577-5490

CHOATE, ALAN GARRICK, b. Detroit, Oct. 16, 1939; B.A., Harvard, 1961; LL.B., U. Mich., 1964. Admitted to D.C. bar, 1965, Pa. bar, 1967; partner firm Pepper, Hamilton & Scheetz, Phila., 1965—; lectr. internat. bus. law Wharton Sch. Fin. and Commerce, U. Pa., Phila., 1969-73. Bd. dirs. Bartlett Exploration Assn., Wynnewood, Pa., 1976—; bd. trustees Nat. Maritime Hist. Soc., 1974—. Mem. Am., Phila., Pa. bar assns., Lawyers Club Phila., Am. Judicature Soc., Maritime Adminstrv. Bar Assn., Internat. Fiscal Assn. Author: Foreign Base Companies, 1976. Office: 123 S Broad St Philadelphia PA 19109 Tel (215) 545-1234

CHOATE, JOHN IRVAN MORITZKY, b. Oklahoma City, Nov. 6, 1946; B.A. (Sun Oil Co. scholar), U. Okla., 1966; J.D., Yale, 1969. Admitted to Calif. bar, 1971, D.C. bar, 1973, Am. Samoa bar, 1973; investment exec. Shearson, Hammill & Co., Beverly Hills, Calif., 1969-71; legal research specialist Asso. Justice Leslie N. Jochimsen, High Ct. of Am. Samoa, Pago Pago, 1973; asst. prof. law U. Pitts., 1974-75, U. Tulsa, 1975—. Pres. Tulsa Stake Quorum of Seventy Ch. of Jesus Christ of Latter-day Saints, 1975—; pres. Yale Law Sch. Assn. of Tulsa, 1975, sec., regional rep. alt., 1976; gov. Ednl. Found. Am. Mem. Assn. Am. Law Schs. (chmn. sect. taxation), Fed. (pres. Tulsa chpt. 1977), Am. bar assns., Town Hall Calif., Phi Delta Phi. Recipient Eagle Scout award Boy Scouts Am., 1962, Am. Jurisprudence prize Coll. Law U. Okla., 1967, Letter of Appreciation, JAGC, 1975; mem. Okla. Law Rev., 1967; asso. editor Samoan Pacific Law Jour., 1973, editor-in-chief, 1973, contbg. editor, pub.: Directory of California Independent Schools, 1973. Home: POB 1683 Beverly Hills CA 90213 Office: U of Tulsa Coll of Law 3120 E 4th Pl Tulsa OK 74014 Tel (918) 939-6351

CHOATE, JOHN SAMUEL, JR., b. Augusta, Ga., Aug. 27, 1947; B.A. in History cum laude, U. Ga., 1971, J.D., 1974. Admitted to Ga. bar, 1974; asso. firm Maguire & Kilpatrick, Augusta, 1974-75; partner firm Bell, Choate & Walker, Augusta, 1975-77, firm Surrett, Thompson, Bell, Choate & Walker, Augusta, 1977—. Mem. Ga. State Bar, Ga., Am. bar assns., Ga. Trial Lawyers Assn., Assn. Trial Lawyers Am., Young Lawyers Club of Augusta (exec. com.), Phi Beta Kappa, Phi Kappa Phi, Phi Delta Phi. Office: 505 1st Nat Bank Bldg Augusta GA 30902 Tel (404) 722-3301

CHOATE, RICHARD L., b. Newport, Ark., Dec. 3, 1924; LL.B., U. Ark., 1951. Admitted to Ark. bar, 1950, N.D. bar, 1952; asso. firm Choate & Temple, Bismark, N.D., to 1953; with Sinclair Oil & Gas Co., 1953-64; individual practice law, 1964-69; asso. firm McKay, Chandler & Choate, Magnolia, Ark., 1969—. Mem. Am., Ark. (chmn. natural resources law sect. 1976-77, recipient Golden Gavel award 1977), Magnolia County bar assns., Am., Ark. trial lawyers assns. Home: 1612 Lakewood St St Magnolia AR 71753 Office: 201 S Jackson Magnolia AR 71753 Tel (501) 234-1036

CHOATE, WILLIAM WESLEY, b. Oklahoma City, July 25, 1939; B.S. in Geological Engring., U. Okla., 1960; J.D., Oklahoma City U., 1973. Admitted to Okla. bar, 1974; civil engr. U.S. Bur. Reclamation, Norman, Okla., 1963-64; civil engring. officer USAF, 1964-69; planning engr., Okla. State Water Resources Bd, 1969-71; civil engr. U.S. Army C.E., 1971-74; individual practice law, Oklahoma City, 1974—; staff JAGC, USAFR, 1974—. Dir. 5th congressional dist. Oklahomans for Life, Inc., 1974—; commr., scoutmaster Boy Scouts Am., 1970—. Mem. Okla. Bar Assn., Nat., Okla. socs. profl. engrs. Contbr. articles in field to profl. jours. Home: 1605 Classen Blvd Oklahoma City OK 73106 Office: 1603 Classen Blvd Oklahoma City OK 73106 Tel (405) 524-6225

CHOLIS, ALEXIS T., b. South Bend, Ind., Oct. 1, 1917; B.S. in Commerce, Notre Dame U., 1941, LL.D., 1942. Admitted to Ind. bar, 1942, U.S. Dist. Ct. bar, 1942; partner firm Cholis & Cholis, S. Bend,

1946—; pub. defender South Bend, 1952-64. Mem. Ind. State, St. Joseph County (sec. 1952-74, pres. 1977-) bar assns. Home: 103 N Sunnyside South Bend IN 46617 Office: 905 St Joseph Bank Bldg South Bend IN 46601 Tel (219) 232-3331

CHOSNEK, EDWARD, b. Wolfrautshausen, Germany, Mar. 6, 1947; B.A., Purdue U., 1969; J.D., Ind. U., 1972; came to U.S., 1949, naturalized, 1955. Admitted to Ind. bar, 1972; partner firm Pearlman & Chosnek, Lafayette, Ind., 1972—. Mem. Am., Ind., Tippecanoe County bar assns., Ind. Trial Lawyers Assn., Am. Arbitration Assn. Home: 1105 W 750 North West Lafayette IN 47906 Office: 203-207 First Federal Bldg Lafayette IN 47902 Tel (317) 742-9081

CHOTINER, KENNETH LEE, b. Los Angeles, Aug. 14, 1937; B.A. in Polit. Sci., U. Calif., Los Angeles, 1959; J.D., Loyola U., Los Angeles, 1969. Admitted to Calif. bar, 1970, U.S. Ct. Customs and Patent Appeals bar, 1971, U.S. Ct. Mil. Appeals bar, 1974, U.S. Supreme Ct. bar, 1975; instr. Am. govt. U. Alaska, 1962; dep. city atty. Los Angeles, 1970-71; individual practice law, Santa Monica, Calif., 1971—; spl. counsel City of Hawthorne (Calif.), 1973—; judge pro tem Los Angeles Municipal Ct., 1975-, Santa Monica Municipal Ct., 1977—. Bd. dirs. So. Calif. ACLU, 1972—. Mem. State Bar Calif. (conf. del. 1972, 73, 76, 77), Santa Monica Bay Dist. (treas., trustee), Am., Los Angeles County, Criminal Cts. bar assns., Am. Arbitration Assn. (panel), Am., Calif. trial lawyers assns., Phi Alpha Delta, St. Thomas More Law Soc. Contbr. articles to legal jours. Office: Garden Suite 1337 Ocean Ave Santa Monica CA 90401 Tel (213) 393-0375

CHOULES, GEORGE THOMAS, b. Driggs, Idaho, Mar. 16, 1928; student Brigham Young U., 1946-47, 1950, U. Utah, 1950-52; LL.B., State U. Iowa, 1956. Admitted to Iowa bar, 1956, Ariz. bar, 1958; law clk. Ariz. Supreme Ct., 1957-58; mem. firm Westover, Mansfield, Westover & Copple (now Westover, Choules, Shadle & Bowen), Yuma, 1958—. Mem. Com. Fourteen, Yuma, 1965—, Western States Water Council, 1970—. Mem. State Bar Ariz. (pres. 1976-77), Nat. Water Resources Assn. (resolutions com.), Iowa, Ariz., Am., Yuma County bar assns., Caballeros de Yuma (pres. 1965), Yuma County C. of C. (dir. 1963-65), Yuma Fine Arts Assn. (dir. 1965-71), Yuma County Hist. Soc. (dir. 1968—). Home: 1483 Gateway Yuma AZ 85364 Office: 190 Madison Ave PO Box 551 Yuma AZ 85364 Tel (602) 783-8321*

CHOWN, NORMAN RALPH, b. San Francisco, Sept. 14, 1922; LL.B., U. San Francisco, 1951. Admitted to Calif. bar, 1953; practice law, Santa Rosa, Calif.; asst. pub. defender Sonoma County (Calif.). Office: 2555 Mendocino Ave Santa Rosa CA 95401

CHRIST, MARCUS HALLSTED, b. New Hyde Park, N.Y., Dec. 19, 1930; B.A. in Pol. Sci., Colgate U., 1953; LL.B., N.Y. U., 1955. Admitted to N.Y. bar, 1957 asso. firm Bleakley, Platt, Schmidt, Hart & Fritz, N.Y.C., 1957-67 partner firm Fritz, Christ, O'Brien & Farrell, Mineola, N.Y., 1967-73; comptroller Nassau County, N.Y., 1973—; justice Village of Muttontown, N.Y., 1967-68. Councilman, Town of Oyster Bay, N.Y., 1969-73 mem. Nassau (County) Govtl. Revision Commn., 1970-75. Mem. Nassau County Bar Assn. (pres. 1970-71), N.Y. State Bar Assn. (chmn. sub-com. on finance 1971—), Nassau Lawyers Assn. Long Island, Am. Jewish Com., NCCJ, Council for Instl. and Govtl. Accounting, Assn. Govtl. Accountants NY. Office: 240 Old Country Rd Mineola NY 11501 Tel (516) 535-3900

CHRISTEN, ARNOLD BUHL, b. Iowa City, Iowa, Oct. 14, 1915; B.S., U. Iowa, 1938; J.D., Georgetown U., 1942. Admitted to D.C. bar, 1942; partner firm Fisher, Christen & Sabol, and predecessors, Washington, 1946—; founding dir. Nat. Patent Devel. Corp., 1958—; pres., dir. A.P. Originals, Ltd.; v.p., dir. Pureco, Ltd. Mem. Am., Fed. bar assns., Am. Chem. Soc., Am. Patent Law Assn., Nat. Aviation Club. Home: 39 Acorn Dr Annapolis MD 21401 Office: 1000 Connecticut Ave Washington DC 20036 Tel (202) 659-2000

CHRISTENSEN, ALBERT SHERMAN, b. Manti, Utah, June 9, 1905; student Brigham Young U., 1923-27; LL.B., Nat. U., 1931; J.D., George Washington U., 1968. Admitted to D.C. bar, 1932, Utah bar, 1933; asst. bus. specialist U.S. Dept. Commerce, 1930-32; practice law, Provo, Utah, 1933-42, 45-54; U.S. Dist. judge Dist. Utah, Salt Lake City, 1954-72, sr. judge, 1972—; mem. Temporary Emergency Ct. Appeals of U.S., 1972—; vis. prof. law U. Utah, 1975, J. Reuben Clark Law Sch., Provo, 1975-77; mem. adv. com. on rules of civil procedure Jud. Conf. U.S., 1972—. Mem. Am., Fed., Utah (pres. 1950-51) bar assns., Am. Judicature Soc., Order of Coif (hon.). Recipient Distinguished Achievement award Brigham Young U., 1955, Abraham O. Smoot Pub. Service award, 1969, outstanding achievement in adminstrn. of justice award Utah State Bar, 1971; contbr. articles profl. jours. Home: 2120 N Temple View Dr Provo City UT 84601 Office: Federal Bldg Salt Lake City UT 84138 Tel (801) 524-5164

CHRISTENSEN, CARL J., b. Salt Lake City, Oct. 11, 1929; student Brigham Young U., 1947-49; B.A., U. Akron, 1954; student St. Mary's U. Sch. Law, San Antonio, 1954-56; LL.B., U. Utah, 1957. Admitted to Nev. bar, 1957, Utah bar, 1967; partner firm Christensen, Bell & Morris, Las Vegas, Nev., 1958-65; stockbroker F. I. Dupont & Co., Salt Lake City, 1966-67; partner firm Fowler, Johnson, Stringham & Christensen, Salt Lake City, 1968; individual practice law, Las Vegas, 1968-71; judge Clark County Dist. Ct., 1971—, chief judge 10 Dept. Ct., 1974. Treas. Boulder Dam council Boy Scouts Am.; nat. bd. dirs. Odyssey House. Fellow Internat. Acad. Trial Judges; mem. Am. Bar Assn. (del. trial judges conf. 1974-75), Am. Judicature Soc., Nev., Utah bars, 9th Circuit Ct. Appeals Bar Assn. Recipient Silver Beaver award Boy Scouts Am., 1975, Spl. recognition Nev. Assn. Legal Secs. Com. on Handbook of Legal Forms, 1976; registered rep. Chgo. Bd. Trade, Am. Stock Exchange, N.Y. Stock Exchange. Home: 3101 Hastings Ave Las Vegas NV 89107 Office: 200 E Carson Ave Las Vegas NV 89101 Tel (702) 386-4011

CHRISTENSEN, CRAIG WANE, b. Lehi, Utah, Mar. 11, 1939; B.S., Brigham Young U., 1961; J.D. magna cum laude, Northwestern U., 1964. Admitted to Ill. bar, 1965 U.S. Supreme Ct. bar, 1973; asso. firm Kirkland, Ellis, Hodson, Chaffetz & Masters, Chgo., 1964-66; exec. asst. to chmn. and pres. C. & N.W. Ry. Co., Chgo., 1966-67; dir. Nat. Inst. for Edn. in Law and Poverty, Chgo., 1967-70; asso. prof. law U. Mich., 1970-71, also legal adviser to pres.; dean, prof. law Cleve. State U., 1971-75; dean, prof. law Syracuse U., 1975—; asst. to chmn. White House Civil Rights Conf., 1966; mem. legal services nat. adv. com. OEO, 1968-70; mem. Am. Right to Legal Services Com., 1970-71. Mem. Am., N.Y. State bar assns., Order of Coif. Home: 501 Bradford Pkwy Syracuse NY 13224 Office: Syracuse Univ Coll Law E I White Hall Syracuse NY 13210 Tel (315) 423-2540

CHRISTENSEN, DAVID LLOYD, b. Atlantic, Iowa, July 15, 1942; B.B.A., U. Iowa, 1967, J.D., 1973. Admitted to Iowa bar, 1973; partner firm Wilson, Bonnett & Christensen, Lenox, Iowa, 1973—. Mem. Taylor County, Iowa State, Am. bar assns., Phi Delta Phi. Office: 103 S Main St Lenox IA 50851 Tel (515) 333-2283

CHRISTENSEN, DONN DOUGLAS, b. St. Paul, June 30, 1929; B.S. Law, U. Minn., 1950, LL.B., 1952. Admitted to Minn. bar, 1952, U.S. Dist. Ct. bar for Dist. Minn., 1955; mem. firm Felhaber, Larson & Fenlon, 1954-60; individual practice law, St. Paul, 1960-68, 70-77; partner firm Christensen & Haglund, 1977—; dep. atty. gen. State of Minn., 1968-70; instr. bus. law Macalester Coll., 1960-67; justice of the peace City of Mendota Heights (Minn.), 1961-66; mem. nat. panel arbitrators Am. Arbitration Assn. Mem. Am., Minn. State (chmn. sect. environ. law 1971-72), Ramsey County bar assns., Execs. Assn. St. Paul (pres. 1966). Home: 676 Schifsky Rd Saint Paul MN 55112 Office: 1210 Commerce Bldg Saint Paul MN 55101 Tel (612) 224-4741

CHRISTENSEN, GEORGE BOWERS, b. Oshkosh, Wis., Apr. 12, 1905; A.B., Lawrence Coll., 1926; J.D., U. Mich., 1929. Admitted to Wis. bar, 1929, Ill. bar, 1929; mem. firm Winston & Strawn, Chgo., 1929—. Fellow Am. Coll. Trial Lawyers; mem. Am., Ill., Chgo. bar assns. Office: One First Nat Plaza Chicago IL 60603 Tel (312) 786-5695

CHRISTENSEN, GERALD D., b. Powell, Wyo., Nov. 24, 1933; B.S., U. Mont., 1959, LL.B., 1961. Admitted to Mont. bar, 1961; with trust dept. Midland Nat. Bank, Billings, Mont., 1961-63; partner firm Jones, Olsen & Christensen, Billings, 1963—. Mem. Mont., Yellowstone County Bar Assns. Home: 3205 Country Club Circle Billings MT 59102 Office: 720 N 30th St Billings MT 59101 Tel (406) 245-6338

CHRISTENSEN, HAROLD GRAHAM, b. Springville, Utah, June 25, 1926; A.B., U. Utah, 1949; J.D., U. Mich., 1951. Admitted to Utah bar, 1952, U.S. Supreme Ct. bar, 1976; partner firm Skeen, Worsley, Snow & Christensen and successors, Salt Lake City, 1956—; v.p., treas., dir. Snow, Christensen & Martineau, P.C. Fellow Am. Coll. Trial Lawyers, Am. Bar Found.; mem. Am., Utah (pres. 1975-76), Salt Lake County (pres. 1972-73) bar assns., Fedn. Ins. Counsel. Home: 2269 Pheasant Way Salt Lake City UT 84121 Office: 7th Floor Continental Bank Bldg Salt Lake City UT 84101 Tel (801) 521-9000

CHRISTENSEN, JOHN WILLIAM, b. Roselawn, Ind., Mar. 14, 1914; A.B., De Pauw U., 1935; J.D. with distinction, Ind. U. Admitted to Ind. bar, 1939, Ohio bar, 1946, U.S. Supreme Ct. bar, 1944; atty., spl. counsel SEC. Phila., 1939-46; asso. and partner firm Dargusch Caren Greek & King, Columbus, Ohio, 1946-52; partner firm Gingher & Christensen, Columbus, 1953—; v.p. gen. counsel, sec., dir. O.M. Scott & Sons Co., Marysville, Ohio, 1952—; v.p., gen. counsel, dir. Columbus Mut. Life Ins. Co., Columbus, 1962—. Gen. counsel, dir. United McGill Corp., Columbus, 1962—; v.p., dir. Brodhead-Garrett Co., Cleve., 1958—; adj. prof. law Ohio State U., 1964-72. Trustee DePauw U., 1964—. Mem. Columbus, Ohio State, Am. bar assns. Home: 2475 Onandaga Dr Columbus OH 43221 Office: 311 E Broad St Columbus OH 43215 Tel (614) 224-6285

CHRISTENSEN, KREGE BOWEN, b. Provo, Utah, Oct. 28, 1942; B.S. in Accounting, U. Utah, 1965, M.B.A., 1967; J.D. with honors, George Washington U., 1973. Admitted to Utah bar, 1973; asso. firm Parsons, Behle & Latimer, Salt Lake City, 1973-75, partner, 1975—; accountant SEC, Washington, 1969-73. Mem. Am., Salt Lake County bar assns., Am. Judicature Soc., Am. Inst. C.P.A.'s, Utah Assn. C.P.A.'s. Home: 3036 Cascade Way Salt Lake City UT 84109 Office: PO Box 11898 79 S State St Salt Lake City UT 84147 Tel (801) 532-1234

CHRISTENSEN, RAY RICHARDS, b. Salt Lake City, July 7, 1922; LL.B., U. Utah, 1944. Admitted to Utah bar, 1944; U.S. Supreme Ct. bar, 1950; enforcement atty. Office of Price Adminstrn., Salt Lake City, 1946; clk. to justice Supreme Ct. Utah, Salt Lake City, 1947-48; partner firm Christensen, Gardiner, Jensen & Evans, and predecessors, Salt Lake City, 1949—; pres. Utah State Bar, 1965-66. Mem. Am. (ho. of dels. 1966-68, 73—), Salt Lake County bar assns., Fedn. Ins. Counsel, Internat. Assn. Ins. Counsel, Am. Coll. Trial Lawyers, Internat. Acad. Trial Lawyers, Salt Lake Jr. C. of C. (dir. 1949-53, v.p. 1950-52). Contbr. articles to legal jours. Home: 861 Monument Park Circle Salt Lake City UT 84108 Office: 900 Kearns Bldg Salt Lake City UT 84101 Tel (801) 355-3431

CHRISTENSEN, SIEGFRIED BENJAMIN, b. New Orleans, Oct. 26, 1907; B.A., Tulane U., 1932; LL.B./J.D., Loyola U. of the South, 1935. Admitted to La. bar, 1935; asso. firm Denechaud et al, New Orleans, 1935-37; partner firm Christensen & Boyle, New Orleans, 1937-40; individual practice law, New Orleans, 1940-43; partner firm Darden & Christensen, New Orleans, 1944-48, Christensen & Christensen, New Orleans, 1953-74; asso. firm Christensen Dean & Perez, Covington, La., 1974—; spl. atty. lands div. U.S. Dept. Justice, New Orleans, 1943-44; atty. constable New Orleans City Ct., 1944-65. Mem. adv. council Loyola U., New Orleans, 1971-73. Mem. Am., Fed., La., New Orleans, Covington, St. Tammany bar assns., La. Notaries Assn., Sigma Pi, Phi Alpha Delta. Home: 181 Country Club Dr Covington LA 70433 Office: 330 N New Hamshire St Covington LA 70433 Tel (504) 892-6330

CHRISTENSON, JIMMY SPENCE, b. Mondovi, Wis., Feb. 7, 1946; B.A., Wis. U., Eau Claire, 1968, J.D., 1973. Admitted to Wis. bar, 1973; asst. dist. atty. Dane County (Wis.), 1973-74; chief gen. counsel sect. Wis. Dept. Natural Resources, Madison, 1974-76, chief gen. counsel sect., 1976—. Mem. Wis. Bar Assn. Home: 6213 Lomax Ln Madison WI 53711 Office: 4610 University Ave Box 7921 Madison WI 53707 Tel (608) 266-1318

CHRISTENSON, TERRANCE P., b. Albany, N.Y., Sept. 14, 1946; B.A. cum laude, Manhattan Coll., 1968; J.D., cum laude, Boston Coll., 1972. Admitted to N.Y. State bar, 1973; asso. firm Cooper, Erving & Savage, Albany, 1973—. Mem. Am., N.Y. State, Albany County bar assns., Capitol Dist. Trial Lawyers Assn., Order of Coif. Contbr. articles to law revs.

CHRISTIAN, ALMERIC LEANDER, b. Christiansted, St. Croix, V.I., Nov. 23, 1919; student U. P.R., 1937-38; A.B., Columbia, 1941, LL.B., 1947. Admitted to V.I. bar, 1947; practiced law, V.I., 1947-62; U.S. dist. atty. for V.I., St. Thomas, from 1962; now judge U.S. Dist. Ct. for V.I., St. Thomas. Dist. commr. Boy Scouts Am., V.I., 1962—; adv. bd. St. Dunstan's Episcopal Sch., St. Croix. Mem. V.I. Bd. Edn., 1961—. Mem. V.I. Bar Assn. Home: Parcel 19-0 Solberg Saint Thomas VI 00801 Office: US Dist Court Saint Thomas VI 00801*

CHRISTIANAKIS, MANUEL, b. New Castle, Pa., Oct. 14, 1929; B.A., Westminster Coll., 1951; J.D., Western Res. U., 1953. Admitted to Ohio bar, 1953; individual practice law Cleve., 1955—. Mem. Cuyahoga County Bar Assn. Office: 33 Public Square Cleveland OH 44113 Tel (216) 621-4964

CHRISTIANSEN, AXEL EINAR, b. Denver, Mar. 9, 1929; B.A., U. Calif., 1950; J.D., Hastings Coll., 1953. Admitted to Calif. bar, 1954; dep. dist. atty. Madera County, Calif., 1954-57; asst. city atty. Redwood City, Calif., 1957-59; mem. firm Bartow and Christiansen, Madera, Calif., 1959—; city atty. City of Madera, 1959—. Mem. Am., Calif. bar assns. Office: 123 E 4th St Madera CA 93637 Tel (209) 674-8588

CHRISTIANSEN, CLARENCE HERBERT, b. Inwood, Iowa, July 2, 1923; B.A. in Econs., U. Iowa, 1947, J.D., 1948. Admitted to Iowa bar, 1948, U.S. Supreme Ct. bar, 1960; partner firm Christiansen & Lowry, Davenport, Iowa, 1948; asso. firm Lambach, Christiansen, Stevenson & Goebel and predecessors, Davenport, 1949-53, partner, 1953-70; individual practice law, Davenport, 1970—; legal officer U.S. Marine Corps, Camp Pendleton, Calif., 1950-51; gen. counsel Bec Industries, Ltd., 1962—, Life Securities of Iowa, Inc., 1964—, Regency Life Ins. Co., 1967-70, Regency Nat., Ltd., 1969—, Am. Security Life Ins. Co., 1967-70, Fin. Holding Corp., 1968—, Fin. Security Life Ins. Co., 1969—. Mem. Am. (vice chmn automobile com. ins. sect. 1965-66, life ins. com. 1970—), Fed., Iowa, Scott County bar assns., Fedn. Ins. Counsel (life ins. com. 1976—), Nat. Lawyers Club, Gamma Eta Gamma. Home: Carriage Club Apt 4 3215 E Locust St Davenport IA 52803 Office: 102 Professional Arts Bldg Davenport IA 52803 Tel (319) 326-2591

CHRISTIANSEN, JAMES RICHARD, b. Columbus, Ohio, Jan. 6, 1930; B.S.E. in Elec. Engring., U. Mich., 1950, LL.B. (Lieke scholar), J.D., 1953; LL.M. in Brit. Constl. Law and Trusts (Fulbright scholar), U. N.Z., Wellington, 1956. Admitted to Mich. bar, 1954, Pa. bar, 1956, Calif. bar, 1957, Hawaii bar, 1975, U.S. Supreme Ct. bar, 1971; mem. elec. engring. faculty U. Mich., 1950-53; asso. firm Morgan, Lewis & Bockius, Phila., 1955-56; dep. atty. gen. State of Calif., Los Angeles, 1956-57; dep. dist. atty. Santa Barbara County, Santa Barbara, Calif., 1957-59; individual practice law, Santa Barbara, 1959—; city atty. City of Carpinteria (Calif.), 1965—; lectr. law U. Calif. Mem. Goleta Union Sch. Bd., 1961-77, pres., 1971-72. Mem. Am. Trial Lawyers Assn., AAUP, State Bar Calif., Los Angeles Bar Assn. Office: 1216 State St Suite 802 Santa Barbara CA 93101 Tel (805) 962-8141

CHRISTIANSEN, JOHN ORROCK, b. Beaver, Utah, Sept. 21, 1924; LL.B., U. Utah, 1949. Admitted to Utah bar, 1950; atty. County of Beaver (Utah), 1951—. Mem. Utah State, So. Utah bar assns. Home: 60 N 400 East St Beaver UT 84713 Office: 105 E Center St Beaver UT 84713 Tel (801) 438-2351

CHRISTIANSON, OSCAR, b. Oslo, Norway, Apr. 29, 1897; student St. Olaf Coll., Northfield, Minn., 1916-18; B.A., U. Wis., 1921, LL.B., 1924. Admitted to Wis. bar, 1924; mem. firm Ela, Christianson, Ela, Esch, Hart & Clark, Madison, Wis., 1924-74; individual practice law, Madison, 1974—. Chmn. Madison Emergency Housing Com., 1942-46. Mem. Wis., Dane County bar assns. Named Man of Year, Am. Dairy Assn., 1970, Wis. Farm Bur., 1971; recipient Silver Gavel award Wis. 4-H Found., 1974; State Appreciation award United Dairy Industry, 1972. Home: 2506 Santa Maria Ct Middleton WI 53562 Office: 122 W Washington Ave Madison WI 53703 Tel (608) 256-5456

CHRISTIANSON, WILLIAM CHRISTIAN, b. Moody County, S.D., Dec. 5, 1892; LL.B., U. Chgo., 1920. Admitted to Minn. bar, 1920; individual practice law, Red Wing, Minn., 1923-46; asso. justice Supreme Ct. Minn., 1946-47; mem. War Crimes Tribunals, Nurenberg, Germany, 1947-49; dist. judge 1st Jud. Dist., Minn., 1949-64. Mem. Am., Minn. bar assns., Am. Legion, Elks, Masons. Home: 535 Summit Ave Red Wing MN 55066

CHRISTIE, GEORGE CUSTIS, b. N.Y.C., Mar. 3, 1934; A.B. Columbia, 1955, J.D., 1957; diploma in internat. law (Fulbright scholar) Cambridge (Eng.) U., 1962; S.J.D., Harvard, 1966. Admitted to N.Y. bar, 1957, D.C. bar, 1958; asso. firm Covington & Burling, Washington, 1958-60; Ford Found. fellow in law teaching Harvard, 1960-61; asso. prof. law U. Minn., Mpls., 1962-65, prof., 1965-66; asst. gen. counsel for Near East and S. Asia, AID Dept. of State, 1966-67; prof. law Duke, 1967—. Mem. Am. Bar Assn., Am. Law Inst., Am. Soc. Internat. Law, Phi Beta Kappa. Author: Jurisprudence: Text and Readings on the Philosophy of Law, 1973; contbr. articles to legal jours.; mem. bd. editors Am. Jour. Legal History, 1971-76. Office: Duke U Sch Law Durham NC 27706 Tel (919) 684-2976

CHRISTIE, JOHN F., b. Bryn Mawr, Pa., July 22, 1940; B.A., Colby Coll., 1962; J.D., Villanova U., 1968. Admitted to Pa. bar, 1969; asso. firm High, Swartz, Roberts & Seidel, Norristown, Pa., 1970—; solicitor Prothonotary Montgomery County (Pa.), Upper Swynedd Twp. Authority. Mem. Am., Pa. bar assns. Home: 1332 Meadowbank Rd Conshohocken PA 19428 Office: 40 E Airy St Norristown PA 19404 Tel (215) 275-0700

CHRISTMAS, PATRICK JOSEPH, b. Jacksonville, Fla., Mar. 17, 1945; B.A., Am. U., 1966; J.D., Georgetown U., 1969. Admitted to D.C. bar, 1969, Md. bar, 1972, U.S. Supreme Ct. bar, 1975; asst. corp. counsel D.C., 1969-71; partner firm Christmas & Schulze, Washington, 1971—; atty. Nat. Labor Labor Conf., Washington, 1969. Mem. D.C. Bar Assn., Plaintiffs Trial Lawyers Am., Am. Arbitration Assn. (panel arbitrators). Home: 5329 Woodlawn Ave Cheve Chase MD 20015 Office: 1010 Vermont Ave NW Washington DC 20005 Tel (202) 783-3511

CHRISTOFFERSEN, VENOY, b. Brigham City, Utah, Dec. 31, 1922; B.A., U. Utah, 1950, J.D., 1952. Admitted to Nev. bar, 1953, Utah bar, 1961; asst. city atty. City of Los Vegas (Nev.), 1953-54; dep. dist. atty. Clark County (Nev.), 1954-58; partner firm Olsen & Christoffersen, Las Vegas, 1959-60; asst. dist. atty. gen. for State of Nev., 1959-60; judge City Ct., Brigham City, Utah, 1961-69; judge 1st Jud. Dist. State of Utah, 1969—; mem. Utah Jud. Com. for Cts., 1965-69; mem. legis. com. Utah Bar on Cts., 1969-73. Bd. dirs. ARC, Brigham City, 1966-70. Mem. Utah, Nebr. bar assns. Recipient Man of Yr. award Rotary Club, Brigham City, 1970, Outstanding Chmn. award Dist. 1 Law Enforcement Planning Council, 1974. Home: 990 N 15th St E Logan UT 84321 Office: 160 N Main St Logan UT 84321 Tel (801) 752-3542

CHRISTOPHER, MAURICE RONALD, b. Cairo, Ill., May 17, 1941; B.A., U. Ky., 1964, J.D., 1967. Admitted to Ky. bar, 1967, U.S. Supreme Ct. bar, 1976; asst. U.S. atty. Western Dist. Ky., 1968-69; partner firm Hurt & Christopher, Murray, Ky., 1969—; Commonwealth's atty. 42d Jud. Dist., 1974. Mem. Am., Fed., Ky., Louisville, Calloway bar assns. Named Outstanding Young Man of

Year Murray Jaycees, 1976. Office: 105 N 6th St PO Box 577 Murray KY 42071 Tel (502) 753-1262

CHRISTOPHER, THOMAS WELDON, b. Duncan, S.C., Oct. 8, 1917; A.B., Washington and Lee U., 1939; LL.B., U. Ala., 1948; LL.M., N.Y. U., 1950, J.S.D., 1957. Admitted to Ala. bar, 1948, Ga. bar, 1955, N.Y. bar, 1961, N.C. bar, 1963, N.Mex. bar, 1968; individual practice law, Tuscaloosa, Ala., 1948-50; prof. law Emory U., 1950-61, asso. dean, 1954-61; individual practice law, N.Y.C., 1960-61; prof. law U. N.C., 1961-65; dean Sch. Law, U. N.Mex., 1965-71; dean, prof. law U. Ala., 1971—; vis. prof. summers U. N.C., 1953, 57, 69, U. Calif. at Berkeley, 1958-59, U. Utah, summer 1963, So. Meth. U., summer 70; mem. nat. adv. food and drug council HEW 1968-70; v.p. Food and Drug Law Found., 1974—. Mem. Am. Bar Assn., Assn. Am. Law Schs., Food and Drug Inst. Author: Cases and Materials on Food and Drug Law, 2d edit., 1973; Constitutional Questions in Food and Drug Laws, 1960; (with Leverett and Hall) Georgia Procedure and Practice, 1957; (with Dunn) Special Federal Food and Drug Laws, 1954; contbr. articles to legal jours. Home: 7 Pinehurst Tuscaloosa AL 35401 Office: PO Box 1435 University AL 35486 Tel (205) 348-5117

CHRISTY, JAMES THOMAS, b. Cin., Nov. 2, 1947; B.B.A., U. Cin., 1969, J.D., 1972. Admitted to Ohio bar, 1973; U.S. Dist. Ct. for so. dist. Ohio bar, 1974, U.S. Supreme Ct. bar, 1976; legis. asst. U.S. Rep., 1973-75; adminstrv. asst. to U.S. Rep., 1975-76; legal counsel, 1976—; asst. public defender, Clermont County, Ohio, 1976—; individual practice law, Milford, Ohio, 1976—. Mem. Ohio State, Cin. bar, assns., U. Cin. Alumni Club Washington, (v.p. 1975-76), Adminstrv. Assts. Assn. of U.S. House of Reps. Contbr. article to law jours. Home: 5338 S Milford Dr Milford OH 45150 Office: 130 Main St Milford OH 45150 Tel (513) 831-5024

CHRZANOWSKI, ROBERT JOSEPH, b. Detroit, Mar. 28, 1935; LL.B., U. Detroit, 1958. Admitted to Mich. bar, 1958; chief trial lawyer Macomb County (Mich.) Prosecutor's Office, 1959-63; chief asst. city atty. City of Warren (Mich.), 1963-68; judge Warren Dist. Ct., 1969-74, Mich. Circuit Ct., 16th Jud. Dist., 1974—. Chmn. Warren Charter Revision Com., 1971. Mem. Mich., Am. Macomb County bar assns., Am. Judicature Soc., Macomb County Traffic Safety Assn. Home: 11359 Greentree St Warren MI 48093 Office: 16th Jud Circuit Mount Clemens MI 48043 Tel (313) 465-1211

CHUCK, WALTER GOONSUN, b. Wailuku, Maui, Hawaii, Sept. 10, 1920; Ed. B., U. Hawaii, 1941; J.D., Harvard, 1948. Admitted to Hawaii bar, 1948; asst. pub. prosecutor, Honolulu County, City, 1949; since practiced law in Honolulu; mem. firm Fong, Miho & Choy, 1950-53, Fong, Miho, Choy & Chuck, 1953-58, Chung, Vitousek, Chuck & Fujiyama, 1967-68, Chuck & Fujiyama, 1968-74, Chuck, Wong & Tonaki, 1974-76, Chuck & Pai, 1976—; dist. magistrate, Honolulu, 1956-63; spl dep. atty. gen. State ot Hawaii; mem. jud. Council; clk. Hawaii Ho. of Reps., 1951-53; senate clk., Hawaii, 1959-62. Chmn. Hawaii Employment Relations Bd., 1955-59. Mem. Am. Bar Assn. (former del. ho. of dels.), Bar Assn. of Hawaii (pres.), Internat. Acad. of Trial Lawyers (former dir.), Law Sci. Inst., Internat Soc. Barristers. Editor Am. Trial Lawyers Assn., 1957. Home: 2691 Aaliamanu Pl Honolulu HI 96813 Office: Suite 200 1022 Bethel St Honolulu HI 96813 Tel (808) 533-3614

CHUMNEY, VERN FRANKLIN, b. Decaturville, Tenn., Nov. 11, 1936; B.S., Memphis State U., 1963, J.D., 1965. Admitted to Tenn. bar, 1965; individual practice law, Memphis, 1965—. Home: 6429 Strathspey Rd Germantown TN 38138 Office: Suite 1003 United Am Bank Bldg 147 Jefferson Ave Memphis TN 38103 Tel (901) 525-4785

CHUPKA, BERNARD THOMAS, b. Pitts., Apr. 29, 1926; student U. Pitts., 1946-50; LL.B., Ohio State U., 1953, J.D., 1965. Admitted to Ohio bar, 1954; individual practice law, Columbus, Ohio, 1954-72; dir. pub. safety City of Columbus, 1972—; asst. atty. gen. Columbus, 1960-61; vice chmn. Ohio Liquor Control Commn., 1961-72; with JAGC, Ohio N.G.; mem. exec. com. Columbus-Franklin County Criminal Justice Coordinating Council. Trustee Mid-Ohio Health Planning Fedn.; chmn. Columbus Med. Services Adv. Council. Mem. Columbus, Ohio State bar assns., Lawyer-Pilots Bar Assn., Judge Advs. Assn. Named an Outstanding Young Man in Central Ohio, Columbus Jr. C. of C., 1961. Home: 955 Norway Dr Columbus OH 43221 Office: City Hall 90 W Broad St Columbus OH 43215 Tel (614) 461-8210

CHURCH, ANDREW, b. Salinas, Calif., Mar. 18, 1936; B.S., U. Calif., 1958, J.D., 1961. Admitted to Calif. bar, 1962, U.S. Ct. Appeals 9th Circuit bar, 1962, U.S. Supreme Ct. bar, 1970; asso. firm Jacob Abramson, Salinas, Calif., 1961-66; partner firm Abramson & Church, Salinas, 1966-71; partner firm Abramson, Church & Stave, Salinas, 1972—. Bd. dirs. United Way, Salinas, 1965-68, v.p., 1967; bd. edn. Salinas City Sch. Dist., 1966-74, pres. 1968-72, 74; bd. dirs. Salinas Council Camp Fire Girls, 1964-70, pres., 1967-70. Mem. State Bar Calif., Am., Monterey bar assns. Office: Crocker Bank Bldg Salinas CA 93901 Tel (408) 758-2401

CHURCH, EDWARDS LEE, b. Evanston, Ill., Mar. 26, 1941; B.A., U. Miami, 1968, J.D., 1971. Admitted to Fla. bar, 1971, U.S. Dist. Ct. for Soc. Dist. Fla. bar, 1971 U.S. Ct. Appeals, 1972, U.S. Dist. Ct. for D.C. bar, 1973; law clk. firm Fleming, O'Brian & Fleming, Ft. Lauderdale, Fla., 1969; legal intern Dade County (Fla.) Pub. Defenders Office, Miami, 1970-71; asst. state atty. 17th Jud. Circuit, Broward County, Ft. Lauderdale, 1971-72; individual practice law, Ft. Lauderdale, 1972—. Mem. Am., Broward County bar assns., Nat. Legal Aid and Defenders Assn., Nat. Dist. Attys. Assn., Fla., D.C. bars. Recipient certificate of Appreciation Notary Club Deerfield Beach, Fla., 1972. Office: Suite 100-B 200 SE 6th St Fort Lauderdale FL 33301 Tel (305) 463-6500

CHURCHILL, WILLIAM PHILIP, b. Dorchester, Mass., Sept. 12, 1908; B.S. in Chem. Engring., U. Maine, 1930; LL.B., George Washington U., 1935. Admitted to D.C. bar, 1934, N.Y. bar, 1939; examiner U.S. Patent Office, 1930-35; mem. firm Fish & Neave and predecessor, N.Y.C., 1935—, partner, 1953—. Chmn. Briarcliff (N.Y.) Planning Bd., 1953-55, Peoples Caucus Briarcliff Manor, 1957-71, Zoning Bd. Appeals, Briarcliff Manor, 1975—; trustee United Fund No. Westchester, 1958-59, Congl. Ch., 1952-57. Mem. Am. Bar Assn., Am., N.Y. patent law assns., Assn. Bar City N.Y., Am. Judicature Soc. Home: 365 Central Dr Briarcliff Manor NY 10510 Office: 277 Park Ave New York City NY 10017 Tel (212) 826-1050

CHVALA, JOSEPH FRANCIS, b. Prentice, Wis., Dec. 9, 1920; student Oshkosh State Coll., 1939-42, Naval Air Coll., Corpus Christi, Tex., 1942; B.S., U. Wis., 1949, LL.B., 1950, J.D., 1950. Admitted to Wis. bar, 1950; v.p. ops. Am. Standard Ins. Co., Madison, Wis., 1950—, also dir.; v.p. Am. Family Ins. Co., Madison; dir. Am. Standard Ins. Co. conducted seminars conf. mut. casualty cos., 1968, 69. Committeeman Our Lady Queen of Peace Council Boy Scouts Am., 1960-71; pres. Sch. and Family Assn., parish council; dir., exec. com. Madison Mustangs Football Team; loaned exec. Red Feather Agency. Mem. Wis. Bar Assn. Home: 518 Edward St Madison WI 53711 Office: 3099 E Washington Ave Madison WI 53701 Tel (608) 249-2111

CHYNOWETH, W(ILLIAM) EDWARD, b. Washington, Sept. 1, 1923; B.S. in Mil. Sci. and Engring., U.S. Mil. Acad., 1946; M.S. in Mech. Engring., U. Calif., Berkeley, 1959; LL.B., Stanford, 1963. Admitted to Calif. bar, 1963; asso. firms Huebner & Worrel, Fresno, Calif., 1963-66, Wild, Christensen, Carter & Hamlin, Fresno, 1966-69; dep. dist. atty. Tulare County, Visalia, Calif., 1969—. Mem. Am., Tulare County bar assns., Calif. Dist. Atty's Assn. Home: 403 S Indianola Ave Sanger CA 93657 Office: Tulare County Courthouse Visalia CA 93277 Tel (209) 733-6411

CIANCI, PETER FRANCIS, b. Reading, Pa., Jan. 28, 1925; B.S., Albright Coll., 1946; J.D., U. Pa., 1949. Admitted to Pa. Supreme Ct. bar, 1950; individual practice law, Reading, 1950-64; partner firm DeLong, Dry, Cianci & Grim, Reading, 1964—; asst. dist. atty. Berks County (Pa.), 1956-61, first asst. dist. atty., 1961-63; first asst. solicitor City of Reading, 1968—. Mem. Am., Pa., Berks County bar assns. Home: 1704 Hill Rd Reading PA 19604 Office: 541 Penn St Reading PA 19601 Tel (215) 376-6721

CIANCI, PETER JOHN, b. Conshohocken, Pa., Nov. 9, 1927; B.S., Villanova U., 1951; LL.B., Temple U., 1955. Admitted to Pa. bar, 1957; partner firm Wisler, Pearlstine, Talone, Craig & Garrity, Norristown, Pa. Mem. Am., Pa., Montgomery County (past dir.) bar assns., Pa. Trial Lawyers Assn. Office: 515 Swede St Norristown PA 19401 Tel (215) 272-8400

CIANCIO, GENE ANDREW, b. Denver, July 29, 1946; B.A., U. Colo., 1969; J.D., U. Denver, 1971. Admitted to Colo. bar, 1972; law clk. to judge Denver Dist. Ct., 1970-72; individual practice law, Denver, 1972-73; partner firms Carroll, Bradley & Ciancio, Denver, 1973-75, DiManna, Eklund & Ciancio, Denver, 1975—; spl. trial counsel City of Northglenn (Colo.), 1974-75; mem. Colo. 17th Jud. Selection Com., 1976—. State treas. Colo. Young Democrats of Adams County, 1965; mem. Adams County Precinct Com. Democratic Party, 1967. Mem. Adams County (pres. 1975-76), Colo. (gov. 1976-77) bar assns., Am., Colo. trial lawyers assns. Home: 1177 Milky Way Denver CO 80221 Office: 50 S Steele St Suite 850 Denver CO 80209 Tel (303) 320-4848

CICCIO, JOSEPH FRANCIS, b. Boston, June 20, 1916; LL.B., Northeastern U., 1940, J.D., 1971. Admitted to Mass. bar, 1941; individual practice law, Boston, 1941-48; atty. Mass. Div. Ins., Boston, 1948-64, gen. counsel, 1964-69, dep. commr. ins. 1969—. Mem. Mass. Govt. Lawyers Assn. (treas. 1971-74). Office: PO Box 8233 Kennedy Station Boston MA 02114 Tel (617) 727-2297

CICCOLELLA, JOHN BARTON, b. Alamogordo, N.Mex., Mar. 2, 1947; B.S., So. Colo. State Coll., 1969; J.D., U. Colo., 1972. Admitted to Colo. bar, 1972; partner firm MacLaughlin, Ciccolella and Barton, Colorado Springs, Colo., 1972—; judge City of Manitou Springs (Colo.), 1975—. Mem. Am., Colo., El Paso County bar assns., Colo., Colorade Springs, Nat. trial lawyers assns., Colorado Springs Criminal Def. Lawyers Assn. Home: 3845 Fetlock Circle Colorado Springs CO 80918 Office: 8 S Nevada Ave Suite 310 Colorado Springs CO 80903 Tel (303) 473-0842

CICERO, FRANK, JR., b. Chgo., Nov. 30, 1935; B.A., Wheaton (Ill.) Coll., 1957; M.P.A., Princeton, 1962; J.D., U. Chgo., 1964. Admitted to Ill. bar, 1965, U.S. Supreme Ct. bar, 1972; asso. firm Kirkland & Ellis, Chgo., 1965-69, partner, 1970—. Del. 6th Ill. Constl. Conv., 1969-70. Mem. Am., Ill. bar assns., Am. Polit. Sci. Assn., Am. Assn. Polit. and Social Sci. Home: 222 Lake St Evanston IL 60201 Office: 200 E Randolph Dr Chicago IL 60601 Tel (312) 861-2216

CICILLINE, JOHN FRANCIS, b. Providence, Aug. 7, 1938; A.B., Providence Coll., 1960; LL.B., Suffolk U., 1964. Admitted to R.I. bar, 1965; partner Bevilacqua & Cicilline, Providence, 1965—. Mem. Am., R.I. bar assns. Home: Palm Beach Ave Narragansett RI 02882 Office: 380 Broadway Providence RI 02903 Tel (401) 274-7444

CICILLINE, STEPHEN EDWARD, b. Providence, Feb. 14, 1942; B.A., Providence Coll., 1963; J.D., Suffolk U., 1970. Admitted to R.I. bar, 1970, U.S. Dist. Ct. bar, 1971, U.S. Tax Ct., 1974; since practiced in Providence, partner firm Bevilacqua & Cicilline, 1970—; staff JA R.I. Air N.G., 1974—; town solicitor Smithfield, R.I., 1972—, mem. 7th senatorial com., 1964-66; town com., 1972—; justice peace, 1970-72. Mem. R.I. Bar Assn. Office: 380 Broadway Providence RI 02909 Tel (401) 274-7444

CICONE, GUY JOSEPH, b. Weirton, W.Va., Sept. 20, 1918; B.S., Loyola U., Balt., 1957; LL.B., U. Md., 1952. Admitted to Md. bar, 1952; asst. city solicitor City of Balt., 1958-59; asst. atty. gen. State of Md., 1962-75; circuit ct. judge Howard County (Md.), 1975—. Mem. Howard County Bar Assn. (pres. 1974-75). Office: Court House Ellicott City MD 21043 Tel (301) 465-5433

CIESIELSKI, JOSEPH STANLEY, b. Chester, Pa., Mar. 26, 1940; A.B., Villanova U., 1961, M.S., 1962, J.D., 1969. Admitted to Calif. bar, 1971; prof., dir. law library U. San Diego, 1969—. Mem. Am., San Diego County bar assns., State Bar Calif., Am. Assn. Law Libraries. Office: Marvin Kratter Law Library U San Diego San Diego CA 92110 Tel (714) 291-6480

CIESLIK, ROBERT THOMAS, b. Detroit, Jan. 4, 1943; B.S., Eastern Mich. U., 1964, J.D., Wayne State U., 1971. Admitted to Mich. bar, 1971; tax specialist Lybrand, Ross and Montgomery, C.P.A.'s, Detroit, 1971-72; supervising atty. Wayne County (Mich.) Legal Services, Inkster, 1973—. Mem. State Bar Mich., Am. Arbitration Assn. Home: 26074 Deerfield St Dearborn Heights MI 48127 Office: 4310 S Middlebelt St Inkster MI 48141 Tel (313) 721-3684

CIMINO, FRANK JOSEPH, b. Youngstown, Ohio, Apr. 3, 1947; A.B., Hiram Coll., 1969; J.D., U. Akron, 1972. Admitted to Ohio bar, 1972; asst. prosecutor Portage County, Ohio, 1972-75, chief criminal div., 1975; law dir. City of Ravenna, Ohio, 1976—; individual practice law, Ravenna, 1976—. Pres. bd. dirs. Portage County Boys Club, 1976—. Mem. Am., Ohio, Portage County bar assns. Articles editor: Akron Law Review, 1971-72, contbr. articles, 1970-72. Office: 113 1/2 E Main St Ravenna OH 44266 Tel (216) 297-7578

CINCOTTA, ANTHONY JOSEPH, b. Mt. Vernon, N.Y., Nov. 24, 1938; B.B.A., St. John's U., Bklyn., 1961, J.D., 1963. Admitted to N.Y. bar, 1963; partner firm Robinson & Cincotta, Oyster Bay, N.Y., 1970—. Mem. Nassau County Bar Assn., Nassau Lawyers Assn. (past sec., chmn. bd.). Office: 34 Audrey Ave Oyster Bay NY 11771 Tel (516) 922-7700

CINDRICH, ROBERT JAMES, b. Washington, Pa., Sept. 22, 1943; A.B., Wittenberg U., 1965; J.D. magna cum laude, U. Pitts., 1968. Admitted to Pa. bar, 1968; trial defender Allegheny County Office of Pub. Defender, 1969-70; trial prosecutor Allegheny County Dist. Atty.'s Office, 1970-72; partner firm McVerry, Baxter, Cindrich, Loughren & Mansmann, Pitts., 1972—; solicitor Robinson Twp., 1976—. Mem. Am., Pa. Allegheny County bar assns., Assn. of Trial Lawyers in Criminal Court (treas.), Am. Arbitration Assn., Order of the Coif. Author: Criminal Ct. Manual, 1970. Home: 741 Shady Ln Pittsburgh PA 15228 Office: 429 Forbes Ave Lawyers Bldg Pittsburgh PA 15219 Tel (412) 765-2500

CION, JUDITH ANN, b. N.Y.C., June 27, 1943; student Smith Coll., 1961-63; A.B., Pomona Coll., 1965; LL.B., Harvard U., 1968. Admitted to N.Y. State bar, 1968; asso. firm Poletti, Freidin, Prashker, Feldman & Gartner, N.Y.C., 1968-71; asso. firm Lovejoy, Wasson, Lundgren & Ashton, N.Y.C., 1971-75, mem., 1975—. Mem. N.Y. State, Am. bar assns., Assn. Bar City N.Y. Office: Lovejoy Wasson et al 250 Park Ave New York City NY 10017 Tel (212) 697-4100

CIPOLLA, JOSEPH SALVATORE, b. Quincy, Mass., Mar. 25, 1921; B.S. in Bus. Adminstrn., Boston U., 1946, LL.B., 1949, LL.M., 1953. Admitted to Mass. bar, 1949, U.S. Dist. Ct. for Dist. Mass. bar, 1951; individual practice law, Quincy, 1949—. Mem. Norfolk County, Quincy bar assns. Home: 75 Emerald St Quincy MA 02169 Office: 1354 Hancock St Quincy MA 02169 Tel (617) 479-4120

CIPOLLA, VINCENT CHARLES, b. Chgo., Nov. 6, 1943; B.S. in Humanities, Loyola U. (Chgo.), 1965; J.D., John Marshall Law Sch., 1974. Admitted to Ill. bar, 1974; caseworker Cook County Dept. Pub. Aid, Chgo., 1965-66; dir. safety and security services Augustana Med. Center, Chgo., 1970-71, adminstrv. asst. Augustana Hosp., 1966-68; asso. firm Judge & Schirott, Park Ridge, Ill., 1974-77; partner firm Schirott, Drew, Cipolla & Kurnik, 1977—; instr. John Marshall Law Sch., 1974-77. Mem. Am., Ill. State, Chgo. (mem. legal edn. com.), NW Suburban bar assns., Am. Arbitration Assn. (arbitrator), Justinian Soc., Ill. Trial Lawyers Assn., Assn. of U.S. Army, Am. Radio Relay League, Tau Epsilon Rho. Recipient Order of John Marshall, 1974; mem. staff John Marshall Jour. of Practice and Procedure, 1974. Home: 1416 Belmont St Arlington Heights IL 60005 Office: 422 N Northwest Hwy Park Ridge IL 60068 Tel (312) 696-2810

CIRILLO, VINCENT ANTHONY, b. Phila., Dec. 19, 1927; A.B., Villanova U., 1951, J.D., LL.B., Temple U., 1955. Admitted to Pa. Supreme Ct. bar, 1956, U.S. Supreme Ct. bar, 1963; law clk. judge of Ct. Common Pleas, 1955-58; practiced in Norristown, Pa., 1955-72; asst. dist. atty. Montgomery County (Pa.), 1958-62, asst. county solicitor, 1964-72; judge Ct. Common Pleas, Montgomery County, Pa., 1972—. Commr. Lower Merion Twp. (Pa.), 1971; mem. awards jury Valley Forge Freedom Found., 1966; mem. exec. bd. Temple U. Law Sch. Mem. Am., Pa., Montgomery County bar assns., Pa. Conf. State Trial Judges, Phi Alpha Delta. Named Man of Year Cath. War Vets., 1975. Home: 825 Bryn Mawr Ave Penn Valley PA 19072 Office: Montgomery County Courthouse Norristown PA 19404 Tel (215) 275-5000

CISLO, DONALD MICHAEL, b. Chgo., Jan. 21, 1935; B.S., Ill. Inst. Tech., 1957; J.D., DePaul U., 1964. Admitted to Ill. bar, 1964, Calif. bar, 1971, U.S. Supreme Ct. bar, 1973; atty. Pure Oil Co., Chgo., 1963-65; asso. firm Mann, Brown & McWilliams, Chgo., 1965-70; partner firm Mahoney, Schick & Cislo, Santa Monica, Calif., 1970—. Mem. Am., Ill., Am. Patent, Calif., Santa Monica, Marina Del Rey bar assns. Office: 401 Wilshire Blvd Santa Monica CA 90401 Tel (213) 870-1163

CITAK, BURTON, b. N.Y.C., Dec. 2, 1927; B.A., Syracuse U., 1949; J.D., Cornell U., 1952. Admitted to N.Y. bar, 1952; with Q.M. Procurement Agy.; mem. firm Grossman & Grossman, N.Y.C. Mem. Am., Queens County bar assns. Office: 475 Fifth Ave New York City NY 10017 Tel (212) 685-3157

CITRON, JEROME DAVID, b. Chgo., June 14, 1948; B.A. in Polit. Sci., No. Ill. U.; J.D., Chgo.-Kent Coll. Law. Admitted to Ill. bar, 1973; asso. firm Pitler & Mandell, Chgo., 1973—. Bd. dirs. Aron Fox Diabetic Found. Mem. Ill., Chgo. bar assns. Office: 230 W Monroe St Chicago IL 60606 Tel (312) 782-9466

CITRON, RICHARD KENT, b. Queens, N.Y., Feb. 9, 1945; B.S., U. Calif., Berkeley, 1966, M.B.A., 1967; J.D., U. Calif., Los Angeles, 1970. Admitted to Calif. bar, 1971, U.S. Supreme Ct. bar, 1975; asst. prof. bus. adminstrn. Calif. State U., Northridge, 1968-73; instr. corps. Western State U., Anaheim, Calif., 1970-72; individual practice law, Los Angeles, 1971—. Mem. Calif., Los Angeles County bar assns., UN Assn. (dir. Los Angeles chpt. 1974—). Office: 1901 Ave of Stars Suite 888 Los Angeles CA 90067 Tel (213) 277-3436

CIVILETTI, BENJAMIN RICHARD, b. Peekskill, N.Y., July 17, 1935; A.B., Johns Hopkins U., 1957; LL.B., U. Md., 1961. Admitted to Md. bar, 1961; asst. U.S. atty. Dist. Md., 1962-64; mem. firm Venable, Baetjer & Howard, Balt., 1964-69, partner, 1969-77; asst. atty. gen. criminal div., U.S. Dept. Justice, 1977—; mem. character com. Ct. Appeals Md., 1970-76; mem. Md. State Legislature Task Force Crime, 1976; lectr. U. Md. Law Sch., 1976—. Mem. Mayor's Com. to Investigate Balt. City Jail, 1972-73. Mem. Am., Md. (chmn. parole aide com. 1971-74) bar assns., Bar Assn. Balt. City, Am. Judicature Soc., Assn. Trial Lawyers Am.

CLABAUGH, ELMER EUGENE, JR., b. Anaheim, Calif., Sept. 18, 1927; B.B.A. cum laude, Woodbury Coll., 1951; B.A. summa cum laude, Claremont Men's Coll., 1958; J.D., Stanford U., 1961. Fgn. service staff U.S. Dept. State, Jerusalem, Tel Aviv, 1951-53; field staff Pub. Adminstrn. Service, El Salvador, Ethiopia, U.S., 1953-57; admitted to Calif. bar, 1961; dep. dist. atty. Ventura County, Calif., 1961-62; mem. firm Hathaway, Clabaugh, Perrett & Webster, Ventura, Calif. 1962—; state inheritance tax referee, 1968—; city atty. City 1000 Oaks, Calif., 1964-69, city Simi Valley, Calif., 1969-71. Bd. dirs. San Antonio Water Conservation Dist., Ventura Community Meml. Hosp.; trustee Ojai Unified Sch. Dist., 1974—; mem. pres.'s adv. council Claremont Men's Coll., 1975—. Mem. Calif. Bar Assn., Am. Arbitration Assn., Phi Alpha Delta. Home: 3510 Santa Paula-Ojai Rd Ojai CA 93003 Office: Hathaway Bldg 5450 Telegraph Rd Ventura CA 93003 Tel (805) 644-7111

CLADOUHOS, HARRY WILLIAM, b. Gt. Falls, Mont., Mar. 9, 1925; ed. City Coll. Mex.; B.S.F.S. magna cum laude, Wash. State Coll., 1951; L.L.B., Harvard, 1954. Admitted to D.C. bar, 1955, U.S. Supreme Ct. bar, 1970; legal asst. office of commr. Fed.

Communications Commn., Washington, 1954-55; officer fgn. service, sec. diplomatic service U.S. Dept. State, Washington, 1955-57; sr. atty. trial sect. antitrust div., U.S. Dept. Justice, Washington, 1957-69; partner firm Peabody Rivlin, Gore, Cladouhos & Lambert, Washington, 1969-73; sr. partner firm Cladouhos & Brashares, Washington, 1973—. Mem. D.C. Bar Assn. Home: 5409 Falmouth Rd Washington DC 20016 Office: 1750 New York Ave NW Washington DC 20006

CLAFLIN, BEECHER NEVILLE, b. Lancaster, Ohio, Mar. 14, 1919; A.B., Miami U., Oxford, Ohio, 1941; LL.B., Columbia, 1947. Admitted to Conn. bar, 1947, Ohio bar, 1966; partner firm Maguire & Cole, Stamford, Conn., 1947-58, Parker Badger & Fisher, Greenwich, Conn., 1958-59; sec., counsel Fafnir Bearing Co., New Britain, Conn., 1959-64, Chase Brass & Copper Co., Cleve., 1964-74; asst. gen. counsel, asst. sec. Arthur G. McKee & Co., Cleve., 1974—. Chmn., New Britain Zoning Bd. Appeals, 1963-64; v.p. Orange Bd. Edn., Cleve., 1968-70. Mem. Am., Ohio, Cleve. bar assns. Home: 29980 Bolingbrook Rd Pepper Pike OH 44124 Office: 6200 Oak Tree Blvd Cleveland OH 44131 Tel (216) 524-9300

CLAGETT, BRICE MCADOO, b. Washington, July 6, 1933; A.B. summa cum laude, Princeton U., 1954; student U. Allahabad, India, 1954-55; J.D. magna cum laude, Harvard U., 1958. Admitted to D.C. bar, 1958, U.S. Supreme Ct. bar, 1962, ICC bar, 1964, U.S. Ct. of Claims bar, 1976; asso. firm Covington & Burling, Washington, 1958-67, partner, 1967—; juridical councellor Cambodian Delegation to the Internat. Ct. of Justice, 1960-62. Bd. trustees Md. Hist. Trust, 1971—, chmn., 1972—; mem. Md. State House Trust, 1972-76; mem., sec. bd. trustees Clagett Sch., Inc., 1974—. Mem. Am., D.C. bar assns., Am. Soc. of Internat. Law, Internat. Law Assn., Washington Inst. of Foreign Affairs. Named comdr. Royal Order of Cambodia, 1962; bd. editors Harvard Law Review, 1956-58; contbr. articles to legal and hist. jours. Home: Holly Hill Friendship MD 20758 Office: 888 16th St NW Washington DC 20006 Tel (202) 452-6306

CLAGETT, JOHN ROBERTSON, b. Sedalia, Mo., July 18, 1908; student Westminster Coll., 1926-28; J.D., Washington U., 1932. Admitted to Mo. bar, 1931, U.S. Supreme Ct. bar, 1944; since practiced in Kansas City, Mo.; atty. Kansas City Pub. Service Co., 1932-33; asso. firm Bowersock, Fizzell & Rhodes, 1933-35; partner firm McVey & Clagett, 1936-46, firm Kemp, Koontz, Clagett & Norquist, 1946-70, firm Lathrop, Koontz, Righter, Clagett, Parker & Norquist, 1970—; pros. atty. War Crimes Trial, Nurnburg, Germany, 1945-46; capt. JAGC, U.S. Army, Washington, 1944-45. Pres., Council on World Affairs, Kansas City, Mo., 1949. Mem. Am., Mo., Kansas City bar assns., Lawyers Assn. (pres. 1958, Distinguished Service award 1959), Am. Judicature Soc., Farmers Club Greater Kansas City (pres. 1954). Home: 616 W 67th Terr Kansas City MO 64113 Office: 1500 Ten Main Center Kansas City MO 64105 Tel (816) 842-0820

CLAIBORNE, HARRY EUGENE, b. McRae, Ark., July 2, 1917; student Ouachita U., 1934-37; LL.B., Cumberland U., 1941, J.D., 1969. Admitted to Ark. bar, 1942, Nev. bar, 1946, U.S. Supreme Ct. bar, 1965; individual practice law Las Vegas, Nev., 1946—; mem. Nev. Assembly, 1949, chmn. judiciary com.; asst. dist. atty. Clark County, Nev., 1946-48; city atty. City of North Las Vegas, 1948-55. Fellow Am. Coll. Trial Lawyers; mem. Nat. Assn. Trial Lawyers, Am. Assn. Criminal Def. Lawyers, Am. Bar Assn., Am. Bd. Trial Advs. (advocate). Home: 500 Rancho Dr Las Vegas NV 89101 Office: 108 S 3d St Las Vegas NV 89101 Tel (702) 384-3553

CLANCY, KENNETH PAUL, b. Milw., May 29, 1943; B.S., Marquette U., 1965, J.D., 1968. Admitted to Wis. bar, 1968, Ariz. bar, 1970; asso. firm Langerman, Begam & Lewis, Phoenix, 1970-72; individual practice law, Phoenix, 1972—. Mem. Am., Wis., Ariz., Maricopa County bar assns., Am., Ariz. Phoenix trial lawyers assns., Am. Bd. Trial Adv. Home: 8211 N 3rd Ave Phoenix AZ 85021 Office: 45 W Jefferson St Phoenix AZ 85003 Tel (602) 258-5749

CLARIE, T. EMMET, U.S. judge; b. 1913; Ph.B., Providence Coll.; LL.B., Hartford Coll. Law. Admitted to bar, 1940; now chief U.S. dist. judge Conn. Mem. Am. Bar Assn. Address: 450 Main St Hartford CT 06103*

CLARK, BAYARD TAYLOR, b. Reserve, Kans., Mar. 7, 1897; LL.B., U. Nebr., 1920, A.B., 1922. Admitted to Nebr. bar, 1920, Fed. Cts. bars, 1920; individual practice law, Falls City, Nebr., 1920—; county atty., 1944-50. Sec. Falls City Bd. Edn., 1926-65. Mem. Nebr. Bar Assn. Home: 2420 Crook St Falls City NE 68355 Office: 1611 Stone St Falls City NE 68355 Tel (402) 245-4325

CLARK, BRUCE MARVIN, b. Fresno, Calif., Aug. 5, 1922; LL.D., U. Mo., 1949. Admitted to Mo. bar, 1948, Hawaii bar, 1949; individual practice law, Honolulu, 1949—. Mem. Hawaii Bar, Am. Bar Assn., Am. Trial Lawyers Assn. Home: 333 Aoloa St Apt 333 Kailua HI 96734 Office: 119 Merchant St Suite 506 Honolulu HI 96813 Tel (808) 538-7434

CLARK, CHAPIN DEWITT, b. Lawrence, Kans., Dec. 27, 1930; B.A., U. Kans., 1952, J.D., 1954; LL.M., Columbia, 1959. Admitted to Kans. bar, 1954, Oreg. bar, 1965; with JAGC, U.S. Army, 1954-58; asst. prof. law U. S.D., 1959-62; asso. prof. law U. Oreg., Eugene, 1962-67, prof., 1967—, dean sch. law, 1974—. Vice chmn., Oreg. Water Policy Rev. Bd., 1975—; mem. Oreg. Gov.'s Commn. on Oceanography, 1967-69; mem. bd. dirs. Water Resources Inst., Oreg. State U., 1966-70; pres. Planned Parenthood Lane County, 1975-76. Mem. Am. Bar Assn., AAUP (pres. U. Oreg. chpt. 1970-71), Am. Judicature Soc., Phi Beta Kappa. Contbr. articles to law revs.

CLARK, CHARLES, b. Memphis, Sept. 12, 1925; student Millsaps Coll., 1943-44, Tulane U., 1944; LL.B., U. Miss., 1948. Admitted to Miss. bar, 1948; mem. firm Wells, Thomas & Wells, Jackson, Miss., 1948-61, Cox, Dunn & Clark, Jackson, 1961-69; spl. asst. to atty. gen. State of Miss., 1961-66; judge U.S. Ct. Appeals, 5th Circuit, 1969—. Mem. Miss. Bar Assn., Am. Law Inst., Am. Coll. Trial Lawyers. Home: Jackson MS Office: US Courthouse Jackson MS 39205 Tel (601) 353-0911

CLARK, CHRISTOPHER JOHN, b. Albany, N.Y., Jan. 1, 1941; B.B.A., St. Bernardine of Siena Coll., 1962; J.D., Villanova U., 1965. Admitted to N.Y. State bar, 1965, Pa. bar, 1971; with Arthur Andersen & Co., N.Y.C., 1965-71; partner firm Lentz, Riley, Cantor, Kilgore & Massey, Paoli, Pa., 1971—. Bd. dirs., sec.-treas. Hill Top Prep. Sc., Inc., Phila., 1971—. Mem. Am., Pa., Chester County bar assns., N.Y. State Soc. C.P.A.'s, Delta Epsilon Sigma. C.P.A., N.Y. Home: 37 Clearview Rd Malvern PA 19355 Office: 30 Darby Rd Paoli PA 19301 Tel (215) 647-3310

CLARK, DAVID MCKENZIE, b. Greenville, N.C., Sept. 1, 1929; B.A., Wake Forest Coll., 1951; LL.B., N.Y. U., 1957. Admitted to N.C. bar, 1958; law clk. to Justice Black, U.S. Supreme Ct., Washington, 1957-59; asso. firm Smith, Moore, Smith, Schell & Hunter, Greensboro, 1959-64; partner firm Stern, Rendleman & Clark, Greensboro, 1964-68, Clark, Wharton, Tanner & Sharp and predecessors, 1968—. Chmn., Guilford County chpt. Nat. Found., 1965; v.p. Children's Home Soc. N.C., 1971-72; mem. ofcl. bd. W. Market St. Methodist Ch., Greensboro, 1974-76; treas. Guilford County Democratic Party, 1970; mem. N.C. Dem. Exec. Com., 1974—; chmn. bd. trustees Greensboro Legal Aid Found., 1965-68; mem. spl. com. on indigent legal services delivery systems N.C. Bar Assn. Found., 1975-76; bd. dirs. Legal Services N.C., 1976—. Mem. Am., N.C., Greensboro (dir. 1974) bar assns. Office: 701 Wachovia Bldg PO Box 1349 Greensboro NC 27402 Tel (919) 275-7275

CLARK, DAVID SCOTT, b. San Diego, Nov. 24, 1944; A.B., Stanford, 1966, J.D., 1969, J.S.M., 1972. Admitted to Calif. bar, 1972; asst. dir. U. Costa Rica Law Project, San Jose, 1970-71; asst. dir. studies in law and devel. Stanford Law Sch., 1973-76; asst. prof. law La. State U., 1976—; lectr. in law U. Santa Clara, 1974-76; hon. mem. Costa Rica bar, 1969-71. Mem. AAUP, Law and Soc. Assn., Author: Renting & Sharecropping in Costa Rica, 1971. Home: 3801 Jolly Dr Baton Rouge LA 70808 Office: Law Center La State U Baton Rouge LA 70803 Tel (504) 388-8701

CLARK, DRENNAN ANTHONY, b. Rochester, N.Y., Aug. 30, 1937; B.S., U. San Francisco, 1959, LL.B., J.D., 1964. Admitted to Nev. bar, 1964, U.S. Supreme Ct. bar, 1974, U.S. Ct. Mil. Appeals, 1975. Law clk. Justice Gordon Thompson, Nev. Supreme Ct., Carson City, 1964-65; asso. firm Guild, Guild & Cunningham, Reno, 1965-69, partner, 1969-70; partner firm Guild, Hagen & Clark, Reno, 1970-72; dir. and officer Guild, Hagen & Clark, Ltd., Reno, 1972—; major, staff judge adv. attached to state hdqrs. Nev. NG, 1972—; mem. Nev. Bd. Parole Commrs., 1976—. Chmn. adv. bd. Vis. Nurse Service, Washoe County Health Dept., 1972-76. Mem. Washoe County (sgt. at arms 1975, treas. 1976), Clark County, Am. bar assns., State Bar Assn. Nev. (chmn. fee arbitration com. 1973—), Phi Alpha Delta, McAuliffe Law Honor Soc. Home: 2545 Sharon Way Reno NV 89509 Office: 102 Roff Way Reno NV 89501 Tel (702) 786-2366 also 302 E Carson Ave Suite 1010 Las Vegas NV 81901 Tel 384-1096

CLARK, EDWARD L., JR., b. Portland, Oreg., Sept. 9, 1923; B.A., Occidental Coll., 1947; LL.B., U. Oreg., 1950. Admitted to Oreg. bar, 1950; partner firm Clark, Marsh & Lindauer, Salem, Oreg. Chmn., Marion-Polk County (Oreg.) Boundary Commn., 1969-76. Mem. Oreg., Marion County bar assns., Oreg. Assn. Defense Counsel. Office: 880 Liberty St NE Salem OR 97301 Tel (503) 581-1542

CLARK, EDWIN MILLIGAN, b. Gilpin Twp., Pa., Aug. 25, 1902; A.B., Muskingum Coll., 1924, L.H.D., 1964; postgrad. U. Mich., 1929-31; J.D., Duquesne U., 1932. Admitted to Pa. bar, 1932, U.S. Dist. Ct. of Western Pa. bar, 1937; mem. firm Holsinger & Clark, Indiana, Pa.; individual practice law, Indiana, Pa., 1932-56; pros. atty. City of Indiana, 1936-48; common pleas judge 40th Jud. Dist. of Pa., Indiana, 1956-76. Bd. dirs. United Fund, Indiana, YMCA, Indiana; trustee J.S. Mack Found. Mem. State Pros. Attys. Assn. (pres. 1940), State Juvenile Ct. Judges Assn. (pres. 1968). Home: 550 Maple St Indiana PA 15701 Office: Holsinger & Clark First Fed Bldg Indiana PA 15701 Tel (412) 463-8791

CLARK, ESTHER FRANCES, b. Phila., Aug. 29, 1929; B.A., Temple U., 1950; J.D., Rutgers U., 1955. Admitted to Pa. bar, 1956; partner firm Clark and Clark, Chester, Pa., 1973-76; asso. prof. Del. Law Sch. Widener Coll., Wilmington, 1976—; lectr. in field; pres. bd. dirs. Del. County Legal Assistance Assn., 1974-76; mem. Pa. State Adv. Com. Law Related Edn., 1974—; mem. juvenile study com. Pa. Joint Council Criminal Justice System, 1974—. Mem. Am., Pa. (chmn. com. youth edn. 1973-74), Del. County bar assns., Am. Trial Lawyers Assn., Nat. Assn. Women Lawyers. Asso. editor Rutgers U. Law Rev., 1954-55; recipient Citizenship award Chester NAACP, 1973. Home: 207 Knoll Rd Wallingford PA 19086 Tel (302) 658-8042

CLARK, FRANCIS JOSEPH, b. Milford, N.H., Dec. 1, 1933; B.S., Northeastern U., 1968; J.D., Suffolk U., 1972. Admitted to Mass. bar, 1973; engr. Kendall Co., Walpole, Mass., 1965—; asso. firm Goldberg & Eskenas, Brockton, Mass., 1976—. Bd. dirs. J.F. Kennedy Sch., 1975-77. Mem. Mass., Boston, Plymouth bar assns. Home: 100 Overton St Brockton MA 02401 Office: 435 Belmont St Brockton MA 02401 Tel (617) 583-0311

CLARK, FRANK HUME, JR., b. Balt., Nov. 9, 1931; B.S., U. Md., 1955; LL.B., U. Balt., 1963. Admitted to Md. bar, 1963; milk market specialist Dept. Agr., Washington. Mem. Md. Bar Assn. C.P.A., Md. Home: 208 Brackenwood Ct Timonium MD 21093

CLARK, FRANK WINSLOW, JR., b. Los Angeles, Nov. 17, 1917; B.S. in Bus. Adminstrn. with honors, U. Calif. at Los Angeles, 1939; LL.B., Hastings Coll. Law, 1946. Admitted to Calif. bar, 1946, since practiced in Los Angeles; partner firm Parker, Milliken, Kohlmeier Clark & O'Hara; exec. v.p., gen. counsel, dir. May Dept. Stores Co. Mem. Zeta Psi. Home: 567 Comstock Ave Los Angeles CA 90024 Office: 606 S Olive St Los Angeles CA 90014*

CLARK, FRED STEPHEN, b. Savannah, Ga., July 10, 1936; B.A., Cornell, 1958; LL.B., U. Ga., 1961. Admitted to Ga. bar, 1960; asso. firm Brannen, Clark & Hester, Savannah, 1961-64, partner, 1966-71; asst. U.S. atty. So. Dist. Ga., Savannah, 1964-66; partner firm Lee and Clark, Savannah, 1972—; asst. atty., police ct. judge pro tem City of Savannah, 1968-70, City of Thunderbolt, 1971-73; atty., police ct. judge City of Savannah Beach, 1973-74. Chmn., Urban Renewal Adv. Com., Savannah, 1968; founder Athens (Ga.) Legal Aid Soc., pres. Legal Aid Soc. Savannah, 1969; chmn. U. Ga. Fund Dr., 1971. Mem. Savannah Bar, State Bar Ga., Am., Fed. (pres. Savannah chpt. 1967) bar assns., Internat. Acad. Trial Lawyers, Fedn. Ins. Counsel, Scribes. Home: 318 Early St Savannah GA 31405 Office: 711 C and S Bank Bldg 300 Bull St Savannah GA 31402 Tel (912) 233-1271

CLARK, FREDERICK ROY, b. Rochester, N.Y., July 22, 1916; LL.B., Bklyn. Law Sch., Niagara U., 1940; M.B.A., Harvard 1947; Admitted to N.Y. State bar, 1940; mem. firm Abbott, Rippey & Hutchens, Rochester, N.Y., 1946, firm Hutchens & Clark, 1947-52; exec. v.p. 1st Comml. Banks, Albany, N.Y., 1972—. Gen. chmn. United Fund, 1964. Home: 90 South Manning Blvd Albany NY 12203 Office: 60 State St Albany NY 12207 Tel (518) 474-7362

CLARK, GLENN WILLETT, b. Montpelier, Idaho, June 8, 1935; student Mass. Inst. Tech., 1952-54; A.B., Harvard, 1959; postgrad. U. Vienna (Austria), 1959-60; LL.B., Yale, 1963. Admitted to Colo. bar, 1963, Iowa bar, 1972; individual practice law, Denver and Des Moines, 1963-76; asst. prof. U. Denver, 1967-70; asso. prof. law Drake U., 1970-73, prof., 1974-76; supt. securities State of Iowa, 1973-74; chief capital markets and debt mgmt. sect., office of gen. counsel U.S. Dept. Treasury, Washington, 1976—; vis. prof. law Brigham Young U., 1975; mem. adv. com. on states jurisdiction and responsibilitigs under the commodity exchange act U.S. Commodity Futures Trading Commn., 1976—; mem. adv. coms. Iowa Uniform Securities Act and Iowa Competition Law, 1973-76. Active Mid-Iowa council Boy Scouts Am.; vol. Mormon Ch.; dir. Des Moines Community Playhouse, 1975—; founding mem., dir. Des Moines Assn. for the Talented and Gifted, 1976. Mem. Am. (chmn. subcom. on cash commodities, sect. corp., banking and bus. law 1976—), Polk County (Iowa) bar assns., Order of Coif, Phi Beta Kappa, Omicron Delta Epsilon. Contbr. articles to legal jours. Home: 6928 Butternut Ct McLean VA 22101 Office: Office Gen Counsel 1414 Main Treasury Washington DC 20220 Tel (202) 566-2558

CLARK, H. SOL, b. Savannah, Ga., Dec. 29, 1906; A.B., Cornell U., 1928, LL.B., 1930. Admitted to Ga. bar, 1929; since practiced in Savannah, Ga., partner firm Brannen, Clark & Hester, and predecessors, 1950-71; judge Ct. of Appeals, 1972-77; partner Lee & Clark, 1977—; asst. city atty., Savannah, 1943-45. Fellow Am. Coll. Probate Counsel, Am. Bar Found., Internat. Acad. Trial Lawyers; mem. Am., Ga., Savannah bar assns., Internat. Soc. Barristers, Scribes. Home: 109 E 44th St Savannah GA 31405 Office: PO Box 8205 Savannah GA 31402 Tel (912) 233-1271

CLARK, JAMES FRANCIS, b. Madison, Wis., Aug. 20, 1920; LL.B., U. Wis., 1948. Admitted to Wis. bar, 1948; U.S. Dist. Ct. Western Dist. Wis. bar, 1950, U.S. Dist. Ct. Eastern Dist. Wis. bar, 1969, U.S. Supreme Ct. bar, 1975; partner firm Ela, Esch, Hart & Clark, Madison and Poynette, Wis., 1948—; gen. counsel Wis. Assn. Sch. Bds., 1961—; lectr. law U. Wis., 1960—; dir. Nat. Council Sch. Attys., 1976—. Mem. Am., Wis., Dane, Columbia County bar assns., Nat. Council Sch. Attys., Wis. Sch. Attys. Assn., Order of Coif, Phi Alpha Delta. Contbr. articles to profl. jours. Home: 208 Old Settlers Trail Poynette WI 53955 Office: 122 W Washington Ave Madison WI 53703 Tel (608) 256-5456

CLARK, JAMES WILLIS, b. Ocala, Fla., Dec. 17, 1944; B.S. in Bus. Adminstrn., U. Fla., 1966, J.D., 1972. Admitted to Fla. bar, 1972, U.S. Supreme Ct. bar, 1976; asso. firm Peavyhouse, Giglio, Grant, Clark & Charlton, Tampa, 1972—. Mem. Am. Bar Assn., Fla., Bay Area trial lawyers assns. Home: 10608 Orange Grove Dr Tampa FL 33618 Office: 1411 N Westshore Blvd Tampa FL 33607 Tel (813) 872-1531

CLARK, JOHN BENTON, b. Laurel, Miss., Sept. 6, 1942; student Millsaps Coll., 1959-61; B.A., U. Miss., 1963; LL.B., U. Va., 1966. Admitted to Miss. bar, 1966; law clk. to Judge James P. Coleman, U.S. Ct. Appeals, 5th Circuit, 1966-67; asso. firm Daniel, Coker, Horton, Bell & Dukes, Jackson, Miss., 1967-69, partner, 1970—. Mem. Jackson, Miss. young lawyers assns., Miss., Hinds County (Miss.) bars, Am. Bar Assn. Home: 2105 Southwood Rd Jackson MS 39211 Office: PO Box 1084 Jackson MS 39205 Tel (601) 352-7607

CLARK, JOHN EUGENE, b. Austin, Tex., June 8, 1933; B.S. in Bus. Adminstrn., Lamar U., Beaumont, Tex., 1954; LL.B., U. Tex., Austin, 1961. Admitted to Tex. bar, 1961, U.S. Dist. Ct. bar, 1965, U.S. Supreme Ct. bar, 1971; asso. law offices of Dan Moody, Austin, 1962-64, partner, 1965-66; asso. firm Graves, Dougherty, Gee, Hearon, Moody & Garwood, Austin, 1966-67; asso. firm Johnson, Jones, Clark & Sheppard and predecessor, Austin, 1967-68, partner, 1968-69; trial atty. govt. ops. sect., criminal div. Dept. Justice, 1969-71; 1st asst. U.S. atty. for Western Dist. Tex., San Antonio, 1971-75, U.S. atty., 1975-77; officer, dir. Cobb, Thurmond, Bain & Clark, Inc., San Antonio, 1977—; mem. Atty. Gen.'s Adv. Com. of U.S. Attys., 1976-77. Mem. Fed. (pres. San Antonio chpt. 1976-77), Travis County, San Antonio bar assns., Phi Alpha Delta. Recipient Outstanding Performance certificate Dept. Justice, 1971, Atty. Gen.'s Spl. Commendation award, 1974; named Outstanding Asst. U.S. Atty., 1973. Home: 11414 Whisper Bluff San Antonio TX 78230 Office: San Antonio TX 78205 Tel (512) 226-0311

CLARK, JOHN RAYMOND, b. New Brunswick, N.J., Mar. 17, 1922; B.A., Rutgers U., 1943; J.D., Harvard U., 1949. Admitted to D.C. bar, 1949, Pa. bar, 1955, U.S. Supreme Ct. bar, 1962; examiner ICC, Washington, 1950-54; asst. gen. solicitor Pa. R.R. Co., Pitts., 1954-56, Phila., 1956-61; individual practice law, Washington, 1961—. Mem. Am., D.C. bar assns., Assn. ICC Practitioners, Motor Carrier Lawyers Assn. Home: 700 New Hampshire Ave NW Washington DC 20037 Office: Suite 1150 600 New Hampshire Ave NW Washington DC 20037 Tel (202) 337-6161

CLARK, JOHN WILLARD, JR., b. Dallas, Nov. 7, 1938; B.A., So. Meth. U., 1960, J.D., 1963. Admitted to Tex. bar, 1963; partner firm Turner, Hitchins, McInerney, Webb & Hartnett, Dallas, 1967—; bd. dirs. State Bar Tex., 1976—. Mem. Am. (bd. govs. 1971-75, ho. of dels. 1971—, standing com. constn. and bylaws 1975—), Dallas bar assns. Office: 1700 Mercantile Bank Bldg Dallas TX 75201 Tel (214) 742-3481

CLARK, JOSEPH MICHAEL, b. Detroit, Nov. 4, 1942; B.A., Fairleigh Dickinson U., 1964; J.D., Rutgers U., 1970. Admitted to N.J. bar, 1971; staff atty. Union County (N.J.) Legal Services, 1970-72; pub. defender City of Englewood (N.J.), 1972, 1974-75; asst. pros. atty. Bergen County (N.J.), 1972-74; municipal ct. judge City of Englewood, 1975—. Trustee, Leonard Johnson Day Care Sch., Social Service Fedn., Child Care Coordinating Council. Mem. Am., N.J., Bergen County bar assns., Phi Alpha Delta. Office: 40 Bergen St Englewood NJ 07631 Tel (201) 568-9390

CLARK, LAWRENCE BROWN, b. Birmingham, Ala., June 29, 1940; B.S. in Commerce and Bus. Adminstrn., U. Ala., 1962, LL.B., 1965. Admitted to Ala. bar, 1965; partner firm Lange, Simpson, Robinson & Somerville, Birmingham, 1970—. Mem. Farrah Law Honor Soc., Phi Alpha Delta. Book rev. editor Ala. Law Rev., 1964-65. Home: 1400 Wellington Rd Birmingham AL 35213 Office: 1700 First Ala Bank Bldg Birmingham AL 35203 Tel (205) 252-5222

CLARK, LESLIE ERNEST, b. Pontiac, Ill., Sept. 24, 1908; B.S., Northwestern U., 1931; J.D., DePaul U., 1933. Admitted to Ill. bar, 1933; personnel officer U.S. Govt., Chgo. and Washington, 1933-44; v.p. personnel Spiegel Inc., Chgo., 1944-66; individual practice law, Deerfield, Ill., 1966—. Address: 640 Thornmeadow Rd Deerfield IL 60015 Tel (312) 945-3626

CLARK, LESTER WILLIAM, b. Hallowell, Maine, Oct. 24, 1911; B.S. in Elec. Engring., George Washington U., 1937; J.D., U. Conn., 1947. Examiner, U.S. Patent Office, 1938-39; patent agt. Honeywell, Inc., 1939-43; patent atty. Chandler-Evans div. Colt Industries, 1943-47, Union Switch div. Westinghouse Air Brake Co., 1947-49; admitted to Conn. bar, 1947, N.Y. bar, 1950; atty. George H. Corey,

N.Y.C., 1949-52; mem. firm Cooper, Dunham, Clark, Griffin & Moran, N.Y.C., 1952—. Mem. Am. Bar Assn., N.Y. Patent Law Assn., N.Y. County Lawyers Assn., IEEE, AAAS, Licensing Exec. Soc., Phi Eta Sigma, Sigma Tau. Home: 9 Birch Close North Tarrytown NY 10591 Office: 30 Rockefeller Plaza New York City NY 10020 Tel (212) 977-9550

CLARK, MARSHALL LOUIS, b. Xenia, Ohio, May 17, 1933; B.A., Miami U., Oxford, Ohio, 1955; LL.B., U. Cin., 1961. Admitted to Ohio bar, 1961; partner firm Miller, Finney & Clark, Xenia, 1963—. Mem. Am., Ohio, Greene County (pres. 1977) bar assns., Ohio Def. Assn., Internat. Assn. Ins. Counsel, Def. Research Inst. Home: 3869 Greenbrier Dr Faiborn OH 45324 Office: 20 King Ave Xenia OH 45385 Tel (513) 372-8055

CLARK, RAMSEY, b. Dallas, Dec. 18, 1927; B.A., U. Tex., 1949; A.M., J.D., U. Chgo., 1950. Admitted to Tex. bar 1951, U.S. Supreme Ct. bar, 1956, D.C. bar, 1969, N.Y. bar, 1970; practiced law, Dallas, 1951-61, N.Y.C., 1970—; asst. atty. gen. U.S. Dept. Justice, 1961-65, dep. atty. gen., 1965-67, atty. gen. U.S., 1967-69. Adj. prof. Howard U., 1969-72, Bklyn. Law Sch., 1973—. Author: Crime in America. Home: 37 W 12th St New York City NY 10011*

CLARK, ROSS BERT, II, b. Lafayette, Ind., Dec. 23, 1932; A.B., U. of South, 1954; J.D., U. Tenn., 1960. Admitted to Tenn. bar, 1961; law clk. U.S. Dist. Ct., Western Dist. Tenn., Memphis, 1961-62; asso. firm Rupert & Ewing, Memphis, 1962-66; asso. firm Laughlin, Watson, Garthright & Halle, Memphis, 1966-68; partner Laughlin, Halle, Regan, Clark & Gibson, Memphis, 1968—; instr. med. and dental jurisprudence, U. Tenn. Sch. Health Scis., Memphis, 1963-72; asst. city atty., Memphis, 1972—. Bd. dirs. Memphis Heart Assn., 1965—; bd. dirs. Family Service of Memphis, 1976—. Mem. Memphis-Shelby County (dir. 1974-76), Tenn., Am. bar assns. Office: 2201 First Nat Bank Bldg Memphis TN 38103 Tel (901) 525-1593

CLARK, RUFUS BRADBURY, b. Des Moines, May 11, 1924; B.A., Harvard U., 1946, J.D., 1951; Dipl.L., Oxford (Eng.) U., 1952. Admitted to Calif. bar, 1952; asso. firm O'Melveny & Myers, Los Angeles, 1951-61, partner, 1962—; dir. Automatic Machinery & Electronics, Inc., Covina, Calif., Brown Internat. Corp., Covina, Econ. Resources Corp., Los Angeles, 1st Charter Fin. Corp., Beverly Hills, Calif., So. Calif. Water Co., Los Angeles. Chancellor, Protestant Episcopal Ch. in Diocese of Los Angeles; bd. dirs. John Tracy Clinic, Los Angeles. Mem. Am., Calif., Los Angeles County bar assns. Author articles in field. Home: 615 Alta Vista Circle S Pasadena CA 91030 Office: 611 W 6th St Los Angeles CA 90017 Tel (213) 620-1120

CLARK, STEPHEN ROBERT, b. Ponca City, Okla., May 21, 1947; B.S., Okla. State U., 1969; J.D., U. Tulsa, 1972. Admitted to Okla. bar, 1972; asst. dist. atty. Tulsa County, 1971-74; asso. firm Hall, Estill, Hardwick, Gable, Collingsworth & Nelson, Tulsa, 1974—; bd. dirs. Travelers Aid Internat.; chmn. Tulsa County Law Day, 1976. Bd. dirs. Tulsa County Republican Party. Mem. Am., Okla., Tulsa County (outstanding jr. mem. 1976) bar assns. Office: 805 Nat Bank Tulsa Bldg Tulsa OK 74103 Tel (918) 585-9161

CLARK, THOMAS PATRICK, JR., b. N.Y.C., Sept. 16, 1943; A.B., U. Notre Dame, 1965; J.D., U. Mo.-Kansas City, 1973. Admitted to Calif. bar, 1973; asso. firm Rutan & Tucker, Santa Ana, Calif., 1973—. Mem. Am., Calif., Orange County (Calif.) bar assns., Bench and Robe, Phi Kappa Phi. Student editor-in-chief Urban Lawyer, 1972-73. Home: 6232 Sierra Palos Irving CA 93665 Office: 401 Civic Center Dr W Santa Ana CA 92701 Tel (714) 835-2200

CLARK, WARD F., b. Phila., Dec. 9, 1927; student Pa. State U.; LL.B., U. Pa., 1952. Admitted to Pa. bar, 1956; clk. firm Duane, Morris & Heckscher, Phila., 1953, Supreme Ct. Pa., Phila., 1955-56; asso. firm Auchey & Power, Doylestown, Pa., 1956-57; clk. to presiding judge Ct. Common Pleas, Burks County, Pa., 1957-58; individual practice law, Doylestown, Pa.; partner firm Lindsay & Clark, New Hope, Pa.; partner firm Pratt, Clark, Gathright & Price, Doylestown, 1972—; asst. dist. atty. Bucks County (Pa.), 1958-65, dist. atty., 1966-72. Mem. Bucks County, Pa. bar assns. Author source book for prosecutors, 1968. Office: 68 E Court St Doylestown PA 18901 Tel (215) 345-1600

CLARK, WILLIAM LEE, b. Farmington, Iowa, Dec. 31, 1936; student Beloit (Wis.) Coll., 1954-55; A.B., U. Ill., 1958; J.D., DePaul U., 1963. Admitted to Ill. bar, 1963, U.S. Supreme Ct. bar, 1966; with law dept. Continental Casulty Co., Chgo., 1961-63; partner firm McClory, Lonchar, Nordigian & Clark, Waukegan, Ill., 1963-70; partner firm Lombardi & Clark, Lake Forest, Ill., 1970-73; individual practice law, Lake Forest, 1974—. Chmn. Lake Bluff March of Dimes, 1969. Mem. Ill. State, Lake County bar assns. Home: 1107 Crestfield St Libertyville IL 60048 Office: 300 E Illinois Rd Lake Forest IL 60045 Tel (312) 234-6590

CLARK, WILLIAM THOMAS, b. Dalton, Ga., Apr. 20, 1925; LL.B., Emory U., 1950. Admitted to Ga. bar, 1950, Ohio bar, 1964; atty., claims mgr. Nationwide Ins. Co., Columbus, Ohio, 1951—. Mem. Am., Ohio, Ga. bar assns., Internat. Claims Assn. Contbr. investment newsletter. Home: 3300 Sciotangy Dr Columbus OH 43221 Office: 246 N High St Columbus OH 43215 Tel (614) 227-6792

CLARKE, ANNE MARIE, b. St. Louis, June 25, 1949; B.A., Northwest Mo. State Coll., 1970; J.D., St. Louis U., 1973. Admitted to Mo. bar, 1974; law clerk Wayman F. Smith and Margaret Bush Wilson, St. Louis, 1973-74; researcher, cons. Arthur D. Little, Inc., Cambridge, Mass., 1974; asst. sec. Northeast Utilities, Berlin, Conn., 1974—. Pres. Black Women's League of Middletown (Conn.), 1975—; bd. dirs. Planned Parenthood League of Conn., Inc., 1976; corporator Middlesex Meml. Hosp., Middletown, Conn., 1976. Mem. Nat., Am. bar assns., Am. Soc. corporate secs. Home: 167 Trolley Crossing Ln Middletown CT 06457 Office: POB 270 Hartford CT 06101 Tel (203) 666-6911

CLARKE, CHARLES FENTON, b. Hillsboro, Ohio, July 25, 1916; A.B. summa cum laude, Washington and Lee U., 1938; LL.B., U. Mich., 1940; LL.D., Cleve. State U., 1971. Admitted to Mich. bar, 1940, Ohio bar, 1946; asso. firm Prescott Coulter & Baxter, Detroit, 1940-42; asso. firm Squire, Sanders & Dempsey, Cleve., 1946-57, partner, 1957—. Chmn. legal com. Cleve. Welfare Fedn., 1969-73; pres. Free Med. Clinic Greater Cleve., 1970—, Cleve. Speech and Hearing Center, 1973; trustee Laurel Sch., 1962-75, Cleve. Citizens League, 1956-62, Legal Aid Soc., 1959-67; bd. dirs. Cleve. Zool. Soc., 1970, Bowman Tech. Sch., 1970; exec. com. Cuyahoga County Republican Orgn., 1950—; pres. alumni bd. dirs. Washington and Lee U., 1972; vice chmn. Cleve. Crime Commn., 1975. Fellow Am. Coll. Trial Lawyers; mem. Nat. Assn. R.R. Trial Counsel (pres. 1966-68), 6th U.S. Circuit Ct. Jud. Conf. (life), Phi Beta Kappa. Contbr. articles to legal jours. Home: 2262 Tudor Dr Cleveland Heights OH 44106 Office: 1800 Union Commerce Bldg Cleveland OH 44115 Tel (216) 696-9200

CLARKE, GEORGE ARTHUR, b. Sioux City, Iowa, Apr. 8, 1918; J.D., U. Wyo., 1967. Admitted to Wyo., Nebr. bars, 1967; U.S. Supreme Ct. bar, 1973. Individual practice law, Lusk, Wyo., 1967—; gen. counsel Wyo. Municipal Power Agy., Lusk, 1973—. Justice of the peace, Niobrara County, 1971—. Bd. dirs. Niobrara (Wyo.) C. of C., Niobrara Hist. Soc., Eastern Wy. Area Council on Aging, Niobrara-Converse Mental Health Assn. Mem. Am., Nebr., Wyo. trial lawyers assns., Nat. Dist. Attys. Assn., Wyo. Minor Ct. Judges Assn. Home: 544 Barrett Blvd Lusk WY 82225 Office: 3 E 3d St Lusk WY 82225 Tel (307) 334-3596

CLARKE, HAROLD G., b. Forsyth, Ga., Sept. 28, 1927; J.D., U. Ga., 1950. Admitted to Ga. bar, 1950; now mem. firm Clarke, Haygood & Lynch, Forsyth; mem. Ga. State Legislature, 1961-71. Mem. Am. Flint Circuit (pres. 1960-61) bar assns., State Bar Ga. (gov. 1971—, exec. com. 1973—, pres. 1976-77), Omicron Delta Kappa. Office: 87 N Lee St PO Box 657 Forsyth GA 31029 Tel (912) 994-5171*

CLARKE, JACK, b. Indpls., Feb. 21, 1939; B.S., U. N.Mex., 1961, J.D., 1971. Officer, U.S. Navy, 1961-69; instr. NROTC Unit, U. N.Mex., 1966-69; admitted to N.Mex. bar, 1971, Ala. bar, 1974; asso. prof. law U. Ala., 1971-76, dir. Rural Law Inst., 1973-76; partner firm Henley and Clarke, P.C., Northport, Ala., 1976—; mem. labor arbitration panels Fed. Mediation and Conciliation Service, Am. Arbitration Assn., 1973—. Mem. Am., Ala., N.Mex. bar assns. Home: 11 Windsor Dr Tuscaloosa AL 35401 Office: 2101 Bridge Ave PO Drawer 450 Northport AL 35476 Tel (205) 339-5151

CLARKE, JAMES CALEB, III, b. Atlanta, July 3, 1946; A.B., U. Ga., 1968; J.D., Emory U., 1971. Admitted to Fla. bar, 1971, Ga. bar, 1972; asso. firm. Savell, Williams, Cox & Angel, Atlanta, 1971-75, partner firm, 1975—. Mem. Am., Fla., Gen., Atlanta bar assns. Home: 2815 Mornington Dr Atlanta GA 30305 Office: 2222 100 Peachtree St Atlanta GA 30307 Tel (404) 521-1282

CLARKE, MERCER KAYE, b. N.Y.C., Sept. 27, 1944; B.A. in Econs., Washington and Lee U., 1966; J.D., U. Fla., 1970. Admitted to Fla. bar, 1971, U.S. Supreme Ct. bar, 1977; partner firm Smothers & Thompson, Miami, Fla., 1975—, asso., 1970-75. Mem. Am., Fla., Dade County (bd. govs. young lawyers sect.) bar assns., Am. Trial Lawyers Assn. Home: 403 Camilo St Coral Gables FL 33134 Office: 1301 Alfred I duPont Bldg Miami FL 33131 Tel (305) 379-6523

CLARKE, RAYMONDE ALEXIS, b. Grand Rapids, Mich., Nov. 3, 1926; student pre law Ind. U.; student Boston Coll. Law Sch., 1948-49; LL.B., U. Miss., 1951. Admitted to Ind. bar, 1952, Miss. bar, 1951; law editor Bobbs-Merrill Co., Indpls., 1951-52; asst. sec. Ind. Senate, 1953 individual practice law, Plymouth, Bremen, Ind., 1952-76; asst. counsel U.S. Senate Banking Com., Washington, 1953-54; mem. Ind. Gen. Assembly 1955-56, mem. judiciary coms.; 1st. dep. prosecuting atty. Marshall County (Ind.), 1965; trial atty. for Ind. Atty. Gen., Marshall County, 1970-72; atty. Farmers' Home Adminstrn., Marshall County, 1969-72; judge Superior Ct., Marshall County, 1977—; atty. Town of Bremen, 1966-76; atty. Bremen Sch. Bd., 1959-68, 1973-74, mem. sch. bd., 1968-72, pres., 1970; mem. Office Bldg. Commn., Ind., 1973; chmn. Wage Adjustment Bd., 1975-76; rec. sec. Bremen Plan Commn., 1966-76. Mem. Ind. Judge Assn., Am., Ind., Marshall County bar assns., Am. Judicature Soc., Phi Delta Phi. Recipient Meritorious Service award Ind. Gov., 1956, Bremen Jaycee distinguished Service award, 1962, outstanding contribution to Voice of Democracy, VFW, 1969-72, 73, appreciation Bremen chpt. Ind. Young Farmers Assn., 1975, award Phi Alpha Delta. Author: Legislative History of the Export Import Bank of Washington, 1953. Home: 545 S Bowen Ave Bremen IN 46506 Office: Courthouse Plymouth IN 46563

CLARKE, WILLIAM NEASE, b. Washington, Pa., Aug. 23, 1917; A.B., Washington & Jefferson Coll., 1939; LL.B., U. Pa., 1942. Admitted to Pa. bar, 1943, N.Y. State bar, 1947; asso. firm Cadawalader, Wickersham & Taft, N.Y.C., 1946-58, partner firm, 1959—; dir. Holiday Inns, Inc., 1961—. Trustee Washington & Jefferson Coll., 1973—; Mem. Am. Bar Assn., Assn. Bar City of N.Y. Home: 164 E 72d St New York City NY 10021 Office: One Wall St New York City NY 10005 Tel (212) 785-1000

CLARKSON, STEPHEN BATCHELDER, b. Hartford, Conn., July 1, 1937; B.A., Yale U., 1959; L.L.B., U. Va. Law Sch., 1962. Admitted to N.Y. bar, 1963, D.C. bar, 1969, U.S. Supreme Ct. bar, 1967; asso. firm Simpson Thacher & Bartlett, N.Y.C., 1962-66, Roth, Carlson, Kwit & Spengler, 1966-68; spl. asst. to gen. counsel and under-sec. U.S. Dept. Commerce, 1968-69; asso. firm Sullivan, Shea & Kenney, Washington, 1969-70; partner firm Beauregard, Clarkson, Moss & Brown, 1970—; mem. advisory bd. Bureau of Nat. Affairs Fed. Contracts Report, 1974-76; editorial cons., 1976—; corp. sec. LogEtronics, Inc., 1970—. Mem. Guild of St. Ives, 1966; Mem. Washington Lawyer's Project, 1969—. Mem. Am. (antitrust, litigation, corp. banking and bus. law, public. contract law, ct. of claims com. sections.), Federal, D.C. bar assns., Assn. Bar City N.Y. Mem. editorial bd. U. Va. Law Rev., 1960-62, notes editor, 1961-62; editor N.Y. State Law Digest, 1965-67. Home: 7101 Heatherhill Rd Bethesda MD 20034 Office: 1800 M St NW Washington DC 20036

CLAUSE, TED GAMBLE, b. Carroll, Iowa, June 12, 1934; A.B., Dartmouth, 1956; LL.B., Stanford, 1962. Admitted to Calif. bar, 1963, Hawaii bar, 1963; asso. firm Case, Kay, Clause & Lynch, Honolulu, 1962-67, partner, 1967—. Mem. Calif., Am., Hawaii State bar assns. Office: 1100 First Hawaiian Bank Bldg Honolulu HI 96813 Tel (808) 526-7261

CLAUSEN, JOHN B., b. Williamstown, Mich., June 12, 1920; A.B., Mich. State U., 1946; J.D., U. Calif., 1951. Admitted to Calif. bar, 1951, U.S. Supreme Ct. bar, 1951; practice law, Walnut Creek, Calif., 1952-53; dep. dist. atty Contra Costa County, Calif., 1953-59, chief asst. dist. atty., 1959-69, acting dist. atty., 1969, county counsel, 1969—. Bd. dirs. Mount Diablo YMCA. Mem. State Bar of Calif., Am., Contra Costa, Mount Diablo bar assns., County Counsels Assn. Calif. (pres.), Nat. Assn. County Ofcls. Office: PO Box 69 County Administration Bldg Martinez CA 94553 Tel (415) 372-2051

CLAUSON, KARL WILLIAM, b. Northampton, Mass., Nov. 22, 1943; A.B., Bowdoin Coll., 1966; J.D., Boston Coll., 1971. Admitted to N.H. bar, 1971; law clk. N.H. Supreme Ct., Concord, 1971-72; asso. Laurence Gardner, Hanover, N.H., 1972-75, partner, 1975—. Mem. Am., N.H. Grafton County bar assns., Order of Coif. Editor Uniform Commercial Code Digest, 1970-71. Home: Greensboro Rd Hanover NH 03755 Office: 1 Maple St Hanover NH 03755 Tel (603) 643-5000

CLAUSS, PETER O., b. Knoxville, Tenn., Sept. 23, 1936; A.B., U. Chgo., 1955; LL.B., Yale U., 1958. Admitted to Pa. bar, 1959, also U.S. Supreme Ct. bar. Asso. firm Clark, Ladner, Fortenbaugh & Young, Phila., 1958-65, partner, 1966—, mem. exec. com., 1967-76, mng. partner, 1968-72, chmn. tax dept., 1968—, chmn. corp. dept., 1970—, chmn. future planning com., 1973—; dir., mem. exec. com. Norcross Inc.; dir. Nutrion Corp., Helcrane Constrn. Corp. Active Wayne (Pa.) Little League Baseball, 1973-75, Ithan (Pa.) Council Boy Scouts Am., 1973-75; treas. Ithan Sch. PTA, 1972-75; sec. Yale Club, Phila., 1974—. Mem. Am. (chmn. com. nonrecognition transactions Tax sect. 1974—), Phila. (chmn. domestic relations com. Tax sect. 1971-74), Pa. bar assns., Juristic Soc. Phila. (bd. govs. 1971-72), Yale Law Sch. Assn. Eastern Pa. (pres. 1974-77), Phi Gamma Delta, (gen. counsel 1972—), Phi Delta Phi. Contbr. articles to legal jours. Home: 758 Darby-Paoli Rd Newtown Square PA 19073 Office: 1700 Widener Bldg Philadelphia PA 19107 Tel (215) 564-5300

CLAUSSEN, FREDERIC PAUL, b. Boston, Feb. 7, 1937; A.B., Harvard, 1959; J.D., Boston U., 1962. Admitted to Mass. bar, 1962; asso. firm Spencer & Stone, Boston, 1962-63; trust officer Old Colony Trust Co., Boston, 1963-68; asso. firm Bowers Fortier & Lakin, Boston, 1969; register of probate Barnstable County, Mass., 1969—. Moderator Cotuit (Mass.) Fire Dist., 1974—. Mem. Mass., Barnstable County bar assns. Recipient Am. Jurisprudence award Boston U., 1962. Home: 910 Main St Cotuit MA 02635 Office: Registry of Probate Barnstable MA 02630 Tel (617) 362-2511

CLAY, ALEXANDER STEPHENS, b. Atlanta, Oct. 23, 1942; B.A., Yale, 1964; LL.D., U. Va., 1967. Law clk. Judge R.S. Body, Eastern Dist. Pa., Phila., 1967-68; admitted to Pa. bar, 1968, Ga. bar, 1970; asso. firm Schnader Harrison Segal & Lewis, Phila., 1968-70; partner firm Kilpatrick, Cody, Rogers, McClatchey & Regenstein, Atlanta, 1975—. Mem. Am., Ga., Atlanta bar assns., Atlanta Lawyer's Club. Recipient Am. Friends Service award, Phila., 1968. Office: 3100 Equitable Bldg Atlanta GA 30327 Tel (404) 522-3100

CLAY, CHARLES GEORGE, b. Catskill, N.Y., Aug. 20, 1926. Admitted to N.Y. bar, 1956; exec. dir. Village of Catskill (N.Y.) Housing Authority, 1956-58; town atty., Catskill, 1958—; asst. atty. gen. N.Y. State, 1959-61; county atty., Greene County, 1963-72; parnter law firm Moon & Clay, Catskill, 1963—. Del., N.Y. State Constl. Conv., 1967; pres. Boys Club of Catskill, N.Y. Mem. Greene County (past pres.), N.Y. State bar assns. Home: RD 9W W Coxsackie NY 12192 Office: 343 Main St Catskill NY 12414

CLAY, JAMES CALVIN, b. Crosby, Miss., July 30, 1940; B.S., The Citidal, 1962; J.D., Cumberland Law Sch., 1968. Admitted to Ala. bar, 1968; asst. dist. atty. Mobile County (Ala.), 1969-71; partner firm Atchison, Clay & Street, Mobile, 1971—; atty., mem. bd. dirs. Health Home Services Bd., City of Mobile, 1975—. Chmn. Mobile Airport Planning and Adv. Com., 1973-75. Mem. Am. Bar Assn., Am., Ala. trial lawyers assns., Am. Def. Lawyers Assn. Home: 7 S Springbank Rd Mobile AL 36608 Office: PO Box 1446 Mobile AL 36601 Tel (205) 438-4751

CLAY, JOHN ERNEST, b. Kansas City, Mo., Nov. 27, 1921; B.A. cum laude, Carleton Coll., 1943; J.D. cum laude, Harvard, 1948. Admitted to Ill. bar, 1949; asso. firm Taylor, Miller, Busch & Magner, Chgo., 1948-51; asso. firm Mayer, Brown & Platt, Chgo., 1951-59, partner firm, 1960—. Treas. Friends of Glencoe Library; chmn. Glencoe Bd. Edn.; pres. Dearborn Pkwy Playground Assn.; pres. Assos. of Inst. for Psychoanalysis; Ill. State chmn., mem. nat. planning com. Am. Vets. Com.; mem. Men for ERA; treas. First Nat. Conf. on Optimum Population and Environment; vice presdl. running mate with Eugene McCarthy in Ill., 1976; co-chmn. Ill. McCarthy Com., 1976. Mem. Chgo. Bar Assn. (chmn. civil rights com., corp. law com.), Chgo. Council Lawyers. Home: 546 W Wellington Chicago IL 60657 Office: 231 S LaSalle St Chicago IL 60604 Tel (312) 782-0600

CLAY, KENDALL OWEN, b. Willis, Va., Jan. 25, 1943; B.S., Va. Poly. Inst. and State U., 1966, M.S., 1968; J.D., U. Va., 1972. Admitted to Va. bar, 1972; individual practice law, Radford, Va., 1972—; dir. 1st Fed. Savs. & Loan Assn. of New River Valley, Pulaski, Va. Bd. dirs. Valley Players, Radford Child Care Center. Mem. Va., Floyd-Montgomery-Radford bar assns., Va. Trial Lawyers Assn. Home: 110 Hammett Ave Radford VA 24141 Office: 1217 Grove Ave Radford VA 24141 Tel (703) 639-9623

CLAY, WILLIAM CALDWELL, JR., b. Mt. Sterling, Ky., Dec. 28, 1915; B.A., Dartmouth, 1937; J.D., Yale, 1940; LL.D., Transylvania Coll., 1973. Admitted to Ky. bar, 1939; spl. atty., anti-trust div. Dept. Justice, Washington, 1938-40; sr. partner firm Clay, Marye & Cowden, Mt. Sterling, 1940—. Chmn. bd. dirs. Exchange Bank of Ky., Mt. Sterling, 1969. Bd. curators, exec. com. Transylvania U.; deacon First Christian Ch., Mt. Sterling. Mem. Mt. Sterling C. of C., Am., Ky. bar assns. Author: Farmer's Tax Manual, 1943; The Dow-Jones-Irwin Guide to Estate Planning, 1976. Home: Virginia Ct Mount Sterling KY 40353 Office: 50 Broadway Mount Sterling KY 40353 Tel (606) 498-2430

CLAYPOOL, ROBERT LOUIS, b. Williamsburg, Iowa, July 9, 1928; B.A., U. Iowa, 1950, J.D., 1952. Admitted to Iowa bar, 1952; partner firm Claypool & Claypool, Williamsburg, 1952—. Mem. Am., Iowa, Iowa County bar assns., Iowa Assn. Sch. Bd. Attys. Home: 304 Long St Williamsburg IA 52361 Office: 505 Court St Williamsburg IA 52361 Tel (319) 668-1170

CLAYTON, CHARLES MORGAN, b. Clayton, Ala., July 26, 1889; A.B., Morehouse Coll., 1914; M.A., Atlanta U., 1936; LL.B., LaSalle U., 1941. Prin., Sylvia Bryant Bapt. Inst., Atlanta, 1916-1931; prin. Herring St. Schs., Decatur, Ga., 1932-53; admitted to Ga. bar, 1944; partner firm Waldern, Herndon, De Antignac, & Clayton, Atlanta, 1953—; legal adviser Decatur Colored Civic League, 1950; mem. Atlanta Housing Appeal Bd., 1974—. Mem. Wheat St. Bapt. Ch., Atlanta, 1915—. Mem. Ga. State, Atlanta, Gate City bar assns. Home: 247 Mellrich Ave NE Atlanta GA 30317 Office: 28 Butler St NE Atlanta GA 30303 Tel (404) 659-0726

CLAYTON, CLAUDE FEEMSTER, JR., b. Tupelo, Miss., June 15, 1948; student Stanton Mil. Acad., 1966; B.A., Tulane U., 1971; J.D., U. Miss., 1973. Staff, U.S. Senate jud. com., 1969; admitted to Miss. bar, 1973, U.S. Ct. Appeals 5th Circuit bar, 1975; asso. firm Mitchell, Rogers & Eskridge, Tupelo, 1973-75; partner firm Mitchell, Rogers, Eskridge, Voge & Clayton, Tupelo, 1975—. Advisor law explorer post Yocana council Boy Scouts Am., 1974-77; sec. Lee County (Miss.) Democratic Exec. com., 1975—; del. Dem. Nat. Conv., 1976; v.p. Lee County Mental Health Assn., 1976—. Fellow Inst. of Politics in Miss.; mem. Am., Miss. (dir. Young Lawyers sect.), Lee County bar assns., Phi Delta Phi (v.p. 1973), Omicron Delta Kappa, Pi Sigma Alpha, Sigma Alpha Epsilon. Contbr. articles to Miss. Law Jour., 1972-73. Home: 909 Hamlin St Tupelo MS 38801 Office: PO Box 29 Tupelo MS 38801 Tel (601) 842-4231

CLAYTON, EDWIN KNIGHT, b. Meridian, Miss., Sept. 18, 1923; student Meridian Jr. Coll., 1946-48, Miss. So. U., 1949; J.D., Vanderbilt U., 1952. Admitted to Miss. bar, 1952; with U.S. Fidelity and Guaranty Co., Jackson, Miss., 1952—, asst. supt. claims, 1976. Active Boy Scouts Am., 1960-68; officer Presbyn. Ch. Mem. Miss. Bar Assn., Meridian (pres. 1964), Miss. (v.p. 1965), Lauderdale County claims assns. Home: 1004 Briarwood Dr Clinton MS 39056 Office: 202 N Congress St Jackson MS 39205 Tel (601) 948-4451

CLAYTON, EVERETT M., III, b. Nashville, July 24, 1945; B.A., U. Louisville, 1968; J.D., Vanderbilt U., 1971. Admitted to Calif. bar, 1972; asso. firm Latham & Watkins, Los Angeles, 1971—. Mem. Am., Calif., Los Angeles bar assns., Order of Coif, Omicron Delta Kappa. Articles editor Vanderbilt Law Rev., 1970-71. Office: 555 S Flower St Los Angeles CA 90071 Tel (213) 485-1234

CLAYTON, HAROLD RICHARD, b. Cushing, Tex., Sept. 13, 1918; J.D., U. Tex., 1943. Admitted to Tex. bar, 1943; asst. city atty., Beaumont, Tex., 1943; individual practice law, Port Arthur, Tex., 1944-51; judge 60th Jud. Dist. Ct., Jefferson County (Tex.), Beaumont, 1951-52, 136th Jud. Ct., Jefferson County, Beaumont, 1955—. Mem. Tex., Jefferson County bar assns. Home: 200 Mockingbird Ln Port Arthur TX 77640 Office: 1149 Pearl St Jefferson County Court House Beaumont TX 77701 Tel (713) 835-8481

CLAYTON, JOE DODSON, b. Bonham, Tex., Nov. 21, 1938; B.B.A., U. Tex., 1960, J.D., 1963. Admitted to Tex. bar, 1963; partner, office mgr. firm Loftis, Rowan, Files, Clayton, Bain & Clark, Tyler, Tex., 1976—. Pres., Montague County Heart Assn., 1963, 64. Fellow Tex. Bar Found. (dir. 1974—); mem. Am. (exec. council young lawyers assn. 1971-72), Smith County bar assns., State Bar of Tex. (dir. 1974—), Tex. Trial Lawyers Assn., E. Tex. Estate Planning Council (pres. 1974). Named Outstanding Young Lawyer, Smith County Jr. Bar assn., 1973-74. Home: 2828 Fry St Tyler TX 75701 Office: 109 W Ferguson St Tyler TX 75701 Tel (214) 595-3573

CLAYTON, JOHN HERMAN, b. Johnston City, Ill., Nov. 29, 1917; B.Ed., So. Ill. U., 1941. Admitted to Ill. bar, 1949; judge City Ct., Johnston City, 1949-58, Cook County (Ill.) Juvenile Ct., 1949-58, Williamson County (Ill.) Ct., 1958-64; asso. judge Circuit Ct., 1st Jud. Circuit, Ill., 1964-70, circuit judge, 1970—, chief judge, 1970-72, 72-74, 74—. Mem. Am., Ill., Williamson County bar assns. Home: 504 S Market St Marion IL 62959 Office: Williamson County Courthouse Marion IL 62959 Tel (618) 997-1234

CLAYTON, WILLIAM FRANCIS, b. Charles City, Iowa, Sept. 20, 1923; B.A., U. Calif., 1948; J.D., U. S.D., 1951. Admitted to S.D. bar, 1951; asso. firm Hamilton & Barron, Sioux Falls, S.D., 1951-54; individual practice law, Sioux Falls., 1954-69; states atty. Minnehaha County, S.D., 1958-65; mem. S.D. House Reps., 1966-69; U.S. atty. Dist. S.D., Sioux Falls, 1969—. Chmn. Minnehaha County Young Republicans, 1956-57, dist. dir., 1958-59; bd. dirs. S.D. Home Handicapped, 1954-58, S.D. Sch. Mentally Retarded, 1964-70. Mem. Fed. Bar Assn. (pres. S.D. chpt. 1972—). Home: 510 E 21st St Sioux Falls SD 57102 Office: 231 Fed Bldg and US Courthouse Sioux Falls SD 57102 Tel (605) 336-2980

CLAYTOR, ROBERT BUCKNER, b. Roanoke, Va., Feb. 27, 1922; A.B. cum laude, Princeton U., 1943; J.D., Harvard U., 1948. Admitted to Mass. bar, 1948, N.Y. State bar, 1949, Va. bar, 1952; atty. AT&T, 1948-51; solicitor N.& W. R.R., Roanoke, 1951-54, asst. gen. solicitor, 1954-56, asst. gen. counsel, 1956-60, gen. solicitor, 1960-64, v.p. law, 1964-68, sr. v.p., 1968-70, exec. v.p., 1970—, also dir.; dir. Del. & Hudson Ry. Co., Dereco, Inc., Norfolk, Franklin & Danville Ry. Co., Richardson-Wayland Elec. Corp. Mem. Am., Va., Roanoke bar assns., Phi Beta Kappa. Home: 836 Wildwood Rd SW Roanoke VA 24014 Office: 8 N Jefferson St Roanoke VA 24042 Tel (703) 981-4611

CLEARY, EDWARD WAITE, b. Jacksonville, Ill., Feb. 21, 1907; A.B., Ill. Coll., 1929; J.D., U. Ill., 1932; J.S.D., Yale, 1933; LL.D., 1973. Admitted to Ill. bar, 1932, Ariz. bar, 1970; individual practice law, Jacksonville, Ill., 1933-44; prof. law U. Ill., Champaign, 1946-67; prof. law Ariz. State U., Tempe, 1967—; reporter Joint Com. on Ill. Civil Practice, 1950-55, Ill. Supreme Ct. Com. Jury Instrns., 1957-63; sec. Ill. Jud. Council, 1957-59; reporter adv. com. Fed. Rules of Evidence, 1965-75. Mem. Am. Law Inst. Author: Handbook of Illinois Evidence, 1963; (with others) McCormick on Evidence, 1972; (with J.W. Strong) Cases on Evidence, 1975. Home: 4818 N 76th Pl Scottsdale AZ 85251 Office: Coll Law Ariz State Univ Tempe AZ 85281 Tel (602) 965-6204

CLEARY, RUSSELL GEORGE, b. Chippewa Falls, Wis., May 22, 1933; student U. Wis., LaCrosse, 1951-54, LL.D., U. Wis., Madison, 1957. Admitted to Wis. bar, 1957; practiced in LaCrosse, 1957-58; atty., dir. sales Hoeschler Realty, LaCrosse, 1958-60; atty. G. Heileman Brewing Co., Inc., LaCrosse, 1960-67, asst. to pres., v.p., 1967-71, pres., chmn. bd. dirs., 1971—; dir., 9th dist. Fed. Res. Bank Mpls., 1976-79, Protection Mut. Ins. Co.; dir. Am. Mut. Adv. Bd., Ill., Wis. Office: G Heileman Brewing Co 925 S 3d St LaCrosse WI 54601 Tel (608) 785-1000

CLEARY, WILLIAM JOSEPH, JR., b. Wilmington, N.C., Aug. 14, 1942; A.B. in History, St. Joseph's Coll., 1964; J.D., Villanova Law Sch., 1967. Admitted to N.J. bar, 1967; law sec. judge N.J. Superior Ct., 1967; asso. firm Lamb, Blake, Hutchinson & Dunne, Jersey City, 1968-72; asst. dep. pub. defender appellate sect. State of N.J., 1972-73; first asst. corp. counsel, Jersey City, 1973-76; individual practice law, Jersey City, 1976—. Mem. Am., N.J., Hudson County bar assns. Home: 2600 Kennedy Blvd Jersey City NJ 07306 Office: 2600 Kennedy Blvd Jersey City NJ 07306 Tel (201) 435-6189

CLEAVER, DAVID CHARLES, b. Sunbury, Pa., Dec. 26, 1941; B.A., U. N.C., 1967; J.D., Dickinson Sch. Law, 1967. Admitted to Pa. bar, 1967, U.S. Supreme Ct. bar, 1971; asso. firm Black & Davison, Chambersburg, Pa., 1967-71; partner firm Sharpe & Sharpe, Chambersburg, 1972—; adj. prof. law Dickinson Sch. Law, Carlisle, Pa., 1971—. Pres., Chambersburg chpt. ARC, 1971, Chambersburg YMCA, 1973-75. Mem. Am., Pa. bar assns., Am. Assn. Trial Lawyers. Author: Cases and Materials on Wills and Decedents Estates, 1975. Home: 455 Overhill Dr Chambersburg PA 17201 Office: 257 Lincoln Way E Chambersburg PA 17201 Tel (717) 263-8447

CLEMENS, DAVID L., b. Dubuque, Iowa, July 8, 1940; B.B.A., J.D., State U. Iowa. Admitted to Iowa bar; partner firm Reynolds, Kenline, Breitbach, McCarthy, Clemens & McKay, Dubuque, 1968—. Chmn. Cancer Dr., 1970; chmn. Dubuque Citizens Adv. Commn., 1974. Mem. Am., Iowa bar assns. Office: 222 Fischer Bldg Dubuque IA 52001 Tel (319) 583-1768

CLEMENS, ERNEST WILLIAM, b. New Braunfels, Tex., Sept. 7, 1897; B.A., U. Tex., 1917; J.D., Harvard, 1921. Admitted to Tex. bar, 1921, U.S. Supreme Ct. bar, 1928; asso. firm Clemens, Spencer, Welmaker & Finck, and predecessors, San Antonio, 1922-26, partner, 1927—. Mayor City of Olmos Park (Tex.), 1948-54; pres. Community Chest, San Antonio, 1951-53, Symphony Soc., San Antonio, 1954-57. Fellow Am., Tex. bar founds.; mem. Am. Law Inst., State Bar Tex., Am. Bar Assn., Am. Judicature Soc. Home: 505 Mandalay Dr E San Antonio TX 78212 Office: 1805 N B C Bldg 430 Soledad St San Antonio TX 78205 Tel (512) 227-7121

CLEMENT, ROBERT CANN, b. Portland, Maine, June 22, 1923; B.S. in Ch.E., Mass. Inst. Tech., 1947; LL.B., Golden Gate U., 1955. Admitted to Calif. bar, 1955, Tex. bar, 1972; successively chem. engr., patent lawyer, gen. mgr. patents and licensing Shell Oil Co., Houston, 1947—. Mem. Am. Bar Assn., Am. Patent Law Assn. Office: 1 Shell Plaza POB 2463 Houston TX 77001 Tel (713) 220-4717

CLEMENT, ROBERT LEBBY, JR., b. Charleston, S.C., Dec. 14, 1928; A.B., The Citadel, 1948; J.D., Duke, 1951. Admitted to N.C. bar, 1951, S.C. bar, 1954; individual practice law, Charlotte, N.C., 1951-53; partner firm Cornish, Clement & Horlbeck, Charleston, 1956-60, firm Hagood, Rivers & Young, Charleston, 1960-65, firm Young, Clement & Rivers, Charleston, 1965—; asst. corp. counsel City of Charleston, 1960; judge municipal ct., 1961-63. Mem. Charleston Zoning and Planning Commn., 1968-75; trustee Charleston Mus., 1970—. Mem. Am., N.C., S.C., Charleston County bar assns. Home: 7 Legare St Charleston SC 29401 Office: 28 Broad St PO Box 993 Charleston SC 29402

CLEMENT, THOMAS EARL, b. Watertown, N.Y., Sept. 9, 1932; B.A., St. Lawrence U., 1954; LL.B., Cornell, 1959. Admitted to N.Y. State bar, 1959, U.S. Dist. Ct. bar, 1959; asso. firm Nixon, Hargrave, Devans & Doyle, Rochester, N.Y., 1959-64, partner, 1965—; dir. Genesee Brewing Co., Inc. Bd. dirs., pres. David Hochstein Meml. Music Sch., Rochester, Mem. Am., N.Y. State (exec. com. banking, corp. and bus. law sect.), Monroe County bar assns. Home: 421 Cobbs Hills Dr Rochester NY 14610 Office: Lincoln First Tower Rochester NY 14603 Tel (716) 546-8000

CLEMENTS, ALLEN CLINTON, JR., b. Macon, Ga., Jan. 15, 1924; B.A., U. Miami, 1948, LL.B. cum laude, 1951, J.D., 1967. Admitted to Fla. bar, 1951; partner firm Clements & Clements, Miami, 1951-53; sr. asso. firm Claude Pepper and predecessors, Miami and Miami Beach, Fla., 1953-73; partner firm Pepper, Clements, Hopkins & Weaver, Miami Beach, 1973—; pros. atty. Town of W. Miami, 1954-56, atty., 1956—; atty. City of S. Miami, 1969-72, Village of Biscayne Park (Fla.), 1972-75. Councilman Town of W. Miami, 1952-53; atty. Dade County (Fla.) Council of Mayors, 1964-72; cons. atty. Dade County League Cities, 1965—; atty. Miami Beach Tourist Devel. Authority, 1969—. Mem. Fla., Dade County bar assns., Phi Delta Phi. Home: 935 NE 75th St Miami FL 33138 Office: 1701 Meridian Ave Miami Beach FL 33139 Tel (305) 532-4853

CLEMENTS, ANNE VICTORIA PHILLIPS, b. Harrodsburg, Ky., Jan. 12, 1921; B.S., U. Ky., 1940; LL.B., U. Louisville, 1950. Admitted to Ky. bar, 1950; statis. clk. U.S. Navy, Pensacola, Fla., 1942-45; ct. reporter, Fort Knox, Ky., 1949-57; atty., Wright-Patterson AFB, 1957-63; depot atty. Lexington-Bluegrass Army Depot, Lexington, Ky., 1963-73. Mem. Ky. Bar Assn., DAR (regent 1977—). Home and Office: 1038 Della Dr Lexington KY 40504

CLEMENTS, JAMIE HAGER, b. Crockett, Tex., Dec. 9, 1930; B.A. with honors, U. Tex., 1952, J.D., 1955. Admitted to Tex. bar, 1956; served as legal officer USMC, 1956-59; asso. firm Cox and York, McAllen, Tex., 1959-60; gen. counsel Scott & White Hosp. Med. Center, Temple, Tex., 1960—; mem. Tex. Ho. of Reps., 1953-61; mayor City Temple, 1970-74; chmn. Tex. Bd. Pub. Welfare, 1976. Former Campaign dir., pres. Temple United Fund; past bd. dirs. Temple Boys' Choir; bd. deacons, bd. elders 1st Presbyn. Ch., Temple; chmn. Temple Planning Commn.; pres. Tex. Municipal League, 1972-73, former exec. bd. Central Tex. Council Govts. Mem. Am., Tex. (chmn. com. liaison med. profession), Bell-Lampasas-Mills Counties (former pres.) bar assns., Am. Soc. Hosp. Atty's. Home: 2644 Marlandwood Circle Temple TX 76501 Office: 2401 S 31st St Temple TX 76501 Tel (817) 778-4451

CLEMENTS, MANNING CHAMBERLAIN, b. Burnet, Tex., Dec. 27, 1908; B.A., Southwestern U., Georgetown, Tex., 1929; LL.B., Houston Law Sch., 1938. With Jesse H. Jones Properties, Houston, 1929-35, United Gas Corp., Houston, 1935-40; admitted to Tex. bar, 1938, U.S. Supreme Ct. bar, 1950; spl. agt. FBI, 1940-70; asst. atty. gen. State of Tex. Div. Crime Prevention, Austin, 1970—. Pi Kappa Delta, Sigma Tau Delta. Editor Atty. Gen's Crime Prevention Newsletter, 1970—. Home: Route 1 PO Box 282 Wimberley TX 78676 Office: Room 302B Supreme Ct Bldg PO Box 12548 Austin TX 78711 Tel (512) 475-2862

CLEMOW, BRIAN, b. Hartford, Conn., Jan. 11, 1944; B.A., Harvard, 1966; LL.B., U. Pa., 1969. Admitted to Conn. bar, 1969; asso. firm Shipman & Goodwin, Hartford, 1969-74, partner, 1974—; adj. prof. Sch. Law, U. Conn., W. Hartford, 1975—. Trustee, Mark Twain Meml., Hartford, 1975—. Mem. Hartford County, Conn. (chmn. labor law com. young lawyers sect. 1972-74), Am. bar assns., Harvard Club No. Conn. (treas. 1974-76, sec. 1976—). Home: 154 Steele Rd W Hartford CT 06119 Office: 799 Main St Hartford CT 06103 Tel (203) 549-4470

CLENDENIN, HARRY HILLIARD, b. Raleigh, N.C., Jan. 6, 1945; B.A., N.C. State U., 1967; J.D. cum laude, Wake Forest U., 1970. Admitted to N.C. bar, 1970; asso. firm Smith, Moore, Smith, Schell & Hunter, Greensboro, N.C., 1970-75, partner firm McNairy, Clifford & Clendenin, 1975—. Mem. Am., N.C. (chmn. coordinating com. young lawyers sect. 1974-75), Greensboro (pres. young lawyers sect. 1974-75) bar assns., N.C. Acad. Trial Lawyers. Home: 2915 Round Hill Rd Greensboro NC 27408 Office: 406 Gate City Bldg 201 W Market St Greensboro NC 27401 Tel (919) 274-3209

CLENDENING, WARREN ELLSWORTH, b. Santa Monica, Calif., June 27, 1932; A.B., U. So. Calif., 1954, LL.B., 1957. Admitted to Calif. Supreme Ct. bar, 1957, U.S. Supreme Ct. bar, 1976; individual practice law, Santa Monica, 1957—. Pres. Legal Aid Soc. of Santa Monica, 1966-68. Mem. Am., Los Angeles County, Santa Monica Bay Dist. (pres. 1970) bar assns., State Bar Calif., U. So. Calif. Legion Lex. Home: 10275 Cresta Dr Los Angeles CA 90064 Office: Suite 400 Union Bank Bldg 2444 Wilshire Blvd Santa Monica CA 90403 Tel (213) 828-4475

CLERMONT, KEVIN MICHAEL, b. N.Y.C., Oct. 25, 1945; A.B., Princeton, 1967; J.D., Harvard, 1971. Admitted to Mass. bar, 1971, N.Y. bar, 1974; law clk. U.S. Dist. Ct. So. Dist. N.Y., N.Y.C., 1971-72; asso. firm Cleary, Gottlieb, Steen & Hamilton, N.Y.C., 1972-74; asst. prof. Cornell Law Sch. Ithaca, N.Y., 1974-76, asso. prof., 1976—. Mem. Am., N.Y. State bar assns. Editor: Harvard Law Review, 1969-71; Fulbright scholar U. Nancy (France) 1967-68. Home: 1 James St Ithaca NY 14850 Office: 263M Myron Taylor Hall Cornell Law Sch Ithaca NY 14853 Tel (607) 256-5189

CLEVENGER, RAYMOND CHARLES, III, b. Topeka, Kans., Aug. 27, 1937; B.A., Yale, 1959, LL.B., 1966. Admitted to D.C. bar, 1967, U.S. Supreme Ct. bar, 1969; since practiced in Washington, D.C., law clk. Mr. Justice White, 1966-67; asso. firm Wilmer, Cutler & Pickering, 1967-72, partner, 1972—. Mem. Am. Bar Assn. Home: 3242 Ellicott St NW Washington DC 20008 Office: 1666 K St NW Washington DC 20006 Tel (202) 872-6071

CLIFFORD, EUGENE THOMAS, b. Utica, N.Y., July 15, 1941; B.A., Boston Coll., 1963; LL.B., 1966. Admitted to N.Y. bar, 1967; asso. firm Chamberlain, D'Amanda, Bauman, Chatman & Oppenheimer, Rochester, N.Y., 1966-72; asso. firm Lamb, Webster, Walz, Donovan & Sullivan, Rochester, 1972-75, partner, 1976—. Bd. dirs. N.Y. State div. Am. Cancer Soc., 1972—, chmn. ad hoc com. on legacies and planned giving, 1976-77. Mem. Am., N.Y. State, Monroe County (N.Y.) bar assns., Am. Judicature Soc. Home: 191 Melrose St Rochester NY 14619 Office: 19 W Main St Rochester NY 14614 Tel (716) 325-2150

CLIFFORD, FRANCIS VINCENT, JR., b. San Francisco, May 5, 1948; B.A., U. San Francisco, 1970, J.D. with honors, 1973. Admitted to Calif. bar, 1973; asso. firm Sedgwick, Detert, Moran & Arnold, San Francisco, 1973-77; partner firm Donohoe, Jones, Brown & Clifford, 1977—. Mem. San Francisco Bar Assn., Calif. Assn. Def. Counsel, Barristers Club. Editorial bd. U. San Francisco Law Rev., 1971-73. Home: 200 Emerystone Terr San Rafael CA 94903 Office: 100 Van Ness Ave San Francisco CA 94102 Tel (415) 982-0303

CLIFFORD, WILLIAM R., b. Anderson, Ind., June 3, 1930; B.S., Ind. U., 1953; J.D., 1955. Admitted to Ind. bar, 1955, Colo. bar, 1956, U.S. Supreme Ct. bar, 1969; mem. trust dept. Denver Nat. Bank, Denver, 1955-57; individual practice law, Denver, Pueblo, Colo., 1957-58; asst. city atty., Denver, 1958-60; asst. trust officer 1st. Nat. Bank of Oreg., Eugene, 1960-63; v.p., trust officer Citizen Banking Co., Anderson, 1964-70; individual practice law, Anderson, 1970-72; chief judge Superior Ct., Madison County Div. 2 (Ind.), 1973—. Dir. Ind. Juvenile Justice Task Force. Mem. Madison County, Ind., Am. bar assns., Ind. Council Juvenile Ct. Judges, Nat. Council Juvenile ct. judges. Home: 413 Stuart Circle Anderson IN 46012 Office: Madison Ct House Anderson IN 46016 Tel (317) 646-9291

CLIFTON, PHILIP KIRKER, b. Breckinridge, Tex., Aug. 2, 1920; B.S., Centenary Coll., 1942; J.D., U. Houston, 1965. Admitted to Tex. bar, 1965, La. bar, 1966; v.p. Williamson Sales Co., Shreveport, La., 1950-62; dir. Williamson Sales and Distbg. Co. Mem. Houston Bar Assn., Comml. Law League. Home: 5620 Holly Springs Houston TX 77056 Office: 5433 Westheimer Suite 213 Houston TX 77056 Tel (713) 621-2638

CLINCH, LEO FRANCIS, b. Greeley, Nebr., Apr. 18, 1920; B.S., Creighton U., 1948, J.D., 1948. Admitted to Nebr. bar, 1948, U.S. Supreme Ct. bar, 1967; individual practice law, Burwell, Nebr., 1948—; county atty. Garfield County (Nebr.), 1950-54. Mem. Am., Nebr. State, Central Nebr. bar assns. Home: 377 Valley Vista Dr Burwell NE 68823 Office: 455 Grand Ave Burwell NE 68823 Tel (308) 346-4284

CLINE, GUY GROVER, b. Ashville, Ohio, July 28, 1915; LL.B., Ohio State U., 1941, LL.D., 1970. Admitted to Ohio bar, 1941; legal officer U.S. Army, 1941-47; pros. atty. Pickaway County (Ohio), Circleville, 1948-52; individual practice law, Ashville, 1952-54; judge Common Pleas, Probate, and Juvenile Cts. Pickaway County, 1954—; solicitor Villages of S. Bloomfield and Ashville. Past pres. Ashville Community Assn.; bd. dirs. Central Ohio council Boy Scouts Am., 1966-71, dist. chmn., 1960-66; bd. dirs. Vets. Service Commn., 1952-55. Mem. Am. Judicature Soc., Ohio Probate Ct. Judges Assn. (past pres.), Nat., Ohio juvenile judges assns., Pickaway County Bar Assn. (Meritorious Service award 1975). Home: 110 Park St Ashville OH 43103 Office: Court House Circleville OH 43113 Tel (614) 474-3950

CLINTON, GORDON STANLEY, b. Medicine Hat, Alta., Can., Apr. 13, 1920; A.B., U. Wash., 1942, J.D., 1947; LL.D. (hon.), U. Puget Sound, 1957, Seattle Pacific Coll., 1960. Admitted to Wash. bar, 1947; dep. atty. King County, Wash., 1947-49; municipal judge pro-tem, Seattle, 1949-52; spl. atty. for city council, Seattle, 1953; mayor City of Seattle, 1956-64; individual practice law, Seattle, 1949—; chmn. Marine Employees Commn., 1965-70. Pres. pres. Nassak Club Seattle, 1953-54, Japan-Am. Soc., Seattle, 1973-74; chmn. Kobe-Seattle Affiliation Com., 1966-72; pres. Am. Municipal Assn., 1962. Mem. Am. Judicature Soc., Seattle/King County, Wash. State, Am. Bar Assns. Decorated Order of Sikatuna, Rank of Maginoo, citation from Philippine govt., 1971, Cordon of the Third Order of the Rising Sun, citation from Japanese govt., 1975; recipient Outstanding Pub. Ofcl. award, 1963, citiation NCCJ, 1964, Seattle/King County Municipal League award, 1964. Home: 7733 58th St NE Seattle WA 98115 Office: 500 Third & Lenore Bldg Seattle WA 98121 Tel (206) 624-6831

CLINTON, WILLIAM JEFFERSON, b. Hope, Ark., Aug. 19, 1946; B.S., Georgetown U., 1968; J.D., Yale, 1973. Admitted to Ark. bar, 1973; individual practice law, Fayetteville, Ark., 1973-76; atty. gen. State of Ark., 1977—; instr. U. Ark., Little Rock, 1975-76; asst. prof. law U. Ark., Fayetteville, 1976-77; exec. dir. Hartford Legis. Action Council, 1971; instr. U. New Haven, 1972. Ark. coordinator Carter for Pres., 1976. Mem. Ark., Am. bar assns., Phi Beta Kappa. Office: Justice Bldg Little Rock AR 72201 Tel (501) 371-2007

CLOHOSEY, THOMAS WEIR, b. N.Y.C., Aug. 19, 1906; A.B., Fordham U., 1927; LL.B., Rutgers U., 1931. Admitted to N.J. bar, 1931, U.S. Supreme Ct. bar, 1966; asso. firm Pomerehne, Laible & Kautz, Newark, 1931-35; mem. firm Rafferty & Clohosey, Newark, 1935-45, firm Clohosey, Lintott & Sant'Ambrogio, Newark, 1945-60, Clohosey & Ford, Newark, 1960-72; individual practice of law, Bloomfield, N.J., 1972—; counsel N.J. Fed. Housing Adminstrn., 1934-43; U.S. Commr. for Dist. N.J., 1946-67; U.S. magistrate, 1967-70; asst. counsel Essex County, 1975—. chmn. planning bd. South Orange, N.J., 1967-73. Mem. Am., N.J. State, Essex County bar assns. Home: 40 Conger St Bloomfield NJ 07003 Office: 554 Bloomfield Ave Bloomfield NJ 07003 Tel (201) 743-5854

CLOKE, KENNETH, b. San Francisco, May 18, 1941; B.A., U. Calif., Berkeley, 1963, J.D., 1966, postgrad. in History and Social Welfare, 1966; candidate in philosophy U. Calif., Los Angeles, 1976.

Admitted to Calif. bar, 1967; asst. editor, asst. dir. Meiklejohn Civil Liberties Library, Berkeley, Calif., 1963-66; law clk., legal researcher Council for Justice, Oakland, Calif., 1964-66; staff counsel Oakland Welfare Rights Orgn., 1966; dir. law student div. Nat. Lawyers Guild, 1966-67, exec. sec., N.Y.C., 1967-68; staff atty. Hawthorne Neighborhood Legal Services (Calif.), 1969; Reginald Heber Smith fellow Venice Neighborhood Legal Services (Calif.), 1969-71; co-chmn. S.E. Asia Mil. Law Project, 1969-71; mem. firm Luke McKissack, Hollywood, Calif., 1971; individual practice law, Santa Monica, Calif., 1971—; prof. law U. San Fernando Valley Coll. Law, 1971—; vis. asst. prof. urban studies Occidental Coll., 1971—; part-time instr. history and polit. sci. El Camino Community Coll., 1973—; prof. law, dir. Center for Study Labor and Law, 1975—; lectr. in field. Mem. State Bar Calif., Soc. Am. Law Tchrs., Am. Soc. Legal History, Am. Hist. Assn., Los Angeles Labor Law Panel, Union for Radical Polit. Econs., Conf. Alternative State and Local Pub. Policies, Orgn. Am. Historians, ACLU, Econ. History Assn., Los Angeles Mil. Law Panel, Westside Lawyers Assn., Nat. Lawyers Guild, Nat. Hist. Soc., Am. Fedn. Tchrs. Author: Military Counseling Manual, 1967, 70; The Law of Welfare, 1967; contbr. articles to mags. and legal jours. Recipient award Constl. Rights Found. and Los Angeles County Bar Assn., 1975. Home: 116 Fraser Ave Santa Monica CA 90405 Office: Univ San Fernando Valley Coll Law 8353 Sepulveda Blvd Sepulveda CA 91343 Tel (213) 396-9801

CLOSE, DAVID PALMER, b. N.Y.C., Mar. 16, 1915; A.B., Williams Coll., 1938; LL.B., Columbia, 1942. Admitted to N.Y. bar, 1942, D.C. bar, 1946; partner firm Dahlgren & Close and predecessor, Washington, D.C., 1946—. Mem. Am., Inter-Am., D.C. bar assns., Bar. Assn. City N.Y., Assn. Trial Lawyers Am. Office: 1000 Connecticut Ave NW Washington DC 20036 Tel (202) 659-1440

CLOSE, GEORGE ROBERT, b. Elkins, W.Va., Jan. 28, 1930; B.B.A. in Mgmt., Tex. Tech. U., Lubbock, 1952; LL.B. with honors, U. Tex., Austin, 1957. Admitted to Tex. bar, 1957; partner firm Lemon, Close, Atkinson & Shearer, Perryton, Tex., 1957—; county atty. Ochiltree County (Tex.), 1960-72. Pres., Perryton and Vicinity YMCA; bd. dirs. Beehive, Inc. mem. Tex. Legislature, 1975—. Mem. Tex. County Attys. Assn. (dir.), Tex. Trial Lawyers Assn. (dir. 1970), Am., Tex., N.E. Panhandle bar assns. Home: 1101 S Drake St Perryton TX 79070 Office: 302 S Main St Perryton TX 79070 Tel (806) 435-6544

CLOSE, GORDON RALPH, b. Chgo., Aug. 18, 1906; Diploma in Commerce, Northwestern U., 1929; LL.B., John Marshall Law Sch., 1931. Admitted to Ill. bar, 1932; asso. firm Lord, Will & Cobb, Chgo., 1932-41; partner firm Lord, Bissell & Brook, Chgo., 1941-74, of counsel, 1974—. Fellow Am. Bar Found., Am. Coll. Trial Lawyers; mem. Am., Ill., Chgo. (past pres.) bar assns., Internat. Assn. Ins. Counsel (past pres.), Soc. Trial Lawyers (past pres.). Recipient citation of merit John Marshall Law Sch., 1966. Home: 127 E 5th St Hinsdale IL 60521 Office: 115 S LaSalle St Chicago IL 60603 Tel (312) 443-0700

CLOSE, MICHAEL JOHN, b. Sandusky, Ohio, Jan. 24, 1943; A.B., Lafayette Coll., 1965; J.D. cum laude, U. Mich., 1968. Admitted to Ohio bar, 1969, N.Y. bar, 1976; ins. agt. A.C. Close Agy., Sandusky, 1963-68; law clk. firm Close & Close, Sandusky, 1965-68; asso. firm Dewey, Ballantine, Bushby, Palmer & Wood, N.Y.C., 1968-76, partner, 1976—; gen. counsel Dayton Safe-Grain Co. (Ohio), 1972—, dir., 1975—; lectr. Practising Law Inst., N.Y.C., Southwestern Legan Found., Dallas. Precinct committeeman Erie County (Ohio) Republican Central Com., 1964-68. Mem. Am., N.Y. State, Ohio bar assns., Assn. Bar City N.Y., Order of Coif, Theta Chi (pres. alumni assn. Alpha Omega chpt. 1971-73, sec. 1973—, gen. counsel 1974—, dir. 1965—). Editor Mich. Law Rev., 1967-68. Home: 554 Birch Ave Westfield NJ 07092 Office: 140 Broadway New York City NY 10005 Tel (212) 344-8000

CLOSE, ROBERT HENRY, b. Denver, Dec. 8, 1911; A.B., Regis Coll., 1934; LL.B., Westminster Law Sch., 1939; J.D., U. Denver, 1960. Admitted to Colo. bar, 1939; partner firm Mueller, Ammons & Close, Denver, 1939-41; litigation atty. Office Price Adminstrn., 1942-43; individual practice law, Denver, 1946-74; judge Denver County Ct., 1974—. Trustee Arapahoe County 4-H Found. Mem. Am., Colo., Denver bar assns. Home: 812 S Milwaukee St Denver CO 80209 Office: City & County Bldg Denver CO 80202 Tel (303) 297-5102

CLOSSIN, JOHN DAVID, b. Frankfort, Ind., Apr. 21, 1946; B.S. in Accounting, Ind. U., 1968, J.D., 1973. Admitted to Ind. bar, 1973; examining atty. Chgo. Title Ins. Co., Indpls., 1973—. Mem. Ind. State, Indpls., Am. bar assns. Tel (317) 639-4481

CLOUD, SANFORD, JR., b. Hartford, Conn., Nov. 27, 1944; student U. Ariz., 1962-64; B.A., Howard U., 1966, J.D. cum laude, 1969. Admitted to Conn. bar, 1969; law clk. firm Covington & Burling, Washington, 1968-69; atty. Aetna Life and Casualty Co., Hartford, 1969; asso. firm Robinson, Robinson & Cole, Hartford, 1970-75, partner, 1975-76; partner firm Cloud & Ibarguen, Hartford, 1977—; mem. Conn. Senate, 1977—; adj. prof. law U. Hartford, 1974-75; adj. lectr. law U. Conn., Hartford, 1975-76. Vice chmn., bd. dirs. Greater Hartford Process, Inc., 1972—; corporator St. Francis Hosp., Hartford, 1972—, Mount Sinai Hosp., Hartford, 1972—, Inst. Living, Hartford, 1973—; chmn. program adv. com. Sta. WFSB-, Hartford, 1977—; bd. regents U. Hartford, 1972—; bd. dirs. Hartford Pub. Library, 1974—. Mem. Am., Conn., Hartford County, bar assns. Contbr. articles to legal jours. Home: 37 Plainfield St Hartford CT 06112 Office: 190 Trumbull St Hartford CT 06103 Tel (203) 278-0700

CLOUSE, ROGER ROY, b. Applecreek, Ohio, Dec. 18, 1907; B.S., Coll. of Wooster, 1929; M.B.A., Northwestern U., 1931, J.D., 1934. Admitted to Ohio bar, 1934; asso. firm Garfield, Daoust, Baldwin and Vrodman, Cleve., 1934-42; sr. v.p., sec., Fed. Res. Bank of Cleve., 1943-72; asso. firm McDonald, Hopkins and Hardy, Cleve., 1973-74; with Kenny Co. Realtors, Cleveland Heights, Ohio. 1974—. Address: 2362 Woodmere Dr Cleveland Heights OH 44106 Tel (216) 932-2126

CLOUSSON, JERRY PAIGE, b. Clarksburg, W.Va., May 31, 1933; A.B., W.Va. U., 1954; LL.B., 1956; LL.M., Georgetown U., 1959. Admitted to W.Va. bar, 1956, Ill. bar, 1960, U.S. Supreme Ct. bar, 1959, Fed. bar, 1963; litigation specialist NLRB, Chgo., 1961-65; labor counsel Am. Newspaper Pubs. Assn., Chgo., 1965-70; asso. firm Naphin, Banta & Cox, Chgo., 1970-76; dir. negotiations AMA, Chgo., 1976—; instr. labor law Loyola U. Law Sch., Chgo., 1972—; hearing examiner Ill. Fair Employment Practices Commn., 1972-73. Commr. Capital Improvements Commn., Glen Ellyn, Ill., 1973-76; pres. United Fund, Glen Ellyn, 1973; treas. Civic Betterment Party, Glen Ellyn, 1972; sec. Jaycee Ednl. Loan Trust Fund., Glen Ellyn, 1970. Mem. Am., Ill. State (chmn. labor law sect. 1972-73, Fed. (pres. Chgo. chpt. 1972-73) bar assns., U.S. C. of C., Indsl. Relations Research Assn. Recipient award merit Ill. Inst. Continuing Legal Edn., 1968; award merit Chgo. chpt. Fed. Bar Assn., 1973. Home: 355 N Park Blvd Glen Ellyn IL 60137 Office: 525 N Dearborn St Chicago IL 60610 Tel (312) 751-6652

CLOUTIER, JOSEPH MICHAEL, b. Bangor, Maine, Nov. 15, 1946; A.B., U. Maine, Orono, 1969; LL.D., Boston Coll., 1973. Admitted to Maine bar, 1973; asso. firm Strout, Payson & Pellicani, Rockland, Maine, 1973-75; partner firm Strout, Payson, Pellicani & Cloutier, Rockland, 1975—; instr. real estate law U. Maine, 1975. Mem. Warren (Maine) Planning Bd., 1976—. Mem. Phi Beta Kappa, Phi Kappa Phi, Pi Sigma Alpha. Home: PO Box 263 Warren ME 04864 Office: 7 Masonic St Rockland ME 04841 Tel (207) 594-8407

CLOUTMAN, EDWARD BRADBURY, III, b. Lake Charles, La., Dec. 8, 1945; J.D., La. State U., 1969. Admitted to La. bar, 1969, Tex. bar, 1971, U.S. Supreme Ct. bar, 1973; lawyer Central La. Legal Aid Service, Alexandria, 1969-70, Dallas Legal Services, 1970-71; partner firm Johnston, Polk, Larson, Cloutman & Dixon, Dallas, 1971-73; mem. firm Mullinax, Wells, Mauzy & Baab, Inc., Dallas, 1973—; bd. dirs. Dallas Legal Services Found., 1971-76. Mem. La., Tex. bar assns. Reginald Heber Smith fellow, 1969-71; certified labor law specialist, Tex. Home: 3317 St John's St TX 75205 Office: 8204 Elmbrook Dr #200 Dallas TX 75247 Tel (214) 630-3672

CLOVER, CARL ESTES, JR., b. Alexandria, LA., June 15, 1944; B.A., U. Tex., 1966, J.D., 1972. Admitted to Tex. bar, 1971, U.S. Dist. Ct. Western Dist. bar; asst. dist. atty. Travis County, Tex., 1971-75; partner firm Conner, Odom & Clover, Sealy, Tx., 1975—; chief prosecutor 147th Dist. Ct., Austin, Tex., 1973-75. Mem. Tex., Austin County bar assns. Home: 103 Westview Sealy TX 77474 Office: Conner Odom & Clover 311 Fowlkes St PO Box 576 Sealy TX 77474 Tel (713) 885-3533

CLOVIS, ALBERT L., b. Canton, Ohio, Oct. 20, 1935; B.A., Yale, 1957; M.A., U. Mich., 1959; LL.B., Harvard, 1962. Admitted to Ohio bar, 1962; asso. firm Day, Ketterer, Raley, Wright & Rybolt, Canton, 1962-65; asst. prof. law Ohio State U., Columbus, 1965-67, asso. prof., 1967-70, prof., 1970—; of counsel firm Wright, Harlor, Morris & Arnold, Columbus, 1973—. Mem. Am., Ohio bar assns., Am. Law Inst. Recipient Distinguished Teaching awards Ohio State U., 1968, 74; author: (with Robert J. Nordstrom) Commercial Paper, 1972. Home: 397 Green Hollow Dr Pataskala OH 43062 43062 Office: 1659 N High St Columbus OH 43210 Tel (614) 422-4740

CLUCK, ELWOOD, b. Dallas, Nov. 24, 1928; A.B., Baylor U., 1950, J.D., 1950; LL.M., U. Mich., 1954. Admitted to Tex. bar, 1950, U.S. Supreme Ct. bar, 1966; partner firms Cluck, Rutherford, Johnson and Wolverton, San Antonio, Cluck and Dodson, Uvalde, Tex.; lectr. St. Mary's U. Sch. Law, 1970—; speaker in field. Mem. San Antonio, Border, Am. bar assns., State Bar Tex. (co-chmn. com. on community property tax problems). Home: 300 E Mandalay St San Antonio TX 78212 Office: 711 Navarro St Suite 222 San Antonio TX 78205 Tel (512) 225-3132

CLUGSTON, SCOTT, b. Denver, June 1, 1932; B.A., U. Utah, 1953; J.D., U. Denver, 1958. Admitted to Colo. bar, 1958; claims examiner Colo. Allstate Ins. Co., Denver, 1958-62, dist. claims mgr. Utah-Montana Allstate Ins. Co., Salt Lake City, 1962-63; practiced in Greeley, Colo., 1963-73; judge Weld County (Colo.) Ct., 1973—; dep. dist. atty. Weld County, 1964; asst. city atty. City of Greeley, 1965-72. Mem. Am., Colo., Weld County bar assns., Colo. County Judges Assn., Nat. Conf. Spl. Cts. Judges, Am. Judicature Soc. Home: 2517 21st Ave Greeley CO 80631 Office: Weld County Courthouse 9th Ave and 9th St Greeley CO 80631 Tel (303) 353-8050

CLUNE, EDWARD CONRAD, b. Jamaica, N.Y., Nov. 17, 1921; B.A., Yale, 1943, J.D., 1945. Admitted to N.Y. bar, 1945, U.S. Supreme Ct. bar, 1961; asso. firm Simpson Thacher & Bartlett, N.Y.C., 1945-47; asso. firm FitzGerald and Clune and predecessor, Tarrytown, N.Y., 1947-55, partner, 1955-66; individual practice law, Tarrytown and Briarcliff Manor, N.Y., 1966—; dep. town atty. Town of Greenburgh, 1955-57, acting police justice Village of Tarrytown, 1958-59; village atty. Village of Briarcliff Manor, 1960-73; spl. asst. dist. atty. Westchester County, N.Y., 1960-73. Pres. Tarrytown Community Chest, 1957-59. Mem. Tarrytown (pres. 1961-62), Westchester County, N.Y. State, Am. bar assns., Tarrytown, North Tarrytown and Irvington (pres. 1960-62) chambers commerce. Home: 200 Scarborough Rd Briarcliff Manor NY 10510 Office: 12 Hamilton Pl Tarrytown NY 10591 Tel (914) 631-1800

CLUNE, JOHN RUSSELL, b. Valley Stream, N.Y., July 11, 1926; B.S., St. Francis Coll., 1948; student Bklyn. Law Sch., 1948-49; N.Y. U. Law Sch., 1949-50. Admitted to N.Y. bar, 1953; law clk. firm Harold P. Clune, N.Y.C., 1949-53, asso., 1953-55; individual practice law, Mineola and Harrison, N.Y., 1955-65; partner firm Clune & O'Brien, Mineola and Harrison, 1965-75, Clune Burns White & Nelson, Mineola and Harrison, 1975—; Candidate for U.S. Congress, 1974. Mem. Def. Research Inst., N.Y. State, Bklyn., Manhattan trial attys. assns., Assn. Ins. Attys., Nassau County Westchester County Rockland County bar assns. Home: 15 Carriage Home Ln Mamaroneck NY 10543 Office: 550 Mamaroneck Ave Harrison NY 10528 Tel (914) 698-8200

CLURFELD, HYMAN, b. Bklyn., Apr. 13, 1926; B.A., Bklyn. Coll., 1949; LL.B., J.D., Harvard, 1952. Admitted to N.Y. State bar, 1953, U.S. Supreme Ct. bar, 1963; asso. firm Falk & Orleans, N.Y.C., 1953-57; individual practice law, N.Y.C.; partner firm Clurfeld, Ross & Krevitz, N.Y.C., 1957—. Mem. industry adv. bd. Nassau County Vocat. Edn. and Extension Bd.; mem. advisory com. Hempstead (N.Y.) Recreation Dept.; pres. Nassau County Assn. for Help of Retarded Children; v.p., gov. N.Y. State Assn. Retarded Children. Mem. Am. Arbitration Assn. (panel arbitrators), Bklyn. Bar Assn. Home: 724 Jeffrey Dr Baldwin NH 11510 Office: 2 Pennsylvania Plaza New York City NY 10001 Tel (212) 279-1371

CLYNES, EDMUND, b. Ithaca, N.Y., Aug. 3, 1900; A.B., Cornell U., 1924, LL.B., 1926. Admitted to N.Y. bar, 1928, U.S. Supreme Ct. bar, 1955; asso. firm Peck and Whitbeck, Rochester, N.Y., 1927-28; law clk. U.S. Dist. judge, 1928-34, 44; trial, appellate work Supreme Ct. U.S., 1944, 2d Circuit Ct. of Appeals, 1935—. Home: 50 Chestnut St Rochester NY 14614 Office: 45 Exchange St Rochester NY 14614 Tel (706) 546-4447

COAD, JAMES KENNEDY, b. Knoxville, Dec. 20, 1931; B.A., Coll. William and Mary, 1953; LL.B., J.D., U. Miami (Fla.), 1957. Admitted to Fla. bar, 1972; adjuster, claims mgr. Phoenix of London, also Phoenix Assurance Co. N.Y., 1958-68; resident adjuster for Broward County (Fla.), Continental Ins. Co. N.Y., 1968-69; nat. claims mgr. Fire & Allied Lines, nat. claims mgr. fire and casualty, claims counsel, asst. v.p. industry relations Am. Bankers Ins. Co. Fla., 1968-75; with litigation div. Helliwell, Melrose & DeWolf, Miami, 1975—. Mem. Am., Fla., Dade County bar assns. Home: 12615 SW 12th St Fort Lauderdale FL 33314 Office: 1401 Brickell Ave 9th Floor Miami FL 33131 Tel (305) 373-7571

COATE, ALFRED BENJAMIN, b. Forsyth, Mont., Mar. 20, 1927; B.A., U. Mont., 1957, LL.B., 1959. Admitted to Mont. bar, 1959, U.S. Dist. Ct. bar, 1960, U.S. Supreme Ct. bar, 1966; asst. atty. gen. Mont., Helena, 1959-67; Dist. Judge, Forsyth, Mont., 1967—; mem. Mont. Criminal Law Revision Commn., 1968-73. Mem. Mont. Bar Assn., Am. Judicature Soc., Mont. Judges Assn. (pres. 1970), Mont. Criminal Justice Project. Home: 462 12th St Forsyth MT 59327 Office: Rosebud County Court House Forsyth MT 59327 Tel (406) 356-7310

COATES, FREDERICK ROSS, b. Etlan, Va., June 27, 1933; B.A., U. Richmond, 1954; J.D., T.C. Williams Sch. Law, 1959. Admitted to Va. bar, 1959; partner firm Coates and Province, Madison, Va., 1974—; commr. accounts Madison County (Va.), 1973—; govt. appeal agt. SSS; mem. adv. bd. Nat. Bank and Trust Co. Deacon, Beth Car Baptist Ch., Madison; Republican committeeman, Madison; mem. Madison Planning Commn., Madison Hwy. Safety Com. Mem. Va. State, Am., Madison-Greene bar assns., Phi Alpha Delta. Home and office: POB 328 Madison VA 22727 Tel (703) 948-5641

COATES, RAYMOND MATTHEW, b. Phoenix, Oct. 1, 1943; B.A., U. San Francisco, 1965, LL.B., 1967. Admitted to Calif. bar, 1967; legal research asst. San Mateo County (Calif.), 1967-68; asso. firm Low, Ball & Lynch, San Francisco, 1968-75, partner, 1975—. Mem. Am., San Francisco bar assns., State Bar Calif., N. Calif. Assn. Def. Counsel. Tel (415) 981-6630

COATES, ROBERT LEO, b. New Britain, Conn., Jan. 24, 1898; LL.B., Union U., 1920. Admitted to Conn. bar, 1921, N.Y. bar, 1924; practice law, Hartford, Conn. and N.Y.C. Home: 107 Hartford Ave Apt 812 New Britain CT 06051 Office: 50 State St Hartford CT 06103 Tel (203) 247-6614

COATES, WALTON, B.S. in Econs., U. Pa., 1938, J.D., 1941. Admitted to Pa. bar, 1942; individual practice law, asso. firms, Glenside, Pa., 1942-45; partner firm McTighe, Markel & Coates, Norristown, Pa., 1946-50, firm High, Swartz, Roberts & Seidel, Norristown, 1967-75; law clk. Ct. Common Pleas, Montgomery County (Pa.), 1953-63, 76—; solicitor Office Controller Montgomery County, 1964-72. Mem. Pa. (chmn. constl. law com. 1976-77), Montgomery County (sec. 1950-70) bar assns. Contbr. articles to legal jours. Office: 40 E Airy St Norristown PA 19404 Tel (215) 275-0700

COATS, ARTHUR WILLIAM, JR., b. Yuba City, Calif., June 22, 1914; A.A., Yuba Coll., 1933; B.A., U. Calif., Berkeley, 1935; J.D., McGeorge Coll. Law, 1942. Admitted to Calif. bar, 1942; mem. firm Manwell and Manwell, Marysville, Calif., 1945-46; mem. firm Coats and Ferrierk, Yuba City, Calif., 1951-52; individual practice of law, Yuba City, Marysville, 1947-50, 1953-62; asst. to atty. gen. of U.S., 1943-45; city atty. Yuba City, Calif., 1946-48; workers compensation judge, State of Calif., 1962-70. Cons. U.S. Delegation to UN Organizational Conf., 1945; mem. Calif. State Assembly, 1948-52; govt. appeal agt. Selective Service Bd., Yuba County, 1953-58. Mem. Am. Bar Assn., Am. Judicature Soc. Home and Office: 719 E Micheltorena St Santa Barbara CA 93103 Tel (805) 963-2839

COAXUM, EDWARD CHRISTOPHER, JR., b. Cleve., Feb. 4, 1944; B.A., Williams Coll., 1966; J.D., Boston U., 1969. Admitted to Ohio bar, 1971; Reginald Heber Smith community law fellow U. Pa. Law Sch., assigned to San Francisco Neighborhood Legal Assistance Found., 1969-70; asso. firm Squire, Sanders & Dempsey, Cleve., 1970-75, Csank & Csank, Cleve., 1975; partner firm Csank, Csank & Coaxum, Cleve., 1976—. Pres., trustee Karamu House, Cleve., 1974-76; trustee Legal Aid Soc., Cleve., 1974—; mem. vis. com. humanities and arts, bd. overseers Case Western Res. U., 1975—; trustee Fedn. for Community Planning, Cleve., 1977—. Mem. Am., Ohio, Greater Cleve. bar assns., Computer Law Assn., Am. Arbitration Assn. (comml. panel). Office: 220 Williamson Bldg Public Sq Cleveland OH 44114 Tel (216) 523-1136

COBB, BERRY BENSON, b. Sherman, Tex., Sept. 8, 1895; B.A., Rustic Coll., 1922; M.A., So. Meth. U., 1931. Admitted to Tex. bar, 1919; practice law, Dallas; instr. comml. law Woodrow Wilson High Sch., Dallas Tech. High Sch., Dallas. Mem. Dallas Bar Assn. (chmn. legal history com., 1936—). Home: 330 Saint John's Dr Dallas TX 75205

COBB, BOBBY LEE, b. Griffin, Ga., May 12, 1933; student N. Ga. Coll., 1951-53, Ga. State Coll., 1953-55; LL.B., Atlanta U., 1961. Admitted to Ga. bar, 1964; adjuster State Farm Ins. Co., Atlanta, 1963-69; partner Cobb, Blandford & Werbin, Chamblee, Ga., 1970—. Mem. Am. Judicature Soc., Am. Bar Assn. Office: 3508 Broad St Chamblee GA 30341 Tel (404) 458-0186

COBB, CHARLES KENCHE, b. Canton, Ga., Aug. 23, 1934; B.S., Ga. Inst. Tech., 1956; M.B.A., Harvard, 1962; postgrad. Emory U., 1962-63, Georgetown U; J.D., Woodrow Wilson Coll. Law. Admitted to Ga. bar, 1969; individual practice law, Atlanta, 1969—; pres. C. Cobb Properties, Inc., 1973—, Sterling Securities, Inc., 1973—. Trustee Reinhardt Coll., Ga. Tech. Alumni Assn.; lay leader Northside Meth. Ch.; fin. chmn. Gadrix for Congress campaign, 1976; bd. dirs. Ga. Tech YMCA. Mem. Ga., Am. bar assns., Assn. Ga. Real Estate Exchangors, Atlanta Bd. Realtors. Home: 2851 Howell Mill Rd NW Atlanta GA 30327 Office: 6650 Powers Ferry Rd NW Atlanta GA 30339 Tel (404) 955-1416

COBB, DALE THOMAS, JR., b. N.Y.C., Aug. 27, 1948; B.A., Clemson U., 1969; J.D., U. So. Calif., 1972. Admitted to S.C. bar, 1972; legal counsel U.S. Army, 1972-74; city atty., Greenville, S.C., 1974-75; pub. defender, Charleston, S.C., 1975—. Mem. Am., S.C., Charleston bar assn. Kiwanian. Office: Pub Defender's Office 134 Meeting St Charleston SC 29401

COBB, EARLE E., JR., b. San Antonio, Nov. 6, 1929; B.A., U. Tex., 1951; J.D., St. Mary's U., San Antonio, 1957. Admitted to Tex. bar, 1957, U.S. Ct. Appeals bar, 5th Circuit, 1965, U.S. Supreme Ct. bar, 1970; asst. dist. atty. Bexar County, Tex., 1958-60; asso. firm Adrian Spears, 1960-62, Davis O'Conner, Pullen & Sugarman, 1962-64; partner firms Gray Gardner Robison Cobb, 1964-70, Cobb Thurman & Bain, San Antonio, 1972—; house counsel Sigmor Corp., 1970-72; foreman Grand Jury, San Antonio, 1972. Home: 11427 Raindrop St San Antonio TX 78216 Office: 1665 Frost Bank Tower San Antonio TX 78205 Tel (512) 226-0311

COBB, HERMAN WARREN, b. Birmingham, Ala., Sept. 28, 1943; A.B., Howard Coll., 1961; J.D., Cumberland Law Sch., Birmingham, Ala., 1968. Admitted to Ala. bar, 1968; law clk. to Judge Virgil

Pittman, U.S. Dist. Ct. for So. and Middle Dists. Ala., 1968-70; asso. firm Dortch, Wright & Cobb, Gadsden, Ala., 1970-73; partner firm Buntin & Cobb, Dothan, Ala., 1973—; instr. in bus. law Jacksonville (Ala.) State U., fall 1972. Mem. Am., Ala., Houston County (Ala.) (sec. 1971-72) bar assns., Ala. Def. Lawyers Assn., Ala. Trial Lawyers Assn. (exec. com.). Home: 909 Derbyshire Dr Dothan AL 36301 Office: PO Box 507 Dothan AL 36301 Tel (205) 794-8526

COBB, HOWELL, b. Atlanta, Dec. 7, 1922; student St. John's Coll., 1940-42; LL.B., U. Va., 1948. Admitted to Ga. bar, 1948, Tex. bar, 1949; mem. firm Kelley & Ryan, Houston, 1949-52, firm Fountain, Cox & Gaines, Houston, 1952-54, firm Orgain, Bell & Tucker, Beaumont, Tex., 1954—. Fellow Tex. Bar Found.; mem. Am., Tex., Jefferson County bar assns., Internat. Assn. Ins. Counsel, Tex. Assn. Def. Counsel. Home: 1385 Thomas Rd Beaumont TX 77706 Office: 400 Beaumont Savs Bldg Beaumont TX 77701 Tel (713) 838-6412

COBB, ISAAC WILLIAM, b. Charlotte, N.C., June 21, 1943; B.A., Presbyn. Coll., 1965; J.D., Mercer U., 1968. Admitted to Ga. bar, 1970; asso. firm Hansell, Post, Brandon & Dorsey, Atlanta, 1970—. Elder, Central Presbyn. Ch., Atlanta, 1970—. Mem. Atlanta, Ga., Am. bar assns., Am. Judicature Soc., Lawyers Club Atlanta, Presbyn. Coll. Alumni Assn. (dir. 1974-76, v.p. 1974-75). Office: 3300 1st Nat Bank Tower Atlanta GA 30303 Tel (404) 934-4380

COBB, LEONARD BENJAMINE, b. Meridian, Miss., Jan. 30, 1947; B.A., Miss. State U., 1970; J.D., U. of Miss., 1973. Admitted to Miss. bar, 1973; partner firm Warner, Ray & Cobb, Meridian, Miss., 1973—. Mem. Am., Miss. State, Lauderdale County bar assns. Home: 2104 Apache Ridge Rd Meridian MS 39301 Office: Box 5633 Meridian MS 39301 Tel (601) 693-1933

COBB, NEUMAN ANDREW, b. Wichita, Kans., Nov. 15, 1888; student Alma Coll., 1903-06; student in engring. U. Mich., LL.B., 1913. Admitted to bar in numerous states and fgn. countries; individual practice law, Battle Creek, Mich., 1913—. Mem. Am., Calhoun County (Mich.) bar assns., State Bar Mich. Home: 16500 Augusta Dr Augusta MI 49012 Office: 279 W Michigan Ave Battle Creek MI 49017 Tel (616) 964-9896

COBIN, HERBERT LEROY, b. Wilmington, Del., June 2, 1908; B.A., U. Del., 1930; LL.B., Harvard, 1933. Admitted to Del. bar, 1934, U.S. Supreme Ct. bar, 1949; practiced in Wilmington; asso. judge Del. Family Ct., 1965—; chief dep. atty. gen. State of Del., 1955-57; chmn. Del. Gov's. Com. State Corrections Program, 1961-63; lectr. in field. Mem. Del., Am. (com. juvenile justice) bar assns., Am. Judicature Soc., Nat. Council Juvenile Ct. Judges, Del. Council on Crime, Justice (pres. 1953-59, chmn. bd. 1959-62), Del. Hist. Soc. Recipient certificate of Merit Del. Council Crime, Justice, 1955, William A. Vrooman award 1960, Layman's award Del. Assn. Health, Phys. Edn., Recreation, 1967; contbr. articles to profl. publs. Home: 902 W 22d St Wilmington DE 19802 Office: Family Ct 6th and Market Sts Wilmington DE 19801 Tel (302) 571-2226

COCCIA, MICHEL A., b. Chgo., Sept. 17, 1922; B.S. in Engring., Ill. Inst. Tech., 1944; LL.B., John Marshall Law Sch., 1951; LL.D., U. Paris, 1965. Admitted to Ill. bar; asso. firm Baker & McKenzie, Chgo., now partner. Fellow Am. Coll. Trial Lawyers; mem. Soc. Trial Lawyers Ill. (past pres.), Internat. Assn. Ins. Counsel (sec.-treas.), Def. Research Inst. (chmn. com. on products liability 1971—), Ill. Def. Counsel, Ill. Trial Lawyers Assn., Am. (chmn. com. on trial practice), Ill. State (gov.), Chgo. bar assns., Ill. Inst. Tech. (past pres., award of Merit 1974), John Marshall Law Sch. (citation of Merit and Distinguished Alumni award 1971, v.p.) alumni assns. Home: 915 Isabella St Evanston IL 60201 Office: 130 E Randolph St Chicago IL 60601 Tel (312) 869-1615

COCCO, LEONARD MICHAEL, b. Bridgeport, Conn., Aug. 25, 1933; B.A., U. Bridgeport, 1955; J.D., Boston U., 1958. Admitted to Conn. bar, 1958; partner firm Cocco & Petrucelli, Bridgeport, 1960-63, Zimmer & Cocco, 1963-75, Conn., Cocco & Melville, Bridgeport, Conn., 1975—; counsel Bridgeport Charter Revision Comm., 1968; asst. city atty., Bridgeport, 1973-75; spl. asst. to speaker Conn. Ho. of Reps., 1961. Campaign chmn. Fairfield County for Nat. Found. March of Dimes, 1970—, state campaign chmn, 1972-76; bd. dirs. U. Bridgeport Alumni Assn.; legal advisor Spanish Mchts. Assn. Mem. Bridgeport, Conn. bar assns. Recipient awards Nat. Found. March of Dimes, Puerto Rican Family Center. Home: 210 Griffin Ave Bridgeport CT 06606 Office: 1115 Main St Bridgeport CT 06604 Tel (203) 367-8491

COCHRAN, ROBERT GEORGE, b. Daytona Beach, Fla., Aug. 19, 1944; A.A., U. Fla., 1964, B.S., 1967, J.D. with honors, 1972. Admitted to Fla. bar, 1972; asso. firm Macfarlane, Ferguson, Allison & Kelly, Tampa, Fla., 1972—. Mem. Fla. Bar, Am., Hillsborough County bar assns., Order of Coif, Phi Kappa Phi. Editorial bd. Fla. Law Rev.; contbr. articles to legal jours. Office: 512 N Florida Ave Tampa FL 33511 Tel (813) 223-2411

COCHRAN, STEVEN KNIGHT, b. Wichita, Kans., Mar. 28, 1934; B.S. in Geology, U. Okla., 1934; LL.B., So. Meth. U., 1962; LL.M., Harvard, 1963. Admitted to Tex. bar, 1962; trial atty. tax div. U.S. Dept. Justice, Washington, 1963-66; asso. firm Rain Harrell Emery Young & Doke, Dallas, 1966—, partner, 1971—. Former dir. Dallas Theatre Center; advt. dir. Maureen Connally Brinker Tennis Found. Ann. Charity Tennis Tournament. Mem. Am., Tex., Dallas bar assns., Order of Woolsack. Home: 2915 Bryn Mawr Dallas TX 75225 Office: Republic National Bank Tower Dallas TX 75201 Tel (214) 742-1021

COCHRAN, THOMAS DEAN, b. Joplin, Mo., Sept. 27, 1934; A.A., Graceland Coll., Lamoni, Iowa, 1954; student Central Mo. State U., Warrensburg, 1955; B.A., U. Mo. at Kansas City, J.D., 1958. Admitted to Mo. bar, 1958; asso. firm Morrison, Hecker, Buck, Cozad & Rodger, 1958-61, Piedimonte & Cochran, Independence, 1962—; asst. pros. atty., 1963; asst. city counselor, 1963-66, 68—. Bd. dirs. Am. Diabetes Assn. Mem. Am. (chmn. young lawyers sect. 1969-70, mem. council family law sect. 1975—), Mo. (pres. 1975—), Kansas City (del. 1972—) bar assns., Graceland Coll. (pres. 1966-70, Distinguished Service citation 1976), U. Mo. at Kansas City (Achievement award 1976) alumni assns. Home: 12810 E 39th St Independence MO 64055 Office: 317 W Kansas Ave Independence MO 64051 Tel (816) 833-1500

COCKE, WILLIAM BOOTH, JR., b. Charlotte, N.C., Nov. 5, 1947; A.B., U. N.C., 1969, J.D., 1972. Admitted to N.C. bar, 1972; partner firm Johnson and Cocke, Newland, N.C., 1972-73; individual practice law, Newland, 1974—; atty. Avery County (N.C.), 1974—, Avery County Sch. Bd., 1974—, Town of Elk Park (N.C.), 1974—. Treas., trustee Crossnore (N.C.) Sch., Inc., 1974—. Mem. N.C., Am. bar assns. Office: POB 606 Newland NC 28657 Tel (704) 733-9538

COCKRIEL, STEPHEN EUGENE, b. Long Beach, Calif., June 8, 1948; B.S., U. So. Calif., 1970; J.D., Loyola U., 1973. Admitted to Calif. bar, 1973; mem. firm Munns, Kofford, Hoffman & Throckmorton, 1974; atty. Thrifty Drug Stores Co., Inc., 1974-76; individual practice law, Long Beach, 1976—. Mem. Calif., Long Beach bar assns., Long Beach Jr. C. of C. (dir. 1976). Office: 500 E 4th St Long Beach CA 90802 Tel (213) 437-2731

COCKRILL, ASHLEY, b. Little Rock, Ark., Dec. 7, 1904; ed. U. Va., LL.B., 1927. Admitted to Ark. bar, 1927; partner firm Cockrill, Armistead & Rector and predecessors, Little Rock, 1928-39, Cockrill & McCehee, and predecessors, Little Rock, 1945—. Mem. Pulaski County, Ark., Am. (gen. chmn. mid-s. regional meeting, 1962) bar assns. Home: 5224 Edgewood Rd Little Rock AR 72207 Office: 201 Pyramid Life Bldg Little Rock AR 72201 Tel (501) 374-4859

COCKRILL, WILLIAM GOODLOE, b. Nashville, Jan. 8, 1948; A.B. in History, Davidson Coll., 1970; J.D., U. Tenn., 1972. Admitted to Tenn. bar, 1973; asso. firm Egerton, McAfee, Armistead, Davis & McCord, Knoxville, Tenn., 1973-76; partner firm McCord & Cockrill, Knoxville, 1976—. Mem. Knoxville, Am., Tenn. bar assns., C. of C. Office: 601 Concord St Knoxville TN 37901 Tel (615) 657-5252

COE, RICHARD THOMAS, b. Detroit, May 10, 1932; A.B., Wheaton Coll., 1953; M.Div., No. Bapt. Theol. Sem., 1957; J.D., U. Detroit, 1965. Admitted to Mich. bar, 1966, U.S. Dist. Ct. bar, 1966, U.S. Ct. Appeals bar, 1967; individual practice law, Detroit, 1966—. Mem. Delta Theta Phi. Home: 18797 Westbrook St Livonia MI 48152 Office: 13938 Inkster Rd Detroit MI 48239 Tel (313) 532-2500

COE, ROBERT VERNON, b. DeRidder, La., Oct. 24, 1909; B.A., Baylor U., 1932, LL.B., 1932. Admitted to Tex. bar, 1932; city atty., Baytown, Tex., 1932-35; asst. atty. gen. State of Tex., 1935-38; 1st asst. city atty., Houston, 1939-40; atty., Shell Oil Corp., Houston, 1940-43; v.p., dir. Traders & Gen. Ins. Co. Dallas, 1943-49; prin., sr. partner firm Thompson, Coe, Cousins & Irons, Dallas, 1950—; gen. counsel, dir. Southwest Indemnity Life Ins. Co. (merged into Lone Star Life Ins. Co.), 1955-70; gen. counsel Timberlawn Psychiat. Hosp., Inc., Dallas, 1954—; gen. counsel, sec., dir. Tecnol, Inc., Dallas, 1976—. Sustaining mem. Circle Ten council Boy Scouts Am.; trustee, sec. Timberlawn Found., Dallas, 1958-62, trustee, pres. 1962-64, chmn. bd. trustees, 1964-74; mem. health facilities adv. com. Dallas Health Planning Council, 1969-71; counsellor Baylor Law Sch., 1974—. Fellow Internat. Acad. Trial Lawyers; mem. Am., Dallas County bar assns., State Bar Tex., Tex. Bar Found., Internat. Assn. Ins. Counsel, World Assn. Lawyers of World Peace through Law Center (founding). Home: 3310 Fairmount #11-C Dallas TX 75201 Office: Suite 1000 2001 Bryan Tower Dallas TX 75201 Tel (214) 742-8621

COE, WARD BALDWIN, JR., b. Riderwood, Md., Aug. 24, 1913; A.B., Princeton, 1936; LL.B., Harvard, 1939. Admitted to Md. bar, 1939; asso. firm Ward B. Coe, 1939-41, John R. Norris, 1940; asso. firm Anderson, Coe & King, and predecessors, Balt., 1945-52, partner, 1952—; mem. Md. State Bd. Law Examiners, 1963-72, sec., 1963-68; asst. atty. gen. State of Md., 1949-52; mem. Gov.'s Commn. to Revise Annotated Code of Md., 1975—. Bd. dirs. Balt. Legal Aid Bur., 1947-53. Fellow Md. Bar Found.; mem. Am., Md. bar assns., Bar Assn. Balt. City, Wednesday Law Club. Home: Route 2 Box 400 Owings Mills MD 21117 Office: 800 Fidelity Bldg Charles St at Lexington St Baltimore MD 21201 Tel (301) 752-1630

COENEN, THEO JULIUS, III, b. Rayville, La., Feb. 5, 1940; A.B., N.E. La. U., 1961; LL.B., Tulane U., 1964. Admitted to La. bar, 1964; partner firm Coenen & Berry, Rayville, 1964—. Mem. Fifth Dist., La., Am. bar assns. Home and Office: PO Drawer 900 Rayville LA 71269 Tel (318) 728-4493

COERPER, MILO GEORGE, b. Milw., May 8, 1925; B.S., U.S. Naval Acad., 1946; LL.B., U. Mich., 1954; M.A., Georgetown U., 1957, Ph.D., 1960. Admitted to Mich. bar, 1954, D.C. bar, 1954, Md. bar, 1960; asso. firm Wilmer & Broun, Washington, 1954-60; asso. firm Coudert Bros., Washington, 1961-63, partner, 1964—. Trustee, Sheridan Sch., chmn. bd., pres., 1974-76; trustee House of Mercy, pres., 1970-74. Mem. Am., D.C. bar assns., Assn. Bar City N.Y., Am. Law Inst., Am. Soc. Internat. Law, Internat. Law Assn. Contbr. articles to legal jours. Home: 7315 Brookville Rd Chevy Chase MD 20015 Office: 1 Farragut Sq S Washington DC 20006 Tel (202) 783-3010

COFFEE, JON NORMAN, b. Dallas, Dec. 15, 1936; A.A., Kemper Coll., 1955; B.B.A., U. Tex., 1959, LL.B., 1960, J.D. Admitted to Tex. bar, 1960, U.S. Supreme Ct. bar; mem. staff Tex. Gen. Land Office, Austin, 1960-61; partner firm Coffee, Goldston & Bradshaw, and predecessors, Austin, 1961—. Mem., sec. Travis County Mental Health Assn.; pres. N.E. Austin Civic Assn. Mem. Tex., Travis County, Am. bar assns., Tex., Am. trial lawyers assns., Am. Judicature Soc. Home: 200 Breezehollow Circle Austin TX 78741 Office: 1000 SW Tower Austin TX 78701 Tel (512) 477-3656

COFFEEN, WILLIAM ALBERT, b. Yuma, Ariz., Oct. 10, 1930; B.S., U. Ariz., 1958, J.D., 1963. Admitted to Ariz. bar, 1963; individual practice law, Yuma, 1963-64, 1967-70; chief dep. county atty. Yuma County, Yuma, Ariz., 1964-67; county atty. County of Greenlee, Ariz., 1971—; town atty. Town of Clifton, Ariz., 1971—. Mem. Am., Ariz. bar assns., Ariz. County Attys. Assn., Nat. Dist. Attys. Assn. Home: Route 1 Box 119 Clifton AZ 85533 Office: POB 727 Clifton AZ 85533 Tel (602) 864-3842

COFFEY, DENNIS PATRICK, b. Racine, Wis., Dec. 13, 1946; student Northwestern U., 1965-67; A.B., U. Wis., 1969, J.D., 1972. Admitted to Wis. bar, 1972, U.S. Supreme Ct. bar; mem. firm Coffey & Coffey, Milw., 1972—. Mem. Am., Milw., Milw. Jr. bar assns., Bar Assn. 7th Fed. Circuit, State Bar Wis. (dir. criminal law sect. 1977-80), Nat. Assn. Criminal Def. Lawyers. Office: 1100 W Wells St Milwaukee WI 53233 Tel (414) 278-7272

COFFEY, GEORGE V., JR., b. Grafton, N.D., Apr. 29, 1941; B.Philosophy, U. N.D., 1963; J.D., U. Ariz., 1971. Admitted to Ariz. bar, 1971; partner firm Richard E. Bailey, Tucson, 1971-72; individual practice law, Tucson, 1972-73; partner firm Bachstein & Coffey, Tucson, 1973—. Pres. Crosstown Optimist Club, Tucson, 1976-77. Mem. Am. Bar Assn., Am. Trial Lawyers, Ariz. Legal Services. Named Optimist of Yr., Sunrise, 1973-74; recipient Pres.'s Heritage award Optimist Internat., 1976. Home: 2211 S Darling Ave Tucson AZ 85710 Office: 316 Transamerica Bldg Tucson AZ 85701

COFFEY, WILLIAM MICHAEL, b. Racine, Wis., Aug. 16, 1932; B.S., U. Wis., 1959, LL.B., 1961. Admitted to Wis. bar, 1961, U.S. Supreme Ct. bar, 1974; atty. U.S. SEC, Chgo., 1961-63; asst. U.S. atty. No. Dist. Ill., Chgo., 1963-64, Eastern Dist. Wis., Milw., 1964-66; partner firm Shellow, Shellow & Coffey, Milw., 1966-69; partner firm Coffey & Coffey, Milw., 1969—; lectr. U. Wis., 1975—. Bd. dirs. Milw. Council on Urban Life, 1970—, Milw. Commando Project I, 1970—, Milw. County Mental Health Assn., 1975—. Mem. Am. Arbitration Assn., Nat. Assn. Criminal Def. Attys., State Bar Wis. (chmn. criminal law sect. 1977), Fed. Bar Assn., Bar Assn. 7th Fed. Curcuit, Wis. Acad. Trial Lawyers (chmn. criminal law sect. 1977), Am. Bar Assn. (task force on criminal justice standards 1977), Am. Judicature Soc. Home: 4444 N Prospect St Shorewood WI 53211 Office: Suite 402 1100 W Wells St Milwaukee WI 53233 Tel (414) 278-7272

COFFIELD, MARCH HENRY, b. El Paso, Tex., Oct. 29, 1935; Sc.B., Tex. Christian U., 1956; LL.B., U. Tex., Austin, 1967; admitted to Tex. bar, 1967; partner firm Seale, Stover & Coffield, Jasper, Tex., 1973—. City councilman, Jasper, 1975—. Mem. Tex., 1st Jud. Dist. bar assns., Am., Tex. trial lawyers assns. Home: 874 Holly Ln Jasper TX 75951 Office: 950 N Wheeler St Jasper TX 75951 Tel (713) 384-3466

COFFIN, FRANK MOREY, b. Lewiston, Maine, July 11, 1919; A.B., Bates Coll., 1940, LL.D., 1959; I.A., Harvard, 1943, LL.B., 1947; LL.D., Bates Coll., 1959, U. Maine, 1967, Bowdoin Coll., 1969, Colby Coll., 1975. Admitted to Maine bar, 1947; individual practice law, Lewiston, Maine, 1947-52; partner firm Verrill, Dana, Walker, Philbrick & Whitehouse, Portland, 1952-56; mem. 85th-86th Congresses from 2d Maine Dist., 1957-60; mng. dir. Devel. Loan Fund, Dept. State, Washington, 1961; dep. adminstr. AID, 1961-64; U.S. permanent rep. devel. assistance com. OECD, 1964-65; judge 1st U.S. Circuit Ct. of Appeals, Portland, 1965-72, chief judge, 1972—; corp. counsel, Lewiston, 1949-52. Trustee Bates Coll. Mem. Am. Law Inst., Am. Bar Assn., Am. Bar Assn., Am. Judicature Soc., Inst. Jud. Adminstrn., Internat. Legal Center (dir.), Overseas Devel. Center (dir.), Examiner Club, Am. Acad. Arts and Scis. Recipient Edwin T. Dahlberg Peace award Am. Baptist Conv., 1970. Home: 1 Ocean Rd South Portland ME 04106 Office: 156 Federal St Portland ME 04112 Tel (207) 775-3131

COFFIN, HUBERT WOODROW, b. Caribou, Maine, Dec. 15, 1914; A.B., Bowdoin Coll., 1938; J.D., Harvard, 1941. Admitted to Mass. bar, 1942; partner firm Kingston & Coffin, Somerville, Mass., 1946—. Mem. Somerville, Middlesex County, Boston, Mass. bar assns., Am. Judicature Soc., Mass. Trial Lawyers Assn., Mass. Conveyancers Assn. Home: 14 Arrowhead Ln Arlington MA 02174 Office: 421 Highland Ave Somerville MA 02144 Tel (617) 625-4322

COFFIN, THOMAS MICHAEL, b. St. Louis, May 30, 1945; B.A., St. Benedicts Coll., 1967; J.D. cum laude, Harvard, 1970. Admitted to Mo. bar, 1970, Calif. bar, 1972; asst. U.S. atty., San Diego, 1971—. Office: 940 Front St San Diego CA 92189 Tel (714) 293-6172

COFFINGER, RICHARD DOUGLAS, b. Phoenix, July 29, 1947; A.A., Phoenix Coll., 1967; B.S. with distinction, Ariz. State U., 1969, J.D., 1972; grad. Nat. Coll. Criminal Def. Lawyers and Pub. Defenders, Houston, 1973. Admitted to Ariz. bar, 1972; dep. pub. defender Maricopa County (Ariz.), 1973-74, pros. atty., 1974; partner firm Wykoff, Charles & Coffinger, Glendale, Ariz., 1974—; mem. panel pvt. attys. for appt. for indigent criminal defendants U.S. Dist. Ct. for Ariz. Mem. Ariz., Maricopa County (pres. young lawyers sect. 1977—), Am. bar assns., Nat. Assn. Criminal Def. Lawyers, Phi Delta Phi, Phi Sigma Kappa, Omicron Delta Epsilon. Home: 5515 N 4th St Phoenix AZ 85012 Office: 7112 N 56th Ave PO Box 1737 Glendale AZ 85311 Tel (602) 939-6546

COFFMAN, FLOYD HURST, b. Overbrook, Kans., July 6, 1918; B.S., Emporia (Kans.) State Coll., 1942; J.D., Washburn U., 1947; law clk. Fed. Dist. Ct. Kans., Kansas City, 1947-48; probate judge Franklin County (Kans.), Ottawa, 1949-53; judge 4th Jud. Dist. Ct., Ottawa, Kans., 1953—. Mem. Am., Kans., Ottawa bar assns., Ottawa C. of C. (pres. 1957). Contbr. articles in field to legal jours. Office: Court Bldg Ottawa KS 66067 Tel (913) 242-6000

COGAR, WILLIAM REA, b. Camden-on-Gauley, W.Va., Mar. 4, 1929; B.A., Washington and Lee U., 1951, LL.B., 1955. Admitted to W.Va. bar, 1955, Va. bar, 1955; asso. firm Mays, Valentine & Danveport & Moore, Richmond, Va., 1955-59, partner, 1959—. Bd. visitors, adv. bd. Med. Coll. Va., 1966-70. Fellow Internat. Soc. Barristers, Am. Coll. Trial Lawyers; mem. Am., Va., Richmond bar assns., Order of Coif, Phi Beta Kappa, Omicron Delta Kappa, Phi Delta Phi. Home: 201 N Wilton Rd Richmond VA 23226 Office: Mays Valentine Danveport & Moore 1111 E Main St PO Box 1122 Richmond VA 23208 Tel (804) 644-6011

COGDILL, GARY WAYNE, b. Borger, Tex., Sept. 14, 1946; B.S., U. Houston, 1968, J.D., 1970. Admitted to Tex. bar, 1970; asst. county atty. Potter County (Tex.), 1970-71; atty. Pioneer Corp., Amarillo, Tex., 1971-75; v.p., gen. counsel Plains Mach. Co., Amarillo, 1976—. Mem. Am., Tex., Amarillo bar assns., Tex. Utility Lawyers, Order of Barons, Delta Theta Phi. Home: 3531 Barclay Amarillo TX 79109 Office: Box 30800 Amarillo TX 79120 Tel (806) 373-3061

COGGAN, HYMAN ALVIN, b. Syracuse, N.Y., Oct. 4, 1911; B.A., Denver U., 1940, LL.B., 1942, J.D., 1970. Admitted to Colo. bar, 1946; individual practice law, Denver, 1946—. Mem. Denver, Colo. bar assns., Colo. Trial Lawyers Assn. Home: 354 Cherry St Denver CO 80220 Office: 666 Sherman St Denver CO 80203 Tel (303) 837-1420

COGHILL, WILLIAM THOMAS, JR., b. St. Louis, July 27, 1927; LL.B. (now J.D.), U. Mo., 1950. Admitted to Mo. bar, 1950, Ill. bar, 1958; spl. agt. FBI, 1951-52; partner firm Smith, Smith & Coghill, Farmington, Mo., 1951-57; asso. firm Coburn & Croft, St. Louis, 1957-58; partner firm Pope and Driemeyer, E. St. Louis, Ill., 1958—. Fellow Am. Coll. Trial Lawyers; mem. Am., Ill., Mo., St. Louis, E. St. Louis, St. Clair County bar assns., Am. Judicature Soc., Ill., Am. assns. trial lawyers, Nat. Assn. R.R. Trial Counsel, Def. Research Inst., Ill. Def. Counsel. Home: 20 Autumn Ln Belleville IL 62223 Office: 1 S Church St Belleville IL 62220 Tel (618) 277-4700

COGSWELL, GLENN DALE, b. Kingman, Kans., Feb. 1, 1922; B.A., Washburn U., 1943, J.D., 1947. Admitted to Kans. bar, 1947, U.S. Supreme Ct. bar, 1957; individual practice law, Topeka, 1947-50, 56-65; partner firm Miller & Cogswell, Topeka, 1950-56, Goodell, Casey, Briman & Cogswell, Topeka, 1965—; judge Ct. of Topeka, 1949-51, probate and juvenile cts. Shawnee County (Kans.), 1951-57. Mem. Topeka (exec. com., chmn. mental health com. 1975—), Kans. (conflict of interest law com. 1975—), Am. bar assns. Home: 2929 SW Lagito Dr Topeka KS 66604 Office: 215 E 8th St Topeka KS 66603 Tel (913) 233-0593

COHAN, JOHN ROBERT, b. Arnhem, The Netherlands, Feb. 10, 1931; came to U.S., 1940, naturalized, 1945; B.S. in Bus. Adminstrn., U. Ariz., 1952; LL.B., Stanford U., 1955. Admitted to Calif. bar, 1956; partner firm Irell & Manella, Los Angeles, 1961—; lectr. taxation U. So. Calif. Sch. Law, Los Angeles, 1961-63; adj. prof. U. Miami Law Sch., 1975—; lectr., writer Calif. Continuing Edn. of Bar Program, 1959—, Practicing Law Inst., 1968—, also various tax and probate insts.; mem. planning com. U. So. Calif. Tax Inst., U. Miami Estate Planning Inst. Trustee Portals House, Inc., Los Angeles, 1962—, pres., 1967-70; trustee Big Bros. Am., 1966—, chmn. internat. expansion movement, 1967—; bd. dirs. Hope for Hearing Research Found., Los Angeles, 1962—; mem. Los Angeles World Affairs Council, 1964—. Fellow Am. Coll. Probate Counsel, Internat. Acad. Probate and Trust Law (exec. com.); mem. Am., Los Angeles County, Beverly Hills bar assns. Editor: Drafting California Revocable Trusts, 1972; Drafting California Irrevocable Trusts, 1973; Inter Vivos Trusts, Shephard's Citations, 1975. Home: 10910 Delco Ave Chatsworth CA 91311 Office: 1800 Ave Stars Suite 900 Los Angeles CA 90067 Tel (213) 277-1010

COHAN, LEON SUMNER, b. Detroit, June 24, 1929; B.A., Wayne State U., 1949, J.D., 1952. Admitted to Mich. bar, 1953; practiced in Detroit, 1954-58; asst. atty. gen. State of Mich., Lansing, 1958-60, dep. atty. gen., 1960-72; v.p. legal affairs Detroit Edison Co., 1973-75, v.p., gen. counsel, 1975—; adj. prof. law Wayne State U., 1974—, mem. com. visitors Law Sch., 1970—, chmn., 1973-74. Mem. Mich. Bd. Ethics, 1973—; bd. dirs. Southeastern Mich. chpt. ARC, Mich. Cancer Found. Mem. State Bar Mich., Detroit, Am. bar assns., Mich. Gen. Counsels Assn. Recipient Distinguished Alumni award Wayne State U. Law Sch., 1972—, Distinguished Service award Wayne State U. Bd. Govs., 1973. Home: 5324 Forest Way Bloomfield Hills MI 48013 Office: 2000 Second Ave Detroit MI 48226 Tel (313) 237-7455

COHAN, RICHARD S., b. Chgo., Mar. 14, 1935; student U. Ill.; J.D., DePaul U., 1959. Admitted to Ill. bar, 1959; staff Legal Aid Bur., 1959-62; asst. atty. gen. State of Ill., 1962-63, spl. asst. atty. gen. for Lake County, 1963-64; individual practice law, Chgo.; mem. panel of arbitrators Am. Arbitration Assn. Mem. Ill. Bar Assn., Ill. Trial Lawyer's Assn., Workman's Compensation Assn. Office: 221 N LaSalle St Suite 748 Chicago IL 60601 Tel (312) 263-3360

COHANE, REGENE FREUND, b. N.Y.C., Oct. 16, 1899; LL.B., Cornell U., 1920; Admitted to Mich. bar, 1920, U.S. Supreme Ct. bar, 1924; individual practice law, Wayne, Oakland and Macomb counties, Mich., 1920-24; partner firm Cohane & Cohane, Detroit, 1924-58; individual practice law, Southfield, Mich., 1958—. Mem. State Bar Mich., Detroit Bar Assn., Sigma Delta Tau. Office: Suite 410 16500 N Park Dr Southfield MI 48075 Tel (313) 559-3080

COHEN, ALEXANDER, b. Camden, N.J., July 4, 1916; B.A. with maj. honors and distinction, U. Pa., 1936, J.D. magna cum laude, 1939, postgrad. (Gowen Memorial fellow in law), 1939-40; certificate Exec. Program, Columbia U., 1965. Admitted to Pa. bar, 1940, N.Y. bar, 1957, U.S. Supreme Ct. bar, 1946; law clk. fed. and state cts., Phila., 1940-42; successively atty., spl. counsel, asst. gen. counsel SEC, Washington, 1945-56; sr. atty. Western Electric Co., Inc., N.Y.C., 1956-61, asst. gen. solicitor, 1961-66, gen. solicitor, 1966-74, asso. gen. counsel, 1975—; lectr. in field. Mem. Am., Fed., N.Y., Phila. bar assns., Exec. Assn. Columbia U., Order Coif. Recipient Spl. Certificate Merit, SEC, 1955; contbr. articles U. Pa. Law Rev., U. Pitts. Law Rev.; editor: U. Pa. Law Rev., SEC Judicial Decisions, Vol. III. Home: 431 Lewelen Circle Engelwood NJ 07631 Office: 222 Broadway New York City NY 10038 Tel (212) 571-2453

COHEN, AVERY SAMUEL, b. Youngstown, Ohio, Nov. 29, 1936; B.A., Western Res. U., 1958; J.D., Harvard U., 1961. Admitted to Ohio bar, 1961; asso. firm Lane, Krotinger, Santora & Stone, Cleve., 1961-62; law clk. to judge U.S. Dist. Ct. No. Dist. Ohio, Cleve., 1962-63; partner firm Guren, Merritt, Sogg & Cohen, and predecessors, Cleve., 1963—; lectr. Cleve. State U. Bd. overseers Case Western Res. U., 1969—; chmn. bd. trustees Hattie Larlham Found., 1976—. Mem. Am., Greater Cleve., Fed., Cuyahoga County bar assns. Home: 4096 Carroll Blvd University Heights OH 44118 Office: 650 Terminal Tower Cleveland OH 44113 Tel (216) 696-8550

COHEN, BERNARD S., b. Bklyn., Jan. 17, 1934; B.B.A., Coll. City N.Y., 1956; J.D., Georgetown U., 1960. Admitted to Va. bar, 1961, Washington bar, 1962, U.S. Supreme Ct. bar, 1964; partner firm Cohen, Vitt & Annand, Alexandria, Va.; labor law adminstrn. advisor U.S. Dept. Labor, Washington, 1960-61. Chmn. Alexandria Democrats Com., 1967-68. Mem. Am., Alexandria bar assns., Assn. Trial Lawyers of Am. (chmn. environ. law sec. 1976). Co-author: Environmental Rights & Remedies, 1972; contbr. articles in field to legal jours. Home: 4001 Fort Worth Ave Alexandria VA 22304 Office: 320 King St Box 117 Alexandria VA 22313 Tel (703) 836-2121

COHEN, DARRYL BRANDT, b. Chgo., Oct. 11, 1944; A.B., U. Ga., 1967; J.D., Mercer U., 1970. Admitted to Fla. bar, 1970, Ga. bar, 1971; mem. states Atty. Office, Miami Fla., 1971; mem. dist. atty. office, Atlanta, Ga., 1971-74; partner firm Cohen, Traub & Mackin, Atlanta, 1974—; bd. dirs. AFTRA, Atlanta Chpt., 1975, Nat. Acad. TV Arts & Scis., 1976; mem. governing council Atlanta Local Screen Actors Guild. Pres. Cross Creek Apts. Resident's Assn., 1975—. Mem. Am., Ga., Fla., Atlanta bar assns. Home: 79 Montre Sq NW Atlanta GA 30327 Office: 229 Peachtree St NE Atlanta GA 30303 Tel (404) 659-8880

COHEN, DAVID NORMAN, b. Troy, N.Y., Aug. 16, 1938; B.A., Harpur Coll., 1959; LL.B., Bklyn. Law Sch., 1962, J.D., 1972. Admitted to N.Y. bar, 1962, U.S. Dist. Ct. for No. Dist. N.Y. bar, 1962, U.S. Dist. Ct. for Western Dist. N.Y. bar, 1967; asso. firm Albert Averbach, Seneca Falls, N.Y., 1963-64; individual practice law, Geneva, N.Y., 1965—; atty., City of Geneva, 1967, 72—; commr. appraisal, urban renewal, 1965-67. Pres., Finger Lakes chpt. Am. Heart Assn., 1971-72; chmn. Ontario County Democratic Com., 1974-77. Mem. N.Y. State, Ontario County bar assns., Lions (past pres. Geneva chpt.). Home: 19 Maplewood Dr Geneva NY 14456 Office: 114 Seneca St Geneva NY 14456 Tel (315) 789-7176

COHEN, DONALD GARY, b. N.Y.C., Oct. 27, 1945; B.S., Cornell U., 1967; J.D., N.Y. U., 1970, LL.M., 1974. Admitted to N.Y. bar, 1971, U.S. Supreme Ct. bar, 1976; asso. firm Leon, Weill & Mahony, N.Y.C., 1970-76, firm Siegel, Chalif & Winn, N.Y.C., 1976—. Mem. commuters com. L.I. R.R., 1976; bd. dirs. Albertson Downs Civic Assn., 1976—. Mem. Assn. Bar City N.Y., Am., N.Y. State bar assns., Bar Assn. Nassau County (trusts and estates com. 1976). Recipient A. Harold Frost award, 1967. Home: 95 Hilldale Rd Albertson NY 11507 Office: 261 Madison Ave Room 1104 New York City NY 10016

COHEN, DONALD W., b. Chgo., Oct. 10, 1934; B.S. in Law, U. Ill., 1955; J.D., Northwestern U., 1957. Admitted to Ill. bar, 1957; asso. firm Asher, Greenfield, Goodstein, Pavalon and Segall, Chgo., 1958-68, partner, 1968—; lectr. in field. Mem. Am., Chgo. bar assns. Home: 1220 Brook Ln Glenview IL 60025 Office: 228 N LaSalle St Chicago IL 60601 Tel (312) 263-1500

COHEN, EZRA HARRY, b. Macon, Ga., Mar. 13, 1942; A.B., Columbia, 1964; J.D. with distinction, Emory U., 1969. Admitted to Ga. bar, 1969, U.S. Supreme Ct. bar, 1975; partner firm Troutman Sanders Lockerman & Ashmore, and predecessor, Atlanta, 1969-76; bankruptcy judge U.S. Dist. Ct. for No. Dist. Ga., 1976—. Mem. Am., Ga., Atlanta bar assns. Office: room 545 US Courthouse 56 Forsyth St Atlanta GA 30303 Tel (404) 526-4258

COHEN, GARY IRWIN, b. New Haven, June 19, 1943; B.A., Yale, 1965; LL.B., U. Va., 1968. Admitted to Conn. bar, 1968, U.S. Dist. Ct. bar, 1968; asso. firm Brown, Jacobson, Jewett & Laudone, Norwich, Conn., 1968-69; partner firm Perehnutter & Cohen, Seymour, Conn., 1969-75; partner firm Gary I. Cohen, Seymour, Conn., 1975—. Chmn. profl. sect. United Way, New Haven, 1974; dir. Jewish Family Service of New Haven. Mem. Conn. Bar. Assn., Conn. Trial Lawyers Assn. (sec.-treas.), Am. Trial Lawyers Assn. Articles editor: Va. Law Review, 1967-68, recipient Order of the Coif, 1968; asso. editor. Conn. Bar Jour., 1970-72. Home: 835 Elm St New Haven CT 06515 Office: 4 Bank St Seymour CT 06483 Tel (203) 888-0577

COHEN, GARY OSMOND, b. Nashville, June 9, 1937; A.B., Vanderbilt U., 1959; J.D., Harvard U., 1963. Admitted to D.C. bar, 1964; atty. div. investment mgmt. SEC, Washington, 1963-68, asst. chief counsel, 1968; asso. firm Freedman Levy Kroll & Simonds, Washington, 1968-73, partner, 1973—. Mem. Am., Fed., D.C. bar assns. Home: 5511 Cedar Parkway Chevy Chase MD 20015 Office: 1730 K St NW Washington DC 20006 Tel (202) 331-8550

COHEN, GEORGE LEON, b. Convington, Ga., June 20, 1930; A.B., Va. Mil. Inst., 1951; LL.B., U. Va., 1956. Admitted to Va. bar, 1956, Ga. bar, 1957, D.C. bar, 1964; asso. firm Sutherland, Asbill & Brennan, Atlanta, 1956-62, partner, 1962—. Mem. Atlanta, Am. bar assns., Lawyers Club Atlanta, State Bar Ga. (chmn. sect. corp. and banking law 1968-69), Am. Law Inst. Home: 294 Camden Rd NE Atlanta GA 30309 Office: 3100 1st Nat Bank Tower Atlanta GA 30303 Tel (404) 658-8725

COHEN, HAROLD, b. Boston, Aug. 10, 1923; J.D., Suffolk U., 1955. Admitted to Mass. bar, 1956; trial atty. firm Coplen & McAvoy, Boston, 1957-68; partner firm Iddings, Kalis, Cohen & Moore, Foxboro, Mass., 1968-74; individual practice law, Foxboro, 1974—; spl. asst. atty. gen. Mass., 1974, 77; spl. asst. dist. atty. Norfolk County, 1975. Chmn., mem. Sharon (Mass.) Sch. Com., 1959-74; trustee Norfolk County Agrl. High Sch., Walpole, Mass.; v.p. Sharon Credit Union. Mem. Am., Mass., Boston, Western Norfolk, Norfolk County bar assns. Home: 32 Oak Hill Dr Sharon MA 02067 Office: 21 Cocasset St Foxboro MA 02035 Tel (617) 543-6353

COHEN, HARRY, b. New Orleans, Apr. 5, 1927; B.A., Tulane U., 1949, J.D., 1951; grad. fellow Yale Law Sch., 1952-53. Admitted to La. bar, 1951, Ala. bar, 1958; law ckl. Civil Dist. Ct., New Orleans, 1951-52; asso. firm Doyle, Smith & Doyle, New Orleans, 1953-54; prof. law U. Ala. at Tuscaloosa, 1954—, dir. admissions Sch. Law, 1967-72; prof. La. State U., 1965, summers 1967, 76; mem. com. on rules of conduct and canons of jud. ethics Ala. Supreme Ct., 1975—. Bd. dirs. Jewish Children's Regional Service, 1976—. Mem. Ala., La. State bar assns., Pi Sigma Alpha, Order of Coif. Recipient Nathan Burkan Meml. prize, 1951; Outstanding Prof. award, 1973. Author: Fundamentals of Land Use Law, 1963; Land Use Law in Alabama, 1974; Floor Plain and Coastal Land Use Controls, 1975. Home: 1232 37th Ave E Tuscaloosa AL 35401 Office: Farrah Hall University Blvd University AL 35486

COHEN, HERBERT ERWIN, b. Utica, N.Y., Nov. 3, 1932; A.B., U. Mich., 1953; J.D., Union U., 1957; LL.M., N.Y. U., 1958. Admitted to N.Y. State bar 1958; asso. firm Strang, Wright, Combs, Wiser & Shaw, Rochester, N.Y., 1958-59; asst. tax mgr. Marine Midland Corp., Buffalo, 1959-61; individual practice law, Albany, N.Y., 1961-64; mem. firm Newkirk Assos., Albany, 1964-65; v.p., gen. counsel Golub Corp., Schenectady, 1965—, sec., 1966—; lectr. Albany Law Sch., 1968-70; dir. Community State Bank, Albany, 1977—. Bd. dirs. Albany Jewish Community Council; trustee Jewish Family Services, 1967—; v.p. Albany Jewish Family Services, 1971-73; pres. 1973-75; bd. trustees Daus. of Sarah Home for the Aged, Troy, N.Y., 1969—. Mem. N.Y. State Bar Assn. (lectr.), Nat. Assn. Food Chains, Practicing Law Inst. (lectr.). Office: 501 Duanesburg Rd Schenectady NY 12306 Tel (518) 355-5000

COHEN, HOWARD MARVIN, b. Bklyn., Mar. 22, 1926; A.B. cum laude, Columbia, 1947; J.D. magna cum laude, Harvard, 1949. Admitted to N.Y. State bar, 1949; asso. firm Greenman, Shea, Sandomire & Zimet, N.Y.C., 1949-51; atty. Office Price Stblzn., Washington, 1951-52; div. counsel Sylvania Elec. Products, Inc., N.Y.C., 1952-57; sec., gen. counsel Sylvania Corning Nuclear Corp., N.Y.C., 1957-60; asso. counsel Gen. Dynamics Corp., N.Y.C., 1960-63; partner firm Kaey Scholer Fierman Hays & Handler, Paris and N.Y.C., 1963-66; v.p. corp. affairs, gen. counsel Revlon, Inc., N.Y.C., 1966-71; partner firm Finley Kumble Underberg Persky & Roth, 1971-73, Cohen & Sandler, N.Y.C., 1973-74, Poletti Freidin Prashker Feldman & Gartner, N.Y.C., 1974—. Trustee Central Synagogue, N.Y.C., 1971—; trustee asso. YM-YWHA's of Greater N.Y., 1972—. Mem. Am. Bar Assn., Assn. Bar City N.Y., Columbia Coll., Harvard Law Sch. alumni assns., Phi Beta Kappa, Zeta Beta Tau. Editorial bd. Harvard Law Rev., 1947-49. Home: 945 Fifth Ave New York City NY 10021 Office: 1185 Ave of the Americas New York City NY 10036 Tel (212) 730-7373

COHEN, IRWIN ROBERT, b. Balt., Sept. 4, 1924; LL.B., U. Balt., 1948. Admitted to Md. bar, 1948; partner firm Cohen & Dackman, Balt., 1952—. Mem. Am., Md. bar assns. Home: 10807 Baronet Rd Owings Mills MD 21117 Office: 19 W Mount Royal Ave Baltimore MD 21201 Tel (301) 332-0222

COHEN, ISRAEL GOODMAN, b. Manchester, Eng., Jan. 1, 1910; J.D., Detroit Coll. Law, 1931. Admitted to Mich. bar, 1931, U.S. Circuit Ct. Appeals bar, 1946, U.S. Supreme Ct. bar, 1965; individual practice law, Detroit, 1931—. Mem. Detroit Bar Assn. (dir. 1975—), State Bar Mich. (assemblyman 1973—, chmn. com. hearings), Mich. (pres. 1959-60), Am. trial lawyers assns., Am. Judicature Soc. Co-author: Detroit Lawyer Federal Trade Commn. Laws of Book Publishers, 1976. Office: 211-214 Ford Bldg Detroit MI 48226 Tel (313) 961-1509

COHEN, JERRY, b. N.Y.C., June 5, 1935; B. in Mech. Engring., Rensselaer Polytech. Inst., 1957; J.D., George Washington U., 1962. Admitted to D.C. bar, 1962, Mass. Bar, 1963; patent examiner Dept. Commerce, Washington, 1957-62; patent atty. Norton Co., Cambridge, Mass., 1962-71; mem. firm Heiken & Cohen, Waltham, Mass., 1971—. Mem. Am., Mass. (bd. dels.) bar assns., Boston Patent Law Assn., ACLU (treas. Mass.). Home: 50 Court St Newton MA 02160 Office: 470 Totten Pond Rd Waltham MA 02154 Tel (617) 890-0110

COHEN, JOEL J., b. N.Y.C., Feb. 8, 1938; B.B.A., Coll. City N.Y., 1959; J.D., Harvard, 1962. Admitted to N.Y. bar, 1963, U.S. Supreme Ct. bar, 1973; with firm Davis Polk & Wardwell, N.Y.C., 1963—, mem., 1969—. Mem. Am. Bar Assn., Bar Assn. City N.Y., Am. Law Inst. Home: 110 East End Ave New York City NY 10028 Office: 1 Chase Manhattan Plaza New York City NY 10005 Tel (212) 422-3400

COHEN, JON STEPHAN, b. Omaha, Nov. 9, 1943; B.A., Claremont Men's Coll., 1965; postgrad. London Sch. Econs., 1963-64; LL.B., Harvard, 1968. Admitted to Ariz. bar, 1968; partnr firm Snell & Wilmer, Phoenix, 1973—. Bd. mgrs. Phoenix YMCA, 1975—. Mem. Ariz., Maricopa County, Phoenix bar assns. Home: 5421 Via Buena Vista Paradise Valley AZ 85253 Office: 3100 Valley Center Phoenix AZ 85073 Tel (602) 257-7211

COHEN, LAWRENCE STEPHEN, b. Boston, Apr. 21, 1939; B.S. in Mech. Engring., Northeastern U., 1962; J.D., Boston U., 1965; spl. student Harvard Law Sch., 1965. Admitted to Mass. bar, 1966, Ill. bar, 1975; with W.R. Grace & Co., Cambridge, Mass., 1968-71; individual practice law, Boston, 1971-73; counsel TRW Inc., Elk Grove, Ill., 1973—. Mem. Framingham, Mass. Town Meeting, 1973; mem. lawyers panel ACLU. Mem. Boston, Ill., Mass., Am., Chgo. bar assns., Am. patent Law Assn. Home: 2958 N Pine Grove St Chicago IL 60614 Office: 1500 Morse Ave Elk Grove IL 60007 Tel (312) 439-8800

COHEN, LEONARD, b. Bklyn., Oct. 3, 1929; A.A., George Washington U., 1961; LL.B., Massey Law Coll., 1970. Admitted to Ga. bar, 1971; individual practice law, Jonesboro, Ga., 1971—; instr. adult edn. Clayton Jr. Coll., Morrow, Ga., 1971—; solicitor, pro hac vice, State Ct. of Clayton County (Ga.), 1975—, judge, pro hac vice, 1976—. Mem. Am., Clayton County, Atlanta bar assns. Office: 112 Smith St Jonesboro GA 30237 Tel (404) 478-2511

COHEN, LEONARD NATHAN, b. N.Y.C., Dec. 22, 1920; B.Social Scis., Coll. City N.Y. N.Y., 1942; LL.B., Columbia, 1949. Admitted to N.Y. bar 1950; Practiced in N.Y.C., 1950-55, 61; law sec. to justice N.Y. Supreme Ct., N.Y. County, N.Y.C., 1955-60; dep. commr. N.Y.C. Marine and Aviation, 1962-65; dep. pres. Borough of Manhattan (N.Y.), 1966-72; judge N.Y.C. Civil Ct., 1973—; acting justice N.Y. State Supreme Ct., 1975; Bronx County Criminal Part, 1976. Mem. Bar Assn. City N.Y., New York County Lawyers Assn., N.Y. State Trial Lawyers Assn. Home: 241 Central Park West New York NY 10024 Office: Civil Courthouse 111 Centre St New York City NY 10013 Tel (212) 374-8063

COHEN, LEWIS ISAAC, b. N.Y.C., July 27, 1932; B.A., U. Calif. at Los Angeles, 1953; LL.B., Columbia U., 1958. Admitted to N.Y. bar, 1959, D.C. bar, 1964, U.S. Supreme Ct. bar, 1966; atty. FCC, Washington, 1959-60, 61-64, CBS, N.Y.C., 1960-61; partner firm Cohen and Berfield, Washington, 1964—. Mem., Fed., D.C., Fed. Communications bar assns. Home: 6315 Swords Way Bethesda MD 20034 Office: 1129-20th St NW Washington DC 20036 Tel (202) 466-8565

COHEN, LOUIS HARMON, b. N.Y.C., Jan. 14, 1912; LL.B., George Washington U., 1936, LL.M., 1937, M.P.L., 1937. Admitted to D.C. bar, 1938, Md. bar, 1950; practiced in Washington, 1938-72, Silver Spring, Md., 1950-72; domestic relation master Md. Circuit Ct. for Montgomery County, 1972—; guest lectr. Am. U. Law Sch., 1975. Mem. Montgomery County (Md.) Revenue Authority, 1960-66. Mem. D.C., Md. State, Montgomery County bar assns. Author: Poetic Potshots at Preachers and People, 1977. Home: 10000 McKenney Ave Silver Spring MD 20902 Office: Montgomery County Circuit Ct for State of Md Rockville MD 20850 Tel (301) 279-8257

COHEN, MANUEL FREDERICK, b. Bklyn., Oct. 9, 1912; B.S., Bklyn. Coll., 1933; LL.B., Bklyn. Law Sch., 1936, also LL.D. (hon.); LL.D. (hon.), Babson Inst., 1968; D.H.L. (hon.), Hebrew Union Coll., 1969. Admitted to N.Y. State bar, 1937, D.C. bar, 1964; staff SEC, 1942-61, mem. commn., 1961-69, chmn., 1964-69; partner firm Wilmer, Cutler & Pickering, 1969—; professorial lectr. in law, George Washington U., 1958—; mem. Council of Adminstrv. Conf. of U.S., 1961-69, 74—; chmn. Commn. on Auditors Responsibilities, 1974—; advisor Am. Law Inst.; mem. bd. editors N.Y. Law Jour. Chmn. advisory bd. Bur. of Nat. Affairs. Mem. Am., Fed., D.C., Internat. bar assns., Assn. Bar City N.Y., Am. Law Inst., Am. Soc. of Internat. Law, Am. Acad. of Polit. and Social Sci., Am. Judicature Soc., Internat. Bar, Order of Coif. Recipient Rockefeller Pub. Service award, Trustees of Princeton U., 1956, Career Service award, Nat. Civil Service League, 1961, Distinguished Service award, SEC, 1965, Brotherhood award, Nat. Conf. of Christians and Jews, 1965; contbr. articles to legal jours. Home: 6403 Marjory Ln Bethesda MD 20034 Office: 1666 K St NW Washington DC 20006 Tel (202) 872-6300

COHEN, MARK PHILIP, b. Balt., Mar. 27, 1946; B.A., U. Md., 1967, J.D., 1970; postgrad. U. Va., Spring 1972, U. San Diego spring 1973, George Washington Law Sch., spring 1974. Admitted to Md. bar, 1971; atty. office of counsel C.E. U.S. Army, Balt. Dist., 1971-75; asst. state's atty. for Balt. City, 1975—. Mem. staff div. young lawyers Asso. Jewish Charities, Balt., 1974—. Mem. Md. State, Am. bar assns. Home: 21 E Centre St Baltimore MD 21202 Office: Room 503 Courthouse Fastte & Calvert Sts Baltimore MD 21202 Tel (301) 396-5020

COHEN, MARVIN SANFORD, b. Akron, Ohio, Oct. 16, 1931; B.A., U. Ariz., 1953, LL.B. (Pima County Bar Aux. scholar), 1957. Admitted to Ariz. bar, 1957; asso. firm Udall & Udall, Tucson, 1957; dep. atty., Pima County, 1958, chief civil dep. atty., 1959-60; 1st asst. city atty., Tucson, 1961; spl. asst. to solicitor Dept. Interior, Washington, 1961-63; asso. firm Bilby, Shoenhair, Warnock & Dolph, Tucson, 1963—; sec. Ariz. Legal Services. Pres. B'nai B'rith Lodge 763, 1957-58; past chmn. young adult div. Combined Jewish Appeal; mem. exec. bd. Jewish Family Service; pres. Tucson Jewish Community Center, 1967-69; chmn. community relations com. Anti-defamation League, 1961, chmn. state league, 1970-73; active Tucson Pub. Sch.'s Com. of 100, UN Assn., Tucson Council for Civic Unity, ACLU; chmn. Interorganizational Mcpl. Pub. Accomodations Com. for Tucson, 1960; asst. cubmaster Pack 122, Boy Scouts Am.; chmn. United Way Guidelines Com., 1972, United Way Planning and Allocations Com., 1973; pres. Ariz. Civic Theatre, 1972-73, 74-75;

pres. Young Democrats Greater Tucson, 1959, Young Dem. Clubs Ariz., 1960; chmn. Pima County Dem. Central Com., 1960; pres. Democrats for Better Govt., 1964; chmn. Ariz. Dem. Telethon Com., 1974; bd. dirs. Tucson Regional Plan; mem. Ariz. Commn. Arts and Humanities; mem. Citizens' Advisory Water Com., Tucson; mem. Citizens' Utilities Advisory Com., also chmn. subcom. rate structures. Mem. Am. Bd. Trial Advs., Am., Ariz. (co-chmn. group and prepaid legal services com.), Pima County bar assns., Phi Beta Kappa, Zeta Beta Tau, Phi Kappa Phi. Recipient Thomas E. Campbell Meml. award U. Ariz., 1950; named Young Man of Year, Bd. Edn., Temple Emmanuel, 1966. Home: 4645 E San Carlos Pl Tucson AZ 85712 Office: 9th Floor Valley Nat Bldg Tucson AZ 85701 Tel (602) 792-4800

COHEN, MELVIN FREDERICK, b. London, Ont., Can., June 28, 1930; A.B., U. Mich., 1951; LL.B., J.D., Harvard U., 1954. Admitted to Calif. bar, 1962; individual practice law, Santa Ana, Calif., 1963-75, Newport Beach, Calif., 1975—; mem. preliminary investigation com. State Bar Calif. Bd. dirs. Orange County chpt. ARC, 1969-76, chmn.; mem. Tustin (Calif.) Park and Recreation Commn., 1965-66. Mem. Orange County, Am. bar assns., Calif. State Bar, Am., Calif. trial lawyers assns., Comml. Law League Am. (council western region). Recipient Lion of Year award, 1976. Office: 1201 Dove St Suite 440 Newport Beach CA 92660 Tel (714) 833-3332

COHEN, MILTON HOWARD, b. Milw., Aug. 9, 1911; A.B., Harvard U., 1932, LL.B., 1935. Admitted to Wis. bar, 1935, Ill. bar, 1947, U.S. Supreme Ct. bar, 1960; with SEC, 1935-46, 61-63; dir. spl. study securities markets, 1961-63; partner firm Schiff, Hardin & Waite, Chgo., 1947-61, 63—; vis. prof. Harvard Law Sch., 1966-67; mem. adv. com. instl. investor study SEC, 1969-71; mem. adv. council U. Pa. Center for Study Fin. Instns.; mem. nat. market adv. bd. SEC. Fellow Am. Bar Found.; mem. Am. Bar Assn., Am. Law Inst. (cons. Fed. Securities Code project), Phi Beta Kappa. Home: 1320 N State Pkwy Chicago IL 60610 Office: 233 S Wacker Dr Chicago IL 60606 Tel (312) 876-1000

COHEN, MURRY BERNIS, b. Houston, Dec. 14, 1945; B.A., George Washington U., 1967; J.D., U. Tex., 1972. Admitted to Tex. bar, 1972, since practiced in Houston; asso. firm Saccomanno, Clegg, Martin & Kipple, Houston, 1972; asst. dist. atty. Harris County (Tex.), 1973-74; individual practice law, 1975—; cons. div. profl. edn. Am. Bar Assn., 1976; lectr. profl. courses. Bd. dirs. Houston chpt. B'nai B'rith Anti-Defamation League, 1975-76. Mem. Houston Bar Assn., Harris County (dir. 1975-76), Tex. criminal def. lawyers assns. Contbr. articles to Tex. Tech Law Rev., 1975. Office: 723 Main St Suite 400 Houston TX 77002 Tel (713) 225-9571

COHEN, MYRON DAVID, b. Boston, May 19, 1935; B.A., Harvard, 1957, LL.B., 1960. Admitted to Mass. bar, 1960, N.Y. bar, 1963; asso. firm Conboy, Hewitt, O'Brien & Boardman, N.Y.C., 1962-69, partner, 1970—. Mem. Assn. Bar City N.Y. Office: 20 Exchange Pl New York City NY 10005 Tel (212) DI4-3131

COHEN, NATHAN JEROLD, b. Pine Bluff, Ark., June 13, 1935; B.B.A., Tulane U., 1957; LL.B., Harvard U., 1961. Admitted to Ga. bar, 1966, N.Y. State bar, 1962, D.C. bar, 1966; asso. firm Cleary, Gottlieb, Steen & Hamilton, N.Y.C., 1961-65, Sutherland, Asbill & Brennan, Atlanta, 1965—; asso. prof. Emory U. Sch. Law, 1967—; lectr. in field. Mem. Community Relations Commn. Atlanta, 1975-76, chmn., 1977—; bd. dirs. ACLU, Atlanta, 1970—, pres., 1973-74; mem. exec. com. Met. Atlanta Lawyers Com. Civil Rights under Law, 1969. Mem. Am. Bar Assn. (vice chmn. com. taxation and its relations to individual right 1976, vice chmn. corp. stockholder relationships com. 1976—), Ga., D.C. bars, Lawyers Club Atlanta. Contbr. articles to legal jours. Office: 3100 1st Nat Bank Tower Atlanta GA Tel (404) 658-8700

COHEN, PHILIP MEYER, b. Los Angeles, Oct. 28, 1947; B.A. in Psychology, San Diego State U., 1969; J.D., U. Calif., Los Angeles, 1972. Student intern Citizen's Communication Center, Washington, 1972; admitted to Calif. bar, 1972; staff atty. Defenders, Inc., San Diego, Calif., 1973—. Mem. San Diego County Bar Assn. Mem. U. Calif. at Los Angeles Law Rev. Office: 1140 Union St San Diego CA 92101 Tel (714) 234-8741

COHEN, ROBERT BERNARD, b. Scranton, Pa., Feb. 13, 1933; A.B., Dickinson Coll., 1954; LL.B., U. Pa., 1957. Admitted to Conn. bar, 1957, U.S. Supreme Ct. bar, 1974; asso. firm Cole & Cole, Hartford, Conn., 1957-63; sr. mem. firm Wilson, Asbel & Channin, Hartford, 1963—. Chmn. W. Hartford (Conn.) Zoning Bd. Appeals, 1975-76. Mem. Am., Conn., Hartford County bar assns. Home: 66 Whetten Rd West Hartford CT 06117 Office: 100 Constitution Plaza Hartford CT 06103 Tel (203) 249-8561

COHEN, ROBERT SAWYER; b. Winthrop, Mass., Oct. 5, 1944; B.A. cum laude Northeastern U., 1967; LL.B., cum laude, Boston Coll., 1970. Admitted to Mass., U.S. Dist. Ct. bars, 1970; partner firm Shenfield & Cohen, Boston, 1970—. Mem. Boston Bar Assn. Recipient Bancroft-Whitney award for Excellence, 1969. Home: 201 Weir St Extension Hingham MA 02043 Office: 31 Fairfield St Boston MA 02116 Tel (617) 782-2860

COHEN, SAUL, b. Los Angeles, June 19, 1927; B.A., U. Calif., Los Angeles, 1950; J.D., Stanford, 1953. Admitted to Calif. bar, 1954, N.Mex. bar, 1971, U.S. Supreme Ct. bar, 1971; practiced law, Beverly Hills, Calif. and Los Angeles, 1954-70; partner firm Selvin & Cohen, 1963-70; partner firm Olmsted & Cohen, Santa Fe, N.Mex., 1971—; lectr. Loyola U. Law Sch., Los Angeles, 1967-70. Mem. Santa Fe Mayor's City Action Com., 1970-74; trustee Inner City Cultural Center, Los Angeles, 1965-69, Community TV So. Calif., 1963-70, Friends of Santa Fe Pub. Library, 1974-76, Santa Fe Prep. Sch., 1974-76, Santa Fe Concert Assn., 1974-76, Santa Fe Pub. Library, 1975-76, Mus. of N.Mex. Found., 1975—, Guadalupe Hist. Found., 1975—; chmn. bd. trustees Old Santa Fe Assn., 1972-75; pres. Friends of U. Calif. Los Angeles Library, 1968-70. Mem. Am., 1st Jud. Dist. bar assns., Am. Arbitration Assn. (mem. N.Mex. adv. council 1971—), N.Mex. State Bar, State Bar Calif. Author: (with John Hogan) An Author's Guide to Scholarly Publishing and the Law, 1965; also numerous articles and essays. Home: Route 4 Box 1-A Santa Fe NM 87501 Office: PO Box 877 237 E Palace Ave Santa Fe NM 87501 Tel (505) 982-3595

COHEN, SEYMOUR, b. Chgo., Sept. 27, 1917; B.S., U. Ind., 1939, J.D., 1941. Admitted to Ind. bar, 1941, Ill. bar, 1948, U.S. Supreme Ct. bar, 1971; atty. NLRB, Washington, 1946-47; individual practice law, Chgo., 1947-53; partner firm Dorfman, DeKoven & Cohen, Chgo., 1953—. Mem. Northbrook (Ill.) Library Bd., 1963-69, pres., 1965-67. Mem. Chgo., Am. bar assns. Contbr. articles to legal jours. Office: One IBM Plaza Suite 3301 Chicago IL 60611 Tel (312) 467-9800

COHEN, SHELDON P., b. Balt., Jan. 11; B.S., Johns Hopkins U., 1960; J.D., U. Md., 1964; M.S., George Washington U., 1968. Admitted to Md. bar, 1964; partner J.K. Lasser & Co., Balt., 1953—. Mem. Am. Bar Assn., Md. Assn. C.P.A.'s. Office: 19A Hamill Rd Baltimore MD 21210 Tel (301) 323-3935

COHEN, SHELDON STANLEY, b. Washington, June 28, 1927; A.B. with spl. honors, George Washington U., 1950, J.D. with highest honors (Charles W. Dorsey scholar), 1952; D.Litt. (hon), Lincoln Coll., 1973. Admitted to D.C. bar, 1952, U.S. Tax Ct. bar, 1956, U.S. Ct. Claims bar, 1969, U.S. Supreme Ct. bar, 1956; legis. atty., chief counsel's office IRS, Washington, 1952-56; asso. firm Paul, Weiss, Rifkind, Wharton and Garrison, Washington, 1956-60; partner firm Arnold, Fortas and Porter, Washington, 1960-63; chief counsel IRS, Washington, 1963-65, commr., 1965-69; partner firm Cohen and Uretz, Washington, 1969—; lectr. Howard U., 1957-58; adj. prof. law U. Miami (Fla.), 1974—; professorial lectr. George Washington U., 1958—. Pres. Jewish Social Service Agy., 1970-72; v.p. Jewish Community Found., 1970-74 Jewish Community Center, 1968-70; pres. Am. Israel Tax Found., 1969—; gen. counsel Dem. Nat. Com., 1972-77, spl. tax. counsel, 1969-72; bd. regents Omar N. Bradley Found., U.S. Army Historic Collection, 1970-73; bd. overseers Jewish Tech. Sem., 1972—; trustee B'nai B'rith Found. U.S.; dir. Jewish Welfare Bd., chmn. pub. affairs com., 1969-74; bd. dirs. United Jewish Appeal for D.C. Mem. Am., D.C., Fed. bar assns., Inter-Am. Center Tax Adminstrs., D.C. Inst. C.P.A.'s. Contbr. articles to profl. jours. Home: 5518 Trent St Chevy Chase MD 20015 Office: 1775 K St NW Washington DC 20036 Tel (202) 293-4740

COHEN, SYLVAN M., b. Phila., July 28, 1914; B.A., U. Pa., 1935, LL.B., 1938. Admitted to Pa. bar, 1939; sr. enforcement atty. Office of Price Adminstrn., Washington, 1941-42; sr. partner firm Cohen, Shapiro, Polisher, Shiekman and Cohen, Phila., 1939—; pres., trustee Pa. Real Estate Investment Trust, Wyncote, 1960—; dir. Indsl. Valley Bank & Trust Co., FPA Corp. Mem. chmn.'s com., trustee United Way, 1963—; pres. Fedn. Jewish Agys. Greater Phila., 1967-70, trustee, 1955—, co-chmn. 75th anniversary com., 1976, chmn. bldg. fund, 1974—; gen. chmn. Phila. Allied Jewish Appeal, 1965; chmn. Israel 25th Anniversary Com. for Greater Phila., 1973; v.p., trustee Albert Einstein Med. Center, 1965-70. Mem. Am., Fed., Pa., Phila. bar assns., Am. Arbitration Assn., Social-Legal Club, Phila. Lawyers Club, Nat. Assn. Real Estate Investment Trusts, (pres. 1976-77), Internat. Council Shopping Centers, Inc. (pres. 1976-77). Contbr. articles to legal jours. Home: C-1014 Cedarbrook Hill III Wyncote PA 19095 Office: 12 S 12th St Rm 2200 Philadelphia PA 19107 Tel (215) WA2-1300

COHEN, WALLACE M., b. Norton, Va., July 11, 1908; Sc.B., Harvard U., 1929, postgrad., 1929-31; LL.B., Cornell U., 1932. Admitted to Mass. bar 1933, D.C. bar 1945, U.S. Supreme Ct. bar, 1945, Md. bar 1955; mem. staff NLRB, Washington, 1938-39, Dept. Labor, Washington, 1939-40; mem. adv. commn. Counsel Nat. Defense, Washington, 1940-41; regional atty. and adminstr. Office Price Adminstrn., Washington, 1941-43; asst. dir. liberated areas Lend Lease Adminstrn., Washington, 1943-45; partner firm Fox, Orlov & Cowin, Washington, 1946-48, Landis, Cohen, Singman and Rauh, and predecessors, 1948—. Mem. adv. bd. Clinch Valley Coll. U. Va., 1972-75; mem. Montgomery County (Md.) Housing Authority, 1965-70; bd. dirs. Am. Jewish Com., 1965. Mem. Am., Mass., D.C., Fed. Bar assns., Fed. Communications Bar Assn., Harvard Club. D.C. Recipient Brandeis U. fellowship, 1947. Author: Unravelments, 1955. Home: 2444 Massachusetts Ave NW Washington DC 20008 Office: 1910 Sunderland Pl NW Washington DC 20036 Tel (202) 785-2020

COHILL, MAURICE BLANCHARD, JR., b. Pitts., Nov. 26, 1929; A.B., Princeton, 1951; LL.B., U. Pitts., 1956. Admitted to Pa. bar, 1957; asso. firm Kirkpatrick, Pomeroy, Lockhart & Johnson, Pitts., 1957-65; judge Juvenile Ct. Allegheny County (Pa.), 1965-68, Ct. Common Pleas Allegheny County, 1969-75, U.S. Dist. Ct., Western Dist. Pa., 1976—; chmn. bd. fellows Nat. Center Juvenile Justice. Active, United Cerebral Palsy Assn. Pitts.; bd. dirs. Shadyside and Kay boys' clubs. Mem. Am., Pa., Allegheny County bar assns., Am. Judicature Soc., Nat. Council Juvenile Ct. Judges. Contbr. articles to profl. jours. Home: 9 Oxford Rd Ben Avon Heights Pittsburgh PA 15202 Office: 733 US Courthouse Pittsburgh PA 15219 Tel (412) 644-6482

COHN, ALICE W., b. N.Y.C., Sept. 2; LL.B., Blackstone Coll. Law, 1948; LL.M., Woodrow Wilson Coll. Law, 1950. Admitted to Ga. bar, 1949; individual practice law, Atlanta. Mem. State Bar Ga., Comml. Law League Am. Office: Alice W Cohn 1052 Hurt Bldg Atlanta GA 30303 Tel (404) 522-9116

COHN, FREDERICK FLOYD, b. N.Y.C., July 2, 1938; A.B., U. Chgo., 1959, J.D., 1962. Admitted to Ill. bar, 1962; U.S. Supreme Ct. bar, 1973; law clk. judge Appellate Ct., Chgo., 1962-63; asso. firm Klein & Thorpe, Chgo., 1963-64; asst. pub. defender Cook County, Chgo., 1964-67; chief atty. North Office Cook County Legal Assistance Found., Evanston, Ill., 1967-68; individual practice law Chgo., 1968-76; dep. dir. tng. and hiring Criminal Def. Consortium of Cook County, Chgo., 1976; dir. Woodlawn Community Defender Office Criminal Defense Consortium of Cook County, Chgo., 1976—; instr. John Marshall Law Sch., Chgo., 1968-75; clin. fellow U. Chgo. Law Sch., 1976-77. Bd. dirs. Edgewater Community Council, Chgo., 1973-77; Central Synagogue, Chgo., 1970-77. Mem. Am., Ill. State, Chgo. bar assns., Chgo. Council Lawyers, Assn. Def. Lawyers, Pub. Defender Assn. Office: 35 E Wacker Dr Chicago IL 60601 Tel (312) 641-0692

COHN, MARCUS, b. Omaha, Sept. 20, 1913; A.B., U. Chgo., 1935, J.D. cum laude, 1938; LL.M., Harvard U., 1940. Admitted to Okla. bar, 1938, D.C. bar, 1949, U.S. Supreme Ct. bar, 1949; mem. staff law dept. FCC, Washington, 1940-44; partner firm Cohn & Marks, Washington, 1944—; lectr. George Washington Law Center, 1967—. Bd. dirs. Greater Washington Ednl. TV Assn., Washington Theater Club, Am. Jewish Com., Arena Stage, Friends Folger Library. Mem. Am. Bar Assn. Contbr. articles to legal jours., popular mags. Home: 4031 Oliver St Chevy Chase MD 20015 Office: 1920 L St NW Washington DC 20036 Tel (202) 293-3860

COHN, MARTIN DAVID, b. Hazleton, Pa., Aug. 31, 1925; B.A., Pa. State U., 1954; LL.B., Harvard, 1950. Admitted to Pa. bar, 1951, U.S. Supreme Ct. bar, 1959; practiced in Hazleton, 1951—; asso. firm James P. Costello, Jr., 1951-53, partner firm Laputka, Bayless, Ecker & Cohn, 1953-72, stockholder, 1973—; spl. asst. atty. gen. Commonwealth of Pa. 1955-63. Pres. Greater Hazleton C. of C. 1969-71; nat. chmn. common. adult Jewish edn. B'nai B'rith, 1971-77; bd. dirs. Jewish Theol. Sem. Am., N.Y.C., 1972—. Mem. Lower Luzerne County, Pa., Am. bar assns., Wilkes-Barre Law and Library Assn. Home: 100 Harding Hazleton PA 18201 Office: 605 Citizens Bank Bldg Hazleton PA 18201 Tel (717) 455-4731

COHN, MELVIN EDWARD, b. San Francisco, Jan. 23, 1917; A.B., U. Calif., 1937, J.D., 1940. Admitted to Calif. bar, 1941; atty. FSA, Washington, 1940-42; partner firm Aaronson, Cohn & Dickerson, San Carlos, Calif., 1946-63; judge Municipal Ct., Redwood City, Calif., 1963-64, Superior Ct., San Mateo County, Redwood City, 1964—; city atty. San Carlos, 1956-63; chmn. Calif. Jud. Criminal Planning Commn., 1975—; lectr. in field. Mem. Calif. Jud. Council (chmn. ct. mgmt. com. 1973-77), Calif. Council Criminal Justice, San Mateo Bar Assn. (pres. 1959), Nat. Conf. Conciliation Cts. (pres. 1970-71), San Carlos C. of C. (pres. 1951). Contbr. articles in field to legal jours. Home: 731 Knoll Dr San Carlos CA 94070 Office: Hall of Justice Redwood City CA 94061 Tel (415) 364-5600

COHN, MILTON LEONARD, b. Bridgeport, Conn., May 4, 1915; B.A., Yale, 1936, LL.B., 1939. Admitted to Conn. bar, 1939; partner firm Bartlett, Keeler & Cohn, Bridgeport, 1939—. Mem. Conn., Bridgeport bar assns., Conn. Estate and Tax Planning Council. Home: 150 Parkwood Rd Fairfield CT 06430 Office: 855 Main St Bridgeport CT 06604 Tel (203) 334-4141

COHN, ROY MARCUS, b. N.Y.C., Feb. 20, 1927; A.B., Columbia Coll., 1946; LL.B., Columbia, 1947. Admitted to N.Y. bar, 1948; asst. U.S. atty. So. Dist. N.Y., 1948-52; spl. asst. to U.S. Atty. Gen. for internal security, Washington, 1952; chief counsel U.S. Senate Investigating Com., Washington, 1952-54; partner firm Curran, Mahoney, Cohn & Stim, N.Y.C., 1954-59; partner firm Saxe, Bacon & Bolan, N.Y.C., 1959—; adj. prof. law, N.Y. Law Sch. Regent St. Francis Coll., 1960—. Mem. Am., Bronx County bar assns. Author: McCarthy, 1968; A Fool for a Client, 1971; McCarthy: The Answer to Tail-Gunner Joe, 1977; recipient annual award Lawyers div. Fedn. Jewish Philanthropies, 1952, Americanism award Am. Legion, 1958, Patriotism award Cath. War Vets., 1975, Patriot award VFW, 1963. Home: Witherell Dr Greenwich CT 06830 Office: 39 E 68th St New York City NY 10021 Tel (212) 472-1400

COKER, DAVID LEE, b. Sumter, S.C., Mar. 16, 1936; A.B., Emory U., 1957, LL.B., 1964. Admitted to Ga. bar, 1964; partner firm King & Spalding, Atlanta, 1964—. Pres. bd. sponsors Alliance Theatre, Atlanta, 1973—; vice chmn. Atlanta Arts Alliance, 1974—; mem. Leadership Atlanta, 1976—. Mem. Am., Atlanta bar assns., State Bar Ga., Lawyers Club of Atlanta. Home: 2489 Montview Dr NW Atlanta GA 30305 Office: 2500 Trust Co Tower Atlanta GA 30303 Tel (404) 572-4600

COKER, JOHN DIAZ, b. San Diego, Feb. 8, 1938; B.A., San Diego State Coll., 1961; LL.D., Golden Gate Coll., 1967. Admitted to Calif. bar, 1967; directing atty. Contra Costa Legal Services Found., Pittsburg, Calif., 1968-71, interim dir., 1976-77; individual practice law, Pittsburg, 1971—; asst. dean Sch. Law Lincoln U., 1976—; instr. law. John F. Kennedy U.; instr. polit. sci. Diablo Valley Coll., 1970-73. Pres. Pittsburg Unified Sch. Dist. Bd. Edn., 1973-77. Mem. Mexican-Am. Bar Assn. Calif., Assn. Mexican-Am. Educators, Mexican-Am. Sch. Bd. Mems., Am., Contra Costa County bar assns., ACLU (legal com. 1968-70). Home: 3788 Enea Dr Pittsburgh CA 94565 Office: 509 Railroad Ave Pittsburg CA 94565 Tel (415) 432-7373

COLANGELO, LOUIS J., JR., b. Bridgeport, Conn., May 7, 1945; A.B., U. Dayton, 1967; J.D., U. Conn., 1970. Admitted to bar; asso. firm Carroll, Land and Reed, Norwalk, Conn., 1970-75, partner, 1976—. Mem. Conn., Am., Norwalk-Wilton (law day chmn. 1975) bar assns. Home: 191 Applegate Rd Fairfield CT 06430 Office: 10 River St Plaza Norwalk CT 06852 Tel (203) 853-6565

COLAPIETRO, BRUNO, b. Endicott, N.Y., Aug. 11, 1935; B.A., Hamilton Coll., 1957; J.D., Cornell U., 1960. Admitted to N.Y. bar, 1960; atty. U.S. Dept. Justice, Washington, 1960-61; partner firm Chernin & Gold, Binghamton, N.Y., 1961—; adj. faculty Cornell U. Law Sch., 1970—; St. Univ. N.Y., Binghamton, 1971—. Pres. Endwell (N.Y.) Rotary Club, 1973; mem. Broome County Bd. Ethics, 1975—; dir. Broome County Mental Health Assn., 1962—. Fellow Am. Acad. Matrimonial Lawyers; mem. Am., N.Y., Broome County (v.p. 1976—) bar assns. Contbr. articles in field to law reviews. Home: 2723 Hamilton Dr Endicott NY 13760 Office: 71 State St Binghamton NY 13902 Tel (607) 723-9581

COLASURD, DONALD MICHAEL, b. Navarre, Ohio, Mar. 31, 1930; B.S. in Commerce, Ohio U., Athens, 1953; LL.B., Cleve.-Marshall Law Sch., 1960. Admitted to Ohio bar, 1960; spl. agt. FBI, 1961-63; asst. atty. gen. State of Ohio, 1963-67, chief workmen's compensation sect. Atty. Gen.'s Office, Columbus, 1964-66, 1st asst., 1967—. Mem. Am., Ohio, Columbus bar assns., Am. Trial Lawyers Assn., Lawyers Club. Home: 685 Chaffin Ridge St Columbus OH 43214 Office: Suite 720 37 W Broad St Columbus OH 43215 Tel (614) 221-0170

COLAVITA, ANTHONY JOSEPH, b. Bronxville, N.Y., Nov. 10, 1935; A.B., Fairfield U., 1957; J.D., Fordham U., 1960. Admitted to N.Y. bar, 1961, U.S. Supreme Ct. bar, 1968; asso. firm Abberley, Kloiman, Amon & Marcellino, N.Y.C., 1960-65; individual practice law, Scarsdale, N.Y., 1965-76, Eastchester, N.Y., 1976—; dep. town atty. Town of Eastchester, 1965-69, town atty., 1969-70, town supr., 1970—. Chmn. drive Eastchester Heart Fund, 1973-76; treas. Eastchester Fire Dist., 1970-75. Mem. Eastchester (pres. 1970-71), Westchester County (N.Y.), N.Y. State, Am. bar assns., Am. Arbitration Assn. (panel arbitrators). Recipient Man of Year award Eastchester C. of C., 1972, Kiwanian of Year award Eastchester Kiwanis Club, 1974, Man of Year award Westchester-Putnam Counties B'nai B'rith, 1974. Office: 575 White Plains Rd Eastchester NY 10707 Tel (914) 793-1222

COLBERT, JOE, b. Columbia, Miss., Apr. 1, 1935; B.S., U. Ala., 1958; LL.B., U. Tex., 1964. Admitted to Tex. bar, 1964; since practiced in Austin, former mem. firm Garey, Colbert & Kidd, now mem. firm Colbert & Mullen. Mem. Tex., Travis County (dir. 1969-70), Austin Jr. (dir. 1966-68) bar assns., Am., Tex. (dir. 1971—) trial lawyers assns. Home: 1804 Vista Ln Austin TX 78703 Office: 115 E 5th St Austin TX 78701 Tel (512) 477-6111

COLBERT, WILLIAM LEE, JR., b. Louisville, June 22, 1944; B.E.E., Miss. State U., 1967; J.D., U. Miss., 1973. Admitted to Miss. bar, 1973; partner firm Satterfield, Allred & Colbert, Jackson, Miss., 1976—; instr. Jackson Sch. Law, 1974-75. Mem. Assn. Trial Lawyers Am., Am., Miss., Hinds County, Jackson Jr. bar assns. Mem. staff Miss. Law Jour., 1973. Home: 940 Bellevue #106 Jackson MS 39202 Office: 1000 Bankers Trust Plaza Bldg Jackson MS 39205 Tel (601) 354-2540

COLBURN, ARCHIE LAMAR, b. Ft. Worth, May 6, 1938; B.A., U. Tex., 1960, LL.B., 1968. Admitted to Tex. bar, 1968; atty. Coastal States Gas Producing Co., 1968-71; asso. firm Porter, Taylor &

Gonzales, Corpus Christi, Tex., 1971-73; partner firm Porter, Taylor, Gonzalez, Thompson & Rogers, Corpus Christi, 1973—. Mem. Tex., Nueces County bar assns. Office: 1800 Guaranty Bank Plaza Corpus Christi TX 78401 Tel (512) 883-6351

COLBURN, JAMES ALLAN, b. Huntington, W.Va., July 5, 1942; A.B., Davidson Coll., 1964; J.D., Rutgers, 1967; postgrad. Marshall U., 1970-72. Admitted to W.Va. bar, 1970, U.S. 4th Circuit Ct. bar, 1974; asso. firm Levy & Patton, Huntington, 1970-72; individual practice law, Huntington, 1973-75; partner firm Baer, Napier & Colburn, Huntington, 1975—; atty., claims examiner N.C. Dept. Ins., Raleigh, 1967-68, W.Va. Dept. Ins., Charleston, 1970. Pres. Family Services Counseling Agy., Huntington; chmn. bd. dirs. Consumer Credit Counseling of Huntington; elder Beverly Hills Presbyterian Ch. Mem. Am., W.Va., Cabell County bar assns., W.Va. State Bar, Huntington Area C. of C. Home: 147 Locust St Huntington WV 25705 Office: 731 5th Ave Huntington WV 25701 Tel (304) 523-8451

COLBURN, JOSEPH BRADLEY, b. Washington, Apr. 10, 1902; LL.B., George Washington U., 1924. Admitted to D.C. bar, 1924, N.Y. bar, 1931, U.S. Supreme Ct. bar, 1944; spl. atty. U.S. Tariff Commn., 1924-28; partner to sr. partner firm Barnes, Richardson & Colburn, N.Y.C., 1935—. Mem. Assn. Bar City N.Y., Am., Inter-Am. bar assns., Assn. Customs Bar (pres. 1966-68). Home: 64 Beach Hill Rd Port Washington NY 11050 Office: 475 Park Ave S New York City NY 10016 Tel (212) 725-0200

COLBY, RICHARD DEATLEE, b. Columbus, Ohio, Aug. 31, 1949; B.A., Ohio State U., 1971; J.D., Capital Law Sch., 1974. Admitted to Ohio bar, 1974, Fed. bar, 1975; pvt. practice law, Columbus, Ohio, 1974—. Chmn. bd. trustees Touchstone Crisis Interaction Center; trustee Oakland Park Community Council. Mem. Franklin County, Ohio, Am. bar assns., Ohio Trial Lawyers Assn. Home: 2870 Kilbourne Ave Columbus OH 43229 Office: 16 E Broad St Columbus OH 43215

COLE, ARNOLD HARVEY, b. Bklyn., Dec. 14, 1927; B.S. in Physics, Coll. City N.Y., 1949; J.D., George Washington U., 1954. Admitted to D.C. bar, 1955, Mo. bar, 1965, U.S. Supreme Ct. bar, 1960; examiner U.S. Patent Office, Washington, 1951-55; atty. USAF, Boston, 1955-S9; sr. atty. Monsanto Co., St. Louis, 1959—. Mem. Pattonville Sch. Dist. Bd. Edn., St. Louis County, 1964-73; mem. exec. bd. St. Louis Area council Boy Scouts Am., 1974-76. Mem. Am. Bar Assn., Am. Patent Law Assn. Home: 74 Willowbrook Dr Creve Coeur MO 63141 Office: 800 N Lindbergh Blvd Saint Louis MO 63166 Tel (314) 694-3131

COLE, BEN THOMAS, II, b. Holly Springs, Miss., Jan. 25, 1947; B.A., Rust Coll., 1969; J.D., Drake U., 1972. Admitted to Ga. bar, 1973, Miss. bar, 1973; Atlanta Legal Aid Soc., Inc., 1972-74; individual practice, 1974-75; mng. atty. Holly Springs office North Miss. Rural Legal Services, Inc., 1976—. Trustee Hopewell Ch., Holly Springs, 1975—. Mem. Ga. State, Miss. State bar assns., Miss. Assn. Minority Attys. Home: 311 W College St Holly Springs MS 38635 Office: 117-A College Ave Holly Springs MS 38635 Tel (601) 252-2278

COLE, CARYL SALOMON, b. N.Y.C., Dec. 22, 1933; B.A., Cornell U., 1955; J.D., Georgetown U., 1967. Admitted to D.C. bar, 1968, U.S. Supreme Ct. bar, 1973; asso. firm Covington & Burling, Washington, 1967-73; atty. Overseas Pvt. Investment Corp., Washington, 1973-74, sr. counsel for ins., 1974-76, asst. gen. counsel for ins., 1976—. Vice pres. Rollingwood Elementary PTA, Chevy Chase, Md., 1972-73. Mem. Fed. Exec. Women, Am., D.C. bar assns., Am. Soc. Internat. Law, Am. Judicature Soc., Phi Beta Kappa, Phi Kappa Phi. Recipient spl. achievement award Overseas Pvt. Investment Corp., 1975. Home: 7211 Delfield St Chevy Chase MD 20015 Office: 1129 20th St NW Washington DC 20527 Tel (202) 632-1766

COLE, CHARLES DUBOSE, b. Monroeville, Ala., May 14, 1938; B.S., Auburn U., 1960; J.D. cum laude, Samford U., 1966; LL.M., N.Y. U., 1971. Admitted to Ala. bar, 1966; asso. firm Porterfield & Scholl, Birmingham, Ala., 1966; prof. law Samford U., 1966-75; instr. Jefferson State Jr. Coll., 1969-70; individual practice law, Jefferson County, Ala., 1969-70; dir. Permanent Study Commn. on Alabama's Jud. System, 1972-74; dir. Ala. Jud. Conf. Criminal Justice Survey, 1972-73, Adv. Commn. on Jud. Article Implementation, 1974-75, Southeastern Regional Office of the Nat. Center for State Courts, Atlanta, 1975. Mem. Am., Ala., Birmingham bar assns., Am. Trial Lawyers Assn., Am. Judicature Soc., Inst. Jud. Adminstrn., Alpha Tau Omega, Phi Alpha Delta. Recipient Outstanding Prof. award Student Bar Assn. Samford U., 1971-72; Outstanding Alumnus award Phi Alpha Delta, Samford U., 1972; inducted into Curia Honoris, Samford U., 1973; Author: (with L. Gwatney) Bench Manual of Probate Judges, 1974; contbr. articles to legal jours. Home: 2584 Briarcliff Rd NE Atlanta GA 30329 Office: 1600 Tullie Circle NE Atlanta GA 30329 Tel (404) 634-3366

COLE, DIANE PHYLLIS CLIVE, b. Winchester, Mass., Sept. 6, 1940; A.B., Brown U., 1962; J.D., George Washington U., 1967. Admitted to Md. bar, 1967; gen. atty. Adminstrv. Office of U.S. Cts., Washington, 1968-73, dep. gen. counsel, 1973—. Mem. Fed., Md. bar assns. Home: 11190 Forest Edge Dr Reston VA 22090 Office: Administrv Office US Cts Washington DC 20544 Tel (202) 393-1640

COLE, HARRY, b. Birmingham, Ala., Feb. 16, 1929; B.A., U. Ala., LL.B., 1959. Admitted to Ala. bar, 1959; partner firm Ball & Ball, Montgomery, Ala., 1961-69, Hill, Hill, Carter, Franco, Cole & Black, Montgomery, 1969—. Mem. Montgomery County Bar Assn. (pres. 1967-68), Ala. Def. Lawyers Assn. (v.p.). Office: Hill Bldg Montgomery AL 36101 Tel (205) 834-7680

COLE, JAMES RAY, b. Reedsburg, Wis., Aug. 14, 1944; B.S. in Am. Instns., 1966, J.D., 1969. Admitted to Wis. bar, 1969, U.S. Supreme Ct. bar, 1973; law clk. to Justice B. Beilfuss, Wis. Supreme Ct., 1969-70; mem. firm Ross & Stevens, Madison, Wis., 1970-73, partner, 1973—; staff counsel OEO Commn. on Calif. Rural Legal Assistance, San Francisco, 1971; lectr. U. Wis. Law Sch., 1972-76; asst. staff counsel Citizens Study Com. on Jud. Orgn., 1973. Mem. bd. trustees 1st Congl. Ch., Madison, 1975-76, mem. personnel bd. City of Madison, 1975—. Mem. Am., Dane County bar assns., State Bar of Wis., Assn. of Trial Lawyers of Am., Wis. Acad. of Trial Lawyers. Home: 7 Blue Spruce Trail Madison WI 53717 Office: 1 S Pinckney St Madison WI 53703 Tel (608) 257-5353

COLE, JOHN LOUIS, b. Los Angeles, July 10, 1923; A.B. with honors, Stanford, 1948, LL.B., 1950. Admitted to Calif. bar, 1951, U.S. Dist. Ct. bar, 1955; asso. firm Loeb & Loeb, Los Angeles, 1951-55, partner, 1956-67; judge Superior Ct., Los Angeles, 1967—. Mem. Am., Los Angeles County bar assns. Office: Superior Ct Los Angeles CA 90012 Tel (213) 974-5791

COLE, KENDALL MARTIN, b. Bangor, Maine, Oct. 25, 1922; A.B., Amherst Coll., 1943; J.D., Harvard, 1948. Admitted to bar; asso., then partner Crowell & Leibman, Chgo., 1948-60; asst. gen. counsel Scott Paper Co., 1960-63; asst. gen. counsel, then v.p., gen. counsel Gen. Foods Corp., 1963-73; asst. gen. counsel Eastman Kodak Co., Rochester, N.Y., 1973-74, v.p., gen. counsel, 1974—, also dir. Mem. Alpha Delta Phi. Home: 592 Allens Creek Rd Rochester NY 14650 Office: 343 State St Rochester NY 14618*

COLE, MORTON EARL, b. Hartford, Conn., Sept. 20, 1902; student U. Conn., 1922-23; LL.B., Boston U., 1926. Admitted to Conn. bar, 1926, Mass. bar, 1930; founder, partner firm Cole & Cole, Hartford, 1930—. Mem. Hartford County, Conn. State, Am., Fed. bar assns., Am. Trial Lawyers Assn. Office: One Constitution Plaza Hartford CT 06103 Tel (203) 246-8561

COLE, RALPH DAVIS, JR., b. Findlay, Ohio, June 12, 1914; B.A., Williams Coll., 1936; J.D., Western Res. U., 1939. Admitted to Ohio bar, 1939; asso. firm Kuth & Trenkamp, Cleve., 1939-42; individual practice law, Findlay, 1946-68; judge Ohio Ct. of Appeals, 3d Dist., 1968—; mem. Ohio Ho. of Reps., 1955-68; city solicitor City of Findlay, 1948-50. Mem. Am., Ohio, Hancock County (Ohio) bar assns., Am. Judicature Soc., Order of Coif, Phi Beta Kappa, Phi Delta Phi. Home: 925 Sixth St Findlay OH 45840 Office: Ct of Appeals Third Appellate Dist of Ohio Allen County Courthouse Lima OH 45801 Tel (419) 223-1861

COLE, ROBERT LANE, b. Jennings, La., Jan. 14, 1941; B.S. in Internat. Trade and Fin. La. State U., 1964, J.D., 1967. Admitted to La. bar, 1967, U.S. Ct. Mil. Appeals, 1968, U.S. Supreme Ct. bar, 1973; with JAGC, USAF, 1967-72; individual practice law, Lafayette, La., 1972—; juvenile defender City of Lafayette, 1972—; mem. Lafayette Parish (La.) Indigent Defender Bd. Bd. dirs. Am. Cancer Soc., Lafayette; v.p. Lafayette PTA. Mem. Lafayette, La bar assns. Home: 904 Omega Dr Lafayette LA 70506 Office: 405 W Main St POB 3261 Lafayette LA 70501 Tel (318) 323-6183

COLE, ROBERT LEWIS, b. Evanston, Ill., May 25, 1929; B.S., U. Ill., 1951, J.D., 1953. Admitted to Ill. bar, 1953, U.S. Ct. Mil. Appeals, 1954; served to 1st lt. JAGC, U.S. Army, 1954-56; asso. firm Vail, Mills & Armstrong, Decatur, Ill., 1956-57; asst. states atty. Macon County (Ill.), 1957-60; partner firm Walden, Cole & Ohlsen, Ltd., Decatur, 1960—; dir. Central Ill. Estate Planning Council, 1976—; lectr. estate planning Ill. Agrl. Assn., 1973. Commr. Decatur Park Dist., 1975—; mem. Decatur City Planning Commn., 1975—, sec., 1976—; v.p. Lincoln Trails council Boy Scouts Am., 1974. Mem. Ill., Decatur bar assns., Ill. Assn. Park Dists. Recipient Silver Beaver award Boy Scouts Am., 1975. Home: 2230 Gary Dr Decatur IL 62526 Office: Suite 206 122 W Prairie St Decatur IL 62523 Tel (217) 429-5237

COLE, ROBERT PETER, b. Chgo., Nov. 3, 1913; A.B., U. Mich., 1937; J.D., John Marshall Law Sch., 1941. Admitted to Ill. bar, 1941, U.S. Supreme Ct. bar, 1971; mem. firm Lord, Bissell & Brook, 1941-69, Foss Schuman & Drake, Chgo., 1961—; Justice of Peace, Palatine Twp., Ill., 1948-53; police magistrate Village Palatine, 1953-61. Mem. Ill., Chgo. bar assns. Home: 1629 E Columbine Dr Schaumburg IL 60194 Office: 11 S LaSalle St Chicago IL 60603

COLE, TERRY PAUL, b. Johnson City, Tenn., July 26, 1945; B.A., Fla. State U., 1967, J.D., 1970. Admitted to Fla. bar, 1971; U.S. game mgmt. agent U.S. Dept. Interior, Atlanta, 1970-72; atty. Fla. Dept. Pollution Control, Tallahassee, 1973, enforcement adminstr., 1973—; enforcement adminstr. Fla. Dept. Environ. Regulation, Tallahassee, 1973-77, dep. gen. counsel, 1977—. Chmn. bd. trustees Tallahassee Heights Methodist Ch., 1974-75, chmn. adminstrv. bd., 1977—. Mem. U.S. Game Mgmt. Assn. Home: 2024 Hill N Dale St Tallahassee FL 32301 Office: 2562 Executive Center Circle E Tallahassee FL 32301 Tel (904) 487-1980

COLE, WILLIAM JAMES, b. Jackson, Miss., June 24, 1948; A.A., Hinds Jr. Coll., 1968; B.Pub. Adminstrn., U. Miss., 1970, J.D., 1974. Admitted to Miss. bar, 1974; spl. asst. atty. gen. Miss. Dept. Justice, Jackson, 1974—; legis. asst. to U.S. rep., Washington, 1972; asst. legis. draftsman Miss. State Senate, 1972. Sect. chmn. Jackson United Way Campaign, 1975. Mem. Am., Miss., Hinds County bar assns. Office: PO Box 220 Jackson MS 39202 Tel (601) 354-7130

COLEMAN, ARTHUR HAROLD, b. N.Y.C., May 24, 1939; B.S. in Econs., U. Pa., 1960; LL.B., Columbia U., 1963. Admitted to N.Mex. bar, 1963; since practiced in Santa Fe, asso. firm Bighee & Byrd, 1963-66; partner firm Valdez & Coleman, 1969; individual practice law, 1966-69, 70-76; partner firm Branch & Coleman, 1976—. Bd. dirs. Goodyear Found.; pres. Santa Fe Girls Club, 1970. Mem. Bar Assn. 1st Jud. Dist. (pres. 1976). Office: PO Box 2525 Santa Fe NM 87501 Tel (505) 982-3501 also 2600 Yale SE Albuquerque NM 87106 Tel (505) 243-1376

COLEMAN, CURTIN ROBERT, JR., b. Atlanta, Jan. 22, 1923; B.A., U. Va., 1944, LL.B., 1949. Admitted to Fla. bar, 1949, U.S. Supreme Ct. bar, 1960; practice law, West Palm Beach, Fla., 1949-51; asso. Stephen C. O'Connell, Ft. Lauderdale, Fla., 1953-55; partner firm Coleman, Leonard & Morrison, and predecessor firms, Fort Lauderdale, 1955—; asst. state atty., 15th Judicial Circuit Ct. Fla., 1960-61; nat. judge adv. Nat. Res. Assn., 1970-72. Mem. Bd. Social Welfare, Dist. 10, Fla., 1956-60; bd. dirs. Community Concert Assn. Ft. Lauderdale. Mem. Broward County, Fla., Am. bar assns., Broward Mfrs. Assn. (chmn. com. on legislation 1969-71), Greater Ft. Lauderdale C. of C. (dir. 1965—), Navy League U.S., Ft. Lauderdale Council (dir. 1974-76). Home: 2621 Castilla Isle Fort Lauderdale FL 33301 Office: 2810 E Oakland Park Blvd Suite 300 Fort Lauderdale FL 33306 Tel (305) 563-2671

COLEMAN, EDWARD EGAN, b. Anoka, Minn., Sept. 9, 1914; B.S., Coll. St. Thomas, 1937; LL.B., U. Minn., 1937. Admitted to Minn. bar, 1937, U.S. Dist. Ct. bar for Dist. Minn., 1937; asso. firm Sam Lipschultz, St. Paul, 1937-38; claims adjuster Employers Mut. Ins. Co. of Wausau, Wis., 1941-48; claim mgr. Allstate Ins. Co., Mpls., 1948-55; practiced in Anoka, 1955-76; spl. judge Municipal Ct., Anoka, Minn., 1953-63; judge Anoka County Probate Ct., 1976—; city atty. City of Anoka, 1963-76. Mem. Anoka County (pres. 1955—), Minn. State, Am. bar assns. Home: 410 Rice St Anoka MN 55303 Office: Anoka County Courthouse Anoka MN 55303 Tel (612) 421-4760

COLEMAN, FRANCIS THOMAS, b. Washington, Apr. 26, 1939; A.B., Georgetown U., 1961, LL.B., 1964, LL.M., 1970. Admitted to D.C. bar, 1965, Md. bar, 1968, U.S. Supreme Ct. bar, 1974; partner firm Loomis, Owen, Fellman & Coleman, Washington, 1968—; adj. prof. labor law Georgetown Law Center, 1973—. Mem. Am., Fed. bar assns., Am. Soc. Hosp. Attys., Barristers. Contbr. articles to legal jours. Home: 8101 Horseshoe Ln Potomac MD 20854 Office: 2020 K St NW Washington DC 20006 Tel (202) 296-5680

COLEMAN, FREDERICK MATTHEW, b. Lilly, Ga., Dec. 27, 1917; student Cleve. Coll. Western Reserve U., 1946-49; J.D., Cleve. Marshall Law Sch., 1953, LL.M., 1957. Admitted to Ohio bar, 1953, Fed. bar, 1953; with U.S. Post Office, Cleve., 1937-57; individual practice law, Cleve., 1953-64; lawyer Pub. Defender's Office, Cleve., 1964-67; judge Cleve. Municipal Ct., 1967-70; U.S. Atty. Cleve., 1970—. Bd. trustees Am. Cancer Soc., 1968—; mem. bd. trustees Blue Cross N.E. Ohio, 1971—; mem. Cleve. Area Manpower Planning Council, 1972—; pres. bd. control Greater Cleve. Safety Council, 1976—; mem. nat. bd. YMCA, 1968—. Mem. Ohio, Cleve., Cuyahoga County bar assns., Fed. Bar Assn., Nat. Bar Assn., Am. Judicature Soc., NAACP (bd. mem. emeritus 1965—), NCCJ. Named Man Year, Nat. Assn. Negro Bus. and Profl. Women's Clubs, 1974, numerous other awards. Office: 400 US Court House Cleveland OH 44114 Tel (216) 522-4392

COLEMAN, HOWARD DAVID, b. Denver, June 8, 1945; A.B., U. Calif., Berkeley, 1967, J.D., 1970. Admitted to Calif. bar, 1970; asso. firm Nossaman, Krueger & Marsh, Los Angeles, 1971-77, partner, 1977—; lectr. U. So. Calif. Sch. Law, 1974—. Mem. Los Angeles County, Am. (chmn. com. internat. aspects of individual rights and responsibilities 1974—, chmn. working group on human right treaties human rights com. sect. internat. law 1974—) bar assns., Am. Soc. Internat. Law, State Bar Calif. Office: 445 S Figueroa St Los Angeles CA 90071 Tel (213) 628-5221

COLEMAN, MARY STALLINGS, b. Forney, Tex.; B.A., U. Md., 1935; J.D., George Washington U., 1939; H.H.D. (hon.), Nazareth Coll.; LL.D. (hon.), Alma Coll., Olivet Coll., Eastern Mich. U., Western Mich. U., Adrian Coll., Detroit Coll. Law. Admitted to D.C. bar, 1940, Mich. bar, 1950; individual practice law, Washington, 1940-50; partner firm Wunsch & Coleman, Battle Creek, Mich., 1950-61; judge Probate and Juvenile Cts., Calhoun County, Marshall, Mich., 1961-73; justice Mich. Supreme Ct., Lansing, 1973—. Mem. Mich. Gov.'s Commn. Crime, 1964-68, Mich. Gov.'s Commn. Delinquency, 1968-70; Mich. Gov.'s Commn. Youth, 1964-70, Gov.'s Commn. Law Enforcement and Criminal Justice, 1968-72. Mem. Nat. Commn., Internat. Womens Year, Washington, 1975-76; trustee Albion Coll., 1973—. Fellow Am. Bar Found.; mem. Am. Bar Assn., Am. Judicature Soc., Nat., Mich. women lawyers assns., Calhoun County Bar Assn., AAUW, P.E.O., Bus. and Profl. Women (Distinguished Woman), Phi Alpha Delta, Beta Sigma Phi, Alpha Delta Kappa. Recipient Service to State award Mich. Probate and Juvenile Ct. Judges Assn., 1972, Outstanding Mich. Alumna award, 1975, Internat. Wyman award, 1975, Alpha Omicron Pi; Distinguished Alumna award U. Md., 1974, Profl. Achievement award George Washington U., 1973, Distinguished Prof. of Year Mich. Assn. Professions, 1973, Distinguished Citizen award Mich. State U., 1977. Home: 355 E Hamilton Ln Battle Creek MI 49015 Office: Mich Supreme Ct POB 30052 Lansing MI 48909 Tel (517) 373-0128

COLEMAN, MICHAEL ROBERT, b. San Francisco, Aug. 1, 1935; A.B., U. Calif. Sch. of Criminology, Berkeley, 1963; J.D., Golden Gate U., San Francisco, 1969. Police officer City and County of San Francisco, 1959-66, adult probation officer, 1966-70; admitted to Oreg. bar, 1970, Calif. bar, 1972; asso. firm Franklin, Des Brisay, Bennett & Jolles, Portland, Oreg., 1970; atty. Office Chief Atty., VA, San Francisco, 1972-73; dep. dist. atty. for Contra Costa County, Calif., 1973—; spl. cons. San Francisco Mayor's Criminal Justice Council, 1971-72; lectr. Golden Gate U., 1973—. Mem. Calif. Bar Assn., Oreg. Bar, Calif. Dist. Attys. Assn. Recipient certificate of meritorious conduct San Francisco Police Dept., 1963, 64, 65, certificate of recognition Golden Gate U. Sch. Law, 1969, advanced certificate Calif. Peace Officers Standards and Tng. Commn., 1969; bd. editors California Law: Trends and Developments, 1967. Home: 1199 Ridge Park Dr Concord CA 94518 Office: Office of Dist Atty Courthouse Martinez CA 94553 Tel (415) 671-4343

COLEMAN, ROBERT BOISSEAU, JR., b. Birmingham, Ala., Mar. 15, 1916; B.S., N.C. State U., 1939; LL.B., Birmingham Sch. of Law, 1952. Admitted to Ala., bar, 1952, Okla. bar, 1953, U.S. Supreme Ct. bar, 1956; Cts. Customs and Patent Appeal, 1964; various chem. engrng. positions Am. Cast Iron Pipe, DuPont, Am. Viscose, So. Research, So. Cement, 1941-53; patent atty. Phillips Petroleum Co., Bartlesville, Okla., 1953-59; individual practice law, Ada, Okla., 1959-64; sr. patent atty. Continental Oil Co., Ponca City, Okla., 1964-70, supr. patents and trademarks, 1970—. Mem. Am., Okla., Ala., Kay County bar assns., Am. Inst. Chem. Engrs., Am. Patent Law Assn. Home: 2513 Mockingbird Ln Ponca City OK 74601 Office: 1000 S Pine St Ponca City OK 74601 Tel (405) 762-3456

COLEMAN, ROBERT FRANKLIN, b. Chgo., Dec. 14, 1944; B.S. in Fin., DePaul U., 1966, J.D., 1969. Admitted to Ill. bar, 1969; atty. gen. antitrust div. State of Ill., Chgo., 1969-73; partner firm Freeman, Atkins & Coleman, and predecessors, Chgo., 1973--. Mem. Am., Chgo. bar assns. Home: 1000 N Marion St Oak Park IL 60302 Office: 100 W Monroe 21st Floor Chicago IL 60603 Tel (312) 782-0337

COLEMAN, ROBERT WINSTON, b. Oklahoma City, Mar. 1, 1942; B.A., Abilene Christian Coll., 1964; J.D. with honors U. Tex., 1968. Admitted to Tex. bar, 1968, Ga. bar, 1970; asso. firm Kilpatrick, Cody, Rogers, McClatchey & Regenstein, Atlanta, 1969-75; asso. firm Stalcup, Johnson, Meyers & Miller, Dallas, 1975—; law clk. U.S. 5th Circuit Ct. Appeals, 1968-69. Mem. Am., Tex., Ga., Dallas, Dallas Jr. bar assns., Am. Judicature Soc.

COLEMAN, RONALD D'EMORY, b. El Paso, Tex., Nov. 29, 1941; B.A., U. Tex., El Paso, 1963, LL.B. (Stevens Estate scholar), 1967. Admitted to Tex. bar, 1969; asst. county atty. El Paso County (Tex.), 1969-71, 1st asst. county atty., 1971-72; individual practice law, El Paso, 1972—; mem. Tex. Ho. of Reps., 1972-74, 74-76, 76—, mem. judiciary com., 1972—. Recipient H.L. Smith-Price award U. Tex., 1967. Office: 1551 Montana St El Paso TX 79902 Tel (915) 544-9232

COLES, ALBERT LEONARD, b. Bridgeport, Conn., Nov. 8, 1909; B.A., Yale, 1931, LL.B., 1933. Admitted to Conn. bar, 1933, U.S. Dist. Ct. Conn. bar, 1942, U.S. 2d Circuit Ct. Appeals bar, 1944, U.S. Supreme Ct. bar, 1955, U.S. Dist. Ct. So. Dist. N.Y. bar, 1961; mem. firm Coles, O'Connell, Dolan & McDonald, Bridgeport, 1941—; mem. Conn. State Senate, 1939-49, majority leader, 1941; judge, City Ct. Bridgeport, 1945-47, 49-51; atty. gen. State of Conn., 1959-63; judge Superior Ct. Conn., 1963-65; dir. People's Savs. Bank, United Illuminating Co., So. New Eng. Telephone Co., Eastern Electric Constrn. Co., Inc. Bd. dirs. United Way Eastern Fairfield County; trustee Park City Hosp., 1968—. Fellow Am. Coll. Trial Lawyers;

mem. Phi Beta Kappa, Phi Alpha Delta. Home: 140 Sailors Ln Bridgeport CT 06605 Office: 855 Main St Bridgeport CT 06604 Tel (203) 368-3475

COLETTA, MARTIN M., b. Salandra, Italy, Mar. 23, 1904; B.A., Trinity Coll., Hartford, Conn., 1926; LL.B., Yale, 1929. Admitted to Conn. bar, 1929; individual practice law, Hartford, 1929-32; research asst. Yale Law Sch., 1932-34; asso. firm Schwolsky, Demezzo & Bracken, Hartford, 1932-40; mem. firm Tracy & Maxwell, Hartford, 1940—. Mem. Am., Conn., Hartford County bar assns. Home: 104 Wood Pond Rd West Hartford CT 06107 Office: 99 Pratt St Hartford CT 06103 Tel (203) 278-6010

COLIE, JOHN EDWIN, b. Jersey City, N.J., Jan. 6, 1925; B.A., Fairleigh Dickinson U., 1958; LL.B., Rutgers U., 1961, also J.D. Admitted to N.J. bar, 1966; with Employers Ins. Wausau (Wis.), 1967-71; N.J. Mfrs. Ins. Co., Trenton, N.J., 1971—. Trustee Passaic Valley Regional High Sch., 1971—, v.p., 1975-76; mem. parish council St. Ann's Ch., West Paterson, N.J., 1974—, chmn., 1975-76. Mem. N.J., Passaic County bar assns. Home: 675 Rifle Camp Rd West Paterson NJ 07424 Office: PO Box 2708 Trenton NJ 08607

COLIN, RALPH FREDERICK, b. N.Y.C., Nov. 18, 1900; A.B., Coll. City N.Y., 1918; LL.B., Columbia, 1921. Admitted to N.Y. bar, 1922; asso. firm Rosenberg & Ball, N.Y.C., 1921, mem. firm, 1926; mem. firm Rosenberg, Goldmark & Colin, and successors, 1926-76; counsel to firm Rosenman Colin Freund Lewis & Cohen, N.Y.C., 1976—; dir., gen. counsel CBS, 1927-69, Columbia Artists Mgmt., Inc.; adminstrv. v.p., gen. counsel Art Dealers Assn. Am.; dir. Maria Bergson Assos., Ltd. Active early devel. art theatres; past dir. Provincetown, Greenwich Village, Actors theatres; dir., trustee, v.p. Philharmonic Symphony Soc. N.Y., 1942-56; trustee, hon. sec. Baron de Hirsch Fund, 1935-56; trustee, v.p. Mus. Modern Art, 1954-69; vice chmn. Internat. Council of Mus. Modern Art; trustee Hosp. Joint Diseases, 1932-52, chmn. bd., 1949-51, pres., 1951-52; mem. vis. com. dept. fine arts and Fogg Mus., Harvard, 1951-73, 75—; bd. visitors Columbia Law Sch., 1961—; bd. dirs. Rockmeadow Found., Richard Rodgers Found., Bernheim Found., Woodheath Found., CBS Found., 1953-69, pres., 1956-69; bd. dirs. Am. Fedn. Arts, 1946-56; chmn. radio broadcasting div. Nat. War Fund, 1943-44. Mem. Assn. Bar City N.Y. (exec. com. 1942-46, chmn. spl. com. on pub. and bar relations 1956-59, v.p. 1960-61, chmn. com. profl. ethics 1961-62), Am., FCC bar assns. Cons. editor Air Law Rev.; contbr. to law revs. and art periodicals. Home 941 Park Ave New York City NY 10028 Office: 575 Madison Ave New York City NY 10022 Tel (212) 644-6950

COLINGO, JOE R., b. Alexandria, La., Aug. 30, 1939; B.B.A., U. Miss., 1961, LL.B., 1964, also J.D. Admitted to Miss. bar; practice law, Pascagoula, Miss. Mem. Am., Miss. trial lawyers assns., Miss. Dist. Attys. Assn. Home: 2124 River Rd Pascagoula MS 29567 Office: 704 Watts Ave Pascagoula MS 39567 Tel (601) 762-8021

COLLENS, LEWIS MORTON, b. Chgo., Feb. 10, 1938; B.S., U. Ill., 1960, M.A., 1963; J.D., U. Chgo., 1966. Admitted to Ill. bar, 1966; asso. firm Ross, Hardies, Chgo., 1966-67; spl. asst. to gen. counsel Equal Employment Opportunity Commn., Washington, 1967-68; asst. prof. Ill. Inst. Tech., Chgo. Kent Coll. Law, 1970-72, asso. prof., 1972-74, prof., 1975—, dean Coll. Law, 1974—. Chmn. bd. dirs. Bar. Rev. Inst., 1967-74; bd. dirs. Ill. Inst. Continuing Legal Edn., 1974—. Mem. Am., Ill., Chgo. bar assns., Am. Law Inst., Order of Coif. Law and Humanities fellow, Harvard, 1973-74. Office: 77 S Wacker Dr Chicago IL 60606 Tel (312) 567-5006

COLLETTA, LAWRENCE RUSSELL, b. Bklyn., May 24, 1931; B.S., Univ. So. Carolina, 1958; J.D., Seton Hall Univ., 1972. Admitted to N.J. bar, 1972; individual practice law, Edison, N.J., 1972—. Mem. Am., N.J., Middlesex County bar assns. Address: 10 Melville Rd Edison NJ 08817 Tel (201) 985-1100

COLLEY, MICHAEL FRANCIS, b. Youngstown, Ohio, Oct. 26, 1936; B.A., Ohio State U., 1958, J.D., 1961; Admitted to Ohio bar, 1961; asst. atty. City of Columbus (Ohio), 1962-64; spl. counsel to atty. gen. State of Ohio, 1963-64; chmn. legal div. United Way., Columbus; chmn. Heart Sunday, Columbus; chmn. bd. dirs. One to One, Columbus; v.p., gen. campaign chmn. Central Ohio chpt. Leukemia Soc. Am. Mem. Am., Ohio, Columbus bar assns., Am. Arbitration Assn., Assn. Trial Lawyers Am. (bd. govs. 6th judicial circuit 1973—, mem. exec. com., 1974—, v.p. 1976—), Ohio Acad. Trial Lawyers (trustee 1968-70, v.p. 1970-71, pres. 1971-72), Franklin County Trial Lawyers Assn. (v.p. 1967-68, pres. 1968-69). Contbr. articles in field to profl. jours. Home: 2685 Canterbury Rd Columbus OH 43221 Office: 536 S High St Columbus OH 43215 Tel (614) 221-1341

COLLIER, ROBERT ALVIS, JR., b. Statesville, N.C., Jan. 13, 1931; A.B., U. N.C., 1957, J.D., 1959. Admitted to N.C. bar, 1959; partner firm Collier, Harris & Collier, Statesville, Mooresville, and Taylorsville, N.C., 1959-68; judge N.C. Superior Ct., 1968—; mem. N.C. Ho. of Reps., 1965-67; dir. 1st Union Nat. Bank. Bd. dirs. Salvation Army, Statesville, Boys Town of N.C.; chmn. Morehead (N.C.) Scholarship Selection Com., 1964—. Mem. Am., N.C. (v.p.) bar assns., Am. Judicature Soc., N.C. Conf. Superior Ct. Judges (pres.). Named Young Man of Year, Statesville, 1964. Home: 315 Earlwood Rd Statesville NC 28677 Office: Hall of Justice Statesville NC 28677 Tel (704) 873-3346

COLLIER, SHIRLEY, b. Taloga, Okla., Aug. 7, 1933; B.S., Okla. State U., 1954; LL.B., George Washington U., 1967. Admitted to Okla. bar, 1973; partner firm Collier & Fakle, Taloga, Okla., 1973—; city atty. Taloga, 1974—. Chmn. Dewey County Dem. party, 1974—. Office: Box 66 Taloga OK 73667 Tel (405) 328-5551

COLLIER, WILLIAM JOSEPH, JR., b. Waterbury, Conn., Aug. 27, 1933; A.B., Coll. Holy Cross, 1955; LL.B., Fordham Law Sch., 1960; LL.M., N.Y. U., 1966. Admitted to N.Y. bar, 1960, Ill. bar, 1966; asso. firm Dillon & O'Brien, N.Y.C., 1960-61, firm McGovern, Vincent & Connelly, New Rochelle, N.Y., 1961-66; v.p., gen. counsel Joyce Beverages, Inc., New Rochelle, 1966—, also dir.; pres. Joyce Assos., Inc. Mem. bd. sch. Insp.'s Ill. Sch. Dist. 86, 1971-74. Mem. Chgo., Westchester bar assns. Office: Joyce Rd New Rochelle NY 10802 Tel (914) 632-7060

COLLIN, DWIGHT RIPLEY, b. White Plains, N.Y., June 6, 1940; B.Gen. Studies, U. Md., 1964; J.D., Syracuse U., 1968. Admitted to N.Y. bar, 1968; asso. firm Nixon, Hargrave, Devans & Doyle, Rochester, N.Y., 1968-75, partner, 1976—. Mem. Monroe County, N.Y. State, Am. bar assns. Home: 4 Bayberry Circle Fairport NY 14450 Office: Lincoln First Tower Rochester NY 14603 Tel (716) 546-8000

COLLINS, DANIEL FRANCIS, b. N.Y.C., Mar. 5, 1942; B.A., Hofstra U., 1964; J.D., Am. U., 1967. Admitted to D.C. bar, 1968; law clk. Hon. E. Barrett Prettyman, U.S. Ct. Appeals, D.C. Circuit, 1967-68; asso. firm Wilner & Scheiner, Washington, 1968-70, Ross, Marsh & Foster, Washington, 1970-74, mem. firm, 1974—. Mem. Am., Fed. Power, D.C. bar assns., Phi Delta Phi. Staff editor Am. U. Law Rev., 1966-67; contbr. articles to profl. jours. Home: 8514 Hazelwood Dr Bethesda MD 20014 Office: 730 15th St NW Washington DC 20005

COLLINS, DAVID EDMOND, b. Oak Park, Ill., June 6, 1934; B.A., U. Notre Dame, 1956; LL.B., Harvard, 1959. Admitted to N.Y. bar, 1962, N.J. bar, 1964; asso. firm Shearman & Sterling, N.Y.C., 1960-62; with Johnson & Johnson, New Brunswick, N.J., 1962—, asst. sec., 1964-70, sec., 1970-75, asso. gen. counsel, 1973-75, gen. counsel, 1975—, v.p., dir., 1976—. Mem. Am., N.J. bar assns., Health Industry Mfrs. Assn. (legal and regulatory sect.), Pharm. Mfrs. Assn. (med. device and diagnostic law sects.). Frederick Sheldon traveling fellow, 1959-60; contbr. articles to profl. jours. Office: 501 George St New Brunswick NJ 08903 Tel (201) 524-6413

COLLINS, DONALD LAMAR, b. Gadsden, Ala., Sept. 8, 1929; B.S., Jacksonville State U., 1952; J.D., U. Ala., 1957. Admitted to Ala. bar, 1957, U.S. Supreme Ct. bar, 1970; law clk. to Supreme Ct. of Ala., 1957; asso. firm Martin and Blakey, Birmingham, Ala., 1958; partner firm Deramus, Johnston, Barton, Proctor and Swedlaw, Birmingham, 1958-70; individual practice law, Gadsden and Birmingham, 1970—; mem. Ala. Ho. of Reps., 1962-66. Co-chmn. Jefferson County (Ala.) Cancer Crusade, 1962-70, chmn., 1971; Ala. at-large del. Republican Nat. Conv., 1976; mem. Etowah County (Ala.) Republican Com. Mem. Ala. (chmn. jr. sect. 1962-63), Am., Birmingham, Gadsden bar assns., Am. Judicature Soc., Omicron Delta Kappa, Phi Alpha Delta (pres. chpt. 1956-57). Recipient award for scholastic achievement Bur. Nat. Affairs, 1957, Sigma Delta Kappa, 1957; asso. editor Ala. Law Rev., 1957. Office: 307 5th St Suite E Gadsden AL 35901 (Tel (205) 543-0275 also 3000 7th Ave South Birmingham AL Tel (205) 323-1571

COLLINS, EPHRAIM, b. N.Y.C., Sept. 29, 1930; A.B., N.Y. U., 1953; J.D., U. Miami, 1957. Admitted to Fla. bar, 1958, U.S. Supreme Ct. bar, 1958; individual practice law, Miami, Fla., 1958-68, Margate, Fla., 1969—; city atty. Deerfield Beach, Fla., 1968-69, Coconut Creek, Fla., 1969-72; city prosecutor North Lauderdale, Fla., 1974—. Mem. Fla. Bar Assn. Home: 420 SE 13th Ave Pompano Beach FL 33060 Office: 6856 W Atlantic Blvd Margate FL 33063 Tel (305) 972-4700

COLLINS, FREIDA GUNN, b. Laurel, Miss., Apr. 30, 1948; B.A., U. Miss., 1969, J.D., 1972, M.L.S., 1975. Admitted to Miss. bar, 1972; individual practice law, Ellisville, Miss., 1972-73; asst. dir. Sea Grant Legal Program, U. Miss., 1973-75; partner firm Collins & Collins, Ellisville, 1975—. Mem. Am. Bar Assn., Fidelia Club, Kappa Beta Phi. Home: 406 Holly St Ellisville MS 39437 Office: PO Box 190 Ellisville MS 39437 Tel (601) 477-9201

COLLINS, JON RICHARD, b. Ely, Nev., May 5, 1923; B.S. in Econs., U. Pa.; S.J.D., Georgetown U. Admitted to D.C. bar, 1950, Nev. bar, 1950; dist. atty. White Pine County (Nev.), Ely, 1950-54; dist. judge Nev. 7th Jud. Dist., 1958-66; justice to chief justice Nev. Supreme Ct., Carson City, 1966-71. Chmn. Nev. Energy Resource Adv. Bd., 1973-76. Mem. Am. Judicature Soc., Am. Bar Assn. Home: 3000 Ashby Ave Las Vegas NV 89102 Office: 1700 Valley Bank Plaza 300 S 4th St Las Vegas NV 89101 Tel (702) 385-2188

COLLINS, KEVIN JOSEPH, b. N.Y.C., Sept. 9, 1939; A.B. in U.S. History, Holy Cross Coll., 1961; LL.B. (now J.D.), Rutgers U., 1964; postgrad. U. Pa. Wharton Sch. Fin., 1972. Admitted to N.J. bar, 1970, U.S. Supreme Ct. bar, 1974; sr. v.p., dir. The First Boston Corp., N.Y.C., 1967-. Chmn. Wyckoff (N.J.) Bicentennial Commn.; trustee Wyckoff Hist. Soc., 1974-; securities industry trustee Wharton Sch., U. Pa. Mem. Am. (securities industry liaison com.), N.J., Bergen County bar assns., Am., N.J., Bergen County hist. assns., Phi Alpha Delta. Home: 556 Miller Rd Wyckoff NJ 07481 Office: 20 Exchange Pl New York City NY 10005 Tel (212) 825-2331

COLLINS, LEROY, b. Tallahassee, Mar. 10, 1909; LL.B., Cumberland U., 1931; LL.D., Rollins Coll., 1955, Fla. State U., 1956, Millikin U., 1963, St. Leo Coll., 1968, U. Fla., 1973. Admitted to Fla. bar, 1931, U.S. Supreme Ct. bar, 1963; mem. Fla. Ho. of Reps., 1934-40, Fla. Senate, 1941-47; gov. State of Fla., 1955-61; pres. Nat. Assn. Broadcasters, 1960-64; dir. Community Relations Service U.S., Washington, 1964; under sec. U.S. Dept. Commerce, Washington, 1965-66; of counsel firm Ervin, Varn, Jacobs, Odom & Kitchen, Tallahassee, 1968—. Chmn., So. Regional Edn. Bd., 1957, Nat., So. gov.'s confs., 1957; permanent chmn. Nat. Democratic Conv., 1960; chmn. Nat. Pub. Adv. Com. on Area Redevel.; mem. Nat. Adv. Com. Jr. Colls.; adv. council Peace Corps, Outdoor Recreation Resources Rev. Commn.; mem. nat. council Boy Scouts Am.; governing council Nat. Municipal League; mem. coll. electors Hall of Fame of Gt. Ams.; trustee Nat. Council Crime and Delinquency, Nat. Assn. Episc. Chs. Mem. Am. (chmn. spl. com. for study legal edn.), Tallahassee bar assns., Fla. Bar (dir. Fla. Legal Services), Phi Delta Phi. Author: Forerunners Courageous, 1976; citation for Christian service Berkeley Div. Sch., New Haven, 1965; Charles Evans Hughes award NCCJ, 1954. Home: The Grove Tallahassee FL 32302 Office: 305 S Gadsden St Tallahassee FL 32302 Tel (904) 224-9135

COLLINS, NATALYN ADELL, b. Rockford, Ill., Mar. 31, 1940; A.A., N. Park Coll., 1959; B.A., U. Ill., 1961; J.D., Tex. Tech. U., 1971. Admitted to Tex. bar, 1971; hearing officer Tex. State Dept. Pub. Welfare, Lubbock, 1971-74; regional atty., 1974—. Mem. Lubbock County Bar Assn. Home: 3406 41st St Lubbock TX 79413 Office: 2424 34th St Lubbock TX 79411 Tel (806) 797-4311

COLLINS, PETER MATTHEW, b. N.Y.C., Aug. 12, 1942; A.B., Holy Cross Coll., 1964; M.A., U. Pa., 1965; J.D., N.Y. U., 1968. Admitted to N.Y. bar, 1969, U.S. Ct. Appeals 2d Circuit bar, 1974; asso. firm White & Case, N.Y.C., 1968—. Mem. N.Y. State Bar Assn., Assn. Bar City N.Y. Home: 67 E 11th St New York City NY 10003 Office: 14 Wall St New York City NY 10005 Tel (212) 732-1040

COLLINS, ULYSSES S., JR., b. Astoria, Ill., May 25, 1917; student Western State Tchrs. Coll., 1935-36, Ill. State Normal U., 1938; J.D. with honors, John Marshall Law Sch., 1942. Admitted to Ill. bar, 1946; individual practice law, Peru, Ill., 1946-48; partner firm Lybarger & Collins, Bushnell, Ill., 1958-72; judge 9th Jud. Circuit Ct. Ill., Macomb, 1972—; asst. atty. gen. State of Ill., 1952-60, spl. asst. atty. gen., 1968-72; city atty. Bushnell, 1959-69. Chmn. Bushnell Swimming Pool Assn., 1959-61; pres. Bushnell Community Recreation Assn., Inc., 1961-64. Mem. Am., Ill. State, McDonough County bar assns., Ill. Judges Assn., Nat. Council Juvenile Ct. Judges, Am. Judicature Soc. Home: 368-W Hurst St Bushnell IL 61422 Office: McDonough County Ct House Macomb IL 61455 Tel (309) 772-3769

COLLINS, WILLIAM COLDWELL, b. El Paso, Tex., June 19, 1921; B.A., U. Tex., 1943, LL.B., 1949. Admitted to Tex. bar, 1949, U.S. Supreme Ct. bar, 1959; asst. atty. El Paso County (Tex.), 1950-54; individual practice law, El Paso, 1954-59; partner firm Collins, Langford & Pine, El Paso, 1959—. Bd. dirs. El Paso Hist. Soc., 1956-59; chmn. ARC, El Paso, 1974-77; bd. dirs. Rio Grande council Girl Scouts U.S.A., 1963-66. Mem. State Bar Tex., Am., El Paso (dir.) bar assns. Home: 4040 N Stanton St El Paso TX 79902 Office: 1100 Bassett Tower El Paso TX 79901 Tel (915) 533-6955

COLLINS, WILLIAM FINN, b. Edgar, Wis., May 5, 1919; B.A., U. Wis., 1942, LL.B., 1942. Admitted to Wis. bar, 1945, N.Y. bar, 1947; asso. firm Cravath, Swaine & Moore, N.Y.C., 1945-52; asst. gen. counsel Revere Copper & Brass, Inc., Rome, N.Y., 1952-55, gen. counsel, N.Y.C., 1955-60, sec., 1960-71, v.p., dir., 1965-67, exec. v.p. legal and fin., 1967-71, pres., mem. exec. com., 1971—, chief exec. officer, 1975—; dir. Servomation Corp. Mem. Copper Devel. Assn. (dir. 1975—), Am., N.Y. State bar assns. Home: 136 E Hunting Ridge Rd Stamford CT 06903 Office: 605 3d Ave New York City NY 10016

COLLISSON, PETER DUNLEVY, b. Washington, Nov. 26, 1945; B.A. in Econs., U. N.C., Chapel Hill, 1966; J.D., Vanderbilt U., 1972. Admitted to Calif. bar, 1972, U.S. Supreme Ct. bar, 1976; asso. firm Paul, Hastings Janofsky & Walker, Los Angeles, 1972—; arbitrator Am. Arbitration Assn., Los Angeles, 1976—; legal adviser Pasadena (Calif.) Unified Sch. Dist., 1974—. Mem. State Bar Calif., Los Angeles County, Orange County (Calif.) bar assns. Office: PO Box 7040 Newport Beach CA 92663 Tel (714) 833-2351

COLOGNE, GORDON BENNETT, b. Long Beach, Calif., Aug. 24, 1924; B.S., U. So. Calif., 1948; LL.B., Southwestern U., 1951. Admitted to Calif. bar, 1951, U.S. Supreme Ct. bar, 1961; atty. Antitrust div. Dept. Justice, Washington and Jacksonville, Fla., 1951; individual practice law, Indio, Calif., 1951-60; partner firm Marsh, Moore & Cologne, Indio, 1960-69, Cologne, Erwin & Angle, Indio, Calif., 1969-72; justice 4th Dist. Ct. of Appeals, Div. One, State of Calif., San Diego, 1972—; adj. prof. law U. San Diego. Mayor, City of Indio, 1954-56; mem. Indio City Council, 1956; mem. Riverside County Bd. of Freeholders, 1957; Calif. state assemblyman, 1963-65; Calif. state senator, 1965-72. Mem. Am. Bar Assn., Inst. Jud. Adminstrn. Recipient Freedom Found. award, 1967; Sears Roebuck Found. Water Conservation award, 1968. Office: 6010 State Bldg San Diego CA 92101 Tel (714) 236-7267

COLOMBO, LOUIS JOSEPH, JR., b. Detroit, Apr. 27, 1911; A.B., U. Mich., 1933, LL.B., 1935; LL.D. (hon), Mercy Coll., Detroit. Admitted to Mich. bar, 1935; asst. atty. gen. State of Mich., 1937; commr.-mayor City of Bloomfield Hills (Mich.), 1963-71. Trustee, Mercy Coll., Beaumont Hosp., Royal Oak, Mich. Fellow Am. Bar Assn.; mem. Mich. (grievance bd. 1954—), Oakland bar assns. Office: 1500 N Woodward St Suite 209 Birmingham MI 48011 Tel (313) 645-9300

COLSON, EARL M., b. Bklyn., Mar. 8, 1930; B.S. magna cum laude, Syracuse U., 1950; LL.B. magna cum laude, Harvard, 1957. Admitted to N.Y. bar, 1958, D.C. bar, 1960; asso. firm Chadbourne, Parke, Whiteside & Wolff, N.Y.C., 1957-60; asso. firm Arent, Fox, Kinter, Plotkin & Kahn, Washington, 1960-68, partner, 1968—; adj. prof. law, Georgetown U., Washington, 1970—. Mem. Am. (tax sect., chmn. estate and gift tax com. 1972-73), D.C. (chmn. tax com. 1971-72) bar assns., D.C. bar (treas, bd. govs. 1974-76), Am. Law Inst., Assn. Bar City N.Y. Author: Capital Gains and Losses, 1975; co-author: Fed. Taxation of Estates, Gifts, and Trusts, 1975; lectr. on tax subjects. Home: 4725 Dorset Ave Chevy Chase MD 20015 Office: 1815 H St NW Washington DC 20006 Tel (202) 857-6205

COLTON, ALBERT JAY, b. Buffalo, N.Y., June 3, 1925; A.B., Dartmouth, 1947, B.Civil Law, Oxford U., 1950; LL.M., Yale, 1951; B.D., Ch. Div. Sch. Pacific, 1963. Admitted to Utah bar, 1952, Calif. bar, 1954; asso. firm Fabian & Clendenin, Salt Lake City, 1951-54, partner, 1954-60, 68—; vice dean Grace Cathedral, San Francisco, 1962-64; rector St. Francis Episcopal Ch., San Francisco, 1964-68; named canon chancellor Diocese of Utah, Episcopal Ch., 1976; chmn. Utah State Bar Examiners, 1973—. Sec., Utah Rhodes Scholarship Selection Com., 1969—; trustee St. Mark's Hosp., Salt Lake City, 1974—, Mount Olivet Cemetery, Salt Lake City, 1973—. Mem. Am., Utah, Calif. bar assns., Salt Lake City C. of C. (bd. govs. 1973-76). Home: 1289 4th Ave Salt Lake City UT 84103 Office: 8th floor Continental Bank Bldg Salt Lake City UT 84101 Tel (801) 531-8900

COLTON, DAVID J., b. N.Y.C., Sept. 20, 1899; A.B., Columbia U., 1920, LL.B., 1922, J.D., 1922. Admitted to N.Y. bar, 1923; asso. firm Gilman & Unger, N.Y.C., 1922-28, partner, 1928-33; individual practice law, N.Y.C., 1933-50; partner firm Colton & Pinkham, N.Y.C., 1951-69; counsel to firm Whitman & Ransom, and predecessors, N.Y.C., 1970—. Founder, La Napoule (France) Art Found. Henry Clews Meml., 1950, trustee, 1950-73, sec., 1951-54, v.p., 1954-62, pres., 1962-73, hon. chmn. bd., 1974—. Home: 930 Fifth Ave New York City NY 10021 Office: 522 Fifth Ave New York City NY 10036 Tel (212) 575-5800

COLTON, JOHN PATRICK, JR., b. Memphis, Feb. 4, 1938; student U. Tenn., 1956-57; B.S., Memphis State U., 1961; LL.B., So. Law Sch. (merged with Memphis State U., 1965), 1964; postgrad. in Law, Northwestern U., 1974. Dep. criminal ct. clk. 15th Jud. Circuit of Tenn., Memphis, 1962-64; admitted to Tenn. bar, 1965; asso. firm Irwin, Owens, Gillock, Memphis, 1965-68, partner, 1968-74; sr. partner firm Colton and Blancett, Memphis, 1974—; asst. pub. defender Shelby County (Tenn.), 1965-76; del. 1971 Constl. Conv. State of Tenn. Bd. dirs. Mental Health Assn., Memphis, 1970—; mem. Tenn. Democratic Exec. Com., 1974—. Mem. Tenn. (chmn. com. continuing legal edn. and admission to bar 1973), Am. bar assns., Am., Tenn. (v.p. 1972-73), Memphis (dir. 1976—) trial lawyers assns., Am. Judicature Soc. Co-reviser: In The Court, 1970. Home: 246 N Rose Rd Memphis TN 38117 Office: 34th Floor 100 N Main Bldg Memphis TN 38103 Tel (901) 523-8005

COLTON, ROGER BYE, b. Bloomington, Ill., Aug. 5, 1937; B.S. in Bus., Ill. Wesleyan U., 1959; J.D., Northwestern U., 1962. Admitted to Fla. bar, 1970; spl. agent FBI, U.S. and P.R., 1962-71; partner firm Foley, Colton and Butler, W. Palm Beach, Fla., 1971—. Bd. dirs. YMCA, Palm Beach Gardens, Fla., 1974. Mem. Am., Fla. bar assns. Home: 11971 Lake Shore Pl North Palm Beach FL 33408 Office: 406 N Dixie St West Palm Beach FL 33401 Tel (305) 832-1744

COLVIN, ROBERT FULTON, JR., b. Charlottesville, N.C., Oct. 19, 1940; B.S., U. Tenn., 1963, J.D., 1970. Admitted to Tenn. bar, 1970, U.S. Supreme Ct. bar, 1974; asst. U.S. atty. Western Dist. Tenn.,

1970-74; mem. firm Fowler, Gardner, Hester & McCrary, Memphis, 1974—. Mem. Am., Tenn., Memphis and Shelby County bar assns. Home: 5725 Chapman Ave Memphis TN 38117 Office: 44 N 2d St Memphis TN 38103 Tel (901) 526-6428

COLWELL, MICHAEL JAMES, b. Aurora, Ill., July 8, 1947; B.A., Loras Coll., 1969; J.D., DePaul U., 1972. Admitted to Ill. bar, 1972; asso. firm Dreyer, Foote & Streit Assos., Aurora, 1971-75, partner firm, v.p., 1975—. Bd. dirs. Fox Valley council Girl Scouts U.S.A., Inc.; mem. Holy Angels Parish Council. Mem. Kane County (treas. 1977—), Ill. State, Am. bar assns., Ill. Trial Laywers Assn., Aurora Jaycees. Editor: Kane County Assn. Newsletter, 1976—. Home: 213 S Gladstone Ave Aurora IL 60506 Office: 900 N Lake St Aurora IL 60506 Tel (312) 897-8764

COMAROW, MURRAY, b. N.Y.C., Jan. 5, 1920; LL.B., Nat. U., 1942. Admitted to U.S. Dist Ct. for D.C. bar, 1947, U.S. Ct. Appeals for D.C. bar, 1949, U.S. Supreme Ct. bar, 1966; with Hdqrs., U.S. Air Force, 1951-58, asst. gen. counsel Office of Sec., 1958-66; exec. dir. FPC, 1966-69, Pres.'s Commn. on Postal Orgn. (on leave from FPC), 1967-68, Pres.'s Council on Exec. Orgn., White House, 1969-70; v.p. Booz, Allen & Hamilton, 1970-72; sr. asst. postmaster gen. U.S. Postal Service, Washington, 1972-74; exec. dir. Interstate Conf., 1974-76; of counsel firm vom Baur, Coburn, Simmons & Turtle, Washington, 1976—; adj. prof. adminstrv. law Am. U., Washington, 1975—. Mem. Nat. Acad. Pub. Adminstrn., Am. Bar Assn., Nat. Press Club. Recipient commendations Sec. U.S. Air Force, 1966, Pres. Johnson, 1968, Chmn. FPC, 1969, Pres. Nixon, 1971. Home: 4910 Western Ave Chevy Chase MD 20016 Office: 1700 K St NW Suite 1100 Washington DC 20006 Tel (202) 833-1420

COMBS, BEN MATTHEW, b. Irvine, Ky., Sept. 6, 1922; A.B., U. Ky., 1946, J.D., 1948. Admitted to Ky. bar, 1948; asso. firms Drake & Howard, Lexington, Ky., 1948-60, Eblen, Howard & Milner, Lexington, 1960-71; adminstrv. law judge HEW, Lexington, 1971—; gen. counsel Ky. Dept. Motor Transp., 1961-62, commr., 1962-67; dep. atty. gen. State of Ky., 1968-69. Mem. Ky., Fayette County (Ky.) bar assns., Fed. Adminstrv. Law Judge Conf., Assn. HEW Adminstrv. Law Judges, Nat. Assn. Regulatory and Utility Commrs. (chmn. 1966—) Home: 330 Glendover Rd Lexington KY 40503 Office: 1500 W Main St Bakhaus Bldg Lexington KY 40505 Tel (606) 252-2312

COMBS, DAN JACK, b. Betsy Layne, Ky., Aug. 22, 1924; student Wooster Coll.; J.D., Cumberland U., 1951. Admitted to Ky. bar, 1951, U.S. Supreme Ct., 1956; individual practice law, Pikeville, Ky. Fellow Internat. Soc. Law and Sci; mem. Am., Ky., Pike County bar assns., Am. Trial Lawyers Assn., Am. Judicature Soc., Nat. Acad. Criminal Defense Lawyers. Office: 207 Caroline Ave Pikeville KY 41501 Tel (606) 437-6218

COMBS, JAMES JOSEPH, b. Springfield, Mo., Oct. 4, 1941; B.A., Harvard U., 1963; diploma in internat. law, Cambridge U., Eng., 1965; LL.B., Columbia U., 1967. Admitted to N.Y. State bar, 1967, D.C. bar, 1968; asso. firm Kirkwood, Kaplan, Russin & Vecchi, Bangkok, Thailand, 1970; asso. firm Dewey, Ballantine, Bushby, Palmer & Wood, N.Y.C., 1971—; served as capt. JAG, USAR, 1968-70; legis. asst. to assemblyman of N.Y. State, 1968. Mem. Am. Bar Assn., N.Y. Legal Aid Soc. Office: 140 Broadway New York City NY 10005 Tel (212) 344-8000

COMBS, NELSON BROWN, b. Lafayette, Ind., Oct. 16, 1934; B.S., Ind. U., 1957; J.D., Golden Gate U., 1972. Admitted to Calif. bar, 1972; individual practice law, San Francisco, 1972-74; partner firm Lia & Combs, San Francisco, 1974—. Mem. Calif. Trial Lawyers Assn., San Francisco Lawyers Club. Office: 676 Chenery St San Francisco CA 94131 Tel (415) 586-6222

COMEN, GERARD SPENCER, b. Balt., Mar. 12, 1940; B.A., U. Balt., 1965, J.D., 1968. Admitted to Md. bar, 1973; detective criminal intelligence div. Balt. City Police Dept., 1960-68; agt. FBI, 1968-70; claims supr. U.S. Fidelity & Guaranty Co., Balt., 1970-74; asst. state's atty. Harford County (Md.), Bel Air, 1974—; instr. principles of criminal law Harford Community Coll. Mem. Bel Air Task Force on Child Abuse and Neglect. Mem. Am., Md., Harford County bar assns. Office: 125 N Main St Bel Air MD 21014 Tel (301) 879-6636

COMISKY, MARVIN, b. Phila., June 5, 1918; B.S.C. summa cum laude, Temple U., 1938; LL.B. cum laude, U. Pa., 1941. Admitted to Pa. bar, 1942; law clk. Pa. Superior Ct., 1941-42, Pa. Supreme Ct., 1946; asso. firm Lemuel B. Schoefield, 1946-54; asso. firm Brumbelow & Comisky, 1954-59; partner firm Blank, Rome, Klaus & Comisky, Phila., 1959—; counsel to Constl. Conv., 1967-68; chmn. Phila. Law Enforcement Council, 1968; mem. Pa. State Bd. Law Examiners, 1974-75. Fellow Am. Coll. Trial Lawyers, Am. Bar Found.; mem. Phila. (vice-chancellor 1963, chancellor 1965), Pa. (pres. 1970), Am. bar assns., Am. Judicature Soc., Nat. Assn. Def. Lawyers in Criminal Cases, Beta Gamma Sigma. Author: Basic Criminal Procedure; contbr. articles in field to profl. jours. Home: 1109 Orleans Rd Cheltenham PA 19002 Office: 1100 Four Penn Center Plaza Philadelphia PA 19103 Tel (215) LO9-3700

COMMETTE, ALBERT S., b. Newport, R.I., Apr. 21, 1911; A.B., Manhattan Coll., 1931; LL.B., Fordham U., 1934. Admitted to N.Y. bar, 1936; asso. firm John P. Smith, N.Y.C., 1936-53; partner firm Budd, Quencer & Commette, 1953-58, partner firm Brown, Quencer & Commette, 1958-72, partner firm Commette, Quencer & Annunziato, 1972—; dir. Midland Ins. Co. Fellow Am. Coll. Trial Lawyers; mem. Am., N.Y. State bar assns., Maritime Law Assn., Am. Arbitration Assn. Office: 60 E 42d St New York City NY 10017 Tel (212) 682-9131

COMPERE, JOHN, b. Abilene, Tex., July 7, 1941; B.A., Tex. Tech. U., 1963; J.D., U. Tex., 1966, certificate U.S. Army Judge Adv. Gen. Sch., 1967. Admitted to Tex. bar, 1966, U.S. Supreme Ct. bar, 1975, U.S. Ct. Mil. Appeals, 1967, U.S. Dist. Ct. for Western Dist. Tex. bar, 1972, U.S. Ct. Appeals for 5th Circuit bar, 1976; partner firm Groce, Locke & Hebdon, San Antonio, 1971—; served to capt. JAGC, U.S. Army, 1966-71, to maj. Res., 1971—. Mem. San Antonio Young Lawyers (dir. 1972-73, pres., 1975-76), San Antonio Family Lawyers (dir. 1976—), San Antonio Bar (dir. 1975-76), Fed., Am. bar assns., State Jr. Bar Tex. (dir. 1976—), State Bar Tex., Tex. Assn. Def. Counsel, Phi Alpha Delta. Office: 2000 Frost Bank Tower San Antonio TX 78205 Tel (512) 225-3031

COMPTON, GARY DARYLL, b. Orangeburg, S.C., Aug. 12, 1947; J.D., Baylor U., 1971. White House intern, 1967; admitted to Tex. bar, 1971; since practiced in Amarillo, briefing atty. 7th Ct. Civil Appeals Tex., 1971-72, asst. city atty., 1972, atty. Pioneer Natural Gas Co., 1972-75; sec., atty. Pioneer Uravan, Inc., Pioneer Coal Co.; v.p. and counsel Pioneer Nuclear, Inc., 1975—. Mem. Am., Tex., Amarillo, Amarillo Jr. bar assns., Wyoming Mining Assn. (legal com.), Phi Alpha Delta. Recipient Am. Legion Americanism award, 1969, Patrick Henry award, 1969; Certificate of Appreciation Childress C. of C., 1965. Home: Route 2 Box 44A-189A Lake Tanglewood TX 79101 Office: PO Box 151 Amarillo TX 79105 Tel (806) 376-4841

COMPTON, GEORGE FREDERICK, JR., b. New Brighton, Pa., Mar. 25, 1948; B.A. in History, Rutgers U., 1970; J.D., U. Akron, 1973. Admitted to Ohio bar, 1973, Fla. bar, 1974; asso. firm Rabb, Axner & Koch, Akron, Ohio, 1973-75; partner firm Koch & Compton, Akron, Ohio, 1975-76; asso. firm McDowall & Whalen, Cuyahoga Falls, Ohio, 1976—. Mem. Am., Ohio, Akron, Fla. bar Assns. Office: POB 8 Cuyahoga Falls OH 44222 Tel (216) 929-4291

COMPTON, JAMES CLEOPHAS, b. Portales, N.Mex., June 23, 1914; student Eastern N.Mex. U., Portales, summer 1934, W. Tex. State U., Canyon, 1935; LL.B., Am. U., Washington, 1940. Admitted to N.Mex. bar, 1941, U.S. Dist. Ct. bar, U.S. Ct. of Appeals; with legal div. Maritime Commn., Washington, 1941; asso. firm Compton & Compton, 1946-68; asst. dist. atty. 9th Dist. N.Mex., 1949-56, dist. atty., 1957-64; judge Dist. Ct., 9th Jud. Dist. N.Mex., Clovis, 1972—; dir. First Nat. Bank, Portales. Scoutmaster, Boy Scouts Am., Portales, 1941-42; chmn. Roosevelt County Salvation Army, 1957-69; dist. advancement chmn. Portales chpt. ARC, 1958, past chmn. Roosevelt County chpt.; Rainbow dad Order Rainbow Girls, Portales, 1959-62, Grand Cross of Color award, 1966-68; chmn. juvenile protection N.Mex. PTA, 1955-57, chmn. safety, 1958-60; adviser for registrants N.Mex. Selective Service Bd. #21, Portales. Mem. Am., N.Mex. bar assns., Legion of Honor, Order DeMolay for Boys, Delta Theta Phi, Sigma Chi. Recipient certificate of appreciation citation Lewis B. Hershey dir. Selective Service System, Presdl. citation Harry Truman, 1952. Home: 1324 S Globe St Portales NM 88130 Office: Dist Ct Courthouse Clovis NM 88130

COMPTON, ROBERT CURRAN, b. El Dorado, Ark., Mar. 27, 1929; B.A., Hendrix Coll., 1949; J.D., U. Ark., 1952. Admitted to Ark. bar, 1952, U.S. Supreme Ct. bar, 1959; spl. agt. FBI, 1952-53; mem. firms Brown & Compton, El Dorado, 1954-63, Brown, Compton & Prewett, El Dorado, 1963—; spl. justice Ark. Supreme Ct., spring 1965; mem. Ark. Penitentiary Study Commn., 1967. Fellow Am. Coll. Trial Lawyers, Internat. Acad. Trial Lawyers; mem. Ark. Bar Assn. (pres. 1975-76). Home: 2504 Forestlawn Dr El Dorado AR 71730 Office: 423 N Washington St El Dorado AR 71730 Tel (501) 862-3478

COMSTOCK, CLYDE NELSON, b. Petoskey, Mich., Feb. 26, 1908; A.B. cum laude, Harvard, 1930, J.D., 1933. Admitted to Mich. bar, 1933, Ohio bar, 1945; individual practice law, Petoskey, 1933-41; mem. firm Andrews, Hadden & Putnam, Cleve., 1945-51; mem. firm Arter & Hadden, Cleve., 1951—, chmn./mng. partner, 1966—; pros. atty. Emmet County, Mich., 1935-39. Mem. bd. mgrs. Cleve. YMCA, 1959-62. Home: 2873 Chatham Rd Pepper Pike OH 44124 Office: Arter & Hadden 1144 Union Commerce Bldg Cleveland OH 44115 Tel (216) 696-1144

COMSTOCK, DAVID COOPER, b. Buffalo, Feb. 10, 1932; B.A., Ohio Wesleyan U., 1954; LL.B., Western Res. U., 1959. Admitted to Ohio bar, 1959; asso. firm Pfau & Pfau, Youngstown, Ohio, 1959-64; partner firm Pfau, Comstock & Springer, Youngstown, 1964—. Trustee, pres. Youngstown Children's and Family Service, 1963-68. Mem. Internat. Assn. Ins. Counsel, Am., Ohio State, Mahoning County (Ohio) bar assns. Home: 4849 Oak Knoll Dr Boardman OH 44512 Office: 900 City Centre One Youngstown OH 44503 Tel (216) 747-3507

COMSTOCK, REGINALD WARREN, b. Madison, Wis., Nov. 15, 1939; B.S. in Chem. Engring., U. Wis., 1963, J.D., 1966. Admitted to Wis. bar, 1966, Ill. bar, 1967; asso. firm Parker, Carter & Markey, Chgo., 1966-69; patent atty. Outboard Marine Corp., Waukegan, Ill., 1969-75, corporate patent counsel, 1975—. Mem. Lake County, Chgo., Ill., Wis., Am. bar assns., Chgo., Am., Milw. patent law assns., Phi Delta Phi. Home: 512 E Scranton Ave Lake Bluff IL 60044 Office: 100 Sea Horse Dr Waukegan IL 60085 Tel (312) 689-5229

COMSTOCK, ROBERT CHARLES, b. Kankakee, Ill. Oct. 28, 1918; A.B., U. Chgo., 1939, J.D., 1941. Admitted to Ill. bar, 1941, Calif. bar, 1954; mem. firm McKnight and Comstock, Chgo., 1942-53; individual practice law, Los Angeles, 1954—. Mem. State Bar Calif., Los Angeles County Bar Assn., Patent Law Assn. Los Angeles, Phi Delta Phi. Office: 2600 Wilshire Blvd Los Angeles CA 90057 Tel (213) 384-3166

CONABOY, RICHARD PAUL, b. Scranton, Pa., June 12, 1925; student, U. Scranton, 1945; LL.B., Cath. U. Am., 1950. Admitted to Pa. bar, 1951; partner firm Powell & Conaboy, Scranton, 1951-54; asso. firm Kennedy, O'Brien and O'Brien, Scranton, 1954-62; judge Pa. Ct. of Common Pleas, 1962—; pres. Pa. Joint Council on Criminal Justice System; mem. Camp Hill Rev. Panel; mam. Nat. Conf. on Juvenile Justice, Nat. Conf. on Corrections. Bd. dirs. Marywood Coll., U. Scranton. Mem. Pa. Conf. State Trial Judges (pres.), Lackawanna, Pa., Am. bar assns., Am. Judicature Soc. Contbr. articles to legal jours. Home: 2115 Prospect Ave Scranton PA 18505 Office: Courthouse Scranton PA 18503 Tel (717) 961-6752

CONAHAN, JAMES PATRICK, b. Hazleton, Pa., May 11, 1941; B.A., Pa. State U., 1965; J.D., Harvard, 1968; Admitted to Hawaii bar, 1968, Samoa bar, 1970; pres., dir. firm Conahan & Conahan, Honolulu; vis. prof. law U. Hawaii, Honolulu, 1975—; instr. Grad. Realtor's Inst., 1971—. Mem. Am., Am. Samoa, Hawaii bar assns. Home: 3725 Diamond Head Rd Honolulu HI 96816 Office: Suite 1500 745 Fort St Honolulu HI 96813 Tel (808) 531-5906

CONANT, MICHAEL, b. Peoria, Ill., Aug. 9, 1924; B.Sc., U. Ill., 1945; A.M., U. Chgo., 1946, Ph.D., 1949, J.D., 1951. Admitted to Ill. bar, 1951; practiced in Chgo., 1951-54; asst. prof. bus. law U. Calif., Berkeley, 1954-60, asso. prof., 1960-66, prof., 1966—; vis. prof. U. Singapore, 1964-65. Mem. Am. Bus. Law Assn., Soc. Pub. Tchrs. Law. Author: Antitrust in the Motion Picture Industry, 1960; Railroad Mergers and Abandonments, 1964; The Constitution and Capitalism, 1974. Home: 9 Norwood Ave Kensington CA 94707 Office: Sch of Bus Adminstrn U of Calif Berkeley CA 94720 Tel (415) 642-1250

CONARD, ALFRED FLETCHER, b. Grinnell, Iowa, Nov. 30, 1911; A.B., Grinnell Coll., 1932, LL.D., 1971; LL.B., U. Pa., 1936; LL.M., Columbia U., 1939, J.S.D., 1942. Admitted to Pa. bar, 1937, Mich. bar, 1967; asso. firm Murdoch, Paxson, Kalish & Green, Phila., 1937-38; asst. prof. U. Kansas City, 1939-41, acting dean, 1941-42; atty. Office Price Adminstrn., Washington, 1942-43; atty. Office Alien Property Custodian, Washington, 1945-46; asso. prof. to prof. U. Ill., Champaign, 1946-54; prof. U. Mich. Ann Arbor, 1954—. Mem. budget and evaluation com. Washtenaw (Wis.) United Way, 1975-77; bd. dirs. Ann Arbor Citizens Council 1969-71. Mem. Am. Bar Assn. (com. corp. laws). Internat. Acad. Comparative Law, Assn. Am. Law Schs. (pres. 1971). Mem. bd. editors Am. Jour. Comparative Law, 1968—, editor-in-chief, 1968-71; bd. editors Am. Bar Found. Research Jour., 1976—; chmn. editorial adv. bd. Bobbs-Merrill law sch. publs. Author: (with others) Enterprise Organization, 2d edit., 1977, Corporations in Perspective, 1976, Cases on Business Organization, 3d edit., 1965, Automobile Accident Costs and Payments, 1964; Studies in the Law of Easements and Licenses in Land, 1942. Recipient Clarence Arthur Kulp award Am. Risk and Ins. Assn., 1965. Home: 16 Heatheridge Ann Arbor MI 48104 Office: 906 Legal Research Bldg U Mich Law Sch Ann Arbor MI 48109 Tel (313) 764-9343

CONCANNON, DONALD O., b. Garden City, Kans., Oct. 28, 1927; A.A., Garden City Jr. Coll., 1948; B.A., Washburn U., 1950, J.D., 1952. Admitted to Kans. bar, 1952, since practiced in Hugoton; county atty. Stevens County (Kans.), 1953-57; city atty. Satanta (Kans.), 1956-62; sec.-treas. Spikes, Inc., Hugoton, 1958-74; pres. Fortune Ins. Co., Inc., Topeka, Kans., 1972-74, chmn. bd., 1974—; dir. 1st Nat. Bank of Attica (Kans.). Chmn., Kans. Republican Party, 1968-70. Mem. Am., Kans., SW Kans. bar assns. Home: 129 N Jackson St Hugoton KS 67951 Office: 120 W 6th St Hugoton KS 67951 Tel (316) 544-4318

CONCANNON, JAMES MICHEAL, III, b. Columbus, Ga., Oct. 2, 1947; B.S., U. Kans., 1968; J.D., 1971. Admitted to Kans. bar, U.S. Dist. Ct. bar, 1971; research atty. Kans. Supreme Ct., Topeka, 1971-73; asst. prof. law Washburn U., Topeka, 1973-76, asso. prof., 1976—; lectr. in field. Mem. Kans., Tex. bar assns., Assn. Trial Lawyers Am., Order of Coif, Phi Alpha Delta. Contbr. articles to legal jours. Home: 2847 Mulvane St Topeka KS 66611 Office: Washburn U Sch Law 1700 College St Topeka KS 66621 Tel (913) 295-6660

CONDE, DALE FRANCIS, b. Rocford, Ill., June 17, 1922; LL.B., Northwestern U., 1948, J.D., 1970. Admitted to Ill. bar, 1948; asst. state's atty. Winnebago County (Ill.), 1948-52; mem. firm Pedderson Menzimer Conde Stoner & Killoren, and predecessors, Rockford, 1952—; instr. law Northwestern U., 1948; instr. law Drake U., 1948. Atty. Loves Park CSC, 1959-63, Loves Park Police Pension Fund, 1959-63, Rock River Fire Protection Dist., 1958-63, Rockford Sch. Dist., 1963—. Mem. Winnebago County (Ill.) (pres. 1975-76), Am., Ill. State bar assns., Order of Coif. Home: 1636 Scottswood Rd Rockford IL 61107 Office: 400 United Center Rockford IL 61101 Tel (815) 987-4000

CONDON, THOMAS P., b. New London, Conn., June 27, 1922; B.S., Providence Coll., 1946; J.D., Georgetown U., 1949. Admitted to Conn. bar, 1950; asso. firm Bascom & O'Brien, New London, 1951-55; partner firm McGarry, Fox & Condon, New London, 1955-62; dept. judge New London City and Police Ct., 1955-61; town counsel, Waterford, Conn., 1953-54; judge Dist. Probate Ct., New London, 1963—; mem. Conn. Ho. of Reps., 1951-52. Fellow Am. Coll. Probate Counsel, Am. Coll. Probate Judges; mem. Am., Conn. (exec. council 1962-65), New London County bar assns., Am. Judicature Soc. Home: 187 Gardner Ave New London CT 06320 Office: Municipal Bldg New London CT 06320 Tel (203) 443-7121

CONDRELL, WILLIAM KENNETH, b. Buffalo, Sept. 19, 1926; B.S., Yale U., 1946; S.M., Mass. Inst. Tech., 1947; LL.B., Harvard U., 1950. Admitted to N.Y. bar, 1951, U.S. Supreme Ct. bar, 1965; with Exec. Office of Pres., Washington, 1951-54; mgmt. cons. McKinsey & Co., Chgo., 1954-55, Gen. Electric Co., Chgo., 1955-59; individual practice law, Washington, 1959-68; partner firm Steptoe & Johnson, Washington, 1968—; chmn. bd. Timber Engring. Co., 1965—. Chmn. Center for Continuing Edn., Washington, 1975—; chmn. parish council Greek Orthodox Ch. of St. George, Bethesda, Md., 1965-69. Mem. Am. Bar Assn., Am. Inst. C.P.A.'s, Soc. Am. Foresters (chmn. natural resources law working group). Editor-in-chief Timber Tax Jour., 1965—. Home: 6601 Michaels Dr Bethesda MD 20034 Office: 1250 Connecticut Ave NW Washington DC 20036 Tel (202) 862-2022

CONFORTI, N. PETER, b. Elizabeth, N.J., Nov. 9, 1943; B.A. in Polit. Sci. magna cum laude, St. Vincent Coll.; J.D., Rutgers U., 1968. Admitted to N.J. bar, 1969, Dist. Ct. N.J., 1969, 3d Circuit Ct. Appeals bar, 1970, U.S. Supreme Ct. bar, 1973; asso. firm Nolan, Lynes, Bell & Moore, 1969-70, Concilio & Brady, 1971-73; individual practice law, 1973-74; partner firm Freytag & Conforti, Sussex, N.J., 1975—; municipal ct. judge Borough of Sussex, 1972—, Sparta Twp., 1974-; atty. to bd. adjustment and planning bd. Branchville Borough, 1976—. Sec. Sussex County Ethics Com., 1973-76. Mem. Am. Judicature Soc., Am., N.J., Sussex County (trustee, treas.) bar assns. Office: 54 Main St Sussex NJ 07461 Tel (201) 875-4196

CONGER, GORDON GENE, b. Idaho Falls, Idaho, May 26, 1935; B.S., Brigham Young U., 1959; LL.D. with honors, U. Wash., 1962. Admitted to Wash. bar, 1962; partner firm Preston, Thorgrimson, Ellis, Holman & Fletcher, Seattle, 1962—. Mem. Seattle-King County, Wash. State, Am. bar assns., Seattle Municipal League, Order of Coif, Phi Delta Phi. Editorial bd. Wash. Law Rev., 1960-62. Home: 2217-123d Ave SE Bellevue WA 98004 Office: 2000 IBM Bldg Fifth Ave and Seneca St Seattle WA 98101 Tel (206) 623-7580

CONGREVE, WILLIAM, III, b. Phila., Oct. 12, 1929; B.S. in Econs., U. Pa., 1953, J.D., 1959. Admitted to Pa. bar, 1961; individual practice law, Allentown, Pa.; asso. house counsel Am. Acceptance Corp., 1963-66, Westinghouse Electric Corp., Pitts., 1966-67, Mack Trucks, Inc., Allentown, 1967-71; atty. City of Allentown, 1971-74. Mem. Am., Pa. Lehigh County (Pa.), Delaware County (Pa.) bar assns. Office: 517 Hamilton St Allentown PA 18101 Tel (215) 439-0577

CONKLIN, KENNETH EDWARD, b. Keota, Iowa, Aug. 21, 1939; B.S., NE Mo. State U., 1966; J.D., Am. U., 1969. Admitted to Md., D.C. bars, 1969, U.S. Supreme Ct. bar, 1973; partner firm Conklin & Noble, Chevy Chase, Md., 1970-77, firm Leighton & Conklin, Washington, 1977—. Mem. Montgomery County, Md., Am., D.C. bar assns., Am. Trial Lawyers Assn. Home: 2208 Osborn Dr Silver Spring MD 20910 Office: suite 800 2033 M St NW Washington DC 20036 Tel (202) 785-4800

CONKLIN, RICHARD JAMES, b. Williston, N.D., Feb. 2, 1930; A.B., Carroll Coll., Helena, Mont., 1952; LL.B., Mont. State U., 1959, J.D., 1970. Admitted to Mont. bar, 1959; individual practice law, White Sulphur Springs, Mont., 1959—; city atty. City of White Sulphur Springs, 1968-75; county atty. County of Meagher County (Mont.), 1968-71; pres., v.p. Mont. Legal Assn., 1970-74; pres. LaPlata Mining Corp., 1970-71; bd. dirs. Reustanco, 1971-75; dir., v.p. Western Mont. Life Inc., 1970-76. Chmn., Democratic Central Com. Meagher County, 1968-76; dir. Meagher County Corp., 1969-75; chmn. Meagher County Devel. Assn., 1965-75. Home: 93 Northern Lights Blvd Kalispell MT 59901

CONKLING, DANIEL CHARLES, b. Balt., Aug. 25, 1940; J.D., U. Balt., 1968. Admitted to Md. bar, 1970; partner firm Naron & Wagner, 1967-69; individual practice law, Glen Burnie, Md., 1969—; pres. Modern Home Builders, Inc., 1976. Pres. Glen Burnie Jaycees, 1973-74; capt. CAP, 1973. Mem. Anne Arundel County Bar Assn., Sigma Delta Kappa. C.P.A., Md. Home: 202 Bell Ave Glen Burnie MD 21061 Office: 32 Balto-Anna Blvd Glen Burnie MD 21061 Tel (301) 761-7522

CONLEY, CHARLES SWINGER, b. Montgomery, Ala., Dec. 8, 1921; B.S., Ala. State U., 1942; M.A. in Edn., U. Mich., 1947, M.A. in History, 1948; J.D., N.Y.U., 1955. Admitted to N.Y. bar, Ala. bar, 1959, U.S. Supreme Ct. bar, U.S. Ct. of Appeals, 5th Circuit, U.S. Dist. Ct., Middle and No. Dist. Ala.; asso. prof. law Fla. A. and M. Coll., Tallahassee, 1956-60; prof. history and polit. sci. Ala. State U., Montgomery, 1962-64; individual practice law, Montgomery, 1960-76; judge Recorder's Ct., Tuskegee, 1968-73, Macon County Ct. Common Pleas, 1973-76, Ala. Dist. Ct., Macon County, 1977—; counsel Congress Racial Equality, N.Y.C., SCLC, Atlanta, ACLU, N.Y.C., S.W. Ala. Farmers Coop. Assn., Inc., Selma, Lawyers Constl. Def. Com., Selma. Mem. Am., Nat. bar assns., Kappa Alpha Psi. Office: 315 S Bainbridge St Montgomery AL 36104 Tel (205) 269-2361

CONLEY, PETER J., b. Fulton, N.Y., June 15, 1934; B.A., U. Notre Dame, 1956; J.D., Albany Law Sch., 1960. Admitted to N.Y. bar; individual practice law, Fulton, 1962—; asst. dist. atty. Oswego County (N.Y.), 1964-70. Mem. N.Y., Oswego and Onontaga Counties bar assns. Office: 306 E Broadway Fulton NY 13069 Tel (315) 592-2446

CONLEY, RAYMOND WILLIAM, b. Council Bluffs, Iowa, Nov. 18, 1943; B.A. in Philosophy, Loras Coll., 1965; J.D., Cath. U. Am., 1974. Intelligence analyst Nat. Security Agy., Ft. Meade, Md., 1965-67, 1970-72; staff asst. Office of Mgmt. Programs, Dept. Justice, Washington, 1972-74; admitted to Iowa bar, 1974; partner firm Conley, Zohn & Needles, Des Moines, 1974—. Legis. campaign mgr., Del., 1972, Iowa, 1976; Iowa coordinator Bread For the World, 1976. Mem. Am., Iowa (chmn. membership com.) assns. trial lawyers, Am. Bar Assn. Recipient Spl. Commendation for outstanding service Dept. Justice, 1973. Home: 651 44th St Des Moines IA 50312 Office: 340 Key Bldg Des Moines IA 50309 Tel (519) 244-6206

CONLON, JOSEPH THOMAS, JR., b. St. Louis, July 24, 1930; A.B., magna cum laude, Notre Dame U., 1952; J.D., Harvard, 1957. Admitted to Mo. bar, 1957; counsel U.S. govt. subcom. Ho. of Reps., Washington, 1957-58; asso. firm Keefe, Schlafly, Griesedieck & Frennel, St. Louis, 1958-59; mem. faculty Notre Dame U., South Bend, Ind., 1960-62; pros. atty. State of Mo., 1963-64; asso. prof. law St. Louis U., 1966—. Mem. Am., St. Louis bar assns., Alpha Kappa Psi, Beta Gamma Sigma. Home: 405 Washington St St Louis MO 63102 Office: 3674 Lindell St St Louis U St Louis MO 63108 Tel (314) CE1-7220

CONN, DAVID GERARD, b. Jersey City, Nov. 18, 1952; B.A. in Chemistry, U. South Fla., 1970; J.D. with honors, U. Fla., 1972. Admitted to Fla. bar, 1973; partner firm Weinstein, Weinberg & Conn, St. Augustine, Fla., 1973—; asst. pub. defender City of St. Augustine, 1975-76. Mem. Am. (vice chmn. com. representation defendants criminal proceedings), Fla., St. Johns County (Fla.) (pres. 1975) bar assns., Acad. Fla. Trial Lawyers. Recipient appreciation certificate Fla. Gov's. Commn. Criminal Justice Standards and Goals, 1975. Office: Weinstein Weinberg & Conn 28 Cordova St Saint Augustine FL 32084 Tel (904) 829-5635

CONN, STEPHEN, b. Newport News, Va., Oct. 21, 1942; B.A., Colgate U., 1964; J.D., Columbia, 1968, M. Internat. Affairs, 1968. Admitted to N.Y. State bar, 1969, N.Mex. bar, 1969, Alaska bar, 1976; atty. Navajo Legal Services, Crownpoint N.Mex., 1968-69, researcher Centro Latino Americano de Pesquisas em Ciencias Socias, Rio de Janeiro, Brazil, 1970; staff atty. Navajo Legal Services, Shiprock, N.Y., 1971; cons. atty. Ramah Navajo High Sch., N.Mex., 1971-72; asso. prof. law U. Alaska, 1972—; asst. dir. bush research programs Criminal Justice Center, 1975—; dir. legal edn. project Alaska Legal Services, 1974-75. Co-organizer Alaska Public Interest Research Group, 1975—; dir. state bd. Alaska chpt. ACLU, 1976—. Mem. Am., Alaska, N.Mex., N.Y. bar assns., Law and Soc. Assn., Orgn. Paralegal Educators, Phi Beta Kappa. Co-author: Law of the People, 1972; Alaska Natives and the Law, 1976; Traditional Eskimo Law Ways and Their Relationship to Bush Justice, 1973; Traditional Athabascan Law Ways and their Relationship to the Contemporary Problems of Bush Justice, 1972; contbr. articles in field to legal jours. Office: 3211 Providence Ave Anchorage AK 99504 Tel (907) 272-5522

CONNARN, JOHN PATRICK, b. Brattleboro, Vt., July 8, 1917; A.B., Norwich U., 1941; LL.B., Portland U., 1952. Admitted to Vt. bar, 1953, U.S. Supreme Ct. bar, 1965; individual practice law, Montpelier, Vt., 1953-64; judge Municipal Ct., Montpelier, 1963, 64; atty. gen. State of Vt., 1965-66; judge U.S. Dist. of Vt., Barre, 1967—; asst. mgr. So. Ariz. Title and Trust Co., 1960-61; mem. Vt. Legislature, 1957-58. Mem. Northfield Sch. Bd., chmn., 1955-59. Mem. Vt., Washington County bar assns. Home: 11 S Main St Northfield VT 05663 Office: Seminary Hill Barre VT 05641 Tel (802) 476-6651

CONNELL, EDWARD PEACOCK, b. Memphis, Apr. 8, 1936; B.B.A. with distinction, U. Miss., 1958, J.D. with distinction, 1961; postgrad. N.Y. U., 1962. Admitted to Miss. bar, 1966, U.S. Supreme Ct. bar, 1966; adj. prof. law U. Miss., 1963-75; asso. firm Holcomb & Curtis, Clarksdale, Miss., 1961-66; partner firm Holcomb, Dunbar, Connell, Merkel, Tollison & Khayat, Clarksdale, 1966—. Mem. Coahoma County (pres. 1969-70), Am. (exec. com. young lawyer's sect. 1966-68) bar assns., Miss. State Bar (2d v.p. 1967-68, pres. young lawyers sect. 1966-67). Home: 111 Cypress Ave Clarksdale MS 38614 Office: 152 Delta Ave Clarksdale MS 38614 Tel (601) 627-2241

CONNELL, MICHAEL JOHN, b. Pasadena, Calif., July 27, 1938; A.B., Harvard U., 1961, LL.B., 1964. Admitted to Calif. bar, 1965; partner firm Paul, Hastings, Jandesky & Walker, Los Angeles, 1964—. Mem. men's council Community TV of So. Calif.; bd. dirs. Connell Found., Los Angeles. Mem. Los Angeles, Calif., Am. bar assns. Office: 555 So Flower St 22d floor Los Angeles CA 90071 Tel (213) 489-4000

CONNELLY, PATRICK, b. Syracuse, N.Y., Feb. 12, 1943; B.S., Lemoyne Coll., 1967; J.D., U. Toledo, 1972. Admitted to N.Y. State bar, 1973; juvenile ct. prosecutor Lucas County (Ohio) Prosecutor's Office, Toledo, 1970-72; legal intern Ohio Supreme Ct., 1971-72; asst. dist. atty. Onondaga County (N.Y.), Syracuse, 1973—; individual practice law, Manlius, N.Y., 1977—; justice Village of Manlius, 1977—. Mem. Onondaga County, N.Y. State, Am. bar assns., Fayetteville-Manlius Jaycees (sec. 1973-74). Recipient Am. Jurisprudence award for Criminal Law, 1971. Home: 601 E Seneca St Manlius NY 13104 Office: Onondaga County Civic Center Syracuse NY 12th Floor 314 E Seneca St Manlius NY 13104 Tel (315) 425-2470 also 682-7340

CONNER, DOUGLAS HENRY, b. Dallas, Mar. 4, 1941; grad. Trinity U., 1964; law degree So. Meth. U., 1969. Admitted to Tex. bar, 1970, U.S. Supreme Ct. bar, 1973; asst. city atty. City of Dallas. Pres. youth fellowship St. Thomas Episcopal Ch. Mem. Dallas Jr., Tex. bar assns. Home: 3316 High Vista Dallas TX 75234 Office: 501 City Hall Dallas TX 75201 Tel (214) 748-9711

CONNER, JAMES CLARY, JR., b. Tampa, Fla., Sept. 3, 1939; B.A., U. Fla., 1964, J.D., 1967. Admitted to Fla. bar, 1967; asso. firm Dye & Joanos, Tallahassee, 1967-68; partner firm Dye & Conner, Tallahassee, 1968-73; individual practice law, Tallahassee, 1973—. Bd. dirs. Municipal Hosp., Tallahassee, 1973—. Mem. Am., Fla. (mem. atty.-realtor liaison com.), Tallahassee bar assns., Leon Club, Tallahassee Jaycees. Home: 2100 Skyland Dr Tallahassee FL 32303 Office: 325 John Knox Rd Suite F-106 Tallahassee FL 32303 Tel (904) 385-1171

CONNER, JON CALVIN, b. Santa Rita, N. Mex., Feb. 11, 1938; B.S., U. Ariz., 1960, J.D., 1967. Admitted to Ariz. bar, 1967; dep. county prosecutor Maricopa County, Ariz., 1967-68; asso. firm Perry & Smith, Phoenix, 1968-69; partner firm Swan & Conner, Phoenix, 1969—. Home: 4411 N 40th St apt 35 Phoenix AZ 85018 Office: 132 S Central Ave Suite 1 Phoenix AZ 85004 Tel (602) 258-6758

CONNER, LEE KENDEL, b. Jackson, Miss., Aug. 3, 1946; B.A., U. Miss., 1967, J.D., 1971. Admitted to Miss. bar, 1971; asso. firm Singley & Morgan, Columbia, 1972-73, county pros. atty. Marion County, 1976-80. Chmn. Marion County March of Dimes, 1974. Mem. Am. Bar Assn., Comml. Law League Am., Miss. Prosecutors Assn., Delta Theta Phi. Home: 415 Dale Columbia MS 39429 Office: POB 366 Columbia MS 39429 Tel (601) 736-2615

CONNER, LEWIS H., JR., b. Chattanooga, Mar. 21, 1938; B.A., Vanderbilt U., 1960, J.D., 1963. Admitted to Tenn. bar, 1963; judge adv. gen. USAR, Fort Campbell, Ky., 1963-66; since practiced in Nashville, partner firm Bailey, Ewing, Dale & Conner, 1966-72, Dearborn & Ewing, 1972—; tchr. Vanderbilt U. Bar Rev., 1967-71. Pres. Nashville Quarterback Club; bd. dirs. Tenn. Jr. Golf Assn.; mem. fin. com. Tenn. Republican Party, 1975—. Mem. Order of Coif, Fed., Nashville, Tenn., Am. bar assns., Tenn., Am. trial lawyers assns.; fellow Coll. Am. Mortgage Attys. Home: 2005 Otter Valley Ln Nashville TN 37215 Office: 1912 Parkway Towers Nashville TN 37219 Tel (615) 259-3560

CONNER, WILLIAM FRED, b. Crandall, Tex., Dec. 8, 1933; B.B.A., U. Houston, 1955; J.D., So. Tex. U., 1969. Admitted to Tex. bar, 1969; accounts supr., economic analyst Tenneco, Inc., Houston, 1955-69; fin. analyst, asst. to v.p. fin. foods div. Coca-Cola Co., Houston, 1969-71; pvt. practice accounting, Houston, 1971-76; partner firm Conner & Cummings, Houston, 1976—; dir. Brittain's Fine Furniture, Brame Constrn., Co., Solar Recording Corp. Dir., Houston Area Men's Brotherhood. Mem. Am. Inst., Tex. Soc. C.P.A.'s. Home: 7726 Pagewood St Houston TX 77063 Office: 2100 W Loop St Suite 815 Houston TX 77027

CONNERAT, WILLIAM SPENCER, JR., b. Savannah, Ga., Oct. 13, 1930; B.A., Yale, 1952; LL.B., U. Ga., 1957. Admitted to Ga. bar, 1958, U.S. Supreme Ct. bar, 1971; pres. Savannah Legal Aid, 1961-63; asso. firm Hunter, Houlihan, Maclean, Exley, Dunn & Connerat, and predecessors, Savannah, 1958-63, mem., 1963—; asst. atty. gen. Eastern Jud. Circuit Ga., 1963. Vestryman, lay reader Christ Episc. Ch., Savannah, 1975—. Mem. Savannah (treas. 1961), Ga., Am. bar assns., Maritime Law Assn. U.S., Am. Judicature Soc. Home: 16 E 56th St Savannah GA 31405 Office: Box 9848 Savannah GA 31402 Tel (912) 236-0261

CONNOLLY, ARTHUR GUILD, JR., b. Wilmington, Del., Sept. 5, 1937; B.S.S., Georgetown U., 1959, J.D., 1962. Admitted to Del. bar, 1962, D.C. bar, 1962; partner firm Connolly, Bove & Lodge, Wilmington, 1962—; mem. Del. State Crime Commn., 1967-68; sec. Bd. Bar Examiners, 1969-74, mem., 1974—. Chmn. profl. unit United Fund, 1970-71. Mem. Am. (corp. law com. 1971—), Del. (chmn. jr. bar com. 1967-69, treas. 1969-71) bar assns. Home: 4615 Weldin Rd Wilmington DE 19803 Office: 1800 Farmers Bank Bldg Wilmington DE 19801 Tel (302) 658-9141

CONNOLLY, EDWARD CHARLES, b. Phila., Apr. 27, 1927; A.B., Villanova U., 1950; LL.B., Cath. U. Am., 1953; postgrad. Temple U., 1976—. Admitted to Pa. bar, 1954, U.S. Supreme Ct. bar, 1963; mem. firm Mullaney & Quinn, Phila., 1955-63; asso. with Walter Jackson, Fairless Hills, Pa., 1963-64; partner firm Connolly, Guerrelli & McAndrews, Warminster, Pa., 1964-67, Connolly & McAndrews, Warminster, 1967-69, Connolly, McAndrews, Kihm & Stevens, Warminster, 1969—; instr. in law Holy Family Coll., 1955-56, Villanova U., 1958-59; dep. asst. atty. gen. State of Pa., 1965-71; solicitor Bucks County Redevel. Authority, 1969-75. Mem. Am., Bucks County (dir. 1973), Pa. bar assns., Am. Judicature Soc. Home: 363 N 2d St Pike Churchville PA 18966 Office: 320 W St Rd Warminster PA 18974 Tel (215) 674-0700

CONNOLLY, JOSEPH JAMES, b. Phila., Sept. 25, 1941; A.B. with honors, U. Pa., 1962, LL.B. magna cum laude, 1965. Admitted to Pa. bar, 1966, U.S. Supreme Ct. bar, 1969; staff counsel Pres's. Commn. on Law Enforcement and Adminstrn. Justice, Washington, 1966; staff asst. Office Sec. of Def., Washington, 1967; asst. solicitor gen. Dept. Justice, Washington, 1967-70; partner firm Goodman & Ewing, Phila., 1970-73, 74—; asst. spl. prosecutor Watergate Spl. Prosecution Force, Washington, 1973-74; adj. prof. constl. law Georgetown U., 1969-70. Mem. Phila., Pa., Am. bar assns., Law Alumni Soc. U. Pa. Law Sch. (sec. 1965—), Order of Coif (bd. mgrs. U. Pa. chpt. 1975—), Phi Beta Kappa. Note editor U. Pa. Law Rev., 1964-65. Office: 1700 Market St Philadelphia PA 19103 Tel (215) 864-7738

CONNOLLY, JOSEPH MICHAEL, b. New Orleans, July 29, 1933; B.B.A., Loyola U., New Orleans, 1955, J.D., 1960. Admitted to La. bar, 1960; partner firm Connolly, Labranche & Lagarde, and predecessors, New Orleans, 1960—; chmn. bd. Century Nat. Bank, New Orleans, 1972—. Bd. dirs. La. Tourist and Conv. Commn., 1970-72. Mem. Am., La., New Orleans bar assns., Am. Judicature Soc. Home: 5978 Louis XIV St New Orleans LA 70126 Office: 3914 Canal St New Orleans LA 70119 Tel (504) 482-5785

CONNOLLY, LEONARD JOHN, b. N.Y.C., July 8, 1937; B.A. magna cum laude, St. Francis Coll., 1959; LL.B., Cornell U., 1963. Admitted to N.Y. bar, 1964; asso. firm Olwine, Connelly, Chase, O'Donnell & Weyher, N.Y.C., 1963-71, partner, 1972—. Mem. Am., N.Y.C. bar assns. Contbr. articles to legal jours. Office: 299 Park Ave New York City NY 10017 Tel (212) 688-0400

CONNOLLY, PAUL KINGSTON, b. Waltham, Mass., June 29, 1906; student Holy Cross Coll., Worcester, Mass., 1925-27; J.D., Boston U., 1930. Admitted to Mass. bar, 1930, U.S. 1st Circuit Ct. Appeals bar, 1935; practiced in Boston, 1930-42, Waltham, 1946-52; judge Waltham Dist. Ct., 1952-70, Mass. Superior Ct., 1970-76, ret., 1976. Chmn. bd. trustees Waltham Pub. Library, 1965—. Mem. Am., Mass., Middlesex, Waltham, Watertown bar assns., Council Judges, Nat. Council Crime and Delinquency. Home: 24 Forest Circle Waltham MA 02154 Office: 637 Main St Waltham MA 02154 Tel (612) 893-6404

CONNOLLY, PAUL RAYMOND, b. Balt., June 28, 1922; A.B. cum laude, Loyola Coll., Balt., 1943, LL.D., 1977; J.D., Georgetown U., 1948, LL.M., 1952. Admitted to Md. bar, 1948, D.C. bar, 1948, U.S. Supreme Ct. bar, 1952, U.S. Tax Ct. bar, 1971, U.S. Ct. of Appeals bar, 1974; asso. firm Hogan & Hartson, Washington, 1948-56, partner, 1956-66; partner firm Williams & Connolly, Washington, 1966-71, Williams, Connolly & Califano, 1971-77, Williams & Connolly, 1977—. Trustee, Pub. Defender Service of D.C., 1969—. Fellow Am. Coll. Trial Lawyers; mem. Am. (litigation sect. council 1973-76, chmn. 1976-77), D.C., Md., Montgomery County bar assns., The Barristers, The Counsellors, Internat. Assn. Ins. Counsel (exec. com. 1967-69). Home: 3005 45th St NW Washington DC 20016 Office: 839 17th St NW Washington DC 20006 Tel (202) 331-5010

CONNOLLY, WALTER BRIGGS, JR., b. Grosse Pointe, Mich., June 10, 1942; student Georgetown U., A.B., U. Detroit, 1964; J.D., U. So. Calif., 1966. Admitted to Mich. bar, 1967; asso. firm Dickinson, Wright & McKean, Detroit; asst. counsel Firestone Tire & Rubber Co., Akron, Ohio, 1972—; adj. prof. Kent State U. Mem. Am., Mich., Detroit bar assns. Author: Practical Guide to Equal Employment Opportunity, 1975; co-author: Practical Guide to Occupational Safety and Health Law, 1976; contbr. numerous articles to law jours. and revs. Home: 3777 Osage Rd Stow OH 44224 Office: 1200 Firestone Pkwy Akron OH 44317 Tel (216) 379-7910

CONNOR, JAMES WILLIAM, b. Seminole, Okla., Aug. 21, 1932; B.S., St. Benedict's Coll., 1954; LL.B., Okla. U., 1959. Admitted to Okla. bar, 1959, U.S. Dist. Ct. for No. Dist. Okla. bar, 1961, for Western Dist. Okla. bar, 1965, U.S. 10th Circuit Ct. Appeals bar, 1972; asst. county atty. Washington County (Okla.), 1959-61, county atty., 1961-63; partner firm Selby, Connor & Coyle and predecessors, Bartlesville, Okla., 1963—; mem. Okla. Ho. of Reps., 1963-71, asst. minority leader 1965-67, minority floor leader, 1967-71; city atty. City of Bartlesville, 1974-75. Mem. state com. Okla. Republican Party, 1963-71; vice chmn. Okla. Commn. on State Fiscal Structure and Procedures, 1965. Mem. Oklahoma County Attys. Assn. (exec. v.p. 1962), Am. Judicature Soc., Washington County (Okla.), Okla., Am. bar assns., Nat. Conf. Legis. Leaders. Recipient Distinguished Service award Bartlesville Jaycees, 1967. Home: 522 E 16th St Bartlesville OK 74003 Office: 416 5th St Bartlesville OK 74003 Tel (918) 336-8114

CONNOR, KENNETH LUKE, b. Atlanta, Apr. 24, 1947; A.A., Chipola Jr. Coll., 1967; B.A. cum laude in Econs. and Internat. Affairs, Fla. State U., 1969, J.D. cum laude, 1972. Admitted to Fla. bar, 1972; since practiced in Lake Wales, Fla., mem. firm Woolfolk, Myers, Curtis, Craig & Gibson, 1972-73, mem. firm Gibson & Connor, 1973—; legis. intern House Com. on Environ. Pollution Control, Fla. Legislature, 1971-72. Mem. Acad. of Fla. Trial Lawyers, Assn. Trial Lawyers of Am., Polk County Criminal Def. Lawyers Assn., Fla. Bar (bd. govs. young lawyers sect. 1977-78). VanDercreek fellow. Home: 834 Campbell Ave Lake Wales FL 33853 Office: 115 N 1st St Lake Wales FL 33853 Tel (813) 676-8584

CONNORS, LEO THOMAS, b. Providence, Apr. 21, 1925; grad. Providence Coll., 1947; J.D., Boston U., 1950. Admitted to R.I. bar, 1952; partner firm Connors & Kilguss, Providence; master in chancery, State of R.I.; town solicitor, Foster, R.I.; chmn. gov.'s Commn. on Emergency Powers, State R.I. Del. R.I. Constl. Conv., 1973, chmn. rules com. Mem. Am. (chmn. legis. council), R.I. (legis. counsel, treas. 1976), New Eng. bar assns., R.I. Trial Lawyers Assn. (pres.), Am. Arbitration Assn. Contbr. articles to legal jours.; editor in chief R.I. Bar Jour. Home: Box 385A S Killingly Rd Fostor RI 02825 Office: 2600 Industrial Bank Bldg Providence RI 02903 Tel (401) 751-3900

CONNORS, STEPHEN WILFRED, b. Monroe, Wis., Mar. 11, 1918; B.S., St. Paul Coll. Law, 1950, LL.B. cum laude, 1952; J.D., William Mitchell Coll. Law, 1969. Admitted to Minn. bar, 1952, Ariz. bar, 1954; individual practice law, Phoenix, 1954—. Mem. Ariz. State Athletic Commn., 1961—; precinct committeeman Democratic Party, 1954-59, 61-72; mem. Ariz. Dem. State Central Com., 1954-59. Mem. Am., Ariz., Minn., Maricopa County, Hennepin County bar assns., Am. Trial Lawyers Assn., Am. Judicature Soc., Internat. Acad. Law and Sci. Home: 3506 N 25th Pl Phoenix AZ 85016 Office: 810 Luhrs Tower Phoenix AZ 85003 Tel (602) 258-5726

CONROY, JAMES PATRICK, b. Chgo., Sept. 8, 1949; B.A. in History cum laude, Ohio State U., 1971, J.D., 1974. Admitted to Ohio bar, 1974; asso. firm Weston, Hurd, Fallon, Paisley & Howley, Cleve., 1974—. Mem. Phi Beta Kappa. Home: 19890 Roslyn Dr Rocky River OH 44116 Office: 2500 Terminal Tower Cleveland OH 44113

CONROY, JOHN PATRICK, b. Bklyn., Mar. 25, 1926; B.S., U.S. Mcht. Marine Acad., 1950; B.S., Fordham U., 1951, J.D., 1957. Admitted to N.Y. bar, 1958; asso. firm Hill, Rivkins, Middleton, Louis & Warburton, N.Y.C., 1957-63, Kelly, Donovan, Robinson & Maloof, N.Y.C., 1963-69; mem. firm McHugh, Heckman, Smith & Leonard, N.Y.C., 1969—; adj. prof. Coll. Ins., N.Y.C., 1972-75. Mem. Maritime Law Assn. U.S. Home: 82 Hampshire Rd Rockville Centre NY 11570 Office: 80 Pine St New York City NY 10005 Tel (212) 422-0222

CONRY, LEONARD MICHAEL, b. Eureka, Calif., Nov. 5, 1922; J.D., U. San Francisco. Admitted to Calif. bar; practice law, Eureka, Calif.; dist. atty., 1958-68. Office: 504 I St Eureka CA 95501 Tel (707) 443-8497

CONSER, LEE CARTER, b. Alliance, Ohio, Dec. 18, 1935; B.A., Ohio Wesleyan U., 1958; J.D., Stetson U., 1961. Admitted to Fla. bar, 1961; individual practice law, Orlando, Fla., 1961-68; justice of the peace, Orlando, 1968-71; county judge Orange County (Fla.), 1971—. Mem. Orlando-Winter Park Camera Club. Recipient three Kodak merit awards. Office: Orange County Court House Room 412 Orlando FL 32801 Tel (305) 420-3616

CONSTAN, CLARENCE RAYMOND, b. Detroit, Feb. 9, 1926; B.S., U. Denver, 1950; J.D., Wayne State U., 1952. Admitted to Mich. bar, 1952; individual practice law, Dearborn Heights, Mich., 1953—; judge Dearborn Twp., 1959-63. Bd. dirs. People's Community Hosp., Wayne, Mich. Mem. Am., Mich. bar assns., Mich. Trial Lawyers Assn., Advocates Club. Office: 23800 Van Born Rd Dearborn Heights MI 48125 Tel (313) 292-4500

CONSTON, HENRY SIEGISMUND, b. Dresden, Germany, Dec. 18, 1928; came to U.S., 1947, naturalized, 1952; B.S. in Bus. Adminstrn., N.Y.U., 1955, J.D., 1958, LL.M., 1961. Admitted to N.Y. bar, 1959; with Calif. Tex. Oil Corp., N.Y.C., 1947-61; asso. firm Walter, Conston, Schurtman & Gumpel, P.C. and predecessors, 1961-62, mem. firm, 1962—. Bd. dirs. Margaret Tietz Center for Nursing, Care, N.Y. Found. Nursing Homes, Inc. Mem. N.Y.C. Bar Assn., Internat. Fiscal Assn. Contbr. articles to publs.; reporter Internat. Fiscal Congress, 1974. Office: 280 Park Ave New York City NY 10017 Tel (212) 682-2323

CONTE, ANTHONY ROCCO, b. Winthrop, Mass., May 26, 1948; B.A. cum laude, Boston U., 1970, J.D., 1973. Admitted to Mass. Supreme Jud. Ct. bar, 1973, U.S. Dist. Ct. bar for Dist. Mass., 1974; partner firm Adair & Conte, Medford, Mass., 1974-76; exec. dir. Mass. Republican State Com., Boston, 1976—; exec. dir. Republicans for an Effective Grass Roots Orgn., Boston, 1975-76. Chmn. Revere (Mass.) Rep. City Com., 1976—; del. Rep. Nat. Conv., 1976. Home: 270 Reservoir Ave Revere MA 02151 Office: 73 Tremont St Room 525 Boston MA 02108 Tel (617) 523-7535

CONTI, RICHARD JOHN, b. Berkeley, Calif., Dec. 13, 1944; B.S., U. Calif., Berkeley, 1967; J.D., Hastings Coll. Law, 1970. Admitted to Calif. bar, 1971; dep. dist. atty. Alameda County, Berkeley, Calif., 1971—. Mem. Alameda County Bar Assn., Criminal Courts Bar Assn. Alameda County (sec., treas.), Lawyers Club of Alameda County. Home: 140 Via Bonita St Alamo CA 94507 Office: 1225 Fallon St Oakland CA 94612 Tel (415) 874-6565

CONTIE, LEROY J., JR., b. Canton, Ohio, Apr. 2, 1920; B.A., U. Mich., 1941, J.D., 1948. Admitted to Ohio bar, 1948, U.S. Supreme Ct. bar, 1968; partner firm Contie & Contie, Canton, 1948-51; city atty., Canton, 1952-60; partner firm Contie & Contie, Canton, 1960-68; judge Ct. of Common Pleas Stark County (Ohio), 1968-71; judge U.S. Dist. Ct. No. Dist. Ohio, Akron, 1971—; chmn. Charter Commn., Canton, 1962. Bd. dirs. Canton chpt. ARC, 1965-68; mem. Stark County Bd. Elections, 1963-68; bd. trustees Legal Aid Soc. Stark County, 1960-71. Mem. Stark County, Ohio, Akron, Am. Cuyahoga County, Fed. bar assns., Am. Judicature Soc., Phi Alpha Delta. Home: 3120 Westmoreland NW Canton OH 44718 Office: 2 S Main St U S Ct House Akron OH 44308 Tel (216) 375-5701

CONVERY, HUGH JAMES, b. Cleve., Feb. 20, 1935; A.B., Bowling Green (Ohio) State U., 1959; J.D., Chase Law Sch., Cin., 1964. Admitted to Ky. bar, 1965; staff claims rep. Allstate Ins Co., Cin., 1964-67; staff atty. Ky. Dept. Highways, Frankfort and Madisonville, 1967-69; individual practice law, Madisonville, 1969—; county atty. Hopkins County (Ky.), 1970-74; city atty. City of Madisonville, 1974-75, city judge, 1975—. Bd. dirs. ARC, Audubon council Boy Scouts Am., chmn. Green River dist., 1976. Mem. Ky., Hopkins County bar assns. Home: 102 Shamrock Dr Madisonville KY 42431 Office: 24 Court St Madisonville KY 42431 Tel (502) 821-2873

CONWAY, BYRON BURTON, b. Wisconsin Rapids, Wis., Jan. 14, 1907; Ph.B., Creighton U., 1928; LL.B., U. Wis., 1930. Admitted to Wis. bar, 1930; individual practice law, Wisconsin Rapids, 1930-50; part-time spl. atty. U.S. Dept. of Justice, 1935-37, 40-42; judge Wood County, Wisconsin Rapids, 1950—. Chmn. South Wood County ARC; mem. bd. advisers, Viterboro Coll., La Crosse, Wis., 1955-70. Mem. Wood County Assn. (pres.), Wis. State Bar Assn. (bd. govs. 1946-50), Nat. Council Juvenile Ct. Judges (pres. 1964-65), Nat. Council on Crime and Delinquency (council of judges 1966-76), Wis. Bd. County Judges, Wis. Bd. Juvenile Ct. Judges, Wis. Bd. Criminal Ct. Judges. Recipient Achievement award for Meritorious Service to Juvenile Cts. of Am., Nat. Council Juvenile Ct. Judges, 1974; contbr. articles to profl. jours. Home: 610 3d St Wisconsin Rapids WI 54494 Office: POB 185 Wisconsin Rapids WI 54494 Tel (715) 423-3000

CONWAY, DONALD ROBERT, b. Bklyn., Apr. 23, 1934; B.S., St. Peter's Coll., 1955; LL.B., Seton Hall U., 1958. Admitted to N.J. bar, 1960, U.S. Supreme Ct. bar, 1968, U.S. Ct. Appeals 3d Circuit bar, 1972; asso. firm Benedict E. Lucchi, Hackensack, N.J., 1960-65; partner firm Lucchi & Conway, Hackensack, 1965-72; prin. Donald R. Conway P.C., 1972—; prosecutor Boro of River Vale, 1963-65, Boro of Westwood, 1965-75; instr. N.J. Continuing Edn.; bd. dirs. Seton Hall Law Sch., 1965-75, Bergen County Legal Services Corp., 1968-72; del. 3d Circuit Judicial Conf., 1968—. Mem. N.J. (pres. 1976-77), Am., Bergen County bar assns., Am., N.J. (trustee) trial lawyers assns. Recipient Hudson County Merit Citation, 1976; named Alumnus of Year, St. Peter's Coll., 1977. Home: 425 2d St Oradell NJ 07649 Office: 25 E Salem St Hackensack NJ 07601 Tel (201) 342-1700

CONWAY, EDMUND VIRGIL, b. Southampton, N.Y., Aug. 2, 1929; B.A. magna cum laude, Colgate U., 1951; LL.B. cum laude, Yale, 1956. Admitted to N.Y. bar, 1956, Circuit Ct. of Appeals bar, 1960; asso. firm Debevoise, Plimpton, Lyons & Gates, N.Y.C., 1956-64; first dep. supt. of banks State of N.Y. and sec. N.Y. State Banking Bd., 1964-67; exec. v.p., trustee Manhattan Savs. Bank, N.Y.C., 1967-68; chmn., pres., trustee The Seamans Bank for Savs., NY.C., 1969—; bd. trustees Consol. Edison Co. of N.Y., Inc., Atlantic Mut. Ins. Co.; bd. dirs. J.P. Stevens & Co., Inc., Centennial Ins. Co., Nat. Securities and Research Corp., Savs. Banks Assn. of the State of N.Y., mem. advisory com. to N.Y. State Supt. of Banks on the supervision of mut. instns., 1967-70. Chmn., Temporary State Commn. on the Water Supply Needs of S.E. N.Y., 1970-75; trustee, Colgate U., 1970-76, Packer Collegiate Inst., Trinity Episcopal Schs. Corp., N.Y. city Police Found., Inc., S. St. Seaport Museum, N.Y. State Maritime Museum Bd.; bd. dirs. N.Y. C. of C. and Industry, Economic Devel. Council of N.Y.C., Inc., Josiah Macy, Jr. Found., Realty Found of N.Y.; v.p. Coalition to Save N.Y.; mem. steering com. Nat. Alliance of Businessmen, Citizens Caucus for Mass Transit; pres. N.Y. Young Rep. Club, 1962-63; del. Rep. State Conv., 1962, 66. Fellow Brandeis U.; mem. Am., N.Y. State bar assns., Assn. of the Bar of the City NY., The Economic Club of N.Y., The Newcomen Soc., Phi Beta Kappa, Order of the Coif, Phi Delta Phi. Editor Yale Law Jour., 1954-56; recipient Brandeis U. medal, 1976. Home: 345 Pondfield Rd Bronxville NY 10708 Office: 30 Wall St New York City NY 10005 Tel (212) 797-5074

CONWAY, EUGENE FRANCIS, b. Evanston, Ill., May 28, 1931; B.S., Xavier Coll., 1953; J.D., Loyola U., 1956. Admitted to Ill. bar, 1956; counsel Continental Casualty Co., Chgo., 1959-69; pres. Eugene F. Conway, Inc., Blue Island, Ill., 1969-76; gen counsel Consumer Credit Ins. Assn., Chgo., 1976—. Mem. Ill. State Bar Assn., Chgo. Athletic Assn. Home: 11801 S Oakley Ave Chicago IL 60643 Office: 307 N Michigan Ave Chicago IL 60601

CONWAY, GERARD LAWRENCE, b. Albany, N.Y., Aug. 30, 1940; B.A., Yale, 1962; J.D., Albany Law Sch., 1965. Admitted to N.Y. bar, 1965; law asst., appellate div. 3rd dept. N.Y. Supreme Ct., 1965-67; asso. firm DeGraff, Foy, Conway and Holt-Harris, Albany, 1967-69, partner, 1969—; asst. to N.Y. Bd. Law Examiners; legis. counsel Med. Soc. N.Y., N.Y. Consumer Fin. Assn., Assn. Adult Care Facilities N.Y., Inc. Democratic committeeman Albany County (N.Y.). Contbr. articles to legal jours. Office: 90 State St Albany NY 12207 Tel (518) 462-5301

CONWAY, JAMES DOMINIC, b. Adams County, Iowa, Oct. 2, 1903; student Loras Coll., Dubuque, Iowa, 1921-23; LL.B., J.D., Creighton U., 1926. Admitted to Nebr. bar; individual practice law, Hastings, Nebr., 1926-41; partner firm Conway & Connelly, and predecessors, Hastings, 1971—; city atty. Hastings, 1935-39; dir. 1st Nat. Bank of Hastings. Nebr. rep. Interstate Oil Compact Commn., 1953-62; chmn. bldg. fund Mary Lanning Meml. Hosp., 1965, trustee, 1970—. Mem. Am., Nebr., 10th Jud. Dist., Adams County bar assns., Delta Theta Phi. Home: RFD 2 11 Village Dr Hastings NE 68901 Office: PO Box 315 Tribune Bldg Hastings NE 68901 Tel (402) 462-5187

CONWAY, JAMES ROBERT, III, b. New Orleans, Mar. 18, 1944; B.B.A., Loyola U., New Orleans, 1965, J.D., 1968. Admitted to La. bar, 1968, U.S. Supreme Ct. bar, 1972; asst. dist. atty. Orleans Parish, New Orleans, 1968-69; asso. of Frank J. Varela, New Orleans, La., 1969-71; partner firm Bridgeman and Conway, Metairie, La., 1971—. Mem. La., Am. bar assns., La. Trial Lawyers Assn. Contbr. article to legal rev. Home: 308 E Livingston Pl Metairie LA 70005 Office: Suite 600 433 Metairie Rd Metairie LA 70005 Tel (504) 837-3200

CONWAY, NEIL MICHAEL, b. Madison, Wis., Apr. 9, 1926; A.B., U. Wis., 1949, LL.B., 1950. Admitted to Wis. bar, 1950; asso. firm Knoll & Wells, Beaver Dam, Wis., 1950, firm Genrich & Terwilliger, Wausau, Wis., 1951-56, Genrich, Terwilliger, Wakeen, Piehler & Conway, Wausau, 1957-72; treas., dir. Terwilliger, Wakeen, Piehler, Conway & Klingberg, Wausau, 1972—, Marathon County Savs. and Loan Assn., Wausau, 1971—; spl. hearing officer Wis. western dist. Dept. Justice, 1958-68. Mem. Wis. Gov.'s Taxation Adv. Com., 1968-70; pres. bd. dirs. Marathon County (Wis.) Social Welfare Coordinating Council, 1959-64; bd. dirs. Wausau Pub. Library, 1964-67. Mem. Wis., Marathon County (pres. 1973-74) bar assns., Phi Alpha Delta. Home: 729 Eau Claire Blvd Wausau WI 54401 Office: 401 4th St Wausau WI 54401 Tel (715) 845-2121

CONWAY, WILLIAM FRANCIS, b. Albany, N.Y., Mar. 28, 1915; B.S., Georgetown U., 1936; J.D., Union U.-Albany Law Sch., 1939. Admitted to N.Y. bar, 1939; mem. firm De Graff, Foy, Conway & Holt-Harris and predecessor, Albany, 1939-51, partner, 1951—; legal asst. N.Y. State Bd. Law Examiners, 1940-60. Mem. adv. bd. Child's Hosp., Albany, 1963-76, trustee, 1976—. Mem. Albany County, N.Y. State, Am. bar assns., Am. Trial Lawyers Assn. Office: 90 State St Albany NY 12207 Tel (518) 462-5301

CONWAY, WILLIAM IGNATIUS, b. Aledo, Ill., Feb. 10, 1900; A.B., Loras Coll., 1924; LL.B., Georgetown U., 1928. Admitted to D.C. bar, 1927, Ill. bar, 1928; spl. agt. FBI, Washington, 1928-33; chief investigator for Atty.-Gen. N.Y., 1938-42; practice law, Chgo., 1946—. Mem. Chgo. Bar Assn. Home: 221 N Kenilworth Ave Oak Park IL 60302 Office: 120 S LaSalle St Chicago IL 60603 Tel (312) 726-3600

COOGLER, MONROE A., JR., b. Brooksville, Fla., Jan. 15, 1939; B.A. in English, U. Fla., 1963; J.D., Fla. State U., 1969. Admitted to Fla. bar, 1970; asso. firm Adams, Sullivan, Coogler & Watson and predecessors, W. Palm Beach, Fla., 1969-71, partner, 1971—; municipal judge City of Boynton Beach, Fla., 1973. Mem. Armed Forces League of the Palm Beaches (sec., pres. 1975-76). Home: 1920 Mediterranean Rd W West Palm Beach FL 33406 Office: 322 First St PO Box 2069 West Palm Beach FL 33402 Tel (305) 659-7200

COOK, CAMILLE WRIGHT, b. Tuscaloosa, Ala., Apr. 14, 1924; A.B., J.D., U. Ala. Admitted to Ala. bar, 1948; asst. prof. Auburn U., until 1968; adminstrv. asst. to dean U. Ala. Sch. Law, 1968-70, asst. dean, lectr. law, 1970-72, asst. dean, dir. continuing legal edn., 1972-75, prof. law, 1975—, asso. dean, dir. continuing legal edn., 1975—. Mem. Assn. Continuing Legal Edn. Adminstrs., U. Ala. Law Sch. Alumni Assn. Home: 32 Ridgeland St Tuscaloosa AL 35401 Office: PO Box CL University AL 35486 Tel (205) 348-6479

COOK, CHARLOTTE SMALLWOOD, b. Union Springs, N.Y., Jan. 24, 1923; B.A., Cornell U., 1944; J.D., Columbia U., 1946. Admitted to N.Y. State bar, 1947, U.S. Ct. Appeals, 1955, U.S. Supreme Ct. bar, 1958, U.S. Dist. Ct. bar, 1952; individual practice law, Warsaw, N.Y., 1947—; mem. firm Smallwood-Cook and Stout, 1975-77, Smallwood-Cook, Stout & Erickson, 1977—; dist. atty. Wyoming County, N.Y., 1950-53. Mem. Am., N.Y. State trial lawyers assns., Wyoming County, N.Y. State (ho. of del.) bar assns. Home: Lamont Gainsville Rd Castile NY 14427 Office: N Main St Warsaw NY 14569

COOK, DANIEL, b. Wilna, Russia, Feb. 28, 1899; B.A., Columbia Coll., 1922, LL.B., 1924. Admitted to N.Y. bar, 1926; since practiced in N.Y.C., individual practice law, 1926-58, tax collector, State N.Y., 1957-68; trial counsel firm Hayt, Hayt & Landau, 1968—; agent, U.S. Govt. Appeal Agency, 1951-54. Mem. N.Y. County Lawyers Assn., Commercial Lawyers Conf. Author: Digest of Commerical Laws of the U.S. Home: 11 Fifth Ave New York City NY 10003 Office: 120 Wall St New York City NY 10005 Tel (212) 425-1179

COOK, DAVID STEWART, b. Logan, Utah, Sept. 20, 1938; J.D., U. Utah, 1962. Admitted to Utah bar, 1962, Idaho bar, 1963; asst. resident counsel Phillips Petroleum Co., Idaho Falls, Idaho, 1962-64; asso. firm Van Cott Bagley Cornwall & McCarthy, Salt Lake City, 1964-66; partner firm Harris & Cook, Shelley, Idaho, 1966-69; asso. firm Nielson, Conder, Hansen, Henriod, 1969-73, partner, 1974-75; mem. firm Stringham & Larsen, P.C., 1975; individual practice law, Bountiful, Utah, 1976—; mem. Moot Ct., Brigham Young U., 1973-75, mem. faculty continuing edn., winter 1975; counsel Utah Legislature. Mem. Am. Bar Assn., Am. Judicature Soc., Order of Coif. Home: 1077 E 75 S Bountiful UT 84010 Office: 85 W 400 St N Bountiful UT 84010 Tel (801) 292-1464

COOK, DOUGLAS EDWARD, b. Trenton, N.J., Jan. 12, 1947; B.A., Dartmouth, 1968; J.D., U. Pa., 1971. Admitted to Pa. bar, 1971; asso. firm. Rambo & Mair, Phila., 1971-73, partner, 1974—. Bd. dirs. Penn. Asylum, 1976—. Mem. Am., Pa., Phila. bar assns. Contbr. articles to profl. jours. Home: 833 Blythe Ave Drexel Hill PA 19026 Office: 220 Witherspoon Bldg Philadelphia PA 19107 Tel (215) 545-3344

COOK, FRANK MILTON, b. Indpls., Sept. 4, 1942; Sc.B., Brown U., 1964; J.D., U. Chgo., 1967. Admitted to Ind. bar, 1968; law clk. to Hon. William E. Steckler, Chief judge U.S. Dist. Ct. for So. Dist. Ind., 1967-68; mem. firm McHale, Cook & Welch, Indpls., 1968-77; individual practice law, Indpls., 1977—. Bd. dirs. Indpls. Jewish Community Relations Council; bd. govs. Indpls. Jewish Welfare Fedn. Mem. Indpls. Bar Assn. Office: 308 Circle Tower Bldg Indianapolis IN 46204 Tel (317) 635-2022

COOK, FRANK ROBERT, JR., b. Washington, Aug. 19, 1923; B.S. in Psychology, Howard U., 1945, postgrad. in psychology, 1946, J.D., 1949; LL.B., Georgetown U., 1955; B.C.S., Southeastern U., 1963, M.C.S., 1964; Ph.D., Western U., 1951, D.D., 1967. Bus. chance broker, Washington, 1941—; real estate broker, Washington, 1942—; ins. broker, Washington, 1943—; pvt. practice accounting, Washington, 1944—; prin. Frank R. Cook, Jr. and Assos., mgmt. cons. co., Seat Pleasant, Md.; admitted to U.S. Ct. Appeals bar, 1949, U.S. Supreme Ct. bar, 1954; U.S. Dist. Ct. bar for Dist. Md., 1976. Minister, Ministry of Salvation, Washington. Mem. Washington Bar Assn., D.C. Unified Bar, Nat. Soc. Pub. Accounts, Am. Assn. Sex Educators and Counselors. Office: 1715 11th St NW Washington DC 20001 Tel (202) DE 2-8108

COOK, HAROLD JAMES, b. Poplar Grove, Ill., Oct. 4, 1905; Ph.B., Marquette U., 1929, LL.B., 1930, J.D., 1968. Admitted to Wis. bar, 1930; individual practice law, Milw., 1930-34; atty. Fed. Home Owners Loan Corp., Madison, Wis., 1934-36; individual practice law, Beloit, Wis., 1936—. Mem. Rock County (Wis.) Bd. Suprs., 1940-46. Mem. Wis., Rock County, Beloit City bar assns. Home: 703 Lilac Rd Beloit WI 53511 Office: 400 E Grand Ave Beloit WI 53511 Tel (608) 362-9000

COOK, HARRY EDWARD, JR., b. Lake Village, Ark., July 18, 1911; B.S. in Elec. Engring., U.S. Naval Acad., 1934; J.D., U. Ark., 1971. Admitted to Ark. bar, 1971; commd. aviation cadet U.S. Navy, 1935, advanced through grades to capt., 1955; ret., 1966; partner firm Evans, Farrar & Callahan, Hot Springs, Ark., 1971-73; asso. firm Wood, Smith & Schnipper, Hot Springs, 1974—. Mem. Am., Ark., Garland County bar assns., Navy League U.S. (pres. Hot Springs 1973-75), Navy League U.S. (Ark. State pres. 1975—). Home: 106 Blue Ridge Dr Hot Srpings AR 71901 Office: 123 Market St Hot Springs AR 71901 Tel (501) 624-1252

COOK, JAMES H., b. Pasadena, Md., Jan. 3, 1918; student Loyola Coll., Balt.; LL.B., U. Md., 1951. Admitted to Md. bar, 1950; now mem. firm Cook, Murray, Howard, Downes & Tracy, Towson, Md. Fellow Am. Coll. Trial Lawyers, Md. Bar Found.; mem. Bar Assn. Balt. City (sec. 1955-56), Baltimore County, Md. State (pres. 1976-77), Am. bar assns., Fedn. Ins. Counsel, Internat. Soc. Barristers, Gamma Eta Gamma. Office: 409 Washington Ave PO Box 5517 Towson MD 21204 Tel (301) 823-4111*

COOK, JAMES JAY, b. St. Paul, Nov. 2, 1940; A.B., Stanford, 1962; J.D. Hastings Coll., 1967. Admitted to Calif. bar, 1968; asso. firm Richards, Watson, Dreyfuss & Gershon, Los Angeles, 1967-72, mng. partner, 1974—. Mem. Am., Calif., Los Angeles County bar assns. Contbr. articles to law jours. Home: 4150 Monterey Rd San Marino CA 91108 Office: 333 S Hope St 38th Floor Los Angeles CA 90071 Tel (213) 626-8484

COOK, JOHN R., JR., b. Lexington, Ky., Jan. 1, 1920; LL.B., U. Ky., 1949. Admitted to Ky. bar, 1949, U.S. Supreme Ct. bar, 1960; individual practice law, 1949-69; partner firm Gess, Mattingly, Saunier & Atchison, Lexington, 1969—; corp. counsel city Lexington, 1954-60, city mgr. 1960-69. Mem. Am., Ky. State bar assns. Home: 501 Clinton Rd Lexington KY 40502 Office: 201 W Short St Lexington KY 40507 Tel (606) 255-2344

COOK, JOSEPH E., b. Denver, Nov. 12, 1921; A.B., Brown U., 1943; M.B.A., U. Pa., 1946; LL.B., Stanford U., 1952. Admitted to Colo. bar, 1952; now mem. firm Welborn, Dufford, Cook & Brown, Denver; mem. Colo. Supreme Ct. Grievance Com., 1969-72. Fellow Am. Coll. Probate Counsel; mem. Denver (pres. 1976-77), Colo. (gov. 1966-70, v.p. 1973-74), Am. bar assns., Lawyer-Pilots Bar Assn., Phi Delta Phi. Office: 1518 United Bank Center 1700 Broadway Denver CO 80202 Tel (303) 861-8013*

COOK, JULIAN ABELE, JR., b. Washington, June 22, 1930; B.A., Pa. State U., 1952; J.D., Georgetown U., 1957. Admitted to Mich. bar, 1958; law clk. to Judge Arthur E. Moore, Oakland County (Mich.) Probate Ct., 1957-58; asso. firms Bledsoe, Ford & Bledsoe, Detroit, 1958-60, Taylor, Patrick, Bailor & Lee, Detroit, 1960-61; partner firms Cooke & Hooe, Pontiac, Mich., 1961-65, Hempstead, Houston, McGrath & Cook, Pontiac, 1965-68, Cook Wittenberg, Curry & Magid, Pontiac, 1965-68, Cook Wittenberg, Curry & Magid, Pontiac, 1975, Cook & Curry, Pontiac, 1976—; individual practice law, Pontiac, 1968-74; mem. Mich. Supreme Ct. Def. Service Com. Chmn. Mich. Civil Rights Commn., 1968-71; pres. Child and Family Services of Mich.; chmn. legis. com., dir. Oakland County (Mich.) Community Mental Health Services Bd.; bd. dirs. Todd-Phillips Childrens' Home, Inc., Detroit, Franklin-Wright Settlement, Inc., Detroit, Pontiac Opportunities Industrialization Orgn., Oakland Youth Symphony, E. Mich. Environ. Action Council; exec. bd. dirs. Camp Oakland, Inc., Oxford, Mich.; mem. Oak Park (Mich.) Compensation Commn. Mem. Am., Nat., Mich. (chmn. com. const. law 1969), Oakland County (chmn. com. continuing legal edn. 1968-69), Wolverine bar assns. Named Distinguished Citizen of Year NAACP, 1970, Boss of Year Oakland County Legal Secs. Assn., 1974; recipient citation of Merit Pontiac Area Urban League, 1971, Resolution of Tribute for work with Civil Rights Commn., 1971. Office: 777 Pontiac Pl 140 S Saginaw St Pontiac MI 48058 Tel (313) 338-6458

COOK, LYLE EDWIN, b. Windham, Maine, Nov. 5, 1908; student Santa Ana Coll., 1925-27; A.B., Stanford, 1929; J.D., U. Calif., Berkeley, 1933. Admitted to Calif. bar, 1933, U.S. Supreme Ct. bar, 1955; dep. collector IRS, Treasury Dept., 1933-37; practiced in Berkeley, Calif., 1937-40, 46-60; served to col. JAGC, U.S. Army, 1940-46; judge Oakland (Calif.)-Piedmont Municipal Ct., 1960-61; judge Alameda County Superior Ct., 1961—, presiding judge, 1969, presiding judge appellate dept., 1973. Mem. Conf. Calif. judges. Recipient Distinguished Alumni award Santa Ana Coll., 1969. Home: 230 Stonewall Rd Berkeley CA 94705 Office: Alameda County Courthouse 1225 Fallon St Oakland CA 94612 Tel (415) 874-6881

COOK, MEYER ALLEN, b. Cleve., Nov. 29, 1905; student Western Res. U., 1927; LL.B., Cleve. Law Sch., 1932. Admitted to Ohio bar, 1932, U.S. Supreme Ct. bar, 1940; individual practice law, Cleve., 1936—; asso. firm Sheehan, Cook and Drain, Cleve.; dep. county clk.

Cuyahoga County (Ohio), 1927-32; asst. law dir. City of Cleve., 1934-35; Torrens examiner Titles for Cts., Cuyahoga County, 1938—. Appeal agt. Draft Bd., Cuyahoga County. Mem. Bar Assn. Greater Cleve., Ohio State Bar Assn. Home: 3725 W 169th St Cleveland OH 44111 Office: 1550 Hanna Bldg Cleveland OH 44115 Tel (216) 696-8860

COOK, OSCAR THOMAS, JR., b. Thomasville, Ga., Dec. 16, 1945; B.A. in Economics, U. Ga., 1967, J.D., 1970. Admitted to Ga. bar, 1970; partner firm Smith, Wiggins, Geer, Brimberry, Hatcher & Cook, Albany, Ga., 1972-73, Hatcher, Cook & Strickland, Albany, 1973—. Mem. Am., Ga., Dougherty bar assns., Albany C. of C., Phi Beta Kappa, Phi Delta Phi. Home: 2324 Hawthorn Dr Albany GA 31707 Office: Suite 504 Albany Towers 235 Roosevelt Ave Albany GA 31702 Tel (912) 883-3737

COOK, RICHARD E., b. Arkansas City, Kans., Mar. 24, 1934; B.A., Washburn U., 1961, LL.B., 1964, J.D., 1970. Admitted to Kans., U.S. Dist. (Kans.) Ct. bars, 1964, U.S. Supreme Ct. bar, 1969; individual practice law, Arkansas City, 1964-67, 1975—; judge Kans. Probate and Juvenile Cts., 1967-75; atty. sch. bd., Cowley County Community Coll., 1967-72. Mem. adv. com. dept. humanities Cowley County Community Coll., 1975-76. Mem. Kans. Bar Assn., Kans. Trial Lawyers Assn. Home: 116 Malwood Ct Arkansas City KS 67005 Office: 110 S A St Arkansas City KS 67005 Tel (316) 442-3350

COOK, ROGER THEODORE, b. Buffalo, June 17, 1915; B.A., Colgate U., 1936; LL.B., U. Buffalo, 1940; J.D., State U. N.Y., 1968. Admitted to N.Y. bar, 1940; partner firms Cook & Cook, Buffalo, 1940-49, Kavinoky, Cook, Hepp, Sandler, Gardner & Wisbaum, Buffalo, 1949-70; justice N.Y. Supreme Ct., Buffalo, 1970—; justice of peace Town of Tonawanda (N.Y.), 1948-59, town atty., 1959-70. Mem. Erie County (N.Y.), N.Y. State, Am. bar assns., Lawyers Club. Recipient Gold Key award Jr. C. of C. Home: 200 Delaware Rd Kenmore NY 14217 Office: Erie County Hall Buffalo NY 14202 Tel (716) 852-1291

COOK, RONALD WALTER, b. Redlands, Calif., Nov. 12, 1943; B.A., U. Calif., Santa Barbara, 1965; J.D., U. Calif., Berkeley, 1968. Admitted to Calif. bar, 1969; asso. firm Price, Postel & Parma, Santa Barbara, 1968-73; mem. firm Hatch & Parent, P.C., Santa Barbara, 1973—; del. to Calif. State Bar Conf. Dels., 1971-72; chmn. Santa Barbara County Continuing Edn. of the Bar, 1969-71. Treas., dir. Family Services Assn., Santa Barbara, 1973—. Mem. Calif., Santa Barbara County bar assns., Barristers Club Santa Barbara (dir. 1971-73). Home: 260 Las Alturas St Santa Barbara CA 93103 Office: 21 E Carrillo St Santa Barbara CA 93102 Tel (805) 963-1971

COOK, WILLIAM DENNIE, b. Lufkin, Tex., Mar. 7, 1944; B.S., Stephen F. Austin State U., 1966; J.D., U. Tex., 1969. Admitted to Tex. bar, 1969, Alaska bar, 1975; judge Lufkin Municipal Ct., 1969-74; individual practice law, Lufkin, 1969-75; trial atty. Tex. Dept. Pub. Welfare, Beaumont, 1975-76; asst. dist. atty. Alaska Dept. Law, Anchorage, 1976—. Mem. adv. bd. Deep E. Tex. Council of Govts. Alcoholism Project, 1972-74. Mem. Alaska Bar Assn., State Bar Tex. Home: Pouch 4-3005 Anchorage AK 99509 Office: Dist Atty's Office 941 W 4th Ave Anchorage AK 99509 Tel (907) 277-8622

COOKE, CHRISTOPHER ROBERT, b. Springfield, Ohio, Dec. 23, 1943; B.A., Yale, 1965; J.D., U. Mich., 1968. Admitted to Ohio bar, 1968, Alaska bar, 1970; asso. firm Taft, Stettinius & Hollister, Cin., 1968; served with VISTA, Kotzebue and Nome, Alaska, 1968-70; staff Alaska Legal Services Corp., Anchorage, 1970-71, Bethel, 1971-73; mem. firm Rice, Hoppner & Hedland, Bethel, 1973-76; judge Alaska Superior Ct., Bechtel, 1976—. Bd. regents U. Alaska, 1975—; mem. adv. bd. Bethel Elementary Sch., 1975—. Mem. Alaska, Bethel (pres.) bar assns. Address: PO Box 555 Bethel AK 99559 Tel (907) 543-2850

COOKE, WILLIAM LEON, b. Aulander, N.C., May 19, 1925; A.B., U. N.C., 1948, LL.B., 1950, J.D., 1969. Admitted to N.C. bar, 1950; partner firm Pritchett, Cooke & Burch, and predecessors, Windsor, N.C., 1951—. Sec.-treas. Bertie County Library, 1952; deacon Baptist Ch., Windsor, N.C., 1974-76; chmn. Bertie March of Dimes, 1951-56; chmn. exec. com. Bertie County Democratic Party, 1974-77. Mem. Am., N.C., Bertie County bar assns., N.C. Bar. Home: 211 W Gray St Windsor NC 27983 Office: 203 Dundee St Windsor NC 27983 Tel (519) 794-3161

COOKSEY, CHARLOTTE MANNING, b. Balt., Oct. 30, 1947; B.A., Newcomb Coll., Tulane U., 1968; J.D., Loyola U., New Orleans, 1971. Admitted to La. bar, 1971, D.C. bar, 1973, Md. bar, 1975; staff atty. New Orleans Local Asst. Corp., 1971-72; staff atty. Legal Aid Bur., Inc., Balt., 1972-74, mng. atty., 1975—; trial atty. div. civil rights Dept. Justice, Washington, 1974-75; mem. Md. Gov.'s Commn. Juvenile Justice, Balt. Mayor's Task Force on Child Abuse and Neglect. Mem. adv. bd. resource project H.E.L.P., Balt., Single Parents, Balt. Mem. La., Am., D.C., Md. State bar assns., Women's Bar Assn. Md. Office: 341 N Calvert St Baltimore MD 21202 Tel (301) 539-5340

COOKSEY, KENNETH E., b. Monticello, Fla., Feb. 9, 1923; student Emory Jr. Coll., 1947; LL.B., Stetson U., 1949. Admitted to Fla. bar, 1949; judge Jefferson County (Fla.), 1953-73, 2nd Jud. Circuit of Fla., Tallahassee, 1973—. Home: PO Box 480 Monticello FL 32344 Office: Ct House Tallahassee FL 32301 Tel (904) 997-3866

COOKSEY, NATHAN LYNN, b. Houston, Apr. 22, 1939; B.A., Abilene Christian Coll., 1965; J.D., Baylor U., 1965. Admitted to Tex. bar, 1967; criminal dist. atty. Texarkana (Tex.), 1971—. Mem. Tex. (com. penal code and criminal procedure), Am., Bowie County bar assns., Tex. Dist. Attys. Assn. Home: 2812 Pine St Texarkana TX 75501 Office: 412 Texas Blvd Texarkana TX 75501 Tel (214) 794-3738

COOKSTON, RAYMOND EUGENE, b. Marion, Ohio, Mar. 1, 1907; J.D., Ohio No. U., 1929. Admitted to Ohio bar, 1930, U.S. Supreme Ct. bar, 1945; asst. v.p. Prentice Hall Corp. Systems, Inc., Cleve.; instr. Cleve. State U., 1971-72. Commdr., Cleve. Power Squadron, 1950. Fellow Ohio State Bar Found.; mem. Ohio (exec. com.), Greater Cleve. bar assns., Soc. Mil. Engrs. Home: 26234 Lake Rd Bay Village OH 44140 Office: 796 Union Commerce Bldg Cleveland OH 44115 Tel (216) 781-3920

COOLEY, GEORGE HENRY, III, b. Buffalo, Oct. 27, 1944; A.B., Marquette U., 1966; J.D., S. Tex. Coll. Law, 1970. Admitted to Tex. bar, 1970; asst. city atty., Galveston, Tex., 1971-73; asst. dist. atty., Galveston County, Tex., 1973—. Mem. State Bar Tex., Nat., Tex. County Dist. Attys. Assns., Galveston County Bar Assn. Home: 6 Tiki Circle Galveston TX 77550 Office: 405 Galveston County Courthouse Galveston TX 77550 Tel (713) 762-8621

COOLEY, THOMAS MCINTYRE, II, b. Detroit, Mar. 5, 1910; A.B., U. Mich., 1932; LL.B., Harvard, 1935. Admitted to Mich. bar, 1935, D.C., Va. bars, 1948, Pa. bar, 1959, also U.S. Supreme Ct. bar; mem. legal staff FCC, Washington, 1936-37; asso. firm Dykema, Jones & Wheat, Detroit, 1937; instr. Western Res. U., 1938-40; asst. prof. law, 1940-41; mem. bd. immigration appeals U.S. Dept. Justice, Washington, 1941-42, asso. dir. alien enemy control unit, 1942-45, dir. alien enemy control unit, chief alien enemy litigation div. 1946-47; dep. dir. div. on displaced persons UNRRA, Washington, 1945-46; counsel imigration and naturalization com. U.S. Ho. of Reps., Washington; counsel Citizens Com. on Displaced Persons, 1947-48; individual practice law, Washington, 1948-50; partner firm Weaver and Glassie Washington, 1950-57; dean, prof. law U. Pitts., 1957-65, 66—; prof. law, U. Ill., 1965-66; counsel labor-mgmt. subcom. U.S. Senate Com. on Labor and Edn., 1948-50; asso. counsel govt. ops. subcom. U.S. Ho. Reps., Washington, 1950; sec. gen. counsel Central Blood Bank Pitts. Mem. Mich., Pa., Va., Allegheny County bar assns., Assn. Immigration and Naturalization Lawyers, ACLU, United World Federalists. Contbr. articles in field to law jours. Home and office: 4644 Filmore Pittsburgh PA 15213 Tel (412) 624-6235

COOLLEY, RONALD BRUCE, b. Manchester, N.H., Feb. 15, 1946; B.S. in Aero. Engring., Iowa State U., 1969; M.B.A., J.D., U. Iowa, 1972. Admitted to Ill. bar, 1973, U.S. Patent Office bar, 1974, U.S. Supreme Ct. bar, 1977; partner firm Mason, Kolehmainen, Rathburn & Wyss, Chgo., 1973—; instr. New Trier High Sch., 1976. Mem. Patent Law Assn. Chgo., Am., Chgo. bar assns. Contbr. article to bus. mag. Home: 534 Deerfield Rd Deerfield IL 60015 Office: 20 N Wacker Dr Chicago IL 60606 Tel (312) 346-1677

COOMBS, ARDEN ERNEST, b. Garland, Utah, Jan. 24, 1930; Asso. Sci., Weber State Coll., 1950; B.S., U. Utah, 1956, J.D., 1957. Admitted to Utah bar, 1957; mem. firm Hermanson & Coombs, Salina, Utah, 1958-59, Tremonton, Utah, 1959-62; mem. firm Coombs & Daines, Brigham City, Utah, 1962-66; individual practice law, Ogden, Utah, 1966—; city atty. Salina, 1958-60, Tremonton, 1960-62, South Ogden, 1968-69; counsel BFM Constructors, Inc.; trustee in bankruptcy No. div. U.S. Dist. Ct. Utah, 1966-74. Mem. Weber County Bar Assn., Am. Assn. Trial Lawyers. Home: 3440 Polk Ave Ogden UT 84403 Office: 2910 Washington Blvd Ogden UT 84401 Tel (801) 621-1585

COONEY, JOHN CHARLES, b. Sopkane, Wash., Nov. 2, 1940; B.A., Gonzaga U., 1963, J.D., 1966. Admitted to Wash. bar, 1966; asst. atty. gen. Wash. State, 1966; pros. atty. City of Spokane, 1967-70; judge U.S. Dist. Ct. for Spokane County, 1970—. Bd. dirs. Sopkane County Corrections Dept. Mem. Wash. State Magistrate Assn. Home: 6020 S Martin St Spokane WA 99203 Office: W 1116 Mallon St Spokane WA 99201 Tel (509) 456-2280

COONEY, JOSEPH PATRICK, b. Hartford, Conn., Aug. 30, 1906; LL.B., Georgetown U., 1929. Admitted to Conn. bar, 1929, U.S. Supreme Ct. bar, 1965; sr. partner firm Cooney, Scully and Dowling, Hartford, 1960—; asst. U.S. Dist. Atty., Dist. of Conn., 1941-43. Mem. Conn. State Senate, 1931-33, 37-41; mem. Hartford County Commn., 1933-39; mem. Hartford Aviation Commn., 1930-31; chmn. Gov.'s Com. on Jud. Selection, 1975—. Mem. Am., Conn. (pres. 1965-66), Hartford County (pres. 1946-48) bar assns., Am. Coll. Trial Lawyers, Internat. Soc. Barristers. Recipient John Carroll award Georgetown U., 1965. Home: 795 Prospect Ave West Hartford CT 06105 Office: 266 Pearl St Hartford CT 06103 Tel (203) 527-1141

COONEY, WILLIAM JOSEPH, b. Oak Park, Ill., June 3, 1937; B.S., Coll. Holy Cross, 1959; LL.B., Georgetown U., 1962. Admitted to Ill. bar, 1962, Mass. bar, 1962; staff atty. SEC, Chgo., 1962-65; asso. firm McBride, Baker, Wienke & Schlosser, Chgo., 1965-70, partner, 1970—; chmn. St. Procopious Legal Aid Clinic, 1973—. Mem. St. Mary's Sch. Bd., 1969-72, pres. bd., 1972; bd. dirs. Riverside Community Fund, 1975-77, pres. bd., 1977; bd. dirs. Chgo. Vol. Legal Services Found., 1973—. Mem. Am., Ill., Chgo., Fed. bar assns. Home: 257 Bartram Rd Riverside IL 60546 Office: 110 N Wacker Dr Chicago IL 60606 Tel (312) 346-6191

COONS, ALLAN HAROLD, b. Ashland, Wis., May 25, 1939; A.B., Stanford, 1961; J.D., U. Calif. Hastings Sch. Law, San Francisco, 1967. Admitted to Calif. bar, 1967, Oreg. bar, 1968; asst. atty. gen. Oreg. Dept. Justice, 1968-69; partner firm Coons, Cole and Anderson, and predecessors, Eugene, Oreg., 1969—. Chmn. Eugene chpt. Sierra Club, 1970-73, 76; sec., bd. dirs. Lane Group Health Services, Lane County, Oreg. Mem. Oreg. Trial Lawyers, Oreg. Workman Compensation Attys., Lane County (chmn. med.-legal com. 1975-76), Oreg. State bars. Home: 2742 Wingate St Eugene OR 97401 Office: 101 E Broadway Suite 303 Eugene OR 97401 Tel (503) 485-0203

COONS, STEPHEN MERLE, b. Indpls., May 27, 1941; A.B., Wabash Coll., Crawfordsville, Ind., 1963; J.D., Ind. U., 1971. Admitted to Ind. bar, 1971; individual practice law, Indpls., 1971-74; asso. firm Compton, Coons, Fetta & Thompson, Indpls., 1974—. Mem. Am., Ind., Indpls. bar assns. Home: 8020 N Meridian St Indianapolis IN 46260 Office: 700 Investors Trust Bldg Indianapolis IN 46204 Tel (317) 634-7680

COONTS, GILBERT GRAY, b. Barbour County, W.Va., Feb. 21, 1919; J.D., W.Va. U., 1948. Admitted to W.Va. bar, 1948; partner firm Hymes & Coonts, Buckhannon, W.Va., 1948—. Mem. Am., W.Va., W.Va. State (chmn. dist. grievance com.), Upshur County (W.Va.) (pres. 1954) bar assns., Buckhannon C. of C. (pres. 1970). Named Employer of Year Buckhannon Bus. and Profl. Women's Club. Home: 2 Highland Dr Buckhannon WV 26201 Office: 23 W Main St Buckhannon WV 26201 Tel (304) 472-1565

COOPER, ALAN JOHN, b. Buffalo, N.Y., Sept. 10, 1942; B.A., U. Notre Dame, 1965; J.D., State U. N.Y., Buffalo, 1968. Admitted to N.Y. bar, 1968, U.S. Supreme Ct. bar, 1971; asso. firm Buerger & O'Connor, Buffalo, 1968; asst. dist. atty. Erie County (N.Y.), 1969-72; partner firm Cooper & Ulaszewski, Cheektowaga, N.Y., 1973-75; individual practice law, Cheektowaga, 1975—; confidential aide N.Y. Supreme Ct. Justice Joseph Kuszynski, 1975—. Mem. Am., N.Y., Erie County bar assns. Home: 30 Sherwood Ln West Seneca NY 14224 Office: 1020 French Rd Cheektowaga NY 14227 Tel (716) 668-1800

COOPER, CARY DAVID, b. Great Falls, Mont., Mar. 29, 1942; B.S., U. Calif., Los Angeles, 1963, M.B.A., 1964, J.D., 1967. Admitted to Calif. bar, 1968; asso. firm Buchalter, Nemer, Fields & Chrystie, Los Angeles, 1967-73, mem., 1973—. Mem. Am., Los Angeles County bar assns. Contbr. articles in field to profl. jours. Office: 700 S Flower St Los Angeles CA 90017 Tel (213) 626-6700

COOPER, CLEMENT THEODORE, b. Miami, Fla., Oct. 26, 1930; A.B., Lincoln U., 1952; postgrad. Boston U., 1954-55; J.D., Howard U., 1958. Admitted to D.C. bar, 1960, Mich. bar, 1960, U.S. Supreme Ct. bar, 1963; individual practice law, Washington, 1960—; legal cons. No. Calif. Mining Assn. Mem. advisory council dept. welfare, Dist. Columbia, 1963-66. Mem. Am. Trial Lawyers Assn., Am. (vice chmn. com. oil natural resources), D.C., Nat. bar assns., ACLU, Am. Judicature Soc., Rocky Mtn. Min. Law Found., Internat. Platform Assn., Am. Lawyers Assn. Author: Sealed Verdict; contbr. articles to legal jours. Home: 728 Dahlia St NW Washington DC 20012 Office: 918 F St NW Washington DC 20004 Tel (202) 393-3900

COOPER, EDWIN DAVIS, b. Jonesboro, Ark., Mar. 13, 1945; B.A., Vanderbilt U., 1967; J.D., Sanford U., 1971. Admitted to Ark. bar, 1971; asst. gen. counsel Cooper Communities, Inc., Bentonville, Ark., 1971—. Mem. Am., Ark. bar assns. Home: 396 Cypress Point Rd #4 W Memphis AR 72301 Office: PO Box 830 101 First Nat Bank Bldg W Memphis AR 72301 Tel (501) 735-3001

COOPER, ERWIN ELLING, b. Boston, Mass., Oct. 7, 1918; A.B., U. Maine, 1939; J.D., Harvard, 1942. Admitted to Mass. bar, 1942, U.S. Tax Ct. bar, 1970, U.S. Ct. of Mil. Appeals bar, 1965, U.S. Supreme Ct. bar, 1965, U.S. Ct. Claims bar, 1971; asso. firm Harry P. Goldstein, Boston, 1946-48; individual practice law, Boston, 1948-53; partner firm Kabatzick Stern & Cooper, Boston, 1953—; adj. prof. law New Eng. Sch. Law, Boston, 1953—; col., JAGC, USAR, active service, 1942-46, res., 1946-74; USAR instr. Harvard Law Sch., 1954-59; Mass. land ct. examiner, 1952—. Mem. Am. Arbitration Assn. (panel 1966—), JAG Assn. Recipient John Kleinberger award, 1939; Lilienthal Distinguished Alumni Service award Tau Epsilon Phi, 1965; Alumni award for Distinguished Faculty Service, New Eng. Sch. Law, 1975. Home: 8 Kirkstall Rd Newtonville MA 02160 Office: 131 State St Boston MA 02109 Tel (617) 523-8181

COOPER, FRED LAVERN, b. Columbia, Miss., Aug. 6, 1940; student U. So. Miss., 1963; LL.B., Jackson (Miss.) Sch. Law, 1969. Admitted to Miss. bar, 1969; individual practice law, Columbia, 1971—. Mem. Miss. Trial Lawyers Assn. Home: Route 2 Box 339 Columbia MS 39429 Office: 203-204 Newsom Bldg Columbia MS 39429 Tel (601) 736-4453

COOPER, GEORGE, b. Balt., May 31, 1937; B.S. in Econs., U. Pa., 1958; LL.B., Harvard, 1961. Admitted to D.C. bar, 1962, U.S. Supreme Ct. bar, 1972, N.Y. State bar, 1975; asso. firm. Covington & Burling, Washington, 1963-66; asst. prof. law Columbia, N.Y.C., 1966-69, asso. prof., 1969-70, prof., 1970—; dir. Center on Social Welfare Policy and Law N.Y.C., 1970-71; vis. prof. Harvard, Cambridge, Mass., 1974-75; co-dir. Employment Rights Project, N.Y.C., 1972—. Co-author: Law and Poverty, 1973; Fair Employment Litigation, 1975; contbr. articles to legal jours. Office: 435 W 116th St New York City NY 10027 Tel (212) 280-4291

COOPER, GORDON REED, b. La Plata, Mo., July 7, 1925; B.S. in Gen. Bus., Ind. U., 1948, LL.B., 1957, J.D., 1967. Admitted to Colo. bar, 1963; individual practice law, Pueblo, Colo., 1964-65, 73-74; asst. dist. atty. Pueblo, 1965-73, county judge, 1974—; sec. Pueblo County Retirement Bd., 1970-74. Mem. Am., Colo., Pueblo County bar assns., Am. Judicature Soc. Office: 320 W 10th St Pueblo CO 81003 Tel (303) 542-0311

COOPER, GRANT BURR, b. N.Y.C., Apr. 1, 1903; student Pace Coll., 1921; J.D., Southwestern U., Los Angeles, Calif., 1926. Admitted to Calif. bar, 1927, U.S. Supreme Ct. bar, 1965; dep. dist. atty. Los Angeles County, 1929-35, chief dep. dist. atty., 1940-43; dep. city atty. City of Los Angeles, 1935-38; asso. Henry Herzbrun, 1938-44, Loeb & Loeb, 1944-46, Stahlman & Cooper, 1946-55, Cooper, Nelson & Moore, 1955-70; individual practice law, 1970-76; of counsel firm Greenberg, Bernhard, Weiss & Karma, Los Angeles, 1977—. Pres. Los Angeles Health Commn., 1944; bd. councilors U. So. Calif. Sch. Law. Fellow Am. Found.; mem. Los Angeles County, Am. bar assns., State Bar Calif., Am. Coll. Trial Lawyers (past pres., bd. regents). Home: 3447 Wrightview Dr Studio City CA 91604 Office: 1880 Century Park E Suite 1150 Los Angeles CA 90067 Tel (213) 553-6111 also (213) 879-1972

COOPER, JOHN CROSSAN, JR., b. Baltimore County, Md., Oct. 16, 1901; A.B., Princeton, 1923; LL.B., Yale, 1927. Admitted to Md. bar, 1927; asso. firm Venable, Baetjer & Howard, Balt., 1927-38, partner, 1938—. Trustee Johns Hopkins U., 1966—, Gilman Sch., 1938—. Fellow Am. Coll. Trial Lawyers; mem. Am., Md. (v.p. 1952-53), Balt. City (past pres.) bar assns. Home: 915 W Lake Ave Baltimore MD 21210 Office: 1800 Mercantile Bank & Trust Bldg 2 Hopkins Plaza Baltimore MD 21201 Tel (301) 752-6780

COOPER, JOHN GORDON, b. Seattle, Dec. 7, 1945; student Whitman Coll., 1963-65; B.A. in Econs. with high honors, U. Calif. at Santa Barbara, 1967; J.D., U. Wash., 1970. Admitted to Wash. bar, 1970, U.S. Supreme Ct. bar, 1974; clk. to judge Wash. State Ct. Appeals, 1970-71; mem. firm Scholfield & Stafford, and predecessor, Seattle, 1971—. Mem. Am., Wash. State, Seattle-King County bar assns., Am., Wash. State trial lawyers assns. Office: 400 Union St Seattle WA 98101 Tel (206) 623-9900

COOPER, JOHN WOODCOCK, JR., b. Eureka, Calif., Dec. 14, 1923; B.M.S., San Francisco Coll. Mortuary Sci., 1945; J.D., Lincoln U., 1970. Admitted to Calif. bar, 1971; owner, pres. Cooper Mortuary, 1945-66; gen. practice law, Eureka, Calif.; arbitrator Am. Arbitration Assn. Mem. Eureka City Council, 1949-50, Eureka Housing Authority, 1946-60; mem. adv. bd. Salvation Army; mem. Republican Central Com. Eureka. Mem. Am., Calif., Humboldt County bar assns., Calif. Trial Lawyers Assn., Am. Inst. Hypnosis. Office: 515 J St Eureka CA 95501 Tel (707) 443-7375

COOPER, LEE EMANUEL, JR., b. Los Angeles, Dec. 17, 1931; A.A., Glendale (Calif.) Coll., 1954; B.S. in Accounting, U. Calif. at Los Angeles, 1957, J.D., 1960. Admitted to Calif. bar, 1961; judge Ventura County (Calif.) Municipal Ct., 1970—, asst. presiding judge, 1975, presiding judge, 1976—; with U.S. Air Force, French Morocco, 1951-52; dep. dist. atty. Ventura County, 1960-62; asso. Robert J. Lagomarsino, Ventura, Calif., 1962-64; partner firm Danch, Ferro, Lagomarsino & Cooper, Ventura, 1965-70; mem. Ventura County Criminal Justice Planning Bd., 1976; mem. adv. bd. Ventura Coll. Law, 1974—. Mem. Ventura County Republican Central Com., 1964, 66, 68; mem. adv. bd. St. Joseph's Convalescent Hosp., Ojai, Calif., 1970; active Ventura Hot Line, 1968-70. Mem. Am., Calif. judges assn., Am. Judicature Soc., Phi Delta Phi. Office: Ventura County Courthouse Ventura CA 93001 Tel (805) 487-7771

COOPER, LEON MELVIN, b. Los Angeles, July 24, 1924; A.B., U. Calif., Los Angeles, 1944; LL.B., Harvard, 1949; LL.M., U. So. Calif., 1965. Admitted to Mass. bar, 1949, Calif. bar, 1950, U.S. Supreme Ct.

bar, 1957; pres. Cooper, Wyatt, Tepper & Plant Profl. Corp. and predecessors, Los Angeles, 1958—; mem. Alcoholic Beverage Control Appeals Bd. Calif., 1965-67, chmn., 1966-67. Chmn. So. Calif. Democratic Central Com., 1968-71. Mem. Am., Mass., Los Angeles, Los Angeles County (arbitrator), bar assns., State Bar Calif. (disciplinary referee), Phi Beta Kappa. Home: 2709 Via Elevado Palos Verdes Estates CA 90274 Office: 611 W 6th St Suite 2700 Los Angeles CA 90017 Tel (213) 680-2180

COOPER, MICHAEL ANTHONY, b. Passaic, N.J., Mar. 29, 1936; B.A., Harvard, 1957, LL.B., 1960. Admitted to N.Y. bar, 1961, U.S. Supreme Ct. bar, 1969; with firm Sullivan & Cromwell, N.Y.C., 1960—, partner, 1968—. Mem. Am., N.Y. bar assns., Assn. Bar N.Y.C., N.Y. County Lawyers Assn., Am. Judicature Soc. Office: 48 Wall St New York City NY 10005 Tel (212) 952-8193

COOPER, NORMAN LEE, b. Birmingham, Ala., Feb. 1, 1940; B.S. in Bus. Adminstrn., U. Ala., 1961, LL.B., 1964. Admitted to Ala. bar, 1964; partner firm Cabaniss, Johnston, Gardner, Dumas & O'Neal, Birmingham, 1966—. Mem. Birmingham (sec. 1972-73), Am., (sec. litigation sect. 1976-77), Ala. (pres. Young Lawyers sect. 1974-75, Merit award 1976) bar assns. Office: First Nat-So Natural Bldg 19th Fl Birmingham AL 35203 Tel (205) 252-8800

COOPER, ROBERT C., b. Detroit, Apr. 6, 1942; student Mich. State U.; B.A., U. South Fla., 1966; J.D., Emory U., 1971. Admitted to Fla. bar, 1971; asso. firm Hoffman, Hendry, Parker & Smith, Profl. Assn., Orlando, Fla., 1971-73; partner firm Earle, Yanchuck & Cooper, Profl. Assn., Orlando, 1973—. Mem. Am., Orange County bar assns., Fla. bar (workmen's compensation sect., trial lawyers sect.), Am. Assn. Trial Lawyers. Home: 304 Wing Ln Winter Park FL 32789 Office: 701 E South St Orlando FL 32801 Tel (305) 896-1451

COOPER, ROBERT ELBERT, b. Chattanooga, Oct. 14, 1920; B.A., U. N.C., 1946; J.D., Vanderbilt U., 1949. Admitted to Tenn. bar, 1948; practiced in Chattanooga, 1949-53; judge Tenn. 6th Jud. Circuit Ct., 1953-60, Tenn. Ct. Appeals, 1960-74, presiding judge eastern div., 1970-74; asso. justice Tenn. Supreme Ct., 1974-76, chief justice, 1976—; chmn. Tenn. Jud. Council, 1967-77; mem. Tenn. Jud. Standards Commn., 1971-77. Elder Presbyn. Ch. in U.S.A.; bd. dirs. Met. YMCA, Chattanooga, 1956-65. Mem. Tenn. Jud. Conf., Am. Tenn. bar assns., Am. Judicature Soc., Order of Coif, Phi Beta Kappa, Phi Alpha Delta. Home: 196 Woodcliff Circle Signal Mountain TN 37377 Office: Hamilton County Justice Bldg Chattanooga TN 37402 Tel (615) 267-0373

COOPER, ROBERT ELLIOTT, b. San Diego, Sept. 6, 1939; A.B. with distinction, Northwestern U., 1961; LL.B., Yale, 1964. Admitted to Calif. bar, 1965, U.S. Supreme Ct. bar, 1972; asso. firm Gibson, Dunn & Crutcher, Los Angeles, 1965-70, partner, 1971—. Mem. Am., Los Angeles County bar assns., Order of Coif, Phi Beta Kappa. Bd. editors, article and book rev. editor Yale Law Jour., 1962-64; contbg. author: Antitrust Adviser, 1971. Home: 14944 La Cumbre Dr Pacific Palisades CA 90272 Office: 515 S Flower St Los Angeles CA 90017 Tel (213) 488-7000

COOPER, ROBERT FRANKLIN, JR., b. Ellisville, Miss., Oct. 19, 1913; A.B., Washington and Lee U., 1935; J.D., U. Louisville, 1938. Admitted to Ky. bar, 1938, U.S. Supreme Ct. bar, 1941, Miss. bar, 1946; spl. agent FBI, Washington, Pitts., Detroit, New Orleans, 1939-67; trust officer First Nat. Bank, Jackson, Miss., 1968—, v.p., 1971—. Mem. Am., Fed., Ky., Miss., Hinds County bar assns., Estate Planning Council Miss., Soc. Former Spl. Agents of the FBI, Inc. Home: 1335 Linden Pl Jackson MS 39202 Office: Room 320 First Nat Bank Bldg 248 E Capitol St Jackson MS 39201 Tel (601) 354-5178

COOPER, ROBERT MAURICE, b. Spokane, Wash., Sept. 27, 1915; LL.D., Gonzaga U., 1941; M.B.A., Kinman Bus. U., 1945. Admitted to Wash. bar, 1941; mem. firm Clark & Cooper, Spokane, 1946-52, Cooper & Roberts, Spokane, 1973—; instr. Wash. Assn. Realtors, Wash. Ednl. Assn., Spokane Bd. Realtors, 1946—; legal counsel Spokane Bd. Realtors, 1972-76, Multiple Listing Service, 1972-76, Spokane Nat. Mines, Columbia Lead & Zinc Mining Co., Uranium Lead and Zinc Mining Co. Mem. Spokane Interstate Fair, Estate Planning Council; v.p., dir. Spokane Lilac Festival; charter mem., pres. Spokane Softball Assn.; exec. dir. Spokane Pro Sports. Mem. Am., Wash. State, Spokane County bar assns., Am. Inst. Accountants. Recipient Eddy award Wash. Assn. Realtors, 1970; recipient Pilgrim Degree of Merit, Loyal Order of Moose, 1962. Home: S 1519 Helena St Spokane WA 99203 Office: N 1522 Washington St Box 5432 Spokane WA 99205 Tel (509) 326-3600

COOPER, SAMUEL, b. N.Y.C., Oct. 27, 1914; B.S. in Edn., City Coll. N.Y., 1936; LL.B., St. Johns U., 1938, J.S.D., 1939; B.S. Johns Hopkins U., 1952. Admitted to N.Y. bar, 1939, Md. bar, 1946; asso. firm Ironside & Mahoney, N.Y.C., 1937-41; housing dir. Dept. Agr., Md., 1941-42; individual practice law, Balt., 1946-71; prof. accounting U. Balt., 1968-71, prof. law, 1971—. Mem. Juvenile Delinquency Com. N.Y.C., 1936; asso. counsel Asso. Jewish Charities Balt., 1948. Mem. Am. Inst. C.P.A.'s (grading advisor), Assn. C.P.A.'s and Lawyers, Assn. Trial Lawyers Am. Home: 6805 Pimlico Dr Baltimore MD 21209 Office: 1420 N Charles St Baltimore MD 21201 Tel (301) 727-6350

COOTER, PAUL ADAM, b. Wichita, Kans., July 26, 1927; LL.B., U. Tex., 1951. Admitted to Tex. bar, 1950, Okla. bar, 1951, N.M. bar, 1956; mem. legal dept. Cities Service Oil Co., Bartlesville, Okla., 1951-52; asso. firm Simon, Jones & Ratliff, Fort Worth, Tex., 1952-55; asso. firm Atwood, Malone, Mann & Cooter, and predecessors, Roswell, N.Mex., 1955—. Trustee Rocky Mountain Mineral Law Found., 1974—. Chmn. Chaves County chpt. ARC, 1966-70. Mem. State Bar N.Mex., State Bar Tex., Okla., Am. bar assns. Home: 702 Sherrill Ln Roswell NM 88201 Office: PO Drawer 700 800 Security Nat Bank Bldg Roswell NM 88201 Tel (505) 622-6221

COPELAN, JESSE THOMAS, JR., b. Greensboro, Ga., July 29, 1941; B.S. in Forestry, U. Ga., 1963, J.D., 1970. Admitted to Ga. bar, 1970; asst. dist. atty. Ocmulgee County (Ga.), 1970-72; partner firm Whitman & Copelan, Eatonton, Ga., 1972-76, firm Copelan & Kopp, Eatonton, 1976—; judge City Ct. Union Point (Ga.), 1970-72. Pres. Ga. Cancer Soc., 1972-74. Mem. Am., Ga., Ocmulgee Jud. (pres. 1973-74) bar assns., Eatonton-Putnam County Jaycees (v.p. 1972-76). Home: 207 Madison Ave Eatonton GA 31024 Office: PO Box 109 Eatonton GA 31024 Tel (404) 485-9410

COPELAND, EDWARD JEROME, b. Chgo., Oct. 29, 1933; B.A., Carleton Coll., 1955; certificate U. London, 1957; J.D., Northwestern U., 1958. Admitted to Ill. bar, 1959; claims adjudicator HEW, Chgo., 1959-60; individual practice law, Chgo., 1960-71; partner firm Foss, Schuman & Drake, Chgo., 1971—; mem. Ill. Ho. of Reps., 1967-70; dir. North Community State Bank, Chgo., 1972-76; chmn. bd. Bank of North Shore, Northbrook, Ill., 1976—. Mem. Ill. Commn. Mental Health, 1971-74; mem. Ill. Bd. Edn., 1974—. Mem. Chgo., Ill., Am. bar assns. Recipient Best Legislators' award Ind. Voters Ill., 1967, 69. Home: 1431 Sherwood Rd Highland Park IL 60035 Office: 11 S LaSalle St Chicago IL 60603 Tel (312) 782-2610

COPELAND, JAMES WILLIAM, b. Woodland, N.C., June 16, 1914; A.B., Guilford Coll., 1934; J.D. with honors, U. N.C.-Chapel Hill, 1937. Admitted to N.C. bar, 1936; individual practice law, Woodland and Murfreesboro, N.C., judge N.C. Spl. Superior Ct., 1961-75; asso. justice N.C. Supreme Ct., Raleigh, 1975—; mem. N.C. State Senate, 1951, 53, 57, 59, chmn. judiciary com., 1957, mem. adv. budget commn., 1957-61, chmn. appropriations com., 1959, legis. counsel to gov., 1961. Mayor, Woodland, N.C., 1938-41, Murfreesboro, 1947-51. Mem. Am. (N.C. del. Nat. Trial Judges Conf. 1969-74), N.C. bar assns. Asst. editor law rev. U. N.C.-Chapel Hill, 1936-37. Home: 407 E High St Murfreesboro NC 27855 Office: PO Box 2448 NC Supreme Ct Raleigh NC 27602 Tel (919) 733-3714

COPELAND, MILTON, b. Hope, Ark., Dec. 30, 1935; B.A., Abilene Christian U., 1958, M.A., 1960; J.D., George Washington U., 1963. Admitted to Calif. bar, 1964, Ark. bar, 1974; asso. firm Kindel & Anderson, Santa Ana and Los Angeles, Calif., 1963-67; partner firm Manatt, Phelps, Copeland & Rothenburg, Los Angeles, 1967-71; asso. prof. Law Sch. U. Ark., 1971-75, prof., 1975—. Mem. Ark. Bar Assn. Recipient Order of the Coif, 1963. Home: 1600 E Shadowridge Fayetteville AR 72701 Office: Law Sch Univ Ark Fayetteville AR 72701 Tel (501) 575-5348

COPLEIN, GORDON DAVID, b. Phila., Mar. 20, 1931; B.S.E.E., U. Pa., 1956; LL.B., N.Y. U., 1959, LL.M. in Trade Regulation, 1962. Admitted to N.Y. bar, 1960; examiner U.S. Patent and Trademark Office, Washington, 1956-58; asso. firm Darby & Darby, N.Y.C., 1958-66, mem., 1966—. Mem. IEEE, Am. Bar Assn., N.Y. Patent Law Assn., Practising Law Inst. (lectr.), Am. Arbitration Assn. Office: 405 Lexington Ave New York City NY 10017 Tel (212) 697-7660

COPLEY, RALPH D., JR., b. 1924; grad. in Engring., Colo. Sch. Mines, 1948; LL.B., U. Denver, 1951. Petroleum engr. Sun Oil Co., 1951-52; asso. firm Gorsuch & Kirgis, 1952-55; adminstrv. asst. to exec. v.p. Seaboard Oil Co., 1955-58; with Getty Oil Co., Los Angeles, 1958—, atty. sub. Tidewater Oil Co., 1958-64, div. atty. western exploration and prodn. div., 1964, western M & M div., 1965, ops. coordinator, then asso. chief counsel, 1966, chief counsel, 1967—, corp. sec., 1971—, v.p., 1973—; dir. Mission Corp., Skelly Oil Corp., Getty Oil Co. (EasternOps) Inc. Office: 3810 Wilshire Blvd Los Angeles CA 90005*

COPPLE, LEONARD WILLIAM, b. Colon, Panama, July 31, 1941; LL.B., U. Ariz., 1965. Admitted to Ariz. bar, 1965, U.S. Ct. Mil. Appeals bar, 1965; capt. JAGC, U.S. Army, 1965-69; asso. firm O'Connor, Cavanagh, Anderson, Westover, Killingsworth & Beshears, Phoenix, 1969-71, Charles M. Brewer, Ltd., Phoenix, 1971-74; individual practice law, Tempe, Ariz., 1974—; instr. legal writing Ariz. State U., Tempe, 1974-76. Mem. adv. bd. Tempe Salvation Army Corps, 1975—; treas. Tempe Sister City Corp., 1974—. Mem. Am., Ariz., Maricopa County bar assns., Am., Ariz. (dir. 1976—) trial lawyers assns. Home: 1922 E Riviera Dr Tempe AZ 85282 Office: 1050 E Southern Ave Suite D-1 Tempe AZ 85282 Tel (602) 968-7771

COPSEY, ORVILLE HOWARD, JR., b. Blackford County, Ind., Oct. 8, 1931; B.S., Ind. U., 1953; LL.B., Chgo.-Kent Coll. Law, 1959. Admitted to Ind. bar, 1960; claim rep. Ins. Co. N.Am., Chgo., 1956-60; claim supv. CNA Ins. Co., Indpls., 1961—. Mem. Ind., Indpls. bar assns. Home: 2009 Schwier Ct Indianapolis IN 46229 Office: 2421 Willowbrook Pkwy Indianapolis IN 46205 Tel (317) 257-3411

CORASH, RICHARD, SR., b. N.Y.C., Mar. 31, 1938; B.A., Harpur Coll. State U. N.Y., 1959; LL.B., Rutgers U., 1963, J.D., 1968; M.A., Bklyn. Law Sch., 1966. Admitted to N.Y. State bar, 1964, Fed. Dist. Ct. bar, 1964, D.C. bar, 1964, U.S. Supreme Ct. bar, 1972; individual practice law, N.Y.C., 1964, S.I., 1964—; spl. asst. atty. gen. for elections State N.Y., 1968; counsel Comml. Bank, 1973—. Trustee Jacques Marchais Center Tibetan Art, S.I., 1972—, vice chmn., 1975—; treas. campaign Ralph J. Lamberti for State Senate, 1976. Mem. N.Y., Richmond County bar assns., N.Y.C. Homebuilders Assn. Home: 340 Lighthouse Ave Staten Island NY 10306 Office: 26 Bay St Staten Island NY 10301 Tel (212) 442-4424

CORBETT, BRUCE REED, b. Rochester, N.Y., July 29, 1944; B.A., U. Pa., 1966; J.D., Cornell U., 1969. Admitted to Calif. bar, 1970; asso. firm Lawler, Felix & Hall, Los Angeles, 1969-75; asso. firm Rutan & Tucker, Santa Ana, Calif., 1975-76, partner, 1977—. Mem. State Bar Calif. Home: 1512 Anita Lam Newport Beach CA 92660 Office: 401 Civic Center Dr Santa Ana CA 92702 Tel (714) 835-2200

CORBETT, CLETUS JOHN, b. Columbus, Ohio, June 18, 1907; LL.B., J.D., Capital U., 1966; postgrad. Ohio State U. Admitted to Ohio bar, 1941; corporate counsel SCOA Industries Inc., Columbus, 1941-42, v.p., sec., 1954-72; mem. firm Porter, Stanley, Platt & Arthur, Columbus, 1971-76, firm Iverson, Yoakum, Pariano & Hatch, Los Angeles, 1976—. Mem. Columbus, Ohio State, Am. bar assns., Am. Judicature Soc. Home: Hancock Turner Park Apt 2D Los Angeles CA Office: 611 W 6th St Los Angeles CA Tel (614) 687-0711

CORBETT, JOHN HARRY, JR., b. Pitts., Aug. 26, 1946; B.A., U. Pitts., 1968, J.D., 1971. Admitted to Pa. bar, 1971; partner firm Karns, Corbett & Kissane, Pitts., 1972—; appellate counsel Allegheny County (Pa.) Pub. Defender's Office, 1972—. Mem. Allegheny County, Pa., Am. bar assns., Pub. Defenders Assn. Pa. Office: 1601 Law and Finance Bldg Pittsburgh PA 15219 Tel (412) 391-6844

CORBETT, WARREN LEE, b. Franklin, Pa., Aug. 26, 1944; B.A., Coll. Wooster, 1966; J.D., Vanderbilt U., 1969. Admitted to Tenn. bar, 1969; partner firm Ingraham, Young & Corbett, Nashville, 1969—. Bd. dirs. Buddies of Nashville. Mem. Am., Tenn., Nashville bar assns., Am., Tenn. trial lawyers assns. Office: 21st Floor Parkway Towers Nashville TN 37219 Tel (615) 244-6632

CORBIN, DONALD LOUIS, b. Hot Springs, Ark., Mar. 29, 1938; A.B., U. Ark., Fayetteville, 1963, J.D., 1966. Admitted to Ark. bar, 1966; individual practice law, Lewisville and Stamps, Ark., 1966—. Vice pres. Ark.-Tex. Center for Human Devel., Texarkana, 1973—; mem. Ark. Ho. of Reps., 1971—. Mem. SW Ark., Am., Ark. bar assns. Home: 408 Patton Dr Lewisville AR 71845 Office: 216 Main St Stamps AR 71860 Tel (501) 533-4492

CORBIN, FRED EAZER, b. New Kensington, Pa., Oct. 3, 1925; B.B.A., U. Pitts., 1953; J.D., U. San Diego, 1964. Admitted to Calif. bar, 1965; mem. staff Legal Aid Soc. San Diego, 1965; asso. firm Carter & Courtney, Corona, Calif., 1965; individual practice law, San Diego, 1965—; mgr. Gen. Electric Co., Bridgeport, Conn., 1953-59; revenue mgr. Gen. Dynamics Corp., San Diego, 1959-65. Mem. adv. bd. city councilman, San Diego, 1972-75. Mem. Calif., Am., San Diego trial lawyers assns., Lawyers for Criminal Justice. Office: 3993 Goldfinch St San Diego CA 92103 Tel (714) 291-4316

CORBIN, ROBERT KEITH, b. Worthington, Ind., Nov. 17, 1928; B.S. in Bus., Ind. U., 1952, J.D., 1956. Admitted to Ind. bar, 1956, Ariz. bar, 1958; individual practice law, Phoenix, 1958-76; county atty. Maricopa County, Phoenix, 1965-68. Mem. county bd. of suprs. Maricopa County, 1973-76, 77-80. Mem. Ariz., Maricopa County bar assns. Home: 1545 West El Caminito Dr Phoenix AZ 85021 Office: Suite 1505 3003 N Central Ave Phoenix AZ 85012 Tel (602) 248-7998

CORBIN, SOL NEIL, b. N.Y.C., Apr. 16, 1927; B.S., Columbia, 1948; J.D. cum laude, Harvard, 1951. Admitted to N.Y. bar, 1952; law sec. to Judge Charles D. Breitel, N.Y.C., 1954-56; counsel to Gov. N.Y., 1962-65; partner firm Corbin & Gordon, N.Y.C., 1970—; spl. counsel to Vice-Pres. of U.S., 1975; chmn. N.Y. State Commn. on Constl. Conv., 1966-67; mem. N.Y. State Banking Bd., 1969-76; mem. N.Y. State Commn. on Local Govt. Powers, 1971-73, Chief Judge's Com. to Recruit State Ct. Adminstr., 1973; chmn. N.Y. State Crime Control Planning Bd., 1974-7S; trustee in bankruptcy Franklin N.Y. Corp., 1974—. Mem. N.Y. Lawyers Club (bd. govs.), Am. Arbitration Assn. (chmn. comml. law subcom.), Am. Law Inst., Am., N.Y. State, N.Y.C. bar assns. Home: 1100 Park Ave New York City NY 10028 Office: 280 Park Ave New York City NY 10017 Tel (212) 682-4300

CORBIN, WILLIAM LOUIS, b. Frederick, Md., Apr. 6, 1940; B.A., U. Md., 1963, J.D., 1971. Admitted to Md. bar, 1972; asso. firm Anderson, Coe and King, Balt., 1971-73; partner firm Corbin, Heller & Warfield, Severna Park, Md., 1973—; mem. staff Ho. of Dels., desk officer, Md. Gen. Assembly, 1975, 76. Mem. Am., Md. State, Anne Arundel County bar assns., Comml. Law League Am. Home: 108 Askewton Rd Severna Park MD 21146 Office: 650 Ritchie Hwy Monumental Title Bldg Severna Park MD 21146 Tel (301) 544-0314

CORBOY, PHILIP HARNETT, b. Chgo., Aug. 12, 1924; student Notre Dame U.; J.D. cum laude, Loyola U., Chgo., 1949. Admitted to Ill. bar, 1949, U.S. Supreme Ct. bar, 1965; now partner firm Philip H. Corboy & Assos., Chgo. Trustee Roscoe Pound Found. Fellow Am. Coll. Trial Lawyers, Internat. Acad. Trial Lawyers, Am., Chgo. (life) bar founds.; mem. Am. (del. 1975—, past com. chmn.), Ill. (past com. chmn.), Chgo. (pres. 1972-73), 7th Fed. Circuit bar assns., Assn. Trial Lawyers Am. (past mem. bd. govs., editor Law Jour.), Am. Judicature Soc. (dir.), Ill. Soc. Trial Lawyers, Ill. Trial Lawyers Assn. (past pres.), Law Sci. Acad., Internat. Soc. Barristers, Inner Circle Advs., Am. Bd. Profl. Liability Attys., Nat. Inst. for Trial Advocacy (vice chmn. 1971-72), Loyola U. Law Alumni Assn. (medal of excellence 1967), Alpha Sigma Nu. Contbr. articles to legal jours. Office: 33 N Dearborn St Chicago IL 60602 Tel (312) 346-3191

CORBRIDGE, JAMES NOEL, JR., b. Mineola, N.Y., May 27, 1934; A.B., Brown U., 1955; LL.B., Yale, 1963. Admitted to N.Y. bar, 1964, Colo. bar, 1975; asso. firm Lord, Day & Lord, N.Y.C., 1964-65; asst. prof. law U. Colo., Boulder, 1965-67, asso. prof., 1967-73, prof., 1973—, v.p. for student affairs, 1970-73, v.p. for student and minority affairs, 1973-74, vice chancellor for acad. affairs, 1974—. Home: 7112 Old Post Rd Boulder CO 80301 Office: Univ Colorado Regent 306 Boulder CO 80309 Tel (303) 492-8195

CORCORAN, JOHN JOSEPH, b. N.Y.C., Aug. 12, 1920; B.S., Georgetown U., 1948, J.D., 1951. Admitted to D.C. bar, 1952, U.S. Supreme Ct. bar, 1973, U.S. Ct. Mil. Appeals bar, 1953; legal cons. Am. Legion Nat. Vets. Affairs Commn., Washington, 1952-56, dir., 1958-67; atty. adviser Nat. Security Agy., Ft. Meade, Md., 1956-57; asst. to gen. counsel VA, Washington, 1967-69, gen. counsel, 1969-77, adminstrv. judge Contract Appeals Bd., 1977—; with JAGC, USAFR, 1960-75. Mem. Am., Fed., D.C. bar assns. Home: 9513 Cable Dr Kensington MD 20795 Office: 941 N Capitol St NE Washington DC 20421 Tel (202) 275-1750

CORDES, ALEXANDER CHARLES, b. Buffalo, Aug. 14, 1925; B.A., Yale, 1947; LL.B., U. Buffalo, 1950. Admitted to N.Y. State bar, 1950; asso. firm Kenefick, Bass, Letchworth, Baldy & Phillips, Buffalo, 1950-54; asst. U.S. atty. Western dist. N.Y., Buffalo, 1954-56; partner firm Phillips, Lytle, Hitchcock, Blaine & Huber, Buffalo, 1956—. Mem. Erie County Bd. Suprs., 1960-61. Fellow Am. Coll. Trial Lawyers; mem. Erie County Trial Lawyers Assn., Am., N.Y. State, Erie County bar assns. Home: 800 W Ferry St Buffalo NY 14222 Office: 3400 Marine Midland Center Buffalo NY 14203 Tel (716) 847-8436

CORDES, CARL H., b. Gettysburg, Pa., Oct. 21, 1930; A.B., Brown U., 1953; LL.B., Dickinson Law Sch., 1956. Admitted to Pa. bar, 1957; Finance and Revenue Bd., Pa., 1957-59; individual practice law, 1959—. Mem. York County, Pa. bar assns. Home: 523 Country Club Rd York PA 17403 Office: 118 E King St York PA 17403 Tel (717) 848-1900

CORDINGLEY, BRUCE ALAN, b. Chgo., Dec. 28, 1946; B.S. in Indsl. Mmgt., Purdue U., 1968; J.D., Harvard U., 1971. Admitted to Mass. bar, 1971, Ind. bar, 1973; asso. firm. Bingham, Dana and Gould, Boston, 1971-73; asso. firm Ice, Miller, Donadio and Ryan, Indpls., 1973—. Home: 600 N Alabama St Suite 2400 Indianapolis IN 46204 Office: 111 Monument Circle Indianapolis IN 46204 Tel (317) 635-1213

CORETTE, JOHN EARL, b. Butte, Mont., Apr. 20, 1908; student U. Mont., 1926; LL.B., U. Va., 1930, J.D., 1971; LL.D. (hon.), Coll. Great Falls (Mont.), 1958, Carroll Coll., Helena, Mont., 1970. Admitted to Mont. bar, 1929; asso. firm Murphy & Whitlock, Missoula, 1930-34; partner firm Corette, Smith & Dean, Butte, 1934—; counsel Mont. Power Co., 1934-44, v.p., asst. gen. mgr. 1944-52, pres., chief exec. officer 1952-67, chmn. bd., chief exec. officer, 1967-73, chmn. bd., 1973—, dir., 1948—; pres. Edison Elec. Inst., 1958-59; dir. Pacific Gas Transmission Co.; mem. adv. council Stanford Research Inst., 1970—; mem. fin. adv. com. Fed. Energy Adminstrn., 1971—. Mem. Butte C. of C. (dir. 1959-62), Am., Mont., Silver Bow County bar assns. Home: 100 Rampart Dr Butte MT 59701 Office: 40 E Broadway Butte MT 59701 Tel (406) 723-5421

CORETTE, ROBERT DRISCOLL, b. Butte, Mont., Jan. 15, 1911; B.A., LL.B., U. Mont., 1934. Admitted to Mont. bar, 1934, U.S. Supreme Ct. bar, 1974; partner firm Corette, Smith & Dean, Butte, 1934—; counsel Mont. Power Co., 1957-75, also dir.; dir. Glacier Gas

Co., Northwest Co., Ray Found. of Mont. Fellow Am. Coll. Trial Lawyers, Am. Coll. Probate Counsel; mem. Am., Silver Bow bar assns., Am. Judicature Soc., Internat. Assn. of Ins. Counsel, Mont. (pres., dir. 1958-62), U.S. (dir. 1966-70) chambers commerce, Amateur Athletic Union of Mont. Home: 1201 W Platinum St Butte MT 59701 Office: Prudential Fed Savs Bldg 49 N Main St Butte MT 59701 Tel (406) 723-3205

COREY, GEORGE HOWARD, b. N. Bend, Oreg., Feb. 16, 1916; B.S., U. Oreg., 1938, J.D., 1940. Admitted to Oreg. bar, 1940, U.S. Supreme Ct. bar, 1960; dist. atty. Umatilla County (Oreg.), 1950-54; partner firm Corey, Byler & Rew, Pendleton, Oreg., 1954—; mem. bd. govs. Oreg. State Bar, 1954-57. Fellow Am. Bar Found., Am. Coll. Trial Lawyers, Am. Coll. Probate Lawyers; mem. Am. Bar Assn., Oreg. State Bar. Home: 200 N W Gilliam St Pendleton OR 97801 Office: 222 S E Dorion Ave Pendleton OR 97801 Tel (503) 276-3331

CORISH, JOSEPH RYAN, b. Somerville, Mass., Apr. 9, 1909; Adj.A., Harvard, 1938; J.D., Boston U., 1932. Admitted to Mass. bar, 1932; individual practice law, Somerville, 1932—; asst. city solicitor Somerville, 1935; counsel to housing authority, Somerville, 1950; pres. New Eng. Assn. Pub. Authority Counsel, 1950; mem. New Eng. Council Legal Task Force. Mem. Mass. Acad. Trial Attys. (dir.), Mass. Trial Lawyers Assn. (dir.), Assn. Trial Lawyers Am., Boston Bar Assn., Mass. Conveyancers Assn. Author: Liability of the Private Hospital, 1937; Gross Negligence, 1934; lectr. to profl. assns. Home: 86 Lawson Rd Winchester MA 02144 Office: 421 Highland Ave Somerville MA 02143 Tel (617) 625-6114

CORLETT, ALLEN NORRIS, b. Cleve., Sept. 3, 1904; A.B., Case Western Reserve U., 1926, LL.B., 1929. Admitted to Ohio bar, 1929, U.S. Supreme Ct. bar, 1950, Ct. of Mil. Appeals bar, 1950; partner firm Weyer & Corlett, Cleve., 1929-42, Roudebush, Brown, Corlett & Ulrich Co. L.P.O., Cleve., 1947—; mem. Ho. of Reps., Ohio, 1931-32; naval legal officer and courts martial judge PTO, 1942-46; mem. Ohio Senate, 1947-48; comdg. officer Naval Law Unit, Cleve., 1949-62; Ohio Presdl. elector, 1952; substitute acting judge Shaker Heights Municipal Ct., 1960-74. Mem. Am., Ohio, Greater Cleve. bar assns., Assn. of Trial Lawyers of Am., Ohio, Cleve. Office: 915 Williamson Bldg Cleveland OH 44114 Tel (216) 696-5200

CORNABY, KAY STERLING, b. Spanish Fork, Utah, Jan. 14, 1936; A.B., Brigham Young U., 1960; postgrad. in Law Heidelberg (Germany) U., 1961-63; J.D., Harvard, 1966. Admitted to N.Y. bar, 1967, Utah bar, 1969; asso. firm Brumbaugh, Graves, Donohue & Raymond, N.Y.C., 1966-69; partner firm Mallinckrodt & Cornaby, Salt Lake City, 1969-72; individual practice law, Salt Lake City, 1972—; mem. Utah Senate, 1977—. Chmn. 2d congl. dist. Utah Republican Party, 1973—; chmn. North and East Regional Council of Neighborhood Councils, Salt Lake City, 1976—. Mem. Am. Bar Assn., Am., N.Y. patent law assns., Assn. Bar City N.Y., Utah State Bar (chmn. com. on law day and Americanization 1975-76). Office: 1406 Deseret Bldg Salt Lake City UT 84111 Tel (801) 532-1600

CORNACHIO, ALBERT WILLIAM, b. N.Y.C., Feb. 16, 1935; B.S., Fordham Coll., 1961, LL.B., 1964, J.D., 1965. Admitted to N.Y. State bar, 1965, U.S. Supreme Ct. bar, 1970; individual practice law, Bronx, N.Y., 1965—; counsel to pub. adminstr. Bronx County (N.Y.), 1969—; asst. prof. Fordham U., 1973—. Bd. dirs. chpt. Am. Cancer Soc., Multiple Sclerosis Soc. Mem. N.Y., Am., Bronx (dir.) bar assns., NE Bronx Businessman's Assn., N.Y. State Trial Lawyers Assn. Contbr. articles to legal jours. Office: 910 Grand Concourse Bronx NY 10451 Tel (212) 681-0900

CORNBLATT, THEODORE BERNARD, b. Balt., Mar. 10, 1943; B.A. with high honors, U. Md., 1964, J.D. with honors, 1966. Admitted to Md. bar, 1966; partner firm Smith, Somerville & Case, Balt., 1966—. Bd. dirs. Balt. Legal Aid Bur., 1971-74. Mem. Am., Md., Balt. (chmn. young lawyers sect. 1976—) bar assns., Assn. Def. Trial Counsel. Casenote editor Md. Law Rev., 1965-66. Home: 9048 Meadow Heights Rd Randallstown MD 21133 Office: 1700 One Charles Center Baltimore MD 21201 Tel (301) 727-1164

CORNELIUS, CLARANCE PRESTON, b. Mooresville, N.C., Mar. 18, 1941; B.S., N.C. State U., Raleigh, 1963; J.D., U. N.C., Chapel Hill, 1967. Admitted to N.C. bar, 1967; partner firm Pope, Brawley & Cornelius, Mooresville, 1967-77; judge N.C. Dist. Ct., 22d Jud. Dist., 1970—. Bd. dirs. N.C. Lung Assn., Tedell County (N.C.) Bd. Social Services, N.C. 4-H Devel. Fund. Mem. N.C., Am. bar assns., N.C. Assn. Dist. Ct. Judges, N.C. Trial Lawyers Assn., Am. Judicature Soc. Recipient 4-H Alumni award N.C. 4-H, 1969, Distinguished Service award Town of Mooresville, 1975. Home: Tanglebriar Estate Mooresville NC 28115 Office: Box 487 Route 4 Mooresville NC 28115 Tel (704) 664-2150

CORNELIUS, WILLIAM JOSEPH, b. Sweetwater, Tex., June 6, 1927; J.D., Baylor U., 1949. Admitted to Tex. bar, 1949, U.S. Supreme Ct. bar, 1972; partner firm Cornelius & Cornelius, Jefferson, Tex., 1949-73; county atty. Marion County (Tex.), 1951-54; dist. atty. 76th Dist. Tex., 1968-70; justice Ct. of Civil Appeals Tex., Texarkana, 1973—; commr. Ct. Criminal Appeals of Tex., 1974—. Trustee East Tex. Bapt. Coll., 1971—, Jefferson Ind. Sch. Dist., 1958-68; mem. exec. bd. Bapt. Gen. Conv. Tex., 1975—; bd. dirs. E. Tex. area council Boy Scouts Am., 1976. Mem. Am. Bar Assn. (mem. council gen. practice sect. 1968), State Bar Tex. (dir. 1964-67, chmn. gen. practice sect. 1969-70), Am. Judicature Soc., Inst. Jud. Adminstrn. Home: PO Box 465 Jefferson TX 75657 Office: Ct Civil Appeals 400 Texas City Bldg Texarkana TX 75501 Tel (214) 794-2576

CORNELL, JULIEN, b. Bklyn., Mar. 17, 1910; B.A. with honors, Swarthmore Coll., 1930; J.D. Yale, 1933. Admitted to N.Y. State bar, 1935, U.S. Supreme Ct. bar, 1944; asso. firm Davies, Auerbach & Cornell, N.Y.C., 1933-40; partner firm Earle & Reilly, N.Y.C., 1942-45; individual practice law, N.Y.C., 1945-50; partner firm Cornell & Cornell, Central Valley, N.Y., 1950—; spl. counsel ACLU, N.Y.C., 1941-50. Pres. Am. Youth Hostels, 1942-48; pres. Monroe-Woodbury (N.Y.) Central Sch. Dist., 1951-53; mem. bd. mgrs. Swarthmore Coll., 1971—. Mem. N.Y. State, Orange County bar assns., Assn. Bar City N.Y., Yale Club N.Y.C. Author: Conscience and the State, 1944; New World Primer, 1947; The Trial of Ezra Pound, 1966; Lexcetera, 1971; A Tale of Treasure Trove, 1977. Home: 270 Dunderberg Rd Central Valley NY 10917 Office: 260 Albany Turnpike Central Valley NY 10917 Tel (914) 928-2235

CORNETT, CHARLES THOMAS, b. Harlan, Ky., July 2, 1938; B.S. in Bus. Adminstrn., Eastern State U., 1960; LL.B., U. Tenn., 1963. Admitted to Ky. bar, 1963; individual practice law, Harlan, Ky., 1963; judge City of Harlan, 1966-72; atty. City of Wallins, Ky., 1974-75. Mem. Ky., Harlan County (pres. 1965) bar assns., Harlan County Jaycees (pres. 1968). Home: Woodland Hills Harlan KY 40831 Office: 1st St and Central St Harlan KY 40831 Tel (606) 573-5497

CORNETT, GRADY STURGEON, b. Paris, Tex., Apr. 15, 1905; LL.B., U. Tulsa, 1930. Admitted to Okla. bar, 1930; individual practice law, Tulsa, 1930-35, 48—; judge pro tem Tulsa County (Okla.), 1933, judge Ct. of Common Pleas, 1935-47. Bd. dirs. Tulsa YMCA. Mem. Tulsa C. of C. (dir.). Home: 210 Pythian Bldg 19 W 5th St Tulsa OK 74103 Office: 210 Pythian Bldg 19 W 5th St Tulsa OK 74103 Tel (918) 582-2826

CORNFIELD, SIDNEY WOODROW, bN.Y.C., Dec. 26, 1912; certificate Coll. City N.Y., 1933; LL.B., St. John's U., Bklyn., 1936. Admitted to N.Y. bar, 1938, U.S. Supreme Ct. bar, 1957, Fla. bar, 1974; partner firm Cornfield, Schneider & Glenn, Bronx, N.Y., 1938-41; individual practice law, N.Y.C., 1941—; trial examiner N.Y.C. Community Sch. Bds., 1972—; chmn. coordinating com. discipline First Jud. Dept. N.Y., 1970-71; former arbitrator N.Y.C. Civil Ct. Small Claims Div.; arbitrator Bronx Civil Ct. Served as oral examiner N.Y. Civil Service Commn. Mem. screening com. for jud. selections Bronx and New York Counties Democratic Party, 1976. Mem. N.Y. State (ho. of dels. 1974—), Bronx County (chmn. grievance com., v.p.), Queens County (N.Y.), Fla. bar assns. Home: 555 Kappock St Bronx NY 10463 Office: 250 W 57th St New York City NY 10019 Tel (212) 245-3250

CORNICK, GERALD ARTHUR, b. Houston, Sept. 12, 1946; B.B.A., U. Houston, 1968; J.D., South Tex. Coll. Law, 1972. Admitted to Tex. bar, 1972; individual practice law, Houston, 1973-74, 75—; asso. firm Caldwell, Cowart & Ginn, Houston, 1974-75; instr. bus. law North Harris County Jr. Coll. Troop advisor Boy Scouts Am. Mem. Am., Houston bar assns., Delta Theta Phi. Home: 6900 Gary St Apt 237 Houston TX 77055 Office: 1249 N Loop W Suite 100A Houston TX 77008 Tel (713) 864-1115

CORNISH, LEBBEUS MORRISON, b. Honolulu, Apr. 20, 1921; A.B., Washburn U., Topeka, 1947, J.D., 1948. Admitted to Kans. bar, 1948; partner firm Glenn, Cornish & Leuenberger, Topeka, 1948—; lectr. bus. law Washburn U., 1951-75; spl. asst. atty. gen. State of Kans., 1973-74; spl. legal counsel Kans. Corp. Commn., 1955-57, Kans. Hwy. Commn., 1955-57, Kans. Alcohol Beverage Control Commn., 1959-60, Kans. Bd. Tax Appeals, 1965-69. Bd. dirs. Topeka United Way, 1960, pres., 1964-66; trustee Topeka Pub. Library, 1964-68; adv. bd. St. Francis Hosp., Topeka, 1965-68; bd. regents Washburn U., 1969-73, chmn., 1972-73. Mem. Topeka, Kans., Am. (vice chmn. com. property ins. law) bar assns. Home: 3621 Holly Ln Topeka KS 66603 Office: 610 1st Nat Bank Tower Topeka KS 66603 Tel (913) 232-0545

CORONTZOS, ROBERT, b. Great Falls, Mont., Oct. 27, 1937; B.S., Coll. Great Falls, 1959; J.D., U. Mont., 1962. Admitted to Mont. bar, 1962; asso. firm Jardine, Stephenson, Blewett & Weaver, Great Falls, 1963-69, partner, 1970—, mng. partner, 1975—. Mem. pres.'s council Coll. of Great Falls; bd. dirs. Great Falls Symphony Assn. Mem. Am. (del. from State Bar Mont. 1970—), Mont., Cascade County bar assns., Am. Judicature Soc. Home: 208 14th St S Great Falls MT 59405 Office: 700 1st Nat Bank Bldg Great Falls MT 59401 Tel (406) 727-5000

CORRELL, TIMOTHY ARMSTRONG, b. Chgo., Mar. 18, 1944; B.A. Carleton Coll., 1965; J.D. Rutgers, 1971. Admitted to Colo. bar, 1971; U.S. Dist. (Colo.) Ct., 1971; U.S. 10th Circuit Ct. Appeals, 1974; law clk. Colo. Supreme Ct., 1971-72; asso. firm Inman, Flynn & Coffee, Denver, 1972-75, partner, 1975—. Sec., Colo. area exec. com. Am. Friends Service Com. Mem. Am., Colo., Denver bar assns., Assn. Trial Lawyers Am., Colo. Trial Lawyers Assn. Home: 1960 Holly St Denver CO 80220 Office: 1040 Capitol Life Center Denver CO 80203 Tel (303) 861-8147

CORRIEA, MARK FREDRIC, b. San Francisco, July 18, 1946; B.A., Calif. State U., 1969; J.D., Golden Gate U., 1972; LL.M., N.Y. U., 1973. Admitted to Calif. bar, 1972; law clk. U.S. Ct. Claims, Washington, 1973-74; tax counsel Bank of Am., San Francisco, 1974—. Mem. Am., San Francisco, Calif. bar assns. Home: 445 Diamond St #4 San Francisco CA 94114 Office: suite 2200 555 Calif St San Francisco CA 94104 Tel (415) 622-5126

CORRIGAN, EDWARD RICHARD, b. Jersey City, Feb. 20, 1916; B.S., St. Peter's Coll., 1938; LL.D., Rutgers U., 1941. Admitted to N.J. bar, 1941; gen. atty. U.S. VA, 1946-74; gen. counsel Morris County (N.J.) Right to Life Assn., 1973—. Address: Rockaway Dr RD 3 Boonton NJ 07005 Tel (201) 263-0683

CORRIGAN, JAMES JOSEPH PATRICK, b. Cleve., July 27, 1901; B.A., John Carroll U., 1922; J.D., Georgetown U., 1925; postgrad. N.Y. U. Inst. Jud. Adminstrn., 1967. Admitted to D.C. bar, 1925, Ohio bar, 1926; practiced in Cleve., 1926-56; judge Ohio Ct. Common Pleas, 1957-63, Ohio Ct. Appeals, 8th Appellate Dist., 1963-69; justice Ohio Supreme Ct., 1969—; lectr. Cleveland-Marshall Law Sch., Cleve. State U. Mem. Ohio Republican Exec. Com.; mem. adv. bd. St. John's Hosp., Cleve. Mem. Ohio State, Cleve., Cuyahoga County (Ohio), Am. bar assns., Am. Judicature Soc., Irish-Am. Cultural Inst., Delta Theta Phi. Home: 11524 Edgewater Dr Cleveland OH 44102 Office: Supreme Ct of Ohio State Office Tower 30 E Broad St Columbus OH 43215 Tel (614) 466-3828

CORRIGAN, MAURA DENISE, b. Cleve., June 14, 1948; B.A. magna cum laude, Marygrove Coll., 1969; J.D. cum laude, U. Detroit, 1973. Admitted to Mich., Ohio bars, 1974; probation officer Detroit Recorder's Ct., 1969-72; law clk. Mich. Ct. Appeals, Detroit, 1973-74; asst. prosecutor Wayne County (Mich.), Detroit, 1974—; lectr. Inst. Continuing Legal Edn., 1976. Exec. bd. Urban Alliance, Detroit, 1973—; bd. dirs. Project Transition, Detroit, 1976—, Interfaith Center for Racial Justice, 1977—. Mem. Detroit, Mich. State, Am. bar assns., Women Lawyers Assn., Marygrove Coll. Alumnae, U. Detroit Law Alumnae. Contbr. articles to legal jours. Home: 1122 Balfour Grosse Pointe MI 48230 Office: 1441 St Antoine #1274 Detroit MI 48226 Tel (313) 224-5777

CORROON, RICHARD FRANCIS, b. Bklyn., Aug. 5, 1913; A.B., Yale, 1935; LL.B., Harvard, 1938. Admitted to N.Y. bar, 1939, Del. bar, 1946; with firm Miller, Owen, Otis & Bailey, N.Y.C., 1938-42; partner firm Potter Anderson & Corroon, and predecessors, Wilmington, Del., 1946—. Dir., v.p. Corroon & Black Corp.; dir. Wellington Fund, Windsor Fund, Exeter Fund, Gemini Fund, W.L. Morgan Growth Fund, Wellsley Fund, Ivest Fund, Westminster Fund, Trustees' Equity Fund, Fund for Fed. Securities, Explorer Fund. Mem. Del. Bd. Bar Examiners, 1951-66; vice chmn. Del. Corp. Law Revision Com., 1964-67. Mem. bd. edn., Wilmington, 1949-53; pres. Diocesan Bd. Edn., Wilmington, 1966-68; mem. Catholic Social Services Wilmington, 1960-66. Bd. dirs. Del. Curative Workshop, 1950-56; trustee Del. Art Mus., 1969—, St. Francis Hosp., Wilmington, 1973—. Decorated Purple Heart. Fellow Am. Coll. Trial Lawyers; mem. Am. Del. (pres. 1975-76) bar assns., Assn. Bar City N.Y., Am. Law Inst. Home: 1105 Westover Rd Wilmington DE 19807 Office: Delaware Trust Bldg Wilmington DE 19801 Tel (302) 658-6671*

CORRY, ROBERT EMMETT, JR., b. Mobile, Ala., Dec. 22, 1935; A.B., U. Ala., 1957; J.D., George Washington U., 1964. Admitted to Ga. bar, 1964; partner firm Nall, Miller, Cadenhead & Dennis, Atlanta, 1964-70; partner firm Dennis, Corry, Webb, Carlock & Williams, Atlanta, 1970—; adj. prof. law Emory U., Atlanta, 1970-73. Mem. State Bar Ga., Atlanta Bar Assn., Atlanta Lawyers Club, Internat. Assn. Ins. Counsel, Ga. Def. Lawyers Assn. Home: 44 Huntington Rd Atlanta GA 30309 Office: 2500 Peachtree Center Atlanta GA 30303 Tel (404) 522-8220

CORSE, CHESTER CLINTON, JR., b. Pitts., Feb. 17, 1940; A.B., U. Pitts., 1962, J.D., 1965. Admitted to Pa. bar, 1965; mem. firm Williamson, Friedberg & Jones, Pottsville, Pa., 1968—; borough solicitor Palo Alto (Pa.), 1973—. Crusade chmn. Schuylkill County unit Am. Cancer Soc. Mem. Am., Pa., Allegheny County, Schuylkill County (dir., treas. 1974—) bar assns., Pa. Trial Lawyers Assn. (chmn. Schuylkill County sect.), Am. Judicature Soc., Schuylkill County Swimming Assn. (pres. 1974-76). Asst. editor Schuylkill Legal Record, 1973—. Home: 203 E Beacon St Palo Alto PA 17901 Office: American Bank Bldg Pottsville PA 17901 Tel (717) 622-5933

CORSI, PHILIP DONALD, b. N.Y.C., Oct. 11, 1928; B.A., Princeton, 1950; J.D., Columbia, 1953. Admitted to N.Y. State bar, 1955; asso. firm Willkie, Farr & Gallagher, N.Y.C., 1955-69, partner, 1969—. Bd. dirs. LaGuardia Meml. House, N.Y.C., 1963—, sec., 1965—. Mem. Am., N.Y. State bar assns. Office: 1 Chase Manhattan Plaza New York City NY 10005 Tel (212) 248-1000

CORSO, FRANK MITCHELL, b. N.Y.C., July 28, 1928; LL.B., St. John's U., 1952. Admitted to U.S. Ct. Mil. Appeals bar, 1954, N.Y. State bar, 1954, U.S. Supreme Ct. bar, 1960, U.S. Dist. Ct. bar, 1963; asso. firm Corso & Petito, Plainview, N.Y., 1967-70, Corso & Engelberg, Jericho, N.Y., 1973—. Mem. Am. (anti-trust and litigation com.), N.Y., Nassau bar assns., Am. Judicature Soc., Assn. Trial Lawyers Am., N.Y. State Trial Lawyers, World Assn. Lawyers (founding). Named Man of Yr., Amer-Itals, Inc., 1966; contbr. articles to legal jours. Home: 5 Suncrest Dr Dix Hills NY 11746 Office: 350 Jericho Turnpike Jericho NY 11753 Tel (516) 822-8600

CORSO, JOSEPH RAYMOND, b. Bklyn., Sept. 11, 1908; LL.B., Fordham U., 1931. Admitted to N.Y. bar, 1932; individual practice, 1932-36; asso. firm Corso & Lucia, Bklyn., 1936-50; assemblyman N.Y. State Legislature, 1949-66; judge Civil Ct., N.Y.C., 1967-68; justice N.Y. State Supreme Ct., Bklyn., 1969—. Mem. N.Y. State, Bklyn. bar assns., Columbian Lawyers Assn., Catholic Lawyers Guild. Office: Supreme Ct Chambers 360 Adams St Brooklyn NY 11201 Tel (212) 643-5874

CORSO, PATRICIA TEITEL, b. Bronx, N.Y., Mar. 2, 1935; ed. St. Johns U. and St. Johns Law Sch. Admitted to N.Y. State bar, 1961; asso. firm Gilman & Schwartz, N.Y.C., 1961-63; partner firm Schotsky, Corso & Teitel, N.Y.C., 1963-64, Corso & Teitel, Huntington, N.Y., 1964-75; individual practice law, Huntington, 1976—. Chmn. advisory bd. for child protective services Suffolk County, N.Y., 1974—; pres. community services Nat. Council Jewish Women, mem. nat. bd. dirs. Mem. Suffolk County Bar Assn. Office: 425 Broadhollow Rd Melville NY 11746 Tel (516) 752-1822

CORTEZ, HERNAN GLENN, b. Harlingen, Tex., Nov. 12, 1934; B.A., U. Tex., 1956, J.D., 1962. Admitted to Tex. bar, 1962; asst. atty. City of Austin, (Tex.), 1962-69, asso. atty., 1969, atty., 1969-70; individual practice law, Austin, 1971—. Bd. dirs. Austin Child Guidance Center, 1971-74. Mem. State Bar Tex., Am., Travis County bar assns., Assn. Trial Lawyers Am., Tex. City Attys. Assn., Am. Judicature Soc. Office: 500 First Federal Plaza Austin TX 78701 Tel (512) 476-8371

COSHAM, DAVID EDWARD, b. Hartford, Conn., Mar. 2, 1946; B.A., Central Conn. State Coll., 1968; J.D., U. Conn., 1972. Admitted to Conn. bar, 1973; asso. Richard C. Parmelee, Middletown, Conn., 1973—; agt. Am. Title Ins. Co., Middletown, 1974—; atty. Chgo. Title Ins. Co., 1976—, FHA, Middletown, 1975—. Hearing officer Middletown Welfare Dept., 1974—. Mem. Am., Conn., Middlesex County bar assns. Home: 1160 S Main St Middletown CT 06457 Office: 547 Main St Middletown CT 06457

COSNER, ALAN, b. Bklyn., Apr. 26, 1945; B.S. in Bus. Adminstrn., Bucknell U., 1966; J.D., Seton Hall U., 1970; LL.M., N.Y. U., 1974. Admitted to N.J. bar, 1970; accountant Lybrand, Ross Bros. & Montgomery, N.Y.C., 1966; field agt. IRS, N.Y.C., 1968-69, Newark, 1969-71; asso. firm Clarick, Clarick & Miller, New Brunswick, N.J., 1971-73; individual practice law, E. Brunswick, 1973—; atty. Middlesex County Conservation Council, 1972; instr. law Rutgers U., Newark, 1975—; arbitrator Am. Arbitration Assn., 1973—; condemnation commr. Middlesex County, 1973—. Mem. Am., N.J., Middlesex County bar assns. Home: 6 Sagamore Ave East Brunswick NJ 08816 Office: 77 Milltown Rd Box 515 East Brunswick NJ 08816 Tel (201) 254-3700

COSNOW, WILLIAM WAYNE, b. Willows, Calif., Sept. 6, 1920; A.A., Sacramento Jr. Coll., 1940; B.S., San Francisco State Coll., 1947; LL.B., J.D., U. Calif. at San Francisco, 1950. Admitted to Calif. bar, 1957; individual practice law, San Francisco, 1951-57, Merced, Calif., 1957-58; city atty., Redding, Calif., 1958-59; individual practice law, Redding, 1961—. Mem. Assn. Def. Counsel, Calif. State Bar, Am. Bar Assn. Home: 3400 Scenic Dr Redding CA 96001 Office: 1428 West St Redding CA 96001 Tel (916) 241-3468

COSTA, JOHN ANTHONY, b. Bklyn., Oct. 6, 1942; B.A., Fairleigh Dickinson U., 1964; J.D., St. John's U., Bklyn., 1970. Admitted to N.Y. bar, 1971; legal adviser legal div. N.Y.C. Police Dept., 1970-72; spl. asst. atty. gen. N.Y. Office Spl. Prosector, N.Y.C., 1973-74; partner firm Costa and Vicari, Congers, N.Y., 1974—; instr. Rockland Community Coll., 1973—, Dutchess Community Coll., 1974-75. Mem. Nyack (N.Y.) Union Free Sch. Dist. 4 Bd. Edn., 1976—. Mem. N.Y. State, Rockland County (N.Y.) bar assns., Rockland County, N.Y. State sch. bds. assns. Home: 779 Brookridge Ct Valley Cottage NY 10989 Office: Costa and Vicari 27 N Route 303 Congers NY 10920 Tel (914) 268-4422

COSTELLO, BARTLEY JOSEPH, III, b. Rockville Centre, N.Y., July 11, 1944; A.B., Coll. Holy Cross, 1966; J.D., Albany Law Sch., 1972. Admitted to N.Y. bar, 1973; asso. firm Hinman, Straub, Pigors & Manning, Albany, N.Y., 1972—. Pres., Pine Hills Neighborhood Assn., Albany; bd. dirs. West Hill Improvement Corp. and Neighborhood Resource Center, Inc., Albany. Mem. Am., N.Y., Albany County bar assns. Home: 37 Bancker St Albany NY 12208 Office: 90 State St Albany NY 12207 Tel (518) 436-0751

COSTELLO, HARRY GEORGE, b. St. Paul, Aug. 11, 1915; student Coll. St. Thomas, St. Paul, 1932-33, 35-36; LL.B. cum laude, William Mitchell Coll., 1940. Admitted to Minn. bar, 1940; mem. firm Moore, Costello & Hart, St. Paul, 1947—; vis. instr. Macalester Coll., 1946-51; mem. State Bd. Law Examiners, 1961—, pres. bd., 1964-67. Mem. Am., Minn., Ramsey County bar assns. Office: Northwestern Bank Bldg 5th and Cedar Sts Saint Paul MN 55101 Tel (612) 227-7683

COSTELLO, JOHN ("JACK") FRANCIS, JR., b. Lindsay, Okla., Mar. 5, 1935; B.B.A., U. Okla., 1957, J.D., 1964. Admitted to Okla. bar, 1964, Tex. bar, 1965; comml. lending officer, sec. to bd. dirs. Fort Worth Nat. Bank, 1964—; v.p., sec., legal liaison Tex. Am. Bancshares Inc., Ft. Worth, 1971—. Bd. dirs., mem. exec. com. Edna Gladney Home, Ft. Worth, 1969—; pres. Tarrant County Easter Seal Soc., 1973-75, bd. dirs., 1970—; treas., mem. exec. com. Van Cliburn Found., 1970—; dir. adv. bd. Tarrant County Jr. Achievement, 1970—; bd. dirs. Ft. Worth Zool. Assn., 1972—. Mem. Am. Soc. Corporate Secs., Assn. Bank Holding Cos. (lawyers com.), Phi Alpha Delta, Sigma Chi. Home: 1313 Shady Oaks Ln Fort Worth TX 76107 Office: POB 9002 Fort Worth TX 76107 Tel (817) 338-8671

COSTELLO, LEO EDWIN, b. Chattanoga, June 6, 1928; student U. Tenn., 1950; LL.B., Birmingham Sch. Law, 1969. Admitted to Ala. bar, 1969, U.S. Supreme Ct. bar, 1976. With Redisco, Inc., 1953-69; individual practice law, Birmingham, Ala., 1969—; faculty Birmingham Sch. Law; lectr. U. Ala. Mem. Am. Trial Lawyers Assn., Comml. Law League, Nat. Assn. Credit Mgrs., Ala. Assn. Credit Execs., Sigma Delta Kappa. Office: 3716 5th Ave South Birmingham AL 35222 Tel (205) 252-9946

COSWAY, RICHARD, b. Newark, Ohio, Oct. 20, 1917; A.B., Denison U., 1939; J.D., U. Cin., 1942. Admitted to Ohio bar, 1942; asst. prof. law U. Cin., 1946-53, asso. prof., 1953-58, prof. U. Wash., 1958—; atty. Dept. Justice, Washington, 1950-51; vis. prof. law So. Meth. U., 1966-67; mem. commn. on Uniform State Laws for Wash., 1967—. Mem. Am., Seattle-King County bar assns. Author: (with Warren Shattuck) Washington Practice, vols. 7 and 8, 1967. Home: 15116 38th Ave NE Seattle WA 98155 Office: Law Sch U of Wash Seattle WA 98195 Tel (206) 543-2644

COTLAR, STEVEN ALLEN, b. Phila., May 26, 1942; B.A., Pa. State U., 1963; J.D., Dickinson Sch. Law, 1969. Admitted to Pa. bar, 1969; clk. to judge Bucks County (Pa.) Ct. Common Pleas, 1969-72; asso. firm Hartzel & Bush, Doylestown, Pa., 1969-72; partner firm Cotlar Mantz Aglow & Elliot, Doylestown, 1972—. Mem. ACLU. Home: 7 Maple Ln Doylestown PA 18901 Office: PO Box 885 Doylestown PA 18901 Tel (205) 343-3600

COTNER, JOHN MICHAEL, b. Lima, Ohio, Mar. 17, 1945; B.A., Ohio No. U., 1967, J.D., 1970. Admitted to Ohio bar, 1970, Fed. Bar So. Dist. Ohio, 1973, Fed. Bar No. Dist. Ohio, 1975; atty. fed. Res. Bank, Cleve., 1970-71; atty. Shipman, Utrecht & Dixon Co., Troy, Ohio, 1972—. Bd. dirs. Miami County (Ohio) Am. Cancer Soc., 1974—; bd. dirs. Lincoln Center, Troy, 1974—; bd. dirs. Troy Recreation Bd., 1974—. Mem. Am., Ohio State, Miami County bar assns. Home: 764 Windsor Rd Troy OH 45373 Office: 12 S Plum St Troy OH 45373 Tel (513) 335-2567

COTRO-MANES, PAUL N., b. Salt Lake City, May 7, 1928; B.A., Westminster Coll., 1949; J.D., U. Utah, 1954. Admitted to Utah bar, 1955; U.S. Supreme Ct. bar, 1962; mem. firm Cotro-Manes, Warr, Fankhauser & Beasley, and predecessors, Salt Lake City, 1955—; staff judge adv. Utah N.G., 1962-75. Mem. Utah Bar Assn., Am. Trial Lawyers Assn., Phi Alpha Delta. Office: 430 Judge Bldg Salt Lake City UT 84111 Tel (801) 531-1300

COTRUVO, FRANCIS PHILLIP, b. Akron, Ohio, Dec. 22, 1919; B.A., U. Akron, 1941; J.D., 1968. Admitted to Ohio bar, 1949, U.S. Supreme Ct. bar, 1954; individual practice law, Akron, 1949-57; asst. atty. gen. State of Ohio, 1957-59; atty. examiner Ohio Indsl. Commn., Columbus, 1959-61; partner firm Cotruvo & Cusack, Columbus, 1961—. Pres., Italian-Am. Civic Assn. of Summit County (Ohio), Akron, 1960—; Italian-Am. rep. Republican Nat. Com., 1960-62. Mem. Ohio, Akron, Columbus bar assns., Franklin County Trial Lawyers Assn. Home: 488 Delmar Ave Akron OH 44310 Office: 50 W Broad St Columbus OH 43215 Tel (614) 224-7888

COTTON, AYLETT BOREL, b. San Francisco, Apr. 10, 1913; B.A., Stanford, 1935, J.D., 1938. Admitted to Calif. bar, 1938, U.S. Supreme Ct. bar, 1959; individual practice law, San Mateo, Calif., 1938-39, San Francisco, 1940-52, Burlingame, Calif., 1952-59; partner firm Cotton, Seligman & Ray and predecessors, San Francisco, 1959—. Founder Crystal Springs Sch., Hillsborough, Calif., 1952, pres. bd. trustees, 1952-57, mem. bd. trustees, 1957—. Mem. Am., Calif., San Francisco (chmn. judiciary com. 1969), San Mateo County bar assns., Stanford Law Soc. of San Francisco (pres. 1974-75). Office: 1400 Alcoa Bldg One Maritime Plaza San Francisco CA 94111 Tel (415) 397-4600

COTTON, EUGENE, b. N.Y.C., May 20, 1914; B.S.S., Coll. City N.Y., 1933; LL.B., Columbia, 1936. Admitted to N.Y. bar, 1936, Ill. bar, 1947, U.S. Supreme Ct. bar, 1942; asso. firm Szold & Brandwen, N.Y.C., 1936-37; atty. N.Y. State Labor Relations Bd., N.Y.C., 1937-41; spl. counsel FCC, Washington, 1941-42; asst. gen. counsel Congress Indsl. Orgns., Washington, 1942-47; partner firms Elson & Cotton, Chgo., 1948-50, Cotton, Watt, Jones, King & Bowlus, Chgo., 1951—; gen. counsel United Packinghouse Workers Am., Chgo., 1947-68, packinghouse dept. Amalgamated Meat Cutters and Butcher Workmen of North Am., 1968—. Mem. Ill. State, Chgo. bar assns., Chgo. Council Lawyers. Note editor Columbia Law Rev., 1935-36. Home: 935 E 49th St Chicago IL 60615 Office: One IBM Plaza Chicago IL 60611 Tel (312) 467-0590

COTTON, HARRIS YALE, b. Harrisburg, Pa., July 25, 1928; B.S. in Biology, Villanova U., 1949; LL.D. cum laude, Rutgers U., 1958. Admitted to N.J. bar, 1958; individual practice law, Woodbury, N.J., 1958-60, 71—; mem. firm Falciani & Cotton, Woodbury, 1960-71; judge Monroe & Elk Twps., N.J.; solicitor Woodbury Heights (N.J.); v.p., atty. Lenape State Bank, West Deptford (N.J.) Twp., Washington; prosecutor Gloucester County (N.J.), 1975—; del. Constl. Conv.; mem. ad hoc com. Del. River Port Authority. Mem. apportionment commn.; pres. Underwood Meml. Hosp., Woodbury. Mem. N.J., Gloucester County, Am. bar assns., Am. Trial Lawyers. Editor Rutgers Law Rev., 1957-58. Home: 9 Buttonwood St Wenonah NJ 08090 Office: 21 Delaward St Woodbury NJ 08096 Tel (609) 848-0100

COTTON, WILLIAM DAVIS, b. Jonesville, La., Feb. 9, 1904; LL.B., La. State U., 1927, J.D., 1968. Admitted to La. bar, 1927, U.S. Supreme Ct. bar, 1946; atty. La. State Land Office, Baton Rouge, 1927-29; individual practice law, Rayville, La., 1929-46; partner firm Cotton & Bolton, Rayville, 1946—; research fellow Southwestern Legal Found., 1964—; mem. La. Senate, 1940-44. Chancellor, La. conf. Meth. Ch., 1968—; pres. La. State U. Alumni Fedn., 1969-70. Fellow Am. Bar Found., Am. Coll. Probate Counsel; mem. Am., La. State (pres. 1965-66) bar assns., La. State Law Inst. (council 1959—). Home: 219 Julia St Rayville LA 71269 Office: PO Box 857 Rayville LA 71269 Tel (318) 728-2051

COTTON, WILLIAM MELVIN, b. Vega, Tex., June 17, 1924; B.S., W. Tex. State U., 1950; J.D., U. Tex., 1953. Admitted to Tex. bar, 1952; staff atty. Phillips Petroleum Co., Amarillo, Tex., 1953-55; asso. and partner firm Stubbeman, McRae, Sealy, Laughlin & Browder, Midland, Tex., 1956-73; partner firm Cotton, Bledsoe, Tighe, Morrow & Dawson, Midland, 1974—; dir. State Jr. Bar of Tex., 1954-55. Mem. Am., Midland County bar assns., State Bar Tex. Editorial bd. Tex. Law Rev., 1952-53. Office: 1930 Wilco Bldg Midland TX 79701 Tel (915) 684-5782

COTTRELL, JAMES LAWRENCE, b. Detroit, Nov. 13, 1943; B.S., Eastern Ky. U., 1967; J.D., U. Ky., 1968. Admitted to Ky. bar, 1969, Fla. bar, 1971, U.S. Supreme Ct. bar, 1973. Staff atty. Ky. Legis. Research Commn., Frankfort, 1969; partner firm Cammack, Cottrell & Fox, Lexington, Ky., 1969-72; ass. firm Pavese, Shields, Garner, Haverfield & Kluttz, Cape Coral, Fla., 1972-73, partner, 1973—; exec. dir. Regional Crime Council, Lexington, 1969-72; city atty., Cape Coral, 1973-76; atty. Cape Coral Health Facilities Authority, 1976—. Bd. dirs. Cape Coral Little League, Inc., 1973—. Mem. Harney Point Kiwanis Club (pres. 1975-76), Cape Coral C. of C. (mem. indsl. devel. com.), Am., Ky., Fla., Lee County bar assns., Lawyers Title Guaranty Fund, Delta Theta Phi, Delta Sigma Rho, Tau Kappa Alpha. Home: 5352 Cobalt Ct Cape Coral FL 33904 Office: PO Box 88 Cape Coral FL 33904 Tel (813) 542-3188

COUCH, ALAN JAY, b. Tulsa, Oct. 17, 1935; B.S. in Bus. Adminstrn., Phillips U., 1957; J.D., Oklahoma City U., 1963; postgrad. U. Nev., 1970, 72-73. Admitted to Okla. bar, U.S. Dist. Ct. bar, Western Dist. Okla., 1963; courtroom dep. U.S. Dist. Ct., Oklahoma City, 1960-63; claim rep. Comml. Union N.Brit. Ins. Group, Oklahoma City, 1963-65; asso. firm Stockwell & Couch, Moore, Okla., 1965-66; claim mgr., atty. Western Casualty & Surety Co., Oklahoma City, 1966-69; spl. dist. judge Cleveland County, Norman, Okla., 1969-72, asso. dist. judge, 1972—; instr. U. Okla., 1970—; instr. Nat. Council Juvenile Ct. Judges, 1974, mem. tng. com., 1975—, faculty adviser 39th Ann. Conf., 1976; faculty adviser Nat. Coll. Juvenile Justice, 1976; bd. dirs., criminal justice adv. com. Assn. Central Okla. Govts., 1975—; faculty Okla. Conf. on Alcohol Abuse and Alcoholism, 1974-75; sec.-treas. steering com. Gov.'s Conf. on Crime and Corrections, 1972—; bd. dirs. Cleveland County Youth Services, 1972—; chmn. pub. agys. and legis. com. Cleveland County Juvenile Delinquency Council, 1974—; established Cleveland County Youth Bur. Citizens Adv. Com., 1975. Congregation pres. Christian Ch., 1971-72, 76—; bd. dirs. Cleveland County chpt. ARC, 1971-76; chmn. profl. adv. bd. dirs. Norman Alcohol Info., Inc., 1972—, pres., 1976—; bd. visitors U. Okla. Mem. Am., Okla., Cleveland County bar assns., Nat. Coll. Probate Judges (adv. council 1974—), Probate Judges Assn. (sec. 1972—), Okla. Jud. Conf. (v.p. 1975—, sec. jud. manpower com. 1971—), Nat. Coll. State Trial Judges, Delta Theta Phi. Recipient Significant Achievement award Rotary, 1971, Community Service citation Juvenile Services, Inc., 1973; contbr. articles to profl. jours. Home: 813 Nancy Lynn Terr Norman OK 73069 Office: Cleveland County Courthouse 200 S Peters St Norman OK 73069 Tel (405) 321-6251

COUCH, JOHN RUSSELL, JR., b. Oklahoma City, Aug. 18, 1942; B.A., Rice U., 1964; M.A., Okla. U., 1968, J.D., 1970. Admitted to Okla. bar, 1970, U.S. Dist. Ct. bar, Western Dist. Okla., 1970; law clk. Hon. William Holloway, U.S. 10th Circuit Ct. Appeals, 1970-71; individual practice law, Stillwater, Okla., 1971-74; judge Okla. Dist. Ct., 6th Jud. Dist., 1974—. Mem. Am., Okla. bar assns. Home: 910 S Stanley St Stillwater OK 74074 Office: Payne County Courthouse Stillwater OK 74074 Tel (405) 372-3889

COUCH, LESLIE FRANKLIN, b. Albany, N.Y., July 22, 1930; A.B., Union Coll., Schenectady, 1952; J.D., Albany Law Sch., 1955. Admitted to N.Y. State bar, 1955, U.S. Dist. Ct. for No. Dist. N.Y. bar, 1955, U.S. Ct. of Appeals for 2d Circuit bar, 1959; practiced in Albany, 1955—; individual practice law, 1955-67; partner firm DiFabio and Couch, profl. corp., 1967—; legal cons. N.Y. Gov. Spl. Asst. Problems of Aged, 1956-58; panelist Am. Arbitration Assn. Trustee Westminster Presbyn. Ch., Albany; bd. dirs. Albany Internat. Center. Mem. Capital Dist. Trial Lawyers Assn. (dir.), Am., N.Y. State, Albany County bar assns. Home: 306 Loudon Rd Loudonville NY 12211 Office: 4 Automation Ln Computer Park Albany NY 12205 Tel (518) 459-1000

COUGHLIN, BARRING, b. Wilkes-Barre, Pa., Dec. 19, 1913; A.B., Princeton U., 1935; LL.B. magna cum laude, Harvard U., 1938. Admitted to D.C. bar 1939, Ohio bar, 1940; law clk. to justice D.C. Ct. Appeals, 1938-39; asso. firm Thompson, Hine and Flory, Cleve., 1939—. Trustee Citizens League, Cleve., 1958-66, Cleve. Homemakers Service Assn., 1966-72. Mem. Am., Ohio, Cleve. (trustee 1966-70) bar assns., Am. Law Inst. Home: 2290 Ardleigh Dr Cleveland Heights OH 44106 Office: 1100 National City Bank Bldg Cleveland OH 44114 Tel (216) 241-1880

COUGHLIN, JOHN JAMES, b. Elizabeth, N.J., Feb. 6, 1906; B.A. with high honors, Swartmore Coll., 1928; J.D., Yale, 1931. Admitted to N.J. bar, 1932, Oreg. bar, 1933, U.S. Supreme Ct. bar, 1952; individual practice law, Portland, Oreg., 1933-40; mem. firm Phillips, Coughlin, Buell, Stoloff & Black, and predecessors, Portland, 1940—; mem. Oreg. Bd. Bar Examiners, 1956-58, chmn., 1958; judge pro tem, 1957; asst. sec. Portland Gen. Electric Co., 1949-74; mem. Oreg. Prepaid Legal Ins., Inc., 1976—. Bd. dirs. Riverdale Sch. Dist., 1956-58, chmn., 1958; bd. dirs. Oreg. Symphony Soc., 1976—. Mem. Oreg., Multnomah County, Am. bar assns., Am. Judicature Soc.; hon. mem. Am., Oreg., Multnomah County med. assns. Home: 2211 SW Park Pl Portland OR 97205 Office: 807 Electric Bldg Portland OR 97205 Tel (503) 222-8821

COULSON, EDWARD DONALD, b. Houston, Apr. 20, 1918; B.A., Tex. A. and M. U., 1938; J.D., U. Tex., 1941. Admitted to Tex. bar, 1941; practiced in Houston, 1941-69; judge Harris County (Tex.) 189th Civil Dist. Ct., 1969-72; asso. justice Tex. 14th Ct. Civil Appeals, 1973—. Mem. Houston, Tex., Am. bar assns., Am. Judicature Soc., Am. Inst. Jud. Adminstrn. Home: 2016 Main St Apt 1922 Houston TX 77002 Office: 105 Civil Cts Bldg 301 Fannin St Houston TX 77002 Tel (713) 228-8311

COULTER, GEORGE PROTHRO, b. El Dorado, Ark., June 8, 1930; B.A., U. Calif. Los Angeles, 1951; J.D., George Washington U., 1957. Admitted to Calif. bar, 1958, Fed. bar, 1958, U.S. Supreme Ct. bar, 1973; with Nat. Security Agy., Washington, 1955-57; asso. firm Gordon & Weinberg, 1958-63; mem. firm Coulter & Coulter, 1963-67, Coulter, Vernoff & Brewer, P.C., 1967—; officer, dir. Parade Properties Inc., 1963—. Mem. Am., Los Angeles County, Pasadena bar assns. Asso. editor Housing Research Found. Jour., 1965-68. Contbr. articles to legal jour. Office: 234 E Colorado Blvd Pasadena CA 91101 Tel (213) 681-4907

COUNCIL, JOHN RAINEY, b. Americus, Ga., Aug. 17, 1939; B.A., U. South Fla., 1968; J.D., U. Fla., 1971. Admitted to Fla. bar, 1971; partner firm Brewton & Council, Dade City, Fla. Mem. Fla., Pasco County bar assns., Dade City C. of C. (dir.). Office: 708 E Meridian Ave Dade City FL 33525 Tel (904) 567-5171

COUNCIL, RONALD ELLIOTT, b. Richmond, Va., May 28, 1936; B.S. in Mech. Engring., Va. Poly. Inst., 1959; J.D., U. Balt., 1966. Admitted to Md. bar, 1968; partner firm Hartman & Crain, Annapolis, Md., 1968—. Mem. Am., Md., Anne Arundel County (chmn. young lawyers sect. 1969-72) bar assns. Office: 222 Severn Ave Annapolis MD 21403 Tel (301) 267-8166 also 269-6190 also 261-2247

COUND, JOHN JAMES, b. Dayton, Ohio, Feb. 7, 1928; B.A., George Washington U., 1949; LL.B., Harvard, 1952. Admitted to D.C. bar, 1952; law clk. U.S. Ct. Appeals, N.Y.C., 1952-53; atty. U.S. Dept. Justice, Washington, 1953-56; prof. law U. Minn., 1956—. Author: (with Friedenthal and Miller) Cases on Civil Procedure, 1968, 1974. Home: 6 Wood Duck Ln St Paul MN 55110 Office: U Minn Law Sch Minneapolis MN 55455 Tel (612) 373-2730

COUNTISS, JOHN RICHARD, III, b. Jackson, Miss., Aug. 26, 1927; B.A., Millsaps Coll., 1950; LL.B. cum laude, Jackson Sch. Law, 1956. Admitted to Miss. bar, 1956, U.S. Supreme Ct. bar, 1972; individual practice law, Jackson, 1956—; U.S. commr., 1963-70, U.S. magistrate, 1971—. Mem. Miss., Am., Hinds County, Fed. bar assns., Am. Judicature Soc., Nat. Assn. U.S. Magistrates. Home: 2022 E Bourne Pl Jackson MS 39211 Office: Federal Bldg Jackson MS 39201 Tel (601) 969-4292

COUNTRYMAN, JOHN WOODS, b. DeKalb, Ill., Nov. 5, 1944; B.A., No. Ill. U., 1967; J.D. with distinction, Ill. Inst. Tech.-Chgo. Kent Coll. Law, 1970. Admitted to Ill. bar, 1970; pub. defender DeKalb County, 1971-73; partner firm Castle, Burns, O'Malley & Countryman, DeKalb, 1973—; spl. asst. atty. gen., 1977—. Pres. bd. dirs. Kishwaukee YMCA, 1974; chmn. DeKalb County Republican Central Com., 1976—. Mem. Am., Ill., Chgo., DeKalb County bar assns., Ill. Trial Lawyers Assn. Home: 1528 Sleepy Hollow Ln DeKalb IL 60115 Office: 363 E Lincoln Hwy DeKalb IL 60115 Tel (815) 756-9571

COUNTS, WILLIAM HUBERT, b. Olive Hill, Ky., May 30, 1907; A.B., Morehead U., 1930; LL.B., U. Ky., 1934. Admitted to Ky. bar, 1934; mem. firm Counts & Counts, Olive Hill, 1934-56; mem. firm Counts & Duval, Olive Hill, 1967-74; served as county atty., Carter County, Ky., 1938-41. Mem. Ky., Carter County bar assns. Home: Route 2 Box 473 Olive Hill KY 41164 Office: Cross St Olive Hill KY 41164 Tel (606) 286-2711

COURTNEY, JOSEPH FRANCIS, b. Bolton, Lancashire, Eng., Mar. 12, 1926; A.B., Northeastern U., 1948; M.A., Boston U., 1950; J.D., Suffolk U., 1963. Admitted to Mass. bar, 1964; individual practice law, Wilmington, Mass., 1964-69; partner firm London & Courtney, Lowell, Mass., 1970—. Dir. Mass. Bur. Program Planning and Research, 1962-64. Mem. Mass., Boston, Lowell, Middlesex County (Mass.) bar assns. Home: 398 Andover St Wilmington MA 01887 Office: 34 Central St Lowell MA 01852 Tel (617) 459-0146

COURTNEY, RICHARD TRAVERS, JR., b. Worcester, Mass., Aug. 12, 1923; J.D., Boston Coll., 1950. Admitted to Mass. bar, 1951, U.S. Dist. Ct. bar, 1955; partner firm Brassard & Courtney, and predecessor, Worcester, Mass., 1953-69; individual practice law, Worcester, 1969—; pub. defender Worcester County, 1960-62. Mem. Worcester County Bar Assn. Home: 20 4th St Worcester MA 01603 Office: 595 Park Ave Worcester MA 01603 Tel (617) 756-0607

COURTNEY, THOMAS FRANCIS, b. Chgo., Aug. 7, 1942; A.B. with honors, U. Ill., Urbana, 1965; J.D., John Marshall Law Sch., Chgo., 1973. Admitted to Ill. bar, 1973; individual practice law, Chgo., 1973—. Mem. Chgo., Ill., Am. bar assns. Office: 12750 S Harlem Ave Palos Heights IL 60462 Tel (312) 881-0809

COUSER, RICHARD BATES, b. Hanover, N.H., Feb. 6, 1941; B.A., Yale, 1963; LL.B., Stanford, 1966. Admitted to N.H. bar, 1966; mem. firm Orr & Reno, Concord, N.H., 1966—; mem. N.H. Bd. Bar Examiners, 1974—. Chmn., Greater Concord United Way, 1973; bd. dirs. A Better Chance, Inc., 1972-76; active Boy Scouts Am. Mem. Am., N.H. bar assns., Am. Trial Lawyers Assn. Contbr. articles to legal jours. Home: RFD 8 Graham Rd Concord NH 03301 Office: 95 N Main St Concord NH 03301 Tel (603) 224-2381

COUTS, CHARLES RAYMOND, b. Wellsville, Ohio, May 28, 1911; A.B. cum laude, Ohio Wesleyan U., 1933; J.D., Harvard, 1936, LL.M., 1937. Admitted to Ohio bar, 1937, Mass. bar, 1938, U.S. Supreme Ct. bar, 1960; asso. firm Nutter, McClennen & Fish, Boston, 1937-38; asst. counsel B.F. Goodrich Co., Akron, Ohio, 1939-58, counsel, 1958-71, asst. sec., 1960-71, corporate sec., 1971-75; arbitrator Am. Arbitration Assn., Cleve., 1975—. Trustee, Ohio No. U., 1967—; mem. Friends Akron U., 1976—. Mem. Am. Soc. Corporate Secs., Am., Boston, Akron bar assns., Phi Beta Kappa, Omicron Delta Kappa, Theta Alpha Phi. Home: 255 N Portage Path Akron OH 44303 Tel (216) 864-6051

COUZENS, JOHN RICHARD, b. Boulder, Colo., June 10, 1910; J.D., U. Wash., Seattle, 1935. Admitted to Calif. bar, 1936; individual practice law, San Francisco, 1937-43, Auburn, Calif., 1946—. Mem. Calif. Bar Assn. Tel (916) 885-7224

COVELLI, DANIEL ANTHONY, b. Chgo., Oct. 14, 1904; J.D., Kent Coll. Law, 1926. Admitted to Ill. bar, 1926; individual practice law, Chgo., 1926-51; asst. state's atty. Cook County (Ill.), 1928-33; judge Circuit Ct. of Cook County, 1951—; dir. 1st Security Trust & Savs. Bank. Office: Civic Center Chicago IL 60602 Tel (312) 443-8243

COVER, ROBERT MELVIN, b. Boston, July 30, 1943; B.A. in History summa cum laude, Princeton, 1965; LL.B. magna cum laude, Columbia, 1968. Asst. prof. law Columbia, 1968-71; prof. law Yale, 1972—; vis. sr. lectr. law, Am. Studies Hebrew U., Jerusalem, Israel, 1971-72, vis. prof. law, autumn 1975. Author: Justice Accused, Antislavery and the Judicial Process, 1975; contbr. articles to law jours. Home: 160 Colony Rd New Haven CT 06511 Office: Yale Law Sch 127 Wall St New Haven Ct 06520 Tel (203) 432-4307

COVERT, MAURICE WILLIAM, b. Houston, Mo., Apr. 9, 1904; LL.B., Washington U., St. Louis, 1925, J.D., 1947. Admitted to Mo. bar, 1925, U.S. Supreme Ct. bar, 1945; mem. firms Covert & Covert, 1925-26, Hiett & Covert, 1951-53, Covert & Hutcheson, Houston, Mo., 1974-76; individual practice, 1977—; pros. atty. Texas County (Mo.), 1929-30, 43-44; asst. atty. gen. State of Mo., 1932, 72-74; mem. Mo. Pub. Service Commn., 1952-53. Mem. Mo., S. Central (pres. 1953) bar assns. Home: 216 Bryan St Houston MO 65483 Office: 109 N Grand St Houston MO 65483 Tel (417) 967-4178

COVINGTON, DEAN, b. Rome, Ga., Mar. 14, 1916; A.B., U. Ga., 1937, LL.B., J.D., 1939. Admitted to Ga. bar, 1939; since practiced law in Rome, mem. firm Leon & Dean Covington, 1939-52, Andrews & Covington, 1952-54, Covington, Kilpatrick & Storey, 1955—; mem. Ga. Ho. of Reps., 1947-52; county atty., 1973. Mem. 7th Dist. Democratic Com. Ga. Mem. Am., Ga., Rome (treas.) bar assns., Am. Judicature Soc., Comml. Law League of Am. Home: 230 Lakeshore Dr Rome GA 30161 Office: 701 Broad St Citizens Fed Bldg Suite 300 Rome GA 30161 Tel (404) 291-8370

COVINGTON, EARL GENE, b. St. Louis, Nov. 10, 1939; B.B.A., U. Tex., 1963; J.D., U. Houston, 1969. Admitted to Tex. Supreme Ct. bar, 1967, U.S. Dist. Ct. bar for So. Dist. Tex., 1974, U.S. Tax Ct. bar, 1976; tax specialist Ernst & Ernst, C.P.A.'s, Houston, 1967-72; asso. firm Urban, Coolidge, Pennington & Scott, Houston, 1973-74; individual practice law, Houston, 1974-76; mem. firm Covington & Reese, P.C., Houston, 1976—; sec. Mariner Corp.; dir. Aquasol, Inc., Houston Research, Inc. Sec.-treas. Tex. Theatre Found.; mem. exec. com. Bayou Woods Civic Club, Houston. Mem. Houston, Am., Tex. bar assns., Am. Inst. C.P.A.'s., Tex. Soc. C.P.A.'s. (dir. Houston chpt. 1974-75), Delta Theta Phi. Home: 9145 Kenilworth St Houston TX 77024 Office: 1700 W Loop South Suite 850 Houston TX 77027 Tel (713) 627-9820

COVINGTON, HEWITT HAYS, b. Nashville, Mar. 30, 1928; B.S. in Commerce, U. Va., 1950, J.D., 1955. Admitted to Va. bar, 1955, Ga. bar, 1956; asso. firm Alston, Miller & Gaines, and predecessors, Atlanta, 1955-60, partner, 1960—; v.p. Citizens and So. Park Nat. Bank, Atlanta, 1966-75; lectr. in field. Mem. Am., Atlanta bar assns. Tel (404) 588-0300

COVINGTON, JOE ETHRIDGE, b. Nashville, Ark., Dec. 14, 1911; B.A., U. Ark., 1932, LL.B., 1940; LL.M., Harvard, 1941, S.J.D., 1952. Admitted to Ark. bar, 1940, Mo. bar, 1959, U.S. Supreme Ct. bar, 1957; faculty U. Ark. Sch. Law, 1941-58, dean, 1954-58; exec. asst. to pres. U. Ark., 1948-51, acting pres. 1951-52, 54, provost, 1951-54; dean U. Mo. Sch. Law, 1958-69, Phi Sheridan Gibson prof. law, 1969—; dir. testing Nat. Conf. Bar Examiners, 1969—. Mem. Am., Boone County (pres. 1962-63) bar assns., Am. Bar Found., Mo. Bar, Am. Judicature Soc., Am. Law Inst. Home: 326 Crown Point St Columbia MO 65201 Office: Law School Univ Mo Columbia MO 65201 Tel (314) 882-7562

COVINGTON, ROBERT NEWMAN, b. Evansville, Ind., Sept. 9, 1936; B.A., Yale, 1958; J.D., Vanderbilt U., 1961. Admitted to Tenn. bar, 1961; asst. prof. law Vanderbilt U., Nashville, 1961-64, asso. prof., 1964-69, prof., 1969—, asso. dean, 1972-75; vis. prof. U. Mich., 1971, U. Calif. at Davis, 1975-76; cons. Tenn. Law Library Commn., 1965-75, Tenn. Dept. Labor, 1971-72; adminstrv. law officer Calif. Agrl. Labor Relations Bd., 1975-76. Mem. Am., Tenn. bar assns., Am. Judicature Soc., Am. Arbitration Assn., Phi Beta Kappa, Order of Coif. Author: (with Wade, Cheatham, Stason, Smedley) Cases on Legal Method, 1969; (with Caghan) Social Legislation, 1st edit., 1971, 2d edit., 1974; (with Jones, Caghan) Discrimination in Employment, 1st edit., (with Jones) 2d edit., 1973, (with Jones, Getman) 3d edit., 1976; contbr. articles to legal jours. Home: 907 Estes Rd Nashville TN 37215 Office: Vanderbilt Law Sch Nashville TN 37240 Tel (615) 322-2615

COWAN, ALVIN RANDALL, b. Bklyn., Jan. 9, 1907; A.B., Cornell U., 1927; J.D., Fordham U., 1930. Admitted to N.Y. State bar, 1931, U.S. Dist. Ct. for Eastern Dist. N.Y. bar, 1937, U.S. Dist. Ct. for So. Dist. N.Y., 1936, U.S. Ct. Appeals for 2d Circuit Ct. bar, 1944, U.S. Supreme Ct. bar, 1968; asso. with H.M. Phillips, 1930-41; asso. firm Weil, Gotshal & Manges, N.Y.C., 1941-43, Olvany, Eisner & Donnelly, N.Y.C., 1943-45; individual practice law, 1945-55; partner firm Abrams & Cowan, N.Y.C., 1955—. Mem. Bar Assn. City N.Y., N.Y. State Bar Assn., New York County Lawyers Assn. Contbr. to Tax Mag., Fin. Chronicle. Home: 2109 Broadway New York City NY 10023 Office: 400 Madison Ave New York City NY 10017 Tel (212) 688-9303

COWAN, ELMER G., b. Youngstown, Ohio, June 11, 1924; LL.B., Cleve.-Marshall Law Sch., 1952, LL.M., 1965. Admitted to Ohio bar, 1952; individual practice law, Cleve., 1952—; law dir. Bay Village (Ohio), 1972—; asst. law dir. N. Olmsted (Ohio), 1972-74; gen. counsel Reliance Chem. Co., Expo, Inc., Electric Power & Maintenance Co., Clark Oil Co. Mem. Ohio, Greater Cleve., Cuyahoga, War Vets. bar assns., Cuyahoga Law Dirs. Home: 29122 Buchanan Dr Bay Village OH 44140 Office: 800 Engineers Bldg Cleveland OH 44114 Tel (216) 696-4272

COWAN, FAIRMAN CHAFFEE, b. Wellesley Hills, Mass., Apr. 22, 1915; A.B., Amherst Coll., 1937; LL.B., Harvard U., 1940, postgrad. Bus. Sch. Admitted to Mass. bar, 1940; asso. firm Goodwin, Procter & Hoar, Boston, 1940-41, 46-52, partner, 1952-54; gen. counsel, clk. Norton Co., Worcester, Mass., 1955-61, sec., 1961—, v.p., 1967—, dir., 1963—; dir. Mechanics Bank, Worcester, Mass. Bus. Devel. Corp. Trustee United Way Worcester, 1975—, Clark U., 1964-76, Meml. Hosp., Worcester, 1967—. Mem. Am., Worcester County, Boston bar assns., Worcester Legal Aid Soc. (dir. 1958—). Home: 48 Berwick St Worcester MA 01602 Office: One New Bond St Worcester MA 01606 Tel (617) 853-1000

COWAN, MARTIN DAVID, b. Bronx, N.Y., Nov. 13, 1914; B.S., Fordham U., 1934; LL.B., St. Lawrence U., 1938. Admitted to N.Y. bar, 1939; individual practice law, N.Y.C., 1939—; Valley Stream, N.Y., 1972—; counsel Gen. Ins. Brokers' Assn. of N.Y., Inc., 1950-70. Pres. Nassau Community Temple, West Hempstead, N.Y., 1974-75. Mem. Gen. Ins. Brokers Assn. N.Y. (pres. 1969-74), Council Ins. Brokers of Greater N.Y. (treas. 1972-77). Recipient awards United Jewish Appeal of Greater N.Y., 1973, Fedn. Jewish Philanthropies, 1972, Reform Jewish Appeal of Union Am. Hebrew Congregations, 1967, 71, 74, Gen. Ins. Brokers Assn. N.Y., 1974. Office: 515 Rockaway Ave Valley Stream NY 11581 Tel (516) 872-6646

COWAN, STUART MARSHALL, b. Irvington, N.J., Mar. 20, 1932; B.S., U. Pa., 1952; LL.B., Rutgers U., 1955. Admitted to N.J. bar, 1957, Hawaii bar, 1962, U.S. Supreme Ct. bar, 1966; mem. firm Greenstein & Cowan, Honolulu, 1962-70, Cowan & Frey, Honolulu, 1970-77; asst. staff legal officer USN, 1957-61. Mem. Hawaii, Am. bar assns., Am. Judicature Soc., Trial Lawyers Assn. Am. (state committeeman for Hawaii 1965-69, bd. govs. 1972-75), Hawaii Trial Lawyers Assn. (v.p. 1972-73). Home: 47-339 Mapumapu Rd Kaneohe HI 96744 Office: 190 S King St Suite 2000 Honolulu HI 96813 Tel (808) 533-1767

COWAN, THEODORE PERRY, b. Chinook, Mont., Dec. 21, 1939; B.S. in Bus. Adminstrn., U. Mont., 1966, J.D., 1969. Admitted to Mont. bar, 1969, U.S. Dist. Ct. bar for Dist. Mont., 1969; law clk. to Asso. Justice John W. Bonner, Mont. Supreme Ct., Helena, 1969-70; partner firm Spoja and Cowan, Lewistown, Mont., 1970-76; individual practice law, Lewistown, 1976—; city atty. City of Lewistown, 1976—. Mem. Central Mont. (treas. 1973—), Am. bar assns., State Bar Mont. (trustee). Office: Suite 208 Bankelectric Bldg Lewistown MT 59457 Tel (406) 538-7844

COWAN, WILLIAM HOWARD, b. Syracuse, N.Y., Mar. 28, 1947; B.A., Johns Hopkins U., 1968; J.D., U. Chgo., 1971. Admitted to Ill. bar, 1972; asso. firm Roan & Grossman, Chgo., 1972—. Mem. Am., Chgo. bar assns. Mem. editorial bd. U. Chgo. Law Alumni Jour., 1974—. Office: 120 S LaSalle St Chicago IL 60603 Tel (312) 263-3600

COWDEN, BARTOW, III, b. Rockmart, Ga., Aug. 26, 1925; B.B.A. in Econs., U. Ga., Athens, 1950, J.D., 1949. Admitted to Ga. bar, 1948; trial atty. with Benton E. Gaines, Atlanta, 1949-50; partner firm Gaines, Champion & Cowden, Atlanta, then partner Gaines & Cowden, Atlanta, 1950-54; individual practice, Atlanta, 1955-67; trial counsel firm Lipshutz, Zusmann, Sikes, Pritchard & Cohen, 1967-77; partner firm Bryant, Davis & Cowden, 1977—. Active Carter campaign for pres., 1975-76. Mem. Am., Ga., Atlanta bar assns., Comml. Law League. Home: 2018 W Lyle Rd College Park GA 30337 Office: Suite 280 2200 Century Pkwy NE Atlanta GA 30345 Tel (404) 325-6846

COWDEN, PAUL DAVID, b. N.Y.C., Aug. 29, 1945; B.A., Williams Coll., 1967; J.D., Vanderbilt U., 1970. Admitted to Ky. bar, 1970; partner firm Clay, Marye & Cowden, Mt. Sterling, Ky., 1970—. Mem. Am., Ky. bar assns. Office: 50 Broadway Mt Sterling KY 40353 Tel (606) 498-2430

COWEN, WILSON, b. nr. Clifton, Tex., Dec. 20, 1905; LL.B., U. Tex., 1928. Admitted to Tex. bar, 1928; pvt. practice, Dalhart, Tex., 1928-34; judge Dallam County (Tex.), 1935-38; Tex. dir. for Farm Security Adminstrn., 1938-40, regional dir., 1940-42; commr. U.S. Ct. Claims, 1942-43, 45-59, chief commr., 1959-64, chief judge, 1964—; asst. adminstr. War Food Adminstrn., 1943-45; spl. asst. to sec. agr., 1945. Past chmn., past trustee Landon Sch. for Boys, Bethesda. Mem. State Bar Tex., Fed., Am. bar assns., Order of Coif, Delta Theta Phi, Nat. Lawyers Club. Home: 2500 Virginia Av NW Washington DC 20037 Office: US Court Claims Washington DC 20005*

COWIN, JUDITH ARNOLD, b. Boston, Apr. 29, 1942; B.A., Wellesley Coll., 1963; J.D., Harvard U., 1970. Admitted to Mass. bar, 1970; asst. legal counsel Mass. Dept. Mental Health, Boston, 1971-72; counsel Dist. Ct. Mass., Newton, Mass., 1972—. Mem. Mass., Boston bar assns. Contbr. article to law jour. Home: 85 Country Club Rd Newton MA 02159 Office: Courthouse West Newton MA 02165 Tel (617) 244-3600

COWLEY, SAMUEL PARKINSON, b. Washington, Mar. 29, 1934; B.S., U. Utah, 1959; J.D., George Washington U., 1962. Admitted to Utah bar, 1962, Nev. bar, 1963, Mo. bar, 1974; staff mem. U.S. Senator Wallace F. Bennett of Utah, Washington, 1959-62; law clk. to E.R. Callister, Utah Supreme Ct., Salt Lake City, 1962, firm Robert Callister, Las Vegas, 1962-63; dep. Office Dist. Atty. Las Vegas, 1963-64; trust adminstr. Bank of Nev., Las Vegas, 1964-65; asso. firm C.W. Coulthard, Las Vegas, 1965; v.p., gen. counsel, sec. Nev. Power Co., Las Vegas, 1965-74; asst. gen. counsel Kansas City Power and Light Co. (Mo.), 1974—. Mem. Mo., Nev., Utah bar assn. Home: 2427 W 63d St Mission Hills KS 66208 Office: 1330 Baltimore Ave Kansas City MO 64105 Tel (816) 471-0060

COWLIN, HENRY LAWRENCE, b. Chgo., June 15, 1924; B.A., U. Mich., 1947; J.D., Wayne State U., 1951. Admitted to Ill. bar, 1952; individual practice law, Huntley and Algonquin, Ill., 1953-59; partner firm Cowlin & Cowlin, Crystal Lake, Ill., 1959-68; mem. firm Cowlin, Cowlin & Ungvarsky, and predecessor, Crystal Lake, 1969—; asst. states atty. McHenry County (Ill.), 1964-68; spl. asst. atty. gen. State of Ill., 1969—. Mem. Am., Ill., McHenry County (past pres.) bar assns., Sigma Phi Epsilon, Delta Theta Phi. Home: 185 Lake Shore Dr Crystal Lake IL 60014 Office: 20 Grant St Crystal Lake IL 60014 Tel (815) 459-5300

COX, ARCHIBALD, b. Plainfield, N.J., 1912; A.B., Harvard, 1934, LL.B., 1937, LL.D., 1975; LL.D., Loyola U., Chgo., 1964, U. Cin., 1967, Rutgers U., 1974, U. Denver, 1974, Amherst Coll., 1974, U. Mich., 1976, Wheaton Coll., 1977. Admitted to Mass. bar, 1937, U.S. Supreme Ct. bar, 1942; law clk. Judge Learned Hand, U.S. Circuit Ct. of Appeals, 1937-38; asso. firm Ropes, Gray, Best, Coolidge & Rugg, Boston, 1938-41; prof. law Harvard Law Sch., Cambridge, Mass., 1945—, now Carl M. Loeb Univ. prof.; solicitor-gen. U.S., 1961-65; spl. prosecutor Watergate, 1973. Chmn., Gov.'s Com. on Jud. Needs, 1976—; bd. overseers Harvard, 1962-65. Mem. Am. Acad. Arts and Scis. Author: Cases in Labor Law, 1948; Law and the National Labor Policy, 1960; (with Howe and Wiggins) Civil Rights, The Constitution and the Courts, 1967; The Warren Court: Constitutional Decision as an Instrument of Reform, 1968; The Role of the Supreme Court in American Government, 1976. Home: Wayland MA 01775 Office: Harvard Law Sch Cambridge MA 02138 Tel (617) 495-3133

COX, C. ROBERT, b. Long Beach, Calif., July 19, 1942; B.A., Stanford U., 1964, J.D., 1968. Admitted to Nev. bar, 1969, Calif. bar, 1972; law clk. Santa Clara County (Calif.) Pub. Defender, San Jose, 1966-67; law clk. Charles E. Cole, Fairbanks, Alaska, 1967; mem. firm Woodburn, Wedge, Blakey, Folsom and Hug, Reno, 1968—. Mem. State Bar Calif., State Bar Nev., Washoe County Bar Assn. Office: 1 E First St Reno NV 89501 Tel (708) 329-6131

COX, CHARLES POSTON, b. Memphis, Mar. 29, 1896; LL.B., Memphis U., 1914. Admitted to Tenn. bar, 1926; with govt. State of Tenn., 1927-28; mem. firm, 1931-72; individual practice law, Memphis, 1972—. Home: 747 Weshak St Memphis TN 38112 Office: Suite 220 114 Madison St Memphis TN 38103 Tel (901) 527-4555

COX, ELIZABETH JUNE, b. Bowling Green, Ohio, June 29, 1932; B.S. in Edn., B.A. magna cum laude, Bowling Green State U., 1954; J.D., Cleve.-Marshall Law Sch., 1967. Admitted to Ohio bar, 1968; mem. firm Cox & Cox, Brook Park, Ohio, 1968—. Mem. Bd. Edn., Berea, Ohio (pres. 1973), 1966-73. Home: 5709 Norwood Dr Brook Park OH 44142 Office: 5709 Norwood Dr Brook Park OH 44142 Tel (216) 734-4140

COX, FRANK JAMES, b. New Orleans, Feb. 24, 1942; B.S., U. Oreg., 1963; J.D., U. San Francisco, 1966. Admitted to Calif. bar, 1966, U.S. Dist. (No. Calif.) Ct. bar, 1966, U.S. 9th Circuit Ct. Appeals bar, 1966; law clk. U.S. Dist. Ct. No. Calif., 1966-67; asst. public defender, Alameda County, Oakland Calif., 1967-71; chief dep. public defender Marin County, San Rafael, Calif., 1971—. Certified specialist in criminal law Calif. Bd. Legal Specialization. Mem. Marin County Bar Assn. (dir.). Office: Public Defender Hall of Justice San Rafael CA 94903 Tel (415) 479-1100

COX, GORDON ELBERT, b. Trenton, Mo., Jan. 15, 1942; B.S. in Bus. Adminstrn., N.E. Mo. State U., 1967; J.D. (Law Found. Scholar), U. Mo., Kansas City, 1973. Admitted to Mo. bar, 1973; research clk. to judge Mo. Ct. Appeals, Kansas City, 1973; asso. firm Cleaveland-Macoubrie, Chillicothe, Mo., 1973-75; partner firm Cleaveland, Macoubrie, Lewis & Cox, Chillicothe, 1976—; research and law clk. firm Stinson, Mag, Thomson, McEvers & Fizzell, Kansas City, 1972. Mem. Livingston County, Mo., Am. bar assns., Delta Theta Phi. Contbr. article to legal inst., 1972. Office: Suite 385 Citizens National Bank Bldg Chillicothe MO 64601 Tel (816) 646-4522

COX, JEROME ROCKHOLD, b. Preston, Md., May 25, 1894; A.B. summa cum laude, Western Md. Coll., 1914; LL.B. (now J.D.), George Washington U., 1922. Admitted to D.C. bar, 1922, Md. bar, 1924, U.S. Supreme Ct. bar, 1927, U.S. Patent Office; atty. Hartford Empire Corp., Curtis Wright Corp., Bendix Aviation Corp.; asso. firm Stevens and Davis, 1944-45; individual practice law, Columbus, Ohio, 1945—. Mem. Am., Ohio, Columbus bar assns., Columbus Patent Assn., Am. Patent Law Assn. Office: 50 W Broad St Columbus OH 43215 Tel (614) 228-5858

COX, JOHN PATRICK, b. Utica, N.Y., July 11, 1922; B.A., Mich. State U., 1949; J.D., Georgetown U., 1951. Admitted to N.Y. bar, 1952; partner firm Jaeckle, Fleischmann, Kelly, Swart & Augspurger, Buffalo, 1952-59; sr. partner firm Cox, Barrell & Walsh, Buffalo, 1959—. Mem. Am., N.Y., Erie County bar assns., Erie County Trial Lawyers Assn. Home: 284 Ruskin Rd EggertsvilleNY 14226 Office: 1000 Rand Bldg Buffalo NY 14203 Tel (716) 856-0153

COX, JOHN SHERMAN, b. Hebardville, Ga., Oct. 5, 1919; B.S. in Bus. Adminstrn., U. Fla., 1943, LL.B., 1947. Admitted to Fla. bar, 1947, U.S. Supreme Ct. bar, 1957; asso. firm E.K. McIlrath, Jacksonville, Fla., 1947-50; asso. firm Fleming, Jones, Scott & Botts, Jacksonville, 1950-55, partner, 1956; partner firm Scott & Cox, Jacksonville, 1957-60; sr. partner firm Cox, Webb & Swain and predecessors, Jacksonville, 1961-72; judge Fla. 4th Jud. Circuit Ct., 1973—; atty. Duval County (Fla.) Civil Service Bd., 1960-68; mem. Fla. Bd. Bar Examiners, 1971-72. Trustee Bapt. Home for Children, Jacksonville, 1972—. Fellow Am. Coll. Trial Lawyers; mem. Am., Jacksonville bar assns., Am. Judicature Soc., Fla. Bar, Phi Alpha Delta, Blue Key. Home: 4459 River Tr Rd Jacksonville FL 32211 Office: 210 Duval County Courthouse Jacksonville FL 32202 Tel (904) 633-6790

COX, JOHN THOMAS, JR., b. Shreveport, La., Feb. 9, 1943; B.S., La. State U., 1965, J.D., 1968. Admitted to La. bar, 1968; asso. firm Sanders, Miller, Downing & Kean, Baton Rouge, 1968-70; asso. firm Blanchard, Walker, O'Quin & Roberts, Shreveport, 1970-71, partner, 1971—; spl. lectr. Centenary Coll. of La. Sch. Bus., 1972—. Mem. Am., La. (jr. bar council rep. 1972—), Shreveport bar assns., La. Law Inst., La. Def. Lawyers Assn., Shreveport C. of C., Order of Coif. Recipient Valley Forge Freedoms Found. award, 1962; co-editor La. Labor Law Newsletter, 1975. Home: 555 Dunmoreland Dr Shreveport LA 71106 Office: 15th floor 1st Nat Bank Tower 400 Texas St Shreveport LA 71101 Tel (318) 221-6858

COX, KENNETH ALLEN, b. Topeka, Kans., Dec. 7, 1916; B.A., U. Wash., 1938, LL.B., 1940; LL.M., U. Mich., 1941. Admitted to Wash. State bar, 1941, D.C. bar, 1972; law clerk Washington Supreme Ct., 1941-42; asst. prof. U. Mich. Law Sch., 1946-48; mem. firm Little, Palmer, Scott & Slemmons and predecessor, Seattle, Wash., 1948-61, partner, 1953-61; spl. counsel in charge TV Inquiry, U.S. Senate Com. on Interstate and Fgn. Commerce, 1956-57; chief, Broadcast Bur., FCC, Washington, D.C., 1961-63, commr., 1963-70; counsel to Haley, Bader & Potts, Washington, 1970—; sr. v.p. MCI Communications Corp., Washington, D.C., 1970—; lectr. U. Wash. Law Sch., 1954, 60; adj. prof. Georgetown Law Center, Washington, D.C., 1971, 72; mem. Nat. Advt. Review Bd., 1971-74, chmn., 1976—. Vice-pres. Mun. League of Seattle and King County, 1960; mem. Seattle World Affairs Council, 1960; pres. Seattle chpt. Am. Assn. for the UN. Mem. Wash. State, Fed. Communications, Am. bar assns., Bar Assn. of the D.C. Recipient Alfred I. DuPont award, Columbia U., 1970; contbr. articles to legal jours. Home: 5836 Marbury Rd Bethesda MD 20034 Office: 1730 M St NW Suite 700 Washington DC 20036 Tel (202) 331-0606

COX, KEVIN D., b. Utica, N.Y., Jan. 27, 1928; B.S., Canisius Coll., 1950; J.D., U. Buffalo, 1954. Admitted to N.Y. bar, 1955, U.S. Supreme Ct. bar, 1974; partner firm Cox, Barrell & Walsh, Buffalo, 1956—; clk. legal dept. Erie County (N.Y.), 1960-63, pub. adminstr., 1965—; legal asst. judge Criminal Ct., 1963-65. Sec., Erie County Republican Com., 1957-60. Mem. N.Y. Bar Assn., Nat. Coll. Probate Judges, Am. Judicature Soc. Home: 115 Dawnbrook Ln Williamsville NY 14221 Office: 1000 Rand Bldg Buffalo NY 14203 Tel (716) 856-0153

COX, LESTER BARRETT, b. Springfield, Mo., Mar. 21, 1947; B.S., Drury Coll., 1969, M.B.A., 1975; J.D., Mo. U., 1973. Admitted to Mo. bar, 1973; v.p., gen. counsel, gen. mgr. Outdoor Recreational Distbg. Co., Springfield, 1973—; v.p., gen. counsel Modern Distbg. Co., Springfield, 1973—, Ozark Motor & Supply Co., Springfield, 1973—, Kansas City Air Conditioning Co., Springfield, 1973—; pres. Southside Marine, Inc., 1976—; individual practice law, Springfield. Home: Route 2 PO Box 49 Ozark MO 65721 Office: 440 E Tampa St Springfield MO 65805 Tel (417) 862-2771

COX, LEWIS CALVIN, JR., b. Fisher, Ark., Jan. 16, 1924; J.D., George Washington U., 1948. Admitted to N.Mex. bar, 1948; asso. firm Quinn & Cox, Clovis, N.Mex., 1948-54; individual practice law, Clovis, 1954-55; partner firm Hinkle, Cox, Eaton, Coffield & Hensley and predecessor, Roswell, N.Mex., 1955—; pres. Rocky Mountain Mineral Law Found., 1973-74. Mem. Am., N.Mex., Chaves County (N.Mex.) bar assns. Office: POB 10 Roswell NM 88201 Tel (505) 622-6510

COX, PAUL B., b. Wichita Falls, Tex., Sept. 4, 1917; J.D., U. Tex., 1940. Admitted to Tex. bar, 1940; partner firm Cox & Cox, Athens, Tex., 1940-42; asso. firm Ryland, Stinson, May and Thompson, Kansas City, Mo., 1942-43; contract adminstr. N. Am. Aviation Corp., Kansas City, Kans., 1943-45; county atty. Cherokee County (Tex.), 1953-64; partner firm Cox & Holcomb, and predecessor, Rusk,

Tex., 1961-76. Pres. Cherokee County (Tex.) Mental Health Assn., 1949-50, Rusk Civic Services, Inc., 1974-76; chmn. official bd. 1st Meth. Ch., Rusk, 1966, 74; chmn. bd. mgrs. Rusk Meml. Hosp., 1969-73. Mem. Tex., Cherokee County (pres.) bar assns., East Tex. Peace Officers Assn. (pres.). Home: RFD #3 Rusk TX 75785 Office: 115 E 6th St Rusk TX 75785 Tel (214) 683-5427

COX, ROBERT WAYNE, b. North Island, Calif., May 10, 1945; B.B.A., U. Tulsa, 1967; J.D., U. Mich., 1970. Admitted to Okla. bar, 1970, Tex. bar, 1973; asso. firm Holliman, Langholz, Runnels & Dorwart, Tulsa, 1970-71; asst. gen. atty. Champlin Petroleum Co., Ft. Worth, 1971-75; sec., gen. counsel Kissinger Petroleum Corp., Denver; bd. advisors Fed. Energy Service, Ft. Worth, 1975. Mem. Benbrook (Tex.) Home Rule Charter Commn., 1975. Mem. Am., Okla., Tex. bar assns., U. Mich. Lawyers Club. Home: 6140 S Monaco Way Englewood CO 80110 Office: 7450 E Progress Pl Englewood CO 80110 Tel (303) 773-0550

COX, ROGER FRAZIER, b. Phila., Sept. 11, 1939; B.A. cum laude, Amherst Coll., 1962; LL.B. cum laude, U. Pa., 1966. Admitted to D.C., Pa. bars, 1967, Calif. bar, 1970; law clk. U.S. Dist. Ct. for So. Dist. N.Y., 1966-67; asst. dist. atty. Phila., 1967-69; staff atty. Alameda County (Calif.) Legal Services, Oakland, 1969-71; asso. firm Blank, Rome, Klaus & Comisky, Phila., 1971-77; lectr. law U. Calif., 1970, Rutgers U., 1974-75. Mem. Am., Pa., Phila. bar assns., Order of Coif. Home: 2510 Pine St Philadelphia PA 19103 Office: 4 Penn Center Plaza Philadelphia PA 19103 Tel (215) LO9-3700

COX, RONALD EDWARD, b. Phila., Jan. 12, 1945; B.S., U.S. Mil. Acad., 1966; J.D., U. Wash., 1973. Admitted to Wash. bar, 1973; asso. firm Preston, Thorgrimson, Ellis, Holman & Fletcher, Seattle, 1973—. Bd. dirs. Children's Home Soc. Wash., Seattle, 1976—. Mem. Am. Bar Assn. Office: 2000 IBM Bldg Seattle WA 98101 Tel (206) 623-7580

COX, ROY WILLIAM, b. Canadian County, Okla., Feb. 6, 1892; B.A., U. Okla., 1914, LL.B., 1916. Admitted to Okla. bar, 1916, U.S. 10th Circuit Ct. Appeals bar, 1932; partner firm Cox & Buhrman, Blackwell, Okla., 1939—; city atty., Blackwell, 1923-32, mun. judge, 1935-39; mem. State bd. Pub. Affairs, State of Okla., 1939-43. Bd. dirs. First Christian Ch. Blackwell, 1921-76. Mem. Am., Okla., Kay County bar assns., Blackwell C. of C. Home: 311 W Bridge Blackwell OK 74631 Office: 1125 1st St Blackwell OK 74631 Tel (405) 363-2980

COX, SANFORD CURTIS, JR., b. El Paso, Tex., July 31, 1929; B.A., Tex. Western Coll., 1951, M.A., 1952; LL.B., U. Tex., 1957. Admitted to Tex. Supreme Ct. bar, 1957, U.S. Ct. Appeals 5th Circuit bar, 1964, Washington Circuit bar, 1975; asso. firm Andress, Lipscomb, Peticolas & Fisk, El Paso, 1957-61; partner firm Lipscomb, Fisk & Cox, El Paso, 1961-74, Fisk & Cox, El Paso, 1974—; mem. Dist. 17 Admissions com. Tex. State Bar, 1976. Mem. State Bar of Tex., El Paso, Am. bar assns., Phi Delta Phi. Mem. editorial bd. Tex. Law Rev., 1956-57. Home: 112 Vista Del Rey El Paso TX 79912 Office: 923 El Paso Nat Bank Bldg El Paso TX 79901 Tel (915) 532-3488

COX, THOMAS MILLS, b. Michigan City, Ind., Mar. 25, 1920; B.S., Washington and Lee U., 1942; J.D., Stanford U., 1951. Admitted to Calif. bar, 1952; dep. dist. atty. Riverside County, Calif., 1952-54; individual practice law, Hemet, Calif., 1952-54; mem. firm Cox Swan Carpenter & Powers, Hemet, 1954—; city atty. San Jacinto, Calif., 1954-65, Hemet, 1954-71. Mem. Am. Bar Assn., Phi Alpha Delta. Home: 41695 Mayberry St Hemet CA 92343 Office: 805 E Florida Ave Hemet CA 92343 Tel (714) 658-2138

COX, WALTER BARRY, b. Forrest City, Ark., Aug. 11, 1941; B.S., U. Ark., 1966, LL.B., 1966. Admitted to Ark. bar, 1966; asso. firm Putman, Davis & Bassett, Fayetteville, Ark., 1966-70, partner, 1970—; reporter Ark. Supreme Ct. Civil Procedure Revision Com., 1975—. Bd. advs. Salvation Army, Fayetteville, 1975—. Mem. Washington County Bar Assn. (pres. 1976—). Home: 2602 Rosewood St Fayetteville AR 72701 Office: 19 E Mountain St Fayetteville AR 72701 Tel (501) 521-7600

COX, WILLIAM HAROLD, JR., b. Jackson, Miss., Nov. 18, 1933; B.A., U. Miss., 1955, LL.B., 1961. Admitted to Miss. bar, 1961; partner firm Cox & Dunn, Jackson, 1961—. Mem. Am., Miss., Hinds County bar assns. Home: 236 Ashcot Circle St Jackson MS 39211 Office: Box 1046 Jackson MS 59201 Tel (601) 354-3783

COY, EDWIN ALLEN, b. Toledo, Mar. 29, 1949; B.A., Capital U., 1971; J.D., Ohio State U., 1974. Admitted to Ohio bar, 1974; asso. firm Robison, Curphey & O'Connell, Toledo, 1974—. Mem. Am., Ohio, Toledo bar assns., Ohio Def. Assn., Order of Coif. Home: 340 Edgewood Dr Perrysburg OH 43551 Office: 425 LOF Bldg Toledo OH 43624 Tel (419) 255-3100

COYLE, CHARLOTTE M., b. Chgo., Oct. 22, 1927; J.D., John Marshall Law Sch., 1955. Admitted to Ill. bar, 1955; atty. Brunswick Corp., 1955—. Mem. Chgo. Bar Assn. Home: 721 Harms Rd Glenview IL 60025 Office: 1 Brunswick Plaza Skokie IL 60076 Tel (312) 982-6000

COYLE, CHRISTOPHER LORAN, b. Los Angeles, Aug. 1, 1945; B.J., Kans. U., 1968, J.D., 1971. Admitted to Okla. bar, 1972; asso. firm Selby & Connor, Bartlesville, Okla., 1971-73; partner firm Selby Connor & Coyle, Bartlesville, 1973—; municipal judge, Bartlesville, 1973-77. Bd. dirs. Bartlesville Jr. Achievement, Bartlesville Jaycees; mem. parish council St. John's Cath. Ch., 1974-77. Mem. Am., Okla., Washington County (pres.) bar assns. Office: 416 E 5th St Bartlesville OK 74003 Tel (918) 336-8114

COYLE, MICHAEL JAMES, b. Mason City, Iowa, Mar. 18, 1945; B.B.A., U. Iowa, 1967, J.D., 1970. Admitted to Iowa bar, 1970; asso. firm Fuerste, Carew, Coyle, Juergens & Sudmeier, Dubuque, Iowa, 1970-73, partner, 1973—. Exec. bd. N.E. Iowa council Boy Scouts Am., 1970—, v.p., 1976—. Mem. Am., Iowa, Dubuque County bar assns., Iowa Trial Lawyers Assn. Home: 1283 Blackhawk St Dubuque IA 52001 Office: 900 Dubuque Bldg Dubuque IA 52001 Tel (319) 556-4011

COYLE, ROBERT EVERETT, b. Fresno, Calif., May 6, 1930; A.B., Calif. State U., Fresno, 1953; J.D., U. Calif. Hastings Coll. Law, San Francisco, 1956. Admitted to Calif. bar, 1956, U.S. Supreme Ct. bar, 1968; dep. dist. atty. Fresno County (Calif.), 1956-58; partner firm McCormick, Barstow, Sheppard, Coyle & Wayte, Fresno, 1958—. Trustee United Givers, Fresno; pres. Fresno Jr. Soccer League, 1975-76; bd. dirs. Fresno Assn. Mentally Retarded; active Boy Scouts Am. Mem. Fresno County Bar Assn. (pres. 1971), 9th Circuit Conf., Calif. State Bar (exec. com. 1973—), No. Calif. Assn. Def. Counsel, Fedn. Ins. Counsel. Home: 1220 E Indianapolis St Fresno CA 93705 Office: 1171 Fulton Mall 4th floor Fresno CA 93721 Tel (209) 442-1150

COYNE, JOHN THOMAS, b. Syracuse, N.Y., Apr. 25, 1937; B.A., Lemoyne Coll., Syracuse, 1959; J.D., Georgetown U., 1964. Admitted to Va. bar, 1964, D.C. and W.Va. bars, 1969, U.S. Supreme Ct. bar, 1969; asst. gen. counsel 1st Va. Bankshares Corp., Arlington, 1967-69; asso. firm Carr, Bonner, O'Connell, Kaplan & Thompson, Washington, 1969-72, partner, 1972-75; partner firm Carr, Jordan, Coyne & Savits, Washington, 1975—; chief investigative atty. Purchasing Practices and Procedures Commn., W.Va. Legislature, 1969-70. Bd. govs. LeMoyne Coll. Alumni, 1973—. Mem. Am., Va., W.Va., D.C., Fed. bar assns., Va. Trial Lawyers Assn. Named an Outstanding Young Man in Am., LeMoyne Coll., 1971. Home: 2009 Fort Dr Alexandria VA 22307 Office: 900 17th St NW Washington DC 20006 Tel (202) 659-4660

CRABILL, FRANK WALLACE, b. Red Cloud, Nebr., Sept. 28, 1913; A.B., U. Nebr., 1935; B.A. (Rhodes scholar), Oxford (Eng.) U., 1938, B.C.L., 1939. Admitted to N.Y. State bar, 1941, U.S. Dist. Ct. bar, 1947; asso. firm Dewey, Ballantine, Bushby, Palmer & Wood and predecessor firms, N.Y.C., 1939-42, 45-51, partner, 1952—. Mem. Am., N.Y. State, N.Y. County bar assns., Assn. Bar City N.Y. Home: 20 Willow Rd Riverside CT 06878 Office: 140 Broadway New York City NY 10005 Tel (212) 344-8000

CRABTREE, BROOKS, b. San Diego, Calif., Aug. 2, 1917; A.B., Pomona Coll., 1939; LL.B., U. Mich., 1942. Admitted to Calif. bar, 1946, Mich. bar, 1946; asso. firm Luce Forward Lee & Kunzel, San Diego, 1946-48; individual practice law, San Diego, 1948-73; partner firm Crabtree & Goodwin, San Diego, 1974—. Mem. Am. Coll. Probate Counsel, Am., Calif. bar assns. Home: 3564 Hugo St San Diego CA 92106 Office: 402 Crabtree Bldg 303 A St San Diego CA 92101 Tel (714) 239-6161

CRABTREE, CHESTER, b. Willette, Tenn., Feb. 22, 1893; M.A., U. Western Ky., 1916; J.D., Cumberland Sch. Law, Samford U., 1913. Admitted to Ky. bar, 1914, Ill. bar, 1931, Tex. bar, 1972; state's atty. Livingston County (Ill.), 1964-68, pub. defender, 1952-64; practice law, McKinney, Tex., 1972—. Chmn., Livingston County Relief Bd., 1933-40; trustee Evenglow Lodge, old peoples home, Pontiac, Ill. Mem. Tex., Northeastern Tex., Livingston County (pres. 1962), Collin County bar assns. Office: 208 E Virginia St McKinney TX 75069 Tel (214) 542-1914

CRABTREE, JAMES WRIGHT, b. Mt. Holly, N.J., Oct. 3, 1943; A.B., U. Fla., 1965, J.D., 1968. Admitted to Fla. bar, 1968, U.S. Supreme Ct. bar, 1972; partner firm Smathers & Thompson, Miami, Fla., 1970—. Mem. Dade County, Fla., Am. bar assns., Phi Delta Phi, Phi Eta Sigma. Editorial bd. U. Fla. Law Rev., 1967-68. Office: 1301 Alfred I DuPont Bldg Miami FL 33131 Tel (305) 379-6523

CRACRAFT, BRUCE NOEL, b. Indpls., Dec. 24, 1921; student Ind. U., 1942, Butler U., 1946; LL.B., Stetson U., 1949. Admitted to Ind. bar, 1949; asso. firm Slaymaker, Locke & Reynolds, Indpls., 1949-55; atty. Ind. Bell Telephone Co., Indpls., 1955-59, gen. atty., 1959-72, v.p., gen. counsel, 1972—; chmn. taxation com. Ind. State C. of C., 1965-. Bd. dirs. Child Guidance Clinic, Marion County, Ind., 1957-65, pres., 1960-61; mem. Ind. Jud. Council on Legal Edn. and Competence at the Bar. Mem. Am., Ind., Indpls. bar assns., Am. Judicature Soc. (chmn. pub. utilities com.), Nat. Tax Assn./Tax Inst. Am., Lawyers Assn. Indpls. (pres. 1960), Am. Right of Way Assn. (pres. 1965). Home: 5253 Shorewood Dr Indianapolis IN 46220 Office: 240 N Meridian St #1829 Indianapolis IN 46204 Tel (317) 265-2141

CRAFT, EDWARD OLIVER, b. Kingsbury, Ind., Nov. 13, 1916; A.B., Ind. U., 1938, J.D. with high distinction, 1940. Admitted to Ind. bar, 1940; practiced in Evansville, Ind., 1940-41; law asst., office legis. counsel U.S. Ho. of Reps., 1941-43, asst. counsel, 1943-62, legis. counsel, 1962-72, ret., 1972; individual practice law, legis. cons., Bloomington, Ind., 1972—; cons. GAO, 1973-75. Mem. Am., Fed., Ind. State, Monroe County (Ind.) bar assns., Am. Judicature Soc., Order of Coif. Student editor Ind. Law Jour., 1938-39, student chmn., 1939-40. Home and Office: 703 S Rose Ave Bloomington IN 47401 Tel (812) 336-4451

CRAFT, JOHN CHARLES, b. Denver, Nov. 28, 1938; A.B., U. Nebr., 1961; J.D., Northwestern U., 1965. Admitted to Mo. bar, 1965; asso. firm Lathrop, Righter, Gordon & Parker, Kansas City, Mo., 1965-69; asst. atty. gen. State of Mo., Jefferson City, 1969-71; asst. U.S. atty. Western Dist. Mo., 1971-72; partner firm Park & Craft, Kansas City, 1972—; sec., atty. Kansas City Bd. Police Commrs. Office: Columbia Union Bank Bldg 900 Walnut St Kansas City NE 65101 Tel (816) 421-2470

CRAFT, LEWIS JOHN, b. Clayton, Ill., Feb. 24, 1927; B.S. in Elec. Engring., B.S. in Mech. Engring., U. Ill., 1949, M.S. in Elec. Engring., 1950; J.D., Kent Coll., 1964. Mgr., Sunbeam Corp., Oakbrook, Ill., 1950—; admitted to Ill. bar, 1964; individual practice law, Villa Park, Ill., 1964—; pres. Reap Investments; sec. Beaver Hills Corp. Pres., Elementary Sch. Bd., Villa Park, 1974—. Mem. Ill., DuPage County bar assns., IEEE. Patentee. Home and office: 0S481 Ardmore Ave Villa Park IL 60181 Tel (312) 834-3555

CRAFT, RONALD RICHARD, b. Hamilton, Ohio, Oct. 6, 1949; B.A., Ohio State U., 1971; J.D., Capital U., 1974. Admitted to Ohio bar, 1974; research asst. Ohio State Bar Assn., Columbus, 1974; asst. staff JAGC, USAF, Holloman AFB, N. Mex., 1975-76, area def. counsel, 1976—. Mem. Ohio State Bar Assn., Phi Alpha Delta. Home: 2846A Quay Loop Holloman AFB NM 88330 Office: Detachment QD3F Holloman AFB NM 88330 Tel (505) 479-6511

CRAHAN, BRIAN DOCKWEILER, b. Los Angeles, June 28, 1935; B.A., Pomona Coll., 1957; LL.B., U. Calif., Los Angeles, 1961. Admitted to Calif. bar, 1963; with Los Angeles City Atty.'s Office, 1963-73, prin. dep. city atty., 1968-70, chief div., 1970-73; judge Municipal Ct., Los Angeles, 1973—. Bd. dirs. Los Angeles Area council Campfire Girls Am. Mem. Los Angeles County Bar Assn., Phi Alpha Delta. Office: 110 N Grand Ave Los Angeles CA 90012 Tel (213) 974-6111

CRAIG, ARLO FRANKLIN, JR., b. Aurora, Iowa, July 21, 1934; B.A., State U. Iowa, Iowa City, 1955, J.D., 1957. Admitted to Iowa bar, 1957; asst. atty. gen. Iowa, Des Moines, 1959-61; individual practice law, Iowa Falls, 1961-63, Independence, Iowa, 1963—; dir. Independence Fed. Savs. and Loan Assn., 1967—. Chmn. Buchanan County United Fund, 1965-66. Mem. Am., Iowa (gov.), Buchanan County (pres. 1973) bar assns., Phi Delta Phi, Phi Beta Kappa. Home: 501 4th Ave SW Independence IA 50644 Office: 316 1st St E Independence IA 50644 Tel (319) 334-6061

CRAIG, DAVID W(ILLIAMSON), b. Pitts., Feb. 17, 1925; A.B., U. Pitts., 1948, LL.B., 1950, J.D., 1968. Admitted to Pa. bar, 1951, U.S. Supreme Ct. bar, 1951; partner firm Moorhead and Knox, Pitts., 1952-61; city solicitor Pitts., 1961-65; dir. Pitts. Dept. Pub. Safety, 1965-69; partner firm Baskin, Boreman, Wilner, Sachs, Gondelman & Craig, Pitts., 1962—; adj. prof. adminstrn. Carnegie-Mellon U. Chmn. Pitts. City Planning Commn., 1959-61; mem. Pitts. City Charter Commn., 1973-74. Mem. Am., Pa., Allegheny County bar assns., Am. Soc. Planning Ofcls., Am. Inst. Planners. Author: Pennsylvania Building and Zoning Laws, 1951. Home: Gateway Towers Apt 14-K Pittsburgh PA 15222 Office: Frick Bldg 10th Floor Pittsburgh PA 15219 Tel (412) 562-8638

CRAIG, HARRY EUGENE, b. Friendship, Tenn., Jan. 5, 1929; B.S. in Arts and Sci., Memphis State U., 1963; J.D., U. Ariz., 1964. Admitted to Ariz. bar, 1964; mem. staff Maricopa County (Ariz.) Atty.'s Office, Phoenix, 1964-65; partner firm Craig, Contreras & Bernstein, Phoenix, 1965-68, firm Craig & Bernstein, Phoenix, 1968-70, firm Craig, Bernstein & Davich, Phoenix, 1970-72; individual practice law, Phoenix, 1972-75; partner firm Craig & Rich, Phoenix, 1975—. Democratic Dist. chmn., 1966-70, Maricopa County chmn., 1972-74. Mem. Am. Trial Lawyers Assn. Home: 1407 E Echo Ln Phoenix AZ 85020 Office: 234 N Central Ave Suite 417 Phoenix AZ 85004 Tel (602) 252-4033

CRAIG, PAUL MAX, JR., b. Munich, Germany, Aug. 8, 1921; B.E.E., Worcester Poly. Inst., 1946; LL.B., Georgetown U., 1950; LL.M., George Washington U., 1952. Admitted to D.C. bar, 1950; mem. firm Craig & Antonelli, and predecessor, Washington, 1952—. Mem. Am., Inter-Am. bar assns., Assn. Internat. for Protection of Indsl. Property, Am. Soc. Internat. Law, Licensing Exec. Soc., Am. Patent Law Assn., IEEE, AAAS. Home: 207 Quaint Acres Dr Silver Spring MD 20904 Office: 2600 Virginia Ave Washington DC 20037 Tel (202) 333-0990

CRAIG, PETER STEBBINS, b. Bklyn., Sept. 30, 1928; B.A., Oberlin Coll., 1950; LL.B., Yale U., 1953. Admitted to D.C. bar, 1953, U.S. Supreme Ct. bar, 1959; spl. asst. jud. com. U.S. Ho. of Reps., Washington, 1951-52; asso. firm Covington & Burling, Washington, 1953-63; commerce counsel So. Ry. Co., Washington, 1964-67; asst. gen. counsel for litigation U.S. Dept. Transp., Washington, 1967-69; gen. atty. So. Ry. Co., Washington, 1969—. Trustee Com. of 100 on the Fed. City, 1965—. Mem. Am., D.C. bar assns., Assn. ICC Practitioners. Named Washingtonian of Year, Washingtonian Mag., 1973. Home: 3406 Macomb St NW Washington DC 20016 Office: So Ry Co McPherson Sq Washington DC 20013 Tel (202) 628-4460

CRAIG, STEPHEN WRIGHT, b. N.Y.C., Aug. 28, 1932; A.B., Harvard U., 1954, J.D., 1959. Admitted to Maine bar, 1959, Calif. bar, 1960, Ariz. bar, 1963, U.S. Supreme Ct. bar, 1962; with office of chief counsel IRS, San Francisco, 1959-61; atty.-advisor U.S. Tax Ct., Washington, 1961-63; partner firm Snell and Wilmer, Phoenix, 1963—; guest lectr. Amos Tuck Sch. Bus., Dartmouth Coll., 1962, Ariz. State U. Tax Inst. Bd., 1968. Chmn. bd. Jane Wayland Child Center; bd. dirs. Central Ariz. Health Planning Agy., Phoenix Community Council; chmn. Task Force on Mental Health Maricopa County; mem. council Episcopal Diocese of Ariz. Mem. Am., Ariz., Calif. bar assns. Contbr. article to Taxes Mag. Home: 7548 Eucalyptus Dr Paradise Valley AZ 85253 Office: 3100 Valley Center Phoenix AZ 85073 Tel (602) 257-7208

CRAIG, WALTER EARLY, b. Oakland, Calif., May 26, 1909; A.B., Stanford, 1931, LL.B., 1934; LL.D., Ariz. State U., 1963, U. San Diego, 1964; S.J.D., Suffolk U., 1964. Admitted to Cal. bar, 1934, Ariz. Bar, 1936; legal dept. regional office HOLC, 1934-36; practice of law, Fennemore, Craig, Allen & Bledsoe, Phoenix, 1936-55, Fennemore, Craig, Allen & McClennen, 1955-64; U.S. judge Ariz. dist., 1964—, chief judge, 1972—. Mem. Ariz. Code Commn., 1951-56; appeal agt. Maricopa County Selective Service, 1945-64; mem. Ariz. Jud. Council, 1950-63; chmn. Nat. Conf. Fed. Trial Judges, 1972-73. Bd. dirs. Sun Angel Found.; exec. com. planning county hosp., offices, 1952-60; bd. visitors Stanford U. Sch. Law, 1958-63; bd. dirs. Maricopa County Hosp. Devel. Assn., 1955-62, Am. Bar Endowment, Ariz. State U. Found.; chmn. bd. visitors Ariz. State U. Coll. Law; trustee Forensic Scis. Found., 1972-75. Decorated Order So. Cross (Brazil). Fellow Am. Bar Found.; mem. Am. Law Inst., Am. (state chmn. jr. bar conf., ho. dels. 1947—, bd. govs. 1958-61, pres. 1963-64), Ariz. (pres. 1951-52), Maricopa County (pres. 1941) bar assns., Am. Judicature Soc. (dir. 1951-61), Inter-Am. (council), Internat. (council), Canadian (hon.) bar assns., Assn. Bar of City N.Y., Am. Acad. Forensic Scis., Ariz. State U. Law Soc. (pres. 1972-74), Ninth Circuit Dist. Judges Assn. (pres. 1973-75), El Ilustre y Nacional Colegio de Abogados de Mexico (hon.), El Colegio de Abogados de la Ciudad de Buenos Aires (hon.). Colegio de Abogados del Uruguay (hon.), Western States Bar Council (pres. 1956-57), Am. Legion, Phi Gamma Delta, Phi Delta Phi. Home: 2020 E Bethany Home Rd Phoenix AZ 85016 Office: US Court House Phoenix AZ 85025*

CRAIGHILL, FRANCIS HOPKINSON, b. Richmond, Va., May 20, 1939; B.A., U. N.C. at Chapel Hill, 1961; LL.D., U. Va., 1964. Admitted to N.C. bar, 1964, D.C. bar, 1967; Ford Found. fellow, legal advisor to Govt. Lesotho, S. Africa, 1964-66; freelance corr., Vietnam, 1967; law clk. to judge U.S. Dist. Ct. D.C., 1966-67; asso. firm Zuckert, Scoutt & Rosengerber, Washington, 1967-70; partner firm Dell, Craighill, Fentress & Benton, Washington, 1970—. Trustee Va. Episcopal Sch., Lynchburg. Mem. D.C., N.C., Am. bar assns., Descs. Signers Declaration Independence. Author: Ballots or Bullets, 1968. Office: 888 17th St NW #1200 Washington DC 20006 Tel (202) 457-8820

CRAIGHILL, G(EORGE) BOWDOIN, JR., b. Washington, Feb. 9, 1914; B.A., U. of the South, 1936; LL.B., George Washington U., 1939. Admitted to D.C. bar, 1939, U.S. Supreme Ct. bar, 1947; practiced in Washington since 1939, mem. firm Craighill, Mayfield & McCally, and predecessors, 1939—; counsel Cathedral Found. Pres. McLean (Va.) Citizens Assn., 1962; chmn. D.C. adv. bd. Salvation Army; chancellor Episcopal Diocese of Washington. Mem. Lawyers Club, Barristers. Home: 19 Second St NE Washington DC 20002 Office: 725-15th St NW Washington DC 20005 Tel (201) 347-4444

CRAIGMILE, DONALD HOLT, b. Oak Park, Ill., Feb. 26, 1933; B.B.A., U. Wis., 1956, LL.B., 1958. Admitted to Ill. bar, 1959; asst. counsel Chgo. Bridge & Iron Co., Oak Brook, Ill., 1961-70, mgr. customer fin., 1970-72, fin. counsel, 1970-76, sec., 1977—. Trustee Kroehler Found., Hinsdale, Ill., 1972—. Mem. Chgo. Bar Assn., The Smithsonian Assos., U.K. Nat. Trust. Home: 15 Princeton Rd Hinsdale IL 60521 Office: 800 Jorie Blvd Oak Brook IL 60521 Tel (312) 654-7088

CRAIGO, RICHARD WARREN, b. Hot Springs Ark., Apr. 30, 1934; B.A. Ark U., 1956; J.D., So. Calif. U., 1966. Admitted to Calif. bar, 1967; atty., DeCastro West & Chodorow, Inc., Los Angeles, Calif., 1967-72; individual practice law, Los Angeles, 1972—, prof., Northrop Inst. Sch. of Law, Inglewood, Calif., 1972-75. Pres. Horseman's Benevolent and Protective Assn. Calif. Mem. Am., Calif., Los Angeles County, Beverly Hills, Century City bar assns. Home: 605 Ocean Front Santa Monica CA 90402 Office: 1800 Ave of the Stars Suite 500 Los Angeles CA 90067 Tel (213) 277-1000

CRAIN, STEPHEN VERN, b. Kansas City, Mo., Apr. 12, 1941; B.A., U. Mo., Columbia, 1963, J.D., 1966. Admitted to Mo. bar, 1966, U.S. Fed. Ct. bar, 1968, U.S. Tax Ct. bar, 1968, U.S. Supreme Ct. bar, 1972; practiced in Kansas City, Mo., 1966—; asso. firm James, McFarland & Trimble, 1966-68; partner firm Snowden, Crain & De Cuyper and predecessor, 1968-76; individual practice Stephen V. Crain, atty. at law, 1977—; sec. Clay County bar, 1971-72. Bd. dirs. Northcross Meth. Ch., 1972—; sec. Kansas City-Clay County Community Center Planning and Zoning Com., 1972—; chmn. Northland Planning Commn., 1973-74. Mem. Am. Bar Assn. Home: 3604 NE Shady Ln Dr Gladstone MO 64119 Office: 6317 NE Antioch Rd Kansas City MO 64119 Tel (816) 455-2300

CRALL, HUGH CHARLES, b. Troy, N.Y., Sept. 17, 1934; B. Chem. Engring., Rensselaer Poly. Inst., 1956; J.D., Suffolk U., 1971. Admitted to Mass. bar, 1971; chem. engr. Union Carbide Chem. Co., Niagara Falls, N.Y. and S. Charleston, W.Va., 1956-59; chem. engr. Foster Grant Co., Inc., Leominster, Mass., 1959-67, staff patent dept., 1967—. Mem. Am., Mass. bar assns., Am. Patent Law Assn. Office: 289 N Main St Leominster MA 01453 Tel (617) 534-6511

CRAMER, DONALD WILLIAM, b. Indpls., Mar. 22, 1929; B.A., Ind. U., 1950, J.D., 1957. Admitted to Ind. bar, 1956, U.S. Supreme Ct. bar, 1976; dep. pros. atty., Marion County, Ind., 1957-58; dep. atty. gen. State of Ind., 1960-61; pvt. practice law, Indpls., 1961-69; trial judge Municipal Ct. of Marion County, 1969-70; presiding judge Municipal Ct., Marion County, Indpls., 1971-77; mem. advisory com. Ind. Criminal Justice Data Div.; mem. bd. advisors Ind. Jud. Center, mem. Ind. State Traffic Safety advisory com.; v.p., dir. Indpls. Lawyers Commn.; vice-chmn. Marion County Criminal Justice Coordinating Council; chmn. steering com. Marion County Criminal Justice Info. Systems. Bd. dirs. Community Service Council of Met. Indpls., Flynn Christian Fellowship Houses; mem. addictions task force Ind. Health Systems Agency. Mem. Am., Ind. State, Indpls. bar assns., Am. Judges Assn., Am. Judicature Soc., Ind. Judges Assn., Indpls. Legal Aid Soc., Lawyers Assn. of Indpls., Phi Alpha Delta. Home: 7145 Burnham Circle Indianapolis IN 46256 Office: One Indiana Sq #2410 Indianapolis IN 46204 Tel (317) 639-5444

CRAMER, JAMES MILTON, b. Sullivan, Ind., Oct. 14, 1931; A.A., Coll. of Marin, 1951; B.A., U. of Redlands, 1956; J.D., U. Calif. at Berkeley, 1960. Admitted to Calif. bar, 1961; with Dist. Attys. Office, County of San Bernardino, Calif., 1961—, dep. dist. atty., 1961-64, chief dep. dist. atty., 1964-73, asst. dist. atty., 1973-75, dist. atty., 1975—. Mem. Am., San Bernardino County (pres.), West End (pres. 1966) bar assns. Office: Room 200 Courthouse San Bernardino CA 92415 Tel (714) 383-2461

CRAMP, JOHN FRANKLIN, b. Ridley Park, Pa., Mar. 14, 1923; B.S. in Bus. Adminstrn., Pa. Mill. Coll. (name changed to Widener Coll.), 1943; LL.B., J.D., Dickinson Sch. of Law, 1948. Admitted to Pa. bar, 1949; asso. firm Hodge, Hodge & Balderston, Chester, Pa., 1949-53; partner firm Hodge, Hodge & Cramp, Media, Pa., 1954-56, sr. partner, 1956-61; sr. partner firm Cramp & D'Iorio, Media, 1962-70; sr. partner firm, pres. Cramp, D'Iorio, McConchie, Forbes & Surrick, Media, 1971—; gen. counsel, sec., pres. Phila. Sub. Transp. Co., now Bryn Mawr Camp Resorts, Inc., 1965—; gen. counsel Widener Coll., 1968—. Mem. SE Pa. Transp. Authority, 1965-66; trustee Child Guidance Clinic, Media, 1961-73; trustee Chester Hosp., 1959-63; trustee Crozer Chester Med. Center, Upland, Pa., 1963—, chmn. bd., 1975-77; trustee Elwyn Inst. (Pa.), 1963-76, vice chmn. bd., 1973-76; trustee Williamson Sch., Lima, Pa., 1966—. Mem. Pa., Am., Del. County bar assns., Am. Judicature Soc., Internat. Soc. Barristers, Def. Research Inst., Nat. Assn. Coll. and Univ. Attys. Mng. editor Dickinson Law Rev., 1947-48; editor Delaware County Legal Jour., 1955-56. Home: Apt 15C Valley Forge Towers 1000 Valley Forge Circle King of Prussia PA 19406 Office: 215 N Olive St Media PA 19063 Tel (215) 565-1700

CRAMPTON, SCOTT PAUL, b. Cleve., Sept. 1, 1913; B.A. cum laude, Am. U., 1935; LL.B., George Washington U., 1939. Admitted to D.C. bar, 1938, U.S. Supreme Ct. bar, 1943; asso. firm George E.H. Goodner, Washington, 1939-51; partner firm Prince, Taylor & Crampton, Washington, 1951-61; partner firm Worth & Crampton, Washington, 1961-71; asst. atty. gen. tax div. U.S. Dept. Justice, Washington, 1971-76; partner firm Hamel Park McCabe & Saunders, Washington, 1976—. Mem. Am. (chmn. sect. taxation 1969-70, mem. council 1968-71), D.C. bar assns., Nat. Lawyers Club, Phi Alpha Delta. Home: 11701 River Dr Lorton VA 22079 Office: 1776 F St NW Washington DC 20006 Tel (202) 785-1234

CRAMTON, ROGER CONANT, b. Pittsfield, Mass., May 18, 1929; A.B., Harvard, 1950; J.D., U. Chgo., 1955. Admitted to Vt. bar, 1956, Mich. bar, 1963; law clk. to judge U.S. Circuit Ct. Appeals for 2nd Circuit, 1955-56, to asso. justice Harold H. Burton, U.S. Supreme Ct., 1956-57; asst. prof. law U. Chgo., 1957-61; asso. prof. law U. Mich., Ann Arbor, 1961-64, prof. law, 1964-70; chmn. Adminstrv. Conf. U.S., 1970-72; asst. atty. gen. Office of Legal Counsel, Dept. Justice, 1972-73; dean, prof. law Cornell U., Ithaca, N.Y., 1973—; chmn. bd. dirs. Legal Services Corp., 1975—; mem. U.S. Commn. on Revision of Fed. Ct. Appellate Systems, 1973-75. Mem. Am. Acad. Arts and Scis., Am. Law Inst. (council), Am. Bar Assn., Order of Coif, Phi Beta Kappa. Contbr. articles to legal jours. Home: 49 Highgate Circle Ithaca NY 14850 Office: Myron Taylor Hall Cornell Law Sch Ithaca NY 14853 Tel (607) 256-3627

CRANDALL, HARRY ALLEN, b. Chgo., May 18, 1939; B.A., U. Ill., 1961; J.D., U. Chgo., 1965. Admitted to Ill. bar, 1969; chief legal clk. U.S. Army, 1965-67; fed. tax editor Commerce Clearing House, Inc., 1967-69; asst. mgr. income tax regulations and hearing div. Ill. Dept. Revenue, Chgo., 1970—. Mem. Am., Ill., Chgo. bar assns. Home: 1318 W Glenlake St Chicago IL 60660 Office: 160 N LaSalle St Chicago IL 60601 Tel (312) 793-3022

CRANE, DAVID JAMES, b. Los Angeles, Nov. 24, 1941; B.A., Humboldt State Coll., 1964; J.D., U. San Francisco, 1970. Admitted to Calif. bar, 1971; asso. firm Dunn, Harland & Gromala, Eureka, Calif., 1970-71; individual practice law, Eureka, 1971—; instr. criminal law Humboldt State U., 1975. Mem. Am., Calif., Humboldt County bar assns., Calif. Trial Laywers Assn. Office: PO Box 1483 369 8th St Eureka CA 95501 Tel (707) 443-6708

CRANE, DONALD RAY, b. Eugene, Oreg., Sept. 7, 1940; B.A., U. Oreg., 1962, LL.B., 1964. Admitted to Oreg. bar, 1964, U.S. Dist. Ct. bar for Dist. Oreg., 1965, U.S. Supreme Ct. bar, 1974; partner firm Proctor, Puckett and Crane, Klamath Falls, Oreg., 1964-66, Crane & Bailey, Klamath Falls, 1972—; asso. firm Richard C. Beesley, Klamath Falls, 1966-67; individual practice law, Klamath Falls, 1967-68; dist. atty. for Klamath County, Oreg., 1969-72. Mem. Klamath Falls Elementary Sch. Bd., 1975—. Mem. Am., Oreg. State, Klamath County bar assns. Office: 325 Main St Klamath Falls OR 97601 Tel (503) 884-1721

CRANE, EDWARD HOLMAN, b. Bklyn., Mar. 26, 1929; B.S., Yale U., 1951, LL.B., 1956. Admitted to Ohio bar, 1956; partner firm Thompson, Hine & Flory, Cleve., 1956-73; gen. counsel Jacobs, Visconsi & Jacobs Co., Cleve., 1973—. Mem. Ohio Bar Assn., Internat. Council Shopping Centers, Tau Beta Pi. Home: 17408 Edgewater Dr Lakewood OH 44107 Office: 25425 Center Ridge Rd Cleveland OH 44145 Tel (216) 871-4800

CRANE, GARY MAL, b. Ogden, Utah, Jan. 1, 1940; B.S., Mont. State Univ., 1961; J.D., Northwestern U., 1964. Admitted to Calif. bar, 1965; asso. tax counsel State of Calif., 1965-67; partner firm Harmer & Crane, Glendale, Calif., 1968-74, Crane, Humphries & Croft, Glendale, 1974—; corporate sec. Central Bank, Glendale, 1972—. Past pres. Glendale Exchange Club, Glendale Rep. Assembly. Mem. Am., Los Angeles County, Glendale (trustee) bar assns., Am. Judicature Soc. Contbr. articles in field to profl. jours. Home: 3601 Figueroa Glendale CA 91206 Office: 411 N Central Ave Suite 302 Glendale CA 91203 Tel (213) 245-5551

CRANE, JOHN FRANCIS, b. N.Y.C., Mar. 5, 1919; A.B., Rutgers U., 1942; LL.B., Harvard, 1948. Admitted to N.J. bar, 1948, U.S. Supreme Ct. bar, 1952; law sec. to Judge Thomas F. Meaney, U.S. Dist. Ct., N.J., 1948-51; counsel depts. banking and ins., civil service, conservation and econ. devel. State of N.J., 1954-57, dep. atty. gen., 1954-57, dep. state treas., 1957-59; 1st asst. prosecutor Essex County (N.J.), 1959-60; judge Essex County, 1960-66, Appellate div., N.J. Superior Ct., 1973—; assignment judge Passaic County Cts., 1966-73. Mem. Am., N.J. State, Essex County, Passaic County bar assns., Am. Judicature Soc. Decorated Silver Star. Home: 17 North Rd Nutley NJ 07110 Office: 520 Broad St Newark NJ 07102 Tel (201) 648-3409

CRANE, ROBERT REED, b. Coldwater, Mich., May 12, 1926; A.B., Yale, 1948; J.D., Capital U., 1962. Admitted to Ohio bar, 1962, U.S. Supreme Ct. bar, 1968; asso. firm Lawrence Ramey, Columbus, Ohio, 1963, firm Freeman T. Eagleson, Columbus, 1964; mem. firm Thompson & Crane, Columbus, 1965-68; partner firm Crane, Heltzel & Berridge, and predecessors, Columbus, 1968—. Former pres. St. Stephens Community House, Estate Planning Group 4; pres. Council of Associated Agys. of United Way. Mem. Am., Ohio State, Columbus (past chmn. bar briefs com.) bar assns. Home: 5720 Aspendale Dr Columbus OH 43224 Office: 7870 Olentangy River Rd Worthington OH 43085 Tel (614) 436-5424

CRANE, RONALD J., b. Oak Park, Ill., Aug. 2, 1934; B.S., Northwestern U., 1955, J.D., 1958; postgrad. Nat. Coll. State Judiciary, 1975. Admitted to Ill. bar, 1958; asso. judge Circuit of Cook County, Chgo. Office: Civic Center Chicago IL 60602 Tel (312) 333-7603

CRANSTON, JOHN MONTGOMERY, b. Denver, Oct. 5, 1909; A.B., Stanford, 1929, J.D., 1932. Admitted to Calif. bar, 1932, U.S. Supreme Ct. bar, 1970; partner firm Gray Cary Ames & Frye, San Diego, 1932—; spl. master So. Div., So. Calif., U.S. Dist. Ct., 1958-61; lectr. in law Stanford U. Law Sch., 1946; mem. exec. com. Conf. State Bar Dels., 1960-64; mem. Calif. Commn. on Jud. Qualifications, 1968-73. Chmn. bd. trustees U.S. Internat. U., San Diego, 1965—; v.p. San Diego chpt. English Speaking Union, 1973—; trustee San Diego County Law Library, 1968-72. Fellow Am. Coll. Probate Counsel, Am. Bar Found.; mem. State Bar Calif. (bd. govs. 1964-67, client security fund com. 1968-75, disciplinary bd. 1976—), Am. (del. to ho. of dels. 1968-74), Internat., San Diego County bar assns., World Assn. Lawyers, Am. Law Inst., Am. Judicature Soc., Order of Coif, Phi Beta Kappa, Phi Alpha Delta. Home: 337 Pacific Ave Solana Beach CA 92075 Office: 2100 Union Bank Bldg San Diego CA 92101 Tel (714) 236-1661

CRAPO, TERRY LAVELLE, b. Idaho Falls, Idaho, July 2, 1939; B.A. with highest honors, Brigham Young U., 1960, M.A., 1960; LL.B. magna cum laude, Harvard, 1963. Admitted to Idaho bar, 1963, U.S. Supreme Ct. bar, 1968; asso. firm Holden, Holden, Kidwell, Hahn & Crapo, and predecessor, Idaho Falls, 1963-68, partner, 1968—; asso. prof. law Brigham Young U., 1975—; mem. Idaho Ho. of Reps., 1966-72, majority leader, 1968-72. Fellow Am. Coll. Probate Counsel; mem. Am. Bar Assn. Contbr. articles to legal jours.; asso. editor Harvard Law Rev., 1963. Home: Route 4 Box 72 Idaho Falls ID 83401 Office: PO Box 129 Idaho Falls ID 83401 Tel (208) 523-0620

CRARY, ELISHA AVERY, b. Grundy Center, Iowa, June 24, 1905; cadet U.S. Mil. Acad., 1922-24, U. Iowa, 1924-26; B.A., U. So. Calif., 1929, J.D., 1929. Admitted to Calif. bar, 1930; asso. firm Meserve, Mumper & Huges, Los Angeles, 1930-36, partner, 1936-61; judge Los Angeles County Superior Ct., 1961-62, U.S. Dist. Ct., Central Dist. Calif., 1962—; dir., pres. Legal Aid Found. of Los Angeles, 1964. Fellow Am. Coll. Trial Lawyers; mem. Am. Law Inst., West Point Soc. Los Angeles (pres. 1952), Am., Los Angeles (trustee 1952-59, pres. 1958) bar assns., Maritime Law Assn. U.S., Chancery Club, Judge Advs. Assn., Phi Kappa Psi, Phi Delta Phi. Decorated Legion of Merit, Bronze Star medal (U.S.), Croix de Guerre (France); named Hon. Consul Govt. Turkey, 1959-61; contbr. article to profl. jour. Home: 901 Via Lido Soud Newport Beach CA 92663 Office: 312 N Spring St Los Angeles CA 90012 Tel (213) 688-3666

CRAVEN, JACK LEE, b. Lincoln, Nebr., Jan. 4, 1927; B.S. in Law, U. Nebr., 1961, LL.B., 1961. Admitted to Nebr. bar, 1961; individual practice law, Crete, Nebr., 1961—; city atty. Crete, 1962-63; Saline County judge, Wilber, Nebr., 1957-61. Mem. Am., Nebr. bar assns., Assn. Trial Lawyers Am. Home: 722 Forest Ave Crete NE 68333 Office: 115 E 13th St Crete NE 68333 Tel (402) 826-3216

CRAVEN, JAMES BRAXTON, III, b. Portsmouth, Va., Dec. 8, 1942; student U.S. Naval Acad., 1960-61; A.B., U. N.C. at Chapel Hill, 1964; J.D., Duke, 1967, postgrad. Div. Sch., 1976. Admitted to N.C. bar, 1967, U.S. Supreme Ct. bar, 1974; trial atty., Civil Rights div. U.S. Dept. Justice, Washington, 1968-69; mem. firm Everett Everett Creech & Craven, Durham, N.C., 1969—; vis. prof. law U. N.C. at Chapel Hill, 1971—; clin. asso. law Duke, 1973—; served as JAGC, USNR. Mem. Am. Law Inst., Am. Bar Assn., U.S. Jud. Conf. of 4th Circuit. Home: 1015 Watts St Durham NC 27701 Office: PO Box 586 Durham NC 27702 Tel (919) 682-5691

CRAWFORD, BURNETT HAYDEN, b. Tulsa, June 29, 1922; B.A., U. Mich., 1944, J.D., 1949. Admitted to Okla. bar, 1949, U.S. Supreme Ct. bar, 1954; law clk. U.S. Dist. Ct., No. Dist. Okla., 1950; asst. prosecutor City of Tulsa, 1951-53; alternate municipal judge, Tulsa, 1953-54; U.S. atty. No. Dist. Okla., 1954-58; asst. dep. atty. gen. U.S. Dept. Justice, Washington, 1958-60; partner firm Crawford and Jackson, Tulsa, 1960—. Mem. Am., Fed., Okla., Tulsa County bar assns., Tulsa Kiwanis (pres. 1961), Reserve Officers Assn. U.S. (nat. pres. 1973-74). Home: 5206 S Harvard Apt 216 Tulsa OK 74135 Office: 1714 1st Nat Bldg Tulsa OK 74103 Tel (918) 587-1128

CRAWFORD, CALVIN, b. Darke County, Ohio, Aug. 30, 1896; A.B., Miami U. of Ohio, 1919; J.D., Harvard, 1922. Admitted to Ohio bar, 1922; practiced in Dayton, Ohio, asso. firm Egan & Delscamp, 1922-24, partner firm Gross & Crawford, 1924-27, partner firm Crawford & Magsig, 1927-35; pros. atty. Montgomery County (Ohio), 1931-35; U.S. Atty. So. Dist. of Ohio, 1939-44; judge Ct. of Common Pleas Montgomery County, 1946-57; judge Ct. of Appeals of Ohio, Dayton, 1957-75, chief justice, 1966-75, judge by assignment of Chief Justice of Supreme Ct. Ohio, Dayton, 1975—. Elder Westminster Presbyterian Ch. Mem. Dayton, Ohio State, Am. bar assns., Phi Beta Kappa, Tau Kappa Alpha. Contbr. articles to legal jours. Home and Office: 531 Belmonte Park N Dayton OH 45405 Tel (513) 222-0529

CRAWFORD, DALE ANTHONY, b. East Orange, N.J., May 5; B.S. in Fin., Ohio State U., 1965, J.D., 1968. Admitted to Ohio bar, 1968, Va. bar, 1970, U.S. Supreme Ct. bar, 1972; exec. sec. Columbus (Ohio) CSC, 1975—; asst. prof. Va. Poly. Inst., 1968-70; asso. firm Dunbar, Kienzle & Murphey, Columbus, 1970-71; sr. asst. city atty. Columbus, 1971-75; part-time prof. Ohio Dominican Coll., Capitol U., 1972-75. Home: 2412 Lytham Rd Columbus OH 43220 Office: Columbus Civil Service Commn 67 N Front St Columbus OH 43215 Tel (614) 461-8300

CRAWFORD, HOMER, b. St. Louis, Nov. 28, 1916; A.B., Amherst Coll., 1938; LL.B., U. Va., 1941. Admitted to N.Y. bar, 1942; asso. firm LeBoeuf, Lamb, Leiby & MacRae, N.Y.C., 1942-54, partner, 1954-56; v.p., sec. St. Regis Paper Co., N.Y.C., 1956—; dir. Howard Paper Mills; dir., sec. St. Regis Paper Co. (Can.) Ltd., Pinetree Universal Ins. Co. (Bermuda) Ltd., Pinetree Gen. Ins. Co. (Bermuda) Ltd. Mem. Am., N.Y. State bar assns., Am. Soc. Corporate Secs., Paper Industry Counsel Group. Home: 1170 Fifth Ave New York City NY 10029 Office: 150 E 42d St New York City NY 10017 Tel (212) 697-4400

CRAWFORD, JOHN, JR., b. Spring Canyon, Utah, May 27, 1925; B.A., J.D., U. Utah, 1949. Admitted to Utah bar, 1949, U.S. Supreme Ct. bar, 1972; individual practice law, Salt Lake City, 1949-56; with Mountain Fuel Supply Co., Salt Lake City, 1957—, fin. v.p., treas., 1972-74, sr. v.p., treas., 1974-76, exec. v.p., 1976—, dir., 1975—. Mem. Bd. Edn. Salt Lake City Sch. Dist., 1971—, pres., 1973-76. Office: 180 E 1st South St Salt Lake City UT 84139 Tel (801) 534-5477

CRAWFORD, JOHN AMES, JR., b. Long Beach, Calif., Sept. 3, 1940; B.A., U.S. Calif., 1962; J.D., Calif. Western U., 1966. Admitted to Calif. bar, 1967, Mich. bar, 1968; claims counsel Airway Underwriters, San Diego, 1967-68; mem. staff criminal div. San Diego City Atty.'s Office, 1969; individual practice, San Diego, 1969—. Mem. Am., Calif., San Diego County bar assns., Phi Delta Phi. Office: 1010 2d St Suite 1825 San Diego CA 92101 Tel (714) 233-7528

CRAWFORD, STEPHEN GREGORY, b. Asheville, N.C., Feb. 4, 1940; A.B., Duke, 1961, LL.B., 1964. Admitted to Ala. bar, 1964; asso. firm Hand, Arendall, Bedsole, Greaves & Johnston, Mobile, Ala., 1964—, partner, 1970—. Mem. Mobile County, Am., Ala. bar assns., Order of Coif. Bd. editors Duke Law Jour.; contbr. articles to continuing legal edn. publs., speaker seminars. Home: 26 Oakland Ave Mobile AL 36608 Office: Box 123 Mobile AL 36601 Tel (205) 432-5511

CRAWFORD, THOMAS HARDY, b. Covina, Calif., Aug. 18, 1937; A.B., Stanford, 1959; LL.B., George Washington U., 1964. Admitted to D.C. bar, 1964, Calif. bar, 1969; with U.S. Fgn. Service, Peru and Dominican Republic, 1964-68, San Francisco Bay Area Rapid Transit Dist., 1969-71; mem. firm Crawford & Haskins, San Francisco, 1971-76; asst. gen. counsel Bay Area Air Pollution Control Dist., San Francisco, 1976—; prof. law Calif. State U., San Jose, 1972—. Trustee Cathedral Sch. for Boys, San Francisco; v.p. San Francisco Tomorrow. Mem. Calif. Bar. Contbr. environ. and environ. law articles to Cry California, Not Man Apart, San Francisco Chronicle, Bicycling Mag. Home: 67 7th Ave San Francisco CA 94118 Office: 939 Ellis St San Francisco CA 94109 Tel (415) 771-6000

CRAWFORD, WILLIAM W., b. 1927; B.S., Georgetown U., 1950; LL.B., Harvard U., 1954. Asso. firm Sullivan & Cromwell, 1954-58; counsel Esso Standard Oil Co., 1958-60; partner firm Alexander & Green, 1960-71; v.p., gen. counsel Internat. Harvester Co., Chgo., 1971—. Office: Internat Harvester Co 401 N Michigan Ave Chicago IL 60611*

CREAGHAN, PAUL S., b. Moncton, N.B., Can., Mar. 27, 1937; B.Com., St. Francis Xavier U., 1958; LL.B., Dalhousie U., Halifax, N.S., Can., 1961; LL.M., Harvard U., 1962. Called to N.B. bar, 1962; asso. firm Edward G. Byrne, 1962; partner firm Creaghan & Creaghan, 1963-67, Leger, Yeoman, Creaghan & Savoie and predecessor, 1967—; minister of health Province of N.B., 1970-72, minister of economic growth, 1972-74, minister of justice, 1974—; mem. N.B. Legis. Assembly from Moncton, 1970—; lectr. U. N.B., 1964-65. Alderman City of Moncton, 1965-67; councillor Westmoreland County (N.B.) Council, 1965-67; mem. Moncton Bd. Trade. Mem. Canadian, N.B. bar assns., Sigma Chi. Home: 12 Lakewood Dr Moncton NB E1E 3L7 Canada Office: Minister of Justice Room 212 Centennial Bldg Fredericton NB E3B 5H1 Canada*

CREBS, PAUL TERENCE, b. St. Louis, Apr. 14, 1938; A.B., Washington U., St. Louis, 1960, J.D., 1962. Admitted to Mo. bar, 1962; partner firm Fordyce & Mayne, St. Louis, 1962-76, Gallop, Johnson, Godiner, Morganstern & Crebs, St. Louis, 1976—. Bd. dirs. Good Shepherd Sch. for Children; mem. Met. St. Louis Regional Commerce Growth Assn., 1970—, Met. St. Louis Council for Developmental Disabilities, 1970—; mem. adv. com. S. Central Regional Center for Deaf-Blind, 1975—. Mem. Am. (chmn. health ins. law com.), Mo., Met. St. Louis bar assns., Internat. Assn. Ins. Counsel. Office: Gallop Johnson Godiner Moganstern & Crebs 7733 Forsyth St Saint Louis MO 63105 Tel (314) 862-1260

CREECH, JAMIE BYRNE, B.A., U. Tex., 1964, J.D., 1969. Admitted to Tex. bar, 1969; individual practice law, San Antonio, 1969—. Mem. Am., Tex., San Antonio bar assns. Home and office: 8827 Pineridge Rd San Antonio TX 78217 Tel (512) 824-6460

CREECH, WILLIAM AYDEN, b. Smithfield, N.C., Aug. 5, 1925; student U. Oslo, Blindern, Norway, summer 1947; A.B. in Polit. Sci., U. N.C., 1948; postgrad. in History and Econs., George Washington U., 1949, 52-53; certificate in English and Comparative Law, City of London Sch., summer 1954; J.D., Georgetown U., 1958. Econ. asst. Am. Embassy, Baghdad, Iraq, 1949-51; internat. economist Near East and African div. Bur. Fgn. Commerce, Dept. Commerce, Washington, 1952-54; econ. officer Am. Embassy, London, 1954-55; profl. staff mem. U.S. Senate Com. on Small Bus., Washington, 1955-58, counsel, 1958-59; admitted to N.C. bar, 1958; individual practice law, Smithfield, N.C., 1959-61, Raleigh, N.C., 1965—; chief counsel, staff dir. U.S. Senate Judiciary Com. Subcom. on Constl. Rights, Washington, 1961-66; mem. N.C. Ho. of Reps., 1974—; mem. N.C. Capital Bldg. Authority. Mem. adv. com. N.C. Symphony Soc., Inc., 1964-67, 73, 74, trustee, 1967—; mem. exec. com., bd. dirs. N.C. Mental Health Assn., 1971—; bd. dirs. Edenton St. United Meth. Child Devel. Center, Raleigh, 1973—, chmn. bd., 1973-75. Recipient Distinguished Service award Smithfield Jr. C. of C., 1961, award for outstanding service Johnston County (N.C.) Hist. Soc., 1965, award for outstanding effort for achievement in accreditation Campbell Coll., 1966; contbr. articles to profl. publs. Home: 1208 College Pl Raleigh NC 27605 Office: PO Box 826 Raleigh NC 27602 Tel (919) 828-0681

CREEDON, JOHN JOSEPH, b. N.Y.C., Aug. 1, 1924; B.S., N.Y. U., 1952, LL.B., 1955, LL.M., 1962. Admitted to N.Y. bar, 1955, U.S. Supreme Ct. bar, 1960; with law dept. Met. Life Ins. Co., N.Y.C., 1955-73, sr. v.p., gen. counsel, 1973-76, exec. v.p., 1976—; adj. prof. N.Y. U. Sch. Law, 1962—; trustee Practising Law Inst., N.Y. U. Law Center Found., Coll. of Ins. Fellow Am. Bar Found. (dir.); mem. Am., N.Y. State bar assns., Assn. Bar City N.Y., Am. Law Inst., Assn. Life Ins. Counsel (v.p.). Editorial bd. N.Y. Law Jour., 1976—; contbr. articles to legal jours. Home: 24 Pine Brook Dr Larchmont NY 10538 Office: 1 Madison Ave New York City NY 10010 Tel (212) 578-2162

CREEKMORE, DAVID DICKASON, b. Knoxville, Tenn., Aug. 8, 1942; A.B., U. Tenn., 1964, LL.B., 1965, J.D., 1965. Admitted to Tenn. bar, 1966, U.S. Ct. Appeals bar, 1967; dep. clk. Gen. Sessions Ct., 1963-65; asst. atty. Knox County (Tenn.), 1966-70; partner firm Creekmore, Thomson & Hollow, 1966-72; appointed judge Gen. Sessions Ct., 1972-74, elected, 1974—; mem. advisory bd. Juvenile Ct. System; lectr. Walters State Coll., 1974—. Mem. Am., Tenn., Knoxville bar assns., Am. Judicature Soc., Am., Tenn. judges assns., Phi Delta Phi. Home: 4734 Sylvan Ln Knoxville TN 37919 Office: 8 Gay St Judges Chambers Knoxville TN 37902 Tel (615) 525-7261

CREEL, JOE, b. Guntersville, Ala., Oct. 23, 1912; A.B., U. Ala., 1932, LL.B., 1934, J.D., 1969. Admitted to Ala. bar, 1934, Fla. bar, 1945, Fed. bar, 1935; individual practice law Guntersville, Ala., 1934-39; partner firm Scruggs & Creel, Guntersville, 1939-44; enforcement atty OPA, Birmingham, Ala., 1943-44; regional litigation atty. S.E. Region OPA, Atlanta, 1944, enforcement atty., chief enforcement atty, Miami Dist. office OPA, Miami, Fla., 1945; spl. asst. U.S. Atty., Birmingham, 1943-44; pvt. practice, Miami, 1945—, partner firm Creel & Glasgow, 1959-77. Mem. Dade County (v.p. 1950-51), Am. (mem. house dels 1969-71) bar assns., The Fla. Bar. Home: 1246 Algardi Ave Coral Gables FL 33146 Office: Suite 600 Univ Fed Bldg 2222 Ponce de Leon Blvd Coral Gables FL 33134 Tel (305) 446-7158

CREGAR, WILLIAM LESLIE, b. Chgo., Jan. 16, 1924; student U. Calif., Los Angeles, 1941-42; U. Chgo., 1942, State U. Iowa, 1943-44; LL.B., John Marshall Law Sch., 1949, J.D., 1970. Admitted to Ill. bar, 1950; partner firm Cregar and Preston, Brookfield, Ill., 1959—; dir. 1st Nat. Bank Brookfield; trustee Chgo. Coll. Osteo. Medicine, Chgo. Osteo. Hosp., 1970—. Mem. West Suburban Bar Assn. (bd. govs. 1961-62, exec. sec. 1963, pres. 1964, Spl. award 1965), Brookfield C. of C. (pres. 1956-58). Office: 3726 Prairie Ave Brookfield IL 60513 Tel (312) 485-9100

CRELLIN, JACK LEE, b. Rawlins, Wyo., Sept. 28, 1926; B.S. in Law, U. Utah, 1951, J.D., 1952. Admitted to Utah bar, 1953, U.S. Supreme Ct. bar, 1970; practiced in Salt Lake City, 1953-68; asst. city atty. Salt Lake City, 1958-68, city atty, 1968-74; asst. atty. gen. State of Utah, 1974—; title analyst, landman with various oil cos., 1953-58. Mem. Salt Lake City Airport Adv. Council, 1968-74. Mem. Utah State Bar Assn., Nat. Inst. Municipal Law Officers (state chmn. 1968-70, dist. chmn. 1971-74). Recipient Resolution of Appreciation Salt Lake City Bd. Commrs., 1974. Home: 2266 Berkeley St Salt Lake City UT 84109 Office: care Utah Atty Gen State Capitol Bldg Salt Lake City UT 84114 Tel (801) 533-5261

CREMIN, JOHN PATRICK, b. Tulsa, Nov. 18, 1944; B.S., U. Tulsa, 1966, J.D., 1973. Admitted to Okla. bar, 1974; asso. firm Hall, Estill, Hardwick, Gable, Collingsworth & Nelson, Tulsa, 1974—. Mem. Greater Tulsa Council; pres. Gilcrease Hills Homeowners Assn.; mem. adv. coms. Tulsa Urban League, Tulsa Jr. Coll., Community Relations Commn. Mem. Tulsa County, Okla., Am. bar assns., Order Barristers, Order Curule Chair. Office: suite 4100 One Williams Center Tulsa OK 74103 Tel (918) 585-9161

CRENSHAW, CRAIG MOFFETT, JR., b. Long Branch, N.J., Nov. 5, 1943; B.A., LaSalle Coll., 1965; J.D. magna cum laude, St. Louis U., 1969. Admitted to Va. bar, 1969, D.C. bar, 1972; atty. Dept. Justice, Washington, 1969-71, 73—; legal officer Govt. of Western Samoa, Apia, 1971-73. Mem. Am. Bar Assn., Va., D.C. bars. Editor-in-chief St. Louis U. Law Jour., 1968-69. Home: PO Box 595 McLean VA 22101 Office: Dept Justice Washington DC 20530 Tel (202) 739-3840

CRENSHAW, JACK, b. Hendersonville, N.C., Aug. 9, 1905; B.A., U. Ala., 1923, student Law Sch., 1923-24; student Harvard Law Sch., 1924-26. Admitted to Ala. bar, 1926; individual practice law, Montgomery, Ala., 1926—; spl. justice Supreme Ct. Ala., 1951; spl. asst. atty. gen. Ala., 1936-39; state atty. OPA, 1942-45; asso. firm Rushton, Crenshaw & Rushton, Montgomery, 1926-38; partner firm Carmichael & Crenshaw, Montgomery, 1938-41, firm Crenshaw & Waller, Crenshaw & Minor, Montgomery, 1973—; individual practice law, 1941-65. Mem. Am., Montgomery County (pres. 1944), Ala. bar assns., Am. Judicature Soc., Assn. Trial Lawyers Am., Trial Lawyers Ala. Author: Organizing Small Corporations, 1971. Home: 3155 Gilmer St Montgomery AL 36105 Office: 643 S Perry St Montgomery AL 36104

CRESPI, MICHAEL ALBERT, b. Bridgeport, Conn., Aug. 23, 1946; B.A., Harvard, 1968; J.D., Cumberland Sch. Law, 1973. Admitted to Ala. bar, 1973, U.S. Supreme Ct. bar, 1976; individual practice law, Birmingham, Ala., 1973-76, Headland, Ala., 1976—. City recorder Headland, 1977—. Mem. Am. Bar Assn., Am. Judicature Soc. Home: Route 1 Headland AL 36345 Office: 9 Grove St Headland AL 36345 Tel (205) 693-3770

CREYKE, GEOFFREY, JR., b. Farmville, Va., Nov. 29, 1910; A.B., George Washington U., 1932, J.D., 1935. Admitted to D.C. bar, 1935, U.S. Supreme Ct. bar, 1938, Md. bar, 1952; partner firm Hudson, Creyke, Koehler & Tacke, Washington, 1935—. Bd. dirs. Salvation Army, 1947—. Fellow Am. Bar Found.; mem. D.C. Bar, Am. (1st chmn. pub. contract law sect.; past mem. ho. of dels.), DC. bar assns. Contbr. articles to legal jours. Office: 1744 R St NW Washington DC 20009 Tel (202) 483-2500

CRIBBON, DANIEL MCNAMARA, b. Youngstown, Ohio, Jan. 27, 1917; B.A., Western Res. U., 1938; J.D., Harvard U., 1941; Admitted to D.C. bar, 1946, U.S. Supreme Ct., 1950; N.Y. bar, 1964; asso. mem. firm Covington & Burling and predecessor, Washington, 1946-49, partner, 1950—; mem. disciplinary bd. D.C. Bar, chmn. 1976—. Fellow Am. Bar Found.; mem. Am. Law Inst. Home: 4655 Hawthorne Ln NW Washington DC 20016 Office: 888 16th St NW Washington DC 20006 Tel (202) 452-6118

CRIKELAIR, PAUL BOGGS, b. Los Angeles, Nov. 22, 1931; A.A., Valley Jr. Coll., 1951; B.S., Los Angeles State Coll., 1955; M.B.A., U. Calif., Los Angeles, 1958, J.D., 1965. Admitted to Calif. bar, 1965, U.S. Supreme Ct. bar, 1972; partner firm Anderson & Crikelair, Ventura, Calif., 1965-70, firm Long & Crikelair, Ventura, 1970-74; individual practice law, Ventura, 1974—. Mem. Ventura County Bar Assn., Ventura Criminal Def. Bar, Calif. Trial Lawyers Assn., Office: 300 S Mills Rd Ventura CA 93003 Tel (805) 644-1838

CRISLIP, STEPHEN RAY, b. Oak Hill, W.Va., Apr. 23, 1948; A.B in Polit. Sci., W. Va. U., 1970, J.D., 1973. Admitted to W.Va. bar, 1973; asso. firm Jackson, Kelly, Holt & O'Farrell, Charleston, W.Va., 1973. Asst. to chmn. W.Va. State Republican. Exec. Com., 1974-76; mem. Citizens Task Force, 1975-76. Mem. Am., W.Va., Kanawha County bar assns., Order of Coif; Phi Beta Kappa. Lead articles editor W.Va. Law Rev., 1972-73. Home: 911 Highland Rd Charleston WV 25303 Office: One Valley Sq Charleston WV 25322 Tel (304) 345-2000

CRISONA, JAMES JOSEPH, b. N.Y.C., Aug. 30, 1907. B.C.S., N.Y.U., 1928, LL.B., 1931. Admitted to N.Y. bar, 1932; sr. partner firm Crisona Bros., N.Y.C., 1940-57; gen. counsel dir. Hudson and Manhattan RR, N.Y.C., 1946-52; v.p. dir. Phoenix Campbell Corp, N.Y.C., 1940-55; mem. N.Y. State Assembly, 1946; N.Y. State Senate, 1955-57; pres. borough Queens, N.Y., 1958; justice N.Y. State Supreme Ct., 1959-76; of counsel firm Netter, Dowd, Ness, Alfieri & Stern, 1976—. Trustee N.Y.U. Constrn. Fund. Mem. Am., N.Y. State, Queens County Bar Assns. Home: 118 E 60th St New York City NY 10022 Office: 660 Madison Ave New York City NY 10021 Tel (212) 486-8600

CRISP, ALFRED REESE, b. Lenoir, N.C., Apr. 9, 1894; A.B., U. N.C., Chapel Hill, 1919; LL.B., Blackstone Inst., 1925; postgrad. in law Wake Forest Coll., 1928. Admitted to N.C. bar, 1927, U.S. Supreme Ct. bar, 1965; partner firm Warren & Crisp, Lenoir, 1930-45; individual practice law, Lenoir, 1945-49, 53—; judge N.C. Superior Ct., 1949-53. Mem. N.C. Bar Assn. Home: 515 Mt View St SW Lenoir NC 28645 Office: Shields Bldg Lenoir NC 28645 Tel (704) 754-3628

CRISP, FLORENCE NELSON BLOUNT, b. Greenville, N.C., Feb. 27, 1938; A.B., Duke U., 1960; J.D., U. N.C., 1967; postgrad. U. Calif., 1961, E. Carolina U., 1962-63. Admitted to N.C. bar, 1968; tchr. English, jr. high sch., San Diego, 1960-63; instr. freshman English, E. Carolina U., Greenville, 1961; asso. firm M.K. Blount, Greenville, 1968-69; individual practice law, Greenville, 1969—; sec.-treas., v.p. Blount Harvey Co., Inc., Greenville; sec. Carolina Dairies, Inc., Greenville, Eastern Lumber & Supply Co., Inc., Winterville, N.C., Stop-N-Go Stores N.C.; treas. Eastern Realty Co., Inc., Greenville; dir. Carolina Dairy Products, Carolina Ice Cream Co., Inc.; dir., v.p. Home Builders Supply Co., Greenville, Lynndale Devel. Co., Greenville; mem. N.C. Commn. Corrections, 1974—. Mem. Am., N.C., Pitt County (N.C.) bar assns. Home: 144 E Longmeadow Rd Greenville NC 27834 Office: Blount & Crisp PO Drawer 7146 119 W 3rd St Greenville NC 27834 Tel (919) 752-6161

CRISPELL, ALBERT EMERY, JR., b. Williamsport, Pa., Oct. 13, 1918; A.B., Washington Square Coll., 1938; LL.B., Harvard, 1941. Admitted to N.Y. bar, 1941, Fla. bar, 1969; asso. firm Renander & Miller, Jamaica, N.Y., 1946-51; individual practice law, St. Petersburg, Fla., 1969—. Pres. Council of Neighborhood Assns., Pinellas County, 1973. Mem. St. Petersburg Bar Assn. Home and office: 970 45th Ave NE St Petersburg FL 33703 Tel (813) 527-3075

CRISPINO, JERRY LOUIS, b. N.Y.C., Apr. 17, 1930; B.A., Manhattan Coll., 1952; LL.B., Fordham U., 1955. Admitted to N.Y. bar, 1955, U.S. Supreme Ct. bar, 1959; law clk. firm Bigham, Englar, Jones and Houston, N.Y.C., 1955; partner firm Helweil and Crispino, N.Y.C., 1956—; mem. N.Y.C. Council, 1975—; asst. counsel joint legis. com. on Study of Alcoholic Beverage Laws in State of N.Y., 1965, to Joseph Zaredski, N.Y. State Senate Minority Leader, 1969-70; asst. commr. N.Y.C. Dept. Real Estate, 1975. Mem. Bronx County (N.Y.), N.Y. State bar assns., Columbia Lawyers Assn., Manhattan Coll., Fordham U. alumni assns. Office: 79 Wall St New York City NY 10005 Tel (212) 344-0062

CRISSMAN, WALTER EDGAR, b. Siloam, N.C., Dec. 11, 1902; A.B., U. N.C., 1926, student in law, 1927-28. Admitted to N.C. bar, 1929; since practiced in High Point, N.C., mem. firm Peacock & Dalton, 1929-31; individual practice law, 1931-49; sr. mem. firm Crissman & Bencini, 1949-54; judge Superior Ct., N.C., 1955—; asst. city atty. High Point, 1939-42; pros. atty. City of High Point, 1946-47; rep. Gen. Assembly State of N.C., 1945-53. Mem. N.C. Conf. Superior Ct. Judges (pres. 1967-68), Am. Judicature Soc., N.C., 18th Jud. Dist., High Point bar assns. (v.p. state assn. 1967-68). Office: City-County Bldg High Point NC 27260 Tel (919) 882-0927

CRISTO, LOUIS, b. Catanzaro, Italy, Mar. 2, 1924; student St. Bonaventure Coll., 1949; LL.B., St. John's U., 1952. Admitted to N.Y. bar, 1952; individual practice law, Rochester, N.Y. Mem. Am. Arbitration Assn., Am., N.Y. bar assns., N.Y., Monroe County trial lawyers assns. Home: 563 1/2 E Wake Rd Ruchville NY 14544 Office: 425 Power Bldg Rochester NY 14614 Tel (716) 546-7462

CRITES, ALBERT WALLACE, b. Chadron, Nebr., Feb. 1, 1915; A.B., U. Nebr., 1946; J.D., Northwestern U., 1949. Admitted Nebr. bar, 1949; asso. firm E.D. & F.A. Crites, Chardon, 1949-53; partner Crites, Shaffer & Slavik, and predecessors, Chadron, 1953-59, 66—; judge 16th Jud. Dist. Nebr., Chadron, 1959-66; state judge advocate Nebr. Nat. Guard, 1968-75. City atty. City of Chadron, 1949-52; chmn. bd. govs. Western Area Tech. and Community Colls., Nebr., 1973—. Mem. Am., Nebr., Dawes County, 16th Jud. Dist. (past pres.) bar assns. Home: 717 Shelton St Chadron NE 69337 Office: 201 E 3d St Chadron NE 69337 Tel (318) 432-3339

CRITTENDEN, THOMAS T., b. San Diego, July 22, 1905; B.S., Oreg. State Coll., 1928; Ph.D., U. Oreg. 1930, M.D., 1932; J.D., Hastings U., 1934. Admitted to Calif. bar, 1934; mgr., owner Pioneer Enterprises, Ltd., San Diego, 1919—; individual practice law, San Diego, 1936-, asso. firm Miller & Crittenden, San Diego, 1964-67; pub. atty., San Diego, 1938-40. Office: PO Box 3056 San Diego CA 92103 also 6117 E 1 Cajon Blvd San Diego CA 92115 Tel (714) 286-1334

CROAK, THOMAS EDWARD, b. Janesville, Wis., July 27, 1937; B.S., Regis Coll., Denver, 1959; J.D., U. Colo., 1966. Admitted to Colo. bar, 1966; asso. firm Marshal Quiat, Denver, 1966-68; partner firm Beck, Fanganello & Croak, Denver, 1968-71; individual practice law, Dillon, Colo., 1971—; county commr. Summit County (Colo.), 1975-77. Address: Box Q Dillon CO 80435 Tel (303) 468-2994

CROAKE, PAUL ALLEN, b. Janesville, Wis., Sept. 1, 1947; B.A., Lawrence U., 1969; J.D., U. Wis., 1972. Admitted to Wis. bar, 1972; asso. firm Ross & Stevens, Madison, 1972, partner, 1975—. Mem. budget com. United Way, 1973—. Mem. Am., Wis., Dane County bar assns. Contbr. articles to law revs. Home: 3105 Cross St Madison WI 53711 Office: 1 S Pickney Madison WI 53703 Tel (608) 257-5353

CROCKER, EDWARD D., b. Fostoria, Ohio, Oct. 21, 1915; A.B., Wittenberg U., 1937; certificate U. Munich, 1938; J.D., Harvard, 1941. Admitted to Ohio bar, 1941, U.S. Supreme Ct. bar, 1955; with firm Arter & Hadden, and predecessors, Cleve., 1941—, partner, 1954—; atty. OPA, 1942. Trustee Cleve. Art Inst., 1976—; bd. advisers Musical Arts Assn., 1975—. Mem. Am., Ohio, Greater Cleve. bar assns., Internat. Assn. Ins. Counsel, Am. Acad. Trial Lawyers, Jud. Conf. 6th Circuit (life). Contbr. articles to legal jours. Home: Saddleback Ln Gates Mills OH 44040 Office: 1144 Union Commerce Bldg Cleveland OH 44115 Tel (216) 696-1144

CROCKER, OTTIS B., b. Houston, Miss., June 27, 1936; LL.B., U. Miss., 1962. Admitted to Miss. bar, 1962; individual practice law, Bruce, Miss., 1962—; town atty. Bruce, 1973. Mem. Calhoun County, Miss. bar assns. Home: PO Box 666 Bruce MS 38915 Office: PO Box 666 Bruce MS 38915 Tel (601) 983-2700

CROCKETT, CHARLES MCDANIEL, b. Dunn, N.C., July 8, 1915; A.B., Wake Forest U., 1939; LL.B., Cumberland U., 1947. Admitted to Tenn. bar, 1948; individual practice law, Elizabethton, Tenn., 1953—; judge Elizabethton City Ct., 1965—. Active ARC, Cancer Soc., Heart Fund; mem. Elizabethton Municipal Airport Commn.; pres. bd. trustees Carter County Rescue Squad, 1977—; legal adviser Carter County React Team. chmn. United Fund, 1963. Mem. Tenn., Carter County (pres. 1957, 68) bar assns. Home: 306 Daytona Pl Elizabethton TN 37643 Office: 116 S Main St Elizabethton TN 37632 Tel (615) 543-3123

CROCKETT, DAVID GIDEON, b. Columbus, Ga., Sept. 29, 1943; B.A., Yale, 1966; J.D., N.Y. U., 1969. Admitted to Ga. bar, 1969; asso. counsel Atlanta Legal Aid Soc., 1969-71, mng. atty., 1972; asso. firm Nall, Miller & Cadenhead, Atlanta, 1973-77; mem. firm Crockett & Zweifel, Ltd., profl. corp., 1977—. Bd. dirs. Southside Day Care Assn., Inc., 1971—; v.p. Fulton County chpt. Ga. Conservancy, 1974-75, chmn. legal com., 1976—. Mem. Am., Ga., Atlanta bar assns., Am. Judicature Soc., Atlanta Lawyers Club. Home: 1714 Pine Ridge Dr Atlanta GA 30234 Office: 1245 Tower Pl 3340 Peachtree Rd NE Atlanta GA 30326 Tel (404) 231-1811

CROCKETT, ED R(AY), b. Tulsa, Sept. 5, 1942; LL.B., U. Tulsa, 1966. Admitted to Okla. bar, 1966, U.S. Supreme Ct., 1976; served to capt. U.S. Army Judge Adv. Gen., 1967-70; pub. defender, Tulsa County, 1971-72; mem. firm Aston & Crockett, Tulsa, 1973-76; individual practice law, 1976—; asst. prof. criminal justice program U. Tulsa. Mem. Okla., Tulsa County Am. bar assns. Home: 5645 S Delaware Pl Tulsa OK 74105 Office: 3733 E 31st St Tulsa OK 74135 Tel (918) 749-2265

CROCKETT, (JOHN) ALLAN, b. Smithfield, Utah, Jan. 19, 1906; LL.B., U. Utah, 1931, B.A., 1946, J.D., 1968. Admitted to Utah bar, 1931; asst. county atty. Salt Lake County, 1933-36; exec. sec. Counsel Pub. Service Commn. Utah, 1938-40; dist. judge, 1941-51; justice Utha Supreme Ct., Salt Lake City, 1951—, chief justice, 1959-61, 67-71; mem. exec. council Nat. Conf. Chief Justices, 1959-62, dir. Nat. Legal Aid, 1955-65. Bd. dirs. Utah Inst. Fine Arts, 1941-51, chmn., 1949-51; bd. dirs. Utah Symphony Orch., 1942-63, pres., 1951-53; bd. dirs. Utah Legal Aid Soc., 1940—; pres., 1967-69; pres. Utah Council on Family Living, 1967-69; chmn. Utah Social Hygiene Assn., 1966-67. Mem. U. Utah Alumni Assn. (Merit Honor award Emeritus Club 1976), Order of Coif, Phi Alpha Delta. Chmn. com. compiled and edited Jury Instruction Forms for Utah, 1957, and similarly Utah Rules of Evidence, 1973; author prose, articles and poetry. Home: 536 13th Ave Salt Lake City UT 84103 Office: Supreme Ct Capitol Bldg Salt Lake City UT 84114 Tel (801) 533-5282

CROCKETT, RICHARD NATHANIEL, b. Wythe County, Va., June 1, 1903; student Roanoke Coll., 1921-23; B.S., U. Va., 1925, LL.B., 1929. Admitted to Va. bar, 1929, N.Y. State bar, 1932; mem. legal staff Cadwalader, Wickersham & Taft, N.Y.C., 1929-48, mem. firm, 1949-74, counsel, 1974—. Pres. Home for Old Men and Aged Couples, N.Y.C., 1959-60; bd. dirs. Samaritan Home for the Aged, 1967-70; gov. The Virginians, 1967-68. Mem. Assn. Bar City N.Y., Am., N.Y. State bar assns., Order of Coif. Home: 1882 Westview Rd Charlottesville VA 22903 Office: 1 Wall St New York City NY 10005 Tel (212) 785-1000

CROCKETT, WILLIAM FRANCIS, b. Wailuku, Hawaii, Sept. 6, 1927; A.B., U. Mich., 1950, LL.B., 1956. Admitted to Hawaii bar, 1956, partner firm Crockett & Crockett, and predecessor, Wailuku, 1959—; with JAGC, U.S. Army, 1946-48, 51-54, col. Res., 1954—. Vice chmn. Maui County (Hawaii) Charter Commn., 1963-64, 66-67; bd. dirs. Cameron Center, Wailuku, 1968—. Mem. Maui County, Hawaii, Am. bar assns. Home: 31 N Kihei Rd Kihei HI 967S3 Office: 38 S Market St Wailuku HI 96793 Tel (808) 244-3796

CROFT, TERRENCE LEE, b. St. Louis, Apr. 13, 1940; A.B., Yale, 1962; J.D., U. Mich., 1965. Admitted to Mo. bar, 1965, Ga. bar, 1970, Fla. bar, 1970; asso. firm Coburn, Croft Shepherd & Herzog, St. Louis, 1965-69, firm Hansell Post, Brandon & Dorsey, Atlanta, 1969-73; partner firm Huie, Ware, Stern, Brown & Ide, and predecessors, Atlanta, 1973—. Mem. Am., Ga., Fla., Atlanta bar assns., Lawyers Club Atlanta. Home: 9 Basswood Circle Atlanta GA 30328 Office: 1200 Standard Federal Bldg Atlanta GA 30303 Tel (404) 522-8700

CROFT, THOMAS LUVERNE, b. Mpls., Feb. 2, 1913; A.B., Wichita State U., 1934; J.D., U. Mich., 1937. Admitted to Mo. bar, 1937; asso. firm Thompson, Mitchell, Thompson & Young, St. Louis, 1937-42, Igoe, Carroll, Keefe & Coburn, St. Louis, 1942, 45-49;

partner firm Coburn, Croft, Shepherd, Herzog & Putzell and predecessors, St. Louis, 1949—; lectr. St. Louis U., 1948-50; mem. Mo. Bd. Law Examiners, 1956-64, pres., 1960-62; sec. Character Com. St. Louis and St. Louis County, 1947-56; mem. com. visitors U. Mich. Law Sch., 1964—; mem. bd. admissions Eastern Dist. Mo., 1975—. Pres. bd. trustees Presbyn. Home for Children of Mo., 1959-60; pres. bd. dirs. Community Sch., 1959-60. Mem. Am., Mo., St. Louis bar assns. Home: 9393 Ladue Rd Ladue MO 63124 Office: 1 Mercantile Center suite 2900 Saint Louis MO 63101 Tel (304) 621-8575

CROKER, RICHARD JAMES, b. Kansas City, Kans., July 18, 1929; B.A., Central Mo. State U., 1956; LL.B., J.D., U. Kans., 1959. Admitted to Kans. bar, 1959, D.C. bar, 1972; asso. firm Boddington & Boddington, 1959-66, sec., asst. treas. United Telecommunication, Inc., Westwood, Kans., 1966-68, v.p., sec., 1968-71, v.p., counsel, Washington, 1971-74, v.p., asso. counsel, Westwood, 1974—. Pres. city council City of Lake Quivira, Kans., 1976—. Mem. Kans. D.C., Am., Fed., Fed. Communications bar assns. Home: 22 Mohawk Dr Lake Quivira KS 66106 Office: 2330 Johnson St Westwood KS 66205 Tel (913) 384-7372

CROMER, RAYMOND WALTER, b. Pitts., Feb. 15, 1923; B.A., U. Pitts., 1944, LL.B., 1949, M.Lit., 1949, J.D., 1949. Admitted to Pa. bar, 1951, U.S. Supreme Ct. bar, 1960; asso. firm Beck, McGinnis & Jarvis, Pitts., 1951-59, partner, 1959—; regional dir. Pa. Labor Relations Bd., 1955-63; asst. atty. gen. Commonwealth of Pa., 1972—; mem. 3d Circuit Jud. Conf. Mem. Whitehall Borough (Pa.) Bd. Adjustment and Appeals, 1954-59. Mem. Allegheny County (Pa.), Pa., Am. bar assns., Assn. Trial Lawyers Am., Am. Judicature Soc. Home: 1590 Williamsburg Rd Pittsburgh PA 15243 Office: 800 Porter Bldg Pittsburgh PA 15219 Tel (412) 281-2738

CROMLEY, BRENT REED, b. Great Falls, Mont., June 12, 1941; A.B., Dartmouth, 1963; J.D., U. Mont., 1968. Admitted to Mont. bar, 1968; law clk. to gen. counsel U.S. Peace Corps, Washington, 1967, to dist. judge, Billings, Mont., 1968-69; asso. firm Hutton, Schiltz & Sheehy, Billings, 1969-73; partner firm Hutton, Sheehy & Cromley, Billings, 1973—; asst. city atty. City of Billings, 1971—. Chmn., Mont. Bd. Personnel Appeals; mem. Yellowstone County Bd. Health, Billings Traffic Commn.; bd. dirs. Billings Campfire Girls, Billings Studio Theater, Mont. Legal Services Assn. Mem. Am., Yellowstone County, Mont. bar assns. Contbr. articles to profl. jours. Home: 235 Parkhill St Billings MT 59101 Office: Fratt Bldg Billings MT 59101 Tel (406) 252-3821

CRONGEYER, ROBERT LEONARD, JR., b. N.Y.C., July 6, 1945; A.B. in English, U. Notre Dame, 1967; J.D., U. Fla., 1971. Admitted to Fla. bar, 1971, U.S. Dist. Ct. No. Dist. Fla., 1971, 5th Circuit Ct. Appeals bar, 1975, U.S. Supreme Ct. bar, 1975; pub. defender intern 8th Circuit, 1970-71; asst. U.S. atty. No. Dist. Fla., 1971-73; partner firm Barksdale, Murphy & Crongeyer, P.A., 1973-75, Barksdale & Crongeyer, 1975-76; U.S. magistrate No. Dist. Fla., Pensacola, 1976—. Dir. Am. Heart Assn., Pensacola, 1975-76; mem. Pres.'s Ad Hoc Com. on Research with Human Subjects, U. West Fla., Pensacola, 1975-76. Mem. Escambia-Santa Rosa Bar Assn., Am. Judicature Soc. Recipient spl. achievement award U.S. Atty. Gen., 1972, outstanding performance citation, 1973. Home: 426 Big Bayou Rd Pensacola FL 32507 Office: POB 1791 Pensacola FL 32598 Tel (904) 434-3211

CRONIN, CHARLES J., b. Bklyn., Dec. 24, 1923; student Western Ky. State Tchrs. Coll.; LL.B., St. John's U., 1953. Admitted to N.Y. bar, 1953, U.S. Dist. Ct. for So. and Eastern N.Y. bar, 1954, U.S. Supreme Ct. bar, 1972; partner firm Cronin & Nicosia, Farmingdale, N.Y., 1967—; judge Village of Farmingdale, 1963—. Mem. Zoning Bd. Appeals, Farmingdale, 1960-63. Mem. Nassau County Bar Assn., L.I. Lawyers Conf., N.Y. State Trial Lawyers Assn., N.Y. State, Nassau County magistrates assns. Home: White Oak Tree Rd Laurel Hollow NY 11791 Office: 145 Merritt Rd Farmingdale NY 11735 Tel (516) CH9-4444

CRONSON, ROBERT GRANVILLE, b. Chgo., Dec. 23, 1924; A.B. in Econs., Dartmouth Coll., 1947; J.D., U. Chgo., 1950. Admitted to Ill. bar, 1951; atty. Daily, Dines, Ross & O'Keefe, Chgo., 1951-53; atty. Ill. Securities Commn., Springfield, 1953-55, commr., 1955-57, asst. sec. of state, 1958-64, dir. planning Office of Sec. State, 1973-74, auditor general, 1974—; mem. firm DeBoice, Greening, Ackerman & Cronson, Springfield, 1957-60; sr. v.p., sec., dir. Chgo. Corp., 1964-73; asso. prof. pub. adminstrn. Roosevelt U., Chgo., 1973-74; chmn. MW Vehicle Proration Compact, 1959-61; dir. Central Nat. Fin. Corp., Central Nat. Life Ins. Co., Jacksonville, Ill. Chmn. William H. Chamberlain Scholarship Fund, Sangamon State U., 1970—. Mem. Midwest Securities Commrs. Assn. (chmn. 1949-64), Securities Industry Assn. (chmn. state legis. com. 1970-72), Am., Ill. bar assns., Phi Kappa Psi. Contbr. articles to profl. jours. Home: 2445 Westchester Blvd Springfield IL 62704 Office: 524 S 2d St Springfield IL 62706 Tel (217) 782-0803

CROOK, DANIEL CLIFFORD, III, b. Balt., Md., May 13, 1941; B.A. cum laude, Hobart Coll., 1959-63; J.D., U. Md., 1966. Admitted to Md. bar, 1966, D.C. bar, 1971, U.S. Supreme Ct. bar, 1975; JAG, USAF, 1967-70; clk. U.S. Dist. Ct., Balt., 1970-71; asso. firm Wilkes & Artis, Washington, 1971-76, partner, 1976—. Mem. Md., Prince Georges County, Montgomery County, D.C. bar assns., Bar Assn. D.C., Barristers, Phi Beta Kappa. Recipient Estates and Trusts award U. Md., 1965. Office: 1666 K St NW Suite 600 Washington DC 20006 Tel (202) 457-7800

CROOKHAM, CHARLES SEWELL, b. Portland, Oreg., Mar. 17, 1923; student Oreg. State U., 1941-43; A.S.T.P., Loyola U., Los Angeles, 1943-44; B.A., Stanford, 1948; J.D., NW Sch. Law, Lewis and Clark Coll., 1951; grad. Nat. Coll. State Trial Judges, 1964. Admitted to Oreg. bar, 1952; asso. firm Vergeer & Samuels, Portland, 1952-62; judge Oreg. Circuit Ct., 4th Jud. Dist., 1963—; served as appellate mil. judge, col. JAGC Res. U.S. Army Ct. Mil. Rev., Washington, 1974-77; faculty advisor Nat. Coll. State Judiciary, 1969. Chmn. Oreg. Mental Health Adv. Bd., 1962-69; mem. Oreg. Criminal Law Revision Commn., 1972-73; vice chmn. Am. Revolution Bicentennial Commn. of Oreg., 1971-76; bd. visitors NW Sch. Law, Lewis and Clark, 1976—. Mem. Oreg. State (author and editor continuing edn. publs.), Multnomah, Am. bar assns., Oreg. Circuit Judges Assn. (pres. 1972), Am. Judicature Soc., Phi Delta Phi. Office: 404 County Courthouse 1021 SW 4th Ave Portland OR 97204 Tel (503) 248-3198

CROOKS, KATHLEEN MORPHEW, b. Beverly, Mass., July 1, 1912; LL.B./J.D., Portia Law Sch., Boston (now New Eng. Sch. Law), 1939, LL.M., 1942. Admitted to Mass bar, 1940, Fed. bar, 1942; house counsel, corporate sec. Riley Stoker Corp. and subs., Worcester, Mass., 1953—; instr. para-legal programs Middlesex Community Coll., Bedford, Mass., 1970, continuing edn. Harvard, Cambridge, Mass., 1950; faculty, dept. bus. law Boston Coll., 1976—. Mem. Boston Big Sister Assn.; bd. dirs. Daniels Found., Worcester. Mem. Am., Mass. bar assns., Assn. Women Lawyers. Author: Manual for Examination of Real Estate Titles, 1956. Home: 21 High Rock Rd Wayland MA 01778 Office: 9 Neponset St Worcester MA 01613 Tel (617) 852-7100

CROOKS, WILLIAM D.K., JR., b. Lynn, Mass., Jan. 14, 1934; A.B., Brown U., 1956; LL.B., New Eng. Law Sch., 1960; LL.M., Suffolk U., 1963. Admitted to Mass. bar, 1960; atty. Boston & Maine R.R., 1965-69; partner firm Crooks, O'Keefe, Stover & Lynch, Marblehead, Mass., 1972—; mem. panel arbitrators Am. Arbitration Commn. Mem. personnel bd. Town of Marblehead, 1975. Mem. Assn. ICC Practitioners. Office: 13 Essex St Marblehead MA 01945 Tel (617) 631-7010

CROSS, BRUCE MICHAEL, b. Washington, Jan. 30, 1942; A.B., Dartmouth, 1964; LL.B.-J.D., Harvard, 1967. Admitted to Wash. bar, 1967, U.S. Supreme Ct. bar, 1974, D.C. bar, 1976; asso. firm Perkins, Coie, Stone, Olsen & Williams, Seattle, 1968-75, partner, 1975—. Mem. Am., Wash., Seattle-King County bar assns. Home: 14056 117th Pl NE Kirkland WA 98033 Office: 1900 Washington Bldg Seattle WA 98101 Tel (206) 682-8770

CROSS, EDWARD GEORGE, b. Ritzville, Wash., Aug. 15, 1909; LL.B., U. Idaho, 1932. Admitted to Wash. State bar, 1933; city treas. City of Ritzville, 1933-43; pros. atty. Adams County (Wash.), 1944-56; individual practice law, Ritzville, 1933—; mem. Wash. State Jud. Council, 1944-50. Chmn., Adams County Republican Central Com., 1948-56. Mem. Am., Wash., Adams County (pres. 1970—), bar assns., Am. Judicature Soc. Home: 406 S Jefferson St Ritzville WA 99169 Office: 120 W Main St Ritzville WA 99169 Tel (509) 659-0600

CROSS, JAMES EDWIN, b. Fort Dodge, Iowa, Aug. 18, 1921; B.S.C., State U. Iowa, 1942; LL.B., U. So. Calif., 1949. Admitted to Calif. bar, 1949, Iowa bar, 1949; since practiced in Los Angeles, asso. firm O'Melveny & Myers, 1949-59, partner, 1960—; dir. Lockheed Aircraft Corp., The TI Corp., Title Ins. & Trust Co., Pioneer Nat. Title Ins. Co., Source Capital, Inc., Enterprise Fund, Inc., Harbor Fund, Inc., Fletcher Fund, Inc., Legal List Investment, Inc., Comstock Fund, Inc., Craig Corp., Pacific Indemnity Co. Trustee Claremont Men's Coll., Los Angeles World Affairs Council, Pacificulture Found.; mem. Town Hall Los Angeles. Mem. State Bar Calif., Los Angeles, C. of C., Los Angeles County, Am. bar assns. Home: 284 Hacienda Dr Arcadia CA 91006 Office: 611 W 6th St Los Angeles CA 90017 Tel (213) 620-1120

CROSS, JOHN BLAKELY, b. Gloversville, N.Y., June 13, 1935; A.B., Cornell U., 1957; J.D., Syracuse U., 1961. Admitted to N.Y. state bar, 1961, U.S. Supreme Ct. bar, 1967; mem. staff N.Y. State Dept. Law, Albany, 1961-63, appellate ct. advocate, 1967; lawyer, pension cons. N.Y. State Dept. Civil Service, Albany, 1963-66, supervising lawyer, 1968-71, chief legal counsel, 1971—; spl. deputy atty. gen. to enforce election law, Albany, 1964-72; sec. Albany County Dist. Atty.'s Readiness Team, 1971-73. Chmn. Albany Independent Movement, 1965; trustee 1st Unitarian Ch. Albany, 1965-67, 70-73; dir. ON Assn., Albany, 1972; pres. Capital Dist. Community Council, 1975; v.p. Albany County Mental Health Assn., 1976; chief spokesman N.Y. State Coalition, 1977; pres. Woodgate Condominium, 1977. Mem. Am., N.Y. State bar assns., Internat. Personnel Mgmt. Assn. Home: 34 Chestnut Rd Delmar NY 12054 Office: 1220 Washington Ave Albany NY 12239 Tel (518) 457-6206

CROSS, THEODORE LAMONT, b. Newton, Mass., Feb. 12, 1924; A.B., Amherst Coll., 1946; LL.B., Harvard U., 1950. Admitted to Mass. bar, 1950, N.Y. bar, 1953; asso. firm Hale and Dorr, Boston, 1950-52; editor-in-chief Bankers mag., N.Y.C., 1962—, Bus. and Soc. Rev., N.Y.C., 1971—; sec., v.p. legal affairs Sheraton Corp. Am., N.Y.C., 1963-68, also dir.; dir. Warren, Gorham & Lamont, Inc., N.Y.C., 1962—; dir. Mgmt. Reports, Inc., Record Pub. Co.; cons. HEW, OEO, 1964-69; co-founder Banking Law Inst., 1965, chmn., 1965—; pub. gov. Am. Stock Exchange, 1972—. Trustee Amherst Coll. Author: Black Capitalism: Strategy for Business in the Ghetto, (McKinsey Found. Book award), 1969; founder, pub. Atomic Energy Law Jour., 1959—; editor Harvard Law Rev., 1948-50. Home: 233 Carter Rd Princeton NJ 08540 Office: 870 7th Ave New York City NY 10019 Tel (212) 977-7412

CROSSETT, EDGAR L., III, b. Long Beach, Calif., June 14, 1944; B.A., Mercer U., 1967; J.D., Oklahoma City U., 1972. Admitted to Ga. bar, 1972; legal intern, law clk. firm Pierce, Duncan, Couch and Hendrickson, Oklahoma City, 1971; law clk. firm Mullis, Reynolds, Marchall, Macon, Ga., 1972; asso. firm Ware, Sterne and Griffin, Atlanta, 1972-73; partner firm Jackson and Crossett, Atlanta, 1973-76, Kiser, Rosser and Crossett, Atlanta, 1976—. Mem. Am. Ga., Atlanta bar assns., Phi Delta Phi. Home: 5020 Nesbit Ferry Ln NE Atlanta GA 30340 Office: 7008 Perimeter Center E Atlanta GA 30346 Tel (404) 393-1640

CROSSON, JAMES DAVID, b. Newberry, S.C., Aug. 9, 1909; Admitted to Ill. bar, 1942; partner firm Gassaway, Crosson, Turner & Parsons, Chgo., 1946-54; referee Municipal Ct., Chgo., 1954-61; adminstrv. asst. to Chief Justice Chgo. Municipal Ct., 1961-62; asso. judge Cook County (Ill.) Municipal Ct., 1962-68; judge Ill. Circuit Ct. of Cook County, 1968—. Trustee John Marshall Law Sch., 1963—, treas., 1967-72; trustee Met. Chgo. YMCA, 1969-76, v.p., 1970-76; trustee Ch. of Good Shepherd Congl., United Ch. of Christ, Chgo. Mem. Ill. Judges Assn., Original Forty Club of Chgo. (pres. 1969-71). Recipient citation of merit John Marshall Law Sch., 1966. Office: 2401 Chgo Civic Center Chicago IL 60602 Tel (312) 443-8382

CROTHERS, JOANNE MARIE, b. Toronto, Ont., Can., May 8, 1946; came to U.S., 1955, naturalized, 1972; B.B.A., U. Miami, 1967; J.D., Stetson U., 1970. Admitted to Fla. bar, 1972, D.C. bar, 1973; partner firm Cross, Murphy & Smith, Washington, 1972-77, firm Crothers & Bernard, Washington, 1973-77, firm Hogue, Crothers & Bernard, Washington, 1977—. Adminstrv. trustee Pan Am. Diagnostic Found., Washington, 1976—. Mem. D.C., Fla. bar assns. Home: 3009 Cathedral Ave NW Washington DC 20008 Office: 1128 16th St NW Washington DC 20036 Tel (202) 857-0261

CROTTY, MICHAEL FRANCIS, b. Balt., Sept. 1, 1947; A.B. with honors, Loyola U., Chgo., 1969; J.D., Northwestern U., 1972. Admitted to Md. bar, 1972, D.C. bar, 1976; served to lt. JAGC, USN, Phila., 1972-76; asst. counsel Am. Bankers Assn., Washington, 1976—; mem. comml. panel arbitrators Am. Arbitration Assn., 1976—, Health Claims Arbitration Panel of Md., 1976—. Mem. Am., Md., D.C. bar assns., Computer Law Assn. Home: 421 Yellow Springs S Laurel MD 20810 Office: 1120 Connecticut Ave NW Washington DC 20036 Tel (202) 467-4370

CROTTY, WILLIAM R., b. Albany, N.Y., Sept. 26, 1920; student Siena Coll., 1927-39, Albany Law Sch., 1945-47, 49. Admitted to N.Y. bar, 1950; asso. firm Towner & Erway, Albany, 1950-63; individual practice law, Albany, 1963—; asso. counsel to chmn. ways and means N.Y. State Assembly, 1964-68; sec. City and County CSC, 1964-66. Mem. N.Y. State Bar Assn., Capital Dist. Trial Lawyers Assn., County Officers Assn. Home: 313 Hackett Blvd Albany NY 12208 Office: 5 Elk St Albany NY 12207 Tel (518) 463-6967

CROUCH, FRANKLIN MADISON, b. Richmond, Va., June 29, 1920; Bs., U. Richmond, 1940; postgrad. U.S. Naval Acad., 1942, Bowdoin Coll., 1942, Mass. Inst. Tech., 1942; J.D., Chgo.-Kent Coll. Law, 1950. Admitted to Ill. bar, 1950, U.S. Patent Office bar, 1951; law clk. firm Carlson, Pitzner, Hubbard & Wofe, Chgo., 1945-50; asso. firm Leydig, Voit, Osann, Mayer & Holt, and predecessors, Chgo., 1950-62, partner, 1962-72, mem., 1972—; instr. physics and aeros. U. Richmond, 1940-41. Commr. Glen Ellyn Park Dist., 1962-75, pres., 1967-73. Mem. Am., Chgo. bar assns., Am., Chgo. patent law assns., U.S. Trademark Assn., Assn. Internationale pour la Protection de la Propriété Industrielle, Internat. Patent and Trademark Assn., Phi Delta Phi, Sigma Pi Sigma. Recipient Outstanding Service awards Girl Scouts U.S.A., 1957, 58, 59. Home: 545 Park Blvd Glen Ellyn IL 60137 Office: One IBM Plaza Suite 4600 Chicago IL 60611 Tel (312) 822-9666

CROUCH, JAMES RAY, b. Lynn Grove, Ky., Jan. 7, 1930; B.S., N.Mex. State U., 1952; J.D., U. Kans., 1957. Admitted to N.Mex. bar, 1957; mem. firm Weir & Crouch, Las Cruces, N.Mex., 1957-68, Crouch, Chalekian, Parr & Valentine, Las Cruces, 1977—. Mem. N.Mex. Bd. Ednl. Fin., 1957-71, Bd. Edn., 1973—. Fellow Am. Bar Found.; mem. N.Mex. Def. Lawyers (past pres.), N.M. State Bar (pres. 1976-77), Am. Bar Assn., Fedn. Ins. Counsel, Las Cruces C. of C. (dir.). Home: 2025 Turentine St Las Cruces NM 88001 Office: PO Box 850 Las Cruces NM 88001 Tel (505) 524-3533

CROUCHER, THOMAS, b. Canandaigua, N.Y., Nov. 22, 1907; A.B., Colgate U., 1929; LL.B., Harvard U., 1932. Admitted to N.Y. State bar, 1933; clk. firm Charles M. Hughes, Schenectady, 1932-34; individual practice law, Canandaigua, 1934—; city judge City of Canandaigua, 1940-44; dist. atty. Ontario County (N.Y.), 1944-56. Mem. N.Y. State, Ontario County bar assns. Office: 70 S Main St Canandaigua NY 14424 Tel (716) 394-2665

CROW, ROBIN CLYDE, b. San Antonio, Dec. 7, 1943; B.A., Southwestern U., 1965; J.D., U. Tex., 1968. Admitted to Tex. bar, 1968; partner firm Eastland, Crow & Dent, Hillsboro, Tex., 1974—; pres. Hill County Bar Assn. 1976, mem. bd. State Jr. Bar Tex. 1976-78. Mem. adminstrv. bd. First United Methodist Church Hillsboro, Tex. Mem. Am., Hill County Bar Assns., State and State Jr. Bar Tex. Home: 418 E Franklin Hillsboro TX 76645 Office: PO Box 840 Hillsboro TX 76645 Tel (817) 582-2284

CROWDER, CHARLES ROGERS, b. Birmingham, Ala., Aug., 1937; B.S., Auburn U., 1959; LL.B., U. Ala., 1962. Admitted to Ala. bar, 1962; formerly clk. to Judge Walter Gewin of U.S. Dist. Ct.; asso. firm Hamilton, Denniston, Butler & Reddick, Mobile, Ala., 1963; partner firm Wilder, Crowder & Hampe, Birmingham, 1969-73; judge Jefferson County (Ala.) Circuit Ct., 10th Jud. Dist., 1973—. Mem. Sigma Delta Kappa, Sigma Phi Epsilon. Editorial bd. U. Ala. Law Rev., 1962-63. Office: Courthouse Birmingham AL 35203 Tel (205) 325-5323

CROWDER, JACK ANDREW, b. Charleston, W.Va., Jan. 2, 1927; B.A., Washington and Lee U., 1948, LL.B. cum laude, 1950. Admitted to Va., D.C. bars, 1950, U.S. Supreme Ct. bar, 1958; individual practice law, Washington, 1950-65; exec. v.p., gen. counsel Nat. Assn. Wool Mfrs., Washington, 1965-67, pres., 1967-70; gen. counsel Am. Textile Mfrs. Inst., Inc., Washington, 1970—; mem. Pres. Mgmt. Labor Textile Adv. Com., 1965—; mem. U.S. Del. to Internat. Wool Textile Orgn., 1965—. Mem. Am., Fed. bar assns., Phi Beta Kappa, Phi Alpha Delta, Omicron Delta Kappa. Home: 3607 Bent Branch Ct Falls Church VA 22041 Office: 1150 17th St NW suite 1001 Washington DC 20036 Tel (202) 833-9420

CROWDER, JAMES F., JR., b. Miami, Fla., Sept. 16, 1939; B.A., Emory U., 1961; LL.B., U. Fla., 1964, J.D., 1967. Admitted to Fla. bar, 1965; now partner firm Bradford, Williams, McKay, Kimbrell, Hamann & Jennings, Miami. Mem. Am., Dade County (pres. 1977—) bar assns., Fla. Bar, Delta Theta Phi. Office: Dade Fed Savs Bldg 9th Floor 101 E Flagler St Miami FL 33131 Tel (305) 358-8181*

CROWE, DANIEL WALSTON, b. Visalia, Calif., July 1, 1940; B.A. in English, U. Santa Clara, 1962; J.D., Hastings Coll. Law, 1965. Admitted to Calif. bar, 1966, U.S. Supreme Ct. bar, 1973; asso. firm Crowe, Mitchell & Crowe and predecessors, Visalia, 1968-74, partner, 1974—; chmn. com. continuing edn. Calif. State Bar, 1976—. Mem. Am., Calif., Tulare County bar assns. Home: 3000 Hyde Way Visalia CA 93277 Office: 2222 W Main St Visalia CA 93277 Tel (209) 733-1125

CROWE, GUTHRIE FERGUSON, b. LaGrange, Ky., July 24, 1910; student U. Ky., 1928-29; LL.B., Cumberland U., 1933. Admitted to Ky. bar, 1933; asso. firm Robert T. Crowe, LaGrange, 1933-37; individual practice law, LaGrange, 1937-42, 46-52; judge U.S. Dist. Ct. for C.Z., Balboa Heights, 1952—; municipal judge, LaGrange, 1938-42; mem. Ky. Ho. of Reps., 1942; commr. Ky. State Police, 1948-52. Past chmn. C.Z. chpt. ARC; chmn. mgmt. com. Armed Services YMCA, Balboa; chmn. admissions com. C.Z. United Fund; v.p., acting pres. council, mem. exec. bd. C.Z. council Boy Scouts Am.; mem. exec. com. C.Z. Heart Assn. Mem. Fed. (past pres. C.Z. chpt.), Ky., C.Z. (hon.) bar assns., Sigma Delta Kappa. Home and Office: PO Box 2006 Balboa Heights CZ Tel 52-7645

CROWE, THOMAS NIKLAUS, b. Hot Springs, Ark., May 15, 1943; B.A. in Econs. Pomona Coll., 1965; J.D., U. Ariz., 1968. Admitted to Ariz. bar, 1968, Calif. bar, 1969, U.S. Supreme Ct. bar, 1972; county atty. Yuma County (Ariz.), 1969; legis. asst. to Rep. John J. Rhodes, Washington, 1969-70; U.S. atty. for Ariz., Phoenix, 1970-76; asso. firm Ryley, Carlock & Ralston, Phoenix, 1977—. Office: 2600 Arizona Bank Bldg Phoenix AZ 85003 Tel (602) 258-7701

CROWE, WILLIAM EUGENE, b. Braymer, Mo., May 6, 1893; A.B., Central Meth. Coll., Fayette, Mo., 1916; LL.B., U. Mo., 1921. Admitted to Mo. bar, 1920, Okla. bar, 1921; individual practice law, Enid, Okla., 1921—; judge Spl. Sessions Ct., Garfield County, Okla., 1960-70. Mem. Am., Okla. (past pres.) bar assns., Am. Judicature Soc., Order of Coif, Phi Alpha Delta. Home: 1931 Live Oaks St Enid OK 73701 Office: 805 Broadway Tower Enid OK 73701 Tel (405) 237-4966

CROWE, WILLIAM LOGAN, b. Gurdon, Ark., Sept. 11, 1930; B.A., La. State U., Baton Rouge, 1952, J.D., 1953. Admitted to La. bar, 1953; asso. firm McKeithen, Mouser & McKinley, Monroe, La., 1956-57; asst. city atty., Monroe, 1959-62; asst. dist. atty., Monroe, 1962-64; acting judge, Monroe City Ct., 1965-67, judge, 1967-70; mem. judiciary commn. La., 1969-70; asst. prof. Loyola U. Law Sch., New Orleans, 1970-72, asso. prof., 1972-75, prof., 1975—. Mem. La. Bar Assn. (bd. govs.), Am. Judicature Soc., Assn. Am. Law Schs. (chmn. elect torts-compensation sect. 1976-78), La. Law Inst. Mem. editorial bd. La. State Bar jour., 1971-73. Home: 1121 Short St New Orleans LA 70118 Office: 6333 Loyola Ave New Orleans LA 70118 Tel (502) 866-8355 ext 8479

CROWELL, ELDON HUBBARD, b. Middletown, Conn., May 15, 1924; A.B., Princeton, 1948; LL.B., U. Va., 1951. Admitted to D.C. bar, 1951, Conn. bar, 1951, U.S. Supreme Ct. bar, 1958; partner firm Sellers, Connor & Cuneo, Washington, 1960-70, firm Jones, Day, Reavis & Pogue, Washington, 1970—; mem. Adminstrv. Conf. U.S., 1972-74; vis. lectr. U. Va., George Washington U. Trustee Williston-Northampton Sch., East Hampton, Mass.; former trustee Madiera Sch. (Va.). Mem. Am., Fed., Conn. bar assns., Order of Coif. Contbr. articles to legal jours. Home: 2315 Bancroft Pl NW Washington DC 20008 Office: 1100 Connecticut Ave NW Washington DC 20036 Tel (202) 452-5800

CROWELL, WILLIAM JEFFERSON, b. Tucson, Aug. 30, 1913; A.B., U. Nev., 1934; LL.B., U. Calif., 1937. Admitted to Nev. bar, 1937; dist. atty. Nye County (Nev.), 1947-54; gen. counsel Nev. Indsl. Commn., Carson City, 1959—. Mem. State Bar Nev. (gov. 1949-55, pres. 1956-57), Am. Bar Assn. Office: 402 N Carson St Carson City NV 89701 Tel (702) 882-1311

CROWLEY, ELLEN, b. Cheyenne, Wyo., July 26, 1916; B.A., U. Wyo., 1938; B.S. in Library Sci., U. Denver, 1942; LL.B., Fordham U., 1948. Admitted to Wyo. bar, 1953; asst. state librarian Wyo., Cheyenne, 1939-42; law librarian law firm, N.Y.C., 1942-49; librarian State of Wyo., 1949-51; law librarian U. Nebr., 1951-53, asst. prof. legal bibliography, 1951-53; individual practice law, Cheyenne, 1953—; asst. atty. gen. State of Wyo., 1955-59, dep. atty. gen., 1959; law clk. U.S. Dist. Ct. Wyo., 1960-69, U.S. Ct. Appeals, 10th Circuit, 1971; mem. Wyo. Ho. of Reps., 1973-74, 77-78. Mem. Am., Wyo., Laramie County (v.p. 1973-74, pres. 1974-75) bar assns., Nat. Assn. Women Lawyers. Home: Carpenter WY 82054 Office: PO Box 287 Cheyenne WY 82001 Tel (307) 634-9669

CROWLEY, FRANCIS LEO, JR., b. Boston, Mass., Sept. 15, 1931; B.S. in Social Scis., Georgetown U., 1952, LL.B., 1955. Admitted to D.C. bar, 1955, Calif. bar, 1969; atty. JAGC, U.S. Army, 1955-60; atty. adviser Office of Gen. Counsel Office of Sec. of Def., Washington, 1960-63; group counsel Litton Industries, Inc., Beverly Hills, Calif., 1963-67, asso. chief counsel, 1969—, v.p., 1976—. Pres., McLean (Va.) Estates Civic Assn., 1959-61. Mem. Am., Calif. bar assns. Home: 18880 Pasadero Dr Tarzana CA 91356 Office: 360 N Crescent Dr Beverly Hills CA 90210 Tel (213) 273-7860

CROWLEY, GEORGE DAVID, b. Chgo., June 17, 1913; A.B., Georgetown U., 1934; J.D., Loyola U., 1937. Admitted to Ill. bar, 1937; atty. SEC, Chgo., 1938-41, Dept. Justice, Washington, 1939-40; atty. Chief Counsel's Office, IRS, Chgo., 1946-49; partner firm Crowley & Goschi, Chgo., 1949—; dir. Bally Mfg. Corp. Fellow Am. Coll. Trial Lawyers; mem. Nat. Coll. Criminal Def. Lawyers and Pub. Defenders (chmn. bd. regents 1976—), Nat. Assn. Criminal Def. Lawyers (pres. elect), Criminal Justice Council, Am., Fed., Chgo. bar assns. Recipient John Carroll award Georgetown U., 1970, medal of excellence Loyola U. Sch. Law, 1976; author: Cross Examination of the Government Technical Tax Expert, 1975; Scientific Evidence and Criminal Advocacy, to 1975; Criminal Tax Fraud-Representing the Taxpayer before Trial, 1976. Home: 1630 Sheridan Rd Wilmette IL 60091 Office: 135 S LaSalle St Suite 758 Chicago IL 60603 Tel (312) 372-3211

CROWLEY, JOHN POWERS, b. Chgo., Oct. 5, 1936; student U. Notre Dame, 1954-57, St. Mary's Seminary, Perryville, Mo., 1955-56; LL.B., DePaul U., 1960; LL.M. in Taxation, N.Y. U., 1961. Admitted to Ill. bar, 1960; asst. U.S. atty. No. Dist. Ill., 1961-65; individual practice law, Chgo., 1965-71; partner firm Crowley, Burke, Nash and Shea, Chgo., 1971-76; U.S. dist. judge No. Dist. Ill., Chgo., 1976—; adj. prof. law DePaul U. Mem. Chgo. (bd. mgrs. 1976-78), Am., Ill., Fed. bar assns., Nat. Assn. Criminal Def. Lawyers, Nat. Lawyers Club. Recipient DePaul U. Distinguished Alumni Award, 1976; Spl. Commendation award, Nat. Assn. Criminal Def. Lawyers, 1976. Contbr. articles in field to profl. jours. Home: 2416 Central Park St Evanston IL 60201 Office: 219 S Dearborn St Chicago IL 60604 Tel (312) 435-5578

CROWLEY, ROBERT EMMET, b. Boston, June 1, 1946; A.B., Georgetown U., 1968, J.D., 1971. Admitted to Maine bar, 1971, Mass. bar, 1972; atty. Boston Legal Aid Soc., 1972-73; mem. firm Crowley & Crowley, Biddeford, Maine, 1973—; instr. real estate law York County Community Coll., Biddeford, 1975—. Mem. Maine, York County bar assns. Home: 103 Main St Kennebunk ME 04043 Office: 57 Graham St Biddeford ME 04005 Tel (207) 284-4563

CROWLEY, ROBERT WHITE, b. Boston, Nov. 30, 1933; B.S.B.A., Boston Coll., 1955; postgrad. Suffolk U. Law Sch., 1961-62; LL.B., Portia Law Sch., Boston, 1965; J.D., New Eng. Law Sch., 1971. Admitted to Mass. bar, 1965, U.S. Dist. Ct. Mass. bar, 1971, U.S. Dist. Ct. Vt., 1975, U.S. Supreme Ct. bar, 1975; devel. specialist Boston Redevelop. Authority, 1961-65; individual practice law, Boston, 1965—. Chmn. Melrose (Mass.) Reorgn. Com., 1973—. Mem. Am. Arbitration Assn. (nat. panel arbitrators 1967—), Mass. Bar, Boston Bar Assn., Mass. Trial Lawyers Assn., Assn. Trial Lawyers Am. Office: One State St Boston MA 02109 Tel (617) 723-8822

CROWN, JOHN JACOB, b. Evanston, Ill., Aug. 10, 1929; B.A., Stanford, 1951, postgrad. Sch. Law, 1950-51; LL.B., Northwestern U., 1955. Admitted to Ill. bar, 1955; asst. states atty. Cook County (Ill.), 1955-56; law clk. to Justice Clark, U.S. Supreme Ct., 1956-57; mem. staff Dept. Justice, Washington, 1957-59; asso. firm Raymond, Mayer, Jenner & Block, Chgo., 1959-63; partner firm Jenner & Block, Chgo., 1964-74; judge Circuit Ct. Cook County, Chgo., 1974—; master in chancery U.S. Dist. Ct. No. Ill., 1961-62; lectr. trial practice Northwestern U. Sch. Law, 1964-68. Bd. dirs. Kendall Coll., Evanston; bd. visitors Stanford Sch. Law; trustee Ill. Inst. Tech., Northwestern Meml. Hosp., Chgo. Editorial bd. Northwestern Law Rev., 1954-55. Office: 1906 Civic Center Chicago IL 60602 Tel (312) 443-8346

CROWTHER, HAROLD FRANCIS, b. Colorado Springs, Colo., July 26, 1920; J.D., Washburn Law Sch., Topeka, 1950. Admitted to Kans. bar, 1950, U.S. Dist. Ct., Kans., 1963, U.S. Ct. Appeals, Tenth Circuit, 1964; individual practice law, Salina, Kans., 1950—, partner with W. B. Crowther, Salina, 1958-60; juvenile ct. probation officer Saline County, Kans., 1956-59; judge pro tempore Probate-Juvenile Ct. Saline County, 1956-59. Sec., treas. Salina Municipal Band, 1960—. Mem. Pearl Harbor Survivors Assn. (life). Prin. flute with Salina Civic Orchestra, 1957—. Home: 646 E Iron Ave Salina KS 67401 Office: 119 S 7th St Salina KS 67401 Tel (913) 823-2576

CROWTHER, MARSHALL LEE, b. Kansas City, Mo., Sept. 2, 1937; A.B., Kans. Wesleyan U., 1962; J.D., U. Kans., 1965. Admitted to Kans. bar, 1966, U.S. Dist. Ct. Kans. bar, 1966; atty. Kans. Pub. Employees Retirement System, Topeka, 1967—; spl. asst. atty. gen. Kans., Topeka, 1969—; gen. legal counsel Kansas Jaycees, 1972-74; corp. sec. Alumni of Kans. Delta Upsion, 1971—. Corp. sec. Boys' Club Lawrence (Kans.), Inc., 1971—; trustee 1st Presbyn. Ch., Lawrence, 1973—. Mem. Am., Kans., Douglas County bar assns., Am. Judicature Soc. Home: 1230 W 29th Ct Lawrence KS 66044 Office: 400 1st Nat. Bank Tower Topeka KS 66603 Tel (913) 296-3921

CRUCE, B.W., JR., b. Bagwell, Tex., Mar. 6, 1930; B.B.A., So. Methodist U., 1956, J.D., 1959. Admitted to Tex. bar, 1959, U.S. Supreme Ct. bar, 1968; asso. firm Burnett & Cruce, Dallas, 1959-64, Cruce, Tatem & Springfield, Mesquite, Tex., 1964-74; individual practice law, Mesquite, 1974—; councilman City of Mesquite, 1959-61, mayor, 1961-65. Mem. Tex., Mesquite (past pres.), Dallas County Criminal bar assns., Tex., Dallas County trial lawyers assns., Mesquite C. of C. (pres. 1965-67). Home: 300 Riggs Circle Mesquite TX 75149 Office: 309 N Galloway St Mesquite TX 75149 Tel (214) 285-8848

CRUEY, BILLY KENNETH, b. Richlands, Va., May 22, 1939; B.S., E. Tenn. State U., 1964; J.D., U. Richmond, 1967. Admitted to Va. bar, 1967; partner firm Cruey, Mason & Patterson and predecessor, Roanoke, Va., 1970—. Bd. dirs. Roanoke Valley Mental Health Services, 1975, Roanoke Valley Mental Health Assn., 1976—. Mem. Va., Roanoke bar assns., Va. Trial Lawyers Assn. Contbr. articles to sports publs. Home: Route 1 Box 65A Union Hall VA 24176 Office: 412 Shenandoah Bldg Roanoke VA 24011 Tel (703) 344-2017

CRUM, JAMES MERRILL, b. Virginia, Ill., Oct. 14, 1912; A.B. with honors, Ind. U., 1937, J.D. with distinction, 1939. Admitted to Ind. bar, 1939, Fla. bar, 1947; asso. firm Kahn & Dees, Evansville, Ind., 1939-40; law clk. U.S. Dist. Ct., So. Dist. Ind., 1941, 46; agt. U.S. Secret Service, 1941-45, acting agt., 1941-45; partner firm McCune, Hiaasen, Crum, Ferris & Gardner, Ft. Lauderdale, Fla., 1947—; city atty. City of Hallandale (Fla.), 1949-53, 57-63, Plantation (Fla.), 1953-59, Miramar (Fla.), 1955-59. Supr., Old Plantation Water Control Dist., Plantation, 1952-74; mem. Broward County (Fla.) Law Library Commn., 1955-56; mem. Miramar City Council, 1955-59. Mem. Fedn. Ins. Counsel, Am., Fla., Broward County bar assns., Order of Coif. Home: 441 Holly Ln Plantation FL 33313 Office: 600 Century Nat Bank Bldg 25 S Andrews Ave PO Box 14636 Fort Lauderdale FL 33302 Tel (305) 462-2000

CRUMLEY, JACK WALTON, b. Tulsa, Dec. 5, 1922; student U. Calif. Berkeley, 1941-43; J.D., U. So. Calif., 1949. Admitted to Calif. bar, 1950; individual practice law, Hollywood, Calif., 1950-52; asst. gen. atty. Union Pacific R.R., Los Angeles, 1952-57; partner firm Luce, Forward, Hamilton & Scripps, San Diego, 1957—. Bd. dirs. Scripps Meml. Hosp., La Jolla, Calif., 1971—. Mem. Am., Calif., San Diego County bar assns., Am. Coll. Trial Lawyers, Am. Bd. Trial Advocates (nat. exec. com.), Nat. Assn. R.R. Trial Counsel, Assn. Bus. Trial Lawyers. Named Calif. Trial Lawyer Year, Am. Bd. Trial Advocates, 1975. Home: 6303 La Jolla Scenic Dr La Jolla CA 92037 Office: 1700 California Plaza 110 W A St San Diego CA 92101 Tel (714) 236-1414

CRUMP, ALFRED WAITER, b. Cin., Nov. 5, 1943; B.S., U. Pa., 1965; J.D., Farleigh-Dickinson U., 1968. Admitted to Pa. bar, 1971, U.S. Dist. Ct. Dist. Pa. bar, 1974, U.S. Tax Ct., 1976; asso. firm Marx, Ruth, Binder, Ward & Crump and predecessors, Reading, Pa., 1970-72, partner, 1972—; asst. solicitor Berks County, Pa., 1974—. Treas., dir. Berks County Unitarian-Universalist Ch., 1973-76. Mem. Am., Pa., Berks County bar assns., Pa. Trial Lawyers Assn. Home: 212 Cherry Dr Wyomissing PA 19610 Office: 520 Washington Reading PA 19601 Tel (215) 376-6794

CRUTCHER, JAMES W., b. Nashville, Feb. 16, 1908; B.A., Vanderbilt U., also LL.B., J.D. Admitted to Tenn. bar, U.S. Supreme Ct. bar; practiced in Nashville, 1932—; served with JAGC. Mem. Tenn., Nashville bar assns. Home: 895 Oak Valley Ln Nashville TN 37220 Office: 935 J C Bradford Bldg Nashville TN 37219 Tel (615) 254-9391

CRUTHIRDS, EARL REDIC, b. Big Creek, Miss., Feb. 24, 1912; B.S., Memphis State U., 1936; LL.B., U. Miss., 1953. Admitted to Miss. bar, 1953; individual practice law, Jackson, Miss., 1953-56, 1960-65; partner firm Robertson, Cruthirds & Wallace, and predecessors, Jackson, 1956-60; partner firm Cruthirds, Nix & Payne, Jackson, 1965-68, Cruthirds and Assos., Jackson, 1968—. Electron commnr. Hinds County (Miss.); lt. gov. Sertoma Internat., 1955-56, Ala.-Miss. Dist. gov., 1958-59, pres. local chpt., Jackson, 1964-65, former sec. Mem. Miss., Hinds County bar assns. Contbr. articles to legal jours. Home: 4580 Old Canton Rd Jackson MS 39211 Office: 1441 Canton Mart Rd Jackson MS 39211 Tel (601) 956-5120

CRYSTAL, GAIL LEE, b. Brookfield, Mo., Jan. 27, 1930; J.D., U. Mo., Kansas City, 1955. Admitted to Mo. bar, 1956; individual practice law, Windsor, Mo., 1956-60; claims atty. Western Casualty Co., Kansas City, 1960-76; magistrate, probate judge Princeton and Mercer Counties (Mo.), 1976—; municipal judge City of Lee Summit (Mo.), 1966-76, City of Lake Lotawana (Mo.), 1975-76. Mem. community council Richards-Gebaur AFB; dir. Prairie Twp. Republican Club. Mem. Mo. Bar, Mo. Municipal Magistrate Judges Assn. Office: 916 Walnut St Kansas City MO 64106 Tel (816) 221-5924

CUBA, BENJAMIN JAMES, b. San Antonio, Dec. 12, 1936; A.A., Temple Jr. Coll., 1957; B.B.A., U. Tex., 1959; J.D., Baylor U., 1963. Admitted to Tex. bar, 1964; sr. partner firm Cuba Johnson & Pickle, Temple, Tex., dir. Temple Savs. Assn. Mem. Am., Bell Lampasas and Mills Counties (pres. 1973-74) bar assns., State Bar Tex., Tex. Assn. Def. Counsel, Tex. Assn. Bank Counsel, Tex. Bar Found., Tex. Assn. Savs. and Loan Counsel, Am. Judicature Soc., Phi Delta Phi. Office: First National Bldg Temple TX 76501 Tel (817) 778-1824

CUDDAHY, JOHN PATRICK, b. Bklyn., Jan. 12, 1930; A.B. magna cum laude, St. Francis Coll., 1951; J.D., Fordham U., 1956; LL.M., N.Y. U., 1972. Admitted to N.Y. bar, 1956, U.S. Tax Ct., 1957; asso. firm Schreiber, Klein & Opton, N.Y.C., 1956-59, firm Austin, Burns, Smith & Walls, N.Y.C., 1959-68; partner firm Davies, Hardy, Ives & Lawther, N.Y.C., 1968-74; sec. East River Savs. Bank, N.Y.C., 1974-76, v.p., gen. counsel, 1976—. Mem. Am. (Robinson-Patman com. Antitrust sect. 1964—), N.Y. State (com. on fed. legis. 1971-76) bar assns. Home: 1736 West End Ave New Hyde Park NY 11040 Office: 26 Cortlandt St New York City NY 10007

CUDDEBACK, CHARLES VANINWEGEN, b. Port Jervis, N.Y., Dec. 22, 1908; B.A., Williams Coll., 1930; LL.B., Harvard U., 1933. Admitted to N.Y. bar, 1933; asso. firm Samuel M. Cuddeback, Port Jervis, 1933-34; partner firm Samuel M. & Charles Van I. Cuddeback, Port Jervis, 1934-39, firm Cuddeback & Cuddeback, Port Jervis, 1939-74, firm Cuddeback, Cuddeback, & Wells, Port Jervis, 1974-77, firm Cuddeback, Cuddeback & Onofry, Port Jervis, 1977—; mem. adv. bd. The County Trust Co. (now Bank of N.Y.), Port Jervis, 1966—. Mem. bd. edn. City Sch. Dist., Port Jervis, 1943-64, pres., 1949-64; dir. Tri-States Area Day Care Center, Port Jervis, 1974—; trustee, asst. sec. Neversink Area Valley Mus., Cuddebackville, N.Y., 1976—; atty. Zoning Bd. Appeals, Town of Deerpark, N.Y., 1970—. Mem. N.Y., Orange County, Port Jervis (past pres.) bar assns. Home: 8 White St Port Jervis NY 12771 Office: 21 Ball St Port Jervis NY 12771 Tel (914) 856-5178

CUDDY, CURTIS EMERY, b. Roanoke, Va., Feb. 2, 1904; J.D., U. Va., 1929. Admitted to Va. bar; individual practice law, Roanoke, 1929-32, 35-42, 62—; asst. Commonwealth atty. City of Roanoke, 1932-35, Commonwealth atty., 1942-62. Mem. Gov.'s Hwy. Safety Com.; dep.-coordinator Roanoke Civil Def.; steward S. Roanoke Methodist Ch. Mem. Commonwealth's Attys. Assn. Va. (past pres.), Va., Roanoke bar assns., U. Va. Alumni Assn. Home: 2135 Carolina Ave SW Roanoke VA 24014 Office: State and City Bldg Suite 409 Roanoke VA 24011 Tel (703) 344-6228

CUDDY, WILLIAM VINCENT, b. Port Chester, N.Y., Jan. 15, 1929; A.B. cum laude, U. Notre Dame, 1952; LL.B., Fordham U., 1956. Admitted to N.Y. bar, 1956, U.S. Supreme Ct. bar, 1962; partner firm Close, Griffiths, McCarthy & Gaynor, White Plains, N.Y., 1956-66; v.p., dir., gen. counsel Bush Universal, Inc., N.Y.C., 1966-70; partner firm Cuddy & Feder, White Plains, 1971—; judge White Plains City Ct., 1975—; adv. council Pace U. Sch. Law, 1976—, Coll. White Plains, 1976—. Bd. dirs. Westchester (N.Y.) Community Service Council, Inc., 1976—. Mem. N.Y., Westchester County, White Plains bar assns., Fordham, Notre Dame law assns., Notre Dame Nat. Alumni Assn. (v.p. 1966, dir. 1964-67, named Man of Year 1962). Home: 9 Oakley Rd White Plains NY 10606 Office: 90 Maple Ave White Plains NY 10601 Tel (914) 761-1300

CULBERTSON, RUTH EVELYN, b. Louisville, Ill., Mar. 25, 1906; LL.B., Okla. City U., 1949. Admitted to Okla. bar, 1949; clk. IRS, Washington, 1936, Little Rock, 1937, Okla. City, 1938-51; mgmt. specialist Tinker AFB, Okla., 1951-66; individual practice law, Oklahoma City, 1966—. Mem. Okla. Bar Assn. Home and office: 6313 S Broadway Ave Oklahoma City OK 73139 Tel (405) 634-8072

CULLEN, RALPH OSBORNE, b. Ocala, Fla., Jan. 9, 1902; A.B., Amherst Coll., 1925; J.D., U. Fla., 1934. Admitted to Fla. bar, 1934; asso. firm Hoffman & Robinson, Miami, Fla., 1935-45; partner firm Knight, Underwood & Cullen, Miami, 1945-50; individual practice law, Miami, 1950-60; circuit judge Dade County, Fla., 1960-72; spl. asst. U.S. atty. gen. So. Fla., 1948-58. Chmn. Dade County Bd. Adjustment, Miami, 1950-51. Mem. Fla. Bar, Phi Delta Phi. Home: 3405 Banos Ct Coral Gables FL 33134

CULLITON, EDWARD MILTON, b. Grand Forks, Minn., Apr. 9, 1906 (parents Canadian citizens) B.A., U. Sask., 1926, LL.B., 1928, D.C.L., 1962. Admitted to Sask. bar. 1930; practice in Gravelbourg, 1930-51; mem. Sask. Legislature, 1935-44, 48-51; provincial sec. Patterson Govt., 1938-41; minister without portfolio, 1941-44; judge Ct. Appeal Sask., 1951-62; chief justice Sask., Regina, 1962—. Chancellor, U. Sask., 1963-69. Home: 3140 Albert St Regina SK S4S 3N8 Canada Office: Court House Regina SK Canada*

CULP, CHARLES WILLIAM, b. Louisville, Nov. 13, 1931; B.A., Yale, 1953, J.D., Harvard, 1958. Admitted to Ind. bar, 1958; asso. firm Cadick, Burns, Duck & Neighbours, Indpls., 1958-63, partner, 1963—; dir. Kofabco, Inc. Mem. Am., Ind., Indpls. bar assns. Home: 8414 Spring Mill Ct Indianapolis IN 46260 Office: 800 Union Federal Bldg Indianapolis IN 46204 Tel (317) 639-1571

CULPEPPER, BOBBY LOYCE, b. Jonesboro, La., July 26, 1941; J.D., La. State U., 1964. Admitted to La. bar, 1965, U.S. Supreme Ct. bar, 1972; law clk. 3rd Circuit Ct. Appeals, Lake Charles, La., 1965-65; partner firm Baker, Culpepper, & Brunson, Jonesboro, 1966—; asst. dist. atty., Jonesboro, 1969-70. Pres., Jackson Parish Farm Bur., 1969-70. Chmn. Jackson Parish chpt. ARC, 1974—. Mem. Am., La., Jackson Parish bar assns., Am., La. trial lawyers assns., Am. Judicature Soc. Office: PO Drawer # E Jonesboro LA 71251 Tel (318) 259-4415

CULPEPPER, LAMAR POLK, b. Alexandria, La., May 12, 1948; student Washington and Lee U., 1966-68; B.A., La. State U., 1970, J.D., 1973. Admitted to La. bar, 1974; asso. firm Polk, Foote, Randolph, Percy & Ledbetter, Alexandria, 1974-75, partner, 1976—. Bd. dirs. Rapides Parish (La.) chpt. ARC, 1975—, vice chmn., 1976—; chmn. asso. vestry, mem. bldg. com. lay reader, chalice bearer St. Timothy's Episcopal Ch., Alexandria, 1976—; vice chmn. Rapides Parish Heart Fund, 1976—; bd. dirs. Alexandria-Pineville YMCA, 1975—, mem. nominating com., 1976—; mem. adv. bd. dirs. Renaissance Home, juvenile detention center, Alexandria, 1975—; mem. La. Trails Adv. Council. Mem. Am. Bar Assn., Alexandria-Pineville C. of C. Home: 3008 Nelson St Alexandria LA 71301 Office: 800 Johnston St Alexandria LA 71301 Tel (318) 487-1790

CULPEPPER, PERRY MELTON, JR., b. Macon, Ga., Nov. 23, 1945; A.B., Mercer U., 1967, J.D., 1970. Admitted to Ga. bar, 1970, Fla. bar, 1970; mem. firm Heyman and Sizemore, Atlanta, 1970-71; mem. firm Mixon, Forrester and Culpepper, Cordele, Ga., 1971—; judge municipal ct. Warwick Ga., 1972—. Past pres. Cordele-Crisp County Hist. Soc., Inc., 1974. Mem. Ga., Fla., Am. bar assns., Cordele-Crisp C. of C. (dir. 1976—, mem. exec. com., v.p. 1976—). Office: 202 12th Ave E Cordele GA 31015 Tel (912) 273-2442

CULVER, RICHARD BENNETT, b. Winston-Salem, N.C., Dec. 1, 1945; B.S. in Bus. Adminstrn., U. Fla., 1967, J.D. with honors, 1973. Admitted to Fla. bar, 1973; asso. firm Rimes, Greaton, Murphy & Batchelder, Ft. Lauderdale, Fla., 1973-75, firm Krupnick & Campbell, Ft. Lauderdale, 1975—. Mem. Am., Fla., Broward County bar assns., Order of Coif, Phi Kappa Phi. Exec. editor U. Fla. Law Rev. Office: Suite 1318 1 Financial Plaza Fort Lauderdale FL 33394 Tel (305) 763-8181

CULVER, ROBERT FRANCIS, b. Belden, Nebr., Feb. 14, 1920; LL.B., Drake U., 1950. Admitted to Iowa bar, 1950, U.S. Tax Ct. bar, 1955; indivudual practice law, Emmetsburg, Iowa, 1951-53, 59-72; partner firm Kelly, Spies & Culver, Emmetsburg, 1953-59; judicial magistrate City of Emmetsburg, 1973—; jud. magistrate County of Palo Alto, Iowa, 1973—. Mem. Am., Iowa, Palo Alto County bar assns., Am. Judicature Soc. Office: Palo Alto County Courthouse Emmetsburg IA 50536 Tel (712) 852-4712

CULVER, RUSSELL LYLE, b. Cooperstown, N.D., May 4, 1926; LL.B., U. Mont., 1950. Admitted to Mont. bar, 1950; asso. firm Al Hansen, Baker, Mont., 1950-63; individual practice law, Baker, 1963—; owner, pres. Fallon County Abstract Co., 1953—. Mem. Baker C. of C., Baker Sch. Bd. Mem. Mont. Bar Assn. Home: 316 W Pleasant Ave Baker MT 59313 Office: Box AA Baker MT 59313 Tel (406) 778-2422

CUMBIE, FRED HARRIS, II, b. Orlando, Fla., June 1, 1947; B.A., U. South Fla., 1969; J.D., Fla. State U., 1972. Admitted to Fla. bar, 1972; asst. state's atty. Fla. 9th Jud. Circuit, 1972; asso. firm Donald D. Lettow, St. Cloud, Fla., 1972-75; partner firm Miles & Cumbie, St. Cloud, 1976—; judge St. Cloud Municipal Ct., 1973—. Bd. dirs. St. Cloud C. of C., 1976—. Mem. Lawyer's Title Guarantee Fund. Home: 625 Avocado St Saint Cloud FL 32769 Office: POB 188 Saint Cloud FL 32769 Tel (305) 892-7171

CUMMING, CLAUDE BARTON, b. Lebanon, Nebr., Nov. 12, 1910; B.A., Hastings Coll., 1931; LL.B., U. Nebr., 1936. Admitted to Nebr. bar, 1936, Calif. bar, 1937, U.S. Ct. Mil. Appeals, 1955, U.S. Supreme Ct. bar, 1955; atty. Gen. Ins. Co. Am., 1937-45; sr. partner firm Murchison & Cumming, Los Angeles, 1945—. Mem. Am., Calif., Los Angeles, Wilshire (pres. 1965) bar assns., Internat. Assn. Ins. Counsel, So. Calif. Def. Counsel, Phi Alpha Delta. Home: 11064 Wrightwood Ln North Hollywood CA 91604 Office: 680 Wilshire Pl Los Angeles CA 90005 Tel (213) 382-7321

CUMMINGS, BENJAMIN BERNARD, JR., b. Wildwood, N.J., July 30, 1945; A.B., Washington & Lee U., 1967, J.D., 1970. Admitted to Va. bar, 1971, U.S. Supreme Ct. bar, 1976; since practiced in Petersburg, Va., asso. firm Lavenstein & Andrews, 1970-73, partner, 1974-75; individual practice law, 1975-76; partner firm Cummings & Levinson, 1977—; commr. in chancery Petersburg (Va.) Circuit Ct., 1973—; substitute judge Petersburg Gen. Dist. Ct., 1974-76; spl. justice 11th Jud. Circuit Ct. Va., 1975—; chmn. Petersburg Legal Aid Soc., 1974-75. Active Petersburg chpt. Am. Cancer Soc., Southside chpt. ARC, 1975; bd. dirs. Temple Brith Achim, sec., 1975; mem. Petersburg City Council, 1976—. Mem. Am., Va. bar assns., Va. Trial Lawyers Assn. Home: 1841 Arch St Petersburg VA 23803 Office: VA Mutual Bldg Petersburg VA 23803 Tel (804) 861-4200

CUMMINGS, LE ROY EDWARD, b. Indpls., Nov. 25, 1946; A.B., Ind. U., 1968; J.D., 1973. Admitted to Ind. bar, 1973; asso. firm Kimmell, Funk & Cummings, and predecessors, Vincennes, Ind., 1973-74, partner, 1975—; chief dep. prosecutor Knox County (Ind.), 1975—. Mem. Ind., Knox County (pres. 1977) bar assns. Home: 1314 Audubon Rd Vincennes IN 47591 Office: 112 N 7th St Vincennes IN 47591 Tel (812) 882-5050

CUMMINGS, WILLIAM BRUCE, b. Bronxville, N.Y., Apr. 26, 1939; B.A. in Econs., Randolph Macon Coll., Ashland, Va., 1961; LL.B., U. Va., 1964. Admitted to Va. bar, 1964; asso. firm Tolbert, Lewis & Fitzgerald, Arlington, 1964-68, partner, 1969-74; partner firm Lewis, Wilson, Cowles, Cummings & Lewis, Ltd., Fairfax, 1974-75; U.S. atty. Eastern Dist. Va., Alexandria, 1975—. Vice chmn. bd. dirs. Arlington YMCA, 1969-74; treas., bd. dirs. Fairfax YMCA, 1974—; bd. dirs. Va. Environ. Endowment. Mem. Arlington Bar Assn. (sec. 1968-72), Alexandria Jr. C. of C. Home: 211 Courthouse Circle Vienna VA 22180 Office: 117 S Washington St Alexandria VA 22314 Tel (703) 557-9100

CUMMINS, ARTHUR BENSON, JR., b. Millington, N.J., May 21, 1941; A.B., Gettysburg Coll., 1963; J.D., Willamette U., 1966. Admitted to Oreg. bar, 1966, U.S. Dist. Ct. for Oreg. bar, 1966, U.S. Ct. Mil. Appeals, 1968, U.S. Ct. Appeals for 9th Circuit bar, 1977; served with JAG, USAF,1966-70; partner firm Rhoten, Rhoten & Speerstra, Salem, Oreg., 1970—; instr. bus. law Chemeketa Community Coll., Salem, 1970—, U. Md. Extension Service, 1968-70. Pres. Child Abuse Study Com., 1974-76. Mem. Am. Bar Assn., Assn. Trial Lawyers Am., Am. Arbitration Assn., Oreg. Trial Lawyers Assn. Tel (503) 364-6733

CUMMINS, DAVID CHARLES, b. Los Angeles, June 19, 1935; B.S., U. Idaho, 1957; J.D., U. Wash., 1960; LL.M., N.Y.U., 1969. Admitted Washington bar, 1960, U.S. Supreme Ct. bar, 1966; asst. atty. gen. State of Wash., 1961-62; mem. firm Dore, Dubuar, Cummins & Badley, Seattle, 1963-68; judge Lake Forest Park Municipal Ct., Wash., 1966-68; asso. prof. law U. Idaho, Moscow, 1969-70; asso. prof. Tex. Tech. U., Lubbock, 1970-72, prof., 1972—. Mem. Am., Wash. bar assns., Soc. Am. Law Tchrs., Order of Coif. Author: Washington State Manual for Real Estate Brokers and Salesmen, 1960; contbr. articles to legal jours. Office: School of Law Texas Tech U Lubbock TX 79409 Tel (806) 742-3785

CUNAN, RICHARD CARL, b. Richmond, Calif., Sept. 27, 1935; B.S., U. Calif. at Berkeley, 1959; J.D., Golden Gate U., 1973. Asst. merchandising mgr. Honig, Cooper & Harrington, 1962; asst. advt. and sales promotion mgr. Calif. Canners & Growers, San Francisco, after 1963, then advt. mgr., asst. corp. sec.; admitted to Calif. bar, 1973. Mem. Am., San Francisco bar assns., San Francisco Lawyers Club. Office: 3100 Ferry Bldg San Francisco CA 94549 Tel (415) 981-0101

CUNNINGHAM, CAMERON MCPHERSON, b. Detroit, Jan. 18, 1939; B.B.A., Tex. Tech. U., 1961; LL.B., U. Tex., 1967. Admitted to Ariz. bar, 1968, Tex. bar, 1969; Reginald Heber Smith fellow Dinebeiina Nahilna Be Agaditahe Legal Services, Window Rock, Ariz., 1967-68; revisor Tex. penal code Tex. Legis. Council, Austin, 1969-70; partner firm Simons, Cunningham, Coleman, Nelson & Howard, Austin, 1969—; co-founder Radical Lawyers Caucus, State Bar Tex., 1970-71. Co-chmn. Travis County (Tex.) Liberal Democrats, 1966. Mem. Nat. Lawyers Guild, Tex. Criminal Def. Lawyers Assn. Contbr. articles Criminal Law Bull., asso. editor, 1971—. Home: 1705 Giles St Austin TX 78722 Office: 501 W 12th St Austin TX 78701 Tel (512) 478-9332

CUNNINGHAM, DAVID WHILEY, b. Lancaster, Ohio, Apr. 25, 1926; B.Sc. in B.A., Ohio State U., 1950, J.D., 1951. Admitted to Ohio bar, 1951, Fla. bar, 1953; asso. firm J. Thomas Gurney, Orlando, Fla., 1953-55; individual practice law, Winter Park, Fla., 1956-69, 71—; partner firm Turnbull, Abner, Daniels & Cunningham, Winter Park, 1969-70; asst. city atty. and prosecutor Winter Park, 1958-68. Mem. Fla., Orange County bar assns. Home: 2838 Red Bug Rd Rt 1 Maitland FL 32751 Office: 411 Park Ave N PO Box 1538 Winter Park FL 32790 Tel (305) 644-4330

CUNNINGHAM, FRANKLIN NEWELL, b. Brookline, Mass., Feb. 7, 1920; A.B., Harvard, 1941, J.D., 1948. Admitted to Mass. bar, 1949; asso. firm Warner & Stackpole, and predecessors, Boston, 1948-60, partner, 1960—. Mem. Am., Boston, Mass. bar assns., Mass. Trial Lawyers Assn. Office: 28 State St Boston MA 02109 Tel (617) 523-6250

CUNNINGHAM, MARY CAROL, b. Waco, Tex., July 13, 1948; B.A. with high honors, Univ. Tex., Austin, 1969, J.D. with honors, 1971. Admitted to Tex. bar, 1972; asst. atty. gen., Tex., 1972-73; individual practice law, 1973—. Mem. Am., Tex. bar assns., Tex. Jr., Travis County Jr. bar assns., Phi Beta Kappa. Address: 7502 Shoal Creek Austin TX 78757 Tel (512) 452-5167

CUNNINGHAM, MORTON CHRISTY, II, b. Austin, Tex., Feb. 19, 1942; B.A., Westminster Coll., 1964; LL.B., U. Mich., 1966. Admitted to Colo. bar, 1966, Okla. bar, 1973; staff atty. legal dept. Phillips Petroleum Co., Denver, 1966-72, Bartlesville, Okla., 1972—. Chmn. support com. Law Explorer Post #41 Boy Scouts Am., Bartlesville, 1973-75. Mem. Colo., Okla., Washington County bar assns. Home: 2608 Oakdale Dr Bartlesville OK 74003 Office: 534 B Frank Phillips Bldg Bartlesville OK 74004 Tel (918) 661-4741

CUNNINGHAM, WARREN PEEK, JR., b. Hampton, Va., Jan. 20, 1915; LL.B., U. Tex., 1937, B.A., 1938; LL.M., Harvard, 1939. Admitted to Tex. bar, 1937, U.S. Supreme Ct. bar, 1941; spl. atty. anti-trust div. U.S. Dept. of Justice, Washington, Tex., 1939-42; individual practice law, Houston, 1947-63; judge 164th Jud. Dist. Ct. Tex., Houston, 1963—; faculty mem. Nat. Coll. State Judiciary, U. Nev., 1968—; chmn. jud. sect. State Bar Tex., 1976-77. Chmn., bd. dirs. Houston Tb Hosp., 1951-52; mem. Houston Community Council, 1956-57. Mem. Am. Bar Assn., Tex. State Bar, Am. Judicature Soc. Author: Civil Proceedings Before Trial, 1976. Home: 11 Farther Point Houston TX 77024 Office: 600 Civil Cts Bldg Houston TX 77002 Tel (713) 221-8316

CUNNINGHAM, WILLIAM PEYTON, JR., b. Natchitoches, La., Feb. 21, 1934; J.D., La. State U., 1960. Admitted to La. bar, 1960; partner firm Cunningham & Cunningham, Natchitoches, 1960-72; judge 10th Jud. Dist. La., Natchitoches and Red River, 1972—. Mem. Am., La., Natchitoches Parish bar assns. Home: 1043 Oma St Natchitoches LA 71457 Office: POB 837 Natchitoches LA 71457 Tel (318) 352-6429

CUPKA, ELLEN MARGARET, b. Newark, Dec. 23, 1948; B.A., Carlow Coll., 1970; J.D., Seton Hall Law Sch., 1974. Admitted to N.J. bar, 1974; asst. dep. pub. defender Office of Pub. Defender, Trenton, N.J., 1975—. Mem. N.J., Essex County bar assns. Office: 520 E State St Trenton NJ 08625

CURETON, WILLIAM E., b. Meridian, Tex., Aug. 5, 1911; grad. U. Tex., 1935. Admitted to Tex. bar, 1936; mem. firm Rogers & Scott, Waco, Tex., after 1938, firm Wilson & Cureton, Waco, after 1945, firm Sheely & Cureton, Waco. Chmn. Waco Pub. Library. Mem. Tex., Waco, McFernon County bar assns. Home: 3404 Chateau St Waco TX 76701 Office: 809 Citizens Tower Waco TX 76701 Tel (817) 754-0987

CURLEY, THOMAS JOSEPH, b. Boston, Dec. 12, 1922; B.S., U.S. Naval Acad., 1944; J.D., U. Md., 1949; grad. Nat. Coll. State Judiciary, 1968, grad. in Criminal Law, 1972. Admitted to Md. bar, 1949; practiced in Md., 1949-64; chief judge People's Ct. of Anne Arundel County (Md.), 1964-71; adminstrv. judge Md. Dist. Ct., Dist. 7, 1971—. Mem. Am., Anne Arundel County (pres. 1963) bar assns. Office: Rowe Blvd and Taylor Ave Annapolis MD 21404 Tel (301) 269-2734

CURRAN, ARTHUR B., b. Rochester, N.Y., June 4, 1925; LL.B., J.D., U. Notre Dame, 1950. Admitted to N.Y. State bar, 1950; legal asst. U.S. Dist. Ct. judge, 1950; individual practice law, Rochester, N.Y., 1951-61; corp. counsel City of Rochester, 1962-65; city mgr., 1965; judge City Ct. of Rochester, 1966—. Mem. Monroe County Bar Assn., Notre Dame Law Sch. Assn. Home: 1705 Highland Ave Rochester NY 14618 Office: City Ct of Rochester Hall of Justice Rochester NY 14614 Tel (716) 428-6718

CURRAN, BARBARA A., b. 1928; B.A., Mass. State Coll. (now U. Mass., Amherst), 1950; J.D., U. Conn., 1953; LL.M., Yale U., 1961. Admitted to Conn. bar, 1953; mem. research staff Am. Bar Found., 1961-76, asso. exec. dir., Chgo., 1976—, also mem. editorial advisory bd. Am. Bar Found. Research Jour., and chmn. staff research rev. com.; mem. advisory com. on truth in lending Fed. Res. Bd.; mem. Ill. Gov.'s Credit Advisory Com.; mem. consumer credit advisory com. Nat. Conf. Commrs. on Uniform State Laws; cons. Task Force on Law and Law Enforcement, Nat. Commn. on Causes and Prevention of Violence, Pres.'s Commn. on Consumer Interests. Mem. Am. Bar Assn. Author: Trends in Consumer Credit Legislation; contbr. articles to profl. jours. Office: 1155 E 60th St Chicago IL 60637 Tel (312) 667-4700*

CURRAN, EDWARD MATTHEW, b. Bangor, Maine, May 10, 1903; A.B., U. Maine, 1928, LL.D., 1970; LL.B., Cath. U. Am., 1927, LL.D. (hon.), 1967; LL.D. (hon.), Georgetown U., 1971. Admitted to D.C. bar, U.S. Supreme Ct. bar; mem. firm King & Nordlinger, Washington, 1928-34; corp. counsel D.C., 1934-36; judge D.C. Police Ct., 1936; atty. U.S. Dept. Justice, Washington, 1940-46; judge D.C. circuit U.S. Dist. Ct., 1946—, chief judge, 1966—, sr. judge, 1970—. Bd. dirs. alumni council Cath. U. Law Sch.; trustee Benedictine Sch. for Exceptional Children. Mem. Am., D.C. bar assns., Soc. Friendly Sons of St. Patrick, John Carroll Soc., Phi Kappa, Gamma Eta Gamma. Recipient Alumni Achievement award Cath. U. Am.; Jud. award Assn. Fed. Investigators; Distinguished Service award D.C. Jr. C. of C. Home: 6607 Western Ave Washington DC 20015 Office: Room 4114 US Courthouse Washington DC 20001 Tel (202) 426-7465

CURRAN, JOHN GERARD, b. Rochester, N.Y., Dec. 22, 1934; B.A. cum laude, U. Notre Dame, 1957, LL.B., 1958, J.D., 1969. Admitted to N.Y. bar, 1958, U.S. Dist. Ct. for Western Dist. N.Y. bar, 1958, Colo. bar, 1960, U.S. Dist. Ct. for Colo. bar, 1960; individual practice law, Rochester, 1961—; councilman-at-large, City of Rochester, 1973—, vice-mayor, 1977. Dem. exec. committeeman, Rochester, 1963-67, 72-73. Mem. Am., N.Y., Monroe County bar assns. Office: 502 Exec Office Bldg Rochester NY 14614 Tel (716) 454-6180

CURRAN, JOHN JAMES, b. Indpls., Apr. 16, 1937; LL.B., Ind. U., 1965, J.D., 1968. Admitted to Ind. bar, 1965; estate tax examiner IRS, Indpls., 1965; contract adminstr., contracting officer Naval Avionics Facility, Indpls., 1965—; individual practice law, Indpls., 1966—. Trustee Marion County City County Bldg Authority, Indpls. Mem. Fed. Bar Assns., St. Thomas More Soc. Office: 6128 E 21st St Indianapolis IN 46219 Tel (317) 356-2814

CURRAN, MARSHALL GLENN, JR., b. New Castle, Pa., Aug. 29, 1928; B.A., Coll. Wooster, 1951; LL.B., Duke, 1954. Admitted to Fla. bar, 1955; asso. firm Carr & O'Quinn, Miami, 1955-59; asst. states atty. Dade County (Fla.), Maimi, 1959-61; partner firm Watkins & Curran, Ft. Lauderdale, Fla., 1961-65; partner firm English, McCaughan and O'Bryan, Ft. Lauderdale, 1965-76, firm Spear Deuschle & Curran, Ft. Lauderdale, 1976—. Mem. Fla. Bar, Am., Broward County bar assns., Acad. Fla. Trial Lawyers, Assn. Trial Lawyers Am. Home: 23 Fort Royal Isle Fort Lauderdale FL 33308 Office: 5554 N Federal Hwy Fort Lauderdale FL 33308 Tel (305) 776-6550

CURRAN, MAURICE FRANCIS, b. Yonkers, N.Y., Feb. 20, 1931; student Cathedral Coll., 1948-50; A.B., St. Joseph Coll. and Sem., 1952; LL.B., Fordham U., 1958. Admitted to N.Y. bar, 1958; mem. firm Kelley, Drye, Newhall & Maginnes, N.Y.C., 1958-60, Wilson & Bave, Yonkers, 1960-65; div. counsel Merck & Co., Rahway, N.J., 1965-69; asst. gen. counsel E.R. Squibb & Sons, Inc., N.Y.C., 1967-70; corp. counsel, chief law dept. City of Yonkers, 1970-72; partner firm Bleakley, Platt, Schmidt & Fritz, White Plains, N.Y., 1972—. Mem. Yonkers Urban Renewal Agy., 1970-72; trial commr., dep. comm. pub. safety, Yonkers, 1972—. Home: 388 Bronxville Rd Yonkers NY 10708 Office: 2 William St White Plains NY 10601 Tel (914) 949-2700

CURRAN, ROBERT OWEN, b. Montpelier, Idaho, Sept. 27, 1913; A.B., U. Calif., Los Angeles, 1935; J.D., U. Mich., 1938. Admitted to Calif. bar, 1938, U.S. Supreme Ct. bar, 1942; asso. firm Goodspeed, Mc Guire, Harris & Pfaff, Los Angeles, 1939-40; asso. firm Robert W. Kenny, Los Angeles, 1940-41; atty. Office of Emergency Mgmt., Washington, 1941-42; dep. atty. gen. State of Calif., Sacramento, 1945-46; dist. atty. Mariposa County (Calif.), 1946-54; city atty. National City (Calif.), 1954-62; partner firm Curran, Golden, McDevitt & Martin, and predecessors, San Diego, 1956-63, 65-73; judge Municipal Ct., San Diego, 1963-65; of counsel Golden, McDevitt & Martin, San Diego, 1965—. Mem. State Bar Calif., Am., San Diego County bar assns. Home: 6128 Waverly Ave La Jolla CA 92037 Office: 716 San Diego Trust and Savings Bldg San Diego CA 92101 Tel (714) 238-1400

CURRAN, TIMOTHY ALEXIS, b. Hartford, Conn., Aug. 16, 1920; B.S. in Advt., U. Fla., 1964; J.D., 1967. Admitted to Fla. bar, 1967; asso. firm Same E. Murrell & Sons, Orlando, Fla., 1967-73; individual practice law, Orlando, 1973—. Mem. Fla., Orange County bar assns. Home: 7120 Lake Dr Orlando FL 32809 Office: 6021 S Orange Ave Orlando FL 32809 Tel (305) 855-7400

CURRIE, F.A., b. Vancouver, B.C., Can., Oct. 17, 1907; LL.B., U. Fla., 1932, J.D., 1967. Admitted to Fla. bar, 1932; practiced in West Palm Beach, Fla., 1932-55; judge City Ct., West Palm Beach, 1943-45, Palm Beach County Small Claims Ct., 1951-55, Small Claims-Magistrate Ct., Palm Beach County, 1955-73, Palm Beach County Ct., 1973-76, ret., 1976. Home: 200 Rugby Rd West Palm Beach FL 33405

CURRIER, THOMAS SHOLARS, b. Shreveport, La., Aug. 18, 1932; student Princeton U., 1950-52, Stanford U., 1952-53; LL.B., Tulane U., 1956. Admitted to La. bar, 1956, U.S. Supreme Ct. bar, 1965, Va. bar, 1967, D.C. bar, 1970, N.Y. bar, 1970; research asso. Yale Law Sch., 1956-57; asso. firm Stone, Pigman & Benjamin, New Orleans, 1957-59; asst. prof. law Tulane U., 1959-62, asso. prof., 1962-64; asso. prof. U. Va., 1964-67, prof., 1967-71; partner firm Mudge Rose Guthrie & Alexander, N.Y.C., 1971—; mem. labor arbitration panels Fed. Mediation and Conciliation Service, Am. Arbitration Assn. Trustee South Kent (Conn.) Sch., 1969-75, Davis and Elkins Coll., 1971—. Mem. La. State, Va. State, N.Y. State, Fed., Am. bar assns. Author: (with Forrester and Moye) Federal Jurisdiction and Procedure, 1962, rev. edit., 1970; contbr. articles to legal jours. Home: 1040 Fifth Ave New York City NY 10028 Office: 20 Broad St New York City NY 10005 Tel (212) 422-6767

CURRIN, ROBERT GRAVES, JR., b. Charleston, S.C., May 25, 1945; A.B., U. N.C., 1967; J.D., U. S.C., 1970. Admitted to S.C. bar, 1970, U.S. Dist. Ct. bar, 1971, U.S. Ct. of Appeals bar, 1974; asso. firm Nelson, Mullins, Grier & Scarborough, Columbia, S.C., 1970-74, partner, 1974—. Chmn. attys. sect. United Way for Richland-Lexington Counties, 1974. Mem. Am. (exec. council young lawyers sect. 1974-76), S.C., Richland County bar assns., S.C. Def. Attys., Am. Judicature Soc. (bd. dirs. 1974-77), Conf. on Personal Fin. Law, Phi Delta Phi, Order of Wig and Robe. Mem. editorial bd. S.C. Law Rev., 1967-70, mem. Barrister Mag., 1976—; recipient Am. Jurisprudence awards, 1967, 69; contbr. articles to legal jours. Home: 1572 Shady Ln Columbia SC 29206 Office: PO Box 11070 Columbia SC 29211 Tel (803) 799-2000

CURRY, DANIEL ARTHUR, b. Phoenix, Mar. 28, 1937; B.S., Loyola U., Los Angeles, 1957, LL.B., 1960; postgrad. U. So. Calif. Law Center, 1965. Spl. asst. to dir. circulation Times Mirror Co., Los Angeles, 1953-61; admitted to Calif. bar, 1961, Hawaii bar, 1972; asso. firm Wolford, Johnson, Pike & Covell, El Monte, Calif., 1964-65; Demetriou & Del Guercio, Los Angeles, 1965-67; counsel corp. staff divisional asst. Technicolor, Inc., Hollywood, Calif., 1967-70; with Amfac, Inc., Honolulu, 1970—, asst. v.p., 1972, corp. sec., 1972—, v.p., 1973—, gen. counsel, 1975—. Trustee Palama Settlement, Honolulu; bd. dirs. Hawaii Med. Library, Honolulu. Mem. Bar Assn. Hawaii (exec. bd.), State Bar Calif., Am. Bar Assn. Office: 700 Bishop St Honolulu HI 96813 Tel (808) 546-8111

CURRY, GRACE MARIE, b. Indpls., Mar. 1, 1928; A.B., Ind. U., 1947, J.D., 1955; M.A., Butler U., 1949. Admitted to Ind. bar, 1955; asso. firm Bingham, Summers, Welsh & Spilman, Indpls., 1957—; librarian Ind. U. Sch. Social Work, 1949-56; ct. reporter Municipal Ct. Marian County (Ind.), 1956-57. Mem. Met. Plan Commn. Marian County, 1966-68, Marian County Bd. Zoning Appeals, 1966-68. Mem. Indpls., Ind. State, Am. bar assns., Phi Beta Kappa, Order of Coif. Office: 2700 Indiana Tower Indianapolis IN 46204 Tel (317) 635-8900

CURRY, MICHAEL MCG., b. Auburn, N.Y., July 7, 1939; B.A., Syracuse U., 1965; LL.B., Yale U., 1968. Admitted to N.Y. bar, 1968, Fla. bar, 1975, U.S. Tax Ct., 1976, U.S. Supreme Ct. bar, 1977, D.C. bar, 1977; resident partner Nixon, Hargrave, Devans & Doyle, Palm Beach, Fla., 1968—. Bd. dirs. Yale Law Sch. Fund. Mem. Am., N.Y. State, Fla., Palm Beach County bar assns., E. Coast Estate Planning

Council. Home: 2121 Palm Circle Juno FL 33408 Office: 247 Royal Palm Way Palm Beach FL 33480 Tel (305) 659-6255

CURRY, ROBERT LEE, b. Lamont, Wis., May 10, 1923; B.S., Lawrence U., 1948; LL.B., U. Wis., 1953. Admitted to Wis. bar, 1953; partner firm Boardman, Suhr, Curry & Field, Madison, Wis., 1956-76; pres. Cuna Mut. Ins. Group, Madison, 1973—, pres., dir. Cuna Credit Union, 1966-70. Chmn. bd. visitors U. Wis. Law Sch., 1965-66. Mem. Am. Law Inst., U. Wis. Law Sch. Alumni Assn. (dir., pres. bd. dirs. 1968-69). Office: PO Box 391 Madison WI 53705 Tel (608) 238-5851

CURTIN, DANIEL FRANCIS, b. Beacon, N.Y., Jan. 13, 1942; B.S. in Bus. Adminstrn., U. Fla., 1963, J.D., 1966. Admitted to Fla. bar, 1966, N.Y. bar, 1969, U.S. Supreme Ct. bar, 1974; asso. prof. U. Va., 1967-68; partner firm Corbally, Gartland & Rappleyea, Poughkeepsie, N.Y., 1968—; instr. bus. law Dutchess Community Coll., 1968—. Bd. dirs. Family Counseling Service, Poughkeepsie, 1975—. Mem. N.Y. State, Dutchess County (pres. young lawyers sect.), Am. (chmn. law day, edn. in law for schs.) bar assns., Am. Bus. Law Assn., Fla. Bar. Home: 10 Old English Way Wappingers Falls NY 12590 Office: 25 Market St Poughkeepsie NY 12601 Tel (914) 454-1110

CURTIN, JOHN T., b. 1921; B.S., Canisius Coll. Admitted to N.Y. bar, 1949; formerly U.S. atty. for Western Dist. N.Y.; judge U.S. Dist. Ct. for Western N.Y., Buffalo, 1967—, now chief judge. Home: 385 Starin Ave Buffalo NY 14216 Office: US Court House Buffalo NY 14202

CURTIN, WILLIAM JOSEPH, b. Auburn, N.Y., Mar. 9, 1931; B.S., Georgetown U., 1953, J.D., 1956, LL.M., 1957. Admitted to D.C. bar, 1956, U.S. Supreme Ct. bar, 1962; asso. firm Morgan, Lewis & Bockius, Washington, 1960-64, partner 1965—. Fellow Am. Bar Found.; mem. Am. Bar Assn. (chmn. spl. com. nat. strikes in transp. industries) Bar Assn. D.C. Recipient outstanding service award Am. Arbitration Assn., 1966; John Carroll award Georgetown U., 1973. Contbr. articles to legal jours. Home: 6216 Kennedy Dr Chevy Chase MD 20015 Office: 1800 M Street NW Washington DC 20036 Tel (202) 872-5000

CURTIS, ALAN W., b. Huntington Park, Calif., Aug. 25, 1943; J.D., Pepperdine U., 1973. Admitted to Calif. bar, 1973; dep. clk. Orange County Superior Ct., 1970-74; individual practice law, Santa Ana, Calif., 1974—; planning commr. City of Santa Ana, 1976—. Bd. dirs. Santa Ana (Calif.) Guild for the Deaf, Operation Speech, Santa Ana. Mem. Am., Calif. bar assns., Assn. Trial Lawyers Am., Calif. Trial Lawyers Assn. Office: 615 Civic Center Dr W Suite 350 Santa Ana CA 92701 Tel (714) 547-8448

CURTIS, ARTHUR STAFFORD, b. Conn., Aug. 11, 1914; J.D., Georgetown U., 1953, LL.M., 1957. Admitted to Va. bar, 1953, D.C. bar, 1958, U.S. Supreme Ct. bar, 1958; individual practice law, Washington, 1953—; gen. counsel Telephone Users Assn., Inc., Washington, 1963—; prof. U.S. Naval Acad., Annapolis, Md., 1944-45; staff mem. subcom. U.S. Senate Banking and Currency Com. Mem. Nat. Press Club. Author: Greatest Army Heroes, 1969; Greatest Air Heroes, 1969; Greatest Navy Heroes, 1968; How to Save Money on Your Telephone Bills, 1972. Office: 816 Nat Press Bldg Washington DC 20045 Tel (202) 628-5696

CURTIS, JAMES ROBERT, b. Fort Worth, Oct. 4, 1905; A.B., Tex. Christian U., 1927, B.E., 1928; M.A. (Arnold fellow), So. Meth. U., 1929; LL.B., Cumberland U., 1930; J.D. (hon.), Samford U., 1969. Instr., Castle Heights Mil. Acad., Lebanon, Tenn., 1929-30; admitted to Tex. bar, 1930, U.S. Supreme Ct. bar, 1939, FCC bar, 1939; health inspector City of Fort Worth, 1930-31, State of Tex., 1931-32; since practiced in Longview, Tex., asso. firm Edwin Lacy & Assos., 1932-35; city judge, 1933-35; apptd. by Gregg County Dist. Ct. as receiver for various oil properties, 1933-35; pres. Sta. KFRO, 1934—; individual practice law, 1930—; sec., mgr. 1st Fed. Savs. & Loan Assn., 1934-36, dir., appraiser, 1936—, v.p., 1955-72, pres., 1972—; pres. Workmen's Oil Co., 1933—; owner, operator Etex Sales Co., 1934-60; sec.-treas. A.A. Canning Co., 1940-42; dir., v.p. Rogers Nat. Bank, Jefferson, Tex., 1942-50; pres. Curtis Found., 1945—, Courtesy Life Ins. Co., 1955-56, Trans-Security Investment Co., 1955-60, Nat. Security Ins. Co., 1945-62; dir. 1st Nat. Bank Longview, 1957-71; dir. Gillespie Paint Co., 1957—, SW Res. Life Ins. Co., 1959-61; chmn. J & L Petroleum Co., 1975—; owner, operator Curtis Enterprises, 1976—. Vice pres. Longview Community Chest, 1935; bd. dirs. Longview Family Counseling Center, 1975—; pres. E. Tex. Area council Girl Scouts U.S.A., 1950-52; v.p., dir. E. Tex. Area council Boy Scouts Am., 1965-67, chmn. Tewakana council, 1959-63; dir. dist. chpt. Am. Cancer Soc., 1957-58; active Tex. Commn. for the Blind, 1959-65, chmn., 1963-65; chmn. Longview Salvation Army, 1960-61, 76—; trustee Tex. Christian U., 1973—. Mem. Am., Tex. bar assns., Longview C. of C. (v.p. 1935-36), Radio Pioneers Assn., Am. Inst. Mgmt., Tex. Ind. Producers and Royalty Owners Assn. (exec. com. 1957-58), Nat. (dir. 1964-66), Tex. (sec.-treas. 1934-46) assns. broadcasters. Recipient Silver Beaver award Boy Scouts Am., 1966; Southwestern Legal Found. fellow, 1976. Home: 2118 E Marshall Ave Longview TX 75601 Office: PO Box 792 Longview TX 75601 Tel (214) 753-4461

CURTIS, LARRY ARTHUR, b. Colorado Springs, Colo., Nov. 22, 1942; B.A. in Econs. with honors, U. Calif., Los Angeles, 1964, J.D., 1967. Admitted to Calif. bar, 1968, U.S. Supreme Ct. bar, 1971; dep. county counsel Los Angeles County, 1968-73; asso. firm Musick, Peeler & Garrett, Los Angeles, 1973-75, partner, 1975—; instr. in pub. sector labor law and legis. U. Calif., Los Angeles, 1973—. Mem. Los Angeles County, Am. bar assns., Indsl. Relations Research Assn. Office: Suite 2000 One Wilshire Blvd Los Angeles CA 90017 Tel (213) 629-3322

CURTIS, RALPH VAN OLINDA, b. Bklyn., Aug. 22, 1914; B.A., Mt. Union Coll., 1936; LL.B. cum laude, Bklyn. Law Sch., 1942. Admitted to N.Y. bar, 1942; asso. firm Mendes & Mount, N.Y.C., 1948-68, partner, 1968—; dir. Phila. Reins. Corp. Trustee 1st Methodist Ch., Astoria, N.Y. Mem. Am. Bar Assn., Phi Delta Phi. Home: 33-34 Crescent St Long Island City NY 11106 Office: Mendes & Mount 27 William St New York City NY 10005 Tel (212) 344-7100

CURTIS, RICHARD DEAN, b. Payette, Idaho, Nov. 14, 1936; B.S., U. Oreg., 1959, J.D., 1961. Admitted to Oreg. bar, 1961; asso. firm Fowler & Curtis, 1962-67, firm Hansen, Curtis & Strickland, 1967-74, firm Curtis, Hendershott & Strickland, Eugene, Oreg., 1974—; municipal judge Springfield, Oreg., 1969—. Mem. Oreg., Lake County bar assns., Municipal Judges Assn. Home: 284 Harvey St Eugene OR 97404 Office: 172 E 8th Ave Eugene OR 97401 Tel (503) 687-1501

CURTIS, ROBERT MCNOWN, b. Tuscaloosa, Ala., Feb. 17, 1919; A.B., U. Ala., 1939; LL.B., U. Fla., 1946. Admitted to Fla. bar, 1946, U.S. Ct. Claims bar, 1953, U.S. Supreme Ct. bar, 1959, Tax Ct. U.S. bar; asso. firm Wallace E. Sturgis, Ocala, Fla., 1946-47; practice law, Ft. Lauderdale, Fla., 1947—; individual practice law, 1947-51, 52-53; mem. firm Robinson & Curtis, 1951-52, Saunders, Curtis & Ginestra, 1953-55, Saunders, Curtis, Ginestra & Gore, 1955-59, sr. mem., 1959; city atty. City of Ft. Lauderdale, 1959; asso. town atty. Town of Lauderdale-By-The-Sea, 1953-55. Bd. dirs. Opera Guild of Ft. Lauderdale, 1975-78; exec. com. Tower Forum, 1977; mem. Broward County Citizens Com. for Quality Edn. (chmn. fin. com.), 1965-67; chmn. North Broward Hosp. Dist., 1961-65; pres. Ft. Lauderdale Youth Center, Inc., 1949; pres. Broward County unit Am. Cancer Soc., 1953-55, Greater Ft. Lauderdale C. of C., 1976, chmn., 1977; chmn. Democratic Exec. Com., 1952-54, 66-72. Mem. Am., Broward County (pres. 1966-67), bar assns., Am., Broward County trial lawyers assns., Acad. Fla. Trial Lawyers, Am. Coll. Mortgage Atty. Home: 833 N Rio Vista Blvd Fort Lauderdale FL 33301 Office: Suite 302 Atlantic Federal Bldg 1750 E Sunrise Blvd Fort Lauderdale FL 33338 Tel (305) 525-0531

CURTISS, JOHN ARTHUR, b. Washington, June 25, 1925; B.A., U. Md., 1950; LL.B., Harvard, 1953. Admitted to D.C. bar, 1953, Fla. bar, 1958; asso. firm Pope, Ballard & Loos, Washington, 1953-58; asso. firm Macfarlane, Ferguson, Allison & Kelly, Tampa, Fla., 1958-62, partner, 1962—. Mem. Am., Tampa, Hillsborough County bar assns., Fla. Bar. Home: 4937 Bay Way Dr Tampa FL 33609 Office: 512 Florida Ave Tampa FL 33601 Tel (813) 223-2411

CURTISS, THOMAS, JR., b. Buffalo, Nov. 4, 1941; B.A., Yale, 1963; J.D., Harvard, 1970. Admitted to Calif. bar, 1971; asso. firm Musick, Peeler & Garrett, Los Angeles, 1970-72, Macdonald, Halsted & Laybourne, Los Angeles, 1972-75, partner, 1976—. Mem. Am., Los Angeles County bar assns. Judge, Hale Moot Ct. Competition U. So. Calif., 1974-75, Roger Traynor Moot Ct. Competition of Barristers, 1976. Home: 2250 Micheltorena St Los Angeles CA 90039 Office: 1200 Wilshire Blvd Suite 600 Los Angeles CA 90017 Tel (213) 481-1200

CURTISS, WILLIS DAVID, b. Sodus, N.Y., May 31, 1916; A.B., Cornell U., 1938, LL.B., 1940. Admitted to N.Y. State bar, 1940, U.S. Supreme Ct. bar, 1946; individual practice, Sodus, 1940-42; dist. atty. Wayne County, N.Y., 1941; asst. prof. law U. Buffalo, 1946-47; asst. prof. law Cornell U., Ithaca, N.Y., 1947-51, asso. prof., 1951-56, prof., 1956—; exec. sec. N.Y. State Law Revision Commn., 1956-60; mem. N.Y. Temporary Comm. on State Ct. System, 1970-73. Mem. Am., N.Y. State, Tompkins County bar assns., Am. Law Inst. Home: 108 Hampton Rd Ithaca NY 14850 Office: Law School Cornell U Ithaca NY 14853 Tel (607) 256-5135

CURTO, ERNEST b. Pentone, Italy, July 28, 1902; student Syracuse U., 1925-26, Niagara U., 1927; U. Buffalo Law Sch. 1928-31. Admitted to N.Y. bar, 1935, U.S. Dist. Ct. Western N.Y., 1937; since practiced in Niagara Falls, N.Y., mem. firms Baker-Cookman, 1935-40, Curto-Palermo, 1941-70; individual practice law, 1970—; judge City Ct., Police Ct., 1941-44; mem. N.Y. State Assembly, 1945-64; pres. Niagara Falls Musicians Assn., 1934-52; sec.-treas. N.Y. State Fedn. Musicians, 1938-44, pres. 1945-50; del. Am. Fedn. Musicians, 1934-52; chmn. Legislative and Orgn. Com., 1944-45; v.p. Niagara Falls Central Trade and Labor Council, 1952-56; mem. Indsl. Relations Assn. Exec. Counsel, 1960-72; cons. Majority Leader, N.Y. Senate, 1968-70. Mem. Niagara Falls Community Chest (v.p. 1958-59); mem. exec. bd. YMCA, 1948-50; Family and Children Soc., 1955-57; Boy Scouts Am., 1948-49; mem. Armed Forces Advisory Com., 1942-45; U.S. Selective Service Bd., 1942-45; Niagara County Recreation Commn., 1964—; Mayor's Com. on Highway Signs, 1965-66; Niagara Falls Budget Commn., 1969—; mem. exec. bd. SPUR (Soc. Promotion, Unification & Redevel. of Niagara, Inc. (chmn. Governmental Affairs Com.), 1970—); bd. mem., exec. bd. mem., v.p. Council Social Agencies, 1963-64; chmn. Mental Health Commn., Community Needs Commn., Free Camp Com.; trustee Niagara County Community Coll., 1964— (chmn. 1969-75); mem. advisory bd. trustees Niagara Univ. 1970-73; Mem. Niagara Falls, Niagara County, N.Y. State, Am. Bar Assns. Home: 782 Van Rensselaer Ave Niagara Falls NY 14305 Office: 1207 United Office Bldg Niagara Falls NY 14303 Tel (716) 285-8437

CURZAN, MYRON PAUL, b. N.Y.C., May 13, 1940; B.A., Columbia U., 1961, LL.B., 1965; M.A., Yale U., 1962. Admitted to Calif. bar, 1966, D.C. bar, 1969; clk. to Chief Justice Roger Trayner, Calif. Supreme Ct., San Francisco, 1965-66; legis. asst. to Senator Robert F. Kennedy, Washington, 1966-67; partner firm Arnold & Porter, Washington, 1967—; dir. Conn. Mut. Life Ins. Co., Scovill Mfg. Co. Advisor, Sch. Home Econs. Interior Design Program, U. N.C., 1975—; bd. overseers dept. history Columbia U., 1976—; adv. bd. Bur. Nat. Affairs Housing and Devel. Mem. Am., Calif., D.C. bar assns. Selected as exec. dir. Task Force Insured or Financed Housing Programs, Nat. Center for Housing Mgmt., Washington, 1972-73; contbr. articles to legal jours. Home: 5519 Uppingham St Chevy Chase MD 20015 Office: 1229 19th St NW Washington DC 20036 Tel (202) 872-6778

CUSACK, JOHN FRANCIS, b. Chgo., Dec. 13, 1904; Ph.B., U. Chgo., 1928, J.D., 1930. Admitted to Ill. bar, 1931; partner firm Cusack & Cusack, Chgo., 1931—; mem. Chgo. Dept. Urban Renewal, 1965—; dir. Hazeltine Research Inc., Chgo. Chmn. Friends of Chgo. Schs. Com., 1966-70; chmn. Motion Picture Appeal Bd., Chgo., 1968—; bd. dirs. South Shore Commn.; mem. Neighborhood Devel. Commn., Chgo., 1973—. Home: 9401 S Hoyne Ave Chicago IL 60620 Office: 11 S LaSalle St Suite 815 Chicago IL 60603 Tel (312) CE 6-9813

CUSACK, MARY JOSEPHINE, b. Canton, Ohio, Mar. 3, 1935; B.A., Marquette U., 1957; J.D., Ohio State U., 1959. Admitted to Ohio bar, 1959, U.S. Supreme Ct. bar, 1962; atty. Ohio Indsl. Commn., Columbus, 1960-61, Ohio Dept. Taxation, Columbus, 1961-65; partner firm Cotruvo & Cusack, Columbus, 1960—; spl. counsel to atty. gen. William J. Brown, Columbus, 1971—; interim instr. Capital U. Coll. Law, 1972-73; mem. legis. com. Ohio Commn. on Status of Women, 1972—. Mem. Ohio State (council dels., past chmn. workmen's and unemployment compensation com.), Columbus bar assns., Franklin County Trial Lawyers Assn., Nat. Assn. Women Lawyers, Women Lawyers of Franklin County (past pres.), Ohio, Franklin County (past v.p.) Democratic attys., Ohio Assn. Attys. Gen. (pres.), Kappa Beta Pi (internat. pres.). Home: 3039 Stadium Dr apt 1 Columbus OH 43202 Office: 50 W Broad St Columbus OH 43215 Tel (614) 224-7888

CUSCIK, CHARLES HARRISON, b. Portland, Oreg., Aug. 8, 1938; B.S., Portland State U., 1963; J.D., Lewis Clark Coll., 1968. Admitted to Oreg. bar, 1968; dep. dist. atty. Multnomah County, Oreg., 1968-69; partner firm Pewsey & Cusick, Lincoln City, 1971-72, firm Cuscik & Poling, Lincoln City, 1972-74; individual practice law, Lincoln City, 1974—; asso. firm Hershiser & Mitchell, Portland, 1968. City councilman Lincoln City, 1974-78; mem. Selective Service Bd., 1971-76. Mem. Oreg. State Bar, Lincoln County Bar (pres. 1976—). Office: 3516 S E Hwy 101 PO Box 806 Lincoln City OR 97367 Tel (503) 996-2541

CUSHENBERY, LEAFORD FRANKLIN, b. Freedom, Okla., July 2, 1908; LL.B./J.D., Washburn U., 1934. Admitted to Kans. bar, 1934; partner firm Tincher, Raleigh & Cushenbery, Hutchinson, Kans., 1934-44, Bremer & Cushenbery, Oberlin, Kans., 1946-55, Cushenbery & Lund, Oberlin, 1955-72; ret., 1972; county atty. Decatur County (Kans.), 1946-47; mem. Kans. State Legislature, 1955-56. Chmn. Oberlin chpt. ARC, 1947-51. Contbr. articles to legal jours. Address: 401 N Wilson St Oberlin KS 67749 Tel (913) 475-3155

CUSHMAN, BERNARD, b. Malden, Mass., Nov. 26, 1911; A.B., Dartmouth, 1934; LL.B., Harvard, 1939; Admitted to Mass. bar, 1939, D.C. bar, 1947, U.S. Supreme Ct. bar, 1948; individual practice law, Mass., 1939-41; staff atty. Mass. Atty. Gen.'s office, 1939-41; asst. to bd. mem. NLRB, 1942-43, trial examiner, 1943-44, spl. asst. to gen. counsel, 1966-69; asst. gen. counsel, disputes sect. Nat. War Labor Bd., 1945; chief legis. and bur. services sect. Dept. Labor, 1946-47; atty. Labor Bur. Middle West, Washington, 1947-60; gen. counsel Amalgamated Assn. of St., Electric Ry. and Motor Coach Employees Am., Washington, 1960-64; ad hoc arbitrator, Washington, 1965; of counsel Bredhoff, Gottesman & Cohen, Washington, 1969-71; partner firm, Bredhoff, Cushman, Gottesman & Cohen, Washington, 1972-77; full-time arbitrator, Silver Spring, Md., 1977—; arbitrator, mem. panels Fed. Mediation and Conciliation Service, 1965—, Am. Arbitration Assn., 1965—, Nat. Mediation Bd., 1973—. Pres., Parkside Civic Assn., Silver Spring, Md., 1960. Mem. Am., D.C. bar assns., Indsl. Relations Research Assn., Soc. Profls. in Dispute Resolution, Phi Beta Kappa. Contbr. articles to legal jours. Home and Office: 9203 Summit Rd Silver Spring MD 20910 Tel (301) 587-4344

CUSHMAN, EDWARD HOWARD, b. Phila., Jan. 22, 1897; LL.B., Temple U., 1920. Admitted to Pa. bar, 1920, Fla. bar, 1970; partner firm Pepper, Hamilton & Scheetz, Phila., 1969—; gen. counsel Nat. Assn. Surety Bond Producers, Washington, 1951—. Mem. nat. exec. com. Union Am. Hebrew Congregations, 1950-63; mem. nat. exec. com. Am. Jewish Com., 1950-59. Mem. Phila. (bd. govs.), Pa. (exec. com.), Am. bar assns., The Fla. Bar. Author: Law of Mechanics' Liens in Pennsylvania, 1926; Bonds on Public Improvements, ann. 1932—; contbr. articles to legal jours. Home: 1108 Harbour House N 10295 Collins Ave Bal Harbour FL 33154 Office: 1000 1st Nat Bank Bldg Miami FL 33131 Tel (305) 358-6300

CUSIMANO, GREGORY STEPHEN, b. Gadsden, Ala., Aug. 18, 1943; B.S., U. Ala., 1965, J.D., 1968. Admitted to Ala. bar, 1968; asso. firm Hawkins & Rhea, Gadsden, 1968-70; partner firm Hawkins, Rhea, Keener & Cusimano, Gadsden, 1970-73, Keener & Cusimano, Gadsden, 1973-76, Keener, Cusimano & Cardwell, Gadsden, 1976—; spl. asst. atty. gen. State of Ala., 1975—; spl. atty. Ala. Dept. Pensions and Security, 1975—; dir. Citizens Bank of Glencoe, 1977—. Bd. dirs. Gadsden YMCA, 1973-76. Mem. Ala. (code of Ala. revision com., exec. com. 1976—), Am., Etowah County (pres. 1977—) trial lawyers assns., Ala., Am. bar assns. Named Outstanding Man of Year Etowah County (Ala.), 1971. Office: 827 Chestnut St Gadsden AL 35901 Tel (205) 547-7583

CUTLER, A. BUDD, b. Haddonfield, N.J., June 25, 1922; B.B.A., U. Md., 1943; J.D. cum laude, U. Miami, 1950, LL.M. in Taxation, 1972. Admitted to Fla. bar, 1950, U.S. Supreme Ct. bar, 1965, U.S. Tax Ct. bar, 1974; partner firm Cohen, Shapiro, Polisher, Shiekman & Cohen, Phila., and Miami, Fla., 1976—; instr. legal aspects of health care Fla. Internat. U., 1974-77. Pres., YM and YWHA of Greater Miami, 1961-64; pres. Fla. Health and Welfare Council, 1968-69, Health Systems Agency of S. Fla., 1975-76. Mem. Am., Dade County, Miami Beach (dir. 1953-55) bar assns., Nat. Health Lawyers Assn., Nu Beta Epsilon, Beta Gamma Sigma. Home: 12940 SW 73d Ave Miami FL 33156 Office: 3050 Biscayne Blvd Miami FL 33137 Tel (305) 573-6111

CUTLER, FELICE REINITZ, b. N.Y.C., Apr. 15, 1937; B.A., Bklyn. Coll., 1957; LL.B., Yale, 1960. Admitted to Calif. bar, 1961; U.S. 9th Circuit Ct. Appeals bar, 1961, U.S. 3rd Circuit Ct. Appeals bar, 1975; dep. atty. gen., Calif., 1960-66; partner firm Cutler & Cutler, Los Angeles, 1966—. Mem. Calif. State Dem. Central Com., 1962-64; Los Angeles County Dem. Com. (treas. 1963-64). Mem. Am., Calif., Los Angeles County Bar Assns., Phi Beta Kappa. Office: 700 S Flower Los Angeles CA 90017 Tel (213) 622-2117

CUTLER, MITCHELL S., b. Quincy, Mass., Sept. 24, 1933; B.S. in Fgn. Service cum laude, Georgetown U., 1955; LL.B. with distinction, George Washington U., 1958. Admitted to D.C. bar, Md. bar; asso. firm Welch, Mott & Morgan, 1958-60; spl. asst. White House, Washington, 1960-61; asso. firm Klagsbrunn, Haynes & Irwin, Washington, 1961-62; house counsel Disc, Inc., Washington, 1962-64; partner firm Foreman, Cutler & Diamond, 1964-69, Danzansky, Dickey, Tydings, Quint & Gordon, Washington, 1970—; adj. prof. law Georgetown U.; cons. real estate adv. com. SEC, 1972. Mem. D.C., Md., Fed., Am. bar assns. Editor in chief George Washington U. Law Rev.; editor and pub. Nat. Property Law Digests; contbr. articles to legal jours. Home: 13 Darby Ct Bethesda MD 20034 Office: 1120 Connecticut Ave NW Washington DC 20036 Tel (202) 331-8700

CUTNER, HELEN H., b. Pitts., Sept. 26, 1933; student Wilmington Coll., N.Y. U., New Sch. for Social Research, 1950-60; B.A. in Social Scis., Temple U., 1964; J.D., 1967. Admitted to Pa., D.C. bars, 1967; asso. firm Dilworth, Paxson, Kalish, Kohn & Levy, Phila., 1967-70, Wolf, Block, Schorr & Solis-Cohen, Phila., 1970-72; sr. litigation atty. for Eastern seabord Atlantic Richfield Co., 1972-75; individual practice law, Phila., 1975—. Mem. Nat. Assn. Women Lawyers, Phila. Bar Assn. Home: 2220 1/2 Lombard St Philadelphia PA 19146 Office: 629 Land Title Bldg Philadelphia PA 19110 Tel (215) LO3-5505

CUTSHAW, JOHN WILLIAM, JR., b. Cambridge City, Ind., Jan. 5, 1932; B.S., Purdue U., 1953; J.D., Ind. U., 1960. Admitted to Ind. bar, 1960, U.S. Supreme Ct. bar, 1974; individual practice law, Cambridge City, 1960—; atty. Cambridge City schs., 1963—, Cambridge City, 1964—. Mem. Selective Service Bd., Wayne County, Inc., 1964-75. Mem. Am., Ind. State, Wayne County bar assns. Home: Rural Route 1 Wagner Rd Cambridge City IN 47327 Office: 15 N Foote St Cambridge City IN 47327 Tel (317) 478-3737

CUTTER, RICHARD AMMI, b. Salem, Mass., May 11, 1902; A.B., Harvard, 1922, LL.B., 1925; S.J.D. (hon.), Suffolk U., 1960. Admitted to Mass. bar, 1926; asso. firm Goodwin, Procter, Field & Hoar, Boston, 1925-27; asst. atty. gen. Mass., 1927-30; adviser to gov. P.R., 1930-31; partner firm Palmer, Dodge, Gardner & Bradford and predecessor, 1931-42, 46-56; asso. justice Mass. Supreme Jud. Ct., 1956-72; miscellaneous assignments as spl. master and arbitrator,

Cambridge, Mass., 1972—. Mem. Am. Law Inst. (pres. 1976—, mem. council 1949—), Am., Mass., Boston bar assns., Harvard Law Sch. Assn. (pres. 1971-73). Home: 62 Sparks St Cambridge MA 02138 Tel (617) 876-0032

CYCMANICK, MICHAEL FLOYD, b. Milw., July 25, 1943; student Orlando Jr. Coll., 1961-64; student Fla. So. U., 1964-65; J.D. cum laude, Stetson U., 1968. Admitted to Fla. bar, 1968, U.S. Supreme Ct. bar, 1972; law clk. to judge U.S. Dist. Ct., Middle Dist. Fla., 1968-70; asso. firm James M. Russ, Orlando, 1970-75; individual practice law, Orlando, 1975-77; judge Orange County (Fla.) Ct., 1977—. Mem. Am., Orange County bar assns., Am. Trial Lawyers Assn., Fla. Bar, Nat. Assn. Criminal Def. Lawyers. Recipient Walter Mann award Stetson U., 1968, Maria G. Martin award, 1968. Home: 9999 Lake Georgia Dr Maitland FL 32751 Office: 46 E Robinson St Orlando FL 32801 Tel (305) 420-3674

CYNAR, WALTER PETER, b. Hamtramck, Mich., Nov. 14, 1919; A.B., Western Mich. U., 1943; postgrad. Georgetown U. Law Sch., 1945, Am. U., 1945; LL.B., U. Detroit, 1949; postgrad. Wayne State U., 1951; grad. Nat. Coll. State Judiciary, 1972. Admitted to Mich. bar, 1949, U.S. Supreme Ct. bar, 1964; asso. firm Jamieson, Erickson, Dyll, Marentay and Van Alburg, Detroit, 1949-59, firm Cynar, Michaels and Olzark, Mount Clemens, Mich., 1959-66; judge Mich. Circuit Ct., 16th Jud. Circuit, 1967—; chmn. Warren (Mich.) Crime Commn., 1968-70; mem. Macomb County (Mich.) Law Enforcement and Criminial Justice Planning Council; past mem. Clinton Twp. Civil Service Commn. Trustee St. Mary's Coll., Orchard Lake, Mich.; regent Orchard Lake Schs.; asst. counsel Detroit Area council Boy Scouts Am.; corp. mem. Boys' Club of Met. Detroit. Mem. Mich. (past dir. negligence sect., treas. family law sect.), Macomb County (past dir.) bar assns., Mich. Judges Assn., Nat. Advs. Soc., Advs. Club Detroit (dir. 1973). Mich. Acad. Named Hon. Alumnus Orchard Lake Sch., 1972, Outstanding Vol. Leader, Boys' Clubs of Met. Detroit, 1975-76; recipient St. George emblem Boy Scouts Am., 1971, award of Merit, 1973, Silver Beaver award, 1975; Polonia award Central Citizens Com., Detroit, 1972; Friend of Boy award, 1973-74; named to Hamtramck High Hall of Honor, 1975. Home: 32012 Aline Dr Warren MI 48093 Office: Macomb County Ct Bldg Mount Clemens MI 48043 Tel (313) 469-5041

CZAJKOWSKI, FRANK HENRY, b. Bklyn., Jan. 7, 1936; B.A., St. John's U., Bklyn., 1957, J.D., 1959; LL.M., George Washington U., 1966. Claims adjustor Hartford Accident & Indsl. Ins. Co., N.Y.C., 1959-60; agt. Equitable Life Assurance Soc., N.Y.C., 1960; admitted to N.Y. bar, 1960, U.S. Supreme Ct. bar, 1964, Pa. bar, 1970, Conn. bar, 1974; atty. Corp. Counsel's Office, N.Y.C., 1960-62, Fgn. Claims Settlement Commn., Washington, 1962-68, Atlantic-Richfield Co., N.Y.C., 1968-70, Phila., 1970-72; employee relations counsel Stauffer Chem. Co., Westport, Conn., 1972—; instr. Fairfield U. Center for Lifetime Learning, 1976; arbitrator Am. Arbitration Assn. Mem. Am., Conn. bar assns., Westchester-Fairfield Corp. Counsel Assn. Office: Stauffer Chem Co Nyala Farms Rd Westport CT 06880 Tel (203) 222-4082

CZARRA, EDGAR FRANK, JR., b. White Rock, Pa., Oct. 4, 1928; B.S., Yale, 1949, LL.B., 1952. Admitted to D.C. bar, 1952, U.S. Supreme Ct. bar, 1959; asso. firm Covington & Burling, Washington, 1952-63, partner, 1963—. Mem. D.C., FCC bar assns. Office: 888 16th St NW Washington DC 20006 Tel (202) 452-6066

DAANE, (GILBERT) WARREN, b. Grand Rapids, Mich., Apr. 15, 1911; B.A., Princeton, 1932; J.D., U. Mich., 1935. Admitted to Mich. bar, 1935, Ohio bar, 1936, U.S. Supreme Ct. bar, 1953; asso. firm Baker, Hostetler & Patterson, Cleve., 1935-50, partner, 1951—. Mem. Bar Assn. Greater Cleve., Ohio State, Am. bar assns., Phi Beta Kappa, Order of Coif, Phi Delta Phi. Office: 1956 Union Commerce Bldg Cleveland OH 44115 Tel (216) 621-0200

DAAR, DAVID, b. Chgo., May 23, 1931; A.B., Sacramento State Coll., 1955; J.D., Loyola U., Los Angeles, 1956. Admitted to Calif. bar, 1956, U.S. Supreme Ct. bar, 1960; with firm David Daar & Assos., Los Angeles, 1956-75; partner firm Daar & Newman, P.C., Los Angeles, 1975—; lectr. in field of maj. litigation, class actions and securities. Mem. Am. (faculty Nat. Coll. Advocacy 1971—), Calif. trial lawyers assns., State Bar Calif. (chmn. com. on fed. cts. 1973). Office: Suite 904 700 S Flower St Los Angeles CA 90017 Tel (213) 629-2111

DABA, RAYMOND JOSEPH, b. San Mateo, Calif., Dec. 17, 1916; A.A., Coll. San Mateo, 1935; A.B., Stanford U., 1937, J.D., 1940. Admitted to Calif. bar, 1940; asso. firm E.E. Hoffmann, San Mateo, 1940-43; mem. firm, 1943-53, partner firm Wagstaffe, Daba & Hulse, and predecessors, Redwood City, Calif., 1953-68; municipal ct. judge City of San Mateo, 1943; state inheritance referee Calif., San Mateo County, 1968—. Vice pres. Calif. State Bd. Edn., 1958-66; trustee Calif. State Coll., 1960-62; mem. Coordinating Council Higher Edn., 1963. Mem. Am., San Mateo County bar assns., State Bar Calif. (gov.). Office: 333 Bradford St POB 5009 Redwood City CA 94063 Tel (415) 366-9594

DACEY, KATHLEEN RYAN, b. Boston; A.B. with honors, Emmanuel Coll., Boston, 1941; M.S. in Library Sci. (Mass. Library Assn. scholar), Simmons Coll., 1942; LL.B., Northeastern U., 1945, J.D., 1945; postgrad. Boston U. Law Sch., 1945-46. Admitted to Mass. bar, 1945, U.S. Supreme Ct. bar, 1957; law clk. to justices Mass. Supreme Jud. Ct., 1945-47; practiced in Boston, 1947-75; asst. atty. gen., chief civil bur. Mass. Dep. Atty. Gen., Boston, 1975—; auditor, master Commonwealth of Mass., 1972-75, Suffolk and Norfolk Counties (Mass.), 1972-75; asst. dist. atty. Suffolk County, 1971-72; mem. panel def. counsel for indigent persons U.S. Dist. Ct., Dist. Mass.; lectr., speaker in field. Bd. dirs. Mission United Neighborhood Improvement Team, Boston; mem. Boston Sch. Com., 1945-46, chmn., 1946-47. Mem. Am., Internat., Boston, Mass., Norfolk, Middlesex bar assns., Am., Mass. trial lawyers assns., Mass., Nat. (pres.) assns. women lawyers, Internat. Fedn. Women Lawyers, Boston U. Law Sch. Alumni Assn. (corr. sec. 1974-76), Boston U. Nat. Alumni Council. Recipient Oratorical Contest prize Am. Legion; named Alumnae Woman of Year Northeastern U. Law Sch. Alumni Assn., 1976; contbr. articles to legal jours., The Standard, New Eng. Ins. Weekly; contbr. poems to Ethos. Office: 100 State St Boston MA 02109 Tel (617) 742-3885

DACHS, NORMAN HOWARD, b. Bklyn., Mar. 5, 1933; B.A., Bklyn. Coll., 1952; J.D., Bklyn. Law Sch., 1954. Admitted to N.Y. bar, 1954; sr. partner firm Shayne, Dachs, Weiss, Kolbrener, Stanisci & Harwood, Mineola, N.Y.; mem. faculty Adelphi U.; lectr. in field; arbitrator N.Y.C. Civil Ct., 1965—. Trustee Hillel Sch., Lawrence, N.Y., Young Israel, Woodmere, N.Y. Mem. N.Y. State, Nassau County bar assns., Am., N.Y. State trial lawyers assns. Co-editor: Art of Evaluating Personal Injury Cases, 1972; contbg. author: Making a Personal Injury Practice Profitable, 1972; contbr. articles to legal jours. Home: 800 Bryant St Woodmere NY 11598 Office: 1501 Franklin Ave Mineola NY 11501

D'ADDARIO, RICHARD PETER, b. N.Y.C., Jan. 29, 1947; A.B., Boston Coll., 1968; J.D., N.Y. U., 1971. Admitted to R.I. bar, 1971; staff atty. mng. atty. R.I. Legal Services, Inc., Providence, 1971-76; legal vol. VISTA, 1971-72. Mem. bd. Child and Family Services of Newport County, pres., 1977—; bd. dirs. VISTA Vols. of Newport County; chmn. legal task force R.I. Coalition for Children's Rights; mem. Human Rights Com. R.I. Mental Health Services for Children; chmn. E. Bay chpt. R.I. affiliate ACLU, 1972-73; mem. R.I. adv. com. U.S. Commn. on Civil Rigts; bd. dirs. Jonnycake Center of Newport County; mem. Newport County Concerned Citizens About Corrections, Foster Family Resource Project. Mem. R.I., Newport County bar assns., Am. Assn. Trial Lawyers. Office: 10 Bull St Newport RI 02840 Tel (401) 847-0171

DADE, MALCOLM, b. Camden, Ark., Mar. 3, 1935; B.A., N. Tex. State U., 1956; LL.B., U. Tex. at Austin, 1962. Admitted to Tex. bar, 1962, U.S. Supreme Ct. bar, 1974; briefing atty. Ct. of Criminal Appeals, Austin, Tex., 1962-63; asst. dist. atty. Dallas County (Tex.), 1963-69; individual practice law, Dallas, 1969—; officer JAGC, USAR, 1965—. Mem. Dallas, Am. bar assns., Dallas County Criminal Bar Assn., Tex. Criminal Def. Lawyers Assn. Office: 1620 Fidelity Union Tower Dallas TX 75201 Tel (214) 744-2283

DADISMAN, STANLEY EVERETT, b. Philippi, W.Va., July 27, 1908; A.B., Broaddus Coll., 1930; LL.B., W.Va. U., 1934, J.D., 1968. Admitted to W.Va. bar, 1934, U.S. Supreme Ct. bar, 1960; sec. to gov. W.Va., 1936-40; mem. firm McClintic, James, Wise, and Dadisman, Charleston, W.Va., 1946-58; prof. law W.Va. U. Coll. Law, Morgantown, 1957-68; sr. law clk. U.S. Dist. Ct. So. Dist. W.Va., Charleston, 1971-75; jud. asst. to justice W.Va. Supreme Ct., 1977—; mem. W.Va. Constl. Revision Com., 1957-63, W.Va. Crime and Delinquency Council, 1964-68; W.Va. state dir. probation and parole, 1939-41; chmn. W.Va. State Bar legal ethics com., 1954-56. Mem. W.Va. Bar Assn., Monongalia Hist. Soc., Am. Legion. Home and Office: 224 Hagans Ave Morgantown WV 26505 Tel (304) 292-4275

D'AGOSTINO, HARRY JOHN, b. Watervliet, N.Y., July 19, 1931; B.A. cum laude, Siena Coll., 1953; LL.B., Albany Law Sch., 1955, J.D., 1968. Admitted to N.Y. state bar, 1955; asso. Brookstein & Zubres and successors, Albany, N.Y., 1955-60, partner, 1960—; justice Town of Colonie (N.Y.), 1960-73; dir., sec. Manufacturers Hanover Trust Co., 1966—. Chmn. Republican Party, Town of Colonie, 1973—; vestryman St. Peter's Episcopal Ch., Albany, 1974—. Mem. Albany County (pres., 1976), N.Y. state, Am. bar assns., N.Y. State Assn Magistrates, Albany-Schenectady County Magistrates Assn., C. of C. (dir.). Office: 90 State St Albany NY 12207 Tel (518) 463-2251

DAHAR, VICTOR WILLIAM, b. Nashua, N.H., Jan. 5, 1930; J.D., Boston Coll., 1958. Admitted to N.H. bar, 1958, Mass. bar, 1958; individual practice law, Manchester, N.H., 1958—; instr. law N.H. Coll., 1961-65. Dir., Info. Center on Immigration, 1963-65; chmn. Manchester chpt. March of Dimes, 1964, Hillsborough County chpt., 1968-69, N.H. chpt., 1970-76; chmn. Manchester chpt. Multiple Sclerosis Soc., 1966, v.p., 1967, pres., 1968, bd. dirs. 1968-76; mem. com. on instruction and curriculum, chmn. site com., mem. joint bd., sch. bd. and alderman com. Manchester Sch. Bd., 1962-66. Mem. Am., N.H., Manchester bar assns., Am. Trial Lawyers Assn. Home: 100 Esty St Manchester NH 03101 Office: 814 Elm St Manchester NH 03101 Tel (603) 622-6595

DAHL, RICHARD CHARLES, b. San Francisco, Nov. 21, 1921; B.A., U. Calif., Berkeley, 1947; B.L.S., 1951; J.D., Catholic U., Wash., D.C., 1958. Admitted to D.C. bar, 1958; law librarian Univ. Calif., Berkeley, 1951-53, Univ. Nebr., Lincoln, 1954-56; with Dept. treasury, Washington, 1961-63; state law librarian State Washington, Olympia, 1963-66; prof., dir. law library Ariz. State Univ., Tempe, 1966—. Author: (with John Whelan) Mil. Dictionary, 1960, (with Connie Bolden) The Am. Judge: A Bibliography, 1968; (with Robert Davis) Effective Speaking for Lawyers, 1969. Home: 6916 E Mariposa Dr Scottsdale AZ 85251 Office: College Law Library Arizona State University Tempe AZ 85281 Tel (602) 965-6141

DAHL, ROBERT EMMETT, b. Grafton, N.D., May 4, 1919; B.C.S., U. N.D., 1941, J.D., 1948. Admitted to N.D. bar, 1948; mem. firm Dahl, Dahl & Greenagel, and predecessor, Grafton, 1948—; atty. City of Grafton, 1954-58, mayor, 1974—. Mem. Walsh County (N.D.) (pres. 1964-65), 2d Jud. Dist. (pres. 1960-62), Am. (chmn. com. on assistance to sole practitioners and small firms sect. gen. practice 1974—, ho. of dels. 1974—) bar assns., U. N.D. Law Found. (pres. 1964-65), State Bar Assn. N.D. (pres. 1965-66), Am. Judicature Soc., Nat. Conf. Bar Pres.'s, Order of Coif, Phi Alpha Delta. Office: PO Box 634 Grafton ND 58237 Tel (701) 352-0470

DAHLGREN, JOHN ONSGARD, b. Missoula, Mont., Sept. 7, 1913; B.A., George Washington U., 1936; J.D., Georgetown U., 1939. Admitted to D.C. bar, 1939, U.S. Supreme Ct. bar, 1950, Md. bar, 1961; chief counsel requisition div. Bd. Econ. Warfare, Washington, 1941-42; partner firm Dahlgren & Close, Washington, 1946—. Pres. Internat. Humanities, Inc., 1960—. Mem. Inter-Am. Bar Found. (dir.), D.C., Am., Inter-Am. (sec. gen. 1967—) bar assns., Bar Assn. D.C., Am. Soc. Internat. Law. Contbg. editor: Lawyer of the Americas, 1973—. Home: 4952 Sentinel Dr Bethesda MD 20016 Office: 1000 Connecticut Ave NW Washington DC 20036 Tel (202) 659-1440

DAHMS, RICHARD WILLIAM, b. Deepwater, Mo., Oct. 4, 1931; B.S.B.A., Central Mo. State U., 1953; J.D., U. Mo., Columbia, 1956. Admitted to Mo. bar, 1956; asst. atty. gen. State of Mo., 1956-58; practiced in Macon, Mo., 1959, St. Joseph, Mo., 1963-66; asst. city atty. City of St. Joseph, 1959-60; asst. pros. atty. Buchanan County, Mo., 1960-62; judge Buchanan County Probate Ct., 1966—. Mem. Mo. Bar Assn., Nat. Coll. Probate Judges, Mo. Assn. Probate Judges. Home: 2109 Lovers Ln Saint Joseph MO 64505 Office: Probate Ct Buchanan County Courthouse Saint Joseph MO 64501 Tel (816) 279-5661

DAIL, JOSEPH GARNER, JR., b. Elloree, S.C., June 15, 1932; B.S., U. N.C., 1953, J.D. with honors, 1955. Admitted to N.C. bar, 1955, D.C. bar, 1959, U.S. Supreme Ct. bar, 1963, Va. bar, 1976; with Turney and Turney, Washington, 1959-66; partner firm Croft and Dail, Washington, 1966-69, Croft, Dail and Vance, 1970-76; individual practice law, McLean, Va., 1976—. Mem. Am., Fed. N.C., Va. bar assns., Assn. ICC Practitioners, Motor Carrier Lawyers Assn. (recipient Distinguished Service award 1976). Asso. editor N.C. Law Rev., 1954-55. Home: 1101 Flor Ln McLean VA 22101 Office: 6810 Fleetwood Rd PO Box 567 McLean VA 22101 Tel (703) 893-3050

DAILEY, LOUIS IRVING, b. Torrance, Miss., Aug. 25, 1902; B.S., U. Miss., 1922, LL.B., 1924. Admitted to Miss. bar, 1924, Tenn. bar, 1951, U.S. Supreme Ct. bar, 1958; sr. field trial atty. ICC, Little Rock, 1938-51; asso. firm Wrape and Hernly, Memphis, 1952-70; individual practice law, Memphis, 1970—. Mem. Memphis-Shelby County, Tenn. bar assns., Motor Carrier Lawyers Assn. Home: 4041 N Rose Rd Memphis TN 38117 Office: 2208 Sterick Bldg Memphis TN 38103 Tel (901) 527-3106

DAILY, ARTHUR CONRAD, b. Washington, Jan. 24, 1941; A.B., N.Y. U., 1965; J.D. (Storke scholar), U. Colo., 1968. Admitted to Colo. bar, 1968; asso. firm Holland & Hart, Colo., 1968-69, Aspen, Colo., 1969—, partner, 1973—; city atty. City of Aspen, 1972-73. Mem. Denver, Colo., Pitkin County bar assns., Order of Coif. Home: 639 Hunter Creek Dr Aspen CO 81611 Office: 434 E Cooper St Aspen CO 81611 Tel (303) 925-3476

DAISLEY, GORDON WALFORD, b. Bklyn., Apr. 2, 1902; B.S., U.S. Naval Acad., 1923; LL.B., George Washington U., 1933. Admitted to D.C. bar, 1932, Va. bar, 1976, U.S. Supreme Ct. bar, 1935, U.S. Ct. Customs and Patent Appeals bar, 1937. Asso. firm Cameron, Kerkam & Sutton, Washington, 1929-38, partner, 1938-72; partner firm Cameron, Kerkam, Sutton, Stowell & Stowell, Washington, 1972—; engr. C&P Telephone Co., Washington, 1924-29. Mem. Am., D.C. bar assns., Am. Patent Law Assn. Home: 6419 Brookside Dr Chevy Chase MD 20015 Office: 2341 Jefferson Davis Hwy Arlington VA 22202 Tel (703) 920-8980

DALE, ERWIN RANDOLPH, b. Herrin, Ill., July 30, 1915; B.A., U. Tex. at El Paso, 1937; J.D., 1943. Admitted to Tex. bar, 1943, D.C. bar, 1953, Mich. bar, 1956, N.Y. state bar, 1960; atty. IRS, Washington, 1943-56, chief reorgn. and dividend br., 1954-56; mem. legal staff Gen. Motors Corp., Detroit, 1956-57; partner firm Chapman, Walsh & O-Connell, N.Y.C. and Washington, 1957-59; partner firm Hawkins, Delafield & Wood, N.Y.C., 1959—; dir. Md. Electronics Mfg. Co., 1948-58, Renaissance Corp., 1968-75, Shamcon Reconstrn. Corp., 1968-75. Mem. Am., Tex., N.Y. State bar assns., Assn. Bar City N.Y., Tax Inst. Am., Nat. Tax Assn. Contbr. numerous articles to profl. jours. Home: 4 Campton Rd Bronxville NY 10708 Office: 67 Wall St New York City NY 10005 Tel (212) 952-4813

DALE, JAMES ALBERT, III, b. Columbus, Miss., Sept. 13, 1940; student Miss. State U., 1958-60; B.A., U. Miss., 1963, J.D., 1966. Admitted to Miss. bar, 1966; partner firm Barnett & Dale, Carthage, Miss., 1966-68; individual practice law, Columbus, Miss., 1968—; city judge Columbus, 1974. Chmn. Lowndes County Heart Fund. Mem. Am., Miss. bar assns., Miss. Trial Lawyers Assn. Office: 512 2d Ave N Columbus MS 39701 Tel (601) 327-1400

DALE, LON JAMES, b. Great Falls, Mont., Nov. 11, 1945; Admitted to Mont. bar; partner firm Milodragovich, Dale & Dye, Missoula, Mont.; dep. county atty. Missoula County, 1973-75. Mem. Am., Mont. bar assns., Am. Judicature Soc. Office: 800 S 3d St Missoula MT 59801 Tel (406) 728-1455

DALES, EDWARD SCOTT, b. Riverside, Calif., Jan. 7, 1923; A.A., N. Mex. Mil. Inst., 1942; LL.B., U. So. Calif., 1950. Admitted to Calif. bar, 1951; asso. firm Best, Best & Krieger, Riverside, 1951; dep. dist. atty. Riverside County, 1951-53, chief trial dep., 1953-54; individual practice law, Riverside, 1954-56; pub. defender Riverside County, 1956-61; judge Riverside Municipal Ct., 1961-66; judge Riverside County Superior Ct., 1966—, presiding judge, 1971, 76-77. Mem. Jud. Council Calif., Conf. Calif. Judges. Recipient Traffic Ct. Procedures award Am. Bar Assn., 1962, Trial Judge of Year award Calif. Trial Lawyers Assn., 1973. Office: 4050 Main St Riverside CA 92501 Tel (714) 787-6101

DALESSANDRO, ARTHUR DOMINICK, b. Pittston, Pa., Aug. 24, 1926; B.S., Wilkes Coll., 1949; LL.D., Dickinson Sch. Law, 1954. Admitted to Pa. bar, 1954; practiced in Luzerne County, Pa., and other locations; judge Luzerne County Ct. of Common Pleas, 1971—. Active Luzerne County Mental Health Assn., Luzerne County Assn. for Retarded Children. Mem. Pa. Conf. State Trial Judges, Am. Judges Assn., Am. Judicature Soc., Pa. Bar Assn., Wilkes-Barre (Pa.) Law and Library Assn., Luzerne County Court En Banc (sec.). Office: Luzerne County Courthouse Wilkes-Barre PA 18702 Tel (717) 823-6161

DALEY, JOHN THOMAS, b. Boston, Mar. 11, 1940; A.B., Harvard, 1961, LL.B., 1964. Admitted to Mass. bar, 1967, U.S. Dist. Ct. Mass. bar, 1968; mem. faculty U. E. Africa, 1964-66; asso. firm Nutter, McClennen & Fish, Boston, 1966-68; mem. faculty New Eng. Sch. Law, 1973—, Suffolk Law Sch., 1976—; asso. firm Dane, Howe & Brown, Boston, 1968-75, partner, 1976—. Mem. W. Local Adv. Council, Boston, 1970-73, v.p., 1971-72; pres. Eire Soc. Boston, 1974-75. Mem. Mass., Boston bar assns. Home: 49 Paul Revere Rd Needham MA 02194 Office: 73 Tremont St Boston MA 02108 Tel (617) 227-3600

DALLAM, ROGER IRVIN, b. New Orleans, Nov. 15, 1943; A.B., Loyola U., 1965, J.D., 1968. Admitted to La. bar, 1968, U.S. Dist. Ct. bar for Eastern Dist. La., 1969, U.S. 5th Circuit Ct. Appeals bar, 1970, U.S. Supreme Ct. bar, 1971; asso. firm Greenberg & Dallam and predecessors, Gretna, La., 1968-71, partner, 1971—. Mem. La. State, Am., Jefferson Parish (La.) bar assns., Am., La. trial lawyers assns. Office: 848 2d St Gretna LA 70053 Tel (504) 366-6491

DALSIMER, VINCENT SIDNEY, b. Cin., Jan. 11, 1921; J.D., magna cum laude, Southwestern U., 1949; LL.D., Pepperdine U., 1975. Admitted to Calif. bar, 1950; dep. atty. gen., Calif., 1951; practice in Bellflower, Calif., 1950, 52-58; dir. Calif. Dept. Consumer Affairs, Sacramento, 1959-61; judge Calif. Superior Ct., 1961—; adj. prof. law Pepperdine U., 1964—, dean Sch. Law, 1965-70, asso. dean, 1970—; Councilman City of Bellflower, 1957, vice-mayor, 1958. Mem. Assn. Calif. Judges. Office: 12720 Norwalk Blvd Norwalk CA 90650 Tel (213) 773-8870

DALTON, EDWARD CARROLL, JR., b. Cambridge, Mass., Apr. 14, 1942; B.S., U. Notre Dame, 1964; J.D., U. Maine, 1967. Admitted to Maine bar, 1967; partner firm Cram & Dalton, Falmouth, Maine, 1967—. Mem. Am., Maine, Cumberland County bar assns., Am., Maine trial lawyers assns. Home: 50C Spunwink Ave Cape Elizabeth ME 04107 Office: 251 US Route 1 Falmouth ME 04105 Tel (207) 781-2830

DALTON, JACK EWALT, b. Sedan, Kans., Mar. 18, 1928; A.B., Kan. U., 1951, LL.B., 1953. Admitted to Kan. bar, 1953, U.S. Supreme Ct. bar, 1972; individual practice law, Jetmore, Kans., 1953-65; partner firm Mangan, Dalton, Trenkle & Gunderson and predecessor, Dodge City, Kans., 1965—; lectr. continuing legal edn. seminars. Chmn. City Mgr. Task Force, Dodge City, 1969, Dodge

City Hosp. Task Force, 1971. Mem. Kans. (pres. 1976), S.W. Kans. (sec.-treas. 1965-66), Am. bar assns., Kans. U. Law Soc. (gov. 1974—), Kans. Jud. Council (co-chmn. com. probate law study 1974). Office: 208 W Spruce St Dodge City KS 67801 Tel (316) 227-8126

DALTON, JOHN JOSEPH, b. N.Y.C., Feb. 7, 1943; B.B.A., Fairfield U., 1964; J.D., Northwestern U., 1967. Admitted to Ill. bar, 1967, Ga. bar, 1970; asso. firm Claussen, Hirsch, Miller & Gorman, Chgo., 1967-69; asso. firm Troutman, Sanders, Lockerman & Ashmore, Atlanta, 1969-73, partner, 1973—. Active state Democratic Party of Ga. Mem. Am., Ga., Ill., Atlanta bar assns., Lawyers Club of Atlanta, Am. Judicature Soc. Home: 2362 Dellwood Dr NW Atlanta GA 30305 Office: 1400 Candler Bldg Atlanta GA 30303 Tel (404) 658-8033

DALTON, JOHN MICHAEL, b. Eureka, Calif., June 5, 1928; student U. Santa Clara, 1946-48; B.A., U. Calif., Berkeley, 1950, J.D., 1957. Admitted to Calif. bar, 1957, U.S. Tax Ct. bar, 1958; partner firm Hill & Dalton, Eureka, 1957-63, Hill, Dalton & Neville, Eureka, 1964-66, Dalton & Nord, Eureka, 1966—. Mem. Am., Calif., Humboldt County (pres. 1971) bar assns., Calif. Trial Lawyers Assn., Phi Delta Phi, Eureka C. of C. (past dir.). Home: 2203 S St Eureka CA 95501 Office: 732 5th St Eureka CA 95501 Tel (707) 443-0878

DALTON, JOHN NICHOLS, b. Emporia, Va., July 11, 1931; A.B., William and Mary Coll., 1953; J.D., U. Va., 1957. Admitted to Va. bar, 1957, U.S. Supreme Ct. bar, 1960; practice law, Radford, Va., 1957—; sr. partner firm Dalton & Jebo, 1975—; mem. Va. Ho. of Dels., 1966-72, Va. Senate, 1972-73; lt. gov. Va., 1974—; mem. Va. Ct. System Study Commn., 1968-72. Vice chmn. alumni bd. dirs. Coll. William and Mary, 1966, recipient Alumni medallion, 1975. Home: 411 4th St Radford VA 24141 Office: PO Box 1089 Radford VA 24141 Tel (703) 639-3984

DALTON, STEPHEN EDWARD, b. Memphis, Sept. 17, 1943; B.A., U. Fla., 1965, J.D., 1967. Admitted to Fla. bar, 1967, U.S. Supreme Ct. bar, 1971; partner firm Pavese, Shields, Garner Haverfield & Kluttz, Ft. Myers, Fla., 1969—; pres., dir. Gulf Abstract & Title, Inc., Ft. Myers, 1975—; arbitrator Am. Arbitration Assn.; chmn. Lee County Law Referral Service, Ft. Myers, 1976. Mem. Am., Fla., Lee County bar assns., Lawyers Title Guarantee Fund, Fla. Acad. Trial Lawyers. Office: 1833 Hendry St Fort Myers FL 33901 Tel (813) 334-2195

DALY, GLENN LAVERNE, b. New Lothrop, Mich., Aug. 31, 1895; student U. Colo., 1913-15; LL.B., Westminster Law Sch., 1927; J.D., U. Denver, 1970. Clk., Continental Oil Co., Denver, 1920-23; claim investigator Union Pacific R.R., Denver, 1923-26; admitted to Colo. bar, 1927, since practiced in Denver; mem. firm Stone & Daly, 1927-28, Hower & Daly, 1928; individual practice law, 1929—; dep. dist. atty. Jefferson County, Colo., 1927-32. Mem. Denver, Colo. bar assns. Home: 3201 Virgil St Golden CO 80401 Office: 942 S Federal Blvd Denver CO 80219 Tel (303) 935-9689

DALY, JOHN JOSEPH, b. Rosemount, Minn., Feb. 22, 1930; B.A., St. Thomas Coll., St. Paul, 1951; J.D., U. Minn., 1954. Admitted to Minn. bar, 1954; practiced law, St. Paul, 1957-63, Burnsville, Minn., 1963-71; judge Municipal Ct., Burnsville, Minn., 1965-71, Dakota County (Minn.) Ct., 1971—. Mem. Am. Bar Assn., Minn. State Bar, Minn. County Judges Assn., Nat. Council Juvenile Ct. Judges. Home: 2401 E 125th St Burnsville MN 55337 Office: 201 Travelers Trail Burnsville MN 55337 Tel (612) 890-1626

DALY, JOHN JOSEPH, b. Hartford, Nov. 5, 1923; B.A., M.A., Trinity Coll., 1947; J.D., U. Conn., 1950. Admitted to Conn. bar, 1950; since practiced in Hartford; prosecutor Hartford Police Ct., 1957-59; judge Circuit Ct., 1961-67, chief judge, 1967-73; judge Superior Ct., 1973—. Mem. Conn. Safety Commn., 1967-73, Conn. Jud. Council, 1967-73, State Drug Adv. Council, State Alcoholism Council, 1969-73, Conn. Planning Com. on Criminal Adminstrn., 1970-73. Mem. Hartford Bd. Edn., 1951-57, pres., 1953-54; bd. regents Wethersfield Sch. Law, 1976—. Mem. Am., Conn., Hartford County bar assns. Co-author: Connecticut Evidence. Home: 257 Terry Rd Hartford CT 06105 Office: 95 Washington St Hartford CT 06101 Tel (203) 566-5234

DALY, JOHN PAUL, b. Pitts., Aug. 6, 1939; B.A., U. Calif., Riverside, 1961; J.D., Loyola U., Los Angeles, 1971. Admitted to Calif. bar, 1972; dep. dist. atty. San Luis Obispo County (Calif.), 1971—; speaker to educators. Mem. Res. Officers Assn. U.S., Calif. State, San Luis Obispo County bar assns. Office: Courthouse Annex San Luis Obispo CA 93401 Tel (805) 543-3464

DAM, KENNETH W., b. Marysville, Kans., Aug. 10, 1932; B.S., U. Kans., 1954; J.D., U. Chgo., 1957. Admitted to N.Y. bar, 1959; law clk. Justice Whittaker, U.S. Supreme Ct., 1957-58; asso. firm Cravath, Swaine & Moore, N.Y.C., 1958-60; faculty U. Chgo. Law Sch., 1960-71, 74—, now Harold J. and Marion F. Green prof.; asst. dir. nat. security and internat. affairs U.S. Office Mgmt. and Budget, 1971-73; exec. dir. U.S. Council on Econ. Policy, 1973. Mem. Am. Bar Assn., Am. Law Inst. Author: (with Lawrence Krause) Federal Tax Treatment of Foreign Income, 1964; The GATT: Law and International Economic Organization, 1970; Oil Resources: Who Gets What How?, 1976; (with George P. Schultz) Economic Policy Beyond the Headlines, 1977. Home: 5609 S Kenwood Ave Chicago IL 60637 Office: U Chgo Law Sch 1111 E 60th St Chicago IL 60637 Tel (312) 753-2393

D'AMATO, ANTHONY A., b. N.Y.C., Jan. 10, 1937; A.B., Cornell U., 1958; J.D., Harvard, 1961; Ph.D., Columbia, 1968. Admitted to N.Y. bar, 1963, U.S. Supreme Ct. bar, 1965; instr. polit. sci. Wellesley (Mass.) Coll., 1965-67; research fellow Social Sci. Research Council, Ann Arbor, Mich., 1967-68; asst. prof. Law Sch. Northwestern Univ., Chgo., 1968-71, asso. prof., 1971-74, prof., 1974—; vis. prof. Univ. Oreg., Eugene, 1973-74. Trustee, Museum Media, N.Y.C., 1968—. Mem. Am., N.Y. bar assns., Internat. League for Rights of Man, Am. Trial Lawyers Assn., N.Y. League Theatres and Producers. Author: The Concept of Custom in Internat. Law, 1971, The Judiciary and Vietnam, 1972, Desegregation from Brown to Alexander: An Exploration of Supreme Ct. Strategies, 1977; co-editor; (with C.W. Beal) The Realities of Vietnam, 1968; contbr. numerous articles in law jours. and reviews. Home: 5807 Lake Shore Ave Holland MI 49423 Office: Northwestern University School Law Chicago IL 60611 Tel (312) 649-8474

DAMBROV, ROBERT LARRY, b. Springfield, Mass., May 15, 1947; B.A. in Govt., U. Mass., 1969; J.D., Boston Coll., 1972. Admitted to Mass. bar, 1972; mem. firm Cooley, Shrair, Alpert & Labovitz, Springfield, 1972—. Bd. dirs. brotherhood Sinai Temple, Springfield, 1973-75, bd. dirs., 1974-76, fin. sec., 1976—; bd. dirs. Springfield Day Nursery, 1976—. Mem. Mass., Hampden County bar assns. Writer, editor Annual Survey Mass. Law, 1970-72. Office: 95 State St Springfield MA 01103 Tel (413) 739-3828

DAMIAN, CARMEN RICHARD, b. Pittsburgh, Pa., Oct. 12, 1928; B.S. in Bus. Adminstrn., Duquesne U., 1951; certificate intelligence investigation, U.S. Counter Intelligence Corps, 1952; certificate German lang. and intelligence, U.S. Army Intelligence Sch., 1952; J.D., Duquesne U., 1965. Spl. agt. U.S. Counter Intelligence Corps, Germany, 1952-54; enforcement supr. U.S. Treasury Dept., Phila., Newark, N.J., Pitts., 1954-66; admitted to Pa. Supreme Ct. bar, 1966, Pa. Superior Ct. bar, 1966, U.S. Ct. of Appeals bar, 1966, U.S. Dist. Ct. bar, 1966; law clk. Allegheny County Common Pleas Ct., 1966-67; partner firm Damian & Damian, Pitts., 1966-67; individual practice law, Pitts., 1967-72; sr. mem. firm Damian & Amato, P.C., Pitts., 1972—; asso. dir. Franklin Fed. Savs. and Loan Assn., 1975—. Coach, Crafton Little League Baseball, 1971-74. Mem. Pa., Allegheny County, Fed. bar assns., Am. Trial Lawyers Assn., Am. Arbitration Assn., Pa. Solicitors Assn., Western Pa. Chiefs of Police Assn. Contbr. note and comment to Duquesne U. Law Rev., 1964-65. Home: 403 Revere Rd Carnegie PA 15106 Office: 1512 Grant Bldg Pittsburgh PA 15219 Tel (412) 261-1900

DAMIANO, AUGUSTINE JOHN, b. Boston, Jan. 24, 1919; B.A., Northeastern U., 1941; LL.B., Boston U., 1947. Admitted to R.I. bar, 1948, U.S. Dist. Ct. bar for Dist. R.I., 1949; individual practice law, Providence. Mem. R.I. Bar Assn. Office: 1104 Indsl Bank Bldg Providence RI 02903 Tel (401) 421-2279

D'AMICO, JOHN, JR., b. Long Branch, N.J., Jan. 24, 1941; A.B. cum laude, Harvard, 1963, J.D., 1966; Admitted N.J. bar, 1966; law clk. to judges Monmouth County Ct., 1966-67; asso. firm Drazin, Warshaw, Auerbach & Rudnick, Red Bank, N.J., 1967-70; atty. Mutual Benefit Life Ins. Co., Newark, 1970-72, Asst. counsel, 1972-74, asso. counsel, 1974—; vol. staff N.J. Pub. Defender Assn., 1967-70. Bd. dirs. Monmouth County Mental Health Assn., 1967-70. Mem. Am., N.J., Monmouth County bar assns., Assn. Life Ins. Counsel, Am. Life Ins. Assn. Home: 53 Wittenburg Ct Oceanport NJ 07757 Office: Mutual Benefit Life Insurance Co 520 Broad St Newark NJ 07101 Tel (201) 481-8152

D'AMICO, MICHAEL LOUIS, b. Buffalo, July 29, 1945; B.A., J.D., State U. N.Y., Buffalo. Admitted to N.Y. bar; adminstrv. asst. to sheriff, Erie County, N.Y., 1970-72, undersheriff, 1974—; mem. firm Gannon & Gannon, Buffalo, 1972-74; instr. Erie County sheriff's dept. tng. acad., 1975—. Mem. Erie County Judges & Police Execs. Conf. Home: 237 S Roycroft Blvd Cheektowaga NY 14225 Office: 10 Delaware Ave Buffalo NY 14202 Tel (716) 846-7614

DAMISCH, JOHN WILLIAM, b. Elgin, Ill., Mar. 10, 1926; B.S., Northwestern U., 1946; J.D., 1950. Admitted to Ill. bar, 1950, U.S. Supreme Ct. bar, 1957; since practiced in Chgo., pres. Barclay, Damisch & Sinson, and predecessors, Chgo., Arlington Heights and Wheaton, Ill., 1950—; legal advisor, head Chgo. office Ill. State Treas., 1953-55, 57-59; justice of peace, Northfield Twp., 1957-65, magistrate Circuit Ct. Cook County, Ill., 1957-65. Active Boy Scouts Am., 1961—; bd. dirs. Washington Meml. Presbyn. Ch., Elgin, Ill., 1970—; sec. 1st Presbyn. Ch., Wilmette, Ill., 1955-57, trustee, 1955-58. Mem. Am., Ill., Chgo., Kane County bar assns., Am. Right of Way Assn., Chgo. Farmers Club (sec. 1973-74, v.p., 1974-75, pres. 1975-76), Am., Ill., Kane County farm burs., Glenview Navy League, Soc. Mayflower Descs. Ill., Northwestern U. Alumni Assn. Recipient Northeastern Ill. Council Pres.'s award, Boy Scouts Am., 1973. Home: 186 Coach Rd Northfield IL 60093 Office: 11 S LaSalle St Chicago IL 60603 Tel (312) 332-2107

DAMMANN, RICHARD WEIL, b. N.Y.C., Oct. 23, 1911; B.A. cum laude, Princeton, 1932; J.D. cum laude, Harvard, 1935. Admitted to N.Y. bar, 1935; since practiced in N.Y.C.; asso. firm Milton Dammann, 1935-42; partner Dammann & Heming and predecessor firms, 1942—. Pres. Bronx House, 1941-42, N.Y. Assn. for New Americans, 1956-60; chmn. United Hosp. Port Chester, N.Y., 1975—. Mem. Am. Bar Assn., Bar Assn. City N.Y. Home: Kirby Ln Rye NY 10580 Office: 380 Madison Ave New York City NY 10017 Tel (212) 687-0880

DAMRON, PHILLIP DEAN, b. Pikeville, Ky., July 22, 1947; B.A., U. Ky., 1969, J.D., 1971. Admitted to Ky. bar, 1972; partner firm Latta, Damron & Fitzpatrick, Prestonsburg, 1972-76; individual practice law, Prestonsburg, 1976—. Mem. Ky., Am. bar assns., Am. Trial Lawyers Assn., Am. Hosp. Lawyers Assn. Home: 236 N Arnold Ave Prestonsburg KY 41653 Office: 12 S Front Ave Prestonsburg KY 41653 Tel (606) 886-9444

DANA, RICHARD WALTON, b. Mattoon, Ill., July 25, 1940; B.S. in Bus., U. Colo., 1963, J.D., 1966. Admitted to Colo. bar, 1966, New Mex. bar, 1967; asso. firm Rowley, Breen & Bowen, Tucumcari, New Mex., 1967; asst. dist. atty. Quay County, N.M., 1967; dep. dist. atty. Araphoe County (Colo.), 1968; asst. dist. atty. Boulder County (Colo.), 1969-70; judge Boulder County Ct., 1971-74, Colo. 20th Jud. Dist. Ct., Boulder, 1975—. Mem. Am., Colo., Boulder County bar assns., State Bar New Mex. Office: 2025 14th St Boulder CO 80302 Tel (303) 441-3744

DANAHER, ROBERT CORNELIUS, JR., b. Washington, Mar. 15, 1947; B.A., Georgetown U., 1969, J.D., 1973. Admitted to Conn. bar, 1973; U.S. Supreme Ct. bar, 1977; asso. firm Danaher, Lewis & Tamoney, Hartford, Conn., 1973-76, partner, 1977—. Mem. West Hartford (Conn.) Town Council, 1975—; chmn. West Hartford Pub. Safety Com., 1975—; bd. dirs. West Hartford Sr. Job Bank, 1975—. Mem. Am., Conn., Hartford County bar assns. Home: 22 Knollwood Rd West Hartford CT 06110 Office: 39 Russ St Hartford CT 06106 Tel (203) 278-2300

DANDO, ALBERT JEFFREY, b. Phila., Dec. 19, 1938; B.C.E., Cornell U., 1961, LL.B., 1964. Admitted to Mass. bar, 1964; partner firm Goodwin Procter & Hoar, Boston; sec. Real Estate Investment Trust Am.; corporator, mem. nominating com. Provident Instn. Savs.; dir. Corcoran Mullins Jonnison, Inc., Real Estate; counsel Town of Essex (Mass.), 1966-69.

D'ANGELO, JAMES PAUL, b. Wilmington, Del., Mar. 15, 1930; grad. U. Del., 1951, Georgetown U. Law Sch., 1955. Admitted to Del. bar, 1955, U.S. Supreme Ct. bar, 1960; practice law, Wilmington; register of wills New Castle County, 1975—; atty. Del. Credit Union League, Inc. Mem. Am., Del. bar assns., Am. Trial Lawyers Assn. (sec.-treas. 1962-63). Home: 30 Golfview Dr Newark DE 19711 Office: 1300 King St Wilmington DE 19801 Tel (302) 678-7101

DANHOF, ROBERT JOHN, b. Grand Rapids, Mich., Aug. 24, 1925; A.B., Hope Coll., 1947; J.D., U. Mich., 1950. Admitted to Mich. bar, 1951; individual practice law, Muskegon, Mich., 1950-53; asst. U.S. atty., Grand Rapids, 1953-60, U.S. atty., 1960-61; del. Mich. Constl. Conv., 1961-62; exec. asst., legal adviser to Gov. George Romney, Lansing, Mich., 1963-68; judge Mich. Ct. of Appeals, Lansing, 1969-76, chief judge, 1976—. Mem. Am., Mich. bar assns., Am. Judicature Soc. (dir.). Home: 710 Pebblebrook Ln East Lansing MI 48823 Office: 200 Washington Sq Bldg Lansing MI 48933 Tel (517) 373-3834

DANIEL, AUBREY MARSHALL, III, b. Monks Corner, S.C., May 16, 1941; B.A., U. Va., 1963; LL.B., U. Richmond, 1966. Admitted to Va. bar, 1966, U.S. Ct. Mil. Appeals, 1969, D.C. bar, 1971; asso. firm Minor, Thompson, Savage, White & Smithers, Richmond, 1966-67; served with Judge Adv. Gen.'s Corps, 1967-71; partner firm Williams & Connolly, Washington, D.C., 1977—. Mem. Va. State, Am. bar assns., Bar Assn. D.C., Va., Am. trial lawyers assns. Recipient Elliott-Black award Am. Ethical Union, 1972; outstanding service award Nat. Dist. Atty.'s Assn., 1971. Home: 2429 Tunlaw Rd NW Washington DC 20007 Office: 1000 Hill Bldg Washington DC 20006

DANIEL, BENJAMINE, b. N.Y.C., Mar. 14, 1936; B.A., Hunter Coll., 1957; J.D., Cumberland Coll., 1970. Admitted to Ala. bar, 1970, Fla. bar, 1971; asst. counsel Liberty National Life Ins. Co., Birmingham, Ala., 1970-72; asst. dist. atty. Jefferson County, Ala., 1972-73; asso. firm Denaburg, Schoel, Meyerson & Ogle, Birmingham, Ala., 1973-75; individual practice law, Birmingham, Ala., 1975—. Mem. Am., Ala., Fla. bar assns. Home: 2521 Gerald Way Birmingham AL 35223 Office: 1135 Brown Marx Bldg Birmingham AL 35203 Tel (205) 252-3741

DANIEL, JOHN BRITT, JR., b. Temple, Tex., Apr. 30, 1916; B.A., U. Tex., 1937, LL.B./J.D., 1940. Admitted to Tex. bar, 1940; individual practice law, Temple, 1940-42; mem. firm Daniel, Traver & Secrest, and predecessors, Temple, 1942—; city atty. Temple, 1942-43. Pres., Temple Sch. Bd., 1952; mem. Temple Charter Commn., 1953, 65, 70. Fellow Tex. Bar Found., Am. Bar Found., Am. Coll. Probate Counsel, Am. Judicature Soc.; mem. Am., Bell-Lampasas-Mills Counties (past pres.) bar assns., State Bar Tex. (past v.p., dir.), Tex. Assn. Def. Counsel (past pres.), Home: 1317 N 9th St Temple TX 76501 Office: 100 W Adams St Suite 301 Temple TX 76501 Tel (817) 773-5215

DANIEL, PRICE, b. Dayton, Tex., Oct. 10, 1910; A.B., Baylor U., 1931, LL.B., 1932, LL.D., 1951. Admitted to Tex. bar, 1932, U.S. Supreme Ct. bar, 1948; individual practice law, Liberty, Tex., 1932-43; mem. Tex. Ho. of Reps., 1939-43, speaker, 1943; atty. gen. State of Tex., 1946-53; mem. U.S. Senate from Tex., 1953-57; gov. State of Tex., Austin, 1957-63; asst. to Pres. for fed.-state relations and dir. Office of Emergency Preparedness, 1967-69; justice Tex. Supreme Ct., Austin, 1971—. Pres. Internat. Christian Leadership, 1956-57; trustee Baylor U., Waco, Tex., Baylor Coll. Medicine, Houston. Mem. Am. Bar Assn., Am. Judicature Soc., Am. Soc. Internat. Law, Internat. Law Assn. Author: (with Mrs. Daniel) Executive Mansions and Capitols of America, 1968. Home: 600 W 10th St #441 Austin TX 78701 Office: PO Box 12248 Capitol Sta Austin TX 78711 Tel (512) 475-4414

DANIEL, WILLIAM FRANCIS, b. Chipley, Fla., Apr. 6, 1928; B.A., U. Fla., 1950, M.Ed., 1951, J.D., 1956. Admitted to Fla. bar, 1956; spl. asst. atty. gen. State of Fla., Tallahassee, 1956-58; partner firm Cotten, Shivers, Gwynn & Daniel, Tallahassee, 1958—; judge Leon County Small Claims Ct., 1959-62; spl. hearing officer U.S. Dept. Justice, 1961-64; commr. No. Dist. Fla. U.S. Dist. Ct., 1964-67; gen. counsel Fla. Edn. Assn., 1965-68; counsel, ethics com. NEA, 1966. Mem. Fla., Am. bar assns., Acad. Fla. Trial Lawyers, Am. Trial Lawyers Assn. Home: 3104 Briarwood Dr Tallahassee FL 32302 Office: 127 E Park Ave PO Box 12 Tallahassee FL 32302 Tel (904) 222-2222

DANIELS, ARTHUR MANLEY, b. Bertha, Minn., July 11, 1900; tchr's. certificate St. Cloud State Coll., 1920; LL.B., St. Paul Coll. Law, 1932. Tchr. pub. schs., Minn., 1920-23. Salesman various cos., 1923-33; admitted to Minn. bar, 1933; atty. Fed. Land Bank, St. Paul, 1933-35; individual practice law, St. Paul, 1935-42; atty. Fort Snelling VA, St. Paul, 1945-48; individual practice in Cass Lake, Minn., 1948—; judge Cass County (Minn.) Ct., 1963-75, ret., 1975, acting judge, 1975—, jud. officer Cass and Hubbard Counties; atty. First Nat. Bank Cass Lake; city atty. City of Cass Lake; title atty. Farmers Home Adminstrn., Cass County. Mem. Nat. Assn. Probate Judges, Cass County, Dist., Minn. bar assns. Home: 207 Basswood St Cass Lake MN 56633 Office: PO Box 155 Cass Lake MN 56633 Tel (218) 335-2405

DANIELS, BRUCE JOEL, b. Denver, Apr. 16, 1935; A.B., Ohio State U., 1957; LL.B., U. Mich., 1961, J.D., 1967. Admitted to Fla. bar, 1961; asst. county atty. Pinellas County (Fla.), 1961-63; trial atty. Fla. Dept. Transp., Tallahassee, 1963-66; asso. firm Levy and Levy, West Palm Beach, Fla., 1966-67; asst. city atty. City of West Palm Beach, 1967-68, asst. pub. defender, 1968-75; individual practice law, 1968-71; atty. firm Lesser, Lesser, profl. assn., West Palm Beach, 1971—. Pres. Big Bros. Assn., West Palm Beach, 1968-69, chmn. adv. council, 1974-76; pres. Muscular Dystrophy Assn. of Greater Palm Beach County (Fla.), 1974-76. Mem. Fla., Palm Beach County bars, Am. Bar Assn. Home: 4213 Magnolia St Palm Beach Gardens FL 33410 Office: 909 N Dixie Hwy West Palm Beach FL 33401 Tel (305) 655-2028

DANIELS, JOHN PETER, b. N.Y.C., Feb. 5, 1937; A.B., Dartmouth Coll., 1959; J.D., U. So. Calif., 1963. Admitted to Calif. bar, 1964; asso. firm Bolton, Groff & Dunn, Los Angeles, 1964-67; partner firm Jones & Daniels, Los Angeles, 1967-70, firm Acret & Perrochet, Los Angeles, 1971—. Mem. Am. Bar Assn., Assn. So. Calif. Def. Counsel, Am. Bd. Trial Advs. Editor Def. Dialogue, 1975—. Office: 11620 Wilshire Blvd Suite 350 Los Angeles CA 90025 Tel (213) 473-9666

DANIELS, WILBUR, b. Detroit, Jan. 23, 1923; B.S., City Coll. N.Y., 1942; J.D., N.Y. U., 1950. Admitted to N.Y. bar, 1950, U.S. Supreme Ct. bar, 1951; asst. dir. research Internat. Ladies' Garment Workers Union, N.Y.C., 1943-50, asso. gen. counsel, 1950-59, asst. to pres., 1959-61, dir. master agreements dept., 1965—, v.p., 1970, exec. v.p., 1973—; partner firm Vladeck and Elias, N.Y.C., 1961-63; exec. sec. Nat. Bd. Coat and Suit Industry, N.Y.C., 1963-65. Mem. Am., N.Y.C., N.Y. bar assns., N.Y. County Lawyers Assn. Home: 242 E 19th St New York City NY 10003 Office: 1710 Broadway St New York City NY 10019 Tel (212) 265-7000

DANIELS, WILLIAM LIONEL, b. Chgo., Oct. 22, 1946; B.A., Ariz. State U., 1968; J.D., Loyola U., Chgo., 1971. Admitted to Ill. bar, 1971; sr. law clk. U.S. Dist. judge Julius A. Hoffman, 1971-72; asst. prof. law, Chgo. Kent Coll. Law, 1972-76; asso. prof. law DePaul, 1976—. Mem. Ill., Am. bar assns., Am. Assn. Law Schs. Contbr.

articles in field to profl. jours. Home: 835 Judson St Evanston IL 60202 Office: 25 E Jackson St Chicago IL 60604 Tel (312) 321-7700

DANIELSON, WALTER GEORGE, b. Anaconda, Mont., July 3, 1903; LL.B., U. Mont., 1929, J.D., 1970. Admitted to Mont. bar, 1929, Calif. bar, 1929; asso. firm Bicksler, Smith, Parke & Catlin, Los Angeles; individual practice law, Westwood, Calif.; asso. firm H. Spencer St. Clair, Los Angeles; partner Danielson, St. Clair, and Davis, Los Angeles; counsul for Sweden, Los Angeles, consul gen. Trustee Calif. Hosp. Med. Center, Los Angeles; bd. dirs. Luth. Hosp. Soc. Mem. Los Angeles County Bar Assn., State Bar Calif. Home: 68 Fremont Pl Los Angeles CA 90005 Office: 615 S Flower St Suite 803 Los Angeles CA 90017 Tel (213) 625-1157

DANIS, DAVID O'NEIL, b. St. Louis, Jan. 5, 1944; J.D., St. Louis U., 1967; LL.M. in Taxation, Washington U., 1975. Admitted to Mo. bar, 1967; asst. prosecuting atty. St. Louis County (Mo.), 1967-69; asst. circuit atty. City of St. Louis, 1969-70; counsel Mo. Judicial Commn. on Retirement, Removal & Discipline, 1973—; pros. atty. City of Ladue, Mo., 1969—; legal advisor Internat. Affairs Div. St. Louis Met. Police Dept., 1975—. Mem. Am., Mo., St. Louis bar assns., St. Louis Defense Counsel Assn. Editor: Legal Events, 1975—. Home: 24 Berkeley Ln Ladue MO 63124 Office: 610 Locust St Saint Louis MO 63101 Tel (314) 241-6530

DANN, WALLACE, b. Washington, Feb. 10, 1921; J.D. cum laude, U. Balt., 1950. Admitted to Md. bar, 1950; asso. counsel Office Gen. Counsel to Quartermaster Gen. U.S. Army, 1953-55; mem. firm Bregel & Bregel, Towson, Md., 1955—, v.p., 1972—; sec.-treas. Wilkes-Barre Iron & Wire Works, Inc. (Pa.), 1970—. Chancellor Epiphany Episcopal Ch. Parish, Timonium, Md., 1974—. Mem. Balt. City, Baltimore County, Md. State, Am. bar assns., Md. Trial Lawyers Assn. (pres. 1969-70). Home: 209 Purlington Rd Timonium MD 21093 Office: 300 W Allegheny Ave Towson MD 21204 Tel (301) 539-2744

DANNEMYER, WILLIAM EDWIN, b. Los Angeles, Sept. 22, 1929; A.B. in Polit. Sci., Valparaiso U., 1950; J.D., U. Calif. at San Francisco, 1952. Admitted to Calif. bar, 1952; asst. city atty. Fullerton (Calif.), 1959-62; dep. dist. atty. Santa Barbara County (Calif.), 1955-57; judge pro tempore N. Orange County (Calif.) Municipal Ct., 1967—, Orange County Superior Ct., 1967—; individual practice law, Fullerton, 1957—; mem. Calif. State Assembly from 69th Dist., 1963-66; mem. Orange County Criminal Justice Council, 1968-72. N. Orange County fin. chmn. Billy Graham Crusade, 1968; active Cub Scouts and Boy Scouts; pres. Orange County Luth. High Sch. Assos., 1975—; bd. dirs. So. Calif. dist. Luth. Ch.-Mo. Synod, 1976. Mem. Am., Calif., Orange County bar assns. Office: 1105 E Commonwealth St Fullerton CA 92631 Tel (714) 871-1046

D'ANTONY, JOSEPH S., b. Akron, Ohio, Jan. 1, 1939; B.S., Ohio No. U., 1962; J.D., Pepperdine U., 1973. Admitted to Calif. bar, 1973; asso. firm Ruston, Nance & DiCaro, Tustin, Calif., 1973—. Mem. Am., Orange County bar assns., So. Calif. Def. Bar, Orange County Trial Lawyers Assn. Office: 17822 17th St Tustin CA 92680 Tel (714) 838-9800

DANTZLER, DERYL DAUGHERTY, b. Macon, Ga., Jan. 26, 1944; A.B. cum laude, Mercer U., 1964, J.D. cum laude, Walter F. George Sch. Law, 1970. Admitted to Ga. bar, 1970; asso. firm Mincey Kenmore & Bennett, Macon, 1970-73; partner firm Bennett & Dantzler, Macon, 1973-77; individual practice law, Macon, 1977—; prof. criminal law Nat. Coll. Criminal Def. Lawyers and Pub. Defenders, Houston, 1975; pres. Macon Legal Aid Soc., 1973-74. Mem. State Bar Ga. (vice chmn. com. on criminal justice 1976—, sec. criminal law sect. 1971-72, 75-76, bd. govs. 1977—), Ga. (charter, v.p. middle dist. 1976), Nat. assns. criminal def. lawyers, Ga. Trial Lawyers Assn. Home: Rl 1 Searcy Dr Juliette GA 31046 Office: 963 Walnut St Macon GA 31201 Tel (912) 742-7318

DARBO, HOWARD HELSETH, b. Wauwatosa, Wis., Dec. 9, 1909; B.S. in Chem. Engring., U. Wis., 1932; J.D., U. Mich., 1935. Admitted to Ill. bar, 1936; staff atty. C.F. Burgess Labs., Inc., Chgo., 1936-38; partner firm Darbo & Vandenburgh, and predecessors, Arlington Heights, Ill., 1938—; dir., sec. Clean Power Systems, Inc.; dir., pres. Portable Cookery, Inc. Chmn. Wheaton (Ill.) Zoning Commn., 1951-59, commr., councilman, 1959-63. Mem. Am., Chgo., DuPage, N.W. Suburban bar assns., Chgo., Am. patent law assns. Home: 1110 N Wheaton Ave Wheaton IL 60187 Office: 15 N Arlington Heights Rd PO Box 670 Arlington Heights IL 60004 Tel (312) 259-4210

DARBY, RICHARD DURHAM, JR., b. Bloomington, Ind., Sept. 27, 1947; A.B., Princeton, 1969; postgrad. Harvard, 1969-70; J.D., Ind. U., 1972. Admitted to Ind. bar, 1972; partner firm Colman, Darby, Lowenthal and Loftman, Bloomington, 1973-76; prin. firm Richard D. Darby, Jr. & Assos., Bloomington, 1976—. Bd. dirs. Ind. Civil Liberties Union, 1974—, Monroe County (Ind.) Juvenile Justice Com., 1974—; mem. Bloomington Environ. Commn., 1974—. Mem. Am., Ind., Monroe County bar assns., Phi Beta Kappa. Author: Lake Monroe: A Legal Handbook for Environmentalists, 1976. Home: Rural Route 2 Box 232A Bloomington IN 47401 Office: 408 E 4th St Bloomington IN 47401 Tel (812) 336-1744

DARBY, ROLAND BERNARD, b. New Iberia, La., Jan. 2, 1945; B.B.A., Lamar U., 1967; J.D., South Tex. Coll. Law, 1970. Admitted to Tex. bar, 1969; partner firm Darby, Harrison & Black, Houston, 1973—. Office: 1455 W Loop S Houston TX 77027 Tel (713) 626-5510

DARBY, WILLIAM THOMAS, b. Vidalia, Ga., May 12, 1914; LL.B., Atlanta Law Sch., 1935. Admitted to Ga. bar, 1935; individual practice law, Vidalia, 1935-36, 42-43, 45-49, 52-69, 73—; mem. firm Jackson & Darby, Vidalia, 1937-41, Darby and Lewis, Vidalia, 1950-51, Darby and Calhoun, Vidalia, 1970-72; city atty. City of Vidalia, 1947-48; county atty. Toombs County (Ga.), 1949-50; solicitor Ga. State Ct. of Toombs County, 1952-56, judge, 1960—. Active Boy Scouts Am., 1936-55. Mem. Am. Judicature Soc., Ga. Trial Lawyers Assn., Human Resources-USA, State Judge's and Solicitor's Assn. (dir. 1974-75). Home: 1007 Center Dr Vidalia GA 30474 Office: PO Box 648 309 Durden St Vidalia GA 30473 Tel (912) 537-7651

D'ARCO, THOMAS RICHARD, b. Detroit, Feb. 15, 1941; B.M.E., U. So. Calif., 1963; M.B.A., U. Pitts., 1964; J.D., Vanderbilt U., 1971. Admitted to Mich. bar, 1971; atty. Touch Ross & Co., Detroit, 1972-73; v.p. F & D Tool Co., Clawson, Mich., 1973—. Mem. Am., Oakland County, Wayne County bar assns. Office: 639 N Rochester St Clawson MI 48017

DARDEN, WILLIAM BYRON, b. Goodwater, Ala., Mar. 28, 1915; student U. Ala., 1937; LL.B., U. Va., 1948. Admitted to N.M. bar, 1948, since practiced in Las Cruces; mem. firm Darden & Caffey, 1958-60, Darden & Mechen, 1960-68, Darden, Mechen & Sage, 1968-70, Darden & Sage, 1970-73, Darden, Sage & Darden, 1973—. Dir. Mut. Bldg. and Loan Assn., Las Cruces. Chmn. Las Cruces Bd. Edn., 1952-73. Named Citizen of Year, Woodmen of World, 1967. Mem. Dona Ana County Bar Assn. (pres. 1954), Nat. Assn. Coll. and Univ. Attys. (1st v.p. 1976-77, pres. 1977-78), Sigma Chi. Home: PO Drawer 578 Las Cruces NM 88001 Office: Darden Sage & Darden 200 W Las Cruces Ave Las Cruces NM 88001 Tel (505) 526-6655*

DARKO, RICHARD JOHN, b. Indpls., Sept. 3, 1943; B.A., U. Notre Dame, 1965; J.D., Ind. U., 1968. Admitted to Ind. bar, 1968, U.S. Supreme Ct. bar, 1974; law clk. U.S. Dist. Ct. So. Dist. Ind., 1968-69; asso. firm Bingham Summers Welsh & Spilman, 1969-73; asst. prof. law U. Ala., 1973-74; partner firm Bingham Summers Welsh & Spilman, Indpls., 1974—. Pres., bd. dirs. St. Vincent Drug Abuse Program, Inc., Indpls., 1975—; active Ind. Civil Liberties Union. Mem. Am., Ind., Indpls., 7th Circuit bar assns. Office: 2700 Indiana Tower Indianapolis IN 46204 Tel (317) 635-8900

DARLING, BRIAN KEVIN, b. Stamford, Conn., Dec. 16, 1946; A.B., Murray State U., 1969, M.B.A., 1971; J.D., U. Louisville, 1973. Admitted to Ky. bar, 1974; individual practice law, Louisville, 1974—; lectr. bus. law and tax law Watterson Coll., Louisville, 1974—, McKendree Coll., 1976—. Mem. Am., Ky., Louisville bar assns., Am. Judicature Soc. Home: 2010 Hounz Ln Louisville KY 40223 Office: 206 Kentucky Towers Louisville KY 40202 Tel (502) 583-1784

DARLING, EDWARD, b. Wilkes-Barre, Pa., Jan. 2, 1906; B.A., Yale, 1927; LL.B., Harvard, 1930. Admitted to Pa. bar, 1930; asso. firm Darling & Mitchell, and predecessors, Wilkes-Barre, 1930-34, partner, 1934—. Mem. Luzerne County (Pa.), Pa., Am. bar assns. Home: 129 Butler St Kingston PA 18704 Office: 848 United Penn Bank Bldg Wilkes-Barre PA 18701 Tel (717) 822-8195

DARLING, HUGH W., b. Tacoma, Sept. 4, 1901; student U. Calif., Berkeley, 1923; LL.B., U. So. Calif., 1928. Admitted to Calif. bar, 1928, U.S. Supreme Ct., 1933; partner firm Darling, Hall, Rae & Gute, and predecessors, Los Angeles, 1928—. Active, Beverly Hills Civil Service Commn., 1953-57; mem. City Council, Beverly Hills, 1957-64, mayor, 1960-61. Mem. Am., Calif. (bd. govs. 1965-68, v.p. 1967-68), Los Angeles County (trustee 1954-60, pres. 1959-60) bar assns., Chancery Club (pres. 1957-58), Order of Coif, Phi Delta Phi. Home: 629 Hillcrest Rd Beverly Hills CA 90210 Office: 523 W 6th St Los Angeles CA 90014 Tel (213) 627-8104

DARNALL, ELEANOR BARCLAY, b. Washington; A.A., Monticello Coll.; A.B., George Washington U.; J.D., U. Tex., 1957. Admitted to Tex. bar, 1956; asso. firm Smith & Shropshire, Austin, Tex., 1958-59, firm Robert C. Howell, Austin, 1959—. Mem. Travis County Bar Assn., State Bar Tex. Home: 3209 Duval St Austin TX 78705 Office: 304 Vaughn Bldg 807 Brazos St Austin TX 78701

DARONCO, RICHARD J., b. Pelham, N.Y., Aug. 1, 1931; B.A., Providence Coll., 1953; LL.B., Union U., Albany, N.Y., 1956. Admitted to N.Y. bar, 1959, U.S. Supreme Ct. bar, 1962; gen. partner firm King, Edwards & O'Connor, White Plains, N.Y., 1959-71; judge Family Ct. of Westchester County, White Plains, 1971-73, adminstrv. judge, 1973; judge Westchester County Ct., White Plains, 1974-76; acting justice N.Y. State Supreme Ct., 1977—; town atty. Town of Pelham (N.Y.), 1963-71; counsel N.Y. State Legis. Com. Commerce, Industry and Econ. Devel., 1969; trustee, acting mayor Village of North Pelham, 1961-66; instr. law Iona Coll., also mem. adv. council on criminal justice. Chmn., Pelham Cancer Crusades, 1968-69; mem. Westchester County Mental Health Bd., 1969-71; Pelham chmn. Boys' Towns of Italy Benefit, 1969-70; adv. com. Pelham Assn. for Kids, 1969-70; sec. N.Y. State Assn. Community Mental Health Bds., 1971; mem. N.Y. State Vol. Fireman's Assn.; bd. dirs. Pelham Civic Assn., Pelham chpt. ARC; trustee St. Catherine's Parish, Pelham. Mem. N.Y. State, Westchester County bar assns., Am. Justinian Soc. Jurists, N.Y. State County Ct. Assn. Office: Court House Grove St White Plains NY 10601 Tel (914) 682-3006

DA ROSA, RONALD ANTHONY, b. Joliet, Ill., June 28, 1943; B.S. in Edn., No. Ill. U., 1965; J.D., John Marshall Law Sch., 1970. Admitted to Ill. bar, 1970; asst. state's atty. DuPage County (Ill.), Wheaton, 1970-71; partner firm Donovan, Atten, Mountcastle, Roberts & DaRosa, Wheaton, 1971—; city prosecutor Downers Grove (Ill.), 1971-75. Mem. Glen Ellyn (Ill.) Zoning Bd. Appeals, 1975-77, chmn., 1976-77; pres. Village of Glen Ellyn (Ill.), 1977—. Mem. Am., Ill., DuPage County (chmn. med.-legal com. 1976) bar assns., Chgo. Hosp. Personnel Mgmt. Assn. (pres. 1969). Home: 600 N Park Glen Ellyn IL 60137 Office: 325 W Wesley St Wheaton IL 60187 Tel (312) 668-4211

DARRAH, JOHN WALTER, b. Chgo., Dec. 11, 1938; B.S., U. Chgo., 1965; J.D., Loyola U., Chgo., 1969. Admitted to Ill. bar, 1969, U.S. Dist. Ct. bar for Northeastern Dist. Ill., 1969; atty.-adviser Chgo. regional office FTC, 1969-71; partner firm Cox, Lyle and Darrah, Glen Ellyn, Ill., 1972-74; chief div. misdemeanor and juveniles Du Page County (Ill.) State's Atty's Office, Addison, 1975—; instr. law Lewis U., 1976—. Mem. Du Page County, Ill. bar assns. Home: ON 748 Peter Rd Wheaton IL 60187 Office: 228 E Lake St Addison IL 60101 Tel (312) 834-9590

DARRAH, JOSEPH EMORY, b. Cody, Wyo., Sept. 25, 1938; B.S. Law, U. Wyo., 1963, J.D., 1965. Admitted to Wyo. bar, 1965; partner firms Dixon and Darrah, Powell, Wyo., 1965-68, Darrah and Anderson, Powell, 1969—; atty. gen. State of Wyo., 1968-69; county and pros. atty. Park County (Wyo.), 1974—. Pres. Powell Athletic Roundtable, 1975. Mem. Wyo. State Bar Assn. (sec.-treas. 1968-73, certificate of appreciation 1974). Home: 415 Sunlight Dr Powell WY 82435 Office: 254 E 2d St Powell WY 82435 Tel (307) 754-2254

DARRELL, NORRIS, b. St. Kitts, B.W.I., Jan. 30, 1899; LL.B., U. Minn., 1923. Admitted to Minn. bar, 1923, N.Y. bar, 1927, U.S. Supreme Ct. bar, 1942; legal sec. Asso. Justice Pierce Butler, U.S. Supreme Ct., 1923-25; asso. firm Sullivan & Cromwell, N.Y.C., 1925—, Paris and Berlin rep., 1928-30, partner, 1934-76, of counsel, 1976—; tech. adviser Fiscal Com. Econ. Devel., 1947-65; adv. bd. Internat. Bur. Fiscal Documentation, 1964-71; past mem. various tax adv. coms. N.Y. State and U.S. govtl. bodies. Trustee Tax Found.; trustee emeritus Practising Law Inst. Fellow Am., N.Y. bar founds.; mem. Am. (ho. dels. 1965—), N.Y. State, Internat. bar assns., Am. Law Inst. (council 1947—, pres. 1961-76, chmn. council 1976—, chmn. or vice chmn. joint com. with Am. Bar Assn. on continuing profl. edn. 1966—), N.Y. County Lawyers Assn., Assn. Bar City N.Y., Council Fgn. Relations, Phi Delta Phi, Order of Coif. Contbr. articles to legal jours.; recipient U. Minn. Law Alumni Assn. award of merit, 1962, U. Minn. Outstanding Achievement award, 1965, Marshall-Wythe medallion Coll. William and Mary, 1967. Home: 1107 Fifth Ave New York City NY 10028 Office: 48 Wall St New York City NY 10005 Tel (212) 952-8096

D'ARRIGO, CHARLES J., b. S.I., Jan. 14, 1928; LL.B., Bklyn. Law Sch., 1954. Admitted to N.Y. bar, 1954; practiced in S.I., 1954-73; judge N.Y.C. Civil Ct., 1974—; mem. Bd. Judges of Civil Ct. Pres. S.I. Inst. Arts and Scis., 1967-69. Mem. Richmond County (N.Y.) Bar Assn. Named Man of Year Richmond County Jr. C. of C., 1959. Office: 927 Castleton Ave Staten Island NY 10310 Tel (212) 442-8000

DARROW, CLARENCE ALLISON, b. Dubuque, Iowa, Mar. 22, 1940; B.S., Loras Coll., Dubuque, 1962; M.S.W., U. Ill., 1966; J.D., Chgo. Kent Coll. Law, 1971. Admitted to Ill. bar, 1971; asst. state's atty. Rock Island County (Ill.), 1971-74; mem. Ill. Legislature, 1974—. Mem. Am., Ill., Rock Island County bar assns. Named Freshman of Year Ill. Edn. Assn., 1976. Office: 1800 3d Ave Rock Island IL 61201 Tel (309) 794-1447

DA SILVA, WILLARD H., b. Freeport, N.Y., Oct. 17, 1923; B.A., N.Y. U., 1946; LL.B., Columbia U., 1949. Admitted to N.Y. bar, 1949, U.S. Supreme Ct. bar, 1969, U.S. Tax Ct. bar, 1969. Individual practice law, N.Y.C., 1949-70; partner firm Goodman & DaSilva, Carle Place, N.Y., 1970-73; individual practice law, Carle Place, 1973-76; partner firm DaSilva and Samuelson, Garden City, N.Y., 1977—; v.p. Marcus Bros. Textile Corp., 1951-63; pres. Cortley Fabrics subs. Cone Mills Corp., N.Y.C., 1964-65; counsel Barandes, Rabbino & Arnold, N.Y.C., 1975—; mem. faculty Practicing Law Inst. Fellow Am. Acad. Matrimonial Lawyers; mem. Am., N.Y. State, Nassau County bar assns., Assn. Am. Trial Lawyers, Am. Arbitration Assn., Phi Beta Kappa. Contbr. articles to legal jours. Office: 585 Stewart Ave Garden City NY 11530 Tel (516) 222-0700

DAUBE, DAVID, b. Freiburg, W.Ger., Feb. 8, 1909; grad. State Exam. in Law, U. Freiburg; J.D. with distinction, U. Gottingen (W.Ger.), 1932; Ph.D., U. Cambridge (Eng.), 1936; M.A., U. Oxford (Eng.), 1955, D.C.L. by decree, 1955. Fellow Caius Coll. U. Cambridge, 1938-46, lectr. in law, 1946-51, hon. fellow in law Gonville and Caius colls., 1974—; prof. jurisprudence U. Aberdeen, 1951-55; Regius prof. civil law U. Oxford, 1955-70, fellow All Souls Coll., 1955-70; prof. law U. Calif., Berkeley, dir. Robbins Collection, 1970—; hon. prof. history U. Konstanz (W.Ger.), 1966—. Pres. Classical Assn. Gt. Brit., 1976—. Fellow Brit. Acad., Gottingen Acad. Scis. (corr.), Bavarian Acad. Scis. (corr.), World Acad. Art and Sci.; mem. Grays Inn, Soc. Pub. Tchrs. Law, Studiorum Novi Testamenti Societas, Société d'Histoire des Droits de L'Antiquité, Société d'Histoire de Droit. Author: Studies in Biblical Law, 1947; The New Testament and Rabbinic Judaism, 1956; Forms of Roman Legislation, 1956; The Exodus Pattern in the Bible, 1963; The Sudden in the Scriptures, 1964; Collaboration with Tyranny in Rabbinic Law, 1965; He that Cometh, 1966; Roman Law, 1969; Civil Disobedience in Antiquity, 1972; Ancient Hebrew Fables, 1973; (with R. Yaron) Ancient Jewish Law, 1976; contbr. articles to legal publs. Office: Sch of Law Boalt Hall U of Calif Berkeley CA 94720 Tel (415) 642-5020

DAUGHERTY, FREDERICK ALVIN, b. Oklahoma City, Aug. 18, 1914; LL.B., Cumberland U., 1934; postgrad. Oklahoma City U., 1934-35, LL.B. (hon.), 1974; postgrad. Okla. U., 1936-37; H.H.D. (hon.), Okla. Christian Coll., 1976. Admitted to Okla. bar, 1937; individual practice law, Oklahoma City, 1937-40; mem. firm Ames, Ames & Daugherty, Oklahoma City, 1946-50, Ames, Daugherty, Byrum & Black, Oklahoma City, 1952-55; judge Dist. Ct. for 7th Jud. Dist. Okla., 1955-61, U.S. Dist. Ct. for Western, Eastern and No. dists. Okla., 1961—, chief judge, 1972—; mem. Jud. Conf. U.S., 1973-76. Sr. warden All Souls Episcopal Ch., 1957; pres. Downtown Kiwanis Club, 1957, lt. gov. dist. 19 Tex.-Okla. Dist., 1959; nat. fund vice-chmn. ARC, 1956-58, chmn. resolutions com. Nat. Conv., 1962, bd. govs. 1963-69; bd. dirs. United Fund Greater Oklahoma City, 1958-62, pres., 1961, trustee, 1963—; bd. dirs. Community Council Oklahoma City and County, 1962-66, pres., 1967-69; pres. Guthrie Scottish Rite Charitable and Ednl. Found., 1971—; bd. dirs. Guthrie Scottish Rite Bldg Co., 1971—; profl. adv. com. Oklahoma County Assn. Mental Health, 1963-70; adv. bd. Okla. Sci. and Arts Found., 1964—; exec. com. Oklahoma City Council on Alcoholism, 1964—, Okla. Med. Research Found., 1966-69; exec. com. Men's Dinner Club of Oklahoma City, 1963-70, pres., 1966-69. Mem. Fed., Am., Okla., Oklahoma County bar assns., Am. Bar Found., Oklahoma City C. of C. (dir. 1960-61, 66-67, 71-72), Phi Delta Phi, Sigma Alpha Epsilon. Recipient award to Mankind, Oklahoma City Sertoma Club, 1962, Outstanding Citizen award Oklahoma City Jr. C. of C., 1965, Citizenship award Big Brothers of Oklahoma County, 1968, Distinguished Service citation U. Okla., 1973, Distinguished Alumni citation Cumberland Sch. Law, Samford U., 1974. Home: 1800 Coventry Ln Oklahoma City OK 73120 Office: Fed Court House Oklahoma City OK 73102 Tel (405) 232-7644

DAUGHERTY, SAMUEL EDWIN, b. Dallas, Apr. 15, 1920; student So. Meth. U., 1946-47, LL.B., 1950. Admitted to Tex. bar, 1950, U.S. Supreme Ct. bar, 1954; asst. dist. atty. Dallas County (Tex.), 1951-52, 53-54; asst. enforcement atty. U.S. 10th Regional Wage Stblzn. Bd., Dallas, 1952-53; asso. firm Martin and Bailey, Dallas, 1954-56; asso. firm Daugherty, Bruner, Merrill & Johnson, and predecessors, Dallas, 1956-67, partner, 1967-72; individual practice law, Dallas, 1954—; U.S. commr. U.S. Dist. Ct., No. Dist. Tex., 1967-68. Mem. Dallas (chmn. bd. dirs. 1962, 63-67, 68), Am. bar assns., Dallas County Criminal Bar Assn. (pres. 1960, Meritorious Service award 1969), State Bar Tex., Tex. Criminal Def. Lawyers Assn. (charter, dir.). Home: 7339 Royal Circle Dallas TX 75230 Office: 1500 Mercantile Bank Bldg Dallas TX 75201 Tel (214) 742-2225

DAUGHTREY, MARTHA CRAIG, b. Covington, Ky., July 21, 1942; B.A., Vanderbilt U., 1964, J.D., 1968. Admitted to Tenn. bar, 1968; asst. U.S. atty. Middle Dist. Tenn., Nashville, 1968-69, asst. dist. atty., Nashville, 1969-72; asst. prof. law Vanderbilt U., Nashville, 1972-75, lectr., 1971-72, adj. prof., 1976—; judge Tenn. Ct. Criminal Appeals, 1975—. Chairperson Nashville Women's Polit. Caucus, 1975-76; v.p. Nashville Area Council Alcoholism, 1971-72. Mem. Am., Tenn., Nashville, Fed. bar assns., NOW, Order of Coif. Contbr. articles to Tenn. Law Rev. Office: Supreme Ct Bldg Nashville TN 37219 Tel (615) 741-2119

DAVENPORT, JOHN EDWIN, b. Nashville, N.C., Apr. 28, 1928; A.B., U. N.C., 1948, J.D., 1951. Admitted to N.C. bar, 1952; partner firm Davenport & Davenport, 1953-57; real property atty. State N.C., 1957-59; asst. trust officer First Citizens Bank, 1959-64; sr. partner Davenport & Fisher, Nashville, 1964—; chmn bd. Sharpsburg Properties, Inc. (N.C.), 1971—; pres. Regency Estates, Inc., Nashville, N.C.; mem. N.C. Ho. of Reps., 1973—, mem. commn. on govtl. ops., 1973—, legis. ethics commn., 1975-77, legis. services commn., 1976—. Chmn. Nash County Democratic Exec. Com., 1966-70; mem. N.C. Dem. Exec. Com., 1970-76; pres. Nashville

Indsl. Devel. Corp., 1964—; bd. dirs. Country Dr. Museum, Bailey, N.C., 1975—. Mem. Nash-Edgecombe (past pres.), 7th Jud. Dist., N.C., Am. bar assns., Nashville C. of C. (dir. 1971—), N.C. Jaycees (past dist. v.p.), N.C. State Bar, Am. Judicature Soc., N.C. Acad. Trial Lawyers, Am. Trial Lawyers Assn. Named Nashville Young Man of Year, Jaycees, 1956. Home: Route 5 Box 117 Rocky Mount NC 27801 Office: 207 Washington St Nashville NC 27856 Tel (919) 459-2124

DAVENPORT, JOHN SIDNEY, III, b. Richmond, Va., Mar. 14, 1905; A.B., Yale U., 1927, LL.B., 1930. Admitted to Va. bar, 1930, U.S. Supreme Ct. bar, 1956; partner firm Edwards & Davenport, Richmond, 1932-39; partner firm Mays, Valentine, Davenport & Moore and predecessor, Richmond, 1939—; staff office gen. counsel War Prodn. Bd., 1942-44; spl. asst. to dep. dir. intelligence, Office Strategic Services, Washington, D.C., 1944-45. Mem. Richmond City Council, 1948-52, vice mayor, 1948-50. Fellow Am. Bar Found., Am. Coll. Trial Lawyers; mem. Richmond (pres. 1960-61), Va. (pres. 1971-72) Am. bar assns. Recipient good govt. award, Richmond 1st Club, 1962; spl. award outstanding community service, Richmond Jaycees, 1962. Home: 23 Chatham Square Richmond VA 23226 Office: PO Box 1122 Richmond VA 23208 Tel (804) 644-6011

DAVENPORT, PETER MALCOLM, b. Joliet, Ill., Nov. 26, 1943; B.A., U. Ky., 1965, J.D., 1966; LL.M., George Washington U., 1973. Admitted to Ky. bar, 1967, U.S. Supreme Ct. bar, 1971; served with JAGC, U.S. Army, 1967-73; partner firm Brock and Davenport, Lexington, Ky., 1974—. Mem. Am., Ky., Fayette County bar assns.; contbr. articles to law jours. Home: Bellevie Farm Paris KY 40361 Office: 177 N Limestone St Lexington KY 40507 Tel (606) 254-5531

DAVID, EDWARD JOSEPH, b. Whiteville, N.C., Sept. 20, 1933; B.S., Notre Dame U., 1956; LL.B., J.D., Wake Forest U., 1958. Admitted to N.C. bar, 1958; served to capt., Judge Adv., USAF, 1959-65; partner firm Downing, David, Vallery and Maxwell, Fayetteville, N.C. Chmn., City of Fayetteville Bd. Appeals. Mem. Fed., N.C. Bar Assns. Home: 4607 Dow Ct Fayetteville NC Office: Box 55 219 Dick St Heritage Sq Fayetteville NC 28301 Tel (919) 483-1319

DAVID, KENNETH DONALD, b. Arkansas City, Kans., Aug. 20, 1929; A.A., Coffeyville Jr. Coll., 1949; B.B.A., Washburn U., 1965; J.D., 1968. Admitted to Kans. bar, 1968; individual practice law, Coffeyville and Independence, 1968-77; asst. county atty. Montgomery County (Kans.), 1969-71; judge Probate and Juvenile Cts., Montgomery County, 1977, Municipal Ct., Independence and Cherryvale, Kans., 1973-76; magistrate City Ct., Independence, 1973-76; asso. dist. judge Montgomery County, 1977—; lectr. on juvenile ct. justice Washburn U., 1973, 74, 77, U. Kans., 1971; lectr. on criminal justice Independence Community Jr. Coll., 1971—; instr. Crisis Intervention Center, Independence, 1973—. Bd. dirs. Children's Group Home, Independence, 1973—; bd. dirs. Kans. Conv. So. Baptists, 1971-73. Mem. Nat. Council Juvenile Justice, Kans. Assn. Spl. Ct. Judges, Delta Sigma Pi, Delta Theta Phi. Home: 1022 N 4th St Independence KS 67301 Office: City Hall Bldg Coffeyville KS 67337 Tel (316) 251-1060

DAVID, KING, b. Alford, Fla., Apr. 5, 1911; J.D., Howard U., 1948. Admitted to D.C. bar, 1957; individual practice law, Washington, D.C., 1957—; tchr. Evening High Sch. 1936-40, social worker, 1934-36, special investigator, 1937-38. Mem. D.C., Nat., Washington bar assns. Home: 3114 Wisconsin Ave NW Washington DC 20016 Office: 1938 Eleventh St NW Washington DC 20001 Tel (202) 265-4410

DAVID, MARY MARLENE, b. Balt., Dec. 29, 1935; B.A., N.Y. U., 1956; J.D., U. Balt., 1964. Admitted to Md. bar, 1965, D.C. bar, 1971, U.S. Supreme Ct. bar, 1970; individual practice law, Balt., 1965-68; atty. Washington Area Field Office, FTC, 1968-70, atty. div. rules and guides, 1970-73, atty. Office Spl. Asst. Dir. for Rulemaking, 1973—; instr. Mt. Vernon Sch. Law (now U. Balt.), 1966-68; spl. counsel to Md. Crime Investigating Commn., 1965-68. Mem. Huxley Inst. for Bio-Social Research, Greater Met. D.C.; sec., trustee Dean Burk Found., Inc.; mem. Md. Physical Fitness Commn., 1964-72. Mem. Nat. Assn. for Women Lawyers, D.C. Bar Assn. for Women, Women's Bar Assn. for Md., AAUW, Nat. Women's Party, Am., Md., D.C., Fed. bar assns., Am. Judicature Soc., Supreme Ct. Hist. Soc. Home: 5550 Columbia Pike Arlington VA 22204 Office: Fed Trade Commission Bldg Washington DC 20580 Tel (202) 724-1192

DAVIDOVICH, JOHN A., b. Chgo., Feb. 9, 1947; B.S., Carrell Coll., 1969; J.D., DePaul U., 1973. Admitted to Ill. bar, 1974; asso. firm Scofield & Main, Hinsdale, Ill., 1974-76; asst. states atty. DuPage County, Wheaton, Ill., 1976—. Elder, clk. Elmhurst Presbyterian Ch., 1971-74. Mem. Ill., DuPage County Bar assns., Hinsdale Jr. C. of C. (bd. dirs. 1976—). Home: 417 S Grant St Hinsdale IL 60521 Office: 207 S Reber St Wheaton IL 60187 Tel (312) 682-7050

DAVIDS, JOHN JACOB, b. Plainfield, N.J., Mar. 12, 1937; LL.B., Golden Gate U. Admitted to Calif. bar, 1966; asso. firm Werchick & Werchick, 1966-69; individual practice law, 1969-70; partner firm Conklin, Davids & Friedman, San Francisco, 1971—. Mem. Calif., San Francisco bar assns., Calif. Trial Lawyers Assn., Am. Arbitration Assn., Assn. Trial Lawyers Am., Calif. Lawyers Ad Hoc Com. on Malpractice. Office: 1200 Gough St Suite 9 PO Box 99406 San Francisco CA 94109 Tel (415) 673-0300

DAVIDSON, BERNARD H., b. Champion, Mich., Aug. 29, 1912; A.B., U. Mich., 1934, LL.B., 1936. Admitted to Ill. bar, 1936, Mich. bar, 1938; staff U.S. Senate Com. on Interstate Commerce Investigating Railroads, Chgo., 1936-38; circuit commr. Marquette County, Mich., 1938-43; prosecuting atty. Marquette County, 1943-44; judge Mich. 25th Jud. Circuit Ct., Marquette, 1963-76; individual practice law, Marquette County, 1938-63. Trustee Francis A. Bell Meml. Hosp., 1952-69, Bay Cliff Health Camp Bd. Mem. Am., Mich., Marquette County bar assns. Home: 17 Lakeview Dr Marquette MI 49855 Office: Peninsula Bank Bldg Ishpeming MI 49849 Tel (906) 486-9981

DAVIDSON, BURCHARD ROSSWELL, b. Russiaville, Ind., Jan. 17, 1921; A.B. in Govt., Ind. U., 1942, J.D., 1949; M.S. in Public Adminstrn., Syracuse U., 1943. Admitted to Ind. bar, 1949; mem. firm Roll and Davidson, Kokomo, Ind., 1953-58; judge Howard County Superior Ct., Kokomo, Ind., 1958-61; prof. polit. sci. Ind. U., Kokomo, 1962—. Mem. Nat. Council YMCAs, 1960-64, 76-78; bd. dirs. Kokomo YMCA, 1955—; gen. bd. Nat. Council Chs., 1960-64; pres. Howard County Council Chs., 1960-62; bd. dirs. Carver Community Center, 1974—. Mem. Am. Polit. Sci. Assn., Howard County Bar Assn., Ind. Judges Assn. Mem. Allied mission to observe Greek elections U.S. Dept. State, 1946; contbr. articles to legal jours. Home: Rural Route 1 Box 285 Kokomo IN 46901 Office: Ind Univ at Kokomo Kokomo IN 46901 Tel (317) 453-2000

DAVIDSON, DONALD ROBERT, III, b. Syracuse, N.Y., July 17, 1946; B.S., Dartmouth Coll., 1968; J.D., George Washington U., 1971. Admitted to Nev. bar, 1972; asso. firm Goodman & Snyder, Las Vegas, Nev., 1971-72; asso. firm Jones, Jones, Bell, LeBaron, Close & Brown, Las Vegas, 1972-75; partner firm Scotty Gladstone, Las Vegas, 1975—. Mem. Am., Nev., Clark County bar assns. Office: 302 E Carson Suite 9000 Las Vegas NV 89101 Tel (702) 382-5036

DAVIDSON, DOUGLAS BRIAN, b. Cleve., Jan. 11, 1947; A.B. in Econs., U. Calif., Irvine, 1968; J.D., U. Calif. Hastings Coll. Law, 1973. Admitted to Calif. bar, 1973; asso. firm Kindel & Anderson, Santa Ana, Calif., 1973—. Sec., legal counsel U. Calif. at Irvine Alumni Assn. Mem. Orange County Bar Assn., Order of Coif. Office: 1020 N Broadway Santa Ana CA 92701 Tel (714) 558-7777

DAVIDSON, IRWIN DELMORE, b. N.Y.C., Jan. 2, 1906; B.S., Washington Square Coll. N.Y. U., 1927, LL.B., 1928. Admitted to N.Y. bar, 1929; practiced in N.Y.C., 1929-48; mem. N.Y. State Assembly, 1935-48; justice Ct. of Spl. Sessions, N.Y.C., 1948-54; mem. 84th Congress from 20th N.Y. Dist.; judge Ct. Gen. Sessions of N.Y.C., 1956-61; justice N.Y. Supreme Ct., N.Y.C., 1961-74, spl. referee, N.Y.C., 1974—. Mem. Am., N.Y. State bar assns., Assn. Bar City N.Y., New York County Lawyers. Author: The Jury is Still Out, 1959. Office: 60 Centre St New York NY 10007 Tel (212) 374-8203

DAVIDSON, JAMES GUY, b. Tulsa, Dec. 28, 1921; B.A., U. Okla., 1943; J.D., Yale, 1947. Admitted to Okla. bar, 1947; individual practice law, Tulsa, 1947—; mem. Okla Ho. of Reps., 1949-50; trustee Gt. Western Investment Trust; dir. First Nat. Bank Turkey, Tulsa. Bd. dirs. Tulsa Council of Social Agencies, 1949-56, Recreation Center for Physically Limited, 1969—. Mem. bd. regents U. Okla., 1960-68, pres., 1967-68; Am., Okla., Tulsa bar assns., Tulsa C. of C., Phi Beta Kappa. Home: 3206 S Birmingham Tulsa OK 74105 Office: 801 Beacon Bldg Tulsa OK 74103 Tel (918) 582-5179

DAVIDSON, JOE RILEY, b. Gatesville, Tex., Oct. 29, 1947; B.A., Southwestern U., 1970; J.D., U. Houston, 1973. Admitted to Tex. bar, 1973; individual practice law, Houston, 1973—. Trustee Southwestern U., 1970-71. Mem. Am., Tex., Houston bar assns., Optimist Internat. Magic Circle Club (v.p.). Home: 2223 W Alabama Townhouse A Houston TX 77098 Office: 3303 Louisiana Suite 211C Houston TX 77006 Tel (713) 526-6603

DAVIDSON, JOHN FREDERICK, b. N.Y.C., Dec. 4, 1905; A.B. magna cum laude, Harvard U., 1927, J.D., 1930. Admitted to N.Y. State bar, 1931; asst. U.S. atty. So. Dist. N.Y., 1934-36; atty. SEC, N.Y.C., 1936-38, sr. atty., 1938-41; spl. litigation atty. Office Price Adminstrn., Washington, 1941-42, regional coordinator, 1942-43, asst. gen. counsel, 1943; individual practice law, N.Y.C., 1946-54; mem. firm Townsend & Lewis, N.Y.C., 1954-73; of counsel firm Thacher, Proffitt & Wood, N.Y.C., 1973—. Mem. Am. Bar Assn., N.Y. County Lawyers Assn. Office: 40 Wall St New York City NY 10005

DAVIDSON, JOHN HENRY, JR., b. Washington, Pa., Dec. 9, 1942; B.A., Wake Forest U., 1964; J.D., U. Pitts., 1967; LL.M., George Washington U., 1972. Admitted to Pa. bar, 1967, S.D. bar, 1972; asso. firm Houston, Houston & Donnelly, Pitts., 1967-68; staff atty. Neighborhood Legal Services, Pitts., 1968-70; teaching fellow George Washington U., 1971; asso. prof. law U. S.D., Vermillion, 1971—. Mem. State Bar S.D. Contbr. articles to legal jours. Home: Rural Route 2 PO Box 109 Vermillion SD 57069 Office: Sch of Law U SD Vermillion SD 57069 Tel (605) 677-5361

DAVIDSON, JOHN TAYLOR, b. Columbus, Ohio, Dec. 24, 1939; B.A., Otterbein Coll., 1963; J.D., Ohio No. U., 1966. Admitted to Ohio bar, 1966; asso. firm Landis & Runyan, Columbus, 1966-67; asst. atty. gen. Ohio Div. Wildlife, Columbus, 1967-71; legal sect. chief Ohio Dept. Natural Resources, Columbus, 1971-75, dep. dir. for resource protection and legal affairs, 1975—; mem. Interstate Oil Compact Commn., 1975—, Gov's. Great Lakes Fisheries Task Force, 1973-74, Franklin County Environ. Planning Commn. Water Task Force, 1971-75; chmn. City of Westerville (Ohio) Boyer Nature Preserve Com., 1974-76. Mem. Ohio Wildlife Mgmt. Assn. Home: 677 Granby Pl S Westerville OH 43081 Office: 1930 Belcher Dr Columbus OH 43224

DAVIDSON, JOSHUA MAURICE, b. N.Y.C., Apr. 1, 1911; student L.I. U., 1929-31; LL.B., Bklyn. Law Sch., 1934. Admitted to N.Y. State bar, 1935, U.S. Supreme Ct. bar, 1958, U.S. Ct. Customs and Patent Appeals, 1958; sr. partner firm Siegel, Mandell & Davidson, N.Y.C., 1935-40; partner firm Tompkins & Davidson, N.Y.C., 1940—. Mem. Assn. Customs Bar (past pres., dir. 1954—), Fed. Bar Council, Am., N.Y. State, Bklyn. bar assns., Am. Importers Assn. (past dir.), Harvar Soc. (past pres.), Iota Theta. Recipient certificate of appreciation Am. Legion, Practising Law Inst., 1972; Scroll of Honor, Internat. Trade div. Wall St. Synagogue, 1969. Contbr. articles to legal jours. Home: 37 W 12th St New York City NY 10011 Office: 1 Whitehall St New York City NY 10004

DAVIDSON, M. BATES, b. Mt. Morris, N.Y., May 29, 1924; B.A., Cornell U., 1948, LL.B., 1950. Admitted to N.Y. bar, 1950, Pa. bar, 1951; atty. Pa. R.R., Pitts., 1950-51; asso. firm Reynolds, Cramer & Donovan, Elmira, N.Y., 1951-54, firm Cramer & Donovan, Elmira, 1954-58; partner firm Cramer, Donovan, Graner & Davidson, Elmira, 1958-62, firm Donovan, Graner, Davidson & Burns, Elmira, 1962-73; individual practice law, 1974—. Mem. Am., N.Y., Chemung County bar assns. Home: 80 Morningside Dr Elmira NY 14905 Office: 243 Lake St Elmira NY 14901 Tel (607) 733-4635

DAVIDSON, MARK LEWIS, b. N.Y.C., May 22, 1945; A.B. magna cum laude, Princeton U., 1966; J.D. cum laude, Columbia U., 1969. Admitted to N.Y. bar, 1969, U.S. Supreme Ct. bar, 1973. asso. firm Kaye, Scholer, Fierman, Hays & Handler, N.Y.C., 1969-71, Milbank, Tweed, Hadley & McCloy, N.Y.C., 1971—; vol. atty. Community Law Office Program, 1969-73. Mem. Harlan Fiske Stone Fellowship com. Columbia Law Sch., 1971, vice chmn. class council, 1974—. Mem. Am. (study dir., sect. com. on effectiveness of relief awarded in sect. 7 actions), N.Y. State bar assns., Assn. Bar City N.Y., Columbia Law Sch. Alumni Assn. (sec. 1974—), Phi Beta Kappa. Harlan Fiske Stone scholar; contbr. articles to legal publs. Home: 144 W 86th St New York City NY 10024 Office: One Chase Manhattan Plaza New York City NY 10005 Tel (212) 422-2660

DAVIDSON, RONALD HAYES, b. Oberlin, Ohio, Aug. 15, 1914; B.S. in Edn., Kent State U., 1937; LL.B., Akron Law Sch., 1950; J.D., Akron U., 1964. Tchr. comml. subjects Lagrange (Ohio) High Sch., 1937-38, Parma (Ohio) High Sch., 1939-40; practice accounting, Akron, 1940-50; admitted to Ohio bar, 1950; tax atty. Firestone Tire & Rubber Co., Akron, 1950—; instr. accounting Hammil-Actual Bus. Coll., Akron, 1950-54; mem. Ohio Pub. Accountants Bd. Mem. Hudson (Ohio) Bd. Zoning Appeals, 1956-68. Mem. Akron, Am. bar assns. Home: 5500 Sullivan Rd Hudson OH 44236 Office: 1200 Firestone Pkwy Akron OH 44317 Tel (216) 379-4587

DAVIDSON, SHELDON, b. Chgo., Feb. 13, 1938; B.S. in Commerce, DePaul U., 1960, J.D., 1962. Admitted to Ill. bar, 1962; trial atty., criminal div. U.S. Dept. Justice, Washington and Chgo., 1962-73, chief Chgo. Strike Force, 1970-73; partner firm Pedersen & Houpt, Chgo., 1973—. Mem. Chgo., Ill. State, Fed. bar assns. Editorial bd. DePaul Law Rev., 1961-62. Office: 180 N LaSalle St Chicago IL 60601 Tel (312) 641-6888

DAVIES, DAVID GEORGE, b. Waukesha, Wis., July 19, 1928; B.S., U. Wis., 1950, J.D., 1953. Admitted to Wis. bar, 1953, Ariz. bar, 1959; trust rep. 1st Nat. Bank Ariz. Phoenix, 1957-58, asst. trust officer, 1958-62, trust officer, head bus. devel. in trust dept., 1962-66, v.p., trust officer, 1966; partner firm Collins, Davies & Cronkhite and predecessors, Phoenix, 1967—; instr. Phoenix Coll., 1968, Maricopa County Jr. Coll., 1975. Pres. Central Ariz. Estate Planning Council; pres. bd. dirs. Visiting Nurses' Assn.; bd. dirs. Ch. Beatitudes, Phoenix chpt. Nat. Hemophilia Found. Mem. Central Assn. Life Underwriters, Am., Wis. bar assns., Estate Planners Council. Home: 4730 E Exeter Blvd Phoenix AZ 85018 Office: Suite 220B 4350 E Camelback Rd Phoenix AZ 85018 Tel (602) 959-9490

DAVIES, JACK, b. Harvey, N.D., Jan. 6, 1932; A.A., Itasca (Minn.) Jr. Coll., 1952; B.A., U. Minn., 1954, J.D., 1960. Admitted to Minn. bar, 1960; asso. firm Fine, Simon and Schneider, Mpls., 1960-65; asst. prof. William Mitchell Coll. Law, St. Paul, 1965-66, asso. prof., 1966-69, prof., 1969—; mem. Minn. Senate, 1959—; mem. Uniform State Laws Commn., 1966—. Mem. Am., Minn., Hennepin County bar assns., AAUP. Author: Legislative Law and Process in a Nutshell, 1975; contbr. articles to legal jours. Home: 3424 Edmund Blvd Minneapolis MN 55406 Office: 875 Summit Ave Saint Paul MN 55105 Tel (612) 227-9171

DAVIES, JOHN LODWICK, b. Columbus, Ohio, May 30, 1909; B.A., Ohio State U., 1930, J.D., 1932. Admitted to Ohio bar, 1932, U.S. Supreme Ct. bar, 1959; asst. atty. City of Columbus, 1932-36; asso. firm Hoskins & Donaldson, 1936-42; individual practice law, Columbus, 1946—. Trustee, sec. Columbus Gallery Fine Arts, 1968-74. Mem. Ohio, Columbus (pres. 1959-60) bar assns. Office: 88 E Broad St Columbus OH 43215 Tel (614) 224-8118

DAVIGNON, ROBERT E., b. Pawtucket, R.I., July 28, 1944; A.B., Providence Coll., 1966; J.D., Suffolk U., 1969. Admitted to R.I. bar, 1969; asso. firm Gladstone & Zarlenga, 1969-73; asso. firm McOsker, Isserlis & Davignon, and predecessors, 1973-74, partner, 1974—; probate judge Town of Foster (R.I.), 1974—. Mem. Foster Democratic Town Com., 1972-74. Mem. Am., R.I. bar assns. Home: 64 Ocean Ave Cranston RI 02825 Office: 131 Waterman St Providence RI 02906 Tel (401) 272-6300

DAVIS, ALLEN ALDRICH, JR., b. Baltimore County, Md., Oct. 22, 1911; A.B., Princeton, 1933; LL.B., Harvard, 1936, J.D., 1954. Admitted to Md. bar, 1936; asso. partner firm Brown and Brune, Balt., 1936-41; lt. col. JAGD, U.S. Army, 1941-45; gen. counsel Monumental Life Ins. Co., Balt., 1946-74; asso. partner firm Niles, Barton and Wilmer, Balt., 1974—; counsel Bd. of Liquor License Commr., Balt., 1938-41. Mem. Am., Md., Balt. bar assns., Assn. Life Ins. Counsel (pres. 1970-72). Home: 1315 Aihtree Rd Towson MD 21204 Office: 929 N Howard St Baltimore MD 21201 Tel (301) 539-3240

DAVIS, ALLYN WHITNEY, b. Lamar, Colo., July 20, 1923; B.S. in Law, U. Denver, 1950, LL.B., 1950. Admitted to Colo. bar, 1950; dep. dist. atty. Gunnison, Rio Grande, Saguache Counties, Colo., 1960, county atty., Saguache and Center Counties, Colo., 1957-62; individual practice law, Pueblo, Colo., 1962—. Mem. Colo., Pueblo County bar assns. Office: 407 Colo Bldg Pueblo CO 81003 Tel (303) 544-7281

DAVIS, ANDREW HAMBLY, b. Fall River, Mass., Feb. 10, 1937; A.B., Brown U., 1959; LL.B., U. Va., 1962. Admitted to Mass. bar, 1962, R.I. bar, 1963, Fed. Dist. Ct. bar, 1964, Fed. Ct. of Appeals bar, 1966; partner firm Swan, Jenckes Asquith & Davis, Providence, 1964—. Pres., Bethany Home of R.I., 1967—; bd. mem. R.I. Philharmonic Orch., 1963—, asst. sec., 1964-74, sec., 1974-76; bd. dirs. Moses Brown Sch., 1968—; bd. dirs. Bradley Hosp., 1974—. Mem. Am., R.I. (lectr. estate planning), Boston bar assns., Estate Planning Council. Home: 9 Harbour Rd Barr RI 02806 Office: 9 Jurks Head Bldg Providence RI 02903 Tel (401) 331-9100

DAVIS, ANTHONY EDWARD, b. Horsham, England, Mar. 1, 1949; B.A., Cambridge (Eng.) U., 1970; M.A., 1974; LL.M. (Fulbright Travel Scholar, Criminal Law Edn. and Research Fellow), N.Y.U., 1971. Admitted to English (Hardwicke and Mansfield Scholar Lincoln's Inn), 1970, N.Y., U.S. Ct. Appeals 2nd Circuit, U.S. Dist. Ct. (Eastern and So. Dists. N.Y.), U.S. Customs Ct. bars, 1975; individual practice law, London, Eng., 1972-73; asst. prof. New York Law Sch., 1974, asst. dean, 1974-75; mem. firm Klotz and Gould, profl. corp., N.Y.C., 1975—, also London, Eng. Mem. Assn. Bar City N.Y., Am., N.Y. State bar assns., N.Y. County Lawyers Assn. Contbr. articles to law jours. and popular periodicals. Home: 210 W 101st St New York City NY 10025 Office: 36 W 44th St New York City NY 10036 also 1 Gray's Inn Sq Gray's Inn London WC1R 5AA England Tel (212) 697-2345

DAVIS, ARNOLD, b. N.Y.C., Jan. 31, 1928; LL.B., Bklyn. Law Sch., 1951, LL.M. summa cum laude, 1954. Admitted to N.Y. bar, 1951, U.S. Supreme Ct. bar, 1959; individual practice law, N.Y.C., 1953—. Vice pres. N.Y. Met. region United Synagogue Am., also mem. adv. council; active Boy Scouts Am. Fellow Am. Assn. Matrimonial Lawyers; mem. Am., N.Y. State, Bklyn. bar assns., N.Y. County Lawyers Assn., Brandeis Assn., Am. Judicature Soc., Internat. Soc. Family Law, Am. Arbitration Assn. (gen. panel arbitrators 1964—). Office: 40 Exchange Pl New York City NY 10005 Tel (212) 344-3399

DAVIS, AYMER DEAN, b. Eldora, Iowa, Mar. 19, 1908; student Grinnell Coll.; B.S. in Commerce, Northwestern U., 1929; LL.B., Ill. Inst. Tech., 1935. Admitted to Ill. bar, 1935; since practiced in Chgo., individual practice law, 1935-73; partner firm Bergstrom, Davis & Olson, 1973—; Mem. Kiwanis Club Oak Park (pres. 1967); active Boy Scouts Am., chmn. troop com., Elmhurst; mem. Elmhurst (Ill.) Planning Commn., 1954-58. Mem. Am., Ill., Chgo. Bar Assns., Delta Theta Phi. Home: 205 Rex Blvd Elmhurst IL 60126 Office: 39 S LaSalle St Chicago IL 60603 Tel (312) 641-1420

DAVIS, BENJAMIN BERNARD, b. Lithuania, June 28, 1902 (parents Am. citizens); Ph.B., U. Chgo., 1921, J.D., 1923. Partner firms Socrates & Davis, Chgo., 1933-37, Davis, Jones & Baer and predecessor, Chgo., 1937—. Mem. Ill., Chgo., Am. bar assns. Home: 1335 Astor St Chicago IL 60610 Office: 120 S La Salle St Chicago IL 60603 Tel (312) ST 2-5949

DAVIS, BENJAMIN WESLEY, b. Eskridge, Kans., Sept. 4, 1889; LL.B., Kans. U., 1913. Admitted to Idaho bar, 1913, 9th Circuit Ct. Appeals bar, 1917, U.S. Ct. Appeals bar, 1956; partner firm Baird & Davis, American Falls, Idaho, 1913-18; individual practice law, Pocatello, Idaho, 1918—; atty. City of Pocatello, 1923-31. Chmn. Idaho Democratic Com., 1938-40. Home: 533 N Hayes St Pocatello ID 83201 Office: PO Box 1073 123 N Arthur Ave Pocatello ID 83201 Tel (208) 2773

DAVIS, BRITTON ANTHONY, b. Highland Park, Ill., Jan. 2, 1936; student Denison U., 1954-57; B.S. in Law, Northwestern U., 1959, LL.B., 1960. Admitted to Ill. Supreme Ct. bar, 1960, U.S. Dist. Ct. for No. Dist. of Ill. bar, 1960, U.S. Ct. of Appeals 7th Circuit bar, 1963, 3d Circuit bar, 1976, U.S. Supreme Ct. bar, 1976; asso. firm Haight, Simmons & Hofeldt, Chgo., 1959-67; partner firm Haight, Hofeldt, Davis & Jambor, Chgo., 1968—. Mem. Am. Bar Assn., Patent Law Assn. Chgo., Bar Assn. 7th Fed. Circuit. Home: 2035 Thornwood Ave Wilmette IL 60091 Office: 55 E Monroe St Suite 3614 Chicago IL 60603 Tel (312) 263-2353

DAVIS, BRUCE GRIFFIN, b. Bainbridge, Ga., Oct. 16, 1925; A.B., Duke, 1947, B.S., 1947; LL.B., U. Fla., 1950, J.D., 1955; postgrad. Fla. State U., 1958. Admitted to Fla. bar, 1950, U.S. Supreme Ct. bar, 1956, U.S. Ct. Mil. Appeals bar; practiced in Tallahassee, 1950—. Mem. Delta Theta Phi, Alpha Phi Omega, Alpha Kappa Psi, Sigma Alpha Epsilon. Home: 413 S Ride St Tallahassee FL 32303 Office: 103 N Gadsden St Tallahassee FL 32301 Tel (904) 385-2548

DAVIS, CHARLES EUGENE, b. Waco, Tex., May 7, 1934; B.S., Trinity U., 1956; LL.B., St. Mary's U., 1959. Admitted to Tex. bar, 1959; partner firm Morriss, Boatwright, Lewis & Davis, San Antonio, 1962—. Mem. Am., Tex., San Antonio bar assns., Am. Judicature Soc. Home: 319 Elizabeth St Terrell Hills TX 78209 Office: 1215 Nat Bank Commerce Bldg San Antonio TX 78205 Tel (512) 227-8304

DAVIS, CHESTER R., JR., b. Chgo., Aug. 30, 1930; grad. Phillips Exeter Acad., 1947; A.B., Princeton, 1951; LL.B., Harvard, 1958. Admitted to Ill. bar, 1958; asso. firm Bell, Boyd, Lloyd, Haddad & Burns, and predecessors, Chgo., 1958-67, partner, 1968—; arbitrator Am. Arbitration Assn., Chgo., 1965—. Sec., bd. dirs. Vascular Disease Research Found., Chgo., 1968—; asso. Rush-Presbyterian-St. Lukes Med. Center, Chgo., 1964—, Adlai Stevenson Inst. Internat. Affairs, Chgo., 1968-74, Newberry Library, Chgo., 1974—; mem. Winnetka Zoning Commn. and Zoning Bd. Appeals, 1974—, Winnetka Plan Commn., 1976—; mem. alumni council Phillips Exeter Acad. Mem. Am., Ill., Chgo. (chmn. com. civil practice 1969-70) bar assns., Am. Judicature Soc., Am. Soc. Internat. Law, Harvard Law Soc. Ill. (past pres.), Harvard Law Sch. Assn. (past nat. v.p.), Law Club Chgo., Legal Club Chgo. Home: 670 Blackthorn Rd Winnetka IL 60093 Office: 135 S LaSalle St Chicago IL 60603 Tel (312) 372-1121

DAVIS, CLIFFORD, b. Dallas, Dec. 5, 1925; B.S., U. Chgo., 1949; LL.B., Harvard, 1952. Admitted to Tex. bar, 1952; clk. Supreme Ct. Tex., 1952-53; individual practice law, San Antonio, 1953-60; instr. St. Mary's U., 1955-60; teaching fellow Harvard, 1960-61; asst. prof., U. Iowa, 1961-64, asst. dean, 1964-66, asso. prof. 1964-68, prof. 1968-69; prof. U. Conn., 1969—; vis. prof. U. Ark., summer 1968, La. State U., summer 1968, U. San Diego, summer 1973, So. Meth. U., spring 1955; judge municipality of Alamo Heights (Tex.), 1956-58; cons. Nat. Water Commn., 1969-71; spl. advisor 2nd Restatement of Torts, 1970—. Mem. Zoning Bd. Appeals Alamo Heights, 1958-60. Mem. Tex., Conn. bar assns. Author: The Iowa Law of Workmen's Compensation (with others), 1967; Eastern Water Rights, 1976; contbr. articles to texts and jours. Home: 26 Fox Den Rd Simsbury CT 06092 Office: 1800 Asylum Ave West Hartford CT 06117 Tel (203) 253-4841

DAVIS, CLIFFORD LEON, b. Mt. Erie, Ill., Jan. 4, 1923; B.S. in B.A., U. Akron, 1948, LL.B., J.D., 1960. Admitted to Ohio bar, 1962, Fla. bar, 1963; asst. sec., mgr. real estate dept. world-wide Firestone Tire & Rubber Co., Akron, Ohio, 1974—. Mem. Fla., Ohio (winner 2d prize for essay), Akron bar assns. Office: 1200 Firestone Pkwy Akron OH 44317 Tel (216) 379-4421

DAVIS, DON WAYNE, b. Madison, Fla., Feb. 7, 1943; B.S. in Journalism, U. Fla., 1965; J.D., Fla. State U., 1969. Admitted to Fla. bar, 1970; judge Madison County (Fla.) Ct., 1971—. Mem. Am. Bar Assn., Nat. Coll. Probate Judges, Conf. County Ct. Judges Fla. (pres. 1976-77). Office: Madison County Courthouse Madison FL 32340 Tel (904) 973-6221

DAVIS, DONALD WAYNE, b. Sapulpa, Okla., Feb. 1, 1934; B.A., U. Colo., 1962; J.D., U. Wyo., 1968. Admitted to Colo. bar, Okla. bar; individual practice law, Oklahoma City, 1969—; asst. asso. municipal judge, Oklahoma City, 1972—. Mem. Nat., Am., Okla., Okla. County bar assns., J.J. Bruce Law Soc. Office: 3709 Springlake Dr Park Plaza Shops Oklahoma City OK 73111 Tel (405) 427-8386

DAVIS, DONALD WILLIAM, b. Washington, Mar. 6, 1943; B.A., U. Va., 1964, LL.B., 1967. Admitted to Ala. bar, 1967; law clk. U.S. Dist Ct. No. Dist. Ala., 1969-70; atty. NLRB, Atlanta, 1970-72, Birmingham, Ala., 1972-77; individual practice law, Birmingham, 1977—. Mem. Fed., Birmingham bar assns. Decorated Bronze Star, Air medal. Contbr. articles in field to legal jours. Home: 2625 Aberdeen Rd Birmingham AL 35223 Office: 821 Frank Nelson Bldg Birmingham AL 35203 Tel (205) 322-7470

DAVIS, DUPREE DANIEL, b. Jackson, Tenn., Mar. 18, 1907; A.B., Morehouse Coll., 1930; B.S., Tenn. State U., 1933; LL.B., LaSalle U.; J.D., Iowa State U., 1944; postgrad. Harvard U., 1945-46. Admitted to Tenn. bar, 1943, Iowa bar, 1944, Ill. bar, 1946, U.S. Supreme Ct. bar, 1969; asst. atty. gen. State of Ill., 1966-69; asst. state's atty. St. Clair County (Ill.), 1946-74; city atty. City of East St. Louis (Ill.), 1960-74, corp. counsel, 1975—. Mem. NAACP. Tel (618) 874-4491

DAVIS, E. LAWRENCE, III, b. Winston-Salem, N.C., Dec. 30, 1937; A.B., Princeton, 1960; LL.B., Duke, 1963; M.B.A., George Washington U., 1966. Admitted N.C. bar, 1963; asso. firm Womble, Carlyle, Sandridge & Rice, Winston-Salem, 1965-69, partner, 1970—; mem. N.C. Ho. of Reps., 1970-74, N.C. Senate, 1974—. Trustee N.C. Bapt. Hosp., N.C., Mental Health Assn. Mem. Am., Forsyth County, N.C. bar assns., Am. Judicature Soc. Named Citizen of Year Winston-Salem Com. Employment Handicapped, 1971, Distinguished Service award Winston-Salem Jaycees, 1972, N.C. Jaycee Freedom Guard award, 1972, U.S. Freedom Guard award, 1973. Home: 321 Banbury Rd Winston-Salem NC 27104 Office: PO Drawer 84 Winston Salem NC 27102 Tel (919) 725-1311

DAVIS, EMILY CLAIRE, b. Kansas City, Mo., Aug. 1, 1913; B.S., Columbia, 1949; J.D., George Washington U., 1967. Admitted to Calif. bar, 1969; individual practice law, Santa Barbara, Calif., 1969—; ops. officer CIA, Washington, 1955-63. Chmn. goals com. Santa Barbara Planning Commn., 1970-74; bd. dirs. Allied Protective and Improvement Assn., Santa Barbara, 1975-76. Mem. Am., Calif. bar assns. Decorated Legion of Merit; named Woman of Yr., Santa Barbara, 1973. Home: 5141 Miembro Laguna Hills CA 92653

DAVIS, ERNEST E., b. Nogalus Prairie, Tex., Oct. 16, 1887; certificate Sam Houston Tchr's. Inst, Huntsville, Tex., 1910; diploma Chadman's Sch. Law, 1920; LL.B., U. Tex., 1926. Prin., coach pub. schs., Tex., 1910-12, 14-16, 16-17, tchr., 1912-13, supt., 1913-14, 17-21, 23-28; county atty. Jasper County (Tex.), 1935-38; dist. justice peace, Liberty County, Tex., 1961; corp. judge City of Dayton (Tex.), 1963-74. Active Boy Scouts Am., 1918—. Mem. Tex. Bar Assn. Recipient Silver Beaver award Boy Scouts Am., 1949. Home: 207 W Barrow St Dayton TX 77535 Office: 510 N Main St Dayton TX 77535 Tel (713) 258-2559

DAVIS, FRANK MYRLE, b. Unicoi, Tenn., Nov. 2, 1921; LL.B., U. Tenn., 1948. Admitted to Tenn. bar, 1948, Mont. bar, 1953; asso. firm McFadden & Davis, Dillon, Mont., 1953-67; individual practice law, Dillon, 1967—; judge 5th Jud. Dist. Mont., Dillon, 1970. Mem. exec. bd. Western Mont. Coll. Mem. Mont. Bar Assn. Recipient Distinguished Service award Jaycees, 1969. Home: 436 S Idaho St Dillon MT 59725 Office: Gleed Bldg Dillon MT 59725 Tel (406) 683-5861

DAVIS, FRANK TRADEWELL, JR., b. Atlanta, Feb. 2, 1938; B.A., Princeton, 1960; J.D., George Washington U., 1963; LL.M., Harvard, 1964. Admitted to Ga. bar, 1963; asso. firm Hansell, Post, Brandon & Dorsey, 1964-68, partner, 1968—; vis. instr. law U. Ga. Sch. Law, 1968-69; dir. Ivan Allen Co., 1971—, Times-Jour. Pub. Co., 1974—; mem. Met. Atlanta Crime Commn., 1974--, chmn., 1977. Legal div. Met. Atlanta United Way, 1971, pub. service unit, 1972; mem. Reading Adv. Bd. City of Atlanta; sec. Atlanta Charter Commn., 1972-73; pres. Research Atlanta, 1972; charter trustee The Westminster Schs. Inc., 1969—; bd. dirs. Met. Atlanta ARC, 1974—. Mem. Internat., Atlanta, Columbia, Ga., Am. bar assns., Atlanta C. of C. (dir. 1975—). Contbr. articles to legal jours. Home: 3229 Chateau Ct NW Atlanta GA 30305 Office: 3300 1st Nat Bank Tower Atlanta GA 30303 Tel (404) 581-8079

DAVIS, FREDERICK BUSH, b. Savannah, Ga., Oct. 16, 1907; LL.B., U. Ga., 1931. Admitted to Ga. bar, 1931; asst. atty. gen. State of Ga., 1943-44; asst. atty. City of Savannah, 1938-40; asso. firm Oliver and Oliver, Savannah, 1937-43; mem. firm Oliver, Oliver and Davis, Savannah, 1943-59; mem. firm Oliver, Davis and Maner, Savannah, 1959-63; individual practice law, Savannah, 1963-73; staff atty. Ga. Indigent Legal Services, Savannah, 1973—. Bd. dirs. Epis. Home for Girls, Savannah. Mem. Am., Ga., Savannah bar assns., Phi Delta Phi. Home: 608 E 56th St Savannah GA 31405 Office: 1723 Bull St Savannah GA 31401 Tel (912) 944-2180

DAVIS, GALE ELWOOD, b. Omaha, July 18, 1909; J.D., U. Nebr., 1931. Admitted to Nebr. bar, 1931; with Mut. of Omaha Ins. Co., 1932-65, exec. v.p., 1958-65; pres. United Benefit Life Ins. Co., 1965-75, dir., 1959—; dir. First Westroads Bank, Omaha, 1966—. Pres., Omaha Home for Boys, dir., 1966—; trustee, dir. U. Nebr. Found., Lincoln, 1967—, Clarkson Hosp., 1954—; bd. dirs. Omaha Indsl. Found., 1974—. Mem. Nebr. Bar Assn. Home: 939 S 106th Plaza Omaha NE 68114 Office: 3301 Dodge St Omaha NE 68131 Tel (402) 342-7600

DAVIS, GARY LYNN, b. Great Falls, Mont., May 6, 1940; B.A., Claremont Men's Coll., 1963; J.D., U. Mont., 1966. Admitted to Mont. bar, 1966; with JAGC, U.S. Army, 1966-70; partner firm Luxan, Murfitt & Davis, Helena, Mont., 1970—. Vice pres. bd. dirs. Helena, United Way, 1975-76; commr. City of Helena, 1976—. Mem. Mont., Am., 1st Jud. Dist. (pres. 1976-77) bar assns. Named Outstanding Young Man, Helena Jaycees, 1976; editorial bd. Mont. Law Rev., 1964-66. Home: 917 Harrison St Helena MT 59601 Office: 312 Northwestern Bank Bldg Helena MT 59601 Tel (406) 442-7450

DAVIS, GEORGE CUNDALL, b. Waupun, Wis., Apr. 28, 1899; A.B., U. Wis., 1923, J.D., 1925. Admitted to R.I. bar, 1926; asso. firm Tillinghast, Collins & Graham and predecessors, Providence, 1926-36, partner, 1936—; pres., chmn., dir. R.I. Blue Cross, 1939-75; dir. R.I. Health Services. Bd. dirs., past pres. R.I. Hist. Soc., bd. dirs. Providence Boys Clubs; sec. R.I. Hosp., Providence, 1940-48; bd. dirs., past pres. R.I. Heritage Found., U. R.I. Found. Fellow Am. Bar Found.; mem. R.I. Bar Assn. (pres. 1962-66, ho. of dels. 1972-74), Am. Law Inst., Am. Judicature Soc. Home: 168 Post Rd Wakefield RI 02879 Office: 2000 Hosp Trust Tower Providence RI 02903 Tel (401) 274-3800

DAVIS, GERALD KENNETH, b. Greensburg, Kans., June 1, 1932; A.B., U. Kan., 1954; J.D., U. Calif., Berkeley, 1959. Admitted to Calif. bar, 1960; asso. firm Baker, Palmer, Wall & Raymond, Bakersfield, 1960-63; partner firm Raymond & Davis, Bakersfield, 1963-65; judge Municipal Ct., Bakersfield Jud. Dist., 1965-76, Kern County Superior Ct., 1976—; mem. Calif. Commn. on Jud., Qualifications, 1968-76. Home: 1621 Country Club Dr Bakersfield CA 93306 Office: 1415 Truxtun Ave Bakersfield CA 93301 Tel (805) 861-2437

DAVIS, GLENN EDWARD, b. Flushing, N.Y., May 27, 1938; B.A. in Sociology Muhlenberg Coll., 1960; J.D., Rutgers U., 1963. Admitted to N.J. bar, 1965, Pa. bar, 1971, D.C. bar, 1971; clerk Kentz, Kentz & Gibson, Summit, N.J., 1963-65; mem. editorial bd. Commerce Clearing House, Clark, N.J., 1965-66; asso. firm Joseph C. Doren, Dunellen, N.J., 1966-70; corp. atty. Gulf Oil Corp., Bala Cynwyd, Pa., 1970—. Mem. Pa., D.C. bar assns., Pa. Trial Lawyers Assn., N.J. Petroleum Council, Am. Petroleum Inst. Office: 1 Presidential Blvd Bala Cynwyd PA 19004 Tel (215) 667-9000

DAVIS, GUY-MICHAEL BENEDICT, b. Toledo, Dec. 10, 1936; B.A. cum laude in Philosophy, Bowdoin Coll., 1959; J.D., U. Toledo, 1966. Admitted to Ohio bar, 1966, D.C., 1966; asso. firm Melrod, Redman & Gartlan, Wash. D.C., 1966-69; asst. to pres., sec.-treas., Sam Davis Co., Inc., Toledo, 1969-70; asst. sec. firm Reose, Wade & Co., Toledo, 1971—; sec. The Reuben Co., Toledo, 1974—. Trustee, Toledo Symphony Orchestra, 1972—, chmn. budget and finance com., 1976—; bd. dirs. Downtown Toledo Assos., 1970; trustee Toledo Modern Art Group, 1970-72; treas. NW Ohio ACLU, 1961-63; chmn., 1963-65; sec., committeeman, Cub Scouts Am., 1972-73. Mem. Toledo, Am. bar assns. Home: 230 Riverside Dr Rossford OH 43460 Office: 620 Madison Ave Toledo OH 43604 Tel (419) 255-3600

DAVIS, HARTWELL, b. Auburn, Ala., Dec. 18, 1906; student U. Fla., 1923-24; B.S., Auburn U., 1928; postgrad. (Woodrow Wilson Meml. scholar) U. Va., 1929-30; J.D., Emory U., 1931. Admitted to Ga., Fla., Ala. bars, 1931; clk. Bradenton Bank & Trust Co., 1924-25; practice law, Opelika and Montgomery, Ala., 1931—; asst. U.S. atty. Middle Dist. Ala., 1932-51, U.S. atty., 1953-62; city atty. Montgomery, 1951-53; spl. asst. atty. gen. Ala., 1964-71. Pres. Montgomery YMCA, 1938-40, bd. dirs., 1935-57; trustee George Wheeler Meml. Scholarship Fund, 1941-71; chmn. ct. honor Tuckabatchee Area council Boy Scouts Am., 1951-52, chmn. merit badge com., 1953; bd. dirs. Ala. Meth. Children's Home, Selma, 1953-76; del. Southeastern Jurisdictional Conf. Meth. Ch., 1948, 52, 56; mem. Meth. Gen. Bd. Evangelism, 1952-56; sec.-treas. bd. lay activities Meth. Ala. Conf., 1945-60. Mem. Am., Fed., Montgomery County bar assns., Ala. State Bar, Am., Ala. trial lawyers assns., Am. Judicature Soc., Phi Alpha Delta. Home: 2216 Allendale Pl Montgomery AL 36111 Office: Suite 609-11 First Alabama Bank Bldg Montgomery AL 36104 Tel (205) 269-1286

DAVIS, HARVEY LEO, b. Birmingham, Ala., Sept. 25, 1911; B.A., U. Akron, 1937; LL.B., So. Meth. U., 1940. Admitted to Tex. bar, 1940, D.C. bar, 1945, U.S. Supreme Ct. bar; spl. agt. FBI, Phila., Chgo., Washington, 1940-46; asso. firm J. Alex Blakeley, Dallas, 1946-49; lectr. law So. Meth. U., Dallas, 1946-49, prof., 1949—, also adviser, coach Moot Ct.; of counsel firm Lancaster & Smith, Dallas, 1975—. Sec., pres. Addison (Tex.) Ind. Sch. Bd., 1955-58; sec., treas. Tex. Consumer Assn., Austin, 1965-73. Mem. Tex., Dallas bar assns., Assn. Am. Law Schs. Contbr. articles to law revs. and jours. Office: Southern Methodist U Sch Law Dallas TX 75275 Tel (214) 692-2569

DAVIS, HEYWOOD HODDER, b. Kansas City, Mo., Sept. 17, 1931; A.B., U. Kans., 1952, LL.B., 1958. Admitted to Kans. bar, 1958, Mo. bar, 1958, U.S. Supreme Ct. bar, 1962; law clk. Justice Charles E. Whittaker, U.S. Supreme Ct., 1958-59; mem. firm Dietrich, Davis, Dicus, Rowlands & Schmitt, Kansas City, 1959—, partner, 1974—; speech instr. U. Kans., 1956-58. Dir., Legal Aid and Defender Soc. of Greater Kansas City, 1962-68, 72—, former pres., sec. and treas. Mem. Am., Kansas City bar assns., Lawyers Assn. of Kansas City, Estate Planning Council of Kansas City (former pres., sec.), Order Coif. Home: 1017 W 67th St Kansas City MO 64113 Office: 1001 Dwight Bldg Kansas City MO 64105 Tel (813) 221-3420

DAVIS, ILUS WINFIELD, b. Kansas City, Mo., Apr. 22, 1917; A.B., U. Kans., 1937; LL.B., U. Mo., 1939. Admitted to Mo. Supreme Ct. bar, 1939, U.S. Supreme Ct. bar, 1968; asso. firm Gossett, Ellis, Dietrich & Tyler, Kansas City, Mo., 1939-40; partner firm Dietrich, Davis, Dicus, Rowlands & Schmitt and predecessors, Kansas City, 1949—, mng. partner, 1971—; councilman City of Kansas City, 1948-55, mayor, 1963-71; chmn. bd. Boatmen's North Hills Bank of Kansas City, 1959—, also Boatmen's Bank and Trust Co. of Kansas City; dir. Boatmen's Bankshares Inc. of St. Louis. Pres. Law Sch. Found. U. Mo. at Columbia, 1974-75; pres. Kansas City Bd. Police Commrs., 1973—. Fellow Am. Bar Found.; mem. Lawyer's Assn., Kansas City, Am. (ho. of dels. 1960-62) bar assns., Am. Judicature Soc., Mo. Bar (pres. 1959, trustee). Home: 1001 W 59th Terr Kansas City MO 64113 Office: 1001 Dwight Bldg 1004 Baltimore St Kansas City MO 64105 Tel (816) 221-3420

DAVIS, JAMES DONALD, b. Danville, Va., Dec. 2, 1938; B.S., Va. Poly. Inst., 1961; LL.B., U. Richmond, 1964; Admitted to Va. bar, 1964; law clk. judge Harry L. Carrico, Va. Supreme Ct., 1964-66; partner firm McCaul, Grigsby & Pearsall, Richmond, 1966—. Active Richmond Civitan Club. Mem. Am., Va., Richmond bar assns., Va. Trial Lawyers Assn., Richmond Estate and Adminstrn. Council. Home: 4215 Kingcrest Pkwy Richmond VA 23221 Office: Box 558 Richmond VA 23219 Tel (804) 644-5491

DAVIS, JAMES EDWIN, b. McAlester, Okla., Jan. 10, 1945; B.A., U. Tex. at Austin, 1967, J.D., 1969. Admitted to Tex. bar, 1969, Ark. bar, 1971, U.S. Supreme Ct. bar, 1973; individual practice law, Texarkana, Tex., 1969—. Bd. dirs. Texarkana Sheltered Workshop, Texarkana Youth Service Corp. Mem. State Bar Tex., S.W. Ark. Bar Assn., Tex. Criminal Def. Lawyers Assn. Office: 711 Pecan St Texarkana AR 75502 Tel (501) 774-2181

DAVIS, JESSE DUNBAR, b. Burden, Kans., June 19, 1908; student U. Okla. Sch. Bus., 1926-28; LL.B., U. Tulsa, 1944. Asst. Mgr. Long-Bell Lumber Co., Muskogee, Okla., 1928-32, gen. mgr., Tulsa, 1933-48, div. mgr., Kansas City, Mo., 1949-57; admitted to Okla. bar, 1944, U.S. Supreme Ct. bar, 1950, Mo. bar, 1959, Fed. bar, 1963; legal officer Supply Corps, USN, 1944-46; individual practice law, Tulsa, 1946—, Joplin, Mo., 1959, Kansas City, Mo., 1960-65, Claremore, Okla., 1969—; v.p., dir. Tamko Asphalt Products, Inc., Joplin, Mo., 1958-59; gen. counsel Southwestern Lumberman's Assn., Kansas City, 1960-65, corporate sec., 1962-65; mgmt. cons., Tulsa, 1965—; realtor, Tulsa; columnist Retail Lumberman Mag., 1962-65; cons. Industry Sch. Forestry, U. Mo., 1962-65; tchr. bus. law U. Mo., 1946-65; tchr. real estate law U. Tulsa, 1969—; v.p., dir., asso. editor Retail Lumberman Pub. Co., Kansas City, 1962-65. Mem. Am. Judicature Soc., Lawyers Assn. Kansas City, Tulsa Bd. Realtors (dir. 1970-72, treas. 1971, corporate sec. 1972), Tulsa C. of C. (Civic award 1939), Res. Officers Assn. U.S. (life), Claremore C. of C. (dir. 1972-74, v.p. 1973-74), Am., Fed., Tulsa County, Rogers County, Kansas City bar assns., SAR, U.S. Navy League, Mid-Am. Lumbermens Assn., Nat. Lumber and Bldg. Material Dealers Assn. (dir. 1962-64), Tulsa County Hist. Soc. (life), Phi Delta Theta, Phi Beta Gamma. Recipient Civic award Tulsa YMCA, 1946-47. Home: 3231 S Utica Ave Tulsa OK 74105 Office: 516 W Will Rogers Blvd PO Box 2 Claremore OK 74017 Tel (918) 266-4234

DAVIS, JIMMY FRANK, b. Lubbock, Tex., June 14, 1945; B.S. in Edn., Tex. Tech. U., Lubbock, 1968; J.D., U. Tex., Austin, 1972. Admitted to Tex. bar, 1972, U.S. Supreme Ct. bar, 1975; asst. criminal dist. atty. Lubbock County, (Tex.), 1973—, adminstrv. asst., 1976—. Mem. Am., Lubbock County bar assns., Lubbock County Jr. Bar (v.p. 1976-77), Tex. Dist. and County Attys. Assn. Recipient Outstanding Young Man of Am. award, 1975. Home: 2311 33d St Lubbock TX 79411 Office: 202 County Courthouse Lubbock TX 79401 Tel (806) 747-0111

DAVIS, JOHN LOYLE, b. St. Louis, May 25, 1942; B.S., Millikin U., 1964; J.D., St. Louis U., 1967. Admitted to Mo. bar, 1967, Ill. bar, 1968; asso. firm Byers & Westfall, 1968-70; asst. pub. defender, Macon County (Ill.), 1969-71; magistrate, asso. circuit Judge 6th Jud. Circuit Ct., Decatur, Ill.; co-founder Vols. in Ct., 1972. Mem. Ill. Bar Assn., Nat. Assn. Juvenile Ct. Judges, Decatur C. of C. (mem. advisory com. 1970). Recipient Certificate of Appreciation AFL-CIO Community Services Bd., 1974; Certificate of Appreciation Lions Club, 1974. Home: 115 Dover Dr Decatur IL 62512 Office: 253 E Wood St Courtroom 6 Decatur IL 62523 Tel (217) 428-9755

DAVIS, JOHN WAYNE, b. Ft. Sill, Okla., Sept. 2, 1943; B.A., U. Wyo., 1964, J.D., 1968. Admitted to Wyo. bar, 1968; asso. firm Bruce Bradley, Sheridan, Wyo., 1968; served with JAGC, U.S. Army, 1969-73; individual practice law, Worland, Wyo., 1973—; ct. commr. Washakie County (Wyo.), 1975—; chmn. Worland Bd. of Adjustment and Planning Commn., 1975—; sec. Environ. Quality Council, Wyo., 1975—. Chmn. Washakie County Dem. Party, 1974—. Mem. Wyo. Bar Assn. Home: 1409 Grace St Worland WY 82401 Office: 212 S 7th St Worland WY 82401

DAVIS, KEN W., b. Foley, Fla., Nov. 14, 1945; B.S. in Bus. Adminstrn., U. Fla., 1967; J.D., Fla. State U., 1970. Admitted to Fla. bar, 1970, U.S. Supreme Ct. bar, 1974; asst. pub. defender 3rd Circuit Fla., 1970-72, pub. defender, 1972-73; partner firm Dansby Davis & Davis, Tallahassee, 1970-72; individual practice law, Tallahassee, 1972-77; partner firm Davis & Judkins, Tallahassee, 1977—. Mem. Am., Tallahassee (pres. 1977) bar assns., Acad. Fla. Trial Lawyers (dir. 1976-78), Assn. Trial Lawyers Am., Nat. Criminal Def. Lawyers Assn., Phi Delta Phi. Home: 2801 Woodside Dr Tallahassee FL 32303 Office: 210 E College Ave Tallahassee FL 32303 Tel (904) 222-6026

DAVIS, KENNETH CULP, b. Leeton, Mo., Dec. 19, 1908; A.B., Whitman Coll., 1931, LL.D., 1971; LL.B., Harvard, 1934. Admitted to Ohio bar, 1935; practiced in Cleve., 1934-35; asst. prof., then asso. prof. W.Va. U., 1935-39; with Dept. Justice, 1939-40; prof. law U. Tex., 1940-48, U. Minn., 1950-61; John P. Wilson prof. law U. Chgo., 1961—. Vis. prof. law Harvard, 1948-50; staff mem. Bd. Investigation and Research, 1942. Mem. Phi Beta Kappa, Delta Sigma Rho, Phi Delta Theta. Author: Administrative Law, 1951; Administrative Law Treatise, 4 vols., 1958, Supplement, 1971; Administrative Law Cases-Text Problems, 5th edit., 1973; Administrative Law and Government, 1960; 2d edit., 1975; Discretionary Justice, 1969; Administrative Law Text, 3d edit., 1972; Police Discretion, 1975. Home: 5830 Stony Island Ave Chicago IL 60637 Office: U Chgo Law Sch 5801 Ellis Ave Chicago IL 60637*

DAVIS, KENT WILSON, b. Syracuse, N.Y., Apr. 28, 1936; A.A., St. Petersburg Jr. Coll., 1958; J.D., S. Tex. Coll., 1965. Admitted to Fla. bar, 1965; title officer W. Coast Title Co., St. Petersburg, Fla., 1965-66; individual practice law, St. Petersburg, 1967; partner firm Foster & Davis, St. Petersburg, 1968—; atty. Town of Redington Beach (Fla.), 1974-75. Mem. Fla. Bar, St. Petersburg Bar Assn. Home: 15810 Gulf Blvd Redington Beach FL 33708 Office: 219-4th St N Saint Petersburg FL 33701 Tel (813) 894-3261

DAVIS, LEE FERGUSON, JR., b. Richmond, Va., May 26, 1939; B.A., Duke U., 1961; M.B.A., U. Va., 1963, LL.B., 1967. Admitted to Va. bar, 1967, U.S. Supreme Ct. bar, 1970; with firm Hunton & Williams, Richmond, 1967-70; asst. atty. gen. State of Va., 1970-72; asso. firm Christian, Barton, Epps, Brent & Chappell, Richmond, 1972-75, partner, 1975—. Mem. Richmond Tax Study Commn., 1970-71; vestryman St. Paul's Episcopal Ch., Richmond, 1971-75; bd. dirs. United Way of Greater Richmond, 1975—. Mem. Am., Va. (chmn. sect. taxation 1971-73), Richmond bar assns. Home: 1314 Lock Lomond Ln Richmond VA 23221 Office: 1200 Mutual Bldg Richmond VA 23219 Tel (804) 644-7851

DAVIS, LEONARD JOHN RODGER, b. Los Angeles, Feb. 17, 1924; B.A., U. Calif., 1948; J.D., U. San Francisco, 1949. Admitted to Calif. bar, 1949, U.S. Ct. Appeals bar, 1949; asso. firm Wallace & Parker, 1949-52; individual practice law, 1952-54, San Francisco, 1968—; partner firm Christin & Davis, 1954-68; lectr. in field; spl. counsel City of Davis (Calif.), also San Francisco Internat. Airport. Mem. Am., San Francisco bar assns., Am. Arbitration Assn. Contbr. articles to legal jours. Office: 100 Bush St Suite 2000 San Francisco CA 94104 Tel (415) GA1-2345

DAVIS, MULLER, b. Chgo., Apr. 23, 1935; B.A., Yale, 1957; J.D., Harvard, 1960. Admitted to Ill. bar, 1960; asso. firm Jenner & Block, Chgo., 1960-67; partner firm Davis, Jones & Baer, Chgo., 1967—. Bd. dirs. Infant Welfare Soc., Chgo., 1975—. Mem. Am., Ill. Chgo., Fed. bar assns., Am. Judicature Soc., Chgo. Estate Planning Council, Am. Trial Lawyers Assn. Contbr. articles to profl. jours. Home: 757 Bluff St Glencoe IL 60022 Office: 120 S LaSalle St Chicago IL 60603 Tel (312) ST2-5949

DAVIS, NOEL CHANDLER, b. Athens, Ohio, Aug. 4, 1941; B.A., Denison U., 1964; J.D., Western Reserve U., 1967. Admitted to Ohio bar, 1967, Ill. bar, 1970, Fed. bar, 1971, U.S. Supreme Ct. bar, 1976; law clk. judge common pleas ct., Cleve., 1967-70; partner firm Hart, Banbury & Banbury, Aurora, Ill., 1970—; spl. asst. atty. gen. State Ill., 1970—. Mem. Ohio, Ill., Kane County, Am., Cuyahoga County bar assns. Home: 1141 Alameda Dr Aurora IL 60506 Office: 122 W Downer Place Aurora IL 60507 Tel (312) 892-7001

DAVIS, RANSOM JEFFERSON, b. Lansing, Mich., May 4, 1942; B.A. with honors, Johns Hopkins, 1964; LL.B. cum laude, Columbia, 1967. Admitted to Md. bar, 1968; law clk. U.S. Dist. Ct. for Md., 1967-68; asso. firm Piper & Marbury, Balt., 1968-70, 73-74; asst. U.S. atty. for Md., 1970-72; asst. atty. gen. State of Md., 1974—. Mem. Am., Md. State bar assns., Bar Assn. Balt. City (mem. exec. com.). Home: 2404 Everton Rd Baltimore MD 21209 Office: 1701 1st Nat Bank Bldg Baltimore MD 21202 Tel (301) 539-6868

DAVIS, RAYMOND MCCURDY, b. Youngstown, Ohio, Mar. 18, 1922; B.B.A., U. Chattanooga, 1949; LL.B., McKenzie Coll. Law, 1957. Admitted to Tenn. bar, 1961, U.S. Supreme Ct. bar, 1971; partner firm Foster & Davis, Chattanooga, 1961-63, Davis & Corn, Cleveland, Tenn., 1963—; judge City of Cleveland, 1971-75. Lay reader St. Luke's Episcopal Ch., Cleveland, 1964-72; chmn. Cleve. chpt. ARC, 1966-68; bd. dirs. Cleveland YMCA, 1965-68, Cleveland Day Care Center, 1967-69; chmn. Cleveland-Bradley County Arthritis Found., 1964-65; pres. Cleveland Community Chest, 1967; campaign chmn. Bradley County Lamar Alexander for Gov., 1974. Mem. Tenn. (chmn. gen. sessions ct. com. 1974-75), Bradley County (pres. 1976-77) bar assns. Home: 221 15th St NW Cleveland TN 37311 Office: 73 1st St NW PO Box 1164 Cleveland TN 37311 Tel (615) 472-3318

DAVIS, RICHARD, b. Miami, Fla., Sept. 12, 1943; B.S. with distinction in Govt. Service, U. Ariz., 1969, J.D., 1972. Admitted to Ariz. bar, 1972; mem. firm Chandler, Tullar, Udall & Richmond, Tucson, 1972—; part-time lectr. U. Ariz. Coll. Law; mem. com. of character and fitness Ariz. State Bar. Treas., bd. dirs. Legal Aid Soc., 1975-76; v.p., bd. dirs. Tucson Urban League, 1975-76. Mem. Pima County, Ariz., Am. bar assns., Alpha Phi Alpha (pres. Eta Psi Lambda chpt.). Home: 5620 E S Wilshire St Tucson AZ 85711 Office: 177 N Church St Suite 1110 Tucson AZ 85701 Tel (602) 623-4353

DAVIS, RICHARD JOSEF, JR., b. Bremerton, Wash., July 25, 1943; A.B., U. Calif., Berkeley, 1965; M.I.S., Claremont Coll., 1967; J.D., U. Calif., Los Angeles, 1970. Admitted to Calif. bar, 1971; research atty. Calif. Ct. Appeals., 1970-71; mem. firm Brundage, Beeson & Pappy, Los Angeles, 1971—. Mem. Am., Los Angeles County bar assns. Contbr. articles to legal jours. Office: 1625 W Olympic Blvd Los Angeles CA 90015 Tel (213) 385-3071

DAVIS, ROBERT SPINK, b. Providence, Dec. 8, 1919; A.B., Yale, 1942; LL.B., Harvard, 1948. Admitted to R.I. bar, 1948; asso. firm Edwards & Angell, Providence, 1948-56, partner, 1956—; dir. Citizens Trust Co., R.I. Tool Co., Colonial Linen Systems, Inc., The Entwistle Co., R.I. Electric Protective Co.; sec. Narragansett Capital Corp., Bus. Devel. Co. of R.I.; asst. sec. Amtel, Inc. Trustee Roger Williams Gen. Hosp., bd. dirs. Providence Athenaeum. Home: 11 Abbotsford Ct Providence RI 02906 Office: 1 Hospital Trust Plaza Providence RI 02903 Tel (401) 274-9200

DAVIS, ROGER EDWIN, b. Lakewood, Ohio, Dec. 29, 1928; A.B., Harvard, 1950; LL.B., U. Mich., 1953. Admitted to Mich. bar, 1953, Fla. bar, 1963; practice in Detroit, 1955—; asso. Langs, Molyneaux & Armstrong, 1955-60; counsel Avis Enterprises, 1961-62; with legal dept. S.S. Kresge Co., 1963-70, v.p., gen. counsel, sec., 1970—. Trustee Arnold Home, Detroit, Detroit Country Day Sch. Mem. State Bar Mich., Fla. Bar, Am. Bar Assn., Am. Soc. Corporate Secs. Office: 3100 W Big Beaver Rd Troy MI 48084 Tel (313) 643-1687

DAVIS, RONALD LEE, b. Rockmart, Ga., Sept. 30, 1935; A.B., Emory U., 1958; J.D., U. Ga., 1963. Admitted to Ga. bar, 1965, U.S. Dist. Ct. bar, 1965; law clk. firm Woodruff, Savell, Lane & Williams, Atlanta, 1963-65, asso., 1965-68; individual practice law, Cartersville, Ga., 1968—; judge City of Cartersville, 1970-74. Mem. Am., Ga. State, Cherokee Circuit (pres. 1976-77) bar assns., Lawyers Club Atlanta, Ga. Trial Lawyers Assn. Home: 23 Cassville Rd Cartersville GA 30120 Office: Box 927 Cartersville GA 30120 Tel (404) 382-8533

DAVIS, RONALD LEE, JR., b. Monroe, La., June 1, 1930; student U. South, Sewanee, Tenn., 1947-49; B.A., La. Poly. Inst., 1951; LL.B., La. State U., 1954. Admitted to La. bar, 1954; asso. firm Theus, Grisham, Davis & Leigh, Monroe, 1954—, now sr. partner. Active various charitable orgns. Mem. Am. Judicature Soc., Am., La. bar assns., Am. Coll. Trial Lawyers, Gamma Eta Gamma. Home: Route 4 Bayou Bend Dr Monroe LA 71201 Office: PO Drawer 4768 1303 Bancroft Circle Monroe LA 71203 Tel (318) 388-0100

DAVIS, ROY, b. Milford, Ohio, Sept. 6, 1920; Chem. Engr., U. Cin., 1950; J.D., Salmon P. Chase Coll. Law, 1954. Admitted to Ohio bar, 1959, U.S. Ct. Customs and Patent Appeals, 1970; patent atty. Nat. Lead Co., Cin. and Toledo, 1954-59; patent atty. Diamond Shamrock Corp., Cleve., 1959-66, gen. patent counsel, 1969—. Mem. Am., Ohio bar assns., Am., Cleve. patent law assns., Alpha Chi Sigma. Home: 5916 Chapel Rd Madison OH 44057 Office: 1100 Superior Ave Cleveland OH 44114 Tel (216) 694-5262

DAVIS, RUSSELL LEWIS, b. Rocky Mount, Va., Mar. 8, 1903; student Roanoke Coll., U. Va. Admitted to Va. bar, 1926; individual practice law, Rocky Mount, 1926—; mem. Va. Ho. of Dels., 1966-72; dir. Peoples Nat. Bank of Rocky Mount. Mem. Phi Alpha Delta, Phi Kappa Phi. Home: 116 Talioferro St Rocky Mount VA 24151 Office: 113 E Court St Rocky Mount VA 24151 Tel (703) 483-5221

DAVIS, THOMAS J., JR., b. Buffalo, July 4, 1938; B.S., State U. N.Y., Buffalo, 1966; J.D., U. Miami, Fla., 1970. Admitted to Fla. bar, 1970; individual practice law, South Miami, Fla., 1970-75; pres. firm Davis, Langer, & McDaniel, South Miami, 1975—. Mem. Am. Bar Assn. Contbr. articles to legal jours. Office: Security Federal Bldg South Miami FL 33143 Tel (305) 665-6985

DAVIS, TINE WAYNE, JR., b. Miami, Sept. 16, 1946; B.S., U. Ala., 1968, J.D., 1971. Admitted to Ala. bar, 1971, Fla. bar, 1972; atty. Winn-Dixie Stores, Inc., Jacksonville, Fla., 1971—; mem. pub. affairs com. Food Mktg. Inst. Mem. Fla. Supermarket Assn. (pres.), Ala. Retail Assn. (dir.), Bd. Associated Industries of Fla., Phi Delta Phi. Tel (904) 783-1800

DAVIS, TRIGG THOMAS, b. Spokane, Wash., July 28, 1945; B.A. in Polit. Sci. with distinction, Wash. State U., 1967; J.D., Stanford U., 1970. Admitted to Calif. bar, 1970, Alaska bar, 1971; law clk. to chief justice Alaska Supreme Ct., 1970-72; partner firm Owen Davis Bantlett, Anchorage, 1972-75; individual practice law, Anchorage, 1975—; mem. Alaska Com. Bar Examiners, 1974, 75, 76, Alaska Probate Com., 1974, 75, 76. Mem. Am., Alaska, Anchorage bar assns. Editor Stanford Law Sch. Jour. Internat. Studies, 1968-69. Home: 4812 Wesleyan Dr Anchorage AK 99504 Office: 519 W 4th Ave Anchorage AK 99501 Tel (907) 278-4655

DAVIS, WARREN JUDSON, b. Fort Worth, Tex., Nov. 7, 1937; B.S., Va. Polytech. Inst., 1962; LL.B., U. Va., 1965. Admitted to Va. bar, 1965, N.C. bar, 1975, U.S. Supreme Ct. bar, 1971; partner firm Wheatly, Mason, Wheatly & Davis, Beaufort, N.C., 1974—; asst. commonwealth atty. State of Va., 1965-67; spl. prosecutor, Fairfax County (Va.), 1967; mem. Fairfax (Va.) City Council, 1968-71; mem. Va. Ho. of Dels., 1971-74; gen. counsel Fairfax County Police Assn., 1967-73; mem. Va. Advisory Legis. Council Spl. Com. on Professions and Occupations, 1971-73; mem. Va. Med. Facilities Commn., 1971-72; commr., bd. dirs. No. Va. Planning Dist. Commn., 1971-72; chmn. No. Va. Recreation and Cultural Authority, 1971-73; Va. rep. Washington Area Met. Council Govts., 1970-72, mem. pub. safety policy com., 1969-71; mem. Fairfax County Hwy. Safety Commn., 1969-71. Vice-chmn. Citizens Com. for Mental Health, 1969-71; mem. advisory bd. No. Va. Big Brothers, 1970-73; bd. dirs. Fairfax Little League, 1970-73, Coop. Sch. for Handicapped Children, 1970-73, Monitor Research & Recovery Found., 1975—, Howland Rock Property Owners, Inc., 1974—. Mem. Am. (mem. exec. council young lawyers sect. 1969-71), Fairfax County (chmn. legal aid for criminal defendants com. 1969-71), Va., N.C., Carteret County bar assns., Am., Va., trial lawyers assns., N.C. Acad. Trial Lawyers, Va. Commonwealth's Attys. Assn., Nat. Dist. Attys. Assn., Am. Judicature Soc., Fairfax C. of C. Home: Route 2 Box 127 Beaufort NC 28516 Office: PO Drawer 360 Beaufort NC 28516 Tel (919) 728-3158

DAVIS, W(EBSTER) BANCROFT, b. Denver, Dec. 8, 1917; B.A., Colo. U., 1947, LL.B., 1950, J.D., 1950. Admitted to Colo. bar, 1950; county atty. Sedgwick County (Colo.), Julesburg, 1960-68; city atty. City of Julesburg, 1970—; dep. dist. atty. 13th Jud. Dist., Julesburg, 1956—. Mem. Colo. Bar Assn. Mem. Rocky Mountain Law Rev., 1948-49. Home: 900 Golf Course Rd Julesburg CO 80737 Office: 217 Cedar St Julesburg CO 80737 Tel (303) 474-2600

DAVIS, WENDELL, JR., b. N.Y.C., June 22, 1933; A.B. cum laude, Harvard U., 1954, LL.B. cum laude, 1961. Admitted to Conn. bar, 1961, N.Y. bar, 1963; individual practice law, Brookfield, Conn., 1961; law sec. to Justice Charles D. Breitel, N.Y.C., 1964-65; mem. firm Scheuermann & Davis, and predecessor, N.Y.C., 1972—. Mem. Am. Law Inst., Am., Conn., N.Y. State bar assns., Assn. Bar City N.Y. Home: 1261 Madison Ave New York City NY 10028 Office: 275 Madison Ave New York City NY 10016 Tel (212) 889-1310

DAVIS, WILEY HOWARD, b. Newman, Ga., Oct. 15, 1913; J.D., U. Ga., 1936. Admitted to Ga. bar, 1937; partner firm Shulman and Davis, Atlanta, 1937-47; editor in chief The Harrison Co., Atlanta, 1947-69; asst. atty. gen. State of Ga., 1970-73; reporter of decisions Ct. of Appeals and Supreme Ct. Ga., Atlanta, 1973—; instr. Atlanta Law Sch., 1973-74. Mem. State Bar Ga., Am. Bar Assn. Author: Georgia Practice and Procedure, 1948, 58. Home: 4525 Stella Dr NW Atlanta GA 30327 Office: 616 State Judicial Bldg Atlanta GA 30334 Tel (404) 255-8950

DAVIS, WILLIAM ALEXANDER, JR., b. Columbus, Miss., Dec. 11, 1941; B.A. cum laude, Amherst Coll., 1963; student (Rotary Found. fellow) U. Ibadan (Nigeria), 1963-64; J.D., Yale, 1968, M. Urban Studies, 1972. Admitted to Mass. bar, 1969, D.C. bar, 1977; exec. The Circle, Inc. Community Devel. Corp., Boston, counsel, 1968-72, pres., 1970-72; asso. prof. law, urban studies Mass. Inst. Tech., Cambridge, 1972—; vis. asso. prof. U. Calif., Berkeley, 1973, 75; asso. firm. Covington & Burling, Washington, 1977—; dir. Commonwealth Mass. Govt. Land Bank, 1975-77; commr. Boston Fin. Comm., 1973-76. Trustee, Amherst (Mass.) Coll., 1974—, Folger Shakespeare Library, Washington, 1974—; bd. dirs. Mass. Found. Humanities and Pub. Policy, 1974-76, Greater Boston Community Devel. Inc., 1973-76, Civil Liberties Union Mass., 1973-75. Mem. Am. Judicature Soc., Am. Bar Assn., Yale Law Sch. Assn. (exec. com.). Named Mellon Found. fellow humanities, Aspen Inst. Humanistic Studies, 1974-75; recipient Ten Outstanding Young Leaders award Boston Jr. C. of C., 1972, Significant Contribution to Black Community award, Roxbury Action Program, 1973. Office: Covington & Burling 888 16th St Washington DC 20006 Tel (202) 452-6000

DAVIS, WILLIAM ARTHUR, b. Cleve., Sept. 22, 1948; B.A., DePauw U., 1970; J.D., Case Western Reserve U., 1974. Admitted to Ohio bar, 1974; asso. firm Komito, Nurenberg, Plevin, Jacobson, Heller & McCarthy, Cleve., 1974—. Mem. Ohio State, Cuyahoga County bar assns., Bar Assn. of Greater Cleve., Am., Ohio acad. of trial lawyers. Office: Engineers Bldg Seventh Floor Cleveland OH 44114 Tel (216) 621-2300

DAVIS, WILLIAM REMALEY, JR., b. Wilkinsburg, Pa., Feb. 18, 1934; B.A., Allegheny Coll., 1956; J.D., U. Pitts., 1959. Admitted to Pa. bar, 1963; analyst, div. real estate U.S. Steel Corp., Pitts., 1960-61; asso. firm George C. Eppinger, Chambersburg, Pa., 1962-65; partner firms inson, Camrsbr 62-65; rtne Mower, Davis and Hoskinson, Chambersburg, 1966-75, Davis and Zullinger, Chambersburg, 1976—; mem. Franklin County (Pa.) Bd. Law Examiners and Censors, 1971—; mem. Pa. Jud. Nominating Commn., 1973—; dir. Valley Bank and Trust Co., Chambersburg, 1973—, chmn. trust comm., 1976—. Mem. ofcl. bd. St. Paul United Meth. Ch., Chambersburg. Mem. Pa., Franklin County (chmn. com. continuing legal edn. 1966-75) bar assns., Am. Soc. Hosp. Attys. Recipient Larabee prize Allegheny Coll., 1956. Home: 254 Norland Ave Chambersburg PA 17201 Office: 5 N Second St Chambersburg PA 17201 Tel (717) 264-6991

DAVIS, WILLIAM RUSSELL, b. Waterbury, Conn., Sept. 15, 1930; B.A., Providence Coll., 1952; LL.B., U. Conn., 1955. Admitted to Conn. bar, 1955; partner firm RisCassi and Davis, Hartford, Conn., 1955—; instr. trial tactics U. Conn. Sch. Law, 1971—. Mem. Am., Hartford County (Conn.) bar assns., Am., Conn. trial lawyers assns., Am. Coll. Trial Lawyers, Am. Judicature Soc. Office: RisCassi & Davis 75 Lafayette St Hartford CT 06103 Tel (203) 522-1196

DAVIS, WYLIE HERMAN, b. Macon, Ga., May 26, 1919; A.B., Mercer U., 1940, J.D. magna cum laude, 1947; LL.M., Harvard, 1948. Admitted to Ark. bar, 1953, Ill. bar, 1958, Ga. bar, 1968, U.S. Supreme Ct. bar, 1957, U.S. Ct. Mil. Appeals, 1957; instr. English, Mercer U., 1946-47; from asst. prof. to prof. law U. Ark., 1948-55; prof. law U. Tex., 1955-56, U. Ill., 1956-67, U. Ga., 1967-70; prof. law U. Ark., 1970—, dean Law Sch., 1973—; of counsel Putman, Davis & Bassett, Fayetteville, Ark., 1976—; summer vis. prof. various univs; chmn. Multistate Bar Exam Com. on Contracts, 1972—. Bd. dirs. Antaeus Lineal Inst., Fayetteville, 1974—. Mem. Am., Ark., Washington County bar assns., Am. Judicature Soc., Am. Law Inst., Phi Alpha Delta, Order of Coif. Dir. Ark. Law Rev., Inc., 1972—; contbr. articles to profl. jours. Home: 1719 Carolyn Dr Fayetteville AR 72701 Office: Sch Law U Ark Fayetteville AR 72701 Tel (501) 575-5600

DAVISON, BURNS HARRIS, II, b. Des Moines, Sept. 15, 1931; B.S., Ind. U., 1953; grad. Sch. Law Drake U., 1958. Admitted to Iowa bar, 1958, U.S. Tax Ct. bar, 1958; asso. firm Holliday & Myers, 1958-60; partner firm Jones, Hoffmann & Davison, Des Moines, 1960—. Pres., Des Moines Community Playhouse, 1967, Hubbell PTA, 1976. Mem. Am., Iowa State, Polk County bar assns., Def. Research Inst., Iowa Def. Counsel Assn. Home: 4812 Algonquin Rd Des Moines IA 50311 Office: 900 Des Moines Bldg Des Moines IA 50309 Tel (515) 243-4148

DAVISON, CALVIN, b. Norwood, Ohio, Jan. 9, 1932; A.B., Miami U., Oxford, Ohio, 1953; J.D., Harvard U., 1959. Admitted to D.C. bar, 1959, U.S. Supreme Ct. bar, 1964; asso. firm Jones, Day, Reavis & Pogue, and predecessors, Washington, 1959-65, partner, 1965—. Mem. Am., Fed. Communications bar assns., D.C. Bar, Am. Soc. Internat. Law. Home: 4950 Quebec St NW Washington DC 20016 Office: 1100 Connecticut Ave NW Washington DC 20036 Tel (202) 452-5871

DAVISON, DENVER NORTON, b. Rich Hill, Mo., Oct. 9, 1891; LL.B., U. Okla., 1915, J.D., 1973. Admitted to Okla. bar, 1915, U.S. Supreme Ct. bar, 1950; practiced law in Ada, Okla., 1915-37; justice Okla. Supreme Ct., 1937—, chief justice, 1973-74. Mem. Will Rogers Commn., supervised bldg. Will Rogers Meml. Bldg., Claremore, Okla. Mem. Phi Delta Phi, Alpha Tau Omega. Home: 1806 Huntington St Oklahoma City OK 73116 Office: State Capitol Bldg Oklahoma City OK 73105 Tel (405) 521-3847

DAVISON, MAXWELL E., b. Shenandoah, Pa., Sept. 4, 1932, B.A. in Govt., Lafayette Coll., 1954; J.D., Dickinson Sch. Law, 1957. Admitted to Pa. bar, 1957; since practiced in Allentown, Pa., mem. Zoning Bd. of Adjustment City of Allentown, 1961-69; solicitor Washington Twp., Lehigh County, 1970-71; spl. asst. atty. gen. Commonwealth of Pa., 1971; judge Ct. of Common Pleas Lehigh County, 1971—. Mem. exec. com. United Way Lehigh County; bd.

trustees Cedar Crest Coll.; bd. assos. Muhlenberg Coll.; bd. dirs. Swain Country Day Sch.; bd. dirs. Jewish Community Center Allentown; bd. dirs. Allentown Police Athletic League; bd. dirs. Boys Club Allentown; mem. advisory bd. Minsi Trails Council Boys Scouts Am.; mem. advisory bd. Vol. Friends Lehigh County. Mem. Pa. Conf. State Trial Judges, Pa., Nat. councils juvenile ct. judges. Home: 2530 Allen St Allentown PA 18014 Office: 455 Hamilton St Allentown PA 18105 Tel (215) 434-9471

DAVITIAN, LOUIE S., b. Williamson, W.Va., July 6, 1935; A.B., W.Va. U., 1957, LL.B., 1959. Admitted to W.Va. bar, 1959; city prosecutor Parkersburg (W.Va.), 1961-67; pros. atty. Wirt County (W.Va.), 1959-72, 74—. Mem. W.Va. Bar, W.Va., Wood County bar assns. Office: Comml Bank Bldg 415 1/2 Market St Parkersburg WV 26101 Tel (304) 428-8207

DAW, WILLIAM JAMES, b. Glasgow, Mont., Apr. 4, 1918; A.B., Reed Coll., 1949; J.D., Willamette U., 1955. Admitted to Oreg. bar, 1955; individual practice law, Portland, Oreg., 1956—; asst. atty. gen. Oreg. Centennial Commn., 1959. Mem. alumni bd. dirs. Reed Coll. Office: 311 NE Killingsworth St Portland OR 97211 Tel (503) 285-8366

DAWE, JAMES NICHOLAS, b. Los Angeles, Aug. 8, 1943; A.B., U. San Francisco, 1965, J.D., 1968. Admitted to Calif. bar, 1969; counsel DiGiorgio Corp., San Francisco, 1969-72; asso. corporate counsel, asst. sec. PVO Internat., Inc., San Francisco, 1972-76, corporate counsel, 1976—; sec. Stockton Elevators, Pacific Oilseeds, Inc. Mem. Am., Calif., San Francisco bar assns. Office: 130 World Trade Center San Francisco CA 94111 Tel (415) 362-0990

DAWES, I.H., b. Stoughton, Wis., Nov. 19, 1907; J.D., U. Wis., 1931. Admitted to Wis. bar, 1932; gen. counsel Clark Oil & Refining Corp., Milw., 1943—. Mem. Wis. Bar Assn. Home and office: Route 2 Ripon WI 54971 Tel (414) 748-3879

DAWKINS, BEN C., JR., b. Monroe, La., Aug. 6, 1911; A.B., Tulane U., 1932; LL.B., La. State U., 1934, J.D., 1968. Admitted to La. bar, 1934; individual practice law, Monroe, 1934-35; sr. mem. firm Blanchard, Goldstein, Walker & O'Quin, Shreveport, La., 1935-53; chief judge U.S. Dist. Ct., Western Dist. La., 1953-73, sr. judge, 1973—; Am. Bar Assn. Research fellow Southwestern Legal Found., 1968—; chmn. com. on legislation Jud. Conf. of 5th Circuit, 1956-60. Mem. Caddo Parish (La.) Sch. Bd., 1949-53, pres., 1950-52; co-chmn. fund dir. ARC, Shreveport, 1952-53; vestryman St. Mark's Episcopal Ch., Shreveport, 1958-62, 67-71. Mem. Shreveport (pres. 1949-50), La. State (sec. sect. jud. adminstrn. 1953), Am. bar assns., Samurai, Phi Delta Phi, Omicron Delta Kappa. Home: 4054 Baltimore Ave Shreveport LA 71106 Office: US Dist Ct Western Dist La Shreveport LA 71101 Tel (318) 226-5263

DAWKINS, JEROME ERSEL, b. Port Arthur, Tex., Mar. 8, 1935; A.B., U. Tex., 1961; LL.B., Baylor U., 1963, J.D., 1969. Admitted to Tex. bar, 1963, N.Y. bar, 1972, Pa. bar, 1975; asst. Dallas County Dist. Atty., 1964-66; atty. Mobil Pipe Line Co., Dallas, 1968-70; sr. atty. Mobil Oil Corp., N.Y.C., 1970-75, regional atty., Valley Forge, Pa., 1975—. Chmn. zoning bd. appeals, Village of Briarcliff Manor, N.Y., 1974-75. Mem. Am., Tex. bar assns. Home: 208 French Rd Newtown Square PA 19073 Office: 10 Executive Mall 530 E Swedesford Rd Valley Forge PA 19482 Tel (215) 293-4351

DAWSON, ALEXANDRA DEGHIZE, b. Balt., May 4, 1931; B.A., Barnard Coll., 1953; J.D., Harvard U., 1966. Admitted to Mass. bar, 1966, Fed. bar, 1977; asso. firm Nutter, McClennen & Fish, Boston, 1966-67; asso. firm McCormack & Zimble, Boston, 1967-72; dir. services Conservation Law Found. of New Eng., Boston, 1973-77; gen. counsel, dir. land use regulations Met. Area Planning Council, 1977—; adj. prof. Tufts U., 1976—; spl. instr. R.I. Sch. Design, 1975—. Mem. Weston Conservation Commn., 1974—. Mem. Mass. Assn. Conservation Commns. (dir.). Author: Mass. Assn. Conservation Commns. Handbook, 1972, 77, Mass. Open Space Law, 1972 supplement. Office: 44 School St Boston MA 02109 Tel (617) 523-2454

DAWSON, DEBRA KAE KING, b. Dallas, Jan. 17, 1948; B.A. in English, So. Meth. U., 1969; postgrad. St. Mary's Sch. Law, San Antonio, 1969-70, Baylor U. Sch. Law, 1970-71; J.D., South Tex. Coll. Law, 1973. Admitted to Tex. bar, 1973, U.S. Supreme Ct. bar, 1976; law clk. firm Sleeper, Williams, Johnson, Helm & Estes, Waco, Tex., 1971; individual practice law, Waco, 1973-74; title examiner Dallas Title & Guaranty Co., 1971; landman Anadarko Oil Co., Houston, 1974; partner firm Dawson, Dawson and Dixon, Dallas, 1975—. Mem. Dallas, Am. (chmn. Woman in Law student div. 1970) bar assns., San Antonio Jaycees (hon.), Phi Alpha Delta. Office: Dallas Fed Savings Tower 8333 Douglas St Mall Dallas TX 75225 Tel (214) 691-4004

DAWSON, FOUNTAIN DE WITT, b. Lenoir County, N.C., Apr. 8, 1915; LL.B., Cumberland U. Law Sch., Lebanon, Tenn., 1937; J.D. Cumberland Sch. Law Samford U.; postgrad. U. N.C. Admitted to Miss. bar, 1954; individual practice law, Greenville, Miss., 1953-74; counsel Internat. Brotherhood Teamsters, Chauffers, Warehousemen and Helpers, Nat. Maritime Union, other unions. Mem. Miss., Am., Fed. bar assns., Assn. Trial Lawyers Am., Comml. Law League, Washington County (Miss.) Bar Assn., Alumnus U. N.C., Nat. Lawyers Club.

DAWSON, GERALD, b. Sapulpa, Okla., June 5, 1935; A.B., San Diego State U., 1959; J.D., U. San Diego, 1963. Admitted to Calif. bar, 1964, U.S. Dist. Ct. bar for So. Dist. Calif., 1964; sr. research atty., law clk. to presiding justice Calif. Ct. of Appeal, 4th Appellate Dist., div. one, 1964-66; lectr. in law U. San Diego, 1964-66, asst. dean Sch. Law, asst. prof. law, 1966, adj. prof., 1967-70; partner firm Procopio, Cory, Hargreaves and Savitch, San Diego, 1968—. Pres. Citizens Coordinator for Century III, San Diego, 1970. Mem. Calif. State Bar (chmn. com. on environment 1976), San Diego County Bar Assn. Office: 530 B St San Diego CA 92101 Tel (714) 238-1900

DAWSON, HOWARD ATHALONE, JR., b. Okolona, Ark., Oct. 23, 1922; B.S. in Commerce, U. N.C., 1946; J.D., George Washington U., 1949. Admitted to D.C. bar, 1949, Ga. bar, 1958; pvt. practice, Washington, 1949-50; atty. civil div. Office Chief Counsel, Internal Revenue Service, 1950-53, asst. regional counsel Atlanta region, 1953-56, regional counsel, 1957, asst. chief counsel adminstrn., Washington, 1958-62; judge U.S. Tax Ct., Washington, 1962—, chief judge, 1973—. Mem. Am., Fed. bar assns., Chi Psi, Delta Theta Phi. Home: 7408 Nevis Rd Bethesda MD 20034 Office: US Tax Ct Washington DC 20044*

DAWSON, JOHN HARLAN, b. Chgo., June 12, 1907; B.A., Stanford, 1929; J.D., Harvard, 1933. Admitted to Calif. bar, 1933; sr. partner firm Holbrook, Taylor, Tarr & Reed, Los Angeles, 1933-37; partner firm Stater & Dawson, Los Angeles, 1937-42; Washington rep.; aircraft, 1943-45; pvt. practice law, San Diego, Santa Ana, Anaheim, Calif., 1956-72, Newport Beach, Calif., 1972—; city atty. City of San Juan Capistrano (Calif.), 1960-69; asst. city atty. City of Anaheim (Calif.), 1960-72. Mem. State Bar Calif., Orange County (Calif.), Am. bar assns., Nat. Inst. Municipal Law Officers. Home: 2152 Vista Dorado Newport Beach CA 92660 Office: 4650 Von Karman St Newport Beach CA 92660 Tel (714) 833-8486

DAWSON, SUZANNE STOCKUS, b. Chgo., Dec. 29, 1941; B.A., Marquette U., 1963; J.D. cum laude, Loyola U., 1965. Admitted to Ill. bar, 1965; asso. firm Kirkland & Ellis, Chgo., 1965-71, partner, 1971—. Mem. Am., Ill. bar assns. Home: 682 Lincoln Ave Winnetka IL 60093 Office: 200 E Randolph Dr Chicago IL 60601 Tel (312) 861-2064

DAY, DAVID BRUCE, b. Chgo., Jan. 13, 1943; B.A., U. Calif., 1966, J.D., 1969. Admitted to Calif. bar, 1970; partner firm Darling, Maclin & Day, Bakersfield, Calif., 1969—. Home: 433 E Belle Terr Pl Bakersfield CA 93307 Office: 2920 H St Suite A Bakersfield CA 93301 Tel (805) 325-5075

DAY, J(AMES) EDWARD, b. Jacksonville, Ill., Oct. 11, 1914; A.B., U. Chgo., 1935; LL.B. cum laude, Harvard U., 1938; LL.D., Ill. Coll. Law, 1962, U. Nev., 1962. Admitted to Ill. bar, 1938, D.C. bar, 1963, Md. bar, 1972, U.S. Supreme Ct. bar, 1964; mem. firm Sidley & Austin, and predecessor, Chgo., 1939-41, 45-73, partner in charge, Washington, 1963-73; asst. to Ill. gov. Adlai Stevenson, 1949-50; mem., sec. Ill. Com. Intergovtl. Cooperation, 1949-53, Ill. Com. on Ins., 1950-53; asso. gen. solicitor Prudential Ins. Co. Am., 1953-56, asso. gen. counsel, 1956, sr. v.p. Western ops., Los Angeles, 1957-61; postmaster gen. U.S.A., 1961-63; partner firm Cox, Langford & Brown, Washington, 1973—, Squire, Sanders & Dempsey, Cleve., 1973—; dir., mem. exec. com. Peoples Life Ins. Co., Washington Med. Mut. Liability Ins. Soc. Md.; trustee Common Stock, Conrail; mem. adv. bd. U.S. Customs Bur., 1966-68; chmn. adv. com. Md. State Ins. Dept., 1967-70; mem. Nat. Civil Service League, 1963-66, pres., 1964-66; chmn. Citizens Conf. on State Legislatures, 1965-70. Chmn. nat. devel. com. Georgetown U., 1970—; trustee Hood Coll., Frederick, Md. Fellow Am. Bar Found.; mem. Am., D.C., Md., Fed. (nat. council 1975) bar assns., Postal Rate Bar Assn. Author: Bartholf Street, 1946; My Appointed Round (929 Days as Postmaster General), 1965; Humor in Public Speaking, 1965; legis. editor Harvard Law Rev. Home: 5804 Brookside Dr Chevy Chase MD 20015 Office: 21 Dupont Circle NW Washington DC 20036 Tel (202) 785-0200

DAY, KIM KYLE, b. Dallas, Dec. 1, 1931; B.S., W. Tex. State U., 1952, M.Ed., 1953; J.D., So. Meth. U., 1965. Admitted to Tex. bar, 1965; credit mgr. Phillips Petroleum Co., Amarillo, Tex., 1953-59; asst. credit mgr. Internat. Credit, Collins Radio Co., Dallas, 1960-64; city prosecutor, Dallas, 1965-67; individual practice law, Dallas, 1967—. Mem. Tex., Dallas bar assns., Dallas Criminal Bar Assn. Home: 4667 Westside Dr Dallas TX 75209 Office: 720 Praetorian Bldg Dallas TX 75201 Tel (214) 742-2281

DAY, MARJORIE WILSON, b. Loch Sheldrake, N.Y., Mar. 10, 1923; LL.B., Western State U., Calif., 1971. Admitted to Calif. bar, 1972; asso. firm Portigal & Hammerton, Santa Ana, Calif., 1972—. Trustee Tustin (Calif.) Unified Sch. Dist., 1974—, pres., 1976—. Mem. Calif. Elected Women, Orange County (Calif.) Women Lawyers, Calif. State Bar, Town Hall. Office: 2021 E Fourth St Santa Ana CA 92705 Tel (714) 558-6991

DAY, REED BLACHLY, b. Washington, Pa., Sept. 20, 1930; B.A., Washington and Jefferson Coll., 1952; J.D., U. Pitts., 1957. Admitted to Pa. bar, 1958; partner firm Peacock, Keller, Yohe & Day, Washington, Pa., 1958—; solicitor Peters Twp. Sch. Dist., Washington County, Pa., 1958—; sch. solicitor Washington (Pa.) Sch. Dist., 1972—. Pres. United Way of Central Washington County, 1975; trustee Washington and Jefferson Coll., 1975—. Mem. Allegheny County (Pa.), Washington County, Pa., Am. bar assns., Nat. Orgn. Legal Problems Edn., Nat. Sch. Bds. Assn., Council Sch. Attys., Gen. Alumni Assn. Washington and Jefferson Coll. (pres. 1973-74). Home: 238 Tepee Rd McMurray PA 15317 Office: 68-70 East Beau St Washington PA 15301 Tel (412) 222-4520

DAY, ROBERT STONE, b. Ezel, Ky., Apr. 16, 1923; B.A., Whitman Coll., 1949; LL.B., Gonzaga U., 1953, J.D., 1967. Admitted to Wash. bar, 1953; partner firm Day & Westland, 1954-57, Gladstone, Day and Day, 1957-60, Peterson, Taylor & Day, Tri-Cities, Wash., 1960—. Fellow Internat. Acad. Trial Lawyers; mem. Am., Wash. (pres. 1975-76, gov. 1971-74), Benton-Franklin Counties bar assns., Wash. Trial Lawyers Assn. Home: 347 Greenbrook Pl Richland WA 99352 Office: 627 W Bonneville St Pasco WA 99301 Tel (509) 547-9555

DAY, WILLIAM LOUIS, b. Antwerp, Ohio, Jan. 3, 1913; J.D., Ohio State U., 1947. Admitted to Ohio bar, 1947; judge Ct. of Common Pleas, Probate Div., Paulding County (Ohio), Paulding, 1963—; city solicitor Villages of Paulding, Oakwood, Antwerp and Grover Hill, Ohio, 1959-62. Mem. Ohio, Northwestern Ohio, Paulding County bar assns., Ohio Probate Judges' Assn., Nat., Ohio juvenile juoges' assns. Home: 733 N Cherry St Paulding OH 45879 Office: Probate Court Court House Paulding OH 45879 Tel (419) 399-4781

DAYE, CHARLES EDWARD, b. Durham, N.C., May 14, 1944; B.A., N.C. Central U., 1966; J.D., Columbia, 1969. Admitted to N.Y. bar, 1970, D.C. bar, 1971, N.C. bar, 1975; law clerk U.S. Ct. Appeals, 6th Circuit, Cin., 1969-70; asso. firm Covington & Burling, Washington, 1970-72; asst. prof. law U. N. C., Chapel Hill, 1972-75, asso. prof., 1975—; spl. asst. Policy Planning Council U.S. State Dept., Washington, 1967; cons. N.C. Dept. Adminstrn., 1975. Chmn. Triangle Housing Devel. Corp., Durham, N.C., 1977—; mem. Community Devel. Task Force, Chapel Hill, 1975. Mem. N. C. Assn. Black Lawyers (pres. 1976-77). Contbr. articles in field to profl. jours. Home: Route 6 Box 89 Chapel Hill NC 27514 Office: Sch Law UNC Chapel Hill NC 27514 Tel (919) 933-5106

DAYS, DREW SAUNDERS, III, b. Atlanta, Aug. 29, 1941; A.B., Hamilton Coll., 1963; LL.B., Yale U., 1966. Admitted to Ill. bar, 1966, N.Y. State bar, 1970, U.S. Supreme Ct. bar, 1969; asso. firm Cotton, Watt, Jones, King and Bowlus, Chgo., 1966; vol. atty. Ill. Civil Liberties Union, 1966-67; vol. Peace Corps, Honduras, 1967-69; cons. AID, 1968-69; interpreter Rockefeller Commn., 1969; first asst. counsel NAACP Legal Def. and Ednl. Fund, Inc., 1969-76; asst. U.S. atty. gen. div. civil rights Dept. Justice, Washington, 1976—; asso. prof. law Temple U., 1973-75, U. Ghana, summer 1975. Mem. steering com. Congl. Black Caucus Nat. Conf. Edn. for Blacks, 1972; pres., bd. dirs. Windham Child Care. Mem. Am. Bar Assn., Nat. Conf. Black Lawyers. Author: Materials on Police Misconduct Litigation. Office: Dept Justice 10th and Pennsylvania Ave NW Room 5643 Washington DC 20530 Tel (202) 739-2151

DAYS, VIRGINIA MAE, b. San Jose, Calif., June 25, 1934; B.A., U. Calif., Berkeley, 1960, LL.B., 1963. Admitted to Calif. bar, 1964; practiced law, San Jose, 1964-75; dir. Calif. Dept. Vets. Affairs, Sacramento, 1975—. Mem. City Council Morgan Hill (Calif.), 1970—, mayor, 1972—; mem. Regional Criminal Justice Planning Bd., 1972-75; mem. Morgan Hill Park and Recreation Commn., Morgan Hill Planning Commn., Santa Clara County Drug Abuse Commn. Mem. Nat. Assn. State Dirs. Vets. Affairs, Santa Clara County Bar Assn. Recipient Justice Byrl R. Salsman award for contbns. to community Santa Clara Bar Assn., 1975; Melvin T. Dixon award for outstanding administrv. leadership, 1976. Office: 1227 O St Sacramento CA 95814 Tel (916) 445-3111

DEACHMAN, ROSS VARICK, b. Plymouth, N.H., Mar. 13, 1942; B.S., U. N.H., 1964; J.D., Boston U., 1967. Admitted to N.H. bar, 1967; asso. firm Burns, Bryant, Hinchey & Nadeau, Dover, N.H., 1967-71, firm Walter L. Murphy, Plymouth, N.H., 1971; partner firm Murphy & Deachman, Plymouth, 1972-75, firm Deachman & Gruber, Plymouth, 1975-76; individual practice law, Plymouth, 1977—; lectr. in field. Mem. Plymouth Planning Bd., 1974-75; chmn. bd. appeals N.H. Labor Dept., 1970—; bd. dirs. Sceva Speare Meml. Hosp., 1975—. Mem. N.H. (bd. govs. 1975-77), New Eng. (dir. 1976—), Grafton County (v.p. 1977—), Am. bar assns., Assn. Trial Lawyers. Office: 7 Russell St Plymouth NH 03264 Tel (603) 536-2520

DEACHMAN, WILLIAM JOHN, b. Woodstock, N.H., Aug. 2, 1923; student U.N.H., 1945-47; LL.B., Boston U., 1954. Admitted to N.H. bar, 1954, U.S. Supreme Ct. bar, 1960; individual practice law, Ashland, N.H., 1954-70; asst. atty. gen. N.H., Concord, 1956-57; minority counsel U.S. Senate Com. Aeronautics and Space Scis., 1959-66; Grafton County (N.H.) prosecutor, 1967-68; legis. counsel revision N.H. Criminal Code, 1970-73; mem. N.H. Eminent Domain Commn., 1972-73; U.S. Atty. N.H., Concord, 1973—. Mem. N.H. Bar Assn. Office: Fed Bldg Concord NH 03301 Tel (603) 225-5588

DEAKTOR, DARRYL BARNETT, b. Pitts., Feb. 2, 1942; B.A., Brandeis U., 1963; LL.B. cum laude, U. Pa., 1966; M.B.A., Columbia, 1968. Admitted to Pa. bar, 1966; asso. firm Goodis, Greenfield, Narin & Mann, Phila., 1968-70, partner, 1971; gen. counsel Life Pa., Fin. Corp., Phila., 1972; asst. prof. law U. Fla., 1972-74, asso. prof. law, 1974—. Chmn., Dist. 3 Human Rights Adv. Com. for the Mentally Retarded, 1977. Home: 1839 NW 31st Terr Gainesville FL 32605 Office: Holland Law Center Gainesville FL 32611 Tel (904) 392-2211

DEAL, JOHN CHARLES, b. Kenton, O., Jan. 5, 1947; B.S., Ohio State U., 1969, J.D. cum laude, 1974. Admitted to Ohio bar 1974; atty. Ohio Div. Banks, Columbus, 1974-76; regional counsel Fed. Deposit Ins. Corp., Columbus, 1976—. Mem. Am., Ohio bar assns. Home: 5764 Freeman Rd Westerville OH 43081 Tel (614) 469-7301

DEAN, ANTHONY ALEXANDER, b. N.Y.C., June 25, 1940; B.A., Yale U., 1962, LL.B., 1965; postgrad. (Fulbright scholar) U. Cologne (Germany), 1965-66. Admitted to N.Y. bar, 1967, U.S. Supreme Ct. bar, 1969; asso. firm Cravath, Swaine & Moore, N.Y.C., 1966-77, firm Dunnington, Bartholow & Miller, N.Y.C., 1977—. Mem. Am., N.Y. State bar assns. Office: Dunnington Bartholow & Miller 161 E 42d St New York City NY 10017 Tel (212) 682-8811

DEAN, ARTHUR H., b. Ithaca, N.Y., Oct. 16, 1898; A.B., Cornell U., 1921, J.D., 1923. Admitted to N.Y. bar, 1923, U.S. Supreme Ct. bar, 1946; with firm Sullivan & Cromwell, N.Y.C., 1923—, partner, 1929-76, of counsel, 1976—; dir. Am. Bank Note Co., Bank of N.Y. Co., Inc., Nat. Union Electric Corp., others; adv. dir. El Paso Co.; U.S. rep. post-armistice negotiations, Panmunjom, 1952; spl. U.S. ambassador to Korea, 1953-54; U.S. rep. UN Confs. on Law of Sea, 1958, 60, Nuclear Test Ban Conf., 1961-62, Disarmament Conf., 1962. Trustee Cornell U., 1945-74, chmn. bd., 1958-68, trustee emeritus, 1974—; bd. dirs. Spanish Inst., 1969—, chmn. bd., 1974—; trustee Adirondack Hist. Assn., Planting Fields Found.; bd. dirs. Teagle Found. Mem. Am., N.Y. State, Inter-Am. bar assns., Am. Bar Found., Am. Coll. Trial Lawyers, Am. Law Inst., Am. Soc. Internat. Law (hon. pres.), Internat. Law Assn., N.Y. County Lawyers Assn. Author: William Nelson Cromwell, 1854-1948, 1957; Test Ban and Disarmament: The Path of Negotiation, 1966. Home: Mill River Rd Oyster Bay NY 11771 Office: 125 Broad St New York City NY 10004 Tel (212) 952-8059

DEAN, DENIS ALLEN, b. Detroit, Jan. 29, 1942; B.A., U. Miami, 1963, J.D., 1966. Admitted to Fla. bar, 1966, U.S. Supreme Ct. bar, 1971; research asst. State Attys Office, Dade County, Fla., 1964-66; asst. state atty. 11th Jud. Circuit of Fla., 1966-70; asso. firm Eugene P. Spellman, Miami, 1970—; instr. criminal law and procedure Dade Jr. Coll., Miami, 1969-71; bd. arbitration N.Y. Stock Exchange, 1973—. Mem. Am., Fed. bar assns., Assn. Trial Lawyers of Am., Acad. Fla. Trial Lawyers, Nat. Assn. Criminal Def. Attys. Home: 12680 Hickory Rd North Miami FL 33181 Office: 240 Dade Federal Bldg Miami FL 33131 Tel (305) 371-3477

DEAN, HENRY WHITE, b. Spokane, Wash., Nov. 23, 1938; B.A. in Bus. Adminstrn., U. Wash., 1960, J.D., 1964. Admitted to Wash. bar, 1965; partner firm Ferguson & Burdell, Seattle, 1965—. Mem. Am., Wash. State, King County, Seattle bar assns. Office: 1700 Peoples Nat Bank Bldg Seattle WA 98171 Tel (206) 622-1711

DEAN, J. THOMAS, b. Cleve., Feb. 22, 1933; B.A., Ohio Wesleyan U., 1956; LL.B., Western Res. U., 1959. Admitted to Ohio bar, 1959; asst. prosecutor, Lake County, Ohio, 1960; asso. firm Blakely and Rand, Painesville, Ohio, 1961-67; partner firm Blakely and Dean, Painesville, 1967-76, partner firm Blakely, Dean, Wilson and Klingenberg, Painesville, 1976—; solicitor North Perry Village, 1970—. Mem. City of Painesville Planning Commn., 1967—, chmn., 1971-76; clk. Painesville Twp. Park, 1962—; mem. Painesville Bd. Zoning Appeals, 1974—; mem. Lake County Bd. Elections, 1964—; county chmn. Lake County Republican Party, 1970-74; mem. Lake County Found. Com., 1976—; bd. dirs. Painesville Sr. Citizen Center, 1975—. Mem. Am., Ohio State, Lake County (sec. 1961) bar assns. Home: 35 Forest Dr Painesville OH 44077 Office: 304 Lake County Fed Bldg Painesville OH 44077 Tel (216) 354-5636

DEAN, JOHN LADD, b. Rollersville, Ohio, Mar. 26, 1905; A.B., Ohio Wesleyan U., 1926; LL.B., Case Western Res. U., 1930. Admitted to Ohio bar, 1930; sr. mem. firm Hahn, Loeser, Freedheim, Dean & Wellman, Cleve., 1930—, partner, 1940—; chmn. Cleve. Ct. Mgmt. Project, 1970-73. Fellow Ohio State (council of dels. 1950, 53, 74—), Am. (ho of dels. 1971-72) bar assns.; mem. Cleve. (pres., 1970-71), Cuyahoga County bar assns., Phi Delta Phi. Recipient Fletcher Reed Andrews Outstanding Alumnus award Case Western

Res. U. Law Sch., 1975. Office: 800 National City E 6th Bldg Cleveland OH 44114 Tel (216) 621-0150

DEAN, JOSEPH WAYNE, b. Nashville, Oct. 19, 1944; B.A., The Citadel, 1966; J.D., Wake Forest Coll., 1969. Admitted to N.C. bar, 1969, U.S. Supreme Ct. bar, 1976; asst. U.S. atty. Eastern Dist. N.C., Raleigh, 1971-77; pvt. practice law, Raleigh, 1977—. Mem. N.C., Wake County bar assns. Named Outstanding Asst. U.S. Atty., U.S. Dept. Justice, 1974, recipient Spl. Commendation award, 1976. Home: 1315 Gardencrest Circle Raleigh NC 27612 Tel (919) 828-9800

DEAN, RUSSELL JENNINGS, b. Indpls., Feb. 17, 1936; A.B., Butler U., 1958; LL.B., J.D., Ind. U., 1961. Admitted to Ind. bar, 1962, U.S. Supreme Ct. bar, 1967; individual practice law, Indpls., 1962-63; dep. prosecutor Marion County, 1963; asst. city atty. City of Indpls., 1967; spl. counsel to Ind. Disciplinary Commn., 1975. Mem. Ind. Ho. of Reps., 1964-66. Mem. Am., Ind. State, Indpls. (chmn. grievance com., 1967-70) bar assns. Mem. Ind. Bd. Law Examiners Com. on Moral Character, 1967—. Home: 1020 N Lesley Ave Indianapolis IN 46219 Office: 136 E Market St Room 915 Indianapolis IN 46204 Tel (317) 631-3171

DEAN, THOMAS FLOYD, b. Hammond, Ind., June 9, 1926; A.B., Ind. U., 1950, LL.B., 1952. Admitted to Ind. bar, 1952, Ill. bar, 1954; asso. prof. Ind. U., 1952-54; asso. firm Holland & Bannigan, 1954-56, Kirkland & Ellis, Chgo., 1956-60; partner firm Kirkland & Ellis, 1960—; lectr. Ill. Continuing Legal Edn. Seminars, DePaul U. Mem. Am. Bar Assn. Home: 30 Strauss Ln Olympia Fields IL 60461 Office: 200 E Randolph Dr Chicago IL 60601 Tel (312) 861-2030

DEAN, WILLIAM TUCKER, b. Chgo., Aug. 31, 1915; A.B., Harvard U., 1937, M.B.A., 1947; J.D., U. Chgo., 1940. Admitted to D.C. bar, 1940, N.Y. State bar, 1949; atty. bituminous coal div. Dept. Interior, Washington, 1940-41; asst. legal adviser, fuel sect. Office of Price Adminstrn., Washington, 1941-42; asst. prof. law U. Kans., Lawrence, 1946-47; asst. prof. N.Y. U., N.Y.C., 1947-52, asso. prof., 1952-53; asso. prof. Cornell U. Law Sch., 1953-58, prof., 1958—; asso. dir. legal research N.Y. State Law Revision Commn., 1963-66; village justice Cayuga Heights (N.Y.), 1962—. Mem. Am., N.Y. State, Tompkins County bar assns., Internat. Acad. Estate and Trust Law, Phi Beta Kappa, Order of Coif, Phi Kappa Phi. Contbr. articles to legal jours. Home: 206 Overlook Rd Ithaca NY 14850 Office: Myron Taylor Hall Cornell U Ithaca NY 14853 Tel (607) 256-3561

DEANGELIS, JOHN R., b. Pitts., Apr. 3, 1945; B.A. in Polit. Sci., U. Dayton, 1968; J.D., Duquesne U., 1972. Admitted to Pa. bar, 1972; asso. firm Watzman, Levenson & Snyder, 1972-76; partner firm Watzman, DeAngelis & Elovitz, Pitts., 1976—. Mem. Am., Pa. trial lawyers assns. Office: 1103 Commonwealth Bldg 316 Fourth Ave Pittsburgh PA 15222 Tel (412) 391-3596

DEANGELUS, DONALD JOHN, b. Schenectady, Mar. 9, 1940; B.B.A. in Accounting cum laude, Siena Coll., 1962; LL.B., Albany Law Sch., 1965, J.D., 1968. Admitted to N.Y. bar, 1965; partner firm De Angelus & De Angelus, Schenectady, 1965—; town atty. Town of Rotterdam (N.Y.), 1974—; lectr. bus. law Siena Coll.; legal adviser Rotterdam Police Dept., 1974—. Mem. N.Y. State, Schenectady County bar assns., Internat. Assn. Chiefs of Police, N.Y. State Defenders Assn., Capital Dist. Trial Lawyers Assn. Office: 170 Lafayette St Schenectady NY 12305 Tel (518) 374-4116

DE ANGELUS, RONALD PATRICK, b. Schenectady, N.Y., May 31, 1935; A.B., Union Coll., 1957; LL.B. cum laude, Albany Law Sch., 1960, J.D. cum laude, 1968. Admitted to N.Y. bar, 1960; clk. to chief judge U.S. Dist. Ct., 9th Circuit, 1960-61; dep. pub. defender Schenectady County, 1966-67, asst. county atty., 1967-68; partner firm De Angelus & De Angelus, Schenectady, 1965—; asst. corp. counsel City of Schenectady. Mem. N.Y. State, Schenectady County bar assns., N.Y. Trial Lawyers Assn., Criminal Defenders Assn. Asso. editor Albany Law Rev,, 1959-60. Office: 170 Lafayette St Schenectady NY 12305 Tel (518) 374-4116

DEARBORN, LUTHER HENRY, b. Lincoln, Ill., Mar. 8, 1941; B.A., U. Ill., 1964, J.D., 1966. Admitted to Ill. bar, 1966; mem. firm Dearborn & Dearborn, Lincoln, Mason City, Ill., 1968-71; asso. judge 11th Jud. Circuit Ct. of Ill., Blommington, 1971-75, circuit judge, 1975—. Mem. Ill., McLean County bar assns. Ill. Judges Assn. Home: 314 Davis St Bloomington IL 61701 Office: Room 410 McLean County Law and Justice Center Bloomington IL 61701 Tel (309) 827-5311

DEARDORFF, MICHAEL KENT, b. Kokomo, Ind., Aug. 5, 1949; B.S., Purdue U., 1971; J.D., Valparaiso U., 1973. Admitted to Ind. bar, 1974; asso. firm Briscoe & Deardorff, Kokomo, 1974-75, firm Ellis, Gamble, Nolan & Deardorff, Kokomo, 1975—; dep. pros. atty. Howard County (Ind.), Kokomo, 1974, dep. pub. defender, 1975—. Bd. dirs. Howard County Mental Health Assn., Shelter Care for Children. Mem. Howard County, Ind., Am. bar assns., Howard County Legal Aid Assn. Home: 212 S Conradt Ave Kokomo IN 46901 Office: 421 W Sycamore St Kokomo IN 46901 Tel (317) 457-3238

DEARING, PETER L., b. Jacksonville, Fla., Aug. 26, 1946; B.A. with honors in polit. sci., U. South, Sewanee, Tenn., 1968; J.D. with honors, U. Fla., 1970. Admitted to Fla. bar, 1971, U.S. Supreme Ct. bar 1974; law clk. to U.S. Dist. Judge, Jacksonville, 1970-71; asst. U.S. atty. Middle Dist. Fla., Jacksonville, 1971-75; mem. firm Mahoney Hadlow & Adams, Jacksonville, 1975—. Legal officer Jacksonville Police Reserve, 1975—. Mem. Fla., Am., Fed. (v.p. Jacksonville chpt.) bar assns., Acad. Fla. Trial Lawyers, Blue Key, Phi Delta Phi, Phi Kappa Phi. Editor: U. Fla. Law Review, 1969-70. Office: 100 Laura St POB 4099 Jacksonville FL 32201 Tel (904) 354-1100

DE ASES, EDUARDO EVARISTO, b. Refugio, Tex., Oct. 26, 1928; A.A., Del Mar Coll., 1955; B.B.A., U. Tex., 1957, LL.B., 1959. Admitted to Tex. bar, 1959; asst. county atty. Nueces County (Tex.), Corpus Christi, 1962-66; individual practice law, Corpus Christi, 1966—; city commr. Corpus Christi, 1969-71, 75-77, mayor pro tem, 1977—. Mem. Nueces County Bar Assn. (pres.). Home: 749 Monette Corpus Christi TX 78412 Office: Suite 206 Guaranty Bank Plaza Corpus Christi TX 78401 Tel (512) 883-7286

DEASON, CHARLES ALBERT, JR., b. Washington, Apr. 27, 1943; A.A., N. Mex. Mil. Inst., 1963; B.A., U. Tex., 1965, J.D., 1968; diploma Comparative Law Inst., Universidad Nacional Autonoma de Mex., 1966. Admitted to Tex. bar, 1968, N. Mex. bar, 1973; served with JAGC, U.S. Army, 1969-71; asso. firm Calhoun, Morton, Deason & Preslar, and predecessors, El Paso, 1971-73, partner, 1973—. Chmn. lawyers div. United Way Campaign, El Paso, 1974. Mem. El Paso Legal Assistance Soc. (dir. 1975—), El Paso Young Lawyers Assn. (pres. 1976—), El Paso Trial Lawyers Assn. (v.p. 1976), State Bar of Tex., State Bar of N. Mex., El Paso, Fed. bar assns., Tex. Trial Lawyers Assn., Am. Trial Lawyers Assn., El Paso Criminal Def. Lawyers Assn. Home: 220 Bird Way El Paso TX 79922 Office: 1604 State National Plaza El Paso TX 79901 Tel (915) 532-3601

DEATHERAGE, WILLIAM VERNON, b. Drumright, Okla., Apr. 17, 1927; B.S., U. Oreg., 1952, LL.B., 1954. Admitted to Oreg. bar, 1954; asso. firm Neff, Frohnmayer & Lowry (now Frohnmayer & Deatherage), Medford, Oreg., 1954-56, partner, 1956—. Chmn. Jackson County (Oreg.) Child Devel., 1972—. Fellow Am. Coll. Trial Lawyers; mem. Am. Bar Assn., Oreg. State (chmn. com. procedure and practice 1972-73), Jackson County bars, Oreg. Assn. Def. Counsel (pres. 1974). Diplomate Am. Bd. Trial Advs. Home: 3715 Princeton Way Medford OR 97501 Office: PO Box 1726 39 S Central St Medford OR 97501 Tel (503) 773-8425

DEATON, WILLIAM WELDON, JR., b. Knoxville, Tenn., Dec. 23, 1930; B.A., U. N.Mex., 1958; J.D., Georgetown U., 1966. Admitted to N.Mex. bar, 1966; partner firm Smith, Ransom & Deaton, and predecessors, Albuquerque, 1968-71; asst. fed. pub. defender N.Mex., Albuquerque, 1972-75, fed. pub. defender, 1975—. Mem. Am., N.Mex., Albuquerque bar assns. Home: PO Box 623 Albuquerque NM 87103 Office: 500 Gold St SW Albuquerque NM 87103

DEATS, PAUL EDWIN, b. Los Angeles, Aug. 20, 1946; B.A., Whittier Coll., 1968; M.A. in Teaching, Whittier Coll., 1971; J.D., U. Notre Dame, 1974. Admitted to Ind. bar, 1974, Mich. bar, 1974, U.S. Supreme Ct. bar, 1977; legal intern South Bend (Ind.) Prosecuting Atty.'s Office, 1972-74, Cass County (Mich.) Prosecuting Atty.'s Office, 1974; asst. prosecuting atty. Cass County, 1974; dir. prosecutor div. U. Notre Dame Legal Aid Clinic, 1973-74; asso. firm O'Connor & Tushla, Cassopolis, Mich., 1975—. Sr. Scout Asso. troup leader Singing Sands Girl Scout Council, 1972-74. Mem. Am., Ind., Mich., Cass County (Mich.) bar assns. Home: Rt 2 Box 349U Edwardsburg MI 49112 Office: 110 S Broadway Cassopolis MI 49031 Tel (616) 455-2427

DEBERARDINE, ROGER B., b. Bklyn., Dec. 30, 1929; B.A., St. John's U., 1951; LL.B., St. John's Law Sch., 1954, J.D., 1968. Admitted to N.Y. State bar, 1954; trial atty. firm Lawless & Lynch, N.Y.C., 1958-62; asso. firm DiTucci Cardone & DeBerardine, Bklyn., 1962-65, DiTucci & DeBerardine, Bklyn., 1975—. Mem. Bd. Edn., Upper Saddle River, N.J., 1972—; pres. Upper Saddle River PTA, 1970-72. Mem. Bklyn. Bar Assn., N.Y. Trial Lawyers Assn., Def. Research Inst. Home: 49 Clover Ln Upper Saddle River NJ 07458 Office: 32 Court St Brooklyn NY 11201 also 21 Hempstead Ave Lynbrook NY 11563 Tel (212) 237-9400

DEBEVOISE, THOMAS MCELRATH, b. N.Y.C., Aug. 10, 1929; B.A., Yale, 1950; LL.B., Columbia, 1954. Admitted to N.Y. bar, 1954, Vt. bar, 1957, D.C. bar, 1963, U.S. Supreme Ct. bar, 1958; asst. U.S. atty. So. Dist. N.Y., 1954-56; individual practice law, Woodstock, Vt., 1957-60; dep. atty. gen. State of Vt., 1959, atty. gen., 1960-62; asst. gen. counsel FPC, Washington, 1962-64; individual practice law, Washington, 1964; partner firm Debevoise & Liberman, Washington, 1965-74, of counsel, 1975—; dean Vt. Law Sch., 1974—; clk. Vt. Constitutional Revision Commn., 1960-61; chmn. legal advisory com. Nat. Power Survey, 1962-63; pub. mem. Adminstrv. Conf. U.S., 1976—. Mem. Am. Law Inst., Am. (council pub. utility sect. 1968-71, spl. com. environ. law 1973-75), Vt. bar assns., Fed Power Bar (exec. com. 1969—, pres. 1973-74), Assn. Bar City N.Y., Am. Judicature Soc., Nat. Lawyers' Com. Civil Rights Under Law, (dir.). Recipient award def. civil liberties N.Y. State, City and County bar assns., 1962. Contbr. to CLE program and profl. jours. Home: Woodstock VT 05091 Office: Vt Law Sch South Royalton VT 05068 Tel (802) 763-8303

DEBLASIO, PETER EDWARD, b. Bklyn., Aug. 20, 1929; A.B., Columbia, 1951, LL.B., 1954. Admitted to N.Y. State bar, 1955; asst. U.S. atty., N.Y., 1955-58; asso. firm Reilly & Reilly, N.Y.C., 1958-61; individual practice law, N.Y.C., 1961-64; partner firm DeBlasio & Meagher and predecessors, N.Y.C., 1964-66; partner firm Kramer Dillof Duhan & DeBlasio, 1966-69, Kramer Dillof DeBlasio & Meagher, 1969—. Mem. N.Y. Bar Assn., Inner Circle of Advocates. Home: 142 West End Ave New York City NY 10011 Office: 233 Broadway New York City NY 10007 Tel (212) 227-6750

DEBOIS, JAMES A., b. Oklahoma City, Dec. 23, 1929; B.A., Okla. State U., 1951; LL.B., U. Okla., 1955. Admitted to Okla. bar, 1954, Mo. bar, 1963, N.Y. bar, 1965, Calif. bar, 1971; atty. Southwestern Bell Telephone Co., Oklahoma City, 1959-63, St. Louis, 1963-64, gen. atty., Oklahoma City, 1965-67, gen. solicitor, St. Louis, 1967-70; atty. Am. Tel. & Tel. Co., N.Y.C., 1964-65; v.p. Pacific Telephone Co., San Francisco, 1970-76, gen. counsel, 1971-76; gen. atty. Am. Tel. & Tel. Co., N.Y.C., 1976—. Mem. Am., Calif., San Francisco, Mo., N.Y. bar assns. Home: 10 Joanna Way Short Hills NJ 07078 Office: 195 Broadway New York City NY 10007 Tel (212) 393-3913

DE BORD, THEODORE LEE, b. Somerset, Ky., Mar. 17, 1908; J.D., U. Wash., 1940. Admitted to Wash. bar, 1940, Calif. bar, 1952; civil dep. to Pierce County (Wash.) Prosecuting Atty., 1941-46; pvt. practice law, Tacoma, and Barstow, Calif.; judge Calif. Dist. Ct., Barstow Jud. Dist., 1966—. Pres. Barstow Kiwanis Club, 1964, Barstow C. of C., 1966-67. Home: 1137 E Williams St Barstow CA 92311 Office: 301 E Mount View St Barstow CA 92311

DE BOW, RUSSELL ROBINSON, b. Lovejoy, Ill., Aug. 5, 1913; B.E., Ill. State Normal U., 1935; postgrad. Georgetown U. Sch. Law, 1951-53; J.D., De Paul U., 1954. Admitted to Ill. bar, 1955, U.S. Supreme Ct. bar, 1958; practiced in Chgo., 1955-62; dep. commr. investigation City of Chgo., 1962-65, adminstrv. asst. to mayor, 1965-67; magistrate Ill. Circuit Ct. of Cook County, 1967-71, asso. judge, 1971, judge, 1971—. Mem. Cook County (Edward H. Wright award 1966, Jud. award of merit 1968), Nat., Am., Chgo. bar assns., Nat. Jud. Council, World Assn. Judges. Recipient Dr. Mary McLeod Bethune Merit award Nat. Council Negro Women, 1973, Distinguished Alumni award Ill. State U., 1976. Home: 8055 S Paxton Ave Chicago IL 60617 Office: Richard J Daley Center Chicago IL 60602 Tel (312) 443-6414

DE CARDY, WILLIAM DENNIS, b. Chgo., May 27, 1942; B.S., U. Ill., 1964, J.D., 1966. Admitted to Ill. bar, 1966, Idaho bar, 1967; law clk. Chief Justice Joseph J. McFadden, Idaho Supreme Ct., 1966-67; asso. firm Zimmerly & Johnson, Champaign, Ill., 1967-69; legis. counsel Ill. State Senate Jud. Com., 1969-71; chief legal counsel W. Russell Arrington, Ill. State Senate Minority Leader, 1971-73; asso. judge Ill. 11th Jud. Circuit Ct., 1973—; mem. legis. advisory com. Ill. Law Enforcement Commn., 1974-75. Mem. McLean County (Ill.), Ill. State bar assns. Home: 1919 Garling Dr Bloomington IL 61701 Office: Courthouse Bloomington IL 61701 Tel (309) 827-5311

DECAS, CHARLES WILLIAM, b. Wareham, Mass., Jan. 19, 1946; B.A., Colby Coll., 1968; J.D., Boston U., 1971. Admitted to Mass. bar, 1971; asso. firm George C. Decas, Wareham and Middleboro, Mass., 1971—. Mem. Mass., Am., Plymouth bar assns. Home: 18 High St Wareham VA 02571 Office: 132 N Main St Middleboro MA 02346 also 219 Main St Wareham MA 02571 Tel (617) 947-4433

DECHERRIE, ROBERT THEODORE, b. Chgo., Feb. 14, 1934; B.S.C., DePaul U., 1956; M.B.A., U. Chgo., 1958; J.D., Chgo.-Kent Coll. Law, 1969. Admitted to Ill. bar, 1969; field rep. U.S. Treasury Dept. IRS, Chgo., 1969—. Mem. Ill. State Bar Assn. Recipient Outstanding Performance award Treasury Dept., 1973, Spl. Act award, 1972. Author: Budget Reports to Management, 1962; Legal Aspects of Discrimination in Private Schools, 1968. Home: 7000 W Roscoe St Chicago IL 60634 Office: 230 S Dearborn St Chicago IL 60690 Tel (312) 253-8592

DECHERT, EDWARD PAUL, b. Warren, Ohio, Mar. 14, 1943; B.B.A., Ohio U.; M.B.A., J.D., Ind. U.; Admitted to Ind. bar, 1973; fin. analyst Ford Motor Co., 1969, Eli Lilly & Co., 1970-71; legal intern Hamilton County (Ind.) Prosecutors Office, 1972; legal advisor Kokomo (Ind.) Police Dept., 1973-75; partner firm Andrews, Dechert & Ferries, Kokomo, 1973—. Mem. Am., Ind. bar assns. Home: 1214 Devon Ct Kokomo IN 46901 Office: 300 N Main St Kokomo IN 46901 Tel (317) 452-0011

DECHTER, NATHAN, b. Rumania, July 1, 1909; LL.B. cum laude, Bklyn. Law Sch., 1936, LL.M. cum laude, 1937. Admitted to N.Y. bar, 1937, U.S. Supreme Ct. bar, 1961; partner firm Dechter and Kornbluth, Woodbury, N.Y.; arbitrator Am. Automobile Assn., 1974—, Civil Ct. Queens, 1976—. Pres. Temple Midway Jewish Center, 1960-61. Mem. Am., Nassau, N.Y. State bar assns., N.Y. State, Am. trial lawyers assns., N.Y. County Lawyers. Home: 5 Wisteria Pl Syosset NY 11791 Office: 7600 Jericho Turnpike Woodbury NY 11797 Tel (516) 921-5040

DE CICCO, ANTHONY JERRY, b. N.Y.C., Dec. 19, 1913; B.S. in Biology, Villanova U., 1934; LL.B., St. John's U., 1938. Admitted to N.Y. bar, 1938; asso. firm Coster & Mc Garey, N.Y.C., 1936-41; atty. firm Rudser & Mulligan, N.Y.C., 1941-54; atty. of record Mass. Bonding Hanover Ins. Co., N.Y.C., 1954-62; partner firm Garbarin, Scher & De Cicco, N.Y.C., 1962—. Mem. Am., N.Y. bar assns., N.Y. State Trial Lawyers, Bar Assn. Nassau County, Soc. Med. Jurisprudence, Nassau and Suffolk County Trial Lawyers Assn. Office: 500 Fifth Ave New York City NY 10036 Tel (212) 354-4222

DECK, ROBERT BYRON, b. Sioux City, Iowa, Oct. 9, 1947; B.S., Morningside Coll., 1970; J.D., U. S.D., 1973. Admitted to Iowa bar, 1973, Neb. bar, 1973; partner firm Deck & Deck, Sioux City. Office: 222 Davidson Bldg Sioux City IA 51101 Tel (712) 255-3573

DECKER, HENRY WALTER, b. Elizabeth, N.J., Dec. 19, 1910; LL.B., N.J. Law Sch., 1934; J.D., Rutgers U., 1970. Admitted to N.J. bar, 1935; judge Municipal Ct. Roselle Park (N.J.), 1945-64; mayor Borough of Roselle Park, 1965-69; legal asst. to Union County Welfare Bd., 1969-71; individual practice law, Elizabeth, 1935—; counsel, dir. Satisfactory Savs. & Loan Assn. Mem. Union County Bar Assn., N.J. Fire Chiefs Assn. Home: 341 Sheridan Ave Roselle Park NJ 07204 Office: 29 Broad St Elizabeth NJ 07201 Tel (201) 354-1661

DECKER, PHILIP GREENE, II, b. Pinehurst, N.C., Oct. 17, 1944; B.A., DePauw U., 1967; J.D., Ind. U., Bloomington, 1970. Admitted to Ind. bar, 1970, U.S. Dsit. Court So. Dist. Ind., 1970; asso. firm Jones, Withers & Adair, Anderson, Ind., 1970-75; gen. partner firm Decker, Lockwood & Swick, Anderson, 1975—; dir. sec., treas. Decker's Inc., Lafayette, Ind.; dir. Edgewood Surg. Co.; gen. counsel Dennis-Hybrid Corp., Windfall, Inc., Richard Overdorf & Assos., Anderson, Parker-Overdorf & Assos., Anderson, Credit Burs. Anderson, Layfayette, and Frankfort, Inc., Rinkers, Inc., North Webster, Ind. Bd. dirs. Jr. Achievement Madison County, Ind., 1972. Mem. Ind., Madison County bar assns. Office: Suite 910 First Savings Tower Anderson IN 46016 Tel (317) 649-9285

DECKER, RICHARD KNORE, b. Lincoln, Nebr., Sept. 15, 1913; A.B., U. Nebr., 1935, J.D., 1938. Admitted to Nebr. bar, 1938, U.S. Supreme Ct. bar, 1941, D.C. bar, 1948, Ill. bar, 1952; atty. antitrust div. U.S. Dept. Justice, Washington, 1938-52; partner firm Lord, Bissell & Brook, Chgo., 1953—. Trustee Village of Clarendon Hills, Ill., 1960-64; chmn. bd. govs. Community House, Hinsdale, Ill., 1976; bd. dirs. Robert Crown Center for Health Edn., Hinsdale, Ill., 1976—. Mem. Am. (chmn. antitrust sect. 1971-72), Chgo. (chmn. antitrust com. 1956-59), Fed., Nebr., Ill. (chmn. antitrust sect. 1965) assns. Home: 20 Waverly Ave Clarendon Hills IL 60514 Office: 115 S La Salle St Chicago IL 60603 Tel (312) 443-0262

DECOSTA, ROBERT LOUIS, b. Fall River, Mass., Mar. 20, 1936; A.B., Providence Coll., 1957; J.D., Boston U., 1964; grad. Nat. Coll. Dist. Attys., 1972, Nat. Inst. Trial Advocacy, 1974, Nat. Coll. Advocacy, 1976. Admitted to Mass. bar, 1965, R.I. bar, 1965; U.S. Supreme Ct. bar, 1973; probate judge City of Bristol (R.I.), 1966-71; spl. asst. atty. gen. State of R.I., Bristol, 1967-71, asst. atty. gen., 1971-75, chief organizer crime sect., 1971-75, partner firm De Costa & Abilhelra, Bristol, 1975—; probate judge Town of Bristol; lectr. Roger Williams Coll., 1975-77. Bd. dirs. Le Baron C. Colt Memorial Ambulance, Inc., Bristol. Mem. Am., Mass., R.I. bar assns., Assn. Trial Lawyers Am. Home: 7 Juniper St Bristol RI 02809 Office: 1052 Main St Warren RI 02885 Tel (405) 245-0070

DEDMAN, BERTRAM COTTINGHAM, b. Columbia, Tenn, Dec. 24, 1914; A.B., U. of South, 1937; J.D., George Washington U., 1941. Admitted to Tenn. bar, 1941; trial atty. antitrust div. Dept. Justice, Washington, 1941-54; trial atty. Texaco, Inc., Los Angeles, 1954-57; asst. counsel, asso. gen. counsel, gen. counsel Ins. Co. N.Am., Phila., 1957-70; v.p., gen. counsel INA Corp., Phila., 1968—; dir. Beta Inac, Inc., Wilmington, Del., Compagnie Financiere INA, Paris, Gamma Inac, Inc., Wilmington, INA Fin. Corp., Wilmington, INAC Corp., N.J., Logan Land Co., Inc., Phila. Former mem. vestry, sec. St. David's (Radnor) Episcopal Ch., Wayne, Pa. Mem. Am. (chmn. com. internat. ins. law), Fed., Phila. bar assns., Am. Judicature Soc., Internat. Assn. Ins. Law (past pres. U.S. chpt.), U. of South Alumni (rep.). Contbr., editor Merger of Insurance Companies, 1972. Home: Timber Ln Devon PA 19333 Office: 1600 Arch St Philadelphia PA 19101 Tel (215) 241-3839

DEDMON, JESSE OSCAR, JR., b. Pine Bluff, Ark., Apr. 13, 1908; B.C.S., Howard U., 1932, LL.B., J.D., 1935. Admitted to Okla. bar, 1937, D.C. bar, 1947, U.S. Supreme Ct. bar, 1944; mem. firm Hall & Dedmon, Tulsa, 1937-40; served to capt. JAGC, U.S. Army, 1941-45; vets. sec. NAACP, Washington, 1945-50; individual practice law, Washington, 1950—; asst. grand-legal advisor Elks; dir. United Nat. Bank. Chmn. bd. 12th St. YMCA, 1965-66; bd. dirs. United Planning

Orgn. Mem. Nat., Wash., D.C., Okla. bar assns., World Assn. Lawyers, D.C. C. of C. (pres. 1966-67). Recipient Man of Year award Howard U. Law Alumni Assn., 1974. Home: 700 7th St SW #227 Washington DC 20024 Office: 611 F St NW Washington DC 20004 Tel (202) 638-4700

DEDRICK, JAMES RUSSELL, b. Kingsport, Tenn., Oct. 23, 1947; B.S., E. Tenn. State U., 1969; J.D., U. Tenn., 1972. Admitted to Tenn. bar, 1972; served with JAGC, U.S. Army, Ft. Bragg, N.C., 1972-74, dep. staff judge advocate, Ft. Hood, Tex., 1974-76; asst. dist. atty. gen., Knoxville, Tenn., 1976—. Mem. Am., Tenn. bar assns., Phi Delta Phi. Home: 5404 Yosemite Trail Knoxville TN 37919 Tel (615) 546-2540

DEELMAN, JAN LAURENS, b. Reading, Pa., Oct. 5, 1913; A.B., Hamilton Coll., 1934; LL.B., U. Pa., 1937, J.D., 1969; postgrad. U. N.C., 1943-44. Admitted to Pa. bar, 1938; individual practice law, Reading, 1938-63, partner firm Levan and Deelman, Reading, 1963—; librarian Berks County (Pa.) Law Library, Reading, 1951-56; law clk. U.S. Dist. Ct. Eastern Dist. Pa., 1956-63; dir. Strasburg R.R. Co., 1958. Sec. redevel. Authority City Reading, 1949-60, chmn., 1960; mem. Sch. Bd. Reading, 1949-51, 52; trustee Reading Pub. Library, 1951—. Mem. Berks County (pres. 1970-71), Pa. bar assns. Office: 500 Berks Title Bldg 607 Washington St Reading PA 19603 Tel (215) 374-4911

DEENY, ROBERT JOSEPH, b. Cedar Rapids, Iowa, Jan. 8, 1941; A.B., Ariz. State U., 1963; J.D., Cath. U. Am., 1970. Admitted to Ariz. bar, 1971; field atty. NLRB, 1971-72; partner firm Shimmel, Hill, Bishop & Gruender, Phoenix, 1972—. Mem. Am. Bar Assn. Office: 10th Floor 111 W Monroe St Phoenix AZ 85003 Tel (602) 257-5500

DEER, JAMES WILLIS, b. Reading, Pa., Mar. 14, 1917; A.B. in Econs., Oberlin Coll., 1938; J.D. with distinction, U. Mich., 1941. Admitted to Mich. bar, 1941, Ohio bar, 1941, N.Y. bar, 1948; asso. firm Cowden, Cowden & Crew, Dayton, Ohio, 1941-42; staff atty. Securities and Exchange Commn., 1942-45; asso. firm Fulton, Walter & Halley, N.Y.C., 1945-47; partner firm Holtzmann, Wise & Shepard, N.Y.C., 1947—. Mem. Am., N.Y. bar assns. Home: 611 Shore Acres Dr Mamaroneck NY 10543 Office: 30 Broad St New York NY 10004 Tel (212) 747-5518

DEES, DON LEON, b. Tulsa, Feb. 24, 1932; LL.B., Tulsa U., 1957. Admitted to Okla. bar, 1957, U.S. Dist. Ct. No. Okla. bar, 1965; atty. U.S. Fidelity and Guaranty Ins. Co., Tulsa, 1955-65; individual practice, Tulsa, 1965—. Bd. dirs. YMCA, Tulsa, 1967-73. Mem. Am., Okla., Tulsa County Bar Assns., Okla., Calif., Trial Lawyers Assns.,Home: 14505 E 12th Pl Tulsa OK 74108 Office: 324 Main Mall Tulsa OK 74103 Tel (918) 583-0121

DEES, MORRIS SELIGMAN, b. Montgomery, Ala., Dec. 16, 1936; B.A., U. Ala., 1958, LL.B., 1960. Admitted to Ala. bar 1960, D.C. bar 1972; partner firm Dees & Fuller, Montgomery, 1960-64; gen. counsel Fuller & Dees Marketing Co., Montgomery, 1964-69; partner firm Levin & Dees, Montgomery, 1969-71; chief trial counsel So. Poverty Law Center, Montgomery, 1971—; Gen Counsel Carter-Mondale Pres. campaign, Atlanta, 1976; nat. finance dir. McGovern Pres. campaign, 1972, Carter Pres. campaign, 1976. Mem. Ala., D.C. Bar assns., ACLU (cooperating atty. 1965-70). Recipient Civil Rights award of Year Tuskegee Inst., 1974. Home: Rolling Hills Ranch Mathews AL 36052 Office: 1001 S Hull St Montgomery AL 36109 Tel (205) 264-0286

DEFILIPPO, FREDERICK JOHN, b. Elmira, N.Y., June 24, 1940; A.B., Princeton, 1962; LL.D., Cornell U., 1965. Admitted to N.Y. bar, 1965, U.S. Tax Ct. bar, 1972; partner De Filippo Bros., Elmira, 1965—; hearing officer N.Y. State Dept. Health, 1972—. Mem. Elmira Heights Central Sch. Dist. Bd. Edn., 1973—, pres., 1976—. Mem. Am., N.Y. State, Chemung County bar assns., Am., N.Y. State assns. trial lawyers, Phi Kappa Phi. Home: 838 Larchmont Rd Elmira NY 14905 Office: 408 E Church St Elmira NY 14901 Tel (607) 734-8175

DEFINO, ANTHONY MICHAEL, b. West New York, N.J., June 25, 1936; B.A. Fairleigh-Dickinson U., 1961; LL.B., Seton Hall U., 1964. Admitted to N.J. bar, 1965; individual practice law, West New York, 1966—. Mayor West New York, 1971-74, 75-79. Mem. Am., N.J., Hudson County bar assns. Home: 6031 Blvd East West New York NJ 07093 Office: 443 60th St West New York NJ 07093 Tel (201) 869-7741

DEFRANCIS, WILLIAM FRANCIS, b. N.Y.C., Feb. 20, 1946; B.A., Lycoming Coll., 1968; J.D. cum laude, N.Y. Law Sch., 1971, LL.M., N.Y. U., 1977. Admitted to N.Y. bar, 1972; asso. firm Jerome F. Woods, Demarest, N.J., 1971-72; sr. asso. firm Brent, Phillips, Dranoff & Davis, Nanuet, N.Y., 1973—; tax and estate planning counsel Rockland County, 1972—. Mem. exec. council Rockland County (N.Y.) council Boy Scouts Am., 1974. Mem. Am., N.Y. State, Rockland County bar assns., Nyack Jaycees (pres. 1972-73). Contbr. articles to law jours.; editor N.Y. Law Forum, 1970-71. Home: 9 Forest Glen Rd Valley Cottage NY 10989 Office: 20 Old Turnpike Rd Nanuet NY 10954 Tel (914) 623-2800

DEGLING, DONALD EWALD, b. Lima, N.Y., Apr., 13, 1928; B. in M.E., Cornell, 1949, LL.B., 1952. Admitted to N.Y. bar, 1952; asso. Fish, Richardson & Neave, N.Y.C., 1955-69; partner firm Fish & Neave, N.Y.C., 1970—. Dir. Rye (N.Y.) Community Concert Assn., 1969—, pres., 1975—. Mem. Am. Bar Assn., Am., N.Y. patent law assns., Assn. Bar City N.Y. Office: 277 Park Ave New York City NY 10017 Tel (212) 826-1050

DEGNAN, EDWARD JEROME, b. N.Y.C., Dec. 9, 1931; B.S., Fordham U., 1954, LL.B., 1959. Admitted to N.Y. bar, 1959, U.S. Supreme Ct. bar, 1964; atty. Fifth Ave. Coachlines, N.Y.C., 1959-62, N.Y. Central R.R., N.Y.C., 1962-64, Record Boston Ins. Group, N.Y.C., 1964-67, dept. corp. law Continental Ins. Co., N.Y.C., 1967-68; individual practice law, Canisteo, N.Y., 1968—; atty. Canisteo Savs. & Loans Assn., 1968—, also dir.; asst. dist. atty. Steuben County (N.Y.), 1972—; atty. towns of Woodhull, Hornellsville, Jasper, Dansville, Almond, Howard and Fremont (all N.Y.); atty. Canisteo Central Sch., Greenwood (N.Y.) Central Sch., Troupsburg (N.Y.) Central Sch., Jasper Central Sch. Mem. Steuben County, N.Y. State bar assns., Am. Arbitration Assn. Office: 2 Depot St POB 25 Canisteo NY 14823 Tel (607) 698-2531

DEGNAN, JAMES GUILLAUME, b. Escanaba, Mich., Sept. 1, 1929; B.A. with distinction, U. Mich., 1951, J.D., 1953. Admitted to Mich. bar, 1953, Calif. bar, 1955; asst. gen. counsel May Co., Los Angeles, 1959-67; partner firm MacFarlane, Schaefer & Haun, Los Angeles, 1967—. Mem. Los Angeles County, Calif. bar assns., Phi Beta Kappa. Home: 700 S Orange Grove Blvd Pasadena CA 91105 Office: suite 2204 One Wilshire Bldg Los Angeles CA 90017 Tel (213) 625-5811

DEGNAN, RONAN EUGENE, b. Lewiston, Minn., Oct. 1, 1924; B.S. in Law, U. Minn., 1950, LL.B., 1952. Admitted to Iowa bar, 1953, Minn. bar, 1955, Utah bar, 1956; prof. law Drake U., 1952-54, U. Utah, 1956-62, U. Calif., Berkeley, 1962—. Mem. Am. Law Inst. Home: 727 Santa Barbara Rd Berkeley CA 94707 Office: 354 Boalt Hall Univ California Berkeley CA 94720 Tel (514) 642-0338

DEGNAN, THOMAS LEONARD, b. Waseca, Minn., Jan. 18, 1909; J.D., Georgetown U., 1930. Admitted to Minn. bar, 1930, N.D. bar, 1933; asso. firm Sexton, Mordaunt, Kennedy and Carroll, St. Paul, 1930-38; founder, mem. firm Degnan, McElroy, Lamb, Comrud, Maddock and Olson, Grand Forks. N.D., 1933—. Pres., nat. committeeman Young Democrats, 1940-48; pres., bd. dirs. Community Chest, 1960-61; bd. dirs. St. James High Sch., 1954-56; mem. adv. bd. Med. Center, 1963-67; pres., dir. Grand Forks Indsl. Found., 1960-74. Mem. N.D. (pres. 1960-61, dir. 1959-62), Am., Grand Forks County (pres. 1952-53), First Dist. (pres. 1957-59) Edward Douglas White Law Club, Pierce Butler Law Club, Sigma Nu Phi. Home: 210 27th Ave S Grand Fords ND 58201 Office: 500 First Nat Bank Bldg Grand Forks ND 58201 Tel (701) 775-5595

DE GRAFF, JOHN TELLER, b. Amsterdam, N.Y., May 25, 1902; B.S. magna cum laude, St. Lawrence U., 1922, LL.D., 1972; LL.B., Albany Law Sch., 1925. Admitted to N.Y. bar, 1925, U.S. Supreme Ct. bar, 1955; mem. firm DeGraff, Foy, Conway & Holt-Harris, Albany, 1939—; mem. N.Y. State Bd. Law Examiners, 1940-69; chmn. N.Y. State Tenure Commn., 1944-61; counsel N.Y. State Legis. Commn. on Extension of Civil Service, 1939-41; pres. Nat. Conf. Bar Examiners, 1951-52. Trustee St. Lawrence U., 1959—. Mem. Am. Law Inst., Am., N.Y. (v.p. 1955-61), Albany bar assns. Mem. editorial bd. N.Y. Law Jour., 1972—. Contbr. articles in field to profl. jours. Home: 136 State St Albany NY 12207 Office: 90 State St Albany NY 12207 Tel (518) 462-5301

DEGRANDI, JOSEPH ANTHONY, b. Hartford, Conn., Jan. 1, 1927; B.S., Trinity Coll., 1949; M.S., George Washington U., 1950, J.D., 1952. Admitted to D.C. bar, 1952, U.S. Supreme Ct. 1956; asso. firm Beveridge, DeGrandi, Kline & Lunsford and predecessors, Washington, 1952—. Mem. adv. bd. Marymount Sch., Arlington, Va., 1967—, pres., 1969-72. Mem. Am., Fed., D.C., Inter-Am. bar assns., Am. Patent Law Assn., Patent Lawyers Club Washington, Patent and Trademark Inst. Can., Chartered Inst. Patent Agts. (Gt. Britain), Thomas More Soc. Home: 1505 Highwood Dr Arlington VA 22207 Office: 1819 H St NW Washington DC 20006 Tel (202) 659-2811

DE GRANDPRE, LOUIS PHILLIPPE, b. Montreal, Que., Can., Feb. 6, 1917; attended Coll. St.-Marie, Montreal; B.A., McGill U., Montreal, 1935, B.C.L., 1938, LL.D., 1972; LL.D., U. Ottawa, 1973. Called to Que. bar, 1938, created king's counsel, 1949; practiced law in Montreal, 1938-73; puisne judge Supreme Ct. of Can., 1974—; batonnier Montreal bar, 1968-69, Province of Que., 1968-69. Mem. Canadian Bar Assn. (pres. 1972-73). Home: 28 Alexandre Tache Blvd Apt 102 Hull PQ J8Y 3K9 Canada Office: Supreme Ct Bldg Wellington St Ottawa ON K1A 0J1 Canada*

DE GUERIN, GEORGE MICHAEL, b. Austin, Tex., Jan. 9, 1945; B.A. in Govt., U. Tex., Austin, 1968; J.D., Tex. Tech. U., 1972. Admitted to Tex. bar, 1972, U.S. Supreme Ct. bar, 1976; law clk. to Judge Wendall A Odom, Tex. Ct. Criminal Appeals, 1972-73, to Judge John V. Singleton, Jr., U.S. Dist. Ct., So. Dist. Tex., 1973-75; asst. fed. pub. defender So. Dist. Tex., 1975—; mem. firm Foreman & DeGuerin, Houston, 1977—; chief justice Jud. Council, Tex. Tech. Sch. Law, 1971; asst. dir. Legal Aid Soc. of Lubbock, Tex., 1971-72. Pres. bd. Montessori Sch. of Houston, 1976. Mem. Houston Bar Assn., Am. Judicature Soc., Phi Delta Theta, Delta Theta Phi. Home: 2113 Kingston St Houston TX 77019 Office: US Courthouse 515 Rusk Ave Houston TX 77002 Tel (713) 226-5901

DE HAAN, PETER ROSS, b. Phila., Nov. 16, 1945; B.S., Pa. State U., 1969; J.D., No. Ky. U., 1974. Admitted to Ohio bar, 1974, U.S. Dist. Ct. bar, 1974; individual practice law, Cin., 1974-76; asso. firm Lutz & DeHaan Co., Cin., 1976—. Mem. Am. Arbitration Assn. (comml. panel arbitrator), Am. Trial Lawyers Assn., Am., Ohio State, Cin. bar assns. Home: 6751 Maple St Cincinnati OH 45227 Office: 8250 Winton Rd Cincinnati OH 45231 Tel (513) 522-8100

DEIMEN, JAMES MALSCH, b. Detroit, Mar. 14, 1938; B.S. in Engring., U. Mich., 1960, M. S., 1962, Ph.D., 1965, J.D., 1967. Admitted to Mich. bar, 1968, U.S. Patent bar, 1970; asso. firm Farley, Forster & Farley, Detroit, 1968-74; individual practice law, Ann Arbor, Mich., 1974—; cons. mech. engr. EPA Motor Vehicle Emissions Lab., Ann Arbor, 1975—. Pres. Portage and Base Lake Property Owners Assn. Inc., 1975—. Mem. Nat., Mich. socs. profl. engrs., Am. Arbitration Assn., Am. Soc. Advancement Sci., Mich., Washtenaw County bar assns. Contbr. articles to profl. jours. Home: 11852 Algonquin Dr Pinckney MI 48169 Office: 407 N Main St Suite 100 Ann Arbor MI 48104 Tel (313) 994-5947

DEIS, LARRY EUGENE, b. Dayton, Ohio, Jan. 24, 1946; B.F.A., U. Cin., 1968, J.D., 1973. Admitted to Ohio bar, 1973; individual practice law, Hamilton, Ohio, 1973—. Mem. Am., Ohio, Cin., Butler County bar assns. Home: 1418 Eualie Dr Fairfield OH 45014 Office: 224 Hamilton Center Bldg 220 High St PO Box 741 Hamilton OH 45011 Tel (513) 863-0664

DEIS, ROBERT FRANKLIN, b. Kansas City, Mo., Aug. 10, 1947; B.A. in Polit. Sci., U. Mo., 1969, J.D., 1972. Admitted to Mo. bar, 1973, Fed. bar, 1973; mem. firm Moore, Lay and Deis, Platte City, Mo., 1973—. Bd, dirs. Northland Symphony Orch. Assn., Parkville, Mo., 1974—, v.p., 1975, treas., 1976—. Mem. Am., Mo. (taxation com. 1973-75, family law com. 1974—), Kansas City, Platte County bar assns. Recipient Divilbiss award Phi Alpha Delta, 1972. Home: 7009 NW 77th St Kansas City MO 64152 Office: PO Box 250 501 Main St Platte City MO 64079 Tel (816) 431-2171

DEITCH, WILLIAM HENRY, b. Elkhart, Ind., Sept. 16, 1916; B.S., Purdue U., 1939; J.D., Duquesne U., 1954. Admitted to Pa. bar, 1959, U.S. Supreme Ct. bar, 1967; chem. engr. Gulf Research & Devel. Co., Pitts., 1939-45; patent atty. Gulf Oil Corp., Oakmont, Pa., 1945-75. Mem. Am., Allegheny County bar assns., Am. Chem. Soc., Am. Pitts. patent law assns. Address: 666 10th St Oakmont PA 15139 Tel (412) 828-8547

DEIZ, MERCEDES FRANCES, b. N.Y.C., Dec. 13, 1917; J.D., Northwestern Coll. Law, Portland, Oreg., 1959. Law library asst. Bonneville Power Adminstrn., Portland, 1949-53; legal sec. Anderson, Franklin, Olsen et. al., Portland, 1954-59; admitted to Oreg. bar, 1960; practiced in Portland, 1960-67; hearing officer Oreg. Workmen's Compensation Bd., Portland, 1968-70; judge Oreg. Dist. Ct. for Multnomah County, 1970-72, Oreg. Circuit Ct. for Multnomah County, 1973—; mem. Oreg. Gov.'s Commn. on Jud. Reform. Mem. adv. com. St. Vincent Hosp., Portland, Portland Community Coll.; bd. dirs. Good Samaritan Hosp., Portland, 1969-74, Oreg. Mental Health Assn., 1960-64, Parry Center for Children, Portland, 1969-74, Lewis and Clark Coll., 1970-76, Oreg. Mus. Sci. and Industry, Portland, 1970-76, Golden Hours, Inc., Portland, 1971—; chmn. Portland Met. Youth Commn., 1958-65, Portland Met. Study Commn., 1960-62. Mem. Am., Nat. bar assns., Oreg. State Bar (chmn. com. minor cts. 1970-71), Nat. Council Juvenile Ct. Judges (chmn. com. status offenses), Am. Judicature Soc. Named Woman of Accomplishment, Portland Jour., 1969; recipient Pres.'s award local chpt. NAACP, 1975. Office: 1021 SW 4th Ave Portland OR 97204

DEJESUS, ANA ELBA, b. Lares, P.R.; B.A., U. P.R., 1951, M.S.W., 1959, J.D., 1963; postgrad. Boston U., 1957—. Admitted to P.R. bar, 1964; family counsellor Superior Ct. San Juan, P.R., 1953-55; Inst. Family Relations, Rio Piedras, P.R., 1955-59; sch. social worker, San Juan, 1959-61; legal counsel State Ins. Fund, San Juan, 1963-65; asst. dist. atty Dept. Justice, San Juan, 1965-67; prof., dir. law library Interam. Univ. P.R., San Juan, 1968-73, prof., dir. center criminal justice Sch. Law, 1973—. Mem. Legal Aid Comm., San Juan, 1971. Mem. Am., P.R., Interam. bar assns., Social Workers Assn. P.R., Nat. Assn. Social Workers, Nat. Assn. Woman Lawyers. Home: 8-1 Palma Real Condominium Miramar PR 00907 Office: 1610 Fdez Juncus Ave Santurce PR 00910 Tel 724-1930

DEKLE, GROVER CLYDE, III, b. Millen, Ga., Dec. 16, 1937; B.A., Emory U., 1960; LL.B., 1963, J.D., 1970. Admitted to Ga. bar, 1964, Fed. bar, 1968; asso. firm Ross & Finch, Atlanta, 1965, Hatcher, Meyerson, Oxford & Irvin, Atlanta, 1966-67, Peek, Whaley, Blackburn, Haldi, Atlanta, 1967-68; mem. firm Calhoun & Dekle, Atlanta, 1969-74; affiliate Swertfeger, Scott & Turnage, P.C., Decatur, Ga., 1975—. Bd. dirs. State YMCA, 1972—. Mem. Ga., DeKalb County, Atlanta bar assns., Ga. Assn. Trial Lawyers. Office: 1000 1st National Bank Bldg Decatur GA 30030 Tel (404) 377-5580

DE KOSTER, LUCAS JAMES, b. Hull, Iowa, June 18, 1918; B.M.E., Iowa State U., 1939; J.D., Cleve.-Marshall Law Sch., 1949. Admitted to Ohio bar, 1949, Iowa bar, 1952; asso. firm J.D. Douglass, Cleve., 1949-51; individual practice law, Hull, 1951—; mem. Iowa Senate, 1964—. Mem. Sioux County, Iowa, Am. bar assns. Office: 1106 Main St Hull IA 51239 Tel (712) 439-2511

DELAHAY, BENJAMIN THOMAS, JR., b. Corsicana, Tex., May 6, 1918; student Trinity U., 1936-39, 45-46; J.D., Harvard U., 1948. Admitted to Tex. bar, 1948, Colo. bar, 1949, Alaska bar, 1964; individual practice law, Colorado Springs, Colo., 1949-54, Steamboat Springs, Colo., 1954-61; with div. engring. Colo. Dept. Hwys., Steamboat Springs, 1961-63; land and mineral adjudicator Bur. Land Mgmt., Dept. Interior, Fairbanks, Alaska, 1963-64; judge Alaska Dist. Ct., Fairbanks; asso. firm Merdes Schaible, Staley & DeLisio, Fairbanks, 1969-70; city atty. City of Fairbanks, 1970-73; borough atty. Kenai Peninsula Borough, Soldotna, Alaska, 1973-76; individual practice law, Kenai-Soldotna, 1976—; dir., sec. Kamar, Inc., BBBC, Inc., Gun Hill, Inc.; mem. joint com. El Paso County (Colo.) Bar Assn. and Colorado Springs Community Fund for establishment of legal aid, 1953. Bd. dirs. All Souls Unitarian Ch., Colorado Springs, 1952-54; chmn. dr. ARC; program chmn. Unitarian-Universalist Fellowship, Alaska, 1964-71. Mem. Am., Alaska, Colo., Kenai Peninsula bar assns. Home: PO Box 2838 Kenai AK 99611 Office: PO Box 1448 Soldotna AK 99669 Tel (907) 262-5838

DE LA MOTTE, MELVIN ANDREW, b. Alameda, Calif., Mar. 22, 1947; B.A., U. Pacific, 1969; M.A., Rutgers U., 1970; J.D., U. Calif. at Davis, 1973; partner firm Wendt, Mitchell, Sinsheimer, de la Motte, & Lilley, San Luis Obispo, Calif., 1973—; chief adminstr. Pub. Defender's Office, San Luis Obispo, 1974—. Regional dir. U. Pacific Alumni Assn., 1976—; pres. Zion Lutheran Ch., San Luis Obispo, 1976. Mem. Calif. State, Am., San Luis Obispo bar assns., Calif. Attys. Criminal Justice, Am. Trial Lawyers Assn. Home: 1616 Huasna St San Luis Obispo CA 93401 Office: 1250 Peach St Suite D San Luis Obispo CA 93401 Tel (805) 543-3287

DELANCY, DAVID PAYTON, b. Richmond, Va., July 29, 1932; LL.B., Western State U., Anaheim, Calif., 1971. Admitted to Orange County bar, 1972; individual practice law, Corona del Mar, Calif., 1972—. Home: 4601 Camden Dr Corona del Mar CA 92625 Office: 2711 E Coast Highway Suite 206 Corona del Mar CA 92625 Tel (714) 675-2711

DELANEY, DEXTER LEE, b. Gt. Falls, Mont., Oct. 21, 1931; B.A., U. Mont., 1955, J.D., 1956. Admitted to Mont. bar, 1956; capt. JAG, USAF, 1956-58; individual practice law, Missoula, Mont., 1958-63; mem. firm Mulroney, Delaney, Dalby & Mudd, Missoula, 1963—; lectr. bus. law U., Mont., 1966-73; chief dep. county atty. Missoula County, 1958-60. Mem. Am., Mont., Western Mont. bar assns., Am., Mont. trial lawyers assns., Am. Judicature Assn., AAUP. Home: 201 Hastings St Missoula MT 59801 Office: Suite 300 Western Bank Bldg Missoula MT 59801 Tel (406) 721-2550

DELANEY, JAMES JOSEPH, b. Mpls., Sept. 17, 1908; B.S., Regis Coll., 1932; J.D., U. Denver, 1942; grad. Nat. Coll. State Trial Judges U. Nev., Reno, 1966, Coll. Juvenile Ct. Judges U. Colo., 1967. Admitted to Colo. bar, 1942; partner firm Delaney and Costello, Denver, 1945-65; judge Colo. Dist. Ct., 17th Jud. Dist., 1965—; forum leader White House Conf. on Children, 1970; trustee, treas. Nat. Juvenile Ct. Found.; mem. advisory bd. children's div. Am. Human Assn.; mem. advisory council Parents Anonymous; mem. Colo. Council Criminal Justice, 1970-74, Colo. Commn. Children and Youth, 1972-75. Bd. dirs. Legal Aid Soc. Met. Denver, 1968-73; mem. Colo. and Adams County Mental Health Assn., 1968—. Mem. Adams County, Am. bar assns., Am. Judicature Soc., Nat. Council Juvenile Ct. Judges (pres. 1968-76, trustee). Contbr. articles to profl. publs. Home: Route 1 POB 312-D Brighton CO 80601 Office: Hall of Justice Brighton CO 80601 Tel (303) 659-1161

DELANEY, JOHN MARTIN, b. Houston, Nov. 10, 1945; B.A., Princeton, 1967; J.D., U. Tex., 1973. Admitted to Tex. bar, 1973; partner asso. firm Dillon, Giesenschlag & Sharp, Bryan, Tex., 1973-76, partner, 1976—. Bd. dirs. Brazos County Girls' Clubs, Twin City Mission, Inc. Mem. State Bar Tex., Am., Brazos County bar assns., Comml. Law League Am., Tex. Trial Lawyers Assn. (exec. council family law com.). Recipient Achievement medal U.S. Navy, 1972. Home: 2308 Avon St Bryan TX 77801 Office: PO Box 711 Bryan TX 77801 Tel (713) 779-7979

DELANEY, JOHN WHITE, b. Springfield, Mass., Feb. 28, 1943; A.B. magna cum laude, Harvard, 1964, J.D., 1967. Admitted to Mass. bar, 1967; law clk. to chief justice and the justices Mass. Superior Ct.,

1967-68; dep. asst. atty. gen. State of Mass., 1968-69, legis. asst. to gov., 1969-73; asst. sec. consumer affairs Commonwealth of Mass., 1973-76; exec. dir. Boston Municipal Research Bur., 1976—; chmn. Mass. Local Election Dists. Rev. Commn., 1972-76; lectr. pub. adminstrn. Suffolk U., Boston, 1976—; moderator Town of W. Springfield (Mass.), 1972-74; mem. bd. dirs. Robert Kennedy Action Corps, Boston, 1973-76. Mem. Mass. Bar Assn. Home: 77 Village Ave Dedham MA 02026 Office: 294 Washington St Boston MA 02108 Tel (617) 482-3626

DELANEY, THOMAS RONALD, b. Marcus, Iowa, Dec. 15, 1905; J.D., Creighton U., 1930. Admitted to Nebr. bar, 1930, Mont. bar, 1938, Iowa bar, 1928; practiced law, Omaha, 1930-32, 34-38, Bayard, Iowa, 1932-34, Polson, Mont., 1938-47, Bellevue, Nebr., 1973—; vol. asst. atty. Welfare Office, Omaha, 1930-34; title examiner Fed. Land Bank, 1934-38; Lake County atty., Mont., 1945-47; mem. prosecution staff Internat. Mil. Tribunal Far East, 1947-48; atty.-advisor U.S. Forces, Japan, 1948-54; counsel U.S. Land Commn. Ryukyus, provost ct. reviewing officer and alt. judge, Okinawa, 1954-56; atty.-contracting officer AID, State Dept., Africa, Mid-East and Washington, 1956-71. Chmn., Bellevue Mayor's Steering Com. for Social Action, 1972-75; mem. Bellevue Planning Commn., 1975-76; chmn. Nebr. joint legis. com. Nat. Ret. Tchrs. Assn., 1974-76. Mem. Fed., Nebr., 2d Jud. Dist. bar assns. Home and Office: 1105 Country Club Ct Bellevue NE 68005 Tel (402) 292-0310

DELAPLAINE, EDWARD SCHLEY, b. Frederick, Md., Oct. 6, 1893; B.A., Washington and Lee U., 1913, postgrad. Law Sch., 1913-14; ed. Law Sch. U. Md., 1914-15. Admitted to Md. bar, 1915, U.S. Supreme Ct. bar, 1932; practice law, Frederick, 1915-38; mem. Md. Ho. of Dels., 1916-18; mem. state councils sect. Council Nat. Defense, Washington, 1918; city atty. City of Frederick, 1919-22; U.S. conciliation commnr., 1934-38; county atty. Frederick County (Md.), 1935-38; chief judge 6th Jud. Circuit Md., Frederick and Montgomery Counties, 1938-44; asso. judge Ct. Appeals Md., 1938-56; mem. First Conf. Chief Justices, St. Louis, 1949. Mem. Md. and Va. Potomac River Commn., 1958. Mem. Am., Md., Frederick County bar assns., Supreme Ct. Hist. Soc. Am. Judicature Soc. Home: 308 Upper College Terr Frederick MD 21701 Office: Pythian Castle Frederick MD 21701 Tel (301) 663-5211

DE LAURANT, BERNHART GEORGE, b. Wolbach, Nebr., Feb. 28, 1918; student Dana Coll., 1936-37; A.B., U. Nebr., 1940, LL.B., 1942; postgrad. U. Miss., 1943, U. Chgo., 1943, U. Mich., 1944. Admitted to Nebr. bar, 1942; adjustor, agt. State Farm Ins. Co., Scotts Bluff, Nebr., 1946-55. Mem. Gering (Nebr.) Sch. Bd., 1962—. Mem. Nebr. Bar Assn. Office: 2014 E 17th St Scotts Bluff NE 69361 Tel (308) 632-6420

DEL DUCA, FRANCES HORAN, b. Phila., Aug. 4, 1928; B.A., Chestnut Hill Coll., 1950; M.A., U. Pa., 1952; J.D., Dickinson Sch. Law, 1966. Admitted to Pa. bar, 1967; mem. firm George B. Faller, Carlisle, Pa., 1967—; dir. Carlisle Area Sch. Bd., 1973—; chmn. juvenile task force Pa. Joint Council on Criminal Justice System, 1974—; mem. exec. com. south central region Pa. Gov.'s Justice Commn., 1974—, Pa. Gov.'s Com. to Study Capital Punishment, 1973; mem. spl. com. Pa. E.R.A. (Equal Rights Amendment), 1976—. Pres. Carlisle League Women Voters, 1957; trustee Carlisle YWCA, 1970-75. Mem. Am., Pa. (mem. council family law sect. 1976—), Cumberland County (exec. com. 1974) bar assns., Nat. Assn. Women Lawyers, Joint Family Law Council, Carlisle Area C. of C. (v.p. 1975—), Dickinson Sch. Law Alumni Assn. (exec. bd. 1974—). Home: 506 S College St Carlisle PA 17013 Office: 10 W High St Carlisle PA 17013 Tel (717) 249-1323

DEL DUCA, LOUIS F., b. Lama Dei Peligni, Chieti, Italy, July 2, 1926; A.B., Temple U., 1950; LL.B., Harvard U., 1952; LL.D., U. Rome, 1954. Admitted to Pa. bar, 1955, U.S. Supreme Ct. bar; asso. firm Montgomery, McCracken, Walker & Rhoods, Phila., 1955-56; with Dickinson Sch. Law, Carlisle, Pa., 1956—, prof. law, dir. admissions; reporter Pa. Bar Assn. and Pa. Conf. State Trial Judges Jt. Council on Standards for Criminal Justice, 1972-74, 76—, Pa. Conf. State Trial Judges, 1976—, Del. Bar Assn. Uniform Comml. Code Implementation Project, 1964-66; mem. adv. commn. on truth in lending Fed. Res. Bd. Govs., 1970—; cons. in field. Chmn. Carlisle ARC, 1962; chmn. law enforcement com. Carlisle Community Workshop on Race Relations, 1968; bd. dirs. Carlisle Police Athletic League, 1957-70, Carlisle Counseling Center, 1976—. Mem. Am. Bar Found., Am. (chmn. sect. local govt. law), Pa. bar assns., Assn. Am. Law Schs. (chmn. sect. comml. contract and consumer law 1973), Pa. Bar Inst. (dir. 1972—). Editor Pa. Bar Assn. Quar., 1968—, Uniform Comml. Code Law Jour., 1970—; co-editor Pa. Jud. Highlights Bull., 1970—. Home: 506 S College St Carlisle PA 17013 Office: Dickinson Sch Law Carlisle PA 17013 Tel (717) 243-4611

DELISIO, STEPHEN SCOTT, b. San Diego, Dec. 30, 1937; B.A., Emory U., 1959; LL.B., Albany Law Sch. Union U., 1962; LL.M., Georgetown U., 1963. Admitted to D.C. bar, 1962, N.Y. bar, 1963, Alaska bar, 1964; asst. dist. atty. Alaska Dept. Law, Fairbanks, 1963-65; asso. firm McNealy & Merdes, Fairbanks, 1965-66; partner firm Merdes, Schaible, Staley & DeLisio, Fairbanks and Anchorage, 1966—, mgr. Anchorage office, 1971—, also dir.; lectr. U. Alaska, 1966-68, 76; trustee U. Alaska Heating Corp., Inc., 1968—; arbitrator Am. Arbitration Assn., 1972—, lectr., 1974, 76. Chmn. dist. 8 Alaska Republican Party, Anchorage, 1974; mem. Republican Precinct Com., Anchorage, 1971-75; bd. dirs. Anchorage Community Chorus, 1975—. Mem. Spenard Bar (pres. 1975-76), Anchorage, Alaska (chmn. com. environ. law 1971-72), Am. bar assns., Am. Judicature Soc., Am. Trial Lawyers Assn., Pi Sigma Phi. Recipient Law Rev. award Am. Patent Assn., 1962; author: (with others) Law and Tactics in Federal Criminal Cases, 1963; asso. editor Albany Law Rev., 1960-62. Home: 5102 Shorecrest Dr Anchorage AK 99502 Office: 2400 Spenard Rd Anchorage AK 99504 Tel (907) 279-9574

DELIZIO, JOSEPH R., b. Staten Island, N.Y., Dec. 23, 1917; B.S., St. John Coll., 1940; LL.B., St. John's U., 1942. Admitted to N.Y. state bar, 1942, Fed. bar, 1959; individual practice law, Bay Shore, N.Y., 1946—. Bd. dirs. Suffolk Rehab. Center Physically Handicapped, Commack, N.Y., 1964-66. Mem. Suffolk County Bar Assn., Islip Lawyers Club, Columbian Lawyers Assn. (dir. 1970-72). Office: 1 E Main St Bay Shore NY 11706 Tel (516) 665-5150

DELIZONNA, HARRY JAMES, b. St. Paul, Mar. 20, 1937; B.S., U. Minn., 1959, J.D., 1965. Admitted to Calif. bar, 1966, U.S. Supreme Ct. bar, 1974; asso. firm Lillick, McHose & Charles, San Francisco, 1966-68; dep. pub. defender Santa Clara County (Calif.), 1968-70; individual practice law, San Jose, Calif., 1970-76; gen. counsel Calif. State Agrl. Labor Relations Bd., Sacramento, 1976—; prof. U. Santa Clara Law Sch., 1970. Mem. San Jose Housing Bd., 1973-74, Santa Clara County Consumer Commn., 1975. Mem. Calif. Trial Lawyers Assn. (v.p. 1976), Calif. State Bar. Editor Santa Clara County Bar Jour., 1973. Office: 915 Capitol Mill Sacramento CA 95874 Tel (916) 322-7017

DELL, DONALD LUNCY, b. Savannah, Ga., June 17, 1938; B.A., Yale U., 1960; LL.B. (Noble Found. fellow), U. Va., 1964. Admitted to D.C. bar, 1964, Va. bar; with firm Hogan & Hartson, Washington, 1965-67; spl. asst. to dir. OEO, Washington, 1967-68; partner firm Dell, Craighill, Fentross & Benton, Washington, D.C., 1969—. Trustee Robert F. Kennedy Meml. Found.; mem. Washington Met. Bd. Trade, 1975-76; sec. Washington Area Tennis Patrons Found., 1970—; hon. bd. govs. Ohio U. Sports Adminstrn. Program. Mem. Am. Council Internat. Sports (dir. 1975—), D.C., Va. bar assns., Yale Scroll and Key Soc., AFTRA. Named Washingtonian Year, 1975. Home: 12200 Stoney Creek Rd Potomac MD 20854 Office: 888 17th St NW Washington DC 20006

DELL, GEORGE MARTIN, b. Washington, Jan. 2, 1925; B.S., U.S. Mil. Acad., 1947; J.D., U. So. Calif., 1953. Admitted to Calif. bar, 1953, U.S. Supreme Ct. bar, 1957; practiced in Los Angeles, 1953-61; commr. Los Angeles Superior Ct., 1961-63; judge Municipal Ct., Los Angeles, Calif., 1963-66; Los Angeles Superior Ct., 1966—. Mem. Calif. Judges Assn., Los Angeles County Bar Assn., Lawyers Club of Los Angeles County, Criminal Cts. Bar Assn., Order of Coif. Editor-in-chief So. Calif. Law Rev., 1952-53. Office: 111 N Hill St Los Angeles CA 90012 Tel (213) 974-1234

DELL'ERGO, ROBERT JAMES, b. Berkeley, Calif., Mar. 2, 1918; B.A. with honors, U. Calif., Berkeley, 1939, LL.B., J.D., 1942. Admitted to Calif. bar, 1946; partner firm Millington, Dell'Ergo & Morrissey, 1946-55; individual practice law, 1955-72; sr. partner firm Dell'Ergo & Tinsley, Redwood City, Calif., 1972—. Trustee Sequoia Union High Sch. Dist., 1952-56. Mem. Am., San Mateo County (pres. 1954) bar assns., Redwood City C. of C. (pres. 1958). Office: Suite 200 Wells Fargo Bank Bldg Broadway St and Main St Redwood City CA 94063 Tel (415) 365-5430

DELLWO, ROBERT DENNIS, b. Polson, Mont., Dec. 10, 1917; B.A., J.D., Gonzaga U., Spokane, Wash. Admitted to Wash. bar, 1943; agent FBI, 1942-48; partner firm Dellwo, Rudolf and Schroeder; individual practice law, Spokane. Mem. Am., Wash., Spokane County bar assns., Am. Judicature Soc. Contbr. articles in field to profl. jours. Home: RFD 1 Colbert WA 99005 Office: 1016 Old National Bank Spokane WA 99201 Tel (509) 624-4291

DE LOLLO, WARREN CARMEN, b. Watervliet, N.Y., May 4, 1918; A.B., Union Coll., 1941; LL.B., Albany Coll., 1948, J.D., 1968. Admitted to N.Y. bar, 1949; individual practice law, Watervliet, 1948—; atty. Watervliet City Sch. Dist., 1967-74; judge Watervliet City Ct., 1974—. Mem. N.Y. State Assn. City Ct. Judges, N.Y. State Assn. Magistrates, Albany-Schenectady Magistrates Assn. Office: 218 19th St Watervliet NY 12189 Tel (518) 273-0071

DELSON, ROBERT, b. N.Y.C., July 18, 1905; A.B., Cornell U., 1926, LL.B., Columbia, 1928. Admitted to N.Y. State bar, 1929, U.S. Dist. Ct. for So. dist. N.Y. bar, 1931, 2d Circuit Ct. Appeals bar, 1956, U.S. Dist. Ct. for D.C. bar, 1968; asso. firm Wise & Seligsberg, N.Y.C., 1929-31; asso. gen. counsel Consol. Film Industries, Inc. and Republic Pictures Corp., N.Y.C., 1931-37; asso. firm Delson & Gordon, N.Y.C., 1937-45, partner, 1945—; counsel Internat. League Human Rights, 1951—. Mem. Am. Law Inst., Am. Soc. Internat. Law, ACLU, Am. Internat., N.Y. State bar assns., N.Y. County Lawyers Assn., Consular Law Soc., Inter-Am. Assn. Democracy and Freedom (U.S. com.), Am. Fgn. Law Assn., Phi Beta Kappa. Contbr. articles to law jours. Home: 11 E 86th St New York City NY 10028 Office: 230 Park Ave New York City NY 10017 Tel (212) 686-8030 also 1900 L St Washington DC

DELTUFO, ROBERT J., b. Newark, Nov. 18, 1933; A.B. in English cum laude, Princeton, 1955; LL.B., Yale, 1958. Admitted to N.J. bar, 1959; legal sec. to Chief Justice Joseph Weintraub, N.J. Supreme Ct., 1958-60; asso. firm Jeffers & Dillon, Morristown, N.J., 1960-63, partner, 1963-74; 1st asst. atty. gen. State of N.J., Trenton, 1974—, dir. div. criminal justice, 1976—; asst. prosecutor Morris County (N.J.), 1963-67, 1st asst. prosecutor, 1965-67; instr. bus. law Fairleigh Dickinson U., 1964; mem. N.J. Bd. Bar Examiners, 1968-74; mem Morris County Coll. Law Enforcement Adv. Com., 1970—. Bd. dirs. ednl. opportunity fund N.J. Dept. Higher Edn., 1968-71, Morristown YMCA, 1970-74; mem. exec. com. United Fund of Morris County, 1966-70, v.p., 1970. Fellow Am. Bar Found.; mem. Am., Morris County, N.J. State bar assns., Am. Judicature Soc., Order of Coif. Contbr. articles to legal jours. Home: Lake Rd Morristown NJ 07960 Office: State House Annex Trenton NJ 08623 Tel (609) 292-4990

DE LUCA, PETER J., b. N.Y.C., Oct. 15, 1927; L.S.Q., Coll. City N.Y., 1951; LL.B. cum laude, N.Y. Law Sch., 1953. Admitted to N.Y. bar, 1954; mem. firm Cravath, Swaine & Moore, N.Y.C., 1953-59; atty. PepsiCo, Inc., Purchase N.Y., 1958-61, v.p., 1963-65, v.p., gen. counsel, sec., 1965-71; v.p., gen. counsel Revlon, Inc., N.Y.C., 1971-72, sr. v.p., gen. counsel, 1973; v.p., gen. counsel Gen. Foods Corp., White Plains, N.Y., 1973-77, sr. v.p., gen. counsel, 1977—. Bd. dirs. Heart Research Found. Cornell Med. Sch.-N.Y. Hosp., Blueberry, Inc.; mem. N.Y. State Gov.'s Advisory Panel. Mem. Am. Bar Assn., N.Y. State Lawyers Assn., Assn. Bar City N.Y. Home: 360 E 72d St New York City NY 10021 Office: 250 North St White Plains NY 10625 Tel (914) 683-2353

DE LUCE, RICHARD D., b. Nanaimo, B.C., Can., Oct. 3, 1928; A.B., U. Calif., Los Angeles, 1950; J.D., Stanford, 1955. Admitted to Calif. bar, 1955, U.S. Supreme Ct. bar, 1963; research atty. Calif. Supreme Ct., 1955-56; asso. firm Lawler, Felix & Hall, Los Angeles, 1956-62, partner, 1962—. Mem. Calif. State, Los Angeles County, Am. bar assns., Phi Beta Kappa. Office: 213 W Olympic Blvd Los Angeles CA 90015 Tel (213) 620-0060

DE MANIO, PETER MICHAEL, b. N.Y.C., Oct. 9, 1935; B.A., U. Pa., 1963; LL.B., Washington and Lee U., 1966. Admitted to Va. bar, 1966, Fla. bar, 1967; asso. firm Lavenstein and Lavenstein, Petersburg, Va., 1966, firm Gurney, Gurney and Handley, Orlando, Fla., 1967; individual practice law, Orlando, 1968; partner firm Bowden and de Manio, Orlando, 1969-71, Bowden, de Manio, Hitt and Hurt, Orlando, 1972; judge Orange County (Fla.) Criminal Ct. of Record, 1972; circuit judge 9th Jud. Circuit Ct., Fla., 1973—. Mem. Fla., Va. bar assns. Office: Orange County Courthouse Orlando FL 32801 Tel (305) 420-3281

DE MARCO, ANTHONY JOSEPH, JR., b. Bklyn., June 27, 1928; B.S., Manhattan Coll., 1952; LL.B., St. John's U., 1968, J.D., 1970. Admitted to N.Y. State bar, 1958; individual practice law, Bklyn., 1959—; trial counsel Gen. Accident Ins., Reliance Ins. Co., N.Y.C.; counsel Heart Fund S.I. Hosp., 1972—; counsel, bd. dirs. S.I. Kidney Found., 1972—. Mem. N.Y. State (exec. com. trial lawyers sect.), Am., Bklyn. bar assns., Met. Trial Lawyers Assn., Columbian Lawyers, Delta Theta Phi. Home: 3 Ismay St Staten Island NY 10314 Office: 26 Court St Brooklyn NY 11242 Tel (212) 858-2284

DE MARCO, JAMES JOSEPH, b. Phila., Mar. 29, 1933; A.B., J.D., Villanova U. Admitteo to Pa. bar, 1960; pvt. practice law, 1961—; mem. draft bd., Pa., 1968-73; hearing examiner Pa. Labor Bd., 1972-74. Bd. dirs. local council Girl Scouts U.S.A., Phila., 1973—, armed services br. YMCA, 1974—. Mem. Am., Pa. trial lawyers assns., Pa., Phila. bar assns. Home: 1514 S Broad St Philadelphia PA 19146 Office: 1617 John F Kennedy Blvd Philadelphia PA 19103 Tel (215) LO-8-8191

DE MASCIO, ROBERT EDWARD, b. Coraopolis, Pa., Jan. 11, 1923; LL.B., Wayne State U., 1951. Admitted to Mich. bar, 1951, since practiced in Detroit; individual practice law, 1951-53, 62-66; asst. U.S. atty. Eastern Dist. Mich., Detroit, 1954-62; judge Detroit Recorder's Ct., 1967-71; U.S. dist. judge, 1971—. Office: US Dist Ct 257 Fed Bldg Detroit MI 48226 Tel (313) 226-7570

DEMASSA, PHILIP ARTHUR, b. San Diego, Mar. 24, 1945; A.B., Occidental Coll., 1967; LL.B., U. San Diego, 1970. Admitted to Calif. bar, 1971, U.S. Supreme Ct. bar, 1975; staff atty. Fed. Defenders of San Diego, Inc., 1971-72; atty. Philip A. Demassa Corp., San Diego, 1972—. Mem. Am., San Diego County bar assns., Calif. Trial Lawyers Assn. Editor U. San Diego Law Rev. Office: 2150 First Ave San Diego CA 92101 Tel (714) 236-0897

DEMATTEO, RAYMOND ETTORE, b. Schenectady, June 10, 1919; student Union Coll., Schenectady, 1937-46; LL.B. (Spear scholar), Albany Law Sch., 1947, J.D., 1950. Admitted to N.Y. State bar, 1951; partner firm De Matteo, De Matteo & De Matteo, Schenectady, 1951—; mem. Schenectady City Council, 1963-67; clk. Schenectady City Ct., 1972-75; asst. counsel Regional Off-Track Betting Corp., 1975—. Mem. Off-Track Betting Commn., Schenectady, 1973-75. Mem. Schenectady County, N.Y. State, U.S. bar assns. Office: 166 Lafayette St Schenectady NY 12305 Tel (518) 393-1311

DE MAY, JOHN ANDREW, b. Phila., Sept. 5, 1925; B.A. in Econs., U. Pitts., 1949, J.D., 1952. Admitted to Pa. bar, 1953, U.S. Dist. Ct. for Western Pa., 1953, U.S. 3d Circuit Ct. Appeals bar, 1960, U.S. 2d Circuit Ct. Appeals bar, 1965, U.S. Supreme Ct. bar, 1965; law clk. Ct. Common Pleas, Pitts., 1952-53; asst. U.S. atty., Pitts., 1953-57; partner firm McArdle, Harrington & McLaughlin, Pitts., 1957-67; individual practice law, Pitts., 1967—. Mem. Am., Pa., Allegheny County bar assns., Acad. Trial Lawyers Allegheny County, Assn. Trial Lawyers Am., Am. Judicature Soc., Pitts. Inst. Legal Medicine. Author: The Plaintiff's Personal Injury Case: Its Trial, Preparation and Settlement. Home: 219 Regency Pl Bethel Park PA 15102 Office: 906 Manor Bldg Pittsburgh PA 15219 Tel (412) 281-4143

DEMBICER, EDWIN HERBERT, b. Bklyn., June 12, 1928; LL.B., N.Y. Law Sch., 1950. Admitted to N.Y. bar, 1950, U.S. Dist. Ct. for Eastern N.Y., 1954, So. N.Y. Dist., 1952, U.S. Supreme Ct. bar, 1959, U.S. Ct. Claims bar, 1959; asso. firm Louis L. Berko, N.Y.C., 1950-51; asso. firm Martin L. Kolbrener, N.Y.C., 1953-56; individual practice law, N.Y.C., Bklyn., 1956-69; partner firm Dembicer & Lederer, Lynbrook, N.Y., Bklyn., 1969—; spl. master Civil Ct., N.Y.C., arbitrator Small Claim div. Civil Ct., N.Y.C. Election dist. leader Democratic party, Hewlett, N.Y., 1965. Mem. Bklyn. Bar Assn., Am. Judges Assn., Am. Arbitration Assn. (arbitrator). Recipient J. Campbell Jeffrey Dean's award, 1950. Home: 36 Steven Dr Hewlett NY 11557 Office: 381 Sunrise Pwy POB 712 Lynbrook NY 11563 Tel (516) 599-9180 also 50 Court St Brooklyn NY Tel (212) 297-4047

DE MENT, IRA, b. Birmingham, Ala., Dec. 21, 1931; A.S., Marion Mil. Inst., 1951; A.B., U. Ala., 1953, LL.B., 1958, J.D., 1969. Admitted to Ala. bar, 1958, U.S. Supreme Ct. bar, 1966; law clk. to asso. justice Ala. Supreme Ct., 1958-59; asst. atty. gen. State of Ala., 1959, spl. asst. atty. gen., 1966-69; asst. U.S. atty. Middle Dist. Ala., 1959-61, acting U.S. atty., 1969, U.S. atty., 1969—; practiced in Montgomery, Ala., 1961-69; instr. Montgomery Police Acad. 1964—; instr., lectr. in field; adj. prof. psychology U. Ala., 1975—; mem. adv. bd. U. Ala. Law Enforcement Acad., 1972—, Auburn U., Montgomery, 1975—; mem. Atty. Gen's. Adv. Com. of U.S. Attys., 1975—; mem. nat. panel Am. Arbitration Assn.; lt. col. JAGC, USAF. Mem. Montgomery Fire Prevention Com., 1975-76. Mem. Montgomery County, D.C., Fed. (charter mem. Montgomery chpt.), Am. bar assns., Ala. State Bar (editorial adv. bd. Ala. Lawyer 1966-72), Nat. Dist. Attys. Assn., Am. Judicature Soc., Fraternal Order Police, Ala. Peace Officers Assn., Res. Officers Assn. U.S., Air Force Assn., Ala. Hist. Assn., Ala. Assn. Chiefs of Police (hon.), Montgomery Firefighters Assn. (hon. mem. local 1444), Phi Alpha Delta. Recipient award for Distinguished Service Internat. Assn. Firefighters, 1975; Rockefeller Pub. Service award Woodrow Wilson Sch. Pub. and Internat. Affairs, Princeton U., 1976. Home: 3437 Warrenton Rd Montgomery AL 36111 Office: PO Box 4163 Montgomery AL 36104 Tel (205) 832-7280

DEMPSEY, MICHAEL DOUGLAS, b. Los Angeles, Mar. 21, 1943; B.A. magna cum laude, Calif. State U., Northridge, 1965; J.D., U. Calif., Los Angeles, 1968. Admitted to Calif. bar, 1969, U.S. Supreme Ct. bar, 1976; asso. firm Lillick, McHose & Charles, Los Angeles, 1968-73, partner, 1974—. Mem. Am., Calif., Los Angeles bar assns., Maritime Law Assn., Order of Coif. Contbr. articles Univ. Calif., Los Angeles Law Review. Office: 707 Wilshire Blvd Los Angeles CA 90017 Tel (213) 620-9000

DEMPSEY, TERENCE MARK, b. Henderson, Minn., Feb. 17, 1932; B.A., Coll. St. Thomas, St. Paul, 1954; J.D., U. Calif., San Francisco, 1962. Admitted to Calif. bar, 1963, Minn. bar, 1963; partner firms McGuire & Dempsey, Montgomery, Minn., 1963-64, Somsen, Dempsey & Schade, New Ulm, Minn., 1964—; asst. pub. defender 5th Jud. Dist. Minn., 1967-69; city atty. City of New Ulm, 1969—; mem. region 9 Gov's Crime Commn., 1975—. Mem. State Bar Calif., Minn. State, 9th Jud. (pres. 1976) bar assns., Minn. City Attys. Assn. (pres. 1973), Am. Judicature Soc. Home: 309 S Minnesota Ave New Ulm MN 56073 Office: State Bond Bldg New Ulm MN 56073 Tel (507) 354-2161

DEMPSEY, THOMAS LAWRENCE, b. Tacoma, July 31, 1935; B.A. Gonzaga U., 1958, LL.B., 1963. Admitted to Wash. bar, 1966, U.S. Ct. Mil. Appeals bar, 1972; clk. Wash. State Supreme Ct., Olympia, 1963-65; asst. atty. gen. State of Wash, 1966; asst. city atty. City of Tacoma, 1967—; served to maj. JAGC, U.S. Army Res., 1968—; guest instr. Seattle U., 1973-74, U. Puget Sound, 1974-76. Mem. Am., Wash. bar assns., Am. Judicature Soc., Nat. Inst. Municipal Law Officers. Home: 9309 Peacock Hill Ave Gig Harbor WA 98335 Office: PO Box 11007 Tacoma WA 98411 Tel (206) 383-2471

DEMPSEY, WILLIAM J., b. N.Y.C., Nov. 19, 1917; B.S., Fordham Coll., 1935, J.D., 1938. Admitted to N.Y. bar, 1940; pvt. practice law, 1940-50; police justice Village of Mineola (N.Y.), 1946-50, Village of Old Westbury (N.Y.), 1948-50; asst. dist. atty. County of Nassau

(N.Y.) Grand Jury and Indictment Bur., 1950-58; judge N.Y. Dist. Ct. for County of Nassau, 1958-63; judge County of Nassau Family Ct., 1963-72, adminstrv. judge, 1972—; mem. Nassau County Criminal Justice Coordinating Council. Mem. N.Y. State Assn. Family Ct. Judges, Nat. Council Juvenile Ct. Judges, Nassau County Bar Assn., Nat. Assn. County Ofcls. Office: Family Ct County of Nassau 1200 Old Country Rd Westbury NY 11590 Tel (516) 292-6033

DE MUTH, CHRISTOPHER CLAY, b. Evanston, Ill., Aug. 5, 1946; A.B., Harvard, 1968; J.D., U. Chgo., 1973. Admitted to Ill. bar, 1973; staff asst. to Pres. U.S., Washington, 1969-70; asso. firm Sidley & Austin, Chgo., 1973-76; asso. gen. counsel Consol. Rail Corp., Phila., 1976—. Home: 317 S American St Philadelphia PA 19106 Office: 6 Penn Center Plaza Philadelphia PA 19104 Tel (215) 594-1169

DEMUTH, RICHARD HOLZMAN, b. N.Y.C., Sept. 11, 1910; A.B., Princeton, 1931; LL.B., Harvard, 1934. Admitted to D.C. bar, 1973, N.Y. bar, 1934; law clk. to judge U.S. Circuit Ct., 1934-35; asso. firm Simpson Thacher & Bartlett, 1935-39; spl. asst. to U.S. Atty. Gen., Office of Solicitor Gen., Washington, 1939-42; with Internat. Bank for Reconstrn. and Devel., Washington, 1946-73, dir. devel. services dept., 1961-73; partner firm Surrey, Karasik and Morse, Washington, 1973—; chmn. Consultative Group Internat. Agrl. Research, 1970-73; chmn. Internat. Bd. for Plant Genetic Resources, 1973—. Bd. dirs. Internat. Inst. Ednl. Planning, Paris, 1964-73. Mem. D.C. Bar Assn., Assn. Bar City N.Y., Soc. Internat. Devel. Home: 5404 Bradley Blvd Bethesda MD 20014 Office: 1156 15th St Suite 1200 Washington DC 20005 Tel (202) 331-4010

DENARO, JACK MATTHEW, b. Rochester, N.Y., July 13, 1943; B.A., St. Bernard Coll., 1964; J.D., Union U., 1967; LL.M., U. Miami (Fla.), 1968, Ph.D., 1972. Admitted to Fla. bar, 1970, U.S. Tax Ct., 1977, U.S. Customs Ct., 1977, U.S. Supreme Ct. bar, 1976; asst. state's atty. Dade County (Fla.), 1970-71, asst. pub. defender, 1971-75; partner firm Black & Denaro, Miami, Fla., 1976—; asso. prof. law U. Miami, 1973—. Mem. Fla. Acad. Trial Lawyers, Am. Bar Assn. Contbr. articles to legal jours. Office: 150 SE 2d Ave Miami FL 33131 Tel (305) 371-6421

DENBO, JAMES RAYMOND, b. Washington, Feb. 18, 1941; B.A., U. Mich., 1963; J.D., George Washington U., 1967. Admitted to U.S. Dist. Ct. for D.C. bar; atty. advice br. NLRB, Washington, 1967-69, field atty., Milw., 1969-71; asso. firm Vedder, Price, Kaufman, Kammholz & Day, Washington, 1971—. Mem. Am. Bar Assn. Home: 5205 Falmouth Rd Bethesda MD 20016 Office: 1750 Pennsylvania Ave NW Washington DC 20006 Tel (202) 298-6445

DENBO, MILTON CARL, b. Camden, N.J., Feb. 24, 1912; A.B., U. Pa., 1932; J.D., U. Mich., 1936. Admitted to D.C. bar, 1937, N.Y. State bar, 1945, U.S. Supreme Ct. bar, 1946; atty. U.S. depts. Agr., Labor and Justice, 1936-44; asso. firm Root, Clark, Buckner & Ballantine, N.Y.C., 1944-45; individual practice law, Washington, 1945-52; partner firm Poole, Shroyer & Denbo, Washington, 1952-56, Shroyer & Denbo, Washington, 1956-71, Vedder, Price, Kaufman, Kammholz & Day, Washington, 1971—; adj. prof. Georgetown U. Law Sch., 1959-61. Bd. dirs. D.C. Mental Health Assn., 1960-70. Mem. Am., Fed., N.Y. State, D.C. bar assns., Assn. Bar D.C., Order of Coif. Contbr. articles to legal jours. Home: 5136 Macomb St NW Washington DC 20016 Office: 1750 Pennsylvania Ave NW Washington DC 20006 Tel (202) 393-5970

DENCE, EDWARD WILLIAM, JR., b. Newport, R.I., Feb. 25, 1938; A.B., Summa cum laude, Providence Coll., 1959; LL.B., Harvard, 1963. Admitted to Mass. bar, 1963, R.I. bar, 1965; sec., gen. counsel Indsl. Nat. Corp., Providence. Trustee, mem. exec. com. R.I. Pub. Expenditure Council, 1969-75; mem. R.I. Commn. on Inter-govtl. Relations, 1970-71; mem. Providence Roman Cath. Diocesan Bd. Edn., 1970-73. Mem. R.I., Am. bar assns. Home: 1485 High Hawk Rd East Greenwich RI 02818 Office: 111 Westminster St Providence RI 02903 Tel (401) 278-5880

DE NEEN, JAMES FRANCIS, b. St. Joseph, Mo., Nov. 27, 1938; B.S. in Bus. Adminstrn., U. Mo., 1961, J.D., 1964. Admitted to Mo. bar, 1964; individual practice law; asst. atty. gen. State of Mo., 1964-66; asst. atty. City of Joplin (Mo.), 1968-70. Home: 1338 Sheridan St Joplin MO 64801 Office: 707 1st Nat Bank Bldg Joplin MO 64801 Tel (417) 623-0350

DENEFE, J. TERRENCE, b. Omaha, July 29, 1947; B.B.A., Drake U., Des Moines, 1969, J.D., 1973. Admitted to Iowa bar, 1973; partner firm Ruschmeyer & Denefe, Ottumwa, Iowa, 1973-76; asst. atty. Wapello County (Iowa), Ottumwa, 1973—; asso. firm Kiple & Kiple, Ottumwa, 1976—. Adviser, K.C., Ottumwa, 1976—. Mem. Am., Iowa, Wapello County bar assns. Home: 181 Northview St Ottumwa IA 52501 Office: 106 N Market St Ottumwa IA 52501 Tel (515) 683-1626

DENHOLM, FRANK EDWARD, b. Andover, S.D., Nov. 29, 1923; B.S., S.D. State U., 1956, LL.B., J.D., 1962; M.S. in Pub. Adminstrn., U. Minn. Admitted to S.D. bar, U.S. Supreme Ct. bar, other fed. bars; formerly farmer and auctioneer; elected sheriff Day County, S.D., 1950; spl. agt. FBI, 1956-62; partner firm Denholm, Glover & Aho, Brookings, S.D., 1962—; former mem. faculty S.D. State U.; mem. 92d-93d Congresses from S.D.; former corp. counsel cities Brookings, Volga, and White. Active United Fund, Boy Scouts Am. Mem. Am. Judicature Soc., Internat. Platform Assn., State Bar Assn. S.D., Am. Bar Assn., S.D. Trial Lawyers Assn., Am. Trial Lawyers Assn., Phi Delta Phi, Gamma Sigma Delta. Contbr. articles to profl. jours. Home: 2127 Elmwood Dr Brookings SD 57006 Office: 418 4th St Brookings SD 57006 Tel (605) 692-2102

DENIRO, PATRICK JOSEPH, b. Bklyn., May 17, 1922; B.A., George Wash. U., 1948; J.D., U. Wyo., 1950. Admitted to Wyo. bar, 1950, Colo. bar, 1958; v.p. law Inter-Am. Petroleum Corp., Denver, 1969—. Chmn. bd. adjustment City Westminster, Colo., 1964. Mem. Denver Bar Assn. Home: 2030 E 11th Ave Denver CO 80206 Office 609 E Speer Blvd Denver CO 80203 Tel (303) 744-1356

DENK, PAUL MICHAEL, b. St. Louis, Jan. 20, 1937; B.S., U. Mo., 1958; J.D., Washington U., St. Louis, 1963, E.E., 1971. Admitted to Mo. bar, 1963—, U.S. Supreme Ct. bar, 1976; individual practice patent law, St. Louis, 1965—. Treas., Legal Aid Soc., St. Louis, 1973-75. Mem. Am., Mo., Met. St. Louis (chmn. young lawyers sect. 1970, treas. assn. 1976, sec. assn., 1977, mem. exec. com. 1974-76) bar assns. Am. Patent Law Assn., Engrs. Club St. Louis. Asso. editor Law Notes, Am. Bar Assn. publ., 1969-73. Home: 8 Burroughs St Ladue MO 63124 Office: 1221 Locust St Saint Louis MO 63103 Tel (314) 241-6668

DENMAN, ALVIN, b. Pawnee, Nebr., May 8, 1895; LL.B., U. Idaho, 1919. Admitted to Idaho bar, 1919; individual practice law, Idaho Falls, 1919—; mem. Idaho Commn. on Uniform Laws, 1930-34; mem. Idaho Senate, 1936-38; spl. legis. atty. Gov. Chase A. Clark of Idaho, 1942; vis. lectr. history Am. law Antioch Coll., 1973, 74, 75. Vice chmn. exec. com. Teton Peaks council Boy Scouts Am., Idaho Falls, 1934-35. Mem. Idaho, Idaho Falls (pres. 1934) bar assns. Home: 945 Terry Dr Idaho Falls ID 83401 Office: 690 Cambridge Dr Idaho Falls ID 83401 Tel (208) 522-2513

DENNEY, EARL LAUDER, JR., b. Jacksonville, Fla., Feb. 18, 1943; B.A., Fla. State U., 1963; J.D., U. Miss., 1967. Admitted to Fla. bar, 1967, Miss. bar, 1967; asso. firm Howell, Kirby, Montgomery D'Aiuto & Dean, W. Palm Beach, Fla., 1968-72, partner, 1972-76, dir., 1973-76; sr. partner firm Montgomery, Lytal, Reiter, Denney & Searcy, W. Palm Beach, 1976—; mem. adv. com., ethics com. Palm Beach County Ct. Mem. Am., Fla. bar assns., Law Sci. Acad., Am. Judicature Soc., Am. Soc. Law and Medicine, Acad. Fla. Trial Lawyers, Am. Arbitration Assn., Phi Alpha Delta. Home: 7124 W Lake Dr Lake Clarke Shores FL 33406 Office: 2139 Palm Beach Lakes Blvd W Palm Beach FL 33402 Tel (305) 686-6300

DENNEY, ROBERT VERNON, b. Council Bluffs, Iowa, Apr. 11, 1916; student Peru State U., U. Nebr., LL.B. cum laude, Creighton U., 1939. Admitted to Nebr. bar, 1939; individual practice law, Fairbury, Nebr., 1939-40, 52-66; spl. agt. FBI, Washington and Chgo., 1940-41; atty. County Jefferson, Nebr., 1947, 48-52; atty. City Fairbury, Nebr., 1951; mem. 90th-91st Congresses from 1st Dist. Nebr., 1966-70; judge U.S. Dist. Ct., Dist. Nebr., Omaha, 1971—. Pres., Fairbury Indsl. Devel. Corp., 1960; mem. Fairbury Sch. Bd., 1956; chmn. Jefferson County Republican Com., 1961-64, Nebr. Rep. Party, 1961-64. Mem. Am., Nebr., Omaha bar assns., Fairbury C. of C. (former pres.), Alpha Sigma Nu. Recipient Merit award Creighton Alumni, 1976. Home: 3020 Paddock Rd Apt 18 Omaha NE 68124 Office: Box 1297 DTS Omaha NE 68101 Tel (402) 221-3615

DENNIS, GERALD EUGENE, b. Ft. Wayne, Ind., Nov. 14, 1926; B.S., Ind. U., 1948, J.D., 1950. Admitted to Ind. bar, 1950, Ill. bar, 1966; mem. firm Tourkow, Dennis & Danehy, Ft. Wayne, 1950-53; spl. atty. IRS, 1953-55; v.p., counsel Great No. Life Ins. Co., 1955-65; counsel Midwestern United Life Ins. Co., 1965-66; sr. v.p., sec., gen. counsel Montgomery Ward Life Ins. Co., Chgo., 1966—, Montgomery Ward Ins. Co., Chgo., 1974—, Forum Ins. Co., Chgo., 1975—. Fellow Life Office Mgmt. Inst.; mem. Am., Ill., Ind., Chgo. bar assns. Home: 950 Huckleberry St Northbrook IL 60062 Office: 140 S State St Chicago IL 60603 Tel (312) 467-8530

DENNIS, WILLIAM LEWIS, b. Ft. Wayne, Ind., May 27, 1914; A.B., Yale U., 1936, LL.B., 1939. Admitted to N.Y. bar, 1942, U.S. Dist. Ct. So. Dist. N.Y. bar, 1943, U.S. Ct. Appeals 2d Circuit bar, 1947, U.S. Supreme Ct. bar, 1966; partner firm Cahill, Gordon & Reindel, N.Y.C., 1943—; mem. faculty Yale U., 1939-43, N.Y. U., 1946—. Home: 20 Pierrepont St Brooklyn NY 11201 Office: 80 Pine St New York City NY 10005 Tel (212) 825-0100

DENNISON, JOHN B., b. Mpls., June 19, 1942; B.A., U. Minn., 1964, J.D., 1967. Admitted to Minn. bar, 1967; atty. Mpls. Star and Tribune Co., Mpls., 1967—. Mem. Univ. Dist. Improvement Assn., Minn. Press Club, U. Minn. Law Alumni Assn. Mem. Am., Minn., Hennepin County (chmn. Lawyer Mag. Com.) bar assns. Home: 700 7th St SE Minneapolis MN 55414 Office: 425 Portland Ave Minneapolis MN 55488 Tel (612) 372-4112

DENNISON, KAREN DENISE, b. Reno, Sept. 26, 1946; B.A. magna cum laude, U. Nev., 1968; J.D., U. San Francisco, 1971. Admitted to Nev. bar, 1971, Calif. bar, 1972; law clk. firm Foucke, Wertsch & Hayes, San Francisco, 1970; asso. firm Hale, Belford, Lane & Peek, Reno, 1972-74, partner, 1974—; instr. Edn. Dynamics Inst., 1973-75. Mem. ad hoc gaming ordnance rev. com. Reno City Council, 1976; trustee Washoe Legal Services Corp., 1973—, chmn. bd., 1975—. Mem. Am., Calif., Nev., Washoe County bar assns. Home: 417 St Lawrence Ave Reno NV 89509 Office: 201 W Liberty St Reno NV 89501 Tel (702) 786-7900

DENNISTON, JOHN BAKER, b. Cin., June 3, 1936; B.Engring. Physics, Cornell U., 1958; J.D., Harvard U., 1962. Admitted to D.C. bar, 1962, U.S. Supreme Ct. bar, 1964, U.S. Ct. Claims bar, 1965; asso. firm Covington & Burling, Washington, 1963-71, partner, 1971—. Mem. D.C. (Young Lawyer of Year 1971), Am. bar assns. Office: 888-16th St NW Washington DC 20006 Tel (202) 452-6388

DENNY, JAMES MCCAHILL, b. Mpls., Oct. 25, 1932; B.A., U. Minn., 1957; LL.B., Georgetown U., 1960. Admitted to N.Y. bar, 1963; asso. firm Dewey, Ballantine, Bushby, Palmer & Wood, N.Y.C. and Paris, 1960-68; asst. counsel Firestone Tire & Rubber Co., Akron, Ohio, 1968-70, asst. treas., 1971-75, treas., 1975—. Trustee Children's Hospital, Akron, 1976. Mem. Am. Bar assn., Assn. Bar City N.Y. Home: 828 Merriman Rd Akron OH 44303 Office: 1200 Firestone Pkwy Akron OH 44317 Tel (216) 379-7953

DENSON, WILLIAM DOWDELL, b. Birmingham, Ala., May 31, 1913; B.S., U.S. Mil. Acad., 1934; LL.B., Harvard, 1937, J.D., 1968. Admitted to Ala. bar, 1937, U.S. Supreme Ct. bar, 1948, D.C. bar, 1953, N.Y. bar, 1958; individual practice law, Birmingham, 1937-42; asst. staff judge advocate, instr. U.S. Mil. Acad., 1942-45, asst. staff judge advocate 3d U.S. Army, 1945-46; chief counsel, prosecutor War Crimes Trials, 1945-47; atty. U.S. AEC, Washington, 1948-52; individual practice law, Washington, N.Y.C., 1952—; trustee, mayor Village of Lawrence, N.Y., 1966-76. Pres. Lawrence Civic Assn., 1965-66; warden Trinity Ch., Hewlett, N.Y. Mem. Am., N.Y. State, D.C. bar assns., Am. Judicature Soc., Bar Assn. City N.Y. Decorated Legion of Honor (France). Home: 290 Narragansett Ave Lawrence NY 11559 Office: 551 Fifth Ave New York City NY 10017 Tel (212) 687-1360

DENT, BOYCE CHILDRESS, b. Lawrence County, Ark., Oct. 3, 1929; A.A. with honors, Eastern Coll. Commerce & Law, 1962; LL.B. with honors, Mt. Vernon Sch. Law, 1964; J.D., U. Balt., 1970. Admitted to Md. bar, 1964; project engr. Koppers Co., Inc., Balt., 1957-62, patent liaison engr., 1962-64, patent atty., 1964-76; legal counsel Ward Machinery Co., Cockeysville, Md., 1976—. Mem. Am., Md. bar assns. Patentee in field. Home: 4 Wakeham Ct Lutherville MD 21093 Office: 10615 Beaver Dam Rd Cockeysville MD 21030 Tel (301) 666-7700

DENT, DEWITT RONALD, b. Savannah Beach, Ga., May 1, 1937; B.S. in Commerce, The Citadel, 1960; J.D., Duke U., 1969. Admitted to Va. bar, 1972, D.C. bar, 1972, Ga. bar, 1973. atty. U.S. Dept. Justice, Washington, 1971-74; individual practice law, Augusta, Ga., 1974—. Mem. Am., D.C., Va., Ga., Augusta bar assns. Home: 3108 Exeter Rd Augusta GA 30909 Office: Suite 102D Bldg D 2623 Washington Rd Augusta GA 30904 Tel (404) 733-1972

DENT, HARRY SHULER, b. St. Matthews, S.C., Feb. 21, 1930; B.A. cum laude, Presbyn. Coll., 1951, LL.D., 1971; J.D., George Washington U., 1957, LL.M., Georgetown U., 1959; D.Polit. Sci., Bapt. Coll., 1971. Admitted to S.C. bar, 1957, D.C. bar, 1973; chief asst. U.S. Senator Strom Thurmond, Washington, 1955-65; sr. partner firm Dent & Kennedy, Columbia, S.C., 1965-68; spl. counsel Pres. Richard Nixon, 1969-72; partner firm Whaley, McCutchen, Blanton & Dent, Columbia, 1973-74; sr. partner, Dent, Kirkland, Taylor & Wilson, W. Columbia, S.C., 1975-77; gen. counsel Republican Nat. Com., Washington, 1973-74. Chmn. S.C. Republican Party, 1965-68, del. Rep. Nat. Conv., 1968, 1976; trustee Freedoms Found. Valley Forge (Pa.); chmn. Sabine River Compact Adminstrn., 1977—. Recipient Distinguished Achievement award Presbyn. Coll., 1970. Home: 2030 Bermuda Hills Rd Columbia SC 29204 Office: Box 528 Columbia SC 29202 Tel (803) 779-7700

DENT, THOMAS AUGUSTINE, b. N.Y.C., Aug. 28, 1920; B.A., Queens Coll., 1942; LL.B., Bklyn. Law Sch., 1948, LL.M., 1957. Admitteo to N.Y.State bar, 1949; asso. firm Dayton & D'Amato, Bayside, N.Y., 1950-54; individual practice law, Flushing, N.Y., 1954-55; partner firm Dent, Goldblum & Witschieben, Flushing, 1956-64, Dent & Witschieben, Flushing, 1964—; adj. prof. law Queens Coll., 1962—; asst. dist. atty. Queens County, N.Y., 1964-66. Pres. No. Queens Child Guidance Center, 1959-62. Home: 32-17 Douglas Rd Douglaston NY 11363 Office: 39-01 Main St Flushing NY 11354 Tel (212) 359-2661

DENTON, DAVID ARNOLD, b. Elkhart, Ind., Nov. 9, 1937; B.S., Ind. U., 1960; LL.B., U.. Md., 1965. Admitted to Ind. bar, 1965; mem. legal dept. CTS Corp., Elkhart, 1965-68; mem. firm Arnold & Denton, Elkhart, 1968—. Bd. dirs. ARC, 1968-74. Mem. Ind. State, Elkhart City, Elkhart County bar assns. Home: 3115 E Lake Dr N Elkhart IN 46514 Office: 222 W Lexington Ave Elkhart IN 46514 Tel (219) 295-4600

DENVER, THOMAS, b. N.Y.C., Oct. 29, 1944; B.A., Syracuse U., 1966; M.S., U. Washington, 1967; J.D., Hastings Coll. of Law, 1973. Admitted to Calif. bar, 1973; mem. firm Hoge, Fenton, Jones & Appel, Inc., San Jose, Calif., 1973—. Mem. Am., Calif. bar assns. Home: 687 Florales St Palo Alto CA 94306 Office: 4 N Second St San Jose CA 95113 Tel (408) 287-9501

DE PASCALE, VINCENT NICHOLAS, b. Ashtabula, Ohio, Sept. 5, 1941; B.A., U. Dayton; J.D., Ohio No. U.; grad. Judge Adv. Gen.'s Sch. Admitted to Ohio bar, 1967, U.S. Supreme Ct. bar, 1971, U.S. Ct. Mil. Appeals, 1967; served with JAGC, U.S. Army, 1967-69; individual practice law, Columbus, Ohio, 1970—; tchr. law, 1966-67. Office: 17 S High St Suite 900 Columbus OH 43215 Tel (614) 464-1991

DE PORTER, DENNIS ALBERT, b. Davenport, Iowa, Nov. 14, 1945; B.A., No. Ill. U., 1967; J.D., U. Ill., 1971. Asst. prof. Western Ill. U., Macomb, 1971-73; admitted to Ill. bar, 1972; asst. state's atty. Knox County (Ill.), Galesburg, 1973-75; partner firm Braud, Warner, Neppl & Westensee, Rock Island, Ill., 1975—. Mem. Am., Ill., Rock Island County, Knox County bar assns., Am. Bus. Law Assn. Home: 54 Blackhawk Hills Dr Rock Island IL 61201 Office: 1703 2d Ave Rock Island IL 61201 Tel (309) 793-1160

DEPPMAN, JOHN C., b. Evanston, Ill., Sept. 25, 1943; A.B., Middlebury Coll., 1965; J.D., Georgetown U., 1969. Admitted to Vt. bar, 1969; since practice in Middlebury, mem. firm Conley & Foote, 1969-72, individual practice law, 1972-73, 75—; state's atty. Addison County (Vt.), 1973-75. Mem. Middlebury Bd. Selectmen, 1971-73; chmn. Middlebury Town Republican Com., 1976—. Mem. Am., Vt., Addison County bar assns. Home: RD 3 Middlebury VT 05753 Office: 7 Court St Middlebury VT 05753 Tel (802) 388-6337

DE PREE, HOWARD JAY, b. Zeeland, Mich., May 22, 1928; B.S. in Mech. Engring., Purdue U., 1949; J.D., U. Notre Dame, 1956; LL.M., John Marshall Law Sch., 1959. Admitted to Ill. bar, 1956, Ind. bar, 1956, U.S. Supreme Ct. bar, 1971; partner firm Bates, De Pree & Bard, Chgo., 1956—. Mem. Spl. Investigating Com. on Engring. Practices of Met. Sanitary Dist. Chgo., 1962; pres. Deerfield (Ill.) Dist. 110 Sch. Bd., 1969; mem. bus. affairs com. Chgo. Presbytery. Mem. Ill. Soc. Profl. Engrs., Ill., Chgo., Am. bar assns. Contbr. articles to engring. jours. Home: 1334 Woodland Dr Deerfield IL 60015 Office: 135 S LaSalle St Chicago IL 60603 Tel (312) 332-3933

DEPUY, DAVID WARREN, b. Livingston, Mont., Sept. 28, 1928; B.S., Mont. State U., 1949. Admitted to Mont. bar, 1966; individual practice law, Livingston, Mont., 1967—; atty, Livingston, 1973-75; atty. DePuty County, 1975—. Chmn. Park County chpt. Am. Cancer Soc., 1970-76; dir. Mont. chpt., 1972-76. Mem. Am., Mont., Park Sweet Grass bar assns. Home: 614 S 8th St Livingston MT 59047 Office: 123 W Lewis St Livingston MD 59047 Tel (406) 222-1524

DERBY, ERNEST STEPHEN, b. Boston, July 10, 1938; A.B. with distinction, Conn. Wesleyan U., 1960; LL.B. cum laude, Harvard, 1965. Admitted to Md. bar, 1965, U.S. Supreme Ct. bar, 1973; clk. to judge U.S. Dist. Ct. Dist. Md. and U.S. Ct. Appeals 4th Circuit, 1965-66; asso. firm Piper & Marbury, Balt., 1966-71, partner, 1973—; asst. atty. gen. State of Md., 1971-73. Mem. policy aov. bd. Martin Luther King, Jr. Center for Parents and Children, Balt.; bd. dirs. Dismas House of Balt., Inc.; trustee Roland Park Country Sch., Inc., Balt., Enoch Pratt Free Library, Balt. Mem. Am., Md. bar assns., Bar Assn. Balt. City. Office: 2000 First Maryland Bldg 25 S Charles St Baltimore MD 21201 Tel (301) 539-2530

DERICKSON, DAVID GREGG, b. Wilmington, Del., Jan. 20, 1945; B.A., Occidental Coll., 1966; J.D., U. Ariz., 1969. Admitted to Ariz. bar, 1969; dep. pub. defender Maricopa County (Ariz.), 1970-73; partner firm Derickson, Kemper & Henze, Phoenix, 1973—. Mem. Ariz., Maricopa County bar assns. Office: 802 Luhrs Bldg 11 W Jefferson St Phoenix AZ 85003 Tel (602) 257-9343

DE RITTER, ELMER, JR., b. Paterson, N.J., Jan. 16, 1942; A.B., Calvin Coll., 1963; LL.B., Rutgers U., 1966, postgrad., 1975—. Admitted to N.J. bar, 1970; adjudicator U.S. VA, Newark, 1969-70, atty., 1970-76, asst. supr. loan guaranty div., 1976—. Mem. Fed. Bar Assn. Home: 7 Downstream Dr Flanders NJ 07836 Office: 20 Washington Pl Newark NJ 07102 Tel (201) 645-3471

DE ROGATIS, DANTE JOSEPH, b. Asbury Park, N.J., Oct. 22, 1943; B.A. in English, St. Peter's Coll., 1965; J.D., Seton Hall U., 1970. Admitted to N.J. bar, 1970; atty. Mut. Benefit Life Ins. Co., Newark, 1971; atty. firm Hiering, Grasso, Gelzer & Kelaher, Toms

River, N.J., 1971-72; asso. counsel Prudential Ins. Co. Am., South Plainfield, N.J., 1972—. Chmn. bd. dirs. Green Island Community Assn., 1976-77; dir. Toms River Little League, 1976-77; bd. dirs., v.p. Toms River Lions Club, 1976-77. Mem. Ocean County, N.J., Am. bar assns. Home: 16 Harbor View Ln Toms River NJ 08753 Office: 1111 Durham Ave South Plainfield NJ 07080 Tel (201) 321-2230

DEROHANNESIAN, PAUL, b. Troy, N.Y., Dec. 29, 1920; student N.Y. State Coll. for Tchrs., 1941-42, Pa. State Coll., 1943-44; LL.B., Union U., Albany, 1952. Admitted to N.Y. State bar, 1953, U.S. Supreme Ct. bar, 1958; individual practice law, Albany, 1953—; research atty. Legis. Index Co., 1953-62; counsel Albany Housing Authority, 1963—; atty. Farmers Home Adminstrn., 1961-70. Vice pres., bd. dirs. Friends of Albany Pub. Library, 1967-68, Americanization Council of Albany, 1967-68. Mem. Am., Albany County, N.Y. State bar assns., Am. Judicature Soc., Capital Dist. Trial Lawyers Assn. (v.p. 1976—). Office: 100 State St Albany NY 12207 Tel (518) 465-6420

DE RONDE, JOHN ALLEN, b. Newburg, N.Y., Dec. 2, 1922; student Cornell U., Siena U., Union U., LL.B., Albany Law Sch., 1951. Admitted to N.Y. bar, 1953, Calif. bar, 1960; commd. Judge Adv. Gen. Corps USAAF, 1942, advanced through grades; ret., 1967; partner firm DeRone & Brewer, Vacaville, Calif.; judge Vacaville Justice Ct.; judge and presiding judge, No. Solano County Jud. Dist. Ct. Mem. Conf. Calif. Judges, Am. Judges Assn. De Ronde Dr. named in recognition of legal services rendered to Travis Unified Sch. Dist., Fairfield, Calif. Office: 550 Union St Fairfield CA 94533 Tel (707) 429-6205

DERR, DAILEY JONATHAN, b. Wilmington, N.C., Nov. 21, 1941; A.B. in Am. History, U. N.C., 1964; A.M. in Govt., George Washington U., 1966, J.D., 1971. Admitted to N.C. bar, 1972, D.C. bar, 1975; law clk. to judge U.S. Dist. Ct., Eastern Dist. N.C., 1972; mem. firm Everett, Everett, Creech & Craven, Durham and Raleigh, N.C., 1972—; supervising atty. clin. trial advocacy program Duke U. Sch. Law, 1973—; legal counsel Durham Jaycees, 1974-75. Mem. Am., N.C. (chmn. com. disaster legal assistance sect. young lawyers 1974-76), Wake County (N.C.) bar assns., Assn. Trial Lawyers Am., N.C. Acad. Trial Lawyers (lectr. family law workshop 1976), Durham Young Lawyers Assn. (pres. 1977—), N.C. 14th Jud. Dist. Bar (2d v.p. 1977—). Home: 3927 Kelly St Durham NC 27707 Tel (919) 682-5691

DERRICK, WILLIAM ALFRED, JR., b. Washington, Oct. 15, 1943; A.B., John Carroll U., 1965; J.D., Howard U., 1968; LL.M., George Washington U., 1970. Admitted to Ohio bar, 1969, U.S. Tax Ct. bar, 1969; staff counsel office of sec. HUD, Washington, 1968; chief staff counsel Model Inner-City Orgn., Inc., Washington, 1969-70; asso. firm Squire, Sanders & Dempsey, Cleve., 1970-72; of counsel firm Kohrman & Jackson, Cleve., 1975—; adj. prof. law Cleve. State U., 1972—; mem. Interracial Council for Bus. Opportunity, Washington, 1969-70; co-founder, trustee Nat. Consumer Info. Center, Washington, 1968-70. Trustee NCCJ, 1974—, Cleve. Area Arts Council, 1974—. Mem. Greater Cleve. (tax com. 1975—), Ohio State, Am. (partnership com. tax sect. 1976—) bar assns., Phi Alpha Delta. Contbr. articles to legal jours. Home: Shaker Heights OH 44120 Office: 1600 Central Nat Bank Bldg Cleveland OH 44114 Tel (216) 696-8700

DERRICK, WILLIAM JAMES, b. El Paso, Tex., Mar. 24, 1934; B.A., U. Tex., 1956, B.B.A., 1958. Admitted to Tex. bar, 1958, U.S. Supreme Ct. bar, 1976; capt. JAGC, USAF, 1958-61; partner firm Kemp, Smith, White, Duncan & Hammond, El Paso, 1962—; conferee Chief Justice Earl Warren Conf. on Advocacy, 1976. Mem. Am. (standing com. specialization), Tex. (chmn. bd. legal specialization 1972-76), El Paso bar assns. Office: Kemp Smith White Duncan Hammond 2000 State National Plaza El Paso TX 79901 Tel (915) 533-4424

DERRYBERRY, LARRY DALE, b. Humphreys, Okla., Apr. 22, 1939; B.A., U. Okla., 1961, J.D., 1963; LL.D. (hon.), New Eng. Sch. Law, 1976. Admitted to Okla. bar, 1963, Fed. bar, 1963, U.S. Supreme Ct. bar, 1971; asso. firm Oden & Oden, Altus, 1963-67; partner firm Oden, Oden & Derryberry, Altus, 1967-70; atty. gen. Okla., Oklahoma City, 1970—; chmn. So. Conf. Attys. Gen., 1976. Mem. Okla. Ho. of Reps., 1962-70, asst. floor leader, 1967, speaker pro tempore, 1969; mem. adv. council elected ofcls. Democratic Nat. Com., 1972. Mem. Am., Okla., Jackson County bar assns., Nat. Assn. Attys. Gen. (com. chmn.), Phi Delta Phi. Recipient Distinguished Service award Jr. C. of C., 1968. Home: North of City Oklahoma City OK 73120 Office: Room 112 State Capitol Oklahoma City OK 73105 Tel (405) 521-3921

DERRYBERRY, THOMAS WARD, b. Denver, Aug. 24, 1945; B.A., U. N.Mex., 1967, J.D., 1970. Admitted to N.Mex. bar, 1970; atty. adviser HUD, San Francisco, 1970-71, Los Angeles, 1971-73; asst. atty. gen. N.Mex. Oil Conservation Commn., Santa Fe, 1973-75, N.Mex. Energy Resources Bd., Santa Fe, 1975-76; asso. firm Ussery Burciaga & Parrish, Albuquerque, 1976—. Mem. N.Mex. State Bar, Albuquerque Bar Assn., Albuquerque Lawyers' Club. Mem. staff Natural Resources Jour., 1968-69, bd. editors, 1969-70. Home: 7805 Raymond Dr NE Albuquerque NM 87109 Office: PO Box 487 Albuquerque NM 87103 Tel (505) 247-0145

DESANTIS, LOUIS JOSEPH, b. N.Y.C., Aug. 6, 1937; B.A., Iona Coll., New Rochelle, N.Y., 1959; J.D., Fordham U., 1962. Admitted to N.Y. bar, 1962; individual practice law, N.Y.C., 1962—; legal counsel Kidney Disease div. Westchester Heart Assn., Inc. Vice pres., mem. exec. com. Westchester Artificial Kidney Center. Mem. N.Y., Bronx County bar assns., Iona Coll. Alumni Assn. (pres.). Office: 4138 Boston Post Rd Bronx NY 10475 Tel (212) 324-8909

DESANTIS, RICHARD A., b. Long Branch, N.J., May 10, 1931; B.A. with honors, Rutgers U., 1953; J.D., Yale, 1958. Admitted to Conn. bar, 1957, Calif. bar, 1960; legal officer United Nat. Command Mil. Armistice Commn., Munsan-Ni, Korea, 1954-56; asst. pub. defender New Haven, Conn., 1954-57; spl. dep. atty. gen., spl. dep. dist. atty. dep. commr. Calif. Div. Corps., Los Angeles, 1960-61; asso. firm Butterworth & Smith, Los Angeles, 1961-62, Zagon, Aaron & Schiff, Beverly Hills, Calif., 1962-63; individual practice law, Los Angeles, 1963—; chmn. bd. Shurtleff Engrng. Corp., 1967-69. Bd. dirs. Lark Ellen Home for Boys, Los Angeles, 1966-70; chmn. bd. Montessori Schs., Inc., Pasadena, 1966-69, Acoustica Assos. Inc., pub. corp., Los Angeles, 1968-70; pres. San Fernando Valley chpt. Calif. Republic League, 1967-74. Mem. Am., Los Angeles County, Beverly Hills, Century City bar assns., Am. Judicature Soc., LaRaza Nat. Lawyers Assn., Nat. Panel Arbitrators, Phi Beta Kappa, Sigma Delta Phi, Phi Alpha Theta, Pi Sigma Alpha, Tau Kappa Alpha. Author: Contract Law and the Uniform Commercial Code, 1960; Negotiable Instruments, 1962. Office: 1901 Avenue of the Stars Suite 790 Los Angeles CA 90067 Tel (213) 553-1901

DE SEVO, ALEX RALPH, b. Jersey City, Mar. 1, 1898; LL.B., N.Y. U., 1922. Admitted to N.J. bar, 1923, U.S. Supreme Ct. bar, 1940; asso. firm Alexander Simpson, Jersey City, 1923-33; individual practice law, Jersey City, 1933—; dir. Legal Aid Soc. of Hudson County, 1965-68. Mem. Hudson County (pres. 1954), N.J. State, Am. bar assns., Hudson County Bar Found. (treas. 1961—). Editor Bulletin, Citator, 1934-77. Home: 158 Jewett Ave Jersey City NJ 07304 Office: 921 Bergen Ave Jersey City NJ 07306 Tel (201) 653-0411

DESHAZO, GARY FORREST, b. Bolivar, Tenn., Feb. 5, 1945; B.A., Tex. Christian U., 1967, M.A., 1970; J.D., U. Tex., 1973. Admitted to Tex. bar, 1973; contract adminstr. Gen. Dynamics Aerospace Corp., Fort Worth, 1968-71; gen. counsel Tex. Criminal Def. Lawyers Assn., Austin, 1974-76; individual practice law, Austin, 1976—; exec. sec. Lawyers Polit. Action Com. of Tex., 1974-76; mem. exec. com., dir. Criminal Def. Lawyers Project, State Bar Tex., 1974—, vice-chmn. vols. in parole com., 1975—. Mem. Tex., Nat. assns. criminal def. lawyers, Travis County Bar Assn. Mng. editor Voice for the Def. Jour., 1974-76. Home: 6305 Highland Hills Dr Austin TX 78731 Office: 508 First Federal Plaza Austin TX 78701 Tel (512) 474-1636

DESMOND, JOHN F., b. Newton, Mass., Feb. 19, 1912; A.B., Boston Coll., 1933; J.D., Harvard U., 1936. Admitted to Mass. bar, 1936, N.Y. bar, 1947; asso. firm Mulcahy, Smith, Canavan & Troy, Boston, 1936-40; with Dept. Justice, 1940-62; gen. atty. New Eng. Tel. & Tel., Boston, 1962—; trustee Hibernia Savs. Bank, Boston, 1965—. Bd. dirs. Family Counseling Guidance Centers, Boston. Office: New Eng Tel & Tel Co 185 Franklin St Boston MA 02107 Tel (617) 743-2323

DESMOND, JOHN PHILIP, b. Pitts., June 3, 1908; B.A. cum laude, Duquesne U., 1929, M.A. cum laude, 1940; LL.B. with honors, U. Wis., 1954. Admitted to Wis. bar, 1954; asso. firm Murphy & Gavin, 1954-56; partner firm Murphy, Gavin, Stolper & Desmond, 1956-66, Murphy, Huiskamp, Stolper, Brewster & Desmond, 1966-73; shareholder firm Murphy, Stolper, Brewster & Desmond, Madison, Wis., 1973—; lectr. U. Wis. Law Sch., 1957. Mem. Am., Wis., Dane County bar assns., Am. Arbitration Assn. (nat. panel arbitrators 1967—), Am. Judicature Assn. Exec. editor Wis. Law Rev., 1954. Home: 3525 Blackhawk Dr Madison WI 53705 Tel (608) 257-7181

DE STEFANO, WILLIAM ANTHONY, b. Bridgeport, Conn., Oct. 6, 1946; B.S., Villanova U., 1968; J.D., Duquesne U., 1971. Admitted to Pa. bar, 1971; trial atty., antitrust div. U.S. Dept. Justice, Phila., 1971-77, asst. U.S. atty. for Eastern Dist. Pa., Phila., 1975-76; mem. firm Pepper, Hamilton & Scheetz, Phila., 1977—; lectr. Temple U., 1974, Mem. Am., Phila. bar assns. Recipient commendation IRS, 1975, Asst. Atty. Gen., 1976. Office: 20th Floor Fidelity Bldg 123 S Broad St Philadelphia PA 19109 Tel (215) 545-1234

DE TARDO, NICHOLAS JAMES, b. Hollywood, Fla., Mar. 29, 1930; B.B.A., U. Ohio, 1950; J.D., U. Miami, 1953. Admitted to Fla. bar, 1953; mem. firm Robbins, Cannova, Watson & DeTardo, Hollywood, 1958-64, DeTardo & Fixel Law Assn., Hollywood, 1964-68; sr. partner firm DeTardo & Longo, Hollywood, 1968-76; city prosecutor Hollywood, 1965-70; municipal judge Hollywood, 1970-76. Pres. Greater Hollywood C. of C., 1963-64; vice-chmn. Broward County Zoning Bd., 1970-76; mem. Jud. Nominating Com. 17th Circuit, 1974—; investigator Client's Sec. Fund, 1975—, chmn. grievance com., 1976—. Mem. Am., Fla, Broward bar assns., Municipal Judges Assn., Phi Alpha Delta, Omicron Delta Kappa. Office: DeTardo Bldg 4747 Hollywood Blvd Hollywood FL 33021 Tel (305) 987-3400

DETCH, PAUL STEWART, b. Clifton Forge, Va., June 4, 1948; A.B., Wittenberg U., 1969; student U. Mo., 1970; LL.B., W.Va. Coll. Law, 1973. Admitted to W.Va. bar, 1973; asso. firm Detch, Detch & Detch, Lewisburg, W.Va., 1973—. Chmn., Greenbrier County chpt. ARC, 1973-75. Mem. Am. Bar Assn., W.Va. Trial Laweyrs Assn. Office: 201 N Court St Lewisburg WV 24901 Tel (304) 645-1993

DETERT, GUNTHER RICHARD, b. Jersey City, Nov. 11, 1912; A.B., Stanford, 1933; LL.B., U. Calif., 1936; postgrad. U. Munich (Germany), 1937. Admitted to Calif. bar, 1937; partner firm Sedgwick, Detert, Moran & Arnold, and predecessors, San Francisco, 1948—. Mem. Am., San Francisco (dir. 1941-42, 45-46, 67-68) bar assns., Def. Counsel Assn., Am. Bd. Trial Attys., Internat. Assn. Ins. Counsel, Attys. Probate Assn., Calif. Vintage Wine Soc. (pres. 1965-75), Napa Valley Wine Library Assn. (pres. 1967-75), San Francisco Wine and Food Soc. (gov.), San Francisco Barristers (past pres.), Phi Alpha Delta. Home: 2533 Filbert St San Francisco CA 94123 Office: 111 Pine St San Francisco CA 94104 Tel (415) 982-0303

DETISCH, DONALD WILLIAM, b. Erie, Pa., May 5, 1941; B.A., Pa. State U., 1963; J.D., U. Calif. at San Francisco, 1970. Admitted to Calif. bar, 1971—; dep. city atty. San Diego, 1971—; claims adjustor Liberty Mut. Ins. Co., Los Angeles, 1964. Mem. Calif. Bar Assn., Hastings Alumni Assn. (pres. 1976). Home: 2538 Quidde Ave San Diego CA 92122 Office: 202 C St San Diego CA 92101 Tel (714) 236-6220

DETTELBACH, THOMAS LEE, b. Lima, Ohio, Mar. 15, 1937; B.S., Ohio State U., 1958; LL.B., Cleve.-Marshall Law Sch., 1966. Admitted to Ohio bar, 1966, U.S. Supreme Ct. bar, 1970; law clk. Cuyahoga County (Ohio) Ct. Common Pleas; asso. Kahn, Kleinman, Yanowitz & Arnson, Cleve., 1969-75, partner, 1975—. Trustee Hebrew Free Loan Assn., 1974—. Mem. Ohio (award of merit 1975), Cuyahoga County (trustee), Greater Cleve. bar assns., Assn. Trial Lawyers Am. Home: 2674 Rochester Rd Shaker Heights OH 44122 Office: 1300 Bond Court Bldg Cleveland OH 44114 Tel (216) 696-3311

DETTMERING, WILLIAM O'NEAL, JR., b. Atlanta, Nov. 10, 1948; student Davidson Coll., 1966-67; B.S., Auburn U., 1970; J.D., U. Ga., 1974. Admitted to Ga. bar, 1974; asso. firm James R. Dollar, Jr., Douglasville, Ga., 1974-75; partner firm Dollar and Dettmering, Douglasville, 1975—. Chmn., Douglas Dist., Atlanta Area council Boy Scouts Am., 1975-77. Mem. Am., Ga. State bar assns., Douglas County C. of C. (dir.), Kappa Delta Pi. Home: 5441 S Lake Dr Douglasville GA 30135 Office: 6508 Spring St PO Box 278 Douglasville GA 30133 Tel (404) 942-5429

DEUTSCH, EADIE, b. Savannah, Ga., Aug. 3, 1921; B.S. cum laude, Northwestern U., 1941; postgrad. (John M. Pixley scholar), U. Calif., Berkeley, 1945-47, M.A., Los Angeles, 1967, Ph.D., 1970; J.D., Loyola U., 1949. Admitted to Calif. bar, 1949; asso. firm Beilenson, Rosenthal and Norton, and successors, Beverly Hills, Calif., 1949-52; individual practice law, Beverly Hills, 1952-57; partner firm Katz, Granof, Maiden and Deutsch, Beverly Hills, 1957-64; asst. prof. Calif. State U., Northridge, 1968-71, spl. asst. to pres. jud. affairs, 1969-70; dean, prof. Coll. Law Univ. San Fernando Valley, Sepulveda, Calif., 1971—. Bd. dir., exec. com. ACLU So. Calif., Los Angeles, 1973—; bd. dirs. Valley Cities Jewish Community Center, Van Nuys, Calif., 1954-63, nominee bd. dir., 1973; bd. dirs., advisory bd. Everywoman's Village, Van Nuys, 1963—; mem. BiCentennial Com. of Constl. Rights Found., Los Angeles. Mem. Am. Bar Assn., AAUP. Contbr. articles to law jours. and mags. Office 8353 Sepulveda Blvd Sepulveda CA 91343 Tel (213) 894-5711

DEUTSCH, FREDERICK MORAN, b. Talmage, Nebr., Sept. 4, 1898; J.D., U. Nebr., 1921. Admitted to Nebr. bar, 1921, U.S. Ct. Appeals 8th Circuit bar, 1925, U.S. Supreme Ct. bar, 1960; individual practice law, David City, Nebr., 1921-23, Norfolk, Nebr., 1923—. Mem. Am., Nebr., 9th Judicial Dist. bar assns., Am. Coll. Trial Lawyers, Am. Coll. Probate Counsel, Internat. Assn. Ins. Counsel, Fedn. Ins. Counsel. Home: 200 Bridge Rd Norfolk NE 68701 Office: 125 Norfolk Ave Norfolk NE 68701 Tel (402) 371-5640

DEUTSCH, IRWIN FREDERICK, b. N.Y.C., July 19, 1932; A.B., Amherst Coll., 1954; J.D., Columbia, 1957; student Universite de Paris, 1951. Admitted to N.Y. bar, 1958, D.C. bar, 1960, U.S. Supreme Ct. bar, 1961; atty. SEC, Washington, 1960-62; asst. counsel to comptroller of the currency, U.S. Treasury, Washington, 1962; partner firm Upham, Meeker & Weithorn, and predecessors, N.Y.C., 1962-76; of counsel firm Abrams & Sassower, N.Y.C., 1976—; spl. dep. atty. gen. State N.Y., 1959. Mem. Assn. Bar City N.Y., Am., Fed., N.Y. State bar assns., Bar Assn. D.C., N.Y. County Lawyers Assn., Practising Law Inst. (lectrs.). Contbr. articles to law jours. Home: 157 E 57th St New York City NY 10022 Office: 598 Madison Ave New York City NY 10022 Tel (212) 688-4200

DEUTSCH, JOEL ALLISTER, b. Moline, Ill., Oct. 5, 1946; B.B.A., U. Wis., Madison, 1968; J.D., U. Ill., Champaign, 1972. Admitted to Ill. bar, 1973; partner firm Deutsch & Deutsch, Rock Island, Ill., 1972—. Mem. Am., Chgo., Ill., Rock Island County bar assns. Home: 8112 8th St W Rock Island IL 61201 Office: 409 1st Nat Bank Bldg Rock Island IL 61201 Tel (309) 788-9541

DEUTSCH, NORMAN TERRY, b. Balt., Dec. 27, 1944; B.A., U. Md., 1967, J.D., 1973. Admitted to Md. bar, 1973; asso. firm Weinberg & Green, Balt., 1974-75; teaching fellow U. Ill., Urbana, 1975-76; asst. prof. law Stetson U., 1976—. Vol., Peace Corps, Somali Republic, 1967-69. Mem. Md. Bar Assn., Order of Coif. Editorial bd. Md. Law Rev., 1971-73. Office: care Stetson Coll Law 1401 61st St S Saint Petersburg FL 33707 Tel (813) 347-2124

DEUTSCH, STUART LEWIS, b. N.Y.C., Dec. 11, 1945; B.A., U. Mich., 1966; J.D., Yale U., 1969; LL.M. (Law Humanities fellow), Harvard U., 1974. Admitted to Calif. bar, 1972; asst. zoning dir. City of New Haven, 1969; asso. firm Olwine, Connelly, Chase, O'Donnell & Weyher, N.Y.C., 1969-70; asst. prof. U. Santa Clara (Calif.) Sch. Law, 1970-73, asso. prof., 1974-76; vis. asso. prof. U. Ill. Coll. Law, Champaign, 1975-76; asso. prof., chmn. grad. urban legal studies program Chgo.-Kent Coll. Law Ill. Inst. Tech., Chgo., 1976—; cons. housing, zoning, fair housing, cities and counties No. Calif., 1970-75. Mem. Am. Bar Assn., Assn. Am. Law Schs. (chairperson law humanities sect.), Phi Beta Kappa. Contbr. articles to legal jours. Home: 2621 Park Pl Evanston IL 60201 Office: Chgo Kent Coll Law Ill Inst Tech 77 S Wacker Dr Chicago IL 60606 Tel (312) 567-5040

DEUTZ, MAX FRANK, b. San Antonio, July 26, 1917; B.S. in Bus. Adminstrn., U. So. Cal., 1939, J.D., 1941. Admitted to Calif. bar, 1942, U.S. Supreme Ct. bar, 1954, Ct. Appeals D.C. bar, 1966; law clerk to chief judge U.S. Dist. Ct. So. Dist. of Calif., 1945-47; asst. U.S. Atty. So. Dist. of Calif., 1947-53; chief civil div., 1953-57, chief asst., 1957-61; with Forest Lawn, Glendale, Calif., 1961-62; mem. firm Pollock & Deutz, Los Angeles, 1962-67; judge Superior Ct. of Los Angeles County (Calif.), Los Angeles, 1967—. Mem. Calif., Los Angeles County bar assns., Am. Judicature Soc., Lawyers Club of Los Angeles, Fed. Bar Assn. Contbr. articles to profl. jours. Home: 800 W First St Los Angeles CA 90012 Office: Superior Ct 111 N Hill St Los Angeles CA 90012 Tel (213) 974-5681

DE VAN, MARK R., b. Cleve., May 30, 1948; A.B., Ashland Coll., 1971; J.D., Cleve. State U., 1974. Admitted to Ohio bar, 1974; law clk. and research asst. firm Summers, Schneider, Burke and Hildebrand, Cleve., 1973, Office of Fed. Defender, Cleve., 1972-74; with pub. defender office of Legal Aid Soc. of Cleve., 1975—. Mem. Ohio State Bar Assn., Nat. Assn. Criminal Defense Lawyers, Ohio Pub. Defender Assn. Office: 2108 Payne Ave Cleveland OH 44114 Tel (216) 621-5980

DE VEAUX, LEROY EUGENE, b. Evergreen Park, Ill., June 21, 1940; B.S. in Psychology, Dana Coll., 1967; J.D., Ariz. State U., 1973; postgrad. Sch. Psychology and Adminstrn., No. Ariz. U. Admitted to Alaska bar, 1973; asso. firm Wanamaker, Dickson, Perry & Jarvi, Anchorage, 1973-74; partner firm Wanamaker & DeVeaux, Anchorage, 1974—. Mem. Am. Acad. Trial Lawyers. Home: 3315 Knik St Anchorage AK 99503 Office: 750 W 2d Ave Anchorage AK 99501 Tel (907) 279-6591

DE VILLE, ROMAN A., b. Wurmannsquick, Germany, Feb. 17, 1946; B.A., Emory U., 1966; J.D., Mercer U., 1969. Admitted to Ga. bar, U.S. Supreme Ct. bar, 1973; individual practice law. Mem. Am. Judicature Soc., Nat. Assn. Criminal Def. Lawyers, Am. Assn. Trial Lawyers, Atlanta, Ga., Am. bar assns., Delta Theta Phi (sec.). Recipient Am. Jurisprudence prize for Excellence in Legal Method, also award for Bills and Notes. Home: 671 W Paces Ferry Rd Atlanta GA 30327 Office: 225 Peachtree St NE Suite 1717 Atlanta GA 30303 Tel (404) 522-9922

DEVINE, EUGENE PETER, JR., b. Albany, N.Y., Oct. 14, 1948; B.A., Villanova U., 1971; J.D., Albany Law Sch., 1975. Admitted to N.Y. bar, 1975; asso. firm Cooper, Erving & Savage, Albany, 1975—; pub. defender Albany County, N.Y., 1975—. Bd. govs. Albany Sons of St. Patrick. Mem. Am., N.Y., Albany County bar assns., K.C. Tel (518) 434-8131

DEVINE, FOY ROBERSON, b. Lynchburg, Va., June 29, 1942; B.A., U. N.C., 1964; LL.B., U. Va., 1967. Admitted to Va., D.C. bars, 1967, Ga. bar, 1970; Prettyman legal intern Georgetown U. Law Center, 1967-68; asst. dep. dir. Legal Aid Agency D.C., 1968-69; asso. firm King & Spalding, Atlanta, 1969-72; partner firm Fierer & Devine, Atlanta, 1972—. Mem. Am., Atlanta bar assns., Va. State Bar, Ga. State Bar, Am. Judicature Soc., Phi Beta Kappa, Order Coif, Omicron Delta Kappa. Mem. editorial bd. Va. Law Review, 1966-67. Author: (with others) Law and Tactics in Sentencing, 1970. Home: 1896

Greystone Rd NW Atlanta GA 30318 Office: 550 N Omni International Atlanta GA 30303 Tel (404) 688-5500

DEVITT, EDWARD JAMES, b. St. Paul, May 5, 1911; LL.B., U. N.D., 1935, B.S., 1936, also LL.D. Admitted to D.C., Minn., Ill. and N.D. bars; practiced in East Grand Forks, Minn., 1935-39, St. Paul, 1946—; municipal judge, 1935-39; asst. atty. gen., Minn., 1939-42; instr. law U. N.D., 1935-39, St. Paul Coll. Law, 1945—; mem. 80th Congress, 4th Minn. Dist.; probate judge Ramsey County, St. Paul, 1950-54; U.S. dist. judge, 1954—, now chief judge. Bd. dirs. Fed. Jud. Center. Decorated Purple Heart. Fellow Am. Bar Found.; mem. Am., Minn., Ramsey County bar assns., Am. Judicature Soc., Am. Legion, V.F.W., D.A.V., Order of Coif, Blue Key, Phi Delta Phi, Beta Gamma Sigma, Delta Sigma Rho. Author: (with Blackmar) Federal Jury Practice and Instructions. Home: 1676 S Mississippi River Blvd Saint Paul MN 55116 Office: Federal Courts Bldg Saint Paul MN 55101*

DEVLIN, GEORGE JOSEPH, b. Lawrence, Mass., Feb. 18, 1918; A.B., Boston Coll., 1939; J.D., Harvard U., 1942. Admitted to Mass. bar, 1942; asso. firm Nutter, McClennen & Fish, Boston, 1946-48; asst. prof. Boston Coll. Law Sch., 1948-50; chief counsel dist. Mass., Office Price Stblzn., Boston, 1950-52; gen. atty. H. P. Hood Inc., Boston, 1953-57, gen. counsel, 1957-70, gen. counsel, clk, sec., v.p., 1970-77; prof. law Suffolk U. Law Sch., Boston, 1977—; lectr., panelist on anti-trust subjects. Mem. Belmont Housing Authority, 1946-48, Norwood Planning Bd., 1955-56; chmn. Norwood Bd. Appeals, 1958-61. Mem. Am., Boston, Mass. bar assns. Home: 11 Hilltop Rd Dover MA 02030 Office: 500 Rutherford Ave Boston MA 02129 Tel (617) 242-0600

DEVLIN, GERARD FRANCIS, b. Boston, May 29, 1933; student Boston Coll., 1951-54; A.B. with honors, Suffolk U., 1959; M.A., U. Md., 1962; J.D., U. Balt., 1969. Admitted to Md. bar, 1972; legis. asst. Rep. Dominick V. Daniels, Washington, 1965-69, adminstrv. asst., 1972-75; asso. firm Ross, Lochte, Murray, Redding & Devlin, Bowie, Md., 1972-75, partner, 1975; mem. Md. Ho. of Dels., 1975—, mem. Ways and Means Com., Joint Com. Mgmt. Pub. Funds; staff mem. staff Office of Md. nat. relations officer, Washington, 1969-72. Vice pres. Prince George's County (Md.) Symphony Orch.; exec. bd. Ballet Concert Theatre, Bowie. Mem. Am., Md., Prince George's County bar assns. Named Outstanding Freshman Legislator, Young Democratic Clubs Md., 1975. Home: 2505 Kitmore Ln Bowie MD 20715 Office: 15518 Annapolis Rd Bowie MD 20715 Tel (301) 262-6000

DEVORE, KENNETH IRVIN, b. Roanoke, Va., Aug. 3, 1927; LL.B., U. Richmond, 1955. Admitted to Va. bar, 1955; individual practice law, Christiansburg, Va., 1955—; mem. Va. Gen. Assembly, 1962-66. Mem. Va., Am. bar assns., Va., Am. trial lawyers assns. Home: Route 2 Christiansburg VA 24073 Office: PO Box 389 Christiansburg VA 24073 Tel (703) 382-4911

DE VRIES, WARREN L., b. Orange City, Iowa, May 28, 1925; student Northwestern Jr. Coll., Orange City, 1942-43, U. Dubuque, 1943-44, Northwestern U., 1944; LL.B., Drake U., 1949. Admitted to Iowa bar, 1949, U.S. Supreme Ct. bar, 1960; individual practice law, Mason City, Iowa, 1950—. Mem. Am., Cerro Gordo County (pres. 1957-58), 12th Jud. Dist. (pres. 1963-64), Iowa (com. pub. relations) bar assns., Iowa Def. Counsel Assn. (chmn. 1968-69), Def. Research Inst., Fedn. Ins. Counsel, Iowa Trial Acad. Home: 615 S Tennessee Pl Mason City IA 50401 Office: 208 1st St NW Mason City IA 50401 Tel (515) 423-1173

DEW, WILLIAM RAY, b. Dalhart, Tex., Mar. 3, 1937; student Westminster Coll., 1956-57; B.A., Iowa U., 1964, J.D., 1966. Admitted to Iowa bar, 1966, U.S. Supreme Ct. bar, 1976; partner firm Griffin & Dew, Ottumwa, Iowa, 1968—; city atty. City of Ottumwa, 1968—. Mem. Am., Iowa, Wapello County (pres. 1976—) bar assns., Municipal Attys. Assn. Iowa (past pres.), Wapello County Legal Aid Soc. (pres. 1976). Office: 211 N Washington St Ottumwa IA 52501 Tel (515) 684-6517

DE WAAY, DONALD GENE, b. Sheldon, Iowa, Oct. 5, 1916; student Sheldon Jr. Coll., 1935-36; B.A., State U. Iowa, 1938, J.D. with distinction, 1940. Admitted to Iowa bar, 1940; partner firm Fisher & DeWaay, Rock Rapids, Iowa, 1940—; dir. Lyon County State Bank, Hawkeye Bancorporation, Des Moines; atty. County of Lyon, 1942-50, atty. City of Rock Rapids, 1950-71. Mem. Am., Iowa (dir. 1958-63), Lyon County bar assns., Iowa Conf. of Bar Assn. Pres. (pres. 1961-62), Assn. Trial Lawyers Am., Iowa Acad. Trial Lawyers. Home: 601 S Union St Rock Rapids IA 51246 Office: Professional Building Rock Rapids IA 51246 Tel (712) 472-3777

DEWELL, JULIAN C., b. San Antonio, Feb. 13, 1930; B.S., Trinity U., San Antonio, 1952; LL.D., U. Wash., 1957. Admitted to Wash. bar, 1957, Calif. bar, 1958; trial atty., antitrust div. Dept. Justice, San Francisco, 1957-59; asso. firm Howe, Davis, Riese & Jones, Seattle, 1959-63; partner firm Anderson, Hunter, Dewell, Baker & Collins, Everett, Wash., 1963—; instr. Am. Inst. Banking, 1964-66 Mem. Everett Sch. Bd., 1967-73, Everett Freeholder's Com. to Redraft City Charter, 1967-68; local adv. com. State Bd. Against Discrimination, 1969-70. Mem. Am., Wash. (young lawyers com. 1959-63, intern com. 1969-70, disciplinary bd. 1974—, sch. atty's bd. 1975—), Calif. bar assns. Co-author Washington Antitrust Laws, 1961. Home: 609 Maulsby Ln Everett WA 98201 Office: 601 1st Nat Bank Bldg Everett WA 98201 Tel (206) 252-5161

DEWEY, PAUL CARPENTER, b. Jenkintown, Pa., Nov. 13, 1931; B.A., Princeton U., 1953; J.D., U. Pa., 1956. Admitted to Pa. bar, 1956, U.S. Dist. Ct. bar, U.S. Supreme Ct. bar; since practiced in Phila., asso. firm Strong, Sullivan, Saylor & Ferguson, 1958-64; exec. dir. Phila. Bar Assn., 1964-67; asso. firm Blank, Rome, Klaus & Comisky, 1967—; dir. F. J. Cooper, Inc., Dewey Investment Corp.; pres., dir. Internat. Gem. Investors Inc. Trustee, Hahneman Med. Coll. & Hosp., 1974-76; dir. Area Council for Economic Edn., 1973-76; pres. Young Am. Preserves, Inc., 1968-76. Mem. Am., Pa., Phila. (vice chancellor) bar assns., Am. Judicature Soc., Tau Epsilon. Office: 11th Floor Four Penn Center Plaza Philadelphia PA 19103 Tel (215) 669-3700

DE WIND, ADRIAN WILLIAM ANDREWS, b. Chgo., Dec. 1, 1913; A.B., Grinnell Coll., 1934; student U. Paris, Sorbonne, 1932-33; LL.B., Harvard, 1937. With Sage, Gray, Todd & Sims, N.Y.C., 1937-43; with U.S. Treasury Dept., 1943-48, asst. tax legislative counsel 1945-47, tax legislative counsel, 1947-48; mem. firm Paul, Weiss, Rifkind, Wharton & Garrison 1948—. Lectr. taxation, N.Y. U., Sch. Law, 1948-54; chief counsel, subcom. on adminstrn. of internal revenue laws, com. on ways and means, Ho. of Reps., Washington 1951-52; chmn. adv. group on city taxation to N.Y.C. Council Pres., 1966; mem. adv. group to Commr. Internal Revenue, 1966-67; mem. Mayor's Task Force on N.Y. Constnl. Conv., 1967; del. Democratic Nat. Conv., 1968. Bd. dirs. Revlon Foundation, Inc., N.A.A.C.P. Legal Def. and Ednl. Fund, Inc. (mem. exec. com.), Met. Applied Research Center, Inc., Nat. Com. Against Discrimination in Housing; bd. overseers Center for N.Y.C. Affairs, chmn., 1975—. Mem. President's Task Force on Tax Policy, 1961. Trustee New Sch. Social Research, Community Service Soc. N.Y. Fellow Am. Bar Found.; mem. Am. Law Inst., Am. Bar Assn. (sect. on taxation), N.Y. County Lawyers Assn., Assn. Bar City N.Y. (v.p. 1975-76, pres. 1976-77), N.Y. State Bar Assn. (tax sect.), spl. Fed. Bar Council. Contbr. articles to legal jours. Home: 37 W 12th St New York City NY 10011 also Sherman CT 06784 also RFD 2 Stowe VT Office: 345 Park Av New York City NY 10022 Tel (212) 644-8000*

DE WITT, EDWARD, III, b. San Juan, P.R., Nov. 20, 1928; A.B., Brown U.; LL.B., Boston U. Admitted to Mass. bar, 1957, U.S. Supreme Ct. bar, 1969; mem. staff Income Found. Fund, Boston, 1957-58; individual practice law, 1958-62; partner firm Tilden and DeWitt, Falmouth, Mass., 1962—; corporator Plymouth Savs. Bank. Sec., Falmouth Fin. Com. Mem. Mass., Barnstable bar assns., Mass. Conveyancers Assn. Home: 318 Elm Rd Falmouth MA 02540 Office: 230 Main St Falmouth MA 02540 Tel (617) 548-2040

DE WITT, FRANKLIN ROOSEVELT, b. Conway, S.C., May 25, 1936; B.S. in Accounting and Bus. Adminstrn., S.C. State Coll., 1962, J.D., 1964; Admitted to S.C. bar, 1964, D.C. bar, 1967; trial atty. U.S. Civil Service Commn., Washington, D.C., 1965-67; city atty. Atlantic Beach, S.C., 1966—; individual practice law, Conway, S.C., 1967—; mem. city council Conway, S.C., 1969-76; adv. to city, Glenarden, Md., 1965-76. Mem. Waccamaw Economic Opportunity Council, Conway, S.C., 1968—, treas. 1973—. Mem. S.C., Fed., Am., Horry County, Nat. bar assns. Home: 1708 Hwy 378 Conway SC 29526 Office: 510 Hwy 278 Conway SC 29526 Tel (803) 248-2308

DEWITT, JACK RICHARD, b. Muskogee, Okla., Dec. 15, 1918; B.A. in Econs., U. Wis., 1940, LL.B., 1942. Admitted to Wis. Supreme Ct. bar, 1942, U.S. Dist. Ct. bar, 1946, U.S. Supreme Ct. bar, 1960; asso. firm Thomas Orr Isaksen & Werner, Madison, Wis., 1946-47; instr. in law U. Wis., Madison, 1947-50, asst. prof. law, 1950-51; acting dist. atty. Dane County (Wis.), 1950; exec. sec. Wis. Jud. Council, Madison, 1951-55; v.p. Marshall Erdman & Assos., constrn. co., Madison, 1955-56; partner firm Immell, Herro, Buehner, DeWitt & Sundby, Madison, 1956-72, DeWitt, McAndrews & Porter and predecessor, Madison, 1972—. Mem. Dane County Vets. Service Commn., 1950-62; bd. dirs. Dane County chpt. ARC, 1972-74. Mem. Dane County (pres. 1960-61), Am. bar assns., State Bar Wis. (pres. 1975-76), Order of Coif (pres. chpt. 1948), Phi Delta Theta (pres. U. Wis. chpt. 1940), Phi Delta Phi (pres. U. Wis. chpt. 1941-42). Decorated D.S.C., Silver Star, Purple Heart; Brit. Mil. Cross; author: (Volz, Pick & Baldwin) Wisconsin Practice Methods, 1949. Home: 113 Longview Ave Mount Horeb WI 53572 Office: 121 S Pickney St Madison WI 53703 Tel (608) 255-8891

DEWITT, SUSAN PIERSON, b. Chgo., May 15, 1947; A.A., Joliet Jr. Coll., 1967; B.S., U. Ill., 1969; J.D., John Marshall Law Sch., 1973. Admitted to Ill. bar, 1973; para-legal counsel firm O'Brien, Garrison, Berard & Kusta, Joliet, Ill., 1970-73, asso. firm, 1973-75; partner firm O'Brien, Garrison, Berard, Kusta & DeWitt, Joliet, 1975—; spl. asst. atty. gen. to William J. Scott, 1972—. Mem. exec. bd., chmn. by-laws com. Salem Village, 1975—; bd. mem. Region II Council Lutheran Welfare Services Ill., 1975—; Ill. State Central Committeewoman, 1974—, mem. exec. bd. Will County Young Republicans, 1974-75; v.p., mem. exec. bd. Zonta Club Joliet Area, 1974—; co-chmn. Will County Bicentennial 76'ers Club, 1976; mem. Citizens Safety Com., C. of C., 1975—, mem. Shoplifting Com., 1973-74; mem. exec. bd. Joliet Drama Guild, 1976; mem. Joliet Jr. Coll. Task Force, 1975; v.p., sec. Joliet Youth Task Force, 1970; active First Presbyn. Ch., 1972—. Mem. Am., Ill. State, Will County bar assns., Alpha Delta Phi. Named Will County Young Republican of Year, 1973, Bus. Prof. Women's Young Career Woman of Year, 1974. Office: 57 W Jefferson St Box 473 Joliet IL 60434 Tel (815) 727-5445

DE WOLFE, JOHN CHAUNCEY, JR., b. Chgo., June 9, 1913; B.S., U. Ill.; J.D., U. Wis., 1939. Admitted to Wis. bar, 1939, Ill. bar, 1940; partner firm DeWolfe, Mills and Markley, and predecessor firms, Chgo., 1946—; trustee Village of Riverside, 1963-70; trustee West Suburban Mass Transit Dist., 1970—, chmn., 1974—. Mem. Am., Ill., Wis., 7th Fed. Dist., Chgo. bar assns. Contbr. articles to profl. jours. Home: 1448 N Lake Shore Dr Chicago IL 60610 Office: 135 S LaSalle St Chicago IL 60603 Tel (312) 726-0320

DEYESO, FREDERICK J., b. Boston, Nov. 24, 1943; B.S., Trinity U., 1967; J.D., St. Mary's U., 1970. Admitted to Tex. bar, 1970, U.S. Supreme Ct. bar, 1973; partner firm Deyeso & Appleberry, Inc., San Antonio, 1973—; instr. San Antonio Coll., 1974—. Mem. San Antonio Bar Assn., San Antonio Trial Lawyers Assn., Tex. Criminal Defense Counsel Assn. Office: Suite 618 901 NE Loop 410 San Antonio TX 78209 Tel (512) 828-0703

DE YOUNG, EDWIN R., b. Atlanta, Oct. 26, 1946; B.A. with honors, U. Tex., 1968, J.D., 1971. Admitted to Tex. bar, 1971, D.C. bar, 1972, U.S. Supreme Ct. bar, 1976; trial atty. U.S. Dept. Justice, Wash., D.C., 1971-72; asso. firm McKenzie and Baer, Dallas, 1972—. Mem. Am. Bar Assn. Recipient Am. Jurisprudence award. Home: 6416 Brookshire Dr Dallas TX 75230 Office: 2222 LTV Tower Dallas TX 75201 Tel (214) 742-1861

DE YOUNG, JAMES WINSTON, b. Evanston, Ill., July 6, 1943; A.B., Washington and Lee U., 1965; J.D., Northwestern U., 1968. Admitted to Ill. bar, 1969; with Baxter Travenol Labs., Inc., Deerfield, Ill., 1969—, asst. to v.p. fin., 1970-72, asst. to sr. v.p. fin., 1972, asst. to exec. v.p. fin., 1972-74, asst. to pres., 1974-76, asst. to vice chmn., 1976-77, mgr. investor relations, 1977—. Trustee Orchestral Assn. Chgo., 1974—; chmn. The Assos., Rush Presbyn. St. Luke's Med. Center, Chgo., 1973, trustee, 1977—; governing mem. Brookfield Zoo, 1977--. Mem. Nat. Investor Relations Inst., Phi Delta Phi. Home: 1448 Lake Shore Dr Chicago IL 60610 Office: One Baxter Parkway Deerfield IL 60015 Tel (312) 948-4102

DE YOUNG, JONATHAN HARVEY, b. Phila., Mar. 4, 1937; B.S. in Social Sci., Georgetown U., 1958; LL.B., Temple U., 1961. Admitted to Pa. bar, 1961; atty. Fox & Fox, Norristown, Pa., 1962-63; partner Torak & DeYoung, King of Prussia, Pa., 1963-69; individual practice law, King of Prussia, 1969—. Area leader Democratic party, 1967-71. Mem. Am., Pa., Montgomery County, Fed. bar assns., Am. Trial Lawyers Assn., Am. Bus. Club. Home: 103 Red Rambler Dr Lafayette Hill PA 19444 Office: 600 DeKalb Pike King of Prussia PA 19406 Tel (215) 265-4600

DEZZANI, DAVID JOHN, b. Oakland, Calif., July 31, 1936; B.A., U. Calif., Berkeley, 1961, J.D., 1965. Admitted to Calif. bar, 1965, Hawaii bar, 1966, U.S. Supreme Ct. bar, 1975; asso. firm Goodsill, Anderson & Quinn, Honolulu, 1965-70, partner, 1970—. Mem. Hawaii State, Am. bar assns., State Bar of Calif., Am. Bd. Trial Advocates (advocate), Honolulu Assn. Defense Counsel (chmn. 1974—). Rotary Found. fellow U. Tübingen (Germany), 1962-63. Office: 1600 Castle & Cooke Bldg Financial Plaza Honolulu HI 96813 Tel (808) 531-5066

DIAL, THOMAS FERRON, b. Idaho Falls, Idaho, Feb. 9, 1938; B.A., Idaho State U., 1969; J.D., U. Idaho, 1967. Admitted to Idaho bar, 1967, U.S. Supreme Ct. bar, 1971; criminal magistrate judge 6th Jud. Dist., Pocatello, Idaho, 1971-74; asso. firm Terrell, Green, Service & Gasser, Pocatello, 1968-71, 74-75; mem. firm Dial & Looze, Pocatello, 1975—; mem. Gov. Council of Criminal Justice Standards, 1973-75; faculty advisor, instr. Am. Coll. Trial Judges, 1973; del. Presdl. Conf. on Nat. Criminal Justice Standards, 1973. Bd. dirs. Legal Aid, Pocatello, 1975, Alcohol Rehab. Center, Pocatello, 1975, Idaho Vol. in Corrections, 6th Dist., Pocatello. Mem. Am., Idaho, 6th Dist. (v.p. 1975, pres. 1976) bar assns., Am., Idaho (bd. govs.) trial lawyers assns., Phi Alpha Delta. Office: PO Box 207 Pocatello ID 83201 Tel (208) 233-0132

DIAMANT, MICHAEL HARLAN, b. Cleve., July 30, 1946; B.S. in Engring. with high honors, Case Western Res. U., 1968; J.D. cum laude, Harvard U., 1971. Admitted to Ohio bar, 1971; asso. firm Kahn, Kleinman, Yamowitz & Arnson, Cleve., 1971—; spl. asst. atty. gen. Ohio, 1974. Mem. Bar Assn. Greater Cleve., Cuyahega City, Ohio State bar assns. Home: 2552 Channing Rd University Heights OH 44118 Office: 1300 Bond Ct Bldg Cleveland OH 44114 Tel (216) 696-3311

DIAMOND, CHARLES MILTON, b. Ashtabula, Ohio, Dec. 18, 1926; J.D., 1951. Admitted to Ohio bar, 1951, Fec. bar, 1962. Partner law firm Diamond & Dubsky, Ashtabula, Ohio, asst. U.S. atty., Cleve., 1961-63; asst. county prosecutor Ashtabula County, 1968-72. Mem. Ohio, Fed., Ashtabula County bar assns. Home: Wamar Ln Ashtabula OH 44004 Office: 355 Prospect Rd Ashtabula OH 44004

DIAMOND, GUSTAVE, b. Burgettstown, Pa., Jan. 29, 1928; A.B., Duke, 1951; J.D., Duquesne U., 1956. Admitted to Pa. 1958; U.S. Ct. Appeals 3d Circuit bar, 1962; law clk. U.S. Dist. Ct. Judge, Pitts., 1955-61; 1st asst. U.S. atty. Western Dist. Pa., 1961-62, U.S. atty., 1963-69; partner firm Cooper, Schwartz, Diamond & Reich, Pitts., 1969-75; individual practice law, Washington, Pa., 1975—; solicitor Washington County (Pa.), 1976—. Mem. Am., Pa., Allegheny County, Washington County, Fed. bar assns. Tel (412) 225-6164

DIAMOND, JOSEPH, b. Washington, Dec. 22, 1935; B.A., Columbia, 1957; LL.B., Cornell U., 1960. Admitted to N.Y. State bar, 1961, D.C. bar, 1964; asso. firm LeBoeuf, Lamb & Leiby, N.Y.C., 1961-63; asso. firm Melrod, Redman & Gartlan, Washington, 1963-65; mem. office of chief counsel Comptroller of the Currency, Washington, 1966-67; partner firm Rogers & Wells, N.Y.C., 1969—. Mem. Assn. Bar City N.Y. Office: 200 Park Ave New York City NY 10017 Tel (212) 972-7000

DIAMOND, LEO AARON, b. N.Y.C., Jan. 8, 1906; Ph.B., U. Chgo., 1927, J.D. cum laude, 1929. Admitted to Ind. bar, 1929, Ill. bar, 1931, N.Y. bar, 1944, D.C. bar, 1953; spl. atty. IRS Chief Counsel Office, 1934-39, asst. to chief counsel, 1939-43; asso. prof. law Rutgers, 1953-56; instr. N.Y. U., 1953-56; partner firm Austin and Diamond, N.Y.C., 1955—. Mem. N.Y. State, N.Y. County bar assns., Assn. Bar City N.Y. Contributing editor: Mertens Law of Federal Income Taxation, 1954-60. Contbr. articles in field to profl. jours. Office: 350 Fifth Ave New York City NY 10001 Tel (212) 695-1727

DIAMOND, LOUIS HOWARD, b. Washington, May 10, 1932; B.A. in Accounting, George Washington U., 1954; J.D. with honors, Georgetown U., 1957, LL.M., 1965. Admitted to D.C. bar, 1957; served with JAGC, U.S. Army, 1957-60; atty. adviser U.S. Tax Ct., Washington, 1960-62; asso. firm Silverstein & Mullins, Washington, 1962-66; partner firm Foreman, Cutler & Diamond, Washington, 1966-70, firm Danzansky, Dickey, Tydings Quint & Gordon, Washington, 1970—; adj. prof. Georgetown U. Law Center, Washington, 1971—. Mem. Am., D.C. bar assns. Contbr. articles to legal jours. Home: 6800 Loch Lomond Dr Bethesda MD 20034 Office: 1120 Connecticut Ave NW Washington DC 20036 Tel (202) 331-8700

DIAMOND, M. JEROME, b. Chgo., Mar. 16, 1942; A.B., George Washington U., 1963; M.A., U. Tenn., 1965, J.D., 1968. Law clk. to U.S. Dist. Judge, 1968-69; state's atty. for Windham County, Vt., 1970-74; atty. gen. State of Vt., 1975—; mem. Vt. Criminal Justice Tng. Council. Past pres. Brattleboro (Vt.) Civic Club; chmn. Putney Zoning Bd. Adjustment, 1971-74. Mem. Nat. Assn. Attys. Gen., Vt. State's Attys. Assn. (past pres.). Office: Atty Gen of Vt Pavilion Office Bldg 109 State St Montpelier VT 05602*

DIAMOND, MURRAY J., b. Bklyn., Dec. 25, 1923; B.A., Bklyn. Coll., 1947; J.D., Bklyn. Law Sch., 1950, J.S.D., 1952. Admitted to N.Y. State bar, 1950, U.S. Supreme Ct. bar, 1956; partner firm Diamond & Dreifuss, N.Y.C., 1950—; adj. lectr. in law U. City N.Y., 1969—; spl. dept. atty. gen., State of N.Y., 1950-59; small claims arbitrator, Civil Ct., N.Y.C., 1962—. Mem. Am. Bar Assn., N.Y. County Lawyers Assn., Am. Bus. Law Assn. Home: 267 Whitman Dr Brooklyn NY 11234 Office: 401 Broadway New York City NY 10013 Tel (212) 925-2697

DIAMOND, PHILIP ERNEST, b. Los Angeles, Feb. 11, 1925; A.B., U. Calif., Los Angeles, 1949, M.A., 1950; J.D., U. Calif., 1953. Admitted to Calif. bar, 1954; law sec. to Justice R. Peters, Calif. Supreme Ct., San Francisco, 1953-55; asso. firm Landels, Weigel & Ripley, San Francisco, 1955-60, partner, 1960-62; partner Landels, Ripley & Diamond, San Francisco, 1962—. Pres. Contra Costa Sch. Bd. Assn., 1967-68; mem. Calif. State Sch. Bd. Governing Conf. Mem. State Bar Calif., San Francisco, Am. bar assns. Home: 1050 Northpoint St San Francisco CA 94109 Office: 450 Pacific Ave San Francisco CA 94133 Tel (415) 788-5000

DIAMOND, ROGER JON, b. Los Angeles, May 17, 1943; B.A., U. Calif., Los Angeles, 1964, J.D., 1966. Admitted to Calif. Supreme Ct. bar, 1967, U.S. Supreme Ct. bar, 1971; asso. firm Graham & James, 1966-69; with firm Hecht & Diamond, Pacific Palisades, Calif., 1969—; instr. law U. West Los Angeles. Mem. Los Angeles County bar assn., Calif. Trial Lawyers Assn. Contbr. articles in field to profl. jours. Office: 15415 Sunset Blvd Pacific Palisades CA 90272 Tel (213) 454-1351

DIB, ALBERT, b. Bklyn., Apr. 6, 1923; B.A., Bklyn. Coll., 1947; J.D., St. John's U., 1951. Admitted to N.Y. bar, 1952, N.J. bar, 1967; asso. firm Buhler, King and Buhler, N.Y.C., 1959—; tchr. Fairleigh Dickinson U. Sch. Constrn. Studies, 1974—, Stevens Inst. Tech., 1975—; contract cons. Princeton U. Plasma Physics Lab., 1976—. Mem. N.Y. County Lawyers Bar Assn., Am. Inst. Chem. Engrs.

(charter chmn. engring. and constrn. contracting com. 1970-72, recipient plaque for spl. contbns.). Author: Forms and Agreements for Architects, Engineers and Contractors, 1976. Home: 169 Euclid Ave Hackensack NJ 07601 Office: 274 Madison Ave New York City NY 10016 Tel (212) 532-9157

DIBBLE, JOHN REX, b. Kaysville, Utah, Mar. 28, 1911; B.S., Utah State U., 1932; LL.B., Stanford, 1936; LL.D., Loyola U., 1968. Admitted to Calif. bar, 1936, U.S. Supreme Ct. bar, 1942; asso. firm Williamson, Hoge, Judson, Los Angeles, 1936-41; partner firm Miller, Chevalier, Peeler & Wilson, Los Angeles, 1941-48; asso. firm Hill, Farrer & Burrill, Los Angeles, 1949-54; prof. law Loyola U., Los Angeles, 1937—, acting dean, 1960-62, dean, 1962-65; asst. counsel War Dept. Price Adjustment Bd., 1944-46; counsel Los Angeles extension Air Force Renegotiation Bd., 1951; mem. Los Angeles Regional Renegotiation Bd., 1952. Mem. Calif., Los Angeles County bar assns., Am. Law Inst. (life), Order of Coif, Phi Delta Phi. Contbr. articles to law jours. Home: 1127 E Del Mar Blvd 335 Pasadena CA 91106 Office: 1440 W 9th St Los Angeles CA 90015 Tel (213) 642-2927

DIBRELL, JOSEPH BURTON, b. Sabinal, Tex., Apr. 20, 1921; LL.D., U. Tex., 1948. Admitted to Tex. bar, 1948; partner firm Dibrell, Tiemann and Irvine, Seguin, Tex., 1948; judge Guadalupe County Ct., 1969—. Mem. Am. Judicature Assn., South Central Tex. Bar Assn. (pres. 1975). Home: 1303 Keller Ln Seguin TX 78155 Office: 207 S Camp St POB 13 Seguin TX 78155 Tel (512) 379-2896

DICARO, JOHN RUSSELL, b. Bklyn., June 16, 1940; B.A., U. Colo., 1962; J.D., U. Calif., Berkeley, 1966. Admitted to Calif. bar, 1966, U.S. Supreme Ct. bar, 197S; asso. firm James J. Duryea and Sydney Weinstock, San Francisco, 1966-68; partner firm Ruston, Nance & Di Caro, Tustin, Calif., 1968—. Mem. Am., Orange County bar assns., Assn. So. Calif. Def. Counsel (dir.), Am. Bd. Trial Advocates (mem. exec. com. Orange County chpt.). Office: 111 Fashion Ln Tustin CA 92680 Tel (714) 832-2220

DICHTER, MARK S., b. Phila., Jan. 22, 1943; B.E.E., Drexel U., 1966; J.D., Villanova U., 1969. Admitted to Pa. bar, 1969; asso. firm Morgan, Lewis & Bockius, Phila., 1969-76, partner, 1976—. Pres., chmn. bd. dirs. Washington Sq. W. Project Area Com.; sec., bd. dirs. Phila. Singers, Inc.; bd. dirs. SE chpt. Ams. for Democratic Action. Mem. Order of Coif, Am. (com. equal employment opportunity law), Pa., Phila. bar assns. Articles editor Villanova Law Rev. Home: 1017 Clinton St Philadelphia PA 19107 Office: 2100 The Fidelity Bldg 123 S Broad St Philadelphia PA 19109 Tel (215) 491-9291

DICKASON, JOHN HAMILTON, b. Wooster, O., June 3, 1931; A.B., Dartmouth Coll., 1953, M.B.A., 1954. With Scott Paper Co., N.Y. state, 1954, 56-58; personnel technician Ill. Civil Service Commn., Springfield, 1958-60; bus. mgr. Ill. Bar Assn., Springfield, 1960-69, asso. dir., 1969-70, exec. dir., 1970—. Pres. Springfield Mental Health Assn. 1965, 66; active Boy Scouts Am.; sr. warden Christ Ch. Parish, Episcopal Ch., Springfield, 1974-75, treas., 1966-69, 76—, chmn. diocesan fin. com., 1975. Mem. A.B.A. (bar exec. asso.), Nat., Ill. (pres. 1972) socs. assn. execs., Nat. Assn. of Bar Execs. (treas. 1966-68, v.p. 1974-75, pres. 1975-77). Home: 11 Boulder Pt Springfield IL 62702 Office: 424 S 2nd St Springfield IL 62701 Tel (217) 525-1760

DICKERSON, CHARLES ADOLPH, b. Rosenberg, Tex., Dec. 2, 1936; B.A., Tex. U., 1959, LL.B., 1963. Admitted to Tex. bar, 1963; county atty. Ft. Bend County (Tex.), 1968-75, dist. atty., 1975-77; judge 240th Jud. Dist., 1977—. Office: Court House Richmond TX 77469

DICKERSON, FREDERICK REED, b. Chgo., Nov. 11, 1909; A.B., Williams Coll., 1931; LL.B., Harvard, 1934; LL.M., Columbia, 1939, J.S.D., 1950. Admitted to Mass. bar, 1934; Ill. bar, 1936, U.S. Supreme Ct. bar, 1943; asso. firm Goodwin, Procter & Hoar, Boston, 1934-35, McNab, Holmes & Long, Chgo., 1936-38; asst. prof. law Washington U., St. Louis, 1939-40; U. Pitts., 1940-42; atty. OPA, 1942-47; asst. legis. counsel U.S. Ho. of Reps., 1947-49; chmn. com. on codification Joint Army-Air Force Statutory Revision Group, dep. asst. gen. counsel U.S. Dept. Def., 1949-58; prof. law Ind. U., 1958—, asso. dean, 1971-75; dist. vis. prof. law So. Ill. U., 1975; chmn. Ind. Commn. on Uniform State Laws, 1969—; mem. Ind. Statute Revision Commn., 1969-70; cons. Dept. Def., 1958-59, 66, FAA, 1960-65, Dept. Transp., 1967-69, Commn. on Govt. Procurement, 1971-72, Pres.'s Com. on Consumer Interests, 1967-68. Pres. Chevy Chase Citizen's Assn 1955-56. Mem. Am. Law Inst., Nat. Conf. Commrs. on Uniform State Laws, Ind. State, Am. bar assns., Order of Coif. Author: Products Liability and the Food Consumer, 1951; Legislative Drafting, 1954; The Fundamentals of Legal Drafting, 1965; The Interpretation and Application of Statutes, 1975; Editor: Legal Problems Affecting Private Swimming Pools, 1961; Products Safety in Household Goods, 1968; (with Nutting and Elliott) Cases and Materials on Legislation, 1969; Professionalizing Legislative Drafting—the Federal Experience, 1973; Recipient Distinguished Civilian Service award U.S. Dept. Def., 1957. Home: 870 Woodscrest Dr Bloomington IN 47401 Ind U Office: Sch Law Bloomington IN 47401 Tel (812) 337-4444

DICKERSON, HENRY PLEASANT, III, b. Newport News, Va., Nov. 11, 1944; B.C.E., Va. Mil. Inst., 1967; J.D., U. Richmond, 1970. Admitted to Va. bar, 1970; asso. firm Elder & Elder, Staunton, Va., 1971—. Mem. Augusta County Bar Assn. Home: 1601 N Belmore Ave Staunton VA 24401 Office: 13 S New St Staunton VA 24401 Tel (703) 886-0763

DICKERSON, JOHN A., b. Anderson, S.C., Aug. 23, 1946; B.S., Clemson U., 1968; J.D., U. Ga., 1971. Admitted to Ga. bar, 1971; staff Ga. Indigent Legal Services, 1971-72; asso. firm McClure, Ramsay, Struble & Dickerson and predecessors, Toccoa, Ga., 1972-73, partner, 1973—. Chmn. bd. Stephens County United Fund, 1975; chmn. Cancer Crusade, 1976. Mem. Am., Ga., Mountain Jud. (sec. treas. 1976—), Stephens County (v.p. 1975-76) bar assns., Am. Assn. Trial Lawyers. Home: 110 Ridgeview Heights Toccoa GA 30577 Office: W Savannah and N Alexander Sts Toccoa GA 30577 Tel (404) 886-3178

DICKEY, DAVID STEELE, b. Chgo., Mar. 28, 1939; A.B., Dartmouth, 1961; J.D., U. Pa., 1964. Admitted to Pa. bar, 1965; dep. atty. gen. State of Pa., 1965-67; atty. SEC, Washington, 1967-68; asst. dist. atty. Franklin County (Pa.), 1969-70; individual practice law, Franklin County, 1969—; dir. First Nat. Bank of Greencastle (Pa.), 1973—. Mem. Am., Pa., Franklin County bar assns. Home: 335 S Ridge Ave Greencastle PA 17225 Office: 11 N Carlisle St Greencastle PA 17225 Tel (717) 597-7161

DICKEY, DON ALLEN, b. Harrison, Ark., Jan. 28, 1945; B.S. in Econs., U. Oreg., 1967; J.D., Williamette U., 1972. Admitted to Oreg. bar, 1972; asso. firm Rhoten, Rhoten & Speerstra, Salem, Oreg., 1972—. Mem. Am., Oreg., Marion County bar assns. Office: 300 Pioneer Trust Bldg Salem OR 97301 Tel (503) 364-6733

DICKEY, LARRY MORGAN, b. Glencoe, Ohio, Nov. 24, 1939; B.A., Youngstown State U., 1965; J.D., Cleve. State U., 1970. Admitted to Ohio bar, 1970; ins. adjuster Nationwide Ins. Co., 1965-70, St. Paul Ins. Co., 1970-71; asst. county prosecutor Columbiana County, 1971-73, judge, 1975—; solicitor Village of Rogers (Ohio), 1973-75. Mem. Am., Ohio, Columbiana County, Mahoning County bar assns., E. Palestine C. of C. (dir. 1974-75). Recipient award for Jud. Excellence, Ohio Supreme Ct., 1975, 76. Home: 1401 N Market St East Palestine OH 44413 Office: 91 W Taggart St East Palestine OH 44413 Tel (216) 426-4121

DICKEY, RICHARD DWIGHT, b. Portsmouth, Ohio, July 29, 1935; B.A. in Polit. Sci., Ohio State U., 1957, J.D., 1960. Admitted to Ohio bar, 1963; asso. firm Merle M. Agin, 1963-75; partner firm Hensal Goldin & Dickey, Wadsworth, Ohio, 1975—; city atty. City of Wadsworth, 1965-66, prosecutor, 1970; judge Medina County (Ohio) Ct., 1974. Chmn. Wadsworth Planning Commn., 1971. Mem. Medina County, Ohio State bar assns. Home: 227 Tanglewood Terr Wadsworth OH 44281 Office: 121 College St PO Box 185 Wadsworth OH 44281 Tel (216) 336-6666

DICKINSON, DANIEL S., JR., b. Binghamton, N.Y., July 25, 1917; B.S., Hartwick Coll., 1939; LL.B., Albany Law Sch., 1949. Admitted to N.Y. State bar, 1950; mem. firm Jenks & Glezen, Whitney Point, N.Y., 1950-54, Glezen & Dickinson, 1955-66; assemblyman N.Y. State Legislature, 1955-66; judge Family Ct. Broome County (N.Y.), 1966—. Mem. Broome County Bar Assn., Family Ct. Judges Assn. (N.Y.). Home: 1314 Chenango St Binghamton NY 13901 Office: Ct House Binghamton NY 13901 Tel (607) 772-2181

DICKINSON, MARTIN BROWNLOW, JR., b. Kansas City, Mo., Apr. 13, 1938; A.B., U. Kan., 1960; M.A., Stanford, 1961; J.D., U. Mich., 1964. Admitted to Colo. bar, 1964, Kans. bar, 1970; asso. firm Holme, Roberts & Owen, Denver, 1964-67; asst. prof. law U. Kans., 1967-69, asso. prof., 1969-71, prof., dean Sch. Law, 1971—; vis. prof. U. Mich., 1970, U. Colo., 1971; dir. 1st Nat. Bank of Lawrence (Kans.). Mem. Lawrence Bd. Zoning Appeals, 1971—; bd. dirs. Douglas County (Kans.) Legal Aid Soc., 1971—. Mem. Douglas County, Kan., Am. bar assns., Order of Coif, Phi Beta Kappa. Woodrow Wilson fellow; author: Materials on Federal Income Taxation, 1976; editor-in-chief Mich. Law Rev., 1963-64. Home: 902 W 27th Terr Lawrence KS 66044 Office: Sch of Law U of Kans Lawrence KS 66045 Tel (913) 864-4550

DICKINSON, MARTIN BROWNLOW, SR., b. Kansas City, Mo., Apr. 26, 1906; A.B., U. Kans., 1926, LL.B., 1928. Admitted to Mo. bar, 1927, U.S. Supreme Ct. bar, 1936, U.S. Tax Ct. bar, 1937; partner firm Dickinson & Dickinson, Kansas City, 1928-46; individual practice law, Kansas City, 1946-74; counsel Dietrich, Davis, Dicus, Rowlands & Schmitt, Kansas City, 1974—. Trustee, treas. Women's Christian Assn. of Kansas City. Mem. Am., Mo., Kansas City bar assns., Lawyers Assn. Kansas City (pres. 1955-56), Phi Beta Kappa, Order of Coif, Delta Tau Delta (pres. 1950-54). Home: 8708 Summit St Kansas City MO 64114 Office: Dwight Bldg 1004 Baltimore St Kansas City MO 64105 Tel (816) 221-3420

DICKINSON, WILSON GORDON, b. Roswell, N.Mex., Apr. 28, 1942; B.A. with honors, U. Tex., 1964, LL.B., 1965. Admitted to N.Mex. bar, 1975, Tex. bar, 1965; asso. firm Crenshaw, Dupree & Milam, Lubbock, Tex., 1965-69; individual practice law, Lubbock, 1969-74, Roswell, 1974—; past dir. State Savs. & Loan Assn., Lubbock; sec.-treas., dir. Dickinson Cattle Co., Amarillo, Tex. Mem. Am., Tex., N.Mex. bar assns. Home: Meadows Dr Roswell NM 88201 Office: 604 W 2nd St Roswell NM 88201 Tel (505) 623-7240

DICKMAN, JAMES LAMAR, b. Fremont, Ohio, Jan. 27, 1933; B.S. in Bus. Adminstrn., Ohio State U., 1956, J.D., 1965. Admitted to Ohio bar, 1965; partner firm Hoshor & Dickman, Hebron, Ohio, 1965-71; individual practice law, Hebron, 1971-73; asso. firm Graham & Graham, Zanesville, Ohio, 1973—; referee Small Claims Ct. Licking County (Ohio), 1970-73. Mem. Ohio State, Muskingum County bar assns. Home: Route 1 Finwood Dr Nashport OH 43830 Office: 200 Citizens Nat Bank Bldg Zanesville OH 43701 Tel (614) 452-8484

DICKSON, DAVID KEITH, b. Ames, Iowa, Nov. 27, 1946; student Luther Coll., Decorah, Iowa, 1965-67; B.B.A., U. Iowa, 1969, J.D., 1972. Admitted to Iowa bar, 1972; asst. county atty. Black Hawk County (Iowa), Waterloo, 1973-76; asso. firm Pickett & Kober, Waterloo, 1973-76; atty. Sidney B. Smith & Co., Des Moines, 1976-77; asso. firm Maurer & Terrill, Ames, 1977—. Parliamentarian, Waterloo Jaycees, 1974. Mem. Am., Story County, Iowa bar assns. Home: 3627 Davisson Rd Des Moines IA 50310 Office: 208 5th St Ames IA 50010 Tel (515) 232-4641

DICKSON, R. G. BRIAN, b. Yorkton, Sask., Can., May 25, 1916; LL.B., Man. Law Sch., 1938; D.Cn.L., St. Johns Coll., 1965; LL.D., U. Man., 1973. Called to bar Man., 1940, created Queens counsel, 1953; asso. firm Aikins, MacAulay & Co., Winnipeg, Man., 1945-63; lectr. Man. Law Sch., 1948-54; judge Ct. of Queens Bench of Man., 1963-67; justice Man. Ct. Appeals, 1967-73, Supreme Ct. Can., 1973—. Trustee, Sellers Found.; chmn. bd. govs. U. Man., 1971-73. Home: Marchmont Dunrobin ON K0A 1T0 Canada Office: Supreme Ct Can Wellington St Ottawa ON K1A 0J1 Canada Tel (613) 992-2366

DICKSON, WILLIAM DAVID, JR., b. Miami, Fla., Jan. 1, 1938; student Ark. State U., 1955-57; B.A., U. Miss., 1960; J.D., Memphis State U., 1968. Admitted to Tenn. bar, 1968; mem. firm Threlkeld & Howard, Memphis, 1968—; instr. Memphis State U., 1971—. Mem. Am., Tenn., Memphis-Shelby County bar assns., Am. Coll. Mortgage Attys. Home: 1602 Vinton St Memphis TN 38104 Office: 175 Tillman St Memphis TN 38111 Tel (901) 458-2533

DICKSTEIN, SIDNEY, b. Bklyn., May 13, 1925; A.B., Franklin and Marshall Coll., 1947; J.D., Columbia U., 1949. Admitted to N.Y. State bar, 1949; law clk. to Joseph Richter, N.Y.C., 1949-50; asso. law office Herman F. Cooper, N.Y.C., 1950-53; founder firm Dickstein & Shapiro, N.Y.C., 1953, now sr. partner successor firm Dickstein, Shapiro & Morin, Washington and N.Y.C., 1972—. Bd. visitors Franklin and Marshall Coll. Mem. Am., D.C. bar assns. Home: 9050 Bradgrove Dr Bethesda MD 20034 Office: 2101 L St NW Washington DC 20037 Tel (202) 785-9700

DICLERICO, JOSEPH ANTHONY, JR., b. Nahant, Mass., Jan. 30, 1941; B.A., Williams Coll., 1963; LL.B., Yale, 1966. Admitted to N.H. bar, 1967, U.S. Supreme Ct. bar, 1975; law clk. N.H. Supreme Ct., Concord, 1967-68; asso. firm Cleveland, Waters & Bass, Concord, N.H., 1968-70; asst. atty. gen. State of N.H., Concord, 1970-76; asso. justice N.H. Superior Ct., 1976—. Pres., Little Sunapee Lake Protective Assn., 1974-76; mem. New London Planning Bd., 1975-76. Mem. Am., N.H. (past mem. com. profl. conduct), Merrimack County (past sec.-treas.) bar assns., Phi Beta Kappa. Home and office: Little Sunapee Rd New London NH 03257 Tel (603) 526-4510

DIDLAKE, WILLIAM WOODFORD, JR., b. Santa Fe, Feb. 11, 1939; B.B.A. in Finance, Tex. Tech. U., 1959; J.D., U. Tex., 1970. Admitted to Tex. bar, 1968; dep. dir. corp. div. Office of Sec. of State, State of Tex., 1969-70, dir. uniform comml. code div., 1970-73, legal counsel, 1973-75, dir. criminal justice div., Austin, 1975—; city atty. City of Rollingwood, Tex., 1969-71. Councilman, City of Rollingwood, 1976—. Mem. Am., Tex. bar assns. Home: 2608 Rollingwood Dr Austin TX 78746 Office: Secretary of State Capitol Bldg Austin TX 78711 Tel (512) 475-3508

DIEKEMPER, JEROME ANTHONY, b. Washington, Dec. 5, 1946; B.A., St. Louis U., 1968, J.D., 1971. Admitted to Mo. bar, 1972; atty. NLRB, St. Louis, 1971-72; partner firm Bartley, Goffstein, Bollato & Lange, St. Louis, 1972—. Mem. Am., St. Louis County, Met. St. Louis bar assns., Mo. Bar. Office: 130 S Bemiston St Clayton MO 63105 Tel (314) 727-0922

DIENER, DAVID, b. Balt., June 5, 1915; B.B.A., Univ. Balt., 1934, LL.B., 1937, C.P.A., 1937. Admitted to Md. bar, 1937. Individual practice law, Balt., 1938—. Mem. Md., Balt. bar assns., Am. Md. assns. of attys.-C.P.A.'s. Home: 3305 Northbrook Rd Baltimore MD 21208 Office: 1124 Fidelity Bldg Baltimore MD 21201 Tel (301) 727-5558

DIES, JACK, b. Washington, May 5, 1936; B.S. in English and Govt., Stephen F. Austin U., 1958; J.D., Baylor U., 1963. Admitted to Tex. bar, 1963, U.S. Supreme Ct. bar, 1973; judge Corp. Ct., Lufkin, Tex., 1963-68; practiced in Lufkin, 1963-73; asst. atty. gen. State of Tex., 1973—, appellate chief of hwys., 1973-74, chief labor div., 1974—; trust officer Houston Citizens' Bank & Trust Co., 1968-69. Bd. govs. Baylor Law Sch. Mem. Tex. State Bar, Am. Bar Assn., Tex. Trial Lawyers Assn., Baylor Law Sch. Alumni Assn. Home: 7623 Rock Point St Austin TX 78731 Office: Supreme Ct Bldg Austin TX 78711 Tel (512) 475-3226

DIETRICH, DONALD PAUL, b. Buffalo, Dec. 27, 1935; B.S., State U. N.Y., Buffalo, 1958; J.D., Duke, 1961. Admitted to N.Y. State bar, 1961, Fla. bar, 1964, U.S. Supreme Ct. bar, 1965; atty., office of gen. counsel SEC, Washington, 1960; staff legal officer U.S. Naval Air Sta., Sanford, Fla., 1961-65; counsel Chenango and Unadilla Telephone Co., Norwich, N.Y., 1965; asso. firm van den Berg, Gay and Burke, Orlando, Fla., 1966-67; individual practice law, Orlando, 1967-74; U.S. magistrate Middle Dist. Fla., 1971—; comdr. JAGC, USNR, 1974—; trustee Orange County (Fla.) Legal Aid Soc., 1970-71. Vice-chmn. central Fla. chpt. ARC, 1973-75. Mem. Am., Fed. (sec. Orlando chpt. 1974-75), Fla., Orange County (exec. council 1970-73) bar assns., Phi Delta Phi, Beta Gamma Sigma. Home: 9 Hopkins Circle Orlando FL 32804 Office: United States Courthouse 80 N Hughey Ave Orlando FL 32801 Tel (305) 420-6362

DIETRICH, RONALD M., b. Hammond, Ind., Nov. 23, 1933; A.B., U. Colo., 1955; J.D., U. Mich., 1961. Admitted to Pa. bar, 1977, D.C. bar, 1973, Ill. bar, 1961; asso. firm McBride, Baker, Wienke & Schlosser, Chgo., 1961-70; gen. counsel OEO, Washington, 1970-71, FTC, Washington, 1971-73; partner firm Pepper, Hamilton & Scheetz, Washington, 1973-76; v.p. law Consol. Rail Corp., Phila., 1976—; dir. Nat. Consumer Law Center, Boston. Mem. Adminstrv. Conf. U.S., D.C., Am. bar assns. Home: 226 W Rittenhouse Sq Philadelphia PA 19103 Office: 1838 Six Penn Center Philadelphia PA 19103 Tel (215) 594-2221

DIETRICH, WILLIAM GALE, b. Kansas City, Mo., Mar. 6, 1925; A.B. with honors, Yale, 1948, LL.B., 1951. Admitted to Mo. bar, 1951; asso. firm Dietrich, Davis, Dicus, Rowlands & Schmidt, and predecessors, Kansas City, Mo., 1951-53, partner, 1953-73; individual practice law, Kansas City, 1973—; gen. counsel Blue Ridge Shopping Center, Inc., 1954-73, Blue Ridge Tower, Inc., 1967-73, A. Reich & Sons, Inc., Sun-Ra Frozen Foods, Inc., A. Reich & Sons Gardens, Inc., 1973—. Treas., vestryman Grace and Holy Trinity Episcopal Cathedral of Kansas City, 1970—; trustee Research Med. Center of Kansas City, 1977—. Mem. Mo. Bar, Kansas City, Am. bar assns., Lawyers Assn. Kansas City. Home: 1000 Huntington Rd Kansas City MO 64113 Office: 900 Blue Ridge Tower Kansas City MO 64133 Tel (816) 358-0039

DIETZ, CHARLTON HENRY, b. Le Mars, Iowa, Jan. 8, 1931; B.A., Macalester Coll., 1953; J.D., William Mitchell Coll. Law, 1957. Admitted to Minn. bar, 1957; with staff pub. relations Minn. Mining and Mfg. Co., St. Paul, 1952-58, atty., 1958-72, sec., asst. gen. counsel, 1972-75, gen. counsel, sec., 1975-76, v.p. legal affairs and gen. counsel, dir., 1976—; dir. Eastern Heights State Bank, St. Paul, 1971—; instr. William Mitchell Coll. Law, 1963-74. Trustee William Mitchell Coll. Law, 1973—; bd. dirs. St. Paul Met. YMCA, 1973—, United Theol. Sem., 1976, Minn. Correctional Services, Mpls., 1976, Mid-Am. Legal Found., 1977. Mem. Am., Minn., Fed. bar assns., Am. Soc. Corporate Secs. Home: One Birch Ln North Oaks MN 55110 Office: 3M Center Saint Paul MN 55101 Tel (612) 733-1190

DIETZ, STANLEY MARTIN, b. N.Y.C., Jan. 21, 1927; A.A., George Washington U., 1948, LL.B., 1951. Admitted to D.C. bar, 1951, U.S. Supreme Ct. bar, 1961; individual practice law, Washington and Md., 1951—. Mem. Am. Bar Assn., Am. Trial Lawyers Assn., Assn. Plaintiffs Trial Attys. of D.C. and Md., First Am. Lawyers Assn. Home: 10008 Battleridge Pl Gaithersburg MD 20760 Office: 1029 Vermont Ave NW Washington DC 20005 Tel (202) 347-6191

DIFABIO, E. MICHAEL, b. Green Island, N.Y., Oct. 27, 1926; B.B.A., Siena Coll., 1950; J.D., Albany Law Sch., 1957. Admitted to N.Y. bar, 1957; prin. firm DiFabio & Couch, Albany, N.Y., 1973—, DiFabio & VanZandt, C.P.A.'s, Albany, 1973—; lectr. taxation Siena Coll., 1959-73, mem. bd. asso. trustees, 1974—. Trustee St. Gregory's Sch. for Boys, Mercy High Sch. Mem. Am., N.Y. State bar assns., Am. Inst. C.P.A.'s, N.Y. State Soc. C.P.A.'s. Office: 4 Automation Ln Albany NY 12205 Tel (518) 459-1000

DI FEDE, JOSEPH, b. Italy, Dec. 8, 1909; B.A., U. Rochester, 1933; LL.B., St. John's U., 1938, J.S.D., 1940. Admitted to N.Y. bar, 1938, U.S. Supreme Ct. bar, 1957; referee N.Y. State Dept. Labor, 1936-44; chief labor officer U.S. Army, Italy, 1944-45; chmn. N.Y. State Labor

Relations Bd., 1954-61; judge Civil Ct., N.Y.C., 1970-71; justice N.Y. State Supreme Ct., Bronx, 1972—; prof. law N.Y. Law Sch., 1955-69, adj. prof. law, 1969—; mem. N.Y. Legislature, 1935. Mem. Am., N.Y. State, Bronx County (pres., past chmn. bd.) bar assns., Assn. Bar City N.Y., Columbian Lawyers Assn., Phi Beta Kappa. Contbr. articles to legal jours.; recipient medal of Freedom (U.S.); Star of Solidarity, First Class (Italy). Office: Supreme Court Bldg 851 Grand Concourse Bronx NY 10451 Tel (212) 293-8000

DIGGES, EDWARD SIMMS, JR., b. Pitts., June 30, 1946; A.B., Princeton, 1968; J.D., U. Md., 1971. Admitted to Md. bar, 1972, U.S. Supreme Ct. bar, 1975; asso. firm Piper & Marbury, Balt., Md., 1971-73, 74-77, partner, 1977—; mem. Gov.'s staff, 1973; lectr. Johns Hopkins U., 1975—, U. Balt. Law Sch., 1976--. Mem. Am. (state membership chmn. 1973—), Md. State (vice-chmn. pattern jury instrn. com. 1973—, chmn. com. on laws 1976—), Balt. City, Anne Arundel County bar assns. Office: 2000 First Maryland Bldg 25 S Charles St Baltimore MD 21201 Tel (301) 539-2530

DI GIACOMO, LOUIS J., b. Phila., Jan. 20, 1926; B.S. in Econs., Villanova U., 1946; LL.B., U. Pa., 1950. Admitted to Pa. bar, 1950; asso. firm. T. Ewing Montgomery, Phila., 1950-57, Zoob, Cohan & Matz, Phila., 1957-62; sr. partner firm Philips, Curtin & DiGiacomo, Phila., 1962—. Mem. Oaklyn (N.J.) Borough Council, 1957-58; justice of peace, Easttown Twp., Pa., 1960-66. Mem. Am., Pa., Phila. bar assns. Recipient Alumni medal Villanova U., 1976. Office: 1000 Western Savs Bank Bldg Broad and Chestnut Sts Philadelphia PA 19107 Tel (215) PE5-5300

DIKEMAN, ROSWELL COLEMAN, b. Goshen, N.Y., May 30, 1922; student Swarthmore Coll., 1940-42; LL.B. cum laude, Albany Law Sch., 1948. Admitted to N.Y. bar, 1948, D.C. bar, 1975; mem. legal staff N.Y. State Comptroller, 1948-54; asso. firm Willkie Farr & Gallagher, and predecessors, N.Y.C., 1955-60; partner, 1961—; mem. Municipal Securities Rulemaking Bd., Washington, 1975—, chmn., 1975-76. Trustee, Albany Law Sch., 1974—. Mem. Am., N.Y., D.C. bar assns., Municipal Analysts Assn., Municipal Forums N.Y. and D.C. Contbr. articles in field to profl. jours. Office: 120 Broadway New York City NY 10005 Tel (212) 248-1000

DILEO, SAMUEL JOHN, JR., b. New Orleans, Oct. 24, 1944; B.A., La. State U., 1968; J.D., Loyola U., 1971; postgrad. Nat. Coll. Dist. Attys., 1973—. Admitted to La. bar, 1972; special counsel to La. State Atty. Gen., Baton Rouge, 1972-74; individual practice law, Hammond, La., 1973-75; sr. partner firm Dileo & Myles, Hammond, 1975—. Mem. Am., La. State, Tangipahua Parish bar assns., St. Thomas Moore Law Club, Phi Alpha Delta. Recipient Am. Jurisprudence award Loyola U. Sch. of Law, 1971. Home: 307 Rue Saint Michael St Hammond LA 70401 Office: 1000 Hwy 51 N Jefferson Ct Suite D Hammond LA 70401 Tel (504) 345-0570

DILEONE, PETER, b. Providence, Feb. 29, 1908; A.B., Case Western Res. U., 1933, LL.B., 1935. Admitted to Ohio bar; individual practice law, Cleve., 1935-37; atty. NLRB, Washington and Cleve., 1937-40; atty. Cleve. Ordnance Contract Sect., War Dept., Cleve., 1942-44; hearing officer War Labor Bd., Cleve., 1944-45. Vice-pres. City Club Forum Found., 1968—. Mem. Ohio, Cuyahoga, Cleve. bar assns. Contbr. articles to legal jours. Home: 17100 Van Aken Blvd Shaker Hts OH 44120 Office: 819 Nat City Bank Bldg Cleveland OH 44114 Tel (216) 621-6070

DILIMETIN, ANTHONY KRIKOR, b. N.Y.C., Feb. 9, 1929; student Bethany Coll., 1950; LL.B., St. John's Coll., 1953. Admitted to N.Y. State bar, 1956; individual practice law, N.Y.C., 1956—; legal officer, dir. Hyecard Realty Corp., N.Y.C., 1964—, Azad, Inc., Phila., 1969—, Etsia, Inc., N.Y.C., 1968—. Pres., Armenian Welfare Assn., N.Y.C., 1962-66; atty. Armenian Diocese N. Am., N.Y.C., 1966-69; mem. Protestant Welfare Assn., N.Y.C., 1965-66. Mem. N.Y. State Bar Assn. Home: 382 Abbey Rd Manhasset NY 11030 Office: 60 E 42nd St New York City NY 10017 Tel (212) 972-0310

DILKS, PARK BANKERT, JR., b. Phila., Mar. 25, 1928; A.B., U. Pa., 1948, J.D., 1951. Admitted to D.C. bar, 1951, Pa. bar, 1952, U.S. Supreme Ct. bar, 1962; asst. dist. atty., Phila., 1952; asso. firm Souser & Schumacher, Phila., 1953-60; asso. firm Morgan, Lewis & Bockius, Phila., Washington and N.Y.C., 1961-64, partner, 1964-71, sr. partner, 1971—, mem. exec. com., 1971—; chmn. bd. trustees U.S. Investment Fund; dir. Arlen Realty, Inc. Mem. Phila., Pa., Am., Fed. bar assns., Phi Beta Kappa. Home: 2604 William Penn House 1919 Chestnut St Philadelphia PA 19103 Office: 2300 Fidelity Bldg 123 S Broad St Philadelphia PA 19109 Tel (215) 491-9228

DILLAHUNTY, WILBUR HARRIS, b. Memphis, June 30, 1928; LL.B. (now J.D.), U. Ark., 1955. Admitted to Ark. bar, U.S. Supreme Ct. bar, 1954; individual practice law, W. Memphis, Ark., 1954-58; atty. City of W. Memphis, 1958-68; U.S. atty. Eastern Dist. Ark., Little Rock, 1968—; atty. Improvement Dists., 1965-68, W. Memphis Utility Commn., 1958-68. Mem. Am., Ark., Crittenden County bar assns., W. Memphis C. of C. (past pres.). Named Young Man of Year, Crittenden County, 1961. Home: 9710 Catskill Rd Little Rock AR 72207 Office: 600 W Capitol St Little Rock AR 72207 Tel (501) 378-5347

DILLARD, HARDY CROSS, b. New Orleans, Oct. 23, 1902; B.S., U.S. Mil. Acad., 1924; LL.B., U. Va., 1927; LL.D., Tulane U., 1971, Washington Coll., 1976. Admitted to Va. bar, 1927; faculty U. Va., Charlottesville, 1927-29, 31-70, James Monroe prof. law, 1958-70, dean. Sch. Law, 1963-68; Carnegie fellow U. Paris, 1930-31; judge Internat. Ct. Justice, The Hague, Netherlands, 1970—; cons. govtl. and pvt. agys., 1945-70; mem. Commn. to Revise Constn. Va., 1968-69. Fellow World Acad. Sci. and Letters; mem. Am. Law Inst. (council 1964—), Am., Va., W.Va. (hon.) bar assns., Am. Soc. Internat. Law (pres. 1962-63). Author: Some Aspects of Law and Diplomacy, 1957; contbr. articles to legal and other jours. Home: 1221 Rugby Rd Charlottesville VA 22903 Office: Peace Palace The Hague Netherlands

DILLARD, J. EDWARD, b. Muskogee, Okla., Jan. 31, 1917; B.S., U.S. Mil. Acad., 1941; LL.B., U. Colo., 1950. Admitted to Colo. bar, 1951, Calif. bar, 1959; claims mgr. Security Life & Accident Co., Denver, 1951-58, asst. counsel, 1951-55, asso. counsel, 1955-58; asso. counsel Pacific Mut. Life Ins. Co., Newport Beach, Calif., 1958-68, asso. gen. counsel, 1968-71, v.p., gen. counsel, 1971—. Mem. Calif., Orange County bar assns., Assn. Life Ins. Counsel (subcom. on punitive damages). Author: The Bomb Fell on California, 1972; California Coastal Commission: Boom or Bust?, 1976; Family Aspect of Life Insurance; contbr. articles to legal jours. Home: 23792 Hillhurst Dr Laguna Niguel CA 92677 Office: 700 Newport Center Dr Newport Beach CA 92663 Tel (714) 640-3323

DILLARD, JACK HANDER, b. Hamlin, Tex., Feb. 24, 1917; B.A., Baylor U., 1938, J.D., 1969. Admitted to Tex. bar, 1969; editor Mexia (Tex.) Daily News, 1938-41; spl. agt. FBI, Newark, Oklahoma City and San Antonio, 1941-47; alumni dir. Baylor U., Waco, Tex., 1947-53, asst. to pres., 1957-67; adminstrv. asst. Gov. of Tex., Austin, 1953-57; asst. atty. gen. State of Tex., Austin, 1969-72; exec. dir., gen. counsel Tex. Center for Judiciary, Austin, 1972—. Mem. State Jud. Educators Nat. Assn. (pres.), Baylor U. Alumni Assn. (nat. pres. 1958). Home: 3502 Lakeland Dr Austin TX 78731 Office: Tex Law Center Box 12487 Austin TX 78711 Tel (512) 475-7087

DILLARD, JACK KELLY, b. Waco, Tex., Apr. 19, 1948; B.B.A., Baylor U., 1972, J.D., 1973. Admitted to Tex. bar, 1973; dep. dir. corporate charter div. Tex. Sec. of State, Austin, 1973; atty. Tenneco, Inc., Houston, 1973—, regional coordinator govt. affairs, 1976—. Gov., Gulf Coast Area, Order of DeMolay, Houston, Mem. State Bar Tex., Houston Bar Assn., Am. Judicature Soc., Tex., Houston jr. bars, Phi Alpha Delta. Home: 2321 Westcreek Ln Houston TX 77027 Office: PO Box 2511 Houston TX 77001 Tel (713) 757-2925

DILLARD, ROBERT LIONEL, JR., b. Corsicana, Tex., Sept. 30, 1913; B.S., So. Meth. U., 1934, J.D., 1935; LL.M., Harvard, 1936. Admitted to Tex. bar, 1935; asso. firm Saner, Saner & Jack, Dallas, 1936-41; asst. city atty. City of Dallas, 1941-45; with Southland Life Ins. Co., Dallas, 1945—, sr. v.p., gen. counsel, 1967-69, sec., 1969-77, exec. v.p., 1970—, also dir.; sec. Southland Fin. Corp., 1972-77, sr. v.p., gen. counsel, 1975—; research fellow Southwestern Legal Found., 1951—. Chmn. bd. Tex. Edn. Service Center, region X, 1968—. Fellow Am. Bar Found., Tex. Bar Found. (charter mem.); mem. Am. Judicature Soc., Nat. Legal Aid Soc., Dallas, Am., Inter-Am. bar assns., State Bar Tex. Named Distinguished Alumnus So. Meth. U., 1963. Home: 6624 Lakewood Blvd Dallas TX 75214 Office: 1105 Southland Center Dallas TX 75201 Tel (214) 653-3536

DILLARD, ROGER LEE, JR., b. Asheville, N.C., Jan. 3, 1945; B.A., U. N.C., 1967, postgrad., 1967-68; J.D., Stanford U., 1972. Admitted to N.C. bar, 1972; salesman Sears Roebuck & Co., Birmingham, Ala., 1968-69; trust officer Birmingham Trust Nat. Bank, 1969-72; partner firm Coward, Coward, Jones & Dillard, Sylva, N.C., 1972—; atty. Smokey Mountain Mental Health Center, 1973—, Swain County, 1974—. Pres. Jackson County (N.C.) Heart Fund, 1974; supt. Sunday sch. First Baptist Ch., Sylva, 1974-76, chmn. bd. deacons, 1976—; mem. N.C. State Banking Commn., 1975—. Mem. N.C., Jackson County, Am. bar assns. Home: 23 Savannah Dr Sylva NC 28779 Office: 43 W Main St Sylva NC 28779

DILLARD, TIMOTHY LEE, b. Montgomery, Ala., Nov. 11, 1946; B.S., U. Ala., 1968; J.D., Samford U., 1971. Admitted to Ala. bar, 1972; partner firm Lindbergh, Leach, Dillard & Ferguson, Birmingham, Ala., 1972—. Mem. Ala. Trial Lawyers Assn., Am. Judicature Soc., Am., Ala., Birmingham bar assns. Home: 3900 Asbury Rd Birmingham AL 35243 Office: 331 Frank Nelson Bldg Birmingham AL 35203 Tel (205) 324-5631

DILLAWAY, STEVEN BRIAN, b. Aberdeen, Wash., Mar. 16, 1945; B.A., U. Wash., 1967; J.D. cum laude, U. San Diego, 1971. Admitted to Calif. bar, 1972; asso. Arthur Young & Co., San Diego, 1971-73; asso. firm Golden, McDevitt & Martin, San Diego, 1973-74; individual practice law, San Diego, 1973-74; partner firm Dilloway, Hughes & Wilson, San Diego, 1974—. Mem. Calif. Assn. Atty.-C.P.A.'s (dir. 1974—), San Diego Young Execs. Assn. (treas. 1974—). C.P.A. Calif. Home: 5108 Canterbury St San Diego CA 92116 Office: 2150 First Ave San Diego CA 92101 Tel (714) 232-7111

DILLE, BRYCE HAGGARD, b. Seattle, Sept. 24, 1939; B.A., U. Wash., 1961; J.D., Gonzaga U., 1966. Admitted to Wash. bar, 1966; asso. firm Stubbs Batali Combs & Small, Tacoma, Wash., 1966-69; partner firm Campbell, Dille, Barnett & McCarthy, Puyallup, Wash., 1969—; city atty. City of Buckley (Wash.), 1968-72. Mem. Puyallup Sch. Bd. and Intermediate Sch. Bd., 1969-72; mem. Tacoma-Pierce County Civic Arts Commn., 1971—; pres. Puyallup Valley Daffodil Festival, 1975-76. Mem. Am., Wash. State, Tacoma-Pierce County bar assns., Tacoma-Pierce County Estate Planning Council, Am., Wash. trial lawyers assns., Puyallup Valley C. of C. (pres. 1974-75). Recipient Achievement award Bur. Nat. Affairs, 1966; editor asso. Gonzaga Law Rev., 1965-66. Home: 209 Dechaux Rd NE Puyallup WA 98371 Office: 319 S Meridian St Puyallup WA 98371 Tel (206) 848-3513

DILLER, THEODORE CRAIG, b. Pitts., Aug. 3, 1904; Ph.B., Kenyon Coll., 1925; LL.B., Harvard, 1928. Admitted to Pa. bar, 1928, Ill. bar, 1929; practiced in Chgo. since 1929, asso. firms Watkins, TenHoor & Gilbert, 1929-34, Concannon & Dillon, 1934-37, Judah, Reichman, Trumbull, Cox & Stern, 1937-39, asso. firm Lord, Bissell & Brook, and predecessor, 1939-45, partner, 1946—. Mem. Am., Ill. State, Chgo. bar assns. Home: 416 Cumnor Rd Kenilworth IL 60043 Office: 115 S LaSalle St Chicago IL 60603 Tel (312) 443-0286

DILLING, KIRKPATRICK W., b. Evanston, Ill., Apr. 11, 1920; student Cornell U., 1939-40, De Paul U., 1946-47; B.S. in Law, Northwestern U., 1942; spl. student l'Ecole Vaubier, Montreux, Switzerland, Sorbonne, U. Paris, others. Admitted to Ill. bar, 1947, U.S. Supreme Ct. bar, 1953; partner firm Dilling & Dilling, Chgo., 1948—; gen. counsel Nat. Health Fedn., 1970—, bd. govs., 1972—; gen. counsel Am. Massage and Therapy Assn., 1966—; counsel Midwest Pharm. Advt. Club, 1973—; pres., dir. P.E.P. Industries, Ltd., 1970—; v.p. Dillman Labs., Ltd., 1966—; dir. Harbil, Inc., Ry. Devel. Corp., Chgo. Truck Leasing Co., others. Bd. dirs. Nat. Safety Council. Mem. Am. (food and drug com.), Ill., Chgo. (chmn. food and drug com. 1976-77) bar assns., Am. Trial Lawyers Assn., Cornell Soc. Engrs. Author publs. in field. Home: 1120 Lee Rd Northbrook IL 60662 Office: 188 W Randolph St Chicago IL 60601 Tel (312) 236-8417

DILLON, CHARLES EDWARD, b. Butler, Pa., Mar. 18, 1920; A.B., U. Notre Dame, 1941; LL.B., U. Pa., 1951. Admitted to Pa. bar, 1952; individual practice law, Butler, 1951-66; partner firm Coulter, Gilchrist, Dillon & McCandless, Butler, 1966-76, firm Dillon, McCandless, King & Kemper, Butler, 1976—; solicitor Butler Area Sch. Dist., 1955—, City of Butler, 1962-66, Mars (Pa.) Area Sch. Dist., 1965—, various other twps. and municipal authorities. Past chmn. fund dr. Butler chpt. ARC; bd. dirs., v.p. Butler County Meml. Hosp., 1960-72. Mem. Am., Pa., Butler County bar assns. Home: 610 E Pearl St Butler PA 16001 Office: 128 W Diamond St Butler PA 16001 Tel (412) 283-2200

DILLON, DON E., b. New Sharon, Iowa, Feb. 15, 1921; LL.B., Drake U., 1943. Admitted to Iowa bar, 1943, Tex. bar, 1946; claims mgr. Aetna Ins. Co., Corpus Christi and Dallas, Tex., 1947-56, ins. agt., Dallas, 1956-60; individual practice law, Bryan, Tex., 1961—; municipal judge, Richardson, Tex., 1958-60. Pres., Brazos Valley Rehab. Center, 1972, Brazos County United Way, 1976—. Mem. Am., Tex., Brazos County (past pres.) bar assns. Office: 409 E 26th St Bryan TX 77801 Tel (713) 779-7979

DILLON, GREGORY RUSSELL, b. Chgo., Aug. 26, 1922; B.A., Elmhurst (Ill.) Coll., 1946; LL.B. (now J.D.) DePaul U., 1948. Admitted to Ill. bar, 1949; jr. partner firm Friedman, Mulligan, Dillon & Urist, and predecessors, Chgo., 1952-61, sr. partner, 1961-62; asst. to pres. Hilton Hotels Corp., Chgo. and Beverly Hills, Calif., 1963-64, v.p., asst. sec., 1964-71, sr. v.p., asst. sec., 1971—, also dir.; exec. v.p. Hilton Inns, Inc., Beverly Hills, 1972—, also dir.; v.p., dir. Hilton-Burns Hotels Co., Inc., Honolulu; trustee Wells Fargo Mortgage Investors Trust, San Francisco. Mem. Nat. Assn. Corporate Real Estate Execs., Am., Ill., Chgo. bar assns., Am. Hotel and Motel Assn., Urban Land Inst. Office: 9880 Wilshire Blvd Beverly Hills CA 90210 Tel (213) 278-4321

DILLON, JOHN JOSEPH, b. Indpls., Aug. 1, 1926; student Xavier U., 1949; LL.B., Ind. U., 1952; LL.D., Marian Coll., 1972. Admitted to Ind. bar, 1952, also U.S. Supreme Ct. bar, U.S. Ct. Mil. Appeals; counsel Indpls. Legal Aid Soc., 1953-56; city atty. Indpls., 1956-64; atty. gen. Ind., 1965-69; mem. firm Dillon, Hardamon & Cohen, Indpls., 1977—. Pres. Marion Coll. Assos., Indpls., 1963, bd. dirs. Indpls. Legal Aid Soc., 1963—; pres., vice chmn. bd. trustees Marion Coll., 1977—, bd. dirs. Catholic Charities Indpls., 1976, Indpls. Civic Ballet Soc., 1977—; trustee Indpls. and English Found., 1975—. Mem. Am., Ind. bar assns., Lawyers Assn. Indpls., 500 Festival Assos., Ind. U. Law Sch. Indpls. Alumni Assn. (dir. 1977—), Aircraft Owners and Pilots Assn., Sigma Delta Kappa. Home: 320 E Kessler Blvd Indianapolis IN 46220 Office: 120 E Market St Indianapolis IN 46204

DILLON, RAYMOND LOWELL, b. Mansfield, Ohio, Feb. 7, 1933; LL.B., Ohio State U., 1957. Admitted to Ohio bar, 1958; mem. firm McDermott & Dillon, and predecessor, Mansfield, 1960—; legal counsel Madison Twp. Zoning Bd. Appeals, Mansfield, 1972—, Richland County Realtors, Mansfield, 1975—; instr. real estate law Ohio State U., Mansfield br. Trustee, Mansfield Cath. Charities, 1972—. Mem. Ohio, Richland County bar assns. Home: 55 Wellington Ave Mansfield OH 44906 Office: 28 Park Ave W Mansfield OH 44902 Tel (419) 524-6911

DILLON, ROBERT C., b. Birmingham, Ala., May 17, 1931; A.B., Jacksonville State U., 1953; LL.B., U. Ala., 1957. Admitted to Ala. bar, 1957; law clk. Ala. Supreme Ct., 1957-58; asst. atty. gen. State of Ala., 1958-59; partner firms Burnham, Klinefelter, & Dillon, Anniston, Ala., 1959-63, Merrill, Porch, Doster & Dillon, Anniston, 1963—. Bd. dirs. Calhoun County (Ala.) chpt. ARC, Choccolocco council Girl Scouts U.S.A.; elder 1st Presbyn. Ch., Anniston. Mem. Calhoun County (pres. 1970-71), Ala. State bar assns., Ala. Def. Lawyers Assn. (dir.), Am. Trial Lawyers Assn. Home: 421 Wildwood Rd Anniston AL 36201 Office: 500 1st Nat Bank Bldg PO Box 580 Anniston AL 36201 Tel (205) 237-2871

DILLON, ROBERT CLABORN, b. Miami, Fla., Nov. 21, 1942; B.B.A., Emory U., 1965, J.D. with distinction, 1972. Admitted to Ga. bar, 1973, since practiced in Atlanta; asso. firm H. Gray Skelton, 1973; gen. counsel Vanguard Properties, Inc., 1973-75; partner firm Merrill & Dillon, 1975—. Mem. Ga., Am. bar assns., Order of the Coif. Home: 2665 Ridgemore Pl NW Atlanta GA 30318 Office: 2045 Peachtree Rd NE Atlanta GA 30309 Tel (404) 351-7200

DILWORTH, ROBERT HOLDEN, b. Evanston, Ill., May 8, 1942; A.B., Harvard U., 1963, LL.B., 1966. Admitted to Ill. bar, 1966, Calif. bar, 1972; mem. firm Baker & McKenzie, Chgo., 1966-71, San Francisco, 1971—. Mem. Bar Assn. San Francisco, State Bar Calif., Am. Bar Assn., Am. Soc. Internat. Law. Office: 555 California St Suite 3950 San Francisco CA 94104 Tel (415) 433-7600

DIM, JACOB, b. St. Paul, Feb. 26, 1918; student U. Minn., 1936-38; B.S. Law, St. Paul Coll. Law, 1940, LL.B. cum laude, 1946. Admitted to Minn. bar, 1942, U.S. Supreme Ct. bar, 1967; practiced in St. Paul, 1946-63; judge U.S. Bankruptcy Ct., St. Paul, 1963—; mem. faculties Fed. Jud. Center, Washington, 1966-68, U. Minn. Continuing Legal Edn., 1974-75, Practicing Law Inst. of N.Y., 1974-75. Mem. Minn. Gov's. Advisory Commn. on Vets'. Affairs, 1955-73; mem. Minn. Gov's. Advisory Commn. on Handicapped, 1965-74; v.p. Jewish Community Relations Council of Minn., 1973-75. Mem. Minn. State (chmn. com. bankruptcy 1972-73), Ramsey County (Minn.), Fed. (pres. Minn. chpt. 1976—) bar assns., Am. Judicature Soc., Recipient citation Bankruptcy Div. Administry. Office U.S. Cts., 1968, Minn. State Bar Assn. and U. Minn., 1974, 75, 76. Man of Year award Jewish War Vets, 1976; author: History of the United States District Court of Minnesota, 1976; contbr. articles to legal publs. Home: 1955 Oakdale St Apt 228 West Saint Paul MN 55118 Office 1-636 US Courthouse Saint Paul MN 55101 Tel (612) 725-7184

DI MENTO, FRANCIS JAMES, b. Boston, Mar. 30, 1927; A.B., Harvard, 1948, LL.B., 1951; Admitted to Mass. bar, 1951, U.S. Ct. Appeals bar 1st Circuit, 1953, 3d Circuit, 1976, 4th Circuit, 1971, 5th Circuit, 1973, U.S. Dist. Ct. bar Dist. Mass., 1952, Dist. Md., 1970, U.S. Tax Ct. bar, 1958, U.S. Supreme Ct. bar, 1965; asso. firm Nutter, McClennen & Fish, Boston, 1951-53; asst. U.S. atty. Dist. Mass., 1953-56; partner firm DiMento & Sullivan, Boston, 1956—. Mem. Boston Bar Assn. Home: 147 Hyslop Rd Brookline MA 02146 Office: 100 State St Boston MA 02109 Tel (617) 523-5253

DIMMITT, LAWRENCE ANDREW, b. Kansas City, Kans., July 20, 1941; B.A., Kans. State U., 1963, M.A., 1967; J.D., Washburn U., Topeka, 1968. Admitted to Kans. bar, 1968, Mo. bar, 1974, N.Y. bar, 1975; law clk. firm Stumbo & Stumbo, Topeka, 1966-67; atty. Southwestern Bell Telephone Co., Topeka, 1968-73, St. Louis, 1973-74; atty. AT&T, N.Y.C., 1974—. Mem. adminstrv. bd. United Meth. Ch., Morristown, N.J., 1976—. Mem. Am. Bar Assn., Phi Alpha Delta. Asso. editor: Washburn Law Jour., 1967-68. Office: 195 Broadway St New York City NY 10007 Tel (212) 393-3553

DIMOFF, RODERICK DIMITRE, b. Seattle, Aug. 18, 1931; B.A., U. Wash., 1952, LL.B., J.D., 1955. Admitted to Wash. bar, 1955, U.S. Dist. Ct. bar for Western Dist. Wash., 1959, U.S. Ct. Appeals bar, 9th Circuit, 1961; asso. firm Greive & Law, Seattle, 1957-63; individual practice law, Seattle, 1963—; adminstrv. law judge Wash. State Employment Security Dept., Seattle, 1971—; legis. bill drafting atty., Olympia, Wash., 1959-69; exec. sec. Wash. Legis. Com. on Indsl. Ins., 1966-67. Treas. Orthodox Cathedral of St. Spiridon, Orthodox Ch. in Am., Seattle, 1959-61, v.p., 1968-77; organizing mem. West Seattle Community Council, 1970-72; organizing mem. Chief Seattle Citizens Advisory Council on Edn., 1971-72. Mem. Wash. State Bar Assn., Am. Judicature Soc., Am. Fed. State, County, Municipal Employees, Assn. Wash. Adminstrv. Law Judges. Home: 10429 Fortieth Ave SW Seattle WA 98146 Office: Suite 606 Securities Bldg 1904 Third Ave Seattle WA 98101 Tel (206) 464-7095

DIMSEY, DENNIS JOHN, b. Washington, Mar. 10, 1943; LL.B., U. Md., 1968; A.B., U. Pa., 1965. Admitted to Md. bar, 1968, U.S. Supreme Ct. bar, 1976; legal officer U.S. Army Depot, Vietnam, 1969-70; atty. criminal sect., civil rights div. Dept. Justice, Washington, 1971-75, atty. appellate sect., 1975—. Recipient Spl. Commendation award Dept. Justice, 1974. Home: 235 G St SW Washington DC 20024 Office: Appellate Sect Civil Rights Div Dept Justice Washington DC 20530 Tel (202) 739-5187

DINEEN, JOHN KELLEY, b. Gardiner, Maine, Jan. 21, 1928; B.A., U. Maine, 1951; J.D., Boston U., 1954. Admitted to Maine bar, 1954, Mass. bar, 1954; partner firm Weston, Patrick & Stevens, Boston, 1954-67, Peabody & Arnold, Boston, 1967-70, Gaston Snow & Ely Bartlett, Boston, 1970—; spl. asst. atty. gen. Commonwealth of Mass, 1967-68. Trustee Cath. Charitable Bur. of Archdiocese of Boston, 1974—, Emmanuel Coll., 1975—. Mem. Boston, Mass., Am. bar assns., U. Maine Alumni Assn. (council, exec. com.). Home: 391 Nahant Rd Nahant MA 01908 Office: Gaston Snow & Ely Bartlett One Federal St Boston MA 02110 Tel (617) 426-4600

DINEEN, MARGUERITE OLIVE RIEDL, b. Milw., May 9, 1949; B.S. cum laude in Elec. Engring., Marquette U., 1971; J.D., 1974. Admitted to Wis. bar, 1974, Va. bar, 1975; law clk. firm Roland Wilde, Milw., 1972-74; adviser patents Office Naval Research, Field Patent Counsel, Dahlgren, Va., 1974-76; atty. adviser Naval Surface Weapons Center, Dahlgreu, 1976—. Mem. Am., Fed., Wis., Va. bar assns., Phi Alpha Delta. Home: 1201 C Potomac Dr Dahlgren VA 22448 Office: Legal Counsel Naval Surface Weapons Center Dahlgren Lab Dahlgren VA 22448 Tel (703) 663-7121

DINEEN, ROBERT EMMETT, b. Syracuse, N.Y., Aug. 12, 1903; LL.B., Syracuse U., 1924, LL.D. (hon.), 1967. Admitted to N.Y. bar, 1926, Wis. bar, 1952; asso. firm Bond, Schoeneck & King, Syracuse, N.Y., 1926-43; supt. ins. state N.Y., 1943-50; v.p. Northwestern Mut. Life Ins. Co., Milw., 1950-65, pres., 1966-67, chmn., 1967-68, chief exec. officer, 1965-68; cons. Nat. Assn. Ins. Commrs., Milw., 1968—. Mem. Am., Wis. bar assns. Contbr. articles and monographs to profl. jours. Home: 3909 N Murray Ave Shorewood WI 53211 Office: 633 W Wisconsin Ave Milwaukee WI 53203 Tel (414) 271-4464

DINEEN, WILLIAM CORNELIUS, b. Milw., June 4, 1922; student U. Notre Dame, 1941-43, 46; LL.B., Marquette U., 1948. Admitted to Wis. bar, 1948; individual practice law, Milw., 1948-73; partner Dineen & Alexander, Milw., 1973—; village atty. Village of River Hills (Wis.), 1955—. Mem. Am., Milw. bar assns., State Bar Wis., Motor Carrier Lawyers Assn. Home: 6128 N Bay Ridge Ave Whitefish Bay WI 53217 Office: 710 N Plankinton Ave Milwaukee WI 53203 Tel (414) 273-7410

DINGUS, LARRY DWAYNE, b. Appleton City, Mo., Aug. 10, 1934; B.S., U. Mo., 1956, LL.B., 1960. Admitted to Calif. bar, 1961; asso. Bohnert, Dingus & McCarthy, and predecessors, San Francisco, 1961-64, partner, 1964-67; partner firm Dingus, Haley & Boring, and predecessors, San Francisco, 1967—. Mem. Am., Calif., San Francisco bar assns., Internat. Assn. Ins. Counsel, Surety Claims Assn. No. Calif. Mng. editor U. Mo. Law Rev. 1959-60; contbr. articles to legal jours. Home: 1 Fawn Ct San Anselmo CA 94960 Office: 1 California St Suite 1760 San Francisco CA 94111 Tel (415) 391-0405

DINKELMEYER, KURT, b. Mineola, N.Y., Mar. 1, 1944; B.A., Allegheny Coll., 1966; J.D., U. Syracuse, 1969. Admitted to Mich. bar, 1970, N.Y. State bar, 1971, N.J. bar, 1972; atty. OEO, Kalamazoo, 1969-70; asso. firm Richard Duigan, N.Y.C., 1971-72, firm Fogarty & Wynee, N.Y.C., 1972-76; mem. firm Kurt Dinkelmeyer, East Orange, N.J., 1976—. Mem. Hudson County Bar Assn., N.Y. County Lawyers Assn. Home: 380 Mountain Rd Union City NJ 07087 Office: 7 Glenwood Ave East Orange NJ 07019 Tel (201) 677-9286

DINKELSPIEL, RICHARD COLEMAN, b. Oakland, Calif., Feb. 13, 1913; A.B., U. Calif. at Berkeley, 1934, J.D., 1937. Admitted to Calif. bar, 1937; individual practice law, Suisun, Calif., 1937-42; partner firm Dinkelspiel, Pelavin, Steefel Levitt, San Francisco, 1946—; city judge Suisun City, 1937-42; justice of peace, Suisun Twp., 1939-42; co-chmn. Gov.'s Commn. on Family, 1966, San Francisco Lawyers Com. for Urban Affairs, 1968-70; exec. commn. Lawyers Com. for Civil Rights under Law, 1968—. Fellow Am. Bar Assn.; mem. Bar Assn. San Francisco (pres. 1968), San Francisco Bar Found. (pres. 1971-73), State Bar Calif. (bd. govs. 1974-77, v.p. 1976-77), St. Thomas More Soc. San Francisco (pres. 1971). Home: PO Box 511 Kentfield CA 94904 Office: One Embarcadero Center 27th Floor San Francisco CA 94111 Tel (415) 391-3900

DINSE, JOHN MERRELL, b. Rochester, N.Y., June 26, 1925; A.B., U. Rochester, 1947; LL.B., Cornell U., 1950. Admitted to N.Y. bar, 1950, Vt. bar, 1951; asso. firm Edmunds, Austin & Wick; and predecessors, Burlington, Vt., 1950-57; partner firm Dinse, Allen & Erdmann, and predecessors, Burlington, 1957—; chmn. Vt. Jud. Nominating Bd., 1967-77. Mem. Lake Champlain Waterways Commn., 1962. Fellow Am. Bar Found.; mem. Am., Vt. (bd. mgrs. 1974—, pres. elect 1977), Chittenden County bar assns., Am. Judicature Soc. (dir. 1975—), Am. Soc. Hosp. Attys., No. New Eng. Def. Counsel Assn. (pres. 1971-72), Assn. Ins. Attys., Internat. Assn. Ins. Counsel, Def. Research Inst. (regional v.p. 1972-75, dir. 1975—), Am. Law Inst. Home: Harbor Rd Shelburne VT 05482 Office: 186 College St Burlington VT 05401 Tel (802) 864-5751

DIONNE, ARTHUR FRANCIS, b. Claremont, N.H., Feb. 11, 1937; B.Mgmt. Engr., Rensselaer Polytechnic Inst., 1959; J.D., Georgetown U., 1965. Admitted to Va. bar, 1965, Mass. bar, 1967; with Am. Cyanamid Co., Washington, 1962-65; partner firm Chapin, Neal & Dempsey, Springfield, Mass., 1965—. Mem. Recreation Study Com., Wilbraham, Mass., 1972; chmn. Playground and Recreation Commn., 1974—. Mem. Mass., Va., Hampden County bar assns. Home: 3 S Park Dr Wilbraham MA 01095 Office: 1387 Main St Springfield MA 01103 Tel (413) 736-5401

DIOTTE, ALFRED PETER, b. Newport, N.H., Apr. 16, 1925; B.S. in Bus. Adminstrn., Marquette U., Milw., 1950; J.D., U. Wis. at Madison, 1953; grad. advanced mgmt. program Harvard Bus. Sch., 1961. Admitted to Wis. bar, 1953; partner firm Fett, Murphy & Diotte, Janesville, Wis., 1953-54; with The Parker Pen Co., Janesville, 1954—, mem. adminstrv. staff, 1954-55, asst. to exec. v.p., 1955-56, 57-59, asst. sec., 1956-62, franchise adminstr., 1956-57, gen. counsel 1959-68, corp sec., 1962-68, v.p., adminstrn., sec. 1968—, dir., 1973—; dir. M & S BanCorp., Janesville, 1973—, Mchts. & Savs. Bank, Janesville, 1974—. Mem. adv. com. U. Wis. Rock County Campus, 1975; campaign chmn. United Way Rock County, 1975; nat. chmn. class agt. div. Ann. Marquette Fund, 1969-71. Mem. Am., Wis., Rock County bar assns. Recipient Bus. Adminstrn. Man of Year award Marquette U., 1976. Office: 219 E Court St Janesville WI 53545 Tel (608) 754-7711

DIPPEL, TIEMAN HENRY, JR., b. Brenham, Tex., Nov. 10, 1945; A.A., Blinn Jr. Coll., 1966; B.B.A., U. Tex., Austin, 1968, J.D., 1971; postgrad. Naval Justice Sch., 1971. Admitted to Tex. bar, 1971, U.S. Supreme Ct. bar, 1974; atty. JAGC, USN, 1971-72; chmn., chief exec. officer Breham Nat. Bank, 1972—; sec.-treas. Brenham Indsl. Found., 1972—; trustee Nat. Livestock Merchandising Inst., 1972—. Mem. Am., Tex. bar assns., Brazos Valley Bankers Assn. (pres. 1975-76), Tex. Law Rev. Assn., East Tex. C. of C. (dir. 1974—), Order of Coif, Chancellors Soc., Washington County (Tex.) Execs. (pres. 1975), Phi Delta Phi, Beta Gamma Sigma, Phi Kappa Phi, Phi Rho Pi. Contbr. article to legal jour. Tel (713) 836-4571

DIRKSMEYER, ANTON CARL, b. Quincy, Ill., June 9, 1922; B.A., Valparaiso U., 1949; J.D., So. Meth. U., 1951. Admitted to Tex. bar, 1951; atty. Allstate Ins. Co., 1952-58, Employers Ins. of Wasau, 1958—. Mem. Tex., Am., Dallas bar assns. Office: 7700 Carpenter Freeway Dallas TX 75247 Tel (214) 638-8830

DISABATINO, ARTHUR FRANK, b. Wilmington, Del., Mar. 24, 1938; A.B., U. Notre Dame, 1959; LL.B., Georgetown U., 1962. Admitted to Del. bar, 1962; asso. firm Killoran & Van Brunt, 1962-71; pub. defender New Castle County, Del., 1965-70; solicitor Town of Odessa, 1966-71, Delaware City, 1968-71, Newark Housing Authority, 1963-71; judge Del. Ct. of Common Pleas, 1971—. Mem. Del. Bicentennial Com., 1969-71; pres. Notre Dame Alumni Club, 1964-66, Deerhurst Civic Assn., 1971; bd. dirs. U.S. Jr. C. of C., 1969-70, Del. chpt. Nat. Multiple Sclerosis Soc., 1969—, Mary Campbell Center, 1972—. Mem. Am., Del. bar assns., Am. Judges Assn., Am. Judicature Soc., Jud. Conf. Del. Named hon. senator Jr. Chamber Internat., 1970, Young Man of Year of Del., 1971. Office Pub Bldg 1020 King St Wilmington DE 19801 Tel (302) 571-2410

DISANDRO, EDMOND A., b. Providence, Aug. 9, 1932; A.B magna cum laude, Providence Coll., 1955; J.D., Boston U., 1960. Admitted to R. I. bar, 1960; asso. firm Goldberg & Goldberg, Providence, 1960-61; sr. asso. counsel firm Kiernan, Connors, Kenyon & Wiley, Providence, 1961-64; partner firm Coia, Hirsch and DiSandro, Providence, 1964-66, DeSimone, Sammartino & DiSandro, Providence, 1966-70; individual practice law, Providence, 1970—. Exec. dir. Smithfield (R.I.) Indsl. Devel. Commn., 1969-70; town chmn. Smithfield Democratic Town Com., 1970-71; bd. dirs. R.I. Legal Services, Inc., 1971-73. Mem. Am. Arbitration Assn. (nat. panel arbitrators), R.I. (chmn. specialization com. 1969-70, 73—, judiciary com. 1975-76), Am., New Eng. bar assns., Am. Judicature Soc., Assn. Trial Lawyers Am. (treas. R.I. chpt. 1968-69), Northeastern Indsl. Developers Assn., Nat. Scholastic Honor Soc. Home: 6 Birch Rd Greenville RI 02828 Office: 1032 Indsl Bank Bldg Providence RI 02903 Tel (401) 521-4970

DISHAROON, JAMES DUDLEY, b. Vicksburg, Miss., Mar. 10, 1949; B.A., Miss. State U., 1970; J.D., U. Miss., 1972. Admitted to Miss. bar, 1972, Fed. bar, 1972; prosecutor intern 14th Circuit Dist., U. Miss. Law Sch., Oxford, 1972; asst. dist. atty. Miss. 14th Circuit Dist., 1973-75; mem. Miss. Ho. of Reps., 1976—; lectr. in field. Mem. Miss. Econ. Council. Mem. Miss. Cattlemen's Assn., Miss. Farm Bur. Fedn., Miss., Am. bar assns., Miss. Prosecutors Assn., Nat. Dist. Atty's Assn., Am. Judicature Soc., Miss. Trial Lawyers Assn., Am., Miss. criminal def. lawyers assns., Copiah County U. Miss. Alumni Assn. (v.p. 1976), Crystal Springs C. of C., Delta Theta Phi. Home: Pinehurst Circle Hazlehurst MS 39083 Office: W Gallatin St Hazlehurst MS 39083 Tel (601) 892-3171

DISICK, DAVID MARTIN, b. Bklyn., Mar. 21, 1940; B.A., Cornell U., 1960; J.D., U. Pa., 1964. Admitted to N.Y. state bar, 1965; law clk. to Judge So. Dist. N.Y., 1964-66; asso. firm Spears & Hill, N.Y.C., 1966-68, Skadden, Arps, Slate, Meagher & Flom, N.Y.C., 1968-70, Wolf, Popper, Ross, Wolf & Jones, N.Y.C., 1971-72; asso. firm Davis & Cox, N.Y.C., 1972-73, partner 1974—. Mem. Assn. Bar City N.Y., N.Y. State, Am. bar assns., Fed. Bar Council. Home: 1020 Park Ave New York City NY 10028 Office: One State St Plaza New York City NY 10004 Tel (212) 425-0500

DISLER, MICHAEL M., b. San Antonio, Nov. 6, 1943; B.S. in Bus. Adminstrn., Ind. U., 1965, J.D., 1971. Co-mgr. Kroger Co., Connersville, Ind., 1965-66; real estate agt. Shell Oil Co., Indpls., 1967-72; admitted to Ind. bar, 1971; individual practice law, Zionsville, Ind., 1972—; judge Zionsville Town Ct., 1973-74; pros. atty. Boone County (Ind.), 1975—. Mem. Am., Ind., Boone County (pres. 1975) bar assns. Home: RR1 POB 109 Zionsville IN 46077 Office: 1000 W Oak St Zionsville IN 46077 Tel (317) 873-4833

DISMUKES, CHARLES LEE, b. Union City, Tenn., July 10, 1933; B.A., Vanderbilt U., 1955, LL.B., 1957; LL.M., Columbia, 1958. Admitted to Tenn. bar, 1957, N.Y. bar, 1959; asso. firm Simpson, Thacher & Bartlett, N.Y.C., 1959-61, Shearman & Sterling, N.Y.C., 1961-65; partner firm Gassera & Hayes, N.Y.C., 1965—. Mem. Assn. Bar City N.Y. Home: 2 5th Ave New York NY 10011 Office: 30 Rockefeller Center New York NY 10020 Tel (212) 247-6800

DISPENZA, SAMUEL ANTHONY, JR., b. Jamestown, N.Y., Mar. 21, 1941; B.A., Syracuse U., 1963, LL.B., 1966. Admitted to N.Y. State bar, 1966; mem. firm Weiner & Lawrence, East Rochester, N.Y., 1973—. Mem. Monroe County, N.Y. State bar assns., N.Y. State Trial Lawyers Assn. Home: 11 Wincanton Dr Fairport NY 14450 Office: 248 W Commercial St East Rochester NY 14445 Tel (716) 586-6280

DISSEN, JAMES HARDIMAN, b. Pitts., Jan. 26, 1942; B.S., Wheeling Coll., 1963, M.B.A., Xavier U., 1966; J.D., Duquesne U., 1972. Admitted to Pa. bar, 1972, W.Va. bar, 1973, U.S. Supreme Ct. bar, 1976; dir. labor relations Columbia Gas Transmission Corp., Charleston, W.Va., 1973—; mgr. personnel Columbia Gas Pa., Inc., Uniontown, 1969-73. Mem. Am., Fed., Pa., W.Va., Allegheny County, Kanawha County bar assns., W.Va. State Bar, Delta Theta Phi. Home: 1 Wood Sedge Way Charleston WV 25302 Office: 1700 MacCorkle Ave SE Charleston WV 25314 Tel (304) 346-0951

DI STEPHAN, FREDERICK SALVATOR, b. Bklyn., Sept. 2, 1937; B.A., St. John's U., L.I., 1959, LL.B., 1962, J.D., 1973. Admitted to N.Y. State bar, 1963; asso. firms Gehrig, Ritter, Coffey & Stein, Hempstead, N.Y., 1963-65, Sprague, Dwyer, Aspland & Tobin, Mineola, N.Y., 1965-75, Joseph W. Conklin, Mineola, 1975—. Mem. Nassau County (N.Y.) Bar Assn. (chmn. com. profl. ethics 1972-76). Office: 222 Station Plaza N Mineola NY 11501 Tel (516) 248-0550

DITTMEIER, ANTHONY THEODORE, b. Louisville, Sept. 30, 1921; J.D., Boston Coll., 1950. Admitted to Mass. bar, 1951, Ohio bar, 1952; practiced in Cin., 1953—. Mem. Assn. Trial Lawyers Am., Ohio Acad. Trial Lawyers, Ohio Cin. bar assns. Home: 2375 Twigwood Ln Cincinnati OH 45237 Office: 2 W Benson St Cincinnati OH 45215 Tel (513) 761-0440

DITTMER, TERRANCE HAROLD, b. Quincy, Ill., Mar. 4, 1945; B.A., Western Ill. U., 1967; J.D., St. Louis U., 1971. Admitted to Mo. bar, 1971, D.C. bar, 1972, Fla. bar, 1976, also U.S. Tax Ct. bar; with ruling sect. IRS, 1972-73, atty., St. Louis, 1973-75, Orlando, Fla., 1975-77; mem. firm Young Turnbull & Linscott, Orlando, 1977—. Mem. Am. Bar Assn., Phi Delta Phi. Home: 620 Beverly Ave Altamonte Springs FL 32701

DI TUCCI, COSMO JOSEPH, b. Bklyn., Dec. 28, 1929; B.A., St. Johns U., 1951, J.D., 1953. Admitted to N.Y. bar, 1953; claim adjuster Allstate Ins. Co., Bklyn., 1954-55; asso. Joseph P. Imperato, Bklyn., 1955-60; partner firm DiTucci & DeBerardine, Bklyn., 1960—; instr. St. Francis Coll., Bklyn., 1972-73, 77; law sec. to Justice Frederic E. Hammer, Supreme Ct., Queens County, 1975-76. Pres., St. Mel's Parish Council, Flushing, 1969; active Christians and Jews United for Social Action, 1960-65; Republican county committeeman 26th Assembly Dist., 1965—; del. Rep. Jud. Conv. 11th Jud. Dist., 1966—; pres. Whitestone Rep. Club, 1967-69; chmn. Rep. County Com. 26th Assembly Dist., 1971—; Rep.-Conservative candidate U.S. Congress, 1970, for N.Y. City Council, 1974, for N.Y.C. Judiciary, 1976; bd. dirs., legal counsel Citizens for a Drug Free Am., Inc. Mem. Def. Research Inst., Inc., Queens County, Bklyn. bar assns., Am. Arbitration Assn., Columbian Lawyers Assn. Office: 32 Court St Brooklyn NY 11201 Tel (212) 237-9400

DIVER, JOHN RANDALL, b. S. Bend, Ind., Sept. 5, 1917; B.S., M.S., Mass. Inst. Tech.; J.D., Northwestern U. Admitted to Ill. bar, 1967; mem. staff Mass. Inst. Tech.; sr. project engr. Gen. Motors Corp.; sr. design engr. Boeing Airplane Co., McDonnell Aircraft Corp.; sr. scientist Borg-Warner Corp.; mem. firm Rummler & Snow, Chgo. Mem. Ill. Bar Assn., Chgo. Assn. Commerce and Industry. Office: 7 S Dearborn St Chicago IL 60603 Tel (312) 236-3418

DIX, RAYMOND VICTOR, b. Cleve., Sept. 26, 1934; A.B., DePauw U., 1956; J.D., Akron U., 1962. Admitted to Ohio bar, 1962; co-publisher Daily Record, Wooster, Ohio, 1965—. Trustee Westminster Ch., Wooster. Mem. Ohio Newspaper Assn., Ohio U.P.I. Editors (pres. 1976-77), Ohio, Wayne County bar assns., Phi Alpha Delta. Office: 212 E Liberty St Wooster OH 44691 Tel (216) 264-1125

DIXON, ALBERT LERUE, III, b. Norfolk, Va., Dec. 14, 1944; B.S., Stephen F. Austin State U., 1967; J.D., Baylor U., 1970. Admitted to Tex. bar, 1970, U.S. Supreme Ct. bar, 1975; asso. firm Box & Adamson, Jacksonville, Tex., 1971-73; individual practice law, Jacksonville, 1973-76; partner Ament & Dixon, Jacksonville, 1976—; dist. atty. 2d Jud. Dist. Tex., 1973—; faculty Nat. Coll. Dist. Attys., 1975; mem. senate com. Dist. Attys. Tex., 1974-75, state and fed. law enforcement com., 1976. Chmn., Thunderbird dist. Boy Scouts Am., 1971, chmn. Ducks Unlimited, Jacksonville, 1976; vestryman Trinity Episc. Ch., Jacksonville, 1975. Mem. Am., Cherokee County (pres. 1975-76) bar assns., Nat., Tex. dist. attys. assns., Tex. Trial Lawyers Assn., Cherokee Pistol League (pres. 1975-76). Home: Route 5 Peeble Beach Jacksonville TX 75766 Office: 217 E Commerce St Jacksonville TX 75766 Tel (214) 586-3561

DIXON, JOHN MORRIS, JR., b. Hopkinsville, Ky., Apr. 3, 1940; B.S., U. Ky., 1962, J.D., 1965. Admitted to Ky. bar, 1965, Ark., bar, 1968; with JAGC, U.S. Army, 1965-68; asso. firm Bridges, Young, Matthews & Davis, Pine Bluff, Ark., 1968-70; partner firm Turner & Dixon, Hopkinsville, 1970—; U.S. magistrate Western Dist. Ky, Middle Dist. Tenn., 1974—. Bd. dirs. Pennyroyal Regional Mental Health/Mental Retardation Center, Hopkinsville, 1972—, chmn. bd., 1976. Mem. Am., Ky., Christian County (v.p. 1976—) bar assns., U.S. Council Magistrates, Nat. Conf. Spl. Ct. Judges. Home: 511 Country Club Ln Hopkinsville KY 42240 Office: 521 Weber St Hopkinsville KY 42240 Tel (502) 886-9453

DIXON, MARDEN GUY, b. Salt Lake City, Oct. 24, 1941; M.D., U. Utah, 1961, J.D., 1965. Admitted to D.C. bar, 1973, U.S. Circuit Ct. of Appeals bar, 1969, U.S. Supreme Ct. bar, 1972, U.S. Ct. of Claims bar, 1974; asso. firm Howard & Lewis, Provo, Utah, 1965-66; individual practice law, Salt Lake City, 1966-72; asst. chief legal medicine sect. Armed Forces Inst. Pathology, Washington, 1972-74; individual practice law, Washington and Silver Spring, Md., 1974—; lectr. Brigham Young U., Provo, Utah, 1965-66; asso. lectr. George Washington U., 1972—; adj. prof. law Georgetown U., 1972-74. Troop leader Boy Scouts Am., 1965-66. Mem. Am., D.C. (co-chmn. med. malpractice com.) bar assns., Am., Utah trial lawyers' assns., Am. Acad. Forensic Scis., Am. Coll. Legal Medicine, AMA, Dist. of Columbia Med. Soc. Author: Legal Medicine, 1967; Drug Product Liability, 1974; contbr. articles in field to profl. jours. Home: 1511 Vivian Pl Silver Spring MD 20902 Office: 803 1725 K St Washington DC 20036 Tel (301) 649-2439

DIXON, ROBERT BERKELEY, b. Toledo, Nov. 30, 1928; B.A. cum laude, U. Toledo, 1950; J.D., U. Mich., 1953. Admitted to Mich. bar, 1953, Ohio bar, 1953, U.S. Supreme Ct. bar, 1960; asst. staff judge adv. James Connally AFB, Waco, Tex., 1954-56; asso. firm Fetterman & Dixon, Toledo, 1956-64, firm Dixon & Schrader, Toledo, 1964—; staff mem. Toledo Bd. Realtors License Sch., 1959—. Mem. Bd. Zoning Appeals Sylvania Twp. (Ohio), 1960-64, chmn. 1964; mem. City of Toledo Citizens Adv. Capital Improvement and Fin. Com., 1961; pres. W. Toldeo Exchange Club, 1960. Mem. Ohio, Toledo, Lucas County (v.p.) bar assns. Home: 5763 Little Rd Sylvania OH 43560 Office: 4024 Lewis Ave Toledo OH 43612 Tel (419) 476-8686

DIXON, STEWART STRAWN, b. Evanston, Ill., Nov. 5, 1930; B.A., Yale, 1952; J.D., U. Mich., 1955. Admitted to Ill. bar, 1957, U.S. Supreme Ct. bar, 1974; mem. firm Kirkland, Ellis, Hodson, Chaffetz & Masters, Chgo., 1957-67; partner firm Wildman, Harrold, Allen & Dixon, Chgo., 1967—; dir. Lord Abbett Managed Funds. Vice pres., trustee Chgo. Hist. Soc., 1972—; trustee Children's Meml. Hosp., Chgo. Zool. Soc.; bd. dirs., past pres. Infant Welfare Soc. Chgo. Mem. Am., Ill., Chgo. bar assns., Am. Judicature Soc., Law Club Chgo., Legal Club Chgo., Soc. Trial Lawyers, Am. Law Inst. Home: 734 E Westminster St Lake Forest IL 60045 Office: One IBM Plaza Chicago IL 60611 Tel (312) 222-0400

DIXON, WALLACE WADE, b. Dunn, N.C., Apr. 8, 1943; B.S. in Bus. Adminstrn., U. N.C., 1965; J.D., Wake Forest U., 1972. Asso. firm Twiford & Abbott, Elizabeth City, N.C., 1972-73; asso. firm Homesley, Jones Gaines & Dixon and predecessors, Statesville, N.C., 1973-76, partner, 1976—. Mem. N.C. State, Iredell County bar assns., N.C. Acad. Trial Lawyers, Masons, Elizabeth City, Statesville Jaycees, Kiwanis. Home: 603 Old Farm Rd Statesville NC 28677 Office: 202-208 Water St PO Box 149 Statesville NC 28677 Tel (704) 873-2172

DIXON, WILLIAM CORNELIUS, b. Dexter, N.Y., July 1, 1904; A.B., U. Mich., 1926, J.D., 1928. Admitted to Ohio bar, 1928, U.S. Supreme Ct. bar, 1946, Calif. bar, 1948; asso. firm Holliday, Grossman & McAfee, Cleve., 1928-32; asst. dir. law City of Cleve., 1932-33; individual practice law, Cleve., 1933-44; judge Ohio Supreme Ct., 1938; spl. asst. U.S. Atty. Gen., Div. Antitrust, Washington, 1944-46, Los Angeles, 1946-54; asst. atty. gen. State of Calif., 1959-63; individual practice law, Los Angeles, 1954-59, 63—. Mem. constl. commn. United Ch. of Christ, 1957-60; moderator Congl. Conf. So. Calif. and S.W., 1960-61. Mem. Calif., Los Angeles bar assns. Home: 1188 Romney Dr Pasadena CA 91105 Office Suite 930 417 S Hill St Los Angeles CA 90013 Tel (213) 628-7755

DIXON, WRIGHT TRACY, JR., b. Raleigh, N.C., Oct. 7, 1921; B.A., Duke, 1946; J.D., U. N.C., 1951. Admitted to N.C. bar, 1951; individual practice law, Raleigh, 1951-55; partner firm Bailey Dixon Wooten McDonald & Fountain, Raleigh, 1955—. Chmn. bd. adjustment City of Raleigh; trustee, mem. exec. com. So. Sem. Jr. Coll., 1960-70. Mem. Wake County (pres.), N.C. (acting sec. 1952) bar assns. Home: 414 Marlowe Rd Raleigh NC 27602 Office: PO Box 2246 Raleigh NC 27602 Tel (919) 828-0731

DIXSON, JOHN JOSEPH, b. Bklyn., Aug. 24, 1914; B.S., St. John's U., 1939, J.D., 1939. Admitted to N.Y. bar, 1940, U.S. Supreme Ct. bar, 1949; mem. legal dept. Travelers Ins. Co., 1936-42; spl. agt., asst. insp. FBI, 1942-67; individual practice law, Keene Valley, N.Y., 1967—; town justice Ct. Spl. Sessions, 1969—. Pres. Town of Keene Sch. Bd., 1970-74; bd. dirs. Keene Valley Hosp., 1969-74, Keene Valley Fire Dept., 1968—. Mem. N.Y. State, Essex County (dir.) magistrates assns., N.Y. State, Essex County bar assns. Home and Office: Keene Valley NY 12943 Tel (518) 576-9878

DOANE, JEFFREY CHARLES, b. N.Y.C., June 8, 1940; B.A., St. Bernard's Coll., 1962; J.D., DePaul U., 1972. Admitted to Ill. bar, 1972, U.S. Supreme Ct. bar, 1976; asst. counsel Ill. Dept. Mental Health, Chgo., 1972-73; dir. legal services Ill. Drug Abuse Program, Chgo., 1972-75; legal counsel Ill. Dept. Corrections, Chgo., 1975—; cons. White House Office on Drug Abuse Prevention, 1973-74; faculty mem. Ill. Inst. Continuing Legal Edn., 1976—. Mem. Am., Ill. State, Chgo. bar assns., Chgo. Council Lawyers. Contbr. articles to legal jours. Home: 210 E Pearson St Chicago IL 60611 Office: 160 N LaSalle St Chicago IL 60601 Tel (312) 793-3017

DOBBS, (CHARLES) EDWARD, b. Richmond, Va., July 15, 1949; A.B., Davidson Coll., 1971, J.D., Vanderbilt U., 1974. Admitted to Ga. bar, 1974; asso. firm Huie, Ware, Sterne, Brown & Ide and predecessors, Atlanta, 1974—. Vol. parole atty. City of Atlanta (Ga.), 1974—. Mem. State Bar Ga. (sec. sect. bankruptcy law 1976-77), Am., Atlanta bar assns., Order of Coif, Omicron Delta Kappa. Articles editor Vanderbilt Law Rev., 1974. Home: 12 Surry County Pl Atlanta GA 30318 Office: 1200 Standard Fed Savs Bldg Atlanta GA 30303 Tel (404) 522-8700

DOBBS, DAN BYRON, b. Ft. Smith, Ark., Nov. 8, 1932; B.A., U. Ark., 1956, LL.B., 1956; LL.M., U. Ill., 1961, J.S.D., 1966. Admitted to Ark. bar, 1956; partner firm Dobbs, Pryor & Dobbs, Ft. Smith, 1956-60; asst. prof. law U. N.C., Chapel Hill, 1966-74, Aubrey L. Brooks prof. law, 1975—; vis. prof. U. Tex., Austin, summer 1962, U. Minn., 1966-67, Cornell U., 1968-69. Author: Remedies, Damages, Equity, Restitution, 1973; Problems in Remedies, 1974; contbr. articles to law revs. Home: 306 Spruce Chapel Hill NC 27514 Office: Sch Law U NC Chapel Hill NC 27514 Tel (919) 933-5106

DOBBS, WILLIAM FISHER, JR., b. Charleston, W.Va., Apr. 26, 1948; B.A. in Polit. Sci., W.Va. U., 1970, J.D., 1973. Admitted to W.Va. bar, 1973; asso. firm Jackson, Kelly, Holt & O'Farrell, Charleston, 1973—. Mem. W.Va. Bar, Am., W.Va. bar assns., Order of Coif. Editor W.Va. Law Rev., 1972-73. Home: 611 Fort Hill Dr Charleston WV 25314 Office: 1 Valley Sq Charleston WV 25314 Tel (304) 345-2000

DOBIN, EDWARD I., b. Binghamton, N.Y., Jan. 30, 1936; B.S. in Econs., Franklin and Marshall Coll., 1957; LL.B., U. Pa., 1960. Admitted to Pa. bar, 1961, U.S. Supreme Ct. bar, 1975; asso. firm Curtin and Heefner, Morrisville, Pa., 1960-66, partner firm, 1967—. Trustee Adath Israel Congregation, Trenton, N.J., 1972—. Mem. Am., Pa. Bucks County (dir. 1971-72, treas. 1973-74) bar assns. Home: RD 1 Woodhill Rd Newtown PA 18940 Office: 250 N Pennsylvania Ave Morrisville PA 19067 Tel (215) 736-2521

DOBKIN, JAMES ALLEN, b. N.Y.C., Sept. 9, 1940; B.Ch.E., Poly. Inst. Bklyn., 1961; J.D., N.Y. U., 1964; LL.M., Georgetown U., 1968. Admitted to N.Y. State bar, 1965, D.C. bar, 1969, U.S. Supreme Ct. bar, 1968; mem. Office of Gen. Counsel, U.S. Army Materiel Command, Washington, 1965-68; asso. firm Arnold & Porter, Washington, 1968-73, partner, 1973—; atty. advisor to Pres.'s Commn. on Govt. Procurement, Washington, 1972-73. Mem. Am., Fed. bar assns. Mng. editor N.Y. U. Law Rev., 1963-64; contbr. articles to legal jours. Home: 8810 Fernwood Rd Bethesda MD 20034 Office: 1229 19th St NW Washington DC 20036 Tel (202) 872-6801

DOBROVIR, WILLIAM AARON, b. N.Y.C., Oct. 25, 1933; A.B. with honors, Trinity Coll., 1957; LL.B. cum laude, Harvard U., 1957. Admitted to N.Y. bar, 1958, D.C. bar, 1960, U.S. Supreme Ct. bar, 1966; mem. staff internat. tax program Law Sch., Harvard U., Cambridge, Mass., 1958-59; mem. adv. task force on taxation to Republic of Colombia, S.Am., 1959; asso. firm Covington and Burling, Washington, 1959-68; adj. prof. law Howard U., Washington, 1968-69; practice law, Washington, 1970—; staff dir. D.C. Com. on Adminstrn. of Justice under Emergency Conditions, 1968-69; cons. AID, 1963, Nat. Commn. on Causes and Prevention of Violence, 1969. Mem. Fed., Am. bar assns., Washington Inst. Fgn. Affairs, Phi Beta Kappa. Fulbright scholar, Chile, 1957-58; co-author books, articles, revs. in legal publs. Office: 2005 L St NW Washington DC 20036 Tel (202) 785-8919

DOCKING, GEORGE RICHARD, b. Topeka, Feb. 10, 1931; B.B.A., U. Kans., 1952, J.D., 1957. Admitted to Kans. bar, 1957, U.S. Supreme Ct. bar, 1962; asso. firm Collins, Hughes, Martin & Pringle, Wichita, Kans., 1957, Rice, Sullivart & Loughborn, Kansas City, Kans., 1958-60; partner firm Loughborn & Docking, Kansas City, 1961-74, Docking & Russell, 1975—; probate judge pro tem Wyandotte County (Kans.), 1960-64, pub. adminstr., 1960-70; vol. atty. Interstate Oil Compact, Oklahoma City, 1962-64. Mem. Kansas City C. of C. (dir. 1968-70), Phi Delta Phi. Office: 430 Brotherhood Bldg Kansas City KS 66101 Tel (913) 321-1400

DOCKRY, JOHN JAMES, b. Kewaunee, Wis., Dec. 22, 1930; B.S., U. Notre Dame, 1952; M.B.A., Ind. U., 1956; LL.D. Fordham U., 1966. Admitted to N.Y. State bar, 1966, Fed. So. and Eastern Dists. N.Y. bars, 1973, Calif. bar, 1976; asst. mgr. tex dept. Pfizer Internat. Inc., 1964-68; mgr. internat. banking and taxation Gulf & Western Industries, Inc., N.Y.C., 1968-72; sr. trial atty. Criminal Def. div. Legal Aid Soc., N.Y.C., 1972-76; individual practice law, N.Y.C., 1976—. Mem. Kings County Criminal, N.Y. State, N.Y.C. bar assns. Office: 155 W 68th St New York City NY 10023 Tel (212) 877-7503

DOCTER, CHARLES ALFRED, b. Hamburg, Germany, Aug. 5, 1931; B.A. magna cum laude, Kenyon Coll., 1953; J.D., U. Chgo., 1956. Admitted to Ohio bar, 1956, D.C., Md. bars, 1959; aide Senator Paul H. Douglas of Ill., 1953-54; individual practice law, Washington, 1959-66; sr. partner firm Docter, Docter & Salus, Washington, 1967—; del. Md. Ho. of Dels., Annapolis, 1967—. Home: 9810 Hillridge Dr Kensington MD 20795 Office: 1707 H St NW Washington DC 20006 Tel (202) 298-9090

DODD, LAWRENCE ROE, b. Alexandria, La., Oct. 17, 1944; B.A., La. State U., 1966, J.D., 1972. Admitted to La. bar, 1973; research asst. Inst. Continuing Legal Edn., La. State U., Baton Rouge, 1971-72; asso. firm Kizer & Kizer, Baton Rouge, 1973-75, partner, 1975-76; individual practice law, Baton Rouge, 1976; partner firm Dodd & Achée, Baton Rouge, 1976—; instr. Am. Inst. Banking, Baton Rouge, 1975—. Mem. Am., La., Baton Rouge bar assns., Am. Trial Lawyers Assn. Editor: (with G.L. Boland) Recent Developments in the Law of Maritime Torts, 1972; contbr. La. Law Rev. Home: 1810 Monterrey Blvd Baton Rouge LA 70815 Office: 4744 Jamestown Dr Baton Rouge LA 70808 Tel (504) 932-3100

DODDO, MICHAEL JOHN, b. Hazelton, Pa., Aug. 18, 1946; B.A., U. Miami, 1968, M.Ed., 1969, J.D., 1972. Admitted to Fla. bar, 1972; asst. fed. pub. defender City of Miami (Fla.), 1972—. Mem. Am., Fla. bar assns. Exec. editor U. Miami Barrister, 1971-72. Tel (305) 350-4391

DODGE, EMILY P., b. Madison, Wis., Feb. 18, 1915; B.A., Swarthmore Coll., 1936; M.A., U. Wis., 1938, J.D., 1943; admitted to Wis. bar, 1943; practiced in Madison; asso. firm Roberts, Roe & Boardman, 1943-46; asst. prof. Law Sch. U. Wis., 1950-56; exec. sec. Wis. Jud. Council, 1959-61; hearing examiner Worker's Compensation Div. State Wis., 1961—. Pres., Altrusa Club Madison, 1956-57. Mem. Dane County, Wis. State bar assns. Contbr. articles to legal jours. Office: 201 E Washington Ave Madison WI 53701 Tel (608) 266-1340

DODSON, JOEL EUGENE, b. Douglasville, Ga., Oct. 5, 1947; B.A. in History, Emory U., 1969, J.D., 1973. Admitted to Ga. bar, 1973; individual practice law, Douglasville, 1974—. Home: 8750 Bowden St Douglasville GA 30134 Office: 8486 Bowden St Douglasville GA 30134 Tel (404) 949-1666

DODSON, RAYMOND GUERRANT, b. S. Charleston, W.Va., Mar. 30, 1947; B.A., Hempden-Sydney Coll., 1969; J.D., W.Va. U., 1972. Admitted to W.Va. bar, 1972; partner firm Dodson & Deutsch, Charleston, W.Va., 1972—; hearing examiner Workmens Compensation, 1973-75; counsel minority leader W.Va. Ho. of Dels., 1975-77. Mem. Am., W.Va. bar assns. Home: 406 Rock Holly Rd Charleston WV 25314 Office: 910 Commerce Sq Charleston WV 25301 Tel (304) 342-6107

DODSON, WILLIAM PEYTON, b. Columbus, Miss., Dec. 10, 1940; B.A., Miss. State U., 1962; J.D., U. Miss., 1970. Admitted to Miss. bar, 1970; law clk. Orma R. Smith, U.S. Dist. Ct. No. Dist. Miss., 1970-71; asso. firm Liston & Upshaw, Winona, Miss., 1971-72; individual practice law, Oxford, Miss., 1972-75; partner firm Dodson, Kelly & Butts, Oxford, 1975—; magistrate U.S. Dist. Ct. western div. No. Dist. Miss., 1972—. Mem. Miss., Am. Fed. bar assns. Home: POB 525 Oxford MS 38655 Office: POB 1084 Oxford MS 38655 Tel (601) 234-4712

DOGGETT, JOHN J., JR., b. Corinth, Miss., June 30, 1919; B.C.S., Benjamin Franklin U., 1943; LL.B., So. Law U. (now Memphis State U.), 1948. Admitted to Tenn. bar, 1948; asso. firm Armstrong Allen Braden Goodman McBride & Prewitt, and predecessor, Memphis, 1950-55, mem., 1955—; agt. IRS, Washington and Nashville, 1948-50. Fellow Am. Coll. Probate Counsel; mem. Am., Fed., Tenn. (past chmn. taxation sect.), Memphis, Shelby County bar assns. Home: 4298 Woodcrest Dr Memphis TN 38111 Office: Armstrong Allen Braden Goodman McBride & Prewitt One Commerce Sq Memphis TN 38103 Tel (901) 523-8211

DOGGETT, KNIGHT EDWARD, b. Shreveport, La., Oct. 6, 1937; B.A., La. Coll., 1959; J.D., La. State U., 1963. Admitted to La. bar, 1964; mem. firm Gravel & Doggett, and predecessors, 1965-69, Doggett & deLaunay, 1969 (all Alexandria, La.); individual practice law, Alexandria, 1970—; spl. counsel to Atty. Gen. La., Baton Rouge, 1964-65. Mem. Rapides Parish (La.) Democratic Com., 1966-70. Mem. Am., La., Alexandria bar assns., Am., La. State trial lawyers assns. Home: 4807 Waverly Blvd Alexandria LA 71301 Office: 720 Jackson St Alexandria LA 71301 Tel (318) 448-0211

DOGGETT, WENDELL JESSE, b. Council Grove, Kans., Jan. 5, 1920; B.A., U. Okla., 1941, LL.B., 1947; LL.M., So. Meth. U., 1963. Admitted to Okla. bar, 1947, Tex. bar, 1959, Kans. bar, 1960; mem. firm Doggett, Doggett & Doggett, Ponca City, Okla., 1947; atty. Magnolia Petroleum Co., Oklahoma City, 1948-56, Dallas, 1956-59; gen. atty. Anadarko Prodn. Co., Liberal, Kans., 1959-60; asst. sec. Panhandle Eastern Pipe Line Co., Kansas City, Mo., 1960-68, gen. atty., Kansas City, 1960-68, gen. atty. Panhandle Eastern Pipe Line Co. and Trunkline Gas Co., Houston, 1968—, v.p., gen. atty., 1975—; dir. Nat. Helium Corp., Kansas City and Houston, 1961-70, 75—, v.p., 1961-67, sec., 1966—. Mem. adminstrv. bd. Chapelwood United Methodist Ch., Houston, 1970-76. Mem. Mid-Continent Oil and Gas Assn., So. Gas Assn., Okla., Tex. (chmn. corporate counsel sect. 1975-76), Kans., Houston, Fed. Power, Am. bar assns., Order of Coif. Phi Delta Phi. Contbr. articles to profl. jours. Home: 12334 Boheme St Houston TX 77024 Office: PO Box 1642 Houston TX 77001 Tel (713) 664-3401

DOHENY, DONALD ALOYSIUS, b. Milw., Apr. 20, 1924; student Notre Dame U., 1942-43; B.M.E., Marquette U., 1947; J.D., Harvard, 1949; postgrad. in indsl. engring. and bus., Washington U., St. Louis, 1950-56. Admitted to Wis. bar, 1949, Mo. bar, 1949, U.S. Supreme Ct. bar, 1970; asso. firm Igoe, Carroll & Keefe, St. Louis, 1949-50; individual practice law, St. Louis, 1950—; lectr. bus. orgn. and adminstrn. Washington U., 1950-74. Mem. Am., Mo., Wis. bar assns., Am. Mktg. Assn. St. Louis (pres.). Home: 10906 Conway Rd Frontenac Saint Louis MO 63131 Office: 2324 Weldon Pkwy Saint Louis MO 63141 Tel (314) 569-3600 also 408 Olive St Suite 400 Saint Louis MO 63102 Tel (314) 231-8000

DOHN, GEORGE THOMAS, b. Chillicothe, Mo., Nov. 6, 1935; A.A.S., Yakima Valley Coll., 1959; B.B.A., U. Wash., 1961, LL.B., J.D., 1963. Admitted to Wash. bar, 1963; asso. firm Tunstall & Hettinger, Yakima, Wash., 1963-65; partner Tunstall, Hettinger & Dohn, 1966-72, McArdle, Dohn, Talbott & Campbell, and predecessor, Yakima, 1973—; arbitrator Am. Arbitration Assn.; city atty. Ellensburg (Wash.), 1964—, Union Gap (Wash.), 1973-74. Bd. dirs., legal counsel Spring Acres Group Home, Inc., 1969-76; bd. dirs., legal cons. Planned Parenthood Assn., Yakima, 1965-75; bd. dirs. Yakima County Young Republicans, 1963-65; adv. bd. Wash. Criminal Justice Edn. and Tng. Center, 1973-74; legal adv. bd. Wash. Found. for Handicapped, 1975—. Mem. Am., Wash., Yakima County bar assns., Wash. Assn. Municipal Attys. (pres. 1972-73), Nat. Inst. Municipal Law Officers, Wash. Govtl. Lawyers Assn., Wash. Assn. Def. Counsel, Def. Research Inst., Phi Theta Kappa, Phi Delta Phi. Home: 506 N 63d Ave Yakima WA 98908 Office: 307 N 3d St Suite 1 Yakima WA 98901 Tel (509) 575-7501

DOI, MASATO, b. Paauhau, Hawaii, Feb. 4, 1921; B.A., Columbia, 1947, LL.B., 1950, J.D., 1970. Admitted to Hawaii bar, 1951; asso. firm Tsukiyama & Yamaguchi, Honolulu, 1951-54; individual practice law, Honolulu, 1955-58; partner firm Doi, Yamada & Shinsato, Honolulu, 1959-65; judge lst Hawaii Circuit Ct., 1966—; mem. Hawaii Territorial Ho. of Reps., 1954-56; mem. Honolulu City Council, 1957-64, chmn., 1960-64. Mem. Hawaii State, Am. bar assns., Jud. Council Hawaii (chmn. com. on criminal law revision 1966-72, Liberty Bell award 1974). Home: 4874 Poola St Honolulu HI 96821 Office: Judiciary Bldg Honolulu HI 96813 Tel (808) 538-6377

DOKE, MARSHALL J., JR., b. Wichita Falls, Tex., June 9, 1934; B.A. magna cum laude, Hardin-Simmons U., 1956; LL.B. magna cum laude, So. Meth. U., 1959. Admitted to Tex. bar, 1959; asso. firm Thompson, Knight, Wright & Simmons, Dallas, 1959, 62-65; founding partner firm Rain Harrell Emery Young & Doke, Dallas, 1965—; gen. counsel Army Contract Adjustment Bd., Washington, 1960-62; gen. counsel Republican Party Tex., 1976—; lectr. So. Meth. U., Dallas, 1965—. Pres. Hope Cottage—Children's Bur., Inc., Dallas, 1969-70; bd. dirs. Dallas Theater Center, 1976—. Mem. Dallas, Tex., Fed., Am. (chmn. sect. pub. contract law 1969-70, mem. ho. of dels, 1970-72, 74—) bar assns., So. Meth. U. Law Alumni Assn. (pres. 1976—). Editor: Am. Bar Assn.'s ann. Developments in Government Contract Law, 1975—. Office: 4200 Republic Bank Tower Dallas TX 75201 Tel (214) 741-1021

DOKSON, ROBERT NEIL, b. Bklyn., Oct. 17, 1944; A.B., Brown U., 1966; J.D., U. Chgo., 1969; LL.M., Harvard, 1972. Admitted to Ga., U.S. Dist. Ct., U.S. Ct. Appeals 5th Circuit bars, 1970, U.S. Supreme Ct. bar, 1974; staff atty. Atlanta Legal Aid Soc., Inc., 1969-71, dep. dir., 1972-74, exec. dir., 1974—; teaching fellow Harvard, 1971-72. Mem. Am., Ga., Atlanta bar assns., Nat. Legal Aid and Defender Assn. Home: 1195 Zimmer Dr NE Atlanta GA 30306 Office: 10 Pryor St Atlanta GA 30303 Tel (404) 577-5260

DOLAN, JAMES BOYLE, JR., b. Memphis, Aug. 1, 1944; A.B., Boston Coll., 1966; J.D., Cornell U., 1969. Admitted to Mass. bar, 1969, U.S. Dist. Ct. bar for Dist. Mass., 1971; asso. firm Badger, Sullivan, Kelley & Cole, Boston, 1969-70, 72—; arbitrator Am. Arbitration Assn., 1975—. Mem. Am., Mass. (arbitrator Fee Disputes Tribunal 1974—, mem. ethics com. 1976—), Boston bar assns., Res. Officers Assn. Office: 84 State St Boston MA 02109 Tel (617) 523-3400

DOLAN, JAMES TIMOTHY, b. St. Louis, July 24, 1927; B.S., St. Louis U., 1950, J.D., 1961. Admitted to Mo. bar, 1962; claims atty. Farmers Ins. Group, St. Louis, 1962-71; legal investigator Mo. Div. Ins., St. Louis, 1971-75; staff atty. Hartford Ins. Group, St. Louis, 1975—. Vol., Cerebral Palsy Assn., 1965-66. Mem. Am. Judicature Assn., Mo. Bar Assn. Home: 1200 Gilbert St St Louis MO 63119 Office: Tel (314) 567-2600

DOLAN, JAMES VINCENT, b. Washington, Nov. 11, 1938; A.B., Georgetown U., 1960, LL.B., 1963. Admitted to Fed. bar, 1964; law clk. to judge U.S. Ct. Appeals, D.C. Circuit, 1963-64; asso. firm Steptoe & Johnson, Washington, 1964-70, partner, 1971—. Mem. Am., D.C., D.C. Jr. (chmn. spl. com. reformation superior ct. 1968) bar assns., Barristers, Counsellors. Contbr. articles to legal jours. Home: 10229 Seven Locks Rd Potomac MD 20854 Office: 1250 Connecticut Ave Washington DC 20036 Tel (202) 223-4800

DOLAN, LOUIS EDWARD, b. Youngstown, Ohio, Feb. 28, 1920; B.A., Youngstown U., 1943; LL.B., Case Western Reserve U., 1947. Admitted to Minn. bar, 1971, Ohio bar, 1948; asso. firm Andrews, Hadden & Putnam, Cleve., 1947-53; with Nationwide Mut. Ins. Co. and sudsidiaries, Columbus, Ohio, 1954-57, The Ohio Co., Columbus, 1957-62; exec. v.p., gen. mgr. Nationwide Corp., Columbus, 1962[65; with Gamble-Skogmo, Inc., Mpls., 1966—, now vice chmn. bd., gen. counsel, dir., co-chmn. exec. com., also pres. and chief exec. officer Gamble's life and casualty ins. ops., dir. Am. Retail Fedn., Washington. Home: 1420 Bohn's Point Rd Wayzata MN 55391 Office: 5100 Gamble Dr Minneapolis MN 55416 Tel (612) 374-6243

DOLBEARE, ROBERT LORING, b. Richmond, Va., Oct. 26, 1936; B. Mgmt. Engring., Rensselaer Poly. Inst., 1958; LL.B., U. Va., 1965. Admitted to Va. bar, 1965; law Clk. U.S. Dist. Ct. Eastern Dist. Va., 1965-66; asso. firm Hunton, Williams, Gay, Powell & Gibson, Richmond, 1966-70; asst. county atty. County of Henrico, Va., 1970-74; partner firm Obenshain, Hinnant, Dolbeare & Beale, Richmond, 1970—; adj. asst. prof. law U. Richmond, 1975—. Mem. bd. mgmt. South Richmond-Chesterfield YMCA, 1972-76; bd. visitors Madison Coll., 1976—. Mem. Am., Va., Richmond bar assns., Assn. Trial Lawyers Am., Va. Trial Lawyers Assn. Home: 8800 Jahnke Rd Richmond VA 23235 Office: 1 N 5th St Richmond VA 23219 Tel (804) 643-3512

DOLE, RICHARD FAIRFAX, JR., b. Lowell, Mass., July 12, 1936; A.B. magna cum laude, Bates Coll., 1958; LL.B. with distinction, Cornell U., 1961, LL.M., 1963; S.J.D., U. Mich., 1966. Admitted to Maine bar, 1961, N.Y. State bar, 1962, Iowa bar, 1966, U.S. Supreme Ct. bar, 1968; asst. prof. law U. Iowa, Iowa City, 1964-67, asso. prof., 1967-69, prof., 1969—; cons. in field; labor arbitrator Am. Arbitration Assn., 1968—. mediator Iowa Pub. Employment Relations Bd., 1975—; adv. mem. Iowa Legis. Uniform Comml. Code Study Com., 1973. Mem. Am. Law Inst., Am. Arbitration Assn., Am. Bar Assn., Nat. Conf. Commrs. on Uniform State Laws, Soc. Profls. in Dispute Resolution. Contbr. articles in field to profl. jours. Home: 242 Ferson Ave Iowa City IA 52240 Office: Coll Law U Iowa Iowa City IA 52242 Tel (319) 353-3502

DOLEAC, MALCOM RONALD, b. Hattiesburg, Miss., Aug. 3, 1948; B.A., U. So. Miss., 1970; J.D., U. Miss., 1972. Admitted to Miss. bar, 1972; partner firm Finch, Wicht and Doleac and predecessors, Hattiesburg, 1975—; pros. atty. City of Hattiesburg,

1975—. Mem. Am. Bar Assn., Miss. State Bar, S. Central Miss. Bar Assn. (treas. 1975), Miss. Prosecutors Assn., Am., Miss. trial lawyers assns. Office: Finch Wicht & Doleac 220 W Pine St Hattiesburg MS 39401 Tel (601) 544-9700

DOLEZAL, HENRY, b. Perry, Okla., Jan. 11, 1905; B.A., U. Okla., 1926, LL.B., 1933. Admitted to Okla. bar, 1933, U.S. Dist. Ct. bar for Western Dist. Okla., 1935, U.S. 10th Circuit Ct. Appeals bar, 1950; individual practice law, Perry, 1933-34, 37-38, 46-69, 75—; county atty. Noble County (Okla.), 1935-36; judge Noble County Ct., 1938-42; asso. judge Okla. Dist. Ct. for Noble County, 8th Jud. Dist., 1969-75, ret. 1975; city atty. City of Perry, 1937-38, mayor, 1947-49, 51-57; mem. Okla. Ho. of Reps., 1957-65. Mem. Am., Okla., Noble County (pres. 1953, 54) bar assns. Home: 1102 Delaware St Perry OK 73077 Office: POB 677 Perry OK 73077 Tel (405) 336-4231

DOLGIN, DAVID AUBRY, b. Toledo, May 24, 1925; B.S., U. Calif., Berkeley, 1948; LL.B., Hastings Coll. Law, 1951. Admitted to Calif. bar, 1952; mem. firm Condon & Dolgin, 1952-68, firm Dolgin, Kully & Jameson, Martinez, Calif., 1968—. Bd. dirs. Contra Costa Legal Services Found. Mem. Am., Calif., Contra Costa County (past pres.) bar assns., Calif., Alameda, Contra Costa Trial Lawyers assns., Am. Judicature Soc. Home: 1117 Ridge Park Dr Concord CA 94518 Office: 900 Thompson St Martinez CA 94553 Tel (415) 228-2300

DOLGIN, KALMON, b. Bklyn., Mar. 19, 1943; A.B., Syracuse U., 1963, J.D., 1966. Admitted to N.Y. bar, 1967; asso. firm Levy & Kornblum, Bklyn., 1966-67; individual practice law, Bklyn., 1967—. Exec. v.p. Kings Point Civic Assn., 1976-77. Mem. Bklyn. Bar Assn., Bklyn. Bd. Realtors. Office: 101 Richardson St Brooklyn NY 11211 Tel (212) 386-7700

DOLIN, ALBERT HARRY, b. Chgo., Nov. 28, 1913; B.C.S., Northwestern U., 1936; LL.B., Loyola U., 1943. Admitted to Ill. bar, 1943, U.S. Supreme Ct. bar, 1950; exec. v.p. Goldblatt Bros., Inc., Chgo., 1968—. Bd. dirs. Civic Fedn. Ill., 1971; gen. counsel Chgo. Heart Research Found., 1962; trustee U. Chgo. Cancer Research Found., 1963; mem. Ill. Internat. Trade and Port Promotion Adv. Com., 1974; chmn. loop div. Community Fund Chgo., 1971; adv. mem. Marquis Biog. Library Soc. Mem. Chgo., Am. bar assns., Decalogue Soc. Lawyers. Home: 68 Lakeview Terr Highland Park IL 60035 Office: 333 S State St Chicago IL 60604 Tel (312) 786-2303

DOLLOFF, ARTHUR DEAN, b. Topsham, Maine, Mar. 25, 1926; A.B., Bowdoin Coll., 1947; J.D., Boston U., 1951. Admitted to Maine bar, 1951; individual practice law, Brunswick, Maine, 1953-58; partner firms Dolloff & Ranger, Brunswick, 1958-64, Spinney Dolloff & Glover, and predecessors, Brunswick, 1964—; recorder Bath (Maine) Municipal Ct., 1953-58; county atty. Sagadahoc County (Maine), 1958-60. Trustee Unitarian-Universalist Assn., Boston, 1969—. Mem. Maine, Sagadahoc County bar assns. Home: 167 Park Row Brunswick ME 04011 Office: 172 Maine St Brunswick ME 04011 Tel (207) 725-5032

DOLPH, WILBERT EMERY, b. Palatka, Fla., Dec. 29, 1923; LL.B., U. Ariz., 1949. Admitted to Ariz. bar, 1949; asst. city atty. Tucson, 1949-50; asst. atty. Ariz., 1950-51; practice in Tucson, 1951—; partner firm Bilby, Shoenhair, Warnock & Dolph, 1953—; counsel jud. com. Ariz. Senate, 1952. Trustee Ariz. Sonora Desert Mus.; trustee, pres. Tucson Med. Center; mem. U. Ariz. Found.; past bd. dirs. Ariz. Heart Assn., Tucson Festival Soc., Ariz. Children's Home Assn., Tucson YMCA. Mem. Am., Ariz., Pima County (exec. com., pres. 1974-75) bar assns., Ariz. Cattle Growers Assn., R.R. Trial Lawyers Assn., Am. Bd. Trial Advs., Navy League (pres.), Phi Delta Phi. Home: 6145 Mina Vista St Tucson AZ 85718 Office: Valley Nat Bldg Tucson AZ 85701 Tel (602) 792-4800

DOLVE, ELMER JOHN, JR., b. Ryegate, Mont., Jan. 13, 1927; LL.B., Blackstone Sch. Law, 1964, LaSalle Extension U., 1970. Admitted to Mont. bar, 1969; individual practice law, Billings, Mont., 1969—; police commr. Billings, 1968—. Mem. Am., Mont. bar assns., Am. Judicature Soc. Home: 3803 Palisades Park Dr Billings MT 59102 Office: 354 Hart Albin Bldg Billings MT 59101 Tel (406) 245-4189

DOMASH, ALVIN EARL, b. Chgo., Mar. 21, 1932; LL.B. with honors, U. Ill., 1955. Admitted to Ill. bar, 1955; served with JAG, U.S. Navy, Norfolk, Va., 1955-57; asst. gen. atty. N.Y. Central Railroad Co., Chgo., 1958-68; partner firm Lord, Bissell & Brook, Chgo., 1968—. Mem. Am., Ill., Chgo. bar assns., Internat. Soc. Barristers, Soc. Trial Lawyers (past dir.), Ill. Def. Counsel, Nat. Assn. Railroad Trial Counsel (past pres. Ill. div.), Am. Arbitration Assn. (arbitrator), Order of Coif. Editor: Ill. Law Forum, 1954-56. Office: 115 S LaSalle St Chicago IL 60603 Tel (312) 443-0219

DOMBROW, ANTHONY ERIC, b. N.Y.C., Apr. 6, 1945; B.A., U. Wis., 1966, J.D., 1969. Admitted to Wis. bar, 1969, Ill. bar, 1973; atty. NLRB, Chgo., 1969-72; partner firm Dorfman, De Koven, Cohen & Laner, Chgo., 1972—. Mem. State Bar Wis., Chgo. Bar Assn. Office: 1 IBM Plaza Suite 3301 Chicago IL 60611 Tel (312) 467-9800

DOMENGEAUX, JEROME ERASTE, b. Lafayette, La., Mar. 3, 1919; B.A., U. S.W. La., 1940; postgrad Georgetown U., 1941; LL.B., Tulane U., 1948, J.D., 1968. Admitted to La. bar, 1948; atty. Lafayette (La.) Parish, 1948-62; mayor City Lafayette, 1956-60; judge 15th La. Dist. Ct., Lafayette, 1962-70, La. Circuit Ct. Appeals, 4th Circuit, New Orleans, 1969-70; judge at large 3d La. Circuit Ct. Appeals, 1970—; mem. Jud. Council La. Supreme Ct., 1965-67. Mem. Am. (Appellate Judges Conf.), La., S.W. La., 15th Jud. Dist., Lafayette Parish bar assns., La. Appellate Judges Conf. Panelist numerous jud. seminars. Home: 1217 Myrtle Pl Blvd Lafayette LA 70501 Office: Box 2096 Lafayette LA 70502 Tel (318) 235-0790

DOMINICK, GAYER GARDNER, II, b. N.Y.C., July 4, 1939; B.A., Yale, 1965; M.A., U. Hawaii, 1968; J.D., U. Mich., 1971. Admitted to Wash. bar, 1972; asst. atty. gen. State of Wash., 1971-73; partner firm Owens, Weaver, Davies & Dominick, Olympia, Wash., 1973—. Trustee Friendship Inc., 1975—, chmn., 1976—; trustee Olympia Community Mental Health, 1976—. Mem. Am., Wash. bar assns. Home: 6345 Murray Ct NW Olympia WA 98502 Office: Bank of Olympia Bldg Olympia WA 98501 Tel (206) 943-8320

DOMRESE, ROBERT JAMES, b. Johnson City, Tenn., May 30, 1944; B.A., Harvard, 1966, J.D., 1971; M.P.A., Princeton, 1968. Admitted to Mo. bar, 1974; gen. counsel subcom. on intergovtl. relations U.S. Senate, Washington, 1971-72; exec. dir. Mo. Pub. Interest Research Group, St. Louis, 1972-74; asso. firm Husch Eppenberger Donohue Elson & Cornfeld, St. Louis, 1974—. Mem. Mo., St. Louis Met. bar assns. Editor Harvard Law Rev., 1969-71. Home: 362 Walton Row Saint Louis MO 63108 Office: 100 N Broadway Saint Louis MO 63102 Tel (314) 421-4800

DONAHER, WILLIAM ANDREW, b. New Kensington, Pa., Jan. 22, 1926; A.B., Cath. U. Am., 1949; LL.B., Harvard, 1952. Admitted to Nebr. Supreme Ct. bar, 1967, Pa. Supreme Ct. bar, 1954, U.S. Supreme Ct. bar, 1959; asst. atty. gen. Commonwealth of Pa., Harrisburg, 1955-59; practiced in Pa., 1959-66; asso. prof. law Creighton U., 1966-70; prof. Duquesne U., 1970—; sr. research asso. Carnegie-Mellon U., 1972—. Mem. Pa. State, Nebr. State bar assns. Author: (with Piehler, Twerski and Weinstein) Product Liability: An Interaction of Law and Technology, 1977; contbr. articles to profl. jours. Home: Apt 7-C Chatham Tower Pittsburgh PA 15219 Office: Duquesne U Sch of Law Pittsburgh PA 15219 Tel (412) 434-6288

DONAHOE, DANIEL JOSEPH, b. Elmira, N.Y., Dec. 31, 1912; A.B., St. Bonaventure U., 1938; LL.B., Syracuse U., 1942, J.D., 1968. Admitted to N.Y. bar, 1946; practiced in Elmira, 1946-55; judge Elmira Recorder's Ct., 1948-54, Chemung County (N.Y.) Children's Ct., 1955-62, Family Ct. of N.Y. State, 1962—, chmn. adv. and rules com., 1973—. Chmn. bd. dirs. St. Joseph Hosp., Elmira, 1971—. Mem. Am., N.Y. State, Chemung County (pres. 1972) bar assns., Jud. Conf. N.Y. State. Home: 625 Newtown St Elmira NY 14904 Office: 203-209 William St Elmira NY 14901 Tel (607) 737-2902

DONAHUE, CHARLES BERTRAND, II, b. Hampton, Iowa, Apr. 17, 1937; A.B., Harvard, 1959; J.D. cum laude, Cleve. Marshall Coll. Law, 1967. Admitted to Ohio bar, 1967, Fla. bar, 1973; contract adminstr. Westinghouse, Pitts., 1962-63; sr. contract adminstr. TRW, Inc., Cleve., 1963-67; asso. firm Calfee, Halter & Griswold, Cleve., 1967-73, partner, 1973—; lectr. law Cleve. Marshall Coll. Law, 1973—. Area class agt., Harvard Coll. Fund. Mem. Am., Fla., Ohio, Greater Cleve. bar assns., Estate Planning Council, Cevel. Soc. Estate Analysts, Phi Delta Theta. Home: 3014 Corydon Rd Cleveland Heights OH 44118 Office: 1800 Central Nat Bank Bldg Cleveland OH 44114 Tel (216) 781-2166

DONAHUE, DENNIS JOSEPH, JR., b. New Haven, July 29, 1935; B.A., U. Conn., 1957, LL.B., LL.D., 1960. Admitted to Conn. bar, 1960, U.S. Supreme Ct. bar, 1965; clerk Circuit Ct. Appeals 2d Circuit, Norwalk, Conn., 1961-62; asso. firm Larash & Gabriel, W. Haven, Conn., 1962-63; partner firm Donahue & Volto, W. Haven, 1964—. Mem. Am., Conn. bar assns., New Haven County Bar. Home: 22 Mills Dr West Haven CT 06516 Office: 415 Main St West Haven CT 06516 Tel (203) 934-6337

DONAHUE, JANE CECELIA, b. Lackawanna, N.Y., Feb. 6, 1919, R.N., Mercy Hosp. Sch. Nursing, Buffalo, 1940; J.D., Cath. U. Am., 1950. Cub reporter Lackawanna Leader, 1936-37; nurse Our Lady of Victory Hosp., Lackawanna, 1940-42; nurse U.S. Army, MTO, ETO, 1942-46; indsl. nurse Linde Air Products Co.; with firm Saft, Schweitzer & Sullivan, Buffalo, 1951-53; admitted to N.Y. State bar, 1953; individual practice law, Buffalo, 1954—; asst. prof. nursing State U. N.Y., Buffalo, 1962-75, asst. clin. prof. preventive medicine, 1972—. Mem. Am., N.Y. State, Erie County (N.Y.) bar assns., Republican Women Lawyers Club (pres. 1965, treas. 1973), Fed. Women's Rep. Clubs N.Y. State, Women Lawyers Assn., Kappa Beta Pi. Home: 731 W Ferry St Buffalo NY 14222 Office: 1056 Ellicott Square Bldg 295 Main St Buffalo NY 14203 Tel (716) 853-2590

DONALDSON, PATRICIA FLEMING, b. Detroit, Mar. 17, 1930; B.A., Marygrove Coll., 1951; J.D., U. Detroit, 1970. Admitted to Mich. bar, 1970; individual practice law, Birmingham, Mich., 1970—; adj. prof. law, Marygrove Coll., 1970-73; adj. prof. law Lawrence Inst. Tech., 1975—. Mem. exec. council Marygrove Coll., 1975—, chmn. deferred giving, 1975—. Mem. Am., Mich., Oakland County bar assns., Nat. Assn. Women Lawyers, Women's Bar Assn. of Oakland County. Home: 16036 Amherst St Birmingham MI 48009 Office: Suite 305 101 Southfield St Birmingham MI 48009 Tel (313) 645-2345

DONALDSON, RICHARD MIESSE, b. Columbus, Ohio, Apr. 8, 1929; B.S., Northwestern U., 1950; J.D., Mich. Law Sch., 1953; LL.M., Harvard U., 1957. Admitted to Ohio bar, 1953; asso. firm McAfee, Hanning, Newcomer, Hazlett & Wheeler, Cleve., 1957-67, jr. partner, 1965-67; gen. partner Squire, Sanders & Dempsey, Cleve., 1967-70; v.p., gen. counsel Standard Oil Co. (Ohio), Cleve., 1970-74, v.p. govt. and pub. affairs, 1974—. Mem. Rocky River (Ohio) Bd. Edn., 1962-69, pres., 1965-69; bd. dirs. Cleve. Internat. Program Youth Leaders Social Workers, 1973—; bd. dirs. Children's Aid Soc.-Cleve., 1962—, pres., 1968-69; bd. dirs. Cleve. Council World Affairs, 1971-75; trustee Ohio Pub. Expenditure Council, 1976—, Govtl. Research Inst., 1977—, Planned Parenthood Cleve., 1966-72, Luth. Med. Center Found., 1977—; com. mem. Young Life in Cleve., 1971-75, chmn., 1971-72; bd. mgrs., treas. The Brush Found., 1977—. Mem. Am., Ohio, Cleve. bar assns., Am. Petroleum Inst. Office: Standard Oil Co 1700 Guildhall Bldg Cleveland OH 44115 Tel (216) 575-5600

DONALDSON, ROBERT JEFF, b. Decatur, Ala., July 14, 1944; B.S., U. Ala., 1967, J.D., 1968. Admitted to Ala. bar, 1968, U.S. Supreme Ct. bar, 1972, U.S. Ct. Mil. Appeals, 1972; individual practice law, Jasper, Ala., 1968—; county solicitor Walker County (Ala.), 1971. Pres. Walker Mental Health Assn., Jasper Kiwanis Club. Mem. Am. Bar Assn., Ala., Am. trial lawyers assns. Home and Office: Box 909 Jasper AL 35501 Tel (205) 387-7748

DONAT, GREGORY JAMES, b. Peru, Ind., Sept. 14, 1947; B.S., Ball State U., 1970; J.D., Ind. U., 1972. Admitted to Ind. bar, 1973; asso. firm Heide Gambs & Mucker, Lafayette, Ind., 1973—. Mem. Am. (com. on representation of defendants in criminal proceedings), Ind. bar assns. Home: 714 S 10th St Lafayette IN 47905 Office: 214 First Fed Bldg Lafayette IN 47901 Tel (317) 742-7381

DON CARLOS, WALDO EMERSON, b. Greenfield, Iowa, Oct. 16, 1909; B.A., Drake U., 1931, LL.B., 1933, J.D., 1968. Admitted to Iowa bar, 1933; individual practice law, Greenfield, 1933-36; partner firm Don Carlos, Don Carlos & Carlberg, and predecessors, Greenfield, 1936—. Mem. Am., Iowa (bd. govs. 1965-69, 73-77), 5B Jud. Dist. (past pres.), Adair County bar assns. Home: 202 SW 5th St Greenfield IA 50849 Office: 113 W Iowa St Greenfield IA 50849

DONDANVILLE, JOHN WALLACE, b. Moline, Ill., Nov. 29, 1937; A.B., Coll. of Holy Cross, 1959; J.D., Northwestern U., 1962. Admitted to Ill. bar, 1962; asso. firm Heineke, Conklin & Schrader, Chgo., 1962-64; asso. firm Baker & McKenzie, Chgo., 1964-70, partner, 1970—. Mem. Am., Ill., Chgo. bar assns., Ill. Soc. Trial Lawyers, Internat. Assn. Ins. Counsel. Home: 622 Arlington Pl Chicago IL 60614 Office: 130 E Randolph Dr Chicago IL 60601 Tel (312) 565-0025

DONLIN, W. PATRICK, b. Madison, Wis., May 12, 1937; B.S., U. Wis., Madison, 1959, LL.B., 1961. Admitted to Wis. bar, 1961, U.S. Dist. Ct. bar for Western Dist. Wis., 1961; individual practice law, Madison and Belleville, Wis., 1961-65, Park Falls, Wis., 1969-74; asso. firm DeBardeleben & Donlin and predecessor, Park Falls, 1965-66, partner, 1966-69; judge Price County (Wis.) Ct., 1974-76; circuit judge 15th Jud. Circuit Wis., 1976—; dist. atty. Price County, 1971-74; mem. Wis. Bd. County Ct. Judges, 1974-76, Bd. Criminal Ct. Judges, Wis. Bd. Juvenile Ct. Judges, 1974-76, Wis. Bd. Circuit Judges, 1976—. Mem. Am. Bar Assn., State Bar Wis., Am. Judicature Soc., 15th Jud. Circuit Bar Assn. Home: 107 Case Ave Park Falls WI 54552 Office: Courthouse Phillips WI 54555 Tel (715) 339-2295

DONNA, JOHN JOSEPH, b. Dalton, Mass., Feb. 5, 1911; B.S., Boston U., 1933, M.A., 1941; LL.B., Northeastern U., Boston, 1946. Admitted to Mass. bar, 1947; individual practice law, Pittsfield, Mass., 1947—. Mem. planning bd. City of Pittsfield, 1959-66, chmn., 1961-66. Fellow Mass. Bar Found.; mem. Am., Mass., Berkshire County (v.p. 1965-66, pres. 1966-67) bar assns. Office: 28 N St PO Box 561 Pittsfield MA 02201 Tel (413) 443-3440

DONNELLY, DAVID C., b. St. Paul, May 11, 1924; B.S. Law, U. Minn., 1947, J.D., 1949. Admitted to Minn. bar, 1949; now mem. firm Oppenheimer, Wolff, Poster, Shepard and Donnelly, St. Paul; mem. Minn. Bd. Profl. Responsibility, 1971-75. Fellow Am. Bar Found.; mem. Ramsey County (Minn.) (pres. 1970), Minn. State (pres. 1976), Am. bar assns., Phi Delta Phi. Office: 1700 First Nat Bank Bldg Saint Paul MN 55101 Tel (612) 227-7271*

DONNELLY, ROBERT TRUE, b. Lebanon, Mo., Aug. 31, 1924; J.D., U. Mo., 1949. Admitted to Mo. bar, 1949; mem. firm Donnelly & Donnelly, Lebanon, 1952-65; city atty. Lebanon, 1954-55; asst. atty. gen. State of Mo., 1957-61; judge Mo. Supreme Ct., Jefferson City, 1965—; bd. govs. Mo. bar, 1957-63. Mem. Lebanon Bd. Edn., 1959-65; trustee Sch. of Religion, Drury Coll., Springfield, Mo., 1958-66; Mo. Sch. of Religion, Columbia, Mo., 1971-72. Mem. Am., Mo. bar assns., Am. Judicature Soc. Home: 3459 Hobbs Ln Jefferson City MO 65101 Office: Supreme Ct Bldg Jefferson City MO 65101 Tel (314) 751-3570

DONNERSBERGER, DAVID RAYELLE, b. Chgo., Nov. 3, 1938; B.A., St. Bonaventure U., 1963; M.A., DePaul U., 1968, J.D., 1972. Admitted to Ill. bar, 1972, Fla. bar, 1972; asst. prof. dept. English, City Coll. Chgo., 1968-75, adj. prof. dept. labor studies, 1975—; asst. states atty. Cook County (Ill.), 1975—. Pres. bd. dirs. Libra Sch., Inc., Riverdale, Ill., 1973-76; mem. sch. bd. St. John of the Cross Sch., Western Springs, Ill., 1975—. Mem. Am., Ill., Chgo., Fla. bar assns. Home: 5128 Ellington St Western Springs IL 60558 Office: 2600 S California St Criminal Courts Bldg Chicago IL 60608 Tel (312) 865-6331

DONOHOE, JOHN PATRICK, b. Bronx, N.Y., Jan. 27, 1945; B.S., St. Peter's Coll., 1967; J.D., Columbia U., 1970. Admitted to N.Y. bar, 1971, N.J. bar, 1974; asso. firm Moses & Singer, N.Y.C., 1970-72; asso. firm Wofsey, Certilmen, Haft & Lebow, N.Y.C., 1962-76, partner, 1977—. Mem. Am. (com. condominiums and coop. ownership apts.), N.Y. State, N.J. bar assns. Home: 1101 Trafalgar St Teaneck NJ 07666 Office: 55 Broad St New York City NY 10004 Tel (212) 425-4320

DONOHUE, MICHAEL J., b. Holyoke, Mass., Dec. 12, 1923; B.A., U. Mass., 1947; LL.B., Boston U., 1950. Admitted to Mass. bar, 1950; practiced in Mass., 1950-63; presiding justice Mass. Dist. Ct., Dist. of Holyoke, 1963—. Mem. Am. Judges Assn. (v.p., editor Hilites 1976—), Am. Judicature Soc. Editor Court Rev., 1969-76; bd. editors Criminal Justice Rev., 1975—. Home: 290 Cabot St Holyoke MA 01040 Office: Dist Ct of Holyoke Holyoke MA 01040 Tel (413) 534-5619

DONOHUE, RICHARD JOSEPH, b. Montclair, N.J., Mar. 13, 1940; B.A., Fairleigh Dickinson U., 1964; LL.B., Seton Hall U., 1967. Admitted to N.J. bar, 1967; asso. firm Gleeson, Nansen, & Pantages, Newark, 1968-69; partner firm Gross, Demetrakis & Donohue, Hackensack, N.J., 1969-74, firm Olson & Donohue, Hackensack, 1974—; borough atty. Rochelle Park (N.J.), 1977—; pros. atty. Hillsdale (N.J.), 1977—. Mem. Hillsdale Planning Bd., Hillsdale Environ. Protection Bd. Mem. Am., N.J., Essex County, Bergen County bar assns., Am. Trial Lawyers Assn., Law Sci. Acad. Home: 49 Plymouth Rd Hillsdale NJ 07642 Office: One Essex St Hackensack NJ 07601 Tel (201) 342-3535

DONOVAN, FRANCIS JOSEPH, b. Bklyn., June 5, 1916; B.A. cum laude, St. Johns Coll., 1939, LL.B. summa cum laude, 1941. Admitted to N.Y. bar, 1941; asso. firm Alexander & Ash, N.Y.C., 1941, 46-47; dep. county atty. Nassau County (N.Y.), 1948-59, judge dist. ct., 1959—; partner firm Donovan & Donovan, Hicksville, N.Y. Home: 101 Duffy Ave Hicksville NY 11801 Office: 129 New Bridge Rd Hicksville NY 11801 Tel (516) 938-1717

DONOVAN, GERARD KIRWAN, b. Champaign, Ill., Jan 28, 1919; A.B., U. Notre Dame, 1940; student U. Chgo. Law Sch., 1946; J.D., U. Tulsa, 1949. Admitted to Okla. bar, 1949, U.S. Supreme Ct. bar, 1964; practiced in Tulsa, 1949—; partner firm Covington & Donovan, 1952-60, Donovan & Rogers, 1962-64, Rogers, Donovan & Rogers, 1964-69, Donovan, Freese & March, 1969—; judge State Indsl. Ct., Oklahoma City, 1950-52; asst. city atty. City of Tulsa, 1949-50; spl. atty. to gov. of Okla., 1954-59; adj. prof. U. Tulsa Law Sch., 1953-63. Chmn. bd. Birthright of Tulsa, 1974—. Mem. Okla., Tulsa bar assns. Contbr. to Okla. Workmen's Compensation Manual. Home: 7232 S Pittsburg St Tulsa OK Office: Suite 700 Mid Continent Bldg 4th and Boston Sts Tulsa OK 74103 Tel (918) 582-3164

DONOVAN, JAMES, b. Napoleon, Ohio, Mar. 13, 1927; A.B., U. Mich., 1950, LL.B., 1953. Admitted to Ohio bar, 1953; partner firm Meekison and Donovan, Napoleon, 1953—. Mem. Am., Ohio bar ass. Home: 63S W Washington St Napoleon OH 43545 Office: 609 N Perry St Napoleon OH 43545 Tel (419) 592-6801

DONOVAN, PAUL FRANCIS, b. Cambridge, Mass., Dec. 15, 1932; A.B., Harvard U., 1955; LL.B., Columbia U., 1958. Admitted to N.H. bar, 1958; asso. firm Hinkley & Donovan, and predecessor, Lancaster, N.H., 1958-63, partner, 1963—; spl. justice Dist. Ct., Lancaster, 1965—; mem. conduct com. N.H. Supreme Ct., 1975—. Chmn. Planning Bd. Lancaster, 1965-72. Mem. Am., N.H. bar assns. Home: PO Box 526 Lancaster NH 03584 Office: 66 Main St Lancaster NH 03584 Tel (603) 788-2525

DONOVAN, PETER ANDREW, b. Boston, Nov. 30, 1935; A.B., Boston Coll., 1957, LL.B., J.D., 1960; LL.M., Georgetown U., 1962, Harvard, 1965. Admitted to Mass. bar, 1960; atty. Dept. Justice, Washington, 1960-63; Ford Found. teaching fellow in law Harvard, 1963-64; asst. prof. law U. Conn., 1964-66; asso. prof. Boston Coll., 1966-68, prof., 1968—; speaker in field; mem. regional sci. task force New Eng. River Basins Commn., 1972-75. Mem. Am. Bar Assn., Nat.

Air Pollution Control Assn., Sierra Club, Order of Coif. Author: (with Curtin, Fine & Brown) The Realities of Franchising: A Guide for the Practicing Attorney, 1970; Editor-in-chief Boston Coll. Indsl. and Comml. Law Rev., 1959-60, Annual Survey of Mass. Law, 1959-60, Environ. Affairs, 1970-72; contbr. articles to legal publs. Office: Sch of Law Boston Coll Newton Center MA 02167 Tel (617) 969-0100

DONOVAN, RICHARD NEIL, b. Granby, N.Y., Oct. 26, 1921; B.A., St. Lawrence U., 1943; LL.B., Syracuse U., 1946, J.D., 1968. Admitted to N.Y. bar, 1946; practiced in Fulton, N.Y., 1947-62; dist. atty. Oswego County, N.Y., 1954-58, judge Surrogate's Ct., 1958-70; justice N.Y. State Supreme Ct., 5th Jud. Dist., 1970—. Home: 1115 Jefferson St Phoenix NY 13135 Office: 200 N 2d St Fulton NY 13069

DONOVAN, RICHARD PRIDDIE, b. N.Y.C., Aug. 14, 1921; A.B., Brown U., 1942; LL.B., J.D., Cornell U., 1948. Admitted to N.Y. State bar, 1948; staff atty. SEC, 1948-50; asst. U.S. atty. So. Dist. N.Y., 1950-53; asso. firm Sullivan, Donovan, Hanrahan & Silliere, and predecessors, N.Y.C., from 1954, now partner; lectr. law Cornell U., Ithaca, N.Y., 1957; asst. prof. Fordham U., N.Y.C., 1957-68. Bd. dirs. Soc. for Prevention Cruelty to Children, N.Y.C., 1970—. Mem. Assn. Bar City of N.Y., N.Y. State Bar Assn., Order of Coif, Phi Beta Kappa. Home: 108 Blvd Pelham NY 10803 Office: 70 Pine St New York City NY 10005 Tel (212) 344-5858

DONOVAN, WILLIAM HOWARD, b. Tuscaloosa, Ala., July 5, 1947; B.A., Birmingham—So. Coll., 1969; J.D., U. Ala., 1972. Admitted to Ala. bar, 1972; law clk. judge Ala. Ct. Criminal Appeals, Montgomery, 1972-73; dep. dist. atty. 10th Jud. Circuit Ala., Birmingham, 1973-75; asso. firm Skinner & Large, Birmingham, 1975—. Mem. Birmingham Bar Assn., Phi Delta Phi. Home: 101 Virginia Dr Birmingham AL 35209 Office: 1407 City Fed Bldg Birmingham AL 35203 Tel (205) 328-9650

DOODY, JOHN THOMAS, JR., b. Evergreen Park, Ill., Jan. 15, 1945; B.A. in Polit. Sci., St. Procopius Coll., 1966; J.D., John Marshall Law Sch., 1974. Admitted to Ill. bar, 1974, U.S. Dist. Ct. for No. Dist. Ill. bar, 1974, U.S. 7th Circuit Ct. Appeals, 1976; law clk. Ill. Appellate Ct., 1974-76; individual practice law, Homewood, 1976—. Mem. Am., Ill. (sec. standing com. on law focused edn.), Chgo. (chmn. law firm econs. com. young lawyers sect., also mem. exec. com. sect.), South Suburban bar assns., Assn. Trial Lawyers Am., Ill. Trial Lawyers Assn., South Suburban Estate Planning Council. Office: 18154 Harwood Ave Homewood IL 60430 Tel (312) 799-7676

DOOLEY, JOHN JOSEPH, b. Canton, Ill., Apr. 18, 1917; B.A., Colo. Coll., 1939; J.D., U. Mich., 1946. Admitted to Colo. bar, 1946; asso. with William A. Carlson, Greeley, Colo., 1946-49; prof. sch. law U. No. Colo., Greeley, 1949-53; asso. firm Houtchens, Houtchens & Dooley, Greeley, 1957-74; county judge Weld County, Colo., 1953-57; asso. firm Stienties & Dooley, Greeley, 1974—. Chmn. Young Republicans Weld County, Colo., 1948; mem. Gov. Colo. Sch. Finance Com., 1951; Colo. State chmn. March Dimes, 1957-58; mem. Greeley Charter Commn., 1959. Mem. Weld., Colo., Am., Def. lawyers assns., Weld County (pres. 1965), Colo. (bd. govs. 1969, chmn. negligence sect. 1971) bar assns., Colo. County Judges Assn. (pres. 1956). Office: 1010 12th St Greeley CO 80631 Tel (303) 353-9000

DOOLITTLE, JESSE WILLIAM, JR., b. Wheaton, Ill., May 19, 1929; A.B. with high distinction, DePauw U., 1951; LL.B. magna cum laude, Harvard, 1954. Admitted to D.C. bar, 1954, U.S. Supreme Ct., 1958; asso. firm Covington & Burling, Washington, 1958-61; asst. to Solicitor Gen., U.S. Dept. Justice, Washington, 1961-63; 1st asst., civil div. U.S. Dept. Justice, 1963-66; gen. counsel U.S. Dept. Air Force, Washington, 1966-68; partner firm Prather Seeger Doolittle Farmer & Ewing, Washington, 1969—; law clk. to justice U.S. Supreme Ct., 1957-58; asst. sec. of Air Force, 1968-69. Chmn. com. on constitution and canons Episcopal Diocese of Washington, 1977—. Mem. D.C. Bar, Bar Assn. D.C., Am. Bar Assn., Am. Law Inst. Home: 4238 50th St NW Washington DC 20016 Office: 1101 16th St NW Washington DC 20036

DOOLITTLE, ROBERT FREDERICK, b. Oberlin, Ohio, June 14, 1902; A.B., Harvard, 1923, LL.B. magna cum laude, 1930; LL.D., Youngstown State U., 1968. Admitted to N.Y. bar, 1932, Ohio bar, 1953; asso. firm Taylor, Blanc, Capron & Marsh, N.Y.C., 1930-32; asso. firm Cotton, Franklin, Wright & Gordon (now Cahill, Gordon & Reindel), N.Y.C., 1932-42; lt. col. AUS, counsel Renegotiation div. Office of Chief of Ordnance, 1942-45; v.p., counsel Baldwin-Lima-Hamilton Corp., Phila., 1948-52; asst. gen. counsel Youngstown Sheet & Tube Co. (Ohio), 1952-59, gen. counsel, 1959-67, v.p., 1964-67, dir., 1967-69; counsel Baker, Hostetler & Patterson, Cleve., 1967—; asst. gen. counsel, gen. counsel Office Contract Settlement, Exec. Office of Pres., Washington, 1945-46. Mem. Ohio Bd. Regents, 1963, vice chmn., 1966—; bd. dirs. World Affairs Council Phila., 1951-52; trustee, mem. exec. com. Cleve. Council World Affairs, 1968—. Mem. Ohio Mfrs. Assn. (pres. 1965-67, exec. com. 1958—). Office: 1956 Union Commerce Bldg Cleveland OH 44115 Tel (216) 621-0200

DOPKIN, MARK DREGANT, b. Balt., Jan. 14, 1943; B.A., Union Coll., 1964; J.D., U. Md., 1967. Admitted to Md. bar, 1967, U.S. Supreme Ct. bar, 1974; asso. firm Blades & Rosenfeld, Balt., 1968-71; asso. firm Kapan, Heyman, Greenberg, Engelman & Belgrad, Balt., 1971-76, partner, 1977—. Trustee Har Sinai Congregation, 1973—, pres. brotherhood, 1973-74; bd. dirs. Asso. Placement and Guidance Bur., Balt., 1974—; mem. Charter Rev. Commn. Baltimore County, 1977—. Mem. Am., Md., Balt. bar assns. Home: 1335 Harden Ln Baltimore MD 21208 Office: Sun Life Bldg 10th Floor Baltimore MD 21201 Tel (301) 539-6967

DOPPELT, LAWRENCE FREDERICH, b. Chgo., Mar. 25, 1935; B.A., Northwestern U., 1956; J.D., Yale, 1959. Admitted to Ill. bar, 1959, U.S. 7th Circuit Ct. Appeals bar, 1971; regional atty., acting supr. NLRB, Chgo., 1959-62; partner firm Dorfman, Dekoven, Cohen & Laner, Chgo., 1962—; asso. prof. law Ill. Inst. Tech.-Chgo. Kent Coll. Law, 1971-74, prof., 1974—; ad hoc and permanent arbitrator to numerous unions and cos., 1970—; hearing officer Ill. Fair Employment Practices Commn., Chgo., 1971-74. Mem. Am., Chgo. bar assns., Am. Judicature Soc., Am. Arbitration Assn. (panel labor arbitrators), Fed. Mediation and Conciliation Service (panel arbitrators), Soc. Profls. Dispute Resolution, Phi Alpha Delta. Contbr. chpts. to books, articles to legal jours. Home: 331 Davis St Evanston IL 60201 Office: 77 S Wacker Dr Chicago IL 60606 Tel (312) 567-5000

DORAN, ROBERT JOSEPH, b. Butte, Mont., July 20, 1931; LL.B., Gonzaga U., 1957, J.D., 1967. Admitted to Wash. bar, 1958, U.S. Supreme Ct. bar, 1968; law clk. Wash. State Supreme Ct., 1957-58; asst. atty. gen. State of Wash., 1958-63, chief asst. atty. gen., 1963-69, dep. atty. gen., 1969-71; judge Wash. Superior Ct., 1971—. Bd. dirs. United Way of Thurston County (Wash.), 1971—, chmn. com. planning and allocation, 1976—. Mem. Wash. State, Mason-Thurston County (Wash.) (hon.) bar assns., Wash. State Superior Ct. Judges' Assn. Home: 2003 Arietta Pl Olympia WA 98501 Office: Thurston County Courthouse Olympia WA 98501 Tel (206) 753-8153

DORAN, WILLIAM KINSON, b. Boone, Iowa, Nov. 28, 1924; B.S., U.S. Naval Acad., 1946; J.D., U. Iowa, 1954. Admitted to Iowa bar, 1954; partner firm Doran, Doran & Courter, Boone, 1954—; dir. Boone State Bank & Trust Co. Mem. Am., Iowa, Boone County (pres. 1961-64) bar assns., Assn. Trial Lawyers Am., Iowa Acad. Trial Lawyers, Order of Coif, Phi Delta Phi. Home: 1003 Kate Shelley Dr Boone IA 50036 Office: 809 8th St Boone IA 50036 Tel (515) 432-1355

DORAZIO, MICHAEL, JR., b. Monogahela, Pa., Aug. 9, 1942; B.A., Pa. State U., 1963; J.D., U. Pitts., 1966. Admitted to Pa. bar, 1966, U.S. Ct. Appeals 3d Circuit bar, 1966, U.S. Dist. Ct. Eastern Dist. Pa. bar, 1966, Calif. bar, 1968, U.S. Ct. Appeals 9th Circuit bar, 1968, U.S. Dist. Ct. Central Dist. Calif. bar, 1968, U.S. Dist. Ct. So. Dist. Calif. bar, 1969; trial atty., atty. gen's. Honors Program, U.S. Dept. Justice, 1966-69; asso. antitrust div. firm Seltzer, Caplan, Wilkins & McMahon, San Diego, 1969-70, partner, 1970—. Mem. Am., Calif., San Diego County bar assns., Calif. Trial Lawyers Assn., Barristers Club. Contbr. articles to law revs. Home: PO Box 1246 Rancho Santa Fe CA 92067 Office: 3003 4th Ave San Diego CA 92103 Tel (714) 291-3003

DORFMAN, JOHN CHARLES, b. Wilkinsburg, Pa., Feb. 3, 1925; B.E. in Elec. Engring., Yale, 1945; J.D., Cornell U., 1949. Admitted to N.Y. bar, 1949, Conn. bar, 1950, Pa. bar, 1956, U.S. Supreme Ct. bar, 1959; counsel Machlett Labs., Springdale, Conn., 1949-54; asso. firm Pennie, Edmonds, Morton, Barrows & Taylor, N.Y.C., 1954-55; Howson & Howson, Phila., 1955-59, partner, 1960-73; partner firm Dorfman, Herrell & Skillman, Phila., 1973—. Mem. IEEE, Am. (mem. council, PTC sec. 1968-72), Pa., Phila. bar assns., Phila (sec. 1962-64, bd. govs. 1968-70, v.p. 1972-74, pres. 1974-76), Am. (bd. mgrs. 1973-76, v.p., nat. council 1976-77) patent law assns., Phi Alpha Delta, Tau Beta Pi. Office: 123 S Broad St Philadelphia PA 19109 Tel (215) KI5-1700

DORFZAUN, RICHARD STEPHAN, b. Morgantown, W.Va., Feb. 22, 1943; B.A., Duquesne U., 1965, J.D., 1968. Admitted to Pa. bar, 1969; asso. firm Dickie, McCamey & Chilcote, Pitts., 1968-74, partner, 1975—; adj. prof. law Duquesne U., 1968-71. Mem. Am. Judicature Soc., Pa., Allegheny County bar assns. Home: 143 Anita Ave Pittsburgh PA 15217 Office: 3180 US Steel Bldg Pittsburgh PA 15219 Tel (412) 281-7272

DORR, IDA LEE, b. Cuyahoga Falls, Ohio, Nov. 8, 1914; B.A., U. Okla., 1935; J.D., Oklahoma City U., 1956. Admitted to Okla. bar, 1956; adjudicator HEW, Balt., 1958-67, Social Security Adminstrn., Balt., 1959-66; cons. firm Rotman & Rotman, Chgo., 1969-72; field rep. Met. Devel. Div., HUD, Chgo., 1966-69. Mem. Okla. Bar Assn., LWV (past pres.), Iota Tau Tau. Recipient Mgmt. award Social Security Adminstrn., 1964, commendation USAF, 1957.

DORR, WILLIAM LENT, b. Auburn, N.Y. Sept. 11, 1940; B.A., Colgate U., 1962; LL.B., Cornell U., 1965. Admitted to N.Y. State bar, 1965; mem. firm Harris, Beach, Wilcox, Rubin & Levey, Rochester, N.Y., 1973—. Mem. Monroe County, N.Y. State bar assns., Am. Assn. R.R. Trial Counsel. Home: 99 Timberbrook Ln Penfield NY 14526 Office: Two State St Rochester NY 14614 Tel (716) 232-4440

DORSEN, NORMAN, b. N.Y.C., Sept. 4, 1930; B.A., Columbia, 1950; LL.B., Harvard, 1953; postgrad. London Sch. Econs., 1956. Admitted to D.C. bar, 1953, N.Y. State bar, 1954, U.S. Supreme Ct. bar, 1958; prof. law N.Y. U., 1961—, of counsel firm Greenbaum, Wolff & Ernst, N.Y.C., 1976—; gen. counsel ACLU, 1969—. Bd. dirs. Am. Friends of London Sch. Econs., 1971-73; chmn. HEW Rev. Panel on New Drug Regulation. Mem. Am. Law Inst., Soc. Am. Law Tchrs. (pres. 1974-75). Author: Political and Civil Rights in the U.S., 1967, 76; (with others) Frontiers of Civil Liberties, 1968; (with L. Friedman) Disorder in the Court, 1973; editor: The Rights of Americans, 1971; (with S. Gillers) None of Your Business: Government Secrecy in America, 1974; contbr. numerous articles to legal jours., popular jours. Home: 146 Central Park W New York City NY 10023Office NY U Law Sch 40 Washington Square S New York City NY 10012 Tel (212) 598-2555

DORSEY, BENJAMIN HENRY, b. Portsmouth, N.H., Feb. 13, 1924; B.S. in Econs., U. Pa., 1945; LL.B., George Washington U., 1948. Admitted to D.C. bar, 1948, Md. bar, 1972; asso. gen. counsel SBA, Washington, 1953-54; practiced in Washington, 1954—; partner firm Brookhart, Becker & Dorsey, 1956-67, Brookhart, Dorsey & Callahan, 1967-70, Dorsey & Callahan, 1970-72; individual practice law, 1972—; dir. Bulova Watch Co. Vice pres. Travelers Aid Soc. Washington. Mem. Am., Fed., D.C. bar assns., Washington Real Estate Investment Trust (trustee). Home: 8 Farmington Ct Chevy Chase MD 20015 Office: Suite 1106 Landow Bldg 7910 Woodmont Ave Washington DC 20014 Tel (301) 654-2140

DORSEY, GRAY LANKFORD, b. Hamilton, Mo., Feb. 16, 1918; A.B., U. Kans., 1941; J.D., Yale, 1948, J.S.D., 1950; m. Jeanne DeVoll, Jan. 1, 1942; 1 dau., Deborah DeVall. Admitted to Mo. bar, 1956, U.S. Supreme Ct. bar, 1967; asst. prof. Sch. of Law, Washington U., St. Louis, 1951-55, asso. prof. 1955-58, prof. 1958—, Charles Nagel prof. jurisprudence and internat. law, 1962—; vis. prof. Nat. Taiwan U. and Soochow U. Law Schs., Taipei, 1952-53; vis. prof. philosophy, U. Hawaii, 1959; cons. Nat. Endowment for Humanities; cons. Naval War Coll., 1962-69. Bd. dirs. U. Centers for Rational Alternatives; adv. bd. Ams. for Effective Law Enforcement. Am. Council Learned Socs. fellow, 1948-50; Center Advanced Study Behavioral Scis. fellow, 1959-60. Mem. Internat. Assn. Philosophy of Law and Social Philosophy (pres.), Am. Soc. Internat. Law, Internat. Law Assn., Am. Soc. Polit. and Legal Philosophy, Am., Mo. bar assns. Contbr. books, articles, teaching materials in field. Home: 8 Conway Springs Dr Chesterfield MO 63017 Office: School of Law Washington Univ St Louis MO 63130 Tel (314) 863-0100

DORSEY, JAMES ELLIOT, b. Cordele, Ga., Aug. 20, 1940; B.C.E., Ga. Inst. Tech., 1962; LL.B., U. Va., 1968. Admitted to Ga. bar, 1968; asso. firm Arnall, Golden & Gregory, Atlanta, 1968-74, partner, 1974—; mem. com. to revise Ga. Corp. Code. Treas., trustee 1st Montessori Sch. Mem. Am., Atlanta bar assns. Office: 1000 Fulton Fed Bldg Atlanta GA 30303 Tel (404) 577-5100

DORSEY, (JOHN) MICHAEL, b. Kansas City, Mo., Feb. 6, 1943; J.D., U. Mo. at Kansas City, 1968, LL.M. in Urban Affairs, 1973. Admitted to Mo. bar, 1968; staff atty. Legal Aid and Defender's Soc. of Greater Kansas City (Mo.), 1969-70, mng. atty., 1970-71, asst. dir., 1971-72; asst. atty. gen. State of Mo., Kansas City, 1973-74; asso. firm Stinson, Mag, Thomson, McEvers & Fizzell, Kansas City, Mo., 1974—. Bd. dirs. George Washington Carver Community Center, Kansas City, Mo., 1974—, Charlie Parker Sq. Housing Corp., Kansas City, Mo., 1975—; pres. Westport Community Council, Kansas City, Mo., 1975—. Mem. Kansas City, Mo., Am. bar assns., Lawyers Assn. of Kansas City. Recipient St. Louis Globe Democrat achievement award, 1974. Home: 3404 Karnes Blvd Kansas City MO 64111 Office: 2100 Ten Main Center Kansas City MO 64105 5 Tel (816) 842-8600

DORSEY, LEIGHTON COLEMAN, b. Wilmington, Del., Oct. 3, 1930; B.A., Dartmouth Coll., 1952; J.D., Harvard U., 1955. Admitted to Del., D.C. bars, 1955; asso. firm William Prickett, Wilmington, 1958; partner firm Dorsey & Dorsey, Wilmington, 1959-70, firm Bader, Dorsey & Kreshtool, Wilmington, 1970—; chmn. Del. adv. com. U.S. Civil Rights Commn., 1969-75. Trustee Children's Beach House, Inc., Wilmington, 1964—; trustee, chmn. fin. com. Pendle Hill, Media, Pa., 1968—; pres. Citizens Housing Alliance of Del., Wilmington, 1975; sec. Greater Wilmington Devel. Council, 1968—; bd. dirs. Grand Opera House, Inc., 1973—. Mem. Am., Del. bar assns. Home: 1224 Tatnall St Wilmington DE 19801 Office: 1102 West St PO Box 2202 Wilmington DE 19899 Tel (302) 656-9850

DORSEY, THOMAS JOSEPH, b. Kingston, Ark., Sept. 19, 1933; B.A., U. Ark., 1959, LL.B. (J.D.), 1962. Admitted to Fla. bar, 1962; field atty. NLRB, Miami, Fla., 1962-65; sr. partner firm Kaplan, Dorsey, Sicking and Hessen, Miami, 1965—. Mem., organizer ACLU, Fla. Mem. Fla. Acad. Labor Lawyers (founder), Fla. Acad. Trial Lawyers, NAACP (staff counsel Fla. 1966-68). Office: Kaplan Dorsey Sicking & Hessen 1951 NW 17th Ave Miami FL 33125 Tel (305) 325-1661

DORT, JAMES MOORE, b. San Diego, Dec. 3, 1933; B.A., Stanford, 1955, LL.B., 1961. Admitted to Calif. bar, 1962, U.S. Supreme Ct. bar, 1970; partner firm Luce, Forward, Hamilton & Scripps, San Diego, 1962—. Mem. Am., San Diego County bar assns., Am. Bd. Trial Advocates, Assn. So. Calif. Def. Counsel. Home: 5181 San Aquario Dr San Diego CA 92109 Office: 110 W A St San Diego CA 92101 Tel (714) 236-1414

DOSCHER, JURGEN HENRY, JR., b. Houston, Jan. 5, 1921; A.B., Amherst Coll., 1942; M.A., Hardin-Simmons U., 1973; J.D., U. Tex., Austin, 1948. Admitted to Tex. bar, 1948; law clk. to Chief Justice Tex. Supreme Ct., 1949; partner firms Wagstaff, Alvis, Pope, Doscher & Charlton, Abilene, Tex., 1950-66, Rhodes, Doscher, Chalk & Heatherly, Abilene, 1967—; prof. legal studies McMurry Coll., 1969—. Bd. dirs. West Tex. Rehab. Center, Abilene, 1969—, Dodge-Jones Found., Abilene, 1972—. Mem. Am., Abilene (pres. 1971-72) bar assns., State Bar Tex. (sec. sect. minerals 1950-51), AAUP, Am. Bus. Law Assn., Phi Delta Phi. Home: 2301 Sayles Blvd Abilene TX 79605 Office: Suite 104 Citizens Bank Bldg Abilene TX 79601 Tel (91S) 677-2493

DOSLAND, CHESTER ALLEN, b. Fargo, N.D., June 14, 1928; student S.D. State Coll., 1945-46; B.S. in Law, U. Minn., 1953, LL.B., 1953. Admitted to Minn. bar, 1953; law clk. Minn. Supreme Ct., St. Paul, 1953-54; partner firm Gislason, Dosland, Malecki, Gislason & Halvorson, New Ulm, Minn., 1954—; mem. Minn. Bd. Law Examiners, 1963—, pres., 1971-77. Pres., New Ulm Library Bd., 1974-77, Unit Ch. Christ of New Ulm Council, 1962-68. Diplomate Am. Bd. Trial Advocates. Fellow Am. Coll. Trial Lawyers; mem. Minn., Am. bar assns., Am. Judicature Soc,, Internat. Assn. Ins. Counsel. Bd. editors Minn. Law Rev., 1950-51. Home: 36 Woodland Dr New Ulm MN 56073 Office: 1 S State St New Ulm MN 56073 Tel (507) 354-3111

DOSLAND, GOODWIN LEROY, b. Moorhead, Minn., July 31, 1903; B.S., Concordia Coll., 1926; J.D., U. Chgo., 1926. Admitted to Ill. bar, 1926, Minn. bar, 1926; pvt. practice law, Chgo., 1926-40, Moorhead, 1945—; asso. firm Dosland, Dosland, Nordhougen & Mickelberg, 1945-68; atty. Clay County, 1946—; chief judge Clay County Ct., Moorhead, 1968-76; ret., 1976; mem. bd. govs. State of Minn. Bd. dirs. Amateur Radio Relay League. Mem. Minn., Clay County bar assns. Home: Rural Route 1 Moorhead MN 56560 Tel (218) 233-0961

DOSS, MARION KENNETH, b. Sebring, Fla., Sept. 25, 1939; student Ga. Inst. Tech., 1957-61; LL.B., U. Ga., 1964; Admitted to Ga. bar, 1965, also fed bars; partner firm Northcutt Edwards & Doss, Atlanta, 1965-71; gen. counsel, v.p. Roy D. Warren Co., Atlanta, 1971-73; partner firm Doss & Sturgeon, Atlanta, 1973-75; atty., law dept. Rollins, Inc., Atlanta, 1975—. Mem. Atlanta C. of C., Atlanta, Fulton County, Ga., Am. bar assns., Am. Trial Lawyers Assn. Office: 2170 Piedmond Rd NE Atlanta GA 30324 Tel (404) 873-2355

DOSTER, SIMUEL FRANKLIN, JR., b. Charleston, S.C., Dec. 21, 1943; A.B. magna cum laude, U. Ga., 1966; LL.B., U. Va., 1969. Admitted to Ga. bar, 1969; partner firm Huie, Brown & Ide, Atlanta, 1973-75, Harland, Cashin, Chambers, Davis & Doster, Atlanta, 1976—. Mem. Lawyers Club Atlanta, Atlanta Council Younger Lawyers (dir. 1974—, pres. 1975-76), Am., Ga., Atlanta (exec. com. 1976—) bar assns., Phi Beta Kappa, Order of Coif. Home: 4254 Lakehaven Dr NE Atlanta GA 30319 Office: 1045 Hurt Bldg Atlanta GA 30303 Tel (404) 522-7360

DOSTER, WILLIAM ERNST, b. Buffalo, May 27, 1941; B.A. cum laude, Baldwin-Wallace Coll., 1963; J.D. with distinction, U. Mich., 1966. Admitted to Fla. bar, 1966; asso. firm Anderson Rush Dean & Lowndes, Orlando, Fla., 1966-69; partner firm Lowndes Peirsol Drosdick & Doster, Orlando, 1969—. Mem. Winter Park (Fla.) Bd. Adjustments, 1975—. Mem. Am., Orange County bar assns., Fla. Bar (mem. 9th Jud. Circuit grievance com. 1973-76, chmn. 1976), Am. Coll. Mortgage Attys. Home: 394 Henkel Circle Winter Park FL 32789 Office: Suite 433 First Federal Bldg PO Box 2809 Orlando FL 32802 Tel (305) 843-4600

DOTSON, ROBERT ADAIR, b. Ames, Iowa, Jan. 21, 1946; B.S. in Econs., Iowa State U., 1968; J.D., U. Iowa, 1971. Admitted to Iowa bar, 1971; asso. firm Hutchison, Buchanan, McClure & Dotson, and predecessor, Algona, Iowa, 1972-73, partner, 1973—; bd. dirs. Kossuth County (Iowa) Med. Center, Inc. Mem. Assn. Trial Lawyers of Iowa, Am., Iowa Kossuth County (sec. 1974-76) bar assns. Home: 801 S Jones St Algona IA 50511 Office: 111 N Dodge St Algona IA 50511 Tel (515) 295-3567

DOTY, DAVID SINGLETON, b. Anoka, Minn., June 30, 1929; B.A., U. Minn., 1961, LL.B., 1961. Admitted to Minn. bar, 1961; asso. firm Felhaber, Larson, Fenlon & Vogt, St. Paul, 1961-62, Popham, Haik, Schnobrich, Kaufuman & Doty, Mpls., 1962—; instr. William Mitchell Coll. Law, 1963-64. Active Commn. Police Regulations,

1976—; trustee Mpls. Library Bd., Mpls. Found. Mem. Am., Minn. (gov. 1976—), Hennepin County (pres. 1975-76) bar assns., Am. Judicature Soc. Home: 146 W Rustic Lodge Ave Minneapolis MN 55409 Office: 4344 IDS Center Minneapolis MN 55402 Tel (612) 335-9331

DOTY, ROBERT WALTER, b. Benton Harbor, Mich., Mar. 9, 1942; B.A. in Psychology, U. Houston, 1964; LL.B., Harvard U., 1967. Admitted to Tex. bar, 1967, Nebr. bar, 1973; asso. firm Fulbright & Jaworski, Houston, 1967-73; asst. prof. law. Creighton U., 1973-75, asso. prof., 1975-76; gen. counsel Municipal Fin. Officers Assn., Washington, 1977—; cons. Kutak, Rock, Cohen, Campbell, Garfinkle & Woodward, Omaha, summer 1974. Mem. Am., Tex., Nebr. bar assns. Contbr. articles and monograph to profl. jours. Office: 1730 Rhode Island Ave NW Suite 512 Washington DC 20036 Tel (202) 466-2014

DOUB, WILLIAM OFFUTT, b. Cumberland, Md., Sept. 3, 1931; B.A., Washington and Jefferson Coll., 1953; LL.B., U. Md., 1956. Admitted to Md. bar, 1956, D.C. bar, 1975; asso. firm Bartlett, Poe & Claggett, Balt., 1958-61; partner firm Niles, Barton & Wilmer, Balt., 1961-71, firm LeBoeuf, Lamb, Leiby & MacRae, Washington and N.Y.C., 1974-77, firm Doub, Purcell, Muntzing & Hansen, Washington, 1977—; people's counsel Md. Pub. Service Commn., 1957-58; chmn. Md. Pub. Service Commn., 1958-71; commr. AEC, 1971-74. Chmn. Balt. City Minimum Wage Commn., 1964-66. Mem. Am., Md., Fed. bar assns. Contbr. articles in field to profl. jours. Home: 6 Warde Ct Potomac MD 20854 Office: 1757 N St NW Washington DC 20036 Tel (202) 457-7500

DOUGHERTY, DANIEL JOHN, b. N.Y.C., Nov. 4, 1928; B.S., Fordham U., 1950; J.D., St. John's U., 1953. Admitted to N.Y. State bar, 1954, Fed. bar, 1956, U.S. Supreme Ct. bar, 1975; partner firm Kirlin, Campbell & Keating, N.Y.C., 1964—; mem. faculty Practising Law Inst., N.Y.C., 1958-. Mem. Maritime Law Assn. U.S. Author: (with Martin J. Norris) Pleasure Boating Legal and Business Problems, 1969; Current Problems and Procedures under the Longshoremen and Harbor Workers' Compensation Act Amendments, 1976. Office: 120 Broadway St New York City NY 10005 Tel (212) 732-5520

DOUGHERTY, JAMES WARREN, b. Jersey City, Mar. 5, 1946; B.A., Fordham U., 1967; J.D. (Hudson County Bar Found. scholar 1971), Seton Hall U., 1971. Admitted to N.J. bar, 1971, U.S. Dist. Ct. for So. Dist. N.Y. bar, 1972, U.S. Dist. Ct. for Eastern Dist. N.Y. bar, 1975; spl. atty., U.S. Dept. Justice, 1972-75; dep. atty. gen., State of N.J., 1975; sr. asst. pros. atty., Passaic County, N.J., 1975—; law sec. U.S. 3d Circuit Ct. Appeals, 1971-72. Mem. Hudson County Bar Assn. Office: Court House Hamilton St Paterson NJ 07505 Tel (201) 525-5000

DOUGHTY, THOMAS PAREMORE, b. Ronceverte, W.Va., Jan. 15, 1942; B.S. in Econs., U. S.C., 1964, J.D., 1968. Admitted to S.C. bar, 1968; individual practice law, Charleston, S.C., 1971—. Mem. S.C. Bar Assn. Home: 211 Collingwood St Charleston SC 29407 Office: 93 Broad St Charleston SC 29401 Tel (803) 723-8958

DOUGLAS, BARTON THRASHER, b. Gainesville, Fla., Mar. 23, 1908; pre-law student U. Fla. at Gainesville, 1926-29, LL.B., 1932, J.D., 1967. Admitted to Fla. bar, 1932, Tex. bar, 1935; judge adv. U.S. Naval Forces, Western Australia, 1943; individual practice law, Gainesville, 1943-74; ret., 1974. Pres., Alachua County Riding Assn.; elder 1st Presbyn. Ch. Mem. Fla., Tex., Am., Eighth Jud. Circuit (past pres.) bar assns., Am. Judicature Soc., Am. Acad. Matrimonial Lawyers, Atlanta Claim Assn., Internat. Acad. Law and Sci., Fed. Bar Assn. Home: 612 NE 4th Ave Gainesville FL 32601 Office: PO Drawer 1228 Gainesville FL 32602 Tel (904) 372-9506

DOUGLAS, BRUCE MICHAEL, b. Detroit, Aug. 17, 1946; A.B., Gettysburg Coll. 1968; J.D. Georgetown U., 1971. Admitted to Colo. bar, 1973; asst. solicitor gen. State of Colo., Denver, 1973—. Mem. Am. Bar Assn. Home: 1131 S Yosemite Way Denver CO 80231 Office: 1525 Sherman St 3d Floor Denver CO 80203 Tel (303) 892-3611

DOUGLAS, CHARLES GWYNNE, III, b. Abington, Pa., Dec. 2, 1942; B.A., U. N.H., 1965; LL.B., Boston U., 1968. Admitted to N.H. bar, 1968; asso. firm McLane, Carleton, Graf, Greene & Brown, Manchester, N.H., 1968-70; partner firm Perkins Douglas & Brock, Concord, N.H., 1970-74; asso. justice N.H. Superior Ct., 1974-76, N.H. Supreme Ct., 1977—; legal counsel to N.H. Gov., 1972-74. Alt. del. Republican Nat. Conv., 1972; mem. N.H. Constl. Conv. Study Commn., 1974; pres. N.H. Task Force on Child Abuse, 1976—. Mem. N.H., Am. bar assns., Nat. Conf. State Trial Judges (exec. com.). Contbr. articles to legal jours. Home: RFD 1 Concord NH 03301 Office: 10 Green St Concord NH 03301 Tel (603) 225-2791

DOUGLAS, JAMES MATTHEW, b. Onalaska, Tex., Feb. 11, 1944; B.A., Tex. So. U., 1966, J.D., 1970; J.S.M., Stanford, 1971. Computer scientist Singer, Inc., Houston, 1966-70, 71-72; admitted to Tex. bar, 1970; asst. prof. law Tex. So. U., 1971-72; asst. prof., asst. dean Cleve. State U. Coll. Law, 1972-75; asso. prof., asso. dean Syracuse U. Coll. Law, 1975—. Active Boy Scouts Am., 1966-68, NAACP, Houston, 1966-72. Mem. State Bar Tex., Am. Bar Assn. Named Outstanding Grad. Tex. So. U., 1972. Home: 4950 Westbrook Hills Dr Bldg 5 Apt 8 Syracuse NY 13215 Office: Coll of Law Syracuse U Syracuse NY 13210 Tel (315) 423-2392

DOUGLAS, JOHN WOOLMAN, b. Phila., Aug. 15, 1921; B.A., Princeton, 1943; LL.B., Yale, 1948; D.Phil., Oxford U., 1950. Admitted to bar, 1948; with firm Covington & Burling, Washington, 1950-51, 52-63, 66—; clk. to Justice Harold H. Burton, U.S. Supreme Ct., 1951-52; asst. atty. gen. civil div. U.S. Dept. Justice, Washington, 1963-66. Mem. D.C. (pres. 1974-75), Am., Fed. bar assns., Nat. Legal Aid and Defender Assn. (pres. 1970-71). Home: 5700 Kirkside Dr Chevy Chase MD 20015 Office: 888 16th St NW Washington DC 20006 Tel (202) 452-6386

DOUGLAS, PAUL L., b. Sioux Falls, S.D., Sept. 19, 1927; B.A., U. Nebr., 1951, J.D., 1953. Practiced law, 1953-56; with Lancaster County (Nebr.) Atty's. Office, 1956-75, county atty., 1960-75; atty. gen. State of Nebr., 1975—; chmn. Nebr. Commn. on Law Enforcement and Criminal Justice. Mem. Lincoln Bar Assn. (past pres.), Nat. Assn. Attys. Gen. Office: Atty Gen of Alaska 2117 State Capitol 1445 K St Lincoln NE 68509*

DOUGLAS, ROBERT ELLIS, b. St. Joseph, Mo., Sept. 30, 1919; A.B., Westminster Coll., 1941; LL.B., U. Kans., 1947. Admitted to Mo. bar, 1947; asso. firm Brown, Douglas & Brown, St. Joseph, 1947-54, partner, 1954—. Pres. St. Joseph Symphony Soc., 1968-70, dir., sec. St. Joseph Indsl. Found., 1961—; bd. dirs. Am. Lung Assn., 1963—, pres., 1977-78, dir. West Mo. br., 1950—; trustee, regent Mo. Western Coll., 1966-75. Mem. Mo., Am. bar assns., Am. Judicature Soc., Order of Coif, Phi Delta Phi. Home: 3 Hawthorn St St Joseph MO 64505 Office: 202-209 Pioneer Bldg St Joseph MO 64501 Tel (816) 232-7748

DOUGLAS, WILLIAM ORVILLE, b. Maine, Minn., Oct. 16, 1898; A.B., Whitman Coll., Walla Walla, Wash., 1920, LL.D. (hon.), 1938; LL.B., Columbia, 1925; M.A. (hon.), Yale, 1932; LL.D. (hon.), Wesleyan U., 1940, Washington and Jefferson Coll., 1942, William and Mary Coll., 1943, Rollins Coll., 1947, Nat. U., 1949, New Sch. for Social Research, 1952, U. Toledo, 1956, Bucknell U., 1958, Dahousie U., N.S., 1958, Colby Coll., 1961, Wayne State U., 1963, U. N.Mex., 1964, W.Va. State Coll., 1964, Parsons Coll., 1964, U. San Fernando Valley, 1967. Admitted to N.Y. bar, 1926; faculty Columbia Law Sch., 1924-28, Yale Law Sch., 1928-36; dir. protective com. study SEC, 1934-36, commr., 1936-39, chmn., 1937-39; asso. justice U.S. Supreme Ct., 1939-75; ret., 1975. Mem. PEN, Overseas Press Club, Phi Beta Kappa, Phi Alpha Delta, Delta Sigma Rho, Beta Theta Pi. Author: America Challenged, 1960; My Wilderness, The Pacific West, 1960; A Living Bill of Rights, 1961; My Wilderness, East to Katahdin, 1961; Muir of the Mountains, 1961; Democracy's Manifesto, 1962; Anatomy of Liberty, 1963; Mr. Lincoln and the Negroes, 1963; Freedom of the Mind, 1964; A Wilderness Bill of Rights, 1965; The Bible and the Schools, 1966; Farewell to Texas, 1967; Toward a Global Federalism, 1969; Points of Rebellion, 1969; International Dissent, 1970; Holocaust or Hemispheric Co-op, 1971; The Three Hundred Year War, 1972; Go East Young Man: The Early Years, 1974; others; contbr. articles to mags. Home: Goose Prairie WA 98929

DOUGLASS, DONALD GUY, b. Phila. Aug. 4, 1943; A.B., Marietta Coll., 1965; J.D., Cornell U., 1968; LL.M. in Taxation, Boston U., 1974. Admitted to Pa. bar, 1968, U.S. Dist. Ct. bar, 1968, U.S. Tax Ct. bar, 1971; practiced in Scranton, Pa., 1968; asso. firm Gelb & Myers, 1969-73; asso. in practice with Henry P. Burke, 1975—; dir. supplies, City of Scranton, 1970-71, asst. solicitor, 1971; lectr. income taxation C.L.U. candidates, 1974. Mem. Am., Pa., Lackawanna County (dir.) bar assns., Am. Judicature Soc., Phi Alpha Delta. Home: 848 N Main Ave Scranton PA 18504 Office: 410 Scranton Electric Bldg Scranton PA 18503 Tel (717) 961-3666

DOUGLASS, WILLIAM DEXTER, b. Pensacola, Fla., Dec. 6, 1929; B.S., U. Fla., 1950, J.D., 1955. Admitted to Fla. bar, 1955; pres., sr. partner Douglass & Powell, Tallahassee, 1955—; pres. jr. bar sect. Fla. Bar, 1961-62, bd. govs. bar, 1960-62. Chmn. bd. trustees Fla. Sch. Deaf & Blind, Tallahassee, 1964—; nat. adv. group Nat. Tech. Inst. Deaf, Rochester, 1971—; bd. govs. Woodward Acad., College Park, Ga., 1970—. Mem. Assn. Trial Lawyers Am., Acad. Fla. Trial Lawyers, Am. Bar Assn. (ins. negligence and compensations sect.). Office: 317 E Park Ave Tallahassee FL 32302 Tel (904) 224-6191

DOUNAY, HERBERT, b. N.Y.C., June 22, 1913; B.S., Coll. City N.Y., 1933; J.D., N.Y.U., 1937. Admitted to N.Y. State bar, 1939, Calif. bar, 1945; individual practice law, Sepulveda, Calif., 1945—. Committeeman Nat. Found. March of Dimes, 1962-68, Am. Cancer Soc., 1965-70; pres. Apt. Owners Assn., San Fernando, 1968. Mem. San Fernando Valley Bar Assn., Am. Legion (Comdr. 1964). Contbr. articles to mags. Home: 12748 Basset St North Hollywood CA 91605 Office: 8600 Sepulveda Blvd Suites 6 and 7 Sepulveda CA 91343 Tel (213) 892-8684

DOUTHWAITE, GRAHAM, b. Johannesburg, South Africa, Oct. 27, 1913; B.A., LL.B., U. Witwatersrand, South Africa; B.C.L., Oxford (Eng.) U., 1940. Admitted to South Africa bar; practiced in Johannesburg, 1936-38; with South African Def. Force, 1940-46; mem. staff South African Dept. External Affairs, London, 1946-49, Pretoria, South Africa, 1950-51, Rome, 1952-55; research editor Bancroft Whitney Pub. Co., San Francisco, 1956-59; asst. prof. law, asso. prof., prof. U. Santa Clara (Calif.), 1959—. Home: 610 Monroe St Santa Clara CA 95050 Office: U Santa Clara Sch Law Santa Clara CA 95053 Tel (408) 984-4559

DOW, WILBUR EGERTON, JR., b. Bklyn., Aug. 5, 1906; student U. Wash., 1925-28, U. So. Calif., 1931-32; LL.B., N.Y. U., 1934. Admitted to N.Y. State bar, 1936; with firm Dow & Symmers, Dow & Stonebridge. Mem. Soc. Naval Architects and Marine Engrs., Maritime Law Assn., Assn. Bar City N.Y., Am. Bar Assn., Marine Soc. City N.Y. (pres. 1971-76), Delta Tau Delta. Home: Pine Point Lake George NY 12845 Office: 80 Broad St New York City NY 10004 also 2800 ITM Bldg New Orleans LA 70130 Tel (504) 586-8777

DOWD, JAMES FRANCIS, b. Bronx, N.Y., Aug. 21, 1941; B.., L.I. U., 1965; J.D., St. John's U., Bklyn., 1968. Admitted to N.Y. bar, 1969; asso. firm Shea, Gould, Climenko & Kramer, N.Y.C., 1968-71, Russell & Russell, N.Y.C., 1971; v.p., gen. counsel, corporate sec. Skandia Group, N.Y.C., 1971—; mem. industry adv. com. N.Y. State Senate Select Com. on Recodification of N.Y. Ins. Laws. Mem. Am., N.Y. State, Nassau County bar assns., Assn. Bar City N.Y. Office: 280 Park Ave New York City NY 10017 Tel (212) 490-0500

DOWD, ROBERT GERALD, b. St. Louis, May 18, 1920; B.S., St. Louis U., 1943, J.D., 1948. Admitted to Mo. bar, 1948; individual practice law, St. Louis, 1948-49; asst. counselor City of St. Louis, 1949-50; magistrate City of St. Louis, 1950-53, judge City Ct., 1953-58; partner firm Dowd and Dowd, St. Louis, 1957-65; circuit judge, State of Mo., St. Louis, 1965-69; judge Mo. Ct. Appeals, 1969—. Chmn. Civic Employment Corp., St. Louis, 1968—; bd. dirs. Met. YMCA, St. Louis, 1972—; mem. Pres.'s U.S. Conf. on Traffic Safety. Mem. Mo. Bar Assn., Lawyers Assn. St. Louis. Award of Honor, 1972. Recipient Alumni Merit award St. Louis U., 1975. Home: 3999 Holly Hills St Louis MO 63116 Office: Civil Cts Bldg 12th and Market Sts St Louis MO 63101 Tel (314) 453-4608

DOWD, THOMAS NATHAN, b. Sioux City, Iowa, Mar. 29, 1917; LL.B., George Wash. U., 1939, J.D., 1942. Admitted to U.S. Dist. Ct. bar, 1942, FCC bar, 1946, Md. bar, 1952, U.S. Supreme Ct. bar, 1957; partner firm Pierson, Ball & Dowd, Washington, 1945-77, mem. counsel, 1977—. Mem. Washington, Am., FCC bar assns., Order of Coif, Phi Beta Kappa, Phi Delta Phi. Home: 13500 Travilah Rd Gaithersburg MD 20760 Office: 1000 Ring Bldg Washington DC 20036 Tel (202) 331-8566

DOWD, WILLIAM TIMOTHY, b. Muskogee, Okla., May 3, 1927; A.B., Xavier U., 1951; LL.B., U. Tulsa, 1957. Admitted to Okla. bar, 1957, U.S. Supreme Ct. bar, 1967; asso. firm Landrith & McGee, Tulsa, 1957-63; partner firm Landrith, McGee & Dowd, Tulsa, 1963-65; partner firm McGee & Dowd, Tulsa, 1965-66; pub. defender Tulsa County, 1958; mem. Okla. House Reps., 1963-64; chief legal officer for Gov. Okla, 1967-69; exec. dir. Interstate Oil Compact Commn., Oklahoma City, 1969—. Mem. Okla. Gov.'s Energy Adv. Council, 1975—, Nat. Petroleum Council Com. Enhanced Recovery, 1976—, Fed. Power Commn. Nat. Gas Survey, 1971—, U.S. Nat. Com. World Energy Conf., 1972-75, Interstate Oil Compact Commn. Task Force Underground Injection Control Programs, EPA, 1975—. Mem. Am., Fed. Power, Okla. bar assns., Oklahoma City Petroleum Club, Assn. Petroleum Writers (associate mem.). Home: 2504 NW 120th St Oklahoma City OK 73120 Office: 900 N E 23d St PO Box 53127 Oklahoma City OK 73105 Tel (405) 525-3556

DOWDY, WILLIAM CLARENCE, JR., McKinney, Tex., Feb. 27, 1925; student N. Tex. Agrl. Coll., 1942-43; B.B.A., U. Tex., Austin, 1949, LL.B., 1951, J.D., 1951. Admitted to Tex. bar, 1951, U.S. Supreme Ct. bar, 1957; asst. dist. atty. Dallas County, Tex., 1951-54; atty. Tex. and Pacific Ry. Co., Dallas, 1954-59, gen. atty., 1959—; gen. atty. Mo. Pacific R.R. Co., Dallas, 1959—; commr. grand jury, Dallas County, 1973. Mem. exec. com. Dallas County Democratic Party, 1964-74; bd. dirs. Democratic Com. for Responsible Govt., 1970—; chmn. 8th Senate Dist. Tex. Dem. Party, 1972-73; elder, trustee John Calvin Presbyterian Ch., Dallas, 1954-65. Mem. Am. Judicature Soc., Am., Tex., Dallas bar assns., Nat. Assn. R.R. Trial Counsel (exec. com. 1972—, v.p. S.W. region 1975—), Phi Alpha Delta. Home: 3308 Duchess Trail Dallas TX 75229 Office: 505 N Industrial Blvd Dallas TX 75207 Tel (214) 748-8181

DOWELL, DOUGLAS ARLEN, b. Melbourne, Mo., Nov. 1, 1937; A.B., Rockhurst Coll., 1963; J.D., U. Mo., Kansas City, 1970. Admitted to Mo. bar, 1970; claims rep. Am. States Ins. Co., Kansas City, Mo., 1964-67; asso. with Clark Ullom, Kansas City, 1970-72; asso. firm Bailey, Maloney & Dowell, Independence, Mo., 1972-74, firm Dowell, Boland, McNearney & Desselle, Independence, 1974—. Bd. dirs. Com. for County Progress, 1972-76. Mem. Mo. Bar, Kansas City, Mo., Eastern Jackson County Bars. Home: 1216 W 72d St Kansas City MO 64114 Office: 3675 Noland Rd Independence MO 64055 Tel (816) 836-3010

DOWELL, JAMES DALE, b. Goose Creek, Tex., July 17, 1932; A.B., Tex. A. and M. U., 1954; LL.B., U. Tex., 1957. Admitted to Tex. bar, 1956, U.S. Supreme Ct. bar, 1969; asso. firm King, Sharfstein & Rienstra, Beaumont, Tex., 1957-63, partner, 1963-68; partner firm Reinstra, Rienstra & Dowell, Beaumont, 1968—. Mem. Tex. Democratic Exec. Com., 1966-68; del. Dem. Nat. Conv., 1976. Mem. Jefferson County (v.p. 1976—), Am. bar assns., State Bar Tex. Home: 6275 Wilchester Ln Beaumont TX 77706 Office: 707 Beaumont Savs Bldg Beaumont TX 77701 Tel (713) 833-5011

DOWELL, MARION RICHARD, b. Du Quoin, Ill., Feb. 28, 1916; A.S. in Engring, Port Arthur Coll., 1943; student Northeastern U., 1944-46, Northwestern U., 1941, U. Ill., 1939-40; B.A., So. Ill. U., 1946; LL.B., Lincoln Coll. of Law, Springfield, Ill., 1948. Admitted to Ill. bar, 1950, Mo. bar, 1963; research asso. Harvard, 1943-46; hearing examiner Ill. Commerce Commn., Springfield, 1946-50; partner firm Dowell and Dowell, Salem, Ill., 1950-52; tax atty. Standard Oil Co. of Indiana, Overland Park, Kans., 1952—; pres. Ill. Tax Reps. Assn., 1963-64. Mem. Mo., Ill., Am., Kansas City bar assns., Am. Judicature Soc., Am. Petroleum Inst. (chmn. Mo. State com., asst. chmn. Nebr. Com.), Mo-Ark. Assn. Tax Reps., Kansas City Tax Club (pres. 1971-72), Mo., Nebr. assessors assns. (asso.), Assn. Assessing Officers. Recipient certificate of appreciation U.S. Office Sci. Research and Devel., 1945, Govt. of Jackson County (Mo.), 1974, letter of appreciation Harvard, 1946. Home: 4734 Harvard Ave Kansas City MO 64133 Office: 8826 Santa Fe Dr Overland Park KS 66201 Tel (816) 968-4148

DOWER, HARRY ALLEN, b. Bethlehem, Pa., Nov. 29, 1918; A.B., Lafayette Coll., 1940; LL.B., Yale, 1948, J.D., 1970. Admitted to Pa. bar, 1949, Fed. bar, 1949, U.S. Supreme Ct. bar, 1974; individual practice law, Allentown, Pa., 1949—; gen. counsel Alpo Pet Foods (Allen Products Co.), 1964-69; sr. partner firm Dower, Yarema & Co., profl. corp., Allentown, 1973—; adj. prof. law Grad. Sch., Coll. Bus., Lehigh U., Bethlehem, 1969—; legal counsel ACLU of Lehigh Valley, 1950—. Trustee Allentown br. NAACP Scholarship Fund, 1965—; bd. dirs. Wiley House, Bethlehem, 1973—. Mem. Pa. Bar Assn., Author: (with Charles Vihon) Cases on Legal Problems of Business in a Free Society, 1973. Home: 1665 Lehigh Pkwy N Allentown PA 18103 Office: Box 950 Allentown PA 18105 Tel (215) 821-1116

DOWLEN, GEORGE EULACE, b. Canyon, Tex., June 12, 1934; B.A., U. Tex., 1957, LL.B., 1960. Admitted to Tex. bar, 1960; asst. city atty. Amarillo (Tex.), 1960-62; partner firm Dowlen & Cox, Canyon, Tex., 1962-66, firm McGlasson & Dowlen, Canyon, 1966-72; criminal dist. atty. Randall County (Tex.), 1964-75; judge 81st Dist. Ct., Potter and Randall Counties, Tex., 1975—. Trustee 1st United Methodist Ch., Canyon, 1964—. Mem. Tex., Amarillo bar assns. Home: Apt 127 Wellington Manor 2700 W 16th St Amarillo TX 79102 Office: 502 Potter County Courthouse Amarillo TX 79101 Tel (806) 372-6221

DOWLING, LEO JEROME, b. Hartford, Conn., Feb. 18, 1898; student Dartmouth Coll., 1918; B.A. Cath. U. Am., 1920; LL.B., Yale U., 1925. Admitted to Conn. bar, 1925, U.S. Dist. Ct. bar for Dist. Conn., 1934; partner firm Dowling and Cosgrove, Hartford, 1925—; dir. Fowler & Hunttine Co., Hartford, 1950—, McNie & Hopkins, Inc., Bloomfield, Conn., 1963—; trustee Preso-Hartford, Inc. Employees Pension Fund, West Hartford, Conn., 1960—. Police commr. City of Hartford, 1931-37; adv. bd. Diocesan Bur. Social Service, Hartford, 1938-42. Mem. Hartford County Bar Assn., Am. Judicature Soc. Decorated Congl. Selective Service award and medal; recipient Half Century award Conn. Bar Assn., 1975. Home: 36 Harmon Dr Suffield CT 06078 Office: 410 Asylum St Hartford CT 06103 Tel (203) 522-2936

DOWLING, RODERICK ANTHONY, b. N.Y.C., Dec. 29, 1940; B.S., Fairfield U., 1962; J.D., Fordham U., 1965. Admitted to N.Y. bar, 1965, Ga. bar, 1973; asso. firm Cahill, Gordon & Reindel, N.Y.C., 1965-72; v.p., gen. counsel U.S. Industries, Atlanta, 1972-73, Fuqua Industries, Inc., Atlanta, 1973—. Mem. Ga., N.Y.C. bar assns. Home: 4475 Harris Trail NW Atlanta GA 30327 Office: 3800 1st Nat Bank Tower Atlanta GA 30303 Tel (404) 658-9000

DOWLING, WILLIAM FRANCIS, b. Utica, N.Y., Dec. 19, 1946; B.A. (N.Y. State Regents scholar), Utica Coll., 1968; J.D. (Alcoa Found. Constl. Law scholar), St. John's U., 1971; postgrad. (Nat. Inst. Trial Advocacy scholar) U. Colo., 1975. Admitted to N.Y. State bar, 1972, U.S. Supreme Ct. bar, 1976; atty. Legal Aid Soc., N.Y.C., 1972—; lectr. in field; judge Moot Ct. N.Y. U. Law Sch. Criminal Law Clinic, 1976. Mem. Am., N.Y. State bar assns., N.Y. Criminal Bar Assn., N.Y. State Defenders Assn., Legal Aid Soc. Assn. Attys., Nat. Legal Aid and Defender Assn., So. Poverty Law Conf. Home: 79 Horatio St New York City NY 10014 Office: 80 Lafayette St New York City NY 10013 Tel (212) 577-3970

DOWNES, ROGER PATRICK, b. Buffalo, Apr. 24, 1940; B.A. (N.Y. State Regents scholar), U. Buffalo, 1962; J.D., U. of Pacific, 1971. Admitted to Calif. bar, 1972; atty. Pacific Tel. & Tel. Co., San Francisco, 1972-76, counsel, San Diego, 1976—; spl. asst. antitrust AT&T, N.Y.C., 1975. Bd. dirs. Time Line, Inc., counseling service, Sacramento, 1973-76. Mem. San Diego, San Francisco, Calif., Am. bar assns. Decorated Air medal, D.F.C. Office: 1720 Union Bank Bldg 525 B St San Diego CA 92101 Tel (714) 238-2896

DOWNEY, ARTHUR HAROLD, b. N.Y.C., Nov. 21, 1938; B.A., Central Coll., Pella, Iowa, 1960; LL.B., Cornell U., 1963. Admitted to Colo. bar, 1963; asso. firm Weller, Friedrich Hickisch & Hazlitt, Denver, 1963-70, partner, 1970—; mem. faculty Nat. Inst. Trial Advocacy, Boulder, Colo., 1973—; lectr. Harvard Law Sch., 1976—. Vice moderator Presbytery of Denver, 1974. Mem. Denver, Colo., Am. bar assns., Am. Coll. Legal Medicine (asso.-in-law), Colo. Def. Lawyers Assn. (pres. 1977—). Office: 900 Capitol Life Center Denver CO 80203 Tel (303) 861-8000

DOWNEY, BRANDT CHASE, III, b. Indpls., Feb. 25, 1945; B.S., Ind. U., 1968; J.D., Stetson U., 1971. Admitted to Fla. bar, 1971; law clk. Fox, George, Loeffler & Downey, Clearwater, Fla., 1970-71, asso., 1971-75, partner, 1975—. Treas., Mental Health Assn. Pinellas County (Fla.), 1973-74, pres., 1974-76, v.p., 1976—; bd. dirs. Big Bros. Pinellas County, Inc. Mem. Clearwater, Am. bar assns., Fla. Bar. Office: 2111 Drew St Clearwater FL 33518 Tel (813) 443-0411

DOWNEY, BRIAN JOSEPH, b. Worcester, Mass., Mar. 29, 1935; B.S., U. Tampa, 1960; J.D., Western New England Coll., 1969. Admitted to Mass. Bar, 1972, U.S. Dist. Ct. Dist. Mass. bar, 1973; individual practice law, Springfield, Mass., 1972—. Mem. Hamdden County Bar Assn. Home: 69 Warwick St Longmeadow MA 01106 Office 31 Elm St Springfield MA 01103 Tel (413) 732-5802

DOWNEY, EDWARD FRANCIS, b. St. Louis, Jan. 19, 1924; LL.B., St. Louis U., 1950, J.D., 1968. Admitted to Mo. bar, 1950, Ill. bar, 1950; individual practice law, St. Louis, 1950-70; adminstrv. law judge U.S. Bur. Hearings and Appeals, St. Louis, 1970—. Mem. Am., Mo. (treas.), St. Louis bar assns. Home: 2091 Shoreham St Florissant MO 63033 Office: 210 N 12th St St Louis MO 63101 Tel (314) 425-4881

DOWNEY, EDWARD F(RANCIS), b. Chgo., Sept. 7, 1930; B.S., Georgetown U., 1952, J.D., 1958. Admitted to Ill. bar, 1958; counsel Assn. Western R.R.'s, Chgo., 1959-60; individual practice law, Chgo., 1961—. Mem. Chgo. Bar Assn. Home: 10238 S Hoyne Ave Chicago IL 60643 Office: 10336 S Western Ave Chicago IL 60643 Tel (312) 233-4040

DOWNEY, JAMES MORRIS, b. Anniston, Ala., June 25, 1943; A.B., Davidson Coll., 1965; J.D., U. Fla., 1968; postgrad. Princeton Theol. Sem., 1968-69. Admitted to Fla. bar, 1968, Colo. bar, 1971; with legal dept. Seaboard Coastline R.R., Jacksonville, Fla., 1968; asso. firm Rodden, Cooper, Woods & Mitchell, Denver, 1971-74; asst. solicitor gen. state of Colo., Denver, 1974-77; asst. county atty. Boulder County (Colo.), 1977—; legal adviser to Colo. Occupational Safety and Health Standards Bd., 1974-77; lectr. Colo. State U. Extension Service, 1975, gov.'s safety congress, 1975; mem. coordinating com. Colo. Extension Rural Farm Safety, 1976. Chmn. Bd. Missions and Social Action, Boulder, Colo., 1976, 77; mem. criminal justice task force Boulder Council Chs., 1975-76. Mem. Am., Fla., Colo., Boulder bar assns. Contbr. article to legal publ. Home: 4880 Lee Circle Boulder CO 80303 Office: 3400 N Broadway Boulder CO 80302 Tel (303) 441-3428

DOWNEY, WILLIAM GERARD, b. Boston, Mar. 27, 1941; B.A., Boston Coll., 1962; J.D., Georgetown U., 1965. Admitted to Mass. bar, 1965, Pa. bar, 1973, U.S. Supreme Ct. bar, 1973; atty. JAGC, USN, 1965-68; asso. firm Edwin Trafton, Boston, 1968-72; asso. firm Clark, Ladner, Fortenbaugh & Young, 1973-75, partner, 1975—. Mem. Am., Pa. bar assns., Maritime Lawyers Soc. U.S. Home: 760 Woodlawn Dr Lansdale PA 19446 Office: 1335 Chestnut St Philadelphia PA 19107 Tel (215) LO4-5300

DOWNEY, WILLIS BATES, b. Hingham, Mass., July 6, 1897; A.B., Brown U., 1919; LL.B., Harvard, 1923. Admitted to Mass. bar, 1923, U.S. Dist. Ct. bar for Dist. Mass., 1928; asso. firm Peabody, Arnold, Batehelder & Luther, Boston, 1923-29; asst. gen. counsel Boston Elevated Railway Co., 1929-37, gen. counsel, 1937-47; gen. counsel Met. Transit Authority, Boston and area, 1947-62, cons., 1962-64; individual practice law, Hingham, 1962—; cons. Mass. Bay Transp. Authority, 1964—. Mem. Hingham Advisory Bd., 1929-44, chmn., 1937-44; mem. Hingham Municipal Light Bd., 1945-54. Mem. Mass., Am. bar assns. Home and office: 45 Lincoln St Hingham MA 02143 Tel (617) 749-1992

DOWNIE, JOHN FRANCIS, b. Lorain, Ohio, Jan. 15, 1934; B.S.S., John Carroll U., 1955; J.D., U. Detroit, 1959. Admitted to Ohio bar, 1959; asso. firm Keep & Scholz, Lorain, 1959-62; atty. Diamond Shamrock Corp., Cleve., 1962-69; v.p., sec., gen. counsel, dir. Cole Nat. Corp., Cleve., 1969—. Address: 29001 Cedar Rd Cleveland OH 44124 Tel (216) 449-4100

DOWNING, JOHN MICHAEL, b. Bklyn., June 18, 1936; B.B.A., St. Francis Coll., 1959; LL.B. cum laude, St. John's U., 1962; postgrad. N.Y. U. Law Sch., 1963-64. Admitted to N.Y. State bar, 1962, U.S. Supreme Ct. bar, 1965; with law dept. Port Authority of N.Y. State and N.J., 1962-64; asso. firm Reilly & Reilly, N.Y.C., 1964-69; individual practice law, N.Y.C., 1969—. Mem. Am., N.Y. State bar assns., N.Y. County Lawyers Assn. Contbr. articles to legal jours.; editor St. John's U. Law Rev., 1962. Home: 17 E 89th St New York City NY 10028 Office: 233 Broadway New York City NY 10007 Tel (212) 227-8090

DOWNING, THOMAS NELMS, b. Newport News, Va., Feb. 1, 1919; B.S., Va. Mil. Inst., 1940; LL.B., U. Va., 1948; LL.D. (hon.), Coll. William and Mary, 1975. Admitted to Va. bar, 1948; substitute judge City of Warwick (now Newport News) (Va.), 1952-58; mem. firm Newman Allan & Downing, Newport News, 1950-55, firm Downing & Andrews, Hampton, Va., 1955-58, firm Bateman, Downing, Redding & Conway, Newport News, 1977—; mem. 86th-94th Congresses from 1st Va. Dist., 1959-76. Bd. dirs. Riverside Hosp., Newport News, 1976—. Mem. Am., Va., Newport News, Hampton bar assns. Home: 27 Indigo Dam Rd Newport News VA 23606 Office: 11048 Warwick Blvd Newport News VA 23601 Tel (804) 596-7627

DOWNS, CHARITY ANN, b. Toms River, N.J., May 7, 1943; B.A., Georgian Ct. Coll., 1966; postgrad. U. Colo., 1966-67; J.D., Rutgers, 1971. Admitted to Vt. bar, 1971, U.S. Dist. Ct. bar, 1972, U.S. Ct. Appeals 2d Circuit bar, 1974; asso. firm Conley & Foote, Middlebury, Vt., 1971—. Mem. planning commn. Town of Wells (Vt.). Mem. Am., Vt., Addison County bar assns. Home: Wells VT 05774 Office: 11 S Pleasant St Middlebury VT 05753 Tel (802) 388-4061

DOWNS, GEORGE WARTHEN, b. Richmond, Va., Dec. 29, 1933; B.S. in Commerce, U. Va., 1957; LL.B., U. Richmond, 1960. Admitted to Va. bar, 1960, Fla. bar, 1973; practiced in Stuart, Va., 1960-65; partner firm Bareford & Downs, Richmond, 1965—; asst. commonwealth's atty. for Henrico County, Va., 1966-71; substitute judge Henrico County Gen. Dist. Ct., 1971—. Mem. Va. State, Richmond bar assns., Richmond Criminal Trial Lawyers Assn. Home: 10 Charnwood Rd Richmond VA 23229 Office: 728 E Main St Richmond VA 23219 Tel (804) 643-9070

DOYLE, HAROLD CARLON, b. Yankton, S.D., Nov. 25, 1926; LL.B., S.D. U., 1950. Admitted to S.D. bar, 1950; State's atty., Yankton County, 1957-61; U.S. atty. for S.D., 1961-69; spl. asst. atty. gen. S.D., 1974. Mem. S.D. Bar Assn. (chmn. criminal law com. 1973-75). Home: 2107 S Phillips Ave Sioux F Falls SD 57105 Office: 412 W 9th St Sioux Falls SD 57104 Tel (605) 336-2565

DOYLE, JAMES EDWARD, b. Oshkosh, Wis., July 6, 1915; B.A., U. Wis., 1937; LL.B., Columbia U., 1940. Admitted to Wis. bar, 1940, also U.S. Supreme Ct. bar; atty. criminal div. Dept. Justice, 1940-41; law clk. to asso. justice James F. Byrnes, U.S. Supreme Ct., 1941-42; cons. Office War Moblzn. and Reconversion, 1945; asst. to counselor Dept. State, 1945-46; asst. U.S. atty., Madison, Wis., 1946-48; partner firm LaFollette, Sinykin & Doyle, Madison, 1948-65; judge U.S. Dist. Ct., Western Dist. Wis., Madison, 1965—; lectr. U. Wis. Law Sch., 1951-53, 58; mem. Jud. Conf. U.S., 1972-75. Nat. co-chmn. Ams. for Democratic Action, 1953-55; chmn. Wis. Dem. Party, 1951-53; exec. dir. Stevenson for Pres. Com., 1960. Mem. Am. Law Inst., Dane County Bar Assn. (pres. 1962-63). Bd. editors Columbia U. Law Rev., 1938-40. Home: 1114 Mohican Pass St Madison WI 53711 Office: Federal Bldg PO Box 591 Madison WI 53701 Tel (608) 252-5151

DOYLE, JOHN CYRIL, b. Buffalo, Feb. 9, 1898; LL.B., Bklyn. Law Sch., 1926, LL.M., 1935; LL.M. in Labor, N.Y. U., 1954. Admitted to N.Y. bar, 1927, U.S. Supreme Ct. bar, 1954; trial counsel Globe Indemnity Co., N.Y.C., 1926-28, Great Am. Co., 1930-40; partner firm Maloney & Doyle, Bklyn., 1940—; village atty. North Haven (N.Y.). Mem. Am., Bklyn. bar assns. Home: 25 Monroe Pl Brooklyn NY 11201 Office: 16 Court St Brooklyn NY 11241 Tel (212) MA 5-1260

DOYLE, JOHN MICHAEL, b. San Antonio, Jan. 11, 1943; B.A., St. Mary's U., San Antonio, 1968, J.D., 1969. Admitted to Tex. bar, 1968; asst. city atty. City of San Antonio, 1968-71; partner firm Doyle & Johnson, San Antonio, 1971—. Mem. Am., Fed., Tex., San Antonio bar assns. Home: 10910 Cedar Elm St San Antonio TX 78230 Office: 1802 NE Loop 410 Room 222 San Antonio TX 78217 Tel (512) 826-2366

DOYLE, JOSEPH ANTHONY, b. N.Y.C., June 13, 1920; B.S. in Social Studies, Georgetown U., 1941; LL.B., Columbia, 1947. Admitted to N.Y. State bar, 1948; asso. firm Shearman & Sterling, N.Y.C., 1947-57, partner firm, 1957—. Mem. N.Y. State, Am. bar assns., Assn. Bar City N.Y. Editor Columbia Law Rev., 1946-47. Home: 32 Washington Sq W New York City NY 10011 Office: 53 Wall St New York City NY 10005 Tel (212) 483-1000

DOYLE, JOSEPH P., b. Pittston, Pa., Apr. 28, 1921; student St. John's U., Bklyn., 1946-47; grad. N.Y. Law Sch., 1949. Admitted to N.Y. bar, 1950, So. Dist. N.Y. U.S. Dist. Ct. bar, 1953; asso. Counsel The Hearst Corp., N.Y.C., 1951-62; corporate sec. and treas. The N.Y. Law Jour., N.Y.C., 1962-65; individual practice law, Plainview, N.Y., 1965—. Chmn. Pub. Employment Relations Bd., Town of Oyster Bay, N.Y., 1968—; mem. panel mediators, fact finders and arbitrators N.Y. State Pub. Employment Relations Bd. and N.J. Pub. Employment Relations Commn. Mem. Am. Arbitration Assn., Fed. Mediation and Conciliation Service, N.J. Mediation Bd., Soc. Profl. in Dispute Resolution. Office: 980 Old Country Rd Plainview NY 11803 Tel (516) 938-8040

DOYLE, RICHARD NASON, b. Kalamazoo, Jan. 26, 1941; A.B., Kalamazoo Coll., 1963; J.D., U. Chgo., 1966. Admitted to Colo. bar, 1966; partner firm Doyle Dominguez & Otis, Greeley, Colo., 1966—. Mem. Greeley Housing Authority, 1971—. Mem. Weld County (chmn. tax sect. 1975—), Colo., Am. bar assns., No. Colo. Estate Planning Council (pres. 1976-77). Home: 2456 Mountair Ln Greeley CO 80631 Office: 1201 10th Ave Greeley CO 80631 Tel (303) 353-6700

DOYLE, TOMMY ETHEN, b. Linden, Tenn., Mar. 2, 1943; B.S., U. Tenn., 1965; J.D., 1967. Admitted to Tenn. bar, 1968; asso. firm Roberts & Deatheridge, Kingston, Tenn., 1968-70; asso. firm Cameron, Oakley & Jared, Coolteville, Tenn., 1970-73; partner firm Humphreys, Taenserd & Doyle, Linden, 1973—; atty. County of Perry (Tenn.), 1974—. Bd. dirs. Perry County Library Bd., South Central Devel. Dist., Meml. Cemetary, Inc. Mem. Am., Tenn. bar assns., Tenn. Trial Lawyers Assn., Phi Delta Phi. Office: Box 216 Linden TN 37096 Tel (615) 589-2167

DRABIN, LEE STEWART, b. Los Angeles, Apr. 5, 1942; B.A., San Fernando Valley State Coll., 1965; J.D., Beverly Coll. Law, 1971. Admitted to Calif. bar, 1972; partner firm Drabin & Drabin, Sherman Oaks, Calif., 1972—. Treas., Los Angeles County chpt. United Cerebral Palsy Assn. Mem. San Fernando Valley Criminal Bar Assn. (pres. 1977), Los Angeles County, Am., San Fernando Valley bar assns. Office: Suite 207 4419 Van Nuys Blvd Sherman Oaks CA 91403 Tel (213) 788-9333

DRABKIN, MURRAY, b. N.Y.C., Aug. 3, 1928; A.B., Hamilton Coll., 1950; LL.B., Harvard U., 1953. Admitted to D.C. bar, 1953, N.Y. State bar, 1966, U.S. Supreme Ct. bar, 1972; counsel Com. Judiciary, U.S. Ho. of Reps., 1957-65, chief counsel spl. subcom. state taxation, 1961-65; spl. cons. tax policy and spl. asst. to mayor N.Y.C., 1966-68; individual practice law, N.Y.C. and Washington, 1968-71; partner firm Kaler, Worsley, Daniel & Hollman, Washington, 1972—; dir. Conn. Revenue Task Force, 1969-71; cons. Blue Ribbon Def. Panel, 1969-70; mem. adv. panel bd. govs. FRS, 1970-71. Mem. D.C. Tax Revision Commn., 1976—. Mem. N.Y. C. of C. (tax com.), Assn. Bar City N.Y., Nat. Bankruptcy Conf., D.C. Bar, Taxation with Representation, Phi Beta Kappa, Delta Sigma Rho. Contbr. articles to legal jours. Office: 1200 18th St NW Washington DC 20036 Tel (202) 331-9100

DRAGON, GARY JOSEPH, b. New Orleans, Oct. 4, 1946; B.S., La. State U., 1968, J.D., 1971. Admitted to La. bar, 1972; asso. firm McBride & Tonry, Chalmette, La., 1972-73; partner firm Tonry, Mumphrey & Dragon, and predecessor, Chalmette, 1973-75; individual practice law, Chalmette, 1975—; pres. Pontchartrain Abstract & Title Co., New Orleans, 1976—. Mem. Am. Soc. Notaries, 25th Jud. Dist. Bar, La., Am. trial lawyers assns. Office: 323 W Judge Perez Dr Chalmette LA 70043 Tel (504) 279-5297

DRAGONETTE, ANTHONY FREDERICK, b. Tucson, Ariz., Sept. 6, 1941; B.A. in Polit. Sci., U. Calif., Santa Barbara, 1963; J.D. U. Calif., Berkeley, 1966; Admitted to Calif. bar, 1966, U.S. Supreme Ct. bar, 1975; asso. firm William J. Connolly, San Francisco, 1966-67; staff atty. Safeco Ins. Cos., Burlingame, Calif., 1967-69; partner firm Ruston, Nance & DiCaro, Tustin, Calif., 1969—. Mem. Am., Orange County bar assns., Calif. State Bar, Am. Bd. Trial Advocates, So. Calif. Def. Counsel. Office: 111 Fashion Ln Tustin CA 92680 Tel (714) 832-2220

DRAHEIM, NEWT, b. Clarion, Iowa, Jan. 21, 1926; B.A., Iowa State Tchrs. Coll., Cedar Falls, 1950; J.D., Drake U., 1954; Prin. elementary and jr. high sch., Madrid, Iowa, 1950-51; admitted to Iowa bar, 1954; appeal referee Iowa Employment Security Commn., 1954-56; partner firm Archerd & Draheim, and predecessor, Clarion, 1957-70; county atty. Wright County (Iowa), 1957-60; judge 2d Jud. Dist. Ct. Iowa, Clarion, 1970—. Past chmn. bd. trustees, past chmn. deaconate bd., moderator First Congl. Ch., Clarion; past mem. credentials com. Iowa Republican Com.; vice chmn. bd. commrs. Clarion Meml. Hosp.; mem. Clarion Zoning and Planning Commn., 1960-70. Mem. Iowa Judges Assn. (sec.-treas., exec. bd., chmn. legis. com.), Iowa (bd. govs., past mem. exec. com.), Wright County (past pres.), 11th Jud. Dist. (past pres.) bar assns. Home: 902 2d Ave NE Clarion IA 50525 Office: Dist Ct Iowa Clarion IA 50525 Tel (515) 532-3695

DRAKE, DONALD WILLIS, b. Corry, Pa., Dec. 19, 1916; LL.B., U. Buffalo, 1954. Admitted to N.Y. bar, 1954; casualty adjuster Allstate Ins. Co., Buffalo, 1954-55, atty., 1955-57; asst. atty. Niagara County (N.Y.), 1957-58; law guardian Niagara County Family Ct., 1959—. Mem. Niagara County, City Niagara Falls bar assns. Home: 511 3rd St Niagara Falls NY Office: 513 3rd St Niagara Falls NY 14301 Tel (716) 285-6989

DRAKE, HOWARD, b. Tryon, Okla, Dec. 27, 1905; A.B., Central Okla. State U., 1932; LL.B., LaSalle U., 1938; J.D., McGeorge Sch. Law, 1954. Admitted to Mont. bar, 1938, Calif. bar, 1955; tchr. pub. schs., Wellston, Okla., 1925-30; with C.E., U.S. Army, 1934-64; adminstrv. asst., atty. State of Calif., Sacramento, 1964-71; individual practice law, Sacramento. Mem. Mont., Calif. bar assns. Home: 5736 Spilman Ave Sacramento CA 95819 Tel (916) 457-3222

DRAKE, HUGH HESS, b. Wayne, Nebr., Apr. 30, 1928; B.S. in Elec. Engring., U. Colo., 1950; J.D., DePaul U., 1957. Admitted to Ill. bar, 1957, D.C. bar, 1963, Colo. bar, 1967; field engr. Gen. Electric Co., Denver, 1950-53; law trainee Washington, 1953-55; agent to sr. patent atty. Zenith Radio Corp., Chgo., 1955-67; individual practice law, Ft. Collins, Colo., 1967—; asst. municipal judge, Ft. Collins, 1969-71. Pres. Madison Sch. PTA, Elmhurst, Ill., 1960-61; councilman City of Elmhurst, 1961-65; trustee St. Luke's Hosp., Denver, 1969-71; capt. Sheriff's Motorized Patrol, Ft. Collins, 1971—. Mem. Colo., Larimer bar assns., Nat. Sheriffs Assn., Star and Sextant, Eta Kappa Nu, Sigma Alpha Epsilon, Delta Theta Phi. Home: Route 1 Livermore CO 80536 Office: 1501 Lemay St Fort Collins CO 80521 Tel (303) 493-0123

DRAKE, ROBERT TUCKER, b. Wilmette, Ill., Feb. 16, 1907; A.B., Dartmouth, 1929; LL.B., Columbia, 1934. Admitted to N.Y. bar, 1934, D.C. bar, 1935, Ill. bar, 1937; atty. Fed. Alcohol Control Adminstrn., Washington, 1934-35, Resettlement Adminstrn., Washington, 1935-36; asso. firm Alden Latham & Young, Chgo., 1937-42; atty. NLRB, Chgo., 1942-47; asso. prof. law U. Idaho, Moscow, 1947-49; individual practice law, Chgo., 1949-60; partner firm Foss, Schuman & Drake, Chgo., 1960—; dir. Wilmette Bank, 1970-77, Bank of North Shore, 1976—. Bd. dirs. Ams. for Democratic Action, Chgo. chpt. World Without War Council; chmn. div. ACLU, 1954-57; mem. U.S. com. Internat. Peace Acad., 1973—; v.p. div. Chgo. chpt. UN Assn., 1975-77. Mem. Am., Ill. State, Chgo. bar assns., Chgo. Council Lawyers. Home: 1225 Whitebridge Ln Winnetka IL 60093 Office: 11 S LaSalle St Chicago IL 60603 Tel (312) 782-2610

DRAKE, RUSSELL JACK, b. Birmingham, Ala., July 3, 1945; J.D., U. Ala., 1969. Admitted to Ala. bar, 1969; staff counsel Selma (Ala.) Inter-religious Project, 1969-71; partner firm Drake and Knowles, Tuscaloosa, Ala., 1971—. Mem. adv. bd. Community Relations Com. Tuscaloosa, 1974-76. Mem. Am., Ala. bar assns., Am., Ala. trial lawyers assns. Contbr. article to law rev. Home: 135 22d St N Tuscaloosa AL 35401 Office: 1509 University Blvd Tuscaloosa AL 35401 Tel (205) 759-1234

DRAKE, WALTER HOMER, JR., b. Colquitt, Ga., Nov. 21, 1932; A.B., Mercer U., 1954, LL.B., 1956. Admitted to Ga. bar, 1956; law clk. to U.S. dist. judge, Atlanta, 1961-64; U.S. bankruptcy judge No. dist. Ga., Atlanta, 1964-76; partner firm Swift, Currie, McGhee & Hiers, Atlanta, 1976—; pres. Nat. Conf. Bankruptcy Judges, 1972-73; advisor and coordinator SE Bankruptcy Law Inst.; adj. prof. law Emory U. Mem. Am., Ga., Atlanta (chmn. bankruptcy law sect. 1976-77) bar assns., State Bar Ga. Home: 16 Fontaine Dr Newnan GA 30263 Office: 771 Spring St NW Atlanta GA 30308 Tel (404) 881-0844

DRAKE, WILLIAM FRANK, JR., b. St. Louis, Mar. 29, 1932; B.A., Principia Coll., 1954; LL.B., Yale, 1957. Admitted to Pa. bar, 1958; asso. firm Montgomery, McCracken, Walker & Rhoads, Phila., 1958-65, partner, 1965-68; sr. v.p., gen. counsel Alco Standard Corp., Valley Forge, Pa., 1968—. Mem. Am., Pa., Phila. bar assns. Office: PO Box 834 Valley Forge PA 19482 Tel (215) 666-0760

DRANE, WALTER HARDING, b. Clarksville, Tenn., Feb. 18, 1915; A.B., U. of South, 1935; postgrad. in bus. Case-Western Res. U., 1936-38. Pres., Banks-Baldwin Law Pub. Co., Cleve., 1960—, also dir.; founder, pres. Walter H. Drane Co., mcpl. code compilers and pubs., Cleve., 1955—, chmn., 1960—. Bd. dirs. Univ. Circle br. YMCA, Cleve., 1958-69. Home: 2312 Delamere Dr Cleveland Heights OH 44106 Office: 1904 Ansel Rd Cleveland OH 44106*

DRAPER, DANIEL CLAY, b. Boston, June 7, 1920; B.S., W.Va. U., 1940, M.A., 1941; LL.B., Harvard, 1947. Admitted to N.Y. State bar, 1947; asso. firm Kelley, Drye, Warren, Clark, Carr & Ellis, N.Y.C., 1947-55; partner firm Cadwalader, Wickersham & Taft, N.Y.C., 1962—; dir. Union Devel. Corp., 1976—; lectr. in field. Campaign mgr. Community Com. candidates, Montclair, N.J., 1964; chmn. Citizens' Advisory Com. Community Improvement, Montclair, 1965-77; trustee Montclair Art Mus., 1966-71, Bloomfield, Coll., 1974—. Mem. Assn. Bar City N.Y. (housing and urban affairs com. 1968-71, real property com. 1972-75), N.Y. County Lawyers Assn. (chmn. banking com. 1969—), Am., N.Y. State bar assns., Fed. Bar

Council. Contbr. articles to profl. jours. Home: 124 Lloyd Rd Montclair NJ 07042 Office: One Wall St New York City NY 10005 Tel (212) 785-1000

DRAPER, GERALD LINDEN, b. Oberlin, Ohio, July 14, 1941; B.A., Muskingum Coll., 1963; J.D., Northwestern U., 1966. Admitted to Ohio bar, 1966; asso. firm Bricker, Evatt, Barton & Eckler, Columbus, Ohio, 1966-71, partner, 1971—. Mem. Am., Ohio State (council dels. 1976—), Columbus (gov. 1975—) bar assns., Am. Judicature Soc., Nat. Assn. R.R. Trial Counsel. Columbus Def. Assn., Am. Arbitration Assn. (panel). Office: 100 E Broad St Columbus OH 43215 Tel (614) 221-6651

DRAPER, JOHN LAFAYETTE, b. Davidson County, Tenn., Jan. 25, 1901; LL.B., Vanderbilt U., 1924. Admitted to Tenn. bar, 1923; judge Gen. Sessions Ct., 1937-60, Criminal Ct. Div. II, Nashville, 1960—. Mem. Nashville, Tenn., Am. bar assns. Home: 117 Myers Ave Goodlettsville TN 37072 Office: 601 Metropolitan Courthouse Nashville TN 37201 Tel (615) 259-6173

DRAPER, ROBERT MARVIN, b. Rosewood, Ohio, Jan. 7, 1906; LL.B., Ohio State U., 1931, J.D., 1971. Admitted to Ohio bar 1932; asso. firm Duffy & Duffy, Columbus, 1931-34; partner firm Bridge & Draper, Columbus, 1934-49; individual practice law, Columbus, 1939-45, 63-66, 69—; partner firm Draper, Lombardo & Morgan, Columbus, 1945-55; judge ct. common pleas, Franklin County, Ohio, 1955-63; U.S. atty. So. Dist. Ohio, Columbus, 1966-69; instr. history Urbana (Ohio) Coll., 1959-60; instr. trial techniques Capital U., Columbus, 1969-71; bar examiner Supreme Ct. Ohio, 1964-69; arbitrator Fed. Mediation and Conciliation Service and Am. Arbitration Assn., 1963—; atty. Center for Sci. and Industry, Pub. Employees Retirees, Inc. Mem. Columbus Bd. Edn., 1940-52, pres., 1941-47; del. Democratic Nat. Conv., 1952, 64; adv. com. Urbana Coll., 1976. Mem. Columbus, Ohio, Fed. bar assns., Phi Alpha Delta. Home: 2178 Yorkshire Rd Columbus OH 43221 Office: 218 E State St Columbus OH 43215 Tel (614) 228-2577

DRAPER, ROBERT SHELLEY, b. Bolder, Colo., Feb. 18, 1942; B.A., U. Calif., Berkeley, 1964, J.D., 1967. Admitted to Calif. bar, 1968; partner firm O'Melveny & Myers, Los Angeles. Grantee Ford Found., 1967-68. Home: 1349 Duende Ln Pacific Palisades CA 90272 Office: 611 W 6th St Los Angeles CA 90017 Tel (213) 629-1120

DRAY, MARK STANLEY, b. Alliance, Ohio, Feb. 8, 1943; B.A., Mt. Union Coll., 1965; J.D., Coll. William and Mary, 1968, M.Law and Taxation, 1969. Admitted to Va. bar; tax sr. Price, Waterhouse & Co., Washington, 1969-70; asso. firm Hunton & Williams, Richmond, Va., 1970-77, partner, 1977—; lectr. taxation U. Richmond, Marshall-Wythe Sch. Law, Coll. William and Mary, also tax confs. Mem. Am., Va. bar assns. Home: 2230 Monument Ave Richmond VA 23220 Office: 707 E Main St Richmond VA 23212 Tel (804) 788-8408

DRAY, WILLIAM PERRY, b. Cheyenne, Wyo., Sept. 20, 1940; B.S. in Law, U. Wyo., 1962, J.D., 1964; LL.M. in Taxation, George Washington U., 1968. Admitted to Wyo. bar, 1965; law clk. firm Hirst, Applegate & Thomas, Cheyenne, Wyo., 1964-65; served with JAGC, U.S. Army, 1965-68; partner firm Hirst, Applegate & Dray, Cheyenne, 1968-75; individual practice law, Cheyenne, 1975-76; partner firm Dray and Madison, Cheyenne, 1976—. Sec. Cheyenne-Laramie County Regional Planning Commn., 1970-74; pres. Indsl. Devel. Assn. Cheyenne, 1974-76; Republican precinct committeeman, Laramie County, 1970-74; bd. dirs. Cheyenne YMCA, 1970—; trustee Laramie County Meml. Hosp., 1976—. Mem. Am., Laramie County, Wyo. bar assns., Am. Trial Lawyers Assn. Contbr. articles to legal jours. Home: 919 Creighton St Cheyenne WY 82001 Office: 329 Majestic Bldg 1603 Capitol Ave Cheyenne WY 82001 Tel (307) 634-8892

DRAYO, DAVID CHARLES, b. Dunkirk, N.Y., Dec. 27, 1940; B.A., Syracuse U., 1962, J.D., 1965. Admitted to N.Y. State bar, 1966; partner firm Drayo and Drayo, Fredonia, N.Y., 1967—; N.Y. State estate tax atty. and appraiser Chautauqua County, N.Y., 1972-75. Pres. United Way of No. Chautauqua County, 1975. Mem. Am., N.Y. State, No. Chautauqua County (pres. 1975) bar assns. Office: 8 Park Pl Fredonia NY 14063 Tel (716) 673-1301

DRAYTON, DOUGLAS LEONARD, b. Hartford, Conn., Dec. 30, 1944; B.S., U. Conn., 1966, J.D., 1969. Admitted to Conn. bar, 1969; partner firm Pomeranz & Drayton, Hartford, 1969—. Mem. Am., Conn., Hartford County bar assns. Home: 393 Brimfield Rd Wethersfield CT 06109 Office: 41 Lewis Hartford CT 06013 Tel (203) 522-3289

DRAZEN, MARTIN, b. N.Y.C., Jan. 8, 1919; LL.B., N.Y. U., 1942, LL.M., 1949, 1950. Admitted to N.Y. bar, 1942; asso. firm Allan R. Campbell, Bronxville, N.Y., 1946-51; individual practice law, Bronxville, 1951-56; partner firm McCarthy, Fingar, Donovan & Glatthaar, and predecessors, White Plains, N.Y., 1956—. Mem. Am., N.Y.C., N.Y., Westchester County (v.p., dir.), White Plains (past pres.) bar assns., Am. Judicature Soc. Home: 26 Blair Rd Armonk NY 10504 Office: 175 Main St White Plains NY 10601 Tel (914) 946-3700

DRAZNIN, ANNE LOUISE, b. Mpls., Mar. 25, 1945; A.B., Earlham Coll., 1966; J.D., U. Ill., 1971. Admitted to Ill. bar, 1971, D.C. bar, 1972; legal honors intern, staff atty. HUD, Washington, 1971-72; staff atty. FTC, Chgo., 1972-76; asso. firm Overton, Schwartz & Yacker, Ltd., Chgo., 1976-77; asst. dir. legal services group Am. Bar Assn., 1977—; arbitrator consumer arbitration program Better Bus. Bur. Met. Chgo., 1974—; judge 7th Circuit, Regional Moot Ct. Competition, 1975. co-chmn. adv. bd. Loop Legal Clinic for Moderate Income Families, 1976—. Mem. Am., Ill., Chgo. (vice chmn. young lawyers sect., 1976-77, dir. young lawyers sect. pub. interest projects and consumer affairs, 1975-76, chmn. young lawyers sect. consumerism and law com., 1974-75, antitrust com. 1976—) bar assns., Am. Judicature Soc., Nat. Assn. Women Lawyers (dir. referrals, 1972). Contbg. editor Consumer Reference Handbook, 1975. Office: 1155 E 60th St Chicago IL 60637 Tel (312) 947-3560

DREIER, WILLIAM ALAN, b. N.Y.C., Sept. 18, 1937; B.S. in Bus. and Engring. Adminstrn., Mass. Inst. Tech., 1958; J.D., Columbia, 1961. Admitted to N.J. bar, 1961, U.S. Supreme Ct. bar, 1969; law sec. Hon. Sidney Goldmann, presiding judge appellate div. Superior Ct. N.J., 1961-62; asso. firm Mackenzie, Welt & Dreier and predecessor, Elizabeth, N.J., 1962-65, partner, 1965-73; judge Union County (N.J.) Dist. Ct., 1973-76, Union County Ct., 1976—; councilman City of Plainfield (N.J.), 1966-68; arbitrator Am. Arbitration Assn., 1967-73; instr. bus. orgns. Inst. Continuing Legal Edn. Rutgers U., 1969-70, lectr., 1976. Treas., mem. Republican City Com., Plainfield, 1962-65; corp. counsel City of Plainfield, 1969-73. Mem. Am., N.J. State, Union County, Plainfield bar assns., Plainfield Patrolmens Benevolent Assn. (hon. Silver Life). Named Outstanding Citizen Plainfield Jaycees, 1972; contbr. articles to legal jours.; supervising editor Municipal Code of the City of Plainfield, 1971. Home: 310 Parkside Rd Plainfield NJ 07060 Office: Union County Ct House Broad St Elizabeth NJ 07207 Tel (201) 353-5000

DREIFUSS, WALTER, b. Cologne, Ger., July 6, 1922; B.S., Northeastern U., 1943; J.D. Bklyn. Law Sch., 1950, J.S.D., 1952. Admitted to N.Y. State bar, 1950, U.S. Supreme Ct. bar, 1956; partner firm Diamond & Dreifuss, N.Y.C., 1950—; lectr. in law Union Free Sch. Dist. 20, Lunbrook, N.Y., 1970—; spl. dep. atty. gen. State of N.Y., 1950-59; small claims arbitrator, referee Civil Ct., N.Y.C., 1962—. Mem. N.Y. County Lawyers Assn. ome: 44 Howland Rd East Rockaway NY 11518 Office: 401 Broadway New York City NY 10013 Tel (212) 925-2697

DRENNAN, JAMES CLIFTON, b. McCormick, S.C., Mar. 23, 1949; B.A. in Polit. Sci. summa cum laude, Furman U., 1971; J.D. with honors, Duke U., 1974. Admitted to N.C. bar, 1974; asst. prof. pub. law and govt. Inst. Govt., U. N.C., Chapel Hill, 1974—. Mem. N.C. Bar Assn., Order of the Coif. Contbr. articles in field to profl. jours; mem. editorial bd. Duke Law Jour. Home: 4155 Deepwood Circle Durham NC 27707 Office: Inst Govt U N C Chapel Hill NC 27514 Tel (919) 933-1303

DRESNER, BYRON, b. N.Y.C., Nov. 13, 1927; B.S., Coll. City N.Y., 1949; LL.B., N.Y. U., 1951. Admitted to N.Y. State bar, 1952, U.S. Supreme Ct. bar, 1961; asso. firm Alexander H. Rockmore, N.Y.C., 1952-57; partner firm Kronish, Dresner & Henle, N.Y.C., 1957-66, firm Dresner & Kenle, N.Y.C., 1966—; spl. master N.Y. State Supreme Ct., 1977—. Treas. Maspeth (N.Y.) Jewish Center, 1959-71; pres. Flushing (N.Y.) Jewish Center, 1971-76; chmn. young adults sect. Nat. Anti-Defamation League, 1954-55; bd. dirs. Queens (N.Y.) Jewish Community Council, 1977—. Mem. Am., Bankruptcy Lawyers bar assns., N.Y. County Lawyers Assn., Brandeis Assn., Comml. Law League Am., B'nai B'rith (pres. young adults sect. Bronx 1952-53, N.Y.C. 1953-54). Home: 45-57 189th St Flushing NY 11358 Office: 475 Park Ave S New York City NY 10016 Tel (212) 679-6240

DRESSEL, WALTER, b. Columbus, Ohio, Oct. 17, 1901; LL.B., Columbus Coll. Law, 1928. Admitted to Ohio bar, 1928; state supt. ins. State of Ohio, 1945-46; mem. Westerville (Ohio) Bd. Zoning Appeals. Address: 723 Birmingham Rd Westerville OH 43081 Tel (614) 882-9690

DRETZIN, DAVID, b. N.Y.C., July 24, 1928; B.A., Reed Coll., 1951; J.D., Yale, 1959. Admitted to N.Y. bar, 1960, U.S. Dist. Ct. for So. Dist. N.Y. bar, 1961; asst. gen. counsel Internat. Ladies Garment Workers Union, N.Y.C., 1959-61; asso. firm Finkelstein, Benton & Soll, N.Y.C., 1962-63; partner firms Heller & Dretzin, N.Y.C., 1963-67, Dretzin & Kauff, N.Y.C., 1971—; individual practice law, N.Y.C., 1968-70. Mem. N.Y.C., Am. bar assns., Phi Beta Kappa. Office: 123 E 62d St New York City NY 10021 Tel (212) 832-2001

DREW, JOHN HAYWARD, b. Edgerton, Wis., June 18, 1947; B.B.A. cum laude, Milton Coll., 1969; J.D., U. Wis., 1972. Admitted to Wis. bar, 1972; asso. firm Steele, Smyth, Klos & Flynn, LaCrosse, Wis., 1972-75, prin., 1975—; lectr. U. Wis., La Crosse, 1975. Chmn. bd. No. Baroque Music Festival, 1973—; bd. dirs. La Crosse Boy Choir, 1976—, Wis. Kidney Found., 1973-75. Mem. Am., La Crosse County bar assns., State Bar Wis., Minn. Trial Lawyers Assn., Assn. Trial Lawyers Am., La Crosse Choral Union (chmn. fin. com. 1976). Home: 223 S 11th St La Crosse WI 54601 Office: 800 Lynne Tower Bldg 318 Main St La Crosse WI 54601 Tel (608) 784-8600

DREXLER, DAVID A., b. N.Y.C., Dec. 25, 1930; B.A., Dartmouth, 1952; LL.B., Yale, 1955. Admitted to N.Y. bar, 1959, Del. bar, 1963; law clk. to U.S. dist. judge for Del., 1958-59; asso. firm Berman & Frost, N.Y.C., 1959-60, Aranow, Brodsky, Bohlinger, Einhorn & Dann, N.Y.C., 1960-62; asso. firm Morris, Nichols, Arsht & Tunnell, Wilmington, Del., 1963-65, partner, 1966—. Pres., Milton and Hattie Kutz Home, Inc., Wilmington, 1972-77. Mem. Am. (chmn. bylaws and resolutions com., charter mem. council sect. litigation), Del. bar assns. Office: Box 1347 12th and Market St Wilmington DE 19899 Tel (302) 658-9200

DREY, NORMAN WALTER, JR., b. Cin., Dec. 8, 1944; B.A. in Polit. Sci., U. Wis., 1966; J.D., Washington U., 1970. Admitted to Mo. bar, 1970; asso. firm Klamen, Summers & Compton, St. Louis, 1970-74; counsel div. savs. and loan supr. Mo. Dept. Consumer Affairs Regulation and Licensing, Jefferson City, 1974—. Mem. Am., Mo., St. Louis Met. bar assns., Mo. Savs. and Loan League. Recipient Am. Jurisprudence award Washington, U., 1970. Home: 12 Magnolia St Saint Louis MO 63124 Office: 308 E High St Jefferson City MO 65101 Tel (314) 751-4243

DREYER, JOHN EDWARD, b. Chgo., Feb. 22, 1929; B.S., Loyola U., Chgo., 1951; J.D., DePaul U., 1953. Admitted to Ill. bar, 1953, U.S. Ct. Appeals 7th Circuit bar, 1953, U.S. Ct. Military Appeals bar, 1954; asso. firm Sears & Streit, Chgo. and Aurora, Ill., 1956-61; jr. partner firm Sears, Streit, Tyler & Dreyer, Chgo., 1961-63; sr. partner Dreyer, Foote & Streit, Aurora, Ill., 1963—. Mem. Am., Ill., Kane County bar assns., Am. Judicature Soc., Ill. Soc. Trial Lawyers, Nat. Assn. RR Trial Counsel, Pi Gamma Mu, Phi Alpha Delta. Mem. editorial bd. DePaul Law Review, 1952-53. Home: Box 68 B Rural Route 1 Sugar Grove IL 60554 Office: 900 N Lake St Aurora IL 60506 Tel (312) 897-8764

DRIESEN, GEORGE BENNETT, b. N.Y.C., Mar. 15, 1933; B.A. magna cum laude, Harvard U., 1954; LL.B., Yale, 1961. Admitted to Conn. bar, 1961, D.C. bar, 1963, U.S. Supreme Ct. bar, 1967; law clk. Chief Judge David L. Bazelon, U.S. Ct. Appeals, D.C., 1961-62; spl. asst. to Gen. Counsel FPC, 1962-63; atty. appellate ct. br. NLRB, Washington, 1962-68; dep. gen. counsel Pension Benefit Guaranty Corp., Washington, 1974-76; partner firm Van Arkel, Kaiser, Gressman, Rosenberg and Driesen, Washington, 1976—; adj. prof. law Georgetown U. Law Center, D.C., 1970-73; vis. lectr. Yale Law Sch., 1976, 77. Mem. D.C., Feb., Am. bar assns., Order of Coif, Phi Beta Kappa. Contbr. articles to profl. jours. Home: 3 Leland Ct Chevy Chase MD 20015 Office: Suite 701 1828 L St NW Washington DC 20036 Tel (202) 466-8400

DRIGGS, CHARLES MULFORD, b. E. Cleve., Jan. 26, 1924; B.S., Yale, 1947, LL.B., 1950. Admitted to Ohio bar, 1951; asso. firm Squire, Sanders & Dempsey, Cleve., 1950-64, partner, 1964—. Pres. Bratenahl (Ohio) Sch. Bd., 1958-62. Mem. Bar Assn. Greater Cleve., Ohio, Am. bar assns., Greater Cleve. Growth Assn., Phi Delta Phi, Tau Beta Pi, Phi Gamma Delta. Home: 3036 Worrell Rd Willoughby Hills OH 44094 Office: 1800 Union Commerce Bldg Cleveland OH 44115 Tel (216) 696-9200

DRINKWATER, ARTHUR, b. Ellsworth, Maine, June 27, 1879; A.B., Harvard, 1900, A.M., 1901, LL.B., 1903. Admitted to Mass. bar, 1903; individual practice law, Boston; mem. Cambridge (Mass.) City Council, 1922-27. Mem. Boston Bar Assn. Home: 993 Memorial Dr Cambridge MA 02138 Office: 53 State St Boston MA 02109 Tel (617) 227-4140

DRISCOLL, JAMES OSCAR, b. Mt. Clemons, Mich., Nov. 26, 1928; A.B., Mich. State U., 1949; J.D., U. Fla., 1957. Admitted to Fla. bar, 1957; asso. firm Anderson & Rush, Orlando, Fla., 1957-59; partner firm Berson Barnes & Inman, Orlando, 1959-64; partner firm Berson, Driscoll, Baugh & LaGrone, Orlando, 1964-65, partner firm Driscoll, Baugh & Lagrone, Orlando, 1965-70; legal counsel City of Maitland, 1960—. Mem. Fla. Bar, Am. Bar Assn., Am. Judicature Soc., Def. Research Inst. Home: 509 Pinar Dr Orlando FL 32807 Office: 3222 Corrine St Orlando FL 32803 Tel (305) 894-8821

DRISCOLL, JOHN JOSEPH, b. Pitts., Feb. 13, 1942; B.S. in Econs., Villanova U., 1963; J.D., U. Pitts., 1966. Admitted to Pa. bar, 1966; asso. firm Pershing Hudock & Driscoll, Greensburg, Pa., 1970-73; individual practice law, Greensburg, 1973—; asst. dist. atty. Westmoreland County (Pa.), 1973. Bd. dirs. Seton Hill Day Care, Inc., Pa. div. Am. Cancer Soc. Mem. Am., Pa. bar assns., Am. Judicature Soc. Home: 9 Briarwood Dr Greensburg PA 16501 Office: 31 N Main St Greensburg PA 15601 Tel (412) 836-2700

DRISCOLL, PERRY FRANCIS, b. Fremont, Ohio, June 6, 1945; B.A., J.D. Admitted to Ohio bar, 1972; individual practice law, Toledo, asst. prosecutor Lucas County, Ohio. Mem. Ohio, Toledo bar assns. Home: 3732 Maxwell St Toledo OH 43613 Office: 2700 Monroe St Toledo OH 43606 Tel (419) 241-6282

DRISCOLL, WILLIAM R., b. Chgo., Apr. 15, 1926; B.S., U. Ill., 1949, J.D., 1950. Admitted to Ill. bar, 1950; atty. Libby, McNeil & Libby, Chgo., 1950-60, asst. gen. counsel, 1960-65, gen. counsel, 1965, v.p., gen. counsel, sec. 1966-69; gen. counsel Inland Steel Co., Chgo., 1969-71, v.p., gen. counsel, 1971—. Mem. Better Bus. Bur.; chmn. planning com. Northwestern Corp. Counsel Inst. Mem. Am., Ill., Chgo. bar assns., Am. Arbitration Assn. Home: 325 N Elm St Hinsdale IL 60521 Office: 30 W Monroe St Chicago IL 60603 Tel (312) 346-0300

DRIVER, L. ROBERT, JR., b. Hanover County, Va., Sept. 30, 1917; A.B. with honors in Econs., Princeton U., 1939; LL.B., Yale U., 1942. Admitted to N.Y. State bar, 1943, U.S. Supreme Ct. bar, 1965; asso. firm Dewey, Ballantine, Bushby, Palmer & Wood, and predecessors, N.Y.C., 1942-55; gen. atty. to trustee Hudson & Manhattan R.R. Co., N.Y.C., 1955-62; gen. counsel Hudson & Manhattan Corp. and Hudson Rapid Tubes Corp., N.Y.C., 1962-73, dir., 1964-71. Home: Pheasant Hill Amwell Rd Hopewell NJ 08525 Office: 120 Broadway New York City NY 10005 Tel (212) 732-0120

DRIVER, PHILIP BROGNARD, JR., b. Ridley Park, Pa., Mar. 13, 1910; B.S., U. Pa., 1931, LL.B., 1934. Admitted to Pa. bar, 1934, U.S. Supreme Ct. bar, 1960; sr. partner firm Harper, George, Buchanan & Driver, Phila., 1934—; solicitor Taylor Hosp., Ridley Park, Ridley Park Sch. Authority, Civil Service Commn. Alternate Pa. del. to Rep. Nat. Conv., 1968, 76. Mem. Am., Pa., Phila. bar assns., Am. Soc. Hosp. Attys., Constl. Club Phila. Home: 24 W Ward Ave Ridley Park PA 19078 Office 1200 Western Savings Bank Bldg Philadelphia PA 19107 Tel (215) PE5-3090

DRIVER, ROBERT TEMPLE, b. Benjamin, Tex., Jan. 24, 1924; B.S., U. Calif., Los Angeles, 1947; LL.B., U. Tex., 1953. Admitted to Tex. bar, 1953; asst. city atty. Wichita Falls (Tex.), 1953-58; judge Wichita County (Tex.), Wichita Falls, 1958-62, 89th Dist. Ct., Wichita County, 1962—; mem. faculty Nat. Coll. Judiciary. Pres. Children's Aid. Soc., Wichita Falls; dir. N.W. Tex. council Boy Scouts Am. Mem. Am., Tex. bar assns., Am. Judicature Soc., Internat. Acad. Trial Judges. Editorial bd. Trial Judges Jour., 1964-69. Home: 4219 Lake Park Dr Wichita Falls TX 76302 Office: County Courthouse Wichita Falls TX 76301 Tel (817) 322-0721

DROLLINGER, WILLIAM CLARENCE, b. Detroit, Sept. 1, 1928; A.B., Wayne State U., 1950, J.D., 1952. Admitted to Mich. bar, 1956, U.S. Supreme Ct. bar, 1962; atty. Patterson Lumber Co., Detroit, 1952-60; atty. Conn. Gen. Life Ins. Co., Southfield, Mich., 1960—. Mem. State Bar Mich., ASCAP. Author: Tax Shelters and Tax Free Income for Everyone, 1972; composer The Jogger's Song, official song of Nat. Jogging Assn., 1969, Michigander, 1971. Home: 4420 Westover Dr Orchard Lake MI 48033 Office: 3000 Town Center Suite 980 Southfield MI 48075 Tel (313) 358-2121

DROPKIN, ALLEN HODES, b. Chgo., Oct. 26, 1930; A.B., U. Chgo., 1948, J.D., 1951. Admitted to Ill. bar, 1951, D.C. bar, 1956; asso. firm Arvey, Hodes & Mantynband (now Arvey, Hodes, Costello & Burman), Chgo., 1951-54, 57-61, partner, 1961—; asst. state's atty. Cook County (Ill.), 1954-56; spl. counsel Subcom. on Housing, Com. on Banking and Currency, U.S. Ho. of Reps., 1956-57. Bd. dirs. Jewish Community Centers of Met. Chgo., 1972-76; pres. Bd. Jewish Edn. of Met. Chgo., 1975—; mem. alumni cabinet U. Chgo., 1976—. Mem. Am., Ill. State, Chgo. bar assns., Decalogue Soc. Home: 87 Graymoor Ln Olympia Fields IL 60461 Office: 180 N LaSalle St Chicago IL 60601 Tel (312) 855-5008

DROPKIN, MARTIN B., b. Boston, Sept. 16, 1932; B.S., Purdue U., 1952; J.D., Harvard U., 1955. Admitted to Mass. bar, 1955, U.S. Supreme Ct. bar, 1962; v.p. Arrow Wholesale Meat Packers, Inc., Boston; sr. partner firm Dropkin & Perlman, Somerville, Mass.; exec. sec. to mayor City of Somerville, 1959-61; spl. asst. dist. atty. Middlesex County (Mass.), 1962. Trustee Recuperative Center, Roslindale, Mass.; chmn. Somerville Charter Change Com., 1968. Mem. Mass., Somerville bar assns., Mass. Trial Lawyers Assn. Home: 486 Clinton Rd Chestnut Hill MA 02167 Office: 1 Davis Sq Somerville MA 02144 Tel (617) 623-2700

DROUGHT, THOMAS JAMES, b. Milw., Dec. 4, 1932; B.A., U. Wis., 1954, LL.B., 1959. Admitted to Wis. bar, 1959; asso. firm Cook & Franke S.C., Milw., 1959-63, mem. firm, 1963—; village atty. Village of Bayside, 1969—. Sec., Milw. County Intergovtl. Coop. Council, 1967-70; village trustee, Bayside, 1961-66, village pres., 1966-69; mem. Fox Point-Bayside Sch. Bd., 1973-76; bd. dirs. Luth. Hosp., 1969-75. Mem. Am., Wis., Milw. (pres. elect) bar assns. Recipient Distinguished Service award North Shore Jr. C. of C. Home: 9029 N Lake Dr Bayside WI 53217 Office: 660 E Mason St Milwaukee WI 53202 Tel (414) 271-5900

DRUCKER, A. NORMAN, b. Bklyn., Aug. 23, 1930; B.S., U. Wis., 1953; J.D., U. Miami, 1958. Admitted to Fla. bar, 1958; individual practice law, Miami Beach, Fla., 1958—; lt. col. JAGC, USAR. Mem.

Am. Acad. Matrimonial Lawyers, Am., Fla. bar assns. Office: 420 Lincoln Rd Suite 601 Miami Beach FL 33139 Tel (315) 538-1401

DRUEN, WILLIAM SIDNEY, b. Farmville, Va., May 5, 1943; A.B., Hamden-Sydney Coll., 1964; LL.B., U. Va., Charlottesville, 1968. Admitted to Va. bar, 1968, Ohio bar, 1970; spl. counsel Gov's. Office, State of Va., 1968-70; partner firm Wagner, Schmidt, McCutchan, Hank & Birkhimer, Columbus, Ohio, 1970-75, sr. partner, 1975—; corp. atty. Nationwide Mut. Ins. Co., Columbus, 1970—; asst. sec. Nationwide Mut. Fire Ins. Co., Nationwide Life Ins. Co., Nationwide Gen. Ins. Co. Mem. Columbus, Ohio, Va. bar assns., Ohio, Am. land title assns. Home: 85 E Deshler Ave Columbus OH 43206 Office: 1 Nationwide Plaza Columbus OH 43216 Tel (614) 227-7640

DRUKE, WILLIAM ERWIN, b. Phoenix, Dec. 5, 1938; B.S., Ariz. State U., 1961; J.D., U. Ariz., 1969. Admitted to Ariz. bar, 1969; law clk. Ct. of Appeals Ariz., Phoenix, 1969; dep. county atty. Pima County (Ariz.), 1970-72; city magistrate, Tucson, 1972-75; judge Pima County Superior Ct., Tucson, 1975—. Mem. Am., Ariz. State, Pima County bar assns., Am. Judges Assn. Office: 111 W Congress St Tucson AZ 85701 Tel (602) 792-8441

DRUMM, BERNHARDT CHARLES, JR., b. St. Louis, Mo., Aug. 29, 1941; B.A. cum laude, Amherst Coll., 1963; J.D., Washington U., St. Louis, 1966. Admitted to Mo. bar, 1966; asso. firm Stein & Seigel, St. Louis, 1969-72; partner firm McAtee & Drumm, Clayton, Mo., 1972-74; individual practice law, Clayton, 1974—; spl. agt. FBI, New Haven and Milw., 1966-69; asst. U.S. atty. Eastern Dist. Wis., Milw., 1969. Mem. St. Louis County Air Pollution Appeal Bd., 1972—, chmn., 1976—. Mem. Am., Mo. bar assns., Bar Assn. Met. St. Louis (chmn. young lawyers sect. 1976—), Lawyers Assn. St. Louis, Phi Delta Phi. Home: 623 Kenilworth Ln Ballwin MO 63011 Office: 11 S Meramec Ave Suite 1400 Clayton MO 63105 Tel (314) 727-0777

DRUMMOND, ADDISON PEAIRS, b. New Concord, Ohio, Feb. 8, 1907; B.Commerce, U. Ala., 1929, LL.B., 1932. Admitted to Miss. bar, 1932, Ala. bar, 1932, Fla. bar, 1933, U.S. Supreme Ct. bar, 1946; individual practice law, Bonifay, Fla., 1933—; county atty. Holmes County (Fla.), 1933-75; col., chief mil. justice Pacific Ocean area JAGC, World War II; mem. Fla. Ho. of Reps., 1937, 39, 59, Fla. Senate, 1941-43; civilian aide to sec. Army, 1961-71. Mem. Am., Fla. bar assns., Am. Legion (state comdr. 1952-53). Recipient Outstanding Civilian Service medal Dept. Army, 1972. Office: 205 E Nebraska Ave Bonifay FL 32425 Tel (904) 547-2651

DRUMMOND, DONALD GALE, b. Pueblo, Colo., Jan. 13, 1938; B.S., Colo. State U., 1964; J.D., U. Colo., 1967. Admitted to Colo. bar, 1967; since practiced in Pueblo; staff Dist. Atty.'s Office, Pueblo County, 1967; asso. firm Kettelkamp & Vento, 1967-75; partner firm Bollinger, Flick, Young & Drummond, 1975—; U.S. magistrate for Colo., 1971-75. Bd. dirs. So. Colo. Mental Health Clinic, 1969-74; Scared Heart Home, Pueblo County Mental Health Clinic; active Colo. Mental Health Assn., Pueblo Legal Aid Soc. Mem. Am., Colo., Pueblo County bar assns. Home: 2931 8th Ave Pueblo CO 81008 Office: 123 W 12th St Pueblo CO 81003 Tel (303) 542-1052

DRUMMOND, WINSLOW, b. Phila., Jan. 29, 1933; A.B., Coll. Wooster, 1954; LL.B., Duke, 1957; Admitted to Ark. bar, 1957; asso. firm Wright, Lindsey & Jennings, Little Rock, 1957-62, partner, 1962—; faculty Hastings Coll. of Trial and Appellate Advocacy, San Francisco, 1974-75; mem. com. on jury instructions Ark. Supreme Ct., 1962. Bd. dirs. Little Rock Bd. Edn., 1966-70; bd. dirs. Urban League Greater Little Rock, 1962-67, pres., 1964-66. Mem. Am., Ark., Pulaski County bar assns., Fedn. Ins. Counsel, Assn. Ins. Attys., Order of Coif. Asso. editor Duke Law Jour., 1956-57. Home: 13001 Crabapple Pl Little Rock AR 72209 Office: 2200 Worthen Bank Bldg Little Rock AR 72201 Tel (501) 371-0808

DRURY, ROBERT EDWARD, b. Detroit, May 19, 1916; LL.B., U. Detroit, 1938, J.D., 1938. Admitted to Mich. bar, 1938; indsl. relations dir. Chrysler Corp., 1946-51; v.p. Controls Corp. Am., 1951-62; group v.p. King Seeley Thermos Co., Ann Arbor, Mich., 1962-74, now dir.; individual practice law, Pigeon, Mich., 1974—; dir. Bayport Bank, Imlay City Bank, Akron Bank. Address: 9030 Crescent Beach Rd Pigeon MI 48755 Tel (517) 856-4266

DRYDEN, ROBERT EUGENE, b. Chanute, Kans., Aug. 20, 1927; A.A., City Coll. San Francisco, 1947; B.S., U. San Francisco, 1951, LL.B., 1954, J.D., 1954. Admitted to Calif. bar, 1955; asso. atty. firm Barfield & Barfield, San Francisco, 1955-65; gen. partner firm Barfield, Barfield & Dryden, San Francisco, 1965-73; v.p. firm Barfield, Barfield, Dryden & Ruane, San Francisco, 1973—; mem. faculty Hastings Nat. Coll. Advocacy; panel mem. Lawyer to Lawyer Consultation Panel; arbitrator San Francisco Pro-Tem Judges Panel, Ct. Arbitration Panel; lectr. Continuing Edn. of the Bar. Diplomate Am. Bd. Trial Advocates. Mem. Assn. Def. Counsel (dir. 1968-69), Am. Judicature Soc., Def. Research Assn., Am. Bar Assn. Office: 1 California St San Francisco CA 94111 Tel (415) 362-6715

DRYE, JOHN WILSON, JR., b. Van Alstyne, Tex., May 28, 1900; LL.B., Washington and Lee U., 1920, LL.D., 1956. Admitted to Tex. bar, 1921, N.Y. bar, 1922; mem. firm Kelley, Drye & Warren, and predecessors, N.Y.C., 1920—, partner, 1930—. Pres., bd. dirs. Juilliard Mus. Found.; bd. dirs. Juilliard Sch., Met. Opera, Lincoln Center for Performing Arts. Mem. Am., N.Y. State, N.Y.C., N.Y. County bar assns. Home: 940 Park Ave New York City NY 10028 Office: 350 Park Ave New York City NY 10022 Tel (212) 752-5800

DUANE, MORRIS, b. Phila., Mar. 20, 1901; A.B., Harvard U., 1923; LL.B., Stetson U., 1927, LL.D., 1965; LL.D., Bucknell U., 1967, LaSalle Coll., 1970, Drexel U., 1976; L.H.D., Women's Med. Coll., 1967; Litt.D., Beaver Coll., 1969. Admitted to Pa. bar, 1928; mem. firm Duane, Morris & Heckscher, Phila., 1931—; ret. dir. Girard Trust Bank, Penn Mut. Life Ins. Co., Phila. Saving Fund Soc.; dir. Phila. Contributionship and other corps., Ednl. Facilities Labs., Inc.; mem. Jud. Conf. 3rd Jud. Circuit. Vice chmn. Cardinal's Com. to Study Phila. Catholic Schs., 1972; mem. Com. on Tri-State Regional Devel. (Pa., N.J., Del.); bd. dirs., past co-chmn. Greater Phila. Movement, chmn. Phila. Adv. Council, 1974-76; bd. dirs. Univ. City Sci. Center, United Fund, 1955-69, Phila. Orch. Corp., 1976 Bicentennial Corp., 1967-71, Phila. Urban Coalition; pres., trustee Presser Found.; pres. bd. trustees Episcopal Acad., 1948-51; bd. dirs. Hosp. Survey Com., Phila., 1960-72, chmn., 1960-64, 72; chmn. Christian R. and Mary F. Lindback Found., 1955—; mem. Harvard Fund Council, 1949-55; former mem. exec. bd. Salvation Army, Phila. Mem. Am., Pa., Phila. bar assns., Assn. Life Ins. Counsel, Juristic Soc., Am. Philos. Soc., Am. Lawn Tennis Assn. (chmn. inter-collegiate com. 1928-33), Delta Psi. Author: New Deal in Court, 1934; contbr. articles to legal jours. Home: 439 Garden Ln Bryn Mawr PA 19010 Office: 100 S Broad St Philadelphia PA 19110 Tel (215) 854-6363

DUBBIN, WILLIAM MYRES, b. San Francisco, May 9, 1934; B.A. in Indsl. Relations, San Jose State Coll., 1957; M.B.A., U. Santa Clara, 1963, J.D., 1968. Admitted to Calif. bar, 1969; partner firm Dreyer, Shulman, Butler, Dubbin & Wilson, San Jose, 1969—; legal officer U.S. Coast Guard Res., San Francisco. Mem. Am., Calif. State, Santa Clara County bar assns., Res. Officers Assn., Navy League, Phi Alpha Delta. Office: 111 W St John St Suite 1010 San Jose CA 95113 Tel (408) 298-5217

DUBBS, ROBERT MORTON, b. Cleve., Aug. 31, 1943; B.S. in Economics, U. Pa., 1965; M.B.A., U. Mich., 1968, J.D., 1968. Admitted to Pa. bar, 1969, U.S. Supreme Ct. bar, 1976; atty. United States Steel Corp., Pitts., 1968-70; asso. gen. counsel Systems Capital Corp., Phila., 1970; chief litigation atty. Sun Oil Co., Phila., 1971—. Mem. Phila. Bar Assn. (chmn. traffic ct. com.), Am. Bar Assn. (mem. antitrust, litigation coms.). Home: 20 Levering Circle Bala Cynwyd PA 19004 Office: 100 Matsonford Rd Radnor PA 19087 Tel (215) 293-6390

DUBIN, BERNARD EDWIN, b. Hartford, Conn., Sept. 5, 1902; B.A. with honors (Holland scholar), Trinity Coll., 1924; LL.B., Yale, 1927, J.D., 1927. Instr. classical and modern langs. pvt. schs., New Haven, 1924-27; admitted to Conn. bar, 1927, U.S. Tax Ct. bar; partner firm Dubin & Dubin, Hartford, 1942—. Mem. Am., Conn., Hartford County bar assns., Am. Soc. for Study Legal History, Conn., N.Y. hist. assns., Am., New Eng. classical assns., Phi Beta Kappa. Home: 10 Middlefield Dr West Hartford CT 06107 Office: 111 Pearl St Hartford CT 06103 Tel (203) 522-3412

DUBIS, MICHAEL FRANCIS, b. Milw., June 30, 1947; B.A., Marquette U., 1969; J.D., 1972. Admitted to bar, 1972; individual practice law, Waterford, Wis., 1972—; trustee in bankruptcy, municipal atty. Town of Waterford, atty. Waterford Sanitary Dist. Mem. Pi Gamma Mu. Recipient Am. Jurisprudence award; mem. staff Marquette Law Review. Home: 1802 Town Line Rd Waterford WI 53185 Office: 208 E Main St Waterford WI 53185 Tel (414) 534-6950

DUBNER, RONALD ALLEN, b. Dallas, Oct. 29, 1942; B.A., So. Meth. U., 1964, LL.B., 1967, M. Comparative Law, 1968. Admitted to Tex. bar, 1967; asso. firm Christopher M. Weil, Dallas, 1968-71; individual practice law, Dallas, 1971-75; shareholder firm Dubner, Weinstein & Bell, Dallas, 1976—. Mem. Am., Tex., Dallas bar assns. Contbr. articles to legal jours. Office: Dubner Weinstein & Bell 2 North Park E Suite 224 Dallas TX 75231 Tel (214) 692-1100

DU BOIS, ROBERT PAUL, b. Lowell, Mass., Sept. 26, 1922; B.S., Boston U., 1953; M.Ed., Boston State Tchrs. Coll., 1964; J.D., New England Sch. Law, 1951. Admitted to Mass. bar, 1961, U.S. Supreme Ct. bar, 1962; individual practice law, Waltham, Mass., 1965—; mem. faculty Harvard U., 1963-65. Mem. Waltham, Watertown, Newton, Weston bar assns. Home: 759 South Ave Weston MA 02193 Office: 680 Main St suite 404 Waltham MA 02154 Tel (617) 891-6444

DUBOISE, GRANT PETERSON, b. San Francisco, Mar. 25, 1937; A.B., U. Calif., Los Angeles, 1958; LL.B., Hastings Coll., 1963. Admitted to Calif. bar, 1964; mem. firm Bronson, Bronson & McKinnon, 1964—. Mem. San Francisco, Am., San Mateo County bar assns., Nat. Assn. R.R. Trial Counsel, Internat. Assn. Ins. Counsel (chmn. life, accident and health com.), Order of the Coif. Office: 555 California St 34th floor San Francisco CA 94104

DUBUC, CARROLL EDWARD, b. Burlington, Vt., May 6, 1933; B.S. in Accounting, Cornell U., 1955; LL.B., Boston Coll., 1962; postgrad. in Bus., N.Y. U., 1966-67. Admitted to N.Y. bar, 1963, D.C. bar, 1972; asso. firm Height, Gardner, Poor & Havens, N.Y.C., 1962-70, partner, 1970-75, resident partner, Washington, 1975—. Vice chmn. Naval Aviation Commandry, 1968. Mem. Am., N.Y. State, Fed. bar assns., Assn. Bar City N.Y., Maritime Law Assn., Internat. Assn. Ins. Counsel, Fedn. Ins. Counsel, Navy League. Home: 2430 Inglewood Ct Falls Church VA 22043 Office: 1819 H St NW Washington DC 20006 Tel (202) 737-7847

DUCKER, WILLIAM LAWRENCE, b. Hattiesburg, Miss., Oct. 23, 1947; B.A., U. So. Miss., 1969; J.D., U. Miss., 1974. Admitted to Miss. bar, 1974; individual practice law, Purvis, Miss., 1974—; city atty. Purvis, 1974-76; county atty. Lamar County (Miss.), 1976—; atty. Lamar County Bd. Edn., 1976—. Dir., Purvis Methodist Youth Fellowship, 1974-76. Mem. Am., Miss. trial lawyers assns., Miss. Prosecutors Assn. (exec. com.), Delta Theta Phi. Decorated Bronze Star. Home: 207 School St Purvis MS 39475 Office: PO Box 217 100 Ohio Ave Purvis MS 39475 Tel (601) 794-8545

DUCKOR, MICHAEL JOHN, b. Los Angeles, Aug. 3, 1945; A.B., U. Calif., Davis, 1967, J.D., 1970. Admitted to Calif. bar, 1970; asso. firm Gray, Cary, Ames & Frye, San Diego, 1970-76; gen. counsel, v.p. fin. William O. Walker & Co., Inc., San Diego, 1976—; instr. in legal research and writing U. San Diego, 1976—; lectr in field. Mem. San Diego County, Am., Calif. State bar assns., Corp. Fin. Council of San Diego. Recipient award for overall contbn. to legal edn. U. Calif., Davis, 1968, 69; Am. Jurisprudence awards, 1968, 69; editor Calif. Continuing Edn. of the Bar Code Legis. Analysis, 1967-69; editor, staff writer U. Calif. at Davis Law Rev., 1968-70. Home: 3543 Inez Terr San Diego CA 92106 Office: 8798 Complex Dr San Diego CA 92123 Tel (714) 560-0327

DUCKWORTH, EDWARD GEORGE, b. N. Attleborough, Mass., Mar. 2, 1921; A.B., U. Maine, 1943; LL.B., U. Denver, 1953. Admitted to Colo. bar, 1953, Wyo. bar, 1964. Geologist, U.S. Geol. Survey, Denver, 1946-47; geologist Geophoto Services, Denver, 1947-51; research dir. Rocky Mt. Mineral Law Found., Boulder, Colo., 1962-63; chief minerals Bur. Land Mgmt., Cheyenne, Wyo., 1963-64; individual practice law, Ft. Collins, Colo., 1953—; atty.-adviser USAF, 1964—; instr. law Met. State Coll., Denver, 1971-76. Mem. Am., Rocky Mt. assn. geologists, Am. Assn. Petroleum Geologists, Color. Sci. Soc., AAAS, Wyo., Fed. bar assns., Phi Delta Phi. Home: 1025 S Adams St Denver CO 80209 Office: FLITE (HQ USAF JAESL) Denver CO 80279 Tel (303) 320-7531

DUCKWORTH, T.A., b. Albany, Mo., Mar. 26, 1912; student Central Coll., 1930-33; LL.B., U. Mo., 1936. Admitted to Mo. bar, 1936, Wis. bar, 1944; with Employers Ins. of Wausau (Wis.), 1936—, pres., chief exec. officer; trustee Am. Inst. Property and Liability Underwriters, Inc., Ins. Inst. Am.; dir. Wausau First Am. Nat. Bank. Bd. dirs. Leigh Yawkey Woodson Art Mus., Inc., Wausau; trustee Lawrence U.; bd. dirs. Student Leadership Services, Inc., Milw.; pres. Wausau Area Chamber Found.; mem. council of assos. Wis. Found. Ind. Colls., Milw.; mem. sr. council Wis. Lung Assn. Mem. Am. Mgmt. Assn. (gen. mgmt. council). Recipient Man of Year award Wausau Jr. C of C, 1946; Merit award Wis. Hosp. Assn., 1971; Presdl. citation State Med. Soc. of Wis., 1974; Distinguished Service award Wis. Assn. Ind. Colls. and Univs., 1975; Citizen of Year award Veterans Labor Day Corp., 1975; Alumni Gold medal U. Mo. Columbia Alumni Assn., 1975; Humanitarian award Ladies Aux. VFW, 1976. Home: 918 McIndoe St Wausau WI 54401 Office: 2000 Westwood Dr Wausau WI 54401 Tel (715) 842-6315

DU COMB, ROBERT JAMES, JR., b. South Bend, Ind., Sept. 3, 1943; B.A., Ind. U., 1964, J.D., 1967. Admitted to Ind. bar, 1967, U.S. Supreme Ct. bar, 1976; partner firm DuComb, Nimtz & DuComb, South Bend, 1969—; mem. Ind. Ho. of Reps., 1972—, majority caucus chmn., 1976—. Mem. adv. bd. Ind. U., 1972—; mem. Alcoholism Council St. Joseph County, South Bend, 1974—. Mem. Ind., St. Joseph County bar assns. Contbr. articles to legal jours. Home: 16146 Brockton Ct Granger IN 46530 Office: 511 W Colfax Ave South Bend IN 46601 Tel (219) 233-3147

DUDINE, WILLIAM FREDERICK, JR., b. Jasper, Ind., Dec. 23, 1931; B.M.E. magna cum laude, Notre Dame U., 1953; J.D., Cornell U., 1960. Admitted to N.Y. State bar, 1960, U.S. Supreme Ct. bar, 1970; partner firm Darby & Darby, N.Y.C., 1960—; co-chmn. N.Y. State Dept. Transp. Task Force, 1976—. Vice-pres. Concerned Citizens of Montauk, Inc., 1973-76; chmn. Ednl. Assembly, Baldwin, N.Y., 1973-74. Mem. Am., N.Y.C. bar assns., N.Y. (chmn. patent law com 1975-76), Am. patent law assns. Office: 405 Lexington Ave New York City NY 10017 Tel (212) OX7-7660

DUDINYAK, RICHARD GEORGE, b. Hazleton, Pa., Mar. 7, 1938; B.S. in Bus. Adminstrn., Pa. State U., 1966, J.D., Villanova U., 1969. Admitted to Pa. Supreme Ct. bar, 1969; asso. firm Mack & Meyer, Wilkes Barre, Pa., 1969-72; individual practice law, Freeland, Pa., 1972—; law clk. to Pres. Judge Bernard C. Brominski, Ct. of Common Pleas of Luzerne County, Pa., 1972—; solicitor Foster Twp, Luzerne County. Mem. Am., Pa., Lower Luzerne County bar assns., Wilkes-Barre Law and Library Assn. Home: 178 Washington St Freeland PA 18224 Office: 608 Centre St Freeland PA 18224 Tel (717) 636-1944

DUDLEY, JAMES BODETTE, b. Escanaba, Mich., Feb. 1, 1937; B.A., Beloit Coll., 1958; M.A., U. Md., 1960, J.D., 1965. Admitted to Md. bar, 1965; asst. state's atty., Balt., 1965-72, Howard County, 1972-73; individual practice law, Ellicott City, Md., 1973—. Mem. Md., Howard County bar assns. Contbr. articles to legal jours. Office: 8351 Court Ave Ellicott City MD 21043 Tel (301) 465-7826

DUE, DANFORD ROYCE, b. Louisville, Sept. 28, 1948; B.A., Vanderbilt U., 1970; J.D. cum laude, Ind. U., 1973. Admitted to Ind. bar, 1973; asso. firm Stewart, Irwin, Gilliom, Fuller & Meyer, Indpls., 1973—. Mem. Am., Ind., Indpls. bar assns. Contbg. author: Indiana Inheritance Tax Rules and Regulations. Home: 6125 S East St Indianapolis IN 46227 Office: 1200 Merchants Bank Bldg Indianapolis IN 46204 Tel (317) 639-5454

DUECY, CHARLES MICHAEL, b. Everett, Wash., Oct. 16, 1912; student U. Wash., 1929-34, Stanford, 1954-55; J.D., U. Ariz., 1957. Admitted to Ariz. bar, 1957, U.S. Supreme Ct. bar, 1965; partner firm Duecy, Moore, Petsch, Robinson & Bennett, Scottsdale, Ariz., 1957—, now sr. partner; spl. counsel to state atty. gen., 1962-64; juvenile counsel Legal Aid Soc., 1960-68; arbitrator Superior Ct. Ariz.; lectr. seminars Ariz. State U. Law Sch., counsel Retarded Children Assn., 1960-66. Counsel St. Barnabas Episcopal Parish, 1960-66; chmn. Gov.'s. Com. Alcoholism, 1966-68; mem. Ariz. Compensation Fund Investment Com. Mem. Am., Internat., Fed. bar assns., Ariz. State Bar, Am. Judicature Soc., Am. Trial Lawyers Assn., Am. Soc. Internat. Law, Phi Delta Phi. Contbr. articles to legal jours. Home: 4229 E Desert Crest Dr Scottsdale AZ 85253 also 323 El Creston St San Carlos Sonora Mexico Office: 3740 Civic Center Plaza Scottsdale AZ 85251 Tel (602) 946-5344

DUENAS, CRISTOBAL CAMACHO, b. Agana, Guam, Sept. 12, 1920; student Aquinas Coll., Grand Rapids, Mich., 1946-48; A.B., U. Mich., 1950, J.D., 1952. Admitted to Guam bar, 1952; asst. atty. gen. Dept. of Law, Govt. of Guam, Agana, 1952-57; dir. dept. of Land Mgmt., Govt. Guam, Agana, 1957-60; judge Island Ct. of Guam, Agana, 1960-69; judge U.S. Dist. Ct. for Guam, Agana, 1969—. Mem. Am., Guam (v.p. 1966-67) bar assns., Am. Judicature Soc. Home: Maite Guam PO Box 203 Agana GU 96910 Office: O Brien St West Agana GU 96910*

DUFF, CHARLES HENRY, b. Houston, Tex., Feb. 11, 1924; B.S., Georgetown U., 1947, J.D., 1950. Admitted to D.C. bar, 1950, Va. bar, 1951; asso. to sr. partner firm Duff, Slenker, Brandt & Jennings, and predecessors, Arlington, Va., 1951-72; judge Circuit Ct. Arlington County, 1972—; instr. law U. Va., 1952-63. Mem. Am., Va., Arlington County (pres. 1962-63) bar assns., Am. Coll. Trial Lawyers, Internat. Assn. Barristers. Office: Court House Arlington VA 22207 Tel (703) 558-2505

DUFF, JEROME JAMES, b. St. Louis, Sept. 30, 1926; LL.D., St. Louis U., 1952. Admitted to Mo. bar, 1952, U.S. Supreme Ct. bar, 1963; partner firm Katcher, Roche, Cloyd and Duff, St. Louis, 1955-62; partner firm Jerome J. Duff and Assos., Inc., St. Louis, 1963—; lectr. labor law Mo. U., Washington U., St. Louis U., 1968—. Mem. Am., Mo., St. Louis bar assns., Lawyers Assn. St. Louis (dir.). Home: 6001 Deerwood Dr Saint Louis MO 63123 Office: 1139 Olive St Saint Louis MO 63101 Tel (314) 621-3833

DUFF, JOHN MILLER, b. Pitts., Dec. 21, 1913; A.B., Princeton U., 1935; LL.B., U. Pitts., 1938. Admitted to Allegheny County Common Pleas and Fed. Dist. Ct. bar, 1939, Supreme Ct. Pa. bar, 1943, Ct. Appeals 3d Circuit bar, 1975; trust officer Potter Title and Trust Co., Pitts., 1941-55, v.p. charge of trusts, 1955-58; v.p., house counsel Fidelity Trust Co., Pitts., 1958-59; v.p. Pitts. Nat. Bank, 1959-63; dep. atty. gen. Western Regional Office Dept. Justice Commonwealth Pa., Pitts., 1971—. Mem. Pa. Bankers Assn. (chmn. trust div. 1962-63). Home: 1174 Murray Hill Ave Pittsburgh PA 15317 Office: 1824 Frick Bldg Pittsburgh PA 15219 Tel (412) 565-7570

DUFFETT, BENTON SAMUEL, JR., b. Kansas City, Mo., Dec. 22, 1936; B.S. in Chemistry, U. Kans., 1959; J.D., U. Mich., 1962. Admitted to D.C. bar, 1963, U.S. Supreme Ct. bar, 1967; since practiced in D.C., asso. firm Burns, Doane, Benedict, Swecker & Mathis, 1963-67, partner firm, 1967-70, partner firm Burns, Doane, Swecker & Mathis, 1970—. Mem. Am. Chem. Soc., Am. Hort. Soc., D.C. Bar, Am. Bar Assn., Am. Patent Law Assn. Home: 9411 Ferry Landing Ct Alexandria VA 22309 Office: 815 Connecticut Ave Washington DC 20006 Tel (202) 298-9185

DUFFY, CHARLES BAIN, b. Point Pleasant, W.Va., May 27, 1900; LL.B., U. Okla., 1922. Admitted to Okla. bar, 1922; practiced in Ponca City, Okla., 1922—; partner firm Duffy & Johnson, Ponca City, 1950—; mem. Okla. Senate, 1934-46, mem. judiciary com., 1934-46; mem. Nat. Commn. on Uniform Laws, 1955-60. Mem. Am. (ho. dels.

1955-58), Okla. (pres. 1955) bar assns., Phi Delta Phi. Home: 221 Virginia Ave Ponca City OK 74601 Office: 320 Security Bank Bldg PO Box 628 Ponca City OK 74601 Tel (405) 765-6666

DUFFY, JAMES HENRY, b. Lowville, N.Y., Feb. 3, 1934; A.B., Princeton, 1956; LL.B., Harvard, 1959. Admitted to N.Y. bar, 1960; asso. firm Cravath, Swaine & Moore, N.Y.C., 1959-67, partner, 1968—. Mem. N.Y. State, Am., Inter-Am. bar assns., Assn. Bar City N.Y. Office: One Chase Manhattan Plaza New York City NY 10005 Tel (212) HA 2-3000

DUFFY, KEVIN THOMAS, b. N.Y.C., Jan. 10, 1933; A.B., Fordham U., 1954, J.D., 1958. Admitted to N.Y. State bar, 1958; law clk. Judge J. Edward Lumbard, U.S. Ct. Appeals 2d Circuit, N.Y.C., 1955-58; asst. chief criminal div. U.S. Atty's Office, So. Dist. N.Y., 1958-61; asso. firm Whitman, Ransom & Coulson, N.Y.C., 1961-66; partner firm Gordon & Gordon, N.Y.C., 1966-69; regional adminstr. SEC, N.Y.C., 1969-72; judge U.S. Dist. Ct., So. Dist. N.Y., 1972—; adj. prof. securities law Bklyn. Law Sch., 1975—. Mem. Fordham Law Sch. Alumni Assn. (trustee 1969—), Assn. Bar City N.Y., N.Y. State, Westchester County (N.Y.) bar assns. Recipient Achievement award in law Fordham Coll. Alumni Assn., 1976. Home: 15 Hewitt Ave Bronxville NY 10708Office: US Courthouse Foley Sq New York City NY 10007 Tel (212) 791-0243

DUFFY, MARY ALICE, b. Phila.; B.S., Chestnut Hill Coll.; LL.B., Dickinson Law Sch. Admitted to Pa. bar, 1954, U.S. Supreme Ct. bar, 1969; partner firm Duffy & Duffy, Phila., 1960—. Mem. Pa. Ho. of Reps., 1957-59. Mem. Nat. Assn. Women Lawyers (v.p. 1976-77, pres. 1977-78), Am., Pa., Phila. (chmn. women's rights com.) bar assns., Am. Trial Lawyers Assn. Contbr. articles in field to legal jours. Home: 5031 Cedar Ave Philadelphia PA 19143 Office: 1710 One E Penn Sq Philadelphia PA 19107 Tel (215) LO8-2576

DUFFY, SARA, b. Phila.; B.S., Temple U.; LL.B., Dickinson Law Sch. Admitted to Pa. bar, 1950, U.S. Supreme Ct. bar, 1969; partner firm Duffy & Duffy, Phila., 1960—. Mem. Am., Pa., Phila. bar assns., Am., Pa. trial lawyers' assns., Nat. Assn. Women Lawyers. Home: 5031 Cedar Ave Philadelphia PA 19143 Office: 1710 One East Penn Sq Philadelphia PA 19107 Tel (215) LO8-2576

DUFFY, THOMAS GRAHAM, b. Racine, Wis., July 18, 1927; B.A., San Diego State U., 1951; J.D., Hastings Coll. Law, U. Calif., San Francisco, 1954. Admitted to Calif. bar, 1955; asso. counsel Union Title Ins. & Trust Co., Calif., 1955-58; dep. city atty., La Mesa, Calif., 1958; partner firm Linley, Duffy, Shifflet & McDougal, El Cajon, Calif., 1958-67; judge Municipal Ct., El Cajon, 1967—; city atty., El Cajon, 1959-67; dist. counsel Rainbow Municipal Water Dist., 1962-67; faculty mem. Calif. Center Jud. Edn. and Research, U. Calif., Berkeley, 1973—. Mem. traffic com. City of El Cajon, 1962-67, bd. dirs. stadium com.; active San Diego County Assn. for Retarded Children. Mem. Am. Judicature Soc., San Diego County Municipal Cts. Assn. (past pres.), Conf. Calif. judges. Office: 110 E Lexington St El Cajon CA 92020 Tel (714) 579-4121

DUFFY, THOMAS JAMES, b. Chgo., Feb. 4, 1919; B.A., U. Notre Dame, 1940; J.D. DePaul U., 1947. Admitted to Ill. bar, 1947; since practiced in Chgo.; partner firm Lane and Duffy, 1947-49, Lane, Duffy & Connell, 1949-57, Duffy & Connell, 1957-64, Duffy and Jordan, 1964—; gen. counsel Ill. Coroners Assn., Ill. Assn. County Clks. and Recorders; legis. counsel Ill. Breeders and Owners Assn., Ill. Savs. and Loan Stock Council and Ill. Legis. counsel Soap and Detergent Assn.; mem. Ill. Commn. on Police Relations, 1967-69; mem. State of Ill. Currency Exchange Adv. Bd., 1970-76. Mem. Ill. State Bar Assn., Chgo. Assn. Commerce and Industry. Recipient Spl. award Ill. Municipal League, 1974; Star of Recognition, Chgo. Police Sgts. Assn., 1972, Chgo. Lts. Assn., 1976. Office: 7 S Dearborn St Chicago IL 60603 Tel (312) 236-4800

DUFFY, WILLIAM J., b. North Branch, Minn., Oct. 29, 1916; B.A., St. Norbert Coll., 1938; LL.B., U. Wis., 1941. Admitted to Wis. bar, 1941; asso. firm Martin, Clifford & Dilweg, Green Bay, Wis., from 1945; partner firm Duffy, Dewone, Miller & Gerlikowski, Green Bay, until 1968; judge 14th U.S. Circuit Ct., Green Bay, 1968—; mem. Wis. State Assembly, 1948-50; mem. Gov.'s Commn. on Human Rights, 1959-65. Mem. Am., Wis., Brown County bar assns., Am. Judicature Soc. Home: 1181 Division St Green Bay WI 54303 Office: Court House Green Bay WI 54301 Tel (414) 437-3211

DUFRESNE, ARMAND ALPHEE, JR., b. Auburn, Maine, Jan. 17, 1909; A.B., U. Montreal, 1930; LL.B., Boston Coll., 1935. Admitted to Maine bar, 1936, since practiced in Lewiston; corp. counsel, Lewiston, 1937-38; asst. county atty., Androscoggin County, 1939-40, county atty., 1941-44, judge of probate, 1945-56; justice Superior Ct. Maine, 1956-65; justice Supreme Jud. Ct. Maine, 1965-70, chief justice, 1970—. Mem. Jud. Council Maine, 1954-65, 70—. Mem. Am., Maine, Androscoggin County bar assns. Home: 12 Sylvan Ave Lewiston ME 04240 Office: Supreme Ct Maine Auburn ME 04210*

DUGAN, FREDERICK DAVID, b. Canandaigua, N.Y., Dec. 27, 1928; B.A., Antioch Coll., Yellow Springs, Ohio, 1952; J.D., Cornell U., 1955; grad. Nat. Coll. State Judiciary U. Nev., 1975. Admitted to N.Y. Supreme Ct. bar, 1956, U.S. Dist. Ct. bar for Western Dist. N.Y., 1956, U.S. 2d Circuit Ct. Appeals bar, 1969, U.S. Supreme Ct. bar, 1961; practiced in Penn Yan, N.Y., 1956-73; judge Yates County (N.Y.) Surrogate and Family Ct., 1973—; adminstrv. judge Family Cts., N.Y. 7th Jud. Dist., 1975—; asst. dist. atty. Yates County, 1957-63; counsel N.Y. State Senate Com. on Taxation, 1964, N.H. Joint Legis. Coms. for Appraisal and Assessment of Publicly Owned Lands, 1964, Joint Legis. Coms. for Unemployment Ins., 1965, N.Y. Constl. Conv., 1967; minority counsel N.Y. State Assembly Com. on Finances, Taxation and Expenditures. Trustee Coll. Center of the Finger Lakes, Corning, N.Y., 1967-72. Mem. Yates County (N.Y.), N.Y. State bar assns., N.Y. State County Judges Assn., Surrogates' Assn., Family Ct. Judges Assn., Nat. Council Juvenile Ct. Judges, Antioch Coll. Alumni Assn (v.p., dir. 1966-69). Home: 2737 Old Country House Rd Penn Yan NY 14527 Office: 108 Court St Penn Yann NY 14527 Tel (315) 536-4013

DUGGAN, EDMUND AUGUSTUS, b. N.Y.C., Sept. 10, 1936; A.A., San Bernardino Valley Coll., 1960; A.B., San Diego State Coll., 1963; J.D., U. San Diego, 1969. Admitted to Calif. bar, 1970; mem. firm Gallardo and Duggan, San Diego, 1970-72; atty. Pacific Telephone Co., San Francisco, 1972—; mem. indigent appeals panel Ct. of Appeals, 1973-76. Chmn. govtl. research San Francisco C. of C., 1976; chmn. govtl. fin. sect. Commonwealth Club Calif., 1975-76. Mem. Maric Bar Assn., Calif. State Bar, Lawyers Club San Francisco. Home: 352 Knight Dr San Rafael CA 94901 Office: 140 New Montgomery St San Francisco CA 94105 Tel (415) 542-3389

DUGGAN, LESTER WILLIAM, JR., b. St. Louis, Jan. 12, 1922; J.D., St. Louis U., 1950. Admitted to Mo. bar, 1950; individual practice law, Ferguson & Florissant, Mo., 1959-67; partner firm Sullivan & Duggan, O'Fallon, Mo., 1967-70; individual practice law O'Fallon, 1970-71, St. Charles, Mo., 1971—; br. claims mgr. Northwestern Mut. Ins. Co., St. Louis, 1953-57, Iowa Nat. Ins. Co., St. Louis 1958-60. Mayor, City of Ferguson, 1960-62. Mem. Mo., N. St. Louis County (past treas.), St. Charles County (past pres.), 11th Jud. Circuit (past pres.) bar assns. Home: 15 Harris Dr Saint Peters MO 63376 Office: 135 S 5th St Saint Charles MO 63301 Tel (314) 946-7538

DUGGER, GEORGE FREDERICK, SR., b. Elizabethton, Tenn., Dec. 28, 1896; student, Tusculum Coll., 1920-21; U. Tenn., 1922; LL.B. U. Ga., 1925. Admitted to Tenn. bar, 1925, Ga. bar, 1925; partner firm Dugger, Bangs & Riner and predecessors, Elizabethton, Tenn., 1925—; mem. Bd. Fed. Law Examinders, 1930-66. Del. Tenn. Constl. Conv., chmn. suffrage com., 1953; trustee Milligan Coll., 1932-48. Mem. Tenn. Bar Assn., Elizabethton C. of C. (pres. 1929, 41). Home: Route 3 Grandview Circle Elizabethton TN 37643 Office: Seiler-Hunter Bldg Courthouse Sq Elizabethton TN 37643 Tel (615) 543-2551

DUGGER, WALTER GRAYSON, b. Greensboro, Ala., Sept. 10, 1895; J.D., Temple U., 1931. Admitted to Pa. bar, 1929; asso. firm Harry Felix, from 1929; asst. dist. atty. Phila., until 1941; individual practice law, 1941—; candidate Judge Common Pleas, 1946. Mem. Phila. Bar Assn. Home: 6363 Woodbine Ave Philadelphia PA 19107 Office: 1 N 13th St Philadelphia PA 19107 Tel (215) LO3-8344

DUGGINS, DAVID D., b. Wichita, Kans., June 9, 1937; student Brown U., 1956; B.A., Tulane U., 1960, LL.B., 1962. Admitted to La. bar, 1962; mem. staff Chevron Oil Co., 1962-65; partner firm Newman, Duggins, Drolla & Gamble, and predecessor, New Orleans, 1965—. Pres. Jeunesse d' Orleans, 1967-70, chmn. bd., 1971; bd. dirs. La. Council for Music and Performing Arts, Inc., 1970-77. Mem. Fed., La. bar assns., Comml. Law League Am. Office: 826 Lafayette St New Orleans LA 70113 Tel (504) 581-2552

DUHL, STUART, b. Chgo., Dec. 3, 1940; B.S. cum laude, Northwestern U., 1962; student law U. Calif., Berkeley, 1962-63; J.D. magna cum laude, Northwestern U., 1965; LL.M., John Marshall Law Sch., 1968. Admitted to Ill. bar, 1965; asso. firm D'Ancona, Pflaum, Wyatt & Riskind, Chgo., 1965-70; partner firm Schwartz & Freeman, Chgo., 1970—; lectr. Northwestern U. Evening Divs., Central YMCA Community Coll. Mem. Am., Ill., Chgo. bar assns., Chgo. Council Lawyers. Contbr. articles to Jour. Taxation. Office: 1 IBM Plaza Suite 4530 Chicago IL 60611 Tel (312) 222-0800

DUITCH, RAYMOND SAMUEL, b. Ames, Iowa, Mar. 25, 1917; B.A., State U. Iowa, 1968, J.D., 1940. Admitted to Iowa bar, 1940, Colo. bar, 1957; individual practice law, Colorado Springs, Colo., 1957—; mem. nat. panel arbitrators Am. Arbitration Assn., 1964. Mem. Colo. Bar Assn. Home: 1530 Woodman Valley Rd Colorado Springs CO 80919 Office: 231 E Vermijo St Colorado Springs CO 80903 Tel (303) 632-3450

DUKE, CHARLES WAYNE, b. Belton, Tex., Dec. 4, 1905; B.B.A., Baylor U., 1928; LL.B., J.D., U. Tex., 1931. Admitted to Tex. bar, 1931; since practiced in San Antonio, mem. firm Dodson and Ezell, 1932-53, Dodson, Duke & Branch, 1953-73, Duke, Branch & Schmidt, 1973—; dir., gen. counsel Handy-Andy, Inc., San Antonio; v.p., dir., gen. counsel Main Savs. Assn., 1964-73; dir. Tex. Turnpike Authority, 1972; dir., past pres. St. Anthony Hotel, San Antonio; exec. com. SW Found. for Research & Edn. Life trustee U. Tex. Law Sch. Found.; bd. regents N. Tex. State U., Denton, 1950-57; bd. dirs. Hemisfair 68; mem. Chancellor's Council, U. Tex., Austin; bd. dirs. San Antonio Zool. Soc., 1967—. Mem. San Antonio (pres. 1948), Tex. (dir. 1948-50), Am. bar assns. Recipient Outstanding Alumnus award U. Tex. Law Sch., 1968. Home: 724 College Blvd San Antonio TX 78209 Office: 650 San Antonio Bank & Trust Bldg San Antonio TX 78205 Tel (512) 226-8274

DUKE, ERSELL CALVIN, b. Lott, Tex., Sept. 19, 1907; LL.B., LaSalle Extension U., Chgo., 1937; diploma Rutgers U. Grad. Sch. Banking, 1948. Bookkeeper, teller First Nat. Bank, Lott, 1927-30; cashier First State Bank, Marlin, Tex., 1930-33; various positions fed. and state govt., Austin, Tex., 1933-38; admitted to Tex. bar, 1938; auditor, individual practice law, Austin, 1939-41; asst. to trust officer, v.p. and trust officer Am. Nat. Bank of Austin, 1942-72. Choir mem., ruling elder, trustee First So. Presbyn. Ch., Austin, 1934—; commr. Austin council Boy Scouts Am.; mem. adv. bd. Gov.'s Com. on Aging for Tex., 1976—; fin. adviser Home of Holy Infancy, Austin, 1936—; treas. Austin corps Salvation Army, 1942-72; trustee Austin United Fund. Mem. Tex. Bankers Assn. (chmn. trust sect. 1952-53), Tex. Bar Assn., Tex. Bd. Pub. Accountancy. Recipient Pro Ecclesia et Pontifice, Pope Paul VI, 1970. Address: 4433 Crestway Dr Austin TX 78731 Tel (512) 452-4423

DUKE, LAWRENCE DANIEL, b. Palmetto, Ga., Jan. 7, 1913; A.B., Oglethorpe U., 1933; LL.B., Atlanta Law Sch., 1938; J.D., Emory U., 1950. Admitted to Ga. bar, 1937, U.S. Supreme Ct. bar, 1946; asst. solicitor gen. Fulton County (Ga.) Superior Ct., 1939-42; asst. atty. gen. State of Ga., 1944-47; partner firm Duke, Durden and Alhadeff, 1945-64; judge Fulton County Criminal Ct., 1964—; judge Ga. State Ct. of Fulton County, 1977—; city atty. City of Fairburn (Ga.), 1943-44, mayor, 1945-46. Mem. Atlanta, Ga., Am. bar assns., Am. Judicature Soc. Named 1 of 10 Outstanding Young Men in Am. Nat. Jr. C. of C., 1946. Home: RFD Tricham Creek Rd Fayetteville GA 30214 Office: Suite 65 Civil-Criminal Ct Bldg 160 Pryor St SW Atlanta GA 30303 Tel (414) 572-2554

DUKE, MELVIN K., b. San Antonio, Nov. 20, 1927; LL.B., U. Ky., 1951. Admitted to Ky. bar, 1951; individual practice law, Hardinsburg, Ky., 1951-71; mem. firm Duke & Brite, Hardinsburg, 1972—. Mem. Ky. Bar Assn. (chmn. ho. dels. 1972-73). Home: PO Box 168 Hardinsburg KY 40143 Office: Court Sq Hardinsburg KY 40143 Tel (502) 756-2184

DUKE, STEVEN BARRY, b. Mesa, Ariz., July 31, 1934; B.S., U. Ariz., 1956, J.D., 1959; LL.M., Yale, 1961. Admitted to Ariz. bar, 1959, U.S. 2d Circuit Ct. Appeals bar, 1967 U.S. Supreme Ct. bar, 1966; law clk. U.S. Supreme Ct., Washington, 1959-60; asst. prof. law Yale, 1961-64, asso. prof. law, 1964-66, prof., 1966—; vis. prof. law U. Calif. Berkeley, 1965-66. Bd. dirs. New Haven Legal Assistance Assn., 1970-73; mem. bd. edn., Woodbridge (Conn.), 1970-72. Mem. Assn. Bar City N.Y. (com. on medico-legal investigations 1976—), Nat. Legal Aid and Defender's Assn., Nat. Assn. Criminal Def. Lawyers, Am. Trial Lawyers. Contbr. articles in field to legal jours. Home: 250 Grandview Ave Hamden CT 06514 Office: 127 Wall New Haven CT 06520 Tel (203) 436-3610

DUKE, TOMMY BRYAN, b. Houston, Apr. 22, 1937; B.B.A., U. Tex., 1962, LL.B., 1965. Admitted to Tex. bar, 1965, Nebr. bar, 1972, Colo. bar, 1974; asso. firm Fulbright & Jaworski, Houston, 1965-72; asso. firm Nelson Harding Marchetti Leonard & Tate, Lincoln, Nebr., 1972-74, partner, Denver, 1974—. Office: 2310 Colo State Bank Bldg Denver CO 80202

DUKES, GENE WALLACE, b. Reevesville, S.C., July 13, 1943; B.S., Clemson U., 1965, M.S., 1967, J.D., 1971. Admitted to S.C. bar, 1971; partner firm Berry & Dukes, St. George, S.C., 1971—; mem. S.C. Ho. of Reps., 1972—. Office: 304 N Parler Ave St George SC 29477 Tel (803) 563-3131

DUKES, WILLIAM FRANCIS, b. Raleigh, Miss., Jan. 15, 1927; B.A. with honors, Miss. So. Coll., 1950; J.D., U. Miss., 1951. Admitted to Miss. bar, 1951; spl. agt. FBI, Washington, Milw., New Orleans and Gulfport, Miss., 1951-68, sr. resident agt., Gulfport, 1958-68; partner firm Daniel, Coker, Horton, Bell and Dukes, Jackson and Gulfport, Miss., 1969—. Mem. Miss. Law Enforcement Officers Assn., Soc. Former Spl. Agts. FBI, Miss. Coast Crime Commn., Fedn. Ins. Counsel, So. Assn. Workmen's Compensation Adminstrs., Am., Harrison County, Fed., Internat. bar assns., Miss. Def. Lawyers Assn. Asso. editor Miss. Law Jour., 1950, bus. mgr., 1951. Home: 123 Bayou Circle St Gulfport MS 39501 Office: 2301 14th St Gulfport MS 39501 Tel (601) 868-1111

DULANY, WILLIAM BEVARD, b. Eldersburg, Md., Sept. 4, 1927; A.B., Western Md. Coll., 1950; postgrad. Mich. Law Sch., 1950-51; LL.B., Md. Law Sch., 1953. Admitted to Md. bar, 1953; asso. firm Baldwin, Jarman & Norris, Balt., 1953-59; partner firm Dulany & Davis, Westminster, Md., 1959—; del. to Md. State Legis., 1962-66, Md. Constl. Conv., 1967-68; chmn. Md. Fair Campaign Practices Commr., 1975—; commr. Md. Human Relations Commn., 1972-74. Vice pres. Am. Heart Assn., 1973-74; bd. trustees Md. Heart Assn., 1966—, Western Md. Coll., 1975—. Mem. Am., Md. (v.p. 1967-68), Carroll County (pres. 1965-67) bar assns., Am. Judicature Soc. Office: 127 E Main St Box 525 Westminister MD 21157 Tel (301) 876-2117

DULIN, JACQUES (JAMES) MATAGNE, b. Toledo, Nov. 23, 1934; B.S. in Biochemistry (LaVerne Noyes scholar), U. Chgo., 1957, postgrad. in chemistry (duPont fellow), 1957-58; J.D. with honors, George Washington U., 1966. Patent examiner U.S. Patent Office, Washington, 1962-64; admitted to Va. bar, 1966, Ill. bar, 1967; law clk., tech. adviser to Hon. I. Jack Martin, judge U.S. Ct. Customs and Patent Appeals, Washington, 1965-66; asso. firm Bair, Freeman, & Molinare, Chgo., 1966-70; partner firm Molinare, Allegretti, Newitt & Witcoff, Chgo., 1971-72; master in accounting U.S. Dist. Ct. for No. Ill., Chgo., 1973-74; pres. firm JM Dulin, P.C., Chgo., 1973—; pres., dir., mem. exec. com. Indsl. Resources, Inc., Chgo. and Denver, 1973—; pres., dir. Indsl. Assets, Inc., Chgo. and Denver, 1973—; lectr. profl. courses, speaker in field. Mem. Deerfield (Ill.) Bd. Police Commrs., 1970-71. Mem. Lawyers for Creative Arts, Am., Ill., Va. bar assns., Patent Law Assn. Chgo., Am. Arbitration Assn. (nat. arbitrator), Order of Coif. 1st pl. winner Van Vleck Moot Ct. Competition, 1964, Nathan Burkan Meml. Competition ASCAP, 1964; patent research editor George Washington Law Rev., 1965-66; contbr. articles to profl. and tech. jours.; patentee field of pollution control. Home: 1333 Imperial Dr Libertyville IL 60048 Office: 135 S LaSalle St Chicago IL 60603 Tel (312) 236-4038

D'ULL, WALTER, b. Vienna, Austria, May 23, 1931; B.A., N.Y.U., 1950; J.D., Yale, 1953. Admitted to N.Y. State bar, 1954, U.S. Supreme Ct. bar, 1967; individual practice law, Bronx, N.Y., 1954—; sr. atty. N.Y. State Div. Housing and N.Y. State Housing Finance Agy., 1961-68. Mem. Bronx County Bar Assn., Tax Cons. of Am. (dir.). Office: 2239 Grand Concourse Bronx NY 10453 Tel (212) 933-0300

DULL, WILBUR ROBBINS, b. Gallatin, Mo., Oct. 4, 1914; B.A, U. Iowa, 1936, J.D. with distinction, 1938. Admitted to Iowa bar, 1938; since practiced in Ottumwa, Iowa, individual practice law, 1938-42; asso. firm Dull, Keith & Beaver, and predecessors, 1942-46, partner, 1946—; legal assistance officer U.S. Naval Advance Base Depot, San Bruno, Calif., 1944-46; mem. Iowa Bd. Bar Examiners, 1967-76, chmn., 1971-72. Mem. Am., Iowa, Iowa State (taxation com., 1954-68; jud. adminstrn. com., 1967-72, chmn. 1969-70; bd. govs. 1962-66), Wapello County (pres. 1955) bar assns. Home: 1577 N Van Buren Ottumwa IA 52501 Office: 211 E 4th St Ottumwa IA 52501 Tel (515) 682-5447

DULSKY, BERYL I., b. London, Ohio, Jan. 24, 1930; A.B., N.Y. U., 1951; LL.B., Fordham U., 1954. Admitted to N.Y. bar, 1956, U.S. Dist. Ct. So. Dist. bar, 1967, U.S. Dist. Ct. Eastern Dist. bar, 1968; mem. firm Suchoff, Kolbell & Dulsky, Hempstead, N.Y., 1957-59; individual practice law, Mineola, N.Y., 1964—; asst. dist. atty. Nassau County, N.Y., 1959-64. Chmn., Roslyn (N.Y.) chpt. Am. Cancer Soc., 1958-59, Roslyn chpt. Am. Heart Fund, 1967-68; pres. Roslyn Republican Club, 1965; v.p., trustee Temple Beth Sholom, Roslyn, 1960-73. Mem. Am., N.Y. State (sec., mem. exec. com. criminal justice sect.), Nassau County bar assns. Office: 146 Old Country Rd Mineola NY 11501 Tel (516) 294-8990

DUMAS, JAMES FREDERICK, b. St. Louis, Mar. 8, 1943; B.A. in English cum laude, Regis Coll., 1965; J.D., Northwestern U., 1968. Admitted to Ind. bar, 1968, Colo. bar, 1969; asso. firm Kennerk, Dumas, Burke & Backs, Ft. Wayne, Ind., 1968; dep. state pub. defender, Littleton, Colo., 1969-73; chief dep. pub. defender, Denver 1973—; alt. to state council on criminal justice; mem. Colo. Commn. Criminal Justice, Standards and Goals. Mem. Am., Colo., Denver bar assns., Colo. Trial Lawyers Assn., Legal Aid and Defender Assn., Western Regional Defender Assn. (Colo. dir.). Home: 1345 Birch St Denver CO 80220 Office: 1575 Sherman St Denver CO 80203 Tel (303) 892-2661

DUMAS, LAWRENCE, JR., b. Talladega, Ala., Oct. 12, 1908; A.B. summa cum laude, Davidson Coll., 1929; J.D., Harvard U., 1932; LL.M., George Washington U., 1933; J.D., Georgetown U., 1935. Admitted to Ala. bar, 1932, D.C. bar, 1933; atty. Fed. Farm Bd. and PWA, 1932-36; practice in Birmingham, Ala., 1936-43, 44—; atty. OPA, asst. U.S. atty., 1943-44; mem. firm Cabaniss, Johnston, Gardner, Dumas & O'Neal; mem. Ala. Constl. Commn., 1970-73; mem. Indsl. Securities Adv. Council; mem. Ala. Ho. of Reps., 1947-55, Ala. Senate, 1959-66; chmn. Ala. Legis. Council, 1955-63. Vice-pres. adv. bd. local Salvation Army, Girl Scouts; bd. dirs. Carraway Meth. Med. Center, Bessemer Carraway Med. Center. Mem. Am. Judicature Soc., Ala. Bar Found., Am. (Ala. chmn. jr. bar conf. 1947), Ala., Birmingham bar assns. Contbr. articles to legal jours. Home: 3251 Dell Rd Birmingham AL 35213 Office: First Nat So Nat Bldg Birmingham AL 35203 Tel 252-8800

DUMONT, MARTIN GARRETH, b. N.Y.C., July 31, 1921; A.B., Union Coll., 1948; LL.B., N.Y. U., 1953, J.D., 1968. Admitted to N.Y. Bar, 1954, Colo. bar, 1958; spl. agt. trial atty. IRS, N.Y.C. and Denver, 1946-58; individual practice law, Glenwood Springs, Colo., 1958—; dep. dist. atty. Glenwood Springs, 1965-67; dist. atty. 9th Jud. Dist. Colo., 1968-73; town atty. Rangeley, Newcastle, Carbondale, Eagle, Minturn, Hudson, Ft. Lupton (all Colo.) Mem. Fed., Colo., Denver, 9th Jud. Dist. bar assns., Am. Trial Lawyers Assn. Author: Manual of Civil Disturbances, 1972; Continuity of Government, 1958. Home and Office: PO Box 188 Glenwood Springs CO 81601 Tel (303) 945-7210

DUNAHOO, MARK, b. Winder, Ga., May 1, 1908; LL.B., Washington Coll. Law, Am. U., 1939, J.D., 1968. Admitted to D.C. bar, 1939, Ga. bar, 1945; with dept. taxation Ga. Revenue Commn., Atlanta, 1930-33; secretarial aide Sen. Richard B. Russell of Ga., Washington, 1933-43; practiced in Winder, 1945-63; judge Ga. Superior Ct., Piedmont Circuit, 1964-77, ret., 1977, now judge emeritus; mem. Ga. Senate, 1951-53. Pres. bd. dirs. 1st Christian Ch., also elder; pres. Statham (Ga.) Civitan Club, 1967-68; mem. state bd. Disciples of Christ Ch., 1977-78. Mem. Ga., Am., Piedmont (pres.) bar assns., Am. Judicature Soc. Home: 1025 E Broad St Winder GA 20680 Office: POB 553 Winder GA 30680 Tel (404) 867-3824

DUNCAN, CHARLES TIGNOR, b. Washington, Oct. 31, 1924; A.B., Dartmouth Coll., 1947; J.D., Harvard U., 1950. Admitted to N.Y. State bar, 1951, D.C. bar, 1953, Md., bar, 1955, U.S. Ct. Appeals D.C. Circuit, 1954, U.S. Supreme Ct., 1954; asso. Resenman Goldmark Colin & Kaye, N.Y.C., 1950-53; partner Reeves, Robinson & Duncan, Washington, 1953-61; prin. asst. U.S. Attorney, Washington 1961-65; gen. counsel U.S. Equal Employment Commn., Washington, 1965-66; corp. counsel, Washington, 1966-70; partner firm Epstein, Friedman, Duncan & Medalie, Washington, 1970-73; dean Howard U. Law Sch., 1973—. Dir. NAACP Legal Defense and Ednl. Fund, 1972—; dir. Nat. Commn. Against Discrimination in Housing, 1973—; dir. Supreme Court Hist. Soc., 1974—. Mem. Nat., Am., D.C. bar assns., D.C. bar, Phi Beta Kappa. Home: 1812 Upshur St NW Washington DC 20011 Office: 2935 Upton St NW Washington DC 20008 Tel (202) 686-6573

DUNCAN, EDWIN WILLIAMS, b. Oakland, Calif., May 11, 1945; A.B., U. Calif. at Berkeley, 1966; J.D., Hastings Coll. Law, 1969. Admitted to Calif. bar, 1970; asso. firm Lawler, Felix & Hall, Los Angeles, 1970-75, partner, 1975—. Mem. Calif., Am., Los Angeles County bar assns., Order of Coif, Thurston Soc., Los Angeles County Barristers (dir. 1971-73), Calif. Barristers Assn. (v.p. 1974-75). Office: 605 W Olympic Blvd Los Angeles CA 90015 Tel (213) 620-0060

DUNCAN, GEORGE RICHARD, b. Minnewaukan, N.D., Feb. 5, 1897; LL.B., Willamette U., 1925. Admitted to Oreg. bar, 1925; individual practice law, Stayton, Oreg., 1927-42; judge Oreg. Circuit Ct., Salem, 1943-64; partner firm Duncan, Duncan & Tiger, and predecessors, Stayton, 1965—; atty. cities of Stayton, Sublimity, Aumsville, 1927-42. Office: 545 3rd St Stayton OR 97383 Tel (503) 769-2115

DUNCAN, HEARST RANDOLPH, b. Center Junction, Iowa, Aug. 28, 1905; J.D., George Washington U., 1931. Admitted to Iowa bar, 1931; state atty. Mitchell County, Iowa, 1932-34; adminstr. Civic Works Adminstrn., Mitchell County, 1934-40; spl. asst. atty. gen. Iowa, 1937; mem. firm Duncan, Jones, Riley & Finley, Des Moines, 1942—. Mem. Am., Iowa State (pres. 1960-61) bar assns., Am. Coll. Trial Lawyers, Order of Coif, Nat. Assn. R.R. Trial Counsel, Delta Sigma Rho. Home: 726 54th St Des Moines IA 50312 Office: 404 Equitable Bldg Des Moines IA 50309 Tel (515) 288-0145

DUNCAN, HEARST RANDOLPH, JR., b. Des Moines, Mar. 15, 1937; B.A., U. Iowa, 1959; postgrad. So. Methodist U., 1961: J.D., Drake U., 1963. Admitted to Iowa bar, 1963; partner firm Duncan, Jones, Riley, & Finley, Des Moines, 1963—; chmn. ethics com. Polk County Bar, 1968, grievance com., 1976; pres. Polk County Jr. Bar, 1967. Chmn., Cerebral Palsy, 1965, March of Dimes, 1970; bd. dirs. Boys Club Des Moines, 1969-72, YMCA Boys Home, Des Moines, 1975—. Mem. Am. Bar Assn., Iowa Def. Counsel Assn., Nat. Assn. R.R. Trial Counsel. Contbr. articles Drake Law Rev. Home: 4240 Foster Dr Des Moines IA 50312 Office: Equitable Bldg 404 Locust St Des Moines IA 50309 Tel (515) 288-0145

DUNCAN, J. DALE, b. Chickasha, Okla., May 1, 1941; B.A., U. Okla., 1962, J.D., 1965. Admitted to Colo. bar, 1966; individual practice law, Colorado Springs, 1966—. Trustee Colo. Springs. Children's Sch., 1974-76, treas., 1974-76; v.p., trustee Colo. Springs. Sch., 1976—. Mem. Am., Colo., El Paso bar assns., Colorado Springs C. of C., Phi Delta Phi. Contbr. articles in field to law jours. Home: 17 El Encanto Dr Colorado Springs CO 80906 Office: 410 Western Fed Savs Bldg Colorado Springs CO 80903 Tel (303) 475-0200

DUNCAN, JOHN ALEXANDER, b. Seattle, May 5, 1937; B.A., U. Wash., 1960; J.D., U. Calif., 1963. Admitted to Calif. bar, 1964, U.S. Tax Ct. bar, 1973, U.S. Supreme Ct. bar, 1973; individual practice law, Santa Ana, Calif., 1968-76, Newport Beach, Calif., 1976—. Mem. Orange County (Calif.) Bar Assn. (sec. probate and trust sect. 1976, chmn. 1977). Office: 610 Newport Center Dr Newport Beach CA 92660 Tel (714) 640-2320

DUNCAN, JOHN CROW, III, b. Middletown, N.Y., Mar. 13, 1939; B.S., Tufts U., 1960; LL.B., George Washington U., 1963. Admitted to Va. bar, 1963, D.C. bar, 1963, U.S. Supreme Ct. bar, 1969; asso. firm Frost & Towers, Washington, 1963-68, partner, 1969-72; asso. firm Douglas, Obear & Campbell, Washington, 1972-73; partner firm McChesney & Pyne, Washington, and Fairfax, Va., 1973—; instr. Strayer Jr. Coll., Washington, 1967, 68. Bd. mem. Mantua Elementary Sch. PTA, 1974-75, pres., 1975-76; bd. mem. St. Matthews United Meth. Ch., 1973, 76, chmn. bd. trustees, 1974, 75; editor Broyhill Crest Community News Letter, 1965, bd. mem., 1966; basketball coach Mantua Elementary Sch. girls team, 1974-76. Mem. Am., D.C. bar assns., Va. State Bar, Va. Trial Lawyers Assn., Bar Assn. of D.C., D.C. Def. Lawyers, The Barristers. Home: 3804 Acosta Rd Fairfax VA 22030 Office: 1000 Connecticut Ave NW Washington DC 20036 Tel (202) 872-8411

DUNCAN, LAURENCE ILSLEY, b. Concord, N.H., Oct. 5, 1906; A.B., Dartmouth, 1927; LL.B., Harvard, 1930. Admitted to N.H. bar, 1930, Mass. bar, 1930; practiced law, Concord, 1930-45; asso. justice N.H. Superior Ct., Concord, 1945-46, N.H. Supreme Ct., Concord, 1946-76; mem. N.H. Bd. Bar Examiners, 1941-44. Del., N.H. Constl. Conv., 1938-41; trustee Concord Hosp., 1944-64, 68—, sec., clk., 1944-64, 68-74. Mem. Am., N.H. bar assns., Am. Judicature Soc., New Eng. Law Inst. (sponsor). Home: 103 Centre St Concord NH 03301

DUNCAN, ROBERT GENE, b. Helena, Mo., Nov. 22, 1932; A.A., Kansas City Jr. Coll., 1951; B.E., Central Mo. State Coll., 1953; J.D., U. Kansas City, 1959. Admitted to Mo. bar, 1959, U.S. Supreme Ct. bar, 1961; asso. firm Quinn, Peebles & Hickman, Kansas City, Mo., 1959-62, Pierce & Duncan, and predecessors, Kansas City, 1962-65, partner, 1965-71; partner firm Duncan & Russell, Gladstone, Mo., 1972—; counsel City of Gladstone, 1961-73; judge Municipal Ct. Gladstone, 1973—; mem. com. standard forms indictments and infos. Mo. Supreme Ct.; tchr. law enforcement Maple Woods Community Coll. Chmn., Sheltered Facilities Bd., Clay County, Mo., 1972—. Mem. Nat. Assn. Criminal Def. Attys, Am. Judicature Soc., Clay County, Kansas City (v.p.), Fed. bar assns., Mo. Municipal Judges Assn., Mo. Police Chiefs Assn., Bench and Bar Soc., Phi Alpha Delta. Home: 5406 N Wyandotte St Gladstone MO 64118 Office: 2700 Kendallwood St Gladstone MO 64119 Tel (816) 454-7300

DUNE, STEVE CHARLES, b. Vithkuqi, Korca, Albania, June 15, 1931; A.B., Clark U., 1953, J.D. (Root-Tilden scholar), N.Y. U., 1956. Admitted to N.Y. State bar, 1957; law clk. U.S. Ct. Appeals 1st Circuit, 1956-57; asso. firm Cadwalader, Wickersham & Taft, N.Y.C., 1957-65, partner, 1965—. Trustee Clark U., Worcester, Mass., 1974—. Mem. Am., N.Y. State bar assns., Fed. Bar Council, N.Y. County Lawyers Assn., Assn. Bar City N.Y. (admiralty com. 1976—), Maritime Law Assn. U.S., Phi Beta Kappa. Office: 1 Wall St New York City NY 10005 Tel (212) 785-1000

DUNFEE, JACK CLINTON, JR., b. South Bend, Ind., July 9, 1934; A.B., Ind. U., 1956, J.D. with distinction, 1962. Admitted to Ind. bar, 1962; partner firm Goheen, Eichler & Dunfee, South Bend, 1962-64; asso. firm Thornburg, McGill, Deahl, Harman, Carey & Murray, South Bend, 1964-69, partner, 1970—; atty. St. Joseph County (Ind.) Health Dept., South Bend, 1963-72, Hist. Preservation Commn., South Bend and St. Joseph County, 1974-76. Pres. Southold Heritage Found., Inc., South Bend, 1976—. Mem. St. Joseph County, Ind., Am. bar assns. Home: 2702 Miami St South Bend IN 46614 Office: Sixth Floor First Bank Bldg South Bend IN 46601 Tel (219) 233-1171

DUNHAM, ALLISON, b. Wessington Springs, S.D., June 19, 1914; A.B., Yankton Coll., 1936; LL.B., Columbia, 1939. Admitted to N.Y. bar, 1940, Ill. bar, 1956; law clk. to Chief Justice Harlan F. Stone, 1939-41; draftsman, reporter Uniform Comml. Code for Am. Law Inst. and Nat. Conf. Commrs. Uniform State Laws, 1947-50; asst. prof. law U. Ind., 1945-47, asso. prof. Columbia, 1947-51, prof. U. Chgo., 1951—, now Arnold I. Shure prof. urban legal studies; exec. dir. Nat. Conf. Commrs. Uniform State Laws, 1962-69; vis. lectr. law Victoria Coll., 1953. Candidate town supr., Westchester, N.Y., 1949. Mem. Am. Law Inst., Am. Bar Assn., Chgo. Bar Assn. Author: Modern Real Estate Transactions, 1952; also articles legal jours. Co-author: Mr. Justice, 1956. Home: 5719 Kenwood Ave Chicago IL 60637 Office: U Chgo Law Sch 5801 Ellis Ave Chicago IL 60637*

DUNIPACE, WILLIAM SMITH, b. Bowling Green, Ohio, June 18, 1908; student Bowling Green State U., 1926-27, U. Ariz., 1939-41, Northwestern U., 1941; J.D., U. Ariz., 1942. Admitted to Ariz. bar, 1942; asso. firm Misbaugh & Fickett, 1942-49; asso. firm Fickett & Dunipace, Tucson, 1949-66; partner firm Fickett, Dunipace & Stewart, Tucson, 1966; partner firm Robertson & Fickett, Tucson, 1966-70; individual practice law, Tucson, 1970—; dep. county atty. planning and zoning Pima County (Ariz.), 1949-57. Librarian Pima County, Tucson, 1935-39; chmn. Tucson Democratic Central Com., 1944-45, 60-62. Mem. Am., Ariz. (mem. com. family law 1973—), Pima County (pres. 1971-72) bar assns., Am. Judicature Soc. Office: 32 N Stone Ave Tucson AZ 85701 Tel (602) 624-0604

DUNKELBERG, ALBERT GIBBS, b. Hull, Iowa, June 29, 1922; LL.B., Drake U., 1952. Admitted to Iowa bar, 1952; practice law, Osage, Iowa; mem. 2d Jud. Dist. Iowa Nominating Commn., 1972—; magistrate appt. commr. Mitchell County (Iowa), 1972—. Sec. Osage Devel. Corp., 1960-61. Mem. Iowa State, 2d Jud. Dist., Mitchell County bar assns., Osage C. of C. (pres. 1958). Home: 804 Poplar St Osage IA 50461 Office: 515 State St Osage IA 50461 Tel (515) 732-3796

DUNKELBERGER, HARRY EDWARD, JR., b. Los Angeles, Apr. 16, 1930; B.A., Yale U., 1954, J.D., 1957. Admitted to D.C. bar, 1957; asso. firm Covington & Burling, Washington, 1957-66, partner, 1966—. Mem. Am., D.C. bar assns. Home: 6718 Melody Ln Bethesda MD 20034 Office: 888 16th St NW Washington DC 20006 Tel (202) 452-6260

DUNKIN, DAVID ALLEN, b. Higgins, Tex., Mar. 31, 1941; B.S., Okla. State U., 1963; J.D., Samford U., 1971. Admitted to Fla. bar, 1971; asso. firm Diez & Dunkin, Englewood, Fla., 1972-75; individual practice law, Englewood, 1975—. Dir. South County Council, 1976; adv. bd. to Sarasota County (Fla.) Sch. Bd., 1973-75. Mem. Sarasota County Bar Assn. (dir. Venice-Englewood sect.). Home: 5 Bridge St Englewood FL 33533 Office: POB 523 Englewood FL 33533 Tel (813) 474-7753

DUNLAP, JOHN KENNEDY, b. Atlanta, Sept. 6, 1939; B.M.E., Ga. Inst. Tech., 1962; LL.B., U. Ga., 1966. Admitted to Ga. bar, 1965; mem. firm Long, Weinberg & Ansley and successors, Atlanta, 1966-70; mem. firm Branch & Swann, Atlanta, 1970; individual practice law, Atlanta, 1971—; prof. law, contracts Atlanta Law Sch., 1971, civil practice and procedure Woodrow Wilson Coll. of Law, 1972—. Mem. Atlanta Bar Assn., State Bar of Ga., Lawyers Club of Atlanta. Recipient of Woodrow Wilson Coll. of Law outstanding tchr. award, 1973-74. Office: Suite 510 The Equitable Bldg 100 Peachtree St NW Atlanta GA 30303 Tel (404) 522-7173

DUNLAP, ROBERT RANKIN, b. St. Paul, July 25, 1915; J.D., U. Minn., 1941. Admitted to Minn. bar, 1941; mem. firm Burkhardt and Dunlap, Plainview, Minn., 1947-62, Dunlap & McHardy, Plainview, 1962-64, Eustis, Price & Dunlap, Rochester, Minn., 1964-70, Price & Dunlap, Rochester, 1970-74, Dunlap, Keith, Collins, Towey, Finseth & Berndt, Rochester, 1974—; atty. Wabasha County, Minn., 1951-52. Mem. Minn. Senate, 1953-67; bd. dirs. Minn. State Coll., 1967-73. Mem. Olmsted County, Minn. State, Am. bar assns. Home: 832 10th St SW Rochester MN 55901 Office: 505 Marquette Bank Bldg Rochester MN 55901 Tel (507) 288-9111

DUNLEAVY, JAMES PATRICK, b. N.Y.C., Sept. 23, 1939; J.D., U. Maine, 1968. Admitted to Maine bar, 1968; individual practice law, Presque Isle, Maine, 1970—; commr. drug abuse State of Maine, 1971-72, bail commr., 1976; instr. U. Maine, Presque Isle, 1975-76. Chmn. adv. com. to Alcoholism Info. and Referral Service, 1975-76; chmn. Aroostook County Democratic Com., 1974-76; mem. Maine State Dem. Com., 1976—; mem. Maine Legislature, 1973-74; probate judge Aroostook County, 1977—. Mem. Am. Judicature Soc., Am., Maine, Aroostook County bar assns., Am., Maine trial lawyers assns. Recipient Outstanding Young Man of Am. award, 1974; conrbr. articles to profl. jours. Home: 125 Cedar St Presque Isle ME 04769 Office: 154 State St Presque Isle ME 04769 Tel (207) 764-4491

DUNN, CECIL FARRA, b. Richmond, Ky., Aug. 2, 1937; student Fla. State U., 1955-58; B.A., Eastern Ky. U., 1960; LL.B., U. Ky., 1965. Admitted to Ky. bar, 1965; law clk. Ky. Ct. Appeals, 1965-66; asso. firm Kincaid, Wilson & Trimble, Lexington, Ky., 1966-71; partner firms Murphy Dunn & Sledd, Lexington, 1971-74, Murphy King Enlow & Dunn, Lexington, 1974—; criminal trial commr. Fayette County (Ky.), 1970-75, asst. county atty., 1975—. Bd. dirs. Blue Grass Mental Health—Mental Retardation Bd., Lexington, 1975—, Ky. Mental Health Adv. Council, 1976—. Mem. Fayette County, Ky., Am. bar assns., Assn. Trial Lawyers Am. Home: 229 Kingsway Dr Lexington KY 40502 Office: 304 Security Trust Bldg Lexington KY 40507 Tel (606) 255-3371

DUNN, EDGAR HART, JR., b. Hyden, Ky., May 10, 1919; J.D., U. Fla., 1947. Admitted to Fla. bar, 1947, also SEC and FPC bars; practiced in St. Petersburg, Fla., 1947-55; sr. v.p., gen. counsel, Fla. Power Corp., St. Petersburg, 1955-68, also dir.; partner firm Bennett and Dunn, St. Petersburg, 1968-74; lectr. U. South Fla. Sch. Law, 1970—; mem. Active Corps Execs., Service Corps of Ret. Execs. of SBA. Mem. Am., Southeastern bus. law assns., Fla. Bar, Phi Delta Phi. Home: 1100 North Shore Dr NE Saint Petersburg FL 33701 Office: U of South Fla 830 First St S Saint Petersburg FL 33701 Tel (813) 898-7411

DUNN, EDWIN RYDELL, b. Boston, July 24, 1942; B.A., U. Notre Dame, 1964; J.D. cum laude, Northwestern U., 1967. Admitted to Ill. bar, 1967; asso. firm Baker & McKenzie, Chgo., 1967-73, partner, 1973—. Mem. Am., Ill., Chgo. bar assns. Office: 2800 Prudential Plaza Chicago IL 60601 Tel (312) 565-0025

DUNN, FRANCIS G., b. Scenic, S.D., Nov. 12, 1913; LL.B., U. S.D., 1937; M.A., George Washington U. Practiced law, Madison, Wis., until 1941; former sec. to U.S. Senator W.J. Bulow; trial atty. Dept. Justice, Washington, 1946-50; asst. U.S. atty. for S.D., 1950-54; asso. firm Doyle, Mahoney and Dunn, Sioux Falls, S.D., 1954-56; judge Sioux Falls Municipal Ct., 1956-59; judge U.S. Circuit Ct., 1959-73; justice S.D. Supreme Ct., 1973—, chief justice, 1974—. Home: Sioux Falls SD Office: Supreme Ct of SD State Capitol Pierre SD 57501*

DUNN, GEORGE JOHNSON, b. Cleve., Apr. 29, 1935; B.S., Yale U., 1957; J.D., Harvard, 1960. Admitted to Ohio bar, 1960; asso. firm McAfee, Hanning, Newcomer & Hazlett, Cleve., 1960-66, Squire, Sanders & Dempsey, 1967-68; v.p., gen. counsel Standard Oil Co. (Ohio), Cleve., 1968—. Trustee Cleve. Council World Affairs, Greater Cleve. Growth Assn. Mem. Am., Ohio, Cleve. bar assns. Office: Midland Bldg Cleveland OH 44115 Tel (216) 575-4560

DUNN, H. STEWART, JR., b. Pitts., July 9, 1929; A.B., Yale U., 1951; LL.B. magna cum laude, Harvard U., 1954. Admitted to D.C. bar, 1954, U.S. Supreme Ct. bar, 1960; asso. firm Ivins, Phillips & Barker, Washington, 1957-61, partner, 1962—; adj. prof. Georgetown U. Law Center, 1976—. Mem. Am. Bar Assn. (vice chmn. sect. taxation 1970-73), Am. Law Inst., D.C. Bar, Bar Assn. D.C. Bd. editors Harvard Law Rev., 1953-54. Office: 1700 Pennsylvania Ave NW Washington DC 20006 Tel (202) 393-7600

DUNN, HARRY LIPPINCOTT, b. Santa Barbara, Calif., Feb. 24, 1894; A.B., U. Calif., 1915; postgrad. Columbia Law Sch., 1916, Harvard Law Sch., 1921. Admitted to N.Y. bar, 1922, Calif. bar, 1925; asso. firm Cravath, Swaine & Moore, N.Y.C., 1921-24; asso. firm O'Melveny & Myers, Los Angeles, 1924-27, partner, 1927-68, counsel, 1968—. Trustee Claremont U. Center, Los Angeles; mem. World Affairs Council. Mem. Los Angeles, Calif. State (com. to revise corp. code), Am., Inter-Am. bar assns., Am. Bar Found. (com. to write mode indenture). Home: 1360 Hillcrest Ave Pasadena CA 91106 Office: 611 W Sixth St Los Angeles CA 90017 Tel (213) 620-1120

DUNN, IRA JOHN, b. Erie, Pa., Aug. 19, 1944; A.B. in Econs., Colo. Coll., 1966; J.D., Dickinson Sch. Law, 1969. Admitted to Pa. bar, 1971; mem. tax staff Arthur Andersen & Co., Denver, 1969-70; asso. firm Dunn & Conner, Erie, Pa., 1971-72, partner, 1973—. Treas., chmn. fin. com. Erie Philharmonic, 1974-75; mem. bd. dirs. and fin. com. Stairways, Inc., 1976; mem. bd. deacons Ch. of the Covenant, 1974-75. Mem. Pa. (zone chmn. young lawyers sect.), Am. bar assns., Pa., Am. Insts. C.P.A.s, Pa. Trial Lawyers Assn. Lic. C.P.A. Home: 1460 South Shore Dr Erie PA 16505 Office: 1111 G Daniel Baldwin Bldg Erie PA 16501 Tel (814) 453-6011

DUNN, JOHN WOOD, b. Peoria, Ill., Oct. 5, 1939; A.B., Wabash Coll., 1961; LL.B., N.Y. U., 1964. Admitted to Colo. bar, 1964; partner firm Cosgriff, Dunn & French, Leadville, Colo., 1969—; county atty. Lake County (Colo.), 1971—. Mem. Am., Continental Divide, Colo. (v.p. fourth dist. 1975-76, Outstanding Young Lawyer 1972) bar assns. Home: 144 W 9th St Leadville CO 80461 Office: 131 W 5th St Leadville CO 80461 Tel (303) 486-1885

DUNN, LEE J., JR., b. Boston, Sept. 16, 1943; A.B., Columbia, 1966, J.D., Case Western Res. U., 1970; LL.M., Harvard, 1971. Admitted to Kans. bar, 1973, U.S. Dist. Ct. Kans. bar, 1973; research asst. Harvard Sch. Pub. Health, 1969-71; staff atty., program dir. Practising Law Inst., N.Y.C., 1971-72; asst. atty. gen. Kans., 1973—; legal counsel to the Med. Center, U. Kans., 1973—. Trustee Boston Latin Sch. Assn., 1971-74. Mem. The Bostonian Soc., Am., Kans., Wyandotte County bar assns., Am. Acad. Forensic Scis., Am. Coll. Legal Medicine, Am. Soc. Law and Medicine, Pitts. Inst. Legal Medicine, Nat. Assn. Coll. and Univ. Attys. Editor: Boston Latin Sch. Alumni Bull., 1972—; contbr. articles in field to profl. jours. Home: 5732 Metcalfe Ct Overland Park KS 66202 Office: 214 Taylor Bldg Rainbow Blvd and 39th St Kansas City KS 66103 Tel (913) 588-7281

DUNN, PAUL JAMES, b. Tiffin, Ohio, Sept. 23, 1939; A.B., Cath. U. Am., 1962; J.D., Ohio State U., 1964. Admitted to Ohio bar, 1965; individual practice law, Tiffin, Ohio, 1965—; city solicitor City of Tiffin, 1973-74. Bd. dirs. Tiffin Community Devel. Corp.; sec., trustee Easter Seal Soc., Tiffin. Mem. Am., Ohio, Seneca County (Ohio) bar assns., Tiffin C. of C. (dir.). Home: 285 Melmore St Tiffin OH 44883 Office: 174 S Washington St Tiffin OH 44883 Tel (419) 447-7422

DUNN, PETER MICHAEL, b. Syracuse, N.Y., Nov. 11, 1936; A.B., Coll. Holy Cross, 1958; LL.B., Fordham U., 1961. Admitted to N.Y. bar, 1961; partner firm Dunn & Dunn, Oneida, N.Y., 1961—. Bd. mgrs. Oneida City Hosp.; gen. chmn. Oneida Community Chest. Mem. N.Y. State, Madison County (pres. 1972) bar assns. Named Young Man of Year, Oneida, 1968. Office: 112 Farrier Ave Oneida NY 13421 Tel (315) 363-4690

DUNN, RALPH, b. Canfield, W.Va., Sept. 11, 1925; J.D., W.Va. U., 1951. Admitted to W.Va. bar, 1951; pros. atty. Nicholas County (W.Va.), 1952-60; partner firm Barber & Dunn, Richwood, W.Va., 1951—. Mem. Nicholas County Bd. Edn., 1974—; chmn. bd. deacons Richwood Presbyterian Ch., 1956, clk. of session, 1964-70, chmn. bd. trustees, 1970—. Mem. Am., W.Va., Nicholas County bar assns. Home: Box 151 Richwood WV 26261 Office: 37 E Main St Richwood WV 26261

DUNN, WALLACE B., b. Chgo., Nov. 28, 1940; B.S., U. Ill., 1963; J.D., De Paul U., 1965. Admitted to Ill. bar, 1965; partner firm Kvistad and Dunn, Chgo., 1966-75; individual practice law, Highwood, Ill., 1975—; corp. counsel City of Highwood; village atty. Village of Wauconda (Ill.). Mem. Deerfield Twp. (Ill.) Republican Precinct Com., 1970-76. Mem. Ill. State, Chgo., N.W. Suburban, Am., Lake County (Ill.) bar assns., Ill. Trial Lawyers Assn. Recipient certificate of award Meehan Soc. of Coll. Law De Paul U., 1963, hon. award for participation 13th Ann. Inst. on Police and Community Relations Mich. State U., 1967, Youth award City of Chgo., 1968. Office: 445 Sheridan Rd Highwood IL 60040 Tel (312) 433-2800

DUNN, WILLIAM ROBERT, SR., b. Shoals Junction, S.C., Mar. 21, 1911; B.S., U. S.C., 1933, LL.B., 1935, J.D., 1970. Admitted to S.C. bar, 1935; individual practice law, Greenwood, S.C., 1935-41, 76—; supt. edn. Greenwood County (S.C.), 1943-71, asst. supt. schs., 1971-76. Mem. S.C., Greenwood County bar assns., Am. Assn. Sch. Adminstrs., NEA, Nat., S.C. ret. tchrs. assns., Am. Legion (adj. 1943-67), Greenwood County Edn. Assn. (pres. 1950-51), S.C. State Assn. County Supts. (past pres.). Recipient Outstanding Educator award Greenwood County Edn. Assn., 1969. Home and Office: 223 Gracemont Dr Greenwood SC 29646 Tel (803) 223-1294

DUNNAN, WEAVER WHITE, b. Paxton, Ill., Sept. 23, 1923; A.B., Harvard U., 1947, LL.B., 1949. Admitted to D.C. bar, 1951, U.S. Supreme Ct. bar, 1954, U.S. Ct. Appeals bar, 1960, U.S. Tax Ct. bar, 1957; law clk. to judge U.S. Ct. Appeals 2d Circuit, N.Y.C., 1949-50; law clk. justice U.S. Supreme Ct., 1950-51; partner firm Covington & Burling, Washington, D.C., 1951—. Mem. bd. govs. St. Albans Sch., Washington, D.C., 1974—; trustee Beauvoir Sch., 1969-74. Mem. Am. Bar Assn., Bar Assn. Washington, D.C., Harvard Law Sch. Assn. Office: 888 16th St NW Washington DC 20006 Tel (202) 452-6248

DUNNE, GERALD THOMAS, b. St. Louis, Sept. 24, 1919; B.B.A., Georgetown U., 1943; LL.B., St. Louis U., 1948. Admitted to Mo. bar, 1948, U.S. Supreme Ct. bar, 1972; with Fed. Res. Bank, St. Louis, 1949-54, gen. counsel, 1954-66, v.p., 1967-73; vis. prof. law U. Mo., 1970-71; lectr. St. Louis U., 1971-72, prof. law, 1973—. Trustee Mo. Hist. Soc., 1973-76; bd. dirs., v.p. St. Louis Mercantile Library, 1972—. Mem. Am., Mo., St. Louis bar assns., Am. Law Inst., Selden Soc., Am. Judicature Soc. Am. Soc. for Legal History (dir.), Phi Beta Kappa. Author: Monetary Decisions of the Supreme Court, 1960; Justice Joseph Story and the Rise of the Supreme Court, 1970; Hugo Black and the Judicial Revolution, 1977. Home: 7301 Princeton St University City MO 63130 Office: 3642 Lindell St Saint Louis MO 63108 Tel (314) 535-3300

DUNNE, JAMES LAWRENCE, b. Glen Cove, N.Y., July 11, 1940; A.B., St. John's U., 1962, LL.B., J.D., 1965. Admitted to N.Y. bar, 1969; spl. agt. FBI, Washington, Charlotte, N.C., Detroit and N.Y.C., 1965-70; partner firm Healy Tuohy & Dunne, N.Y.C., 1970—. Mem. Nassau County Environ. Mgmt. Council, 1975—; pres. N.Shore Youth Council, Town of Oyster Bay, 1970-74; mem. Youth Bd. Village of Sea Cliff, 1970-74; mem. Sea Cliff Bicentennial Commn., 1975-76; pres. Sea Cliff Chamber Players, N.Shore Kiwanis; bd. dirs. Harbor Day Care Center. Mem. Nassau County, Nassau-Suffolk Criminal bar assns., N.Shore Lawyers Assn. (chmn. 1974-75), Phi Delta Phi, St. John's Law Sch. Alumni Assn. (v.p. Nassau County, treas.). Office: 425 New York Ave Huntington NY 11743 also 215 Glen Cove Ave Sea Cliff NY 11579 Tel (516) 427-9120

DUNNER, DONALD ROBERT, b. Bklyn., May 12, 1931; B.S.Ch.E., Purdue U., 1953; J.D., Georgetown U., 1958. Admitted to U.S. Dist. Ct. bar for D.C., 1958, U.S. Supreme Ct. bar, 1963. Examiner U.S. Patent Office, Washington, 1955-56; law clk. Chief Judge Noble J. Johnson, Ct. Customs and Patent Appeals, 1956-58; since practiced in Washington; asso. firm Strauch, Nolan & Neale, 1958-59; asso. firm Diggins & LeBlanc, 1959-60, partner, 1961-62; partner firm Lane, Aitken, Dunner & Ziems, 1962—; professorial lectr. in law George Washington U., 1969—. Pres. Chevy Chase (Md.) Gardens Citizens Assn., 1965-66. Mem. D.C. Bar (chmn. steering com. div. 14 1976—), Bar Assn. of D.C. (bd. dirs. 1965-66, patent, trademark and copyright sect. sec.-treas. 1961-63, chmn. 1964-65), Am. Bar Assn. (chmn. coms. 1966-68, 73-74), Am. Patent Law Assn. (treas. and bd. mgrs. 1970-73, 2d v.p. 1976—). Co-author: Patent Law Perspectives, 1970—; Court Review of Patent Office Decisions, 1969, 73. Office: 1828 L St NW Washington DC 20036 Tel (202) 466-8090

DUNPHY, JAMES MCGAUGHEY, b. Indpls., Nov. 24, 1926; B.A., Duke, 1948; J.D., Franklin U. (now Capital U.), 1962. Admitted to Ohio bar, 1962; asst. atty. gen. State of Ohio, Columbus, 1963-65; individual practice law, Westerville, Ohio, 1965-70; master commr. Ohio Supreme Ct., Columbus, 1970-71; asst. pros. atty. Franklin County (Ohio), Columbus, 1971—. Mem. Columbus Bar Assn. Home: 150 N West St Westerville OH 43081 Office: 80 E Fulton St Columbus OH 43215

DUNST, ALAN IRA, b. Newark, June 6, 1947; B.A. Morris Harvey Coll., 1969; J.D., N.Y. Law Sch., 1972. Admitted to N.J. bar, 1972; jud. clk. Middlesex County Superior Ct., 1972-73; asso. firm Cohen, Hoagland, Keefe & Oropollo, New Brunswick, N.J., 1973-75, partner, 1976-77; partner firm Hoagland, Longo, Oropollo & Moran, New Brunswick, 1977—. Mem. Am., N.J., New Brunswick bar assns., Middlesex County Trial Lawyers Assn. Home: 565 Fairfield Rd East Windsor NJ 08520 Office: 96 Bayard St New Brunswick NJ 08903 Tel (201) 545-4717

DUNWORTH, JAMES RICHARD, b. E. St. Louis, Ill., Aug. 11, 1936; B.S., U.S. Mcht. Marine Acad., 1958; J.D., Hastings Coll., 1973. Admitted to Calif. bar, 1974, C.Z. bar, 1976; individual practice law, San Francisco, 1974-75; admiralty atty. Office of Gen. Counsel Panama Canal Co., Balboa Heights, C.Z., 1975—. Cubmaster, Marin County (Calif.) Boy Scouts Am., 1974-75; chmn. cubpack com. C.Z. council Boy Scouts Am., 1976—. Mem. Calif, C.Z. bar assns., Naval Res. Lawyers Assn., Order of Coif. Home: PO Box 206 Balboa Heights CZ Office: PO Box M Balboa Heights CZ Tel (CZ) 52-7511

DUPLANTIER, ADRIAN GUY, b. New Orleans, Mar. 5, 1929; J.D., Loyola U. Admitted to La. bar, 1950, U.S. Supreme Ct. bar, 1955; 1st asst. dist. atty. Orleans Parish (La.), 1954-56; judge Orleans Parish Civil Dist. Ct., div. B., 1974—; mem. La. Senate, 1960-74; lectr. Loyola U. Law Sch., 1952—; mem. La. State Law Inst. Council, 1960—. Del. Democratic Nat. Conv., 1964; bd. dirs. Interracial Council for Bus. Opportunity, 1970—, co-chmn., 1972—. Mem. New Orleans, La. State, Am. bar assns. Editor-in-chief Loyola Law Rev., 1948-49. Home: 5601 Charlotte Dr New Orleans LA 70122 Office: 421 Loyola Ave New Orleans LA 70112 Tel (504) 523-4920

DUPLESSIE, RICHARD D., b. Waterville, Maine, Sept. 24, 1949; B.A., Creighton U., 1971, J.D., 1973. Admitted to Wis. bar, 1974; asso. firm Wilcox & Wilcox, Eau Claire, Wis., 1974-76, partner, 1976—. Mem. Westcentral Wis. Health Planning Council, 1975—. Mem. Am., Wis., Eau Claire County bar assns. Office: 131 S Barstow St Eau Claire WI 54701 Tel (715) 832-6645

DUPUY, HOWARD MOORE, JR., b. Portland, Oreg., Mar. 15, 1939; B.B.A., U. Portland, 1951; LL.B., Lewis and Clark Coll., 1956. Admitted to Oreg. bar, 1956; asso. firm Green Richardson Green & Griswold, Portland, 1956-57; partner firm Morton Crowther & Dupuy, Portland, 1957-61, Morton & Dupuy, Portland, 1961-68, Phillips Coughlin Buell & Phillips (now Phillips Coughlin Buell Stoloff & Black), Portland, 1968—. Mem. Portland C. of C. (past mem. taxation com.), Am. Trial Lawyers Assn., Am. Arbitration Assn. (nat. panel). Home: 16116 NE Stanton St Portland OR 97213 Office: 807 Electric Bldg 621 SW Adler St Portland OR 97205 Tel (503) 222-9821

DURAN, ALFREDO G., b. Havana, Cuba, Aug. 16, 1936; B.S., La. State U., 1957; J.D., U. Miami, 1967. Admitted to Fla. bar, 1967; mem. firm Acosta and Duran, Miami, 1967-75; individual practice law, Miami, 1975—; mem. firm Duran, Cantera, Kalish, Schere & Press, profl. assn. Past chmn. Dade County Community Relations Bd.; past mem. Dade County Sch. Bd., Health Planning Council; chmn. Democratic Party, State of Fla. Mem. Interam., Am., Fla., Dade County bar assns. Home: 3550 Rockerman Rd Miami FL 33133 Office: 619 NW 12th Ave Miami FL 33136 Tel (305) 324-5040

DURANT, HARRY L., b. Pensacola, Fla., May 23, 1925; LL.B., U. Miami, 1949. Admitted to Fla. bar, 1949; asst. county solicitor Dade County (Fla.), 1953-54, asst. state atty., 1954-55; partner firm Smathers & Thompson, Miami, Fla., 1964—. Mem. Dade County, Am., Fla. bar assns., Am. Judicature Soc., Assn. Trial Lawyers Am., Comml. Law League Am., Internat. Bar Assn. Editor U. Miami Law Quar., 1948. Home: 13404 S W 58th Ave South Miami FL 33136 Office: 1301 Alfred I DuPont Bldg Miami FL 33131 Tel (305) 379-6523

DURANT, NAPOLEON JOSEPH, JR., b. Pensacola, Fla., Nov. 4, 1928; A.B. magna cum laude, U. Miami, Coral Gables, Fla., 1953, LL.B. cum laude, 1956. Dep. clk. Fla. Circuit Ct. of Dade County, 1943-45; city mgr. North Bay Village, Fla., 1949; admitted to Fla. bar, 1956; asso. firm Snyder and young, North Miami Beach, Fla., 1957-59; asst. state atty. Fla. 11th Jud. Circuit, 1959-70, chief asst. state atty., 1970-75; judge Fla. 11th Jud. Circuit Ct., 1975—; legal counsel Dade County Grand Jury, 1966-75. Mem. Fla. Bar, Nat. Dist. Attys. Assn., Fla. Prosecuting Attys. Assn., Fla. Conf. Trial Judges. Recipient commendation Dade County Grand Jury, 1973, Outstanding Citizenship award Grand Jury Assn. Fla., 1974; author: (with Philipp Hubbard) Florida Rules of Criminal Procedure, 1970. Home: 7808 Mindello Ave Coral Gables FL 33143 Office: Room 315 Metro Justice Bldg 1351 NW 12th St Miami FL 33125 Tel (305) 547-5493

DURANTE, JAMES PETER, b. N.Y.C., July 17, 1914; LL.B., St. John's U., 1938. Admitted to N.Y. State bar, 1939, U.S. Supreme Ct. bar, 1955; partner firm Lewis, Durante & Bartel, N.Y.C., 1960-63, firm Reavis & McGrath, N.Y.C., 1963—; lectr. labor law Wagner Coll., N.Y.C., 1965-66. Mem. Am. Bar Assn. Author: Law of Sports, 1946. Home: 222 E 39th St New York City NY 10016 Office: 345 Park Ave New York City NY 10022 Tel (212) 752-6830

DURBIN, PAUL JAMES, b. Clarkson, Ky., June 25, 1917; A.B., U. Ky., 1940, LL.B., 1941. Admitted to Ky. bar, 1941, U.S. Ct. Mil. Appeals bar, 1954, U.S. Supreme Ct. bar, 1954, Hawaii bar, 1970; individual practice law, Fulton, Ky., 1946-48; commr. Ky. Ry. Commn., 1947; commd. capt. JAGC, U.S. Army, 1941, advanced through grades to col., 1968; individual practice law, Fulton, 1969, Honolulu, 1970—. Mem. Am., Ky., Hawaii State bar assns. Home: 1462 Kalanikai Pl Honolulu HI 96821 Office: 735 Bishop St Honolulu HI 96813 Tel (808) 531-7924

DURDEN, HOMER SYLVESTER, JR., b. Swainsboro, Ga., May 16, 1919; B.S. in Commerce, U. Ga., 1940, LL.B., 1943, J.D., 1963. Admitted to Ga. bar, 1943, U.S. Supreme Ct. bar, 1961; judge State Ct. Emanuel County (Ga.), 1962—, Juvenile Ct. Emanuel County, 1962—; mem. criminal adv. bd. Central Savannah River expenditure fed. funds to fight crime. Mem. Emanuel County Bar Assn., Ga. Bar Assn. (vice chmn. traffic com.). Contbr. to Ency. Ga. Laws, articles to legal jours. Home: 318 Watson St Swainsboro GA 30401 Office: 128 S Main St Swainsboro GA 30401 Tel (912) 237-8962

DURGIN, JOHN CHARLES, JR., b. Malden, Mass., Feb. 16, 1926; J.D., Suffolk U., 1951. Admitted to Mass. bar, 1953; prin. John C. Durgin, Jr., Boston, 1957—; partner firm Durgin, Josephson & Raymond, Stoneham, Mass., 1969—. Pres. Atlantic Community Drug Program, Stoneham, 1970-75. Mem. Middlesex, 4th Dist. Ct. bar assns. Home: 3 Rose Ln Stoneham MA 02180 Office: 84 State St Boston MA 02109 also 5 Central Sq Stoneham MA 02180 Tel (617) 438-7700

DURHAM, HARRY BLAINE, III, b. Denver, Sept. 16, 1946; A.B. cum laude, Colo. Coll., 1969; J.D., U. Colo., 1973. Admitted to Wyo. bar, 1973, U.S. Tax Ct. bar, 1974, 10th Circuit Ct. Appeals bar, 1976; asso. firm Brown, Drew, Apostolos, Massey & Sullivan, Casper, Wyo., 1973—. Bd. dirs. Natrona County United Way, 1975—, pres., 1977-78; bd. dirs. Casper Symphony Assn., 1974—; sec. Casper Amateur Hockey Club, 1970—. Mem. Am., Wyo., Natrona County Bar Assns., Phi Beta Kappa. Articles editor U. Colo. Law Rev. Home: 3101 Hawthorne St Casper WY 82601 Office: Suite 512 Petroleum Bldg Casper WY 82601 Tel (307) 265-9210

DURHAM, JAMES DAVID, JR., b. Paris, Tex., May 18, 1941; A.A., Paris Jr. Coll., 1962; LL.B., Baylor U., 1966. Admitted to Tex. bar, 1966, N.Mex. bar, 1967; asso. firm Esther Smith, Clovis, N.Mex., 1966-68; mem. firm Tom Upchurch, Amarillo, Tex., 1968-73; individual practice law, Amarillo, 1973—. Mem. Tex. Trial Lawyers Assn., Tex. Criminal Defense Lawyers Assn., Am. Bar Assn. Home: 3121 Fleetwood St Amarillo TX 79109 Office: 510 S Polk St Amarillo TX 79101 Tel (806) 373-3054

DURICA, TERRENCE DAVID, b. Cleve., Dec. 21, 1949; B.A., Kenyon Coll., 1971; J.D., Case Western Res. U., 1974. Admitted to Ohio bar, 1974; asso. firm Dachman & Dachman, Cleve. Mem. Ohio, Cuyahoga County (Ohio) bar assns. Home: 11820 Edgewater St Lakewood OH 44107 Office: Dachman & Dachman 807 Engineers Bldg Cleveland OH 44114 Tel (216) 621-2244

DURICK, BRYAN TIMOTHY, b. Crosby, N.D., Mar. 31, 1945; B.A., U. Notre Dame, 1967; J.D., U. Minn., 1971. Admitted to N.D. bar, 1971; spl. asst. atty. gen. State of N.D., Bismarck, 1971-73; partner firm Wheeler, Wolt, Wefald & Durick, Bismarck, 1973-75, Pearce, Anderson, Thames & Durick, Bismarck, 1976—; asst. judge Bismarck Municipal Ct., 1976. Mem. N.D. Bar Assn. Home: 1800 Masterson Ave Bismarck ND 58501 Office: Box 400 Bismarck ND 58501

DURKEE, BERT REID, b. Chatham, Ont., Can., Mar. 11, 1912; LL.B. cum laude, U. Nebr., 1938. Admitted to Nebr. bar, 1938, Ill. bar, 1938; partner firm Hansgen & Durkee, Rock Island, Ill., 1938-46, firm Katz, McAndrews, Durkee & Telleen, and predecessors, Rock Island, 1946—. Mem. Am., Ill. State, Rock Island County bar assns. Home: 1336 21st Ave Rock Island IL 61201 Office: 200 Cleaveland Bldg 1705 2d Ave PO Box 66 Rock Island IL 61201 Tel (309) 788-5661

DURLAND, WILLIAM REGINALD, b. N.Y.C., Mar. 28, 1931; A.B., Bucknell U., 1953; LL.B., Georgetown U., 1959, J.D., 1966; M.A., U. Notre Dame, 1975; Ph.D., Union U., 1977. Admitted to Wis. bar, 1960, D.C. bar, 1961, U.S. Supreme Ct. bar, 1963, Va. bar, 1965, Ind. bar, 1973; asst. to dir. U.S. Commn. on Internat. Rules of Jud. Procedure, 1959-60; trial atty. HEW, Washington, 1960-61; individual practice law, 1962-73; mem. Va. legislature, 1966-70. Pres., Mason Neck Conservation Com., 1966-68; bd. dirs., v.p. Va. Citizens' Consumer Council, 1966-70; bd. dirs. Va. Assn. Mental Retardation, 1966-70; pres. Matthew 25 Assn., 1976—. Mem. Am. Bar Assn., AAUP. Recipient Civitan award Va. State Legislature, 1966; author: No King but Caesar, 1975; Ethical Issues, 1975; contbr. articles in field to profl. jours. Home: 3625 Elwood Dr Fort Wayne IN 46805 Office: POB 2214 Fort Wayne IN Tel (219) 484-5439

DURO, TERRY C., b. Jamestown, N.Y., Dec. 28, 1925; B.A., Alfred U., 1950; LL.B., U. Buffalo, 1953, J.D., 1968. Admitted to N.Y. bar, 1955, Fla. bar, 1963, U.S. Supreme Ct. bar, 1958; dist. atty. Chautauqua County Legal Services, Inc., Dunkirk, N.Y., 1969—. Founding dir. Albanian-Am. Orgn., pres., 1948; pres. St. Elia Albanian Orthodox Ch., 1975—. Mem. No. Chautauqua County, Fla. bar assns., Legal Services Corp. (project dirs. adv. group). Author: 10,000 Reasons Why My Husband Should Not Be Allowed to Visit the Children; I Knew Right Away the Minute I Saw You That I Needed a Lawyer. Office: 321 Central Ave Dunkirk NY 14048 Tel (716) 366-3934

DUROCHER, JOSEPH WILLIAM, b. Long Beach, Calif., June 8, 1938; B.S., Villanova U., 1960; J.D., U. Fla., 1967. Admitted to Fla. bar, 1967; partner firm Panico & DuRocher, Orlando, Fla., 1967-70; dir. Legal Aid Soc., Orlando, 1970-71; judge Juvenile Ct. Orange County (Fla.), 1971-72, 9th Circuit Ct., Fla., 1973-76; partner firm DuRocher & Walsh, Orlando, 1976—. Mem. Orange County, Am. bar assns., Fla. Acad. Trial Lawyers. Home: 3563 Emerywood Ln Orlando FL 32806 Office: 326 N Fern Creek Ave Orlando FL 32803

DURR, ELDON WENDELL, b. Granite City, Ill., Oct. 2, 1937; B.S. in Psychology, U. Ill., 1960, J.D., 1961. Admitted to Ill. bar, 1962; partner firm Durr and Durr, Edwardsville, Ill., 1962-72, owner, 1972—; asst. states atty. Madison County (Ill.), 1964, park dist. atty., 1968-75, village atty., 1970-73, city atty., 1965—; del. Ill. Constl. Conv., 1970; author, lectr. Ill. Inst. Continuing Legal Edn. Office: Durr & Durr 910 N Main St Edwardsville IL 62025 Tel (618) 656-6030

DURYEA, LESLIE NOYES, b. Chgo., May 21, 1926; B.S. in Mech. Engring. and B.S. in Naval Sci. and Tactics, Purdue U., 1947; postgrad. DePauw U.; LL.B., Stanford U., 1950. Admitted to Calif. bar, 1950; individual practice law, San Francisco, 1950-56; counsel Beckman Instruments, Inc., 1956-63; partner firm Adams, Duque & Hazeltine, Los Angeles, 1963-65; partner firm Duryea, Randolph, Malcolm & Daly, Newport Beach, Calif., 1965—; dir. numerous varied mfg., service and investment cos. Pres., chmn. World Affairs Council Orange County; asso. county and state central coms. Republican party. Mem. Orange County, Los Angeles, Am. (mem. council, corp., banking and bus. law sect.) bar assns., Phi Alpha Delta. Home: 841 Madera Place Fullerton CA 92635 Office: 4301 Mac Arthur Blvd Newport Beach CA 92663 Tel (714) 833-0730

DURYEE, SAMUEL SLOAN, b. N.Y.C., Nov. 18, 1903; B.A., Yale, 1917; LL.B. cum laude, Fordham U., 1923. Admitted to N.Y. State bar, 1924; mem. firm Parker & Duryee, and predecessors, N.Y.C.; now of counsel firm Parker, Duryee, Zunipo, Malone & Carter, N.Y.C. Gov. N.Y. Hosp., N.Y.C.; past pres. Hosp. for Spl. Surgery; chmn. Yale Alumni Fund. Mem. Am. Bar Assn., Assn. Bar City N.Y. Office: 1 E 44th St New York City NY 10017 Tel (212) 573-9340

DUSIC, RALPH CHARLES, JR., b. Cumberland, Md., Feb. 24, 1938; A.B., W.Va. U., 1961, LL.B., 1964. Admitted to W.Va. bar, 1964; asso. firm Kay, Casto & Chaney, Charleston, W.Va., 1964-73; partner firm Friedman & Dusic, Charleston, 1973—. Mem. vestry St. Matthews Episcopal Ch., 1968-71, registrar, 1968-71; chmn. Gov.'s com. to provide legal assistance to victims of Buffalo Creek Disaster; mem. W.Va. Bd. Probation and Parole, 1975—. Mem. Am. (nat. officer young lawyers sect. 1972-74), W.Va. (bd. govs., chmn. young lawyers sect. 1970-71, chmn. membership com. 1971-72), Kanawha County (treas. 1969-70, chmn. Frank C. Haymond Testimonial Dinner) bar assns., W.Va. U. Alumni Assn. (v.p. Kanawha County chpt.). Recipient citation of merit Exec. Office Pres., Office Emergency Preparedness, 1973; named Kanawha Legal Secs. Boss of Year, 1971. Office: 804 Commerce Sq Charleston WV 25301 Tel (304) 342-7128

DUTSON, ROGER SAMUEL, b. Roberts, Idaho, Aug. 5, 1937; B.S., Utah State U., 1962; LL.B., J.D., George Washington U., 1965. Admitted to Va. bar, 1965, Utah bar, 1968; served with JAGC, U.S. Navy, 1965-68; individual practice law, Ogden, Utah, 1968—; dep. city atty. Ogden, 1968-70; legal adviser Ogden Police, 1970-71; atty. Roy City, 1971—. Bd. dirs. Weber County (Utah) Legal Services; mem. adv. bd. Law Enforcement Planning Agy. Div. II. Mem. Utah Municipal Attys. Assn. (pres 1974-75), Weber County Bar Assn., Utah State Bar. Home: 1455 28th St Ogden UT 84403 Office: 863 25th St Ogden UT 84401 Tel (801) 621-2630

DUTTON, DIANA C., b. Sherman, Tex., June 27, 1944; B.S., Georgetown U., 1967; J.D., U. Tex., Austin, 1971. Admitted to Tex. bar, 1971; atty. enforcement div. Region VI, EPA, Dallas, 1971-73, asst. regional counsel Office Gen. Counsel, 1973-75, regional counsel, 1975—. Chmn. women's com. Fed. Exec. Bd., Dallas-Fort Worth, 1974-76. Mem. Am., Fed. bar assns., Dallas Jr. Bar, State Bar Tex.

(chmn. environ. law sect. 1975-76). Recipient Bronze Medal EPA, 1973; asso. editor: Tex. Law Rev. Office: 1201 Elm St Environmental Protection Agency Dallas TX 75270 Tel (214) 749-1821

DUTTON, STEPHEN JAMES, b. Evergreen Park, Ill., Sept. 20, 1942; B.S., Ill. Inst. Tech., 1965; J.D. cum laude, Ind. U., 1969. Admitted to Ind. bar, 1969; mem. firm McHale, Cook and Welch, Indpls., 1969—; exec. sec. Ind. Jud. Study Commn. and Ind. Jud. Conf., 1968-69. Treas. Indpls. Day Nursery Assn., Inc. Mem. Indpls., Ind., Am. bar assns., Bar Assn. Seventh Circuit Ct. Appeals, Am. Judicature Soc. Home: 5235 Roland Dr Indianapolis IN 46208 Office: 1122 Chamber of Commerce Bldg Indianapolis IN 46204 Tel (317) 634-7588

DUTY, TONY EDGAR, b. Golinda, Tex., May 14, 1928; B.B.A., Baylor U., 1952, J.D., 1953. Admitted to Tex. bar, 1954; individual practice law, Waco, Tex., 1954-56; 1st asst. city atty., Waco, 1957-63; mem. firm Valentine, Valentine & Duty, Waco, 1964—; asst. municipal judge, Waco, 1957—; municipal judge, Woodway, Tex., 1964—, Bellmead, Tex., 1965—, Beverly Hills, Lacy-Lakeview, Tex., 1976—; instr. bus. law Hankamer Sch. Bus., Baylor U., 1976—; partner Indian Creek Estates, Hewitt, Tex.; v.p. Shannon Devel. Co., Inc., Telco Systems, Inc.; dir. Sun Valley Water & Devel. Co., Inc., Hewitt Devel. Co., Inc. Mem. Waco Plan Commn., 1966-69; mem. Waco Fire and Police CSC, 1975—, chmn., 1977—; mem. Waco-McLennan County Library Commn., 1968-72, chmn., 1971-72; exec. com., chmn. Heritage 76 com. Am. Revolution Bicentennial Commn. Waco, 1974-76; mem. McLennan County Hist. Survey Com., McLennan County Hist. Commn.; past chmn. bd. dirs. Ft. House Mus.; past bd. dirs. Waco Heritage Soc., Historic Waco Found.; bd. dirs. Gun Mus., Confederate Research Center, Hill Jr. Coll., Hillsboro, Tex.; pres. Friends of Moody Tex. Ranger Meml. Library. Mem. Tex., Waco-McLennan County bar assns., Delta Theta Phi. Author articles on hist. subjects. Home: 613 Camp Dr Waco TX 76710 Office: 508 Franklin Ave Waco TX 76701 Tel (817) 752-8379

DUVAL, ROBERT, b. Bronx, N.Y., June 23, 1937; B.S., Cornell U., 1959; LL.B., St. John's U., 1967. Admitted to N.Y. bar, 1968, U.S. Supreme Ct. bar, 1971, Pa. bar, 1976; mem. firms Gates & Laber, Kelley, Drye & Warren, Hart & Hume, N.Y.C., 1967-75; atty. Westinghouse Electric Corp., Pitts., 1976—. Mem. Am., N.Y. bar assns., Am. Arbitration Assn. (arbitrator). Home: 1350 Old Meadow Rd Pittsburgh PA 15241 Office: Westinghouse Bldg Gateway Center Pittsburgh PA 15222 Tel (412) 255-3652

DUVARAS, JAMES, JR., b. San Francisco, May 3, 1927; A.B., U. Calif., Berkeley, 1950; J.D., U. Calif., San Francisco. Admitted to Calif. bar, 1955; partner firm Racanelli, Duvaras & Trepel, Sunnyvale, Calif., 1955-63; judge Municipal Ct., Sunnyvale-Cupertino Jud. Dist., 1963-72, Superior Ct., County of Santa Clara, San Jose, 1972—; mem. judges joint com. for adminstrn. of criminal justice. Chmn. Sunnyvale Personnel Bd., 1959; pres., mem. Sunnyvale Sch. Bd., 1959-63. Mem. Conf. Calif. Judges (exec. bd. 1976—), Santa Clara County Municipal Ct. Judges' Assn. (pres. 1968). Recipient Distinguished Service award Sunnyvale Tchrs. Assn., 1963; certificate of recognition Navarino Messemian Soc., 1974. Office: 191 N 1st St San Jose CA 95113 Tel (408) 299-1121

DUXBURY, JOHN ROGERS, b. N. Adams, Mass., Sept. 17, 1928; B.A., Boston U., 1951, LL.B., 1954. Admitted to Mass. bar, 1955; pub. liability claims supr. Travelers Ins. Co., Boston, 1954—. Home: 15 Smith Rd Hingham MA 02043 Office: 125 High St Boston MA 02110 Tel (617) 423-5304

DWECK, JACK S., b. Bklyn., Aug. 15, 1938; B.B.A., Coll. City N.Y., 1958; B.B.A., N.Y. U., 1961. Admitted to N.Y. bar, 1961, Fla. bar, 1973; asso. firm Epstein, Burke & Shapiro, N.Y.C., 1961-62, Raymond Gitlin, N.Y.C., 1962-64, Jay Leo Rothschild, N.Y.C., 1964-67; partner firm Dweck & Sladkus, N.Y.C., 1968-74, Ploscowe, Dweck & Sladkus, N.Y.C. and Miami, Fla., 1974—; lectr. in field. Mem. Am. Arbitration Assn. (nat. panel 1969—), N.Y. State, Am. bar assns., Assn. Bar City N.Y., Fla. Bar. Contbr. articles to legal jours. Office: 666 Fifth Ave New York City NY 10019 Tel (212) 246-6666 also 1110 Brickell Ave Miami FL 33131 (305) 377-2777

DWIGHT, JOSEPH LOVEJOY, JR., b. Honolulu, Jan. 16, 1922; B.S., Williamette U., 1952, LL.B., 1955. Admitted to Hawaii bar, 1955; dep. pub. prosecutor, Honolulu, 1955-57; dep. atty. gen. Hawaii, 1957-60; commr. Honolulu Liquor Commn., 1960-62; rep. Hawaii State Legislature, 1960-63; now individual practice law, Honolulu; pres. W. L. F. Corp., Honolulu, 1957—. Mem. Hawaii Bar Assn. Office: 765 Queen St Honolulu HI 96813 Tel 537-6372

DWORKIN, ROGER BARNETT, b. Cin., Jan. 19, 1943; A.B., Princeton, 1963; J.D., Stanford, 1966. Admitted to Calif. bar, 1967; asso. firm Hewitt, Klitgaard & Sharkey, San Diego, 1966-68; asst. prof. law Ind. U., 1968-71, asso. prof., 1971-74, prof., 1974—; vis. prof. biomed. history U. Wash. Sch. Medicine, 1974-75, summer 1976. Mem. Soc. for Health and Human Values, Inst. Society, Ethics and Life Scis. (asso.), AAAS, Order of Coif, Phi Beta Kappa, Phi Delta Phi. Office: Ind U Sch Law Bloomington IN 47401 Tel (812) 337-4951

DWORKIN, SIDNEY LEONARD, b. Bridgeport, Conn., Jan. 19, 1933; A.B., Boston U., 1954; LL.B., U. Conn., 1958. Admitted to Conn. bar, 1958; asso. firm Dworkin and Dworkin, Bridgeport, 1958-69, Dworkin and Minogue, Bridgeport, 1969-76, mem. firm Dworkin, Minogue and Bucci, Bridgeport, 1976—; judge of probate Dist. Bridgeport, 1971-75. Mem. Charter Revision Commn., Bridgeport, 1968, mem. Zoning Commn., 1968-71, Fin. Advisory Bd., 1974—; mem. Bridgeport Mayor's Pension Rev. Commn., 1975. Mem. Bridgeport, Conn., Am. bar assns. Home: 546 W McKinley Ave Bridgeport CT 06604 Office: 955 Main St No 609 Bridgeport CT 06601 Tel (203) 335-0197

DWORSHAK, CALVIN GEORGE, b. Burley, Idaho, Nov. 9, 1928; LL.D., George Washington U., 1952. Admitted to D.C. bar, 1952, Idaho bar, 1953; asso. firm Colladay & Colladay, Washington, 1952-54; mem. firm Worthwine & Dworshak, Boise, Idaho, 1954-64; individual practice law, Boise, 1964—. Mem. Idaho State Bar (chmn. ethics com.), Third Dist. Bar Assn. (pres. 1960). Office: 10 S Latah St Boise ID 83705 Tel (208) 344-7848

DWYER, JACK HENRY, b. Grand Junction, Colo., Aug. 7, 1929; B.S., U. Denver, 1954, J.D., 1956. Admitted to Colo. bar, 1957; individual practice law, Denver, 1957—; asso. municipal judge, Thorton, Colo., 1972-76. Mem. Nat. Found. March of Dimes, 1951-73, metro campaign chmn., 1969; zoning adminstr. City and County of Denver, 1962-63; treas. Metro Area Bd. Cath. Edn., 1972-73. Mem. Am., Colo., Denver bar assns., Colo. Trial Lawyers Assn., Assn. Trial Lawyers Am., Am. Judicature Soc., Nat. Assn. Criminal Def. Lawyers, Colo. Municipal Judges Assn. (sec.-treas. 1975-76, v.p. 1976—), Nat. Council Alcoholism, Phi Alpha Delta. Home: 1121 Milwaukee Denver CO 80206 Office: 2520 Lincoln Center Denver CO 80203 Tel (303) 892-5511

DWYER, JAMES BERNARD, b. Buffalo, N.Y., Apr. 24, 1915; Ph.B., U. Notre Dame, 1937; LL.B., Harvard, 1940. Admitted to Pa. bar, 1940; partner firm Quinn, Leemhuis, Plate & Dwyer, Erie, Pa., 1945-64; judge Orphans Ct., Erie, 1964—. Bd. dirs. Villa Marie Coll., Erie, 1960-64, Mercyhurst Coll., Erie, 1960-65; trustee St. Vincent Hosp., Erie, 1960-64. Mem. Pa., Erie County bar assns., Pa. State Trial Judges' Assn., Jud. Council of Pa. Home: 3750 Drexel Dr Erie PA 16506 Office: County Court House Erie PA 16501 Tel (814) 452-3740

DWYER, JOHN JOSEPH, b. Somerville, Mass., Jan. 10, 1919; A.B., George Washington U., 1948, LL.B., 1950, LL.M., 1952. Admitted to D.C. bar, 1950, Va. bar, 1952, U.S. Supreme Ct. bar, 1955; partner firms Dwyer & Dwyer, Washington, 1950-65, Dwyer & Lamb, Washington, 1965-68; individual practice law, Washington, 1968—. Mem. D.C. Bar Assn. U.S. Trial Lawyers Assn., Va. Trial Lawyers. Home: Black Rock Farms Flint Hill VA 22747 Office: 1621 Connecticut Ave NW Washington DC 20009 Tel (202) 332-1800

DWYER, MARTIN, JR., b. Newark, Mar. 25, 1922; A.B., Yale, 1944; LL.B., N.Y. U., 1952. Admitted to N.Y. bar, 1952; mem. firm Sprague, Dwyer, Aspland & Tobin, Profl. Corp., Mineola, N.Y., 1962—, sr. partner, 1965—; chmn. bd., pres. Jamaica Water Properties Inc., Lake Success, N.Y., 1968-; chmn., chief exec. officer Jamaica Water Supply Co., Lake Success, 1973—, Sea Cliff Water Co., Lake Success, 1973—; chmn. Orbit Internat., Inc., San Juan, P.R., 1973—; dor. Hobe Sound Co. (Fla.), Hobe Sound Water Co. Bd. dirs., pres. Police Relief Assn. Nassau County (N.Y.); bd. dirs. Legal Aid Soc. Nassau County; vice chmn. bd. trustees L.I. U.; trustee United Fund L.I. Home: Box 1860 Hobe Sound FL Office: 220 Old Country Rd Mineola NY 11501 Tel (516) 746-5700

DWYER, PAMELA SUSAN, b. Perth Amboy, N.J., Sept. 19, 1946; B.A., Smith Coll., 1968; J.D., Columbia, 1972. Admitted to N.Y. State bar, 1973, N.J. bar, 1973; law clk. to judge 3d Circuit U.S. Ct. Appeals, 1972-73; asso. firm Sullivan & Cromwell, N.Y.C., 1973—. Mem. Am. Bar Assn. Home: 952 Fifth Ave New York City NY 10021 also 31 Mason Dr Edison NJ 08817 Office: 48 Wall St New York City NY 10005 Tel (212) 952-8100

DWYER, ROBERT KEAN, b. Memphis, July 9, 1923; LL.B., So. Law U., 1950. Admitted to Tenn. bar, 1950; staff Shelby County (Tenn.) Atty. Gen's. Office, 1951-69; judge Ct. Criminal Appeals, Memphis, 1969—. Mem. Shelby County Bar Assn. Office: 170 N Main St Memphis TN 38103 Tel (901) 534-6696

DYAL, LUCIUS MAHLON, JR., b. Gadsden, Ala., Mar. 30, 1937; B.C.E., Auburn U., 1959; J.D., U. Fla., 1966. Admitted to Fla. bar, 1966; mem. firm Shackleford, Farrior, Stallings & Evans, Tampa, Fla., 1966—; atty. Greater Tampa C. of C., 1976—; chmn. Interam. Lawyer Exchange Program, 1970—. Chmn., Tampa World Trade Council. Fellow Acad. Fla. Labor Mgmt.; mem. Am., Interam., Fla. (vice chmn. labor law com.), Honduras (hon.), Lima, Peru (hon.) bar assns. Office: Box 3324 Tampa FL 33601 Tel (813) 228-7621

DYCHES, A. FLETCHER, b. Augusta, Ga., Nov. 3, 1938; A.B., U. Ga., 1961; J.D., Stetson U., 1969. Admitted to Fla. bar, 1969; since practiced in Tampa, mem. firm Gibbons Tucker McEwen Smith Cofer & Taub, 1969-70, Pope & Burton, 1970-73, Gibbons Tucker McEwen Smith Cofer & Taub, 1973—. Mem. The Fla. Bar, Am., Hillsborough County bar assns., Am. Trial Lawyers Assn. Home: 3310 S San Miguel St Tampa FL 33609 Office: 606 Madison St Tampa FL 33602 Tel (813) 228-7841

DYCUS, JEWEL EUGENE, JR., b. Fort Worth, Nov. 19, 1944; B.A., Tex. Christian U., 1966, M.A., 1970; J.D., Baylor U., 1973. Admitted to Tex. bar, 1973; served with JAGC, U.S. Army, 1974—. Home: 2711 Green St Fort Worth TX 76109 Office: HHC 2d Inf Div SJA Camp Casey Korea 96224

DYE, DEWEY ALBERT, JR., b. Bradenton, Fla., June 12, 1926; student Duke U., 1943-44; B.A., U. Fla., 1947, LL.B., 1949. Admitted to Fla. bar, 1949, since practiced in Bradenton; sr. partner Dye, Cleary, Scott & Deitrich, 1969—; county atty. Manatee County (Fla.), 1954-56; gen. counsel West Coast Inland Nav. Dist. Fla., 1954—; mem. nominating commn. 12th Jud. Circuit Trial Ct. Pres. Fla. Waterways Assn., 1965-66; dir. Hist. Commn.; pres. DeSoto Hist. Soc., 1958; dir. Bradenton C. of C. Mem. Am. Coll. Probate Counsel, Am., Fla. (exec. council environ. law sect.), Manatee County (pres. 1959-60) bar assns., Phi Delta Phi. Contbr. articles to profl. jours. Office: Suite 55 Southeast Nat Bank Bldg Box 9480 Bradenton FL 33506 Tel (813) 747-4911

DYE, HAROLD VAN, b. Cut Bank, Mont., Mar. 3, 1946; B.S. in Bus. Adminstrn., U. Mont., 1968, J.D., 1971. Law clk. to judge U.S. Dist. Ct., Billings, Mont., 1971-72; county atty. Missoula County (Mont.), 1972-75, dep., 1972-73, chief dep., 1973-75; partner firm Deschamps, Andrews & Dye, Missoula, 1973-75, firm Milodragovich, Dale & Dye, Missoula, 1975—; counsel Missoula local govt. study commns., 1975-76. Mem. Am., Western Mont. bar assns., Assn. Trial Lawyers Am., State Bar Mont., Missoula Young Lawyers. Author pamphlet: Montana Juvenile Law, 1972. Home: Box 2983 Missoula MT 59806 Office: Drawer R Missoula MT 59806 Tel (406) 728-1455

DYE, LEWIS WILLIAM, b. Marion, Ohio, Oct. 23, 1944; B.A., B.S., Ohio State U., 1967; J.D., Ohio No. U., 1971. Admitted to Ohio bar, 1972; asst. prosecutor City Atty.'s Office, Columbus, Ohio, 1971-72; individual practice law, Columbus, 1972—. Mem. Am., Ohio bar assns. Home: 9680 Sunbury Rd Columbus OH 43081 Office: 534 S Pearl St Columbus OH 43215 Tel (614) 224-7298

DYE, LUTHER VAUGHN, b. Winston-Salem, N.C., Sept. 26, 1933; B.S., N.C. A. and T. State U., 1955; LL.B., Bklyn. Law Sch., 1960. Admitted to N.Y. State bar, 1960, also U.S. Supreme Ct. bar; U.S. Dist. Ct. for Eastern and So. Dist. N.Y. bars; title officer Chgo. Title Ins. Co., N.Y.C., 1958-69; asso. firm Demov, Morris, Levin & Shein, N.Y.C., 1969-73; asst. counsel N.Y. Life Ins. Co., N.Y.C., 1974—; adminstrv. hearing officer Parking Violations Bur., City of N.Y.; Mem. local draft bd., SSS, Jamaica, NY, 1968-76. Mem. N.Y. State, Queens County bar assns., Bklyn. Law Sch. Alumni Assn. Home: 99-03 205th St Hollis NY 11423 Office: 51 Madison Ave New York City NY 10010 Tel (212) 576-6845

DYE, RALPH DEAN, JR., b. Zanesville, Ohio, Sept. 10, 1931; B.S. in Adminstrn., Ohio State U., 1953; LL.B., Youngstown U., 1958. Admitted to Ohio bar, 1958; individual practice law, McConnelsville, Ohio, 1958—; dir. Malta (Ohio) Savs. and Loan Co., 1958—. Auditor, Morgan County ARC, 1958-75. Mem. Jr. C. of C. Home: 87 S 11th St McConnelsville OH 43756 Office: PO Box 178 McConnelsville OH 43756 Tel (614) 962-4031

DYE, WILLIAM ELLSWORTH, b. Detroit, Oct. 15, 1926; B.A., U. Wis., 1948, J.D., 1951. Admitted to Wis. bar, 1951; individual practice law, Racine, 1951-74; partner firm Heft, Dye, Heft & Paulson, Racine, 1975—. Bd. dirs. Racine Theatre Guild, 1973—, Prairie Sch., 1966—. Mem. Am., Racine County bar assns., State Bar Wis. (bd. govs. 1973—), Order of Coif. Home: 3308 Rosalind Ave Racine WI 53405 Office: 827 S Main St Racine WI 53403 Tel (414) 634-3366

DYER, GARY SPENCER, b. Sedalia, Mo., Oct. 21, 1945; B.S., SW Mo. State U., 1968; J.D., U. Mo., 1971. Admitted to Mo. bar, 1971; partner firm Lathrop, Koontz, Righter, Clagett, Parker & Norquist, Kansas City, Mo., 1971—. Bd. dirs. Citizens Assn. Kansas City. Mem. Am., Kansas City bar assns., Lawyers Assn. Kansas City. Office: 1500 Ten Main Center Kansas City MO 64105 Tel (816) 842-0820

DYER, GEORGE COLEMAN, b. Warrenton, Mo., Aug. 24, 1906; A.B. cum laude, Central Wesleyan Coll., 1925; J.D., Washington U., St. Louis, 1928. Admitted to Mo. bar, 1928, U.S. Supreme Ct. bar, 1938; asst. U.S. atty. Eastern Dist. Mo., 1929-34; chief atty. Office Price Adminstrn., Eastern Dist. Mo., 1943-44; sr. partner firms Dyer, Coffey & Boland, St. Louis, 1957-59, Dyer & Weitzman, 1959-75. Trustee William Woods Coll. Mem. Mo., St. Louis, Am. bar assns. Alt. Rhodes Scholar, 1924; participant in five internat. debates, Oxford, and Cambridge Univs. (Eng.), U. Australia; author: Constitutionality of Federal Anti-Lynching Legislation, 1928. Office: Suite 900 1015 Locust Bldg Saint Louis MO 63101 Tel (314) 241-5620

DYER, GEORGE LEWIS, JR., b. Detroit, Dec. 30, 1931; B.A., Cornell U., 1955; LL.B. cum laude, Harvard, 1961. Admitted to Hawaii bar, 1961; since practiced in Honolulu, asso. firm Goodsill, Anderson & Quinn, 1961-66, partner, 1967—; dir. Legal Aid Soc. Hawaii, 1969-72; editor Hawaii Bar Journal, 1965-66. Mem. rules com., del. Republican Nat. Conv., 1972, 76; 4th vice-chmn. Rep. party Hawaii, 1971-73; chmn. Rep. party Hawaii State Conv., 1972; chmn. Hawaii Lawyers com. to Re-elect the Pres., 1972; chmn. rules com. Rep. Party Hawaii, 1970-73; mem. ofcl. observors primary and gen. elections Hawaii, 1974, chmn., 1976; mem. election adv. com., 1974-76, chmn., 1976—; bd. dirs. Friends of Hawaii Pub. TV, 1977—. Mem. Am., Hawaii State bar assns. Home: 101 Koohoo Pl Kailua HI 9673 Office: PO Box 3196 Honolulu HI 96801 Tel (808) 531-5066

DYER, IRBY LLOYD, b. Pecos, Tex., Aug. 26, 1916; student Schreiner Inst., 1934-36, U. Tex., 1940. Admitted to Tex. bar, 1940; asso. firm Hubbard & Kerr, Pecos, 1940-42; partner firm Turpin, Smith, Dyer & Saxe, Midland, Tex., 1945—; gen. counsel, dir. Petroleum Exploration and Devel. Funds, Inc., Midland, 1967—; dir. Adobe Oil and Gas Corp., Midland, DST Exploration Corp., Midland. Chmn. Midland County chpt. ARC, 1948. Mem. Midland County (pres. 1969-70), Am. bar assns., State Bar Tex. Home: 2100 Wadley St Midland TX 79701 Office: 1st Nat Bank Bldg Midland TX 79701 Tel (915) 682-2525

DYER, THOMAS ROSS, b. Nashville, May 19, 1941; J.D., U. Tenn. Admitted to Tenn. bar, 1967; asso. firm Walt, Dyer & James and predecessors, 1967-72, partner, 1972—. Chmn. large gifts com. Memphis Mus.; mem. adv. council Coll. Law, U. Tenn.; bd. dirs. Boys Club, Memphis, 1974—. Mem. Am., Tenn. (bd. govs.), Memphis and Shelby County bar assns. Young Lawyers Tenn. (pres.). Home: 1597 Carr St Memphis TN 38104 Office: 158 Madison St Memphis TN 38103 Tel (901) 526-6488

DYER, WAYNE PADDOCK, b. Kankakee, Ill., May 14, 1917; A.B., U. Ill., 1938, LL.B. with honors, 1948. Admitted to Ill. bar, 1942; atty. U.S. Treasury Dept. Gen. Counsel's Office, Washington, 1943-46; practiced in Kankakee, 1946-68; partner firm Dyer & Dyer, 1946-57; individual practice law, 1957-68; asso. judge Circuit Ct., 1968-71, judge, 1971—. Mem. Kankakee County Bar Assn., Order of the Coif. Contbr. articles in field to profl. jours. Home: 12 Croydon Pl Kankakee IL 60901 Office: Ct House Kankakee IL 60901 Tel (815) 937-2920

DYESS, BOBBY DALE, b. Waxahachie, Tex., Jan. 27, 1935; B.A., N.Tex. State U., 1956; J.D., So. Meth. U., 1959. Admitted to Tex. bar, 1959, U.S. Supreme Ct. bar, 1977; asso. firm Brundidge Fountain Elliott & Churchill, Dallas, 1963-65; partner firm Elliott Churchill Hansen Dyess & Maxfield, Dallas, 1965—; dir. Combined Am. Ins. Co., Dallas, 1973—; chmn. bd. Rainbow Sound, Inc., Dallas, 1975—; judge adv. U.S. Air Force, 1960-63. Bd. mgmt. E. Dallas YMCA, 1974—, chmn. fund dr., 1977, chmn. bd. mgmt., 1977-78; chief YMCA Indian Guides, 1971; chmn. pack com. Boy Scouts Am., 1970. Mem. Am., Tex., Dallas bar assns., N. Tex. Weimaraner Club, Am. Soc. Writers on Legal Subjects (pres. 1976, dir. 1977), Scribes. Home: 6808 Meadow Lake Circle Dallas TX 75214 Office: 35th floor Southland Center Dallas TX 75201 Tel (214) 741-1143

DYGERT, JERRY GLENN, b. Mpls., Aug. 21, 1940; B.A. magna cum laude, U. Minn., 1962, LL.B. magna cum laude, 1964. Admitted to Minn. bar, 1964, N.Y. bar, 1966; asso. firm Cleary, Gottlieb, Steen & Hamilton, N.Y.C., 1965-68; asst. prof. law Rutgers State U., Camden, N.J., 1968-71; partner firm Dygert & Dygert, Mpls., 1971—. Mem. Hennepin County, Minn., Am. bar assns. Home: 5056 Colfax Ave S Minneapolis MN 55419 Office: 414 Title Insurance Bldg Minneapolis MN 55401 Tel (612) 333-2411

DYK, TIMOTHY BELCHER, b. Boston, Feb. 14, 1937; B.A., Harvard U., 1958, LL.B., 1961. Admitted to N.Y. State bar, 1962, Washington Dist. Ct., 1964, Ct. of Appeals, 1972; spl. asst. to asst. atty. gen., Dept. Justice, Washington, 1963-64; asso. firm Wilmer, Cutler & Pickering, Washington, 1964-68, partner, 1969—; law clk. to Chief Justice Warren, 1961-63; law clk. to Justices Reed, Burton, 1961-62. Chmn., Migrant Legal Action Program, Inc. Contbr. publs. to Law Review. Home: 1825 O St NW Washington DC 20009 Office: 1666 K St Washington DC 20006

DYKSTRA, DANIEL JAMES, b. Mich., Feb. 25, 1916; B.S., Wis. State U., River Falls, 1938; LL.B., U. Wis., 1948; S.J.D., 1950. Admitted to Wis. bar, 1948, Utah bar, 1952; asso. prof. law U. Utah, 1949-52, prof. law, 1952-66, dean Coll. Law, 1954-61, acad. v.p., 1961-63; prof. law U. Calif., Davis, 1966—, dean, 1971-74; vis. prof. U. Pa., 1963-64, Stanford, 1966-67, U. Wis., summers 1957, 58, U. Minn., summer 1950, U. Tex., summer 1969. Mem. Am. Bar Assn., Nat. Acad. Arbitrators, Am. Law Inst. Recipient Distinguished Alumnus award Wis. State U., River Falls, 1970; Fulbright prof. U. Melbourne (Australia), 1959. Home: POB 2524 El Macero CA 96618 Office: Sch Law U Calif Davis CA 95616 Tel (916) 752-3262

EADS, JOHN WESLEY, JR., b. Medford, Oreg., May 31, 1947; B.S., U. Oreg., 1969, J.D., 1972. Admitted to Oreg. bar, 1972; asso. firm Brophy, Wilson, & Duhamie, Medford, 1972-74; city atty., Medford, 1974—. Mem. Am., Oreg. bar assns., Nat. Inst. Municipal Law Officers. Recipient Distinguished Achievement award Internat. Acad. Trial Lawyers, 1972. Home: 38 Geneva Medford OR 97501 Office: 411 W 8th St Medford OR 97501 Tel (503) 776-7508

EAGAN, F. OWEN, b. Hartford, Conn., Oct. 2, 1930; B.S. in Social Studies, Georgetown U., 1952, LL.B., J.D., 1956. Admitted to D.C. bar, 1956, Conn. bar, 1957; asso. firm Massey & Manion, Hartford, 1957-62; asst. U.S. Atty., Hartford, 1962-64; partner firm Eagan, Jackson, O'Keefe & Murray, W. Hartford, 1964-75; magistrate U.S. Dist. Ct. Conn., Hartford, 1975—; past dir. Citizens Bank & Trust Co.; interviewer Georgetown U. applicants. Past pres. St. Timothy's Ch.; former chmn. fin. com. NW Catholic High Sch. Mem. Hartford County, Conn. (co-chmn. criminal law com.), Am., Fed. bar assns., Cranwell Alumni Assn. (past pres., dir.). Home: 58 Hartwell Rd West Hartford CT 06117 Office: 450 Main St Fed Bldg Hartford CT 06103 Tel (203) 244-2567

EAGAN, JAMES EDWARD, b. N.Y.C., June 28, 1941; student Pace Coll., Cath. Coll. Minon Sem.; LL.B., N.Y. Law Sch., 1966. Admitted to N.Y. bar, 1966; individual practice law, N.Y.C., 1967-72; mem. firm Eagan & Rudick, N.Y.C., 1972—; asso. counsel N.Y. State Senate, 1971-73; legal advisor Aux. Police Benevolent Assn., N.Y.C., 1974—. Mem. New York County Lawyers Assn. Recipient Appreciation award Aux. Police Benevolent Assn., 1975. Office: 150 Broadway New York City NY 10038 Tel (212) 732-4277

EAGEN, MICHAEL JOHN, b. Jermyn, Pa., May 9, 1907; grad. St. Thomas Coll., 1927; postgrad. Harvard Law Sch., 1927-28. Admitted to Pa. bar, 1931; dist. atty., Lackawanna County, Pa., 1938-42; judge Ct. of Common Pleas of Lackawanna County, 1942-60; justice Supreme Ct. Pa., Scranton, 1960—, chief justice, 1977—. Pres., Coll. Presdl. Electors Pa., 1940, Lackawanna United Fund. Recipient awards ARC, 1944, Scranton-Dunmore Community Chest, 1944, Friendly Sons of St. Patrick of Lackawanna County, 1946, Golden Deeds award Exchange Club Scranton, 1950, awards Lackawanna United Fund, 1958, Koch-Conley Post 121, Am. Legion, 1959, Americanism award B'nai B'rith Amos Lodge 136, 1969; knight Equestrian Order Holy Sepulchre of Jerusalem, 1960. Home: 711 Taylor Ave Scranton PA 18510 Office: Lackawanna County Court House Washington Ave Scranton PA 18503 Tel (717) 346-9263

EAGLE, DELBERT PFAFF, b. Gary, Ky., Oct. 29, 1902; A.B., Berea Coll., 1932; M.A., U. Ky., 1934; student law U. Ky., U. Louisville 1938-40. Admitted to Ky. bar, 1941; judge Garrard County, Ky., 1946-52; mem. firm Eagle, Cox and Smith, Lancaster, Ky., 1951—; circuit judge 13th Jud. Dist. Ky., 1967-71. Mem. Ky. Tb Commn., 1954-67, Ky. Health Planning Council, Ky. Mental Retardation Planning Commn., Blue Grass Regional Planning Commn.; chmn. bd. Garrard County Meml. Hosp., Lancaster, Ky., 1956-70; mem. Ky. Republican Central Com.; trustee Methodist Ch., Lancaster, 1941-77. Mem. Ky. Bar Assn., Phi Delta Phi, Tau Kappa Alpha. Named Outstanding Citizen Garrard County, Ky., 1972. Office: 318 Richmond St Lancaster KY 40444 Tel (606) 792-2614

EAKELEY, DOUGLAS SCOTT, b. Morristown, N.J., Mar. 2, 1946; B.A. In Econs. with honors summa cum laude, Yale, 1968; J.D., 1972; B.A. in Jurisprudence (Rhodes scholar), Oxford (Eng.) U., 1970. Admitted to N.Y. bar, 1973; asso. firm Debevoise, Plimpton, Lyons & Gates, N.Y.C., 1972, 1973—; law clk. to Hon. Harold R. Tyler, Jr., So. Dist. N.Y., 1972-73. Spl. counsel N.Y.C. Bd. Corrections, 1974. Mem. Assn. Bar City N.Y., N.Y. State Bar Assn. Spl. com. profl. economics and efficency research Ford Found. grantee, 1974. Author: A Lawyer at a Price People Can Afford, 1975. Office: 299 Park Ave New York City NY 10017 Tel (212) 752-6400

EALY, F. RONALD, b. Effingham, Ill., Dec. 7, 1934; J.D., DePaul U., 1961. Admitted to Ill. bar, 1961, U.S. Supreme Ct. bar, 1972; asso. firm Sennett, Levin, Craine & Stride, Chgo., 1961-65; individual practice law, Effingham, 1965-75; partner firm Ealy & Bower, Effingham, 1975—; spl. asst. to atty. gen. Ill., 1966-68; field counsel Fed. Nat. Mortgage Assn., also Govt. Nat. Mortgage Assn., 1970—; escrow atty. Farmers Home Adminstrn., 1970—; instr. Lakeland Coll., 1975—. Bd. dirs. Effingham County Mental Health Assn., 1970-74, Effingham County Mental Health Center, 1972—, United Fund, 1975—; mem. Effingham County Mental Health Bd., 1972-75, Effingham Community Unit Sch. Bd., 1973—. Mem. Am., Ill. (individual rights and responsibility council 1975—), Effingham County (sec. 1966-68, v.p. 1975-76, pres. 1976—) bar assns., Ill. Inst. Continuing Edn. (area rep., mem. jud. adv. polls com. 1967-68), Am., Ill. trial lawyers assns., Am. Judicature Soc. Home: PO Box 97 Effingham IL 62401 Office: PO Box 97 113 E Jefferson St Effingham IL 62401 Tel (217) 342-2290 also (217) 347-7323

EARL, MARION BRADLEY, b. Bunkerville, Nev., Sept. 13, 1897; B.S., U. Utah, 1922; LL.B. with honors, George Washington U., 1931. Admitted to Nev. bar, 1932, U.S. Supreme Ct. bar, 1964; sr. partner firm Earl & Earl, Las Vegas, Nev., 1946—; justice peace, Las Vegas Twp., 1935-39. Mem. Clark County Draft Bd., 1940-48, chmn., 1948-67; mem. Nev. State Appeal Bd. Selective Service, 1968-72. Fellow Am. Coll. Probate mem. Nev., Am., Clark County (pres. 1945-46) bar assns., Order Coif. Home: 3111 Bel Air Dr apt 19D Las Vegas NV 89109 Office: 228 S 4th St Las Vegas NV 89101 Tel (702) 385-1421

EARLE, JOSEPH HAYNSWORTH, JR., b. Washington, Apr. 15, 1918; B.A., Furman U., J.D., U. Va., 1942. Admitted to Va. bar, 1942, S.C. bar, 1946; asso. atty. U.S. Maritime Commn., Washington, 1942-43; partner firm Cain & Earle, Greenville, S.C., 1948-56, Earle & Bozeman, Greenville, 1956-58, Earle, Bozeman & Grayson, Greenville, 1958-77; individual practice, Greenville, 1977—; county atty. Greenville County, 1975—. Mem. S.C. Ho. of Reps., Greenville, 1953-54, Greenville County Council, 1968-72; pres. Greenville County Hist. Soc. Mem. Am., Greenville County bar assns., Res. Officers Assn. Home: 357 Riverside Dr Greenville SC 29605 Office: 18 Beattie Pl Greenville SC 29601 Tel (803) 271-6506

EARLE, RICHARD ALAN, b. N.Y.C., Apr. 30, 1941; B.B.A., U. Mich., 1963, M.B.A., 1964, J.D., 1968. Admitted to Mich. bar, 1968, D.C. bar, 1969; asso. firm Patton, Boggs & Blow, Washington, 1968-74, partner, 1975—. Mem. Am., Fed. bar assns., Am. Soc. Internat. Law, Washington Fgn. Law Soc. An editor Prospectus, Jour. Law Reform. Home: 6760 Brigadoon Dr Bethesda MD 20034 Office: 1200 17th St NW Washington DC 20036 Tel (202) 223-4040

EARLE, RICHARD TILGHMAN, JR., b. Centreville, Md., Oct. 24, 1915; A.B., St. John's Coll., Annapolis, Md., 1938; LL.B., Harvard, 1941. Admitted to Fla. bar, 1941; since practiced in St. Petersburg; chmn. Pinellas County (Fla.) Charter Commn., 1965; mem. Fla. Constn. Revision Commn., 1967; mem. Fla. Jud. Qualifications Commn., 1967—, also chmn. Fellow Am. Bar Found.; mem. St. Petersburg (pres. 1955), Am. bar assns. Recipient Herbert Harley award Am. Judicature Soc. Home: 1522 Seventh St N Saint Petersburg FL 33704 Office: 447 Third Ave N Saint Petersburg FL 33701 Tel (813) 898-4474

EARLE, RONALD DALE, b. Fort Worth, Feb. 23, 1942; A.B., U. Tex., 1964, J.D., 1967. Admitted to Tex. bar, 1967; legal asst. to Gov. John Connally, 1967-69; judge Municipal Ct., Austin, Tex., 1969-72; chief counsel Tex. Civil Jud. Council, Austin, 1972-73; individual practice law, Austin, 1973-76; mem. Tex. Ho. of Reps., 1973-76; dist. atty. Travis County (Tex.), 1977—; pres. Community Corrections Council Travis County Adult Probation Dept., 1969-72. Bd. dirs. Devel. Assistance for Rehab., Austin, 1974—; mem. Tex. Adv. Commn. on Intergovtl. Relations, 1973—. Mem. Tex. State, Tex. State Jr., Travis County bar assns., Am. Judicature Soc. Named Outstanding Young Lawyer, Travis County Jr. Bar Assn., 1975. Office: Travis County Courthouse Austin TX 78701 Tel (512) 476-2655

EARLE, WILLIAM GEORGE, b. Monroe, Mich., July 10, 1940; student Yale; B.A., U. Mich., 1963, LL.B., 1966. Admitted to Fla. bar, 1967, 5th Circuit bar, 1967, U.S. Supreme Ct. bar, 1970, 2d Circuit bar, 1976; law clk. to Hon. David W. Dyer, U.S. Ct. Appeals 5th Circuit, 1966-67; trial atty. U.S. Dept. Justice, Washington and Miami, 1967-69; asso. firm Kelly, Black, Black & Kenny, Miami, 1969-73, partner, 1973—; mem. nat. com. U. Mich. Law Sch. Pres. U. Mich. Alumni Club of Miami, 1967-70. Mem. Fla. Bar (chmn. com. on eminent domain 1975-77), Am., Dade County, Fla., Fed. (vice chmn. com. on real property 1977—) bar assns., Phi Delta Phi. Author: Florida Eminent Domain Practice and Procedure, 3d edit., Defenses to the Taking, 1976. Home: 280 Harbor Dr Key Biscayne FL 33149 Tel (305) 358-5700

EARLEY, JEROME ANTHONY, b. Pitts., Feb. 26, 1924; B.S. in Bus. Adminstrn., U. Pitts., 1948, LL.B., 1950. Admitted to Pa. bar, 1950; gen. atty. to asst. to v.p. corporate devel. Rockwell Mfg., Pitts., 1953-73, staff v.p. strategic planning, 1973-75, staff v.p. corporate devel., 1975, v.p. corporate devel. Rockwell Internat., Pitts., 1975—; dir. AVM Corp., Babcock Lumber Co. Bd. dirs. Greater Pitts. Guild for the Blind. Mem. Am., Allegheny County bar assns. Office: Rockwell International 600 Grant St Pittsburgh PA 15219 Tel (412) 565-7209

EARLY, ALEXANDER RIEMAN, b. Phila., Sept. 22, 1917; student St. John.'s Coll., Annapolis, Md., 1934-36; B.A., Cornell, 1938; LL.B., Harvard, 1941. Admitted to Calif. bar, 1946, U.S. Supreme Ct. bar, 1969; individual practice law, Los Angeles, 1946-50; sr. atty. Calif. Div. Hwys., 1950-55; asst. U.S. atty., Los Angeles, 1955-57; asst. county counsel County of Los Angeles, 1957-71; judge Los Angeles Superior Ct., 1972—; adj. prof. law Southwestern Law Sch., Los Angeles, 1968—. Mem. Am. Security Council, Navy League U.S., Am. Bd. Trial Advocates, Am., Calif., Los Angeles bar assns., Conf. Calif. Judges, Am. Right of Way Assn. Office: 111 N Hill St Los Angeles CA 90012 Tel (213) 974-5607

EARLY, BERT HYLTON, b. Kimball, W.Va., July 17, 1922; student Marshall U., 1940-42; A.B., Duke U., 1946; J.D., Harvard U., 1949. Admitted to W.Va. bar, 1949, Ill. bar, 1963, U.S. Supreme Ct. bar, 1960; asso. firm Fitzpatrick, Marshall, Huddleston & Bolen, Huntington, W.Va., 1949-57; instr. Marshall U., 1950-53; asst. counsel Island Creek Coal Co., Huntington, 1957-60, asso. gen. counsel, 1960-62; dep. exec. dir. Am. Bar Assn., Chgo., 1962-64, exec. dir., 1964—; mem. vis. com. U. Chgo. Law Sch., 1975—. Mem. W.Va. Jud. Council, 1960-62, Huntington City Council, 1961-62; bd. dirs. Huntington Pub. Library, 1951-60, Huntington Galleries, 1961-62, Robert Crown Center, Hinsdale, Ill., 1970-76, United Charities Chgo., 1970—, Community Renewal Soc. Chgo., 1965-75; trustee Morris Meml. Hosp., 1953-60, David & Elkins Coll., 1960-63. Fellow Am. Bar Found.; mem. Am. (chmn. Jr. Bar Conf. 1958, ho. of dels. 1958-59), W.Va., Chgo., Internat. (asst. sec.-gen. 1967—), Inter-Am. bar assns., Am. Law Inst., Econ. Club Chgo. Home: 136 S Oak St Hinsdale IL 60521 Office: 1155 E 60th St Chicago IL 60637 Tel (312) 947-4040

EARLY, CHARLES EDWARD, b. Sarasota, Fla., Aug. 24, 1926; J.D. with high honors, U. Fla., 1950. Admitted to Fla. bar, 1950, U.S. Supreme Ct. bar, 1959; mem. firm Early & Early, Sarasota, 1950—; atty. Sarasota-Fruitville Drainage Dist., 1954-61; dir. probate and trust law div., real property, probate and trust sect. Fla. Bar, 1975—, jr. bd. govs., 1951. Vice pres. Sunnyland council Boy Scouts Am.; v.p. Fla. W. Coast Symphony Orch., 1970-72. Mem. Sarasota County, Am. bar assns., Am. Coll. Probate Counsel, Fla. Blue Key, Phi Kappa Phi, Phi Delta Phi. Contbr. articles to legal jours. Office: Suite 920 United First Fed Bldg 1390 Main St Sarasota FL 33577 Tel (813) 366-2707

EARLY, JIM, b. Lynchburg, Va., Jan. 8, 1944; B.S., U. Ky., 1972, J.D., 1973. Admitted to Ky. bar, 1973; clk. firm McCauley, Wilhoit & Elam, Versailles, Ky., 1972; with Ky. Office Pub. Defender, Frankfort, 1972—, in charge criminal trial sect., 1976—. Mem. Am., Ky. bar assns. Home: 788 Marcella St Versailles KY 40383 Office: 625 Leawood Dr Frankfort KY 40601 Tel (502) 564-3754 also (606) 873-8992

EARLY, JOHN COLLINS, b. N.Y.C., Jan. 24, 1919; A.B., Princeton, 1940; J.D., Harvard, 1947. Admitted to N.Y. bar, 1947, U.S. Supreme Ct. bar, 1951; asso. firm McCanliss & Early, N.Y.C., 1947-48, partner, 1950—; asso. firm Conboy Hewitt O'Brien and Boardman, N.Y.C., 1948-50. Past pres. United Campaign of Madison and Florham Park, N.J.; past v.p., trustee Kent Place Sch., Summit, N.J. Mem. Am., N.Y. State bar assns., Assn. Bar City N.Y. Home: Dellwood Park Madison NJ 07940 Office: 140 Broadway New York City NY 10005 Tel (201) 943-0280

EASLER, WILLIAM RANDOLPH, b. Seneca, S.C., Sept. 30, 1946; B.A., U. S.C., 1967, J.D., 1970. Admitted to S.C. bar, 1970. U.S. Supreme Ct. bar, 1972; asso. firm Cox & Brooks, Spartanburg, S.C. Mem. Spartanburg City Council, 1976—. Mem. S.C., Spartanburg County bar assns., Comml. Law League. Recipient award Am. Jurisprudence Soc., 1968. Office: PO Box 426 Spartanburg SC 29304 Tel (803) 582-8906

EASLEY, MACK, b. Akins, Okla., Oct. 14, 1916; student Northeastern State Coll., Tahlequah, Okal., 1935-39; LL.B., U. Okla., 1947. Admitted to Okla., bar, 1947, N.Mex. bar, 1948; practiced in Hobbs, N.Mex., 1948-74; judge N.Mex. Dist. Ct., 5th Dist., 1974-76; justice N.Mex. Supreme Ct., 1976—; asst. dist. atty. Lea County, N.Mex., 1949-50; mem. N.Mex. Ho. of Reps., 1951-52, 55-62, speaker of house, 1959-60; lt. gov. State of N.Mex., 1963-66; mem. N.Mex. Senate, 1967-70, majority whip, 1969-70. Mem. Lea County, N.Mex., Am. bar assns., Am. Judicature Soc., Am. Trail Lawyers' Assn. Home: 817 Zia Rd Santa Fe NM 87501 Office: Supreme Ct Bldg Santa Fe NM 87502 Tel (505) 827-2812

EAST, GARY W., b. Ogden, Utah, June 16, 1942; B.S., U. Utah, 1964, J.D., 1967. Admitted to Utah bar, 1967, Wash. bar, 1969; asso. firm Mabey, Bradford & Marsden, Salt Lake City, Utah, 1966-68, asso. Transam. Title Ins. Co., Seattle, Wash., 1968-69; asso. John W. Underwood, Bellevue, Wash., 1969-70, partner firm Kelleher & East, Seattle, 1970-73, individual practice law, Seattle, 1973—. Office: 17723 15th Ave NE Seattle WA 98155 Tel (206) 367-0600

EAST, THOMAS FERNS, b. Oclona, Miss., Sept. 4, 1923; A.B., U. N.C., 1948; LL.B., Wake Forest U., 1953. Admitted to N.C. bar, 1953; individual practice law, Franklin County, N.C., 1953—. Home: 119 Person St Louisburg NC 27549 Office: 109 S Main St Louisburg NC 27549 Tel (919) 496-5771

EASTMAN, JAMES COBURN, b. Carlinville, Ill., Dec. 30, 1938; B.S., Pa. State U., 1961; J.D., Am. U., 1966. Admitted to D.C. bar, 1966, Va. bar, 1966, Md. bar, 1970; mgmt. intern Dept. Labor, 1963; staff asst. Pres.'s Com. on Juvenile Delinquency, Washington, 1964; program coordinator United Planning Orgn., Washington, 1965-66; asso. firm Pledger & Mahoney, Washington, 1966-71; partner firm Lamb, Eastman & Keats, Washington, 1972—. Mem. Va., Md., Am. (mem. standing com. on legislation 1976—) bar assns., D.C. Bar (chmn. continuing legal edn. 1975—), Bar Assn. D.C. (dir. 1973-74), Nat. Legal Aid and Defender Assn. Home: 3409 Bradley Ln Chevy Chase MD 20015 Office: 1742 N St NW Washington DC 20036 Tel (202) 785-4822

EASTMAN, RONALD DAVID, b. San Antonio, Nov. 7, 1942; B.A., U. Tex., 1963; LL.B., Harvard U., 1966. Admitted to Tex. bar, 1966, D.C. bar, 1969; Office of Gen. Counsel Fed. Power Commn., Washington, 1967-69; asso. firm Verner, Liipfert, Bernhard & McPherson, Washington, 1969—; gen. counsel Democratic Nat. Com., 1977—. Bd. dirs. Hemisports, Inc. Mem. Tex., D.C., Fed. Power bar assns. Office: Suite 1000 1660 L St NW Washington DC 20036 Tel (202) 452-7436

EASTON, ROBERT GEORGE, b. Rochester, N.Y., July 24, 1936; B.S., Princeton U., 1958; M.B.A., Columbia U., 1960; J.D., Georgetown U., 1974. With controllers div. Eastman Kodak Co., Rochester, 1960-64; sec. Farrington Mfg. Co., N.Y.C., 1964-74, pres., Washington, 1971-74; admitted to Ill. bar, 1975; asst. exec. dir. Am. Bar Assn., Chgo., 1974—. Mem. Am., Ill. bar assns., Am. Soc. Corporate Secs. Home: 800 N Washington St Hinsdale IL 60521 Office: 1155 E 60th St Chicago IL 60637 Tel (312) 947-4030

EASTON, WILLIAM STARK, b. Lowville, N.Y., Aug. 22, 1936; A.B., Hamilton Coll., 1958; J.D., U. Chgo., 1961. Admitted to N.Y. bar, 1961, Mich. bar, 1969; partner firm Ohlin, Damon, Morey, Sawyer & Most, Buffalo, 1961-69; staff atty. Upper Peninsula Legal Services, Marquette, Mich., 1969-70, sr. staff atty., 1970-75; judge Mich. Dist. Ct., 96th Dist., 1975—; instr. No. Mich. U., 1969-70, guest lectr., 1970—. Bd. dirs. Upper Peninsula Area-Wide Health Planning Assn., Mich. chpt. ACLU. Mem. State Bar Mich., Marquette County Bar Assn., Nat. Legal Aid, Defender Assn. Home: 1207 West Ave Marquette MI 44855 Office: Courthouse Marquette MI 49855 Tel (906) 225-1301

EATHERTON, LEWIS HAMILTON, III, b. Tulsa, Dec. 10, 1932; B.S. in Petroleum Engring., U. Tulsa, 1958; LL.B., George Washington U., 1964. Admitted to Va. bar, 1964, Tex. bar, 1967; atty. FPC, 1964-65; patent examiner U.S. Trademark Patent Office, 1965-67; atty. Exxon Prodn. Research Co., Houston, 1967—. Home: 2314 Winrock St Houston TX 77057 Office: Exxon Prodn Research Co PO Box 2189 Houston TX 77001 Tel (713) 965-4065

EATON, BERRIEN CLARK, JR., b. Chgo., Feb. 12, 1919; student William Coll.; B.S., U. Va., 1940, LL.B., 1948, J.D., 1970. Admitted to Mich. bar, 1948, Ariz. bar, 1969, Ga. bar, 1971; asso. firm Miller, Canfield, Paddock & Stone, Detroit, 1948-58, partner, 1959-69; mem. firm Leibsohn, Eaton, Gooding & Romley, P.C., Phoenix, 1971—; lectr. law Wayne State U., 1954-69, Ariz. State U., 1969-71; prof. law U. Ga., 1970-71; dir. numerous small corps., mainly in Mich., including Panax Corp., Pontchartrain Hotel Co. Mem. Am., Maricopa County (Ariz.) bar assns., State Bar Ariz., Am. Law Inst., Ariz. Estate Planning Council, Assn. Profs., Newcomen Soc. Author: Professional Corporations and Associations, 1970; bd. editors Estate Planning, Community Property mags. contbr. articles to legal publs. Office: 3343 N Central Ave Phoenix AZ 85012 Tel (602) 264-9221

EATON, FREDRICK M., b. Akron, Ohio, May 21, 1905; A.B., Harvard, 1927, LL.B., 1930. Admitted to N.Y. bar, 1932; mem. firm Cotton & Franklin, 1930-40, Shearinan & Sterling, N.Y.C., 1946—. Counsel War Product Bd., 1940-45. Office: 53 Wall St New York City NY 10005 Tel (212) 483-1000

EATON, GEORGE STRATFORD, b. Bklyn., June 17, 1925; LL.B., Fordham U., 1946. Admitted to N.Y. bar, 1946, U.S. Supreme Ct. bar, 1954, U.S. Dist. Ct. Eastern and So. Dist. N.Y. bar, 1965; individual practice law, Mineola, N.Y., 1946-49, Glen Head, N.Y., 1949-53, Mineola, 1953—; sr. atty. N.Y. State Bldg. Code Commn., N.Y.C., 1952-53; justice of Village Ct., Mineola, 1950—; instr. comml. law Hofstra U., 1958-59. Clk. Mineola Union Free Sch. Dist., 1950—; pres. Mineola Republican Club, 1956-57, Mineola Community Civic Assn., 1966-68. Mem. Cath. Lawyers Guild Diocese of Rockville Center (pres. 1965-67), Nassau County Bar Assn. (chmn. ethics com. 1976—), N.Y. State (exec. com. 1975—), Nassau County (pres. 1974-76) magistrates assns., N.Y. State Pub. Defenders Assn., Nassau County Criminal Cts. Bar Assn., Nassau Lawyers Assn. L.I., Delta Theta Phi. Office: 176 Mineola Blvd Mineola NY 11501 Tel (516) 746-0400

EATON, HAVEN MCCRILLIS, b. Youngstown, Ohio, Sept. 26, 1926; B.B.A., Case Western Res. U., 1947; J.D., Duquesne U., 1959. Admitted to Pa. bar, 1960; asso. firm Kirkpatrick, Pomeroy, Lockhart & Johnson, Pitts., 1959-60; sales Terryphone Corp., Pitts., 1959-60, asst. sec., Harrisburg, Pa., 1960-61, sec., 1961-62, treas., 1962-63, v.p., Camp Hill, Pa., 1963-64; v.p., chief counsel, sec., dir. ITT Terryphone Corp., Harrisburg, 1964—. Bd. dirs. Paxton Crossing Home Owner's Assn., 1974—, pres., 1974, 75; Mem. Am., Pa. (chmn. com. on corp. law depts. 1974—), Dauphin County bar assns., Harrisburg, Pa. chambers commerce, Air Force Assn. (past state v.p.), N.Am. Telephone Assn. (dir., exec. com. 1973—). Office: ITT Terryphone Corp 300 E Park Dr Harrisburg PA 17111 Tel (717) 564-4343

EATON, JAMES SAMUEL, b. Gulfport, Miss., June 11, 1912; B.A., Vanderbilt U., 1933; LL.B., U. Miss., 1935. Admitted to Miss. bar, 1935; partner firm Eaton, Cottrell, Galloway and Lang, Gulfport.

Chmn. Gulfport Sch. Bd., 1950-71. Mem. Miss. State Bar, Am., Fed. Power bar assns. Home: 1515 Kelly Ave Gulfport MS 39501 Office: 2300 14th St Gulfport MS 39501 Tel (601) 864-2682

EATON, JONATHAN CHASE, JR., b. Fargo, N.D., Feb. 26, 1927; B.S., Northwestern U., 1949; LL.B., Stanford U., 1952. Admitted to Calif. bar, 1952, N.D. bar, 1952, U.S. Ct. Claims, 1971; partner firm Funke & Eaton, Minot, N.D., 1960-71, firm Eaton & Van de Streek, Minot, 1974—; judge Minot Municipal Ct., 1954-60; owner Eaton Ranch, Denbigh, N.D. Chmn. Mouse River Irrigation Dist., 1968-72, Home Rule Charter Commn., 1970, State Real Estate Commn., 1966-76; pres. State Library Assn., 1960, Minot Library Bd., 1958-62; mem. Garrison Dist. Conservancy Bd. Mem. N.D., Am. bar assns., Am. Trial Lawyers Assn. Home: 807 13th St NE Minot ND 58701 Office: 312 Midwest Federal Savings and Loan Bldg Minot ND 58701 Tel (701) 852-4837

EATON, RICHARD BEHRENS, b. Albany, Oreg., Dec. 22, 1914; A.B., Stanford, 1934, J.D., 1938. Admitted to Calif. bar, 1938; law clk. Carter, Barrett, Finley & Carlton, Redding, Calif., 1939-40; asso. firm Glenn D. Newton, Redding, 1939-40; individual practice law, Redding, 1940, 46-51; U.S. commr., Redding, 1948-51; judge City Ct. of Redding, 1950-51; justice of peace, 1950-51, judge Superior Ct. of Calif. for Shasta County, 1951-76. Bd. dirs. Redding Mus., 1963—; lay reader Episcopal Ch., 1946—. Mem. Calif. State, Shasta-Trinity bar assns., Shasta Hist. Soc. (dir. 1958—). Recipient Silver Beaver award Boy Scouts Am., 1956, George Washington medal Freedoms Found., 1957, hon. Legion of Honor De Molay, 1968, Continuing Service award PTA, 1976, commendation Calif. Legislature, 1977. Home: 1520 West St Redding CA 96001

EATON, WILLIAM MELLON, b. N.Y.C., Oct. 5 1924; B.S., Duke, 1945; J.D., Harvard, 1949. Admitted to N.Y. bar, 1949, U.S. Dist. Ct. for So. N.Y. bar, 1949, U.S. Supreme Ct. bar, 1961; since practiced in N.Y.C.; asso. firm White & Case, 1949-60; partner firm Hardy, Peal, Rawlings, Werner & Maxwell, 1960-65; sr. partner firm Eaton, VanWinkle, Greenspoon & Grutman, 1965—; pres., dir. BT Capital Corp. subs. Bankers Trust N.Y. Corp., 1972—. Trustee Skowhegan Sch. Painting and Sculpture, 1976—. Mem. Assn. Bar City N.Y., Am. (chmn. com. on investment securities 1969-73), N.Y. State (chmn. investment com.), Internat. bar assns. Home: 17 E 89th St New York City NY 10028 Office: 600 3d Ave New York City NY 10016 Tel (212) 867-0606

EAVENSON, LEON CHANDLER, b. Atlanta, Sept. 24, 1927; LL.B. magna cum laude, Woodrow Wilson Coll. Law, Atlanta, 1950, LL.M., Atlanta Law Sch., 1951. Admitted to Ga. bar, 1951; spl. agt. FBI, Albany, N.Y., 1952-54, Milw., 1954-56; mgr. security dept. Rich's, Atlanta, 1956—, mem. Ga. Bd. Pvt. Detective and Pvt. Security Agencies, 1973—; mem. guards and investigators com. Pvt. Security Adv. Council, Law Enforcement Assistance Adminstrn., U.S. Dept. Justice, 1975—. Mem. Internat. Assn. Chiefs Police (asso.), Am. Soc. Indsl. Soc., Met. Atlanta Police Assn., Am., Ga. bar assns., Soc. Former Spl. Agts. FBI, Nat. Retail Mchts. Assn. (bd. dirs. security services group 1975—). Home: 3552 N Druid Hills Rd Decatur GA 30033 Office: Rich's 45 Broad St S W Atlanta GA 30302 Tel (404) 586-2616

EAVES, GRADY JYLES, b. Louisville, Miss., Nov. 6, 1933; B.A., Miss. State U., 1960; J.D., U. Miss., 1962. Admitted to Miss. bar, 1962; sr. partner firm Eaves & Eaves, Louisville and Jackson, Miss., 1963—; dist. atty. 5th Circuit Ct. Dist. Miss., 1967-72; judge City of Louisville, 1974—. Mem. Miss. Bar Found., Am. Judicature Soc., Am., Fed., Miss., Hinds County, Winston County bar assns., Phi Alpha Delta. Office: 114 S Columbus Ave Louisville MS 39339 Tel (601) 773-3540

EBER, MARTIN HARVEY, b. N.Y.C., Mar. 24, 1943; A.B., U. Calif., Berkeley, 1964, J.D., Hastings Coll. Law, San Francisco, 1972. Spl. asst. to exec. dir. Housing Authority of San Francisco, 1970-74; admitted to Calif. bar, 1973; individual practice law, San Francisco, 1975—. Home: 354 30th Ave San Francisco CA 94121 Office: 2806 Van Ness Ave San Francisco CA 94109 Tel (415) 776-4545

EBERLEIN, FREDERIC CHARLES, b. Shawano, Wis., Jan. 25, 1919; B.A., St. Norbert's Coll., 1940; LL.B., U. Wis., 1946. Admitted to Wis. bar, 1946; mem. firm Eberlein & Eberlein, Shawano, Wis., 1946-74; partner firm Eberlein & Gansen, Shawano, 1974—; dist. atty. Counties of Shawano and Menominee (Wis.), 1953-62; labor negotiator, Shawano, Menominee, Oconto, Bayfield counties, Wis., 1963—. Mem. State Bar Wis. (chmn. dist. grievance com. 1972—), Wis., Shawano County bar assn. Office: 117 N Main St Shawano WI 54166 Tel (715) 526-3030

EBERLY, JOHN E., b. Rochester, N.Y., June 13, 1937; B.S., Pa. Mil. Coll., 1961; J.D., Case Western Res. U., 1964. Admitted to Pa. bar, 1965; individual practice law, Warren, Pa., 1966-74; partner firm Harper, Clinger & Eberly, Warren, 1975—; asst. dist. atty. Warren County (Pa.), 1968-71. Mem. Warren County Sch. Bd., 1967-75; chmn. Warren County Emergency Med. Services Commn., 1976—; bd. dirs. Warren YMCA, 1967-73, pres., 1973. Mem. Am., Pa., Warren County bar assns. Office: 701 Pennbank Bldg Warren PA 16365 Tel (814) 723-8660

EBERSPACHER, EDWARD CHRISTIAN, b. Shelby County, Ill., Dec. 18, 1908; B.A., U. Ill., 1930, J.D., 1937. Admitted to Ill. bar, 1937; individual practice law, Shelbyville, Ill., 1937-64; justice Ill. Appellate Ct., 1964—; mem. Ill. Ct. Commn., 1970—; mem. Ill. Ho. of Reps., 1954-60, Ill. Senate, 1960-64; chmn. Ill. Sch. Problems Commn., 1962-64. Mem. Ill. State, Am. bar assns. Home: 219 N Washington St Shelbyville IL 62565 Office: 246 E Main St Shelbyville IL 62565 Tel (217) 774-4041

EBERT, MICHAEL, b. N.Y.C., Jan. 9, 1917; B.S., Coll. City N.Y., 1940; LL.B., N.Y. Law Sch., 1952. Patent advisor Radar Labs., Belmar, N.J., 1942-44, Radiation Lab., Mass. Inst. Tech., 1944-46; chief dept. electronics patents N. V. Philips of Holland, Irvington, N.Y., 1946-53; admitted to N.Y. bar, 1953, Customs and Patent Appeals Ct. bar, 1954; asso. firm Kenyon & Kenyon, N.Y.C., 1953-60; partner firms Lewy, Rosoff & Stern, N.Y.C., 1960-66, Hopgood & Calimafole, N.Y.C., 1966—. Pres. East Side Democrats, N.Y.C., 1955-57; mem. bd. advisors N.Y. Community Coll., 1976—. Mem. N.Y. Patent Law Assn., IEEE. Home: 565 Alda Rd Mamaroneck NY 10543 Office: 60 E 42d St New York City NY 10017 Tel (212) YU 6-2480

EBERWEIN, TONY LEW, b. St. Louis, Dec. 30, 1941; A.B., Central Mo. State U., 1963; J.D., U. Mo., 1966. Admitted to Mo. bar, 1966; city atty., Maplewood, Mo., 1966—; individual practice law, Clayton, Mo., 1966-77; partner firm Eberwein & Bigler, Clayton, 1972—; St. Louis adminstrv. asst. to Congressman Symington, 1969-71. Chmn. edn. United Ch. of Christ, 1974—, mem. ch. council, pres. ch., 1976-77; mem. St. Louis Mid-County Jaycees. Mem. Fed., St. Louis County bar assns., Met. Bar. St. Louis. Recipient St. Louis Mid-County Jaycees distinguished service award, 1974. Office: 7733 Forsyth St Clayton MO 63105 Tel (314) 862-8600

EBERZ, JAMES GERARD, b. Phila., Sept. 24, 1943; A.B., Marquette U., 1965; J.D., Fordham U., 1968. Admitted to N.Y. bar, 1968, U.S. Supreme Ct. bar, 1976; staff atty. Joel H. Lichtenstein, N.Y.C., 1968-72; asso. firm Kramer, Dillof & Tessel, N.Y.C., 1972; asso. with Joseph T. Mirabel, Huntington, N.Y., 1972—. Mem. Am., N.Y. State, Suffolk County bar assns., Nat. Health Lawyers Assn. Home: 625 Cardinal Rd Peekskill NY 10566 Office: 56 E Carver St Huntington NY 11743 Tel (516) 271-3800

EBY, WILSON GUY, b. Cassopolis, Mich., June 12, 1915; A.B., Kalamazoo Coll., 1938; LL.B., J.D., Detroit Coll. Law, 1942; Admitted to Mich. bar, 1946; partner firm Eby & Eby, Cassopolis, 1946-56; commr. Cass County Circuit Ct., 1947-53; practiced in Cassopolis, 1946-70; judge Cass County (Mich. (Mich.) Probate Ct., 1965—; village atty. Cassopolis Village, 1951-53. Bd. dirs. Cass County Assn. Retarded Children, Inc., 1960. Mem. Am. Mich. State, Cass County (pres. 1963-64) bar assns., Am. Judicature Soc., Mich. Probate, Juvenile Ct. Assn., Nat. Council Juvenile Ct. Judges, Children's Charter of Mich., Inc. Recipient William G. Howard award Kalamazoo Coll., 1937. Home: 108 Michigan St Dowagiac MI 49047 Office: Courthouse Cassopolis MI 49031 Tel (616) 445-8621

ECHARD, ROBERT ANDREW, b. Portsmouth, Va., Jan. 10, 1940; B.S. in Bus. Mgmt., Brigham Young U., 1965; J.D., U. Utah, 1968. Admitted to Utah bar, 1968; partner firm Patterson, Phillips, Gridley & Echard, Ogden, Utah, 1968—; dep. dist. atty. 2d Jud. Dist. Utah, 1969-71; atty. Morgan County (Utah), 1971-73; city atty. Harrisville (Utah), 1971—, Pleasant View (Utah), 1974—; mem. council consumer credit State Utah, 1976—. Mem. Utah Bar Assn., Am. Trial Lawyers Assn. Home: 249 W 4350 North St Ogden UT 84404 Office: 427 27th St Ogden UT 84404 Tel (801) 394-7706

ECHELBERRY, JOSEPH DAY, b. Battle Creek, Mich., Aug. 3, 1945; A.B. in Econs., U. Mich., 1967; J.D., Wayne State U., 1972. Admitted to Mich. bar, 1972; asst. corp. counsel law dept. City of Detroit, 1972-77; 3d dep. chief for labor relations Detroit Police Dept., 1977—; instr. Wayne State U., Detroit. Mem. State Bar Mich., Detroit Bar Assn., Am. Arbitration Assn., Internat. Assn. Chiefs Police, Internat. Personnel Mgmt. Assn., Mich. Pub. Employer Labor Relations Assn. Office: 8045 2d Ave Detroit MI 48202 Tel (313) 224-4449

ECHELES, JULIUS LUCIUS, b. Chgo., June 17, 1915; A.A., Crane Jr. Coll., Chgo., 1933; student Chgo. Law Sch., 1933-35, John Marshall Law Sch., 1935-36. Admitted to Ill. bar, 1936, U.S. Supreme Ct. bar, 1949; individual practice law, Chgo., 1936—. Mem. Am., Ill. bar assns., Def. Lawyers Assn. (bd. mgrs.). Office: 35 E Wacker Dr Chicago IL 60601 Tel (312) 782-0711

ECHEVERRIA, PETER, b. Shoshone, Idaho, June 29, 1918; B.A., U. Nev., 1943; LL.B., Stanford, 1949, J.D., 1953. Admitted to Nev. bar, 1949, U.S. Ct. Appeals 9th Circuit bar, 1953, U.S. Supreme Ct. bar, 1963; asso. firm Pat McCarran, Reno, 1949-51; partner firm Echeverria & Young, Reno, 1951-53; with firm Woodburn, Foreman & Woodburn, Reno, 1953-56; individual practice law, Reno, 1956-66; partner firm Echeverria & Osborne, Reno, 1966—; dep. atty. gen. State of Nev., 1951-53, senator, 1959-63; mem. Nev. State Planning Bd., 1963-73, chmn., 1973; chmn. Nev. State Gambling Commn., 1973-77. Fellow Am. Coll. Trial Lawyers, Basque Acad. Preservation of Basque Language and Culture; mem. Nev. Trial Lawyers (pres. 1970), Am. Bd. Trial Advocates (nat. pres. 1977—). Home: 546 Court St Reno NV 89501 Office: 555 S Center St Reno NV 89501 Tel (702) 786-4800

ECHTMAN, IRWIN M., b. N.Y.C., June 21, 1937; B.A., Hunter Coll., N.Y.C., 1958; LL.B., Yale U., 1961. Admitted to N.Y. State bar, 1961, U.S. Supreme Ct. bar, U.S. Ct. Appeals 2d Circuit bar; asso. Gainsburg, Gottlieb, Levitan & Cole, N.Y.C., 1961-64; asso. firm Herman Odell, N.Y.C., 1964-65; partner firm Easton & Echtman, P.C., N.Y.C., 1965—; arbitrator Civil Ct. City N.Y., Bronx County. Chmn. Roslyn (N.Y.) Environ. Assn.; del. Democratic Nat. Conv., 1968. Mem. N.Y. State, Bronx County bar assns. Home: 30 Bluebird Dr Roslyn Heights NY 11577 Office: 122 E 42d St New York City NY 10017 Tel (212) 687-0140

ECK, ROBERT JOSEPH, b. St. Louis, Mo., Mar. 10, 1939; B.S.C.E., Washington Univ., 1961, J.D., 1964. Admitted to Mo. Supreme Ct. bar, 1964, U.S. Supreme Ct. bar, 1970; individual practice law, St. Louis, 1964-71; trademark counsel The Seven-Up Co., St. Louis, 1971—. Mem. Internat., Inter-Am., Am., Met. St. Louis bar assns., U.S. Trademark Assn., Licensed Exec. Soc., Inter-Am. Assn. Protection Indsl. Property. Contbr. articles in field to profl. jours. Home: 5869 Delor St Louis MO 63109 Office: 121 S Meramec St Louis MO 63105 Tel (314) 863-7777

ECKARDT, RICHARD WILLIAM, b. St. Charles, Ill., Mar. 8, 1938; B.A., Ohio State U., 1959; J.D., U. So. Calif., 1966. Admitted to Calif. bar, 1967, U.S. Dist. Ct. No. and Central Dist. Calif., 1967, U.S. Supreme Ct. bar, 1972; legal staff Pacific Lighting Corp., 1968-70; asso. firm Mitchell and Mitchell, Los Angeles, 1970-71, Sprague and Clements, Los Angeles, 1971-73; individual practice law, Los Angeles, 1973—. Mem. Los Angeles County, Am. bar, assns., State Bar Calif., Am. Judicature Soc., Phi Alpha Delta. Club: University (Los Angeles). Office: 1520 Crocker Bank Plaza 611 W 6th St Los Angeles CA 90017 Tel (213) 680-1061

ECKERLE, THOMAS CRAIG, b. Mauston, Wis., Aug. 30, 1939; B.S., U. Wis., 1961, J.D., 1964. Admitted to Wis. bar, 1964, U.S. Supreme Ct. bar, 1971; asst. U.S. atty. Western Dist. Wis., 1966-68; partner firm Risser, Risser & Eckerle, Madison, 1969—. Mem. Wis., Dane County bar assns. Home: 5906 Old Middleton Rd Madison WI 53705 Office: 140 W Wilson St Madison WI 53703 Tel (608) 255-2956

ECKERT, WILLIAM ALTHEN, JR., b. New Orleans, Sept. 1, 1919; B.A., La. State U., 1939; LL.B. with honors, U. Ark., 1948. Admitted to Ark. bar, 1948, U.S. Supreme Ct. bar, 1967; partner firm Crumpler & Eckert, Magnolia, Ark., 1948-53; partner firm Keith, Clegg & Eckert, Magnolia, 1956—; individual practice law, Magnolia, 1953-55; dept. pros. atty. Columbia County (Ark.), 1950-52; judge Municipal Ct., Magnolia, 1956—. Mem. Am., Ark., Columbia County bar assns. Home: 528 Margaret St Magnolia AR 71753 Office: 201 McAlester Bldg Magnolia AR 71753 Tel (501) 234-3550

ECKERT, WILLIAM HENRY, b. Pitts., Mar. 27, 1900; B.S. in Econs. summa cum laude, U. Pitts., 1921, LL.B. with high honors, 1924. Admitted to Pa. bar, 1924, U.S. Supreme Ct. bar, 1929; asso. firm Eckert, Seamans, Cherin & Mellott, and predecessors, Pitts., 1924-30, partner, 1930-75, sr. partner, 1976—; mem. adv. com. on law of decedents' estates and related subjects Pa. Legislature, 1945—, chmn., 1972—; mem. procedural rules com. Pa. Supreme Ct., 1945—. Chmn., Rosslyn Farms (Pa.) Zoning Appeals Bd., 1965—. Recipient 1st Distinguished Alumnus award U. Pitts. Law Sch., 1972; named Man of Year in Law, Pitts. Jaycees, 1975. Mem. Allegheny County (Pa.) (pres. 1945-46), Pa. (pres. 1969), Am. bar assns. Home: 410 Kings Hwy Rosslyn Farms Carnegie PA 15106 Office: 42d Floor US Steel Bldg 600 Grant St Pittsburgh PA 15219 Tel (412) 566-6000

ECKHARDT, AUGUST GOTTLIEB, b. Sylvan, Wis., Aug. 8, 1917; B.A., U. Wis., 1939, LL.M., 1946, S.J.D., 1951; LL.B., George Washington U., 1942. Admitted to D.C. bar, 1941, Wis. bar, 1946, Ariz. bar, 1974; practiced in Merrill, Wis., 1946-47, 50-52; asst. prof. law George Washington U., 1947-49; prof. U. Wis., 1954-72, U. Ariz., 1972—; dir. Wis. Continuing Legal Edn., 1954-60, Mem. Am. Bar Assn., state bars Wis., Ariz. Author: Workbook for Wisconsin Estate Planners, 1961; Meeting the Educational Needs of the Newly Admitted Lawyer, 1967. Home: 2002 E 3d St Tucson AZ 85719 Office: Coll of Law U of Ariz Tucson AZ 85721 Tel (602) 884-1881

ECKHART, HENRY WORLEY, b. Columbus, Ohio, Nov. 12, 1932; B.S. in Bus. Adminstrn., Ohio State U., 1954; J.D., U. Mich., 1958. Admitted to Ohio bar, 1958; individual practice law, Columbus, 1958—; chmn. Pub. Utilities Commn. Ohio, 1971-73. Mem. Ohio Democratic Party State Exec. Com., 1968-74; mem. Dem. Nat. Com. Charter Commn., 1973-74. Mem. Columbus, Ohio State bar assns. Home: 1850 Upper Chelsea Upper Arlington OH 43215 Office: 88 E Broad St Columbus OH 43215 Tel (614) 461-0984

ECKHART, MORRIS L., b. Vinton, Iowa, Dec. 22, 1948; B.A., U. No. Iowa, 1971; J.D., Drake U., 1973. Admitted to Iowa bar, 1974; partner firm Milroy & Eckhart, Vinton, 1974—; asst. atty. Benton County (Iowa), 1974-75. Mem. Eastern Iowa Area Crime Commn., 1974-76; crusade chmn. Benton County chpt. Am. Cancer Soc., 1975; elder Presbyterian Ch. of Vinton, 1975—. Mem. Iowa, Benton County bar assns., Iowa Municipal Attys. Assn. Home: 1608 G Ave Vinton IA 52349 Office: 218 W 4th St Vinton IA 52349 Tel (319) 472-4711

ECKHOFF, JAMES DAVID, b. St. Louis, Apr. 28, 1944; B.S. in Bus. Adminstrn., Washington U., St. Louis, 1966, J.D., 1970. Admitted to Mo. bar, 1970; partner firm Fordyce & Mayne, St. Louis, 1970—. Mem. Am., Mo. bar assns., Bar Assn. Met. St. Louis. Home: 424 Steeplechase Ln Saint Louis MO 63131 Office: 120 S Central St Suite 1100 Saint Louis MO 63105 Tel (314) 863-6900

ECKL, WILLIAM WRAY, b. Florence, Ala., Dec. 2, 1936; B.A., U. Notre Dame, 1959; LL.B., U. Va., 1962. Admitted to Va. bar, 1962, Ala. bar, 1962, Ga. bar, 1964; partner firm Swift, Currie, McGhee & Hiers, Atlanta, 1968—. Mem. Ala., Va., Ga., Am. bar assns. Office: 771 Spring St NW Atlanta GA 30342 Tel (404) 881-0844

ECKLER, JOHN ALFRED, b. Elyria, Ohio, July 2, 1913; A.B., Ohio Wesleyan U., 1935; J.D., U. Chgo., 1939. Admitted to Ill. bar, 1939, Ohio bar, 1945; asso. firm Knapp, Allen & Cushing, Chgo., 1939-43; adminstrv. asst. to Senator John W. Bricker of Ohio, Washington, 1947-49; practice law, Columbus, Ohio, 1946—; partner firm Bricker, Evatt, Barton & Eckler, 1954—; mem., chmn. Ohio Bd. Bar Examiners, 1954-59; chmn. Nat. Conf. Bar Examiners, 1960, Standing Com. on Multi-State Bar Exam., 1968-74, Standing Com. on Fed. Bar Exam., 1975—. Trustee, gen. counsel World Neighbors, Oklahoma City, 1952—; chmn. trustee Ohio Wesleyan U., Delaware, 1958—; bd. visitors U. Chgo. Law Sch., 1968-73. Fellow Am., Ohio (pres. 1976—) bar founds.; mem. Am. (chmn. spl. com. ct. congestion 1958-60, mem. ho. of dels. 1960-69, mem. law lists com. 1968-73), Ohio (mem. modern cts. com.), Columbus (past pres.) bar assns., Am. Coll. Trial Lawyers, Nat. Assn. R.R. Trial Lawyers, Am. Judicature Soc. (trustee 1977-), Order of Coif, Phi Beta Kappa. Home: 2105 Lower Chelsea Rd Columbus OH 43212 Office: 100 E Broad St Columbus OH 43215 Tel (614) 221-6651

ECKMAN, DAVID WALTER, b. Ogden, Utah, Oct. 23, 1942; B.A. with honors, U. Tex., Austin, 1964, J.D., 1967. Admitted to Tex. bar, 1967, Calif. bar, 1976; assisting trial atty. Exxon Co., U.S.A. div. Exxon Corp., Houston, 1967-68, atty. South Tex. div., Corpus Christi, Tex., 1968-70, atty., counsel East Tex. div., Houston, 1971-74, counsel Southeastern div., New Orleans, 1974, Prudhoe Bay Law Task Force, Houston and Los Angeles, 1974-75, Pacific Region, Los Angeles, 1975-77. Vestryman, dir. Christian edn. All Saints Episcopal Ch., Corpus Christi, 1968-70; leader adult study St. Marks Episcopal Ch., Houston, 1971-74; mem. St. Patrick's Sch. Bd., Thousand Oaks, Calif., 1976-77. Mem. Am., Houston, Los Angeles County bar assns., Calif., Tex. bars. Recipient Am. Jurisprudence award in antitrust law, 1967; Sam D. Hanna scholar, 1964-65. Address: 7315 Greenbriar Dr Houston TX 77030 Tel (713) 665-1290

ECKMAN, RAGNAR VERN, b. Center City, Minn., Sept. 16, 1899; B.A., Gustavus Adolphus Coll., 1920; J.D., U. Mich., 1926. Admitted to Minn. bar, 1926; individual practice law, Duluth, Minn., 1926-47, partner firm Eckman & Eckman, 1947-67, firm Eckman, Mellum & Fillenworth, 1967—; dir., atty. Duluth Nat. Bank, 1939-70. Chmn., U.S. Selective Service Bd., Duluth, 1940-50; vice consul for Sweden at Duluth, 1960-70. Mem. Minn., 6th Dist. bar assns. Decorated knight Order of Vasa by King of Sweden, 1970. Home: 2915 Greysolon Rd Duluth MN 55812 Office: Duluth National Bank Bldg Duluth MN 55806 Tel (218) 722-7715

EDDLEMAN, WILLIAM ROSEMAN, b. Shelby, N.C., May 21, 1913; student U. N.C., 1930-34; LL.B., Gonzaga U., 1939; postgrad. Parker Sch. Internat. Law, Columbia, 1964; Licenciado en Derecho, Universidad Nacional Autonoma de Mexico, 1968. Admitted to Wash. bar, 1939, Mexico bar, 1968, Tex. bar, 1972; individual practice law, Garfield, Wash., 1939-46; mem. firm Eddleman & Wheeler, Seattle, 1948-63; mem. firm Perez-Verdia Eddleman, Mexico City, 1963—; mem. firm Carp & Eddleman, Dallas, 1972—; De La Fuente Eddleman, Mexico, 1977—. Mem. Am. (nat. chmn. Young Lawyers, 1948-49), Internat., Inter-Am., Wash. State, Tex., Dallas bar assns., Selden Soc. Contbr. articles to legal publs. Home: 7149 Northaven St Dallas TX 75230 Office: 4014 Republic Nat Bank Tower Dallas TX 75201 Tel (214) 741-3109

EDEE, JAMES PHILIP, b. Pawnee City, Nebr., Oct. 12, 1929; B.S. in Law, U. Nebr., 1952, J.D., 1954; M.B.A., Ga. State U., 1971; LL.M. in Taxation, Emory U., 1975. Admitted to Nebr. bar, 1954, Ga. bar, 1958; legal officer USAF, 1954-56; trust rep. 1st Nat. Bank of Atlanta, 1956-60; atty. IRS, Atlanta, 1961-73; individual practice law, Atlanta, 1973-76; partner firm Floyd, Edee & Stanford, Atlanta, 1976—. Mem. Am., Nebr., Ga. bar assns., Nebr. Alumni Assn. (pres. Atlanta chpt.).

U. Nebr. Regent's scholar, 1947-48. Home: 2639 Battle Overlook NW Atlanta GA 30327 Office: 3340 Peachtree Rd NE Atlanta GA 30326 Tel (404) 231-1355

EDELBERG, IRVING MUNROE, b. Saranac Lake, N.Y., Jan. 11, 1915; B.A., U. Mich., 1937, J.D., 1940. Admitted to N.Y. State bar, 1941; individual practice law, Saranac Lake, 1946—; police judge Saranac Lake, 1949-70; prof. bus. law Paul Smith's (N.Y.) Coll., 1963—. Trustee Village of Saranac Lake, 1946-49. Mem. Essex, Franklin County bar assns. Home: 146 Park Ave Saranac Lake NY 12983 Office: Hotel Saranac Arcade Saranac Lake NY 12983 Park Ave Saranac Lake NY 12983 Office: Hotel Saranac Arcade Saranac Lake Tel (518) 891-1660

EDELMAN, BARRY H., b. Dallas, Jan. 29, 1942; B.B.A., U. Tex., 1962; J.D., St. Mary's U., San Antonio, 1970. Admitted to Tex. bar, 1969; accountant Lichtenstein & Rosow, C.P.A.'s, San Antonio, 1962-67; chief accountant Turbine Support div. Chromalloy Am. Corp., San Antonio, 1967-68; sr. accountant Concentrated Employment program Econ. Opportunities Devel. Corp., San Antonio, 1968; accountant Karpel & Panfeld, C.P.A.'s, San Antonio, 1969; partner Karpel, Panfeld & Edelman, C.P.A.'s San Antonio 1970-74, Panfeld, Edelman & Co., C.P.A.'s, San Antonio, 1974—; instr. accounting St Mary's U., 1968. Treas., dir. San Antonio chpt. Am. Jewish Com.; mem. budget com. Jewish Social Service Fedn., San Antonio, 1973-75. Mem. Am., Tex., San Antonio bar assns., San Antonio Estate Planners Council (pres. 1974-75, dir. 1973-76), Am. Inst. C.P.A.'s, Tex., San Antonio socs. C.P.A.'s. Home: 2506 Old Gate Rd San Antonio TX 78230 Office: 1800 NE Loop 410 Plaza W Suite 300 San Antonio TX 78217 Tel (512) 828-6381

EDELMAN, LENORE A.; B.A., Adelphi Coll., 1949; LL.B., Bklyn. Law Sch., 1957, J.D., 1967. Admitted to N.Y. bar, 1958; asso. firm Morris A. Edelman, N.Y.C., 1958—; conf. atty. Family Ct. N.Y.C., 1976—; hearing officer Small Claims Ct., Bklyn., 1975—. Mem. N.Y. Lawyers Assn. Office: 111 Broadway New York City NY 10006 Tel (212) RE2-8696

EDELMAYER, ROBERT JOHN, b. Phila., Nov. 7, 1947; A.B. in Social Scis., Villanova U., 1969, J.D., 1972. Admitted to Pa. bar, 1972; asso. firm McLafferty & Edelmayer, Norristown, Pa., 1972—; asst. pub. defender Montgomery County (Pa.), 1973-76. Mem. Am., Pa., Montgomery County (vice chmn. Young Lawyers sect. 1975, chmn., 1976) bar assns., Pa. Trial Lawyers Assn. Home: 645 9th Ave Warminster PA 18974 Office: 325 Swede St Norristown PA 19401 Tel (215) 279-2440

EDELSTEIN, DAVID NORTHON, b. N.Y.C., Feb. 16, 1910; B.S., A.M., LL.B., Fordham U. Admitted to N.Y. State bar, practiced in N.Y.C.; atty. claims div. Dept. Justice, 1944; asst. U.S. atty., So. Dist. of N.Y., 1945-47, spl. asst. to atty. gen. in charge lands div., 1947; asst. atty. gen. in charge of customs div. Dept. Justice, 1948; U.S. dist. judge So. Dist. N.Y., 1951—, now chief judge. Assisted Pres.'s Temporary Commn. on Employee Loyalty, chmn. in preparation of its report, 1946. Mem. legislative com. Attys. Gen. Conf. on Crime, 1950. Mem. Fed. (past pres. Empire chpt. past nat. del.), Am. (past alternate del. ho. of dels. for Fed. Bar Assn.) bar assns., Bar Assn. City N.Y. (jud. mem.), Bklyn.-Manhattan Trial Lawyers Assn., Maritime Lawyers Assn., Am. Trial Lawyers Assn., Nat. Lawyers Club (hon.). Author: The History and Scope of The Fair Labor Standards Act of 1938, 1941. Home: 1040 Park Ave New York City NY 10028 Office: US Court House Foley Square New York City NY 10007*

EDELSTEIN, HARRY, b. Bklyn., July 24, 1924; student U. Utah, L.I. U., 1945-47; LL.B., Bklyn. Law Sch., 1949. Admitted to N.Y. bar, 1951; asso. firm Fuchsberg & Fuchsberg, N.Y.C., 1952-53, O'Donnell & Schwartz, N.Y.C., 1953-62; individual practice law, Haverstraw, N.Y., 1960-74; judge Rockland County (N.Y.) Ct., New City, 1975—. Vol. counsel Exceptional Child PTA, Rockland County, NAACP, Spring Valley, N.Y., Planned Parenthood, W. Nyack, N.Y., Hi-Tor Animal Shelter, Pomona, N.Y.; former pres. Nanuet Hebrew Center, Nanuet, N.Y., Am. Cancer Soc., New City, Rockland Cdunty Vet. Coordinating Council. Mem. Am., N.Y. bar assns., N.Y. State Trial Lawyers Assn. (dist. gov.). Home: 35 Glenwood Rd New City NY 10956 Office: County Office Bldg New City NY 10956 Tel (914) 638-0500

EDELSTEIN, MORTIMER SIDNEY, b. Paterson, N.J., Mar. 1, 1904; B.S. in Econs., U. Pa., 1926; J.D., Cornell U., 1931. Admitted to N.Y. bar, 1932, U.S. Supreme Ct. bar, 1960; asst. gen. counsel Port of N.Y. Authority, 1944, asst. to exec. dir., 1945; asso. firm Olcott Holmes Glass Paul & Havens, N.Y.C., 1931-35; partner firm Paul Weiss Wharton & Garrison, N.Y.C., 1945-49, firm Young Kaplan Edelstein, N.Y.C., 1949—; vis. lectr. Duke U., 1966, Wharton Sch. U. Pa., 1975; lectr. Practising Law Inst., 1960-66. Mem. Assn. Bar City N.Y., N.Y. State, Am. bar assns., Order of Coif, Phi Kappa Phi. Bd. editors Cornell Law Quar., 1930-31. Home: 245 E 72d St New York City NY 10021 Office: 277 Park Ave New York City NY 10017 Tel (212) 826-0313

EDEN, NATHAN ELLIS, b. Key West, Fla., Mar. 24, 1944; B.A., U. Fla., 1966, J.D. magna cum laude, Stetson U., 1969. Admitted to Fla., U.S. Dist. Ct. Middle Dist. Fla. bars, 1969, U.S. Dist. Ct. So. Dist. Fla. bar, 1969; asso. firm Nelson, Stinnet, Surfus, Korp & Payne, Sarasota, 1970-71; partner firm Feldman, Eden and Allen and predecessors, Key West, 1971—; asst. pub. def. Monroe County, Fla., 1970, asst. county solicitor, 1970-73; county solicitor, 1973-74, chief asst. state atty, 1974-76, U.S. magistrate, So. Dist. Fla., 1976—; bd. govs. Fla. Bar, 1977—. Mem. Fed., Fla. bar assns., Fla. Acad. Trial Lawyers. Home: 1701 White St Key West FL 33040 Office: 417 Eaton St Key West FL 33040 Tel (305) 294-5588

EDERER, RONALD FRANK, b. Corpus Christi, Tex., Aug. 25, 1943; B.B.A., N.Tex. State U., 1965; J.D., St. Mary's U., 1969. Admitted to Tex. bar, 1971; law clk. to U.S. Dist. Ct. judge, 1971-72; asst. U.S. atty. for Western Tex., 1972-76; individual practice law, El Paso, Tex., 1976—; U.S. magistrate, 1976—. Mem. El Paso, Fed. bar assns., El Paso Young Lawyers Assn., El Paso Trial Lawyers Assn. Tel (915) 532-5471

EDGAR, JOHN MAURICE, b. Bonham, Tex., Sept. 25, 1943; B.S. in Bus. Adminstrn., U. Kans., 1965; J.D., U. Mo., Kansas City, 1968. Admitted to Mo. bar, 1968; partner firm Stinson, Mag, Thomson, McEvers & Fizzell, Kansas City, Mo., 1972—. Mem. Am., Mo., Kansas City bar assns., Lawyers Assn. Kansas City.

EDGE, JULIAN DEXTER, JR., b. Newport News, Va., June 7, 1942; B.S. in Indsl. Mgmt., Ga. Inst. Tech., 1960, J.D., Emory U., 1973. Admitted to Ga. bar, 1973; asso. firm Henkel & Lamon, Atlanta, 1973—. Mem. Order of Coif, Omicron Delta Kappa. Home: 1274 Oak Grove Drive Decatur GA 30033 Office: 229 Peachtree St NE Atlanta GA 30303

EDHLUND, SANDRA ANN, b. Mankato, Wis., Apr. 8, 1942; B.A., Milw. Downer Coll., 1964; M.A., U. Wis., 1967, J.D., 1970. Admitted to Wis. bar, 1970; asso. firm Greenberg, Karp, and Heitzman, Milw., 1970-72; partner firm Edhlund & Bales, Milw., 1972—; tchr. U. Wis. Law Sch., 1976; commr. Wis. Gov.'s Commn. Status Women, 1976—; mem. Wis. Council Criminal Justice Goals and Standards Com., 1976. Bd. dirs. Wis. Civil Liberties Union, 1975—, Milw. Legal Services, 1975—. Mem. State Bar Wis., Milw., Milw. Jr. bar assns. Contbr. articles to legal jours. Office: suite 300 536 W Wisconsin Ave Milwaukee WI 53203 Tel (414) 273-1040

EDINGER, DONALD PAUL, b. St. Louis, Apr. 20, 1948; B.J., U. Mo., Columbia, 1970, J.D., 1974. Admitted to Mo. bar, 1974; supervising trust examiner div. finance State of Mo., Kansas City, 1974—, supr., 1976—. Mem. Am., Mo. bar assns. Home and office: 525 N Osage St Apt 8 Independence MO 64050 Tel (816) 836-0378

EDMISTEN, RUFUS L., b. Watauga County, N.C., July 12, 1941; B.A. with honors, U. N.C.; law degree with honors, George Washington U. Admitted to N.C. bar, D.C. bar; former chief aide to U.S. Senator Sam J. Ervin; former dep. chief counsel Senate Select Com. on Presdl. Campaign Activities (Watergate Com.); former chief counsel, staff dir. Senate Judiciary Subcom. on Separation of Powers; former counsel to Senate Judiciary Subcom. on Constl. Rights; atty. gen. State of N.C., 1974—. Bd. advisers Lees-McRae Coll. Mem. Am., N.C., D.C., Fed. bar assns., Nat. Assn. Attys. Gen. (vice chmn. com. on office of atty. gen.). Office: Atty Gen of NC Dept of Justice Bldg Raleigh NC 27602*

EDMISTON, PAUL DAVID, b. Lexington, Ky., Nov. 23, 1948; B.S., Purdue U., 1970; J.D., Ind. U., 1973. Admitted to Ind. bar, 1973; partner firm Power, Little & Edmiston, Frankfort, Ind., 1974—. Membership chmn. Boy Scouts Am., 1975-76; drive chmn. Am. Heart Fund, 1974-75; unit leader United Way, 1974; counsel Ind. Jaycees, 1975, Council on Aging, 1976. Mem. Am., Ind., Clinton County bar assns. Office: 253 N Jackson St Frankfort IN 46041 Tel (317) 654-4340

EDMUNDS, J. OLLIE, b., Higgston, Ga., Mar. 1, 1903; A.B., Stetson U., 1927, J.D., 1928; numerous hon. degrees. Admitted to Fla. bar, 1927, Fed. bar, 1929; asso. firm Hull, Laudis & Whitahair, 1927-29; individual practice law, Jacksonville, Fla., 1929-31; county judge Duval County (Fla.) 1931-45; pres. Stetson U., 1948-68, chancellor, 1968—. Pres. Jacksonville Council Social Agys., 1937; active Boy Scouts Am., YMCA. Mem. Jacksonville, Fla. bar assns. Home: 405 N Arnelia St DeLaud FL 32720 Office: 1560 Lancaster Terr Jacksonville FL 32204 Tel (904) 354-5162

EDMUNDS, JOHN SANFORD, b. Los Angeles, Jan. 3, 1943; A.B., Stanford, 1964; J.D., U. So. Calif., 1967. Admitted to Hawaii bar, 1968, U.S. Supreme Ct. bar, 1972; practiced in Honolulu, 1968—; chief dep. pub. defender State of Hawaii, 1970-72; vis. prof. law U. Hawaii, 1976; bd. dirs. Legal Aid Soc. Hawaii, 1974-75. Mem. ACLU of Hawaii (dir. 1969-73, pres. 1971-73, adv. council 1974—), Am., Hawaii State (chmn. prepaid legal services com. 1974-75) bar assns., Assn. Trial Lawyers Am. (state committeeman 1976). Contbr. to Hawaii Bar Jour., 1975. Office: 225 Queen St Honolulu HI 96813 Tel (808) 524-2000

EDMUNDS, PALMER DANIEL, b. Terre Haute, Ill., Oct. 29, 1890; A.B., Knox Coll. 1912, LL.D. (hon.), 1945; LL.B., Harvard U., 1915; LL.D., Piedmont Coll., 1974. Admitted to Ill. bar, 1915, Fed. bar, 1928; chief clk., counsel Ill. Service Recognition Bd., 1922-25; commr. Supreme Ct. Ill., 1929-32; compliance commr. War Prodn. Bd. and Civilian Prodn. Adminstrn., 1944-47; hearing commr. Defense Prodn. Adminstrn., 1951-53; mem. firm Dodd & Edmunds, Chgo., 1925-58; mem. faculty John Marshall Law Sch., Chgo., 1926-76; vis. prof. law Knox Coll., 1944-57; Mem. Chgo., Ill., Am., Indian bar assns., Am. Judicature Soc., Am. Soc. Internat. Law, Am. Polit. Sci. Assn., World Peace Through Law Center, World Assn. Lawyers. Author: (with Walter F. Dodd) Illinois Appellate Procedure, 1929; Edmunds Common Law Forms, 1931; Edmunds Illinois Civil Practice Forms, 1933; Edmunds Federal Rules of Civil Procedure, 1938; Cyclopedia of Federal Procedure Forms, 1939; Law and Civilzation, 1959. Address: PO Box 317 Gilman IL 60938 Tel (815) 686-2473

EDSON, CHARLES LOUIS, b. St. Louis, Dec. 14, 1934; A.B., Harvard, 1956, LL.B., 1959. Admitted to Mo. bar, 1959, U.S. Supreme Ct. bar, 1966, D.C. bar, 1967; asso. firm Lewis, Rice Tucker, Allen & Chubb, St. Louis, 1959-65; chief ops. Legal Services Program OEO, Washington, 1966-67; gen. counsel Pres.'s Commn. on Postal Orgn., Washington, 1967-68; chief pub. housing sec. Office of Gen. Counsel, HUD, Washington, 1968-70; partner firm Lane and Edson, P.C., Washington, 1970—; adj. prof. law Georgetown U. Law Center, 1970—; HUD coordinator Pres. Carter's Transition Staff, 1976-77. Councilman, Town of Somerset, Md., 1976. Mem. Am., D.C. bar assns., Harvard Law Sch. Assn. (pres. D.C. 1972-73). Alt. White House fellow, 1965; co-author: A Practical Guide to Low and Moderate Income Housing, 1972; A Leased Housing Primer, 1975; A Section 8 Deskbook, 1976; co-editor Housing and Devel. Reporter, 1970—. Home: 5515 Uppingham St Chevy Chase MD 20015 Office: 1800 M St Suite 400 S Washington DC 20036 Tel (202) 457-6800

EDSON, LYLE RICH, b. Ogden, Utah, Mar. 26, 1917; B.S. cum laude, U. San Francisco, 1943, J.D. cum laude, 1948. Admitted to Calif. bar, 1949; asso. firm McCutchen, Thomas, Matthew, Griffiths & Greene, San Francisco, 1948-51; atty. Office Price Stabilization, San Francisco, 1951-53; chief dep. dist. atty. County of San Mateo (Calif.), 1953-64; judge Municipal Ct. of San Mateo County, 1964-69, San Mateo County Superior Ct., 1969—. Mem. Conf. Calif. Judges. Office: Hall of Justice Redwood City CA 94063 Tel (418) 364-5600

EDWARDS, BINGHAM DAVID, b. Decatur, Ala., Apr. 6, 1943; B.A., U. of the S., 1965; J.D., U. Ala., 1968. Admitted to Ala. bar, 1968; partner firm Hutson, Elrod, Edwards & Belser, Decatur, 1973—. Senator State of Ala., Lawrence and Morgan Counties, Ala., 1974—. Mem. Decatur C. of C., Morgan County, Ala., Am. bar assns. Office: 205 Holly St NE Decatur AL 35601 Tel (205) 355-3731

EDWARDS, C. WYTHE, b. Herald, Va., Dec. 13, 1923; J.D., U. Tenn., 1953. Admitted to Tenn. bar, 1961; partner firm Masengill & Edwards, Blountville, Tenn. Mem. Tenn., Kingsport, Bristol, Blountville bar assns. Home: 1617 Fairfield Ave Kingsport TN 37660 Office: PO Box 85 Blountville TN 37617 Tel (615) 323-4414

EDWARDS, CHARLES ARCHIBALD, b. Lumberton, N.C., Sept. 19, 1945; A.B., Davidson Coll., 1967; J.D., U. N.C., 1970. Admitted to Ga. bar, 1970, U.S. Supreme Ct. bar, 1973; asso. firm Hunter, Houlihan, Maclean, Exley, Dunn & Connerat, Savannah, Ga., 1970-71, mem., 1972-76; partner firm Constangy, Brooks & Smith, Atlanta, 1976—; instr. Am. history and govt. Armstrong State Coll., Savannah, 1971-74. Mem. Am., Atlanta bar assns., State Bar Ga., Def. Research Inst., Am. Soc. Personnel Adminstrs. Contbr. articles to legal jours. Office: 1900 Peachtree Center 230 Peachtree St NW Atlanta GA 30303 Tel (404) 525-8622

EDWARDS, DANIEL PAUL, b. Enid, Okla., Apr. 15, 1940; B.A., U. Okla., 1962; J.D., Harvard, 1965. Admitted to Colo. bar, 1965; partner firm Cole, Helox, Tolley, Edwards & Keene, Colorado Springs, Colo., 1968—; lectr. bus. law Colo. Coll., 1976—. Bd. dirs. Springs Area Beautiful Assn., Broadmoor Improvement Soc. Mem. Am. Colo. bar assns., Phi Beta Kappa. Home: 5 Cheyenne Mountain Blvd Colorado Springs CO 80906 Office: 3 S Tejon St Colorado Springs CO 80903 Tel (303) 473-4444

EDWARDS, ELTON, b. Wayne County, N.C., Aug. 14, 1923; A.B., U. N.C., 1943, J.D., 1948. Admitted to N.C. bar, 1948, U.S. Ct. Mil. Appeals bar, 1959; practiced in Greensboro, N.C., 1949—; individual practice law, 1949-54; partner firm Moseley & Edwards, 1954-71; sr. partner firm Edwards, Greeson and Toumaras, 1971—; mem. N.C. Ho. of Reps., 1964-68, N.C. Senate, 1968-70. Chmn. Morehead Meml. Commn., Greensboro, Handiclean Family Found., Greensboro. Mem. Greensboro, N.C., Am. bar assns. Home: 309 N Tremont Dr Greensboro NC 27403 Office: PO Box 210 Greensboro NC 27402 Tel (919) 373-8761

EDWARDS, GARY KIP, b. Wichita, Kans., Jan. 28, 1947; B.B.A., U. Wash., 1968; J.D., U. Calif., 1971. Admitted to Calif. bar, 1972; teaching fellow Stanford Law Sch., 1971-72; asso. firm Orrick, Herrington, Rowley & Sutcliffe, San Francisco, 1972—. Mem. State Bar Calif., Am. Bar Assn., ACLU, Boalt Hall Alumni Assn., Order of Coif. Home: 310 W 37th Ave San Mateo CA 94403 Office: 600 Montgomery St San Francisco CA 94111 Tel (415) 392-1122

EDWARDS, GEORGE, b. Dallas, Aug. 6, 1914; B.A., So. Meth. U., 1933; M.A., Harvard, 1934; J.D., Detroit Coll. Law, 1949. Rep. UAW-CIO, Detroit, 1937, dir. dept. welfare, 1938-39; dir. sec. Detroit Housing Commn., 1940-41; mem. Detroit Common Council, 1941-49, pres., 1945-49; admitted to Mich. bar, 1944; partner firm Rothe, Marston, Edwards and Bohn and predecessor, Detroit, 1946-51; probate judge charge Wayne County (Mich.) Juvenile Ct., 1951-54; judge Mich. Circuit, Ct., 3d Jud. Circuit, 1954-56; justice Mich. Supreme Ct., 1956-62; commr. of police City of Detroit 1962-63; judge U.S. Ct. Appeals, 6th Circuit, 1963—; chmn. com. adminstrn. criminal laws Jud. Conf. U.S., 1966-70; men. Nat. Com. Reform Fed. Criminal Laws, 1967-71. Chmn. SE Mich. Cancer Crusade, 1950-51; chmn. 13th Congl. Dist. Wayne County Democratic Party, 1950-51. Mem. Am., Mich., Detroit bar assns., Nat. Council Judges, Nat. Council Crime, Delinquency, Inst. Jud. Adminstrn., Phi Beta Kappa, Kappa Sigma. Recipient award for community work Workmen's Circle, 1949, St. Cyprian's Episcopal Ch., 1950; Americanism award Jewish War Vets., 1953, award for outstanding achievement VFW, 1953, St. Peter's medal St. Peter's Episcopal Ch., Detroit, 1956, Judiciary award Assn. Fed. Investigators, 1971; author: The Police on the Urban Frontier, 1968; (with others) The Law of Criminal Correction, 1968; Pioneer-at-Law, 1974; contbr. articles to profl. jours. Home: 4057 Egbert St Cincinnati OH 45220 Office: US Courthouse Cincinnati OH 45202 Tel (513) 684-2961

EDWARDS, HUGH ROBERTSON, JR., b. Searcy, Ark., Aug. 12, 1947; B.A., U. Ark., 1969, J.D., 1972. Admitted to Ark. bar, 1972, U.S. Dist. Ct. Eastern Dist. Ark. bar, 1974; individual practice law, Searcy, 1972—; dep. pros. atty. White County, Ark., 1975; dir. White County Guaranty Savs. & Loan Assn., 1973—. Mem. Am., Ark., White County bar assns. Home: 9 Meadowlane Searcy AR 72143 Office: 302 W Center Ave Searcy AR 72143 Tel (501) 268-8689

EDWARDS, JACK LARRY, b. Lubbock, Tex., Dec. 14, 1947; B.A. in Econs., Tex. A. and M. U., 1969; J.D., Tex. Tech. U., 1972. Admitted to Tex. bar, 1972; since practiced Dimmitt, Tex., asso. firm Burkett, Ross & Edwards, 1972-75, partner, 1975—; city atty. Dimmitt, 1972—; city atty. Nazareth (Tex.), 1974—. Mem. Dimmitt C. of C. (dir. 1972, pres. 1976), Jr. C. of C. (dir. 1972, 74), Tex., 64th Jud. Dist. bar assns. Home: 1605 Sunset Circle Dr Dimmitt TX 79027 Office: 114 S Broadway Dimmitt TX 79027 Tel (806) 647-2131

EDWARDS, JOSEPH EDWARD, JR., b. Dallas, Jan. 4, 1940; B.S., U. Houston, 1965, J.D., 1967. Admitted to Tex. bar, 1966, Colo. bar, 1968; individual practice law, Aspen, Colo., 1968-70; mem. firm Shellman, Carney & Edwards, Aspen, individual practice law, Aspen, 1971—; commr. Pitkin County (Colo.), 1973—. Mem. Tex., Colo. bar assns. Office: PO Box 1541 Wheeler Opera House Aspen CO 81611 Tel (303) 925-7116

EDWARDS, KNIGHT, b. Providence, Dec. 22, 1923; A.B., Brown U., 1945; LL.B., Harvard, 1948. Admitted to R.I. bar, 1949; asso. firm Edwards & Angell, Providence, 1948-56, partner, 1956—; dir. Freedom Fund, Independence Fund, Boston, 1974—; dir. Travelers Equities Fund, Hartford, 1968—. Trustee Loomis Inst., Windsor, Conn., 1967—; pres., bd. trustees Providence Pub. Library, 1973—; hon. trustee Andover-Newton Theol. Sch., 1969—; trustee emeritus Brown U., 1976—. Mem. R.I., Am. bar assns. Office: 2700 Hospital Trust Tower Providence RI 02903 Tel (401) 274-9200

EDWARDS, MAX NIXON, b. Wichita, Kans., Dec. 4, 1921; A.B., Dartmouth Coll., 1947; LL.B., U. Ariz., 1950. Admitted to N.Mex. bar, 1950, Ariz. bar, 1950, U.S. Supreme Ct. bar, 1960, D.C. bar, 1969; practiced law, Hobbs, N.Mex., 1950, 54-60; mem. firm Edwards & Reese, 1954-60; asst. dist. atty. 5th Jud. Dist. N.Mex., 1951-53; gen. counsel N.Mex. Senate, 1959; asst. to sec., legis. counsel Dept. Interior, Washington, 1961-67, asst. sec. water quality and research, 1967-69; partner firm Shannon, Rill, Edwards & Scott, Washington, 1969—; trustee Environics Internat., Notre Dame, Ind., 1969—. Mem. Am., Inter-Am., N.Mex., Ariz., D.C. bar assns. Author: Role of Federal Government in Controlling Oil Pollution at Sea from Oil on the Sea, 1969; Oil Pollution and the Law from Oil Pollution, 1969; recipient Distinguished Service medal Dept. Interior, 1967. Home: 2905 P St NW Washington DC 20007 Office: 1055 Thomas Jefferson St NW Suite 308 Washington DC 20007 Tel (202) 337-6000

EDWARDS, ROBERT BROOKS, b. Knoxville, Tenn., Nov. 7, 1937; B.S., U. Richmond, 1958; LL.B., U. Va., 1962. Admitted to Va. bar, 1962; served with JAG Corps., U.S. Army, 1963-66; partner firm Edwards & Edwards, Smithfield, Va., 1966—; judge Isle of Wight County (Va.) Gen. Dist. Ct., 5th Jud. Dist., now chief judge. Active Smithfield Baptist Ch. Mem. Va. State Bar, Va. State Bar Assn., Assn.

Judges. Home: 209 Moonefield Dr Smithfield VA 23430 Office: 302 Main St Smithfield VA 23430 Tel (804) 357-3834

EDWARDS, VERN DOWNING, b. Superior, Wis., May 23, 1916; LL.B., U. Wis., 1939, Ph.D., 1968, LL.D., 1968. Admitted to Wis. bar, 1939; atty. tax dept. Wis. Dept. Revenue, Madison, 1940-45; mem. firm Edwards, Becker, Lynch, Parke & Heim, LaCrosse, Wis., 1945—; pub. advisor to Regional Commrs. Office, Chgo., 1968-69, to legis. counsel State of Wis., 1974-75; chmn. bd. Coulee State Bank, LaCrosse, 1962—. Mem. Am. Bar Assn. Contbr. articles to legal jours. Home: 1327 Cass St La Crosse WI 54601 Office: 502 Exchange Bldg La Crosse WI 54601 Tel (608) 784-1605

EFIRD, ROBERT EARL, b. Albemarle, N.C., Feb. 19, 1908; student Wake Forest (N.C.) Coll. (now in Winston-Salem, N.C.), 1927-29. Admitted to N.C. bar, 1929; practiced in Albemarle, 1929-42; with VA Regional Office for N.C., Winston-Salem, 1945-72, adjudicator-clk. div. finance, 1951-56, adjudication clk., 1956-72. Mem. panel Better Bus. Bur., Winston-Salem, 1974-76. Mem. N.C. Bar Assn. Home: 1069 Irving St Winston-Salem NC 27103 Tel (919) 722-3342

EFRON, SAMUEL, b. Lansford, Pa., May 6, 1915; B.A., Lehigh U., 1935; LL.B., Harvard, 1938. Admitted to Pa. bar, 1938, D.C. bar, 1949, N.Y. bar, 1967; atty. forms and regulations div., SEC, Washington, 1939-40; office solicitor U.S. Dept. Labor, Washington, 1940-42; asst. chief real and personal property sect. Office Alien Property, U.S. Dept. Justice, Washington, 1942-43, chief debt claims and asst. chief claims branch, 1946-51; asst. gen. counsel internat. security affairs U.S. Dept. Def., Washington, 1951-53, cons., 1953-54; partner firm Surrey, Karasik, Gould & Efron, Washington, 1954-61; exec. v.p. Parsons & Whittemore, Inc., N.Y.C., 1961-68; partner firm Arent, Fox, Kintner, Plotkin & Kahn, Washington, 1968—. Mem. Am., Fed., Inter-Am., D.C. bar assns., Am. Soc. Internat. Law, Assn. Bar City N.Y., Soc. for Internat. Devel., Phi Beta Kappa. Decorated Order of the Lion, Finland, 1975; author: The Military Assistance Program and the Mobilization Base, 1953; Foreign Taxes on U.S. Expenditures, 1954; The Payment of American Creditors from Vested Assets, 1948; The Operation of Investment Incentive Laws with Emphasis on the U.S. of A. and Mexico, 1977. Home: 3537 Ordway St NW Washington DC 20016 Office: 1815 H St NW Washington DC 20006 Tel (202) 857-6275

EFTHIMIOU, GUS, JR., b. Miami, Fla., Sept. 23, 1926; J.D., U. Miami, 1951. Admitted to Fla. bar, 1951; individual practice law, Miami, 1951—; fee counsel SBA, 1963-64; asst. atty. gen. State of Fla., 1965-71; gen. counsel Clerk of Ct. Dade County (Fla.), 1973—; gen. counsel Miami Inter-City Bd., Inc., 1973—, Miami River Regatta, 1973—. Mem. econ. adv. bd. City of Miami, 1962-66. Mem. Fla., Dade County bar assns., Am. Arbitration Assn., S. Miami C. of C. Office: 807 duPont Bldg 169 E Flagler St Miami FL 33131 Tel (305) 373-0602

EFURD, ROBERT T., JR., b. Atlanta, May 28, 1932; B.B.A., Ga. State U., 1958, M.B.A., 1960; LL.B., Emory U., 1953. Admitted to Ga. bar, 1953; individual practice law, Atlanta. C.P.C.U. Home: 460 Riverside Pkwy NW Atlanta GA 30328 Office: 1010 First Federal Bldg Atlanta GA 30303 Tel (404) 522-7144

EGAN, EDWARD JOSEPH, b. Southington, Conn., Aug. 9, 1913; A.B., Cath. U., 1939; J.D. Admitted to N.Y. bar, 1942, D.C. bar, 1940; asso. firm Egan & Weitzner, 1946-56; partner firm Egan & Bliss, 1956-74; individual practice law, N.Y.C., 1974—; counsel firm Plunkett, Wetzel & Jaffee, N.Y.C., 1976—, East Hudson Pkwy. Authority, Westchester County, N.Y., 1960—. Trustee Iona Coll., Saints John and Paul Ch.; bd. dirs. New Rochelle Hosp. Med. Center. Mem. Am., N.Y., Westchester County bar assns. Home: 33 Byron Ln Larchmont NY 10538 Office: 250 Park Ave New York City NY 10017 Tel (212) 986-7420

EGAN, JAMES B., b. Chgo., Oct. 25, 1914; LL.B., John Marshall, 1937, J.D., 1970; B.S., DePaul Univ., 1939. Admitted to Ill. bar, 1937, since practiced in Chgo.; individual practice law, 1937-47, 72—; mem. firm West & Egan, 1947-71. Bd. dirs. Chgo. Regional Blood Program. Mem. Ill. Bar Assn. Home: 11415 S Maplewood St Chicago IL 60655 Office: 11750 S Western Ave Chicago IL 60643 Tel (312) 239-6800

EGAN, JAMES EDMUND, b. Chgo., Aug. 29, 1945; B.S. in Mktg., U. Ill., 1968; J.D., Chgo-Kent Coll. Law Ill. Inst. Tech., 1973. Admitted to Ill. bar, 1973; asso. firm Galowich, Galowich, McSteen & Phelan, Joliet, Ill., 1973—; asst. pub. defender Will County, Ill., 1974—. Mem. Am., Ill. State, Will County bar assns. Home: 525 Cornelia St Joliet IL 60435 Office: 57 N Ottawa St Joliet IL 60431 Tel (815) 727-4575

EGAN, JOHN JOSEPH, b. Springfield, Mass., Sept. 25, 1945; A.B., Holy Cross Coll., 1966; J.D., Boston Coll., 1969. Admitted to Mass. bar, 1969; partner firm Egan, Flanagan & Egan, Springfield, 1969—; pub. defender Hampden County (Mass.), Springfield, 1970-72, spl. asst. dist. atty. Western Dist. Mass., 1974-75; spl. asst. atty. gen. Commonwealth of Mass., 1976—; instr. law Western New Eng. Coll., 1973-75. Bd. dirs. Springfield Boys' Club, Heart Assn. Western Mass., Alcoholism Services Greater Springfield, Goodwill Industries Hartford-Springfield, Hope Home Western Mass. Mem. Am., Mass., Hampden County bar assns. Home: 18 Duxbury Ln Longmeadow MA 01106 Office: 31 Elm St Springfield MA 01103 Tel (413) 737-0269

EGAN, MICHAEL JOSEPH, b. Savannah, Ga., Aug. 8, 1926; A.B., Yale U., 1950; LL.B. cum laude, Harvard U., 1955. Admitted to Ga. bar, 1955, D.C. bar, 1961; asso. firm Sutherland, Asbill & Brennan, Atlanta and Washington, 1955-61, partner, 1961—; lectr. in law Emory U., 1958-59; mem. Ga. Ho. of Reps., 1965-77, minority leader, 1971-77; asso. atty. gen. U.S., 1977—. Mem. State Bar Ga., Am., Atlanta bar assns., Lawyers Club Atlanta, Am. Coll. Probate Counsel. Chief reporter Am. Bar Assn.-Am. Law Inst. publ. Problems of Federal Taxation of Estates-Gifts-Trusts, 1966.

EGER, HARVEY JAY, b. Nevada City, Calif., Oct. 12, 1943; B.B.A., Kent State U., 1967; J.D., Duquesne U., 1970; LL.M., N.Y.U., 1971. Admitted to Pa. bar, 1970; asso. firm Berkman Ruslander Pohl Lieber & Engel, Pitts., 1971-76; gen. counsel Resource Investments, Inc., Pitts, 1976-77; adj. prof. Robert Morris Coll., 1977—; lectr. Pa. Bar Inst.; spl. cons. Tax Mgmt., Inc. Mem. Am., Pa., Allegheny County bar assns., Allegheny Tax Soc. (past chmn., mem. exec. bd.). Contbr. articles to legal jours. Home: 18 Ridgecrest Dr Pittsburgh PA 15235 Office: 1215 Frick Bldg Pittsburgh PA 15219 Tel (412) 281-1980

EGGERS, WILLIAM JACOB, III, b. Oakland, Calif., Feb. 18, 1939; B.A., U. Calif., Berkeley, 1962; LL.B., J.D. (Dept. Interior scholar), Hastings Coll., San Francisco, 1966. Admitted to Hawaii bar, 1967, U.S. Supreme Ct. bar, 1973; adminstrv. asst. Dillingham Corp., Honolulu, 1966-67; dep. pros. atty. City and County of Hololulu, 1967-69; sr. counsel Hawaii Office Consumer Protection, 1969-72; asst. U.S. atty. Dist. Hawaii, Honolulu, 1972—; mem. Honolulu Pacific Fed. Exec. Bd., 1972—; organized crime and racketeering liaison atty. Dept. Justice, Honolulu, 1972—. Trustee, Honolulu Theatre for Youth, 1972-73. Mem. Fed. Bar Assn. (pres. local chpt. 1975-76), Am. Trial Lawyers Assn., Am. Judicature Soc., Phi Delta Phi. Home: 1016 Kealoolu Ave Honolulu HI 96816 Office: 320 Federal Bldg Honolulu HI 96809 Tel (808) 546-7170

EGLER, FREDERICK NORTON, b. Pitts., May 27, 1922; B.A., Duquesne U., 1943; LL.B., U. Pitts., 1947. Admitted to Pa. bar, 1948; mem. firm Egler & Reinstadtler, Pitts., 1948—. Chmn. bd. dirs. Allegheny County (Pa.) Sanitary Authority, Pitts., 1974—. Fellow Am. Coll. Trial Lawyers, Internat. Acad. Trial Lawyers; mem. Internat. Assn. Ins. Counsel, Acad. Trial Lawyers of Alleghany County (pres. 1968), Am., Pa., Allegheny County (bd. govs. 1967-69) bar assns., 3d Circuit Judicial Conf. (del.). Office: 2100 Lawyers Bldg Pittsburgh PA 15219 Tel (412) 281-9810

EGLIT, HOWARD CHARLES, b. Chgo., Sept. 20, 1942; B.A., U. Mich., 1963; J.D., U. Chgo., 1967. Admitted to Ill. bar, 1967, D.C. bar, 1972, 7th Circuit Ct. Appeals bar, 1973, No. Dist. Ill. bar, 1973; instr. law U. Mich., 1967-68; atty. Office Gen. Counsel, OEO, Washington, 1968-69; legislative asst. Rep. William F. Ryan, Washington, 1969-71; counsel com. on the judiciary U.S. Ho. of Reps., Washington, 1971-73; legal dir. Roger Baldwin Found., ACLU, Chgo., 1973-75; asso. prof. Ill. Inst. Tech.-Chgo. Kent Coll. Law, 1975—. Bd. dirs. John Howard Assn., Chgo., 1975-77. Mem. Chgo. Council Lawyers (gov. 1976—), Phi Beta Kappa, Order of Coif. Contbr. articles in field to profl. jours. Office: 77 S Wacker Dr Chicago IL 60606 Tel (312) 567-5000

EHRHARDT, CHARLES WINTON, b. Elkader, Iowa, Oct. 24, 1940; B.S., Iowa State U., 1962; J.D., U. Iowa, 1964. Admitted to Iowa bar, 1964, Fla. bar, 1972; law clerk to Hon. M.D. Van Dosterhout, U.S. Ct. Appeals, St. Louis, Mo., 1964-65; asst. U.S. Atty. No. Dist. Iowa, Sioux City, 1965-67; asst. prof. law Fla. State U., Tallahassee, 1967-70, asso. prof., 1970-74, prof., 1974—; reporter on evidence code Fla. Law Revision Council, 1973—. Named Outstanding Prof. Fla. State U. Coll. Law, 1971. Home: 3700 Bellwood Dr Tallahassee FL 32303 Office: Coll Law Fla State U Tallahassee FL 32306 Tel (904) 644-4010

EHRHART, JOHN HESSE, b. Quincy, Ill., Feb. 27, 1945; A.B., U. Detroit, 1967; J.D., U. Iowa, 1970. Admitted to Iowa bar, 1970; law clk. chief judge U.S. Dist. Ct. No. Dist. Iowa, Cedar Rapids, 1970-72; asst. dir. Linn County Legal Assistance, Cedar Rapids, 1972-75; asst. county atty. Linn County, Cedar Rapids, 1975—; partner firm Fisher, Yarowsky, Martin & Ehrhart, Cedar Rapids, 1972—. Dir., Citizens Com. Alcohol and Drug Abuse, 1972—. Mem. Am., Iowa (com. lawyer referral and legal aid 1974—), Linn County bar assns. Home: 2303 26th St Dr SE Cedar Rapids IA 52403 Office: 420 Paramount Bldg Cedar Rapids IA 52401 Tel (319) 366-7794

EHRLICH, BERNARD HERBERT, b. Washington, Apr. 3, 1927; LL.B., George Washington U., 1949, M.A., 1950. Admitted to D.C. bar, 1949; asso. firm Posner, Berge, Fox & Arent, Washington, 1947-52; partner firm Posner & Ehrlich, Washington, 1952-63; individual practice law, Washington, 1963—; legal counsel Nat. Home Study Council, 1950—, Nat. Assn. Trade and Tech. Schs., 1965—, Nat. Assn. Cosmetology Schs., 1968—, Inst. Indsl. Launderers, 1958—. Mem. Pres.'s Commn. on Employment of Handicapped, 1965-69. Mem. Am. Bar Assn., Bar Assn. of D.C., Phi Beta Kappa, Nu Beta Epsilon. Home: 507 Bonifant St Silver Spring MD 20910 Office: 919 18th St NW Washington DC 20006

EHRLICH, CHARLES WALTER, b. Istanbul, Turkey, Nov. 4, 1944; B.A., Dickinson Coll., Carlisle, Pa. 1967; J.D., Stetson U., 1971. Admitted to Fla. bar, 1971; asst. state's atty. Fla. 6th Jud. Circuit, St. Petersburg, 1971-72; asso. firm John A. Lloyd, Jr., St. Petersburg, 1972-74; individual practice law, St. Petersburg, 1974—. Mem. Pinellas County (Fla.) Opportunity Council, 1975-76. Mem. Am. Bar Assn., Fla. Bar, Am. Arbitration Assn., Fla., Pinellas acads. trial lawyers, Pinellas Criminal Def. Lawyers. Office: 4753 Central Ave Saint Petersburg FL 33713 Tel (813) 381-0454

EHRLICH, GERD WILLIAM, b. Berlin, June 22, 1922; student U. Geneva (Switzerland), 1944-46; B.A., Coll. Idaho, 1948; M.A., State U. Wash., 1950; J.D., U. Md., 1954; Ph.D., Johns Hopkins U., 1972. Admitted to Md. bar, 1954; partner firm Ehrlich, Evelius & Blosfelds, Balt., 1954-59; asst. prof. law Morgan State U., 1949-54; asso. prof. Essex Community Coll., 1959-66; prof. Towson State U., 1966—; guest prof. Padagogische Hochschule, Berlin, 1973-74, U. Bamberg (Germany), summer 1976. Mem. Am. Bar Assn., AAUP, Am. Polit. Sci. Assn. Author: Gegenwrst im Ruckblick, 1971. Office: Towson State U Towson MD 21204 Tel (301) 823-2956

EICHEL, CHARLES RICHARD, b. N.Y.C., June 16, 1932; A.B., Williams Coll., 1954; LL.B., N.Y.U., 1957. Admitted to N.Y. bar, 1957, Fla. bar, 1958, U.S. Supreme Ct., 1967, Vt. bar, 1973. individual practice law, N.Y.C., 1960—, Manchester Center, Vt., 1973—. Sec., bd. govs., Boys Athletic League, Inc., N.Y.C., 1961—; bd. trustee Ethan Allen Community Coll., Manchester Center, Vt., 1975—. Mem. Vt., Fla. bar assns., N.Y., Bennington County lawyers assns. Home: Route 30 South Dorset VT 05263 Office: 71 Park Ave New York City NY 10016 also Main St Manchester Center VT 05255 Tel (212) 689-1338 also (802) 362-2410

EICHELBAUM, MELVIN N., b. N.Y.C., Aug. 3, 1942; A.A., San Antonio Coll., 1962; B.B.A., St. Mary's U., 1964; J.D., U. Tex., 1967. Admitted to Tex. bar, 1967, U.S. Supreme Ct. bar, 1971; since practiced in San Antonio, Tex.; mem. Bexar County Legal Aid Assn., 1968-72, mem. firm Adams, Eichelbaum & Sanders, 1972-75, LeLaurin, Adams, Eichelbaum & Sanders, 1975—; municipal judge city of Leon Valley, Tex., 1976—. City Councilman Leon Valley, Tex., 1974-76. Mem. Tex., San Antonio bar assns., Tex., Am. trial lawyers, Commercial Law League Am. Contbr. articles to legal jours. Home: 6127 Forest Wood San Antonio TX 78240 Office: 2100 Alamo Nat Bldg San Antonio TX 78205 Tel (512) 226-4131

EICHLER, JOHN ALFRED, b. Wash., D.C., Jan. 28, 1935; B.S., U. Md., 1957; J.D. with honors, George Wash. U., 1962; LL.M., Harvard, 1964. Admitted to Md. bar, 1962, D.C. bar, 1964, Tex. bar, 1973, Va. bar, 1975, U.S. Supreme Ct. bar, 1972; law clk. judge Oscar H. Davis, U.S. Ct. Claims, Washington, 1962-63; asso. firm Arnold & Porter, Wash., D.C., 1964-69; individual practice law, Rockville, Md., 1969-72; asso. firm Stalcup, Johnson, Meyers & Miller, Dallas, 1972-74; atty. Ethyl Corp., Richmond, Va., 1974—. Mem. Am., Va., Richmond City, D.C. bar assns., Tax. Execs. Inst., Am. Inst. CPA's, Order of Coif. Office: 330 S 4th St Richmond VA 23219 Tel (804) 644-6081

EICHSTEADT, HAROLD ALVIN, b. Wautoma, Wis., July 8, 1917; student Tulane U., 1946-49, Willamette U., 1949-50; J.D., Willamette U., 1950. Admitted to Oreg. bar, 1950; individual practice law, Woodburn, Oreg., 1950-69; partner firm Eichsteadt, Bolland & Engle, Woodburn, 1969—; reviser Oreg. Statutes, 1950-53; city atty. Woodburn, 1953-59, Gervais, Oreg., 1953-67, Hubbard, Oreg., 1953-67; justice peace, Woodburn, 1955-57; atty. SSS, 1968-72; spl. asst. U.S. Atty. San Francisco, 1971-72. Mem. Marion County, Oreg., Am. bar assns., Ky. Cols., Phi Delta Phi. Office: 345 N 2d St Woodburn OR 97071 Tel (503) 981-0155

EIDE, ALLEN JULLEEN, b. Ramona, S.D., Nov. 17, 1946; B.S. in History, S.D. State U., 1968; J.D. cum laude, U. S.D., 1971. Admitted to S.D. bar, 1971; asso. firm Gribbin Burns & Eide, Watertown, S.D., 1973-74, partner, 1975—; dep. states atty. Codington County (S.D.), 1977—. Mem. State Bar S.D., Codington County (sec.-treas. 1974—) bar assns. Recipient award Outstanding Student Article, S.D. Law Rev., 1971. Office: 6 1/2 S Broadway Watertown SD 57201 Tel (605) 886-5885

EIDEM, RAYMOND WILMAR, b. Fargo, N.D., Jan. 19, 1915; Ph.B., U. Toledo, 1942, J.D., 1956. Admitted to Ohio bar, 1957; dist. mgr. Social Security Adminstrn., Steubenville, Ohio, 1958-71, retired, 1971. Home: 803 Euclid Ave Toronto OH 43964

EIGENBROD, WALTER FREDERICK, b. New Orleans, Dec. 5, 1912; B.A., La. State U., 1935; J.D., Tulane U., 1941. Admitted to La. bar, 1941, Ala. bar, 1947; individual practice law, Huntsville, Ala., 1947—; mem. Presdl. Emergency Bd., 1962; adv. 5th session Trade and Devel. Bd., UN Conf. Trade and Devel., Geneva, 1967; mem. arbitration panel Fed. Mediation and Conciliation Service. Mem. Huntsville-Madison County (pres. 1963-64), La., Ala., Am. (mem. com. on labor arbitration and law of collective bargaining agreements, com. internat. labor law) bar assns., Nat. Acad. Arbitrators, Am. Arbitration Assn. (labor and comml. arbitration panel), Am. Trial Lawyers Assn. Home: 1009 Cleermont Dr Huntsville AL 35801 Office: 508 Terry Hutchens Bldg Huntsville AL 35801 Tel (205) 539-2771

EIGER, NORMAN NATHAN, b. Chgo., Aug. 6, 1903; LL.D., DePaul U., 1924. Admitted to Ill. bar, 1924; mem. exec. staff, capital stock tax assessor, atty. Ill. Tax Commn., 1932-36; asst. to corp. counsel City of Chgo., 1936-47; chmn. Ill. Bd. Rev., Dept. of Labor, 1948-52; judge Mcpl. Ct. of Chgo., 1952-64; asso. judge Circuit Ct. of Cook County, 1964—, circuit judge, 1971—; lectr. DePaul U. Coll. Law. Hon. life trustee Temple Isaiah Israel; exec. sec. Patriotic Found. of Chgo.; v.p. Adult Edn. Council Met. Chgo.; v.p., trustee Coll. Jewish Studies; v.p., hon. life trustee Bd. Jewish Edn.; chmn. Lawyers div. Combined Jewish Appeal; v.p. Chgo. B'nai B'rith Council, past pres. Jackson Park lodge; past co-chmn. Conciliation Commn., Chgo. Fedn., United Am. Hebrew Congregations. Mem. Am. Assn. Arbitration, Ill., Chgo. bar assns., Ill. Asso. Judges Assn. (past pres.), Ill. Judges Assn. (dir., chmn. ann. conv. 1973-77), Ill. Inst. Continuing Edn. (com. family law), Nu Beta Epsilon (grand chancellor), Alpha Epsilon Pi. Home: 505 N Lake Shore Dr Chicago IL 60611 Office: 11 S LaSalle St Chicago IL 60602

EILERS, JOHN WAGNER, JR., b. Cin., Nov. 21, 1939; B.A. in Econs., Marietta Coll., 1961; J.D., Chase Coll. Law, 1967. Admitted to Ohio, Fed., U.S. Supreme Ct. bars, 1967; asst. to Hamilton County (Ohio) pros. atty., 1968-69; asso. Paxton & Seasongood, Cin., 1969-74; trust officer Fifth Third Bank Cin., 1974—; lectr. in field; participant Ohio Continuing Legal Edn. Seminars. Trustee, Counsel Better Housing League, Cin., 1972—; trustee Multiple Sclerosis Soc., Cin., 1974—. Mem. Am., Cin., Ohio bar assns. Home: 1131 Beverly Hill Dr Cincinnati OH 45226 Office: PO Box 478 Trust Div Cincinnati OH 45201

EINHORN, HERBERT ARTHUR, b. N.Y.C., Feb. 5, 1913; A.B. cum laude, Ohio U., 1933; LL.B., Columbia U., 1935. Admitted to N.Y. State bar, 1935; sr. counsel investigation Ins. Fund, N.Y. State, 1938-40, spl. counsel, 1940-41; asst. atty. gen. N.Y. State, 1943-46; sr. partner firm Aranow, Brodsky, Bohlinger, Benetar & Einhorn, N.Y.C., 1946—; lectr. Am. Mgmt. Assn., Practising Law Inst. Chmn. bd. dirs. Camp Loyaltown, N.Y.C. and Huntertown, N.Y., 1965—; mem. Trustees Acad., Ohio U., 1966—. Mem. Assn. Bar City N.Y., N.Y. County Lawyers Assn., N.Y. State, Am. bar assns., Fed. Bar Council. Author: (with Edward R. Aranow) Proxy Contests for Corporate Control, 1957, rev. edit., 1963; Tender Offers for Corporate Control, 1973; contbr. articles to profl. publs. Home: 12 Glen Eagles Dr Larchmont NY 10538 Office: 469 Fifth Ave New York City NY 10017 Tel (212) 889-1470

EINHORN, JOSEPH HAROLD, b. N.Y.C., May 1, 1906; A.B., Union Coll., 1928; LL.B./J.D., Albany Law Sch., 1931. Admitted to N.Y. bar, 1932, U.S. Supreme Ct. bar, 1965, U.S. Immigration Appeals bar, 1948, ICC bar, 1958; partner firm Halter, Sullivan & Einhorn, Albany, N.Y., 1933-42; individual practice law, Albany, 1943—. Referee incompetent accounts Albany County, 1935-45; mem. Albany County Bd. Suprs., 1966-68, Albany County Democratic Com., 1935-70. Mem. Am., N.Y. State, Albany County bar assns., Assn. Immigration and Nationality Lawyers, Am. Trial Lawyers Assn., Chem. Warfare Vets. Assn. (nat. judge adv.), Am. Legion. Recipient Covenant award for Humanitarian Service, B'nai B'rith, 1953. Home: 152 Rosemont St Albany NY 12206 Office: 90 State St Albany NY 12207 Tel (518) 465-1431

EISELE, GARNETT THOMAS, b. Hot Springs, Ark., Nov. 3, 1923; student U. Fla., 1940-42, Ind. U., 1942-43; A.B., Washington U., 1947; LL.B., Harvard, 1950, LL.M., 1951. Admitted to Ark. bar, practiced in Hot Springs, 1951-52, Little Rock, 1953-69; asso. firm Wootten, Land and Matthews, 1951-52, Owens, McHaney, Lofton & McHaney, 1956-60; asst. U.S. atty., Little Rock, 1953-55; individual practice, 1961-69; U.S. dist. judge, Little Rock, 1970—, now chief judge; legal adviser to gov. Ark., 1966-69. Del. Ark. 7th Constl. Conv., 1969-70. Trustee U. Ark., 1969-70. Mem. Am., Ark., Pulaski County bar assns., Am. Judicature Soc. Home: 7 Cantrell Rd Little Rock AR 72207 Office: US Post Office and Courthouse Little Rock AR 72203*

EISEN, SOLOMON SIDNEY, b. N.Y.C., Sept. 12, 1911; B.S., Fordham U., 1932, LL.B., 1934; Admitted to N.Y. bar, 1934, U.S. Dist. Ct. So. Dist. N.Y., 1944, U.S. Supreme Ct. bar, 1945, U.S. Dist. Ct. Eastern Dist. N.Y. bar, 1956, U.S. Dist. Ct. Eastern Dist. Mich., 1944, U.S. Ct. Appeals, 1976; since practiced in N.Y.C.; assoc. firm Milton P. Bauman Assocs., 1935-41, sr. partner, 1941—; partner Eisen & Mitchell, 1965—. Mem. Assn. interstate Commerce Commn. Practitioners, Motor Carriers Lawyers Assn., Traffic Club of N.Y., Am. Soc. of Traffic & Transportation, Inc. Speaker various insts. and

Seminars. Home: 7510 193rd St Flushing NY 11366 Office: 370 Lexington Ave New York City NY 10017 Tel (212) 532-5100

EISENBERG, DAVID STANLEY, b. Atlanta, Feb. 21, 1925; LL.B., U. Ga., 1950. Admitted to Ga. bar; since practiced in Atlanta, asso. firm McKenzie & Kaler, 1950-52, mem. firm Parks & Eisenberg, 1953-73, mem. firm Parks, Eisenberg & Weinstein, 1973—. Home: 1724 Dunwoody Terr NE Atlanta GA 30324 Office: 455 E Paces Ferry Rd NE Atlanta GA 30305 Tel (404) 261-6442

EISENBERG, LAWRENCE HENRY, b. Los Angeles, Jan. 16, 1936; A.A., Los Angeles City Coll., 1958; B.S. in Pub. Accounting, U. So. Calif., 1962, J.D., 1966. Auditor, GAO, Los Angeles, 1962-63; admitted to Calif. bar, 1966, U. S. Supreme Ct. bar, 1970; asso. firm Ward & Heyler, Beverly Hills and Century City, Calif., 1966-71; individual practice law, Sherman Oaks, Calif., 1971—; examiner Calif. State Bar, 1970-72, mem. local adminstrv. com., 1972-74; judge pro tempore Los Angeles and Beverly Hills municipal cts., 1972—; examiner Los Angeles Police Dept. oral selection unit, 1973—. Bd. dirs. Legion Lex, U. So. Calif. Law Center support group, 1970—. Mem. Am., Calif., Los Angeles County, Beverly Hills, San Fernando Valley bar assns., Calif. Acad. Appellate Lawyers, Phi Alpha Delta. Office: 14724 Ventura Blvd Sherman Oaks CA 91316 Tel (213) 788-0354

EISENBERG, MEYER, b. Bklyn., Dec. 15, 1931; B.A., Bklyn. Coll., 1953; LL.B., Columbia, 1958. Admitted to N.Y. State bar, 1960, D.C. bar, 1970, U.S. Supreme Ct. bar, 1963; law clk. to Chief Justice William McAllister, Supreme Ct., Oreg., Salem, 1958-59; atty. SEC, Washington, 1959-70, asst. gen. counsel, 1966-68, exec. asst. to chmn., 1968-69, asso. gen. counsel, 1969-70; with firm Lawler, Kent & Eisenberg, Washington, 1970—; cons. in field; adj. prof. law George Washington U., 1972-75. Mem. Md. Commn. Aid to Non-Pub. Schs., 1968-70; chmn.; Nat. Law Commn.; mem. Nat. Civil Rights Exec. Com., Anti-Defamation League of B'nai B'rith. Mem. Fed., Am., D.C. bar assns. Contbr. to publs. in field. Office: 1156 15th St NW Washington DC 20005 Tel (202) 293-2240

EISENBERG, ROBERT ST., b. Jersey City, Apr. 8, 1931; B.A., Brandeis U., 1953; J.D., N.Y. U., 1957. Admitted to N.J. bar, 1958, U.S. Supreme Ct. bar, 1964; asst. prosecutor Hudson County, N.J., 1963-65; individual practice law, Jersey City, 1958—. Vice pres., legal counsel Leukemia Soc. N.J., 1963-65; bd. dirs. Central Jersey Jewish Fedn., 1973-76. Mem. N.J. (mem. correction reform com.), Hudson County (chmn. com. municipal cts.) bar assns., Nat. Assn. Criminal Def. Lawyers, Trial Attys. N.J. Office: 26 Journal Sq Jersey City NJ 07306 Tel (201) 653-5159

EISENDRATH, RALPH HENRY, b. Chgo., Dec. 31, 1906; LL.B., Chgo.-Kent Coll. Law, 1939, J.D., 1969. Admitted to Ill. bar, 1939, U.S. Ct. Appeals bar, 1959, U.S. Supreme Ct. bar, 1965; individual practice law, Chgo., 1939—; gen. counsel Kenwood C. of C. Bd. trustees Du Sable Mus., Chgo. Fellow Am. Acad. Matrimonial Lawyers; mem. Chgo., Ill. State, Am. bar assns. Recipient Good Neighbor award Hyde Park-Kenwood Community Conf., 1955. Home: 5232 Hyde Park Blvd Chicago IL 60615 Office: 5232 Hyde Park Blvd Chicago IL 60615 Tel (312) MU4-5050

EISENSTEIN, STANLEY, b. Chgo., Nov. 30, 1946; B.A., U. Ill., 1968, J.D., 1973. Admitted to Ill. bar, 1973; asso. firm Harold E. Collins & Assos., Chgo., 1973-74; asso. firm Katz & Friedman, Chgo., 1974—. Mem. Ill. State, Chgo. bar assns., Decalogue Soc. Home: 1327 W Greenleaf St Chicago IL 60626 Office: 7 S Dearborn St Chicago IL 60603 Tel (312) 263-6330

EISWERT, LEONARD JAMES, b. Balt., Mar. 22, 1943; B.S., Loyola Coll., Balt., 1965; J.D., U. Balt., 1972. Admitted to Md. bar, 1972; asst. state's atty. Baltimore City, 1972-77; partner firm Burnett & Eiswert, Oakland, Md., 1977—. Mem. Md., Garrett County bar assns. Home: 5100 Thomas Ave Baltimore MD 21236 Office: 1000 Thayer Center Oakland MD 21550 Tel (301) 334-9480

ELA, WILLIAM MACHARG, b. Grand Junction, Colo., May 11, 1923; LL.B., Harvard, 1949. Admitted to Colo. bar, 1949; mem. firm Adams Heckman Traylor & Ela, and predecessors, 1949-65; judge dist. ct., 1965—. Mem. county planning commn., water bd., fire bd. Mem. Am., Colo., Mesa County (Colo.) bars, Am. Judicature Soc. Home: 3142 F Rd Grand Junction CO 81501 Office: PO Box 520 Grand Junction CO 81501 Tel (303) 242-4761

ELAM, JOHN CARLTON, b. Fort Wayne, Ind., Mar. 6, 1924; B.A., U. Mich., 1948, J.D. with distinction, 1949. Admitted to Mich. bar, 1949, Ohio bar, 1950; asso. firm Vorys, Sater, Seymour & Pease, Columbus, Ohio, 1949-54, partner, 1954—, presiding partner, 1968—. Chmn. campaign United Way of Franklin County (Ohio), Inc., 1975; moderator Columbus Town Meeting; mem. com. visitors U. Mich. Law Sch. Fellow Am. Coll. Trial Lawyers (regent); mem. 6th Circuit Jud. Conf. (life), Am. (ho. of dels. and council litigation sect.), Ohio, Columbus (pres. 1964) bar assns., Assn. Ins. Attys. (pres. 1967-68), Columbus Area C. of C. (dir., chmn. bd. 1971). Home: 5000 Squirrel Bend Columbus OH 43220 Office: 52 E Gay St Columbus OH 43215 Tel (614) 464-6271

ELBER, GEORGE A., b. N.Y.C., Apr. 1, 1916; B.S., Columbia, 1936, J.D., 1937. Admitted to N.Y. bar, 1973, Calif. bar, 1968; atty. firm Davis & Gilbert, 1937-55, partner, N.Y.C., 1955-60; exec. v.p. Four Star Television, Los Angeles, 1961-67; individual practice law, Los Angeles, 1968—; lectr. assns. and clubs. Mem. Los Angeles County, Criminal Cts., San Fernando Valley Criminal Cts., Juvenile Ct. bar assns., Am. Arbitration Assn. (panel arbitrators). Author: (with others) Television Agreements, 1956; producer TV program Twenty Questions, 1952-54. Home: 148 E Chestnut Hill Pl Claremont CA 91711 Tel (213) 657-1021

ELCONIN, RICHARD CONRAD, b. Milw., Feb. 1, 1929; B.A., U. Mich., 1950, J.D., 1953. Admitted to Wis. bar 1953, Mich. bar, 1956; atty. Chrysler Corp., Highland Park, Mich., 1955-58; individual practice law, Monroe, Mich., 1958—; asso. firm Elconin, Czeryba, Dulany & Luchansky; chief asst. pros. atty. Monroe County (Mich.), 1958-60; atty. Mich. Harness Horsemen's Assn., 1963—. Mem. State Fair Campaigns Practice Commn., 1962; pres. Monroe Sertoma Club, 1963. Mem. Monroe County Bar Assn. Office: 31 Washington St Monroe MI 48161 Tel (313) 242-3434 also 8078 Secor Rd Lambertville MI 48144 Tel (313) 856-6755

ELDEN, GARY MICHAEL, b. Chgo., Dec. 11, 1944; B.A., U. Ill., 1966; J.D., Harvard, 1969. Admitted to Ill. bar, 1969, U.S. Supreme Ct. bar, 1973; partner firm Kirkland & Ellis, Chgo., 1969—. Mem. Chgo. (sec. com. appellate rules 1975-76), Am., Ill. State bar assns., Chgo. Council Lawyers, Appellate Lawyers Assn. (dir. 1975-76). Home: 3020 N Sheridan Rd Chicago IL 60657 Office: 200 E Randolph Dr Chicago IL 60601 Tel (312) 861-2192

ELDER, JAMES ROBERT, b. Tulsa, Aug. 16, 1946; A.A., Okla. Mil. Acad., 1967; B.A., Northeastern State Coll., 1969; J.D., Tulsa U., 1971. Admitted to Okla. bar, 1972; individual practice law, Tulsa, 1972; asso. firm Morehead, Savage, O'Donnell, McNulty & Cleverdon, Tulsa, 1973—; atty. City Jenks (Okla.), 1975—. Mem. Okla. Trial Lawyers Assn., Am. Judicature Soc., Am., Okla., Tulsa bar assns. Office: 201 W 5th St Suite 500 Tulsa OK 74103 Tel (918) 584-4716

ELDREDGE, LAURENCE HOWARD, b. Cold Spring, N.J., Mar. 18, 1902; B.S., Lafayette Coll., 1924, Litt. D., 1970; J.D., U. Pa., 1927. Admitted to Pa. bar, 1928, U.S. Supreme Ct. bar, 1933, Calif. bar, 1972; asso. firm Roberts & Montgomery, Phila., 1927-38; prof. law Temple U., 1928-33, adj. prof. law, 1947-52; prof. law U. Pa., 1938-44; partner firm Norris, Lex, Hart & Eldredge, Phila., 1944-56; individual practice law, Phila., 1956-71; prof. law Hastings Coll. Law, U. Calif. San Francisco, 1970—; vis. prof. law Columbia, 1941, 46; lectr. U. Pa. Med. Sch., 1940-68; reporter of decisions Supreme Ct. Pa., 1942-68; spl. dep. atty. gen. Pa., 1948-49. Mem. Am. Law Inst. (life), Am., Calif., Pa. (editor Quar. 1938-42), Phila. (chmn. bd. govs. 1960-61), San Francisco bar assns., Am. Judicature Soc., Order of Coif (pres. U. Pa. chpt. 1959-61). Author: Modern Tort Problems, 1941; Trials of a Philadelphia Lawyer, 1968; contbr. articles to law jours. Home: 3741 Broderick St San Francisco CA 94123 Office: 198 McCallister St San Francisco CA 94102 Tel (415) 557-2495

ELIAS, RAPHAEL LIVINGSTON, b. Charleston, S.C., Aug. 9, 1905; A.B., Coll. Charleston, 1925; LL.B., Harvard, 1928. Admitted to N.Y. State bar, 1928, U.S. Supreme Ct. bar, 1957; practiced in N.Y.C., 1928—; asso. firm Leo Oppenheimer and successors, 1928-35; sr. partner firm Elias Sokolski & Melzer, 1935-65, firm Elias Schewel & Schwartz, 1965—. Mem. Bar Assn. City N.Y. Home: 610 Seney Ave Mamaroneck NY 10543 Office: 122 E 42d St New York City NY 10017 Tel (212) 693-3140

ELIAS, SYLVAN HOWARD, b. N.Y.C., Feb. 20, 1909; B.A., Coll. City N.Y., 1930; LL.B., Fordham U., 1933, Dr. of Law, 1968. Admitted to N.Y. State bar, 1933, U.S. Supreme Ct. bar, 1952; individual practice law, N.Y.C., 1943; asst. corp. counsel City of N.Y., 1943-45; asso. firm Conrad & Smith, N.Y.C., 1945-49; partner firm Vladeck, Elias, Vladeck & Lewis, and predecessors, N.Y.C., 1949-74, prin., 1974—; tchr. labor relations Fairleigh Dickinson U., 1973-76; mem. panel of arbitrators N.Y., N.J. bds. mediation, Am. Arbitration Assn. Mem. Assn. Bar City N.Y., N.Y., Westchester bar assns., Am. Arbitration Assn., N.Y. County Lawyers Assn., Internat. Found. of Employee Benefit Plans. Home: 8 E 83d St New York City NY 10028 Office: 1501 Broadway St New York City NY 10036 Tel (212) 354-8330

ELIASBERG, MARTIN D., b. N.Y.C., 1934; B.A., U. Colo., 1950; LL.B., N.Y.U., 1957, J.D., 1968. Admitted to N.Y. bar, 1957; since practiced in N.Y.C., partner firm Eliasberg, Bzura & Finkelstein. Mem. Am., N.Y. State bar assns. Home: 23 Richfield St Plainview NY 11803 Office: 565 5th Ave New York City NY 10017 Tel (212) 682-1955

ELIU, E. ROMERO, b. Arrovo Hondo, N.Mex., Sept. 13, 1926; B.A., U. N.Mex., 1948; LL.B. U. Denver, 1954. Admitted to N.Mex. bar, 1956; gen. counsel 1st No. Savs. and Loan Asso. of Taos (N.Mex.), dir.; organizer Centinel Bank of Taos, counsel, chmn. bd.; owner, operator Sierra Morena Ranch, Taos Art Center; chmn. bd. Devel. Corp. of Albuquerque, Holy Cross Hosp., Taos, Embudo Presbyn. Hosp., Questa Health Center, Sangre De Cristo Health Center, San Luis, Colo., Health Center, Cuba. Chmn. N. Mex. Adv. Council to SBA; mem. SBA Adv. Council for Minority Bus. Enterprises. Mem. N.Mex. State, Am. bar assns., N.Mex., Am. trial lawyers assns., Am. Arbitration Assn., Am. Judicature Soc., Pan Am. Bankers Assn. (chmn.). Home and Office: PO Box 1932 Taos NM 87571 Tel (505) 758-2297

ELKIND, ARNOLD B., b. N.Y.C., Dec. 15, 1916; B.S., N.Y. U., 1937, LL.B., 1939. Admitted to N.Y. bar, 1939, D.C. bar, 1959; asso. Gerald F. Finley, N.Y.C., 1940-50; individual practice law, N.Y.C., 1950-55; partner firm Zelenko & Elkind, N.Y.C., 1955-65; individual practice law, N.Y.C., 1965-70; partner firm Elkind, Lampson & Sable, N.Y.C., 1973-74, Elkind & Lampson, N.Y.C., 1975—; chmn. Nat. Commn. on Product Safety, Washington, 1968-70; chmn. editorial adv. bd. Fed. Consumer Product Safety Service, Washington, 1974-76; lectr. in field. Mem. Assn. Bar City N.Y., Am., N.Y. State bar assns., Internat. Acad. Trial Lawyers, Assn. Trial Lawyers Am. (Citation of Exceptional Merit 1968). Author: (with J.W. Cotchett) Federal Courtroom Evidence, 1975. Office: 122 E 42d St New York City NY 10017 Tel (212) 986-4921

ELKOURI, FRANK, b. Byron, Okla., Sept. 3, 1921; B.A., U. Okla., 1943, LL.B., 1947; LL.M., U. Mich., 1948, S.J.D., 1951. Admitted to Okla. bar, 1947; partner firm Quinlan & Elkouri, Oklahoma City, 1948-51; enforcement atty. Nat. Wage Stablzn. Bd., Washington, 1951, Dallas, 1951-52; prof. law U. Okla., Norman, 1952—, advisor to pres. office, 1952-57; spl. justice Okla. Supreme Ct., Oklahoma City, 1967; mem. nat. def. exec. res. Dept. Labor, 1963—. Mem. Okla. Bar Assn., Nat. Acad. Arbitrators, Am. Arbitration Assn. Author: (with Edna Asper Elkouri) How Arbitration Works, 1st edit., 1952, 2d edit., 1960, 3d edit., 1973; Trade Regulation Cases and Materials, 1957; contbr. articles to legal jours. Home: 1001 Whispering Pines Dr Norman OK 73069 Office: 300 Timberdale Rd Norman OK 73019 Tel (405) 325-3911

ELLENBERG, RICHARD DENNIS, b. N.Y.C., June 9, 1947; B.A. cum laude, Brown U., 1969; J.D. cum laude, Harvard, 1972. Admitted to Ga. bar, 1972; atty. Atlanta Legal Aid Soc., Inc., 1972-76; partner firm Ellenberg, Wildau & Stagg, Atlanta, 1976—. Mem. Am., Ga., Atlanta bar assns. Recipient InterFaith, Inc. award, 1976. Office: 1950 Peachtree Summit 401 Peachtree St NW Atlanta GA 30308 Tel (404) 681-1950

ELLENBOGEN, HENRY, b. Vienna, Austria, Apr. 3, 1900; student Royal Imperial U. Vienna, 1918-21; A.B., Duquesne U., J.D., 1924. Admitted to Pa. bar, 1926; practiced in Pitts., 1926-38; mem. 73d-75th Congresses from 33d Pa. Dist.; judge Pa. Ct. of Common Pleas of Allegheny County, 1938-63, presiding judge, 1963—; adj. prof. pub. adminstrn. U. Pitts., 1972—. Mem. Allegheny County, Pa., Am., Inter-Am. bar assns., Pa. Conf. State Trail Judges, Internat. Acad. Law and Sci., Am. Judicature Soc., Assn. Former Mems. Congress, Jud. Council Pa., Nat. Conf. Metropolitan Cts. Office: 618 City-County Bldg Pittsburgh PA 15219 Tel (412) 355-5406

ELLENBOGEN, SEYMOUR, b. Elizabeth, N.J., Dec. 24, 1906; student N.Y. U., 1923-25; LL.B., Albany, Law Sch., 1928. Sr. partner firm Hirschfeld, Ellenbogen & Ellenbogen and predecessors, Albany, 1928—; admitted to N.Y. bar, 1929, U.S. Supreme Ct. bar, 1936; counsel N.Y. State Legis. Bill Drafting Commn., Albany, 1929-68. Mem. Am., N.Y. State, Albany County bar assns. Home: 82 S Pine Ave Albany NY 12208 Office: 75 State St Albany NY 12207 Tel (518) 463-6668

ELLERBEE, O. WAYNE, b. Ft. Benning, Ga., Mar. 21, 1938; B.S., Fla. State U., 1962; LL.B., U. Ga., 1965. Admitted to Ga. bar, 1965; mem. firm Young, Young & Ellerbee, Valdosta, Ga., 1965—; judge Juvenile Ct. Lowndes County (Ga.), Valdosta, 1971—. Mem. Am., Ga. bar assn., Valdosta Bar Assn. (pres. 1975). Home: 2003 Woodvalley Dr Valdosta GA 31601 Office: PO Box 820 331 N Ashley St Valdosta GA 31601 Tel (912) 242-2520

ELLETT, ALBERT HAYDEN, b. Huntsville, Ala., Feb. 4, 1898; LL.B., Blackstone Coll. Law, 1930; B.A., U. Utah, 1956. Admitted to Utah bar, 1930; individual practice law, Salt Lake City, 1930-32; mem. firm Black Ellett & Henriod, Salt Lake City, 1933; dep. county atty. Salt Lake County, 1933-34; judge Salt Lake City Ct., 1934-40, 3d Jud. Dist. Utah, 1941-66; justice Utah Supreme Ct., 1967-76, chief justice, 1977—; mem. faculty Nat. Coll. State Trial Judges, Boulder, Colo., 1964, 66, Phila., 1967; tchr. pub. schs., Tex., La. and Utah, 1916-23, prin., Lake Shore, Utah, 1920-21, 22-23. Bd. dirs. Salvation Army, Salt Lake City, Family Service Soc., Salt Lake City. Mem. Utah State Bar, Order of Coif, Phi Beta Kappa, Phi Kappa Phi. Author: (with others) Trial Judges Handbook, 1964. Home: 920 E 550 N Bountiful UT 84010 Office: 332 State Capitol Salt Lake City UT 84114 Tel (801) 533-5283

ELLICK, ALFRED GEORGE, b. Omaha, June 24, 1917; A.B., U. Mich., 1939, J.D., 1941. Admitted to Nebr. bar, 1941; asso. firm Ellick, Fitzgerald & Smith, Omaha, 1941-46; partner firm Ellick, Spire & Jones, and predecessors, Omaha, 1946—; pres. Legal Aid Soc. of Omaha, 1966-68; asso. prof. med. jurisprudence U. Nebr. Coll. Medicine, Omaha. Pres. Family and Child Service of Omaha, 1953. Mem. Omaha (pres. 1962), Nebr. State (pres. 1976), Am. bar assns. Home: 607 N 65th St Omaha NE 68132 Office: 712 Farm Credit Bldg Omaha NE 68102 Tel (402) 341-4133

ELLICKSON, ROBERT CHESTER, b. D.C., Aug. 4, 1941; A.B., Oberlin Coll., 1963; LL.B., Yale, 1966. Admitted to D.C. bar, 1967, Calif. bar, 1971; atty. advisor Pres.'s Com. on Urban Housing (Kaiser Com.), D.C., 1967-68; mgr. urban affairs, coordinator operations group Levitt & Sons, Inc., Lake Success, N.Y., 1968-70; asst. prof. law U. So. Calif., Los Angeles, 1970-72, asso. prof., 1972-75, prof., 1975—; vis. asso. prof. law U. Chgo., 1974-75; vis. prof. law Stanford, 1977. Mem. County of Los Angeles Beach Adv. Com., 1971-75.

ELLIOTT, ARCHIE, JR., b. Portsmouth, Va., Oct. 9, 1941; B.S. in Accounting, Va. State Coll., 1965; J.D., magna cum laude, N.C. Central U., 1971. Admitted to Va. bar, 1971; of counsel Equal Employment Opportunity Commn., Washington, 1971; asst. commonwealth atty. Portsmouth, 1972-74; individual practice law, Portsmouth, 1974—. Councilman City of Portsmouth, 1974—. Mem. Nat., Va., Old Dominion bar assns., Va. Trial Lawyers Assn. Home: 902 Taft Dr Portsmouth VA 23701 Office: 605 Green St Portsmouth VA 23704 Tel (804) 399-7683

ELLIOTT, CLIFTON LANGSDALE, b. Kansas City, Mo., Oct. 26, 1938; B.A., Dartmouth Coll., 1960; J.D., Northwestern U., 1963. Admitted to Mo. bar, 1963, U.S. Ct. Appeals 4th Circuit bar, 1967, 8th Circuit bar, 1964, 10th Circuit bar, 1976; partner firm Spencer, Fane, Britt & Browne, Kansas City, 1968—; mem. ad hoc advisory com. Am. Hosp. Assn. Mem. Am. Bar Assn., Kansas City, Mo. bar. Office: 1000 Power and Light Bldg 106 W 14th St Kansas City MO 64105 Tel (816) 474-8100

ELLIOTT, DANIEL ROBERT, JR., b. Cleve., Mar. 15, 1939; B.A. with honors, distinction, Conn. Wesleyan U., 1961; J.D., U. Mich., 1964. Admitted to N.Y. bar, 1965, Ohio bar, 1970; asso. firm Cravath, Swaine & Moore, N.Y.C., 1964-68; adminstrv. asst. Congressman Ogden Reid, N.Y.C., 1968-69; asso. firm Jones, Day, Reavis & Pogue, Washington and Cleve., 1969-72, partner, 1972-76; v.p. law White Consol. Industries, Inc., Cleve., 1976—. Chmn., Greater Cleve. Project; pres. Cleve. Tenants Orgn.; chmn. pub. social policy com. Neighborhood Center Assn., Cleve.; active study group racial isolation Cleve. Pub. Schs. Contbr. notes to law rev. Office: 1177 Berea Rd Cleveland OH 44111 Tel (216) 252-3700

ELLIOTT, HOWARD EDWARD, JR., b. Balt., Aug. 29, 1921; B.S., U. Md., 1942; J.D., U. Balt., 1970. Admitted to Md. bar, 1963. Claims rep. State Automobile Mutual Ins. Co., Balt., 1949—. Home: 8515 Oakleigh Rd Baltimore MD 21234 Office: 7215 York Rd Baltimore MD 21212 Tel (301) 825-5100

ELLIOTT, J(AMES) ROBERT, b. Gainesville, Ga., Jan. 1, 1910; Ph.B., Emory U., 1930, LL.B., 1934. Admitted to Ga. bar, 1934; practiced in Columbus, Ga., 1934-62; judge U.S. Dist. Ct., Middle Dist. Ga., 1962—, chief judge, 1972—. Mem. Ga. Jr. C. of C. (pres. 1941-42), Ga. Bar Assn., Lambda Chi Alpha, Phi Delta Phi. Home: 2612 Carson Dr Columbus GA 31906 Office: PO Box 2017 Columbus GA 31902 Tel (404) 324-4118

ELLIOTT, JOSEPH BARDWELL, b. Yazoo City, Miss., Nov. 21, 1930; B.B.A., U. Miss., 1953, LL.B., 1954, J.D., 1968. Admitted to Miss. bar, 1954; asso. firm Neal & Houston, 1958-63; partner firm Neal, Houston, Elliott & Barnett, 1963-68; individual practice law, Jackson, Miss., 1968—; mgr. Chgo. Title Ins. Co., 1971-73. Mem. Miss., Hinds County bar assns. Home: 5329 Briarfield Rd Jackson MS 39211 Office: 1344 Capital Towers 125 S Congress St Jackson MS 39205 Tel (601) 969-6611

ELLIOTT, LOUIE CECIL, JR., b. Duke, Okla., Aug. 20, 1925; LL.B. with high distinction, Wayne U., 1956. Admitted to Okla. bar, 1957, N.H. bar, 1971; U.S. Dist. Ct. N.H., 1973, U.S. Tax Ct. bar, 1975; served to lt. col. USAF, 1943-69; individual practice law, Stillwell, Okla., 1969-71; partner firm Edes & Elliott, Newport and Woodsville, N.H., 1971-76; individual practice law, Newport, 1976-77; partner firm Elliott & Jasper, Newport, 1977—. Bd. dirs. Upper Valley-Lake Sumapee Region Assn., Planning Council, 1973-76, sec., 1975-76; bd. dirs. Sullivan City Environ. Engring. Review Council, 1973-76, pres. 1973-74; bd. dirs. Newport Devel., Inc., 1975-77, Housing for Elderly, 1975-77, Newport Area Home Health Agency, 1975—; trustee Newport Hosp., 1974—. Mem. Am., N.H. (gov. 1974-76, sec. 1976-77), Sullivan County, Grafton County bar assns. Home: Pike Hill Rd Newport NH 03773 Office: 35B Main St Newport NH 03773 Tel (603) 863-4105

ELLIOTT, NORMAN DALE, b. Grinnell, Iowa, Nov. 14, 1922; student Upper Iowa U., 1940; A.B., Drake U., 1948; LL.B., U. Miami, Coral Gables, Fla., 1950, J.D., 1951. Admitted to Fla. bar, 1950, Iowa bar, 1952; individual practice law, Miami, Fla., 1950-53, Des Moines, 1953-73; judge Iowa Dist. Ct., Polk County, 1973—; city atty. City of Des Moines, 1957; gen. counsel Nat. Travelers Ins. Co., 1965-71; instr. Des Moines Community Coll., 1974. Bd. dirs. United Cerebral Palsey, 1970. Mem. Am. Judicature Soc., Phi Alpha Delta. Tel (515) 284-6412

ELLIOTT, RICHARD GIBBONS, JR., b. Wilmington, Del., May 28, 1940; B.S., Washington & Lee U., 1963; LL.B., U. N.C., 1966. Admitted to Del. bar, 1966; dep. atty. gen. State of Del., 1967-68; partner firm Richards Layton & Finger, Wilmington, 1968—; dir. ROMP, Inc. Mem. Am., Del. bar assns. Contbr. articles to legal jours. Home: 913 Stuart Rd Wilmington DE 19807 Office: 4072 duPont Blvd Wilmington DE 19899 Tel ((302) 658-6541

ELLIOTT, RICHARD KARL, b. Buffalo, Nov. 8, 1928; student Am. U.; B.A., Denison U., 1951; LL.B., U. Mich., 1956. Admitted to Mich. bar, 1957, Ohio bar; asso. firm Tubbs & Grettenberger, Grand Rapids, Mich., 1956; mem. staff prosecutor's office Kent County (Mich.), Grand Rapids, 1959-60; individual practice law, Hastings, Mich., 1960-62; legal staff INA, 1963-64; asso. firm Griffith, Elliott & Smith, Columbus, Ohio; legal staff Buckeye Union; warden Ohio State Ins. Dept., Columbus, 1963-65. Mem. Ohio State, Columbus, Mich., Grand Rapids bar assns., Def. Assn. Columbus, Def. Assn. Ohio. Home: 6480 Evening St Worthington OH 43085 Office: PO Box 351 700 High St Worthington OH 43085

ELLIOTT, ROBERT CONE, b. Columbia, S.C., July 26, 1949; B.A., U.S.C., 1970, J.D., 1973. Admitted to S.C. bar, 1973; individual practice law, Columbia, 1973-74; partner firm Hyatt, Nielsen & Elliott, Columbia, 1974-76; partner firm Hyatt & Elliott, Columbia, 1976—; instr. govt., criminal justice Palmer Coll., Midlands Tech. Coll., 1974-75; recorder Town of Eastover, 1975—. Mem. Richland County, S.C. bar assns., Richland County Criminal Trial Lawyers Assn. Mem. criminal justice advisory com. Midlands Tech. Coll., 1976-77. Home: Rt 1 Box 25-A Eastover SC 29044 Office: 1107 Barringer Bldg Columbia SC 29201 Tel (803) 799-9402

ELLIOTT, ROBERT RAYMOND, b. Buffalo, Feb. 26, 1941; A.B. magna cum laude, Harvard Coll., 1963, LL.B., 1966. Admitted to N.Y. State bar, 1968, D.C. bar, 1968; gen. counsel HUD, Washington, 1974-77; partner firm Dechert, Price & Rhoads, Washington, 1977—; dir. Fed. Nat. Mortgage Assn. Pres. Gainesville/Antioch (Va.) Parents Tchr. Orgn., 1976; pres. Chile Found., 1973-74. Mem. Am., D.C. bar Assns., Am. Judicature Soc. Home: 7500 Cerro Gordo Rd Gainesville VA 22065 Office: 888 17th St NW Washington DC 20006 Tel (202) 872-8600

ELLIOTT, ROBERT WILLIAM, b. Ripley, Miss., Apr. 10, 1936; B.A., U. Miss., 1958, LL.B., 1962, J.D., 1968. Admitted to Miss. bar, 1962, U.S. Ct. Appeals 5th Circuit bar, 1970; individual practice law, Ripley, 1962—. Pres. Ripley PTA. Mem. Ripley C. of C., Am., Miss., 3d Circuit (past pres.) bar assns., Am. Judicature Soc., Miss. Def. Lawyers Assn., U. Miss. Alumni Assn. (dir.), Home: Route 1 Forrest Rd Ripley MS 38663 Office: 103 N Main St Ripley MS 38663 Tel (601) 837-5831

ELLIOTT, RUFUS EDWARD, III, b. Birmingham, Ala., July 26, 1944; B.S., U. Ala., 1966; J.D., Cumberland Law Sch. Samford U., 1972. Admitted to Ala. bar, 1972; law clk. Ala. Ct. Civil Appeals, Montgomery, 1972-73; partner firm Williams & Elliott, Birmingham, 1973—. Mem. Am., Ala., Birmingham bar assns. Office: 812 Massey Bldg Birmingham AL 35205 Tel (205) 324-8525

ELLIOTT, W. G., b. Cuthbert, Ga., July 28, 1931; A.B., Emory U.; J.D., U. Ga. Admitted to Ga. bar, 1959; judge Superior Ct., So. Jud. Circuit Ga., 1975—. Office: Box 1349 Valdosta GA 31601

ELLIOTT, WARREN GRANT, b. Pueblo, Colo., Jan. 3, 1927; J.D., U. Mich., 1952; LL.B., U. Colo., 1974. Admitted to Colo. bar, 1952, Conn. bar, 1976; asst. city mgr., city atty., Pueblo, Colo., 1955-61; legis. counsel, adminstrv. asst. to U.S. Senator, Washington, 1956-68; ass. gen. counsel Life Ins. Assn. Am., Washington, 1961-68; gen. counsel Aetna Life and Casualty Co., Hartford, 1968—; mem. asso. bd. Conn. Bank and Trust Co. Mem. Fed. Bar Assn., Assn. Life Ins. Counsel, Conn. Bus. and Industry Assn. (govt. relations com.). Home: 1414 Asylum Ave Hartford CT 06105 Office: 151 Farmington Ave Hartford CT 06156 Tel (203) 273-3431

ELLIS, ANDREW JACKSON, JR., b. Ashland, Va., June 23, 1930; A.B., Washington and Lee U., 1951, LL.B., 1953. Admitted to Va. bar, 1952; partner firm Campbell, Ellis & Campbell, Ashland, 1955-70, firm Mays, Valentine, Davenport & Moore, Richmond, 1970—; mem. Ashland Town Council, 1956-63; mayor Town of Ashland, 1958-63; substitute judge Hanover County (Va.) Ct., 1958-63; commonwealth's atty. for Hanover County, 1963-70, county atty., 1970—. Mem. Richmond, Va., Am. bar assns., Va. Trial Lawyers Assn. Home: Route 2 POB 218 Beaverdam VA 23015 Office: POB 1122 Richmond VA 23208 Tel (804) 644-6011 1122 Richmond VA 23208 Tel (804) 644-6011

ELLIS, COURTENAY, b. Cottingham, Eng., Jan. 4, 1946; B.A., Oxford (Eng.) U., 1967, M.A., 1974; LL.M., George Washington U., 1972. Solicitor, Supreme Ct. Eng. and Wales, 1970; admitted to D.C. bar, 1973; solicitor firm Farrer & Co., London, 1970; asso. firm Covington & Burling, Washington, 1972-76, firm Akin, Gump, Hauer & Feld, Washington, 1976—; atty. Neighborhood Legal Services Program, Washington, 1974. Mem. Am., D.C. bar assns., Am. Soc. Internat. Law, Law Soc. London. Home: Apt 722 1200 S Washington St Alexandria VA 22314 Office: Suite 1100 1155 15th St NW Washington DC 20005 Tel (202) 457-7706

ELLIS, COURTNEY FORD, b. Chgo., Jan. 30, 1933; B.A., Yale, 1955; J.D., U. Ky., 1965. Admitted to Ky. bar, 1966; asso. firm Hurst & Burnett, Lexington, Ky., 1966-68, Miller, Griffin & Marks, Lexington, 1968-71; individual practice law, Lexington, 1971—. Mem. Lexington-Fayette County Hist. Survey and Planning Commn., 1969-70; bd. dirs. Lexington Children's Theatre, 1964-68, Child Guidance Center, Lexington, 1966-69; trustee Comprehensive Care Center, Lexington, 1968-71, Alice Lloyd Coll., Pippa Passes, Ky., 1967-72, Caney Creek Community Center, Pippa Passes, 1967-72. Mem. Ky., Fayette County bar assns. Office: 404 N Limestone St Lexington KY 40508 Tel (606) 252-5123

ELLIS, DAVID BURTON, b. Boston, Feb. 23, 1933; B.A., Boston U., 1954, LL.B., 1957; LL.M., N.Y. U., 1958. Admitted to Mass. bar, 1957; atty. NLRB, Newark, 1958-60, Boston, 1960-67; partner firm Foley, Hoag & Eliot, Boston, 1967—. Mem. Needham (Mass.) Personnel Bd., 1970-74. Mem. Boston (co-chmn. labor law com. 1973—), Am. bar assns. Home: 30 Wildwood Dr Needham MA 02192 Office: 10 Post Office Sq Boston MA 02109 Tel (617) 482-1390

ELLIS, DEL JAMES, b. Cherokee, Iowa, Sept. 20, 1940; B.S., Regis Coll., 1962; J.D., Creighton U., 1965. Admitted to Nebr. bar, 1965, Colo. bar, 1965; legis. asst. to Sen. Peter Dominick, 1965-67; asst. atty. gen. Colo., 1968-73; mem. firm Cody & Ellis, Denver, 1974—. Sec., City of Wheatridge (Colo.) Home Rule Charter Commn. Mem. Colo., 1st Jud. Dist. bar assns. Recipient Wall St. Jour. award, 1962. Office: 260 Lakeside National Bank Bldg Denver CO 80212 Tel (303) 458-1330

ELLIS, DORSEY DANIEL, JR., b. Cape Girardeau, Mo., May 18, 1938; B.A., Maryville Coll., 1960; J.D., U. Chgo., 1963. Admitted to N.Y. bar, 1967, Iowa bar, 1976; asso. firm Cravath, Swaine & Moore, N.Y.C., 1963-68; asso. prof. law U. Iowa, 1968-71, prof., 1971—, spl. asst. to pres., spring 1974, acting asst. dean faculties, 1974-75; vis. mem. sr. common room Mansfield Coll., Oxford (Eng.) U., 1972-73, 75. Trustee Montessori Sch., Iowa City, 1970-72, v.p., 1970-71, pres., 1971-72; mem. Johnson County (Iowa) Law Enforcement Adv. Commn., 1971-72. Mem. Am., Internat., Iowa bar assns., Selden Soc., Am. Soc. Legal History. Home: 428 Ferson St Iowa City IA 52240 Office: Coll of Law U of Iowa Iowa City IA 52242 Tel (319) 353-6985

ELLIS, EDWARD EVAN, b. Tallahassee, Sept. 13, 1931; B.A. in Math., Washington and Lee U., 1952, LL.B. magna cum laude, 1956. Admitted to N.Y. bar, 1957, Ky. bar, 1970; actuarial asst. Acacia Mut. Life Ins. Co., Washington, 1952-53; asso. firm Davis, Polk & Wardwell, N.Y.C., 1956-63; internat. counsel The Interpublic Group, N.Y.C. and Switzerland, 1963-69; v.p., gen. counsel, sec. Ky. Fried Chicken, Louisville, 1969-75; pres., gen. mgr. Spring Valley Farms, Inc., Louisville, 1975—. Bd. dirs. Louisville Metro YMCA, 1974—. Mem. Am., Ky. bar assns., Assn. Bar City N.Y., Order of Coif, Phi Beta Kappa. Home: 2502 Longest Ave Louisville KY 40204 Office: 1939 Goldsmith Ln Suite 210 Louisville KY 40218 Tel (502) 459-9913

ELLIS, EDWARD PRIOLEAU, b. Atlanta, May 31, 1929; A.B. U. Ga., 1951; LL.B., Harvard, 1956. Admitted to Ga. bar, 1956; partner firm Alston, Miller & Gaines, Atlanta, 1956—; pres. 1st Security & Exchange Co. Mem. Am., Atlanta bar assns., State Bar Ga., Am. Coll. Probate Counsel. Home: 2804 Habersham Rd NW Atlanta GA 30305 Office: 1220 C and S National Bank Bldg Atlanta GA 30303 Tel (404) 588-0300

ELLIS, ELGAR PERCY, b. Ft. White, Fla., Sept. 28, 1901; LL.B., U. Fla., 1924, J.D., 1967. Admitted to Fla. bar, 1924; mem. firm Walsh, Beckham & Ellis, Miami, Fla., 1925-36, firm Walsh & Ellis, Miami, 1937-48; individual practice law, Coral Gables, Fla., 1949—. Mem. Fla., Dade County bar assns. Home and Office: 619 Altara Ave Coral Gables FL 33146 Tel (305) 665-2172

ELLIS, FRANK CORLEY, JR., b. Columbiana, Ala., Feb. 24, 1940; A.B., Ala. Coll., 1962; LL.B. magna cum laude, U. Ala., 1964. Admitted to Ala. bar, 1964; asso. firm Wallace, Ellis, Head & Fowler, Columbiana, Ala., 1964-67, partner, 1967—. Dir. Intra-Governmental Planning Commn. on Consumer Affairs. Mem. Ala. (mem. Inst. for Continuing Legal Edn.), Shelby County (pres. 1977), Am. bar assns., Ala., Am. trial lawyers assns. Contbr. articles to legal publs. Home: Route 1 Box 15 C Columbiana AL 35051 Office: Box 587 Columbiana AL 35051 Tel (205) 669-6783

ELLIS, GEORGE HAYWOOD, b. St. Louis, July 27, 1938; A.B., Stanford 1959; J.D., U. Calif., 1965. Admitted to Calif. bar, 1966; asso. firm Forster, Gemmill & Farmer, Los Angeles, 1966-68; dep. pub. defender Los Angeles County, 1968-71; mem. firm Morgan, Wenzel & McNicholas, Los Angeles, 1971—; dean Calif. Coll. Law, 1969-70; judge pro tem Los Angeles Municipal Ct. Mem. State Bar Calif. Home: 219 N Norton Ave Los Angeles CA 90004 Office: 1545 Wilshire Blvd Los Angeles CA 90017 Tel (213) 483-1961

ELLIS, GLEN JAMES, b. Kaysville, Utah, Aug. 14, 1930; B.S., U. Utah, 1962, J.D., 1964. Admitted to Utah bar, 1964; corp. counsel City of Provo (Utah), 1965—; mem. firm Maxfield, Gammon, Ellis & Dalebout, Provo, 1967—; dir. Indsl. Western, Inc. Mem. Am. Bar Assn. Office: PO Box 1097 Provo UT 84601 Tel (801) 375-1822

ELLIS, GLYN DIAL, b. Logan, W.Va., Oct. 20, 1921; B.A., U. Miami, 1955, LL.B., 1957. Admitted to Fla. bar, 1957, W.Va. bar, 1957; individual practice law, Logan, W.Va., 1957—, Coral Gables, Fla., 1970—. Mem. Dade County, Miami, Logan County, Logan bar assns. Home: 1522 Alegriano Ave Coral Gables FL 33146 Office: 316 Aragon Ave Suite 317 Coral Gables FL 33134 Tel (305) 448-4651

ELLIS, GUY KENNER, JR., b. Greenville, Miss., Aug. 29, 1941; B.A., U. Miss., 1963, J.D., 1965. Admitted to Miss. bar, 1965; atty. City of Greenville, 1968—. Mem. Miss. Trial Lawyers Assn., Miss. Prosecutors Assn., Miss. City Attys. Assn., Miss., Washington County bar assns. Home: 912 S Main St Greenville MS 38701 Office: PO Box 452 313 Washington Ave Greenville MS 38701 Tel (601) 378-3355

ELLIS, JOHN AUSTIN, b. Amarillo, Tex., Dec. 28, 1937; B.A., U. Calif., Los Angeles, 1960; LL.B., Hastings Coll. Law, 1964. Admitted to Calif. bar, 1965; asso. firm Bautzer, Irwin & Schwab, Beverly Hills, Calif., 1965-66, Hindin, McKittrick & Marsh, Beverly Hills, 1968-70; individual practice law, Beverly Hills, 1967-68; partner firm Raskin, Lichtig & Ellis, Los Angeles, 1970—. Mem. Calif. State Bar, Los Angeles County, Beverly Hills bar assns. Office: Suite 714 1880 Century Park E Los Angeles CA 90067 Tel (213) 553-6171

ELLIS, JOHN DONALD, JR., b. Bklyn., July 28, 1944; B.A., The Citadel, 1966; J.D., So. Meth. U., 1969; M.S. in Forensic Sci., George Washington U., 1973, LL.M. in Tax, 1974. Admitted to Tex. bar, 1969, U.S. Ct. Mil. Appeals bar, 1969, U.S. Supreme Ct. bar, 1974, U.S. Dist. Ct. So. Dist. Tex. bar, 1976; with JAG, U.S. Army, 1969-72, counsel to Dir. Armed Forces Inst. Pathology, Washington, 1973-74; partner firm Wyckoff, Russell, Dunn & Frazier, Houston, 1974—; asst. prof. George Washington U., 1973-74; asst. prof. forensic pathology U. Tex. Med. Sch., 1975—, mem. med. ethics com. Health Scis. Center. Advisor Montgomery County (Md.) Com. on Juvenile Drug Abuse, 1972-73; bd. dirs. Ashford Community Assn. Mem. Am., Houston (co-chmn. com. med. legal dilemma 1975), Houston Jr. (chmn. luncheons and speakers bur. 1975-76, sec. 1976—) bar assns., State Bar Tex., Am. Coll. Legal-Medicine (com. to develop a med.-legal curriculum for med. schs. 1975—), Phi Alpha Delta. Home: 12410 Brandywyne Dr Houston TX 77077 Office: 800 First City Nat Bank Bldg Houston TX 77002 Tel (713) 658-8585

ELLIS, JOHN WEBSTER, b. Ellicottville, N.Y., Nov. 22, 1883; LL.B., U. Buffalo, 1904. Admitted to N.Y. bar, 1905; practice law, Ellicottville, 1905—; justice of the peace Town of Ellicottville, 1907-13; clk. Village of Ellicottville, 1905, 11, 12; asst. revision clk. N.Y. State Assembly, 1913; spl. dep. atty. gen. N.Y. State, 1923-25; dist. atty. Cattaraugus County, 1926; mayor Village of Ellicottville, 1927; atty. Fed. Land Bank Cattaraugus County, 1933-75; sec.-treas. Iroquois Nat. Farm Loan Assn. Cattaraugus and Allegheny Counties, 1935-45; pres. Ellicottville Real Estate Corp., 1930. Chmn., Democratic Com. Cattaraugus County, 1920-21; govt. appeal agt. local bd. SSS, 1940-48; dir. U.S. Hwy. 219 Assn., 1950-65. Mem. N.Y. State, Cattaraugus County (Pub. Service award 1975, life mem.) bar assns., Ellicottville C. of C. (dir. 1948-52, pres. 1951; recipient Community Service award), Center for Study of Democratic Instns., Nat. Council Sr. Citizens, Am. Assn. Ret. Persons. Recipient Bronze medal for faithful and loyal service SSS, World War II; Bronze medal for meritorious service St. John's Episcopal Ch., Ellicottville, 1960. Home: 4 W Washington St Ellicottville NY 14731 Office: 17 Washington St Ellicottville NY 14731 Tel (716) 699-4774

ELLIS, MARTIN BAER, b. Hampton, Va., Sept. 30, 1945; B.Arch., U. Cin., 1968; J.D. with honors, U. Md., 1973. Archtl. draftsman Clark, Buhr & Nexsen, Architects and Engrs., Norfolk, Va., 1963-65; designer John Hackler & Co., Architects, Peoria, Ill., 1966-69, Nelson, Salabes Inc., Architects, Balt., 1969-70, Morris Steinhorn, Architect, Balt., 1970; thcr. 7th grade math. Balt. City Pub. Schs., 1969-70; tchr. 12th grade math. Sch. Without A Bldg., 1970-71; law clk. Md. Dept. Natural Resources, Annapolis, 1971, firm Piper & Marbury, Balt., 1971-73; admitted to Md. bar, 1973; asso. firm Weinberg and Green, Balt., 1973-77; v.p., gen. counsel Equitable Trust Bank, Balt., 1977—. Mem. Md. State Bar Assn., Nat. Consumer Fin. Assn., Order of Coif. Recipient Honor award in Criminal Law Lawyers Coop. Pub. Co., 1969, Honor award in Civil Procedure, 1971. Home: 6204 Cross Country Blvd Baltimore MD 21215 Office: Munsey Bldg Calvert and Fayette Sts Baltimore MD 21203 Tel (301) 547-4253

ELLIS, THOMAS SELBY, III, b. Bogota, Colombia, May 15, 1940; B.S.E., Princeton U., 1961; J.D., Harvard U., 1969; diploma in law Magdalen Coll., Oxford U., 1970. Admitted to Va. bar, 1969; partner firm Hunton & Williams, Richmond, Va., 1970—. Bd. dirs. Va. Lung Assn. Mem. Va. Trial Lawyers Assn., Am. Bar Assn. Harvard Knox fellow, 1969-70. Home: 4267 Cheyenne Rd Richmond VA 23235 Office: 707 E Main St PO Box 1535 Richmond VA 23212 Tel (804) 788-8453

ELLIS, WILLIAM HAWKINS, b. Birmingham, Ala., Aug. 26, 1902; student Birmingham So. Coll.; LL.B., U. Ala., 1925. Admitted to Ala. bar, 1925, U.S. Supreme Ct. bar, 1937; asso. firm Murphy, Hanna, Woodall & Lindbergh, Birmingham, 1926-39; partner firm Ellis, Lindbergh & Ellis, Birmingham, 1939-46; individual practice law, Birmingham, 1946—. Mem. Am., Ala., Birmingham bar assns. Home: 206 Malaga Ave Birmingham AL 35209 Office: 1412 John A Hand Bldg Birmingham AL 35203 Tel (205) 322-0668

ELLISON, NEWELL WINDOM, b. Parrottsville, Tenn., Oct. 4, 1894; A.B., George Washington U., 1917, LL.B., 1921, LL.D. (hon.), 1957; J.D. (hon.) Tenn. Wesleyan Coll., 1964. Admitted to D.C. var, 1921; mem. firm Covington & Burling, Washington, 1921-26, partner, 1926—; dir. N.J. Zinc Co., 1943-69, mem. exec. com. 1959-69; dir. Union Trust Co., Washington, D.C., 1952-75. Chmn. D.C. Commn. Judicial Disabilities and Tenure, 1971-75; chmn. com. Adminstrn. Justice, 1968-71; chmn. bd. elections D.C., 1955-56; chmn. Com. Juvenile Crime of Council on Law Enforcement D.C., 1953-55; mem. bd. govs. St. Albans Sch. Boys, Washington, 1966-72; trustee Supreme Ct. Hist. Soc.; trustee George Washington U., 1943—, chmn. bd. trustees, 1959-65. Mem. Am. Bar Assn. (chmn. standing com. facilities of law library Congress 1950-53), D.C. Bar, Bar Assn. D.C. (named lawyer year 1969, distinguished service award 1969), Am. Judicature Soc., Lawyers Club Washington, Washington Inst. Fgn. Affairs, Washington Fgn. Law Soc. (co-founder 1952, pres. 1953-54), Sigma Alpha Epsilon, Phi Delta Phi, Order Coif, Omicron Delta Kappa. Recipient distinguished alumnus award George Washington Law Assn., 1967. Home: 2323 Wyoming Ave NW Washington DC 20008 Office: 888 16th St NW Washington DC 20006 Tel (202) 452-6142

ELLISON, PATRICIA LEE, b. Elizabeth, N.J., Oct. 17, 1943; B.A., Denison U., 1965; M.A., U. Calif., 1967; J.D., U. San Diego, 1973. Admitted to Calif. bar, 1973; research atty. San Diego County Dist. Atty.'s Office, 1974; asso. firm Butler, Ruff & Harrigan, San Diego, 1974; partner firm Ellison, Eichten & Bell, San Diego, 1975—; instr. U. San Diego Sch. Law, spring 1976. Mem. Calif., San Diego County bar assns. Mem. U. San Diego Moot Ct. Bd., 1972-73. Office: 233 A St suite 903 San Diego CA 92101 Tel (714) 232-6124

ELLMAN, HARRY S., b. Detroit, Mar. 5, 1947; B.A., Mich. State U., 1964; J.D. cum laude, Wayne State U., 1971. Admitted to Mich. bar, 1971; asso. firm Kratze, Greenbaum & Littman, 1971-72; partner firm Crane & Ellman, 1973-74; individual practice law, Southfield, Mich., 1975—. Mem. Mich., Oakland County, Detroit, Southfield bar assns. Home: 25062 Glynholm St Birmingham MI 48010 Office: 25130 Southfield Rd Suite 212 Southfield MI 48075 Tel (313) 557-5657

ELLNER, RICHARD NORTON, b. N.Y.C., Apr. 12, 1929; A.B. cum laude, Harvard, 1951, J.D., 1954. Admitted to N.Y. bar, 1954, D.C. bar, 1962, Calif. bar, 1966; atty. br. of enforcement SEC, N.Y.C., 1957-59, sr. atty. div. corp. fin., Washington, 1959-61; asso. firm Morison, Murphy, Clapp & Abrams, Washington, 1962-63; v.p., gen. counsel Polrized Corp. Am., Beverly Hills, Calif., 1962-65; asso. firm Hahn, Cazier, Hoegh & Leff, Los Angeles, 1966-68, partner, 1968-76; partner firm Cummins, White & Breidenbach, Los Angeles, 1977—; mem. faculty Northrup U. Sch. Law, 1976—. Mem. bus. exec. adv. com. So. Calif. Research Council. Mem. State Bar Calif., Am., Fed., Los Angeles bar assns. Contbr. articles to law jours. Home: 426 S McCadden Los Angeles CA 90020 Office: 688 W 6th St Los Angeles CA 90017 Tel (213) 624-3431

ELLS, THEODORE FISCHER, b. New Haven, Dec. 24, 1939; B.A., Amherst Coll., 1961; LL.B., U. Va., 1964. Admitted to Conn. bar, 1964, N.Y. State bar, 1968; asso. firm Gumbart, Corbin, Tyler & Cooper, New Haven, 1965-67, Seward & Kissel, N.Y.C., 1967-69, Patterson, Belknap & Webb, N.Y.C., 1969-71; asst. gen. counsel, asst. sec. U.S. Industries, Inc., N.Y.C., 1971—. Elder 1st Presbyterian Ch. Brooklyn, 1975—; chmn. bd. advisors Bklyn. Music Sch., 1974—. Mem. N.Y. State Bar Assn. Home: 13 Garden Pl Brooklyn NY 11201 Office: 250 Park Ave New York City NY 10017 Tel (212) 697-4141

ELLWOOD, SCOTT, b. Boston, July 8, 1936; A.B., Eastern Mich. U., 1958; LL.B., Harvard, 1961. Admitted to Iowa bar, 1961, Ill. bar, 1961; asso. firm McBride, Baker, Wienke & Schlosser, Chgo.,

1961-67, partner firm 1968—, exec. com., 1970-74, sec., 1972—; dir. Decorations Unlimited, Inc., 1965-70, Appleton Chair Co., 1966-68, Rigidbilt, Inc., 1971—; pres. Miller Investment Co.; dir., v.p., sec. 110 N. Wacker Dr. Found., 1974—. Mem. Winnetka Caucus Com., 1974-76; chmn. Park Dist. Candidates' Com., Policies and Procedures Com. Mem. Am., Iowa State, Ill. State, Chgo. (chmn. trust law spousal rights subcom., chmn. trust law com. div. II, trust law com. exec. com.) bar assns. Home: 205 Scott Ave Winnetka IL 60093 Office: 110 N Wacker Dr Chicago IL 60606 Tel (312) 346-6191

ELLYSON, WILLIAM GAINES, b. Richmond, Va., Jan. 5, 1938; B.A., Trinity Coll., Hartford, 1963; LL.B., U. Richmond, 1966. Admitted to Va. bar, 1966, since practiced in Richmond; partner firm Martin & Ellyson, 1966-69, Bell, Ellyson & Wilkins, 1970—. Chmn., Offender Aid and Restoration of Richmond, Inc., 1974-75; bd. dirs. Richmond chpt. ARC, 1974—, Fan Dist. Assn., 1973-75. Mem. Am., Va. (ethics com. 1974—), Richmond (chmn. real estate sect. 1974-75) bar assns. Home: 1511 Hanover Ave Richmond VA 23220 Office: 605 Mutual Bldg Richmond VA 23219 Tel (804) 649-7021

ELMAN, BARRY DONALD, b. Chgo., Apr. 10, 1930; B.B.A. in Accounting, U. Wis., 1952; J.D., Northwestern U., 1954. Admitted to Ill. bar, 1954; partner firm Berger, Newmark & Fenchel, Chgo., 1961—. Mem. Chgo. Bar Assn. Office: 180 N LaSalle St Chicago IL 60601 Tel (312) 782-5050

ELMAN, PHILIP, b. Paterson, N.J., Mar. 14, 1918; A.B., Coll. City of N.Y., 1936; LL.B., Harvard U., 1939. Admitted to N.Y. State bar, 1940, D.C. bar, 1948, U.S. Supreme Ct. bar, 1946; law clerk Judge Calvert Magruder, U.S. Ct. Appeals, Boston, 1939-40; atty., FCC, 1940-41; law clerk Justice Felix Frankfurter, U.S. Supreme Ct., 1941-43; asst. chmn. Office of Foreign Economic Coordination, Dept. State, 1943-44; legal adviser Office of Mil. Govt., Berlin, Germany, 1945-46; asst. to solicitor gen. of U.S., 1944-61; commr. FTC, Washington, D.C., 1961-70; prof., Georgetown U. Law Center, Washington, 1970-76; of counsel firm Wald, Harkrader & Ross, Washington, 1971—; mem. advisory bd. Antitrust and Trade Regulation Report, 1970—; trustee, past chmn. Inst. for Pub. Interest Representation, Georgetown U. Law Center, 1971—; mem. litigation review com. Environ. Defense Fund, 1971-74; bd. dirs. Nat. Inst. for Consumer Justice, 1971-73. Mem. Am., Fed., D.C. bar assns., Am. Law Inst., Am. Judicature Soc., Phi Beta Kappa. Recipient Rockefeller Pub. Service award, 1967; editor Harvard Law Rev., Of Law and Men, 1956; contbr. articles to legal jours. Home: 6719 Brigadoon Dr Bethesda MD 20034 Office: 1320 19th St NW Washington DC 20036 Tel (202) 296-2121

ELMER, BRIAN CHRISTIAN, b. Washington, Apr. 18, 1936; A.B., Cornell U., 1960; LL.B., U. Mich., 1962. Admitted to Mich. bar, 1963, D.C. bar, 1963, U.S. Supreme Ct. bar, 1968; law clk. U.S. Ct. Appeals, D.C. Circuit, 1962-64; partner firm Jones, Day, Reavis & Pogue, Washington, 1964—. Mem. Am., D.C. bar assns., Phi Delta Phi. Home: 3843 N 26th St Washington VA 22207 Office: 1100 Connecticut Ave NW Washington DC 20036 Tel (202) 452-5846

ELMS, LARRY ALVIN, b. Walla Walla, Wash., Jan. 1, 1945; B.S., W. Tex. State U., 1966, M.A., 1968; J.D., U. Houston, 1972. Admitted to Tex. bar, 1972; asso. firm Kimmel & Elms, Lubbock, Tex., 1977—. Mem. State Bar Tex., Lubbock County Bar Assn., Tex. Trial Lawyers Assn. Home: 5708 15th St Lubbock TX 79416 Office: 2223 34th St Lubbock TX 79411 Tel (806) 744-2353

ELROD, CHARLES ELLISON, JR., b. Charleston, S.C., Feb. 22, 1943; A.B. in Economics, U. N.C., 1964, J.D. with honors, 1967. Admitted to N.C. bar, 1967, U.S. Supreme Ct. bar, 1971, Ga. bar, 1972; trial atty. Office of Chief Counsel Tax Ct. Div. IRS, Washington, 1967-71; asso. firm Hansell, Post, Brandon & Dorsey, Atlanta, 1971-73; asso. firm Henkel & Lamon, Atlanta, 1973-74, mem., 1974—. Mem. Am., Ga., Atlanta bar assns. Contbr. articles in field to profl. jours. Home: 356 Woodward Way Atlanta GA 30305 Office: 229 Peachtree St Atlanta GA 30303 Tel (404) 659-2500

ELROD, WILLIAM HARVEY, JR., b. Opelika, Ala., May 29, 1925; A.B., Birmingham-So. Coll., 1948; LL.B., U. Mich., 1953. Admitted to Ala. bar, 1953; U.S. Supreme Ct. bar, 1966; asso. firm Deramus, Fitts, Johnston & Mullins, and predecessors, Birmingham, Ala., 1953-58, partner, 1958-63, dep. atty. gen. State of Ala., Montgomery, 1963-67; partner firm Hutson, Elrod, Edwards & Belser, and predecessors, Decatur, Ala., 1967—. Mem. Am., Birmingham, Morgan County bar assns., Am. Trial Lawyers Assn. Office: 140 Citizens Industrial Bank Bldg Decatur AL 35601 Tel (205) 355-3731

ELSBERG, LAWRENCE BRUCE, b. Sioux City, Iowa, Sept. 14, 1945; B.A., U. Nebr., 1967, M.A., 1970, J.D., 1973. Admitted to Ind. bar, 1974; asso. law firm Dann Pecar Newman Talesnick & Kleiman, Indpls., 1974—. Mem. Ind. State, Am. bar assns., Comml. Law League Am. Home: 6310 Sunset Ln Indianapolis IN 46260 Office: 151 N Delaware St Indianapolis IN 46204

ELSEN, SHELDON HOWARD, b. Pitts., May 12, 1928; A.B., Princeton, 1950; A.M., Harvard, 1952, J.D., 1958. Admitted to N.Y. bar, 1959, U.S. Supreme Ct. bar, 1971; asso. firm Strasser, Spiegelberg, Fried and Frank, N.Y.C., 1958-60; asst. U.S. atty., So. Dist. N.Y., 1960-64; asso. firm Phillips, Nizer, Benjamin, Krim and Ballon, N.Y.C., 1964-65; partner firm Orans, Elsen & Polstein, N.Y.C., 1965—; lectr. law Columbia Law Sch., 1966-69, adj. prof., 1969—; chief counsel N.Y. Moreland Act Commn., 1975-76; cons. Pres's. Commn. Law Enforcement Adminstrn. Justice, 1967; mem. faculty Nat. Inst. Trial Advocacy, 1973. Mem. Phi Beta Kappa. Contbr. articles to legal jours. Office: Orans Elsen & Polstein 1 Rockefeller Plaza New York City NY 10020 Tel (212) 586-2211

ELSING, WILLIAM TADDES, b. Bisbee, Ariz., May 8, 1910; student Stanford U., 1928, U. Calif., Berkeley, 1929; J.D., U. Ariz., 1933. Admitted to Ariz. bar, 1933, Calif. bar, 1946; individual practice law, Prescott, Ariz., 1933-38, Phoenix, 1938—. Chmn. bd. govs. Ariz. Dept. Mineral Resources, Phoenix, 1971-76. Mem. Am., Calif., Ariz., Maricopa County bar assns., Soc. Mining Engrs., Am. Inst. Mining, Metall. and Petroleum Engrs. Home: 6545 N 13th St Phoenix AZ 85014 Office: 34 W Monroe St Suite 712 Phoenix AZ 85003 Tel (602) 253-2191

ELSON, ALEX, b. nr. Kiev, Russia, Apr. 17, 1905; came to U.S., 1906, naturalized, 1913; Ph.B., U. Chgo., 1926, J.D., 1928. Admitted to Ill. bar, 1928; atty. Legal Aid Bur., Chgo., 1927-34; asso. firm Tolman, Chandler & Dickinson, Chgo., 1934-38; regional atty. Wage-Hour Div., Chgo., 1938-41; regional atty., asst. gen. counsel Office Price Adminstrn., Chgo., 1941-45; individual practice law, 1945-62; sr. mem. firm Elson, Lassers & Wolff, Chgo., 1962—; lectr. Yale, 1946; vis. prof. labor relations Northwestern U. Law Sch., 1961-65; vis. prof. law Ariz. State U., 1971; chmn. com. profl. standards discipline Am. Bar Found. Vice pres. Law in Am. Soc. Found., 1965—; pres. Inst. for Psychoanalysis, Chgo., 1975—. Fellow Am. Bar Found.; mem. Am., Ill., Chgo. (mgr.) bar assns., Fed. Bar Assn., Am. Judicature Soc., Am. Law Inst., Nat. Acad. Arbitrators (gov. 1973-76), Am. Law Inst. Author: Civil Practice Forms, 1934; Civil Practice Forms, Illinios-Federal, 1952, (with Willard J. Lassers and Aaron S. Wolff) rev. edit., 1965; contbr. articles to legal jours. Home: 5642 Dorchester Ave Chicago IL 60637 Office: 11 S LaSalle St Room 3200 Chicago IL 60603 Tel (312) 372-5461

ELSON, WILLIAM B., b. St. Louis, Jan. 2, 1914; Ph.B., U. Chgo., 1933; J.D. cum laude, U. Chgo., 1935; certificate Advanced Mgmt. Program Harvard Bus. Sch., 1969. Admitted to Ill. bar, 1935; asso. firm A.H. & H. Veeder, Chgo., 1935-41; atty. Swift & Co., Chgo., 1941-47, mgr. corp. and property div., 1947-67, asst. gen. counsel, 1967-73; asst. gen. counsel Esmark Inc., Chgo., 1973—. Mem. Am., Chgo. bar assns. Mem. editorial bd. U. Chgo. Law Rev. Home: 4800 S Chicago Beach Dr Chicago IL 60615 Office: 55 E Monroe St Chicago IL 60603 Tel (312) 431-3640

ELSTEIN, HENRY, b. Bridgeport, Conn., Apr. 19, 1934; B.A., Yale, 1956, LL.B., 1959. Admitted to Conn. bar, 1959; partner firm Magilnick, Simko & Elstein, Bridgeport; chmn. Fairfield (Conn.) Municipal Employees Contract Study Com. Formerly dep. moderator, chmn. coms. on pub. works, planning, legislation and adminstrn. Fairfield Rep. Town Meeting; dist. leader Democratic party, Fairfield; trustee, Park Ave. Temple, Fairfield. Mem. Conn., Bridgeport (formerly chmn. com. on continuing legal edn.) bar assns. Home: 58 Stirrup Hill Rd Fairfield CT 06430 Office: 955 Main St Bridgeport CT 06604 Tel (203) 367-4421

ELTON, ROGER HENRY, b. Summit, N.J., June 16, 1941; B.E.E., Mass. Inst. Tech., 1963; M.B.A., Harvard U., 1965; J.D., U. Santa Clara, 1970. Admitted to Calif. bar, 1971, Nev. bar, 1972; with Raytheon Corp., 1965-67, Watkins Johnson Co., 1967-71, Pacific Co., 1972-74; with Bernard & Hildahl, C.P.A.'s, 1974-76; individual practice law, Reno, 1976—. Mem. Am. Bar Assn., Am. Inst. C.P.A.'s, Assn. Attys. and C.P.A.'s, Fin. Execs. Inst. Home: 155 Markelo Dr Reno NV 89511 Office: 155 W 2d St PO Box 2959 Reno NV 89505 Tel (702) 786-3226

ELTZROTH, CLYDE ALFRED, JR., b. Savannah, Ga., Aug. 4, 1948; B.A., The Citadel, 1970; J.D., U. of S.C., 1973. Admitted to S.C. bar, 1973, U.S. Ct. of Appeals, 1974; mem. firm Murdaugh, Peters, Parker & Eltzroth, Hampton, S.C., 1973—. Mem. Am., S.C., Hampton County (sec.-treas. 1975—) bar assns., S.C. Trial Lawyers Assn. Home: Box 463 Varnville SC 29944 Office: Box 457 Hampton SC 29924 Tel (803) 943-2111

ELVERMAN, TIMOTHY JOHN, b. Kenosha, Wis., Dec. 11, 1948; B.A., Dominican Coll. of Racine (Wis.), 1971; J.D., Marquette U., 1974. Admitted to Wis. bar, 1974, Minn. bar, 1975; dir. Bemidji State U. Student Legal Assistance Center, 1974-76; ombudsman, home sec. to Rep. Les Aspin, Janesville, Wis., 1976—. Mem. State Bar Wis., Minn., Am. bar assns. Home: 2309 Harvard Dr Janesville WI 53545 Office: 210 Dodge St Janesville WI 53545 Tel (608) 752-9074

ELWELL, JOHN MIKE, b. Wichita, Kans., Oct. 28, 1942; B.A., U. Kans., 1965; J.D., 1967. Admitted to Kans. bar, 1967; asst. county atty. Douglas County (Kans.), 1968-69, county atty., 1972-76; judge Juvenile Ct. Douglas County, 1976—, County Ct., 1976—, Probate Ct., 1976—; asso. dist. judge 7th Jud. Ct., 1976—; mem. Kans. Gov.'s Com. on Criminal Justice. 1976. Mem. Lawrence Mayor's Com. on Drug Abuse, 1971, Douglas County Drug Abuse Council, 1974. Mem. Nat. Sculpture Soc., Nat. Council Juvenile Ct. Judges. Home: Rural Route 2 Lawrence KS 66044 Office: 11th and Massachusetts Sts Lawrence KS 66044 Tel (913) 841-7700

ELWOOD, W. DOUGLAS, b. Williamsport, Ind., June 11, 1911; A.B., Butler U., 1933; LL.B., Ind. U., 1936. Admitted to Ind. bar, 1936; prosecuting atty. Benton County, Ind., 1939-43; judge Benton Circuit Ct., 1943-59; atty. Benton County Plan Commn., 1970-73, Benton Community Sch. Corp., 1973-77. Home: 604 Park Dr Fowler IN 47944 Office: 205 N Madison Ave Fowler IN 47944 Tel (317) 884-0364

ELWYN, HUGH ROSS, b. Woodstock, N.Y., Aug. 4, 1914; A.B., Union Coll., 1935; LL.B., Albany Coll., 1939, J.D., 1968. Admitted to N.Y. bar, 1939, U.S. Supreme Ct. bar, 1961; partner firm Fowick & Elwyn, 1945-49; individual practice law, 1950-63; judge Spl. City Ct., Kingston, N.Y., 1962-63, judge Family Ct., 1963—. Pres. Kingston Library. Mem. Am., N.Y. bar, assns., Nat. Council Juvenile Ct. Judges, N.Y. State Family Ct. Judges Assn. (dir.), Am. Judicature Soc., Phi Beta Kappa. Home: 335 Pearl St Kingston NY 12401 Office: 240 Fair St Kingston NY 12401 Tel (914) 331-9300

ELY, FORREST E., b. Batavia, Ohio, Apr. 1, 1901; A.B., U. Cin., 1924; LL.B., 1927, J.D., 1928. Admitted to Ohio bar, 1927, U.S. Supreme Ct. bar, 1945; partner firm Ely & Ely, and predecessor, 1927-42, Ely White & Davidson, 1947-59, Ely Moore & Telbury, Batavia, 1959—; prosecuting atty., 1928-32; asst. prosecuting atty., 1933-41; asst. atty. gen. State of Ohio, 1941-43; city solicitor City of Batavia, 1946-69. Del., Republican Nat. Conv., 1936, 40-48; pres. bd. edn., 1940-42. Mem. Internat. Assn. Ins. Counsel, Am. Coll. Trial Lawyers, Ohio Trial Lawyers Assn., Ohio Def. Counsel Assn., Ohio, Am. bar assns., Cin. Soc. Decorated Bronze Star medal; named Ky. col. Home: 90 N 5th Ave Batavia OH 45103 Office: 257 Main St Batavia OH 45103 Tel (513) 732-2140

ELY, JAMES WALLACE, JR., b. Rochester, N.Y., Jan. 20, 1938; A.B., Princeton, 1959; LL.B., Harvard, 1962; Ph.D., U. Va., 1971. Admitted to N.Y. State bar, 1962; asso. firm Harris, Beach and Wilcox, Rochester, N.Y., 1962-67; instr. U. Va., Charlottesville, 1970; instr., then asst. prof., Va. Commonwealth U., Richmond, 1970-73; asst. prof. law Vanderbilt U., Nashville, Tenn., 1973-75, asso. prof., 1975—. Mem. Am. Soc. Legal History, Orgn. Am. Historians, So. Hist. Assn. Author: The Crisis of Conservative Virginia: The Byrd Organization and the Politics of Massive Resistance, 1976; editor: The Legal Papers of Andrew Jackson. Home: 112 Lynwood Terr Nashville TN 37205 Office: Vanderbilt Law Sch Nashville TN 37240 Tel (615) 322-2705

ELY, NATHANIEL JEREMIAH, b. Balt., May 28, 1910; J.D., Johns Hopkins U., 1936; LL.D. (hon.), Georgetown U., 1977. Admitted to Md. bar, 1936, U.S. Supreme Ct. bar, 1943, D.C. bar, 1944; individual practice law, Washington, Md., 1936—; judge appeal tax ct., Rockville, Md., 1955-65; counsel to pres. Georgetown U. U.S. rep. to World Bank as conciliator mem. to Internat. Center for Settlemand of Investment Disputes. Mem. Am., Fed., Md., D.C. bar assns. Home: 7316 Helmsdale Rd Bethesda MD 20034 Office: 7300 Loch Lomond Dr Bethesda MD 20034 Tel (301) 229-0500

ELY, NORTHCUTT, b. Phoenix, Sept. 14, 1903; A.B., Stanford U., 1924; J.D., 1926. Admitted to Calif. bar, 1927, N.Y. bar, 1927, D.C. bar, 1931, U.S. Supreme Ct. bar, 1932; exec. asst. to Sec. Interior, 1929-33; individual practice law, Calif. and Washington, 1933—; sr. partner firm Northcutt Ely, Washington; spl. asst. atty. gen. State of Calif., 1963-64; Mem. Am. (ho. of dels.), Inter-Am., Internat. bar assns., Am. Law Inst. (life). Author: Hoover Dam Contracts, 1933; Oil Conservation through Interstate Agreement, 1933; The Hoover Dam Documents, 1948; Summary of Mining and Petroleum Laws of the World, 1961, 70; Authorization of Federal Water Projects, 1972; Law of International Drainage Basins; AIME Handbook on Mining Law; Economics of Mineral Industries, 1964, 73. Office: Watergate 600 Bldg Washington DC 20037 Tel (202) 337-0200

ELY, SAMUEL CHESNUT, b. Ainsworth, Nebr., Jan. 9, 1910; A.B., U. Nebr., 1931, LL.B., 1934, J.D., 1968. Admitted to Nebr., 1934; practiced in Bassett, Nebr., 1935-41, Ainsworth, 1947-73; atty. criminal div. Dept. Justice, Washington, 1941-47; city atty., Ainsworth, Nebr., 1951-55, county atty., Brown County, Nebr., 1959-69; county judge 15th Jud. Dist., Nebr., 1973—. Mem. Nebr., County Judges' Assn. (pres. 1976—), Nebr. Bar Assn. (ho. of dels. 1967-73), Am. Bar Assn., Phi Delta Phi, Alpha Sigma Phi. Home: 341 E 2d St Ainsworth NE 69210 Office: Courthouse Ainsworth NE 69210 Tel (402) 387-2864

ELY, THEODORE BENJAMIN, b. Erie, Pa., Nov. 4, 1945; B.A., Bethany Coll., 1968; J.D., Duquesne U., 1972. Admitted to Pa. bar, 1972; partner firm Silin, Eckert, Burke, Ely & Bernard, Erie; solicitor Erie County Recorder of Deeds, 1973-76. Mem. Erie County, Pa. bar assns., Pa. Trial Lawyers Assn. Home: 429 W 7th St Erie PA 16502 Office: 255 W 10th Erie PA 16505 Tel (814) 452-4473

EMANUELSON, MILLARD EDWARD, b. Monson, Maine, May 13, 1914; B.S., Colby Coll., 1936; J.D., Boston U., 1951. High sch. tchr., athletic coach, Maine, 1936-51; admitted to Maine bar, 1951; partner firm Emanuelson, Barris & Michael, Portland, Maine, 1952-74; judge Municipal Ct., Portland, 1960-65; U.S. Commr., Portland, 1967-71; U.S. Magistrate, Portland, 1972-74; judge Maine Dist. Ct., Machias, 1974—; prof. law U. Maine, 1956-74. Mem. Pine Tree Legal Assn. Maine (1st pres.), Am., Maine, Cumberland County bar assns., Am. Judicature Soc., Am. Judges Assn. Home: 123 Coyle St Portland ME 04103 Office: Maine Dist Ct Machias ME 04654 Tel (207) 255-3044

EMENS, JOHN RICHARD, II, b. Jackson, Mich., May 3, 1934; B.A., DePauw U., 1956; J.D., U. Mich., 1959. Admitted to Mich. bar, 1959, Ohio bar, 1964, U.S. Supreme Ct. bar, 1968; partner firm W.K. McInally, Jackson, 1959-64, Emens & Ashworth, Marion, Ohio, 1964-67; individual practice law, Marion, 1967-68; partner firm Tingley, Hurd & Emens, Columbus, Ohio, 1968—; dir. Patrick Petroleum Co., Standard Savs. & Loan Assn.; mem. legal com., Ohio reporter Interstate Oil Compact Commn.; trustee Ohio Oil and Gas Assn.; atty., mem. Ohio Oil and Gas Bd. Rev., 1965-75, sec., 1966-75; lectr. Former pres., dir. Friends of Libraries of Ohio State U.; co-chmn. legal div. Columbus United Way, 1976. Mem. Am., Ohio, Columbus bar assns., Rocky Mountain Mineral Law Found., Southwestern Legal Found. Contbr. articles to legal jours. Office: 250 E Broad St Columbus OH 43215 Tel (614) 221-6527

EMERLING, STANLEY JUSTIN, b. Cleve., Feb. 3, 1926; student Case Inst. Tech., 1944; A.B., U. Mich., 1949; LL.B., Cleve-Marshall Law Sch., 1955. Pres., Greenbaum Bros. Co., Cleve., 1953—; atty. No. Ohio Hotel and Restaurant Meat Purveyors Assn., 1963-75. Mem. Cleve., Ohio State bar assns., Phi Beta Kappa, Phi Eta Sigma, Phi Kappa Phi. Co-editor Cleve.-Marshall Law Rev., 1954-55, contbr. articles, 1955. Home: 41 Maple St Chagrin Falls OH 44022 Office: 509 Bolivar Rd Cleveland OH 44115 Tel (216) 781-3760

EMERSHAW, GEORGE JOSEPH, b. Kingston, Pa., Aug. 3, 1940; B.A., Kings Coll., 1962; J.D., U. Akron, 1968. Admitted to Ohio bar, 1968; med. rep. Burroughs Wellcome & Co., 1962-67; asst. prof. fin. and bus. law U. Akron, 1967-68; individual practice law, Akron, 1968—. Mem. Am., Ohio, Akron bar assns. Office: 27 S Forge St Akron OH 44304 Tel (216) 376-4122

EMERSON, FRANK DANA, b. Marion, Ohio, May 28, 1916; A.B., U. Akron, 1938; J.D., Case Western Res. U., 1940; LL.M., N.Y. U., 1956. Admitted to Ohio bar, 1940, Ky. bar, 1963; practiced in Cleve., 1940-44; interpretative atty. SEC, Cleve., 1944-54; asst. prof. law U. Cin., 1954-66; prof. law Cleve. State U., 1966—; lectr. Case Western Res. U., 1951-53; cons. in field. Author: (with Latcham) Shareholder Democracy, 1954; Modernzing Our Corporation Laws, 1977; contbr. articles to legal jours. Home: 1801 E 12th St apt 1116 Cleveland OH 44114 Office: Coll Law Cleveland State U Cleveland OH 44115 Tel (216) 687-2324

EMERSON, IRVIN DALE, b. Plains, Kans., Oct. 4, 1920; LL.B., St. Louis U., 1951. Admitted to Mo. bar, 1951; asst. atty. Jefferson County, Mo., 1953-57, 59-61; judge Probate Ct. Jefferson County, Hillsboro, 1963—. Bd. dirs. Hillsboro R-3 Sch. Bd., 1954-62, Sch. for Retarded Children, 1956-59; moderator Jefferson Baptist Assn., 1969-70. Mem. Mo., Jefferson County bar assns., Mo. Assn. Probate Magistrates and Judges (pres.), Nat. Coll. Probate Judges, Am. Judicature Soc. Home: 18 Juvette Terr Hillsboro MO 63050 Office: POB 326 Hillsboro MO 63050 Tel (314) 789-3911

EMERSON, ROBERT FERRELL, b. Chgo., Dec. 28, 1932; B.S., U. Ill., 1956, LL.B., 1958. Admitted to Ill. bar, 1959; counsel Firemans Fund Ins. Co., Chgo., 1960-72, Montgomery Ward Life Ins. Co., Chgo., 1972-74; asso. gen. counsel and asst. sec. Globe Life Ins. Co., Chgo., 1974—. Mem. Am., Ill. bar assns., Assn. Life Ins. Counsel. Tel (312) 782-0720

EMERSON, THOMAS IRWIN, b. Passaic, N.J., July 12, 1907; A.B., Yale, 1928, LL.B., 1931, M.A., 1946; LL.D., U. Pa., 1976, Amherst Coll., 1976. Admitted to N.Y. State bar, 1932, U.S. Supreme Ct. bar, 1936; asso. firm Engelhard, Pollak, Pitcher & Stern, N.Y.C., 1931-33; asst. counsel Nat. Recovery Adminstrn., 1933-34; prin. atty. NLRB, 1934-36, asst. gen. counsel, then asso. gen. counsel, 1937-40; prin. atty. Social Security Bd., 1936-37; spl. asst. to atty. gen. U.S. Dept. Justice, 1940-41; asso. gen. counsel Office Price Adminstrn., 1941-43, dep. adminstr. for enforcemnt, 1943-45; gen. counsel Office of Econ. Stblzn., 1945; gen. counsel Office War Moblzn. and Reconversion, 1945-46; prof. law Yale, 1946—; Lines prof. law, 1955—; Guggenheim fellow, 1943; vis. prof. London Sch. Econs. and Polit. Sci., 1953-54; vis. prof. Brookings Inst., 1960-61; lectr. U. Tokyo, 1974-75. Mem. Conn. Commn. on the Status of Women, 1975—. Mem. Nat. Lawyers Guild (pres. 1950-51), Soc. Am. Law Tchrs. (bd. govs. 1974—). Author (with David Haber and Norman Dorsen) Political and Civil Rights in the United States, 1952, 4th edit., 1976; Toward a General Theory of the First Amendment, 1966; The System of Freedom of Expression, 1970; contbr. to profl. periodicals.

Home: 2271 Ridge Rd North Haven CT 06473 Office: Yale Law Sch New Haven CT 06520 Tel (203) 436-2666

EMERY, MARGARET HENCKEL, b. Cleve., Sept. 23, 1904; student Western Res. U., 1922-24; A.B. with distinction, U. Mich., 1926, J.D., 1931. Admitted to Ill. bar, 1933; real estate mgmt. for Chgo. Title & Trust Co., 1932-34; law offices E.H. McDermott, Chgo., 1934—. Trustee, Village of Winnetka (Ill.), 1967-71, hearing officer open housing ordinance, 1971-74, mem. architecture and environment bd., 1974; mem. bd. steering com. Ill. Constl. Conv., New Trier Twp., 1968, New Trier Citizens League, 1963-72; bd. dirs. U. Mich. Law Sch. Devel. Council. Mem. Fed., Ill. bar assns., Nat. Assn. Women Lawyers, Kappa Beta Pi, Delta Sigma Rho, Pi Lambda Theta. Home: 680 Green Bay Rd #204 Winnetka IL 60093

EMIL, GERALD RAYMOND, b. Doylestown, Pa., Feb. 14, 1949; A.B. in Polit. Sci., Queens Coll., City U. N.Y., 1971; student law U. Dijon (France), 1972; J.D., U. Miss., 1973. Admitted to Miss. bar, 1973; legal advisor Police Dept. Harrison County (Miss), 1973; asst. dist. atty. 2d Jud. Dist., Harrison County, 1974; mem. firm Ladner & Emil, Gulfport, Miss., 1976—; master in chancery. Mem. Am. Judicature Soc., Am. (vice chmn. membership com. young lawyers sect., state del. 1976), Miss. (conv. chmn., dir. young lawyers sect.) bar assns., Am., Miss. Trial Lawyers Assns. Home: 226 Oakwood St Gulfport MS 39501 Office: 2301 14th St Suite 206 Gulfport MS 39501 Tel (601) 864-3926

EMLEY, CHRISTOPHER FIELDING, b. N.Y.C., Dec. 15, 1943; B.A., U. Calif., 1964, J.D., 1967. Admitted to Calif. bar, 1967; staff atty. San Francisco Legal Aid Soc., 1967-71; partner firm Jenkins & Emley, San Francisco, 1971-73, individual practice law, San Francisco, 1973—; cons. Children's Hosp. of East Bay, Oakland, Calif., 1973—; mem. Calif. Gov.'s Task Force on Child Abuse, 1973; bd. dirs. San Francisco Child Abuse Council, 1973-76, Legal Services for Children, Inc., 1976—. Mem. San Francisco Bar Assn. (chmn. juvenile justice sect. 1975, 76, chmn. lawyer referral service com. 1977). Office: 1959 Ocean Ave San Francisco CA 94127 Tel (415) 334-2555

EMMENS, DAVID PECK, b. Ashland, Ohio, Apr. 9, 1948; A.B. cum laude, Kenyon Coll., 1970; J.D., Ohio State U., 1973. Admitted to Ohio bar, 1974; atty. Shelby Mut. Ins. Co. (Ohio), 1974—. Mem. Ohio State, Richland County (Ohio) bar assns. Home: 645 Yale Dr Mansfield OH 44907 Office: 19 Mansfield Ave Shelby OH 44875 Tel (419) 347-1880

EMMERLING, JOHN WILLIAM, b. Milw., Aug. 31, 1916; Ph.B., U. Wis., 1937, LL.B., 1939, J.D., 1939. Admitted to Wis. bar, 1939, U.S. Dist. Cts. for Eastern and Western Dists. Wis. bar, 1939, U.S. 7th Circuit Ct. Appeals bar, 1949, U.S. Supreme Ct. bar, 1950; practiced in Milw., 1939-41; supervising investigator Office Price Adminstrn., Milw., 1942-43; spl. trial atty. Office Price Adminstrn.-Office Price Stablzn., Milw. and St. Paul, 1945-47; individual practice law, Milw., 1947—. Mem. Am. Judicature Soc., Am., Fedn., Milw. bar assns., State Bar Wis. Office: 152 W Wisconsin Ave Milwaukee WI 53203 Tel (414) 271-5250

EMMERMAN, HOWARD C., b. Chgo., May 21, 1945; B.S., U. Ill., 1967; J.D., DePaul U., 1970. Admitted to Ill. bar, 1970, U.S. Dist. Ct. for No. Ill. bar, 1970, U.S. Tax Ct. bar, 1974; since practiced in Chgo., asso. firm Friedman & Koven, 1970-71; asso. firm Frederick S. Stein, 1971-74; partner firm Rudnick & Wolfe, 1974—. Vice pres., bd. dirs. Woodfield Jewish Congregation. Mem. Chgo. Bar Assn. (mem. circuit ct. ops. com., uniform comml. code com.). Contbr. articles to legal jours. Office: 30 N LaSalle St Chicago IL 60602 Tel (312) 368-4012

EMMET, RICHARD PERRINO, b. Albertville, Ala., Apr. 13, 1929; B.S., U. Ala., 1953, J.D., 1956. Admitted to Ala. bar, 1956; partner firm Emmet & Franco, Montgomery, Ala., 1956-60; judge Ala. Circuit Ct., 15th Circuit, Montgomery, 1960—. Mem. Am., Ala. bar assns., Am. Judicature Soc. Contbr. articles Ala. Lawyer, Va. Law Quart. Home: 2324 Woodley Rd Montgomery AL 36106 Office: Courthouse Montgomery AL 36104 Tel (205) 269-1261

EMMETT, KATHRYN, b. Los Angeles, Dec. 13, 1944; B.A. magna cum laude, Radcliffe Coll., 1966; LL.B., Yale, 1970. Admitted to Conn. bar, 1970, U.S. Supreme Ct. bar, 1975, Calif. bar, 1976; asso. firm Koskoff, Koskoff, Rutkin & Bieder, Bridgeport, Conn., 1970-76; prin. firm Kathryn Emmett, Stamford, Conn., 1976—. Mem. Calif., Conn., Stamford, Bridgeport bar assns., Nat. Lawyers Guild, Assn. Trial Lawyers Am., Conn. Trial Lawyers Assn. Office: 322 Main St Stamford CT 06901 Tel (203) 357-8130

EMMONS, CLARENCE SCOTT, b. Manning, Iowa, Sept. 16, 1908; A.B., Willamette U., 1931, LL.B., 1931. Admitted to Oreg. bar, 1931; practiced in Salem, Oreg., 1931-38; asst. atty. gen. State of Oreg., Salem, 1938-44, 46-48; practiced in Albany, Oreg., 1948—, partner firms Willis, Kyle and Emmons, 1948-68, Emmons, Kyle, Kropp and Kryger, 1968—. Mem. Oreg. State Bar (pres. 1960), Am. Bar Assn. Tel (503) 928-6171

ENDIEVERI, ANTHONY FRANK, b. Syracuse, N.Y., May 21, 1939; A.B., Syracuse U., 1961, J.D., 1965. Admitted to N.Y. bar, 1967, U.S. Supreme Ct. bar, 1970; individual practice law, Camillus, N.Y., 1967—; chief pros. atty. City of Syracuse, 1970-74. Mem. criminal appeals div. Hiscock Legal Aid Soc., Syracuse, 1968. Mem. Am., N.Y., Onondaga County bar assns. Home: 205 Emann Dr Camillus NY 13031 Office: 5104 W Genesee St Camillus NY 13031 Tel (315) 487-9458

ENDSLEY, J. PATRICK, b. Indpls., Jan. 19, 1928; B.S. with distinction, Ind. U., 1950, J.D., 1956. Admitted to Ind. bar, 1956, U.S. Supreme Ct. bar, 1961; clk., treas., Lawrence, Ind., 1956-59, asst. city prosecuter, 1960-62; pub. defender, Marion County, Ind., 1962; chief dep. Ind. Atty. Gen., 1965-69; individual practice law, Indpls., 1956-74; partner firm Endsley, Timmons & Endsley, 1968-75; judge, Marion County Circuit Ct., 1975—; sec. Lawrence (Ind.) Bd. Zoning Appeals, Planning Commn., 1956—; dir. Sueman Coleman Agency, Indpls. Bd. dirs., counsel, Mud Creek Players, 1970-73; mem. Marion Coll. Assos., Ind. U. Alumni Assn. Mem. Ind. Judges Assn., Am., Ind., Indpls. bar assns., Ind., Am. trial lawyers assns., Lawyers Assn. of Indpls., Marion County Bar Assn. (ct. liason com., legislative com.), Phi Alpha Delta, Chi Gamma Iota. Recipient JFK Meml. award, Marion County, 1970; elected to Sagamore of the Wabash State of Ind., 1968. Home: 7033 Fremont Ct Indianapolis IN 46256 Office: W-506 City-County Bldg Indianapolis IN 46204 Tel (317) 633-3235

ENDSLEY, THOMAS C., b. Indpls., Jan. 6, 1930; B.S. in B.A., Tri-State Coll., 1955; J.D., U. Louisville, 1968. Admitted to Ind. bar, 1968; asso. firm Endsley, Whitecotton & Endsley, Indpls., 1968-73; partner firm Timmons, Endsley, Chavis, DuMond & Baker, Indpls., 1974—; dep. pros. atty. Marion County, Ind., 1969-71; chief dep. securities commr. State of Ind., 1971-74; commr. Marion County Probate Ct., 1974—. Mem. Indpls. Bar Assn. Home: 6649 E 52d Pl Indianapolis IN 46226 Office: 120 E Market St Suite 777 Indianapolis IN 46204 Tel (317) 632-8513

ENG, PATRICK JOSEPH, b. San Francisco, Sept. 12, 1945; B.S., U. Mo., 1968, B.J., 1970, J.D., 1973. Admitted to Mo. bar, 1973, U.S. Dist. Ct. bar for Western Dist. Mo., 1973; partner firm Welliver, Atkinson & Eng, Columbia, Mo., 1973—. Mem. Columbia Human Rights Commn., 1971—. Mem. Boone County (Mo.), Mo., Am. bar assns. Recipient Willie Bean Norton Scholastic Diligence award Bean Law Found., 1973. Home: 302 W Boulevard S Columbia MO 65201 Office: 317 Guitar Bldg Columbia MO 65201 Tel (314) 449-0854

ENGBER, MICHAEL DAVID, b. Columbus, Ohio, June 10, 1942; B.S. in Fin., Ind. U., Bloomington, 1964, J.D., 1967; M.A. in Mgmt., Ball State U., Muncie, Ind., 1973. Admitted to Ind. bar, 1970; asso. prof. bus. law Ball State U., 1967—, also individual practice law, Muncie, 1970—; adminstrv. asst. to chmn. dept. fin. Ball State U., 1972-75. Mem. steering com., legal cons. Muncie Internat. Cultural Centre. Mem. Am., Tri-State Regional bus. law assns. Recipient bus. research grants Ball State U., 1975-77. Home: 3904 W Godman St Muncie IN 47304 Office: Dept Fin Ball State U Muncie IN 47306 Tel (317) 285-6053

ENGEBRETSEN, ARDEN B., b. San Francisco, Dec. 2, 1931; B.S., U. Utah, 1953, J.D., 1955. Admitted to Utah bar, 1956, Del. bar, 1969; legis. asst., Staff of Gov. Utah; asst. atty. gen. State of Utah, 1958; adminstrv. asst. to plant mgr. Bacchus Works Hercules Inc., Wilmington, Del., 1959-68, counsel legal dept., 1968-71, sr. counsel, 1971-74, asst. treas., 1974-75, treas., 1975—. Active, Utah Republican Central Com., 1964-67, also chmn., Salt Lake County, Utah. Mem. Am., Del., Utah bar assns., Utah Self-Insurers Assn. (bd. dirs. 1967-68). Home: 607 Haverhill Rd Wilmington DE 19803 Office: 910 Market St Wilmington DE 19899 Tel (302) 575-5250

ENGEBRETSON, ANDREW PETER, b. Starbuck, Minn., Aug. 21, 1932; B.A., St. Olaf Coll., 1954; J.D., U. Minn., 1959. Admitted to Minn. bar, 1960; asso. firm Rudolph L. Swore, Alexandria, Minn., 1959-62, Ernest H. Steneroden, St. Paul, 1962-69; individual practice law, St. Paul, 1969-76; partner firm Engebretson, Galena & Ulleberg, St. Paul, 1976—. Mem. Am., Minn. bar assns., Am. Trial Lawyers Assn., Delta Theta Phi. Home: 715 E Montana St Saint Paul MN 55106 Office: 304 McColl Bldg Saint Paul MN 55101 Tel (612) 224-5801

ENGEL, ALBERT JOSEPH, b. Lake City, Mich., Mar. 21, 1924; A.B., U. Mich., 1948, LL.B., 1950. Admitted to Mich. bar, 1950; partner firm Engle and Engel, Muskegon, Mich., 1951-66; judge Mich. Circuit Ct., 14th Circuit, Muskegon, 1967-71, U.S. Dist. Ct., Western Dist. Mich., Grand Rapids, 1971-74, U.S. Ct. Appeals, 6th Circuit, Grand Rapids, 1974—. Mem. Am. Bar Found., Am., Muskegon County, Grand Rapids, Cin., Fed. bar assns., Am. Judicature Soc. Home: 7287 Denison Dr SE Grand Rapids MI 49506 Office: Federal Bldg Grand Rapids MI 49503 Tel (616) 456-456-2550

ENGEL, CARL RUDOLPH, b. Cleve., July 13, 1916; A.B., Western Res. U., 1939, LL.B., 1941. Admitted to Ohio bar, 1942; with Republic Steel Corp., Cleve., 1941-43, Gen. Motors Corp., Cleve., 1943-48; employment mgr. Ohio Indsl. Commn., Cleve., 1948-49; safety adviser Addressograph-Multigraph Corp., Cleve., 1949-51; asst. personnel mgr. Ohio Indsl. Commn., Cleve., 1951-61; atty.-examiner Workmen's Compensation Service Co., Cleve., 1961—. Mem. Ohio Bd. Bldg. Appeals, 1963-71, chmn., 1975—. Mem. Ohio Bar Assn., Am. Soc. Safety Engrs. Home: 3363 Warrensville Center Rd Shaker Heights OH 44122 Office: 1410 National City Bank Bldg Cleveland OH 44114 Tel (216) 621-7551

ENGEL, DAVID CHAPIN, b. N.Y.C., Oct. 6, 1931; B.A., St. Lawrence U., 1954; LL.B., N.Y. U., 1956. Admitted to N.H. bar, 1956, U.S. Dist. Ct. N.H., bar, 1956, Mass. bar, 1967, U.S. Dist. Ct. Mass. bar, 1967; law clk. atty. gen., Concord, N.H., 1956-58; asso. firm Shute, Engel & Frasier, Exeter, N.H., 1958-60, partner, 1960—. Dir. recreation dept. competitive swim team, Exeter, 1973-76; mem. Kensington (N.H.) Bd. Adjustment, 1965-68; bd. dirs. Greenland (N.H.) Community Ch., 1975—, Exeter Day Sch. 1952-55, Exeter Hist. Soc., 1973—; scoutmaster, Exeter Council Boy Scout Am., 1959-64. Mem. Am., Mass., N.H. (chmn. legislation com.), Rockingham County (sec. 1960-61) bar assns., Assn. Trial Lawyers Am., Am. Judicature Soc., Am. Arbitration Assn., Nat. Trust for Hist. Preservation, Internat. Platform Assn. Home: 47 Park Ave Greenland NH 03840 Office: 1 Center St Exeter NH 30883 Tel (603) 772-3738

ENGEL, EDWARD IGNATIUS, b. Portland, Oreg., Feb. 18, 1926; A.B., U. Portland, 1949; J.D., Northwestern Sch. Law, Lewis and Clark Coll., 1954. Admitted to Oreg. bar, 1955; individual practice law, Portland, 1955-67; partner firm Goldsmith, Siegel, Engel & Littlefield, Portland, 1967—; circuit judge pro tempore Multnomah County, Oreg., 1969; dist. judge pro tempore, 1969-74; sec., treas. Multnomah Bar Found., 1972-73, chmn., 1973—. Bd. dirs. Met. Portland area YMCA, 1965-66, Downtown Br. Portland YMCA, 1959-66, chmn., 1963-64. Mem. Oreg. State Bar (sec. disciplinary rules and procedures com. 1964-65), Am., Multnomah bar assns. Recipient Service to Youth award Portland YMCA, 1964, Award of Honor, Oreg. Jr. C. of C., 1961, Outstanding Service award Multnomah County Bar Assn., 1970. Home: 6209 SW Tower Way Portland OR 97221 Office: 875 Boise Cascade Bldg Portland OR 97201 Tel (503) 226-4185

ENGEL, RONALD L., b. Gary, Ind., Jan. 16, 1938; B.S. in Chem. Engring. with honors, U. Ill., 1959; J.D. with honors, U. Chgo., 1962. Admitted to Ill. bar, 1962, U.S. Supreme Ct. bar, 1973; partner firm Kirkland & Ellis, Chgo. Mem. Am., Ill. bar assns., Am., Chgo. patent law assns., U.S. Trademark Assn., Order of Coif, Tau Beta Pi, Phi Lambda Upsilon. Home: 233 E Walton Pl Chicago IL 60611 Office: 200 E Randolph Dr Chicago IL 60601 Tel (312) 861-2130

ENGELBERG, ALFRED BENJAMIN, b. Derby, Conn., Aug. 26, 1939; B.S. in Chem. Engring., Drexel U., 1961; LL.B. cum laude, N.Y.U., 1965. Admitted to N.Y. bar, 1965, U.S. Supreme Ct. bar, 1973; examiner U.S. Patent Office, 1961-62; patent agt. Exxon Research & Engring. Co., Linden, N.J., 1962-65; trial atty., civil div., patent sect. U.S. Dept. Justice, 1965-68; asso. firm Amster & Rothstein, N.Y.C., 1969-72, partner, 1972—. Mem. Assn. Bar City N.Y. (patent com.), N.Y. Patent Law Assn. (patent law revision com.), Tau Beta Pi, Order of Coif. Office: 50 E 42d St New York City NY 10017 Tel (212) 697-5995

ENGELHARD, SHELDON, b. Bklyn., Nov. 4, 1935; B.S. in Bus. Adminstrn., Lehigh U., 1957; J.D., George Washington U., 1960. Admitted to N.Y. bar, 1961; asso. firm Vladeck, Elias, Vladeck & Lewis, N.Y.C., 1961-69, mem., 1969—. Pres. 5th Ward Democratic Club, 1966-67; pres. Oceanside Jewish Center, 1975-77; mem. B'nai B'rith. Mem. Am. Bar Assn., Assn. Bar City N.Y., N.Y. County Lawyers Assn., Phi Alpha Delta, Am. Arbitration Assn. (arbitrator 1968—, labor panel arbitrators N.Y. State Mediation Bd. 1974). Home: 160 Beatrice Ave Oceanside NY 11572 Office: 1501 Broadway St New York City NY 10036 Tel (212) 354-8330

ENGLE, DONALD EDWARD, b. St. Paul, Mar. 5, 1927; B.A., Macalester Coll., 1948; B.S.L., J.D., U. Minn., 1952. Admitted to Minn. bar, 1952, U.S. Supreme Ct. bar, 1967, Mo. bar, 1972; law clerk Atty. Gen., Minn., 1951-52; atty., asst. gen. counsel Great No. Ry., St. Paul, 1953-70; asso. gen. counsel Burlington No., Inc., St. Paul, 1970-72; v.p., gen. counsel St. Louis-San Francisco Ry. Co., St. Louis, 1972—; lectr. continuing edn. U. Minn.; dir. Clarkland, Inc., Clarkland Royalty, Inc., Frisco Transp. Co., 906 Olive Corp., (all St. Louis), Quanah, Acme & Pacific Ry Co. (Tex.). Bd. dirs. YMCA, 1965; pres. PTA chpt., 1966; active United Fund. Mem. Nat. Assn. R.R. Trial Counsel, Minn. R.R. Def. Counsel (pres.), Def. Inst., Am. Arbitration Assn., Am., Ramsey County, Mo., Met. St. Louis bar assns., Phi Delta Phi. Home: PO Box 205 Christmas Valley Rd Chesterfield MO 63017 Office: 906 Olive St Saint Louis MO 63101 Tel (314) 241-7800

ENGLE, ISADORE, b. Eagle, Wis., Aug. 17, 1920; Ph.B., U. Wis., 1942, J.D., 1944; Admitted to Wis. bar, 1944, U.S. Supreme Ct. bar, 1944; staff atty. NLRB, Washington, 1945-47, Fed. Security Agy., Balt., 1947-48; individual practice law, Waukesha, Wis., 1948—; pvt. practice psychology, 1942—. Mem. exec. com. NCCJ, 1960-65; v.p. Congregation Agudas Achim Synagogue, 1970—. Mem. Tau Epsilon Rho, Psi Chi. Home: 3924 N 68th St Milwaukee WI 53216 Office: 211 South St Waukesha WI 53186

ENGLER, WILLIAM JOSEPH, JR., b. Fountain Springs, Pa., May 7, 1940; A.B., LaSalle Coll., Phila., 1962; J.D., Boston Coll., 1965. Admitted to Conn. bar, 1965, Pa. bar, 1966; law clk. to judge U.S. Dist. Ct. Conn., 1965-66; asso. firm Duane, Morris & Heckscher, Phila., 1966-71; gen. solicitor Rochester & Pitts. Coal Co., Indiana, Pa., 1971-72, gen. counsel, 1973—. Mem. Indiana Area Bd. Edn., 1975—. Mem. Am., Pa., Fed., Indiana bar assns. Office: 655 Church St Indiana PA 15701 Tel (412) 465-5621

ENGLERT, HAMILTON EDWARD, b. Valley City, N.D., Jan. 31, 1909; B.A., U. N.D., 1933; degree in teaching Valley City State Coll., 1932; certificate in ct. reporting Gregg Coll., Chgo., 1935. Admitted to N.D. bar, 1949; ct. reporter N.D. Dist. Ct., 1st Jud. Dist., 1935-62; practiced in Valley City, 1949-63; judge N.D. Dist. Ct., 1st Jud. Dist., 1963—; mem. N.D. Jud. Council, 1963—, chmn. pretrial com., 1974—. Mem. Am., N.D., Barnes County (N.D.) bar assns., Am. Judicature Soc., Nat. Council Juvenile Ct. Judges, State Trial Judges Assn. (Am. Bar del. 1972-76), Sigma Chi. Recipient Community Leaders and Noteworthy Ams. award News Pub. Co., 1975. Home: 506 4th Ave SW Valley City ND 58072 Office: POB 993 Barnes County Courthouse Valley City ND 58072 Tel (701) 845-0681

ENGLISH, GEORGE W., b. Vienna, Ill., Feb. 19, 1898; B.S., U. Ill., 1921; J.D., Harvard, 1924; H.H.D., Nova U.; LL.D., Fla. So. Coll. Admitted to Ill. bar, 1924, Fla. bar, 1925; city atty. Ft. Lauderdale, Fla., 1928-39; of counsel English, McCaughan & O'Bryan, Ft. Lauderdale; chmn. exec. com. Landmark 1st Nat. Bank Ft. Lauderdale; chmn. bd. Landmark Bank of North Ft. Lauderdale; dir. Landmark Bank of Plantation (Fla.), 1st Fed. Savs. & Loan Assn. of Broward County, Fla. Power & Light Co., Wright & Putnam, Inc., Harbor Beach Cos., Utilities Operating Co. Mem. bd. control Fla. Instns. Higher Learning, 1952-55; trustee U. Fla. Found., 1959-69; trustee Nova U. Advanced Tech., 1964-69, now hon; hon trustee Pine Crest Prep. Sch., Broward Community Coll; trustee U. Ill. Found., U. Fla. Presidents Council. Fellow Am. Coll. Probate Counsel; mem. Broward County Bar Assn., Ft. Lauderdale Hist. Soc. (trustee), Newcomen Soc., U. Fla. Alumni Assn. (hon.). Recipient U. Ill. Alumni Achievement award, 1977. Home: 1636 SW 15th Ave Fort Lauderdale FL 33312 Office: PO Box 14098 Fort Lauderdale FL 33302 also 1st Fed Bldg Fort Lauderdale FL 33301

ENGLISH, H. ELWOOD, b. Greybull, Wyo., Aug. 3, 1945; B.A. in Polit. Sci., Ottawa (Kans.) U., 1967; J.D., Harvard, 1973. Admitted to Mont. bar, 1974, D.C. bar, 1974; legal intern firm Church, Harris, Johnson & Williams, Great Falls, Mont., 1972; legal asst. Robert L. Stephens, Jr. and Cate & Lynaugh, Billings, Mont., 1973-74, Sandall, Moses, Cavan & Kampfe, Billings, 1974, Crowley, Kilbourne, Haughey, Hanson & Gallagher, Billings, 1974; asso. firm Crowley, Haughey, Hanson, Gallagher & Toole, Billings, 1974—; instr. Rocky Mountain Coll. Trustee, youth sponsor, mem. by-laws com., adult camp dir. 1st Baptist Ch., Billings. Mem. Am. Bar Assn., Am. Judicature Soc. Home: 926 Ave C Billings MT 59102 Office: 500 Electric Bldg Billings MT 59101 Tel (406) 252-3441

ENGLISH, HARRY GORDON, b. N.Y.C., June 10, 1921; B.B.A. (N.Y. State Regents scholar), St. John's U., Bklyn., 1946; M.B.A., N.Y. U., 1949; LL.B., N.Y. Law Sch., 1951, S.J.D., 1965, J.D., 1969; postgrad. (Coll. scholar) Wellesley Coll. Summer Inst. Social Progress, 1952. Underwriter, Royal Ins. Co., N.Y.C., 1940-41; staff accountant Nat. Biscuit Co., N.Y.C., 1941-42; accountant Gulf Oil Co., N.Y.C., 1942-43, Alex Grant & Co., C.P.A.'s, N.Y.C., 1943-46; dir. internal audit div. CARE, N.Y.C., 1946-53; asst. v.p., controller H. L. Green Co., Inc., N.Y.C., 1953-54; admitted to N.Y. bar; asst. v.p., comptroller Weisglass Milk Corp., S.I., N.Y., 1954-55; partner firm Restaine & English, Bklyn., 1955-56; partner English, English & Hansen, pub. accountants, tax cons., Bklyn., 1956—; individual practice law, Bklyn., 1959—; pres. Bliss Realty Co., 1951—; asst. prof. bus. fin. Connelly Coll. L.I. U., 1964-65, adj. asso. prof., 1968-75, adj. asst. prof. Sch. Bus., 1965-68, adj. asso. prof., 1969-75, mem. faculty Weekend Coll., 1975—, instr. in charge real estate courses St. Francis Coll., Bklyn. Bd. Realtors, 1974—. Bd. dirs. ARC. Mem. Bay Ridge Real Estate Bd., Am. Trial Lawyers Assn., Bay Ridge Lawyers Assn. (pres. 1965-66), Inst. Internal Auditors, Am. Bar Assn., Nat. Soc. Pub. Accountants. Home: 219 Bay Ridge Pkwy Brooklyn NY 11209 Office: 7219 Third Ave Brooklyn NY 11209 Tel (212) 238-3360

ENGLISH, JAMES H., b. Altoona, Pa., Nov. 24, 1947; B.A., Westminster Coll., 1969; J.D., U. Pitts., 1972. Admitted to Pa. bar, 1972; since practiced in Altoona, mem. firm Mullen & Casanave, 1972-75, individual practice law, 1975—; mem. staff Blair County Public Defenders Office, 1974—, Trial Ct. Nominating Commn., Blair County 1973-75. Mem. Am., Pa., Blair County bar assns. Home: 1106 13th Ave Altoona PA 16601 Office: 539-540 Central Trust Bldg Altoona PA 16601 Tel (814) 946-1289

ENGLISH, JOHN EDWARD, b. Joplin, Mo., Jan. 3, 1935; B.B.A., Washburn U., Topeka, 1957; J.D., Northwestern U., 1959. Admitted to Ill. bar, 1959, Mich. bar, 1961; field atty. NLRB, Detroit, 1959-61; asso. firm Beaumont, Smith & Harris, Detroit, 1961-65; Fildew Degree, Gilbride & Smith, Detroit, 1965-71; mem. firm Fitzgerald Peters, English & Damm, Detroit, 1971-73, English and van Horne, Detroit, 1973—; adj. prof. law U. Detroit Law Sch., 1970—; dir. numerous Mich. corps.; mem. Mich. State Bar Rep. Assembly, 1976—. Mem. advisory bd. Vista Marie Sch., Detroit, 1972—. Mem. Am., Mich., Ill., Detroit (trustee), Fed., Macomb County bar assns., Assn. Immigration and Naturalization Attys., K.C., Detroit Athletic Club. Home: 90 Tonnancour Pl Grosse Pointe Farms MI 48236 Office: 4472 City Nat Bank Bldg Detroit MI 48226 Tel (313) 961-5100

ENGLISH, JOHN WILLIAM, b. Erie, Pa., Apr. 20, 1915; A.B., Georgetown U., 1937; LL.B., Harvard, 1940. Admitted to Pa. bar, 1940, since practiced in Erie; mem. firm English, Quinn, Leemhuis & Plate, 1940-46, English & Baker, 1946-49, English, Gilson, Baker & Bowler, 1950-60, English, Bowler & Jenks, 1960—; pres. Sir Walter TV, Raleigh, N.C., 1953-57; pres. Great Lakes TV Co., formerly v.p., dir., 1963-76; v.p. XYZ TV, Grand Junction, Colo., 1967—; mem. Pa. State Bd. Law Examiners. Trustee Gannon Coll.; pres., chmn. bd. NW Pa. Heart Assn.; mem. St. Vincent Hosp.; bd. incorporators Hamot Hosp. Mem. Erie County, Pa., Am., Fed. Communications bar assns., Am. Arbitration Assn., Nat. Conf. Bar Examiners (bar exam. com.). Home: 2050 S Shore Dr Erie PA 16505 Office: 162 W 6th St Erie PA 16501 Tel (814) 454-4533

ENGLISH, RICHARD GILDERSLEEVE, b. Hartford, Conn., Jan. 1, 1947; A.B., Middlebury Coll., 1969; J.D., Cornell U., 1972. Asso. firm Conley and Foote, Middlebury, Vt., 1972-74; admitted to Vt. bar, 1973; state's atty. for Addison County (Vt.), Middlebury, 1975—. Mem. Vt., Am. bar assns., Nat. Dist. Attys. Assn. Home: Munger St New Haven VT 05443 Office: 3 Court Sq Middlebury VT 05753 Tel (802) 388-7931

ENGSTROM, DAVID FREDRIK, b. Lenoir, N.C., Jan. 29, 1940; B.S., Southeastern U., Washington, 1967; J.D., U. Balt., 1970. Admitted to Md. bar, 1970; atty., adviser Office of Gen. Counsel, U.S. GAO, Washington, 1970-75, sr. atty., 1975-76, dep. asst. gen. counsel, 1976—. Vestryman, Holy Trinity Episcopal Ch., Bowie, Md., 1971-74, investment treas., 1975—. Mem. Fed., Md. bar assns. Recipient Meritorious Service award GAO, 1970, Outstanding Performance certificate, 1975, certificate of appreciation, 1976; Presidential Mgmt. Improvement award Pres. Nixon, 1972. Home: 2706 Largo Pl Bowie MD 20715 Office: Office of General Counsel US Gen Accounting Office Washington DC 20548

ENNIS, BRUCE CLIFFORD, b. Dover, Del., Mar. 22, 1941; B.A., W.Va. Wesleyan Coll., 1963; J.D., Dickinson Sch. Law, 1966. Admitted to Del. bar, 1969; asso. firm Schmittinger & Rodriguez, Dover, 1969—; instr. Wesley Coll., Dover, 1971—. Mem. Del. State, Kent County (sec. 1970-73) bar assns. Office: 414 S State St Dover DE 19901 Tel (302) 674-0140

ENOCH, DAVID WILLIAM, b. Chanute, Kans., Aug. 7, 1924; A.B., U. Wichita, 1948; J.D., U. Colo., 1951. Admitted to Kans. bar, 1951, Colo. bar, 1952; practiced in Wichita, Kans., 1951, Colorado Springs, Colo., 1952-61, 66-70; judge Colo. 4th Jud. Dist. Ct., 1961-64, presiding judge, 1965; asso. judge Colo. Ct. of Appeals, 1970—. Mem. Internat. div. Nat. YMCA, 1968—; pres. bd. dir. Sch. Dist. 12, Colorado Springs, 1958-61, Family Service Agy., Colorado Springs, 1955-60, Symphony Assn., Colorado Springs, 1959-61. Mem. Colo. Bar (chmn. com. youth edn. 1973—), El Paso County (pres. 1969), Denver County, Am., Inter-Am. bar assns. Named Outstanding Law Enforcement Officer of Year Dad Bruce chpt. Internat. Footprinters Assn., 1965; recipient Service to Youth award Colorado Springs YMCA, 1966, Service to Mankind award Sertoma Internat., 1967. Home: 350 Gilpin St Denver CO 80218 Office: 1575 Sherman St Suite 613 Denver CO 80203 Tel (313) 892-2648

ENRIGHT, RICHARD T., b. St. Louis, June 4, 1926; LL.B., St. Louis U., 1951. Admitted to Mo. bar, 1951; individual practice law, Mo., 1951-62; magistrate judge 6th Dist. Ct. St. Louis County (Mo.), 1963-76; judge Circuit Ct. St. Louis County, Clayton, 1976—. Mem. Mo., St. Louis County, No. County, Met. St. Louis bar assns., Lawyers' Assn. St. Louis. Home: 6970 Lake Valley Dr Florissant MO 63033 Office: 7900 Carondelet St Clayton MO 63105 Tel (314) 889-2681

ENSLEN, FREDERICK TERRELL, JR., b. Montgomery, Ala., Oct. 5, 1941; B.S., U. Ala., 1963, J.D., 1966. Admitted to Ala. bar, 1966, law clk. Ala. Ct. Appeals, 1966; partner firm Salmon & Enslen, Montgomery, 1968-74, Odom, Argo & Enslen, Montgomery, 1974—; instr. bus. adminstrn. Troy State U., 1970—. Dir. Montgomery Riverboat Commn., 1973—; co-chmn. Montgomery City-County Consolidation Study Commn., 1976—. Mem. Am., Ala., Montgomery County bar assns., Phi Kappa Sigma. Home: 3056 Highfield Dr Montgomery AL 36111 Office: PO Box 1550 Montgomery AL 36102 Tel (205) 834-2460

ENSOR, THOMAS RICHARD, b. Evanston, Ill., Sept. 28, 1946; A.B. in History, Ind. U., 1968, J.D., 1971. Admitted to Ill. bar, 1971, Colo. bar, 1972; staff atty., VISTA vol. Adams County (Colo.) Legal Aid Soc., 1971-73; dep. dist. atty. Adams County, Brighton, 1973—; instr. dept. bus. Community Coll. Denver, 1972—. Mem. Adams County Council for Youth, 1972-73; mem. adv. bd. Community Coll. Denver, 1974—. Mem. Adams County (sec.), Colo. bar assns., Nat. Dist. Atty's Assn. Office: 450 S 4th St Brighton CO 80601 Tel (303) 659-7720

ENTIN, DAVID, b. New Bedford, Mass., Mar. 3, 1911; B.S. in Bus. Adminstrn., Boston U., 1931, LL.B., 1934, J.D., 1934. Admitted to Mass. bar, 1934, U.S. Supreme Ct. bar, 1959; pres. firm Entin & Entin, Inc., Fall River, Mass.; corp. counsel City of Fall River, 1958-64; atty. Fall River Housing Authority, 1964-67. Dir. ARC; chmn. Cancer Dr., Cerebral Palsy Dr., Heart Fund Dr.; dir. Animal Rescue League. Mem. Mass., Fall River, Bristol County bar assns. Home: 509 Madison St Fall River MA 02720 Office: 41 N Main St Fall River MA 02720 Tel (617) 674-3501

ENTWISLE, ROBERT MORGAN, JR., b. Pitts., May 26, 1916; B.A., Princeton, 1938; LL.B., U. Pitts., 1941. Admitted to Pa. Supreme Ct. bar, 1942, Pa. Superior Ct. bar, 1942; asso. firm Paul, Lawrence & Wills, Pitts., 1946-50; partner firm Wills, Entwisle & Hill, Pitts., 1950-56; Miller, Entwisle & Duff and predecessors, Pitts., 1956—; dep. atty. gen. State of Pa., 1950-51. Pres. Churchill Borough Council, 1954-58. Mem. Am., Pa., Allegheny County (sec. 1959-64) bar assns., Phi Delta Phi. Recipient Man of Year award Churchill Borough Town Meeting, 1958. Office: 728 Frick Bldg Pittsburgh PA 15219 Tel (412) 391-3211

EOVALDI, WILLIAM GEORGE, b. DuQuoin, Ill., Mar. 4, 1904; LL.B., U. Ill., 1930, LL.D., 1930. Admitted to Ill. bar, 1931; practiced in Benton, Ill., 1931—; U.S. commr. Eastern dist. Ill., 1942-49; judge City Ct., Benton, Ill., 1954-68, Ill. Circuit Ct., 2d Jud. Circuit, 1968-75. Mem. Ill. State, Franklin County (Ill.), Am. bar assns., Bar of 7th Jud. Circuit, Am. Acad. Matrimonial Lawyers, U. Ill. Alumni Assn., Justinian Soc. Lawyers, Sigma Delta Kappa. Office: C A Jackson Bldg POB 186 Benton IL 62812 Tel (618) 439-4991

EPHRAIM, CHARLES, b. Chgo., Sept. 18, 1924; Ph.D., U. Chgo., 1948, J.D., 1951. Admitted to D.C. bar, 1951, U.S. Supreme Ct. bar 1954; asso. firm Berge, Fox & Arent, Washington, 1951-53; mem. firm Ephraim & Polydoroff, and predecessors, Washington, 1953—; sec., dir. Herner & Co., 1963—. Bd. dirs. Christ Ch. Child Center, Bethesda, Md., 1961-68, chmn. bd., 1961-62; bd. dirs. Bethesda Fellowship House, 1976—, v.p. bd., 1976—. Mem. Am., D.C. bar assns., Motor Carrier Lawyers Assn. (pres.-elect 1976-77), Phi Beta Kappa, Order of Coif. Mng. editor U. Chgo. Law Rev., 1950-51; contbr. articles to legal jours. Home: 5604 Western Ave Chevy Chase MD 20015 Office: Suite 600 1250 Connecticut Ave NW Washington DC 20036

EPP, HENRY CLARENCE, b. Cleve., Nov. 8, 1945; B.B.A., Kent State U., 1969; J.D., Case Western Res. U., 1972. Admitted to Ohio bar, 1972; asso. firm Weitzmen & Grabow, Cleve., 1972—. Mem. Am., Ohio Cleve., Cuyahoga County bar assns. Home: 321 S Island Rocky River OH 44116 Office: 502 Lincoln Bldg Cleveland OH 44114

EPPENBERGER, FRED ARNOLD, b. Chgo., Oct. 30, 1906; J.D., Washington U., St. Louis, 1928. Admitted to Mo. bar, 1928; partner firm Husch, Eppenberger, Donohue, Eilson & Cornfield and predecessors, St. Louis, 1936—; trustee, chmn. Mo. Bar Found., 1962—. Chmn. St. Louis County Human Relations Commn., St. Louis County Civil Service Commn.; vice chmn. Joint Manpower Commn., mem. citizens adv. com. St. Louis Juvenile Ct. Fellow Am. Bar Found.; mem. Am. (ho. of dels.). St. Louis (v.p.) bar assns., Mo. Bar (pres.) Am. Judicature Soc., Am. Coll. Probate Counsel, Nat. Assn. Coll. Attys., Order Coif, Phi Beta Phi. Recipient alumni citation Washington U., 1962. Contbr. articles to legal jours. Home: 7141 Washington Ave University City MO 63130 Office: 100 N Broadway St St Louis MO 63102 Tel (314) 421-4800

EPSTEIN, BERNARD STEPHEN, b. N.Y.C., May 18, 1934; B.A., Bklyn. Coll., 1955; LL.B., Bklyn. Law Sch., 1957. Admitted to N.Y. bar, 1957; individual practice law, N.Y.C., 1957-68; mem. firm Epstein & Epstein, N.Y.C., 1968—. Mem. N.Y. State Trial Lawyers Assn., N.Y. State Bar Assn. Home: 155 W 68th St New York City NY 10023 Tel (212) 868-3050

EPSTEIN, DAVID, b. San Antonio, June 19, 1935; A.B., Harvard U., 1957, LL.B., 1960. Admitted to Tex. bar, 1960, D.C. bar, 1962, U.S. Supreme Ct. bar, 1967; gen. atty. Nat. Capital Planning Commn., Washington, 1962; asst. U.S. atty., Washington, 1962-66; partner firm Cole and Groner, Washington, 1966-72, firm Berry, Epstein & Sandstrom, Washington, 1972—; adj. prof. Georgetown U. Law Center, 1970-75; mem. Disciplinary Bd. D.C., 1972-77; roster of arbitrators Fed. Mediation and Conciliation Service; cons. Ct. Mgmt. Studies. Cabinet mem. Greater D.C. United Jewish Appeal Fedn., 1976; research asst. Senate staff U.S. Sen. Ralph W. Yarborough, 1958; gen. counsel Ohio McGovern-Shriver Campaign, 1972; campaign organizer for U.S. Sen. Paul Sarbanes, 1976. Mem. D.C., Fed., Am., bar assns. Contbr. articles in field to profl. jours. Home: 7407 Wyndale Rd Chevy Chase MD 20015 Office: Suite 670 1700 Pa Ave NW Washington DC 20006 Tel (202) 393-6242

EPSTEIN, HARRY, b. N.Y.C., Dec. 16, 1904; B.S., N.Y. U., 1926, J.D., 1930. Admitted to N.Y. bar, 1931; individual practice law, N.Y.C., 1931-60, Long Beach, N.Y., 1973—; mem. firm Schultz & Epstein, Long Beach, 1960-77. Mem. Long Beach Lawyers Assn. Address: 45 W Park Ave Room 1 Long Beach NY 11561 Tel (516) 432-0800

EPSTEIN, LEONARD, b. Jersey City, June 30 1938; A.B., U. Pa., 1958; J.D., Harvard U., 1961. Admitted to N.Y. bar, 1962; since practiced in N.Y.C., asso. firm Kaye, Scholer, Fierman, Hays & Handler, 1962-68, asst. gen. counsel Internat. Playtex Corp., 1968-69; partner firm Berlack, Israels & Liberman, 1969—. Mem. Am., N.Y. State bar assns., Assn. Bar City N.Y., N.Y. County Lawyers Assn. Office: 26 Broadway New York City NY 10004 Tel (212) 248-6900

EPSTEIN, MARK BARRY, b. Chgo., July 13, 1946; B.A., U. Chgo., 1967; J.D., Northwestern U., 1970. Admitted to Ill. bar, 1970; instr. clin. legal edn. Northwestern U., 1970-72; dir. Mental Health Legal Service Project, Chgo., 1973-74; partner firm Epstein and Kesselman, Chgo., 1974—; guest instr. law and ethics Northwestern Law Sch., 1977. Mem. Am., Ill., Chgo. bar assns., Decalogue Soc. Lawyers. Reginald Heber Smith Community Lawyer fellow, 1970-72. Author: Northwestern Legal Assistance Clinic Welfare Manual, 1971; Nat. Endowment for Humanities scholar, 1977. Office: 134 N LaSalle St Chicago IL 60602 Tel (312) 782-3193

EPSTEIN, PAULINE, b. Bklyn., Aug. 17, 1907; LL.B., Southwestern U., 1933. Admitted to Calif. bar, 1933; individual practice law, Sherman Oaks, Calif., 1972—; atty., social worker State Relief Adminstrn., Los Angeles, 1936-38. Chmn., Exceptional Children's Opportunity Sch., Los Angeles; mem. Nat. Conf. on Social Welfare, ACLU. Fellow Am. Assn. Mental Deficiency; mem. Internat. Fedn. Women Lawyers, Los Angeles County Bar Assn., Lawyers Club Los Angeles County, Am. Judicature Soc., Assn. Trial Lawyers Am. Office: 14615 Ventura Blvd Sherman Oaks CA 91403 Tel (213) 872-3474

EPSTEIN, SHELDON LEE, b. Chgo., July 16, 1938; B.E.E. and Indsl. Mgmt., Mass. Inst. Tech., 1961; J.D., Columbia U., 1964; postgrad U. Chgo., 1977—. Admitted to Ill. bar, 1964, U.S. Patent Office bar, 1964, U.S. Supreme Ct. bar, 1971; individual practice law, Chgo. and Evanston, Ill., 1964-67; project mgr. Booz Allen Applied Research Inc., Chgo., 1967-68; new bus. and product evaluation asso. Brunswick Corp., Skokie, Ill., 1968-71, sr. patent and licensing atty., 1971—. Mem. ednl. council Mass. Inst. Tech., 1966—. Mem. IEEE, Am. Bar Assn., Licensing Execs. Soc. Home: PO Box 400 Wilmette IL 60076 Office: 1 Brunswick Plaza Skokie IL 60076 Tel (312) 982-6000

EPSTEIN, STANLEY MURRAY, b. Lowell, Mass., Jan. 10, 1918; A.B., Harvard, 1939, LL.B., 1942. Admitted to Mass. bar, 1942, U.S. Supreme Ct. bar, 1955; law clk. Hon. Charles E. Wyzanski, Jr., U.S. Dist. Ct., Boston, 1943-44; asso. firm Mintz, Levin and Cohn, Boston, 1944-46; individual practice law, Boston, 1946-65; partner firm Epstein, Salloway & Kaplan, Boston, 1965—. Chmn. United Fund, Newton, Mass., 1964; chmn. fin. com. Mass. Bay Red Cross Chpts., 1971-75; mem. nat. conv. resolutions com. Am. Nat. Red Cross, 1974; mem. adv. bd. Paralegal Inst., Bentley Coll., 1974—; trustee Social Law Library, Boston. Mem. Am., Mass., Boston bar assns., Am. Trial Lawyers Assn., Boston C. of C., Phi Beta Kappa. Home: 32 Fairview Rd Weston MA 02193 Office: 131 State St Boston MA 02109 Tel (617) 742-5400

EPSTEIN, WILLIAM WARREN, b. Atlanta, Mar. 18, 1933; B.A., U. Va., 1955; LL.B., Emory U., 1960. Admitted to Ga. bar, 1960; partner firm Troutman, Sanders, Lockerman, & Ashmore, Atlanta, 1967—. Mem. exec. com. Muscular Dystrophy Assn., Atlanta, 1973—. Mem. Am., Atlanta bar assns., State Bar Ga., Lawyers Club Atlanta. Home: 231 Peachtree Battle Ave NW Atlanta GA 30305 Office: 1500 Candler Bldg Atlanta GA 30303 Tel (404) 658-8039

EPTING, ROBERT LEE, b. High Point, N.C., July 18, 1945; A.B., U. N.C., 1967, J.D., 1970. Admitted to Ohio bar, 1970, N.C. bar, 1972, U.S. Supreme Ct. bar, 1974; asso. firm Schottenstein, Garel, Swedlow & Zox, 1970-71; asst. dir. inst. govt. U. N.C., Chapel Hill., 1971-72; partner firm Epting, Hackney & Long, Chapel Hill, 1972—. Mem. bd. aldermen, Chapel Hill., 1975—. Mem. Am., N.C. bar assns., Am. Assn. Trial Lawyers. Contbr. articles to law revs. Office: 214 W Rosemary St Chapel Hill NC 27514 Tel (919) 929-0323

ERBSTEIN, KEITH S., b. N.Y.C., Mar. 6, 1946; B.A., U. Buffalo, 1967; J.D., Temple U., 1970. Admitted to Pa. bar, 1970; asso. firm Beasley, Hewson, Casey, Colleran and Stopford, Phila., 1970—. Mem. Am., Pa., Phila. bar assns., Am., Pa., Phila. trial lawyers assns. Editor Temple Law Quar., 1969-70. Office: 21 S 12th St 5th floor Philadelphia PA 19107 Tel (215) 665-1000

ERENS, JAY ALLAN, b. Chgo., Oct. 18, 1935; B.A. summa cum laude, Yale U., 1956; LL.B. magna cum laude, Harvard U., 1959. Admitted to Ill. bar, 1959; law clk. Justice John M. Harlan, U.S. Supreme Ct., 1959-60; individual practice law, Chgo., 1960-64; partner firm Levy and Erens, Chgo., 1964—; lectr. law Northwestern U., 1961-63; spl. asst. atty. gen. State of Ill., 1964-69; dir. Upper Ave. Nat. Bank, Chgo., Popeil Bros., Inc., Chgo. Trustee Latin Sch. Chgo., 1975—. Mem. Am., Chgo. bar assns. Note editor Harvard Law Rev., 1958-59. Office: 208 S LaSalle St Chicago IL 60604 Tel (312) 368-9500

ERICKSON, ALF LEIF, b. Wilmington, Del., Dec. 31, 1938; B.S., U. Wis., 1960; J.D., U. Calif. at Berkeley, 1964; LL.M., U. London, 1970. Admitted to Calif. bar, 1965, Fla. bar, 1967, U.S. Supreme Ct. bar, 1968; asst. dist. atty. Modesto (Calif.), 1965-67; pres. Fed. Bakeries, LaCrosse, Wis., 1967-70; prof. Fla. Internat. U., Miami, 1972—. Bd. govs. Univ. Sch. Nova U., Ft. Lauderdale, Fla., 1975—. Mem. Am. Bar Assn. (com. arms control and disarmament), Interam. Bar Assn. (com. on space law), Am. Soc. Internat. Law, Internat. Inst. Strategic Studies, Calif., Fla. bar assns. Home: 509 Flamingo Dr Fort Lauderdale FL 33301 Office: Sch Bus Fla Internat Univ Miami FL 33199 Tel (305) 552-2571

ERICKSON, CLAUD ROBERT, b. Manistee, Mich., Jan. 8, 1900; B.S., Mich. State U., 1922, M.E., 1927, E.E. 1933, C.E., 1934. Admitted to Mich. bar, 1936, U.S. Supreme Ct. bar, 1963; pvt. practice law; with Lansing (Mich.) Bd. Water and Light, 1920-73, gen. mgr., 1966-73. Mem. Lansing Charter Commn., 1975—; del. Mich. Constl. Conv., 1961-62; chmn. for Ingham County Savs. Bond div. U.S. Dept. Treasury, 1941—; bd. dirs. Lansing Center for the Arts, St. Lawrence Hosp., Lansing; pres. Lansing Area Safety Council, 1976—. Mem. Ingham County Bar Assn. Named Man of Year, Am. Pub. Works Assn., 1968. Home: 1307 Cambridge Rd Lansing MI 48910 Office: 360 Hollister Bldg Lansing MI 48933 Tel (517) 489-6221

ERICKSON, GEORGE EVERETT, JR., b. Fort Scott, Kans., July 20, 1937; B.S., U.S. Naval Acad., 1959; J.D., Washburn U., 1966. Admitted to Kans. bar, 1966, Okla. bar, 1966; with legal dept. Amerada Petroleum Corp., Tulsa, 1966-69; partner firm Cosgrove, Webb & Oman, Topeka, 1969-73; individual practice law, Topeka, 1973—; asso. prof. law Washburn U., 1973-74; city atty. Auburn (Kans.), 1976—. Mem. Am., Kans., Topeka bar assns., Am. Trial Lawyers Assn., Selden Soc. Contbr. articles to legal jours. Home: 6000 Urish Rd Topeka KS 66604 Office: 420 W 33rd Topeka KS 66611 Tel (913) 266-4220

ERICKSON, HARVEY, b. Spokane, Wash., Nov. 20, 1907; LL.B., Gonzaga U., 1934. Admitted to Wash. bar, 1934, U.S. Supreme Ct. Bar, 1950; dep. pros. atty. City of Spokane, 1935-40; asst. U.S. atty., Eastern Dist. Wash., 1940-46, 46-53; asst. prof. law Gonzaga U., 1948-52; individual practice law, Spokane, 1952—. Trustee Eastern Wash. State Coll., 1958-69. Mem., Am., Wash., Spokane County (pres. 1962-63) bar assns. Home: W424 29th Ave Spokane WA 99203 Office: 315 Pacific Nat Bank Bldg Spokane WA 99201 Tel (509) 624-2347

ERICKSON, LLOYD EDWIN, b. Klamath Falls, Oreg., Feb. 6, 1930; B.A., U. Calif., Berkeley, 1952, J.D., 1955; LL.M., U. So. Calif., 1966. Admitted to Calif. bar, 1958, U.S. Dist. Ct. for So. Dist. Calif. bar, 1958; asso. firm Iverson & Hogoboom, Los Angeles, 1958-59; dept. city atty. Los Angeles City Atty.'s Office, 1959-63; individual practice law. Mem. Calif. State Bar, Am. Bar Assn. Home: 17534 Index St Granada Hills CA 91344 Tel (213) 486-6145

ERICKSON, STANLEY EUGENE, b. Clatskanie, Oreg., Jan. 18, 1938; B.S., Lewis and Clark Coll., 1961; J.D., Northwestern Sch. Law, 1968. Underwriter, Standard Ins. Co., Portland, Oreg., 1961-67, asst. mgr., 1967-68; admitted to Oreg. bar, 1968, U.S. Supreme Ct. bar, 1973; asso. firm Reiter, Day, Wall & Bricker, 1968-69; partner firm Wilson & Erickson, 1970-74; individual practice law, Portland, 1974-75; partner firm Erickson & Geer, Tualatin, Oreg., 1976—. Mem. Am., Oreg., Multnomah County (Oreg.), Washington County (Oreg.) bar assns., Am. Trial Lawyers Assn. Home: 1210 Elliott Rd Newberg OR 97132 Office: Erickson & Greer 18735 SW Boones Ferry Rd Tualatin OR 97062 Tel (503) 638-9855

ERICKSON, VINCENT N., b. Mpls., Nov. 25, 1919; A.A., Pasadena Jr. Coll., 1940; A.B., U. So. Calif., 1942, LL.B., 1948. Admitted to Calif. bar, 1949; asst. U.S. atty. So. Dist. Calif., 1949-52; practiced in Los Angeles, 1952-63; judge Los Angeles Municipal Ct., 1963—, asst. presiding judge, 1972, presiding judge, 1973—; tchr., lectr. on trial testimony. Mem. Municipal Ct. Judges Assn. of Los Angeles County (chmn. 1973), Los Angeles County Bar Assn., U. So. Calif. Law Alumni, Delta Theta Phi. U. So. Calif. scholar; editorial bd. So. Calif. Law Rev., 1946-47. Office: Div 44 Criminal Cts Bldg 210 W Temple St Los Angeles CA 90012 Tel (213) 974-6043

ERICKSON, WILLIAM HURT, b. Denver, May 11, 1924; Petroleum Engr., Colo. Sch. Mines, 1947; J.D., U. Va., 1950. Admitted to Colo. bar, 1951, U.S. Supreme Ct. bar, 1953; justice Colo. Supreme Ct. Chmn., Pres.'s Nat. Commn. for Rev. Fed. and State Laws Relating to Wiretapping and Electronic Surveillance; mem. council Am. Law Inst.; mem. nat. adv. council Practicing Law Inst.; mem. cts. task force Nat. Adv. Commn. on Criminal Justice Standards and Goals; co-chmn. Colo. task force on cts. Colo. Commn. on Criminal Justice Standards and Goals; mem. Adv. Com. on Revision of Uniform Rules of Criminal Procedure; hon. chmn. Nat. Edn. Inst.; mem. adv. com. for promulgation of juvenile justice standards Inst. Justicial Adminstrn. Fellow Am. Bar Found., Am. Coll. Trail Lawyers, Internat. Acad. Trail Lawyers (past dir., sec.-treas.), Internat. Soc. Barristers (past pres.); mem. Am. Bar Assn. (mem. fed. rules com. 1969-71, chmn. council criminal justice sect. 1971-72, criminal justice sect. del. Ho. of Dels. 1972-74, chmn. spl. com. on adminstrn. criminal justice 1973-76, Colo. bar assn. del. Ho. of Dels. 1974-76, bd. govs. 1975—, judicial mem. at large, dep. chmn. com. to implement standards for criminal justice, chmn. com. to implement standards for criminal justice for 10th circuit), Colo. Bar Assn. (chmn. negligence sect. 1961, bd. govs. 1968-72, founder, past chmn. criminal law sect., mem. council judiciary sect.), Denver Bar Assn. (pres. 1968-69, trustee), Nat. Legal Aid and Defender Assn. (past state dir.), Scribes (v.p., dir.), Nat. Assn. Def. Lawyers in Criminal Cases (past dir.), Am. Judicature Soc. (dir.), Order of Coif. Home: 10 Martin Ln Englewood CO 80110 Office: 303 State Capitol Bldg Denver CO 80203 Tel (303) 892-2418

ERICKSTAD, RALPH JOHN, b. Starkweather, N.D., Aug. 15, 1922; B.S.L., LL.B., U. Minn. Admitted to N.D. bar, 1949; municipal judge, Devils Lake, N.D.; state's atty. Ramsey County, N.D.; mem. N.D. Senate, 1957-63; asso. justice N.D. Supreme Ct., 1963-73, chief justice, 1973—; past mem. legis. research com. N.D. State Budget Bd.; past mem. Gov.'s spl. Com. on Labor. Former commr. Mo. Valley council Boy Scouts Am.; chmn. bd. trustees Mo. Valley Family YMCA. Mem. State Bar Assn. N.D., Burleigh County, Am. bar assns., Am. Judicature Soc., Am. Law Inst., Conf. of Chief Justices (exec. council). Recipient Sioux award U. N.D., 1973. Home: 1266 W Highland Acres Rd Bismarck ND 58501 Office: Supreme Ct of ND State Capitol Bismarck ND 58505 Tel (701) 224-2221

ERICSSON, LLOYD BAYLES, b. Salina, Kans., Aug. 12, 1939; B.A. in Economics, U. Kans., 1962; LL.B., U. Va., 1965. Admitted to Va. bar, Oreg. bar, U.S. Ct. Appeals 9th Circuit bar, U.S. Supreme Ct. bar; asso. firm Dusenbery, Martin, Beatty & Parks, 1965-68; jr. partner firm Dusenbery, Martin, Beatty, Bishoff & Templeton, 1968-73; sr. partner firm Martin, Bischoff, Templeton, Biggs & Ericsson, Portland, 1973—. Mem. Am., Va., Oreg., Multnomah County, Lawyer Pilots (v.p.) bar assns., Phi Delta Phi, Order of Coif. Contbr. articles in field to profl. jours. Home: 830 SW 84th Ct Portland OR 97225 Office: 2908 First National Tower Portland OR 97201 Tel (503) 224-3113

ERIKSSON, ANN MEIKLE, b. Harrisburg, Pa., Feb. 24, 1927; B.A., Wilson Coll., Chambersburg, Pa., 1948; J.D., Dickinson Sch. Law, 1951. Admitted to Pa. bar, 1952, Ohio bar, 1967; with firm Rupp & Meikle, Harrisburg, 1952-59; chief legal services Ohio Legis. Service Commn., Columbus, 1960-71; dir. Ohio Constl. Revision Commn., Columbus, 1971—. Mem. Am., Ohio, Columbus bar assns., Am. Judicature Soc., Am. Soc. Pub. Adminstrn. (Outstanding Pub. Employee Central Ohio 1967), Am. Acad. Polit. and Social Sci. Home: 2342 Tremont Rd Columbus OH 43221 Office: 41 S High St Columbus OH 43215 Tel (614) 466-6293

ERISMAN, JAMES ALBERT, b. Wilmington, Del., Jan. 29, 1940; B.S., U. Del., 1963; J.D., Dickinson Sch. Law, 1966. Admitted to Del. bar, 1966, U.S. Supreme Ct. bar, 1972; served with Judge Adv. Gen. Corps, U.S. Marine Corps, 1967-70; dep. atty. gen. State of Del., Wilmington, 1970-72; partner firm Conner, Daley, Erisman, Wilmington, 1972—; spl. counsel Del. Pub. Service Commn., 1972-73. Mem. Am., Del. bar assns., Del. Trial Lawyers Assn. (sec.), Assn. Trial Lawyers Am., Am. Judicature Soc., Del. Alumni Assn. Dickinson Sch. Law (pres.). Office: 1224 King St Wilmington DE 19801 Tel (302) 652-3501

ERLICHMAN, JOSEPH, b. Brussels, Belgium, Jan. 11, 1940; B.A., U. Conn., 1964; J.D., St. John's U., N.Y.C., 1967. Admitted to N.Y. State bar, 1967, U.S. Dist. Ct. bar, 1968, Ariz. bar, 1968, U.S. 9th Circuit Ct. Appeals bar, 1976; practiced in Phoenix, 1968—; dep. atty. Maricopa County (Ariz.), 1968-71; partner firm Erlichman and Southern, Ltd., 1971-74; partner firm Erlichman Fagerberg & Margrave and predecessors, 1974—. Mem. Ariz. State Bar (mem. pub. relations com.), Am. (mem. criminal law sect., criminal justice com.), Maricopa County (pres. young lawyers sect. 1975-76) bar assns., Am., Ariz. trial lawyers assns. Office: Suite 2100 Valley Bank Center Phoenix AZ 85073 Tel (602) 257-5161

ERLITZ, STEPHEN N., b. Bklyn., Oct. 21, 1937; B.A., Bklyn. Coll., 1959, J.D., 1967. Admitted to N.Y. State bar, 1963, Fla. bar, 1973; mem. firms Shapiro & Brown, N.Y.C., 1963-64, Daniel Segal, 1964-65, Murray M. Segal, 1966; individual practice law, Bklyn., 1967-69; partner firm Bacine & Erlitz, Bklyn., 1969—. Mem. N.Y., Bklyn. bar assns. Home: 16A Murdock Rd E Rockaway NY 11518 Office: 407 Utica Ave Brooklyn NY 11213 Tel (212) 772-2351

ERSHICK, JANET B., b. Toledo, Ohio, July 9, 1915; LL.B., U. Toledo, 1940. Admitted to Ohio Supreme Ct. bar, 1941, U.S. Dist. Ct. bar, 1967; tax counsel The Electric Auto, Lite Co., Toledo, 1942-63; asst. sec. Am. Lincoln Corp., 1963-67, asso. mem. firm Cobourn, Smith, Rohrbacher & Gibson, Toledo, 1967-72, partner, 1972—. Trustee YWCA, Toledo, 1977. Mem. Toledo, Ohio, Am. bar assns. Home: 3242 Talmadge Rd Toledo OH 43606 Office: 624 Adams St Toledo OH 43604

ERSKINE, BLAKE CHARLES, b. Mexia, Tex., Oct. 17, 1945; B.A., U. Tex., 1967; J.D., Baylor U., 1969. Admitted to Tex. bar, 1969; partner firm Kenley, Boyland, Hawthorn, Starr & Coghlan, Longview, Tex., 1976—. Active Greater Longview United Fund. Mem. Am., Tex., Gregg County bar assns. Home: 608 Woodcrest Ln Longview TX 75601 Office: 500 Petroleum Bldg 202 Whaley St PO Box 312 Longview TX 75601 Tel (214) 757-2636

ERTSGAARD, DUANE RICHARD, b. Sisseton, S.D., Apr. 19, 1929; B.A., Willamette U., 1951, J.D., 1958. Admitted to Oreg. bar, 1958; individual practice law, Salem, Oreg., 1958-61, 65-69; partner firm Burt and Ertsgaard, Salem, 1962-64; county counsel Marion County (Oreg.), 1969-72; judge Marion County Circuit Ct., 1973—. Mem. Marion County (pres. 1973), Oreg. State, Am. bar assns., Oreg. Circuit Judges Assn., Phi Delta Phi. Office: Marion County Courthouse Salem OR 97301 Tel (503) 588-5051

ERVIN, ROBERT MARVIN, b. Marion County, Fla., Jan. 19, 1917; B.S., B.A., U. Fla., 1941, J.D., 1947. Admitted to Fla. bar, 1947, U.S. Supreme Ct. bar, 1960; partner firm Ervin, Varn, Jacobs, Odom & Kitchen, and predecessors, Tallahassee, Fla., 1947—. Mem. Fla. Constitution Revision Commn., 1966-68; trustee U. Fla. Law Center Assn., 1967; chmn. bd. visitors Fla. State U. Coll. Law, 1974-76. Fellow Am. Coll. Trial Lawyers, Internat. Acad. Trial Lawyers, Am., Fla. bar founds.; mem. Fla. Bar (pres. 1965-66, bd. govs. 1959-66), Tallahassee (pres. 1954-55), Am. (ho. of dels. 1966—, chmn. sect. criminal justice 1975-76) bar assns., Am. Law Inst., Am. Judicature Soc. Office: 305 S Gadsden St Tallahassee FL 32302 Tel (904) 224-9135

ERVIN, SAMUEL JAMES, III, b. Morganton, N.C., Mar. 2, 1926; B.S., Davidson Coll., 1948; LL.B., Harvard, 1951, U.S. Dist. Ct. bar for Western Dist. N.C., 1953; individual practice law, Morganton, 1952-57; mem. firm Patton, Ervin & Starnes and predecessors, Morganton, 1957-67; judge Superior Ct. 25th Jud. Dist. of N.C., 1967—; solicitor Burke County (N.C.) Criminal Ct., 1954-56. Pres. Davidson Coll. Nat. Alumni Assn., 1973-74; vice chmn. bd. trustee Grace Hosp., Morganton. Mem. Morganton C. of C. (pres. 1962). Named Morganton Young Man of Year Morganton Jr. C. of C., 1954. Home: 4 Woodside Pl Morganton NC 28655 Office: Burke County Courthouse Morganton NC 28655 Tel (704) 433-5000

ERWIN, WILLIAM MARSH, b. Pontiac, Ill., Oct. 28, 1921; B.A. cum laude, Knox Coll., 1943; J.D., U. Fla., 1966. Funeral dir. Erwin Funeral Home, Pontiac, Ill., 1946-52; asst. sec., Fla. office mgr. Inter-county Constrn. Corp., Fort Lauderdale, 1953-64; admitted to Fla. bar, 1966, U.S. Supreme Ct. bar, 1971; individual practice law, Ft. Lauderdale, 1966—; mem. panel of arbitrators Am. Arbitration Assn., 1970—; lectr. continuing legal edn. Bd. dirs. Doctors Gen. Hosp., Plantation, Fla., 1967—, pres., 1972-73, v.p., 1974—. Mem. Fla. Bar (exec. council sect. family law). Home: 223 Hendricks Isle Fort Lauderdale FL 33301 Office: 1523 NE 4th Ave Fort Lauderdale FL 33304 Tel (305) 764-7271

ESAREY, MARY LOGAN, b. Tobinsport, Ind., Apr. 15, 1898; B.A., Ind. U., 1919, LL.B., 1924. Admitted to Ind. bar, 1924, Fla. bar, 1927; tchr. comml. law Palm Beach County (Fla.) High Sch., West Palm Beach, 1924-25; asso. firm Winters, Foskett & Wilcox, West Palm Beach, 1925-30; individual practice law, West Palm Beach, 1930—. First pres. West Palm Beach Zonta Club of the Palm Beaches, 1947-49. Home: 252 Forest Hill Blvd West Palm Beach FL 33401 Office: 702 Downtown Square Bldg West Palm Beach FL 33401 Tel (305) 655-0665

ESCHBACH, JESSE ERNEST, b. Warsaw, Ind., Oct. 26, 1920; B.S., Ind. U., 1943, J.D. with distinction, 1949. Admitted to Ind. bar, 1949; partner firm Graham, Rasor, Eschbach & Harris, Warsaw, 1949-62; city atty., Warsaw, 1952-53; dep. pros. atty. 54th Jud. Circuit Ct. Ind., 1952-1954; judge U.S. Dist. Ct. Ind., 1962-74, chief judge, 1974—. Pres. Endicott Church Furniture, Inc., 1960-62; sec., gen. counsel Dalton Foundries, Inc., 1957-62. Trustee, Ind. U., 1965-70. Hastings scholar, 1949; recipient U.S. Law Week award, 1949. Mem. U.S. (labor relations com. 1960-62), Warsaw (pres. 1955-56) chambers commerce, Nat. Assn. Furniture Mfrs. (dir. 1962), Ind. Mfrs. Assn. (dir. 1962), Am., Ind. (bd. mgrs. 1953-54, ho. dels. 1950-60, 7th Circuit Fed. bar assns., Am. Judicature Soc., Order of Coif. Editorial staff Ind. Law Jour., 1947-49. Home: 2000 N Bay Dr Warsaw IN 46580 Office: US Post Office and Court House Fort Wayne IN 46802*

ESHOO, GEORGE PAUL, b. Turlock, Calif., Dec. 8, 1937; B.S., U. Calif., Berkeley, 1961, J.D., Hastings Coll. Law, San Francisco, 1966. Admitted to Calif. bar, 1966, U.S. Dist. Ct. bar for No. Dist. Calif., 1966, U.S. Ct. Appeals bar, 9th Circuit, 1966; asso. firm Hoge Fenton, Jones & Appeal, San Jose, Calif., 1966-67; partner firm Wilhelm, Blatt, Gross & Eshoo, 1967-72; individual practice law, Redwood City, Calif., 1972—; counsel Atherton Police Assn., Westates Ins. Agy., Weststates Financial Group, Calif. Hawaii Corp.; gen. counsel Assyrian Am. Fedn. Am., 1972-74. Mem. spl. finance com. Convent of Sacred Heart, 1975. Mem. State Bar Calif., Am., San Mateo, Santa Clara bar assns., Calif., Am., San Mateo trial lawyers assn. Office: 500 Allerton St Redwood City CA 94063 Tel (415) 364-7030

ESKRIDGE, DOUGLAS BRENNER, b. Kansas City, Mo., Oct. 10, 1942; B.A., U. Mo. at Columbia, 1964; J.D., U. Kans., 1971. Admitted to Mo. bar, 1972; chief asst. pros. atty. Platte County (Mo.), 1971-72; individual practice law, Platte City, Mo., 1972—. Bd. dirs. Friends Mus. Mem. Platte County (treas.), Am., Kansas City, Mo. bar assns., Platte County Hist. Soc. (v.p.), Western Platte Jaycees (v.p.). Home: Rt 2 Weston MO 64098 Office: 601 Marshall Rd Platte City MO 64079 Tel (816) 431-5141

ESLER, MICHAEL JOHN, b. Chgo., Oct. 8, 1945; B.A., U. Ill., 1967, J.D., 1971. Admitted to Oreg. bar. Mem. Am., Oreg., Multnomah County bar assns., Am. Trial Lawyers Assn. Office: 2626 First National Tower Portland OR 97201 Tel (503) 223-2626

ESLICK, GORDON STANLEY, b. Mishawaka, Ind., Feb. 9, 1938; B.S. in Bus. with distinction, Ind. U., 1960, J.D., 1963. Admitted to Ind. Supreme Ct. bar, 1963, U.S. Supreme Ct. bar, 1966; mem. firm Thornburg, McGill, Deahl, Harman, Carey & Murray, Elkhart, Ind., 1967-73, partner, 1973—. Bd. dirs. Assn. for Disabled of Elkhart County, Inc., 1974—. Mem. Elkhart City, Elkhart County, Ind. State (ho. of dels. 1971—, chmn. legal ethics sub-com. 1976—), Am. bar assns. Chmn. editorial com. Uniform Commercial Code Forms, 1974. Office: 305 First Nat Bank Bldg Elkhart IN 46514 Tel (219) 293-0681

ESLIEN, HOWARD JEROME, b. Oconto, Wis., Apr. 18, 1941; B.A., Marquette U., Milw., 1966, J.D., 1969. Admitted to Wis. bar, 1970; partner firm Eslien & Eslien, Oconto Falls, Wis., 1972—. Vol. Peace Corps., 1969-72. Mem. Wis. Bar Assn., Oconto Falls Bus. Assn., Oconto Falls Jr. C. of C. (legal advisor 1975-77), Kiwanis Club (pres. 1975-76), K.C. (chmn. com. on Mentally Retarded Fund Dr. 1975-76). Office: 208 E Central Ave Oconto Falls WI 54154 Tel (414) 846-3261

ESPINOZA, ANN SHARP, b. Fairmont, W.Va., Aug. 12, 1928; B.S., Columbia U., 1964, LL.B., 1967. Admitted to N.Y. bar, 1967, Calif. bar, 1971; asso. firm Pennie & Edmonds, N.Y.C., 1967-71; mem. firm Limbach, Limbach & Sutton, San Francisco, 1971-76; individual practice law, Berkeley, Calif., 1976—; Mem. Phi Beta Kappa. Home and Office: 1475 LeRoy St Berkeley CA 94708 Tel (415) 843-8264

ESPOSITO, JOHN VINCENT, b. Logan, W.Va., Dec. 25, 1946; B.A. magna cum laude in Arts and Scis. (Claude Worthington Benedum scholar, Bd. Govs. Achievement scholar), W.Va. U., 1968, J.D. (Bd Govs. Grad. scholar), 1971. Admitted to W.Va. bar, 1971; legis. aide to Congressman Ken Hechler 4th Dist. W.Va., 1971; individual practice law, Logan, W.Va., 1972—; counsel to Hon. Hans McCourt, pres. W.Va. State Senate, 1972; instr. So. W.Va. Community Coll., 1972-74; arbitrator United Mine Workers Am. and Coal Operators Assn.; spl. judge, Commr. in Chancery, Circuit Ct. Logan County (W.Va.); judge Municipal Ct., Chapmanville, W.Va. Mem. Am, W.Va. (chmn. young lawyers sect.) bar assns., Am., W.Va. trial lawyers assns., Am. Judicature Soc. Scholar, Coll. of Advocacy, Hastings Coll. Law U. Calif., 1976; co-author: Laws for Young Mountaineers, 1974. Home: 607 Stratton St Logan WV 25601 Office: 401 Stratton St Logan WV 25601 Tel (304) 752-7300

ESPOSITO, JOSEPH ANTHONY, b. Spokane, Wash., Oct. 4, 1941; B.A., Gonzaga U., Spokane, 1963, J.D., 1969. Admitted to Wash. bar, 1969; law clk. to chief judge Ct. Appeals, Spokane, 1969-70; mem. firm Delluo, Rudolf & Grant, Spokane, 1970-73, partner, 1973—; partner firm Trezona, Lorenz, Parry & Esposito, Spokane, 1973—. Bd. dirs. Spokane Comprehensive Health Counsel, 1973-74, St. Josephs Children's Home, Spokane, 1974—. Mem. Wash., Spokane County (dir.) bar assns., Spokane Jr. C. of C. (dir.). Office: 302 Fidelity Bldg Spokane WA 99201 Tel (509) 747-6173

ESPOSITO, STANLEY E., b. Bklyn., July 27, 1938; B.A., L.I. U., 1960; LL.B., Bklyn. Law Sch., 1963. Admitted to N.Y. State bar, 1964; mem. firm Hendler, Murray & Watson, N.Y.C., 1963-67; individual practice law, Thornwood, N.Y., 1967—; atty. Hawthorne Improvement Dist., 1972—, Hawthorne Fire Dist., 1975—. Mem. Westchester County, N.Y. State bar assns. Home: 467 Old Sleepy Hollow Rd Pleasantville NY 10570 Office: 645 Marble Ave Thornwood NY 10594

ESQUIVEL, EDWARD H., b. Austin, Tex., Oct. 26, 1941; B.B.A., U. Tex., Austin, 1964, LL.B., 1967. Admitted to Tex. bar, 1967; asst. atty. gen. State of Tex., Austin, 1967-71; asso. firm Dumas, Huguenin, Boothman & Morrow, Dallas, 1971-77, partner, 1977—. Mem. Am., Dallas bar assns. Office: 1212 United National Bank Bldg Dallas TX 75201 Tel (214) 741-3458

ESS, HENRY NEWTON, III, b. Kansas City, Mo., Aug. 17, 1921; A.B., Princeton, 1942; LL.B., Harvard, 1944. Admitted to N.Y. bar, 1945, U.S. Supreme Ct. bar, 1961; asso. firm Sullivan & Cromwell, N.Y.C., 1944-53, partner, 1953—; trustee William Nelson Cromwell Found., 1961—, Vincent Astor Found., 1973—; Animal Med. Center N.Y.C., 1974—, Princeton Library in N.Y.C., 1970—. Mem. Am., N.Y. State bar assns., N.Y. County Lawyers Assn. (pres. 1973-75), Am. Bar Found., Assn. Bar N.Y.C., Adjudicature Soc., Am. Coll. Probate Counsel. Home: 80 Park Ave New York City NY 10016 Office: 250 Park Ave New York City NY 10017 Tel (212) 952-8411

ESSER, JOSEPH JACOB, b. Milw., Oct. 21, 1924; A.A., St. Lawrence Sem., Mt. Calvary, Wis., 1945; J.D., Marquette U., 1952. Admitted to Wis. bar, 1952; adjuster, supervising adjuster Travelers Ins. Co., Milw., 1952-57; individual practice law, Milw., 1957-62; asst. corp. counsel Milwaukee County (Wis.), 1962-70; individual practice law, Menomonee Falls, Wis., 1970—; municipal justice Village of Menomonee Falls, 1962—. Mem. Wis., Waukesha County bar assns., Wis. Municipal Justice Assn., Nat. Right of Way Assn., Am. Judicature Soc., Nat. Judges Assn. Home: W152 N7327 Westwood Dr Menomonee Falls WI 53051 Office: N84 W 15959 Appleton Ave PO Box 596 Menomonee Falls WI 53051 Tel (414) 251-5700

ESSIG, WILLIAM JOHN, b. South Bend, Ind., July 13, 1938; B.A., Yale U., 1959; J.D., U. Chgo., 1965. Admitted to Ill. bar, 1966; atty. Lawyers Title Ins. Corp., Chgo., 1966-67; title officer Pioneer Nat. Title Ins. Co., Chgo., 1967-69; asso. firm Ralph E. Brown, Chgo., 1969-71; asst. gen. counsel Benefit Trust Life Ins. Co., Chgo., 1971—. Mem. Chgo., Ill. State, Am. bar assns. Home: 2942 Greenleaf Ave Wilmette IL 60091 Office: 1771 Howard St Chicago IL 60626 Tel (312) 274-8100

ESTES, JOHN B., b. Davis, Okla., Feb. 23, 1936; B.B.A., U. Okla., 1957; J.D., Okla. City U., 1973. Admitted to Okla. bar, 1973; engaged in banking, 1959-70. Mem. Am., Okla. trial lawyers assns., Okla. City C. of C. (pres.). Office: 2915 Lincoln St Oklahoma City OK 73105 Tel (405) 524-2268

ETELSON, ARNOLD PHILIP, b. Suffern, N.Y., Nov. 13, 1937; B.A., Syracuse U., 1959; LL.B., Bklyn. Law Sch., 1962. Admitted to N.Y. bar, 1962; asso. firm Etelson & Fassberg, Spring Valley, N.Y., 1962-75, mem. firm, 1975—; village justice Village of Spring Valley, 1967-75; town justice Town of Ramapo (N.Y.), 1976—. Vice chmn., bd. dirs., atty. Arts Council Rockland, Spring Valley, 1973—. Mem. Am., N.Y. State, Rockland County (N.Y.) (1st adminstr. Assigned Counsel Plan 1966-67) bar assns., N.Y. State Trial Lawyers Assn. Home: 2 Catherine Ct Suffern NY 10901 Office: 300 N Main St Spring Valley NY 10977 Tel (914) 356-0448

ETHEREDGE, ROBERT FOSTER, b. Birmingham, Ala., July 14, 1920; A.B., U. Ala., 1946, LL.B., 1949. Admitted to Ala. bar, 1949; since practiced in Birmingham, partner firm Spain, Gillon, Riley, Tate & Etheredge, 1949—; mem. adv. com. Family Ct. Bd. Dirs., Ala.; mem. Ala. Ho. of Reps., 1963-66. Mem. Ala. Soc. for Crippled Children and Adults, pres., 1972-73; dir. North Central Ala. Rehab. Com., 1969-75. Mem. Ala. Law Inst., Am., Ala., Birmingham bar assns., Farrah Law Soc., Am. Judicature Soc., Ala. Claims Assn., Am. Legion, VFW, Ala. Def. Lawyers Assn., Internat. Assn. Ins. Counsel. Home: 3748 Locksley Dr Birmingham AL 35223 Office: 800 John A Hand Bldg Birmingham AL 35203 Tel (205) 328-4100

ETHERIDGE, JACK PAUL, b. Atlanta, Mar. 16, 1927; B.S., Davidson Coll., 1949; J.D., Emory U., 1955. Admitted to Ga. bar, 1954, U.S. Supreme Ct. bar, 1965; asso. firm Kilpatrick, Cody, Rogers, McClatchey & Regenstein, Atlanta, 1955-57; partner firm Huie, Etheridge & Harland, Atlanta, 1957-66; judge Superior Ct., Atlanta Jud. Circuit, 1967-77, sr. judge, 1977—; asso. prof. U. S.C., 1977—. Mem. Ga. Ho. of Reps., 1962-66; mem. faculty Nat. Coll. State Judiciary, Reno, 1975; cons. Nat. Endowment for Humanities; adj. prof. law Emory U. Mem. Internat. Acad. Trial Judges, Am. Hist. Assn., Selden Soc., Am. Soc. Legal History, Nat. Conf. State Trial Judges (exec. com.). Home: 4715 Harris Tr NW Atlanta GA 30327 Office: Fulton County Courthouse Pryor St Atlanta GA 30303 Tel (404) 572-3136

ETHRIDGE, THOMAS RAMAGE, b. West Point, Miss., May 2, 1918; B.A., U. Miss., 1940, J.D., 1946, M.A., 1951. Admitted to Miss. bar, 1946; partner firm Ethridge & Ethridge, Oxford, Miss., 1946-54; partner firm Ethridge & Grisham, 1961-71, counsel, 1971—; U.S. atty. U.S. Dist. Ct. for No. Dist. Miss., Oxford, 1954-61; prof. law U. Miss., 1971—; mem. Miss. Senate, 1948-54. Trustee Mary Buie Mus., Oxford, 1968—, Oxford-Lafayette County Hosp., 1974-76. Mem. Lafayette County (Miss.), Miss. (commr.), Am. bar assns., Am.

Judicature Soc., Miss. Bar Found. (v.p. 1975-76, pres. 1976-77), Miss. Jud. Coll. (gov.), Miss. Inst. Continuing Legal Edn. (bd. govs.). Home: 1011 S 11th St Oxford MS 38655 Office: Sch of Law U of Miss University MS 38677 Tel (601) 232-7361

ETIENNE, MYRON E., b. Pasadena, Calif., June 22, 1949; J.D., Hastings Coll., 1952. Admitted to Calif. bar, 1953, Dist. Columbia bar, 1953; legal research aide Dist. Ct. Appeal Div. 1, 1953-54; deputy dist. atty. Monterey County, 1954-55; mem. firm Noland, Hamerly, Etienne & Hoss, Salinas, Calif., 1955—; instr. Real Estate & Tax Law U. Calif., bd. dirs., past pres. Hastings Law Sch. Alumni Assn., mem. exec. com. U. Calif. Alumni Council. Chmn. bd. Harbor Commissioners Moss Landing Harbor Dist., 1957-64; bd. dirs., past pres. Calif. Rodeo, Salinas; mem. Monterey County Republican Central Com., 1962-66, vice chmn. 12th Congressional Dist. Com.; gen. counsel, mem. Monterey Jazz Festival; bd. dirs. Salinas Valley Fair, chmn. advisory com, bd. dirs. Rodeo Cowboys Assn.; mem. Center City Authority, Rancheros Visitadores. Mem. Monterey County, Los Angeles, San Francisco, Am. bar assns., Psi Upsilon, Phi Alpha Delta. Recipient Outstanding Young Man Year Jr. C. of C. Home: 23799 Salinas Monterey Hwy Salinas CA 93901 Office: 333 Salinas St Salinas CA 93901 Tel (408) 424-1414

ETTIEN, J(OHN) CHAN(DICE), b. Deer Lodge, Mont., Oct. 8, 1916; student Gonzaga U., 1937-39; J.D., U. Mont., 1942. Admitted to Mont. bar, 1942, U.S. Supreme Ct. bar, 1959; individual practice law, Philipsburg, Mont., 1946-50; mem. firm Ettien & Hanifen, Philipsburg, 1950-53; county atty. Granite County (Mont.), 1947-50; state senator Granite County, 1951-54; city atty. Philipsburg, 1953; dep. county atty. Hill County, Mont., 1957-67; tribal counsel Fort Bellknap Indian Reservation, 1961-67; Eastern screening panel, malpractice, joint Mont. legis. com., Mont. Med. Assn., 1969-71. Chmn., Hosp. Fund Drive, Granite County, 1951-52, Red Cross Drive, Hill County, Mont., 1959; mem. Havre City-County Planning Bd., 1959-60; mem. adv. com. Havre High Sch., 1975—; trustee Mont. Cath. Conf., 1977—. Mem. Am., Mont., 12th Jud. Dist. bar assns., Am. Judicature Soc., Asso. Trial Lawyers Am. Recipient Justin Miller prize U Mont. Law Sch., 1942; contbr. articles to legal jours. Home: 700 First Ave Havre MT 59501 Office: 339 Third St POB 1070 Havre MT 59501 Tel (406) 265-4396

ETTINGER, JOSEPH ALAN, b. N.Y.C., July 21, 1931; B.A., Tulane U., 1954, J.D., 1956. Admitted to La. bar, 1956, Ill. bar, 1960; served with Judge Adv. Gen. Corps, 1956-59; state's atty. Cook County, Ill., 1960-63; individual practice law, Chgo., 1962-73; partner firm Ettinger & Lake, Chgo., 1973—; asso. prof. law Ill. Inst. Tech., 1973—. Chmn. Olympia Fields (Ill.) Zoning Bd. Appeals, 1969-76; chmn. panel on corrections Welfare Council Met. Chgo., 1969-71. Mem. Chgo. Bar Assn., Assn. Criminal Def. Lawyers (gov. 1970-72). Contbr. articles to law revs. Home: 1540 N LaSalle St Chicago IL 60610 Office: 100 N LaSalle St Chicago IL 60602 Tel (312) ST2-8435

ETTINGER, WARREN L., b. Cleve., May 7, 1929; B.S., U. So. Calif., Los Angeles, 1952, LL.B., 1955. Admitted to Calif. bar, 1956; dep. dist. atty. Los Angeles, 1956-58; individual practice law, Beverly Hills, Los Angeles, 1958-66; judge Municipal Ct. Pasadena, Calif., 1966—; mem. Jud. Council State of Calif., 1971-74; lectr. Nat. Judges Coll., Reno, 1974, Calif. Coll. Trial Judges, 1970-75, U. So. Calif. Law Sch., 1972-76. Bd. dirs. Pasadena Urban League, 1976. Mem. Calif. (advisor, com. on criminal law and procedure 1966-68), Los Angeles (criminal law trial law sec. 1955-70), Criminal Cts. (pres. 1966) bar assns. Home: 1415 Chamberlain Rd Pasadena CA 91103 Office: 200 North Garfield St Pasadena CA 91101 Tel (213) 796-9361

EUBANK, JAMES HARDY, b. Corpus Christi, Tex., Apr. 15, 1940; B.A., Tex. Tech. U.; LL.B., U. Tex. Admitted to Tex bar; former partner firm Hill, Daugherty and Eubank, Shamrock, Tex.; atty. Texaco, Inc., Wichita Falls, Ft. Worth and Midland, Tex.; individual practice law, Midland, 1967—. Mem. Am., Midland County bar assns., State Bar of Tex., Pi Sigma Alpha. Office: 619 W Texas St Midland TX 79701 Tel (915) 683-4253

EUBANK, ROBERT BENJAMIN, b. Alexandria, La., May 30, 1942; A.B., Princeton, 1964; J.D., Harvard, 1967; LL.M., N.Y. U., 1973. Admitted to La. bar, 1968, Ala. bar, 1973; clk. U.S. Dist. Ct. for Western La., Lake Charles, 1967-68; atty. So. Natural Gas Co., Birmingham, Ala., 1968-72; mem. firm Sirote, Permutt, Friend, Friedman, Held & Apolinsky, Birmingham, 1973—; prof. Cumberland Sch. Law, Samford U., 1974—. Mem. Am., Ala., La. bar assns. Home: 4833 Old Leeds Rd Birmingham AL 35213 Office: 2222 Arlington Ave S Box 3364A Birmingham AL 35205 Tel (205) 933-7111

EUBANKS, GARY LEROY, b. North Little Rock, Ark., Nov. 25, 1933; J.D., U. Ark., 1960. Admitted to Ark. bar, 1960, since practiced in Little Rock; partner firm Bailey, Jones & Eubanks, 1960-63, Eubanks & Dean, 1963-65, Eubanks & Hood, 1965, Eubanks, Hood & Files, 1965-70, Eubanks Files & Hurley, 1970-76, Haskins, Eubanks & Wilson, 1976—. Mem. Ark. Ho. of Reps., 1963-67; mem. Pulaski County Sch. Bd., 1967. Mem. Am., Ark., Pulaski County, North Pulaski County bar assns., Am., Ark. trial lawyers assns. Home: 4 Wayside Dr Little Rock AR Office: 1690 Union Nat Plaza Little Rock AR 72201 Tel (501) 372-2224

EUBANKS, LEON STEWART, JR., b. Phila., July 10, 1941; B.A., So. Meth. U., 1964, LL.B., J.D., 1967. Admitted to Tex. bar, 1967, U.S. Dist. Ct. bar for No. Dist. Tex., 1967; asso. firm Irion, Cain, Magee & Davis, Dallas, 1966-68; asst. dist. atty. for Dallas County, 1968—, chief felony prosecutor, 1970—; lectr. Tex. Criminal Justice Council. Bd. dirs. Dallas Civic Opera, United Fund, Dallas. Mem. Tex., Dallas bar assns., Tex. Dist. and County Attys'. Assn. Recipient Am. Jurisprudence award, 1967. Office: Office of Dist Atty Dallas County Govt Center Dallas TX 75202 Tel (214) 749-8511

EUBANKS, RAYMOND CONVERSE, JR., b. Spartanburg, S.C., Dec. 18, 1933; A.B., Wofford Coll., 1956; LL.B., U. S.C., 1959. Admitted to S.C. bar, 1959; asst. gen. counsel U.S. Senate Judiciary Subcom. Trading with Enemy Act, 1959-60; mem. staff Judge Adv. Gen. Dept., USAF, Moody AFB, Ga., 1960-63; partner firm Brown & Eubanks, Spartanburg, 1963-68; mem. S.C. Ho. of Reps., 1964-68; partner firm Cauthen & Eubanks, Spartanburg, 1968-76, Jim Smith & Assos., Inc., Spartanburg, 1977—; mem. com. to study S.C. uniform consumer credit code, 1969-70. Home: 233 Holly Dr Spartanburg SC 29301 Office: 601 W Main St Spartanburg SC 29301

EUGENE, NEAL TURK, b. Bklyn., Jan. 26, 1934; B.S., L.I. U., 1955; LL.B., Bklyn. Law Sch., 1960, J.D., 1967. Admitted to N.Y. bar, 1961; individual practice law, Bklyn., 1961—. Pres. jr. high sch., Bklyn.; v.p. United Parents Assn. of N.Y.C. Mem. N.Y., Am. bar assns., Am. Trial Lawyers Assn. Home and Office: 1796 E 29th St Brooklyn NY 11229 Tel (212) 258-8623

EUPHRAT, LOUIS, b. Cin., Dec. 22, 1924; J.D., U. Cin., 1949. Admitted to Ohio bar, 1950; with claims dept. Employers Liability Assurance Co., Ltd., 1951; br. claims mgr. So. Ohio Adjustment Services, Inc., 1952; claim dept. and supervising examiner Fed. Mut. Ins. Co.-Kemper Ins., 1952-64; claims atty. Nationwide Mut. Ins. Co., Canton, Ohio, 1964—, also regional rehab. coordinator Northeastern Ohio region. Mem. Ohio Bar Assn., Internat. Assn. Laryngectomies, Ohio Def. Assn. (charter). Contbr. articles to legal jours. Home: 8778 Colton St NW Massillon OH 44646 Office: PO Box 8379 1014 Market Ave N Canton OH 44711 Tel (216) 456-9551

EURE, DELMAN HODGES, b. Norfolk, Va., July 5, 1928; B.A., Coll. William and Mary, 1952, B.C.L., 1954; LL.M., N.Y. U., 1955. Admitted to Va. bar, 1955, N.Y. bar, 1963; with Office of Chief Counsel, IRS, Washington, 1955-58, trial atty., Milw., 1958-61, asst. regional counsel, Chgo., 1961-62; asso. firm Dunnington, Bartholow & Miller, N.Y.C., 1962-67; partner firm Vandevander, Black, Meredith & Martin, Norfolk, 1967-69, Christian, Barton, Epps, Brent & Chappel, Richmond, Va., 1969—. Mem. Va. State, City of Richmond, N.Y. State, N.Y.C., Am., Fed. bar assns. Home: 503 Gaskins Rd Richmond VA 23233 Office: 1200 Mutual Bldg Richmond VA 23219 Tel (804) 644-7851

EUSEY, CHARLES JOSEPH, b. Worcester, Mass., July 22, 1946; A.B., Atlantic Union Coll., 1969; J.D., Villanova U., 1972. Admitted to Ind. bar, 1972, Mich. bar, 1974, Pa. bar, 1975; dep. prosecutor, Vermillion County, Ind., 1972-74; individual practice law, Newport, Ind., 1972-74; dir. trust services Pa. Conf. Seventh-Day Adventists, Reading, 1975—. Dir. religious liberty, Pa. Conf. Seventh-Day Adventists, 1976—. Mem. Ind., Mich., Pa., Berks County bar assns. Home: Governor Mifflin Apt 114-I Shillington PA 19607 Office: 720 Museum Rd Reading PA 19611 Tel (215) 374-8331

EUSON, RICHARD ALLER, b. Chgo., Oct. 16, 1948; B.A., U. Kans., 1970; J.D., Washburn U., Topeka, 1973. Admitted to Kans. bar, 1974; asso. firm Dresie, Jorgensen & Wood, Wichita, Kans., 1974-76, partner, 1976—; counsel Wichita Jaycees, 1975-76. Office: 433 N Broadway St Wichita KS 67202 Tel (316) 267-4231

EUSTACE, FRANK JAMES, JR., b. Phila., Mar. 26, 1903; A.B., U. Pa., 1924; LL.D., Temple U., 1924. Admitted to Pa. bar, 1924; asso. firm Gibbons & Whitaker, Phila., 1924, firm Wilson & McAdams, Phila., 1925-38; partner firm McAdams & Eustace, Phila., 1938-58; individual practice law, Phila., 1958-71; partner firm Gibbons Eustace & Obert, Phila., 1971—. Mem. Phila. Human Relations Bd., 1966-72; bd. govs. U. Pa. Coll. Alumni, 1968—; pres. St. Joseph's Prep. Alumni, 1946-48, Temple U. Law Alumni, 1950-52, U. Pa. Class of 1924 Alumni, 1957—; Mem. Phila. Trial Lawyers Assn. (pres. 1960-61), Phila. Bar Assn. (censor 1962-64, treas. 1964-66), St. Thomas More Soc. (pres. 1958). Office: 1442 Fidelity Bldg Philadelphia PA 19109 Tel (215) PE5-4868

EVAN, CHARLES, b. Domazlice, Czechoslovakia, Oct. 4, 1905; JUDr, Charles U. (Czechoslovakia), 1929; LL.B., Bklyn. Law Sch., 1943. Admitted to Czechoslovak bar as candidate, 1929, as adv., 1934, N.Y. bar, 1947; adv., Czechoslavakia, 1934-39; with U.S. Office War Info., Dept. State, 1943-47; individual practice law, N.Y.C., 1947—; faculty mem. Sch. Law N.Y. U., N.Y.C., 1950—. Mem. Am. Bar Assn., Am. Trial Lawyers Assn., Internat. Law Assn. (com. chmn.), Am. Soc. Internat. Law, Am. Fgn. Law Assn. Contbr. articles to legal jours. and revs. Office: 295 Madison Ave New York City NY 10017 Tel (212) LE2-2673

EVANS, CHESTER EARL, b. Witt, Ill., July 15, 1915; B.S., U. Ill., 1949, U.D., 1950. Admitted to Ill. bar, 1950; asso. Omer Poos, Hillsboro, Ill., 1950-58; individual practice law, Hillsboro, 1958-73; partner firm Evans & Evans, Hillsboro, 1973—; spl. asst. atty. gen. State of Ill., 1968—. Mem. Ill., Montgomery County bar assns. Home: 506 Jefferson St Hillsboro IL 62049 Office: 218 S Main St Hillsboro IL 62049 Tel (217) 532-6154

EVANS, DONALD JOHN, b. Springfield, Mass., Jan. 29, 1926; A.B., Dartmouth, 1947; J.D., Harvard, 1952. Admitted to Mass. bar, 1952; asso. firm Goodwin, Procter & Hoar, Boston, 1952-59, partner, 1960—; officer, dir. various cos.; participant forums Practising Law Inst., New Eng. Law Inst. Bd. dirs. World Affairs Council, Inc., Boston, 1957—, Boston Opera Assn., Inc., 1974—; corporator New Eng. Bapt. Hosp., Boston, 1969—, Big Bros. Assn. of Boston, 1974—; trustee, corporator Bundy Found., Inc., Waitsfield, Vt., 1970—; chmn. leadership gifts South Area United Way of Massachusetts Bay, 1976. Mem. Am. (past chmn. sect. corp., banking and bus. law, chmn. com. on counsel responsibilities 1973—), Boston, Mass. bar assns., Am. Law Inst. Contbr. articles to legal jours. Home: 72 N Main St Cohasset MA 02025 Office: 28 State St Boston MA 02109 Tel (617) 523-5700

EVANS, DORSEY, b. Kansas City, Kans., Dec. 7, 1930; Mus.B., U. Kans., 1952; J.D., Howard U., 1958. Admitted to Kans. bar, 1960, D.C. bar, 1960; individual practice law, Washington, 1960—; v.p. Homemaker Service, Inc., Washington, 1972-75, dir., 1971-75. Pres. Woodridge Civic Assn., Washington, 1962-64; treas., campaign advisor D.C. Del. Congressman Walter E. Fauntroy, 1971—; mem. adv. bd. concillior U. D.C., 1976—; mem. adv. com. Superior Ct. Rules Civil Procedure D.C., 1971-74; pres. Young Dem. Club D.C., 1962-63. Mem. Nat., Am., D.C. bar assns., Am. Judicature Soc., Am. Arbitration Assn. (adv. council 1971—). Home: 2840 Davenport St NW Washington DC 20008 Office: 1025 Connecticut Ave NW Suite 506 Washington DC 20036 Tel (202) 659-4343

EVANS, EUGENE HARRY, b. Phila., July 19, 1942; B.B.A., Pa. Mil. Coll., 1964; J.D., Villanova U., 1967. Admitted to Pa. bar, 1967; asso. Raymond E. Larson, Media, Pa., 1967-68, Freonfield, deFuria & Petrikin, Media, 1970-76; partner firm Goldberg & Evans, West Chester, Pa., 1976—; solicitor Radnor Twp., Delaware County, Pa., 1974—; solicitor Thornbury Twp. (Pa.) Zoning Hearing Bd., 1976—. Bd. dirs. Briar Lyn Civic Assn., Radnor, 1970—. Mem. Am., Pa., Delaware County, Chester County bar assns. Home: 2 Earle's Ln Newtown Square PA 19073 Office: 131 W Market St West Chester PA 19380 Tel (215) 436-6220

EVANS, FRANK OWEN, b. Gordon, Ga., Dec. 15, 1910; B.S. in Econs., Washington and Lee U., 1930; LL.B., Mercer U., 1933. Admitted to Ga. bar, 1933, U.S. Supreme Ct. bar, 1953; practiced in Milledgeville, Ga., 1933-53, 61—; U.S. atty. Middle Dist. Ga., 1953-61. Mem. Ga., Am. bar assns. Home: 220 E Montgomery St Milledgeville GA 31061 Office: PO Box A Milledgeville GA 31061 Tel (912) 452-1324

EVANS, GOMER ALLAN, b. Tulsa, July 21, 1944; B.B.A., U. Okla. at Tulsa, 1966; J.D., U. Tulsa, 1968. Admitted to Okla. bar; asso. firm Oliver, Evans, & Wallis, Tulsa, 1969—. Mem. Okla. Trial Lawyers Assn. Office: 1410 4th Nat Bank Bldg Tulsa OK 74119 Tel (918) 585-8181

EVANS, GORDON EMIL, b. Douglas, Ariz., Sept. 1, 1932; student Tex. Western Coll., 1950-51; B.J., U. Ariz., 1958, J.D., 1970. Admitted to Ariz., Alaska bars, 1970; law clk. to presiding judge Superior Ct., Juneau, Alaska, 1970-71; partner firm Engstrom and Evans, Juneau, 1971-77, Ely, Guess & Rudd, Juneau, 1977—. Chmn., Greater Juneau Democratic Com., 1973-76; state chmn. Alaska Dem. Party, 1976—. Mem. Am., Alaska, Juneau (sec. 1971-72, pres. 1974-75) bar assns., State Bar Ariz., Am. Trial Lawyers Assn. Home: 604 Gold St Juneau AK 99801 Office: Mendenhall Bldg Juneau AK 99801 Tel (907) 586-3210

EVANS, HAROLD BRADLEY, JR., b. Watertown, N.Y., Oct. 12, 1937; B.A., Yale, 1959; LL.B., Georgetown U., 1966. Admitted to Va. bar, 1966; asso. firm Boothe, Dudley, Kountz, Blakinship & Stump, Fairfax, Va., 1967-68; partner Evans & Economou, Alexandria, Va., 1969—. Mem. Va., Fairfax County, Alexandria bar assns., Am., Va. No. Va. (pres. 1974-75, v.p. 1973-74, mem. bd. dirs. 1970-75) trial lawyers assns. Contbr. articles to field to profl. jours. Home: 1136 Custis St Alexandria VA 22303 Office: 122 S Royal St Box 701 Alexandria VA 22313 Tel (703) 354-5710

EVANS, HENRY DARLING, b. Washington, Apr. 3, 1914; LL.B., Nat. U. Law, 1942. Admitted to Va. bar, 1969; U.S. probation officer Dist. Ct., Washington, 1943-44, Richmond, Va., 1944-70; judge D.C. Bankruptcy Ct., 1970-75. Recipient numerous photography awards, 1947—.

EVANS, JAMES THOMAS, b. Tulsa, Aug. 10, 1943; B.B.A., U. Houston, 1965, J.D. cum laude, 1968. Admitted to Tex. bar, 1968, U.S. Supreme Ct. bar, 1974; asso. firm Baer, Cryan, Keen & Kelly, Houston, 1969-70; partner firm Evans & Birnberg, Bellaire, Tex., 1970—, sr. partner, 1972—; judge City of Friendswood (Tex.), 1970—. Judge adv. Am. Legion. Mem. Am., Tex., Houston bar assns., Am. Judges Assn. Home: 1919 W McKinney St Houston TX 77019 Office: 5959 W Loop S Bellaire TX 77401 Tel (713) 664-7782

EVANS, JEREMY HARRISON, b. Cleve., Sept. 29, 1931; B.A., San Diego State Coll., 1953; LL.B., Southwestern Law U., 1963. Admitted to Calif. bar, 1966; individual practice law, Redondo Beach and Torrance, Calif. Planning commr. City of Manhattan Beach (Calif.), 1972-74. Mem. Redondo Beach C. of C. (v.p. 1975-76), S. Bay Bar Assn. (dir. 1967—, sec.). Office: 925 Union Bank Tower 21515 Hawthorne Blvd Torrance CA 90503 Tel (213) 540-3377

EVANS, JOHN DAVID, b. Council Bluffs, Iowa, Dec. 14, 1946; B.A., Rutgers U., 1969; J.D., Columbia U., 1972. Admitted to N.Y. State bar, 1973; asso. firm Davies, Hardy, Ives & Lawther, N.Y.C., 1972—. Mem. Assn. Bar City N.Y., Am., N.Y. bar assns., Legal Aid Soc. Office: 2 Broadway New York City NY 10004 Tel (212) 422-6610

EVANS, JOHN THORNLEY, b. Salt Lake City, Mar. 14, 1938; J.D., U. Utah, 1965. Admitted to Utah bar, 1965; law clk. to chief justice Utah Supreme Ct., 1964-65; dep. atty. Salt Lake County, 1965-66; asst. Atty. Gen. State of Utah, 1968-73; partner firm Clyde & Pratt, Salt Lake City, 1968—; chmn. condemnation sect. Utah State Bar, 1973-74; lectr. Nat. Inst. Municipal Law Officers. Neighborhood commr. Greater Salt Lake council Boy Scouts Am., 1969-71; del. Salt Lake County Republican Convs., 1968, 74. Mem. Am. (com. on condemnation and condemnation procedure, sec. local govt. law 1973—), Salt Lake County bar assns., Phi Delta Phi. Home: 1032 Douglas St Salt Lake City UT 84105 Office: 351 S State St Salt Lake City UT 84111 Tel (801) 322-2516

EVANS, LAWRENCE JACK, JR., b. Oakland, Calif., Apr. 4, 1921; diplomate Near East Sch. Theology, Beirut, 1951; M.A., Am. U., Beirut, 1951; Ph.D., Brantridge Forest Sch., Sussex, Eng., 1968; J.D., Ariz. State U., 1971. Admitted to Ariz. bar, 1971, U.S. Supreme Ct. bar, 1975; individual practice law, Tempe, Ariz., 1971, Phoenix, 1972; chief hearing officer Ariz. Corp. Commn., Phoenix, 1972-76; individual practice law, Tempe, 1976—. Vice pres., bd. dirs. Tempe Republican Men's Club, 1971-72. Mem. Princeton Council for Fgn. and Internat. Studies, Ariz., Maricopa County bar assns., Ret. Officers Assn., Nat. Rifle Assn. Author: Legal Aspects of Land Tenure in the Republic of Lebanon, 1951; (with Helen Miller Davis) International Constitutional Law, Electoral Law and Treaties of Near and Middle East, 1953. Home: 539 E Erie Dr Tempe AZ 85282 Office: Tempe AZ 85282 Tel (602) 966-4329

EVANS, LODGE, b. Putnam, Va., May 16, 1919; LL.B., U. Tenn., 1942, J.D., 1942; B.S., E. Tenn. State U., 1948. Admitted to Tenn. bar, 1942, U.S. Supreme Ct. bar, 1971; asso. firm Testerman, Ambrose & Badgett, Knoxville, Tenn., 1942; partner Evans & Evans, Elizabethton, Tenn., 1946-58; city atty. City of Elizabethton, 1956-58; dist. atty. gen. 1st Circuit, Tenn., 1958-66; individual practice law, Elizabethton, 1966—; city atty. City of Watauga, Tenn., 1975—. Bd. trustees, bd. dirs. Appalachian Christian Village, 1964-72; legal asst. E. Tenn. Christian Home, 1966-76. Mem. Tenn., Carter County (past pres.) bar assns. Home: 306 Elm St Elizabethton TN 37643 Office: 609 Elk Ave Elizabethton TN 37643 Tel (615) 542-4551

EVANS, MARK LEWIS, b. Bklyn., Dec. 2, 1942; A.B., Hamilton Coll., 1964; J.D., Cornell U., 1968. Admitted to N.Y. bar, 1968, D.C. bar, 1969, U.S. Supreme Ct. bar, 1971; law clk. U.S. Ct. Appeals D.C. Circuit, 1968-69; asso. firm Shea & Gardner, Washington, 1969-72; asst. to Solicitor Gen., U.S. Dept. Justice, Washington, 1972-76; gen. counsel ICC, 1976—. Mem. Am., Fed. bar assns., Order of Coif. Home: 2436 39th St NW Washington DC 20007 Office: ICC Washington DC 20423 Tel (202) 275-7312

EVANS, MELVIN RAY, b. Inkerman, W.Va., June 14, 1909; pre law certificate Eastern Coll. Commerce and Law, Balt., 1952, LL.B., 1954. Admitted to Md. bar, 1954, U.S. Supreme Ct. bar, 1962; agt. IRS, Balt., 1938-46, conferee, 1946-52, appellate officer, 1952-68; bus. claims examiner inner harbor project City of Balt., 1968-72. Mem. Md., Garrett County bar assns. Address: Route 2 Box 215 Dry Run Rd Swanton MD 21561 Tel (301) 245-4422

EVANS, NEIL KENNETH, b. Harbor Creek, Pa., Nov. 22, 1936; A.B. with honors in History, U. Rochester, 1958; LL.B., U. Pa., 1964. Admitted to Ohio bar, 1964; asso. firm Hahn, Loeser, Freedheim, Dean and Wellman, Cleve., 1964-72, partner, 1972—. Chmn. bd. trustees Presbytery of Western Res.; co-chmn. subcom. aging comml. areas Cleve. Heights Citizens' Adv. Com. on Redevel. Mem. Ohio, Am., Greater Cleve. (chmn. continuing legal edn. com. 1975-76, Appreciation award 1975) bar assns., Am. Judicature Soc. Office: 800 National City E 6th Bldg Cleveland OH 44114 Tel (216) 621-0150

EVANS, ORINDA DALE, b. Apr. 23, 1943; A.B., Duke, 1965; J.D. with distinction, Emory U., 1968. Admitted to Ga. bar, 1968; asso. firm Fisher & Phillips, Atlanta, 1968; asso. firm Alston, Miller & Gaines, 1969-74, mem., 1974—; adj. prof. law Emory U., 1974—; counsel to Atlanta Crime Commn., 1970-71; mem. Emory Law Sch. Council, 1976. Dir. Ansley Park Civic Assn., 1975. Mem. Am., Atlanta bar assns., Emory U. Alumni Assn. (treas. 1974-75). Contbr. articles in field to legal jours; editor Jour. Pub. Law, 1967-68. Office: 1200 C & S Nat Bank Bldg Atlanta GA 30303 Tel (404) 588-0300

EVANS, ORRIN BRYAN, b. Baraboo, Wis., Oct. 6, 1910; B.A., U. Wis., 1931, LL.B., 1935; J.S.D., Yale, 1940. Admitted to Wis. bar, 1935, Mo. bar, 1940; asst. prof. law U. Idaho, 1937-38; asst. prof. U. Mo., Columbia, 1938-42, asso. prof., 1942-45, prof., 1945-47; Bruce prof. U. So. Calif., Los Angeles, 1947—, asso. dean Sch. of Law, 1952-62, dean, 1962-67; vis. prof. law Yale, 1946, Northwestern U., Evanston, Ill., 1948, U. Calif., Berkeley, 1956, U. Wis., Madison, 1960, U. Calif., Los Angeles, 1973. Mem. Am., Los Angeles County bar assns., State Bar Wis., State Bar Mo., Order of Coif, Phi Kappa Phi. Home: 5947 W Colgate Ave Los Angeles CA 90036 Office: Law Center U Southern California Los Angeles CA 90007 Tel (213) 746-2107

EVANS, PAUL VERNON, b. Colorado Springs, Colo., June 19, 1926; B.A. cum laude, Colo. Coll., 1953; LL.B. (Law Sch. scholar), Duke, 1956, J.D., 1956. Field mgr. Keystone Reader's Service, Dallas, 1946-50; admitted to Colo. bar, 1956, U.S. Supreme Ct. bar, 1971; practiced in Colorado Springs since 1956, individual practice law, 1956-60, partner firms Goodbar, Evans & Goodbar, 1960-63, Evans & Briggs, and predecessors, 1963—; city atty. City of Fountain (Colo.), 1958-62, City of Woodland Park (Colo.), 1962—; atty. Rock Creek Mesa Water Dist., 1963—. Mem. Republican Precinct Com., El Paso County, Colo., 1956-72. Mem. Am. Judicature Soc., Colo. Mining Assn., Am., Colo., El Paso County bar assns., Am., Colo. trial lawyers assns., Nat. Inst. Municipal Law Officers, Colo. Municipal Attys., Phi Beta Kappa, Phi Delta Phi, Tau Kappa Alpha (pres. 1953). Office: Suite 222 Mining Exchange Bldg 8 S Nevada Ave Colorado Springs CO 80903 Tel (303) 473-4660

EVANS, RANDALL EDWARD, b. Marlin, Tex., Aug. 11, 1947; B.A., U. Tex. at Austin, 1970; J.D., Baylor U., 1971; LL.M. in Taxation, N.Y. U., 1973. Admitted to Tex. bar, 1971; mem. firm Foreman, Dyess, Prewett, Rosenberg & Henderson, Houston, 1974—; counsellor Baylor U. Sch. Law, 1974—. Mem. Tex. Soc. C.P.A.'s, Tex., Am. bar assns. Asso. editor Baylor Law Rev., 1970-71. Home: 2801 Nottingham St Houston TX 77005 Office: 2900 Entex Bldg Houston TX 77002 Tel (713) 658-8500

EVANS, SHERLOCK HOLMES, b. Massillon, Ohio, Mar. 4, 1906; student Columbia and Am. Acad. Dramatic Arts, 1925-28; LL.B. cum laude, Cleve. Law Sch., 1936. Admitted to Ohio bar, 1936, U.S. Supreme Ct. bar, 1970; clk. Massillon Municipal Ct., 1932-40; solicitor City of Massillon, 1940-41; chief dep. Probate Ct. of Stark County, Ohio, 1942-43; practice law, Massillon. Fellow Ohio Bar Found.; mem. Internat. Platform Assn., Am. Judicature Soc., Am., Ohio (past del., exec. com.), Stark County (past pres.) bar assns., Massillon Lawyers Club (pres. 1936). Office: 501 Massillon Bldg Massillon OH 44646 Tel (216) 833-4234

EVANS, STANLEY ROSS, b. Pittsfield, Mass., Sept. 9, 1920; B.S., Northwestern U., 1944, J.D., Harvard, 1948. Admitted to Calif. bar, 1949; law clk. to justice Dist. Ct. of Appeals, San Francisco, 1949; partner firm Moerdyke, Anderson, Evans & Rhodes, Palo Alto, Calif., 1950-61; judge Municipal Ct., Palo Alto Calif. Mountain View Jud. Dist., 1961-63; judge Santa Clara County (Calif.) Superior Ct., 1963-68, presiding judge, 1968-73, presiding judge appellate dept., 1973—; mem. Palo Alto City Council, 1957-62; vice mayor City of Palo Alto, 1958-59. Mem. Palo Alto Planning Commn., 1953-57, chmn., 1956-56. Mem. Calif Judges Assn. Named Palo Alto's Young Man of Year U.S. Jr. C. of C., 1954. Office: 191 N 1st St San Jose CA 95113 Tel (408) 299-3411

EVANS, TERRY MEREDITH, b. Quincy, Ill., Dec. 24, 1944; B.S. in Pub. Adminstrn., U. Mo., 1968, J.D., 1971. Admitted to Mo. bar, 1971; partner firm Stockard, Andereck, Hauck, Sharp & Evans, Trenton, Mo. Mem. Am., Mo. bar assns. Home: 731 W 12th St Trenton MO 64683 Office: PO Box 549 Trenton MO 64683 Tel (816) 359-2244

EVANS, WILLIAM ALLEN, b. Shelby, Ohio, July 1, 1940; B.S., U.S. Mil. Acad., West Point, 1962; J.D. with honors, U. Fla., 1969; Admitted to Fla. bar, 1970, N.Y. State bar, 1972; asso. firm Rimes, Greaton & Murphy, Fort Lauderdale, Fla., 1970-71; partner firm Price, Miller & Evans, Jamestown, N.Y., 1973—; instr. law Jamestown Community Coll., 1972-73; asso. corp. counsel City of Jamestown, N.Y., 1972-73; legislator Chatauqua County, N.Y., 1976—, asst. minority leader, 1976—. Pres. Lakewood (N.Y.) PTA, 1974-75; bd. dirs. Jamestown United Fund and Easter Seal Soc., 1976—. Mem. Jamestown Estate Planning Council (pres. 1975-76), Am., N.Y. State, Jamestown Bar Assns., Phi Kappa Phi, Omicron Delta Kappa, Blue Key, Order of Coif. Home: 5 Brigg St Lakewood NY 14750 Office: 500 Fenton Bldg Jamestown NY 14701 Tel (716) 614-7414

EVANS, WILLIAM RICHARD, b. Flint, Mich., Apr. 30, 1935; B.S. in Engring., U. Mich., 1956, J.D., 1959; diploma Flint (Mich.) Bible Inst., 1975. Admitted to Mich. bar, 1959; since practiced in Mt. Morris; partner firm Evans & Evans, 1960-68; city atty. City of Mt. Morris, 1961-68; judge 67th Dist. Ct., Genesee County, 1969—. Pres., Flint Christian Sch. Bd.; bd. dirs. Flint Bible Inst. Mem. Genesee County Bar Assn., Mich. Dist. Judges' Assn. (dir.). Home: 2249 E Mt Morris Rd Mt Morris MI 48458 Office: 11820 N Saginaw St Mt Morris MI 48458 Tel (313) 686-7140

EVERDELL, WILLIAM, b. N.Y.C., May 29, 1915; A.B., Williams Coll., 1937; LL.B., Yale, 1940. Admitted to N.Y. bar, 1941; asso. firm Debevoise, Plimpton, Lyons & Gates, N.Y.C., 1940-49, partner, 1949—. Corporator, WoodsHole (Mass.) Oceanographic Inst.; trustee St. Paul's Sch., Concord, N.H., 1960-65; bd. dirs. Community Hosp., Glen Cove, N.Y., 1955-66; trustee The Green Vale Sch., Glen Head, N.Y., 1951-59. Mem. Am., N.Y. State bar assns., Assn. Bar City N.Y., Pilgrims of the U.S. Contbr. articles to legal jours. Home: 1 E 66th St New York City NY 10021 Office: 299 Park Ave New York City NY 10017 Tel (212) 752-6400

EVERETT, C. CURTIS, b. Omaha, Aug. 9, 1930; B.A. cum laude, Beloit Coll., 1952; J.D., U. Chgo., 1957. Admitted to Ill. bar, 1957; asso. firm Bell, Boyd, Lloyd, Haddad & Burns, Chgo., 1957-64, partner, 1965—. Mem. Am., Ill., Chgo. bar assns., U. Chgo. Law Sch. Alumni Assn. (dir. 1973-76), Law Club, Legal Club Chgo., Order of Coif. Editorial bd. U. Chgo. Law Rev., 1956-57. Home: 2302 MacDonald Ln Flossmoor IL 60422 Office: 135 S LaSalle St Chicago IL 60603 Tel (312) 372-1121

EVERETT, STEPHEN EDWARD, b. Shreveport, La., Jan. 16, 1944; B.A., La. Tech. U., 1965; J.D., Tulane U., 1967. Admitted to La. bar, 1967; asso. firm Montgomery, Barnett, Brown & Read, New Orleans, 1967-69; asso. firm Gravel, Roy & Burnes, Alexandria, La., 1969-73; individual practice law, Alexandria, 1973—; spl. lectr. mental health and law La. State U. Sch. Nursing, 1972—. Mem. Am. (mem. sect. taxation, com. on sales, exchange and basis 1974—, mem. subcom. dispositions 1974—), La., Alexandria bar assns., Am. Judicature Soc., La. Trial Lawyers Assn. Central La. Estate Planning Council. Home: 8512 Fairway Dr Pineville LA 71360 Office: 525 Johnson St Alexandria LA 71301 Tel (318) 442-4409

EVERS, WILLIAM DOHRMANN, b. San Francisco, May 6, 1927; B.A., Yale, 1949; J.D., U. Calif. at Berkeley, 1952. Admitted to Calif. bar, 1953; asso. firm Chickering & Gregory, San Francisco, 1953-55; asst. to commr. SEC, Washington, 1955-57; asso. firm Allan, Miller, Groezinger, Kesling & Martin, San Francisco, 1957-61; partner firm Pettit, Evers & Martin, San Francisco, 1961—. Vice-chmn. San Francisco Bay Conservation and Devel. Commn., 1968-73, chmn., 1973-76; pres. San Francisco Planning and Urban Renewal Assn., 1975—. Mem. Am., Calif., San Francisco bar assns. Office: 600 Montgomery St San Francisco CA 94111 Tel (415) 434-4000

EVERSTINE, CARL NICHOLAS, b. Cumberland, Md., June 8, 1909; A.B., U. Md., 1930, LL.B., 1947; Ph.D., Johns Hopkins U., 1938. Admitted to Md. bar, 1947; asst. dir. Md. Dept. Legis. Reference, Balt., 1948-52, acting dir., 1952, dir. 1953—; asso. mem. Commissioners Uniform State Laws 1952—. Mem. Am., Md. State, Baltimore City bar assns. Editor 30 Codes pub. local laws. Home: 5732 Cross Country Blvd Baltimore MD 21209 Office: 90 State Circle Annapolis MD 21401 Tel (301) 269-2361

EVERTZ, BARRY GRAY, b. Hackensack, N.J., Apr. 14, 1943; B.A., Rutgers, 1965, J.D., 1968. Admitted to N.J. bar, 1968; asso. firm Winne & Banta, Hackensack, N.J., 1968-69; asst. prosecutor Bergen County (N.J.), 1971-76; partner firm Evertz & McClure, Hackensack, 1977—. Bd. dirs. Teaneck (N.J.) Group Care Home, 1972—, v.p.; vice chmn. Teaneck Youth Guidance Council, 1972—. Mem. N.J., Bergen County bar assns. Home: 464 Ogden Ave Teaneck NJ 07666 Office: 1 Essex St Hackensack NJ 07601 Tel (201) 489-3555

EWALD, WILLIAM JOHN, b. Marinette, Wis., June 15, 1945; B.S., U. Wis., 1968, J.D., 1971. Admitted to Wis. bar, 1971; asso. firm Denissen, Kranzush, Mahoney & Ewald, and predecessors, Green Bay, Wis., 1971-73, partner, 1973—. Bd. dirs. Family Services Assn. of Brown County, Inc., Green Bay, 1976—. Mem. State Bar Wis., Am., Brown County (sec.-treas. 1975—) bar assns., Phi Delta Phi. Home: 127 E Briar Ln Green Bay WI 54301 Office: PO Box 1106 3000 Riverside Dr Green Bay WI 54301 Tel (414) 435-4391

EWERS, JAMES FRANKLIN, b. Gratiot, Ohio, Apr. 21, 1899; student Tex. U., 1920, 25. Admitted to Tex. bar, 1926; mem. firm Strickland & Ewers, Mission, Tex., 1929—; mem. firm Ewers & Toothaker, McAllen, Tex., 1949—; city atty. Mission, 1928-30, Weslaw, Tex., 1933-45. Mem. Hidalgo Bar Assn. Home: Route 2 Box 184 Weslaw TX 78501 Office: 1630 N 10th St McAllen TX 78501 Tel (512) 686-3771

EWING, RICHARD STUART, b. Chgo., July 27, 1942; A.B. in Polit. Sci., DePauw U., 1964; J.D., Ind. U., 1967. Admitted to Ind. bar, 1967, U.S. Ct. Mil. Appeals bar, 1968; chief prosecutor, dir. mil. justice, spl. ct. martial judge JAGC, USAF, 1967-71; partner firm Stewart Irwin Gillion Fuller & Meyer, Indpls., 1972—; prof. Legal Research Learning in the Cities program Lily Found., 1975. Vice pres., dir. Fall Creek Valley Republican Club, 1974—. Mem. Am., Ind., Indpls. bar assns. Home: 7001 Fairwood Dr Indianapolis IN 46256 Office: 1200 Merchants Bank Bldg Indianapolis IN 46204 Tel (317) 639-5454

EWING, ROBERT, b. Little Rock, July 18, 1922; B.A., Washington and Lee U., 1943; LL.B., Yale U., 1945. Admitted to Conn. bar, 1945; asso. firm Shipman & Goodwin, Hartford, Conn., 1945-50, partner, 1950—; asst. pros. atty. West Hartford (Conn.), 1953-55. Incorporator Hartford Hosp., Mt. Sinai Hosp.; sr. deacon Asylum Hill Congregational Ch., Hartford, 1972-75; vice chmn. Greater Hartford chpt. ARC, 1976-77. Mem. Am. Law Inst., Am., Conn. (chmn. com. on fed. bench-bar relations), Hartford County bar assns. Home: 28 Birch Rd West Hartford CT 06119 Office: 799 Main St Hartford CT 06103 Tel (203) 549-4770

EYERMAN, EDWARD LOUIS, b. St. Louis, Dec. 20, 1909; A.B., Washington U., St. Louis, 1934, LL.B. with honors, 1934; admitted to Mo. bar, 1933; spl. agt. FBI, San Francisco, 1934; asso. firm Fordyce White Mayne & Williams, St. Louis, 1934-36, Eagleton Waechter Elam & Clark, St. Louis, 1937-42; price atty., dist. price exec. OPA, St. Louis, 1942-47; individual practice law, St. Louis, 1947-71; partner firm Millsap Weil Eyerman & Schenberg, Clayton, Mo., 1971—. Mem. St. Louis Bd. Health, 1958-70; pres. St. Louis Civic Music League, 1962-68. Mem. Am., Mo., Met. St. Louis Bar Assns. Home: 3729 Utah Pl Saint Louis MO 63116 Office: 7777 Bonhomme Ave Suite 2300 Clayton MO 63105 Tel (314) 726-6545

EYLES, THOMAS HENRY, b. Leominster, Mass., Aug. 13, 1936; B.S. cum laude, Boston U., 1958; J.D., Stanford, 1961. Admitted to D.C. bar, 1961, Mass. bar, 1961, Conn. bar, 1964, R.I. bar, 1970; partner firm Copp, Brenneman & Tighe, New London, Conn., 1964-69, firm Harris & Eyles, Pawcatuck, Conn., 1969—; town atty. Town of Stonington (Conn.), 1972-74. Mem. Stonington Bd. Police Commrs., 1974—. Mem. R.I., Mass. bar assns. Home: RD 1 Collins Rd Stonington CT 06378 Office: 6 Mechanic St Pawcatuck CT 02891 Tel (203) 599-5574

EYMANN, DAN BECKNER, b. Fresno, Calif., Nov. 13, 1921; A.A., Reedley Coll. (Calif.), 1941; B.A., Stanford, 1943; J.D. U. San Francisco, 1947. Admitted to Calif. bar, 1947; dep. dist. atty. Fresno County (Calif.), 1948-50, chief asst. dist. atty., 1950-51; dist. counsel Office of Price Stblzn., Fresno, 1951-52; individual practice law, Fresno, 1952-54; judge Fresno Municipal Ct., 1954—; dean San Joaquin Coll. Law, 1969—. Pres. Fresno County Safety Council, Fresno Cancer Soc., Fresno YMCA Found., Boys' Club of Fresno. Mem. Conf. Calif. Judges. Recipient Man of Year award Boys' Club, 1958; Cancer Soc. award of Merit, 1961. Home: 3382 N Wishon St Fresno CA 93704 Office: POB 1241 Fresno CA 93715 Tel (209) 488-3463

EYRAUD, GEORGE VICTOR, JR., b. Coal Valley, Ala., Aug. 11, 1928; B.S., U. Ala., 1951, LL.B., 1955; LL.M., N.Y. U., 1956. Admitted to Ala. bar, 1955; asso. firm Spain, Gillon & Young, Birmingham, Ala., 1956-57; atty. Vulcan Materials Co., Birmingham, 1959-60; individual practice law, Birmingham, 1960—; instr. tax law, Birmingham Sch. Law., 1961-63; arbitrator Fed. Mediation and Conciliation Service. Mem. Ala., Am. Bar Assn. Kenessan fellow, 1956. Home: 3304 Brookwood Rd Mt Brook AL 35223 Office: 1127 City Federal Bldg Birmingham AL 35203 Tel (205) 323-3489

EYSTER, WILLIAM BIBB, b. Decatur, Ala., June 21, 1921; B.A. with honors, U. So., 1941; postgrad. Law Sch., U. Va., 1941-42; LL.B., U. Ala., 1947. Admitted to Ala. bar, 1947; partner firm Eyster, Eyster & Key, and predecessors, Decatur, 1947—; mem. Bd. Bar Commrs. State of Ala., 1954-66. Bd. trustees U. South Sewanee, Tenn., 1970-75. Fellow Am. Coll. Trial Lawyers; mem. Morgan County, Ala., Am. bar assns., Decatur C. of C. Home: 2010 Country Club Rd SE Decatur AL 35601 Office: PO Box 1607 Decatur AL 35602 Tel (205) 353-6761

EZER, MITCHEL JULIAN, b. Chgo., Jan. 3, 1935; B.S., Northwestern U., 1956; J.D., Yale, 1959. Admitted to Calif. bar, 1959; teaching asso. Sch. Law U. Calif., Los Angeles, 1959-60; asso. firm Hastings & Lasker, Los Angeles, 1960-63; staff atty. Universal Studios. Los Angeles, 1964; partner firm Rich & Ezer, Los Angeles, 1964—; lectr. Sch. Law Loyola U., 1963-67. Mem. Beverly Hills Bar Assn., Am. Judicature Soc., Scribes, Am. Arbitration Assn. (mem. nat. panel arbitrators), Yale Law Sch. Assn., Phi Alpha Delta. Contbr. chpts., articles to legal publs. Office: 1888 Century Park E Los Angeles CA 90067 Tel (213) 277-7747

EZRATTY, HARRY AARON, b. N.Y.C., Aug. 25, 1933; B.A., N.Y.U., 1955; LL.B., Bklyn. Law Sch., 1958. Admitted to N.Y. bar, 1958, D.C. bar, 1971, P.R. bar, 1970; individual practice law, N.Y.C., 1960-64, San Juan, P.R., 1964—. Chmn., Human Rights Council, San Juan, 1970-73. Mem. Am., N.Y., Bronx bar assns. Contbr. articles to profl. jours. Home: 30 Washington San Juan PR 00906 Office: 306 Ponce De Leon San Juan PR 00906 Tel (809) 723-8640

EZRIN, HERBERT STANLEY, b. Washington, Oct. 11, 1938; B.C.S., Benjamin Franklin U., 1958, M.C.S., 1959; B.S. in Bus. Adminstrn., Am. U., 1964, J.D., 1966; LL.M., Georgetown U., 1970. Admitted to Md. bar, 1966, D.C. bar, 1967, U.S. Supreme Ct. bar, 1970; asso. firm Sachs, Greenebaum & Frohlich, Washington, 1966-70; individual practice law, Washington, 1970-71; partner firm Ezrin & West., Washington, 1971-72; partner firm Levitan, Ezrin, Cramer, West & Weinstein, Chevy Chase, Md., 1972—. Mem. D.C. Inst. C.P.A.'s, Am., Fed., Md., D.C.; Montgomery County bar assns., D.C. Bar, Phi Delta Phi. Case note editor Am. U. Law Rev., 1965-66. Home: 11501 Hornfair Ct Potomac MD 20854 Office: 5454 Wisconsin Ave Chevy Chase MD 20015 Tel (301) 656-0915

FABER, PETER LEWIS, b. N.Y.C., Apr. 29, 1938; A.B., Swarthmore Coll., 1960; LL.B. cum laude, Harvard, 1963. Admitted to N.Y. State bar, 1964; asso. firm Harter, Secrest & Emery, Rochester, N.Y., 1963-65, partner, 1966—; mem. firm Parker, Chapin & Flattau, N.Y.C., 1965-66; instr. pension planning Am. Coll. Life Underwriters, Rochester, N.Y., 1968-69; mem. subchpt. C adv. group Am. Law Inst. Mem. Am. (chmn. subcom. on redemptions com. on corp. stockholder relationships 1972-74), N.Y. State (chmn. tax sect. 1976-77), Monroe County (chmn. tax sect. 1972-74) bar assns., Estate Planning Council Rochester. Contbr. articles to legal jours. Office: 700 Midtown Tower Rochester NY 14604 Tel (716) 232-6500

FABKE, JOHN EDWARD, b. South Milwaukee, Wis., Apr. 24, 1929; Ph.B., Marquette U., 1951, J.D., 1954; B.S.M.E., U. Wis., Madison, 1963. Admitted to Wis. bar, 1954, Ill. bar, 1966; practiced in Milw., 1954-60; patent atty. Corning Glass Works (N.Y.), 1963-65, Chemetron Corp., Chgo., 1966-69; asso. firm Brown, Jackson, Boettcher & Dienner, Chgo., 1965-66; patent counsel Parker Pen Co., Janesville, Wis., 1969—; chmn. com. pub. offender study Rock County (Wis.) Bd., 1973-74. Pres. Janesville Community Day Care Center, 1973—; mem. exec. bd. Janesville-Beloit Symphony Orch., 1975—. Mem. Patent Law Assn. Chgo., Milw. Patent Law Assn., Am. Bar Assn. Home: Route 2 White Pine Farm Milton WI 53565 Office: 219 East Court St Janesville WI 53545 Tel (608) 754-7711

FABY, RAYMOND MICHAEL, b. Balt., June 26, 1930; B.A., Western Md. Coll., 1953; LL.B., U. Balt., 1960. Admitted to Md. bar, 1960; since practiced in Balt., asso. firm Rollins, Smalkin, Weston and Andrew, 1962-65; asst. state's atty., 1965-68; partner firm Faby & Milburn, 1968—; asst. pub. defender, 1972; mem. Md. Ho. of Dels., 1973-74. Mem. Am., Balt. City bar assns. Home: 5416 St Albans Way Baltimore MD 21212 Office: 4930 Belair Rd Baltimore MD 21206 Tel (301) 483-4400

FACTOR, ALFRED, b. Providence, June 27, 1931; B.S., U. R.I., 1956; J.D., Boston U., 1956. Admitted to R.I. bar, 1956; asso. firm Kirshenbaum & Kirshenbaum, Providence, 1956-68, partner, 1968—. Mem. Am. Arbitration Assn. (panel), Am. Trial Lawyers Assn. (v.p. local chpt.), R.I. Bar Assn. Recipient Am. Jurisprudence award Boston U., 1956; editorial staff Boston U. Law Rev. Home: 57 Chatham Rd Cranston RI 02920 Office: 86 Weybosset St Providence RI 02903 Tel (401) 421-9439

FADELEY, EDWARD NORMAN, b. Williams, Mo., Dec. 13, 1929; A.B., U. Mo., Columbia, 1951; J.D. with honors, U. Oreg., 1957. Admitted to Oreg. bar, 1957, U.S. Supreme Ct. bar, 1968; individual practice law, Eugene, Oreg., 1957—; mem. Oreg. Ho. of Reps., 1961-63, Oreg. Senate, 1963—. Chmn. Democratic Party of Oreg., 1966-68; pres. Lane County (Oreg.) Assn. Retarded, 1966-68. Mem. Am. Bar Assn., Oreg. State Bar, Nat. Conf. State Legislature (criminal law and consumer affairs task force). Home: 260 Sunset Eugene OR 97403 Office: 801 E Park St Eugene OR 97401 Tel (503) 342-5804

FADEM, JERROLD ALAN, b. St. Louis, Jan. 19, 1926; student Washington U., St. Louis, 1943-44; B.S. in Indsl. Mgmt. and Econs., U. Calif., Los Angeles, 1947; J.D., Loyola U., Los Angeles, 1953. Admitted to Calif. bar, 1953, U.S. Supreme Ct. bar, 1970; partner firm Fadem, Berger & Norton, Beverly Hills, Calif., 1953—; spl. cons. Calif. Lands Commn., 1965; cons. Assembly Transp. Com. on Airport Noise, 1969; mem. adv. com. to city atty. City of Los Angeles, 1973; cons. Calif. Law Revision Commn., 1970—. Mem. Democratic State Central Com., 1964-66, Los Angeles Dem. Central Com., 1968-70; chmn. Fairfax High Sch. Adv. Council, 1971. Mem. Am., Calif., Los Angeles, Beverly Hills bar assns. Contbr. articles to legal jours. Home: 328 18th St Santa Monica CA 90402 Office: 501 Santa Monica Blvd Santa Monica CA 90401 Tel (213) 451-9951

FAGG, GEORGE GARDNER, b. Eldora, Iowa, Apr. 30, 1934; B.S., Drake U., 1956, J.D., 1958; grad. Nat. Coll. Judiciary, 1973. Admitted to Iowa bar, 1958; asso. firm Cartwright, Druker, Ryden & Fagg, Marshalltown, Iowa, 1958-72; judge 2d Jud. Dist. Ct. Iowa, Marshalltown, 1972—. Mem. Am., Iowa, Marshall County (pres.

1970-71) bar assns., Iowa Judges Assn., Order of Coif, Omicron Delta Kappa, Delta Sigma Pi, Beta Gamma Sigma. Recipient Marshalltown Distinguished Service award, 1967; editor: Drake Law Rev., 1957-58. Home: RFD 4 Marshalltown IA 50168 Office: Marshall County Courthouse Marshalltown IA 50158 Tel (515) 752-6369

FAHL, THOMAS ROBERT, b. Milw., Aug. 27, 1940; B.A., Marquette U., 1962; J.D., U. Wis., 1965. Admitted to Wis. bar, 1965; asso. firm Porter & Porter, Madison, Wis., 1965-66; mem. firm Brendel, Flanagan & Sendik, Wauwatosa, Wis., 1966—. Pres., Parish Council, St. Therese Congregation, Milw. Mem. Assn. Trial Lawyers Am., Milw. Bar Assn. Home: 1080 Indianwood Dr Brookfield WI 53005 Office: 6324 W North Ave Wauwatosa WI 53213 Tel (414) 771-7000

FAHLE, PAULINE COLLIER, b. Taloga, Okla., July 15, 1935; B.S., Okla. State U., 1955, M.S., 1959; J.D., U. Okla., 1968. Admitted to Okla. bar, 1968; asst. prof. Southwestern State U., 1968—; mem. firm Collier & Fahle, Taloga, 1973—. Home: 515 N Caddo Weatherford OK 73096 Office: PO Box 66 Taloga OK 73667 Tel (405) 328-5551

FAHRENKOPF, FRANK J., JR., b. Bklyn., Aug. 28, 1939; B.A., U. Nev., 1962; J.D., U. Calif. at Berkeley, 1965. Admitted to Nev. bar, 1965; mem. firm Fahrenkopf Mortimer Sourwine Mousel & Pinkerton, Reno, 1976—; tchr. criminal law U. Nev. at Reno, 1967—; judge pro tempore Reno Municipal Ct., 1973—; lectr. Nat. Coll. State Judiciary, Reno, 1974—. Bd. dirs. Nev. Cancer Soc., 1970—, Washoe County unit Nev. Cancer Soc., 1968—, Reno YWCA, 1974—, Nev. Opera Guild, 1974—, Sierra Sage council Camp Fire Girls, 1974-75; state chmn. Nev. Republican Party, 1975—, gen. counsel, 1973-75; mem. exec. bd. Washoe County Rep. Central Com., 1969—, Nev. Rep. Central Com., 1972—. Mem. Am., Washoe County (past pres.) bar assns., Am., No. Nev. (past v.p.) trial lawyers assns., Am. Judicature Soc., Nev. Barristers Club (past dir. and v.p.), Comml. Law League. Home: 1040 LaRue Ave Reno NV 89502 Office: 333 Marsh Ave Reno NV 89509 Tel (702) 323-8633

FAHRNEY, DANIEL BURDETT, b. Dayton, Ohio June 19, 1940; B.A., Ohio State U., 1966; J.D., U. Denver. Admitted to Colo. bar, 1971; chief dep. dist. atty. Golden (Colo.), 1971, dep dist. atty., 1971-74, chief dep. dist. atty., 1975—. Mem. Colo. Dist. Attys. Assn., Colo. Bar Assn., Nat. Sheriffs Assn. Recipient Am. Jurisprudence award of Excellence, U. Denver, 1971. Home: 11551 W Tennessee Pl Lakewood CO 80226 Office: 1700 Arapaho Golden CO 80419 Tel (303) 279-6511

FAHY, CHARLES, b. Rome Ga., Aug. 27, 1892; student U. Notre Dame, 1910-11; LL.B., Georgetown, U., 1914, LL.D., 1942. Admitted to D.C. bar, 1914, U.S. Supreme Ct. bar, 1920, N. Mex. bar, 1924; practiced in Washington, 1914-17, 19-24, 47-49, in Santa Fe, 1924-33; 1st asst. solicitor, mem. chmn., Petroleum Adminstrv. bd. Dept. Interior, Washington, 1933-35; gen. counsel NLRB, Washington, 1935-40; asst. solicitor gen. of U.S., Washington, 1940-41, solicitor gen. of U.S., 1941-45; mem. Pres's. Naval and Air Base Commn. to London, 1941; adviser to U.S. Del. to San Francisco Conf. UN, 1945; legal adviser to Mil Gov., dir. legal div. Mil. Gov., Germany, 1945-46; legal adviser Dept. State, Washington, 1946-47; adviser U.S. delegation to Gen. Assembly UN, N.Y.C., 1946, del., 1947-49; judge U.S. Ct. Appeals, Washington, 1949-67, sr. judge, 1967—; chmn. Pres's. Com. Equality Treatment and Opportunity Armed Services, 1948-50; chmn. personnel security rev. bd. AEC, 1949; chmn. Pres's. Spl. Mediation Panel, 1967. Pres. Cath. Assn. Internat. Peace, 1950-51, gov., 1964-67; pres. Washington League of Laymen's Retreats, 1960-63. Decorated Navy Cross, medal for Merit; recipient Robert S. Abbot Meml. award Chgo. Defender, 1951, John Carroll award Georgetown U., 1952, Russman award Nat. Newspaper Publishers Assn., 1953, Distinguished Service award Bar Assn. D.C., 1969. Office: US Courthouse Washington DC 20001 Tel (202) RE7-0321

FAIER, MARTIN, b. Omaha, July 18, 1930; B.S., Northwestern U., 1952; J.D., 1953; postgrad., Stanford. Admitted to Ill. bar, 1953, U.S. Dist. Ct. bar, 1954, U.S. Ct. of Appeals bar, 1955, U.S. Supreme Ct. bar, 1960, U.S. Patent Office bar, 1960; asso. firm Kegan & Kipnis, Chgo., 1953-54, individual practice law, Chgo., 1954—; partner, Faier Properties, Omaha, and Chgo., 1951—; sec. and dir. Little Giant Products, Inc., 1960—, Little Giant Europa N.V., Berse, Belgium, 1968—, Little Giant Products (Western), Inc., Fullerton, Calif., 1973—, S.A. Little Giant de Mexico, Monterrey, N.L., Mexico, 1972-74, Little Giant Canada Ltd., Cooksville, Ont., 1970-73; partner, Villa on the Lake Devel., 1972-74, The Chgo., Group, Chgo. and Palatine, 1973-75; pres., Chem. Devel. Corp., 1968-73; sec. and dir. Boardwalk, Inc., 1970-73. Mem. Ill., Chgo. bar assns. Office: 120 S LaSalle St Chicago IL 60603 Tel (312) 332-2060

FAIGIN, LARRY BERNARD, b. Cleve., Nov. 10, 1942; A.B., Western Res. U., 1965, J.D., 1968. Admitted to Ohio bar, 1968, N.Y. State bar, 1969, Ga. bar, 1972; asso. firm Willkie, Farr & Gallagher, N.Y.C., 1968-72, Alston, Miller & Gaines, Atlanta, 1972-75; v.p., gen. counsel Shapell Industries, Inc., Beverly Hills, Calif., 1976—; lectr. Yale, 1973, 74. Mem. Am. (criminal practice and procedure com. of antitrust sect.), N.Y. State, N.Y.C., Ga., Atlanta bar assns. Home: 454 Holt Ave Los Angeles CA 90048 Office: 8383 Wilshire Blvd Suite 700 Beverly Hills CA 90211 Tel (213) 655-7330

FAIN, RALPH EDWIN, b. Murray, Ky., Aug. 10, 1917; LL.B., U. Tex., 1948. Admitted to Tex. bar, 1948; with Prudential Ins. Co. Am., Houston, 1951—, counsel southwestern home office. Home: 4502 Waynesboro St Houston TX 77035 Office: PO Box 2075 Houston TX 77001 Tel (713) 790-0771

FAIR, ANDREW JOSEPH, b. Phila., Aug. 1, 1942; B.A., LaSalle Coll., Phila., 1964; M.A., N.Y. U., 1965; J.D., N.Y. Law Sch., 1972. Admitted to N.Y. bar, 1973; asso. firm Shapiro, Shiff, Beilly Fox & Fair, and predecessors, N.Y.C., 1973, 74, partner, 1975—; spl. lectr. continuing edn. program Hofstra U. Mem. Am., N.Y., Nassau County bar assns., Am. Soc. Pension Actuaries, N.Y. County Lawyers Assn. Mem. editorial advisory bd. Pension and Profit Sharing Jour., 1975—. Contbr. articles in field to profl. jours. Home: 168 Rim Ln Hicksville NY 11801 Office: 225 Broadway St New York City NY 10007 Tel (212) 267-9020

FAIR, EUGENE LOVE, b. Jackson, Miss., Apr. 27, 1946; B.A., U. Miss., 1966, J.D., 1968. Admitted to Miss. bar, 1968, U.S. Dist. Ct. bar for No. Dist. Miss., 1968, for So. Dist. Miss., 1973, Tex. bar, 1972, U.S. Supreme Ct. bar, 1975; with Judge Adv. Gen. Corps USN, 1968-72; partner firm Rogers, Morris & Fair, Profl. Assn., Hattiesburg, Miss., 1972—. Mem. bd. deacons Westminster Presbyn. Ch., Hattiesburg, 1974-76, chmn., 1976. Mem. South Central Miss. (pres. sect. young lawyers 1975-76, sec. 1977), Miss. State (chmn. com. state-wide reassessment study sect. young lawyers), Am. (vice chmn. com. law and media sect. young lawyers 1976—) bar assns., Miss., Tex. state bars. Home: PO Box 455 112 Lakeshore Dr Hattiesburg MS 39401 Office: PO Box 109 522 Main St Hattiesburg MS 39401 Tel (601) 544-1111

FAIR, ROBERT J., b. Detroit, Oct. 15, 1919; A.B., George Washington U., 1947, J.D. with honors, 1949. Admitted to Ind. bar, 1949, D.C. bar, 1950; spl. agt. FBI, 1950-53; now mem. firm Fair, Stilwell & Palmer, Princeton, Ind.; county atty. Gibson County, Ind., 1954-55, pros. atty., 1959-66; city atty. City of Princeton, 1956-59; mem. Ind. Senate, 1967—; mem. Ind. Jud. Study Commn., 1969—. Mem. Gibson County, Ind. State (pres. 1977—), Am. bar assns., Assn. Trial Lawyers Am. Office: 223 W State St Princeton IN 47670 Tel (812) 385-5233*

FAIRBAIRN, JAMES D., b. Atlantic City, Aug. 16, 1938; B.S., Am. U., 1961; J.D., Washington Coll. Law, 1967. Admitted to D.C. bar, 1967; engaged in individual practice law, Washington; mem. faculty U. Md. Sch. Business Adminstrn., 1968—. Mem. D.C. Bar Assn., Am. Assn. Trial Lawyers. Office: 1511 K St S-843 Washington DC 20005

FAIRCHILD, THOMAS E., b. Milw., Dec. 25, 1912; student Princeton, 1931-33; A.B., Cornell U., 1934; LL.B., U. Wis., 1938. Admitted to Wis. bar, 1938, practiced Portage, Wis., 1938-41, Milw., 1945-48, 53-56; atty. OPA, Chgo., Milw., 1941-45, hearing commr., Chgo. Region, 1945; atty. gen., Wis., 1948-51; U.S. atty. for Western Dist. Wis., 1951-52; justice Supreme Ct. Wis., 1957-66, U.S. Ct. Appeals for 7th circuit, 1966—, now chief judge. Dem. candidate Senator from Wis., 1950, 52. Mem. Am., Wis., Fed., Milw. bar assns., Am. Judicature Soc., Am. Law Inst., Phi Delta Phi. Office: Ct Appeals 219 S Dearborn Chicago IL 60604*

FAIRWEATHER, CHARLES WALTER, III, b. Lovington, N.Mex., June 5, 1936; A.B., U. Calif., Los Angeles, 1960; J.D., So. Meth. U., 1963. Admitted to Tex. bar, 1963; 1st asst. county atty. Potter County (Tex.), 1964—; partner firm Fairweather & Hale, Amarillo, Tex., 1967—. Trustee Ralph Wilson Pub. Trust, Amarillo. Mem. Amarillo, Am. trial lawyers assns., Nat. Assn. Def. Lawyers in Criminal Cases, Tex. Criminal Def. Lawyers Assn. (charter), Phi Beta Kappa, Phi Delta Phi. Home: 2210 S Hayden St Amarillo TX 79109 Office: 310 W 6th St Amarillo TX 79101 Tel (806) 372-5711

FAISON, JAMES WINFRED, III, b. Clinton, N.C., Dec. 25, 1946; B.A., Tex. Coll., 1969, J.D., So. Methodist U., 1972. Admitted to N.J. bar, 1972, U.S. Supreme Ct. bar, 1976; law clk. to judge Superior Ct. N.J., Camden County, 1972-73, asst. prosecutor, 1973-74, 76—; asst. city atty. City of Camden, 1974-76; individual practice law, Camden, 1974-76. Bd. dirs. Nat. Bus. League, Camden, 1976—; mem. Juvenile Conf. Com. Camden County, 1975-76. Mem. N.J., Garden State, U.S. Supreme Ct. bar assns., N.J. Prosecutors Assn., N.J. Asst. Prosecutors Assn. Home: 371 Burwood Ave Camden NJ 08105 Office: Camden County Prosecutor 3d Floor Parkade Bldg 518 Market St Camden NJ 08102 Tel (609) 757-8400

FAISS, ROBERT DEAN, b. Centralia, Ill., Sept. 19, 1934; B.A., Am. U., 1969; J.D., Washington Coll., 1972. Admitted to Nev. bar, 1972, D.C. bar, 1973; partner firm Lionel Sawyer & Collins, Las Vegas, 1973—; asst. to pres. Lyndon B. Johnson, 1968-69. Mem. Am. bar Assn., State Bar Nev. Office: 1700 Valley Bank Plaza Las Vegas NV 89101 Tel (702) 385-2188

FALAHEE, JAMES BURNS, b. Jackson, Mich., May 31, 1924; A.B., U. Mich., 1948, J.D., 1950. Admitted to Mich. bar, 1950; atty. Consumers Power Co., Jackson, 1950-58, gen. atty., 1958-76, v.p., gen. counsel, 1976—. Pres. St. Joseph Home for Boys, Jackson, 1971; bd. dirs. Foote Hosp., Jackson, 1976—. Mem. Jackson County, Am., Mich. bar assns., Fed. Power Bar Assn. Office: 212 W Michigan Ave Jackson MI 49201 Tel (517) 788-0820

FALCONER, HAZEL LUCILLE, b. Bismarck, N.D., Aug. 1, 1921; student Dickinson State Tchrs. Coll., 1941, Bismarck Jr. Coll., 1939-41; U. N.D., 1946-47, U. Okla., 1950-51; read law under Hon. Judge W. J. Austin, Ct. of Increased Jurisdiction, 1965-69. Admitted to N.D. bar, 1969; tchr. Aurora Sch. No. 1, Goodrich, N.D., 1941-42; property clk. old age assistance div. N.D. Welfare Bd., 1948-50; sec. State Printer's Office, Bismarck, 1942-43, 44-46; sec. geol. div. Cities Service Oil Co., Bismarck, 1951-54; sec. to office mgr. Gerlach's Sheet Metal Works, Bismarck, 1954-69; individual practice law, Bismarck, 1969—. Mem. N.D., Burleigh County bar assns. Home: Route 2 Box 123 Bismarck ND 58501 Office: Route 2 Box 123 Bismarck ND 58501 Tgl (701) 223-6362

FALER, WILLIAM D., b. Independence, Kans., Apr. 1, 1947; B.A., U. Kans., 1969, J.D., 1972. Admitted to Idaho bar, 1972, U.S. Dist. Ct. bar, 1972; partner firm Holden Holden Kidwell Hahn & Crapo, Idaho Falls, Idaho, 1972—. Pres. Idaho Falls Civitan Club, 1976, Bonneville County (Idaho) chpt. Am. Cancer Soc., 1975-77. Mem. Am., Idaho State bar assns., Idaho Assn. Def. Counsel, Am. Trial Lawyers Assn., Phi Delta Phi. Editorial bd. U. Kans. Law Rev. Home: 1870 McKenzie St Idaho Falls ID 83401 Office: PO Box 129 Idaho Falls ID 83401 Tel (208) 523-0620

FALES, HALIBURTON, II, b. N.Y.C., Aug. 7, 1919; student Harvard, 1938-41; LL.B., Columbia U., 1947. Admitted to N.Y. bar, 1948, U.S. Supreme Ct. bar, 1957; asso. firm White & Case, N.Y.C., 1947-58, partner, 1959—. Chmn. Bedminster Twp. Planning Bd., Somerset County, N.J., 1971-75; sr. warden St. Luke's Ch., Gladstone, N.J.; sr. v.p. St. Barnabas Hosp., Bronx, N.Y.; sec., trustee Pierpont Morgan Library, N.Y.C. Fellow Am. Coll. Trial Lawyers; mem. Am., Internat., N.Y. State (ho. of dels.) bar assns., Am., N.Y. bar founds., Am. Judicature Soc., Am. Law Inst., Am. Soc. Internat. Law, Assn. Bar City N.Y., Down Town Assn., Fed. Bar Council, Internat. Law Assn., Internat. Legal Aid and Defender Assn., Inst. Judicial Adminstrn., N.Y. County Lawyers Assn. Contbr. articles to legal jours. Home: Pottersville Rd Gladstone NJ 07934 Office: 14 Wall St New York City NY 10005 Tel (212) 732-1040

FALK, ARNOLD ROSS, b. Rochester, N.Y., Oct. 6, 1947; B.A. in English, State U. N.Y., Buffalo, 1969; J.D., Columbia, 1972. Admitted to N.H. bar, 1973, U.S. Dist. Ct. bar for Dist. N.H., 1973; asso. firm Bell & Kennedy, Keene, N.H., 1973-75; partner firm Bell & Falk, Keene, 1975—. Bd. dirs. N.H. Legal Assistance, 1975-76. Mem. Am., N.H., Cheshire County (N.H.) bar assns. Tel (603) 352-5950

FALK, E. GAIL, b. N.Y.C., Sept. 14, 1943; A.B., Radcliffe Coll., 1966; J.D., Yale, 1971. Admitted to Conn. bar, 1971, W.Va. bar, 1971; counsel Legal Aid Soc. Charleston (W.Va.), 1971-73, United Mine Workers Am., Charleston, 1973-76; individual practice law, Charleston, 1976—. Office: 808 Union Bldg Charleston WV 25301 Tel (304) 343-5541

FALK, WILLIAM EDWARD, b. Moline, Ill., Jan. 2, 1926; B.A., State U. Iowa, 1947, J.D., 1953; student U. Louisville, 1944-45. Admitted to Iowa bar, 1953; partner firm Ferguson, Ferguson & Falk, Shenandoah, Iowa, 1954-60, Ferguson, Clovis & Falk, Shenandoah, 1960-66, Clovis, Falk & Norris, Shenandoah, 1966-76, Falk & Norris, Shenandoah, 1976—. Atty. Page County (Iowa), 1956-60. Mem. Page County, Iowa bar assns. Home: 1304 Southmoreland Pl Shenandoah IA 51601 Office: 601 W Sheridan Ave Shenandoah IA 51601 Tel (712) 246-1924

FALLGATTER, CURTIS SCOTT, b. Fargo, N.D., Jan. 19, 1948; B.S. in Math., U. Okla., 1970, J.D., 1973. Admitted to Okla. bar, 1973, Fla. bar, 1976. With JAGC, U.S. Navy, 1973-76, head trial counsel Naval Legal Service Office, Jacksonville, Fla., 1976; asst. U.S. atty. Middle Dist. Fla., 1977—. Counsel local homeowner's assn. Mem. Am., Okla., Fla. bar assns. Recipient Am. Jurisprudence award, 1973. Home: 8 Jonathan Ct Orange Park FL 32073 Office: US Atty 311 W Monroe St Jacksonville FL 32202 Tel (904) 791-2624

FALLON, CHRISTOPHER CHAFFEE, JR., b. Alexandria Bay, N.Y., Sept. 2, 1948; B.A., psych., King's Coll., 1970; J.D. cum laude, Syracuse Univ., 1972. Admitted to Pa. bar, 1973; asso. firm LaBrum & Doak, Phila., 1973-75, partner, 1975—. Mem. bd. dirs. Phila. chpt. Syracuse Law Coll. Assn., mem. product liability reform com. Pa. C. of C. Mem. Am., Pa., Phila. bar assns., Def. Research Inst., Phi Alpha Delta. Named Outstanding Young Men of Am., 1974. Home: 438 W Montgomery Ave Haverford PA 19041 Office: 1500 Seven Penn Center Plaza Philadelphia PA 19103 Tel (215) 561-4400

FALLS, RAYMOND LEONARD, JR., b. Youngstown, Ohio, Feb. 24, 1929; B.A., Coll. of Wooster, 1950; LL.B., Harvard, 1953. Admitted to N.Y. bar, 1957, U.S. Supreme Ct. bar, 1961; law clk. to judge U.S. Ct. Appeals for 2d Circuit N.Y., 1955-56; asso. firm Cahill, Gordon & Reindel, N.Y.C., 1956-63, partner, 1963—; asso. adj. prof. N.Y. U. Law Sch., 1967-73. Mem. Mayor's Task Force on Reorgn. N.Y.C. Govt., 1965-66. Office: 80 Pine St New York City NY 10005 Tel (212) 825-0100

FALSTROM, KENNETH EDWARD, b. San Luis Obispo, Calif., June 25, 1946; A.B. in Econs., U. Calif., Los Angeles, 1967; J.D., U. Calif., Berkeley, 1970. Admitted to Calif. bar, 1971; asst. Center for Study of Democratic Instns., Santa Barbara, Calif., 1970-71; with law offices Christopher Zajic, Santa Barbara, 1971-72; individual practice law, Santa Barbara, 1972—. Mem. bd. govs. Hope Sch. Dist., Santa Barbara, 1972—; bd. dirs. Pacific Coast Community Video, Santa Barbara. Mem. State Bar Calif., Santa Barbara County Bar Assn. Recipient Am. Jurisprudence award, Constl. Law, Bancroft-Whitney, 1969. Office: 1 Fairtree Mews 906 Garden St Santa Barbara CA 93101 Tel (805) 966-3434

FALTERMAN, ANTHONY GERARD, b. Napoleonville, La., Mar. 6, 1946; student Nicholls State U., 1964-67; J.D., La. State U., 1970. Admitted to La. bar, 1970; mem. firm Falterman & Joffrion, Pierre Part, La.; sheriff Assumption Parish, La., 1976—; mem. Council on Peace Officer Standards and Tng. Chmn. fin. campaign com. Assumption Red Cross, 1975, 76, 77. Mem. Nat., La. sheriff's assns., La. Juvenile Assn., Sellea, Metlac law assns. Named Outstanding Young Man Am., 1976. Home: Box 283 Napoleonville LA 70390 Office: Box 69 Napoleonville LA 70390 Tel (504) 369-7281

FAMILO, EDWARD DOUGLAS, b. Detroit, July 15, 1921; A.B., Western Res. U., 1943, LL.B., 1948. Admitted to Ohio bar, 1948, since practiced in Cleve., asso. firm Grossman, Schlesinger & Carter, 1948-53, partner firm, 1953-64, partner firm Stotter, Familo, Cavitch, Elden & Durkin, and predecessors, 1964—; pres., dir. Am. Lawyers Co., Cleve.; lectr. fed. practice and bankruptcy Cleve.-Marshall Law Sch., 1952-62. Trustee Lakewood (Ohio) Hosp. Found., 1975—. Mem. Am., Cleve. (mem. exec. com. 1959-62), Ohio State bar assns., Cuyahoga County Law Library, Adelbert Coll., Western Res. U. (pres. 1952) alumni assns., Delta Kappa Epsilon (pres. No. Ohio 1969). Asso. editor Ohio Transaction Guide, Mathew Bender, 1976. Home: 22811 Laramie Dr Rocky River OH 44116 Office: 1401 E Ohio Bldg Cleveland OH 44114 Tel (216) 621-7860

FANDEL, ROBERT FRANCIS, b. Milton, Mass., Sept. 25, 1933; B.S. in Econs., Coll. of Holy Cross, Worcester, Mass., 1955; LL.B., Suffolk U., 1964. Admitted to Mass. bar, 1964; trial atty. Mass. Defenders Com., Brockton, 1964-67, sr. trial atty., 1967-69, 1st asst. to chief counsel, 1969-73, atty. in-charge Plymouth County office, 1973—; chmn. Mass. Mental Health Legal Advisers Com., 1974—. Mem. Mass., Norfolk County (Mass.), Plymouth County bar assns. Home: 11 Richard Rd Hingham MA 02043 Office: 232 Main St Brockton MA 02401 Tel (617) 583-5316

FANNING, STEPHEN A(LOYSIUS), JR., b. Washington, Nov. 4, 1929; A.B., Providence Coll., 1950; J.D., Boston Coll., 1955. Admitted to R.I. bar, 1956, U.S. Supreme Ct. bar, 1974; clk. firm Edwards & Angell, Providence, R.I., 1955, asso., 1956-63, partner, 1964—. Mem. fathers council, past pres. Salve Regina Coll., Newport, R.I., 1974—. Mem. Am., R.I., Pawtucket (past pres.) bar assns., Providence Coll. Alumni Assn. (past pres.) Home: 50 Quincy St Providence RI 02908 Office: 2700 Hospital Trust Tower Providence RI 02903 Tel (401) 274-9200

FANNING, STEVEN ERLE, b. Bryan, Tex., Aug. 20, 1944; B.B.A. in Economics, J.D., U. Ga. Admitted to Ga. bar, 1973; partner firm Farmer & Fanning, Newnan, Ga., 1973—. Mem. Am., Ga. trail lawyers assns., Newnan-Coweta Bar Assn. (sec. 1976), Ga., Nat. assns. criminal def. lawyers. Home: 17 Festiva Dr Newnan GA 30263 Office: 32 S Court Square Newnan GA 30263 Tel (404) 253-3282

FANNING, THOMAS JOSEPH, III, b. Ft. Brady, Sault Ste. Marie, Mich., Feb. 5, 1907; B.A., St. Mary's Coll., Calif., 1932; J.D., U. Calif., 1936. Admitted to Calif. bar, 1936; asso. with Joseph P. Fallon, Jr., San Francisco, 1936-39; individual practice law, Yreka, Calif., 1939-41; examiner area rent control Office of Price Adminstrn., San Diego, 1942-51; dep. city atty. City of San Diego, 1943-51, also acting chief trial dep., acting. asst. city atty., atty. for Mission Bay Aquatic Park; spl. asst. to U.S. Atty., So. Dist. Calif., San Diego, 1951-52; asso. with firm Morrision, Henderson, Fanning and Morrision, San Diego, 1952-62; individual practice law, San Diego, 1962—; acting dean, prof. contracts U. San Diego, 1954-55; dir. Panel Lock Fence Co., Wahrenbrocks Book House, Weiser Sporting Goods, Grove Equipment and Office Supply Co., Lee-Mar Aquarium and Pet Supply, Rocky Rd., E.F. Waten Corp. Auctioneers. Incorporator, Boat, Handling and License Preparation Sch.; dir. San Diego Hist. Days, 1952; incorporator, v.p., dir. United Cerebral Palsy Found., San Diego, 1953; chmn. advisory com. San Diego Mental Health Clinic, 1955-57. Mem. State Bar Calif., San Diego County Bar Assn., Phi Alpha Delta. Home: 382 San Fernando St San Diego CA 92106 Office: 233 A St Suite 1108 San Diego CA 92101 Tel (714) 234-8307

FANNING, WILLIAM EDWARD, b. Ashland, Ky., July 8, 1912; J.D., U. Ky., 1935. Admitted to Ky. bar, 1935; practiced in Ashland, 1935-43; naturalization examiner Immigration and Naturalization Service, Dept. Justice, Cin. and Columbus, Ohio, 1943-46; mem. firm Nickell, Fannin and Rose and predecesssor, Ashland, 1946-70; chief judge 32d Jud. Circuit of Ky., Catlettsburg, 1970—. Election commr. Boyd County (Ky.), 1937-42. Mem. Boyd County, Ky., Am. bar assns., Jud. Council Ky. Home: 2537 Bradley Dr Ashland KY 41101 Office: Boyd County Courthouse Catlettsburg KY 41129 Tel (606) 739-5844

FANT, FRANCIS RODGERS, JR., b. Anderson, S.C., Oct 28 1940; B.A., Erskine Coll., 1964; J.D., U. S.C., 1964. Admitted to S.C. bar, 1964; asso. firm Fant & Rogers, Anderson, 1964-67, Fant & Doyle, Anderson, 1967-69; partner firm Fant, Doyle, Glenn, & Vaughan, Anderson, 1969-72, firm Doyle, Fant, Vaughan & Palmer, Anderson, 1972-74; individual practice law, Anderson, 1974—; v.p. Nevitt-Forest, Inc., 1968—. Vice-chmn. Anderson County ARC, 1972-73. Mem. Am., S.C., Anderson County bar assns. Home: Westwind Way Rt 7 Anderson SC 24621 Office: 122 W Whitner St Anderson SC 29621 Tel (803) 226-3444

FANT, RICHARD OWEN, JR., b. Tuscaloosa, Ala., Feb 26, 1916; B.A., U. Ala., 1936, M.A. in History, 1940, LL.B., 1948. Admitted to Ala. bar, 1948; individual practice law, Tuscaloosa; legal officer Ala. wing CAP, 1955—, then lt. col. Mem. Tuscaloosa County Bar Assn. Home: 818 S Lurleen Wallace Blvd Tuscaloosa AL 35401 Office: 705 First Nat Bank Bldg Tuscaloosa AL 35401 Tel (205) 758-3453

FARABEE, KENNETH RAY, b. Wichita Falls, Tex., Nov. 22, 1932; B.B.A., U. Tex., 1957, LL.B., 1961. Admitted to Tex. bar, 1961; partner firm Fillmore, Lambert, Farabee, Purtle & Lee, Wichita Falls, 1961—; mem. Tex. Senate, 1975—, vice chmn. Tex. Coordinating Commn. State Health and Welfare Services. Pres., Sta. KIDZ-TV, Wichita Falls, Mem. Am., Wichita County (pres. 1968-69), Tex. Jr. (v.p. 1969-70) bar assns. Recipient Senate Mem. Outstanding Legis. Service award, Tex. Farmers Union, 1975. Home: 1512 Buchan St Wichita Falls TX 76309 Office: 816 7th St Wichita Falls TX 76307 Tel (817) 723-0981

FARAGE, DONALD JAMES, A.B., U. Pa., 1930, LL.B. with honors, 1933; LL.D., Dickinson Sch. Law, 1966. Admitted to Pa. bar, 1933; asst. to Prof. Francis H. Bohlen, 1933-36; prof. law Dickinson Sch. Law, 1934-46, 50—, George Washington U., 1948-50; vis. prof. med. jurisprudence Jefferson Med. Coll., 1948-76; sr. partner firm Farage & Shrager, Phila. Fellow Law Sci. Acad., Internat. Soc. Barristers (dir. 1971-74), Am. Coll. Trial Lawyers, Internat. Acad. Law and Sci., Southwestern Legal Found., Internat. Acad. Trial Lawyers (pres. 1970-71); mem. Am. (council sect. ins., negligence and compensation), Pa. (ho. dels.), Phila. bar assns., Lawyers Club Phila., Assn. Trial Lawyers Am. (v.p. Pa. chpt. 1956-58), 3d Circuit Jud. Conf., Am. Law Inst., Order of Coif, Phi Alpha Delta. Office: Suburban Station Bldg Philadelphia PA 19103 Tel (215) LO 3-3973

FARBER, ABNER ABRAHAM, b. West Hoboken, N.J., Nov. 11, 1909; certificate Dana Coll. of Newark, 1929; LL.B., N.J. Law Sch. (now Rutgers U.), 1932, J.D., 1970. Admitted to N.J. bar, 1935, U.S. Supreme Ct. bar, 1956; individual practice law, Union City, N.J., 1935—; legal counsel Weehawken-Union City Trunk Sewer Bd., 1958—; acting judge Union City, Secaucus and Guttenberg Municipal Cts., 1962-74. Mem. N. Hudson Lawyers Club, Hudson County Bar Assn. Home: 1315 Bergenline Ave Union City NJ 07087 Tel (201) 865-7547

FARBER, IRVING OLIVER, b. Santurce, P.R., Sept. 19, 1941; B.A., Wagner Coll., S.I., 1965; LL.B., Bklyn. Law Sch., 1967. Admitted to N.Y. bar, 1968, U.S. Supreme Ct. bar, 1975, also U.S. 2d Circuit Ct. Appeals, U.S. Eastern Dist., U.S. So. Dist. Ct., U.S. No. Dist. bars; asso. firm Coppola & Lawless, Bklyn., 1968-72, Clark, Gagliardi & Miller, White Plains, N.Y., 1972-76, Kahan, Meiselman & Farber, Poughkeepsie, N.Y., 1976—; guest speaker in field. Mem. Westchester (county, N.Y.), N.Y. State bar assns. Home: 2 Grace Ct Brooklyn NY 11201 Office: 313 Mill St Poughkeepsie NY 12601

FARBER, STEVEN WAYNE, b. Denver, Sept. 21, 1943; B.A., U. Colo., 1965, J.D., 1968. Admitted to Colo. bar, 1968; partner firm Brownstein, Hyatt, Farber & Madden, Denver, 1968—. Trustee Am. Cancer Research Center, Lakewood, Colo., 1976—. Mem. Am., Colo., Denver bar assns., Am., Colo. trial lawyers assns., U. Colo. Alumni Assn. (dir. 1974-75). Recipient Am. Jurisprudence awards in torts, 1966, adminstrv. law, 1968; contbr. articles to legal jours.; bd. editors U. Colo. Law Rev., 1966-68. Home: 75 Sedgwick Pl Englewood CO 80110 Office: Suite 1700 1660 Lincoln St Denver CO 80203 Tel (303) 534-6335

FARBSTEIN, DONALD FRANCIS, b. San Francisco, Jan. 22, 1928; B.S. cum laude, U. San Francisco, 1948, LL.B., 1951. Admitted to Calif. bar, 1952; asso. firm Barfield & Barfield, San Francisco, 1953-54; partner firm Connolly & Farbstein, San Francisco, 1954-61; individual practice law, San Mateo, Calif., 1961-64; partner firm Hession, Creedon, Hamlin, Kelly, Hanson & Farbstein, San Mateo, 1964—. Pres. San Francisco Archdiocesan Council Cath. Men, 1960-61. Mem. San Mateo County (chmn. conf. of dels. 1972-73), Am. bar assns., Fedn. Ins. Counsel, Trial Lawyers Am., Bar Assn. San Francisco State Bar Calif., Assn. Def. Trial Counsel, No. Calif. Assn. Def. Counsel (sec. treas. 1968-69), Lawyers Club San Francisco, San Mateo C. of C. (pres. 1974-77), Phi Alpha Delta.

FARDAL, HAROLD STERLING, b. Webster City, Iowa, Mar. 3, 1930; B.A., St. Olaf Coll., 1951; M.A., U. Wis., 1954; J.D., Yale, 1958. Admitted to Wash. bar, 1958; asso. firm Keller, Rohrback, Waldo & Hiscock, Seattle, 1958-64, partner, 1964—. Bd. dirs. Mercer Island Sch. Dist., 1971—, pres., 1975. Mem. Am., Wash., Seattle-King County bar assns. Home: 6920 96th Ave SE Mercer Island WA 98040 Office: 1220 IBM Bldg Seattle WA 98101 Tel (206) 623-1900

FARDON, DOROTHY FAVREAU, b. St. Louis, Sept. 7, 1902; A.A., William Woods Coll., 1922; student Kans. U., 1922, U. Mo., Kansas City, 1938, Rockhurst Coll., 1940; J.D., U. Mo., Kansas City, 1939. Admitted to Mo. bar, 1939, U.S. Supreme Ct. bar, 1954; partner firm Kimball, Fardon & Madden, 1939-41; asso. city atty. City of Kansas City (Mo.), 1941-67, aviation atty., 1947-67; individual practice law, Lake Lotawana, Mo., 1967—, also city atty. City of Lake Lotawana, 1974—. Former mem. state bd. Mo. LWV; former mem. internat. bd. Zonta, Internat. Mem. Am., Mo., Kansas City bar assns., Phi Alpha Delta, Phi Theta Kappa. Recipient ASCAP award, 1939, alumnae award of distinction William Woods Coll., 1959; named an achiever Women's C. of C., 1974. Home and Office: Z57 Lake Lotawana MO 64063 Tel (816) 578-4346

FARIS, ESRON MCGRUDER, b. Norfolk, Va., May 24, 1925; B.S. in Bus. Adminstrn., Washington and Lee U., 1949, J.D., LL.M., Duke U., 1954. Admitted to Va. bar, 1952, N.C. bar, 1960; asst. prof. law Washington and Lee U., 1951-57; asso. prof. law Wake Forest U., 1957-62, prof., 1962—; individual practice law, Williamsburg, Va., 1965-67; cons. in field, 1960—; organizer, dir. Exeter (Eng.) Legal Studies Program, 1967-69. Mem. Va., N.C. bar assns., Lexington Jaycees, Phi Delta Phi. Contbr. to various law revs.; author: Accounting for Lawyers, 1975. Home: 933 Goodwood Rd Winston Salem NC 27106 Office: Wake Forest U Law Sch Winston Salem NC 27109 Tel (919) 761-5434

FARIS, WAYNE GORDON, b. Ottowa, Ont., Can., Dec. 15, 1941; B.A., Wheaton Coll., 1964; J.D., U. Minn., 1970. Admitted to Minn. bar, 1970; asso. firm Oppenheimer, Wolff, Foster, Shepard & Donnelly, St. Paul, 1970-75, partner, 1976—. Commr. Minn. Uniform Conveyancing Blanks Commn., 1971-74; mem. adv. com. Ramsey County (Minn.) Lung Assn., 1976—. Mem. Am., Minn. bar assns. Home: 4531 Dupont Ave S cinneapolis MN 55409 Office: 1700 First Nat Bank Bldg Saint Paul MN 55101 Tel (612) 227-7271

FARKAS, ROBERT A., b. Trenton, Feb. 17, 1942; B.S. in Econs., Villanova U., 1964, J.D., 1967. Admitted to N.J. bar, 1967; atty. Nationwide Ins. Co., Haddonfield, N.J., 1968-69; asst. prosecutor in charge Mercer County (N.J.) Narcotics Strike Force, Trenton, 1975-76; project dir. Mercer County-Trenton Organized Crime Strike Force, 1971-76; asst. prosecutor Mercer County, Trenton, 1969-76, 1st asst. prosecutor, 1976—; asst. prof. law Rider Coll., 1973-75; lectr. organized crime seminar N.J. Police Dept., 1973—; cons. dept. law and pub. safety U.S. V.I., 1976. Mem. Am., N.J., Mercer County bar assns., Nat. Dist. Attys. Assn. Home: 160 Abernethy Dr Trenton NJ 08618 Office: 209 S Broad St Mercer County Court House Trenton NJ 08607 Tel (609) 989-6307

FARLEY, DONALD STEPHEN, b. Chgo., Jan. 15, 1928; B.S., U.S. Merchant Marine Acad., 1949; LL.D., U. Wis., 1952. Admitted to Ill. bar, 1955; trust officer First Nat. Bank Chgo., 1954-63; v.p. trust dept. First Nat. Bank Neenah, Wis., 1963-69; v.p. trust dept. Nat. City Bank of Mpls., 1969-70; sr. v.p. trust dept. Northwestern Nat. Bank of St. Paul, 1970—. Dir. deferred giving com. United Fund; bd. dirs. St. Paul chpt. ARC. Mem. Wis., Ill., Minn. bar assns. Tel (612) 291-2112

FARLEY, DONALD WILLIAM, b. Cleve., Feb. 20, 1930; B.S.S., John Carroll U., 1952; LL.B., Case Western Reserve U., 1957. Admitted to Ohio bar, 1957; since practiced in Cleve.; asso. firm Ralph Vince, 1957-65; partner firm Burke, Haber & Berick, 1965—. Advisory bd. mem. St. Alexis Hosp., Cleve. Mem. Ohio Bar Assn., Bar Assn. of Greater Cleve. Home: 2621 Courtland Oval Shaker Heights OH 44118 Office: 1500 Central National Bank Bldg Cleveland OH 44114 Tel (216) 771-2700

FARLEY, JACK EMORY, b. Pikeville, Ky., Jan. 4, 1939; B.A., U. Ky., 1962; J.D., Am. U., 1967. Admitted to D.C. bar, 1968, Ky. bar, 1969; analyst Dept. Def., Washington, 1962-67; trial atty. Dept. Justice, Washington, 1967-68; exec. dir. Pike County C. of C., Pikeville, 1968-72; individual practice law, Pikeville, 1970-75; state pub. defender Ky., 1975—; counsel Pikeville-Pike County Airport Bd., 1969-74, Pikeville Urban Renewal Agy., 1970-75. Chmn., Pike County Headstart Policy Com., 1970-71; v.p. Eastern Highlands Tourism Region, 1970-72; bd. dirs. Big Sandy Area Devel. Council, 1970-72. Mem. Am., Fed., Ky. bar assns. Home: 917 Brookhaven Dr Frankfort KY 40601 Office: 625 Leawood Dr Frankfort KY 40601

FARLEY, THOMAS TANCRED, b. Pueblo, Colo., Nov. 10, 1934; B.S., U. Santa Clara, 1956; LL.B., U. Colo., 1959. Admitted to Colo. bar, 1959; partner firm Petersen & Fonda, Pueblo, 1959—; mem. Colo. Ho. Reps., 1965-74, minority leader, 1967-74; commr. div. wildlife Colo. Dept Nat. Resources, 1975—. dir. United Bank Pueblo, Sunset Plaza Shopping Center, Inc., Pueblo Cablevision. Bd. dirs. Colo. Wildlife Fedn.; trustee Farley Found., 1972—, Holy Cross Abby, Canon City, Colo., 1975—. Mem. Am., Colo., Pueblo County bar assns., Pueblo C. of C., Colo. Broadcasters Assn. Home: 117 E Orman Ave Pueblo CO 81004 Office: 650 Thatcher Bldg Pueblo CO 81003 Tel (303) 545-9330

FARMER, EDGAR T., b. St. Louis, Apr. 25, 1929; A.B., St. Louis U., 1951, J.D. cum laude, 1957. Admitted to Mo. bar, 1957; now mem. firm Fordyce & Mayne, St. Louis; mem. comml. panel Am. Arbitration Assn.; mem. faculty St. Louis U. Sch. Law, 1958—; area rep. Judge Adv. Gen. USAF, 1965-67; bd. dirs. Legal Aid Soc. of St. Louis and St. Louis County, 1971—, treas., 1973-75. Fellow Am. Coll. Probate Counsel; mem. Bar Assn. Met. St. Louis (v.p. 1963, 74, exec. com. 1966—, pres. 1976-77), Mo. Bar, Am. Bar Assn. (chmn. com. on probate law and estate planning sect. gen. practice 1974-75), Am. Judicature Soc., Lawyers Assn. St. Louis, St. Louis Bar Found. (pres. 1975-76), Order Woolsack (pres. 1969-71), Scribes, Am. Soc. Writers on Legal Subjects, Phi Delta Phi, Alpha Sigma Nu. Editor St. Louis U. Law Jour., 1956-57, St. Louis Bar Jour., 1964-67. Office: 120 S Central St Suite 1100 Saint Louis MO 63105 Tel (314) 863-6900*

FARMER, EDWARD CAMPBELL, JR., b. Muskegon, Mich., Aug. 20, 1918; A.B., Dartmouth, 1941; J.D., Northwestern U., 1951. Admitted to Mich. bar, 1951; practiced in Muskegon, 1951-68; judge Mich. Dist. Ct., 60th Dist., 1969—, presiding judge, 1970, 73, 75. Mem. exec. bd. West Mich. Shores council Boy Scouts Am. Mem. Am. Bar Assn., Am. Judicature Soc. Editor-in-chief The Reporter, 1950-51. Home: 1665 Jefferson St Muskegon MI 49441 Office: County Bldg Muskegon MI 49440 Tel (616) 724-6250

FARMER, FRANCES, b. Keysville, Va., Dec. 5, 1909; B.A., Westhampton Coll., 1931; LL.B., U. Richmond, 1933, Litt.D. (hon.), 1976. Admitted to Va. bar, 1933; law librarian U. Richmond, 1938-42; law librarian, prof. U. Va., Charlottesville, 1942-76, prof. emeritus, library cons. to dir. Center for Oceans Law and Policy, 1976—. Mem. Va. State Bar, Va. Bar Assn., Am. Assn. Law Libraries (pres. 1959-60, contbr. to jour.), Order of the Coif, Phi Beta Kappa. Home: 2031 Hessian Rd Charlottesville VA 22903 Office: Sch Law U Va Charlottesville VA 22901 Tel (804) 924-7930

FARMER, GUY OTTO, b. Foster Falls, Va., Sept. 13, 1912; B.A., W.Va. U., 1934, LL.B., 1936; postgrad. civil law (Rhodes scholar) Oxford U., 1936-37. Admitted to W.Va. bar, 1936, D.C. bar, 1946, U.S. Supreme Ct. bar; asso. gen. counsel NLRB, 1943-45, chmn., 1953-55; partner firm Steptae & Johnson, Washington, 1955-60, Farmer, Shibley, McGuinn & Flood, Washington, 1960—. Mem. Am., D.C., Supreme Ct., W.Va. bar assns. Office: 1120 Connecticut Ave Washington DC 20036 Tel (202) 331-7311

FARNEY, BENJAMIN FRANKLIN, b. Kiowa, Kans., Jan. 30, 1933; A.B. in Chemistry, U. Kans., 1954, LL.B., 1957. Admitted to Kans. bar, 1957, Mo. bar, 1958; asso. firm Fishburn and Gold, Kansas City, Mo., 1957-58; individual practice law, Overland Park, Kans., 1958-65; judge Johnson County (Kan.) Juvenile Ct., 1965-73, Probate Ct., 1965-76; mem. firm Bouska and Allen, Overland Park; asst. prof. law Washburn Law Sch., 1976—. Bd. dirs. Nat. Council Alcoholism, Community Alcohol Program, Pilot House, Stand-by House, local YMCA. Mem. Johnson County Bar Assn., Kan. Spl. Ct. Judges Assn., Am. Judicature Soc., Nat. Coll. Probate Judges. Home: 5301 W 57th Terr Roeland Park KS 66205 Office: Bouska & Allen Gen Square Bldg 9800 Metcalf St Overland Park KS 66212 Tel (913) 381-8180

FARNEY, DUNCAN RICHARD, b. Carthage, N.Y., Oct. 30, 1941; A.B., Hamilton Coll., 1963; LL.B., Syracuse U., 1966. Admitted to N.Y. State bar, 1966; asso. firm Wiser, Shaw, Freeman, Van Graafeiland, Harter & Secrest, Rochester, N.Y., 1966-73; asso. firm Johnson, Reif & Mullan, Rochester, 1973-76, mem, 1976—; instr. adult edn. Greece Central Sch. Dist., Rochester, 1969—. Trustee Fairport (N.Y.) Pub. Library, 1970-75. Mem. N.Y. State, Monroe County bar assns., Community Assns. Inst., Justinian Law Soc., Phi Kappa Phi. Comments editor Syracuse Law Rev., 1965. Office: 47 S Fitzhugh St Rochester NY 14614 Tel (716) 262-5700

FARNHAM, CLAYTON HENSON, b. New Brunswick, N.J., Aug. 18, 1938; B.A., U. of South., 1961; LL.B., U. Ga., 1967. Admitted to Ga. bar, 1968; law clk. to judge U.S. Dist. Ct. No. Dist. Ga., 1967-69; asso. firm Swift, Currie, McGhee & Hiers, Atlanta, 1969-74, partner, 1974—; sec., counsel Atlanta Landmarks, Inc., 1975-76. Chmn. Transp. Study Com. of Senator Paul Coverdell of Ga., 1972. Mem. State Bar Ga., Am., Atlanta bar assns., Internat. Assn. Arson Investigators. Editor student editorial bd. Ga. State Bar Jour., 1966-67. Home: 30 Inman Circle NE Atlanta GA 30309 Office: 771 Spring St NW Atlanta GA 30308 Tel (404) 881-0844

FARNSWORTH, E(DWARD) ALLAN, b. Providence, June 30, 1928; B.S., U. Mich., 1948; M.A., Yale, 1949; LL.B. (Ordronaux prize), Columbia, 1952. Admitted to D.C. bar, 1954, N.Y. State bar, 1956; faculty Columbia, N.Y.C., 1954-59, prof. law, 1959-70, Alfred McCormack prof., 1970—; vis. prof. various univs., U.S.A., Europe, 1965-74; del. UN Commn. Internat. Trade Law, 1968—. Spl. counsel N.Y.C. Council, 1966-68. Mem. Am., N.Y.C. bar assns., Am. Law Inst. (reporter Restatement, Second, Contracts), Assn. Am. Law Schs. (dir. orientation program 1965-68), Phi Beta Kappa. Author: (with W. Young, H. Jones) Cases and Materials on Contracts, 1972; (with J. Honnold) Cases and Materials on Commercial Law, 1976; Cases and Materials on Commercial Paper, 1976; An Introduction to the Legal System of the United States, 1963. Home: 201 Lincoln St Englewood NJ 07631 Office: 435 W 116th St New York City NY 10027 Tel (212) 280-2661

FARR, G. NEIL, b. Los Angeles, Jan. 9, 1932; A.B., U. Calif., 1957, J.D., 1960. Admitted to Calif. bar, 1961; dep. dist. atty. Solano County (Calif.), 1961-66, Kern County (Calif.), 1966-69; asso. firm Young, Wooldridge, Paulden & Self, Bakersfield, Calif., 1969—. Recreation commr. City of Fairfield (Calif.), 1964-66. Mem. Calif. Applicants Assn., Am. Arbitration Assn., Kern County Bar Assn., State Bar Calif., Calif., Los Angeles trial lawyers assns. Office: Young Wooldridge Paulden & Self 1600 M St Bakersfield CA 93301 Tel (805) 327-9661

FARRAND, JAMES RIDLEY, b. Altadena, Calif., Sept. 6, 1945; A.B., Pomona Coll., 1967; M.S., U. Wis., 1968; J.D., U. Calif., Berkeley, 1971. Admitted to Calif. bar, 1972, D.C. bar, 1972; asso. firm Wilmer Cutler and Pickering, Washington, 1972—. Mem. Am. Bar Assn. Contbr. articles to legal publs. Home: 5109 Duvall Dr Bethesda MD 20016 Office: 1666 K St NW Washington DC 20006 Tel (202) 872-6380

FARRAR, ARCHIBALD ALEXANDER, b. Summerville, Ga., Sept. 6, 1921; student Davidson Coll., 1940-43; LL.B., U. Ga., 1948, J.D., 1969. Admitted to Ga. bar, 1948; individual practice law Summerville, Ga., 1946—; served to capt. JAGC, 1948—; mem. Ga. Senate, 1951-52; juvenile ct. referee, 1949-73; solicitor State Ct. Chattooga County (Ga.), 1964-70. Mem. Lookout Mountain Bar Assn. Club: Masons. Contbr. articles to sports mags. Home: 108 Virginia Dr Summerville GA 30747 Office: POB 171 8 W Washington St Summerville GA 30747 Tel (404) 857-3497

FARRELL, FRANK SAMUEL, b. Duluth, Minn., Nov. 29, 1920; B.S., U. Minn., 1947, LL.B., 1948; grad. Advanced Mgmt. Program, Harvard U., 1972. Admitted to Minn. bar, 1949, U.S. Supreme Ct. bar, 1963; asst. atty. No. Pacific Ry. Co., 1949-53; asst. commerce counsel, 1953-57, commerce counsel, 1957-60, asst. gen. solicitor, 1960-61, gen. solicitor, 1961-68, v.p., gen. counsel, 1968-70; v.p., gen. counsel Burlington No. Inc., St. Paul, 1970-74, v.p.-law, 1974—. Bd. dirs. St. Paul Civic Center Authority, 1969—, St. Paul Jr. Achievement, 1965—; mem. Minn. Gov.'s Crime Commn., 1967-68, Minn. Gov.'s Reapportionment Com., 1964-66. Mem. Am., Minn., Ramsey County bar assns. Recipient Regents award U. Minn., 1968. Home: 56 N Mississippi River Blvd Saint Paul MN 55104 Office: 176 E 5th St Saint Paul MN 55101

FARRELL, LOUIS, JR., b. Manila, Philippines, Jan. 27, 1911; A.B., U. Calif., Berkeley, 1932, LL.B., 1935, J.D., 1972. Admitted to Tenn. bar, 1935; since practiced in Nashville, partner firm Farrell & Farrell, 1935-42, 46-49, White Gullett Farrell & Phillips, 1949-57, Farrell & Neil, 1957-65, Farrell & McCoy, 1975—; instr. YMCA Night Law Sch., Nashville, 1948-51; cons. Tenn. Law Rev., 1939-68. Mem. Am., Nashville (past pres.) bar assns., Am. Judicature Soc. Chmn., Tenn. Supreme Ct. Commn. on Bar Unification, 1974-76. Home: Route 4 Franklin TN 37064 Office: 921 JC Bradford Bldg Nashville TN 37219 Tel (615) 255-1113

FARRELL, MARTIN PETER, b. Mt. Vernon, S.D., Oct. 21, 1912; grad. U. S.D., Springfield, 1937; J.D., U. S.D., 1940. Admitted to S.D. bar, 1940; individual practice law, Hot Springs, S.D., 1946—. Fellow Am. Coll. Probate Counsel; mem. Assn. Trial Lawyers Am. Office: 441 N River St Hot Springs SD 57747 Tel (605) 745-5161

FARRELL, NEAL FRANCIS, b. Chgo., Sept. 7, 1934; B.C.S., DePaul U., 1962; J.D., John Marshall Law Sch., Chgo., 1969. Admitted to Ill. bar, 1969; tax counsel Borg-Warner Corp., Chgo., 1974-75, asst. gen. counsel, 1975-77, dir. taxes, 1977—. Mem. adv. com. Chgo. Civic Fedn., 1974—; mem. taxation com. Chgo. Assn. Commerce and Industry, 1974—. Mem. Am., Ill., Chgo. bar assns. Office: 200 S Michigan Ave Borg-Warner Corp Chicago IL 60604 Tel (312) 663-8860

FARRELL, RICHARD JAMES, b. Uniontown, Pa., Nov. 7, 1916; B.S., Washington and Jefferson Coll., 1938; J.D., U. Pa., 1941; grad. Advanced Mgmt. Program, Harvard, 1954; LL.D., Washburn U. Topeka, 1970. Admitted to Pa. bar, 1942, N.Y. bar, 1947, Ill. bar, 1955, also Fed. Cts. and ICC; practice gen. and corp. law Cadwalader,

Wickersham & Taft, N.Y.C., 1941-42; atty. Standard Oil Co. (Ind.), 1942, asst. gen. counsel, 1957, asso. gen. counsel, 1959-60, gen. counsel, 1963-72, dir., 1963—, v.p. law and pub. affairs, 1965—; v.p., dir. Midwest Oil Corp.; dir. Wilmette Bank. Mem. adb. bd. Internat. Oil and Gas Ednl. Center (chmn.), Southwestern Legal Found., Internat. and Comparative Law Center. Trustee Am. Enterprise Inst., Ravinia Festival Assn.; bd. dirs. Nat. Legal Aid and Defender Assn., Hwy. Users Fedn.; bd. govs. Aspira Ill. Mem. Am., Ill. bar assns., Assn. Bar City N.Y., Am. Judicature Soc., Assn. Gen. Counsel, Am. Petroleum Inst. (com. on pub. affairs), Am. Arbitration Assn. (dir.), Northwestern U. Assos., Practicing Law Inst. (nat. adv. council for corporate law depts.), Pi Sigma Alpha, Delta Sigma Rho, Lambda Chi Alpha. Home: 1299 Hackberry Lane Winnetka IL 60093 Office: Standard Oil Co 200 E Randolph Dr Michigan Ave Chicago IL 60601*

FARRINGTON, JOHN MICHAEL, b. Wakefield, Mass., May 2, 1944; A.B. magna cum laude, Tufts U., 1966; postgrad. in Am. History, Brown U., 1966-67; J.D., Boston Coll., 1970. Admitted to Mass. bar, 1970; atty. State Mut. Life Assurance Co. Am., Worcester, Mass., 1970-72, asst. counsel, 1972-76, asst. sec., 1974—, asso. counsel, 1976—. Mem. Am., Boston bar assns., St. Vincent De Paul Soc. Home: 1450 Worcester Rd Framingham MA 01701 Office: 440 Lincoln St Worcester MA 01605 Tel (617) 852-1000

FARRIS, JAMES MARTIN, b. Houston, Oct. 10, 1932; B.B.A., Baylor U., 1953, J.D., 1959. Admitted to Tex. bar, 1959; asst. atty. gen. State of Tex., Austin, 1959-61; asst. dist. atty. City of Beaumont (Tex.), 1961-69; judge Jefferson County (Tex.) Ct. at Law 2, 1969—; speaker in field. Mem. Jefferson County Bar Assn., Tex. State Bar, Nat. Council Juvenile Ct. Judges (chmn. planning com. 1974-75), Juvenile Ct. Judges of Tex. (chmn. 1973-75). Home: 1830 Chevy Chase St Beaumont TX 77706 Office: County Court at Law 2 Courthouse Beaumont TX 77701 Tel (713) 835-8428

FARRIS, JOHN LAUCHLAN, b. Vancouver, B.C., Can., Sept. 5, 1911; B.A., U. B.C., 1931; LL.B., Harvard, 1934. Admitted to B.C. bar, 1935; past partner firm Farris, Vaughan, Wills & Murphy, Vancouver; chief justice B.C., 1973—. Lectr. comml. law U. B.C., 1945-50; past dir. Kelly, Douglas Co. Ltd., Sun Pub. Co. Ltd., Loomis Armored Car Service Ltd., Pacific Petroleums Ltd., Toronto-Dominion Bank, B.C. Telephone Co. Chmn. bd. govs. Crofton House Sch., 1959-63. Fellow Am. Coll. Trial Lawyers; mem. Canadian (council 1955-58, vice chmn. 1960-61, v.p. for B.C. 1962-64, pres. 1971-72, exec. com. 1966—), Vancouver (exec. council 1954-62, pres. 1959-60), Am. (hon.) bar assns., Law Soc. B.C. Home: 1403 Angus Dr Vancouver BC V6H 1V2 Canada Office: Court House 800 W Georgia St Vancouver BC V6C 1P6 Canada*

FARRIS, JOSEPH JEROME, b. Birmingham, Ala., Mar. 4, 1930; B.S., Morehouse Coll., 1951; M.S.W., Atlanta U., 1955; J.D., U. Wash., 1958; grad. Appellate Judges' Seminar, 1972, Nat. Coll. State Judiciary U. Nev., Reno, 1973. Admitted to Wash. bar, 1958; sr. partner firm Farris, Bangs & Horowitz, Seattle, 1965-69; judge 1st div. Wash. Ct. Appeals, 1969-76, chief judge, 1977—; chmn. Wash. Council of Nat. Council on Crime and Delinquency, 1970-72; mem. vis. com. Sch. Social Work, Seattle Found. mem. Wash. Child Welfare Advisory Com., 1972-73; mem. King County (Wash.) Youth Commn., 1969-70; mem. King County Mental Health-Mental Retardation Bd., 1967-69; del. White House Conf. on Children and Youth, 1970. Mem. Seattle-King County Bar Assn. (trustee 1969), Wash. State Jr. C. of C. (pres. 1965-66, Clayton Frost award 1966, Distingusihed Service award 1965). Home: 1908 34th Ave S Seattle WA 98144 Office: 11th floor Pacific Bldg Seattle WA 98104 Tel (206) 464-7659

FARTHING, EDWIN GLENN, b. Greensboro, N.C., July 2, 1947; B.A., U. N.C., 1969, J.D., 1972. Admitted to N.C. bar, 1972; partner firm Smathers, Ferrell & Farthing, Hickory, N.C., 1972-73; partner firm Smathers & Farthing, Hickory, 1973—. Chmn. Catawba County Bd. Elections, 1976—. Mem. Am., N.C., Catawba County bar assns., Def. Research Inst. Home: 1401 4th St NW Hickory NC 28601 Office: PO Box 1708 216 2d St NW Hickory NC 28601 Tel (704) 322-8376

FASS, PETER MICHAEL, b. Bklyn., Apr. 11, 1937; B.S., U. Pa., 1958; J.D., Harvard, 1961; LL.M., N.Y.U., 1964. Admitted to N.Y. bar, 1962; partner law firm Carro, Spanbock, Londin, Rodman & Fass (and predecessor firms), N.Y.C., 1961—; adj. asst. prof. real estate N.Y. U., 1977—; lectr. Practicing Law Inst., 1972—. Mem. Am., N.Y. State, Fed. bar assns., Assn. Bar of N.Y.C. Recipient, Haskins award, 1964. Contbr. articles to profl. jours. Office: 1345 Ave of Americas New York City NY 10019 Tel (212) 757-2400

FATZER, HAROLD R., b. Fellsburg, Kans., Aug. 3, 1910; student Kans. State U., 1928-30; LL.B., Washburn Coll., 1933, J.D., 1970, LL.D. (hon.), 1971. Admitted to Kans. bar, 1933; individual practice law, Kinsley, Kans., 1933-41; county atty. Edwards County (Kans.), 1934-41; chief counsel Kans. Bd. Social Welfare, 1941-43; asst. atty. gen. Kans., 1943, 45-49, atty. gen., 1949-56; justice Supreme Ct. Kans., 1956—, now chief justice; lectr. legal ethics Washburn Law Sch., 1964-68; mem. appellate judges seminar N.Y. U. Sch. Law, 1959. Chmn., Edwards County Debt Conciliation Com., 1935, Edwards County chpt. ARC, 1937; pres. Edwards County Young Republican Club, 1938; bd. dirs. Kans. Hist. Soc.; trustee Washburn Coll. Mem. Am., Kans. bar assns., Am. Judicature Soc. (dir., Herbert Lincoln Harley award 1972), Kans. County Attys. Assn. (pres. 1939), Nat. Assn. Attys. Gen. (pres. 1952-53), Washburn Alumni Assn. (pres. 1966), Washburn Law Sch. Assn. (Distinguished Service award 1967), Inst. Jud. Adminstrn., Kans. Dist. Ct. Judges Assn. (Meritorious Achievement award 1973), Conf. Chief Justices (exec. council 1975—), Santa Fe Trails Found. (dir.), Delta Theta Phi. Recipient Distinguished Service award Washburn U., 1964. Home: 1415 Ward Pkwy Topeka KS 66604 Office: State Capitol Topeka KS 66612 Tel (913) 234-0212

FAUBION, MARCUS E., b. Houston, July 8, 1948; B.A., U. Houston, 1970, J.D., 1973. Admitted to Tex. bar, 1973; asso. firm Denson & Swain, Houston, 1973-76; partner firm Faubion, Brady & Hammonds, Houston, 1976—. Mem. State Bar Tex., Houston Jr., Houston bar assns. Home: 7907 Rockhill St Houston TX 77061 Office: PO Box 34706 Houston TX 77034 Tel (713) 944-9931

FAULK, BOB J., b. Huntsville, Ala., Nov. 10 1939; B.S. in Mktg., Austin P. State U., Clarksville, Tenn., 1963; J.D., U. Ala., 1971. Admitted to Ala. bar, 1971; asst. dist. atty. 26th judicial circuit, Phenix City, Ala., 1971-73; partner firm Phillips, Funderburk and Faulk, Phenix City, 1973-74; individual practice law, Phenix City, 1974—. Mem. Russell County Chpt. Am. Cancer Soc., 1975-76, Setoma Club, 1974—, Civitan Club, 1974—; bd. trustees, sr. warden, Church of the Resurrection, 1974-75. Mem. Ala. (pres. assn. memberships), Russell County (sec.) bar assns., Ala. Trial Lawyers, Assn. Trial Lawyers Am. Named Outstanding Young Man of Year, Phenix City Jaycees, 1975. Home: 4100 Surrey Lane Phenix City AL 36867 Office: PO Box 837 Phenix City AL 36867 Tel (205) 297-1222

FAULKNER, CHARLES BRIXEY, b. Springfield, Mo., Feb. 11 1934; B.S., U. Ark., 1955; LL.B., U. Mo., 1960. Amditted to Mo. bar, 1960; partner firm Ratican & Faulkner, Aurora, Mo., 1960-72; legal advisor U.S. Bur. Prisons, U.S. Med. Center for Fed. Prisoners, Springfield, 1972-74; regional legal advisor U.S. Bur. Prisons, Kansas City, Mo., 1974—; pros. atty, counsel Lawrence County (Mo.), 1960-70; atty. City of Marionville (Mo.), 1960-72, City of Aurora, 1970-72. Chmn. bd. dirs. Lawrence County (Mo.) chpt. ARC, 1963-65. Mem. 39th Jud. Circuit Bar Assn. (v.p. 1966-70), Beta Gamma Sigma. Recipient Kansas City Bank and Trust award, 1960. Editorial bd. Mo. Law Rev., 1958-60. Home: 4700 NW 82nd St Kansas City MO 64151 Office: 8800 NW 112th St Kansas City MO 64153 Tel (816) 243-5680

FAULKNER, JOHN BRYANT, b. Waco, Tex., Oct. 14, 1928; B.S., Tex. Christian Univ., 1951; J.D., Tex. Univ., 1958. Admitted to Tex. bar, 1958; partner firm Edwards, Faulkner, Giles & Makowsky, Waco. Trustee, Waco Ind. Sch. Dist., 1966-76. Mem. Am., Tex. Waco-McLennan County bar assns., Am. Trial Lawyers Assn. Home: 2325 Rosewood St Waco TX 76710 Office: 620 Columbus Ave Waco TX 76701 Tel (817) 756-2193

FAULKNER, ROBERT WESLEY, b. Malvern, Ark., Feb. 4, 1938; B.A., Ouachita Bapt. U., 1960; LL.B., U. Ark., 1965; student George Washington U., 1956-57. Admitted to Ark. bar, 1966; individual practice law, Malvern, 1966-68, Little Rock, 1971-73; gov.'s rep. to Ark. Claims Commn., 1967-69, legis. liaison, 1968-69; asst. campaign mgr. Gov. Winthrop Rockefeller, 1968; exec. sec. to gov. Ark., 1969-71; part-time U.S. magistrate, 1971-73, full-time, 1973—. Mem. Am. Bar Assn. (ho. of dels.). Home: 9909 Catskill Rd Little Rock AR 72207 Office: 521 US Post Office and Courts Bldg Little Rock AR 72203 Tel (501) 378-6107

FAULKNER, THOMAS PLUNKETT, b. Chgo., Oct. 27, 1922; J.D., DePaul U., 1948. Admitted to Ill. bar, 1949, U.S. Dist. Ct. bar for N.E. Ill., 1951, U.S. Supreme Ct. bar, 1953; partner firm Faulkner & Faulkner, Joliet, Ill., 1948-61; individual practice law, Joliet, 1961-62; asso. firm Gray, Thomas, Wallace & O'Brien, Joliet, 1962-65; partner firm O'Brien, Faulkner & Garrison and predecessor, Joliet, 1965-71; asso. judge Ill. Circuit Ct., 12th Jud. Circuit, 1971—. Mem. Will County (Ill.), Ill. (sec.-treas. Will County chpt. 1960-62) bar assns. Home: Diamond K Ln Joliet IL 60433 Office: Will County Courthouse Joliet IL 60431 Tel (815) 722-8558

FAULKNER, WALTER THOMAS, b. New Haven, Sept. 17, 1928; A.B., Providence Coll., 1952; LL.B., Columbia U., 1955. Admitted to N.Y. bar, 1956, U.S. Supreme Ct. bar, 1961; asso. firm Putney, Twombly, Hall & Skidmore, N.Y.C., 1955-59; asso. firm Rogers, Hoge & Hills, N.Y.C., 1959-69, partner, 1969—; dir. Raymond Internat. Inc.; corporate sec., dir. Bacardi Corp.; corporate sec. Sterling Drug, Inc. Mem. Assn. Bar City N.Y. (mem. grievance com. 1973—), Am., N.Y. State bar assns. Office: 90 Park Ave New York City NY 10016 Tel (212) 953-9217

FAULWETTER, WILLIAM CHARLES, b. Fond du Lac, Wis., Sept. 27, 1928; J.D., Stanford, 1957; B.A., U. Calif. at Berkeley, 1951. Admitted to Calif. bar, 1959; dep. county counsel San Diego County, 1959-61; individual practice law, La Mesa, Calif., 1961—. Mem. governing bd. Grossmont Community Coll. Dist., El Cajon, Calif., 1969—, pres., 1975—; bd. dirs. Spring Valley (Calif.) Fire Protection Dist., 1961-69, pres., 1965-69. Mem. Calif., Foothills (pres. 1967) bar assns. Home: 10986 Explorer Pl La Mesa CA 92041 Office: 7373 University Ave Suite 111 La Mesa CA 92041 Tel (714) 463-9906

FAUNCE, SHERMAN POWERS, b. Detroit, Sept. 23, 1938; B.B.A., U. Iowa, 1960; J.D., Wayne State U., 1963. Admitted to Mich. bar, Fed. bar, 1963; individual practice law, Detroit, 1963-65; asst. pros. atty. Macomb (Mich.) Prosecutor's Office, 1965-66; asst. city atty. City of Warren (Mich.), 1966-69, chief asst. city atty., 1969-70, city atty., 1970-75; judge 37th Jud. Dist. Ct., Warren, 1975—. Mem. Am. Judges' Assn. Home: 31280 Shaw Dr Warren MI 48093 Office: 8300 Common Rd Warren MI 48093 Tel (313) 573-9130

FAUNTLEROY, JOHN DOUGLASS, b. Washington, Sept. 6, 1920; B.S., Am. U., 1953, LL.B., 1941. Admitted to D.C. bar, 1942; individual practice law, Washington, 1947-67; judge D.C. Juvenile Ct., 1967-71, D.C. Superior Ct., 1971—; mem. D.C. Spl. Police Trial Bd., 1966-67; law mem. D.C. Bd. Appeals and Rev., 1960-67; mem. D.C. Commrs. Council on Human Relations, 1963-67; comdr. JAGC, U.S. Navy Res., 1973—; del. Superior Ct. to Nat. Conf. State Trial Judges, 1972—. Bd. dirs. United Planning Orgn., Washington, 1965—, pres., 1971-72; chmn. nat. bd. govs. Am. U., 1971-72; mem. nat. vis. com. Sch. Social Work, Howard U., 1976—; mem. nat. adv. bd. Am. Vets. Com., 1967—; bd. dirs. Capital View Devel. Corp., 1967—, Potomac Law Sch., 1976—; trustee Tabor Presbyn. Ch., Washington, 1946-57; elder NE Presbyn. Ch., Washington, 1976—. Mem. Nat., Washington (past pres.) bar assns., Bar Assn. D.C. Recipient Bill of Rights award D.C. chpt. Am. Vets Com., 1962; Norris Civil Rights award Anti-Defamation League and B'nai B'rith, 1965; Outstanding Service award to Community, Washington Bar Assn., 1968. Office: 613 G St NW Washington DC 20001 Tel (202) 727-1020

FAUST, ANNE SONIA, b. Honolulu, Aug. 27, 1936; B.A., U. Hawaii, 1960; J.D., Harvard, 1964. Admitted to Hawaii bar, 1964; intern in pub. affairs Coro Found., San Francisco, 1960-61; dep. corp. counsel City and County of Honolulu, 1964-66; asst. researcher Legis. Reference Bur., Honolulu, 1966-69; asso. counsel Legal Aid Soc., Honolulu, 1969-70; dept. atty. gen. State of Hawaii, 1970-72; atty., exec. officer Hawaii Pub. Employment Relations Bd., Honolulu, 1972—; mem. Hawaii Bd. Bar Examiners, 1975—. Mem. Am. bar Assn. (chmn. membership Hawaii 1965), Bar Assn. Hawaii, Indsl. Relations Research Assn. Hawaii (dir. 1974-76, sec. 1977), Phi Beta Kappa, Phi Kappa Phi. Home: 1251 Heulu St Honolulu Hi 96822 Office: 550 Halekauwila St Honolulu HI 96813 Tel (808) 548-6267

FAUST, DAVID E., b. Allentown, Pa., Apr. 10, 1942; B.S., Northwestern U., 1964; J.D., 1967. Admitted to Pa. bar, 1968; atty. Penn Central Transp. Co., Phila., 1971-74, asst. gen. atty., 1974-76; mem. law dept. Conrail Corp., Phila., 1976—; mem. firm Post & Schell, Phila., 1976—. Mem. Phila. Bar Assn., Pa. Def. Inst., Nat. Assn. R.R. Trial Counsel, Am. Arbitration Assn. Office: Post & Schell 2 Penn Center Plaza Philadelphia PA 19102 Tel (215) 561-0420

FAUST, LELAND HOWARD, b. Los Angeles, Aug. 30, 1946; A.B., U. Calif., 1968; J.D., Harvard, 1971. Admitted to Calif. bar, 1972; asso. firm Taylor, Winokur, Schoenberg & Maier, San Francisco, 1971-75; partner firm Taylor & Faust, San Francisco, 1975—. Mem. Am., San Francisco bar assns. Home: 47 Malta Dr San Francisco CA 94131 Office: 1 California St San Francisco CA 94111 Tel (415) 421-9535

FAUVER, SCRIBNER LEE, b. Elyria, Ohio, June 1, 1931; B.A., Dartmouth Coll., 1953; LL.B., Harvard Coll., 1956. Admitted to Ohio bar, 1956; asso. firm Jones, Day, Reavis & Pogue, Cleve., 1956-60; partner firm Fauver & Fauver, Elyria, 1960—. Mem. Ohio Legislature, 1975—; mem. Elyria City Council, 1970-75. Mem. Am., Cleve., Ohio State, Lorain County bar assns. Office: 1002 Lorain County Bank Bldg Elyria OH 44035 Tel (216) 322-6373

FAWCETT, DWIGHT WINTER, b. Springfield, Ohio, Sept. 24, 1927; A.B., Ind. U., 1948; J.D., Harvard, 1951. Admitted to Ill., Ohio bar, 1951; partner Mayer, Brown & Platt, Chgo., 1951—. Chmn. legal aid com. United Charities Chgo.; trustee Seabury Western Theol. Sem. Mem. Am. (mem. banking com. of sect. corp., banking and bus. law), Chgo. bar assns. Home: 711 Locust St Winnetka IL 60093 Office: 231 S LaSalle St Chicago IL 60604 Tel (312) 782-0600

FAWELL, MICHAEL KENT, b. Aurora, Ill., Jan. 13, 1940; B.S., North Central Ill. Coll., 1962; J.D., Chgo.-Kent Coll. of Law, 1969. Admitted to Ill. bar, 1969, U.S. Dist. Ct. bar, U.S. Supreme Ct. bar, 1973; asst. state's atty., DuPage County, Ill., 1969-70; partner firm Botti & Fawell and predecessors, Wheaton, Ill., 1972-76; sr. partner firm Fawell & Ward, Wheaton, 1976—; spl. asst. atty. gen. State of Ill., 1973—. Mem. Am., Ill. bar assns., Am. Judicature Soc. Contbr. articles to legal jours. Office: 316 E Liberty Dr Wheaton IL 60187 Tel (312) 653-3550

FAWKE, WILLIAM ROBERT, b. Oakland, Calif., Jan. 2, 1945; B.A. in Polit. Sci. and History, Loma Linda U., 1966; J.D., Golden Gate U., 1969. Admitted to Calif. bar, 1970; asso. firm David Kikkert & Assos., San Francisco, 1970, Sprague, Milligan & Beswick, San Bernardino, Calif., 1973; Superior Ct. trial dep. Dist. Atty.'s Office, San Bernardino County, 1970—; instr. Loma Linda U., 1974, 75, guest lectr. med. sch., 1975, 76. Chmn. bd. North Highland Improvement Assn., 1975-76; mem. San Bernardino City Unified Sch. Bd., 1977—. Mem. Calif. Dist. Attys. Assn., Am. Soc. Internat. Law, Am. Trial Lawyers Assn., Calif., San Bernardino County bar assns. Office: 316 Mountain View St San Bernardino CA 92415 Tel (714) 393-1700

FAY, EDWARD DWIGHT, JR., b. Montgomery, Ala., Aug. 25, 1937; B.S., U. Ala., 1959; J.D. cum laude, Samford U., 1969. Admitted to Ala. bar, 1969, U.S. 5th Circuit Ct. Appeals bar, 1959, U.S. Dsit. Ct. bar 1959; partner firm Lutz, Fay & Foley, Huntsville, Ala. Mem. Huntsville Symphony Orch. Assn., Huntsville Art League and Mus. Assn. Mem. Am., Ala. trial lawyers assns., Phi Delta Phi. Contbr. articles to law jours. Home: 2309 Big Cove Rd Huntsville AL 35801 Office: Suite 52 Central Bank Bldg Huntsville AL 35801 Tel (205) 539-2178

FAY, RICHARD JOSEPH, b. River Edge, N.J., Mar. 1, 1929; A.B., Holy Cross Coll., 1951; J.D., George Washington U., 1954. Admitted to D.C. bar, 1955, N.J. bar, 1956; law clk. to judge U.S. Dist. Ct., D.C., 1954-55; practice law, Belmar, N.J., 1956—. Mem. ethics com., Monmouth County, N.J., 1967-69, 74-76, chmn., 1969. Mem. Am., N.J. bar assns., Monmouth Bar Assn. (past treas., 3rd v.p.), Order of Coif. Asso. editor George Washington Law Rev., 1954. Home: 215 Monmouth Ave Spring Lake NJ 07762 Office: 712 10th Ave Belmar NJ 07719 Tel (201) 681-1100

FAY, ROBERT JESSE, b. Cleve., Apr. 9, 1920; B.S., Mass. Inst. Tech., 1942; J.D., Case Western Res. U., 1948. Admitted to Ohio bar, 1949, U.S. Supreme Ct. bar, 1951, D.C. bar, 1963; mem. firm Fay and Sharpe, Cleve., 1951—; lectr. Law Sch. Case Western Res. U., 1963, 65, 66, 68, 70-75. Contbr. articles to legal jours. Office: 1113 East Ohio Bldg Cleveland OH 44114 Tel (216) 861-5582

FAY, THERESA URBAN, b. Houston, Mar. 25, 1944; B.B.A., U. Tex., 1965; J.D., U. Houston, 1969. Admitted to Tex. bar, 1968; mem. staff Dallas Title Ins. Co., Houston, 1969 and following; asst. dist. atty. Dallas County, 1974; atty. Lone Star Gas Co., Dallas; registrar Indian lands, leasing officer Canadian Fed. Govt., Ottawa, Ont., 1970-74. Mem. Dallas Bar Assn Assn. Office: 301 S Harwood St Dallas TX 75201 Tel (214) 741-3711

FAY, THOMAS FORTUNE, b. N.Y.C., Apr. 16, 1940; A.B., U. Notre Dame, 1961; LL.B., Rutgers U., 1965, J.D., 1968. Admitted to D.C. bar, 1967, Md. bar, 1971, U.S. Supreme Ct. bar, 1975; resident counsel Wilmington (Del.) Savs. Fund Soc., 1967-68; individual practice law, Washington, 1968-75, Md., 1971-75; mem. firm Fay, Fenney and Donald, 1975—; mem. panel or arbitrators Am. Arbitration Assn., 1974—. Mem. Am., Md. State bar assns., Assn. Trial Lawyers Am., D.C. Bar, Bar Assn. D.C., Assn. Plaintiffs Trial Attys. Met. Washington (pres.), Md. Trial Lawyers Assn. Home: 3701 Roseneath St Olney MD 20832 Office: 5454 Wisconsin Ave Suite 1455 Chevy Chase MD 20015 Tel (301) 652-8566

FAYSSOUX, JAMES WALTER, b. Greenville S.C., Sept. 24, 1947; B.A., Furman U., 1969; J.D., U. S.C., 1972. Admitted to S.C. bar, 1972; partner firm Hill, Wyatt & Fayssoux, Greenville, 1974—. Mem. Am. Bar Assn., S.C. State Bar, S.C. Trial Lawyers Assn. Home: 204 Ravensworth Rd Taylors SC 29687 Office: 100 Williams St Greenville SC 29602 Tel (803) 242-5133

FAZIO, D. FREDRICO, b. Bradford, Pa., July 25, 1940; B.S., Fla. State U., 1962; J.D., U. Miami, 1967. Admitted to Fla. bar, 1967; asso. firm Hawkesworth & Kay, 1967-69; sr. partner firm Fazio, Dawson & Thompson, Ft. Lauderdale, Fla., 1969—. Bd. dirs. Boys Town of Fla. Mem. Am. Trial Lawyers Assn., Acad. Fla. Trial Lawyers, Fla., Broward bar assns. Home: 2887 Riverland Rd Fort Lauderdale FL 33354 Office: 200 SE 6th St Fort Lauderdale FL 33301 Tel (305) 463-0585

FEAGIN, ROBERT DOUGLAS, b. Macon, Ga., Sept. 5, 1937; B.A., Emory U., 1959, J.D., 1962. Admitted to Ga. bar, 1961, U.S. Supreme Ct. bar, 1971; law clk to Judge Griffin B. Bell, U.S. 5th Circuit Ct. Appeals, Atlanta, 1961-63; asst. U.S. atty. No. dist. Ga., Atlanta, 1963; mem. firm Gambrell & Mobley, Atlanta, 1963—; U.S. commr. No. dist. Ga., 1965-71; spl. hearing officer U.S. Dept. Justice, Atlanta, 1964-68. Legal chmn. Ga. Heart Assn., 1974. Mem. Am., Atlanta bar assns., State Bar Ga., Lawyers Club Atlanta. Home: 42 Blackland Rd NW Atlanta GA 30342 Office: 3900 First Nat Bank Tower Atlanta GA 30303 Tel (404) 658-9150

FEAGLER, DAVID H., b. Auburn, Ind., July 7, 1933; B.A., DePaw U., 1955; J.D., Ind. U., 1963. Admitted to Ind. bar, 1963, U.S. Dist. Ct. bar, 1963; partner firms Stevens, Wampler, Travis & Feagler,

Plymouth, Ind., 1963-68, Feagler, Sowinski & Easterday, Plymouth, Ind., 1968—; past gen. counsel U.S. Jaycees; past pres. Marshall-Starke Devel. Center, Plymouth. Chmn. commn. on stewardship and finance First Meth. Ch., Plymouth, 1966-70. Mem. Marshall County (Ind.), Ind. State bar assns., Ind. Trial Lawyers Assn. Home and office: 225 W Jefferson St Plymouth IN 46563 Tel (219) 936-4937

FEATHERSTONE, DAVID MICHAEL, b. Mt. Holly, N.C., Jan. 14, 1941; A.B., Davidson Coll., 1963; J.D., U. S.C., 1970; LL.M., U. Ga., 1971; certificate Nat. Juvenile Ct. Judges Coll., U. Nev., 1975. Vice pres. Mercer W. Simmons Inc., Lincolnton, N.C., 1965-67; admitted to S.C. bar, 1970; instr. U. Ga., 1970-71; asst. prof. law Mercer U., 1971-72; asso. prof. U. Miss., 1972—; adviser S.C. Commn. on Child Abuse, 1968-70, Miss. Law Commn. on Edn., 1973-76. Scoutmaster Piedmont council Boy Scouts Am., Lincolnton. Mem. Am., S.C. bar assns. Named Outstanding Grad., S.C. Law Sch., 1970; author: Comparative Analysis—Criminal Law, 1973; Law: A Way of Life in Mississippi, 1975; contbr. articles to profl. jours. Home: POB 682 University MS 38677 Office: Law Sch U of Miss University MS 38677 Tel (601) 232-7421

FECZKO, ALBERT GEORGE, JR., b. Homestead, Pa., Sept. 2, 1939; student John Carroll U., 1957-59; B.S. in Math. U. Detroit, 1961; LL.B., Duquesne U., 1964. Admitted to Pa. bar, 1966, U.S. Supreme Ct. bar, 1975; asso. firm Mercer & Buckley, Pitts., 1967-70; partner firm Feczko & Seymour, Pitts., 1970—; solicitor Glenfield (Pa.) Borough, 1973—. Pres. tng. div. Little League Baseball of St. Louise Parish, Upper St Clair, Pa., 1973; bd. dirs. Med. Eye Bank of Western Pa., 1973-76; v.p. St. Louise Parish Council, 1976. Mem. Allegheny County (Pa.), Pa., Am. bar assns. Book rev. editor Duquesne Law Rev., 1963-64. Home: 2656 Monterey Dr Upper Saint Clair PA 15241 Office: 800 Lawyers Bldg Pittsburgh PA 15219 Tel (412) 261-4970

FEDDE, GABRIEL BERNHARD, b. Bklyn., Mar. 7, 1909; A.B., Williams Coll., 1930; J.D., Univ. Oreg., 1936; M.A., Oreg. State Univ., 1964. Admitted to Oreg. bar, 1936, U.S. Supreme Ct. bar, 1969; Asso., firm Robert T. Jacob, Portland, Oreg., 1936-38; individual practice law, Eugene, Oreg., 1938-43, Portland, 1955-69, 1970-73; adj. prof. history, internat. law, Portland State Univ., 1956—; partner firm Cole, Fedde & Peterson, Portland, 1969, firm Shepherd, Fedde & Miller, Portland, 1973—; Legal advisor Lutheran World Fedn. in Palestine, 1949-50; exec. sec. Portland Am. Friends Service Com.; chmn. sect. Nansen Symposium on Refugees, Bergen, Norway, 1971; v.p. Portland Chpt. Oreg. United Nations Assn., 1976—; dir. World Without War Council, Portland, 1976—. Mem. Oreg., Multnomah County bar assns., AAUP, Hague Acad. Internat. Law Assn. of Lawyers. Author: The Norwegian-Swedish Crisis of 1905, 1965; Frequent lectr. on refugees, draft, Scandinavian History. Home: 1919 NW Ramsey Crest Portland OR 97229 Office: 3040 First National Bank Tower Portland OR 97201 Tel (503) 221-1492

FEDER, ALVIN MARTIN, b. Bklyn., Nov. 13, 1930; B.A., Columbia, 1952, LL.B., 1954. Admitted to N.Y. bar, 1956; partner firm Feder, Kaszovitz & Weber, and predecessor, N.Y.C., 1966—. Mem. N.Y. County Lawyers Assn. Home: 170 Westminster Rd Brooklyn NY 11218 Office: 450 7th Ave New York City NY 10001 Tel (212) 239-4610

FEDER, ROBERT STANTON, b. Newark, Mar. 30, 1931; B.S., Syracuse U., 1952; J.D., Harvard, 1955. Admitted to N.J. bar, 1955, U.S. Supreme Ct. bar, 1965; asso. firm Milmed & Rosen, Union City, N.J., 1957-59, partner firm Milmed & Feder, Union City, 1959-66; individual practice law, Union City, 1966—. Mem. N.J., Hudson County bar assns., North Hudson Lawyers Club. Home: 2000 Linwood Ave Ft Lee NJ 07024 Office: 400 38th St Union City NJ 07087 Tel (201) 865-2617

FEDER, SAUL E., b. Bklyn., Oct. 8, 1943; B.S., N.Y. U., 1965; J.D., Bklyn. Law Sch., 1968. Admitted to N.Y. bar, 1969, U.S. Ct. Appeals 2d Circuit bar, 1969, U.S. Supreme Ct. bar, 1972, U.S. Ct. Claims, 1970, U.S. Customs Ct. bar, 1972, U.S. Ct. of Customs and Patent Appeals bar, 1974; mng. atty. Queens Legal Services, Jamaica, N.Y., 1970-71; partner firm Previte, Glasser, Feder & Farber, Jackson Heights, N.Y., 1972-73; asso. firm Hein, Waters, Klein & Feder, Far Rockaway, N.Y., 1973-75, partner, 1975—; spl. investigator Bur. Elections Frauds Atty. Gen. Office State of N.Y., 1966-67, spl. dep. atty. gen., 1969-70; arbitrator, consumer counsel small claims part Civil Ct. City of N.Y., 1974-75. V.p., dir. Young Israel of Briarwood (N.Y.), 1972—; dir. Queens Legal Services, Jamaica, 1975—; Republican candidate N.Y. State Assembly, 1976. Mem. Am., Queens County, Nassau County bar assns., Am. Judges Assn., N.Y. Trial Lawyers Assn., Internat. Acad. of Law and Sci., Am. Judicature Soc., Soc. of Med. Jurisprudence. Home: 147-29 84 Dr Briarwood NY 11435 Office: 1600 Central Ave Far Rockaway NY 11691 Tel (212) 327-6800

FEDERA, HENRY APPLETON, b. Louisville, May 19, 1913; A.B., U. Louisville, 1935, LL.B. magna cum laude, 1937. Admitted to Ky. bar, 1936, Pa. bar, 1948, N.Y. bar, 1950, Tex. bar, 1973; atty. Dept. Revenue of Ky., Frankfort, 1937-40, asst. atty. gen. State of Ky., Frankfort, 1940-42; served to capt. JAGD, U.S. Army, 1942-45; atty. U.S. Steel Corp., Pitts. 1946-50; sec. and counsel Orinoco Mining Co., N.Y.C., 1950-52; gen. counsel, corporate sec. Raymond Internat. Inc., Houston, 1952—, gen. counsel, 1954—, dir., 1964—, sr. v.p., 1971—. Chmn. bd., Delta Epsilon, 1959-62, pres., 1962-65. Mem. Am., Ky., Tex., N.Y. bar assns., Am. Soc. Corporate Secs. Home: 11502 Habersham Lane Houston TX 77024 Office: 2801 S Post Oak Rd Houston TX 77027 Tel (713) 623-1457

FEDERICO, DOMENIC, b. Cleve., Jan. 10, 1941; A.B., Western Res. U., 1962; LL.B., U. Mich., 1965. Admitted to Ohio bar, 1965; partner firm Federico, Myers & Enz, Columbus, Ohio, 1970—; pres. Ohio Food Systems, Inc., Columbus, 1969—. Mem. Columus, Ohio, Am. bar assns. Office: 100 E Broad St Suite 2301 Columbus OH 43215 Tel (614) 469-1124

FEDERICO, PASQUALE J., b. Monessen, Penn., Mar. 25, 1902; B.S., Case Western Res. U., 1923; M.A., George Washington U., 1925; J.D., Am. U., 1933. Admitted to D.C. bar, 1932, U.S. Supreme Ct. bar, 1935; examiner, U.S. Patent Office, Washington, 1923-46, mem. bd. appeals, 1947-70; asso. firm Cushman, Darby & Cushman, Washington, 1971—; writer lectr. in field; U.S. del. various patent treaties. Mem. Am. Bar Assn., Am. Patent Law Assn. Recipient awards gold medal Dept. Commerce, 1949, Thomas Jefferson gold medal, N.J. Patent Law Assn., 1953, patent, Am. Inst. Chemists, 1969. Mem. advisory bds. Internat. Rev. Indsl. Property and Copyright Law, 1970—, Bur. Nat. Affairs Patent, Trademark and Copyright Jour., 1970—. Home: 3634 Jocelyn St NW Washington DC 20015 Office: 1801 K St NW Washington DC 20006

FEDOR, GEORGE EDWARD, b. Czechoslovakia, Mar. 28, 1909, came to U.S., 1913, naturalized, 1921, B.A., Western Reserve U., 1931; LL.B. magna cum laude, Cleve. Law Sch., 1939. Admitted to Ohio bar, 1940, U.S. Supreme Ct. bar, 1963; asso. firm Fedor & Fedor, Cleve., 1963—; law dir. city Lakewood, Ohio, 1956-59; mem. Ohio House Reps., 1949-52; mem. city Lakewood Planning Commn., 1953-55. Mem. Am. Judicature Soc., Cleve., Cuyahoga County, Ohio State, Am. bar assns., 1st Cath. Slovak Union, 1st Cath. Slovak Ladies Assn., Nat. Slovak Soc., Cath. Slovak Sokol. Recipient outstanding alumnus award Cleve. Marshall Law Sch., 1964. Office: 1026 Terminal Tower Cleveland OH 44113 Tel (216) 696-0650

FEDOTA, MARK CLARKE, b. Chgo., Apr. 15, 1944; A.B., Loyola U., Chgo., 1966; J.D., Georgetown U., 1969. Admitted to Ill. bar, 1969; asso. firm Philip H. Corboy & Assos., Chgo., 1969-73; asso. firm Wildman, Harrold, Allen & Dixon, Chgo., 1973-76, partner firm, 1977—; arbitrator Am. Arbitration Assn., 1975—. Mem. Chgo. Bar Assn., Assn. Trial Lawyers Am., Trial Lawyers Club Chgo. Office: 1 IBM Plaza Chicago IL 60611 Tel (312) 222-0400

FEDYNSKYJ, JURIJ, b. Velyki Mosty, Ukraine, Sept. 19, 1912; Magister juris, Lvov U. (USSR), 1934; J.D., Innsbruck (Austria) U., 1943; M.L.S., Columbia, 1957; J.D., Ind. U., 1965. Admitted to Polish bar, 1934, USSR bar, 1940; individual practice law, Stanyslaviv, Lviv, Poland, 1934-39, asst. prof. Lviv U., 1939-41; teaching asso. Innsbruck U., 1945-49; lectr. Graz (Austria) U., 1946-47; legal advisor IRO, Innsbruck, 1948-49; sec.-gen. Shevchenko Sci. Soc., N.Y.C., 1952-57; asst. law librarian U. Notre Dame, 1957-59, Ind. U., 1959-66; asso. law librarian, 1966—, asst. prof., 1966-69, asso. prof., 1969—. Mem. Internat. Assn. Law Librarians (sec. 1962-65), Am. Assn. for Study Comparative Law (dir. 1973—), Société de legislation Comparée (Paris). Author: Rechtstatsachen auf dem Gebiete des Erbrechts im Gerichtsbezirk Innsbruck, 1968; contbr. articles to legal jours. Home: 706 S Rose Ave Bloomington IN 47401 Office: Ind U Sch Law Bloomington IN 47401 Tel (812) 337-9666

FEELY, PALLISTER HAMILTON, b. Bklyn., Oct. 2, 1907; LL.B., Fordham U., 1933. Admitted to N.Y. State Bar, 1934; asso. Walter Jeffreys Carlin, N.Y.C., 1934-52; partner firm Carlin, Merriam, Feely & Donohue, N.Y.C., 1952-68; partner firm Wrenn & Schmid, Bklyn., 1968—; dir. Lafayette Nat. Bank, 1958-65. Mem. Am., Bklyn. bar assns., Lawyers Club Bklyn. (pres. 1945-46). Home: 235 Adams St Brooklyn NY 11201 Office: 26 Court St Brooklyn NY 11242 Tel (212) 852-6700

FEENEY, FLOYD FULTON, b. Franklin, Ind., Sept. 26, 1933; B.S., Davidson Coll., 1955; LL.B., N.Y. U., 1960. Admitted to N.C. bar, 1960, D.C. bar, 1961; asso. firm Covington & Burling, Washington, 1960-61; law clk. to Justice Black, U.S. Supreme Ct., 1961-62; spl. asst. to solicitor Dept. Labor, Washington, 1962-63; spl. asst. to adminstr. AID, Washington, 1963-67; asst. dir. Pres's. Commn. on Law Enforcement and Adminstrn. Justice, Washington, 1967; prof. law, exec. dir. Center on Adminstrn. Criminal Justice U. Calif., Davis, 1968—; mem. criminal justice advisory bd. Sacramento Regional Area Planning Commn. Mem. Am. Bar Assn., Law and Soc. Assn. Author: (with Weir) The Prevention and Control of Robbery, 1973; (with Baron) Juvenile Diversion Through Family Counseling, 1976. Home: 1228 Colby Dr Davis CA 95616 Office: Center on Adminstrn Criminal Justice U of Calif Davis CA 95616 Tel (916) 752-2893

FEENEY, JOHN MICHAEL, b. Pitts., July 3, 1927; A.B., U. Pitts., 1950, LL.B., 1953, J.D., 1966. Admitted to Pa. bar, U.S. Supreme Ct. bar, 1963; asso. firm Moorehead & Knox, Pitts., 1954-57; partner firm McCardle, Harrington & Feeney, Pitts., 1957-67, Harrington, Feeney & Schweers, Pitts., 1967—. Mem. Am., Pa., Allegheny County (v.p. 1973-76) bar assns., Acad. Trial Lawyers Allegheny County (pres. 1971), Order of Coif. Office: Mellon Bank Bldg Pittsburgh PA 15219 Tel (412) 391-3477

FEENEY, JOSEPH FRANCIS, b. Boston, May 26, 1918; student George Washington U., 1941-42, 46-47; J.D., Boston U., 1951. Admitted to Mass. bar, 1951, D.C. bar, U.S. Ct. Appeals bar; asst. U.S. atty., Mass., 1952-53; asst. dist. atty. Suffolk County, Boston, 1954-57; legis. clerk U.S. Ho. of Reps., 1953-57; spl. justice Municipal Ct. S. Boston, 1957—; partner firm Feeney & Freeley, Boston, 1973—; chief sec., spl. counsel to Speaker John W. McCormack, U.S. Ho. of Reps., 1946-53, 68-70. Pres. Assn. Spl. Justices Com., Mass., 1972—, S. Boston Citizens Assn., 1966-68. Bd. dirs. Cerebral Palsy Council Greater Boston; chmn. Boston Sch. Commn., 1964-66; trustee Bethany Sch. for Deaf, 1976—. Mem. Am., Mass., Boston bar assns., Am. Trial Lawyers Assn. (treas. 1974), Am. Judicature Soc. Mass. Judges Conf. (vice chmn., chmn. com. legislation 1977). Named one of Greater Boston Ten Outstanding Young Men, 1952; Man of Year, Taxi Industry Scholarship Fund, 1976; Histarut Scholarship award, 1976. Home: 294 Highland St Milton MA 02186 Office: 131 State St Boston MA 02109 Tel (617) 523-5010

FEENEY, THOMAS WILLIAM, b. Lewiston, Idaho, July 31, 1922; J.D., U. Idaho, 1950. Admitted to Idaho bar, 1950; individual practice law, Lewiston, 1950-64; partner firm Blake, Feeney & Clark, and predecessors, Lewiston, 1965—; gen. counsel Port of Lewiston Commn., 1958—. Pres. Lewis-Clark Valley Boy's Clubs, Lewiston, 1963-64, bd. dirs., 1955—, mem. exec. bd., 1963-72; chmn. Nez-Perce County Republican Central Com., 1952-53; mem. Lewiston Traffic Com., 1971—. Mem. Idaho State Bar (chmn. unauthorized practice of law com. 1962-63, mem. exec. com. bar exam. preparation and grading team 1971—), Am., Clearwater (pres. 1959-60) bar assns., Lewiston C. of C. (dir. 1966-72, pres. 1969, chmn. govtl. affairs com. 1973-75), Bench and Bar, Am. Legion, Alpha Tau Omega. Home: 2136 2d St Lewiston ID 83501 Office: 1901 Idaho St Lewiston ID 83501 Tel (208) 743-9516

FEGAN, DAVID ALBERT, b. Washington, July 13, 1918; student Harvard, 1938; J.D., George Washington U., 1943. Admitted to D.C. bar, 1943, S.C. bar, 1943, Md. Bar, 1949; partner firm Morris, Pearce, Gardner & Pratt, Washington, 1943-60; individual practice, Washington, 1960—; v.p., dir. Calvert Bank & Trust Co., 1961—, Mar-Ber Devel. Corp., 1960—; v.p., chmn. bd. Capitol Clay Products, Inc., 1970—. Mem. Am., D.C. bar assns., Reciprocity Club. Home: 8709 Seven Locks Rd Bethesda MD 20034 Office: 1000 Vermont Ave NW Washington DC 20005 Tel (202) 347-8200

FEGAN, DAVID COYLE, b. Washington, July 9 1944; B.A., Washington Coll., 1967; J.D., U. Md., 1970; LL.M., George Washington U., 1974. Admitted to Md. bar, 1970; tax law specialist, individual income tax br. IRS, Washington, 1970-75, with Office of Chief Counsel, 1975—. Home: 8709 Seven Locks Rd Bethesda MD 20034 Office: Nat Office IRS Washington DC 20224 Tel (202) 566-3554

FEHELEY, LAWRENCE FRANCIS, b. Phila., Oct. 9, 1946; B.A., Cornell U., 1969, J.D. with distinction, 1973. Admitted to Ohio Supreme Ct. bar, 1973, U.S. Tax Ct. bar, 1973, U.S. Dist. Ct. bar; asso. firm Tingley, Hurd & Emens, Columbus, Ohio, 1973—; special counsel Dept. Adminstrv. Services State of Ohio, 1975; lectr. in field. Mem. jr. council Columbus Gallery Fine Arts, 1975—. Mem. Am. (subcom. state labor law devels. sect. labor relations law), Ohio (subcom. pub. employee collective bargaining, subcom. civil rights legislation labor law sect.), Columbus (admissions to bar com., prepaid legal services com.) bar assns., Order Coif. Contbr. articles to legal jours. Home: 1474 Yorktown Rd Columbus OH 43227 Office: 250 E Broad St Columbus OH 43215 Tel (614) 221-6527

FEHLBERG, JAMES HAROLD, b. Racine, Wis., Dec. 9, 1940; B.S., U. Wis., 1962, LL.B., 1965. Admitted to Wis. bar, 1965, Ill. bar, 1965; mem. staff 1st Wis. Nat. Bank of Madison, 1965-67, Conn. Mut. Ins. Co., Bloomington, Minn., 1967—. Mem. Chartered Life Underwriters, Mpls. Life Underwriters, Phi Beta Kappa. Home: 4501 Bruce Ave S Edina MN 55424 Office: 1 Appletree Square Suite 1041 Bloomington MN 55420 Tel (602) 854-0600

FEHLHABER, ORVILLE WALTER, b. Wausau, Wis., Mar. 16, 1903; B.A. in Commerce, U. Wis., 1923, LL.B., 1928. Admitted to Wis. bar, 1928; individual practice law, Wausau, 1928-65; U.S. commr., Wausau, 1933-40, 51-59; mem. Wis. State Legislature, Madison, 1940-42. Mem. Marathon County Bar Assn. (pres. 1950), State Bar Wis. Home: 1109 Grand Ave Wausau WI 54401 Tel (715) 842-1907

FEHR, EDWARD THOMAS, b. Rochester, Pa., Jan. 2, 1947; B.A., So. Meth. U., 1968; J.D., U. Ill., 1971. Admitted to Ill. bar, 1971; law clk. firm Webber, Balbach & Thies, Urbana, Ill., 1969-71, asso., 1971-72, 76—, also dir.; with JAGC, USAF, 1972-76. Mem. Ill. State, Am., Champaign County (Ill.) bar assns., Am. Judicature Soc. Home: 2210 S Lynn St Urbana IL 61801 Office: 202 Lincoln Urbana IL 61801 Tel (217) 367-1126

FEICK, HANS-GEORG K., b. Berlin, Feb. 24, 1940; LL.B., U. Munich (Germany), 1963; LL.M., U. Calif., Berkeley, 1966; J.D., Chgo.-Kent Coll. Law, 1970. Admitted to Ill. bar, 1970, Frankfurt (Germany) bar, 1972; partner firm Baker & McKenzie, Chgo. Mem. Am., German, Ill. bar assns. Home: 4 Minnholzweg Kronberg West Germany 6242 Office: 50 54 Bethmannstrasse Frankfurt Main West Germany 6000 Tel (0611) 20791

FEIDLER, MARIE MYNSTER, b. Wausau, Wis., July 11, 1909; A.B., U. N.D., 1931, B.S. in Edn., 1931, M.A., 1941, J.D., 1953, J.D. with distinction, 1969. Admitted to N.D. bar, 1953; tchr. English and fgn. langs. N.D., 1931-51; mgr. Bendeke Abstract Co., Grand Forks, N.D., 1954-55; asso. firm Ulseth & Feidler, Grand Forks, 1955-58; partner firm Feidler, & Feidler, Grand Forks, 1958—; tchr. bus. law Central High Sch., Grand Forks, 1962-66. Mem. Grand Forks, N.D. bar assns., Phi Beta Kappa. Compiler, editor: In Retrospect, Teaching in North Dakota, 1976. Home: 607 Walnut St Grand Forks ND 58201 Office: 101 N 3d St Suite 306 Grand Forks ND 58201 Tel (701) 775-7361

FEIDLER, ROBERT AUGUST, b. Superior, Wis., Sept. 3, 1919; B.J., U. N.D., 1948, J.D., 1969. Admitted to N.D. bar, 1947; individual practice law, Grand Forks, N.D., 1947-48; states atty. Sioux County (N.D.), 1949-60; partner firm Feidler & Feidler, Grand Forks, 1960—; municipal judge Larimore and Northwood (N.D.), 1973—. Mem. N.D., Grand Forks bar assns. Home: 607 Walnut St Grand Forks ND 58201 Office: 101 N 3d St Suite 306 Grand Forks ND 58201 Tel (701) 775-7361

FEIDLER, THEODORE ROOSEVELT, b. David City, Nov. 8, 1904; A.B., U. Nebr., 1931, LL.B., 1933, J.D., 1968. Admitted to Nebr. bar, 1933; individual practice law, Scottsbluff, Nebr., 1933-41; justice of the peace, Scottsbluff, 1933-35; police judge City of Scottsbluff, 1935-41; judge Scottsbluff County Ct., 1941-61; judge Dist. Ct., 17th Jud. Dist. Nebr., Gering, 1961-77. Mem. Nebr. Bar Assn. Home: 2420 3d Ave Scottsbluff NE 69361

FEIERBACH, ADOLPH, b. Oakland, Calif., Aug. 30, 1901; LL.B., Golden Gate Coll., 1925, also J.D. Admitted to Calif. bar, 1925; individual practice law, Visalia, Calif., 1926—. Mem. Tulare County Bar Assn. Home: 610 N Encina St Visalia CA 93277 Office: 1640 W Mineral King Ave Visalia CA 93277 Tel (209) 732-5685

FEIGE, HANS CHARLES OTTO, b. Rotterdam, Netherlands, Jan. 15, 1947; B.A., Clemson U., 1968; J.D., Fla. State U., 1972. Admitted to Fla. bar, 1972, U.S. Supreme Ct. bar, 1976; partner firm Patterson, Maloney & Shankweiler, Ft. Lauderdale, Fla., 1972—; adj. prof. law Nova U., 1975—; mem. Broward County (Fla.) Law Day Com., 1974-76. Mem. Am., Fla., Broward County bar assns., Fla. Acad. Trial Lawyers, Broward County Trial Lawyers Assn. Home: 1312 SE 11th St Fort Lauderdale FL 33316 Office: 3101 N Federal Hwy Fort Lauderdale FL 33306 Tel (305) 565-0351

FEIN, ROBERT EDWARD, b. Springfield, Mass., July 16, 1923; B.A., U. Mass., 1948; J.D., Boston U., 1951. Admitted to Mass. bar, 1951; asst. clk. Dist. Ct. of Springfield, 1951-73, clk., 1973—; tchr. Springfield Tech. Community Coll. Mem. Mass., Hampden County (exec. com.) bar assns., Assn. Clks. and Asst. Clks. Dist. and Municipal Cts. of Mass., Mass. Assn. Clks. (sec.). Office: District Court of Springfield 50 State St Springfield MA 01101 Tel (413) 781-8100

FEIN, ROGER GARY, b. St. Louis, Mar. 12, 1940; student Washington U., St. Louis, 1959, N.Y. U., 1961; B.S., U. Calif., Los Angeles, 1962; J.D., Northwestern U., 1965; M.B.A. in Fin. Mgmt., Am. U., 1967. Admitted to Ill. bar, 1965, U.S. Dist. Ct. No. Dist. Ill bar and U.S. Ct. Appeals 7th Circuit bar, 1968, U.S. Supreme Ct. bar, 1970; atty. div. corp. fin. SEC, Washington, 1965-67; partner firm Arvey, Hodes, Costello & Burman, Chgo., 1967—; chmn. securities adv. com. to Ill. Sec. of State, 1973—; spl. asst. atty. gen. State of Ill., 1974—; lectr. Mem. Bd. Edn., Northfield, Ill., 1977—; bd. dirs. Northfield Community Fund, 1976—. Mem. Am. Judicature Soc., Fed., Ill. (gov. and mem. assembly 1976—), Chgo. (certificate of appreciation 1976) bar assns. Recipient Pub. Service award Ill. Sec. of State, 1976, citation of merit Sta. WAIT, 1976; contbr. articles to legal publs. Home: 1661 North Ln Northbrook IL 60062 Office: 180 N LaSalle St Suite 3800 Chicago IL 60601 Tel (312) 855-5010

FEINBERG, H(ASKEL) ROBERT, b. New Brunswick, N.J., Mar. 13, 1929; B.S., N.Y. U., 1950; LL.B., Harvard, 1953. Admitted to N.Y. State bar, 1956; asso. firm Jacobs, Persinger & Parker, N.Y.C., 1956-62, partner, 1962-76; partner firm Monasch Chazen Stream & Feinberg, N.Y.C., 1976—; lectr. in field. Mem. Am., N.Y. State bar assns., Assn. Bar City N.Y. Office: 777 Third Ave New York City NY 10017 Tel (212) 759-7220

FEINBERG, PAUL HERER, b. Yonkers, N.Y., Nov. 24, 1938; A.B., U. Pa., 1960; LL.B. cum laude, Harvard, 1963; LL.M., N.Y.U., 1970. Admitted to N.Y. State bar, 1965; asso. firm Webster, Sheffield, Fleischmann, Hitchcock & Brookfield, N.Y.C., 1965-71; asst. gen. counsel Ford Found., N.Y.C., 1971—. Mem. Assn. Bar City N.Y., N.Y. State Bar Assn. Contbg. author: The Local Economic Development Corporation, 1970. Home: 867 President St Brooklyn NY 11215 Office: 320 E 43d St New York City NY 10017 Tel (212) 573-4710

FEINSAND, HOWARD L., b. N.Y.C., Jan. 12, 1948; A.B., Econs., Temple U., 1968; J.D., St. Johns U., 1971. Admitted to N.Y. bar, 1973, U.S. Ct. Appeals bar 2d Circuit, 1974, U.S. Tax Ct. bar, 1975; asso. firm Barrett Smith Schapiro & Simon, N.Y.C., 1971-76, Feit & Ahrens, N.Y.C., 1976—. Mem. Am., N.Y. State bar assns., Assn. Bar City N.Y. Home: 500A E 87th St New York City NY 10028 Office: 488 Madison Ave New York City NY 10022 Tel (212) 371-6220

FEINSCHREIBER, ROBERT ANDREW, b. N.Y.C., Apr. 18, 1943; B.A., Trinity Coll., 1964; M.B.A., Columbia, 1967; LL.B., Yale, 1967; LL.M., N.Y.U., 1973. Admitted to N.Y. State bar, 1971; asst. prof. law Wayne State U., 1967-69; tax supr. Chrysler Corp., Detroit, 1969-70; dir. taxation NAM, N.Y.C., 1970; partner firm Robert Feinschreiber & Assos., N.Y.C., 1970—; sr. internat. tax adviser World Trade Inst., N.Y.C., 1973—; dir. Internat. Tax Inst., 1971—. Mem. Am. Bar Assn., N.Y. County Lawyers Assn. Editor Internat. Tax Jour., 1974—, Bus. Ops. Tax Jour., 1975—, cons. editor U.S. Taxation of Internat. Ops.; author: Tax Incentives for U.S. Exports, 1975; Tax Depreciation Under the Class Life ADR System, 1975; contbr. articles in field to profl. jours. Office: Penthouse A 823 Park Ave New York City NY 10021 Tel (212) 734-3119

FEINSCHREIBER, SELVEN FREDERICK, b. N.Y.C.; B.S., L.I. U., 1931; J.D., Blkyn. Coll., 1935. Admitted to New York bar, 1936; registered agt. Dept. Justice for Republic of Ghana, Accra, 1957; counsellor to Uganda, Kampala, 1957-63, cons. to gov.-gen. of Eritrea, Asmara, 1964; adviser to pres. Imperial Council of Ethiopia, Addis Ababa, 1965, cons. to chief exec. of Kenya, Nairobi, 1965-68, adviser to archbishop of Haiti, Port Au Prince, 1966; adviser NBC Internat. Ednl. TV, N.Y.C., 1968-73; chmn. bd. Instructional TV Systems Corp., N.Y.C. 1973—. Mem. nat. adv. council Center for Study of the Presidency, N.Y.C., 1976—. Mem. N.Y. County Lawyers' Assn., L.I. Univ. Alumni Assn. (former pres.). Co-author Constitution of Uganda. Office: 15 Park Row St New York City NY 10038 Tel (212) RE2-4580

FEINSTEIN, ARNOLD LESTER, b. Meridian, Miss., July 3, 1947; B.A., Tulane U., 1969, J.D., Harvard, 1973. Admitted to Ga. bar, 1973; asso. firm Jones, Bird, & Howell, Atlanta, 1973—. Mem. Am., Atlanta bar assns., State Bar Ga., Phi Beta Kappa. Office: 75 Poplar St NW Haas-Howell Bldg Atlanta GA 30303 Tel (404) 522-2508

FEINSTEIN, FRED, b. Chgo., Apr. 6, 1945. B.S., DePaul U., J.D., 1970. Admitted to Ill. bar, 1970; asso. firm, McDermott, Will & Emery Chgo., 1970-77, partner, 1977—. Mem. Chgo. Bar Assn., Deborah Goldfine and Reva Smilgoff Meml. Club for Cancer Res., Ill. State Bar Assn., Beta Gamma Sigma, Beta Alpha Psi, Pi Gamma Mu, Lex Legio. Author: Partition Suits-Quiet Title Actions, Real Estate Litigation, 1976; contbr. articles to legal jours. Home: 8611 Prairie Rd Skokie IL 60076 Office: 111 W Monroe St Chgo IL 60603 Tel (312) 372-2000

FEINSTEIN, MILES ROGER, b. Camden, N.J., June 25, 1941; B.A., Rutgers U., 1963; LL.B., Duke, 1966. Admitted to N.J. bar, 1966; law clk. to judge N.J. Superior Ct.; asso. firm Cole, Berman & Garth, Paterson, N.J., 1967-68; individual practice law, Passaic, N.J., 1969—; mem. Passaic Criminal Justice Planning Bd., 1972. Mem. Passaic County (chmn. com. on law enforcement and adminstrn. justice 1973-74, 75-76, award 1975), N.J., Fed., Am. bar assns., N.J., Am. trial attys. assns., Phi Beta Kappa, Phi Alpha Theta. Named Man of Year Passaic Bad Guys, charitable assn., 1974, Passaic Boy Scout Council, 1976, Passaic Heart Fund, 1976; Henry Rutgers scholar, 1963. Office: 40 Passaic Ave Passaic NJ 07055 Tel (201) 779-1124

FEINSTEIN, PAUL DAVID, b. N.Y.C., May 15, 1943; B.A., L.I. U., 1965; J.D., Union U., 1968. Admitted to N.Y. State bar, 1968; asso. firm Herrick, Feinstein, Mendelson & Abramson, N.Y.C., 1968-71; pres. Vantage Mgmt. Corp., N.Y.C., 1971-73; partner firm Kroll, Levy, Baron & Feinstein, N.Y.C., 1973—; guardian of incompetent, N.Y. State Supreme Ct., N.Y.C., 1977, receiver of real property, 1975-77; dep. atty. gen. State of N.Y., 1971-74. Mem. N.Y. State, N.Y.C. bar assns. Recipient Philanthropic award Muscular Dystrophy Assn. Home: 102 Sunnyside Dr Yonkers NY 10705 Office: 600 5th Ave New York City NY 10020 Tel (212) 489-6220

FEIRICH, JOHN COTTRILL, b. Chgo., Jan. 2, 1933; student Northwestern U., 1951-53; J.D., U. Ill., 1956. Admitted to Ill. bar, 1956, U.S. Dist. Ct. bar for Eastern Dist. Ill., 1956, U.S. Supreme Ct. bar, 1962; partner firm Feirich, Feirich & Green, Carbondale, Ill., 1956-68; pres. John C. Feirich Assos., Chartered, Carbondale, 1968—; mem. Chgo.-Ill. State bar assns. joint com. on Ill. Cts. Commn.; mem. Nat. Com. for Effective Adminstrn. Justice; supr., judge Lincoln Award Competition. Bd. dirs. Carbondale YMCA, 1958-65, chmn. bd., 1958-62; mem. Carbondale Grade Sch. Com. on Sch. Problems, 1968; mem. Carbondale Community High Sch. Dist. 165 Bd. Edn., 1969-74; pres. So. Ill. Sailing Sch., Carbondale, 1968. Fellow Am. Coll. Trial Lawyers; mem. Ill. State (chmn. spl. com. on jud. assignment, mem. exec. council sect. on civil practice and procedure and sect. mineral law), Am. (nat. chmn. coms. on lawyers title guaranty fund and ct. improvement Jr. Bar Conf.), St. Louis, Jackson County (Ill.) (pres. 1966-67) bar assns., Am. Judicature Soc. (dir.), U. Ill. Law Alumni (pres. 1973-74), U. Ill. Law Forum (Council Practicing Lawyers), Def. Research Inst., Ill. Def. Cdunsel, Ill. Trial Lawyers Assn., Assn. Ins. Attys., Scribes. Author: State Conferences on Judicial Selection and Court Administration, 1961; (with others) Illinois Pattern Instructions, 1971, 77; contbr. articles to legal jours. Office: 206 W College St PO Box 2677 Carbondale IL 62901 Tel (618) 549-0761

FEIST, MALCOLM WEILLER, b. Shreveport, La., Nov. 18, 1905; B.A., Wash. U., 1923; LL.B., Tulane U., 1926. Admitted to La. bar, 1926, U.S. Supreme Ct. bar, 1943; individual practice law, Shreveport, 1926—. Mem. Shreveport (pres. 1972), La. State bar assns., Phi Beta Kappa. Office: 806 Mid South Towers Shreveport LA 71101 Tel (318) 424-2644

FEIT, ELLIOT MICHAEL, b. N.Y.C., Jan. 30, 1942; B.B.A., Coll. City N.Y., 1963; J.D., Bklyn. Coll., 1966; LL.M., N.Y.U., 1969. Admitted to N.Y. State bar, 1966, U.S. Supreme Ct. bar, 1972; partner firm Johnson, Tannen, Katzman, Brecher, Fishman & Feit, N.Y.C., 1969—. Mem. Community Planning Bd. 12, N.Y.C. Mem. Bklyn. (chmn. Workman's Compensation Com. 1975—), Nassau County, N.Y. State Workman's Compensation bar assns., N.Y. County Lawyers Assn. Home: 1075 Ocean Pkwy Brooklyn NY 11230 Office: 401 Broadway New York City NY 10013 Tel (212) WA5-4567

FEITELSON, ROBERT JOEL, b. Yonkers, N.Y., Jan. 6, 1935; student U. Vt., 1953-55; B.S., N.Y. U., 1956, LL.B., 1962. Admitted to N.Y. State bar, 1963; individual practice law, Yonkers, 1963—. Mem. N.Y. State Bar Assn., N.Y. Assn. Atty.-C.P.A.'s, Am. Assn. Atty-C.P.A.'s. Office: 20 S Broadway Yonkers NY 10701 Tel (914) 969-5400

FELANDO, AUGUST JOHN, b. San Pedro, Calif., Feb. 11, 1929; LL.B., Loyola U., Los Angeles, 1954, B.B.A., 1955. Admitted to Calif. bar, 1956, So. Dist. U.S. Dist. Cts. bar, 1956; served with Judge Adv. Gen. Corps, USAF; asso. firm Overton, Lyman & Prince, Los Angeles; individual practice law, San Pedro, Calif., 1959-60; gen. mgr. Am. Tuna Boat Assn., San Diego, 1960—; mem. U.S. Law of Sea Delegation, 1971—; advisor fisheries orgns. Mem. Am., Calif., San Diego County bar assns. Office: 1 Tuna Ln San Diego CA 92101 Tel (714) 233-6405

FELD, BENJAMIN, b. N.Y.C., Feb. 7, 1917; B.S. in Social Sci., Coll. City N.Y., 1937; LL.B., St. Lawrence U., 1941, S.J.D., 1948; Ph.D., Georgetown U., 1960. Admitted to N.Y. bar, 1942, Md. bar, 1953, D.C. bar, 1970; asso. prof., dir. admissions Bklyn. Law Sch. of St. Lawrence U., 1946-53; adj. prof. Georgetown U. Law Center, 1965-68; adj. prof. Center Adminstrn. Justice, Am. U., Washington, 1965—, also commr. U.S. Ct. Mil. Appeals, 1953—. Trustee Alta-Vista Elementary Sch., 1958-67; del. Montgomery County (Md.) Council PTA's, 1966-68; pres. local civic assn. Mem. Fed. Bar Assn., Phi Sigma Alpha. Author: A Manual of Courts-Martial Practice and Appeal (1st prize for lit. award Mil. Law Inst.), 1958; (with others) A Practical Guide to Legal Research, 1950; Criminal Justice and the Constitution, 1971; contbr. articles to legal jours. Home: 5115 Wickett Terr Bethesda MD 20014 Office: 450 E St NW Washington DC 20442 Tel (202) 693-7100

FELDACKER, BRUCE S., b. East St. Louis, Ill., June 26, 1940; A.B., Washington U., St. Louis, 1962; J.D., U. Chgo., 1965; LL.M., Georgetown U., 1969. Admitted to Mo., Ill. bars, 1965; asso. firm Katz & Friedman, Chgo., 1965; served as capt. JAGC, U.S. Army, Pentagon, Washington, 1966-69; asso. firm Schuchat, Cook & Werner, St. Louis, 1969-74, partner 1974-76; individual practice law, St. Louis, 1976—; adj. asso. prof. law U. Mo., 1977—. Mem. Human Relations Commn. University City (Mo.), 1972—. Mem. Am., Mo., Ill., St. Louis (chmn. labor law com. 1974-75) bar assns. Contbr. articles to legal jours. Home: 7322 Cornell St University City MO 63130 Office: 706 Chestnut St Saint Louis MO 63101 Tel (314) 241-3535

FELDER, JOHN GRESSETTE, b. Orangeburg, S.C., Sept. 4, 1944; B.A., Wofford Coll., 1966; J.D., U. S.C., 1969. Admitted to S.C. bar, 1969; mem. firm Gressette & Gressette, St. Matthews, S.C., 1969-73, Felder & Culclasure, St. Matthews, 1975-76; individual practice law, St. Matthews, 1973-74, 76—; tchr. comml. law Orangeburg-Calhoun Tech. Coll. Chmn. bd. trustees St. Matthews Schs., 1973; bd. dirs. St. Matthews chpt. Am. Cancer Soc.; adv. bd. Home Health Services; mem. adminstrv. St. Paul Methodist Ch. Mem. Am., S.C. bar assns. Recipient Friend of Edn. award, 1975, Heart Fund award, 1974. Home: Pine Hill Rd St Matthews SC 29135 Office: PO Box 437 US Hwy 601 N St Matthews SC 29135 Tel (803) 874-2010

FELDER, RAOUL LIONEL, b. N.Y.C., May 15, 1934; B.A., N.Y.U., 1955, J.D., 1959; postgrad. U. Bern (Switzerland), 1955-56. Admitted to N.Y. bar, 1959, U.S. Dist. Ct. for So. and Eastern N.Y., 1962, U.S. 2d Circuit Ct. Appeals bar, 1962, U.S. Supreme Ct. bar, 1970; individual practice law, N.Y.C., 1959-61; 64—; asst. U.S. atty., 1961-64. Mem. Assn. Bar City N.Y. (mem. spl. com. matrimonial law), Am., N.Y. State bar assns., N.Y. State Dist. Attys. Assn., N.Y. State Trial Lawyers Assn. (former chmn. matrimonial law 1974-75), Nat. Criminal Def. Lawyers Assn., N.Y. State Soc. Med. Jurisprudence, Am. Judicature Soc., Am. Acad. Matrimonial Lawyers, Am. Arbitration Assn., Nat. Council on Family Relations. Author: Divorce, The Way Things Are, Not The Way Things Should Be, 1971; contbr. articles to legal jours. Home: 985 Fifth Ave New York City NY 10021 Office: 711 Fifth Ave New York City NY 10022 Tel (212) 832-3939

FELDHEIM, DAVID ALLEN, b. Cleve., Dec. 14, 1947; B.A., Sch. Internat. Service, Am. U., 1969; J.D., N.Y. U., 1972. Admitted to Pa. bar, 1972; jud. law clk. Ct. of Common Pleas Montgomery County (Pa.), 1972-74; atty. Sun Oil Co., Phila., 1974—. Mem. Am., Pa., Montgomery County bar assns. Recipient Am. Jurisprudence award, 1971. Home: 27 Scarlet Oak Dr LaFayette Hill PA 19444 Office: 1600 Walnut St Philadelphia PA 19103 Tel (215) 972-4135

FELDMAN, DEBORAH GREENBERG, b. London; student Am. Inst. Banking, Boston U.; J.D., Northeastern U., 1941, LL.M., 1943. Admitted to Mass. bar, 1945; with Boston Safe Deposit and Trust Co., asst. trust officer, 1958-62, legal officer, 1962—; lectr. in field. Mem. Town Meeting, Brookline, Mass., 1968-70; vice chmn. lawyers group Combined Jewish Philanthropies; past pres. bus. and profl. group Hadassah, Jewish Women Coll. Club. Mem. Nat. Assn. Bank Women, Mass., Boston bar assns., Mass. Women Lawyers (past pres.), Kappa Beta Pi (past dean). Contbr. articles to legal jours. Home and Office: 141 Sea St Quincy MA 02169

FELDMAN, EARL NELSON, b. Cleve., June 22, 1943; B.S. cum laude, U. Calif., Los Angeles, 1965, M.B.A., 1966; J.D., Harvard, 1969. Admitted to Calif. bar, 1970, U.S. Supreme Ct. bar, 1972; summer field audit intern IRS, San Diego, 1964, summer legal intern chief counsel's office, Washington, 1968; sr. tax accountant Coopers & Lybrands, San Francisco, 1969-71; asso. firm Friedman, Heffner, Kahan & Dysart, San Diego, 1971-73; asso. firm Augustine & Delafield, San Diego, 1973-74, partner, 1975—; lectr. in field. Bd. dirs. San Diego Hebrew Home for the Aged, San Diego United Jewish Fedn. Mem. Am., San Diego bar assns., Calif. Bar, Am. Inst. C.P.A.'s., Calif. C.P.A.'s., Atty-C.P.A. Assn. Recipient Ernst & Ernst Accounting award U. Calif. at Los Angeles, 1966; editor Harvard Jour. on Legilslation, 1968-69; certified specialist in taxation law. Office: 111 Elm St San Diego CA 92101 Tel (714) 236-1125

FELDMAN, EUGENE, b. N.Y.C., May 24, 1927; B.S., Coll. City N.Y., 1948; J.D., Harvard, 1952; LL.M., N.Y. U., 1961. Admitted to N.Y. State bar, 1952, U.S. Supreme Ct. bar, 1966; asso. firm Booth, Lopton & Lipton, N.Y.C., 1952-54; mem. firm John J. Tullman, N.Y.C., 1955-56; individual practice law, N.Y.C., 1956—; asst. prof. Queens Coll., 1963—; asst. dist. atty. Queens County, 1962-66. Mem. N.Y. State Bar Assn., Dist. Attys. Assn. Home: 736 Carroll St New York City NY 11215 Office: 217 Broadway New York City NY 10007 Tel (212) 732-7570

FELDMAN, FRANKLIN, b. N.Y.C., Nov. 12, 1927; B.A., N.Y. U., 1948; LL.B., Columbia, 1951. Admitted to N.Y. bar, 1952; mem. office of gen. counsel U.S. Air Force Dept. Def., Washington, 1951-53; atty. office of counsel to gov. State of N.Y., 1954; asso. firm Stroock Stroock & Lavan, N.Y.C., 1955-64, partner, 1965—; editor-in-chief Columbia Law Rev., 1950-51; mem. Temporary N.Y. Commn. on Constl. Conv.; cons. in field. Mem. Am., N.Y. State bar assns., Assn. Bar City N.Y., N.Y. County Lawyers Assn., Internat. Found. for Art Research (pres. 1971-76). Author: (with Stephen E. Weil) Art Works: Law, Policy and Practice, 1974; contbr. articles to law jours. Home: 15 W 81st St New York City NY 10024 Office: 61 Broadway New York City NY 10006 Tel (212) 425-5200

FELDMAN, HAROLD LAWRENCE, b. Tyler, Tex., Apr. 18, 1941; B.A., U. Okla., 1963; LL.B., So. Meth. U., 1966, J.D., 1968. Admitted to Tex. bar, 1966; with tax dept. Peat, Marwick & Mitchell, Dallas, 1966-67; asso. firm Marks, Times & Aranson, Dallas, 1967-68; adj. prof. U. Dallas, 1968; individual practice law, Dallas, 1968-71; sr. partner Feldman O'Donnell & Neil, Dallas, 1971—. Bd. dirs. Temple Shalom Brotherhood, Dallas, 1976. Mem. Tex. Trial Lawyers Assn. Home: 6204 Shadycliff Dr Dallas TX 75240 Office: 1960 Fidelity Union Tower Bldg Dallas TX 75201 Tel (214) 748-7848

FELDMAN, HYMAN, b. Chgo., Oct. 15, 1906; LL.B., DePaul U., 1927, J.D., 1972. Admitted to Ill. bar, 1928; practiced in Chgo., 1928-37; asst. corp. counsel City of Chgo., 1937-45; asst. state's atty. Cook County (Ill.), 1945-54; judge Chgo. Municipal Ct., 1955-64, Ill. Circuit Ct. in Cook County, 1964—. Mem. Chgo. Bar Assn., Decalogue Soc. Lawyers. Home: 340 Diversey Blvd Chicago IL 60657 Office: 1802 Civic Center Chicago IL 60602 Tel (312) 935-0167

FELDMAN, MILTON A., b. Phila., Feb. 24, 1931; B.S. in Econs., U. Pa., 1952, LL.B., J.D., 1955; asso. firm Sterling, Magaziner, Stern & Levy, Phila., 1957-64; partner firm Hamilton, Darmopray & Malloy, Phila., 1964-68, firm Townsend, Elliott & Munson, Phila., 1968-74; counsel firm Clark, Ladner, Fortenbaugh & Young, Phila., 1976—; arbitrator Am. Arbitration Assn. Trustee, mem. exec. com., sec. Chestnut Hill Hosp., Phila.; bd. dirs., exec. com. Planned Parenthood Assn. Southeastern Pa.; mem. devel. com., spl. gifts chmn. Phila. div. Am. Cancer Soc., 1977; mem. acad. affairs com. Germantown Acad.; mem. exec. com. Pa. Republican Fin. Com.; commr. Pa. Commn. Acad. Facilities, 1970-71; chmn. Operation Alphabet, 1960-61; chmn. child care budget sect. United Fund, 1965, mem. allocations com., 1966-68. Mem. Am., Pa., Phila. bar assns., Sociol. Club. Contbr. articles to legal jours. Office: 1700 Widener Bldg 1339 Chestnut St Philadelphia PA 19107 Tel (215) 564-5300

FELDMAN, MORTON, b. Atlantic City, July 3, 1939; B.S.E., U. Pa., 1959; LL.B., Rutgers U., 1963. Admitted to N.J. bar, 1967, D.C. bar, 1967; tax specialist IRS Fed. Triangle, Washington, 1967; individual practice law, Atlantic City, 1967—; instr. law Atlantic Community Coll.; counsel Environ., Taxpayer and Civic Research Found., Atlanta, City. Contbr. articles in field to profl. jours. Office: 1 S New York Ave Atlantic City NJ 08401 Tel (609) 344-3185

FELDMAN, MYER, b. Phila., June 22, 1917; B.S. in Econs., U. Pa., 1935, LL.B., 1938. Admitted to D.C. bar, 1965, Pa. bar, 1939, U.S. Supreme Ct. bar, 1949; spl. counsel, exec. asst. to chmn. SEC, 1946-54; counsel banking and currency com. U.S. Senate, 1955-57; legislative asst. to Sen. John F. Kennedy, 1958-61; dep. spl. counsel to Pres. John F. Kennedy, 1961-63; counsel to Pres. Lyndon B. Johnson, 1964-65; partner firm Ginsburg, Feldman & Bress, Washington, 1965—; dir. Tiger Internat., Inc., Nat. Savs. & Trust Co., Music Fair, Inc., Key Stas., WWBA, Inc., WLLH, Inc., WLAM, Inc. Bd. govs. Weizmann Inst. Sci.; trustee United Jewish Appeal, Jewish Publ. Soc.; trustee Eleanor Roosevelt Meml. Found.; overseer Coll. of the Virgin Islands; dir. Flame of Hope, Inc.; v.p. Congressional Leadership for Future, 1970; pres. McGovern for Pres. Com., 1971-72; fin. chmn. Bayh for Pres. Com., 1975-76. Mem. Am. Bar Assn., Am. Law Inst. Contbr. articles profl. jours., Standard Pennsylvania Practice (4 vols.). Office: 1700 Pennsylvania Ave NW Washington DC 20006 Tel (202) 637-9100

FELDMAN, ROGER DAVID, b. Worcester, Mass., Aug. 2, 1945; A.B., Harvard, 1967; J.D., Boston U., 1970. Admitted to Mass. bar, 1970; asso. firm Gaston Snow & Ely Bartlett, Boston, 1970—. Mem. Boston Bar Assn. Home: Cedar Rd Lincoln MA 01773 Office: One Federal St Boston MA 02110 Tel (617) 426-4600

FELDSTEIN, ALAN RICHARD, b. Rochester, N.Y., Aug. 17, 1944; B.A., State U. N.Y., Buffalo, 1966, J.D., 1969. Admitted to N.Y. bar, 1970; since practiced in Rochester; law clk. N.Y. Supreme Ct., 1969-71; asso. firm Martin, Dutcher, Cooke, Mousaw & Vigdor, 1971-73; partner firm Wegman, Mayberry, Burgess & Feldstein, 1973—; personal law clk to Justice Witmer, Appellate div. 4th dept. N.Y. State Supreme Ct., Rochester, 1973—; dir. Continuing Developmental Services, Inc., Rochester, 1977—. Mem. N.Y. State, Monroe County bar assns. Contbr. articles to law revs. Home: 668 Eastbrook Ln Rochester NY 14618 Office: Suite 701 One Exchange St Rochester NY 14614 Tel (716) 454-6000

FELDSTEIN, JAY HARRIS, b. Elizabeth, Pa., June 23, 1937; B.A., Pa. State U., 1959; J.D., Yale, 1962. Admitted to Pa. bar, 1963, Fla. bar, 1963, U.S. Supreme Ct. bar, 1967; individual practice law, Pitts., 1963-68; pres. Feldstein Greenberg, Stein & McKee, Pitts., 1969—; asst. gen. counsel Pa. Human Relations Commn., 1969-76; solicitor Borough of Elizabeth, Allegheny County, Pa., 1970—. Co-counsel and bd. dirs. Elizabeth-Foward Student Aid Scholarship Fund, 1968—; exec. bd. Alumni Assn. Pa. State U., 1971—. Mem. Am., Allegheny County bar assns., Western Pa. Trial Lawyers Assn., Pitts. Inst. Legal Medicine. Named Outstanding Young Man in Pitts. Area, Pitts. Jr. C. of C., 1969. Home: 592 Sandrae Dr Mount Lebanon PA 15243 Office: 707 Law and Finance Bldg Pittsburgh PA 15219 Tel (412) 471-0677

FELHABER, RICHARD SOULE, b. Mpls., July 23, 1905; B.A., U. Minn., 1928, LL.B., 1928. Admitted to Minn. bar, 1928, U.S. Supreme Ct. bar, 1968; mem. firm Weickert, Lohmann & Felhaber, St. Paul, 1928-36, firm Elmquist, Felhaber, & Elmquist, St. Paul, 1936-42, firm Felhaber, Larson, Fenlon & Vogt, St. Paul, 1942—. Mem. Am., Minn., Ramsey County bar assns. Home: 11 Dogwood Ln North Oaks MN 55110 Office: W 1080 First Nat Bank Bldg Saint Paul MN 55101 Tel (612) 222-6321

FELIG, NORMAN JOSEPH, b. N.Y.C., June 15, 1919; B.S., St. John's U., 1939; LL.B., N.Y. Law Sch., 1943. Admitted to N.Y. bar, 1946; partner firm Felig & Felig, N.Y.C., 1946-71; asst. dist. atty. Kings County (N.Y.), 1950-54; law sec. to justice N.Y. State Supreme Ct., Kings County, 1954-71; judge N.Y.C. Criminal Ct., 1972-76; acting justice N.Y. Supreme Ct., Kings County, 1976—. Mem. N.Y. State, Bklyn. bar assns., Kings County Criminal Bar Assn., Am. Judicature Soc., Am. Judge Assn. Office: 120 Schermerhorn St Brooklyn NY 11201 Tel (212) 875-0500

FELLER, DAVID EDWARD, b. N.Y.C., Nov. 19, 1916; A.B., Harvard, 1938; LL.B., 1941. Admitted to Mass. bar, 1941, D.C. bar, 1941, U.S. Supreme Ct. bar, 1950; lectr. law and economics, U. Chgo., 1941-42; atty. Dept. justice Washington, 1945-48; law clk. U.S. Supreme Ct., Washington, 1948-49; partner firm Goldberg, Feller and Bredhoff and successor firms, Washington, 1949-67; gen. counsel United Steel Workers of Am., 1961-65; indsl. union dept. AFL-CIO, 1961-66; prof. law U. Calif. Berkeley, 1967—; dir. legal def. fund NAACP, 1955—. Mem. Am. Bar Assn., AAUP (dir. 1975—). Contbr. articles to law reviews. Home: 728 Santa Barbara Rd Berkeley CA 94707 Office: Univ Calif Sch Law Berkeley CA 94720 Tel (415) 642-0629

FELLER, KATHERINE CHRISTINE, b. Cleve., Aug. 3, 1909; B.A., Flora Stone Mather Coll., 1931; J.D., Cleve.-Marshall Law Sch., 1944. Admitted to Ohio bar, 1944; med. technologist Univ. Hosps. of Cleve., 1935-60, radium technologist, 1935-37, head radium dept., 1937-47, asso. dir. sch. med. technology, 1960-75. Mem. Ohio State, Am. bar assns., Cleve. Women Lawyers Assn., Kappa Beta Pi. Home: 6079 Middle Ridge Rd Madison OH 44057

FELLING, DARRELL EDWARD, b. Terre Haute, Ind., June 12, 1947; B.A., DePauw U., 1969; J.D., Ind. U., 1972. Admitted to Ind. bar, 1972, U.S. Dist. Ct. So. Dist. Ind. bar, 1972; pres. firm Felling, Tabor and Crawford, and predecessors, Terre Haute, 1972—; student legal counselor Ind. State U., Terre Haute, 1972—. Pres. Program Headstart, Terre Haute, 1974-75; v.p. Terre Haute Jaycees, 1973-75; v.p. Community Action Program, 1975-76; pres. Dixie Bee PTA, 1974, Vigo County PTA, 1976—; bd. dirs. Hyte Community Center, Vigo County unit Am. Cancer Soc., Planned Parenthood Wabash Valley, Assn. Retarded Citizens; mem. Ind. Legislature from 50th dist., 1977-78. Mem. Am., Ind. State, Terre Haute bar assns., Phi Delta Phi. Recipient State and Nat. award U.S. Jaycees, 1975. Home: 7005 Dixie Bee Rd Terre Haute IN 47802 Office: 103 S 3d St Terre Haute IN 47807 Tel (812) 238-1408

FELLOWS, DOUGLAS MAC, b. Pomeroy, Wash., Aug., 27, 1940; B.S., U. Oreg., 1962; J.D., Lewis and Clark Coll., 1968. Admitted to Oreg. bar, 1968; asso. firm Fellows, McCarthy & Zikes, and predecessors, Portland, Oreg., 1968-70, partner firm, 1970—; mem. Oreg. State Bar Com. on Disciplinary Rules and Procedures, 1970-74. Mem. Oreg. State, Am. bar assns., Am. Trial Lawyers Assn., Delta Theta Phi. Office: 808 Am Bank Bldg Portland OR 97205 Tel (503) 226-3031

FELLOWS, THEODORE EDWIN, b. Hardwick, Minn., Apr. 15, 1904; LL.B., U. Minn., 1930. Admitted to Minn. bar, 1930; municipal judge City of Pipestone (Minn.), 1931-72; individual practice law, 1930—. Home: 312 3d Ave SE Pipestone MN 56164 Office: A & S Drugs Bldg Main St Pipestone MN 56164 Tel (507) 825-3262

FELS, JAMES ALEXANDER, b. Chgo., Nov. 13, 1944; B.S., Butler U., 1970; J.D. magna cum laude, Ind. U., 1974. Admitted to Ind. bar, 1974; asso. firm Wilson, Tabor & Holland, Indpls., 1974—. Mem. Am., Ind., Indpls. bar assns., Am. Ind. trial lawyers assns., Lawyer Pilot Bar Assn. Home: 6223 Washington Blvd Indianapolis IN 46220 Office: 850 Fort Wayne Ave Indianapolis IN 46204 Tel (317) 632-7393

FELT, JAMES HENRY, b. Oak Park, Ill., July 21, 1920; B.S., U. Ill., 1942; J.D., Harvard, 1948; postgrad. Northwester U., 1948-51. Admitted to Ill. bar, 1948, Mass. bar, 1955; asso. firm Kixmiller, Baar, & Morris, Chgo., 1948-49; tax mgr. Arthur Andersen & Co., C.P.A.s, Chgo., 1950-53, Boston, 1953-55; asso. firm Seyfarth, Shaw, Fairweather & Geraldson, Chgo., 1955-58; sec., legal counsel Acme Steel Co., Chgo., 1958-62; judge Circuit Ct. of Cook County (Ill.), 1963—. Pres. Better Govt. Assn. Chgo., 1961-62; bd. dirs. Bellwood (Ill.) Boys Club, 1964-73, U. Ill. Alumni Assn., 1964-70; pres. U. Ill. Coll. Commerce Alumni Assn., 1963-64. Mem. Am., Ill., Chgo. bar assns., Am. Judicature Soc. C.P.A., Ill., Mass. Home: 1773 Pheasant Trail Inverness Palatine IL 60067 Office: Civic Center Chicago IL 60602 Tel (312) 443-8378

FELTER, EDWIN LESTER, b. Des Moines, N. Mex., Aug. 24, 1927; student U. N.Mex., 1936-37, George Washington U., 1937-40; J.D., Am. U., 1944. Admitted to D.C. bar, 1944, U.S. Supreme Ct. bar, 1972; individual practice law, Santa Fe, 1946-71; judge N. Mex. Dist. Ct., 1st Dist., Santa Fe, 1971—. Home: 800 Lomita St Santa Fe NM 87501 Office: County Courthouse Santa Fe NM 87501 Tel (505) 827-2385

FELTON, ROBERT JOHN, b. Titusville, Pa., May 17, 1943; B.S. cum laude, St. Bonaventure U., 1965; J.D., Duquesne U., 1968. Admitted to Pa. bar, 1969, U.S. Supreme Ct. bar, 1972; with JAGC, U.S. Army, 1969-73; asso. firm Jack, Kookogey & Schug, Titusville, 1973—; asst. dist. atty. Crawford County (Pa.), 1976—. Mem. Titusville Recreation Commn., 1975—; bd. dirs. Titusville YMCA, 1975—. Mem. Pa., Crawford County bar assns. Home: 649 Maxwell Dr Titusville PA 16354 Office: 144 W Spring St Titusville PA 16354 Tel (814) 827-2788

FEMIA, VINCENT JAMES, b. Phila., July 26, 1936; B.A., George Washington U., 1959, J.D., 1961. Admitted to Md. Ct. Appeals bar, 1961, U.S. Supreme Ct. bar, 1966, U.S. Dist. Ct. bar for D.C., 1962, for Dist. Md., 1964; individual practice law, Oxon Hill, Md., 1961-69; asst. state's atty. for Prince Georges County (Md.), 1963-69, dep. state's atty., 1969-72; judge Md. Dist. Ct. Dist. 5, 1972—; instr. Prince Georges Community Coll. Mem. Md., Prince Georges County bar assns. Home: 15454 Old Marshall Hall Rd Accokeek MD 20607 Office: Courthouse Upper Marlboro MD 20870 Tel (301) 952-4020

FENDERSON, RALPH LEON, JR., b. Los Angeles, Jan. 17, 1919; B.A., U. Calif., Los Angeles, 1942; J.D., George Washington Univ., 1949. Admitted to D.C. bar, 1949, Ariz. bar, 1955; asst. atty. gen., Phoenix, 1959-61; dep. county atty., Maricopa County Ariz., 1961-70, 73—; asst. city atty., Scottsdale, Ariz., 1970-73. Mem. Ariz. Bar Assn., Nat. Dist. Attys. Assn. Home: 7103 N Via de Mas Scottsdale AZ 85258 Office: 125 W Washington St AZ 85003 Tel (602) 262-3727

FENDLER, OSCAR, b. Blytheville, Ark., Mar. 22, 1909; B.A., U. Ark., 1930; LL.B., Harvard, 1933. Admitted to Ark. bar, 1933, U.S. Supreme Ct. bar, 1941; individual practice law, Blytheville, 1933—; spl. judge Trial Cts. Ark., 1965—; spl. justice Ark. Supreme Ct., 1965. Mem. Mississippi County Democratic Central Com., 1948—, Mississippi County Election Commn., 1952-56; mem. Ark. Bd. Pardons and Paroles, 1970-71. Fellow Am., Ark. bar founds., Am. Coll. Probate Counsel; mem. Am. Judicature Soc. (dir. 1964-68), Am. Bar Assn. (chmn. sect. gen. practice 1966-67, mem. standing com. edn. about Communism 1967-70, standing com. legal aid and indigent defendants 1970-73, chmn. standing com. on law lists 1973-74, mem. 1973-76, mem. ho. dels. 1968—, exec. council nat. conf. bar pres.'s 1962-64), Ark. (pres. 1962-63), Blytheville (pres. 1957-58) bar assns., Ark. Conf. Local Bar Assns. (pres. 1958-60). Pres. bd. dirs. Ark. Law Rev., 1961-67; recipient Lawyer Citizen award Ark. Bar Assn. and Ark. Bar Found., 1973-74; contbr. articles to profl. jours. Home: 1062 W Hearn St Blytheville AR 72315 Office: 104 N 6th St PO Box 548 Blytheville AR 72315 Tel (501) 763-6891

FENERTY, FRANK BURKE, b. New Orleans, Jan. 24, 1927; B.B.A., Loyola U. of South, 1951, LL.B., 1952. Admitted to La. bar, 1952; individual practice law, New Orleans, 1952-54; atty. Prudential Ins. Co., New Orleans, 1954-59; asst. gen. counsel, 2d v.p. Pan Am. Life Ins. Co., New Orleans, 1959—. Active Vieux Carre Commn., New Orleans, 1970—, Historic La. Dists. Study Com., 1974-75. Mem. Am., La. bar assns., Am. Judicature Soc., Am. Life Ins. Assn., La. Bar (dir. corp. law sect. 1968-70). Home: 61 S Wren St New Orleans LA 70124 Office: 2400 Canal St New Orleans LA 70119 Tel (504) 821-2510

FENSTAMAKER, RICHARD LISLE, b. Williamsport, Pa., Feb. 24, 1937; A.B., Coll. William and Mary, 1959; J.D. (scholastic), U. Iowa, 1963. Admitted to Iowa bar, 1963, N.Y. bar, 1964, Pa. bar, 1968, U.S. Supreme Ct. bar, 1967; asso. firm Pell, Butler, Curtis & LeViness, N.Y.C., 1963-65; house counsel Radiant Steel Products Co., Williamsport, 1965—, pres., chmn. bd., 1969—. Mem. Loyalsock Twp. (Pa.) Zoning Bd. Appeals, 1972-75; mem. UN/U.S.A. Com. of UN, 1976-77; mem. United Way Allocations Bd., Williamsport, 1970-73. Mem. Assn. Bar City N.Y. (merit award for legal aid work 1965), N.Y. State, Pa., Lycoming County (Pa.) bar assns. Home: 1621 Sheridan St Williamsport PA 17701 Office: 205 Locust St Williamsport PA 17701 Tel (717) 322-7828

FENSTERMAKER, NORMAN KEITH, b. Pickerington, Ohio, Dec. 13, 1921; B.S., Ohio State U., 1944, LL.B., 1950. Admitted to Ohio bar, 1949, W.Va. bar, 1950; W.Va. claim mgr. Allstate Ins. Co., 1958-62; partner firm Jenkins & Fenstermaker, Huntington, W.Va., 1962—. Pres. Huntington Church Basketball League, 1967-73. Mem. Am., Ohio State, W.Va., Cabell County (chmn. ethics com. 1976) bar assns. Home: Route 1 Box 221 Chesapeake OH 45619 Office: Suite 1100 Coal Exchange Bldg Huntington WV 25701 Tel (304) 697-2100

FENSTERWALD, BERNARD, b. Nashville, Aug. 2, 1921; B.S., LL.B., Harvard U. Admitted to D.C., Mass. bars.; with Dept. State, 1950-56; U.S. Senate staff, 1957-68. Home: 811 Prince St Alexandria VA 22314 Office: 2101 L St NW Washington DC 20037 Tel (202) 785-1636

FENTON, NORMAN S., b. N.Y.C., June 16, 1923; LL.D., Syracuse U., 1947. Admitted to N.Y. bar, 1947, Ariz. bar, 1961; individual practice law, N.Y.C., 1947-57; mem. firm Fenton & Schorr, Tucson; chief magistrate Tucson City Ct., 1963-67; judge Ariz. Superior Ct. for Pima County, 1967—; presiding judge Pima County Conciliation Ct., 1971—; jud. mem. Ariz. Interagy. Coordinating Council on Drug and Alcohol Abuse, 1974; chmn. com. ct. rules Nat. Conf. State Trial Judges, 1969; faculty adviser Trial Judges Coll., Reno, 1972, 76. Mem. Ariz. Gov's. Adv. Commn. on Alcoholism and Drug Abuse, 1966; mem. planning com. and faculty U. Ariz. Southwestern Sch. Alcohol Problems, 1967-70; pres. Boys' Club of Tucson, 1963; chmn. Pima County Council on Alcoholism; mem. second century com. St. Mary's Hosp., 1967. Mem. Pima County, Ariz. State, Am. (chmn. subcom. on edn. and tng., family cts. and family law judges) bar assns., Ariz. State Municipal Judges Assn. (pres. 1967, Spl. award 1968), Nat. Assn. Family Conciliation Cts. and Services (pres. 1975-76); chmn. Gov.'s Task Force on Marriage and the Family, 1976-77. Office: Courthouse Tucson AZ 85701 Tel (602) 792-8169

FENTRESS, ARTHUR LEE, b. Niagara Falls, N.Y., Apr. 27, 1941; B.A., Tulane U., 1963; LL.B., U. Va., 1966. Admitted to Va., D.C. bars, 1967; asst. U.S. atty. for D.C., 1967-68. Trustee Robert F. Kennedy Meml. Found. Mem. Bar. Assn. D.C., Va. State Bar, Fed., Am. bar assns., Md. State Bar, Am. Judicature Soc. Home: 10704 Alloway Dr Potomac MD 20854 Office: Suite 1200 888 17th St NW Washington DC 20006 Tel (202) 457-8830

FENWICK, EDWARD GULAGER, JR., b. Washington, Feb. 22, 1927; B.A., U. Va., 1950; M.A., Am. U., 1954; LL.B., George Washington U., 1955. Admitted to Va. bar, 1957, D.C. bar, 1958, U.S. Supreme Ct. bar, 1962; mem. firm Mason, Fenwick & Lawrence, Washington, 1955—, partner, 1963—. Mem. Am. Bar Assn., Bar Assn. D.C., Am. Patent Law Assn. Home: 6719 N 26th St Arlington VA 22213 Office: 1730 Rhode Island Ave NW Washington DC 20036

FERBER, DAVID I., b. N.Y.C., July 31, 1942; B.S. in Econs., Wharton Sch. Finance and Commerce U. Pa., 1963; LL.B., N.Y. U., 1966. Instr. finance N.Y. Inst. Tech., 1966-68; admitted to N.Y. bar, 1967, U.S. Dist. Ct. for So. Dist. N.Y. bar, 1975; asso. firms Delson & Gordon, N.Y.C., 1968-71, Graubard, Moskovitz, McGoldnick, Dannett & Horowitz, N.Y.C., 1972-73; partner firm Kantor, Davidoff, Winston & Ferber, P.C., N.Y.C., 1973—; Mem. panel arbitrators Am. Arbitration Assn. Mem. Assn. Bar City N.Y., N.Y. State Bar Assn. Named to sr. bd. Moot Ct. Bd. N.Y. U. Office: 200 Park Ave New York City NY 10017 Tel (212) 682-8383

FERBER, JAMES M. L., b. N.Y.C., July 21, 1947; B.A., Pa. State U., 1968; J.D., Temple U., 1971. Admitted to Pa. bar, 1971, Ohio bar, 1974; atty. NLRB, Pitts., 1971-73; asso. firm Weintraub & DeHart, Memphis, 1973-74, Schottenstein, Garel, Swedlow & Zox, Columbus, Ohio, 1974—. Mem. Columbus, Ohio State, Pa., Fed., Am. bar assns., Am. Judicature Soc. Home: 8863 Stonehenge Dr Pickerington OH 43147 Office: 250 E Broad St Columbus OH 43215 Tel (614) 221-3211

FERBER, KENNETH STANLEY, b. N.Y.C., Mar. 11, 1930; LL.B., Bklyn. Law Sch., 1951, LL.M., 1952. Admitted to N.Y. State bar, 1952, U.S. Mil. Ct. Appeals bar, 1954, U.S. Supreme Ct. bar, 1958, Eastern and So. Dist. U.S. Fed. Ct. bar, 1954; partner firm Ferber and Ferber, N.Y.C., 1952—; spl. dep. atty. gen. N.Y. State, 1956-59; referee Municipal Ct., N.Y.C., 1958-62, Civil Ct., N.Y.C., 1962-76. Mem. Narcotics Panel Radio Sta. WWRL, N.Y.C., 1964; chmn. Westchester County (N.Y.) Conservative Interim Com., 1967-68; chmn. Conservative Citizens Forum, Westchester County, 1969-76; nat. chmn. Com. for Nelson Rockefeller for vice pres., 1974; vice chmn. Youth Bd., Mt. Vernon, N.Y., 1973—. Named hon. dep. sheriff, Westchester County; recipient SSS medal, 1976. Mem. Bklyn., Westchester County bar assns. Tel (212) WO2-5562

FERGUS, NELLIE MARGARET, b. Pitts., Oct. 22, 1919; A.B., Mount Holyoke Coll., 1941; J.D., U. Pitts., 1943; Admitted to Pa. bar, 1944, U.S. Supreme Ct. bar, 1953; since practiced in Pitts.; asso. firm Reed, Smith, Shaw & McClay, 1943-52; individual practice law, 1952—. Dir. Met. YWCA, Pitts., 1947-52; treas. Fort Soc., Pitts., 1969-74; co-chmn. bequest and annuities coms., Mt. Holyoke Coll., 1974-76, chmn., 1976—. Mem. Am. (mem. com. on state and local bar liasion 1976), Pa. State, Allegheny County (mem. membership com., 1945-76, vice chmn. membership com. 1977—) bar assns., Civic Club Allegheny County (mem. legis. com, chmn. exceptionally able youths com. 1958-60), Phi Beta Kappa. Recipient Alumnae Medal of Honor, Mt. Holyoke Coll., 1966. Home and office: 776 Valleyview Rd Pittsburgh PA 15243 Tel (412) 341-9993

FERGUSON, DALLAS EUGENE, b. Blackwell, Okla., Dec. 20, 1945; B.A., Cornell Coll., Mt. Vernon, Iowa, 1968; J.D., Columbia U., 1971. Admitted to Okla. bar, 1971; Ct. law clk. judge U.S. Ct. Appeals 10th Circuit, 1971-72; asso. firm Doerner, Stuart, Saunders, Daniel & Langenkamp, Tulsa, 1973—; mem. Okla. adv. council Nat. Legal Services Corp., 1976. Mem. Am., Okla., Tulsa County bar assns. Home: 2965 S Cincinnati St Tulsa OK 74114 Office: 1200 Atlas Life Bldg Tulsa OK 74103 Tel (918) 582-1211

FERGUSON, DOUGLAS PEDDER, b. Oakland, Calif., Sept. 29, 1939; student Harvard, 1957-60; LL.B., Stanford, 1963. Admitted to Calif. bar, 1963; asso. firm Ackerman, Johnston, Norberg & Parkinson, San Francisco, 1964-67; atty. AID, Washington, 1968-69; partner firm Ferguson, Hoffman, Henn & Mandel, San Francisco, 1969—. Adv. bd. Save San Francisco Bay Assn., 1969—; pres. Ecumenical Assn. for Housing, 1969-70; bd. dirs. Trust for Pub. Land, 1974—. Mem. Calif., San Francisco bar assns. Office: 1365 Columbus Ave San Francisco CA 94133 Tel (415) 673-8300

FERGUSON, G. DOUGLAS, b. Santa Ana, Calif., Feb. 3, 1943; B.S., U. Wash., 1966, M.B.A., 1967, J.D., 1973. Admitted to Wash. bar, 1973, U.S. Dist. Ct. Western Dist. Wash. bar, 1974, U.S. Ct. Appeals 9th Circuit bar, 1975; asso. firm Anderson, Hunter, Dwell, Baker & Collins, P.S., Everett, Wash. 1973—. Pres. Drug Abuse Council, Everett, 1974-76. Mem. Am., Wash., Snohomish County bar assns., Am. (essay award 1971), Wash. trial lawyers assns. Office: 1st National Bank Bldg Everett WA 98201 Tel (206) 252-5161

FERGUSON, GEORGE HERBERT, b. Lorain, Ohio, Dec. 2, 1930; A.B. cum laude, U. Notre Dame, 1953; J.D., Ohio State U., 1956. Admitted to Ohio bar, 1956; judge adv. USAF, 1957-60; asso. firm Wilcox & Wilcox, Elyria, Ohio, 1961-75; partner firm Ferguson, Lowther, Coey & Ashbaugh, Elyria, 1975—. Solicitor City of Elyria, 1976—, South Amherst Village, 1969—; legal advisor Eaton, Elyria, Grafton Twps.; legal officer (lt. col.) Ohio Air NG; chmn. Legal Aid Soc., 1967-76, Catholic Social Service adv. bd., 1969-76, Lorain County Welfare adv. bd., 1961-76, Troop 133 Firelands council Boy Scouts Am., 1971-74. Mem. Ohio State, Lorain County bar assns. Home: 359 Miami Ave Elyria OH 44035 Office: 802 Elyria Savings & Trust Bank Bldg Elyria OH 44035 Tel (216) 323-7433

FERGUSON, GEORGE ROBERT, b. Learned, Miss., Aug. 13, 1933; B.S., Miss. State U., 1955; LL.B., Jackson Sch. of Law, 1965. Admitted to Miss. bar, 1965; individual practice law, Raymond, Miss., 1965—; mem. Miss. Ho. of Reps., 1968—. Elder Presbyterian Ch. Mem. Am., Miss., Hinds County bar assns., Hinds County, Miss. trial lawyers assns. Home and office: PO Box 89 Raymond MS 39154 Tel (601) 857-5282

FERGUSON, HAROLD LAVERNE, JR., b. Cleveland, Miss., Dec. 3, 1938; B. Public Adminstrn., U. Miss., 1960; J.D., Samford U., 1973. Admitted to Ala. bar, 1973; asso. firm Hardin, Stuart & Moncus, Birmingham, Ala., 1973; asso. firm Spain, Gillon, Riley, Tate & Etheredge, Birmingham, Ala., 1973—. Mem. Am., Ala., Birmingham Bar Assns. Home: 440 Hillwood Dr Birmingham AL 35209 Office: 800 John A Bldg Birmingham AL 35203 Tel (205) 328-4100

FERGUSON, JOHN TYE, b. Atlanta, Dec. 1, 1931; A.B., Emory U., 1951; LL.B., Harvard, 1954. Admitted to Ga. bar, 1953, U.S. Supreme Ct. bar, 1960; dep. asst. and asst. atty. gen. State of Ga., Atlanta, 1956-60; partner firm Bolton & Ferguson, Griffin, Ga., 1960; asso. firm Sheats, Parker & Ferguson, Atlanta, 1965—; asst. and asso. county atty. Fulton County, Ga., 1964—. Mem. Am., Atlanta bar assns., State Bar Ga., Lawyers Club Atlanta. Office: 150 Peachtree Center-Cain Tower 229 Peachtree St NW Atlanta GA 30303 Tel (404) 588-0888

FERGUSON, PAUL FRANCIS, b. Danvers, Mass., Feb. 16, 1925; A.B., Harvard, 1947; J.D., Boston U., 1953; M.S. in Library Sci., Our Lady of Lake Coll., 1970. Admitted to Mass. bar, 1953; librarian Essex County Law Library, Mass., 1953-66; law library dir., prof. law St. Mary's U. Sch. of Law, San Antonio, 1966—. Mem. Am. Assn. Law Libraries, Tex. Library Assn., Essex County Bar Assn. (sec. 1956-66). Editor: Boston U. Law Rev., 1953. Home: 914 Fabulous St San Antonio TX 78213 Office: 2700 Cincinnati Ave St Mary's Univ Sch Law San Antonio TX 78284 Tel (512) 436-3435

FERGUSON, ROBERT WILLIAM, b. Portland, Maine, Dec. 3, 1935; B.S., Gordon Coll., 1960; J.D., U. Maine, 1963. Admitted to Maine bar, 1963; partner firm Williams & Ferguson, Springvale, Maine, 1963—; dir. Mutual Title Ins. Co., 1972—. Mem. planning bd. Shapleigh, Maine, 1971—, chmn. 1971-75; deacon, mem. adv. bd. 1st Bapt. Ch., Sanford, Maine, 1958—. Mem. Am., Maine (title standards com. 1974—), York County bar assns. Home: Back Rd Shapleigh ME 04076 Office: POB 97 Springvale ME 04083 Tel (207) 324-5357

FERGUSON, WILLIAM EDWARD, b. Denver, Sept. 17, 1923; B.A., Pomona Coll., 1943; LL.B., U. Calif., 1949. Admitted to Calif. bar, 1949; partner firm Ferguson, Ferguson & Newburn, La Jolla, Calif., 1949—. Bd. dirs., pres. Scripps Meml. Hosp., La Jolla, 1968—. Mem. State Bar Calif., Am. Coll. Probate Counsel, Internat. Acad. Estate and Trust Law. Home: 6223 Avenida Cresta La Jolla CA 92037 Office: 7848 Ivanhoe St La Jolla CA 92037 Tel (714) 454-4233

FERMAN, IRVING, b. N.Y.C., July 4, 1919; B.S., N.Y. U., 1948; J.D., Harvard, 1948. Admitted to La. bar, 1949, U.S. Supreme Ct. bar, 1952, D.C. bar, 1974; mem. firm Provensal, Faris & Ferman, New Orleans, 1949-52; dir. ACLU, Washington, 1952-59; exec. vice chmn. Pres.'s Com. on Govt. Contracts, Washington, 1959-60; v.p. Internat. Latex Corp., Dover, Del., 1960-67; pres. Piedmont Theatres Corp., Lynchburg, Va., 1967-69; prof. law Howard U., 1969—; vis. prof. law Am. U., 1972—; chmn. Police Complaint Rev. Bd., Washington, 1965-73; mem. adv. com. U.S. Commn. on Govt. Security, 1967;

mem. reviewing authority HEW, 1969—. Mem. Am. Bar Assn. Office: 2935 Upton St Washington DC 20009 Tel (202) 686-6562

FERNAN, JOHN ROBERT, b. Rockford, Ill., Jan. 31, 1942; B.S. in Accounting and Fin., St. Vincent Coll., 1964; J.D., Duquesne U., 1967. Admitted to Pa. bar, 1968; partner firm Cartright, Fernan & Whitney, Ridgeway, Pa., 1968—; incorporated Health Systems Agy., Inc., Erie, Pa., 1975—. Chmn. adv. bd. Salvation Army, Ridgeway 1973—, dir. Elcam Vocat. Rehab. Center, Inc., St. Marys, Pa., 1974—; fin. chmn. Elk County Republican Party, 1971—; chmn. parish council St. Leo Magnus Ch., Ridgway, 1974-76. Mem. Am., Pa., Elk County, Allegheny bar assns., Elk-Ridgway C. of C. (dir. 1975—). Home: 118 Metoxet St Ridgway PA 15853 Office: Masonic Temple Bldg Ridgway PA 15853 Tel (814) 776-6191

FERNANDEZ, MANUEL ADAM, b. New Orleans, Oct. 15, 1942; grad. U. Southwestern La., 1964; LL.B., Loyola U., 1967. Admitted to bar; partner firm Perez, Fernandez, Seemann & Egan, Chalmette, La., 1967—; mem. La. Ho. Reps., 1976—. Mem. St. Mark's Sch. Bd., 4th Ward Civic Assn.; advisory bd. St. Bernard Council on Aging. Mem. La. Bar Assn., Chalmette (La.) C. of C. Office: 1310 E Judge Perez Dr Chalmette LA 70044 Tel (504) 271-8461

FERO, DEAN JOHN, b. Rochester, N.Y., July 1, 1930; B.A., Hobart Coll., 1953; LL.B., Syracuse U., 1956, J.D., 1968. Admitted to N.Y. bar, 1956, U.S. Dist. Ct. for Western Dist. N.Y., 1957, U.S. 2d Circuit Ct. Appeals bar, 1957; partner firm Damico, Fero & Cook, Rochester, N.Y. Mem. N.Y. State, Monroe County bar assns. Phi Delta Phi. Home: 154 Warren Ave Rochester NY 14618 Office: 1 Exchange St Suite 802 Rochester NY 14614 Tel (716) 325-1827

FERR, PAUL JOHN, b. Milw., Oct. 23, 1932; LL.B., Marquette U., 1960. Admitted to Wis. bar, 1960; partner firm Murn, Ferr & Gumina, West Allis, Wis., 1967—. Mem. Wis. Bar Assn. Home: 7330 W Eden Pl Milwaukee WI 53220 Office: 1429 S 70th St Milwaukee WI 53214 Tel (414) 774-0135

FERRARI, DAVID GEORGE, b. San Jose, Calif., May 31, 1939; LL.B., U. Santa Clara, 1964. Admitted to Calif. bar, 1965; asso. firm DeKlotz and Hayes, San Jose, 1965-66, Hayes, Dunn and Ferrari, San Jose, 1968-71, Dunn and Ferrari, San Jose, 1971—. Mem. Calif. State, Santa Clara County bar assns. Home: 1731 Emory St San Jose CA 95126 Office: Suite 600 101 Park Center Plaza San Jose CA 95113 Tel (408) 286-4850

FERRARI, RICARDO BRANDAO, b. N.Y.C., Oct. 14, 1940; B.A., Northwestern U., 1963; J.D., Stanford, 1968. Admitted to Utah bar, 1969; asso. firm Van Cott, Bagley, Cornwall & McCarthy, Salt Lake City, 1968-73, partner, 1973—; lectr. law U. Utah, 1976; mem. faculty 16th Ann. Advanced Antitrust Law Seminar, Practising Law Inst., 1977. Vestryman, St. Mark's Episcopal Cathedral, 1976—. Mem. Am., Salt Lake County, Utah State bar assns., Stanford Alumni Assn., Stanford Law Soc. Contbr. articles to legal jours. and handbooks. Home: 1780 S Woodside Dr Holladay UT 84117 Office: 141 E 1st S Salt Lake City UT 84111 Tel (801) 532-3333

FERRELL, RUTH MORRIS, b. Portsmouth, Va., Apr. 29, 1928; B.A., Agnes Scott Coll., 1949; M.A., Emory U., 1952; J.D., U. Pa., 1960. Admitted to Del. bar, 1960, U.S. Supreme Ct. bar, 1964, D.C. bar, 1975; law clk. to judges Del. Ct. Chancery and Del. Superior Ct., 1961-62; dep. atty. gen. State of Del., 1963-70, head civil div. Del. Atty. Gen's. Office, 1967-70, state solicitor, 1969-70; individual practice law, Wilmington, Del., 1971—. Mem. Del. Gov's. Commn. on Status of Women., 1963-68; mem. European adv. council State Dept., 1971-72. Mem. Am. (council, chmn. com. budget and fin. com. social services sect. local govt.), Del., Fed. bar assns., Nat. Assn. Women Lawyers (del.), AAUW, Christina Bus., Profl. Women's Club (pres.), Mortar Bd., Phi Beta Kappa. Recipient Outstanding Pub. Service award N.E. Regional Women's Conf., 1967; contbr. articles to profl. jours. Home and Office: 17 Cragmere Rd Wilmington DE 19809

FERRIN, WILLIAM JOSEPH, b. Chgo., Jan. 29, 1930; B.S., Northwestern U., 1951; J.D., U. So. Calif., 1959. Accountant, Baumann, Finney & Co., Chgo., 1950-51, 54-55, Haskins & Sells, Los Angeles, 1956-58; dep. gen. controller Capitol Records, Inc., Hollywood, Calif., 1958-62; admitted to Calif. bar, 1960, U.S. Dist. Ct. bars for So. and Central Dists. Calif., 1961, U.S. Tax Ct. bar, 1969; sec., controller, dir. Kaufman & Broad, Inc., and subs., Phoenix and Los Angeles, 1962-64; v.p. finance Lee-Lasky Cos., Los Angeles, 1965-67; practice in Sherman Oaks, 1967—; judge pro-tem Los Angeles Municipal Ct., 1971—; dir. Hartford Devel. Co., many small corps. Pres. bd. dirs. Tarzana (Calif.) Little League; mem. World Affairs Council, Los Angeles, Town Hall. Mem. Am. Inst. C.P.A.'s, Am., Calif., Los Angeles County, San Fernando Valley bar assns., Assn. Bus. Trial Lawyers, Legion Lex, Am. Arbitration Assn. (arbitrator). Home: 4829 Ellenita Ave Tarzana CA 91356 Office: 15233 Ventura Blvd Sherman Oaks CA 91403 Tel (213) 788-0590

FERRIS, ALFRED GEORGE, b. Pittsfield, Mass., Sept. 7, 1936; A.B. cum laude (Holmes and Narver, Gamble and Gant scholar), Stanford, 1958, J.D., 1963. Admitted to Calif. bar, 1964; law clk. to chief judge U.S. Dist. Ct., So. Dist. Calif., 1963-64; asso., then partner firm Procopio, Cory, Hargreaves and Savitch, San Diego, 1964-68; pres. firm Ferris, Weatherford and Brennan, P.C., San Diego, 1968—; judge pro-tem Calif. trial cts.; adj. prof. law U. San Diego Sch. Law, 1976—. Mem. Am. Bar Assn., State Bar Calif. (conf. of dels. 1974, 75), Bar Assn. San Diego (chmn. client relations com. 1975, editor jour. 1977), Am. Arbitration Assn. (nat. bd. arbitrators 1973—), Indsl. Relations Research Assn. (advisor 1970—), Corporate Fin. Council, Nat. Cable TV Assn., Am. Judicature Soc., Harvard, Stanford law socs., Phi Delta Phi. Contbr. articles to Jour. Bar Assn. San Diego. Office: 1200 3d Ave San Diego CA 92101 Tel (714) 233-3131

FERRIS, BOYD B., b. Mansfield, Ohio, July 28, 1942; B.S. in Bus. Adminstrn., Ohio State U., 1964, J.D., 1967. Admitted to Ohio bar, 1967; served with JAGC, U.S. Army, 1967-71; sec. Ohio Pub. Utilities Commn., 1972-74; partner firm Muldoon, Pemberton & Ferris, Columbus, 1974—. Mem. Columbus, Ohio, Fed. bar assns., Am., Ohio motor carrier lawyers assns. Home: 6685 Berend St Worthington OH 43085 Office: 50 W Broad St Columbus OH 43215 Tel (614) 464-4103

FERRIS, COLLINS HAKES, b. Waukesha, Wis., Dec. 20, 1918; student in Bus., U. Wis., 1936-37, LL.B., 1948, J.D., 1966; student in Hotel Mgmt., Mich. State Coll., 1937-40. Admitted to Wis. bar, 1948; U.S. Tax Ct. bar, 1948; practiced in Waukesha, 1948-51; v.p. firm Marshall Erdman & Assos., Madison, Wis., 1954-55; v.p. Madison Bank and Trust Co., 1955-58, exec. v.p., 1958-62; pres., 1962-68; pres. Mid-Wis. Bankshares, Inc. (name changed to United Banks of Wis., Inc.), 1968—; chmn. bd. United Bank and Trust of Madison, United Bank of Westgate, Madison. Active United Way, Madison, 1955-70; bd. dirs. Madison YMCA, 1958-72, Madison ARC, 1968-72. Mem. State Bar Wis., Dane County (Wis.) Bar Assn., Assn. Bank Holding Cos., Bank Mktg. Assn., Wis., Am. bankers assns. Decorated Legion of Merit, D.F.C., Air medal with 5 oak leaf clusters (U.S.); Croix de Guerre (France). Home: 500 Farwell Dr Madison WI 53704 Office: 222 W Washington Ave Madison WI 53703 Tel (608) 252-3560

FERRIS, JOHN GREGORY, b. Detroit, June 20, 1922; Ph.B., U. Detroit, 1942, LL.B., 1948. Admitted to Mich. bar, 1948, Fla. bar, 1958; practiced in Detroit, 1948-57, Broward County, Fla., 1962-63; supr. claims Allstate Ins. Co., Ft. Lauderdale, Fla., 1957-59; judge Municipal Ct., Miramar, Fla., 1958-63; asst. county solicitor Broward County, 1959-62; judge Broward County Ct. of Record, 1963-72, presiding judge, 1970-71; judge Fla. 17th Jud. Circuit Ct., 1972—, chief judge, 1973-75; mem. Miramar City Council, 1959-62. mem. Miramar Airport Zoning Bd., 1960-63; chmn. Miramar United Fun, 1963. Mem. Delta Theta Phi (Scholarship certificate and Key 1948). Recipient Gamma Eta Gamma award U. Detroit Law Sch., 1942. Home: 664 SW 8th Terr Fort Lauderdale FL 33315 Office: Courthouse 201 SE 6th St Fort Lauderdale FL 33301 Tel (305) 765-4653

FERRIS, SANTO JOSEPH, b. Milw., June 26, 1928; B.A., Carroll Coll., Waukesha, Wis, 1952; LL.B., Marquette U., Milw., 1956, J.D., 1970. Admitted to Wis bar, 1956, Fed. Ct. bar, 1956; individual practice law Milw., 1956—. Mem. Wis. State Bar Assn. Home: 7045 Aetna Ct Wauwatosa WI 53213 Office: 536 W Wisconsin Ave Suite 610 Milwaukee WI 53203 Tel (411) 272-4023

FERRIS, THOMAS GEORGE, b. Chappell, Nebr., Jan. 31, 1926; B.S., U. Wash., 1949; J.D., Georgetown U., 1963. Admitted to Md. bar, 1965, U.S. Patent Bar, 1968, U.S. Supreme Ct. bar, 1969; research biochemist, Naval Med. Research Inst., Bethesda, Md., 1958-67; patent examiner, U.S. Patent Office, Washington, 1967-68; patent atty., HEW, Bethesda, 1968—. Pres. Maplewood Citizens Assn., Bethesda, 1967-68, St. Andrew's Soc. of Washington, 1950—. Mem. Govt. Patent Lawyers Assn. Home: 5420 Alta Vista Rd Bethesda MD 20014 Office: Patent Branch HEW Westwood Bldg Room 5A-03 Nat Insts of Health Bethesda MD 20014 Tel (301) 496-7056

FERRIS, TONY, b. West Frankfort, Ill., Jan. 23, 1928; A.B., Wayne State U., 1949; J.D., Wayne U., 1951. Admitted to Mich. bar, 1951, U.S. Supreme Ct. bar, 1958; individual practice law, Detroit, 1953-56, Warren and Mt. Clemens, Mich., 1963—; partner firm Parris & Ferris, Warren, 1956-61; chief asst. pros. atty. Macomb County, Mich., 1961-63. Mem. Am., Mich. trial lawyers assns., Macomb County, Mich. State bar assns. Office: 158 Cass Ave Mount Clemens MI 48043 Tel (313) 468-2619

FERRISS, FRANKLIN, b. St. Louis, Nov. 11, 1911; A.B., Yale, 1933; M.A., Columbia, 1935; LL.B., Washington U., St. Louis, 1938. Admitted to Mo. bar, 1938; asso. firm Salkey & Jones, St. Louis, 1938-41, 46-51, firm Jones, Hocker, Gladney and Grand, St. Louis, 1951-54; judge St. Louis County (Mo.) Circuit Ct., Div. 6, 1954—. Mem. Clayton Twp., St. Louis County Republican Central Com., 1950-54; pres. St. Louis Council on World Affairs, 1970-72. Mem. St. Louis, St. Louis County, Am. bar assns., Washington U. Law Alumni Assn. (pres. 1950-51), Phi Delta Phi. Home: 8425 Colonial Ln Clayton MO 63124 Office: 7900 Carondelet St Clayton MO 63105 Tel (314) 889-2690

FERRO, ANTHONY JOSEPH, b. San Antonio, Sept. 14, 1928; LL.B., St. Mary's U., 1953. Admitted to Tex. bar, 1953; partner firm Ferro & Chavarria, San Antonio, 1970—; asst. criminal dist. atty. Bexar County (Tex.), 1953-62. Mem. San Antonio Bar Assn., Tex. Criminal Def. Lawyers Assn., Tex. Trial Lawyers Assn. Home: 153 Rosemont St San Antonio TX 78228 Office: Villita Sq 120 Villita St San Antonio TX 78205 Tel (512) 227-4186

FERRO, ARIOSTO MICHAEL, b. Salt Lake City, Mar. 12, 1909; B.A., U. Utah, 1929; LL.B., U. Chgo., 1931. Admitted to Utah bar, 1931; individual practice law, Salt Lake City, 1951—; U.S. magistrate, 1971-75; U.S. Commr., 1969-71; atty. for indsl. commn. of Utah Dept. Employment Security, 1936-51; adminstr. Utah dist. Office Price Adminstrn., 1941-46; price atty., 1946-47. Mem. Am. Bar Assn. Home: 1166 S 5th E Salt Lake City UT 84105 Office: 414 Walker Bank Bldg Salt Lake City UT 84111 Tel (801) 322-2408

FERRO, FRANCIS EUGENE, b. N.Y.C., Jan. 27, 1942; A.B., Marist Coll., Poughkeepsie, N.Y., 1965; J.D., St. Mary's U., San Antonio, 1971; LL.M., N.Y.U., 1974. Admitted to N.Y. State bar, 1972, Fla. bar, 1973; asst. atty. gen. N.Y. State Dept. Law, N.Y.C., 1972-75; sr. atty. N.Y. State Atty. Gen.'s Office, N.Y.C., 1975—. Alt. del. Republican Nat. Conv., 1976; founder Marlboro-Milton (N.Y.) Med. Center, 1967. Mem. Am., N.Y. State, Fla. bar assns., Nat., N.Y. State dist. attys. assn., Am. Judicatrue Assn., Am. Arbitration Assn., Phi Alpha Delta. Home: Old Indian Rd Milton NY 12547 Office: 2 World Trade Center New York City NY 10047 Tel (212) 488-3345

FERST, BARTON EUGENE, b. Phila., Jan. 23, 1920; B.S. in Econs., U. Pa., 1940, LL.B., 1944; M.A. in Govt., La. State U., 1941. Admitted to Pa. bar, 1944; asso. firm Herman H. Krekstein, Phila., 1944-52, firm Blank & Rudenko, Phila., 1952-55; partner firm Blank, Rome, Klaus & Comisky, Phila., 1955—; lectr. in field. Vice pres. Fedn. Jewish Agys. of Greater Phila., 1973-76; bd. dirs. United Way, Phila., 1974—. Mem. Am., Pa., Phila. bar assns., Order of Coif. Co-author: Basic Accounting for Lawyers, 1976. Office: 4 Penn Center Plaza Philadelphia PA 19103 Tel (215) LO 9-3700

FERTITTA, ROBERT STEPHEN, b. Balt., Oct. 26, 1940; A.B., U. Md., 1963, J.D., 1964. Admitted to Md. bar, 1964, Tex. bar, 1974; asst. State's Atty's Office, Balt., 1966-71; asso. dean Nat. Coll. Dist. Attys., at U. Houston Coll. Law, 1971—, adj. asst. prof. law U. Houston, 1972—; research atty. Am. Bar Found., Chgo., 1968. Mem. Am. Bar Assn., Nat. Dist. Atty's. Assn., Houston, Tex bars. Home: 13219 Indian Creek St Houston TX 77079 Office: Nat Coll Dist Attys Coll of Law U of Houston Houston TX 77004 Tel (713) 749-1571

FESSENDEN, JOHN STIRLING, b. Portland, Maine, Apr. 22, 1931; A.B., Dartmouth Coll., 1952; LL.B. with distinction, George Washington U., 1959. Admitted to Maine bar, 1959, D.C. bar, 1959, U.S. Supreme Ct. bar, 1962, Va. bar, 1976; asso. firm Rice, Carpenter & Carraway, Washington, 1959-62, partner, Arlington, Va., Washington, 1962—; legis. asst. to U.S. Senator from Maine, 1955-59. Mem. Am., Maine, Va. bar assns., D.C. Bar, Motor Carrier Lawyers Assn. (treas. 1976-78), Order Coif. Home: 4603 Exeter St Annandale VA 22003 Office: 1600 Wilson Blvd Arlington VA 22209 Tel (703) 522-0900

FEUCHTWANGER, SAMUEL ADLER, b. N.Y.C., Apr. 3, 1905; LL.B., St. Lawrence U., 1927. Admitted to N.Y. bar, 1928; asso. firm Stein & Salant, N.Y.C., 1928-55; individual practice law, N.Y.C., 1955—. Sec., trustee, counsel Tremont Temple, Bronx, N.Y. Mem. Bronx Bar Assn. Home: 215 E 201st St Bronx NY 10458 Office: 47 W 34th St New York City NY 10001 Tel (212) WI 7-6580

FEUER, HERBERT JEROME, b. N.Y.C., Sept. 6, 1923; B.A., St. Johns U., 1949; J.D., N.Y. Law Sch., 1949. Admitted to N.Y. State bar, 1950; sr. practitioner, N.Y.C., 1950-65; sr. partner firm Feuer & Bryer, N.Y.C., 1965—; commr. Bd. Elections City N.Y., 1973—, pres., 1974-75. Mem. N.Y. State Assembly, 1966. Leader 76th Assembly Dist. Democratic Party, N.Y., 1972—. Mem. N.Y. State, Bronx County bar assns., Lawyers Squire Club. Home: 1066 Ogden Ave Bronx NY 10452 Office: 200 E 42d St New York City NY 10017 Tel (212) 642-0790

FEUERSTEIN, HARVEY SAUL, lawyer; b. N.Y.C., Dec. 22, 1937; A.B., Columbia Coll., 1958; J.D., Harvard, 1962. Admitted to N.Y. bar, 1963, U.S. Supreme Ct., 1966, 2d Circuit Ct. Appeals, 1966, So. Dist. N.Y., 1969, Eastern Dist. N.Y., 1969; asso. law firm Becker, Ross & Stone, N.Y.C., 1963-69; asso. firm Hecrick, Feinstein, Mendelson & Abramson, N.Y.C., 1969, partner, 1970—. Chmn. membership com. Park East Synagogue, N.Y.C., 1976—. Mem. Am., N.Y. State bar assns. Home: 505 E 79th St New York City NY 10021 Office: 2 Park Av New York City NY 10016

FEUTZ, JAMES FOSTER, b. Tacoma, Nov. 27, 1942; B.A., Whitman Coll., 1965; J.D., U. Calif., 1968. Admitted to Calif. bar, 1968, Wash. bar, 1969; asso. firm Davies, Pearson, Anderson, Seinfeld, Gadbow, Hayes and Johnson, Tacoma, 1969-70; partner firm Landels, Ripley and Diamond, San Francisco, 1970—. Mem. San Francisco Bar Assn. Office: 450 Pacific Ave San Francisco CA 94133 Tel (415) 788-5000

FIALA, DAVID MARCUS, b. Cleve., Aug. 1, 1946; B.B.A., U. Cin., 1969; J.D., No. Ky. State Coll., 1974. Admitted to Ohio bar, 1974; U.S. Dist. Ct. So. Dist. Ohio bar, 1974. Asso. firm Walker & Chatfield, Cin., 1974—. Mem. exec. com., corp. underwriting chmn. WCET-TV, Cin., 1976-77; trustee, Contemporary Dance Theater, Cin., 1976, mem. exec. com., 1974—; trustee, mem. exec. com., Mental Health Service West, Cin., 1974—. Mem. Am., Ohio, Cin. bar assns. Home: 7859 Foxtort Dr North Bend OH 45052 Office: 522 Dixie Terminal Bldg Cincinnati OH 45202 Tel (513) 621-1506

FICARROTTA, JOSEPH H., b. Tampa, Fla., Jan. 19, 1947; B.S., U. Fla., 1969; J.D., U. Miami, 1972. Admitted to Fla. bar, 1973; law clk. Hillsborough County (Fla.) State Atty.'s Office, Tampa, 1972-73, asst. state atty., chief felony div., 1974—; law clk. to chief justice Fla. Supreme Ct., 1973-74. Home: 4616 Beach Park Dr Tampa FL 33609 Office: Hillsborough County State Attys Office Courthouse Annex Tampa FL 33602 Tel (813) 272-5400

FICHTNER, RAE ANN, b. San Antonio, Mar. 31, 1930; A.B., Tex. Woman's U., 1950; J.D., George Washington U., 1952; LL.M., So. Meth. U., 1972. Admitted to D.C. bar, 1952, Tex. bar, 1954, U.S. Supreme Ct. bar, 1956; individual practice law, Dallas, 1954-71; instr. Tex. Womans U., 1963-64, So. Meth. U. Sch. Law, Dallas, 1971-73, Dallas Police Acad., 1972-, N. Tex. Regional Police Acad., 1972-76; asst. city atty. Dallas, 1973—; police legal adviser Dallas Police Dept., 1973—. Bd. dirs. Dallas Council Alcoholism, 1975-, George Washington Law Sch., 1971-75. Mem. Am., Tex., Dallas bar assns., Am. Judicature Soc., Nat. Assn. Women Lawyers, Internat. Assn. Chiefs Police. Recipient Outstanding Alumni award Tex. Woman's U., 1975. Author: Needed Legislative Changes in Juvenile Code, 1977. Contbg. author: Police Procedures, 1976. Home: 5509 Tanbark Rd Dallas TX 75229 Office: Legal Liaison Div Dallas Police Dept City Hall Dallas TX 75201 Tel (214) 748-9711

FICURELLI, JOSEPH PATRICK, b. N.Y.C., Mar. 18, 1939; B.B.A., Coll. City N.Y., 1960; postgrad. Harvard Law Sch., 1963. Admitted to Mass. bar, 1963, Calif. bar, 1971; asso. firm Burns & Levinson, Boston, 1963-64; asst. gen. counsel and asst. sec., Sonesta Internat. Hotels, Boston, 1964-70; gen. counsel and asst. sec., Rocor Internat., Palo Alto, Calif., 1971—. Mem. Am., Calif. bar assns. Home: 18 Buena Vista Terr San Francisco CA 94117 Office: 260 Sheridan Ave Suite 200 Palo Alto CA 94306 Tel (415) 327-3208

FIDALGO, WILLIAM FRANCIS, b. Providence, July 21, 1920; Ph.B., Providence Coll., 1942; J.D., Boston U., 1948. Admitted to R.I. bar, 1948; individual practice law, East Providence, R.I., 1949—; legal counsel E. Providence Sewer Commn., 1957-59, R.I. Dept. Pub. Works, 1959-61, E. Providence Housing Authority, 1962-74; trial counsel R.I. Dept. Pub. Works, E. Providence, 1963-69; judge of probate City of E. Providence, 1974-76. Mem. Am., R.I. bar assns., Assn. Trial Lawyers Am. Home: 2486 Pawtucket Ave East Providence RI 02914 Office: 2486 Pawtucket Ave East Providence RI 02914 Tel (401) 434-4405

FIDDES, RICHARD CORBETT, b. Chgo., July 23, 1945; B.A. cum laude, Knox Coll., 1967; J.D. cum laude, Northwestern U., 1970. Admitted to Ill. bar, 1970; asso. firm Wilson & McIlvaine, Chgo., 1970—. Home: 614 Carriage Dr Batavia IL 60510 Office: 135 S LaSalle St Chicago IL 60603 Tel (312) 263-1212

FIDLER, MILTON MANNING, b. N.Y.C., Feb. 22, 1919; LL.B., St. John's U. Coll., 1947. Admitted to N.Y. bar, 1947; asso. Rober Moers, N.Y.C., 1947-48; asso. firm Solomon, Shein, Hausman & Rosenbaum, N.Y.C., 1948-49; mem. firm Fidler & Mirabel, Bklyn., 1949-60; individual practice law, Bklyn., 1960—; hearing officer N.Y.C. Dept. Transp., 1970—; referee N.Y.C. Civil Ct., 1960—; arbitrator Am. Arbitration Assn., N.Y.C., 1970—; trial examiner N.Y.C. Bd. Edn., 1973—; asso. chmn. community bd., N.Y.C., 1970—; hon. pres. 67th Police Precinct Community Council, 1973—. Mem. Bklyn. Bar Assn., St. John's Law Alumni Assn. Office: 26 Court St Brooklyn NY 11242 Tel (212) 875-0643

FIELD, CYRUS ADAMS, b. Fergus Falls, Minn., Oct. 27, 1902; A.B., U. Minn., 1923; J.J.D., Harvard, 1926. Admitted to Minn. bar, 1926, U.S. Supreme Ct. bar, 1969; mem. firm Field, Arvesen, Donoho, Lundeen & Hoff and predecessors, Fergus Falls, Minn., 1926-76, sr. mem., 1952-76; ret., 1976; trustee Minn. Bar Found., 1968-76; mem. adv. com. to Supreme Ct. Minn. on rules of practice and procedure, 1950—; dir. Western Minn. Savs. & Loan. Past pres. Community Chest; trustee Wright Hosp., Lake Region Hosp. Mem. Minn. (pres. 1962-63, bd. govs. 1963-66), Am. (ho. of dels. 1963-66) bar assns. Home: 334 Alcott Ave E Fergus Falls MN 56537 Office: 125 S Mill St Fergus Falls MN 56537 Tel (218) 736-5457

FIELD, DAVID ANTHONY, b. Bklyn., Mar. 5, 1934; B.A. magna cum laude, Tufts U., 1955; LL.B., Columbia, 1958; LL.M., N.Y. U., 1965. Admitted to N.Y. State bar, 1958; partner firm DiFalco, Field & Lomenzo, N.Y.C., 1959—. Pres. Hewlett Park Civic Assn., 1963-64; pres. lodge B'nai B'rith, 1964-65. Mem. N.Y. County

Lawyers Assn., Young Men's Philanthropic League (bd. dirs.). Office: 605 3d Ave New York City NY 10016 Tel (212) 986-2434

FIELD, HENRY AUGUSTUS, JR., b. Wisconsin Dells, Wis., July 8, 1928; student Western Mich. Coll., 1946-47; Ph.B., Marquette U., 1950; LL.B., U. Wis., 1952. Admitted to Wis. bar, 1952; asst. U.S. atty. Western Dist. Wis., 1956-57; asso. firm Roberts, Boardman, Suhr, Bjork & Curry, Madison, Wis., 1957-62; partner firm Roberts, Boardman, Suhr & Curry, Madison, 1962-70; partner firm Boardman, Suhr, Curry & Field, Madison, 1970—; mem. State of Wis. Judicial Council, 1974—. Bd. dirs. Family Service Soc., 1969-75, treas., 1971-72, pres., 1973-74. Fellow Am. Coll. Trial Lawyers; mem. Dane County (pres., 1971-72), Am. bar assns., State Bar Wis. (chmn. negligence sect., 1971-75, chmn. legis. com., 1969-71), Bar Assn. Seventh Fed. Circuit, Order of Coif, Phi Delta Phi, Sigma Tau Delta. Home: 4410 Keating Terr Madison WI 53711 Office: 131 W Wilson St Madison WI 53703 Tel (608) 257-9521

FIELD, HENRY FREDERICK, b. Weston, Mass., June 3, 1941; B.A., Harvard, 1962; J.D., U. Chgo., 1965. Admitted to Ill. bar, 1965, D.C. bar, 1966, U.S. Supreme Ct. bar, 1971; law clk. Mr. Justice Walter V. Schaefer Ill. Supreme Ct., 1965-66; asst. U.S. atty., Washington, 1966-67; spl. asst. Pres. U. Chgo., 1968-69; asso. firm Mayer, Brown & Platt, Chgo., 1969-74, partner, 1975—. Dir. Taylor Inst., Chgo., 1976—. Mem. Chgo. Council of Lawyers (dir. 1969-75). Contbr. articles in field to profl. jours. Home: Apt 1403 345 Fullerton Pkwy Chicago IL 60614 Office: 231 S LaSalle St Chicago IL 60604 Tel (312) ST2-0600

FIELD, JERE, b. Cartersville, Ga., Aug. 5, 1917; LL.B., U. Ga., 1939. Admitted to Ga. bar, 1940; judge, recorder's ct., Monroe, Ga., 1945—. Mem. Ga. State, Alcovy bar assns., Am. Judicature Soc. Office: 416 S Broad St Monroe GA 30655 Tel (404) 267-5311

FIELD, MILTON MORTIMER, b. Bklyn., Mar. 25, 1925; B.E.E., U. Nebr., 1948; LL.B., George Washington U., 1952. Admitted to D.C. bar, 1952; examiner U.S. Patent Office, Washington, 1948-61, law examiner Office of Solicitor, Washington, 1957, 58; since practiced in Washington, asso. firm Shapiro & Shapiro, 1961-65, partner, 1966-71, individual practice law, 1972—. Mem. D.C., Am. bar assns., Am. Patent Law Assn., Patent Office Soc., Vol. Lawyers for the Arts. Home: 2212 White Oaks Dr Alexandria VA 22306 Office: Suite 750 Washington Bldg Washington DC 20005 Tel (202) 783-0900

FIELD, MORTON R., b. Chgo., July 28, 1923; B.A., U. Ill., 1945; LL.B., DePaul U., 1948. Admitted to Ill. bar, 1948, Calif. bar, 1951, D.C. bar, 1957; atty. SEC, Washington, 1948-51; partner firm Wallenstein & Field, Los Angeles, 1957-73, Jackson & Goldstein, Los Angeles, 1973—; capt. JAGC, U.S. Army. Mem. Am. Arbitration Assn. (arbitrator), Am., Fed., Los Angeles, Ill. State, Calif. bar assns. Home: 306 S Bronwood Ave Los Angeles CA 90049 Office: 1901 Ave of Stars Los Angeles CA 90067 Tel (213) 277-0200

FIELDER, PARKER CLINTON, b. Chgo., Oct. 20, 1918; B.S., Northwestern U., 1941; LL.B., U. Tex., 1948. Admitted to Tex. bar, 1948, U.S. Supreme Ct. bar, 1955; asso. prof. law U. Tex., Austin, 1948-53, W.H. Francis, Jr. prof. law, 1961—; partner firm Turpin, Kerr, Smith & Dyer, Midland, Tex., 1953-61; vis. prof. U. Pa., 1964-65; vis. cons. tax dept. Exxon Corp., 1969; cons. Legis. Property Tax Com. Tex., 1974-75; vis. prof. U. Utah, 1976. Bd. dirs. Human Opportunities Corp., Austin, 1968-72. Mem. Am. Bar Assn., Am. Law Inst., Ex-Editors Assn. Tex. Law Rev. Home: 906 Terrace Mountain Dr Austin TX 78746 Office: 2500 Red River St Austin TX 78705 Tel (512) 471-5151

FIELDMAN, NEIL, b. Springfield, Mass., Sept. 19, 1931; B.A., Brandeis U., 1953; J.D., Boston U., 1959. Admitted to Mass. bar, 1959, U.S. Dist. Ct. bar for Dist. Mass., 1961. Mem. Hampden County (Mass.), Mass. bar assns. Office: 1387 Main St Springfield MA 01103 Tel (413) 785-1321

FIELDS, ALAN BOYD, JR., b. Miami, Fla., Nov. 13, 1931; B.S., U. Fla., 1957, J.D., 1966. Admitted to Fla. bar, 1966, U.S. Dist. Ct. for No. Fla., 1966, U.S. 5th Circuit Ct. Appeals bar, 1968, U.S. Dist. Ct. for Middle Fla. bar, 1969, U.S. Supreme Ct. bar, 1969, U.S. Dist. Ct. for So. Fla. bar, 1975; asso. firm Jones & Sims, Pensacola, Fla., 1966-67, partner, 1967-69; partner firm Dowda and Fields, Profl. Assn. (and predecessor firms), Palatka, Fla., 1969—; mem. Gov.'s Com. on Cold War Edn., State of Fla., 1963; dir. Fla. Tourism Council, 1963; Fla. Council for Econ. Edn., 1963; chmn. Putnam County (Fla.) Water Conservation Com., 1973-74. Bd. govs. United Fund Pensacola, 1962; pres. San Mateo (Fla.) Recreation Club, 1974—; trustee St. Leo Coll., 1974—. Mem. Am., Fla. (Outstanding pres. 1974), Putnam County (pres. 1973), John Marshall bar assns., Soc. Bar 1st Jud. Circuit, Am. Judicature Soc., VFW, Fla. Pub. Relations Assn., Am. Assn. Retired Persons, Elks. Recipient Farmers Home Adminstrn. award Dept. Agr., 1972; Civic Betterment award, Elks club # 1232, 1975. Home: Oaklane Ranch San Mateo FL 32088 Office: 413 St Johns Ave Palatka FL 32077 Tel (901) 325-2041

FIELDS, MICHAEL JOHNSON, b. Columbus, Ohio, Oct. 23, 1943; B.A. in History, U. Mo. at Columbia, 1965, J.D., 1969. Admitted to Mo. bar, 1969; asso. firm Head & Nettleton, Columbia, 1971-72; asst. city counselor Columbia, 1972-74; asso. counsel Mo. Div. Ins., Dept. Consumer Affairs, Regulation and Licensing, Columbia, 1974—. Mem. Mo., Cole and Boone County bar assns. Home: 34 Leatherwood Hills Columbia MO 65201 Office: 415 E High St Jefferson City MO 65201 Tel (314) 751-2619

FIELDS, MILTON PALMER, b. Halifax County, N.C., Jan. 17, 1926; A.B., E. Carolina U., 1949; postgrad. Emory U., 1949-52; J.D., Wake Forest U., 1953. Admitted to N.C. bar, 1953; pros. atty. City of Rocky Mount (N.C.), 1955-56; individual practice law, Rocky Mount, 1953—. Mem. N.C., Nash-Edgecombe bar assns., Am. Trial Lawyers Assn., N.C. Acad. Trial Lawyers. Home: 3504 Sheffield Dr Rocky Mount NC 27802 Office: Box 4538 Rocky Mount NC 27801 Tel (919) 442-3115

FIENMAN, HARRY HENRY, b. Boston, Sept. 29, 1915; B.S. in Bus. Adminstrn., Boston U., 1940; LL.B., New Eng. Sch. Law, 1950. Admitted to Mass. bar, 1951; mem. firm Heimberg, Rudnick & Fienman, Brookline, Mass., 1954-57; asst. to dir. Mass. Civil Def. Agy., 1960-69; asst. dir. corp. records Mass. Sec. of State, 1969-76. Bd. dirs. Alumni N E Sch. of Law, 1965—, Mass. Half-Way Houses Inc., 1965-76, Brighton YMCA, 1973; pres. Fed. Credit Union for Ex-Convicts, 1972. Mem. Boston Bar Assn. Decorated Purple Heart; named to Hall of Fame, Boston U., 1940. Office: 231 St Paul St Brookline MA 02146 Tel (617) 277-4562

FIGG, ROBERT MCCORMICK, b. Radford, Va., Oct. 22, 1901; A.B., Coll. Charleston, 1920, Litt.D., 1970; postgrad. Columbia Law Sch., 1920-22; LL.D., U. S.C., 1954. Admitted to S.C. bar, 1922, U.S. Supreme Ct. bar, 1931; practiced in Charleston, S.C., 1922-62, partner firms Rutledge Hyde Mann & Figg, 1924-34, Figg, Gibbs & Grimball, 1959-62, individual practice law, 1934-59; mem. S.C. Ho. of Reps., 1932-34; dean U. S.C. Law Sch., 1959-70; sr. counsel firm Robinson McFadden Moore & Pope, Columbia, S.C., 1971—; solicitor S.C. 9th Judicial Circuit, 1935-47; spl. circuit judge Ct. Common Pleas, 1957, 75, 76; gen. counsel S.C. State Ports Authority, 1942-72; chmn. S.C. Reorgn. Commn., 1951-55, 71-75; mem. Reardon Com. Fair Trial-Free Press; speaker in field. Mem. Columbia Mus. Art Commn.; trustee, pres. Saul Alexander Found., Charleston; hon. life chmn. Coll. Charleston Found. Fellow Am. Coll. Trial Lawyers; mem. Am. Law Inst., Am. (ho. dels. 1971-72), S.C. (pres. 1971), Charleston County (pres. 1953), Inter-Am. bar assns., Blue Key, Phi Beta Kappa, Phi Delta Phi. Author: (with others) Civil Trial Manual, 1974; contbr. articles to legal jours. Home: 1522 Deans Ln Columbia SC 29205 Office: Suite G Jefferson Sq Columbia SC 29202 Tel (803) 779-5323

FILARDI, CONSTANTINE BASIL, b. White Plains, N.Y., Dec. 6, 1930; B.B.A., Fordham U., 1952, J.D., 1959. Admitted to N.Y. bar, 1959; asso. Louis Fusco, Jr., N.Y.C., 1959-63; individual practice law, Armonk, N.Y., 1963—. Legis. asst. N.Y. State Assembly, 1959-65; justice Town Justice Ct., Town of North Castle (N.Y.), 1969-75; mem. North Castle Conservation and Recreation Bd., 1963-69. Mem. Westchester, No. Westchester bar assns. Home: 23 Creemer Rd Armonk NY 10504 Office: 500 Main St Armonk NY 10504

FILAROWITZ, THOMAS CHESTER, b. Perth Amboy, N.J., Jan. 18, 1947; B.A. in Polit. Sci., Rider Coll., 1969; J.D., Bklyn. Law Sch., 1972. Admitted to N.Y. bar, 1973, N.J. bar, 1974; individual practice law, Perth Amboy, 1973—; of counsel Bobich Deutsch & Schlesse, N.Y.C., 1971—; research analyst N.J. Dept. Community Affairs, Trenton, 1969; internist S. Bklyn. Legal Services, 1969-71. Address: 153 State St Perth Amboy NJ 08861 Tel (201) 442-1709

FILES, GORDON LOUIS, b. Ft. Dodge, Iowa, Mar. 5, 1912; A.B., U. Calif., Los Angeles, 1934; LL.B., Yale, 1937. Admitted to Calif. bar, 1937; law clk. to U.S. 8th Circuit judge, St. Louis, 1937-38; mem. firm Freston & Files, Los Angeles, 1938-59; enforcement atty. OPA, San Francisco, 1942; judge Superior Ct., Los Angeles, 1959-62; justice Calif. Ct. of Appeal, 1962, presiding justice 2d Dist., Div. 4, 1964—; lectr. U. Calif. Extension, Los Angeles, 1953, 61, 68, U. So. Calif. Law Sch., 1959-65; mem. Calif. Jud. Council, 1964-71, 73-77. Mem. Am., Calif. (bd. govs. 1957-59), Los Angeles bar assns., Conf. State Bar Dels. (chmn. 1954), Inst. Jud. Adminstrn., Am. Judicature Soc., Order of Coif, Phi Beta Kappa, Phi Delta Phi, Phi Kappa Sigma. Home: 154 S Arroyo Blvd Pasadena CA 91105 Office: 3580 Wilshire Blvd Los Angeles CA 90010 Tel (213) 736-2623

FILIATRAULT, ROBERT MURRAY, b. Cleve., Oct. 19, 1944; student U. Notre Dame, U. Detroit; J.D., Detroit Coll. Law, 1970. Law clk. U.S. Dist. Ct., Eastern Dist. Mich., Detroit, 1969-71; admitted to Mich. bar, 1970; partner firm Allen, James, Snow & Filiatrault, Detroit, 1971-73; prof. law Detroit Coll. Law, 1973—. Mem. Am. Judicature Soc., Am., Mich., Detroit, Fed. (asst. treas. Detroit chpt. 1971-72) bar assns. Home: 2352 Bratton Ave Bloomfield Hills MI 48013 Office: 136 E Elizabeth St Detroit MI 48201 Tel (313) 965-0150

FILICE, CHARLES FRANK, b. Lansing, Mich., Feb. 9, 1944; B.B.A., Western Mich. U., 1965; J.D., Wayne State U., 1968. Admitted to Mich. bar, 1968; law intern Neighborhood Legal Services, Detroit, 1967-68; chief trial atty., head criminal div. Ingham County (Mich.) Pros. Atty's. Office, Lansing, 1968-71; judge Mich. Dist. Ct. 54-A, Lansing, 1971—. Mem. pub. serivce advisory bd. Sta. WJIM TV and Radio, Lansing, 1973—; mem. Northside adv. council Boys' Club of Lansing, 1975—; bd. dirs. local chpt. Nat. Council on Alcoholism, Lansing. Mem. State Bar Mich., Ingham County Bar Assn., Mich. Dist. Judges Assn. Named Top Bus. Mgmt. Student Western Mich. U., 1965, Outstanding Young Person for City of Lansing Lansing Jr. C. of C., 1974. Office: City Hall Lansing MI 48933 Tel (517) 487-1350

FILLNER, RUSSELL KENNETH, b. Forsyth, Mont., Apr. 18, 1926; LL.B., U. Mont., 1952, J.D., 1968. Admitted to Mont. bar, 1952, U.S. Dist. Ct. for Mont. bar, 1956, U.S. 9th Circuit Ct. Appeals bar, 1956; atty. Rosebud County, Mont., 1952-66; asso. firm Sandal, Moses & Cavan, Billings, Mont., 1967-72; partner firm Fillner, Snyder & Mudd, Billings, Mont., 1972-75; individual practice law, Billings, 1975—; mem. Mont. Criminal Law Revision Commn., 1964-73. Alderman, City of Billings, 1971-74, pres. city council, 1972-74. Mem. Am., Mont. bar assns., Am. Judicature Soc., Mont. County Attys Assn. (pres. 1957). Home: 211 Clark Ave Billings MT 59101 Office: 2906 2d Ave N Suite 212 Billings MT 59101 Tel (406) 248-7824

FINAN, JOHN PATRICK, b. N.Y.C., Apr. 3, 1934; A.B., Fordham U., 1956; J.D., Columbia, 1961; postgrad. Harvard, 1963, N.Y.U., 1964; U. Calif. Berkeley, 1966. Admitted to N.Y. State bar, 1961, Ill. bar, 1967, Ohio bar, 1975; asso. firm Hawkins, Delafield & Wood, N.Y.C., 1962-63; asst. prof. law Ohio No. U., 1963-65, Loyola U., Chgo., 1965-67; prof. law U. Akron (Ohio), 1967-69, 75—, asst. dean, 1969-72, asso. dean, 1972-74. Mem. Akron, Ohio State bar assns., League Ohio Law Schs. Contbr. articles in field to profl. jours. Home: 2295 Woodpark Rd Akron OH 44313 Office: U Akron Sch Law Akron OH 44325 Tel (216) 375-7331

FINAN, LILLIAN, b. Middletown, Conn., Feb. 6, 1921; J.D., U. So. Calif., 1956, postgrad. Med. Sch., 1965-66. Admitted to Calif. bar, 1957, U.S. Supreme Ct. bar, 1976; individual practice law, Los Angeles, 1957—. Bd. dirs. Salerni Collegium for Med. Sch. U. So. Calif. Mem. Calif. Bar, Los Angeles, Century City bar assns., Calif. (dir.), Los Angeles (dir.) trial lawyers assns., NOW, Calif. Women's Lawyers Assn., Legion Lex. Office: 1801 Century Park E Suite 1700 Los Angeles CA 90067 Tel (213) 556-3400

FINCH, JAMES AUSTIN, JR., b. St Louis, Nov. 13, 1907; A.B., U. Mo., 1930, J.D., 1932, LL.D., 1966. Admitted to Mo. bar, 1931; asst. atty. gen. State of Mo., 1932; mem. firm Finch, Finch & Knehans and predecessor, Cape Girardeau, Mo., 1933-64; justice Mo. Supreme Ct., 1965—, chief justice, 1971-73; pros. atty. Cape Girardeau County (Mo.), 1941-42; dir. Nat. Center for State Cts., 1971—, pres., 1975-77. Bd. curators U. Mo., 1951-65, pres., 1954-64; chmn. Mo. Gov's. Council on Higher Edn., 1959-63. Mem. Am. Bar Assn., Mo. Bar, Appellate Judges Conf. (exec. com. 1972-76, sec., 1973-77), Am. Law Inst., Am. Judicature Soc., Inst. Jud. Adminstrn., Acad. Mo. Squires, Order of Coif, Phi Beta Kappa. Home: 404 Crystal View Jefferson City MO 65101 Office: Supreme Ct Bldg Jefferson City MO 65101 Tel (314) 751-3477

FINCH, NATHAN C., b. Los Angeles, Aug. 14, 1909; A.B., Stanford U., 1931, LL.B., 1934. Admitted to Calif. bar, 1934; partner firm Howe & Finch, after 1938, now Finch, Sauers, Player & King. Pres. Palo Alto (Calif.) Bd. Edn., 1954-57. Mem. Am., Calif., Santa Clara County bar assns. Tel (415) 321-6560

FINCH, WALTER GILCHRIST, b. Balt., Jan. 25, 1918; B. Engring., Johns Hopkins, 1940, M. Engring., 1950; J.D., Temple U., 1949, M.B.A., 1950; LL.M., George Washington U., 1949; grad. Command and Gen. Staff Coll., 1953, Nat. War Coll., 1965, Indsl. Coll. Armed Forces, 1965. Admitted to Md. bar, 1947, D.C. bar, 1951, U.S. Supreme Ct. bar, 1951; jr. instr. engring. Johns Hopkins, 1940-41, instr. civil engring., 1947-49; design engr. Glenn L. Martin Co., Balt., 1946; asst. to chief physicist Office Chief Ordnance, U.S. Army, Washington, 1946-47, capt. 2402d Research and Devel. Tng. Group, 1949-50; patent lawyer firm Roberts B. Larson, Washington, 1950-51; asst. counsel Applied Physics Lab., Johns Hopkins, 1951-57, univ. patent counsel, 1953—; individual practice law, Balt., 1957—. Dist. commr. Old Glory council Boy Scouts Am., Balt., 1953-56, mem. exec. bd. Balt. area council, 1965—; pres. adv. council Catonsville Community Coll. Mem. Md. Hist. Soc., Md. Acad. Scis., English Speaking Union, Balt. Assn. Commerce, Fed., Balt., Md., Inter-Am., Internat., Am. bar assns., Internat. Patent and Trademark Assn., World Peace Through Law Center, Am. Patent Law Assn., Am. Ordnance Assn., Res. Officers Assn., Am. Inst. C.P.A.'s, Md. Assn. C.P.A.'s, ASME, Nat., Md. socs. profl. engrs. Registered profl. engr., D.C.; C.P.A., Md. Author: (with Paul A. Twamley) The Romance of Invention of the Eastern and Western Worlds, 1977; contbr. articles to legal jours. Office: 1501-04 Fidelity Bldg Baltimore MD 21202 Tel (301) 539-8170

FINCK, ROBERT JOHN, SR., b. Jamaica, L.I., N.Y., Nov. 11, 1946; A.A., St. Petersburg Jr. Coll., 1966; B.A., U. Fla., 1968, J.D., 1971. Admitted to Fla. bar, 1971, U.S. Supreme Ct. bar, 1976; asst. dist. counsel U.S. Army Corps of Engrs., Jacksonville, Fla., 1971-72; asso. firm Masterson, Sundberg & Rogers, St. Petersburg, 1972-73; staff counsel and dir. Legal Aid Soc. of St. Petersburg, Inc., 1973-77; adj. prof. Stetson U. Coll. of Law, St. Petersburg, 1974-77; asso. firm Jenkins, Fischer, Brook & Brown, St. Petersburg, 1977—. Mem. Am., St. Petersburg bar assns. Home: 1501 Alcazar Way S St Petersburg FL 33705 Office: 695 Central Ave St Petersburg FL 33701 Tel (813) 822-5342

FINDER, THEODORE ROOSEVELT, b. N.Y.C., Oct. 28, 1914; A.B., Columbia U., 1936, J.D., 1938. Admitted to N.Y. bar, 1938; asso. firm Fearey, Allen, Johnston & Smyth, and successors, N.Y.C., 1938-42; asso. firm Beekman & Bogue, N.Y.C., 1945-49, partner, 1950—; v.p., asst. sec., dir. B. Fischer & Co., Inc., N.Y.C., 1951-54, asst. sec., dir., 1957-64; pres., dir. Asher Am., Inc., Calgary, Alta., Can., 1952-53, asst. sec., 1953-58; dir. Redwater Am., Inc., Calgary, 1952-55, pres., 1953, asst. sec., 1953-55; v.p., dir. Gen. Fertilizer Corp., Walla Walla, Wash., 1958-64; asst. sec., dir. Calvan Am., Inc., Calgary, 1951-61, asst. treas., 1952-61; asst. sec., dir. Cola Beverage Corp., Jacksonville, Fla., 1958-64; dir. Studebaker Packard Corp., South Bend, Ind., 1958-60, mem. fin. com., 1958-59, mem. personnel com., 1958-60, mem. exec. com., 1959-60. Mem. Am., N.Y. State, N.Y. County, N.Y.C. bar assns. Home: 136 E 76th St New York City NY 10021 Office: 5 Hanover Sq New York City NY 10004 Tel (212) 422-4060

FINE, HERBERT LEONARD, b. N.Y.C., May 25, 1921; LL.B., St. Johns U., 1943. Admitted to N.Y. bar, 1943; mem. firm Rubinton & Coleman, Bklyn., 1943; asst. corp. counsel City N.Y., 1943-45; asso. firm Douglas & Douglas, Bklyn., 1943-50; asso. firm Harry Zeitlan, N.Y.C., 1950-55; partner firm Starkman & Fine, N.Y.C., 1955-69; partner firm Isaacson, Robustelli, Fox, Fine & Greco, N.Y.C., 1969—. Pres. Dogwood Civic Assn., Franklin Square, N.Y.; pres. Franklin Square (N.Y.) Jewish Center pres. bd. trustee Franklin Square Library. Mem. Am., N.Y. trail lawyers assns., Nassau County, N.Y. County bar assns. Office: 277 Broadway St New York City NY 10007 Tel (212) WO2-1200

FINE, JOSEPH JULIUS, b. Macon, Ga., Nov. 11, 1908; LL.B., U. Ga., 1930. Mem. Ga. bar, 1930; individual practice law, Atlanta, 1930—. Mem. Am., Atlanta, Ga. bar assns., FCC Bar Assn., Am. Judicature Soc., Atlanta C. of C. Home: 22 Chatham Rd NW Atlanta GA 30305 Office: 100 Colony Sq Suite 1905 Atlanta GA 30361 Tel (404) 892-7160

FINE, NEAL HARVEY, b. Indpls., Dec. 25, 1944; B.A., U. Buffalo, 1966; J.D., Am. U., 1969. Admitted to Va. bar, 1969, D.C. bar, 1971, U.S. Supreme Ct. bar, 1975; tax law specialist IRS, 1969-70; staff counsel Am. Fedn. of Govt. Employees, Washington, 1970-73, Nat. Treasury Employees Union, Washington, 1974-75; asst. chief labor relations U.S. Govt. Printing Office, Washington, 1975—. Mem. Am. Bar Assn., Soc. Fed. Labor Relations Profls. (sec. 1973). Home: 5620 Freshaire Ln Columbia MD 21044 Office: 732 N Capitol St Washington DC 20001 Tel (202) 275-2938

FINE, RICHARD ISAAC, b. Milw., Jan. 22, 1940; B.S., U. Wis., 1961; J.D., U. Chgo., 1964; Ph.D., U. London, 1967. Admitted to Ill. bar, 1964, D.C. bar, 1972, Calif. bar, 1973; asso. Coudert Bros., London, 1968; trial atty., atty. adv. Fgn. Commerce sect. U.S. Dept. Justice Antitrust Div., Washington, 1968-72; asso. firm Swerdlow, Glikbarg & Shimer, Los Angeles, 1972-73; chief antitrust div. City of Los Angeles, 1973-74; individual practice law, Los Angeles, 1974—; prof. U. Syracuse Law Sch. Overseas Program summer, 1970-72. Spl. Counsel Govt. Efficiency Com. Los Angeles City Council, 1973. Mem. Am., Los Angeles County bar assns., Am. Soc. Internat. Law, Internat. Law Assn., Brit. Inst. Internat. and Comparative Law, Am. Fgn. Law Assn. Contbr. articles to profl. jours. Home: 14013 Captains Row Marina del Rey CA 90291 Office: 1801 Century Park E 26th Floor Los Angeles CA 90067 Tel (213) 277-5833

FINE, ROBERT GEORGE, b. N.Y.C., June 15, 1931; B.A., Syracuse U., 1953; LL.B., Columbia, 1956. Admitted to N.Y. bar, 1956; atty. Atty Gen.'s Office, State N.Y., 1956-58; partner firm Fine, Finkelstein, Saminsky, Olin & Stern, N.Y.C., 1959—. Mem. N.Y. Workmen's Compensation Bar Assn. (dir.), N.Y. County Lawyers Assn.

FINEBERG, DAVID L., b. Hartford, Conn., Nov. 21, 1931; B.A., Colgate U., 1953; LL.B., Columbia, 1956. Admitted to Conn. bar, 1956, Fla. bar, 1976; since practiced in Hartford, mem. firm Schatz & Schatz, 1956-76, firm Albrecht & Richman, 1976—. Councilman City of Bloomfield (Conn.), 1965-67. Mem. Am., Conn., Fla. bar assns., Comml. Law League Am. Home: 49 Hurdle Fence Dr Avon CT 06001 Office: 410 Asylum St Hartford CT 06003 Tel (203) 522-5295

FINEFROCK, RICHARD HARVEY, b. Barberton, Ohio, Feb. 4, 1919; B.A., Ohio Wesleyan U., 1940; LL.B., Cornell U., 1942; postgrad. Nat. Coll. Judiciary, Reno, Nev., 1966, 70, 73. Admitted to

Ohio bar, 1942; asso. firm Squire, Sanders & Dempsey, Cleve., 1942; partner firm Campbell, Thompson & Finefrock, Bellefontaine, Ohio, 1946-55; individual practice law, Bellefontaine, 1955-58; judge Common Pleas Ct. of Logan County, Ohio, 1958—; solicitor City of Bellefontaine, 1949-53. Mem. Phi Delta Phi, Alpha Tau Omega (province chief 1954-60). Home: 618 E Sandusky St Bellefontaine OH 43311 Office: Court House Bellefontaine OH 43311 Tel (513) 592-2926

FINERMAN, RALPH, b. N.Y.C., Oct. 21, 1935; B.S. in Econs., U. Pa., 1956; LL.B., Columbia, 1959; LL.M., N.Y. U., 1967. Admitted to N.Y. State bar, 1959; asso. firm Kaye, Scholer, Fierman, Hays & Handler, N.Y.C., 1966-68; partner firm Simonoff, Peyser, & Citrin, N.Y.C., 1968-73; partner firm Clarence Rainess & Co., N.Y.C., 1973—. Mem. N.Y. State Bar Assn., N.Y. County Lawyers Assn., N.Y. Soc. of CPA's, Am. Inst. CPA's. Office: 1515 Broadway New York City NY 10036 Tel (212) 869-8100

FINGER, JOHN HOLDEN, b. Oakland, Calif., June 29, 1913; A.B., U. Calif., 1933, LL.B., 1937. Admitted to Calif. bar, 1937; individual practice law, San Francisco, 1937-42; chief mil. commn. sect. Far East Hdqrs. War Dept., Toyoko, 1946-47; mem. firm Hoberg, Finger & Brown, San Francisco, 1947—; dir. 1st Fed. Savs. and Loan Assn. of Fresno. Trustee Pacific Sch. Religion, 1959—, bd. chmn. 1969—; bd. dirs. Calif. Maritime Acad., San Francisco Legal Aid Soc., 1955-70; bd. visitors Judge Adv. Gen. Sch., Charlottesville, Va., 1964—, Stanford Law Sch., 1969-71; pres. Laymen's Fellowship No. Calif. Conf. Congl. Chs., 1951-53, moderator, 1954-55. Fellow Am. Bar Found., Am. Coll. Trial Lawyers; mem. Am. Judicature Soc., Am. Bar Assn. (ho. of dels. 1970—, council jud. adminstrn. div. 1972—, nat. chmn. lawyers conf. com. appellate advocacy 1976—), Bar Assn. San Francisco (dir. 1960-62), Judge Adv. Assn. (dir. 1957—, pres. 1964-65), Lawyers Club San Francisco (pres. 1953), State Bar Calif. (gov. 1965-68, pres. 1967-68), Sierra Club (exec. com. legal def. fund), Phi Alpha Delta, Sigma Phi Epsilon. Home: 12675 Skyline Blvd Oakland CA 94619 Office: 703 Market St San Francisco CA 94103 Tel (415) 543-9464

FINGERMAN, ALBERT R., b. Cin., Sept. 29, 1920; LL.B., U. Cin., 1948. Admitted to Ohio bar, 1948; now mem. firm Schmidt, Effron, Josselson & Weber, Cin.; trustee Ohio Legal Services Plan, 1974—. Mem. Cin. (pres. 1976-77), Ohio State (chmn. com. on profl. econs. 1969-72), Am. bar assns., Cin. Lawyers Club (pres. 1955). Office: 700 Atlas Bank Bldg 524 Walnut St Cincinnati OH 45202 Tel (513) 241-4037*

FINK, BRUCE REUBEN, b. Detroit, July 19, 1938; B.S. in Engring., U. Calif., 1965; J.D., cum laude, Pepperdine U., 1970. Admitted to Calif. bar, 1971; individual practice law, Santa Ana, Calif., 1971—. Vice pres. Placentia (Calif.) Boys' Club, 1973. Mem. Los Angeles County, Orange County bar assns.

FINK, IRVING LEON, b. Youngstown, Ohio, Mar. 25, 1920; B.S., Northwestern U., 1941; J.D., U. Mich., 1948. Admitted to Ohio bar, 1948, Ind. bar, 1949; individual practice law, Indpls., 1949—; pres. Indpls. Lawyers Commn., 1977. Pres. Polio Found., 1951, Indpls. Children's Bur., 1968, Am. Jewish Congress, 1955-57, Jewish Community Relations Council, 1972-75; bd. Ind. Civil Liberties Union, Robert J. Risk award, 1970; bds. Legal Services Orgn., Jewish Welfare Fedn. Recipient Brotherhood award NCCJ, 1971. Mem. Am., Ind. State, Indpls. (v.p. 1974-75) bar assns. Recipient David M. Cook award, 1968, Christian Theol. Sem. award, 1975. Home: 5445 N Park Dr Indianapolis IN 46220 Office: 602-5 Board of Trade Bldg Indianapolis IN 46204 Tel (317) 636-5425

FINKE, ROBERT FORGE, b. Chgo., Mar. 11, 1941; A.B., U. Mich., 1963; J.D., Harvard, 1966. Admitted to Ill. bar, 1966, U.S. Supreme Ct. bar, 1970; law clk. U.S. Dist. Ct., Chgo., 1966-67; asso. firm Mayer, Brown & Platt, Chgo., 1967-72, partner, 1973—. Bd. dirs. Lyric Opera of Chgo. Guild. Mem. Am. (vice-chmn. sect. legal edn. and admissions to the bar 1976-77, mem. antitrust, litigation sects.), Chgo. bar assns. Office: 231 S LaSalle St Chicago IL 60604

FINKEL, BENJAMIN, b. Bklyn., Sept. 10, 1905; student N.Y. U., 1923-24; LL.B., Fordham U., 1927. Admitted to N.Y. bar, 1929; partner firm Buitenkent & Finkel, to 1934, Finkel & Goldstein, and predecessors, N.Y.C., 1936—. Mem. Bklyn., N.Y. State bar assns. Recipient awards B'nai B'rith and United Jewish Appeal. Home: 2000 Kings Hwy Brooklyn NY 11229 Office: 401 Broadway New York City NY 10013 Tel (212) CA 6-6904

FINKEL, BERNARD, b. Bklyn., Feb. 3, 1928; LL.B., J.D., St. John's U., 1950. Admitted to N.Y. bar, 1950, U.S. Supreme Ct. bar, 1957; partner firm Argiriou & Finkel, N.Y.C., 1950—. Mem. N.Y. State, Kings County bar assns., N.Y. State Trial Lawyers Assn. Home: 9920 Ave K Brooklyn NY 11236 Office: 310 Madison Ave New York City NY 10017 Tel (212) 697-0620

FINKELMAN, EMANUEL DAVID, b. Kiev, Russia, July 7, 1905; student law in Office of Zalkin & Cohen, N.Y.C., 1925-29. Admitted to N.Y. State bar, 1929, U.S. Supreme Ct. bar, 1967; clk. Joseph Hilton Clothiers, N.Y.C., 1920-22; clk. firm Zalkin & Cohen, N.Y.C., 1924-26, mng. clk., 1926-30; asso. house counsel Curtiss-Wright Airplane Div., Buffalo, N.Y., 1944-46; asso. firm Stillman & Stillman, N.Y.C., 1957-64; asso. firm Blum, Haimoff, Gersen, Lipson & Szabad, N.Y.C., 1965—, mng. atty., 1970—. Trustee Congregation Beth Elohim, Bklyn., 1959—; mem. exec. bd. Met. Conf. Jewish Chautauqua Soc., N.Y.C. Mem. N.Y. State Bar Assn., N.Y. County Lawyers Assn. Home: 75 Henry St Brooklyn NY 11201 Office: 270 Madison Ave New York City NY 10016 Tel (212) 683-6383

FINKELSTEIN, HERBERT L., b. Bklyn., Dec. 29, 1932; B.A., Columbia, 1955, J.D., 1957. Admitted to N.Y. State bar, 1957, U.S. Dist. Ct. Eastern and So. Dist. N.Y. bar, 1958; practiced in N.Y.C., 1957—; asso. firm Botein, Hays, Sklar & Herzberg, 1957-60; asso. firm Jaffin, Schneider & Conrad, 1960-66, partner, 1966—. Mem. N.Y. State, N.Y.C., Am. bar assns. Home: 19 Eldridge Ave Ossining NY 10562 Office: 350 Madison Ave New York City NY 10017 Tel (212) 661-4480

FINLEY, GEORGE, b. Aspermont, Tex., Dec. 28, 1915; student Tex. Tech. U., 1932-34; B.B.A., U. Tex., 1948, LL.B., 1950, J.D., 1950. Admitted to Tex. bar, 1950; since practiced in Kermit, Tex., individual practice law, 1950-58; partner firm Finley and Scogin, 1958—; city atty., 1951; county atty. Winkler County, Tex., 1953-56., Am., Tex., Trans-Pecos bar assns., Tex. Bar Found., Tex. Landowners Protective Assn., Am. Judicature Soc., Am., Tex. trial lawyers assns., Am. Coll. Probate Counsel, Tex. Soc. C.P.A.'s, Delta Sigma Pi, Beta Gamma Sigma, Phi Delta Phi, Beta Alpha Psi. Home: 215 S Ave H Kermit TX 79745 Office: PO Box 920 Kermit TX 79745 Tel (915) 586-3417

FINN, ARTHUR, b. Boston, Oct. 23, 1909; certificate Staley Coll., 1929; J.D., Boston Coll., 1935. Admitted to Mass. bar, 1936; individual practice law, Boston and Waltham, Mass., 1936—. Fence viewer City of Waltham, 1956—; pres. Beth Israel Temple, Waltham. Mem. Mass., Middlesex, Waltham, Watertown, Weston, Newton bar assns. Home: 26 Mary Ellen Rd Waban MA 02168 Office: 681 Main St Waltham MA 02154 Tel (617) 894-3000

FINN, FRANK, b. Dallas, Sept. 20, 1928; B.A. in Econs., U. Notre Dame, 1949; LL.B., U. Tex., 1956. With career tng. program FBI, Washington, 1949-51; instr. dept. speech U. Tex., 1955-56; admitted to Tex. bar, 1956, asso. firm Thompson, Knight, Simmons & Bullion, Dallas, 1956-63, partner, then sr. partner, 1963—; chmn. Southwestern Legal Found. Short Course Environ. Law and Litigation. Mem. Dallas Environ. Quality Com. Mem. State Bar Tex., Dallas, Am. bar assns., Am. Bd. Trial Advs. (pres. Dallas chpt. 1973-74), Fedn. Ins. Counsel. Named Man of Year U. Notre Dame, 1975. Office: 2300 Republic Nat Bank Bldg Dallas TX 75201 Tel (214) 655-7545

FINNEGAN, B. JAMES, b. San Francisco, July 14, 1941; A.B., San Jose State U., 1963; J.D., U. San Francisco, 1972. Admitted to Calif. bar, 1972, U.S. Dist. Ct. bar, 1972, U.S. Ct. of Appeals bar, 1972, U.S. Supreme Ct. bar, 1976; asso. firm Kiernan & Finnegan, and predecessor, San Francisco, 1972-73, partner, 1973—. Mem. McAuliffe Soc. Home: 360 Summit Ave San Rafael CA 94901 Office: 16 California St San Francisco CA 94111 Tel (415) 981-6561

FINNEGAN, MARCUS BARTLETT, b. Morristown, N.J., Sept. 15, 1927; B.S., U.S. Mil. Acad., 1949; J.D., U. Va., 1955; LL.M., George Washington U., 1957. Admitted to Va. bar, 1955, D.C. bar, 1955, U.S. Supreme Ct. bar, 1960, N.Y. bar, 1960; commd. 2d lt. U.S. Army, 1949, advanced through grades to capt. Judge Adv. Gen. Corps, 1954; assigned Army Patents Div., Pentagon, Washington 1955-57, U.S. patent adviser, Tokyo, Japan, 1957-59, ret., 1959; mem. firms Morgan, Finnegan, Durham & Pine, N.Y.C., 1959-63, Irons, Birch, Swindler & McKie, Washington, 1963-65; sr. partner firm Finnegan, Henderson, Farabow & Garrett, Washington, 1965—; professorial lectr. law George Washington U., 1971—; lectr. in field; cons. UNIDO, Vienna, Austria, 1971—, UNCTAD, Geneva, Switzerland, 1974—; adviser tech. transfer Govt. Mexico, 1972—; del. inter-Am. working group on sci. and transfer of tech. Dept. State, 1974-75; cons. U.S.-USSR Joint Working Group on Intellectual Property, 1974—; mem. expert study panel on ERDA Patent Policy, 1975—; adviser White House Council Internat. Econ. Policy, 1975—; del. numerous internat. confs. Mem. Internat., Am. (chmn. patent com. adminstrv. law sect. 1974), Fed., D.C., Va., Inter-Am. bar assns., Licensing Execs. Soc. U.S.A. (pres. 1973-74), Licensing Execs. Soc. Internat. (pres. 1975), Am. (bd. mgrs. 1974—), N.Y., N.J. patent law assns., Raven Soc., Assn. Bar City of N.Y., N.Y. County Lawyers Assn., Patent Lawyers Club Washington, World Peace Through Law Center, World Assn. Lawyers, World Assn. Law Profs. (life), Soc. Am. Law Tchrs., Am. Soc. Internat. Law, Patent and Trademark Inst. Can., Internat. Patent and Trademark Assn., Inter-Am. Assn. Indsl. Property, Internat. Studies Assn., Supreme Ct. Hist. Soc., Assn. Trial Lawyers Am., Inst. Mil. Law, Internat. Legal Soc. Japan, Ligue Internationale Contre La Concurrence Deloyale, Nat., Patent lawyers clubs, Order of Coif, Omicron Delta Kappa, Phi Delta Phi. Co-author: Patent-Antitrust, Compliance and Confrontation, 1972; author and co-editor: The Law and Business of Licensing, 1974; author and editor: The Law and Business of Patent and Know-How Licensing, 1971, 3d edit. 1975; contbr. articles to profl. jours; editorial advisory bd. Patent, Trademark, Copyright Jour., 1972—; recipient Internat. gold medal Licensing Execs. Soc., London, 1977. Home: 9017 Clewerwall Dr Bethesda MD 20034 Office: 1775 K St NW Washington DC 20006 Tel (202) 293-6850

FINNEGAN, THOMAS JOSEPH, JR., b. Wilkes-Barre, Pa., Aug. 14, 1935; A.B., Fordham U., 1957; J.D., Columbia, 1961. Admitted to N.Y. bar, 1961, Mass. bar, 1967; asso. firm Townsend & Lewis, N.Y.C., 1961-66; asst. counsel Mass. Mut. Life Ins. Co., Springfield, 1966-67, asso. counsel 1967-71, counsel, 1971-72, sec., asst. gen. counsel, 1972—; sec. MML Investment Co., Inc., Springfield, 1971-76. Mem. Am. Bar Assn. Home: 5 Wright Pl Wilbraham MA 01095 Office: 1295 State St Springfield MA 01111 Tel (413) 788-8411

FINNERTY, JOHN FRANCIS, b. Boston, Mar. 31, 1917; B.A., Boston Coll., 1938, J.D., 1947. Admitted to Mass. bar, 1947; partner firm Finnerty & Finnerty, Boston; 1972—; vis. lectr. N.Am. Clin. Dermatology Soc., Mass. Dental Soc., Am. Trial Lawyers Assn. Co-chmn. Newton (Mass.) March of Dimes, 1950. Mem. Am., Mass. bar assns., Internat. Assn. Ins. Counsel. Office: 40 Broad St Boston MA 02109 Tel (617) 426-6730

FINNERTY, JOSEPH GREGORY, JR., b. Balt., Jan. 25, 1937; B.S. in Physics cum laude, Loyola Coll., Balt., 1958; postgrad. in Engring. Physics (Celanese fellow) Cornell U., 1958-59; J.D. with honors, U. Md., 1963. Admitted to Md. bar, 1963, U.S. Supreme Ct. bar, 1972; law clk. Supreme Bench of Balt. City, 1960-63; asso. firm Piper & Marbury, Balt., 1963-66, partner, 1971—; asso. firm Tydings, Rosenberg & Gallagher, Balt., 1966-68; partner firm Gallagher, Evelius and Finnerty, Balt., 1968-71; lectr. U. Balt. Law Sch., 1968-71. Bd. dirs. Health and Welfare Council of Md., Inc., 1970—; mem. advisory bd. Villa Julie Coll., 1973—. Mem. Am., Md. State, Balt. City bar assns. Home: 4100 Saint Paul St Baltimore MD 21218 Office: 2000 First Md Bldg 25 S Charles St Baltimore MD 21201 Tel (301) 539-2530

FINNIGAN, THEODORE JOHN, b. Buffalo, June 25, 1927; A.B., Colgate U., 1948; LL.B., Cornell U., 1951, J.D., 1969. Admitted to N.Y. State bar, 1954; atty., Niagara Mohawk Power Corp., Buffalo, 1951—; asst. sec. Maryner Redevel. Corp. Inc., Buffalo, 1969-72; bd. dirs. Western Div. Credit Union, 1975—. Mem. Erie County (N.Y.) Bar Assn., Western N.Y. Utilities Assn. (charter). Office: 500 Electric Bldg 535 Washington St Buffalo NY 14223 Tel (716) 856-2424

FINZ, LEONARD LEIGH, b. N.Y.C., Aug. 17, 1924; B.A., N.Y. U., 1949, J.D., 1951. Admitted to N.Y. bar, 1953, U.S. Supreme Ct. bar, 1960; individual practice law, N.Y.C., 1953-65; chmn. Urban Renewal Commn. Queens County, 1961-62; asst. counsel N.Y. State Joint Legis. Com. on Professions, 1963-64; judge Civil Ct. City of N.Y., 1966-73, also co-chmn. community relations com. Bd. Judges; justice Supreme Ct. State of N.Y., Jamaica, 1974—; adj. prof. law Queens Coll., City U. N.Y., N.Y. Law Sch., 1975—; faculty Nat. Coll. State Judiciary, U. Nev., N.Y. Acad. Trial Lawyers; vis. lectr. N.Y. Law Sch., St. Johns Law Sch. Founder, chmn. bd. Brandeis Assn., Inc. Mem. Am., N.Y., Queens County Criminal Cts. bar assns., New York County Lawyers Assn., N.Y. State Assn. Trial Lawyers, Am. Judicature Soc. Recipient awards Boy Scouts Am., ARC, N.Y. U. Sch. Law, Brandeis Assn., Fedn. Jewish Philanthropies; contbr. articles to legal jours. Office: Supreme Ct NY 88-11 Sutphin Blvd Jamaica NY 11435 Tel (212) 520-3754

FIORELLA, ALBERT JOSEPH, b. N.Y.C., Jan. 23, 1927; B.A., Fordham U., 1950; LL.B., Bklyn. Law Sch., 1953. Admitted to N.Y. bar, 1955, U.S. Supreme Ct. bar, 1973; trial counsel Allstate Ins. Co., N.Y.C., 1955-66, atty. of record N.Y.C. and L.I., 1957-66; individual practice law, Mineola, N.Y., 1967—. Mem. Nassau-Suffolk (dir. 1962-66), Am. trial lawyers assns., Nassau County (com. on cts. 1973—), Suffolk County (unlawful practice of law com. 1970-72), Am., N.Y. State bar assns., Nat. Assn. Criminal Def. Lawyers, N.Y. State Criminal Defender Assn. Home: 26 Hayes Hill Dr Northport NY 11768 Office: 1565 Franklin Ave Mineola NY 11501 Tel (516) 741-0311

FIORENTINO, CARMINE, b. Bklyn., Sept. 11, 1932; LL.B., Blackstone Sch. Law, Chgo., 1954; LL.B., John Marshall Law Sch., Atlanta, 1957. Admitted to Ga. bar, 1958, D.C. bar, 1971; individual practice law, Atlanta, 1959-63; trial atty. HUD, Atlanta and Washington, 1963—. Mem. State Bar Ga., Atlanta, D.C., Am. bar assns., Am. Judicature Soc. Home: 2164 Medfield Trail NE Atlanta GA 30345

FIORILLO, ALBERT LEOPOLD, b. Caserta, Italy, Nov. 1, 1898; LL.B., Fordham U., 1920. Admitted to N.Y. bar, 1922; pvt. practice law, Yonkers, N.Y., 1923—; pres. Yonkers (N.Y.) Bd. Alderman, 1938-39; councilman Yonkers, N.Y., 1945-46; city judge Yonkers N.Y., 1947-62; judge Family Ct., State N.Y., Westchester County, 1962-68; trustee, Peoples Savs. Bank of Yonkers, 1948-74. Mem. N.Y. State, Westchester County bar assns., Yonkers Lawyers Assn. Recipient B'nai B'rith Citizen of Yr. award, 1957; named Yonkers Man of Outstanding Achievement, 1945. Home: 279 N Broadway Yonkers NY 10701 Office: 20 S Broadway Yonkers NY 10701

FIRESTEIN, CHARLES LEWIS, b. Phoenix, Oct. 14, 1945; B.S. in Bus. Adminstrn., U. Ariz., 1968, J.D., 1971. Admitted to Calif. bar, 1972, Ariz. bar, 1972, U.S. Supreme Ct. bar, 1976; asso. firm Cohen, Whitfield & Osborne, Oxnard, Calif., 1971-72; mem. firm Dietsch, Gates, Morris & Merrell, Los Angeles, 1972—. Mem. Los Angeles County, Am. bar assns., State Bar Calif., State Bar Ariz. Contbr. articles to legal publs. Office: 800 Wilshire Blvd Los Angeles CA 90017 Tel (213) 680-0140

FIRESTONE, JACOB, b. Wasserberg, Germany, Mar. 14, 1947; B.A. with highest honors, San Diego State U., 1970; J.D., U. Calif., 1973. Admitted to Calif. bar, 1973, U.S. Tax Ct. bar; law clk. to Fed. Magistrate So. Dist. Calif., 1972-73; legal researcher to acting pres. San Diego State U., 1973; individual practice law, San Diego, 1974-75; partner firm Campbell & Firestone, San Diego, 1975—. Mem. Am. Bar. Assn., Calif., Am. trial lawyers assns., Phi Kappa Phi. Office: 4060 Oakcrest Dr San Diego CA 92105 Tel (714) 282-3306

FIRMAGE, EDWIN BROWN, b. Provo, Utah, Oct. 1, 1935; B.S. summa cum laude, Brigham Young U., 1960, M.S. in History, 1962; J.D. (Nat. Honors scholar), U. Chgo., 1963, LL.M., 1964, J.S.D., 1964. Admitted to Utah bar, 1963, U.S. Supreme Ct. bar, 1966; prof. law. U. Mo., 1964-65, U. Utah, 1966—; White House fellow, mem. staff Vice-Pres. H.H. Humphrey, Washington, 1965-66. Internat. Affairs fellow Council of Fgn. Relations, Geneva, Switzerland, 1970-71; UN vis. scholar, N.Y.C., 1970-71; fellow in law and humanities Harvard, 1974-75. Mem. Am., Utah bar assns., White House Fellows Assn., Am. Judicature Soc., Am. Soc. Internat. Law, Council on Fgn. Relations. Contbr. chpts. to International Law of Civil War, 1971, Law and Civil War in the Modern World, 1974, The Vietnam War and International Law, 1976; contbr. articles in field to law jours. Home: 2171 Arbor Ln Salt Lake City UT 84117 Office: Coll Law Univ Utah Salt Lake City UT 84112 Tel (801) 581-7819

FIRST, HARRY, b. Phila., Jan. 17, 1945; B.A. cum laude with distinction, U. Pa., 1966, J.D., cum laude, 1969. Admitted to Pa. bar, 1969; law clk. to Justice Samuel J. Roberts, Supreme Ct. Pa., 1969-70; atty. Antitrust div. U.S. Dept. Justice Washington, 1970-72; asst. prof. Coll. Law Univ. Toledo, 1972—; vis. asso. prof. Law Sch. N.Y. U., 1976—. Mem. Order of Coif, Phi Beta Kappa. Contbr. articles to legal periodicals. Home: 3422 Pelham Rd Toledo OH 43606 Office: Department Law University Toledo Toledo OH 43606 Tel (419) 537-2960

FIRTH, PETER ALAN, b. Rockville Center, N.Y., Jan. 7, 1943; A.B. in Econs., Georgetown U., 1964; LL.B., Albany Law Sch., 1967. Admitted to N.Y. bar, 1967; partner firm LaPann, Reardon, Fitzgerald & Firth, Glen Falls, N.Y., 1967—; asst. dist. atty. Warren County (N.Y.), 1973-74. Mem. Am., N.Y., Warren County bar assns., Am. Arbitration Assn. (panel). Mem. Albany Law Rev., 1966-67. Office: 55 Elm St Glen Falls NY 12801 Tel (518) 792-5894

FISANICK, VASIL, b. Barnesboro, Pa., Jan. 30, 1925; student St. Francis Coll., 1945-48; LL.B., J.D., U. Richmond, 1950; LL.M., Duke, 1951. Admitted to Va. bar, 1950, Pa. bar, 1951, Fed. bar, 1956; mem. firm Fisanick & Solomon, Ebensburg, Pa. and Barnesboro, Pa., 1951—; spl. asst. dep. atty. gen., Harrisburg, Pa., 1958-64; adminstrv. law judge hearing examiner Pa. Labor Relations Bd., 1974-76. Pres., Miners Hosp. of No. Cambria, 1973-75, Pa. Sch. Bd. Solicitors Assn., 1977, Barnesboro Lions Club, 1974. Mem. Am., Pa. bar assns., Am., Pa. trial lawyers assns. Recipient Chrostwaite award, Pa. Assn. of Boroughs, 1952, McNeil Law Soc. award, 1949, Delta Theta Phi Scholarship award, 1950, Barnesboro Pub. Library Civic award, 1974. Home and Office: 1111 Philadelphia Ave Barnesboro PA 15714 Tel (814) 948-9290

FISCH, JOSEPH, b. N.Y.C., Apr. 7, 1939; B.A. in History, Tufts U., 1960; J.D., N.Y.U., 1963, LL.M., 1969. Admitted to N.J. bar, 1964, U.S. Dist. Ct. bar, 1964, U.S. Supreme Ct. bar, 1969; law clk. to judge of Hudson County Ct., Jersey City, 1963-64; asso. firm Hannoch, Weisman, Stern & Besser, Newark, 1964-65, Blume & Kalb, Newark, 1965-66; individual practice law, Somerset, N.J., 1966—; co-adj. asst. prof. bus. law Rutgers U., New Brunswick, N.J., 1967—. Pres. Franklin Housing and Neighborhood Devel. Corp., 1975—; trustee Temple Beth El, Somerset, 1970-72. Mem. Am., N.J., Somerset County bar assns., Am. Arbitration Assn., Am. Trial Lawyers Assn., Franklin Township Jaycees (past pres., dir., chmn. bd.). Office: 812 Hamilton St Somerset NJ 08873 Tel (201) 846-2039

FISCH, RALPH, b. Havana, Cuba, July 4, 1937; B.B.A., U. Miami, 1958, J.D., 1962. Admitted to Fla. bar, 1962; asso. firm Ammerman & Landy, Miami, Fla., 1962-65; partner firm Tobin & Fisch, Miami, 1965—; sr. judge Municipal Ct., Medley, Dade County, Fla., 1967-71. Pres., Moshe Dyan br. Farband Labor Zionist Orgn.; pres. B'nai Israel and Greater Miami Youth Synagogue. Mem. Fla. Bar. (internat. law com.), Am. Arbitration Assn. Recipient Scroll of Friendship, City of Miami, 1970; certificate Honor award Sta. WQBA, Miami, 1968; Merit award Cuban Liceum, 1970. Office: 825 S Bayshore Dr Miami FL 33131 Tel (305) 371-4544

FISCHBACH, DONALD RICHARD, b. Ventura, Calif., Sept. 26, 1947; B.S. with honors, Calif. State Poly. Coll., 1969; J.D., U. Calif. Hastings Coll. Law, San Francisco, 1972. Admitted to Calif. bar, 1972; asso. firm Baker, Manock & Jensen, Fresno, Calif., 1972-75, partner, 1975—. Mem. Fresno County (pres. 1974-75, dir. 1974—), Calif. (dir. young lawyers assn. 1976—) barristers assns., Am., Fresno County (dir. 1974-75) bar assns. Contbr. articles to legal jours. Home: 6470 N Flora St Fresno CA 93710 Office: 6th floor Security Bank Bldg Fresno CA 93721 Tel (209) 442-0550

FISCHBEIN, CARL, b. N.Y.C., Aug. 26, 1921; B.S. in Accounting, U. Okla., 1943, J.D., 1948. Admitted to Okla. bar, 1949; revenue agt. IRS, 1948-51; partner Sartain Fischbein & Co., C.P.A.'s, Tulsa, 1951—. Mem. Gov's. Adv. Com. on Advalorem Tax, 1966-67; bd. dirs. Arthritis Found., Congregation B'nai Emunah; mem. Tulsa C. of C. C.P.A., Okla. Mem. Okla., Tulsa County bar assns., Am. Inst. C.P.A.'s, Okla., Ark., Tulsa, Socs. C.P.A.'s, Am. Assn. Atty. C.P.A.'s, Tulsa Estate Planning Forum (pres. 1975-76). Office: 1710 Fourth Nat Bank Bldg Tulsa OK 74119 Tel (918) 583-2111

FISCHER, BARRY ROBERT, b. Albany, N.Y., Mar. 4, 1942; A.B., Princeton, 1964; J.D., Albany, 1967. Admitted to N.Y. State bar, 1967, U.S. Supreme Ct. bar, 1976; asso. firm O'Connel & Aronowitz, Albany, 1967-69, partner, 1969-72, mem., 1972—; spl. counsel Asso. Industries, N.Y., 1967-70; village atty. Voorheesville, N.Y., 1970-71. Mem. Am., N.Y. State, Albany County bar assns., Captial Dist. Trial Lawyers Assn. Home: 7 South Helderberg Parkway Slingerlands NY 12159 Office: 100 State St Albany NY 12207 Tel (518) 462-5601

FISCHER, DAVID ARNOLD, b. St. Louis, May 10, 1943; A.A., Lincoln (Ill.) Coll., 1963; A.B., U. Mo., Columbia, 1965, J.D., 1968. Admitted to Mo. bar, 1968; with JAGC, U.S. Army, 1968-72; asst. prof. law U. Mo., Columbia, 1972-76, asso. prof., 1976. Home: 702 Marion Dr Columbia MO 65201 Office: 114 Tate Hall Sch of Law U Mo Columbia MO 65201 Tel (314) 882-2727

FISCHER, PAUL DAVID, b. Chgo., Feb. 17, 1943; B.B.A., Loyola U., Chgo., 1966, J.D., 1967. Mem. staff Arthur Andersen & Co., Chgo., 1967-69; admitted to Ill. bar, 1968, U.S. Dist. Ct. for No. Dist. Ill. bar, 1969, U.S. Ct. Appeals bar, 1972, U.S. Supreme Ct. bar, 1972; partner firm Crane & Kravets, Chgo., 1976—; hearing officer Ill. Pollution Control Bd., 1973—. Mem. Ill. State, Chgo. bar assns. Home: 1114 S Wesley St Oak Park IL 60304 Office: 100 W Monroe St Chicago IL 60603 Tel (312) 236-0788

FISCHER, RICHARD LAWRENCE, b. Pitts., Oct. 22, 1936; A.B. in Econs., U. Pitts., 1958, J.D., 1961; LL.M., Georgetown U., 1965. Admitted to Pa. bar, 1963; D.C. bar, 1963; atty. Aluminum Co. of Am., Pitts., 1965-69, gen. atty., 1969-72, internat. counsel, 1973-74, asst. gen. counsel, 1974—; spl. agt. FBI, 1961-65; supervising dir. P. T. Alcoa Minerals of Indonesia, 1969—. Mem. Pa., Am., Allegheny County, Internat. Inter-Am. bar assns., Internat. Fiscal Assn., Am. Soc. Internat. Law, World Assn. Lawyers. Contbr. articles to profl. jours. Office: 1501 Alcoa Bldg Pittsburgh PA 15219 Tel (412) 553-4741

FISCHER, ROBERT FREDERICK, b. Balt., Feb. 29, 1932; B.A., U. Md., 1954; LL.B., U. Balt., 1961. Admitted to Md. bar, 1961; partner Pierson & Pierson, Balt., 1962-69; individual practice law, Ellicott City, Md., 1969-73; county solicitor, Howard County, Md., 1972-73; judge Dist. Ct. Md., 1973—. Bd. dirs. Howard County Gen. Hosp., 1974—. Mem., Am. Judicature Soc., Md., Howard County bar assns. Home: 8605 Chapelview Rd Ellicott City MD 21043 Office: Court House Ellicott City MD 21043 Tel (301) 465-7664

FISCHER, ROGER MAX, b. Erie, Pa., June 28, 1934; B.A., Pa. State U., 1955; J.D., U. Pitts., 1958. Admitted to Pa. bar, 1958, U.S. Dist. Ct. bar, 1958; partner firm Kahn, D'Ambrosio & Fischer, Erie, 1958-63, firm Gifford, Lay, Fischer & Kennedy, Erie, 1963-68, Lund, Fischer, Kennedy & Schleicher, Erie, 1968—; chief atty. Erie Legal Aid Soc., 1961-63; register of wills Erie County, Pa., 1964—. Chmn. Erie County Democratic Com., 1968—; bd. incorporators Legal Services Northwestern Pa., 1971-74. Mem. Am., Pa., Erie County bar assns., Am. Judicature Soc. Home: 353 E 41st St Erie PA 16504 Office: 332 E 6th St Erie PA 16507 Tel (814) 452-2209

FISCHER, STANLEY HENRY, b. N.Y.C., July 29, 1943; B.A., Queens Coll., 1964; J.D., N.Y. U., 1967. Admitted to N.Y. bar, 1968, U.S. Supreme Ct. bar, 1971; sr. partner firm Fischer and Burstein, N.Y.C., 1976—; sec. INS of Queens. Mem. Queens Bar Assn., Brandeis Assn., Moot Ct. Justices Assn. Office: 565 Fifth Ave New York City NY 10017 Tel (212) 490-1870

FISCHMAN, BERNARD DAVID, b. N.Y.C., Feb. 26, 1915; LL.B., N.Y.U., 1936. Admitted to N.Y. State bar, 1937; sr. partner firm Shea, Gould, Climenko & Casey, N.Y.C., 1950—. Office: 330 Madison Ave New York City NY 10017 Tel (212) 661-3200

FISH, ALLEN JOE, b. Los Angeles, Nov. 12, 1942; A.B. magna cum laude, Yale U., 1965, LL.B., 1968. Admitted to Tex. bar, 1968, U.S. Supreme Ct. bar, 1976; asso. firm McKenzie & Baer, Dallas, 1968—. Mem. Dallas, Tex., Am. bar assns. Office: 2222 LTV Tower Dallas TX 75201 Tel (214) 742-1861

FISH, BURTON LEROY, b. Erie, Pa., Feb. 15, 1940; B.A., Allegheny Coll., 1962; J.D., U. Pa., 1965. Admitted to Pa. bar, 1966; individual practice law, Erie, 1967—; asso. Erie Bd. Realtors. Mem. Am., Pa., Erie County bar assns., Pa. Trial Lawyers Assn. Sears Roebuck Nat. Merit scholar, 1958-62. Tel (814) 452-3311

FISH, EUGENE CHARLES, b. Phila., Jan. 2, 1910; B.S. in Economics, U. Pa., 1931, J.D., 1934. Admitted to Pa. bar, 1937; mng. sr. partner firm Romeika, Fish & Scheckter, Phila., 1941—; mng. sr. partner Tax Assos., Phila., 1939—; chmn. Eastern Foundry Co., Boyertown, Pa., 1949—, also dir.; pres. Peerless Industries, Inc., Boyertown, 1949—, also dir.; dir. Hull Corp., Alex C. Fergusson Co. Past pres. Jenkintown Sch. Bd., YMCA; pres. Washington Crossing Found.; trustee Lebanon Valley Coll.; v.p. bd. trustees Jenkintown Methodist Ch. Home: Washington Ln and Wyncote Rd Jenkintown PA 19046 Office: 215 S Broad St Philadelphia PA 19107 Tel (215) KI5-4592

FISH, HELEN MARY, b. Newton, Mass., July 18, 1912; LL.B., Northeastern U., 1935, LL.M., 1938, J.D., 1936; postgrad. Boston U., 1940. Admitted to Mass. bar, 1936, U.S. 1st Circuit Ct. Appeals, 1948; individual practice law, Boston, 1942-76, Roslindale, Mass., 1976—. Sec. Guild of Our Lady of Ransom, law appeals and rehab. prisoners, Walpole, Mass., 1946—; bd. dirs. Cath. Charitable Bur., 1950—. Mem. Mass., Norfolk bar assns., Mass. Assn. Women Lawyers. Home and office: 817 South St Roslindale MA 02131 Tel (617) 325-4691

FISH, JEROME SULLIVAN, b. St. Louis, Mo., July 9, 1927; B.A., Berea Coll., 1951; LL.B., George Washington U., 1955. Admitted to Ky. bar, 1956; practice law, Berea, Ky. Mem. Am., Ky. bar assns. Home: 329B Center St Berea KY 40403 Office: 122 Main St Berea KY 40403 Tel (606) 986-8157

FISHBURN, JOHN CHARLES, b. Muscatine, Iowa, Nov. 9, 1918; B.A., U. Iowa, 1940, J.D., 1947. Admitted to Iowa bar, 1947; partner firm Fishburn & Fishburn, Muscatine, 1947—; asst. atty. Muscatine County, 1970-71, zoning adminstr., 1970-71. Mem. Iowa, Muscatine County bar assns., Phi Beta Kappa. Bd. editors Iowa Law Rev., 1947. Home: 716 Mulberry Ave Muscatine IA 52761 Office: 221 Med Arts Bldg Muscatine IA 52761 Tel (319) 263-7861

FISHBURNE, BENJAMIN POSTELL, III, b. S. Bend, Ind., Nov. 14, 1943; B.A. cum laude, U. Notre Dame, 1965; LL.B., U. Va., 1968. Admitted to Va. bar, 1968, D.C. bar, 1971; served with JAGC, U.S. Army, 1968-72; asso. firm Surrey, Karasik and Morse, Washington, 1968, 1972-75, partner, 1976—. Mem. Am. Bar Assn., Am. Soc. Internat. Law, Order of Coif. Home: 3807 Gramercy St NW Washington DC 20016 Office: 1156 NW 15th St Washington DC 20005 Tel (202) 331-4014

FISHEL, GLADYS LEECH, b. Montgomery, Ala., Jan. 18, 1931; B.A., George Washington U., 1954, M.A., 1956, J.D., 1965. Admitted to D.C. bar, 1965, Va. bar, 1965; staff atty. Congresswoman Martha Griffiths of Mich., Washington, 1965; individual practice law, Arlington, Va., 1965—; adult edn. tchr. Arlington County Schs. Mem. Washington Women's (pres. 1974), Arlington County, D.C., D.C. Unified bar assns., No. Va. Estate Planning Council, Kappa Beta Pi. Home: 3819 N Albemarle St Arlington VA 22207 Office: 2060 N 14th St Court House Sq Arlington VA 22201 Tel (703) 522-5634

FISHEL, GRACE JOHNSON, b. Concordia, Kans., Dec. 21, 1942; B.A., U. Kans., 1965; M.S., Northwestern U., 1966; J.D., U. Mich., 1969. Admitted to Ill. bar, 1970, U.S. Patent bar, 1971, Mo. bar, 1973; atty. Quaker Oats Co., Barrington, Ill., 1969-73; asso. firm Haverstock & Heywood, St. Louis, 1973-74; partner firm Pope & Fishel, St. Louis, 1974—. Mem. Am., Ill., Mo. bar assns., Bar Assn. Met. St. Louis., Phi Beta Kappa. Home: 558 Bonhomme Forest St Olivette MO 63132 Office: 818 Olive St Saint Louis MO 63101 Tel (314) 241-8465

FISHER, A. B., b. Johnson City, Tenn., May 28, 1907; LL.B., E. Tenn. Law Sch. Admitted to Tenn. bar, 1945; individual practice law, Johnson City. Address: 429 W Maple St Johnson City TN 37601 Tel (615) 926-2249

FISHER, ADAM, JR., b. Columbus, Ga., Dec. 10, 1940; B.S. in Chem. Engring., Purdue U., 1962; J.D., U. S.C., 1969. Admitted to S.C. bar, 1969; mem. various firms, 1969-75; individual practice law, Greenville, S.C., 1975—; asst. municipal judge City of Greenville, 1973-76; municipal judge City of Fountaininn, 1975—, City of Travelers Rest, 1976—; city prosecutor City of Mauldin, 1974—. Mem. Am., S.C., Greenville bar assns. Home: 103 Lionel Ct Simpsonville SC 29681 Office: 109 E North St Greenville SC 29603 Tel (801) 271-2656

FISHER, BENJAMIN CHATBURN, b. Coos Bay, Oreg., Feb. 6, 1923; A.B. with highest honors, U. Ill., 1948; J.D. magna cum laude, Harvard U., 1951. Admitted to D.C. bar, 1951; law clk. to Judge Learned Hand, 2d circuit, N.Y.C., 1951-52; mem. firm Fisher, Wayland, Southmayd & Cooper, Washington, 1952—. Mem. Audit Hearing Bd., U.S. Office Edn., 1973—; mem. Adminstrv. Conf. U.S., 1970-76; chmn. bd. dirs. Center Adminstrv. Justice, Washington, 1972—; gen. counsel Commn. Population Growth and the Am. Future, 1970-72. Mem. Am. (chmn. adminstrv. law sect. 1968-69, mem. ho. of dels. 1970-72, 73-75), Fed. Communications (pres. 1967-68), D.C. bar assns., Phi Beta Kappa, Phi Kappa Phi. Contbr. legal articles to legal jours. Home: 5118 Cammack Dr Washington DC 20016 Office: 1100 Connecticut Ave NW Washington DC 20036 Tel (202) 659-3494

FISHER, CHARLES EDWARD, b. Mt. Carmel, Ill., Dec. 5, 1943; B.S. in Accounting, U. Ill., 1962, J.D., 1969. Admitted to Ill. bar, 1969; nat. sales counsel Kemper Fin. Services, Inc.; revenue litigation and gen. law divs. Office of Ill. Atty. Gen., Chgo., 1969-72; supr. Investors Services, Inc., Chgo., 1972—. Mem. Am., Ill. bar assns., Chgo Assn. Fin. Planners. Home: 5 S661 Mockingbird Ct Naperville IL 60540 Office: 120 S LaSalle St Chicago IL 60603 Tel (312) 346-3223

FISHER, CHARLES OSBORNE, JR., b. Oceanport, N.J., Sept. 1, 1943; A.B., Loyola Coll., Balt., 1965; J.D., U. Md., Balt., 1969. Admitted to Md. bar, 1969; law clk. to chief judge Supreme Bench Balt. City, 1968-69; asst. state's atty., Balt., 1969-72; mem. firm. Walsh, Fisher & Gilmore, Westminster, Md., 1972—. Bd. dirs. Carroll County Heart Assn., 1975—, Carroll County Pastoral Counseling Service, 1974—; vice chmn. Democratic Central Com. Carroll County, 1974—. Mem. Am., Md., Carroll County bar assns., Md. Dist. Attys. Assn. Home: 137 E Green St Westminster MD 21157 Office: 179 E Main St Westminster MD 21157 Tel (301) 848-9200

FISHER, DAVID LEWIS, b. Chgo., Dec. 27, 1929; B.S., U. Ill., 1950; J.D., Northwestern U., 1953. Admitted to Ill. bar, 1953; partner firm Prince, Schoenberg, Fisher & Newman, and predecessors, Chgo., 1953—; exec. v.p. Elec. Industry Show Corp., Chgo., 1974—; exec. dir. Elec. Industries Assn., distbr. products div. central region, Chgo., 1974—. Chmn. elec. and chem. group Chgo. Crusade of Mercy, 1959-60; trustee North Shore Congregation Israel, 1972—. Mem. Am., Ill., Chgo. bar assns. Home: 445 Lincoln Ave Glencoe IL 60022 Office: Suite 1600 222 S Riverside Plaza Chicago IL 60606 Tel (312) 648-1600

FISHER, EDWARD JOSEPH, b. Ft. Leavenworth, Kans., Apr. 22, 1943; B.A., So. Ill. U., 1967; J.D., John Marshall Sch. Law, Chgo., 1971. Admitted to Ill. bar, 1971, U.S. Dist. Ct. bar, 1971; partner firm Nehrt, Sachtleben & Fisher, Chester, Ill., Red Bud, Ill., 1971—; pub. defender Randolph County, Ill., 1973-74. Mem. Am., Ill., Randolph County bar assns., Ill. Trial Lawyers' Assn., Chester C. of C. (dir. 1976-79). Home: 1158 George St Chester IL 62233 Office: Herschbach Bldg Chester IL 62233 Tel (618) 826-5021

FISHER, FRED, b. Phila., June 26, 1929; B.S. in Elec. Engring., Drexel Inst. Tech., 1952; J.D. with honors, George Washington U., 1956. Admitted to D.C. bar, 1956, Pa. bar, 1960; mem. patent staff RCA, Washington, D.C., 1952-56, Camden, N.J., 1956-58; patent atty. Univac Div. Sperry Rand Corp., Blue Bell, Pa., 1958-66; patent atty. Western Electric Co., Inc., Allentown, Pa., 1966-70; individual practice law, Allentown, 1970—; patent counsel Bunker Ramo Corp., Oak Brook, Ill., 1975-76; elec. engr. Philco Corp., Phila., 1952-53. Sch. dir. Salisbury (Pa.) Twp., 1969-75; mem. joint operating com. Lehigh County Area Vocat. Tech. Sch., 1969-75. Mem. Am., Phila. patent law assns., Am., Pa., Lehigh County bar assns., IEEE. Home: 2910 Meadowbrook Circle N Allentown PA 18103 Office: 530 Hamilton St Allentown PA 18101 Tel (215) 432-4620

FISHER, GARRY VERNON, b. Butte, Mont., Aug. 11, 1926; B.A., U. Mont., 1951, J.D., 1951. Admitted to Mont. bar, 1951, U.S. Ct. Claims bar, 1952; trial atty. U.S. Dept. Justice, Washington, 1951-53; adminstrv. law judge, adminstrv. counsel U.S. Dept. Interior, Billings, Mont., 1954—. Mem. Mont. Bar Assn. Home: 2502 Burlington St Billings MT 59102 Office: Room 3319 316 N 26th St Billings MT 59101 Tel (406) 657-6663

FISHER, GERARD NATHAN, b. Seattle, Mar. 12, 1922; B.S. in Laws, U. Wash., 1949, J.D., 1950. Admitted to Wash. bar, 1950; asso. firm Garland & Garland, Bremerton, 1950-52; individual practice law, 1952-64; partner firm Gerard N. Fisher & Lawrence Soriano, Bremerton, 1964-67; city atty. City of Bremerton, 1964-67; judge Kitsap County (Wash.) Dist. Ct., 1967—; mem. Wash. State Jud. Council. Mem. Am., Wash. State, Kitsap County (pres. 1958) bar assns., Wash. State Magistrates Assn. (pres. 1973). Home: Star Route 1 POB 175 Seabeck WA 98380 Office: Kitsap County Courthouse 614 Division St Port Orchard WA 98380 Tel (206) 876-7144

FISHER, HARRY NOBLE DEFOLDESSY, b. Grand Forks, N.D., June 15, 1931; A.B. with honors, U. Chgo., 1950, J.D., 1953. Admitted to Iowa bar, 1953, Mo. and Fed. bars, 1957; clk. legal dept. Marathon Oil Co., Findlay, Ohio, 1952; served with JAGC, U.S. Air Force, 1953-57; asso. firm Stolar, Kuhlmann & Meredith, St. Louis, 1957-59; account exec. Lemoine Skinner, Jr., Pub. Relations, Inc., 1959-63; pub. relations dir. Stemmler, Fisher & Assos., St. Louis, 1963—; dir. Archway Publs., Inc., Rutledge Advt. Co.; tchr. bus. law So. Ill. U., 1963. Pub. relations dir. U.S. Youth Games, 1968; program coordinator Miss. River Tricentennial Com. Key 73 Easter Sunrise Music Festival. Mem. Bar Assn. St. Louis, Pub. Relations Soc. Am., Mo. Bar Assn. Author: Advice to Divers and Other Poems, Songs and Hymns, 1975; North Slope and Other Poems, 1976; contbr. to The New Style in Election Campaigns (ed. Agranoff), 1972, 76; contbr. articles to mags.; lyricist hymns and anthems. Home: 6 Godwin Ln Saint Louis MO 63124 Office: 8007 Clayton Rd Saint Louis MO 63117 Tel (314) 721-3556

FISHER, HERBERT K., b. Uniontown, Pa., Dec. 29, 1927; B.A., N.Y. U., 1950; LL.B., Temple U., 1953. Admitted to Pa. bar, 1953; partner firm Brown, Ocks & Fisher, Phila., 1965—. Mem. Phila. Bar Assn. Home: Center City One Juniper and Spruce Sts Apt 3003 Philadelphia PA 19107 Office: 1822 Spruce St Philadelphia PA 19103 Tel (215) KI6-7100

FISHER, JAMES H., b. South Bend, Ind., Sept. 5, 1934; B.S., U. Notre Dame, 1956; LL.D., Fordham U., 1962. Admitted to N.Y. bar, 1962; asso. firm Connelly & Connelly, 1963-65; asst. district atty. Ulster County, 1965-71; pres. James H. Fisher, P.C., Kingston, N.Y., 1973—; individual practice law Kingston, N.Y., 1963—; spl. dep. atty. gen., 1965-70, counsel agrl. com. N.Y. State Senate, 1974—. Mem. Ulster County, N.Y. State, Am. bar assns., N.Y. State Trial Lawyers Assn. Home: 10 Laurel Kingston NY 12401 Office: 261 Fair Kingston NY 12401 Tel (914) 338-1120

FISHER, JOE JEFFERSON, b. Bland Lake, Tex., Apr. 16, 1910; student Stephen F. Austin Coll., 1929; LL.B., U. Tex., 1936. Admitted to Tex. bar, 1936; county atty. San Augustine County, 1936-39; dist. atty. 1st Jud. Dist. Tex., 1939-46; practice law, Jasper, Tex., 1946-57; dist. judge 1st Jud. Dist. Tex., 1957-59; U.S. dist. judge for Eastern Dist. Tex., 1959-67, chief judge, 1967—. Trustee, Trinity United Methodist Ch., Beaumont, Schlesingers Geriatric Center; dist. gov., bd. dirs. Lions Internat., mem. exec. bd., mem. Tex. Lions Hall of Fame; pres. Tex. Gulf. Hist. Soc.; mem. adv. bd. Southwestern U. St. Elizabeth Hosp. Mem. Am. (chmn. jud. sect. 1957), 1st Jud. (pres. 1956), Tex. bar assns., Am. Judicature Soc., Ex-Students Assn. U. Tex. and Stephen F. Austin State U. (Hall of Fame), E.Tex., Jasper and Beaumont chambers commerce, Sons Republic of Tex., Delta Kappa Epsilon. Recipient Silver Beaver award Boy Scouts Am., 1954. Home: 130 C Caldwood St Beaumont TX 77707 Office: PO Box 88 Beaumont TX 77704 Tel (713) 838-0271

FISHER, LARRY ROBERT, b. Marion, Ind., Sept. 29, 1939; B.S. with distinction, Ind. U., 1965, J.D., 1968. Admitted to Ind. bar, 1968, U.S. Supreme Ct. bar, 1973; asso. firm Stuart, Branigin, Ricks & Schilling, Lafayette, Ind., 1968-73, partner 1973—. Mem. Am., Ind. State, Tippecanoe County bar assns. Staff Ind. Law Jour., 1967-68. Office: 8th floor The Life Bldg Lafayette IN 47902 Tel (317) 423-1561

FISHER, LAWRENCE LEE, b. Mt. Sterling, Ohio, Jan. 4, 1941; student U. Bonn, Ger., 1962-63; B.S., Ohio State U., 1964, J.D., Harvard U., 1967. Admitted to Ohio bar, 1967; asso. firm Vorys, Sater, Seymour & Pease, Columbus, Ohio, 1967-74, partner, 1974—. Founding trustee Columbus Assn. Performing Arts, 1969—; pres. Jefferson Center Assn., 1975—. Mem. Am., Columbus (recipient community service award 1976-77), Ohio State (vice chmn. bd. govs. probate and trust law sect. 1976) bar assns. Recipient Outstanding Young Man award Columbus Jaycees, 1973. Home: 495 Tucker Dr Worthington OH 43085 Office: 52 E Gay St Columbus OH 43215 Tel (614) 464-6283

FISHER, LILLIAN S., b. N.Y.C., June 18, 1921; B.S., Bklyn. Coll., 1942; J.D., U. Airz., 1963. Admitted to Ariz. bar, 1963, U.S. Supreme Ct. bar, 1975; individual practice law, Tucson, 1963-74; judge Pima County (Ariz.) Superior Ct., Tucson, 1975—; former counsel Tucson Bot. Gardens. Former pres. Cerebral Palsy Found. Mem. Ariz., Pima County bar assns., World Peace Through Law. Home: Rt 8 Box 582 Tucson AZ 85710 Tel (602) 792-8241

FISHER, LLOYD EDISON, JR., b. Medina, Ohio, Oct. 23, 1923; B.S. in Bus. Adminstrn., Ohio State U., 1947, J.D. cum laude, 1949. Admitted to Ohio bar, 1950; mem. gen. hearing bd. Ohio Dept. Taxation, 1951-52; trust officer The Huntington Nat. Bank of Columbia, 1953-61; mem. firm Alexander, Ebinger, Holschuh, Fisher & McAlister, Columbus, 1961—; adj. prof. Ohio State U. Coll. Law, 1967-69. Mem. Am., Ohio State, Columbus bar assns. Past editor Ohio State U. Law Jour. Home: 174 DeSantis Dr Columbus OH 43214 Office: 17 S High St Columbus OH 43215 Tel (614) 221-6345

FISHER, LOUIS JOSEPH, JR., b. High Point, N.C., 1935; B.A., U. N.C., 1957, J.D. with hons., 1960. Admitted to N.C. bar, 1960; capt. JAGC, U.S. Air Force, 1960-63; mem. firm Fisher, Fisher & McAllister, High Point, N.C., 1963—. Chmn. Civil Service Commn., 1972-76, High Point (N.C.) Bd. Alcoholic Beverage Control, 1976—. Fellow Internat. Soc. Barristers; mem. Assn. Trial Lawyers Am., Am., N.C. (councilor bd. govs., pres. High Point), Judicial (pres. 18th dist.) bar assns., Phi Beta Kappa. Author: Constitutional Law, Police Power,

1959; asso. editor N.C. Law Review, 1959-60. Home: 1100 Brookwood St High Point NC 27260 Office: Suite 800 1st Citizens Bank Plaza High Point NC 27262

FISHER, MELVILLE, b. Albany, N.Y., Sept. 22, 1911; student Union Coll., Schenectady, 1929-30, 31-32, Ohio State U., 1930-31; LL.B., Albany Law Sch., 1935. Admitted to N.Y. bar, 1936, U.S. Supreme Ct. bar, 1937; partner firm Freedman & Fisher, Albany, N.Y., 1938-43, Tepedino and Fisher, Albany, 1947-73, Fisher and Safranko, Albany, 1973—. Mem. N.Y. State, Capital Dist. trial lawyers assns., Am., N.Y. State, Albany County (N.Y.) bar assns. Office: 74 State St Albany NY 12207 Tel (518) 465-1421

FISHER, MITCHELL SALEM, b. Hoboken, N.J., Apr. 5, 1903; A.B., N.Y. U., 1923; M.A., Columbia, 1927, LL.B. (James Beck Hon. fellow), 1933, Ph.D., 1946. Admitted to N.Y. bar, 1933, U.S. Supreme Ct. bar, 1942; asso. firm Guggenheimer & Untermyer, N.Y.C., 1933-45; individual practice law, N.Y.C., 1945-68; sr. partner firm Mitchell Salem Fisher & Kemper, and predecessors, N.Y.C., 1968—; gen. counsel N.Y. Bd. Rabbis, 1952—; lectr. in field. Mem. Assn. Bar City N.Y. (chmn. city ct. com. 1959), N.Y. State Bar Assn. (chmn. sect. family law 1970-71, Spl. award 1971), Am. Bar Assn., Am. Acad. Matrimonial Lawyers (pres. N.Y. State chpt. 1971-73, nat. gov. 1974—, Spl. award of N.Y. State chpt. 1973). Recipient Ordronaux prize Columbia, 1933, Spl. award on lectureship Practising Law Inst., 1967. Author: Robert Boyle-Devout Naturalist, 1929; contbr. articles to legal jours. Home: 1050 Park Ave New York City NY 10028 Office: 122 E 42d St New York City NY 10017 Tel (212) 661-6750

FISHER, MORTON POE, JR., b. Balt., Aug. 17, 1936; A.B., Dartmouth, 1958; LL.B., Yale, 1961. Admitted to Md. bar, 1961; law clk. chief judge U.S. Dist. Ct. Dist. Md., 1961-62; asso. firm Piper & Marbury, Balt., 1962-68; asso. gen. counsel The Rouse Co., Columbia, Md., 1968-73; partner firm Frank, Bernstein, Conaway & Goldman, Balt., 1973—; instr. U Md. Sch. Law, 1975-76; instr. ALI-ABA-CLE-TV series, Washington, 1973. Mem. Am. Law Inst., Am., Md. State, Balt. City bar assns. Contbr. articles to legal jours. Home: 1325 Harden Ln Pikesville MD 21208 Office: 1300 Mercantile Bank and Trust Bldg 2 Hopkins Plaza Baltimore MD 21201 Tel (301) 547-0590

FISHER, ROBERT MORTON, b. St. Paul, Oct. 15, 1938; A.B., Harvard, 1960, J.D., 1963; Ph. D., London Sch. Econs. and Polit. Sci. U. London, 1967. Admitted to Minn. bar, 1963, Calif. bar, 1970; prof. criminology U. Calif. at Berkeley, 1965-71; staff atty. Contra Costa Legal Services Found., 1971; pres. John F. Kennedy U., Orinda, Calif., 1974—; partner firm Fisher, Bernstein, & Barde, Lafayette and Oakland, Calif., 1974—. Mayor, councilman City Lafayette, 1968-76; chmn. Local Agency Formation Commn., 1975, Criminal Justice Agy., 1970-75. Mem. Am., British socs. criminology, Minn., Calif., Am. bar assns. Contbr. articles to legal jours. Home: 3932 N Peardale Dr Lafayette CA 94549 Office: John F Kennedy U Orinda CA 94563 Tel (415) 254-0200

FISHER, SOLOMON, b. Phila., Apr. 4, 1935; B.S., Temple U., 1957, J.D., 1960. Admitted to Pa. bar, 1960, D.C. bar, 1964, U.S. Supreme Ct. bar, 1964; trial atty. tax div. Dept. Justice, Washington, 1960-64; asso. firm Dilworth, Paxson, Kalish & Levy, Phila., 1964-68, partner, 1968—; lectr. grad. program Temple U. Sch. Law, 1976—. Pres. Phila. chpt. Am. Jewish Com., 1970-72, chmn., 1972-74, nat. bd. govs., 1976—; v.p. Phila. Jewish Community Relations Council, 1975—; trustee Fedn. Jewish Agys. of Greater Phila., 1976—. Mem. Am., Fed., Pa., D.C., Phila. (sec.-treas. tax sect.) bar assns. Office: 2600 Fidelity Bldg 123 S Broad St Philadelphia PA 19109 Tel (215) KI 6-3000

FISHER, STANLEY MILTON, b. Mansfield, Ohio, Dec. 23, 1921; J.D., Wayne State U., 1949. Admitted to Mich. bar, 1949; with Abstract and Title Guaranty Co., Detroit, 1940-51; individual practice law, Lincoln Park, Mich., 1951-55; exec. v.p. Am. Title Ins. Co., Detroit and Miami, 1955-74. Mem. Am., Detroit bar assns., State Bar Mich. Home: 68 Greenbrair Ln Grossee Pointe Shores MI 48236 Office: 17150 Kercheval Ave Grosse Pointe MI 48230 Tel (313) 882-2644

FISHGOLD, HERBERT, b. N.Y.C., May 28, 1941; B.A., City Coll. N.Y., 1963; LL.B., Yale U., 1966; LL.M., Sydney (Australia) U., 1970. Admitted to N.Y. bar, 1967, D.C. bar, 1975; atty. NLRB, Office Gen. Counsel, Appellate Ct. Br., Washington, 1967-71; counsel for labor relations Office of Solicitor, U.S. Dept. Labor, Washington, 1971-73; gen. counsel Fed. Mediation and Conciliation Service, Washington, 1973—. Mem. Am., Fed. bar assns., Phi Beta Kappa. Home: 7810 Friars Ct Alexandria VA 22306 Office: 2100 K St NW Washington DC 20427 Tel (202) 653-5305

FISHLEIGH, CLARENCE TURNER, b. Chgo., July 31, 1895; B.E.E., U. Mich., 1917; J.D., Detroit Coll. Law, 1939. Admitted to Mich. bar, 1939; Ill. bar, 1952; mech. prodn. Ford Motor Co., Detroit, 1919-22; exptl. motor testing, asst. prodn. mgr. Am. Car and Foundry Co., Chgo., also Rich Tool Co., Detroit, 1923-24; mgr. Clarence T. Fishleigh Co., Chgo., 1924-30; asso. engr., cons. engr. Walter T. Fishleigh, Detroit, 1930-47; cons. engr. Detroit, 1947-51, Chgo., 1951—. Mem. Nat., Ohio socs. profl. engrs., Soc. Automotive Engrs., ASME, Western Soc. Engrs., Engring. Soc. Detroit, Am., Mich. patent law assns., Am., Chgo., Ill., Mich. bar assns. Address: 920 Kenton Rd Deerfield IL 60015 Tel (312) 945-0694

FISK, HAYWARD DAN, b. Las Vegas, Nev., Mar. 5, 1943; B.S. in Bus. Adminstrn., U. Kans., 1965, J.D., 1968; LL.M., U. Mo., 1971. Admitted to Kans. bar, 1968, Pa. bar, 1972; law clk. to judge Shawnee County (Kans.) Dist. Ct., Topeka, 1967; gen. atty. United Telecommunications, Inc., Shawnee Mission, Kans., 1968-71; gen. counsel United Telephone System, Eastern Group, Carlisle, Pa., 1971-72, sec., gen. counsel, 1972—; sec., dir. Le-Mo Cable Co., Kansas City, Mo., 1968-71; asst. sec. United Computing Systems, Inc., Kansas City, 1969-71; sec. United Transmission, Inc., Kansas City, Kans., 1968-69; v.p., legal sec., treas., dir. Newville (Pa.) Builders Supply & Mfg., Inc., 1972—. Vice pres., dir. Vernon Place Home Assn., Merriam, Kans., 1970-71; trustee Scott Eckert Conservation Meml. Found., Carlisle, Pa., 1974—; city councilman, Merriam, 1971. Mem. Am., Kans., Pa. bar assns., C. of C., Sigma Alpha Epsilon, Phi Delta Phi. Home: R D 4 Box 241 Carlisle PA 17013 Office: 1170 Harrisburg Pike Carlisle PA 17013 Tel (717) 249-6346

FITZ, HERBERT HENRY, b. San Francisco, June 21, 1934; A.B., Stanford, 1956; J.D., U. Calif. at San Francisco, 1963. Admitted to Calif. bar, 1964; asso. firm Spray, Gould & Bowers, Los Angeles, 1964-70; prof. Southwestern U. Sch. Law, Los Angeles, 1970—. Mem. Am. Bd. Trial Advocates, Assn. So. Calif. Def. Counsel, Am. Arbitration Assn. (arbitrator 1969—), Am., Los Angeles County bar assns. Office: 675 S Westmoreland Ave Los Angeles CA 90005

FITZER, NORMAN B., b. Syracuse, N.Y., June 18, 1912; B.A., Syracuse U., 1934, J.D., 1937. Admitted to N.Y. bar, 1937; individual practice law, Wellsville, N.Y., 1938-73; justice Town of Wellsville, 1946-53, dist. atty. Allegeny County N.Y., 1953-60; judge, 1961-63; justice N.Y. Superior Ct., 1962-65, judge N.Y. State Ct. Claims, 1973—; supervising justice Spl. Narcotics and Predicate Felony Parts Supreme Ct., 1974-76. Mem. N.Y. State, Allegeny County (pres.) bar assns. Office: Room 758 111 Center St New York City NY 10013 Tel (213) 374-8000

FITZGERALD, HUGH FRANCIS, b. Bklyn., Dec. 17, 1913; A.B., U. Notre Dame, 1934; LL.B., Columbia, 1937. Admitted to N.Y. bar, 1937, U.S. Dist. Ct. bar, 1946, U.S. Supreme Ct. bar, 1958; partner firm Coudert Bros., N.Y.C., 1960—. Mem. Am., N.Y. State, N.Y.C. bar assns., U. Notre Dame Law Assn. (pres. 1974-75). Office: 200 Park Ave New York City NY 10017 Tel (212) 973-5802

FITZGERALD, JOHN DESMOND, b. N.Y.C., May 17, 1923; B.S. cum laude, St. John's U., 1942; J.D., Columbia, 1949. Admitted to Calif. bar, 1950; jr. partner firm DeMeo & DeMeo, Santa Rosa, Calif., 1950-54; sr. partner firm Fitzgerald, von der Mehden, Gowen & Fitzgerald, Santa Rosa, 1955—; instr. trial preparation and practice U. Calif., 1953-56, tax aspects of real estate law, 1959-62, Calif. Continuing Edn. of Bar Program, 1956. Mem. City of Santa Rosa Pub. Housing Authority, 1958; trustee Rincon Valley Sch. Dist., Sonoma County, Calif., 1951-58; bd. dirs. Santa Rosa Symphony Assn., 1975—. Mem. Am., Sonoma County, Calif. State bar assns., Am. Bd. Trial Advocates. Home: 3538 Fir Dr Santa Rosa CA 95405 Office: 1041 College Ave Santa Rosa CA 95404 Tel (707) 542-6976

FITZGERALD, JOHN MOONAN, b. Rochester, Minn., Jan. 20, 1923; B.S.L., U. Minn., 1946, LL.B., 1948; grad. Trial Judges' Coll., postgrad., 1970. Admitted to Minn. bar, 1948; practiced in New Prague, 1948-63; judge 1st Jud. Circuit, Minn. Dist. Ct., 1963—; city atty. City of New Prague (Minn.), 1950-55; mem. Minn. Ho. of Reps., 1957-62. Trustee Minn. Soldier's Home, Mpls., 1954-56. Mem. Minn., Am. bar assns. Home: 201 Sunrise Ave New Prague MN 56071 Office: Scott County Courthouse Shakopee MN 55379 Tel (612) 445-7750

FITZGERALD, JOHN ROHDE, b. Danbury, Conn., June 26, 1927; B.A., U. Conn., 1951, J.D., 1953. Admitted to Conn. bar, 1953, U.S. Supreme Ct. bar, 1959; pros. atty. Manchester (Conn.), 1955-57; partner firm Howard, Kohn, Sprague & Fitzgerald, Hartford, Conn., 1955—; lectr. law U. Conn., 1953—. Chmn. Manchester Charter Revision Commn., 1968-69, 72-73; sec. Manchester Conservation Commn., 1974—; pres. Unitarian Universalist Soc. Manchester, 1971-72. Mem. Am., Conn., Hartford County (sec. 1977), Manchester (pres. 1973) bar assns. Co-author: Connecticut Law of Torts, 1968. Office: 229 Buckingham St Hartford CT 06100 Tel (203) 525-3101

FITZGERALD, JOHN WARNER, b. Grand Ledge, Mich., Nov. 14, 1924; B.S., Mich. State U., 1947; J.D., U. Mich., 1954. Admitted to Mich. bar, 1954; legal counsel Mich. Senate, Lansing, 1954-58; mem. Mich. Senate, 1958-64; chief judge pro tem Mich. Ct. Appeals, 1965-74; justice Mich. Supreme Ct., 1974—, dep. chief justice, 1977—. Mem. State Bar Mich., Am. Bar Assn., Inst. Jud. Adminstrn., Am. Judicature Soc. Office: Law Bldg Mich Supreme Ct Lansing MI 48901 Tel (517) 373-0123

FITZGERALD, JOSEPH MICHAEL, JR., b. Norfolk, Va., Oct. 9, 1943; B.S., Mt. St. Mary's Coll., Emmitsburg, Md., 1965; J.D., Cath. U. Am., 1970; LL.M. in Ocean Law, U. Miami, 1973. Admitted to Fla. bar, 1970; asso. firm Joseph M. Fitzgerald, Profl. Assn., Miami, Fla., 1970-71, 71—; legal officer Broward County (Fla.) Pollution Control Bd., 1971; legal adviser office environ. affairs Fla. Dept. State, 1971-72; spl. asst. state atty. for environ. crimes Broward County, 1973-75; spl. counsel Broward County Environ. Quality Control Bd., 1973-76. Mem. Miami Bicentennial Com., 1975-76; trustee Fla. Ind. Colls. and Univs. Found., 1976. Mem. Fla. Bar, Dade County (Fla.), Am. bar assns., Am. Judicature Soc. Home: 618 NE 58th St Miami FL 33137 Office: 700 Brickell Ave Miami FL 33131 Tel (305) 358-7143

FITZGERALD, MARY F., b. Boston, Feb. 25, 1945; A.B. summa cum laude, Boston U. Coll. Liberal Arts, 1967, J.D. cum laude, Sch. Law, 1969. Admitted to Mass. bar, 1969, U.S. Dist. Ct., 1971; staff atty. Boston Legal Aid Soc., 1969-71; asso. law firm Michaels, Adler & Wilson, Boston, 1971-75; asst. clk. 3d Dist. Ct. Plymouth (Mass.); pvt. practice law, Plymouth, 1975—. Mem. Mass., Plymouth Dist., Boston bar assns. Home: 11 Sassamon Rd Scituate MA 02066 Office: 31 North St Plymouth MA 02360

FITZGERALD, MICHAEL DAVID, b. Cape Vincent, N.Y., Feb. 8, 1941; A.B., Georgetown U., 1962; J.D., Harvard, 1965. Admitted to N.Y. bar, 1966, U.S. Supreme Ct. bar, 1972; asso. firm Quimby, Gosier & Hrabchak, Watertown, N.Y., 1966-68, individual practice law, Adams, N.Y., 1968—; gen. counsel Jefferson County Assn. Deaf and Handicapped, S. Jefferson C. of C., Adams Fire Dept., Worth Fire Dept. Chmn. bd. Historical Assn. S. Jefferson, mem. S. Jefferson Ecumenical Council 1972-75, mem. com. Handicapped 1973—. Mem. Jefferson County, Am. bar assns., Commercial Law League Am. Home: 5248 Doxtator St Adams NY 13605 Office: 3090 N Main St Adams NY 13605

FITZ-GERALD, ROGER MILLER, b. N.Y.C., July 13, 1935; B.S. with honors, U. Ill., 1957, J.D. with honors, 1961. Admitted to Ill. bar, 1961, U.S. Dist. Ct. No. Dist. Ill., 1961, U.S. Patent and Trademark Office bar, 1965; asso. firm Kirkland, Ellis, Hodson, Chaffetz & Master, Chgo., 1961-64; mgr. fgn. patent dept. Fitch, Even, Tabin & Luedeka, Chgo., 1964-72; patent atty. Bell & Howell Co., Chgo., 1972-74, sr. patent atty., 1974-75, group patent atty., 1975-76, group patent counsel, 1976—; gen. counsel 43d Ward Republican Orgn., Chgo., 1964-70. Constl. revision chmn. Ill. Young Republicans, 1968-70; pres. 43d Ward Young Reps., Chgo., 1967-68. Mem. Ill., Chgo. bar assns., Patent Law Assn. Chgo., Am. Patent Law Assn., Order of Coif, Phi Beta Kappa, Pi Eta Sigma. Author: (with F.J. Zeni) Precinct Captain's Guide, 1958; contbr. to Materials on Legislation, 1973; contbr. articles profl. jours.; bd. editors U. Ill. Law Forum, 1958-61. Office: 7100 McCormick Rd Chicago IL 60645 Tel (312) 262-1600

FITZGERALD, TERENCE JAMES, b. Worcester, Mass., Dec. 2, 1943; A.B., Worcester State Coll., 1966; M.A., U. Conn., 1967; J.D., Boston Coll. Admitted to Mass. bar, 1973; staff Mass. Defenders Com., Worcester, 1973-76; individual practice law, Worcester, 1977—. Mem. Worcester County, Mass., Am. bar assns. Home: 41 Newell Hill Rd Sterling MA 01564 Office: 340 Main St Worcester MA 01608 also Route 117 Lancaster MA Tel (617) 754-3291

FITZGERALD, THEODORE ANDREW, b. Chgo., Sept. 19, 1938; B.B.A., Notre Dame U., 1960, J.D., 1962. Admitted to Ind. bar, 1962, U.S. Ct. Appeals bar, 7th Circuit, 1971, U.S. Dist. Ct. bar for No. Dist. Ind., 1972; clk. Ind. Supreme Ct., 1962-63; asso. firm Petry & Fitzgerald, Hebron, Ind., 1965-67, partner, 1967—; mem. Ind. Supreme Ct. Com. on Character and Fitness; dir. 1st Nat. Bank of Valparaiso (Ind.). Mem. Ind., Am., Porter County (pres. 1973-74) bar assns. Home: PO Box 335 Hebron IN 46341 Office: PO Box 95 107 Main St Hebron IN 46341 Tel (219) 996-2300

FITZGERALD, WILLIAM JUSTIN, b. Mineola, N.Y., July 10, 1934; B.A., Cath. U. Am., 1955; LL.B., Georgetown U., 1962. Admitted to Va. bar, 1962, D.C. bar, 1962; asso. firm Collins & Finney, Washington, 1962-65; mem. firm Collins & Fitzgerald, Washington, 1965—. Pres. Ashton Heights Civic Assn., Arlington, Va., 1968-70; mem. Arlington County Democratic Com., 1966-70. Mem. Va., D.C., Arlington County bar assns. Office: Shoreham Bldg 806 15th St NW Washington DC 20005 Tel (202) 638-2418

FITZGERALD, WILLIAM PETZOLDT, b. Billings, Mont., Mar. 30, 1941; B.A., U. Mont., 1965; LL.B., Harvard, 1968. Admitted to Mass. bar, 1968, Mont. bar, 1974; asso. firm Robinson, Donovan, Madden & Berry, Springfield, Mass., 1968-69; dir. Western Mass. Legal Services Inc., Holyoke, 1969-73; partner firm Cate, Lynaugh & Fitzgerald, Billings, Mont., 1974—. Mem. Mass., Mont. (mem. ethics com. 1975-77, trustee 1976-77) bar assns. Home: 107 Avenue C Billings MT 59101 Office: Suite 500 Midland Bank Bldg Billings MT 59101 Tel (406) 252-3461

FITZGIBBON, DANIEL HARVEY, b. Columbus, Ind., July 7, 1942; B.S. in Engring., U.S. Mil. Academy, 1964; J.D., Harvard, 1972. Admitted to Ind. bar, 1972; asso. firm Barnes, Hickam, Pantzer & Boyd, Indpls., 1972—. Mem. Ind. State, Am., bar assns. Home: 5833 Eastview Ct Indianapolis IN 46250 Office: 1313 Merchants Bank Bldg Indianapolis IN 46204 Tel (317) 638-1313

FITZPATRICK, ALBERT JOHN, b. Washington, Nov. 16, 1932; B.S. in Bus., Va. Commonwealth U., 1960; J.D., U. Richmond, 1963. Admitted to Va. bar, 1963; asst. title officer Lawyers Title Ins. Corp., Richmond, Va., 1964-67; asst. atty. City of Richmond, 1967—; asst. counsel Indsl. Devel. Authority City of Richmond, Richmond Supplemental Retirement System. Mem. McNeil Law Soc. Home: 4705 Calumet Rd Richmond VA 23226 Office: 300 City Hall Richmond VA 23219 Tel (804) 780-4912

FITZPATRICK, JOHN M., b. Phila., Nov. 26, 1932; B.S., St. Joseph's Coll., 1954; LL.B., Temple U., 1961. Admitted to Pa. bar, 1962; with Ins. Co. N.Am., Phila., 1962-63, Liberty Mut. Ins. Co., Phila., 1963-66; partner firm Dilworth, Paxon, Kalish & Levy, Phila., 1966—; solicitor Haverford (Pa.) Sch. Dist., 1973-75. Pres. Coopertown Civic Assn.; v.p. Haverford Twp. Civic Council, 1974-76. Mem. Am., Pa., Phila. bar assns., Def. Research Inst., Phila. Ins. Claims Assn. Home: 41 Meadows Ln Haverford PA 19041 Office: Fidelity Bldg Philadelphia PA 19109 Tel (215) 546-3000

FIX, BRIAN DAVID, b. Rochester, N.Y., May 31, 1944; B.A. cum laude, Columbia, 1965, J.D., 1968. Legis. aide to Sen. Kenneth B. Keating, Washington, 1964; admitted to N.Y. bar, 1968, D.C. bar, 1969; asso. firm Surrey Karasik & Morse, Washington, 1968-71, partner, 1976—, resident partner Middle East office, Beirut, 1975-76; asso. firm Surrey Karasik Morse & Goekjian, Paris, 1971-73, partner, 1974-75. Mem. Am., D.C. bar assns., Am. Soc. Internat. Law. Office: 1156 Fifteenth St NW Washington DC 20005 Tel (202) 331-4048

FIZZELL, ROBERT BRUCE, b. Taylorville, Ill., Sept. 20, 1889; A.B., U. Ill., 1910, LL.B., 1913. Admitted to Mo. bar, 1913, U.S. Supreme Ct. bar 1972; asso. firm Bowersock, Hall & Hook, Kansas City, 1913-24; mem. firm Bowersock, Fizzell & Rhodes and predecessors, 1924-44; partner firm Stinson, Mag, Thomson, McEvers & Fizzell and predecessor, Kansas City, 1944—. Trustee Kansas City Art Inst. Mem. Am., Mo., Kansas City bar assns., Friends of Art Kansas City (pres. 1937-39), Lawyers Assn. Kansas City (pres. 1947), Phi Beta Kappa, Delta Sigma Rho. Home: 1228 W 68th Terr Kansas City MO 64113 Office: 2100 Ten Main Center Kansas City MO 64105 Tel (816) 842-8600

FJORD, HILLIARD JAMES, b. Kankakee, Ill., Sept. 26, 1924; B.A., DePauw U., 1947; J.D., U. Mich., 1949; M.B.A., Xavier U., 1965. Admitted to Ill. bar, 1950, Ohio bar, 1953; title officer Lawyers Title Ins. Corp., Columbus, Ohio, 1953-56; asso. counsel Western-So. Life Ins. Co., Cin., 1956-60, asst. treas., 1960-63, treas., 1963-64, 2d v.p., 1964-68, v.p., 1968-73; exec. v.p., sec. So. Ohio Bank, Cin., 1973—. Trustee, treas. Mental Health Assn. Cin. Area; trustee Edgecliff Coll., 1973—. Mem. Cin. Bar Assn., Bankers Club. Home: 3817 Petoskey Ave Cincinnati OH 45227 Office: 515 Main St Cincinnati OH 45202 Tel (513) 852-2511

FLACK, EVELYN ROBERTS, b. Tallahassee, Fla., Aug. 19, 1928; B.S., Fla. State U., 1948; J.D., U. Fla., 1966. Admitted to Fla. bar, 1966; legal research asst. to judge Dist. Ct. of Appeals for 2d Dist. Fla., Lakeland, 1966-68; clk. Dist. Ct. of Appeals for 4th Dist. Fla., West Palm Beach, 1968-71; asso. law offices Ronald Sales, Palm Beach, 1971-72; chief Appelate div. Office Pub. Defender, West Palm Beach, 1972-73; individual practice law, Palm Beach, 1972-74; asso. firm Johnson, Ackerman & Bakst, West Palm Beach, 1974; judge Wakulla County Ct., Crawfordville, 1974—. Mem. Am., Fla., Tallahassee bar assns. Home and Office: POB 132 Crawfordville FL 32327 Tel (904) 926-7997

FLACK, ROBERT LLOYD, b. Syracuse, N.Y., Oct. 2, 1926; A.B., Princeton, 1948; LL.B., Syracuse U., 1951, J.D., 1968. Admitted to N.Y. bar, 1952, U.S. Supreme Ct. bar, 1958; individual practice law, Syracuse, 1952-62, Watkins Glen, N.Y., 1962—; village atty. Watkins Glen, 1963-67, village justice, 1967-73; dist. atty. Schuyler County (N.Y.), 1975—; N.Y. State transfer tax atty. Schuyler County, 1975—. Chmn. Zoning Bd. Appeals Watkins Glen, 1968-70. Mem. Am., N.Y. State, Schuyler County (v.p.), Onondaga County bar assns., Am. Judicature Soc. Home: 101 Grand View Ave Watkins Glen NY 14891 Office: 113 E 6th St Watkins Glen NY 14891 Tel (607) 535-4412

FLAHERTY, CARRIE JEANETTE THOMPSON, b. Vidalia, La., July 19, 1936; B.S. in Sci. Edn., So. U., 1959; postgrad. Mich. State U., 1964-65; J.D., Wayne State U., 1972. Admitted to Mich. bar, 1972; tchr. biology, Vicksburg, Miss., 1959-60; tchr., chmn. sci. dept., Pontiac, Mich., 1962-67; congl. intern Detroit Office of Congressman John Conyers, Jr., 1971-72; atty. Nat. Labor Relations Bd., Detroit, 1972; atty. legal aid research div. Juvenile Defenders Office, Detroit, 1972; individual practice law, Detroit, 1974—. Mem. Am., Mich., Detroit, Wolverine, Nat. (dir. women's div.) bar assns., Am. Mich. trial lawyers assns., Women Lawyers Assn., Greater Detroit C. of C.,

NAACP, NOW. Office: 2703 David Stott Bldg Detroit MI 48226 Tel (313) 964-0515

FLAHERTY, PETE F., b. Pitts., June 24, 1925; J.D., U. Notre Dame, 1951; M.B.A., U. Pitts., 1967. Admitted to Pa., Fla. bars; practiced law, 1951-57; asst. dist. atty. Allegheny County (Pa.), 1957-65; mem. Pitts. City Council, 1965-69; mayor City of Pitts., 1970-77; dep. atty. gen. U.S., Washington, 1977—. Mem. legis. action com. U.S. Conf. Mayors. Pres. Pa. League of Cities; trustee U. Notre Dame, U. Pitts., Carnegie Mellon U. Office: US Dept Justice Constitution Ave and 10th St NW Washington DC 20530

FLAHERTY, PETER JAMES, III, b. Bristol, Pa., Nov. 12, 1948; A.B., Loyola U., New Orleans, 1970; J.D., U. Ky., 1973. Admitted to Ky. bar, 1973; law clk. 25th Jud. Circuit, 1972-73; asso. firm Shumate, Shumate & Flaherty, Richmond, Ky., 1973-75, ltd. partner, 1976—; adj. instr. police adminstrn. Eastern Ky. U., 1976-77. Mem. Am., Ky., Madison County (v.p. 1976) bar assns., Am. Judicature Soc. Home: 23 Martin Dr Rt 10 Stateland Richmond KY 40475 Office: 221 W Irvine St Richmond KY 40475 Tel (606) 623-3049

FLAHERTY, VINCENT DONALD, b. Norwalk, Conn., June 14, 1920; B.S. cum laude, Niagara U., 1943; LL.B. cum laude, St. John's U., 1948. Admitted to Conn. bar, 1948, U.S. Supreme Ct. bar, 1960; asso. firm Keogh & Candee, Norwalk, 1948-50; individual practice law, Norwalk, 1950-66; partner firm Flaherty and Vallerie, Norwalk, 1966—; corp. counsel City of Norwalk, 1955-57; counsel Norwalk Redevel. Agy., 1955—. Mem. Norwalk-Wilton, Conn., Am. bar assns., Am. Right-of-Way Assn. Home: 19 Merrill Rd Norwalk CT 06851 Office: 500 West Ave Norwalk CT 06852 Tel (203) 838-6589

FLAKE, JAY VINCENT, b. Olympia, Wash., Dec. 23, 1941; B.B.A., Ariz. State U., 1966; J.D., U. Ariz., 1969. Admitted to Ariz. bar, 1969; partner firm Davis & Flake, Showlow, Ariz., 1969-76; individual practice law, Snowflake, 1976—; city atty. City of Snowflake, 1969-77; dep. county atty. Navajo County, Ariz., 1974-77, county atty., 1977—. Chmn. fund drive Boy Scouts Am., 1974, 75. Mem. State Bar Ariz. Home and office: Box 85 Snowflake AZ 85937 Tel (602) 536-4487

FLANAGAN, WILLIAM S., JR., b. Tulsa, Aug. 1, 1947; B.A., Western State Coll. of Colo. 1969; J.D., U. Tulsa, 1971. Admitted to Okla. bar, 1972; partner firm Dyer Powers & Marsh, Tulsa and Collinsville, Okla., 1971—; exec. v.p. Am. Exchange Bank, Collinsville, 1976. Mem. Tulsa County Bar Assn., Am. Bankers Assn., Internat. Rodeo Assn. Address: POB 189 Collinsville OK 74021 Tel (918) 371-2655

FLANDERS, GILBERT LEE, b. San Diego, Calif., Sept. 18, 1935; student U. San Diego, 1954-57; J.D., Southwestern U., 1964. Admitted to Calif. bar, 1965; asso. firm. H.H. Hiestand, Los Angeles, 1965-66; asso. firm English & MacDowell, Lynwood, Calif., 1966-68; individual practice law, Downey Calif., 1968—; bd. dirs. Fed. Legal Services, S.E. Los Angeles, 1970—; counsel Mexican-Am. Political Assn., 1965-68; mem. Los Angeles Dist. Atty. Adv. Council, 1967-70, Calif. Atty. Gen. Adv. Council, 1970-77; adviser to registrants SSS, 1972. Pres. Oralingua Found. Deaf Children, Los Angeles, 1973-74; trustee Oralingua Sch. Deaf Children, 1974-75. Mem. Am., Calif. trial lawyers assns., Am., Southeast, Los Angeles County bar assns., Themis Legal Soc. Office: 11510 S Downey Ave Downey CA 90241 Tel (213) 923-9238

FLANDERS, HAROLD HERBERT, b. Denver, Feb. 2, 1938; B.S. in Engring. Physics, U. Colo., 1960; J.D., George Washington U., 1966. Engring physicist Dow Chem. Corp., Rocky Flats (Colo.) AEC Plant, 1960-61; admitted to Va. bar, 1966, Patent Office bar, 1967, Tex. bar, 1973; examiner U.S. Patent Office, Washington, 1963-66; asso. patent counsel Xerox Corp., Rochester, N.Y., 1966-68; patent mgr. J.M. Huber Corp., Borger, Tex., 1968—. Mem. Borger Cable Communications Commn., 1975—. Mem. Am., Fed., Va., Tex., Hutchinson County bar assns., Dallas-Ft. Worth Patent Law Assn., Assn. Advancement Invention Innovation, Am. Patent Law Assn. Home: 625 Evergreen St Borger TX 79007 Office: POB 2831 Borger TX 79007 Tel (806) 274-6331

FLANNERY, DANIEL GELBERT, b. Pittston, Pa., Jan. 6, 1942; A.B. cum laude, King's Coll., Pa., 1963; LL.B., Georgetown U., 1966. Admitted to Pa. bar, 1966; law clk. to justice Pa. Supreme Ct., Phila., 1966-67; mem. firm Rosenn, Jenkins & Greenwald, Wilkes-Barre, Pa., 1967—; solicitor Sugar Notch Borough, Luzerne County, Pa., 1972-76. Bd. dirs. Wyoming Valley chpt. ARC, 1976—. Mem. Am., Pa. bar assns., Wilkes-Barre Law and Library Assn., Am., Pa. trial lawyers assns. Home: 530 Hoyt St Pringle PA 18704 Office: 1000 Blue Cross Bldg Wilkes-Barre PA 18711 Tel (717) 829-0511

FLANNERY, KYRAN JOSEPH, JR., b. Albany, N.Y., Aug. 29, 1944; A.B., Holy Cross Coll., 1966; J.D., Albany Law Sch., 1969; Admitted to N.Y. State bar, 1969, U.S. Dist Ct. for No. Dist. N.Y. bar, 1969; mem. firm Zubres D'Agostine & Hoblock, Albany, 1969—. Mem. Am., N.Y. State, Albany County bar assns. Home: 183 Colonial Ave Albany NY 12208 Office: 90 State St Albany NY 12207 Tel (518) 463-2251

FLANNERY, ROSEMARY MCCARRON, b. Phila., June 11, 1921; A.B., Chestnut Hill Co., 1943; LL.B., Villanova U., 1965. Admitted to Pa. bar, 1965; asso. firm Wisler, Pearlstine, Talone, Craig & Garrity, and predecessor, Norristown, Pa., 1965-73, partner, 1973—. Dem. committeewoman, 1962—, Dem. municipal chmn., 1973-; mem. Selective Service Bd., 1972-75; trustee Eastern State Sch. and Hosp. of Pa. Mem. Am., Pa., Montgomery (sec. 1971—) bar assns., Am. Judicature Soc., Montgomery County Trial Lawyers Assn., Montgomery County Estate Planning Council (exec. com., second v.p.), Phila. Bar Assn. (asso.). Home: 666 Midway Ln Blue Bell PA 19422 Office: 515 Swede St Norristown PA 19401 Tel (215) 272-8400

FLATE, RONALD ALLEN, b. Cleve., Nov. 26, 1937; B.S., U. Wis., 1960; J.D., Calif. Western Sch. Law, 1966. Admitted to Calif. bar, 1967, U.S. Supreme Ct. bar, 1974; atty.-agt. IRS, Los Angeles, 1966-68; supervisory atty. SBA, Los Angeles, 1971-72; sr. partner firm Ronald A. Flate, Los Angeles, 1968-71, 72—; owner Ron Realty. Mem. Am., Calif., Los Angeles (mem. coms. tax, real estate, probate, bus. corp.) bar assns., Nat. Assn. Realtors, Los Angeles Bd. Realtors, Phi Delta Phi. Contbr. articles to legal jours.; lectr. bus. assns., civic orgns. Office: 4929 Wilshire Blvd #700 Los Angeles CA 90010 Tel (213) 933-7141

FLATLEY, ROBERT HUGH, b. Chgo., July 3, 1908; J.D., U. Wis., 1935. Admitted to Wis. bar, 1935, U.S. Supreme Ct. bar, 1961; agt. FBI, Boston, N.Y.C. and Chgo., 1942-45; partner firm Flatley & Jacques, Green Bay, Wis. Mem. Green Bay Bd. Edn., 1957-63, pres., 1962-63. Mem. Assn. Trial Lawyers Am., Brown County Bar Assn. (former pres.). Home: 918 S Jackson St Green Bay WI 54301 Office: 140 S Madison St PO Box 1053 Green Bay WI 54305 Tel (414) 437-9168

FLATTEN, DANIEL VINCENT, b. San Antonio, Mar. 1, 1942; B.A., U. Tex., 1964, LL.B., 1966. Admitted to Tex. bar, 1966, Okla. bar, 1970, U.S. Supreme Ct. bar, 1973, U.S. Ct. Appeals 5th Circuit bar, 1974; served to judge adv. U.S. Air Force, 1966-70; shareholder firm Mehaffy, Weber, Keith & Gonsoulin, Beaumont, Tex., 1970—. Mem. Am., Jefferson County (treas. 1974, dir.) bar assns., State Bar Tex., State Bar Okla., Tex. Assn. Def. Counsel, Ass. Ins. Attys., Maritime Law Assn. U.S. Office: 1400 San Jacinto Bldg Beaumont TX 77701 Tel (713) 835-5011

FLATTERY, PAUL CHARLES, b. Jamaica, N.Y., Apr. 15, 1935; B.S.E.E., U. Notre Dame, 1957; J.D., Georgetown U., 1964. Admitted to N.Y. bar, 1965, Ill. bar, 1976; patent examiner U.S. Patent Office, Washington, 1960-62; clk. Browne Schuyler & Beveridge, Washington, 1962-64; partner firm Fish & Neave, N.Y.C., 1964-75; chief patent counsel Travenol Labs., Inc., Deerfield, Ill., 1975—. Mem. Am., Ill. bar assns., Am., N.Y., Chgo. patent law assns., Assn. Corp. Patent Counsel. Office: Travenol Laboratories 1 Baxter Pkwy Deerfield IL 60015 Tel (312) 948-4940

FLATTERY, THOMAS LONG, b. Detroit, Nov. 14, 1922; B.S., U.S. Mil. Acad., 1947; J.D., U. Calif., Los Angeles, 1955; LL.M., U. So. Calif., 1965. Admitted to Calif. bar, 1955, U.S. Patent Office bar, 1957, U.S. Supreme Ct. bar, 1974; gen. counsel, asst. sec. McCulloch Corp., Los Angeles, 1957-64; sec., corp. counsel Technicolor, Inc., Hollywood, Calif., 1964-70; v.p., sec., gen. counsel Amcord, Inc., Newport Beach, Calif., 1970-72, Schick, Inc., Los Angeles, 1972-75; counsel, asst. sec. C. F. Braun & Co., Alhambra, Calif., 1975-76; v.p., asst. gen. counsel, asst. sec. Automation Industries, Inc., Los Angeles, 1976—; author, lectr. in field. Mem. State Bar Calif., Los Angeles County (chmn. corp. law dept. com. 1966-67), Am., Century City bar assns., Patent Law Assn. of Los Angeles, Fgn. Law Assn. of So. Calif., Am. Soc. Corp. Secs. (pres. Los Angeles regional group, 1973-74), Phi Alpha Delta Internat. Recipient 3d prize Fletcher Found. Patent Essay Contest, 1955. Home: 439 Via de la Paz Pacific Palisades CA 90272 Office: care Automation Industries Inc 1901 Ave of the Stars suite 2000 Los Angeles CA 90067 Tel (213) 879-2222

FLAX, RICHARD ELDEN, b. Columbus, Ohio, Dec. 5, 1948; B.S., Miami U., Oxford, Ohio, 1971; J.D. summa cum laude, Ohio State Coll., 1974. Admitted to Ohio bar, 1974; asso. firm Phau, Comstock & Springer, Youngstown, Ohio, 1974-76; asso. firm Lucas, Prendergast, Albright, Gibson, Brown & Newman, Columbus, 1976—. Mem. Am., Ohio, Franklin County bar assns. Home: 990 Corbin Ct Westerville OH 43081 Office: 42 E Gay Columbus OH 43215 Tel (614) 228-5711

FLEAK, ARTHUR BERL, JR., b. Tulsa, Oct. 14, 1947; B.S., Okla. State U., 1970; J.D., U. Tulsa, 1972; postgrad. Nat. Coll. Criminal Def. Lawyers and Pub. Defenders, Houston, 1975. Admitted to Okla. bar, 1973, U.S. Dist. Ct. bar, 1973, U.S. 10th Circuit Ct. Appeals bar, 1975; asst. pub. defender, Tulsa County, Okla., 1972-75; individual practice law, Tulsa, 1975—. Mem. Okla. Criminal Def. Lawyers Assn. Contbr. articles in field to profl. jours. Home: 3626 S Sandusky St Tulsa OK 74135 Office: 1141 E 37th St Tulsa OK 74105 Tel (918) 747-8001

FLECK, CONRAD LEE, b. Washington, Oct. 10, 1944; B.S. in Chemistry, U. Md., 1967, J.D., 1973. Admitted to Md. bar, 1973, U.S. Dist. Ct., Md. bar, 1974; individual practice law, Silver Spring, Md., 1973-74; asso. firm Carney & Fleck, Silver Spring, 1974-75. Mem. Am., Md., Prince Georges County bar assn. Home: 2115 Saranac St Adelphi MD 20783 Office: 6505 Belcrest Rd Suite 3 Hyattsville MD 20782 Tel (301) 699-8200

FLECK, DANIEL JOSEPH, b. Pitts., May 22, 1947; B.A., Duquesne U., 1969, J.D., 1972. Admitted to Pa. bar, 1972, U.S. Supreme Ct. bar, 1976; asso. firm Will & Keisling, Pitts., 1973-75; individual practice law, Pitts., 1976—; solicitor 1st Fed. Savs. & Loan Assn. of Carnegie (Pa.). Mem. Pa., Am., Allegheny County (Pa.) bar assns. Home: Hope Hollow Rd Charles Dr Carnegie PA 15106 Office: 1110 Grant Bldg Pittsburgh PA 15219 Tel (412) 391-3760

FLECK, HARRY ALLEN, b. Lowell, Ohio, Apr. 14, 1880; student Chgo. Law Sch., 1903-06. Admitted to Ill. bar, 1906; asst. corp. counsel City of Chgo., 1921-27; individual practice law, Chgo., 1927—. Mem. Am., Ill. bar assns. Home: 5740 N Campbell St Chicago IL 60659 Office: 11 S LaSalle St Chicago IL 60603 Tel (312) CE 6-2578

FLEET, ERWIN, b. Boston, Sept. 25, 1927; B.S. U. Fla., 1949, J.D., 1950; grad. Nat. Coll. State Judiciary U. Nev., 1975. Admitted to Fla. bar, 1950, since practiced in Ft. Walton Beach; asst. states atty. 1st Jud. Circuit, 1955-57; first resident circuit judge Okaloosa County, 1957-58; U.S. commr. with trial jurisdiction Eglin AFB, Fla., 1959-71, U.S. magistrate, 1971-73; circuit judge 1st Jud. Circuit, 1973—; atty. Okaloosa County Sch. Bd., 1962-72. Cubmaster, scoutmaster, Sea Explorer adviser Boy Scouts Am.; head chaperone Choctawhatchee High Sch. Band, 1971-75; active United Fund Campaigns. Mem. Am. (v.p. com. on econs. of law practice), Fla., Okaloosa-Walton (past pres.) bar assns., Soc. Bar First Jud. Circuit (past pres.), Am. Judicature Soc., Am. Trial Lawyers Assn., Acad. Fla. Trial Lawyers, Ft. Walton Beach C. of C. (past pres., dir.). Home: 622 Lakeview Rd NW Fort Walton Beach FL 32548 Office: Courthouse Annex Shalimar FL 32579 Tel (904) 651-3710

FLEGEL, JOHN LAWRENCE, b. San Mateo, Calif., May 30, 1948; B.A., Claremont Men's Coll., 1970; J.D., Santa Clara Sch. Law, 1973. Admitted to Calif. bar, 1973; partner firm Dormody & Flegel, Menlo Park, Calif., 1974—. Mem. City Menlo Park Housing Commn., Menlo Park Housing and Community Development Act Com. Mem. Calif. State, San Mateo County, Am. bar assns. Home: 111 E Creek Dr Menlo Park CA 94025 Office: 1155 Crane St Suite 7 Menlo Park CA 94025 Tel (415) 320-8240

FLEISCHAKER, MARC L., b. Cin., Feb. 22, 1945; B.S. in Econs., U. Pa., 1967; J.D., George Washington U., 1971. Admitted to D.C. bar, 1971, U.S. Supreme Ct. bar, 1974. Asso. firm Arent, Fox, Kintner, Plotkin & Kahn, Washington, 1971—. Mem. Am., D.C., Fed. (chmn. adminstrv. law and procedure com. 1974-75, chmn. council on fed. law, agys. and practice 1975—) bar assns., Am. Judicature Soc. Contbr. articles to legal jours. Home: 6308 Broad Branch Rd Chevy Chase MD 20015 Office: 1815 H St NW Washington DC 20006 Tel (202) 857-6053

FLEISCHLI, FRANZ KARL, III, b. Springfield, Ill., Apr. 29, 1943; B.S., Purdue U., 1965; M.B.A., Washington U., 1973, J.D., 1973. Admitted to Ill. bar, 1973, U.S. Tax Ct. bar, 1975, U.S. Dist. Ct. bar, 1976, U.S. Ct. Appeals bar, 1976; with Ill. State's Atty.'s Office, Springfield, 1973; asso. firm Robert C. Walbaum, Springfield, 1973-74; partner Walbaum, Hayes & Fleischli, Springfield, 1974—; instr. Am. Inst. Banking, 1974, Lincoln Land Community Coll., 1975—. Mem. Ill., Sangamon County bar assns., Am., Ill. trial lawyers assns. Home: 1943 Illini Rd Springfield IL 62704 Office: 1231 S 8th St PO Box 1365 Springfield IL 62705 Tel (217) 789-0911

FLEISCHLI, GEORGE ROBERT, b. Springfield, Ill., Aug. 23, 1940; B.S. in Mgmt., U. Ill., 1962, J.D. with honors, 1965, M.S. in Labor Relations, 1970. Admitted to Ill. bar, 1965, Wis. bar, 1971. Research asst. Inst. Labor and Indsl. Relations, U. Ill., Champaign, 1965-66, 70; with JAGC, USAF, 1966-69; labor mediator-arbitrator-hearing examiner Wis. Employment Relations Commn., Madison, 1970-75, gen. counsel, 1976—; mem. labor arbitration panel Fed. Mediation and Conciliation Service, 1973—, Am. Arbitration Assn. labor arbitration panel, 1974—. Mem. Nat. Acad. Arbitrators, Indsl. Relations Research Assn., Soc. Profls. in Dispute Resolution, Order of Coif. Home: 15 Hiawatha Circle Madison WI 53711 Office: 30 W Mifflin St Room 910 Madison WI 53702 Tel (608) 266-1381

FLEISCHMAN, EDWARD HIRSH, b. Cambridge, Mass., June 25, 1932; student Harvard; LL.B., Columbia, 1959. Admitted to N.Y. bar, 1959; asso. firm Beekman & Bogue, N.Y.C., 1959-67, partner, 1968—; adj. asso. prof. N.Y. U., 1976—. Mem. Am. Law Inst., Am. Bar Assn. (chmn. ad hoc subcom. rule 144, 1970-72, chmn. subcom. broker-dealer matters 1973—). Contbr. articles to legal jours. Office: 5 Hanover Sq New York City NY 10004 Tel (212) 422-4060

FLEISCHMAN, JEROME BENNETT, b. Bklyn., July 26, 1931; B.A., Rutgers U., 1953; J.D., Harvard, 1956. Admitted to N.Y. bar, 1957; asst. staff judge adv. USAF, Portsmouth, N.H., 1956-58, now lt. col. JAGC Res.; asst. to justice N.Y. State Supreme Ct., Smithtown, 1958-60; research asst. N.Y. Law Sch., 1960-61; individual practice law, N.Y.C., 1961—; atty. Long Beach (N.Y.) Pub. Library, 1965—. Pres., East End Civic Assn., 1970-72; county committeeman Democratic Party, 1965—, chmn. Long Beach County Dem. County Com., 1975—; bd. dirs. Am. Cancer Soc., Inter-Racial Council. Mem. N.Y. State Bar Assn., Long Beach Lawyers Assn. Contbr. articles to profl. jours. Recipient 4th Ann. Brotherhood award Inter-Racial Council. Home: 57 Armour St Long Beach NY 11561 Office: 370 7th Ave New York City NY 10001 Tel (212) 868-3434

FLEISCHMANN, ARNOLD, b. Bayreuth, Germany, Nov. 7, 1925; A.B., U. Md., 1951, J.D., 1954. Admitted to Md. bar, 1954; U.S. Supreme Ct. bar, 1961, U.S. Tax Ct. bar, 1961; Law clk. to judge U.S. Dist. Ct., 1954-55; asso. firm Smalkin, Hessian, Martin & Taylor, 1955-58; asso. firm Nyburg, Goldman & Walter, 1958-59, partner, 1960-65; partner firm Fisher & Fleischmann, 1968-70; Fleischmann, Needle, Ehudin & Schwarz, Towson, Md., 1977—. Chmn. Balt. County Planning Bd., 1975—; mem. Commn. To Revise Zoning Laws, 1960, Baltimore County Zoning Revision Com., 1966. Mem. Am., Fed., Md., Balt. County, Balt. City bar assns. Editorial bd. Md. Law Rev., 1954. Home: 11202 Woodland Dr Lutherville MD 21093 Office: Suite 505 102 W Pennsylvania Ave Towson MD 20204 Tel (301) 321-0300

FLEISCHMANN, KARL, b. N.Y.C., Jan. 19, 1937; A.B., Columbia, 1957; J.D., Harvard, 1960. Admitted to Conn. bar, 1960, U.S. Supreme Ct. bar, 1971; practiced in Hartford; partner firm Satter & Fleischmann, 1964-70, Satter, Fleischmann & Sherbacow, 1971-75, Fleischmann & Sherbacow, 1975—; lectr. law U. Conn. Law Sch., 1968-73. Mem. West Hartford Town Plan and Zoning Commn., 1970-73. Mem. Conn. (chmn. profl. ethics com. 1975—), Hartford County bar assns. Home: 1055 Prospect Ave West Hartford CT 06105 Office: 60 Washington St Hartford CT 06106 Tel (203) 547-0120

FLEISS, MILTON LESTER, b. Bklyn., Nov. 7, 1908; B.A., Columbia Coll., 1928, LL.B., 1930, J.D., 1930. Admitted to N.Y. bar, 1931, U.S. Supreme Ct. bar, 1963, U.S. Ct. Appeals bar, 1967; individual practice law, Bklyn. Mem. Am., N.Y. State, Bklyn. bar assns., N.Y. State Trial Lawyers Assn. Home: 75 Henry St Brooklyn NY 11201 Office: 188 Montague St Brooklyn NY 11201 Tel (212) 624-3200

FLEMING, CLARENCE JOSEPH, b. Springfield, Ill., Mar. 29, 1930; A.A., Springfield Jr. Coll., 1950; B.C.E., U. Ill., 1952; LL.B., George Washington U., 1962. Admitted to Ill. bar, 1962; asso. firm Greist, Lockwood, Greenewalt & Dewey, Chgo., 1962-69; partner firm McDougall, Hersh, & Scott, Chgo., 1969—. Mem. Am. Bar Assn., Chgo. Patent Law Assn. Home: 1247 Chestnut Ave Wilmette IL 60091 Office: 135 S LaSalle St Chicago IL 60603 Tel (312) 346-0338

FLEMING, JAMES G., b. Jackson, Mich., Nov. 5, 1929; A.A., Jackson Community Coll., 1950; J.D., U. Detroit, 1954. Admitted to Mich. bar, 1954, U.S. Supreme Ct. bar, 1959; circuit ct. commr., 1954-58; individual practice law, Jackson, 1954-74; commr. Jackson City, 1956-58; chief asst. pros. atty. Jackson County (Mich.), 1958-60, pros. attys., 1960-66; mem. Mich. Senate, 1967-74; mem. firm Fleming, Fleming & Treciak, Jackson, 1970-74; judge Circuit Ct. Jackson County 4th Mich. Jud. Circuit, Jackson, 1974—. Mem. Am., Mich., Jackson County bar assns. Home: 5335 Deer Ridge Rd Jackson MI 49201 Office: 312 S Jackson St The Ct House Jackson MI 49201 Tel (517) 787-4380

FLEMING, JOHN GUNTHER, b. Berlin, July 6, 1919; B.A., Oxford (Eng.) U., 1939, M.A., 1943, Ph.D., 1948, D.C.L., 1959. Admitted to English bar, 1947; prof. law, dean Australian Nat. U., Canberra, 1949-60; Shannon Cecil Turner prof. law U. Calif., Berkeley, 1960—. Mem. Am. Law Inst., Internat. Assn. Legal Sci. (v.p. 1975—), Internat. Acad. Comparative Law. Author: Introduction to the Law of Torts, 1967; Law of Torts, 5th edit., 1977; editor-in chief Am. Jour. Comparative Law, 1971—; contbr. articles to legal jours. Home: 836 Spruce St Berkeley CA 49707 Office: School of Law U Calif Berkeley CA 94720 Tel (415) 642-1870

FLEMING, JULIAN DENVER, JR., b. Rome, Ga., Jan. 12, 1934; student U. Pa., 1951-53; B.Ch.E. with highest honors, Ga. Inst. Tech., 1955, Ph.D., 1959; J.D. with distinction, Emory U., 1967. Admitted to Ga. bar, 1966, D.C. bar, 1967; asso. firm Sutherland, Asbill & Brennan, Atlanta and Washington, 1967-71, partner, 1971—; instr. Ga. Inst. Tech., 1955-59, asst. prof., 1959-61, asso. prof., 1961-66, research engr., prof. chem. engring., 1966-67; staff cons. Oak Ridge Nat. Lab., 1962-67; mem. gov.'s advisory counsel on Mental Health and Mental Retardation, 1976. Fellow Am. Inst. Chemists, AAAS; mem. Am. Bar Assn., Bar Assn. Dist. Columbia, State Bar Ga., Lawyers Club Atlanta, Mental Health Assns. Ga., Met. Atlanta (dir. 1970—; pres. 1974-75). Registered profl. engr. Ga., Calif.; contbr. articles to profl. jours. Home: 2238 Hill Park Ct Decatur GA 30033 Office: 3100 1st Nat Bank Tower Atlanta GA 30303 Tel (404) 658-8700

FLEMING, ROBBEN WRIGHT, b. Paw Paw, Ill., Dec. 18, 1916; B.A., Beloit Coll., 1938, LL.D., 1968; LL.B., U. Wis., 1941, LL.D., 1969; LL.D., Mich. State U., 1967, U. Mich., 1967, Mich. Tech. U., 1968, U. Ill., Chgo. Circle, 1968, Western Mich. U., 1968, Cleve. State U., 1969, Wayne State U., 1970, Hawaii Loa Coll., 1971, Millikin U., 1971, Albion Coll., 1971, U. Ariz., 1971; Litt. D., No. Mich. U., 1968; L.H.D., Coll. Wooster, 1971, Detroit Coll. Bus., 1973, U. Fla., 1974. Admitted to Wis. bar, 1941; dir. Indsl. Relations Center U. Wis., 1947-52; dir. Inst. Labor and Indsl. Relations U. Ill., 1952-58, faculty law U. Ill., 1958-64; chancellor U. Wis., Madison, 1964-67; pres., prof. U. Mich., 1968—; exec. dir. Nat. Wage Stabilization Bd., Washington, 1951. Mem. Wis. Bar Assn., Nat. Acad. Arbitrators (pres. 1966-67), Am. Council Edn., Assn. Am. Univs., Nat. Assn. Land Grant Colls., State Univs. Author books; contbr. articles to profl. jours. Home: 815 S University St Ann Arbor MI 48109 Office: 2068 Adminstrn Bldg U of Mich Ann Arbor MI 48109

FLEMING, ROBERT BURKE, b. Pitts., Dec. 18, 1921; B.M.E., U. Minn., 1943; LL.B., U. Buffalo, 1951. Admitted to N.Y. bar, 1951; teaching fellow Harvard, 1952-53; asst. prof. law St. Louis U., 1953-56; asso. prof. law U. Buffalo, 1956-59; partner firm Lipsitz, Green, Fahringer & Fleming, Buffalo, 1959-62; prof. law State U. N.Y., Buffalo, 1962-76, asso. dean, 1962-66, 1974-76; prof., dean sch. law Pace U., 1976—; chief counsel com. on labor N.Y. Constl. Conv., 1967; research cons., draftsman N.Y. Bus. Corp. Law, 1956-59; gen. counsel Nat. Cath. Council on Civil Liberties, 1960-65; counsel, dir. Mental Health Manpower and Tng., Inc., Buffalo, 1974-76. Registered profl. engr., Minn. Home: 86 Stratford Ave White Plains NY 10605 Office: Pace Law Sch 78 Broadway White Plains NY 10603 Tel (914) 682-8260

FLEMING, WILLIAM MARVIN, JR., b. Winston-Salem, N.C., Oct. 20, 1924; LL.B., U. Ga., 1950. Admitted to Ga. bar, 1950; partner firm Nicholson & Fleming, Augusta, Ga., 1951-68; judge Superior Ct. Ga., Augusta, 1968—; mem. Ga. Gen. Assembly, 1959-68. Mem. Ga., Augusta Circuit, Augusta bar assns., Am. Trial Lawyers Assn. Home: 615 Scotts Way St Augusta GA 30904 Office: 305 City-County Municipal Bldg Augusta GA 30902 Tel (404) 722-1524

FLETCHER, DANIEL LOUIS, b. Los Angeles, Nov. 23, 1918; B.A., U. So. Calif., 1946; LL.B., Southwestern U., Los Angeles, 1949. Admitted to Calif. bar, 1950; partner firm Snyder & Fletcher, South Pasadena, Calif., 1950-53; dep. dist. atty. County of Los Angeles, 1953-66; judge Municipal Ct., Pasadena, Calif., 1966-71, Los Angeles County Superior Ct., 1971—. Pres. Optimist Club, South Pasadena, 1952; v.p. Lions Club, West Covina, Calif., 1962. Mem. Criminal Ct. Bar Assn., Pasadena Bar Assn., Delta Theta Phi. Home: 3655 Fairmeade Rd Pasadena CA 91107 Office: 111 N Hill St Los Angeles CA 90112 Tel (213) 974-5741

FLETCHER, FRANK UTLEY, b. N.C., Feb. 7, 1912; student N.C. State Coll., 1927-29; LL.B. cum laude, Wake Forest U., 1932; postgrad. Duke U., 1932-34. Admitted to N.C. bar, 1933, D.C. bar, 1939; atty. FCC, Washington, 1934-39; asso. firm Spearman & Roberson, Washington, D.C., 1939-42; individual practice law, Washington, 1945-53; sr. partner firm Fletcher, Heald, Rowell, Kenehan & Hildreth, Washington, 1953—; co-owner radio sta. WARL, Arlington, Va., 1946-51; chmn. communications industry com. Bus. Adv. Council Fed. Reports; mem. planning council World Peace Through Law Center, 1965-77. Mem. Nat. Assn. Broadcasters, Am., Fed., D.C. bar assns., Fed. Communications Bar Assn. (pres. 1960, exec. com. 1954-55), Am. Judicature Soc., Broadcast Pioneers (bd. dirs. 1976—, chmn. D.C. chpt. 1976—). Home: 4201 Cathedral Ave NW Washington DC 20016 Office: 1225 Connecticut Ave NW Washington DC 20036 Tel (202) 659-9100

FLETCHER, JOHN STUART, II, b. Washington, Feb. 22, 1938; B.S., U. N.C., Chapel Hill, 1961, J.D., 1964; LL.M., N.Y. U., 1969. Admitted to N.C. bar, 1964; individual practice law, Greenville, N.C., 1964-69, Swan Quarter, N.C., 1972—; asst. prof. East Carolina U., Greenville, 1965-67; dir. police sci. Pitt Tech. Inst., Greenville, 1967-69; asst. prof. law U. Ottawa (Can.), 1970-71; dir. Hyde Co. Bd. dirs. People to Hold Jocky's Ridge; Hyde County del. So. Albemarle Assn. Mem. N.C. Bar Assn., Phi Alpha Delta. Home: Oyster Creek Rd Swan Quarter NC 27885 Office: POB 81 Swan Quarter NC 27885 Tel (919) 926-7911

FLETCHER, NORMAN LEE, b. Newellton, La., Feb. 17, 1937; B.A., Calif. State U., Fresno, 1958; J.D., U. Calif., Hastings, 1967. Admitted to Calif. bar, 1968; dep. dist. atty. Fresno County (Calif.), 1968-70; individual practice law, Fresno, 1970—; torts prof. law San Joaquin Law Sch., 1975—. Bd. dirs. Family Service Center, Fresno, 1974-76. Mem. Fresno County and City C of C (dir.), Am., Calif., Fresno County bar assns., Calif. Trial Lawyers Assn. Home: 6264 N Van Ness Ave Fresno CA 93711 Office: 1015 Security Bank Bldg Fresno CA 93721 Tel (209) 485-5960

FLETCHER, RAYMOND RUSSWALD, JR., b. Schenectady, June 7, 1929; B. Chem. Engring., Rensselaer Poly. Inst., 1949; LL.B., Harvard, 1956. Admitted to N.Y. bar, 1956; asso. atty. Chadbourne, Parke, Whiteside & Wolff, N.Y.C., 1956-63; with Trans World Airlines, Inc., 1963—, v.p., gen. counsel, 1969—. Decorated Air medal. Mem. Am., N.Y. State bar assns., Assn. Bar City N.Y. Home: RD 1 Mount Kisco NY 10549 Office: 605 3d Ave New York City NY 10016*

FLETCHER, WALTER SINCLAIR, b. Birmingham, Ala., Sept. 24, 1923; student So. Coll. Birmingham, 1941-42, 1946-47; LL.B., U. Ala., 1949. Admitted to Ala. bar, 1949; partner firm Dominick, Fletcher, Yeilding, Dominick & Acker, and predecessors, Birmingham, 1949—; instr., lectr. various insts.; dir. So. Nat. Bank. Pres. Vis. Nursing Assn., 1971-72; mem. bd. edn. Mountain Brook, Ala., 1968—; chmn. adminstrv. bd. First United Meth. Ch., Birmingham., 1972-74; pres. Birmingham Civic Opera Assn., 1974-76. Mem. Am., Ala., Birmingham bar assns., Am. Judicature Soc. Home: 3548 Brookwood Rd Mountain Brook AL 35223 Office: 927 Brown-Marx Bldg Birmingham AL 35203 Tel (205) 322-0653

FLICK, JAY EDWARD, b. Meadville, Pa., Sept. 25, 1942; B.A., U. Colo., 1963, J.D., 1966. Admitted to Colo. bar, 1966; atty. Pueblo County (Colo.) Legal Services, Pueblo, 1966-68; individual practice law, Pueblo, 1968-72; partner firm Bollinger, Flick and Young, Pueblo, 1972-75; pres. Bollinger, Flick, Young and Drummond, 1975—. Mem. Pueblo Area Scholar. Found., Inc. (pres. 1976). Mem. Colo., Pueblo bar assns., Colo. Trial Lawyers Assn. (dir.), Assn. Trial Lawyers Am. Home: 2030 Oakland St Pueblo CO 81004 Office: 123 W 12th St Pueblo CO 81003 Tel (303) 542-1052

FLICK, JOHN EDMOND, b. Franklin, Pa., Mar. 14, 1922; student U. Pa., 1945; student Northwestern U., 1941-44, LL.B., 1948; postgrad. in law U. Va., 1960-61. Admitted to Ill. bar, 1948, Calif. bar, 1971, U.S. Supreme Ct. bar, 1973; asst. prof. law Calif. Western U. Law Sch., 1949-50; lt. col. JAGC, U.S. Army, 1950-63; faculty dept. law U.S. Mil. Acad., 1954-57; corp. counsel Litton Industries, Beverly Hills, Calif., 1963-67; sr. v.p., gen. counsel, sec. Bangor Punta Corp., Greenwich, Conn., 1967-70, also dir.; v.p., gen. counsel, sec. Times Mirror Co., Los Angeles, 1970—; dir. Tejon Ranch Co., Sporting News. Mem. Am. (Academic award 1961), Calif., Los Angeles County bar assns., Am. Soc. Corporate Secs., Northwestern U. Wigmore Club (life). Home: 23680 Park Sevilla Calabasas Park CA 91302 Office: Times Mirror Co Times Mirror Sq Los Angeles CA 90053 Tel (213) 486-3831

FLICKINGER, WALTER GARRETT, b. Erie, Pa., July 9, 1929; B.A., Yale, 1950; J.D., U. Mich., 1953. Admitted to N.Y. State bar, 1956, Ky. bar, 1969; asso. firm White & Case, N.Y.C., 1955-60; asst. prof. law Boston U., 1960-63; asso. prof. law U. Ky., Lexington, 1964-67, prof., 1967-75; prof. law U. N. Mex., Albuquerque, 1975—; univ. acad. ombudsman U. Ky., 1971-72; chmn. U. Ky. Senate Council, 1972. Mem. Council Legal Edn. Opportunities (dir.), Am., N.Y.C., Ky. bar assns., AAUP, Am. Hist. Soc., Phi Beta Kappa. Contbr. articles in field to legal jours. Home: 20 Lakeshore Dr NE Albuquerque NM 87112 Office: U N Mex Sch Law 1117 Stanford St NE Albuquerque NM 87131 Tel (505) 277-4654

FLIEHLER, RAYMOND HENRY, b. Strawberry Point, Iowa, May 11, 1912; B.A., State U. Iowa, 1936. Admitted to Iowa bar, 1938; individual practice law, Strawberry Point, 1942—; city atty., Strawberry Point, 1975-77. Mem. Clatyon County (Iowa) Bd. of Edn., 1968-74. Office: 118 W Mission St Strawberry Point IA 52076 Tel (319) 933-4980

FLINN, RICHARD DECAMP, b. Pitts., Mar. 28, 1923; B.A., U. Pitts., 1950, LL.B., 1951. Admitted to Pa. bar, 1951; with Trust dept. Mellon Bank, Pitts., 1951—, v.p. legal div., 1965—; dir. Monogahela Light and Power Co. Mem. Pa., Alleghany County bar assns. Home: 945 Florida Ave Mount Lebanon PA 15228 Office: 2531 Mellon Bank Bldg Mellon Square Pittsburgh PA 15230 Tel (412) 232-4418

FLINT, ROBERT BRYAN, b. Washington, Mar. 10, 1939; B.A., in Econs., Yale, 1960; LL.B., Georgetown U., 1963. Admitted to Va. bar, 1963, Alaska bar, 1964; asst. atty. gen. City of Juneau (Alaska), 1964; asst. dist. atty. 3d Jud. Dist., Anchorage, 1964-65; asso. firm Robison, McCaskey & Lewis, Anchorage, 1965-66; legis. asst. to Rep. Howard W. Pollock, Washington, 1967-68; partner firm Wohlforth & Flint; and predecessor, Anchorage, 1969—. Pres. Cath. Social Services, Inc., Anchorage, 1975—. Mem. Alaska Bar Assn. Home: 2515 Telequana Dr Anchorage AK 99503 Office: 645 G St Anchorage AK 99503 Tel (907) 272-9489

FLOBERG, JOHN FORREST, b. Chgo., Oct. 28, 1915; A.B., Loyola U., 1936; LL.B., Harvard, 1939. Admitted to Ill. bar, 1939, D.C. bar, 1953, Ohio bar, 1961; asso. firm Kirkland, Fleming, Green, Martin & Ellis, Chgo., 1939-41, 46-49, partner, Washington, 1953-57; asst. sec. navy for air, 1949-53; mem. U.S. AEC, 1957-60; gen. counsel Firestone Tire & Rubber Co., Akron, Ohio, 1960—, sec., 1962—. Mem. Akron-Canton Airport Authority, 1965—, pres., 1971, 73; mem. Tri-County Planning Commn., 1971-75, Summit County Emergency Med. Services Com., 1972—, Lake Erie Regional Transp. Rev. Bd., 1973—, Summit County Anti-Pollution Rev. Bd., 1974-76, N.E. Ohio Five-County Planning and Devel. Orgn., 1975—. Mem. Am., Ill., Chgo., Ohio, Akron bar assns., Am. Judicature Soc. Home: 4240 Ira Rd Bath OH 44210 Office: 1200 Firestone Pkwy Akron OH 44317 Tel (216) 379-6432

FLOCKS, KARL WILHELM, b. N.Y.C., Apr. 27, 1910; B.M.E., Johns Hopkins U., 1930; J.D., George Washington U., 1934. Admitted to D.C. bar, 1933, U.S. Ct. Customs and Patent Appeals, 1934, U.S. Supreme Ct. bar, 1955; mem. exam. staff U.S. Patent Office, Washington, 1930-37; sr. mem. firm Karl W. Flocks & Assos., Washington, 1940—. Mem. Am. Bar Assn., Bar Assn. D.C., Am. Trial Lawyers Assn., Am. Patent Law Assn., Internat. Assn. Protection of Indsl. Property, Internat. Patent and Trademark Assn., The Chartered Inst. Patent Agts. (London). Office: 1226 Munsey Bldg Washington DC 20004

FLOMENHOFT, HOWARD CHARLES, b. Phila., Nov. 29, 1940; B.A., Cornell U., 1962; J.D., U. Chgo., 1965. Admitted to Ill. bar, 1965; asso. firm Quinn, Jacobs & Barry, Chgo., 1965; estate and gift tax atty. IRS, Chgo., 1965-68; mem. firm Levenfeld, Kanter, Baskes & Lippitz, Chgo., 1968-74; individual practice law, Chgo., 1974—; lectr. in field. Mem. United Jewish Appeal Young Leadership Cabinet, 1976—. Mem. Am., Chgo., Ill. State, Fed. bar assns., Chgo. Council Lawyers. Home: 3257 Prestwick Ln Northbrook IL 60062 Office: 180 N LaSalle St Suite 1905 Chicago IL 60601 Tel (312) 782-6690

FLOOD, DAVID ALLAN, b. Phila., July 19, 1938; B.A., Pa. State U., 1960; LL.B., Temple U., 1964. Admitted to Pa. bar, 1965; partner firm Little, Gettig, Flood, Lee & Martin, Bellefonte, Pa., 1965—; home office claims supt. Gen. Accident & Ins. Co., Phila., 1964-65; borough solicitor Bellefonte, 1966—; U.S. commr., 1965-70; asst. gen. counsel Am. Philatelic Soc. Pres. Bellefonte Area Community Fund, 1968; chmn. personnel com. Centre Community Hosp., 1969. Mem. Am., Pa. bar assns., Bellefonte Area C. of C. (pres. 1970-71), Lambda Sigma Kappa. Tel (814) 355-4769

FLOOR, RICHARD EARL, b. Lynn, Mass., Aug. 3, 1940; A.B., Fairfield U., 1962; LL.B., Harvard, 1965. Admitted to Mass. bar, 1965; law clk. U.S. 6th Circuit Ct. Appeals, 1965-66; asso. firm Goodwin, Procter & Hoar, Boston, 1966-75, partner, 1975—; dir. several pvt. cos. Mem. Am. Bar Assn. Contbr. articles to legal jours. Office: Goodwin Procter & Hoar 28 State St Boston MA 02109 Tel (617) 523-5700

FLORA, FRED LESLIE, JR., b. Tucson, Feb. 5, 1947; B.S. in Bus. Adminstrn., U. N.C., 1969, J.D., 1972. Admitted to N.C. bar, 1972, Fed. Dist. Ct. bar, 1973; asso. firm Ammons & Maxwell, Fayetteville, N.C., 1972-73; partner firm Ammons & Flora, Fayetteville, 1973—. Mem. Am., N.C. Cumberland County (v.p. real property sect., v.p. young lawyers sect.) bar assns., N.C. Acad. Trial Lawyers, Delta Theta Phi. Home: 116B Lofton Dr Fayetteville NC 28301 Office: Box 1177 Fayetteville NC 28301 Tel (919) 483-1033

FLORA, WILLIAM GROVER, b. Neelyville, Mo., Mar. 12, 1923; LL.B., J.D., U. Mo. at Columbia, 1950. Admitted to Mo. bar, 1950; ins. claims worker State Mutual, U.S.F. & G. Ins. Co., 1951-56; partner firm Clancy D. Tull, Mo., 1956-59; individual practice law, Independence, Mo., 1959—. Mem. sch. bd., Lancaster, Mo., 1950. Mem. Mo., Kansas City bar assns. Sub. police judge, Kansas City, 1967-68; police judge Blue Summit, Mo., 1972. Home: 129 E Bridlespur Dr Kansas City MO 64114 Office: 554 S Ash St Independence MO 64053 Tel (816) 254-6070

FLORENCE, HENRY JOHN, b. Hempstead, N.Y., Dec. 11, 1934; B.S., Villanova U., 1956; LL.D., Fordham U., 1961. Admitted to N.Y. bar, 1962, Ariz. bar, 1963; atty. Navajo Legal Aid, Window Rock, Ariz., 1962-63; dep. atty. Maricopa County (Ariz.), Phoenix, 1964-65, civil chief dep., 1965-67; partner firm Stewart & Florence, Phoenix, 1967-73; sr. partner firm Henry J. Florence Ltd., Phoenix, 1973—. Pres., New Ariz. Family, Inc., 1974—, Ariz. Drug Abuse Adv. Council, Phoenix, 1976—. Mem. N.Y., Ariz. State bar assns., Am. Trial Lawyers Assn., Nat. Assn. Criminal Def. Lawyers, Calif. Attys. for Criminal Justice. Office: 13 W Jefferson St Phoenix AZ 85003 Tel (602) 258-5375

FLORES, NESS, b. Rio Hondo, Tex., Dec. 13, 1942; B.S., U. Wis., 1967; J.D., Baylor U., 1969. Admitted to Wis. bar, 1970; mem. firm Langill & Flores, Waukesha, 1970-71; dir. legal services United Migrant Opportunity Services, Inc., Milw.; dir. migrant legal services and Latin criminal def. Milw. Legal Services, Inc., 1971-74; exec. dir. Gov's. Commn. on Migrant Labor, Madison, Wis., 1974—. Mem. Wis. Equal Rights Council, Wis. Local Affairs and Devel. Council, Waukesha Police and Fire Commn.; bd. dirs. Migrant Legal Action Program, Washington, Wis. Legal Services. Mem. State Bar Wis., Chicano Lawyers Assn. Co-author: Advocacy for Latinos, 1976; also govt. reports. Home: 125 N Charles St Waukesha WI 53186 Office: 201 E Washington Ave Madison WI 53701

FLORY, ROBERT LEHR, b. St. Edward, Nebr., July 19, 1918; B.S. in Bus. Adminstrn., U. Nebr., 1940, J.D., 1942. Admitted to Nebr. bar, 1942; individual practice law, Fremont, Nebr., 1946-61; judge 6th Jud. Dist., Nebr., 1961-77. Mem. Nebr. State, Am. bar assns., Am. Judicature Soc. Home: 2141 Phelps St Fremont NE 68025 Office: Ct House Fremont NE 68025

FLOTA, CHARLES THERMAN, b. Norris City, Ill., Jan. 4, 1894; LL.B., Chgo. Kent Coll. Law, 1918, LL.M., Blackstone Coll., 1919, J.D., 1920. Admitted to Ill. bar, 1919, New Mex. bar, 1950; individual practice law, Harrisburg, Ill., 1919-50, Truth or Consequences, N.Mex., 1950—; Ill. state's atty., Harrisburg, 1924-28; city atty., Harrisburg, 1935-36, corp. counsel, 1936-40; municipal judge, Truth or Consequences, 1976—. Mem. N. Mex. Bar Assn. Author: Life Yesterday, Today, Tomorrow, 1970. Home: 802 Marie St Truth or Consequences NM 87901 Tel (505) 894-3688

FLOURNOY, J. MICHAEL, b. Williams, Ariz., Apr. 5, 1937; B.S. in Bus. Adminstrn., U. Ariz., 1959, J.D., 1962. Admitted to Ariz. bar, 1962; partner firm Preston, Flournoy, Flick and Challis, and predecessors, Flagstaff, Ariz., 1962—; atty. Coconino County (Ariz.), 1969-76. Chmn. Red Cross Dr.; chmn. Heart Assn. Mem. Assn. Trail Lawyers Am., Assn. Trial Lawyers Ariz., Nat. Dist. Attys. Assn., Ariz. County Attys. Assn., Ariz. Sheriffs and County Attys. Assn. Home: 5340 E Mount Pleasant Dr Flagstaff AZ 86001 Office: 202 Arizona Bank Bldg PO Box E Flagstaff AZ 86002 Tel (602) 774-7386

FLOYD, DAVID KENNETH, b. Buffalo, July 11, 1932; B.A., Trinity Coll., Hartford, Conn., 1954; J.D., U. Chgo., 1960. Admitted to N.Y. State bar, 1960; asso. firm Phillips, Lytle, Hitchcock, Blame & Huber, Buffalo, 1960-65, partner, 1965—; justice Town of Aurora (N.Y.), 1964—. Mem. Erie County (N.Y.), N.Y. State, Am. bar assns. Office: 3400 Marine Midland Center Buffalo NY 14203 Tel (716) 847-8460

FLOYD, JAMES B., III, b. Booneville, Miss., June 28, 1942; B.S., Miss. State U., 1960; J.D., Jackson Sch. Law, 1970. Admitted to Miss. bar, 1970; individual practice law, Tupelo, Miss., 1970—. Trustee, Tupelo Sch. Bd. Mem. Am., Miss. bar assns., Mis. Prosecutors Assn. Office: PO Box 1781 Tupelo MS 38801 Tel (601) 844-4324

FLOYD, JASON HOUSTON, b. Panola County, Miss., Sept. 27, 1908; student Vanderbilt U., 1925-27; LL.B., U. Miss., 1930. Admitted to Miss. bar, 1930, Tenn. bar, 1931; practiced in Memphis, 1930-31, Senatobia, Miss., 1935-42, Gulfport, Miss., 1946—, mem. firm Floyd & Holleman, 1952-61; partner firm Floyd & Floyd, 1967-77; mem. Miss. Ho. of Reps., 1936-40. Mem. Am., Miss. State, Harrison County (Miss.) bar assns. Home: 200 Southern Circle Gulfport MS 39501 Office: 310-12 Hewes Bldg Gulfport MS 39501 Tel (601) 863-0522

FLOYD, JAY HAWKINS (TIMBER), JR., b. Big Spring, Tex., Aug. 21, 1943; B.A. in History, U. Tex., 1967; J.D., South Tex. Coll. Law, 1970. Admitted to Tex. bar, 1970; with JAGC, U.S. Army, 1970-72; individual practice law, Midland, Tex., 1972—. Bd. dirs. LaFlorecita Day Care Center, Midland, 1972—. Mem. State Bar Tex., Am., Midland bar assns., Midland Jaycees, Midland C. of C. Office: 200 W Texas St Suite 111 PO Box 1852 Midland TX 79701 Tel (915) 683-5213

FLOYD, TERRY KIMSEY, b. Jasper, Ga., Oct. 16, 1948; B.A. in History, Emory U., 1970; J.D., U. Ga., 1973. Admitted to Ga. bar, 1973; partner firm Jenkins & Landrum, Jasper, 1973-77, firm Landrum & Floyd, Jasper, 1977—. Vice chmn. Pickens County (Ga.) Democratic Exec. Com., 1974—; mem. Ga. Dem. Exec. Com., 1976—. Mem. State Bar Ga., Blue Ridge Bar Assn. (sec.-treas.). Home: 1460 Oglethorpe Mountain Rd Bent Tree Jasper GA 20143 Office: 201 N West St Jasper GA 30143 Tel (404) 692-6464

FLYNN, ALVIN NASH, b. Tyler, Tex., Dec. 19, 1946; B.A., Baylor U., 1970, J.D., 1973. Admitted to Tex. bar, 1973; asso. with Charles H. Clark, Tyler, 1973—. Mem. Tex., Smith County bar assns. Home: 3526 Betts St Tyler TX 75701 Office: Citizens Bank Bldg POB 98 Tyler TX 75701 Tel (214) 593-2514

FLYNN, CHARLES PHILLIP, b. Chgo., Apr. 17, 1943; B.A., Willamette U., 1965; LL.B., Harvard, 1968. Admitted to Alaska bar, 1969; asso. firm Burr, Pease & Kurtz, Anchorage, 1968-70, partner, 1970—. Mem. Alaska (chmn. com. on ethics 1973—), Anchorage, Am. bar assns. Office: 825 W 8th Ave Anchorage AK 99501 Tel (907) 279-2411

FLYNN, JOHN LAURENCE, JR., b. Los Angeles, July 21, 1926; B.S., U. Calif., Los Angeles, 1960; J.D., Southwestern U., 1957. Admitted to Calif. bar, 1958; staff Calif. State Bar, 1958-70; municipal ct. judge Central Orange County Jud. Dist., 1970-72; judge Superior Ct. Orange County (Calif.), Santa Ana, 1972—. Mem. Am. Bd. Trial Advocates. Office: 700 Civic Center Dr Santa Ana CA 92701 Tel (714) 834-3886

FLYNN, JOSEPH P., b. Ansonia, Conn., Oct. 19, 1940; J.D., Georgetown U. Admitted to Conn. bar, 1965; mem. firm Buckley & Flynn, Ansonia, 1965—; mem. exec. bd. Conn. Jr. Bar, 1967-68; staff U.S. Senator Conn.; mem. subcom. juvenile delinquency Senate Judiciary Com.; mem. Conn. State Senate, 1974—, counsel to majority leader, 1971-74. Mem. Am., Conn., New Haven County,

Valley bar assns. Home: 4 Finney St Ansonia CT 06401 Office: 366 Main St Ansonia CT 06401 Tel (203) 735-7447

FLYNN, JOSEPH PATRICK, b. Mineola, N.Y., Oct. 2, 1939; B.S. in Polit. Sci., Benedictine Coll., 1962; J.D., Washburn U., 1965; M. Internat. Mgmt., Am. Sch. Internat. Mgmt., 1973. Admitted to Kans. bar, 1965; atty. AEC, Albuquerque, 1965-66; corp. atty. Garvey, Inc., Wichita, Kans., 1966-68; gen. counsel Pizza Hut, Inc., Wichita, 1968-72, v.p. internat. div., 1972—. Mem. Wichita Crime Commn., 1973-76. Mem. Am., Kans., Wichita bar assns. Contbr. articles to profl. jours. Office: 10225 E Kellogg Wichita KS 67201 Tel (816) 685-8261

FLYTHE, JOSEPH JOHNSON, b. Conway, N.C., June 6, 1930; B.A., High Point Coll., 1951; LL.B., U. of N.C., 1958. Admitted to N.C. bar, 1958; atty., Northampton County, N.C., 1958-66; asso. firm Cherry, Cherry & Flythe, Ahoskie, N.C., 1966—; solicitor of recorders Northampton County Ct., 1960-62. Mem. N.C. Bar Assn. Home: 433 Carolina St Ahoskie NC 27910 Office: 119 W Main St Ahoskie NC 27910 Tel (919) 332-4094

FODEMAN, ALAN BERNARD, b. Bridgeport, Conn., Mar. 17, 1938; B.A., U. Conn., 1959; LL.B., Boston U., 1962. Admitted to Conn. bar, 1962; individual practice law, Bridgeport, 1962—. Alderman City of Bridgeport, 1971-72. Mem. Bridgeport Bar Assn. Home: 109 Random Rd Fairfield CT 06432 Office: 1101 E Main St Bridgeport CT 06609 Tel (203) 367-6345

FOGEL, EDWARD ALLAN, b. Chgo., Sept. 17, 1912; student DePaul U., Chgo., 1933-35; LL.B., St. John's U., 1939; postgrad. Columbia U., 1946-47. Admitted to N.Y. bar, 1940, U.S. 2d Circuit Ct. Appeals bar, 1941; individual practice law, N.Y.C., 1940—; prof. law taxation Grad. Sch. Pace U., 1959—; lectr. taxation law. Trustee Scarsdale Adult Sch., 1970-77; mem. nat. com. Harvard U. Center for Jewish Studies, 1975—. Mem. Am. Bar Assn., Assn. Bar City N.Y., Fed. Bar Council, Fedn. Jewish Philanthropies (trustee), Am. Jewish Soc. for Service. Author: Your Tax Guide; columnist Bus. Week Newsletter, 1969-72; contbr. articles to profl. and popular mags. Home: 86 Carthage Rd Scarsdale NY 10583 Office: 500 5th Ave New York City NY 10036 Tel (212) 564-1727

FOGEL, JO BENSON, b. Richmond, Va., Apr. 13, 1945; B.A., Duke, 1966; J.D., George Washington U., 1970. Admitted to Md. bar, 1970, D.C. bar, 1971, U.S. Supreme Ct. bar, 1974; law clk. to asso. judge 7th Jud. Circuit, Upper Marlboro, Md., 1970; consumer affairs coordinator Electronic Industries Assn., Consumer Electronics Group, Washington, 1970-71; asso. firm Dukes & Troese, Landover, Md., 1971-75, partner, 1976; guest lectr. community domestic relations course Prince George's County Community Coll.; individual practice law, Kensington and Hyattsville, Md., 1977—; counsel Prince George's County Senate Del., 1976, 77. Mem. Am., Md., D.C., Montgomery County, Prince George's County bar assns., Md. Women's Bar Assn. (pres.), Prince George's County Women's Law Caucus, Pi Sigma Alpha. Home: 2428 E Gate Dr Silver Spring MD 20906 Office: 5303 Baltimore Ave Hyattsville MD 20781 also 10605 Concord St #301A Kensington MD 20795 Tel (301) 699-8585

FOGEL, SHELDON LESLIE, b. Bklyn., Mar. 2, 1942; B.A., U. N.C., 1963, J.D., 1965. Admitted to N.C. bar, 1965, U.S. Supreme Ct. bar, 1971, U.S. Ct. Appeals bar, 1974; asso. firm Johnson, Gamble & Hollowell, Raleigh, N.C., 1965-66; partner firm Potter & Fogel, Raleigh, 1967-69, McDaniel & Fogel, Raleigh, 1970—. Vice pres. B'nai B'rith Soc., Raleigh, 1967. Mem. Raleigh C. of C., Am., N.C. bar assns., N.C. Acad. Trial Lawyers, Am. Trial Lawyers Assn. Home: 4505 Edwards Mill Rd Raleigh NC 27612 Office: 1305 Millbrook Rd Raleigh NC 27609 Tel (919) 872-4920

FOGLE, FREDRIC DEAN, b. Newark, Nov. 18, 1936; B.E.E., Ohio State U., 1959; J.D., Rutgers U., 1970. Admitted to N.J. bar, 1970; v.p. Q.V.S. Inc., East Orange, N.J., 1963-70, gen. counsel, 1970—; individual practice law, East Orange, 1970—; dir. Products Liability Prevention Conf., Newark, 1973-74; participant Products Liability Prevention Conf., Design Engring. Show, Reliability Conf. Mem. Roseland (N.J.) Bd. Edn., 1968-71. Mem. Essex County Bar Assn., IEEE. (com. chmn.). Home: 2 Overlook Ln Mendham NJ 07945 Office: 20 N 15th St East Orange NJ 07017 Tel (201) 673-3955

FOGLEMAN, JOHN ALBERT, b. Memphis, Nov. 5, 1911; LL.B., U. Memphis, 1934. Admitted to Ark. bar, 1934; dep. circuit ct. clk. Crittenden County (Ark.), 1933-34; individual practice law, Marion, Ark., 1934-44; partner firm Hale & Fogleman, Marion and West Memphis, Ark., 1944-66; dep. pros. atty. Crittenden County, 1946-57; asso. justice Ark. Supreme Ct., Little Rock, 1967—; chmn. Ark. Judiciary Commn., 1963-65; mem. Ark Constl. Revision Commn., Ark. Criminal Code Revision Commn. Fellow Am. Coll. Trial Lawyers; mem. Ark., (past pres.), Am. bar assns. Home: 67 Cherry St Marion AR 72364 Office: Justice Bldg Little Rock AR 72201 Tel (501) 372-5643

FOHRMAN, BURTON H., b. Chgo., July 9, 1939; B.A., U. So. Calif., 1960; J.D., U. Calif., Los Angeles, 1963. Admitted to Calif. bar, 1964; asso. firm Martin S. Stolzoff, Beverly Hills, Calif., 1963-64, Hennigan, Ryneal & Butterwick, Riverside, Calif., 1964-66, Redwine & Sherrill, Riverside, 1966—. Vice pres., trustee Riverside Art Center and Mus., 1976—; pres. Temple Beth El, Riverside, 1968—; chmn. United Jewish Appeal campaign, 1973. Mem. Am., Calif., Riverside County, Los Angeles County (chmn. com. real estate fin. 1977—) bar assns. Office: 3737 Main St Suite 1020 Riverside CA 92501 Tel (714) 684-2520

FOLEY, DERMOT G., b. N.Y.C., Apr. 8, 1931; B.S., Columbia, 1957, LL.B., 1960. Admitted to N.Y. State bar, 1961, Md. bar, 1968, U.S. Supreme Ct. bar, 1971, other circuit and dist. ct. bars; litigation atty. Burlingham Hupper & Kennedy, N.Y.C., 1960-61, Hill Betts Yamaoka Freehill & Longcope, N.Y.C., 1961-62, Kaplan Kilsheimer & Foley, N.Y.C., 1964—; legal counsel Nat. League of Families of Am. Prisoners and Missing in S.E. Asia, Washington and N.Y.C., 1974—; spl. law asst. to bd. justices N.Y. State Supreme Ct., N.Y.C., 1962-64. Mem. N.Y. State, Bronx County, N.Y.C. bar assns., Fed. Bar Council. Home: 10 Ocean Ave Larchmont NY 10538 Office: 122 E 42d St New York City NY 10017 Tel (212) 687-1980

FOLEY, FRANCIS FREDERICK, b. Boston, May 26, 1917; A.B., Harvard U., 1939; LL.B., Boston U., 1954. Admitted to Mass. bar, 1954; mem. firm Merritt U. Aldrich, Mass., 1955-65, James D. Casey, Mass., 1965-67, Roger Babb, 1967-69; individual practice law, Brockton, Mass., 1969—; law instr. Suffolk U., 1972—. Mem. Mass. Bar Assn. Home: Winnetuxet Rd Olympton MA 02367 Office: One Centre St Brockton MA 02401 Tel (617) 588-6100

FOLEY, JAMES JOSEPH, b. Des Moines, Nov. 15, 1935; B.S., Iowa State U., 1958; J.D., Drake U., 1961; M.B.A., U. Dayton, 1965; M.A. in Internat. Relations, U. So. Calif., 1967. Admitted to Iowa bar, 1961, Calif. bar, 1970; trial atty. U.S. Air Force, Washington, 1961-65, staff judge adv., London, 1965-68, prof. Judge Adv. Sch. Inst. Profl. Devel., Air U., Montgomery, Ala., 1968-69; counsel McDonnell Douglas Corp., Huntington Beach, Calif., 1970—. Mem. Fed., Am., Orange County bar assns. Office: 5301 Balsa Ave Huntington Beach CA 92647 Tel (714) 896-2567

FOLEY, JOHN BERNARD, b. N.Y.C., June 21, 1935; A.B., Holy Cross Coll., 1957; LL.B., Fordham U., 1960. Admitted to N.Y. bar, 1961; asso. firm McCormick, Dunne & Foley, N.Y.C., 1961-66, partner, 1966—. Mem. Am., Queens County bar assns., Long Island City (pres. 1974), N.Y. County lawyers assns. Office: 55 Liberty St New York City NY 10005 Tel (212) RE2-5136

FOLEY, JOHN FIELD, b. Tulsa, Aug. 6, 1931; A.B., Stanford U., 1953, J.D., 1956. Admitted to Calif. bar, 1956, U.S. Supreme Ct. bar, 1967; asso. firm Wool & Richardson, San Jose, Calif., 1957-62; individual practice law, San Jose, 1962—. Mem. adv. bd. Calif. State Collection Agy., 1971-76, sec. 1974, vice chmn., 1975; mem. Vis. Nurse Assn., 1969—, chmn. 1972; mem. Republican Central Com., 1962-71, chmn. 1969-71; mem. Santa Clara County Young Reps., chmn. 1961; councilman Monte Sereno, Calif., 1976—. Mem. Barristers Club Santa Clara County (pres. 1963), Am., Calif., West Valley bar assns., Stanford U. Law Soc. Santa Clara County (pres. 1974-76). Home: 18441 Hernandez Ln Monte Sereno CA 95030 Office: 2 N 2d St San Jose CA 95113 Tel (408) 287-6287

FOLEY, JOHN FRANCIS, b. Milw., Sept. 4, 1929; B.S., U. Wis., 1952, M.S., 1953, J.D., 1955. Admitted to Wis. bar, 1955, Fed. ct. bars, 1955; partner firm Valenti, Flessas & Foley, Milw., 1955-68; judge Milwaukee County Ct., 1968-71, 2d Wis. Circuit Ct., 1971-76; chief judge Family, Children and Probate Cts., Milwaukee County, 1976—. Mem. Milw. Sch. Bd., 1959-68, pres., 1965-66, 66-67. Mem. Am., Wis., Milw. bar assns., Order Coif. Recipient numerous community achievement awards. Home: 609 N 115th St Wauwatosa WI 53226 Office: Milwaukee County Courthouse 901 N 9th St Milwaukee WI 53233 Tel (414) 278-4504

FOLEY, JOSEPH LLEWELLYN, b. Phila., Oct. 22, 1937; B.S., Pa. State U., 1960; J.D., Temple U., 1968. Admitted to Pa. bar, 1968, U.S. Dist. Ct. bar, 1968, U.S. Ct. of Appeals bar, 1968, U.S. Supreme Ct. bar, 1974; asso. firm Detweiler, Hughes & Kokenos, Phila., 1968-72, firm Durben and Moore, Morrisville, Pa., 1972-73; individual practice law, Abington, Pa., 1973—; pub. defender Montgomery County, Pa., 1972-75. Mem. Am., Pa., Montgomery County (membership com.) bar assns., Pa. Trial Lawyers Assn., Montgomery County Estate Planning Council. Office: 1219 York Rd Abington PA 19001 Tel (215) 884-5879

FOLEY, PATRICK JOSEPH, b. N.Y.C., Oct. 2, 1930; A.B., Iona Coll., 1957, J.D., N.Y. U., 1961. Admitted to N.Y. bar, 1961, fed. bar, 1966, U.S. Supreme Ct. bar, 1971, U.S. Tax Ct. bar, 1971, U.S. Customs Ct. bar, 1971, U.S. Ct. Appeals bar, 1971; asst. underwriter Atlantic Mut., 1958-60; account exec. Hagedorn and Co., 1960-62; with Am. Home Assurance Group, 1963, asst. gen. counsel, 1974; asst. counsel Am. Home Assurance Co. and Ins. Co. State of Pa., 1964, counsel, 1967; counsel Am. Internat. Life Ins. Co. N.Y., 1967, sec., 1968; sec., counsel Nat. Union Fire Ins. Co. and Birmingham Fire Ins. Co., 1969, v.p., gen. counsel, 1970; v.p., gen. counsel Lexington Ins. Co., 1972—; now v.p., gen. counsel Am. Home Assurance Co., AIU Ins. Co., Am. Internat. Life Assurance Co. N.Y., Birmingham Fire Ins. Co. Pa., Commerce and Industry Ins. Co., Del. Am. Life Ins. Co., Life Ins. Co. N.H., Nat. Union Fire Ins. Co. Pitts., Trans Atlantic Reins. Co., Ins. Co. State Pa., Pacific Union Life Ins. Co., Am. Internat. Aviation, Inc. Mem. Am., Westchester County, Yorktown, Bronx County, N.Y. State bar assns., Am. Arbitration Assn. Home: 2 Fox Meadow Ln Scarsdale NY 10583 Office: 102 Maiden Ln New York City NY 10005 Tel (212) 791-7437

FOLEY, ROGER D., b. 1917; LL.B., U. San Francisco. Admitted to Nev. bar, 1946; atty. gen. Nev.; chief judge U.S. Dist. Ct., Nev. Dist., Las Vegas. Mem. Am. Bar Assn. Office: Federal Bldg Las Vegas NV 89101*

FOLGER, ALONZO DILLARD, b. Mt. Airy, N.C., Nov. 15, 1922; student U. N.C., 1938-40; J.D., Wake Forest U., 1949. Admitted to N.C. bar, 1949; asso. firm Price & Osborne, Eden, N.C., 1949-51; mem. firm Folger and Fulp, and predecessors, Madison, N.C., 1951-75, firm Folger & Tucker, Madison, 1975—; past mem. N.C. Cts. Commn., N.C. State Bar Council. Mem. bd. stewards Madison Meth. Ch. exec. com., bd. dirs. Hope Valley Inc. Mem. Am., N.C. bar assns., N.C. State Bar, Am. Judicature Soc., Pan-Helenic Council, Phi Alpha Delta. Home: 206 S Market St Madison NC 27025 Office: 102 E Murphy St Madison NC 27025 Tel (919) 548-2309

FOLGER, WORTH BARNARD, b. Dobson, N.C., Jan. 6, 1917; LL.B., U. N.C., 1948. Admitted to N.C. bar, 1948; individual practice law, Sparta, N.C., 1948-74; partner firm Folger & Murray, Sparta, 1974—; town atty. Town of Sparta, 1948—; founder, developer Mahogany Rock Recreation & Resort Homes Community. Office: NW Bank Bldg Sparta NC 28675 Tel (919) 372-5541

FOLLICK, ROBERT LEE, b. Cambridge, Mass., July 20, 1940; B.S., Purdue U., 1962; LL.B., Bklyn. Law Sch., 1966, J.D., 1967. Admitted to N.Y. State bar, 1967; customs examiner, import specialist and acting law specialist U.S. Customs Service, N.Y.C., 1962-67; asso. firm Serko & Sklaroff, N.Y.C., 1967, firm Sharretts, Paley, Carter & Blauvelt, N.Y.C., 1968-71, firm Siegel, Mandell & Davidson, N.Y.C., 1971-76, partner firm Follick & Furman, N.Y.C., 1977—. Commr. football program Huntington Boys' Club, 1971-77; past pres. Half Hollow Hills Little League. Mem. Assn. Customs Bar, N.Y. County Lawyers Assn. Office: 55 Liberty St New York City NY 10005 Tel (212) 233-6630

FOLTZ, CHARLES ROBERT, b. Evanston, Ill., April 18, 1938; B.A., Harvard, 1960; D.S., U. Paris, 1961; LL.B., Harvard, 1964. Admitted to Ill. bar, 1965; asso. firm Woodson Pattishall & Garner, Chgo., 1964-65; asso. firm Chapman and Cutler, Chgo., 1965-73, partner, 1973—. Mem. Ill. bar assn. Home: 1380 N Elm Tree Rd Lake Forest IL 60045 Office: 111 W Monroe St Chicago IL 60603 Tel (312) 726-6130

FONDI, MICHAEL EUGENE, b. Ely, Nev., Apr. 4, 1937; B.A., Stanford, 1959; J.D., Hastings Coll., 1962. Admitted to Calif. bar, 1963, Nev. bar, 1964; adminstrv. asst. to gov. Nev., Carson City, 1963-65; dep. atty. gen. State of Nev., Carson City, 1965-66; chief dep. dist. atty. City and County of Carson City, 1967-70; dist. atty. Carson City, 1971—; mem. small county allocation com. Nev. Crime Commn., 1976—. Mem. 1st Jud. Dist. (pres. 1968-69), Nev., Calif., Am. bar assns., Nev. (pres. 1972), Nat. dist. attys. assns. Home: 2210 Ash Canyon Rd Carson City NV 89701 Office: 208 N Carson St Carson City NV 89701 Tel (702) 882-1619

FONER, HAROLD BERNARD, b. N.Y.C., July 23, 1923; A.B., N.Y. U., 1948, M.A., 1949; J.D., Bklyn. Law Sch., 1950, LL.M., 1956. Admitted to N.Y. bar, 1950, U.S. Supreme Ct. bar, 1956; individual practice law, N.Y.C., 1950—; counsel N.Y.C. Police Dept. Traffic Squad Benevolent Assn., 1958—; counsel Patrolmen's Benevolent Assn., N.Y.C., 1973—, counsel to pres., 1977—; gen. counsel Stationary Firemen, City of N.Y. local 1795, AFL-CIO, 1973—, Baseball Broadcasters Assn. Am., 1973—; mem. mayor's com. on emergency criminal justice, N.Y.C.; mem. Police Square Club of City of N.Y., St. George Assn. of N.Y.C. Police Dept., City Club of City of N.Y. Mem. Bklyn. Bar Assn. (chmn. com. on human rights 1965-72, chmn. com. on criminal ct. City N.Y., 1972-75, chmn. spl. action com. on Pres's. report 1968-70). Lectr., coordinator in police phase of criminal justice adminstrn., N.Y. U. Sch. Law, 1970. Home: 160 E 38th St New York City NY 10016 Office: 188 Montague St Brooklyn NY 11201 Tel (212) 624-5775

FONG, FRANKLIN DEA, b. Hong Kong, June 21, 1920; A.B., U. Md., 1948; LL.B., George Washington U., 1950. Admitted to D.C. bar, 1951, Va. bar, 1968; individual practice law, Washington, 1952—. Chmn., Chinese Consol. Benevolent Assn., Washington 1974-76. Home: 8502 Doyle Dr Alexandria VA 22308 Office: 850 Nat Press Bldg 529 14th St NW Washington DC 20004 Tel (202) 347-0776

FONG, WESLEY FRANCIS, b. Honolulu, July 6, 1943; B.A. in Polit. Sci., U. Hawaii, 1965; J.D., U. Ill., 1968. Admitted to Hawaii bar, 1968; dep. atty. gen. Hawaii Transp. Div., Honolulu, 1968, Hawaii Anti-Trust Div., Honolulu, 1971; trial and def. counsel U.S. Army, Ft. Sam Houston, Tex. and Republic of Vietnam, 1969, dep. staff JAGC 29th Inf. Brigade, 1971; dep. corp. counsel City and County of Honolulu, 1972—; chief mil. justice IX Corps USAR, 1972—; real estate broker, Honolulu, 1973; v.p., legal counsel Hawaii Camp Fire, Inc., 1974; chmn. Maryknoll Sch. Adv. Bd. Mem. Hawaii Res. Officers Assn. (judge adv. 1973—), Am. Judicature Soc., Am., Hawaii bar assns., Hawaii Young Lawyers Assn., Honolulu Bd. Realtors, Chinese C. of C., Hawaii Jaycees (past v.p.). Decorated Bronze Star with oak leaf cluster (U.S.); Cross of Gallantry (Vietnam). Office: Dept of Corp Counsel City Hall Honolulu HI 96813 Tel (808) 523-4702

FOONBERG, JAY G., b. Chgo., Oct. 29, 1935; B.S. in Accounting, U. Calif. at Los Angeles, 1957, J.D., 1963. Admitted to Calif. bar, 1964; individual practice law, Beverly Hills, Calif., 1964-70; partner firm Foonberg & Frandzel, Beverly Hills, 1970-72, pres., prin., 1972—; auditor Calif. Bd. Equalization, 1957-59; accountant Seidman & Seidman, Beverly Hills, 1959-60, Lever & Anker, Beverly Hills, 1960-63; judge protem Beverly Hills Municipal Ct., 1969-71; lectr. econs. of law practice. Mem. Brazil Calif. Trade Assn. (pres. 1976, 77), Am. (council mem. econs. of law practice sect. 1976-77), Beverly Hills (bd. govs. 1972-75) bar assns., Am., Calif. (pres. 1970, 74) assns. attys.-C.P.A.'s. Author: How to Start and Build a Law Practice, 1976. Recipient Order of So. Cross, Brazil, 1974. Home: 716 N Rexford Dr Beverly Hills CA 90210 Office: 8530 Wilshire Blvd Beverly Hills CA 90211 Tel (213) 659-2611

FOONMAN, G(OTSHALL) COVINGTON, b. Woodland, Calif., Apr. 11, 1940; A.A., Coll. of the Sequoias, 1959; B.S., S.E. La. Tchrs. Coll., 1963; J.D., Western States Coll. Law, 1970. Admitted to Calif. bar, 1973, D.C. bar, 1974; staff atty. Pres.'s Commn. on Bingo Parlors, 1972; research atty. Blythe (Calif.) Justice Ct., 1973; partner firm Foonman & Krelmin, San Diego, 1974—. Mem. Death Valley Bar Assn. Home: 3711 Bandersnach Ave Space 317A San Diego CA 92101 Office: 110 C St Suite 1375 San Diego CA 92109 Tel (714) 233-0003

FOOTE, JACK CLAYTON, b. Cleve., Sept. 29, 1908; B.A., Western Res. U., 1931; LL.B., Harvard, 1934. Admitted to Ohio bar, 1934, Minn. bar, 1937; asst. gen. counsel FHA, Washington, 1934-37; partner firm Doherty, Rumble & Butler, St. Paul, 1942—; dir. Am. Hoist & Derrick Co., First Trust Co. of St. Paul, Toro Co.; trustee Minn. Mut. Life Ins. Co. Mem. Am., Minn. bar assns., Am. Judicature Soc. Home: 1585 Dodd Rd Saint Paul MN 55118 Office: 1500 First Nat Bank Bldg Saint Paul MN 55101 Tel (612) 291-9333

FOOTE, MARVIN WELLS, b. Chgo., Aug. 16, 1913; A.B., Colo. State Coll., 1940, M.A., 1941; J.D., U. Mich., 1949. Admitted to Mich. bar, Colo. bar, 1950; individual practice law, Englewood, Colo., 1950-54, 55-60; judge Dist. Ct., 18th Jud. Dist. Colo., 1954, 61-70, chief judge, 1970—. Mem. Am., Colo., Arapahoe County bar assns., Am. Judicature Soc., Nat. Conf. State Trial Judges (chmn. 1973-74). Recipient Alumnus award Colo. State Coll., 1965. Office: Arapahoe County Court House Littleton CO 80120 Tel (303) 794-9281

FOOTE, RALPH ALBERT, b. Proctor, Vt., Jan. 22, 1923; B.A., Amherst Coll., 1943; LL.B., Union U., 1949. Admitted to Vt. bar, 1950; individual practice law, Middlebury, 1950-54; partner firm Conley & Foote, Middlebury, 1955-73, sr. partner, 1973—; state's atty. State of Vt., Addison County, 1950; mem. Vt. Ho. of Reps., 1957-60; lt. gov., State of Vt., 1961-64; trustee, bd. dirs. Vt. Legal Aid, 1969—. Moderator Middlebury Village, 1956-64; mem. sch. bd. Middlebury Union High Sch., 1965—. Mem. Am., Vt. (pres. 1972-73), Addison County (pres. 1966-67) bar assns. Home: 5 Blinn Ln Middlebury VT 05753 Office: Drawer 391 Middlebury VT 05753 Tel (802) 388-4061

FOOTE, ROGER WILLIAM, b. Gainesville, Fla., Oct. 7, 1937; B. Engring., U. Fla., 1960; J.D., U. N.C., 1969. Admitted to Fla. bar, 1969, N.C. bar, 1969, U.S. 5th Circuit Ct. and all Fed. Dist. Ct. bars Fla., 1970, U.S. Supreme Ct. bar, 1973; individual practice law, Tallahassee, Fla., 1973—; asst. atty. gen. Fla., 1969-72; pros. atty. Leon County, Fla., 1972. Mem. bus. adv. com. Leon County, 1973-75. Mem. Am., Fla., N.C., Tallahassee bar assns. Office: PO Box 587 Tallahassee FL 32302 Tel (904) 224-3141

FORAN, JAMES THOMAS, b. Orange, N.J., Aug. 9, 1943; B.S., St. Peter's Coll., 1966; J.D., Seton Hall U., 1971. Admitted to N.J. bar, 1971; dep. atty. gen. State of N.J., Newark, 1971-74; corporate atty. Pub. Service Electric & Gas Co., Newark, 1974—; spl. prosecutor N.J. Atty. Gen.'s Office, 1974-75; lectr. criminal fin. transactions seminar N.J. Atty. Gen. and N.J. Prosecutors Assn., 1974—. Chmn., Borough of Verona (N.J.) Bd. Ethics, 1976—; bd. dirs. Mt. Carmel Guild, Roman Catholic Archdiocese of Newark, 1976—. Mem. Am., N.J. bar assns., Nat. Assn. Dist. Attys. Home: 117 Linden Ave Verona NJ 07044 Office: 90 Park Pl Newark NJ 07101 Tel (201) 622-7000

FORBES, HAROLD GEORGE, b. Greenwood County, Kans., Jan. 5, 1912; J.D., Washburn U., 1934. Admitted to Kans. bar, 1935; individual practice law, Yates Center, Kans., 1935-39; partner firm Forbes & Pohl, and predecessor, Eureka, Kans., 1939—. Mem. Kans., SE Kans., Greenwood County bar assns. Home: 1601 Madison St Eureka KS 67045 Office: 417 N Main St Eureka KS 67045 Tel (316) 583-5508

FORBES, SEELY PERRY, b. Rockford, Ill.; B.A., Yale, 1929, J.S., 1932. Admitted to Ill. bar, 1933; practiced in Rockford, 1933-42; with JAGC, U.S. Army, 1942-46; probate judge, 1946-64; asso. circuit judge 17th Jud. Circuit, 1964-68, circuit judge, 1968-77; mem. Rockford City Council from 3d Ward, 1939-42; past mem. Ill. Cts. Commn., Supreme Ct. Rules Com. Mem. Gov.'s Com. and del. White House Conf. on Children and Youth, 1950; past pres. Rockford Goodwill Industries; past bd. dirs. Winnebago County Mental Hygiene Soc., Protestant Welfare Service, Rockford Big Bros., Rockford adv. bd. Ill. Childrens Home and Aid Soc. Mem. Am., Ill., Winnebago County bar assns., Am. Bar Found., Ill. Judges Assn. Am. Judicature Soc., Ill. Judges Assn. (past pres.). Home: 1401 National Ave Rockford IL 61103

FORBES, THEODORE MCCOY, JR., b. Atlanta, Oct. 28, 1929; B.S. in Chemistry, Ga. Inst. Tech., 1950; LL.B., U. Va., 1953. Admitted to Ga. bar, 1952, D.C. bar, 1972; asso., then partner firm Gambrell, Russell, Killorin & Forbes and predecessors, Atlanta, 1953—. Bd. dirs. Travelers Aid Met. Atlanta, 1974—, pres., 1975-76; bd. dirs. Ga. Arthritis Assn., 1961-68. Mem. State Bar Ga. (chmn. adminstrv. law sect. 1967-68, chmn. internat. law sect. 1976-77), Am., Atlanta bar assns., D.C. Bar, Lawyers Club Atlanta, Am. Judicature Soc., Order of Coif. Home: 1760 Marlborough Dr Dunwoody GA 30338 Office: 4000 1st National Bank Tower Atlanta GA 30303 Tel (404) 394-4151

FORBIS, CLINTON SHERMAN, JR., b. High Point, N.C., Dec. 21, 1944; A.B., High Point Coll., 1967; J.D., Wake Forest U., 1972. Admitted to N.C. bar, 1972; asso. firm Rutledge & Friday, Kannapolis, N.C., 1972-77; individual practice law, Kannapolis, 1977—. Sec. Kannapolis Businessmen's Club, 1973; mem. exec. com. High Point Coll. Alumni Assn. Forsyth County, Winston-Salem, N.C., 1972. Mem. Cabarrus County, N.C. (com. on spl. observances), Am. (real property and probate sect.) bar assns., Phi Alpha Delta. Home: 1010 Robinhood Ln PO Box 111 Kannapolis NC 28081 Office: 218 Oak Ave Kannapolis NC 28081 Tel (704) 938-4643

FORBIS, JOHN T., b. Childress, Tex., May 24, 1926; LL.B., So. Meth. U., 1950. Admitted to Tex. bar, 1950; partner firm Williams, Broughton & Forbis, Childress, 1950—; city atty. City of Childress, 1950-57; dist. atty. 100th Jud. Dist. Tex., 1957-64. Pres. bd. devel. Childress, 1952-53; chmn. Childress County ARC, 1953-54. Mem. Tex., 100th Jud. Dist. bar assns. Author: What Parents Should Know About Horses, 1976; contbr. articles to profl. jours.; named Man of Year, Childress C. of C., 1971. Home: 1000 Hillcrest St Childress TX 79201 Office: 127 Ave B NW Childress TX 79201 Tel (817) 937-2516

FORBUS, LADY WILLIE, b. Zeiglerville, Miss., Aug. 24, 1892; B.A., U. Miss., 1915; LL.B., U. Mich., 1918. Admitted to Wash. bar, 1919; individual practice law, Seattle, 1918—; asst. atty. gen. State of Wash., 1943-46; mem. U.S. Senate, 1942-46. Pres. Seattle br. Florence Crittenden Home. Mem. Wash. Bar. Assn. Contbr. articles to legal jours. Home: 2580 Magnolia Blvd W Seattle WA 98199 Office: PO Box 99001 Seattle WA 98199 Tel (206) 282-2849

FORD, ASHLEY LLOYD, b. Cin., Mar. 10, 1939; A.B., Princeton, 1960; J.D., Yale, 1963. Admitted to Ohio bar, 1963; asso. firm Dinsmore, Shohl, Coates & Deupree, Cin., 1964-69; with legal div. Procter & Gamble Co., Cin., 1969—, counsel, 1969-71, div. counsel, divs. toilet goods and paper products, 1971—. Sec., Cin. Summer Opera Assn., 1967-74, Cin. Opera Guild, Inc., 1974—. Mem. Cin., Ohio, Am. bar assns., Order of Coif, Phi Beta Kappa. Office: Legal Div Procter & Gamble Co PO Box 599 Cincinnati OH 45201 Tel (513) 562-3106

FORD, BYRON EDWARD, b. Columbus, Ohio, Apr. 22, 1901; A.B., Ohio State U., 1923, LL.B., 1925, J.D., 1973. Admitted to Ohio bar, 1925, U.S. Supreme Ct. bar, 1945; partner firm Vorys, Sater, Seymour & Pease, Columbus, 1932—. Fellow Am. Bar Found., Am. Coll. Trial Lawyers; mem. Columbus (pres., 1945-46), Ohio State (exec. com., 1956-60), Am. bar assns., Phi Alpha Delta. Home: 5050 Kitzmiller Rd New Albany OH 43054 Office: 52 E Gay St Columbus OH 43215 Tel (614) 464-6277

FORD, DONALD ROBERT, b. Warren, Ohio, Nov. 8, 1931; B.A., Bethany (W.Va.) Coll., 1953; J.D., U. Mich., 1956. Admitted to Ohio bar, 1957; individual practice law, Warren, 1957—; asst. county prosecutor Trumbull County (Ohio), 1962-68; spl. counsel Trumbull County Bd. Commrs., 1969-72, Trumbull County Hwy. Engr., 1968-72; judge Warren Municipal Ct., 1972-76, Trumbull County Ct. Common Pleas, 1976—. Bd. dirs. Trumbull County Crippled Children's Soc., Trumbull County March of Dimes, Trumbull County Mental Health Center, Trumbull County Council on Alcohol; Cub scout chmn. Western Res. council Boy Scouts Am.; pres. PTA, Morgandale Sch. Mem. Trumbull County, Ohio State, Am. bar assns. Named Man of Year Trumbull County Democrat, 1972, Distinguished Citizen Warren Urban League, 1975. Home: 3564 Kimberly Dr Warren OH 44483 Office: High St NW Warren OH 44481 Tel (216) 399-8811

FORD, FREDERICK WAYNE, b. Bluefield, W.Va., Sept. 17, 1909; A.B., W.Va. U., 1931, J.D., 1934. Admitted to W.Va. bar, 1934, U.S. Supreme Ct. bar, 1954, D.C. bar, 1968; asso. firm Stathers & Cantrall, 1934-39; asst., gen. counsel's office Social Security Bd., 1939-41, OPA, 1941-42, 46-47; atty., gen. counsel's office, chief hearing div. FCC, Washington, 1948-52, commr., 1957-65, chmn. commn., 1960-61; 1st asst. Office Legal Counsel, Dept. Justice, Washington, 1953-56, acting asst. atty. gen., 1956, asst. dept. atty. gen., 1957; pres. Nat. Cable TV Assn., Washington, 1965-69; partner firm Pittman, Lovett, Ford & Hennessey, Washington, 1970—. Mem. Am. Law Inst., W.Va. State Bar, Am. Bar Assn., Fed. Communications Bar Assn. Home: 519 S Lee St Alexandria VA 22314 Office: 1819 H St NW Suite 1000 Washington DC 20006 Tel (202) 293-7400

FORD, GEORGE LOGAN, b. Dallas, Oct. 19, 1906; B.A. in Math. and Chemistry, So. Meth. U., 1927, LL.B., 1930. Admitted to Tex. bar, 1930, U.S. Supreme Ct. bar, 1944; asso. firm Burford, Ryburn & Ford, Dallas, 1930-38, partner, 1938—. Mem. Am., Tex., Dallas bar assns., Am. Coll. Trial Lawyers, Tex., Dallas assns. def. counsel, Trial Attys. Am. Contbr. articles to legal jours. Office: Suite 1511 Fidelity Union Life Bldg Dallas TX 75201 Tel (214) 741-5811

FORD, JOHN CALVIN, b. Cooke County, Tex., Apr. 11, 1917; B.B.A., U. Tex., Austin, 1941, LL.B., 1941. Admitted to Tex. bar, 1942; asst. city atty. City of Dallas, 1946-53; asst. U.S. atty. No. Dist. Tex., 1953-58; asst. regional adminstr. SEC, Ft. Worth, 1958-61; judge U.S. Bankruptcy Ct., Ft. Worth, 1961-72, Dallas, 1972—. Mem. Dallas, Fed., Am. bar assns. Home: 5808 Biscayne Ct Fort Worth TX 76117 Office: 1100 Commerce St Dallas TX 75202 Tel (214) 7491871

FORD, LARRY ALBERT, b. Portsmouth, Ohio, Feb. 8, 1939; B.A., B.S. in Edn., Ohio State U., 1962, J.D., 1965. Admitted to Calif. bar, 1966, Ohio bar, 1972, also U.S. Supreme Ct. bar; asso. firm Walker, Wright, Tyler and Ward, Los Angeles, 1966-69; div. counsel Ashland Chem. Co. div. Ashland Oil, Inc., Columbus, Ohio, 1969-72; partner firm Alden and Ford, Columbus, 1972—; mem. Worthington (Ohio) City Council, 1973—. Mem. Mid-Ohio Regional Planning Commn., Columbus, 1975—. Mem. Am., Ohio, Calif., Columbus bar assns. Home: 320 Longfellow Ave Worthington OH 43085 Office: Suite 115 1395 E Dublin-Granville Rd Columbus OH 43229 Tel (614) 846-2781

FORD, LEE ELLEN, b. Auburn, Ind., June 16, 1917; Ph.D., Iowa State U.; J.D., U. Notre Dame. Admitted to Ind. bar, 1972; atty. Butler (Ind.) Park Bd., 1972-75; personal aide to Gov. of Ind., Indpls., 1973-75; individual practice law, Butler, 1976—. Mem. Butler City Planning Commn., 1975—; mem. exec. bd. Ind.-Ky. Lutheran Ch. Am. Mem. Am., DeKalb County bar assns., Nat. Assn. Women Lawyers. Editor: Women's Legal Handbook Series, 1975—; Animal Welfare Encyclopedia, 1971—; founder, editor New Dimensions in Legislation, 1971-72. Office: 701 S Federal Ave Butler IN 46721 Tel (219) 868-5331

FORD, MICHAEL R., b. Pitts., Jan. 9, 1942; B.S., Villanova U., 1964; J.D., Duquesne U., 1967. Admitted to Pa. bar, 1968, U.S. Supreme Ct. bar, 1972; individual practice law, Pitts., 1969—. Mem. Allegheny County, Pa., Am. bar assns. Home: 17 Stancey Rd Pittsburgh PA 15220 Office: 818 Frick Bldg Pittsburgh PA 15219 Tel (412) 288-9595

FORD, MICHAEL RAYE, b. Blackwell, Okla., Sept. 1, 1945; B.A., U. Okla., 1967, J.D., 1970; LL.M. in Taxation, George Washington U., 1974. Admitted to Okla. bar, 1970; atty. legal dept. Cities Service Oil Co., Tulsa, 1970; served as capt. U.S. Army JAGC, Washington, 1971-73, trial atty. regulatory law div., 1973-74; asso. firm Gable, Gotwals, Rubin, Fox, Johnson & Baker, Inc., Tulsa, 1974—. Deacon, bd. First Christian Ch., Falls Church, Va., 1973-74; deacon, bd., com. chmn. First Christian Ch., Tulsa, 1976—; pres. jr. officers council Hdqrs. Mil. Traffic Mgmt. and Terminal Services, D.C., 1972-73. Mem. Am. Bar Assn. (mem. taxation, corp., banking, bus. sec.), Okla. Bar Assn. (mem. taxation young lawyers sect.), ICC Practitioners Assn. Tulsa County Bar Assn., Order of Coif, Phi Delta Phi. Articles and book rev. editor Okla. Law Rev., 1969-70; contbr. articles to legal jours. Home: 7017 E 77th St Tulsa OK 74133 Office: 20th Floor 4th Nat Bank Bldg Tulsa OK 74119 Tel (918) 582-9201

FORD, PAUL HOWARD, b. Balt., Dec. 13, 1930; B.S., U. Md., 1951; J.D., George Washington U., 1967. Analyst H. Zinder and Assos., Inc., Washington, 1951-56; Washington rep. Ebasco Services, Inc., 1956-61, Pennzoil Co., 1961-68; admitted to Md. bar, 1967, D.C. bar, 1968; atty. Washington Gas Light Co., 1968—. Sec., Temple Sinai, Washington, 1972-75, trustee, 1972-75, mem. sch. bd., 1969-72; 1st v.p. Springbrook High Sch. PTA, Silver Spring, Md., 1976—; pres. emeritus Key Jr. High Sch. PTA, Silver Spring, 1975-76, pres., 1974-75; pres. Cresthaven Sch. PTA, Silver Spring, 1970-71, trustee, 1971-74; mem. exec. bd. West Hillandale Citizens Assn., 1970-75. Mem. Md., D.C., Prince George's County bar assns., Phi Delta Phi. Home: 1008 Robroy Dr Silver Spring MD 20903 Office: 1100 H St NW Washington DC 20080 Tel (202) 624-6665

FORD, RAYMOND CHARLES, b. Hermansville, Mich., July 21, 1899; B.A., St. Francis Sem., 1924; J.D., Marquette U., 1929. Admitted to Wis. bar, 1930; circuit ct. reporter, br. 4 Circuit Ct., Milw., 1935-44; adjudicator claims service Regional Office VA, Milw., 1946-48; registration officer, Vets. Rehab. and Edn., Milw., 1948-51; fiduciary accounts analyst, chiefy atty. div., regional office VA, Milw., 1951-67. Mem. Delta Theta Phi (emeritus). Office: Milwaukee WI

FORD, RICHARD, b. Ypsilanti, Mich., Nov. 22, 1903; A.B., Eastern Mich. U., 1923; J.D., U. Mich., 1926. Admitted to Mich. bar, 1926, U.S. Supreme Ct. bar, 1933; asso. firm McKay, Wiley, Streeter, Smith & Tucker, 1926-30; mem. firm Wiley, Streeter & Ford, 1930-42; partner firm Fischer Franklin & Ford, Detroit, 1942—; asso. prof. law Detroit Coll. Law, 1955—. Fellow Am. Coll. Trial Lawyers. Home: 4555 Pickering Rd Birmingham MI 48010 Office: 1700 Guardian Bldg Detroit MI 48226 Tel (313) WO 2-5210

FORD, RICHARD EDMOND, b. Ronceverte, W.Va., May 3, 1927; student U. N.C., 1950; B.S., W.Va. U., 1951; LL.B., 1954. Admitted to W.Va. bar, 1954; partner firm Haynes, Ford and Guills, and predecessors, Lewisburg, W.Va., 1954—; mem. W.Va. Legislature, 1960-64; commr. Commn. on Uniform State Bars, 1964—. Trustee Greenbrier Coll. for Women, 1960-73; bd. dirs. W.Va. U. Found., 1972—. Mem. Am., W.Va., Greenbrier County bar assns., Phi Beta Kappa. Home: Buckingham Acres Lewisburg WV 24901 Office: 203 W Randolph St Lewisburg WV 24901 Tel (304) 645-1858

FORDHAM, JEFFERSON BARNES, b. Greensboro, N.C., July 8, 1905; A.B., U. N.C., 1926, M.A., J.D. with honors, 1929, LL.D., 1952; J.S.D., Yale, 1930; LL.D., Franklin and Marshall Coll., 1960; L.H.D., U. Pa., 1970. Admitted to N.C. bar, 1929, N.Y. State bar, 1937, Ohio bar, 1949, Pa. bar, 1955, Utah bar, 1974; asst. prof. law W.Va. U., 1930-31, asso. prof., 1931-34, prof., 1934-35; spl. asst. to sec. labor, 1935; asso. firm Reed, Hoyt & Washburn, N.Y.C., 1935-38; mem. legal div. U.S. Pub. Works Administrn., Washington, 1938-39, counsel, chief bond atty., 1939-40; prof. La. State U., 1940-46, Vanderbilt U., 1946-47; prof., dean Coll. of Law, Ohio State U., 1947-52; prof. law U. Pa., 1952-72, prof. emeritus, 1972—, dean Sch. Law, 1952-70, dean emeritus, 1972—; prof. law U. Utah, 1972-74, Distinguished prof., 1974—; mem. Permanent Com. for Oliver Wendell Holmes Devise, 1961-69. Past pres. Phila. Housing Assn.; past pres. Phila. Fellowship Commn., hon. life pres; co-chmn. Utah Joint Legis. Com. on Energy Policy, 1976. Mem. Am. Law Inst. (council), Am. Bar Assn. (chmn. sect. local govt. law 1949-51, 1st chmn. sect. individual rights and responsibilities 1966-68, ho. of dels. 1952-54, 68-69), Assn. Am. Law Schs. (pres. 1970), Order of Coif, Phi Beta Kappa, Phi Kappa Phi (hon.). Recipient Distinguished Service awards Yale Law Sch. Assn., 1968, U. N.C. Law Sch., 1969, U. Pa. Law Alumni Soc., 1970. Author: Local Government Law, 1949, revised edit., 1975; A Larger Concept of Community, 1956; The State Legislative Institution, 1957; (with Horace Read, John MacDonald & William Pierce) Materials on Legislation, 2d edit., 1959, 3d edit., 1973; editor-in-chief N.C. Law Rev., 1928-29; Jefferson B. Fordham professorship established at U. Pa. Law Sch., 1973. Home: 584 16th Ave Salt Lake City UT 84103 Office: U of Utah Coll of Law Salt Lake City UT 84112 Tel (801) 581-7352

FORDYCE, CLIFTON POWELL, b. Little Rock, Mar. 15, 1901; A.B., Harvard U., 1923, LL.B., 1926. Admitted to Mo. bar, 1927, U.S. Supreme Ct. bar, 1932, U.S. Tax Ct. bar, 1932; mem. firm Fordyce and Mayne and predecessor firms, St. Louis; lectr. Benton Coll. Law. Mem. Am. (coms. on taxation, real property, probate and trust law), Mo., St. Louis bar assns., C. of C. Met. St. Louis. Contbr. articles to legal jour. Home: 27 Lenox Pl St Louis MO 63108 Office: Chromalloy Plaza 120 S Central Ave St Louis MO 63105 Tel (314) 863-6900

FOREHAND, OLIVER CLYDE, b. Sylvester, Ga., Aug. 9, 1927; B.S., U. Ala., 1945; LL.B., John Marshall Law Sch., Atlanta, 1950. Admitted to Ga. bar, 1950; individual practice law, Sylvester. Address: 104 E Pope St Sylvester GA 31741 Tel (912) 776-2046

FOREMAN, JOSEPH EDWARD, b. Wadsworth, Ohio, Nov. 23, 1936; A.B., Ohio Wesleyan U., 1958; J.D., Ohio State U., 1964. Admitted to Ohio bar, 1965; trust officer Citizens Bank & Trust Co., Wadsworth, 1966-70; mem. firm Foreman & McMannis, Wadsworth, 1965-66; individual practice law, Wadsworth, 1970-72; partner firm Luck Palecek McIlvaine & Foreman, Wadsworth, 1972—; city solicitor City of Wadsworth, 1968-73. Sec. Wadsworth Community Improvement Corp. Mem. Ohio State, Medina County (Ohio) (pres. 1975) bar assns. Office: 210 Citizens Bank Bldg Wadsworth OH 44281 Tel (216) 336-2727

FOREMAN, PERCY, b. Polk County, Tex., June 21, 1902; LL.B., U. Tex., 1927. With Nat. Lyceum, then Chautauqua lectr.; admitted to Tex. bar, 1927, since practiced in Houston, partner firm Foreman & DeGuerin. Mem. Am., Tex., Houston bar assns., Nat. Assn. Def. Lawyers Criminal Cases (pres. 1963-64). Home: 200 Carnarvon St Houston TX 77022 Office: Foreman & DeGuerin First Nat Life Bldg 800 Main St Houston TX 77002*

FOREMAN, SAMUEL IRVING, b. Kiev, Russia, Dec. 2, 1903; B.S. in Edn., U. Pa., 1928; LL.B., Temple U., 1933, M.S. in Edn., 1948. Admitted to Pa. bar, 1935; individual practice law, Phila., 1935—. Tel (215) LI 8-1431

FOREN, WILLIAM DOUGLAS, b. Detroit, June 28, 1949; B.A., Oakland U., 1971; J.D., Detroit Coll. of Law, 1974. Admitted to Mich. bar, 1974; staff atty. Oakland County Legal Aid Soc., 1974—. Mem. Mich., Oakland, Am. bar assns. Home: 23593 Valley Starr Rd Novi MI 48050 Office: 10 W Huron St Pontiac MI 48050 Tel (313) 332-9176

FORER, LOIS GOLDSTEIN, b. Chgo., Mar. 22, 1914; A.B., Northwestern U., 1935, J.D., 1938. Admitted to Ill. bar, 1938, Pa. bar, 1942; mem. legal staff U.S. Senate Commn. on Edn. and Labor, 1938-39; with REA, 1940-41; law clk. U.S. Ct. of Appeals 3d Circuit, Phila., 1942-46; mem. legal staff Office Price Stblzn., Phila., 1950-51; dep. atty. gen. State of Pa., Harrisburg, 1954-63; atty. in charge Community Legal Services Office of Juveniles, Phila., 1966-68; individual practice law, Phila., 1946-71; judge Ct. of Common Pleas, Philadelphia County, Pa., 1971—; lectr. in law U. Pa., 1953-59. Mem. White House Conf. on Children and Youth, 1960, 70; advisor to Urban League Child Advocacy Program. Mem. Women Organized Against Rape, Com. on Child Abuse Reporting Law, ACLU. Recipient Ross Essay award, Am. Bar Assn., 1953. Author: No One will Listen: How our Legal System Brutalizes the Youthful Poor, 1970; The Death of the Law, 1975. Home: Philadelphia PA Office: Room 1004 1 E Penn Sq Bldg Philadelphia PA 19107 Tel (215) 686-7328

FORESTER, JOHN GORDON, JR., b. Wilkesboro, N.C., Jan. 14, 1933; B.S. in Indsl. Relations, U. N.C., Chapel Hill, 1955; LL.B., George Washington U., 1962. Admitted to D.C. bar, 1962, U.S. Supreme Ct. bar, 1968; law clk. to judge U.S. Dist. Ct. D.C., 1963-64; individual practice law, Washington, 1964—; mem. firms Forester & Perkins, Washington, 1969-72, Forester & Smith, Washington, 1973-76. Pres., Barrister Inn Washington, 1976-77, Friendly Citizens Assn., 1962, Gonzaga Fathers Club, 1975-76; dir. Sursum Corda Neighborhood Assn., 1975-77. Mem. D.C., Am. bar assns., The Counselors, Phi Delta Phi. Home: 9810 Indian Queen Point Rd Oxon Hill MD 20022 Office: 1101 17th St NW Washington DC 20036

FORGANG, MARTIN J., b. Bklyn., Sept. 17, 1906; student Columbia, 1926; LL.B., Bklyn. Law Sch., 1929, LL.M., 1930. Admitted to N.Y. bar, 1931, since practiced in N.Y.C.; partner firm Ernstoff & Forgang, N.Y.C., 1940-55; individual practice law, 1955—; hearing officer N.Y.C. Parking Violations Bur., N.Y.C. Taxi and Limousine Commn. Mem. N.Y. County Lawyers Assn., Bklyn. Lawyers Club. Office: 253 Broadway New York City NY 10007 Tel (212) CO7-3741

FORGNONE, ROBERT, b. Paterson, N.J., Dec. 4, 1936; J.D., Loyola U., Los Angeles, 1970. Admitted to Calif. bar, 1971; partner firm Gibson, Dunn & Cratcher, Los Angeles, 1970—. Mem. Am., Los Angeles County bar assns., Lawyer-Pilots Bar Assn., State Bar Calif. Office: 515 S Flower St Los Angeles CA 90071 Tel (213) 488-7494

FORGOTSON, EDWARD HERMAN, b. Albuquerque, May 10, 1934; B.A., U. Tex., 1953, J.D., 1960; M.D., Wash. U., 1957; LL.M., U. Mich., 1963. Admitted to Tex. bar, 1960, D.C. bar, 1964, U.S. Supreme Ct. bar, 1964, Calif. bar, 1967; asst. to commr. U.S. AEC, Washington, 1960-62; research asso. W.E. Meyer Research Inst. of Law, New Haven, 1963; dep. spl. asst. to U.S. Pres., Washington, 1964-65; asso. prof. pub. health U. Calif. at Los Angeles, 1965-70; asso. firm Stroud & Smith, Dallas, 1970-73; asso. firm Worsham, Forsythe & Sampels, Dallas, 1973—; cons. Nat. Adv. Commn. on Health Manpower, 1966-67. Mem. Dallas, Am. bar assns., Am. Judicature Soc., State Bar Tex., State Bar Calif. Contbr. articles to legal jours. Home: 10205 Epping Ln Dallas TX 75229 Office: 2500 2001 Bryan Tower Dallas TX 75201 Tel (214) 748-9365

FORINGER, JOHN WILLIAM BEIGHLEY, b. Franklin, Pa., Mar. 3, 1907; B.E., Valparaiso (Ind.) U., 1928; LL.B., U. Ind., 1931. Admitted to Ind. bar, 1931, Tex. bar, 1934, Ill. bar, 1954; individual practice law, Hammond, Ind., 1931-34, San Antonio, 1934-36, Bedford, Ind., 1966—; legal staff Owens Ill. Glass Co., San Francisco, 1936-39; asst. to v.p., Carnegie Ill. Steel Corp., Pitts., 1939-41; atty., dir. indsl. relations U.S. Steel Corp., U.S. Steel Supply Co., Chgo., 1941-47; v.p. Kansas City Power & Light Co. (Mo.), 1947-52; ranch operator, Douglas, Ariz., 1952-57; counsel Appleton Electric Co. (Ill.), 1957-60; accounting v.p. Walter E. Heller Co., Chgo., 1960-65; pvt. practice law, cattle farm operator, Bedford, Ind., 1966—. Mem. Am. Bar Assn., State Bar Ind., Ill., Tex. judicature socs., Am. Trial Lawyers Assn., Delta Theta Phi. Home: 126 Edgewood Dr Bedford IN 47421 Tel (812) 279-2220

FORLENZA, PHILIP RUSSELL, b. N.Y.C., Feb. 24, 1942; J.D., Fordham U., 1966. Admitted to N.Y. bar, 1967; asso. firm Cahill, Gordon & Reindel, N.Y.C., 1966-71; partner firm Hawkins, Delafield & Wood, N.Y.C., 1971—. Mem. Am., N.Y. State bar assns. Office: 67 Wall St New York City NY 10005 Tel (212) 952-4777

FORMAN, DAVID AVRUM, b. Atlantic City, Apr. 1, 1942; B.A., Rutgers U., 1964; J.D., U. Minn., 1970. Admitted to N.J. bar, 1970; asst. pros. atty. Atlantic County (N.J.), 1971—; instr. criminal law Atlantic Community Coll., 1972-75. Mem. Atlantic County, N.J., Am. bar assns. Home: 2639 Pacific Ave Atlantic City NJ 08401 Office: 600 Guarantee Trust Bldg Atlantic City NJ 07201 Tel (609) 344-0277

FORMAN, PHILLIP, b. N.Y.C., Nov. 30, 1895; LL.B., Temple U., 1919. Admitted to N.J. bar, 1917, since practiced in Trenton; partner firm Forman & Levy, 1919-32; asst. U.S. atty., 1923-28, U.S. atty., 1928-32; U.S. Dist. Ct. judge, 1932-52, chief judge, 1952-59; judge 3d Circuit Ct. of Appeals, 1959-61, sr. judge, 1961—. Mem. Am., Fed., Mercer County bar assns., Am. Judicature Soc. Home: 5 Belmont Circle Trenton NJ 08618 Office: U S Fed Court Bldg 402 E State St Trenton NJ 08605 Tel (609) 695-6675

FORNELLI, FRANCIS JOSEPH, b. Sharon, Pa., Aug. 1, 1941; A.B. magna cum laude, U. Notre Dame, 1963; postgrad. U. Concepcion, 1964; J.D., N.Y. U., 1966. Admitted to Pa. bar, 1966; partner Cusick, Madden, Joyce & McKay, Sharon, Pa., 1966—; bd. trustees N.W. Legal Services Pa., 1976—. Bd. trustees Mercer County Drug Council, 1971—, 1st v.p., 1975—; chmn. legis. com. Christian Assos. Shenango Valley, 1973—; chmn. Mercer County Deanery Council, 1972—; active Mercer County People for Life Assn., 1976—; bd. trustees Shenango Valley Home for Sr. Citizens, 1973—; mem. exec. com. Mercer County Democratic Party, 1971. Mem. Am., Mercer County (chmn. com. on criminal rules 1976—) bar assns., Pa. Trial Lawyers Assn., Hickory Profl. and Businessmen's Assn. Home: 190 Todd Ave Sharon PA 16146 Office: 1st Fed Bldg Sharon PA 16146 Tel (412) 981-2000

FORNEY, KENT MASON, b. Hull, Iowa, Sept. 17, 1932; B.A., State U. Iowa, 1956, J.D., 1958. Admitted to Iowa bar, 1958; partner firm Bradshaw, Fowler, Proctor & Fairgrave, Des Moines, 1958—; pres. Polk County Legal Aid Soc., 1968. Mem. Am., Polk County (past pres.), Iowa (gov.) bar assns., Iowa Acad. Trial Lawyers (v.p.), Iowa Def. Counsel Assn., Internat. Assn. Ins. Counsel, Internat. Soc. Barristers. Contbr. articles to legal jours. Home: 913 Cummins Pkwy Des Moines IA 50312 Office: Bradshaw Fowler Procter & Fairgrave Des Moines Bldg Des Moines IA 50309 Tel (515) 243-4191

FORREST, HERBERT EMERSON, b. N.Y.C., Sept. 20, 1923; B.A. with distinction, George Washington U., 1948, J.D. with highest honors, 1952. Admitted to Va. bar, 1952, D.C. bar, 1952, U.S. Supreme Ct. bar, 1956, Md. bar, 1959; law clk. to Bolitha J. Laws chief judge U.S. Dist. Ct. for D.C., 1952-55; asso. firm Welch & Morgan, Washington, D.C., 1955-63, partner, 1963-65; partner firm Steptoe & Johnson, Washington, 1965—; chmn. Criminal Justice Act Adv. Bd., 1971-74; sec. com. on admissions and grievances U.S. Ct. Appeals, 1973—; mem. Title I Audit Hearing Bd., U.S. Office Edn., 1976—; mem. comml. panel Am. Arbitration Assn., 1976—. Pres., Whittier Woods Elementary Sch. P.T.A., Bethesda, Md., 1970-71. Mem. Am. (chmn. com. reports, vice chmn. agy. rule making adminstrv. law sect.), Fed. Communications (chmn. Legal Aid program, mem. exec. com.), D.C., Fed. bar assns., D.C. Bar (bd. govs., chmn. Employment Discrimination Complaint Service), Am. Judicature Soc., Va. State Bar, Computer Law Assn., Washington Council Lawyers, Phi Beta Kappa, Order of the Coif. Recipient Thomas F. Walsh award in Irish History, 1952, Morgan Richardson Goodard award in Commerce, 1952; bd. advisors Duke Law Jour., 1969-75; contbr. articles to legal jours. Home: 7001 Whittier Blvd Bethesda MD 20034 Office: 1250 Connecticut Ave NW Washington DC 20036 Tel (202) 223-4800

FORRESTER, WALTER IRVING, b. Memphis, July 13, 1910; LL.B., So. Law U., 1940. Admitted to Tenn. bar, 1940; individual practice law, Memphis, 1940—, mem. Tenn. Ho. of Reps., 1952-56. Mem. Memphis, Shelby County, Tenn. bar assns. Home: 3474 Joslyn St Memphis TN 38128 Office: 1010 Exchange Bldg Memphis TN 38103 Tel (901) 526-1171

FORRESTER, WILLIAM RAY, b. Little Rock, Ark., Jan. 14, 1911; A.B., U. Ark., 1933, J.D., U. Chgo., 1935; LL.D. (hon.), U. Ark., 1963. Admitted to Ill. bar, 1936, N.Y. bar, 1970; asso. firm Defrees, Buckingham, Jones & Hoffman, Chgo., 1935-41; prof. law Tulane U., 1943-49, dean, W.R. Irby Prof. Law, 1952-63; prof. law, dean Vanderbilt U., 1949-52; dean, prof. law Cornell U., 1963-73, Robert S. Stevens Prof. Law, 1973—; arbitrator Fed. Mediation and Conciliation Service, Washington, 1943—; prof. law U. Calif. Hastings Sch. Law, 1976—; commr. Uniform State Laws Commn., 1956-63; mem. Regional Wage Stblzn. Bd., Nashville, 1951-52; pub. mem. Nat. Advt. Review Bd., N.Y.C., 1975—; trustee Food and Drug Law Inst., Washington, 1963—; del. Argentina Conf. on Pol. Sci., Buenos Aires, 1960. Mem. Am., Tompkins County bar assns. Author: Forrester's edition of Dobie & Ladd, Federal Jurisdiction & Procedure, 1951; Cases and Materials on Constitutional Law, 1959; (with Currier) Cases and Materials on Federal Jurisdiction and Procedure, 1962; (with Currier and Moye) Cases & Materials on Federal Jurisdiction and Procedure, 1972; (with Moye) Cases and Materials on Federal Jurisdiction and Procedure, 1977. Home: 218 Fall Creek Dr Ithaca NY 14850 Office: Myron Taylor Hall Cornell Law Sch Ithaca NY 14853 Tel (607) 256-3379

FORROW, BRIAN DEREK, b. N.Y.C., Feb. 7, 1927; A.B., Princeton U., 1947; J.D., Harvard U., 1950. Admitted to bar, 1950; mem. firm Cahill, Gordon, Sonnett, Reindel & Ohl, Morristown, N.J., 1950-68; v.p., gen. counsel Allied Chem. Corp., Morristown, 1968, dir., 1969—. Mem. nat. adv. council Episcopal Ch. Found. Mem. Am., Conn., N.J., N.Y. State, Internat. bar assns., Assn. Bar City N.Y., Am. Soc. Corp. Secs., Practising Law Inst., Am. Judicature Soc. Contbr. articles to legal jours. Home: 704 Lake Ave Greenwich CT 06830 Office: PO Box 3000R Morristown CT 07960 Tel (201) 455-4212

FORSBERG, THOMAS GERALD, b. Appleton, Minn., Jan. 14, 1927; B.S.L., U. Minn., 1950, J.D., 1952. Admitted to Minn. bar, 1952; partner firm Hall, Smith, Juster, Forsberg & Feikema, Minn., 1958-68; county municipal judge, 1968-71, county ct. judge, 1971-72, dist. judge, 1972—; judge city of Coon Rapids, Minn., 1954-68; atty. City of Blaine, Minn., 1954-68. Sec. Blaine Met. Planning Commn., 1960-64. Mem. Am., Minn., 18th Jud. (pres.), Anoka County bar assns., Minn. State Municipal Judges Assn. (sec.), Coon Rapids C. of C. Home: 10571 Flora St Coon Rapids MN 55433 Office: Anoka County Courthouse Anoka MN 55433

FORSETER, BERNARD, b. Bklyn., Feb. 24, 1945; B.A., Bklyn. Coll., 1967; J.D., N.Y. U., 1969; LL.M. in Taxation, George Washington U., 1974. Admitted to N.Y. bar, 1969, Md. bar, 1971, D.C. bar, 1972; summer intern, excise tax br., nat. office IRS, Washington, 1968, tax law specialist pension trust br., 1969-70, estate tax atty. office internat. ops., 1970-71; asst. regional dir. pension div. Aetna Life Ins. Co., Washington, 1971-74; individual practice law, N.Y.C. and Washington, 1971-74; v.p., counsel, pres. DCP Adminstrs., Inc., Washington, 1975—; partner firm Sussman & Forseter, N.Y.C. and Washington, 1975—. Mem. Am., Fed., Md., D.C. (tchr. continuing legal edn. program 1976—) bar assns., Am. Soc. Pension Actuaries, Am. Pension Conf., Am. Soc. C.L.U.'s. Editorial cons. Pension Plan Guide, 1974—. Home: 3109 Woodhollow Dr Chevy Chase MD 20015 Office: 604 Washington Bldg Washington DC 20005 Tel (202) 783-3000

FORSLUND, CURTIS DUANE, b. Roseau, Minn., July 15, 1933; B.A., U. Minn., 1962, LL.B., 1962. Admitted to Minn. bar, 1962, Calif. bar, 1971, U.S. Supreme Ct. bar, 1971; partner firm Gray, Plant, Mooty, Mooty & Bennett, Mpls., 1975—; solicitor gen. State of Minn., 1972, chief dep. atty. gen., 1973-74. Mem. Minn. State, Hennepin County bar assns. Editor Minn. Law Rev., 1961-62. Home: 6618 Parkwood Ln Minneapolis MN 55436 Office: 300 Roanoke Bldg Minneapolis MN 55402 Tel (612) 339-9501

FORSTADT, JOSEPH LAWRENCE, b. Bklyn., Feb. 21, 1940; B.A., Coll. City N.Y., 1961; LL.B., N.Y. U., 1964. Admitted to N.Y. State bar, 1965, U.S. Supreme Ct. bar, 1968, since practiced in N.Y.C.; dept. commr. N.Y.C. Dept. Licenses, 1967-68, acting commr., 1968-69; acting commr. N.Y.C. Dept. Consumer Affairs, 1969; asst. adminstr. Econ. Devel. Adminstrn., 1969; asso. firm Stroock & Stroock & Lavan, 1969-75, partner, 1976—; lectr. in trial practice N.Y. County Lawyers Assn. Mem. Fed. Bar Council, Am. Judicature Soc., Assn. Trial Lawyers Am., N.Y. Trial Lawyers Assn. Recipient Judge Jacob Markowitz Scholarship, 1963; Benjamin F. Butler Meml. Prize, 1964. Office: 61 Broadway New York City NY 10006 Tel (212) 425-5200

FORSTER, CLIFFORD, b. N.Y.C., July 6, 1913; B.A., Yale U., 1935, LL.B., 1938. Admitted to New York State bar, 1939; staff and spl. counsel ACLU, N.Y.C., 1940-54; counsel Internat. League for Rights of Man, N.Y.C., 1955-65. Mem. Assn. Bar City N.Y., Am. Bar Assn., Am. Judicature Soc. Decorated comdr. Order of Merit (W.Ger.). Home: 301 E 7th St New York City NY 10021 Office: 1212 Ave of Americas New York City NY 10036 Tel (212) 586-4700

FORSTER, ROBERT SHARP, b. San Salvador, El Salvador, Central Am., June 24, 1945; B.A., U. N.H., 1967; J.D., U. Miss., 1970. Admitted to Miss. bar, 1970, La. bar, 1971; asst. counsel Pan Am. Life Ins. Co., New Orleans, 1970, counsel internat. ops., 1972—, 2d v.p., 1977—; v.p., counsel Jersey Settlers, Kingston, Miss., 1973—. Mem. La., Miss., Am. bar assns. Home: 22 Wisteria Tchefuncta Estates Covington LA 70433 Office: 2400 Canal St New Orleans LA 70119 Tel (504) 821-2510

FORSTNER, JAMES ALLAN, b. Balt., Feb. 17, 1936; B.S. cum laude, Loyola U., Balt., 1958; M.S., Carnegie Inst. Tech., 1961, Ph.D., 1962; J.D., U. Md., 1969. Admitted to D.C. bar, 1969, Del. bar, 1969; research chemist E.I. duPont de Nemours & Co., Inc., Wilmington, Del., 1962-65, patent agt., 1965-69, patent atty., 1969-73, sr. atty., 1974—; asst. pub. defender State of Del., 1972-73. Mem. allocations com. Del. United Way, 1976—; chmn. spl. projects Del. Found. for Retarded Children, 1972—; bd. dirs. N. Mill Creek Assn., 1975—. Mem. Am., Del., D.C. bar assns. Home: 207 N Spring Valley Rd Wilmington DE 19807 Office: Legal Dept EI duPont de Nemours & Co Inc Market and 10th Sts Wilmington DE 19898 Tel (302) 774-8618

FORTAS, ABE, b. Memphis, June 19, 1910; A.B., Southwestern Coll., Memphis, 1930; LL.B., Yale, 1933. Admitted to Conn. bar, 1934, U.S. Supreme Ct. bar, 1940, D.C. bar, 1945; faculty Yale U. Law Sch., 1933-38; ofcl. SEC, 1933-39; with Dept. Interior, 1939-42, undersec. interior, 1942-46; mem. firm Arnold, Fortas & Porter, Washington, 1946-65; asso. justice U.S. Supreme Ct., 1965-69; mem. firm Fortas & Koven, Washington, 1970—; adviser U.S. Del. to UN. Trustee, Carnegie Hall, John F. Kennedy Center for Performing Arts. Mem. Am., Fed., FCC bar assns. Office: 1200 29th St NW Washington DC 20007 Tel (202) 337-5700

FORTENBERRY, ERNEST EDWARD, b. Jasper, Tex., Dec. 24, 1933; B.B.A., U. Tex., 1954, LL.B., 1955. Admitted to Tex. bar, 1955, Calif. bar, 1971; gen. counsel Tex. Employment Commn.; sr. counsel Texaco, Inc.; partner firm Heily, Blase & Ellison, Oxmond, Calif., 1969-74, Cutrer, Jefferson & Fortenberry, Houston, 1974—. Office: 2100 W Loop St S Houston TX 77027 Tel (713) 626-7800

FORTUNE, JOHNNY ALLEN, b. Crestview, Fla., Oct. 30, 1928; B.S., Fla. State U., 1952, M.S., 1956; LL.B., U. Fla., 1960, J.D., 1967. Admitted to Fla. bar, 1960; asso. firm Philip Barton, Gainesville, Fla., 1960-61; partner firm Estergren, Fortune, Anchors & Powell, Ft. Walton Beach, Fla., 1961—. Bd. dirs. YMCA, Ft. Walton Beach. Mem. Fla. Bar, Am. Bar Assn., Fla. Trial Lawyers Assn. Home: 109 Meigs Dr Shalimar FL 32579 Office: PO Box F Fort Walton Beach FL 32548 Tel (904) 243-7184

FORTUNE, PHILIP LEE, b. High Point, N.C., Nov. 11, 1945; B.A., U. N.C., Chapel Hill., 1967; J.D., U. Toledo, 1970. Admitted to Ga. bar, 1971; partner firm Smith, Currie & Hancock, Atlanta; mem. panel of arbitrators Am. Arbitration Assn.; instr. in field Emory U., 1972. Sec., Buckhead-Atlanta Exchange Club, 1973; sec., asst. treas. Leafmore-Creek Park Community Club, Inc. Mem. Am., Ga., Atlanta bar assns., Am. Judicature Soc., Gamma Beta Phi. Mem. editorial staff U. Toledo Law Rev., 1969-70. Office: 2600 Peachtree Center Harris Tower 233 Peachtree St NE Atlanta GA 30303 Tel (404) 521-3800

FORTUS, SIDNEY, b. St. Louis, Nov. 21, 1921; B.J., U. Mo., 1947; LL.B., Wash. U., 1951. Admitted to Mo. bar, 1951; partner firm Fortus & Anderson, St. Louis; asst. atty. gen. State Mo., 1964-68. Mem. Assn. Trial Lawyers Am. Recipient Distinguished Service award Am. Soc. Composers, Authors and Pubs., 1951. Home: 1522 Strollways Dr Ballwin MO 63011 Office: 120 S Central Ave St Louis MO 63105 Tel (314) 862-6800

FOSSUM, LEE LEIF, b. Farmington, Minn., Oct. 27, 1934; B.A., St. Olaf Coll., 1956; J.D., William Mitchell Coll. Law, 1967. Law clk. firm Burns, O'Connor, Collins & Abrahamson, St. Paul, 1966-68; admitted to Minn. bar, 1968; partner firm Sawyer & Lampe, Northfield, Minn., 1968-71, Lampe Fossum Jacobson & Borene, Northfield, 1971—; atty. City of Northfield, 1969-75. Bd. dirs. Northfield Indsl. Corp., 1969—, pres., 1975-76; chmn. Northfield Bi-Centennial Com., 1974-76; mem. alumni bd. St. Olaf Coll., 1975—. Mem. Rice County (Minn.) (sec.-treas. 1969-70), Am. bar assns., Minn. State Bar, Northfield Hist. Soc. (v.p. 1975-76), Minn. Trial Lawyers Assn. Office: 501 E 5th St Northfield MN 55057 Tel (507) 645-4411

FOSTEL, MICHAEL LEONARD, b. San Diego, Aug. 12, 1945; B.A. in Journalism, Tex. Christian Univ., 1967; J.D., Tex. Tech Univ., 1970. Admitted to Tex. bar, 1970; asso. firm Calvin Wesch, Kermit, Tex., 1970-71; partner firm Finley & Scogin, Kermit, 1971-72; individual practice law, Kermit, 1972—; county atty. Winkler County, 1972—. Chmn. Winkler County W. Tex. Boys Ranch, 1974—, Tex. Heart Assn., 1973-75. Mem. Tex. Bar Assn., Tex. Trial Lawyers Assn., Tex. Dist. and County Attys. Assn. Home: 913 E San Antonio Kermit TX 79745 Office: Austin and Poplar Sts Kermit TX 79745 Tel (915) 586-3781

FOSTER, BERNARD A., III, b. Washington, Nov. 25, 1942; B.A., U. South, 1964; LL.B., George Washington U., 1967. Admitted to D.C. bar, 1968; asso. firm Ross, Marsh & Foster, Washington, 1967-74, partner, 1974—. Vice pres. Wood Acres Citizens Assn., 1973. Mem. Am., Fed., Fed. Power bar assns., Bar Assn. D.C. Office: 730 15th St NW Washington DC 20005 Tel (202) 628-2623

FOSTER, CHARLES EDWARD, b. Utica, N.Y., Jan. 5, 1935; B.A., Colgate U., 1956; LL.B., Univ. Ariz., 1964. Admitted to Ariz. bar, 1964, Calif. bar, 1970; asso. firm Lewis & Roca, Phoenix, 1964-68, firm Powers, Boutell, Fannin & Kurn, Phoenix, 1969—; counsel Litton Industries, Inc., Beverly Hills, Calif., 1969-76, Occidental Petroleum Corp., Los Angeles, 1976—. Mem. Am., Ariz., Calif., Los Angeles County, Beverly Hills bar assns. Home: 16942 Bollinger Dr Pacific Palisades CA 90272 Office: 10889 Wilshire Blvd Los Angeles CA 90024 Tel (213) 879-1700

FOSTER, DAVID SMITH, b. Wilmington, Del., May 20, 1927; B.A., U. Va., 1951; J.D., Tulane U., 1964. Admitted to La. bar, 1964; partner firm Voorhies & Labbe, Lafayette, La., 1964-71; individual practice law, Lafayette, 1971—; instr. mineral law U. Southwest La.; dir. Offshore Logistics, Inc. Mem. external services City of Lafayette, also mem. traffic planning bd.; bd. dirs. La. Cemetary Bd. Mem. La. (speaker seminars), Am., Lafayette, 15th Judicial Dist. bar assns., Lafayette Landman's Assn., Am. Assn. Petroleum Landmen. Office: PO Box 52389 Lafayette LA 70505 Tel (318) 232-9313

FOSTER, HENRY HUBBARD, JR., b. Norman, Okla., Dec. 3, 1911; A.B., U. Nebr., 1933, LL.B. cum laude, 1936; LL.M., Harvard, 1941; LL.M., U. Chgo., 1960. Admitted to Nebr. bar, 1936, Okla. bar, 1949, Pa. bar, 1961, N.Y. State bar, 1966, U.S. Supreme Ct. bar, 1958; atty., NLRB, Kansas City, Mo., Washington, 1937-40; spl. atty. U.S. Dept. Justice, Washington, Denver, San Francisco, 1941-46; prof. law U. Idaho, 1946-47; prof. law U. Okla., 1947-50, vis. distinguished prof., 1975; prof. law U. Nebr., 1950-54, U. Pitts., 1954-62, N.Y.U., 1962—; vis. prof. law U. Wis., 1952, Northwestern U., 1962, U. Tex., 1965, U. Luxemberg, 1963; cons. in field; advisor Divorce Reform Commns. Hon. fellow Am. Psychiat. Assn.; mem. Am. Law Inst., Order of the Coif, Am. (chmn. family law sect. 1976-77), N.Y. State bar assns., Assn. Bar City N.Y., N.Y. County Lawyers Assn. Author: Society and the Law, 1962; Law and The Family, 1966, 72; Family Law, 1972; Children and the Law, 1972; A Bill of Rights for Children, 1974. Contbr. articles in field to profl. jours. Home: 100 Bleecker St New York City NY 10012 Office: 40 Washington Sq S New York City NY 10012 Tel (212) 598-2574

FOSTER, JAMES JOHN, b. Pitts., Oct. 27, 1945; B.S., Mass. Inst. Tech., 1967; J.D., Harvard, 1970. Admitted to N.Y. bar, 1971; asso. firm Cahill, Gordon & Reindel, N.Y.C., 1970—. Office: 80 Pine St New York City NY 10005 Tel (212) 825-0100

FOSTER, JAMES L., b. 1940; A.B., LL.B., U. Alta. (Can.). Called to Alta. bar, 1965; now atty. gen. Province of Alta.; now minister of justice and mem. Alta. Legis. Assembly from Red Deer Dist. Mem. Canadian Bar Assn. Office: Madison Bldg 9919 105th St Edmonton AB T5K 2E8 Canada*

FOSTER, PHILIP CAREY, b. Salisbury, Md., Jan. 5, 1947; A.B., Coll. of Wooster, 1969; J.D., Vanderbilt U., 1972. Admitted to D.C. bar, 1973, Md. bar, 1973; atty. advisor, office of hearings and appeals Dept. Interior, Arlington, Va., 1972-73; asso. firm Henry, Hairston and Price, Easton, Md., 1973-75; asst. state's atty. Talbot County (Md.), Easton, 1975-77, dep. state's atty., 1977—; individual practice law, Easton, 1975—. Chmn. Easton Heart Fund Dr., 1976; elder Easton Presbyn. Ch., 1975—; chmn. Talbot County Democratic Central Com., 1974—; chmn. Eastern Shore Assn. Dem. Central Coms., 1974—. Mem. Talbot County, Md., D.C., Am. bar assns., Izaak Walton League, Easton Jaycees. Office: Stewart Bldg Box 661 Easton MD 21601 Tel (301) 822-1700

FOSTER, STANLEY DELMONT, b. Sumner, Maine, Apr. 3, 1890; J.D., Northeastern U., 1919. Admitted to Mass. bar, 1920, U.S. Dist. Ct. bar, 1921, Maine bar, 1929, U.S. Supreme Ct. bar, 1940; individual practice law, Boston and Abington, Mass., 1920—; mem. legal staff Mass. Inheritance Tax Div., Boston, 1925-60, dir. div., 1953-60, ret., 1960. Chmn., Abington Bd. Appeals, 1942-45; asso. mem. adv. bd. for registrants U.S. SSS, 1941-43. Mem. Plymouth County (Mass.) Bar Assn. Home and office: 750 Plymouth St Abington MA 02351 Tel (617) 878-2669

FOSTER, THOMAS ARNOLD, b. Kansas City, Mo., Oct. 5, 1938; B.S., U. Mo., Columbia, 1961; J.D., U. Mo., Kansas City, 1968. Admitted to Mo. bar, 1968; asso. firm Hubbell, Lane & Sawyer, Kansas City, Mo., 1968-70; trust officer estates div. trust dept. 1st Nat. Bank Kansas City (Mo.), 1970-72, personal trust div., 1972-73, v.p., coordinator trust new bus. for 1st nat. charter corp. banks, 1976—. Chmn. bd. dirs. Renaissance West, Inc., 1973-76. Mem. Mo., Kansas City (mem. probate com. 1975-76) bar assns., Mo. Bankers Assn., Estate Planning Assn., Corporate Fiduciaries, Lawyers Assn., Phi Delta Phi. Home: 7219 Ward Pkwy Kansas City MO 64114 Office: 14 W 10th St Kansas City MO 64105 Tel (816) 221-2800

FOSTER, THOMAS LEVERNE, b. Talladega, Ala., May 16, 1945; B.S. in Indsl. Relations, U. Ala., 1967; J.D., Stanford, 1971. Admitted to Ala. bar, 1972; city judge, Talladega, 1971-72; adminstrv. asst. to congressman, Washington, 1972-73; asso. firm Skinner, Large, & Corley, Birmingham, Ala., 1973-75; individual practice law, Birmingham, 1975—. Mem. Am., Ala., Birmingham bar assns., Birmingham Trial Lawyers. Decorated Bronze Star. Home: 1400 Pinetree Dr Birmingham AL 35215 Office: 2010 City Federal Building Birmingham AL 35203 Tel (205) 328-9000

FOSTER, THOMAS MICHAEL, b. St. Louis, July 28, 1939; B.A., U. Tampa, 1962; J.D., Stetson U., 1965. Admitted to Fla. bar, 1965, D.C. bar, 1969; trial atty. U.S. Dept. Justice, Washington, 1965-67; staff atty., asst. dir., then dir. Fla. Rural Legal Services, Inc. (formerly

S. Fla. Migrant Legal Services), Ft. Myers, 1967-69; asst. state atty. Fla., Tampa, 1970-74, chief asst. state atty., 1974-76; asso. firm Wagner Cunningham Vaughan & Genders, Tampa, 1976—; asst. spl. prosecutor Statewide Grand Jury, 1974-75; mem. Tampa Mayor's Task Force on Rape, 1974—; adv. bd. Hillsborough County Stop Rape, Inc. Mem. Tampa-Hillsborough County Bar Assn. Office: 708 E Jackson St Tampa FL 33602 Tel (813) 223-7421

FOSTER, VINCENT WALKER, JR., b. Hope, Ark., Jan. 15, 1945; A.B., Davidson Coll., 1967; J.D. with high honors, U. Ark., 1971. Admitted to Ark. bar, 1971, U.S. Supreme Ct. bar, 1974; asso. firm Rose, Nash, Williamson, Carroll, Clay & Giroir, Little Rock, 1971-73, partner, 1973—; chmn. Ark. adv. council Legal Services Corp., 1976—. Mem. Ark. (ho. dels. 1973-76, chmn. legal aid com. 1975—), Am. bar assns. Mng. editor Ark. Law Review, 1970, also contbr. articles to profl. jours. Office: 720 W 3d St Little Rock AR 72201 Tel (501) 375-9131

FOSTER, WILLIAM EDWARD, b. Laramie, Wyo., Feb. 24, 1931; LL.B. cum laude, U. Wyo., 1955. Admitted to Colo. bar, 1956, Wyo. bar, 1955; mem. firm Keller & Bloomenthal, Denver, 1955-56; atty. Wilshire Capital Co., Grand Junction, Colo., 1956-57; individual practice law, Grand Junction, 1957—; v.p., gen. counsel, dir. Dixson, Inc., Grand Junction, 1963—; chmn. bd., dir. Powderhorn Ski Corp., Inc.; dir. Best Quality Plastics Co., Denver; pres., dir. Thermo Dynamics, Inc., Shawnee Mission, Kans.; pres., dir. CBW Builders Inc., Grand Junction, 1968—; mem. Colo. Ho. of Reps., 1964-66. Mem. Colo. Commn. Higher Edn., 1970-75; chmn. Colo. 4th Congressional Dist., 1969-73; pres., bd. dirs. Grand Junction Eagles Baseball team, 1963-68. Mem. Am., Colo. bar assns., Sigma Chi, Omicron Delta Kappa. Recipient One of Three Outstanding Young Men Award in Colo., Colo. Jr. C. of C., 1966. Home: 1701 Orchard Ave Grand Junction CO 81501 Office: Valley Fed Plaza Suite 601 Grand Junction CO 81501 Tel (303) 243-4232

FOUGNER, ROBERT SELMER, b. N.Y.C., Jan. 26, 1913; A.B., Lafayette Coll., 1934; LL.B., Harvard U., 1937. Admitted to N.Y. bar, 1938, U.S. Supreme Ct. bar, 1950; mem. firm Middlebrook & Sincerbeaux, N.Y.C., 1938-41; with Office Price Adminstrn., Washington, 1942-43, chief regional rent atty. N.Y. Region; sr. atty. U.S. Anti-trust div. Dept. Justice, N.Y.C., 1946-49; mem. firm Shanley McKegney & Fougner, N.Y.C., 1949-51, McLaughlin & Fougner, N.Y.C., 1951—. Mem. Am., Fed., Nassau County bar assns., Assn. Bar City N.Y., N.Y. County Lawyers Assn. Home: 132 Elderfields Rd Manhasset NY 11030 Office: 666 Fifth Ave New York City NY 10019 Tel (212) 541-8866

FOULKROD, SAMUEL WALTER, III, b. Phila., Aug. 2, 1941; B.A., U. Pa., 1962; J.D., Temple U., 1966. Admitted to Pa. bar, 1966, U.S. Supreme Ct. bar, 1970; partner firm Butler, Beatty, Greer and Johnson, Media, Pa., 1970-72; sec., asst. gen. counsel Reliance Ins. Cos., Phila., 1973-76; mem. firm Pepper, Hamilton & Scheetz, Harrisburg, Pa., 1976—; com. chmn. Ins. Fedn. Pa., 1975-76. Mgr., Media Little League Assn.; trustee, lay leader United Methodist Ch. of Media. Mem. Am., Pa., Phila., Dauphin County bar assns., Pa. Profl. Liability Joint Underwriters Assn. (chmn. bd. 1976). Recipient Lucas Hirst award Temple U. Law Sch., 1964. Office: 10 S Market Sq Harrisburg PA 17108 Tel (717) 233-8483

FOUST, MICHAEL VAL, b. Great Bend, Kans., May 19, 1943; B.A., U. Kans., 1966; J.D., Washburn Law Sch., 1972. Admitted to Kans. bar, 1972; partner firm Sparks, Foust & Vignery, Goodland, Kans., 1973—. Mem. NW Kans. (mem. ethics and disciplinary com. 1974—), Sherman County (sec. 1972-73), Kans., Am. bar assns., Kans., Am. assns trial lawyers, Washburn U. Sch. Law, Law Jour. Assn. Mng. editor Washburn Law Jour. 1971-72; contbr. articles to legal jours. Home: 820 E 15th St Goodland KS 67735 Office: 1015 Main St Goodland KS 67735

FOWLER, CALEB LEIGHTON, b. Wilmington, Del., May 20, 1942; B.A., U. Pa., 1964, M.B.A., 1967; J.D., Temple U., 1968. Admitted to Pa. bar, 1969; with Ins. Co. N.Am. and INA Corp., Phila., 1968—, contracts counsel, 1973-76, v.p., claims counsel, 1976—; lectr. law Temple U., 1969-71; mem. bd. ethical inquiry Am. Inst. Property and Liability Underwriters, 1977—; bd. dirs. Legal Aid Soc. Mem. Phila., Pa., Am. bar assns. Recipient Sara A. Shull award Temple U. Sch. Law; award for greatest contbn. to law sch. Temple U. Sch. Law Class of 1936. Office: 1600 Arch St Philadelphia PA 19101 Tel (215) 241-3480

FOWLER, CHARLES REX, b. Kansas City, Mo., May 23, 1938; B.A., U. Kans., 1960; postgrad. U. South Hampton, 1960-61; J.D., Stanford, 1964. Admitted to Mo. bar, 1964; partner firm Dietrich, Davis, Dicus, Rowlands & Schmitt, Kansas City, Mo., 1964—; judge municipal ct. N. Kansas City, Mo., 1966. Bd. govs. Bacchus Ednl. Found., 1973—; pres. Clay, Platte and Ray Counties Mental Health Assn., 1973; bd. dirs. Kansas City Assn. Mental Health, 1973-76; publicity dir. Clay County Charter Commn., 1969; mem. exec. staff KCPT (TV) Auction, Kansas City, 1974-76; bd. dirs. St. Joseph Hosp., Kansas City, 1975. Mem. K.C. Lawyers Assn., Editor-Lawyers Assn. News and Announcements, K.C. Bar Assn. (chmn. tax sect.), Heart of Am. Tax. Inst. (co-chmn.), Estate Planning Assn. Kansas City (pres. 1976), Am. Royal Assn. (bd. govs.). Home: 501 NE Poplar Dr Kansas City MO 64118 Office: 1001 Dwight Bldg 1004 Baltimore Ave Kansas City MO 64105 Tel (816) 221-3420

FOWLER, CONRAD MURPHREE, b. Montevallo, Ala., Sept. 17, 1918; B.S., U. Ala., 1941, J.D., 1947. Admitted to Ala. bar, 1948; partner firm Ellis & Fowler, Columbiana, Ala., 1948-53; dist. atty. 18th Jud. Circuit Ala., 1953-59; probate judge, Shelby County, 1959-77; dir. pub. affairs West Point Pepperell, Inc. (Ga.), 1977—; chmn. Ala. Constl. Commn., 1970-76; mem. Presdl. Adv. Commn. on Intergovtl. Relations, 1970-77. Bd. dirs. Am. Lung Assn. Mem. Ala. Law Inst., Nat. Assn. Counties (pres. 1969), Assn. Probate Judges Ala. (pres. 1966). Home: PO Box 1395 Columbiana AL 35051 Office: West Point Pepperell Inc PO Box 71 West Point GA 31853

FOWLER, DAVID ANDERSON, b. N.Y.C., May 16, 1920; A.B., Princeton, 1942, LL.B., Harvard, 1948. Admitted to N.Y. bar, 1949, Pa. bar, 1955; asso. firm Harrison, Coughlin, Dermody & Ingalls, Binghamton, N.Y., 1949-52; counsel Scott Paper Co., 1952-60; asso. firm Saul, Ewing, Remick & Saul, Phila., 1960-67, Morgan, Lewis & Bockius, Phila., 1967—. Pres., Bryn Mawr (Pa.) Civic Assn., 1973-75, Fedn. Lower Merion (Pa.) Civic Assns., 1976; chmn. Ind. Schs. Fund Phila., 1973-74. Mem. Am., Pa., Phila. bar assns. Office: 123 S Broad St Philadelphia PA 19109 Tel (215) 491-9285

FOWLER, GEORGE WILLIAM, b. Rensselaer, Ind., May 17, 1945; B.B.A., U. Tex., El Paso, 1968; J.D., St. Mary's U., 1970. Admitted to Tex. bar, 1971, U.S. Supreme Ct. bar, 1974; asst. atty. El Paso County (Tex.), 1971-72; legal examiner gas utilities div. R.R. Commn. Tex., Austin, 1972-76; individual practice law, Austin, 1976—; counsel Tex. Gas Assn., 1976—. Mem. Am. Bar Assn. Contbr. articles St. Mary's Law Jour., Pub. Utility Law Anthology. Home: 2108 Matterhorn Ln Austin TX 78704 Office: 1200 SW Tower Bldg Austin TX 78701 Tel (512) 474-2426

FOWLER, JAMES ALEXANDER, JR., b. Clinton, Tenn., Feb. 27, 1897; A.B., U. Tenn., 1916; LL.B. cum laude, Harvard, 1919. Admitted to N.Y. bar, 1920, U.S. Supreme Ct. bar, 1943; asso. firm Cadwalader, Wickersham & Taft, N.Y.C., 1919-21, McAdoo, Cotton & Franklin, N.Y.C., 1921-26; partner firm Cahill Gordon & Reindel, and predecessors, N.Y.C., 1926-65, ret. partner, 1965—; counsel Bur. Naval Personnel, Dept. Navy, 1942-44. Fellow Am. Bar Found., Am. Coll. Trial Lawyers; mem. Am. Law Inst., Practicing Law Inst. (trustee 1947-75, pres. 1960-69, chmn. 1970-75), Am., N.Y. bar assns., Assn. Bar City N.Y., N.Y. County Lawyers Assn., Am. Judicature Soc., Harvard Law Sch. Assn. (nat. fund chmn. 1955-57, pres. 1961-63). Home: 91-A Enfield Ct Leisure Village Ridge NY 11961 Office: 80 Pine St New York City NY 10005 Tel (212) 825-0100

FOWLER, JOEL ALFRED, b. Atlanta, Mar. 13, 1948; B.A., Presbyn. Coll., Clinton, S.C., 1970; J.D., Mercer U., 1973. Admitted to Ga. bar, 1973, Ct. Mil. Appeals, 1974; served as capt. JAGC, U.S. Army, 1973—; mem. office staff judge adv. Ft. Lee, Va., 1973; instr. law U.S. Army Mil. Police Sch., Ft. Gordon, Ga., 1974-75; chief, legal assistance and trial counsel, magistrate's ct., office staff judge adv. Ft. McClellan, Ala., 1975—; lectr. in field. Mem. Ga., Am. bar assns., Phi Alpha Delta. Home: 3824 Vermont Rd NE Atlanta GA 30319 Office: SJA Fort McClellan AL 36205 Tel (205) 238-5334

FOWLER, JOHN RICHARD, b. Elkins, W.Va., Oct. 2, 1942; A.B., W.Va. U., 1964, LL.B., 1967, J.D., 1969. Admitted to W.Va. bar, 1967, U.S. Supreme Ct. bar, 1972; asso. firm Steptoe & Johnson, Charleston, W.Va., 1969-70, Preiser & Wilson, Charleston, 1970-72; sr. partner firm Fowler and Lane, Charleston, 1972—. Mem. Am. Bar Assn., Am. Trial Lawyers Assn. Home: 1205 Summit Dr Charleston WV 25302 Office: 930 Charleston National Plaza Charleston WV 25301 Tel (304) 344-9869

FOWLER, WILLIAM EDWARD, JR., b. Pitts., Apr. 20, 1919; B.S., Sheffield Sci. Sch. Yale, 1942; J.D. with distinction, U. Mich., 1948. Admitted to Ohio bar, 1948, U.S. Dist. Ct. for Eastern Div. No. Dist. Ohio bar, 1949, 6th Circuit bar, 1955; asso. firm Harrington, Huxley & Smith, Youngstown, Ohio, 1948-55, partner, 1956—. Mem. Youngstown Bd. Edn., 1960-75, pres., 4 years. Fellow Ohio State Bar Found., Am. Bar Found.; mem. Mahoning County (Ohio), Ohio State (council of dels., exec. com. 1963-66, chmn. com. group legal services), Am. bar assns. Home: 50 Forest Hill Rd Youngstown OH 44512 Office: 1200 Mahoning Bank Bldg Youngstown OH 44503 Tel (216) 744-1111

FOX, ARTHUR EDWARD, b. N.Y.C., Sept. 3, 1920; B.B.A., Coll. City N.Y., 1940; LL.M./J.D. cum laude, U. Miami, 1954; postgrad. Nat. Inst. Trial Advocacy, U. N.C., 1975-76. Admitted to Fla. bar, 1954; individual practice law and accounting, Miami, Fla., 1954—; tchr. fed. income taxes Peninsular Inst., Miami, 1954-55; lectr. fed. taxes, estate planning, trusts, others. Mem. Am., Fla., Dade County bar assns., Am., Fla. insts. C.P.A.'s. Author: How to Settle the Estate Tax Return on the Administrative Level, 1973; How to Use Sprinkling Trusts to Best Advantage, 1968. Editorial bd., founder Mgmt. Services Mag., 1964-65. Office: 245 SE First St Miami FL 33131 Tel (305) 373-8706

FOX, CHARLES DUNSMORE, III, b. Roanoke, Va., Aug. 25, 1929; B.A., U. N.C., 1951; LL.B., U. Va., 1957. Admitted to Va. bar, 1957; pres. firm Hunter, Fox & Wooten, Inc., Roanoke, 1957—. Chmn. Roanoke Valley Red Cross, 1966, Roanoke Valley United Fund, 1966, Roanoke Valley Council, Community Services, 1971, Roanoke Valley Trouble Center, 1973-75. Mem. Va. Bar, Am. Bar Assn., Va. State Bar (chmn. sect. bus. law, chmn. com. on cooperation with Va. Soc. C.P.A.'s.). Home: 3711 Peakwood Dr SW Roanoke VA 24014 Office: Seven-O-Seven Bldg Roanoke VA 24024 Tel (703) 343-2451

FOX, DONALD THOMAS, b. Council Bluffs, Iowa, June 12, 1929; A.B. magna cum laude, Harvard, 1951; LL.B., N.Y. U., 1956; Brevet de Traduction et de Terminologie Juridiques, U. Paris, 1957, Diplôme de Droit Comparé, 1960. Admitted to N.Y. bar, 1957; asso. firm Davis, Polk, Wardwell, Sunderland & Kiendl, N.Y.C., 1958-67; partner firm Fox, Glynn & Melamed, N.Y.C., 1968—; instr. Inst. Comparative Law N.Y. U., 1957-59; dir. Washington Sq. Legal Services, Inc., N.Y.C., 1974—; trustee N.Y. U. Law Center Found., 1975—. Mem. Am. Law Inst., Council on Fgn. Relations, Center Inter Am. Relations. Contbr. articles to legal jours. Office: 299 Park Ave New York City NY 10017 Tel (212) 593-6600

FOX, ELEANOR MAE, b. Trenton, N.J., Jan. 18, 1936; B.A., Vassar Coll., 1956; LL.B., N.Y. U., 1961. Admitted to N.Y. State bar, 1961, U.S. Supreme Ct. bar, 1965; asso. firm Simpson Thacher & Bartlett, N.Y.C., 1962-69, partner, 1970-76, of counsel, 1976—; asso. prof. N.Y. U. Sch. Law, N.Y.C., 1976—. Mem. adv. bd. Bur. Nat. Affairs Antitrust and Trade Regulation Reporter, 1977—; trustee N.Y. U. Law Center Found., 1975—; bd. dirs. Antitrust Inst., 1976—. Mem. Am. (chairperson merger com. antitrust sect. 1974-77), N.Y. State (vice chairperson antitrust sect. 1977—) bar assns., Fed. Bar Council (v.p. 1974—), Assn. Bar City N.Y. (exec. com. 1977—, chairperson trade regulation com. 1974-77), N.Y. U. Law Alumni Assn. (dir. 1974—). Co-author: Corporate Acquisitions and Mergers, 3 vols.; bd. editors N.Y. Law Jour., 1976—; contbr. articles to legal jours. Home: 69 W 89th St New York City NY 10024 Office: 40 Washington Sq S New York City NY 10012 Tel (212) 598-2016

FOX, ERIC R., b. Jackson Heights, N.Y., July 4, 1939; B.A., Amherst Coll., 1961; LL.B. cum laude, Harvard, 1964. Admitted to N.Y. bar, 1964, D.C. bar, 1965, U.S. Supreme Ct. bar, 1973, U.S. Tax Ct. bar, 1965; atty., legal adviser's office U.S. Dept. State, 1964-65; asso. firm Ivins, Phillips & Barker, Washington, 1965-70, partner, 1971—. Bd. dirs. Washington Performing Arts Soc., 1971—, gen. counsel, 1975—; chmn. lawyers div. United Jewish Appeal Fedn. Greater Washington, 1974-75, trustee, 1974—, exec. com., 1975—, asso. chmn. Vanguard div., 1976-77; bd. dirs. Washington chpt. Interracial Council Bus. Opportunity, 1968-73, co-chmn., 1970-73, nat. dir., 1970-73; bd. dirs. Washington Ballet Co., 1977—. Mem. Am., D.C. bar assns. Home: 3056 Ellicott St NW Washington DC 20008 Office: 1700 Pennsylvania Ave NW Washington DC 20006 Tel (202) 393-7600

FOX, FRANCIS, b. Montreal, Que., Can., Dec. 2, 1939; B.A., LL.L., D.E.S., U. Montreal; LL.M., Harvard, 1963; M.A., Oxford U., 1965. Called to Que. bar, 1963; asso. firm Tansey & DeGrandpry, Montreal; mem. Parliament, 1972-76, sec. to minister justice, 1975; solicitor gen. Can., Ottawa Ont., 1976—. Mem. Can. Bar Assn. Address: 340 Lauier Ave W Ottawa ON K1A 0P8 Canada

FOX, FRED L., II, b. Charleston, W.Va., Aug. 12, 1938; A.B., Davis & Elkins Coll., 1960; J.D. W.Va. U., 1967. Admitted to W.Va. bar, 1967; mem. firm Furbee, Amos, Webb & Critchfield, Fairmont, W.Va., 1967-70; served with JAG, USMC, 1968-69; judge 16th Jud. Circuit, W.Va., Fairmont, 1970—; instr. W.Va. Coll. Law, 1974-75. Bd. dirs. United Fund; commr. Babe Ruth League. Mem. Marion County, W.Va., Am. bar assns., Am. Trial Lawyers Assn., W.Va., Am. jud. assns., Am. Judicature Assn. Recipient Fraternal Order Police award, 1974. Home: 103 Hallhurst Rd Fairmont WV 26554 Office: Marion County Ct House Fairmont WV 26554 Tel (304) 366-2831

FOX, G. RICHARD, b. Galveston, Tex., Feb. 17, 1942; B.S., St. Louis U., 1964, J.D., 1967. Admitted to Mo. bar, 1969, U.S. Dist. Ct. bar Eastern Dist. Mo., 1971, U.S. Ct. Appeals bar 8th Circuit, 1971; asso. firm Rooney, Webbe, Davidson & Schlueter, St. Louis, 1971-76; partner firm Kell & Fox, St. Louis, 1976—; pros. atty. City of Ballwin, Mo., 1975—; dir. Devel. By Design Corp., Holloway Industries, Inc. (Sullivan, Mo.). Dir. Camp Wyman, Inc., Eureka, Mo., 1975—. Mem. Am., Mo. bar assns., Bar Assn. Met. St. Louis, Am. Trial Lawyers Assn., Phi Delta Phi. Office: 722 Chestnut St Saint Louis MO 63101 Tel (314) 241-7888

FOX, GENEVIEVE KUBREENER, b. Chgo., Feb. 3, 1908; student Northwestern U., 1927-29, DePaul U., 1929-30, U. Chgo. Law Sch., 1930-31; J.D., Loyola U., 1931. Admitted to Ill. bar, 1931; partner firm Fox and Fox, Chgo., 1931—; lectr. bus. law U. Ill., 1966-68, U. Wis., 1968-70, Roosevelt U., 1973-77. Mem. Nat., Chgo. (sec.-treas. 1957-59) bus. law assns. Friends Am. Writers. Home: 175 E Delaware Pl Chicago IL 60611 Office: 875 N Michigan Ave Chicago IL 60611 Tel (312) 944-0123

FOX, HAROLD WILLIAM, b. Oak Park, Ill., Nov. 6, 1927; B.S., U. Ariz., 1952, LL.B., 1958. Admitted to Ariz. bar, 1958; asso. firm Snell & Wilmer, Phoenix, 1958-66, partner, 1966—. Mem. Maricopa County (Ariz.), Am. bar assns., State Bar Ariz., Internat. Assn. Ins. Counsel, Am. Bd. Trial Advocates, Phi Delta Phi. Home: 6030 N 2d St Phoenix AZ 85012 Office: 3100 Valley Center Phoenix AZ 85073 Tel (602) 257-7286

FOX, HARRY, b. Chattanooga, Oct. 5, 1944; B.A., U. Md., 1962, J.D., 1969. Admitted to Md. bar, 1969; sr. atty. Central Legal Aid Bur., Balt. Mem. Am., Md., Balt. City bar assns. Home: 3607 Sussex Rd Baltimore MD 21207 Office: Court Square Bldg Suite 1021 Baltimore MD 21202

FOX, HERBERT LAWRENCE, b. Charlottesville, Va., July 28, 1939; B.A., U. Va., 1961. LL.B., 1964; LL.M., N.Y. U., 1965. Admitted to Va. bar, 1964, D.C. bar, 1969; law clk., counsel for comdt. USMC Dept. Navy, Washington, 1964; with legis. and regulation div. Chief Counsels Office IRS, Washington, 1965-69, asst. br. chief, 1968-69; asso. firm Pepper, Hamilton & Scheetz, Phila., Washington, 1969-72, mem., 1972-77, mng. partner Washington office, 1976-77; mem. firm Cadwalader, Wickersham & Taft, 1977—. Lectr. tax policy seminars. Mem. Am., Va. bar assns. Washington columnist, Jour. Corporate Taxation, 1974—, Rev. Taxation, 1976—; contbr. tax and environ. articles to legal jours. Home: 1612 Stonebridge Rd Alexandria VA 22304 Office: 11 Dupont Circle Suite 450 Washington DC 20036 Tel (202) 387-8100

FOX, JACOB LOGAN, b. Chgo., Apr. 20, 1921; B.A., U. Chgo., 1942, J.D., 1947. Admitted to Ill. bar, 1947; asso. firm Brown, Fox & Blumberg, Chgo., 1947-53, partner, 1953-76; partner firm Altheimer & Gray, Chgo., 1976—; dir., chmn. exec. com. Wylain, Inc.; dir. Republic Industries, Inc., Raco Steel Co., Inlander-Steindler Paper Co., Fin. Mktg. Services Co., Fasano Pie Co. Trustee Columbia Coll., Chgo., 1976—; trustee Chgo. Youth Centers, 1955—, pres., 1962-64. Mem. Chgo., Ill., Am. bar assns. Office: Suite 3700 One IBM Plaza Chicago IL 60611 Tel (312) 467-9600

FOX, JOHN HENRY, III, b. Clinton, Miss., June 22, 1927; B.A., U. Miss., 1949, LL.B., 1951. Admitted to Miss. bar, 1951, U.S. Ct. Mil. Appeals bar, U.S. Supreme Ct. bar, 1966; dep. sec. state securities, 1958-59; asst. dist. atty. 7th Circuit Ct. Dist. Miss., 1960-68; city atty. Clinton (Miss.), 1963—; atty. Clinton Municipal Separate Sch. Dist., 1970—. Mem. Hinds County, Fed., Am., Miss. State bar assns., Hinds County, Miss. trial lawyers assns., Am. Judicature Soc. Office: PO Drawer 22547 Jackson MS 39205 Tel (601) 948-4848

FOX, JOHN PATRICK, JR., b. Chgo., Dec. 14, 1918; A.B., Loyola U., Chgo., 1941, J.D., 1949. Admitted to Ill. bar, 1948; atty. Beatrice Foods Co., Chgo., 1948, gen. atty., 1965, gen. counsel, 1969, v.p., 1971, sr. v.p., asst. to chmn. bd., 1975—; gen. counsel Boyle Ice Co. of Del., Chgo., 1950-74, also dir., sec. Mem. Am., Chgo. (anti-trust com., chmn. corp. law dept. 1974) bar assns. Home: 201 Kedzie St Evanston IL 60202 Office: 120 S LaSalle St Chicago IL 60603 Tel (312) 782-3828

FOX, MICHAEL EDWARD, b. Chgo., Apr. 14, 1938; B.S. in Accountancy with high honors, U. Ill., 1959; J.D., Harvard, 1962. Admitted to Ill. bar, 1962; asso. firm Rusnak, Deutsch & Gilbert, Chgo., 1963-65; staff atty. Congl. Joint Com. on Internal Revenue Taxation, Washington, 1965-68; asso. firm Seyfarth, Shaw, Fairweather & Geraldson, Chgo., 1968-72, partner, 1972-74; partner firm Adams, Fox, Marcus & Adelstein, Chgo., 1974—. Bd. dirs., trustee Goodwill Industries of Chgo. and Cook County, Ill., Inc., 1973—. Mem. Chgo., Ill., Fed., Am. bar assns. C.P.A., Ill. Office: 208 S LaSalle St Chicago IL 60604 Tel (312) 346-7731

FOX, NOEL PETER, b. Kalamazoo, Aug. 30, 1910; Ph.B., Marquette U., 1933, J.D., 1935. Admitted to Wis. bar, 1935, Mich. bar, 1935, also U.S. Supreme Ct.; asso. firm Bunker & Rogoski, 1935-39, Fox & Beers, 1945-49; pvt. practice, 1935-44, 46-51; asst. pros. atty., Muskegon County, 1937-39; circuit judge 14th Jud. Circuit of Mich., 1951-62; U.S. dist. judge Western Dist. Mich., 1962—, chief U.S. dist. judge, 1971—. Mem. faculty Fed. Jud. Center for Seminars for Newly Apptd. Dist. Judges, 1970-72. Mem. Mich. Judges Assn. (past pres.), State Bar Mich. (past chmn. ct. adminstrn. com.), Nat. Jesuit Scholastic and Hon. Soc., Fed., Am., Muskegon, Grand Rapids bar assns., Jud. Conf. Com. Trial Practice and Techniques, Am. Judicature Soc. Home: 2162 Robinson Rd SE Grand Rapids MI 49506 Office: Federal Bldg Grand Rapids MI 49502*

FOX, RECTOR KERR, II, b. N.Y.C., Sept. 25, 1934; A.B., Harvard U., 1956; J.D., Stanford U., 1963. Admitted to Calif. bar, 1964, U.S. Supreme Ct. bar, 1974; dep. city atty. San Diego, 1964-69; corporate counsel Travelodge Internat., Inc., El Cajon, Calif., 1970-73; city atty. Fullerton (Calif.), 1973—. Home: 1830 Mariposa Ln Fullerton CA 92633 Office: 303 W Commonwealth Fullerton CA 92632 Tel (714) 525-7171

FOX, RICHARD PAUL, b. N.Y.C.; B.A., U. Calif., Los Angeles; J.D., Loyola U., Los Angeles. Admitted to Calif. bar, 1970, U.S. Ct. Mil. Appeals, 1973, U.S. Ct. Claims, 1973, U.S. Supreme Ct. bar, 1974; individual practice law, Los Angeles, 1970-73, partner firm Fox and Gest, Los Angeles, 1973—. Mem. Los Angeles County Bar Assn., Nat. Lawyers Guild, Christian Legal Soc. Office: 1888 Century Park East Suite 225 Los Angeles CA 90067 Tel (213) 553-2700

FOX, ROBERTA FULTON, b. Phila., Nov. 25, 1943; B.A., U. Fla., 1964, J.D., 1967. Admitted to Fla. bar, 1968; asso. firm Goldin & Jones, Gainesville, Fla., 1968; field atty. Migrant Legal Services, Miami, 1968-69, Legal Services of Greater Miami, 1970-72; mem. firm Gold & Fox, P.A., Coral Gables, Fla., 1972—; mem. Fla. Ho. of Reps., 1976—; counsel NOW, Women's Action Center, Inc.; counsel and dir. Planned Parenthood of S. Fla.; instr. Miami-Dade Community Coll.; guest lectr. various univs. Chairperson, Family Law Task Force, Commn. on Status of Women, Dade County; chairperson Dade County Women's Polit. Caucus, NOW State Legal Referral Com.; bd. dirs. YMCA Affirmative Action Com.; dir. Girl Scout Council of Tropical Fla.; dir. Community Action agency advisory bd.; treas., Transition, Inc., NOW; 1st v.p. Fla. Women's Polit. Caucus. Mem. Fla. Women's Lawyers Assn., Fla. Bar Assn., AAUW, ACLU, U. Fla. Law Center Assn., Common Cause. Recipient John Marshall Bar Assn. award, 1967. Office: 4651 Ponce de Leon St Coral Gables FL 33146 Tel L305) 667-2512

FOX, SAMUEL, b. Chgo., Mar. 18, 1908; Ph.B., U. Chgo., 1924, M.B.A., 1947; J.D., Loyola U., 1927, LL.M., 1928; Ph.D., U. Notre Dame, 1950. Admitted to Ill. bar, 1927; asso. firm Luster & Luster, Chgo., 1927, asso. firm Fox and Fox, Chgo., 1928-39; U.S. Regional Enforcement atty. OPA, Chgo. region, 1943-46; lectr. in law Loyola U. Law Sch., Chgo., 1928-32; prof. managerial jurisprudence U. Ill., Chgo., 1965-73; prof. Walter Heller Coll. Bus. Adminstrn., Roosevelt U., 1973—; cons. AID, U.S. Dept. State, Lima, Peru, 1967; Fulbright-Hays lectr. Al-Hikma U., Baghdad, Iraq., 1966-67. Fellow Internat. Acad. Law and Sci.; mem. Am. (exec. v.p. 1963-64), Chgo. (1st pres. 1957-59) bus. law assns., Ill. State Bar Assn., Am. Assn. Attys.—CPAs, Am. Judicature Soc., Am. Taxation Assn. Author: Law of Decedents's Estates, 1938; Management and the Law, 1968; Managerial Law Workbook, 1971. Home: 175 E Delaware Place Chicago IL 60611 Office: 875 N Michigan Ave Chicago IL 60611 Tel (312) 944-0123

FOX, SANFORD JACOB, b. N.Y.C., Sept. 28, 1929; A.B., U. Ill., 1950; LL.B., Harvard U., 1953. Admitted to D.C. bar, 1953, N.Y. bar, 1958; teaching fellow law Harvard U., 1957-58; asst. dir. Project for Effective Justice, Columbia U., 1958-59; prof. law Boston Coll., 1959—; vis. prof. law U. Tex., 1965; cons. Nat. Center Child Abuse and Neglect, HEW, 1977—; cons. on juvenile ct. Pres.'s Commn. Law Enforcement and Adminstrn. of Justice, 1966-67; mem. adv. com. juvenile delinquency Nat. Commn. Criminal Justice Standards and Goals, 1972-73; chmn. adv. com. Mass. Dept. Youth Services, 1972-75; chief counsel Maine Criminal Law Revision Commn., 1972-76; chief counsel Vt. Com. to Revise Criminal Code, 1973-75. Ford Found. Law Faculty fellow, 1961-62, 63-64; Nat. Endowment for Humanities sr. fellow, 1971-72; recipient grants NIMH, 1960-61, Nat. Inst. Law Enforcement and Criminal Justice, 1970, NSF, 1973-75; author: Modern Juvenile Justice, 1972; The Law of Juvenile Courts in a Nutshell, 1971; Science and Justice: The Massachusetts Witchcraft Trials, 1968; contbr. articles law jours. Home: 44 Sumner Rd Brookline MA 02146 Office: 885 Centre St Newton Centre MA 02159 Tel (617) 969-0100

FOX, SHAYLE PHILLIP, b. Chgo., July 20, 1934; B.S., U. Ill., 1954; J.D., DePaul U., 1957. Admitted to Ill. bar, 1957, U.S. Supreme Ct. bar, 1967; asso. firm McKay, Moses & McGarr, Chgo., 1958-61; asso. firm Lederer, Fox and Grove, Chgo., 1961-63, partner, 1963—. Vice-pres., bd. dirs. Young People's div. Jewish United Fund, Chgo., 1965; bd. dirs. Schwab Rehab. Hosp., 1970-73, Jewish Community Centers of Chgo., 1977—. Mem. Ill., Chgo., Am. bar assns., Am. Judicature Soc., Chgo. Assn. Commerce and Industry, Ill. Soc. C.P.A.'s, Ill. C. of C. C.P.A., Ill. Home: 1 Rockgate Ln Glencoe IL 60622 Office: Sears Tower 233 S Wacker Dr Chicago IL 60606 Tel (312) 876-0500

FOX, THOMAS EDWARD, b. Carters Creek, Tenn., Nov. 19, 1912; B.S., Middle Tenn. State U., 1940; LL.B., U. Tenn., Knoxville, 1948. Admitted to Tenn. bar, 1948, U.S. Supreme Ct. bar, 1965; partner firm Fox and Humphrey, Columbia, Tenn., 1948-56; mem. Tenn. State Senate, 1950-54; asst. atty. gen. State of Tenn., Nashville, 1956-67, dep. atty. gen., 1967-71; individual practice law, Franklin, Tenn., 1971—. Office: 218 E Main St Franklin TN 37064 Tel (615) 794-0807

FOX, THOMAS PHILIP, b. Appleton, Wis., May 27, 1946; B.A., Coll. St. Thomas, 1968; J.D., U. Wis., 1971. Admitted to Wis. bar, 1971; chief clk. Wis. State Assembly, Madison, 1970-72; partner firm Hawkes & Fox, Washburn, Wis., 1972-75; dist. atty. Bayfield County (Wis.) Washburn, 1975—. Chmn. bd. Wis. Dept. Natural Resources, 1976—, mem., 1973—. Mem. Wis., Ashland-Bayfield Counties bar assns., Nat., Wis. dist. attys. assns. Home: 229 E 3d St Washburn WI 54891 Office: Bayfield County Courthouse Washburn WI 54891 Tel (715) 373-5339

FOX, WARREN G., b. Paxton, Ill., May 5, 1923; student Wright Jr. Coll., 1941-43, U.S. Naval Acad., 1943-44; A.B., Lake Forest Coll., 1947; J.D., John Marshall Law Sch., 1956. Admitted to Ill. bar, 1956; corp. exec., 1947-61; individual practice law, 1961-63; corp. mgmt. exec., 1963-68; exec. dir. Lake County (Ill.) Legal Aid, 1968-71; asso. judge Ill. Circuit Ct., 19th Circuit, 1971—. Pres. Young Republican Club of New Trier Twp. (Ill.); pres. Allen Park (Mich.) Indsl. Assn.; v.p. Ill. Legal Aid Dirs. Assn.; chmn. com. criminal law Ill. Asso. Judges' Seminar. Mem. Ill. State (chmn. com. pub. services), Lake County (chmn. com. law reform) bar assns. Office: Courthouse Waukegan IL 60085 Tel (312) 689-6358

FOXMAN, STEPHEN MARK, b. Youngstown, Ohio, Aug. 10, 1946; certificate London (Eng.) Sch. Econs., 1967; B.S. in Econs. cum laude, U. Pa., 1968; J.D., Harvard U., 1971. Admitted to Pa. bar, 1971, D.C. bar, 1973; law clk. to J. Sydney Hoffman, Superior Ct. Pa., 1971-72; asso. firm Ewing & Cohen, Phila., 1972-74, asso. firm Goodman & Ewing, Phila., 1974-76, partner, 1976—; referral atty. Pub. Interest Law Center of Phila. and Community Legal Services, Phila.; faculty Inst. Paralegal Tng., Phila. Mem. Am., Phila., D.C. bar assns. Office: 1700 Market St Philadelphia PA 19103 Tel (215) 864-7722

FOY, DUDLEY BRYAN, JR., b. Baird, Tex., Nov. 28, 1925; B.S., U. Tex., 1946, LL.B. with honors, 1949. Admitted to Tex. bar, 1949; asso. firm Kemp, Lewright, Dyer & Sorrell, Corpus Christi, Tex., 1949-53; partner firm Branscomb and Foy, Corpus Christi, 1953-60; individual practice law, Corpus Christi, 1960—. Fellow Am. Coll. Trial Lawyers; mem. State Bar Tex., Nueces County (pres. 1962-63), Am. bar assns., Am. Judicature Soc., Tex. Assn. Def. Counsel, Order of Coif. Home: 336 Meldo St Corpus Christi TX 78411 Office: 1602 Guaranty Bank Plaza Corpus Christi TX 78401 Tel (512) 884-6305

FOY, EDWARD DANIEL, JR., b. Phila., Dec. 27, 1940; B.S., Villanova U., 1963, LL.B., 1966. Admitted to Pa. bar, 1966; law clk. to judge Ct. Common Pleas Bucks County (Pa.), 1966; partner firm Liederbach, Elmer & Rossi, Richboro, Pa., 1966—. Bd. dirs. Council Rock Youth and Community Center, 1967-70; chmn. Northampton Twp. Republican Com., 1970-71; solicitor Lower Southampton Teens, Inc., 1971—. Mem. Am., Pa., Bucks County bar assns., Am. Trial Lawyers Assn., Am. Arbitration Assn. Home: 74 E Robin Rd Holland PA 18966 Office: 892 2d St Pike Richboro PA 18954 Tel (215) 357-4920

FOY, HENRY GRATTAN, b. High Point, N.C., Feb. 6, 1942; A.B., U. N.C., 1964, J.D., 1968. Admitted to N.C. bar, 1968; asso. firm Frink & Gore, Southport, N.C., 1968-69; partner firm Frink & Foy, Southport, 1969-72, Frink Foy & Gainey, Southport, 1972—. Mem. Brunswick County Hosp. Authority, 1975-76, Brunswick County Airport Authority, 1971-76. Mem. Am., 13th Jud. Dist. (past pres.), Brunswick County (past sec.), N.C. bar assns., Am. Judicature Soc., N.C. Acad. Trial Lawyers. Office: 120 Moore St Southport NC 28461 Tel (919) 457-5284

FOZZARD, HARRY BROWARD, b. Jacksonville, Fla., Feb. 6, 1905; student U. Fla., 1923-25; LL.B., Washington and Lee U., 1929, J.D., 1969. Admitted to Fla. bar, 1929; law clk. Giles J. Patterson, Jacksonville, Fla., 1930, A. D. McNeill, Jacksonville, Fla., 1930-31, Frank J. Heintz, Jacksonville, 1931, Rogers & Towers, Jacksonville, 1931-33; individual practice law, Jacksonville, Fla., 1933—; asst. city atty. Jacksonville, 1941-46, spl. tax atty., 1946-56, atty. city council, 1956-66. Mem. Jacksonville, Fla. State bar assns., Am. Young Men's Bar Assn. (orgn. com. nationwide 1931), Southeastern Admiralty Law Inst. Home: 4436 Ortega Blvd Jacksonville FL 32210 Office: 1045 Riverside Ave Jacksonville FL 32204 Tel (904) 355-2554

FRACASSE, GEORGE, b. Providence, Dec. 16, 1917; student St. Michael's Coll., 1937-39, Providence Coll., 1940-42; A.B., U. So. Calif. Sch. Law, 1956. Admitted to Calif. bar, 1961; individual practice law, Los Angeles, 1961—. Mem. Calif. Trial Lawyers Assn. Home: 2359 N Cameron Ave Covina CA 91724 Office: 7322 Avalon Blvd Los Angeles CA 90003 Tel (213) 752-3716

FRAILEY, CHARLES WOODROW, b. Elizabethtown, Ill., May 29, 1913; J.D., Chgo.-Kent Coll. Law, 1950. Admitted to Ill. bar, 1951; atty. casualty dept. gen. offices Armour & Co., Chgo., 1950-54; individual practice law, Hardin County, Ill., 1954-66; judge 2d Jud. Circuit Ct. of Ill., Elizabethtown, 1966—; asst. atty. gen. Hardin, Pope, Johnson and Pulaski Counties, 1960-66. Mem. SE Ill. Bar Assn. Home and office: Elizabethtown IL 62931 Tel (618) 287-2066

FRAILEY, ROBERT BELL, b. Phila., Dec. 12, 1923; B.M.E., U. Pa., 1945, LL.B., 1949. Admitted to Pa. bar, 1949, D.C. bar, 1949; asso. firm Paul & Paul, Phila., 1950-53, partner, 1954-73; individual practice law, Haverford, Pa., 1974—. Pres. Council Civic Assns., Newtown Twp., Pa., 1965-67; mem. Bd. Suprs. Newtown Twp., 1968-72, chmn., 1968-71. Mem. Am., Phila. (sec. 1974-76) patent law assns., Phila., Pa. bar assns. Recipient Amran prize for Pa. practice U. Pa., 1949. Home: 353 Echo Valley Ln Newtown Square PA 19073 Office: 349 Lancaster Ave Haverford PA 19041 Tel (215) 649-5095

FRAMENT, WILLARD J., b. Mechanicville N.Y., June 26, 1918; A.B., State U. N.Y., 1940; LL.B., Union U., 1946; M.B.A., Siena Coll., 1955; C.L.U., Am. Inst., 1956-60; Admitted to N.Y. bar, 1946; individual practice law, Cohoes, N.Y., 1947—; prof. law and fin., Siena Coll., Loudonville, N.Y., 1947—. Mem. Cohoes, Albany County, N.Y. bar assns. Home: Masten Ave Cohoes NY 12047 Tel (518) 237-6141

FRAMPTON, CHARLES WINSLOW, b. Winslow, Pa., Feb. 9, 1907; A.B., Bucknell U., 1931; J.D., Temple U., 1935. Admitted to Pa. bar, 1938, U.S. Supreme Ct. bar, 1970; ct. adminstr. Orphans' Ct. of Phila., 1963-69, dep. ct. adminstr. Orphans' Ct. div., 1969-73; trustee chpt. XIII procs. Bankruptcy Ct., Eastern Dist. Pa., 1963-75; individual practice law, 1938—. Mem. Am., Pa., Phila. bar assns., Am. Judicature Soc., Law Alumni of Temple U. Author: (Frampton revision) Remick Orphan's Court Practice and Procedure, Vols. I and II, 1976, Vols. III and IV, 1977. Home and Office: 823 Herschel Rd Philadelphia PA 19116 Tel (215) 673-0478

FRANCIOSA, MICHAEL VINCENT, b. Phila., Oct. 10, 1931; B.A., U. Md., 1953; J.D., U. Pa., 1958; grad. Nat. Coll. State Trial Judges, 1971. Admitted to Pa. bar, 1959; mem. staff legal dept. Pa. R.R., Phila., 1958-59; asst. city solicitor City of Easton (Pa.), 1960-64, city solicitor, 1964-68; 1st asst. dist. atty. Northampton County (Pa.), 1967-69; individual practice law, Easton, 1959-69; judge Northampton County Ct. Common Pleas, 1970—, Juvenile Ct., 1974—; mem. Northampton County Legal Aid and Pub. Defender's Staff, 1959-62. Mem. Easton-Phillipsburg Area Commn. on Human Relations, Pa. Gov's. Justice Commn.; exec. com. Minsi Trail council Boy Scouts Am., mem. St. Anthony's Youth Council, Easton. Mem. Northampton, Pa., Am. bar assns., Nat. Coll. State Trial Judges, Pa. Conf. State Trial Judges, Nat. Council Crime and Delinquency. Office: 231 Spring Garden St Easton PA 18042 Tel (215) 258-3131

FRANCIS, ALAN, b. Saskatoon, Sask., Can., Feb. 5, 1920; B.A., U. B.C., J.D., Pacific Coast U. Admitted to Calif. bar, 1972; asso. firm Early Maslach Boyd & Leavey, Los Angeles, 1973-75; prof. law Pacific Coast U., Long Beach, Calif., 1975—. Mem. Long Beach Bar Assn. Home and Office: 329 Claremont Ave Long Beach CA 90803 Tel (213) 439-5426

FRANCIS, JACK STANLEY, b. New Martinsville, W.Va., Jan. 30, 1921; J.D., W.Va., U., 1949. Admitted to W.Va. bar, 1949, U.S. Ct. Appeals bar, 4th Circuit, 1950, U.S. Dist. Ct. bar No. Dist. W.Va., 1950; partner firm Brennan & Francis, New Martinsville and Sistersville, W.Va., 1967—, sr. partner, 1977—. Fellow Am. Coll. Trial Lawyers; mem. Fedn. Ins. Counsel, W.Va. State Bar (gov.), W.Va. Law Sch. Assn. (gov. 1975—), W.Va., Am. bar assns. Office: PO Drawer 68 New Martinsville WV 26155 Tel (304) 455-1751

FRANCIS, JOE, b. Chgo., Apr. 26, 1921; A.B., U. Okla.; LL.B., Georgetown U. Admitted to Okla. bar; practice law, Tulsa, 1949—; atty., trustee Max and Tookah Campbell Found., 1956—; atty. Am. Title Ins. Co., 1956—; dir. Corrosion Services Inc., Petroleum Electronics Inc. Mem. Phi Beta Kappa, Phi Eta Sigma. Home: 2216 E 20th St Tulsa OK 74114 Office: 1610 1st Nat Bldg Tulsa OK 74103

FRANCIS, JOHN JOSEPH, b. Orange, N.J., June 19, 1903; LL.B./J.D., Rutgers U., 1925; LL.M., N.Y. U., 1947; LL.D., Rutgers U., 1959. Admitted to N.J. bar, 1926; asso. various firms, Newark, 1926-37; partner firm Foley & Francis, Newark, 1937-47; adv. master Ct. of Chancery, Newark, 1947-48; judge Essex County (N.J.) Ct., 1948-53; appellate div. N.J. Superior Ct., 1953-57; asso. justice N.J. Supreme Ct., 1957-72; lectr. Rutgers U. Law Sch., 1972-73; spl. counsel N.J. State Commn. Investigation, 1952-53; counsel firm Apruzzese & McDermott, Springfield, N.J., 1973—; chmn. N.J. Supreme Ct. Adv. Com. on Jud. Conduct, 1974—, mem. com. on jud. pensions, 1966-76. Mem. Am., N.J., Essex County (past pres.) bar assns. Asso. editor N.J. Law Jour., 1943-47, 72—. Contbr. articles to legal jours. Home: 9 Keasby Rd South Orange NJ 07079 Office: 500 Morris Ave Springfield NJ 07081 Tel (201) 467-1776

FRANCIS, JUDSON CHARLES, JR., b. Dallas, Nov. 25, 1930; student Baylor U., 1949-53; LL.B., So. Meth. U., 1956. Admitted to Tex. bar, 1956; mem. firm Gallagher, Francis, Bean, Wilson & Berry, Dallas, 1958-63; partner firms Bean, Francis, Ford, Francis & Wills, Dallas, 1963-73, Francis, Coffin, Francis & Kolenovsky, Dallas, 1973—. Chmn. bd. Dallas Country Day Sch., 1969-72; bd. dirs. Help Is Possible, Dallas, 1970-74. Mem. Tex. Trial Lawyers Assn. (pres. 1969-70), Assn. Trial Lawyers Am. (gov., chmn. dep. state relations). Home: 5618 W Caruth St Dallas TX 75209 Office: 3700 Cedar Springs Rd Dallas TX 75219 Tel (214) 522-6920

FRANCIS, ROBERT ALAN, b. Cin., Mar. 29, 1940; B.A., Ind. U., 1962; J.D., U. Mich., 1968. Admitted to Mich. bar, 1968, Colo. bar, 1971; staff atty. Washtenaw County (Mich.) Legal Aid. Soc., 1968-69; partner firms Toomey & Francis, Ann Arbor, Mich., 1969-71, Moore, Francis & Van Domelen, and predecessors, Aspen, Colo., 1971-75; individual practice law, Aspen, 1975—; dep. dist. atty. Pitkin County (Colo.), 1971-75. Mem. Mich., Colo. State, Washtenaw County, Pitkin County (pres. 1976—) bar assns. Home: PO Box 3098 Aspen CO 81611 Office: 440 E Main St Aspen CO 81611 Tel (303) 925-6150

FRANCK, THOMAS MARTIN, b. Berlin, July 14, 1931; B.A., U. B.C., LL.B., 1953; 1952; LL.M., Harvard U., 1954, S.J.D., 1956. Asst. prof. law U. Nebr., 1956-57; asso. prof. N.Y. U., 1957-60, prof., 1960—, dir. Center Internat. Studies, 1965-73; vis. prof. U. East Africa, Tanzania, 1963, Stanford U., 1963, York U., Toronto, 1972, 74-75; cons. in field constl. adviser govts. Tanganyika, 1963, Zanzibar, 1963, 64, Mauritius, 1965; mem. Sierra Leone Govt. Commn. Legal Edn., 1964. Mem. Can. Council Internat. Law, Internat. Law Assn. (exec. com. Am. chpt. 1968—, v.p.), Carnegie Endowment Internat. Peace (dir. internat. law program), African Law Assn. (dir. 1970-73), Assn. Am. Law Schs., U.S. Inst. Human Rights (dir. adv. council). Author: Race and Nationalism, 1960; The Role of the United Nations in the Congo, 1963; African Law, 1963; East African Unity Through Law, 1965; Comparative Constitutional Process, 1968; The Structure of Impartiality, 1968; A Free Trade Association, 1968; Why Federations Fail, 1968; Word Politics, Verbal Strategy Among the Superpowers, 1971; Secrecy and Foreign Policy, 1974; Resignation in Protest, Political and Ethical Choices Between Loyalty to Team and Loyalty to Conscience in American Public Life, 1975; bd. editors Am. Jour. Internat. Law; contbr. articles in field to profl. jours; Guggenheim fellow, 1973-74; recipient Christopher award, 1976. Home: 15 Charlton New York City NY 10014 Office: 40 Washington Sq S New York City NY 10012 Tel (212) 598-7644

FRANCKE, ALBERT, III, b. N.Y.C., Nov. 10, 1934; B.A. in History, Yale U., 1956; LL.B., Stanford U., 1961. Admitted to N.Y. Ct. Appeals 1st Circuit bar, 1962, U.S. Dist. Ct. for D.C. bar, 1967; partner firm Curtis, Mallet-Prevost, Colt & Mosle, N.Y.C., 1968—; lectr. Practising Law Inst. N.Y., 1969—; mem. adv. council Interagy. Task Force SEC, U.S. Treasury Dept., Fed. Reserve Bd., U.S. State Dept., 1971-72. Mem. Am., N.Y. bar assns., Fed. Bar Assn. for N.Y., N.J., Conn., Bar Assn. City of N.Y., Am. Soc. Internat. Law, Council Fgn. Relations. Home: 4 E 70th St New York City NY 10021 Office: 100 Wall St New York City NY 10005 Tel (212) 248-8111

FRANCKLYN, REGINALD ENDICOTT, b. Barcelona, Spain, Dec. 17, 1925; A.B., Yale, 1950; LL.B., U. Va., 1955. Admitted to Conn. bar, 1955; asso. firm Robinson, Robinson & Cole, Hartford, Conn., 1955-60, partner, 1960—; counsel Town of Avon (Conn.), 1960-62. Corporator Hartford Hosp., St. Francis Hosp., Newington Children's Hosp.; trustee Avon Old Farms Sch., 1968—; mem. Greater Hartford Community Council, 1970—. Fellow Am. Acad. Matrimonial Lawyers; mem. Hartford County, Conn. State, Am. bar assns., Phi Alpha Delta. Home: 408 Deercliff Rd Avon CT 06001 Office: 799 Main St Hartford CT 06103 Tel (203) 278-0700

FRANCO, JOHN CESARE, b. Detroit, June 7, 1945; B.B.A., Detroit Inst. Tech., 1969; J.D., Detroit Coll. Law, 1973. Admitted to Mich. bar, 1973, fed. bar, 1973; individual practice law, Southfield, Mich., 1973—. Mem. Oakland County Bar Assn. Office: 21840 W 9 Mile Rd Suite 3 Southfield MI 48220 Tel (313) 353-0890

FRANCO, RALPH ABRAHAM, b. Montgomery, Ala., Dec. 27, 1921; B.S., U. Ala., 1943, J.D., 1948. Admitted to Ala. bar, 1948, U.S. Supreme Ct. bar, 1951; asso. firm Hill, Hill, Stoval & Carter, and successor, Montgomery, 1948-53, partner, 1953—. Pres. Jewish Fedn. Montgomery, 1956-57. Mem. Am., Ala. State (chmn. Law Day 1966-68, chmn. jr. bar sect. 1955-56) bar assns., U. Ala. Law Sch. Found. (dir. 1971—), U. Ala. Law Sch. Alumni Assn. (pres. 1958), Farrah Law Soc. (dir. 1971—); fellow Am. Bar Found. Home: 3609 Thomas Ave Montgomery AL 36111 Office: 2nd Floor Hill Bldg Montgomery AL 36104 Tel (205) 834-7600

FRANDSEN, GORDON KENT, b. Aurora, Ill., Apr. 28, 1927; B.S. Bradley U., 1950; J.D., Ind. U., 1965. Admitted to Ind. bar, 1965; asst. dean Sch. Law, asso. prof. law Ind. U., 1965—; judge Lebanon (Ind.) City Ct., 1969—; chief counsel staff Office Ind. Atty. Gen., 1969; mem. Ind. Criminal Law Study Commn., 1970-75. Mem. Am., Ind. State, Boone County (Ind.) (pres. 1972-73), Indpls. bar assns., Order of Coif. Recipient Black Cane award Student Bar Assn., 1967; contbr. articles to Ind. Law Rev. Home: 1300 Sunnybrook Ln Lebanon IN 46052 Office: 735 W New York St Indianapolis IN 46202 Tel (317) 264-8523

FRANETOVICH, FLORIO NICHOLAS, b. Bel Air, Md., Mar. 15, 1927; B.B.A., Upsala Coll., 1950; M.B.A., N.Y. U., 1953; LL.B., U. Md., 1960. Admitted to Md. bar, 1960; project finance mgr. Martin Marietta Corp., Middle River, Md., 1953-64; individual practice law, Bel Air, Md., 1964—; asst. states atty. Harford County (Md.), 1965—; asst. prof. comml. law Harford Community Coll., 1964—. Commr. Town of Bel Air, 1962-66; trustee John Carroll Sch., Bel Air. Mem. Nat. Assn. Dist. Attys., Am. Trial Lawyers Assn., Harford County Bar Assn. Home: 505 S Giles St Bel Air MD 21014 Office: 25 Courtland W Bel Air MD 21014 Tel (301) 838-8186

FRANK, ARTHUR JUDD, b. Chgo., Mar. 18, 1946; B.S. in Bus. Adminstrn., Babson Coll., 1967; J.D., U. Ill., 1971. Admitted to Ill. bar, 1971; partner Frank Assos., Ltd., Chgo., 1971—. Mem. Am. (com. on advt. young lawyers sect.), Ill., Chgo. (chmn. creative arts com. 1974, chmn. commn. profl. responsibility 1975, mem. spl. com. instnl. advt. 1976, dir. young lawyers sect. 1976, chmn. elect 1977) bar assns., Lawyers for Creative Arts (pres. 1975-76). Office: 180 N LaSalle St Chicago IL 60601 Tel (312) 368-4460

FRANK, BEN WILLIAM, b. Lampasas, Tex., Oct. 23, 1929; B.A., U. Tex., 1956; LL.B., U. Ark., 1964. Admitted to Ark. bar, 1964; claims mgr. Comml. Union Assurance Co., Little Rock, 1964—. Mem. Traskwood (Ark.) Booster Club. Mem. Ark. Bar Assn., Ark. Adjuster Assn., Little Rock Claim Mgrs. Council. Home: Route 1 Box 16A Traskwood AR 72167 Office: 1100 N University Little Rock AR 72207

FRANK, BENJAMIN, b. Phila., July 21, 1902; B.A., U. Pa., 1922; student Penn Law Sch., 1922-24. Admitted to Pa. bar, 1926, U.S. Supreme Ct. bar, 1926; individual practice law, Norristown, Pa.; asst. atty. gen. Pa. Dept. Edn., 1966-73. Founder, 1st pres. Curtis Hills Civic Assn., Montgomery County, Pa., 1955-56. Mem. Phila., Montgomery County, Pa. bar assns. Home: 310 S Easton Rd Glenside PA 19038 Office: 515 Swede St Norristown PA 19401 Tel (215) 272-8400

FRANK, BERNARD, b. Wilkes-Barre, Pa., June 11, 1913; Ph.B., Muhlenberg Coll., 1935; J.D., U. Pa., 1938. Admitted to Pa. Supreme Ct. bar, 1941, U.S. Supreme Ct. bar, 1971; individual practice law, Allentown, Pa., 1939—; pres. firm Frank, Frank & Wishchuk, P.C., Allentown, 1970—; asst. U.S. atty for Eastern Dist. Pa. 1950-51; asst. city solicitor City of Allentown, 1956-60. Chmn. Allentown Housing Bd. Rev., 1960-70. Mem. Lehigh County (Pa.), Pa., Am., Internat. (chmn. ombudsman com. 1973—), Inter-Am. bar assns., World Assn. Lawyers. Contbr. articles to profl. jours. Home: 745 N 30th St Allentown PA 18104 Office: 832 Hamilton Mall POB 419 Allentown PA 18105 Tel (215) 435-8091

FRANK, BERNARD ALAN, b. Rochester, N.Y., Nov. 12, 1931; B.S., Northwestern U., 1953, J.D., 1955. Admitted to N.Y. bar, 1955, Ill. bar, 1955. Partner law firm Frank, Garrity and Tiernan Rochester, N.Y.; dir. Monroe Abstract & Title Co. Gen. counsel ACLU, 1971-73. Mem. N.Y. State, Monroe County bar assns. Club: U.S. Lawn Tennis Assn. (hon. life). Home: 25 San Rafael Dr Rochester NY 14618 Office: 1050 Crossroads Bldg Rochester NY 14614 Tel (716) 325-7616

FRANK, ELI, JR., b. Balt., Aug. 29, 1902; B.A., Johns Hopkins U., 1922; LL.B., Harvard U., 1925. Admitted to Md. bar, 1925; asso. firm Beeuwkes Skeen & Oppenheimer, Balt., 1925-34; chief counsel U.S. Bur. Customs, Washington, 1934-36; asst. gen. counsel Dept. Treasury, Washington, 1936; partner firms Lauchheimer & Frank, Balt., 1936-54, Frank, Bernstein, Conway & Goldman, and predecessors, Balt., 1946—; mem. rules com. Md. Ct. Appeals 1947-58. Balt. trustee Johns Hopkins U., 1960-75; pres. Balt. Bd. Sch. Commrs., 1962-68. Mem. Am., Md. (pres. 1967-70) bar assns., Am. Law Inst., Am. Judicature Soc. Home: 5415 Greenspring Ave Baltimore MD 21209 Office: 2 Hopkins Plaza Baltimore MD 21201 Tel (301) 547-0500

FRANK, HARRY HERSCHEL, b. Newcastle, Pa., Sept. 18, 1903; B.S., U. Pitts., 1926, LL.B., 1929. Admitted to Pa. bar, 1929, U.S. Supreme Ct. bar, 1938; asso. firm Graham, Matthews & Jameson, Newcastle, 1929-35; asst. counsel Pub. Utility Commn., Pa., 1935-43; partner firm McNees, Wallace & Nurick, Harrisburg, Pa., 1943—; asst. dist. atty. Lawrence County, Pa., 1929-35. Mem. Am. Law Inst., Motor Carrier Lawyers Assn., Assn. of ICC Practitioners, World Peace Through Law Center, Pa. (chmn. Pub. Utility sect. 1952-53, chmn. Adminstrv. Law sect. 1954-55), Am. (vice chmn. Devel. sect. 1954) bar assns., Order Coif, Beta Gamma Sigma, Masons, B'nai B'rith. Home: 3505 N Front St Harrisburg PA 17110 Office: 100 Pine St PO Box 1166 Harrisburg PA 17108 Tel (717) 236-9341

FRANK, JACK, b. Chgo., June 26, 1915; B.B.S., U. Toledo, 1938, J.D., 1950. Admitted to Ohio bar, 1950; partner firm Winter & Frank, Toledo, 1950-57; individual practice law, Toledo, 1957-66; gen. counsel Toledo Legal Aid Soc., 1966-70; asso. firm Frank & Epstein, Toledo, 1970—. Mem. Am., Ohio, Toledo, Lucas County bar assns., Assn. Trial Lawyers Am. Home: 2304 Cheltenham St Toledo OH 43606 Office: 234 Spitzer Bldg Toledo OH 43604 Tel (419) 243-5271

FRANK, JOHN J., b. St. Louis, Jan. 21, 1935; student U. Mo., 1953-56; LL.B., J.D., St. Louis U., 1962. Admitted to Mo. bar, 1962; asso. firm Hullverson, Hullverson & Frank, Inc. and predecessor, St. Louis, after 1962, now partner; lectr. products liability Washington U., St. Louis, 1970-74; jud. commr. 22d Jud. Commn. Mo., 1975—; port commr. City of St. Louis, 1976. Leader, Boy Scouts Am. Mem. Fed., Mo. (torts sect.), St. Louis (trial sect.) bar assns., Am. (state committeeman), Mo. assns. trial lawyers, Am. Judicature Soc. (mem. ct. en banc com. on civil dockets), Lawyers Assn. St. Louis (exec. com.). Contbr. articles to profl. jours. Home: 5878 Walsh St St Louis MO 63109 Office: 722 Chestnut St Suite 1100 St Louis MO 63101 Tel (314) 421-2313

FRANK, NEIL ALLEN, b. N.Y.C., Oct. 28, 1946; B.A., Hunter Coll. U. City N.Y., 1967; J.D., Fordham U., 1972. Admitted to N.Y. State bar, 1973, U.S. Dist. Cts. for Eastern and So. Dists. N.Y. bars, 1974, U.S. Supreme Ct. bar, 1976; law asst. judges of Family Ct. of N.Y. State, Jamaica, 1973-76, judges of Supreme Ct., Bronx County, 1976—. Mem. N.Y. State Bar Assn., Assn. Law Assts. of Civil, Criminal and Family Cts. Notary pub., N.Y. Contbr. articles to law jours. Home: 530 W 236th St Riverdale NY 10463 Office: 851 Grand Concourse Bronx NY 10451 Tel (212) 293-8030

FRANK, PAUL RICHARD, b. N.Y.C., Nov. 29, 1933; A.B., Columbia, 1955, LL.B., 1958. Admitted to N.Y. State bar, 1959, U.S. Supreme Ct. bar, 1970; asso. firm Landis, Feldman, Reilly & Akers, N.Y.C., 1958-64; asso. firm Poletti, Freidin, Prashker, Feldman & Gartner, N.Y.C., 1964-66, partner, 1966—. Mem. Am., N.Y. State bar assns., Assn. of the Bar of City of N.Y. Home: 310 West End Ave New York City NY 10023 Office: 1185 Ave of the Americas New York City NY 10036 Tel (212) 730-7373

FRANK, RAYMOND MICHAEL, b. Balt., Jan. 21, 1940; B.A., U. Md., 1961; J.D., Cornell U., 1975. Admitted to Conn. bar, 1965, D.C. bar, 1966, U.S. Ct. Mil. Appeals, 1966, Ohio bar, 1970, U.S. Ct. Appeals for D.C., 1972, 6th circuit, 1973, U.S. Supreme Ct. bar, 1977; mem. firm McKissick & Burt, Durham, N.C., 1965; atty. Neighborhood Legal Services Washington, 1966-67, asst. project dir., 1968; exec. dir. Advs. for Basic Legal Equality, Toledo, 1969—; founder Found. for Law in the Pub. Interest, 1976. Mem. Toledo City Council Citizen Com. on Housing, 1971, on Consumer Rights, 72, on Water Rates, 1976. Mem. Toledo Bar Assn. Recipient Civil Liberties Award ACLU of NW Ohio, 1970-71. Home: 2232 Scottwood Ave Toledo OH 43620 Office: 740 Spitzer Bldg Madison & Huron Sts Toledo OH 43604 Tel (419) 255-0814

FRANK, ROBERT R., b. N.Y.C., Apr. 20, 1923; B.B.A., U. Miami, 1950, J.D., 1952. Admitted to Fla. bar, 1952; asso. firm Sommer, Frank & Weston, Miami Beach, Fla., 1952-63, firm Frank, Strelkow & Marx, Miami Beach, Fla., 1963-72, firm Frank, Strelkow & Gay, Miami Beach, Fla., 1972—. Mem. Am., Fla., Miami Beach, Internat. bar assns., Comml. Law League. Office: 1666 Kennedy Causeway Miami Beach FL 22141 Tel (305) 868-4711

FRANK, WILLIAM SAMUEL, b. Mineola, N.Y., Sept. 18, 1939; B.A. in Econs., C.W. Post Coll., 1963; J.D., Bklyn. Law Sch., 1967. Admitted to N.Y. bar, 1967, Fla. bar, 1974; dir. properties TWA, N.Y.C., 1971-74; asst. gen. counsel Howard Johnson Co., N.Y.C., 1968-71; sr. real estate analyst ITT, N.Y.C., 1974—. Founding dir. Concerned Parents of Jamaica Day Care Center, Jamaica, N.Y., 1971. Mem. Assn. Bar City N.Y., Phi Delta Phi, Pi Gamma Mu. Home: 36 W 84th St New York City NY 10024 Office: 320 Park Ave New York City NY 10022 Tel (212) 752-6000

FRANKE, DONALD THEODORE, b. Eyota, Minn., Aug. 16, 1921; A.A., Rochester Jr. Coll., 1941; B.A., U. Minn., 1946, LL.B., 1952. Dir. pub. relations Central Wash. Coll., Ellensburg, 1947-48; realtor, Rochester, Minn., 1948-50; admitted to Minn. bar, 1953, Fla. bar, 1973; partner firm Frank & Steiner, Rochester, 1959-64; judge Minn. State Dist., Rochester, 1964-75; mem. firm Neinas Goodlette & Franke, Naples, Fla., 1976—; pres. Probationed Offenders Rehab. and Tng. Community Corrections Pioneer Program, Rochester, 1973; mem. Minn. Ho. of Reps., 1957-63. Mem. exec. com. Rochester Meth. Hosp., 1962-75. Mem. Minn., Fla. bar assns., Am. Judicature Soc. Home: 223 Pine Valley Circle Naples FL 33940 Office: 3174 E Tamiami Trail Naples FL 33940 Tel (813) 774-2870

FRANKE, PAUL MARION, JR., b. Gulfport, Miss., Dec. 18, 1937; student U. Miss., 1956-58, 63-64; B.S., U. So. Miss., 1961; LL.B., Jackson Sch. Law, 1966. Admitted to Miss. bar, 1966; adminstrv. judge Miss. Workmen's Compensation Commn., Jackson, 1966-69, commr., 1969-70; partner firm White & Morse, Gulfport, 1970—. Mem. Nat. Seashore Adv. Commn., Miss. State Port Authority. Mem. Am., Miss., Harrison County bar assns., Miss. Def. Lawyers Assn., Am. Trial Lawyers Assn., Internat. Assn. Accident Bds. and Commns., U. SE Miss., U. Miss. alumni assns., Sigma Delta Kappa. Home: 1515 Bert Ave Gulfport MS 39501 Office: PO Drawer 100 Gulfport MS 39501 Tel (601) 863-9821

FRANKEL, IRV, b. N.Y.C., Nov. 3, 1926; B.A., U. Calif., Los Angeles, 1949; J.D., Bklyn. Law Sch., 1953. Admitted to N.Y. bar, 1953; individual practice law, Islip, N.Y., 1969-72; partner firm Gliboff & Frankel, Islip, 1972—; bd. dirs. Suffolk County (N.Y.) Prepaid Legal Services Corp. Mem. Nassau County, Suffolk County bar assns. Office: Gliboff & Frankel 1 Grant Ave Islip NY 11751

FRANKEL, MARK DAVID, b. York, Pa., Jan. 12, 1948; B.A., U. Md., 1970; J.D., Am. U. Washington Coll. Law, 1973. Admitted to Pa. Supreme Ct. bar, 1973; individual practice law, York, 1973; partner firm Frankel & Abrahamsen, asst. chief counsel Pa. Personal Income Tax Bur., asst. atty. gen Commonwealth of Pa., 1973—; lectr. York Coll. of Pa. Co-chmn. York County fund dr. Leukemia Soc. Am., 1975; bd. dirs. Colonial York. Mem. York County, Am., Pa. bar assns., U. Md. Alumni Assn. (dir. Central Pa. area 1975—), Phi Delta Pi. Office: 14 W King St York PA 17401 Tel (717) 845-9211

FRANKL, ARTHUR ALBERT, b. Springfield, Mass., Jan. 25, 1930; A.B., Yale, 1952; LL.B., Harvard, 1955. Admitted to Mass. bar, 1955, D.C. bar, 1964; individual practice law, Springfield, Mass., 1955-62, 68-76, Washington, 1964-68; partner firm Fein, Sheehy, Brooslin, Maskell and Frankl, Springfield, 1976—; with antitrust div. U.S. Dept. Justice, Washington, 1962-63; master in English and history and debate coach Wilbraham (Mass.) Acad., 1956-57. Mem. Hampden County Bar Assn. Home: 49 Pennsylvania Ave Springfield MA 01118 Office: 52 Mulberry St Springfield MA 01105 Tel (413) 781-5400

FRANKLIN, BENJAMIN, b. Buffalo, Dec. 30, 1902; student U. Mich., 1922-25; LL.B., U. Buffalo 1928. Admitted to N.Y. State bar, 1929, U.S. Treasury Dept. bar, 1963; individual practice law, Buffalo, 1929—. Home: 43 Jewett Pkwy Buffalo NY 14214 Office: 334 Brisbane Bldg 403 Main St Buffalo NY 14203 Tel (716) 854-3042

FRANKLIN, BLAKE TIMOTHY, b. San Mateo, Calif., Sept. 28, 1942; A.B., Dartmouth Coll., 1963; J.D., Harvard, 1966. Admitted to Calif. bar, 1966, D.C. bar, 1969, U.S. Supreme Ct. bar, 1970, N.Y. State bar, 1976; contractor AID, vol. Peace Corps, 1966-68; asso. firm Coudert Bros., Washington, 1969-74, partner, N.Y.C. and San Francisco, 1975—; vis. prof. U. Costa Rica, 1967-68; legal counsel Bolivian State Oil Co., 1970—. Trustee Jose Limon Dance Found., N.Y.C., 1976—, v.p., 1977—. Mem. Am., Inter-Am. bar assns., Am. Soc. Internat. Law. Office: 200 Park Ave New York City NY 10017 Tel (212) 973-5556 also 3 Embarcadero Center San Francisco CA Tel (415) 981-5115

FRANKLIN, LEE, b. Bklyn., Aug. 9, 1909; Ph.B., Brown Coll., 1931; LL.B., J.D., Yale, 1934. Admitted to N.Y. Supreme Ct. bar, 1934, U.S. Supreme Ct. bar, 1960; formerly with firm Child & Handel; Office of Alien Property Custodian, 1938-43; individual practice law, N.Y.C., 1943—; mgr. mines, Nigeria, 1951-53; pres., chmn. bd. firm Newtown, Jackson Co., Inc., Port Washington, N.Y., 1947—. Mem. Phi Beta Kappa. Home: 79 Longview Rd Port Washington NY 11050 Tel (516) 883-1648

FRANKLIN, LEONARD LORING, b. Boston, Apr. 13, 1928; B.A., U. Calif. at Los Angeles, 1948; J.D., Bklyn. Law Sch., 1956. Admitted to N.Y. bar, 1957, Tex. bar, 1962; individual practice law, Mt. Vernon, N.Y., 1958-60; corp. counsel Tenax, Inc., N.Y.C., 1960-62; individual practice law, Austin, Tex., 1962-75; corp. counsel U.S. Surg. Corp., N.Y.C., 1976—; judge Westlake Hills, Tex., 1965-71, 74-75. Trustee Eanes Ind. Sch. Dist. Westlake Hills, 1971-74, pres. bd., 1974. Mem. Am. Bar Assn. Home: 56 E 66th St New York City NY 10021

FRANKLIN, MITCHELL, b. Montreal, Que., Can., Feb. 19, 1902; A.B., Harvard, 1922, J.D., 1925, S.J.D., 1928. Admitted to N.Y. State bar, 1930, La. bar, 1943; law clk. Supreme Jud. Ct. of Mass., 1925-28; practice law, N.Y.C., 1928-30; W.R. Irby prof. law Tulane U., New Orleans, 1930-67, emeritus, 1967—; vis. prof. law State U. N.Y. at Buffalo, 1967-68, prof. law and philosophy, 1968-74, emeritus, 1974—, charter mem. Emeritus Center State U. N.Y. Buffalo, 1976—; legal officer UN, UNRRA (SE Europe). Contbr. numerous articles to legal and philos. jours. Home: Apt 710 675 Delaware Ave Buffalo NY 14202 Office: John Lord O'Brian Hall State Univ NY Buffalo NY 14260 also Tulane Law Sch New Orleans LA 70118 Tel (504) 636-2495

FRANKLIN, ROBERT DRURY, b. Mead, Okla., June 6, 1935; B.S., U. Okla., 1957; LL.B., So. Methodist U., 1964. Admitted to Tex. bar, 1964; petroleum engr. Mobil Oil Corp., Healdton, Okla., 1957-59; asst. prodn. mgr. Bayview Oil Corp., Dallas, 1959-64; sec.-treas., dir. Siboney Corp., Dallas, 1964-70; pres., dir. Northland Oils Ltd., Dallas, 1970—, Costa Resources Inc., Dallas, 1973—. Mem. AIME, Ind. Petroleum Assn. Am., Tex.-Mid Continent Oil and Gas Assn., Am. Petroleum Inst., Tex., Dallas bar assns. Home: 6781 Eastridge St Apt 2076 Dallas TX 75231 Office: 3303 Lee Pkwy Dallas TX 75219 Tel (214) 522-6780

FRANKLIN, ROBERT NIXON (NICK), b. Hobbs, N.Mex., Mar. 25, 1943; B.A. in Govt., N.Mex. State U., 1965; J.D., George Washington U., 1968. Admitted to N.Mex. bar, 1969, D.C. bar, 1969; partner firms Franklin & Ahaya, Albuquerque, 1969-70, Lamb, Metzgar, Franklin & Lines, Albuquerque, 1970—; chief legis. aide and legal adviser to Gov. N.Mex., Santa Fe, 1975—; chmn. N.Mex. Gov.'s Council on Criminal Justice Planning, Santa Fe, 1975—; liaison for N.Mex. Gov. to N.Mex. State Bar Assn.; mem. State Bar N.Mex. legis. and jud. selection coms. Pres. bd. dirs. 1st Unitarian Ch., Albuquerque, 1973-74; mem. N.Mex. Democratic Central Com., 1973—; vol. govt. counselor N.Mex. Boys' State program. Mem. N.Mex., Albuquerque, D.C., Am. bar assns. Recipient Service award State Bar N.Mex., 1976. Home: 14 La Villita Circle NE Albuquerque NM 87112 Office: 1010 Bank of N Mex Bldg PO Box 987 Albuquerque NM 87103 Tel (505) 247-0107

FRANKLIN, ROBERT VERNON, b. Toledo, Jan. 6, 1926; B.A., Morehouse Coll., Atlanta, 1947; J.D., U. Toledo, 1950. Admitted to Ohio bar, 1950; individual practice law, Toledo, 1950-60; judge Toledo Municipal Ct., 1960-68; judge Lucas County (Ohio) Common Pleas Ct., Toledo, 1969—; pros. atty. City of Toledo, 1953-59. Mem. Ohio, Toledo, Lucas County, 2d Nat. bar assns., Ohio Common Pleas Judges Assn. (v.p.), Phi Alpha Delta. Home: 5018 Chatham Valley St Toledo OH 43615 Office: Lucas County Court House Toledo OH 43624 Tel (419) 259-8773

FRANKS, DONALD, b. Wheeler, Miss., June 4, 1908; student U. So. Miss., 1928-30; grad. Sch. Law U. Miss., 1936. Admitted to Miss. bar, 1936; individual practice law, Booneville, Miss., 1936—; pres. Mfgs. Warehousing Co., 1968—, Prentiss Community Devel., Inc., 1972—; dir. Miss. Textiles, JLM Realty, and numerous other companies. Mem. Am., Miss., Prentiss County bar assns., Miss. Trial Lawyers Assn. Columnist Booneville Banner-Independent. Home: 1100A South Second Booneville MS 38829 Office: 215 1/2 West College Booneville MS 38829 Tel (601) 728-4494

FRANKS, HERSCHEL PICKENS, b. Savannah, Tenn., May 28, 1930; J.D., U. Tenn., 1957; postgrad. Nat. Coll. State Judiciary U. Nev., 1971. Admitted to Tenn. bar, 1959, U.S. Supreme Ct. bar, 1968; claims atty. USF&G Co., Knoxville, Tenn., 1957-59; mem. firm Moon, Harris & Dineen, Chattanooga, 1959-65, Harris, Moon, Meacham & Franks, Chattanooga, 1965-70; judge probate and chancery ct. 3d chancery div. State of Tenn, Chattanooga, 1970—. Mem. Hamilton County Records Commn.; mem. estate planning council, Chattanooga. Mem. Am. (recipient award for Law Day Programs), Tenn., Chattanooga (pres. 1968-69, dir. 1965-70, chmn. past presidents com. 1977-78) bar assns., Nat. Conf. State Trial Judges (Tenn. rep.), Am. Judicature Soc., Tenn. Jud. Conf., Am. Judges Assn., Tenn. Trial Judges Conf. Recipient Bancroft-Whitney award in constl. law, 1956. Home: 703 Brown's Ferry Rd Chattanooga TN 37409 Office: Room 210 Courthouse Chattanooga TN 37402 Tel (615) 757-2658

FRANKS, LEONARD PETER, b. Cleve., Nov. 13, 1910; B.A., Ohio State U., 1938, J.D., 1938. Admitted to Ohio bar, 1939; practice law, Cleve., 1939—. Office: 3692 E 71st St Cleveland OH 44105 Tel (216) 341-0110

FRANZE, ANTHONY JAMES, b. Albany, N.Y., Sept. 22, 1941; B.S. in Pharmacy, St. John's Coll., 1963, J.D., 1966. Admitted to N.Y. bar, 1966, U.S. Patent bar, 1971; counsel Norwich Pharmacal Co., Norwich, N.Y., 1970—; asst. sec. Morton Norwich Products, Inc., Norwich. Mem. N.Y., Am. pharm. assns., Am., N.Y. bar assns., Am., Central N.Y. patent law assns., U.S. Trademark Assn., Am. Judicature Soc. Home: 70 Cortland St Norwich NY 13815 Office: 17 Eaton Ave Norwich NY 13815 Tel (607) 335-2283

FRASCH, DAVID EDWARD, b. Columbus, Ohio, Mar. 28, 1947; B.A., Lawrence U., 1969; J.D., U. Mich., 1972; LL.M., U. London, 1973. Admitted to Ohio bar, 1972, Wis. bar, 1974; asso. firm Lane, Alton & Horst, Columbus, 1973-74; partner firm Wiley and Frasch, Chippewa Falls, Wis., 1974—. Mem. Am., Wis., Chippewa County (v.p.) bar assns. Home: 204 W Spruce St Chippewa Falls WI 54729 Office: 119 1/2 N Bridge St Chippewa Falls WI 54729 Tel (715) 723-2247

FRASCONA, JOSEPH LOHENGRIN, b. N.Y.C., Nov. 11, 1910; B.S., Coll. City N.Y., 1932; J.D., Harvard, 1935. Admitted to N.Y. bar, 1937, Colo. bar, 1947, Fed. Dist. N.Y. bar, 1940, Fed. Dist. Colo. bar, 1958; asso. firm Walton, Bannister & Stitt, N.Y.C., 1937-40; asso. atty. Office Atty. Gen. U.S., Washington 1942-46; gen. counsel, dept. to acting field commr. Dept. State, London, 1945-46; asst. prof. bus. law U. Colo., 1946-48, asso. prof., 1948-55, prof., 1955—; dir. Colo. Sch. Banking, 1959—; arbitrator Am. Arbitration Assn., 1971—. Bd. dirs. Way, Inc., Boulder, Colo., Denver Coalition Ventures, Inc. Mem. N.Y., Colo., Boulder County bar assns., Res. Officers Assn. U.S. (pres. Boulder chpt. Colo. Dept.), Am. Bus. Law Assn. (pres. 1955-56), Beta Gamma Sigma. Author: Visit Search, and Seizure on The High Seas: A Proposed Convention of International Law on the Regulation of this Belligerent Right, 1938; (with Walter B. Franklin) Statutory Materials For the Study Of Commercial Law, 1951; Agency, 1964; C.P.A. Law Review, Under the Uniform Commercial Code, 5th edit., 1977; contbr. to Ency. Americana. Home: 420 Ponderosa Dr Boulder CO 80303 Office: Coll of Bus and Adminstrn U of Colo Boulder CO 80309 Tel (303) 443-1950

FRASER, EVERETT MACKAY, b. Mpls., July 20, 1921; B.A. in Math. and Physics, U. Minn., 1943; LL.B., Columbia, 1948. Admitted to Minn. bar, 1949, Mass. bar, 1968; patent atty. ITT, N.Y.C., 1948-50; patent adviser S.C. U.S. Army, Belmar, N.J., 1950-51; legal counsel Harlan H. Bradt Assos., N.Y.C., 1952-54; mgr. N.Y. patent operation Burroughs Corp., N.Y.C., 1954-59; chief patent counsel LFE Corp., Waltham, Mass., 1959-62, gen. counsel, 1962—, sec., 1963—, v.p., 1970—; mem. town meeting Town of Arlington (Mass.), 1976—. Mem. Am., Mass. bar assns., Am., Boston patent law assns., Am. Soc. Corporate Secs. Home: 23 Sheraton Park Arlington MA

02174 Office: LFE Corp 1601 Trapelo Rd Waltham MA 02154 Tel (617) 890-2000

FRASER, GEORGE BROADRUP, b. Washington, May 9, 1914; A.B., Dartmouth, 1936; J.D., Harvard, 1939; LL.M., George Washington U., 1941. Admitted to D.C. bar, 1939, Oklahoma bar, 1952; individual practice law, Washington, 1939-41; V.A. atty., Boise, Idaho, 1946; prof. law U. Idaho, Moscow, 1946-49, U. Okla., Norman, 1949—, Boyd prof. law, 1959—; advisor Okla. Legis. Council, 1968-69. Mem. Am., Okla., D.C. bar assns. (mem. civil procedure com. Okla. assn. 1951—). Contbr. articles in field to legal jours. Home: 1206 Greenbriar Ct Norman OK 73069 Office: 300 Timberdell Rd Norman OK 73019 Tel (405) 325-3911

FRASER, PETER, b. Albion, N.Y., June 22, 1941; A.B., Columbia U., 1964; J.D., Fordham U., 1968. Admitted N.Y. State bar, 1968, Calif. bar, 1971; partner firm Friedman, Kahan Dysart & Fraser, San Diego. Mem. Am., N.Y. State, San Diego County (chmn. corps. legis. subcom.) bar assns., Defenders Programs San Diego (dir., treas. 1974—). Contbr. articles to legal jours. Office: 1800 Financial Sq San Diego CA 92109 Tel (714) 238-1010

FRASER, ROBERT WILLIAM, b. Seattle, Oct. 5, 1924; student Franklin U., Marshall Coll., 1943-44, Washington and Lee U., 1942-43; J.D., Northeastern U., 1949. Admitted to Mont. bar, 1949, Calif. bar, 1950, U.S. Supreme Ct. bar, 1955; partner firm Fraser, Brown & Hewett, Santa Ana, Calif., 1952-55, firm Fraser, Hewett & Rickles, Santa Ana, 1955-60; individual practice law, Santa Ana, 1960—; govt. appeals agt., 1968-73; judge pro tem Superior Ct. Mem. Orange County Bar Assn. (pres. 1962-63), Am. Bd. Trial Lawyers (adv.), Orange County Trial Lawyers Assn., Orange County Criminal Justice Counsel, Clan Fraser Assn. for Calif. (founder, 1st chmn.). Home: Round Potrero San Juan Capistrano CA Office: 811 N Broadway Santa Ana CA 92701 Tel (714) 558-8888

FRATCHER, WILLIAM FRANKLIN, b. Detroit, Apr. 4, 1913; A.B. with distinction, Coll. City Detroit, 1933; A.M., Wayne State U., 1938; J.D. with distinction, U. Mich., 1936, LL.M., 1951, S.J.D., 1952; grad. U.S. Army Command and Gen. Staff Sch., 1944; postgrad. U. Paris, 1945. Admitted to Mich. bar, 1936, U.S. Supreme Ct. bar, 1942, Mo. bar, 1958; asso. firm Lewis & Watkins, Detroit, 1936-39, mem., 1939-41; with JAGC, U.S. Army, 1941-47, chief war crimes br. legal div. Office Mil. Govt. for Germany (U.S.), Berlin, 1945-46; asso. prof. law U. Mo., 1947-49, prof., 1949—, R.B. Price Distinguished prof., 1971—; vis. prof. U. Mich., 1952, N.Y. U., 1954-55, 63, 65, U. Calif., 1976; Ford Found. Law Faculty fellow in internat. legal studies, hon. mem. faculty laws U. London King's Coll., 1963-64; research counsel N.Y. State Temporary Commn. on Estates, 1963. Fellow Am. Coll. Probate Counsel (acad.); mem. Am. Bar Assn. (vice chmn. coms.), Mo. Bar (council com. probate and trusts), Soc. Pub. Tchrs. Law, Am. Soc. Legal History, Selden Soc. Author: The National Defense Act, 1945; Perpetuities and Other Restraints, 1955; (with Simes) Fiduciary Administration, 1956; Trusts and Estates in England, 1968; Veterinary Jurisprudence, 1968; (with others) Uniform Probate Code, 1970, Uniform Probate Code Practice Manual, 1972; Trust, 1974; contbr. articles to legal jours.; reporter Uniform Probate Code, 1963-70; gen. reporter Internat. Ency. Comparative Law, 1966—, Mo. Probate Laws Revision Project, 1973—; editor pocket parts Simes & Smith on Future Interests, 1961—. Office: Tate Hall U of Mo Columbia MO 65201 Tel (314) 882-6558

FRATIES, GAIL ROY, b. Carmel, Calif., Mar. 1, 1928; B.A. in Polit. Sci., Stanford U., 1952; B.A. in Fgn. Trade, Am. Inst. Fgn. Trade, 1954; J.D., U. San Francisco, 1966. Admitted to Calif. bar, 1966, Alaska bar, 1969; pres. firm Gregg, Fraties, Petersen, Page & Baxter, Anchorage; dep. dist. atty. Monterey County (Calif.), 1967-68; asst. atty. gen. State of Alaska, 1969; dist. atty. 1st Jud. Dist. Alaska, 1969-70; lectr. U. Alaska. Mem. Am. Bar Assn., Am. Trial Lawyers Assn., Calif., Alaska bars, Am. Judicature Soc. Home: 4325 Macalister St Anchorage AK 99502 Office: 720 M St Anchorage AK 99501 Tel (907) 276-3464

FRAUENSHUH, RONALD RAY, SR., b. St. Paul, July 7, 1936; B.A., Macalster Coll., 1960; LL.B., William Mitchel Coll., 1964. Admitted to Minn. bar, 1964; atty. City of Paynesville, Minn., 1972—, City of Brooten, 1972—; partner firm Weis & Frauenshuh, Paynesville, 1964-72; atty. City of Eden Valley, 1972-74, 75—; partner firm Frauenshuh & Fahlberg, 1974—. Pres., Paynesville Jaycees, 1971-72, Paynesville Lions, 1976. Mem. Am., Minn., Stearns County bar assns., Minn. Assn. Trial Lawyers, Am. Judicature Soc., Comml. Law League. Home: 803 Washburne Ave Paynesville MN 56362 Office: 113 Washburne Ave Paynesville MN 56362 Tel (612) 243-3748

FRAWLEY, WILLIAM HENRY, b. Eau Claire, Wis., Feb. 15, 1911; B.A., U. Wis., 1934, J.D., 1934. Admitted to Wis. bar, 1934; U.S. Conciliation Commr., Eau Claire, 1934-36; spl. atty. div. land utilization Dept. Justice, Eau Claire, 1936-39, Circuit Ct. Commr., Eau Claire, 1943-49; U.S. Commr., Eau Claire, 1949-71; dir. Wis. Bar Found., 1955-64; judge Bankruptcy Ct., Eau Claire, 1962—; U.S. magistrate, Eau Claire, 1971—. Mem. Police and Fire Commn., Eau Claire, 1947-62. Mem. Am., Eau Claire County, 7th Circuit Ct. Appeals bar assns., State Bar Wis., Am. Arbitration Assn. (mem. Nat. panel arbitrators). Home: 513 E Lexington Blvd Eau Claire WI 54701 Office: 3031/2 S Barstow St Eau Claire WI 54701 Tel (715) 832-1721

FRAZIER, ROBERT HAINES, b. Greensboro, N.C., Jan. 8, 1899; student Guilford Coll., 1917-18; A.B., U. N.C., 1922; postgrad. Columbia, 1929; LL.D., N.C. Agrl. and Tech. State U., 1970. Admitted to N.C. bar, 1922, D.C. bar, 1947; practiced in Greensboro, 1922-25; partner firm Frazier & Frazier, 1925-74, Frazier, Frazier, Mahler & Walker, 1974—; sr. atty. OPA, 1943, chief counsel Office Export-Import, 1944-47; with Am. Fgn. Service, 1918-20; vice counsul Oslo, Norway, Murmansk, Russia, and Havre, France. Mem. Am. Friends Service Com., chmn. Southeastern region, 1948-54; mem. Guilford County Bd. Health, 1951-55; mem. permanent bd. N.C. Yearly Meeting of Friends, 1940-64, Friends World Com., 1953-69, rep. to Friends World Conf., 1934, 52, 67; chmn. John Motley Morehead Meml. State Commn., 1959-72; mem. Regional Export Expansion Council, 1972-75. Councilman, mayor pro-tem City of Greensboro, 1949-51, mayor, 1951-55; rep. U.S. Conf. Mayors at Internat. Conf., Rome, 1955; chmn. bd. Greensboro Pub. Library, 1941-49; pres. Greensboro Community Chest, 1950; trustee Guilford Coll., 1932-74, chmn., 1950-69, emeritus, 1974—; trustee N.C. Agrl. and Tech. State U., chmn., 1957-70; trustee Oak Ridge Acad. Found., 1965—, Wooglin Found. Fellow Am. Bar Found., Am. Coll. Probate Counsel (regent 1967-74); mem. N.C. Soc. Preservation Antiquities (dir., v.p. 1954-69), Fed., Internat., Am. (chmn. sect. on real property, probate and trust law 1961-62, mem. ho. of dels. 1962-64), N.C., Greensboro (pres. 1950-51) bar assns., S.A.R. (pres. chpt. 1949), NCCJ (pres. chpt. 1949), Am. Judicature Soc. (dir. 1966-69), Am. Soc. Internat. Law, Am. Law Inst., Beta Theta Pi (nat. trustee, v.p. 1936-42), Phi Delta Phi. Editor: U. N.C. Law Rev., 1922. Home: 620 Woodland Dr Greensboro NC 27408 Office: 206 Southeastern Bldg Greensboro NC 27402 Tel (919) 272-2274

FRAZIER, THOMAS ALEXANDER, JR., b. Clarksdale, Miss., Jan. 3, 1934; A.B., U. Va., 1954, LL.B., 1959. Admitted to Va. bar, 1959, D.C. bar, 1962, U.S. Supreme Ct. bar, 1965; trial atty. tax div. Dept. Justice, Washington, 1959-62; asso. firm Ivins, Phillips & Barker, Washington, 1962-67; partner firm Alvord & Alvord, Washington, 1968-76, Haynes & Miller, Washington, 1976—. Vestryman St. Alban's Ch., Washington, 1966-69. Mem. Am., D.C., Va. bar assns., Phi Beta Kappa. Office: Suite 401 1156 15th St NW Washington DC 20005 Tel (202) 466-5000

FRAZIER, WILLIAM M., b. Huntington, W.Va., Mar. 9, 1929; A.B., Marshall U., 1951; J.D., W.Va. U., 1954. Admitted to W.Va. bar, 1954; organizer Valley Nat. Bank of Huntington, 1966, now sec., dir.; dir. Guaranty Nat. Bank of Huntington. Home: 151 Camelot Dr Huntington WV 25701 Office: Suite 400 First Huntington Bldg Huntington WV 25701 Tel (304) 697-4370

FREDENBERGER, WILLIAM ERWIN, JR., b. Louisville, Sept. 5, 1942; A.A., George Washington U., 1962, B.A., 1964; J.D., Am. U., 1967. Admitted to Md. bar, 1967, D.C. bar, 1971, U.S. Supreme Ct. bar, 1972; legal asst. to John H. Fanning, NLRB, Washington, 1967-69; field atty. Region 20, NLRB, San Francisco, 1969-70; asso. firm Mulholland, Hickey & Lyman, Washington, 1971-75; gen. counsel Nat. Mediation Bd., Washington, 1975—. Mem. Am., Md., D.C. bar assns. Home: 9422 Goshen Ln Burke VA 22015 Office: 1425 K St NW Suite 910 Washington DC 20572 Tel (202) 523-5944

FREDERICK, HELEN RICE, b. Memphis, Aug. 1, 1927; J.D., Southwestern U., Los Angeles, 1971. Admitted to Calif. bar, 1972, U.S. Supreme Ct. bar, 1976; individual practice law, Compton, Calif., 1972-77, Lynwood, Calif., 1977—; property services advisor Los Angeles County Civil Service, 1967-72. Bd. dirs., v.p. SE Legal Aid Soc., Compton, 1975—. Mem. Los Angeles County, S. Central Dist. (pres.) bar assns., Assn. Black Women Lawyers, Assn. Women Lawyers, Women for Good Govt. (hon., Mary Church Terrell award for outstanding contbn. in community and women's rights 1971), John M. Langston Bar Assn. Office: 3543 E Imperial Hwy Lynwood CA 90262 Tel (213) 774-8150

FREDERICK, RAYMOND EARL, b. Washington, D.C., June 5, 1923; student Balt. Polytechnic Inst., 1942; A.A., U. Balt., 1948; LL.B., 1951. Admitted to Md. bar, 1951; individual practice law, Towson, Md., 1951—. Mem. Balt. County Bar Assn. Home: Corinthia Farm Box 125 Route 1 Millers MD 21107 Office: 24 W Pennsylvania Ave Towson MD 21204 Tel (301) 825-1298

FREDERICKS, DALE EDWARD, b. Springfield, Ill., Mar. 12, 1943; B.S. with honors, Bradley U., 1965; J.D., U. Ill., 1968. Admitted to D.C. bar, 1969, Calif. bar, 1971, U.S. Ct. Mil. Appeals bar, 1969, U.S. Supreme Ct. bar, 1976; mem. firm Sedgwick, Detert, Moran & Arnold, San Francisco, 1972—. Mem. Am. Bar Assn., State Bar Calif., Bar Assn. San Francisco. Home: 192 Oak Knoll Loop Walnut Creek CA 94596 Office: Sedgwick Detert Moran & Arnold 111 Pine St San Francisco CA 94111 Tel (415) 982-0303

FREDERICKS, FRANK OSCAR, b. N.Y.C., Jan. 24, 1919; B.S., N.Y. U., 1940; LL.B., Columbia, 1947. Admitted to N.Y. bar, 1948, U.S. Supreme Ct. bar, 1961; with firm Frank and Fredericks, and predecessors, N.Y.C., 1948—, mem., 1948-58, sole proprietor, 1958—. Pres. Roquefort Assn., Inc., N.Y.C., 1960—; Mem. Am. Bar Assn. Office: 41 E 42d St New York City NY 10017 Tel (212) 682-0767

FREDRICKS, CONRAD BRADLEY, b. Helena, Mont., Apr. 10, 1934; B.S. in Chemistry, Mont. State U., 1955; J.D., U. Mont., 1962. Admitted to Mont. bar, 1962, U.S. Dist. Ct. for Mont. bar, 1962; asso. firm Loble, Picotte & Fredricks and predecessor firm, Helena, 1962-65, partner, 1965-67; individual practice law, Helena, 1967-68; partner firm Josephson & Fredricks, Big Timber, Mont., 1968—; mem. Gov.'s Advisory Com. on Air Pollution Control Legislation, 1966; mem. Criminal Law Commn., 1971-73; atty. Sweet Grass County, Mont., 1970-74. Mem. Am., Mont., Park-Sweet Grass County bar assns, Big Timber Lions Club (pres. 1971-72), Helena Jaycees (dir. 1963-64, v.p. 1964-65; state dir. 1965-66), Phi Delta Phi. Home and office: PO Box 1047 Big Timber MT 59011 Tel (406) 932-2184

FREDSTON, ARTHUR H., b. Chgo., July 25, 1929; B.B.A., U. Mich., 1949; LL.B., Yale U., 1954. Admitted to N.Y. bar, 1954; asso. firm Winthrop, Stimson, Putnam & Roberts, N.Y.C., 1954-61, partner, 1962—. Mem. Assn. Bar City N.Y., Order of Coif. Home: 3 Cedar Island Larchmont NY 10538 Office: Winthrop Stimson Putnam & Roberts 30 Rockefeller Plaza New York City NY 10020 Tel (212) 943-0700

FREED, DORIS JONAS, b. St. Louis, Nov. 12, 1920; B.A., N.Y. U., 1951, LL.B., 1953, LL.M., 1954, J.S.D., 1958. Admitted to N.Y. bar, 1954, Md. bar, 1955, U.S. Supreme Ct. bar; individual practice law, N.Y.C., 1964—. Mem. Am. (exec. com., officer family law sect., chmn. com. divorce law and procedures), N.Y. State bar assns., Assn. Bar City N.Y., Internat. Fedn. Women Lawyers, N.Y. County Lawyers Assn., Am. Acad. Matrimonial Lawyers, Am. Arbitration Assn. Co-author: Law and the Family, 1967, rev. edit., 1972; The American Law of Charities and Foundations, 1974; Cases and Materials on Family Law, 1972; Annual Surveys of N.Y. Law, 1976; Etats-Unis, Les Etats Regis Par La Common Law, 1975; contbr. articles to legal jours.; co-author column N.Y. Law Jour. Office: 60 E 42d St Suite 2022 New York City NY 10017 Tel (212) 687-3493

FREED, HOWARD ALVIN, b. Dickinson, N.D., Mar. 14, 1926; B.A., Coll. St. Thomas, 1950; LL.B., Marquette U., 1953. Admitted to Wis. bar, 1953, N.D. bar, 1953; partner firm Freed, Dynes, Malloy & Reichert, Dickinson, 1953—; state's atty. Stark County, N.D., 1955-59; mem. N.D. State Senate, 1966—. Bd. regents Mary Coll., Bismarck, N.D., 1968—. Fellow Am. Coll. Probate Counsel; mem. Am., N.D. bar assns. Home: 926 7th Ave W Dickinson ND 58601 Office: 235 Sims St Dickinson ND 58601 Tel (701) 225-6711

FREEDMAN, BARRY HOWARD, b. N.Y.C., Sept. 30, 1943; B. of Engring., City Coll. N.Y., 1965; J.D., N.Y. U., 1968. Admitted to D.C. bar, 1970, N.J. bar, 1971, U.S. Patent and Trademark Office bar, 1972; mem. patent staff Bell Telephone Labs., Holmdel, N.J., 1970—. Mem. N.J. Bar Assn., Tau Beta Pi, Eta Kappa Nu. Home: 5 Vincent Ct East Brunswick NJ 08816 Office: Bell Telephone Laboratories Room 4B 206 Holmdel NJ 07733 Tel (201) 949-6043

FREEDMAN, EDWIN JULIEN, b. Freeport, N.Y., Dec. 12, 1914; LL.B., Bklyn. Law Sch., 1937. Admitted to N.Y. bar, 1938, U.S. Supreme Ct. bar, 1954; partner firm Freedman, Weisbein, Levy & Novick, and predecessors, Freeport Mineola, N.Y., 1938—; justice Village of Freeport, 1962-77, village atty., 1961. Mem. Nassau County (1st v.p.), N.Y. State, Women's, Criminal Ct., Fed. bar assns., Fedn. Lawyers Club Nassau County (past pres.), Nassau Lawyers Assn. L.I. (past pres.), Nassau Magistrates Assn. (past pres.). Recipient Arthur I. Coan Humanitarian award Central Nassau Anti-Defamation League, 1971. Home: 7 W Forest Ave Freeport NY 11520 Office: 114 Old Country Rd Mineola NY 11501 Tel (516) 294-6666

FREEDMAN, ELLIS JOSEPH, b. Albany, N.Y., May. 3, 1921; B.A., Cornell U., 1941, LL.B., 1943. Admitted to N.Y. bar, 1943; asso. firm Ernst, Gale, Bernays, Falk & Eisner and successors, N.Y.C., 1943-54; partner firms Bernays & Eisner and successors, N.Y.C., 1954-73, Lowenthal, Freedman, Landau, Fischer & Todres, N.Y.C., 1973-76, Freedman & Kolins, N.Y.C., 1976—. Sec., The Koussevitzky Music Fornd. Library Congress, N.Y.C., 1972—; sec., treas., dir. The Charles Ives Soc., N.Y.C., 1972—; pres. Am. Friends of Aldeburgh N.Y.C., 1973—. Mem. Assn. Bar N.Y.C., Cornell Law Assn. Office: 645 Fifth Ave New York City NY 10022 Tel (212) PL2-5300

FREEDMAN, GARY JAY, b. Bloomington, Ill., Oct. 1, 1942; A.B., U. Ill., 1964; J.D., Hastings Coll. Law, 1967. Admitted to Calif. bar, 1968; dep. atty. gen., Los Angeles, 1967-68; asso. firm Smith & Wilson, Los Angeles, 1968-71; partner firm Goldman, Gilbert & Freedman, Los Angeles, 1971-74; partner firm Diller & Freedman, Los Angeles, 1974—. Mem. Am., Los Angeles, Beverly Hills bar assns. Office: 1880 Century Park E Los Angeles CA 90067 Tel (213) 553-6411

FREEDMAN, JAMES OLIVER, b. Manchester, N.H., Sept. 21, 1935; A.B., Harvard, 1957; LL.B., Yale, 1962. Admitted to N.H., bar, 1962, Pa., bar, 1971; prof. law U. Pa., 1964—. Univ. Ombudsman U. Pa., 1973-76. Pres. bd. dirs. Mental Health Assn. Southeastern Pa., 1972; bd. dirs. Mental Health Assn. Pa., 1970—. Mem. Am. Law Inst., Am. Arbitration Assn. (nat. panel arbitrators). Nat. Endowment for the Humanities fellow for ind. study and research vis. fellow Clare Hall Cambridge (Eng.) U., 1976-77; contbr. articles to profl. jours. Home: 428 S 47th St Philadelphia PA 19143 Office: 3400 Chestnut St Philadelphia PA 19104 Tel (215) 243-7068

FREEDMAN, JAY WEIL, b. Washington, May 19, 1942; B.A., Williams Coll., 1964; J.D., Yale, 1967. Admitted to D.C. bar, 1968, U.S. Supreme Ct., 1973; atty. Gen. Counsel's Office, FCC, Washington, 1967-68; partner firm Freedman, Levy, Kroll & Simonds, Washington, 1968—. Mem. exec. bd. Washington chpt. Am. Jewish Com.; bd. dirs. Washington Hebrew Congregation. Mem. Bar Assn. D.C., Fed. Bar Assn. Office: 1730 K St NW Washington DC 20006 Tel (202) 331-8550

FREEDMAN, MONROE HENRY, b. Mt. Vernon, N.Y., Apr. 10, 1928; A.B., Harvard, 1951, LL.B., 1954, LL.M., 1956. Admitted to Mass. bar, 1954, Pa. bar, 1957, D.C. bar, 1960, U.S. Supreme Ct. bar, 1960; faculty asst. Harvard, 1954-56; asso. firm Wolf, Block, Schorr & Solis Cohen, Phila., 1956, 58; prof. law George Washington U., 1958-73; partner firm Freedman & Temple, Washington, 1969-73; dir. Stern Community Law Firm, Washington, 1970-71; prof. law Hofstra U., 1973—, dean, 1973—; mem. nat. bd. ACLU, 1971—; cons. in field. Mem. D.C. Bar (chmn. legal ethics com., 1974—), Fed., Am. (certificate merit) bar assns., Am. Law Inst., Soc. Am. Law Tchrs. (mem. governing bd., 1974—, exec. com., 1976—). Author: Lawyers' Ethics in an Adversary System; contbr. articles in field to profl. jours. Home: 100 Ash Dr East Hills NY 11576 Office: Hofstra Law School Hempstead NY 11550 Tel (516) 560-3634

FREEDMAN, RICHARD ALAN, b. N.Y.C., Aug. 10, 1940; B.A., Cornell U., 1961; J.D., Yale U., 1964. Admitted to N.Y. bar, 1965, U.S. Ct. Mil. Appeals bar, 1966, U.S. 2d Circuit Ct. Appeals bar, 1972, U.S. Supreme Ct. bar, 1972; served with JAGC, U.S. Air Force, Keesler AFB, Miss., 1965-68; atty. Western Union Telegraph Co., N.Y.C., 1968-72; atty. L.I. Lighting Co., Mineola, N.Y., 1972—. Mem. Am., N.Y. State, Nassau County bar assns. Home: 35 Suncrest Dr Dix Hills NY 11746 Office: 250 Old Country Rd Mineola NY 11746 Tel (516) 228-2194

FREEDMAN, ROBERT BRANDEIS, b. Los Angeles, Dec. 12, 1943; B.A., U. Calif., Los Angeles, 1965, J.D., U. Calif., Berkeley, 1968. Admitted to Calif. bar, 1969, U.S. Supreme Ct. bar, 1973; mem. firm Wald & Freedman, and predecessor, Oakland, Calif., 1969-71, partner, 1971—; instr. legal asst. program Merritt Coll., 1973-76, John F. Kennedy U. Sch. Law, 1976. Pres. Consumers Group Legal Services Inc., Berkeley, 1972, bd. dirs., 1971-74; bd. dirs. Bay Area Lawyers for the Arts, Inc., Berkeley, 1975—. Mem. State Bar Calif., Am., Alameda County (Calif.) bar assns. Author: Basic Legal Problems for the Artist, 1975. Office: 528 Grand Ave Oakland CA 94610 Tel (415) 835-4822

FREEDMAN, SAMUEL, b. Russia, April 16, 1908; migrated to Can., 1911; B.A. (hons.), U. Man., 1929; LL.B., Man. Law Sch., 1933; LL.D., U. Windsor, 1960, N.D. State U., 1965, U. Toronto, 1965, Hebrew U. Jerusalem, 1964, U. Man., 1968, Brock U., 1968, McGill U., 1968, Dalhousie U., 1971, Queen's U., 1969, York U., 1971, Trent U., 1972, William Mitchell Coll. Law, St. Paul, 1973; D. Canon Law, St. John's Coll., Winnipeg, 1967; D.C.L., U. Western Ont., 1973. Called to Canadian bar, 1933; created Queen's counsel, 1944; mem. firm Steinkopf, Lawrence & Freedman, 1933-45, Freedman & Golden, 1946-52; judge Ct. of Queen's Bench of Man., 1952-60; judge Ct. of Appeal Man., 1960—, chief justice, 1971—; lectr. Man. Law Sch., 1941-59; chancellor U. Man., 1959-68. Pres. YMHA of Winnipeg, 1936-37, Winnipeg Lodge B'nai B'rith, 1943-44; chmn. Rhodes Scholarship Selection Com. Man., 1956-66; co-chmn. central div. Canadian Council Christians and Jews, 1955-58; chmn. Winnipeg chpt. Canadian Friends of Hebrew U., 1953-68; mem. adv. bd. Centre Criminology, U. Toronto. Bd. dirs. Confdn. Centre of Arts, Charlottetown, P.E.I., Can.; trustee John W. Dafoe Found., 1955—; bd. govs. Hebrew U. Jerusalem, 1955—. Hon. pres. U. Man. Students Union, 1949-50; recipient Man of Year award Sigma Alpha Mu, 1957. Mem. Man. Bar Assn. (pres. 1952), Medico-Legal Soc. Man. (pres. 1954-55), Law Soc. Man. (bencher 1949-52). Home: 425 Cordova St Winnipeg 1 MB R3N 1A5 Canada Office: Law Cts Winnipeg 1 MB Canada*

FREEDMAN, SAMUEL SUMNER, b. Bridgeport, Conn., July 5, 1927; student U. Conn., 1946-48; A.B. in Govt., George Washington U., 1950; J.D., Yale U., 1954. Admitted to Conn. bar, 1954; partner firm Freedman, Peck & Freedman, and predecessors, Bridgeport, 1955-77, sr. partner, 1977—; individual practice law, Westport, Conn., 1964—; spl. pub. defender County of Fairfield (Conn.), 1959-61; vis. lectr. polit. sci. Sacred Heart U., Bridgeport, 1974-75;

vis. lectr. Yale U. Law Sch., New Haven, 1977; mem. Conn. Ho. of Reps., 1973-75; legis. commr. State of Conn., 1975—; bd. dirs., legal counsel County Service Corp.; mem. spl. task force on sex crimes Conn. Permanent Commn. on Status of Women, 1974. Vice pres., mem. exec. bd. Nationalities Service Center, Bridgeport, 1955-60; pres., mem. exec. bd. Bridgeport chpt. Am. Assn. UN, 1955-60; Parliamentarian, Republican State Rules Conv., 1975, Rep. State Conv., 1976. Mem. Westport, Bridgeport, Conn. (exec. com. civil justice sect.) bar assns., Nat. Assn. Criminal Def. Lawyers, Phi Beta Kappa, Pi Gamma Mu. Columnist Westport News, 1964—; contbr. articles to Brookfield Jour. and Lakefield Jour. Named Outstanding Freshman Legislator, Conn. Legislature, 1973. Home: 17 Crawford Rd Westport CT 06880 Office: 256 Post Rd E Westport CT 06880 Tel (203) 226-4225

FREEDMAN, STUART JOEL, b. Brookline, Mass., Oct. 14, 1939; B.A., Rutgers Coll., 1962; J.D., Columbia, 1965. Admitted to N.J. bar, 1965, U.S. Supreme Ct. bar, 1975; law sec. to sr. judge appellate div. N.J. Superior Ct., 1965-66; asso. firm Sills, Beck, Cummis, Radin & Tischman, Newark, 1966-68; corp. sec. and counsel Cadence Industries Corp., West Caldwell, N.J., 1969—. Mem. Assn. Bar City N.Y., Am., N.J. bar assns., Am. Soc. Corp. Secs., Assn. Corp. Counsel N.J., Phi Beta Kappa. Henry Rutgers scholar, Harlan Fiske Stone scholar. Office: 21 Henderson Dr West Caldwell NJ 07006 Tel (201) 227-5100

FREEDMAN, WALTER, b. St. Louis, Mo., Oct. 30, 1914; A.B., Washington U., St. Louis, 1937, J.D., 1937; LL.M., Harvard U., 1938. Admitted to Mo. bar, 1937, U.S. Supreme Ct. bar, 1940, Ill. bar, 1945, D.C. bar, 1946; atty. SEC, 1938-40; chief legal sect. Bituminous Coal div., 1940-42; chief counsel Office Export Control, Bd. Econ. Warfare, 1942-44, dir., 1944-45; sr. partner firm Freedman, Levy, Kroll & Simonds and predecessors, Washington, 1948—. Mem. Am., D.C., Fed. bar assns., Am. Law Inst., Phi Beta Kappa, Omicron Delta Kappa, Pi Sigma Alpha. Home: 4545 W St NW Washington DC 20007 Office: 1730 K St NW Washington DC 20006 Tel (202) 331-8550

FREEDMAN, WILLIAM EMERSON, b. Chgo., Sept. 24, 1928; J.D., Hastings Coll. Law U. Calif., San Francisco, 1953. Admitted to Calif. bar, 1954, Nev. bar, 1956; staff Nev. Atty. Gen.'s. Office, 1956-60; chief counsel Nev. Dept. Hwys., 1957-60; dep. city atty. City of Reno, 1960-61; dep. dist. atty. Clark County (Nev.), 1962-64; partner firms Boyd, Leavitt & Freedman, 1964-69, Boyd & Freedman, 1969-75, Freedman & Whelton, Las Vegas, Nev., 1975—. Bd. dirs. YMCA, 1966-70. Mem. Calif., Nev. bar assns., Am. Trial Lawyers Assn., Am. Judicature Soc. Office: 309 S Third St Suite 316 Las Vegas NV 89101 Tel (702) 385-4720

FREELAND, JOSEPH STEPHEN, b. Paducah, Ky., Mar. 19, 1915; LL.B., U. Ky., 1938, J.D., 1970. Admitted to Ky. bar, 1937, U.S. Ct. Appeals bar 6th Circuit, 1949, U.S. Supreme Ct. bar, 1959; individual practice law, Paducah, Ky., 1938—; mem. Ky. Workmen's Compensation Bd., also ex-officio mem. Ky. Bd. Claims, 1960-68; pub. defender McCracken County, Ky., 1973-76. Mem. Am., Ky., McCracken County bar assns., Assn. Trial Lawyers Am., Ky. Trial Lawyers Assn., Order of Coif. Contbr. articles Ky. Law Jour., Ky. Bar Jour. Home: 272 Old Orchard Rd Paducah KY 42001 Office: Citizens Bank and Trust Co Bldg Paducah KY 42001 Tel (502) 442-0121

FREELAND, RALPH LYNN, JR., b. Lovell, Okla., Dec. 17, 1917; A.B. in Engring., Stanford, 1939, M.E., 1941; J.D., George Washington U., 1947. Test engr. Gen. Electric Co., Schenectady, 1941-43, engr. field service, 1943-45, patent law clk., 1945-47; admitted to D.C. bar, 1947, Calif. bar, 1948; patent atty. Calif. Research Corp. (name later changed to Chevron Research Co.), San Francisco, 1952-59, departmental atty., 1957-59, supervising atty., 1959-72, mgr. div. oil field and mech., 1972—; asso. firm Woodcock & Phelan, Phila., 1951-52. Mem. San Francisco (pres. 1969-70), Am. (bd. mgrs. 1972-75) patent law assns., Calif. State Bar (chmn. sect. trademark and copyright 1973-74). Office: care Chevron Research Co 575 Market St San Francisco CA 94105 Tel (415) 894-2052

FREELAND, T. PAUL, b. Princeton, Ind., Sept. 26, 1916; A.B., DePauw U., 1937; LL.B., Columbia, 1940. Admitted to N.Y. bar, D.C. bar, Mass. bar; asso. firm Cravath, deGersdorff, Swaine & Wood, N.Y.C., summer 1939, Dunnington, Bartholow & Miller, N.Y.C., 1940-42; atty. Office Chief Counsel, IRS, 1945-48; partner firm Wenchel, Schulman & Manning, Washington, 1948-62, Sharp & Bogan, Washington, 1962-65, Bogan & Freeland, Washington, 1965—. Trustee Embry-Riddle Aero. U. Mem. Am., Inter-Am., Fed., D.C. bar assns., Internat. Fiscal Assn., Phi Delta Phi. Home: 5525 Pembroke Rd Bethesda MD 20034 Office: 1000 16th St Washington DC 20036 Tel (202) 223-4260

FREELAND, VERNE LEE, b. Mt. Hope, W.Va., Aug. 13, 1925; J.D., U. Miami (Fla.), 1953. Admitted to Fla. bar, 1953; asso. firms Walsh, Simmonite, Budd & Walsh, Miami, Fla., 1953-57, Silver Squarcia, Miami, 1957-60, Fuller Warren, Miami, 1960-73; corp. counsel Westland Meats, Inc., Pompano Beach, Fla., 1973—. Home: 1011 NW 195th St Miami FL 33169 Office: PO Box 693652 Miami FL 33169 Tel (305) 946-2898

FREEMAN, ANDREW, b. Budapest, Hungary, July 19, 1916; came to U.S., 1949, naturalized 1960; Dr. Laws, Dr. Polit. Scis., U. Budapest, 1938; LL.B., St. John's U., 1951. Mem. Bar of Budapest, 1941-48; admitted to N.Y. State bar, 1960, Fed. bar, 1960; partner firm Regosin, Edwards, Freeman & Stone, N.Y.C., 1960—. Mem. Am. Fgn. Law Assn. (v.p. 1975, treas. 1972), Consular Law Soc. N.Y. (v.p. 1971), Assn. Bar City N.Y. Contbr. articles to legal jours. Home: 136 E 56th St New York City NY 10022 Office: 30 Broad St New York City NY 10004 Tel (212) 425-5551

FREEMAN, BRIAN AROLD, b. Erie, Pa., Oct. 30, 1940; A.B., Oberlin Coll., 1962; J.D., Ohio State U., 1965. Admitted to Ohio bar, 1965, U.S. Supreme Ct. bar, 1970; asst. atty. gen. State of Ohio, 1966-67; asst. prof. law Capital U., Columbus, Ohio, 1967-72, asso. prof., 1972-73, prof., 1973—; cons. Ohio Dept. Edn., 1972-74, Ohio Municipal League, 1973-74. Alt. del. at large Republican Nat. Conv., 1968. Mem. Am., Ohio, Columbus bar assns., Am. Judicature Soc. Co-author: Model General Offense Code, 1973. Home: 65 Meadow Park Ave Columbus OH 43209 Office: 2199 E Main St Columbus OH 43209 Tel (614) 236-6395

FREEMAN, CHARLES EDWARD, b. Pensacola, Fla., July 21, 1931; B.S. in Bus. Adminstrn., Fla. State U., 1957; J.D., U. Fla., 1963. Admitted to Fla. bar, 1964; indsl. relations adviser Gulf Oil Corp., Pitts., 1965-67; div. mgr. indsl. relations, Rockwell Mfg. Co., Atchison, Kans., 1967-68; corp. mgr. labor relations Emerson Electric Co., St. Louis, 1969-71; gen. counsel, asst. to pres. Conco, Inc., Mendota, Ill., 1971-73; chmn. Fla. Pub. Employees Relations Com., Tallahassee, 1974-75; individual practice law, Tallahassee, 1975—. Mem. Am., Fla., Tallahassee bar assns., Indsl. Relations Research Assn., Am. Arbitration Assn. Home: T-2 Forest Green Dr Corapolis PA 15108 Office: 311 Executive Center Dr Tallahassee FL 32301 Tel (412) 262-2267

FREEMAN, EUGENE PAUL, b. St. Louis, Aug. 7, 1921; J.D., St. Louis U., 1950. Admitted to Mo. bar, 1950, U.S. Supreme Ct. bar, 1971; individual practice law, 1950-53; asst. circuit atty., asso. city counselor City of St. Louis, 1956-67, dep. city counselor, 1967—; regional counsel Citizens for Decent Lit., 1960-66; co-organizer Mo. Lawyers for Life, 1973—; Law Sch. Moot Ct. judge St. Louis U.; speaker Great Issues Program, St. Louis U. Mem. Mo. Bar Integrated, Met. Bar Assn. St. Louis, Assn. Def. Counsel City and County of St. Louis, Delta Theta Phi. Home: 6735 Delor St St Louis MO 63109 Office: 1200 Market St City Hall St Louis MO 63103 Tel (314) 453-3366

FREEMAN, FORSTER WEEKS, JR., b. Paterson, N.J., July 14, 1899; LL.B., N.Y. U., 1921. Admitted to N.J. bar, 1921, U.S. Supreme Ct. bar, 1957; partner firm Freeman & Freeman, Paterson, 1921-55, Freeman, Reilly & Freeman, Paterson, 1955-73; of counsel firm Evans, Hand, Allabough & Amoresano, West Paterson, N.J., 1973—; counsel Gen. Conv. of New Jerusalem, 1956-76. Bd. dirs. Swedenborg Found., Inc., 1949—, v.p., 1965—; trustee Paterson YMCA. Mem. Passaic County (pres. 1937), N.J. State (pres. 1954), Am. (ho. of dels. 1958-66), Inter-Am., Internat., Fed. bar assns., Nat. Conf. Bar Presidents, Am. Judicature Soc., Greater Paterson C. of C. (pres. 1950). Home: 606B Lake Point Dr Lakewood NJ 08701 Office: care Evans Hand Allabough & Amoresano & Garret Mountain Plaza West Paterson NJ 07509 Tel (201) 881-1100

FREEMAN, FREDERICK ROE, b. Arkansas City, Kans., July 11, 1914; A.B., Southwestern Coll., 1952; J.D., U. Mo., Kansas City, 1954. Admitted to Mo. bar, 1954, U.S. Supreme Ct. bar, 1965; individual practice law, Kansas City, Mo., 1954—; v.p., dir. Jones & Babson, Inc., 1959—; sec.-treas. David L. Babson Investment Fund, Inc., 1959—, v.p., treas., 1976—; pres., dir. Income & Retirement Security Corp., 1973—. Mem. Kansas City Bar Assn., Lawyers Assn. Kansas City. Home: 6023 Wyandotte St Kansas City MO 64113 Office: Garden 15 2440 Pershing Rd Crown Center Kansas City MO 64108 Tel (816) 471-4534

FREEMAN, LEE ALLEN, JR., b. Chgo., July 31, 1940; B.A magna cum laude, Harvard U., 1962, J.D. magna cum laude, 1965. Admitted to Ill. bar, 1966, U.S. Ct. Appeals bar D.C., 1967, 7th Circuit, 1971, 9th Circuit, 1973, 2d Circuit, 1975, 6th Circuit, 1975, U.S. Dist. Ct. bar, D.C., 1967, No. Dist. Ill., 1968, Eastern Dist. Wis., 1973, U.S. Supreme Ct. bar, 1969; law clk. to Justice Tom C. Clark, U.S. Supreme Ct., 1965-66; asst. U.S. atty. D.C., 1966-68; spl. asst. atty. gen. States of Ill. and W.Va., 1969—; hearing examiner State of Ill. Pollution Control Bd., 1972; spl. asst. atty. gen. for Master Key Antitrust Litigation, States of Mich., Colo., Wis., Minn., Pa., Ky. and S.D., 1974—; spl. corp. counsel City of Chgo.; partner firm Freeman, Rothe, Freeman & Salzman, Chgo., 1970—. Pres. bd. dirs. Chgo. Lyric Opera Guild; pres. Fine Arts Music Found. Chgo.; governing life mem. Art Inst. Chgo.; mem. vis. com. dept. humanities U. Chgo. Mem. Am., Chgo., Ill. bar assns., Chgo. Council Lawyers. Home: 232 E Walton St Chicago IL 60611 Office: 1 IBM Plaza Suite 3200 Chicago IL 60611 Tel (312) 467-6540

FREEMAN, MELVYN, b. Phila., Jan. 7, 1936; student Wharton Sch., U. Pa., 1953-57, LL.B., 1960-63. Asso. firm Cravath, Swaine & Moore, N.Y.C., 1963-71; admitted to N.Y. bar, 1964; partner firm Freeman, Meade, Wasserman & Schneider, N.Y.C., 1972—. Mem. N.Y., Am. bar assns. Home: 77 Duffield Dr South Orange NJ 07079 Office: 551 Fifth Ave New York City NY 10017 Tel (212) 697-6464

FREEMAN, MICHAEL ERNEST, b. Hannover, Germany, Mar. 13, 1937; B.A., U. Mich., 1958, LL.B., Harvard, 1961. Admitted to Ill. bar, 1961, Wis. bar, 1962; asso. firm Quarles, Herriott & Clemons, Milw., 1962-68; gen. counsel Manpower, Inc., Milw., 1969-73; individual practice law, Milw., 1974—. Mem. Am., Wis., Milw. bar assns., Am. Judicature Soc. Office: 700 N Water St Milwaukee WI 53202 Tel (414) 276-4080

FREEMAN, PALMER, JR., b. Charlotte, N.C., July 25, 1944; B.S., Davison Coll., 1966; J.D., U. S.C., 1971. Admitted to S.C. bar, 1971; intern Justice Dept., Washington, summer 1970; asso. firm Mack, Mack & Freeman, Ft. Mill, S.C., 1971-72, partner, 1972—; mem. S.C. Ho. of Reps., 1977—. Mem. Am., S.C. bar assns., York County (S.C.) Bar (v.p. 1972-73, treas., 1973—). Recipient Outstanding Young Man award U.S. Jaycees, 1976. Staff S.C. Law Rev., 1968-71. Home: POB 682 Fort Mill SC 29715 Office: POB 128 Fort Mill SC 29715 Tel (803) 547-2032

FREEMAN, ROGER PAUL, b. Pomona, Calif., Mar. 27, 1946; B.A. cum laude, U. Redlands, 1968; J.D., U. Calif., Los Angeles, 1971. Admitted to Calif. bar, 1972, U.S. Dist. Ct. bar for Central Dist. Calif., 1972; dep. city atty. City of Torrance (Calif.), 1972—; counsel Torrance Planning Commn., 1972-75, Torrance Environ. Rev. Bd., 1973-76. Mem. Calif., Am., Los Angeles County, South Bay bar assns. Office: 3031 Torrance Blvd Torrance CA 90503 Tel (213) 328-5310

FREEMAN, RUSSELL ADAMS, b. Albany, N.Y., July 22, 1932; B.A., Amherst (Mass.) Coll., 1954; J.D., Albany Law Sch., 1957; LL.M., U. So. Calif., 1966. Admitted to N.Y. bar, 1957, Calif. bar, 1960; asso. John W. Manning, Albany, 1957-59; with Security Pacific Nat. Bank, Los Angeles, 1959-74, v.p., asst. sec., 1965-68, v.p., counsel, 1968-72, sr. v.p., counsel, 1972-74; gen. counsel Security Pacific Corp., Los Angeles, 1973—. Mem. Am., Calif., Los Angeles County bar assns., Assn. Bank Holding Cos. (lawyers com.), Calif. Bankers Assn. (exec. com. state govt. relations div.). Co-author: California Bankers Guide to the Uniform Commercial Code, 1964; California Commercial Law, 1966. Office: 333 S Hope St 52d Floor Los Angeles CA 90071 Tel (213) 613-6880

FREEMAN, WAYNE W., b. Graves County, Ky., Dec. 25, 1912; B.S., Murray State U., 1936; LL.B., J.D., U. Louisville; postgrad. U. Georgetown Law Sch. Admitted to Ky. bar, 1944; mem. Ky. Ho. of Reps., 1939, 40, Ky. Senate, 1951-55, 1955-59; railroad commr., Ky., 1959-71; prin. atty. Dept. Transp. for Ky., Mayfield, 1975—. Mem. Graves County, Ky. bar assns. Office: Mangrum Bldg 427 E Broadway Mayfield KY 42066 Tel (502) 247-5520

FREESE, ROGER DEAN, b. Cedar Rapids, Iowa, Apr. 12, 1944; B.S., Iowa State U., 1966; J.D., U. Iowa, 1968. Admitted to Iowa bar, 1968; partner firm Norton & Freese, Lowden and Clarence, Iowa, 1968—; jud. magistrate 7th Jud. Dist. Iowa, 1973—. Dir., sec., treas. Cedar County Work Activity Center, Inc., Tipton, Iowa; pres. Clarence-Lowden Commn. Sch. Bd. Edn., 1974—. Mem. Am., Iowa, Cedar County bar assns., Order of Coif, Phi Kappa Phi. Home: Piatt St Clarence IA 52216 Office: 515 Lombard St Clarence IA 52216 Tel (319) 452-3713

FREIER, ERNEST WALTER, b. Chgo., Dec. 28, 1926; B.S., DePaul U., 1948, J.D., 1951. Admitted to Ill. bar, 1951; since practiced in Chgo., individual practice law, 1951-56; partner firm Freier, Gardner & Pavalon, 1956-61, Freier & Comberg, 1961-65; pres. Freier & Stoumen, Ltd., 1965—; dir. Ill. div. Am. Assn. Attys. & C.P.A.'s. Mem. Chgo. Bar Assn. (fed. tax com.), Am. Assn. Attys. & C.P.A.'s. C.P.A., 1950. Office: 228 N La Salle St Chicago IL 60601 Tel (312) 332-1344

FREILICHER, IRA LEE, b. Bklyn., Aug. 5, 1937; A.B., Columbia, 1959; J.D., Harvard, 1963. Admitted to N.Y. bar, 1964; atty. legal dept., L.I. Lighting Co., Mineola, N.Y., 1963-74, sr. policy coordinator, 1974, exec. asst. to pres., 1974-75, v.p. pub. affairs, 1975—. Mem. Energy Assn. N.Y., N.Y. Com. Job and Energy Independence. Home: 63 Old Farm Rd East Hills NY 11577 Office: 250 Old Country Rd Mineola NY 11501 Tel (516) 228-2027

FREIMAN, SAMUEL FREDERIC, b. N.Y.C., July 30, 1942; A.B., Syracuse U., 1964; J.D., John Marshall Law Sch., 1970. Admitted to Ill. bar, 1972, also Fed. bar; tech. advisor, supr. Ill. Dept. Revenue, Chgo., 1969-70; enforcement atty. corp. and securities div. Ill. Sec. State, Chgo., 1972-73; asst. atty. gen. State of Ill., 1973-75; individual practice law, Chgo., 1975—; legis. asst. Ill. Ho. of Reps., 1976-77. Chmn. 44th Ward Community Zoning Bd., 1974—; bd. dirs. U.S. SSS, 1970-75. Mem. Am., Chgo. bar assns., Midwest (pres. 1969—), Nat. (dir. 1977-81) Syracuse U. alumni assns. Recipient Decadrachm award Syracuse U., 1975; named Outstanding Young Man of Year Jaycees, 1976. Home: 711 W Melrose St Chicago IL 60657 Office: Suite 910 100 N LaSalle St Chicago IL 60602 Tel (312) 372-7355

FREIMUTH, MARC WILLIAM, b. Duluth, Minn., Sept. 23, 1946; B.A., U. Minn., 1968, J.D. magna cum laude, 1971. Admitted to Ohio bar, 1971; asso. firm Squire, Sanders & Dempsey, Cleve., 1971—. Aux. trustee Park Synagogue, Cleve., 1974-76, Agnon Sch., Cleve., 1976-77. Mem. Am., Ohio, Greater Cleve. bar assns. Office: 1800 Union Commerce Bldg Cleveland OH 44115 Tel (216) 696-9200

FREISEM, GEORGE HAMILTON, b. New Orleans, Oct. 7, 1947; B.A., Tulane U., 1969; J.D., Emory U., 1972. Admitted to Ga. bar, 1972, Fla. bar, 1972; asst. to chief enforcement atty. SEC, 1971; staff atty. Atlanta Legal Aid Soc., 1971; asso. firm Galkin, Katz & Tye, Atlanta, 1973-75; individual practice law, Atlanta, 1975—; staff JAGC, U.S. Army, 1972-73. Mem. Am. (mem. younger lawyers sect. and taxation sects.), Ga. (younger lawyers sect., real estate sect.), Atlanta, Fla. bar assns. Contbr. article to law jour. Home: 1216 Bellaire Dr Atlanta GA 30319 Office: D-110 1401 W Paces Ferry Rd Atlanta GA 30327 Tel (404) 266-2873

FREISER, LAWRENCE MORTON, b. Bklyn., Mar. 3, 1942; B.A., N.Y.U., 1963, LL.B., 1966, J.D., 1967. Admitted to N.Y. bar, 1966, Calif. bar, 1972, U.S. Supreme Ct. bar, 1970; assoc. firm Kaufman, Taylor, Kimmel, & Miller, N.Y.C., 1967-68; assoc. firm Ruben Schwartz, N.Y.C., 1968; individual practice law, N.Y.C., 1968-72; atty. Hughes Air Corp, San Mateo, Calif., 1972-73; individual practice law, Pleasant Hill, Calif., 1973, N.Y.C., 1973-74, Los Angeles, 1974-75; assoc. firm Alvin B. Green, Los Angeles, 1975—. Mem. Am., New York County, Los Angeles County, Calif. bar assns. Contbr. articles in field to law reviews. Home: 11669 Mayfield Ave Los Angeles CA 90049 Office: 10850 Wilshire Blvd Los Angeles CA 90024 Tel (213) 474-9515

FREISHTAT, DAVID DANNY, b. Washington, Oct. 11, 1942; B.A., Am. U., 1964; J.D., U. Balt., 1968. Admitted to Md. bar, 1968, D.C. bar, 1974; staff counsel Washington Suburban Sanitary Commn., Hyattsville, Md., 1968-71; asso. gen. counsel Md. Nat. Capital Park and Planning Commn., Riverdale, 1971-73; asso. firm Linowes and Blocher, Silver Spring, Md., 1973—. Mem. Am., Md. State, Prince George's County (Md.), Montgomery County (Md.) bar assns. Home: 13009 Bellevue St Beltsville MD 20705 Office: 8720 Georgia Ave 600 Silver Spring MD 20910 Tel (301) 588-8580

FREITAG, PAUL WILLIAM, b. Reno, Aug. 21, 1940; B.A., U. Nev., 1963; J.D., George Washington U., 1966. Admitted to Nev. bar, 1966; dep. dist. atty. Washoe County (Nev.), 1967-71; atty. City of Sparks (Nev.), 1971—. Govt. chmn. United Fund, 1972; bd. dirs. Easter Seals, 1972—. Mem. Nev., Washoe County bar assns. Office: 431 Prater Way Sparks NV 89431 Tel (702) 359-2700

FRELS, JACK CURTIS, b. Ft. Worth, June 15, 1945; B.B.A., St. Edward's U., 1968; J.D., S. Tex. Coll. Law, 1971. Admitted to Tex. bar, 1971; briefing atty. 13th Ct. Civil Appeals, Corpus Christi, Tex., 1971-72; asst. dist. atty. Harris County, Houston, 1972—. Mem. Tex., Houston Jr. bar assns., Nat. Dist. Attys. Assn., Tex. Dist. and County Attys. Assn. Office: 301 San Jacinto St Houston TX 77002 Tel (713) 221-5843

FRENCH, CARROLL DAVIES, b. Jersey City, June 20, 1928; B.A., Yale, 1950; J.D., Harvard, 1956. Admitted to N.Y. State bar, 1957; asso. firm Dewey, Ballantine, Bushby, Palmer & Wood, N.Y.C., 1956-62; asso. firm Reid & Priest, N.Y.C., 1962-67, partner, 1968-69; atty. Am. Can Co., Greenwich, Ct., 1969-72, asst. gen. counsel, asst. sec., 1972—. Mem. Am., N.Y. State bar assns., Westchester-Fairfield Corp. Counsel Assn. (treas., dir. 1973-74), Am. Arbitration Assn. (mem. panel). Home: 6 Winterberry Ln Ridgefield CT 06877 Office: American Ln Greenwich CT 06830 Tel (203) 552-3245

FRENCH, FRANK WALTER, JR., b. Oakland, Calif., Sept. 30, 1906; jr. certificate Loyola U., Los Angeles, 1927; LL.B., Hastings Coll. Law U. Calif., San Francisco, 1930. Admitted to Calif. bar, 1930; individual practice law, Santa Monica, Calif.; legal aide to comdt. Mare Island Navy Yard, Vallejo, Calif., World War II. Mem. State Bar Calif., Santa Monica Bar Assn. (past pres.). Home and office: 833 Cedar St Santa Monica CA 90405 Tel (213) 399-4797

FRENCH, JOHN DANIEL, b. Mpls., June 2, 1915; LL.B., U. Mont., 1939, J.D., 1970. Admitted to Mont. bar, 1939; individual practice law, Ronan, Mont., 1939—; atty. Lake County (Mont.), 1940-42, 46-53; city atty. Ronan, 1953-67. Bd. regents Mont. Bd. Edn., 1962-74; bd. dirs. Ronan Hosp., 1947-57. Mem. Mont., Western Mont. bar assns., Am. Legion (comdr. 1951-52). Home and Office: PO Box 648 Ronan MT 59864 Tel (406) 676-4470

FRENCH, MILLARD FILMORE, b. Spanishburg, W.Va., Aug. 7, 1907; LL.B., U. Louisville, 1933. Admitted to Ky. bar, 1934; with claims dept. Bituminous Casualty Corp., Louisville, 1937-42; investigator U.S. Civil Service, Cin., Chgo., 1942-43; atty. U.S. VA, Louisville, 1945-73; councilman, St. Matthews, Ky., 1957—. Mem.

Ky. State Bar Assn. Home and office: 3938 Nanz Ave Louisville KY 40207

FRENCH, ROBERT BRYANT, JR., b. Howell, Tenn., Sept. 16, 1933; B.S., Sch. Commerce and Bus. Adminstrn., U. Ala., 1959, J.D., U. Ala., 1963. Admitted to Ala. bar, 1963, U.S. Supreme Ct. bar, 1971; partner firm Williams, McDuff & French, Tuscaloosa, Ala., 1963-64, Traylor & French, Fort Payne, Ala., 1964-68, French & Nelson, Fort Payne, 1968-72; individual practice law, Fort Payne, 1972—. Mem. Am., DeKalb County (v.p. 1967, pres. 1968), Ala. (local bar activities com. 1969, econs. of law practice com. 1970—) bar assns., Am. Judicature Soc., Farrah Law Soc. Named One of Outstanding Young Men Am., Nat. Jaycees, 1963, DeKalb County Man of Year, 1968, One of Four Outstanding Young Men of Ala., Ala. Jaycees, 1968; recipient award for Civic Service, Fort Payne Jaycees, 1967, Distinguished Service award Fort Payne Jaycees, 1968. Home: Scenic Road Fort Payne AL 35967 Office: 308 Alabama Ave S Fort Payne AL 35967 Tel (205) 845-2250

FRENCH, SUSAN FLETCHER, b. Palo Alto, Calif., Sept. 26, 1943; B.A., Stanford, 1964; J.D., U. Wash., 1967. Admitted to Wash. bar, 1967; asso. firm Preston, Thorgrimson, Starin, Ellis & Holmar, Seattle, 1967-71; asso. firm Martin, Niemi, Burch & Mentele, Seattle, 1971-75; acting prof. law U. Calif., Davis, 1975—. Mem. Am. Bar Assn., Order of Coif. Articles editor: U. Wash. Law Review, 1966-67. Office: Law School University California Davis CA 95616 Tel (916) 752-2756

FRENZ, PAUL DIETER, b. Indpls., Dec. 24, 1941; A.B., Ind. U., 1962, J.D., U. Mich., 1967. Admitted to Ill. bar, 1968, U.S. Supreme Ct. bar, 1972; asso. firm McBride, Baker, Wienke & Schlosser, Chgo., 1967-74, partner, 1974—. Vice pres., dir. Project LEAP Ednl. and Research Fund, Inc., Chgo., 1973—. Mem. Am., Ill., Chgo. bar assns., Chgo. Council of Lawyers. Office: 110 N Wacker Dr Chicago IL 60606 Tel (312) 346-6191

FREUD, NICHOLAS STEVEN, b. N.Y.C., Feb. 6, 1942; A.B., Yale U., 1963, J.D., 1966. Admitted to N.Y. bar, 1968, Calif. bar, 1970; asso. firm Hughes, Hubbard, Blair & Reed, N.Y.C., 1966-68; asso. firm Severson, Werson, Berke & Melchior, San Francisco, 1968-73, partner, 1974—. Treas. Planned Parenthood, San Francisco-Alameda; bd. dirs. Canon Kip Community House, San Francisco; mem., dept. fin. Diocese of Calif. Mem. San Francisco, Calif., N.Y. State, Am. bar assns., Assn. Bar City N.Y. Contbr. articles to profl. jours. Office: One Embarcadero Center San Francisco CA 94111 Tel (415) 398-3344

FREUDENFELD, BERNARD NEAL, b. Milw., Aug. 15, 1916, B.A., U. Wis., 1938; J.D., Marquette U., 1946. Admitted to Wis. bar, 1946; individual practice law, Milw., 1946—. Mem. Am., Wis., Milw., Sheboygan County bar assns., Am. Arbitration Assn., Am. Trial Lawyers' Assn. Home: Rural Route 2 Elkhart Lake WI 53020 Office: 536 W Wisconsin Ave Milwaukee WI 53203 Tel (414) 273-5774

FREUND, ALLAN GRANT, b. Newark, Dec. 21, 1929; A.B., Drake U., 1952; J.D., Harvard U., 1955. Admitted to N.J. bar, 1955, D.C. bar, 1955; asso. firm Carpenter, Bennett & Morrissey, Newark, 1955-65; gen. counsel Mercedes-Benz of N.Am., Inc., Montvale, N.J., 1965—, sec., 1971, asst. v.p., 1971. Mem. Am. Bar Assn., Harvard Law Sch. Assn. Home: 3 Farmstead Rd North Caldwell NJ 07006 Office: 1 Mercedes Dr Montvale NJ 07645 Tel (201) 573-2225

FREUND, CHARLES GIBSON, b. Chgo., Oct. 8, 1923; B.S., Aero. U. Chgo., 1948; J.D., John Marshall Law Sch., 1956. Admitted to Ill. bar, 1956; with Natural Gas Pipeline Co. Am., Chgo., 1956-69, sec., 1961-66, v.p. finance, 1966-69; v.p., sec., treas. People's Gas Co., Chgo., 1969—. Mem. Loyola U. Citizens Bd. and Investment Com., Chgo. Mem. Tex. Mid-Continent Oil, Gas Assn., Ill. C. of C., Chgo. Assn. Commerce, Industry, Pub. Utility Securities Club Chgo., Am. Soc. Corp. Secs., Inc., Financial Execs. Inst., Nat. Investor Relations Inst. Office: 122 S Michigan Ave Chicago IL 60603 Tel (312) 431-4412

FREUND, PAUL ABRAHAM, b. St. Louis, Feb. 16, 1908; A.B., Washington U., 1928, LL.D., 1956; LL.B., Harvard, 1931, S.J.D., 1932; LL.D., Columbia, 1954, U. Louisville, 1956, U. Chgo., 1961, Boston U., 1964, Queen's U., Ont., 1970, Brown U., 1972, Yale, 1972, Brandeis U., 1974, Williams Coll., 1974; L.H.D., Hebrew Union Coll., 1961; Litt.D., Cornell Coll., 1968, Bates Coll., 1973, Temple U., 1973, Yeshiva U., 1975; D.C.L., Union Coll., 1968. Admitted to D.C. bar, 1935, Mass. bar, 1947; law clerk to Mr. Justice Brandeis, 1932-33; legal staff Treasury Dept. and R.F.C., 1933-35, spl. asst. to atty. gen., Office of Solicitor Gen., Justice Dept., 1935-39, 1942-46; lectr. law, Harvard Law Sch., 1939-40, prof. law, 1940-50, Charles Stebbins Fairchild prof., 1950-57; Royall prof. law Harvard U., 1957-58; Carl M. Loeb U. prof. Harvard, 1958—; Pitt. prof. Am. history and institutions Cambridge U., 1957-58, fellow Trinity Coll., 1957-58; fellow Center for Advanced Study in Behavioral Scis., 1969-70; Jefferson lectr. Nat. Endowment for Humanities, 1975. Dir. Salzburg Sem. Am. Studies. Trustee Washington U. Recipient Research award Am. Bar Found., 1973. Fellow Am. Acad. Arts and Scis. (past pres.); mem. Am. Judicature Soc., Mass. Hist. Soc. (v.p.), Am. Philos. Soc., Am. Bar Assn., Am. Law Inst., Harvard Soc. Fellows, Signet Soc., Phi Beta Kappa, Pi Sigma Alpha. Author: On Understanding the Supreme Court, 1949 (Rosenthal lectures, Northwestern U.); The Supreme Court of the U.S., 1961; On Law and Justice, 1968. Editor: Experimentation with Human Subjects, 1970. Co-editor: Cases on Constitutional Law, 1962. Editor-in-chief: History of Supreme Court. Contbr. Ency. Brit., Ency. Social Sci., legal periodicals. Home: 1010 Memorial Dr Cambridge MA 02138 Office: Harvard Law Sch Cambridge MA 02138*

FREY, ALAN MICHAEL, b. Bklyn., Jan. 30, 1942; B.S. in Mgmt., Mass. Inst. Tech., 1963; LL.B., U. Va., 1966. Admitted to Va. bar, 1966, D.C. bar, 1969; trial atty. FTC, Bur. Restraint of Trade, Washington, 1966-69; partner firm Bierbower & Rockefeller, Washington, 1969—. Mem. Am. (mem. anti-trust sect., vice-chmn. legis. com.), Fed. (chmn. antitrust council), Va. bar assns. Contbr. articles in field. Office: 1625 K St NW Washington DC 20006 Tel (202) 347-1900

FREY, CHARLES DAVID, b. Hocking County, Ohio, Oct. 4, 1939; B.S. in Civil Engring., Ohio U., 1961; J.D., Northwestern U., 1970. Admitted to Ohio bar, 1970; asso. firm Lavelle & Yanity, Athens, Ohio, 1970-74; staff counsel Ohio Valley Health Services Found., Athens, 1974-76; pros. atty. Athens County (Ohio), 1977—. Mem. Ohio State, Athens County bar assns. Home: 37 Utah Pl Athens OH 45701 Office: PO Box 206 Athens OH 45701 Tel (614) 592-4474

FREY, PHILIP SIGMUND, b. Los Angeles, July 31, 1941; A.B. with honors, Calif. State U. at Long Beach, 1964; postgrad. U. So. Calif., 1964-65; J.D., Stanford, 1968. Admitted to Hawaii bar, 1969; asso. firm Padgett, Greeley, Marumoto & Steiner, Honolulu, 1968-70; partner Ames-Frey Co., Los Angeles, 1965-70; partner, bus. mgr. Cowan & Frey, Honolulu, 1970—; pres. Hawaii Blossoms Ltd., 1974-75; dir. various corps., Hawaii. Fellow Roscoe Pound-Am. Trial Lawyers Found.; mem. Internat. Platform Assn., Am. Judicature Soc., Am. Bar Assn. (sustaining), Am. Trial Lawyers Assn. (sustaining; state committeeman for Hawaii 1972—), Bar Assn. Hawaii (chmn. med.-legal com. 1972-73), Stanford U. Law Assn. (treas. 1967-68), Supreme Ct. Hist. Soc. (founding mem.). Phi Kappa Phi. Home: 443 Portlock Rd Honolulu HI 96825 Office: Pacific Trade Center 190 S King St Honolulu HI 96813 Tel (808) 533-1767

FREY, ROBERT MARK, b. Quakertown, Pa., June 22, 1928; LL.B., Dickinson Coll., 1950, J.D., 1953. Admitted to Pa. bar, 1954; individual practice law, Carlisle, Pa., 1955. Mem. Carlisle Borough Council, 1960-70. Home: 1010 Drayer Ct Carlisle PA 17013 Office: 5 South Hanover St Carlisle PA 17013 Tel (717) 243-5838

FRIBERG, JOHN EDWARD, b. Boston, May 12, 1942; B.A., Colby Coll., 1964; LL.B., Boston U., 1967. Admitted to N.H. bar, 1967, Mass. bar, 1967; judge advocate U.S. Air Force, Robins AFB, Ga., also Thailand, 1967-71; asso. firm Wadleigh, Starr, Peters, Dunn & Kohls, Manchester, N.H., 1972-75, partner, 1975—. Mem. Am., N.H. bar assns. Editor Boston U. Law Rev., 1966-67. Office: 95 Market St Manchester NH 03101 Tel (603) 669-4140

FRIDAY, ELMER OTTO, JR., b. Bartow, Fla., Feb. 23, 1924; student La. Poly. Inst., 1944-45, U. Okla. at Norman, 1945-46; LL.B., U. Fla. at Gainesville, 1949, J.D., 1949. Admitted to Fla. bar, 1949, U.S. Supreme Ct. bar, 1969; county judge Lee County (Fla.), 1957-61; mem. Fla. State Senate, 1962-70; individual practice law, 1949-66, 70—; partner firm Roberts, Watson, Taylor & Friday, Ft. Myers, Fla., 1966-70; trustee Spessard L. Holland Law Center, U. Fla., 1967-72, chmn. Indsl. Relations Commn., Appellate Jurisdiction of Workmen's Compensation, 1974; pres. Lawyers Title Guaranty Fund, Orlando, Fla., 1951-55, constitution adv. commn., 1955, constitution revision commn., 1968. Office: 1321 Executive Center Dr Tallahassee FL 32301 Tel (904) 488-4082

FRIDAY, HERSCHEL HUGAR, b. Lockesburg, Ark., Feb. 10, 1922; student Little Rock Jr. Coll., 1939-41, U. Minn., 1943; LL.B., J.D., U. Ark., 1947. Admitted to Ark., bar, 1947; law clk. U.S. Judge John E. Miller, Western Dist. Ark., Ft. Smith, 1947-52; sr. partner firm Friday, Eldredge & Clark, Little Rock, 1952—; lectr. U. Ark., Fayetteville, 1951-52; dir. First Nat. Bank in Little Rock, Allied Telephone Co., Met. Nat. Bank, Mo. Pacific R.R. Co., St. Louis. Pres., Ark. Assn. for Retarded Children, 1967-69; pres. bd. trustees Ark. Childrens Hosp., 1962-64; pres. Exchange Club of Little Rock, 1955-56, Pleasant Valley Country Club, 1964-65. Fellow Am. Bar Found.; mem. Am. (Ark. del. 1954-68, 71—, chmn. standing com. 1973-76), Ark. (Outstanding Lawyer award 1971, pres. 1976—) bar assns., Am. Judicature Soc., Am. Coll. Trial Lawyers, Am. Law Inst., Adminstrv. Conf. U.S. Named Man of Year in Ark., Ark. Democrat, 1971, Distinguished Alumnus, U. Ark. at Little Rock Alumni Assn., 1976. Home: 172 Pleasant Valley Dr Little Rock AR 72212 Office: First Nat Bldg Little Rock AR 72201 Tel (501) 376-2011

FRIDAY, JOHN RALPH, b. Dallas, N.C., Nov. 15, 1926; B.S., Wake Forest Coll., 1948; LL.B., U. N.C., 1951. Admitted to N.C. bar, 1951; practiced in Lincolnton, N.C., 1955-68; judge 27th Dist. Ct., 1968-70, N.C. Superior Ct., 1970—; judge Dallas (N.C.) Recorders' Ct., 1955, Lincoln County (N.C.) Recorder's Ct., 1957-67. Elder 1st Presbyterian Ch., Lincolnton; pres. Lincoln County (N.C.) United Fund. Mem. N.C., Lincoln County, 27th Dist. bar assns. Home: Lithin Inn Rd POB 371 Lincolnton NC 28092 Office: County Courthouse Lincolnton NC 28092 Tel (704) 735-2232

FRIED, DONALD DAVID, b. N.Y.C., Feb. 28, 1936; B.A., Coll. City N.Y., 1956; LL.B., Harvard U., 1959. Admitted to N.Y. bar, 1959; asso. firm Conboy, Hewitt, O'Brien & Boardman, N.Y.C., 1960-68, partner, 1968—. Home: 37 W 12th St New York City NY 10011 Office: 600 Madison Ave New York City NY 10022 Tel (212) 758-8000

FRIED, HARVEY JULIEN, b. N.Y.C., Aug. 3, 1937; B.S., Coll. City N.Y., 1958; LL.B., Columbia, 1961, J.D., 1967. Admitted to N.Y. bar, 1961; partner firm Fried, Greenbaum & Scher, N.Y.C., 1969; partner firm Blum, Hainoff, Gersen & Seabad, N.Y.C., 1965-69; town judge Harrison (N.Y.), 1974—, town atty., 1968-74. Mem. Westchester County, N.Y. State bar assns., Fed. Bar Council, Am. Judicature Soc., Magistrates Assn. Office: 271 Madison Ave New York City NY 10016 Tel (212) 889-1250

FRIED, MARTIN LEON, b. N.Y.C., Feb. 11, 1934; B.A., Antioch Coll., 1955; LL.B., Columbia, 1958; LL.M., N.Y.U., 1968. Admitted to N.Y. State bar, 1959; individual practice law, N.Y.C., 1959-68; assn. prof. law Syracuse U., 1968-72, prof. law, 1972—; vis. prof. law, U. Iowa, 1971-72, U. Cin., 1974. Mem. N.Y. State Bar Assn. Author: Taxation of Securities Transactions, 1971; contbr. articles in field to profl. jours. Home: 1111 E Colvin St Syracuse NY 13210 Office: Syracuse Univ Coll Law Syracuse NY 13210 Tel (315) 423-3678

FRIEDBERG, HARRY J., b. N.Y.C., Nov. 27, 1937; B.A., Wittenberg Coll., 1959; LL.B., N.Y. Law Sch., 1962. Admitted to N.Y. State bar, 1962, U.S. Supreme Ct. bar, 1967, U.S. Ct. Appeals bar, 2d Circuit, 1971, U.S. Dist. Ct. bar for So. and Eastern Dist. N.Y., 1963; partner firm Olitt & Friedberg, N.Y.C., 1970-77; individual practice law N.Y.C., 1977—. Mem. Assn. Bar City N.Y., N.Y. State Bar Assn., ACLU, Phi Mu Delta. Office: 551 Fifth Ave New York City NY 10017 Tel (212) 867-0755

FRIEDBERG, MICHAEL ROBERT, b. Chgo., June 27, 1946; student Tulane U., 1964-66; B.A., Northwestern U., 1968; J.D., U. Chgo., 1971. Admitted to Ill. bar, 1971, U.S. Tax Ct. bar, 1976, U.S. Ct. Claims bar, 1976; with trust dept. Continental Ill. Nat. Bank & Trust Co. of Chgo., 1971-72; mem. firm Levenfeld, Kanter, Baskes & Lippitz, Chgo., 1972—. Mem. Am. Bar Assn. Office: 10 S LaSalle St Chicago IL 60603 Tel (312) 346-8380

FRIEDERICH, RAY RUBEN, b. Fredonia, N.D., Sept. 20, 1921; B.C.S., U. N.D., 1943; B.S. in Law, U. Minn., 1947; LL.B., U. N.D., 1948. Admitted to N.D. bar, 1948; practiced in Rugby, N.D., 1948-60; judge N.D. 2d Jud. Dist. Ct., 1961—; pros. atty. Pierce County (N.D.), 1950-56, asst. pros. atty., 1957-60; mem. Jud. Council on Juvenile Ct. Procedure. Mem. adv. council Social Services Bd., Bismarck, N.D. Mem. Bar Assn. N.D., N.D. Jud. Council, Dist. Judges Assn. N.D. (pres. 1972-73). Home: 313 3d Ave SW Rugby ND 58368 Office: Courthouse PO Box 72 Rugby ND 58368 Tel (701) 776-5266

FRIEDLUND, HERBERT RAYMOND, b. Detroit, Apr. 23, 1908; pre-legal certificate Detroit Inst. Tech., 1933; LL.B., Detroit Coll. Law; grad. Nat. Coll. State Trial Judges, U. Nev., 1969. Admitted to Mich. bar, 1938, Ill. bar, 1941; individual practice law, Detroit, 1938-41; partner firm Friedlund, Levin and Friedlund, Chgo., 1941-62; judge Ill. Circuit Ct. of Cook County, 1962—. Trustee, pres. West Ridge United Methodist Ch., Chgo., 1955-76; gov. Hi-Ridge YMCA, Chgo. Mem. Chgo., Ill. bar assns., Nordic Law Club, Lawyers Shrine Club, Sigma Delta Kappa. Contbr. articles to legal publs. Home: 5034 W Coyle St Skokie IL 60076 Office: Chicago Civic Center Chicago IL 60602 Tel (312) 443-8340

FRIEDMAN, ALAN EDWARD, b. N.Y.C., May 5, 1946; B.A., Amherst Coll., 1967; J.D., Stanford, 1970. Admitted to Calif. bar, 1971; asso. firm Tuttle & Taylor Incorporated, Los Angeles, 1970-75; mem. firm, 1975—. Mem. State Bar Calif., Am., Los Angeles County bar assns. Office: 609 S Grand Los Angeles CA 90017 Tel (213) 683-0600

FRIEDMAN, ALLEN DAVID, b. Chgo., Dec. 5, 1927; Ph.B., U. Chgo., 1949; LL.B., Chgo.-Kent Coll. Law, 1952; J.D., Ill. Inst. Tech., 1967. Admitted to Ill. bar, 1952; since practiced in Chgo., gen. counsel Am. Photocopy Equipment Co., Evanston, Ill., 1957-59; sec.-treas. Ontario Contracting & Service Co., Chgo., 1962—; pres. Keystone Electric Constrn. Co., Chgo., 1962—. Mem. adv. bd. Chgo.-Kent Coll. Law, 1973—. Mem. Am., Ill. bar assns., Nat. Elec. Contractors Assn. Office: 100 N LaSalle St Chicago IL 60602 Tel (312) 346-0646

FRIEDMAN, ARTHUR D., b. N.Y.C., May 28, 1932; B.A., Tufts Coll., 1954; J.D., N.Y. U., 1954. Admitted to Conn. bar, 1960, U.S. Dist. Ct. Conn. bar, 1960, U.S. Dist. Ct. So. dist. N.Y., 1969, U.S. 2nd Circuit Ct. Appeals bar, 1971, U.S. Supreme Ct. bar, 1966; mem. firm Friedman & Friedman, Bridgeport, 1958—, now partner; atty. Town of Trumbull, Conn., 1963-73. Chmn., Trumbull United Fund; dir. United Jewish Appeal Greater Bridgeport; active Republican party, 1960—; dir. Greater Bridgeport Ballet Co. Mem. Conn., Bridgeport bar assns., Def. Research Inst. Home: 24 Inverness Rd Trumbull CT 06611 Office: 1 Lafayette Circle Bridgeport CT 06604 Tel (203) 367-7446

FRIEDMAN, AVERY SAMUEL, b. Walla Walla, Wash., Aug. 5, 1945; A.B., U. Louisville, 1968; J.D., Cleve. State U., 1972. Admitted to Ohio bar, 1973, U.S. Supreme Ct. bar, 1977; individual practice law, Cleve., 1973—; asso. dir. Am. Bar Assn. Lawyers for Housing, Cleve., 1973-75; chief counsel The Housing Advs., Inc., Cleve., 1975—; lectr. in law, HUD, 1973—; adj. prof. law Cleve. State U., 1973—; adj. asst. prof. urban affairs, Cleve. State U., 1975—; vis. lectr. U. Tex., 1974, U. N.C., 1975, Duquesne U., 1974, Case Western Res. U., 1975. Trustee and sec. Cleve. Area Arts Council, 1974—. Mem. Bar Assn. Greater Cleve., Cuyahoga County, Am. bar assns. Recipient spl. tribute for pursuit of improvement of legal writing in Am., SCRIBES, 1972, U.S. Fair Housing Achievement award HUD, 1976; named Outstanding Young Man Am., 1975, 1 of Ten Outstanding Young Men of Greater Cleve., 1973, Ten Outstanding Young Citizens Cleve., 1975; contbr. articles to legal jours. Home: 23625 Duffield Rd Shaker Heights OH 44122 Office: 706 Citizens Bldg Cleveland OH 44114 Tel (216) 621-9292

FRIEDMAN, BENJAMIN JACOB, b. Detroit, Jan. 19, 1931; LL.B., Wayne State U., 1960. Admitted to Mich. bar, 1961, U.S. Dist. Ct. bar, 1961; partner firm Friedman & Cohen, to 1974; municipal judge, Oak Park, Mich., 1969-75; judge 45th Judicial dist., 1975—. Mem. Am. Judges Assn., Mich. Dist. Ct. Judges Assn., Mich., Oakland County bar assns. Recipient Distinguished Alumnus award Wayne State U., 1976. Home: 25911 Stratford Pl Oak Park MI 48237 Office: 13600 Oak Park Blvd Oak Park MI 48237 Tel (313) 542-7042

FRIEDMAN, BRUCE ALAN, b. Los Angeles, June 6, 1935; B.A., U. Calif., Los Angeles, 1957; J.D., U. Calif., Berkeley, 1960. Admitted to Calif. bar, 1961, U.S. Supreme Ct. bar, 1976; law clk. Calif. Ct. Appeal, 1960-61; individual practice law, Beverly Hills, Calif., Los Angeles, 1961—; instr. Southwestern Sch. Law, 1964-65; guest speaker in field. Mem. Hollywood Bowl Assn., 1966. Mem. Am., Los Angeles County bar assns., Assn. Trial Lawyers Am., Los Angeles Trial Lawyers Assn., Med.-Legal Soc. So. Calif., Phi Alpha Delta. Office: 727 W 7th St Suite 600 Los Angeles CA 90017 Tel (213) 625-0711

FRIEDMAN, CHARLES BARRY, b. Cleve., July 29, 1945; BA., U. Wis., 1967, M.A., Yale, 1969; J.D., U. Chgo., 1973; postgrad. (Woodrow Wilson scholar) Oxford (Eng.) U. Admitted to Ill. bar, 1973; asso. firms Fink Coff and Nudelman, 1973-75, Tenney and Bentley, Chgo., 1975—. Cons. New Britain (Conn.) Housing Authority, 1969-70; mem. Cleve. Voter Registration Com., 1971. Mem. Am. Bar Assn., Chgo. Bar, Phi Beta Kappa, Phi Kappa Phi, Phi Eta Sigma. Home: 3800 N Lake Shore Chicago IL 60613 Office: 69 W Washington St Chicago IL 60602 Tel (312) CE-6-4787

FRIEDMAN, DANIEL MORTIMER, b. N.Y.C., Feb. 8, 1916; A.B., Columbia, 1937, LL.B., 1940. Admitted to N.Y. bar, 1941, U.S. Supreme Ct. bar, 1948; individual practice law, N.Y.C., 1940-42; mem. staff SEC, 1942-51; with appellate sect., antitrust div. Dept. Justice, Washington, 1951-59, asst. chief, 1954-59, with Office Solicitor Gen., 1959—, 2d asst. to solicitor gen., 1962-68, 1st dep. solicitor gen., 1968—. Mem. Am., Fed. (Tom C. Clark award D.C. chpt. 1976) bar assns., Am. Law Inst. Recipient Career Service award Nat. Civil Service League, 1976; contbr. articles to legal jours. Home: 3249 Newark St NW Washington DC 20008 Office: US Dept Justice 10th St and Pennsylvania Ave NW Washington DC 20530 Tel (202) 739-2208

FRIEDMAN, EDWARD DAVID, b. Chgo., May 2, 1912; A.B. with honors, U. Chgo., 1935, J.D. cum laude, 1937. Admitted to Ill. bar, 1937, D.C. bar, 1969, U.S. Supreme Ct. bar, 1969; law clk. to fed. master in chancery, Chgo., 1937-38, firm Rosenberg, Toomin & Stein, Chgo., 1938-39; mem. gen. counsel staff SEC, 1939-42; chief counsel OPA, 1942-43; spl. asst. to dep. solicitor and solicitor Dept. Labor, Washington, 1943-48; chief law officer 5th regional office, also asst. gen. counsel NLRB, 1948-60; labor counsel to Senator John F. Kennedy, 1960-61, Senator Wayne Morse, 1961-65, U.S. Sen. Labor and Pub. Welfare Com., 1961-65; counsel to majority and minority floor mgrs. Senators Clark and Case on Civil Rights Bill, 1964; spl. asst. fgn. farm labor program sec. labor, 1964, dep. solicitor of labor, 1965-69; partner firm Bernstein, Alper, Schoene & Friedman, Washington, 1969-76, Highsaw, Mahoney & Friedman, 1976—; U.S. del. to OECD, Paris, 1968;Mem. town council Garrett Park, Md., 1954-58, mayor, 1960-66. Mem. Am., Fed. bar assns., Order of Coif. Asso. editor U. Chgo. Law Rev., 1936-37; James Nelson Reymond fellow, 1937. Office: 1050 17th St NW Washington DC 20036 Tel (202) 296-8500

FRIEDMAN, EDWARD IRWIN, b. Bklyn., Dec. 26, 1930; student Bklyn. Coll., 1948-49, L.I. U., 1949-50; LL.B., St. John's Law Sch., 1953. Admitted to N.Y. State bar, 1953; asso. firm Dreyer & Traub, Bklyn., 1955, firm Guzik & Boukstein, N.Y.C., 1956-60; mem. firm Cohen, Friedman, Goldstein & Raphael, N.Y.C., 1960—. Mem. exec. com. Hartsdale Civic Assn., 1963-65; mem. steering com. for Town of North Castle, United Towns for Home Rule, 1974. Mem. N.Y. State, Bronx County bar assns., N.Y. County Lawyers Assn., N.Y. State Trial Lawyers Assn. Office: 975 Amsterdam Ave New York City NY 10025 Tel (212) MO 3-0700

FRIEDMAN, ERROL NATHAN, b. New Orleans, Feb. 4, 1945; B.J., E. Tex. State U., 1967; J.D., Tex. Tech. U., 1970. Admitted to Tex. bar, 1970, Ark. bar, 1970; partner firm Harkness, Friedman & Kusin, Texarkana, Tex., 1970—. Mem. NE Tex., Texarkana, Bowie County bar assns., Tex. (dir.), Am. trial lawyers assns., State Bar Tex., State Bar Ark. Home: 1 Cindywood St Texarkana TX 75501 Office: 406 Texas Blvd Texarkana TX 75501 Tel (214) 794-2561

FRIEDMAN, EUGENE STUART, b. N.Y.C., Apr. 5, 1941; B.A., N.Y. U., 1961; LL.B., Columbia U., 1964. Admitted to N.Y. State bar, 1965; atty. NLRB, San Francisco 1965-67; partner firm Cohen, Weiss & Simon, N.Y.C., 1968—. Mem. N.Y. State Bar Assn., Fed. Bar Council. Office: 605 3d Ave New York City NY 10016 Tel (212) 682-6077

FRIEDMAN, FRED, b. Salzburg, Austria, Oct. 5, 1926; B.S., N.Y.U., 1950; J.D., Bklyn. Law Sch., 1954. Admitted to N.Y. State bar, 1955, U.S. Supreme Ct. bar, 1961; mem. firm Friedman & Root, Akron, N.Y., 1955—; village atty., Arkon, 1955-59. Mem. Am. Bar Assn. (vice chmn. internat. legal exchange com. gen. practice sect.), N.Y. State, Erie, Genesee assns., Clarence C. of C. (dir., past pres. 1970-72), Buffalo World Hospitality Assn. (treas. 1975-77). Home: 9319 Hunt Valley Rd Clarence NY 14031 Office: 74 Main St Akron NY 14001 Tel (716) 542-5444

FRIEDMAN, HARBERT MARC, b. N.Y.C., Jan. 3, 1931; A.B., Syracuse U., 1952; LL.B., Columbia, 1957, J.D., 1969. Admitted to N.Y. bar, 1958; defense counsel, trial counsel AUS, 1953-54; with N.Y. State Dept. Audit Control, Albany, 1958—, law apprentice, 1958-63, jr. atty., 1963-65, atty., 1965-75, sr. atty., 1975-76, asso. atty., 1973-76, asso. counsel, 1976—. Active Boy Scouts Am.; area chmn. Columbia Law Sch. Fund, 1966—. Mem. N.Y. State Bar Assn., Columbia Law Sch. Alumni Assn. Contbr. articles to profl. jours. Home: 26 Broad St Kinderhook NY 12106 Office: Governor A E Smith State Office Bldg Albany NY 12236 Tel (518) 474-8698

FRIEDMAN, HOWARD MARTIN, b. Springfield, Ohio, Sept. 26, 1941; B.A., Ohio State U., 1962; J.D., Harvard, 1965; LL.M., Georgetown U., 1967. Admitted to Ohio bar, 1965; atty. SEC, Washington, 1965-67; asst. prof. law U. N.D., 1967-69; atty. U.S. Indian Claims Commn., Washington, 1969-70; asso. prof. law U. Toledo, 1970-74, prof., 1974—. Chmn. community relations com. Toledo Jewish Welfare Fedn., 1975—. Mem. Am., Ohio, Toledo bar assns., AAUP. Contbr. articles in field to profl. jours. Home: 2461 Cheltenham Rd Toledo OH 43606 Office: University of Toledo College of Law Toledo OH 43606 Tel (419) 537-2911

FRIEDMAN, HYMAN, b. N.Y.C., Mar. 25, 1923; B.S. in Accounting, L.I. U., 1952; LL.B., Bklyn. Law Sch., 1956, J.D., 1967. Admitted to N.Y. bar, 1957; partner firm Kleinberg & Friedman, N.Y.C., 1960—. Mem. Am. Trial Lawyers Assn. Office: 225 Broadway Room 3303 New York City NY 10007

FRIEDMAN, ISIDORE, b. N.Y.C., July 4, 1922; A.B., City Coll. N.Y., 1941; J.D., Harvard, 1947. Admitted to N.Y. State bar, 1948; asst. corp. counsel N.Y.C., 1954-60; practice law, N.Y.C., 1960—. Mem. N.Y. County Lawyers Assn. Home: 242-23 54th Ave Douglaston NY 11362 Office: 10 E 40th St New York City NY 10016 Tel (212) 532-4626

FRIEDMAN, JANE MARCEE GOLDBARG, b. St. Paul, July 23, 1941; B.A., U. Minn., 1962, J.D., 1965. Admitted to Minn. bar, 1965, Mich. bar, 1974; trial atty. U.S. Justice Dept. Civil div., Washington, 1966-69; asst. gen. counsel Fed. Commn. on Obscenity, Washington, 1969-70; asst. prof. Wayne State U., Law Sch., Detroit, 1971-72, asso. prof., 1972-75, prof., 1975—; cons. Migrant Legal Action Program, Washington, 1970; lectr. Center for Adminstrn. of Justice, 1973—. Mem. Am. Bar Assn., Soc. Am. Law Tchrs. Contbr. articles to legal periodicals. Home: 1513 Brooklyn Ave Ann Arbor MI 48104 Office: 468 W Ferry Wayne State Univ Law Sch Detroit MI 48202 Tel (313) 577-3950

FRIEDMAN, JAY FRED, b. Ft. Smith, Ark., Sept. 20, 1934; student U. Tex., 1952-53, U. Ark., 1956-59; LL.B., So. Law U., 1962. Admitted to Tenn. bar, 1964; sr. partner firm Friedman, Rosenberg & Wiener, Memphis. Mem. Am., Tenn., Memphis and Shelby County bar assns., Am. Trial Lawyers Assn., Tenn. Assn. Criminal Def. Lawyers. Home: 2350 Thornwood St Memphis TN 38138 Office: 261 Chelsea Bldg Memphis TN 38107 Tel (901) 527-6518

FRIEDMAN, JERRELL DON, b. Pell City, Ala., June 6, 1945; B.S., Troy State U., 1967; J.D., Stetson U., 1973. Admitted to Fla. bar, 1973, U.S. Tax Ct. bar, 1973; law clk. U.S. 10th Circuit Ct. Appeals, 1973-74; partner firm O'Brien & Friedman, St. Petersburg, Fla., 1974—; city pros. Maderra Beach (Fla.), 1974—; instr. Fla. Inst. Tech., 1977. Mem. Am., Fla., St. Petersburg bar assns., Am. Judicature Soc. Home: 5411 17th Ave N Saint Petersburg FL 33710 Office: 3443 5th Ave N Saint Petersburg FL 33710 Tel (813) 821-0406

FRIEDMAN, LAWRENCE M., b. Chgo., Apr. 2, 1930; A.B., U. Chgo., 1958, J.D., 1951, LL.M., 1953. Admitted to Ill. bar, 1951; individual practice law, Chgo., 1955-57; instr. St. Louis U., 1957-61, U. Wis., 61-67; prof. law Stanford U., 1968—, Marion Rice Kirkwood prof., 1976—. Mem. Law and Soc. Assn. (trustee, 1970) Am. Soc. for Legal Hist. Author: Contract Law in America, 1965; Government and Slum Housing, 1968; A History of American Law, 1973; The Legal System, A Social Science Perspective, 1975; Law and Society: an Introduction, 1977; co-editor; (with Stewart Macaulay) Law and the Behavioral Sciences, 1969 2d edit., 1977; recipient Triennial Coif Book award, 1976. Home: 724 Frenchman's Rd Stanford CA 94305 Office: Stanford Law Schl Stanford CA 94305 Tel (415) 497-3072

FRIEDMAN, LEON, b. N.Y.C., Feb. 6, 1933; B.A., Harvard, 1954; LL.B., 1960. Admitted to N.Y. State bar, 1961; asso. firm Haye, Scholer, Fienman, Hays and Handler, N.Y.C., 1960-67; gen. counsel Chelsea House Pubs., N.Y.C., 1967-70; asso. dir. spl. com. on courtroom conduct Assn. Bar City, N.Y., 1970-73; staff atty. ACLU, N.Y.C., 1973-74; prof. law Hofstra U., Hempstead, N.Y., 1974—. Mem. N.Y.C. Bar Assn. Author: Disorder in the Court, 1974; The Wise Minority, 1971; Justices of the Supreme Court, 1789-1969; Their Lives and Major Opinions, 1970; recipient Scribes award, 1970; contbr. articles in field to profl. jours. Home: 103 E 86th St New York City NY 10028 Office: Hofstra University School of Law Hempstead NY 11550 Tel (516) 560-3859

FRIEDMAN, LILLIAN SIEGEL, b. N.Y.C., Jan. 3, 1906; LL.B., Albany Law Sch., Union U., 1958; postgrad. Practicing Law Inst., 1961, Russell Sage Coll., 1961. Admitted to N.Y. bar, 1961; individual practice law, Schenectady, 1961—; mem. Schenectady Pub. Defender's Staff; law guardian appellate div. Schenectady Family Ct.; law guardian examiner Schenectady Surrogate's Ct. Past pres., bd. dirs. Schenectady sect. Nat. Council Jewish Women; past pres. nat. women's com. Brandeis U.; chmn., organizer women's aux. Jewish Home for Aged, Daus. of Sarah; past bd. dirs. Jewish Community Center, Planned Parenthood, Sr. Citizens of Schenectady; past pres. Sisterhood Temple Gates of Heaven Congregation. Mem. N.Y. State, Schenectady County (past law day chmn., past lawyer's day chmn., mem. legal aid com.) bar assns., Nat. Assn. Women Lawyers, Schenectady Bd. Realtors, Am. Arbitration Assn. Licensed real estate broker. Named Patroon of Schenectady, 1976. Home: 1019 Wendell Ave Schenectady NY 12308 Office: 124 Clinton St Schenectady NY 12305 Tel (518) 374-5327

FRIEDMAN, MARVIN ROSS, b. Mpls., July 13, 1941; B.B.A., U. Miami, 1963, J.D., 1966. Admitted to Fla. bar, 1966; individual practice law Miami, Fla., 1961-71; partner firm Friedman & Lipcon, Coral Gables, Fla., 1971—. Mem. Fla. Acad. Trial Lawyers, Assn. Trial Lawyers Am., Am. Bar Assn. Office: 2600 Douglas Rd Suite 1011 Coral Gables FL 33134 Tel (305) 446-6485

FRIEDMAN, MELVIN, b. St. Louis, Dec. 10, 1923; student U., Mo. 1941-42, Washington U., St. Louis, 1946—; J.D., St. Louis U., 1948; postgrad. in Law, Tulane U., 1948-49. Admitted to Mo. bar, 1948; partner firm Steinberg & Friedman, St. Louis, 1949-57, Friedman & Fredericks, Clayton, Mo., 1957—; dir., mem. exec. com. Comml. Bank of St. Louis County, 1973—. Bd. dirs. Jewish Children's and Family Services, Jewish Children's Home. Mem. Am., Mo., St. Louis County bar assns., St. Louis Lawyers Assn. Home: 11 Upper Barnes Rd Ladue MO 63124 Office: 7730 Carondelet Ave Clayton MO 63105 Tel (314) 725-3322

FRIEDMAN, MELVIN IRVING, b. N.Y.C., Nov. 4, 1930; B.A., Coll. City N.Y., 1953; LL.B., N.Y. U., 1956. Admitted to N.Y. State bar, 1956; editor Matthew Bender & Co., N.Y.C., 1956-70; partner firm Kreindler & Kreindler, N.Y.C., 1972—. Mem. N.Y. State Bar Assn., Am. Trial Lawyers Assn. (vice chmn. aviation sect. 1976—), Assn. Bar City N.Y. Author: (with Frumer) Products Liability, 1960; research editor N.Y. U. Law Rev., 1955-56; asso. editor Personal Injury Newsletter, 1958-68; co-editor Personal Injury Ann., 1961-69. Home: 395 Ardsley Rd Scarsdale NY 10583 Office: 99 Park Ave New York City NY 10016 Tel (212) 687-8181

FRIEDMAN, MICHAEL, b. San Francisco, July 26, 1939; A.B., U. Calif., Berkeley, 1961; J.D., U. S.D., 1965; postgrad. U. Oxford, 1965-68. Admitted to Calif. bar, 1965, U.S. Supreme Ct. bar, 1968; asso. firm Werchick & Werchick, San Francisco, 1968-71; partner firm Conklin, Davids & Friedman, San Francisco, 1971—. Mem. Calif., San Francisco bar assns., Calif., San Francisco trial lawyers assn., Lawyers Club San Francisco. Contbr. article to legal jour. Home: 1875 Mountain View Tiburon CA 94920 Office: PO Box 99406 San Francisco CA 94109 Tel (415) 673-0300

FRIEDMAN, MILTON REUBEN, b. Hartford, Conn., Jan. 16, 1904; B.A., Yale U., 1925, LL.B., 1928. Admitted to Conn. bar, 1928, N.Y. bar, 1929; asst. probation officer Hartford Police Ct., 1927, 28; law clk. to Judges Learned Hand and Thomas W. Swan Fed. Circuit Ct., 1928-29; with firm Taylor, Blanc, Capron & Marsh, N.Y.C., 1929-58; partner firm Parker, Duryee, Benjamin, Zunino & Malone, N.Y.C., 1958-76; individual practice law, N.Y.C., 1976—; lectr. in field; adviser restatement law of property Am. Law Inst. Mem. Am. Bar Assn., Assn. Bar City N.Y. (chmn. real property law). Author: Friedman on Leases, 3 vols., 1974-77; Contracts and Conveyances of Real Property, 3d edit., 1975; contbr. articles to legal jours. Office: 115 W 73d St New York City NY 10023 Tel (212) 787-0028

FRIEDMAN, NICHOLAS L., b. N.Y.C., July 24, 1901; LL.B., Drake U., 1922, J.D., 1968. Admitted to Iowa bar, 1922; individual practice law, Des Moines, 1922—. Home: 2706 Holcomb St Des Moines IA 50310 Office: Empire Bldg Suite 618 Des Moines IA 50309 Tel (515) 282-9594

FRIEDMAN, RICHARD LAWRENCE, b. Newark, Apr. 25, 1946; B.A., Rutgers U., 1968, J.D., 1971. Admitted to N.J. bar, 1971; atty. City of Camden (N.J.), 1971; spl. asst. in charge of narcotics Camden County (N.J.) Prosecutors Office, 1972-75; asso. firm Avena & Hendren, Camden, 1975—. Mem. Am., N.J., Camden County bar assns. Home: 1125 Thackary Ct Voorhees NJ 08043 Office: 530 Cooper St Camden NJ 08101 Tel (609) 964-0103

FRIEDMAN, SIMON LEE, b. Springfield, Ill., Nov. 18, 1921; A.B., U. Ill., 1943, LL.D., 1944. Admitted to Ill. bar, 1944; govt. atty., Springfield, Ill., 1944-46; practiced in Springfield, 1946-72; judge Ill. Circuit Ct., 7th Jud. Circuit, 1972—; asst. legal advisor Office Supt. Pub. Instruction of Ill., Springfield, 1958-62. Mem. Springfield Symphony Orch. Bd.; mem. spl. com. Springfield Bd. Higher Edn. Mem. Ill. State, Sangamon County (Ill.), Chgo. bar assns. Office: County Bldg Springfield IL 62701 Tel (217) 753-6813

FRIEDMAN, SOLOMON PHILIP, b. N.Y.C., June 7, 1931; B.B.A., Coll. City N.Y., 1952; LL.B., Bklyn. Law Sch., 1961. Admitted to N.Y. bar, 1961; asso. firm Strasser, Spiegelberg, Fried & Frank, N.Y.C., 1962-67; asso. firm Davis & Gilbert, N.Y.C., 1967-69, partner, 1969—. Mem. Am., N.Y. bar assns., Assn. Bar City N.Y. Contbr. articles to legal jours. Home: 35 Sutton Pl New York City NY 10022 Office: 500 Fifth Ave New York City NY 10036 Tel (212) 564-3530

FRIEDMAN, STANLEY JAY, b. N.Y.C., Aug. 28, 1939; B.A., U. So. Calif., 1962; LL.B., U. Calif., Berkeley, 1965. Admitted to Calif. bar, 1966; partner firms Herzstein, Maier, Friedman & Lippett, San Francisco, 1966-70, Friedman & Sloan, San Francisco, 1970—. Mem. Berkeley Police Rev. Commn., 1973-76; bd. dirs., chmn. legal com., mem. exec. com. ACLU of No. Calif. Mem. Bar Assn. San Francisco (bd. dirs., chmn. criminal justice adv. council). Office: 680 Beach St Suite 436 San Francisco CA 94109 Tel (415) 776-3070

FRIEDMAN, STEVEN LEWIS, b. Phila., Mar. 28, 1946; B.A., Yale, 1968; J.D., U. Pa., 1971. Admitted to Pa. bar, 1971; law clk. Pa. Supreme Ct., Phila., 1971-72; partner firm Dilworth, Paxson, Kalish & Levy, Phila., 1972—; rep. auditor gen. of Pa. on Del. River Port Authority, 1975—; mem. Pa. Hwy. and Bridge Authority. Mem. Kent State Task Force Pres. Commn. on Campus Unrest, 1970. Mem. Am., Pa., Phila. bar assns. Office: 2600 Fidelity Bldg Philadelphia PA 19109 Tel (215) 546-3000

FRIEDMAN, STEVEN MICHAEL, b. St. Louis, Dec. 13, 1939; student U. Colo., 1957-59; A.B., Washington U., St. Louis, 1962, J.D., 1965; postgrad. N.Y. U., 1965-66. Admitted to Mo. bar, 1966, Ariz. bar, 1966, U.S. Supreme Ct. bar, 1972; asso. firm Gorey & Ely, Phoenix, 1966-67, Green & Lurie, Phoenix, 1967-70; partner firm Lurie & Friedman, Phoenix, 1970-73; individual practice law, Phoenix, 1973-77; partner firm Shortridge Friedman and Foster, Phoenix, 1977—; co-founder, chmn. bd. dirs. Hacienda de Los Angeles, 1969-75, mem. bd. dirs., 1969—. Mem. Maricopa County, Am. bar assns., Assn. Trial Lawyers Am., Ariz. Trial Lawyers Assn. (dir. 1975-76). Office: 4008 N 15th Ave Phoenix AZ 85015 Tel (602) 264-0234

FRIEDMAN, WILBUR HARVEY, b. N.Y.C., May 2, 1907; B.A., Columbia, 1927, LL.B., 1930. Admitted to N.Y. bar, 1931; law clk. U.S. Supreme Ct. Justice Harlan F. Stone, 1930-31; atty. U.S. Solicitor Gen. Office, Dept. Justice, 1931-32; asso. firm Proskauer, Rose, Goetz & Mendelsohn, N.Y.C., 1932-40, partner, 1940-55, sr. partner, 1955—; lectr. N.Y. U. Insts. on Fed. Taxation, 1943-65. Mem. Internat., Am., N.Y. State bar assns., Assn. Bar City N.Y., New York County Lawyers Assn. (pres. 1975—). Author: (with J.K. Lasser) Estate Tax Handbook, 1976; contbr. articles to legal jours. Home: 1016 Fifth Ave New York City NY 10028 Office: 300 Park Ave New York City NY 10022 Tel (212) 593-9210

FRIEDMAN, WILLIAM S., b. Springfield, Ohio, Mar. 19, 1941; B.A., U. Dayton, 1963; J.D., U. Cin., 1966. Admitted to Ohio bar, 1966; asst. Atty. Gen. of Ohio, 1966-68; dept. asst. to Gov. of Ohio, 1968-69; asso. firm Sebastian, Durst & Marsh, Ohio, 1969-73; partner firm Lewis and Friedman, Columbus, Ohio, 1973—. Mem. task force New Careers Program of New Dimensions, Columbus, 1969; mem. community relations com., Columbus, 1969-70; chmn. young leadership, Columbus, 1970-71. Mem. Ohio, Columbus bar assns., Am. Trial Lawyers Assn. Home: 1000 Urlin Ave Columbus OH 43212 Office: 360 S 3d St Columbus OH 43215 Tel (614) 221-3938

FRIEL, BERNARD PRESTON, b. St. Paul, Aug. 23, 1930; B.S. in Law, U. Minn., Mpls., 1954, LL.B., 1954. Admitted to Minn. bar, 1954; asso. firm Briggs and Morgan, and predecessor, St. Paul, 1956-61, mem. firm, 1961—, also dir.; lectr. in field. Chmn. adv. bd. Faribault (Minn.) State Hosp., 1973-76; mem. Minn. Ind. Sch. Dist. 197 Sch. Bd. Edn., 1967-69; mem. Minn. Higher Edn., Facilities Authority, 1971—, also chmn., chmn. gen. bus. div. Greater St. Paul United Fund, 1971—. Mem. Am., Minn., Ramsey County (Minn.) bar assns., Am. Trial Lawyers Assn. Recipient Community Service award Greater St. Paul United Fund, 1964; named 1 of 10 Outstanding Young Men in Minn.; 1965. Home: 750 Mohican Ln Mendota Heights MN 55120 Office: W-2200 First Nat Bank Bldg Saint Paul MN 55101 Tel (612) 291-1215

FRIEND, CHARLES ERNEST, b. Lexington Va., Feb. 10, 1935; B.A., George Washington U., 1957; B.F.T., Am. Grad. Sch. Internat. Mgmt., 1965; J.D., William & Mary Coll., 1969. Admitted to Va. bar, 1969, mem. firm, Christian, Barton, Parker, Epps & Brent, Richmond Va., 1969-70; individual practice law, Yorktown Va., 1970-72; prof. of law, Richmond, 1972—; pres. York County Bar Assn., 1971-72; asso. Judge, York County Ct., 1972; Editor, Va. Bar Assn. Journal, 1974—. Trustee, Jamestown Found., 1971—; legal advisor Va. Fedn. of Humane Soc., 1975;. Mem. Va., Williamsburg bar assns., Peninsula Corrections Council. Outstanding Educator award, Richmond U., 1975. Home: 10651 Clearpoint Dr Chesterfield VA 23832 Office: Richmond U Richmond VA 23173 Tel (804) 285-6370

FRIEND, EDWARD ARMAND, b. Toledo, Sept. 26, 1921; A.B., U. Chgo., 1943; LL.B., Harvard, 1949. Admitted to Calif. bar, 1950; asso. firm Emmett R. Burns, San Francisco, 1950-52; individual practice law, San Francisco, 1952—. Bd. dirs. Midtown Terr. Homeowners Assn., 1959-66, pres., 1960, 1966. Mem. San Francisco Bar Assn. (jud. plebiscite com., 1972-73, edn. of youth com.), Harvard Law Sch. Assn. Home: 25 Midcrest Way San Francisco CA 94131 Office: Suite 1606 703 Market St San Francisco CA 94103

FRIEND, EDWARD MALCOLM, JR., b. Birmingham, Ala., May 1, 1912; A.B., U. Ala., 1933, LL.B., 1935. Admitted to Ala. bar, 1935; since practiced in Birmingham; asso. firm J.P. Mudd, 1935-40; partner firm Sirote, Permutt, Friend, Friedman, Held & Aplinsky., 1945—; pres. Legal Aid Soc. Birmingham, 1954-55; chmn. com. for study of State Correctional Insts. and Procedures, 1976; co-chmn. Human Rights Com., 1976; pres. Ala. Law Sch. Fedn., 1971-72; rep. lawyers and courts on the distbn. comm. Greater Birmingham Found. Co-chmn., Jefferson County United Appeal, 1960, v.p. dist. council Boy Scouts Am.; mem. pres' cabinet U. Ala., 1976-77. Mem. Am., Ala., Birmingham (pres. 1971) bar assns., Am. Judicature, Omicron Delta Kappa, Phi Beta Kappa. Recipient Daniel Meador Outstanding Alumnus award, U. Ala., 1971. Club: Rotary (pres. 1975). Home: 22 Woodhill Rd Birmingham AL 35213 Office: 2222 Arlington Ave Birmingham AL 35205 Tel (205) 933-7111

FRIEND, HENRY CHARLES, b. Milw., Mar. 30, 1909; B.A., Harvard, 1931, LL.B., 1934. Admitted to Wis. bar, 1934, U.S. Supreme Ct. bar, 1976; asso. atty. Home Owners Loan Corp., Chgo., 1934-36; practiced in Milw., 1936-42, 43—; atty. Office Price Administrn., Washington, 1942-43. Mem. Am., Milw. bar assns., Am. Counsel Assn., State Bar Wis. Contbr. numerous articles to legal, hist. jours. Home: 1714 E Kane Pl Milwaukee WI 53202 Office: 238 W Wisconsin Ave Milwaukee WI 53203 Tel (414) 276-1310

FRIERSON, JAMES GORDON, b. Jonesboro, Ark., Apr. 9, 1940; B.S. in Econs., Ark. State U., 1962, M.B.A., 1969, J.D., 1965. Admitted to Ark. bar, 1965; asso. firm Frierson, Walker & Snellgrove, Jonesboro, 1965-66; instr. bus. law Ark. State U., 1965-67; asst. prof. bus. adminstrn. Kans. State Coll., Pittsburg, 1967-73; asso. prof. bus. adminstrn. E. Tenn. State U., Johnson City, 1973—. Mem. Am. Bar Assn., Am. Bus. Law Assn. Contbr. articles in field to profl. jours. Home: 608 N Hills Dr Johnson City TN 37601 Office: Box 23440A East Tennessee State University Johnson City TN 37601 Tel (615) 929-4433

FRIERSON, SARAH STEWART, b. Mobile, Ala., Feb. 8, 1949; B.S., U. Ala., 1969, J.D., 1972. Admitted to Ala. bar, 1972; trust officer Birmingham Trust Nat. Bank, Ala., 1972—. Summer intern legal div. FDIC, Washington, 1970-71; pres. Magic City BPW Club, Birmingham, 1974-75. Mem. Ala., Am., Birmingham Bar Assns., Am. Inst. of Banking, Ala. Bankers Assn. (trust div.). Home: 3780 Montevallo Rd Birmingham AL 35213 Office: PO Box 2554 Birmingham AL 35290 Tel (205) 254-5710

FRIES, PAUL STOWE, b. Bronsdale, Minn., Oct. 7, 1905; B.A., Cornell Coll., Iowa, 1927; LL.B., U. Colo., 1930. Admitted to Colo. bar, 1930, Ariz. bar, 1955. Editor, Rocky Mountain Law Review, Boulder, 1930; partner firm Dudley & Fries, Colorado Springs, 1937-38; trust officer So. Ariz. Bank, Tucson, 1958-59. Mem. Colo., Ariz., Pima County bar assns., Phi Alpha Delta. Office: 8760 E Wrightstown Rd Tucson AZ 85715 Tel (602) 298-1132

FRISBIE, CHARLES, b. Kansas City, Mo., June 1, 1939; A.B. (Nat. Merit Scholar), Princeton, 1961; J.D. with honors, U. Mich., 1964. Admitted to Mo. bar, 1964; U.S. Supreme Ct. bar, 1968; asso. firm Lathrop, Koontz, Righter, Clagett, Parker & Norquist and predecessors, Kansas City, 1964-70, partner, 1971—. Mem. Am., Mo. bar assns., Order of Coif, Phi Delta Phi. Home: 808 Romany Rd Kansas City MO 64113 Office: 1500 Ten Main Center Kansas City MO 64105 Tel (816) 842-0820

FRISBIE, CURTIS LYNN, JR., b. Greenville, Miss., Sept. 13, 1943; B.S., U. Ala., 1966; J.D., St. Mary's U., San Antonio, 1971. Admitted to Tex. bar, 1971, Ga. bar, 1972; trial atty. antitrust div. Dept. Justice, Atlanta, 1971-74; mem. firm King & Spalding, Atlanta, 1974—. Mem. Am., Ga., Atlanta bar assns., Phi Alpha Delta. Office: 2500 Trust Company Tower Atlanta GA 30303 Tel (404) 572-4600

FRISBIE, DUANE C., b. Stevensville, Mont., Jan. 16, 1913; B.A., Stanford, 1934; LL.B., Harvard, 1937. Admitted to Wash. bar, 1938; pres. Internat. Motor Assn.; pres. Western Internat. Yacht & Boat Assn., Ltd.; pres. Western Prepaid Legal Services, Seattle. Home: 5715 63d NE Seattle WA 98105 Office: 4900 25th St NE Seattle WA 98105 Tel (206) 524-8650

FRISCH, E. ROGER, b. N.Y.C., Dec. 30, 1933; B.A., Yale, 1955; J.D., U. Mich., 1960. Admitted to N.Y. bar, 1961, U.S. Supreme Ct. bar, 1965; asso. Sullivan & Cromwell, N.Y.C., 1960-65; partner firm Walsh & Frisch, N.Y.C., 1965—. Office: 250 Park Ave New York City NY 10017 Tel (212) 687-6100

FRISINA, DOMENIC FRANK, b. Ravenna, Ohio, Apr. 2, 1948; B.A. cum laude, Kent State U., 1970; J.D., Georgetown U., 1973. Admitted to Ohio bar, 1973, U.S. Dist. Ct. bar No. Dist. Ohio, 1973; asso. firm Hahn, Loeser, Freedheim, Dean & Wellman, Cleve., 1973—; adj. prof. law Cleve. State U., 1976—. Steering com. Cleve. Fedn. Community Planning; sec.-treas. Cleve. chpt. Nat. Jr. Tennis League, 1974-76. Mem. Am., Ohio, Greater Cleve. (exec. com. young lawyers sect.) bar assns., Blue Key, Nat. Thespian Soc., Delta Theta Phi, Omicron Delta Kappa, Phi Alpha Theta, Pi Sigma Alpha, Epsilon Nu Gamma. Home: 3661 Traynham Rd Shaker Heights OH 44122 Office: 800 National City E 6th Bldg Cleveland OH 44114 Tel (216) 621-0150

FRITSCH, REGENNAS ELLIOTT, b. Columbus, Ind., May 9, 1944; B.S. in Econs., Ind., State U., 1968, M.S. in Econs., 1969; J.D., Ind. U., 1972. Admitted to Ind. bar, 1973; compensation and benefits cons. Cummins Engine Co., Columbus, 1969—. Mem. Ind., Bartholomew County bar assns., NAACP. Home: 4224 River Rd Columbus IN 47201 Office: 1000 5th St Columbus IN 47201 Tel (812) 379-5971

FRITZ, THOMAS GARY, b. Mitchell, S.D., June 30, 1946; B.A., U. S.D., 1968, J.D., 1971, M.A., 1976. Admitted to S.D. bar, 1971; clk. U.S. Dist. Ct. S.D., 1971-72; partner firm Lynn Jackson, Shultz, Ireland & Lebrun, Rapid City, S.D., 1973—. Mem. Am., S.D. trial lawyers assns. Contbr. articles to legal jours. Home: 4829 Powderhorn Dr Rapid City SD 57701 Office: 724 Saint Joseph St Rapid City SD 57701 Tel (605) 342-2592

FRITZ, THOMAS V., b. Pitts., July 6, 1934; B.B.A., U. Pitts., 1960; J.D., Duquesne U., 1964; LL.M., N.Y. U., 1966; A.M.P., Harvard, 1975. Admitted to Pa. bar, 1965; mng. partner Arthur Young & Co., Pitts., 1973—; adj. prof. Duquesne U. Sch. Law, Pitts., 1966—; mem. Estate Planning Council Pitts. Recipient Hon. Wallace S. Gourley award Acad. Trial Lawyers, 1964. Office: Arthur Young Co 2400 Koppers Bldg Pittsburgh PA 15219 Tel (412) 281-1559

FRITZINGER, JOHN GEORGE, JR., b. Abington, Pa., Dec. 10, 1936; B.A., Yale, 1958; LL.B., Harvard, 1961. Admitted to N.Y. bar, 1962; asso. firm Dewey, Ballantine, Bushby Palmer & Wood., N.Y.C., 1961-69, partner, 1969—. Mem. Assn. Bar City N.Y., N.Y. State bar assn. Bd. dirs. Adirondack Trail Improvement Soc. Office: 140 Broadway New York City NY 10005 Tel (212) 344-8000

FRIZLEN, WILLIAM DUDLEY, b. Phila., Aug. 10, 1932; A.B. in Govt., Lafayette Coll., 1953; J.D., U. Pa., 1958. Admitted to Pa. Supreme Ct. bar, 1959; asso. firm Jenkins, Bennett & Jenkins, Phila., 1959-60; estate planner Central Penn Nat. Bank, Phila., 1960-61; atty. Am. Water Works Service Co., Inc., Phila., 1961-67, counsel, div. corp. sec., 1961-68, Pitts., 1969—. Mem. Am., Pa., Allegheny County bar assns. Home: 731 Pinetree Rd Pittsburgh PA 15243 Office: 250 Mount Lebanon Blvd Pittsburgh PA 15234 Tel (412) 343-0400

FROEHLICH, FREDERICK ELI, b. Glenbeulah, Wis., Apr. 21, 1922; B.A., Valparaiso U., 1945, LL.B., 1947, J.D., 1967. Admitted to Wis. bar, 1948, U.S. Supreme ct. bar, 1972, mem. firm Brummund & Froehlich, Appleton, Wis., 1957-62; individual practice law, Appleton, 1948-51, 62—; dist. atty. Outagamie County (Wis.), 1951-57; city atty. City of Appleton, 1962-66. Mem. Am. Bar Assn., Wis. Bar, Am. Trial Lawyers Assn. Recipient Distinguished Service award Appleton Jr. C. of C., 1951. Office: 103 W College Ave Appleton WI 54911 Tel (414) 734-9839

FROHLICHER, JOHN HANAWALT, b. St. Paul, Dec. 12, 1937; A.B., Harvard U., 1959; M.B.A., U. Pa., 1961; J.D., Georgetown U., 1966. Admitted to D.C. bar, 1966; law clk. U.S. Dist. Ct. for D.C., 1966-67; asso. firm Glassie, Pewett, Beebe & Shanks, and predecessor, Washington, 1967-73, partner, 1973—; lectr. Cath. U. Am., 1975. Home: 1009 Independence Ave SE Washington DC 20003 Office: 1737 H St NW Washington DC 20006 Tel (202) 466-4310

FROHNMAYER, DAVID BRADEN, b. Medford, Oreg., July 9, 1940; A.B. magna cum laude, Harvard, 1962; B.A. (Rhodes scholar) Oxford, 1964; M.A., 1971; J.D., Univ. Calif., Berkeley, 1967. Admitted to Oreg. bar, 1971, Calif. bar, 1967; asso. firm Pillsbury, Madison & Sutro, San Francisco, 1967-69; asst. to sec. HEW, 1969-70; prof. law, spl. asst. to pres. Univ. Oreg., Eugene, 1971—; rep. Oreg. Legis. Assembly, 1975-77; cons. Civil Rights div. U.S. Dept. Justice, 1973-74. Mem. Oreg. Field Burning Com., 1973-74, Gov.'s Com. on Conflict of Interest Legis., 1974. Mem. Am., Oreg., Calif. bar assns., Am. Assn. Rhodes Scholars. Recipient Detur Prize, Harvard, Samuel Pool Weaver Constl. Law Essay award Am. Bar Found., 1972, 74. Home: 2875 Baker Blvd Eugene OR 97403 Office: University of Oreg School of Law Eugene OR 97403 Tel (503) 686-3855

FROHOCK, THOMAS NAYLOR, b. St. Louis, Dec. 4, 1934; B.A., Williams Coll., 1956; LL.B., Yale, 1959. Admitted to D.C. bar, 1959; U.S. Supreme Ct. bar, 1972; served with JAGC, U.S. Army, 1959-61; asso. firm McKenna, Wilkinson & Kittner, Washington, 1961-64, partner, 1964—. Mem. Am., FCC bar assns., Phi Beta Kappa. Home: 1200 S Arlington Ridge Rd Arlington VA 22202 Office: 1150 17th St NW Washington DC 20036 Tel (202) 296-1600

FROLICH, JOHN NOEL, b. Phila., May 18, 1915; B.S., St. John's U., N.Y.C., 1934, LL.B., 1936, LL.M., 1937; certificate in engring. Chamberlain Inst. Tech., 1941; LL.D., U. Calif., Los Angeles, 1948. Admitted to N.Y. bar, 1937, Calif. bar, 1947, U.S. Supreme Ct. bar, 1965; spl. hearing judge OPA, 1943; atty-commentator Legal Clinic of the Air, radio program, Sta. KXLA, 1948-49; gen. counsel Community Taxpayers Assn. Calif., 1965—. Mem. Am., Internat. bar assns., Los Angeles County Bar, Lawyers Club of Los Angeles, Calif. Trial Lawyers Assn., Am. Judicature Soc. Author screenplay: Crime Without Punishment, 1947. Office: 727 W 7th St Suite 626 Los Angeles CA 90017 Tel (213) 622-8104

FROSH, BRIAN ESTEN, b. Washington, Oct. 8, 1946; B.A., Wesleyan U., 1968; J.D., Columbia U., 1971. Admitted to Md. bar, 1972, D.C. bar, 1973; state legis. liaison Md. Dept. Employment and Social Services, 1971-72; legis. asst. Sen. Harrison A. Williams, Jr., Washington, 1972-76; partner firm Kass, Skalet & Frosh, Washington, 1976—; dir. State Nat. Bank, Rockville, Md., 1976—. Bd. dirs. ACLU, Montgomery County, Md., 1973—. Home: 3627 R St NW Washington DC 20007 Office: 1225 19th St NW Washington DC 20036 Tel (202) 659-3436

FROSH, STANLEY B., b. Denver, Jan. 9, 1919; B.S., Northwestern U., 1939, J.D., 1942. Admitted to Ill. bar, 1942, D.C. bar, 1945, Md. bar, 1949; sr. litigation atty. O.P.A., Chgo., 1942, Washington, 1945-47; partner firm Camalier, Frosh, Sperling & Dorsey, Washington and Montgomery County, Md., 1947-75; asso. judge 6th Jud. Dist. of Md., Rockville, 1975—; chmn. bd., gen. counsel State Nat. Bank of Md., 1958-76; dir. Gibralter Savs. & Loan Assn., Silver Spring, Md., 1958-70; lectr. Am. U., 1949-53; lectr., Am. law specialist for U.S. Dept. State and USIA, Africa, 1964, Phillipines, Vietnam and S. Korea, Republic of China, 1966, Cyprus, Malta and Portugal, 1976. Mem. Montgomery County Council, 1958-62, pres. pro tem, 1961-62; bd. dirs. Dag Hammarskjold Coll., 1972-75, Washington Planning and Housing Assn., 1958-66, Montgomery County Community Chest, Montgomery County C. of C., 1963-65, Jewish Community Center of Greater Washington, 1958-73; chmn. bd. dirs. Montgomery County chpt. ACLU, 1970-72. Mem. Am., Md., Montgomery County, D.C. bar assns., Am. Trial Lawyers Assn. Home: 6100 Bradley Blvd Bethesda MD 20034 Office: Court House Rockville MD 20850 Tel (301) 279-1923

FROST, OTIS LAMONT, JR., b. Wynnewood, Okla., May 26, 1917; B.A., Vanderbilt U., 1938; J.D., U. Calif. at Berkeley, 1941; LL.M., U. So. Calif., 1947. IRS agt. U.S. Treasury Dept., Los Angeles, 1946-48; with Occidental Life Ins. Co., Los Angeles, 1948—, v.p., 1965-75, exec. v.p., gen. counsel, 1975—, also dir.; v.p. Transam. Corp., Los Angeles, 1968—, also dir.; sr. v.p., gen. counsel, dir. Transam. Ins. Corp., Los Angeles, 1969—. Mem. Calif. Constn. Revision Commn., 1967—. Bd. dirs., treas. Coro Found.; Cal. state v.p. Am. Life Conv. Mem. Assn. Calif. Life Ins. Cos. (dir. 1961—), Health Ins. Assn. Am., Calif. Ins. Fedn. (v.p., dir. 1960—), Nat. Assn. Ins. Commrs., Assn. Life Ins. Counsel, Am., Calif. State, Los Angeles County bar assns., Los Angeles Area C. of C., Calif. C. of C. Home: 2740 Monte Mar Terr Los Angeles CA 90064 Office: Occidental Center Los Angeles CA 90054*

FRUE, WILLIAM CALHOUN, b. Pontiac, Mich., Dec. 29, 1934; A.B., Washington and Lee U., 1956; J.D., U. N.C., 1960. Admitted to N.C. bar, 1960; partner firm Wright & Shuford, 1965-69; partner firm Shuford, Frue & Best, and predecessors, Asheville, N.C., 1969—. Mem. Am., Buncombe County bar assns.

FRUG, GERALD ELLISON, b. Berkeley, Calif., July 31, 1939; A.B., U. Calif., Berkeley, 1960; LL.B., Harvard, 1963. Admitted to Calif. bar, 1965, N.Y. State bar, 1969; law clk. to Roger Traynor, chief justice of Calif., San Francisco, 1964-65; asso. firm Heller, Ehrman, White & McAuliffe, San Francisco, 1965-66; spl. asst. to chmn. U.S. Equal Employment Opportunity Commn., Washington, 1966-69; asso. firm Cravath, Swaine & Moore, N.Y.C., 1969-70; 1st dep. adminstr. N.Y.C. Health Services Adminstrn., 1970-73, adminstr., 1973-74; asso. prof. law U. Pa., Phila., 1974—. Frank Knox fellow, 1963-64. Contbr. articles in field to legal jours. Home: 717 N Mt Pleasant Rd Philadelphia PA 19119 Office: 3400 Chestnut St Philadelphia PA 19119 Tel (215) 243-6190

FRUIN, JOHN GIBSON, b. Waterbury, Conn., June 27, 1891; B.S., Fordham U., 1913, LL.B., 1916. Admitted to N.Y. bar, 1916; individual practice law, N.Y.C., 1916—. Office: 1170 Broadway New York City NY 10001 Tel (212) MU-4-3359

FRUTKIN, ARTHUR MARVIN, b. Alliance, Ohio, Aug. 30, 1908; Ph.B., U. Chgo., 1929, J.D., 1931. Admitted to Ill. bar, 1931, Ohio bar, 1932; individual practice law, Alliance, 1932-74, Canton, Ohio, 1955—. Mem. Ohio, Stark County bar assns., Comml. Law League Am. Home: 3718 Kaiser Ave NE Canton OH 44705 Office: 626 Renkert Bldg Canton OH 44702 Tel (216) 456-0083

FRY, ROBERT G., b. Tulsa, Dec. 19, 1941; B.A., Mich. State U., 1964; J.D., U. Tulsa, 1967; postgrad. Northwestern U., 1969. Admitted to Okla. bar, 1968, U.S. Dist. Ct. for No. Dist. Okla., 1968, U.S. 10th Circuit Ct. Appeals bar, 1968; individual practice law, Tulsa, 1969—; pub. defender Tulsa County, Okla., 1969-70. Mem. Okla. Trial Lawyers Assn., Tulsa Alumni of Sigma Chi (pres. 1976), Phi Alpha Delta. Named Outstanding Young Lawyer, Tulsa County, 1971. Office: 411 Mayo Bldg Tulsa OK 74103 Tel (918) 585-1107

FRYE, RICHARD ARTHUR, b. Akron, Ohio, Sept. 3, 1948; B.A., Wittenberg U., 1970; J.D., Ohio State U., 1973. Admitted to Ohio bar, 1973; asst. atty. gen. State of Ohio representing Ohio Dept. Natural Resources, Columbus, 1973-74; asso. firm Knepper, White, Arter & Hadden, Columbus, 1974—; spl. counsel to atty. gen. Ohio, 1974-75; lectr. Ohio Legal Center Inst., 1975. Mem. Am., Fed., Ohio, Columbus bar assns., Ohio Def. Assn., Ohio State U. Franklin County Alumni Club (gov. 1975—). Co-author: Supplement to Knepper's Ohio Civil Practice, 1975; Ohio Eminent Domain Practice, 1977. Home: 184 Chatham Rd Columbus OH 43214 Office: 180 E Broad St Columbus OH 43215 Tel (614) 221-3155

FRYER, HUGH NEVIN, b. Phila., June 11, 1938; A.B., Brown U., 1960; LL.B., U. Pa., 1963. Admitted to N.Y. bar, 1966, U.S. Supreme Ct. bar, 1969; asso. firm Dewey, Ballantine, Bushby, Palmer & Wood, N.Y.C., 1963-71, partner, 1971—. Mem. Assn. Bar City N.Y., N.Y. State, Am., Internat. bar assns., Am. Judicature Soc., N.Y. Law Inst. Home: Hunter Ln Rye NY 10580 Office: 140 Broadway New York City NY 10005 Tel (212) 344-8000

FRYER, JOEL JAMES, b. Cleve., Dec. 1, 1928; B.B.A., U. Ga., 1949, LL.B., 1951. Admitted to Ga. bar, 1951, U.S. Dist. Ct. bar for No. Dist. Ga., 1951; mem. staff atty. gen., Atlanta, Ga., 1954-55; asso. firm McKenzie, Kaler and Shulman, Atlanta, 1955-56, firm Sam Dettelbach, Atlanta, 1956-61; partner firm Fryer & Harp, Atlanta, 1961-68; partner firm Arnall, Golden & Gregory, Atlanta, 1968-74; judge Fulton County (Ga.) Civil Ct., 1971-74, Fulton County Superior Ct., 1974—. Mem. Am., Atlanta, Ga. bar assns., Am. Judicature Soc. Office: 512 Courthouse 136 Pryor St SW Atlanta GA 30303 Tel (404) 572-2968

FRYHOFER, GEORGE WILLIAM, b. Washington, Mar. 8, 1927; student Vanderbilt U., 1944, N.C. Coll. Agr. and Engring., 1945; A.B., Emory U., 1949, LL.B., 1950. Admitted to Ga. bar, 1951, U.S. Supreme Ct. bar, 1965; asso. Fulcher law firm, Augusta, Ga., 1951-54; individual practice law, Waynesboro, Ga., 1954—; solicitor Ga. State Ct. of Burke County, 1961-63, judge, 1963—. Pres. Augusta Choral Soc., 1952. Mem. Am., Ga., Augusta Area trial lawyers assns., Ga. Assn. Plaintiffs Trial Lawyers (pres. 1967), Am. Bar Assn., Ga. Assn. Trial Lawyers, Am. Legion, Waynesboro Exchange Club (past pres.), Omicron Delta Kappa. Home: Wood Valley Rd Waynesboro GA 30830 Office: 114 E 6th St PO Box 66 Waynesboro GA 30830 Tel (404) 554-5151

FRYLING, RICHARD, JR., b. Orange, N.J., Dec. 10, 1941; A.B., Cornell U., 1964; LL.B., Steton Hall U., 1967. Admitted to N.J. bar, 1967, U.S. Supreme Ct. bar, 1976; asso. firm Carpenter, Bennett & Morrissey, Newark, 1967-71; atty. Pub. Service Electric and Gas Co., Newark, 1971-75, asst. gen. solicitor, 1975—; atty. Bernards Twp. Bd. Health. Mem. N.J., Essex County, Fed. Power bar assns. Office: 80 Park Pl Newark NJ 07101 Tel (201) 622-7000

FU, PAUL SHAN, b. Shen-Young, China, Sept. 7, 1932; LL.B., Soochow U., 1960; M.C.L. (fellow), U. Ill. Coll. Law, 1962; M.L.S., Villanova U., 1968. Asst. law librarian, lectr. in law Detroit Coll. Law, 1968-69; law librarian, asso. prof. law Ohio No. U. Coll. Law, Ada, 1969-72; law librarian Supreme Ct. Ohio, Columbus, 1972—; cons. county law library assns., Hancock County (Ohio), Findlay, 1973, Clinton County (Ohio), Wilmington, 1975, vice chmn. State and Ct. Law Libraries U.S. and Can. Mem. Am. (certiified law librarian), Ohio regional assns. law libraries, ALA, Am. Soc. Internat. Law, Am. Trial Lawyers Assn. Author: Law Library Handbook of the Supreme Court of Ohio, 1975; contbr. articles to legal library jours. Home: 940 Evening St Worthington OH 43085 Office: 30 E Broad St Columbus OH 43215 Tel (614) 466-2044

FUCHS, ELDON LOUIS, b. Farmersville, Ill., Sept. 19, 1912; student Ill. State Normal U., 1930-32; LL.B., Lincoln Coll., 1950. Admitted to Ill. bar, 1951; individual practice of law, Farmersville, 1951—; asso. firm Traynor & Hendricks, Springfield, Ill., 1957-71; pres. State Bank of Virden (Ill.), 1968—; dir. various banks, 1968—. Chmn. March of Dimes, 1959-69. Mem. Ill. State, Montgomery County (pres. 1962) bar assns. Home and Office: Box 216 Farmersville IL 62533 Tel (217) 227-3294

FUCHS, STANLEY, b. July 21, 1934; B.A. with spl. honors, City Coll. N.Y., 19—; LL.B., J.D., Bklyn. Law Sch., 1959; M.B.A., L.I. U., 1969. Admitted to N.Y. bar, 1960, U.S. Supreme Ct. bar, 1968; corp. counsel, asst. to pres. Paramount Publications, 1966-70; asst. prof. bus. law Fordham U., 1970—; individual practice law, N.Y.C.; hearing officer transp. adminstrn. parking violations bur., N.Y.C. Mem. Am. Bus. Law Assn., Bklyn. Bar Assn., Am. Arbitration Assn. Contbr. articles to law jours. Home: 43 Gladstone Rd New Rochelle NY 10804 Office: Fordham U Rose Hill Campus Bronx NY 10458 Tel (212) 933-2233

FUCHSBERG, ABRAHAM, b. N.Y.C., July 6, 1915; B.A., Coll. City N.Y., 1935, M.S. in Edn., 1936; LL.B., J.D., St. John's U., 1950; partner Fuchsberg & Fuchsberg, N.Y.C., 1950—; lectr. in field. Chmn., bd. dirs. Mut. Housing Assn. Mem. Am., N.Y. State trial lawyers assns., Bronx Bar Assn. Editor-in-chief Trial Lawyers Quar., 1973—. Home: 3850 Sedgwick Ave New York City NY 10463 Office: 250 Broadway New York City NY 10007 Tel (212) WO2-2800

FUGAZZI, FRED EDWARD, JR., b. Lexington, Ky., July 30, 1947; B.S., U. Ky., 1969, J.D., 1972. Admitted to Ky. bar, 1972; mem. firm Brown Sledd & McCann, Lexington, Ky., 1972, Landrum Patterson & Dickey, Lexington, 1972-75; asst. fed. pub. defender Eastern dist. Ky., Lexington, 1975—. Mem. Am., Fayette County bar assns. Home: 225 Catalpa St Lexington KY 40502 Office: POB 1489 111 Church St Lexington KY 40501 Tel (606) 252-2312

FUJIWARA, GARY YORITOSHI, b. Waialua, Oahu, Hawaii, May 9, 1918; student, Waseda Univ. Law Sch., Tokyo, 1940-41; LL.B., Yale, 1951, J.D., 1971. Admitted to Hawaii bar, 1952, 9th Circuit Ct. Appeals bar, 1957, U.S. Supreme Ct. bar, 1957; naturalization examiner U.S. Immigration & Naturalization Service, Honolulu, 1954-60, gen. atty., 1960-75, trial atty., 1975—. Mem. Hawaii Bar Assn. Recipient Outstanding Performance award U.S. Immigration & Naturalization Service, 1965. Home: 1561 Kanunu St Apartment 1405 Honolulu HI 96814 Office: 595 Ala Moana Blvd Honolulu HI 96813 Tel (808) 546-2149

FUKUSHIMA, YASUTAKA, b. Honolulu, June 3, 1916; B.A., U. Hawaii, 1937; J.D., Harvard, 1940. Admitted to Hawaii bar, 1940; practiced in Honolulu, 1940-67; judge Hawaii Circuit Ct., 1st Circuit, 1967—; asst. pub. prosecutor City and County of Honolulu, 1948-49; del. Hawaii Constl. Conv., 1949; mem. Hawaii Territorial Ho. of Reps., 1950-59, Hawaii Senate, 1959-66. Mem. Hawaii, Am. bar assns., Am. Judicature Soc. Home: 2386 E Manoa Rd Honolulu HI 96822 Office: Judiciary Bldg Honolulu HI 96813 Tel (808) 537-6556

FULD, STANLEY HOWELLS, b. N.Y.C., Aug. 23, 1903; B.A., N.Y.C. Coll., 1923, LL.D., 1972; LL.B., Columbia, 1926, LL.D., 1959; LL.D., Hamilton Coll., 1949, Union Coll., 1961, N.Y. U., 1963, Syracuse U., 1967, others. Admitted to N.Y. bar, 1926, U.S. Supreme Ct. bar, 1933; asst. dist. atty. N.Y. County, chief Indictment, Appeals Burs., 1935-44; partner firm Hartman, Craven & Fuld, N.Y.C., 1944-46; asso. judge Ct. Appeals, N.Y., 1946-66; chief judge State N.Y., Ct. Appeals, Albany, 1967-73; spl. counsel firm Kaye, Scholer, Fierman, Hays & Handler, N.Y.C., 1974—; dir. Greater N.Y. Mut. Ins. Co.; chmn. Nat. Comm. New Tech. Uses of Copyrighted Works, Washington, 1975—; Nat. News Council, N.Y.C., 1974-76, New

York Fair Trial Free Press Conf., 1967-73. Bd. visitors Columbia Law Sch., 1951—; chmn., bd. dirs. Jewish Theol. Sem. Am., N.Y.C., 1966-74; bd. dirs. Beth Israel Med. Center, N.Y.C., 1971—; chmn. bd. visitors City Coll. N.Y., 1973—; bd. dirs. Benjamin N. Cardozo Sch. Law Yeshiva U., 1976—; Fellow Am. Acad. Arts Scis.; mem. Am., N.Y. State, N.Y.C., bar, assns., N.Y. County Lawyers Assn., Order Coif (hon.). Recipient chief justice Hardan Fiske Stone award Assn. N.Y. Trial Lawyers, 1966, medal for excellence Columbia Law Sch. Alumni Assn., 1967, John Peter Zenger award N.Y. Soc. Newspaper Editors, 1970, John H. Finley award Alumni Assn. City Coll. N.Y., 1971, Earl Warren medal Jewish Theol. Sem. Am., 1972, Martin Luther King medal City Coll. N.Y. 1974, others. Mem. Order of Coif. Bd. editors N.Y. Law Jour., 1976—; contbr. numerous articles to legal jours. Home: 211 E 70th St New York City NY 10021 Office: 425 Park Ave New York City NY 10022 Tel (212) 759-8400

FULK, WINTON DREW, b. Oak Park, Ill., July 5, 1938; B.E.E., Ill. Inst. Tech., 1962; J.D., Chgo.-Kent Coll. Law, 1969. Admitted to Ill. bar, 1970, U.S. Supreme Ct. bar, 1973; prin. elec. engr. Met. San. Dist. of Chgo., also individual practice law, Skokie, Ill., 1970—; atty. Luth. Gen. Hosp., Park Ridge, Ill., 1971—; mem. Am. Arbitration Assn. Panel of Judges, Chgo., 1975—. Mem. Skokie Mayor's Commn. for Beautification and Improvement, 1970-71. Mem. Ill. State Bar Assn., Delta Theta Phi. Registered profl. engr. Home and Office: 9451 N Kostner Ave Skokie IL 60076 Tel (312) 676-2170

FULKER, JOHN EDWARD, b. Troy, Ohio, Apr. 13, 1929; B.A., Miami U., 1950; J.D., Columbia, 1953. Admitted to Ohio bar, 1953, Fed. bar, 1957; individual practice law, Troy, 1953-72; partner firm Faust, Harrelson, Fulker & McCarthy, Troy, 1972—; asst. prosecuting atty. Miami County, Ohio, 1954-64. Mem. Am., Ohio State, Miami County (pres. 1970) bar assns., Ohio Acad. Trial Lawyers, Assn. Trial Lawyers Am. Home: 1270 Pine St Troy OH 45373 Office: 12 S Cherry St Troy OH 45373 Tel (513) 335-3887

FULLAGAR, WILLIAM WATTS, b. Chgo., July 3, 1914; B.S., Northwestern U., 1937; LL.B., Chgo.-Kent Coll. Law, 1942. Admitted to Ill. bar, 1942; partner firm Rooks, Pitts, Fullagar and Poust, and predecessors, Chgo. Mem. Am., Ill., Chgo. bar assns. Home: 2320 Isabella St Evanston IL 60201 Office: 208 S LaSalle St Chicago IL 60604 Tel (312) 372-5600

FULLEM, JOSEPH WILLIAM, JR., b. Utica, N.Y., Jan. 23, 1938; B.A., U. Notre Dame, 1959; J.D., Villanova U., 1962. Admitted to Pa. bar, 1963; asso. firm Bennett, Bricklin & Saltzburg, Phila., 1963-66, partner firm, 1967—; lectr. in field. Mem. Notre Dame Club Phila., Am., Pa., Phila. bar assns., Def. Research Inst., Phila. Assn. Def. Counsel, Lawyer's Club Phila., Am. Arbitration Assn. Home: 4115 Meadow Ln Newtown Sq PA 19073 Office: 1700 Market St Suite 1800 Philadelphia PA 19103 Tel (215) 561-4300

FULLEM, LAWRENCE ROBERT, b. Jersey City, Aug. 16, 1929; B.A., Colgate U., 1951; LL.B., Harvard U., 1954. Admitted to D.C. bar, 1954, N.Y. State bar, 1958; mem. firm Dewey, Ballantine, Bushby, Palmer & Wood, N.Y.C., 1958-63, partner firm, 1963—; dir. Tesoro Petroleum Corp., San Antonio, Commonwealth Oil Refining Co., Inc., San Antonio. Mem. Am. Bar Assn., N.Y. State Bar Assn., Assn. Bar City N.Y. Home: 236 Upper Mountain Ave Upper Montclair NJ 07043 Office: Dewey Ballantine et al 140 Broadway New York City NY 10005 Tel (212) 344-8000

FULLER, DAVID OTIS, JR., b. Grand Rapids, Mich., May 28, 1939; A.B., Wheaton Coll., 1961; J.D., Harvard, 1964; certificate in French, U. Paris, 1966. Admitted to Mich. bar, 1964, N.Y. bar, 1967, U.S. Supreme Ct. bar, 1968; asso. firm Amberg, Law & Fallon, Grand Rapids, 1964-65; asst. dist. atty. N.Y. County, 1966-72; law sec. to justice Supreme Ct. N.Y. County, 1972-73; legal dept. Pan Am. World Airways, Inc., N.Y.C., 1973-74, The Readers Digest Assn., Inc., N.Y.C., 1974—; counsel Tuckahoe (N.Y.) Parking Authority, 1975—. Bd. dirs. Heartsease Home, Inc., 1971-76. Mem. Am., N.Y. State bar assns., Assn. Bar City N.Y. Contbr. articles to legal jours. Home: 4 Gifford St Tuckahoe NY 10707 Office: 200 Park Ave New York City NY 10017 Tel (212) 972-6180

FULLER, DAVID WILBUR, b. Southwest Harbor, Maine, Jan. 5, 1907; A.B., U. Maine, 1928; postgrad. Harvard Law Sch., 1928-30. Admitted to Maine bar, 1932; individual practice law, Bangor, Maine, 1931-42, 45—; house counsel Webber Oil Co., Bangor, 1954—; mem. city council city of Bangor, 1946-48; mem. Maine Ho. of Reps., 1951-54; mem. legis. research commn., 1951-52. Mem. Am., Maine, Penobscot County (Maine) bar assns. Office: 96 Harlow St Bangor ME 04401 Tel (207) 942-8384

FULLER, DONALD ORIN, b. Mesa, Ariz., Mar. 18, 1945; B.S., Ariz. State U., 1969, J.D., 1972. Admitted to Ariz. bar, 1972; partner firm Smith, Riggs, Buckley, Riggs & Fuller, Mesa, Ariz., 1972—. Mem. Tri-City (dir.), Ariz. (mem. com. creditors and debtors rights) bar assns. Office: 231 N Alma School Rd Mesa AZ 85201 Tel (602) 834-3344

FULLER, PERRY LUCIAN, b. Central City, Nebr., Oct. 26, 1922; student U. Chgo. Law Sch., 1946-47; B.A., U. Nebr., 1947, J.D., 1949. Admitted to Ill. bar, 1950, U.S. Supreme Ct. bar, 1960; sr. partner firm Hinshaw, Culbertson, Moelmann, Hoban & Fuller, Chgo., 1956—; lectr. U. Chgo. Law Sch., 1970-76. Chmn., Cook County Civil Service Commn., 1967-69; spl. asst. atty. gen. Ill. Hwy. Trust Authority, 1969-70, Ill. Dept. Mental Health, 1970-72; commr. Ill. Law Enforcement, 1972-73, mem. exec. com., 1973, standing com. on cts., 1972-73; trustee Legal Defenders, Inc.; pres. Law in Am. Soc. Found. Fellow Am. Bar Found.; mem. Am., Fed., Ill., Chgo., DuPage County bar assns., Am. Coll. Trial Lawyers, Ill. Soc. Trial Lawyers (pres. 1977), Am. Judicature Soc., Am. Law Inst., Bar Assn. 7th Fed. Circuit, Def. Research Inst., Internat. Assn. Ins. Counsel, NAACP Legal Def. Fund, Scribes. Office: 69 W Washington St Suite 2700 Chicago IL 60602 Tel (312) 630-4408

FULLER, ROBERT ARMSTRONG, b. N.Y.C., Jan. 24, 1940; B.A., Dartmouth, 1961; LL.B., U. Pa., 1964. Admitted to Conn. bar, 1964, U.S. Dist. Ct. for Conn. bar, 1965, U.S. Supreme Ct. bar, 1971; asso. firm Keogh, Candee & Burkhart, Norwalk, Conn., 1965-69; asso. firm Schwartz & Knight, New Haven, 1969-70; partner firm Lovejoy, Cuneo & Curtis, Wilton, and Norwalk Conn., 1970—; asst. counsel Town of Wilton, 1971-73, counsel, 1973—. Mem. Charter revision commn., Wilton, 1971. Mem. Am., Conn. (mem. exec. com., planning & zoning sect.) bar assns. Office: 31 Center St Wilton CT 06897 Tel (203) 762-5536

FULLER, WARREN ROBERT, b. Chgo., Aug. 2, 1942; B.B.A., Loyola U., Chgo., 1965, J.D., 1967. Admitted to Ill. bar, 1967; asso. firm, Finn, VanMell & Penney, Chgo., 1967-69; asso. firm, Crowley & Goschi, Chgo., 1969—. Mem. Plan Commn. of the Village of South Barrington, Ill. Mem. Chgo. Bar Assn., Windemere Assn. (pres.). Home: 2738 Canterbury Ct South Barrington IL 60010 Office: 135 S La Salle St Chicago IL 60603 Tel (312) 372-3211

FULLER, WAYNE PAUL, b. Buhl, Idaho, Aug. 19, 1932; B.A. with great distinction, Stanford, 1954, LL.B., 1957. Admitted to Idaho bar, 1957; asso. firm Moffat and Thomas, Boise, Idaho, 1958; dep. pros. atty. Canyon County (Idaho), 1959-60; partner firm Fuller & Radke, and predecessors, Caldwell, Idaho, 1959—. Bd. dirs. Idaho Legal Aid Services, Inc., Boise, 1968—, pres., 1974-75; dist. chmn. canyon dist. Ore-Ida council Boy Scouts Am., 1974-75. Mem. Am., Idaho, 3rd Dist. (pres. 1971-72) bar assns. Contbr. article Idaho Law Rev. Home: 1910 Ray St Caldwell ID 83605 Office: Box 130 Caldwell ID 83605 Tel (208) 459-1681

FULLER, WILLIS, JR., b. Athens, Ga., Oct. 16, 1940; B.S. in Bus. Adminstrn., The Citadel, 1962; LL.B., U. S.C., 1965. Admitted to S.C. bar, 1965; served with JAG, USAF, 1965-68; asso. firm Altman & Fuller and predecessors, North Charleston, 1969-70, partner, 1970—. Bd. dirs. Charleston Legal Assistance Program, 1974-75; chmn. Charleston Democratic Party, 1973. Mem. Am., S.C. trial lawyers assns., S.C., Charleston County bar assns., Charleston C. of C. (dir. 1976). Home: 9 St Michael's Alley Charleston SC 29401 Office: 3972 Rivers Ave N Charleston SC 29405 Tel (803) 554-6664

FULLERTON, BYRON, b. Aug. 18, 1922; B.S., U. Tex., 1946, LL.B., 1956; M.Ed., U. Colo., 1950. Tchr. pub. schs.; admitted to bar; asst. atty. gen. State of Tex.; asst. prof. law U. Tex., Austin, 1963-69, asso. prof., 1969—, asst. dean Sch. Law, 1963-69, asso. dean, 1969—. Mem. Nat. Advisory Council for Edn. Professions Devel., 1970, Nat. Advisory Council on Extension and Continuing Edn., 1972; mem. advisory bd. Children's Home, Cherokee, Tex.; state co-chmn. Tex. Hi-Y Youth and Govt. Model Legislature; bd. dirs. Adult Probation Project of Travis County (Tex.). Mem. Travis County, Am. bar assns., State Bar Tex. (chmn. pub. relations), Assn. Continuing Legal Edn. Adminstrs., Phi Delta Kappa, Delta Theta Phi. Home: Route 2 PO Box 43 Liberty Hill TX 78642 Office: Dept of Law U of Tex Austin TX 78712

FULLERTON, PHILIP CHARLES, b. Chgo., Sept. 26, 1931; B.A., Duke, 1953; LL.D., Stanford, 1956. Admitted to Calif. bar, 1957, U.S. Supreme Ct. bar, 1976; asso. firm Kimble, Thomas, Snell, Jamison & Russell, Fresno, Calif., 1956-58; partner firm Fullerton, Lang, Richert & Patch and predecessors, Fresno, 1958—, sr. partner, 1958—; v.p. Stanford Law Fund, 1969-75; speaker Calif. Council Judges. Pres. Bullard chpt. Am. Field Service, 1976—, Multiple Sclerosis Soc. of Fresno, 1976—; treas. Fresno Mayor's Prayer Breakfast. Mem. State Bar Calif., Fresno County Bar Assn., Am. Bd. Trial Advs. Editorial bd. Stanford Law Rev., 1955. Office: Suite 500 United Calif Bank Bldg Fresno CA 93721 Tel (209) 486-3011

FULLERTON, ROBERT PERINE, b. Denver, Apr. 1, 1929; A.B., Dartmouth Coll., 1951; LL.B., U. Denver, 1954. Admitted to Colo. bar, 1955; individual practice law, Denver, 1955-58; judge Denver County (Colo.) Ct., 1958-63, Denver Dist. Ct., 1963-65, 73—, Colo. Dist. U.S. Bankruptcy Ct., Denver, 1965-73; lectr. Nat. Seminar Bankruptcy Judges; instr. law Met. State Coll., U. Denver; commr. uniform state laws, 1977. Pres. Crestmoor Homeowners Assn., Denver, 1976—; exec. com. Denver area council Boy Scouts Am., Denver, 1972—. Mem. Colo., Denver bar assns., Dist. Judges Assn. Named Outstanding Young Man, Jr. C. of C., 1963. Office: City-County Bldg Denver CO 80202 Tel (303) 297-3604

FULLIN, JAMES LAWRENCE, b. Newark, Ohio, Feb. 23, 1923; B.A., John Carroll U., 1944; LL.B. (now J.D.) Ohio State U., 1947. Admitted to Ohio bar, 1948; research atty. Ohio Case Revision Commn., 1948-53; atty., examiner, adminstrv. asst. Pub. Utilities Commn. of Ohio, Columbus, 1953-63; sr. counsel, asst. sec. Columbia Gas Distbn. Co., Columbus, 1963—. Mem. Am., Ohio, Columbus bar assns. Office: 99 N Front St Columbus OH 43215 Tel (614) 460-2553

FULLINGIM, JACKIE WORTH, b. Lorenzo, Tex., July 24, 1928; B.A., Howard Payne U., 1949; J.D., U. Tex., Austin, 1956. Admitted to Tex. bar, 1955, U.S. Dist. Ct. No. Dist. Tex. bar, 1957, U.S. Dist. Ct. Western Dist. Tex. bar, 1965, U.S. Ct. Appeals 5th Circuit bar, 1972; since practiced in Lubbock, Tex., asst. city atty., 1956-62, 73—; dist. counsel SBA, 1962-70; partner firm Fullingim & Fullingim, 1970-73. Mem. Exec. Council Second Baptist Ch., 1963-64, (mem. publicity com. 1975—). Mem. Tex., Lubbock County bar assns., Alpha Chi. Home: 3024 67th St Lubbock TX 79413 Office: PO Box 2000 Lubbock TX 79413 Tel (806) 762-6411

FULTON, GEORGE CLYDE, b. Astoria, Oreg., Mar. 14, 1919; LL.B., Northwestern Coll., 1952. Admitted to Oreg. bar, 1953; partner firm Anderson, Fulton, Lavis & VanThiel, Astoria, Oreg., 1968—. Mem. Oreg., Am. bar assns. Home: 1050 34th St Astoria OR 97103 Office: 968 Commercial St Astoria OR 97103 Tel (503) 325-5911

FULTZ, ROBERT EDWARD, b. Columbus, Ohio, May 24, 1941; B.A. cum laude, Ohio State U., 1963; J.D. with distinction, U. Mich., 1965. Admitted to Ohio bar, 1966; partner firm Wright, Harlor, Morris & Arnold, Columbus, 1971—. Trustee, pres. Central Community House; past trustee, sec. United Cerebral Palsy of Columbus, Franklin County, Ohio; trustee Columbus Law Library Assn.; gov. Goodwill Industries Central Ohio; active Upper Arlington Civic Assn., Ohio Hist. Soc., Colo. Hist. Found., Inc. Mem. Columbus, Ohio State, Am. bar assns., Ohio State U. Assn., U. Mich. Alumni Assn., Phi Beta Kappa, Delta Upsilon. Home: 4630 Burbank Dr Columbus OH 43220 Office: 37 W Broad St Columbus OH 43215 Tel (614) 224-4125

FUNAKI, JAMES TAMIO, b. Olaa, Hawaii, May 20, 1930; A.B., Grinnell Coll., 1952; M.B.A., U. Mich., 1953, J.D., 1959. Admitted to Hawaii bar, 1959; with firm Okumura, Takushi, Funaki & Wee, and predecessors, Honolulu, asso., 1959-63, partner, 1963—; atty. Hawaii Ho. of Reps., 1963-64, chief atty., 1965—; atty. Hawaii Constl. Conv., 1968; atty. Hawaii Legis. Reapportionment Commn., 1973. Mem. Am., Hawaii bar assns. Home: 374 Puamamane Honolulu HI 96821 Office: 1015 Bishop St Honolulu HI 96813 Tel (808) 536-1791

FUNK, LARRY EDWARD, b. Washington, Oct. 4, 1947; B.A., U. Md., 1969, J.D., 1972. Admitted to Md. bar, 1972, D.C. bar, 1974; served with JAGC, U.S. Air Force, 1973-77; atty. Washington Gas Light Co., 1977—. lectr. bus. law Belleville Area Coll., 1974-76, Park Coll., 1975-76, U. Md., 1976—. Mem. Am., Md., D.C. bar assns., Phi Beta Kappa. Contbr. article to legal jour. Office: Law Dept Washington Gas Light Co 11th and J Sts NW Washington DC 20001

FUNK, MARY VASHTI (JONES), b. Duncan Falls, Ohio, Aug. 19, 1896; B.Ph., Denison U., 1917; student Ohio State U., 1924. Admitted to Ohio bar, 1923, U.S. Supreme Ct. bar, 1936; mem. firm Jones, Jones & Goldcamp, Zanesville, Ohio, 1923-41, Jones, Goldcamp & Funk, Zanesville, 1942-65, Jones, Funk & Payne, 1965—; mgr. Fed. Land Bank Assn. of Zanesville, 1927—. Advisory bd. Salvation Army, 1942—; bd. edn. Zanesville, 1948-60; bd. Avondale Children's Home, 1935-40; advisory bd. Ohio U., Zanesville, 1974—; trustee Bethesda Hosp., 1974—; trustee, v.p. Bethesda Hosp. Found. Mem. Muskingum County Assn., Ohio Fedn. Bus. Profl. Womens Clubs (state pres.), Ohio Fedn. Farm Loan Assns. (state pres.), Phi Alpha Delta, Delta Omicron, Delta Kappa Gamma, Kappa Alpha Theta. Home: 1251 Marwood Dr Zanesville OH 43701 Office: 45 N 4th St Zanesville OH 43701 Tel (614) 452-5403

FUNK, OTTO EUGENE, b. Funk's Lake, Ill., May 19, 1916; B.S., U. Ill., 1938, LL.B., 1940, J.D., 1968. Admitted to Ill. bar, 1940; individual practice law, Hillsboro, Ill., 1940-48; law clk. U.S. Circuit Ct. Appeals, Chgo., 1942; states atty. Montgomery County (Ill.), 1948-68; individual practice law, Hillsboro, 1968—; founder and pres. Security Savs. and Loan Assn., Hillsboro, 1962—, Fidelity Loan Corp., Hillsboro. Mem. Ill., Montgomery County bar assns., Ill. States Attys. Assn. (pres. 1960). Office: Courthouse Sq Hillsboro IL 62049 Tel (217) 532-2177

FUNKHOUSER, DAVID EDWARD, b. Fort Madison, Iowa, Nov. 11, 1941; B.B.A., U. Iowa, 1964, J.D., 1967. Admitted to Iowa bar, 1967; law clk. to Justice Supreme Ct. Iowa, Des Moines, 1967-68; partner firm Brown, Kinsey & Funkhouser, Mason City, Iowa, 1968—; mem. Iowa Supreme Ct. Commn. on Continuing Legal Edn., 1975-79. Civil service commr., Mason City, 1972—; bd. dirs. Mason City Pub. Library, 1974—. Mem. Iowa Acad. Trial Lawyers, Iowa Assn. Trial Lawyers, Am., Iowa bar assns. Contbr. articles to legal jours. Home: 231 Lakeview Dr Mason City IA 50401 Office: 19 1/2 E State St Mason City IA 50401 Tel (515) 423-6223

FURCOLO, FOSTER, b. New Haven, July 29, 1917; B.A., Yale, 1933, LL.B., 1936. Admitted to Mass. bar, 1937; partner firm Noonan & Furcolo, Springfield, Mass.; mem. 81st-82d Congresses from 2d Mass. Dist.; treas. State of Mass., 1952-55, gov., 1957-61; asst. dist. atty. Middlesex County (Mass.), 1967-73; U.S. adminstrv. law judge, 1975—; Commonwealth prof. Mass. State Coll. System, 1973-75. Author: Let George Do It; Pills, People, Problems; Rendezvous at Katyn; Law for You. Decorated knight comdr. Order of Polonia Restituta (Free Poland), Star of Solidarity (Italy), St. Dennis of Zante medal (Greece). Address: 11-11 Stearns Hill Waltham MA 02154

FURDOCK, RONALD MICHAEL, b. DuBois, Pa., Jan. 3, 1941; A.A., Otero Jr. Coll., 1960; B.A., Colo. Coll., 1962; J.D., Dickinson Sch. Law, 1965; postgrad. Armed Forces Staff Coll., 1971-72, Indiana (Pa.) U., 1965-66, U. Tex., 1975-76. Admitted to Pa. bar, 1965, N.J. bar, 1974, Ct. Mil. Appeals bar, 1966; commd. lt. j.g. U.S. Navy, 1965, advanced through grades to lt. comdr., 1971; asst. legal officer Naval Air Sta., Pensacola, Fla., 1966-68; dep. judge adv. Comdr. Naval Air Basic Tng., Pensacola, 1968; legal officer U.S.S. Independence, 1969-70, Naval Sta., Mayport, Fla., 1970-71; staff judge adv. Commandant 4th Naval Dist., Phila., 1972-75; counsel for naval petroleum and oil shale reserves, Colo., Utah and Wyo., 1975—. Pres., Clearfield County (Pa.) Young Republicans, 1964-65; wrestling coach Woodbury Heights Boys Club, Gloucester County, N.J., 1972-75 asst. wrestling coach Lanier High Sch., Austin, Tex., 1975-76. Mem. Am., Pa., N.J. bar assns. Office: Naval Petroleum and Oil Shale Reserves Casper WY Tel (307) 265-5550 X5411

FUREY, SHERMAN FRANCIS, JR., b. Pocatello, Idaho, June 1, 1919; B.A., U. Idaho, 1946, LL.B., 1947. Admitted to Idaho bar, 1947; asst. atty. gen. State of Idaho, Boise, 1947-48; asst. U.S. atty. for Dist. Idaho, Dept. Justice, Boise, 1948-49, U.S. atty., 1953-57, 69-70; partner firm Doane & Furey, Boise, 1949-51; individual practice law, Salmon, Idaho, 1951-53, 57-69, 70—; mayor City of Salmon, 1959-61. Mem. Idaho State Bar Assn. (chmn. com. on unauthorized practice of law 1960-64, chmn. citizens com. legis. compensation 1976—). Home: POB 1127 Salmon ID 83467 Office: POB 1127 New Thrasher Bldg Salmon ID 83467 Tel (208) 756-2577

FURIN, GARY CARL, b. Berea, Ohio, Apr. 15, 1938; A.B., John Carroll U., 1959; J.D., Duke, 1963. Admitted to Ga. bar, 1964, U.S. Supreme Ct. bar, 1977; asso. firm Wilson, Branch, Barwick & Vandiver, Atlanta, 1963-66; gen. counsel and asst. sec. United Trust Life Ins. Co., Atlanta, 1966-67; asso. firm Lipshutz, Macey, Zusmann & Sikes, Atlanta, 1967-69, partner, 1970-72; individual practice law, Atlanta, 1972—. Pres. Serra Club of Met. Atlanta, 1974-75, trustee, 1975—; mem. Cathedral Parish Council, 1970—, chmn., 1972-73, 77—; chmn. Atlanta John Carroll U. Alumni, 1969—. Mem. Am., Ga., Atlanta bar assns., Lawyers Club Atlanta, Assn. Immigration and Nationality Lawyers (sec. Atlanta chpt. 1974-77). Author: Legal Considerations with Respect to Formation of a REIT, 1970; Immigration Law: Alien Employment Certification, 1977. Home: 2837 Alpine Rd NE Atlanta GA 30305 Office: 2970 Peachtree Rd NW Atlanta GA 30305 Tel (404) 262-2962

FURLONG, ROBERT STAFFORD, b. St. John's, Nfld., Can., Dec. 9, 1904; attended St. Bonaventure's Coll., St. John's; read law with James L. McGrath. Called to Nfld. bar, 1926, created king's counsel, 1944; chief justice Nfld. Ct. Appeal, Supreme Ct., 1959—; appt. mem. Bd. Broadcast Govs. of Can., 1958. Mem. Law Soc. Nfld. (past treas.), Nfld. Hist. Soc., Medico-Legal Soc. (London), Royal Commonwealth Soc. (London). Decorated comdr. Order Brit. Empire, knight comdr. Order St. Gregory, officer Order St. John of Jerusaleum. Home: Winter Ave Saint John's NF Canada Office: Law Courts Saint John's NF Canada*

FURLOW, WALTER SAMUEL, JR., b. Rochester, Minn., Aug. 5, 1925; A.B., Princeton U., 1945; LL.B., Harvard, 1951. Admitted to D.C. bar, 1951, Md. bar, 1953; asst. counsel Bur. Ships, Dept. Navy, Washington, 1951-55; partner firm Lambert, Furlow, Elmore & Heidenberger, and predecessors, Washington, 1955—; lectr. wills and trusts Cath. U. Am., 1975—. Mem. Am., Fed., Md., D.C. bar assns. Home: 7925 Orchid St NW Washington DC 20012 Office: 1629 K St NW Suite 200 Washington DC 20006 Tel (202) 296-7080

FURMAN, JOHN PRYOR, b. Newark, Nov. 4, 1920; A.B. summa cum laude, Princeton U., 1942; LL.B. cum laude, Yale U., 1946; M.A., Am. U., 1954. Admitted to D.C. bar, 1946, U.S. Supreme Ct. bar, 1954, Md. bar, 1959; economist Office Internat. Trade Policy, U.S. Dept. State, 1946-48, atty-adv. Legal Adviser's Office, 1949-56; economic cons. Foster Assos., Inc., Washington, 1956-62, gen. mgr., 1958-62; individual practice law, Washington, 1962—; legal adv. to U.S. dels. to conf. of deputy fgn. ministers Austria, 1949, intergovtl. study group on Germany, 1950-51; asso. counsel Pres. Com. to Study U.S. Mil. Assistance Program, 1959. Mem. exec. com. Princeton U. Grad. Council, 1943-45, mem. Princeton U. Fund, 1946; pres.

Western Bethesda (Md.) Community Planning Assn., 1958-59. Mem. Am. (Ross Prize Essay award 1957), Fed., Fed. Energy bar assns., Am. Soc. Internat. Law. Editor-in-chief Yale Law Jour., 1944-45; contbr. articles to profl. jours. Office: 1701 Pennsylvania Ave NW Washington DC 20006 Tel (202) 298-8700

FURRER, PATRICK JAMES, b. Medford, Oreg., Mar. 10, 1942; B.S., U. Oreg., 1964; J.D., U. Pacific, 1971. Admitted to Oreg. bar, 1971, Calif. bar, 1971; individual practice law, Tigard, Oreg., 1971—. Bd. dirs. Com. Experiences for Career Edn., Inc., 1976—. Mem. C. of C., Am., Washington County bar assns. Co-editor: Continuing Legal Edn.; Oreg. State Bar-Land Use Planning, 1975-76. Home: 8720 SW Fannowood Ln Beaverton OR 97005 Office: 12492 SW Main St Tigard OR 97223 Tel (503) 620-4540

FURTH, ALAN COWAN, b. Oakland, Calif., Sept. 16, 1922; A.B., U. Calif. at Berkeley, 1944, LL.B., 1949; grad. Advanced Mgmt. Program, Harvard, 1959. Admitted to Cal. bar. U.S. Supreme Ct. bar; with S.P. Co., 1949—, gen. counsel, 1963—, now exec. v.p.-law, also dir.; dir., mem. exec. com. St. Louis Southwestern Rwy. Co.; gen. counsel Pacific Motor Trucking Co., So. Pacific Land Co., So. Pacific Pipe Lines, Inc. Trustee Head-Royce Schs., Pomona Coll., Human Resources Research Orgn. Mem. Am. (council pub. utilities sect.), San Francisco bar assns., State Bar Cal., Assn. ICC Practitioners, San Francisco C. of C. (bd. dirs. 1967-69). Home: 54 Sotelo Av Piedmont CA 94611 Office: 1 Market St San Francisco CA 94105*

FUSCO, ANDREW GENE, b. Punxsutawney, Pa., Jan. 11, 1948; B.S./B.A. in Finance, W.Va. U., 1970, J.D., 1973. Admitted to W.Va. Supreme Ct. Appeals bar, 1973, U.S. Supreme Ct. bar, 1977; individual practice law, Morgantown, 1973—; mem. firm Fusco & Newbraugh, Morgantown, W.Va., 1974-75; pros. atty. Monongalia County, W.Va., 1977—; instr. W.Va. U. Law Center and Coll. Commerce. Bd. dirs. W.Va. Career Colls., 1971—. Mem. Am., Monongalia County bar assns., W.Va. Bar, W.Va. State Bar, Am., W.Va. trial lawyers assns., Comml. Law League, Baker St. Irregulars of N.Y. Recipient Am. Jurisprudence award Bancroft-Whitney Pub. Co., 1971; editor, contbg. author: Twenty Feet From Glory (John R. Goodwin), 1970; Business Law (John R. Goodwin), 1972; Beyond Baker Street (Michael Harrison), 1976. Home: 158 Hoffman Ave Morgantown WV 26505 Office: 220 Pleasant St Morgantown WV 26505 Tel (304) 296-1793 also Courthouse Morgantown WV 26505 Tel (304) 292-6351

FUSCO, JOHN JOSEPH, b. N.Y.C., Sept. 11, 1931; B.B.A., Manhattan Coll., 1953; LL.B., St. John's U., 1958, J.D., 1968. Admitted to N.Y. bar, 1959; pvt. practice law, Yonkers, N.Y., 1959—. Asst. corp. counsel City of Yonkers, 1964-65; city justice City of Yonkers, 1967—; lt. def. counsel bds. spl. court martial USNR. Mem. N.Y. State, Westchester magistrates assns., N.Y. State, Westchester County bar assns., Assn. Trial Lawyers Am., Yonkers Lawyers Assn. Home: 7 Brook Rd Bronxville NY 10708 Office: 30 S Broadway Yonkers NY 10701

FUSCO, OTTO F., b. Phila., Jan. 1, 1912; B.A., Fordham Coll., 1937; LL.B., St. Johns U., 1940. Admitted to N.Y. bar, 1941; individual practice law, N.Y.C., 1941-70; partner firm Fusco & Fusco, Bronx, 1970—. Mem. Am., N.Y. State, Bronx bar assns., N.Y. State Trial Lawyers Assn., Am. Legion (post judge adv. 1946-65), Confederate War Vets. (post judge adv. 1946-66). Contbr. articles to profl. publs. Home: 31 Brendon Hill Rd Scarsdale NY 10583 Office: 196 E 161st St Bronx NY 10451 Tel (212) CY2-7711

FUSCO, RALPH LOUIS, b. Perth Amboy, N.J., June 8, 1911; LL.B., Rutgers U., 1934. Admitted to N.J. bar, 1936, Korean Supreme Ct. bar, 1945, U.S. Supreme Ct. bar, 1946; practiced in Perth Amboy, N.J., 1936-61; spl. prosecutor Bergen County (N.J.), 1954-55, Passaic County (N.J.), 1955-56; pres. Pub. Utilities Commn., Newark, 1956-61; mem. N.J. Gov's. Cabinet, 1959-61; judge Superior Ct., 1961—. Chmn. Perth Amboy (N.J.) Civil Defense, 1940-42; dir. Community Fund, Perth Amboy, 1946-50. Mem. Perth Amboy, Middlesex County (N.J.) (pres. 1954-55), N.J. State, Am. bar assns. Author: Manual on Municipal Court Practice, 1954. Home: 28 Eileen Way Edison NJ 08817 Office: 706 Essex County Cts Bldg Newark NJ 07102 Tel (201) 961-7277

FUSELIER, LOUIS ALFRED, b. New Orleans, Mar. 26, 1932; B.A., La. State U., 1953; LL.B. (now J.D.), Tulane U., 1959. Admitted to La. bar, 1959, Miss. bar, 1964, U.S. Supreme Ct. bar, 1965; atty. NLRB, New Orleans, 1959-62; partner firm Fuselier, Ott, McKee & Flowers, Jackson, Miss., 1962—. Mem. Miss Wildlife Fedn. (pres. 1975-76), Am., La., New Orleans, Miss., Hinds County, Fed. bar assns., Am. Law Inst. Miss. Bar Found., Jackson C. of C., Am. Judicature Soc. Accredited personnel diplomate. Office: 2100 Deposit Guaranty Plaza Jackson MS 39201 Tel (601) 948-2226

FUTRELL, TIM, b. Cadiz, Ky., Oct. 12, 1948; B.A., U. Ky., 1970; J.D., Harvard, 1973. Admitted to Ky. bar, 1973; law clk. to chief judge U.S. Ct. Appeals 6th Circuit, Ky., 1973-74; asso. firm Wyatt, Grafton & Sloss, Louisville, 1974; lectr. Vanderbilt U., 1973-74, U. Louisville, 1974-77; lectr. seminars. Chmn., Louisville UN Day Comn., 1976; trustee U. Ky., 1969-70, fellow, 1976. Mem. Am., Fed., Ky., Louisville bar assns. Home: 2308 Tuckaho Rd Louisville KY 40207 Office: 2800 Citizens Plaza Louisville KY 40202 Tel (502) 589-5235

FUTTERMAN, STANLEY NORMAN, b. N.Y.C., Aug. 18, 1940; A.B., Columbia, 1961; LL.B., Harvard, 1964, M.Pub.Adminstrn., 1969. Admitted to N.Y. State bar, 1966; law clk. to judge U.S. Ct. Appeals, Boston, 1964-65; spl. asst. to legal adviser U.S. Dept. State, Washington, 1965-67, asst. legal adviser for spl. polit. affairs, 1967-68, asst. legal adviser for East Asian and Pacific affairs, 1969-71; asso. prof. law N.Y.U., 1971-76, vis. prof. law U. Wis., Madison, 1976; asso. firm Poletti Freidin Prashker Feldman & Gartner, N.Y.C., 1976—. Treas. Larchmont (N.Y.) Democratic Com., 1974—. Mem. Assn. of Bar City N.Y., Am. Soc. Internat. Law. Contbg. author: The Constitution and the Conduct of Foreign Policy, 1976; None of Your Business, 1974. Home: 17 Cherry Ave Larchmont NY 10538 Office: 1185 Ave of Americas New York City NY 10036 Tel (212) 730-7373

FUZAK, VICTOR THADDEUS, b. Buffalo, Mar. 29, 1926; A.B., Williams Coll., 1948; LL.B., Harvard, 1951. Admitted to N.Y. State bar, 1952, U.S. Dist. Ct. Western Dist. N.Y. bar, 1954, U.S. Supreme Ct. bar, 1975; partner firm Hodgson, Russ, Andrews, Woods & Goodyear, Buffalo, 1951—; vis. instr. U. Buffalo, 1953-58; spl. hearing officer U.S. Dept. Justice, 1953-56; contbr. N.Y. Pattern Jury Instrns.; dir. Gaymar Industries, Inc., Kenford Co., Inc., Joseph Malecki, Inc.; counsel to Indsl. Power Consumers Conf. Mem. Am., Erie County bar assns., Am. Law Inst. Home: 3 Doncaster Rd Kenmore NY 14217 Office: 1800 One M & T Plaza Buffalo NY 14203 Tel (716) 856-4000

GAAR, NORMAN EDWARD, b. Kansas City, Mo., Sept. 29, 1929; student Baker U., 1947-49; A.B., U. Mich., 1955, J.D., 1956. Admitted to Mo. bar, 1957, Kans. bar, 1962, U.S. Supreme Ct. bar, 1969; asso. firm Stinson, Mag, Thomson, McEvers & Fizzell, Kansas City, Mo., 1956-59, partner, 1959—; mem. faculty N.Y. Practicing Law Inst., 1967-74; judge Westwood (Kans.) Municipal Ct., 1959-63; mayor City of Westwood, 1963-65; mem. Kans. Senate, 1965—, majority leader, 1976—. Mem. Kansas City, Mo., Am. bar assns., Kansas City Lawyers Assn. Home: 2340 W 51st St Shawnee Mission KS 66205 Office: 2100 Ten Main Center Kansas City MO 64105 Tel (816) 842-8600

GABBERT, MYRON DANIEL, JR., b. Chgo., Feb. 13, 1943; B.A., Bradley U., Peoria, Ill., 1967; J.D., U. Ill., 1967. Admitted to Ill. bar, 1967, Idaho bar, 1968; law clk. Idaho Supreme Ct., 1967-68; individual practice law, Boise, Idaho, 1968-70; partner firm Wallis, Chruchill & Gabbert, Boise, 1970-71; asso. firm Moffatt, Thomas, Barrett & Blanton, Boise, 1971-73; prin., 1973—. Mem. Idaho, Boise bar assns. Office: Box 829 Boise ID 83701 Tel (208) 345-2334

GABBERT, ROY ELLIS, b. Portsmouth, Ohio, Apr. 4, 1925; student Oahu U., 1946; B.A., Ohio State U., 1949, LL.B., 1951, J.D., 1967. Admitted to Ohio bar, 1952; individual practice law, West Union, Ohio, 1952-76; mem. firm. Gabbert & Caldwell, West Union, 1976—; librarian Adams County Law Library; asst. attorney gen. State of Ohio, 1959-63, spl. counsel, 1973—; dep. dir. Adams County Civil Def., 1960-70. Mayor, West Union, 1953; chmn. Adams County chpt. ARC, 1964; chmn. credentials com. Ohio Democratic Party, 1962, chmn. exec. com., 1959-63. Mem. Adams County (pres. 1970 sed. 1953—), Ohio (fellow) bar assns. Office: 301 N Market St West Union OH 45693 Tel (513) 544-2831

GABLE, G. ELLIS, b. Kerens, Tex., Mar. 7, 1905; life tchrs. certificate Northeastern State Coll., Tahlequah, Okla., 1922; J.D., Okla. U., 1926. Admitted to Okla. bar, 1926; since practiced in Tulsa, mem. firm Gable, Gotwals, Rubin, Fox, Johnson & Baker, 1946—; judge pro tempore Tulsa County Ct., 1938-39. Past mem. Tulsa Bd. Edn., pres., 1956-57; mem. Okla. State Regents for Higher Edn., 1958-76. Mem. Am. (mem. Fellows), Okla. (pres. 1954), Tulsa County (pres. 1949) bar assns., Phi Delta Phi. Home: 2004 E 38th St Tulsa OK 74105 Office: 2010 Fourth Nat Bank Bldg Tulsa OK 74119 Tel (918) 582-9201

GABRIEL, EBERHARD JOHN, b. Bucarest, Rumania, Mar. 22, 1942; B.A., St. Joseph's Coll. (Ind.), 1963; J.D., Georgetown U., 1966. Admitted to Md. bar, 1966, U.S. Supreme Ct. bar, 1972; atty. Fgn. Claims Settlement Commn., Washington, 1966-68; corp. counsel Govt. Employees Ins. Co., Washington, 1968-70; sr. v.p., gen. counsel, Govt. Employees Fin. Corp., Denver, 1970—; sec.-treas., dir. Indsl. Bank Savs. Guaranty Corp. Colo., Denver, 1973—. Mem. Am., Md. bar assns., Nat. Consumer Finance Assn. (mem. law forum), Lakewood (Colo.) C. of C. (chmn. civic affairs council 1974-75; govtl. affairs council 1975-76). Home: 7546 S Wadsworth Ct Littleton CO 80123 Office: 7751 W Alameda Ave POB 5555 Denver CO 80217 Tel (303) 237-6911

GABRIEL, GARY ELMER, b. Toledo, Ohio, Aug. 3, 1929; B.A., U. Toledo, 1950, J.D., 1955. Admitted to Ohio bar, 1956; practiced in Toledo, Ohio, 1956-70; judge Toledo Municipal Ct., 1970—. Mem. advisory bd. Vols. of Am., Toledo, 1972—; mem. exec. bd. Toledo Area council Boy Scouts Am., 1972—. Mem. Am., Ohio State, Lucas County (Ohio), Toledo bar assns., Am. Judges Assn., Ohio Municipal Judges Assn. Recipient Superior Jud. award Ohio Supreme Ct., 1975, 76. Home: 1715 Fallbrook Rd Toledo OH 43614 Office: 555 N Erie St Toledo OH 43624 Tel (419) 247-6053

GABRIELLI, DOMENICK L., b. Rochester, N.Y., Dec. 13, 1912; B.S., St. Lawrence U., 1936, LL.D., 1973; J.D., Albany Law Sch., 1936; LL.D., Union U., 1973, Bklyn. Law Sch., 1976; L.H.D., Siena Coll., 1975. Admitted to N.Y. bar, 1937; corp. counsel City of Bath, 1940-53; dist. atty. Steuben County, N.Y., 1953-57, county judge, 1957-61; justice N.Y. Supreme Ct., 1957-61, mem. appellate divs., 1967-72; judge N.Y. Ct. Appeals, Bath, 1973—. Mem. Am., N.Y. State, Steuben County bar assns., Am. Law Inst. Home: 120 W Washington St Bath NY 14810 Office: 19 E Pulteney Sq Bath NY 14810 Tel (607) 776-7005

GABY, GENE PAUL, b. Greeneville, Tenn., Sept. 15, 1942; J.D., Tusculum Coll. U. Tenn., 1966. Admitted to Tenn. bar, 1966; partner firm Milligan, Coleman, Fletcher and Gaby, Greeneville, 1966—. Mem. Greene County (Tenn.) Tenn., Am. bar assns. Home: Route 8 POB 36 Greeneville TN 37743 Office: 1st Nat Bank Bldg Greeneville TN 37743 Tel (615) 638-4159

GADBOIS, RICHARD ARTHUR, JR., b. Omaha, June 18, 1932; A.B., St. John's Coll., 1954; J.D., Loyola U., Los Angeles, 1958; postgrad. in legal study U. So. Calif., 1958-60. Admitted to Calif. bar, 1959, U.S. Supreme Ct. bar, 1966; dep. atty. gen., Los Angeles, 1959-60; asso. firm Forster, Gemmill & Farmer, Los Angeles, 1960-62; partner firm Musick, Peeler & Garrett, Los Angeles, 1962-68; v.p., gen. counsel, sec. Denny's Inc., La Mirada, Calif., 1968-71; judge Municipal Ct., Los Angeles, 1971-72, Superior Ct. Los Angeles County, 1972—; bd. dirs. Legal Aid Found.; bd. dirs. Regional Criminal Justice Planning Commn. Mem. Am., Los Angeles County (trustee 1966-67) bar assns., Conf. Calif. Judges (chmn. juvenile cts. com.). Office: 111 N Hill St Los Angeles CA 90012 Tel (213) 974-1234

GADDIS, LARRY ROY, b. Pratt, Kans., Nov. 8, 1941; B.A., U. Colo., 1963, J.D., 1969. Admitted to Colo. bar, 1969; staff atty. Pikes Peak Legal Services, Colorado Springs, 1969-71, dir., 1971-73; partner firm Walta, Gaddis & Kin, Colorado Springs, 1973—; instr. police sci. El Paso Community Coll., Colorado Springs; vis. lectr. U. Colo., 1973, 74. Bd. dirs. Pikes Peak Family Counseling and Mental Health Center, Colorado Springs, 1972—, pres., 1974; chmn. allocations United Way, Colorado Springs, 1973-76. Mem. Am., Colo. (gov. 1976—), El Paso County (trustee) bar assns., Phi Kappa Alpha. Office: Suite 220 105 E Vermijo St Colorado Springs CO 80903 Tel (303) 471-3848

GADY, NATHAN DAVID, b. Pitts., Apr. 11, 1924; B.S., U. Pitts., 1950; J.D., Pepperdine U., 1970. Engr., Bucyrus Erie Co., Erie, Pa., 1955-58; admitted to Calif. bar, 1971; prof. law Western State U., Calif., 1971-76; judge pro-tempore Westminster and Habor Dist., Calif., 1973-75; individual practice law, Anaheim, Calif., 1971—. Mem. Orange County Bar Assn. Home: 1421 E Bell Ave Anaheim CA 92805 Office: 2030 W Lincoln Ave Anaheim CA 92801 Tel (714) 956-1702

GAEDE, ANTON HENRY, JR., b. Charlotte, N.C., Dec. 20, 1939; B.S., Yale U., 1961; LL.B., Duke U., 1964. Admitted to Ala. bar, 1964; asso. firm Bradley, Arant, Rose & White, Birmingham, Ala., 1964-71, partner, 1971—; lectr. U. Ala. Law Sch., 1969—. Pres., Community, Inc., 1972-76, v.p., 1976—. Mem. Am., Ala. (constrn. com., com. on correctional Instns. and procedures labor law sect.), Birmingham (grievance com.) bar assns. Contbr. article to legal jour. Mem. editorial bd. Duke Law Jour. Office: 1500 Brown-Mark Bldg Birmingham AL 35203 Tel (205) 252-4500

GAERTNER, GARY M., b. St. Louis, Aug. 11, 1937; J.D., St. Louis U., 1961. Admitted to Mo. bar, 1961, Ill. bar, 1966, U.S. Supreme Ct. bar, 1965; individual practice law, St. Louis, 1961-64, asst. city counselor, St. Louis, 1961-64, asso. city counselor, 1964-67, city counselor, 1968-69; judge Circuit Ct. of Mo., St. Louis, 1969—, juvenile judge, 1972-75. Dist. chmn., mem. exec. bd. Boy Scouts Am.; chmn. Mo. Council on Criminal Justice. Mem. Am., Mo. Met. St. Louis bar assns., Khoury Internat. League (v.p.), Mo. Council Juvenile Ct. judges, Lawyers Assn. of St. Louis, Am. Judicature Soc. Contbr. articles to profl. jours. Office: Civil Cts Bldg St Louis MO 63101 Tel (314) 453-3011

GAFFNEY, BILL GRANT, b. Texarkana, Tex., June 16, 1922; LL.B., So. Meth. U., 1949. Admitted to Tex. bar, 1949; founder Nat. Claims Service, also gen. counsel, 1954; pres. Wright Land Co., Houston, 1962—. Nat. dir. U.S. Jaycees, 1956-62; pres. Internat. Knights of Round Table, 1964. Mem. Am., Tex., Houston bar assns., Comml. Law League Am. Home: 10118 Lynbrook Hollow St Houston TX 77042 Office: 4801 Richmond Ave Nat Claims Bldg Houston TX 77027 Tel (713) 621-5181

GAFFORD, FRANCIS JOHNS, b. Phillipsburg, N.J., Dec. 31, 1909; A.B. summa cum laude, Lafayette Coll., 1931; J.D., U. Pa., 1934. Admitted to Pa. bar, 1934, U.S. Supreme Ct. bar, 1942, U.S. Ct. Mil. Appeals, asso. firm Smith & Paff, Easton, Pa., 1934-42; served to lt. col. JAGC staff Supreme Comdr. U.S. Army, 1942-46; dep. atty. gen. State of Pa., Harrisburg, 1947-55, 64-71; asst. to Sec. Treas., Washington, 1956-61; atty. ICC, Washington, 1961-64. Mem. Judge Adv. Assn. (life), Pa. Bar Assn. (life), Phi Beta Kappa. Decorated Bronze Star; contbr. articles to legal jours. Home: 1504 Ferry St Easton PA 18042 Office: 115 North St Apt 510 Harrisburg PA 17101 Tel (717) 232-8305

GAFFORD, GEORGE NELSON, b. Cleve., Mar. 25, 1916; A.B. with honors, Yale, 1936; J.D., Case-Western Res. U., 1939. Admitted to Ohio bar, 1939; mem. SEC, 1939-41; partner firm Kiefer, Waterworth, Hunter & Knecht, Cleve., 1946-68; asst. atty. gen. State of Ohio, 1949-51; of counsel firm Weston, Hurd, Fallon, Paisley & Howley, Cleve., 1969-74; prof. law Calif. Western Sch. Law, San Diego, 1969—; vis. prof. Adelbert Coll. Case-Western Res. U., 1947-51, Ohio Coll. Podiatric Medicine, Cleve., 1949-69, Cleve. State U., 1947-59, Case Western Res. U., Cleve., 1958-60; dir. McLoughlin Med. Mfg. Co. Active Cleve. United Appeal, 1946-69; mem. men's commn. La Jolla Mus., 1969—; bd. trustees Forest City Hosp., Cleve., 1959-69. Mem. Am., Cleve., San Diego bar assns., Order of Coif, Order of Barristers, Phi Delta Phi. Home: 5270 Chelsa St La Jolla CA 92037 Office: 350 Cedar St San Diego CA 92101 Tel (714) 239-0391

GAGE, CHARLES QUINCEY, b. Bluefield, W.Va., Jan. 20, 1946; B.S. in Bus. Adminstrn., W.Va. U., 1967, J.D., 1970. Admitted to W.Va. bar, 1970; partner firm Jackson, Kelly, Holt & O'Farrell, Charleston, W.Va., 1970—. Mem. Am., Kanawha County bar assns. Home: 2902 Noyes Ave SE Charleston WV 25304 Office: PO Box 553 Charleston WV 25322 Tel (304) 345-2000

GAGE, FRED KELTON, b. Mpls., June 20, 1925; B.S.L., U. Minn., 1948, LL.B., 1950. Admitted to Minn. bar, 1950; asso. firm Wilson, Blethen & Ogle, Mankato, Minn., 1950-55; partner firm Blethen, Gage, Krause, Blethen, Corcoran, Berkland & Peterson, and predecessors, Mankato, 1955—; mem. Minn. Senate, 1966-72; mem. State Bd. Profl. Responsibility, Minn. Supreme Ct., 1974—. Mem. Mankato Sch. Bd., 1957-66, Minn. State Coll. Bd., 1960-64. Mem. Am., Minn. State (chmn. tax sect. 1965-66, pres. 1977) bar assns. Home: 133 Belmont St Mankato MN 56001 Office: 206 Hickory St Mankato MN 56001 Tel (507) 387-1166

GAGE, GASTON HEMPHILL, b. Charlotte, N.C., June 16, 1930; B.A., Duke, 1953; LL.B., U. N.C., 1958. Admitted to N.C. bar, 1958, U.S. Ct. Appeals 4th Circuit bar, 1964, U.S. Supreme Ct. bar, 1965; partner firm Grier, Parker, Poe, Thompson, Bernstein, Gage and Preston, and predecessors, Charlotte, 1964—. Pres. Boys Town of N.C., Charlotte, 1974—. Mem. Am., N.C. bar assns. Home: 324 Lockley Dr Charlotte NC 28207 Office: 1100 Cameron Brown Bldg Charlotte NC 28204 Tel (704) 372-6730

GAGE, GERALD DAVID, b. Galveston, Tex., Aug. 3, 1939; B.B.A., U. Tex., 1961, LL.B., 1963. Admitted to Tex. bar, 1963, Ariz. bar, 1964, U.S. Supreme Ct. bar, 1971; partner firm Divelbiss & Gage, Phoenix, 1966—. Republican chmn. Maricopa County, 1971-73. Mem. Am., Maricopa County bar assns., Am. Ariz. (pres. 1974-75), Phoenix (pres. 1973-74) trial lawyers assns. Office: 45 W Jefferson St Phoenix AZ 85003 Tel (602) 257-8367

GAGE, WILLIAM HENRY, b. Chgo., Mar. 4, 1912; B.A., Yale, 1934, J.D., 1937. Admitted to N.Y. bar, 1938, Ill. bar, 1945; asso. firm Moot, Sprague, Marcy & Gulick, Buffalo, 1938-47, partner, 1947-63; asst. exec. sec. grievance com. Erie County Bar Assn., 1963-74, chief atty. 4th Dept. Discipline unit, 1974—. Mem. Am., N.Y., Erie County, Internat. bar assns., Nat. Orgn. Bar Counsel. Office: 1036 Ellicott Sq Bldg Buffalo NY 14203 Tel (716) 855-1191

GAGLIARDI, LEE PARSONS, b. Larchmont, N.Y., July 17, 1918; B.A., Williams Coll., 1941; J.D., Columbia, 1947. Admitted to N.Y. bar, 1948; asst. to gen. atty. N.Y. Central R. R. Co., N.Y.C., 1948-55; partner firm Clark, Gagliardi, Gallagher & Smyth, White Plains, N.Y., 1955-72; judge U.S. Dist. Ct., So. Dist. N.Y., 1972—. Chmn. bd. police commrs. Town of Mamroneck (N.Y.), 1969-72. Office: US Courthouse Foley Square New York City NY 10007 Tel (212) 791-0905

GAHAGAN, HENRY COLE, JR., b. Brownwood, Tex., Sept. 15, 1945; B.S., La. State U., 1969, J.D., 1970. Admitted to La. bar, 1970; asso. firm Gahagan & Gahagan, Natchitoches, La., 1970-72, partner, 1973—; chmn. Natchitoches City Charter Study Commn., 1975. Mem. adminstrv. bd. 1st United Methodist Ch., Natchitoches, 1974—; bd. dirs. Natchitoches Assn. for Retarded Children, 1972-75, Natchitoches Parish Council on Aging, 1974-75. Mem. Am., La. (vice chmn. continuing legal edn. com.), Natchitoches Parish bar assns., Am. Judicature Soc., Natchitoches Parish C. of C. (pres. 1976—), Natchitoches Jaycees (past v.p.). Home: 812 Parkway Dr

Natchitoches LA 71457 Office: 123 St Denis St Natchitoches LA 71457 Tel (381) 352-2069

GAHAGAN, MARVIN FREEMAN, b. Natchitoches, La., Aug. 28, 1932; J.D., La. State U., 1955. Admitted to La. bar, 1955, U.S. Dist. Ct. bar, Western Dist. La., 1955, U.S. Ct. Appeal, 1976, U.S. Supreme Ct. bar, 1977; partner firm Gahagan & Gahagan, Natchitoches, 1955—; judge Natchitoches City Ct., 1960—; chmn. Notary Pub. Exam. Com., Natchitoches, 1969—, indigent defender com. 10th Jud. Dist. Ct., 1971—. Bd. dirs. Natchitoches Parish Hosp. Mem. Am., La., Natchitoches-Red River bar assns., Am. Trial Lawyers Assn., Am. Judicature Soc., La. City, N.Am., Juvenile Ct. (La. council) judges assns., La. Assn. Def. Counsel, Assn. Trial Lawyers. Home: 301 Bird Ave Natchitoches LA 71457 Office: PO Box 70 Natchitoches LA 71457 Tel (318) 352-6666

GAILOR, FRANK ROBERT, b. Estelline, S.D., May 19, 1940; B.S. cum laude, S.D. State U., 1962; M.P.A. with distinction, Syracuse U., 1963; J.D. with honors, George Washington U., 1970. Admitted to D.C. bar, 1971; analyst Office of Sec., HUD, Washington, 1964-66; adminstrv. asst. to U.S. Rep., Washington, 1966-70; resident partner firm Duryea, Carpenter & Barnes, Washington, 1971; partner firm Gailor & Elias, Washington, 1972—; gen. counsel Nat. Assn. State Savs. and Loan Suprs., 1972—. Ruling elder Bush Hill Presbyn. Ch., 1973-75. Mem. Fed. (chmn. savings assn. law com. 1973-74, mem. nat. council 1974), D.C. bar assns. Editor: Savings and Loan Stock Conversions, 1974. Office: 700 E St SE Washington DC 20003 Tel (202) 543-1700

GAINES, BENNETT GILBERT, b. Balt., Mar. 16, 1947; student Columbia U., 1965-67; B.A., John Hopkins U., 1970; J.D., U. Md., 1973. Admitted to Md. bar, 1973; staff atty. U.S. Commn. Revision Fed. Ct. Appellate System, Washington, D.C., 1973-74; asso. Adelberg, Adelberg & Rudow, Balt., 1974—; lectr. Johns Hopkins U., 1974—. Mem. Md. State, Am. Bar Assns., Bar Assn. Baltimore City. Contbr. articles to legal jours. Home: 5746 Cross Country Blvd Baltimore MD 21209 Office: 10 Light St Baltimore MD 21202 Tel (301) 539-5195

GAINES, HOWARD CLARKE, b. Washington, Sept. 6, 1909; LL.B., Catholic U. Am., 1936. Admitted to D.C. bar, 1936, U.S. Supreme Ct. bar, 1946, Calif. bar, 1948; with U.S. Govt., Washington, 1943-46; individual practice law, Washington, 1938-43, 46-47, Santa Barbara, Calif., 1948-51; asso. firm Price, Postel & Parma, Santa Barbara, 1951-54, partner, 1954—. Chmn. Santa Barbara Police and Fire Commn., 1948-52; bd. dirs. Santa Barbara Mental Health Assn., 1957-59, v.p., 1959; pres. Santa Barbara Found., 1976—; mem. Santa Barbara Com. on Alcoholism; bd. dirs. Santa Barbara Humane Soc.; trustee Santa Barbara Bot. Garden. Fellow Am. Bar Found.; mem. Am. Judicature Soc., Santa Barbara County Bar (pres. 1957-58), Am. Bar Assn., State Bar of Calif. (gov. 1969-72, v.p., treas. 1971-72). Home: 1306 Las Alturas Rd Santa Barbara CA 93103 Office: 200 E Carrillo Santa Barbara CA 93102 Tel (805) 962-0011

GAINES, IRVING DAVID, b. Milw., Oct. 14, 1923; B.A., U. Wis., 1943, J.D., 1947; postgrad. U. Pa., 1943-44. Admitted to Wis. bar, 1947, Fla. bar, 1971; since practiced in Milw.; individual practice law, 1947-64; partner Gaines & Saichek, 1964—; lectr. trial practice U. Wis., 1970-72. Mem. Am., Milw. (mem. exec. com.), Broward County (Fla.), Dade County bar assns., State Bar Wis., Fla. Bar (editorial bd. jour. 1972—), Acad. Fla. Trial Lawyers, Wis. Acad. Trial Lawyers (pres. 1970-71), Assn. Trial Lawyers Am., Am. Judicature Soc., Bar Assn. 7th Fed. Circuit, Inter-Am. Bar Assn., Am. Arbitration Assn. (panel), Am. Acad. Forensic Sciences, World Peace Through Law, Internat. Acad. Forensic Scis., Am. Soc. Law and Medicine. Contbr. articles to legal jours. Home: 2107 N Terrace Ave Milwaukee WI 53202 Office: 161 W Wisconsin Ave Milwaukee WI 53203 Tel (414) 271-1938 also 3300 Spanish Moss Terr suite 401 Fort Lauderdale FL 33319 Tel (305) 735-9210

GAINES, KENNETH ROY, b. Chgo., July 4, 1943; B.A., Williams Coll., 1965; J.D., Northwestern U., 1968. Admitted to Ill. bar, 1968; asso. firm Altheimer & Gray, Chgo., 1969-75, partner, 1975—; law clk. to judge U.S. Dist. Ct., Chgo., 1968-69; instr. Ill. Inst. Tech.—Chgo. Kent Coll. Law, 1975-76. Mem. Am., Ill. Chgo. bar assns., Chgo. Council Lawyers. Contbg. author: Federal Civil Practice in Illinois, 1974. Office: 1 IBM Plaza Suite 3700 Chicago IL 60611

GAINES, RICHARD DAVID, b. Elgin, Ill., July 15, 1944; B.A., DePauw U., 1966; J.D., U. Ill., 1969. Admitted to Ill. bar, 1969, U.S. Dist. Ct. bar, 1973; asso. firm Welsh, Holmstrom, Jacobson, Worden & Gaines, Rockford, Ill., 1971-75, partner, 1976—. Mem. Am., Ill. (sec. young lawyers sect. 1977-78), Winnebago County bar assns. (active various coms. state and county assns.). Co-author: Third Party Practice: Skyclimber & Beyond, 1974. Office: 800 N Church St PO Box 589 Rockford IL 61105 Tel (815) 962-7071

GAINES, TRACY JACKSON, b. Campobello, S.C., Dec. 5, 1909; A.B., Furman U., 1937; LL.B., LaSalle U., 1946. Admitted to S.C. bar, 1946; individual practice law; pres. Bell Fed. Savs. & Loan Assn., Spartanburg; mem. S.C. Legislature, 18 years, served as speaker pro tem, 2 years. Mem. Am., County bar assns. Mem. Spartanburg County Democratic Exec. Com. Home: 29 Littlefield St Inman SC 29349 Office: 150 Archer St Spartanburg SC 29301 Tel (803) 472-6300

GAINES, WEAVER HENDERSON, JR., b. Fort Meade, S.D., Aug. 31, 1943; A.B., Dartmouth, 1965; LL.B., U. Va., 1968. Admitted to N.Y. bar, 1969; asso. firm Dewey, Ballantine, Bushby, Palmer & Wood, N.Y.C., 1971—. State dir. N.Y. Lawyers Com. to Re-elect Pres. Mem. Am., N.Y.C. bar assns., Fed. Bar Council, Order of Coif. Office: Room 4500 140 Broadway New York City NY 10005 Tel (212) 344-8000

GAITENS, LARRY PATRICK, b. Sturgeon, Pa., Mar. 2. 1938; B.A., Duquesne U., 1960, J.D., 1965. Admitted to Pa. bar, 1965, U.S. Supreme Ct. bar, 1970; asso. firm Spinelli, McLean & Witt, Pitts., 1965-66; partner firm Lucchino, Gaitens & Hough, Pitts., 1966—; pub. defender Allegheny County (Pa.), 1965-69; solicitor-prothonotary Allegheny County, 1969-70; solicitor N. Fayette Twp. (Pa.), 1967—; solicitor Carylnton Sch. Dist., Carnegie, Pa., 1975—; mayor Crafton Borough (Pa.), 1970-74; mem. Home Rule Study Commn., Crafton Borough, 1973-74. Del., Dem. Nat. Conv., 1976. Mem. Allegheny County Bar Assn., Criminal Trial Lawyers Assn. Allegheny County (trustee 1969—). Office: Suite 1204 Lawyers Bldg Pittsburgh PA 15219 Tel (412) 391-6920

GALANE, MORTON ROBERT, b. N.Y.C., Mar. 15, 1926; B.E.E., Coll. City N.Y., 1946; LL.B., George Washington U., 1950. Admitted to D.C. bar, 1950, Nev. bar, 1955, Calif. bar, 1975; patent examiner U.S. Patent Office, Washington 1948-50; spl. partner firm Roberts & McInnis, Washington, 1950-54; partner firm Galane & Tingey, Las Vegas, 1955—; spl. counsel to Gov. Nev., 1967-70. Mem. Am. Law Inst., IEEE, Am. Bar Assn., State Bar Nev., State Bar Calif., D.C. Bar. Home: 2019 Bannies Ln Las Vegas NV 89102 Office: 302 E Carson Ave Las Vegas NV 89101 Tel (702) 382-3290

GALASSO, JOHN MICHAEL, b. Glen Cove, N.Y., Dec. 26, 1944; B.A. in History and Polit. Sci., C.W. Post Coll., L.I. U., 1966; J.D., St. John's U., 1969. Admitted to N.Y. bar, 1969, U.S. Supreme Ct. bar; asst. dist. atty. Nassau County, N.Y., 1969—. Mem. Nassau County Police Dept. Holy Name Soc., Am. Com. on Italian Migration. Mem. Am., N.Y. State, Nassau County bar assns., Nat., N.Y. State dist. attys. assns., Cath. Lawyers Guild. Home: 23 Underhill Ave Oyster Bay NY 11771 Office: 262 Old Country Rd Mineola NY 11501 Tel (516) 535-4800

GALATI, FRANK THOMAS, b. Bridgeport, Conn., Aug. 13, 1948; B.A. in Govt., U. Ariz., 1970, J.D., 1973. Admitted to Ariz. bar, 1973; asst. atty. gen. State Ariz., Phoenix, 1973-76; dep. atty. Maricopa County (Ariz.), 1976—. Mem. Am., Maricopa County bar assns. Winner of Roger L. Perry legal writing competition State Bar Ariz., 1974; contbr. article to legal jour. Office: 101 W Jefferson Ave Maricopa County Attorney's Office Phoenix AZ 85003 Tel (602) 262-3411

GALATZ, NEIL GILBERT, b. N.Y.C., Jan. 22, 1933; B.A., Adelphi Coll., 1953; J.D., Columbia, 1956. Admitted to N.Y. bar, 1957, Nev. bar, 1958, Ariz. bar, 1961; sr. trial dep. dist. atty. Clark County (Nev.), 1959-61; mem. firm Galatz, Earl & Biggar, Las Vegas, Nev., 1976—. Fellow Internat. Acad. Trial Lawyers (dir.), Internat. Soc. Barristers; mem. Assn. Trial Lawyers Am., Am., Ariz., Nev., N.Y. bar assns. Office: 710 S 4th St Las Vegas NV 89101 Tel (702) 386-0000

GALBRAITH, JOHN ALAN, b. Washington, July 3, 1941; B.A., Harvard, 1963; J.D., U. Mich., 1966. Admitted to Mass. bar, 1966, Calif. bar, 1967, U.S. Supreme Ct. bar, 1972; mem. firm Williams & Connolly, Washington, 1968—. Mem. Am., D.C. bar assns. Home: 3529 Ordway St NW Washington DC 20016 Office: 839 17th St NW Washington DC 20006 Tel (202) 311-5022

GALBREATH, CHARLES FORD, b. Nashville, Jan. 12, 1925; J.D., Cumberland Law Sch., 1947. Admitted to Tenn. bar, 1947, U.S. Supreme Ct. bar, 1963; practiced in Nashville, 1947-68; judge Tenn. Ct. Criminal Appeals, 1968—; mem. Tenn. Ho. of Reps., 1960-68; pub. defender City of Nashville and Davidson County (Tenn.), 1962-64. Mem. Am., Tenn., Nashville bar assns. Contbr. numerous opinions to Southwestern Reporter, 1969—. Home: 727 Summerly Dr Nashville TN 37209 Office: Supreme Ct Bldg Nashville TN 37219 Tel (615) 741-3278

GALBUT, HOWARD NATHANIEL, b. Miami Beach, Fla., July 31, 1941; B.B.S., U. Miami, 1962, J.D., 1965. Admitted to Fla. bar, 1965; partner firm Galbut and Galbut, Miami Beach, 1965—; asso. govt. appeal agt. Selective Service Bd., Miami, 1974; mem. Dade County (Fla.) Probate Com.; bd. dirs. Dade County Bar Jud. Trust Fund. Active Miami Beach Civic Club, Miami Beach Democratic Club. Mem. Fla., Miami Beach, Dade County bar assns. Home: 777 NE 62d St Apr C403 Miami FL 33138 Office: 721 Washington Ave Miami Beach FL 33139 Tel (305) 672-3100

GALE, FOURNIER JOSEPH, III, b. Mobile, Ala., Aug. 3, 1944; B.A. in Polit. Sci. with honors, U. Ala., 1966, J.D., 1969. Admitted to Ala. bar, 1969, U.S. Supreme Ct. bar, 1974; asso. firm Cabaniss, Johnston, Gardner & Clark (now Cabaniss, Johnston, Gardner, Dumas & O'Neal), Birmingham, Ala., 1969-75, partner, 1975—. Mem. Am. (del. young lawyers sect. 1975, 76), Ala. (chmn. sect. on environ. law, pres.-elect. young lawyers sect.), Birmingham (chmn. law day 1975) bar assns., Farrah Law Soc. (trustee 1975—), Farrah Order Jurisprudence, Order of Coif. Editor-in-chief Ala. Law Rev., 1969. Home: 4017 Little Branch St Birmingham AL 35243 Office: 1900 First National-So Natural Bldg Birmingham AL 35203 Tel (205) 252-8800

GALE, GEORGE ALEXANDER, b. Quebec, Que., Can., June 24, 1906; B.A., U. Toronto (Ont., Can.), 1929; called to Bar at Osgoode Hall Law Sch., Toronto, 1929-32; LL.D., McMaster U., 1968, York U., 1969. Called to bar Ont., 1932, created king's counsel, 1945; read law with firm Donald, Mason, White & Foulds, Toronto, 1929-32; partner firm Mason, Foulds, Davidson & Gale, 1944-46; justice Supreme Ct. Ont., Toronto, 1946-63, Ct. Appeal for Ont., 1963-64; chief justice High Ct. Justice for Ont., 1964-67; chief justice of Ont., 1967-76; mem. Com. on Rules of Practice for Ont., 1941-76, chmn., 1967—; vice chmn. Ont. Law Reform Commn., 1977—; hon. lectr. Osgoode Hall Law Sch.; former lectr. Faculty of Medicine, U. Toronto. Former chmn. Rhodes Scholarship Selection Com.; bd. govs. Wycliffe Coll., U. Toronto, Upper Can. Coll., Toronto. Mem. Canadian Bar Assn. (former chmn., past mem. council), State Bar Ga. (hon.), Lawyers Club of Toronto (pres. 1940, hon. pres. 1968), Phi Delta Phi. Editor: Practice and Procedure in Ontario, 6th edit., 1968. Home: 2 Brookfield Rd Willowdale ON Canada Tel 488-0252

GALERSTEIN, GEORGE, b. N.Y.C., Oct. 7, 1922; B.M.E., Coll. City N.Y., 1944; LL.B., So. Meth. U., 1954. Admitted to Tex. bar, 1954, U.S. Ct. Claims bar, 1962, U.S. Patent Office bar, 1962; with Bell Helicopter Textron, Ft. Worth, 1952—, chief legal counsel, 1974—; sec. Bell Helicopter Internat., Inc., Bell Ops. Corp.; cons. to industry. Mem. Dallas Civil Service Bd., 1976—. Mem. Am., Tex. bar assns., Dallas-Ft. Worth Patent Law Assn., Assn. Am Trial Lawyers, Mfrs. Aircraft Assn., Aerospace Industries Assn. Am., Def. Research Inst., Pi Tau Sigma, Order of the Woolsack. Contbr. to So. Meth. U. Law Jour., 1953-54. Office: Bell Helicopter Textron PO Box 482 Fort Worth TX 76101 Tel (817) 280-3221

GALES, ROBERT ROBINSON, b. N.Y.C., Feb. 15, 1941; B.A., Ohio Wesleyan U., 1962; J.D., Syracuse U., 1965; LL.M., George Washington U., 1966; postgrad. in fgn. affairs U. Philippines, 1969; certificate in nat. security mgmt. Indsl. Coll. Armed Forces, 1971. Admitted to N.Y. bar, 1966, D.C. bar, 1973; asst. staff judge adv. U.S. Air Force, Tacoma, 1966-68, Vietnam, 1968-69; dep. dir. internat. law 13th Air Force, Pampanga, Philippines, 1969-71; asst. legal adviser U.S. del. Renegotiation of Philippines-U.S. Status of Forces Agreement, 1969-71; chief civil law Tactical Air Command, U.S. Air Force, Hampton, Va., 1971-72, chief adminstrv. law, 1972-73; asso. firm Herzfeld & Rubin, N.Y.C., 1973-77; task force coordinator Volkswagen Am., Inc., 1977—. Mem. Wash. State Soccer Commn., 1967-68; pres. Ossining Hist. Soc., 1974-76; bd. dirs. Westchester Soc. Prevention of Cruelty to Animals, 1974—; mem. Westchester Republican County Com., 1975—. Mem. Assn. Bar City of N.Y. (com. on mil. justice and mil. affairs 1974—), N.Y. County Lawyers Assn. (com. on law reform 1973—, com. on mil. justice 1974—), N.Y. State, Westerchester County, D.C. bar assns., Am. Judicature Soc., Phi Alpha Delta, Delta Phi Epsilon. Recipient Bronze Star medal, Meritorious Service medal, Air Force Commendation medal. Contbr. articles to legal jours. Home: 10 S State Rd Briarcliff Manor NY 10510 Office: Volkswagen Am Inc 818 Sylvan Ave Englewood Cliffs NJ 07632 Tel (201) 894-6253

GALFOND, DAVID CHARLES, b. Johnstown, Pa., Jan. 16, 1931; student George Washington U., 1949-50; J.D., Catholic U. Am., 1966. Admitted to D.C. bar, 1967, Md. bar, 1968; individual practice law, Washington, 1967-75; partner firm Rhodes, Galfond & Mininberg, Washington, 1975-77; lectr. real estate firms and Montgomery County (Md.) Bd. Realtors, 1967-77. Pres. Civic Assn. Takoma Park, Md., 1954-56; mem. joint com., Citizen's Assn., Takoma Pk., 1955-57. Mem. Am., D.C. bar assns. Editorial bd. Catholic U. Law Review, 1964-66; contbr. articles to jours. Home: 8301 Loring Dr Bethesda MD 20034 Office: 1100 17th St NW Washington DC 20036 also 7315 Wisconsin Ave Bethesda MD 20014 Tel (202) 331-0700 also (301) 654-6160

GALINSON, MURRAY LAWRENCE, b. Mpls., May 8, 1937; B.A. cum laude, U. Minn., 1958, J.D. cum laude, 1961; Ph.D., U.S. Internat. U., 1976. Admitted to Minn. bar, 1961; asst. U.S. atty. Minn., 1961-63; partner firm Mullin, Galinson, Swirnoff & Weinberg, Mpls., 1964-71; prof. law Calif. Western Sch. Law, San Diego, 1972—; councilman St. Louis Park, Minn., 1968-71; asst. state pub. defender, Minn., 1966-71; chmn. sect. on family and juvenile law Assn. Am. Law Schs., 1975, vice-chmn., 1974; chmn. criminal law com. Hennepin County Bar Assn., 1970-71. Chmn. Minn. Com. Gun Control, 1968-69; mem. St. Louis Park (Minn.) Planning Commn. and Bd. Zoning Appeals, 1969-70. Mem. Minn., San Diego bar assns., Assn. Am. Law Schs. Contbr. articles in field. to legal jours. Home: 1555 El Camino del Teatro La Jolla CA 92037 Office: 350 Cedar St San Diego CA 92101 Tel (714) 239-0391

GALIP, RONALD GEORGE, b. Youngstown, Ohio, Feb. 28, 1934; B.A., Youngstown State U., 1955; J.D., Ohio State U., 1957. Admitted to Ohio bar, 1957; gen. counsel, corp. sec. Cafaro Co., shopping center devel. co., Youngstown, 1957—; speaker, lectr. in field; mem. faculty Univ. of Shopping Centers, 1973-76; chmn. U.S. Law Conf., Internat. Council Shopping Centers, Boca Raton, Fla., 1975, Carlsbad, Calif., 1976. Chmn. Liberty Twp. (Ohio) United Appeal, 1974. Mem. Mahoning County (Ohio), Ohio State, Am. bar assns., Phi Delta Phi. Home: 3445 Logan Way Youngstown OH 44505 Office: 2445 Belmont Ave Youngstown OH 44504 Tel (216) 747-2661

GALLAGHER, HAROLD JOHN, b. Clinton, Iowa, Dec. 29, 1894; LL.B., U. Iowa, 1916; student Harvard Law Sch., 1916-17; LL.D., St. John's U., N.Y.C. Admitted to Iowa bar, 1916, N.Y. bar, 1919; asso. firm Hornblower, Miller, Garrison & Potter, N.Y.C., 1917-25, mem., 1925-76, counsel, 1976—; bd. dirs. Am. Bar Endowment, 1951-71, pres., 1963-65. Mem. Am. (pres. 1949-50, N.Y., Internat., Inter-Am. bar assns., Assn. Bar City N.Y., N.Y. County Lawyers Assn., Nat. Legal Aid and Defender Assn., Am. Bar Found. (dir. 1961-73). Home: Northgate Apts Alger CT Bronxville NY 10708 Office: 277 Park Ave N New York City NY 10017 Tel (212) 248-1000

GALLAGHER, JAMES CORNELIUS, b. Lyndonville, Vt., June 16, 1945; A.B., Tufts U., 1967; J.D., Cornell U., 1971. Admitted to Vt. bar, 1971; asso. firm Downs, Rachlin & Martin, St. Johnsbury, Vt., 1971-75, partner, 1975—. Chmn., Caledonia County (Vt.) Democratic Com., 1971-72, Vt. State Dem. Com., 1971-72. Mem. Vt., Am., Caledonia County bar assns., Assn. Trial Lawyers Am., Def. Research Inst. Asso., Cornell Law Rev., 1970, editor, 1971. Home: Box 126 Lyndon VT 05849 Office: 9 Prospect St Saint Johnsbury VT 05819 Tel (802) 748-8324 also 100 Dorset St Burlington VT 05401 Tel (802) 863-2375

GALLAGHER, JOSEPH EDWARD, b. Scranton, Pa., Jan. 14, 1917; B.A., U. Scranton, 1938; J.D., Fordham U., 1941. Admitted to Pa. bar, 1947, U.S. Supreme Ct. bar, 1976; individual practice law, Scranton, 1947-56; partner firm O'Malley, Bour & Gallagher and predecessor firm, Scranton, 1956—. Fellow Am. Coll. Trial Lawyers, Am. Bar Found.; mem. Am. (del. 1975—), Pa. (pres. 1976—), Lackawanna (pres. 1974) bar assns., Am. Judicature Soc., Third Circuit Jud. Conf. Home: 1112 E Gibson St Scranton PA 18510 Office: 310 Scranton Electric Bldg Scranton PA 18503 Tel (717) 346-0745

GALLAGHER, MARIAN GOULD, b. Everett, Wash., Aug. 29, 1914; student Whitman Coll., 1931-32; A.B., U. Wash., 1937, LL.B., 1937, M.L.S., 1939. Admitted to Wash. bar, 1937; law librarian, instr. law U. Utah, 1939-44; law librarian U. Wash., 1944—, asst. prof. 1944-48, asso. prof. law, 1948-53, prof. law, 1953—. Fellow Am. Bar Found., mem. Am., Washington State, Seattle-King County Bar Assns., Am. Assn. Law Libraries (pres. 1954-55) (Distinguished Service Award, 1966), ALA, Order of the Coif. Home: 1000 8th Ave Seattle WA 98104 Office: Law Library Univ Wash Condon Hall JB-20 1100 NE Campus Pkwy Seattle WA 98105 Tel (206) 543-4089

GALLAGHER, MICHAEL LANTAFF, b. LeMars, Iowa, Apr. 14, 1944; B.A., Ariz. State U., 1966, J.D., 1970. Admitted to Ariz. bar, 1970; partner firm Snell & Wilmer, Phoenix, 1970—. Mem. Am., Ariz., Maricopa bar assns., Phoenix Assn. Def. Counsel (dir.), Assn. Profl. Ballplayers Am., Ariz. State U. Law Soc. (dir.). Home: 5605 N 4th St Phoenix AZ 85012 Office: 3100 Valley Center Phoenix AZ 85073 Tel (602) 257-7254

GALLAGHER, MYLES FRANCIS, b. Cleve., Dec. 20, 1926; B.A., John Carroll U., 1955; LL.B., Cleve. Marshall Law Sch., 1957. Admitted to Ohio bar, 1957; pvt. practice law, Fairview Park. Mem. Am., Ohio, Greater Cleve., Cuyahoga County bar assns. Office: 4610 Concord Dr Fairview Park OH 44126 Tel (216) 671-0928

GALLAGHER, RAYMOND JOSEPH, b. Pitts., Nov. 6, 1922; B.A., Duquesne U., 1950; J.D., U. Pitts., 1955. Admitted to Pa. bar, 1967; individual practice law, Pitts., 1967—. Mem. Am., Pa., Allegheny County bar assns. Home: 1873 Brandywine Dr Allison Park PA 15101 Office: 818 Frick Bldg Pittsburgh PA 15219 Tel (412) 288-9595

GALLAGHER, THOMAS ALLEN, b. Cleve., Sept. 15, 1942; B.E.E., Tulane U., 1965; J.D. with honors, George Washington U., 1968. Admitted to Md. bar, 1968, Calif. bar, 1970; patent examiner U.S. Patent Office, Washington, 1965-67; patent adviser Naval Ordinance Lab., Office of Naval Research, U.S. Navy, White Oak, Md., 1967-68; staff atty. Communications Satellite Corp., Washington, 1968-69; asso. firm Limbach, Limbach, & Sutton, San Francisco, 1969-72, partner, 1972—. Mem. Am., San Francisco bar assns., Am. Patent Law Assn. Office: 2001 Ferry Bldg San Francisco CA 94111 Tel (415) 433-4150

GALLAGHER, THOMAS FRANCIS, b. Faribault, Minn., Nov. 24, 1897; B.A., U. Minn., 1919, J.D., 1921. Admitted to Minn. bar, 1921, U.S. Supreme Ct. bar, 1936; with firm Tappan & Gallagher, Mpls.,

1921-28; individual practice law, Mpls., 1921-42; asso. justice Minn. Supreme Ct., St. Paul, 1942-66; investments, Mpls., 1966—. Mem. nat. emergency bds. ry. labor disputes, 1948, 50; pres. Minn. Safety Council, 1955-60; pres. U. Minn. Law Sch. Alumni Assn., 1954; Democratic nominee for gov. Minn., 1938; del. at large Dem. Nat. Conv., 1940. Mem. Am., Minn. bar assns., Phi Delta Phi. Recipient nat. award for outstanding service in judiciary Am. Trial Lawyers Assn., 1967. Home: 2200 Newton Ave S Minneapolis MN 55405 Tel (612) 337-9112

GALLAGHER, WILLIAM FRANCIS, b. New Haven, June 28, 1937; B.S., Fairfield U., 1959; LL.B., U. Conn., 1963. Admitted to Conn. bar, 1963, U.S. Supreme Ct. bar, 1969; individual practice law, New Haven, 1963—; asst. corp. counsel City of West Haven (Conn.), 1969-71; spl. asst. states atty. New Haven County, 1974—. Mem. Am., Conn., New Haven County bar assns., Am. Trial Lawyers Assn., Am. Judicature Soc. Home: 33 Forest Hills Rd West Haven CT 06516 Office: 265 Church St New Haven CT 06510 Tel (203) 624-4165

GALLANT, EUGENE GERALD, b. Pawtucket, R.I., May 8, 1920; A.B. cum laude, Brown U., 1950; LL.B., Harvard, 1953. Admitted to R.I. bar, 1954, U.S. Dist. Ct. bar, 1956; exec. counsel to gov. R.I., Providence, 1955-58; individual practice law, Providence, 1958-68; justice R.I. Superior Ct., Providence, 1968—; mem. R.I. Jud. Council, 1966-68. Mem. Am., R.I. bar assns., Am. Judicature Soc., Harvard Law Sch. Alumni Assn. R.I. (pres.). Home: 5 Nancy St Pawtucket RI 02860 Office: Superior Ct 250 Benefit St Providence RI 02903 Tel (401) 277-3250

GALLANT, WADE MILLER, JR., b. Raleigh, N.C., Jan. 12, 1930. LL.B. summa cum laude, Wake Forest U., 1952, J.D. cum laude, 1955. Admitted to N.C. bar, 1955; asso. firm Womble, Carlyle, Sandridge & Rice, Winston-Salem, N.C., 1955-63, partner, 1963—; dir. Brenner Industries, Inc., Thomas Built Buses, Inc., Wacayman Bank and Trust Co., Cayman Reef Devel. Co. Ltd., Wacayman Banking Corp., Ltd.; lectr. continuing legal edn. program N.C. Bar Found., 1966—. Pres. Winston-Salem Symphony Assn., 1965-66, Forsyth (county, N.C.) Mental Health Assn., 1972-73; v.p. N.C. Mental Health Assn., 1973, pres., 1975-76. Mem. Internat., Am., N.C., Forsyth County bar assns., Am. Council Assn. (hon.). Home: 224 Roslyn Rd Winston-Salem NC 27104 Office: 2400 Wachovia Bldg Winston-Salem NC 27102 Tel (919) 725-1311

GALLASPY, JOHN NORMAN, b. Pelican, La., Nov. 8, 1932; B.A., La. State U., 1952, J.D., 1958. Admitted to La. Supreme Ct. bar, 1958; asso. firm Hall, Raggio and Farrar, Lake Charles, La., 1958-61; sr. partner firm Gallaspy and Paduda, Bogalusa, La., 1975—; 2d asst. dist. atty. 22d Jud. Dist., 1969—. Chmn. Bogalusa Bd. Adjustments, 1963-65, Bogalusa Community Affairs Com., 1965-66, ofcl. bd. Elizabeth Sullivan Meml. Meth. Ch., Bogalusa, 1967-69. Mem. Am., La. State bar assns., La. Dist. Atty's Assn., Washington Parish (La.) Bar Assn. (pres. 1972). Recipient Distinguished Service award Bogalusa Jaycees, 1966. Home: 1737 Gaylord Dr Bogalusa LA 70427 Office: 327 Memphis St Bogalusa LA 70427 Tel (504) 732-4268

GALLEGOS, JAKE EUGENE, b. Tucumcari, N.Mex., Oct. 19, 1935; B.A., U. N.Mex., 1956, J.D., 1960. Admitted to N.Mex. bar, 1961, U.S. Supreme Ct. bar, 1966; asst. U.S. Atty., Albuquerque, 1961; asst. atty. gen. State of N.Mex., Santa Fe, 1962; asso. firm O. Russell Jones, Sante Fe, 1963-65; partner firm Jones, Gallegos, Snead & Wertheam, and predecessors, Santa Fe, 1965—; mem. bd. advisers Mountain Bell Co. N.Mex.; mem. N.Mex. Bd. Bar Examiners, 1974—, N.Mex. Bar Judiciary Com. Chmn. bd. St. Vincent's Hosp., 1971-74; bd. dirs. Cath. Charities Bur., Council of Ind. Colls. N.Mex. Mem. Am., N.Mex. bar assns. Office: 215 Lincoln Ave Santa Fe NM 87501 Tel (505) 982-2691

GALLINA, GINO E., b. N.Y.C., Feb. 24, 1935; B.S., Villanova U., 1956; J.D., N.Y. U., 1964. Admitted to N.Y. State bar, 1965; asso. firm Poles, Tublin & Patastedies, N.Y.C., 1964; dist. atty. N.Y. County, 1965-70; partner firm Lenefsky, Gallina, Mass & Hoffman, N.Y.C., 1970-75; individual practice law, N.Y.C., 1976—. Mem. Mayor's Task Force on Child Abuse, 1970-74. Mem. N.Y. State, Am. bar assns., Trial Lawyers Assn., Nat. Dist. Attys. Assn. Office: 30 Broad St New York City NY 10004 Tel (212) 425-1060

GALLO, JON J., b. Santa Monica, Calif., Apr. 19, 1942; B.A., Occidental Coll., 1964; J.D., U. Calif., Los Angeles, 1967. Admitted to Calif. bar, 1967; practiced law, Los Angeles, 1967—; partner firm Greenberg & Glusker, Los Angeles, 1971—; mem. exec. council, steering com. Law in A Free Soc. coop. project State Bar Calif., U. Calif. and Schs. Law of U. Calif., 1970-73, 75—, vice chmn., 1975—; lectr. profl. courses. Mem. Am., Los Angeles County, Beverly Hills (gov. 1970-74, sec. probate com. 1972) bar assns., State Bar Calif. (com. on econs. of law practice 1971-72), Calif. Barristers Assn. (gov. 1971-74, v.p. 1973-74), Barristers Beverly Hills Bar Assn. (gov. 1969-74, pres. 1973-74); fellow Assn. Tax Counselors. Contbr. articles to legal publs.; recipient citation for meritorious services U.S. Dept. Def., 1973. Home: 17540 Margate St Encino CA 91316 Office: 1900 Ave of the Stars Suite 2000 Los Angeles CA 90067 Tel (213) 553-3610

GALLOP, DONALD PHILIP, b. St. Louis, Aug. 28, 1932; B.A., U. Mo., 1954; J.D., Washington U., St. Louis, 1959. Admitted to Mo. bar, 1959; partner firm Gallop & Gallop, St. Louis, 1959-68, Shifrin, Treiman, Schermer & Gallop, St. Louis, 1968-73, Susman, Stern, Agatstein & Heifetz & Gallop, St. Louis, 1973-75, Gallop, Johnson, Godiner, Morgenstern & Crebs, St. Louis, 1976—; pres. Assos. Jewish Hosps., 1970-71. Bd. dirs. Jewish Fedn. St. Louis, Mem. Am., Mo., St. Louis bar assns. Home: 49 Granada Way St Louis MO 63124 Office: 7733 Forsyth Blvd Suite 1800 St Louis MO 63105 Tel (314) 862-1200

GALLOWAY, E. DEXTER, b. Grosse Ile, Mich., Sept. 25, 1930; A.B., Hillsdale Coll., 1952; J.D., U. Mich., 1957. Admitted to Mich. bar, 1957, Kans. bar, 1958, U.S. Supreme Ct. bar, 1967; individual practice law, Hutchinson, Kans., 1957—; pres. Reno County (Kans.) bar, 1975. Mem. Am., Kans. bar assns., Kans. Trial Lawyers Assn. (bd. govs. 1976—). Editorial contbr. Hutchinson News, Am. Bar Jour. Home: 7300 Monroe St Hutchinson KS 67501 Office: 401 First National Center Hutchinson KS 67501 Tel (316) 662-0191

GALLOWAY, HENRY HOLLAND, SR., b. Fargo, N.D., Mar. 31, 1932; Ph.B., U. N.D., 1955, J.D., 1957. Admitted to N.D. bar, 1957; claims rep. State Farm Mut., Fargo, 1958-63; asso. firm O'Grady Edwards & Galloway, Grand Forks, N.D., 1963-68; individual practice law, Grand Forks, 1968—; atty. for Grand Forks County Water Mgmt. Dist., 1966—; alt. municipal judge, Grand Forks, 1968—. Mem. Am., N.D. State, Grand Forks County bar assns., Phi Delta Phi. Home: 3124 Chestnut St Grand Forks ND 58201 Office: 1832 S Washington St Grand Forks ND 58201 Tel (701) 775-8173

GALSTON, NINA MOORE, b. N.Y.C., Mar. 2, 1914; A.B., Vassar Coll., 1935; LL.B., Columbia, 1938. Admitted to N.Y. State bar, 1938; asso. firm Milbank, Tweed & Hope, 1938-39; asso. comparative law Columbia U., N.Y.C., 1953—, adj. prof. comparative law, 1971—; vol. atty. N.Y. Legal Aid Soc., 1940-42, 43-46, bd. dirs., 1946-71, mem. exec. com., 1947-71, mem. spl. bd. for neighborhood offices, 1967—. Mem. Assn. Bar City N.Y., Am. Fgn. Law Assn., Am. Soc. Internat. Law, Union internationale des avocats. Editor: (monograph series) Bilateral Studies in Private International Law, 1965; Professional Responsibility of the Lawyer, 1976. Home: 338 Woodbury Rd Huntington NY 11743 Office: Box 62 Law Sch Columbia U 435 W 116th St New York City NY 10027 Tel (212) 280-2692

GALTON, DAVID S., b. N.Y.C., Nov. 22, 1901; A.B., Columbia U., 1921, B.S., 1922, M.A., 1922, M.S., 1923, LL.B., 1926. Admitted to N.Y. State bar, 1926, U.S. Dist. Ct. bar, 1928; sr. partner firm Benjamin & Galton, 1929-38, Benjamin, Galton & Robbins, 1938-60, Benjamin, Galton, Robbins & Flato, 1960-66, Robbins, Galton & Bondi, 1966-71; gen. counsel Jewish Theol. Sem. Am., 1969—; spl. counsel N.Y. Infirmary, 1969—. Mem. Am., N.Y. State bar assns. Home: 119 W 71st St New York City NY 10023 Office: 3080 Broadway New York City NY 10027 Tel (212) 749-8000

GALUSZKA, WALTER L., b. Manchester, Conn., Nov. 6, 1917; A.B., Union Coll., 1946; J.D., Catholic U., 1951. Admitted to Conn. bar, 1952; prosecutor City of Hartford, Ct., 1955-58; atty. for Gen. Law Com., Conn. State Legislature. Chmn. Govt. Action Com., Polish Am. Congress, 1972-76. Mem. Am., Conn., Hartford County bar assns. Home: 45 High Gate Rd Newington CT 06111 Office: 50 State St Hartford CT 06103 Tel (203) 522-6207

GALVIN, MICHAEL JOHN, JR., b. Winona, Minn., July 8, 1930; B.A., Coll. St. Thomas, 1952; LL.B., U. Minn., 1957. Admitted to Fed. Dist. Ct. bar, 1957, 8th Circuit Ct. Appeals bar, 1957, Minn. Supreme Ct. bar, 1957, U.S. Supreme Ct. bar; co-founder, co-chmn. U. Minn. Law Sch. Legal Aid Clinic, 1956-57; asso. firm Briggs and Morgan, St. Paul, 1957—. Pres. St. Paul Winter Carnival Assn., Inc., 1970; chmn. St. Thomas Coll. Nat. Alumni Fund Dr., 1971; trustee Coll. St. Thomas, 1973—. Mem. Ramsey County (Minn.) (chmn. legis. com.), Minn. State, Am. (chmn. unauthorized practice com. sect. jr. bar) bar assns., Ramsey County Jr. Bar Assn. (pres.), Coll. St. Thomas Alumni Assn. (pres. 1965). Named Outstanding Young Man of City of St. Paul, St. Paul Jaycees, 1964, Outstanding Young Man of Minn., Minn. Jaycees, 1964. Home: 1303 Bohland Pl Saint Paul MN 55116 Office: W-2200 1st Nat Bank Bldg Saint Paul MN 55101 Tel (612) 291-1215

GALWAY, RICHARD EDWARD, b. Columbus, Ga., Jan. 21, 1944; B.A., U. N.H., 1966; Fulbright scholar, Eng., 1966-67; J.D., Boston U., 1970. Admitted to N.H. bar, 1970; partner firm Devine, Millimet, Stahl & Branch, Manchester, N.H. Dir. Neighborhood Info. and Referral Service, 1972-74. Mem. Am., N.H., Manchester bar assns. Home: South Rd Deerfield NH 03037 Office: 1850 Elm St Manchester NH 03105 Tel (603) 669-1000

GAMBEL, WILLIAM CHRISTIAN, b. New Orleans, Jan. 14, 1942; LL.B., Loyola U. of South, 1964; LL.M. in Taxation, Boston U., 1965. Admitted to La. bar, 1964; asso. firm Milling, Benson, Woodward, Hillyer & Pierson, New Orleans, 1965-69, partner, 1969—; lectr. on taxation Loyola U. Sch. Law, New Orleans, 1969—. Bd. dirs. Boys' Club of Greater New Orleans; mem. bd. devel. Mercy Hosp., New Orleans. Mem. New Orleans, La., Am. bar assns., Am. Judicature Soc., Nat. Tax Assn., Tax Inst. Am. Contbr. articles to Loyola U. of South Law Rev. Home: 1415 Octavia New Orleans LA 70115 Office: 1100 Whitney Bldg New Orleans LA 70130 Tel (504) 581-3333

GAMBINO, JOSEPH ANTHONY, b. Cleve., Dec. 4, 1945; B.S., Bowling Green State U., 1968; J.D., Cleve. State U., 1972. Admitted to Ohio bar, 1972; asso. firm Friedman, Kovacs & Agnello, Cleve., 1972—; pros. atty. City of Strongsville (Ohio), 1974—. Mem. Am., Ohio State, Cuyahoga County bar assns., Bar Assn. Greater Cleve. Office: 412 Citizens Bldg Cleveland OH 44114 Tel (216) 621-7593

GAMBLE, CAMERON CALVIN, b. New Orleans, Jan. 6, 1938; LL.B., Tulane U., 1963. Admitted to La. bar, 1963; partner firm Newman, Duggins, Drolla & Gamble, New Orleans, 1974—; dir. New Orleans Legal Referral Service, Inc. Vice chmn. citizens adv. com. Vol. Services Orleans Parish Sch. Bd., 1976—. Mem. Am., La., New Orleans bar assns., Am., La. trial lawyers assns. Tel (504) 581-2552

GAMBLE, EDWARD ANDREW, b. Mercer County, Pa., Jan. 11, 1934; B.A., U. Calif., Los Angeles, 1958; J.D., Georgetown U., 1964. Admitted to Calif. bar, 1965, Pa. bar, 1968; asso. firm Pillsbury, Madison, Sutro and Howard, Prim, Smith, Rice & Downs, San Francisco, 1964-68; asso. firm Gilbert D. Levine, Esq., New Castle, Pa., 1968-69; partner firm Gamble & Verterano & Mojock, New Castle, 1969—; gen. counsel Redevel. Authority, City of New Castle, 1969—. Mem. Am. (coms. corps., probate and trust law), Pa., Calif. bar assns. Home: Destinaire Stock Farm New Wilmington PA Office: 12 W Washington St New Castle PA 16101 Tel (412) 658-3708

GAMBRELL, DAVID HENRY, b. Atlanta, Dec. 20, 1929; B.S., Davidson Coll., 1949; LL.B., cum laude, Harvard, 1952. Admitted to Ga. bar, 1951; teaching fellow Harvard, 1954-55; asso., then partner King & Spalding, Atlanta; partner firm Gambrell & Mobley, Atlanta, 1963—; mem. U.S. Senate, 1970-72. Bd. dirs. Ga. YMCA, 1965; trustee Atlanta Commn. Crime and Delinquency, 1966-68. Mem. Legal Aid and Defender Assn. (dir. 1965), Am. (del. 1976), Ga. (pres. 1967-68), Atlanta (pres. 1965-66) bar assns., Lawyers Club Atlanta. Home: 3820 Castlegate Dr NW Atlanta GA 30327 Office: 3900 1st Nat Bank Tower Atlanta GA 30303 Tel (404) 658-9150

GAMBRELL, EMMETT ATLEY, b. Newton, Miss., Aug. 13, 1926; A.B., Tougaloo Coll.; M.S., Kans. State U.; J.D., Marquette U. Admitted to Wis. bar, 1967; since practiced law in Milw., asso. firm Phillips & Phillips, 1967-70, mem. firm Phillips & Gambrell, 1971-73, mem. firm Phillips, Gambrell & Jones, 1974—. Mem. Wis. Black Lawyers Assn., Nat. Bar Assn., Alpha Phi Alpha. Home: 2942 N 2d St Milwaukee WI 53212 Office: 606 W Wisconsin Ave Suite 1306 Milwaukee WI 53203 Tel (414) 224-0888

GAMER, BARBARA TUTTLE, b. New Rochelle, N.Y., Nov. 20, 1943; B.A., U. Calif. Los Angeles, 1966, J.D., 1970. Admitted to Calif. bar, 1971; dep. dist. atty. San Diego County, Calif., 1970-72; asso. prof. law Calif. Western Sch. of Law, San Diego, 1973—. Bd. mem. State, Fed. and Appellate Defenders of San Diego. Mem. Calif., San Diego Bar Assns., Lawyers Club. Contbr. to profl. jours., law reviews. Office: 350 Cedar St San Diego CA 92101 Tel (714) 239-0391

GAMMAGE, ROBERT ALTON, b. Houston, Mar. 13, 1938; A.A., Del Mar Coll., 1958; B.S., U. Corpus Christi, 1963; M.A., Sam Houston State U., 1965; J.D., U. Tex., 1969. Admitted to Tex. bar, 1969, U.S. Supreme Ct. bar, 1973; individual practice law, Houston, 1969—; mem. Tex. Ho. of Reps., 1971-73, Tex. Senate, 1973-76, U.S. Ho. of Reps., 1976—. Recipient CONSUL award U. Tex. Sch. Law, 1969. Mem. Houston, Tex. (Distinguished Service award 1975), Am. bar assns., Am. Judicature Soc., Assn. Trial Lawyers Am., Phi Alpha Delta. Office: 7718 Bellfort St Houston TX 77061 Tel (713) 644-8011

GAMMILL, WARREN PRICE, b. Fort Smith, Ark., Jan. 21, 1947; A.B., Dartmouth Coll., 1969; J.D., Vanderbilt U., 1972. Admitted to Fla. bar, 1972; asso. firm Salley, Barns, Pajon and Primm, Miami, 1972-74; asso. firm Smathers & Thompson, Miami, 1974-77; individual practice law, Miami, 1977—. Mem. Dade County, Fla. bar assns. Home: 11685 Canal Dr Apt 402 North Miami FL 33181 Office: 1699 Coral Way Suite 315 Miami FL 33145 856-8896

GAMPELL, RALPH J., b. Salford, Eng., Dec. 9, 1916; M.D., U. Manchester (Eng.), 1940; LL.B., Stanford U., 1957. Admitted to Calif. bar, 1957; now mem. firm Gampell & Teter, San Jose, Calif. Mem. Am. Bar Assn., State Bar Calif. (pres. 1976-77). Office: San Jose Plaza Suite 1400 2 N Second St San Jose CA 95113 Tel (408) 998-1500*

GAMSER, HOWARD GRAHAM, b. N.Y.C.; B.S.S., Coll. City N.Y., 1940; M.A., Columbia, 1941; LL.B., N.Y. Law Sch., 1952, J.D., 1972. Admitted to N.Y. State bar, 1952, D.C. bar, 1963; individual practice law, N.Y.C., 1952-61, Washington, 1969—; partner firm Bobroff, Olonoff & Scharf, N.Y.C., 1952-61; counsel Dutton, Zumas & Wise, Washington, 1969-73; lectr. London Sch. Econs., 1952-53; chief counsel Ho. of Rep. Com. on Edn. and Labor, 1961-63; chmn. Nat. Mediation Bd., 1963-69; adj. prof. law Georgetown U., 1964—. Mem. D.C., Fed. bar assns. Office: 1140 Connecticut Ave NW Washington DC 20036 Tel (202) 223-4455

GANDAL, ROBERT, b. Cleve., Feb. 9, 1928; B.B.A., Case Western Res. U., 1950; J.D., Cleve. State U., 1954. Admitted to Ohio bar, 1955; mgr. residential lighting dept. Midland Electric Co., 1960-65, asst. sales mgr. maj. appliance div., 1950-60; gen. mgr. Citrus Fruit Juice Co., 1965-67; v.p., sec., corp. counsel Mgmt. Recruiters Internat., Inc., Cleve., 1967—. Mem. Am., Ohio bar assns. Home: 6805 Mayfield Rd Apt 1217A Mayfield Heights OH 44124 Office: 1015 Euclid Ave Suite 600 Cleveland OH 44115 Tel (216) 696-8066

GANDRUD, RONALD GEORGE, b. Benson, Minn., July 25, 1932; B.A., Concordia Coll., Moorhead, Minn., 1954; LL.B., U. Minn., 1958. Admitted to Minn. bar, 1958; asso. firm Hulstrand & Langsjoen, Willmar, Minn., 1959-61; v.p., asso. counsel, mgr. Met. ops. Title Ins. Co. of Minn., Mpls., 1961. Pres. St. James Lutheran Ch., Crystal, Minn., 1975. Mem. Am., Minn., Hennepin County (chmn. real property sect. 1972-73) bar assns. Home: 3155 Yukon Ave N Minneapolis MN 55427 Office: 400 2d Ave S Minneapolis MN 55401 Tel (612) 371-1111

GANDY, EDYTHE EVELYN, b. Hattiesburg, Miss., Sept. 4, 1922; student U. So. Miss., 1939-40; LL.B., U. Miss., 1944. Admitted to Miss. bar, 1944; practiced law, Hattiesburg, Miss., 1947; mem. Miss. State Legislature, 1948-52; atty. Miss. State Dept. Pub. Welfare, 1952-58; asst. atty. gen. State of Miss., 1959, state treas., 1964-67, commr. of ins., 1972-76, lt. gov., 1976—; mem. State Bldg. Commn., Commn. of Budget and Accounting, Agrl. and Indsl. Bd.; past chmn. Pub. Employees Retirement Bd., State Bd. Savs. and Loan Assns., State Ins. Commn., State Fire Fighters Sch. Bd. Mem. Am., Miss. State, Forrest County, Hinds County bar assns. Home: 727 Arlington St Jackson MS 39202 Office: PO Box 1787 New Capitol Bldg Jackson MS 39205 Tel (601) 354-6788

GANDY, H. CONWAY, b. Washington, D.C., Nov. 3, 1934; B.A., Colo. State U., 1962; J.D., U. Denver, 1968. Admitted to Colo. bar, 1969; claims rep. Continental Casualty Co., Denver, Colo., 1962-69; asso. firm Paul E. Wenke, Ft. Collins, Colo., 1969-70; individual practice law, Ft. Collins, 1970-74; sr. partner firm Gandy & Roberts, Ft. Collins, 1974—; dir. Choice Care Health Services, 1976. Bd. dirs. Foothills-Gateway Rehab. Center, Inc., Ft. Collins, 1970-76, pres. bd., 1975-76, v.p. and bd. mem. Ft. Collins Sertoma Club, 1970-76. Mem. Am., Colo., Larimer County bar assns., Colo. Trial Lawyers Assn. Recipient Centurion, Tribune and Senator awards, Sertoma Internat., 1973-75. Home: 1045 Montview Rd Fort Collins CO 80521 Office: Suite 440 Savings Bldg POB 2306 Fort Collins CO 80522 Tel (303) 482-5482

GANDY, MICHAEL CHARLES, b. Bryan, Tex., June 3, 1945; B.B.A., U. Tex., 1967; J.D., Baylor U., 1970. Admitted to Tex. bar, 1970, U.S. Supreme Ct. bar, 1973; asst. city atty. Waco (Tex.), 1970-72; individual practice law, Bryan, 1972-75; asso. gen. counsel Tex. Sec. of State, 1975-76; partner firm McVey, Gandy & Mauro, Bryan, 1976—. Mem. Brazos County Bar Assn. (sec.-treas. 1976), State Bar Tex., Tex. Trial Lawyers Assn. Home: 2704 Apple Creek Bryan TX 77801 Office: PO Box 3786 Bryan TX 77801 Tel (713) 779-2222

GANG, LEONARD IRWIN, b. N.Y.C., July 30, 1935; B.S., Cornell U., 1960; J.D., N.Y. U., 1963. Admitted to Nev. bar, 1964, also Fed. Dist. Ct. bar, U.S. Ct. Appeals bar; law clk. Nev. Supreme Ct., 1963-64; dep. dist. atty. Clark County, Nev., 1965-66, dep. pub. defender, 1967; mem. firms Singleton, DeLanoy and Jemison, Las Vegas, 1966-67, Dickerson, Miles and Gang, 1969—; individual practice law, Las Vegas, 1967-69; judge Nev. Dist. Ct., 8th Jud. Dist., for Clark County, 1971-74. Mem. Clark County, Am. bar assns., State Bar Nev., Am. Judicature Soc., Nat. Council Juvenile Ct. Judges. Home: 3235 E Oguendo Rd Las Vegas NV 89120 Office: 316 E Bridger St Las Vegas NV 89101 Tel (702) 385-3761

GANGEL, PHYLLIS BEVERLY, b. N.Y.C.; B.A., Bklyn. Coll., 1951; J.D., N.Y. U., 1966. Admitted to N.Y. State bar, 1966; asso. firm Tucker, Kalman & Starr, N.Y.C., 1967-74; individual practice law, N.Y.C., 1974—. Mem. Assn. Bar City N.Y., Am. Arbitration Assn. (arbitrator), N.Y. County Lawyers Assn., Women's bar assn. Condr. seminar matrimonial law Women's Sch. Home and Office: 502 Park Ave New York City NY 10022 Tel (212) PL 4-1284

GANNETT, DAMON LYNN, b. Amarillo, Tex., Apr. 29, 1947; B.A. in Bus. Adminstrn., U. Mont., 1969, J.D., 1972. Admitted to Mont. bar, 1972; atty. Missoula County, Mont., 1972; served with JAGC, USAF, 1972-76; asso. firm Jones, Olsen & Christensen, Billings, 1976—. Mem. Am., Mont. bar assns. Home: 1929 Ave D Billings MT 59102 Office: 720 N 30th St Billings MT 59102 Tel (406) 245-6338

GANNON, JAMES PATRICK, b. Phila., Jan. 4, 1941; A.B., U. Notre Dame, 1962; J.D., Villanova U., 1966. Admitted to Pa. bar, 1966, U.S. Supreme Ct. bar, 1975; asso. firm Liebert, Harvey, Herting & Short, Phila., 1966-70; individual practice law, Media, Pa., 1970-75; partner firm Beagan, Gannon, & Barnard, Media, 1975—; solicitor

Borough of Brookhaven (Pa.), 1972—. Mem. Am., Pa., Delaware County bar assns. Home: 817 Lincoln Dr Brookhaven PA 19015 Office: PO Box 666 Media PA 19063 Tel (215) 566-2870

GANSON, CHARLES MACKAY, b. New Rochelle, N.Y., Dec. 8, 1908; grad. Phillips Acad., 1928; B.A., Yale, 1932; LL.B., Harvard, 1935. Admitted to Mass. bar, 1936; partner firm Taylor, Ganson & Perrin, Boston, 1936—; clk., treas. George Lawley & Son Corp., 1953-57; clk. Fisher-Pierce Co., South Braintree, Mass., 1939-55; clk., dir. Sigma Instruments, Inc., South Braintree, 1943-55; clk. Photon, Inc., Wilmington, Mass., 1948-73; dir., clk. Cambridge Acoustical Assos., Inc., 1959—, Chmn. Products Corp., East Providence, R.I., 1955-71, Concord Control, Inc., Boston, 1956-71; clk., dir. Samson Cordage Works, Boston, 1957—; dir. Gauley Coal Land Co. Mem. fin. com. Town of Weston (Mass.), 1944-50; mem. Weston Bd. Selectmen, 1950-56; commr. Trust Funds for Weston, 1957—; mem. Weston Town Forest Com., 1957-75; hon. trustee, sec. Concord (Mass.) Acad., 1958—; asso. trustee New Eng. Conservatory Music, Boston. Mem. Am., Middlesex, Boston bar assns., Newcomen Soc. Home: 118 Chestnut St Weston MA 02193 Office: 100 Federal St Boston MA 02110 HU2-4070

GANSON, NORRIS LLOYD, b. Buffalo, Jan. 8, 1929; LL.B., U. Cin., 1958. Admitted to Ohio bar, 1959, U.S. Supreme Ct. bar, 1966, Ariz. bar, 1970; individual practice law, Cin., 1959-69, Tucson, 1970-75; sr. partner Ganson, Powell & Hays, Tucson, 1975—; spl. ct. commr. County-Ariz. Superior Ct., 1975. Bd. dirs. Victim-Witness Advocacy program Pima County, Ariz., 1976—. Mem. Ariz. State, Pima County, Cin. bar assns., Am. Arbitration Assn. (mem. nat. panel 1965—). Office: 32 N Stone Ave Suite 1001 Tucson AZ Tel (602) 622-4715

GANTZ, D. CHARLES, b. Indpls., Oct. 2, 1943; A.B., Indiana U., 1966, J.D., 1971. Admitted to Ind. bar, 1971; pros. atty. 8th Judicial Circuit of Ind., 1975—. Mem. Am., Indpls., Ind. State, Johnson County bar assns. Home: 816 Knollwood Dr Greenwood IN 46142 Office: 944 Fry Rd Greenwood IN 46142 Tel (317) 882-2901 also 783-9218

GARABEDIAN, CHARLES BAGDASAR, b. Mar. 19, 1917; A.B. in History, Tufts Coll., 1939; postgrad. Harvard, 1939-40; J.D., Boston U., 1943. Admitted to Mass. bar, 1943, U.S. Supreme Ct. bar, 1963, U.S. Ct. Mil. Appeals, 1970; faculty law sch. Suffolk U., 1944—, prof., dir. outside clin. studies, 1969—; regional atty. Office Price Stblzn. Mass., 1950-52. Mem. central com. Am. Armenian Gen. Benevolent Union Am., Inc., 1967—, mem. New Eng. dist. com., 1967-68; mem. parish council Armenian Holy Trinity Ch. Greater Boston, 1944-56; charter mem., organizer Trinity Men's Union Armenian Holy Ch. Greater Boston, 1950—; Armenian Ch. Youth Am.; del. dicesan assembly Armenian Ch. N.Am., 1956-72, mem. dicesan bd. trustees, 1970—. Mem. Am., Mass., Middlesex County, Boston bar assns., Am., Mass. trial lawyers assns., Harvard Law Sch., Boston U. Law Sch. alumni assns., Boston U. Law Rev. Assn., Ct. Practice Inst., Am. Soc. Writers on Legal Subjects, Nat. Dist. Attys. Assn. Contbr. articles to law revs. Home: 9 Ginn Rd Winchester MA 01890 Office: Suffolk Univ Sch Law 41 Temple St Boston MA 02114 Tel (617) 723-4700

GARABEDIAN, JOANNE MARIE, b. Worcester, Mass., July 3, 1940; B.A., Russell Sage Coll.; J.D., New Eng. Sch. Law. Admitted to Mass. bar, 1966; mem. firm A. Aram Garabedian, Worcester, 1966-67; individual practice law, Worcester, 1967—. Mem. Am., Mass., Worcester (bi-centennial com.) bar assns. Home and Office: 8 Southwood Rd Worcester MA 01609 Tel (617) 755-0353

GARB, ISAAC SMITH, b. Trenton, N.J., June 19, 1929; B.A., Rutgers U., 1951; LL.B., U. Pa., 1956. Admitted to Bucks County (Pa.) bar, 1958; asso. firm Cadwallader, Darlington & Clarke, Morrisville, Pa., 1958-63, firm Power, Bowen & Valimont, Doylestown, Pa., 1965-66; pub. defender Bucks County, 1960-63; asst. U.S. atty., 1963-65; judge Ct. of Common Pleas, 1966—. Chmn. Mental Health, Mental Retardation Bd., 1968—, S.E. regional planning council Gov. Pa.'s Justice Comm., 1971—, Drug and Alcohol Commn., 1972—; bd. dirs. Bucks County Blind Assn., 1968—; mem. Juvenile Ct. Judges Commn., 1975—; mem. exec. bd. Bucks County council Boy Scouts Am., 1974—. Home: Route 4B Buckingham PA 18912 Office: Courthouse Doylestown PA 18901 Tel (215) 348-2911

GARBARINO, ROBERT PAUL, b. Wanaque, N.J., Oct. 6, 1929; B.B.A. cum laude, St. Bonaventure U., 1951; J.D. summa cum laude, Villanova U., 1956. Admitted to Pa. bar, 1957; law clk. to judge U.S. Dist. Ct., Phila., 1956-57; asst. counsel Phila. Electric Co., 1957-61, asst. gen. counsel, 1961-62; partner firm Kania & Garbarino and predecessors, Bala Cynwyd, Pa., 1962—; trustee in bankruptcy Tele-Tronics Co., 1963-64; cons. Edison Electric Inst., 1960-62; mem. bd. consultors Law Sch. Villanova (Pa.) U., 1968—, chmn., 1973-75. Chmn. pres.'s adv. council St. Bonaventure (N.Y.) U., 1977—. Mem. Am., Fed., Fed. Power, Pa., Phila., Montgomery bar assns., Assn. of Army, Thomas Moore Soc., Order of Coif, Phila. Lawyers Club. Contbr. articles to legal jours. Home: 302 Conestoga Rd Wayne PA 19087 Office: 2 Bala Cynwyd Plaza Bala Cynwyd PA 19004 Tel (215) 667-3240

GARBER, KENNETH A. NEIMAN, b. Phila., May 18, 1939; B.S. in Econs., U. Pa., 1960; J.D., Villanova U., 1963; postgrad. Temple U. Law Sch. Admitted to Pa. bar, 1964, U.S. Supreme Ct. bar, 1968; law clk. firm Levin, Levin and Stock, Phila., 1962-63; asst. treas. Martel's Supermarkets, Inc., Swarthmore, Pa., 1963-64; mem. firm Costigan, Garber & Rubin, Phila., 1964—; v.p., pres. subs. Strong Wear Hosiery Co., Inc., Camden, N.J., 1969-73. Ward leader (county committeeman) 63rd Ward Democratic Party, 1974—, ward treas., 1970-74, committeeman, 1966-76; v.p. Delaware County Young Democrats, 1957-59. Mem. Phila., Pa., Am. bar assns., Am. Arbitration Assn. (panel mem.); recipient Criminal Law prize, also Moot Ct. Competition award Phila. Bar Assn., 1963. Home: 8520 Verree Rd Philadelphia PA 19111 Office: 300 Penn Sq Bldg Philadelphia PA 19107 Tel (215) 568-2572

GARBOSE, WILLIAM, b. Athol, Mass., Mar. 11, 1915; B.S. in Bus. Adminstrn., Boston U., 1936, LL.B., 1939; postgrad. U. Va., 1945, Yale, 1945. Admitted to Mass. bar, 1946, U.S. Supreme Ct. bar, 1961; justice Mass. Dist. Ct., Winchendon, 1968—. Mem. Am. Judicature Soc., Mass., Worcester County bar assns. Home: 1192 Main Athol MA 01331 Office: 80 Central Winchendon MA 01475 Tel (617) 297-0156

GARCIA, PEDRO P., b. Encino, Tex., Jan. 18, 1940; B.A., U. Tex., Austin, 1963, J.D., 1974. Admitted to Tex. bar, 1965; practice law, Corpus Christi, Tex. Pres. Cath. Sch. Bd., Corpus Christi, 1974-76. Mem. Tex. Bar, Am. Bar Assn., Tex., Am. trial lawyers assns. Office: 4466 S Staples St Corpus Christi TX 78412 Tel (512) 854-2305

GARCIA, RICHARD ARTHUR, b. Los Angeles, May 16, 1936; LL.B., Calif. Coll. Law, 1968. Claims mgr. Provident Mut. Life Ins. Co., Los Angeles, 1965-70, United Family Life Ins. Co., Atlanta, 1970-73; admitted to Ga. bar, 1972; asso. firm Edwin Marger, Atlanta, 1973-75, partner, 1975-76; partner firm Garcia and Kennedy, Atlanta, 1976—. Bd. dirs. Latin-Am. Assn., 1975—. Mem. Am., Ga., Atlanta bar assns., Ga. Trial Lawyers Assn. Home: 705 Lakestone Ct Roswell GA 30076 Office: Suite 211 6666 Powers Ferry Rd Atlanta GA 30339 Tel (404) 252-9710

GARCIA-MARTINEZ, ALFONSO LUIS, b. Salinas, P.R., July 7, 1919; B.S. in Pharmacy, U. P.R., 1939, LL.B., 1954; postgrad. Tulane U., 1971-72. Admitted to P.R. bar, 1954; U.S. Dist. Ct. for P.R., 1957; U.S. Ct. Appeals, 1st Circuit bar, 1957; law clk. Supreme Ct. P.R., 1954-56; asst. atty. gen. P.R., 1956-57; atty. Dept. Justice for Commonwealth of P.R., 1957-60; atty. P.R. Urban Renewal and Housing Corp., 1960-63; judge Superior Ct. P.R., 1963-72; prof. law Inter-Am. U., 1972—. Bd. govs. Ateneo Puertorriqueno, 1974-75. Mem. P.R. Bar Assn. (bd. govs. 1973-74; pres. law rev. commn. 1958-61, advisor 1961—), P.R. Pharm. Assn. Author: Idioma y Politica (Language and Politics), 1976. Home: Calle A-10 Urb Garcia Rio Piedras PR 00926 Office: Apartado 285 Hato Rey PR 00919 Tel 790-2061

GARCIA-PEDROSA, JOSE RAMON, b. Havana, Cuba, May 2, 1946; B.A., Harvard U., 1968, J.D., 1971. Admitted to Fla. bar, 1971, U.S. Supreme Ct. bar, 1974; asso. firm Smathers & Thompson, Miami, Fla., 1971—. Mem. Am., Dade County (ethics com. 1975—) bar assns., Fla. Bar (v.p. bicentennial com. 1975-76, chmn. law week and Am. citizenship com. 1976—). Home: 1234 S Greenway Dr Coral Gables FL 33134 Office: 1301 Alfred I DuPont Bldg Miami FL 33131 Tel (305) 379-6523

GARDEN, RICHARD PAUL, b. Norfolk, Nebr., Apr. 2, 1935; B.S. in Law, U. Nebr., 1961, LL.B., 1963. Admitted to Nebr. bar, 1963; asso. firm Hutton & Hutton, Norfolk, 1963-65, Hutton, Hutton & Garden, 1965-71, Hutton and Garden, 1971—; instr. bus. law N.E. Nebr. Tech. Community Coll. Active Norfolk United Fund, YMCA. Mem. Madison County, 9th Jud., Nebr., Am. bar assns. Home: 1211 N 18th St Norfolk NE 68701 Office: 601 S 13th St Norfolk NE 68701 Tel (402) 371-3140

GARDINER, LESTER RAYMOND, JR., b. Salt Lake City, Aug. 20, 1931; B.S. with honors, U. Utah, 1954; J.D., U. Mich., 1959. Admitted to Utah bar, 1959; law clk. to u U.S. Dist. judge Utah Dist., 1959; partner firm VanCott, Bagley, Cornwall & McCarthy, Salt Lake City, 1960-67, Pugsley, Hayes, Rampton & Watkiss, Salt Lake City, 1967, Gardiner and Johnson, Salt Lake City, 1968-71, Christensen, Gardiner, Jensen and Evans, Salt Lake City, 1971—; reporter, mem. com. adoption uniform rules of evidence Utah Supreme Ct. 1970-73, mem. com. on revision criminal code, 1975—. Mem. Salt Lake City Bd. Edn., 1971-72; bd. dirs. Salt Lake City Pub. Library, 1974-75; mem. Republican State Central Com. of Utah, 1960-72; mem. Utah Rep. Exec. Com., 1975—. Mem. Am., Utah, Salt Lake County, Fed. bar assns., Am. Judicature Soc., Am. Assn. Trial Lawyers. Office: 900 Kearns Bldg Salt Lake City UT 84101 Tel (801) 355-3431

GARDNER, ALLEN, b. Mathiston, Miss., Jan. 31, 1930; A.A., Wood Coll., 1954; B.S. in Pub. Affairs, Miss. State U., 1955; LL.B., U. Miss., 1958; postgrad. Northwestern U., 1961. Admitted to Miss. bar, 1958, Tenn. bar, 1961; trust officer 1st Nat. Bank, Memphis, 1960-62; asso. firm Nelson, Norvel, Wilson & Thomason, Memphis, 1962-63; partner firm Udelsohn, Trunage, Hester, Gardner & Blaylock, Memphis, 1963-70; partner firm Gardner & Hester, 1970-73; partner firm Fowler, Gardner, Hester & McCrary, Memphis, 1973—; asso. dir. placement and fin. aids U. Miss., 1958-59; mem. Miss. Ho. Reps., 1958-60; v.p. Mid-South Sight Service, 1968-69. Mem. Am., Tenn., Miss. bar assns., Southeast Memphis Lions Club (pres. 1967) Masons, Jaycees, Phi Alpha Delta. Home: 5518 Forsyth Dr Memphis TN 38118 Office: 44 N 2nd St Memphis TN 38103 Tel (901) 526-6428

GARDNER, CONRAD EARL, b. St. Louis, Feb. 16, 1938; A.B., Dartmouth, 1960; LL.B., Stanford, 1963. Admitted to Calif. bar, 1963, Colo. bar, 1964, U.S. Supreme Ct. bar, 1967; partner firm Fleming, Pattridge, Hacking & Gardner, Golden, Colo., 1965—; acting atty. Jefferson County (Colo.), 1968; asst. judge City of Golden, 1970-73. Active Jefferson County Library Bd. Mem. Am., Colo., Jefferson County, Calif. bar assns., Colo. Trial Lawyers Assn. Home: 5095 Pine Ridge Dr Golden CO 80401 Office: 1200 Arapaho St Golden CO 80401 Tel (303) 279-2563

GARDNER, FREDERICK EUGENE, b. Steubenville, Ohio, Mar. 19, 1948; A.B., W. Va. U., 1970, J.D., 1973. Admitted to W. Va. bar, 1973, U.S. Dist. Ct. bar, 1973; asso. firm Rickey, Chase, Chase & Hyre, Moundsville, W. Va., 1973-76, partner, 1976—; city atty., Benwood, W. Va., 1974-76. Dept sheriff, Marshall County, W.Va.; mem. Civil Service Commn., 1975-76. Mem. Am., W. Va., Marshall County bar assns. Home: 820 Echo Valley St Glen Dale WV 26038 Office: 509 7th St Moundsville WV 26041 Tel (304) 845-5100

GARDNER, JAMES FRANCIS, b. Boston, Apr. 19, 1918; LL.B., Northeastern U., 1939. Admitted to Mass. bar, 1939, Tex. bar, 1947, U.S. Supreme Ct. bar, 1951; spl. agt. FBI, 1940-48; individual practice law, San Antonio, 1948-51, 53—. Chmn. bd. Salvation Army, San Antonio, 1955-56. Mem. Nat. Contract Mgrs. Assn., Tex., Am., San Antonio, Fed. bar assns. Home: 106 E Gramercy Pl San Antonio TX 78212 Office: 1800 Plaza West Suite 100 1800 NE Expressway San Antonio TX 78217 Tel (512) 828-6166

GARDNER, JOHN DEXTER, b. Boston Apr 3, 1947; A.B., Johns Hopkins U., 1969; J.D. summa cum laude, Ohio State U., 1973. Admitted to Ind. bar, 1974; asso. firm Baker and Daniels, Indpls., 1973—. Mem. Am. (sect. taxation), Ind. State, Indpls. bar assns. Contbr. note to legal jour. Home: 2111 E 91st St Indianapolis IN 46240 Office: 810 Fletcher Trust Bldg Indianapolis IN 46204 Tel (317) 636-4535

GARDNER, JOHN JAY, b. Cortland, N.Y., Sept. 5, 1914; A.B., Cornell U., 1938; LL.B., Union U., 1938, J.D., 1968. Admitted to N.Y. bar, 1938; individual practice law, Cortland, 1938—; research counsel N.Y. State Commn. on Modernization, Revision and Simplification of Law of Estates, 1962-64; town atty. Town of Cortlandville (N.Y.), 1964—; atty. McGraw (N.Y.) Central Sch. Dist., 1965—. Sec. Cortland Municipal CSC, 1940-42; treas. Cortland Mem. Hosp., Inc. Mem. Cortland County, N.Y. State, Am. bar assns. Home: 332 Groton Ave Extension Cortland NY 13045 Office: 100 Grange Pl Cortland NY 13045 Tel (607) 753-3081

GARDNER, MARTIN RALPH, b. Salt Lake City, Nov. 3, 1944; B.S., U. Utah, 1969, J.D., 1972. Admitted to Utah bar, 1972; instr. law Ind. U., Bloomington, 1972-73; asst. prof. law U. Ala., University, 1973-77, U. Nebr., Lincoln, 1977—. Harvard fellow in law and humanities, 1975-76; contbr. articles in field to legal jours. Office: U Nebr Coll Law Lincoln NE 68583 Tel (402) 472-2161

GARDNER, MITCHELL, b. New Britain, Conn., Oct. 19, 1930; B.S., Bochnell U., 1953; LL.B., U. Conn., 1960. Admitted to Conn. bar, 1960; practice law, New Britain. Home: 208 South Mountain Dr New Britain CT 06051 Office: 272 Main St New Britain CT 06051 Tel (203) 225-4631

GARDNER, REECE ALEXANDER, b. Columbia, Mo., Oct. 6, 1911; A.B., Harvard, 1933, J.D., 1936. Admitted to Mo. bar, 1936, Kans. bar, 1941, U.S. Supreme Ct. bar, 1946; asso. firm Stinson, Mag, Thompson, McEvers & Fizzell, and predecessor, Kansas City, Mo., 1936-39, partner, 1939—. City clk. City of Mission Hills (Kans.), 1959-70. Mem. Am., Fed., Kansas City bar assns., Am. Judicature Soc., Am. Law Inst., Lawyers Assn. Kansas City, Mo. Bar. Contbr. articles to legal jours. Home: 5049 Wornall Rd Kansas City MO 64112 Office: 2100 Ten Main Center Kansas City MO 64105 Tel (816) 842-8600

GARDNER, RICHARD ELLIS, JR., b. New Orleans, Sept. 30, 1941; B.A., Ark. Polytech. Coll., 1964; J.D., U. Tulsa, 1969. Admitted to Ark. bar, 1970; mem. firm Williams & Gardner, 1970—. Mem. bd. C. of C. Russellville, Ark. 1973-76. Mem. Ark., Am., Pope-Yell County bar assns., Am. Trial Lawyers Assn. Office: Box 866 110 S Denver Russellville AR 72801 Tel (501) 968-5333

GARDNER, RICHARD JACOB, b. Quincy, Fla., Apr. 10, 1912; B.A., U. Fla., 1933, J.D. with honors, 1935. Admitted to Fla. bar, 1935; asso. firm Thomas B. Adams, Jacksonville, Fla., 1935-37; asso. firm Gardner & Lines, Quincy, 1937-42; 42-68; individual practice law, Quincy, 1968—; legal aide Fla. Gov. Leroy Collins, 1955-60; chmn. Fla. Bd. Bar Examiners, 1968-69; mem. Fla. Jud. Council, 1953-59. Pres. Fla. State U. Found., Tallahassee, 1968-69. Mem. Fla. Bar, Am. Bar Assn., Am. Judicature Soc., Am. Coll. Probate Counsel, So. Acad. Letters, Arts and Scis., Blue Key, Phi Alpha Delta, Phi Kappa Phi. Home: 905 Myrtle Ave Quincy FL 32351 Office: 4 E Washington Quincy FL 32351 Tel (904) 627-9291

GARDNER, RICHARD NEWTON, b. N.Y.C., July 9, 1927; A.B., Harvard, 1948; J.D., Yale, 1951; Ph.D., Oxford (Eng.) U., 1954. Admitted to N.Y. bar, 1952; asso. firm Coudert Bros., N.Y.C., 1954-57, spl. counsel, 1969—; asso. prof. law Columbia, 1957-65, Henry L. Moses prof. law and internat. orgn., 1965-77; dep. asst. sec. state U.S. Dept. State, Washington, 1961-65; U.S. ambassador to Italy, 1977—. Mem. mem. Group of High Level Experts on the Restructuring of the UN System, N.Y.C., 1975; mem. Pres.'s. Commn. on Internat. Trade and Investment Policy, Washington, 1969-71; mem. U.S. Advisory Com. on the Law of the Sea, 1971—; U.S. mem. bd. trustees UN Inst. for Training and Research, 1969-73. Mem. Century Assn. N.Y.C., Met. Club Washington, AAAS, Freedom House (dir.), Atlantic Council (dir.), UN Assn. (dir.). Author: The Global Partnership, Internat. Agencies and Econ. Devel., 1968; Blueprint for Peace, 1966; In Pursuit of World Order, 1966; Sterling-Dollar Diplomacy, 1969; co-author: reports of Trilateral Commn., 1974, 75. Guggenheim Found. fellow, 1974-75; Rhodes scholar, 1954; recipient Arthur S. Flemming award, 1963. Home: 1150 Fifth Ave Apt 11A New York City NY 10028 Office: Columbia Law Sch 435 W 116th St New York City NY 10027 Tel (212) 280-2642

GARDNER, ROBERT, b. Arlington, Wash., Dec. 27, 1911; A.B., U. So. Calif., 1933, LL.B., 1936. Admitted to Calif. bar, 1936; practiced in Santa Ana, Calif., 1936-46; judge Superior Ct., Orange County, Calif., 1947-70; presiding justice Calif. 4th Appellate Dist., 2d Dist., San Bernardino, 1970—. Home: 320 Evening Canyon Rd Corona Del Mar CA 92625 Office: State Bldg San Bernardino CA 92401 Tel (714) 383-4443

GARDNER, ROBERT FRANCIS, b. Cin., Apr. 8, 1930; B.A., U. Cin., 1954; LL.B., Salmon P. Chase Coll. of Law, 1958; M.A., Xavier U., 1962. Admitted to Ohio bar, 1958; individual practice law, Columbus, Ohio, 1970—; jr. accountant C.J. Keller & Co., Cin., 1954-55; field agt. IRS, Cin., 1955-56; with 1st Nat. Bank of Cin., 1956-64; asst. treas. State of Ohio, 1964-70, dept. treas., 1969—. Mem. Am., Ohio State, Columbus bar assns. C.P.A., Ohio. Home: 1046 Medhurst Rd Columbus OH 43220 Office: 601 S High St Columbus OH 43215 Tel (614) 221-0749

GARDNER, RUSSELL MENESE, b. High Point, N.C., July 14, 1920; A.B., Duke, 1942, LL.B., 1948. Admitted to Fla. bar, 1948; mem. firm McCune, Hiaasen, Crum, Ferris & Gardner, and predecessors, Fort Lauderdale, Fla., 1948—. Home: 2412 NE 14th St Fort Lauderdale FL 33304 Office: 2626 E Oakland Park Blvd Fort Lauderdale FL 33306 Tel (305) 462-2000

GARDNER, THOMAS JOSEPH, III, b. Jackson, Miss., Feb. 12, 1936; B.A., Millsaps Coll., 1960; J.D., U. Miss., 1966. Admitted to Miss. bar, 1966; asso. firm Mitchell, McNutt & Bush, Tupelo, Miss., 1966-71; individual practice law, Tupelo, 1971—; asst. dist. atty. 1st Dist. State of Miss., 1976—; city prosecutor City of Tupelo. Mem. Miss. Trial Lawyers Assn., Nat. Assn. Dist. Attys., Miss. Bar Assn. Home: 1412 Pinecrest Dr Tupelo MS 38801 Office: Thomas Bldg Tupelo MS 38801 Tel (601) 844-4754

GARDNER, THOMAS VAUGHN, JR., b. Monroe, La., Feb. 10, 1948; B.A., NE La. U., 1970; J.D., La. State U., 1973. Admitted to La. bar, 1973; law clk. Wright & Joyce, Monroe, La., 1972-73, asso., 1973-75; individual practice law, Monroe, 1975—. Mem. La. State, 4th Jud. Dist. bar assns., La., NE La. trial lawyers assns. Office: 3012 Lee Ave Monroe LA 71202 Tel (318) 322-7842

GARDNER, WARNER WINSLOW, b. Richmond, Ind., Sept. 25, 1909; A.B., Swarthmore Coll., 1930; M.A., Rutgers U., 1931; LL.B., Columbia, 1934. Admitted to N.Y. bar, 1935, U.S. Supreme Ct. bar, 1938, D.C. bar, 1947; law clk. to Justice Harlan F. Stone, U.S. Supreme Ct., 1934-35; mem. staff Office Solicitor Gen., Washington, 1935-41, 1st asst., 1938-41; solicitor Dept. Labor, Washington, 1941-42; solicitor Dept. Interior, Washington, 1942-43, 45-46, asst. sec., 1946-47; mem. firm Shea & Gardner, Washington, 1947—; spl. Supreme Ct. counsel Fed. Maritime Bd., 1956. Mem. Am., D.C. bar assns., Am. Law Inst., Maritime Adminstrv. Bar Assn. (pres. 1962-64), Adminstrv. Conf. U.S. (chmn. com. on informal action 1968-76), Phi Beta Kappa. Decorated Legion of Merit (U.S.); Croix de Guerre (France); contbr. articles to legal jours. Home: 6903 Armat Dr Bethesda MD 20034 Office: 734 Fifteenth St NW Washington DC 20005 Tel (202) 737-1255

GARDNER, WILLIAM COURTLEIGH, b. Springfield, Ohio, Oct. 19, 1917; A.B., Howard U., 1948; J.D., Harvard Law Sch., 1951. Admitted to U.S. Dist. Court for the Dist. Columbia, 1951, Dist. Columbia Court of Appeals bar, 1951, Superior Court for the Dist. Columbia, 1951, U.S. Court of Appeals for the Dist. Columbia Circuit bar, 1953, U.S. Supreme Court bar, 1957, U.S. Court Appeals for Sixth Circuit bar, 1962; partner firm Houston and Gardner, Washington, 1951—; commr. Nat. Conference Commrs. Uniform State Laws; mem. com. grievances U.S. Dist. Court; mem. com. admissions Dist. Columbia Court of Appeals; mem. commn. Judicial Disabilities and Tenure, Dist. Columbia; mem. U.S. Court Appeals Com. Admissions and Grievances; mem. bd. trustees Public Defender Services; bar examiner Dist. Columbia. Mem. Dist. Columbia Citizen's Traffic Bd., 1963-66; Dist Columbia Hacker's Appeal Bd., 1963-67; mem. Special Police Trial Bd., 1966-69; mem. bd. dirs. Neighborhood Legal Services Program, 1967-70; mem. bd. Appeals and Review of Dist. Columbia, 1969-75. Fellow Am. Coll. Trial Lawyers; mem. Am. Bar Assn., Bar Assn. D.C. (dir. 1971-72), Trial Lawyers Assn., Assn. Plaintiffs' Trial Attys. Met. Washington, The Counsellors, Harvard Law Sch. Assn., Alpha Phi Alpha. Home: 4366 Argyle Terr NW Washington DC 20011 Office: 615 F St NW Washington DC 20004 Tel (202) 628-7058

GARDNER, WILLIAM F., b. Birmingham, Ala., Apr. 24, 1934; B.A., U. Ala., 1956; LL.B., U. Va., 1959. Admitted to Ala. bar, 1959; asso., partner Cabaniss, Johnston, Gardner, Dumas & O'Neal, Birmingham, 1959—. Mem. Am. Bar Assn., Def. Research Inst. Tel (205) 252-8800

GARDNER, WOODFORD LLOYD, JR., b. Pryor, Okla., Feb. 4, 1945; B.S., Western Ky. U., 1967; J.D., U. Ky., 1969. Admitted to Ky. bar, 1969; law clk. Judge Mac Swinford U.S. Dist. Ct., 1969; partner firm Redford, Redford & Gardner, Glasgow, Ky., 1971—; asst. commonwealth's atty. 43d Circuit Ky., 1976. Mem. Am., Ky., Barren County bar assns., Phi Delta Phi. Contbr. articles in field to profl. jours. Home: Route 7 Box 140 Glasgow KY 42141 Office: 202 E Washington St Glasgow KY 42141 Tel (502) 651-8346

GARETY, ROGER PATRICK, b. San Francisco, Oct. 21, 1920; B.S., U. Santa Clara, 1942; LL.B., U. San Francisco, 1949. Admitted to Calif. bar, 1949; with Dist. Atty.'s Office, San Francisco, 1949; asso. firm Shirley, Saroyan, Shearer & Sullivan, San Francisco, 1950; dep. dist. atty. Marin County (Calif.), San Refael, 1950-60, dist. atty., 1960-64; mem. firm Buresh, Garety, Vallarino & Costamagna, San Rafael, 1964-71, Myers, Praetzel & Garety, San Rafael, 1971—. Mem. Calif. Welfare Commn., 1962, Calif. Alcoholic Beverage Control Appeals Bd., 1967-68; chmn. Marin County Housing for Elderly Com.; mem. Bay Area Social Planning Council. Mem. Am., Calif., Marin County (past pres.) bar assns., Am. Bd. Trial Advs., Marin Council Adminstrn. Justice. Home: 829 S Eliseo Dr Greenbrae CA 94904 Office: 1615 5th Ave San Rafael CA 94901 Tel (415) 453-7121

GAREY, JACK, b. Brady, Tex., Jan. 20, 1930; B.B.A., U. Tex., 1955, LL.B., 1957. Admitted to Tex. bar, 1956, U.S. Dist. Ct. bar, 1958, U.S. Ct. Appeals bar, 1959; sr. partner firm Garey, Colbert & Kidd, Austin, Tex., 1966-70, firm Garey, Morris & Ausley, 1970—. Mem. Austin Jr. (pres. 1960-61), Travis County (dir. 1961-62) bar assns., Tex. Trial Lawyers Assn., Phi Delta Phi. Author: Handling A Workman's Compensation Claim, 1968. Home: Route 2 Box 22-B Round Rock TX 78664 Office: 1010 Brown Bldg Austin TX 78701 Tel (512) 255-2526

GARFINKEL, PAUL WARREN, b. Charleston, S.C., Aug. 10, 1944; A.B., U. S.C., 1967, J.D., 1970. Admitted to S.C. bar, 1970; individual practice Law, Charleston, 1970—. Chmn. bd. dirs. Addlestone Hebrew Acad., 1973-75; sec. Brith Sholom Beth Israel, 1973—. Mem. Am., S.C., Charleston County bar assns., Nat. Assn. Home Builders. Home: 241 Confederate Circle Charleston SC 29407 Office: POB 206 Charleston SC 29402 Tel (803) 577-6583

GARFINKLE, GERALD DAVID, b. Phila., Mar. 5, 1939; B.A., Pa. State U., 1961; J.D., Temple U., 1967. Admitted to Pa. bar, 1968; contract adminstr. U.S. Def. Supply Agency, 1962-66; law clk. to John P. Fullam U.S. Dist. Ct. Eastern Dist. Pa., 1966-68; former partner firm Fine, Staud, Grossman and Garfinkle, Phila.; now partner (Garfinkle & Corbman, Phila.; chief justice Temple U. Law Sch. Moot Ct., 1965-68; lectr. in field. Counsel, Plymouth Hill Civic Assn. Mem. Phila. Bar Assn., Am., Phila., Pa. (treas.) trial lawyers assns., Am. Arbitration Assn. Recipient Criminal Law, Criminal Procedure, Family Law prizes, Temple Univ. Law Sch. Home: 2901 Henley Rd Norristown Pa 19403 Office: 106 S 16th St Philadelphia PA 19102 Tel (215) 568-5510

GARGIULO, ANDREA W., b. Hartford, Conn., Apr. 26, 1946; B.A., Smith Coll., 1968; J.D. cum laude, Suffolk U., 1972. Admitted to Mass. bar, 1972, U.S. Dist. Ct. for Mass. bar, 1975; legal intern Atty. Gen.'s office, State of Mass., 1971; asst. dist. atty., Middlesex County, Mass., 1972-75; asso. firm Richard A. Gargiulo, Boston, 1976—; chmn. Boston Fin. Commn., 1975-77, Boston Licensing Bd., 1977—. Mem. Boston, Mass. bar assns. Recipient Am. Jurisprudence award, 1972; contbr. articles to legal jours. Office: 1 Court St Boston MA 02108 Tel (617) 742-3833

GARGIULO, WILLIAM CARMINE, b. Cleve., July 19, 1935; A.B., Ohio U., 1957; postgrad. John Carroll U., 1958-61; J.D., Cleve. State Coll. Law, 1969. Admitted to Ohio bar, 1969; partner firm Manley and Gargiulo, Willoughby, Ohio, 1969-76, firm Patterson and Gargiulo, Willoughby, 1976—; asst. Lake County prosecutor, 1972-74; dir. Lake/Geauga County Narcotic Unit, 1972-74; instr. law enforcement Lakeland Community Coll. Chmn. Wickliffe Civil Service Commn., 1976—. Mem. Am., Ohio, Cuyahoga, Lake County bar assns. Home: 29037 Homewood Dr Wickliffe OH 44092 Office: 33579 Euclid Ave Willoughby OH 44094 Tel (216) 943-4700

GARLAND, ABE J., b. St. Louis, Nov. 23, 1913; A.B., Washington U., St. Louis, J.D., 1936. Admitted to Mo. bar, 1936; mem. firm Lewis Rice Tucker Allen & Chubb, St. Louis, 1936—. Mem. Am., Mo., St. Louis Met. bar assns., Order of Coif, Phi Beta Kappa. Office: Lewis Rice Tucker Allen & Chubb 611 Olive St Saint Louis MO 63101 Tel (314) 231-5833

GARLAND, ALEC, b. Sewanee, Tenn., Mar. 18, 1946; B.S., Tenn. Tech. U., 1968; J.D., U. Tenn. at Knoxville, 1971. Admitted to Tenn. bar, 1971; individual practice law, Manchester, Tenn., 1971-75; mem. firm Harrison, Garland & Fisher, Manchester, 1975—; city judge Manchester, 1973—. Mem. Coffee County Bar Assn. (pres. 1975-76). Home: Fredonia Rd Manchester TN 37355 Office: Box 486 214 N Spring St Manchester TN 37355 Tel (615) 728-0900

GARLAND, BENJAMIN BYRD, b. Barnesville, Ga., June 18, 1911; Emory U., 1931. Admitted to Ga. bar, 1932; individual practice of law, Atlanta, Jackson, Ga., 1943-73; mem. firm Garland & Garland, Jackson, 1973—; solicitor gen. Flint Judicial Circuit, 1949-53, city atty., 1962-73, city recorder, 1972-73. Mem. Ga. Gen. Assembly, 1948-49; former chmn. bd. deacons, 1st Baptist Ch., Jackson. Office: 300 W 3rd St Jackson GA 30233 Tel (404) 775-3188

GARLAND, EDWARD THOMAS MOON, b. Atlanta, June 10, 1941; B.A., U. Ga., 1963, LL.B., 1965. Admitted to Ga. bar, 1964; partner firm Garland, Garland & Garland, Atlanta, 1965-73; partner firm Garland, Nuckolls & Kadish, Atlanta, 1973-76, Mem. Garland, Nuckolls, Kadish, Cook & Weisensee, 1976—. Atlanta, bar assns., Am., Ga. trial lawyers assn., Ga. Assn. Criminal Def. Atty.s Home: 2660 Howell Mill Rd NW Atlanta GA 30327 Office: 1012 Candler Bldg 125 Peachtree St Atlanta GA 30303 Tel (404) 577-2225

GARLAND, JOHN BYRD, b. Atlanta, Mar. 22, 1947; B.B.A., U. Ga., 1970; J.D., Mercer U., 1973. Admitted to Ga. bar, 1973; partner firm Garland & Garland, Jackson, Ga., 1973—. Mem. Ga. Bar Assn. Home: 225 Fox Hollow Wood Jackson GA 30233 Office: 300 W 3d St Jackson GA 30233 Tel (404) 775-3188

GARLAND, NORMAN MICHAEL, b. Chgo., Aug. 28, 1939; B.S. in Bus. Adminstrn., Northwestern U., 1961, J.D., 1964; LL.M., Georgetown U., 1965. Admitted to D.C. bar, 1965, Ill. bar, 1965; asso. firm Howery, Simon, Baker & Marchison, Washington, 1965-68; asst. prof. law, asst. dean Northwestern U., 1968-72, asso. prof. law, 1972-75; prof. law Southwestern U., 1975—. Mem. Am. Bar Assn., Themis Soc., Order of the Coif. Contbr. articles to law jours. Office: 675 S Westmorland Ave Los Angeles CA 90005 Tel (213) 380-4800

GARLAND, SYLVIA DILLOF, b. N.Y.C., June 4, 1919; B.A., Brooklyn Coll., 1939; J.D., New York Law Sch., 1960. Admitted to N.Y. State bar, 1960, also U.S. Supreme Ct. bar, others; asso. firm, Borden, Skidell, Fleck & Steindler, Jamaica, N.Y., 1960-61; asso. firm, Field, Zimmerman, Skodnick & Siegal, Jamaica, 1961-65; asso. firm, Marshall, Bratter, Green, Allison & Tucker, N.Y.C., 1965-68; legal sec., N.Y. Supreme Ct. Justice, Riverhead, N.Y., 1968-70; partner firm, Hofheimeimer, Gartlir, Gottlieb & Gross, N.Y.C., 1970—; adj. prof., N.Y. Law Sch., 1972—. Mem. Am., N.Y., Queens County bar assns. Editor in chief New York Law Forum, 1959-60; asso. editor, Queens County Bar Bull., 1964-70; recipient Dean Gutman award, Trustee award, 1960, Moot Ct. award, 1960; author: A Lawyer is A Girl's Best Friend, 1975, Complex Issues of A Simple Will, 1965. Home: 31 Country Village New Hyde Park NY 11040 Office: 100 Park Ave New York City NY 10017 Tel (212) 725-0400

GARLINGHOUSE, F. MARK, b. Topeka, Kans., Dec. 4, 1914; student U. Chgo., 1932-33; Ph.B., Washburn U., 1936; LL.B., 1939, J.D., 1939. Admitted to Kans. bar, 1939, N.Y. State bar, 1941, Mo. bar, 1950, U.S. Supreme Ct. bar, 1945, Fed. bar, 1975; v.p., gen. counsel Southwestern Bell Telephone Co., St. Louis, 1953-65; v.p., Am. Telephone and Telegraph Co., N.Y.C., 1965-72, v.p., gen. counsel, N.Y.C., 1972—. Pres. Ladue (Mo.) Sch. Bd., 1959-65; pres., chmn. St. Louis Soc. Crippled Children, 1959-63. Fellow Am. Bar Found.; mem. Am. Bar Assn. (chmn. pub. utility sect. 1972-73). Home: 328 Hartshorn Dr Short Hills NJ 07078 Office: 195 Broadway St New York City NY 10007 Tel (212) 393-3346

GARLINGTON, JAMES CLARKE, b. Missoula, Mont., Mar. 24, 1908; A.B., LL.B., U. Mont., 1930. Admitted to Mont. bar, 1929; partner firm Pope and Garlington, Missoula, 1930-35; asso. firm Murphy & Witlock, Missoula, 1935-39; partner firm Murphy, Garlington & Pauly, Missoula, 1939-54, Garlington, Lohn & Robinson, Missoula, 1954—; atty. City Missoula, 1935; participant permanent lawyers com. Fed. Ninth Circuit Jud. Conf., 1960-75; prof. law U. Mont., 1946-60; mem. Mont. Bd. Law Examiners, 1966—; dir. Western Mont. Nat. Bank, Missoula, 1954-74, Intermountain Lumber Co., Missoula, 1970-74, Helena br. Fed. Reserve Bank Mpls., Missoula, 1975—. Trustee Missoula Sch. Dist. #1, Missoula County High Sch.; del. State Mont. Constl. Conv., 1972, Gen. Conv. Episc. Ch., 1964, 1967, 1970, 1972. Mem. Mont. (pres. 1949-50), Am. bar assns., Am. Law Inst., Am. Coll. Probate Lawyers, Phi Delta Phi. Home: 1600 Arthur Ave Missoula MT 59801 Office: 199 W Pine St Missoula MT 59801 Tel (406) 728-1200

GARMENT, LEONARD, b. Bklyn., May 11, 1924; grad. Bklyn. Law Sch., 1949. Admitted to N.Y. bar, 1949; mem. firm Mudge, Rose, Guthrie & Alexander, N.Y.C., 1949-60, 76—; spl. cons. to Pres. Nixon, 1969-73, acting counsel, 1973-74; asst. to Pres. Ford, 1974; vice chmn. Adminstrv. Conf. U.S., 1973-74; U.S. rep. UN Commn. on Human Rights, 1975-77. Home: 40 Willow Pl New York City NY 11201 Office: Mudge Rose et al 20 Broad St New York City NY 10005 Tel (212) 422-6767

GARMON, HOLLIS DEE, b. Point, Tex., Oct. 21, 1929; M.S., East Tex. State U., 1949; J.D., Tex. and Houston Law Sch., 1954; grad. Nat. Coll. Trial Judges, 1971. Admitted to Tex. bar, 1957; with Garmon Realty, 1950-54; staff Galena Park Pub. Schs., 1955-57; asso. firm Garmon & Roy, Houston, 1957-60; individual practice law, Greenville, Tex., 1961-62; asso. firm Garmon, Horton & Miller, Greenville, 1964-67; state dist. atty. Tex. 8th Jud. Dist., 1969; judge Tex. Dist. Ct., 196th Jud. Dist., 1969—; vis. prof. East Tex. U., 1974-75. Mem. ofcl. bd. United Methodist Ch., Greenville, 1966-67. Mem. State Bar Tex. (dir. N.Tex. 1963-65), Am. Bar Assn. (chmn. North Tex. area 1962-64). Office: County Courthouse Bldg Greenville TX 75401 Tel (214) 455-5600

GARNER, MARCELLUS CRAIG, JR., b. Raleigh, N.C., May 6, 1948; student George Washington U., 1968; A.B., Davidson Coll., 1970; J.D., Washington and Lee U., 1974. Admitted to S.C. bar, 1974, U.S. Dist. Ct. S.C., 1975, 4th Circuit Ct. Appeals, 1976; mem. Staff U.S. Ho. of Reps. Com. on D.C., Washington, 1970-71; asso. firm McNair, Konduros, Corley, Singletary & Dibble, Columbia, S.C., 1974—. Mem. S.C., Richland County, Am. bar assns. Office: POB 11895 Suite 1820 Bankers Trust Tower Columbia SC 29211 Tel (803) 799-9800

GARNER, REX WALLACE, b. East Prairie, Mo., Apr. 4, 1937; B.S., S.E. Mo. State U., 1963; LL.B., Atlanta Law Sch., 1969, J.D., 1976. Admitted to Ga. bar, 1972, U.S. Supreme Ct. bar, 1976; individual practice law, Rome, Ga., 1972-73, 74—; asst. dist. atty. Rome Jud. Circuit of Ga., 1973-74. Pres. Floyd County (Ga.) Democratic Assn., 1975-76. Mem. Rome, Am. bar assns., State Bar Ga. Home: 16 Luminosa Terr Rome GA 30161 Office: 100 W 5th Ave Rome GA 30161 Tel (404) 291-4750

GARNER, ROBERT EDWARD LEE, b. Bowling Green, Ky., Sept. 26, 1946; B.A., U. Ala., 1968; J.D., Harvard, 1971. Admitted to Ga. bar, 1971; staff JAGC, 1971-72; asso. firm Gambrell, Russell, Killorin & Forbes, Atlanta, 1972-76, partner, 1976—. Mem. DeKalb County Rep. Party, DeKalb County Young Reps. Mem. Am., Ga., Atlanta bar assns., Lawyers Club Atlanta, U. Ala. Nat. Alumni Assn., Harvard Alumni Assn. Phi Alpha Theta, Pi Sigma Alpha. Home: 1641 Executive Park Ln Atlanta GA 30329 Office: 4000 First Nat. Bank Tower Atlanta GA 30303 Tel (404) 658-1620

GARNER, THOMAS ARNOLD, JR., b. Ector, Tex., June 24, 1935; B.A., U. Tex., 1961; LL.B., U. Houston, 1964. Admitted to Tex. bar, 1964; asso. firm George Fred Rhodes, Port Lavaca, Tex., 1964-66; partner firm Rhodes & Garner, 1966-75, Rhodes, Garner & Roberts, Port Lavaca, 1975—; chmn. flood ins. study com. Commnrs. Ct. Calhoun County (Tex.), 1971. Bd. dirs. Guadalupe-Blanco River Authority, 1969-75, chmn., 1972; bd. dirs. Golden Crescent Council Govts., Victoria, Tex., 1970—; 3d v.p., 1971, 2d v.p., 1972, 1st v.p., 1973-74, pres., 1975; advisory com. Tex. Costal Mgmt. Program, 1975—; exec. sec. Housing Authority City Seadrift (Tex.), 1976. Mem. Calhoun County Bar Assn. (sec.-treas. 1965-68, pres. 1969). Recipient W. St. John Garwood award U. Houston, 1962, 63, 64; named Outstanding Young Man, Calhoun County, 1971; asso. editor, bus. mgr. Houston Law Review, 1963-64. Home: 1021 N San Antonio St Port Lavaca TX 77979 Office: 202 S Ann St Port Lavaca TX 77979

GARNETT, RICHARD WINGFIELD, III, b. Thomasville, Ga., Oct. 25, 1943; B.A. in Greek, Swarthmore Coll., 1965; LL.B., U. Va., 1968. Admitted to Pa. bar, 1969, Alaska bar, 1971; research asso. Va. Constl. Revision Commn., 1968; asso. firms Drinker Biddle & Reath, Phila., 1969, MacCoy, Evans & Lewis, Phila., 1969-71, Ely Guess & Rudd, Anchorage, 1973-74; asst. atty. gen. Alaska Atty. Gen., Juneau, 1971-73, Anchorage, 1974-75; individual practice law, Anchorage, 1975; municipal atty. City of Anchorage, 1975—; counsel Anchorage Charter Commn., 1975; Alaska chmn. Nat. Inst. Municipal Law Officers. Mem. Am., Alaska, Anchorage bar assns. Home: 1342 W 12th St Anchorage AK 99501 Office: Pouch 6-650 Anchorage AK 99501 Tel (907) 279-3123

GARR, LEE DOUGLAS, b. Chgo., July 16, 1943; B.A., Coe Coll., 1965; J.D., Chgo.-Kent Coll. Law, 1971. Admitted to Ill. bar, 1971. asst. atty. gen. Ill., 1971-72; partner firm Brundage & Garr, Chgo., 1972-74, firm Hines, Garr & DeMaertelaero, Elk Grove Village, Ill., 1974—. Mem. bd. counselors Alexian Bros. Med. Center, 1975—. Mem. Ill., NW Suburban bar assns., NW Suburban Bd. Realtors, Elk Grove Assn. Industry and Commerce. Recipient Presdl. award of honor Elk Grove Village Jaycees, 1974. Office: 31 Profl Arcade Park and Shop Center Elk Grove Village IL 60007 Tel (312) 593-8777

GARRETSON, ALBERT HENRY, b. Tacoma, Wash., Mar. 30, 1910; B.A., Whitman Coll., 1931, LL.D., 1976; M.A., Am. U., 1932; B.A. (Jur.), Oxford (Eng.) U., 1934; LL.B., Syracuse U., 1942, J.D., 1959. Admitted to N.Y. State bar, 1942, U.S. Supreme Ct. bar, 1958; sr. atty. Dept. Justice, 1942-43; chief gen. intelligence unit div. econ. warfare Am. Embassy, London, 1943-44; dep. chief econ. sect. Supreme Hdqrs. AEF, Versailles, France, 1944-45; asst. legal adviser Dept. State, Washington, 1945-46; legal adviser Imperial Ethiopian Govt., Addis Ababa, 1947-57; asst. prof. law N.Y. U., 1946-47, prof., 1957—, dir. Inst. Internat. Law, 1959—, Fgn. Law Insts., 1971—; legal cons. UN Devel. Fund, 1972-75; hon. prof. law King's Coll. U. London, 1964—. Mem. Bar Assn. City N.Y., Am. Bar Assn., Am. Soc. Internat. Law, Internat. Law Assn. Editor Jour. Maritime Law and Commerce, 1969-71. Home: 33 Washington Square W New York City NY 10011 Office: NYU Law Sch 40 Washington Square S New York City NY 10012 Tel (212) 598-2531

GARRETT, DUDLEY WILLIAM, JR., b. Atlanta, Nov. 14, 1935; B.B.A., Ga. State Coll., 1959; B.Laws, Atlanta Law Sch., 1967, postgrad. U. Ga. and U.S. Bur. Narcotics Drug Investigation Workshop, 1969, Pros. Attys. course Northwestern U., 1969, Nat. Dist. Attys. Assn. and Coll. Dist. Attys. Police and Prosecutor Inst., 1974. Admitted to Ga. bar, 1969; criminal investigator Dist. Atty. of Atlanta Jud. Circuit, 1964-69, asst. dist. atty., 1969-70; partner firm Spence, Garrett & Spence, Alpharetta, Ga., 1970—. Coach Alpharetta Youth Program, 1975—; founder North Fulton Met. Atlanta Recreational Com., 1976. Mem. Ga., Am., Atlanta bar assns., Am. Judicature Soc., N.Fulton C. of C. (charter). Home: 14680 Freemanville Rd Alpharetta GA 30201 Tel (404) 475-4538

GARRETT, JOHN THOMAS, b. Paducah, Ky., Nov. 6, 1921; LL.B., U. Ky., 1949. Admitted to Ky. bar, 1949; individual practice law, Paducah, 1949—; mem. Ky. Senate, 1962—, caucus chmn., 1970-72, majority leader, 1974-76. Pres., Ky. Young Democrats, 1960-61. Mem. Ky., McCracken County (pres. 1974) bar assns. Home: 700 Hillgate Rd Paducah KY 42001 Office: 206-10 Guthrie Bldg Paducah KY 42001 Tel (502) 443-2409

GARRETT, JUDSON PAUL, JR., b. Charleston, S.C., Oct. 26, 1937; A.B., St. Mary's Sem. and U. Balt., 1960; LL.B., U. Md., 1968. Probation Counselor children's div. Domestic Relations Ct. of Charleston County (S.C.), 1960-61; juvenile probation officer Circuit Ct. of Cecil County (Md.), 1961-67; regional supr. Md. Dept. Juvenile Services, 1967-69; admitted to Md. bar, 1969, U.S. Supreme Ct. bar, 1973, 4th Circuit bar, 1973, 3d Circuit bar, 1975; asso. firm Rollins & Calvert, Elkton, Md., 1969-71; asst. atty. gen. State of Md., 1971—; counsel Md. Gen. Assembly, 1976—. Mem. Md. State Bar Assn. Recipient certificate of appreciation U.S. Pres., 1971; co—author: Continuing Legal Education Handbook, 1971. Home: 663 Rhone Ct Glen Burnie MD 21061 Office: 104 Legislative Services Bldg 90 State Circle Annapolis MD 21401 Tel (301) 269-3786

GARRETT, MICHAEL TERRELL, b. Lubbock, Tex., Apr. 21, 1940; B.B.A., U. N.Mex. and Tex. Tech. U., 1962; J.D., So. Meth. U., 1965; LL.M., Harvard, 1966. Admitted to Tex. bar, 1965, N.Mex. bar, 1966; clk. firm Thompson, Knight, Wright & Simmons, Dallas, 1965; partner firm Garrett & Hartley, Clovis, N.Mex., 1970-73, Garrett, Hartley & Tatum, Clovis, 1974-75; sr. atty. firm Michael T. Garrett, Clovis, 1976—; spl. atty. gen., Clovis, 1968—; asst. prof. Eastern N.Mex. U., 1970-71. Mem. Am., N.Mex., Tex. bar assns., Am. Trial Lawyers Assn. Editor of Southwestern Law Jour., 1964-65. Home: 1119 Fairway Terr Clovis NM 88101 Office: 400 Pile Pl Suite 100 Clovis NM 88101 Tel (505) 762-4545

GARRETT, RICHARD GLENN, b. N.Y.C., Oct. 16, 1948; B.A. magna cum laude, Emory U., 1970, J.D., 1973. Admitted to Ga. bar, 1973; asso. firm Haas Holland Levison & Gibert, Atlanta, 1973-77, partner, 1977—. Mem. Am., Ga. bar assns. Editor: Emory U. Law Jour., 1973. Home: 37 La Rue Pl NW Atlanta GA 30327 Office: 2700 1st Nat Bank Tower Atlanta GA 30303 Tel (404) 658-1811

GARRETT, ROGER EARL, b. Tucson, Nov. 29, 1942; B.S. in Bus. Edn., U. Ariz., 1964, J.D., 1967. Admitted to Ariz. bar, 1967; partner firm Chester & Garrett, Phoenix, 1967-74; individual practice law, Phoenix, 1974—; dep. atty. Maricopa County, Ariz., 1967-69; legal counsel to speaker, majority leader Ariz. Ho. of Reps., 1969-74. Mem.

Am. Trial Lawyers Assn., Ariz., Maricopa County bar assns. Office: 2035 N Central Ave Suite 206 Phoenix AZ 85004 Tel (602) 258-8601

GARRETT, THEODORE LOUIS, b. New Britain, Conn., Sept. 4, 1943; B.A., Yale U., 1965; J.D., Columbia U., 1968. Admitted to N.Y. State bar, 1968, U.S. Supreme Ct. bar, 1973; law clk. to Hon. J. Joseph Smith, Second Circuit Ct., 1968-69; spl. asst. to Asst. Atty. Gen. William H. Rehnquist, 1969-70; law clk. to Chief Justice Warren E. Burger, U.S. Supreme Ct., 1970-71; asso. firm Covington & Burling, Washington, 1971-76, partner, 1976—. Mem. Am. Bar Assn., Bar Assn. of D.C. Home: 7206 Lenhart Dr Chevy Chase MD 20015 Office: 888 16th St NW Washington DC 20006 Tel (202) 452-6112

GARRETT, VIRGINIA BONNER, b. Valdosta, Ga., Sept. 22, 1927; B.S., South Ga. Jr. Coll., 1944-46; postgrad. West Ga. Coll., 1975—; J.D., Woodrow Wilson Coll. Law, 1972, LL.M., 1973. Admitted to Ga. bar, 1973, U.S. Dist. Ct. bar for No. Dist. Ga., 1973, U.S. Ct. Appeals bar, 5th Circuit, 1975; individual practice law, Douglasville, Ga., 1973; partner firm Garrett, Brown & Smith, P.C., and predecessor, Douglasville, 1974—. First v.p. Douglas County (Ga.) Democratic Exec. Com., 1975—. Mem. Ga. Trial Lawyers Assn., Ga. Assn. Criminal Def. Lawyers, Am., Ga., Tallapoosa Jud. Circuit bar assns. Office: POB 337 8479 Pray St Douglasville GA 30133 Tel (404) 949-1381

GARRISON, RAY HARLAN, b. Allen County, Ky., Aug. 6, 1922; B.A., Western Ky. U., 1942; M.A. (Fellow), U. Ky., 1944; postgrad. Northwestern U., 1945-46; J.D., U. Chgo., 1949. Admitted to Ky. bar, 1951, Ill. bar, 1962, U.S. Tax Ct. bar, 1962; supr. escheats Ky. Dept. Revenue, 1944-45; fiscal analyst, 1945; lectr. Loyola U., Chgo., 1949-51; spl. atty. U.S. Treasury Dept., St. Louis, 1952-57, spl. asst. 1957-59, asst. regional counsel, 1959-61; sr. atty. Internat. Harvester Co., Chgo., 1961—. Del., Ill. Constl. Conv., 1969-70; mem. Ill. Racing Bd., 1975—; adv. bd. Ill. Thoroughbred Breeders Fund, 1976—. Mem. Am., Ill., Ky., Chgo. bar assns., Nat. Tax Assn., NAM, Nat. Assn. State Racing Commrs. Contbr. articles in field to profl. jours. Home: 2625 Hawthorne Ln Flossmoor IL 60422 Office: 401 N Michigan Ave Chicago IL 60611 Tel (312) 670-2170

GARRISON, ROBERT CARLTON, b. Birmingham, Ala., Dec. 4, 1904; LL.B./J.D., U. Ala., 1926. Admitted to Ala. bar, 1926; gen. county adminstr. Jefferson County (Ala.), Birmingham, 1946—; instr. Birmingham Sch. Law, 1943-44. Mem. Birmingham, Ala. bar assns., Am. Judicature Soc. Home: 28 Beechwood Rd Birmingham AL 35213 Office: 920 Frank Nelson Bldg Birmingham AL 35203 Tel (205) 324-7556

GARRISON, WILLIAM SEYMOUR, b. Newburgh, N.Y., Oct. 31, 1934; A.A.S., Orange County Community Coll., 1954; B.A., U. Md., 1967; J.D., Ind. U., 1970. Admitted to Ind. bar, 1970; partner firm Hynes, Marsh & Garrison, Muncie, Ind., 1970-75; individual practice law, Muncie, 1975—. Mem. Ind. State Bar Assn., DAV. Winner Will Drafting Contest, Estate Planning Seminar, Ind. U. Sch. Law, 1970. Office: 311 W Jackson St Muncie IN 47305 Tel (317) 289-8656

GARRITY, PAUL JOSEPH, b. Boston, Sept. 2, 1934; A.B. in Econs. cum laude, Suffolk U., 1961; M.B.A., Babson Coll., 1963; J.D., Suffolk U., 1968. Admitted to Mass. bar, 1968; contracts positions staff Dept. Def., Boston, 1963-66; contracting officer NASA, Cambridge, Mass., 1966-70; regional fin. mgmt. officer HUD, Boston, 1970-77. Mem. budget com. Mass United Community Services, Boston, 1972-73; bd. dirs. South Shore Council Campfire, Inc., 1972-76. Mem. Mass. Bar Assn. Recipient numerous outstanding service awards HUD. Home: 7 Talbot Rd Hingham MA 02043 Office: John Fitzgerald Kennedy Fed Bldg Boston MA 02203 Tel (617) 223-4347

GARST, CLAFLIN, JR., b. Bradenton, Fla., Feb. 7, 1935; B.S. in Forestry, U. Fla., 1960, LL.B., 1963, also J.D. Forester, Fish and Wildlife Service, St. Marks, Fla., 1960-61; personnel mgr. African Pavilion, New York World's Fair, 1964; admitted to Fla. bar, 1964; asso. firm Paderewski, Cramer & Robinson, Sarasota, 1964-66; partner firm St. Laurent & Garst, Bradenton, 1966-67; individual practice law, Bradenton, 1967-68; county judge, Manatee County, 1969-72; judge County Ct., Manatee County, Bradenton, 1973—; chmn. Manatee County Zoning Bd. of Appeals, 1968. Pres., Manatee County Taxpayers Assn., 1968; bd. dirs. Manatee County Hist. Soc., 1969-70, 2d v.p., 1970-74, 1st v.p., 1974-75; bd. dirs. sr. council Manatee County Youth Center, 1974-75, v.p., 1975, pres., 1976. Mem. Fla., Manatee County bar assns., Fla. Judges Conf. Office: Manatee County Courthouse Bradenton FL 33505 Tel (813) 747-4545

GARTH, LEONARD I., b. Bklyn., Apr. 7, 1921; B.A., Columbia, 1942; LL.B., Harvard, 1952. Admitted to N.J. bar, 1952; mem. firm Cole, Berman & Garth and predecessors, Paterson, N.J., 1952-70; judge U.S. Dist. Ct. for N.J., Newark, 1970-73, U.S. Circuit Ct. Appeals, 3d Circuit, Newark and Phila., 1973—; mem. N.J. Bd. Bar Examiners, 1964-68; mem. com. on revision of gen. and admiralty rules Fed. Dist. Ct. N.J.; lectr. Inst. Continuing Legal Edn. Mem. Am., Fed., N.J., Passaic County (N.J.) (pres. 1967-68) bar assns., Harvard Law Sch. Assn. (nat. v.p. 1963-64), Am. Law Inst. Home: 17 Greenview Way Upper Montclair NJ 07043 Office: PO Bldg and Courthouse Newark NJ 07101 also 20316 Courthouse Philadelphia PA 19106 Tel (201) 645-3356

GARTNER, MURRAY, b. N.Y.C., Sept. 23, 1922; B.A., N.Y. U., 1942; LL.B., Harvard, 1945. Admitted to N.Y. State bar, 1946, Calif. bar, 1948; law clk. to Justice Robert H. Jackson, U.S. Supreme Ct., 1945-47; asso. firm Pillsbury Madison & Sutro, San Francisco, 1947-51, Roosevelt & Freidin and predecessor, N.Y.C., 1953-59; asst. to gen. counsel Office of U.S. Spl. Rep., Paris, 1951-53; partner firm Poletti Freidin Prashker Feldman & Gartner and predecessors, N.Y.C., 1959—; instr. in law Hastings Coll. Law U. Calif., San Francisco, 1948-49. Mem. Assn. Bar City N.Y. Home: 520 E 86th St New York City NY 10028 Office: 1185 Ave of the Americas New York City NY 10036 Tel (212) 730-7373

GARTZKE, PAUL COULTER, b. Milw., Oct. 6, 1927; B.A., State U. Iowa, 1949; LL.B., Harvard U., 1952. Admitted to Wis. bar, 1952, U.S. Supreme Ct. bar, 1964; partner firm Bieberstein, Cooper, Bruemmer, Gartzke & Hanson, Madison, Wis., 1952—; lectr. law U. Wis., 1973—; pres. Bayview Found., Inc., Madison, 1970-73. Mem. Am., Wis., Dane County bar assns., Motor Carrier Lawyers Assn. Home: 1709 Hoyt St Madison WI 53705 Office: 121 W Doty St Madison WI 53703 Tel (608) 256-0606

GARVER, THEODORE MEYER, b. Buffalo, July 29, 1929; B.A., Williams Coll., 1954; LL.B., Cornell U., 1954. Admitted to N.Y. bar, 1954, Ohio bar, 1957; spl. asst. to atty. gen., tax div., U.S. Dept. Justice, Washington, 1954-56; mem. firm Jones, Day, Reavis & Pogue, Cleve., 1956—. Mem. Cleve., Am. bar assns. Home: 12010 Lake Ave Cleveland OH 44107 Office: 1700 Union Commerce Bldg Cleveland OH 44115 Tel (216) 696-3939

GARY, CHARLES ELMER, b. Elvins, Mo., July 23, 1919; student Flat River Jr. Coll., 1937-38, U. Hawaii, 1940-41; LL.B., Washington U., 1947. Admitted to Mo. bar, 1947, Fed. bar, 1948, U.S. Supreme Ct. bar, 1954; partner firm Inman, Dyer, Gray & Dreher, St. Louis, 1947-53, firm Schoenbeck & Gray, St. Louis, 1954-56, firm Gray & Ritter, St. Louis, 1970—; pres. The Don-ite Corp., 1968—; sec., gen. counsel Don V. Davis Co., 1960—. Mem. Mo. Appellate Judicial Commn., 1970-76; mem. Mo. Supreme Ct. Rules Com., 1969—. Fellow Internat. Acad. Trial Lawyers (dir. 1964); mem. Am. Coll. Trial Lawyers, Internat. Soc. Barristers (state chmn. 1966), Am., Mo., St. Louis bar assns., Phi Delta Phi. Contbr. articles to legal jours. Home: 12 Clifside Dr Glendale MO 63122 Office: 1015 Locust St St Louis MO 63101 Tel (314) 241-5620

GARY, HOLLAND MERRICK, b. Zanesville, Ohio, Dec. 11, 1911; B.A., Yale, 1933, J.D., 1936. Admitted to Ohio bar, 1936, U.S. Dist. Ct. bar, 1937, U.S. Supreme Ct. bar, 1945; practiced in Zanesville, Ohio, 1936—; individual practice law, 1936-50; partner firm Gary & Kinkade, 1950-54; judge Ct. of Common Pleas, Probate and Juvenile Divs., 1955—. Pres., Ohio Legal Services Assn., Columbus, Ohio, 1970-72; pres. bd. trustees Ohio Soldiers and Sailors Orphans Home, Xenia, Ohio, 1970-75; mem. adv. com. to Ohio Youth Commn.; vice chmn. bd. dirs. Nat. Action for Foster Children; bd. fellows Nat. Center for Juvenile Justice, Pitts. Mem. Am., Ohio, Muskingum County bar assns., Ohio Assn. Probate Ct. Judges (pres. 1962-64), Nat. Council Juvenile Ct. Judges (pres. 1973-74), Internat. Assn. Youth Magistrates (v.p.). Contbr. articles in field to profl. jours. Home: 500 Abbey Pl Zanesville OH 43701 Office: Probate Ct Court House Zanesville OH 43701 Tel (614) 454-0177

GARY, JAMES WARREN, b. Cameron, Tex., Sept. 22, 1929; B.A., Rice U., 1951; LL.B., U. Tex., 1956. Admitted to Tex. bar, 1956; asso. Gary, Thomasson, Hall & Marks, and predecessor, Corpus Christi, Tex., 1956-60, partner, 1960—. Mem. Nueces County, Tex., Am. bar assns., Corpus Christi, Am. assns. petroleum landmen, Nat. Orgn. Legal Problems in Edn., Nat. Sch. Bds. Assn. Council Sch. Attys. Home: 4933 Cherry Hills St Corpus Christi TX 78413 Office: 200 Hawn Bldg Corpus Christi TX 78401 Tel (512) 884-1961

GARZA, REYNALDO G., b. Brownsville, Tex., July 7, 1915; B.A., LL.B., U. Tex.; LL.D. (hon.), U. St. Edwards, Austin, Tex., 1965. Admitted to Tex. bar, 1939; pvt. practice, 1939-42, 46-50; partner firm Sharpe, Cunningham & Garza, 1950-60, Cunningham, Garza & Yznaga, 1960-61; U.S. dist. judge So. dist. Tex., Brownsville, 1961—, now chief judge. Treas. Cameron County Child Welfare Bd., 1950-52; mem. Tex. Good Neighbor Commn., 1957-61. Commr., City Brownsville, 1947-49. Trustee Brownsville Ind. Sch. Dist., 1941-42. Recipient Pro Ecclesia et Pontifica medal Pope Pius XII, 1952; decorated knight Order St. Gregory the Great, Pope Pius XII, 1954. Mem. Am., Cameron County bar assns., State Bar Tex. Home: 234 Calle Retama Brownsville TX 78520 Office: Post Office Bldg Brownsville TX 78520*

GASAWAY, LAURA NELL, b. Searcy, Ark., Feb. 24, 1945; B.A., Tex. Woman's U., 1967, M.L.S., 1968; J.D., U. Houston, 1973. Admitted to Tex. bar, 1974; catalog librarian, U. Houston, 1968-72, asst. law librarian, 1972-73, law librarian, asst. prof. law, 1973-75; dir. law library, asso. prof. law, U. Okla., Norman, 1975—. Mem. Am. Assn. Law Libraries, Spl. Libraries Assn., Am. Bar Assn., State Bar Tex. Contbr. articles to jours. Home: 2213 NW 29th St Oklahoma City OK 73107 Office: 300 Timberdell Rd Norman OK 73019 Tel (405) 325-4313

GASH, ROBERT TALIAFERRO, b. Brevard, N.C., Oct. 6, 1924; A.A., Brevard Coll., 1943; A.B., U. N.C., 1948, J.D., 1950. Admitted to N.C. bar, 1950; mem. N.C. Senate, 1953-54; judge Transylvania County, Brevard, N.C., 1961-66; judge 29th Dist. Ct., Brevard, 1968—, chief judge, 1970—. Pres. Episcopal Found. of Western N.C., 1976—. Mem. Am. Bar Assn., Am. Judicature Soc., Chief Judges Conf. (past pres.), N.C. Assn. Dist. Ct. Judges (past pres.). Home: 118 Laurel Ln Brevard NC 28712 Office: Box 347 Brevard NC 28712 Tel (704) 883-9046

GASIOROWSKI, FRANCIS WILLIAM, b. Bayonne, N.J., Nov. 8, 1944; B.S. in Econs., St. Peter's Coll., 1966; J.D., Seton Hall U., 1973; grad. Keeler Polygraph Sch., Chgo., 1974. Investigator prosecutor's detective bur. Union County (N.J.) Prosecutor's Office, Elizabeth, 1971-74; admitted to N.J. bar, 1974; asst. county prosecutor Union County, 1974—; counsel N.J. State Polygraph Assn., 1976—. Mem. N.J. State, Union County bar assns., N.J. State Patrolman's Benevolent Assn. (hon. life). Office: 2 Broad St Elizabeth NJ 07207 Tel (201) 353-8000

GASK, MICHAEL MASON, b. Bklyn., Nov. 6, 1934; B.A., Coll. City N.Y., 1966; J.D., Fordham U., 1971. Admitted to N.Y. State bar, 1972; law clk. firm Guzik & Boukstein, N.Y.C., 1970-71; title reader Chgo. Title Ins. Co., N.Y.C., 1972-73, research atty. eastern region, 1974—. Mem. Am., Bronx bar assns., N.Y. County Lawyers Assn. Recipient Am. Jurisprudence prize in internat. law Fordham U. Law Sch., 1971. Home: 255 E 176th St Bronx NY 10457 Office: Chicago Title Ins Co 233 Broadway New York City NY 10007 Tel (212) 285-4039

GASSER, EMMETT CLARK, b. Pocatello, Idaho, Mar. 2, 1929; B.A., St. Marys Coll. of Calif., 1951; LL.B., George Washington U., 1956, J.D., 1970. Admitted to D.C. bar, 1957, Idaho bar, 1957, U.S. Supreme Ct. bar, 1972; partner firm Terrell and Gasser, Pocatello, 1957-62, firm Terrell, Green, Service and Gasser, Pocatello, 1962—; mem. Idaho State Bar Examining Com., 1968-75, co-chmn., 1972-74. County chmn. Easter Seal Soc., 1958-60; master Boy Scouts Am., 1959-62; pres. Campfire Girls of Pocatello, 1963; chmn. St. Josephs Adv. Bd., 1969-70; mem. Pocatello Planning and Zoning Commn., 1970-72; chmn. Pocatello Bd. Adjustments, 1972-73; bd. dirs. Pocatello chpt. ARC, 1973; adv. bd. St. Anthony Hosp., 1974-75; bd. dirs. Indsl. Lands, 1974—. Mem. Am., Idaho bar assns., Am. Judicature Soc., Am. Trial Lawyers Assn., Def. Research Inst. Home: 420 S 12th St Pocatello ID 83201 Office: C-1 Center Plaza Pocatello ID 83201 Tel (208) 232-4471

GAST, DAVID WESLEY, b. Cedar Rapids, Iowa, June 15, 1946; B.A., Carleton Coll., Northfield, Minn., 1968; J.D., U. Chgo., 1971; M.S. in Indsl. Relations, U. Chgo., 1977. Admitted to Ill. bar, 1971, U.S. Supreme Ct. bar, 1976; asso. firm Chadwell, Kayser, Ruggles, McGee & Hastings, Chgo., 1971-74; atty. Household Fin. Corp., Chgo., 1974-77, gen. atty., 1977—. Mem. Am., Fed., Ill. State, Chgo. bar assns., Indsl. Relations Research Assn., Phi Delta Phi. Home: 730 Monroe Ave River Forest IL 60305 Office: 3200 Prudential Plaza Chicago IL 60601 Tel (312) 944-7174

GASTON, IAN FREDERICK, b. Washington, Oct. 20, 1944; A.B., U. of the South, 1965; J.D., U. Ala., 1968. Admitted to Ala. bar, 1968; partner firm Gaston, Bryant & Gaston, Mobile, Ala., 1968—; asst. city atty. City of Mobile, 1970. Mem. vestry St. Paul's Episcopal Ch., 1975—. Mem. Ala., Am. trial lawyers assns., Am., Judicature Soc., Mobile County Bar Assn. (pres. young lawyers sect. 1975-76, exec. com. 1975-76), Ala. Law Inst. (exec. com. 1974—), Order of Coif, Phi Beta Kappa, Omicron Delta Kappa. Asst. editor Ala. Law Rev., 1967-68. Home: 4113 Highpoint Dr S Mobile AL 36609 Office: PO Drawer 1465 Mobile AL 36601 Tel (205) 432-4671

GASTON, JOHN FLETCHER, b. Sewickley, Pa., Feb. 10, 1908; student Cornell Coll., Mt. Vernon, Iowa, 1926-28. Admitted to Iowa Supreme Ct. bar, 1940, U.S. Supreme Ct. bar, 1966; gen. atty. Iowa Electric Light and Power Co., Cedar Rapids, 1963—. Mem. Am. (chmn. energy resources com. 1975-77), Iowa bar assns. Home: 214 24th St Dr SE Cedar Rapids IA 52403 Office: 1100 I E Tower PO Box 351 Cedar Rapids IA 52406 Tel (319) 398-4499

GASTON, WILLIAM ROBERT, b. Sparta, Ill., Feb. 16, 1938; LL.B., U. Ill., 1967. Admitted to Ill. bar, 1968; asst. state's atty. Champaign County (Ill.), 1968, 69-72, Saline County (Ill.), 1968-69; asso. firm Mathis & Turnbow, Rantoul, Ill., 1969; partner firm Gaston & Goldstein, Urbana, Ill., 1973—. Mem. Ill., Champaign County bar assns. Office: 303 W Green St Urbana IL 61801 Tel (217) 367-5411

GASTWIRTH, STUART LAWRENCE, b. N.Y.C., Feb. 26, 1939; B.A., Hofstra Coll., 1959; J.D., Cornell U., 1962. Admitted to N.Y. State bar, 1963; asso. firm Cole & Deitz, and predecessor, N.Y.C., 1962-67; counselor at law, house counsel Central State Bank, N.Y.C., 1967-69; partner firm Semon, Gastwirth & Braverman, and predecessor, Jericho, N.Y., 1969-75; individual practice law, Jericho, 1975—. Mem. Am., N.Y. State, Nassau County bar assns., N.Y. County Lawyers Assn., Bank Lawyers Conf., L.I. Bank Lawyers Assn. Home: 9 Plymouth Rd Great Neck NY 11023 Office: 333 Broadway Jericho NY 11753 Tel (516) 938-0007

GATCHEL, JOHN KENNETH, b. Tell City, Ind., Nov. 27, 1931; B.A. Ind. U., 1959, LL.B., 1962. Admitted to Idaho bar, 1963; individual practice law, Payette, Idaho, 1963—. Mem. Am., Idaho bar assns., Am. Trial Lawyers Assn. Home: 1115 1st Ave S Payette ID 83661 Office: Center Ave and 9th St Payette ID 83661 Tel (208) 642-4411

GATES, LAWRENCE STUART, b. Providence, Nov. 15, 1934; A.B., Tufts Coll., 1956; LL.D., Boston U., 1959, LL.M., 1962. Admitted to R.I. bar, 1959; of counsel Zietz, Sonkin & Radin, Providence; legal counsel Gov. State of R.I., 1967-68. Pres. R.I. Big Bros., 1961-62, Gordon Sch., East Providence, R.I., 1972-73, Young Leadership Jewish Fedn., R.I., 1962-63; trustee Jewish Family and Children's Service of R.I.; mem. allocation com. United Fund, Providence; sec. Temple Beth-El, Providence; mem. com. personnel and med. matters Miriam Hosp., Providence. Mem. R.I., Am. bar assns., Am. Health Care Lawyers. Home: 200 Lorimer Ave Providence RI 02906 Office: 131 Wayland Ave Providence RI 02906 Tel (401) 861-7600

GATES, SAMUEL KENT, b. Roaring Spring, Pa., Aug. 3, 1938; B.S., Pa. State U., 1960; J.D., Dickinson Sch. Law, Carlisle, Pa., 1971. Admitted to Pa. bar, 1971; individual practice law, York, Pa., 1971—. Mem. Pa., Am. bar assns. Author: Divorce in Pennsylvania, 1975. Home: RD 1 Spring Grove PA 17336 Office: 2 W Market St York PA 17401 Tel (717) 843-9669

GATES, STEPHEN FRYE, b. Clearwater, Fla., May 20, 1946; B.A., Yale U., 1968; J.D., Harvard U., 1972, M.B.A. (Knox fellow 1972-73), 1972. Admitted to Mass., Fla. bars, 1973; asso. firm Choate, Hall & Stewart, Boston, 1973—. Mem. Am. Bar Assn. Office: Choate Hall & Stewart 28 State St Boston MA 02109 Tel (617) 227-5020

GATHINGS, EZEKIEL CANDLER, b. Prairie, Miss., Nov. 10, 1903; student U. Ala., 1923-26; LL.B., U. Ark., 1929, J.D., 1969. Admitted to Ark. bar, 1929, U.S. Supreme Ct. bar, 1940; partner firms Robertson and Gathings, Helena, Ark., 1929-30, Cooper and Cathings, Earle and West Memphis, Ark., 1931-33, Shafer and Gathings, West Memphis, 1933-39; individual practice law, Earle, 1930-31, West Memphis, 1969—; mem. Ark. Senate, 1935-39; mem. U.S. Ho. of Reps. from 1st Dist. Ark, 1939-69. Mem. West Memphis Port Authority, 1974—; mem. West Memphis Flood Control Com., 1975-76. Mem. Ark., bar assns., Ark. Trial Lawyers Assn., Am. Judicature Soc., Ark. Bar Found., East Ark. Estate Council. Recipient 50th Anniversary medal Fed. Land Bank, 1967, citation for being Watch Dog of Treasury Nat. Assn. Businessman, 1968, citation for meritorious service Ark. Farm Bur. Fedn., 1968. Home: 421 W Barton St West Memphis AR 72301 Office: 11C Holiday Plaza Mall West Memphis TN 72301 Tel (501) 735-2630

GAUGHAN, JOHN EMMET, III, b. Lake Village, Ark., Nov. 12, 1948; B.A. in Zoology, U. Ark., 1970, J.D., 1973; Admitted to Ark. bar, 1973; asso. firm Gaughan, Barnes, Roberts, Harrell & Laney, Camden, Ark., 1973—. Mem. Am., Ark., Ouachita County bar assns. Office: 303 Jackson Camden AR 71701 Tel (501) 836-5771

GAUL, DEWIE JOSEPH, b. Earling, Iowa, Sept. 18, 1928; A.B. maxima cum laude, Loras Coll., 1950; J.D. Georgetown U., 1955. Admitted to Iowa bar, 1955; since practiced in Sioux City, Iowa, asso. firm Sifford & Wadden, 1955-63, partner, 1963-69; partner firm Davis, Jacobs & Gaul, 1969-74, Jacobs, Gaul, Nymann & Green, 1974—; Jud. Hospitalization referee Woodbury County, 1976—. Trustee Sioux City Pub. Library, 1972—; chmn. Woodbury County Democratic Central Com. 1962-66. Mem. Woodbury County, Iowa State, Am. bar assns. Home: 1906 Iowa St Sioux City IA 51104 Office: 383 Orpheum Electric Bldg Sioux City IA 51101 Tel (712) 258-0101

GAUTIER, REDMOND BUNN, JR., b. Miami, Fla., Apr. 3, 1909; student Washington and Lee U. Admitted to Fla. bar, 1932; partner firm Worley, Gautier & Sams, Miami, 1932—; dir., chmn. bd. Greater Miami Fed. Savs. and Loan Assn.; dir. City Nat. Bank. Trustee U. Miami, Pub. Health Trust Dade County (Fla.); mem. Fla. Legislature, 1943-49, U.S. Senate, 1949; mem. Fla. Devel. Commn., 1958-61. Home: The Island House 200 Ocean Lane Dr Key Biscayne FL 33149 Office: Greater Miami Fed Bldg 200 SE 1st St Miami FL 33131 Tel (305) 377-4501

GAVIN, ROBERT LEE, b. Roseboro, N.C., May 22, 1916; A.B., U. N.C., 1945, LL.B., 1956. Admitted to N.C. bar, 1946; practiced in Sanford, 1946-54; partner firm Gavin, Jackson & Gavin, 1946-54; asst. U.S. atty., Middle Dist. N.C., 1954, U.S. atty., 1957-58; city atty. Sanford, 1965—; judge Superior Ct. N.C., 1975—; dir. So. Nat. Bank, N.C., Sanford. Mem. N.C. State Constn. Study Commn., N.Y. State Zool. Adv. Bd.; del. Republican Nat. Conv., 1960, 64; Rep. candidate for gov. N.C., 1960, 64; chmn. N.C. Rep. Exec. Com. Mem. Am.,

N.C. bar assns., N.C. State Bar, 4th Circuit Jud. Conf. (life mem.), Sanford C. of C. (dir., v.p.), Phi Delta Phi. Home: 227 N Vance St Sanford NC 27330 Office: 114 Wicker St Sanford NC 27330

GAVIN, WILLIAM FRANCIS, b. Milw., Feb. 17, 1922; student Trinity Coll., Hartford, Conn., 1939-41; grad. Fordham U. Sch. of Law, 1945. Admitted to N.Y. bar, 1946, Calif. bar, 1955, U.S. Supreme Ct. bar, 1971; asso. firm Holland, Armstrong, Bower & Carlson, N.Y.C., 1946-49; asso. Coopers & Lybrand, C.P.A.'s, Los Angeles, 1954-56; individual practice law, San Diego, 1956-62, 63—; chief counsel Legal Aid Soc., San Diego, 1962-63. Mem. State Bar Calif., San Diego County Bar Assn. Recipient award Am. Civil Liberties Union of So. Calif., 1974. Home: 7661 Hillside Dr La Jolla CA 92037 Office: 455 Spreckels Bldg 121 Broadway St San Diego CA 92101 Tel (714) 234-3673

GAW, JOHN GOODWIN, JR., b. Charlotte, N.C., Oct. 28, 1945; B.S., Presbyterian Coll., 1968; J.D., U. S.C., 1971. Admitted to N.C. bar, 1971, S.C. bar, 1971; asst. dist. atty. 1st Jud. Dist. N.C., 1971-72; mem. firm LeRoy, Wells, Shaw, Hornthal, Riley & Shearin, Elizabeth City and Kitty Hawk, N.C., 1973—. Chmn. disaster com. Dare County chpt. ARC. Mem. N.C., S.C. bar assns., N.C. Acad. Trial Lawyers. Office: Kitty Dunes Profl Bldg Kitty Hawk NC 27949

GAY, GORDON BERTRAM, b. Washington, Nov. 21, 1943; B.A., Washington and Lee U., 1965, LL.B., J.D., 1968. Admitted to Va. bar, 1969; with Fed. Reserve Bank of Richmond Communications Center, Culpeper, Va., 1969-70; individual practice law, Fredericksburg, 1970—; asst. commonwealth atty. Spotsylvania County, Va., 1975-76. Mem. Am., Va., 15th Judicial Circuit bar assns., Am., Va. trial lawyers assn. Office: 121 Prince St Falmouth VA 22401 Tel (703) 373-5666

GAY, JAMES FERBEE, b. Norfolk, Va., Dec. 9, 1942; B.S. in Chemistry, Norfolk State Coll., 1965; J.D., U. Va., 1968. Admitted to Va. bar, 1968; with legal internat. div. Allied Chem. Corp., N.Y.C., 1968-69; asst. to pres. Nat. Bus. League, Washington, 1969-70, gen. counsel, 1974—; pres. Coastal Pharm. Co., Norfolk, 1970—; pres. Tidewater Area Bus. League, Norfolk, 1972. Bd. dirs. Norfolk State Coll. Found.; mem. advisory by. Urban Mass Transit Authority. Mem. Am., Va. State, Old Dominion Twin City bar assns., Am. Judicature Soc. Recipient Pres.'s award Bus. League, 1973. Home: 237 Lucian Ct Norfolk VA 23502 Office: 2909 Granby St Norfolk VA 23517 Tel (804) 622-3377

GAY, RICHARD GALLATIN, b. Winchester, Va., Feb. 9, 1941; B.A., W.Va. Weslyan Coll., 1964; J.D., W.Va. Coll. Law, 1967. Admitted to W.Va. Supreme Ct. of Appeals bar, 1967, Pa. Supreme Ct. bar, 1969, Ohio Supreme Ct. bar, 1974; asso. firm Kump & Nuzum, Elkins, W.Va., 1967-68; gen. atty. H. J. Heinz Co., Pitts., 1968-72; house legal counsel Beverage Mgmt., Inc., Columbus, Ohio, 1972—, asst. sec., 1973—, gen. counsel, 1974—, v.p., 1975—, also dir.; counsel Trinity Episcopal Ch., Columbus, Ohio. Mem. W.Va. State, Pa. State, Ohio State, Columbus, Am. bar assns., Am. Trial Lawyers Assn. Home: 1830 N Devon Rd Upper Arlington OH 43212 Office: 1001 Kingsmill Pkwy Columbus OH 43229 Tel (614) 846-9800

GAYLE, GIBSON, JR., b. Waco, Tex., Oct. 15, 1926; A.B., LL.B., Baylor U., 1950. Admitted to Tex. bar, 1950; sr. partner firm Fulbright & Jaworski, Houston. Bd. dirs. Am. Bar Endowment; bd. govs. Harris County Center for Retarded, 1956-76. Fellow Am., Tex. bar founds.; mem. Am. (del. 1960—, sec. 1963-67, bd. editors Jour. 1967-72), Internat. (council), Tex. (pres. 1976-77), Houston bar assns., Am. Judicature Soc. Recipient Outstanding Young Lawyer in Tex. award, 1964, Baylor U. Lawyer of Year award, 1975. Office: 800 Bank of Southwest Bldg Houston TX 77002 Tel (713) 651-5151

GAYNOR, JAMES KENNETH, b. Greensburg, Ind., Aug. 11, 1912; B.S., Ind. U., Bloomington, 1946, J.D., 1950; LL.M., George Washington U., 1953, S.J.D., 1967. Admitted to Ind. bar, 1950, Ohio bar, 1967, Ky. bar, 1973; commd. 1st lt. U.S. Army, advanced through grades to col., 1962; chief new trial div. Office of JAG, 1951-54; staff judge adv. Ryukyus Command, Okinawa, 1954-57; chief legis. div. Office of Sec. Army, 1957-60; mem. Army Bd. Rev., 1960-61; staff judge adv., Ft. Knox, Ky., 1961-63, 1st U.S. Army, Ft. Meade, Md., 1966-67; legal adviser U.S. European Command, Paris, 1963-66; ret., 1967; asso. prof. law Cleve.-Marshall Law Sch., 1967-68, prof., dean, 1968-71; prof. Chase Law Sch., Cin., 1971-72, Chase Law Sch. No. Ky. U. (formerly No. Ky. State Coll.), 1972—. Mem. Am., Ind. State, Ohio State, Ky., Cin. bar assns., Judge Advs. Assn. (life), Phi Delta Phi. Author: Profile of the Law, 1973; editor: Military Jurisprudence, 1951. Home: 324 N Broadway Greensburg IN 47240 Office: Chase Coll of Law No Ky U 1401 Dixie Hwy Covington KY 41011 Tel (616) 292-5353

GAZZIGLI, JOSEPH ANTHONY, b. Port Chester, N.Y., Sept. 20, 1940; B.S., Calif. State U., Los Angeles; J.D., Whittier Coll. Law, 1969. Admitted to Calif. bar, 1970; law clk., asso. firm Paul Caruso, Beverly Hills, Calif., 1968-70; dep. dist. atty. Los Angeles County, 1970-72, Shasta County (Calif.), Redding, 1972-74; partner firm Tocher & Gazzigli, Redding, 1974—; instr. law Los Angeles Community Coll., Shasta Coll.; chmn. Juvenile Justice Commn. Shasta County, 1976. Mem. Am., Shasta-Trinity bar assns. Home: 2395 Oriole Ln Palo Cedro CA 96073 Office: 1900 Gold St Redding CA 96001 Tel (916) 241-6900

GEAREN, JOHN JOSEPH, b. Wareham, Mass., Sept. 1, 1943; B.A., U. Notre Dame, 1965; M.A. (Rhodes scholar), Oxford U., 1967; J.D., Yale U., 1970. Admitted to Ill. bar, 1972; law clk. U.S. Ct. Appeals D.C., 1970-71; asso. firm Mayer, Brown & Platt, Chgo., 1971—. Environ. adv. commr. Oak Park (Ill.), 1975—; Dutch Elm Disease commr. Oak Park, 1975; mem. Ill. Rhodes Scholarship Selection Bd., 1973-76. Mem. Ill. State Bar Assn., Yale U. Law Sch. Alumni Assn. (pres. 1976—). Home: 179 Linden Ave Oak Park IL 60302 Office: 231 S LaSalle St Suite 1955 Chicago IL 60604 Tel (312) 782-0600

GEARHART, JANE ANNETTE, b. Seibert, Colo., Mar. 2, 1918; A.B., U. Denver, 1940, LL.B., 1942, J.D., 1970. Admitted to Colo. bar, 1942, Oreg. bar, 1956; cons. to State of Oreg., individual practice law, Salem, Oreg., 1973—. Tel (503) 390-0219

GEARHISER, CHARLES JOSEF, b. Dyersburg, Tenn., Aug. 14, 1938; LL.B., U. Tenn., 1961; B.S., Austin Peay State U., 1965. Admitted to Tenn. bar, 1962, U.S. 6th Circuit Ct. Appeals bar, 1964, U.S. Supreme Ct. bar, 1974, U.S. 5th Circuit Ct. Appeals bar, 1974; asso. firm Strang, Fletcher, Carriger & Walker, Chattanooga, 1962-63; law clk. to Judge Frank W. Wilson, U.S. Dist. Ct., Chattanooga, 1963-64; asst. U.S. atty. Dept. Justice, Chattanooga, 1964-66; mem. firm Stophel, Caldwell & Heggie, Chattanooga, 1966-74; partner firm Gearhiser, Carpenter & Peters, Chattanooga, 1974—; U.S. commr. Eastern Dist. Tenn., 1967-70, 1971—. Chmn. bd. dirs. Golden Gloves Assn. Chattanooga, 1968—. Mem. Chattanooga (pres. 1973), Tenn., Am. bar assns., Chattanooga, Tenn., Am. trial lawyers assns., Order of Coif. Editorial staff U. Tenn. Law Rev., 1960-61. Home: 12 N Crest Rd Chattanooga TN 37404 Office: 807 Chestnut St Chattanooga TN 37402 Tel (615) 756-5171

GEARTY, EDWARD JOSEPH, b. Mpls., Mar. 17, 1923; B.A., St. Thomas Coll., 1952; LL.B., Georgetown U., 1955. Admitted to D.C. bar, 1955, Minn. bar, 1956; individual practice law, Mpls., 1958—; mem. Minn. Ho. of Reps., 1963-70; mem. Minn. Senate, 1971—, pres., 1977—. Mem. Minn., Hennepin County bar assns. Home: 3810 Xerxes Ave N Minneapolis MN 55412 Office: 1102 W Broadway Minneapolis MN 55411 Tel (612) 521-3503

GEARY, JOSEPH WILLIAM, b. Dallas, Feb. 2, 1924; B.A., So. Meth. U., 1946, LL.B., 1947, J.D., 1948. Admitted to Tex. bar, 1947; asst. dist. atty. Dallas County, 1947-51; individual practice law, 1951-S6; partner firm Geary, Stahl, Koons, Rohde & Spencer and predecessors, Dallas, 1956—; mem. Dallas City Council, 1959-61. Mem. Am., Tex. State, Dallas bar assns. Home: 5929 Club Oaks Dr Dallas TX 75248 Office: 2800 One Main Pl Dallas TX 75250 Tel (214) 748-9901

GEB, LEONARD GILBERT, b. Racine, Wis., Aug. 14, 1917; A.A., No. Okla. Jr. Coll., 1937; LL.B., U. Okla., 1944. Admitted to Okla. bar, 1943; atty. Kay County (Okla.), 1945-46; asst. dist. atty. Okla. County, 1973—. Chmn. Democratic Dist. Com. Okla., 1966; chmn. Kay County Dem. Com., 1965. Mem. Ponca Jr. C. of C. (pres. 1954), Am. (v.p. 1960), Okla. (pres. 1959) trial lawyers assn. Home: 3161 NW 24th Oklahoma City OK 73102 Office: 320 Robert Kerr Blvd Oklahoma City OK 73102 Tel (405) 326-2727

GEBHARDT, ROBERT CHARLES, b. Old Forge, N.Y., Nov. 23, 1937; A.B., State U. N.Y., Albany, 1961; J.D., Georgetown U., 1967. Admitted to N.Y. State bar, 1967; asso. firm Harris, Beach & Wilcox, Rochester, N.Y., 1967-70; v.p., sec., gen. counsel Lincoln 1st Banks Inc., Rochester, 1970—. Mem. N.Y. State, Monroe County (N.Y.) bar assns., Assn. Bank Holding Cos. Editor Georgetown U. Law Jour., 1965-67. Home: 33 Village Trail Honeoye Falls NY 14472 Office: One Lincoln First Square Rochester NY 14643 Tel (716) 262-2463

GEDAN, JOSEPH MORTON, b. Chgo., May 20, 1934; student U. Ill.; LL.B., DePaul U., 1958. Admitted to Ill. bar, 1958; Hawaii bar, 1960; asst. U.S. atty. Hawaii, 1961-64, 1966-72; dep. atty. gen. Hawaii, 1964-66; individual practice law, Honolulu, 1972—. Mem. Am., Hawaii bar assns. Home: 3703 Round Top Dr Honolulu HI 96822 Office: Suite 810 333 Queen St Honolulu HI 96813 Tel (808) 521-7434

GEDULDIG, MARTIN, b. N.Y.C., Oct. 5, 1941; B.A., Ohio State U., 1963; LL.B., Georgetown U., 1966. Admitted to N.Y. State bar, 1967; atty. criminal div. Legal Aid Soc., 1967-71; counsel to chmn. N.Y. State Sen. Com. on Crime and Corrections, Albany, 1971-72; mem. firm Redieaf Ain Geduldig & Farinacci, Floral Park, N.Y., 1974—. Mem. Nassau and Queens County Bar Assn., Nassau and Queens County Criminal Bar Assn. Editorial bd., contbr. articles to Nassau County Law Jour. Office: 260-09 Hinside Ave Floral Park NY 11004 Tel (516) 437-7675

GEE, THOMAS GIBBS, b. Jacksonville, Fla., Dec. 9, 1925; student The Citadel, 1942-43; B.S., U.S. Mil. Acad., 1946; LL.B., U. Tex., 1953. Admitted to Tex. bar, 1953; asso. firm Baker & Botts, Houston, 1953-54; asso. firm Graves, Daugherty, Gee, Hearon, Moody & Garwood, Austin, Tex., 1954, partner, to 1973; judge U.S. Ct. Appeals for 5th Circuit Tex., Austin, 1973—. Mem. State Bar Tex., Am., Travis County bar assns., Am. Law Inst., Am. Judicature Soc., Tex. Bar Found., Phi Delta Phi, Order of Coif. Home: 4603 Ridge Oak Dr Austin TX 78731 Office: 200 W 8th St Austin TX 78701 Tel (512) 397-5844

GEEKER, NICHOLAS PETER, b. Pensacola, Fla., Dec. 15, 1944; B.A. in English, La. Poly. Inst., 1966; J.D., Fla. State U., 1969. Admitted to Fla. bar, 1969, U.S. Dist. Ct. bar, 1970; asso. firm Merritt & Jackson, Pensacola, 1969; law clk. U.S. Dist. Judge D.L. Middlebrooks, Tallahassee, 1970-73; asst. state atty. Fla. 1st Jud. Circuit, 1973; asst. U.S. atty. No. Dist. Fla., 1973-76, U.S. atty., 1976—; mem. Fed.-State Joint Com. on Law Enforcement. Mem. Fla. Bar Assn., Fla. Trial Lawyers Assn. (editor Newsletter 1975), Phi Delta Phi. Home: 150 Munro Rd Pensacola FL 32503 Office: PO Box 12313 Pensacola FL 32581 Tel (904) 434-3251

GEERDES, DAVID BRUCE, b. San Diego, Aug. 2, 1943; B.A., U. Calif., 1965, J.D., 1968. Admitted to Calif. bar, 1969, U.S. Supreme Ct. bar, 1976; asso. firm Gray, Cary, Ames & Frye, San Diego, 1968-74, partner, 1974—. Mem. Calif. State Bar, Am., San Diego County bar assns., Indsl. Relations Research Assn. (San Diego chpt. exec. bd.). Office: 2100 Union Bank Bldg San Diego CA 92101 Tel (714) 236-1661

GEESLIN, GARY L., b. Grenada, Miss., Oct. 31, 1940; B.A., Miss. State U., 1962; J.D., U. Miss., 1968. Admitted to Miss. bar, 1968; mem. firm Threadgill & Smith, Columbus, Miss., 1968—. Mem. Am., Miss., Lowndes County bar assns. Case note, comment editor Miss. Law Jour., 1968. Home: Pine Knoll Columbus MS 39701 Office: 215 5th St N Columbus MS 39701 Tel (601) 328-2316

GEHL, WILLIAM DANIEL, b. Milw., May 1, 1946; A.B. in Econs., U. Notre Dame, 1968; J.D., U. Wis., 1971; M.B.A., Wharton Sch. U. Pa., 1974. Admitted to Wis. bar, 1971, Fla. bar, 1973; individual practice law, West Bend, Wis., 1976—. Author: Photographs As Evidence, 1971. Office: 143 N 6th Ave West Bend WI 53217 Tel (414) 338-0649

GEHMAN, LARRY KERMIT, b. Allentown, Pa., July 18, 1943; B.A., Wheaton (Ill.) Coll., 1965; J.D., Northwestern U., 1968. Admitted to Pa. bar, 1968, Ill. bar, 1971; asst. gen. counsel Seeburg Corp., 1971-72; chief tech. advisor Ill. Civil Service Commn., 1972—; asst. judge adv. U.S. Army, 1968-70. Mem. Am., Ill., Chgo. bar assns. Office: Illinois Civil Service Commission 425 1/2 S 4th St Springfield IL 62701 Tel (312) 782-7373

GEIGER, JAMES NORMAN, b. Mansfield, Ohio, Apr. 5, 1932; B.A., Ohio Wesleyan U., 1954; LL.B., Emory U., 1962. Admitted to Ga. bar, 1961; partner firm Nunn, Geiger & Pierce and predecessors, Perry, Ga., 1964—. Bd. trustees Westfield (Ga.) Schs., 1970-74; pres. Perry Club Council, 1966-67; mem. civilian adv. bd. Warner Robins AFB, 1976. Mem. Am., Ga., Cobb County, Houston County bar assns., Perry Area C. of C. (pres. 1976), Phi Delta Phi. Office: 1007 Jernigan St Perry GA 31069 Tel (912) 987-2952

GEIGLE, STEPHEN ALEXANDER, b. Phila., June 3, 1945; B.B.A., Wake Forest U., 1967; J.D., U. Ark., 1970. Admitted to Ark. bar, 1970, U.S. Dist. Ct. bar, 1970; asst. gen. counsel Cooper Communities, Inc., Bella Vista, Ark., 1970-71; individual practice law, Rogers, Ark., 1971—; judge Municipal Ct., Rogers, Ark., 1972—. Mem. Ark. Bar Assn., Ark. Municipal League, Rogers C. of C. Home: 924 S 27th St Rogers AR 72756 Office: 1039 W Walnut Box 193 Rogers AR 72756 Tel (501) 636-1057

GEIMAN, J. ROBERT, b. Evanston, Ill., Mar. 5, 1931; B.S., Northwestern U., 1953; J.D., U. Notre Dame, 1956. Admitted to Ill. bar, 1956, U.S. Supreme Ct. bar, 1959, U.S. Tax. Ct. bar, 1972; asso. firm Peterson, Ross, Schloerb & Seidel, and predecessors, Chgo., 1956-64, partner, 1964—. Mem. bd. lay advisors Cath. Charities of Archdiocese Chgo., 1973—. Mem. Ill. State (sec., mem. bd. govs. 1969-71), Chgo., Am. bar assns., Bar Assn. 7th Fed. Ct., Legal Club Chgo., Law Club Chgo., Soc. Trial Lawyers, Notre Dame Club Chgo. (dir. 1957-59), Chgo. Athletic Assn. (pres. 1973), Cath. Lawyers Guild. Home: 1034 Seminole Rd Wilmette IL 60091 Office: 73d Floor 200 E Randolph Dr Chicago IL 60601 Tel (312) 861-1400

GEISLER, JAMES CHARLES, b. Madison, Wis., May 19, 1915; Ph.B., U. Wis., 1937, LL.B., 1940. Admitted to Wis. bar, 1940; individual practice law, 1946-61; partner firm Geisler & Kay, Madison, Wis., 1961—; atty. Shorewood Hills, 1956-67, 73-. Mem. Optimist Club, Madison, Wis., (pres. 1958-59); Blackhawk Country Club (pres. 1950). Am. Am., Wis., Dane County (past pres.) bar assns. Home: 2929 Colgate Rd Madison WI 53705 Office: 433 W Washington Ave Madison WI 53703 Tel (608) 257-4401

GELB, JUDITH ANNE, b. N.Y.C., Apr. 5, 1935; B.A., Bklyn. Coll., 1955; J.D., Columbia U., 1958. Admitted to N.Y. State bar, 1959, Ct. Mil. Appeals bar, 1962; asst. to editor N.Y. Law Jour., N.Y.C., 1958; confdl. asst. to U.S. atty. Eastern Dist. N.Y., Bklyn., 1959-61; asso. firm Whitman and Ransom, N.Y.C., 1961-70, partner, 1971—. Mem. N.Y. State Bar Assn., N.Y. Dist. Attys. Assn., N.Y. Women's Bar Assn., Fed. Bar Council. Home: 169 E 69th St New York City NY 10021 Office: 522 Fifth Ave New York City NY 10036 Tel (212) 575-5800

GELBAND, STEPHEN LAURENCE, b. N.Y.C., Feb. 13, 1931; A.B., Yale, 1952; J.D., Harvard, 1955. Admitted to N.Y. bar, 1955, D.C. bar, 1961; staff Office U.S. Atty. So. Dist. N.Y., 1955; legal assistance adviser U.S. Army, Ft. Myer, Va., 1956-57; trial atty. CAB, Washington, 1957-60; mem. firm Fisher, Gelband & Sinick, and predecessors, Washington, 1963—. Mem. Somerset (Md.) Town Council, 1967-70. Mem. Am., Fed., D.C. bar assns. Home: 6510 River Rd Bethesda MD 20034 Office: 1522 K St NW Washington DC 20005 Tel (202) 223-4600

GELBER, DON JEFFREY, b. Los Angeles, Mar. 10, 1940; student U. Calif., Los Angeles, 1957-58, Reed Coll., 1958-59; A.B., Stanford, 1961, LL.B., 1963. Admitted to Calif. bar, 1964, Hawaii bar, 1964; asso. firm Greenstein, Yamane & Cowan, Honolulu, 1964-67; reporter penal law revision project Hawaii Jud. Council, Honolulu, 1967-69; partner firm Burgess & Gelber, 1972-73; individual practice law, Honolulu, 1974—; legal counsel Hawaii Senate Judiciary Com., 1965, Edn. Com., 1967, 68; adminstrv. asst. to majority floor leader Hawaii Senate, 1966; majority atty. Hawaii Ho. of Reps., 1974. Mem. Hawaii, Am. bar assns., Hawaii Estate Planning Council. Office: Suite 2117 745 Fort St Honolulu HI 96813 Tel (808) 524-0155

GELBER, WALTER JOSEPH, b. Vienna, Austria, Feb. 8, 1924; J.D., Washington U., St. Louis, 1951. Admitted to Mo. bar, 1952, U.S. Supreme Ct. bar, 1960; mem. firm Lyng, McLeod & Davison, 1952-54; atty. Aetna Casualty Co., 1954-58; pres. firm Walter J. Gelber, Inc., Clayton, Mo., 1958—; of counsel firm Gerald Bamberger, St. Charles, Mo., 1975—, Stephen Kennedy, St. Charles, 1975—. Mem. Am., Mo. bar assns., Lawyers Assn. St. Louis (v.p. 1961, treas. 1962-63), Am. (recipient Recognition award 1973), Mo. (gov. 1970-75) trial lawyers assns., Am. Judicature Soc. Office: 111 S Bemiston Ave Clayton MO 63105 Tel (314) 721-8144

GELFMAN, RICHARD DAVID, b. Northampton, Mass., Oct. 26, 1947; B.S., U. Mass., Amherst, 1969; J.D., U. Md., 1972. Admitted to Md. bar, 1973, D.C. bar, 1973, U.S. Dist. Ct. Md., 1973; chief atty. Mental Health Project, Legal Aid Bur. Balt., 1972-74; partner firm Gelfman & Gelfman, Ellicott City, Md., 1974—; lectr. U. Balt. Sch. Law, 1975—. Mem. Md. State, Am., D.C. bar assns., Am., Md. trial lawyers assns. Contbr. articles to legal jours. Home: 10532 Jason Ln Columbia MD 21044 Office: 9051 Baltimore Nat Pike Ellicott City MD 21043 Tel (301) 465-1824

GELFOND, RICHARD BRUCE, b. Newark, Dec. 22, 1946; B.A magna cum laude with honors, Kenyon Coll., 1969; J.D., N.Y. U., 1973. Admitted to N.J. bar, 1973; clk. to judge Superior Ct. N.J., Jersey City, 1973-74; dep. atty. gen. State of N.J., Trenton, 1974-77; asso. firm Simon & Allen, Newark, 1977—. Mem. Am., N.J. bar assns., Phi Beta Kappa, Phi Alpha Delta. Office: 744 Broad St Newark NJ 07102 Tel (201) 621-2230

GELLER, MARC BRUCE, b. Los Angeles, Mar. 19, 1948; B.A., U. So. Calif., 1970; J.D., U.S. Internat. U., 1973; Admitted to Calif. bar, 1973; partner firm Hagerstrom & Geller, San Diego, 1973—. Mem. San Diego County Bar Assn., ACLU, Nat. Lawyers Guild. Office: 1144 State St San Diego CA 92101 Tel (714) 239-9457

GELMAN, ANDREW RICHARD, b. Chgo., June 20, 1946; B.A., U. Pa., 1967; J.D., U. Va., 1970. Admitted to Va. bar, 1970, Ill. bar, 1971; asso. firm McBride Baker Wienke & Schlosser, Chgo., 1974—. Mem. Chgo. (chmn. young lawyers sect.) past editor Young Lawyers Jour.), Ill., Am., Va. bar assns., Chgo. Council Lawyers. Vice-chmn., Jr. Med. Research Inst. Council, Michael Reese Hosp., 1976—. Home: 512 W Belden St Chicago IL 60614 Office: 110 N Wacker Dr Suite 500 Chicago IL 60606 Tel (312) 346-6191

GELMAN, DAVID, b. Bklyn., June 5, 1939; B.S., N.Y. U., 1964; M.B.A., Coll. City N.Y., 1966; J.D., West New Eng. Coll., 1975. Admitted to Mass. bar, 1975. Mem. Hampden County Bar Assn. Tel (413) 525-7873

GELNETTE, JEFFREY ALTON, b. Brookville, Pa., Apr. 29, 1948; B.A., Pa. State U., 1970; J.D., U. Pitts., 1973. Admitted to Pa. Supreme Ct. bar, 1973, U.S. Ct. Appeals bar, 3d Circuit, 1973; asso. firm Dennison & Matson, Brookville, Pa., 1973-74; individual practice law, Brookville, 1974—; instr. law Pa. State U., 1976—. Bd. dirs. Miss Teenage Brookville, 1975—. Mem. Am., Pa. bar assns. Home and Office: 70 Pickering St Brookville PA 15825 Tel (814) 849-5318

GEMPELER, MARK STEPHEN, b. Sparta, Wis., Jan. 3, 1949; B.A., No. Ill. U., 1971; J.D., Marquette U., 1974; postgrad U. Wis., Milw., 1974. Admitted to Wis. bar, 1974; 1st asst. dist. atty. Waukesha County (Wis.) Dist. Attys. Office, 1974—; faculty advisor Nat. Coll. Dist. Attys., 1977. Mem. Wis., Milw., Waukesha County bar assns. Office: 515 W Moreland Blvd Waukesha WI 53226 Tel (414) 544-8066

GENBERG, IRA, b. Newark, July 27, 1947; A.B. magna cum laude, Rutgers U., 1969; J.D., U. Pa., 1972. Admitted to Ga. bar, 1972; mem. firm Haas, Holland, Levison & Gibert, Atlanta, 1972-75, firm Stokes & Shapiro, Atlanta, 1975—. Mem. Am., Ga., Atlanta bar assns., Phi Beta Kappa. Editor moot ct. bd. U. Pa. Home: 2209 Briarcliff Rd Atlanta GA 30329 Office: 2 Peachtree St Atlanta GA 30303 Tel (404) 658-9050

GENDE, SUSAN BANDLOW, b. Chgo., Feb. 19, 1937; B.A., U. Ill., 1959, LL.B., 1963; M.S.W., U. Iowa, 1965. Admitted to Ill. bar, 1963; psychiatric social worker E. Moline (Ill.) State Hosp., 1963-64; asst. state's atty, Juvenile Ct. Rock Island County (Ill.), 1965-68; chief social worker Rock Island County Assn. for Retarded Children and Adults, Moline, 1970-74, asst. state's atty. Juvenile Ct., 1974—; asst. prof. U. Iowa Grad. Sch. Social Work, Iowa City, 1966-68; lectr. Marycrest Coll., Davenport, Iowa, 1972. Mem. adv. bd. Children at Risk, Rock Island, 1976—; bd. dirs. United Way, Rock Island, 1975—, Project Now, 1973-76; mem. adv. council State of Ill. Hosps., 1974—, State of Ill. Juvenile Justice and Delinquency Prevention to Ill. Law Enforcement Commn., 1975-76; mem. Delinquency Prevention Commn., 1975—. Mem. Ill. State Bar Assn., Nat. Assn. Social Workers, Ill. Assn. Children with Learning Disabilities. Home: 3523 39th St Moline IL 61265 Office: Rock Island County Courthouse Rock Island IL 61265 Tel (309) 786-4451

GENESEN, LAWRENCE I., b. Chgo., Feb. 23, 1922; B.A., U. Ill., 1946, J.D., 1948. Admitted to Ill. bar, 1948, U.S. 7th Circuit Ct. Appeals bar, 1949; asst. state's atty. for Cook County (Ill.), 1950-67; magistrate Ill. Circuit Ct. of Cook County, 1967-71, assoc. judge, 1971-76, judge, 1976—. Mem. Chgo. Bar Assn. (chmn. com. mental health). Author: Search and Seizure, 1955, rev. edit., 1961. Home: 550 Pleasant St Glenwood IL 60425 Office: Civic Center Randolph and Clark Sts Chicago IL 60602 Tel (312) 443-5500

GENEVA, LOUIS BRION, b. Wilmington, Del., Feb. 2, 1947; B.A., Miami U., Oxford, Ohio, 1969; J.D., Suffolk U., 1973; LL.M., N.Y. U., 1974. Admitted to Ohio bar, 1973, Conn. bar, 1977; instr. law N.Y. U., 1974-76; asso. firm Bergman, Horowitz & Reynolds, New Haven, 1976—. Mem. Am. Bar Assn. Office: 900 Chapel St New Haven CT 06510 Tel (203) 789-1320

GENNET, SAMUEL ADAIR, b. Newark, June 10, 1912; B.A., Univ. Heights Coll. N.Y. U., 1933; J.D. Harvard, 1936. Admitted to N.J. bar, 1936, U.S. Supreme Ct. bar, 1963; individual practice law, Newark, N.J., 1936-70, East Orange, N.J., 1970—; trustee Harvard Law Sch. Assn. N.J., 1974—; mem. Essex County (N.J.) Ethics Com., 1975—, chmn., 1977. Nat. trustee, N.J. chmn. Nat. Jewish Hosp. and Research Center, 1970—. Mem. Essex County, N.J., Am. Fed. bar assns., Fedn. Ins. Counsel. Contbr. articles to N.J. Law Jour. Audio Digest. Home: 39 Greenview Way Upper Montclair NJ 07043 Office: 55 Washington St East Orange NJ 07017 Tel (201) 672-7100

GENRICH, WILLARD ADOLPH, b. Buffalo, Feb. 19, 1915; LL.B., U. Buffalo, 1938; L.H.D., Medaille Coll., 1973; LL.D., Canisius Coll., 1974. Admitted to N.Y. bar, 1939; spl. agent FBI, 1942-46; individual practice law, Amherst, N.Y., 1946—; pres. Genrich Builders, Inc., Buffalo, 1966—; dir. N.Y. State Higher Edn. Assistance Corp. Bd. dirs. Northeast Br. YMCA, Amherst, N.Y.; delegate N.Y. State Constitutional Conv., 1967; bd. regents U. State N.Y. and State Edn. Dept., 1973—. Mem. Am., N.Y. State, Eric County bar assns., Am. Judicature Soc. Recipient Daemen Colls. 1st Annual Pres. award, 1975; DeVeaux Sch. Distinguished Citizen award, 1976. Home: 66 Gezville Rd Amherst NY 14226 Office: 4287 Main St Buffalo NY 14226 Tel (716) 832-7484

GENSBURG, ROBERT A., b. Watertown, N.Y., Sept. 3, 1939; B.A., U. Pa., 1961; LL.B., Union U., 1967. Admitted to Vt. bar, 1967; asso. firm John A. Swainbank, St. Johnsbury, Vt., 1967-69; partner firm Swainbank, Gensburg, Morrissette & Neylon, St. Johnsburg, 1970-76, Gensburg & Axelrod, St. Johnsbury, 1976—; states atty. Caledonia County (Vt.), 1969-70; spl. pros. atty. State of Vt., 1974-76; chmn. Vt. Transp. Authority, Montpelier, 1973, adv. bd., 1974; chmn. Vt. Transp. Bd., 1975-77. Chmn., Caledonia County Bd. Tax Appeals, 1970; lister Town of Peacham (Vt.), 1969-70. Mem. Assn. Trial Lawyers Am., Vt. Bar Assn., Assn. ICC Practitioners. Home: RFD E Burke VT 05832 Office: 101 Eastern Ave St Johnsbury VT 05819 Tel (802) 748-8161

GENTRY, JOHN A., III, b. Lake Worth, Fla., Jan. 6, 1936; B.A. in English, Vanderbilt U., 1960; LL.B., U. Fla., 1964, J.D., 1967. Admitted to Fla. bar, 1965; partner firm Moyle, Gentry, Jones, Flanigan & Groner, W. Palm Beach, Fla., 1965—. Bd. dirs. Mental Health Assn. Palm Beach County, 1969-71, pres., 1970-71. Mem. Am. Bar Assn., The Fla. Bar, Palm Beach County Bar Assn., Am. Trial Lawyers Assn., Acad. Fla. Trial Lawyers, Delta Theta Phi, Alpha Tau Omega. Home: 220 Russlyn Dr West Palm Beach FL 33405 Office: 707 N Flagler Dr PO Box 3888 West Palm Beach FL 33402 Tel (305) 659-7500

GENTZ, WILLIAM ARTHUR, b. Mt. Clemens, Mich., Oct. 9, 1920; LL.B., Detroit U., 1951. Admitted to Mich. bar, 1952, U.S. Supreme Ct. bar, 1959; since practiced in Mt. Clemens, Mich., partner firm Starkey & Gentz, 1952-57, individual practice law, 1968—; atty. Clinton Twp., 1955-59; New Baltimore (Mich.), 1957-59; Chippewa Valley Sch. Dist., 1955-59. Bd. dirs United Found., Mt. Clemens, Mich., 1959; pres. Zion United Ch. Christ, Mt. Clemens, 1965. Mem. Mich., Macomb County bar assns. Home: 546 Wellington Crescent Mt Clemens MI 48043 Office: 15 Gratiot Ave Mt Clemens MI 48043 Tel (313) 463-0597

GEOCARIS, JAMES ALEXANDER, b. Chgo., Nov. 11, 1930; B.A., U. Chgo., 1949; J.D., DePaul U., 1953. Admitted to Ill. bar, 1953; partner firm D'Angelo, Baim, Dahl & Geocaris, Chgo., 1956-62; atty. Village of Niles (Ill.), 1962-65; judge Cook County (Ill.) Circuit Ct., Presiding judge 3d Municipal Dist., Niles, 1965—. Mem. Ill., Chgo. bar assns. Office: 7166 Milwaukee Ave Niles IL 60648 Tel (312) 647-7320

GEOGHEGAN, WILLIAM ALOYSIUS, b. Cin., Jan. 3, 1925; A.B., U. Cin., 1951; LL.B., Harvard, 1949. Admitted to Ohio bar, 1949, U.S. Supreme Ct. bar, 1963, D.C. bar, 1965; partner firm Geoghegan, Levy and Daly, Cin., 1949-55; asso. firm Dinsmore, Shohl, Sawyer and Dinsmore, Cin., 1955-57, partner, 1958-61; asst. dep. atty. gen., U.S. Dept. Justice, Washington, 1961-65; partner firm Pierson, Ball & Dows, Washington, 1965—; chief counsel, select com., U.S. Ho. of Reps., 1967, com. on standards of official conduct, 1976. Mem. Am., D.C., Fed. bar assns. Decorated Bronze Star medal, Purple Heart. Home: 9612 Accord Dr Potomac MD 20854 Office: 1000 Ring Bldg 1200 18th St NW Washington DC 20036 Tel (202) 331-8566

GEORGE, ALEXANDER ANDREW, b. Missoula, Mont., Apr. 26, 1938; B.S. in Bus. Adminstrn., U. Mont., 1960, J.D., 1962; postgrad. John Marshall Law Sch., 1966. Admitted to Mont. bar, 1962; individual practice law, Missoula, 1966—; partner firm George, Williams & Benn, and predecessors, Missoula, 1966—; lectr. U. Mont. Tax Inst. Pres. Missoula Civic Symphony, 1974; pres. Greek Orthodox Ch., Missoula. Mem. State Bar Mont. (trustee), Western Mont. Bar Assn. (past pres.), Mont. Soc. C.P.A.'s, Estate Planning Council Western Mont., Phi Delta Phi. Named Outstanding Young Man of Community, Missoula, 1973. Home: 4 Greenbrier Ct Missoula MT 59801 Office: 310 Western Bank Bldg Missoula MT 59801 Tel (406) 728-4310

GEORGE, CLAUD REID, b. Birta, Ark., Nov. 12, 1906; LL.B., U. Ark., 1929, J.D., 1969. Admitted to Ark. bar, 1928, U.S. Supreme Ct. bar, 1969; judge Yell County, Ark., 1942, dist. atty., 1943-46; city atty. Danville (Ark.), 1938-77, municipal judge, 1977—, also City of Dardanelle (Ark.). Home: 307 W 5th St Danille AR 72833 Office: 410 Main St Danville AR 72833 Tel (501) 495-2281

GEORGE, HARRIET PAVLES, b. Jamaica, N.Y., Dec. 6, 1930; B.A., Hofstra Coll., 1951; LL.D., Fordham U., 1954. Admitted to N.Y. bar, 1955, U.S. Supreme Ct. bar, 1976; individual practice law, Jamaica, N.Y., 1955-77; counsel to State Senator Frank Padavan, 1973-77; housing officer, judge Civil Ct. City N.Y. Chmn. Cyprian Relief Fund St. Demetrios Ch., Jamaica; Republican state committeewoman for 24th Assembly Dist. Queens County (N.Y.), chmn. Rep. County Com., 1976-77; nat. bd. dirs. Greek Orthodox Ladies Philoptochos Soc. of Archdiocese. Mem. Queens County Women's Bar Assn. (past pres.), Queens County Bar Assn., Columbian Lawyers Assn., Greek-Am. Lawyers Assn. Home: 18448 Grand Central Pkwy Jamaica Estates NY 11432

GEORGE, LAWRENCE PHILIP, b. Utica, N.Y., Feb. 23, 1948; B.A., Syracuse U., 1969, J.D., 1971. Admitted to N.Y. bar, 1973; partner firm George & Puleo, Utica, N.Y., 1973—; instr. bus. law Mohawk Valley Community Coll., 1973-76; 1st asst. corp. counsel City of Utica, 1974-75. Mem. charter revision commn. City of Utica, 1975; 2d vice chmn. Utica Democratic Com., 1976—. Mem. N.Y., Oneida County bar assns. Home: 1006 Rudolph Pl Utica NY 13501 Office: 425 James St Utica NY 13501 Tel (315) 797-8980

GEORGE, NEWELL ADOLPHUS, b. Kansas City, Mo., Sept. 24, 1904; LL.B., Nat. U., Washington, 1934, LL.M., 1935, M.P.L., 1935. Admitted to D.C. bar, 1935, Kans. bar, 1943; mem. firms Green, Bray & George Washington, 1934-35, Miller & George, Kansas City, Kans., 1953—; regional atty. Fed. Security Agy., Kansas City, Mo., 1935-52; chief dep. county atty. Wyandotte County, Kans., 1953-58; mem. 86th Congress from 2d Kans. Dist.; U.S. atty. for Dist. Kans., 1961-68; mem. Kans. Gov's. Com. on Criminal Adminstrn. and Cts. Sub-com., 1966-75; Kans. gov's rep. Pub. Land Law Rev. Commn., 1969-70; mem. pub. lands com. Interstate Oil Compact Commn., 1970-74. Mem. Kansas City (Kans.) Civil Service Commn., 1970—; mem. Kans. State Govtl. Ethics Commn., 1974—. Mem. Am., Kans., Fed., Wyandotte County (Kans.) (Meritorious award 1971) bar assns., Am. Judicature Soc., Delta Theta Phi. Named Law Enforcement Man of Year Rockne Club of Am., 1965; contbr. articles to Kans. U. Law Rev. Home: 1831 New Jersey Ave Kansas City KS 66102 Office: 804 Huron Bldg Kansas City KS 66101 Tel (913) 342-5917

GEORGE, RALPH NATHANIAL, JR., b. N.Y.C., Nov. 17, 1942; B.B.A., Iona Coll., 1964; J.D. cum laude, N.Y. U., 1972. Admitted to N.Y. State bar, 1973; IRS agt. U.S. Treasury Dept., N.Y.C., 1964-69; asst. v.p., tax. dir., asst. to the counsel Bowery Savs. Bank, N.Y.C., 1964-69; pres. Institutional Pension Cons., Inc., N.Y.C., 1975—; cons. in field. Advisor Bronx Com. of Thirty, Bronx, N.Y., 1965-70; mem. Cambria Heights (N.Y.) Civic Assn., 1974-75. Mem. Am., N.Y. State, Queens County bar assns., Tax Execs. Inst., Savs. Bank Assn. N.Y. (pension cons. 1975—). Home: 115-10 230 St Cambria Heights NY 11411 Office: 1212 Ave of the Americas New York City NY 10036 Tel (212) 869-8305

GEORGE, ROBERT ELIAS, b. Burlington, Vt., Apr. 27, 1936, B.S. in Bus. Adminstrn., New Haven U., 1967; J.D., Western New Eng. Coll., 1972. Admitted to Mass. bar, 1973; individual practice law, Sturbridge, Mass., 1973—. Chmn. Heart Fund, 1975; bd. dirs. Am. Cancer Soc., S. Central Mass., 1976-77; mem. St. Anne's Parish Council, 1975-77; budget com. United Way, 1976-77; bd. dirs. S. Central Mass. Elder Bus, Inc., 1973-76, Southbridge Credit Bur., 1976-77. Mem. Mass., Worcester County, S. Central Worcester County bar assns. Recipient Distinguihsed Service award, Mass. Heart Assn., 1969, Outstanding Service award, 1975; Whitcomb Athletic award, 1954; Hyde Book prize for Civic Achievement, 1954. Home: Stallion Hill Rd Sturbridge MA 01518 Office: Main St PO Box F Sturbridge MA 01518 Tel (617) 347-7240

GEPHARDT, RICHARD ANDREW, b. St. Louis, Jan. 31, 1941; B.S., Northwestern U., 1962; J.D., U. Mich., 1965. Admitted to Mo. bar, 1965; partner firm Thompson & Mitchell, St. Louis, 1965-76; mem. U.S. Ho. of Reps. from 3d Mo. Dist., 1976—. Mem. devel. bd. St. Louis Children's Hosp., 1975-76, pres. Children's United Research Effort, 1974-76; alderman City of St. Louis, 1971—; pres. CURE, St. Louis, 1972; bd. dirs. St. Louis Boy Scouts, 1975—. Mem. Mo., St. Louis bar assns. Recipient Am. Spirit Honor medal, 1966, Distinguished Service award St. Louis Jaycees, 1974, St. Louis Sr. Citizens Appreciation award, 1976. Home: 4121 Fairview St Saint Louis MO 63116 Office: 509 Cannon House Office Bldg Washington DC 20515 Tel (202) 225-2671

GERAGHTY, JOHN JAMES, b. Weehawken Heights, N.J., Feb. 12, 1908; B.A., Columbia, 1933, LL.B., 1935. Admitted to N.Y. State bar, 1935, Ga. bar, 1944, N.C. bar, 1953, U.S. Supreme Ct. bar, 1965, U.S. Ct. Claims bar, 1967; staff mem. Office of Asst. Atty. Gen. N.Y., 1935-37; asso. firm Duke and Landis, and predecessor, N.Y.C., 1937-42, 46-51; chief of legal div. U.S. Army Chem. Warfare Service, Atlanta, 1944, chief contract termination, Washington, 1944-46; partner firm Poyner, Geraghty, Hartsfield & Townsend, Raleigh, N.C., 1951—; lectr. in law Sch. Fin., N.Y. U., 1946-51. Mem. Am., N.C., Wake County bar assns. Home: 1003 James Pl Raleigh NC 27605 Office: 615 Oberlin Rd Raleigh NC 27605 Tel (919) 834-5241

GERARD, DONALD KEITH, b. N.Y.C., Feb. 4, 1937; B.B.A., J.D., Washington U., St. Louis. Admitted to Mo. bar, 1964; individual practice law, Kansas City, Mo., Elsberry, Mo., Clayton, Mo. Bd. dirs. Musculary Dystrophy Assn., Big Bros. Assn. St. Louis; trustee Children's Christmas Found. Mem. Am., St. Louis bar assns. Office: 7751 Carondelet St Clayton MO 63105 Tel (314) 726-1288

GERARD, JULES BERNARD, b. St. Louis, May 20, 1929; A.B., Washington U., St. Louis, 1957, J.D., 1958. Admitted to N.Y. bar, 1959; asso. firm Donovan, Leisure, Newton & Irvine, N.Y.C., 1958-60; asst. prof. law U. Mo., 1960-62; asst. prof. law Washington U., 1962-64, assoc. prof., 1964-67, prof., 1967—. Mem. Am. Bar Assn., Phi Beta Kappa. Ford Found. fellow U. Wis., 1963. Author: (with Van Alstyne and Karst) Sum and Substance of Constitutional Law, 1976. Home: 12912 Bellerive Estates Dr Creve Coeur MO 63141 Office: Sch Law Washington U St Louis MO 63130 Tel (314) 863-0100

GERARD, WHITNEY IAN, b. N.Y.C., Oct. 31, 1934; B.A., Princeton U., 1956; J.D., Harvard U., 1963. Admitted to N.Y. State bar, 1964; asso. firm Alexander & Green, N.Y.C., 1963-70, partner, 1970—; dir. The Dreyfus Fund, Dreyfus Spl. Income Fund, Dreyfus Liquid Assets, Kay Corp. Mem. N.Y. State Bar Assn. Home: 940 Park Ave New York City NY 10028 Office: 299 Park Ave New York City NY 10017 Tel (212) 758-6900

GERBER, CHARLES EVANS, b. Chgo., Dec. 29, 1941; B.A., So. Meth. U., 1963; J.D., U. Ill., 1966. Admitted to Ill. bar, 1966, D.C. bar, 1970; asso. firm Friedman & Koven, Chgo., 1966-69, partner, 1969—. Mem. Am., Ill., Chgo. bar assns., Am. Judicature Soc. Office: 208 S LaSalle St Chicago IL 60604

GERBER, SAMUEL ROBERT, b. Hagerstown, Md., Aug. 22, 1898; student Valparaiso (Ind.) U., 1917-18; M.D., Cin. E. Med. Coll., 1922; LL.B., Cleve. Marshall Law Sch., 1949. Physician in charge, med. service, Warrensville (Ohio) Correction Farm, 1925-28; physician div. child hygiene Cleve. Dept. Health, 1927-33; acting chief physician Cleve. Parochial Schs., 1928-33; coroner County of Cuyahoga (Ohio), 1937—; admitted to Ohio bar, 1949, U.S. Supreme Ct. bar, 1955, U.S. Dist. Ct. No. Ohio., 1961; asso. in legal medicine, Sch. Medicine Western Res. U., Cleve.; co-founder, co-dir. Law-Medicine Center, Cleve. Home: 2112 Acacia Park Dr Lyndhurst OH 44124 Office: 2121 Adelbert Rd Cleveland OH 44106 Tel (216) 721-5610

GERDE, CARLYLE NOYES (CY), b. Long Beach, Calif., Oct. 22, 1946; A.B., Purdue U., 1967; J.D., Ind. U., 1970. Admitted to Ind. bar, 1971, U.S. Supreme Ct. bar, 1976; individual practice law, Lafayette, Ind., 1971-72; partner firm Hanna and Gerde, Lafayette, Ind., 1972—; adj. prof. indsl. engring., Purdue U., 1973—. Bd. govs. Tippecanoe County Hist. Assn., 1976—; chmn. Erwin for Congress Com., 1976; sect. chmn. United Way Tippecanoe County, Tippecanoe County Cancer Soc.; mem. Carriage Assn. Am., Ohio Valley Carriage Assn., Am. Driving Soc., Ind. State Hist. Assn., Wabash Valley Hist. Trust. Mem. Am., Ind. State, Tippecanoe County Bar Assns., Am. Trial Lawyers Assn., Am. Arbitration Assn. Office: 50 B Lafayette Bank and Trust Bldg Lafayette IN 47901 Tel (317) 742-5005

GERHARDT, RICHARD LEE, b. Circleville, Ohio, Nov. 25, 1941; B.A., Ohio No. U., 1963; J.D., Georgetown U., 1966. Admitted to Ohio bar, 1966; individual practice law, Circleville, 1966—; pros. atty. Pickaway County, Ohio, 1972-77; mayor, Circleville, 1968-72. Mem. council Boy Scouts Am., 1976; chmn. Pickaway County Hist. Soc., 1975-76. Mem. Circleville C. of C., Am., Ohio, Pickaway County bar assns., Nat. Dist. Atty. Assn. Contbg. editor Ohio Prosecutor's Handbook, 1975. Home: 572 Willow Ln Circleville OH 43113 Office: 113 S Court St Circleville OH 43113 Tel (614) 474-7575

GERHART, EUGENE CLIFTON, b. Bklyn., Apr. 7, 1912; A.B., Princeton, 1934; LL.B., Harvard, 1937. Admitted to N.J. bar, 1938, N.Y. bar, 1945; practiced in Newark, 1938-43, Binghamton, N.Y., 1946—; sr. partner firm Coughlin and Gerhart; sec. to Judge Manley O. Hudson, Secretariat League of Nations, Geneva, 1934; lectr. U. Newark, 1942-43, Triple Cities Coll., Endicott, N.Y., 1946-48, Harpur Coll., Endicott, 1953-55, Cornell U., 1946; chmn. bd., gen. counsel, dir. Columbian Mut. Life Ins. Co., Binghamton; mem. N.Y. State Joint Com. on Ct. Reorganization, 1973—; mem. arbitration panel N.Y. State Mediation Bd. Mem. council State U. N.Y., Cortland, 1967—, chmn., 1971-77. Fellow Am. Bar Found., Am. Coll. Probate Counsel; mem. Am. (bd. editors jour. 1946-67, recipient Ross Essay award 1946), N.Y. State (editor in chief jour. 1961—), Broome County (pres. 1961-62) bar assns., Assn. Bar City N.Y., Am. Law Inst., Am. Judicature Soc. (dir. 1954-59), Assn. Life Ins. Counsel, Am. Trial Lawyers Assn., Am. Arbitration Assn. (nat. panel), Harvard Law Sch. Assn. (pres. Upstate N.Y. 1955-57), Selden Soc. (rep. Upstate N.Y. 1961—). Author: American Liberty and Natural Law; America's Advocate: Robert H. Jackson; Robert H. Jackson, Lawyer's Judge; Quote It! Memorable Legal Quotations; also articles; editor The Lawyer's Treasury. Home: 34 West End Ave Binghamton NY 13905 Office: 1 Marine Midland Plaza Binghamton NY 13901 Tel (607) 723-9511

GERITY, PATRICK LEONARD, b. Cleve., Dec. 17, 1919; student Cleve. Marshall Law Sch., 1957-58, J.D., 1973; A.B., John Carroll U., 1969. With Cleve. Police Dept., 1942-71, capt., 1963-68, insp. detectives, 1968, chief police, 1968-70; admitted to Ohio bar, 1973; individual practice law, Cleve., 1973—; safety and security cons. Vice-pres. Cleve. Safety Council, 1968-70; mem. Criminal Justice Coordinating Com., 1969-70, Com. on Sch. and Local Community Relations, 1974-75; candidate for mayor, Cleve., 1971; trustee Univ. Circle, Inc., 1969-72. Mem. Am., Ohio, Cuyahoga County, Greater Cleve. bar assns., Citizens League, Fraternal Order Police, Am. Legion, Alpha Sigma Lamda (hon.), Delta Theta Phi. Home: 29100 Osborn Rd Bay Village OH 44140 Office: Suite 800 Fidelity Bldg Cleveland OH 44114 Tel (216) 771-0560 also 871-1103

GERLACH, NORMAN HARBRIDGE, b. Oak Park, Ill., June 1, 1904; LL.B., Chgo.-Kent Coll. Admitted to Ill. bar, 1926, U.S. Supreme Ct. bar, 1972; practice law, Chgo. Mem. Chgo., Am. patent law assns. Home: 3550 N Lake Shore Dr Chicago IL 60657 Office: 105 W Adams St Chicago IL 60603 Tel 332-6930

GERLASH, JOHN MIDDLETON, b. Tarkio, Mo., May 10, 1903; B.S., Tarkio Coll., 1924; J.D., U. Mo., 1927. Admitted to Mo. bar, 1926; mem. firm Gerlash and Gerlash, Tarkio, 1927—. Office: Farmers and Valley Bank Bldg Tarkio MO 64491 Tel (816) 736-4157

GERLIN, ROBERT ARTHUR, b. Bayside, N.Y., June 27, 1932; B.A., St. Lawrence U., 1955; LL.B., Columbia, 1960. Admitted to N.Y. bar, 1961, Conn. bar, 1968, U.S. Supreme Ct. bar, 1965; asso. firm Rogers, Hoge & Hills, N.Y.C., 1961-65, firm Coudert Bros., London, 1965-67, firm Maguire, Cole, Bentley & Babson, Stamford, Conn., 1967-69; asso. firm Cross Broderick & Chipman, Stamford, 1969, partner, 1970; counsel firm Gregory & Adams, Wilton, Conn., 1970-74, partner, 1975—; asst. town counsel Town of Wilton, 1970-71. Selectman, Town of Wilton, 1972-73; mem. Wilton Charter

Rev. Commn., 1971-72; trustee and sec. Wilton Land Conservation Trust, 1971—; bd. dirs. Wilton Town Assn., 1970-71; sec. Wilton Interfaith Council, Inc., 1975—; bd. dirs., sec. Youth Employment Service of Wilton, 1975—; mem. mgmt. com. Weir Nature Preserve, The Nature Conservancy, Wilton, 1975—; bd. dirs. Wilton Trails Assn., Inc., 1970—. Mem. Assn. Bar City N.Y., Conn., N.Y. State, Norwalk-Wilton bar assns. Home: 121 Millstone Rd Wilton CT 06897 Office: PO Box 547 Old Ridgefield Rd Wilton CT 06897 Tel (203) 762-5543

GERMAIN, ALBERT EDWIN, b. Saginaw, Mich., Feb. 2, 1934; B.S. in Accounting, Notre Dame U., 1955; LL.B., Mich. U., 1958; LL.M., N.Y. U., 1959. Admitted to Mich. bar, 1958, Pa. bar, 1959; atty. Alcoa Co., Pitts., 1959-64, gen. atty., 1965-68, tax counsel, 1968—, asst. officer, 1974—; Nat. officer Tax Execs. Inst., 1974; lectr. in field. Mem. Am., Pa. bar assns., Contbr. articles to legal jours. Office: 1501 Alcoa Bldg Pittsburgh PA 15219 Tel (412) 553-4232

GERMAIN, TERENCE JOSEPH, b. Syracuse, N.Y., Nov. 12, 1935; student LeMoyne Coll, 1953-54, B.A., St. Bernard's Seminary, 1959; LL.B., Syracuse U. Coll., 1966. Admitted to N.Y. State bar, 1967; mem. firm Brandt & Laughlin, Westfield, N.Y., 1966-67, Robert M. Weldon, Watertown, N.Y., 1967-69, Conboy, McKay, Bachman & Kendall, 1969-71; individual practice law, Watertown, N.Y., 1971—; asst. atty. Jefferson County 1974-76. Dir. No. N.Y. Heart Assn., 1975-77. Mem. Jefferson County, N.Y. State bar assns. Editor: Syracuse Law Rev., 1965-66. Home: 138 Ward St Watertown NY 13601 Office: 216 Washington St Watertown NY 13601 Tel (315) 788-5508

GERMAN, EDWARD C., b. Phila., Dec. 28, 1922; J.D., Temple U., 1950. Admitted to Pa. bar, 1951; since practiced in Phila., asso. firm LaBrum and Doak, 1951-54; partner, 1955—; mem. Pa. Rules of Civil Procedure Com., 1963-71, Common Ct. Pleas Com., 1964-71. Dist. dir. United fund campaign, 1960; solicitor-counsel Civil Assn. Delaware County, Pa., 1955-60; coach Episcopal Acad. Ice Hockey team, 1973-74. Mem. Am. Pa., Phila. bar assns., Fed. Bench-Bar Conf., Fedn. Ins. Counsel (bd. govs. 1960-62, v.p. 1962-63, sec.-treas. 1963-65, exec. v.p. 1965-66, pres. 1966-67, chmn. 1967-68), Internat. Assn. Ins. Counsel, Pa. Def. Research Inst., Def. Research Inst. Profl. Liability-Inst., Pa., Phila. chambers commerce, Scribes, Phila. Def. Counsel Assn., Internat. Assn. Humble Humbugs, Phi Delta Phi. Contbr. articles to law revs. Home: 1208 Ormond Ave Drexel Hill PA 19026 Office: 1500 7 Penn Center Plaza Philadelphia PA 19103 Tel (215) 561-4400

GERMANI, ELIA, b. Providence, Feb. 5; A.B. magna cum laude, U. R.I., 1957; J.D., Harvard, 1961. Admitted to R.I. bar, 1962; asso. firm Graham, Reid, Ewing & St. Apleton, Providence, 1961-68; asst. sec., counsel The Narragansett Electric Co., Providence, 1968-76; partner firm Tillinghast, Collins & Graham, Providence, 1976—. Mem. Am., R. I. bar assns., Harvard Law Sch. Assn. R.I. (pres. 1973-74). Home: 22 Cedar Pond Dr Apt 7 Warwick RI 02886 Office: 2000 Hospital Trust Tower Providence RI 02903 Tel (401) 274-3800

GERMANOTTA, JOHN JOSEPH, b. Milw., Aug. 7, 1946; B.A., De Pauw U., 1968; J.D., Marquette U., 1971. Admitted to Wis. bar, 1971; staff atty. Milwaukee County Pub. Defender Office, 1971-74; asso. firm Steve Enich, Milw., 1974; partner firm Ziino, Pulito & Germanotta, Milw., 1975—. Sec.-treas. Bradystreet Mchts. Assn. Inc., Milw., 1976; pres. 1st Neighborhood Credit Union, Milw., 1976—. Mem. Milw., Milw. Jr. bar assns. Home: 5320 N Berkeley St Whitefish Bay WI 53217 Office: 1700 N Farwell St Milwaukee WI 53202 Tel (414) 272-2295

GERMANY, JOHN, b. Daviston, Ala., Jan. 16, 1923; B.A., U. Fla., 1944; LL.B./J.D., Harvard, 1950; LL.D. (hon.), Stetson U., 1974. Admitted to Fla. bar, 1950; asso. firm Fowler White Gillen Yancey & Humpkey, Tampa, Fla., 1950-52; partner firm Coles, Himes and Germany, Tampa, 1952-59; judge 13th Jud. Circuit Fla., Tampa, 1959-66; partner firm Knight Jones Whitaker & Germany, Tampa, 1966-68, Holland, Knight & Germany, Tampa, 1966—; legal asst. to Gov. Fla., 1955, 57; mem. Fla. Bd. Bar Examiners, 1967-76, vice chmn., 1969-70, chmn., 1970-71. Pres., Tampa Friends of Library, 1965; chmn. Mayor's Com. for Improvement of Tampa, 1965; pres. bd. trustees U.S. Fla. Found., 1952-54; chmn. bd. visitors Fla. State U. Law Sch., 1974-75. Fellow Am. Bar Assn.; mem. Nat. Conf. Bar Examiners (chmn. 1974-76), Am. Bar Assn. (chmn. standing com. on admiralty and maritime law 1975—), Fla. Bar. Recipient medallion for Community Services, U. South Fla., 1962. Home: 3415 Morrison Ave Tampa FL 33609 Office: PO Box 1288 Tampa FL 33601 Tel (813) 223-1621

GERMER, LAWRENCE LOUIS, b. Waco, Tex., Oct. 28, 1941; B.A., U. Tex., 1963, J.D., 1966. Admitted to Tex. bar, 1966; mem. firm Orgoin, Bell & Tucker, Beaumont, Tex., 1966—, partner, 1972—. Pres., Beaumont Symphony Soc., 1975-77; bd. dirs. West End YMCA, 1973. Mem. Am., Jeff Davis County (pres. jr. bar 1973), Tex. bar assns., Tex. assn. Def. Counsel. Office: Beaumont Savings Bldg Beaumont TX 77701 Tel (713) 838-6412

GERMINO, DONALD OWEN, b. Los Banos, Calif., Oct. 1, 1939; A.B., U. So. Calif., 1961; LL.D., U. Calif., Berkeley, 1964. Admitted to Calif. bar, 1965; individual practice law, Los Banos, 1965; city atty. Los Banos, 1971—, Dos Lapos (Calif.), 1976—. Chmn. Merced County Republican Central Com., 1968-70. Mem. Am., Calif., Merced County bar assns. Office: 1341 E Pacheco Blvd Los Banos CA 93635 Tel (209) 826-5024

GERNS, PETER HARRY, b. Mannheim, Germany, Apr. 4, 1922; A.B. with honors in Polit. Sci., U. N.C., 1948, LL.D. with honors, 1956. Admitted to N.C. bar, 1956, U.S. Supreme Ct. bar, 1970; individual practice law, Charlotte, N.C., 1956—; judge Charlotte City Ct., 1957-59. Sec. Better Bus. Bur. Greater Mecklenburg; bd. mem. N.C. Employment Security Commn. Adv. Council, Mecklenburg County Transp. Task Force, Contact Counseling Service; chmn. bd. Charlotte Area Fund, 1972-76, Charlotte Rehab. Homes, 1969-71, Nevins Center Retarded Children, 1963-66, County Mental Retardation Adv. Bd., 1972; mem. Mayor's Com. to Employ Handicapped, 1961-63; mem. bd. 1st Methodist Ch., 1960-65. Mem. Am., N.C., Mecklenburg County bar assns., N.C. Acad. Trial Lawyers, Am. Inst. Parliamentarians (dist. dir.), Charlotte Sales and Mktg. Execs. Named N.C. Toastmaster of Year, 1974, Rotarian of Year, 1976. Home: 3125 Mountainbrook Rd Charlotte NC 28210 Office: 1200 American Bldg Charlotte NC 28286 Tel (704) 374-1200

GERRARD, KEITH, b. Malden, Mass., Feb. 8, 1935; A.B., Harvard, 1956, LL.B., 1963. Admitted to Wash. bar, 1963; asso. firm Perkins, Coie, Stone, Olsen & Williams, Seattle, 1963-70, partner, 1970—. Mem. Am., Wash. State, Seattle-King County bar assns. Home: 618 W Highland St Seattle WA 98119 Office: 1900 Washington Bldg Seattle WA 98101 Tel (206) 682-8770

GERRIE, ROBERT BRUCE, b. Oak Park, Ill., Feb. 28, 1924; B.S., Northwestern U., 1948, J.D., 1951. Admitted to Ill. bar, 1951, U.S. Tax Ct., 1960; asso. firm McBride, Baker, Wienke & Schlosser, Chgo., 1951-57, partner, 1958-73; v.p. legal affairs, gen. counsel Morton-Norwich Products Inc., Chgo., 1974—, sec., 1974-76. Commnr., Wilmette (Ill.) Park Dist., 1965-77, pres., 1967-71; pres. New Trier Citizens League, Winnetka, Ill., 1969-73; chmn. New Trier Twp. Com. on Youth, Winnetka, 1972-74. Mem. Chgo., Ill. State, Am. bar assns., Law Club Chgo., Legal Club Chgo., Phi Delta Phi. Office: 110 N Wacker Dr Chicago IL 60606 Tel (312) 621-5682

GERRY, NORMAN BERNARD, b. N.Y.C., Nov. 19, 1946; B.A., U. Okla., 1968, J.D., Vanderbilt U., 1971. Admitted to Tenn. bar, 1971, Ga. bar, 1973; asso. firm Martin, Tate, Morrow, & Maston, Memphis, 1971-72; asso. firm Stack & O'Brien, Atlanta, 1972-75, partner, 1975-76; partner firm Stack, Rogers & Gerry, Atlanta, 1976—. Mem. State Bar Ga., Am., Atlanta bar assns., Order of Coif. Case and notes editor Vanderbilt Law Rev. Home: 1153 Fielding Way Marietta GA 30067 Office: 1401 W Paces Ferry Rd NW Atlanta GA 30327 Tel (404) 231-1313

GERSHENGORN, WENDIE ILENE, b. N.Y.C., Jan. 29, 1943; B.A., Ohio U., 1963; LL.B., Columbia, 1966. Admitted to Mass. bar, 1972; legal dept. Met. Life Ins. Co., N.Y.C., 1970-71; criminal atty. Mass. Defenders Com., Boston, 1972-75; mem. Mass. State Parole Bd., Boston, 1975—; clin. instr. Boston Coll. Law Sch., 1974-75. Mem. Am. Judicature Soc., Mass. Bar Assn. Office: 100 Cambridge St Boston MA 02202 Tel (617) 727-3281

GERSHENSON, HARRY, b. St. Louis, July 8, 1902; LL.B., Benton Coll. Law, 1934. Admitted to Mo. bar, 1923, U.S. Supreme Ct. bar, 1951; Gershensen & La Tourette, 1923-36, Gershenson & Gershenson, St. Louis, 1964—; prof. law St. Louis U., 1948-54. Bd. dirs. Salvation Army, St. Louis. Mem. Am. (gov. 1961-64, mem. Lawyers Guaranty Fund 1962—, past mem. various coms.), Mo. (pres. 1957-58, merit award 1966), St. Louis (pres. 1946-47, merit award 1966) bar assns., Am. Coll. Probate Counsel (pres. 1945-46), Am. Bar Found. (life), Scribes (pres. 1959-60). Home: 542 Warder Ave University City MO 63130 Office: 7733 Forsyth St St Louis MO 63105 Tel (314) 725-2545

GERSHENSON, MILTON GABRIEL, b. N.Y.C., June 25, 1910; B.S., Coll. City N.Y., 1930; LL.B., Bklyn. Law Sch., 1933, S.J.D., 1934, LL.D., 1977. Admitted to N.Y. State bar, 1933, U.S. Supreme Ct. bar, 1960; prof. law Bklyn. Law Sch., 1938—; spl. hearing officer U.S. Dept. Justice, 1956-68; lectr. Practicing Law Inst., 1956—; advisor N.Y. Legis. Commn. on Family Law, 1960-65; chief reporter State of N.Y. Criminal Jury Instrn. Com., 1975—. Mem. N.Y.C. Bar Assn. Home: 170 Shepherd Ln Roslyn Heights NY 11577 Office: Bklyn Law Sch 250 Joralemon St Brooklyn NY 11201 Tel (212) 625-2200

GERSON, ALLAN, b. Uzbekistan, USSR, June 19, 1945; B.A., U. Buffalo, 1966; J.D., N.Y.U., 1969; LL.M., Hebrew U. of Jerusalem, 1972; J.S.D. (Univ. Consortium fellow), Yale, 1976. Admitted to N.Y. State bar, 1970; asso. prof. law New Eng. Sch. Law, Boston, 1974—. Mem. Am. Bar Assn., Soc. Am. Law Tchrs., Am. Soc. Internat. Law. Contbr. articles to legal jours. Home: 33 Concord Ave Cambridge MA 02138 Office: 126 Newbury St Boston MA 02116 Tel (617) 267-9655

GERSON, HERBERT EDWARD, b. Atlanta, Aug. 21, 1948; B.A., Emory U., 1970, J.D., 1973. Admitted to Tenn. bar, 1973; asso. firm Canada Russell & Turner, Memphis, 1973—; adj. prof. bus. law Memphis State U. Sch. Bus. Adminstrn., 1974. Mem. Am., Tenn. bar assns., Omicron Delta Kappa, Pi Sigma Alpha. Office: 12th Floor Planters Nat Bank Bldg Memphis TN 38103 Tel (901) 521-1111

GERSON, ROBERT WALTHALL, b. Macon, Ga., Aug. 6, 1935; A.B. in Law, Emory U., 1959, LL.B., 1960, J.D., 1960. Admitted to Ga. bar, 1960; atty. Ga. Pub. Service Commn., 1960-65; counsel Ryder Truck Lines, Inc., Jacksonville, Fla., 1965-68; partner firm Troutman, Sanders, Lockerman & Ashmore, Atlanta, 1968—; instr. Ga. State U. Mem. Atlanta Lawyers Club, Motor Carrier Lawyers Assn., Atlanta Bar Assn., State Bar Ga. Home: 1622 Arnaud Ct Atlanta GA 30308 Office: 1400 Candler Bldg 127 Peachtree St Atlanta GA 30303 Tel (404) 658-8045

GERSTEIN, JOE W., b. Atlanta, July 29, 1927; A.B., Duke, 1949; LL.B., 1952, J.D., 1970. Admitted to Ga. bar, 1953, U.S. Supreme Ct. bar, 1967; sr. partner firm Gerstein Carter & Chestnut, Doraville, Ga., 1962-76; individual practice law, Doraville, 1976—; city atty., Doraville, 1973-76. Mem. Am., Ga., Atlanta, Decatur-DeKalb bar assns., Atlanta Estate Planning Council, Comml. Law League Am. (sec.). Home: 222 Burdett Rd NW Atlanta GA 30327 Office: 6485 Peachtree Industrial Blvd Doraville GA 30360 Tel (404) 457-8244

GERSTEN, JOSEPH JULIUS, lawyer; b. Simsbury, Conn., Nov. 4, 1917; LL.B., Nat. U., 1941; J.D., George Washington U., 1941. Admitted to D.C. bar, 1942, Fla. bar, 1947; pvt. practice law, Miami, Fla., 1942—; judge City of Miami Mcpl. Ct., 1964-66; mem. Fla. Bd. Bar Examiners, 1972-76, chmn., 1975-76; chmn. Fla. Supreme Ct. News Media Com., 1975—; mem. Fla. Supreme Ct. Traffic Review Com., 1976—. Mem. Am., Fla., Dade County bar assns., Am. Judicature Soc., Blue Key. Established Annual Joseph J. Gersten Key award for outstanding U. Fla. Law Sch. Sr., also Judge Joe Morris annual ward for two outstanding grads. of Stetson U. Law Sch. Home: 5640 Collins Av Miami Beach FL 33140 Office: 1050 Spring Garden Rd Miami FL 33136

GERSTEN, SANDRA PESSIN, Hartford, Conn., June 21, 1936; B.A., Vassar Coll., 1957, LL.B., U. Conn., 1960. Admitted to Conn. bar, 1960; individual practice law, West Hartford, Conn., 1960—. Pres. Greater Hartford Orgn. for Rehab. through Tng., 1968-69. Mem. Am., Conn., Hartford County bar assns., Am. Arbitration Assn. Home: 25 Pioneer Dr West Hartford CT 06117 Tel (203) 561-2233

GERSTLEY, KIEFER NEWMAN, b. Phila., Oct. 12, 1926; B.S. in M.E., Cornell U., 1948; J.D., U. Pa., 1952. Admitted to U.S. Dist. Ct. bar, 1953, Pa. Supreme Ct. bar, 1953, Phila. Common Pleas Ct. bar, 1953, Montgomery County Common Pleas bar, 1959; asso. firm Wolf, Block, Schorr & Solis-Cohen, Phila., 1953-59; asso. firm Wisler, Pearlstine, Talone & Gerber, Morristown, Pa., 1959-66; partner firm Schachtel, Einhorn & Gerstley, Phila., 1966—. Bd. dirs. Eagleville (Pa.) Hosp. and Rehab. Center, 1952—, pres., 1966-69, chmn. exec. com., 1969-72; asst. treas. The Philip H. and A.S.W. Rosenbach Found., Phila., 1954—; trustee Fedn. Jewish Ags., Phila., 1966-72. Mem. Am., Pa., Phila., Montgomery County bar assns., Phila. Estate Planning Council. Office: 3220 PSFS Bldg 12 S 12th St Philadelphia PA 19107 Tel (215) WA2-1400

GERSTMAN, ALFRED M., b. Phoenix, Feb. 3, 1932; LL.B., Bklyn. Law Sch., 1954. Admitted to N.Y. bar, 1954, U.S. Dist. Ct. bar, 1954, U.S. Supreme Ct. bar, 1958, U.S. Circuit Ct. Appeals bar, 1969; partner firm Gerstman & Gerstman, Mountaindale, N.Y., 1956-60, Krieger & Gerstman, Woodridge, N.Y., 1960-68, Krieger, Gerstman & Orseck, Woodridge, 1968-70. Krieger, Kesten, Gerstman & Ledina, Monticello, N.Y., 1971-73, Kesten Gerstman & Ledina, Monticello, N.Y., 1973—; urban renewal atty., Town of Fallsburg, N.Y., 1970-73. Councilman, Town of Fallsburg, 1959-60. Mem. Am., N.Y. State, Sullivan County bar assns. Home: PO Box 263 Mountaindale NY 12763 Office: PO Box 844 Monticello NY 12701 Tel (914) 794-1000

GERSTMAN, GEORGE HENRY, b. N.Y.C., July 25, 1939; B.E.E., U. Ill., 1960; J.D. with honors, George Washington U., 1963. Patent examiner U.S. Patent Office, 1960-63; admitted to Ill. bar, 1964, U.S. Patent Office bar, 1964, U.S. Supreme Ct. bar, 1970; practiced in Chgo., 1964—; asso. firm Dressler, Goldsmith, Clement and Gordon, 1963-70; partner firm Lettvin and Gerstman, 1970-75, Pigott & Gerstman, 1976—; govt. appeal agt. SSS, 1967-73. Mem. Bd. Zoning Appeals, Village of Northbrook (Ill.), 1971—. Mem. Am., Chgo. bar assns., Patent Law Assn. Chgo., Order of Coif. Asst. patent editor George Washington Law Rev., 1962-63; Mary Covington Meml. scholar, 1962. Home: 4041 Picardy Dr Northbrook IL 60062 Office: 135 S LaSalle St Chicago IL 60603 Tel (312) 263-4350

GERSTMAN, LOUIS, b. N.Y.C., Sept. 24, 1914; student Bklyn Coll., 1931-34; LL.B., St. John's U., 1938, LL.M., 1939, J.D., 1972. Admitted to N.Y. bar, 1939; dir. birth certificate, correction div. N.Y.C. Dept. Health, Bklyn., 1937-46; practice law, Bklyn., 1946—; mem. firm Gerstman & Gerstman; arbitrator N.Y. Civil Ct. Small Claims, 1972—; hearing examiner Parking Violations, Bur. Transp. Adminstrn., 1972—; conf. officer Family Ct., Queens County, N.Y., 1976—. Mem. Queens County Bar Assn., Brandeis Assn. Queens County (treas. 1976—). Home: 70-29 173d St Flushing NY 11365 Office: 215 Rogers Ave Brooklyn NY 11225 Tel (212) 773-0002

GERTMENIAN, RUSSELL MESROP, b. N.Y.C., July 22, 1947; B.A., Rutgers Coll., 1969; J.D., Columbia, 1972. Admitted to Ohio bar, 1972; asso. firm Vorys, Sater, Seymour & Pease, Columbus, Ohio, 1972—. Trustee Columbus Regional Info. Service. Mem. Columbus, Ohio, Am. bar assns. Office: 52 E Gay St Columbus OH 43215 Tel (614) 464-6317

GERTNER, ABRAHAM, b. Toronto, Can., Feb. 7, 1909; B.A. with honors and high distinction in Polit. Sci., Ohio State U., 1929, J.D. summa cum laude, 1935; M.A. (Cowles fellow 1930-32), Yale U., 1930, Ph.D., 1934. Admitted to Ohio bar, 1935, U.S. Supreme Ct. bar, 1959; individual practice law, Columbus, Ohio, 1935-68; partner firm Gertner & Gertner, 1968-72; adminstrv. law judge Columbus Bur. Hearings and Appeals, 1972—; spl. counsel Atty. Gen. State Ohio, 1963-70; dir., owner A.B. Gertner Bar Review Sch., Columbus, 1935-61. Mem. Am., Ohio, Columbus (bd. govs. 1955-59) bar assns., Assn. Trial Lawyers Am. (hon.), Assn. Adminstrv. Judges, Order of Coif, Phi Beta Kappa, Tau Epsilon Rho (supreme chancellor 1962). Author, editor: Leading Cases on Ohio Law, 1935. Home: 2753 Plymouth Ave Columbus OH 43209 Office: 50 W Broad St Suite 1006 Columbus OH 43215 Tel (614) 469-7388

GERTZ, ELMER, b. Chgo., Sept. 14, 1906; Ph.B., U. Chgo., 1928, J.D., 1930. Admitted to Ill. bar, 1930, U.S. Supreme Ct. bar; mem. firm McInerney, Epstein & Arvey, Chgo., 1930-44; individual practice law, Chgo., 1944-73; partner firm Gertz & Giampietro, 1973-75; faculty John Marshall Law Sch., Chgo., 1971—; mem. adv. com. chief justice Mcpl. Ct. Chgo. Mem. Mayor's Housing Com., 1945-49; chmn. Bill of Rights Com., 6th Ill. Constl. Conv., 1969-70. Mem. Am., Fed., Ill., Chgo., 7th Circuit bar assns., Am. Jud. Assn., First Amendment Lawyers (nat. v.p.), Appellate Lawyers Assn.; Decalogue Soc. Lawyers (past pres.). Author books and articles in field. Home: 6249 N Albany Ave Chicago IL 60659 Office: John Marshall Law Sch 315 S Plymouth Ct Chicago IL 60659 Tel (312) 427-2737

GERWIG, DEAN, b. Elkins, W. Va., Sept. 29, 1920; A.B., W.Va. Wesleyan Coll., 1942; LL.B., U. Va., 1948. Admitted to Va. bar, 1947, W.Va. bar, 1948, Ky. bar, 1961, Ohio bar, 1973; atty. Charleston (W.Va.) Group Co., Columbia Gas System, 1948-73; sr. atty. Columbia Gas of W.Va., Inc., 1973—. Mem. Ohio Ky., Va., W.Va. state bars, Am., Columbus, W.Va. bar assns. Office: 99 N Front St Columbus OH 43215 Tel (614) 460-2559

GESMER, HENRY, b. Quincy, Mass., Apr. 1, 1912; B.S. magna cum laude, Harvard U., 1933, J.D., 1936. Admitted to Mass. bar, 1936; mem. firm Brown, Rudnick, Freed & Gesmer, Boston, 1960—, sr. partner, 1960—. Hon. trustee Combined Jewish Philanthropies; past pres. Jewish Family and Children's Service; pres. Associated Jewish Community Centers, N.E. sect. Nat. Jewish Welfare Bd. Mem. Mass., Boston bar assns., Mass. Trial Lawyers Assn. Home: 111 Danehill Rd Newton Highlands MA 02161 Office: Brown Rudnick Freed & Gesmer 85 Devonshire St Boston MA 02109 Tel (617) 726-7800

GESTON, MARK SYMINGTON, b. Atlantic City, June 20, 1946; A.B. in History, Kenyon Coll., Gambier, Ohio, 1968; J.D., N.Y. U., 1971. Admitted to Idaho bar, 1971, Fed. Dist. Ct. Idaho bar, 1971; asso. atty. firm Eberle, Berlin, Kading, Turnbow & Gillespie, Boise, Idaho, 1971—; writer; novels include: Lords of the Starship, 1967; Out of the Mouth of the Dragon, 1968; The Day Star, 1972; The Seige of Wonder, 1976. Mem. Am., Idaho bar assns., Sci. Fiction Writers Am. Office: Box 1368 Boise ID 83701 Tel (208) 344-8535

GETMAN, GEORGE HERBERT, b. Ilion, N.Y., Sept. 24, 1922; A.B., Cornell U., 1944, J.D., 1948; postgrad. Yale, 1945-46; U. Mich., 1946-47. Admitted to N.Y. bar, 1948, U.S. Supreme Ct. bar, 1958; partner firm Getman & LaRaia and predecessors, Ilion, N.Y., 1950—; atty. Ilion (N.Y.) Central Sch. Dist., 1949-72, Village of Ilion, 1949-57, Ilion Bd. Water Commrs., 1955—; atty. Town German Flatts, N.Y., 1950; counsel Herkimer County for N.Y. State Tax Commn., 1963-75. Pres. United Fund of Herkimer, Ilion and Mohawk, 1960-61, v.p. (hon.) dir., 1962—; officer Ilion-Frankfort (N.Y.) chpt. ARC, 1950-55; mem. advisory bd. Salvation Army, 1972—; dir. Blue Shield, 1971—; dir. Presbyterian Home, 1975—. Mem. Am., N.Y. State (Ho. Dels. 1974-75) Herkimer County (pres. 1974-75) bar assns., N.Y. State Lawyers Assn. Recipient DeMolay Cross of Honor, 1966, Legion of Honor, 1970, Medal of Appreciation, 1974; named Mohawk Valley Father of the Year, 1971; potentate, Ziyara Temple (Shriners), 1970; grand marshal, Masons, 1976. Home: 22 John St Ilion NY 13357 Office: 38 Morgan St Ilion NY 13357 Tel (315) 894-9976

GETMAN, JULIUS GERSON, b. N.Y.C., Aug. 21, 1931; A.B., Coll. City N.Y., 1953; J.D., Harvard, 1958, LL.M., 1959. Admitted to D.C. bar, 1959, Ind. bar, 1970; atty. U.S. Dept. Navy, 1958-59; atty. NLRB, 1959-61; teaching fellow Sch. Law, Harvard, Cambridge, Mass., 1961-63; prof. Sch. Law, Ind. U., Bloomington, 1963-75; prof. Sch.

Law Stanford, 1976—; Ford Found. cons. legal edn. India, 1967-68; vis. prof. Sch. Law U. Chgo., 1972; arbitrator labor disputes, 1965—. Hearing officer, Stanford, 1970-75; cons. Ind. Employment Relations Bd., 1974-76; chmn. bd. inquiry Health Care Industry, Calif., 1975. Mem. Am. Bar Assn., AAUP, Nat. Acad. Arbitrators (legislature com.), Indsl. Relations Research Assn. Author: Union Representation Elections Law and Reality, 1976; contbr. articles to legal jours. Office: Stanford Law Sch Stanford CA 94305 Tel (415) 497-4069

GETTE, ROGER L., b. Devils Lake, N.D., Aug. 30, 1948; B.A., U.N.D., 1969, J.D., 1972. Admitted to N.D. bar, 1972, Wis. bar, 1973; staff atty. Wis. Judicare, Inc., Wausau, Wis., 1972-76; bd., cons. Community Tng. & Devel., Inc., Fond du Lac, Wis., 1973-76; dir. Legal Assistance of N.D., Inc., Bismarck, N.D., 1977—. Mem. Wis. (sec. to bd. young lawyers div.), Am. bar assns. Home: 1503 Oakland Dr Bismarck ND 58501 Office: 420 N 4th St Bismarck ND 58501 Tel (701) 258-4270

GETTLE, DONALD W., b. Big Stone Gap, Va., Aug. 24, 1930; A.B., Catawba Coll., 1956; J.D. with honors, Emory U., 1962. Admitted to Ga. bar, 1961; engr. So. Bell Tel. & Tel., 1956-58, supr. tax staff, 1958-60; asso. firm Fisher & Phillips, Atlanta, 1961-63; partner firm Gettle, Jones & Fraser, Atlanta, 1963-70, Gettle & Fraser, Atlanta, 1970—; lectr. law Atlanta Law Sch., 1963—. Mem. State Bar Ga., Atlanta Bar Assn., Am. Judicature Soc., Bryan Soc., Phi Alpha Delta. Home: Box 766 Cartersville GA 30120 Office: 1401 West Paces Ferry Rd NW Atlanta GA 30327

GETTNER, VICTOR SALOMON, b. N.Y.C., Feb. 18, 1906; B.S., Princeton, 1927; J.D., Harvard, 1930. Admitted to N.Y. bar, 1931; assoc. firm Olvany, Eisner & Donnelly, N.Y.C., 1930-33; individual practice law, N.Y.C., 1933-35; partner firm Gettner, Simon & Asher, N.Y.C., 1935-63; individual practice law, N.Y.C., 1963-75, White Plains, N.Y., 1975—; mem. legal adv. bd. Nat. Recovery Adminstrn., N.Y.C., 1933; spl. hearing officer Office Price Adminstrn., 1943-45; lectr. Practising Law Inst., 1954-64; mem. comml. arbitration panel Am. Arbitration Assn., 1942—. Mem. joint appeals bd. Work Projects Adminstrn., N.Y. City Arts Porject, 1936-38; bd. dirs. N.Y. Civil Liberties Union, 1932—, vice-chmn., 1955-60, chmn., 1960-67; bd. dirs. Civil Liberties Ednl. Found., N.Y.C., 1957-63; chmn. Free Speech Assn. Com, ACLU, 1970—; sec. Young Dem. Club N.Y., 1934; pres. Internat. Psychiat. Research Found., N.Y.C., 1967—. Mem. N.Y. State, White Plains, Westchester County bar assns., Assn. Bar City N.Y. Home: 1001 North St White Plains NY 10605 Office: 188 E Post Rd White Plains NY 10601 Tel (914) 761-8866 also (212) 933-4878

GETTY, GERALD WINKLER, b. Chgo., June 17, 1913; J.D., DePaul U., 1938l Admitted to Ill. bar, 1938, Ind. bar, 1938; partner firm Getty & Getty, Dolton, Ill., 1948-53; lectr. real estate law Roosevelt U., Chgo., 1944-54; asst. pub. defender Cook County (Ill.), 1954-72, pub. defender, 1972—; police and fire commr. Village of Dolton, 1971—. Mem. S. Suburban Bar Assn. Author: Public Defender, 1974. Office: 15000 S Dorchester St Dolton IL 60419 Tel (312) 841-9000

GETZ, STANLEY, b. Balt., Oct. 4, 1933; A.A., U. Balt., 1954, LL.B., 1957. Admitted to Md. bar, 1957, U.S. Supreme Ct. bar, 1965; patner firm Getz, Getz and Getz, Bel Air, Md., 1957—; trial magistrate, People's Ct. Judge Harford County, 1959-71. Pres. Lions Club of Bel Air, 1960. Mem. Am., Md. trial lawyers assns., Am., Md., Harford County (pres. 1972-73) bar assns. Office: 26 S Main St Bel Air MD 21014 Tel (301) 838-4135

GETZEN, WILLIAM EUGENE, b. Elkhorn, Wis., May 9, 1932; B.S. in Engring., U. Ill., 1954, LL.B., J.D., 1959. Admitted to Fla. bar, 1959; partner firm Williams, Parker, Harrison, Dietz & Getzen, Sarasota, Fla., 1959—; dir. Ellis Am. Bank, Sarasota. Mem. Sarasota County (pres. 1974-75), Am. bar assns., Fla. Bar. Home: 1421 Westbrook Dr Sarasota FL 33579 Office: 1550 Ringling Blvd Sarasota FL 33577 Tel (813) 366-4800

GEWANTER, SIDNEY MARTIN, b. N.Y.C., Jan. 31, 1928; B.A., N.Y. U., 1947; J.D., Harvard, 1949. Admitted to N.Y. State bar, 1949, Mass. bar, 1953, U.S. Supreme Ct. bar, 1958; atty. U.S. Govt., N.Y.C., 1950-52; individual practice law, N.Y.C., 1952-69; counsel N.Y.C. Fin. Adminstrn., Income Tax Bur., 1966-69; asso. counsel Gulf & Western Industries, Inc., 1969-73; asso. gen. counsel J. Henry Schroder Banking Group, N.Y.C., 1973—; prof. taxation and internat. bus. Pace U., 1955—, N.Y. U., 1964—; prof. law N.Y. Law Sch., 1974—. Mem. tax adv. com. City of N.Y. Fin. Adminstrn. Mem. Am., N.Y. State, Mass. bar assns., N.Y. County Lawyers' Assn., AAUP. Contbr. articles to profl. jours. Home: 40 E 10th St New York City NY 10003 Office: One State St Plaza New York City NY 10004 Tel (212) 269-6500

GEWIRTZ, MICHAEL IAN, b. N.Y.C., Oct. 2, 1946; B.A., U. Md., 1969; J.D., George Washington U., 1972. Admitted to Md. bar, 1972, D.C. bar, 1973; law clk. D.C. Ct. Appeals, 1972-73; asst. U.S. atty. Dept. Justice, Washington, 1973—. Office: US Atty US Courthouse Washington DC 20001 Tel (202) 426-7115

GEZELSCHAP, CARL GEORGE, b. Milw., Jan. 19, 1919; Ph.B., Marquette U., 1941, J.D., 1943; postgrad. Harvard U., 1946. Admitted to Wis. bar, 1943, Fla. bar, 1948; asso. firm Lines, Spooner & Quales, Milw., 1943-46; individual practice law, Milw., 1947-48; instr. bus. adminstrn. Marquette U., 1947-48; partner firm Paty, Warwick & Paul, West Palm Beach, Fla., 1948-51, Gringle, Gezelschap & Grand, Delray Beach, Fla., 1951-53; individual practice law, Delray Beach, 1953-73; pres., treas. Gezelschap & Chapin, Delray Beach, 1973—; commr. Town of Ocean Ridge (Fla.), 1953-56. Mem. Am., Fla., Wis. bar assns. Office: 1045 E Atlantic Ave Delray Beach FL 33444 Tel (305) 278-2833

GHIARDI, JAMES DOMENIC, b. Gwinn, Mich., Nov. 10, 1918; Ph.B., Marquette U., 1940, J.D., 1942. Admitted to Wis. bar, 1942; prof. law Marquette U., 1946—; dir. Def. Research Inst., Milw., 1962-72; of counsel Kluwin, Dunphy, Hankin, & McNulty, Milw., 1972—. Mem. Am., Wis. (pres. 1970-71), Milw. bar assns., Am. Judicature Soc., Am. Law Inst. Recipient Pere Marquette Award for Teaching Excellence, 1971. Home: 5437 N Santa Monica Blvd Milwaukee WI 53217 Office: 1103 W Wisconsin Ave Milwaukee WI 53233 Tel (414) 224-7095

GHIGLIERI, BERNARD J., JR., b. Toluca, Ill., Sept. 25, 1922; A.B., U. Notre Dame, 1943; LL.B., Georgetown U., 1949. Admitted to Ill. bar, 1950; practiced in Peoria, Ill., 1950—; asst. state's atty. Peoria County, 1954-58; U.S. commr., 1965-70; U.S. magistrate, Peoria, 1970—. Bd. dirs. Expn. Gardens, Peoria, 1950-56. Mem. Ill. State, Peoria County, Am. bar assns., Am., Ill. trial lawyers assns., Am. Judicature Soc. Named Notre Dame Man of Year, 1966. Home: 4117 N Ashton Ave Peoria IL 61614 Office: 615 1st Nat Bank Bldg Peoria IL 61602 Tel (309) 676-5531

GHIZ, THEODORE HARVEY, b. Logan, W.Va., Oct. 24, 1924; B.A., W.Va. U., 1948, J.D., 1951. Admitted to W.Va. bar, 1951; asso. firm Jones & Ghiz, Charleston, W.Va., 1951-60; individual practice law, Charleston, 1960-67; asso. firm Kaufman & Ghiz, Charleston, 1967-72, firm Goad, Ghiz & Vealey, Charleston, 1972-74, firm Ghiz & Vealey, Charleston, 1974—; trial examiner W.Va. Dept. Employment Security, 1960—; mem. Fed. Mediation and Conciliation Service, 1969—. Dir., W.Va. Safety Responsibility, Charleston, 1958-60. Mem. W.Va., Kanawha County bar assns. Home: 1409 Connell Rd Charleston WV 25314 Office: 800 Kanawha Blvd E Charleston WV 25301 Tel (304) 346-0718

GHOLSON, HUNTER MAURICE, b. Columbus, Miss., Feb. 19, 1933; B.A., U. Miss., 1954, LL.B., 1955, J.D., 1955. Admitted to Miss. bar, 1955, U.S. Ct. of Claims bar, 1971, U.S. Supreme Ct. bar, 1974, D.C. bar, 1976; U.S. Navy Judge Advocate, 1956-59; mem. firm Burgin, Gholson, Hicks & Nichols, and predecessors, Columbus, Miss., 1959—; bd. dirs., exec. com. and sec. Nat. Bank of Commerce of Miss.; gen. counsel Gulf States Mfg., Moretti-Harrah Marble Co. Dir., Columbus-Lowndes C. of C., 1970-73, YMCA, 1976—. Mem. Am., Miss., Lowndes County (pres. 1973-74), D.C. bar assns. Editor in chief Miss. Law Jour., 1954-55. Home: 1100 N Sixth St Columbus MS 39701 Office: 518 N Second Ave Columbus MS 39701 Tel (601) 328-4721

GIAMPIETRO, WAYNE BRUCE, b. Chgo., Jan. 20, 1942; B.A., Purdue U., 1963; J.D., Northwestern U., 1966. Admitted to Ill. bar, 1966, U.S. Supreme Ct. bar, 1971; asso. firm Elmer Gertz, Chgo., 1966-73, partner, 1974-75; individual practice law, Chgo., 1975-76; partner firm Ligtenberg, DeJong, Poltrock & Giampietro, Chgo., 1976—; cons. atty. Looking Glass div. Traveler's Aid Soc., Chgo., 1971-73. Mem. Chgo. 47th Ward Young Republicans, 1967-70, ch. council St. Mark Lutheran Ch., Chgo., 1970-73, Ravenswood Conservation Commn., Chgo., 1972-74. Mem. Am., Ill., Chgo. bar assns., Ill. Trial Lawyers Assn., Appellate Lawyers Assn. Ill., First Amendment Lawyers Assn., Bar Assn. Seventh Fed. Circuit. Asst. mng. editor Northwestern Univ. Law Rev., 1965-66; contbr. articles to Northwestern Univ. Law Rev., DePaul Law Rev., Ill. State Bar Jour., Loyola Law Rev. Home: 1023 Wilmot Rd Deerfield IL 60015 Office: 134 N LaSalle St Suite 1100 Chicago IL 60602 Tel (312) 236-0606

GIANNINI, GARY VINCENT, b. San Jose, Calif., July 18, 1939; B.A., U. Oreg., 1961; J.D., U. Santa Clara, 1964. Admitted to Calif. bar, 1965; partner firm Johnston, Miller & Giannini, San Jose, 1965—. Mem. Santa Clara County Bar Assn. Office: Crocker Plaza Suite 800 84 W Santa Clara St San Jose CA 95113 Tel (408) 294-9046

GIANOULAKIS, JOHN, b. St. Louis, Nov. 22, 1938; A.B., Washington U., St. Louis, 1960; LL.B., Harvard, 1963. Admitted to Mo. bar, 1963, U.S. Dist. Ct. Eastern Dist. Mo. bar, 1963, U.S. Ct. Appeals 8th Circuit oar, 1974, U.S. Supreme Ct. bar, 1974; asso. firm Thompson, Walther & Shewmaker, St. Louis, 1963-69, partner, 1970; partner firm Kohn, Shands & Gianoulakis, St. Louis, 1971-73, Kohn, Shands, Elbert, Gianoulakis & Giljum, St. Louis, 1973—; instr. bus. law Washington U., 1971-73; mem. 22d Judicial Circuit Bar Com., 1976—. Bd. dirs. Legal Aid Soc. City and County of St. Louis, 1972—, v.p., 1976—; mem. University City (Mo.) Bd. Edn., 1970-76, v.p., 1970-71, pres., 1971-73, 75-76. Mem. Am., Mo. bar assns., Bar Assn. Met. St. Louis. Home: 7039 Washington St Saint Louis MO 63130 Office: 411 N 7th St Saint Louis MO 63101 Tel (314) 241-3963

GIBB, RONALD JOHN, b. Niagara Falls, N.Y., Apr. 25, 1943; B.A., Niagara U., 1967; J.D., State U. N.Y., Buffalo, 1970. Admitted to N.Y. State bar, 1971; individual practice law Mayville, N.Y., 1971—; first asst. pub. defender Chautauqua County, N.Y.; atty. Town of Clymer, N.Y.; atty. Mayville Central Sch. Dist.. Mem. N.Y. State Defender Assn., No. Chautauqua County Bar Assn., Mayville Area C. of C. (pres. 1974) Office: 34 S Erie St Mayville NY 14757 Tel (716) 753-2915

GIBBONS, JOHN JOSEPH, b. Newark, Dec. 8, 1924; B.S., Holy Cross Coll., 1947; LL.B. cum laude, Harvard, 1950. Admitted to N.J. bar, 1950; clk. McCarter, English & Studer, Newark, 1949; mem. firm Crummy & Consodine, Newark, 1950-54; partner firm Crummy, Gibbons & O'Neill and predecessor firm, Newark, after 1954; now U.S. circuit judge 3d Circuit Ct. of Appeals Newark; faculty Seton Hall Law Sch., 1951-58, 72—, Suffolk U. Sch. Law, summer 1976-77, Rutgers U. Law Sch., 1977—; chmn. N.J. Bd. Bar Examiners, 1963-64; permanent del. 3d Circuit Jud. Conf.; mem. adv. com. on appellate rules Jud. Conf., 1976; dir. Newark Air Service, Inc. Active N.J. Gov.'s Select Commn. on Civil Disorders, 1967-68, N.J. Council Against Crime, 1968-70; pres., bd. dirs. Cerebral Palsy of Essex County and West Hudson, 1950-60; trustee Holy Cross Coll., St. Benedicts Prep. Sch., Newark. Mem. Am. (del. 1968—, chmn. legal adv. com. 1970-73), N.J. (trustee 1961-64, pres. 1967-68), Essex County (trustee 1960-64) bar assns., N.J. Inst. for Continuing Legal Edn. (trustee), Practicing Law Inst. (trustee), Gen. Alumni Assn. Holy Cross Coll. (dir. 1963-70). Contbr. articles to legal jours. Home: 50 Grosvenor Rd Short Hills NJ 07078 Office: Post Office and Courthouse Bldg Newark NJ 07101 Tel (201) 624-2930

GIBBONS, JOHN MARTIN, b. Houston, Aug. 21, 1938; B.S., U. Houston, 1962; J.D. with honors, George Washington U., 1970. Admitted to D.C. bar, 1970; law clk. Judge Oliver Gasch U.S. Dist. Ct. for D.C., 1970-71; asso. firm Stroock & Stroock & Lavan, Washington, 1971—. Mem. D.C. Bar, Bar Assn. D.C., Am., Fed. bar assns., Washington Fgn. Law Soc. Mem. editorial bd. George Washington Law Review, 1969-70. Office: 1150 17th St NW Washington DC 20036 Tel (202) 452-9250

GIBBS, CHARLES FREDERICK, b. Paterson, N.J., Mar. 1, 1934; A.B., Seton Hall U., 1956; LL.B., Fordham U., 1962. Admitted to N.Y. bar, 1963, N.J. bar, 1976; asso. firm Davis Polk & Wardwell, N.Y.C., 1962-72; partner firm Breed Abbott & Morgan, N.Y.C., 1973—; adj. prof. law N.Y. Law Sch., 1976. Mem. N.Y. State Bar Assn. Home: 829 Scioto Dr Franklin Lakes NJ 07417 Office: 1 Chase Manhattan Plaza New York City NY 10005 Tel (212) 676-0800

GIBBS, DELBRIDGE LINDLEY, b. Jacksonville, Fla., Jan. 13, 1917; B.S. in Bus. Adminstrn., U. Fla., 1939; LL.B., 1940, J.D., 1967. Admitted to Fla. bar, 1940; mem. firm Boggs, Gibbs & Smith, Jacksonville, 1948-56; mem. firm Marks, Gray, Conroy & Gibbs, Jacksonville, 1957—. Mem. First Appellate Dist. Jud. Nomination Commn., Fla., 1973-76. Mem. Fla. Bar (pres. 1963-64), Jacksonville (pres. 1956), Am. (del. 1964-68) bar assns., Fellow Am. Bar Found., Am. Coll. Trial Lawyers; Duval County Legal Aid Assn. (past pres.). Home: 4101 Venetia Blvd Jacksonville FL 32210 Office: POB 447 Jacksonville FL 32201 Tel (904) 355-6681

GIBBS, WILLIAM JOSEPH, b. Springfield, Ill., Apr. 23, 1931; B.A., Georgetown U., 1957, J.D., 1959. Admitted to Ill. bar, 1959; with State's Attys. Office, Sangamon County, Ill., 1958-59; corporate counsel City of Springfield, Ill., 1966; individual practice law, 1970—; rep. Ill. Legislature, 1971-74. Bd. dirs. Boys Club, Nat. Crime and Delinquency Commn. Mem. Am. Judicature Soc., Ill., Sangamon County bar assns., Ill. Trial Lawyers Assn. Home: 3 Homewood Ct Springfield IL 62704 Office: Illinois Bldg Springfield IL 62701 Tel (217) 528-5058

GIBLIN, PAMELA MARJORIE, b. N.Y.C., June 7, 1946; B.A. with honors, U. Tex., 1967, J.D., 1970. Admitted to Tex. bar, 1970; chief counsel Tex. Air Control Bd., Austin, 1971-76; asso. firm McGinnis, Lochridge & Kilgore, Austin, 1976—. Chmn. Mayor's Commn. on Electric Rates, Austin, 1975-76. Mem. State Bar Tex. (vice chmn. pub. law sect., dir. environ. law sect.). Home: 3107 Carlisle Dr Austin TX 78731 Office: 900 Congress Ave Austin TX 78789 Tel (512) 476-6982

GIBSON, DAN MCDONNELL, b. Birmingham, Ala., Feb. 23, 1943; B.S., U. Ala., 1968, J.D., 1971. Admitted to Ala. bar, 1971; asst. dir. Ala. Law Inst., Tuscaloosa, 1971-72; partner firm Roberts, Davidson & Gibson, Tuscaloosa, 1972-76; asso. counsel U. Ala., Tuscaloosa, 1976—; spl. asst. atty. gen. State of Ala., 1975. Mem. Ala. Tuscaloosa County bar assns., Am. Judicature Soc. Home: 31 Windsor Dr Tuscaloosa AL 35401 Office: POB 1675 Tuscaloosa AL 35401 Tel (205) 348-5490

GIBSON, DONALD EUGENE, b. Marion, Ind., Sept. 6, 1941; B.A., Northwestern U., 1963, J.D., Ind. U., 1971. Admitted to Ind. bar, 1971, U.S. Dist. Ct. bar, 1971, U.S. Ct. Appeals bar, 1976; individual practice law, Veedersburg, Ind., 1971—. Gen. chmn., Veedersburg Centennial, 1972. Mem. Ind., Fountain County bar assns., Ind. Pub. Defenders Assn., Order of Barristers, Veedersburg Jaycees (v.p. 1972). Home and office: 108 E 2d St Veedersburg IN 47987 Tel (317) 294-4433

GIBSON, FLOYD ALFRED, b. W. Union, S.C., Nov. 11, 1933; B.S. in Textile Engring., Clemson U., 1956; J.D., Am. U., 1960. Admitted to Va. bar, 1960, N.C. bar, 1961; examiner U.S. Patent Office, Washington, 1956-59; patent advisor U.S. Naval Weapons Plant, Washington, 1959-60; partner firm Bell, Seltzer, park & Gibson, and predecessors, Charlotte, N.C., 1960—. Mem. Am., N.C., Va. bar assns., Am. Patent Law Assn., U.S. Trademark Assn. Home: 5031 Parview Dr Matthews NC 28105 Office: 1211 E Morehead St POB 10337 Charlotte NC 28237 Tel (704) 377-1561

GIBSON, FLOYD ROBERT, b. Prescott, Ariz., Mar. 3, 1910; A.B., U. Mo., 1931, J.D., 1933. Admitted to Mo. bar, 1932; practiced in Independence, Mo., 1933-37, Kansas City, Mo., 1937-61; mem. firm Johnson, Lucas, Bush & Gibson, and predecessor, 1954-61; judge U.S. Dist. Ct., Western Dist. Mo., 1961-65, chief judge, 1962-65; judge U.S. Ct. Appeals, 8th Circuit, 1965—, chief judge, 1974—; mem. Nat. Conf. Commrs. Uniform State Laws, 1957—; mem. Mo. Ho. of Reps., 1940-46; mem. Mo. Senate, 1946-61, majority floor leader, 1952-54, pres. pro tempore, 1956-60; pres. Nat. Legis. Conf., 1960—61. Trustee U. Mo., Kansas City, Kansas City Philharmonic Assn.; bd. dirs., trustee Jacob Loose Million Dollar Charity Fund, Kansas City, Mo.; del. Democratic Nat. Conv., 1956, 60. Mem. Appellate Judges Conf. (chmn. 1973-74), Kansas City, Fed., Am. bar assns., Lawyers Assn. Kansas City, Inst. Jud. Adminstrn. Named 2d Most Valuable Mem. Mo. Legislature, Globe-Democrat, 1958, Most Valuable Mem., 1960; recipient Faculty-Alumni award U. Mo., 1968; named to Mo. Acad. Squires, 1974; named Man of Year Phi Kappa Psi, 1974. Tel (816) 842-9450

GIBSON, GEORGE DANDRIDGE, b. Richmond, Va., May 8, 1904; B.A., U. Va., 1924; A.M., Harvard, 1925, LL.B., 1928. Admitted to Va. bar, 1928; since practiced in Richmond, asso. firm Hunton & Williams, and predecessors, 1931-34, partner, 1934—; gen. counsel Va. Electric & Power Co., 1958-75. Mem. Va. Commn. Arts and Humanities, 1968-74. Fellow Am. Bar Found.; mem. Richmond (chmn. com. portraits justices, 1957-61), D.C., Am. (chmn. sect. pub. utility law 1940-41, sect. corp. banking and bus. law 1959-60, chmn. com. corporate laws 1962-65, chmn. com. sec. projects 1965-70, editor The Bus. Lawyer 1957-58) bar assns., Am. Law Inst., Am. Judicature Soc., Assn. Bar City N.Y., Edison Electric Inst. (chmn. legal com. 1965-67), English Speaking Union (nat. dir. 1964-71), Phi Beta Kappa (dir. assos. 1971—), Phi Kappa Sigma. Contbr. articles to legal jours. Home: 9 River Rd Richmond VA 23226 Office: 707 E Main St Richmond VA 23212 Tel (804) 788-8320

GIBSON, GEORGE EDWARD, b. Grove, Okla., Aug. 19, 1909; A.B., U. Okla., 1934; LL.B., George Washington U., 1937. Admitted to D.C., Okla. bars, 1937, Mo. bar, 1953; atty. IRS, D.C., 1938-41, Chgo., 1942-43, St. Louis, 1946-51, Indpls., 1952; asso. firm Stinson, Mag, Thomson, McEvers & Fizzell, Kansas City, Mo., 1953-55, partner, 1956-74, cons. partner, 1974—. Mem. Am., Mo., Kansas City bar assns., Lawyers Assn. Kansas City, Order of Coif. Home: 910 Pennsylvania St Kansas City MO 64105 Office: 2100 TenMain Center Kansas City MO 64105 Tel (816) 842-8600

GIBSON, HERBERT CUMMINS, b. West Palm Beach, Fla., Jan. 13, 1945; B.A. cum laude (John G. Ruge honor scholar), U. of the South, 1967; J.D., U. Fla., 1970. Admitted to Fla. bar, 1970; asso. firm Gibson, Gibson & Sheehan, Profl. Assn. and predecessor, West Palm Beach, 1971-73, partner, 1973—; with Judge Adv. Gen. Corps USAR, 1971—. Bd. dirs. YMCA Central Br., West Palm Beach, 1973—, sec., 1975-76; bd. dirs. Palm Beach (Fla.) Blood Bank, 1975—; mem. West Palm Beach Planning Bd., 1976—; trustee U. of South, 1974, 75. Mem. Fla. Bar, Am. Bar Assn., Am. Trial Lawyers Assn., Fla. Acad. Trial Lawyers, Am. Soc. Hosp. Attys., Phi Delta Phi. Home: 361 Colonial Rd West Palm Beach FL 33405 Office: 209 S Olive Ave PO Box 1629 West Palm Beach FL 33402 Tel (305) 655-8686

GIBSON, HUGH, b. Tomnolen, Miss., Feb. 15, 1946; B.A., Miss. State U., 1968; J.D., Jackson Sch. Law, 1972; J.D., U. Miss., 1972. Admitted to Miss. bar, 1972; research asst. Miss. Supreme Ct., 1972-73; casualty claims supr. Home Ins. Cos., 1973-74; partner firm Listen, Crull & Gibson, Eupora, Miss., 1974—. Pres., treas. Eupora Jaycees, 1975-77. Mem. Am., Miss. bar assns., Am., Miss. trial lawyers assns. Home: Eupora MS 39744 Office: PO Drawer G Eupora MS 39744 Tel (601) 258-7855

GIBSON, HUGH FRANCIS, b. Kingston, Ont., Can., Dec. 12, 1916; B.A., Queen's U., Kingston, 1937, B.Comm., 1938; Barrister-at-Law, Osgoode Hall, Toronto, 1942. Called to Ont. bar, 1942, created Queen's counsel, 1960; asso. firm Gibson, Sands & Flanigan, Kingston, 1946-64; asso. crown atty. County of Frontenac, 1946-52; solicitor City of Kingston, 1950-64; judge Exchequer Ct. of Can., 1964—; chmn. Fed. Airport Inquiry Royal Commn., 1973; judge pres. Martial Appeal Ct. Can., 1964; mem. trial div. Fed. Ct. Can.,

1971. Mem. Phi Delta Phi. Home: 300 The Driveway S Ottawa ON K: 3M6 Canada Office: Suite 59 Supreme and Fed Cts Bldg Wellington St Ottawa ON K1A 0H9 Canada Tel (613) 992-5963

GIBSON, JAMES, b. Salem, N.Y., Jan. 21, 1902; B.A., Princeton, 1923; LL.B., Albany Law Sch., 1926; LL.D., Union Coll., 1970. Admitted to N.Y. State bar, 1926, since practiced in Hudson Falls; asso. firm Rogers and Sawyer, 1926-29; partner firm Sawyer and Gibson, 1929-36; individual practice law, 1936-53; dist. atty. Washington County, N.Y., 1936-53; justice N.Y. Supreme Ct., 1953-69, 73—, presiding justice appellate div., 1964-69; asso. judge Ct. of Appeals, N.Y., 1969-72; mem. adminstrv. bd. Jud. Conf. State N.Y., 1964-69. Trustee Albany Law Sch. of Union U. Mem. Washington County, N.Y. State (chmn. jud. sect. 1970-71, exec. com. 1970-71, Distinguished Service award 1973), Am. bar assns. Contbr. articles to legal jours. Home: 93 Pearl St Hudson Falls NY 12839 Office: Maple St Hudson Falls NY 12839 Tel (747) 4115

GIBSON, JAMES DICK, b. McKeesport, Pa., Nov. 7, 1898; B.S., U. Ill., 1921, J.D., 1924. Admitted to Okla. bar, 1924, ICC bar, 1926; asst. gen. atty. Midland Valley Ry., K.O. & G. Ry. Co. and OCAA Ry. Co., 1925-30, gen. atty., 1941-64; individual practice, 1930-41, Muskogee, Okla., 1972—; trust officer First Nat. Bank and Trust Co. of Muskogee, 1964-72. Active Muskogee Gen. Hosp. Bd., 1943—. Mem. Am., Okla., Muskogee County (pres. 1937) bar assns. Home: 2305 Boston St Muskogee OK 74401 Office: 504 Court St Muskogee OK 74401 Tel (918) 682-7864

GIBSON, JOHN ROBERT, b. Springfield, Mo., Dec. 20, 1925; A.B., U. Mo., 1949, J.D., 1952. Admitted to Mo. bar, 1952; asso. firm Morrison, Hecker, Curtis, Kuder & Parrish, Kansas City, Mo., 1952-58, partner, 1958—. Vice chmn. Jackson County Charter Transition Com., 1971-72; mem. Jackson County Charter Commn., 1970; v.p. Bd. Police Commrs., Kansas City, Mo., 1973—. Mem. Am., Mo. (pres. 1977-78), Kansas City (pres. 1970-71) bar assns. Mo. Bar (bd. govs. 1972—, v.p. 1975-76, Pres.'s award 1974), Phi Beta Kappa, Omicron Delta Kappa. Home: 207 E 110th St Kansas City MO 64114 Office: 1600 Bryant Bldg Kansas City MO 64106 Tel (816) 842-5910*

GIBSON, JOHNSON RUSSELL, III, b. Troy, Ala., Apr. 26, 1947; B.A., U. Ala., 1971, J.D., 1973. Admitted to Ala. bar, 1974; law clk. Ala. Ct. Civil Appeals, Montgomery, 1973-74; asso. firm Phelps and Owens, Tuscaloosa, Ala. Bd. dirs. Vol. Action Center, 1976—. Mem. Tuscaloosa County, Ala. State, Am. bar assns., Am. Judicature Soc., Farah Law Soc. Office: Suite 426 First Fed Bldg Tuscaloosa AL 35401 Tel (205) 345-5100

GIBSON, JOSEPH EDWIN, b. Upperville, Va., Aug. 26, 1923; B.A. in Econs., U. Va., 1951, J.D., 1954. Admitted to Va. bar, 1953; individual practice law, Charlottesville, Va., 1954—; of counsel Paxson Marshall and Smith, 1962-68; instr. commerce and taxation U. Va., 1955-56, asst. prof., 1956-61, asso. prof., 1961-71, prof., 1972—; lectr. Am. Inst. C.P.A.'s. Vice chmn. Albemarle County (Va.) Bd. Suprs., 1968-72. Mem. Charlottesville-Albemarle, Va., Am. bar assns., Raven Soc., Beta Gamma Sigma, Beta Alpha Psi, Omicron Delta Kappa. Named Alumni Distinguished Prof. U. Va., 1975; editor: Michie's Federal Tax Handbook, 1970-77 edits. Home: W Leigh Dr Charlottesville VA 22901 Office: Monroe Hall U of Va Charlottesville VA 22903 Tel (804) 924-3175

GIBSON, MARY ROBERTA, b. Kansas City, Mo., Jan. 29, 1947; B.A., U. Mo., Kansas City, 1969, J.D., 1972. Admitted to Mo. bar, 1972; legal intern Greater Kansas City Legal Aid & Defender Soc., 1971-72; legal intern Chgo. Title Ins. Co., Kansas City, 1973-76, mgr. Platte City, Mo., 1976—. Mem. Am., Mo., Platte County bar assns.

GIBSON, MELVIN EARL, JR., b. Charlottesville, Va., Dec. 30, 1946; B.A., U. Va., 1969, J.D., 1972. Admitted to Va. bar, 1972; asso. firm Tremblay & Smith, Charlottesville, 1972-75, partner, 1975—. Bd. dirs., v.p., sec. Charlottesville-Albemarle Assn. Retarded Citizens, 1972—; chmn. profl. div. United Way, Charlottesville, 1975-76. Mem. Am. Bar Assn., Va. State Bar. Home: 1431 Grove Rd Charlottesville VA 22901 Office: 105-109 E High St Charlottesville VA 22901 Tel (804) 977-4455

GIBSON, RANKIN MACDOUGAL, b. Unionville, Mo., Oct. 9, 1916; LL.B., U. Mo., 1939; B.S. in Law, St. Paul Coll., 1948; LL.M., George Washington U., 1950. Admitted to Mo. bar, 1939, U.S. Supreme Ct. bar, 1951, Ohio bar, 1954; individual practice law, Unionville, Mo., 1939-40; atty. T.H. Mastin & Co., St. Louis, 1940-42; atty. VA, 1945-51; atty. Nat. Wage Stabilization Bd., 1951; asso. prof. law U. Toledo, 1951-56; mem. firm DiSalle, Green, Haddad & Lynch, Toledo, 1956-59; now partner firm Lucas, Prendergast, Albright, Gibson, Brown & Newman, Columbus, Ohio; asst. to Gov. Ohio, 1959-61; judge Supreme Ct. Ohio, 1963-65; adj. prof. law Franklin Law Sch. Capital U., 1960—. Mem. Am. Judicature Soc., Franklin County Trial Lawyers Assn., Fed. (pres. Columbus chpt. 1967-68), Columbus (pres. 1972-73), Ohio bar assns. Contbr. articles in field to profl. jours. Home: 2690 Fishinger Rd Columbus OH 43221 Office: 42 E Gay St Columbus OH 43215 Tel (614) 228-5711

GIBSON, ROBERT LAW, JR. (ROBIN), b. Port of Spain, Trinidad, Nov. 8, 1936 (parents Am. citizens); B.A., U. Fla., 1959, J.D., 1962. Admitted to Fla. bar, 1962; asso. firm Nichols, Gaither, Beckham, Colson & Spence, Miami, 1962-66; partner firm Woolfolk, Myers, Curtis, Craig & Gibson, Lake Wales, Fla., 1966-73, Gibson & Connor, Lake Wales, 1973—; lectr. in field. Chmn., Downtown Devel. Commn., 1968—, Charter Revision Sub-Com., 1975-76, Lake Wales. Mem. Am., Fla. (gov. 1968-70, gov. young lawyers sect. 1965-70, pres. 1969-70) bar assns., 10th Jud. Circuit Bar (pres. 1971-72), Assn. Trial Laweyrs Am., Acad. Fla. Trial Lawyers (past dir.), Lake Wales C. of C. (past dir.). Named Outstanding Young Man, City of Lake Wales, 1970, Citizen of Yr., 1974; contbr. articles to profl. publs. Office: 225 E Stuart Ave Lakes Wales FL 33853 Tel (813) 676-8584

GIBSON, WARREN WOLCOTT, b. Akron, Ohio, June 26, 1927; B.B.A., Kent State U., 1959; LL.B., Case Western Res. U., 1952, J.D., LL.M., 1967. Admitted to Ohio bar, 1952, Fla. bar, 1970; practice law, Cuyahoga Falls, Ohio. Service dir. City of Cuyahoga Falls, Ohio. Mem. Am., Fla., Ohio, Inter-American, Sarasota, Akron bar assns. Home: 543 Broad Blvd Cuyahoga Falls OH 44221 Office: 234 W Portage Trail Cuyahoga Falls OH 44221 Tel (216) 929-0507

GIDLEY, THOMAS DUNNE, b. Orange, N.J., March 13, 1934; B.A., Dartmouth Coll., 1956; LL.B., Yale, 1959. Admitted to R.I. bar, 1960, U.S. District Ct. bar, 1962, U.S. Supreme Ct. bar, 1964, 1st Circuit U.S. Ct. of Appeals bar, 1968; asso. firm Hinckley, Allen, Salisbury & Parsons, Providence, R.I., 1960-66, partner, 1966—. Mem. Am., R.I. bar assns., R.I. Defense Counsel Assn., Internat. Assn. of Ins. Counsel Am. Soc. Hosp. Attys. Home: 350 Olney St Providence RI 02906 Office: 2200 Industrial Bank Bldg Providence RI 02903 Tel (401) 274-2000

GIERACH, JAMES ELROY, b. Madison, Wis., Oct. 26, 1944; B.A., Mich. State U., 1966; J.D., DePaul U., 1969. Admitted to Ill. bar, 1969; delegate Ill. Constl. Conv., 6th Dist., 1969-70; asst. state's atty. Cook County (Ill.), 1970-73; partner firm Gierach, Stambulis & Schussler, Oak Lawn, Ill., 1974—. Bd. dirs. Trinity Lutheran Church, Oak Lawn, 1970-74; bd. dirs., chmn. campaign Oak Lawn Community Chest, 1971—. Mem. Am., Ill., Chgo., S. Side bar assns., Am. Trial Lawyers Assn., Oak Lawn C. of C. (dir.). Office: 9500 S 50th Ct Oak Lawn IL 60453 Tel (312) 424-1600

GIERACH, WILL EDWIN, b. Cedarburg, Wis., Feb. 19, 1923; B.A., U. Wis., 1943; J.D., DePaul U., 1947. Admitted to Wis. bar, 1945, Ill. bar, 1947, U.S. Ct. Appeals bar, 7th Circuit, 1949; economist, atty. War Labor Bd., Chgo., 1943-45; asst. to regional dir. War Assets Adminstrn., Chgo., 1945-46; instr., lectr. Ill. Inst. Tech., 1946-47; individual practice law, Oak Lawn, Ill., 1946-76; partner firm Gierach, Stambulis & Schussler, Ltd., and predecessors, Oak Lawn, 1976—. Elder, tchr. Trinity Lutheran Ch., Oak Lawn, 1948-75; bd. dirs. S.W. Suburban YMCA, Oak Lawn, 1957—, chmn., 1960; bd. dirs. High Sch. Outreach, Oak Lawn, 1968-74. Mem. Chgo., Ill., Am. bar assns., Am. Trial Lawyers Assn. Office: 9500 S 50th Ct Oak Lawn IL 60453 Tel (312) 424-1600

GIERKE, HERMAN FREDRICK, III, b. Williston, N.D., Mar. 13, 1943; B.A., U. N.D., 1964, J.D., 1966. Admitted to N.D. bar, 1966; served to capt. JAGC, U.S. Army, 1967-71; partner firm Tschetter & Gierke, Watford City, N.D., 1972-73; individual practice law Watford City, 1973—; state's atty., McKenzie County, N.D., 1974—; city atty., Watford City, 1974—. Mem. Upper Mo. Bar Assn., State Bar Assn. N.D. (exec. com. 1977—), Assn. Trial Lawyers Am., N.D. Trial Lawyers Assn., (gov. 1977—), N.D. State's Attys. Assn. (treas. 1976—), Am. Judicature Soc., 5th Jud. Dist. Bar Assn. (pres. 1977—), Nat. Dist. Attys. Assn., Am. Bar Assn., Grievance Com. West. Decorated Bronze Star. Home: Gierke Ranch Watford City ND 58854 Office: 101 N Main Watford City ND 58854 Tel (701) 842-3621

GIESE, GARY L., b. Grand Island, Nebr., Oct. 2, 1943; A.B., U. Nebr., 1967, J.D., 1970. Admitted to Nebr. bar, 1970; dep. atty. Buffalo County, Nebr., 1970-71; individual practice law, Kearney, Nebr., 1971—. Mem. Am., Nebr., Buffalo County bar assns. Home: 1414 W 37th Kearney NE 68847 Office: 205 W 30th Kearney NE 68847 Tel (308) 234-9872

GIFFIN, DONALD WALTER, b. Kansas City, Kans., June 8, 1930; A.B., U. Kans., 1951, LL.B., 1953; LL.M., Yale U., 1957. Admitted to Kans. bar, 1953, Mo. bar, 1954; asst. staff judge adv. Ft. Campbell, Ky., 1954-55, staff judge adv., 1956; trial atty. firm Spencer, Fane, Britt and Browne, Kansas City, 1957—; mem. Mo. Bar. Govs., Jefferson City, 1973—. Chmn. bd. mgrs. Johnson County YMCA, 1971. Mem. Am. Trial Lawyers Assn., Western Mo. Def. Lawyers, Kans., Mo., Kansas City, Am. bar assns., Yale Law Alumni Assn. Home: 8109 Grandea Prairie Village KS 66208 Office: 1000 Power and Light Bldg 106 W 14th St Kansas City MO 64105 Tel (816) 474-8100

GIFFORD, PATRICIA J., b. Indpls., Apr. 13, 1938; A.B., Coll. William and Mary, 1960; J.D., Ind. U., 1968. Admitted to Ind. bar, 1968, since practiced in Indpls.; asso. firm Runnels & Rademacher, 1968-69; dep. atty. gen., Indpls., 1969-70, asst. atty. gen., 1970-72; dep. prosecutor Marion County, 1972-74; partner firm Moriarty & Gifford, 1972-76; individual practice law, 1976—; referee Marion County Juvenile Ct., 1975—. Bd. dirs. Bd. Ch. Extension, Disciples of Christ. Mem. Ind., Indpls. bar assns. Home: 5014 N Central Ave Indianapolis IN 46205 Office: One Indiana Sq Suite 3300 Indianapolis IN 46204 Tel (317) 634-3880

GIFFORD, ROBERT GENUNG, b. Hackensack, N.J., Sept. 23, 1928; B.S. in History, Holy Cross U., 1949; LL.B., Fordham U., 1956. Admitted to N.Y. bar, 1957; asso. firm Reid & Priest, N.Y.C., 1956-68, partner, 1969—. Mem. Maritime Law Assn., Am. Bar Assn., N.Y. State Bar. Recipient George L. Bacon award Fordham U., 1955-56. Office: 40 Wall St New York City NY 10005 Tel (212) 344-2233

GIFFORD, WILLIAM CARLETON, b. Aurora, Ill., Sept. 18, 1941; A.B., Dartmouth Coll., 1963; LL.B., Harvard, 1966. Admitted to Ill. bar, 1966, D.C. bar, 1968, N.Y. State bar, 1976; asso. firm Ivins, Phillips & Barker, Washington, 1967-72, partner, 1972-74, of counsel, 1974—; asso. prof. law Cornell U., Ithaca, N.Y., 1974—; vis. asst. prof. law U. Ala., Tuscaloosa, 1966-67. Mem. Am. Bar Assn., Internat. Fiscal Assn., Taxation with Representation. Author: International Tax Planning, 1974. Home: 121 Linn St Ithaca NY 14850 Office: Cornell U Law School Myron Taylor Hall Ithaca NY 14853 Tel (607) 256-3604

GIGLIO, VINCENT EUGENE, b. Tampa, Fla., Jan. 16, 1934; A.A., U. Fla., 1952, B.A., 1954; J.D., Stetson U., 1961. Admitted to Fla. bar, U.S. Dist. Ct. bar, 1961, U.S. Supreme Ct. bar, 1970; asso. firm William T. Fussell, Tampa, Fla., 1961-62; individual practice law, Tampa, 1962-64; partner firm Spicola, Luckey & Giglio, Tampa, 1964-69, Peavyhouse, Giglio, Grant, Clark & Charlton, and predecessors, Tampa, 1973—; asst. atty. gen. State of Fla., Tallahassee, 1961; asst. pub. defender, Tampa, 1962-69, chief asst. state's atty., Tampa, 1969-73. Committeeman Democratic Precinct, Tampa, 1962; pres. Interbay Civitan Club, Tampa, 1967-68. Mem. Am., Fla., Hillsborough County, Tampa bar assns. Recipient Am. Jurisprudence award Phi Delta Phi, 1961. Office: Suite 100 1411 N Westshore Blvd Tampa FL 33607 Tel (813) 872-1531

GIGNOUX, EDWARD THAXTER, b. Portland, Maine, June 28, 1916; A.B. cum laude, Harvard U., 1937, LL.B. magna cum laude, 1940; LL.D., Bowdoin Coll., 1962, U. Maine, 1966, Colby Coll., 1974, Nasson Coll., 1974. Admitted to D.C. bar, 1942, Maine bar, 1946; practiced in Buffalo, 1940-41, Washington, 1941-42; partner firm Verrill, Dana, Walker, Philbrick & Whitehouse, Portland, 1946-57; judge U.S. Dist. Ct., Dist. of Maine, Portland, 1957—; mem. Portland City Council, 1949-55, chmn., 1952; chmn. law faculty Salzburg Seminar in Am. Studies, 1972. Trustee Maine Med. Center; adv. trustee Portland Symphony Orch.; bd. overseers Harvard U., 1971—, chmn. vis. com. Law Sch., 1972—. Mem. Am. Judicature Soc. (dir. 1973—), Inst. Jud. Adminstrn., Am. Law Inst. (council 1966—, 2d v.p. 1976), Am., Maine State, Cumberland County (Maine) bar assns. Decorated Bronze Star, Legion of Merit; editor Harvard Law Rev., 1939-40. Home: 15 Starboard Ln Cumberland Foreside Portland ME 04110 Office: 156 Federal St Portland ME 04112 Tel (207) 774-2512

GILBAR, HAROLD JAMES, JR., b. Cambridge, N.Y., Aug. 26, 1942; J.D., Albany Law Sch., 1971. Admitted to N.Y. bar, 1971, Vt. bar, 1972; practiced in Slingerlands, N.Y., 1973—. Mem. Vt. Bar Assn. (pres. Bennington County chpt.). Office: 1397 New Scotland Rd Slingerlands NY 12159 Tel (518) 439-9936

GILBERT, FREDERICK PEEK, b. Tulsa, Nov. 9, 1937; A.B. in Physics, Harvard Coll., 1959; LL.b., Harvard, 1965. Admitted to Okla. bar, 1965, U.S. Patent Office bar, 1969, U.S. Supreme Ct. bar, 1970; asso. Farmer, Woolsey, Flippo & Bailey, Tulsa, 1965-67; asso. William S. Dorman, Tulsa, 1967-69, 71—; public defender Tulsa County, 1969; law clk. to Justice McInerney, Okla. Supreme Ct., 1970-71; capt. JAGC, USAR, 1966—. Home: 1722 S Carson Ave Tulsa OK 74119 Office: 1401 NBT Bldg Tulsa OK 74103 Tel (918) 582-8201

GILBERT, IAN R., b. Washington, Dec. 10, 1942; B.A., Haverford Coll., 1963; J.D., Columbia, 1967. Admitted to N.Y. State bar, 1967, U.S. Supreme Ct. bar, 1971, D.C. bar, 1975; asso. firm Rogers & Wells, N.Y.C., 1967-72; counsel Foremost-McKesson, Inc., N.Y.C., 1972—; also asst. sec.; counsel McKesson Wine & Spirits Co., N.Y.C., 1973—; sec. 21 Brands, Inc.; v.p., sec. Mohawk Liqueur Corp.. Mem. Am., N.Y. State, D.C. bar assns., Assn. Bar of the City of N.Y. Office: 155 E 44th St New York City NY 10017 Tel (212) 557-0270

GILBERT, JAMES BENJAMIN, b. Washington, D.C., Mar. 4, 1912; A.B., Harvard U., 1933, LL.B., 1937. Admitted to D.C. bar, 1936, Md. bar, 1938; individual practice law, Bethesda, Md., 1936—. Mem. Md., D.C. bar assns., Harvard Law Sch. Assn. Home: 4604 Sleaford Rd Bethesda Md 20014 Office: 7758 Wisconsin Ave Bethesda MD 20014 Tel (301) 652-6786

GILBERT, PAUL ENSIGN, b. San Diego, Sept. 16, 1943; B.S., Brigham Young U., 1968, J.D., U. Calif. at Berkeley, 1971. Admitted to Ariz. bar, 1972; mem. firm Jennings, Strouss & Salmon, Phoenix, 1971-74, partner, 1974—. Mem. Ariz., Am. bar assns. Home: 4501 E Lafayette Blvd Phoenix AZ 85018 Office: 111 W Monroe St Phoenix AZ 85003 Tel (602) 262-5840

GILBERT, RICHARD E., b. Washington, Dec. 26, 1946; B.A., Am. U., 1968, J.D., 1973; LL.M. in Taxation, N.Y. U., 1974. Admitted to Md. bar, 1973, Washington bar, 1974, Calif. bar, 1976; law clk. to judge U.S. Tax Ct., 1974-76; asso. firm Paul, Hastings, Janofsky & Walker, Los Angeles, 1976—. Office: 555 S Flower St 22d Floor Los Angeles CA 90071 Tel (213) 489-4000

GILBERT, STEPHEN ALAN, b. N.Y.C., Feb. 20, 1939; A.B., Cornell U., 1960, J.D., 1962. Admitted to N.J. bar, 1963, Fla. bar, 1964; asso. firm Carpenter, Bennetee & Morrissey, Newark, 1961-63; asso. firm Milton M. & Adrian M. Unger, Newark, 1963-67; v.p., asso. gen. counsel Motor Club of Am., Newark, 1967—. Active Boys Clubs of Newark, Inc., 1970—, pres., 1977; active Newark Mus. Council, 1975—. Mem. N.J., Fla., Am., Essex County bar assns., Fed. Bar. of N.J., Fedn. of Ins. Counsel. Home: 8909 Francis Pl North Bergen NJ 07047 Office: 484 Central Ave Newark NJ 07107 Tel (201) 733-4077

GILBREATH, CHARLES LEACH, b. Alice, Tex., Dec. 27, 1937; B.B.A., S.W. Tex. State Coll., 1968; J.D., S. Tex. Coll., 1972. Admitted to Tex. bar, 1971; mem. firm, 1971-75, partner firm, 1976—, Stovall, Wilhite & Gilbreath, Inc., Houston. Mem. Houston Bar Assn. Home: 26 S Cheska St Houston TX 77024 Office: 1814 Memorial St Houston TX 77007 Tel (713) 861-2171

GILCHRIST, THOMAS BYRON, JR., b. Bklyn., Mar. 1, 1912; A.B., Yale, 1933; LL.B., Columbia, 1936. Admitted to N.Y. bar, 1938, Fed. Dist. Ct. bar, 1955, U.S. Ct. of Appeals bar, 1955; staff asst. Hon. Thomas E. Dewey, spl. prosecutor New York County, 1937-38; dep. asst. dist. atty., New York County, 1938-40; mem. firm Cadwalader, Wickersham & Taft, N.Y.C. 1940-46, Bleakley, Platt, Gilchrist & Walker, N.Y.C., 1947-55; spl. asst. atty. gen. N.Y., 1952-53; chief asst. U.S. atty. for So. Dist. N.Y., 1955-57; mem. firm Bleakley, Platt, Schmidt & Fritz, N.Y.C., 1957—; town atty., New Castle, N.Y., 1957-62; commr. for bingo control inquiry N.Y. State Moreland Act, 1961-62; counsel N.Y. State Citizens Com. on Reapportionment, 1964; owner, operator Oxbow Garden Center, Inc., Vista, N.Y.; dir. The MONY Fund, Inc., N.Y.C.; mem. The MONY Variable Account-A Com.; trustee Manhattan Savs. Bank. Active mem. Vista Fire Dept., 1965—; commr. Vista Fire Dist.; bd. dirs. Greater N.Y. councils, hon. mem. exec. bd. Manhattan council Boy Scouts Am.; chmn. Lewisboro (N.Y.) Republican Town Com., 1966-76; bd. dirs. United Fund of No. Westchester, 1963-69, Temple of Understanding, Washington, 1967—, Internat. Schs. Services, N.Y., 1963-73, Speedwell Services for Children, Inc., N.Y.C., 1963-73; chmn. bd. trustees Loomis Chaffee Sch., 1974—; trustee Loomis Sch., Windsor, Conn., 1962-68. Fellow Am. Coll. Trial Lawyers; mem. Am., N.Y. State, N. Westchester, Westchester County bar assns., Assn. Bar City N.Y., Fed. Bar Council, Am. Arbitration Assn. (panelist), SR (v.p., bd. mgrs. 1965-74). Home: RR 2 Box 88 Elmwood RD South Salem NY 10590 Office: 80 Pine St New York City NY 10005 Tel (212) 732-2000

GILDEA, AUSTIN CORNELIUS, b. Elkhart, Ind., Sept. 7, 1906; LL.B., Notre Dame U., 1930, also J.D. Admitted to Ind. bar, 1930; justice of peace, Concord Twp., Ind., 1930-33; local counsel HOLC, 1933-42; city atty. Elkhart, Ind., 1942-51; mem. firm Gildea and Stuart, Elkhart, 1950—. Pres. Rehab. Center, Inc.; past pres. Elkhart Symphony Soc. Mem. Am., Ind., Elkhart City and County (past pres.) bar assns. Recipient Outstanding Citizen award Rehab. Center, 1974. Home: 5 St Joseph Manor Elkhart IN 46514 Office: 106 W Lexington Ave Elkhart IN 46514 Tel (219) 293-5581

GILDENHORN, JOSEPH BERNARD, b. Washington, Sept. 17, 1929; B.S., U. Md., 1951; LL.B., Yale, 1954, J.D., 1954. Admitted to D.C. bar, 1954, Md. bar, 1957; mem. Office of Gen. Counsel, SEC, Washington, D.C., 1954-56; mem. firm Brown, Gildenhorn & Jacobs, Washington, 1956—; guest lectr. George Washington U. Law Sch. Pres. Hebrew Home of Greater Washington, 1975-77; bd. dirs. Greater Washington Jewish Found. Mem. D.C. Bar Assn. Order of the Coif. Home: 7000 Loch Lomond Dr Bethesda MD 20034 Office: 1220 19th St Washington DC 20036 Tel (202) 296-8600

GILDER, DON LOVLESS, b. Bokchito, Okla., Feb. 7, 1924; B.S., Northeastern State Coll., Tahlequah, Okla. 1950; J.D. U. Tulsa Sch. Law, 1955. Admitted to Okla. bar, 1955; partner firm Walker & Gilder, Tulsa, 1955-65; individual practice law, Tulsa, 1965—. Mem. Okla. Bar Assn., Okla. Trial Lawyers Assn. Home: 4820 S Florence Ave Tulsa OK 74105 Office: 206 Beacon Bldg Tulsa OK 74103 Tel (918) 584-3591

GILES, HOMER WAYNE, b. Noble, Ohio, Nov. 9, 1919; A.D., Adelbert Coll., 1941; LL.B., Western Reserve U., 1943, LL.M., 1959. Admitted to Ohio bar, 1943, Supreme Ct. Ohio bar, 1943, Fed. bar, 1946; mem. firm Davis & Young, Cleve., 1942-43; mem. firm William L. Moon, Port Clinton, Ohio, 1946-48; law clk. Ohio 8th Dist. Ct. Appeals, 1955-58; partner firm Kuth & Giles, Cleve., 1958-68; partner firm Walter, Haverfield, Buescher & Chockley, Cleve., 1968—. Chmn. bd. trustees Am. Econ. Found., N.Y.C., 1973-76; chmn. exec. com. Citizens League, 1973—. Mem. Am. Bar Assn., Am. Arbitration Assn., World Law Assn. Editor: Skeel's Ohio Appellate Procedure Manuel, 1958; Baldwin's Ohio Legal Forms, 1961. Home: 2588 S Green Rd University Heights OH 44122 Office: 1215 Terminal Tower Cleveland OH 44113 Tel (216) 781-1212

GILES, JACK, b. Marion Junction, Ala., Nov. 21, 1915; J.D., U. Ala., 1948. Admitted to Ala. bar, 1948, since practiced in Huntsville; partner firm Payne & Giles, 1955-58, Thomas, Giles & Manning, 1958-60, Morring, Giles, Willisson & Cartron, 1964-75, Giles & Bryan, 1975—; register in chancery 23d Jud. Circuit Ala., 1950-52; municipal judge City of Huntsville, 1955-57, city atty., 1958-62; dir. Ala. Dept. Indsl. Relations, 1963-64. Chmn., Ala. Space Sci. Commn.; bd. dirs. Ala. Arts Council; trustee Troy State U. Mem. Ala., Huntsville-Madison County (past pres.) bar assns., Farrah Law Soc. Mem. Ala. Senate, 1966-71; mem. cabinet gov. Ala., 1963-64. Home: 5832 Criner Rd SE Huntsville AL 35802 Office: 213 Randolph Ave SE Huntsville AL 35801 Tel (205) 539-6501

GILES, JAMES DELBERT, b. Shawnee, Okla., Nov. 14, 1911; LL.D., Georgetown U., 1938. Admitted to Okla. bar, 1939; practiced in Oklahoma City, 1940-50, 60-66; div. counsel Tenneco, Oklahoma City, 1950-60; referee Okla. Supreme Ct., Oklahoma City, 1966—. Office: 252 State Capitol Oklahoma City OK 73105 Tel (405) 521-3849

GILES, PAUL HOLT, b. Alexandria, Va., June 16, 1948; B.A. in Polit. Sci., Va. Poly. Inst., 1970; J.D., Coll. William and Mary, 1973. Admitted to Va. bar, 1973; asso. firm Compton, Latimer, Compton & Compton, Woodbridge, Va., 1973—; lectr. in bus. law No. Va. Community Coll. Mem. Prince William County (Va.), Am. bar assns. Office: 14914 Jefferson Davis Hwy Woodbridge VA 22191 Tel (703) 494-2106

GILES, WILLIAM CLEMENT, JR., b. Springfield, Mass., July 1, 1921; A.B., Brown U., 1942; J.D. Harvard, 1948. Admitted to Mass. bar, 1948; of counsel firm Bulkley, Richardson, Ryan and Gelinas, Springfield, 1966—; atty. Monarch Life Ins. Co., Springfield, 1952-68, chmn. bd., 1968—, dir., 1964—; asso. gen. counsel Springfield Life Ins. Co., 1959-65, dir., 1965—, chmn. bd., 1968—; chmn. bd. Monarch Capital Corp., Springfield, 1968—; dir. Valley Bank and Trust Co., Springfield. Chmn. bd. trustees Am. Internat. Coll.; trustee Baystate Med. Center; bd. dirs. Mass. Taxpayers Found. Mem. Am., Mass. (bd. dels.), Hampden County (Mass.) bar assns., Life Ins. Assn. Mass. (dir.), Ins. Econs. Soc. Am. (1st v.p.). Home: 237 Longmeadow St Longmeadow MA 01106 Office: 1250 State St Springfield MA 01133 Tel (413) 785-5811

GILL, GREGORY BARRY, b. Neenah, Wis., Feb. 20, 1949; B.A., Regis Coll., 1967; J.D., U. Miss., 1974. Admitted to Miss. bar, 1974, Wis. bar, 1974; asso. Gill Law Offices, Appleton, Wis., 1974, partner, 1976—. Chmn. project inquiry NCCJ. Mem. Assn. Trial Lawyers Am., Am., Outagamie County bar assns., Phi Alpha Delta. Office: 427 W College St Appleton WI 54911 Tel (414) 739-1107

GILL, JAMES POWELL, b. Latrobe, Pa., Nov. 25, 1925; B.A., U. Pitts., 1951, LL.B., 1952, J.D., 1965. Admitted to Pa. bar; individual practice law, Pitts., 1952-60; partner firm Spotts Gill & Morrow, Pitts., 1960—; gen. counsel corps. Mem. Am. Trial Lawyers Assn. (past officer), Am., Pa., Allegheny County bar assns., Acad. Trial Lawyers. Home: RD 1 Mary Reed Rd Baden PA 15005 Office: 802 Frick Bldg Pittsburgh PA 15219 Tel (412) 281-2268

GILL, JOHN PATRICK, b. N.Y.C., Apr. 30, 1935; B.B.A. in Accounting, Iona Coll., 1956; J.D., N.Y.U., 1959. Admitted to N.Y. State bar, 1960; sr. accountant Price Waterhouse & Co., 1960-66; asst. controller Ogilvy & Mather, Inc., 1968-70, asst. treas., 1970—; controller Ogilvy & Mather Internat. Inc., N.Y.C., 1971—. Mem. N.Y. State Bar Assn., Am. Inst. C.P.A.'s, Fin. Execs. Inst. C.P.A., N.Y. Home: 230 Pennsylvania Ave Crestwood NY 10707 Office: 2 E 48th St New York City NY 10017 Tel (212) MU8-6100

GILL, KEITH HUBERT, b. Pocatello, Idaho, May 31, 1929; B.A., Idaho State Coll., 1952; M.B.A., U. Calif. at Los Angeles, 1962; J.D., U. So. Calif., 1968. Admitted to Calif. bar, 1969, U.S. Supreme Ct. bar, 1973; asso. firm Kadison, Pfaelzer, Woodard, Quinn and Rossi, Los Angeles, 1968-73, partner, 1973—. Sec. state and local govt. sect. Town Hall of Calif.; pres. Calabasas Park Homeowners Assn.; active Los Angeles County Art Mus.; pres. Woodland Hills Mormon Sunday Sch. Mem. State Bar Calif., Calif. Conf. Dels., Los Angeles County Bar Assn., Los Angeles Trial Lawyers Assn., Am. Bar Assn., World Affairs Council, U. So. Calif. Legion Lex, Phi Alpha Delta. asso. editor U. So. Calif. Law Rev., 1966-68. Office: 611 W 6th St Los Angeles CA 90017 Tel (213) 626-1251

GILL, KENNETH JACK, b. Mpls., Jan. 25, 1921; B.S. in Edn., U. Minn., 1946, J.D., 1953. Admitted to Minn. bar, 1953, U.S. Supreme Ct. bar, 1957; chief referee Family Ct. Div. 4th Jud. Dist. Ct. of Minn., 1959-73; judge Hennepin County Municipal Ct., Mpls., 1973—. Bd. dirs. Antioch Coll., Mpls. Mem. Minn. State, Am. bar assns. Home: 3541 Fremont Ave S Minneapolis MN 55408 Office: 637 Hennepin County Govt Center Minneapolis MN 55487 Tel (612) 348-3205

GILL, LAWRENCE D., b. Pocatello, Idaho, May 24, 1934; B.A. (Coll. Nat. scholar), Columbia, 1956; J.D. (Root-Tilden scholar), N.Y. U., 1962; postgrad. in Law Western Res. U. Admitted to Ohio bar, 1962, Colo. bar, 1970; asso. firm Baker, Hostetler & Patterson, Cleve., 1962-69; asso. firm Ireland, Stapleton, Pryor & Holmes, P.C., Denver, 1969-71, mem., 1971-74; mem. Gill P.C., Denver, 1974—; dir. bus. corps.; trustee trusts; lectr. U. Wyo. Inst. Bishop Ch. of Jesus Christ of Latter-day Saints, 1971-75. Mem. Am., Colo., Denver bar assns., Rocky Mountain Estate Planning Council. Home: 5655 E Piedmont Dr Englewood CO 80110 Office: 3525 S Tamarac St Suite 222 Denver CO 80237 Tel (303) 770-3040

GILL, LYLE BENNETT, b. Lincoln, Nebr., May 11, 1916; B.A., Swarthmore Coll., 1937; LL.B., U. Nebr., 1940. Admitted to Nebr. bar, 1940, U.S. Ct. Appeals 8th Circuit bar, 1960, U.S. Supreme Ct. bar, 1960; individual practice law, Fremont, Nebr., 1945—; atty. City of Fremont, 1959-62, 67—. Chmn. Dodge County (Nebr.) Republican Party, 1945-51; chmn. Dodge County Vets. Service com., 1948—; vice-chmn. Dodge County chpt. ARC, 1953-59. Mem. Am., Nebr., Omaha, Dodge County (pres. 1962) bar assns., Am. Trial Lawyers Assn. Office: 308 First Nat Bank Bldg Fremont NE 68025 Tel (402) 721-7550

GILL, PATRICK DAVID, b. N.Y.C., Apr. 27, 1944; B.A., Queens Coll., 1965; J.D., N.Y. U., 1968. Admitted to N.Y. bar, 1968, U.S. Customs Ct., 1968, U.S. Ct. Customs and Patent Appeals, 1969; trial atty., customs sect., civil div. Office Asst. Atty. Gen., U.S. Dept. Justice, N.Y.C., 1968-73; partner firm Rode & Qualey, N.Y.C., 1973—. Mem. Am. Bar Assn. (sect. taxation subcom. on customs law), Assn. Customs Bar (com. on practice, procedure and legis. 1974—). Home: 1393 Long Beach Rd Rockville Centre NY 11570 Office: 21 E 40th St New York City NY 10016

GILL, ROBERTA LOUISE, b. Balt., June 25, 1947; B.A., Am. U., 1969; postgrad. U. Chgo., 1969-71; J.D., U. Md., 1972; M.P.H., Johns Hopkins, 1976. Admitted to Md. bar, 1972; law clk. various law firms, Balt., 1970-73; partner firm Mitchell, Pettit & Gill, Balt., 1973-75; individual practice law, Balt., 1976—; equal employment opportunity cons. Md. Dept. Transp., 1974-75; legal cons. East Balt. Community Corp., 1976. Troop leader Girl Scouts U.S.A., Balt., 1975-76. Mem. Monumental, Nat. bar assns., Balt. Urban League, Lifestream, Inc., Delta Sigma Theta (Outstanding Achievement award 1976). Home and office: 3415 Callaway Ave Baltimore MD 21215 Tel (301) 728-8256

GILL, TOM IRVIN, b. Chautauqua, N.Y., Sept. 27, 1910; A.B., Allegheny Coll., 1930; A.M., Harvard, 1935, LL.B., 1936. Admitted to Va. bar, 1937, Supreme Ct. Korea, 1946, Pa. bar, 1957; individual practice law, Danville, Va., 1937-42, 48-57; civilian legal advisor Dept. of Justice, U.S. Mil. Govt., Korea, 1946-47; partner firm Gill, Lederer, Rayback & Price, State College, Pa., 1957—; served to lt. col. JAGC, USAR, ret.; examiner Pa. Bd. Law Examiners, 1963-67, asst. supervising examiner, 1968—; dir. Pa. Bar Inst., 1975—. Mem. Am., Pa., Centre County bar assns., Va. State Bar, Am. Judicature Soc.

GILLEECE, MARY ANN, b. Effingham, Ill., Sept. 30, 1940; B.A., U. Conn., 1962; J.D., Suffolk U., 1972. Admitted to Mass. bar, 1972; asso. firm Garguilo & Holian, Cambridge, Mass., 1972—; asst. atty. gen. Commonwealth of Mass., until 1975. Mem. Mass., Boston, Middlesex bat assn. Home: 8 Whitter Pl Apt 21F Boston MA 02114 Office: 678 Massachusetts Ave Cambridge MA 02139 Tel (617) 227-1429

GILLES, ANNE MARIE, b. Cleve., Jan. 11, 1949; J.D., U. San Francisco, 1972. Admitted to Calif. bar, 1973; atty. Hewlett-Packard Co., Palo Alto, Calif., 1972—. Mem. Am., San Mateo County, Santa Clara County (head corp. counsel sect.) bar assns. Office: 1501 Page Mill Rd Palo Alto CA 94304 Tel (415) 493-1501

GILLESPIE, GEORGE JOSEPH, III, b. N.Y.C., May 18, 1930; A.B. magna cum laude, Georgetown Coll., 1952; LL.B. magna cum laude, Harvard, 1955, postgrad. (Frederick Sheldon fellow), 1955-56. Admitted to N.Y. State bar, 1957; asso. firm Cravath, Swaine & Moore, N.Y.C., 1956-63, partner, 1963—; trustee Practising Law Inst.; dir. Cia. Fundidora Monterrey, S. A., The Washington Post Co., Pinkerton's, Inc. Bd. dirs. Nat. Multiple Sclerosis Soc., Madison Sq. Boys' Club. Mem. Am., N.Y. State bar assns., Assn. Bar City N.Y. Home: Sterling Rd Harrison NY 10528 Office: 1 Chase Manhattan Plaza New York City NY 10005 Tel (212) 422-3000

GILLESPIE, HAL KEITH, b. Orlando, Fla., Oct. 21, 1947; B.A. with honors, U. Tex., 1969, J.D. with honors, 1972. Admitted to Tex. bar, 1972, U.S. Ct. Mil. Appeals bar, 1973, U.S. 5th Circuit Ct. Appeals bar, 1976; asso. firm Mullinax, Wells, Mauzy & Baab, Dallas, 1972—, partner, 1976—; served with JAGC, USAF, 1973-74. Mem. Am., Tex., Dallas bar assns., Southwest Legal Found. Contbr. articles to legal jours. Home: 5938 Vanderbilt Dallas TX 75206 Office: 8204 Elmbrook Dr Suite 200 Dallas TX 75247 Tel (214) 630-3672

GILLESPIE, JAMES WOODROW, b. Haw River, N.C., Nov. 6, 1914; B.A., Elon Coll., 1939; J.D., U. N.C., 1954. Admitted to N.C. bar, 1955, U.S. Supreme Ct. bar, 1967; individual practice law, Burlington, N.C., 1955—. Mem. N.C., Am., 15th Jud., Alamance County bar assns., N.C. State Bar. Home: 1213 Warwick Dr Burlington NC 27215 Office: 134 W Front St PO Box 893 Burlington NC 27215 Tel (919) 226-9081

GILLESPIE, ROBERT G., b. Madison, Ala., Sept. 17, 1903; ed. Huntsville Jr. Coll., U. Ala. Law Sch. Admitted to Miss. bar, 1927; individual practice law, Meridian, 1927-34; spl. agt. FBI, after 1934; then partner with Thomas Bailey, to 1943; individual practice law, 1943-54; judge Miss. Supreme Ct., Jackson, 1954—, presiding justice, 1966-71, chief justice, 1971—; chancellor 2d Chancery Dist. Miss., 1939; mem. Miss. Council State Govts. Bd. dirs. Southwestern Coll., Memphis; trustee Miss. Old Mens Home, Powers Found.; mem. awards jury Freedoms Found., 1959. Mem. Am., Miss. bar assns., Am. Judicature Soc., Delta Tau Delta. Home: 1355 Belvoir Pl Jackson MS 39202 Office: PO Box 117 Jackson MS 39205 Tel (601) 354-6021

GILLIAM, CARRELL LEWIS, b. Union, S.C., Sept. 25, 1929; A.B., U. of S.C., 1949, M.A., 1950; J.D. with highest honors, Geo. Wash. U., 1957. Admitted to D.C. bar, 1957, U.S. Supreme Ct. bar, 1961; asso. firm Dow, Lohnes & Albertson, Washington, 1957-64; partner firm Grove, Jaskiewicz, Gilliam & Cobert, Washington, 1964—; mem. audit hearing bd. Office of Edn., HEW, 1976; lectr. programs Southwestern Legal Found., Rocky Mt. Mineral Law Insts., Am. Bar Assn. Nat. Insts. Mem. Am. (chmn. nat. resources law sect. 1977—, council adminstrv. law sect. 1973-75, standing com. environ. law), Fed. Power (pres. 1975-76), D.C. bar assns., Order Coif, Phi Beta Kappa. Recipient John Bell Larner award George Washington U., 1957. Home: 4104 Aspen St Chevy Chase MD 20015 Office: 1730 M St NW Washington DC 20036 Tel (202) 296-2900

GILLIAM, NANCY TROWBRIDGE RICHARDSON, b. Seattle, Sept. 28, 1946; B.A., U. West Fla., 1970; J.D., Fla. State Coll. Law, Tallahassee, 1972. Admitted to Fla. bar, 1973; asst. pub. defender Pensacola (Fla.) Office of Pub. Defender, 1973; individual practice law, Pensacola, 1973—; adj. prof. polit. sci. U. West Fla., 1974, 76. Mem. Fla. Gov's. Commn. on Status of Women, 1974-76; bd. dirs. Escambia Blood Bank, Pensacola, 1976. Office: 226 S Palafox St Pensacola FL 32501 Tel (904) 433-5468

GILLIAM, STEVEN PHILIP, b. Los Angeles, Feb. 5, 1949; B.B.A., U. Ga., 1971, J.D. cum laude, 1974. Admitted to Ga. bar, 1974; asso. firm Smith, Smith & Frost, Gainesville, Ga., 1974—; instr. legal research and writing U. Ga. Sch. Law, 1973-74. Bd. dirs. Gainesville Jaycees, Gainesville-Hall County Girls' Club. Mem. Am., Gainesville-Northeastern Ga. (sec.-treas.) bar assns., State Bar Ga., Am. Trial Lawyers Assn. Home: Route 12 Hardy Rd Gainesville GA 30501 Office: Smith Smith & Frost 112 Washington St SE Gainesville GA 30501 Tel (404) 536-3381

GILLIARD, ALLEN FLETCHER, JR., b. Morgantown, W.Va., June 27, 1943; B.A., Yale, 1965; LL.B., U. Pa., 1968. Admitted to Ill. bar, 1971, U.S. Dist. Ct. bar for No. Dist. Ill., 1971; asso. firm Braun, Corbett and Ryan and predecessors, Chgo., 1971—. Mem. Chgo., Ill. State, Am. bar assns. Home: 122 S Quincy St Hinsdale IL 60521 Office: 66 E South Water St Chicago IL 60601 Tel (312) FR 2-1818

GILLIES, DONALD ALLASTAIR, b. Evanston, Ill., Sept. 15, 1931; B.A., Denison U., 1953; J.D., Northwestern U., 1956. Admitted to Ill. bar, 1956; asso. firm Winston & Strawn, Chgo., 1956-61; asso. firm Altheimer & Gray, Chgo., 1961-66, partner, 1966—. Trustee Bapt. Theol. Union, Chgo., 1965—, pres., 1974—; mem. vis. com. Div. Sch. U. Chgo., 1974—. Mem. Chgo., Ill. State, Am. bar assns., Law Club Chgo., Legal Club Chgo., Am. Coll. Probate Counsel, Am. Judicature Soc., Chgo. Estate Planning Council. Contbr. articles to legal jours. Home: 555 Willow Rd Winnetka IL 60093 Office: One IBM Plaza Suite 3700 Chicago IL 60611 Tel (312) 467-9600

GILLIS, JOHN HERBERT, b. Detroit, Feb. 2, 1923; student Spring Hill Coll., 1941-42; student U. Detroit, 1946-48, J.D., 1951. Admitted to Mich. bar, 1952; mem. firm DeBaeke, Ellis, Frohlich & Gillis, Detroit, 1952-64; judge Mich. Ct. Appeals, 1965—; mem. Mich. Jud. Tenure Commn., 1969—, chmn., 1969-75. Mem. State Bar Mich., Am. Bar Assn., Am. Judicature Soc. Home: 9 Colonial Rd Grosse Point Shores MI 48236 Office: 900 First Fed Bldg Detroit MI 48226 Tel (313) 256-2785

GILLIS, JOHN LAMB, JR., b. St. Louis, June 13, 1939; A.B., Washington U., St. Louis, 1965; LL.B., Stanford, 1968. Admitted to Mo. bar, 1968; asso. firm Armstrong, Teasdale, Kramer & Vaughan, St. Louis, 1968-75, partner, 1975—. Bd. dirs. St. Louis U. Div. Sch., 1969-75, chmn., 1971-74; bd. dirs. Edgewood Childrens Center, St. Louis, 1970—, 1st v.p., 1975—. Mem. Am., Mo., Met. St. Louis bar assns. Home: 1 Fielding Rd St Louis MO 63124 Office: 611 Olive St St Louis MO 63101 Tel (314) 621-5070

GILLMAN, BARRY STEPHEN, b. N.Y.C., Oct. 27, 1944; A.B., Bklyn. Coll., 1965; J.D., N.Y. U., 1968. Admitted to N.Y. bar, 1969; mem. firm Sahn, Shapiro & Epstein, N.Y.C., 1970—. Mem. Council N.Y. Law Assos., N.Y. County Lawyers Assn., Order of Coif. Office: Sahn Shapiro & Epstein 350 Fifth Ave New York City NY 10001 Tel (212) 695-3270

GILLMOR, JOHN EDWARD, b. Phila., Oct. 26, 1937; B.A., Swarthmore Coll., 1959; LL.B., U. Pa., 1962. Admitted to D.C. bar, 1962, N.Y. State bar, 1963, Tenn. bar, 1972; asso. firm Dewey Ballantine Bushby Palmer & Wood, N.Y.C., 1962-63, 66-71; v.p., sec., corporate counsel Hosp. Affiliates Internat., Inc., Nashville, 1971—. Mem. Am., N.Y. State, Nashville bar assns., Assn. Bar City N.Y. Home: 6700 Rodney Ct Nashville TN 37205 Office: 4525 Harding Rd Nashville TN 37205 Tel (615) 383-4444

GILLMOR, PAUL EUGENE, b. Tiffin, Ohio, Feb. 1, 1939; B.A., Ohio Wesleyan U., 1961; J.D., U. Mich., 1964. Admitted to Ohio bar, 1965; mem. firm Tomb & Hering, Tiffin, 1967—; mem. Ohio Senate, 1967—; mem. Ohio Constl. Revision Comm., 1971—. Mem. Am., Ohio Bar assns. Home: 2253 Sand Rd Port Clinton OH 43452 Office: 88 S Washington Tiffin OH 44883 Tel (419) 447-2521

GILLON, JOHN WILLIAM JR., b. Sherman, Tex., Apr. 24, 1900; A.B., Miss. Coll., 1922; LL.B., U. Ky., 1925. Admitted to Ky. bar, 1925, Ala. bar, 1925, U.S. Supreme Ct. bar, 1961; asso. firm Spain, Gillon, Riley, Tate & Ethredge and predecessor, 1925-33, partner, 1933—. Chmn. bd. Med. Clinic Birmingham, 1966-69. Mem. Am., Ala., Birmingham (pres. 1960) bar assns., Ala. Law Inst., Farrah Law Soc., Estate Planning Council Birmingham. Recipient Lafferty medal U. Ky., 1925; contbr. articles to law jours. Home: 1260 S 33d St Birmingham AL 35205 Office: 800 John A Hand Bldg Birmingham AL 35203 Tel (205) 328-4100

GILMAN, DAVID ELLIS, b. South Bend, Ind., Feb. 19, 1941; B.A., Ind. U., 1962, M.B.A., 1964, J.D., 1970. Admitted to Ind. bar, 1970; asso. firm Sommer, Tinkham, Barnard & Freiberger, Indpls., 1970-73; partner firm Rifkin & Gilman, Indpls., 1973—. Chmn. subcom. bequests and memorials of fund-raising com. Ind. chpt. Am. Diabetes Assn., 1976—, bd. dirs., 1976—; mem. Jewish Community Relations Counsel, 1975-77. Mem. Am., Ind., Indpls. bar assns., B'nai B'rith. (pres. Indpls. chpt. 1977—). Home: 5250 N Meridian St Indianapolis IN 46208 Office: 3634 Mission Dr Indianapolis IN 46224 Tel (317) 299-8198

GILMARTIN, HUGH JOSEPH, b. Bklyn., Jan. 18, 1930; A.B., Washington Sq. Coll.; N.Y. U., 1956; J.D., Seton Hall U., 1970. Chemist, Allied Chem. Co., Elizabeth, N.J., 1956-58; with Hoffman La Roche, Nutley, N.J., 1958—, mem. chem. ops. mgmt. group, 1976—; admitted to N.J. bar, 1970; individual practice law, Wanaque, 1971—. Mem. Wanaque Bd. Adjustment, 1960-65, Wanaque Indsl. Commn., 1959-60. Mem. N.J., Passaic County, Am. bar assns. Home: 71 Willow Way Wanaque NJ 07465 Office: 395 A Ringwood Ave Wanaque NJ 07465 Tel (201) 835-3016

GILMORE, DURWARD WILSON, b. East Prairie, Mo., Dec. 25, 1911; student U. Mo., 1933-37; LL.B., Washburn U., 1948. Admitted to Mo. bar, 1938, Kans. bar, 1938, U.S. Supreme Ct. bar, 1945; individual practice law, Benton, Mo., 1939-41, 1945-52; pros. atty. Scott County (Mo.), 1947-49; mem. Mo. Senate, 1949-51; judge Circuit Ct. 28th Jud. Ct. Mo., 1952-55; asso. council Kansas City Life Ins. Co., 1955-58, v.p., counsel, 1958-65, sr. v.p., gen. counsel, 1965-66, sr. v.p., 1966-73, sr. v.p., sec., 1973—, vice-pres. bd. police commrs. Kansas City, 1966-72; mem. Mo. Elections Commn., 1975—; dir. Agr. Hall Fame, Bonner Springs, Kans., 1975— trustee U. Mo. Kansas City, 1967; bd. regents Rockhurst Coll. Mem. Mo., Kansas City bar assns., Assn. Life Ins. Counsel, Am. Council Life Ins. Home: 1250 W 61st Terr Kansas City MO 64113 Office: PO Box 139 Kansas City MO 64141 Tel (816) 753-7000

GILMORE, GRANT, b. Boston, Apr. 8, 1910; A.B., Yale, 1931, Ph.D., 1936, LL.B., 1942. Admitted to N.Y. bar, 1943; asso. firm Milbank, Tweed & Hope, N.Y.C., 1942-44; prof. law Yale, New Haven, 1946-65, Sterling Prof. law, 1972—; prof. law U. Chgo., 1965-72. Mem. Order of the Coif. Author: Security Interests in Personal Property, 1965 (recipient Ames prize 1966, Coif award 1967); The Death of Contract, 1974; (with C.L. Black, Jr.) The Law of Admiralty, 2d edit., 1975; The Ages of American Law, 1977; contbr. articles in field to legal jours. Home: Brigham Hill Rd Norwich VT 05055 Office: Yale Law Sch New Haven CT 06520 Tel (203) 436-0288

GILMORE, HORACE WELDON, b. Columbus, Ohio, Apr. 4, 1918; A.B., U. Mich., 1939, J.D., 1942. Admitted to Mich. bar, 1946; spl. asst. U.S. atty., Detroit, 1952-54; mem. Mich. Bd. Tax Appeals,

Detroit, 1954-55; dep. atty. gen. State Mich., Lansing, 1955-56; judge Wayne County (Mich.) Circuit Ct., 3d Circuit, Detroit, 1956—; chmn. Mich. Com. to Revise Criminal Code, Criminal Procedure Code; mem. Mich. Jud. Tenure Comm., 1969-76; adj. prof. law Wayne State U.; vis. lectr. U. Mich. Mem. Am., Detroit bar assns., Am. Judicature Soc., Am. Law Inst., Nat. Conf. State Trial Judges, Nat. Coll. State Judiciary. Author: Michigan Civil Procedure Before Trial, 1964; 2d edit., 1975; contbr. articles to legal jours. Home: 1113 Harvard Grosse Pointe Park MI 48230 Office: 1611 City-County Bldg Detroit MI 48226 Tel (212) 224-5204

GILMORE, PATRICK JOSEPH, JR., b. Ketchikan, Alaska, Jan. 10, 1911; Ph.B., Gonzaga U., 1932; LL.B., Georgetown U., 1938, J.D., 1967. Admitted to U.S. Dist. Ct. bar for D.C., 1938, for Ter. Alaska, 1939. U.S. Dist. Ct. Appeals bar, D.C., 1938, U.S. Ct. Appeals bar, 9th Circuit, 1953, U.S. Supreme Ct. bar, 1950; asst. U.S. atty. Dept. Justice, Ketchikan and Juneau, Alaska, 1939-43, U.S. atty., Juneau, 1946-54; practice law, Ketchikan, 1954—. Past chmn. bd. Alaska Heart Assn.; mem. advisory com. Alaska U.S. Commn. on Civil Rights, 1960-63. Mem. Alaska Bar Assn. Tel (907) 225-4200

GILPATRIC, ROSWELL LEAVITT, b. Bklyn., Nov. 4, 1906; B.A., Yale, 1928; LL.B., Franklin and Marshall Coll., 1931, LL.D. (hon.), 1962; LL.D., Bowdoin Coll., 1963. Admitted to N.Y. bar, 1932, U.S. Supreme Ct. bar, 1935; partner firm Cravath, Swaine & Moore, N.Y.C., 1940-51, 53-61, 64—; chmn. bd. Fairchild Camera & Instrument Corp., 1975-77, Fed. Res. Bank of N.Y., 1971-75; dir. Eastern Air Lines, CBS, Inc., Bedford-Stuyvesant D and S Corp.; asst. sec. Air Force, 1951, undersec., 1951-53; dep. sec. def., 1961-64. Bd. dirs. Sherman Fairchild Found.; trustee Met. Mus. Art, N.Y. Pub. Library, Inst. Fine Arts N.Y. Mem. Am., N.Y. State bar assns. Recipient citation of merit Yale Law Sch., 1963; named Hotchkiss Man of Year, 1962. Home: 3 E 77th St New York City NY 10021 Office: 1 Chase Manhattan Plaza New York City NY 10005 Tel (212) HA2-3000

GILROY, WILLIAM GEORGE, b. Providence, July 16, 1929; A.B., Providence Coll., 1953; LL.B., Suffolk U., 1958. Admitted to R.I. bar, 1959, U.S. Dist. Ct. R.I. bar, 1960, 1st Circuit U.S. Ct. Appeals bar, 1966; mem. firm Gilroy, McDonough & Sheehan, Providence, 1961—; staff atty. R.I. Legislative Council, 1966-71, asst. dir. 1972-75; exec. counsel to gov. state R.I., 1971-72; counsel to Speaker Ho. of Reps., R.I., 1976—; judge of probate, Glocester, R.I., 1974-75. Mem. Home Rule Charter Commn., North Providence, R.I., 1966-67, R.I. Aeros. Advisory Bd., 1972—, Democratic Town Com., N. Providence, 1966—; exec. com. Democratic State Central Com., 1972-75. Mem. Am., R.I. bar assns., Am. Soc. Law and Medicine. Home: 43 Gaudet St North Providence RI 02911 Office: 906 Industrial Bank Bldg Providence RI 02903 Tel (401) 351-1190

GILVAR, BARRY STEVEN, b. Boston, Apr. 1, 1938; A.B., Bates Coll., 1961; LL.B. cum laude, Boston U., 1964; P.M.D., Harvard Sch. Bus. Adminstrn., 1974. Admitted to Mass. bar, 1964; law clk. to chief justice Mass. Superior Ct., 1964-65; asst. v.p., counsel Liberty Mut. Ins. Co., Boston, 1965—. Sec. Boston Urban Coalition, Inc., 1968-69, Mass. Residential Programs, Inc., Cambridge, 1973-76; asso. mem. Wayland (Mass.) Conservation Commn., 1972. Mem. Boston Bar Assn., Assn. Life Ins. Counsel. Editor Boston U. Law Rev., 1962-64. Home: 6 Cameron Rd Wayland MA 01778 Office: 175 Berkeley St Boston MA 02117 Tel (617) 357-9500

GIMBEL, FRANKLYN MELROYE, b. Milw., Mar. 18, 1936; B.B.A., U. Wis., 1958; J.D., Marquette U., 1960. Admitted to Wis. bar, 1960, U.S. Supreme Ct. bar, 1966; asst. U.S. atty. Eastern Dist. Wis., 1963-68; partner firm Gimbel, Gimbel & Boyle, Milw., 1968-71, Gimbel, Gimbel & Reilly, 1971—. Mem. Fed. (pres. Milw. chpt. 1967-68), Wis., Milw. (pres. 1976—) bar assns. Recipient U.S. Atty. Gen.'s Superior Performance award, 1967. Home: 1626 W Prospect Ave Milwaukee WI 53202 Office: 270 E Kilbourn Ave Milwaukee WI 53202 Tel (414) 271-1440

GIMBEL, SEYMOUR, b. Milw. Nov. 25, 1927; B.S., U. Wis., 1952, J.D., 1955. Admitted to Wis. bar, 1955, U.S. Supreme Ct. bar, 1966; individual practice law, Milw., 1955—. Mem. Am., Wis., Milw. bar assns. Home: 9440 N Spruce Rd Milwaukee WI 53217 Office: 744 N 45h St Milwaukee WI 53203 Tel (414) 271-4380

GINES, RALPH JUNIOR, b. Woodland, Utah, May 8, 1933; B.S., Brigham Young U., 1958; J.D., George Washington U., 1965. With Peat Marwick Mitchell & Co., Provo, Utah, 1960-62; admitted to Oreg. bar, 1966, Idaho bar, 1969; asso. with Garthe Brown Atty., Portland, Oreg., 1966-67; asso. firm Pattullo and Gleason, Portland, 1967, Carter, Gines & Rice, Boise, Idaho, 1972—; prof. taxation, accounting, Boise State U., 1967-75. Mem. Idaho Ho. of Reps., 1972-76. Mem. Oreg., Idaho state bars. CPA, Utah, Oreg. Office: PO Box 447 Boise ID 83701 Tel (208) 343-3656

GINN, ALEXANDER, b. Cleve., Jan. 2, 1913; B.A., Princeton, 1934; postgrad. Oxford (Eng.) U., 1934-35; LL.B., Yale, 1938. Admitted to Ohio Supreme Ct. bar, 1939; partner firm Jones, Day, Reavis & Pogue and predecessor, Cleve., 1938-42, 45—. Mem. Am., Ohio State bar assns., Am. Judicature Soc., Bar Assn. Greater Cleve. Home: SOM Center and Cedar Rds Chagrin Falls OH 44022 Office: 1700 Union Commerce Bldg Cleveland OH 44115 Tel (216) 696-3939

GINSBERG, WILLIAM ROY, b. N.Y.C., June 10, 1930; B.A., Antioch Coll., 1952; J.D., Yale, 1955. Admitted to N.Y. bar, 1956, Fed. Dists. for So. and Eastern Dist. N.Y. bars, 1960; house counsel Empire Millwork Corp., N.Y.C., 1956-57; asso. firm Riesner & Jawitz, N.Y.C., 1957-59; partner firm Ginsberg, Schwab & Goldberg, N.Y.C., 1959-68; dep. and acting exec. asst. Pres. N.Y.C. Council, 1966-67; commr., 1st dep. adminstr. N.Y.C. Parks, Recreation and Cultural Affairs Adminstrn., 1968-70; counsel, dir. research N.Y. State Temporary Commn. on Powers of Local Govt., 1970-73; asso. prof. law Hofstra U., 1974—. Vice pres. dir. Catskill Center for Conservation, Devel.; chmn. com. on pub. policy Citizens Housing and Planning Council of N.Y., 1976—; bd. dirs. L.I. Environ. Council. Mem. Assn. Bar City N.Y., Natural Resources Def. Council. Home: 40 E 83d St New York City NY 10028 Office: Sch of Law Hofstra U Hempstead NY 11550 Tel (516) 560-3249

GINSBURG, ALLEN JAY, b. Chgo., July 5, 1944; B.S., Northwestern U., 1965, J.D. cum laude, 1968. Admitted Ill. bar, 1969; partner firm Rudnick & Wolfe, Chgo., 1973—. Mem. Chgo., Ill. bar assn., Chgo. Council of Lawyers. Asso. editor Jour. of Criminal Law; C.P.A., Ill. Office: 30 N LaSalle St Chicago IL 60602 Tel (312) 368-4025

GINSBURG, RUTH BADER, b. Bklyn., Mar. 15, 1933; A.B., Cornell U., 1954; postgrad. Harvard U., 1956-58; LL.B., J.D., Columbia U., 1959; LL.D., (Hon.), Lund U. (Sweden), 1969. Admitted to N.Y. bar, 1959, D.C. bar, 1975, U.S. Supreme Ct. bar, 1967, U.S. 2d Circuit Ct. Appeals bar, 1961, U.S. 5th Circuit Ct. Appeals bar, 1975, U.S. Dist. Cts. for So. and Eastern Dists. N.Y. bars, 1961; law sec. U.S. Dist. Ct., 1959-61; research asso., asso. project dir. Columbia Law Sch., 1961-63; asst. prof. law Rutgers U., 1963-66, asso. prof., 1966-69, prof., 1969-72; prof. law Columbia, 1972—; gen. counsel ACLU, 1973—, nat. bd. dirs., 1974—; mem. editorial bd. Am. Jour. Comparative Law, 1966-72. Mem. Am. Bar Assn. (bd. editors jour. 1972—, mem. council sect. individual rights and responsibilities 1975—), Assn. Bar City N.Y. (mem. exec. com. 1974—), Am. Fgn. Law Assn. (v.p. 1973-76, dir. 1970—), Assn. Am. Law Schs. (mem. exec. com. 1972), Am. Law Inst., Council on Fgn. Relations, Women's Law Fund, Women's Equity Action League, Women's Action Alliance, Fedn. Orgns. for Profl. Women, Urban Inst. Center for Policy Research on Women, Soc. Am. Law Tchrs. (mem. exec. com., bd. govs.). Phi Beta Kappa, Phi Kappa Phi. Author: (with Anders Bruzelius) Civil Procedure in Sweden, 1965; A Selective Survey of English Language Studies on Scandinavian Law, 1970; (with Herma Hill Kay and Kenneth M. Davidson) Text, Cases and Materials on Sex-Based Discrimination, 1974; Constitutional Aspects of Sex-Based Discrimination, 1974; co-author: The Legal Status of Women Under Federal Law, Report to the U.S. Commn. on Civil Rights, 1974; co-translator (with Anders Bruzelius) Swedish Code of Judicial Procedure, 1967; volume editor: Business Regulation in the Common Market Nations, vol. 1, 1970; contbr. articles to law reviews. Home: 150 E 69th St New York City NY 10021 Office: Law Sch Columbia Univ New York City NY 10027

GINTHER, FERGUS MAHONY, b. El Dorado, Ark., Nov. 26, 1936; student So. Methodist U., 1957; B.B.A., U. Houston, 1959, J.D., 1962. Admitted to Tex. bar, 1962; partner Ginther-Davis Interests, Houston, 1971—; owner, mgr. Ginther Ins. Agency, Houston; individual practice law, Houston; owner, counselor Ginther Gas Processing Plants, Houston. Mem. Am., Tex., Houston bar assns., Houston C. of C., Delta Theta Phi. Home: 5379 Lynbrook St Houston TX 77056 Office: 4600 Post Oak Place Dr Suite 202 Houston TX 77027 Tel (713) 627-0202

GINTZ, RALPH EDWARD, b. Milw., Oct. 18, 1910; LL.B., U. Wis., 1935, J.D., 1966. Admitted to Wis. bar, 1935; individual practice law, Milw., 1935-36; unemployment compensation examiner State of Wis., Sheboygan, 1936-43, workmen's compensation hearings examiner, Madison, 1947-56, adminstr. workmen's compensation, Madison, 1956-73; cons. in field to Saudi Arabia, 1974; mem. Wis. Civil Service Exam. Bds., 1975—; election inspector State of Wis., Madison, 1973—. Mem. Internat. Assn. Indsl. Accident Bds. and Commns. (hon. life, pres. 1967-68), Wis., Dane County bar assns. Recipient Legal Edn. award Wis. Bar Assn., U. Wis., Marquette U., 1966. Home and office: One Hempstead Pl Madison WI 53711 Tel (608) 271-5419

GIPSON, HARVEY LOFTON, b. Memphis, Feb. 18, 1931; B.B.A., Memphis State U., 1959; LL.B., So. Law U., 1962. Admitted to Tenn. bar, 1963; asso. Walter Buford Memphis, 1965-67; partner firm Friedman & Gipson, Memphis, 1967-71, firm Gipson & Tucker, Memphis, 1971—. Mem. Am., Tenn. bar assns., Am. Trial Lawyers Assn., Am. Judicature Soc. Home: 3036 Glengarry Rd S Memphis TN 38128 Office: Suite 1104 Exchange Bldg Memphis TN 38103 Tel (901) 525-6331

GIRTH, MARJORIE LOUISA, b. Trenton, N.J., Apr. 21, 1939; A.B., Mt. Holyoke Coll., 1959; LL.B., Harvard, 1962. Admitted to N.J. bar, 1963, U.S. Supreme Ct. bar, 1969, N.Y. bar, 1976; individual practice law, Trenton, 1963-65; research asso. Brookings Institution, Washington, 1965-70; asso. prof. law State U. N.Y., Buffalo, 1971—. Bd. dirs. YWCA of Buffalo & Erie County (N.Y.), 1972-76; mem. Commn. on Peace, Justice and Human Rights of Internat. Assn. Religious Freedom, Frankfurt, W. Germany, 1976—. Mem. Law and Soc. Assn. (trustee 1976—), So. Am. Law Tchrs., Am., N.Y., Erie County bar assns. Author: (with David T. Stanley) Bankruptcy: Problem, Precess, Reform, 1971; Poor People's Lawyers, 1976. Office: 626 O'Brian Hall State Univ N Y North Campus Buffalo NY 14260 Tel (716) 636-2103

GISI, LYLE DEVON, b. Roscoe, S.D., Dec. 30, 1940; LL.B., Creighton U., 1964. Admitted to Nebr. bar, 1964, S.D. bar, 1964, Calif. bar, 1969; served to maj. JAGC, U.S. Army, 1964-69; asso. firm Gray, Hewitt & Lenhard, Marysville, Calif., 1969-71; partner firm Berrian & Gisi, Marysville, 1971-72, Powell, Offutt, Coolidge & Gisi, Marysville, 1972-75, Offutt, Coolidge, Gisi & Jones, Marysville, 1976—; dep. pub. defender County of Yuba (Calif.), 1969-72. Mem. St. Isidore's Parish Council Sch. Bd., 1976—; bd. dirs. Amici Italiani Club, 1974—. Mem. Nebr., S.D., Yuba-Sutter bar assns., State Bar Calif., Calif. Trial Lawyers Assn. Home: 1591 Peach Tree Ln Yuba City CA 95991 Office: 630 B St POB 286 Marysville CA 95901 Tel (916) 743-6582

GISLASON, DANIEL ADAM, b. New Ulm, Minn., Oct. 13, 1944; B.A., U. Minn., 1966, J.D., 1969. Admitted to Minn. bar, 1969; asso. firm Gislason, Dosland, Malecki, Gislason & Halvorson, New Ulm, 1972-75, partner, 1975—. Mem. Am., Minn., 9th Dist. Minn. bar assns. Home: 1407 10th St New Ulm MN 56073 Office: 1 S State St New Ulm MN 56073 Tel (507) 354-3111

GISLASON, SIDNEY PAYSON, b. Minneota, Minn., May 22, 1908; LL.B., U. Minn., 1935. Admitted to Minn. bar, 1935; partner firm Streissguth & Gislason, New Ulm, Minn., 1936-42; partner firm Young & Gislason, 1942-50; dist. judge, 9th Dist. Minn., 1950-52; partner firm Gislason & Reim, New Ulm, 1952—; asst. county atty. Brown County (Minn.), 1936-42; govt. appeal agt. SSS, 1941-67. Bd. dirs. Minn. State Coll. System, 1967-73; trustee Courage Found., 1972—. Fellow Am. Bar Found.; mem. Am., Minn. (pres. 1954) bar assns., Internat. Acad. Trial Lawyers (pres. 1959), Am. Coll. Trial Lawyers, Fedn. Ins. Counsel. Home: 600 Summit Ave New Ulm MN 56073 Office: 1 S State St New Ulm MN 56073 Tel (507) 354-3111

GISSBERG, JOHN GUSTAV, b. Seattle, May 6, 1943; B.S. cum laude (Territorial Sportsmen scholar), U. Wash. Coll. Fisheries, 1965; Ford Found. fellow Stanford U. Center, 1966-67; postgrad. Tokyo U., 1967; J.D., U. Mich., 1970, Ph.D. in Fisheries (NDEA fellow), 1971. Admitted to Mich. bar, 1971, Alaska bar, 1971; guest investigator Marine Policy Affairs and Ocean Mgmt. Program, Woods Hole Oceanographic Inst., 1971; postdoctoral asso. U. Mich., S.E. Asia Coastal Environment Resource Studies Program; lectr. Faculty Law, U. Singapore, 1972; asso. firm Cole, Hartig, Rhodes & Norman, Anchorage, 1972-74; spl. cons. Japanese land law and policy Conservation Found., 1975; asst. atty. gen. State of Alaska, Anchorage, 1976; mem. Gov.'s Commn. on Conf. of Law of the Sea, 1974; participant Japan and U.S. seminars. Mem. Am., Alaska (co-chmn. environ. law com. 1973-74), Anchorage (chmn. lawyers referral service com. 1973-74), Mich. bar assns., Am. Fisheries Soc. (chmn. student fgn. study com. 1970, mem. internationalism com. 1977), Am. Soc. Internat. Law, Japan Environ. Law Soc. (asso.), Japan Land Law Assn., Pioneers of Alaska, Phi Eta Sigma. Rockefeller Found. fellow in Environ. Affairs, 1975; recipient William F. Thompson award Coll. Fisheries, U. Wash., 1964, Am. Jurisprudence award U. Mich. Law Sch., 1970. Office: 360 K St Anchorage AK 99501 Tel (907) 272-1551

GIST, HOWARD BATTLE, JR., b. Alexandria, La., Sept. 17, 1919; student Washington and Lee U., 1936-38; B.A., Tulane U., 1941, LL.B., J.D., 1943. Admitted to La. bar, 1943; mem. firm. Gist, Methvin & Trimble, and predecessors, Alexandria, 1946—; dir. Security 1st Nat. Bank. Bd. dirs. St. Frances Cabrini Hosp., Inc., Alexandria. Mem. La. State (pres. 1977—), Alexandria (pres. 1967) bar assns., La. City Attys. Assn. (past pres.), La. Def. Attys. Assn. (past pres.), Internat. Assn. Ins. Counsel, Assn. Ins. Attys., Am. Coll. Trial Lawyers, La. State Law Inst. (council). Home: 2009 Polk St Alexandria LA 71301 Office: 803 Johnston St Alexandria LA 71301 Tel (318) 448-1632

GITCHEL, WALLACE DENTY, b. Little Rock, Ark., July 19, 1941; B.A., Hendrix Coll., 1963; J.D., U. Ark., 1969. Admitted to Ark. bar, 1969; asso. firm Wright, Lindsey & Jennings, Little Rock, 1969-70; individual practice law, Little Rock, 1971; partner firm Haley, Young, Bogard & Gitchel, 1972-73; partner firm Cearley, Gitchel, Bogard & Mitchell, Little Rock, 1973—. Ark. coordinator Nat. Orgn. for Reform Marijuana Laws, 1975—; bd. dirs. Westside YMCA, Little Rock, 1974—, Pulaski County United Way, 1975—. Mem. Am., Ark., Pulaski County bar assns., Assn. Am. Trial Lawyers, Assn. Ark. Trial Lawyers, Am. Judicature Soc. Home: 4911 Woodlawn St Little Rock AR 72205 Office: 370 Tower Bldg Little Rock AR 72201 Tel (501) 374-4801

GITELMAN, MORTON, b. Chgo., Feb. 7, 1933; J.D., DePaul U., 1959; LL.M., U. Ill., 1965. Admitted to Ill. bar, 1959, U.S. 10th Circuit Ct. Appeals bar, 1963, Ark. bar, 1972, 8th Circuit bar, 1972, U.S. Dist. Ct. for Ark. bar, 1972, U.S. Supreme Ct. bar, 1974; teaching fellow U. Ill., 1959-60; research asso. Duke, 1960-61; asst. prof. law U. Denver, 1961-65; prof. U. Ark., 1965—; vis. prof. U. Ill., 1970-71. Mem. adv. com. U.S. Commn. on Civil Rights, 1966—, chmn., 1972—; mem. Fayetteville (Ark.) Planning Commn., 1967-76, chmn., 1974-76. Mem. Ill., Ark., Washington County bar assns., ACLU (pres. Ark. chpt. 1969-70, nat. dir. 1969-72). Author: Unionization Attempts in Small Enterprises, 1963; (with Wright) Land Use-Cases and Materials, 1976. Office: Law Sch U of Ark Fayetteville AR 72701 Tel (501) 575-2708

GITELSON, BRUCE LAWRENCE, b. Los Angeles, June 4, 1941; A.B. magna cum laude, Stanford, 1963, J.D., 1964. Admitted to Calif. bar, 1964; teaching asst. law sch. Stanford, 1964-65, instr., 1970-71; instr. sch. law Southwestern U., 1967, U. So. Calif., 1968, 69, 70; asso. firm Gibson, Dunn & Crutcher, Beverly Hills, Calif., 1965-70, partner, 1971—; mem. faculty U. West Los Angeles Sch. Paralegal Studies, 1974—; adj. prof. Loyola Law Sch., 1973—. Dir. Constl. Rights Found., mem. lawyers adv. bd. edn. council. Mem. Am. (sects. legal edn. and admissions to the bar, and banking and bus. law), Los Angeles, Beverly Hills bar assns., State Bar Calif., Am. Assn. Law Teachers, Order of Coif, Phi Beta Kappa. Lectr., panelist seminars and insts.; editorial adv. bd. Jour. Fin. Planning. Office: 9601 Wilshire Blvd Suite 800 Beverly Hills CA 90210 Tel (213) 273-6990

GITTER, ALLAN REINHOLD, b. Yonkers, N.Y., Aug. 26, 1936; B.A., Washington and Lee U., 1958; LL.B., U. Mich. 1961. Admitted to N.C. bar, 1963; partner firm Womble, Carlyle, Sandridge & Rice, Winston-Salem, N.C.; lectr. in field; chmn. N.C. Appellate Rules Com., 1977. Pres., Childrens Center Physically Handicapped, Winston-Salem, 1973-75. Mem. N.C., Forsyth County bar assns., Internat. Assn. Ins. Counsel. Home: 1067 E Kent Rd Winston-Salem NC 27104 Office: PO Drawer 84 Winston-Salem NC 27102 Tel (919) 725-1311

GITTINGS, THOMAS MORTON, JR., b. Frederick, Md., Aug. 31, 1927; A.A., George Washington U., 1948, LL.B., 1951. Admitted to D.C. bar, 1951, Md. bar, 1951, U.S. Supreme Ct. bar, 1967; law clk. to judges U.S. Ct. Claims, 1951-52; asso. firm King & King, Washington, 1952-56, partner, 1957-67; individual practice law, Washington, 1967—. Mem. Am., Fed. bar assns., D.C. Bar, Bar Assn. D.C. Home: 9420 River Rd Potomac MD 20854 Office: Suite 425 Shoreham Bldg 806-15th St NW Washington DC 20005 Tel (202) 628-2878

GIUNTINI, E. ROBERT, b. Pawtucket, R.I., Aug. 27, 1923; B.A., St. John's U., 1951, J.D., 1951. Admitted to N.Y. bar, 1951, U.S. Supreme Ct. bar, 1970; individual practice, N.Y.C., 1952-64, White Plains, N.Y., 1964—; prin. E. Robert Giuntini, Profl. Corp., White Plains, 1973—. Trustee bd. edn. Union Free Sch. Dist., Harrison, N.Y., 1955-58. Mem. N.Y. State, Westchester County, White Plains bar assns., N.Y. County Lawyers Assn., N.Y. State Trial Lawyers Assn. Office: 175 Main St White Plains NY 10601 Tel (914) 949-5505

GIUTTARI, THEODORE RICHARD, b. Jersey City, Feb. 4, 1931; B.A., Fordham U., 1952, LL.B., 1958; M.A., Columbia U., 1958, Ph.D., 1969. Admitted to N.Y. bar, 1958, N.J. bar, 1959; asso. prof. polit. sci. Rutgers U., 1963-75; internat. atty. Am. Home Products Corp., N.Y.C., 1973—. Mem. Internat. Law Assn. (hon. sec.-treas. Am. br. 1970-73). Author: The American Law of Sovereign Immunity, 1970. Address: 1973 Kennedy Blvd Jersey City NJ 07305 Tel (212) 986-1000

GIVAN, RICHARD MARTIN, b. Indpls., June 7, 1921; LL.B., Ind. U., 1951. Admitted to Ind. bar, 1952; dep. pub. defender, Ind., 1952-53; dep. atty. gen. State of Ind., 1953-64; partner firm Bowen, Myers, Northam & Givan, 1960-69; dep. pros. atty. Marion County (Ind.), 1965-66; justice Ind. Supreme Ct., Indpls., 1969—. Mem. Ind. Ho. of Reps., 1967-68. Mem. Ind., Indpls. bar assns., Ind. Soc. Chgo., Newcomen Soc. N.Am., Internat. Arabian Horse Assn. (dir., chmn. ethical practices rev. bd.), Ind. Arabian Horse Club (pres. 1971-72), Sigma Delta Kappa. Home: Rural Route 2 Box 376 Indianapolis IN 46231 Office: 324 State House Indianapolis IN 46204

GIVEN, THOMAS ALLEN, b. Cleve., Aug. 18, 1945; A.B., Northwestern U., 1967; J.D., Case Western Res. U., 1970. Admitted to Ohio bar, 1970; asso. firm Pickands, Mather and Co., Cleve., 1970—. Mem. Am., Ohio bar assn. Office: 1100 Superior Ave Cleveland OH 44114 Tel (216) 694-5478

GIVENS, THOMAS PRESTON, b. Sunflower County, Miss., Aug. 2, 1937; B.A., Delta State U., 1959; LL.B., Miss. Coll., 1964. Claim rep. U.S. Fidelity and Guaranty Ins. Co., Meridian and Jackson, Miss., 1960-66; admitted to Miss. bar, 1964; asso. firm Brewer, Brewer & Luckett, Clarksdale, Miss., 1966-69; adminstrv. judge Miss. Workmen's Compension Commn., Jackson, 1969-76; adminstrv. law judge Bur. of Hearings and Appeals, Social Security Adminstrn., Memphis, 1976—. Mem. Miss. State, Hinds County (Miss.) bar assns., Fed. Adminstrv. Law Judges Conf., Assn. Adminstrv. Law Judges HEW. Office: Suite 604 Mid-Memphis Tower 1407 Union Ave Memphis TN 38104 Tel (901) 521-2671

GLADDEN, THOMAS D., b. McDonald, Pa., Nov. 8, 1932; A.B., Allegheny Coll., 1954; J.D., Dickinson Sch. Law, 1957. Admitted to Pa. bar, 1957; asso. firm Bloom, Bloom Rosenberg and Bloom, Washington, Pa., 1959-71; judge Common Pleas Ct. 27th Jud. Dist., Washington, Pa., 1971—; mem. criminal procedural rules com. Pa. Supreme Ct., 1975—. Dist. chmn. Iroquois council Boy Scouts Am., 1972-73; founding mem. Vols. in Probation; active Family Service, Washington, Pa. Mem. Washington County, Pa. bar assns., Pa. State Trial Judges Assn. (co-chmn. criminal rules com. 1976). Nominee of both parties in contested primary election, 1973. Home: 687 Elmhurst Dr Washington PA 15301 Office: Courthouse Washington PA 15301 Tel (412) 225-0100

GLADFELTER, PHILLIP ELLMORE, b. Phila., June 24, 1933; A.B., Princeton, 1955; LL.B., Harvard, 1961. Admitted to Wash. bar, 1962; asso. firm Perkins, Coie, Stone, Olsen & Williams, Seattle, 1961-71; asst. counsel PACCAR Inc., Bellevue, 1971—. Chmn. schs. com. Seattle King County Municipal League, 1969, mem. adv. council, 1970-72. Mem. Am., Wash., Seattle King County bar assns. Home: 1959 Perkins Ln W Seattle WA 98199 Tel (206) 283-9161

GLADNEY, SAMUEL R., b. B.A., U. Mo., 1951, LL.B., 1953. Admitted to Mo. bar, 1953; individual practice law, Raytown, Mo., 1953—. Home: 10700 E 56th Terr Raytown MO 64133 Office: 9503 E 63d St Raytown MO 64133 Tel (816) 356-7878

GLAISTER, AMY BUTLER, b. London, Mar. 14, 1907; A.B., Cornell U., 1929, M.A., 1933; J.D., Loyola U., Chgo., 1939. Admitted to Ill. bar, 1938, Wis. bar, 1956; individual practice law, Chgo. and Mt. Prospect, Ill. and Neenah, Wis., 1938—. Bd. dirs. John Nelson Bergstrom Art Center and Mus., Neenah, 1958—; trustee Neenah Pub. Library, 1960—. Mem. Women's Bar Chgo., Am., Wis., Winnebago County bar assns., AAUW. Home and Office: 603 E Wisconsin Ave Neenah WI 54956 Tel (414) 722-8865

GLAISTER, PAUL JOSEPH, b. Montclair, N.J., June 29, 1907; E.E., Cornell U., 1931; J.D., Loyola U., Chgo., 1937. Admitted to D.C. bar, 1935, Ill. bar, 1937, Wis. bar, 1956; asso. firm Soans, Pond & Anderson, Chgo., 1936-43; mem. firm Soans, Glaister & Anderson, Chgo., 1950-56; patent and trademark counsel Kimberly-Clark Corp., Neenah, Wis., 1956-68, asst. v.p., 1959-68, cons., 1968—; of counsel firm Wolfe, Hubbard, Voit & Osann, Chgo., 1968-71. Mem. Am., Chgo., Wis., Winnebago County bar assns., Am., Chgo. patent law assns. Office: 603 E Wisconsin Ave Neenah WI 54956 Tel (414) 722-8865

GLANDER, CHARLES EMORY, b. West Alexandria, Ohio, Mar. 5, 1903; B.A., Ohio State U., 1925, J.D., 1930. Admitted to Ohio bar, 1930; practiced in Columbus, 1930-40, 51—, partner firms Wright, Harlor, Morris, Arnold & Glander, 1953-71, Glander, Brant, Ledman & Newman, 1971—; atty. Ohio Div. Securities, Columbus, 1940; exec. sec. to Gov. Ohio, Columbus, 1941-45; tax commr. State of Ohio, Columbus, 1945-51; lectr. Ohio State U. Coll. Law, adj. prof., 1948-74. Pres. Council Social Agys., Columbus, 1955-57; mem., pres. Ohio Citizen's Council of Health and Welfare, 1959-61. Mem. Am., Ohio, Columbus bar assns., Nat. Tax Assn. (pres. 1962-63), Nat. Assn. Tax Admnstrs. (pres. 1948-50), Ohio State U. Assn. (pres. 1957-59), Ohio C. of C., Citizens Research, Inc. Contbr. articles to profl. publs. Home: 4660 Haymarket Ct Columbus OH 43220 Office: 250 E Broad St Columbus OH 43215 Tel (614) 221-2121

GLANSTEIN, JOEL CHARLES, b. Jersey City, N.J., May 16, 1940; B.A., Lehigh U., 1962; LL.B., N.Y.U., 1965, LL.M. in Labor Law, 1969. Admitted to N.Y. bar, 1967, D.C. bar, 1975; partner law firm Markowitz & Glanstein, N.Y.C., 1972—. Mem. Am. (mem. sect. on labor law, mem. com. on internat. labor law 1976-77, mem. com. on labor arbitration and collective bargaining 1976-77), N.Y. State (sec. labor law, com. labor arbitration and collective bargaining 1976-77) bar assns., N.Y. County Lawyers Assn., D.C. bar. Office: 50 Broadway New York City NY 10004 Tel (212) 943-6148

GLANZ, SADIE, b. Hartford, Conn.; A.B., Wellesley Coll., 1928; LL.B., Columbia, 1932. Admitted to Conn. bar, 1932; atty. R.R. Retirement Bd., Washington, 1936-42; chief price atty. Conn. office, Office Price Adminstrn., Hartford, 1942-45; individual practice law, Hartford, 1948—. Mem. Hartford Zoning Bd. Appeals, 1959-69, Capital Region Planning Agy., 1969-72, Conn. Regional Mktg. Authority, 1950-55. Mem. Conn., Hartford County bar assns. Home: 31 Woodland St Hartford CT 06105 Office: 266 Pearl St Hartford CT 06103 Tel (203) 522-9377

GLANZER, MONA NAOMI SORCHER, b. N.Y.C., July 29, 1931; student Adelphi Coll.; LL.B., Bklyn. Law Sch., 1953. Admitted to N.Y. bar, 1954, U.S. Supreme Ct. bar, 1976; mem. legal staff Commerce Clearing House, Chgo., 1953-54; mem. panel mediators and fact finders N.Y. State Pub. Employment Relations Bd., 1969—; partner firm Pogrebin Rains & Scher, Mineola, N.Y., 1973—. Bd. govs. Lawrence Village Assn.; bd. edn. Temple Beth El, Cedarhurst, N.Y., 1975—. Mem. Am., Nassau County bar assns., Nassau County, Suffolk County women's bar assns. Contbr. articles to legal jours. Office: 210 Old Country Rd Mineola NY 11501 Tel (516) 742-2470

GLASCOFF, DONALD GEORGE, JR., b. Indpls., Apr. 23, 1945; B.A., Yale, 1967; J.D., Cornell, 1970. Admitted to N.Y. State bar, 1972; asso. firm Cadwalader, Wickersham & Taft, N.Y.C., 1972-73, 75—; asso. dep. gen. counsel HUD, Washington, 1973-75; adj. asso. prof. Del. Law Sch., 1974. Mem. Am. Bar Assn., N.Y. County Lawyers Assn. (chmn. com. housing and urban renewal). Home: 38 Shady Terr Wayne NJ 07470 Office: 1 Wall St New York City NY 10005 Tel (212) 785-1000

GLASER, ROBERT EDWARD, b. Cin., Jan. 12, 1935; B.S. in Bus. Adminstrn., Xavier U., 1955; LL.B., U. Cin., 1960; LL.M. (M.C.L.), U. Chgo., 1962; postgrad. U. Tuebingen (Germany), 1961. Admitted to Ohio bar, 1960, U.S. Dist. Ct. bar, 1963, U.S. Circuit Ct. bar, 1964, U.S. Tax Ct. bar, 1970, U.S. Customs Ct. bar, 1971; asso. firm Arter & Hadden, Cleve., 1963-69, partner, 1970—; lectr. Cleve. Tax Inst., 1966—; arbitrator Cuyahoga County Ct. of Common Pleas, 1972—. Officer Bay View Hosp., 1972—; trustee Hill House, 1975—. Mem. Am., Ohio, Cleve. bar assns., Am. Judicature Soc., Am. Arbitration Assn. (arbitrator 1969—). Contbr. articles in field to legal jours. Home: 22895 Mastick Rd Fairview Park OH 44126 Office: 1144 Union Commerce Bldg Cleveland OH 44115 Tel (216) 696-1144

GLASGOW, JAMES MONROE, b. Dresden, Tenn., Feb. 17; J.D., U. Tenn., 1948. Admitted to Tenn. bar, 1947, U.S. Supreme Ct. bar, 1956; individual practice law, Dresden, 1948-51; asst. atty. gen. Tenn., 1952-61; asst. gen. counsel Nat. Life and Accident Inst. Co., Nashville, 1962-63; mem. firm Elom, Glasgow, Tonner & Acree, Union City Tenn., 1964—; mem. adv. com. on rules to civil procdure Tenn. Supreme Ct., 1975—. Pres. Obion County United Fund, 1968-69, Union City-Obion County C. of C., 1971-73; chmn. devel. com. U. Tenn., Martin, 1974-75; mem. devel. council U. Tenn., 1975—. Mem. Obion County, Tenn. (bd. govs. 1975—), Am. bar assns. Home: 1212 Armstrong Rd Union City TN 38261 Office: First and Church Sts Union City TN 38261 Tel (901) 885-2011

GLASGOW, ROBERT JOE, b. Stephenville, Tex., Feb. 28, 1942; B.A., Tarleton State U., 1967; J.D., U. Tex., 1969. Admitted to Tex. bar, 1969; adminstrv. asst. to Tex. Gov. Preston Smith, 1969-71; partner firm Glasgow & Jones, Stephenville, 1971—; dist. atty. 29th Jud. Dist., 1974—. Active Am. Heart Assn., Erath County Heart Assn., Erath County Assn. Retarded Citizens. Mem. Am., Tex., Erath County bar assns., Am., Tex. trial lawyers assns., Tex. Dist., Erath County attys. assns., Stephenville C. of C., Erath County Livestock Assn. Home: 2051 Crestridge St Stephenville TX 76401 Office: 211 N Belknap St Stephenville TX 76401 Tel (817) 965-5069

GLASGOW, ROBERT SAMUEL, JR., b. Adamsville, Ala., July 3, 1907; A.B., Birmingham-So. Coll., 1928; LL.B., U. Ala., 1933. Admitted to Ala. bar, 1933; individual practice law, Adamsville and Birmingham, Ala., 1933—; compliance atty. Office of Price Adminstrn. rent div., Birmingham, Ala., 1945-46; chief area atty. Office of Housing Expediter, Birmingham, 1946-50; gen. atty., trial atty. Office of Price Stblzn., Birmingham, 1951-53; sr. title agt. Ala. Power Co., Birmingham, 1955-62; adminstrv. law judge Bur. Hearings and Appeals Social Security Adminstrn., Birmingham, 1962-77; mayor City of Adamsville, 1953-55; city atty., Adamsville, 1956-57, Brookside, Ala., 1955-58. Chmn. Adamsville Bicentennial Community, 1976; chmn. Indsl. Devel. Bd., Adamsville, 1974-75; past chmn. bd. trustees Crumly Methodist Ch.; treas. bd. trustees Midway Cemetery, Inc. Mem. Birmingham Ala., Am. bar assns., Ged. Adminstrv. Law Judges Conf., Phi Alpha Delta. Contbr. articles to legal jours.; editor, pub. The Western Jeffersonian, 1929-30; former columnist Ala. Christian Adv. Home: 5012 Adams Ave Adamsville AL 35005 Office: 104 Spring St Adamsville AL 35005 Tel (205) 674-6496 Oxmoor Rd Birmingham AL 35209 Tel (205) 254-1543

GLASS, CARSON MCELYEA, b. Farmersville, Tex., Oct. 8, 1915; B.A., U. Tex., 1941, LL.B., 1938. Admitted to Tex. bar, 1937, D.C. bar, 1950; atty. Justice Dept., 1938-39, Dept. Labor, 1939; spl. atty. antitrust div. Justice Dept., 1939-47; spl. asst. to atty. gen. U.S., 1947-48; partner firm Fischer, Wood, Burney & Glass, Corpus Christi, Tex., 1949-50; mem. firm Clifford & Miller, Washington, 1950-68; partner firm Clifford, Glass, McIlwain & Finney, and predecessor, Washington, 1968—; lectr. econs. U. Corpus Christi, 1948-50. Mem. Am., Fed. (nat. Council 1961-69) bar assns., Bar Assn. D.C., State Bar Tex., White House Hist. Assn. (atty. adviser 1961—, dir. 1975—), Sat. Morning Coffee Soc. (Corpus Christi); founding mem. Nat. Lawyers Club, U.S. Supreme Ct. Hist. Soc. Contbr. articles to legal jours. Home: 2550 28th St NW Washington DC 20008 Office: 815 Connecticut Ave Washington DC 20006 Tel (202) 298-8686

GLASS, EDMUND GERALD, b. Newark, Mar. 6, 1943; B.A., Tulane U., 1964; postgrad. L'Inst. D'Etudes Politiques, Paris, 1962-63; LL.B., N.Y. U., 1967. Admitted to N.Y. State bar, 1968; asso. firm Cravath, Swaine & Moore, N.Y.C., 1967-73; asso. firm Poletti, Friedin, Prashker, Feldman & Gartner, N.Y.C., 1973-75; asso. counsel Olin Corp. Chem. Group, Stamford, Conn., 1975—; dir. Halle Industries, N.Y.C. Mem. Westchester-Fairfield County Counsel Assn., Assn. of Bar of City of N.Y., N.Y. State Bar Assn. Home: 168 E 74th St New York City NY 10021 Office: 120 Long Ridge Rd Stamford CT 06504 Tel (203) 356-2987

GLASS, GEORGE WILLIAM RILEY, b. Winchester, Va., Mar. 6, 1943; B.A., U. Va., 1965; J.D., U. Richmond, 1968. Admitted to Va. bar, 1968; partner firm Hundley Taylor and Glass, Richmond, Va., 1968—. Mem. Va., Richmond, Am. bar assns., Va. Trial Lawyers Assn. Home: 7701 Hollins Rd Richmond VA 23229 Office: 20 N 8th St Richmond VA 23219 Tel (804) 649-9193

GLASS, GERALD DURAND, b. Balt., June 4, 1942; B.S., U. Md., 1964; J.D., U. Balt., 1968. Admitted to Md. bar, 1970; asst. states atty., Balt., 1970-75; asst. city solicitor, Balt., 1970-76; asst. fed. defender Dist. Md., Reisterstown, 1976—; faculty advisor Nat. Coll. Dist. Attys., Houston, 1972-73. Mem. Am., Md. bar assns., Nat. Assn. Dist. Attys., Am. Judicature Soc. Home: 115 Sunnydale Way Reisterstown MD 21136 Office: 101 W Lombard St US Ct Ho Baltimore MD 21202 Tel (301) 962-3962

GLASS, JOHN DUEL, JR., b. Oklahoma City, Aug. 17, 1931; B.B.A., U. Tex., Austin, 1952, LL.B., 1955. Admitted to Tex. bar, 1955; partner firm Glass & Glass, Tyler, Tex., 1955-76; individual practice, 1976—. Mem. Smith County (Tex.) Bar Assn., State Bar Tex. Home: 1009 Santa Rosa St Tyler TX 75701 Office: 917 Peoples Bank Bldg Tyler TX 75702 Tel (214) 597-4967

GLASS, STUART MICHAEL, b. Bklyn., Apr. 6, 1934; B.A., Columbia, 1956, J.D. 1960. Admitted to N.Y. bar, 1966; v.p. Avon Watch Case Co., Inc., Bklyn., 1959-65; legal cons. Office of the Mayor, N.Y.C., 1965-66; house counsel Columbia U., 1966-71; individual practice law, Margaretville, N.Y., 1971-75, Port Chester, N.Y., 1975—. Mem. Assn. Bar City N.Y., N.Y., Westchester, Delaware County bar assns. Office: 345 Westchester Ave Port Chester NY 10573 Tel (914) 937-3880

GLASSCOCK, CHARLES NEIL, b. Cullman, Ala., June 3, 1933; B.S., U. North Ala., 1956; postgrad. Tulane U. Law Sch., 1956-57; M.A., U. Ala., 1959; LL.B., Atlanta Law Sch., 1972, LL.M., 1973. Admitted to Ga. bar. 1972; criminal investigator U.S. Treasury Dept., Atlanta, 1959-66; spl. asst. to dir. internal security IRS, Atlanta, 1966-70, group mgr., 1970-75; sr. instr. criminal law Fed. Law Enforcement Tng. Center, Glynco, Ga., 1975—. Recipient Spl. Achievement award U.S. Treasury, 1973. Mem. Am., Ga. bar assns., Assn. Fed. Investigators (Atlanta v.p. 1967-68), Fed. Criminal Investigators Assn. Home: 110 Gould St Saint Simons Island GA 31522 Office: Federal Law Enforcement Training Center Glynco GA 31520 Tel (912) 265-6611

GLASSER, ISRAEL LEO, b. N.Y.C., Apr. 6, 1924; LL.B., Bklyn. Law Sch., 1948; B.A., U. City N.Y., 1976. Admitted to N.Y. bar, 1948; fellow Bklyn. Law Sch., 1948-49, instr., 1950-52, asst. prof. law, 1952-53, asso. prof., 1953-55, prof., 1955-74, adj. prof., 1974—; judge N.Y. State Family Ct., N.Y.C., 1969—. Mem. Am. Bar Assn. Office: 283 Adams St Brooklyn NY 11201 Tel (212) 643-2849

GLASSMAN, MARTIN ELLIOTT, b. Chgo., Sept. 26, 1948; B.S. in Bus. Mgmt., Bradley U., 1969; J.D., Loyola U., Chgo., 1972. Admitted to Ill. bar, 1972; sr. extern Ill. Supreme Ct., 1971-72; individual practice law, Chgo., 1972—. Mem. Am., Ill bar assns. Office: 221 N LaSalle St Chicago IL 60601 Tel (312) 726-2772

GLAUBERMAN, MELVIN LEONARD, b. Bklyn., Nov. 3, 1927; B.A., Bklyn. Coll., 1948; LL.B., J.D., Harvard, 1951. Admitted to N.Y. State bar, 1951, U.S. Dist. Ct. bar, 1953, U.S. Supreme Ct. bar, 1972; partner firm Berman Glauberman & Bernstein and predecessors, 1957—; mem. panel of arbitrators Am. Arbitration Assn. Mem. N.Y. State Trial Lawyers Assn. Home: 28 Parkwold Dr W Valley Stream NY 11580 Office: 253 Broadway New York City NY 10007 Tel (212) 964-5070

GLAVES, DONALD WILLIAM, b. Chgo., Mar. 1, 1935; B.A., Ill. Coll., 1956; J.D., U. Chgo., 1962. Admitted to Ill. bar, 1962; asso. firm Ross, Hardies, O'Keefe, Babcock & Parsons, Chgo., 1962—; clk. to Judge Carl McGowan, U.S. Ct. Appeals, D.C. Circuit, 1963. Active Am. Cancer Soc., 1971—, chmn. bd. North Shore unit Ill. div., 1974-76. Mem. Am. Law Inst., Chgo., Am. bar assns. Office: One IBM Plaza Suite 3100 Chicago IL 60611 Tel (312) 467-9300

GLAVIN, A. RITA CHANDELLIER, b. Schenectady, May 11, 1937; A.B. cum laude, Middleburg Coll., 1958; LL.B., Union U., 1961, J.D., 1968. Admitted to N.Y. bar, 1961, U.S. Tax Ct. bar, 1965; asso. firm Eugene J. Steiner, Albany, N.Y., 1961-64; mem. firm Glavin & Glavin, Waterford, Schenectady and Albany, 1965—; asso. Helen Fox Chandellier, Schenectady, 1965-76; confdl. law clk. to judges N.Y. State Ct. Claims, 1968-71; del. Jud. Conv., 4th Jud. Dist., 3rd dept. N.Y., 1966; spl. lectr. in law Middlebury Coll., 1976. Co-chmn. Waterford Cancer Dr., 1964; mem. nat. exec. com. Albany Law Sch. expansion fund, 1967; bd. dirs., officer Bellevue Maternity Hosp., Schenectady, 1966—; mem. maternity and pediatric task force and maternity and pediatric care com. Regional Hosp. Rev. and Planning Council of Northeastern N.Y., 1974, 76; mem. maternity and pediatric tech. adv. group H.S.A. of Northeastern N.Y., 1976—; bd. dirs. Jr. League Schenectady, 1974, 76. Mem. N.Y. State, Schenectady, Saratoga County bar assns., Phi Beta Kappa. Editor Albany Law Rev., 1960, 61. Home: 66 Saratoga Ave Waterford NY 12188 Office: 69 Second St PO Box 40 Waterford NY 12188 Tel (518) 237-5505

GLAVIN, JAMES HENRY, III, b. Albany, N.Y., Oct. 6, 1931; A.B., Villanova U., 1953; LL.B., Albany Law Sch., 1956, J.D., 1966. Admitted to N.Y. bar, 1956, U.S. Supreme Ct. bar, 1959; served with JAGC, USAF, 1957-60; partner firm Glavin and Glavin, Waterford and Albany, 1960—; spl. counsel Waterford (N.Y.), 1968—; atty. Waterford Water Commn., 1961—; regional dir. Nat. Comml. Bank & Trust Co., 1968—, chmn. bd., 1976—. Mem. Waterford Planning Com., 1961-68. Chmn. Saratoga County (N.Y.) Democratic Com., 1964-68, Dem. Jud. Conv., 1967; upstate campaign coordinator N.Y. State Dem. Com., 1965; trustee St. Mary's Ch., Waterford, 1974—; bd. dirs. Waterford Central Cath. Sch., 1969—, Bellevue Maternity Hosp., Schenectady, 1969—; trustee Waterford Rural Cemetery, 1969—. Mem. Am. Acad. Polit. and Social Sci., Am. Soc. Law and Medicine, Internat. Soc. Gen. Semantics, Am. Psychology-Law Soc., Am. Soc. Hosp. Attys., ICC Practitioners Assn., Nat. Health Lawyers Assn., Estate Planning Council Eastern N.Y., Motor Carrier Lawyers Assn., Judge Advs. Assn., Assn. Trial Lawyers Am., Am., Fed., N.Y. State, Albany County, Saratoga County, Rensselaer County bar assns., N.Y. State Trial Lawyers Assn., Air Force Assn. Author: The Tour Broker and the Interstate Commerce Commission, 1977. Home: 66 Saratoga Ave Box 40 Waterford NY 12188 Office: 69 2d St Waterford NY 12188 and 74 State St Albany NY 12207 Tel (518) 237-5505

GLAZE, THOMAS ARTHUR, b. Joplin, Mo., Jan. 14, 1938; B.A., U. Ark., 1960, J.D., 1964. Admitted to Ark. bar, 1965, since practiced in Little Rock; exec. dir. Election Research Council, Inc., 1964-65, legal advisor to Winthrop Rockefeller, 1965-66, dep. Office Ark. Atty. Gen., 1967-70, exec. dir. Election Laws Inst., Inc., 1970—, individual practice law, 1970—; chmn. spl. advisory com. Ark. State Election Commn., 1970-71, lect. U. Ark., 1971-72, legal advisor Pulaski County Election Commission 1971-73, cons. subcom. elections House Adminstrn. Com. 1974, initiated Consumer Protection Div. Atty. Gen. Office and assisted drafting legislation creating Consumer Program, 1969-70. Bd. dirs. Community Mental Health Center Little Rock, 1975-77. Mem. Ark., Pulaski County, Am. bar assns. Co-author: Arkansas Election Code. Home: 2400 McCain Bldg North Little Rock AR 72116 Office: One Spring Bldg Suite 310 Little Rock AR 72201 Tel (501) 374-2400

GLAZER, FRANK, b. McKees Rocks, Pa., Aug. 26, 1924; student U. Pitts., 1941-43, Knox Coll., 1943; J.D., U. Chgo., 1949. Admitted to Ill. bar, 1949; asso. firm Bercham Schwantes & Thuma, Chgo., 1951-53; mgr. legal dep. Hartford Ins. Group, Chgo., 1956-71; partner firm Glazer & Cohan, Ltd., Chgo., 1971-75; individual practice law as Frank Glazer Ltd., Chgo., 1975—; atty. Village of Dolton (Ill.), 1967-69; served with JAG, U.S. Air Force, 1951-53. Mem. Soc. Trial Lawyers, Trial Lawyers Club Chgo., Am., Ill., Chgo. bar assns., Ill. Inst. Continuing Legal Edn. (editorial rev. bd.). Home: 735 E 167th St South Holland IL 60473 Office: 185 N Wabash Ave Chicago IL 60601 Tel (312) 726-1907

GLAZER, MICHAEL, b. Los Angeles, Oct. 10, 1940; B.S., Stanford, 1962; M.B.A., Harvard, 1964; J.D., U. Calif., Los Angeles, 1967. Admitted to Calif. bar, 1967; clk. to chief justice Calif. Supreme Ct., San Francisco, 1967-68; mem., officer firm Tuttle & Taylor, Los Angeles, 1968—. Commr., Los Angeles Dept. Water and Power, 1973-76; chmn. Calif. Water Commn., 1976—. Mem. Calif., Los Angeles County bar assns. Office: 609 S Grand Ave Los Angeles CA 90017 Tel (213) 683-0600

GLAZER, RONALD BARRY, b. Phila., Jan. 13, 1943; A.B., Dickinson Coll., 1964; LL.B., U. Pa., 1967. Admitted to Pa. bar, 1967, U.S. Dist. Ct. Eastern Dist., Pa., 1975, Fla. bar, 1976; mem. firm Cohen, Shapiro, Polisher, Shiekman & Cohen, Phila., 1967—. Mem. Am., Pa., Phila., Fed. bar assns., Am. Judicature Soc. Asso. editor: The Retainer, 1973-75; author Pennsylvania Condominium Law and Practice, 1975; recipient Outstanding Young Men Am. award, 1977. Office: Suite 2200 12 S 12th St Philadelphia PA 19107 Tel (215) 922-1300

GLAZNER, LARRY EUGENE, b. Lubbock, Tex., Sept. 6, 1942; B.S., Southwestern U., 1966; J.D., Tex. Tech. U., 1972. Admitted to Tex. bar, 1973; mem. editorial staff Tex. Appellate Form Book, Lubbock, 1972; asst. criminal dist. atty. for Lubbock County, Tex., 1973-74; asso. firm Quinn Brackett, Lubbock, Tex., 1974; exec. dir. Legal Aid Soc. of Lubbock, Inc., 1974—; individual practice law, Lubbock, 1974—. Mem. Am., Lubbock County bar assns. Mem. editorial staff, contbr. articles to Tex. Tech. Law Sch. newspaper, 1972-73. Home:

1616 59th St Apt 4 Lubbock TX 79412 Office: 18 Briercroft Office Park Lubbock TX 79412 Tel (806) 765-5767

GLEASON, DONALD WILLIAM, b. Wrightstown, Wis., Dec. 6, 1907; B.Ed., Oshkosh State Tchrs.'. Coll., 1928; J.D. magna cum laude, Marquette U., 1934. Tchr. pub. high schs., Manitowoc, Milw. and Green Bay, Wis., 1928-31, 34-35; admitted to Wis. bar, 1934; spl. agt. FBI Dept. Justice, 1935-36; practiced in Green Bay, Wis., 1934-35, 36-44; dist. atty. Brown County (Wis.), 1941-44; judge Brown County Municipal Ct., 1944-61, Wis. 14th Jud. Circuit Ct., 1962-76; chief judge for seven counties 10th Adminstrv. Jud. Dist. Wis., 1976—; mem. Judicial Planning Com. Wis. Supreme Ct., 1976—. Mem. Wis. Gov.'s. Commn. on Human Rights, 1954-56. Mem. Wis. State, Brown County, 14th Jud. Circuit bar assns. Recipient Fellowship award B'nai B'rith, 1957, Distinguished Alumni award Wis. State U.-Oshkosh, 1969; Civic award Order of Eagles, 1974, Mil. Order Purple Heart, 1950, Community Service Green Bay Jr. C. of C., 1970. Mem.Am. Trial Lawyers Assn. Home: 2636 Beaumont St Green Bay WI 54301 Office: Brown County Courthouse Green Bay WI 54301 Tel (414) 437-3221

GLEASON, JAMES ARTHUR, b. Cleve., Feb. 20, 1905; A.B., Georgetown U., 1928; J.D., Case Western Res. U., 1931. Admitted to Ohio bar, 1932; practiced law in Cleve., 1932-41, 46—; dir. Automatic Auto-Park, Inc., N.Y.C. Mem. bd. govs. senate Georgetown U., Washington, 1953—. Mem. Am. (ho. of dels. 1943—, chmn. standing com. lawyers in armed forces, 1974-76), Cleve., Ohio State (del. internat. bar conf. Madrid, 1952; gen. chmn. conv. com. 1966), Internat. (del. conf. 1966), Inter-Am., Cuyahoga County (mem. fed. ct. probate ct. taxation com. 1966-67), Fed. (pres. Cleve. chpt. 1961-62), bar assns., Judge Advs. Assn., Am. Soc. Internat. Law, Mil. Order World Wars, Am. Legion, Res. Officers Assn., Assn. U.S. Army. Home: 172 N County Rd at Park Ave PO Box 564 Palm Beach FL 33480 also 13605 Shaker Blvd Cleveland OH 44120 Office: Room 1209 215 Euclid Ave Cleveland OH 44114 Tel (216) 771-2525

GLEAVES, A. FRANK, III, b. Indpls., Oct. 30, 1938; B.S., Butler U., 1960; J.D., Ind. U., 1971. Admitted to Ind. bar, 1971, U.S. Supreme Ct. bar, 1974: dept. atty. gen., Ind., 1971-76; individual practice law, Indpls., 1976—. Bd. dirs. Mary Rigg Center, Indpls. Mem. Am., Ind., Indpls. bar assns. Office: 1165 S Warman Ave Indianapolis IN 46221 Tel (317) 634-4666

GLECKMAN, ROGER J., b. Providence, Sept. 14, 1941; B.A., U. Mass., 1963; J.D., U. Calif., Los Angeles, 1968. Admitted t Calif. bar, 1969; asso. firm Kessler & Drasin, Los Angeles, 1969-71; partner firm Gleckman & Prescott, Los Angeles, 1971—. Mem. Los Angeles County Bar Assn. (chmn. com. immigration 1976—), Los Angeles Trial Lawyers Assn., Calif. Trial Lawyers Assn., Assn. Immigration, Nationality Lawyers (sec. Los Angeles chpt. 1976—). Office: 3435 Wilshire Blvd Suite 1400 Los Angeles CA 90010 Tel (213) 381-7741

GLEIN, RICHARD JERIEL, b. Los Angeles, Aug. 20, 1929; student U. Wash. Admitted to Wash. bar, 1963; dep. pros. atty., King County, Wash., 1963-65; asso. firm Clinton, Fleck, Glein & Brown, Seattle, 1965-68, partner, 1968—. Mem. Am., Wash., King County-Seattle bar assns., Wash. State Def. Attys. Assn., Internat. Footprint Assn. (pres. Seattle chpt. 1969-70). Home: 12040 28 NE A07 201 Edmonds WA 98020 Office: 500 3rd and Lenora Bldg Seattle WA 98121 Tel (206) 624-6831

GLEISNER, WILLIAM CHARLES, III, b. Milw., Sept. 19, 1946; B.A., Marquette U., 1970, J.D. (St. Thomas scholar), 1974. Admitted to Wis. bar, 1974; asso. firm Puls & Puls, Milw., 1974—; chief village prosecutor Village of Menomonee Falls (Wis.), 1974—. Mem. Milw. Bar Assn. (editorial bd. jour. Gavel, sr. asso. editor jour. Briefs, editor-in-chief Milw. Lawyer 1977—), Scribes, Phi Alpha Delta. Recipient 1st place award Nat. Moot Ct. Competition, 1972; contbr. articles to legal jours.; co-editor-in-chief Marquette Oyer, 1974 (recipient 1st pl. award Nat. Law Sch. Newspaper Competition 1974). Office: 212 W Wisconsin Ave Milwaukee WI 53203 Tel (414) 251-6860

GLENDON, MARY ANN, b. Pittsfield, Mass., Oct. 7, 1938; B.A., Univ. Chgo., 1959, J.D., 1961, M.Comparative Law, 1963. Admitted to Ill. bar, 1964; legal intern European Common Market, Brussels, 1962-63; asso. firm Mayer, Brown & Platt, Chgo., 1963-68; prof. law Boston Coll., 1968—; lectr. Internat. Faculty Comparative Law, Strasbourg, France, 1972—; vis. prof. law Harvard, 1974-75. Mem. Am. Comparative Law Assn. Author: (with Max Rheinstein) The Law of Decedents' Estates; contbr. articles in field to profl. jours. Office: 885 Centre St Newton MA 02159 Tel (617) 969-0100

GLENN, ARNOLD BENNETT, b. N.Y.C., Oct. 27, 1926; B.S., Ohio State U., 1945; J.D., N.Y. U., 1949; M.Sc., L.I. U., 1962. Admitted to N.Y. bar, 1949, U.S. Supreme Ct. bar, 1977; staff atty. Legal Aid Soc., N.Y.C., 1950-51; partner firm Lehmann & Glenn, N.Y.C., 1955-64; individual practice law, N.Y.C., 1964-68, Eastchester, N.Y., 1971—; partner firm Glenn & Heiler, N.Y.C., 1968-70; Moot Ct. judge N.Y. U. Sch. Law, 1970—. Mem. Am. Arbitration Assn. (arbitrator 1968—), N.Y. County Lawyers Assn., Eastchester Bar Assn. (treas. 1976-77). Home: 4 Huntley Rd Eastchester NY 10709 Office: 575 White Plains Rd Eastchester NY 10707

GLENN, JOHN EVERETT, b. Delmar, N.Y., Aug. 30, 1902; B.A., Union Coll., 1924; LL.B., St. Lawrence U., 1927; J.D., Blyn. Law Sch., 1967. Admitted to N.Y. State bar, 1927, U.S. Dist. Ct., No. Dist. N.Y., 1932, U.S. Supreme Ct. bar, 1970; asso. William A. Glenn, 1927-54; partner firm Glenn & Kimmey, 1954-70, Glenn, Bergan & Murphy, Albany, 1970—; counsel N.Y. State Sch. Bds. Assn., 1949-54, N.Y. State Tchrs. Assn., 1954-67. Mem. Bethlehem Central Sch. Dist., Albany County, 1942-58; mem. adv. bd. Salvation Army, 1941—, hon. life mem., 1976—; mem. Bd. Coop. Ednl. Services of Albany, Schoharie and Schenectady counties, 1952-71; bd. chancellor Episcopal Diocese of Albany, 1966-77, emeritus, 1977—. Mem. Nat. Orgn. Legal Problems of Edn. (hon. life), Am. (life mem.), N.Y. State, Albany County bar assns. Co-author: Handbook on Personnel Practices for Teachers, 1970. Home: 15 Meadowbrook St Delmar NY 12054 Office: 11 N Pearl St Albany NY 12207 Tel (518) 465-1403

GLENN, MARTIN RICHARDSON, b. Frankfort, Ky., Dec. 16, 1905; B.A., U. Ky., 1930, LL.B., 1932. Admitted to Ky. bar, 1932, U.S. Supreme Ct. bar, 1936; individual practice law, Madisonville, Ky., 1932-34; atty., asst. gen. counsel Fed. Land Bank of Louisville, 1934-45; individual practice law, Louisville, 1946-56, 68-72; clk. U.S. Dist. Ct., Western Dist. Ky., 1956-68; asst. to mayor City of Louisville, 1972-74; asst. dir law City of Louisville, 1974—. Mem. Ky., Louisville bar assns., Phi Alpha Delta, Sigma Delta Chi. Contbr. articles to legal jours. Home: 1293 Cherokee Rd Louisville KY 40204 Office: 200 City Hall 6th and Jefferson Sts Louisville KY 40202 Tel (502) 587-3511

GLENN, ROBERT EASTWOOD, b. Catlettsburg, Ky., Dec. 24, 1929; B.A. in Accounting cum laude, Washington and Lee U., 1951, J.D. cum laude, 1953. Admitted to Va. bar, 1952; judge adv. USAF, 1953-57; partner firm Eggleston & Glenn, and predecessors, Roanoke, Va., 1957—. Chmn. Roanoke City Republican Com., 1968-70; bd. visitors Radford Coll., 1972—, rector, 1975—; chmn. Roanoke Valley chpt. ARC, 1974-76. Mem. Am., Va., Roanoke bar assns., Phi Delta Phi. Home: 3101 Allendale St SW Roanoke VA 24014 Office: 315 Shenandoah Bldg Roanoke VA 24001 Tel (703) 342-1851

GLENN, THOMAS JOSEPH, JR., b. Darby, Pa., Nov. 12, 1942; B.A. in Econs., Kings Coll., 1964; J.D., Catholic U., 1967. Admitted to Pa bar, 1968; judge adv. USMC, Vietnam, 1968-71; practice law, 1971—; partner firm Glenn and Schoen, Wilkes-Barre, Pa., 1974—; asst. dist. atty. Luzerne County, Pa., 1974—; asst. prof. criminal justice Kings Coll., 1975—. Mem. Am., Pa., Luzerne County bar assns. Recipient Naval Achievement medal, 1970. Home: 3 Rebel Hill Rd Mountaintop PA 18707 Office: 65 W Jackson Wilkes-Barre PA 18702 Tel (717) 822-3968

GLENNON, PAUL WILLIAM, b. Worcester, Mass., July 22, 1910; B.B.A., Northeastern U., 1932, LL.B., 1940; M.B.A., Boston U., 1936; LL.M., N.Y.U., 1944, J.S.D., 1946. Admitted to Mass. bar, 1948; prof. law Northeastern U., Boston, 1946-54; dean Becker Jr. Coll., Worcester, 1954-62; bankruptcy judge U.S. Dist. Ct., Mass., 1962—. Chmn., Woods Hole, Marthas Vineyard, Nantucket Steamship Authority, 1956-59. Mem. Am., Worcester County bar assns. Office: 1128 Federal Bldg Boston MA 02109 Tel (617) 223-2934

GLENNON, ROBERT JEROME, JR., b. Newton, Mass., Aug. 27, 1944; A.B., Boston Coll., 1966, J.D., 1969; M.A., Brandeis U., 1972. Admitted to Mass. bar, 1969; law clk. judge A. Julian, U.S. Dist. Ct., Boston, 1969; asso. prof. Wayne State U., Detroit, 1973—; vis. asso. prof. U. Ill., Champaign, 1975; legal intern Mass. atty. gen. Elliot Richardson, Boston, 1968, ACLU, Chgo., 1967. Bd. dir., ACLU Mich. Mem. Am. Bar Assn., Am. History Assn., Orgn. Am. Historians, Am. Soc. Legal History, Order of Coif. Am. Bar Found. fellow, 1976-77, Faculty Research award, Wayne State U., 1975. Tel (313) 577-3947

GLIBOFF, DAVID, b. Bronx, N.Y., Feb. 27, 1929; B.A., L.I. U., 1948; LL.B., BKlyn. Law Sch., 1951. Admitted to N.Y. State bar, 1950, U.S. Supreme Ct. bar, 1959; individual practice law, Islip, N.Y., 1953; asso. firm Kramer and Gliboff, Islip, 1964-71, Gliboff & Frankel, Islip, 1973—. Bd. dirs. Suffolk County council Girl Scouts U.S.A.; pres. Brightwaters Manor Civic Assn. Mem. Suffolk County Bar Assn., Estate Planners Council Suffolk County, Islip Town Lawyers Club (pres. 1964-65), Islip C. of C. (dir. 1972—). Office: 1 Grant Ave Islip NY 11751 Tel (516) 581-1111

GLICK, PAUL MITCHELL, b. N.Y.C., Dec. 7, 1948; B.A. with distinction, U. Wis., 1970; J.D. cum laude, DePaul U., Chgo., 1973; postgrad. (NSF grantee) Columbia U., 1966. Admitted to Ill. bar, 1973, U.S. Tax Ct., 1973, U.S. Supreme Ct. bar, 1976; asso. firm Friedman & Koven, Chgo., 1973—; lectr. in field. Mem. Am., Ill., Chgo. bar assns. Office: 208 S LaSalle St Chicago IL 60604 Tel (312) 346-8500

GLICKHOUSE, LOUIS, b. N.Y.C., Feb. 16, 1908; B.A., Washington Sq. Coll., 1929; J.D., N.Y. U., 1931. Admitted to N.Y. bar, 1931, U.S. Supreme Ct. bar, 1943; with Edbro Realty Corp., N.Y.C., 1934; with Morgage Commn. State of N.Y., 1935-40; with N.Y.C. Housing Authority, 1950-73, trial officer, 1973—; individual practice law, N.Y.C., 1932—. Chmn. Manhattan Local Community Planning Bd. #3, 1970; bd. dirs. Lower East Side Neighborhood Assn., 1955-70. Mem. N.Y. County Lawyers Assn., Citizens Housing and Planning Assn., Citizens Union, Nat. Assn., Housing and Redevel. Ofcls. Home and Office: 457 FDR Dr New York City NY 10002 Tel (212) 673-3732

GLICKMAN, ANNE LEE, Bklyn., Feb. 4, 1936; A.B., Bklyn. Coll., 1955; LL.B., N.Y.U., 1958. Admitted to N.Y. State bar, 1959, So. and Eastern Dists., Fed. Ct. bar, 1966; asso. firm Freeman & Hyman, Queens, N.Y., 1958-59; counsel N.Y. State Dept. Labor, N.Y.C., 1959-60, N.Y.C. Legal Aid Soc., 1960-61; mem. firm Jelenick & Glickman, N.Y.C., 1961-63; asso. firm Schwall & Carroll, New City, N.Y., 1964-65; chief atty. and dir. Rockland County Legal Aid Soc., New City, N.Y., 1965-73; asso. prof. law Ramapo Coll. N.J., Mahwah, 1973—; individual practice law, Suffern, N.Y., 1973-76; mem. firm Glickman & McAlevey, New City, 1976—. Counsel to Spring Valley NAACP; bd. dirs. Rockland Civil Liberties Union, Rockland Legal Aid Soc., Child Advocacy Council. Mem. N.Y. State, Rockland County bar assns. Home: One Galileo Ct Suffern NY 10901 Office: 130 N Main St New City NY 10956 Tel (914) 634-8884

GLICKMAN, SYLVIA KAUFER, b. Wilkes Barre, Pa., Oct. 9, 1923; B.B.A., U. Mich., 1944; J.D., Seton Hall U., 1964. Admitted to N.J. State bar, 1964; individual practice law, Somerset, N.J., 1965-75; tchr. Franklin Twp. Bd. Edn., Somerset, 1955-61, 64-75, staff asst. Affirmative Action, 1975-76, Affirmative Action officer, 1976—. legal counsel Housing Authority Franklin Twp., 1967-72. Mem. NEA, N.J. Edn. Assn., N.J. State Bar Assn., Am. Judicature Soc., Internat. Assn. Jewish Lawyers and Jurists. Home: 15 Holly St Somerset NJ 08873 Office: 1 Railroad Ave Somerset NJ 08873 Tel (201) 873-2400

GLICKSON, JUSTIN, b. Norwalk, Conn., Aug. 19, 1915; A.B., Harvard, 1936; LL.B., Yale, 1939. Admitted to Conn. bar, 1939, N.Y. bar, 1941; chmn. exec. com., gen. counsel Presdl. Realty Corp., White Plains, N.Y., 1946—. Mem. Norwalk (Conn.) Bd. Edn., 1960-66, chmn., 1964, mem. charter revision commn., 1974; mem. Conn. Bd. Regional Community Colls., 1967-71. Contbr. to legal publs. Office: Presidential Realty Corp 180 S Broadway White Plains NY 10605

GLIDDEN, JOHN REDMOND, b. Sanford, Maine, July 24, 1936; B.S., Coe Coll., 1958; LL.B., U. Iowa, 1961. Admitted to Iowa bar, 1961, Ill. bar, 1965; judge adv. U.S. Air Force, 1961-65; asso. firm Williams & Hartzell, Carthage, Ill., 1965-67; partner firm Hartzell, Glidden, Tucker & Neff, and predecessor, Carthage, 1967—; city atty. Carthage, 1969—. Bd. dirs. Carthage Indsl. Div. Mem. Ill., Fed., Iowa, Hancock County bar assns., Ill. (governing bd. 1971—), Am. (nat. coll. advocacy) trial lawyers assns. Home: Rural Route 3 Carthage IL 62321 Office: Williams Bldg Carthage IL 62321 Tel (217) 357-3121

GLIEBERMAN, SHELDON LEONARD, b. Chgo., July 26, 1924; B.S., Roosevelt U., 1947; J.D., Northwestern U., 1950. Admitted to Ill. bar, 1950; individual practice law, Chgo., 1950—. Office: 19 S LaSalle St Suite 1600 Chicago IL 60603 Tel (312) 782-9777

GLOCK, CARL EDWARD, b. Pitts., Sept. 22, 1918; B.A., Williams Coll., 1939; J.D., Harvard U., 1946. Admitted to Pa. bar, 1947; U.S. Supreme Ct. bar, 1966, also U.S. Ct. Claims U.S. Tax Ct.; asso. firm Reed, Smith, Shaw & McClay, Pitts., 1946-58, partner, 1958—. Mem. Allegheny County Planning Commn., 1952-76, acting chmn., 1970-73; mem. Southwestern Pa. Regional Planning Commn., 1962-76, chmn., 1969-70; bd. dirs. Family and Children's Service Allegheny County, pres. 1959-62; trustee Community Services Pa.; mem. citizens assembly, various coms. Allegheny County Health and Welfare Assn.; mem. com. Revision Adoption Law Adv. Com. to Pa. Dept. Welfare. Fellow Am. Bar Found.; mem. Allegheny County (bd. govs. 1963-65, 75-76, treas. 1975-76), Pa. (pres.-elect, bd. govs. 1976-77), Am. (ho. of dels.) bar assns., Am. Law Inst. Home: 1450 Wightman St Pittsburgh PA 15217 Office: 747 Union Trust Bldg Pittsburgh PA 15219 Tel (412) 288-3146

GLOCK, EARL F., b. Johnstown, Pa., July 21, 1924: A.B., Harvard, 1948, J.D., 1951. Admitted to Pa. bar, 1952; individual practice law, Johnstown, 1952—; counsel Cambria County (Pa.) Med. Soc., 1957—; solicitor Southmont Borough, 1958—, Greater Johnstown Water Authority, 1963—, Mercy Hosp., Johnstown, 1971—. Pres., Cambria County Easter Seal Soc., 1956; bd. dirs. Johnstown Symphony Orch., 1965—. Mem. Pa., Cambria County bar assns., Am. Judicature Soc. Office: 703 United States Bank Bldg Johnstown PA 15901 Tel (814) 536-0701

GLOD, STANLEY JOSEPH, b. Altoona, Pa., June 28, 1936; A.B. with high honors, John Carroll U., 1958; J.D., Georgetown U., 1961; certificate Hague Acad. Internat. Law, Holland, 1964; S.J.D., U. Munich, Ger., 1967. Admitted to D.C. bar, 1962, Va. bar, 1970, U.S. Supreme Ct. bar, 1969; adj. instr. bus., internat., and mil. law U. Md., European Div., Verdun, France, 1965, Munich, 1965-67; maj. JAGC, U.S. Army, 1962-69; asso. prof. internat. and comparative law JAG Sch., U. Va., Charlottesville, 1968-69; partner firm Sutton & O'Rourke, Washington, 1969-71; Boner & Glod, Washington, 1971-72; individual practice law, Washington, 1972-77; of counsel firm Weitzman & Houser, Washington, 1977—. Chmn. 1st and 2d Polonia Press Confs., Washington, 1974, 75: mem. Presdl. Adv. Com. for Trade Negotiations, 1975; mem. Presdl. trade del. to Polish Ministry of Fgn. Trade, 1975. Mem. Am. (chmn. working group on internat. trade cts. 1970-73), Fed., Internat., Inter-Am. bar assns., D.C. Unified Bar, Va. State Bar., Am. Soc. Internat. Law, Internat. Law Assn., World Peace Through Law Center (Geneva), Assn. Alumni Hague Acad. Internat. Law, Judge Adv. Assn., Polish Inst. Arts and Scis. Am., Internat. Soc. Mil. Law and Law of War, Washington Fgn. Law Soc., Am. Fgn. Law Assn., Grotius Found., Polish-Am. Arts Assn. Washington, Nat. Advocates Soc. (nat. sec.-treas. 1975-77, v.p. 1977—), Polish Am. Congress (bd. dirs. Washington chpt. 1975-77), Alpha Sigma Nu, Phi Alpha Delta. Contbr. articles to profl. jours. Home: 3160 Woodland Ln Alexandria VA 22309 Office: 1735 K St NW Washington DC 20006 Tel (202) 467-5424

GLOE, H. NICK, b. Cedar Rapids, Iowa, June 12, 1941; B.A., U. Iowa, 1964, J.D., 1967. Admitted to Iowa bar, 1967; mem. firm Faches Klinger & Gloe, Cedar Rapids, 1969—. Bd. dirs. Vol. Action Center. Mem. Phi Delta Phi. Office: 318 Paramount Bldg Cedar Rapids IA 52401 Tel (319) 366-7675

GLOJEK, FERDINAND ALVIN, b. W. Allis, Wis., Oct. 22, 1914; J.D., Marquette U., 1937. Admitted to Wis. bar, 1937; asst. atty. City of W. Allis, 1946-49, city atty., 1949-50; v.p., dir. W. Allis State Bank, 1948—, Southwest Bank, 1972—; sec., dir. Bancopr. of Wis., Inc., 1977—; dir. Maintenance Service Corp., Chgo. Machine Rebuilders, Inc., Milw. Mfg. Co. Mem. W. Allis Library Bd., 1946-47; commr. W. Allis Police and Fire, 1965-75, pres., 1971-72; pres. Milw. County Park Commn., 1970-72, mem., 1968—; dir. Villa Clement Nursing Home, W. Allis, 1973—; bd. dirs. United Way, Milw., 1973—. Mem. Wis., Milw. bar assns. Home: 11917 W Appleton Ave Milwaukee WI 53224 Office: 6212 W Greenfield Ave West Allis WI 53214 Tel (414) 774-3414

GLOS, GEORGE ERNEST, b. Poznan, Poland, Dec. 31, 1924; B.A., Lycee Prague (Czechoslovakia), 1943, LL.B., 1948; J.U.D., Charles U., Prague, 1948; LL.B. (Commonwealth scholar), U. Melbourne (Australia), 1956, LL.M., 1959; J.S.D. (Sterling-Ford fellow), Yale, 1960. Admitted to Czechoslovakia bar, 1948; called to Victoria (Australia) bar, 1957; individual practice law, Prague, 1948-49; asso. in law Charles U., 1948-49; individual practice law, Melbourne, 1955-58; lectr. Law U. law U. Singapore, 1960-63; mem. firm Pennie & Edmonds, N.Y.C., 1963-64; asso. prof. St. Mary's U., San Antonio, 1964-69, prof., 1969—. Mem. Soc. Pub. Tchrs. Law. Author: International Rivers, 1961; contbr. articles to legal jours. Office: One Camino Santa Maria San Antonio TX 78284 Tel (512) 436-3424

GLOSSER, JEFFREY MARK, b. Windsor, Ont., Can., June 29, 1936; B.A. in Econs. with distinction, U. Pa., 1958; LL.B., Harvard, 1961. Admitted to D.C. bar, 1962; law clk. U.S. Ct. Claims, 1963-64; asso. firm Emery & Wood, 1965-69; partner firm Pasternak & Kaufmann, Washington, 1969—. Mem. Am. (mem. council sect. adminstrv. law), Fed. bar assns., Bar Assn. D.C. Office: 4400 Jenifer St NW Suite 350 Washington DC 20015 Tel (202) 362-4060

GLOSSER, MARK LOUIS, b. Johnstown, Pa., Mar. 26, 1946; B.B.A., Case Western Reserve U., 1968; J.D., Duquesne U., 1973. Admitted to Pa. Supreme Ct. bar, 1973; asso. firm Cooper, Schwartz, Diamond & Reich, Pitts., 1973-75; partner firm Samuel J. Reich, P.C., Pitts., 1975—; lectr. legal research and writing Duquesne U., 1972-73. Mem. Pa., Am. Allegheny County bar assns., Am. Trial Lawyers Assn. Asso. Duquesne U. Law Rev., 1972-73. Home: 5656 Melvin St Pittsburgh PA 15217 Office: 1321 Frick Bldg Grant St Pittsburgh PA 15219 Tel (412) 391-6222

GLOSSER, WILLIAM LOUIS, b. Johnstown, Pa., Aug. 30, 1929; B.S. Temple U., 1951, LL.B., U. Pa., 1954. Admitted to Pa. bar, 1954, Fla. bar, 1957; asso. Broad & Cassel, Miami Beach, Fla., 1958; individual practice law, Coral Gabies, Fla., 1950-61; asst. treas. Glosser Bros., Johnstown, Pa., 1962—; U.S. commr. U.S. Dist. Ct. for Western Pa., 1964-67, U.S. magistrate 1973—. Mem. Pa. Human Relations Commn., 1970—, chmn., 1977—; pres. Johnstown Jewish Community Council, 1971-76; bd. dirs. Johnstown YMCA, 1975—, Johnstown Symphony Orch., 1964-70, Johnstown Community Chest, 1970-73, Johnstown Area Arts Council, 1965-67. Mem. Am., Pa., Cambria County, Fla. bar assns., Am. Arbitration Assn., Am. Jurisprudence Soc. Home: 521 Luzerne St Johnstown PA 15905 Office: Franklin and Locust Sts Johnstown PA 15901 Tel (814) 536-6633

GLOVER, CHARLES CARROLL, III, b. Washington, Apr. 9, 1918; B.A., Yale, 1940; LL.B., Harvard, 1943. Admitted to Mass. bar, 1943, D.C. bar, 1946; partner law firm Cox, Langford, Stoddard & Cutler, Washington, 1946-62, firm Wilmer, Cutler & Pickering, Washington, 1962—. Bd. dirs. Eugene and Agnes E. Meyer Found. Mem. Bar Assn. D.C., Am., D.C. bar assns. Home: 5235 Duvall Dr Bethesda MD 20016 Office: 1666 K St NW Washington DC 20006

GLOWACKI, FRANK EDMUND, b. Chgo., June 1, 1928; B.A., Grinnell Coll., 1952; J.D., DePaul U., 1956. Admitted to Ill. bar, 1956; house counsel Hardware Mut. Ins. Co., Chgo., Ill., 1959-61; gen. atty. Chgo. & Eastern Ill. R.R., Chgo., 1961-67; individual practice law, Chicago Heights, Ill., 1967—; corp. counsel, Chicago Heights, 1970-74. Mem. Ill., Am. bar assns. Home: 169 W Elmwood St Chicago Heights IL 60411 Office: 100 First Nat Plaza Suite 201 Chicago Heights IL 60411 Tel (312) 755-5515

GLOWACKI, JOHN WILLIAM, b. Detroit, July 18, 1932; Ph.B., U. Detroit, 1958, M.A., 1961; J.D., Detroit Coll. of Law, 1969. Admitted to Mich. bar, 1969; individual practice law, Detroit, 1969-71, East Detroit, 1971—; instr. bus. law Detroit Pub. Schs., 1969, Wayne County Community Coll., 1970. Mem. Am., Mich., Detroit, Macomb County bar assns., Am. Arbitration Assn., Assn. Trial Lawyers. Office: 18850 E Nine Mile Rd East Detroit MI 48021

GLUCK, DANIEL JOSEPH, b. Toledo, Apr. 9, 1914; Ph.B., U. Toledo, 1935; J.D., U. Mich., 1938. Admitted to Ohio bar, 1938, Ill. bar, 1948; sr. partner firm Arnstein, Gluck, Weitzenfeld & Minow, Chgo., 1948—. Mem. Chgo., Ill. State, Am. bar assns. Home: 790 Heather Ln Winnetka IL 60093 Office: 75th Floor Sears Tower Chicago IL 60606 Tel (312) 876-7100

GLUSAC, MICHAEL M., b. Highland Park, Mich, July 28, 1930; B.A., Wayne State U., 1953, J.D., 1956. Admitted to Mich. bar, 1956; individual practice law, Highland Park, 1956-70; corp. counsel City of Detroit, 1970-74; exec. dir. S.E. Mich. Council of Govts., Detroit, 1974—; councilman City of Highland Park, 1963-65, mayor, 1965-68, council pres., 1968-70; instr. bus. adminstrn. Wayne State U., 1959-61; exec. chmn. Detroit-Wayne County Criminal Justice System Coordinating Council, 1972-73; mem. Govt.'s Spl. Commn. on Local Govt., 1971-72, Gov.'s Task Force on Option Process, 1972-73; mem. staff dir.'s adv. council Nat. Assn. Regional Councils, 1975-77; mem. Mich. Econ. Action Council, 1975-76. Pres. Mich. Municipal League, 1969-70; mem. Wayne County Bd. Suprs., 1967-68. Mem. Am. Judicature Soc., Detroit, Mich., Am., Highland Park (past pres.) bar assns. Home: 90 Meadow Ln Grosse Pointe Farms MI 48236 Office: 810 Book Bldg Detroit MI 48226 Tel (313) 961-4266

GLYNN, WILLIAM EDWARD, b. Schenectady, N.Y., July 7, 1923; B.S., U.S. Mil. Acad., 1945; LL.B., Harvard, 1953. Admitted to Conn. bar, U.S. Dist. Ct. bar, 1954; asso. firm Day, Berry & Howard, Hartford, Conn., 1953-59, partner, 1959—. Mem. Hartford Housing Authority, 1957-61; mayor of Hartford, 1961-63, 63-65; vice chmn. distribution com. Hartford Found. Pub. Giving, pres. Hartford Pub. Library, 1973—. Mem. Am., Conn., Hartford County bar assns. Home: 84 Westerly Terr Hartford CT 06105 Office: One Constitution Plaza Hartford CT 06103 Tel (203) 278-1330

GOATER, RICHARD ALFRED, b. Rochester, N.Y., Nov. 9, 1921; A.B., Ohio Wesleyan U., 1947; J.D., U. Cin., 1949. Admitted to Ohio bar, 1949; practiced in Piqua, Ohio, 1949-74; judge probate and juvenile div., Miami County (Ohio) Common Pleas Ct., 1974—; city commr., mayor City of Piqua, 1956-57. Mem. Ohio Bar Assn., Ohio, Nat. assns. probate and juvenile ct. judges. Home: 1113 Maplewood Dr Piqua OH 45356 Office: Miami County Safety Bldg Troy OH 45373 Tel (513) 335-8341

GOBBEL, LUTHER RUSSELL, b. Durham, N.C., May 17, 1930; A.B., Duke, 1952; J.D., Harvard, 1955. Admitted to Tenn. bar, 1955, Md. bar, 1972; asst. counsel Bur. Ordnance, Navy Dept., Washington, 1955-59, asst. counsel Bur. Naval Weapons, San Diego, 1959-65; sr. atty. electronic div. Gen. Dynamics Corp., Rochester, N.Y., 1965-70; sec., gen. counsel Litton Bionetics, Inc., Kensington, Md., 1970—; counsel Amecom div. Litton Systems, Inc., College Park Md., 1970—; panel arbitrators Am. Arbitration Assn., 1969—; del. 9th Circuit Jud. Conf., 1964. Mem. Harper's Choice Village Bd., Columbia, Md., 1972-75; chmn. Columbia Combined Bds., Md., 1973; mem. Howard County (Md.) Criminal Justice Task Force, 1975-76; mem. Howard County Police Tng. Adv. Bd., 1976—. Mem. Am., Md., Fed. (nat. council 1962-71, nat. v.p. 9th dist. 1963-64, pres. San Diego chpt. 1962-63) bar assns., Nat. Security Indsl. Assn. (procurement advisory com., legal and spl. task sub-com). Adv. bd. Bur. Nat. Affairs Fed. Procurement Reports. Home: 10931 Swansfield Rd Columbia MD 21044 Office: 5115 Calvert Rd College Park MD 20740 Tel (301) 864-5600

GOBER, HENRY FRED, b. Gainesville, Ga., Apr. 30, 1917; A.B., Columbia, 1939; LL.B., 1942. Admitted to Ga. bar, 1945, U.S. Supreme Ct. bar, 1974; asso. firm Dunaway, Riley & Howard, Atlanta, 1946-50; gen. counsel Atlanta Legal Aid Soc., 1950-55; partner firm Arnall, Golden & Gregory, Atlanta, 1955—; instr. Ga. Inst. Tech., 1950-60; lectr. law Emory Univ., 1955-65; mem. Ga. Court Commn., 1965, Fulton County Court Commn., 1974. Pres. East Lake Civic Club, Atlanta, 1948. Mem. Ga., Atlanta bar assns., Lawyers Club of Atlanta. Editor Supplemental Code, City of Atlanta Compendium of Laws-Armed Forces, 1954; contbr. articles in field to profl. jours. Home: 4358 Northside Dr NW Atlanta GA 30327 Office: 1000 Fulton Federal Building Atlanta GA 30303 Tel (404) 577-5100

GOCHMAN, ARTHUR MORTON, b. N.Y.C., Jan. 18, 1931; B.S., Trinity U., San Antonio, 1951; LL.B., U. Tex., Austin, 1954. Admitted to Tex. bar, 1954, U.S. Supreme Ct. bar, 1970; partner firm Maverick, Tynan & Gochman, San Antonio, 1958-68, firm Gochman & Weir, San Antonio, 1968—. Mem. State Bar Tex., Am., Tex. trial lawyers assns., Am. Judicature Soc., Am. Bar Assn. Editor Tex. Law Rev., 1953-54. Home: 314 Joliet Ave San Antonio TX 78209 Office: Suite 555 711 Navarro St San Antonio TX 78205 Tel (512) 226-9102

GOCHNAUER, LOIS ANN, b. Mason City, Wash., May 29, 1942; B.A. magna cum laude, Butler U., 1964; J.D., State U. N.Y., Buffalo, 1969; LL.M., Free U. Brussels, 1977. Admitted to N.Y. bar, 1970; atty. FCC, Washington, 1969-70, FPC, 1971, HEW, Washington, 1970—. Mem. Am. Bar Assn., Phi Kappa Phi. Recipient Am. Jurisprudence awards, 1968, 69; Glamour Mag. Outstanding Young Working Women award, 1976. Mem. Nat. Ballet Can., 1964-66, San Francisco Ballet, 1964. Home: Oakmont North Garden VA 22959 Office: Office Gen Counsel HEW Washington DC 20201 Tel (202) 245-8952

GODA, ALAN MASATO, b. Rivers, Ariz., Feb. 25, 1945; B.B.A., U., Hawaii, 1967; J.D., U. Mich., 1970. Admitted to Hawaii bar, 1970; law clk. Supreme Ct. Hawaii, Honolulu, 1970-71, dep. atty., 1971-73; partner firm Padgett, Greeley & Marumoto, Honolulu, 1973-75; asso. firm Kobayashi, Koshiba & Watanabe, Honolulu, 1975—. Commn. Hawaii Environ. Quality Com., 1974—. Mem. Hawaii Bar Assn. Office: 814 Hawaii Bldg 745 Fort St Honolulu HI 96813 Tel (808) 524-5700

GODBOLD, GENE HAMILTON, b. Mullins, S.C., June 14, 1936; A.B., Furman U., 1958; LL.B., Tulane U., 1963. Admitted to Fla. bar, 1963; asso. firm Maguire, Voorhis & Wells, Orlando and Winter Park, Fla., 1963—; dir. Attys. Title Services, Inc., Orange County, 1970-73, pres., 1972-73; pres. Legal Aid Soc. Orange County, Inc., 1971, 72. Bd. dirs. Participation Enriches Sci., Arts and Cultural Orgns., Winter Park, 1968, 76, v.p., 1968. Mem. Orange County (exec. com. 1968-73, pres. 1971-72), Fla. (co-chmn. conv. com. 1975-76) bar assns. Home: 2148 Via Tuscany Winter Park FL 32789 Office: 180 Park Ave N Winter Park FL 32789 Tel (305) 843-4421

GODBOLD, JOHN COOPER, b. Coy, Ala., Mar. 24, 1920; B.S., Auburn U., 1940; J.D., Harvard, 1948. Admitted to Ala. bar, 1948; practiced in Montgomery, 1948-66; judge U.S. Ct. Appeals for 5th Circuit, 1966—. Home: 3590 Thomas Ave Montgomery AL 36111 Office: Fed Courthouse Montgomery AL 36102 Tel (205) 832-7211

GODDARD, SAMUEL PEARSON, JR., b. Clayton, Mo., Aug. 8, 1919; A.B., Harvard Coll., 1941; LL.B., U. Ariz., 1949. Ariz. bar, 1949; partner firm Goddard & Ahearn, Tucson, 1975—; gov. State of Ariz., 1965-66. Bd. govs. United Way Am., 1972—; Democratic nat. committeeman Ariz., 1977. Mem. Am., Ariz., Pima, Maricopa County bar assns., Res. Officers Assn., Air Force Assn., Nat. Rowing Found., Phi Alpha Delta. Address: Ariz Bank Bldg 101 N 1st Ave Phoenix AZ 85003

GODFREY, MICHAEL FITZGERALD, b. Litchfield, Ill., June 11, 1921; B.A., U. Notre Dame, 1942, LL.B., 1948. Admitted to Ill. bar, 1949, Mo. bar, 1949; practiced in East Saint Louis, Ill., 1949-51, Litchfield, 1951-53, St. Louis, 1954-65; judge Mo. Circuit Ct., 22d Jud. Circuit, 1965—; spl. judge Mo. Supreme Ct. and St. Louis Ct. Appeals, 1965-70. Chmn. Litchfield chpt. ARC, 1952; active St. Louis area council Boy Scouts Am., 1965-68. Mem. Mo. Bar Integrated, Met. Bar Assn. St. Louis Lawyers Assn., Am. Judicature Soc., Delta Phi. Recipient Knight of Year award K.C., 1965. Home: 6247 Westway Pl Saint Louis MO 63109 Office: Civil Cts Bldg 10 N 12th St Saint Louis MO 63101 Tel (314) 453-3011

GODFREY, OTIS HICKMAN, JR., b. St. Paul, Nov. 16, 1924; B.A., Yale, 1947; LL.B., U. Minn., 1950. Admitted to Minn. bar, 1950; individual practice law, St. Paul, 1950-61; spl. asst. atty. gen., Minn., 1951-53; municipal judge, St. Paul, 1961-68; judge Minn. Dist. Ct., St. Paul, 1968—. Bd. dirs. St. Paul chpt. ARC, 1963—; active YMCA, St. Paul, 1963—, Hallie G. Brown Community House, 1961-73. Mem. Minn., Hennepin County bar assns., Internat. Acad. Trial Judges (regent) Home: 772 Fairmont Ave St Paul MN 55105 Office: 1539 Courthouse St Paul MN 55102 Tel (612) 298-4710

GODLIN, HAROLD NATHANIEL, b. Stamford, Conn., Oct. 24, 1926; A.B., Brown U., 1950; J.D., Harvard, 1953. Admitted to Conn. bar, 1953, U.S. Supreme Ct. bar, 1960; asso. firm Beizer & Beizer, Hartford, 1953-54; partner firm Godlin, Rondos & Godlin, Stamford, 1954—; dir. Gerber Life Ins. Co., 1973—. Pres. Stamford Pop Warner Football League, 1960-61. Mem. Stamford, Conn., Am. bar assns. Home: 18 Toms Rd Stamford CT 06906 Office: 832 Bedford St Stamford CT 06901 Tel (203) 324-7383

GODOFSKY, STANLEY, b. N.Y.C., May 24, 1928; A.B. Columbia U., 1949, J.D., 1951. Admitted to N.Y. bar, 1951, U.S. Supreme Ct. bar, 1961; asso. Rogers and Wells and predecessor firms, N.Y.C., 1951-64, partner, 1965—; special asst. counsel N.Y. State Crime Commn., 1952. Mem. Assn. Bar City N.Y., Am., N.Y. State bar assns., Fed. Bar Council, Am. Judicature Soc., Internat. Bar Assn., Union Internationale de Avocats, World Assn. Lawyers, Internat. Assn. Jewish Lawyers and Jurists. Mem. bd. editors Columbia Law Review, 1950, revising editor, 1951. Home: 22 Holbrooke Rd White Plains NY 10605 Office: 200 Park Ave New York City NY 10017 Tel (212) 972-3978

GODSON, FRANK GEORGE, b. Elizabeth, N.J., Apr. 20, 1928; B.A., Colgate U., 1948; J.D., Yale, 1951. Admitted to N.Y. bar, 1951, U.S. Dist. Ct. bar for Western Dist. N.Y., 1961, U.S. Ct. Appeals bar, 2d Circuit, 1975; asso. firm Dudley, Stowe & Sawyer, Buffalo, 1951-61; asso. firm Smith, Murphy & Schoepperle, Buffalo, 1961-65, partner, 1966—. Mem. Erie County (N.Y.) bar assn., Erie County Trial Lawyers Assn., Am. Arbitration Assn. Home: 57 Koster Row Eggertsville NY 14226 Office: 786 Ellicott Square Bldg Buffalo NY 14203 Tel (716) 852-1544

GOEBEL, WILLIAM MATHERS, b. Jacksonville, Ill., Nov. 5, 1922; A.B., Ill. Coll., 1946; J.D., U. Mich., 1949. Admitted to Ill. bar, 1949; partner firm Conger, Elliott, Goebel & Elliott, Carmi, Ill., 1949-59; asst. gen. counsel Ill. Agrl. Assn. and affiliated cos., 1959-64; partner firm Dunn, Brady, Goebel, Ulbrich, Morel and Jacob, Bloomington, 1964—; lectr. dept. ednl. adminstrn. Ill. State U.; instr. Ill. Wesleyan U. Mem. Ill. Citizens Com. for Uniform Comml. Code; mem. Ill. Sch. Problems Commn., 1965-69; bd. dirs. Bloomington-Normal Symphony Soc., 1967-73; trustee Brokaw Hosp., Normal, Ill., 1964-69; sec. bd. trustees, mem. exec. com. Ill. Wesleyan U., Bloomington. Mem. Am. Judicature Soc., Am., Ill. (past council chmn. comml. banking and bankruptcy law sect.), McLean County bar assns. Contbr. to U. Ill. Law Forum, 1962. Home: 1311 E Washington St Bloomington IL 61701 Office: 600 Peoples Bank Bldg Bloomington IL 61701 Tel (309) 828-6241

GOEKJIAN, SAMUEL VAHRAM, b. Syra, Greece, Aug. 22, 1927, came to U.S., 1948, naturalized, 1954; B.A., Syracuse U., 1952; J.D., Harvard U., 1957. Admitted to N.Y. State bar, 1958, D.C. bar, 1960; asso. atty. Chase Manhattan Bank Head Office, N.Y.C., 1957-58; counsel Devel. Loan Fund. U.S. Dept. State, Washington, 1958-60; asso. firm Surrey, Karasik & Morse, and predecessors, Washington, 1960-62, mng. partner, Washington, 1962-68, sr. resident partner Beirut, Lebanon, 1968-70, sr. resident partner, Paris, France, 1970—; cons. AID, Washington, 1963, cons. to UN on establishment African Devel. Bank, 1962; lectr. George Washington U. Grad Sch. Pub. Law, 1963-68; lectr. Georgetown Inst. Internat. and Fgn. Trade Law, 1974—. Mem. D.C., Fed., Am., Inter-Am. bar assns., World Peace Through Law Center (charter mem.), Am. Soc. Internat. Law. Contbr. articles to legal jours. Home: 14 Ave Voltaire 78600 Maisons Laffite France Office: 53 Ave Montaigne 75008 Paris France Tel 359-2349

GOELDNER, RALPH HUGO, b. Sigourney, Iowa, Aug. 17, 1908; B.A., U. Iowa, 1931, J.D., 1933. Admitted to Iowa State bar, 1931; individual practice law, Sigourney, 1933-40; partner firm Goeldner & Goeldner, Sigourney, 1940—; atty. Keokuk County (Iowa), 1934-46. Mem. Iowa State, Am. bar assns. Home: 302 W Elm St Sigourney IA 52591 Office: 22 S Main St PO Box 67 Sigourney IA 52591 Tel (515) 622-3300

GOERING, MARLO E., b. Newton, Kans., June 5, 1933; B.S., Bethel Coll., 1956; J.D., Washburn U., 1966. Admitted to Kans. bar, 1966; spl. securities asst. Kans. Corp. Commn., 1966-69; pres. Century Investment Corp., Wichita, Kans., 1969-70; individual practice law, Wichita, 1971—. Treas., West Heights Methodist Ch., Wichita, 1973-74. Mem. Am. Inst. C.P.A.'s, Kans. Bar Assn. Home: 1349 W 135th St Wichita KS 67235 Office: 9100 W Central St Wichita KS 67212 Tel (316) 722-3391

GOERING, ROBERT ALFRED, b. LaPorte, Ind., Nov. 1, 1935; B.A., Yale, 1957; J.D., Salmon P. Chase Coll. Law, 1962. Admitted to Ohio bar, 1962; buyer Proctor & Gamble Co., Cin., 1957-63; asst. prosecutor Hamilton County, Ohio, 1963-64; partner firm Wilke & Goering, Cin., 1964—; adj. prof. law Salmon P. Chase Coll. Law, Covington, Ky., 1971—. Chmn. bd. United Cerebral Palsy Cin., 1967-71; sec. Living for Developmentally Disabled, Inc., 1974-76. Mem. Ohio, Cin. bar assns. Recipient award of merit Ohio Legal Center, 1971. Home: 1 Emery Ln Cincinnati OH 45227 Office: 128 E 6th St Cincinnati OH 45202 Tel (513) 621-0912

GOERINGER, JOAN MOSER, b. Balt., Sept. 16, 1934; A.B., Goucher Coll., 1955; J.D., Georgetown U., 1972. Admitted to Md. bar, 1973; individual practice law, Rockville, Md., 1977—. Mem. Am., Md., Montgomery County bar assns., Phi Delta Phi. Home: 6801 Buttermere Ln Bethesda MD 20034 Office: 354 Hungerford Dr Rockville MD 20850 Tel (301) 424-2828

GOETSCHIUS, FRANCIS ABRAM, b. Suffern, N.Y., Aug. 4, 1912; LL.B., Fordham U., 1937. Admitted to N.Y. bar, 1939; staff officer, labor relations counselor U.S. Maritime Commn., Washington, 1941-49; individual practice law, Suffern, N.Y., 1949—; village justice Villages of Shoatsburg and Suffern, 1950-60, Village of Suffern, 1967—. Mem. Romapo Central Sch. Dist., Hillburn (N.Y.) Bd. Edn., 1961—, pres., 1971-72. Mem. Rockland County (N.Y.), N.Y. State magistrates assns., Rockland County, N.Y. State bar assns., Am. Arbitration Assn. (nat. panel 1945—). Home: 11 Pothat St Sloatsburg NY 10974 Office: 31 Park Ave Suffern NY 10901 Tel (914) 357-0050

GOETTEL, GERARD LOUIS, b. N.Y.C., Aug. 5, 1928; B.A., Duke, 1950; LL.D. Columbia, 1955. Admitted to N.Y. bar, 1955, U.S. Supreme Ct. bar, 1959; asst. U.S. atty., N.Y.C., 1955-58; dep. chief atty. gen.'s spl. group on organized crime Dept. Justice, N.Y.C., 1958-59; asso. firm Lowenstein, Pitcher, Hotchkiss, Amann & Parr, N.Y.C., 1959-62; counsel N.Y. Life Ins. Co., N.Y.C., 1962-68; with firm Natanson & Reich, N.Y.C., 1968-69; asso. gen. counsel Overmyer Co., N.Y.C., 1969-71; U.S. magistrate So. Dist. N.Y., 1971-76; judge U.S. Dist. Ct., So. Dist. N.Y., 1976—; asst. counsel N.Y. Ct. on the Judiciary, 1971. Mem. Council Fresh Air Fund, N.Y.C. 1961-64; bd. dirs. Yonkers (N.Y.) Community Action Program, 1964-66; pres. Sprain Lake Civil Assn., Yonkers, 1966. Mem. Am., Westchester County (N.Y.) bar assns., Nat. Conf. Spl. Ct. Judges, Assn. Bar City N.Y. Contbr. articles to legal jours. Home: 6 Chamberlain St Rye NY 10580 Office: US Dist Ct So Dist NY Foley Square New York City NY 10007 Tel (212) 791-0151

GOETZ, CLARENCE EDWARD, b. Balt., Feb. 4, 1932; A.A., U.Balt., 1961, LL.B., 1964. Admitted to Md. bar, 1964; asso. firm Hackney & Yourtee, Anne Arundel County, Md., 1965-66; asst. U.S. atty. for Md., 1966-70; U.S. magistrate for Md., 1970—; asst. prof. law U. Balt., 1975, Towson State Coll., 1976. Mem. Nat. Council U.S. Magistrates. Office: Room 218 US Courthouse 101 W Lombard St Baltimore MD 21202 Tel (301) 962-4560

GOETZL, THOMAS MAXWELL, b. Chgo., May 31, 1943; A.B., U. Calif., Berkeley, 1965, J.D., Boalt Hall, 1969. Admitted to Calif. bar, 1970, Fed. bar, 1970; asso. firm Fleischmann & Farber, San Francisco, 1970-72; asst. prof. law Golden Gate U., San Francisco, 1972-74, asso. prof., 1975—; asso. prof. law Willamette U., Salem, Oreg., 1974-75. Mem. Calif. State Bar Assn., ACLU, Artists Equity (dir. N. Calif. chpt.), Order of Coif. Home: 1019 Keith Ave Berkeley CA 94708 Office: 536 Mission St San Francisco CA 94105 Tel (415) 391-7800

GOFF, ROBERT WILLIAM, JR., b. Houston, Apr. 22, 1946; B.B.A., Tex. Tech. U., 1968; J.D., U. Tex., 1971. Admitted to Tex. bar, 1971; partner firm Sherrill, Pace, Rogers, Crosnoe & Morrison, Wichita Falls, Tex., 1971—. Bd. dirs. Beacon Lighthouse for the Blind, 1974—; mem. phys. bd. YMCA of Wichita Falls, 1973—. Mem. Am., Tex., Wichita County (dir.) bar assns. Home: 350 Morningside Dr Wichita Falls TX 76301 Office: 1100 Hamilton Bldg Wichita Falls TX 76301 Tel (817) 322-3145

GOFFIN, SUMNER J., b. Portland, Maine, June 15, 1919; ed. U. Iowa; LL.B., Peabody Law Sch. Admitted to Maine bar, 1942; practiced in Portland, 1942-73; justice Maine Superior Ct., 1973—; mem. faculty Portland U. Law Sch., 1949-57; mem. Maine Panel of Mediators, 1956-73; chmn. Maine Employees Appeals Bd., 1967-73. Chmn. Yarmouth (Maine) Town Council, 1966-67; bd. dirs. Community Counseling Center, Portland, 1970-74, Blind Children's Resource Center, Portland, 1970—; life bd. dirs. Maine Sight Conservation Assn. Mem. Cumberland, Maine State, Am. bar assns., Nat. Acad. Arbitrators, Am. Arbitration Assn. Home: 45 Eastern Promenade Portland ME 04101 Office: 142 Federal St Courthouse Portland ME 04111 Tel (207) 773-7067

GOFREED, HOWARD, b. N.Y.C., June 16, 1947; B.A., George Washington U., 1969; J.D., U. Md., 1973. Admitted to Md. bar, 1973; asso. firm Xavier, Aragona, Oxon Hill, Md., 1973-76; partner firm Yochelson & Gofreed, Oxon Hill, 1976—. Mem. Am., Md., Prince George's County bar assns. Office: 10905 Fort Washington Rd Suite 102 Oxon Hill MD 20022 Tel (301) 292-5505

GOGEL, WILLIAM ALAN, b. Bklyn., June 5, 1942; B.A., Western Res. U., 1964; J.D., Boston U., 1967. Admitted to N.Y. State bar, 1968; asst. dist. atty., Kings County, N.Y., 1968-70; asso. counsel Patrolmen's Benevolent Assn., N.Y.C., 1970-72; partner firm Corso, Agulnick & Gogel, Bklyn., 1972—; cons. Mobil Oil Corp. Mem. N.Y. State, Nassau County, Kings County bar assns. Home: 25 Woodgreen Ln East Hills NY 11577 Office: 32 Court St Brooklyn NY 11201 Tel (212) 624-6650

GOGGINS, ROBERT JAMES, b. Fond du Lac, Wis., June 10, 1936; B.S., Wis. State U., Oshkosh, 1962; J.D., William Mitchell Coll. Law, 1967. Admitted to Wis. bar, 1968, Minn. bar, 1968; asso. firm C.J. Schloemer, West Bend, Wis., 1968-69; partner firm O'Neill, Goggins & Traxler, New Prague, Minn., 1969—; asst. Scott County (Minn.) atty., 1969-74; city atty. City of New Prague, 1969—. Mem. Am. Judicature Soc., Nat. Dist. Attys. Assn. (asso.), 8th Dist. Bar Assn. (pres. 1976). Home: Rural Route 2 Box 286 New Prague MN 56071 Office: Law Bldg 222 E Main St New Prague MN 56071 Tel (612) 758-2568

GOICOECHEA, ROBERT BRIAN, b. Wendell, Idaho, June 22, 1945; B.S., Loyola U., Chgo., 1967; J.D., U. Utah, 1970. Admitted to Utah bar, 1970, Nev. bar, 1972, U.S. Supreme Ct. bar, 1974; law clk. Chief Justice J. Allan Crockett Utah Supreme Ct., 1969-70; asso. firm Roe, Fowler, Jerman & Dart, Salt Lake City, 1970-71; asso. firm Vaughan, Hull, Marfisi, Goicoechea & Miller, Elko, Nev., 1972-73, partner, 1974-75; partner firm Goicoechea & di Grazia, Elko, 1976—; atty. City of Wells, Nev., 1976—, City of Carlin, Nev., 1976—; chief judge TeMoak Bands of the Western Shoshone, 1976—. Mem. Nev. State Republican Central Com., 1974; chmn. Elko County Heart Fund, 1974; mem. Nev. Humanities Com. of Nat. Endowment for Humanities, 1974—. Mem. Am., Utah, Elko County bar assns., State Bar Nev., Elko C. of C. Home: 354 W Oak St Elko NV 89801 Office: 463 5th St Elko NV 89801 Tel (702) 738-8091

GOLBERT, ALBERT SIDNEY, b. Denver, Nov. 26, 1932; B.S., U. So. Calif., 1954; J.D., U. Denver, 1956; LL.M., U. Mich., 1964; D. es Sc., U. Geneva, 1968. Admitted to Colo. bar, 1957, Calif. bar, 1958, U.S. Supreme Ct. bar, 1964, Mich. bar, 1970; assoc. firm Oxman & Snyder, Denver, 1957-58; served to capt. JAGC, USAF, 1958-61; sr. atty. Chrysler Corp., Detroit, 1961-70; counsel Paul & Gordon, Los Angeles, 1970-71, Diamond, Tilem, Colden & Emery, Los Angeles, 1971-74; partner firm Forry Golbert & Singer, Los Angeles and San Francisco, 1974—; adj. prof. law Southwestern U., 1970-71, asso. prof., 1971-73, prof. law, head dept. internat. legal studies, 1973-77, adj. prof., 1977—. Mem. Am., Internat., Calif., Colo., Mich. bar assns., Internat. Law Assn., Am. Soc. Internat. Law (asso. editor-in-chief jour. The Internat. Lawyer), Hague Internat. Lawyers Inter-Group. Author: (with Arthur I. Rosett) Cases and Materials on International Trade and Investment, 1973; Inter-American Law and Institutions (with Yenny Nun Gingold), 1974; contbr. articles to legal jours. Home: 301 Conway Ave Los Angeles CA 90024 Office: 1800 Century Park E Los Angeles CA 90067 Tel (213) 277-0300

GOLD, HOWARD ARTHUR, b. Bronx, N.Y., May 8, 1945; B.A. in Govt. and Pub. Adminstrn., Am. U., 1967; J.D., U. Cin., 1970. Admitted to N.Y. bar, 1971, D.C. bar, 1971, Ga. bar, 1974; research asso. So. Edn. Found., Washington, 1968; staff atty. Indian Claims Commn., Washington, 1971-72; individual practice law, Washington, 1972-74; partner firm Nadler, Gold & Beskin, Atlanta, 1974—; cons. Atlanta Pub. Defender Program, 1975—; legal counsel Am.-Vietnamese Assn. of Ga., 1975—. Mem. Atlanta, Ga., D.C. bar assns., Criminal Trial Lawyers Assn., Am.-Vietnamese Assn. Home: 1105 Rosedale Dr Atlanta GA 30306 Office: 2500 Nat Bank of Ga Atlanta GA 30303 Tel (404) 522-6778

GOLD, LAWRENCE MICHAEL, b. Atlanta, Jan. 5, 1944; B.A., U. Va., 1965, LL.B., 1968. Admitted to Ga. bar, 1968; mem. firm Powell, Goldstein, Frazer & Murphy, Atlanta, 1969—. Mem. Am., Ga. bar assns. Office: 1100 C&S National Bank Bldg Atlanta GA 30303 Tel (404) 521-1900

GOLD, MARTIN ELLIOT, b. N.Y.C., Jan. 6, 1946; A.B., Cornell U., 1967; J.D., Harvard, 1970, M.Pub. Adminstrn., 1971. Admitted to N.Y. State bar, 1972; research fellow Internat. Legal Center, Ceylon, 1971-72, Cambridge, Mass., 1972-73; asso. firm Debevoise, Plimpton, Lyons & Gates, N.Y.C., 1973—; atty. Community Law Office, N.Y.C., 1974—, Sierra Club, 1975—; judge moot ct. finals Am. Soc. Internat. Law, 1975. Mem. Asia Soc., Sri Lanka Council, Bar. Assn. City N.Y., Legal Aid Soc., Am. Econ. Assn., Law and Soc. Assn. Author: Law and Social Change: A Study of Land Reform in Sri Lanka, 1977. Contbr. articles to legal and econ. jours. Home: 330 W 72d St New York City NY 10023 Office: 299 Park Ave New York City NY 10017 Tel (212) 752-6400

GOLD, MYRON MIKE, b. N.Y.C., July 4, 1930; B.B.A., U. Miami, 1951, J.D., 1953. Admitted to Fla. bar, 1953, U.S. Supreme Ct. bar, 1961; asst. state atty. State of Fla., Miami, 1955-61; mem. firm Huysman, Engel & Gold, 1961-71, firm Gold & Fox, Miami, 1971—; vol. pub. defender Miami, 1974—. Mem. Democratic exec. com., Miami, 1977—, precinct capt., 1974-76. Mem. NOW, Men for ERA, ERA Coalition, LWV. Office: 4651 Ponce de Leon Blvd Coral Gables FL 33146 Tel (305) 667-2512

GOLDBAUM, ARTHUR, b. Bklyn., June 25, 1910; LL.B., St. Lawrence U., 1931. Admitted to N.Y. State bar, 1932, Ariz. bar, 1948; practiced in N.Y. State, 1932-47; individual practice law, Tucson, 1948-69; partner firm Goldbaum & Goetz, Tucson, 1969—. Pres., Pima County (Ariz.) Legal Aid Soc., 1973-75. Mem. Am., Pima County (pres., 1960) bar assns. Home: 5221 E Holmes St Tucson AZ 85711 Office: 1403 Home Fed Tower 32 N Stone St Tucson AZ 85701 Tel (602) 622-7483

GOLDBERG, ALAN JOEL, b. Bklyn., Jan. 22, 1943; B.B.A., U. Miami, 1965, J.D., 1968. Admitted to Fla. bar, 1968; asso. firm Goldberg, Young & Goldberg, P.A., and precedessors, Ft. Lauderdale, 1968-75, sr. partner, 1975—; atty. City of Margate (Fla.), 1969-70, City of Tamarac (Fla.), 1970-71. Mem. Am., Fla. bar assns. Office: 2881 E Commercial Blvd Fort Lauderdale FL 33308 Tel (305) 771-8550

GOLDBERG, ARTHUR ABBA, b. Jersey City, N.J., Nov. 25, 1940; A.B. with honors, Am. U., 1962; LL.B., Cornell U., 1965. Admitted to N.J. bar, 1965, Conn. bar, 1966, U.S. Supreme Ct. bar, 1968; intern, mem. staff to senator, 1962; law clk. firm DeSevo & Cerutti, Jersey City, 1964; adminstrv. asst. to congressman, Ohio, 1966-67; individual practice law Jersey City, 1965—; asst. prof. law U. Conn., 1965-67; dep. atty. gen. State of N.J., 1967-70; counsel N.J. Dept. Community Affairs and Housing Fin. Agency, 1967-70; gen. counsel N.J. chpt. Municipal Fin. Officers Assn., 1969-73, N.J. chpt. Nat. Assn. Housing and Redevelopment Ofcls., 1968-74; v.p., mgr. municipal fin. dept. Matthews & Wright Inc., N.Y.C., 1970—; lectr. Practicing Law Inst., N.Y.C., 1970—; adj. lectr. Rutgers U., 1972—; v.p., Alfus Corp., Jersey City, 1965—; managing partner Bank Bldg. Assos., Jersey City, 1975—; dir. Titan Industries, 1975—; Cooperating atty. NAACP Legal Defense Fund, 1965—; mem. exec. com. N.J. Commn. on Discrimination in Housing, 1968-74; chmn. Nat. Leased Housing Assn., 1973—; bd. dirs. S. Bronx Community Housing, Inc., 1975—; mem. urban advisory council Anti-Defamation League, 1971-74; spl. cons. on zoning Nat. Com. Discrimination in Housing, 1967-72; chmn. Com. for Absorption of Soviet Emigres, 1975—; pres. The New Synagogue, Jersey City, 1972—; treas. Hebrew Free Loan of N.J.; dir. Jersey City Hebrew Free Loan Assn., 1968—; chmn. Met. N.Y. Com. Soviet Jewry, 1976—. Mem. Conn. Assn. Municipal Attys. (mem. exec. com. 1966-67, editor Newsletter 1967), Nat. Housing Conf., Am., N.J. (chmn. com. on housing and urban renewal 1972-75), Conn., Hudson County bar assns., Am. Polit. Sci. Assn., Nat. Acad. Polit. and Social Sci., Council Jewish Orgns. Jersey City (treas. 1975-76), Omicron Delta Kappa, Pi Gamma Mu, Pi Sigma Alpha, Pi Delta Epsilon. Author: Financing Housing and Urban Development, 1972; Zoning and Land Use, 1972; Tax-Exempt Financing of Industrial Development and Pollution Abatement Facilities, 1973. Contbr. articles to legal jours. Home: 83 Montgomery St Jersey City NJ 07302 Office: Matthews & Wright 14 Wall St New York City NY 10005 Tel (212) 248-8890

GOLDBERG, ARTHUR IRWIN, b. N.Y.C., July 24, 1932; B.S., Bklyn. Coll. Pharmacy, L.I. U., 1953; LL.B., N.Y. U., 1959, LL.M., 1962. Admitted to N.Y. bar, 1962, U.S. Supreme Ct. bar, 1964; asso. firm Lader, Waldman & Schuh, Jamaica, N.Y., 1959-60, Louis Wallach, Jamaica, 1961; partner firm Jacobson & Goldberg, Mineola and Garden City, N.Y., 1961—; prof. pharmacy adminstrn. L.I. U., 1965-70; village justice, East Hills, N.Y., 1970—. Trustee L.I. U. Sch. Pharmacy. Mem. Nassau County Bar Assn., N.Y. State, Nassau County (dir.) magistrates assns. Contbr. legal articles to publs. Home: 94 Entrance Rd East Hills NY 11577 Office: 591 Stewart Ave Garden City NY 11530 Tel (516) 222-2330

GOLDBERG, ARTHUR JOSEPH, b. Chgo., Aug. 8, 1908; A.A., Coll. City Chgo., 1926; B.S.L., Northwestern U., 1929, J.D. summa cum laude, 1930. Admitted to Ill. bar, 1929, U.S. Supreme Ct. bar, 1937, D.C. bar, 1952, N.Y. bar, 1968; sr. partner firm Goldberg, Devoe, Shadur & Mikva, Chgo., 1945-61, Goldberg, Feller & Bredhoff, Washington, 1952-61; gen. counsel CIO, 1948-55, United Steelworkers Am., 1948-61; spl. counsel AFL-CIO, 1955-61; sec. Dept. Labor, 1961-62; asso. justice U.S. Supreme Ct., Washington, 1962-65; ambassador to UN, 1965-68; sr. partner firm Paul, Weiss, Goldberg, 1962-65; ambassador to UN, 1965-68; sr. partner firm Paul, Weiss, Goldberg, Rifkind, Wharton & Garrison, N.Y.C., 1968-71; individual practice law, Washington, 1971—; Charles Evans Hughes prof. Princeton, 1968-69; distinguished prof. Columbia, 1969-70; prof. law and diplomacy Am. U., Washington, 1972-73; vis. distinguished prof. Hastings Coll. Law, San Francisco, 1974—. Former chmn. pres.'s Com. Migratory Labor, Pres.'s Missile Sites Labor Commn., Pres.'s Com. on Youth Employment, Employer-Mgmt. Relations Program, Workers Adv. Com. on U.S., Pres.'s Adv. Com. on Labor-Mgmt. Policy, Pres.'s Com. on Equal Employment Opportunity; former ex-officio mem. and ad hoc participant NSC; former pres. Internat. Edn. Assn.; hon. pres. Am. Jewish Com. Mem. Am., Ill., Chgo., D.C. bar assns., Assn. Bar City N.Y. Author: AFL-CIO Labor United, 1956; Defenses of Freedom, 1966; Equal Justice; the Warren Era of the Supreme Court, 1972; contbr. articles to legal jours. Office: 1101 17th St NW Washington DC 20036 Tel (202) 293-3868

GOLDBERG, ARTHUR ROBERT, b. Washington, Mar. 28, 1947; A.B., Princeton, 1969; J.D., Georgetown U., 1972. Admitted to Md. bar, 1973, D.C. bar, 1974; law clk. Pa. Supreme Ct., 1972-73; asso. firm Sachs, Greenebaum & Tayler, Washington, 1973—. Office: 1620 I St NW Washington DC 20006 Tel (202) 872-9090

GOLDBERG, CHARLES, b. Denver, July 28, 1939; B.A., U. Colo., 1961; J.D., U. Denver, 1964. Admitted to Colo. bar, 1964, since practiced in Denver; partner firm Goldberg and Pred, 1964-65; asso. firm Van Cise, Freeman, Phillips & Goldberg and predecessors, 1965-67, partner, 1968-74; dist. judge 2d Jud. Dist. Colo., 1974—. Trustee Nat. Asthma Center, 1968—. Mem. Colo., Denver (chmn. Young lawyers sect. 1969-70) bar assns. Office: City and County Bldg Denver CO 80202 Tel (303) 297-5559

GOLDBERG, EDWARD CHARLES, b. Norwich, Conn., Sept. 19, 1942; B.A., U. Conn., 1964, J.D., W.Va. U., 1967. Admitted to W.Va. bar; individual practice law, Charleston, W.Va., 1969—; asst. prof. W. Va. State Coll., 1969-74, asso. prof., 1974—; served with JAGC, USNR. Mem. Am., W.Va. State, Kanawha County (W.Va.) bar assns. Home: 1955 Parkwood Rd Charleston WV 25314 Office: Commerce Square Suite 910 Charleston WV 25301 Tel (314) 342-6107

GOLDBERG, JACQUELINE MAE, b. New Orleans, Dec. 10, 1943; B.S. in Bus. Adminstrn., U. New Orleans, 1966; J.D., Loyola U., 1972. Admitted to La. bar, 1972, U.S. Supreme Ct. bar, 1976, U.S. Customs Ct., 1972; individual practice law, New Orleans, 1972—. Mem. Am., La. bar assns., Am., La. trial lawyers assns., Hadassah Council Jewish Women, U. New Orleans Alumni Assn. (dir. 1974-75). Office: 4655 Michoud Blvd Suites 2 and 4 New Orleans LA 70129 Tel (504) 254-1482

GOLDBERG, JEROME ALLAN, b. Chgo., Feb. 3, 1932; B.S., U. Ill., 1957; J.D., DePaul U., 1963. Admitted to Ill. bar, 1963, Calif. bar, 1973; partner firm Goldberg & Goldberg, Chgo., 1967—; fed. estate tax atty., 1963-66; lectr. in field. Mem. Fed., Am., Ill., Calif., Chgo. bar assns., Decalogue Soc. Lawyers. Office: 11 S LaSalle St Chicago IL 60603 Tel (312) 368-0255

GOLDBERG, LEE H., b. Pitts., May 14, 1942; B.S., W.Va. U., 1964; J.D., U. Pitts., 1970. Admitted to Pa. bar, 1970; asso. firm Flaherty & Bloch, Pitts., 1970-72, firm Berkman, Ruslander, Pohl, Lieber & Engel, Pitts., 1972-74; partner firm Goldberg & Snodgrass, Pitts., 1974—. Bd. dirs. A Better Chance, 1974—; chief adviser, nat. coordinator Nat. Task Force Phys. Fitness. Mem. Am., Pa., Allegheny County bar assns., Allegheny County Tax Soc., Am. Arbitration Assn. Contbr. articles to legal jours. Office: 1312 Frick Bldg Pittsburgh PA 15219

GOLDBERG, LEO MONROE, b. Providence, Feb. 28, 1907; A.B., Brown U., 1928; LL.B., Yale, 1931. Admitted to R.I. bar, 1931, Mass. Bar, 1936, U.S. Dist. Ct., R.I., 1932; U.S. Dist. Ct. Mass., 1949, U.S. 1st Circuit Ct. Appeals, 1952; asso. firm Voigt, O'Neil & Monroe and predecessor firm, Providence 1931-34; partner firm Goldberg & Goldberg, Providence, 1935—; pub. defender R.I. Superior Ct., 1936-37. Mem. Am., R.I., Mass. bar assns. Home: 52 Lorraine Ave Providence RI 02906 Office: 36 Kennedy Plaza Providence RI 02903 Tel (401) 331-6221

GOLDBERG, LOUIS SAMUEL, b. N.Y.C., Apr. 27, 1897; LL.B., Fordham U., 1919. Admitted to Iowa bar, 1925, U.S. Supreme Ct. bar, 1968; sr. partner Goldberg, Wilkinson & Redshaw, Sioux City, Iowa, C.P.A.'s, 1928-76; sr. partner firm Goldberg, Mayne, Probasco, Berenstein & Yeager, Sioux City, 1928-76. Bd. dirs. Travelers Aid Soc. Sioux City, 1950-70. Mem. Am. Bar Assn., Am. Inst. C.P.A.'s, Iowa Soc. C.P.A.'s (past pres.), Am. Assn. Atty. C.P.A.'s (hon. past pres., dir.). Author: Tax Planning Manual, 1973; Book of American Family Poetry, 1976; contbr. articles to profl. jours. Home: 2 37th St Pl Sioux City IA 51104 Office: Commerce Bldg Sioux City IA 51101 Tel (712) 252-3226

GOLDBERG, MARTIN STANFORD, b. Youngstown, Ohio, July 11, 1924; B.S. in Bus. Adminstrn., Ohio State U., 1952, J.D., 1952. Admitted to Ohio bar, 1952, U.S. Supreme Ct. bar, 1961; individual practice law, Youngstown, 1952—. Mem. Am., Mahoning County, Ohio State bar assns., Ohio State Trial Lawyers, Am. Trial Lawyers Assn. Home: 5750 Lockwood Blvd Youngstown OH 44512 Office: 20 1/2 W Boardman St Youngstown OH 44503 Tel (216) 743-2659

GOLDBERG, MAX FREDERICK, b. Globe, Ariz., Apr. 11, 1899; B.S., Harvard, 1922, LL.B., 1925; Admitted to Ill. bar, 1925; asso. firm Levinson, Becker, Frank, Glenn & Barnes, Chgo., 1925-29; asso. with John P. Barnes, Chgo., 1929-31; partner firm King, Barnes & Goldberg, Chgo., 1931-33; individual practice law, Chgo., 1933-38; partner firm Goldberg & Lawrence, Chgo., 1938-47; partner firm Lawrence, Goldberg, Lawrence & Lewin, Chgo., 1947-72; of counsel firm Lawrence, Lawrence, Kamin, & Saunders, Chgo., 1972—. Mem. Am., Ill. State, Chgo. bar assns., Zeta Beta Tau. Home: 1520 Sheridan Rd Highland Park IL 60035 Office: 209 S LaSalle St Chicago IL 60604 Tel (312) 372-1947

GOLDBERG, MORTON DAVID, b. Chgo., May 27, 1929; A.B. magna cum laude, Harvard, 1951; LL.B., Yale, 1954. Admitted to N.Y. State bar, 1955, U.S. Supreme Ct. bar, 1959; partner firm Schwab & Goldberg, N.Y.C., 1962—; mem. working group on new technologies and copyright Com. on Sci. and Tech. Info., Fed. Council Sci. and Tech., 1969-72; mem. copyright adv. com. Office Edn., 1968-70; cons. in field. Mem. Copyright Soc. U.S.A. (past pres., hon. trustee 1974—), Am. Bar Assn. (chmn. com. on copyright and new tech. 1974-75, chmn. com. on trade secrets 1975-76, chmn. com. unfair competition 1976—), Computer Law Assn., U. S. Trademark Assn. (chmn. lawyers adv. com. 1972-74), Assn. Bar City N.Y. (chmn. com. on copyright and literary property 1966-69), Am. (bd. mgrs. 1972-75, chmn. copyright com. 1969-72), N.Y. (chmn. copyright com. 1970-71, bd. govs. 1972-75) patent law assns., Info. Industry Assn., Am. Soc. Info. Sci., Assn. Computing Machinery, Nat. Micrographics Assn., Phi Beta Kappa. Author: (with Harriet F. Pilpel) A Copyright Guide, 4th edit. 1969; editorial adv. bd. Patent, Trademark & Copyright Jour., Bur. Nat. Affairs, 1971—; contbr. articles to legal jours. Home: 14 Ridge Rd Chappaqua NY 10514 Office: 1185 Ave of Americas New York City NY 10036 Tel (212) 575-8150

GOLDBERG, PAUL JOSEPH, b. N.Y.C., July 18, 1937; A.B., Brown U., 1959; LL.B., Columbia, 1962. Admitted to N.Y. State bar, 1963; asso. firm Chester C. Davis, N.Y.C., 1962-68; partner firm Davis & Cox, N.Y.C., 1968-71, Lea, Goldberg & Spellun, Profl. Corp., N.Y.C., 1971-77, Kissam, Halpin & Genovese, N.Y.C., 1977—. Mem. Am., N.Y. State bar assns., N.Y. County Lawyers Assn. Home: 28 W Horseshoe Dr East Hills NY 11577 Office: 120 Broadway New York City NY 10005 Tel (212) 962-2000

GOLDBERG, STEVEN DAVID, b. Wilmington, Del., Feb. 3, 1946; B.A., U. Del., 1968; J.D. with honors, George Washington U., 1971. Admitted to Del. bar, 1971; partner firm Theisen, Lank, Mulford & Goldberg, Wilmington. Chmn. bd. dirs. Albert Einstein Acad., 1975—; bd. dirs. Jewish Nat. Fund of Del., 1975—; bd. dirs. Beth Shalom Congregation, 1976. Mem. Am., Del. bar assns., Phi Alpha Delta. Home: 4406 Tennyson Rd Brandywine Hills Wilmington DE 19802 Office: 1118 Wilmington Trust Bldg PO Box 1470 Wilmington DE 19899 Tel (302) 656-7712

GOLDBERG, STEVEN JAMES, b. Springfield, Mass., Sept. 4, 1945; B.B.A., Boston U., 1967; J.D., 1970. Admitted to Mass. bar, 1970, D.C. bar; staff atty. FTC, Washington, 1970-72; individual practice law, Boston, 1972—; partner firm Litner & Goldberg, Boston. Mem. Am., Mass., Boston bar assns. Office: 19 Milk St Boston MA 02109 Tel (617) 482-2218

GOLDBERGER, CHARLES A., b. N.Y.C., Apr. 10, 1939; A.B., U. Rochester, 1961; J.D., Bklyn. Law Sch., 1964. Admitted to N.Y. bar, 1964, U.S. Supreme Ct. bar, 1971; partner firm Fredericks & Goldberger, White Plains, N.Y., 1968—. Mem. Westchester County, White Plains (pres. 1974) bar assns. Home: Lake Dr Somers NY 10589 Office: 175 Main St White Plains NY 10601 Tel (914) 949-5921

GOLDBERGER, KIM HARVEY, b. Highland Park, Mich., July 16, 1947; B.A., Western Mich. U., 1969; J.D., U. Toledo, 1972. Admitted to Colo. bar, 1972, U.S. Dist. Ct. of Colo., U.S. Ct. Appeals 10th Circuit bar, 1972; individual practice law, Evergreen, Colo., 1972-75; judge Jefferson County (Colo.) Ct., Golden, 1975—. Chmn. bd. dirs. Evergreen Devel. Center, Inc., 1973-75; mem. Evergreen Vol. Fire Dept., 1972-76, pres., 1973-74. Mem. Evergreen C. of C. (pres. 1975-76), Colo., Am., Denver bar assns., First Judicial Dist. Bar Assn. (chmn. Young Lawyers sect.), Assn. County Ct. Judges, Am. Judicature Soc. Office: Hall of Justice Golden CO 80401 Tel (303) 297-7443

GOLDBERGER, MILTON W., b. N.Y.C., Apr. 24, 1913; A.B., N.Y. State Tchrs. Coll., 1935; LL.B., J.D., Harvard U., 1939. Admitted to N.Y. bar, 1939, U.S. Supreme Ct. bar, 1950; sr.partner, mng. partner firm Goldberger, Pedersen & Hochron, Binghamton, N.Y., 1950—. Mem. Broome County, N.Y. State, Am. bar assns., Am. Judicature Soc. Author: Enforcement of Money Office: 19 Chenango St Binghamton NY 13901 Tel (607) 722-7214

GOLDBERGER, PAUL ALAN, b. N.Y.C., May 6, 1941; B.A., Tufts U., 1963; J.D., LL.B., St. Johns U., 1966. Admitted to N.Y. bar, 1966; since practiced in N.Y.C., asst. dist. atty. N.Y. County, 1966-70; partner firm Licht, Asness and Goldberger, 1970-71, firm Goldberger, Feldman and Breitbart, 1971—; advisor N.Y. Cts., 1969-71. Officer United Leukemia Fund, 1975—. Mem. Am., N.Y. State bar assns., N.Y. County Lawyers Assn., N.Y. Criminal Bar Assn., Fed. Bar Council, Assn. Trial Lawyers Am. Home: 9 Pinetree Dr Kings Point NY 11024 Office: 401 Broadway New York City NY 10013 Tel (212) 925-2105

GOLDBERGER, ROBERT ROOSEVELT, b. N.Y.C., May 16, 1908; B.A., Yale U., 1930, LL.B., 1933. Admitted to Conn. bar, 1933, U.S. Dist. Ct. Conn., 1935; individual practice law, Bridgeport, Conn., 1933—. Mem. Conn., Greater Bridgeport (exec. com. 1972-75, chmn. Law Day, 1975, pres. 1976-77) bar assns. Home: Office: 955 Main St Bridgeport CT 06604 Tel (203) 334-2106

GOLDEN, BRUCE PAUL, b. Chgo., Dec. 4, 1943; S.B., Mass. Inst. Tech., 1965, S.M., 1966; J.D., Harvard, 1969. Admitted to Ill. bar, 1969, No. Dist. Ill. bar, 1969; asso. firm McDermott, Will & Emery, Chgo., 1970-75, partner, 1976—. V.p., dir. Positive Action for Cancer Elimination, Am. Cancer Soc., Chgo., 1975—. Mem. Chgo. Bar Assn., Sigma Xi, Tau Beta Pi, Eta Kappa Nu. Office: 111 W Monroe St Chicago IL 60603 Tel (312) 372-2000

GOLDEN, EDWARD RUFUS, b. Moultrie, Ga., June 4, 1936; B.S. in Indsl. Mgmt., Ga. Inst. Tech., 1960; LL.B., Emory U., 1967. Admitted to Ga. bar, 1967; trust officer Trust Co. of Ga., Atlanta, 1967-73; individual practice law, Decatur, Ga., 1974—. Mem. exec. com. Republican Party of DeKalb County (Ga.), 1967—; mem. DeKalb County Bd. Elections, 1975—. Mem. Am., Atlanta, Decatur-DeKalb bar assns., State Bar Ga., Phi Alpha Delta. Home:

1495 Sagamore Dr NE Atlanta GA 30345 Office: 526 Decatur Fed Bldg Decatur GA 30030 Tel (404) 378-1417

GOLDEN, HARVEY LAURANCE, b. Bklyn., Oct. 15, 1929; LL.B., U. S.C., 1954, B.A., 1953. Admitted to S.C. bar, 1954; asso. firm Edens and Woodward, Attys. at Law, Columbia, S.C., 1954-55; mem. firm E.B. Ussery & Assos., Attys. at Law, Columbia, 1956; sr. partner firm Golden & Lourie, Attys. at Law, Columbia, 1957-60; prin firm Harvey L. Golden, Atty. at Law, Columbia, 1960—; former spl. county ct. judge; lectr. divorce, negotiations, pleading, U. S.C. Law Center. Pres. Beth Shalom Synagogoue, Columbia, 1975-77; co-founder dir. Workshop Theatre S.C.; co-founder Columbia City Ballet. Mem. Am. Bar Assn. (vice. chmn. mid-south region family law sect. 1976-77, outstanding achievement award 1976), Richland County (S.C.) Bar Assn. (chmn. torts sect.); fellow Am. Acad. Matrimonial Lawyers. Editor-in-chief S.C. Law Rev.; contbg. columnist family law S.C. Trial Lawyers Newsletter, 1976—. Home: 6240 Lakeshore Dr Columbia SC 29206 Office: 2742 River Dr Columbia SC 29201 Tel (803) 779-3700

GOLDEN, HAWKINS, b. Morton, Miss., June 24, 1905; B.A., Vanderbilt U., 1926; M.A., Harvard, 1927; J.D., So. Meth. U., 1930. Admitted to Tex. bar, 1930, U.S. Supreme Ct. bar, 1943; asso. firm Golden Potts Boeckmann & Wilson, and predecessors, Dallas, 1931-35, partner, 1935—. Chmn. bd. Highland Park (Tex.) Meth. Ch., 1955. Mem. Dallas (pres. 1950), Tex., Am. bar assns. Home: 8931 Preston Rd Dallas TX 75225 Office: 2300 Republic Bank Tower Dallas TX 75201 Tel (214) 742-8422

GO DEN, HENRY DAVIS, b. Walnut Grove, Miss., Jan. 23, 1937; B.S., Miss. Coll., 1966, M.B.A., 1975; J.D., Jackson (Miss.) Sch. Law, 1970. Admitted to Miss. bar, 1970; with utility sect. Miss. Hwy. Dept., Jackson, 1966—. Office: Woolfolk State Office Bldg Jackson MS 39205 Tel (601) 354-6350

GOLDEN, HOWARD NORMAN, b. N.Y.C., Apr. 22, 1920; B.A., N.Y. U., 1941; LL.B., Yale U., 1947. Admitted to N.Y. bar, 1948; asso. firm Sullivan and Cromwell, N.Y.C., 1948-50; partner firm Golden, Wienshienk and Mandel, N.Y.C., 1950—. Mem. Assn. Bar City N.Y. Home: 19 Mayhew Ave Larchmont NY 10538 Office: 10 E 40th St Room 1600 New York City NY 10016 Tel (212) 679-3760

GOLDEN, JONATHAN, b. Atlanta, June 13, 1937; A.B., Princeton, 1959; LL.B., Harvard, 1962. Admitted to Ga. bar, 1961; partner firm Arnall, Golden & Gregory, Atlanta, 1962—; instr. U. Ga., 1966-67; adj. prof. law Emory U., 1974. Mem. State Bar Ga., Am. Judicature Soc., Am., Atlanta bar assns. Home: 4580 Jettridge Dr Atlanta GA 30327 Office: 1000 Fulton Fed Bldg Atlanta GA 30303 Tel (404) 577-5100

GOLDEN, RICHARD A., b. Detroit, July 15, 1941; B.S. in Elec. Engring., Wayne State U., 1965, J.D., 1971. Staff engr. nuclear scis. and space power dept. Aerospace Systems div. Bendix Corp., Ann Arbor, Mich., 1965-69; chief civil clk. 48th Dist. Ct. Mich., 1969; admitted to Mich. bar, 1971; individual practice law, Southfield, Mich., 1971—. Mem. Republican State Central Com., 1975—; Rep. nominee State Senate, 1974, U.S. Congress, 1976. Mem. Am., Oakland County, Southfield bar assns., Am. Judicature Soc., IEEE, State Bar Mich. Home: 77 W Hancock St Detroit MI 48201 Office: 17117 W Nine Mile Rd Suite 536 Southfield MI 48075 Tel (313) 559-5443

GOLDEN, ROBERT HENRY, b. Detroit, May 2, 1938; A.B., Wayne State U., 1958, J.D., 1961. Admitted to Mich. bar, 1961, U.S. Supreme Ct. bar, 1966. mem. firm Golden and Lakind, Southfield, Mich. Mem. Oakland County, Mich. State bar assns., Am. Trial Lawyers Assn., Am. Soc. Law and Medicine. Office: 350 Congress Bldg 30555 Southfield Rd Southfield MI 48076 Tel (313) 645-2101

GOLDEN, SOL I., b. Lithuania, Oct. 15, 1899; A.B., Oglethorpe U., 1920; M.A., Columbia U., LL.B., 1926. Admitted to Ga. bar, 1926, U.S. Supreme Ct. bar; mem. firm Golden & Haas, 1945-49, Arnall, Golden & Gregory, Atlanta, 1949—; lectr. Oglethorpe U., 1947-49. Mem. Atlanta, Am. bar assns., Lawyers Club, Am. Judicature Soc., Bryan Soc. Home: 3090 Arden Rd Atlanta GA 30305 Office: 1000 Fulton Federal Bldg Atlanta GA 30303 Tel (404) 577-5100

GOLDEN, THOMAS FULLER, b. New Orleans, May 24, 1942; B.S., Okla. State U., 1965; J.D., Tulsa U., 1968. Admitted to Okla. bar, 1968, U.S. Supreme Ct. bar, 1972; partner firm Hall, Estill, Hardwick, Gable, Collingsworth & Nelson, Tulsa, 1971; gen. counsel Williams Bros. Overseas Co., Ltd., Toronto, Ont., Can., 1971-75; gen. counsel Arctic Constructors, Fairbanks, Alaska, 1974—. Group chmn. fund dr. Tulsa council Boy Scouts Am.; bd. dirs. Tulsa Boys Home, Inc. Mem. Am., Okla., Tulsa County bar assns., Order of Curule Chair. Villard Martin scholar, 1967. Mng. editor: Tulsa Law Jour., 1967-68. Home: 2826 E 48th St Tulsa OK 74105 Office: 4100 Bank of Okla Tower Tulsa OK 74103 Tel (918) 588-2700

GOLDENBERG, JAY SAMUEL, b. Bklyn., Dec. 14, 1938; B.A., Shimer Coll., 1957; J.D. with honors, John Marshall Law Sch., 1966. Admitted to Ill. bar, 1966; estate and gift tax atty. IRS, Chgo., 1966-71; chief, legal support sect. EPA, Chgo., 1971-73; individual practice law, Chgo., 1973-75, 75—; asso. firm Howard C. Flomenhoft, Chgo., 1975; cons. Ill. EPA, Springfield, 1973; instr. lawyers asst. program Roosevelt U., Chgo., 1977—. Mem. Am., Ill., Chgo. Fed. bar assns. Home: 5524 S Everett St Chicago IL 60637 Office: 180 N LaSalle St Chicago IL 60601 Tel (312) 346-7899

GOLDENBERG, MICHAEL PHILIP, b. Phila., May 1, 1947; B.A. with honors, U. Md., 1969; J.D., Georgetown U., 1972. Admitted to D.C. bar, 1973, U.S. Ct. Appeals D.C. Circuit bar, 1975, U.S. Supreme Ct. bar, 1977; law clk. firm Sharon, Pierson, Semmes, Crolius & Finley, Washington, 1971-73; asso. firm Lowe & McGillan, Washington, 1973-75; individual practice law, Washington, 1976—. Mem. D.C. Bar Assn. Home: 426 Girard St Apt 302 Gaithersburg MD 20760 Office: 3520 Connecticut Ave NW Washington DC 20008 Tel (202) 362-8000

GOLDENFARB, SONDRA GAMOW, b. Bklyn., Apr. 25, 1942; B.A., Radcliffe Coll., 1964; J.D., Harvard, 1967. Admitted to Mass. bar, 1967, Fla. bar, 1973; researcher Atlanta Legal Aid Soc., 1968-69; asso. firm Donahey & Furnell Clearwater, Fla., 1973-76; asso. firm Joseph G. Donahey, Jr., Clearwater, 1976—. Mem. S. Ward. Sch. adv. com., 1976-77; asst. dist. leader Pinellas County (Fla.) Democratic Exec. Com., 1976. Mem. Fla., Clearwater bar assns., Gifted Assn. Pinellas, Inc. (pres. 1976-77). Home: 316 Eastleigh Dr Belleair FL 33516 Office: Suite 1 Legal Arts Bldg 501 S Harrison Ave Clearwater FL 33516 Tel (816) 442-5121

GOLDENRING, IRA, b. N.Y.C., Apr. 13, 1924; B.B.A., Woodbury Coll., 1950; J.D., Southwestern U., 1973. Admitted to Calif. bar, 1963; prof. law U. San Fernando Valley, 1974; individual practice law, Sherman Oaks, Calif., 1963—. Bd. dirs. Valley Cities Jewish Community Center, Van Nuys, Calif., Jewish Centers Assn., Build Rehab. Industries, North Hollywood, Calif. Mem. Calif., Los Angeles trial lawyers assns., Los Angeles County, San Fernando Valley bar assns. Office: 13016 Erwin St Van Nuys CA 91401 Tel (213) 286-8909

GOLDFARB, BERNARD SANFORD, b. Cleve., Apr. 15, 1917; A.B., Case Western Res. U., 1938, J.D., 1940. Admitted to Ohio bar, 1940; partner firm Goldfarb & Reznick, Cleve., 1965—, sr. partner, 1965—; spl. counsel Atty. Gen. of Ohio, 1950, 1970-74. Mem. Ohio Commn. for Uniform Traffic Rules, 1973—. Mem. Am., Ohio, Cleve., Cuyahoga, Fed. bar assns., Am. Judicature Soc., Motor Carrier Lawyers Assns. Home: 39 Pepper Creek Dr Pepper Pike OH 44124 Office: 1825 The Illuminating Bldg Cleveland OH 44113 Tel (216) 781-0383

GOLDFARB, RONALD L., b. Jersey City, Oct. 16, 1933; A.B., Syracuse U., 1954, LL.B., 1956; LL.M., Yale, 1957, J.S.D., 1960. Admitted to N.Y. State bar, Calif. bar, D.C. bar; served to capt. JAG, U.S. Air Force, 1957-60; partner firm Goldfarb, Singer & Austern, and predecessors, Washington, 1966—; spl. prosecutor Dept. Justice, 1961-64; chmn. spl. rev. com. U.S. Dist. Ct. of D.C. to rev. compliance with decision concerning services to migrant workers, 1975-76; cons., lectr. in field. Speech writer for Robert F. Kennedy; adviser McGovern for Pres. Campaign, fall 1972, Udall for Pres. Campaign, spring 1976; v.p. Washington Service Bur., 1966—; pres. D.C. Citizens's Council for Criminal Justice Ins., 1971, 72; trustee Syracuse U. Library Assos. Mem. N.Y., Calif., Fed., Am. bar assns., Common Cause Am. Jewish Com. (dirs.), Nat. Alliance for Safer Cities (nat. bd. dirs.), Law-Sci. Council (chmn. bd. dirs. 1971—), Am. Judicature Soc., Am. Acad. Polit. and Social Sci. Author: The Contempt Power, 1963, paperback, 1971; Ransom: A Critique of the American Bail System (awards Fed. Bar Assn. 1965-66, N.J. Edn. Assn. 1966), 1965, paperback, 1967; (with Alfred Friendly) Crime and Publicity, 1967, paperback, 1968; (with Linda Singer) After Conviction—A Review of the American Correction System, 1973, paperback, 1977; Jails: The Ultimate Ghetto, 1975, paperback, 1976. Contbr. numerous articles to legal jours., popular mags., and newspapers. Home: 7312 Rippon Rd Alexandria VA 22307 Office: 918 16th St NW Suite 503 Washington DC 20006 Tel (202) 466-3030

GOLDIN, EDWARD SEYMOUR, b. Providence, Apr. 13, 1930; B.S., U. R.I., 1952; J.D., Boston U., 1955. Admitted to R.I. bar, 1955; individual practice law, Providence, 1956-65; partner firm Pucci & Goldin, Providence, 1965—. Councilman City of Providence, 1962-74; chmn. laws com. Temple Beth-El, Providence, 1967—. Mem. Am., R.I. (com. on liason with accountants) bar assns., Comml. Law League Am., Am. Trial Lawyers Assn. Home: 51 Harwich Rd Providence RI 02906 Office: 624 Industrial Bank Bldg Providence RI 02903 Tel (401) 861-7400

GOLDMAN, ABRAHAM R., b. New Haven, July 17, 1904; A.B., Brown U., 1926; J.D., Cornell U., 1929. Admitted to Conn. bar, 1930, N.Y. bar, 1931, Mass. bar, 1934; asso. firm Charles T. McClure, New Haven, 1931-34; since practiced in Westfield, Mass., individual practice law, 1934-58, 66—; partner firm Goldman & Ferriter, 1959-66. Mem. Hampden County (mem. exec. bd. 1968), Westfield (pres. 1966-68) bar assns. Home: 40 Southview Terr Westfield MA 01095 Office: 2 School St Westfield MA 01085 Tel (413) 562-3320

GOLDMAN, ALVIN LEE, b. N.Y.C., Feb. 27, 1938; B.A., Columbia, 1959; LL.B., N.Y.U., 1962. Admitted to N.Y. bar, 1963, Ky. bar, 1969; asso. firm Parker, Chapin & Flattau, N.Y.C., 1962-65; asst. prof. law U. Ky., 1965-68, asso. prof., 1968-72, prof., 1972—; prof. in residence Nat. Labor Relations Bd., Zagoria staff, 1967-68; vis. prof. U. Calif., Davis, 1976-77. Labor arbitrator, 1967—; bd. mem. Ky. Civil Liberties Union. Mem. Am. Bar Assn., Labor Law Group, Law and Soc. Assn., Internat. Soc. for Labor Law and Social Legislation, Internat. Studies Assn. Author: Processes for Conflict Resolution, 1972, The Supreme Ct. and Labor-Mgmt. Relations Law, 1976. Office: Coll of Law U Ky Lexington KY 40506 Tel (606) 257-2825

GOLDMAN, EDWARD BRUCE, b. Detroit, Aug. 13, 1943; B.A. with honors, U. Mich., 1965, J.D. cum laude, 1968. Admitted to Mich. bar, 1968; asso. firm Keywell & Rosenfeld, Detroit, 1968-69; asst. city atty. City of Ann Arbor (Mich.), 1969-73; adj. asst. prof., dir. clin. law program U. Mich., 1973-75, lectr. in law, 1976—; partner firm Harris, Lax, Goldman & Gregg, Ann Arbor, 1975—; arbitrator Nat. Labor Panel, Am. Arbitration Assn., 1974—. Bd. dirs. Summit St. Med. Center; sec. Washtenaw County ACLU; adv. bd. Washtenaw County Juvenile Ct. Mem. Mich. Bar Assn. (com. on mentally disabled). Author: U. Mich. Clin. Law Manual, 1975; Counseling the Divorce Client, 1975; contbr. articles in field to profl. jours. Home: 3708 Middleton Dr Ann Arbor MI 48105 Office: Suite 320 City Center Bldg Huron St Ann Arbor MI 48108 Tel (313) 994-3000

GOLDMAN, HARRY DOUGLAS, b. Rome, N.Y., Mar. 27, 1903; B.A., Syracuse U., 1925; postgrad. Harvard, 1925-28; LL.B., Bklyn. Law Sch., 1930. Admitted to N.Y. bar, 1931; individual practice law, Rochester, 1931-56; asso. firm Sherman, Ribman, Griffin & Goldring, N.Y.C., 1929-31; sr. partner firm MacFarlane, Harris & Goldman, Rochester, 1931-52, Goldstein Goldman & Goldman, 1952-56; justice 7th Jud. Dist., N.Y. State Supreme Ct., Rochester, 1956-57, asso. justice appellate div., 1957-69, 74—, pres. justice, 1969-74. Directing trustee appellate div. 4th dept. N.Y. Supreme Ct. Library, 1957—; v.p., bd. dirs. Rochester Hosp. Service Corp.-Blue Cross, 1959—; impartial chmn. Rochester Joint Bd. Retail Retirement Fund, 1960—; mem. Nat. Conf. on the Met. Cts., 1962—; mem. adminstrv. bd. Jud. Conf., 1969-74; mem. guidelines com. N.Y. Free Press-Fair Trial Conf., 1969—; formed Goldman Panel on Attica Prison uprising, 1971. Bd. dirs. Rochester Community Chest, 1945—, mem. exec. com., 1950—; founder Friends Rochester Pub. Library, 1953, treas., 1953-56, chmn. lit. awards com., 1961—; chmn. research adv. com. Council Social Agys., Rochester, 1959—; active NCCJ, 1936—; mem. adv. com. Rochester Lend-A-Hand, 1965—; mem. exec. bd. N.Y. Salvation Army, 1952—; active Otetiana council Boy Scouts Am., 1952—; del. N.Y. Constl 08v., 1967; bd. dirs. Health Council Monroe County (N.Y.), 1966—, Jewish Community Council, 1937—; trustee St. John Fisher Coll., Alfred U., Brighton Meml. Library, Rochester Regional Research Library Council. Mem. Internat. (patron), Am., N.Y. (com. on criminal justice, Root/Stimson award 1976), Monroe County bar assns., Am. Judicature Soc., Nat. Legal Aid. Rochester C. of C. (Civic Devel. award in govt. 1974), NAACP, Urban League. Recipient Silver Beaver award Boy Scouts Am.; named Rochester Citizen of Yr. 1966; contbr. articles to profl. jours. Home: 210 Pelham Rd Rochester NY 14610 Office: 501 Hall of Justice Rochester NY 14614 Tel (716) 232-6220

GOLDMAN, IRVING, b. Plattsburgh, N.Y., Sept. 3, 1916; B.A., Williams Coll., 1937; LL.B., Yale, 1940, J.D., 1971. Admitted to N.Y. bar, 1941; asso. firm Kaufman & Cronan, N.Y.C., 1941-42; partner firm Goldman & Goldman, Plattsburgh, 1950-64; judge Plattsburgh City Ct., 1956-65; surrogate judge Clinton County (N.Y.) Ct., 1965—; mem. No. region adv. bd. Nat. Comml. Bank & Trust Co. Exec. v.p. Champlain Valley Physicians Hosp. Med. Center, Plattsburgh, 1965-74; pres. Temple Beth Israel, Plattsburgh, 1966-68; chmn. No. N.Y. United Jewish Appeal Fund, 1961-62. Mem. N.Y. State, Clinton County (pres. 1963-64) bar assns., N.Y. State Magistrates Assn., N.Y. State Surrogates Assn. (sec.-treas. 1976—), Nat. Assn. Probate Judges, Am. Judicature Soc. Home: 4 Ridgewood Dr Plattsburgh NY 12901 Office: Surrogate's Ct Chambers Govt Center Plattsburgh NY 12901 Tel (518) 561-8800

GOLDMAN, LAWRENCE SAUL, b. Phila., Mar. 25, 1942; B.A., Brandeis U., 1963; LL.B., Harvard, 1966. Admitted to N.Y. bar, 1966, U.S. Dist. Ct. bar, 1971, U.S. Ct. of Appeals, U.S. Supreme Ct. bars, 1972; asst. dist. atty. N.Y. County, 1966-71; asst. gen. counsel Temporary N.Y. State Study Commn. for N.Y.C., 1972-73; partner firm Goldman & Hafetz, N.Y.C., 1972—; cons. in field; mem. Gov.'s Task Force on Drug Reform & Alcoholism, 1974-75. Mem. Am., N.Y. State bar assns., Assn. Bar City N.Y., N.Y. Criminal Bar Assn. (mem. exec. com.). Home: 65 W 90th St New York City NY 10024 Office: 60 E 42d St New York City NY 10017 Tel (212) 682-8337

GOLDMAN, MARK, b. Platling, W. Ger., Jan. 20, 1949; B.A., Rutgers U., 1970, J.D., 1973. Admitted to N.J. bar, 1973; atty. Newark Legal Services, 1973—; mem. N.J. Consumer Task Force. Mem. N.J., Bergen County bar assns. Home: 151 Prospect Ave Hackensack NJ 07601 Office: 449 Central Ave Newark NJ 07107 Tel (201) 484-4010

GOLDMAN, MARTIN MAYER, b. Plattsburgh, N.Y., Dec. 7, 1910; B.A., Williams Coll., 1932; student law Harvard U., 1932-34; J.D., Boston U., 1935. Admitted to N.Y. bar, 1936, U.S. Dist. Ct. bar No. Dist. N.Y., 1937, U.S. Customs Ct. bar, 1965, Bd. Immigration Appeals bar, 1950; individual practice law, Plattsburgh, 1937—. Acting city judge City of Plattsburgh, 1942-46, city judge, 1952-56; inheritance tax atty. Clinton County, N.Y., 1938-42, 54-58; adminstrv. hearing officer N.Y. State Employees Retirement System. Mem. panel arbitrators Am. Arbitnation Assn. Mem. N.Y. State, Clinton County (pres. 1969) bar assns., Assn. Trial Lawyers Am., N.Y. State Magistrates Assn (pres. 1958), Comml. Law League Am. Home: 75 Park Ave Plattsburgh NY 12901 Office: 60 Margaret St Plattsburgh NY 12901 Tel (518) 561-2900

GOLDMAN, MARVIN GERALD, b. Los Angeles, June 1, 1939; A.B. in Econs., U. Calif. at Los Angeles, 1960, J.D., 1963; LL.M. in Comparative Law, N.Y. U., 1964. Admitted to Calif. bar, 1964, N.Y. bar, 1966, U.S. Supreme Ct. bar, 1970, U.S. Customs Ct., 1972; asso. firm Reid & Priest, N.Y.C., 1965-73, partner 1974—. Mem. Am. Arbitration Assn., Am. Soc. Internat. Law, Assn. Bar City N.Y., Inter-Am., Am. bar assns. Contbr. articles to legal jours. Office: Reid & Priest 40 Wall St New York City NY 10005 Tel (212) 344-2233

GOLDMAN, MICHAEL DAVID, b. Jersey City, Oct. 16, 1942; A.B., Pa. State U., 1964; J.D., Villanova U., 1967. Admitted to Del. bar, 1968; law clk. Ct. of Chancery State of Del., 1967-68; asso. firm Potter Anderson & Corroon, Wilmington, Del., 1968-73, partner, 1974—. Mem. Del. state exec. bd. Muscular Distrophy Assn., 1974—. Mem. Am. (mem. corp. banking and bus. law sect.), Del. State (asst. sec. 1973-74, chmn. com. cts. and procedures 1972-74, chmn. com. on adminstrn. of justice 1974-75, vice chmn. 1975—, chmn. coll. student orientation program 1973-74, mem. com. on gen. corp. law 1975—, com. on med.-legal and dental legal relations 1974—) bar assns., Order of Coif. Recipient award Bur. Nat. Affairs, 1967, Silverberg award, 1967. Home: 3350 Morningside Rd Wilmington DE 19810 Office: Box 951 350 Delaware Trust Bldg Wilmington DE 19899 Tel (302) 658-6771

GOLDMAN, RUTH, b. Chgo., July 6, 1921; B.S., U. Chgo., 1942, J.D., 1947. Admitted to Ill. bar, 1948; legal aid atty. Jewish Family and Community Service, Chgo., 1948-50; asso. firm Devoe, Shadur, & Krupp, Chgo., 1969-77, partner, 1977—; mem. faculty Greenerfields, Inc., Northfield, Ill., 1972—. Mem. Public. Bldg. Commn., Lake County, Ill., 1975—, Bd. Edn., 1963-69. Mem. Chgo. Bar Assn., Chgo. Council Lawyers. Home: 953 Wildwood Ln Highland Park IL 60035 Office: 208 S LaSalle St Chicago IL 60604 Tel (312) 263-3700

GOLDMAN, THOMAS EDWARD, b. Rochester, N.Y., Dec. 25, 1939; A.B., Bucknell U., 1962; LL.B., Syracuse U., 1965. Admitted to N.Y. bar, 1965; asso. firm Fix, Spindelman & Turk, Rochester, 1965-67; asso. firm Brennan, Centner, Palermo & Blauvelt, Rochester, N.Y., 1967-70, partner, 1970—; town justice Pittsford (N.Y.), 1967—; adminstrv. judge Monroe County, 1974—. Active Boy Scouts Am., 1976—; mem. United Community Chester Greater Rochester, 1975—, task force chmn., 1974—; mem. Brighton Fire Dept., 1967—, capt., 1974-75. Mem. Justices and Magistrates Assn. Monroe County (pres. 1975), N.Y. State Assn. Magistrates, Monroe County, N.Y., State bar assns. Home: 3805 E Ave Rochester NY 14618 Office: 500 Reynolds Arcade Bldg Rochester NY 14614 Tel (716) 546-6474

GOLDMAN, WILLIAM LEWIS, b. Phila., May 13, 1919; B.S., Temple U., 1942, J.D., 1951. Admitted to Pa. bar, 1951, D.C. bar, 1951; individual practice law, Doylestown, Pa., 1951—, Levittown, Pa., 1960—, Richboro, Pa., 1975—. Mem. state com. family law sect. Pa. Bar Assn. to revise marriage and divorce laws in Pa. Fellow Am. Acad. Matrimonial Lawyers; mem. Am., Fed., Inter-Am., Bucks County (past pres., treas. and v.p.) bar assns., Am., Phila. trial lawyers assns., Comml. Law League Am., Nat. Assn. Defense Lawyers in Criminal Cases, N.Y. Trial Lawyers Assn., Am. Judicature Soc., Am. Arbitration Assn., Phi Alpha Delta. Office: 90 E State St Doylestown PA 18901 Tel (215) 348-2605 also 1 Stonybrook Dr Levittown PA Tel (215) 949-2828 also 770 2d St Pike Richboro PA Tel (215) 322-2100

GOLDRING, IRWIN DONALD, b. Los Angeles, Mar. 26, 1931; B.S. in Accounting, U. Calif. at Los Angeles, 1953, J.D., 1956. Admitted to Calif. bar, 1957; served with JAG, U.S. Air Force, 1956-58; asso. firm Charles Goldring, Los Angeles, 1958-65; individual practice law, Los Angeles, 1965-67, Beverly Hills, Calif., 1970—; corporate counsel Kleiner, Bell & Co., Inc., Beverly Hills, 1967-70. Vice pres. Great Western council Boy Scouts Am., 1966-76; treas. UN Assn., Los Angeles, 1969-75. Mem. Beverly Hills, Los Angeles, Calif., Am. bar assns. Contbr. articles to legal jours. Home: 13208 Bloomfield St Sherman Oaks CA 91423 Office: 433 N Camden Dr Suite 770 Beverly Hills CA 90210 Tel (213) 273-7444

GOLDSBOROUGH, NICHOLAS, b. Balt., Nov. 14, 1934; B.A., U. Va., 1959; LL.B., George Washington U., 1964. Admitted to Md. bar, 1964, D.C. bar, 1968, U.S. Supreme Ct. bar, 1974; asso. firm McWilliams & Melvin, Annapolis, Md., 1965, firm Wray, Serio & Hopper, Annapolis, 1965-72; partner firm Blumenthal, Goldsborough, May & Downs, and predecessors, Annapolis, 1973—. Pres. Anne Arundel County chpt. Am. Cancer Soc., 1971-72; bd. dirs. Severn Sch., 1975—, Annapolis Community Chest United Fund, 1966-72, Arundel Nursing Center, Crownsville, Md., 1968—. Mem. Am., Md., Anne Arundel County bar assns., Balt. Estate Planning Council. Home: 1608 Winchester Rd Annapolis MD 21401 Office: 182 Duke of Gloucester St Annapolis MD 21401 Tel (301) 268-7707

GOLDSMITH, EARL ARTHUR, b. Chgo., May 5, 1939; B.S., Northwestern U., 1961, J.D., 1964. Admitted to Ill. bar, 1965, Ga. bar, 1973; staff atty. Legal Aid Bur., Chgo., 1967-68; dir. Nat. Council Juvenile Ct. Judges, Chgo., 1968-69; sr. advisory title officer Pioneer Nat. Title Ins. Co., Waukegan, Ill. and Atlanta, 1971-76; with firm Wallace B. Dunn, Highwood, Ill., 1976—. Mem. Ill., Lake County, Chgo. bar assns. Office: 445 Sheridan Rd Highwood IL 60040 Tel (312) 433-2800

GOLDSMITH, MARTIN NEIL, b. N.Y.C., Oct. 30, 1942; B.A., L.I. U., 1964; LL.B., Bklyn. Law Sch., 1967, J.D., 1967. Admitted to Ohio bar, 1969; corp. counsel Arby's Inc., Youngstown, Ohio, 1968-71; asst. corp. counsel SCOA Industries, Inc., Columbus, Ohio, 1971-76; corp. counsel Merry Go Round Enterprises, Inc., Balt., 1976—. Mem. Am., Ohio bar assns. Author anti-trust monogram series Robinson-Patman Act-Lawful Price. Office: 1220 E Joppa Rd Towson MD 21204 Tel (301) 828-1000

GOLDSMITH, WILLIAM WALLACE, b. Newark, May 17, 1893. Admitted to bar; practice law, Charleston, W.Va.; now ret. Home: 1105 Highland Rd Charleston WV 25302

GOLDSTEIN, ABRAHAM, b. Providence, May 25, 1916; A.B., Brown U., 1938; LL.B., Boston Coll., 1952. Admitted to R.I. bar, 1952, U.S. Supreme Ct. bar, 1965; individual practice law, Providence, 1952—; Cranston, R.I., 1952—; asst. city solicitor, Cranston, 1961-62, probate judge, 1971-74; legal counsel R.I. Ho. Rep. Judiciary Com., 1976—. Mem. R.I. Bar Assn. Home: 72 Massasoit Ave Cranston RI 02905 Office: 76 Westminster St Providence RI 02903 Tel (401) 331-8647

GOLDSTEIN, ABRAHAM SAMUEL, b. N.Y.C., July 27, 1925; B.B.A. cum laude, Coll. City N.Y., 1946; LL.B., Yale, 1949, M.A. (hon.), 1961; M.A. (hon.) Cambridge (Eng.) U., 1964. Admitted to D.C. bar, 1949, U.S. Supreme Ct. bar, 1954; law clk. U.S. Ct. Appeals, Washington, 1949-51; asso. firm Cook and Berger, Washington, 1949; partner firm Donohue and Kaufmann, Washington, 1951-56; asso. prof. law Yale, 1956-61, prof., 1961-70, dean law sch., 1970-75, Sterling Prof. law, 1975—; cons. Pres.'s Commn. on Law Enforcement, 1966-67; mem. Gov's Planning Commn. on Criminal Adminstrn., 1967-71; mem. Conn. Bd. Parole, 1968-70; mem. Jud. Council Conn., 1970-75; vis. fellow Inst. Criminology, Cambridge U., 1964-65; vis. prof. Hebrew U., 1976. Mem. Am., Conn. bar assns., AAAS. Guggenheim fellow, 1964-65, 75-76. Author: The Insanity Defense, 1971; (with J. Goldstein) Crime, Law & Society, 1971; (with L. Orland) Criminal Procedure, 1974. Home: 545 Ellsworth Ave New Haven CT 06511 Office: 127 Wall St New Haven CT 06520 Tel (203) 432-4308

GOLDSTEIN, ABRAHAM Z., b. N.Y.C., Oct. 6, 1908; student Columbia U.; LL.B., Bklyn. Coll., 1931. Admitted to N.Y. bar; individual practice law, Kew Gardens, N.Y., 1933—. Mem. Queens Criminal Bar Assn., Immigration and Naturalization Lawyers Assn. Office: 120-10 Queens Blvd Kew Gardens NY 11415 Tel (212) 261-1414

GOLDSTEIN, ARTHUR, b. Jackson Heights, N.Y., Sept. 25, 1932; B.A., Syracuse U., 1953; LL.B., cum laude, N.Y. U., 1956. Admitted to N.Y., D.C. bars, 1956; atty. U.S. Dept. Justice, Washington, 1956-58, spl. atty., 1958-59; partner firm Goldstein & Rubinton, Huntington, N.Y., 1968—; dep. atty. Huntington Twp. (N.Y.), 1963-67, atty., 1968-70; counsel S. Huntington Pub. Library, 1966—. Chmn. Huntington Narcotics Guidance Council, 1970-75; bd. dirs. Huntington YMCA, 1973—; trustee Heckscher Art Mus. Huntington, 1972—. Mem. N.Y., Am. bar assns., Suffolk County Trial Lawyers Assn., Huntington C. of C. (dir. 1970-73). Author: District and Civil Court Procedure, 1963; co-author: Criminal Procedure in State N.Y., 1960. Home: 1 Farragut Pl Huntington NY 11743 Office: 177 Main St Huntington NY 11743 Tel (516) 421-9051

GOLDSTEIN, BERNARD HERBERT, b. N.Y.C., June 7, 1907; B.S., Coll. City N.Y., 1927; LL.B., Columbia, 1930. Admitted to N.Y. State bar, 1932; asst. gen. counsel Liggett Drug Co., N.Y.C., 1933-44; partner firm Roy M. Stern & Bernard H. Goldstein, N.Y.C., 1944-47, Gettner, Simon & Ashe, N.Y.C., 1948-59, Tenzer, Greenblatt, Fallon & Kaplan, N.Y.C., 1959—. Mem. citizens adv. com. Housing and Devel. Adminstrn., City of N.Y., 1969—. Mem. Am., N.Y., N.Y.C. (com. chmn.) bar assns., World Peace Through Law Center, N.Y. County Lawyers Assn. Contbr. articles Ency. Brit., various legal publs. Home: 21 Colonial Rd Port Washington NY 11050 Office: 100 Park Ave New York City NY 10017 Tel (212) 953-1828

GOLDSTEIN, FRANK ROBERT, b. Balt., July 31, 1943; A.B., Duke U., 1964; LL.B., U. Md., 1967. Admitted to Md. bar, 1967; law clk. Hon. Roszel C. Thomsen, Chief Judge U.S. Dist. Ct. Dist. Md., 1967-68; asso. firm Piper & Marbury, Balt., 1968-74, partner, 1974—. Pres. Tidesfall Assn., Inc., 1972-73. Mem. Am., Md. (chmn. sect. legal edn. and admissions 1975-76), Balt. bar assns., Order of the Coif. Case note editor: Md. Law Review, 1966-67. Home: 10319 Wilde Lake Terr Columbia MD 21044 Office: 25 S Charles St Baltimore MD 21201 Tel (301) 539-2530

GOLDSTEIN, HARVEY L., b. N.Y.C., May 21, 1930; B.A., Bklyn. Coll., 1952, LL.B., 1954, J.D., 1967. Admitted to N.Y. State bar, 1956, U.S. Dist. Ct. Eastern and So. Dist. N.Y. bar, 1958; U.S. Ct. Appeals bar, 1964, U.S. Supreme Ct. bar, 1964; partner firm Finkel & Goldstein and predecessor, N.Y.C., 1956—. Mem. Gov.'s Council for Mgmt., 1968; bd. dirs. temple. Mem. N.Y. County Lawyers Assn., N.Y. State Bar Assn. (lectr.). Contbr. articles to profl. jours. Home: 82 Bounty Ln Jerico NY 11753 Office: 401 Broadway New York City NY 10013 Tel (212) 226-6904

GOLDSTEIN, JACK CHARLES, b. Ft. Worth, May 11, 1942; B.M.E., Purdue U., 1964; J.D. with honors, George Washington U., 1968. Admitted to Ill. bar, 1968, Tex. bar, 1968, D.C. bar, 1969; patent examiner U.S. Patent and Trademark Office, Washington, 1964-67; patent advisor Office Naval Research, Washington, 1967-68; law clk. U.S. Ct. Customs and Patent Appeals, Washington, 1968-69; asso. firm Arnold, White & Durkee, Houston, 1969-74; mem., 1974—; adj. prof. copyright law S. Tex. Coll. Law, 1974—. Mem. adv. council The Little Sch. House, Houston, 1975—. Mem. Am., Fed., Houston bar assns., Am., Houston patent law assns., State Bar Tex., D.C. Bar. Home: 6231 S Braeswood Blvd Houston TX 77096 Office: 2100 Transco Tower Houston TX 77056 Tel (713) 621-9100

GOLDSTEIN, JONATHAN LANCE, b. N.Y.C., Feb. 16, 1941; student Wharton Sch. Fin. and Commerce, U. Pa., 1962, N.Y. U. Sch. Law, 1965. Admitted to N.Y. bar, 1966, N.J. bar, 1970; U.S. atty. Dist. N.J., Newark, 1974—. Mem. Am., N.Y. State, N.J., Essex County bar assns., Assn. Fed. Bar State N.J. (pres.). Recipient Arthur S. Fleming award, 1971, Superior Performance award U.S. atty. gen., 1971, Younger Fed. Lawyer award Fed. Bar Assn., 1972, Spl. commendation for outstanding service Dept. Justice, 1972, Atty. Gen.'s award for distinguished service, 1973, Distinguished Service award Newark Jr. C. of C., 1975; named One of Ten Outstanding Young Men Am., U.S. Jr. C. of C., 1975. Office: 970 Broad St Newark NJ 07102 Tel (201) 645-2289

GOLDSTEIN, JOSEPH, b. Springfield, Mass., May 7, 1923; A.B., Dartmouth, 1943; Ph.D. (Fulbright scholar), London Sch. Econs., 1950; LL.B., Yale, 1952; postgrad. Western New Eng. Inst. for Psychoanalysis, 1968. Admitted to Va. bar, 1963; law clk. to Judge David L. Bazelon, U.S. Ct. Appeals, Washington, 1952-53; acting asst. prof. law Stanford, 1954-56; Russell Sage resident, vis. scholar Harvard Law Sch., 1955-56; asso. prof. Yale, 1956-59, prof. 1959—, Justus H. Hotchkiss prof. law, 1968-69, Walton Hall Hamilton prof. law, sci. and social policy, 1969—; mem. Com. on Life Scis. and Social Policy NRC, 1968-75; law fellow U. Wis., 1958; mem. Salk Inst. Council on Biology in Human Affairs, 1969-72; mem. Com. for Study Incarceration, 1971-75; mem. Commn. to Revise Criminal Statutes of State of Conn., 1970; Fulbright vis. lectr. Hitotsubashi U., Research and Tng. Inst. for Family Ct. Probation Officers, Japan Supreme Ct., 1973. Bd. dirs. Vera Inst. of Justice, N.Y.C., Sigmund Freud Archives, N.Y.C. Author: The Government of A British Trade Union, 1952, Am. edit., 1953; (with Richard Donnelly and Richard Schwartz) Criminal Law, 1962; (with Jay Katz) The Family And The Law, 1965; (with Jay Katz and Alan Dershowitz) Psychoanalysis, Psychiatry and Law, 1966; (with A. S. Goldstein) Crime, Law And Society, 1971; (with Anna Freud and A. J. Solnit) Beyond The Best Interests Of The Child, 1973; (with Alan M. Dershowitz and Richard D. Schwartz) Criminal Law, Theory and Process, 1974; contbr. articles to profl. publs. Office: Yale Law Sch 127 Wall St New Haven CT 06520 Tel (203) 436-2665

GOLDSTEIN, MARTIN EDWARD, b. St. Louis, Nov. 23, 1934; B.S. in Chem. Engring., U. Ill., 1955; J.D. with honors, George Washington U., 1964. Admitted to D.C. bar, 1965, N.Y. bar, 1965; patent lawyer Gen. Electric Co., Waterford, N.Y., 1964-65; partner firm Kane Dalsimer Kane Sullivan Kurucz & Goldstein and predecessors, N.Y.C., 1966-73, McAulay Fields Fisher & Goldstein and predecessor, N.Y.C., 1973—. Dist. leader New Rochelle (N.Y.) Republican Party, 1974—; pres. New Rochelle Neighborhood Assn., 1971-74; active Beth El Synagogue, New Rochelle. Mem. Am. Patent Law Assn., Am., D.C. bar assns., Assn. Bar City N.Y., Order Coif, Phi Delta Phi. Office: 20 Exchange Pl New York City NY 10005 Tel (212) 248-5330

GOLDSTEIN, MICHAEL JAMES, b. N.Y.C., July 29, 1933; B.A., Pa. State U., 1955; LL.B., Bklyn. Law Sch., 1958, J.D., 1967. Admitted to N.Y. bar, 1958; partner firm Samuel Goldstein & Sons, N.Y.C. and Mineola, N.Y., 1958—; with Judge Adv. Gen. Corps USAF, 1959-62; mem. legis. com. N.Y. Real Estate Bd., 1976—. Treas. Peoples Village Party of Lake Success (N.Y.), 1970—; mem. Lake Success Bd. Zoning Appeals, 1974—. Mem. Nassau, Queens, Bklyn. bar assns., Nassau Lawyers Assn. of L.I., N.Y. Tax Rev. Bar Assn., Assn. Bar City N.Y. Contbr. articles to N.Y. Law Jour. Home: 7 Old Field Ln Lake Success NY 11020 Office: 217 Broadway New York City NY 10007 Tel (212) 732-5433

GOLDSTEIN, MORTON NORMAN, b. Washington, May 15, 1936; B.A., U. Md., 1957; grad. George Washington U. Law Sch., 1961. Admitted to D.C. bar, 1962, Md. bar, 1973; asst. corp. counsel D.C. Govt., 1962-67; asso. firm Donnelly & Golin, Washington, 1967-70; asso. firm Newrath, Snyder & Meyer, Washington, 1970-74; partner firm Kearney & Goldstein, Rockville, Md., 1974—; instr. Para Legal Inst., 1973—. Mem. Comml. Law League Am., D.C. Bar, Bar Assn. D.C. Fed., Montgomery County bar assns., Am. Aribtration Assn. (mem. panel arbitrators). Home: 14801 Cobblestone Dr Silver Spring MD 20904 Office: 22 W Jefferson St Rockville MD 20850 Tel (301) 762-4998

GOLDSTEIN, NORTON AARON, b. Boston, Mar. 21, 1929; A.A., Northeastern U., 1949, LL.B., 1953. Admitted to Mass. bar, 1954, U.S. Supreme Ct. bar, 1964; asso. firm James Levensohn, Boston, 1954-55; individual practice law, Boston, 1955-64; partner firm Epstein, Goldstein & Feldman, Boston, 1964—. Pres. Temple Beth Shalom, Needham, 1964-65; v.p. Associated Synagogues Mass., 1974—. Mem. Boston, Mass. bar assns., Mass. Trial Lawyers Assn. Home: 236 Parish Rd Needham MA 02194 Office: 100 State St Boston MA 02109 Tel (617) 523-7573

GOLDSTEIN, PETER ALAN, b. N.Y.C., Oct. 31, 1945; B.A., U. Colo., 1967, J.D., 1970. Admitted to Colo. bar, 1970; law clk. to Chief Justice Edward E. Pringle, Colo. Supreme Ct., Denver, 1970-71; mem. firm Agee, Ewing & Goldstein, Colorado Springs, Colo. Mem. Colo., El Paso County bar assns., Colo., El Paso County trial lawyers assns. Office: 512 S 8th St Colorado Springs CO 80905 Tel (303) 473-1515

GOLDSTEIN, STEVEN IRA, b. N.Y.C., Jan. 2, 1943; A.B., U. N.C., 1964, J.D., 1967. Admitted to N.C. bar, 1967; asso. firm Lee, Lee & Cogburn, Asheville, N.C., 1967-69, Patla, Straus, Robinson & Moore, P.A., Asheville, 1969—. Mem. Am., N.C. bar assns., Comml. Law League. Office: 29 N Market St Asheville NC 28807 Tel (704) 255-7641

GOLDSTEIN, WILLIAM M., b. Ft. Owens, Mass., Oct. 11, 1944; B.S., U. Ill., 1966, J.D., 1969. Admitted to Ill. bar, 1969; asst. state's atty. Champaign County (Ill.), 1969-72; partner firm Gaston & Goldstein, Urbana, Ill., 1972—; guest instr. Police Tng. Inst. U. Ill., 1970—; instr. Parkland Coll., Champaign, Ill., 1971-76. Mem. adv. bd. Champaign County Youth Home, 1972-76. Mem. Ill., Champaign County (dir. bd. govs. 1973-75, v.p. bd. govs. 1974-75) bar assns. Home: 807 W University St Champaign IL 61820 Office: 303 W Green St Urbana IL 61801 Tel (217) 367-5411

GOLDSWORTHY, DONALD JOSEPH, b. Beloit, Wis., July 1, 1947; B.S., U. Wis., Whitewater, 1969, J.D., Madison, 1972. Admitted to Wis. bar, 1972, U.S. Dist. Ct. bar for Western Dist. Wis., 1972; partner firm Junig & Goldsworthy, Beloit, 1972-76; atty. fiduciary, inheritance and gift tax bur. Wis. Dept. Revenue, Madison, 1976—. Mem. Equal Opportunities Commn. of Beloit (Wis.), 1976. Mem. State Bar Wis., Am. Bar Assn. Home: 450 Woodside Terr Madison WI 53711 Office: POB 74 4638 University Ave Madison WI 53711 Tel (608) 266-2157

GOLLER, RONALD REESE, b. Bridgeport, Conn., Jan. 10, 1945; B.A., Fla. State U., 1967, J.D., 1970. Admitted to Fla. bar, 1970; research aide 4th Dist. Ct. Appeals, West Palm Beach, Fla., 1971; asso. firm Berryhill, Avery, Schwenke & Williams, Ft. Lauderdale, 1972-73; partner firm McCutcheon, Rowan & Goller, St. Petersburg, Fla., 1974-77, Hartke and Klein, St. Petersburg, Sarasota, Fla., Washington, N.Y.C., 1977—; asst. to counsel Fla. Assn. Ct. Clks., Tallahassee, 1969-70. Mem. Fla. Bar, Lawyers Title Guaranty Fund, Nat. Ry. Hist. Soc. (counsel Tampa Bay chpt. 1976—), Phi Alpha Delta. Home: 3427 39th Ln S St Petersburg FL 33711 Office: Suite 341 3251 3d Ave N St Petersburg FL 33713 Tel (813) 823-5419 also 2051 Main St Sarasota FL 33577 also 600 Watergate Washington DC 20037 also 230 Park Ave Suite 460 New York City NY 10017

GOLOB, DENNIS EDWARD, b. Chgo., June 14, 1942; B.S., U. Calif., Los Angeles; J.D., U. So. Calif. Admitted to Calif. bar, 1967; mem. firm Spiegelman and Raisch; then asso. firm Harshman, Marantz, Comsky & Deutsch; now asso. firm Bernhard, Weiss & Karma, Inc., Los Angeles. Mem. Am., Calif. State, Los Angeles County bar assns. Office: 10850 Wilshire Blvd Los Angeles CA 90024 Tel (213) 475-0504

GOLUB, GERALD BRUCE, b. Cleve., Apr. 2, 1948; B.A., Ohio State U., 1970; J.D., U. Cin., 1973. Admitted to Ohio bar, 1973; individual practice law, Hamilton, Ohio, 1973—; hearing examiner Butler Met. Housing Authority, 1975—. Trustee Center for Forensic Psychiatry, 1974—. Mem. Ohio, Butler County bar assns. Home: 446 Emerson Ave Hamilton OH 45013 Office: 1st National Bank Bldg Hamilton OH 45011 Tel (513) 867-0264

GOMBERG, BERNARD JACK, b. Bklyn., Apr. 2d27, 1929; B.A., Washington Sq. Coll., 1948; LL.B., N.Y. U., 1951. Admitted to N.Y. State bar, 1952; mem. firm Booth Lipton & Lipton, N.Y.C., 1951-52; mem. firm Norman Kaliski, N.Y.C., 1952-54; individual practice law, N.Y.C., 1955—. Mem. Am. (adminstrv. asst. to pres. 1964-66, chmn. com. on ins. research 1964-66), N.Y. State, Met. trial lawyers assns., N.Y. County Lawyers Assn. Office: 20 Vesey St New York City NY 10007 Tel (212) 732-5505

GOMEZ, ROLAND HERMAN, b. Bklyn., Aug. 3, 1938; B.A., U. Fla., 1960, LL.B., 1963. Admitted to Fla. bar, 1963; partner firm Ress, Gomez, Rosenberg & Berke, North Miami, Fla., 1963—. Mem. Am., Fla. trial lawyers assns., Am. Arbitration Assn., Am., Fla. Dade County (Fla.), North Dade bar assns. Home: 7460 Twin Sabal Dr Miami Lakes FL 33014 Office: 1700 Sans Souci Blvd North Miami FL 33181 Tel (305) 893-5506

GOMPERS, JOSEPH ALAN, b. Wheeling, W.Va., Jan. 21, 1924; A.B., Mt. St. Mary's Coll., Emmitsburg, Md.; LL.D., U. Va., Charlottesville. Admitted to W.Va. bar, 1948; partner firm Gompers & Gompers, Wheeling, 1948-57, Gompers & Buch, Wheeling, 1957-74, Gompers, Buch & McCarthy, Wheeling, 1975—; pros. atty. Ohio County, 1953-57, commr. accounts, 1958-68, 73—. Mem. W.Va. Ho. of Dels., 1951-52; chmn. adv. bd. W.Va. Alcohol Beverage Control Commn., 1969—; pres. Oglebay Inst., 1965-66. Mem. Am., W.Va., Ohio County (past pres.) bar assns., Am. Trial Lawyers Assn. Home: 222 Washington Ave Wheeling WV 26003 Office: Board of Trade Bldg Wheeling WV 26003 Tel (304) 233-2450

GOMPF, CLAYTON NORVIN, JR., b. Ft. Riley, Kans., Oct. 24, 1946; student Dickinson Coll., Carlisle, Pa., 1965-67; B.A. in Polit. Sci. and Philosophy, Furman U., 1969; J.D., U. S.C., 1972, postgrad in Criminal Justice, 1975—. Admitted to S.C. bar, 1972; asso. firm Franchot A. Brown and Assos., Columbia, S.C., 1972; staff counsel S.C. Human Affairs Commn., Columbia, 1973, dept. commr., gen. counsel, 1974—. Mem. S.C. Law Enforcement Officer's Assn., Nat. Assn. Human Rights Workers, Am. Bar Assn., S.C. State Bar, Carolina Jazz Soc. Home: 3404 Keenan Dr Columbia SC 29201 Office: State Human Affairs Commn PO Box 11300 Capitol Station Columbia SC 29211 Tel (803) 758-2748

GONDREE, HOWARD FRANK, b. Glen Gardner, N.J., May 14, 1943; B.A., State U. N.Y. at Buffalo, 1967, J.D., 1969, B.S. in Bus. Adminstrn., 1971. Admitted to N.Y. State bar, 1970, U.S. Dist. Ct. Western Dist. N.Y. bar, 1970, U.S. Tax Ct. bar, 1970; accountant Touche Ross & Co., Buffalo, 1970-73; partner firm Phillips, Brown & Gondree and predecessors, Buffalo, 1973—. Mem. N.Y., Am. assns. atty.-C.P.A.'s, N.Y. State, Erie County bar assns., N.Y. State Soc. C.P.A.'s, Nat. Assn. Accountants, C.P.A., N.Y. Home: 1159 Elmwood Ave Buffalo NY 14222 Office: 936 Ellicott Sq Bldg Buffalo NY 14203 Tel (716) 852-6267

GONSHAK, DAVID MANUEL, b. Newark, Feb. 4, 1928; J.D., U. Miami, 1953. Admitted to Fla. bar, 1953, since practiced in Miami. Mem. Fla., Dade County bar assns., Tau Epsilon Rho. Home: 8901 SW 21st Terr Miami FL 33165 Office: 1497 NW 7th St Miami FL 33125 Tel (305) 642-0722

GONSON, SAUL DONALD, b. Buffalo, June 13, 1936; A.B., Columbia, 1958; J.D., Harvard, 1961; postgrad. (Fulbright scholar), U. Bombay (India), 1961-62. Admitted to Mass. bar, 1962; instr. law Boston U., 1963-65; mem. firm Hale and Dorr, Boston, 1962—, sr. partner, 1972—; trustee Boston Five Cents Savs. Bank; dir., chmn. Mass. Community Devel. Fin. Corp. Bd. dirs. Cambridge Family and Children's Service, Inc. Mem. Am. Bar Assn. Home: 32 Hubbard Park Cambridge MA 02138 Office: 28 State St Boston MA 02109 Tel (617) 742-9100

GONZALES, SERVANDO HIGINIO, JR., b. Benavides, Tex., Sept. 24, 1940; A.A., Del Mar Coll., 1964; B.B.A., Tex. A. & I. U., 1965; J.D., St. Mary's U., 1969. Admitted to Tex. bar, 1969, U.S. Dist. Ct. So. Dist. Tex. bar, 1971, U.S. Ct. Appeals bar, 1972, U.S. Supreme Ct. bar, 1976; asst. dist atty. State Tex., Edinburg, 1970; dep. dir. Tex. Rural Legal Aid, Edinburg, 1971, bd. dirs., 1972—; partner firm Judin, Ellis, Gonzales & Barron and predecessor firm, McAllen, Tex., 1972—. Bd. dirs. McAllen United Way, 1975—, Tex. Rural Legal Aid. Edinburg, Tex., 1972—, Valley Youth for Christ, McAllen, 1976—. Mem. Am., Tex., Hidalgo County bar assns., Tex. Trial Lawyers Assn., Tex. Criminal Def. Lawyers Assn., Phi Delta Phi. Mng. editor St. Mary's Law Jour., 1969. Home: 1501 Iris St McAllen TX 78501 Office: 920 N Main St McAllen TX 78501 Tel (512) 682-0111

GONZALEZ, ALEXANDER RAMON, b. Ft. Stockton, Tex., June 17, 1932; B.A., Sul Ross State U., 1958, M.A., 1960; student law Am. U., 1966-67; J.D., U. Tex., Austin, 1971. Admitted to Tex. bar, 1971;

individual practice law, Ft. Stockton, 1971—; city atty. City of Ft. Stockton, 1973—; justice of peace Pecos County, Tex., 1963-64; adminstrv. asst. to Congressman Richard C. White, 1965-67, liaison officer, 1969-71; exec. officer Peace Corps, Peru, 1967-69; mem. legis. com. West Tex. C. of C. Mem. Am., Trans-Pecos, Pecos County bar assns., Nat. Inst. Municipal Law Officers, Tex. Criminal Def. Lawyers Assn., Delta Theta Phi. Home: 201 N Gillis St Fort Stockton TX 79735 Office: 104 W Callaghan St Fort Stockton TX 79735 Tel (915) 336-5900

GONZALEZ, CHARLES AUGUSTINE, b. San Antonio, May 5, 1945; B.A., U. Tex., 1969; J.D., St. Mary's U., 1972. Admitted to Tex. bar, 1972; individual practice law, San Antonio, 1972—; referee Bexar County (Tex.) Juvenile Ct., 1974. Mem. Alamo Area council Camp Fire Girls, 1973—; active United Way, 1975—, Easter Seals Soc., 1976—, Arthritis Found., 1975. Mem. Tex., Am., San Antonio bar assns., ACLU, Am., Tex. trial lawyers assns., Tex. Criminal Def. Lawyers Assn. Home: PO Box 407 Helotes TX 78023 Office: 314 Bank of San Antonio Bldg San Antonio TX 78205 Tel (512) 222-1247

GOOCH, JOEL EDWARD, b. Houma, La., June 16, 1942; B.A., U. Southwestern La., 1966; J.D., Tulane U., 1967. Admitted to La. State bar, 1968; spl. agt. FBI, 1967-71; mem. firm Allen, Gooch & Bourgeois, Ltd., Lafayette, La., 1971—; commr. Lafayette Harbor, Terminal and Indsl. Devel. Dist., 1973—, mem. exec. com., 1976—. Mem. La. State (mem. ho. of dels. 1976-77), Lafayette Parish (treas. 1976-77) Bar assns. Office: 1015 St John St Lafayette LA 70501 Tel (318) 233-5056

GOOD, G. MORTON, b. Atlanta, May 10, 1929; A.B., Emory U., 1951; LL.B., George Washington U., 1958. Admitted to Va. bar, 1958, Fla. bar, 1959; partner firm Smathers & Thompson, Miami, Fla., 1959—. Mem. Dade County, Va. Fla., Am. bar assns., Maritime Law Assn. U.S. Home: 5601 100th St Miami FL 33156 Office: 1301 Alfred I DuPont Bldg Miami FL 33131 Tel (305) 379-6523

GOOD, NED, b. Chgo., June 6, 1928; B.S., U. So. Calif., 1949, LL.B., 1951. Admitted to Calif., Fla. bars, 1952, Ill. bar, 1954, Korea bar, 1953; practiced in Los Angeles, 1955—; prin. law offices Ned Good, Los Angeles; judge pro-tem Los Angeles Superior Ct.; faculty U. So. Calif. Law Sch.; lectr. in field. Mem. Am. (v.p. Calif., past sec. aviation sect.), Calif. (past pres., chmn. aviation com.), Los Angeles (past pres., Trial Lawyer of Year 1976) trial lawyers assns., Los Angeles Bar Assn., Profl. Helicopter Pilots Assn. Calif. (asso.), Lawyer-Pilots Bar Assn., Calif. Aviation Counsel, Aircraft Owners and Pilots Assn., Aircraft Owners and Pilots Assn. Calif. (legis. liaison com.), Inner Circle Advs. Asso. editor Calif. Trial Lawyers Assn. Jour., 1960—; contbr. numerous articles to legal jours. Office: 333 S Hope St Suite 3600 Los Angeles CA 90071 Tel (213) 683-0880 also 615 Civic Center Dr W Suite 305 Santa Ana CA Tel (714) 973-1122

GOODE, JOHN LAYMAN, b. Benton, Ill., Nov. 21, 1903; student Okla. Baptist U., 1920-22, U. Ill., 1922; A.B., U. Okla., 1925, LL.B., 1925. Admitted to Okla. bar, 1925; mem. firms Goode, Dierker & Goode, Shawnee, Okla., 1929-38, Goode & Goode, Shawnee, 1938-53, Goode, Goode & Henson, 1953-56, Goode & Henson, Shawnee, 1956-75, city commr., Shawnee, 1946-50, mayor, 1948-50; mem. Okla. Securities Commn., 1963-66. Trustee Okla. Bapt. U., 1958-59. Mem. Am., Okla., Potawattamie (pres. 1966-67) bar assns., Phi Delta Phi, Delta Sigma Rho. Home: 1835 N Minnesota St Shawnee OK 74801 Office: 513 Federal National Bank Bldg Shawnee OK 74801

GOODE, MICHAEL TAYLOR, b. Norfolk, Va., Feb. 12, 1944; B.A., Washington and Lee U., 1966; J.D., U. Richmond, 1970. Admitted to Va. bar, 1970; asst. commonwealth's atty. State of Va., Portsmouth, 1970-73; asso. firm Cooper, Davis, Kilgore, Parker, Leon and Fennell, Portsmouth, 1973—. Pres. Portsmouth YMCA, 1975—; bd. dirs. Portsmouth USO. Mem. Va. Bar Assn. Home: 114 East Rd Portsmouth VA 23707 Office: PO Drawer 10 Portsmouth VA 23705 Tel (804) 397-3481

GOODELL, SOL, b. St. Louis, Aug. 24, 1906; A.A., El Paso Jr. Coll., 1925; J.D. with highest honors, U. Tex., 1929. Admitted to Tex. bar, 1929; asso. firm Thompson, Knight Simmons, Bullion, and predecessors, Dallas, 1930-40, partner, 1940—; instr. law U. Tex. at Austin, 1929. Mem. Dallas, Tex., Am. bar assns. Editor-in-chief Tex. Law Rev., 1929. Home: 5927 Joyce Way Dallas TX 75225 Office: 2300 Republic Nat Bank Bldg Dallas TX 75201 Tel (214) 655-7605

GOODELLE, FRED BELDEN, b. Waterloo, N.Y., Sept. 27, 1901; student Syracuse U., 1921-24; LL.B., Cornell U., 1926. Admitted to N.Y. bar, 1927; asso. firm Wile, Oviatt and Gilman, Rochester, N.Y., 1926-29, sr. asst. corp. counsel, 1929-34; individual practice law, Rochester, 1934-42; dept. corp. counsel City of Rochester, 1942-55, city ct. judge, 1956-62; partner firm Goodelle, Newman & Dutcher, and predecessor, Rochester, 1963—. Mem. Am., N.Y. State, Monroe County bar assns., Cornell Law Assn. Home: 11 B Brook Hill Ln Rochester NY 14625 Office: 520 Temple Bldg Rochester NY 14604 Tel (716) 454-3058

GOODFARB, STANLEY ZACHARY, b. N.Y.C., Nov. 1, 1930; B.A., U. Ariz., 1952, J.D., 1954. Admitted to Ariz. bar, 1954; practiced in Phoenix, 1957-59; asst. atty. gen. State of Ariz., Phoenix, 1959-76; judge Ariz. Superior Ct., 1976—; lectr. in field. Mem. State Bar Ariz., Am. Bar Assn., Am. Right of Way Assn. (pres. Phoenix chpt. 1970, internat. bd. dirs. 1971-72). Contbr. articles to profl. jours., including numerous articles to Am. Right of Way mag. Office: 120 W Jefferson St Phoenix AZ 85020 Tel (602) 262-3471

GOODFRIEND, HERBERT JAY, b. N.Y.C., Sept. 9, 1926; A.B., N.Y. U., 1947, LL.B., 1950, LL.M. in Taxation, 1953. Admitted to Appellate Div. 1st Dept. N.Y. bar, 1950, U.S. Dist. Ct. for So. Dist. N.Y. bar, 1951, for Eastern Dist. N.Y. bar, 1951, U.S. 2d Circuit Ct. Appeals bar, 1952, U.S. Tax Ct. bar, 1953; asso. firm Otterbourg, Steindler, Houston & Rosen, profl. corp., N.Y.C., 1950-55, partner, 1955—, chmn. bd., 1970—. Trustee Temple Beth El, Great Neck, N.Y., 1975—. Mem. N.Y. County Lawyers Assn. (com. on arbitration, com. on unauthorized practice of law 1975—), Am. Bar Assn. (sect. econ. practice chmn. com. on communication systems and equipment 1974—, sect. council 1976—). Editorial bd. N.Y. U. Law Rev., 1948-50. Office: 230 Park Ave New York City NY 10017 Tel (212) 679-1200

GOODHART, DAVID, b. Chgo., Aug. 19, 1929; B.B.A., U. Miami, Coral Gables, Fla., 1951, J.D., 1960. Admitted to Fla. bar, 1960, U.S. Supreme Ct. bar, 1971; practiced in Miami, 1960-62; asst. state atty. Dade County, Fla., 1962-72, exec. asst. state atty., 1966-72; judge Fla. Circuit Ct., 11th Jud. Circuit, 1973-76; partner firm Goodhart & Rosner, Miami, Fla., 1976—. Mem. Am. Bar Assn., Fla. Bar, Nat. Dist. Attys. Assn. Recipient Spl. award Dade County Grand Jury, 1971. Home: 11231 SW 69th Ct Miami FL 33156 Office: 28 W Flagler St Suite 1000 Miami FL 33130 Tel (305) 358-7100

GOODHUE, MARY BRIER, b. London, July 24, 1921; B.A., Vassar Coll., 1942; LL.B., U. Mich., 1944. Admitted to N.Y. bar, 1945, Mich. bar, 1944; asso. firm Root, Clark, Buckner & Ballantine, N.Y.C., 1945-48, asst. counsel N.Y. State Crime Commn., 1951-53, Moreland Commn., 1953-54; partner firm Goodhue, Lange & Arons, and predecessors, Mt. Kisco, N.Y., 1955—; mem. N.Y. State Assembly, 1975—. Bd. dirs. Mgrs. Episcopal Mission Soc. N.Y., 1964—, No. Westchester Hosp., Mt. Kisco, 1974—. Mem. Am., Westchester, No. Westchester bar assns. Home: McLain St Mount Kisco NY 10549 Office: 61 Smith Ave Mount Kisco NY 10549 Tel (914) 666-8033

GOODING, ROYAL GARY, b. Neenah, Wis., July 14, 1944; B.S. in Econs., U. Wis., 1966; J.D., John Marshall Law Sch., 1972. Admitted to Ill. bar, 1972; claims adjuster, supr. Aetna Life & Casualty Co., Aurora, Ill., 1966-72; partner firm Gooding & Vanderwater, Aurora, 1972—; part-time asst. state's atty., 1972-75; spl. prosecutor Kane County (Ill.), 1974. Rep., Boulder Hill Civic Assn.; Republican committeeman, Aurora. Mem. Am., Ill. State, Kane County, Kendall County bar assns. Home: Rte 3 Box 226 Oswego IL 60543 Office: 111 W Downer Suite 302 Aurora IL 60507 Tel (312) 896-5595

GOODMAN, ALFRED NELSON, b. N.Y.C., Jan. 21, 1945; B.S. in Mech. and Aero. Scis., U. Rochester, 1966; J.D., Georgetown U., 1969. Admitted to N.Y. state bar, 1970, D.C. bar, 1971, U.S. Patent Office bar, 1973; examiner patents U.S. Patent Office, Washington, D.C., 1969-71; asso. atty. firm Roylance, Abrams, Berdo & Kaul, Washington, D.C., 1971-74, partner 1975—. Mem. Am., D.C. bar assns., Bar Assn. D.C., Am. Patent Law Assn. Office: 1225 Connecticut Ave NW Washington DC 20036 Tel (202) 659-9076

GOODMAN, BENJAMIN MAX, b. New Orleans, Mar. 5, 1913; B.A., Tulane U., 1932, LL.B., 1935. Admitted to La. bar, 1935; individual practice law, New Orleans, 1935—. Bd. dirs. Jewish Community Center, New Orleans, 1950-52, Gates of Prayer Congregation, New Orleans, 1939-41. Mem. New Orleans, La. bar assns. Index editor Tulane Law Rev., 1933-35. Home: 2100 Saint Charles Ave New Orleans LA 70130 Office: 700 N Broad Ave New Orleans LA 70119 Tel (504) 821-3723

GOODMAN, ELLIOTT IRVIN, b. Chgo., Mar. 28, 1934; B.S., Northwestern U., 1955, J.D., 1958. Admitted to Ill. bar, 1958; asso. firm Gottlieb & Schwartz, Chgo., 1959-66, partner, 1966—; sec. T C Mfg. Co., Evanston, Ill., 1969—; sec.-treas. Ind. Basketball Players Assn., 1971-74; sec. E Z Paintr Corp., Milw., 1972-73; permanent arbitrator Amalgamated Social Benefits Plan, 1975—. Sec.-treas. Athletes for Better Edn. Found., 1975—. Mem. Am., Chgo. bar assns. Certified pub. accountant, Ill. Home: 549 County Line Rd Highland Park IL 60035 Office: 120 S LaSalle St Chicago IL 60603 Tel (312) 726-2122

GOODMAN, EZRA NORMAN, b. Bklyn., Jan. 27, 1943; B.A., Yeshiva U., 1964; J.D., Harvard, 1967. Admitted to N.Y. bar, 1968; partner firm Szold, Brandwen, Meyers & Altman, N.Y.C., 1974—. Trustee P.E.F. Israel Endowment Funds, Inc., N.Y.C., Mem. N.Y.C., N.Y. County bar assns. Office: Szold Brandwen et al 30 Broad St New York City NY 10004 Tel (212) 422-1777

GOODMAN, HERBERT, b. Bklyn., May 26, 1939; B.S., N.Y.U., 1961; LL.B., Bklyn. Law Sch., 1964, J.D., 1967. Admitted to N.Y. bar, 1965; individual practice law, N.Y.C., 1966—. C.P.A., N.Y. Office: 225 W 34th St New York City NY 10001 Tel (212) 594-8165

GOODMAN, IRVIN GUY, b. Sterling, Ill., Jan. 25, 1933; B.S. in Ceramic Engring., U. Ill., 1956; J.D., John Marshall Law Sch., 1973. Supt. melting and metallurgy Midland-Ross Corp., Melrose Pk., Ill., 1956-70; admitted to Ill. bar, 1973; asst. dir. environ. research Businessmen for the Pub. Interest, Chgo., 1973-75; mem. Ill. Pollution Control Bd., Chgo., 1975—. Mem. Am., Ill., Chgo. bar assns., Air Pollution Control Assn., Lake Mich. Fedn., Water Pollution Control Assn. Home: 22 W 081 Hickory Ct Medinah IL 60157 Office: 309 W Washington St Chicago IL 60606 Tel (312) 793-3620

GOODMAN, JAMES FLATT, b. Waco, Tex., May 27, 1923; B.S., U. Ill., 1943, J.D., 1948; M.B.A., U. Tex., 1951. Admitted to Ill. bar, 1949, Tex. bar, 1950; sr. partner firm Goodman Nielsen & Pakis, Waco, 1953-62; individual practice law, Houston, 1964-72; pres. Data Mate Computer Systems, Inc., Houston, 1972—. Trustee Linolean Ch., Houston. Mem. State Bar Tex. C.P.A., Tex. Home: 5400 Memorial Dr Houston TX 77007 Office: Memorial Towers Houston TX 77007 Tel (713) 869-5531

GOODMAN, JAY SYLVAN, b. N.Y.C., Nov. 5, 1923; B.A., Queens Coll., 1947; J.D., N.Y. Law Sch., 1953. Admitted to N.Y. bar, 1954, since practiced in N.Y.C.; tax counsel Siegel, Matson & Lasky, N.Y.C., 1974—. Pres., Great Neck (N.Y.) Estates Civic Assn., 1972-73; trustee Village of Great Neck Estates, 1975-76. Mem. N.Y. State Bar Assn., N.Y. County Lawyers Assn. Office: 230 Park Ave New York City NY 10017 Tel (212) 682-8840

GOODMAN, JEROME DANIEL, b. Annapolis, Md., June 1, 1913; A.B., St. John's Coll., 1934; LL.B., Harvard, 1937. Admitted to Mass. bar, 1938, U.S. Dist. Ct. bar, 1939; individual practice law, Boston, 1938—; master Mass. Superior Ct.; asst. dist. atty. Norfolk County (Mass.), 1958-60; spl. town counsel, Brookline, Mass., 1960-70. Mem. Brookline Town Meeting, 1948-74; trustee Temple Israel, Boston, 1968—, pres. Brotherhood, 1968-70; pres. Jewish Big Brother Assn., Boston, 1955-57, Brookline Citizens Com., 1972—. Mem. Am., Mass., Boston, Norfolk County bar assns., Mass. Trial Lawyers Assn. Author: What Are My Rights: A Guide to Labor Relations, 1938. Recipient award Am. Arbitration Assn., 1973, Combined Jewish Philanthropies of Greater Boston, 1956. Home: 100 Shaw Rd Chestnut Hill MA 02167 Office: 85 Devonshire St Boston MA 02109 Tel (617) 542-1081

GOODMAN, MAX A., b. Chgo., May 24, 1924; Herzl Jr. Coll., 1943; J.D., Loyola U., Los Angeles, 1948. Admitted to Calif. bar, 1948; individual practice law, Los Angeles, 1948-53; partner firm Goodman, Hirschberg & King, Los Angeles, 1953—; prof. law Southwestern U., 1966—. Mem. Am., Wilshire, Los Angeles County bar assns. Editor: Family Law Symposium Handbook, 1975, 76; contbr. articles in field to profl. jours. Home: 328 S Elm Dr Beverly Hills CA 90212 Office: 3850 Wilshire Blvd Suite 307 Los Angeles CA 90010 Tel (213) 389-2174

GOODMAN, MEYER FOX, b. N.Y.C., Sept. 8, 1912; LL.B., St. John's U., 1934. Admitted to N.Y. bar, 1935, U.S. Supreme Ct., 1954; pvt. practice law, Carle Place, N.Y., 1971. Mem. Nassau County, N.Y. State, Am. bar assns., Am. Acad. Matrimonial Lawyers, Am. Arbitration Assn. (mem. panel arbitrators 1968—), N.Y. State Trial Lawyers Assn., N.Y. State Assn. Home: 215 W Fulton Ave Roosevelt NY 11575 Office: 1 Old Country Rd Carle Place NY 11514

GOODMAN, MORTIMER, b. N.Y.C., Jun 11, 1910; Sc.B., N.Y. U., 1931, J.D., 1933. Admitted to N.Y. State bar, 1933, U.S. Supreme Ct. bar, 1959; individual practice law, N.Y.C., 1934-40; asso. firm Rosston, Hort & Brussel, N.Y.C., 1940-47; partner Grandefeld & Goodman, N.Y.C., 1948—; pub. mem. Securities Industry Conf. on Arbitration, 1977—. Chmn., United Jewish Appeal of Flushing, 1958; pres. Free Synagogue of Flushing, 1953-56. hon. pres., 1967—, trustee, 1951—; trustee N.Y. Fedn. Reform Synagogues, 1970—; v.p. YM & YWHA of Greater Flushing, 1976—, bd. dirs., 1957—; founder State of Israel Bond Orgn., 1951. Mem. Am., Queens County bar assns., N.Y. County Lawyers Assn. Office: 39 Broadway New York City NY 10006 Tel (212) 422-0045

GOODMAN, PAUL JAY, b. N.Y.C., Aug. 3, 1933; B.A., Dartmouth, 1955, J.D., Yale, 1958; LL.M., N.Y.U., 1976. Admitted to N.Y. bar, 1959; practiced in Mineola, 1959-60; with firm Priest & Carson, Forest Hills, N.Y., 1960—, sr. partner, 1974—. Mem. Queens County Bar Assn. (family law com.). Contbr. articles to legal jours. Home: 210 Greenway South Forest Hills NY 11375 Office: 71-23 Austin St Forest Hills NY 11375 Tel (212) BO8-9090

GOODMAN, WAYNE MITCHELL, b. Chicago, Ill., Dec. 14, 1946; B.S., U. Ill., Champaign, 1969; J.D., DePaul U., Chgo., 1972. Admitted to Ill. bar, 1972, U.S. Dist. Ct. bar, 1972; asso. firm Allen S. Pesmen, Chgo., 1972-75, partner Pesmen, Goodman & Weil, Chgo., 1975—. Mem. Am., Ill., Chgo. bar assns. Office: 29 S LaSalle St Chicago IL 60603 Tel (312) 641-3333

GOODMAN, WILLIAM PENN, b. Kyles Ford, Tenn., Apr. 29, 1922; J.D., U. Tenn., 1949. Admitted to Tenn. bar, 1949, U.S. Supreme Ct. bar, 1954; with JAGC, U.S. Army, 1950-66; dep. law dir. City of Knoxville (Tenn.), 1966-67; asso. prof. bus. law Tenn. Tech. U., 1967—. Mem. Tenn., Fed. bar assns., Nat. Assn. Bus. Law Tchrs., Am. Bus. Law Assn. Home: 675 Woodlawn Dr Cookeville TN 38501 Office: Box 5152 TTU Sta Cookeville TN 38501 Tel (615) 528-3359

GOODMAN, ZENIA SACHS, b. Chgo., Aug. 18, 1921; B.A. cum laude, Columbia, 1942; J.D. cum laude, U. Chgo., 1948. Admitted to Ill. bar, 1949; asst. states atty. Cook County (Ill.), 1949-51; asso. firm Katz & Friedman, Chgo., 1968-74; arbitrator Indsl. Commn. State of Ill., 1974—, pres., 1977—. Trustee, Village of Glencoe (Ill.), 1972-76; bd. dirs. Congregation Am. Shalom. Mem. Ill., Chgo., Women's bar assns., Nat. Assn. Women Lawyers, Decalogue Soc. (bd. mgrs.), Order of Coif, Phi Beta Kappa. Office: 160 N LaSalle St Chicago IL 60601 Tel (312) 435-6516

GOODNOUGH, ROGER ALLEN, b. Franklin, N.H., Sept. 13, 1946; B.A. cum laude, U. N.H., 1968; J.D., Columbia, 1971. Admitted to N.Y. bar, 1972, U.S. Dist. Ct. So. Dist. N.Y. bar, 1973, U.S. Ct. Appeals 2d Circuit, 1976; asso. firm Hart & Hume, N.Y.C., 1972-75, sr. asso., 1976—. Mem. N.Y. State, Am. Bar Assns. Contbr. articles to legal publs. Home: 165 Pinehurst Ave New York City NY 10033 Office: 10 E 40th St New York City NY 10016 Tel (212) 686-0920

GOODPASTURE, HENRY, b. Nashville, Oct. 3, 1898; LL.B., Cumberland U., Lebanon, Tenn., 1921. Admitted to Tenn. bar, 1921; partner firm Goodpasture Carpenter Wood and Sasser and predecessors, Nashville, 1929—. Pres. bd. Salvation Army, Nashville, Children's Mus., Nashville, 1972—. Mem. Nashville (past pres.), Tenn., Am. bar assns., Tenn. Hist. Soc. (pres. 1970-71). Home: Old Town St Franklin TN 37064 Office: 6th Floor Am Trust Bldg Nashville TN 37203 Tel (615) 352-4524

GOODRICH, GEORGE HERBERT, b. Charlestown, W.Va., June 19, 1925; B.A., Williams Coll., 1949; LL.B., U. Va., 1952. Admitted to D.C. bar, 1953, Md. bar, 1958; practiced in Washington, 1953—; asso. firm Guggenheimer, Untermyer & Goodrich, 1952-62; asso. firm Heffelfinger, Schweitzer & Goodrich and predecessor, 1962-67, partner, 1967-69; asso. judge Superior Ct. D.C., 1969—; former faculty mem. Am. Inst. Banking; former comml. law lectr. Am. U.; adj. prof. civil procedure Potomac Sch. Law. Past pres. Homemakers Service, Washington; past vice chmn. Hillcrest Children's Center, Washington; past bd. dirs. ARC, Washington. Mem. Am., D.C. (sec. 1962-68, chmn. various coms.) bar assns., Am. Law Inst., Nat. Coll. State Judiciary (faculty advisor), Williams Coll. Alumni Assn. (past pres.). Contbr. articles in field to legal jours. Home: 6003 Corbin Rd NW Washington DC 20016 Office: 4th and E Sts NW Suite 219 Washington DC 20001 Tel (202) 727-1055

GOODRICH, LAURANCE VILLERS, b. Ann Arbor, Mich., Apr. 6, 1929; B.A. in Econs. magna cum laude, Harvard, 1950; J.D., Columbia, 1953. Admitted to N.Y. bar, 1953; asso. firm Cravath Swaine & Moore, N.Y.C., 1957-66; partner firm Barrett Knapp Smith & Shapiro, N.Y.C., 1966-70, firm Sage Gray Todd & Sims, N.Y.C., 1970-73; individual practice law, Bklyn., 1974—. Mem. N.Y. State Bar Assn., Assn. Bar City N.Y. Tel (212) 858-5996

GOODRICH, LAURENCE IVAN, b. Savannah, Ga., Jan. 21, 1932; A.B., U. Fla., 1954, J.D., 1957. Admitted to Fla. bar, 1957; asso. firm Carlton, Fields, Ward, Emanuel, Smith & Cutler, Tampa, Fla., 1957-58; asst. county solicitor, Hillsborough County, Tampa, 1958-60; partner firm Liles, Edwards & Goodrich, Tampa, 1960-64; asst. city atty., Tampa, 1962-63, 1968-72; atty. Hillsborough County Bd. Pub. Instrn., Tampa, 1964; judge 13th Jud. Circuit of Fla., Tampa, 1973—; lectr. bus. law U. South Fla., Tampa, 1960-61; U. Tampa, 1975; part-time asst. prof. bus. law, Hillsborough Community Coll., Tampa, 1973—. Mem. Fla. Bar Assn., Fla. Conf. Circuit Judges. Home: 3318 McKay Ave Tampa FL 33609 Office: Room 380 Hillsborough County Ct House Tampa FL 33602 Tel (813) 229-1745

GOODRUM, WAYNE LOUIS, b. Ft. Worth, Dec. 8, 1934; B.B.A., Hardin-Simmons U., 1958; J.D., U. Tex., Austin, 1971. Admitted to Tex. bar, 1972; div. mgr. Gen. Telephone Co. SW, Seymour, Tex., 1967-69, sr. atty., San Angelo, Tex., 1972-76; gen. counsel Gen. Telephone Co. of Ky., Lexington, 1976—. Dist. chmn. NW Tex. council Boy Scouts Am., 1966; deacon Baptist Ch., Seymour, 1967-69, San Angelo, 1972-76. Mem. State Bar Tex., Tom Green County (Tex.) Bar Assn. Home: 3362 Pepperhill St Lexington KY 40502 Office: 2001 Harrodsburg Rd Lexington KY 40504 Tel (606) 277-6115

GOODSON, JOHN FERDINAND, b. Phoenix, Ariz., Nov. 4, 1931; B.A., U. Ariz., 1953, LL.B., 1961, J.D., 1961. Admitted to Ariz. bar, 1961; bailiff Superior Ct. Ariz., 1961; asso. firm Jennings, Strouss, Salmon & Trask, Phoenix, 1961-63; founding partner Cunningham, Goodson & Tiffany, Ltd. and predecessor firms, Phoenix, 1963—;

evening instr. Phoenix Coll., 1975—; prof. law of office mgmt., real estate, estate planning, bus. orgns. Founding mem. Valley Big Bros., 1967-68; chmn. restructure com. Maricopa County Presbytery, 1966; dir. sec PAK Found., 1968—; founding mem., dir. Primate Found. Ariz.; founding mem., bd. dirs. YMCA. Mem. Am., Maricopa County bar assns., State Bar Ariz., Am. Trial Lawyers Assn., Am. Judicature Soc., Central Ariz. Estate Planning Council, Hosp. Fin. Mgmt. Assn., Am. Arbitration Assn., Internat. Bar Assn., Legion, Phoenix Alumni Assn. U. Ariz., Phi Delta Theta. Author: Legal Aspects of Doing Business in Arizona. Contbr. articles to legal jours. Home: 1117 W Coronado Phoenix AZ 85007 Office: 9th Floor Luhrs Bldg Jefferson and Central Sts Phoenix AZ 85003 Tel (602) 254-5104

GOODSON, RALPH RAYMOND, b. Los Angeles, May 20, 1933; B.S. in Accounting, U. So. Calif., 1958, J.D., 1961. Admitted to Calif. bar, 1961; mgr. real estate Litton Industries, Beverly Hills, Calif., 1961-67; assigned to Calif. State Survey on Govt. Efficiency and Cost Control-Edn. Study Team, 1967; sr. financial specialist -Litton-Greece, 1967-68; dir. adminstrn. Litton Internat. Inc., 1968-70; individual practice law, Los Angeles, 1971—; pres. Lake Tulloch Corp., 1972-73; chmn. bd. Am. Multiplex System, Inc., 1975—. Mem. Calif. Recreational Trails Com., 1971—, vice-chmn. 1975; bd. dirs. Pres.'s Circle U. So. Calif., 1976. Mem. Am., Calif. bar assns., Am. Arbitration Assn., (arbitrator), U. So. Calif. Alumni Assn. Office: 1800 Ave of the Stars Los Angeles CA 90067 Tel (213) 277-6133

GOODSTEIN, MAURICE MAC, b. Denver, July 27, 1909; B.A., U. Calif., Los Angeles, 1931; LL.B., Loyola U., Los Angeles, 1935. Admitted to Calif. bar, 1936; individual practice law, Los Angeles, 1936-42; partner firms Goodstein & Moffitt, Los Angeles, 1949-71, Jackson & Goodstein, Los Angeles, 1971—. Trustee, U. Calif. at Los Angeles Found., 1970—. Mem. Am., Los Angeles County (chmn. sect. natural resources 1975-76), Calif. bar assns., Am. Judicature Soc. Decorated Bronze Star with oak leaf cluster; recipient Achievement award U. Calif. at Los Angeles, 1964. Home: 405 N Palm Dr Beverly Hills CA 90212 Office: 1901 Ave of the Stars Suite 1600 Los Angeles CA 90067 Tel (213) 277-0200

GOODWIN, ALFRED THEODORE, b. Bellingham, Wash., June 29, 1923; B.A., U. Oreg., 1947, J.D., 1951; LL.D. (hon.), Lewis and Clark Coll., 1976. Admitted to Oreg. bar, 1951; asso. firm Darling & Vonderheit, Eugene, Oreg., 1951-55; judge Oreg. Circuit Ct., Eugene, 1955-60; asso. justice Oreg. Supreme Ct., 1960-69; U.S. dist. judge for Oreg., 1969-71; judge U.S. Ct. Appeals for 9th Circuit, 1971—; mem. Oreg. Constl. Revision Commn., 1961, 62. Mem. Am. Bar Assn., Am. Judicature Soc., Am. Law Inst. Recipient Distinguished Service award U. Oreg., 1972. Office: US Circuit Ct Pioneer Courthouse Portland OR 97204 Tel (503) 221-2184 also Room 416 US Ct Appeals San Francisco CA 94101

GOODWIN, HUGH WESLEY, b. Steelton, Pa., May 6, 1921; A.B., Howard U., 1943; LL.B., Harvard, 1948. Admitted to Calif. bar, 1949; partner firm Maddox & Goodwin, Los Angeles, 1949-51; individual practice law, Fresno, Calif., 1952-67; asst. pub. defender County of Fresno, 1967-76; judge Fresno Municipal Ct., 1976—. Pres. Fresno Rescue Mission, 1974—; bd. dirs. Alcoholics Victorious, Fresno, 1975—; mem. Fresno Mayor's Prayer Breakfast Com.; deacon Second Bapt. Ch., Fresno. Mem. Calif., Fresno County, Nat. bar assns. Home: 3160 W Kearney Bldg Fresno CA 93706 Office: 1100 Van Ness Ave Fresno CA 93721 Tel (209) 488-3385

GOODWIN, JACK, b. McCurtain, Okla., Nov. 17, 1921; B.S., U. Calif., Los Angeles, 1950; J.D., U. So. Calif., 1965. Admitted to Calif. bar, 1968; dep. savs. and loan commr. Calif. Dept. Savs. and Loan, Los Angeles, 1969—. Mem. Am. Bar Assn. Home: 10100 Halbrent Ave Mission Hills CA 91345 Office: 600 S Commonwealth Ave Los Angeles CA 90005 Tel (213) 736-2801

GOODWIN, JOHN ROBERT, b. Morgantown, W.Va., Nov. 3, 1929; B.S. in Edn., W.Va. U., 1952, J.D., 1964. Admitted to W. Va. bar, 1964, U.S. Supreme Ct. bar, 1972; prof. bus. law W.Va. U., 1964—; city atty. Monongalia County, W.Va., 1966-68, spl. pros. atty., 1968. Mayor City of Morgantown, 1964-66; chmn. Morgantown San. Bd., 1964-66; mem. Morgantown Library Commn., 1960-66. Mem. W.Va. Bar Assn., Beta Gamma Sigma. Named one of 1000 outstanding West Virginians, 1970; author: Twenty Feet from Glory, 1970; Business Law, Principles, Documents and Cases, 1972-76. Home: 427 Mildred Ave Morgantown WV 26505 Tel (304) 296-3771

GOODWIN, LEONARD JAMES, b. Stockton, Calif., Feb. 11, 1943; A.B., U. Calif., Berkeley, 1964; J.D., St. John's U., Bklyn., 1969; LL.M. in Labor Law, N.Y. U., 1970. Admitted to N.Y. bar, 1970, U.S. Supreme Ct. bar, 1975; mgr. labor relations Trans World Airlines, Inc., N.Y.C., 1970-72; asso. counsel N.Y.C. Bd. Higher Edn., 1974-76; asso. gen. counsel Office Municipal Labor Relations of Mayor of N.Y.C., 1976—; gen. counsel 7th Ave. Betterment Com., Inc., N.Y.C., 1974—. Pres. temple action group Union Temple of Bklyn., 1976—, asso. trustee temple, 1977—. Mem. Am., Bklyn. bar assns., Fed. Bar Council. Home: 839 President St Brooklyn NY 11215 Office: 250 Broadway New York City NY 10007 Tel (212) 566-6076

GOODWIN, RONALD RAY, b. Phillips, Tex., Jan. 9, 1941; B.B.A., Baylor U., 1963, J.D., 1969. Admitted to Tex. bar, 1969; since practiced in San Angelo, Tex.; trust officer 1st Nat. Bank, Odessa, Tex., 1969-70; partner firm Griffis, Williams, Goodwin & Harrison, 1970-72, Kerr, Gayer, Gregg & Goodwin, 1972-75, Goodwin & Hawthorne, 1975—; Trustee San Angelo Independent Sch. Dist., 1976—, chmn. Civil Service Commn., 1972-75; bd. dirs. March of Dimes, 1973-75, YMCA, 1974-76. Mem. Tom Green County, Am. bar assns., State Bar Tex. (mem. com. admissions 1974—), Baylor Law Sch. Alumni Assn. (dir. 1974—) Home: 3702 Sul Ross San Angelo TX 76901 Office: PO Drawer 31 San Angelo TX 76901 Tel (915) 655-7331

GOODWIN, WILLIAM LLOYD, b. Hattiesburg, Miss., July 22, 1944; B.A. magna cum laude, Vanderbilt U.; LL.B., U. Va., 1969. Admitted to Ga. bar, 1970; asso. firm Powell, Goldstein, Frazer & Murphy, Atlanta, 1976—. Mem. Atlanta Bar Assn., Phi Beta Kappa. Mem. editorial bd. Va. Law Rev. 1967-69. Home: 5930 Kayron Dr Atlanta GA 30328 Office: 1100 Citizens and Southern National Bank Building Atlanta GA 30308 Tel (404) 521-1900

GOOGINS, ROBERT REVILLE, b. Cambridge, Mass., June 2, 1937; B.S., U. Conn., 1958, J.D., 1961; M.B.A., U. Hartford, 1970. Admitted to Conn. bar, 1961; atty. Conn. Mut. Life Ins. Co., Hartford, 1961-62, asst. counsel, 1964-67, asso. counsel, 1967-70, counsel, 1970-72, counsel, sec., 1972-74, v.p., counsel, sec., 1974-75, v.p., gen. counsel, sec., 1975—; lectr. U. Conn. Law Sch., 1966—; mem. report coordinating group SEC, 1974—. Chmn. Glastonbury Sewer Commn., 1973-75; vice chmn. Glastonbury (Conn.) Town Council, 1975—. Mem. Am., Conn. bar assns., Am. Council Life Ins. (chmn. com. variable contracts 1975—), Nat. Assn. Securities Dealers (bd. govs. 1976—). Home: 74 Forest Ln Glastonbury CT 06033 Office: 140 Garden St Hartford CT 06109 Tel (203) 549-4111

GOOLRICK, ROBERT MASON, b. Fredericksburg, Va., Mar. 25, 1934; B.A. with distinction, U. Va., 1956, J.D., 1959. Admitted to Va. bar, 1959, D.C. bar, 1960; with firm Steptoe & Johnson, Washington, 1959—, partner, 1966—. Mem. Am. Bar Assn., Order of Coif, Phi Beta Kappa. Contbr. articles to legal jours. Home: 9312 Briarwood Pl Fairfax VA 22030 Office: 1250 Connecticut Ave Washington DC 20036 Tel (202) 862-2158

GOOSTREE, ROBERT EDWARD, b. Montgomery County, Tenn., Sept. 23, 1923; A.B., Southwestern U., Memphis, 1943; M.A., State U. Iowa, 1948, Ph.D., 1950; J.D., Am. U., 1962. Admitted to D.C. bar, 1962, U.S. Supreme Ct. bar, 1966; instr. polit. sci. state U. Iowa, 1946-50, U. Md., 1951-53; asst. prof. Sch. Govt., Am. U., Washington, 1953-71, prof. law and govt., 1963-71, acting dean Sch. Govt., 1958-62, acting dean Sch. Law, 1970-71; prof. law Capital U., Columbus, 1971—, dean Sch. Law, 1971—; individual practice law, Washington, 1968-69; cons. in field. Mem. Am., Fed. bar assns., Am. Polit. Sci. Assn., Am. Trial Lawyers Assn., Nat. Lawyers Club Washington. Contbr. articles to legal jours. Home: 999 Matterhorn Reynoldsburg OH 43068 Office: 2199 E Main St Capital U Law Sch Columbus OH 3209 Tel (614) 236-6395

GOPLEN, ARNOLD OLAF, b. Binford, N.D., July 15, 1907; B.S. in Edn., U. N.D., 1929, M.A., 1935. Admitted to N.D. bar, 1942; spl. asst. atty. gen. N.D. State Dept. Health, Bismarck, 1949-66; legal counsel Lutheran Hosps. and Homes Soc. Am., Fargo, N.D., 1966-74, legal cons., 1974—; tchr. pub. schs., Northwood, N.D., 1929-34, Jamestown, N.D., 1934-36, Crookston, Minn., 1936-37; historian Nat. Park Service, Bismarck and Medora, N.D., 1937-39; state personnel dir. Youth Employment Nat. Youth Adminstrn., Bismarck, 1939-43; dir. div. hosps. N.D. State Dept. Health, Bismarck, 1948-66. Treas. Burleigh County Council Aging, 1976—. Mem. N.D. Bar Assn., Soc. Hosp. Attys., Am. Hosp. Assn., Am. Assn. Hosp. Planning. Contbr. articles to mags. Home: 1220 N 1st St Bismarck ND 58501 Tel (701) 223-2167

GORAN, JAY, b. Chgo., May 15, 1915; LL.B., Chgo. Kent Coll. Law, 1937. Admitted to Ill. bar, 1937; individual practice law, 1937-43; mem. firm Crane & Goran, 1946-56; individual practice law, Chgo., 1956—. Pres. Chgo. Parents of the Deaf, 1954; bd. dirs. Henner Speech and Hearing Clinic, 1971-73. Mem. Chgo., Ill. bar assns. Editor: Food and Drug Jour., 1946. Office: 19 S LaSalle St Chicago IL 60603 Tel (312) RA 6-6616

GORDER, CHARLES FRANKLIN, b. Aberdeen, S.D., Nov. 9, 1925; B.S., U.S. Naval Acad., 1947; J.D., George Washington U., 1955, LL.M., 1967. Commd. ensign USN, 1947, advanced through grades to comdr., 1962; ret., 1967; admitted to Va. bar, 1955, Calif. bar, 1962, U.S. Supreme Ct. bar, 1966; asso. firm Higgs, Jennings, Fletcher & Mack, San Diego, 1967-70, partner, 1971; mem. firm Jennings, Engstrand & Henrikson, San Diego, 1971—. Bd. mgrs. John A. Davis Family YMCA, La Mesa, Calif., 1975—. Mem. Am., San Diego County, Foothills (pres. 1972) bar assns., State Bar Calif., Bar Commonwealth Va., Omicron Delta Kappa. Recipient Bell Larner Scholarship award George Washington U. Law Sch., 1955; named Boss of Year San Diego Legal Secs. Assn., 1975; editor in chief George Washington Law Rev., 1954-55. Office: 2255 Camino del Rio S San Diego CA 92108 Tel (714) 291-0840

GORDON, ALEXANDER SIDNEY, b. Chelsea, Mass., Apr. 29, 1913; B.S., B.A., Boston U., 1933, LL.B., 1936, S.J.D., 1971. Admitted to Mass. bar, 1936, Fla. bar, 1945; individual practice law, Mass., 1936-39, Miami and Miami Beach, Fla., 1945—; spl. agent FBI, 1939-45; mem. Fed. Mediation and Conciliation Service. Mem. Bd. Commrs., Dade County, Fla., 1958-72. Mem. Am., Fla. bar assns., Am. Trial Lawyers, Am. Arbitration Assn. Home: 2450 Meridian Ave Miami Beach FL 33139 Office: 1206 Alfred I duPont Building 169 E Flagler St Miami FL 33131 Tel (305) 371-3437

GORDON, BENJAMIN EDWARD, b. Lawrence, Mass., Oct. 12, 1909; A.B., Boston U., 1930; LL.B., Harvard, 1933, J.D., 1968. Admitted to Mass. bar, 1933; U.S. Supreme Ct. bar, 1944; regional atty. Fed. Emergency Relief Adminstrn., Washington, 1935; regional atty. Resettlement Adminstrn. Northeastern Region, New Haven, 1935-36; New Eng. counsel Nat. Park Service, Cambridge, Mass., 1936-37; litigation counsel NLRB, Washington 1937, regional counsel, Pitts. and Boston, 1937-41; individual practice law, 1941—; founder firm Gordon, Leiter & Turney, Boston, 1964, Labor counsel Asso. Wholesale Food Distbrs., Boston, 1941—, Lewiston-Auburn (Maine) Shoe Mfrs., 1947-74; gen. counsel Smaller Bus. Assn. New Eng., 1966-73; lectr. labor relations Stonehill Coll., Easton, Mass., 1968-71; lectr. in field. Mem. Boston U. Coll. Liberal Arts Alumni Assn. (pres. 1965-67), Nat. Alumni Council Boston U., Am., Mass., Boston bar assns., Am. Arbitration Assn., Mass. Trial Lawyers Assn. Contbr. articles to legal jours. Home: 131 Beaver Rd Weston MA 02193 Office: 31 State St Boston MA 02109 Tel (617) 227-4900

GORDON, CHARLES EDWARD, b. N.Y.C., Sept. 21, 1946; B.A., Rollins Coll., 1968, M.C.S., 1970; J.D., Emory U., 1972. Admitted to Fla. bar, 1973; asst. states atty. Jud. Circuit Ct., Sanford, Fla., 1973—. Mem. Am., Fla., Orange County bar assns., Nat. Dist. Attys. Assn., Fla. Pros. Attys. Assn. Home: 1841 Englewood Rd Winter Park FL 32789 Office: 280 Canton Ave W suite 200 PO Box 956 Winter Park FL 32789 Tel (305) 628-1414

GORDON, EDGAR GEORGE, b. Detroit, Feb. 27, 1924; A.B., Princeton, 1947; J.D., Harvard, 1950. Admitted to Mich. bar, 1951, U.S. Supreme Ct. bar, 1953; asso. firm Poole, Warren & Littell, Detroit, 1950-54, partner, 1954-63; gen. counsel Hygrade Food Products Corp., Detroit, 1963-69, sec., 1966-69, v.p., 1968-69; v.p., counsel City Nat. Bank Detroit, 1969—; v.p., sec., gen. counsel No. State Bancorp., Detroit, 1970—; dir. Kelly Mortgage & Investment Co., Bloomfield Hills, Mich. Mem. Am., Mich., Detroit bar asssns. Home: 210 Lothrop Rd Grosse Pointe Farms MI 48236 Office: Suite 3900 400 Tower Renaissance Center Detroit MI 48243 Tel (313) 965-1900

GORDON, EUGENE ANDREW, b. Guilford County, N.C., July 10, 1917; A.B., Elon Coll., 1938; LL.B., Duke, 1941. Admitted to N.C. bar, 1941; practiced law, 1946-64; mem. firm Young, Young & Gordon, Burlington, 1947-64; solicitor Alamance Gen. County Ct., 1947-54; county atty., Alamance County, 1954-64; U.S. judge Middle Dist. N.C., 1964—, now chief judge. Former chmn. adv. bd. Salvation Army. Former nat. committeeman N.C. Young Democrats; former pres. Alamance County Young Democrats; chmn. Alamance County Dem. Exec. Com., 1954-64. Mem. Alamance County Bar Assn. (past pres.), Burlington-Alamance County C. of C. (past pres.), Burlington Jr. C. of C., Phi Delta Phi. Home: 1001 Pebble Dr Greensboro NC 27410 Office: Greensboro NC 27402*

GORDON, GEORGE ROBERT, b. San Anselmo, Calif., May 25, 1910; B.S. magna cum laude, St. Mary's Coll., Moraga, Calif., 1931; certificate in secondary edn. U. Calif., 1932; LL.B., Oakland Coll. Law, 1938. Admitted to Calif. bar, 1938; partner firm Carlson, Collins & Gordon, Richmond, Calif., 1939-42, 46-54, firm Gordon & Welch, 1954-60, Gordon, Waltz, De Fraga, Watrous & Pezzaglia, and predecessor, Martinez, Calif., 1960—. Trustee Contra Costa Community Coll. Dist., 1949-77, pres.; regent St. Mary's Coll., Moraga, 1965—, trustee, pres. bd. trustees. Mem. Contra Costa, Am., Richmond bar assns. Recipient Pres's. award St. Mary's Coll., 1966. Home: 1980 Pine St Martinez CA 94553 Office: 611 Las Juntas St Martinez CA 94553 Tel (415) 228-1400

GORDON, HARLAN MEYER, b. Cleve., Jan. 31, 1943; A.B., Case Western Res. U., 1965, J.D., 1968; postgrad. Coll. of Law, U. Ill., 1968-69. Admitted to Ohio bar, 1968, U.S. Supreme Ct. bar, 1976; law clk. to Hon. Thomas D. Lambros of Fed. Dist. Ct., Cleve., 1969-73; with fed. pub. defender's office, Cleve., 1973-74; asso. firm Komito, Nurenberg, Plevin, Jacobson, Heller and McCarthy, Cleve., 1974—. Mem. Ohio State, Cleve. bar assns., Assn. Trial Lawyers Am., Order of Coif. Home: 3579 Washington Blvd Blvd Cleveland Heights OH 44118 Office: 7th Floor Engineers Bldg Cleveland OH 44114 Tel (216) 621-2300

GORDON, HOWARD D., b. Cleve., Mar. 24, 1944; B.S. in Indsl. Engrng., Purdue U., 1967; J.D., Cleve. State U., 1971. Admitted to Ohio bar, 1971; sr. patent atty. Eaton Corp., Cleve. Mem. Am., Ohio State, Cleve. bar assns. Office: 100 Erieview Plaza Cleveland OH 44114 Tel (216) 523-5170

GORDON, IVAN H., b. Bklyn., Sept. 15, 1907; LL.B., St. John's U., 1929. Admitted to N.Y. bar, 1931; individual practice law, 1931—; arbitrator Am. Arbitration Assn., Small Claims Ct., N.Y. Civil Ct. Mem. N. Am. Judges Assn., N.Y. County Lawyers Assn. Office: 95 Madison Ave New York City NY 10016 Tel (212) 684-4863

GORDON, JAY F., b. N.Y.C., Feb. 5, 1926; student Coll. City N.Y., 1941-43, Cornell U., 1943-44; LL.B., St. John's U., 1948. Admitted to N.Y. bar, 1949, U.S. Supreme Ct. bar, 1965; asso. firm Harte & Natanson, N.Y.C., 1949-54; partner firm Natanson, Gordon & Reich, and predecessors, N.Y.C., 1954-68; sr. partner firm Gordon, Goldman, Cooperman & Buchalter, Hempstead and N.Y.C., 1969-71; partner firm Phillips, Nizer, Benjamin, Krim & Ballon, N.Y.C. and Washington, 1972—; mem. nat panel arbitrators Am. Arbitration Assn., 1968—; mayor Village of Lawrence (N.Y.), 1966-69, trustee, 1964-66. Mem. Nassau County Bar Assn. Home: 116 Causeway Lawrence NY 11559 Office: 40 W 57th St New York City NY 10019 Tel (212) 977-9700

GORDON, JOHN ROY, b. Denver, Sept. 8, 1942; B.A., U. Mont., 1964, J.D. with honors, 1967. Admitted to Mont. bar, 1967, N.D. bar, 1968; law clk. to judge 9th Circuit U.S. Ct. Appeals, San Francisco, 1967-68; asso. firm Bjella & Jestrab, Williston, N.D., 1968-70; partner, 1970-76; asso. firm Murray, Donahue, & Kaufman, Kalispell, Mont., 1976—; sec., treas. State Bar N.D., 1970-72. Chmn. bd. dirs. N.W. Human Resource Center, Williston, 1970-76. Mem. Am., Mont., N.D. bar assns., Am. Judicature Soc. Home: 18 Konley Dr Kalispell MT 59901 Office: 240 1st Ave W Kalispell MT 59901

GORDON, JOSEPH KELLER, b. Phila., June 9, 1925; A.B., in English, Princeton, 1948; LL.B., U. Pa., 1951. Admitted to Pa. bar, 1952; since practiced in Phila., asso. firm Ballard, Spahr, Andrews & Ingersoll, 1951-59; resident Phila. Nat. Bank, counsel, 1959-61, v.p., 1961-70, sr. v.p., 1970-74; sr. v.p. chief counsel Phila. Nat. Corp., 1974—; dir. sec. Phila. Internat. Bank; Congress Factors Corp.; dir. Colonial Mortgage Service Co.; sec. PNB Mortgage and Realty Investors. Mem. Middle Atlantic Com. Project Hope, (chmn. 1967-69); dir. allocations com. Nat. and State Services Div. United Fund Phila. Area, 1964-69; dir. Voluntary Defender Assn. Phila., 1969-71; dir. Children's Service, Inc., 1955-72, pres. 1960-63; mem. advisory panel YWCA, Phila., 1972—; bd. dirs. Haverford Civic Assn.; trustee Episcopal Acad., Lankenaw Hosp., Hosp. Survey Com. Mem. Pa. C. of C. (mem. comml. law com.), Urban League, Fellowship Commn., World Affairs Phila., Scotch-Irish Soc. U.S. Am. (mem. exec. com.), trustee. Mem. Phila., Pa., Am. bar assns., Phila. Bar Found. (pres. 1974). Office: Broad and Chestnut Sts Philadelphia PA 19101 Tel (215) 629-3821

GORDON, L. JAMES, b. Phila., Mar. 17, 1927; B.A., Denison U., Granville, Ohio, 1950; LL.B., Yale, 1953. Admitted to Ohio bar, 1953; asso. firm E. Clark Morrow, Newark, Ohio, 1953-59; partner firm Morrow, Gordon & Byrd, Newark, 1960—. Mem. Granville (Ohio) Exempted Village Bd. Edn., 1969—, pres., 1971—; pres. United Way of Licking County (Ohio), 1971-72. Mem. Am., Ohio, Licking County (pres. 1968) bar assns., Phi Beta Kappa, Phi Alpha Delta, Order of Coif. Home: 732 Mount Parnassus Granville OH 43023 Office: 33 W Main St Newark OH 43055 Tel (614) 345-9764

GORDON, LAWRENCE ROBERT, b. Los Angeles, Apr. 27, 1940; student U. Calif. at Los Angeles, 1961; J.D., Loyola U., Los Angeles, 1964. Admitted to Calif. bar, 1965; partner firm Gordon, Weinberg & Gordon, Century City Calif., 1965. Mem. Am., Century City, Los Angeles bar assns. Author: Practical Lawyer, 1973; Lawyers News Letter, 1974, Case and Comment, 1974. Home: 4432 Libbit Ave Encino CA 91316 Office: 1901 Ave of Stars 800 Century City Los Angeles CA 90067 Tel (213) 277-8822

GORDON, MORRIS JAY, b. Lynn, Mass., Mar. 17, 1928; B.S., McGill U., 1952; LL.B., Boston U., 1955. Admitted to Mass. bar, 1955; asso. firm Ralph Goldstein, Boston, 1955-56; individual practice law, Lynn, 1956—. Vice pres. N. Shore Jewish Community Center; bd. dirs. Neighborhood Legal Services, Lynn. Mem. Lynn, Essex County, Boston bar assns. Editor Boston U. Law Rev. Home: 300 Atlantic Ave Marblehead MA 01945 Office: 60 Lewis St Lynn MA 01902 Tel (617) 595-1800

GORDON, PHILLIP, b. Potgietersrust, S.Africa, July 11, 1943; B.A., U. Witwatersrand, 1964, B.A. (hon.), 1965; B.A., Oxford (Eng.) U., 1967, M.A., 1973; J.D., U. Chgo., 1969. Admitted to Ill. bar, 1969, N.Y. bar, 1973; asso. firm Winthrop, Stimson, Putnam & Roberts, N.Y.C., 1969-73; asso. firm Altheimer & Gray, Chgo., 1973-76, partner, 1976—; teaching asso. Northwestern U. Sch. Law, 1967-68; lectr. close corps. Ill. Inst. Continuing Legal Edn.; lectr. panel on opinion letters Chgo. Bar Assn. Bd. dirs. Internat. Rescue Com., Inc. Editor, Corp. Securities Law Newsletter, Ill. Bar Assn. Contbr. article to legal jour. Office: Altheimer & Gray 1 IBM Plaza Suite 3700 Chicago IL 60611 Tel (312) 467-9600

GORDON, RAYMOND JOHN, b. N.Y.C., Apr. 8, 1935; B.A. magna cum laude, William Jewell Coll., 1963; J.D., U. Mo., 1966. Admitted to Mo. bar, 1966, U.S. Dist. Ct. bar, 1968; partner firm Dabney & Gordon, Liberty and Pineville, Mo., 1966-68; atty. complaint div. Mo. Dept. Ins., Jefferson City, 1968-69; partner firm Yocom & Gordon, Pineville, 1969-71; atty. Hickory County (Mo.), Hermitage, 1971-74; magistrate, probate judge St. Clair County (Mo.), Osceola, 1975—; mem. Ozark Gateway Law Enforcement Council, Joplin, Mo., 1969-71; mem. Osage Council Criminal Justice, Clinton, Mo., 1972—. Mem. Sr. Citizens Policy Adv. Council, Lanagan, Mo., 1968-69. Mem. Am., Mo. bar assns., Am. Trial Lawyers' Assn., Am. Judicature Soc., Mo. Municipal Judges' Assn., Mo. Probate Judges' Assn., Pi Gamma Mu, Pi Kappa Delta, Delta Theta Phi. Office: POB 271 Osceola MO 64776 Tel (417) 646-2421

GORDON, RICHARD ALAN, b. Paterson, N.J., Feb. 16, 1946; B.S. in Commerce, U. Va., 1967; J.D., Boston U., 1970. Admitted to Ga. bar, 1971, also U.S. Dist. Ct. bar N. Ga., U.S. Ct. Appeals bar 5th Circuit, U.S. Tax Ct. bar; asso. firm Gettle, Jones & Fraser, Atlanta, 1971-74; partner firm Gettle, Fraser, Berthold & Gordon, Atlanta, 1975, Berthold & Gordon, Atlanta and Smyrna, Ga., 1975—; lectr. Atlanta Law Sch., 1972-73; lectr., counselor Small Bus. Adminstr., SCORE, ACE, S.E. Inst. Entrepreneurship and Mgmt., 1975—; mem., counselor Ga. Vol. Lawyers for the Arts. Mem. Ga. Bar Assn. Office: 1707 Spring St Atlanta GA 30080 Tel (404) 433-2900

GORDON, ROBERT EARL, b. Chgo., July 2, 1937; J.D., DePaul U., 1962. Admitted to Ill. bar, 1962; mem. firm Gordon, Brustin & Schaefer, Ltd., Chgo., 1962-77; sr. mem. firm Gordon, Schaefer & Gordon, Ltd., 1977—. Trustee Village of Northbrook, Ill., 1975—; founder, pres. Sutton Point Homeowners Assn., 1967-69; co-founder, chmn. Greater Northbrook Homeowners Assn., 1968; mem. Northbrook Zoning Bd. of Appeals, 1969, Northfield Twp. Park Dist. Legal Com., 1974; mem. bus. com. Sch. Dist. #27, 1968; bd. dirs. Northbrook B'nai B'rith, Concerned Citizens for a Better Northbrook. Mem. Ill., Am., Chgo. bar assns., Ill., Am. Trial Lawyers Assns., Trial Lawyers Club Chgo., Am. Arbitration Assn. (mem. Nat. Panel Arbitrators). Recipient Northbrook Park Dist. Spl. Achievement award, 1974, Northbrook B'nai B'rith Membership award, 1975; named Man of Year, Sutton Point Homeowners Assn., 1973, 74, 75. Home: 4001 Rutgers St Northbrook IL 60062 Office: 228 N La Salle St Chicago IL 60601 Tel (312) 332-2490

GORDON, ROBERT EUGENE, b. Los Angeles, Sept. 20, 1932; A.A., U. Calif., Los Angeles, 1952, A.B., 1954, LL.M., Berkeley, 1959, J.D., 1964; postgrad. U. Hamburg (Germany), 1959-60. Admitted to Calif. bar, 1960; asso. firm Lillick, Geary, McHose, Roethke & Myers, Los Angeles, 1960-64; partner firm Baerwitz & Gordon, Beverly Hills, Calif., 1965-69; partner firm Ball, Hart, Hunt, Brown & Baerwitz, Beverly Hills, 1970-71; of counsel firm Jacobs, Sills & Coblentz, San Francisco, 1972—; partner firm Gordon & McCabe, San Francisco, 1974—; lectr. Internat. Faculty of Comparative Law, Luxembourg, 1960. Mem. Am., San Francisco bar assns., Practicing Law Inst., Los Angeles Copyright Soc. Home: 35 Elaine Ave Mill Valley CA 94941 Office: 555 California St 3100 San Francisco CA 94104 Tel (415) 391-4800

GORDON, ROBERT MARION, JR., b. Manila, Mar. 22, 1933; B.S., U. Rochester, 1962; J.D., U. Denver, 1966. Admitted to Colo. bar, 1967; individual practice law, Golden, Colo., 1970—. Mem. Am., Colo., 1st Colo. Jud. Dist. bar assns. Office: Golden Savings and Loan Bldg Golden CO 80401 Tel (303) 278-1443

GORDON, STEPHEN F., b. N.Y.C., Jan. 30, 1940; LL.B., N.Y. U., 1963. Admitted to N.Y. bar, 1963, U.S. Supreme Ct. bar, 1969; asso. firm Frankenthaler and Kohn, N.Y.C., 1963-69, firm Delson & Gordon, N.Y.C., 1966-71; partner firm Mirkin, Barre, Saltzstein & Gordon, P.C., Great Neck, N.Y., N.Y.C. and Suffolk County, Hauppauge, 1972. Founder Greater Westbury Community Coalition, 1972. Mem. Am. N.Y. State (chmn. subcom. on prepaid legal plans of pension welfare and related plans com. of labor law sect.), Nassau County bar assns. Developer group prepaid legal services plans N.Y. Met. Area; guest speaker confs. on Ednl. Conf. Health, Welfare and Pension Plans, N.Y.C. Mayor's Consumer Conf., 1976. Co-author: Prepaid Legal Services: An Approach that Works, 1976. Home: 310 Laurel Ln Laurel Hollow NY Office: 98 Cutter Mill Rd Great Neck NY 11021 Tel (516) 466-6030

GORDON, THEODORE HOWARD, b. Oakland, Calif., May 2, 1946; A.A., Merritt Coll., 1966; B.S. in Bus. Adminstrn., San Jose State Coll., 1969, M.B.A., 1971; J.D., U. Calif., San Francisco, 1973. Admitted to Calif. bar, 1974; v.p. Phildon, Inc., Walnut Creek, Calif., 1971-72; law clk. firm Davidson & Graham, San Rafael, Calif., 1972-73; partner firm Graham, Gordon, McFarlan & Stewart, San Rafael, 1973—; instr. City Coll. San Francisco, 1976—, Golden Gate U., 1976—. Mem. Am., Calif., Marin County bar assns. Author: Summary California Real Estate Law, Cases and Materials, 1976; 3rd degree black belt in Ju-Jitsu, 1971; instr. 1966—. Home: 283 Flagstone Terr San Rafael CA 94903 Office: A280 Redwood Hwy Suite 10 San Rafael CA 94903 Tel (415) 479-8635

GORDON, THOMAS CHRISTIAN, JR., b. Richmond, Va., July 14, 1915; B.S., U. Va., 1936, LL.B., 1938. Admitted to Va. bar, 1937; asso. firm Parrish, Butcher & Parrish, Richmond, 1938-40; asso. firm McGuire, Woods & Battle, and predecessor, Richmond, 1940-49, partner, 1949-65, 72—; justice Supreme Ct. Va., Richmond, 1965-72; lectr. law sch. U. Va., 1970-71. Trustee Crippled Children's Hosp., pres., 1954-59; vestryman Episcopal Ch. Fellow Am. Bar Found., Am. Law Inst.; mem. Am., Va. State (pres. 1963-64) bar assns., Richmond Bar. Mem. bd. editors Va. Law Rev., 1937-38. Home: 300 W Franklin St Richmond VA 23220 Office: 1400 Ross Bldg Richmond VA 23219 Tel (804) 644-4131

GORE, BERNARD, b. N.Y.C., July 7, 1911; B.A., Fordham U., 1931, LL.B., 1934. Admitted to N.Y. bar, 1935; individual practice law, N.Y.C., 1947-66; partner firm Gore & Freiberg, Bronx, N.Y., 1962-76; arbitrator N.Y.C. Civil Ct., Am. Arbitration Assn.; mem. panel for indigent defendants Appellate Div., 1st Dept. Mem. N.Y. State, Bronx bar assns., N.Y. State Trial Lawyers Assn., New York County Lawyers Assn., Bronx Criminal Bar Assn., Am. Arbitration Assn. Home: 2121 Saint Raymond Ave Bronx NY 10462 Office: 391 E 149th St Bronx NY 10455 Tel (212) WY-3-2228

GORE, CLARK HUGHES, b. Rock Port, Mo., Jan. 17, 1909; LL.B., U. Colo., Boulder, 1932. Admitted to Mo. bar, 1932; practiced in Rock Port, Mo., 1932-68; pub. adminstr. Atchison County (Mo.), 1938-42, pros. atty., 1946-50; city atty. City of Rock Port, 1946-50; judge Probate Ct., Atchison County, 1968—, Magistrate Ct., Atchison County, Rock Port, 1968—; mem. Rock Port City Council, 1936-40. Chmn. Atchison County chpt. ARC, 1936-40, Atchison County Tb Assn., 1938-42. Mem. Mo., Nat., Internat. assns. probate judges. Home: 611 Calhoun St Rock Port MO 64482 Office: Courthouse Rock Port MO 64482 Tel (816) 744-2700

GORE, GEORGE FRANCIS, b. New Haven, Oct. 26, 1939; B.A., U. Notre Dame, 1961; J.D., Western Res. U., 1964. Admitted to Ohio bar, 1964; mem. Gen. Counsel's Office HEW, Washington, 1966-67; partner firm Arter & Hadden, Cleve., 1967—. Chmn. charter review commn. City of Richmond Heights (Ohio), 1973, mem. Civil Service Commn., 1976, chmn., 1977. Mem. Internat. Assn. Ins. Counsel, Def. Research Inst., Ohio Bar Assn., Bar Assn. Greater Cleve. Home: 4870 Donald Ave Richmond Heights OH 44143 Office: 1144 Union Commerce Bldg Cleveland OH 44115 Tel (216) 696-1144

GORE, GEORGE HENRY, b. Oak Park, Ill., June 22, 1923; J.D., U. Notre Dame, 1948; LL.M., N.Y. U., 1950. Admitted to Fla. bar, 1948; asso. firm Saunders, Buckley & O'Connell, Ft. Lauderdale, Fla., 1950; individual practice law, Ft. Lauderdale, 1951-54; partner firm Saunders, Curtis, Ginestra & Gore, Ft. Lauderdale, 1954—; dir. Century Nat. Bank of Broward, Ft. Lauderdale, 1968—. Mem. law advisory council U. Notre Dame, Ind., 1965—. Dir. Ft. Lauderdale Oral Sch., Inc., 1956—; mem. council Village of Sea Ranch Lakes, Ft. Lauderdale, 1959-63; trustee Holy Cross Hosp., Ft. Lauderdale, 1960—. Mem. Fla. Bar (exec. council tax sect. 1955-57), Broward County Bar Assn., Broward County Estate Planning Council, Artists Equity Assn. Home: 23 Minnetonka Rd Village of Sea Ranch Lakes Fort Lauderdale FL 33308 Tel (305) 525-0531

GORE, RICHARD STUART, b. Chgo., Apr. 21, 1941; B.A., U. Ill., 1963; J.D., DePaul U., 1965. Admitted to Ill. bar, 1965; asso. firm Barbera & Friedlander, Chgo., 1965-67; asso. firm Haft, Shapiro & Haft, Chgo., 1967-70; partner firm Berry & Gore, Ltd., Chgo., 1970—. Mem. Am., Chgo. bar assns., Ill. Trial Lawyers Assn., Decalogue Soc. Lawyers. Office: 221 N LaSalle St Chicago IL 60601 Tel (312) 644-8880

GORE, STANLEY NORMAN, b. Chgo., Sept. 29, 1942; B.S., U. Wis., 1965; J.D., DePaul U., 1968. Admitted to Ill. bar, 1968; asso. firm King, Robin, Gale and Pillinger, Chgo., 1968-72, partner, 1970-72; asso. firm Rudnick and Wolfe, Chgo., 1972—, partner, 1974—. Mem. Chgo., Ill. State, Am. bar assns. Contbr. articles to legal jours. Home: 75 Ellendale Rd Deerfield IL 60015 Office: 30 N LaSalle St Chicago IL 60602 Tel (312) 368-4000

GORELICK, ALLAN, b. Los Angeles, May 16, 1930; B.A., U. Calif., Berkeley, 1954; J.D., Golden Gate U., 1967. Admitted to Calif. bar, 1967; asst. pub. defender Alameda County (Calif.), Oakland, 1970-73; mem. firm Braverman & Gorelick, Oakland and Hayward, Calif., 1976—. Mem. Calif., Alameda-Contra Costa attys. criminal justice, Alameda County Bar Assn. Certified specialist criminal law Calif. Bd. Legal Specialization. Home: 582 Montclair Ave Oakland CA 94607 Office: 225 W Winton St Hayward CA 94544 and 12th and Oak St Bldg Oakland CA 94607 Tel (415) 785-1444 also 465-0844

GORELICK, WALTER LEE, b. Los Angeles, Mar. 30, 1945; A.B. in History, U. Calif., Los Angeles, 1967; J.D., Golden Gate U., 1970. Admitted to Calif. bar, 1971; dep. pub. defender, Tulare County, Calif., 1971-74, asst. pub. defender, 1974—. Mem. Tulare County Bar Assn. (bd. dirs.), Tulare County Trial Lawyers Assn. (dir.), Calif. Attys. for Criminal Justice (state bd. govs.). Pub. and editor For the Defense. Office: 113 N Church St Visalia CA 93277 Tel (209) 732-8331

GOREN, RALPH MARSHALL, b. Chgo., Aug. 1, 1929; A.A., Chgo. City Jr. Coll., 1949; J.D., U. Chgo., 1952. Admitted to Ill. bar, 1952, U.S. Supreme Ct. bar, 1963; partner Goren, Horka & Lindell, and predecessors, Chgo., 1953-59; asst. state's atty. Cook County (Ill.), Chgo., 1965-69; individual practice law, Chgo., 1960—; tchr. Malinckrodt Coll., Wilmette, Ill., 1974—. Bd. dirs. Internat. Visitors Center, Chgo., 1975—. Mem. Am., Ill., Chgo. (chmn. arbitration com. 1976) bar assns. Home: 317 Hibbard Rd Wilmette IL 60091 Office: 11 S La Salle St Chicago IL 60603 Tel (312) 332-4469

GORFINKLE, ROBERT ALLEN, b. Boston, June 28, 1935; A.B., Boston U., 1957, LL.D., Boston Coll. Law Sch., 1960; LL.M. in Taxation, N.Y.U., 1961. Admitted to Mass. bar, 1960; mem. firm Friedman, Atherton, Sisson and Kozol, Boston, 1961-65; partner firm Schair, Duquet & Gorfinkle, Braintree, Mass., 1965—; lectr. Boston Coll. Law Sch., 1965-71, various profl. groups. Mem. Norfolk County, Mass., Am. bar assns. Home: 95 Old Country Way Braintree MA 02184 Office: 1000 Washington St Braintree MA 02184 Tel (617) 843-5030

GORHAM, BRADFORD, b. Providence, Mar. 7, 1935; A.B., Dartmouth, 1957; J.D. cum laude, Harvard, 1964. Admitted to R.I. bar, 1964; partner firm Gorham & Gorham, Providence, 1964—; solicitor, Town of Foster (R.I.), 1964-74, Town of Exeter (R.I.), 1966-70; rep. R.I. Gen. Assembly, 1968-70, 77—; probate judge Town of Exeter, 1968-70, Town of Glocester (R.I.), 1971-73. Mem. Am., R.I. bar assns. Home: Cucumber Hill Rd Foster RI 02825 Office: 58 Weybosset St Providence RI 02903 Tel (401) 421-7680

GORKIN, MITCHELL ASA, b. N.Y.C., June 25, 1945; B.A., Hofstra U., 1967; J.D., Suffolk U., 1970. Admitted to Mass. bar, 1972, N.Y. bar, 1973; staff atty. U.S. Fidelity & Guaranty Co., N.Y.C., 1971-73; asst. counsel Nat. Council Compensation Ins., N.Y.C., 1973; asso. firm Fuchsberg & Fuchsberg, N.Y.C., 1973-76, firm Arum, Friedman & Katz, N.Y.C., 1976—. Mem. Am., N.Y., N.Y.C. bar assns. Office: 450 Park Ave New York City NY 10022 Tel (212) 644-9800

GORMAN, ALBERT SALAMON, b. Cin., Sept. 11, 1912; LL.B., St. John's U., 1935, LL.M., 1936. Admitted to N.Y. State bar, 1936, U.S. Supreme Ct. bar, 1968; individual practice law, N.Y.C., 1936—. Mem. Bklyn. Bar Assn. Home: 3823 Beach 38th St Brooklyn NY 11224 Office: 1325 Surf Ave Brooklyn NY 11224 Tel (212) 372-0864

GORMAN, EDWARD G., b. Jamaica, N.Y., Oct. 13, 1931; B.A., St. John's U., 1953, LL.B., 1962. Admitted to N.Y. bar, 1963, Calif. bar, 1971, U.S. Supreme Ct. bar, 1972; with CIA, Washington, 1956-64, 66-70; partner firm Francis & Gorman, Cuba, N.Y., 1964-65, Brogdon, Gorman & Miller, Redondo Beach, Calif., 1971—; exec. advisor, cons. Rockwell Internat., Anaheim, Calif., 1970—; mem. panel of arbitrators Am. Arbitration Assn. Mem. Los Angeles County, S. Bay bar assns., Los Angeles Trial Lawyers' Assn. Home: 2607 Pinale Ln Palos Verdes Estates CA 90274 Office: 1801 S Catalina Ave Suite 103 Redondo Beach CA 90277 Tel (213) 378-0288

GORMAN, EDWARD JOSEPH, JR., b. Syracuse, N.Y., May 27, 1929; B.S. summa cum laude, LeMoyne Coll., 1951; J.D., Georgetown U., 1954. Admitted to U.S. Supreme Ct. bar, 1972, Md. bar, 1961; law clk. to judge U.S. Dist. Ct. Washington, 1956-57; atty. firm Macleay, Lynch & Macdonald, Washington, 1957-63; partner firm Butler & Gorman, Washington and Silver Spring, Md., 1963-70; individual practice law, Washington and Bethesda, Md., 1970-76; partner law, Washington and Bethesda, Md., 1970-76; partner firm Gorman & Canfield, Washington, 1976—. Bd. dirs. March of Dimes, Washington, 1965-67; trustee LeMoyne Coll., 1970—. Mem. D.C., Md., Am., Montgomery County bar assns., Am. Judicature Soc., Def. Lawyers Assn. Home: 5316 Woodlawn Ave Chevy Chase MD 20015 Office: Suite 355 4400 Jenifer St NW Washington DC 20015 also Suite 1000 4720 Montgomery Ave Bethesda MD 20014 Tel (202) 244-5695

GORMAN, GERALD WARNER, b. North Kansas City, Mo., May 30, 1933; A.B. cum laude, Harvard, 1954, LL.B. magna cum laude, 1956. Admitted to Mo. bar, 1956; asso. firm Dietrich, Davis, Dicus, Rowlands & Schmitt, and predecessors, Kansas City, Mo., 1956-63, partner, 1963—; dir. North Kansas City State Bank, 1967—. Trustee Citizens Bond Com. of Kansas City (Mo.), 1972—. Mem. Mo. Bar, Lawyers Assn. Kansas City (exec. com. 1968-71), Am., Clay County (Mo.), Kansas City bar assns., Harvard Law Sch. Assn. of Mo. (pres. 1972-73). Home: 917 E Vivion Rd Kansas City MO 64118 Office: 1001 Dwight Bldg Kansas City MO 64105 Tel (816) 221-3420

GORMAN, JOSEPH GREGORY, JR., b. Chgo., Sept. 27, 1939; A.B., U. Calif., Berkeley, 1961, M.B.A., Los Angeles, 1963, J.D., 1966. Admitted to Calif. bar, 1967; asso. firm Sheppard, Mullin, Richter & Hampton, Los Angeles, 1966-72, partner, 1972—; lectr. in field. Mem. State Bar Calif. (exec. com. tax sect. 1975—, chmn. com. death and gift tax, tax sec. 1976—), Los Angeles County (chmn. com. death and gift tax 1974-75), Am. bar assns. Home: 2710 Doresta Rd San Marino CA 91108 Office: 333 S Hope St 48th floor Los Angeles CA 90071 Tel (213) 620-1780

GORMAN, JOSEPH TOLLE, b. Rising Sun, Ind., Oct. 1, 1937; B.A., Kent State U., 1959; LL.B., Yale U., 1962. Admitted to Ohio bar, 1962; asso. firm Baker, Hostetler and Patterson, Cleve., 1962-68; with TRW Inc., Cleve., 1968—, sec., 1970-72, 73—, v.p., 1972—, sr. counsel, 1972-76, v.p., gen. counsel, 1976—, dir., officer subs's. Trustee Govtl. Research Inst., Shaker Heights Library, Univ. Circle, Inc. Mem. Assn. Gen. Counsel, Am. Soc. Corp. Secs., Am., Ohio, Cleve. bar assns. Home: 2849 Glengary Rd Shaker Heights OH 44120 Office: 23555 Euclid Ave Cleveland OH 44117 Tel (216) 383-3205

GORMAN, LOUIS WILLIAM, b. Fulton, N.Y., Apr. 28, 1910; LL.B., Cumberland U., 1941. Admitted to Ky. bar, 1943; mem. firm Gorman, Sheehan & Hogan, Covington, Ky., 1949—; magistrate First Dist., Covington, 1954-58. Active Kenton County Dem. Club, pres., 1954. Mem. Kenton County Bar Assn. Home: 1915 Fortside Circle Fort Mitchel KY 41017 Office: 106 E 8th St Covington KY 41011 Tel (606) 581-7645

GORMAN, ROBERT HERANCOURT, b. Cin., Aug. 2, 1935; B.A., Brown U., 1957; LL.B., U. Cin., 1960. Admitted to Ohio bar, 1960; served with JAGC U.S. Air Force, Portland, Oreg., 1961-64; partner firm Gorman, Davis, Hengelbrok & Price, Cin., 1964-72; judge Hamilton County (Ohio) Municipal Ct., 1973-77; judge Hamilton County Ct. of Common Pleas, 1977—. Mem. Ohio Gen. Assembly, 1965-66. Mem. Am., Ohio State, Cin. bar assns., Am. Judicature Soc., Am. Judges Assn., Ohio Jud. Conf. Recipient award for superior jud. services Ohio Supreme Ct., 1975. Home: 1010 Brayton Ave Cincinnati OH 45215 Office: 564 L Hamilton County Courthouse Cincinnati OH 45202 Tel (513) 632-8342

GORMAN, WALTER THOMAS, b. Binghamton, N.Y., Oct. 2, 1926; A.B., Holy Cross Coll., 1951; LL.B., Georgetown U., 1954. Admitted to N.Y. State bar, 1955; asst. dist. atty. Broome County (N.Y.), 1962-66; judge Binghamton City Ct., 1966-74, N.Y. State Ct. Claims, Binghamton, 1974—. Mem. N.Y. State, Broome County bar assns. Home: 79 Bennett Ave Binghamton NY 13905 Office: 111 Centre St New York City NY 10013 Tel (212) 374-8007

GORMIN, GARY PAUL, b. St. Paul, July 5, 1943; B.A., U. Minn., 1965; J.D., Ohio State U., 1970. Admitted to Ohio, Fla. bars, 1970; instr. Ohio State Coll. Law, Columbus, 1970; partner firm Gormin, Geoghegan, Easley, Granese & Bauman, Clearwater, Fla., 1971—; instr. in criminal and constl. law St. Petersburg Jr. Coll., 1972—. Bd. dirs. Rational Living, Inc., 1972—; trustee Temple B'nai Israel, 1972-76. Mem. Ohio, Fla., Clearwater bar assns. Office: 1212 S Highland Ave Clearwater FL 33516 Tel (813) 447-4547

GORMLEY, R(OBERT) JAMES, b. Oak Park, Ill., July 23, 1921; B.S.C., Northwestern U., 1942, M.B.A., 1950, J.D., 1950. Admitted to Ill. bar, 1950; asso. firm Bell, Boyd, Lloyd, Haddad & Burns, Chgo., 1950-S8, partner, 1958—. Mem. Am., Fed., Chgo. bar assns., Law Club, Legal Club of Chgo. C.P.A., Ill. Office: 135 S LaSalle St Chicago IL 60603 Tel (312) 372-1121

GORNICK, ALAN LEWIS, b. Leadville, Colo.; A.B., Columbia, 1935; J.D., 1937. Admitted to N.Y. State bar, 1937, Mich. bar, 1948; asso. firm Baldwin, Todd & Young, N.Y.C., 1937-41; with firm Milbank, Tweed, Hope & Hadley, N.Y.C., 1941-47; asso. counsel Ford Motor Co., Dearborn, Mich., 1947-49, dir. tax affairs, tax counsel, 1949-64; pres. Hidden Valley, Inc., Perry-Davis, Inc., Meadow Brook Park Devel. Co.; v.p., dir. Bloomfield Center, Inc., Seagate Hotel, Inc.; spl. lectr. bus. adminstrn. U. Mich., Ann Arbor, 1949-53. Mem. adv. bd. Detroit area council Boy Scouts Am., 1960—; pres. Mich. Assn. Emotionally Disturbed Children, 1962; v.p. Archives of Am. Art.; mem. fin. com. Mich. Heart Assn. Mem. Council on World Affairs (trustee Detroit chpt.), Am., Fed., Mich., Detroit, N.Y.C. bar assns., Am. Law Inst., Tax Inst. Inc. (past pres.), U.S. Nat. Tax Assn. (exec. com.), Internat. Fiscal Assn., Internat. Law Assn., Auto Mfrs. Assn., Tax Execs. Inst. (past pres.), Phi Delta Phi. Recipient Spl. award Gov. State of Colo., 1952. Author: Divorce, Separation and Estate Taxes, 1952, Arrangements for Separation and Divorce: Handbook of Tax Techniques, 1952, Taxation of Partnerships, Estates & Trusts, revised edition, 1952; contbr. articles to legal jours. Home: 150 Lowell Ct Bloomfield Hills MI 48013 Office: 1565 Woodward Ave Suite 8 PO Drawer J Bloomfield Hills MI 48013 Tel (313) 636-4347

GOROVE, STEPHEN, b. Transylvania; J.D., U. Budapest (Hungary), 1939; postgrad. (Brit. Council fellow), Oxford (Eng.) U., 1948; LL.M., Yale U., 1950, J.S.D., 1952, Ph.D., 1955. Research asso. Yale U., 1951-52, Georgetown U., 1952-53, Columbia U., 1957-58; prof. law N.Y. Law Sch., U. Akron, U. Denver; prof. U. Miss., chmn., dir. grad. program Sch. Law, 1965—; spl. adviser Miss. State Bar. Mem. Am. Soc. Internat. Law, Internat. Law Assn., Inter-Am., Am. bar assns., Internat. Inst. Space Law. Sterling fellow; Yale U. fellow; Carnegie fellow, 1948; author: Law and Politics of the Danube: An Interdisciplinary Study, 1964. Office: U Miss Law Center University MS 38677 Tel (601) 232-7421

GORRELL, FLOYD DAWSON, b. Powell, Wyo., May 30, 1919; B.S. in Accounting, U. Wyo., 1942, J.D., 1947. Admitted to Wyo. bar, 1947, since practiced in Worland; mem. firm O'Mahoney & Gorrell, 1947-59; individual practice law, 1959—; city atty. City of Worland, 1948—; mem. Wyo. Bar Commn., 1958-59. Pres. Worland C. of C., 1960; vestryman St. Alban's Episcopal Ch., Worland. Mem. 5th Jud. Bar Assn. (pres. 1951-52), Phi Delta Theta, Alpha Kappa Psi. Home: 919 Obie Sue St Worland WY 82401 Office: PO Box 526 121 S 9th St Worland WY 82401 Tel (307) 347-2562

GORRELL, FRANK CHEATHAM, b. Russellville, Ky., June 20, 1927; B.S., Vanderbilt U., 1949, J.D., 1952. Admitted to Tenn. bar, 1952; asso. firm Bass, Berry & Sims, Nashville, 1952-56, partner, 1956—; mem. Tenn. Senate, 1963-71, chmn. judiciary com., 1965-67, speaker, 1967-71, lt. gov., 1967-71; vice chmn. Tenn. Jud. Council, 1967-71. Vice chmn. Tenn. Gov.'s Sci. Adv. Com., 1970; trustee Acquinas Jr. Coll., 1973-76; co-chmn. for Tenn. Pres.'s Com. for Revenue Sharing. Mem. Am., Tenn., Nashville bar assns., Am. Judicature Soc., Tenn., Am. trial lawyers assns., Am. Coll. Trial Lawyers Assn. Hosp. Attys. Home: Route 2 Columbia Pike Thompson Station TN 37179 Office: 2700 First Am Center Nashville TN 37238 Tel (615) 244-5370

GORRONO, LOUIE, b. Emmett, Idaho, Mar. 2, 1919; B.S. in Bus., U. Idaho, 1942, LL.B., 1949. Admitted to Idaho bar, 1949; individual practice law, Emmett, 1949—. Mem. Gem. County C. of C. (pres. 1955), Am., Idaho bar assns. (pres. dist. chpt.), Am. Judicature Soc. Home: 1016 E 2d St Emmett ID 83617 Office: 105 N Hayes St Emmett ID 83617 Tel (208) 365-2421

GORSKI, GERALD MICHAEL, b. Chgo., Mar. 23, 1943; B.A., N. Central Coll., 1966; J.D., DePaul U., 1970. Admitted to Ill. bar, 1970; with trust dept. 1st Nat. Bank Chgo., 1970-71; asso. firm Rathie, Woodward, Dyer & Burt, Chgo., 1971-75, partner, 1976—. Vice pres., dir. DuPage County Legal Assistance Found. Mem. Ill., DuPage County (chmn. legal aid com. 1974-75) bar assns. Home: 6525 S Main St Downers Grove IL 60515 Office: 203 E Liberty Dr Wheaton IL 60187 Tel (312) 668-8500

GORTATOWSKY, JULIAN EHRLICH, b. Albany, Ga., Mar. 20, 1911; A.B., Vanderbilt U., 1932; LL.B., U. Ga., 1935. Admitted to Ga. bar, 1935; since practiced in Atlanta; asso. firm Harold Hirsch and Marion Smith, 1935-39; asso. firm Smith, Kilpatrick, Cody, Rogers & McClatchey, 1939-46; partner firm Willingham & Gortatowsky and predecessor firms, 1946-66; individual practice law, 1966—; prof. law Atlanta Law Sch., 1947-49, Woodrow Wilson Coll. Law, 1966—. Trustee Vis. Nurses Assn., 1964-71. Mem. Am., Ga., Atlanta bar assns., Lawyers Club Atlanta (mem. exec. com. 1955-64, pres. 1962), Old War Horse Club. Home: 3553 Kingsboro Rd NE Atlanta GA 30319 Office: 1024 Hurt Bldg Atlanta GA 30303 Tel (404) 523-2844

GORTON, SLADE, b. Chgo., Jan. 8, 1928; A.B., Dartmouth, 1950; LL.B. (Harlan Fiske Stone scholar) Columbia, 1953. Admitted to Wash. bar, 1953; mem. Wash. State Legislature, 1959-69, majority leader, 1967-69; individual practice law, Seattle, 1953-69; partner firm Little, Gandy, Palmer, Slemmons & Holcomb, Seattle, 1965-69; atty. gen. Wash., Olympia, 1969—. Trustee Pacific Sci. Center, Seattle, 1970-76; mem. Wash. Gov.'s Com. on Law and Justice, 1969—, chmn., 1969—; Chmn. Wash. State Criminal Justice Tng. Commn., 1974-76. Mem. Nat. Assn. Atty.'s Gen. (pres. 1976—). Office: Temple of Justice Olympia WA 98504 Tel (206) 753-2550

GOSE, RICHARD VERNE, b. Hot Springs, S.D., Aug. 3, 1927; B.S., U. Wyo., 1950, M.E., 1959; M.S., Northwestern U., 1955; LL.B., George Washington U., 1967, J.D., 1967. Admitted to U.S. Supreme Ct. bar, 1976, N.Mex. Supreme Ct. bar, 1967, U.S. Ct. Appeals 10 Circuit bar, 1968; exec. asst. U.S. Senator J.J. Hickey, Washington, 1960-62; mgr. E.G. & G., Inc., Washington, 1962-67; spl. asst. atty. gen. State of N. Mex., Santa Fe, 1967-70; individual practice law, Santa Fe, 1967—. Mem. N.Mex., 1st Jud. (past pres.) bar assns., Pi Tau Sigma, Sigma Tau. Home: 815 Don Gaspar St Santa Fe NM 87501 Office: PO Box 1391 Santa Fe NM 87501 Tel (505) 983-9145

GOSHIEN, DAVID BARNEY, b. New Bedford, Mass., July 20, 1937; A.B. magna cum laude, Brown U., 1959; J.D., U. Chgo., 1962. Admitted to N.C. bar, 1962, Ohio bar, 1976; individual practice law, Charlotte, N.C., 1962-67; instr. U. N.C., Chapel Hill, 1966-67; asst. prof. law U. Okla., Norman, 1967-68; asso. prof. law Cleve. State U., 1968-72, prof. 1972—; cons. Equal Employment Opportunity Commn., 1968-69; 1969, 71-72. Home: 2691 Edgehill Rd Cleveland Heights OH 44106 Office: Cleveland State Coll Law Cleveland OH 44115 Tel (216) 687-2325

GOSHORN, EVERETT ELWIN, b. Huntington, Ind., Jan. 15, 1945; B.S., Purdue U., 1967; J.D., Ind. U., 1970. Admitted to Ind. bar, 1970; asso. firm Edris Edris & Dale, Bluffton, Ind., 1970-74; pros. atty. Wells County (Ind.), 1974—; bd. dirs. Region II Ind. Criminal Justice Planning Agy. Bd. dirs. Wells County Mental Health Assn. Mem. Am., Ind., Wells County (past pres.) bar assns., Ind. Pros. Attys. Assn., Nat. Dist. Attys. Assn. Home: Route 4 Bluffton IN 46714 Office: Courthouse Bluffton IN 46714 Tel (219) 824-4102

GOSS, MICHAEL MAYER, b. Phila., Dec. 26, 1942; B.A. in Polit. Sci., Pa. State U., 1964; J.D., Villanova U., 1967. Admitted to Pa. bar, 1967; mem. firm Weinstein, Goss and Katzenstein, Phila., 1967—. Past pres. Wm. J. Blitman Lodge B'nai B'rith; commr. Boy Scouts Am.; past v.p. Upper Moreland (Pa.) Bicentennial Com. Mem. Phila. Bar Assn., Am., Pa. trial lawyers assns., Am. Arbitration Assn. (arbitrator), Pi Sigma Alpha. Home: 240 Buckboard Rd Willow Grove PA 19090 Office: 1000 Penn Sq Bldg 1317 Filbert St Philadelphia PA 19107 Tel (215) LO3-5953

GOSSELS, CLAUS PETER ROLF, b. Berlin, Ger., Aug. 11, 1930, came to U.S., 1941, naturalized, 1952; A.B., Harvard, 1951, LL.B., 1954. Admitted to Mass. bar, 1955, U.S. Supreme Ct. bar, 1965; asso. firm Sullivan & Worcester, Boston, 1956-65; partner firm Zelman, Gossels & Alexander Boston, 1965-72; partner firm Weston, Patrick, Willard & Redding, Boston, 1972—; lectr. internat. bus. law Boston U., 1965-70. Town counsel Wayland, Mass., 1968, Boxborough, Mass., 1974—; counsel to planning bd. Sudbury, Mass., 1971; asst. town counsel, Brookline, Mass., 1976; mem. finance com. Wayland, 1966-68; cons. spl. commn. taxation of commonwealth Mass., 1955. Mem. Am., Mass., Boston bar assns., City Solicitors and Town Coounsels Assn., Am. Soc. Internat. Law. Contbr. articles to legal jours. Home: Hampshire Rd Wayland MA 01778 Office: 84 State St Boston MA 02109 Tel (617) 742-9310

GOSSETT, DENTON DELAPLANE, b. Norman, Okla., Sept. 23, 1924; LL.B., U. Okla., 1948, J.D., 1970. Admitted to Okla. bar, 1948; asst. county atty., Durant, Okla., 1948-52; office atty. Md. Casualty Co., Oklahoma City, 1952-62; legal asst. Okla. Supreme Ct., 1962-65; adminstrv. law judge Bur. Hearing and Appeals, HEW, 1965—. Mem. Fed. Adminstrv. Law Judges' Conf. Assn. of Adminstrv. Law Judges HEW. Home: 304 Saunier Way McAlester OK 74501 Office: 104 E Carl Albert Pkwy McAlester OK 74501 Tel (918) 423-1102

GOSTIN, IRWIN, b. N.Y.C., July 22, 1927; A.B., U. Calif., Los Angeles, 1948; J.D., Harvard, 1951. Admitted to Calif. bar, 1952; partner firm Gostin & Katz, Inc., San Diego, 1957—. Pres., San Diego chpt. ACLU, 1966-67, chmn. legal panel, 1959-66. Mem. Assn. Trial Lawyers Am., Calif., San Diego (pres. 1966-67) trial lawyers assns., San Diego County Bar Assn. Office: 2550 5th Ave San Diego CA 92103 Tel (714) 233-7705

GOTTFRIED, PHILIP HOWARD, b. N.Y.C., Jan. 10, 1941; B.S. Coll. City N.Y., 1965; J.D., Bklyn Law Sch., 1969; LL.M., George Washington U., 1971. Admitted to N.Y. state bar, 1969, D.C. bar, 1970, U.S. Patent Office bar, 1971; asso. firm Lane, Aitken, Dunner & Ziems, Washington, 1969-71, Amster & Rothstein, N.Y.C., 1971—. Mem. Am., D.C., Rockland County bar assns., Am. Patent Law Assn. Home: 24 York Dr New City NY 10956 Office: 50 E 42d St New York City NY 10017 Tel (212) 697-5995

GOTTLIEB, ARTHUR JOSEPH, b. Mt. Vernon, N.Y., Apr. 7, 1929; B.A., U. Calif., Los Angeles, 1951; LL.B., Pacific Coast U., 1961. Tchr., Redlands (Calif.) Unified Sch. Dist., 1953; contract adminstr. North Am. Aviation Co., Los Angeles, 1953-64, Europe, 1962-63; admitted to Calif. bar, 1962; partner firms Gyler & Gottlieb, Inc., Long Beach, Calif., 1964-72, Gottlieb, Gottlieb & Stein, Inc., Long Beach, 1973—. McGovern del. Democratic Nat. Conv., 1972; pres. Long Beach chpt. Am. Field Service, 1972; bd. dirs. Long Beach Hoffman Halfway House, 1975—; advisor Long Beach Elderly Nutrition Program 1975—. Mem. Calif., Los Angeles County, Long Beach bar assns., Calif. Trial Lawyers. Home: 215 Prospect Ave Long Beach CA 90803 Office: 675 E Wardlow Rd Long Beach CA 90807 Tel (213) 424-0427

GOTTLIEB, DANIEL MARSHALL, b. Chgo., May 11, 1940; B.S., U. So. Calif., Los Angeles, 1962; J.D., U. Calif., Berkeley, 1965. Admitted to Calif. bar, 1966; dist. atty. Los Angeles County, 1965-70; sr. partner firm Gottlieb, Locke & Leeds, Los Angeles, 1970—; pres. Bus. Mgmt. Co. Office: 10100 Santa Monica Blvd suite 1040 Los Angeles CA 90067 Tel (213) 556-1011

GOTTLIEB, EDWARD N., b. Phila., July 31, 1907; B.S., U. Pa., 1928; grad. Temple U., 1933. Admitted to Pa. bar, 1934; spl. asst. atty. gen. Dept. Health and Welfare, Phila., 1957-76; individual practice law, 1976—. Mem. Phila. Lawyers Club, Fed. bar Assn., Am. Arbitration Assn. Office: 1000 Penn Sq Bldg Philadelphia PA 19107 Tel (215) LO3-2625

GOTTLIEB, GIDON ALAIN GUY, b. Paris, Dec. 9, 1932; LL.B. with honors, London Sch. Econs., 1954, Trinity Coll., Cambridge (Eng.) U., 1956, diploma in comparative law, 1958; LL.M., Harvard U., 1957; J.S.D., Harvard U., 1962. Admitted to Lincoln Inn, 1958; lectr. govt. Dartmouth Coll., 1960-61; asso. firm Shearman and Sterling, N.Y.C., 1962-65; prof. law N.Y. U., 1965-76; Leo Spitz prof. internat. law U. Chgo., 1976—; UN rep. Amnesty Internat., 1966-72; mem. founding com. World Assembly for Human Rights, 1968; cons. Pres's. Commn. for Human Rights Year, 1968; chmn. com. humanitarian law Am. chpt. Internat. Law Assn.; reporter panel on humanitarian law Am. Soc. Internat. Law; mem. adv. bd. Internat. League for Rights of Man. Mem. U.S. Inst. Human Rights. Author: The Logic of Choice: An Investigation of the Concepts of Rule and Rationality, 1968. Office: U Chgo Sch Law 1111 E 60th St Chicago IL 60637 Tel (312) 753-2401

GOTTLIEB, IRA LEONARD, b. N.Y.C., Sept. 3, 1938; B.A., Coll. City. N.Y., 1960; J.D., U. Wis., 1968. Admitted to Oreg. bar, 1969; law clk. Oreg. Supreme Ct., 1968; supervising atty. Legal Aid, Multnomah County (Oreg.), 1968-71; individual practice law, Portland, 1971—; prof. family law Lewis and Clark Law Sch., 1971. Mem. Oreg. State Bar, Multnomah County Bar Assn., Internat. Soc. Family Law. Office: 933 American Bank Bldg Portland OR 97205 Tel (503) 224-7563

GOTTLIEB, LEO, b. N.Y.C., June 21, 1896; Ph.B., Yale, 1915; LL.B., Harvard, 1920. Admitted N.Y. State bar, 1921, D.C. bar, 1947; since practiced law in N.Y.C., asso. firm Root, Clark, Buckner & Howland, 1920-25, partner firm and successor firms, 1925-46; partner firm Cleary, Gottlieb, Friendly & Cox, successor firm Cleary, Gottlieb, Steen & Hamilton, 1946-74, counsel, 1974—. Fellow Am., N.Y. State bar founds.; mem. Assn. Bar City N.Y. (v.p. 1968-70), N.Y. County Lawyers' Assn. (pres. 1963-65), Am., N.Y. State bar assns. Home: 120 E 81st St New York City NY 10028 Office: 1 State St Plaza New York City NY 10004 Tel (212) 344-0600

GOTTSCHALD, ROBERT ALEXANDER, b. St. Paul, Sept. 25, 1943; B.A., Mankato (Minn.) State Coll., 1966; J.D., Drake U., 1970. Admitted to Iowa bar, 1970; individual practice law, Indianola, Iowa, 1971—; county atty. Warren County, Indianola, 1971-74, jud. hospitalization referee, 1976—. Mem. Am., Iowa, Warren County (sec.), 5A (pres.) bar assns., Am. Assn. Trial Lawyers, Nat. Dist. Attys. Assn. Home: 602 N Buxton St Indianola IA 50125 Office: 207 W 1st Ave Indianola IA 50125 Tel (515) 961-7445

GOTWALS, CHARLES PLACE, JR., b. Muskogee, Okla., May 19, 1917; A.B., U. Okla., 1938, J.D., 1940. Admitted to Okla. bar, 1940; asso. firm Yancey, Spillers & Bush, Tulsa, 1940-42; served to maj. JAGC, U.S. Army, 1942-46; since practiced law in Tulsa, mem. firm Bush, Gable & Gotwals, 1946-50, Gable & Gotwals, 1950, Gable, Gotwals, Rubin, Fox, Johnson & Baker, and predecessors, 1951—. Mem. Tulsa County (sec. 1948), Okla., Am. bar assns., Am. Judicature Soc. Home: 1108 Woodward Blvd Tulsa OK 74114 Office: 2010 4th Nat Bank Bldg Tulsa OK 74119 Tel (918) 582-9201

GOUDY, HARRY CHESTER, b. Balt., July 29, 1934; B.S., Coll. Bus. and Pub. Adminstrn., U. Md., 1957, LL.B., Sch. Law, 1961, J.D., 1969. Admitted to Md. bar, 1961; asso. firm F. Gray Goudy, Balt., 1961-65; dep. state's atty. Anne Arundel County (Md.), 1965-70; partner firm Goudy, Lechowicz & Loney, Glen Burnie, Md., 1970—; arbitrator Am. Arbitration Assn. Bd. govs. Severn Sch., Severna Park, Md., 1973; bd. dirs. Severna Park Found. Mem. Anne Arundel County (exec. com. 1975, atty. grievance commn. 1976—), Md., Am. bar assns. Office: 100 Baltimore-Annapolis Blvd NW PO Box 849 Glen Burnie MD 21061 Tel (301) 766-0090

GOUDY, MAYNARD POWELL, b. Salt Lake City, Feb. 26, 1926; B.S.E., U. N. Mex., 1946; LL.B., U. Ariz., 1954. Admitted to Ariz. bar, 1954; law clk. to justice Ariz. Supreme Ct., 1954-55; asso. firm Snell & Wilmer, Phoenix, 1955-61, partner, 1962—. Bd. dirs. John C. Lincoln Hosp., 1972—; trustee Chester H. Smith Meml. Scholarship Fund; ruling elder Orangewood Presbyn. Ch., 1968-74. Mem. Am., Maricopa County bar assns. Home: 602 W Belmont St Phoenix AZ 85021 Office: 3100 Valley Center St Phoenix AZ 85073 Tel (602) 257-7250

GOUGH, AIDAN RICHARD, b. Los Angeles May 22, 1934; A.B., Stanford U., 1956, A.M., 1957; J.D., U. Santa Clara, 1962; LL.M. (Ford Found. fellow), Harvard, 1966. Admitted to Calif. bar, 1963, U.S. Supreme Ct. bar, 1966; probation officer Santa Clara County (Calif.) Juvenile Ct., 1956-60; prof. law Univ. Santa Clara, Calif., 1962—; exec. dir. Calif. Gov.'s Comm. Family, staff sec. Calif. Gov. Edmund G. Brown, Sr., Sacramento, 1966; vis. prof. law Stanford, 1972; academic visitor London Sch. Economics and Polit. Sci. U. London, 1973; reporter Nat. Joint Comm. Juvenile Justice Standards; alt. referee Santa Clara County Juvenile Ct. Mem. med. quality review com. State Calif. Bd. Med. Quality Assurance, 1976—; mem. profl. standards com., com. medicine and humanities Santa Clara County Med. Soc., San Jose. Mem. Am., Santa Clara County bar assns., Nat. Council Juvenile Ct. Judges, Am. Coll. Legal Medicine, Internat. Soc. Family Law (exec. council). Bd. editors; Family Law Quarterly, 1965; contbr. numerous articles, book reviews to legal jours. Home: 1219 Thurston Ave Los Altos CA 94022 Office: School Law University Santa Clara Santa Clara CA 95053 Tel (408) 984-4088

GOULD, BENJAMIN Z., b. Chgo., July 27, 1913; A.B., U. Chgo., 1935, J.D., cum laude, 1937. Admitted to Ill. bar, 1937; since practiced in Chgo.; asso. firm Gould & Ratner and predecessor firms, 1937, partner to 1949, sr. partner, 1949—; sec., gen. counsel, dir. Henry Crown (Ill.) & Co.; sec., gen. counsel Material Service Corp. subs. Gen. Dynamic Corp., Marblehead Lime Co., Freeman United Coal Mining Co., Arie & Ida Crown Meml., Sioux City and New Orleans Terminal Corp., Sioux City and New Orleans Barge Lines, Inc., Thomas B. Bishop Co., Santa Barbara Research Park div. University Exchange Corp., Utah Marblehead Lime Co., Oils, Inc., div. Exchange Bldg. Corp.; sec., gen. counsel, dir. Century-Am. Corp., Follansbee Metals Co., Stickney Terminal Corp., University Exchange Corp., San Francisco., Mascar Corp., Monticello Realty Corp., Burton Dixie Corp.; v.p., sec., gen. counsel, dir. Standard Forgings Corp., Exchange Bldg. Corp.; sec., gen. counsel, mem. exec. com., dir. Central Enterprises, Inc., Chgo. Bd. dirs. Hebrew Theol. Coll. Mem. Navy League U.S., Execs. Club, 100 Club, Am., Internat., Ill., Chgo. bar assns., Am. Judicature Soc., Am. Soc. Corporate Secs., Am. Arbitration Assn. (mem. nat. panel), Am. Inst. Mgmt. (asso.)., Phi Beta Kappa. Home: 1170 N Michigan Ave Wilmette IL 60091 Office: 300 W Washington St Chicago IL 60606 Tel (312) 236-3003

GOULD, DIRK SAMUEL, b. N.Y.C., Jan. 18, 1933; B.A., Queens Coll., 1955; J.D., N.Y.U., 1960, LL.M., 1964. Admitted to N.Y. bar, 1960, U.S. Dist. Ct. for So. N.Y. bar, 1962, U.S. Tax Ct. bar, 1963; since practiced in N.Y.C.; asso. firm Sereni, Herzfeld & Rubin, 1960-62, firm Squadron Alter & Weinrib, 1962-65, firm Pross, Smith, Halpern & Lefevre, 1966-68; partner, sec. firm Alter, Lefevre, Raphael, Lowry & Gould, and predecessor firm, 1968—; lectr. City U. N.Y., 1961-64. Mem. Am. Bar Assn. (mem. sects. on law labor and patent Trademark and and Copyright law), N.Y. County Lawyers Assn. (mem. com. on patents, trademarks and copyrights 1976—), Am. Arbitration Assn. (arbitrator). Home: 6 Sarah Dr Dix Hills NY 11746 Office: 530 Fifth Ave New York City NY 10036 Tel (212) 687-4426

GOULD, FRANKLIN PURNELL, b. Balt., Jan. 9, 1908; B.S., Johns Hopkins U., 1930; LL.B., U. Balt., 1933. Admitted to Md. bar, 1934, U.S. Ct. Mil. Appeals bar, 1952, D.C. bar, 1955, U.S. Supreme Ct. bar, 1959; mem. legal dept. U.S. Fidelity & Guaranty Co., Balt., 1934-35; asst. state counsel Home Owners Loan Corp., Balt., 1935-39; partner firm France & Gould, Balt., 1939-42; law specialist U.S.Navy, 1942-46; individual practice law, Balt., 1946-50; served to comdr. JAGC, USNR, 1950-54; partner firm Partridge & Gould, Washington, 1955-69; staff counsel, legis. liaison FPC, Washington, 1969—. Mem. Am., Fed., D.C., Inter-Am. bar assns. Home: University Club 1135 16th St NW Washington DC 20036 Office: FPC 825 N Capitol St NE Washington DC 20426 Tel (202) 275-4891

GOULD, FREDRICK GERALD, b. Chgo., Aug. 22, 1943; B.A., Washington U., St. Louis, 1965; J.D. cum laude, Northwestern U., 1968. Admitted to Ill. bar, 1968; asso. firm Gould & Ratner, Chgo., 1968-74, partner firm, 1974—. Mem. Ill., Chgo., Am. bar assns. Mem. editorial bd. Northwestern U. Law Rev., 1967-68. Home: 334 Barry Ave Chicago IL 60657 Office: 300 W Washington St Chicago IL 60606 Tel (312) 236-3003

GOULD, JUSTINUS, b. Germany, Aug. 12, 1901; student Johns Hopkins U., 1925, postgrad., 1930-31; LL.B., U. Md., 1927; S.J.D., George Washington U., 1934. Admitted to Md. bar, 1927, U.S. Supreme Ct. bar, 1942; individual practice law, Balt., 1927-48; police magistrate City of Balt., 1939-42; research cons., sec. Md. Commn. Revision State Motor Vehicle Laws, 1942-43; legal research cons. Md. Com. Motor Vehicle Regislation, 1943-46; trial atty. criminal div. U.S. Dept. Justice, Washington, 1948-53; spl. asst. to atty. gen. U.S., Washington, 1950-53; counsel Com. on Small Bus., U.S. Ho. of Reps., Washington, 1955-74, dep. gen. counsel, 1974-76, gen. counsel, 1976-77. Mem. Fed. (pres. Capitol Hill chpt. 1968-69, nat. council 1968—), Md., Balt. bar assns. Author: Law of Pleading in Criminal Cases in Maryland, 1936; History and Accomplishments of the Select Committee on Small Business, 1973; also monographs and articles. Recipient certificate of merit Md. State Guard, 1943; Certificate for Outstanding and Meritorious Service to Congress and Pub., 1974. Home: 2807 Bartol Ave Baltimore MD 21209

GOULD, ROBERT FRANKLIN, b. Cleve., Jan. 24, 1942; student U. Miami, 1959; B.A., Case Western Res. U., 1962, J.D., 1966. Admitted to Ohio bar, 1966; fgn. service officer U.S. Dept. State, 1967-72; legis. liaison Ohio EPA, Columbus, 1973-74; asst. atty. gen. State of Ohio, Columbus, 1974-75; senate majority counsel Ohio Senate, Columbus, 1976—. Recipient U.S. AID Superior Achievement award, 1969. Office: Ohio Senate Statehouse Columbus OH 43215 Tel (614) 466-4822

GOULD, RODNEY ELLIOTT, b. Boston, June 3, 1943; A.B., Colby Coll., Waterville, Maine, 1965; J.D., Columbia U., 1968. Admitted to N.Y. bar, 1968, D.C. bar, 1969, Mass. bar, 1976, U.S. Customs Ct. bar, 1974; asst. regional dir. Boston office FTC, 1975—; asso. firm Covington & Burling, Washington, 1969-75. Mem. Am., Boston (antitrust com.) bar assns. Office: 150 Causeway St Boston MA 02114 Tel (617) 223-6621

GOULD, STANLEY EDWARD, b. N.Y.C., Dec. 9, 1928; B.A., U. Mich., 1951; J.D. cum laude, Cornell U., 1954. Admitted to N.Y. bar; individual practice law, N.Y.C., 1958—. Active Boy Scouts Am. Mem. Bklyn. Bar Assn., Am., N.Y. State trial lawyers assns. Office: 475 Fifth Ave New York City NY 10017 Tel (212) MU9-2608

GOULD, WILLIAM DAVID, b. Los Angeles, Nov. 21, 1938; B.A., Loyola U., Los Angeles, 1960; J.D., U. Calif. at Los Angeles, 1963. Admitted to Calif. bar, 1964; partner firm O'Melveny & Myers, Los Angeles, 1971—; lectr. Continuing Edn. of the Bar. Mem. Am., Los Angeles County (editor-in-chief bar bull. 1970-71) bar assns. Co-author chpt. for Operating Problems of California Corporations, 1977. Office: 1800 Century Park E Los Angeles CA 90067 Tel (213) 553-6700

GOULDEY, M. MARTIN, b. Boston, Mass., Mar. 7, 1899; LL.B., Suffolk Law Sch., 1929. Admitted to Mass. bar, 1929; individual practice law, Edgartown, Mass., 1929—. Mem. Am., Mass. bar assns., Am. Judicature Soc., Mass. Conveyancers Assn. Office: Gouldey Office Bldg Edgartown MA 02539 Tel (617) 627-4400

GOULDIN, DAVID MILLEN, b. Binghamton, N.Y., Mar. 8, 1941; A.B., Princeton, 1963; J.D., Cornell, 1966. Admitted to N.Y. bar, 1966; partner firm Levene, Gouldin & Thompson, Binghamton, 1966—. Mem. Planned Parenthood of Broome County, Inc., 1971—, pres., 1973-75; pres. Broome County Young Republican Club, 1972-73; pres. Binghamton Parks and Recreation Comm., 1976; trustee Wyoming Seminary, Kingston, Pa., 1973—, Tabernacle United Methodist Ch., Binghamton, N.Y., 1974—. Mem. N.Y., Broome County bar assns., Fedn. Bar 6th Judicial Dist. (pres. 1974-75). Home: 85 Highland Ave Binghamton NY 13905 Office: 902 Press Bldg Binghamton NY 13902 Tel (607) 772-9200

GOULET, LIONEL JOSEPH, b. Chgo., June 27, 1922; B.A., U. Ill., 1943; LL.B., Georgetown U., 1954. Admitted to D.C. bar, 1954, U.S. Ct. Mil. Appeals bar, 1955, Ill. bar, 1967; commd. ensign USN, 1944, advanced through grades to comdr., 1959; legis. atty. Office Legis. Affairs, Dept. Navy, Washington, 1964-65; ret., 1965; labor counsel Universal Oil Products Co., Des Plaines, Ill., 1966-71; dir. labor relations Sunbeam Corp., Oak Brook, Ill., 1971-73, mgr. indsl. relations, 1973-75, dir. corporate relations, 1975-77, v.p. corporate relations, 1977—. Bd. dirs. N.W. Suburban council Boy Scouts Am., 1967-72; mem. youth council Village of Arlington Heights (Ill.), 1969-71. Mem. Am., Fed., Ill. State bar assns., Indsl. Relations Assn. Chgo. Home: 720 S Kaspar Ave Arlington Heights IL 60005 Office: 2001 S York Rd Oak Brook IL 60520 Tel (312) 654-1900

GOULET, WALLACE RICHARD, JR., b. Santa Monica, Calif., July 29, 1948; B.B.A., U. Notre Dame, 1970; J.D., U. N.D., 1973. Admitted to N.D. bar, 1973; mem. firm DePuy, O'Connor & Goulet, Ltd., Grafton, N.D., 1973—; asst. city atty. Grafton, 1973—; asst. state's atty. Walsh County, N.D., 1975-77. St. John's Parish Council, 1975—. Mem. N.D., Walsh County (pres. 1975—) bar assns., Phi Delta Phi. Recipient Distinguished Service award City of Grafton, 1975. Home: 1544 Griggs Ave Grafton ND 58237 Office: Walsh County Bank Bldg Grafton ND 58237 Tel (701) 352-2320

GOVERNALI, JOSEPH PAUL, b. N.Y.C., Oct. 22, 1934; A.B., Columbia, 1956; LL.B., Fordham U., 1959, J.D., 1968. Admitted to N.Y. bar, 1960, N.Y. State Ct. Appeals bar, 1961, U.S. Ct. for So. Dist. N.Y., 1968, U.S. Supreme Ct. bar, 1968; individual practice law, N.Y.C., 1960—. Mem. New Fairfield (Conn.) Fin. Bd., 1969—; justice of the peace, New Fairfield, 1966—. Mem. N.Y. State, Bronx County bar assns. Office: 1443 E Gun Hill Rd New York City NY 10469 Tel (212) 379-7800

GOWEN, CHARLES LATIMER, b. Fayette County, Iowa, Jan. 31, 1904; LL.B., U. Ga., 1925. Admitted to Ga. bar, 1925, U.S. Supreme Ct. bar, 1951; partner firm Gowen, Conyers, Fendig & Dickey and predecessors, Brunswick, Ga., 1925-61; partner firm King & Spalding, Atlanta, 1962—; judge Glynn County (Ga.) Juvenile Ct., 1935-42; mem. Judicial Council Ga., 1946-49, 51-54. Mem. Ga. Gen. Assembly, 1939-54, 57-60; chmn. State Commn. on Compensation, 1971—. Trustee Richard B. Russell Found. Fellow Am. Bar Found., Am. Coll. Trial Lawyers; mem. Am. Judicature Soc., Lawyers Club Atlanta, Am., Ga. (past pres.), Atlanta bar assns. Office: 2500 Trust Company Tower Atlanta GA 30303 Tel (404) 572-4600

GOZIGIAN, EDWARD, b. Syracuse, N.Y., Nov. 9, 1931; B.S., Syracuse U., 1954, LL.B., 1959. Admitted to N.Y. bar, 1959; asso. firm Van Horne & Feury, Cooperstown, N.Y., 1959-64; individual practice law, Cooperstown, 1964-70; partner firm Van Horne, Feury & Gozigian, Cooperstown, 1970—. Village atty. Cooperstown, 1960-70. Mem. Otsego County, N.Y. State, Am. bar assns. Home: 40 Nelson St Cooperstown NY 13326 Office: 101 Main St Cooperstown NY 13326

GRACE, GERALD, JR., b. N. Tonawanda, N.Y., Feb. 16, 1947; B.A., St. John Fisher Coll., 1969; J.D., State U. N.Y., Buffalo, 1972. Admitted to N.Y. bar, 1973; asso. firm Cox, Barrell & Walsh, Buffalo, 1972—. Mem. N.Y. State, Erie County bar assns. Home: 14 Groveland St Buffalo NY 14214 Office: 1000 Rand Bldg Buffalo NY 14203 Tel (716) 856-0153

GRACE, WALTER CHARLES, b. Elmira, N.Y., Mar. 4, 1947; B.A., Duke U., 1969; J.D., U. Tenn., 1972. Admitted to Ill. bar, 1972; asst. state's atty. Jackson County (Ill.), 1972, pub. defender, 1974—; asso. firm Donald R. Mitchell, Carbondale, Ill., 1972-74; mem. adv. com. law enforcement Sch. Tech. Careers So. Ill. U. Mem. Greater Egypt Regional Planning and Devel. Commn. Mem. Am., Ill., Jackson County bar assns., Nat. Legal Aid and Def. Assn., Ill. Pub. Defender Assn. (legis. com. 1975—). Home: 1504 Taylor Dr Carbondale IL 62901 Office: Pub Defenders Office Courthouse Murphysboro IL 62966 Tel (618) 684-2151

GRACH, BRIAN STEWART, b. Chgo., May 29, 1945; B.S., U. Ill., 1967, J.D., 1970. Admitted to Ill. bar, 1970; asso. firm Diver, Brydges, Bollman, Grach & Riseborough, Waukegan, Ill., 1970-74, partner, 1975—. Bd. dirs. United Way of Lake County, 1973-75, Temple Am. Echod, Waukegan 1975-76. Mem. Am., Ill., Lake County bar assns., Am. Assn. Atty.-C.P.A.'s. Recipient Silver award United Way 1976; contbr. articles to legal jours. Office: 111 N County St Waukegan IL 60085 Tel (312) 662-8611

GRAD, JEFFREY STUART, b. Haverhill, Mass., Oct. 8, 1941; A.B., Princeton, 1963; LL.B., Columbia, 1966. Admitted to Mass. bar, 1966, Calif. bar, 1972, Hawaii bar, 1974; asso firm Ely, Bartlett, Brown & Proctor, Boston, 1966-72; asst. gen. counsel Boise Cascade Corp., Palo Alto, Calif., 1972-74; partner firm Finney & Grad, Honolulu, 1974—; devel. mgr. Waikaloa, Kamuela, Hawaii, 1973-74. Dir. Hawaii Council Culture & Arts, 1975-76. Mem. Mass., Boston, Hawaii, Calif. bar assns. Office: 841 Bishop St Suite 2001 Honolulu HI 96813 Tel (808) 521-4757

GRADDIS, ALBERT HAROLD, b. N.Y.C., Nov. 5, 1914; B.S. in Chem. Engring., N.Y.U., 1934; M. in Chem. Engring., Bklyn. Polytech. Inst., 1936; LL.B., N.Y.U., 1941. Admitted to D.C. bar, 1940, N.Y. State bar, 1942, N.J. bar, 1972; examiner U.S. Patent Office, Washington, 1936-39; atty. Celanese Corp., N.Y.C., 1939-52; counsel Nepera Chem. Co., Inc., Yonkers, N.Y., 1952-56; patent counsel Warner-Lambert Co., Morris Plains N.Y., 1957—; lectr. patent inst. Fairleigh Dickinson U., Madison, N.Y., 1976—. Mem. United Fund budget com. Mem. Am., N.Y., N.J. patent law assns., Assn. of Corp. Patent Counsel. Home: 57 Old Glen Rd Convent Station NJ 07961 Office: 201 Tabor Rd Morris Plains NJ 07950 Tel (201) 540-2576

GRADISON, HELEN MARTIN, b. Cin., Dec. 25, 1929; B.S., Tufts U., 1951; J.D., U. Cin., 1971. Admitted to Ohio bar, 1972; individual practice law, Cin., 1972—; pub. defender juvenile div. Hamilton County Ct. Common Pleas. Cin., 1972—. Trustee Cin. Adolescent Clinic, Inc., 1975-77; mem. contract compliance adv. com. U. Cin., 1975—; mem. justice vol. adv. com., 1975—. Mem. Ohio, Am., Cin. bar assns. Office: 893 Ohio Pike Cincinnati OH 45245 Tel (513) 752-7600

GRADY, ALBERT EDWARD, b. Brockton, Mass., Apr. 8, 1944; B.S., King's Coll., 1965; J.D., Cath. U., 1968. Admitted to Mass. bar, 1968; individual practice law, Brockton, 1968—. Mem. Plymouth County Bar Assn., Mass. Acad. Trial Lawyers. Home: 172 Silver St Hanover MA 02148 Office: 142 Main St Brockton MA 02401 Tel (617) 583-8562

GRADY, JOHN STEPHEN, b. Wilmington, Del., Jan. 17, 1944; A.B., St. Joseph's Coll., 1966; J.D., Georgetown U., 1969. Admitted to Del. bar, 1969, U.S. Supreme Ct. bar, 1974; staff atty. Community Legal Aid, Wilmington, 1969-72; asso. firm Bader Dorsey & Kreshtool, Dover, Del., 1972—. Mem. Am., Del., Kent County bar assns., Am. Judicature Soc. Home: 424 N Bradford St Dover DE 19802 Office: 314 S State St Dover DE 19901 Tel (302) 678-1265

GRADY, THOMAS CHRISTIAN, b. St. Louis, Feb. 4, 1945; A.B., St. Louis U., 1966, J.D., 1969. Admitted to Mo. bar, 1970; asso. firm Whalen, O'Connor & Danis, St. Louis, 1970-76; magistrate judge 5th Dist. City of St. Louis, 1976—; provisional judge City Ct. of St. Louis, 1976; chief adviser on historic dist. legis. Office Mayor St. Louis, 1969-70; mem. St. Louis Landmarks and Urban Design Commn., 1970-76, Citizens Adv. Com. on Parks Bonds, 1974. Bd. dirs. Landmarks Assn. St. Louis, Inc., 1969—. Mem. St. Louis Met. Bar Assn. (founding chmn. com. on correctional facilities), Mercantile Library Assn., Soc. Archtl. Historians, Nat. Trust for Historic Preservation. Office: Civil Cts Bldg 10 N 12th St Saint Louis MO 63101 Tel (314) 453-3584

GRADY, WARREN ALBERT, b. Port Washington, Wis., Mar. 3, 1924; B.S., Northwestern U., 1947; LL.B., U. Wis., 1950. Admitted to Wis. bar, 1950; partner firm Grady Law Office, Port Washington, Wis., 1950-62; judge br 2 Ozaukee County (Wis.) Ct., 1962—; mem. Wis. State Assembly, 1953-61; mem. Wis. Jud. Council, 1963-67, chmn. 1966-67; del. Nat. Conf. State Trial Judges, 1975-76; chmn. Wis. Bd. County Judges. Mem. Ozaukee County, Am. bar assns., State Bar Wis. Home: 908 W Grand Ave Port Washington WI 53074 Office: Courthouse Port Washington WI 53074 Tel (414) 284-9411

GRAETZ, MICHAEL JAY, b. Atlanta, Nov. 20, 1944; B.B.A., Emory U., 1966; J.D., U. Va., 1969. Admitted to Va. bar, 1969; advisor to asst. sec. of treasury, Washington, 1969-72; prof. Sch. Law U. Va., Charlottesville, 1972—; adj. prof. Law Sch. Georgetown U., Washington, 1971-72; vis. prof. Law Sch. U. So. Calif., Los Angeles, 1976-77; cons. U.S. Dept. Treasury, 1976—. Mem. Va. State Bar, Am. Bar Assn., Nat. Tax Assn. Author: (with Erwin N. Griswold) Federal Income Taxation: Principles and Policies, 1976; recipient Dept. Treasury Exceptional Service award, 1972; contbr. articles to publs. Home: 128 Observatory Ave Charlottesville VA 22902 Office: Univ Va Sch Law Charlottesville VA 22901 Tel (804) 924-3222

GRAF, JACK RICHARD, JR., b. Columbus, Ohio, Apr. 20, 1947; certifcate de langue francaise U. Paris, 1969; B.A., Ohio State U., 1970; J.D., Captial U., 1973. Admitted to Ohio bar, 1973; partner firm Britt Graf Campbell & Nagel, Columbus, Ohio, 1976—; asst. county prosecutor Franklin County, Ohio, 1972. Mem. Upper Arlington (Ohio) Planning Commn., 1975, 76. Mem. Am., Ohio, Columbus bar assns., Franklin County Trial Lawyers Assn., Am. Judicature Soc. Office: 501 S High St Columbus OH 43215 Tel (614) 224-8339

GRAFF, JOHN FRANCIS, b. Worthington, Pa., Dec. 28, 1888; grad. Mercersburg Acad., 1907; A.B., Princeton, 1911; student Harvard Law Sch., 1913-14; LL.B., U. Pitts., 1915; LL.D. Thiel Coll., 1954. Admitted to Pa. bar, 1915; partner firm Ralston & Graff, Kittanning, Pa., 1915-24; pres. judge Ct. Common Pleas of Armstrong County, Pa. 33d Judicial Dist., 1924-72; sr. judge, 1972—. Bd. dirs. Armstrong County Meml. Hosp., Kittanning, 1925-75; trustee YMCA, Kittanning, 1954—; mem. council St. John's Lutheran Ch., Kittanning. Mem. Pa. Bar Assn., Armstrong County C. of C. (dir.). Recipient Benjamin Rush award, 1966; Pa. State Am. Legion award for Meritorious Service, 1965, Jaycees of Armstrong County Outstanding Citizen award, 1971; Salvation Army Meritorious Service award, 1965; B'nai B'rith award, 1965. Home: 125 Hazel St Kittanning PA 16201 Office: Armstrong County Court House Kittanning PA 16201 Tel (412) 542-2711

GRAGLIA, LINO ANTHONY, b. Bklyn., Jan. 22, 1930; B.A., Coll. City N.Y., 1952; LL.B., Columbia, 1954. Admitted to N.Y. State bar, 1954, D.C. bar, 1957; atty. U.S. Dept. Justice, Washington, 1954-57; individual practice law, N.Y.C., and Washington, 1957-66; Rex G. Baker and Edna Heflin Baker prof. Constl. law U. Tex., 1966—. Author: Disaster by Decree, the Supreme Court Decisions on Race and the Schools., 1976. Office: 2500 Red River Austin TX 78705 Tel (512) Gr 1-5151

GRAHAM, ARNOLD HAROLD, b. N.Y.C., Dec. 29, 1917; B.S. with honors, N.Y.U., 1945, J.D. with honors, 1952. Admitted to N.Y. State bar, 1953, U.S. Tax Ct. bar, 1959, U.S. Supreme Ct. bar, 1959, U.S. Ct. Appeals 2d Circuit bar, 1960; practiced in N.Y.C., 1953—; dep. atty. gen. State of N.Y., 1952-54; individual practice law, 1952-75; asst. dean N.Y. Law Sch., 1976—. Trustee Kings Hwy. Bd. Trade, Temple Ahavath Sholom; bd. advisors United Jewish Appeal. Mem. Am. Assn. Atty.-C.P.A.s, Am. Bar Assn., N.Y. State Trial Lawyers Assn., N.Y. County Lawyers Assn., Fed. Bar Council, N.Y. State Soc. C.P.A.'s. C.P.A., N.Y. Home: 2223 Ave T Brooklyn NY 11229 Office: New York Law Sch 57 Worth St New York City NY 10013 Tel (212) 966-3500

GRAHAM, EDMUND LOWELL, b. Sanford, N.C., July 17, 1937; B.A., U. N.C., 1960; J.D., U. Calif. at Los Angeles, 1968. Admitted to Calif. bar, 1969, U.S. Supreme Ct. bar, 1969; partner firm Kelly & Graham, Torrance, Calif., 1969—; sec., dir. Vacation Industries, Inc., 1971—; mem. adv. bd. dirs. Torrance Nat. Bank, 1975—. Mem. Los Angeles, Calif. trial lawyers assns., Los Angeles County Bar Assn. Office: 21515 Hawthorne Blvd Suite 1130 Torrance CA 90503 Tel (213) 371-3535

GRAHAM, HARDY MOORE, b. Meridian, Miss., Oct. 21, 1912; student U. So. Calif., summer 1932; B.A., LL.B., U. Miss., 1934. Admitted to Miss. bar, 1934, U.S. Supreme Ct. bar, 1943, Tenn. bar, 1946; partner firm Graham & Graham, Meridian, Miss., 1934-43; atty. FTC, Washington, 1943-44; legal assistance officer USN, Washington, 1945-46; individual practice law, Union City, Tenn., 1946—; mayor Union City, 1950-58. Mem. Union City Sch. Bd., 1958-66, U. Tenn. Devel. Council, 1970-75; trustee Union U., Jackson, Tenn., 1959-61, 61-63, 63-65. Mem. Tenn., Am., Union City Obion County (pres. 1948-49) bar assns., Am., Judicature Soc. Named Young Man of Year in Union City Jaycees Citizens Com., 1948. Home: 630 E Main St Union City TN 38261 Office: 1915 Reelfoot Ave Union City TN 38261 Tel (901) 885-1214

GRAHAM, PETER JOHN, b. N.Y.C., July 4, 1930; B.S., St. Francis Coll., 1952; J.D., St. John's U., 1955. Admitted to N.Y. bar, 1958, U.S. Supreme Ct. bar, 1973; atty. Hartford Accident and Indemnity Co., Bay Shore, N.Y., 1958-65; partner firm Costigan & Graham, Port Jefferson, N.Y., 1965-71; individual practice law, Port Jefferson, 1971—; acting village judge Village of Port Jefferson, 1967—. Trustee Port Jefferson Free Library, 1974—. Mem. N.Y. State, Suffolk County bar assns., Suffolk Trial Lawyers Assn., Suffolk County Magistrates Assn., Suffolk County Criminal Bar Assn., Columbian Lawyers Assn., N.Y. State Assn. Magistrates. Office: 1500 Main St Port Jefferson NY 11777 Tel (516) 473-4900

GRAHAM, RICHARD THOMAS, b. Indianna, Pa., Aug. 20, 1948; B.A., Ashland Coll., 1970; J.D., Cleve.-Marshall, 1974. Admitted to Ohio bar, 1974, N.J., 1976; child support counselor, Cuyahoga County Juvenile Ct., Cleve., 1973, referee, 1974-76; individual practice law, Madison, N.J., 1976-77, Brooklyn, Ohio, 1977—. Mem. N.J., Ohio, Cuyahoga County bar assns. Home and office: 4100 Westbrook Dr Brooklyn OH 44144 Tel (216) 398-9863

GRAHAM, SELDON BAIN, JR., b. Franklin, Tex., Apr. 14, 1926; B.S., U.S. Mil. Acad., 1951; J.D., U. Tex., 1970. Petroleum engr. Atlantic-Richfield Co., Tulsa, 1954-60, Mobil Oil Corp., Corpus Christi, Tex., 1961-67, Tex. R.R. Commn., Austin, 1967-70; admitted to Tex. bar, 1970; atty. Exxon Corp., Houston, 1970—. Mem. Am. Bar Assn., State Bar Tex., Soc. Petroleum Engrs. Home: 14303 Broadgreen St Houston TX 77079 Office: PO Box 2180 Houston TX 77001 Tel (713) 656-2696

GRAHAM, THEODORE WILLIAM, b. San Bernardino, Calif., Sept. 17, 1939; A.B., Stanford U., 1961, LL.B., 1963. Admitted to Calif. bar, 1964; asso. firm Luce, Forward, Hamilton & Scripps, San Diego, 1963-70, partner, 1970—; v.p. Stanford Law Soc. San Diego; pres. Comml. Lawyers Group San Diego, 1975-76. Pres. Presidio Little League, 1976-77; mem. steering com. Ducks Unltd. San Diego. Mem. San Diego County, Calif., Am. bar assns. Speaker programs, seminars. Office: 110 West A St San Diego CA 92101 Tel (714) 226-1414

GRAHAM, WAYNE MARKHAM, b. Kansas City, Mo., May 24, 1944; B.A., U. Kans., 1966; J.D., U. Mo.-Kansas City, 1969. Admitted to Mo. bar, 1970; with Fireman's Fund Ins. Cos., Kansas City, Mo. and Detroit, 1969-71; individual practice law, Independence, Mo., 1971-72; asst. counsel Competitive Livestock Mktg. Assn., Kansas City, Mo., 1972-75; asst. pres. atty. Jackson County, 1975—. Bd. dirs. Jr. Achievement, 1974—; mem. Jackson County Bicentennial Com., 1975—. Mem. Am., Mo. bar assns. Home: 4312 S Pleasant Independence MO 64055 Tel (816) 881-4489

GRAHAM, WILLIAM THOMAS, b. Waynesboro, Va., Oct. 24, 1933; A.B. in Econs., Duke, 1956; J.D., U. Va., 1962. Admitted to N.C. bar, 1962, Va. bar, 1962, D.C. bar, 1970, U.S. Supreme Ct. bar, 1970; asso. firm Craige, Brawley and predecessors, Winston-Salem, N.C., 1962-64; partner firm Craige, Brawley, Horton & Graham, Winston-Salem, 1965-69, Billings and Graham, Winston-Salem, 1971-75; asst. gen. counsel U.S. HUD, Washington, 1969-70; judge N.C. Superior Ct., 1975—. Home: 1000 Arbor Rd Winston Salem NC 27104 Office: PO Box 1411 Forsyth County Hall Justice Winston Salem NC 27102 Tel (919) 761-2420

GRAHAME, ORVILLE FRANCIS, b. Palo, Iowa, Apr. 2, 1904; B.A., U. Iowa, 1925, J.D., 1929. Admitted to Iowa bar, 1929, N.Y. bar, 1932, Mass. bar, 1940, U.S. Supreme Ct. bar, 1954; text writer Am. Law Book Co., N.Y.C., 1929; law asst., asst. sec. Guardian Life, N.Y.C., 1930-40; with Paul Revere Life Ins., Worcester, Mass., 1940—, v.p. gen. counsel, 1945-67, cons., 1968—; v.p., gen. counsel ins. Avco Corp., Greenwich, Conn., 1967-70. Mem. White House Conf. Aging, 1959-61, 71-72; mem. Mass. Pension Study Commn., 1953-55; mem. Worcester Bd. Zoning Appeals, 1958-63; bd. dirs. Worcester Red Cross, 1957-63, 66-74, U. Iowa Found., 1968-74. Mem. Am., Mass., Worcester bar assns., Bar Assn. City N.Y., N.Y. County Lawyers Assn., Am. Arbitration Assn., Order of Coif. Recipient Distinguished Service award Iowa, 1964. Contbr. articles to profl. jours. Home: 6 Boncroft Tower Rd Worcester MA 01609 Office: 18 Chestnut St Worcester MA 01608 Tel (617) 799-4441

GRAMLICH, CHARLES JOHN, b. Springfield, Ill., July 20, 1938; B.S., Bradley U., 1963; J.D., John Marshall Law Sch., Chgo., 1966. Admitted to Ill. bar, 1967; asst. state's atty. Sangamon County (Ill.), 1966-68, pub. defender, 1971; state's atty. Edgar County (Ill.), 1968-71; legal adviser Ill. Sec. of State, 1971-72; individual practice law, Springfield, 1971—. Trustee Springfield Park Dist., 1975—. Mem. Ill., Sangamon County bar assns., Ill. Trial Lawyers Assn. Home: 45 Westwood Terr Springfield IL 62702 Office: 918 E Capitol Ave Springfield IL 62701 Tel (217) 525-0901

GRAMLING, WILLIAM EARL, b. Milw., Mar. 2, 1913; J.D., Marquette U., 1936. Admitted to Wis. bar, 1936; mem. firm Gramling & Gramling, Milw., 1936-41; agt. FBI, 1941-45; mem. firm Love, Davis & Gramling, Waukesha, Wis., 1946-52; judge Waukesha County (Wis.), 1952-58; judge Circuit Ct. of Wis., Waukesha, 1958—; chief judge Waukesha County, 1971-75. Chmn. Republican. party, Waukesha County, 1948-52. Mem. Waukesha County, Wis. bar assns. (pres. Waukesha County 1952), C. of C. (dir.); Home: 325 S Greenfield St Waukesha WI 53186 Office: Ct House Waukesha WI 53186

GRAMZA, ALLEN EDWARD, b. Racine, Wis., July 23, 1921; LL.B., then J.D., Marquette U., 1948. Admitted to Wis. bar, 1948, U.S. Ct. Appeals bar, 1952, U.S. Supreme Ct. bar, 1952; individual practice law, Racine, 1948-58; staff atty. Air Line Pilots Assn., Chgo., 1958-61, dir. legal dept., Chgo. and Washington, 1964-69; dir. legal dept. Allied Pilots Assn., N.Y.C., 1969-70; U.S. adminstrv. law judge

Social Secuirty Adminstrn. HEW, 1970-71, adminstrv. law judge in charge, Milw., 1971-75, regional chief adminstv. law judge, Chgo., 1975—. Mem. Wis. Bar Assn., Adminstrv. Law Judge Assn. in HEW, Fed. Conf. Adminstrv. Law Judges. Home: 1130 Emmetsen Rd Racine WI 53406 Office: 300 S Wacker Dr Chicago IL 60606 Tel (312) 353-0631

GRANADIER, GERALD EDWARD, b. Detroit, Mar. 2, 1930; B.A., Wayne State U., 1952, LL.B., 1954. Admitted to Mich. bar, 1955; individual practice law, Detroit, 1955—; arbitrator State of Mich. Police and Fire Fighters Arbitration Panel. Mem. Mich. Bar Assn., Am. Arbitration Assn. (arbitrator 1961). Home: 7202 Lindenmere St Birmingham MI 48010 Office: 1935 1st National Bldg Detroit MI 48226

GRANAI, CORNELIUS O., b. N.Y.C., July 11, 1897; student Vt. Coll.; LL.B., Syracuse U., 1923. Admitted to Vt. bar, 1926; practice law, Barre, Vt.; served as judge adv. U.S. Army, 1943-46. Mayor City of Barre; mem. Vt. State Legislature, 1947-49, 51-57, 63-68; trustee U. Vt., 1953-59, Vt. Coll., 1949-57. Home: 46 Beacon St Barre VT 05641 Office: 107 N Main St Barre VT 05641 Tel (802) 476-7131

GRAND, PAUL ROBERT, b. St. Louis, Dec. 23, 1933; B.A., Harvard, 1955; LL.B. (Harlan Fiske scholar, James Kent scholar), Columbia, 1960. Admitted to N.Y. bar, 1960, U.S. 2nd Circuit Ct. Appeals bar, 1962, U.S. Dist. Ct. So. Dist. N.Y., 1962, U.S. Dist. Ct. Eastern Dist. N.Y. bar, 1974; asso. firm Sullivan & Cromwell, N.Y.C., 1960-64; asst. U.S. atty., N.Y.C., 1964-69, chief securities fraud unit, 1968-69; partner firm Poletti, Freidin, Prashker, Feldman & Gartner, N.Y.C., 1969-76; partner firm Grand & Ostrow, N.Y.C., 1976—; mem. U.S. Ct. Appeals Criminal Justice Act Screening Com. Mem. Assn. Bar City N.Y. (mem. com. proposed new fed. criminal code), Am. Bar Assn. Editor: Columbia Law Rev. Home: 7 W 81st St New York City NY 10024 Office: 375 Park Ave New York City NY 10022 Tel (212) 832-3611

GRANDE, CORINNE PAULINE, b. Providence, June 29, 1928; J.D., Northeastern U., 1952. Admitted to Mass. bar, 1952, R.I. bar, 1953, U.S. Supreme Ct. bar, 1966; practiced in Providence, 1953-69; spl. asst. atty. gen. State of R.I., 1960-67; judge R.I. Dist. Ct., 1969—. Bd. dirs. Blue Cross of R.I., 1973-76; trustee Roger Williams Coll., YWCA, Greater R.I.; v.p. Health Planning Council of R.I. Mem. R.I. Bar Assn., R.I. Women Lawyers Assn. Home: 262 Waterman St Providence RI 02906 Office: RI Dist Ct Providence RI 02909 Tel (401) 331-1603

GRANDE, RICHARD ALAN, b. Providence, May 31, 1944; A.B., George Washington U., 1967; J.D., U. Pa., 1972; spl. student Yale Law Sch., 1971-72. Admitted to N.Y. bar, 1974, Fla. bar, 1976; asso. firm Haight, Gardner, Poor & Havens, N.Y.C., 1972-75, firm Smathers & Thompson, Miami, 1975-77; individual practice law, Miami Shores, Fla., 1977—. Mem. Am., Fla., Dade County bar assns. Tel (305) 754-0304

GRANESE, ANTHONY PATRICK, b. Madison, N.J., Mar. 17, 1946; B.A., Seton Hall U., 1968; J.D., Stetson U., 1972. Admitted to Fla. bar, 1972; asso. firm Gormin, Geoghegan, Easley, Granese & Bauman, Clearwater, Fla., 1972-74, partner, 1974—. Home: 530 Richards Ct Clearwater FL 33515 Office: 1212 S Highland Ave Clearwater FL 33516 Tel (813) 447-4547

GRANGER, DAVID IRELAND, b. Washington, Sept. 4, 1932; A.B., Princeton, 1954; LL.B., Harvard, 1959. Admitted to D.C. bar, 1959; asso. firm Ross, Marsh & Foster, Washington, 1959-61; atty. tax div. Dept. Justice, 1961-65; asso. firm Clifford, Warnke, Glass, McIlwain & Finney, Washington, 1965-69, partner, 1970—. Trustee Landon Sch., 1967-70; bd. dirs. Peirce-Warwick Adoption Service, 1968-72, pres., 1970-72; trustee Potomac Sch., 1971—, chmn., 1974-76. Mem. D.C., Am., Fed. bar assns. Office: 815 Connecticut Ave NW Washington DC 20006 Tel (202) 298-8686

GRANGER, DELBERT WILLIAM, b. Salt Lake City, Aug. 24, 1925; B.S., U. Utah, 1950, LL.B., 1951, J.D., 1967. Admitted to Utah bar, 1951, Ariz. bar, 1960, U.S. Supreme Ct. bar, 1966; individual practice law, Salt Lake City, 1951-53; staff claims dept. State Farm Ins. Co., Salt Lake City and Phoenix, 1953-60; mem. firm Lewis & Roca, Phoenix, 1960—, partner, 1965—. Mem. Fedn. Ins. Counsel, Internat. Assn. Ins. Counsel, Am. Bd. Trial Advs., Phoenix Assn. Def. Counsel (past pres.). Home: 7013 E Belleview St Scottsdale AZ 85257 Office: 1st National Bank Plaza 100 W Washington St Phoenix AZ 85003

GRANT, BARRY M., b. Detroit, Jan. 16, 1936; B.A., Mich. State U., 1957; J.D., Wayne State U., 1960; postgrad. Northwestern U., 1974. Admitted to Mich. bar, 1960, U.S. Supreme Ct. bar, 1966; individual practice law, Southfield, Mich., 1965—; asst. pros. atty. Oakland County (Mich.), 1961-64, legal investigator Probate Ct., Oakland County Clk., Oakland County Probate Ct., 1960; Probate Ct. referee, 1960, 74; mem. Oakland County Criminal Justice Coordinating Council, 1977. Trustee, treas. Southfield Bd. Edn., 1964-68; mem. Gov.'s Traffic Safety Commn., 1964; chmn. lawyers com. Torch Dr., 1968; bd. dirs. Oakland County Hist. Soc., 1967; exec. sec. Southfield Beautification Com., Parent Youth Guidance Commn., 1961-64. Mem. Nat. Dist. Attys. Assn., Am., Mich. (state bar rep. assembly), Oakland County bar assns. Office: 21751 W 11 Mile Rd Suite 212 Southfield MI 48076 Tel (313) 358-4828

GRANT, CHRISTOPHER JOHN, b. Tulsa, Aug. 29, 1949; B.S. in Edn., U. Tulsa, 1971, J.D., 1973. Admitted to Okla. bar, 1974, U.S. Dist. Ct. bar for No. Dist. Okla., 1974; ct. clk. Dist. Ct. of Tulsa County, 1972-73; clk., intern, asso. firm Baker, Baker & Martin, Tulsa, 1973-74; asso. firm Howe and Grant, Tulsa, 1974-77; asso. firm Williams, Fransein and Savage, Tulsa, 1977—. Mem. Okla., Tulsa County bar assns., Am. Judicature Soc., Delta Theta Phi (Distinguished Service award T. Austin Gavin Senate 1974). Office: 204 Denver Bldg Tulsa OK 74119 Tel (918) 585-8112

GRANT, GARRETT JAY, b. Moraga, Calif., Nov. 16, 1942; B.A. in Anthropology, U. Calif., Berkeley, 1964; J.D., Golden Gate Law Sch., 1970. Admitted to Calif. bar, 1972; dept. dist. atty. Contra Costa County (Calif.), Richmond, 1972—. Mem. San Francisco Lawyers Club, Calif. Dist. Attys. Assn., Bay Area Prosecutors Assn. Office: 100 37th St Richmond CA 94553 Tel (415) 233-7060

GRANT, GARY ALAN, b. Easton, Maine, May 6, 1935; B.A., Bob Jones U., 1956; J.D., U. Denver, 1968. Admitted to Colo. bar, 1968; since practiced in Denver, with Cobusco, Inc., 1960—, Sec., asst. treas., counsel, 1969—; partner firm Menin & Grant, 1968-71; individual practice law, 1971—. Mem. Colo. Epilepsy Assn., (dir. 1972). Mem. Colo., Denver bar assns., Rocky Mountain Assn. Credit Mgmt., Order of St. Ives. Office: POB 5846 Denver CO 80217 Tel (303) 934-5601

GRANT, JAMES KIRKLAND, b. Monroe, Mich., Feb. 14, 1943; B.B.A., U. Mich., 1965, J.D. cum laude, 1967. Admitted to Mich. bar, 1968, N.Y. state bar, 1971, S.C. bar, 1975; asst. prof. law Ga. State U., Atlanta, 1967-69; asst. prof. law, asst. dean U. Toledo, 1969-70; asso. firm Sullivan & Cromwell, N.Y.C., 1970-72; prof. law U.S.C., Columbia, 1972—; reporter S.C. Corp. Law Revision, 1973—; cons. corporate law securities, commodities and related regulation. Mem. Am. Bar Assn. (mem. sects. on corp. law, legal edn.). Contbr. articles in field to legal jours. Home: 130 S Waccamaw Ave Columbia SC 29205 Office: Law Sch USC Columbia SC 29208 Tel (803) 777-4155

GRANT, JAMES WILLIAM, b. Ronan, Mont., Oct. 3, 1914; Ph.B., Gonzaga U., 1936, LL.B., 1938. Admitted to Wash. bar, 1938; credit analyst Peoples Nat. Bank of Wash., Seattle, 1938-42; commd. ensign USNR, 1942, advanced through grades to capt., 1959, ret., 1962; gen. counsel PACCAR, Inc., Bellevue, Wash., 1963—. Mem. Wash. State, Am., Seattle-King County bar assns. Home: 5721 S Eddy St Seattle WA 98118 Office: POB 1518 Bellevue WA 98009 Tel (206) 455-7518

GRANT, RONALD ELGIN, b. Dallas, Oct. 20, 1947; B.A., So. Meth. U., 1969, J.D., 1972. Admitted to Tex. bar, 1972; asso. firm Welz, Anderson and Peters, Dallas, 1972-74; partner firm Grant, Stevenson and Franklin, Dallas, 1974—; intern U.S. Atty. Office, No. Dist. Tex., 1971. Counselor, Ute Trail Boys' Camp, Powderhorn, Colo., 1967-68; asst. dir. Red Cloud Camp, Lake City, Colo., 1969; coach YMCA Softball, Dallas, 1971. Mem. State Bar Tex., Dallas Bar Assn., Tex. Trial Lawyers Assn., Phi Delta Phi. Contbr. articles in field to profl. jours. Home: 7502 Fair Oaks 2109 Dallas TX 75231 Office: 3131 Turtle Creek 208 Dallas TX 75219 Tel (214) 521-5830

GRATHWOL, JAMES NORBERT, b. St. Paul, Dec. 19, 1930; student U. Vienna, Austria, 1952; U. Minn., 1953; B.A. magna cum laude, Coll. St. Thomas, 1953; LL.B. cum laude, William Mitchell Coll. Law, 1958. Admitted to Minn. bar, 1958; mem. firm Grathwol, Ploetz, Oberhauser & Thompson, Excelsior and Wayzata, Minn. Bd. dirs. Lake Minnetonka Conservation Dist., 1966-75; precinct chmn. Republican Com., Excelsior, 1969. Mem. Am., Minn., Hennepin County bar assns., Excelsior C. of C. (pres. 1966). Home: 200 2d St Excelsior MN 55331 Office: 1421 E Wayzata Blvd Suite 210 Wayzata MN 55391 Tel (612) 475-2401

GRAUBART, JEFFREY LOWELL, b. Chgo., Aug. 18, 1940; B.S., U. Ill., 1962; J.D., Northwestern U., 1965. Admitted to Ill. bar, 1965, Calif. bar, 1968; asso. firm Curtis, Friedman & Marks, Chgo., 1965-68; staff atty. Capitol Records, Inc., Los Angeles, 1968-70; individual practice law, San Francisco, 1970—; sec. Paramount Growers, Inc., McFarland, Calif., 1969-70; sec., v.p. London Internat. Artists, Ltd., Los Angeles, 1969-70; instr. Coll. Rec. Arts, Garden State U., San Francisco, Family Light Music Sch., Sausalito, Calif.; gov. San Francisco chpt. Nat. Acad. Rec. Arts and Scis., 1973—; del. Calif. Bar Conf. Dels., 1973-75. Mem. Bar Assn. San Francisco, Lawyers Club San Francisco (bd. govs.), Patent Law Assn. San Francisco. Contbr. articles to legal jours. Office: 900 North Point San Francisco CA 94109 Tel (415) 441-1211

GRAUF, NORVIN LYLE, b. Keokuk, Iowa, Feb. 10, 1926; B.A., Stanford, 1950, LL.B., J.D., 1952. Admitted to Calif. bar, 1952; individual practice law, San Deigo, 1952—. Mem. Am., Calif., San Diego (probate chmn. Superior Ct. com.) bar assns., Phi Alpha Delta. Office: 110 W C St Suite 1405 San Diego CA 92101 Tel (714) 239-2221

GRAVEL, CAMILLE FRANCIS, JR., b. Alexandria, La., Aug. 10, 1915; student U. Notre Dame, 1931-35, La. State U., 1937, Catholic U. Am., 1939. Admitted to La. bar, 1940, U.S. Supreme Ct. bar; asst. dist. atty. Rapides Parish, La., 1942; asst. city atty. Alexandria, 1946-48; partner firm Gravel, Roy, Burnes, Alexandria; atty. La. Tax Commn. 1948-52; mem. La. gov.'s spl. counsel on health, 1967; gen. counsel State La. Labor Mgmt. Commn. Inquiry, 1967; spl. legislative counsel to Gov. La., 1972—; exec. counsel to Gov., 1975—; mem. La. Bd. Tax Appeals. Vice-chmn. Constitutional Conv. Com. La. State Bar Assn., 1953-56; mem. Gov.'s Adv. Commn. La. Workmen's Compensation Laws and Tax Laws La., 1966-67; mem. La. Interdepartmental Health Policy Commn., 1967-68; mem. La. Democratic State Central Com., 1948-64, presdl. elector, 1952, nat. committeeman La. 1954-60, rep. 12 so. states on exec. com. Dem. Nat. Com., 1955-60, chmn. La. Del. to Dem. Nat. Conv., 1956, mem. nat. adv. council Dem. party, 1956-60, chmn. site selection com., co-chmn. credentials com., mem. arrangements com. 1960 Dem. Nat. Conv., Los Angeles, 1960, del. to Dem. Nat. Conv., 1956, 60, 64, 72. Fellow Internat. Acad. Trial Lawyers; mem. Notre Dame Law Assn., Law Sci. Acad., Internat. Soc. Barristers, Am. Judicature Soc., Nat. Assn. Criminal Defense Lawyers, Am. Trial Lawyers Assn., Phi Delta Phi. Home: 3214 Carol Court Alexandria LA 71301 Office: 711 Washington St Alexandria LA 71301 Tel (318) 487-4501

GRAVEL, CLARKE ALBERT, b. Burlington, Vt., Dec. 26, 1916; A.B., St. Michael's Coll., 1938; J.D., Boston Coll., 1941. Admitted to Vt. bar, 1941, U.S. Dist. Ct. Vt., 1942, U.S. Ct. Appeals 2d Circuit bar, 1964, U.S. Supreme Ct. bar, 1965; state's atty., Chittenden, Vt., 1942-47; judge of probate, Chittenden, 1947-53; partner firm Gravel, Shea & Wright and predecessors, Burlington, 1963—; asst. clk. Vt. Ho. of Reps., 1951-53; mem. Nat. Conf. Commrs. on Uniform Laws, 1956-63, 69—; sec. Joint Editorial Bd. for Uniform Probate Code, 1970—. Former pres. Burlington Boys Club, United Way. Fellow Am. Coll. Probate Counsel (state chmn. 1975-76); mem. Am. Judicature Soc., Am. Coll. Pro-Counsel, Am. (chmn. com. adminstrn. and distbn. decedents' estates of sect. real estate, trust and probate sect.), Vt. (pres. 1976-77) bar assns. Home: Office: 109 S Winooski Ave Burlington VT 05401 Tel (802) 658-0220

GRAVELEY, CHARLES ALLAN, b. Bremerton, Wash., Oct. 28, 1944; A.B., Carroll Coll., 1966, J.D., U. Mont., 1973. Admitted to Mont. bar, 1973; dep. county atty. Lewis and Clark County (Mont.), 1973-77, county atty., 1977—; individual practice law, Helena, Mont., 1973—. Mem. Helena Airport Adv. Bd., 1975—; v.p. Helena '77 Rodeo Assn., 1974—. Mem. State Bar Mont., First Jud. Dist. Bar Assn., Helena Young Lawyers (pres. 1975). Home: 1821 Peosta St Helena MT 59601 Office: 1420 Cedar-Airport Way Helena MT 59601 Tel (406) 442-1700

GRAVEN, DAVID LAUREN, b. Mpls., July 22, 1929; B.A., St. Olaf Coll., 1950; LL.B., U. Minn., 1953. Admitted to Minn. bar, 1953; served to 1st lt. JAGC, U.S. Air Force, 1954-57; partner firm Olson & Graven, Albert Lea, Minn., 1957-63, firm Holmes, Kircher & Graven, Mpls., 1974—; prof. law U. Minn., 1963-74; mem. Minn. Uniform Law Commn., 1958-61; sec. Minn. Jud. Council, 1965-70; chmn. drafting com. Minn. Supreme Ct. Adv. Commn. for Rules of Criminal Procedure, 1971—. Bd. dirs. Citizens League, 1967-74, 75—; mem. Twin Cities Area Met. Council, 1971-75; chmn. Twin City Area Transp. Adv. Bd., 1977—. Mem. Am., Minn., Hennepin County bar assns. Contbr. articles to legal jours. Home: 417 Tarrymore St Minneapolis MN 55419 Office: 4610 IDS Bldg Minneapolis MN 55402 Tel (612) 371-3900

GRAVES, CHARLES EDWARD, b. S.I., N.Y., Mar. 22, 1931; B.A., Duke U., 1953; LL.B., U. Colo., 1959. Admitted to Colo., Wyo. bars, 1959, U.S. Supreme Ct. bar, 1970; partner firm Graves & Hacker, and predecessors, Cheyenne, Wyo., 1960—; gen. counsel Wyo. Edn. Assn., 1964—. Exec. sec. Wyo. Youth Council, 1960-63; sec. Cheyenne Housing Authority, Cheyenne Urban Renewal Bd., 1966—; treas. Wyo. Easter Seal Soc., 1966-68; bd. dirs. Community Action of Laramie County (Wyo.), 1968-70; chmn. Cheyenne Model Cities Application Com., 1970; mem. Cheyenne Laramie County Planning Commn., 1975-76, vice chmn., 1977. Mem. Am., Colo., Wyo., Laramie County (sec.-treas. 1963-64) bar assns., Wyo. Trial Lawyers Assn., Nat. Assn. Tchrs. Attys. Home: 1809 E 20th St Cheyenne WY 82001 Office: 604 First Wyoming Bank Tower Cheyenne WY 82001 Tel (307) 8811

GRAVES, EBEN MONTGOMERY, b. Saginaw, Mich., Apr. 1, 1903; B.S. in Chem. Engring., U. Mich., 1926; LL.B., Fordham U., 1930. Admitted to N.Y. bar, 1931, U.S. Supreme Ct. bar, 1960; partner firm Brumbaugh, Graves, Donohue & Raymond, N.Y.C., 1935—; mem. internat. indsl. property panel Dept. State, 1969-70. Mem. Am. Bar Assn., Bar Assn. City N.Y., Am. (pres. 1967-68), N.Y. patent law assns., Am. Judicature Soc. Home: Sasco Point Southport CT 06409 Office: 30 Rockefeller Plaza New York City NY 10020 Tel (212) 489-3311

GRAVES, H. BRICE, b. Charlottesville, Va., Sept. 1, 1912; B.S., U. Va., 1932, M.S., 1933, Ph.D., LL.B., 1938. Admitted to N.Y. bar, 1940, Va. bar, 1949; asso. firm Cravath, Swaine & Moore, N.Y.C., 1938-42, 1945-48; partner firm Hunton & Williams, Richmond, Va., 1949—; lectr. in field; planning com. Univ. Va. Ann. Tax Conf., 1971—. Mem. Richmond, Va. (chmn. taxation com., 1971-73), Am. (chmn. com. exempt orgns. tax sect., 1963-65, com. mem., 1975—) bar assn., Am. Law Inst., Richmond Estate Planning Council. Contbr. articles William and Mary Law Rev., Jour. Taxation. Home: 6024 St Andrews Ln Richmond VA 23226 Office: 707 E Main St Richmond VA 23212 Tel (804) 788-8404

GRAY, ARTHUR W., JR., b. Los Angeles, July 2, 1928; B.A., Valparaiso U., 1950; J.D., U. Calif., San Francisco, 1952. Admitted to Calif. bar, 1953, U.S. Supreme Ct. bar, 1973; now mem. firm Carden & Gray, Anaheim, Calif. Mem. Anaheim Library Bd., 1958-65. Mem. Am., Orange County (pres. 1976-77) bar assns., State Bar Calif. Office: Center Law Bldg 914 W Lincoln Ave Anaheim CA 92805 Tel (714) 535-1157*

GRAY, DALE OSBORN, b. West Stewartstown, N.H., July 27, 1941; B.A., U. Vt., 1964; LL.B., U. Maine, 1967. Admitted to Vt. bar, 1967; atty. Vt. Legal Aid, Inc., St. Johnsbury, 1969-70; state's atty. Caledonia County, Vt., 1970—. Mem. Vt. State's Atty's Assn. (pres. 1974-75), Nat. Dist. Atty's Assn., Am. Bar Assn. Office: 83 Eastern Ave St Johnsbury VT 05819 Tel (802) 748-9258

GRAY, FRANK, JR., b. Franklin, Tenn., Feb. 25, 1908; LL.B., Cumberland U., 1928. Admitted to Tenn. bar, 1928; practice in Franklin, 1928-61; U.S. judge Middle Dist. Tenn., 1961—, chief judge, 1970—. Mayor of Franklin, 1947-61. Mem. Am., Tenn. (bd. govs. 1956-58) bar assn., Am. Judicature Soc., Order of Coif. Home: 1003 Adams St Franklin TN 37064 Office: US Courthouse Nashville TN 37203*

GRAY, FRANK TRUAN, b. Prince Frederick, Md., Oct. 22, 1920; A.B., Princeton, 1942; student Cambridge (Eng.) U., 1945; LL.B., Harvard, 1948. Admitted to Md. bar, 1949; asso. firm Piper & Marbury, Balt., 1948-56, partner, 1957—; asst. atty. gen. State of Md., 1955-56; pres. Balt. Estate Planning Council, 1975-76. Pres., Citizens Planning and Housing Assn., Balt., 1958-60; bd. dirs. Balt. Neighborhoods, Inc., 1959—; trustee Provident Hosp., Inc., 1961-74. Fellow Md. Bar Found.; mem. Am., Md. State, Balt. City bar assns., Am. Law Inst. Editor Harvard Law Rev., 1947-48. Office: 2000 First Maryland Bldg Baltimore MD 21201 Tel (301) 539-2530

GRAY, FRED DAVID, b. Montgomery, Ala., Dec. 14, 1930; B.S., Ala. State U.; LL.B., Western Res U., 1954. Admitted to Ala. bar., 1954, Ohio bar, 1954; sr. partner firm Gray, Seay and Langford, Montgomery and Tuskegee, Ala., 1967—; mem. Ala. Ho. of Reps., 1970-74; mem. Ala. adv. com U.S. Commn. on Civil Rights. Mem. Com. for a Greater Tuskegee; bd. dirs. Southwestern Christian Coll., Terrell, Tex.; minister Chs. of Christ., 1942—. Mem. Am., Nat., Ohio, Ala. bar assns., NAACP, Omega Psi Phi, Sigma Pi Phi. Recipient Const. Law award Ala. Civil Liberties Union, 1968; Capitol Press Corps award, 1972. Home: 2112 Ethel Dr Tuskegee Inst Ala 36088 Office: PO Box 239 Tuskegee AL 36083 Tel (205) 727-4830

GRAY, HENRY LATHAM, JR., b. Gainesville, Fla., Nov. 15, 1931; B.A. with honors, U. Fla., 1958, LL.B., 1961, J.D., 1967. Admitted to Fla. bar, 1961, D.C. bar, 1976; mem. firm Chandler, O'Neal, Gray, Lang & Haswell, and predecessors, Gainesville, 1961—. Pres. United Fund Gainesville, 1968. Mem. Fla. Bar (bd. govs. young lawyers sect. 1964-68), Am. Trial Lawyers Assn., Am., 8th Jud. Circuit (pres. 1970) bar assns., Acad. Fla. Trial Lawyers. Office: 211 NE 1st St Gainesville FL 32601 Tel (904) 376-5226

GRAY, JAN CHARLES, b. Des Moines, June 15, 1947; B.A., U. Calif. at Berkeley, 1969; J.D., Harvard U., 1972. Admitted to Calif. bar, 1972, D.C. bar, 1974; law clk. firm Kindel & Anderson, Los Angeles, 1971-72; asso. firm Halstead, Baker & Sterling, Los Angeles, 1972-75; dir. legal dept. and counsel Ralphs Grocery Co., Los Angeles, 1975—; instr. bus. U. Calif., Los Angeles, 1976—; real estate broker, Los Angeles, 1973—. Mem. Am., Calif., Los Angeles County, San Fernando Valley (chmn. real property sec. 1975—) bar assns., Am. Econ. Assn., Los Angeles World Affairs Council, Ephebian Soc. Los Angeles, Town Hall Los Angeles, U. Calif. Alumni Assn., Harvard Club So. Calif., Phi Beta Kappa. Contbg. author: Life or Death: Who Controls?, 1976. Contbr. articles to legal jours. Home: PO Box 407 Beverly Hills CA 90213 Office: PO Box 54143 Los Angeles CA 90054 Tel (213) 637-7791

GRAY, JAN STEPHEN, b. Salisbury, N.C., Oct. 8, 1947; B.A., Catawba Coll., 1969; J.D., Wake Forest U., 1972. Admitted to N.C. bar, 1972; individual practice law, Salisbury, N.C., 1972-73; sr. partner firm Gray and Whitley, Salisbury, 1973—. Mem. N.C. Acad. Trial Lawyers, Am. Acad. Trial Lawyers, N.C. Bar Assn., Nat. Assn. Criminal Defense Lawyers, Phi Alpha Delta. Office: 207 Law Bldg Salisbury NC 28144 Tel (704) 637-1111

GRAY, JOHN LATHROP, b. Elizabeth, N.J., Mar. 20, 1905; A.B. cum laude, Harvard, 1927, LL.B. cum laude, 1930. Admitted to N.Y. bar, 1932, U.S. Dist. Ct. Eastern Dist., 1934, So. Dist., 1935, Treasury Dept. bar, 1944, Tax Ct. of U.S., 1959; asso. firm Dewey, Ballantine, Bushby, Palmer & Wood, and predecessors, N.Y.C., 1930-41, mem., 42—; mem. adv. com. N.Y. State Commn. on Estates, 1960-66. Bd. dirs. Greenwich (Conn.) Community Chest and Council, 1949-55, pres., 1954-55; trustee Rosemary Hall Found. Girls Sch., Greenwich, 1958-71, William R. Kenan, Jr. Charitable Trust, N.Y.C., 1965—. Fellow Am. Coll. Probate Counsel; mem. Am., N.Y. State bar assns., Assn. Bar City N.Y., N.Y. County Lawyers Assn., Am. Judicature Soc. Recipient Appreciation certificate for outstanding service in continuing legal edn. N.Y. Practicing Law Inst., 1961. Office: 140 Broadway New York City NY 10005 Tel (212) 344-8000

GRAY, KENNETH EDWARD, b. Yonkers, N.Y., June 25, 1944; B.A., Iona Coll., 1966; J.D., Harvard, 1969, M.P.A., 1970. Admitted to Ill. bar, 1970; asso. firm Ross, Hardies, O'Keefe, Babcock & Parsons, Chgo., 1970-72; asst. prof. law Ill. Inst. Tech., 1972-76; asso. prof. law DePaul U., 1976—; mem. adminstrv. rev. bd. Ill. Sec. State, 1974—. Bd. dirs. Rogers Park Community Council. Mem. Am., Ill., Chgo. bar assns., Chgo. Council Fgn. Relations. Contbr. articles in field to profl. jours. Home: 6301 N Sheridan Rd Apt 7-B Chicago IL 60660 Office: 25 E Jackson Blvd Chicago IL 60604 Tel (312) 274-0602

GRAY, LAWRENCE CHARLES, b. Joliet, Ill., Dec. 16, 1944; B.A., Knox Coll., 1967; J.D., DePaul U., 1971. Admitted to Ill. bar, 1971; asso. firm Thomas, Wallace, Feehan & Baron, Joliet, 1971—. Chmn. lawyers' div. ARC, Will County, Ill., 1975, 76. Mem. Am. Trial Lawyers Assn., Will County (sec.-treas. 1973-77), Ill. (sec. environ. law council 1974-77) bar assns. Office: 5 E Van Buren St Joliet IL 60431 Tel (815) 727-4511

GRAY, MILTON HEFTER, b. Chgo., Dec. 10, 1910; B.A., Northwestern U., 1931, J.D. magna cum laude, 1934. Admitted to Ill. bar, 1934; asso. and partner firm Gardner, Carton & Douglas, 1934-43; individual practice law, Chgo., 1943-60; sr. partner firm Altheimer & Gray, Chgo., 1960—; spl. master U.S. Dist. Ct., 1973—; commr. Ill. Supreme Ct., 1957-62, 66-68, 70-73; v.p., sec., dir. Blackstone Mfg. Co., Inc.; sec., dir. Noma-World Wide, Inc.; sec. Alloy Mfg. Co.; lectr. Am. Inst. Banking, 1943-45, U. Ill., 1953, Northwestern U., 1956, Harvard U., 1967. Pres., N.E. Ill. council Boy Scouts Am., 1957-59, hon. pres., 1977—, exec. bd. region VII, 1959—, vice chmn., 1966-68, chmn., 1968-70, mem. nat. exec. bd., 1968-70, mem. nat. adv. council, 1970—. Recipient Silver Beaver award Boy Scouts Am., 1959, Silver Antelope award, 1963, Distinguished Eagle Scout Citizens award, 1969; award of merit Northwestern U., 1973. Mem. Internat., Am. (com. state regulation securities 1961—, com. fed. regulation securities 1963—, com. corporate law and accounting 1973—), Ill. (past chmn. corp. and securities laws sect.), Chgo. (past chmn. corp. law com., past chmn. securities law com., bd. mgrs. 1966-68, 1st v.p. 1970-71, pres. 1971-72) bar assns., World Assn. Lawyers, Order of Coif. Editorial bd. Ill. Bus. Corp. Act Annotated, 1947; contbr. articles to legal jours. Home: 420 Lakeside Pl Highland Park IL 60035 Office: 1 IBM Plaza Chicago IL 60611 Tel (312) 467-9600

GRAY, OSCAR SHALOM, b. N.Y.C., Oct. 18, 1926; A.B., Yale, 1948, J.D., 1951. Admitted to Md. bar, 1951, D.C. bar, 1952, U.S. Supreme Ct. bar, 1952; atty.-adviser legal adviser's office, U.S. Dept. State, Washington, 1951-57; sec. Nuclear Materials and Equipment Corp., Apollo, Pa., 1957-64, treas., 1957-67, v.p., 1964-71, dir., 1964-67; spl. counsel presdl. task force on communications policy, Washington, 1967-68; cons. U.S. Dept. Transp., Washington, 1967-68, acting dir. office of environ. impact, Dept. Transp., 1968-70; adj. prof., lectr. Law Center Georgetown U., Washington, 1970-71; lectr. Sch. Law Cath. U. Am., Washington, 1970-71; asso. prof. Sch. Law U. Md., Balt., 1971-74, prof. law, 1974—; individual practice law, Washington, 1970—, Balt., 1971—. Vis. prof. Sch. Law U. Tenn., Knoxville, 1977. Past pres. Apollo (Pa.) C. of C. Mem. Am. Law Inst., D.C. Bar, Md. Bar Assn., Assn. Trial Lawyers Am., Order of Coif, Phi Beta Kappa. Author: Cases and Materials on Environmental Law, 1970, 2d edit., 1973; supplements, 1974-77; (with H. Shulman and F. James, Jr.) Cases and Materials on the Law of Torts, 3d edit., 1976; contbr. articles to legal jours. Office: 500 W Baltimore St Baltimore Md 21201 Tel (301) 528-7174 also 1225 19th St NW Suite 800 Washington DC 20036 Tel (202) 223-4006

GRAY, WHITMORE, b. Monroe, Mich., Nov. 6, 1932; A.B., Principia Coll., 1954; J.D., U. Mich., 1957; postgrad. U. Paris, 1957-58. Admitted to Mich. bar, 1958; asso. firm Casey, Lane & Mittendorf, N.Y.C., 1958-60; prof. Sch. Law, U. Mich., Ann Arbor, 1960—; vis. prof. Stanford U., Munster U., Tubingen U., Kyoto U. Mem. Am. Bar Assn., Am. Fgn. Law Assn., Internat. Acad. Comparative Law (asso.). Translator: Russian Republic Civil Code, 1965; editor in chief Mich. Law Review, 1956-57; mem. bd. editors Am. Jour. Comparative Law. Home: 909 Heather Way Ann Arbor MI 48104 Office: Hutchins Hall Univ Mich Ann Arbor MI 48109 Tel (313) 764-0536

GRAY, WILLIAM DOUGLAS, b. Orangeburg County, S.C., Apr. 24, 1941; B.J., U. S.C., 1963, J.D., 1966. Admitted to S.C. bar, 1966; asso. firm Watkins, Vandiver, Kirven, Long & Gable, Anderson, S.C., 1966-70, partner, 1970—. Bd. dirs. Anderson Community Found. Mem. Am., S.C., Anderson County bar assns. Home: 2810 Echo Trail Anderson SC 29621 Office: 500 S McDuffie St Anderson SC 29621 Tel (803) 225-2527

GRAY, WILLIAM OXLEY, b. Iowa Falls, Iowa, Nov. 23, 1914; B.A., Coe Coll., 1936; J.D., U. Iowa, 1938. Admitted to Iowa bar, 1938; partner firm Silliman, Gray & Stapleton, Cedar Rapids, Iowa, 1938—; spl. agt. FBI, 1942-46. Chmn. Iowa State Hwy. Commn., 1969-73; past chpt. chmn. Linn County cht. ARC; former dir. Iowana council Camp Fire Girls and Camp Good Health; former dir. Cedar Rapids C. of C.; trustee Herbert Hoover Presdl. Library Assn., Coe Coll. Mem. Am., Iowa, Linn County (past pres.) bar assns., Linn County Law Club (past pres.), Soc. Former Spl. Agts. FBI (nat. pres. 1970-71). Home: 509 Knollwood Dr SE Cedar Rapids IA 52403 Office: American Bldg Cedar Rapids IA 52401 Tel (319) 364-1535

GRAYBILL, LEO CARLISLE, JR., b. Belt, Mont., Mar. 28, 1924; B.A., Yale, 1947, J.D., 1950; J.D., U. Mont., 1952. Admitted to Mont. bar, 1952; partner firm Graybill, Ostrem, Warner & Crotty, Great Falls, Mont., 1952—; instr. bus. law Coll. Great Falls, 1971—; pres. Mont. Constl. Conv., 1971-73. Chmn., Great Falls Internat. Airport Commn., 1967-72. Office: 400 1st National Bank Bldg Great Falls MT 59401 Tel (406) 452-8579

GRAYSON, JOHN ALLAN, b. Lowell, Ind., Oct. 14, 1930; B.S.S., Northwestern U., 1952; J.D., U. Mich., 1955. Admitted to Mich. bar, 1955, Ind. bar, 1955; asso. firm Ice Miller Donadio & Ryan, Indpls., 1955-65, partner, 1966—; vis. asst. prof. Ind. U. Sch. Law, Bloomington, 1957-58. Dir., Crossroads Rehab. Center, Inc., Indpls., 1972—, pres., 1975—. Mem. Am., Ind. State, Indpls. bar assns., Indpls. Bar Found., hon. mem. Ind. Land Title Assn. Office: 111 Monument Circle Indianapolis IN 46204 Tel (317) 635-1213

GRAYSON, ROBERT ARTHUR, b. Glendale, Calif., Mar. 2, 1940; B.A., U. Redlands, 1962; J.D., Harvard, 1965. Admitted to Nev. bar, 1966; law clk. Nev. Supreme Ct., Carson City, 1965-66; asso. firm Springer & Newton, Reno, 1966-67; dept. atty. gen., Carson City, 1967-70; individual practice law, Carson City, 1970—. Mem. First Judicial Dist. Bar Assn. (pres.). Office: 305 N Carson St POB 1308 Carson City NV 89701 Tel (702) 882-5447

GRAYSON, SPENCE MONROE, b. Savannah, Ga., Dec. 7, 1900; student Ga. Inst. Tech., 1919-20; LL.B., U. Ga., 1924. Admitted to Ga. bar, 1924, U.S.Dist. Ct. bar, 1924; land examiner Superior Ct., Savannah 1927-31; mem. Ga. Ho. of Reps., 1927-31, 34-44; mem. Ga. Senate, 1945-52, 61-62, pres. pro tem, 1945-46, 49-52; atty. City of Savannah, 1937-46, Coastal Hwy. Co-mn. Ga., 1949-64, U.S. magistrate So. Dist. Ga., Savannah, 1970—. Mem. Savannah C. of C. (dir. 1945), State Bar Ga. (gov. 1946-49), Ga. Municipal Assn. (v.p. 1940), Savannah Bar Assn., Nat. Council U.S. Magistrates. Recipient Lucas Trophy award City of Savannah, 1949. Home: Box 1108 Wilmington Island Savannah GA 31410 Office: PO Box 9480 Savannah GA 31402 Tel (912) 232-0163

GRAYSON, WALTON, III, b. Shreveport, La., Aug. 18, 1928; A.B. in Economics, Princeton U., 1949; LL.B., Harvard U., 1952. Admitted to Tex. bar, 1952; asso. firm Atwell, Grayson & Atwell, Dallas, Tex., 1953-61, partner, 1961-69; partner firm Grayson & Simon, 1969-73; dir. Southland Corp., Dallas, 1962—, v.p. and gen. counsel, 1965-72, exec. v.p. corp. adminstrn. and services, 1972—; asst. counsel Gt. Nat. Life Ins. Co., 1954-69; of counsel firm Simon and Twombly, 1973—. Mem. Am., Tex., Dallas bar assns. Home: 10525 Strait Land St Dallas TX 75229 Office: 2828 N Haskell Ave Dallas TX 75204 Tel (214) 828-7201

GREAGER, HAROLD COOPER, b. Hyattsville, Md., Feb. 20, 1910; B.S., U. Colo., 1941; LL.B. (now J.D.), Westminister Law Sch., 1947. Admitted to Colo. bar, 1947; owner, mgr. Greager Motor Service, 1934-39; pub. accountant Ernst & Ernst, Denver, 1941-42, 46-47; individual practice law, Ft. Collins, Colo., 1947—; dir. Whitneys, Inc., Ft. Lupton, Colo. Mem. Am., Colo., Larimer County bar assns., Am. Inst. C.P.A.'s, Colo. Soc. C.P.A.'s, Calif. Thoroughbreeders Assn., Beta Alpha Psi, Delta Sigma Pi. Home: 3624 E Mulberry St Fort Collins CO 80521 Office: 333 W Mountain Ave Fort Collins CO 80522 Tel (303) 482-2179

GREATHEAD, RICHARD SCOTT, b. Santa Monica, Calif., May 18, 1946; A.B., Princeton, 1968; J.D., U. Va., 1972. Admitted to N.Y. State bar, 1974; asso. firm Lord, Day & Lord, N.Y.C., 1972—. Bd. dirs., sec. N.Y. Lawyers for Pub. Interest, Inc., N.Y.C., 1976—; bd. dirs. Fund for New Priorities in Am., N.Y.C., 1974—. Mem. Assn. Bar City N.Y. (com. on mil. justice and mil. affairs 1976—), Am. Bar Assn., The Council N.Y. Law Assos. (chmn. steering com. 1976—). Home: 8 Montague Terr Brooklyn NY 11201 Office: 25 Broadway New York City NY 10004 Tel (212) 344-8480

GREAVES, THOMAS GUY, JR., b. Lynchburg, Va., Apr. 19, 1918; B.S. in Econs., Wharton Sch. U. Pa., 1939; LL.B., U. Ala., 1947. Admitted to Ala. bar, 1948, since practiced in Mobile; partner firm Hand, Arendall, Bedsole, Greaves & Johnston, 1952—. Pres. Mobile County chpt. A.R.C., 1966-68; pres. Episcopal Churchmens Assn. Ala., 1960-61; mem. Ala. Bar Found., U. Ala. Law Sch. Found. Fellow Am. Bar Found.; mem. Ala. State Bar (pres. 1975-76), Am. (ho. dels. 1959-74, bd. govs. 1966-69, chmn. standing com. Am. citizenship 1960-63, com. documents of title 1959-62; chmn. rules and calendar com. ho. of dels. 1970-72, vice chmn. com. draft of ho. of dels. 1960-63; chmn. bar activities sect. 1965-66; mem. exec. council young lawyers sect. 1953-55; mem. adv. bd. jour. 1961-63; 1st v.p. 1974-75; chmn. law day adv. com.), Ala. (young lawyers sect. 1948-49), Mobile County (pres. 1968, chmn. youth edn. for citizenship 1972-74) bar. assns., Am. Judicature Soc. (dir. 1959-63), Fedn. Ins. Counsel (dir. 1963-65), Am. Counsel Assn. (exec. com. 1960-63), U. Ala. Law Sch. Alumni Assn. (pres. 1963-64), Am., Ala. law insts., English Speaking Union (pres. 1970), Farrah Order Jurisprudence, Delta Kappa Epsilon, Phi Delta Phi, Phi Eta Sigma. Home: 77 Clarise Circle Mobile AL 36608 Office: First Nat Bank Bldg Mobile AL 36602 Tel (205) 432-5511*

GRECO, ALFRED VINCENT, b. N.Y.C., Sept. 12, 1935; B.A., Hunter Coll., 1957; J.D. Fordham U., 1960. Admitted to N.Y. State bar, 1961; with SEC, 1962-65; individual practice law, N.Y.C., 1965—. Mem. Am., N.Y. State bar assns. Office: 630 5th Ave New York City NY 10020 Tel (212) 757-4025

GRECO, AMEDEO, b. Long Branch, N.J., Jan. 27, 1942; B.A., Upsala Coll., 1964; J.D., U. Wis., 1967. Admitted to N.J. bar, 1967, D.C. bar, 1968, Wis. bar, 1973; legal asst. to chmn. NLRB, Washington, 1967-70, legal asst. to mem., 1970-71, trial atty., Milw., 1971-73; arbitrator, mediator, hearing examiner Wis. Employment Relations Commn., Madison, 1973—; tchr. U. Wis., 1973—. Mem. NLRB Profl. Assn. (pres. 1968-69). Home: 5310 Fairway Dr Madison WI 53711 Office: Room 910 30 W Mifflin St Madison WI 53703 Tel (608) 266-8331

GREELY, MICHAEL TRUMAN, b. Great Falls, Mont., Feb. 28, 1940; B.A., Yale, 1962; J.D., U. Mont., 1967. Admitted to Mont. bar, 1967; asst. atty. gen. State of Mont., Helena, 1967-70; dep. atty. Cascade County (Mont.), 1970-76; individual practice law, Great Falls, 1970-77; atty. gen. Mont., Helena, 1977—; chmn. Mont. Gov.'s Council on Criminal Justice Standards and Goals, 1975-76; mem. Mont. Ho. of Reps., 1971-74, Mont. Senate, 1975-76. Mem. Mont. Mental Health Council, 1975, Cascade County Mental Health Adv. Council. Mem. Mont., Cascade County bar assns. Office: Capitol Bldg Helena MT 59601 Tel (406) 449-2026

GREEN, ANDREW WILSON, b. Harrisburg, Pa., May 17, 1923; student Princeton, 1940-43; B.S., N.Y. U., 1944; LL.B., Dickinson Sch. Law, 1948; M.B.A., U. Pa., 1961, Ph.D., 1968; Diploma, U. Amsterdam (Holland), 1967. Admitted to D.C. bar, 1949, Pa. bar, 1950; adminstrv. asst. Pa. Pub. Utility Comm., Harrisburg, 1950-51; individual practice law, Harrisburg, 1951-61; research assn. Pa. Economy League, Phila., 1962, Center Strategic & Internat. Studies Georgetown Univ., Brussels, Belgium, 1967-69, Foreign Policy Research Inst. Univ. Pa., Brussels, 1969-70; asso. prof. dept. bus., economics W. Chester (Pa.) State Coll., 1970-74, prof., chmn. dept., 1974—; prof. Delaware Law Sch., Wilmington, 1973-76, adjunct prof., 1976—; hearing officer Selective Service System, Harrisburg, 1952-58. Mem. Am., Pa. bar assns., Am. Bus. Law Assn., Nat. Assn. Bus. Law Tchr's., Am. Polit. Sci. Assn., Am. Economic Assn., Soc. Pub. Tchrs. Law. Author: Polit. Integration by Jurisprudence, The Ct. of Justice of European Communities, 1969, Bibliography of British Legal Edn., 1974, Survey of Bus. Law Teaching in U.S., 1976. Office: Dept Business & Economics West Chester State College West Chester PA 19380 Tel (215) 436-2236

GREEN, ARNOLD BORIS, b. N.Y.C., May 30, 1938; B.S., N.Y.U., 1960; J.D., Bklyn. Law Sch., 1963. Admitted to N.Y. State bar, 1963; field auditor IRS, N.Y.C., 1963-65; mem. firm James Dempsey, White Plains, N.Y., 1965-67; partner firm Bacharach, Green & Bass, White Plains, 1967—; arbitrator Am. Arbitration Assn. Chmn. Greenburgh Narcotic Guidance council, Greenburgh, N.Y., 1974-75. Mem. White Plains, Westchester County bar assns.; recipient Outstanding Jaycee award, 1968. Home: 28 Scott Pl Hartsdale NY 10530 Office: 200 Mamaroneck Ave White Plains NY 10601 Tel (914) 761-2030

GREEN, DALE MONTE, b. Outlook, Wash., Apr. 27, 1922; B.A. in Econs. and Bus., U. Wash., 1947, B.S. in Law, 1949, J.D., 1950. Admitted to Wash. bar, 1950; asso. firm Graves, Kizer & Graves, Spokane, Wash., 1950-54; asst. U.S. Dist. Atty. for Eastern Dist. Wash., 1954-56, U.S. atty., 1958-61; trial atty. civil div. Dept. Justice, Washington, 1956-58; partner firm Sherwood, Tugman & Green, Walla Walla, Wash., 1961-69; judge Wash. State Ct. Appeals, div. 3, 1969—; mem. Wash. Pattern Jury Instruction Com., 1971—, Nat. Council Crime, Delinquency, 1972—, Wash. State Bd. Jud. Tng. Standards, 1974—. Mem. Am. Judicature Soc., Appellate Judges' Conf., Nat. Legal Aid, Defender Assn. Home: 3914 S Cook St Spokane WA 99203 Office: Wash State Ct Appeals Div III Broadway Centre Bldg Broadway and Jefferson Sts Spokane WA 99201 Tel (509) 456-3922

GREEN, DENSLOW BROOKS, b. Madera, Calif., Feb. 4, 1922; B.A. cum laude, Stanford, 1943, J.D. Admitted to Calif. bar, 1947, U.S. Surpeme Ct. bar, 1957; partner firm Sherwood & Denslow Green, Madera, 1947—; gen. counsel Madera Irrigation Dist., Chowchilla Water Dist., La Branza Water Dist., Broadview Water Dist., Farmers Water Dist., Tranquillity Irrigation Dist., Fresno Slough Water Dist.; dir. Berry Constrn. Co., Security Seed Co. Mem. Madera County, Calif. bar assns. Office: 219 S D St Madera CA 93637 Tel (209) 674-5656

GREEN, DOUGLAS GUSTAVE, b. Washington, Jan. 9, 1947; B.A., Bowdoin Coll., 1968; M.A. in English, U. Va., 1969; J.D., Georgetown U., 1973. Admitted to D.C. bar, 1973, U.S. Supreme Ct. bar, 1977; asso. firm Arent, Fox, Kintner, Plotkin & Kahn, Washington, 1973—; mem. pub. contracts law com. Nat. Acad. Sci. Mem. Am., D.C. bar assns. Asso. editor Pub. Contract Law Jour.; editor Georgetown U. Law Jour. Office: 1815 H St NW Washington DC 20006 Tel (202) 857-6060

GREEN, DOYE ENGRID, b. Soperton, Ga., Aug. 14, 1932; B.A., Mercer U., 1960, J.D., Walter F. George Sch. Law, 1962. Admitted to Ga. bar; asso. firm McKenna, House, Lancaster & Green, and predecessors, Macon, Ga., jr. partner, sr. partner, 1975—. Pres. brotherhood, deacon Tatnall Square Baptist Ch., Macon; bd. mgrs., bd. govs. River North Acad., Macon, 1974—. Mem. Am., Macon (pres. 1970-71) bar assns., State Bar Ga., Am. Trial Lawyers Assn., Delta Theta Phi (pres. local chpt. 1960), Sigma Alpha Epsilon. Recipient Meritorious Service award Mercer U. Alumni Assn., 1976. Home: 5691 Kentucky Downs Dr Macon GA 31204 Office: 200 Am Fed Bldg PO Box 1058 Macon GA 31202 Tel (912) 746-9683

GREEN, GEORGE DERK, b. Marceline, Mo., Aug. 11, 1904; J.D., Washington U., St. Louis, 1925. Admitted to Mo. bar, 1925, U.S. Dist. Ct. bar, 1926, U.S. Supreme Ct. bar, 1960; individual practice law, Marceline, 1925-40; city atty. Marceline, 1926-38; pros. atty. Linn County (Mo.), 1936-40; judge 9th Circuit Ct. Mo., Brookfield, 1940—. Home: 1118 Sunset Hill Rd Brookfield MO 64628 Office: 309 1/2 N Main St Brookfield MO 64628 Tel (816) 258-3121

GREEN, GERALDINE DOROTHY, b. N.Y.C., July 14, 1938; student in Accounting, Coll. City N.Y., 1962-64; J.D., St. John's U., Bklyn., 1968. Tax accountant Coopers & Lybrand, N.Y.C., 1966-68; staff atty. IBM Corp., Armonk, N.Y., 1968-69, Gaithersburg, Md., 1969-71, Los Angeles, 1971-72; atty., asst. corp. sec. Atlantic Richfield Co., Los Angeles, 1972—; counsel to exec. dir. on spl. matters Los Angeles Urban League. Vice pres. Beverly Hills/Hollywood (Calif.) br. NAACP, 1973-76, treas., 1977—; mem. Los Angeles Bd. Traffic Commrs., 1976—. Mem. Am., Calif., Nat. bar assns., Black Women Lawyers Calif., Fin. Lawyers Conf., Langston Law Club, Women Lawyers of Los Angeles, Calif., Los Angeles world affairs councils, Nat. Legal Aid and Defender Assn., So. Poverty Law Center, U.S. Olympic Soc. Recipient Freedom award citation NAACP, 1973, Community Service award Los Angeles Urban League, 1973, certificate of Achievement YWCA, 1976. Office: 515 S Flower St Suite 3000 Los Angeles CA 90071 Tel (213) 486-1451

GREEN, HALCOTT PRIDE, b. Middlebury, Vt., Nov. 15, 1943; A.B., Yale, 1966; J.D., Vanderbilt U., 1969. Admitted to S.C. bar, 1969; asso. firm McCants, Nelson and Green and predecessors, Columbia, S.C., 1969-72, partner, 1972—. Mem. Am., S.C., Richland County (S.C.) bar assn., Comml. Law League. Home: 120 S Waccamaw Ave Columbia SC 29206 Office: 900 Security Fed Bldg Columbia SC 29201 Tel (803) 799-9911

GREEN, HARLAND NORTON, b. Los Angeles, Feb. 14, 1930; B.S. in Bus. Adminstrn. with honors, U. Calif., Los Angeles, 1951, J.D., 1954; LL.M., U. So. Calif., 1962. Admitted to Calif. bar, 1955, U.S. Supreme Ct. bar, 1963; accountant J. Arthur Greenfield & Co., C.P.A.'s, Los Angeles, 1956-58; asso. firm Rosenthal & Green and predecessors, Beverly Hills, Calif., 1958-61, partner, 1961-68; individual practice law, Beverly Hills, 1969-72; pres. firm Harland N. Green, profl. corp., Beverly Hills, 1972—. Vice chmn. bd. trustees So. Calif. chpt. Nat. Multiple Sclerosis Soc. Mem. Am., Calif., Beverly Hills bar assns., Assn. Attys.-C.P.A.'s, Los Angeles Copyright Soc., Order of Coif, Phi Beta Kappa, Beta Gamma Sigma. Named Outstanding Trustee So. Calif. chpt. Nat. Multiple Sclerosis Soc., 1966, Most Valuable Trustee, 1976; contbr. articles to U. Calif. at Los Angeles Law Rev.; certified tax specialist. Office: 8383 Wilshire Blvd Beverly Hills CA 90211 Tel (213) 658-7888

GREEN, HAROLD PAUL, b. Wilkes-Barre, Pa., Feb. 23, 1922; A.B., U. Chgo., 1942, J.D., 1948. Admitted to Ill. bar, 1949, D.C. bar, 1954, Md. bar, 1960; asso. firm Gottlieb, Schwartz & Friedman, Chgo., 1948-50; atty. Office Gen. Counsel AEC, Washington, 1950-54; acting counsel Subcom. Reorgn. Senate Com. Govt. Ops., Washington, 1955; partner firm Fried, Frank, Harris, Shriver & Kampelman, Washington, 1957—; prof. law, dir. law, sci. and tech. program George Wash. U. Nat. Law Center, Washington, 1964—. Mem. Am. (spl. com. on energy law 1976—), Fed. bar assns. Author: (with Alan Rosenthal) Government of the Atom: The Integration of Powers; numerous articles for legal, sci. and tech. mags. Home: 2500

Virginia Ave NW Washington DC 20037 Office: 600 New Hampshire Ave NW Washington DC 20037 Tel (202) 965-9400

GREEN, JAMES SAMUEL, b. Danville, Pa., May 24, 1947; A.B., Princeton, 1969; J.D., Villanova U., 1972. Admitted to Del. bar, 1972, Pa. bar, 1973; asso. firm Connolly Bove & Lodge, Wilmington, Del., 1972-75, 76—; dep. atty. gen. Del., 1975-76. Mem. Del. Bar Assn. Home: 2442 W 18th St Wilmington DE 19806 Office: 1800 Farmers Bank Bldg Wilmington DE 19899 Tel (302) 658-9141

GREEN, JOHN ORNE, b. Erie, Pa., Jan. 1, 1922; A.B., Yale, 1943; J.D., Harvard, 1948. Admitted to N.Y. bar, 1950, N.J. bar, 1960, Conn. bar, 1975; asso. firm Mudge, Rose, Guthrie & Alexander, N.Y.C., 1948-51; gen. atty., asst. sec. Johnson & Johnson, New Brunswick, N.J., 1951-62; asst. sec., asst. gen. counsel Richardson-Merrell Inc., Wilton, Conn., 1962-65, sec., asst. gen. counsel, 1965-66, gen. counsel, 1966—, v.p., 1970. Mem. Am. Soc. Corporate Secs., Pharm. Mfrs. Assn., Proprietary Assn. Office: Richardson-Merrell Inc Ten Westport Rd Wilton CT 06897 Tel (203) 762-2222

GREEN, JOYCE HENS, b. N.Y.C., Nov. 13, 1928; B.A., U. Md., 1949; J.D., George Washington U., 1951. Admitted to D.C. bar, 1951, Va. bar, 1956, U.S. Supreme Ct. bar, 1956, U.S. Ct. of Claims bar, 1958; individual practice law, Washington, 1951-68, Arlington, Va., 1956-68; asso. judge Superior Ct. of D.C., 1968—; mem. advisory bd. D.C. Law Students in Court, 1976—. Trustee D.C. div. Am. Cancer Soc., 1963-76. Fellow Am. Acad. Matrimonial Lawyers; mem. Am., D.C., D.C. Women's (pres. 1960-62) bar assns., Am. Judicature Soc., Nat. Conf. State Trial Judges, Exec. Women in Govt. (sec. 1976, chmn. 1977), Kappa Beta Pi, Phi Delta Phi (hon.). Recipient Certificate of Merit, D.C. Profl. Panhellenic Assn.; Achievement award George Washington U., 1975; Women's Legal Def. Fund award, 1976. Office: 400 E St NW Rm 218 Washington DC 20001 Tel (202) 727-1060

GREEN, MICHAEL B., b. N.Y.C., Mar. 17, 1903; LL.B., St. John's U., 1928. Admitted to N.Y. State bar, 1930, U.S. Dist. Ct. So. N.Y. bar, 1931, U.S. Dist. Ct. Eastern Dist. N.Y., bar, 1932, U.S. Ct. Appeals 2d Circuit bar, 1935; practiced in N.Y.C., 1930—; mem. staff Surrogate Ct., 1923-28, N.Y. State Mortgage Commn., 1938-39, N.Y. State Mortgage Tax Bur., 1939-41, N.Y. State Estate Tax Bur., 1941-62, Surrogate Ct., N.Y. County, 1962-73. Mem. Bronx County Bar Assn. Author: Pocket Manuel on Wills & Estates, 1939; contbr. articles in field to profl. jours. Home and Office: 2185 Valentine Ave Bronx NY 10457 Tel (212) 733-2188

GREEN, MILTON DOUGLAS, b. May 16, 1903; A.B., U. Mich., 1926, J.D., 1928; J.Sc.D., Columbia, 1944. Admitted to Colo. bar, 1929; Wash. bar, 1947, Mo. bar, 1954; individual practice law, Denver, 1929-37; prof. U. Colo., 1937-38, 40-45; asso. prof. U. Utah, 1938-40; prof. U. Wash., 1945-53; prof., dean Washington U., St. Louis, 1953-59; prof. N.Y. U., 1959-67, Hastings Coll. Law, San Francisco, 1967—. Mem. Am., St. Louis bar assns. Author: Basic Civil Procedure, 1972; contbr. articles in field to profl. jours. Home: 2030 Vallejo St San Francisco CA 94123 Office: 198 McAllister St San Francisco CA 94102 Tel (415) 921-2020

GREEN, OLIVER LAIN, JR., b. Charleston, S.C., Nov. 19, 1932; B.S., U. Ala., 1957; J.D., Stetson U., 1958. Admitted to Fla. bar, 1958; partner firm Oxford, Oxford & Green, Lakeland, Fla., 1958-7; judge Municipal Ct., Lakeland, 1971, Polk County (Fla.) Magistrate Ct., 1971-72, 10th Jud. Circuit Ct. of Fla., 1973—. Mem. Am., Fla. Lakeland bar assns., Polk County Legal Aid Soc. (dir. exec. com.), Pi Kappa Phi, Phi Delta Phi. Recipient Good Govt. award Lakeland Jaycees, 1973. Home: 415 Lake Miriam Dr Lakeland FL 33803 Office: PO Box 987 Bartow FL 33830 Tel (813) 533-0411

GREEN, PHILIP PALMER, JR., b. Fort Benning, Ga., July 24, 1922; A.b., Princeton, 1943; J.D., Harvard, 1949; diploma U.S. Army Command & Gen. Staff Coll., 1964; diploma U.S. Army War Coll., 1970. Admitted to N.C. bar, 1949; U.S. Dist. Ct. for eastern Dist. N.C. bar, 1953, U.S. Supreme Ct. bar, 1964; asst. dir. Inst. Govt. U. N.C., Chapel Hill, 1949—, prof., 1957—, vis. lectr. Law Sch., 1950-52, 65-68, 72; mem. N.C. Gov.'s Tech. Advisory Com. on Area Devel., 1960-61, N.C. Gov.'s Advisory Com. on Low-income Housing, 1966-68; dir. N.C. Low Income Housing Devel. Corp., 1967—; mem. N.C. Task Force on Rural Housing, 1970—. Chmn. Chapel Hill Community Chest, 1954; treas., dir. Chapel Hill Day Care Center, 1966-69. Mem. Am., N.C. State bar assns., Am. Soc. Planning Ofcls. Recipient Distinguished Service award N.C. chpt. Am. Inst. Planners, 1976; Pershing award U.S. Army Command and Gen. Staff Coll., 1964; contbr. articles to law jours. Home: 100 Fern Ln Chapel Hill NC 27514 Office: Inst Govt U NC Chapel Hill NC 27514 Tel (919) 966-5381

GREEN, RAYMOND BERT, b. Hartford, Conn., July 12, 1929; B.A., Yale, 1951, LL.B., 1954. Admitted to Conn. bar, 1954, U.S. Ct. Appeals 2nd Circuit bar, 1966, U.S. Ct. Mil. Appeals bar, 1974; asso. firm Camp, Williams & Richardson, New Britain, Conn., 1954-55; served with Judge Adv. Gen. Corps U.S. Navy, 1955-58; asso. firm Day, Berry & Howard, Hartford, 1958-65, partner, 1966—; judge of probate Dist. of Canton (Conn.), 1962—. Sec. YMCA of Met. Hartford, Inc., 1973—. Mem. Hartford County (chmn. ethics com. 1972-76), Conn., Am. (vice-chmn. litigation of estates com.) bar assns., Judge Advs. Assn., Am. Judicature Soc., Phi Beta Kappa. Home: West Rd Collinsville CT 06022 Office: 1 Constitution Plaza Hartford CT 06103 Tel (203) 728-1330

GREEN, ROBERT WARD, b. Kansas City, Kans., Aug. 21, 1942; B.A., Kans. State U., 1964, J.D., 1967. Admitted to Kans. bar, 1967; since practiced in Ottawa, Kans., asso. Winter & Green, and predecessor, 1968-69, partner, 1970-73; individual practice law, 1973—. Vice-pres. Ottawa (Kans.) Rotary Club, 1976—; mem. Ottawa C. of C.; pres. Franklin County (Kans.) Shrine Club, 1973-74. Mem. Am. Bar Assn. (chmn. young lawyers membership sect. 1971), Kans., Franklin County (sec.-treas. 1975—) bar assns. Home: 1027 Olive St Ottawa KS 66067 Office: 109 W 2d St Ottawa KS 66067 Tel (913) 242-2783

GREEN, ROBERT WILLIAM, b. Sioux City, Iowa, Jan. 7, 1945; B.S., Morningside Coll., 1966; M.A. in Corp. Fin., U. Nebr., 1970; J.D., U. S.D., 1972. Project dir. Sioux City Urban Renewal Dept., 1968, 70; admitted to Iowa bar, 1973; asso. firm Kindig, Beebe, McCluhan, Rawlings & Nieland, 1973-74; asso. firm Jacobs, Gaul, Nymann & Green, and predecessor, Sioux City, 1974, partner, 1974—; adj. prof. bus. law and real estate Morningside Coll., 1974—. Chmn. Woodbury County (Iowa) Vets. Affairs Commn., 1975—. Mem. Woodbury County, Iowa, Am. bar assns., Assn. Trial Lawyers Iowa. Home: RFD 1 Lawton IA 51030 Office: 383 Orpheum Electric Bldg Sioux City IA 51102 Tel (712) 258-0101

GREEN, THOMAS ANDREW, b. N.Y.C., Mar. 18, 1940; A.B., Columbia, 1961; Ph.D., Harvard, 1970, J.D., 1972. Asst. prof. history Bard Coll., Annandale, N.Y., 1967-69; asst. prof. law U. Mich., 1972-75, asso. prof., 1975-77, prof. law and legal history, 1977—. Mem. Am. Soc. Legal History (bd. editors Am. Jour. Legal History 1976—), Medieval Acad. Am., Selden Soc. Home: 1100 Berkshire Ann Arbor MI 48104 Office: 931 Legal Research U Mich Law Sch Ann Arbor MI 48109 Tel (313) 764-1457

GREEN, THOMAS CHARLES, b. Mpls., Feb. 7, 1941; B.A., Dartmouth Coll., 1962; LL.B., Yale U., 1965. Admitted to Minn. bar, 1965, D.C. bar, 1967, U.S. Supreme Ct. bar, 1968, U.S. Ct. Mil. Appeals, 1968; asst. U.S. Atty., D.C., 1967-70; partner firm Ginsburg, Feldman & Bress, Washington, D.C., 1975—. Mem. regional bd. B'nai B'rith. Mem. D.C. Bar, Bar Assn. D.C. (mem. exec. council young lawyers sect. 1972-73), Am. Bar Assn., Asst. U.S. Attys. Assn. D.C. (pres. 1972-73), Judicial Conf. D.C. Office: 1700 Pennsylvania Ave NW Washington DC 20006 Tel (202) 637-9140

GREEN, TIMOTHY MICHAEL, b. Hubbard, Nebr., June 12, 1921; A.B., Trinity Coll., Sioux City, Iowa, 1942; J.D., U. Notre Dame, 1947. Admitted to Mich. bar, 1948; practiced in St. John's, Mich., 1948-73; judge Clinton County (Mich.) Probate Ct., 1947—. Mem. Am., Clinton-Gratiot County bar assns., Am. Judicature Soc., Mich. State Bar. Office: Courthouse Saint Johns MI 48879 Tel (517) 224-6761

GREEN, VERNON NELSON, b. Moriah, N.Y., Dec. 6, 1925; LL.B., Albany Law Sch., 1951. Admitted to N.Y. state bar, 1951; asso. firm Francis W. McGinley, Glens Falls, N.Y., 1952-54; individual practice law, Glens Falls, 1954—; village police justice Village South Glens Falls, N.Y., 1955-75; town atty. Moreau, 1956—; atty. South Glens Falls Central Sch. Dist., 1961—. Mem. Warren County, Saratoga County, N.Y. State, Am. bar assns. Home: 6 Charles St South Glens Falls NY 12801 Office: 87 Main St South Glens Falls NY 12801 Tel (518) 793-4464

GREEN, WILLIAM OSCAR, JR., b. Kerrville, Tex., July 23, 1933; student Davidson Coll., 1951-53, U. Houston, 1954; B.B.A., So. Methodist U., 1956; LL.B., Emory U., 1960, J.D., 1970. Admitted to Ga. bar, 1960, U.S. Dist. Ct. bar, 1960, U.S. Ct. Appeals bar 5th Dist., 1960, U.S. Supreme Ct. bar, 1965; asso. firm Fullbright & Duffey, Rome, Ga., 1960-64; partner firm Payne, Barlow & Green, Austell, Ga., 1964-73; sr. partner firm Green, Force and Alderman, Austell, 1973-76, Green & Butler, 1976—; dir. Springtime, Inc.; lectr. U. Ga. Mem. State Bar of Ga. (vice chmn. penal reform com. 1972-73, chmn. 1973-75), Am. Bar Assn., Am., Ga. (lectr.) trial lawyers assns., Mountain Retreat Assn. (dir.), Kappa Sigma, Phi Delta Phi. Contbr. articles to legal jours. Home: Floyd Rd Austell GA 30001 Office: Suite 355 Park Plateau Office Complex 300 Wendell Ct SW Atlanta GA 30336 Tel (404) 691-7630 also 6713 Church St Douglasville GA

GREENAWALT, KENNETH WILLIAM, b. Boulder County, Colo., Oct. 9, 1903; LL.B., Cornell U., 1927. Admitted to N.Y. State bar, 1929, U.S. Supreme Ct. bar, also U.S. dist. cts. and cts. of appeal; practice law, N.Y.C., 1927—; asso. firm Sackett, Chapman, Brown & Cross, 1927-30; asso. firm Davies, Auerbach & Cornell and successor firms, 1930-44, mem. firm, 1944—. Mem. Edmont Sch. Dist. Bd. Edn., Scarsdale, N.Y., 1957-62; bd. regents L.I. Coll. Hosp., Bklyn., 1962—. Fellow Soc. Values in Higher Edn. (dir.); mem. Bar Assn. City N.Y., N.Y. State, Am. bar assns., Am Coll. Trial Lawyers, Cornell Law Assn., Am. Judicature Soc., Sphinx, Phi Sigma Kappa. Recipient Gavel award Am. Bar Assn., 1962, George Washington honor medal Freedoms Found., 1962, awards for legal assistance in merger of Congregational Chs. and United Ch. of Christ; contbr. articles to Boys' Life mag., also legal jours.; guest participant radio and TV programs relating to the law. Home: 65 High Ridge Rd Hartsdale NY 10530 Office: Two Broadway New York City NY 10004 Tel (212) 422-6559

GREENAWALT, ROBERT KENT, b. N.Y.C., June 25, 1936; A.B., Swarthmore Coll., 1958; B.Phil., Oxford (Eng.) U., 1960; LL.B., Columbia, 1963. Admitted to N.Y. State bar, 1963, U.S. Ct. of Appeals bar, 1969, U.S. Supreme Ct. bar, 1970; law clk. to Justice John M. Harlan, U.S. Supreme Ct., Washington, 1963-64; asst. prof. law Columbia, N.Y.C., 1965-68, asso. prof., 1968-69, prof., 1969—; spl. asst. AID, 1964-65; asso. dir. N.Y. Inst. Legal Edn., summer 1969; dep. solicitor gen. U.S., 1971-72; cons. Office of Telecommunications Policy, 1974-76. Mem. Am. Law Inst., Am. Soc. Legal and Polit. Philosophy (v.p.). Contbr. articles to legal jours. Home: 435 Riverside Dr New York City NY 10025 Office: 435 W 116th St New York City NY 10027 Tel (212) 280-2637

GREENBAUM, ELI DORI, b. Tel Aviv, Israel, Sept. 2, 1945; B.A., Wayne State U., 1967, J.D., 1972. Copywriter, Young & Rubicam Internat., Detroit, 1968-69, Sheldon Marks Assos., Beverly Hills, Calif., 1969-70; admitted to Mich. bar, 1972; individual practice law, Troy, Mich., 1974-77; legal counselor Common Ground Counseling Center, Birmingham, Mich., 1974-77. Founder Greater Detroit Drama & Poultry Soc., Official La Bamba Baseball League. Mem. State Bar of Mich., Oakland County Bar Assn. Office: 2820 W Maple Rd Troy MI 48084 Tel (313) 649-1260

GREENBAUM, JEROME BRYON, b. Detroit, May 20, 1937; A.B., U. Mich., 1958, LL.B., 1961. Admitted to Mich. bar, 1961, U.S. Supreme Ct. bar, 1966; partner firm Greenbaum & Greenbaum, Detroit, 1961-67; asst. U.S. Atty., Detroit, 1967-69; partner firm Kratze, Greenbaum & Littman, Detroit, 1969-73; individual practice, Southfield, Mich., 1973—. Asso. chmn. Met. Div. Allied Jewish Campaign, Detroit, 1975—; bd. dirs. Detroit Service Group, Jewish Welfare Fedn., Detroit, 1977—. Mem. Detroit, Mich., Am. bar assns. Office: 24901 Northwestern Hwy Ste 413A Southfield MI 48075 Tel (313) 353-1022

GREENBAUM, SAMUEL MEYER, b. Washington, July 15, 1916; J.D., Georgetown U., 1939, LL.M., 1942. Admitted to D.C. bar, 1939, U.S. Ct. Appeals, 1945, U.S. Supreme Ct. bar, 1950; individual practice law, Washington, 1939—; now sr. mem. firm Greenbaum, Gins & Goldstein, 1939—; lectr. creditors rights George Washington U., 1961, Catholic U., 1965-73, American U., 1977; alt. chmn., atty., mem. Commn. on Mental Health U.S. Dist. Ct. D.C., 1962-72; adj. prof. law creditors rights and bankruptcy, secured transactions Georgetown U. Law Center, 1971, American U., Washington Coll. Law, 1971-74; 77. Mem. D.C., Am. bar assns. Home: 2840 Brandywine St NW Washington DC 20008 Office: One Thousand Connecticut Ave Suite 301 Washington DC 20036 Tel (202) 785-9123

GREENBERG, JACK MANDEL, b. Chgo., Sept. 28, 1942; B.S. in Commerce, DePaul U., 1964, J.D., 1968. Admitted to Ill. bar, 1968; with Arthur Young & Co., Chgo., 1964—, mgr., 1969-72, prin., 1972-74, partner, 1974-75, tax dir. Chgo. office, 1975—; instr. DePaul U. Mem. Ill. Soc. C.P.A.'s, Chgo. Bar Assn., Chgo. Assn. Commerce and Industry. Office: 1 IBM Plaza Chicago IL 60611 Tel (312) 751-3073

GREENBERG, MARTIN FRED, b. N.Y.C., Apr. 19, 1936; B.S., N.Y.U., 1960; J.D., U. Miami (Fla.), 1968. Admitted to Fla. bar, 1968; individual practice law, Miami 1968; sr. partner firm Greenberg, Donsky & Mills, Miami, 1969—. Mem. Am., Fla., Dade County insts. C.P.A.'s, Am. Arbitration Assn., Am. Assn. Atty-C.P.A.'s, Lawyers Title Guaranty Fund, Am., Fla., Dade County bar assns. C.P.A., N.Y., Fla. Office: 1 Biscayne Tower Suite 1920 2 S Biscayne Blvd Miami FL 33131 Tel (305) 358-9010

GREENBERG, MELVIN NATHANIEL, b. Newark, Oct. 22, 1928; B.A., N.Y. U., 1949, LL.M., 1955; J.D. with honors, U. Fla., 1952. Admitted to Fla. bar, 1952; individual practice law, Miami, 1952-55; partner firm Morehead, Forrest, Gotthardt and Greenberg, Miami, 1955-60, Greenberg and Saks, Miami, 1960-67, Greenberg, Traurig, Hoffman, Lipoff, Quentel & Wright, Miami, 1967—; mem. Greater Miami Tax Inst., 1961; lectr. Ariz. State. U., Stetson U., numerous profl. insts.; adj. prof. Sch. Law, U. Miami, 1966-75. Mem. pres.'s council U. Fla.; chmn. Miami Citizens Adv. Bd.; trustee U. Miami; bd. visitors Fla. State U. Contbr. U. Miami Law Rev. Quar.; presented numerous papers to insts. Home: 4770 Davis Rd Miami FL 33143 Office: 1401 Brickell Ave Miami FL 33131 Tel (305) 377-3501

GREENBERG, ROGER BRUCE, Detroit, Oct. 16, 1944; B.A., U. Calif., Los Angeles, 1966; J.D., U. Tex., 1970. Admitted to Tex. bar, 1970, U.S. Supreme Ct. bar, 1974; partner firm Richie, Greenberg & Brackman and predecessor, Houston, 1970—. Active ACLU, Common Cause. Mem. Fed., Am. (co-chmn. 5th Circuit Fed. practice com. sect. litigation), Tex., Houston, Houston Jr. bar assns., Am., Tex. (exec. council state bar liaison com.) trial lawyers assns. Home: 7711 Bankside St Houston TX 77071 Office: 1200 S Post Oak Rd Suite 520 Houston TX 77056 Tel (713) 627-2720

GREENBERGER, HOWARD LEROY, b. Pitts., July 16, 1929; B.S. magna cum laude, U. Pitts., 1951; LL.B. cum laude, N.Y. U., 1954; L.Dip., Univ. Coll., Oxford U., 1955. Admitted to D.C. bar, 1954, Pa. bar, 1955, N.Y. bar, 1969, U.S. Supreme Ct. bar, 1964; served as capt. JAGC, USAR, 1955-58; law clk. chief judge U.S. Ct. Appeals Third Circuit, Phila., 1958-60; asso. firm Kaufman & Kaufman, Pitts., 1960-61; prof. Sch. Law N.Y. U., N.Y.C., 1961-72, 75—, asst. dean, 1961-68, asso. dean, 1968-72; dean and dir. Practicing Law Inst., N.Y.C. 1972-75; univ. sen. N.Y. U., 1975—; v.p., cons. Nat. Center for Paralegal Tng., N.Y.C.; cons. Legal Edn. Inst., U.S. CSC. Chmn. nat. legal com., pres. N.Y. chpt. Am. Jewish Com., 1975—; vice-chmn. exec. com. Community Action for Legal Services, N.Y.C., 1976—; chmn. devel. campaign N.Y. U. Sch. Law, 1976; bd. dirs. Early Am. Industries Assn. Mem. Am. Law Inst., Law Center Found. (dir.), Washington Sq. Legal Services Corp. Chmn. bd. advisers Jour. Legal Edn., 1975—; contbr. articles to legal jours. Office: 40 Washington Square S New York Univ Sch Law New York City NY 10012 Tel (212) 598-2535

GREENBERGER, I. MICHAEL, b. Scranton, Pa., Oct. 30, 1945; A.B., Lafayette Coll., 1967; J.D., U. Pa., 1970. Admitted to D.C. bar, 1971, U.S. Supreme Ct. bar, 1975; law clk. to judge U.S. Ct. Appeals, D.C., 1970-71; asso. firm Wald, Harkrader & Ross, Washington, 1971-72; legis. asst. Congresswoman Elizabeth Holtzman, Washington, 1973; atty. advisor Atty. Gen. Dept. Justice, Washington, 1973; asso. firm Shea & Gardner, Washington, 1973-77, partner, 1977—. Mem. Am. Bar Assn. (vice chmn. consumer protection subcom. sect. adminstrv. law 1976—). D.C. Bar, Washington Council Lawyers, Am. Jewish Com. Contbr. articles to legal jours.; editor-in-chief U. Pa. Law Rev., 1969-70. Home: 2757 Brandywine St NW Washington DC 20008 Office: 734 15th St NW Washington DC 20005 Tel (202) 737-1255

GREENBERGER, TOMAS, b. Czechoslavakia, June 27, 1947; came to U.S., 1948, naturalized, 1954; B.A., Bklyn. Coll., 1970; J.D., St. John's U., 1972. Admitted to N.Y. bar, 1973; asso. firm Mariash, Levy, and Super, Bklyn., 1973-74, firm Sommers and Gross, Bklyn., 1972-73; individual practice law, Bklyn., 1974—. Mem. Am., N.Y. State, Bklyn. bar assns. Home: 1056 50th St Brooklyn NY 11219 Office: 5103 New Utrecht Ave Brooklyn NY 11219 Tel (212) 438-7000

GREENBLATT, IRA JOSEPH, b. Bklyn., Oct. 5, 1932; A.B., Cornell U., 1953; J.D., N.Y. U., 1957. Admitted to N.Y. bar, 1957; partner firm Tenzer, Greenblatt, Fallon & Kaplan, N.Y.C., 1956—. Trustee, Univ. Settlement, 1964-70, Peninsula Counseling Center, Woodmere, N.Y., 1974—; bd. dirs. S.Shore div. United Jewish Appeal, 1972—; trustee Brandeis Sch., Lawrence, N.Y., 1960—, pres., chmn. bd., 1964-70. Mem. N.Y. County Lawyers Assn., Am., N.Y. State bar assns., Assn. Bar City N.Y. Office: Tenzer Greenblatt et al 100 Park Ave New York City NY 10017 Tel (212) 953-1800

GREENE, ALLEN STANLEY, b. Prophetstown, Ill., May 20, 1924; B.A., Beloit Coll., 1949; J.D., Chicago-Kent Coll. of Law, 1951. Admitted to Ill. bar, 1951; spl. atty. State Ill. Dept. Transp., 1952-58. Mem. Am., Ill., DuPage County bar assns. Office: 1325 N Main St Wheaton IL 60187 Tel (312) 668-4590

GREENE, BENNETT EVANS, b. Brockton, Mass., Oct. 26, 1941; A.B., Middlebury Coll., 1963; J.D., Boston U., 1966. Admitted to Vt. bar, 1966, U.S. Supreme Ct. bar, 1976; law clk. U.S. Dist. Judge Bernard J. Leddy, Burlington, Vt., 1966-67; pros. atty. Burlington City Grand Juror, 1967-69; individual practice law, Burlington, 1969-76; legis. draftsman State of Vt., Montpelier, 1970-72; instr. bus. law Champlain Coll., Burlington, 1973; individual practice law, Essex Center, Vt., 1976—. Bd. dirs. Josephine B. Baird Children's Center, 1970-76, v.p. bd., chmn. legal com., 1974-76; justice of peace, Burlington, 1970-75; mem. Burlington Democratic City Com., 1970-75, Chittenden County Dem. Com., 1970-75. Mem. Am., Vt., Chittenden County bar assns., Assn. Trial Lawyers Am. Home: RD 2 Milton VT 05468 Office: PO Box 367 Essex Center VT 05451 Tel (802) 879-6321

GREENE, DON DARIUS, b. Morristown, Tenn, Oct. 2, 1940; B.S., E. Tenn. State U., 1962; J.D., U. Tenn., 1966. Admitted to Tenn. bar, 1966; atty. Union Carbide Corp., Oak Ridge, Tenn., 1966-70; individual practice law, Morristown, 1970—; judge juvenile ct. Hamblen County, Tenn., 1974—. Bd. dirs. Morristown-Hamblen Library, 1968-71, Morristown Boys Club. Mem. Tenn., Hamblen County (sec.-treas.) bar assns., Jaycees, Morristown C. of C. Home: 1311 Walters Dr Morristown TN 37814 Office: 303 N Fairmont Box 1646 Morristown TN 37814 Tel (615) 581-3100

GREENE, EDWARD H., b. Logan, W.Va., Jan. 28, 1913; A.B., Marshall U., 1937; J.D., W.Va. U., 1940. Admittgd to W.Va., bar, 1940; asso. firm Greene, Ketchum & Mills, Huntington, W.Va.,

1957—; pros. atty. Cabell County (W.Va.), 1943-53; mem. state bd. control, 1956. Mem. W.Va. Bd. Regents, 1969—, pres., 1976—. Mem. Cabell County, W.Va. State, Am. bar assns. Author: West Virginia School Guide, 1962; Guide to Notaries Public, 1965; The Law and Your Dog, 1969; The Law and Your Horse, 1971. Home: 162 Honeysuckle Ln Huntington WV 25701 Office: 419 11th St Huntington WV 25701 Tel (304) 525-9115

GREENE, FRIEND BOSSER, b. Fremont, Mo., Aug. 8, 1891; grad. Chillicothe Bus. Coll., 1911. Admitted to Mo. bar, 1932; individual practice law, Van Buren and Eminence, Mo., 1932-49; city atty., Van Buren, Mo., 1939-41, Eminence and Winona, Mo., 1942-70, Birch Tree, Mo., 1946-70; mayor Eminence, 1947-49; prosecuting atty. Shannon County (Mo.), 1949-67; judge Probate and Magistrate Cts., Eminence, 1970—. Chmn. Ration Bd. Shannon County, 1942-45. Mem. Mo., Shannon County bar assns. Home: Greene Rd Eminence MO 65466 Office: Court House Eminence MO 65466 Tel (314) 226-5515

GREENE, JAMES COFFIN, b. San Francisco, Feb. 18, 1915; B.A., Yale, 1936; LL.B., 1939. Admitted to Calif. bar, 1940; asso. firm O'Melveny & Myers, Los Angeles, 1939-53, partner, 1953—; dir. Great Western Fin. Corp., Great Western Savs. and Loan Assn., Am. Mut. Fund, Inc. pres. Honnold Library Soc., Claremont, Calif., Los Angeles Com. on Fgn. Relations; trustee Pacific Oaks, Pasadena, Calif., Thacher Sch., Ojai, Calif. Mem. Am., Los Angeles County bar assns., State Bar Calif. Home: 1085 Glen Oaks Blvd Pasadena CA 91105 Office: 611 W 6th St Los Angeles CA 90017 Tel (213) 620-1120

GREENE, JOHN ASHLEY, b. Ashville, Ala., Jan. 15, 1898; LL.B., John Marshall Law Sch., Chgo., 1933, J.D., 1969. Admitted to Ill. bar, 1933, Oreg. bar, 1939, U.S. Ct. Mil. Appeals bar, U.S. Supreme Ct. bar; individual practice law, Chgo., 1933-39, Portland, Oreg., 1939-50, Oregon City, Oreg., 1952-73, Woodburn, Oreg., 1973—; asst. atty. gen. State of Ill., 1934-39; dep. U.S. atty. Office of Price Adminstrn., Oreg. and S.W. Wash., 1950-52. Mem. Am., Multnomah County, Clackamas County (past pres.) bar assns., Delta Theta Phi, Res. Officers Assn. (past chpt. pres.). Address: 1340 Randolph Rd Woodburn OR 97071 Tel (503) 982-9672

GREENE, JOHN THOMAS, JR., b. Salt Lake City, Nov. 28, 1929; B.A., U. Utah, 1952, J.D., 1955. Admitted to Utah bar, 1955, U.S. Supreme Ct. bar, 1964; clk. Utah Supreme Ct., 1955-56; partner firm Callister, Green & Nebeker and predecessors, Salt Lake City, 1957—; asst. U.S. atty. Dist. Utah, 1957-59; spl. asst. atty. gen. State of Utah, from 1968; spl. counsel Salt Lake City Grand Jury, 1969; chmn. judiciary com. Utah State Bar, 1971-77; Utah del. Nat. Council State Cts., 1972-73. Pres. Community Services Council, Salt Lake City area, 1971-74; mem. advisory panel Nat. Legal Services Corp., 1976—. Mem. Utah State (pres. 1970-71), Am. (chmn. spl. com. environ. law, mem. ho. of dels., mem. council G.P. Sect.) bar assns., Order of Coif, Phi Beta Kappa. Law rev. editor U. Utah Law Sch., 1953-55; contg. author: American Law of Mining, 1965; various law revs. and legal periodicals. Home: 1923 Browning Ave Salt Lake City UT 84108 Office: 800 Kennecott Bldg Salt Lake City UT 84133 Tel (801) 531-7676

GREENE, JOSEPH E., JR., b. Phila., Jan. 4, 1931; B.S., U. Pa., 1952, LL.B., 1957. Admitted to Pa. bar, 1958; partner firm Guest & Greene, Phila., 1968—. Trustee The Wyndcroft Sch., Pottstown, Pa., 1974—. Mem. Am., Pa., Phila. bar assns. Home: Conestoga Rd Chester Springs R D 1 PA 19425 Office: 1604 The Fidelity Bldg Philadelphia PA 19109 Tel (215) 735-6636

GREENE, MICHAEL ALAN, b. Chgo., Sept. 18, 1946; A.B. in History, Stanford, 1968, J.D., 1972. Admitted to Calif. bar, 1972, Idaho bar, 1972, U.S. Supreme Ct. bar, 1975; sr. teaching fellow Stanford Law Sch., 1972; asso. firm Eberle, Berlin, Kading, Turnbow & Gillespie, Boise, Idaho, 1972-77, partner, 1977—; mem. bar exam. com. Idaho Supreme Ct., 1972-73, mem. appellate rules com., 1975-76; instr. Boise State U., 1977. Mem. Am., Calif., Idaho bar assns., Am. Trial Lawyers Assn. Home: 2309 Ellis St Boise ID 83702 Office: PO Box 1368 Boise ID 83701 Tel (208) 344-8535

GREENE, RICHARD DORWYN, b. Wheaton, Ill., Oct. 7, 1925; A.B., Cornell Coll., Mt. Vernon, Iowa, 1948; J.D., U. Denver, 1957. Admitted to Colo. bar, 1957, U.S. Supreme Ct. bar, 1970, U.S. Ct. of Appeals bar, 1970; since practiced in Littleton, Colo.; dep. dist. atty. 18th Jud. Dist., 1960-70; chief dep. state pub. defender, 1970-71; judge Dist. Ct., 18th Jud. Dist., 1971—. Mem. Colo., Arapahoe County bar assns. Home: Office: 2069 W Littleton Blvd Littleton CO 80120 Tel (303) 794-9281

GREENE, ROBERT FRANK, b. Covington, Ky., Mar. 28, 1931; J.D., U. Cin., 1959. Admitted to Ohio bar, 1959, Ky. bar, 1959; individual practice law, Burlington, Ky., 1959—, judge Ct. of Appeals of Ky., 1976. Mem. Am., Ky., Boone County (past pres.) bar assns., Am. Judicature Soc. Home: 827 Limaburg Rd Hebron KY 41048 Office: 3 W Washington St Burlington KY 41005 Tel (606) 586-6188

GREENE, ROBERT MICHAEL, b. Buffalo, Jan. 14, 1945; A.B. magna cum laude, Canisius Coll., 1966; J.D., U. Notre Dame, South Bend, Ind., 1969; LL.M., N.Y. U., 1971. Admitted to N.Y. State bar, 1970; vol. VISTA, N.Y.C., 1969-71; asso. firm Phillips, Lytle, Hitchcock, Blaine & Huber, Buffalo, 1971-75, partner, 1976—. Trustee Canisius Coll., 1971-77; chmn. law com., mem. exec. com. Erie County (N.Y.) Democratic Com., 1974, 76—; mem. council State U. N.Y. Agrl. and Tech. Coll., Alfred, 1975—. Mem. Am., N.Y. State, Erie County bar assns., Thomas More Guild (pres. 1976-77), Marshall Club (pres. 1975-76), Canisius Coll. Alumni Assn. (pres. 1976-77). Named Man of Year Canisius Coll., 1966. Home: 110 Beard Ave Buffalo NY 14214 Office: 3400 Marine Midland Center Buffalo NY 14203

GREENE, RONALD JAMES, b. Omaha, Nebr., Nov. 29, 1942; A.B., Harvard, 1964, LL.B. summa cum laude, 1968. Admitted to D.C. bar, 1968; law clk. Mr. Justice Marshall U.S. Supreme Ct., 1968-69; asst. to gen. counsel Dept. Army, 1969-72; asso. firm Wilmer, Cutler & Pickering, Washington, 1972-75, partner, 1976—; spl. counsel Commn. on CIA Activities, 1975. Mem. D.C. Bar. Home: 6312 Beachway Dr Falls Church VA 22044 Office: 1666 K St NW Washington DC 20006 Tel (202) 872-6282

GREENE, VINCENT ALVIN, b. Cleveland Heights, Ohio, Dec. 13, 1924; B.M.E., Case Inst. Tech., 1949; LL.B., Georgetown U., 1952. Admitted to D.C. bar, 1953, Ohio bar, 1954; patent atty. McCoy, Greene & TeGrotenhuis, Cleve., 1953-67; patent atty. McCoy, Greene & Howell, Cleve., 1967-72, Bosworth, Sessions & McCoy, Cleve., 1972—. Mem. Cleve., Am. bar assns., Am., Cleve. patent law assns., Tau Beta Pi. Home: 589 Saddleback Ln Gates Mills OH 44040 Office: 625 National City Bank Bldg Cleveland OH 44114

GREENE, WILLIAM HERBERT, b. Chgo., Mar. 5, 1938; B.S., U. Pa., 1959; J.D., John Marshall Law Sch., 1963; postgrad. in history, U. Nev., 1967-68. Admitted to Ill. bar, 1967, Nev. bar, 1969, U.S. Supreme Ct. bar, 1970; founder, pres. Am. Equities Group, Chgo. and San Francisco, 1960-74; real estate developer, San Francisco, 1970—; licensed pvt. detective, 1970—; hon. consul gen. Senegal, 1972—. Home and Office: Rancho Verdi Mill Valley CA 94941

GREENEBAUM, LEONARD CHARLES, lawyer; b. Langgeons, Germany, Feb. 6, 1934; B.S. cum laude, Washington & Lee U., 1956, LL.B., J.D. cum laude, 1959. Admitted to D.C. bar, 1959, Commonwealth of Va. bar, 1959, Md. bar, 1965. Asso. law firm Sachs, Greenebaum & Taylor (and predecessor firms), Washington, 1959-64, partner, 1964—; arbitrator Am. Arbitration Assn., 1975—; 2d v.p., mem. exec. com. Goodwill Industries, 1976—; dir. Hebrew Home for Aged Men's Club, 1961-64. Mem. Am. Judicature Soc., Am., Md., Va. bar assns., Judl. Conf. D.C. Circuit. Home: 6121 Shady Oak Ln Bethesda MD 20034 Office: 1620 Eye St NW Washington DC 20006

GREENFELDER, GLEN EDWARD, b. Detroit, Mar. 19, 1943; A.A., St. Leo Coll., 1963; B.S., Loyola U., Chgo., 1966, M.S., 1968, J.D., 1971. Admitted to Fla. bar, 1971; indsl. engr. Motorola Inc., Franklin Park, Ill., 1963-67; salesman Hytrol Converyers Co. Midwest, La Grange, Ill., 1967-71; partner firm McClain, Hobby & Greenfelder, Dade City, Fla., 1971—; city atty. City of San Antonio (Fla.), 1975—. Youth dir. Dade March of Dimes, 1973—; chmn. charity ball Jackson Meml. Hosp., 1974. Mem. Am., Fla., Pasco County (past pres.) bar assns., Am. Judicature Soc. Recipient awards Loyola U. Alumni Assn., 1974, Ct. Practice Inst., Chgo., 1975, Outstanding Citizen of Year award Jaycees, 1975. Home: 2109 Marion Ln Dade City FL 33525 Office: PO Box 4 Dade City FL 33525 Tel (904) 567-5636

GREENFIELD, EDWARD J., b. N.Y.C., Dec. 8, 1922; B.A. magna cum laude, N.Y. U., 1943; J.D., Harvard, 1948. Admitted to N.Y. State bar, 1949, U.S. Supreme Ct. bar, 1955; mem. firm Glatzer, Glatzer & Diamond, N.Y.C., 1948-55; law sec. presiding justice appellate div. 1st dept., N.Y.C., 1956-60; mem. firm Proskauer, Rose, Goetz & Mendelsohn, N.Y.C., 1960-63; judge Civil Ct., N.Y.C., 1964-68; justice Supreme Ct. of N.Y. State, N.Y.C., 1969—, supervising justice criminal div. N.Y. County Supreme Ct., 1974-76. Mem. Assn. Supreme Ct. Justices (1st v.p. N.Y.C.), Am. Judicature Soc., Bar Assn. City N.Y. Home: 55 East End Ave New York City NY 10028 Office: 60 Centre St New York City NY 10007 Tel (212) 374-4733

GREENFIELD, GERALD, b. Cohoes, N.Y., Sept. 9, 1939; B.A., Union Coll., 1961; LL.B., Albany Law Sch., Union U., 1964, J.D., 1968. Admitted to Ill. bar, 1973, N.Y. State bar, 1964; partner firm Jenner & Block, Chgo.; lectr. Ill. Inst. Continuing Legal Edn. Mem. Am., Ill., N.Y., Chgo. bar assns., Chgo. Mortgage Attys. Assn. Contbr. articles in field to profl. jours. Office: One IBM Plaza Chicago IL 60611 Tel (312) 222-9350

GREENFIELD, IRVING HYAM, b. Russia, Nov. 15, 1902; LL.B., Bklyn. Law Sch., 1924. Admitted to N.Y. State bar, 1924; asst. sec., counsel Metro-Goldwyn-Mayer, Inc., N.Y.C., 1924-54, sec., counsel, 1954-68; mem. firm Greenfield Lipsky & Bress, N.Y.C., 1968—. Mem. N.Y. County Lawyers Assn. Home: 275 Central Park W New York City NY 10024 Office: 310 Madison Ave New York City NY 10017 Tel (212) 867-1616

GREENFIELD, LESLIE HAROLD, b. N.Y.C., Oct. 12, 1934; B.B.A., U. Miami, 1956; M.S. in Indsl. Relations, Loyola U., Chgo., 1959; LL.B., Southwestern U., Los Angeles, 1964. Admitted to Calif. bar, 1965, U.S. Supreme Ct. bar, 1973; partner firm Cogan & Greenfield, Los Angeles, 1965-68, Greenfield & Moray, 1968-73, Brady & Greenfield, Beverly Hills, Calif., 1973-76; individual practice law, Van Nuys, Calif., 1976—. Mem. Am. Arbitration Assn., Am., Calif., Los Angeles trial lawyers assns., Am., Los Angeles County, San Fernando Valley bar assns., Assn. Bus. Trial Lawyers. Office: 15236 Burbank Blvd Van Nuys CA 91411 Tel (213) 786-1153

GREENFIELD, MICHAEL C., b. Chgo., May 4, 1934; B.A., U. Ill., 1955; J.D., Northwestern U., 1957. Admitted to Ill. bar, 1957, U.S. Supreme Ct. bar, 1974; asst. states atty. Cook County (Ill.), 1957-59; partner firm Asher, Greenfield, Goodstein, Pavalon & Segall, Chgo., 1959—; mem. inquiry bd. Ill. Supreme Ct. Disciplinary Commn., 1973—. Mem. Assn. Pvt. Pension and Welfare Plans (dir. 1975—), Internat. Found. Employee Benefit Plans (advisory dir. 1977—), Am., Ill., Chgo. bar assns. Home: 211 Green Bay Rd Highland Park IL 60035 Office: 228 N LaSalle St Chicago IL 60601 Tel (312) 263-1500

GREENFIELD, MICHAEL M., b. Chgo., Aug. 21, 1944; A.B., Grinnell Coll., 1966; J.D., U. Tex., Austin, 1969. Asst. prof. law Washington U., St. Louis, 1969-72, asso. prof. 1972-76, prof., 1976—; vis. prof. U. Calif., Davis, 1974-75. Contbr. articles in field to profl. Office: Sch Law Washington U St Louis MO 63130 Tel (314) 863-0100

GREENFIELD, ROBERT KAUFFMAN, b. Phila., Mar. 30, 1915; B.A., Swarthmore Coll., 1936; J.D., Harvard, 1939. Admitted to Pa. bar, 1939; asso. firm Goodis, Greenfield, Henry & Edelstein and predecessors, Phila., 1939-46, partner, 1947—; trustee GREIT Realty Trust; dir. Bankers Securities Corp.; mem. Lloyd's of London. Bd. dirs. Pa. Coll. Podiatric Medicine, 1967—; v.p. Marriage Council of Phila., 1973—; pres., chmn. bd. Moss Rehab. Hosp., Phila., 1969—; chmn. finance Inst. Contemporary Art, Phila., 1974—; trustee Pa. Coll. Pediatric Medicine. Mem. Phila., Pa., Am. bar assns., Socialegal. Home: 8221 Fairview Rd Elkins Park PA 19117 Office: 1234 Market St Philadelphia PA 19107 Tel (205) 563-5678

GREENFIELD, STANLEY WILLIAM, b. Pitts., Dec. 12, 1933; B.A. summa cum laude, U. Pitts., 1955, LL.B., 1959. Admitted to Pa. bar, 1959, U.S. Supreme Ct. bar, 1969; asst. U.S. atty. Western Dist. Pa., Pitts., 1962-66, 1st asst. U.S. atty., 1966-69; partner firm Greenfield & Minsky, Pitts., 1969—; adj. prof. law Duquesne U., 1970—; co-chmn. Joint Council Standards Criminal Justice Pa. Bd. dirs. Pitts. Ballet, 1976—. Mem. Am., Pa., Allegheny County (treas., past chmn. fin. com.) bar assns. Home: 6315 Beacon St Pittsburgh PA 15217 Office: 412 Carlton House Pittsburgh PA 15219 Tel (412) 281-8801

GREENHILL, JOE ROBERT, b. Houston, July 14, 1914; B.A., B.B.A., U. Tex., 1936, LL.B., 1939, LL.D. (hon.), So. Meth. U., 1977. Admitted to Tex. bar, 1938, U.S. Supreme Ct. bar, 1949; briefing atty. Tex. Supreme Ct., 1941, 46; asst. atty. gen. Tex., 1947-50, first asst. atty. gen., 1948-50; partner firm Grayes, Dougherty & Greenhill, Austin, 1950-57; asso. justice Tex. Supreme Ct., 1957-72, chief justice, 1972—. Fellow Tex. Bar Found., mem. Am. Judicature Soc. (past dir.), Am. Law Inst. (adviser), Tex. Bar Assn. (past chmn. jud. sect. and natural resources sect.), Order of Coif, Phi Beta Kappa, Phi Delta Phi. Recipient George Washington Gold medal Freedoms Found. at Valley Forge, 1971, Rosewood Gavel award St. Marys Law Sch., 1969; named Distinguished Alumnus, Coll. Bus. Adminstrn., U. Tex., 1974, Sch. Law, 1977; editor Tex. Law Rev., 1938-39; adviser S.W. Law Jour., 1973—. Home: 3204 Bridle Path Austin TX 78703 Office: Supreme Court Bldg PO Box 12248 Austin TX 78711 Tel (512) 475-2416

GREENHUT, KENNETH ROBERT, b. Rockville Centre, N.Y., Jan. 18, 1947; B.S., N.Y. Inst. Tech., 1967; J.D., Bklyn. Law Sch., 1970; LL.M., N.Y. U., 1973. Admitted to N.Y. bar, 1971; asso. firm Ernst & Ernst, N.Y.C., 1970-72; partner firm Harold M. Kaufman & Co., N.Y.C., 1972—; lectr. N.Y. Inst. Tech., N.Y.C., 1975. Mem. N.Y. Bar Assn., N.Y. State Soc. C.P.A.'s. Contbr. articles to N.Y. State CPA Jour. Home: 15 Gary Rd Syosset NY 11791 Office: 200 Park Ave New York City NY 10017 Tel (212) 687-1500

GREENSFELDER, EDWARD, JR., b. St. Louis, Feb. 15, 1937; A.B., Yale, 1959; J.D., U. Chgo., 1962; LL.M., N.Y.U., 1963. Admitted to Mo. bar, 1963, D.C. bar, 1964; atty., tax div. U.S. Dept. Justice, Washington, 1963-67. Mem. Am., Mo., D.C. bar assns., Home: 4401 Cathedral Ave NW Washington DC 20016 Office: 888 17th St NW Washington DC 20008 Tel (202) 785-0270

GREENSPAN, JOHN PAUL, b. N.Y.C., May 23, 1940; A.B., Lawrence U., 1962; J.D., U. Md., 1966. Admitted to Md. bar, 1968, D.C. bar, 1974; staff atty. Legal Aid Bur. Balt., 1968-73, Office Gen. Counsel, FCC, Washington, 1973—; evening staff program dir. Sta. WBJC-FM, Balt., 1969-71. Mem. Am., D.C., Md. bar assns. Home: 2324 Micarol Rd Baltimore MD 21209 Office: 1919 M St NW Washington DC 20554 Tel (202) 632-6990

GREENSPAN, LEON JOSEPH, b. Phila., Feb. 10, 1932; B.A., Temple U., 1955, LL.B., 1958. Admitted to N.Y. bar, 1959; individual practice law, White Plains, N.Y., 1959-64, partner firm Greenspan and Aurnou, White Plains, 1964-77, firm Greenspan, Kanarek, Jaffe & Funk, White Plains, 1977—; atty. Tarrytown (N.Y.) Housing Authority. Mem. Am., Westchester County, White Plains bar assns., N.Y. State Trial Lawyers Assn., Criminal Cts. Bar Assn. Westchester County. Home: 14 Pine Brook Dr White Plains NY 10605 Office: 14 Mamaroneck Ave White Plains NY 10601 Tel (914) 946-2500

GREENSTEIN, MARTIN RICHARD, b. Boston, Dec. 29, 1944; B.S. in Elec. Engring. magna cum laude, Tufts U., 1965; M.S. in Elec. Engring., Princeton U., 1966; J.D. with honors, John Marshall Law Sch., 1971. Admitted to Ill. bar, 1971, U.S. Patent Office bar, 1971; mem. tech. staff Ill. Bell Tel. Labs., Naperville, 1965-70, mem. patent staff, 1970-71; asso. firm Baker & McKenzie, Chgo., 1971—; instr. John Marshall Law Sch., Chgo., 1971—. Mem. Am., Ill., Chgo. bar assns., Am. Patent Law Assn., Patent Law Assn. Chgo., Tau Beta Pi, Eta Kappa Nu. Mem. editorial bd., ann. report com. The Trademark Reporter, 1972—. Home: 4 S 775 Pinehurst Dr Naperville IL 60540 Office: 2700 Prudential Plaza Chicago IL 60601 Tel (312) 565-0025

GREENWALD, ALVIN G., b. N.Y.C., Dec. 16, 1920; B.A., U. Calif. Los Angeles, 1942; J.D., U. So. Calif., 1946. Admitted to Calif. bar, 1946, U.S. Supreme Ct. bar, 1954; since practiced in Los Angeles, individual practice law, 1946-60; partner firm Greenwald and Baim, and predecessor, 196C—. Pres. Carthay Homeowners Assn., 1950; mem. exec. com. Nat. Conf. Urban Environment, 1974—. Mem. Am., Los Angeles County bar assns. Contbr. articles to legal jours. Office: 6300 Wilshire Blvd Los Angeles CA 90048 Tel (213) 653-3970

GREENWALD, ANDREW ERIC, b. N.Y.C., May 31, 1942; B.S., U. Wis., 1964; J.D., Georgetown U., 1967. Admitted to D.C. bar, 1968, Md. bar, 1969, U.S. Supreme Ct. bar, 1971; with NLRB, Washington, 1967-68; asst. corp. counsel, Govt. D.C., 1968-69; partner firm Kaplan, Smith, Joseph, Greenwald and Laake, Langley Park, Md., 1975—; former instr. for Bar Rev. Sch.; lectr. U. Md. and Univ. Coll., 1970—; guest faculty symposium Children's Hosp. Nat. Med. Center, 1976. Mem. Md. State, Montgomery County, Prince George's County, D.C. bar assns., Am. Trial Lawyers Assn., Am. Arbitration Assn. (panel). Office: 1345 University Blvd E Langley Park MD 20783 Tel (301) 439-3900

GREENWALD, LEONARD, b. Bklyn., Oct. 5, 1932; B.S., Cornell U., 1954; J.D., U. Chgo., 1959. Admitted to N.Y. State bar, 1960; U.S. Supreme Ct. bar, 1964; partner firm Abramson, Lewis & Greenwald, N.Y.C., 1960-67; spl. counsel Internat. Ladies Garment Workers Union, AFL-CIO, N.Y.C., 1967-69; partner firm Frankle & Greenwald, N.Y.C., 1969—; adj. prof. York Coll., N.Y.C., 1971-73; vis. lectr. Cornell U. Sch. Indsl. and Labor Relations, N.Y.C., 1974-75; mem. labor arbitration panel Am. Arbitration Assn. 1970-77; panel mem. N.Y. State Mediation Service, 1970-77. Ad hoc counsel N.Y.C. Mayor's Com. Against Exploitation of Minorities, 1963-65. Mem. Am. Bar Assn., Assn. Bar City N.Y. Office: 80 8th Ave New York City NY 10011 Tel (212) 242-0200

GREENWALD, MARTIN LAWRENCE, b. Newburgh, N.Y., Aug. 13, 1927; A.B., Brown U., 1950; J.D., Boston U., 1959. Admitted to R.I. bar, 1960, U.S. Supreme Ct. bar, 1974; news broadcaster Sta. WJAR, Providence, 1954-68, Sta. WJAR-TV, Providence, 1954-68; partner firm Feiner, Winsten & Greenwald, Providence, 1968—. Mem. R.I. Bar Assn. Office: 15 Westminster St Providence RI 02903

GREENWOOD, DAVID ALLEN, b. Salt Lake City, Aug. 9, 1946; B.A. (hon.), U. Utah, 1970; J.D., U. Chgo., 1973. Admitted to Utah bar, 1973; asso. firm Van Gott, Cornwall & McCarthy, Salt Lake City, 1973—. Mem. Am., Utah State, Salt Lake County bar assns., Phi Beta Kappa, Phi Kappa Phi. Home: 1121 Second Ave Salt Lake City UT 84102 Office: 141 E First St Salt Lake City UT 84111 Tel (801) 532-3333

GREENWOOD, HERMAN EDWARD, b. Indpls., July 21, 1942; B.S., Ind. U., 1965, J.D., 1968. Admitted to Ind. bar, 1968; individual practice law, Speedway, Ind., 1968—. Mem. Democratic election bd., Speedway, 1975, Dem. vice-committeeman, 1975—. Mem. Am., Ind., Ind. State bar assns. Named Optimist of Year, 1972; recipient citation for meritorious service Town of Speedway, 1975. Home: 1102 N Lyndhurst St Speedway IN 46224 Office: 5135 W 10th St Speedway IN 46224 Tel (317) 243-7567

GREER, DANIEL JAMES, b. Evanston, Ill., Aug. 11, 1941; B.A., Ohio Wesleyan U., 1963; LL.D., U. Ill., 1966. Admitted to Ill. bar, 1966; individual practice law, Springfield, Ill., 1968—. Mem. Ill., Sangamon County bar assns. Home: 2112 Barberry St Springfield IL

62704 Office: 617 E Monroe St Springfield IL 62705 Tel (217) 544-3477

GREER, RAY VAUGHN, b. San Francisco, July 16, 1937; B.S., Memphis State U., 1966, J.D., 1970; LL.M., U. Tex., 1977. Admitted to colo. bar, 1971, Tex. bar, 1976; individual practice law, Ft. Collins, Colo., 1971-76; regional atty. Forest Oil Corp., Corpus Christi, Tex., 1976-77; gen. counsel Geodynamics Oil & Gas Corp., Corpus Christi, 1977—. Mem. Colo. Larimer County, Am., Tex., Nueces County bar assns., Am., Corpus Christi assns. petroleum landmen. Author: The Associated Problems of Ownership and Development of Geothermal Resources in Texas: Something New Under the Sun, 1977. Office: 1420 The 600 Bldg Corpus Christi TX 78401 Tel (512) 882-3682

GREEVY, CHARLES FRITCHER, b. Williamsport, Pa., May 2, 1914; Ph.B., Dickinson Coll., 1936; J.D., Dickinson Sch. Law, 1939. Admitted to Pa. Supreme Ct. bar, 1939, U.S. Dist. Ct. for Middle Dist. Pa. bar, 1940; practiced in Williamsport, 1939-52; partner firm Greevy, Greevy & Knittle and predecessor, 1939-52; pres. judge Ct. Common Pleas, 29th Jud. Dist. Pa., 1952—. Pres. Williamsport Cleft Palate Clinic, 1960—; mem. Pa. Council Crime and Delinquency; pres. New Covenant United Ch. of Christ, Williamsport. Mem. Lycoming County, Pa., Am. bar assns., Pa. Assn. Probation and Corrections. Recipient Silver Beaver award Boy Scouts Am., 1964, Alumni award Theta Chi, 1963, Nat. Brotherhood award Nat. Conf. Christians and Jews, 1963. Home: 1224 Campbell St Williamsport PA 17701 Office: Courthouse 48 W 3d St Williamsport PA 17701 Tel (717) 323-9811

GREEVY, LESTER LEROY, JR., b. Williamsport, Pa., July 1, 1943; B.A., Dickinson Coll., 1965, J.D., 1968. Admitted to Pa. bar, 1969; 1970; asso. firm Greevy, Knittle & Mitchell, Williamsport, 1968-72, Greevy & Mitchell, Williamsport, 1972-75; partner firm Greevy, Greevy & Greevy, Williamsport, 1975—; atty. examiner Pa. Dept. Revenue, 1970—. Chmn. Lycoming Democratic County (Pa.), 1970-71; Dem. committeeman State of Pa., 1972—, mem. Dem. Exec. Com., 1972—. Mem. Lycoming Law Assn., Pa., Am. bar assns., Pa. Trial Lawyers Assn., Pa. Def. Inst. Home: Rural Delivery 2 Jersey Shore PA 17740 Office: 29 W 4th St Williamsport PA 17701 Tel (717) 326-6561

GREFE, ROLLAND EUGENE, b. Ida County, Iowa, June 27, 1920; B.A., Morningside Coll., 1941; J.D., State U. Iowa, 1946. Admitted to Iowa bar, 1946, U.S. Supreme Ct. bar, 1960; asso. firm Schaetzle Swift Austin & Stewart, and predecessor, Des Moines, 1946-54; partner firms Schaetzle, Austin & Grefe, Des Moines, 1954-61, Austin, Grefe & Sidney, Des Moines, 1961-71, Grefe & Sidney, Des Moines, 1971—. Bd. dirs. Des Moines Area Community Coll., Ankeny, Iowa, 1966-75, pres., 1968-75. Mem. Polk County (Iowa) (pres. 1971-72), Iowa State (chmn. com. taxation 1955-57, mem. grievance com. 1970-72, bd. govs. 1972-76, v.p. 1976-77, pres. elect 1977-78), Am. bar assns. Home: apt 917 3000 Grand Ave Des Moines IA 50312 Office: Suite 1980 Financial Center 666 Walnut St Des Moines IA 50309 Tel (515) 245-4300

GREGG, HAROLD, b. Cleve., Nov. 11, 1944; B.S. in Bus. Adminstrn., Syracuse U., 1966; J.D., Case Western Res. U., 1969. Admitted to Ohio bar, 1969; asso. firm Peltz and Lipson, Cleve., 1970-75, firm Mays Fant & Gregg, Cleve., 1975—; mem. arbitration panel Ohio region, Ohio Motor Carrier Labor Relations Assn., 1969-71; mem. comml. and personal injury panels Am. Arbitration Assn., Cleve., 1972—; guest lectr. Sunbeam Sch. for Physically Handicapped, Cleve. Sch. Dist. Co-chmn. legal com. Al Sirat Grotto Circus, Cleve., 1975—. Mem. Cleve., Ohio State, Cuyahoga County bar assns. Office: 23811 Chagrin Blvd Suite 130 Cleveland OH 44122 Tel (216) 464-3030

GREGG, JAMES C., b. Ebensburg, Pa., Dec. 26, 1924; A.A., George Washington U., 1948, LL.B., 1950. Admitted to D.C. bar, 1950, Va. bar, 1953; partner firm Gregg & Tait, Washington, 1950-57, Macleay, Lynch, Bernhard & Gregg, Washington, 1957—. Mem. D.C., Va. bar assns., Def. Research Inst., Phi Delta Phi. Home: 3156 N 21st St Arlington VA 22201 Office: 1625 K St NW Washington DC 20006 Tel (202) 393-3390

GREGORY, ARTHUR, b. Savannah, Ga., Mar. 22, 1940; A.B., Duke, 1963; J.D., U. S.C., 1968. Admitted to S.C. bar, 1968, Ga. bar, 1969; asso. firm Candler, Cox McClain and Andrews, Atlanta, 1968-70; asso. firm McClain, Mellen, Bowling & Hickman, Atlanta, 1970-73, partner, 1973—; lectr. law Atlanta Law Sch., 1970—. Mem. Am., Atlanta (chmn. com. travel) bar assns., State Bar S.C., State Bar Ga., Lawyers Club, Duke (pres. Atlanta chpt. 1974-76), U. S.C. (pres. Atlanta chpt. 1976, exec. com. alumni council 1976-77) alumni assns. Home: 1150 Collier Rd NW Apt B-8 Atlanta GA 30318 Office: PO Drawer 56505 Atlanta GA 30343 Tel (404) 577-9411

GREGORY, BILLY BOB, b. Longview, Tex., Dec. 9, 1931; A.A., Kilgore Jr. Coll., 1951; B.S., Tex. A. and M. U., 1954; J.D., Baylor U., 1961. Admitted to Tex. bar, 1961; with Hwy. Dept., State of Tex., 1961; asso. law firm, Irving, Tex., 1961-62; ins. adjuster State Farm Ins. Co., Atlanta, 1962—; ins. broker, Dallas, 1963; asso. firm Victor Sellars, Garland, Tex., 1964; individual practice law, Garland, 1964—. Mem. Garland Bar Assn. (v.p.), Garland C. of C. Home: 3305 S Glenbrook Garland TX 85041 Office: 2329 S Garland Ave Garland TX 75041 Tel (214) 278-6146

GREGORY, DAVID MICHAEL, b. Lawton, Okla., Apr. 29, 1945; B.B.A., U. Tex., Austin, 1967, J.D., 1970. Admitted to Tex. bar, 1970, U.S. Supreme Ct. bar, 1974; served as capt. JAGC, USMC, 1970-74; partner firm Kelsey, Wood & Gregory and predecessor, Denton, Tex., 1974—; instr. bus. law, legal rights of women Tex. Woman's U., Denton, 1974, 75; instr. bus. law N. Tex. State U., Denton, 1975—. Dir. Services Program for Aging Needs, Denton County, 1975—, Big Bros.-Big Sisters of Denton County, 1975—. Mem. Tex., Denton County bar assns. Recipient Am. Jurisprudence award U.S. Supreme Ct. Seminar, 1969; certified family law specialist. Home: 2109 Northwood Terr Denton TX 76201 Office: 611 1st State Bank Bldg Denton TX 76201 Tel (817) 387-9551

GREGORY, DRAPER B., b. Phila., Sept. 3, 1929; B.S., U.S. Mil. Acad., 1954; M.S. in Engring., Stanford U., 1975; J.D., U. Calif. at Berkeley, 1960. Admitted to Calif. bar, 1961; individual practice law, San Francisco, 1965—. Mem. ASME, Am. Soc. Metals, Calif. Trial Lawyers Assn., Am., San Francisco bar assns. Office: 220 Montgomery St Suite 1500 San Francisco CA 94104 Tel (415) 989-8796

GREGORY, GEORGE G., b. Whittier, Calif., Dec. 21, 1932; B.A. Harvard, 1954, LL.B., 1957. Admitted to Calif. bar, 1957; asso. firm Gibson, Dunn & Crutcher, Los Angeles, 1957-66; partner firm, 1966-69; vice pres., gen. counsel, sec. Cordura Corp., Los Angeles, 1969-74; partner firm Collins, Gregory & Rutter Inc., Los Angeles, 1974—. Mem. Am., Calif., Beverly Hills, Los Angeles County bar assns., Los Angeles Town Hall, World Affairs Council, Phi Beta Kappa. Office: 1900 Ave of The Stars Los Angeles CA 90067 Tel (213) 879-9494

GREGORY, HENRY WATT, III, b. Pine Bluff, Ark., Jan. 16, 1942; A.B., Vanderbilt U., 1963; LL.B., U. Ark., 1966. Admitted to Ark. bar, 1966, U.S. Supreme Ct. bar, 1970; asso. firm Rose, Nash, Williamson, Carroll, Clay & Giroir, Little Rock, 1966-70, mem. firm, 1971—. Mem. Pulaski County, Am., Ark. (chmn. standing com. on unauthorized law practice) bar assns. Office: 720 W Third St Little Rock AR 72201 Tel (375-9131

GREGORY, JAMES PETER, b. Hartford, Conn., May 27, 1934; A.B. Brown U., 1956; J.D., George Washington U., 1961. Admitted to D.C. bar, 1961, Conn., 1963; chief law clk. U.S. Ct. Claims, Washington, 1961-62; asso. Cummings & Lockwood, Stamford, Conn., 1962-64; corp. atty. Pfizer, Inc., N.Y.C., 1964-66; gen. counsel Perkin-Elmer Corp., Norwalk, Conn., 1966—. Chmn. Zoning bd. Appeals, Ridgefield, Conn., 1972-74. Mem. Conn., (mem. profl. ethics com.), D.C. bar assns. Home: 47 Pierrepont Dr Ridgefield CT 06877 Office: Perkin-Elmer Corp Main Ave Norwalk CT 06856 Tel (203) 762-4976

GREGORY, WILLIAM ANTHONY, b. Cleve., May 15, 1943; B.A., Case Western Reserve U., 1965; M.A., U. Mich., 1966; J.D., Harvard, 1969. Admitted to Calif. State bar, 1970; individual practice of law, Los Angeles, 1970-71; atty. Pacific Lighting Corp. law dept., Los Angeles, 1971-73; asso. prof. U. Tulsa Coll. of Law Tulsa, 1973-76, vis. prof. law St. Mary's U., San Antonio, 1976—. Office: St Mary's U San Antonio TX 78284 Tel (512) 696-1931

GREIF, HARVEY EDWARD, b. N.Y.C., Nov. 22, 1938; B.B.A. summa cum laude, Coll. City N.Y., 1960; J.D., Harvard U., 1964. Admitted to N.Y. bar, 1965, Mass. bar, 1970; tax specialist Touche Ross & Co., C.P.A.'s, N.Y.C., 1964-68; tax partner Laventhol & Horwath, C.P.A.'s, Boston, 1968-76; mem. Dellorfano & Greif, Boston, 1976—. Mem. Boston Estate and Bus. Planning Council, Am. Inst. C.P.A.'s, Mass. Soc. C.P.A.'s, N.Y. State Soc. C.P.A.'s (Gold medal 1966). C.P.A., N.Y., Mass. Home: 9 Yorkshire Rd Marblehead MA 01945 Office: Two Center Plaza Boston MA 02108 Tel (617) 523-3856

GREIG, WALTER, b. Austin, Tex., Nov. 16, 1906; student U. Tex., 1924-28, student Law Sch., 1928-30; B.S. (hon.), Cleary Coll., 1949, B.B.A., 1960, M.B.A., 1961, Sc.D. (hon.), 1962; D.C.S., Drake Coll. Fla., 1964. Admitted to Tex. bar, 1931, U.S. Supreme Ct. bar, 1942, Mich. bar, 1946; individual practice law, Austin, 1931-41, Detroit, 1946-47, 49; exec. v.p., Cleary Coll., 1949-70, pres., 1970-74; cons. in field, 1974—; exec. sec. Mich. Liquor Control Commn., Lansing, 1974-49. Chmn. Ypsilanti Compensation Commn., 1973—; mem. bd. dirs. Ypsilanti Fireman and Police Pension Commn., 1973—; chmn. Ypsilanti Bd. Rev., 1977—. Mem. Mich., Tex. bar assns. Named Outstanding Citizen, Mayor of Ypsilanti, 1974; recipient commendation Mich. Legislature, 1974. Contbr. articles to profl. jours. Home and office: 1223 Washtenaw Ave Ypsilanti MI 48197 Tel (313) 482-2852

GREINER, KEITH ALLEN, b. Hunter, Kans., Feb. 24, 1940; B.A., Emporia (Kans.) State Coll., 1962; LL.B., U. Va., 1966. Admitted to Kans. bar, 1966; mem. firm Keith A. Griever and predecessor firms, Emporia, Kans., 1966—. Treas. Kans. div. Am. Cancer Soc., 1974—; trustee Emporia State Coll. Endowment Assn., Inc.; chmn. Lyon County Republican. Com., 1968—. Mem. Am., Kans. (chmn. citizenship com.), Lyon County bar assns. Office: Citizens Bank Bldg Emporia KS 66801 Tel (316) 342-1157

GREINKE, GARY ARTHUR, b. Hastings, Nebr., Feb. 1, 1941; B.A., Valparaiso U., 1963; J.D., U. Nebr., 1966. Admitted to Nebr. bar, 1966; instr. polit. sci. Concordia Coll., Seward, Nebr., 1966-68, asst. prof., 1968-73, asso. prof., 1973—, asst. to pres., 1968—, dir. planning, 1973—. Chmn. Seward Republican party, 1970, 72, 74; Nebr. central Republican committeeman, 1974-76. Mem. Nebr. Bar Assn. Am. Council on Edn. fellow, 1976—. Home: 158 E Hillcrest St Seward NE 68434 Office: Weller 108-C Concordia Coll 800 N Columbia St Seward NE 68434 Tel (402) 643-3651

GRENIER, ARTHUR SYLVESTER, JR., b. N.Y.C., Aug. 24, 1914; A.B., Princeton, 1936; LL.B., U. Tex., 1939. Admitted to Tex. bar, 1939, N.Y. bar, 1941; asso. firm Reid & Priest, N.Y.C., 1939-42; atty. So. Union Gas Co., Dallas, 1946-56, atty., asst. sec., 1960-67, v.p., gen. atty., sec., 1967-74, v.p., gen. counsel, sec., 1974-76; v.p., gen. counsel, sec. So. Union Co., Dallas, 1976—. Mem. adv. bd. Internat. Oil and Gas Ednl. Center, Southwestern Legal Found. Mem. Am., Tex. (adv. council pub. utility law sect.), Dallas bar assns., Tex. Utility Lawyers (past pres.), Am. Soc. Corporate Secs. (past pres. Dallas regional group, nat. dir.). Home: 4317 Stanhope Ave Dallas TX 75205 Office: 1800 First Internat Bldg Dallas TX 75270 Tel (214) 748-8511

GRENIER, EDWARD JOSEPH, JR., b. N.Y.C., Nov. 26, 1933; B.A. summa cum laude, Manhattan Coll., 1954; LL.B. magna cum laude, Harvard U., 1959. Admitted to D.C. bar, 1959, U.S. Surpeme Ct. bar, 1966; law clk. to chief judge U.S. Ct. Appeals D.C. Circuit, 1959-60; asso. firm Covington & Burling, Washington, 1960-68; partner firm Sutherland, Asbill & Brennan, Washington, 1968—; v.p. Internat. Council Computer Communications, 1977—, bd. govs., 1975—; adj. prof. law Georgetown U. Law Center, 1974—. Trustee, mem. exec. com. Connelly Sch. Holy Child, Potomac, Md., 1976—; bd. dirs. D.C. Rec. for the Blind, 1977—; v.p., Heritage Farm Homeowners Assn., Potomac, 1973-74; pres. Adelphi Citizens Assn., 1965-66. Mem. Am. (council sect. administrv. law 1975—), D.C., Fed. Power, Fed., FCC bar assns., Bar Assn. D.C. (vice-chmn. adminstrv. law sect. 1971-72, chmn. 1972-73; dir. assn. 1973-74), Assn. Computing Machinery, Computer Law Assn. (dir. 1973—, v.p. 1977—), Harvard Law Sch. Assn. D.C. (v.p. 1976-77, pres. 1977—). Contbr. articles to legal jours.; editor Harvard Law Rev., 1957-59. Home: 9420 Duxford Ct Potomac MD 20854 Office: 1666 K St NW Washington DC 20006 Tel (202) 872-7827

GRESSMAN, EUGENE, b. Lansing, Mich., Apr. 18, 1917; A.B., U. Mich., 1938, J.D., 1940. Admitted to U.S. Supreme Ct. bar, 1945, D.C. bar, 1948, Mich. bar, 1940, Md. bar, 1959; atty. SEC, Washington, 1940-43; law clk. U.S. Supreme Ct., 1943-48; partner firm Van Arkel, Kaiser, Gressman, Rosenberg & Driesen, Washington, 1948-77, of counsel, 1977—; William Rand Kenan prof. law N.C. Law Sch., 1977—; vis. prof. law George Washington Law Sch., 1971-77, Mich. Law Sch., 1969, Ohio State Law Sch., 1967, Ind. Law Sch., 1976; judge Appeal Tax Ct. Montgomery County (Md.), Rockville, 1959-62. Mem. Am., Fed., D.C. bar assns., Am. Judicature Soc., Phi Beta Kappa, Order of Coif. Author: (with Robert L. Stern): Supreme Court Practice, 5th edit., 1977; (with Charles A. Wright et al) Federal Practice and Procedure, Vol. 16, 1977; contbr. articles to legal jours.

GREW, ROBERT RALPH, b. Metamora, Ohio, Mar. 25, 1931; A.B. in Letters, Law, U. Mich., 1953, J.D., 1955. Admitted to Mich. bar, 1955, N.Y. bar, 1958; asso. firm Carter, Ledyard & Milburn, N.Y.C., 1957-68, partner, 1968—. Mem. N.Y., Fed., Am., Internat. bar assns., Assn. Bar City N.Y. Home: 8 E 96th St New York City NY 10028 Office: 2 Wall St New York City NY 10005 Tel (212) 732-3200

GRIDLEY, WILLIAM CARTER, b. Orlando, Fla., Nov. 26, 1941; B.A., U. Fla., 1963, J.D., 1965. Admitted to Fla. bar, 1966; practiced in Orlando, 1966-70; asst. pub. defender Orange County (Fla.), 1970-72; judge Orange County Juvenile Ct., 1972-73, Fla. 9th Circuit Ct., 1973—. Bd. dirs. Boys' Club of Central Fla., Greenhouse Family Counseling, Inc., Orlando. Mem. Fla. (past mem. com. juvenile rules), Am. bar assns. Home: 619 Darcey Dr Winter Park FL 32792 Office: Orange County Courthouse Orlando FL 32801 Tel (305) 420-3645

GRIESER, CHARLES RICHARD, b. Springfield, Ohio, Sept. 15, 1920; B.S., Ohio State U., 1942; LL.B., Harvard, 1948, J.D., 1969. Admitted to Ohio bar, 1949, U.S. Supreme Ct. bar, 1954; individual practice law, Columbus, Ohio, 1949—; sr. mem. firm Richards, Grieser & Schafer Co., LPA, Columbus. Mem. Am., Ohio, Columbus (chmn. negligence com.) bar assns., Am. Coll. Trial Lawyers, ICC Bar. Contbr. articles on negligence, pleadings and products liability to legal jours. Office: 8 E Broad St Columbus OH 43215 Tel (614) 221-5192

GRIFFEN, THOMAS GAINES, b. Gainesville, Tex., June 15, 1945; B.A., Hope Coll., Holland, Mich., 1967; J.D., Albany Law Sch. of Union U., 1972. Admitted to N.Y. bar, 1973; mem. firm Meyers, Griffen and Whitbeck, Hudson, N.Y., 1975—; legal advisor City of Hudson, 1974—; town atty. Town of Kinderhook, N.Y., 1976—; asst. public defender Columbia County, N.Y., 1974-75. Mem. bd. dir. Hudson Area Library, 1974—; mem. bd. trustees Friends of Olana, Inc., 1974—; pres. Columbia County Young Republicans, 1976. Mem. Am., N.Y., Columbia County bar assns. Home: 29 Broad St Kinderhook NY 12106 Office: 542 Warren St Hudson NY 12534 Tel (518) 828-3669

GRIFFENBERG, E. DICKINSON, JR., b. Wilmington, Del., Feb. 26, 1931; B.A., Williams Coll., 1952; LL.B., Harvard U., 1957. Admitted to Del. bar, 1957; asso. firm Killoran & Van Brunt, Wilmington, 1957-69; partner firm Potter, Anderson & Corroon, Wilmington, 1969—; asst. atty. New Castle County (Del.), 1964-69. Mem. Del., Am. bar assns. Home: 2309 Ridgway Rd Wilmington DE 19805 Office: 350 Delaware Trust Bldg Wilmington DE 19801 Tel (302) 658-6771

GRIFFETH, RONALD CLYDE, b. Athens, Ga., Jan. 5, 1935; B.A., U. Ga., 1957; J.D., Augusta (Ga.) Law Sch., 1972. Admitted to Ga. bar, 1972; individual practice law, Augusta, 1972—; v.p.-claims, corporate counsel First of Ga. Ins. Group, Augusta, 1966—; adjuster/br. mgr. Gen. Adjustment Bur., Inc., West Palm Beach, Fla. and Augusta, 1958-66. Mem. Am., Ga., Augusta bar assns., Assn. Trial Lawyers Am., Christian Legal Soc., Southeastern, Augusta claims assns. Home: 1848 Bolin Rd North Augusta SC 29841 Office: POB 1895 Augusta GA 30903 Tel (404) 738-0114

GRIFFIN, HANCOCK, JR., b. Albany, N.Y., Aug. 21, 1912; A.B. cum laude, Williams Coll., 1934; LL.B., Yale, 1938. Admitted to N.Y. bar, 1939, Maine bar, 1967, U.S. Supreme Ct. bar, 1949; asso. firm Kelley, Drye & Warren, and predecessors, N.Y.C., 1938-55, mem. firm, 1955-66; mem. firm Fenton, Griffin, Chapman & Burrill, and predecessor, Bar Harbor, Maine, 1967—. Former mem. Sch. Bd., Smithtown, L.I., N.Y.; former trustee Fisk U. Mem. Am., N.Y. State, Maine, Hancock County bar assns., Assn. Bar City N.Y., N.Y. County Lawyers Assn., Am. Judicature Soc. Home: Harbor Ln Bar Harbor ME 04609 Office: 109 Main St Bar Harbor ME 04609 Tel (207) 288-3331

GRIFFIN, HAROLD HAM (HATCH), b. Atlanta, July 12, 1928; B.S., U. Fla., 1950, J.D., 1968. Admitted to Fla. bar, 1968, Ga. bar, 1969; C.P.A., Turnburke, Brock & Raines, Clearwater, Fla., 1959-61; comptroller Evans Packing Co., Dade City, Fla., 1961-63; C.P.A., sr. accountant Jetstar project control Lockheed Aircraft Co., Marietta, Ga., 1963-70; mem. firm Robert Wilson, Clearwater, 1970-73; sr. mem. firm Griffin, Uber & Halisky, Clearwater, 1973—. Pres. Mease Hosp. Devel. Bd., Dunedin, Fla., 1976. Mem. Fla. Inst. C.P.A.'s, Am., Ga., Fla., Clearwater bar assns. Home: 450 S Gulfview Blvd Apt 402 Clearwater FL 33515 Office: 1455 Court St PO Box 6086 Clearwater FL 33518 Tel (813) 446-3015

GRIFFIN, HARRY LEIGH, JR., b. Charlotte, N.C., May 1, 1935; B.A. magna cum laude, Harvard, 1957; LL.B., Duke, 1963. Admitted to N.C. bar, 1963, Ga. bar, 1964; law clk. to Judge J. Spencer Bell, U.S. 4th Circuit Ct. Appeals, 1963-64; partner firm Currie & Hancock, Atlanta, 1965—; lectr. in field Ga. Inst. Tech., Colo. State U. Bd. dirs. Atlanta Legal Aid Soc., Atlanta chpt. March of Dimes, Atlanta Lawyers Com. for Civil Rights Under Law. Mem. Am. Bar Assn. (Ga. rep. asso. and adv. com. fed. legislation 1972-73, vice chmn. bd. contract appeals, pub. contract law sect. 1971-72; vice chmn. socioeconomic rights and remedies public contract law sect. 1971-72). Co-author: Opportunity for Urban Excellence, 1966; contbr. articles to law jours. Office: 2600 Peachtree Center-Harris Tower 233 Peachtree St NE Atlanta GA 30303 Tel (404) 521-3800

GRIFFIN, HENRY MCHENRY, b. Owensboro, Ky., Dec. 26, 1921; LL.B., U. Ky., 1949, J.D., 1970. Admitted to Ky. bar, 1949, since practiced in Owensboro; police judge, 1954-59; county atty. Daviess County, 1960-68; circuit judge Daviess County, 1968—. Mem. Am., Ky., Daviess County (pres. 1964) bar assns., Am. Judicature Soc., Ky. Circuit Judges' Assn. Home: 203 W 17th St Owensboro KY 42301 Office: Court House Owensboro KY 42301 Tel (502) 684-9812

GRIFFIN, JAMES LAWRENCE, b. Chgo., Nov. 18, 1911; A.B., Villanova U., 1933; J.D., DePaul U., 1938. Admitted to Ill. bar, 1938, U.S. Supreme Ct. bar, 1950; partner firm Griffin & Gallagher, Chgo., 1942-71; asso. judge Circuit Ct. Cook County (Ill.), Chgo., 1971-76; judge Circuit Ct., Cook County, Ill., 1976—. Mem. Am., Chgo. bar assns. Home: 6209 S Campbell Ave Chicago IL 60629 Office: 5240 W James St Oak Lawn IL 60453 Tel (312) 636-6100

GRIFFIN, JOHN ALFRED, b. Glendale, Calif., June 6, 1922; student U. So. Calif., 1947-50; LL.B., Southwestern U., 1950. Admitted to Calif. bar, 1952; partner firm Erb, French, Picone & Griffin, Beverly Hills, Calif., 1953-56; individual practice law, Beverly Hills, 1956-73, Orange, Calif., 1966-73; judge South Orange County (Calif.) Municipal Ct., 1973—; instr. real estate law Calif. State U., Fullerton. Mem. Orange County Bar, Am. Bd. Trial Advocates. Office: 30143 Crown Valley Pkwy Laguna Niguel CA 92677

GRIFFIN, WENTWORTH E., b. Kansas City, Mo., Feb. 22, 1917; A.B., Westminster Coll., 1938; J.D., Washington U., 1941. Admitted to Mo. bar, 1941, U.S. Supreme Ct. bar, 1952; mem. firm Reeder, Griffin, Dysart, Taylor & Penner, and predecessors, Kansas City, 1937—. Mem. Kansas City Bd. Edn., 1956-70, pres., 1960-62. Mem. Am., Kansas City, Mo. bar assns., Motor Carrier Lawyers Assn. (v.p. 1959-62, pres. 1963). Home: 3523 Eastvale Dr Shawnee Mission KS 66205 Office: 1221 Baltimore Ave Kansas City MO 64105 Tel (816) 221-1464

GRIFFIN, WILLIAM HANCOCK, b. Huntsville, Ala., June 10, 1930; student U. Ala., 1948-49, 53-57; LL.B., Birmingham Sch. Law, 1958. Admitted to Ala. bar, 1958; partner firm Griffin & Griffin, Huntsville, Ala., 1958—; city prosecutor, Huntsville, 1958-59, city recorder, 1959-72, presiding recorder, 1972—. Mem. Ala. Municipal Judges Assn. (charter). Home: 1703 Fagan Circle SE Huntsville AL 35801 Office: 408 Franklin St SE Huntsville AL 35801 Tel (205) 536-6691

GRIFFITH, BLAIR A., b. Buffalo, Jan. 7, 1926; A.B., Duquesne U., 1949; LL.B., U. Pitts., 1954. Admitted to Pa. bar, 1955, U.S. Supreme Ct. bar, 1970; individual practice law, Greensburg, 1955-67; dir. Pa. Bur. Land Records, 1967-69; first asst. U.S. atty., Pitts., 1969-75, U.S. atty., 1975—. Mem. Am., Pa., Fed. (pres. Pitts. chpt. 1976) bar assns., Am. Judicature Soc. Recipient Outstanding Performance awards Dept. Justice, 1972, 73, 74, Sustained Performance award, 1972. Home: PO Box 2472 Pittsburgh PA 15230 Office: 633 US Post Office and Courthouse Grant St St Pittsburgh PA 15219 Tel (412) 644-3500

GRIFFITH, DAVID MILLER, b. Warren, Ohio, Sept. 14, 1917; A.B., Miami U., 1940; LL.B., U. Cin., 1943. Admitted to Ohio bar, 1943; pros. atty. Trumbull County, Ohio, 1968-71; judge Common Pleas Ct., Warren, Ohio, 1971—. Mem. Ohio State, Trumbull County bar assns. Home: 4205 E Market St Warren OH 44484 Office: Court House High St Warren OH 44481 Tel (216) 399-8825

GRIFFITH, ELWIN JABEZ, b. Barbados, W.Indies, Mar. 2, 1938; student Harrison Coll., Barbados, 1950-55; B.A., L.I. U., 1960; J.D., Bklyn. U., 1963; LL.M., N.Y. U., 1964. Admitted to N.Y. Bar, 1963; tchr. Modern High Sch., Barbados, 1955-56; individual practice law, N.Y.C., 1964-72; asst. dean, asst. prof. Drake U., 1972-73; asso. dean, prof. law U. Cin., 1973—; asst. counsel Chase Manhattan Bank, N.Y.C., 1964-71, Tchrs. Ins. & Annuity Assn., N.Y.C., 1971-72; lectr. L.I. U., 1965; asst. prof. law Cleveland-Marshall Law Sch., 1968; vis. prof. Black exec. exchange program Nat. Urban League, N.Y.C., 1971, 75. Mem. Am., N.Y. State bar assns., Am. Arbitration Assn., Bedford-Stuyvesant Jr. C. of C. (former counsel). Contbr. articles to legal jours. Office: U Cin Cincinnati OH 45221 Tel (513) 475-6805

GRIFFITH, GARTH ELLIS, b. Cleve., July 1, 1928; A.B., Ohio Wesleyan U., 1950; J.D., U. Mich., 1953; LL.M., Case Western Res. U., 1964. Admitted to Ohio bar, 1953, U.S. Supreme Ct. bar, 1968; with Judge Adv. Gen. Corps U.S. Army, Austria, Germany, 1953-57; with Chesapeake and Ohio Railway Co., Cleve., 1957—, gen. atty. 1970-75, corp. sec., 1975—, gen. solicitor, 1975—; with Chessie System, Cleve., 1973—, corp. sec. 1975—, gen. solicitor, 1975—. Mem. Am., Ohio, Greater Cleve. bar assns., Am. Soc. Corp. Secs. Office: POB 6419 Cleveland OH 44101 Tel (216) 623-2410

GRIFFITH, GEORGE WILLIAM, b. Alice, Tex., Jan. 22, 1948; A.B. in Polit. Sci., U. Ga., 1969, J.D., 1972. Admitted to Ga. bar, 1972; asso. firm Ballard & Thigpen, Covington, Ga., 1972-74; partner firm Ballard, Thigpen & Griffith, Covington, 1974-76, firm Griffith, DeGonia, & Payne, Covington, 1976—. Mem. adminstrv. bd. 1st United Methodist Ch., Covington, 1975—. Mem. Ga., Alcovy bar assns., Ga. Trial Lawyers Assn., Newton-Rockdale Lawyers Club. Home: 6157 Crestview Dr Covington GA 30209 Office: 3146 Hwy 278 Covington GA 30209 Tel (404) 787-2550

GRIFFITH, HORACE ERNEST, b. Loraine, Tex., Nov. 24, 1915; B.A., Tex. Tech U., 1935; LL.B., Georgetown U., 1939. Admitted to D.C. bar, 1939, Tex. bar, 1940; asst. counsel Alley Dwelling Authority, Washington, 1939-41; partner firm Thompson & Griffith, Colorado City, Tex., 1945-46; with VA, Lubbock, Tex., 1946-50, OPS, 1950-52; individual practice law, Lubbock, 1952-60; title atty. Lubbock Abstract & Title Co., 1960—; approved atty. Lawyers Title Ins. Corp., 1960—; instr. Am. govt. Tex. Tech U., 1952-73. Pres. Colorado City Jaycees, 1946. Mem. Am., Tex., Lubbock County (pres. 1961-62) bar assns. Office: 1215 Texas Ave Lubbock TX 79401 Tel (806) 763-1204

GRIFFITH, JAMES ARTHUR, b. Cleve., Feb. 28, 1933; B.B.A., Case Western Res. U., 1954, J.D., 1958. Admitted to Ohio bar, 1958; asso. firm Calfee, Halter, Cleve., 1958-63; house counsel, Central Cadillac Co., Cleve., 1963-74; mem. firm Roudebush, Brown, Corlett and Ulrich, Cleve., 1974—. Pres. Western Res. Coll. Assn.; mem. vis. com., bd. overseers Case Western Res. U.; bd. dirs. Cleve. Athletic Club. Mem. Am., Ohio State, Greater Cleve. bar assns. Office: 915 Williamson Bldg Cleveland OH 44114 Tel (216) 696-5200

GRIFFITH, JOE EDGAR, b. Port Arthur, Tex., Sept. 14, 1936; B.A., So. Meth. U., 1959, LL.B., 1961. Admitted to Tex. bar, 1961, US. Supreme Ct. bar, 1964; asso. firms J. B. Sallas, Crockett, Tex., 1961-62, Sallas, Griffith & Meriwether, Crockett, 1965-76; with JAGC, U.S. Army, 1962-65; individual practice law, Crockett, 1976—. Mem. Tex. Bar Assn., Am. Trial Lawyers Assn. Home: 210 Homewood Dr Crockett TX 75835 Office: 120 N 5th St Crockett TX 75835 Tel (713) 544-2065

GRIFFITH, STEVE CAMPBELL, JR., b. Newberry, S.C., June 14, 1933; B.S., Clemson U., 1954; LL.B., U. S.C., 1959. Admitted to S.C. bar, 1959, N.C. bar, 1966; mem. firm Blease & Griffith, Newberry, 1959-64; asst. gen. counsel Duke Power Co., Charlotte, N.C., 1964-71, sec., asso. gen. counsel, 1971-74, gen. counsel, 1975—, v.p., 1977—; mem. S.C. Gen. Assembly, 1961-62. Mem. Am., Fed. Power, N.C., S.C., 26th Jud. bar assn. Home: 2325 Croydon Rd Charlotte NC 28207 Office: 422 S Church St Charlotte NC 28242 Tel (704) 373-4380

GRIFFITH, STEVEN FRANKLIN, SR., b. New Orleans, July 14, 1948; B.B.A., Loyola U. of the South, 1972, J.D., 1975. Admitted to La. bar, 1972, U.S. Supreme Ct. bar, 1976; asso. firm Oubre & Griffith, and predecessor, Norco, La., 1972-73, partner, 1973-75; individual practice law, Destrehan, La., 1975—; legal counsel Am. Legion Post 366, 1972—, St. Charles Parish (La.) Sheriff's Dept., Hanville, 1976—, River Rd. Hist. Soc. Mem. bd. commrs. Pontchartrain Levee Dist., 1973-75. Mem. Acad. New Orleans Trial Lawyers, 29th Jud. Dist., Am., La. State bar assns., Assn. Trial Lawyers Am., La. Trial Lawyers, Am. Soc. Notaries, Comml. Law League, Greater New Orleans C. of C. (dir. River Area council 1974—). Home: 34 Shadow Ln Destrehan LA 70047 Office: 8892 River Rd PO Drawer G Destrehan LA 70047 Tel (504) 525-1064

GRIFFITH, THOMAS JEFFERSON, b. Ackerman, Miss., Dec. 12, 1923; B.A., U. of N.C., 1943; LL.B., U. Miss., 1948. Admitted to Miss. bar, 1948, Tex. bar, 1950, Republic of Korea bar, 1952, U.S. Ct. Appeals 5th Circuit bar, 1954, U.S. Supreme Ct. bar, 1968; partner firm Nason & Griffith, Ackerman, 1948, Crenshaw & Griffith, Lubbock, 1953-54, Brister & Griffith, Lubbock, 1970—; individual practice law, Columbus, Miss., 1949-50, Lubbock, 1953-70; dir. Census Bur. 1st Dist. Miss., 1949-50; instr., Lubbock, 1953-62; sr. counsel Tex. Civil Liberties Union, 1973—. Chmn. Democrats of Miss. for Truman-Barkley, 1948; tchr. adult Sunday sch. Baptist Ch., Lubbock, 1958-74. Mem. Lubbock County (pres. 1963-64), Am. (advocacy com. 1974—) bar assns., State Bar Tex., Phi Alpha Delta, Beta Theta Pi, Eta Sigma Phi. Home: 4405 14th St Lubbock TX 79416 Office: Lubbock Nat Bank Bldg Suite 6F Lubbock TX 79401 Tel (806) 762-0275

GRIGER, HARRY MAX, b. Des Moines, Mar. 13, 1941; B.A., U. Iowa, 1963, J.D. with distinction, 1966. Admitted to Iowa bar, 1966; with West Pub. Co., 1966-67; asst. atty. gen. Iowa Atty. Gen's. Office, Des Moines, 1967-71, 71—; asst. atty. gen. Va. Atty. Gen., 1971. Mem. Iowa, Polk County (Iowa) bar assns. Home: 3320 Brookview Dr Des Moines IA 50265 Office: Lucas State Office Bldg Des Moines IA 50319 Tel (515) 281-5846

GRILL, RAYMOND J., JR., b. Los Angeles, Oct. 19, 1940; B.A., St. Mary's Coll., 1966; J.D., U. Tex., Austin, 1969. Admitted to Tex. bar, 1969; spl. prosecutor Travis County (Tex.) Juvenile Ct., 1969-71, dir. juvenile pub. defenders, 1971-73, referee, 1973—. Bd. dirs. Boys' Club, Austin, Tex., 1973—. Mem. Am. Bar Assn., Tex. Corrections Assn. (program com. 1969, 75-76, Gold Seal mem.). Certified specialist family law Tex. Bd. Legal Specialization. Office: 2515 S Congress Ave Austin TX 78704 Tel (512) 442-6733

GRILLIOT, HAROLD JOHN, b. Dayton, Ohio, Sept. 5, 1937; B.S., U. Dayton, 1960; J.D., U. Cin., 1967. Admitted to Ohio bar, 1967; asso. prof. bus. U. Cin., 1974—. Mem. Am. Bar Assn., Am. Inst. C.P.A.'s. C.P.A., Ohio. Author: Introduction to Law and the Legal System, 1975. Office: Coll Bus Adminstrn U Cin Cincinnati OH 45221 Tel (513) 475-6876

GRIM, DOUGLAS PAUL, b. Bellingham, Wash., May 12, 1940; B.A., Lawrence Coll., 1962; LL.B., Stanford, 1965; LL.M. in Taxation, N.Y. U., 1966. Admitted to Calif. bar, 1966; asso. firm Hanna & Morton, Los Angeles, 1966-72; of counsel firm Harris Noble Uhler & Gallop, Los Angeles, 1972-75; partner firm Nicholas Kolliner Myers D'Angelo & Givens, Los Angeles, 1975; prin. Douglas P. Grim, Los Angeles, 1975—; instr. Golden Gate U. Sch. Law, 1975. Vice pres., dir. Los Angeles Jr. C. of C., 1966-75; chmn. fin. com. Rosewood Meth. Ch., Los Angeles, 1966-72; chmn. exec. com. troop 35 Los Angeles Area council Boy Scouts Am., 1967-72. Mem. State Bar Calif., Los Angeles County, Am. bar assns. Recipient Michael F. Tobey award Los Angeles Jr. C. of C., 1972. Home: 247 S Lorraine Blvd Los Angeles CA 90004 Office: 523 W Sixth St Los Angeles CA 90014 Tel (213) MA-9-4502

GRIM, LE RUE JAMES, b. Dexter, Mo., June 22, 1928; LL.B., Lincoln U., 1965. Admitted to Calif. State bar, 1966; individual practice of law, San Francisco, 1966—. Mem. Am., San Francisco bar assns. Office: 877 Bryant St San Francisco CA 94103 Tel (415) 621-8071

GRIMAUD, GERALD CASSIMERE, b. Concord, N.H., July 27, 1942; B.A., Atlantic Union Coll., 1965; LL.B., York U., Toronto, Ont., Can., 1971. Admitted to Pa. bar, 1971; asst. atty. gen. for environ. protection State of Pa., 1971-74; individual practice law, Tunkhannock, Pa., 1974—; pub. defender Wyoming and Sullivan Counties (Pa.), 1974—; cons. Pa. Environ. Council, 1974—. Bd. dirs. United Services Agy., 1974-76, Home Health Services Northeastern Pa., 1974-76, Wyoming County Heart Soc., 1974—. Mem. Pa., Wyoming County bar assns. Contbr. article to legal rev. Home and Office: 69 Putnam St Tunkhannock PA 18657 Tel (717) 836-4668

GRIMES, ROBERT L., b. Oxnard, Calif., Nov. 10, 1946; A.B., San Diego State Coll., 1969; J.D., U. San Diego, 1972. Admitted to Calif. bar, 1972; asso. firm James H. Pasto, San Diego, 1972-73; partner firm Grimes & Warwick, San Diego, 1974—. Alumni adviser Sigma Chi Frat. San Diego State Coll., 1969—; mem. Mission Beach Precise Planning Com., 1971. Mem. Calif. Attys. for Criminal Justice, Am., San Diego County bar assns., San Diego Trial Lawyers Assn., Blue Key. Home: 5404 Chelsea St La Jolla CA Office: 2664 4th Ave San Diego CA 92103 Tel (714) 232-2014

GRIMES, STEPHEN HENRY, b. Peoria, Ill., Nov. 17, 1927; B.S.B.A., U. Fla., 1950, J.D., 1954; Admitted to Fla. bar, 1954, U.S. 5th Circuit Ct. Appeals bar, 1965, U.S. Tax Ct. bar, 1965, U.S. Supreme Ct. bar, 1972; asso. firm Holland & Knight, Bartow, Fla., 1954-56, partner, 1956-73; judge Fla. 2d Dist. Ct. Appeal, 1973—. Trustee Polk Community Coll., 1967-70, chmn., 1970; mem. Bartow Library Bd., 1968—. Mem. Am., 10th Jud. Circuit (pres. 1966) bar assns. Fla. Bar, Am. Coll. Trial Lawyers, Am. Judicature Soc., Order of Coif, Phi Delta Phi. Editor U. Fla. Law Rev., 1951. Home: 1950 El Paso St E Bartow FL 33830 Office: 1005 E Memorial Blvd Lakeland FL 33802 Tel (813) 682-5336

GRIMSLEY, JAMES OTIS, b. Asheboro, N.C., Jan. 18, 1945; B.S., Wake Forest U., 1967; J.D., U. N.C., 1972. Admitted to N.C. bar, 1972; asso. firm Frank P. Holton, Jr., Lexington, N.C., 1972-74; mem. firm Ivey & Grimsley, Asheboro, 1974—. Pres. Randolph County (N.C.) unit Am. Cancer Soc.; bd. dirs. Mainstream, Inc.; pres. Lindley Park Sch. PTA, Asheboro; active YMCA Capital Funds Campaign; dir. dept. youth 1st Bapt. Ch., Asheboro. Mem. N.C., Am. bar assns., N.C. State Bar, Lexington (N.C.) Jaycees, N.C. Acad. Trial Lawyers. Home: 1031 Worth St Extension Asheboro NC 27203 Office: 111 Worth St Asheboro NC 27203 Tel (19) 625-3043

GRINDELAND, GENE CURRAN, b. Hatton, N.D., Aug. 19, 1931; B.S., N.D. State U., 1959; J.D., U. N.D., 1962. Admitted to N.D. bar, 1962; individual practice law, Mayville, N.D., 1965—; asst. atty. gen., N.D., 1964; state's atty., Traill County, N.D., 1967-71; Traill County justice, 1971—. Mem. City of Mayville Council. Mem. Am., N.D. bar assns. Home: 429 1st St Mayville ND 58257 Office: 23 W Main St Mayville ND 58257 Tel (701) 786-2360

GRINDLE, JOHN, JR., b. Washington, Aug. 24, 1916; B.S., Harvard, 1939, LL.B., 1947. Admitted to D.C. bar, 1947; Washington rep. firm Milbank, Tweed, Hadley & McCloy, N.Y.C. and Washington, 1947-53, 54-74; gen. asst. to sec. U.S. HEW, 1953-54; of counsel firm Watson, Cole, Grindle & Watson, Washington, 1974—. Mem. Health and Welfare Council of D.C., 1955-65; vice chmn. bus. com. Nat. Symphony Orch. Sustaining Fund, 1957-59. Mem. Am., D.C. bar assns., Harvard Law Sch Assn (nat. v.p. 1964-65, pres. D.C. assn. 1962-63), English Speaking Union (bd. govs. Washington br. 1958—), Harvard Alumni Assn. (dir. 1970-72). Home: 4215 7th St NW Washington DC 20011 Office: 1909 K St NW Washington DC 20006 Tel (202) NA 8-0088

GRINDLINGER, JAMES ELLIOTT, b. Oakland, Calif. Apr. 23, 1948; A.B., in Polit. Sci., U. Calif. Berkeley, 1969, J.D., Boalt Hall, 1972. Admitted to Calif. bar, 1972; legal editor Matthew Bender & Co., San Francisco, 1973-74; law clk. to U.S. Dist. Judge, San Francisco, 1974—. Mem. Am., Alameda County bar assns., State Bar of Calif. Boalt Hall Alumni Assn., Calif. Alumni Assn. Tel (415) 556-3973

GRINDSTAFF, EVERETT J., b. Abilene, Tex., May 7, 1931; B.B.A., Baylor U., 1952, J.D., 1954. Admitted to Tex. bar, 1954; mem. firm Grindstaff & Grindstaff, Ballinger, Tex., 1954—; city atty. Ballinger, 1957—; bd. dirs. State Bar Tex. 1972-75; chmn. Upper Colo. River Authority, 1974—. Pres. Tex. Lions Camp Crippled Children. Home: 501 6th St Ballinger TX 76821 Office: Box 576 707 Hutchings Ave Ballinger TX 76821 Tel (915) 365-3515

GRINSTED, ALBERT, b. San Diego, Aug. 22, 1917; B.E.E., U. Nebr., 1951; J.D., Fla. State U., 1972. With personnel and accounting dept. Chgo. Burlington & Quincy R.R. Co., Chgo., 1936-43; research and devel. mgr. USAF, 1943-69; admitted to Fla. bar, 1973; individual practice law, Shalimar, Fla., 1973—; part-time pub. defender 1st Circuit Fla., 1973-75. Bd. dirs. Okaloosa Guidance Clinic, Fort Walton Beach, Fla., 1974-76. Mem. Am., Fla., Okaloosa-Walton (pres. 1975) bar assns. Home: 45 Meigs Dr Shalimar FL 32579 Office: Eglin Pkwy at Old Ferry Rd PO Drawer 915 Shalimar FL 32579 Tel (904) 651-2015

GRISCOM, RICHARD ANDREW, b. Phila., May 12, 1935; B.A., Wesleyan U., 1957; J.D., Harvard U., 1961. Admitted to D.C. bar, 1962, N.Mex. bar, 1972; asst. atty. gen. N.Mex., 1971-72; gen. counsel N.Mex. Dept. Health and Social Services, Santa Fe, 1972-76; chief party Robert R. Nathan Assos., Inc., cons. group, La Paz, Bolivia, 1976—; founder, dir. Peace Corps Program in Paraguay, 1965-68; dir. Peace Corps Tng. Center, Escondido, Calif., 1969-71; bd. dirs. Santa Fe Legal Aid Soc., 1971-73. Past pres., bd. dirs. Galisteo (N.Mex.) Community Corp. Mem. N.Mex., D.C. bar assns. Co-author: Escondido Papers—Experiences in Training, 1971. Home and Office: Casilla Postal 5115 La Paz Bolivia S Am Tel 54145

GRISEZ, JOHN PATRICK, b. Modesto, Calif., Dec. 28, 1943; B.S., U. Calif., Davis, 1965, J.D., 1973; M.S., Oreg. State U., 1967. Admitted to Calif. bar, 1973; dep. pub. defender, Stanislaus County, Calif., 1973—. Mem. Newman-Crows Landing Sch. Bd., 1974—. Mem. Am. Bar Assn., Calif. Trial Lawyers' Assn., Calif. Pub. Defenders' Assn., Calif. Attys. for Criminal Justice. Office: 1016A 12th St Modesto CA 95354 Tel (209) 526-6844

GRISHAM, LOWELL EDWARD, b. Tishomingo County, Miss., Aug. 27, 1925; LL.B., U. Miss., 1950, J.D., 1968. Admitted to Miss. bar, 1950; individual practice law, Iuka, Miss., 1950-51; spl. agt. supr. Washington hdqrs. FBI, 1954-55, spl. agt., Washington, 1951, Portland, Oreg., 1951-52, Los Angeles, 1952-54; mgr. personnel and security Reynolds Metals Co., Sheffield, Ala., 1955-59; asst. U.S. atty. for No. Miss., 1959-61; partner firm Ethridge & Grisham, Oxford, Miss., 1961—; mem. Miss. Ho. of Reps., 1948-51; with JAGC, U.S. Air Force Res., 1951-56; city atty. Oxford (Miss.), 1971-72. Fellow Miss. Bar Found.; mem. Miss. Def. Lawyers Assn. (charter), Am., Fed. bar assns., Def. Research Inst., Oxford-Lafayette C. of C., Phi Delta Phi. Home: 200 Vivian St Oxford MS 38655 Office: 1001 Jackson Ave Oxford MS 38655 Tel (601) 234-3626

GRISHMAN, DAVID BENJAMIN, b. New Orleans, June 21, 1944; B.A., U. Ala., 1966, J.D., 1970; LL.M. in Taxation, N.Y. U., 1971. Admitted to Tex. bar, 1971, Miss. bar, 1971; partner firm Watkins Pyle Ludlam Winter & Stennis, Jackson, Miss., 1976—. Mem. Miss., Tex. state bars, Jackson Young Lawyers Assn., Am. Bar Assn. (council sect. gen. practice). Editor: Docket Call, 1976. Home: 1978 Plantation Blvd Jackson MS 39211 Office: PO Box 427 Jackson MS 39205 Tel (601) 354-3456

GRISWOLD, ERWIN NATHANIEL, b. East Cleveland, Ohio, July 14, 1904; A.B., Oberlin Coll., 1925, A.M., 1925; LL.B., Harvard U., 1928, S.J.D., 1929. Admitted to Ohio bar, 1929, U.S. Supreme Ct. bar, 1932, Mass. bar, 1935, D.C. bar, 1973; asso. firm Griswold, Green, Palmer & Hadden, Cleve., 1929; with Office Solicitor Gen. U.S., 1929-34; faculty Harvard Law Sch., 1934-67, dean, 1946-67; solicitor gen. U.S., 1967-73; partner firm Jones, Day, Reavis & Pogue, Washington, 1973—. Mem. U.S. Commn. on Civil Rights, 1961-67, Commn. to Investigate Domestic Activities of CIA, 1975. Mem. Am. (del. 1957—), Mass., D.C. bar assns., Am. Law Inst., Am. Bar Found. (dir.), Inner Temple England (hon. bencher). Author: Spendthrift Trusts, 1936; The Fifth Amendment Today, 1954; Law and Lawyers in the United States, 1964; contbr. articles to profl. jours. Home: 36 Kenmore Rd Belmont MA 02178 Office: 1100 Connecticut Ave NW Washington DC 20036 Tel (202) 452-5880

GRISWOOD, H. ALAN, b. Riverside, Calif., Oct. 9, 1924; LL.B., So. Meth. U., 1950. Admitted to Tex. bar 1950, U.S. Supreme Ct. bar, 1968; asst. dist. atty. Dallas County (Tex.), 1950; mem. firm Biggers, Baker & Lloyd, Dallas, 1951-57; gen. counsel S.W. ter. Sears, Roebuck & Co., Dallas, 1957—; research fellow Southwestern Legal Found., 1960—. Mem. Drug Abuse Council Dallas, 1973. Mem. Tex. Retail Assn. (pres. 1976-77). Office: 1000 Belleview St Dallas TX 75295 Tel (214) 565-4766

GROBE, CHARLES STEPHEN, b. Columbus, Ohio, May 5, 1935; B.A., U. Calif. Los Angeles, 1957; J.D., Stanford, 1961. Admitted to Calif. bar, 1962; since practiced in Los Angeles, asso. firm Halstead and Crocker, 1963-66; individual practice law, 1966-70; partner firm Grobe, Reinstein, Freid & Katz, 1970-76; corporate partner Grobe & Bazar, 1976—; lectr. law, U. Calif. Los Angeles, 1972, Loma Linda U., 1971-76. Licensed C.P.A., Calif.; certified specialist taxation law, Calif. Bd. Legal Specialization. Mem. Am., Calif. Los Angeles, Beverly Hills, bar assns., Calif. Soc. C.P.A.'s., Nat. Health Lawyers Assn., Soc. Hosp. Attys. Am. Hosp. Assn. Author: Guide to Investing Pension and Profit-Sharing Trust Funds, 1973; Guardianship, Conservatorship and Trusts on Behalf of persons Who are Mentally Retarded - An Assessment of Current Applicable Laws in the State of California, 1974; Using an Individual Retirement Savings Plan and the Related Rollover Provisions of the Pension Reform Act of 1974, 1976; Guide to Setting Up a Group Term Life Insurance Program Under IRC Section 79, 1976. Office: 1880 Century Park E Los Angeles CA 90067 Tel (213) 553-4500

GROCE, JOSH HALBERT, b. Waxahachie, Tex., Aug. 10, 1901; A.B., Va. Mil. Inst., 1922; J.D., U. Tex., 1925. Admitted to Tex. bar, 1925, U.S. Supreme Ct. bar, 1950; practice law, Waxahachie, 1925-28, San Antonio, 1928—; mem. firm Groce, Locke & Hebdon. Fellow Am. Coll. Trial Lawyers; mem. Def. Research Inst. (pres. 1961-65, chmn. bd. 1965-66), Tex. State Bar (past chmn. ins. sect.), Nat. Assn. R.R. Trial Counsel (past v.p.), Am., San Antonio bar assns., Internat. Assn. Ins. Counsel, Fedn. Ins. Counsel, Asssn. Ins. Attys., Tex. Assn. Def. Cousnel, Phi Delta Phi. Mem. Tex. Law Rev. Home: 302 W Kings Hwy San Antonio TX 78212 Office: 2000 Frost Bank Tower San Antonio TX 78205 Tel (512) 225-3031

GRODSKY, IRVIN, b. Mobile, Ala., Sept. 12, 1946; B.A., Va. Mil. Inst., 1968; J.D. (Harlan Stone scholar), Columbia, 1971. Admitted to Ala. bar, 1971; asso. firm Feibelman, Silver & Grodsky, Mobile, 1973-75; individual practice law, Mobile, 1976—. Active Mobile County Alcoholism Rehab. and Edn., 1976—; bd. dirs. Mobile Chamber Music Soc., 1975—; bd. dirs., com. chmn. Dauphin St. Synagogue, Mobile. Mem. Am., Ala. bar assns., Comml. Law League, Trial Lawyers Assn. Am., Am. Judicature Soc. Office: Box 112 Mobile AL 36601 Tel (205) 433-3657

GROENING, WILLIAM ANDREW, b. Saginaw, Mich., Nov. 20, 1912; A.B., U. Mich., 1934, J.D., 1936; LL.D., Saginaw Valley State Coll., 1974. Admitted to Mich. bar, 1936, U.S. Supreme Ct. bar, 1954; atty. Dow Chem. Co., Midland, Mich., 1937—, asst. gen. counsel, 1951-67, gen. counsel, 1968-77, v.p., 1971—, spl. counsel, 1977—, mem. finance com., 1972-77, sec., dir. Dow Corning Corp., 1961—, Kartridg Pak Co., 1966—. Mem. Midland City Council, 1946-52; mayor City of Midland, 1950-52; chmn. bd. Saginaw Valley State Coll., 1963-73. Mem. Midland County (pres. 1951-52), Am. bar assns., State Bar Mich. (chmn. sect. antitrust law 1967-68), Am. Judicature Soc. (dir.), World Assn. Lawyers, Assn. Gen. Counsel. Home: 4204 Arbor Dr Midland MI 48640 Office: 2030 Dow Center Midland MI 48640 Tel (517) 636-1957

GROGAN, PHILLIP RAY, b. Bowling Green, Ky., Jan. 1, 1944; J.D., U. Ky., 1969. Admitted to Ky. bar, 1970; partner firm Garman & Grogan, Bowling Green, 1970-73; individual practice law, Bowling Green, 1973—; asst. commonwealth atty. 8th Jud. Dist. Ky., Warren County, 1972-76. Home and Office: 938 College St Bowling Green KY 42101 Tel (502) 781-5737

GROLLMAN, GEORGE GILBERT, b. Easton, Pa., May 21, 1911; A.B., Muhlenberg Coll., 1932; LL.B., Fordham U., 1938, J.D., 1975. Admitted to Pa. bar, 1940, N.Y. bar, 1945; closing atty. War Dept. N. Atlantic div., 1942-45; authorizer VA, 1945-47; individual practice law, 1947—; counsel Fordham U. Employees Assn., 1968-69. Active Community Chest, Easton, Pa., 1940-42; mem. Friends of N.Y. Philharmoic, Met. Opera Guild; sponsor Circle in the Sq., N.Y.C., 1976-77; mem. Murray Hill Com., N.Y.C., 1976-77. Mem. N.Y. State, Am. trial lawyers assns., N.Y.C. Assn. Trial Lawyers. Home: 220 Madison Ave New York City NY 10016 Office: 475 Fifth Ave New York City NY 10017 Tel (212) MU4-1414

GROMAN, ARTHUR, b. Los Angeles, Sept. 13, 1914; A.B., magna cum laude, U. So. Calif., 1936; J.D., Yale U., 1939. Admitted to Calif. bar, 1939, U.S. Supreme Ct. bar, 1971; gen. counsel office Dept. Treasury, Washington, 1939-41; chief counsel's office, IRS, Washington, 1941-42, div. counsel's office, N.Y.C., 1942-44; asso. firm Mitchell, Silberberg & Knuhl, Los Angeles, 1944-48, partner, 1948—; dir. Occidental Petroleum Corp., Los Angeles, 1957—; co-founder U. So. Calif. Tax Inst., 1948; bd. counselors U. So. Calif. Law Sch., 1970—; instr. law U. So. Calif. Pres., Calif. Inst. Cancer Research, 1974—; Los Angeles chmn., nat. v.p. Am. Jewish Com., 1966-69. Mem. Am., Calif., Los Angeles County, Beverly Hills bar assns.; fellow Am. Coll. Trial Lawyers. Contbr. articles to legal jours. Home: 520 Stonewood Dr Beverly Hills CA 90210 Office: 1800 Century Park E Los Angeles CA 90067 Tel (213) 553-5000

GROMEN, FREDERICK EDWARD, b. Martins Ferry, Ohio, Aug. 3, 1939; A.B., Wittenberg U., 1961; J.D., Ohio No. Coll. Law, 1966. Admitted to Ohio bar, 1966; asst. atty. gen. State of Ohio, Columbus, 1966-69; asso. firm Cinque, Banker and Linch, Bellaire, Ohio, 1969-71; partner firm Cinque, Banker, Linch, Gromen and White, Bellaire, 1971—. Mem. Bellaire Area C. of C., Am., Ohio, Belmont County bar assns., Ohio Acad. Trial Lawyers, Assn. Trial Lawyers Am. Office: 808 First National Bank Bldg Bellaire OH 43906 Tel (613) 676-2111

GRONER, BEVERLY ANNE, b. Des Moines, Jan. 31, 1922; student Drake U., 1939-40; LL.B., Catholic U., 1956; LL.B. (later J.D.), Washington Coll. Law, 1959. Admitted to Md. bar, 1959, D.C. bar, 1965, U.S. Supreme Ct. bar, 1963; mem. firm Groner & Groner, Bethesda, Md., 1962—; lectr. Montgomery Coll., Rockville, Md., 1972-73; chmn. Md. Gov.'s Commn. on Domestic Relations Laws, 1977—; mem. Md. Gov.'s Commn. to Study Implementation Equal Rights Amendment 1974—. Mem. faculty domestic relations div. Montgomery-Prince George's Continuing Legal Edn. Inst., 1974; guest lectr. Montgomery Coll. Adult Edn. Community Services Curriculum, 1976—, Mount Vernon Coll., 1976, Am. U. Washington Coll. Law, 1975. Fellow Am. Acad. Matrimonial Lawyers; mem. Md. (chmn. sect. council family and juvenile law 1975-77, 3d Appellate Jud. Circuit rep. 1977—), Montgomery County (chmn. membership com. 1970-71, chmn. domestic relations com. 1975-76), Am. (chmn. fee arbitration panel 1974-76) bar assns., D.C. Bar, Am. Judicature Soc., Am. U., Cath. U. alumni assns., Nat. Paraplegia Found. Contbr. to Md. Bar Jour. Home: 6710 Western Ave Chevy Chase MD 20015 Office: Suite 304 Perpetual Bldg 7401 Wisconsin Ave Bethesda MD 20014 Tel (301) 657-2828

GRONER, SAMUEL BRIAN, b. Buffalo, Dec. 27, 1916; A.B., Cornell U., 1937, LL.B. (J.D.), 1939; M.A. in Economics, Am. U., 1950. Admitted to N.Y. state bar, 1939, D.C. bar, 1952, Md. bar, 1953, U.S. Supreme Ct. bar, 1944; individual practice law, Buffalo, N.Y., 1939-40; atty-adv. U.S. Dept. Justice, Washington, D.C., 1946-53; asst. to commr. FCC, Washington, D.C., 1953; individual practice law, Md., and Washington, D.C., 1953-63; partner firm Groner, Stone & Greiger, Washington, 1955-57; partner firm Groner & Groner, Silver Spring, Bethesda, Md., 1959—; asst. counsel Naval Ship Systems Command, Washington, D.C., 1963-73; trial atty. Office Gen. Counsel Navy, Washington, D.C., 1973-74, asso. chief trial atty., 1974—; instr. Terrell Law Sch., Washington, D.C., 1948; mem. faculty U.S. Dept. Agr. Grad. Sch., 1973—. Active P.T.A., civic assns., Jewish Community Council, Community Chest. Mem. Am. (vice chmn. pub. contract law sec. com. on bds. contract appeals 1976—), Fed., Montgomery County, Md. bar assns., Bar Assn. D.C., Cornell Law Assn (pres. D.C. chpt. 1947-54), Govt. Adminstrv. Trial Lawyers Assn., Phi Beta Kappa. Contbr. articles to legal jours.; asso. editor Fed. Bar Jour., 1948-55. Home: 6710 Western Ave Chevy Chase MD 20015 Office: Office Gen Counsel Navy Washington DC 20360 Tel (202) 692-0990

GROOMS, HARLAN HOBART, JR., b. Birmingham, Ala., May 30, 1931; B.S., U. Ala., 1954, J.D., 1955. Admitted to Ala. bar, 1955, U.S. Supreme Ct. bar, 1965; asso. firm Spain, Gillon, Riley, Tate & Etheredge, 1958-65, partner, 1965—; Judge Adv. Gen., USMC, 1955—. Mem. Ala. Republican State Exec. Com.; past chmn. Birmingham Legal Aid Soc., bd. dirs. Aletheia House, Inc. Mem. Ala., Birmingham (exec. com; pres. 1977-78) bar assns., Internat. Assn. Ins. Counsel, Fed. Mediation and Conciliation Service and Arbitration Rev. Bd., Omicron Delta Kappa. Recipient Algernon Sydney Sullivan award U. Ala., 1955. Office: 1700 John Hand Bldg Birmingham AL 35203 Tel (205) 328-4100

GROSBY, ROBERT NACHMAN, b. N.Y.C., Jan. 13, 1927; A.B., Harvard, 1947; LL.D., Cornell U., 1950. Admitted to N.Y. bar, 1950, Conn. bar, 1950; U.S. Supreme Ct. bar, 1953, Bar Ct. Mil. Appeals, 1953; partner firm Grosby & Hohn, profl. corp. Norwalk, Conn.; clk. Conn. Ho. of Reps., 1957-58, counsel, 1963-65; part-time pub. defender Conn. Ct. Common Pleas, 1965-77. Mem. Norwalk (pres. 1976), Conn., Fed. bar assns. Home: East Rocks Rd Norwalk CT 06851 Office: 21 Isaac St Norwalk CT 06852 Tel (203) 866-4457

GROSE, CLINT JOHN, b. Kittson, Minn., Dec. 20, 1923; B.S. in Law, 1948, LL.B., 1950. Admitted to Minn. bar; sr. partner firm Grose, Von Holtum, Von Holtum, Sieben & Schmidt, Mpls. Mem. Am., Minn. (v.p.) trial lawyers assns., Minn. Bar Assn., Nat. Assn. Compensation Attys. (pres.). Contbr. articles to legal jours. Office: Suite 558 4940 Viking Dr Minneapolis MN 55435 Tel (612) 835-2575

GROSS, AVRUM M., b. N.Y.C., Feb. 25, 1936; B.A., Amherst Coll., 1957; J.D., U. Mich., 1960. Staff counsel Alaska Legis. Affairs Agy., 1960-61; asst. atty. gen., chief appellate sect. dept. law State of Alaska, Juneau, 1961-63, atty. gen., 1974—; asso. firm Faulkner, Banfield, Doogan, Gross & Holmes and predecessor, Juneau, 1963-64, partner, 1965-74; Mem. Alaska Supreme Ct. Criminal Rules Revision Com., 1973-75, chmn., 1973-74. Mem. Alaska Bar Assn. (gov. 1968-71, v.p. 1970-71). Office: Atty Gen Dept of Law 410 State Capitol 120 4th St Pouch K Juneau AK 99801*

GROSS, BAETY ONEAL, JR., b. Durahm, N.C., Nov. 18, 1947; B.A., Wofford Coll., 1969; J.D., U. S.C., 1972. Admitted to S.C. bar, 1972; asso. firm Younts, Reese & Cofield, Fountain Inn, S.C., 1973-74, firm William H. Gibbes, Columbia, S.C., 1974-75; partner firm Younts, Spivey & Gross, Fountain Inn, 1975—; judge Simpsonville (S.C.) Municipal Ct., 1976—. Mem. Am., Greenville County (S.C.) bar assns., S.C. Bar. Office: PO Box 566 Fountain Inn SC 29644 Tel (803) 862-2528

GROSS, DAVID BRYAN, b. Oxford, Miss., Apr. 16, 1921; B.S., U. Ala.; J.D., U. Miss. Admitted to Miss. bar, 1947, La. bar, 1946, Tex. bar, 1973; individual practice law, Laurel, Miss., 1947-54; with legal dept. Shell Oil Co., New Orleans, 1954-60, mgr. legal dept., Denver, 1969-71, office head legal dept., Houston, 1971-73, mgr. indsl. relations dept., Houston, 1973—; mem. Miss. Legislature, 1948-52. Bd. dirs. Meth. Hosp., New Orleans, 1965-69. Mem. Am., La., Miss., Tex. bar assns., Bus. Roundtable, Labor Policy Assn. Home: 214 Stonewall Jackson Conroe TX 77301 Office: PO Box 2463 Houston TX 77001 Tel (713) 220-3614

GROSS, ERNEST ARNOLD, b. N.Y.C., Sept. 23, 1906; S.B., Harvard, 1927, LL.B., 1931. Admitted to N.Y. bar, 1933; partner firm Curtis, Mallet-Prevost Colt & Mosle, N.Y.C., 1954-75, of counsel, 1975—; adj. prof. internat. law Fletcher Sch Internat. Law and Diplomacy, 1976; legal adviser Dept. State, Washington, 1947-48, asst. sec. of state, 1948-49; dept. U.S. rep. to UN, 1949-53. Trustee Carnegie Fund for Internat. Peace. Mem. Bar Assn. N.Y.C., Am. Bar Assn. Author: United Nations; Structure For Peace, 1962; contbr. numerous articles on fgn. affairs to legal jours. Home: 340 E 72d St New York City NY 10021 Office: 100 Wall St New York City NY 10021 Tel (212) 248-8111

GROSS, JAMES HOWARD, b. Springfield, Ohio, Sept. 21, 1941; B.A. summa cum laude, Ohio State U., 1963; LL.B., Harvard U., 1966. Admitted to Ohio bar, 1966, D.C. bar, 1975; asso. firm Vorys, Sater, Seymour & Pease, Columbus, Ohio, 1966-74, partner, 1975—, resident partner Washington office, 1975—; White House fellow, spl. asst. to sec. HUD, 1972-73. Trustee, officer Franklin County (Ohio) Mental Health Assn., 1972-75, recipient Distinguished Service award, 1975; trustee Ohio Assn. Mental Health, 1974-75. Mem. Fed., Ohio, D.C. bar assns. Home: 200 Vassar Pl Alexandria VA 22314 Office: 1701 K St NW Washington DC 20006 Tel (202) 296-2929

GROSS, JUSTIN ARTHUR, b. Berkeley, Calif., Sept. 9, 1932; student U. Calif. at Berkeley, 1951-53; LL.B., Golden Gate Coll., 1960. Admitted to Calif. bar, 1961; with Kaiser Industries Corp., Oakland, Calif., 1961-69; dir. trusts Pacific Maritime Assn., San Francisco, 1969—. Office: 635 Sacramento St San Francisco CA 94111 Tel (415) 362-7973

GROSS, MALCOLM JOSEPH, b. Allentown, Pa., Oct. 2, 1940; A.B. cum laude, Muhlenberg Coll., 1962; J.D., Villanova U., 1965. Admitted to Pa. bar, 1965; law clk to justice Pa. Supreme Ct., 1965-66; partner firm Brennen & Gross, Allentown, 1966-71; sr. partner firm Gross & Brown, Allentown, 1972-76, firm Gross, McGinley & McGinley, Allentown, 1976—; asst. pub. defender Lehigh County (Pa.), 1969-72; solicitor Lehigh County Children's Bur., 1973—; lectr. law Muhlenberg Coll., 1974—; mem. disciplinary bd. Supreme Ct. Pa., 1975—. Bd. dirs. YMCA, Allentown, 1972—; bd. dirs. Lehigh Valley Child Care, Inc., 1973—, pres., 1973-75. Mem. Pa. Soc., Pa., Lehigh County bar assns. Editor Vilanova Law Rev. 1965. Home: 2653 Allen St Allentown PA 18104 Office: 137 N 5th St PO Box 1398 Allentown PA 18105 Tel (215) 820-5450

GROSS, MARC STUART, b. N.Y.C., July 19, 1934; B.S. in Chem. Engring., Mass. Inst. Tech., 1955; J.D., George Washington U., 1959. Admitted to D.C. bar, 1959, N.Y. bar, 1960; patent examiner U.S. Patent Office, Washington, 1955-58; law clk. to judge U.S. Ct. Customs and Patent Appeals, Washington, 1958-59; asso. firm Sweedler & Zucker, N.Y.C., 1959-62; asso. firm Ostrolenk, Faber, Gerb & Soffen, N.Y.C., 1962-68, partner, 1968-72; individual practice law, N.Y.C., 1972-73; partner firm Hubbell, Cohen, Stiefel & Gross, N.Y.C., 1974—; lectr. Practising Law Inst., 1968—. Ednl. councillor Mass. Inst. Tech., bd. govs. N.Y. Alumni Center. Mem. Am. Bar Assn., Am., N.Y. State, N.J. patent law assns. Home: 3 Franklin Ct Ardsley NY 10502 Office: 551 Fifth Ave New York City NY 10017 Tel (212) 687-1360

GROSS, MAYNARD ARTHUR, b. Long Island, N.Y., July 11, 1940; B.A., Georgetown U., 1963; J.D. cum laude, U. Miami, 1967. Admitted to Fla. bar, 1967; with Dade County State Attys. Office, Miami, 1967-69; mem. firm Gross & Krause, Miami, 1969-73; individual practice law, Miami, 1973-76; partner firm Whitman, Wolfe & Gross, Miami, 1976—; prosecutor Town of Medley, Fla. Mem. Fla. Bar Assn., Comml. Law League. Home: 9149 SW 96th Ave Miami FL 33176 Office: 9595 N Kendall Dr Miami FL 33176 Tel (305) 279-7000

GROSS, REUBEN ELLIOT, b. N.Y.C., Aug. 6, 1914; A.B., City U. N.Y., 1935; J.D., Harvard, 1938, A.M., Wagner Coll., 1955. Admitted to N.Y. State bar, 1938, Israel bar, 1970, N.J. bar, 1976; individual practice law, S.I., N.Y., 1940-44, 45-68, 70—; mem. Israel Ministry of Communications, Jerusalem, 1970; pres. Freedom Fin. Co., Inc., S.I., 1967—; arbitrator Civil Ct. City of N.Y., 1974—. Mem. Richmond County Bar Assn. Home: 79 Howard Ave Staten Island NY 10301 Office: 30 Bay St Staten Island NY 10301 Tel (212) 447-8006

GROSS, RICHARD ALAN, b. Chgo., Jan. 6, 1949; B.A. (Horace Reed Baldwin fellow 1970), Wesleyan U., 1970; J.D., Harvard U. 1973. Admitted to Mass. bar, 1973; mng. atty. Boston Legal Assistance Project, 1973-75; asst. atty. gen., dep. chief Consumer Protection Div. Dept. Atty. Gen., Commonwealth Mass., Boston, 1975—, instr. Harvard U. Law Sch., 1976—. Office: One Ashburton Pl Boston MA 02108 Tel (617) 727-4475

GROSS, ROBERT NORMAN, b. Boston, Apr. 28, 1939; B.A., Norwich U., 1960; J.D. cum laude, Suffolk U., 1969. Admitted to Mass. bar, 1969; asst. dist. atty. Suffolk Dist. Atty., Boston, 1969-73; asso. firm Schair, Duquet & Gorfinkle, Braintree, Mass., 1973-75; partner firm Gross & Galvin, Weymouth, Mass., 1975—. Mem. Am., Mass., Norfolk County, Weymouth bar assns. Office: 49 Pleasant St South Weymouth MA 02190 Tel (617) 331-0200

GROSS, ROBERT WILLIAM, b. Sullivan, Ind., Sept. 9, 1947; A.B., DePauw U., 1969; J.D., Vanderbilt U., 1972. Admitted to Tenn. bar, 1972, Ind. bar, 1973; asst. on staff Gov. Tenn., 1971-72; clk. to judge U.S. Ct. Appeals 6th Dist., 1972-73; partner firm Krieg, Devault, Alexander & Capehart, Indpls., 1973—. Mem. Tenn., Ind., Am. bar assns. Office: One Indiana Sq Suite 2860 Indianapolis IN 46204 Tel (317) 636-4341

GROSS, SANFORD, b. Cleve., Nov. 29, 1940; B.B.A., Case Western Res. U., 1963, J.D., 1966. Admitted to Ohio bar, 1966, U.S. Dist. Ct. bar No. Dist. Ohio, 1967, U.S. Ct. Appeals bar 6th Circuit, 1976; asso. firm Metzenbaum, Gaines, Krupansky, Finley & Stern, Cleve., 1965-68; trial atty. U.S. Dept. Labor, Office of the Solicitor, Cleve., 1968-69, Office of Gen. Counsel, NLRB, Cleve., 1969-72; partner firm Rosenfeld & Gross, Cleve., 1972—; instr. legal research and writing Case Western Res. U., 1965; instr. continuing legal edn. program Ohio Legal Center, Inc., 1977. Mem. Cuyahoga County (Ohio) Republican Exec. Com., 1972—, Greater Cleve. Growth Assn. Mem. Fed., Ohio (award), Cleve. bar Rev., Indsl. Relations Research Assn., Order of Coif. Recipient Shelly Halpern award, 1964, Rebecca Grant Meml. award, 1965, award of merit Ohio Legal Center Inst., 1977. Home: 24920 Sittingbourne Ln Beachwood OH 44127 Office: 1326 Terminal Tower Cleveland OH 44114 Tel (216) 781-3434

GROSS, SEYMOUR, b. Cleve., Nov. 19, 1927; B.B.A., Case Western Res. U., 1949, LL.B., 1952, J.D., 1968. Admitted to Ohio bar, 1952; individual practice law, Cleve., 1952—. Mem. Cleveland Acad. Trial Attys. (v.p. 1977—), Assn. Trial Lawyers Am., Greater Cleve., Ohio State bar assns. Office: 636 Engineers Bldg Cleveland OH 44114 Tel (216) 696-5060

GROSS, STEVEN ROSS, b. N.Y.C., June 15, 1946; B.A. (Kellett fellow, Chanler fellow), Columbia, 1968, M.A., 1969; LL.B., Cambridge (Eng.) U., 1971; J.D., Yale, 1973. Admitted to N.Y. bar, 1974; asso. firm Debevoise, Plimpton, Lyons & Gates, N.Y.C., 1973—. Mem. Am. Bar Assn., Assn. Bar City N.Y., Phi Beta Kappa. Editor, Yale Law Jour., 1972-73. Office: Debevoise Plimpton Lyons Gates 299 Park Ave New York City NY 10017

GROSS, WILLIAM BARNES MARTIN, b. Chgo., Sept. 9, 1936; B.A., Amherst Coll., 1958; LL.B., Harvard U., 1961. Admitted to Ill. bar, 1961; asso. firm Martin, Craig, Chester & Sonnenschein, Chgo., 1961-68, partner, 1968—. Pres. sch. bd. dist. 181, Hinsdale, Ill. Mem. Am., Ill., Chgo. bar assns. Office: 115 S LaSalle St Chicago IL 60603 Tel (312) 368-9700

GROSSBERG, RICHARD MALCOLM, b. St. Louis, July 30, 1922; student Washington U., St. Louis, 1940, U. Calif. at Los Angeles, 1941-43, 46, Sorbonne, 1945-46; J.D., U. So. Calif., 1950. Admitted to Calif. bar, 1951, Fed. bar, 1951, U.S. Supreme Ct. bar, 1975; dep. legis. counsel State Calif., 1951-53; individual practice law, Sacramento, 1953-70, San Diego, 1971—. Mem. Calif. Democratic Central Com., 1954-55; chmn. Urban Govt. Commn., Sacramento, 1955-56. Mem. San Diego Trial Lawyers Assn., Mensa Internat. Home: 2625 Pirinpos Way #227 Carlsbad CA 92008 Office: 1168 Union St #202 San Diego CA 92101 Tel (714) 231-1042

GROSSE, WILBUR JACK, b. Cin., Apr. 3, 1923; J.D., Chase Coll. Law, 1962; M.B.A., Xavier U., 1954; LL.M., Case Western Res. U., 1969; LL.D., No. Ky. U., 1972. Admitted to Ohio bar, 1962, Ky. bar, 1972; prof. Chase Coll. Law, Cin., 1962-64, Clarkson Coll. Tech., Potsdam, N.Y., 1965-66; dean, prof. Chase Coll. Law, Cin. and Covington, Ky., 1966-68, 70-76; prof. Xavier U., 1968-70; individual practice law, Cin., 1962-64. Bd. dirs. Pro-Seniors, Cin., 1974-76; mem. adv. com. Family Service, Covington, 1975-76. Mem. Am., Ky., Ohio bar assns. Home: 837 Wakefield Dr Cincinnati OH 45226 Office: 1401 Dixie Hwy Covington KY 41011 Tel (606) 292-5343

GROSSMAN, AARON DAVID, b. Bridgeport, Conn., Dec. 2, 1941; B.A., U. Mich., 1963, J.D., 1966. Admitted to Calif. bar, 1966; atty. U.S. AEC, Berkeley, Calif., 1966-69, Singer Bus. Machines, San Leandro, Calif., 1969-71; gen. counsel U.S. Leasing Real Estate Investors, San Francisco, 1971-76, The Gap Stores, Inc., Burlingame, Calif., 1976—. Licensed real estate broker. Office: 875 Mahler Rd Barlingame CA 94010 Tel (415) 692-5450

GROSSMAN, ALLAN IRVIN, b. Bklyn., Oct. 13, 1945; B.S., Bklyn. Coll., 1966; J.D., Harvard, 1969. Admitted to Calif. bar, 1970; clerk to Judge John W. Kern III, Dist. Columbia Ct. Appeals, Washington, 1969-70; asso. firm Sheppard, Mullin, Richter & Hampton, Los Angeles, 1970-76, mem. 1976—. Mem. Am., Los Angeles County bar assns., Calif. State Bar. Editor: Harvard Law Review, 1967-69. Office: 333 S Hope St 48th Floor Los Angeles CA 90071 Tel (213) 620-1780

GROSSMAN, EMILE, b. Berkeley, Calif., Feb. 26, 1904; J.D., U. Calif., 1927. Admitted to Calif. bar, 1927, U.S. Supreme Ct. bar, 1970; asst. legis. counsel, Sacramento, 1929; asso. firm Burbank & Spence, San Francisco, 1927-32, H. Boyarsky, Oakland, Calif., and M.F. Ryan, Oakland, 1932-60. Mem. State Bar Calif. Tel (415) 832-8286

GROSSMAN, MARSHALL BRUCE, b. Omaha, Mar. 24, 1939; student U. Calif., Los Angeles, 1957-59; B.S. Law, U. So. Calif., 1964, LL.B., 1964. Admitted to Calif. bar, 1965; asso. firm Schwartz, Alschuler & Grossman, Los Angeles, 1965-67, partner, 1967—; lectr. in field. Chmn. com. on law and legis. Los Angeles Jewish Fedn., 1973-74. Mem. Am., Los Angeles, Beverly Hills (gov. 1971-76, pres. Barristers 1972-73) bar assns., Assn. Bus. Trial Attys. (gov. 1974-75), Order of Coif, Tau Delta Phi, Phi Alpha Delta. Office: 1880 Century Park E 1212 Los Angeles CA 90067 Tel (213) 277-1226

GROSSMAN, MORTON, b. Bklyn., Dec. 25, 1926; B.S., Coll. City N.Y., 1948; LL.B., N.Y. U., 1950. Admitted to N.Y. bar, 1950, U.S. Supreme Ct. bar, 1957; mng. atty. Emanuel Silverman, N.Y.C., 1950-55; individual practice law, N.Y.C., 1955-70; partner firm Grossman & Zafrin, N.Y.C., 1970—. Past mem. law and legis. com. Nat. Council Young Israel; mem. bd. edn. Rabbi Harry Halpern Day Sch.; adv. com. to bd. trustees E. Midwood Jewish Center, Bklyn. Mem. Bklyn. Bar, Bronx County Bar Assn., N.Y. U. Law Alumni Assn. Office: 170 Broadway New York City NY 10038 Tel (212) 962-1276

GROSSMAN, ORIN GENE, b. Blyn., July 15, 1941; A.B., N.Y. U., 1963; LL.B., U. Tex., 1968. Admitted to Nev. bar, 1969, U.S. Supreme Ct. bar, 1973; individual practice law, Las Vegas. Nev., 1971—. Mem. State Bar Nev. (chmn. securities div. 1975). Office: 401 S Third St Suite 301 Las Vegas NV 89101 Tel (702) 382-3134

GROSSMAN, PAUL, b. Palo Alto, Calif., Aug. 26, 1939; B.A., Amherst Coll., 1961; LL.B., Yale, 1964. Admitted to Calif. bar, 1965; partner firm Paul, Hastings, Janofsky & Walker, Los Angeles, 1964—; instr. law U. So. Calif., 1975—. Bd. dirs. Los Angeles chpt. ARC, 1976—; trustee Greater Los Angeles Zoo Assn., 1974—. Mem. Am., Los Angeles County bar assns., Legal Aid Found. Los Angeles (dir.). Co-author: Employment Discrimination Law, 1976. Office: 555 S Flower St Los Angeles CA 90071 Tel (213) 489-4000

GROSSMAN, RHEA PINCUS, b. Bklyn., July 25, 1941; A.B., U. Miami, 1965, J.D., 1965. Admitted to Fla. bar, 1965; individual practice law, Miami Beach, Fla., 1965-68; judge indsl. claims Circuit Ct., Miami, 1970—. Mem. Bus. & Profl. Women's Clubs (Miami chpt.) Conf. Circuit Judges (exec. com. 1975-76, chmn. rules com. 1975-76, chmn. trial judges handbook 1975-76). Office: 416 Dade County Ct House Miami FL 33130 Tel (305) 579-5482

GROTH, RAYMOND CLARENCE, b. West Bend, Wis., Jan. 5, 1947; B.B.A., U. Wis., 1969; J.D., Yale U., 1972. Admitted to N.Y. bar, 1973; asso. firm Cravath, Swaine & Moore, N.Y.C., 1972—. Office: One Chase Manhattan Plaza New York City NY 10005 Tel (212) 422-3000

GROUT, ROBERT WAYNE, b. Memphis, Nov. 2, 1944; B.A. in Econs., Vanderbilt U., 1966; LL.B., U. Va., 1969, U.S. Supreme Ct. bar, 1975; partner firm Troutman, Sanders, Lockerman & Ashmore and predecessor, Atlanta, 1969—. Bd. stewards Peachtree Rd. United Meth. Ch., Atlanta, 1976. Mem. Am., Atlanta bar assns., Lawyers Club of Atlanta. Home: 4885 Westfalia Ct NE Atlanta GA 30342 Office: 1400 Candler Bldg Atlanta GA 30303 Tel (404) 658-8049

GROVE, KALVIN MYRON, b. Chgo., Aug. 27, 1937; B.A., U. Mich., 1958; J.D., DePaul U., 1961. Admitted to Ill. bar, 1961, Fla. bar, 1961; U.S. Supreme Ct. bar, 1971; field atty. NLRB, Tampa, Fla., 1962-63, Miami, Fla., 1963-64, Chgo., 1964-65; mem. manpower adv. com. Gov. Ill., 1966-68; mem. firm Lederer Fox and Grove, Chgo.; arbitrator Am. Arbitration Assn., Fed. Mediation and Conciliation Service. Mem. Ill. State, Am. bar assns., The Fla. Bar, Am. Judicature Soc. Contbr. articles to profl. jours. Home: 3846 Medford Circle Northbrook IL 60062 Office: 233 S Wacker Dr Suite 7916 Chicago IL 60606 Tel (312) 876-0500

GROVE, RUSSELL SINCLAIR, JR., b. Marietta, Ga., Dec. 25, 1939; B.S., Ga. Inst. Tech., 1963; LL.B. with distinction, Emory U., 1964. Admitted to Ga. Supreme Ct. bar, 1965, U.S. Supreme Ct. bar, 1971; Fulbright research grantee U. Melbourne (Australia) Faculty of Law, 1965-66; asso. firm Smith, Currie & Hancock, Atlanta, 1966-67; partner firm Binford, Joiner & Grove, Atlanta, 1967-68; asso. firm Hansell, Post, Brandon & Dorsey, Atlanta, 1968-72, partner, 1972—. Mem. So. Council on Internat. Pub. Affairs, Atlanta Com. on Fgn. Relations, Community Relations Council, all Atlanta. Mem. Am., Ga., Atlanta bar assns., Am. Judicature Soc., Omicron Delta Kappa. Editor-in-chief Jour. Pub. Law, 1963-64. Office: 3300 1st Nat Bank Tower Atlanta GA 30303 Tel (404) 581-8000

GROVER, THOMAS GEORGE, b. Fond du Lac, Wis., Dec. 15, 1944; B.S. in Bus. Adminstrn., Marquette U., Wis., 1968, J.D., 1972. Admitted to Wis. bar, 1972; asso. firm Gwin & Fetzner, Hudson, Wis., 1972-73, firm Fetzner Law Offices, 1973-74; partner firm Winter & Grover, Shawano, Wis., 1974-76; county judge Br. 2 Shawano-Menonine County Ct., Shawano, Wis., 1976—. Vice pres. Shawano County Arts Council, 1975—; bd. govs. Mielke Theatre, 1975—; chmn. profl. div. Shawano United Way, 1974—, sec., 1977—, bd. dirs. Mem. Wis., Shawano County bar assns., Wis. Young Layers Assn. dir. 1975), Shawano Jr. C. of C. (dir. 1974-75, v.p. 1973-74). Home: RTE 2 Box 197 Shawano WI 54116 Office: Courthouse Shawano WI 54166 Tel (715) 526-2978

GROVES, JAMES KIRK, b. Grand Junction, Colo., Aug. 29, 1910; A.B., U. Colo., 1932, LL.B., 1935. Admitted to Colo. bar, 1935; practiced in Grand Junction, 1935-68; justice Colo. Supreme Ct., 1968—. Mem. Am. (ho. of dels. 1958—, chmn. 1972-74), Colo. (award of Merit), Denver, Arapahoe County (Colo.), Mesa County (Colo.) bar assns., Order of Coif. Recipient William Lee Knous award U. Colo., 1969. Contbr. articles to legal jours. Home: 6814 S Detroit Circle Littleton CO 80122 Office: State Capitol Denver CO 80203 Tel (303) 892-2417

GRUENISEN, ALLAN GEORGE, b. Oshkosh, Wis., Dec. 19, 1919; Ph.B., U. Wis., 1944, J.D., 1946. Admitted to Wis. bar; exec. v.p. Am. Standard Ins. Co. Wis., Madison, 1960-65, dir., sec., v.p. legal dept., 1965—; sec., v.p. legal, dir. Am. Family Ins. Group, Madison, 1965—. Dir. Wis., Minn. Med. Malpractice Plan, Wis., Minn. Ins. Insolvency Bd.; mem. Wis. Gov.'s Task Force No Fault Ins. Mem. Am. Bar Assn., Internat. Assn. of Ins. Counsel, Ins. Alliance (chmn. 1969-70, 1975), State Bar Wis., Nat. Assn. Ind. Insurers (past chmn. com. auto repair costs, gen. liability markets). Home: 6437 Antietam Ln Madison WI 53707 Office: 3099 E Washington Ave Madison WI 53704 also Box 7430 Madison WI 53707 Tel (608) 249-2111

GRUNDHOEFER, MARVIN LANDY, b. St. Paul, Aug. 19, 1927; B.A., Coll. St. Thomas, 1948; LL.B., St. Paul Coll. Law, 1952, J.D., 1969. Admitted to Minn. bar, 1952; individual practice law, Northfield, Minn., 1952—; asst. atty. Rice County (Minn.), 1966-68; lawyer mem. rev. bd. Cambridge (Minn.) State Hosp., 1970—; spl. municipal judge City of Northfield, 1959-65. Mayor, Northfield, 1968-72. Mem. Rice County, Minn. bar assns., Northfield C. of C. (pres. 1962). Home: 408 College St Northfield MN 55057 Office: 319 Division St Box 7 Northfield MN 55057 Tel (507) 645-5644

GRUNFELD, DAVID IRA, b. Phila., June 23, 1943; B.S., Lehigh U., 1965; J.D., U. Pa., 1968. Admitted to Pa. bar, 1968, U.S. Supreme Ct. bar, 1972; asso. firm Steinberg, Greenstein, Gorelick & Price, Phila., 1968-73, partner firm, 1973—. Mem. Pa., Phila., Am. bar assn., Jaycees (pres. Phila., 1975-76), Tau Epsilon Rho. Recipient Outstanding Young Man of Am. Award, 1973; editor of book revs. The Legal Intelligencer, 1973-75. Home: 124 Shasta Rd Plymouth Meeting PA 19462 Office: 818 Widener Bldg Philadelphia PA 19107 Tel (215) 564-3880

GRUSH, JULIUS SIDNEY, b. Los Angeles, Dec. 4, 1937; B.S. in Bus. Adminstrn., U. Calif., Los Angeles, 1960; LL.B., Southwestern U., 1964. Admitted to Calif. bar, 1965; city atty. Los Angeles, 1965-67; partner firm Morton & Grush, Los Angeles, 1967-68, Salute, Grush & Segalove, Los Angeles, 1968-72; individual practice law, Los Angeles, 1972—; judge pro tem Los Angeles Jud. Dist., Van Nuys. Mem. Calif., Los Angeles, Beverly Hills bar assns. Office: 1880 Century Park E Suite 817 Los Angeles CA 90067 Tel (123) 553-4337

GRUSON, MICHAEL, b. Berlin, Germany, Sept. 17, 1936; LL.B., U. Mainz (Germany), 1962; M.C.L., Columbia, 1963, LL.B., 1965; Dr. Law, Freie Universitaet, Berlin, 1966. Admitted to N.Y. bar, 1969; asso. firm Shearman & Sterling, N.Y.C., 1966-72, partner, 1973—; mem. faculty Legal Aspects of Internat. Bus. Transactions for Latin Am. Attys., U. Ill., Urbana. Bd. dirs. Deutsche Sprachschule N.Y., Inc. Mem. Assn. Bar City N.Y., Am., N.Y. bar assns., Am. Soc. Internat. Law, Deutsche Gesellschaft für Rechtsvergleichung. Author: Die Beduerfniskompetenz, 1967; also articles. Office: 53 Wall St New York City NY 10005 Tel (212) 483-1000

GUANDOLO, JOHN, b. Conway, Pa., Sept. 11, 1919; A.B. in Econs., U. Ill., 1940; J.D., U. Md., 1943, J.D., 1969. Admitted to D.C. bar, 1944, Md. bar, 1952, Ill. bar, 1956, Mo. bar, 1962; U.S. Supreme Ct. bar, 1949; trial atty. antitrust div. U.S. Dept. Justice, Washington, 1947-56; gen. atty. Rock Island R.R., 1956-57; practice law, Washington, 1957-62; commerce atty. M.P. R.R., 1962-63; partner firm MacDonald and McInerny, Washington, 1963—; lectr., Am. U., 1968-73. Mem. Am., Fed., D.C. bar assns., Motor Carriers Lawyers Assn., Assn. ICC Practitioners (pres. 1976-77), World Peace Through Law. Author: Transportation Law, 1965, 73; co-author: Regulation of Transportation, 1964, Transportation Regulation, 1972; co-author, author vols. of Federal Procedure Forms, 1949, 3 vol. edit., 1961, author supplements, 1950-58; contbr. book chpts.; editor-in-chief ICC Practitioners Jour., 1959-75. Home: 10905 Rosemont Dr Rockville MD 20852 Office: 1000 6th St NW Washington DC 20036 Tel (202) 783-8131

GUARINO, ALFRED A., b. White River Junction, Vt., June 14, 1914; LL.B. cum laude, Boston U., 1938. Admitted to Vt. bar, 1938; individual practice law, 1938-42, 46-70; sr. partner firm Guarino & Bean, White River Junction, 1970—; dep. state's atty. Windsor County, 1939-40; judge Hartford Municipal Ct., 1947-51; legal agent Town of Hartford. Moderator Town of Hartford, (Vt.), 1951-66, trustee pub. funds, 1972—; dir. Hartford Sch. Dist., 1961-65. Fellow Am. Probate Coll.; mem. Am., Vt., Windsor County bar assns. Home: 5 Half Penny Rd White River Junction VT 05001 Office: 28 N Main St White River Junction VT 05001 Tel (802) 295-2575

GUARINO, PATRICK HAROLD, JR., b. N.Y.C., Nov. 5, 1932; B.A., Coll. City N.Y., 1959; J.D., Bklyn. Law Sch., 1961. Admitted to N.Y. bar, 1962; individual practice law, Bronx, N.Y., 1962—; asst. counsel N.Y. State Assembly Housing Com., 1975-76; counsel, advisor Simpson St. Devel. Assn., 1970—; New Community Democratic Club, 1970—. Mem. Southeast Bronx Community Orgn., Inc., 1973—; vice chmn. N.Y. Center for Ethnic Affairs, 1975—. Mem. Bronx County Bar Assn., Colombian Lawyers Assn. Office: 2125 Williamsbridge Rd New York City NY 10461 Tel (212) 823-1212

GUARNIERI, DONALD LEWIS, b. Warren, Ohio, May 8, 1924; B.A., Hiram Coll., 1956; LL.B., Cleve. State U., 1960, LL.M., 1963, J.D., 1965. Admitted to Ohio bar, 1960; asso. firm Guarnieri and Secrest, Warren, 1960—. Mem. Trumbull County, Ohio, Am. bar assns., Am. Judicature Soc. Office: 151 E Market St Warren OH 44481

GUARNIERI, FRED RAYMOND, b. Niles, Ohio, May 2, 1911; A.B., Cath. U. Am.; LL.B., Case Western Res. U. Admitted to Ohio bar, 1934; practice law, Warren, Ohio; asst. prosecutor, 1950-52. Home: 235 Bonnie Brae St NE Warren OH 44483 Office: 140 E Market St Warren OH 44481 Tel (206) 395-6402

GUBBRUD, JOHN DEXTER, b. Sioux Falls, S.D., June June 23, 1941; B.B.A., U. S.D., 1963, J.D., 1966. Admitted to S.D. bar, 1966; asso. firm Christenson & Christenson, Elk Point, S.D S.D., 1966-67; partner firm Beck & Gubbrud, Alcester, S.D., 1967—. Mem. S.D. Task Force on R.R. Policy, 1974—. Mem. Am., S.D. (real property probate and trust com.) bar assns. Home: Alcester SD 57001 Office: POB 97 Alcester SD 57001 Tel (605) 934-2140

GUBLER, MARION EMIL, b. St. George, Utah, June 29, 1930; B.S., U. Utah, 1958, J.D., 1960. Admitted to Utah bar, 1960, Calif. bar, 1962; clk. to chief justice Supreme Ct. Utah, 1960; tax atty. U.S. Treasury Dept., Los Angeles, 1961-63; asso. firm Rogan & Radding, Burbank, Calif., 1963-73; judge Burbank Municipal Ct., 1973—, presiding judge, 1975—; mem. Burbank Lawyers' Reference and Legal Aid Com., 1966-73. Bus. chmn. United Crusade, City of Burbank, 1966; mem. Bi-centenial Com. City of Glendale, 1976. Mem. Calif. Judges Assn., Los Angeles County Municipal Ct. Judges Assn., Burbank Bar Assn. (sec. 1973). Home: 1362 Highland Ave Glendale CA 91202 Office: 300 E Olive Ave PO Box 750 Burbank CA 91503 Tel (213) 842-2171

GUBLER, V. GRAY, b. Santa Clara, Utah, Jan. 11, 1910; B.A., U. Utah, 1932, LL.D., 1935. Admitted to Nev. bar, 1936; asst. dist. atty. Clark County (Nev.), 1941-43, dist. atty., 1943-47; practice law, Las Vegas, Nev., 1947—. Pres., Clark County chpt. March of Dimes, 1957; supt. Las Vegas 6th Ward Sunday sch. Ch. of Jesus Christ of Latter-day Saints, 1966, 67, supt. Las Vegas E. Stake Sunday Sch., 1968-70. Mem. Nev. (pres. 1955), Am., Clark County (pres. 1942) bar assns., Am. Coll. Probate Counsel, Order of Coif, Tau Kappa Alpha, Phi Kappa Phi. Home: 1139 S 5th Pl Las Vegas NV 89104 Office: 300 E Carson Suite 601 Las Vegas NV 89101 Tel (702) 382-4343

GUBOW, LAWRENCE, b. Detroit, Jan. 10, 1919; A.B., U. Mich., 1940, LL.B., 1950. Admitted to Mich. bar, 1951; asso. firm Rosin and Kobel, Detroit, 1951-53; U.S. atty. for Eastern Dist. Mich., Detroit, 1961-68; judge U.S. Dist. Ct., Detroit, 1968—; dir. of investigations Mich. Corp. and Securities Commn., 1953, dep. commr., 1953-56, commr., 1956-61. Mem. Am., Mich., Detroit bar assns., Am. Judicature Soc. Home: 4397 Sunningdale Dr Bloomfield Hills MI 48013 Office: 740 Federal Bldg Detroit MI 48226 Tel (313) 226-7950

GUEDRY, JAMES WALTER, b. Morgan City, La., Jan. 7, 1941; A.B. magna cum laude, Georgetown U., 1962. postgrad. U. Brussels, 1962-63; LL.B., U. Va., 1966. Admitted to N.Y. bar, 1967; asso. firm Lord, Day & Lord, N.Y.C., 1966-76; counsel Internat. Paper Co., N.Y.C., 1976—. Mem. Assn. Bar City N.Y. Home: 79 Charles St New York City NY 10014 Office: 220 E 42d St New York City NY 10017 Tel (212) 490-6437

GUENTHER, JACK EGON, b. San Antonio, Dec. 14, 1934; B.B.A., U. Tex. at Austin, 1956; LL.B. magna cum laude, St. Mary's U., 1959; LL.M. in Taxation, N.Y. U., 1960. Admitted to Tex. bar, 1959, U.S. Supreme ct. bar, 1962; practiced in San Antonio, 1960—; asso. firm Cox, Smith, Smith, Hale & Guenther and predecessors, 1961—, partner, 1965—; adj. prof. St. Mary's U., San Antonio, 1961-65. Mem. San Antonio, Tex., Am. bar assns., Tex. Soc. C.P.A.'s. Office: 500 Nat Bank Commerce Bldg San Antonio TX 78205 Tel (512) 224-4281

GUENZER, PHILIP JOSEPH, b. Cinc., Apr. 2, 1939; B.M.E., Cornell U., 1961; LL.B., U. Md., 1966. Admitted to Md. bar, 1966, D.C. bar, 1973; engr. and accountant Westinghouse, Balt., 1961-70; partner firm Wonneman, Styles & McConkey, Arbutus, Md., 1970-73; asso. firm William Wilson Bratton, Elkton, Md., 1973-76; individual practice law, Elkton, 1976—; asst prof. bus. Catonsville (Md.) Community Coll., 1970-73. Dist. dir. Manpower; officer Cecil County council Boy Scouts Am. Mem. Md., Cecil County, 2d Jud. Circuit bar assns. Office: 146 E Main St Elkton MD 21921 Tel (301) 398-9090

GUERNSEY, HUGH GALE, b. Plano, Iowa, Aug. 10, 1892; B.A., U. Iowa, 1916, LL.B., 1920. Admitted to Iowa bar, 1920; county atty. Appanoose County (Iowa), 1932-36; mem. Iowa State Senate, 1936-40; partner firm Guernsey & Drake, and predecessors, Centerville, Iowa, 1939—. Mem. Am., Iowa, Appanoose, 8th Jud. Dist. bar assns. Home: 610 Park Ave Centerville IA 52544 Office: 303 W State St Centerville IA 52544 Tel (515) 856-8624

GUERNSEY, JOHN THOMAS, b. Fostoria, Ohio, July 23, 1917; A.B., U. Mich., 1938, J.D., 1940. Admitted to Ohio bar, 1940; practiced in Lima, Ohio, 1940-57; judge Ct. Appeals, 3d Appellate Jud. Dist. of Ohio, 1957—, presiding judge, 1961-63, 67-69, 73-75; sec. Cts. of Appeals of Ohio, 1966, chief justice, 1967, sr. judge, 1975—; asst. pros. atty. Allen County (Ohio), 1949-57. Mem. Ohio Jud. Conf., Ohio, Allen County bar assns., Am. Judicature Soc., Inst. Jud. Adminstrn. Home: 2845 Fort Amanda Rd Lima OH 45805 Office: Ct of Appeals Courthouse Lima OH 45801 Tel (419) 223-1861

GUERRI, WILLIAM GRANT, b. Higbee, Mo., Mar. 30, 1921; A.B., Central Meth. Coll., Fayette, Mo., 1943; LL.B., Columbia, 1946. Admitted to N.Y. State bar, 1946, Mo. bar, 1947, U.S. Supreme Ct. bar, 1960; partner firm Thompson & Mitchell, St. Louis, 1956—; dir. Pott Industries Inc., St. Louis, 1963—. Bd. dirs. St. Louis Heart Assn., 1963—, chmn., 1972-73. Mem. Am., Mo., St. Louis, N.Y.C. bar assns., Am. Law Inst., Am. Judicature Soc. Bd. editors Columbia Law Rev., 1945-46. Home: 1993 Windmoor Pl St Louis MO 63131 Office: Thompson & Mitchell 1 Mercantile Center St Louis MO 63101 Tel (314) 231-7676

GUESS, WILLIAM MARION, b. Atlanta, Oct. 16, 1907; LL.B., Emory U., 1931. Admitted to Ga. bar, 1931; individual practice law, Atlanta, 1931-59. Mem. Stone Mountain (Ga.) City Council, 1937-39, 54-56; city atty., Stone Mountain, 1931-76, mayor, 1940-44; judge recorder's Ct. of DeKalb County (Ga.), 1967-76. Mem. Ga. Bar Assn. Home and Office: 5417 Park Circle Stone Mountain GA 30083

GUEST, MICHAEL KURT, b. Ypsilanti, Mich., Apr. 14, 1949; A.B. with distinction and honors, Ind. U., 1971, J.D. cum laude, 1974. Admitted to Ind. bar, 1974, also dist. and circuit bars; mem. firm McHale, Cook & Welch, P.C., Indpls., 1974—. Mem. Am. Judicature Soc., Am., Ind., Indpls. bar assns., Phi Beta Kappa, Phi Eta Sigma. Note editor Ind. Law JOur., 1973-74; contbr. article to legal jour. Office: Chamber of Commerce Bldg Indianapolis IN 46204 Tel (317) 634-7588

GUEST, PAUL IVINS, b. Camden, N.J., May 2, 1916; A.B., Ursinus Coll., 1933, LL.D., 1972; J.D., U. Pa., 1941. Admitted to Pa. bar, 1942; since practiced in Phila., asso. firm Newbourg & Grubb, 1941-49, partner Newbourg, Grubb & Junkin, 1950-54, Grubb, Guest & Littleton, 1955-65, Grubb & Guest, 1965-67, Grubb, Guest & Greene, 1967-71, Guest & Greene, 1972—; sec., dir. Irwin & Leighton, Inc., Bickley Furnaces, Inc., Mira-Ball, Inc.; dir. Delaware Fund Group, Phila. Gear Corp., Phila Mixers Corp., Whitins Patterson Co., Inc., Plasaica Co., Inc. Trustee Methodist Hosp., 1952—, pres., 1960—; pres. bd. dirs. Phila. Hosp. Services, Inc., 1962—; bd. dirs. Delaware Valley Hosp. Council, 1964-70, 72—, chmn., 1973—; bd. dirs. Hosp. Assn. Pa., 1966-69, 73—; 1st. v.p. Ursinus Coll., 1969—; bd. dirs., v.p. Russell C. Ball Found. Mem. Pa., Phila., Am. bar assns. Bus. mgr. The Shingle, 1958-67, editor, 1968-69. Home: 1316 Colton Rd Gladwyne PA 19035 Office: Fidelity Bldg Philadelphia PA 19109 Tel (215) 735-6636

GUEVARA, ANDREW R., b. El Paso, Tex., Aug. 23, 1941; A.B. in Econs., Georgetown U., 1963; LL.B., U. Tex., 1967. Admitted to Tex. bar, 1967; partner firm Guevara, Rebe & Baumann, El Paso, 1968—; sec., dir. Continental Nat. Bank, Mission Fed. Savs. & Loan Assn. Vice pres. Goodwill Industries, El Paso, 1972. Mem. Tex., El Paso bar assns., El Paso bar assns., El Paso C. of C., El Paso Bd. Realtors (past pres.). Office: PO Box 2009 El Paso TX 79950 also 601 N Mesa St Suite A El Paso TX 79901 Tel (915) 544-6646

GUGGENHEIM, EVE B., b. Stuttgart, Ger., June 22, 1928; B.A., Westminster Coll., 1949; M.S., Columbia, 1952; J.D., U. Toledo, 1967. Admitted to Ohio bar, 1967, Pa. bar, 1969; individual practice law, Pitts., 1971—. Home: 201 Grant St Sewickley PA 15143 Office: 1425-A Grant Bldg Pittsburgh PA 15219 Tel (412) 288-9012

GUGGENHEIM, MALVINA HALBERSTAM, b. Kempno, Poland, May 2, 1937; came to U.S., 1947, naturalized, 1952; B.A. cum laude, Bklyn. Coll., 1957; J.D. (Kent scholar, Stone scholar), Columbia, 1961, M.Internat. Affairs, 1964. Admitted to N.Y. State bar, 1962, U.S. Supreme Ct. bar, 1966, Calif. bar, 1968; law clk. Fed. Dist. Ct., So. Dist. N.Y., 1961-62; research asso. Columbia Sch. Law, 1962-63; asst. dist. atty. N.Y. County, 1963-67; individual practice law, Los Angeles, 1967-69; sr. atty. Nat. Legal Program on Health Problems of the Poor, U. Calif., Los Angeles, 1969-70; prof. Loyola U. Law Sch., Los Angeles, 1970-76; vis. prof. U. Va., 1975-76, U. So. Calif., 1972-73, U. Tex. summer 1974; prof. law Benjamin N. Cardoza Sch. Law, Yeshiva U., 1976—. Mem. Am., N.Y., Calif. bar assns., Am. Soc. Internat. Law, Columni Law Alumni Assn., Phi Beta Kappa. Contbr. articles to legal jours. Home: 4940 Goodridge Ave Riverdale NY 10471 Office: 55 Fifth Ave New York City NY 10003 Tel (212) 255-5600

GUGLIELMINO, ROSARIO JOSEPH, b. Buenos Aires, Argentina, Apr. 3, 1911; came to U.S., 1920, naturalized, 1932; A.B. with honors, Cornell U., 1934, J.D., 1936. Admitted to N.Y. State bar, 1936; individual practice law, Rochester, N.Y., 1936—; exec. dir. and counsel Police Adv. Bd., 1963-70; counsel Eye Bank Assn. Am., 1963-70, Assn. Blind of Rochester and Monroe County, Inc., 1975—. Mem. bd. visitors Albion State Tng. Sch. and Western Reformatory for Women, 1956-66; founder, pres. Rochester Eye and Human Parts Banks, Inc., 1952, pres. emeritus, 1954—; founder, pres. Eye Bank Assn. Am., 1961-63; pres. Children's Meml. Scholarship Fund., 1958-60; mem. Rochester Council State Commn. Against Discrimination, 1956-66; bd. dirs. Assn. Blind of Rochester and Monroe County, Inc., 1973—. Mem. Monroe County (pres. 1969), N.Y. State, Am. bar assns., N.Y. State Trial Lawyers Assn., Am. Judicature Soc., Phi Beta Kappa, Phi Kappa Phi. Named Citizen of Year Valguarnera Soc., 1977; recipient Heise award Eye Bank Assn. Am., 1975. Home: 68 Fairlane Dr Rochester NY 14626 Office: 925 Crossroads Bldg Rochester NY 14614 Tel (716) 454-2596

GUGLIELMINO, RUSSELL JOHN, b. Rochester, N.Y., July 29, 1940; B.A., Cornell U., 1965, J.D., 1968. Admitted to N.Y. bar, 1968; asso. firm Reavis & McGrath, N.Y.C., 1968-74, partner, 1974—. Trustee Franklin Twp. (N.J.) Pop Warner, Inc., 1973—, treas., 1973-74; exec. v.p. N.J. Jaycees, 1975-76; trustee N.J. Jaycees Found., 1976—. Mem. Am., N.Y. State bar assns., Cornell Law Assn. Named Outstanding Project Chmn., Franklin Twp. Jaycees, 1973, Outstanding Chpt. Officer, 1974; Outstanding Chpt. Pres. N.J. Jaycees, 1975; editor, bus. mgr. Cornell Law Rev., 1967-68. Home: 6 Denise Ct Somerset NJ 08873 Office: 345 Park Ave New York City NY 10022 Tel (212) 269-7600

GUITAR, EARL BEAL, JR., b. San Angelo, Tex., Nov. 29, 1929; B.A. in Econs. with honors, U. of the South, 1951; J.D., U. Tex., 1957. Admitted to Tex. bar, 1957, Okla., bar, 1958; staff atty. Phillips Petroleum, Bartlesville, Okla., 1957-61; sr. atty., 1962-67, v.p., gen. counsel, Europe, Africa, Brussels, Belgium, London, Eng., 1967-71, sr. v.p., Europe, Africa, 1971-74, mgr. internat. affairs, Bartlesville, 1974-76, mng. dir. Europe and Africa Natural resources div., London, 1976—. Mem. regulator practices com., Interstate Oil Compact Commn., 1974-76; chmn. bd. Am. Sch., London, 1971-74; bd. dirs. Internat. Sch. of Brussels, 1968-70. Mem. Tex., Okla., Am. bar assns., Am.-U.K. C. of C. (dir. 1977—). Office: Phillips Petroleum Port House Stag Pl London SW1 United Kingdom Tel 828-9766

GUITTAR, DONALD JAMES, b. Canton, Ohio, Aug. 18, 1932; B.A., Kent State U., 1954; J.D., Western Reserve Law Sch., 1960. Admitted to Ohio bar, 1960, U.S. Supreme Ct. bar, 1967; mem. firm Smoot & Riemer, Cleve., 1960-62; asst. dir. law City of Cleve., 1962-71; asst. atty. gen. chief transp., Columbus, Ohio, 1971—. Mem. adv. bd. Cleve. Womens Orchestra, Cudell Arts and Crafts adv. bd. Home: 6956 Starfire Dr Reynoldsburg OH 43068 Office: 25 S Front St Columbus OH 43215 Tel (614) 466-4656

GUITTARD, CLARENCE ALWIN, b. Waco, Tex., Mar. 17, 1917; A.B., Baylor U., 1940, J.D., 1940. Admitted to Tex. bar, 1940; practiced in Alice, Tex., 1940-41; briefing atty. Tex. Supreme Ct., 1941-43; asso. firm Burford, Ryburn & Ford and predecessor, Dallas, 1944-45, partner, 1945-61; judge Dallas County Dist. Ct., 14th Dist., 1961-70; asso. justice Tex. Ct. Civil Appeals, 1971-76, chief justice, 1977—; lectr. in field; mem. Tex. Supreme Ct. Advisory Com. on Rules of Civil Procedure, 1961—; mem. Tex. Jud. Qualifications Commn., 1970. Mem. Tex. Democratic Exec. Com., 1960-61. Mem. Dallas, Am. bar assns., State Bar Tex. (pres.'s award 1974), Am. Judicature Soc., Inst. Jud. Adminstrn. Contbr. articles to legal jours. Home: 6306 Desco Dr Dallas TX 75225 Office: Ct of Civil Appeals 600 Commerce St Dallas TX 75202 Tel (214) 749-8381

GULDIN, JOHN RICHARD, b. Shenandoah, Pa., Sept. 1, 1940; B.A., Heidelberg Coll., 1962; J.D., U. Akron, 1967. Admitted to Ohio Supreme Ct. bar, 1967, U.S. Ct. Appeals 6th Circuit bar, 1970, U.S. Supreme Ct. bar, 1972; staff atty. Summit County (Ohio) Legal Aid Soc., Akron, 1967-69, asst. gen. counsel, 1969-70, exec. dir., gen. counsel, 1970-72; partner firm Guldin, Dickey & Bauders, Wadsworth, Ohio, 1972—; prosecutor City of Wadsworth, 1973, solicitor, 1974; acting judge Medina County Ct., 1973. Mem. Akron, Medina County, Ohio State, Am. bar assns. Home: 4119 Bagdad Rd Medina OH 44256 Office: 121 College St Wadsworth OH 44281 Tel (216) 335-2507

GULOTTA, FRANK ANDREW, b. Bklyn., June 4, 1907; A.B., Columbia, 1929; LL.B., St. John's U., 1931. Admitted to N.Y. State bar, 1932, U.S. Supreme Ct. bar, 1950; dist. atty. Nassau County (N.Y.), 1949-59; justice N.Y. State Supreme Ct., 1959—; presiding justice appellate div., 2nd Jud. Dept., 1974—. Mem. Am., N.Y. State, Nassau County bar assns. Recipient Gold medal Nassau County Bar Assn., 1975. Home: 155 Walnut St Lynbrook NY 11563 Office: 45 Monroe Pl Brooklyn NY 11201 Tel (212) 875-1300

GUMBINER, KENNETH JAY, b. Chgo., Sept. 2, 1946; B.S. in Indsl. Engring., Purdue U., 1968; J.D., U. Ill., 1971. Admitted to Ill. bar, 1971; asso. firm Pendleton, Neuman, Williams & Anderson, Chgo., 1971-72, Pedersen & Houpt, Chgo., 1974—; asst. atty. gen. environ. div. State of Ill., Chgo., 1972-74. Mem. Am., Ill., Chgo. bar assns. Office: 180 N LaSalle St Chicago IL 60601 Tel (312) 641-6888

GUMBS, JERE ALAN, b. Perth Amboy, N.J., Sept. 21, 1945; B.A., Rutgers U., 1967, J.D., 1971. Admitted to N.J. bar, 1971; individual practice law, Perth Amboy, 1971—. Chmn. Perth Amboy Community Devel. Policy Council, Housing Devel. Corp. Mem. Am., N.J., bar assns., Middlesex County (N.J.) Trial Lawyers Assn. Home and Office: 184 Meade St Perth Amboy NJ 08861 Tel (201) 442-1175

GUNDERSEN, HARRY F., b. Omaha, Nov. 30, 1924; B.S., U. Wis., 1949, LL.D., 1954. Admitted to Wis. bar, 1954; asso. firm Wigderson & Lindholm, Madison, Wis., 1954; individual practice law, Grantsburg, Wis., 1955; judge Burnett County (Wis.) Ct., 1956—; mem. Bd. Criminal/Ct. Judges, State Bd. County Judges, State Bd. Juvenile Ct. Judges. Mem. State Bar Wis., Inter-County Bar. Home: Route 2 Grantsburg WI 54840 Office: Courthouse Grantsburg WI 54840 Tel (715) 463-5346

GUNDERSON, HARVEY ALFRED, b. Hayti, S.D., Apr. 3, 1913; student S.D. State Coll., 1931-33; LL.B., U. S.D., 1936. Admitted to S.D. bar, 1936; partner firm Gunderson & Evenson, Clear Lake, S.D., 1947—; atty. City of Clear Lake, 1948—; states atty. Deuel County (S.D.), 1951-55; mem. S.D. Bd. of Bar Commn., 1963-66. Mem. State Bar S.D., Am. Bar Assn. Office: Clear Lake SD 57226 Tel (605) 874-2111

GUNN, EDWIN NORMAN, b. Chgo., Nov. 20, 1925; student Northwestern U., Chgo., 1945, Princeton, 1945, U. Notre Dame, 1943-44; B.S., U. Ill., Champaign, 1947, J.D., 1950. Admitted to Ill. bar, 1950; asso. B.S. Quigley, Chgo., 1950-52; individual practice law, Chgo., 1952-54; partner firm Gunn, Davidson & Brantman, Chgo., 1954-68, Gunn & Michaels, Chgo., 1968—; arbitrator Am. Arbitration Assn., 1967—. Vice pres. Wilmette Civic Responsibility Assn., 1969—. Mem. Am., Ill., Chgo. bar assns., Am. Judicature Soc., Am. Trial Lawyers Assn. Home: 2046 Brandon Rd Glenview IL 60025 Office: 120 W Madison St Chicago IL 60602 Tel (312) 782-9309

GUNN, GEORGE F., JR., b. Ft. Smith, Ark., Oct. 29, 1927; A.B., Westminster Coll., 1950; J.D., Washington U., 1955. Admitted to Mo. bar, 1955; asso. firm Gleick & Strauss, St. Louis, 1955-56; atty. Wabash R.R. Co., St. Louis, 1956-58; partner firm Rebman, LaTourette & Gunn, St. Louis, 1958-68; city atty. City of Brentwood (Mo.), 1963-71; counsel Terminal R.R. Assn., St. Louis, 1968-71; county counselor St. Louis County (Mo.), 1971-73; judge Rock Hill (Mo.) Municipal Ct., 1971, St. Louis dist. Mo. Ct. Appeals, Clayton, 1973—; Chmn. South County Region ARC, St. Louis, 1971-74; bd. mgrs. Mid County YMCA, St. Louis, 1961—; bd. dirs. World Congress Equality and Freedom, 1975. Mem. Am., Met. St. Louis bar assns., Washington U. Law Alumni (pres. 1974), Phi Delta Phi. Office: St Louis County Courthouse Clayton MO 63105 Tel (314) 889-3507

GUNN, HAROLD ROSS, b. Humboldt, Tenn., Jan. 1, 1944; B.S., Memphis State U., 1965; J.D., U. Tenn., 1967. Admitted to Tenn. bar, 1968; individual practice law, Humboldt, Tenn., 1968—. Pres. Civitan Club, 1970-72. Mem. Am., Tenn. bar assns., Am., Tenn. trial lawyers assns. Home: 1605 Osborne St Humboldt TN 38343 Office: 1211 Main St Humboldt TN 38343 Tel (901) 784-2000

GUNN, JOHN HOUSTON, b. Ft. Scott, Kans., Nov. 24, 1918; A.B., U. Ark., 1938; postgrad. U. Colo. Law Sch.; LL.B., U. Mo., 1941. Admitted to Mo. bar, 1941, Fla. bar, 1948; asso. firm Murrell, Fleming & Flowers, Miami, Fla., 1948-50; partner firm Rosemond & Gunn, Miami, 1950-55; partner firm Gunn, Verney & Buhler, Miami, 1956—. Bd. dirs. Inst. for Mayan Studies, Miami, 1975-77, Grove House, Inc., Miami, 1976—. Mem. Dade County (Fla.) (chmn. com. on bankruptcy 1955-56, 57-65), Fed., Am. bar assns., Fla. Bar (chmn. sect. banking and bus. law 1971-72). Home: 4102 University Dr Coral Gables FL 33146 Office: Suite 1525 DuPont Bldg Hagler St Miami FL 33131 Tel (305) 371-1346

GUNN, WILLIAM CORY, b. Tulsa, Nov. 19, 1947; B.B.A., So. Meth. U., 1970; J.D., U. Denver, 1973. Admitted to Colo. bar, 1973; asso. Fischer & Beatty, Ft. Collins, Colo., 1973-75; partner firm Fischer, Brown, Huddleson and Gunn, Ft. Collins, 1975—. Bd. dirs. Ft. Collins. Com. on Drug Edn., 1974, Ft. Collins Sertoma Club, 1976—. Mem. Ft. Collins C. of C., Am., Colo., Larimer County bar assns. Office: PO Box J Fort Collins CO 80522 Tel (303) 482-1056

GUNNELL, FRANKLIN LANOEL, b. Logan, Utah, Feb. 16; B.S., Utah State U.; J.D., U. Utah. Admitted to Utah bar, 1967; partner firm Hillyard and Gunnell, Logan. Mem. Utah State, Cache County bar assns., Jaycees (pres. Logan chpt. 1969), Cache C. of C. (dir.). Recipient Distinguished Service award. Contbr. article to newspaper. Home: 6597 S 2400 W Mount Sterling UT 84321 Office: 175 E 1st N Logan UT 84321 Tel (801) 752-2610

GUNNELS, HENRY JAY, JR., b. Paola, Kans., Nov. 1, 1922; B.S., Sch. Bus. U. Kans., 1944; J.D., U. Mo., Kansas City, 1948. Admitted to Mo. bar, 1948, Kans. bar, 1949; individual practice law, Kansas City, Mo., 1948—. Mem. Republican Ward Com., Fairway, Kans.; chmn. Johnson County (Mo.) Am. Revolution Bicentennial Com.; deacon 2d Presbyn. Ch., Kansas City, 1962. Mem. Am., Mo., Kans., Kansas City (Mo.) bar assns., Lawyers Assn. Kansas City (life), Alumni Assn. U. Mo. at Kansas City, Mo. (life), Kans. (life) hist socs., Phi Alpha Delta (dist. justice alumni chpt. 1958-62, justice Kansas City 1959). Home: 5445 Chadwick St Fairway KS 66205 Office: 1130 Westport Rd Kansas City MO 64111 Tel (816) 931-6545

GUNNING, FRANCIS PATRICK, b. Scranton, Pa., Dec. 10, 1923; student City Coll. N.Y., 1941-43, St. John's Coll., 1946-47; LL.B., St. John's U., 1950. Admitted to N.Y. bar, 1950; legal editor Prentice-Hall Pub. Co., N.Y.C., 1950; exec. v.p., gen. counsel Tchrs. Ins. & Annuity Assn. Am., N.Y.C., 1951—; trustee, mem. finance and audit coms. Mortgage Growth Investors. Mem. Am., N.Y. State bar assns., Am. Law Inst., Assn. Bar City N.Y., Assn. Life Ins. Counsel, Am. Land Title Assn., Nat. Assn. Coll. and Univ. Attys. Contbr. articles to profl. jours. Office: 730 3d Ave New York City NY 10017 Tel (212) 490-9000

GUNTER, JAMES HOUSTON, JR., b. Atlanta, Mar. 8, 1943; B.B.A., Tex. A. and M. U., 1965; J.D., U. Houston, 1972. Admitted to Tex. bar, 1972, Ark. bar, 1973; partner firm Gunter & Walker, Hope, Ark., 1973—; pros. atty. 8th Dist. Ark., 1977—. Trustee Ark. Eye and Kidney Bank, Little Rock, 1976-77; bd. dirs. Ark. Enterprises for the Blind, Little Rock, 1975—. Mem. State Bar Tex., Am., Ark., Houston, Hempstead County bar assns., Nat. Dist. Attys. Assn., Ark. Trial Lawyers Assn., Ark. Pros. Attys. Assn., Southwest Ark. Assn., Delta Theta Phi. Home: RTE 4 Box 332 S Grady St Hope AR 71801 Office: PO Box 591 E 3d St and Edgwood St Hope AR 71801 Tel (501) 777-8621

GUNTER, ROBERT LEROY, b. Tacoma, Wash., Aug. 25, 1945; B.A., Seattle Pacific Coll., 1967; J.D., U. Washington, 1970. Admitted to Wash. bar, 1970; law clk. to justice Wash. State Supreme Ct. and U.S. Dist. Ct. Western Dist. Wash., 1970-71; instr. Seattle Pacific U., 1971—; partner firm Thorgrinnson, Ellis, Holman & Fletcher, Reston and Seattle, Wash., 1971—. Bd. dirs. Center for Law and Religious Freedom, Christian Legal Soc., 1975—, Seattle Youth for Christ, 1974—, N.W. Teen Jamboree, 1973—. Mem. Am. (vice chmn. land use planning and zoning subcom. local govt. law sect. 1974-75), Seattle-King County, Wash. State bar assns., Seattle Pacific U. Alumni Assn. (pres. 1975-77). Mem. Washington Law Review, 1969-70. Home: 9845 N E 20th St Bellevue WA 98004 Office: 2000 IBM Bldg Seattle WA 98101 Tel (206) 623-7580

GUNTER, WILLIAM BARRETT, b. Commerce, Ga., Apr. 20, 1919; A.B., U. Ga., 1940, LL.B. cum laude, 1942. Admitted to Ga. bar, 1941; partner firm Kenyon, Gunter, Hulsey & Sims and predecessor, Gainesville, Ga., 1946-71; asso. justice Ga. Supreme Ct., 1972—; mem. Ga. Ho. of Reps., 1952-58; city atty. City of Gainesville, 1959-70; mem. Ga. Bd. Bar Examiners, 1965-70. Mem. Democratic Nat. Com. for Ga., 1971. Fellow Am. Bar Found.; mem. State Bar Ga., Am. Bar Assn., Phi Beta Kappa, Phi Kappa Phi. Home: 710 Hillside Dr Gainesville GA 30501 Office: 533 State Jud Bldg Atlanta GA 30334 Tel (404) 656-3477

GUPTA, RUTH CHURCH, b. Orland, Calif., June 4, 1917; B.A., Mills Coll., 1938; J.D., Hastings Coll., 1948. Admitted to Calif. bar, 1949, U.S. Supreme Ct. bar, 1969; partner firm Gupta & Gupta, San Francisco, 1949—; mem. Calif. Constl. Revision Commn., 1964-74. Active Calif. State Bd. Control, Sacramento, 1976—; Calif. Water Quality Control Bd., Sacramento, 1964-67; mem. advisory council Bay Area Air Pollution Control Dist., San Francisco, 1971—, chmn, 1976—. Mem. Am. Bar Assn., Lawyers Club San Francisc (pres. 1976), Bar Assn. San Francisco, Queen's Bench (pres. 1953), Nat. Assn. Women Lawyers Office: 2237 Chestnut St San Francisco CA 94123 Tel (415) 567-8140

GUREN, SHELDON B., b. Cleve., Oct. 25, 1924; B.B.A., Western Reserve U., 1944; J.D., Harvard, 1948. Admitted to Ohio bar, 1948; partner firm Guren, Merritt, Sogg & Cohen, Cleve., 1948—; trustee U.S. Realty Investments, Cleve., 1961—, pres., 1971—; pres. Trans Comml. Industries, Inc., Cleve., 1973—. Mem. Am., Greater Cleve. bar assns. Home: 32810 Creekside Dr Pepper Pike OH 44124 Office: 650 Terminal Tower Cleveland OH 44113 Tel (216) 696-8550

GUSMAN, ROBERT CARL, b. N.Y.C., Nov. 17, 1931; B.A., N.Y.U., 1953; J.D., Cornell U., 1956. Admitted to N.Y. State bar, 1957, D.C. bar, 1960, Calif. bar, 1962; atty. Dept. Navy, Washington, 1956-58, spl. counsel Navy Fleet Ballistic Missile program, 1958-60; asst. gen. counsel Aerojet Gen. Corp., El Monte, Calif., 1960-70; corp. counsel Lockheed Aircraft Corp., Burbank, Calif., 1970—; instr. law Loyola U., Los Angeles, 1971-72; spl. advisor to the commn. on govt. procurement under P.L. 91-129, 1970-71; mem. Fed. Contracts Adv. Bd., 1969-74, cons., 1974—. Mem. Cornell Law Assn., Am. Bar Assn. Contbr. articles to law jours. Office: Lockheed Aircraft Corp 2555 N Hollywood Way Burbank CA 91520 Tel (213) 847-6502

GUSTAFSON, CHARLES HAROLD, b. Wheeling, W.Va., Aug. 10, 1937; B.S., U. Buffalo, 1959; J.D., U. Chgo., 1962. Admitted to N.Y. bar, 1964, D.C. bar, 1969; lectr. law, Maxwell fellow Ahmadu Bello U., Zaria, No. Region, Nigeria, 1962-63; asso. firm Shearman & Sterling, N.Y.C., 1964-66; atty., adviser Office of Legal Adviser, Dept. State, Washington, 1966-69; asso. frim Surrey, Karasik & Morse, Washington, 1969-72; asso. prof. law Georgetown U., 1972—; cons. Adminstrv. Conf. of U.S., 1975; Privacy Protection Study Commn., 1976. Mem. Am., D.C. bar assns., Bar Assn. City N.Y., Am. Soc. Internat. Law, Order of Coif. Articles editor: U. Chgo. Law Rev. 1961-62. Home: 3401 Fulton St Washington DC 20007 Office: 600 New Jersey Ave NW Washington DC 20001 Tel (202) 624-8299

GUSTAFSON, GALE ROBERT, b. Whitehall, Mont., Feb. 18, 1947; B.A. in Bus. Adminstrn., U. Mont., 1969, J.D., 1972; postgrad. Coll. of Advocacy Hastings Coll. Law, U. Calif., 1974. Admitted to Mont. bar, 1972; partner firm Keil and Gustafson, Conrad, Mont., 1972—; city atty. City of Conrad, 1973—; instr. Coll. Great Falls, 1972, 74; hearings officer Mont. Human Rights Commn., 1976—. Mem. Pondera County (Mont.) Mus. Com., 1975—; pres., chmn. bd. P-T Activities Inc. for tng. and housing developmentally disabled, 1975—. Mem. Mont., Am., 9th Jud. Dist. bar assns., Municipal Atty.'s Assn., Conrad Jaycees, Phi Delta Phi. Recipient Outstanding Law Day award Mont. Bar Assn., 1974. Home: POB 95 Route 3 Conrad MT 59425 Office: POB 1318 315 S Main St Conrad MT 59425 Tel (406) 278-5575

GUSTAVESON, ROBERT CARL, b. Los Angeles, Feb. 3, 1928; B.S., Utah State U., 1951, M.S., 1954; LL.B., U. Utah, 1958. Admitted to Calif. bar, 1959; practiced in Downey, Calif., 1959, Pomona, Calif., 1960-72; city atty. City of Ponoma (Calif.), 1963-73; judge Municipal Ct., Pomona Jud. Dist., 1973—. Chmn. Sunset dist. Old Baldy council Boy Scouts Am., 1975. Mem. Calif. Conf. Judges, Municipal Ct. Judges Assn. Los Angeles, Los Angeles County Bar Assn. (chmn. sect. local govt. 1972). Contbr. articles to legal jours. Office: Municipal Ct Div III 350 W Mission St Pomona CA 91766 Tel (714) 623-6811

GUSTE, WILLIAM JOSEPH, JR., b. New Orleans, May 26, 1922; A.B., Loyola, New Orleans, 1942, LL.B., 1943, LL.D., 1974. Admitted to La. bar, 1943; asso. firm Guste, Barnett & Redmann, 1943, 46-56, Guste, Barnett & Little, 1956-70, Guste, Barnett & Colomb, 1970-72; mem. La. Senate, 1968-72; atty. gen. State La., New Orleans, 1972—. Co-owner Antoine's Restaurant, New Orleans; chief counsel Housing Authority New Orleans, 1957-71. Pres., New Orleans Cancer Assn., 1960-62; nat. pres. United Cancer Council, 1965-67; pres. Met. Crime Commn., 1956-57, Asso. Cath. Charities, 1960-62; chmn. Juvenile Ct. adv. com. Orleans Parish, 1961-63. Mem. City New Orleans Street Paving Study Com., 1965-66. Trustee, Xavier U., 1967—, also chmn. bd. lay regents. Named Outstanding Young Man City New Orleans, Nat. Jr. C. of C., 1951; recipient John F. Kennedy Leadership award Young Dems. La. State U., 1973. Mem. Am. Assn. Small Bus. (dir.), Nat. Assn. Housing and Redevel. Ofcls. (dir.), Am. Judicature Soc., Legal Aid Bur., Am., La., New Orleans bar assns., St. Thomas More Cath. Lawyers Assn., Internat. House, Blue Key, Sigma Alpha Kappa. Home: 4 Richmond Pl New Orleans LA 70115 Office: 234 Loyola St New Orleans LA 70112*

GUSTIN, RALPH LIVINGSTON, JR., b. West Somerville, Mass., Mar. 7, 1918; A.B., Harvard, 1940, LL.B., 1943, grad. Advanced Mgmt. Program, 1960. Admitted to Calif. bar, 1947, Mass. bar, 1953, U.S. Supreme Ct. bar; asso. McCutchen, Thomas, Matthew, Griffiths & Greene, San Francisco, 1947-53; asso. counsel John Hancock Mut. Life Ins. Co., Boston, 1953-57, 2d v.p., counsel, 1957-62, v.p., gen. solicitor, 1962-65, v.p., gen. counsel, 1965-66, sr. v.p., gen. counsel, 1967—. Sec., bd. dirs. United Fund of Greater Boston, also Mass. Bay United Fund, 1957-73. Mem. Am., Mass., Boston bar assns., Cal. State Bar Assn., Life Ins. Counsel (pres. 1976-77), Nat. Assn. Securities Dealers (bd. govs., vice chmn. 1971-74). Home: 27 Colgate Rd Wellesley MA 02181 Office: 200 Berkeley St Boston MA 02117*

GUSTKE, ARTHUR NORMAN, b. Parkersburg, W.Va., Nov. 1, 1928; A.B., W.Va. U., 1953, J.D., 1956. Admitted to W.Va. bar, 1956; atty. legal div. W.Va. Tax Commr., Charleston, 1956-59; mem. firm Cather, Renner & Parker, Parkersburg, 1959-62; municipal judge city Parkersburg, 1962-65; asso. firm Hardman & Gustke, Parkersburg, 1965-74; circuit judge 4th Judicial Circuit, Wood and Wirt Counties, W.Va., 1975—. Mem. adv. council Wood County Emergency Services, 1971—; mem. adv. bd. Parkersburg Community Coll., 1971-76. Mem. W.Va., Wood County, bar assns., Am. Judicature Soc., W.Va. Judicial Assn., W.Va. Juvenile Judges Assn. (asst. sec. treas. 1976—), W.Va. Law Sch. Assn. Recipient key man award Jaycees,

1960. Home: 25 N Hills Dr Parkersburg WV 26101 Office: Wood County Courthouse Parkersburg WV 26101 Tel (304) 485-3150

GUTERSON, MURRAY BERNARD, b. Seattle, Dec. 17, 1929; B.S. in Law, U. Wash., 1951, LL.B., 1952. Admitted to Wash. bar, 1953, U.S. Supreme Ct. bar, 1971; dept pros. atty. King County (Wash.), 1953-55; asst. U.S. atty. for Western Dist. Wash., 1955-58; partner firm Culp, Dwyer, Guterson & Grader, Seattle, 1958—. Chmn. B'nai B'rith Anti-Defamation League, Seattle, 1962-64. Mem. Am. Coll. Trial Lawyers, Am., Wash. State, King County (pres.) bar assns. Home: 7040 39th St NE Seattle WA 98115 Office: 13th Floor Hoge Bldg Seattle WA 98104 Tel (206) 624-7141

GUTH, PAUL CONRAD, b. Vienna, Austria, Nov. 8, 1921; B.A., Columbia, 1947, LL.B., 1947. Admitted to N.Y. bar, 1948; asso. firm Cleary Gottlieb Friendly & Cox, N.Y.C., 1947-49; asso firm Lauterstein & Lauterstein, N.Y.C., 1950-52, partner, 1952—; asst. prosecutor in charge of evidence Dauchau and Mauthausen War Crimes Trials, World War II, 1946-47, chief investigator war crimes br. 3d Army Intelligence Center, 1946. Bd. dirs. Robert Lehman Found. Mem. N.Y.C. Bar Assn., Am. Judicature Soc. Home: 955 Fifth Ave New York City NY 10021 Office: One Rockefeller Plaza Lauterstein & Lauterstein New York City NY 10020 Tel (212) 757-4900

GUTH, PAUL DAVID, b. Phila., July 19, 1932; B.S. in Econs., Wharton Sch., U. Pa., 1953, J.D., 1956. Admitted to Pa. bar, 1957; partner firm Blank, Rome, Klaus & Comisky, Phila., 1956—. Bd. dirs. Am. Friends Hebrew U., Phila., 1974—. Mem. Am., Pa., (co-chmn. home com. 1974), Phila. (vice chmn. profl. guidance com. 1977—) bar assns., Order of Coif, Beta Gamma Sigma, Beta Alpha Psi (treas. 1952-53). Home: RD 1 Box 17A New Hope PA 18938 Office: 4 Penn Center Plaza Philadelphia PA 19103 Tel (215) 569-3700

GUTHMAN, SEYMOUR SOLOMON, b. Chgo., Dec. 28, 1906; Ph.B., U. Chgo., 1929, J.D., 1930. Admitted to Ill. bar, 1931, D.C. bar, 1932, U.S. Supreme Ct. bar, 1940; asst. to Congressman Adolph J. Sabath, 1930-32, to Congressman Emanuel Celler, 1932-40; practice law, Washington, 1944—. Pres. Jewish Nat. Fund, Washington, 1956. Mem. D.C. Bar Assn., Nat. Lawyers Club, Decalogue Soc. Lawyers, Contbr. biography of U.S. Supreme Ct. Justice Louis Dembitz to Universal Jewish Ency., 1939. Home: 2450 Virginia Ave NW Washington DC 20037 Office: 1101 17th St NW Suite 908 Washington DC 20036 Tel (202) 833-1611

GUTHRIE, ELEANOR YOUNG, b. Annawan, Ill., Aug. 12, 1915; A.B., U. Ill., 1937; J.D., Chgo.-Kent Coll. Law, 1940. Admitted to Ill. bar, 1940; editor Commerce Clearing House, Inc., Chgo., 1940-42; asso. firm Defrees & Fiske, Chgo., 1942-52, partner, 1952—; mem. hearing bd. atty. disciplinary system Ill. Supreme Ct., 1974—. Parliamentarian Ill. Fedn. Bus. and Profl. Women's Clubs, Inc., 1958—; v.p. YWCA of Metropolitan Chgo., 1972—; bd. dirs. Community Fund Chgo. Mem. Chgo., Am. bar assns., Women's Bar of Ill., Nat. Assn. Women Lawyers, Nat. Assn. Parliamentarians, AAUW, Zeta Phi Eta. Office: 72 W Adams St Chicago IL 60603 Tel (312) 372-4000

GUTHRIE, RANDOLPH HOBSON, b. Richmond, Va., Nov. 5, 1905; B.S., The Citadel, 1925, LL.D. (hon.), 1976; LL.B., Harvard U., 1931. Admitted to N.Y. bar, 1932, D.C. bar, 1972; partner firm Mudge Rose Guthrie & Alexander, and predecessors, N.Y.C., 1931—; chmn. bd. dirs. Studebaker-Worthington, Inc., 1963-71, chmn. exec. com., 1971—; chmn. bd. UMC Industries, Inc., 1969-76, chmn. exec. com., 1976—. Mem. Am., N.Y. State, N.Y.C. bar assns. Home: 43 Beach Lagoon Dr S Sea Pines Plantation Hilton Head Island SC 29928 Office: Mudge Rose Guthrie & Alexander 20 Broad St New York City NY 10005 Tel (212) 422-6767

GUTHRIE, ROBERT LEE, b. Salado, Tex., Feb. 13, 1900; B.A., Baylor U., 1921; M.A., Brown U., 1922; postgrad. Princeton, 1923-24; B.A. (Rhodes scholar), Oxford U. (Eng.), 1926, B.C.L., 1927. Admitted to Tex. bar, 1927, U.S. Supreme Ct. bar, 1954; asso. firm Thompson, Knight, Baker & Harris, Dallas, 1927-35; partner firm Guthrie & Guthrie, Dallas, 1935-42, Johnson, Guthrie, Nash & Shanklin, 1954—; mem. staff JAG, USAAF, 1942-48; U.S. judge Allied High Commn., Germany, 1948-54. Mem. Dallas Civil Service Bd., 1935-39. Mem. Tex., U.S. Supreme Ct. bar assns. Home: 6623 Park Ln Dallas TX 75225 Office: 1410 Republic Bank Bldg Dallas TX 75201 Tel (214) 741-2464

GUTHRIE, RODNEY M., b. 1908; B.A., LL.B., U. Wyo. Admitted to Wyo. bar, 1931; now chief justice Supreme Ct. of Wyo. Mem. Am. Bar Assn. Office: Supreme Ct Cheyenne WY 82001*

GUTMAN, ROBERT, b. Bklyn., Dec. 15, 1928; B.A., N.Y. U., 1949; J.D., 1951, LL.M., 1952. Admitted to N.Y. State bar, 1952, U.S. Supreme Ct. bar, 1961, U.S. Dist. Ct. bar; with firm Colin & Millstein, N.Y.C., 1951-52, Judge Adv. Gen.'s Office, U.S. Army, 1952-54; partner Sanders & Gutman (now Sanders & Gutman, P.C.), Bklyn., 1960—. Mem. Am. Arbitration Assn. (arbitrator 1976—), Bklyn. Bar Assn., N.Y. State Trial Lawyers Assn. Home: 7 Warren Pl Plainview NY 11803 Office: 41 Schermerhorn St Brooklyn NY 11201 Tel (212) 522-0666

GUTOF, RICHARD STEWART, b. Chgo., July 30, 1940; B.A., U. Ill., 1962; J.D., DePaul U., 1964. Admitted to Ill. bar, 1964, U.S. Supreme Ct. bar, 1971; asst. state's atty. Cook County (Ill.), 1964-69; individual practice law, Evanston, Ill., 1969—. Mem. Am., Ill., N. Suburban, NW Suburban, Chgo. bar assns., Decalogue Soc. Lawyers, Am. Judicature Soc., Nat. Dist. Attys. Assn. Home: 607 Lavergne St Wilmette IL 60091 Office: 1580 Sherman Ave Suite 424 Evanston IL 60201 Tel (312) 869-7404

GUTTAG, ALVIN, b. N.Y.C., Sept. 2, 1918; B.S. in Chemistry, Mass. Inst. Tech., 1940; postgrad. Carleton Coll., 1941-42, U. Richmond, 1943-45; LL.B., Georgetown U., 1948, J.D., 1948. Chemist, E.E. Bartos Co., Locust Valley, N.Y., 1941; grad. asst. Carleton Coll., 1941-42; admitted to Va. bar, 1946, D.C. bar, 1954, U.S. Supreme Ct. bar, 1960, Ct. of Customs and Patent Appeals bar, 1946; examiner U.S. Patent Office, Richmond, Va. and Washington, 1942-53; asso. firm Cushman, Darby & Cushman, Washington, 1953-57, partner, 1957—. Mem. Am. Bar Assn., Am. Patent Law Assn., Internat. Patent and Trademark Assn., Va. State Bar, Bar Assn. D.C., D.C. Bar. Patentee in field (20). Home: 6612 Whittier Blvd Bethesda MD 20034 Office: 1801 K St NW Washington DC 20006 Tel (202) 833-3000

GUTTERMAN, BARRY NEIL, b. Louisville, Ky. Apr. 14, 1943; B.S. in Bus. Adminstrn., Roosevelt U., 1966; J.D., John Marshall Law Sch., 1969. Admitted to Ill. bar, 1969; asst. gen. counsel Seeburg Corp., Chgo., 1970; gen. atty. Burlington No. Inc., Chgo., 1971—. Mem. Ill., Am., Chgo., Fed. bar assns. Am. Judicature Soc., Nat. Assn. R.R. Trial Counsel (sec. Ill. div.), Home: 820 King Richards Ct Deerfield IL 60015 Office: 547 W Jackson Blvd Chicago IL 60606 Tel (312) 435-4448

GUTTERMAN, SAMUEL, b. N.Y.C., May 21, 1903; LL.B., St. Lawrence U. Admitted to N.Y. State bar, 1925; individual practice law, N.Y.C. Mem. Am., N.Y. County, Bronx County bar assns. Office: 60 E 42d St New York City NY 10017 Tel (212) YU6-7180

GUY, ADDELIAR DELL, b. Chgo., Nov. 1, 1923; LL.B., Loyola U. at Chgo., 1957. Admitted to Ill. bar, 1957, U.S. Dist. Ct. for No. Ill. bar, 1958, U.S. 7th Circuit Ct. Appeals bar, 1964, U.S. Supreme Ct. bar, 1964, Nev. bar, 1966, U.S. 9th Circuit Ct. Appeals bar, 1973; asst. corp. counsel City of Chgo., 1964; research asst. Dist. atty.'s office Clark County, Nev., 1964, adminstrv. asst., 1964-66, dep. dist. atty., 1966-73, chief dep. dist. atty., 1973-75; judge dist. ct., 1975, juvenile dist. ct., 1976. Active, March of Dimes, A.D. Guy Boys Club; mem. Clark County Democratic Central Com., Housing Authority, City of Las Vegas. Mem. Ill., Nev., Clark County bar assns., Nev. Dist. Judge's Assn., VFW, NAACP, Jr. C. of C., Am. Legion. Office: 200 E Carson Las Vegas NV 89101 Tel (702) 386-4011

GUY, CHARLES BRYANT, b. Memphis, Dec. 23, 1918; LL.B., U. Memphis. Admitted to Tenn., D.C., Tex., U.S. Supreme Ct., U.S. Ct. Mil. Appeals bars.; commd. USMC, advanced through grades to lt. col.; ret.; dir. claims Continental Trailways Co., Dallas; mem. Mil. Ct. Rev., 1964-66. Mem. Tex., Dallas, Fed., Am. bar assn., Fed. Ins. Council. Home: 1100 Navaho Trail Richardson TX 75080 Office: Suite 318 1500 Jackson St Dallas TX 75201 Tel (214) 744-1912

GUY, DANIEL SOWERS, b. Columbus, Ohio, July 12, 1928; B.A., Ohio Wesleyan U., 1949; J.D., Ohio No. U., 1952; LL.M., U. Mich., 1956, S.J.D., 1970. Admitted to Ohio bar, 1952, U.S. Supreme Ct. bar, 1962; asst. atty. gen. of Ohio, Columbus, 1957-58; asst. prof. law Ohio No. U., Ada, 1959-62, asso. prof., 1962-65, prof., 1965-73, asst. dean, 1964-73; prof. law U. N.D., Grand Forks, 1973—; staff dir. Crime Prevention Task Force, N.D. Criminal Justice Commn., Grand Forks, 1974-75. Mem. Am. Bar Assn., Am. Judicature Soc., League of Ohio Law Schs. (pres. 1968-69), Phi Beta Kappa, Order of Coif. Author: State Highway Condemnation Procedures, 1971; contbr. articles in field to legal jours. Home: 715 25th Ave S Grand Forks ND 58201 Office: Sch Law U North Dakota Grand Forks ND 58202 Tel (701) 777-2961

GUY, GEORGE FREDRIK, b. Cheyenne, Wyo., May 4, 1904; J.D., U. Wyo., 1927. Admitted to Wyo. bar, 1927, Supreme Ct. of Philippines bar, 1945, U.S. Supreme Ct., 1941. High Ct. (hon.) Am. Samoa bar, 1971; asst. atty. Laramie (Wyo.) County, 1928-29; city police jude, Cheyene, 1930-31; city atty., Cheyenne, 1948-52; atty. gen. Wyo., 1955-57; Judge Advocate Gen. N.G., Wyo., 1949-61; mem. Wyo. Legislature, 1949-51. Mem. Wyo. Bicentinnial Commn., 1973-77. Mem. Wyo. (pres. 1966-67), Laramie County (pres. 1964-65), Am. bar assns. Recipient Wyman award outstanding atty. gen. U.S., Nat. Assn. Atty. Gens., 1957; contbr. articles to law jours. Home: 4019 Carey Ave Cheyenne WY 82001 Office: 1600 Van Lennen Ave Cheyenne WY 82001

GUZZETTI, LOUIS ADOLPH, JR., b. Yonkers, N.Y., Mar. 25, 1939; B.A., Williams Coll., 1961; LL.B. cum laude, Harvard, 1964. Admitted to N.Y. State bar, 1965, U.S. Supreme Ct. bar, 1977; asso. firm Breed, Abbott & Morgan, N.Y.C., 1964-67; atty. Celanese Corp., N.Y.C., 1967-69, sr. atty., 1969-73, asst. gen. counsel, 1973; corp. counsel Gen. Host Corp., N.Y.C., 1973, gen. counsel, 1973—, v.p., 1974-77, sec., 1976—, v.p. adminstrn., 1977—. Mem. Am., N.Y. State bar assns., Assn. of the Bar of the City of N.Y. Home: 440 E 62nd St New York City NY 10021 Office: 22 Gatehouse Rd Stamford CT 06902 Tel (203) 357-9900

GWIRTZMAN, MILTON SAUL, b. Rochester, N.Y., Mar. 17, 1933; B.A. summa cum laude, Harvard U., 1954; J.D., Yale U., 1958. Admitted to D.C. bar, 1959; legis. asst. U.S. Senate, Washington, 1959-64; partner firm Dutton, Gwirtzman, Zumas & Wise, Washington, 1964-73; of counsel firm Stroock, Stroock & Lavan, Washington, 1974—; adviser on spl. issues to Pres. J.F. Kennedy, 1963; issues adviser to Pres. J. Carter, 1976; mem. sr. adv. bd. Inst. Politics John F. Kennedy Sch. Govt., Cambridge, Mass., 1976—. Mem. Washington adv. bd. Am. Jewish Com., 1972—. Mem. D.C. Bar, Fed. City Club, Am. C. of C. in France, Phi Beta Kappa. Author: On His Own, Robert Kennedy, 1964-68; contbr. articles to profl. jours, mags. Office: 1150 17th St NW Washington DC 20036 Tel (202) 452-9250

GYLER, EMANUEL, b. N.Y.C., Oct. 17, 1919; B.S., U. Minn., 1948, J.D., 1949. Admitted to Minn. bar, 1949, Calif. bar, 1954, U.S. Supreme Ct. bar, 1963; asso. firm Robins, Davis & Lyons, Mpls., 1949-53; individual practice law, Long Beach, Calif., 1954-57, 74—; partner firm Gyler & Gottlieb, Long Beach, 1957-73. Bd. dirs. Long Beach Community Welfare Council; pres. Long Beach Jewish Community Center, 1962-64. Mem. Calif., Long Beach bar assns. Recipient Torch of Liberty award Anti-Defamation League B'nai B'rith, 1973. Tel (213) 433-9973

HAAKH, GILBERT EDWARD, b. Rotterdam, Netherlands, July 25, 1923; A.B., U. Calif., 1947; LL.B., Harvard, 1950. Admitted to Calif. bar, 1952, Mass. bar, 1952, U.S. Supreme Ct. bar, 1971; asso. firm O'Melveny & Myers, Los Angeles, 1952-60; partner firm Swanwick, Donnelly & Proudfit, Los Angeles, Donnelly, Clark, Chase & Haakh, Los Angeles, 1961-72; partner firm Macdonald, Halsted & Laybourne, Los Angeles, 1973—. Mem. Am., Los Angeles County (exec. com., bus. and corp. law sec.) bar assns. Home: 1021 S Orange Grove Blvd Pasadena CA 91105 Office: 1200 Wilshire Blvd Los Angeles CA 90017 Tel (213) 481-1200

HAAR, CHARLES M., b. Antwerp, Belgium, Dec. 3, 1921; A.B., N.Y. U., 1940; M.A., U. Wis., 1941; LL.B., Harvard, 1948; LL.D., Lake Erie U., 1968. Admitted to N.Y. State bar, 1948, Fed. bar, 1949; individual practice law, N.Y.C., 1948-51; asst. prof. Harvard Law Sch., Cambridge, 1951-54, prof., 1954-72, Louis D. Brandeis prof. law, 1972—; asst. sec. U.S. Dept. HUD, Washington, D.C., 1966-68. Chmn. Mass. Housing Fin. Agy, 1976—, Gov.'s Mgmt. Task Force, 1976—; dir. New Communities Corp., 1975—. Mem. Am. Acad. Arts and Scis., Am. Law Inst. Author: Casebook on Land-Use Planning, 1976; Between the Idea and the Reality, 1975; Suburban Reader, 1975; Federal Credit and Private Housing, 1966. Home: 1 Kennedy Rd Cambridge MA 02138 Office: Harvard Law Sch 300 Faculty Office Bldg Cambridge MA 02138 Tel (617) 868-4574

HAAS, FIELDING DALE, b. Fort Gibson, Okla., Sept. 9, 1924; LL.B., U. Okla., 1951. Admitted to Okla. bar, 1950, U.S. Supreme Ct. bar, 1971; dist. landman Lion Oil div. Monsanto Chem. Co., Liberal, Kans., 1954-57; chief land dept., counsel An-Son Petroleum Corp., Oklahoma City, 1957-59; individual practice law, Norman, Okla., 1960—; counsel City of Norman, 1964-70, 1973-75, Norman Municipal Hosp., 1964—; spl. justice Supreme Ct., 1970; spl. lectr. in law Okla. U. Law Sch., 1969-70. Trustee First Presbyn. Ch., Norman, 1963-65. Mem. Okla., Cleveland County bar assns., Phi Delta Phi, Sigma Phi Epsilon. Home: 1871 Rolling Hills Norman OK 73069 Office: 202 City Nat Bank Bldg Norman OK 73069 Tel (405) 364-7710

HAAS, GLENN RAY, b. Oak Park, Ill., Oct. 9, 1942; B.A., U. Ill., 1963; J.D., Chgo.-Kent Coll. Law, 1966. Admitted to Ill. bar, 1966; individual practice law, Villa Park, Ill., 1970—. Office: 23 E Park Blvd Villa Park IL 60181 Tel (312) 279-9311

HAAS, LOUIS NATHANIEL, b. San Francisco, July 12, 1941; B.A., U. Calif., Berkeley, 1963; J.D., Stanford, 1966. Admitted to Calif. bar, 1966; served with JAGC, U.S. Army, 1967-71; asso. firm Mendelson & Fastiff, San Francisco, 1971-73; sr. partner firm Haas & Najarian, San Francisco, 1973—. Trustee, Common Coll., 1972—. Mem. Am., Fed., San Francisco bar assns. Home: 12 Addison St San Francisco CA 94131 Office: 451 Jackson St San Francisco CA 94111 Tel (415) 788-6330

HAAS, MORTIMER, b. N.Y.C., May 14, 1909; LL.B., St. Johns Coll., 1930. Admitted to N.Y. bar, 1931; individual practice law, N.Y.C., 1931—; arbitrator Civil Ct. N.Y.C., 1965—; panel of arbitrators Am. Bar Assn., N.Y.C., 1960—. Mem. N.Y. Bar Assn., Assn. Arbitrators. Office: 299 Broadway New York City NY 10007 Tel (212) 964-1234

HAAS, STEPHEN CHARLES, b. Evansville, Ind., Nov. 6, 1937; B.S., Ind. U., 1959, J.D., 1963. Admitted to Ind. bar, 1963, U.S. Dist. Ct. bar for So. Dist. Ind., 1963, U.S. Supreme Ct. bar, 1970; adjuster Aero Mayflower Transit Corp., Indpls., 1963-65; law clk. to Judge Benjamin Buente, Vanderburgh Superior Ct., 1965-66; atty. Legal Aid Soc. of Evansville (Ind.), 1966-67; individual practice law, Evansville, 1967—; chief dep. prosecutor Vanderburgh County, Ind., 1967-70; pub. defender Vanderburgh Superior Ct., 1975—. Bd. dirs. Legal Aid Soc. of Evansville. Mem. Evansville Bar Assn., Ind. Trial Lawyers Assn., Am. Arbitration Assn. Home: 1241 Shiloh Square Evansville IN 47715 Office: 1421 N Main St Evansville IN 47711 Tel (812) 425-5208

HAASE, CHARLES JAMES, b. Memphis, Aug. 14, 1929; B.S., Yale, 1952; B.S., Mass. Inst. Tech., 1956; J.D., Denver U., 1971. Admitted to Colo. bar, 1971; individual practice law, Colorado Springs, Colo., 1971—; mktg. mgr. KAMAN Scis. Corp., Colorado Springs, 1967-70; pres., gen. mgr. Space Instrumentation Corp., Santa Monica, Calif., 1959-67. Chmn. El Paso County Planning Commn., 1972—. Mem. El Paso County, Am. bar assns. Home: 3780 McKay Rd Colorado Springs CO 80906 Office: 105 E Vermijo Ave #360 Colorado Springs CO 80903 Tel (303) 473-4790

HAASE, KATHELEEN KOEHLER, b. Wyandot County, Ohio, May 5, 1925; B.S.C., Tiffin U., 1948; J.D., Ohio State U., 1952. Admitted to Ohio bar, 1952, U.S. Dist. Ct. bar, 1964, Sixth Circuit Ct. of Appeals bar, 1968, Tax Ct. of the U.S. bar, 1965, U.S. Supreme Ct. bar, 1969; asst. elections counsel Sec. of State of Ohio, 1952-55, elections counsel, 1955-60; asst. to dir. fin. State of Ohio, 1960-63; asso. firm Summer, Hoffman & Bowsher, Columbus, Ohio, 1963-73; individual practice law, Columbus, 1973—. Mem. Am., Ohio State, Columbus bar assns. Office: 22 E Gay St Columbus OH 43215 Tel (614) 221-0857

HAASE, M. CRAIG, b. Evanston, Ill., Mar. 3, 1943; student U. Wis., Madison, 1961-64; B.A. in Geology, Northwestern U., 1965; J.D., U. Ill., 1971. Admitted to Nev. bar, 1972; asso. firm Adams, Reed, Bowen & Murphy, Reno, Nev., 1972-73; asso. firm Sanford, Sanford, Fahrenkopf & Mousel, Reno, 1973-75; partner firm Hawkins, Rhodes, Sharp & Barbagelata, Reno, 1976—; instr. real estate law U. Nev., Reno, 1973-74; spl. dep. atty. gen. State of Nev., 1972-73; lectr.-in-chief Nev. Bar Rev., 1973; instr. bus. law U. Ill., 1970-71; faculty advisor Nat. Coll. State Judiciary, Reno, 1974; mem. legal asst. advisory staff Reno Jr. Coll. Bus., 1973—; law clk. to Judge Bruce R. Thompson, U.S. Dist. Ct., Reno, 1971-72. Mem. Rocky Mountain Mineral Law Found., Geol. Soc. Am. Asso., editor U. Ill. Coll. Law Law Forum; Nev. del., 9th Circuit Judicial Conf., 1976. Contbr. articles to legal jours. Office: 1 E Liberty St Reno NV 89509 Tel (702) 786-4646

HAASE, NORMAN LEWIS, b. Englewood, N.J., Aug. 28, 1943; B.A., Gettysburg Coll., 1965; J.D., Villanova U., 1968. Admitted to Pa. bar, 1968, U.S. Supreme Ct. bar, 1975; asso. firm Cramp & D'Iorio, Media, Pa., 1968-69, Fronefield, deFuria, Petrikin, Media, 1969-74, Hinkson & Brennan, Chester, Pa., 1974—; mem. Merit Selection Trial Ct. Nominating Com., Delaware County, Pa., 1975-78; sec. Joint Council on Criminal Corrections, 1973-74; founder, initial chmn. Pa. Vol. Parole Aide program, 1973-75. Pres. A Better Chance, high sch. scholarship program for disadvantaged minorities, Swarthmore, Pa.; v.p. Banneker House, neighborhood community center in financially depressed area, 1974—. Mem. Pa., Delaware County (sec. 1974-75) bar assns., Delco Young Lawyers Assn. (pres. 1974). Home: 310 Dartmouth Ave Swarthmore PA 19081 Office: 19 W 5th St Chester PA 19013 Tel (215) 876-6168 also 343 Dartmouth Ave Swarthmore PA 19081

HABER, JOEL ABBA, b. N.Y.C., Sept. 17, 1943; B.S., U. Buffalo, 1964; J.D., U. Wis., 1967. Admitted to Wis. bar, 1967, Ill. bar, 1968, U.S. Supreme Ct. bar, 1973; trial atty. SEC, Washington and Chgo., 1967-70; asso. firm Schiff, Hardin & Waite, Chgo., 1970-71; partner firm Chatz. Sugarman, Abrams & Haber, 1972—. Mem. Am., Chgo., Wis. bar assns., Chgo. Council Lawyers. Home: 1156 Ridgewood Dr Highland Park IL 60035 Office: Suite 3000 105 W Adams St Chicago IL 60603 Tel (312) 346-7500

HABER, KENNETH AARON, b. Cleve., May 12, 1941; B.A., Case-Western Res. U., 1963; J.D., Cleve. State U., 1968. Tax analyst, dept. trust tax Cleve. Trust Co., 1965-68; admitted to Wis. bar, 1969, Ariz. bar, 1971; probate adminstr. 1st Nat. Bank of Madison (Wis.), 1968-70; trust officer So. Ariz. Bank and Trust Co., Tucson, 1970-73; asso. firm Waterfall, Economidis, Caldwell & Hanshaw, Tucson, 1973—. Mem. Wis., Ariz., Am., Pima County (Ariz.) bar assns., Phi Alpha Delta. Home: 7511 E Pima St Tucson AZ 85715 Office: 5151 E Broadway St Suite 1600 Tucson AZ 85711 Tel (602) 790-5828

HABER, ROBERT JAY, b. N.Y.C., Apr. 27, 1942; A.B., U. Pa., 1963; LL.B., N.Y.U., 1966, LL.M., 1967. Admitted to N.Y. bar, 1966; asso. firm Bondy & Schloss, N.Y.C., 1969-74, partner, 1974—. Mem. Assn. of the Bar City of N.Y., N.Y. State Bar Assn., N.Y. County Lawyers Assn. Home: 1111 Park Ave New York City NY 10028 Office: 6 East 43rd St New York City NY 10017 Tel (212) 661-3535

HABIF, ISAAC NACE, b. Atlanta, June 4, 1922; B.C.S., Ga. State U., 1946; LL.B., Woodrow Wilson Coll. Law, Atlanta, 1948; LL.M., John Marshall Law Sch., Atlanta, 1949. Admitted to Ga. bar, 1949; partner Habif Arogeti & Wynne, C.P.A.'s, Atlanta, 1951—. Mem. Am. Inst. C.P.A.'s, Am., Atlanta bar assns., Ga. Soc. C.P.A.'s. Home: 1260 Kittredge Ct NE Atlanta GA 30329 Office: 1073 W Peachtree St NE Atlanta GA 30309 Tel (404) 872-9651

HACHEY, RONALD EDWARD, b. Grand Rapids, Minn., Dec. 18, 1909; LL.B., William Mitchell Coll. Law, 1943. Admitted to Minn. bar, 1943; asst. U.S. atty. Minn., 1951-53; judge Minn. Dist. Ct., 2d Jud. Dist., 1955—, chief judge, 1974—; instr. William Mitchell Coll. Law, 1956—, pres. bd. trustees, 1973—. Chmn. planning council St. Paul United Fund, 1961-64; trustee Holy Spirit Ch., St. Paul, 1969—; chmn. Archbishop's Appeal Bd., 1972-73. Mem. Minn. State, Am. bar assns., Am. Judicature Soc., Dist. Judges Assn. (pres. 1964-65). Recipient Outstanding Citizen award St. Paul United Fund Planning Council, Outstanding Alumnus award William Mitchell Coll. Law, Outstanding Achievement award Archbishop W. Brady. Home: 1080 Palace Ave Saint Paul MN 55105 Office: 1421 Courthouse Saint Paul MN 55102 Tel (612) 298-4109

HACHTMAN, SAMUEL JOSEPH, b. Chgo., Apr. 25, 1900; grad. U. Chgo., 1921; J.D., Northwestern U., 1922. Admitted to Ill. bar, 1922; individual practice law,Chgo.; law, Chgo.; sr. counselor State of Ill. Mem. Am., Ill. State, Chgo. bar assns., Am. Judicature Soc. Patentee health industry methods. Home: 1108 N Harlem Ave River Forest IL 60305 Tel (312) 227-7676

HACK, CHARLES WILLIAM, b. Paris, Tex., Dec. 22, 1929; B.S. in Chem. Engring., U. Tex., 1951, M.S., 1953; J.D., Tulsa U., 1973. Admitted to Okla. bar, 1974; with Cities Service Co., 1955-69; legal intern firm Dyer, Power and Marsh, 1973-74, firm Best, Sharp, Thomas & Glass, 1973-74; atty. firm Capenter & Guthrie, Tulsa, 1974; partner firm Carpenter, Guthrie & Hack, Tulsa, 1975, firm Carpenter, Ellson & Hack, Tulsa, 1976—. Mem. Am., Okla. bar assns. Office: 4111 S Darlington St Mercantile Bank Bldg Tulsa OK 74135 Tel (918) 664-2602

HACK, STANLEY FEIN, b. Milw., Feb. 3, 1936; B.A. in Econs., U. Pa., 1958; LL.B., U. Wis., 1961. Admitted to Wis. bar, 1961, N.Y. bar, 1962; asso. firm Kaye, Scholer, Fierman, Hayes & Handler, N.Y.C., 1961-62; instr. U. Wis., 1962-63; asso. firm Laiken, Jacobson & Sweitlik, Milw., 1963-66; individual practice law, Milw., 1966—; instr. U. Wis., Milw., 1966-67. Bd. dirs. Milw. Found., 1973—, chmn. found. 1976—. Mem. Wis., Milw. bar assns. Contbr. articles to law reviews. Home: 8643 N Fielding Rd Milwaukee WI 53217 Office: 161 W Wisconsin Ave Milwaukee WI 53203 Tel (414) 271-6364

HACKETT, ROBERT V., b. Detroit, Mar. 30, 1916; A.B., Wayne State U., 1938; J.D., U. Mich., 1941. Admitted to Mich. bar, 1941; legal staff Gen. Motors Co., Mich., 1942-54; individual practice law, Bloomfield Hills, Mich., 1954—. Mem. Am., Mich., Oakland County bar assns. Office: 21 E Long Lake Rd Ste 200 Bloomfield Hills MI 48013 Tel (313) 645-9159

HACKLER, EUGENE THEODORE, b. Tampa, Kans., Jan. 17, 1924; A.B., Washburn U., 1947, J.D., 1949. Admitted to Kans. bar, 1949, U.S. Dist. Ct. bar, Dist. Kans., 1949, U.S. Supreme Ct. bar, 1969; partner firm Hackler, Londerholm, Speer, Vader & Austin Charter and predecessors, Olathe, Kans., 1949—; lectr. continuing legal edn. Treas., Evang. Luth. Good Samaritan Soc., Sioux Falls, S.D., 1957-69; pres. Am. Assn. Homes for the Aging, Washington, 1970-73; del. White House Conf. on Aging, 1971. Fellow Am. Coll. Trial Lawyers; mem. Washburn Law Sch. Assn. (pres. bd. govs. 1973-75), Johnson County (pres. 1955), Kans. (chmn. com. profl. relations 1968), Am. bar assns., Am. Judicature Soc., Am. Soc. Hosp. Attys., Delta Theta Phi. Recipient Distinguished Service award U.S. Jaycees, 1954, award of Honor Am. Assn. Homes for the Aging, 1974; author Legal News Letter for gen. bd. health and welfare ministries United Meth. Ch., Evanston, Ill.; contbr. articles to Concern in the Care of the Aging. Home: 685 W Cedar St Olathe KS 66061 Office: 201 N Cherry St POB 1 Olathe KS 66061 Tel (913) 782-1000

HACKLEY, DAVID KENNETH, b. Chgo., Mar. 31, 1940; B.A., Miami U., Oxford, Ohio, 1960; M.A. in Am. Studies, U. Wyo., 1961; J.D. cum laude, U. Minn., 1965. Admitted to Minn. bar, 1965; law clk. to Hennepin County (Minn.) Dist. Ct., 1965-66; individual practice law, Mpls., 1966—; licensed real estate broker, Minn.; active Legal Advice Clinics, Ltd., 1968-74; referee Hennepin County Family Ct., summer 1975. Chmn., Mpls. Bd. of Housing Appeals, 1967—. Mem. Minn., Hennepin County bar assns., Am. Trial Lawyers Assn. Office: 816 Title Insurance Bldg 400 Second Ave S Minneapolis MN 55401 Tel (612) 332-6569

HACKMAN, MARY COOK MACATEE, b. Huntington, W.Va., Dec. 2, 1911; J.D., Am. U., 1960. Admitted to Va. bar, 1962, D.C. bar, 1971, U.S. Supreme Ct. bar, 1972; individual practice in Arlington, Va., 1962-76; mem. firm Hackman, Ellis & Hackman, Ltd., 1977—; columnist No. Va. Sun newspaper, 1956-57; pub. Arlington Citizen Weekly, 1956-57; mem. advisory bd. Fidelity Nat. Bank, Arlington, 1965-66. Vice chmn. No. Va. Regional Park Authority, 1959-70; mem. advisory bd. Consortium Colls. and Univs. No. Va., 1977. Mem. Am., Arlington, Va., bar assns., D.C. Women's Bar, Kappa Beta Pi. Recipient trophy for civic endeavor Washington Evening Star, 1957. Home: 3104 N Inglewood St Arlington VA 22207 Office: 2009 N 14th St Arlington VA 22201 Tel (703) 524-9544

HACKMANN, FRANK HENRY, b. St. Louis, Jan. 22, 1945; B.S. in Chem. Engring., U. Ill., 1967; J.D., St. Louis U., 1972. Admitted to Mo. bar, 1972, Ill. bar, 1973; process engr., Environ. engr. Mansanto Co., Sauget, Ill., 1967-73; atty. Ralston Purina Co., St. Louis, 1973-76, dir. environ. affairs, 1976—. Mem. Clayton (Mo.) Bd. Edn., 1976—. Mem. Am. Bar Assn., Bar Assn. Met. St. Louis, Am. Inst. Chem. Engrs. Mem. St. Louis U. Law Jour. Office: Checkerboard Sq Saint Louis MO 63188 Tel (314) 982-2619

HACKNEY, BARRY ALBERT, b. Norfolk, Va., Jan. 7, 1946; B.A., Hampden Sydney Coll., 1967; J.D., Williams Law Sch., 1970. Admitted to Va. bar; asso. firm May Garrett & Miller, Richmond, Va., 1970-73, Hieschler & Fleischer, Richmond, 1973—. Mem. Am., Richmond (exec. com. young lawyers sect.) bar assns. Home: 1705 Park Ave Richmond VA 23220 Office: Heischler & Fleischer 644-6041 4th and Main Sts Richmond VA 23219

HACKNEY, VIRGINIA HOWITZ, b. Phila., Jan. 11, 1945; B.A., Hollins Coll., 1967; J.D., U. Richmond, 1970. Admitted to Va. bar, 1970; asso. firm Hunton & Williams, Richmond, Va., 1970—; sec. 3d dist. com. Va. State Bar, 1976—; pres. Met. Richmond Women's Bar, 1973-74. Mem. Va., Richmond, Va. Women's, Am. bar assns., Nat. Assn. Women Lawyers, Va. Trial Lawyers Assn., McNeil Law Soc. Office: 707 E Main St Richmond VA 23219 Tel (804) 788-8263

HADDAD, FRANK E., JR., b. Louisville, June 23, 1928; LL.B., U. Louisville, 1952. Admitted to Ky. bar, 1952, U.S. Supreme Ct. bar, 1959, U.S. Circuit Ct. Appeals bar, 6th Circuit, 1963; individual practice law now in Louisville. Pub. adminstr. and guardian Jefferson County, Ky., 1963-66. Fellow Internat. Acad. Trial Lawyers, Am. Coll. Trial Lawyers; mem. Legal Aid Soc. Louisville (pres. 1967-71), Louisville (pres. 1964), Ky. (pres. 1977—), Am. bar assns., Am. Judicature Soc., Nat. Assn., Criminal Def. Lawyers (pres. 1973-74), Ky. Trial Lawyers Assn. (pres. 1966), Assn. Trial Lawyers Am. Office: 529 Ky Home Life Bldg Louisville KY 40202 Tel (502) 583-4881*

HADDEN, ARTHUR ROBY, b. San Antonio, Feb. 13, 1929; B.B.A., U. Tex., 1952, LL.B., 1957. Admitted to Tex. bar, 1957; asso. firm Ramey, Flock, Deveroux and Hutchins, Tyler, Tex., 1957-70; U.S. atty. Eastern Dist. Tex., 1970—. Office: 310 Federal Bldg Tyler TX 75701 Tel (214) 597-8146

HADDOCK, DOUGLAS RAY, b. Idaho Falls, Idaho, Apr. 7, 1942; B.A., U. Utah, 1967, J.D., 1970. Admitted to U.S. Supreme Ct. bar, 1976; law clk. to justice Minn. Supreme Ct., 1970-71; asso. Briggs and Morgan, St. Paul, 1971-75; prof. law Hamline U., St. Paul, 1975—; legis. draftsman Minn. Revisor of Statutes, 1972-73. Mem. high council St. Paul stake Ch of Jesus Christ of Latter-day Saints. Mem. Am., Minn. bar assns., Order of Coif, Phi Beta Kappa. Contbr. publs. in field. Home: 2136 Bradley St St Paul MN 55117 Office: 1536 Hewitt Ave St Paul MN 55104 Tel (612) 641-2071

HADDOCK, JAMES HOLMES, b. Stonewall, Miss., Apr. 28, 1918; B.A., U. Miss., 1940, LL.B., 1941, J.D., 1968; postgrad. U. So. Miss., 1951-52. Admitted to Miss. bar, 1946, U.S. Supreme Ct. bar, 1946; spl. agt. FBI, various cities, 1941-44; individual practice law, 1946-72; chief atty., gen. counsel Miss. State Tax Commn., Jackson, 1972—. Mayor City of Philadelphia (Miss.), 1951-56; bd. dirs. Pearl River Basin, Jackson, 1964-70. Mem. Miss. State, Hinds County bar assns., U.S. Assn. Tax Attys. Home: 5330 N State St Jackson MS 39206 Office: Woolfork State Office Bldg NW St Jackson MS 39202 Tel (601) 354-7268

HADDOCK, LAWRENCE PAGE, JR., b. Jacksonville, Fla., Nov. 1, 1945; B.A., Harvard, 1967; J.D., U. Fla., 1970; postgrad. Nat. Coll. for State Judiciary, 1975. Admitted to Fla. bar, 1970; asso. firm Dawson, Galant, Maddox, Boyer, Sulik & Nichols, Jacksonville, 1970-73; asst. state atty. 4th Circuit, Jacksonville, 1972-74; police legal advisor City of Jacksonville, 1973; judge County Ct., Jacksonville, 1974—. Bd. dirs. Child Guidance Clinic of Duval County (Fla.), 1975. Mem. Am., Fla. trial lawyers assns. Office: 330 E Bay St Jacksonville FL 32216 Tel (904) 633-6780

HADE, VICTOR, b. N.Y.C., Apr. 24, 1935; B.S., N.Y. U., 1960; LL.B., N.Y. Law Sch., 1964. Admitted to N.Y. State bar, 1965; asst. corp. counsel City. of N.Y., 1967-69, 1970-72; law sec. to N.Y. Civil Ct. judge, 1969—; mem. firm Scwartz & Weiss, N.Y.C., 1972—. Mem. N.Y. State, Bronx County bar assns., Real Estate Tax Certiorari Bar Assn. Home: 14 Fairfield Dr Dix Hills NY 11746 Office: 521 Fifth Ave New York City NY 10017 Tel (212) 687-5725

HADEN, MABEL DOLE, b. Lynchburg, Va., Feb. 17; B.S., Va. State Coll., 1941; LL.M., Howard U., 1948, J.D., 1948; LL.M., Georgetown U., 1956. Admitted to D.C. bar, 1948; tchr. pub. schs., Washington, 1941-48; individual practice law, Washington, 1948—. Mem. Am., Nat. bar assns., D.C. Bar Unified, Nat. Assn. Black Women Attys., Iota Phi Lambda. Contbr. articles to legal publs. Office: 506 5th St NW Washington DC 20001 Tel (202) 638-0907

HADJI-MIHALOGLOU, SERGE BASIL, b. Thessaloniki, Greece, Sept. 25, 1942; B.A., State U. N.Y., Buffalo, 1965; J.D., Detroit Coll. Law, 1968; LL.M. in Internat. Law, N.Y. U., 1969. Admitted to Mich. bar, 1968, N.Y. bar, 1970, U.S. Supreme Ct. bar, 1974; asso. firm Rogers, Hoge & Hills, N.Y.C., 1970—; lectr. N.Y. U., 1975—. Trustee Anatolia Coll., Greece, 1974—, Hellenic U. Graduates Assn., N.Y.C., 1973— (hon.). Mem. Assn. Bar City N.Y., Am. Soc. Internat. Law, Am., N.Y. State bar assns. Office: 90 Park Ave New York City NY 10016 Tel (212) 953-1796

HADLEY, JAMES FREDERICK, b. Morenci, Mich., Sept. 18, 1939; B.A., U. Mich., 1961; J.D., Duke, 1964. Admitted to Fla. bar, 1964, Ohio bar, 1966, U.S. Tax Ct. bar, 1968; asso. firm Anderson, Rush, Dean & Lowndes, Orlando, Fla., 1964-65; asst. atty. gen. State of Ohio, 1965-67; asso. firm Gingher & Christensen, Columbus, Ohio, 1967-71; individual practice law, Columbus, 1971-74; partner firm Hadley & Wollett, Worthington, Ohio, 1974-76, firm Moritz, McClure Hughes & Hadley, Columbus, 1976—. Mem. Am., Ohio, Columbus bar assns., Am. Judicature Soc., Fla. Bar, Columbus Lawyers Club, Estate Planning Council, Phi Delta Phi. Home: 4294 Randmore Rd Columbus (Upper Arlington) OH 43220 Office: 155 E Broad St Columbus OH 43215 Tel (614) 224-0888

HADLEY, STEPHEN MERRILL, b. Ogden, Utah, June 23, 1932; A.A., Boise Jr. Coll., 1952; B.A., San Jose State U., 1954; J.D., U. Utah, 1962. Admitted to Utah bar, 1962; intern auditor Touche, Niven, Bailey & Smart, Los Angeles, 1957; real estate salesman A.A.A. Realty, Salt Lake City, 1960; life ins. salesman Bonneville Life Ins. Co., Salt Lake City, 1960; clk. Utah Supreme Ct., Salt Lake City, 1962-63; partner firm Rigtrup & Hadley, Salt Lake City, 1963-65, firm Rigtrup, Hadley, Livingston & Newman, Salt Lake City, 1965-67; commr. workmen's compensation State of Utah, 1967—. Mem. Internat. Assn. Indsl. Accident Bds. and Commns. (pres. 1975, dir. 1971-74). Home: 583 E 1700 S Bountiful UT 84010 Office: 350 E 500 S Salt Lake City UT 84111 Tel (801) 533-6411

HADLOW, EARL BRYCE, b. Jacksonville, Fla., July 29, 1924; student Clemson Coll., 1941-43; A.B., Duke, 1947, LL.B., 1950. Admitted to Fla. bar, 1950, U.S. Supreme Ct. bar, 1965; asst. county solicitor, 1952-53; with firm Mahoney, Hadlow & Adams, and predecessors, Jacksonville, 1955—, partner, 1956—; dir. Barnett Banks, Fla.; chmn. Fed. Judicial Nominating Commn. of Fla. Sec., counsel Children's Home Soc. of Fla., 1960-69; trustee Jacksonville U., 1966—, chmn., 1974-75. Fellow Am. Coll. Probate Counsel, Am. Bar Found., Am. Judicature Soc. (dir. 1976—, chmn. com. implementation of standards and codes, sec. sect. bar activities 1976); mem. Fla. Bar (bd. govs. 1967-72, pres. 1973-74, chmn. designation coordinating com. 1976—), Jacksonville Bar (pres. 1966), Am. Bar Assn. (mem. ho. of dels. 1974—, mem. exec. com. 1976—). Contbg. author Fla. Legal Ency. Florida Law and Practice. Home: 2171 River Rd Jacksonville FL 32207 Office: PO Box 4099 Jacksonville FL 32201 Tel (904) 354-1100

HAEFELI, RICHARD THOMAS, b. Flushing, N.Y., Apr. 16, 1940; A.B., Providence Coll., 1962; J.D., St. John's U., Bklyn., 1968; LL.M. in Taxation, N.Y. U., 1972. Admitted to N.Y. State bar, 1969, U.S. Supreme Ct. bar, 1973; asso. firm Meyer & Wexler, Smithtown, N.Y., 1969-76; partner firm McNulty, DiPietro, Nesci & Haefeli, Riverhead and Southampton, N.Y., 1976—. Mem. Rensenberg-Speonk Sch. Bd. Mem. Suffolk County (N.Y.) Bar Assn. Home: Matthews Dr Remsenberg NY 11960 Office: 130 Ostrander Ave Riverhead NY 11901 Tel (516) 727-8200

HAERING, ARLO EDGAR, b. Chaska, Minn., Sept. 26, 1902; student U. Minn.; B.A., St. Paul Coll. Law, 1927. Admitted to Minn. bar, 1927, U.S. Supreme Ct. bar, 1960; individual practice law, Waconia, Minn., 1928-53; judge Minn. Dist. Ct., 1953-72, ret., 1972, under assignment, 1972—; city atty. City of Waconia, 1928; county atty. Carver County (Minn.), 1934-38. Mem. 8th Dist., Minn., Am. bar assns., Minn. State Dist. Judges Assn. (past pres.), Am. Judicature Soc.

HAERTLE, EUGENE MICHAEL, b. Milw., Apr. 28, 1906; J.D. cum laude, Marquette U., 1929. Admitted to Wis. bar, 1929, U.S. Supreme Ct. bar, 1973; partner firm Mayer, Wilde & Haertle, Milw., 1929-35, Zimmers, Randall & Zimmers, 1935-40; probate counselor Milw. County Cts., 1940-56, ct. legal asst., 1956-59, register in probate, 1959-73; individual practice law, 1973—; tchr. Am. Inst. Banking, Milw., 1949-64; guest lectr. Marquette U. Law Sch., 1953-71; mem. Wis. Registers Probate, 1958-73, pres., 1965-67. Mem. Wis. (bd. govs.), Milw. bar assns., Thomas More Soc., Am. Soc. Pub. Adminstrn., Delta Theta Phi. Author: Probate Practice in Wis., 1964; Adoption and Birth Records in Wisconsin, 1967; bd. editors Gavel, Milw. Bar Assn., 1950-76, editor, 1970-71; contbr. articles to legal jours. Home and office: 8533 Glencoe Circle Wauwatosa WI 53226 Tel (414) 453-5583

HAFERKAMP, HUGH JOHN, b. Des Moines, Aug. 8, 1927; B.A., U. N.Mex., 1950; J.D., U. Mich., 1955. Admitted to Calif. bar, 1956, U.S. Supreme Ct. bar, 1975; trial atty. legal dept. Allstate Ins. Co., Los Angeles, 1956-63, mng. atty., 1960-63; with firm Cavalleto, Webster, Mullen & McCaughey, Santa Barbara, Calif., 1963-76; individual practice law, Santa Barbara, 1976—. Pres. Santa Barbara Council on Crime, 1970-71. Mem. Am., Calif., Santa Barbara County bar assns. Office: 1335 State St Santa Barbara CA 93101 Tel (805) 963-0838

HAFFER, LOUIS PAUL, b. Boston, May 19, 1914; J.D. cum laude, Boston U., 1937. Admitted to Mass. bar, 1937, U.S. Supreme Ct. bar, 1945, D.C. bar, 1949; law sec. to justices Mass. Supreme Jud. Ct., Boston, 1937-39; atty. Fed. Wage-Hour Adminstrn., Washington, 1939-42, FDA, Washington, 1942; trial atty. U.S. Dept. Justice, Washington, 1943-48; practice law, Washington, 1948—; sr. partner firm Haffer and Alterman, Washington, 1975—; exec. v.p., counsel Air Freight Forwarders Assn.; lectr. Catholic U. Sch. Law, 1955-65; mem. consumer adv. bd. CAB, 1970-72. Mem. Am., D.C. bar assns., Nat., Internat. aviation clubs. Editor-in-chief Boston U. Law Rev., 1936-37. Home: 4711 MacArthur Blvd NW Washington DC 20007 Office: 1730 Rhode Island Ave NW Washington DC 20036 Tel (202) 293-1030

HAFFEY, DAVID ALLEN, b. Canal Winchester, Ohio, Sept. 15, 1947; B.A., Cedarville Coll., 1969, Central State U., Wilberforce, Ohio, 1969; J.D., U. Notre Dame, 1972. Admitted to Ohio bar, 1973; asso. firm Miller, Finney & Clark Co., Xenia, Ohio, 1973—; instr. Cedarville Coll., 1973—. Chmn. bd. deacons Southgate Bapt. Ch., Springfield, Ohio. Mem. Am., Ohio, Greene County (Ohio) bar assns., Christian Legal Soc. Home: 168 Creamer Dr Cedarville OH 45314 Office: 20 King Ave PO Box 610 Xenia OH 45385 Tel (513) 372-8055

HAFFNER, ALFRED LOVELAND, JR., b. Brooklyn, Sept. 11, 1925; B.S.E., U. Mich., 1950, J.D., 1956. Admitted to New York State bar, 1958, U.S. Supreme Court bar, 1961; asso. firm of Kenyon & Kenyon, N.Y.C., 1957-60; asso. firm of Ward, McElhannon, Brooks & Fitzpatrick, N.Y.C., 1960-61, partner, 1961-71; partner firm Brooks Haidt Haffner & Delahunty, N.Y.C., 1971—. Treas. Strathmore Assn. Westchester, Scarsdale, N.Y., 1976—. Mem. Am., New York State bar assns., Am., New York (bd. govs. 1964-72, pres. 1970-71), patent law assns., Nat. Council Patent Law Assns. (chmn. 1973-74), Phi Gamma Delta, Phi Alpha Delta. Home: 1 Gainsborough Rd Scarsdale NY 10583 Office: 99 Park Ave New York NY 10016 Tel (212) 697-3355

HAFFNER, WALTER SOL, b. Cleve., July 18, 1915; B.A., Ohio State U., 1941; J.D., Harvard, 1948. Admitted to Ohio bar, 1948, U.S. Supreme Ct. bar, 1962; mem. firm Sindell & Sindell, Cleve., 1948-50; individual practice law, Cleve., 1950—; mem. Ohio Ho. of Reps., 1953-54. Mem. Ohio, Cuyahoga County, Greater Cleve. bar assns. Home: 4972 Oakland Dr Lyndhurst OH 44124 Office: 1008 Standard Bldg 1370 Ontario St Cleveland OH 44113 Tel (216) 241-6443

HAFNER, THOMAS MARK, b. Evansville, Ind., Aug. 8, 1943; B.A., Valparaiso U., 1965, J.D., 1968. Admitted to Ind. bar, 1968, U.S. Customs Ct. bar, 1971, U.S. Supreme Ct. bar, 1975; asso. firm Nieter, Smith, Blume, Wyneken & Dixon, Ft. Wayne, Ind., 1968-70; atty. Magnavox Co., Ft. Wayne, 1970, asst. counsel, 1971, asso. counsel, 1972, group counsel, 1973-76; sr. counsel N.Am. Philips Corp., Ft. Wayne, 1976—. Bd. dirs. Shepherd of the City Lutheran Ch., Ft. Wayne, 1973-76. Mem. Am., Ind. bar assns. Office: 1700 Magnavox Way Fort Wayne IN 46804 Tel (219) 432-6511

HAFT, ROBERT JOSEPH, b. N.Y.C., July 12, 1930; B.A. cum laude, Coll. City N.Y., 1951; LL.B., J.D., Columbia, 1954. Admitted to N.Y. bar, 1955; law clk. to judge U.S. Dist. Ct., N.Y.C., 1954-55; asso. firm Goldstein, Judd, Gurfein, N.Y.C., 1955-61; partner firm Stamer & Haft, N.Y.C., 1961-73, Kronish, Lieb, Shainswit, Weiner & Hellman, N.Y.C., 1973—. Mem. Fed. Bar Council, Am., N.Y. State bar assns., Assn. Bar City N.Y. Author: Tax Sheltered Investments, 1975; contbr. articles to profl. jours. Office: 1345 Ave of the Americas New York City NY 10019 Tel (212) 765-6000

HAGAN, ALFRED CHRIS, b. Moscow, Idaho, Jan. 27, 1932; B.A., U. Idaho, 1953, J.D., 1958. Admitted to Idaho bar, 1958; asst. atty. gen. State Idaho, Boise, 1958; dep. pros. atty. Ada County, Idaho, 1959; mem. firm Clemons, Skiles & Green, Boise, Idaho, 1960-67; atty. City Boise, 1967; judge Dist. Ct. 4th Dist., Boise, 1967—; participant Nat. Conf. Commr's. on Uniform State Laws, 1969—. Office: Box 877 Boise ID 83701 Tel (208) 384-8907

HAGAN, CHARLES FRANCIS, b. N.Y.C., Nov. 18, 1923; B.S., Georgetown U., 1946; LL.B., Fordham U., 1949, LL.M., N.Y.U., 1958. Admitted to N.Y. bar, 1949; asso. firm Kirlin, Campbell & Keating, N.Y.C., 1949-55; asst. gen. counsel Pfizer, Inc., N.Y.C., 1955-74; gen. counsel Am. Home Products Corp., N.Y.C., 1974—. Mem. Am., N.Y. State bar assns., Mfg. Chemists Assn. (past chmn.

food, drug and cosmetic com.), Pharm. Mfrs. Assn. (past chmn. law sect.), Nat. Pharm. Council (past chmn. law sect.), Drug, Chem. and Allied Trades Assn. (past gen. counsel). Contbr. articles to profl. jours. Home: 94 Claydon Rd Garden City NY 11530 Office: 685 3d Ave New York City NY 10017 Tel (212) YU-6-1000

HAGAN, WILLIAM ALOYSIUS, JR., b. Bklyn., Aug. 31, 1932; B.S., Georgetown U., 1954; J.D., Columbia, 1960. Admitted to N.Y. bar, 1960; asso. firm Willkie Farr & Gallagher, N.Y.C., 1960-64; asso. gen. atty. Western Electric Co., N.Y.C., 1964-65; gen. counsel Thomas J. Lipton, Englewood Cliffs, N.J., 1965-66; partner firm Shea Gould Climenko & Casey, N.Y.C., 1967—; dir. Security State Bank of Pompano Beach, 1972—; gen. counsel Central State Bank, 1972-75. Mem. Assn. Bar City of N.Y. (banking law com.), N.Y. State, (banking law com.), Am. bar assns. Home: 155 Sussex Dr Manhasset NY 11030 Office: 330 Madison Ave New York City NY 10017 Tel (212) 661-3200

HAGEMANN, JOHN FREDERICK, b. Fort Atkinson, Wis., Feb. 12, 1939; A.B., Lawrence Coll., 1961; J.D., U. Wis., 1968. Tchr., Rich Central High Sch., Olympia Fields, Ill., 1961-65; admitted to Wis. bar, 1968, U.S. Supreme Ct. bar, 1972; asso. prof. Sch. Law U. S.D., Vermillion, 1968-77, prof., 1977—. Mem. State Bar Wis. Contbr. article to legal jour. Home: PO Box 163 Vermillion SD 57069 Office: U SD Sch Law Vermillion SD 57069 Tel (605) 677-5361

HAGEN, KENNETH EDWARD, b. Berkeley, Calif., Dec. 29, 1929; B.A. in Speech, U. Calif. at Berkeley, 1952, J.D., 1955. Admitted to Calif. bar, 1956; atty. Bechtel Corp., San Francisco, Australia and Can., 1956-64, Ralph M. Parsons Corp., Los Angeles, 1965-68, McDonnell Douglas Corp., Huntington Beach, Calif., 1968-71; individual practice law, Fullerton, Calif., 1971—. Mem. citizens adv. bd. fin. Fullerton Union High Sch. Dist. Mem. Assn. Bus. Trial Lawyers, Calif., Assn. Trial Lawyers Am., Orange County trial lawyers assns., Am., Calif., Orange County bar assns. Address: 1559 W Commonwealth Ave Fullerton CA 92633 Tel (714) 879-7070

HAGER, CHARLES READ, b. N.Y.C., Aug. 16, 1937; B.A., Harvard, 1959; LL.B., 1962. Admitted to N.Y. bar, 1962; asso. firm Dewey, Ballantine, Bushby, Palmer & Wood, N.Y.C., 1962-71, partner, 1971—; mem. bd. N.Y.C. Legal Aid Soc. Mem. Assn. Bar City N.Y. (com. on bankruptcy and corporate reorgn., com. on housing and urban devel.). Home: 357 W 11th St New York City NY 10014 Office: 140 Broadway New York City NY 10005 Tel (212) 344-8000

HAGERMAN, JOHN DAVID, b. Houston, Aug. 1, 1941; B.A. in Accounting, So. Meth. U., 1963; LL.B., U. Tex., 1966. Admitted to Tex. bar, 1966; partner firm Hagerman & Seureau, Houston, 1965—; dep. pros. atty. Harris County (Tex.). Mem. Am., Tex., Houston bar assns. Office: 225 S Heights Houston TX 77007 Tel (713) 869-6444

HAGGARD, JERRY LEROY, b. El Dorado, Kans., Aug. 17, 1936; B.S., U. Kans., 1959; J.D., Am. U., 1965. Admitted to Kans. bar, 1965, D.C. bar, 1966, Ariz. bar, 1970; individual practice law, Washington, 1965-67; atty. Pub. Land Law Rev. Commn., Washington, 1967-70; partner firm Evans, Kitchel & Jenckes, Phoenix, 1970—. Active Ariz. Environ. Planning Commn., Phoenix, 1973-75. Mem. Am., Ariz., Maricopa County bar assns., Rocky Mountain Mineral Law Inst. (trustee). Office: 363 N 1st Ave Phoenix AZ 85003 Tel (602) 262-8832

HAGGERTY, JAMES JOSEPH, b. Scranton, Pa., June 12, 1936; A.B. in Econs., Holy Cross Coll., 1957; J.D., Georgetown U., 1960. Admitted to Pa. bar, 1961; asso. firm Farrell, Butler, Kearney and Parker, Scranton, 1960-62; law clk. to chief judge William J. Neolon of U.S. Dist. Ct. Middle Dist. Pa., 1963-64; mem. firm Haggerty & Mcdonnell, and predecessor, Scranton, 1966-72, partner, 1972—; dir. First Nat. Bank, Dunmore, Pa. Mem. Am. Arbitration Assn., Am., Pa. (com. ethics and profl. responsibility), Lackawanna County (dir.) bar assns., Pa., Am. trial lawyers assns. Home: 1524 Adams Ave Dunmore PA 18509 Office: Jordan Bldg 203 Franklin Ave Scranton PA 18503 Tel (717) 344-9845

HAGLER, JOHN HARBELL, b. Denver, Tex., Aug. 19, 1944; B.A., Northwestern U., 1966; J.D., U. Tex., 1969. Admitted to Tex. bar, 1969, Ill. bar, 1972; asst. city atty. Dallas, 1972; asst. dist. atty. Dallas County, 1972—. Mem. Tex. Dist. and County Attys. Assn. Home: 6838 Shady Brook Ln Apt 1016 Dallas TX 75231 Office: Dallas County Dist Attys Office Dallas County Courthouse Dallas TX 75202 Tel (213) 749-8511

HAGOOD, GEORGE BAILEY, b. Marietta, Ga., Mar. 6, 1940; B.A., Emory U., 1962; J.D., Mercer U., 1971. Admitted to Ga. bar, 1971, U.S. Supreme Ct. bar, 1976; mem. firm Downing, McAleer & Gaskin, Savannah, Ga., 1974—. Mem. Ga., Savannah bar assns., Ga. Trial Lawyers Assn., Savannah Plaintiff Trial Lawyers Assn., Am. Judicature Soc. Home: 421 E 53d St Savannah GA 31405 Office: 24 E Oglethorpe Ave Savannah GA 31401 Tel (912) 236-4428

HAGOORT, NICHOLAS H., JR., b. Paterson, N.J., Apr. 26, 1930; A.B., Harvard U., 1951, J.D., 1954. Admitted to N.J. bar, 1954; sec. to Judge Alexander P. Waugh, 1955; now mem. firm Booth, Bate, Hagoort, Keith & Harris, Montclair, N.J. Mem. Montclair and West Essex (sec. 1958), Essex County (pres. 1976-77), N.J. State (gen. council 1970—, jud. selection com. 1973—), Am. bar assns., Harvard Club N.J. (pres. 1970-71), Harvard Law Sch. Assn. N.J. (v.p. 1975-76). Office: 31 Park St Montclair NJ 07042 Tel (201) 744-1900*

HAGSTROM, DAVID DEAN, b. Schenevus, N.Y., Oct. 24, 1940; A.B., Oberlin Coll., 1962; J.D., U. Pa., 1965. Admitted to N.Y. State bar, 1966, Ohio bar, 1971; asso. firm Hornburg, Diggs & Hornburg, Olean, N.Y., 1965-66, 67-70; law clk. to judge U.S. Dist. Ct., Middle Dist. Pa., 1966-67; counsel Diamond Shamrock Corp., Cleve., 1970-71; partner firm Van De Water & Van De Water, Poughkeepsie, N.Y., 1971—. Active United Way of Dutchess County, N.Y., 1973-76; Republican county committeeman Dutchess County, 1975—; town atty., Poughkeepsie, 1977—. Mem. Am., N.Y., Ohio, Dutchess County bar assns., Def. Research Inst. Home: 20 Horizon Hill Dr Poughkeepsie NY 12603 Office: 54 Market St PO Box 112 Poughkeepsie NY 12602 Tel (914) 452-5900

HAGSTROM, RONALD GLENN, b. Oak Park, Ill., Apr. 29, 1938; J.D., Northwestern U., 1963. Admitted to Ill. bar, 1964, U.S. Supreme Ct. bar, 1970; individual practice law and real estate, Oak Park, 1964—; appointed to Ill. Adv. Council, 1971; cons. Village of Oak Park, 1974. Mem. Eagle rev. and advancement com. Thatcher Woods Area council Boy Scouts Am., Oak Park, 1970-74. Mem. Am., Ill. State, Chgo. bar assns., Am. Judicature Soc., Nat. Assn. Real Estate Bds., Oak Park Bd. Realtors (dir., sec. 1972-73, v.p. 1974-75), Ill., Wis. realtors assns. Office: 115 N Oak Park Ave Oak Park IL 60301 Tel (312) 386-4126

HAGUE, GREGORY D., b. Cin., Sept. 30, 1948; B.S., Miami U., 1971; J.D., Am. U., 1974. Admitted to Ohio bar, 1974; with Hague Realtors, Cin., 1970—. Mem. Ohio, Cin. bar assns., Cin. Bd. Realtors, Nat., Ohio assns. realtors, Soc. Real Estate Appraisers, Am. Assn. Trial Lawyers. Home: 8543 Landen Cove Ln Cincinnati OH 45239 Office: 7321 Montgomery Rd Cincinnati OH 45236 Tel (513) 891-5555

HAHESY, WILLIAM CARRICK, b. Tulare, Calif., Oct. 31, 1932; B.A., Fresno State Coll., 1954; J.D., U. Calif., Berkeley, 1957. Admitted to Calif. bar, 1957, U.S. Dist. Ct. No. Dist. Calif., 1957, U.S. Cts. of Appeal for 9th Circuit, 1957; dep. dist. atty. County of Tulare, 1958-59; mem. firm Hahesy & Hahesy, Tulare, 1960-62; individual practice law, Tulare, 1962-71, 75—; mem. firm Hahesy & Ward, 1971-75; judge Tulare Jud. Dist. Ct., 1969—. Active, Tulare Plaza Project, 1946-65, Tulare City Planning Commn., 1960-69, Tulare County Alcoholism Council, 1971-72; chmn. Tulare Redevel. Agy., 1967—; bd. dirs. Tulare County Legal Services, 1964-67, Tulare County Tng. Center for Handicapped, 1962-72; v.p., bd. dirs. Tulare Local Devel. Co. Mem. Calif., Tulare County bar assns., Calif. Trial Lawyers Assn., Greater Tulare C. of C. (dir. 1966-69, chmn. task force com. 1967, Man of Year 1974). Home: 1086 Manor St Tulare CA 93274 Office: 225 North M St Tulare CA 93274 Tel (209) 686-8633

HAHN, GILBERT, JR., b. Washington, Sept. 12, 1921; A.B., Princeton, 1943; LL.B., Yale, 1948. Admitted to D.C. bar, 1948, also Md. bar, 1958; asso., then partner firm Trobiner, Trobiner & Hahn; partner firm Amram, Hahn, Sendground & Santerelli and predecessors, Washington, 1954-76, firm Wolf, Block, Schorr & Solis-Cohen, Washington, 1976—; chmn. D.C. City Council, 1969-72; dir. U.S. Shoe Corp. Mem. Republican Nat. Finance Com., 1964-68; chmn. D.C. Rep. Com., 1968-69; pres. bd. dirs. Washington Hosp. Center Research Found., 1964-66, Washington Hosp. Center, 1966-69. Mem. D.C., Md., U.S. Supreme Ct. bar assns. Decorated Purple Heart. Office: 2000 K St NW Washington DC 20006

HAHN, JEROME, b. Pitts., May 14, 1920; B.A., U. Pitts., 1942, LL.B., 1947. Admitted to Pa. bar, 1948; city solicitor, Pa., 1962-72; individual practice law, 1972—; solicitor Twp. Home: 595 McKinley Ave Washington PA 15301 Office: 247 Washington Trust Bldg Washington PA 15301 Tel (412) 225-4900

HAID, DONALD J., b. Winnipeg, Man., Can., Jan. 27, 1927; B.A., Emory U., 1950; J.D., George Washington U., 1971. Enlisted in U.S. Army, 1950, advanced through grades to lt. col., 1966; chief Army Aviation Human Research Unit, Ft. Rucker, Ala., 1961-64; comdg. officer 501st Aviation Bn., Viet Nam, 1965-66; ret., 1970; admitted to Tex. bar, 1971; asso. firm Henry Klepak, Dallas, 1971-75; partner firm Haid & Kyle, Inc., Dallas, 1975—. Mem. Am., Tex., Dallas bar assns., Assn. U.S. Army, Ret. Officers Assn., Army Aviation Assn. Am. Decorated Legion of Merit (2), Bronze Star, Air medal (11). Home: 2943 Las Campanas St Dallas TX 75234 Office: 4835 LBJ Freeway Dallas TX 75234 Tel (214) 387-4830

HAIGNEY, JOHN EUSTACE, b. N.Y.C., Feb. 15, 1912; B.S., N.Y. U., 1933; LL.B., St. Johns U., 1936. Admitted to N.Y. bar, 1937; since practiced in N.Y.C., asso. firm Scandrett, Tuttle & Chaiaire, 1937-49, partner firm Ide & Haigney, 1949—; dir. Clevepak Corp., Glyco Chem. Inc., Chas. L. Huisking & Co., W.R. Grace & Co., Inc. Trustee Leonard Tingle Found., Huisking Found. Mem. Am., N.Y. State bar assns., Assn. Bar City N.Y., N.Y. County Lawyers Assn. Home: 37 Larchmont Ave Larchmont NY 10538 Office: 41 E 42nd St New York City NY 10017 Tel (212) 682-2590

HAIGWOOD, THOMAS DAVID, lawyer; b. Columbia, S.C., Nov. 9, 1945; LL.B., U. N.C., 1970. Admitted to N.C. bar, 1970, Fed. bar, 1970, U.S. Supreme Ct., 1974; law clk. U.S. Dist. Ct., Eastern Dist. N.C., 1970-71; asst. dist. solicitor, New Bern, N.C., 1971-73; partner firm Owens, Browning & Haigwood, Greenville, N.C., 1973-75; asst. dist. atty., 3d Judicial Dist., Greenville, 1975—. Mem. N.C., Am., Pitt County bar assns., N.C. Dist. Atty.'s Assn. Kiwanian (pres. 1975-76). Office: Pitt County Courthouse PO Box 643 Greenville NC 27834

HAILEY, JOE C., b. Nashville, Sept. 19, 1943; B.B.A., Memphis State U., 1965, J.D., 1968. Admitted to Tenn. bar, 1968; individual practice law, Selmer, Tenn., 1968-69; partner firm Hailey & Whitlow, Selmer, 1970—. Mem. Am., Tenn. bar assns., Rotary. Case editor: Memphis State Law Review, 1967-68. Office: W Houston Ave Selmer TN 38375 Tel (901) 645-6147

HAIMS, BRUCE DAVID, b. N.Y.C., Nov. 25, 1940; B.S. in Econs., U. Pa., 1962; LL.B. magna cum laude, Harvard, 1965; LL.M., N.Y. U., 1972. Admitted to Conn. bar, 1965, N.Y. bar, 1967; asso. firm Debevoise, Plimpton, Lyons & Gates, N.Y.C., 1967-72, partner, 1973—. Mem. N.Y. State Bar Assn. (employee benefit com., tax sect.), Assn. Bar City N.Y., Beta Gamma Sigma, Beta Alpha Psi. Office: Debevoise Plimpton et al 299 Park Ave New York City NY 10017 Tel (212) 752-6400

HAIN, BRUCE VALENTINE, b. Selma, Ala., Sept. 3, 1915; A.B., Vanderbilt U., 1938; LL.B., U. Ala., 1941. Admitted to Ala. bar, 1941; individual practice law, Selma, 1941-59; partner firm Hobbs and Hain, Selma, 1959—; mem. Ala. Ho. of Reps., 1954-70. Bd. dirs. Sturdivant Museum, Selma. Mem. Dallas County (Ala.), Am. bar assns., Ala. State Bar, Ala. Law Inst. (council 1972—). Home: 109 Hooper Dr Selma AL 36701 Office: 100 Church St Selma AL 36701 Tel (205) 874-4694

HAINES, ANDREW WILLIAM, III, b. New Orleans, Sept. 9, 1944; A.B., U. Minn., 1966; J.D., U. Mich., 1969; postgrad. (Reginald Heber Smith Community Lawyer fellow), 1969. Admitted to La. bar, 1970, Minn. bar, 1971; atty. New Orleans Legal Assistance Corp., 1969-70; atty. Legal Assistance of Ramsey County (La.), 1970-71; asso. firm Doherty, Rumble & Butler, St. Paul, 1971-73; asst. prof. law William Mitchell Coll., 1973—. Mem. Metro Econ. Devel. Assn., Mpls., 1972—, State Bd. Human Rights, St. Paul, 1971-75, Mpls. Commn. Human Relations, 1974-76, Twin Cities Fed. Exec. Bd. Minority Bus. Devel. Com., 1975—. Mem. La., Minn., Ramsey County bar assns., Am. Assn. Law Schs. Home: 5726 Garfield Ave S Minneapolis MN 55419 Office: 2100 Summit Ave Saint Paul MN 55105 Tel (612) 698-3885

HAINES, RICHARD SAWYER, b. Lakewood, N.J., Jan. 10, 1947; A.B., Kenyon Coll., 1968; J.D., Boston U., 1971. Admitted to Mass. bar, 1971, N.J. bar, 1973; asso. firm Haines, Schuman & Butz, Toms River, N.J., 1973-75, partner, 1975—; municipal prosecutor Stafford Twp., 1975. Mem. Am., Ocean County, N.J. bar assns., Assn. Trial Lawyers Am. Home: 1430 Summit Ave Toms River NJ 08753 Office: 214 Washington St Toms River NJ 08753 Tel (201) 349-4400

HAINLINE, FORREST ARTHUR, JR., b. Rock Island, Ill., Oct. 20, 1918; A.B., Augustana Coll., 1940; J.D., U. Mich., 1947, LL.M., 1948. Admitted to Ill. bar, 1942, Mich. bar, 1943, Fla. bar, 1970, also U.S. Supreme Ct.; mem. firm Cross, Wrock, Miller & Vieson, and predecessor, Detroit, 1948-71, partner, 1957-71; v.p., gen. counsel Am. Motors Corp., Detroit, 1971—, sec., 1972—. Chmn., Wayne County Regional Interagy. Coordinating Com. for Developmental Disabilities, 1972—; chmn. grievance com. U.S. Tennis Assn., 1970—, mem. exec. com., 1972—; pres. Catholic Social Services of Oakland County, 1972—, Western Tennis Assn. Mich., Ill., Ind., Wis., Ohio, Ky., 1972-74, Western Improvement Assn., 1969—. Bd. dirs. Augustana (Ill.) Coll. Mem. Am., Fed., Mich., Ill., Fla., Detroit bar assns., Am. Judicature Soc., Mich. Assn. Professions, Augustana (Ill.) Coll. Alumni Assn. (pres. bd. dirs. 1973-74), Phi Alpha Delta. Home: 26308 Ivanhoe Rd Detroit MI 48239 Office: 27777 Franklin Rd Southfield MI 48076*

HAIR, MATTOX STRICKLAND, b. Coral Gables, Fla., Jan. 18, 1938; B.S., Fla. State U., 1960; J.D., U. Fla., 1964. Admitted to Fla. bar, 1964; asst. atty. gen. State of Fla., Tallahassee, 1964-65; partner firm Marks, Gray, Conroy & Gibbs, Jacksonville, Fla., 1965—; mem. Fla. House of Reps., Tallahassee, 1972-74; mem. Fla. Senate, Tallahassee, 1974—. Mem. Am., Fla., Jacksonville bar assns. Recipient Jacksonville Jaycees Good Govt. award, 1974. Home: 2950 Saint Johns Ave Jacksonville FL 32205 Office: 231 E Forsyth St Jacksonville FL 32202 Tel (904) 355-6681

HAIRSTON, ANDREW JASPER, b. Clemons, N.C., July 8, 1932; B.A., Paul Quinn Coll., 1955, B.S., 1956; B.D., Tex. Christian U., 1961, Th.M., 1971; J.D., John Marshall Law Sch., 1969; LL.M., Woodrow Wilson Law Sch., 1970; postgrad. Atlanta U., 1961-63. Admitted to Ga. bar, 1971; ordained to ministry Ch. of Christ, 1951; pastor S. 8th St. Ch. of Christ, Waco, Tex., 1957-61, Lake Como Ch. of Christ, Fort Worth, 1957-61, Simpson St. Ch. of Christ, Atlanta, 1961—; salesman Louie C. Hill Realty Co., Atlanta, 1968-71, asso. broker, v.p., 1971-73; asso. broker Charles Clark Properties, Inc., Decatur, Ga., 1973-74, Realty Dynamics, Inc., Atlanta, 1974—; individual practice law, Atlanta, 1971-76; asst. solicitor gen. Fulton County (Ga.) State Ct., Atlanta, 1976—; instr. law John Marshall Law Sch., Atlanta, 1971—. Coordinator Give God a Chance, Monrovia, Liberia, 1969; coordinator 26th Nat. Lectureship, Chs. of Christ, 1970, organizer S.E. lectureship, 1973—, coordinator, 1973—. Mem. NAACP, SCLC, Operation Breadbasket, Nat. Bus. League, Am., Nat., Ga., Atlanta, Gate City bar assns., Ga. Conf. Black Lawyers, Christian Council. Home: 245 E Simon Terr NW Atlanta GA 30318 Office: 2485 Bankhead Hwy NW Atlanta GA 30318

HAITBRINK, RICHARD F., b. Salina, Kans., Sept. 7, 1941; B.A. in Econs., U. Kans., 1963, J.D., 1966. Admitted to Kans. bar, 1966, Mo. bar, 1968; legis. asst. for U.S. Sen. James B. Pearson of Kans., Washington, 1966-68; asso. firm Brewer & Myers, Kansas City, Mo., 1968-69; partner firm Herntzen, Haitbrink & Moore, Kansas City, 1969—. Active Kansas City United Fund, 1969-73. Mem. Am., Kans., Kansas City, Mo. bar assns., Lawyers Assn. Kansas City, Estate Planning Council of Kansas City, Order of Coif. Home: 8171 Monrovia St Lenexa KS 66215 Office: 1140 Ten Main Center Kansas City MO 64105 Tel (816) 221-5025

HAJEWSKI, CYRIL MARTIN, b. Milw., Nov. 12, 1916; B.M.E., Marquette U., 1939, J.D., 1947. Admitted to Wis. bar, 1947, U.S. Supreme Ct. bar, 1961; sr. atty. Kearney & Trecker Corp., West Allis, Wis., 1947—. Mem. Am., Wis. bar assns., Am., Milw. patent law assns., Internat. Patent and Trademark Assn., Licensing Execs. Soc. Home: 12209 W Holt Ave West Allis WI 53227 Office: 11000 Theodore Trecker Way West Allis WI 53214 Tel (414) 476-8300

HAKIM, VICTOR PHILIP, b. N.Y.C., Mar. 14, 1944; B.A., U. Miami, 1964; LL.B., Bklyn. Law Sch., 1967, J.D., 1968; postgrad. U.S. Treasury Law Enforcement Sch., 1968. Admitted to N.Y. bar, 1968, U.S. Dist. Cts., 1968; spl. agt. intelligence div. U.S. Treasury Dept., N.Y.C., 1967-71; partner firm Hakim & Landau, N.Y.C., 1971—; gen. counsel Future Foods Corp., N.Y.C., 1975—. Mem. Am., N.Y. bar assns., Am., N.Y. trial lawyers assns., Am. Judicature Soc., Fed. Investigators Assn., N.Y. Assn. Chiefs of Police. Office: 340 E 63d St New York City NY 10021 Tel (212) 688-2472

HALAMKA, DAGMAR MARIE VANAGS, b. Riga, Latvia, July 15, 1942; came to U.S., 1950, naturalized, 1956; student Grandview Jr. Coll., 1961-62, El Camino Coll., 1968-69, Calif. State Coll., 1968-70; J.D., Loyola U., 1973. Admitted to Calif. bar, 1973; asso. with Hiram W. Kwan, Los Angeles, 1973—; partner firm Halamka & Halamka, Torrance, Calif., 1976—; dir. legal asst. program El Camino (Calif.) Coll., 1976—, prof. bus. law, 1974—; prof. bus. law U. So. Calif., Los Angeles, 1974—. Leader Women's Rights Sem. and Workshops, Ceritos and El Camino Jr. Colls., 1975—. Mem. Los Angeles Bar Assn., Women Lawyers Assn. Author: Joy of Law; More Joy of Law; recipient award Am. Jurisprudence Soc., 1972. Office: 3220 W Sepulveda Suite A Torrance CA 90505 Tel (213) 539-1431

HALBACH, EDWARD CHRISTIAN, JR., b. Clinton, Iowa, Nov. 8, 1931; B.A., U. Iowa, 1953; J.D., 1958; LL.M., Harvard, 1959; LL.D., U. Redlands, 1971. Admitted to Iowa bar, 1958; individual practice law, Clinton, 1958-59; acting asso. prof. law U. Calif., Berkeley, 1959-62, prof., 1962—, dean Sch. of Law, 1966-75. Mem. Am. Bar Assn., Am. Law Inst., Am. Coll. Probate Counsel, Internat. Acad. Estate and Trust Law, Order of Coif. Author: (with E. Scoles) Materials on Decedents' Estates and Trusts, 2d edit., 1973; Uses of Trusts in Estate Planning, 1975; contbr. articles to legal jours. Home: 679 San Luis Rd Berkeley CA 94707 Office: School of Law Univ of Calif Berkeley CA 94720 Tel (415) 642-1829

HALBACH, VICTOR MARION, JR., b. Memphis, Sept. 5, 1939; B.S., Fla. State U., 1961; J.D., U. Fla., 1965. Admitted to Fla. bar, 1966; partner firm Marks, Gray, Conroy & Gibbs, Jacksonville, Fla., 1966—. Bd. govs. Fellowship of Christian Athletes, 1974—; com. chmn. Greater Jacksonville Open Golf Tournament, 1974—. Mem. Am., Fla., Jacksonville (bd. govs. 1973—) bar assns., Fla. Def. Lawyers Assn., Assn. Ins. Attys. Contbg. author Fla. Civil Practice Damages Manual, 1968. Office: PO Box 447 Jacksonville FL 32201 Tel (904) 355-6681

HALBERSTADT, BERTRAM STANLEY, b. Bklyn., May 21, 1939; B.A., Queens Coll., 1959; M.A. in Psychology, U. Mich., 1961; J.D., Columbia, 1964. Admitted to N.Y. State bar, 1965, Del. bar, 1969; atty. Anti-Defamation League, N.Y.C., 1965-67, Bristol Myers Co., N.Y.C., 1967-69; mem. firm Connolly, Bove & Lodge, Wilmington, Del., 1969-76, Murdoch & Walsh, Wilmington, 1976—; prof. law Goldey Beacom Coll., Wilmington, 1975—. Mem. Del., N.Y. State bar assns., Am. Bar Assn. (mem. Supreme Ct. Del. adv. commn. to implement standards of criminal justice), Am. Trial Lawyers Assn., Soc. Med. Jurisprudence. Home: 1112 Grinnell Rd Wilmington DE 19803 Office: Murdoch and Walsh Bank of Del Bldg Wilmington DE 19899 Tel (302) 658-8661

HALBERT, SHERRILL, b. Terra Bella, Calif., Oct. 17, 1901; A.B., U. Cal., Berkeley, 1924, J.D., 1927. Admitted to Calif. bar, 1927; individual practice law, Porterville, Calif., 1927-42; asso. firm McCutchen, Olney, Mannon & Greene, San Francisco, 1942-44; individual practice law, Modesto, Calif., 1944-49; dist. atty. Stanislaus County, Calif., 1949; judge Superior Ct. of State of Calif., 1949-54; judge U.S. Dist. Ct., Eastern Dist. Calif., Sacramento, 1954—; chmn. McGeorge Sch. of Law bd. advisors. Mem. Selden Soc., Phi Delta Phi. Contbr. author: Lincoln for the Ages, 1960, Lincoln: A Contemporary Portrait, 1962. Home: 4120 Los Coches Way Sacramento CA 95825 Office: 2042 U S Ct House 650 Capitol Mall Sacramento CA 95814 Tel (916) 440-2211

HALBREICH, JEFFREY WILLIAM, b. N.Y.C., Oct. 2, 1941; B.A., Bethany Coll., 1963; LL.B., N.Y. Law Sch., 1966. Admitted N.Y. State bar, 1967; asso. firm Leinwand, Maron & Hendler, N.Y.C., 1967-68; atty., asst. sec. Prentice-Hall Corp., N.Y.C., 1968—. Mem. com. on rent control Village of Freeport, N.Y., 1969. Mem. N.Y. County, N.Y. State bar assns. Home: 53 Stratford Rd Rockville Centre NY 11570 Office: 521 Fifth Ave Room 900 New York City NY 10017 Tel (212) 687-7660

HALBRIN, HENRY STEINER, b. N.Y.C., May 5, 1924; LL.B., U. Va., 1949, J.D., 1970. Admitted to N.Y. bar, 1949, Conn. bar, 1967, U.S. Supreme Ct. bar, 1961; atty. Legal Aid Soc., N.Y.C., 1950-51; spl. dep. asst. atty. gen. State of N.Y., N.Y.C., 1952; asst. counsel N.Y. State Temporary Housing Rent Commn., N.Y.C., 1972-73; asso. J. Leo Rothschild and partner firm Kahaner, Norman & Halprin, N.Y.C., 1952-55; asso. counsel N.Y. State Joint Legis. Com. on Charitable and Philanthropic Orgns., 1955; asst. counsel, acting chief ops., asst. regional dir. for spl. programs U.S. Housing and Home Fin. Agy., N.Y.C., 1955-61; asso. firm Demov & Morris, N.Y.C., 1961-64, partner, 1964-65; partner firm Halprin & Goler, Bridgeport, Conn., 1965—. Mem. Am., Conn. bar assns., N.Y. County Lawyers Assn., Bar Assn. City N.Y., B'nai Brith (chmn. anti-defamation league). Office: 855 Main St Bridgeport CT 06604 Tel (203) 334-0444 also 60 E 42d St New York City NY 10017 Tel (212) 986-4181

HALBY, WILLIAM GRANDJEAN, b. Marion, Ohio, June 27, 1931; A.B., U. Mich., 1953, J.D., 1955. Admitted to Mich. bar, 1955, N.Y. bar, 1956; asso. firm White & Case, N.Y.C., 1955-63; asso. firm Wickes, Riddell, Bloomer, Jacobi & McGuire, N.Y.C., 1963-67, partner, 1968-73; asso. gen. counsel Equitable Life Assurance Soc., N.Y.C., 1973—, v.p., 1975—. Mem. Am. Bar Assn., Assn. Life Ins. Counsel, Assn. of N.Y. Life Ins. Cos., Am. Council Life Ins. (co. tax subcom.), Order of Coif. Office: 1285 Ave of Americas New York City NY 10019 Tel (212) 554-4908

HALE, ALLAN MURRAY, b. Plymouth, Mass., Feb. 21, 1914; LL.B., Northeastern U., 1939, LL.D. (hon.), 1972; J.D. (hon.), New Eng. Sch. Law, 1975. Admitted to Mass. bar, 1940; asst. dist. atty., Plymouth County, 1951-54; justice Superior Ct. Mass., Boston, 1967—, chief justice Appeals Ct., 1972—. Mem. Middleboro (Mass.) Fin. Com., 1938-41; chmn. Middleboro Housing Authority, 1949-67, Middleboro chpt. ARC. Home: 35 Peirce St Middleboro MA 02346 Office: 1500 New Courthouse Boston MA 02108 Tel (617) 742-1140

HALE, BENJAMIN WILKES, JR., b. Logan, W.Va., June 21, 1944; B.B.A., Marshall U., 1967; J.D., Ohio State U., 1970. Admitted to Ohio bar, 1970; asso. firm Smith Stobin, Columbus, Ohio, 1970-72, partner, 1972—. Mem. Bexley (Ohio) Planning Commn., 1976—; active Columbus Area Leadership Program. Mem. Am., Ohio, Columbus bar assns., Am. Judicature Soc. Home: 2361 Bryden Rd Columbus OH 43209 Office: 37 W Broad St Columbus OH 43215 Tel (614) 221-4255

HALE, CHARLES RUSSELL, b. Talpa, Tex., Oct. 17, 1916; A.B., Stanford, 1939; J.D., Fordham U., 1950. Supr., United Geophys. Co., Pasadena, Calif., 1940-46; mem. patent staff Bell Telephone Labs., N.Y.C., 1947-48, Sperry Gyroscope Co., Great Neck, N.Y., 1948-51; admitted to N.Y. State bar, 1950, Calif. bar, 1953; individual practice law, Pasadena, 1951-54; mem. firm Christie, Parker & Hale, Pasadena, 1954—. Mem. Am., Los Angeles, Pasadena bar assns., Am. Patent Law Assn., Am. Soc. Internat. Law, AAAS, IEEE. Office: 201 S Lake Ave Pasadena CA 91101 Tel (213) 795-5843

HALE, DOUGLAS ALLAN, b. Middleboro, Mass., Mar. 14, 1945; B.A., Boston U., 1967, J.D., 1970. Admitted to Mass. bar, 1970, U.S. Dist. Ct. for Mass. bar, 1974; asso. firm Kisloff, Hoch, Schuman & Flanagan, Boston, 1973-74; dist. atty., Suffock County, Boston, 1974-75; partner firm Huntoon, Hale and Hennessey, Wareham, Mass., 1975-77; partner firm Hale and Hale, Middleboro, 1976—. Pres. Citizens Scholarship Found., Middleboro, 1974—. Mem. Am., Mass, Plymouth County bar assns. Home: 31 School St Middleboro MA 02346 Office: Route 28 Office Bldg W Grove St Middleboro MA 02346 Tel (617) 947-7056

HALE, HAMILTON ORIN, b. Crystal Lake, Ill., Sept. 15, 1906; B.S., U. Ill., 1928; J.D., Northwestern U., 1931. Admitted to Ill. bar, 1931, U.S. Ct. Claims bar, 1935, N.Y. bar, 1940, U.S. Ct. Appeals 2d Circuit bar, 1964, U.S. Dist. Ct. for D.C. bar, 1965; partner firm Bennett & Hale, McHenry County, Ill., 1931; asso. firm Pruitt & Grealis, Chgo., 1932-40; partner firm Pruitt, Hale & MacIntyre, N.Y.C., 1940-48; founding partner firm Hale & Stimson (now Hale, Russell, Gray, Seaman & Birkett), N.Y.C. and Washington, 1948-70; of counsel firm Joslyn & Green, Woodstock, Ill., 1970—. Home: 317 S Valley Hill Rd Woodstock IL 60098 Office: 145 Virginia St Crystal Lake IL 60014 Tel (815) 459-8440

HALE, J. KEVIN, b. Kansas City, Mo., Mar. 7, 1947; B.A., U. Notre Dame, 1970; J.D., U. Mo., 1973. Admitted to Mo. bar, 1973, N.Mex. bar, 1973; asso. firm Wade Beavers, Farmington, N.Mex., 1973-76; individual practice, Farmington, 1976—; chief pub. defender San Juan County (N.Mex.). Bd. dirs. San Juan County Econ. Opportunity Council. Mem. Am., San Juan County (sec.) bar assns., Phi Delta Phi. Office: 1000 W Apache Farmington NM 87401 Tel (505) 325-8813

HALE, MICHAEL EUGENE, b. Dallas, Dec. 27, 1941; B.B.A., 1965, J.D., 1968. Admitted to Ark. bar, 1968, U.S. Supreme Ct. bar, 1975; asso. firm Barber, McCaskill, Amsler & Jones, Little Rock, 1968—. Mem. Pulaski County (Ark.), Ark., Am. bar assns. Home: 3019 Charter Oak St Little Rock AR 72201 Office: 1500 Union Nat Plaza Little Rock AR 72201 Tel (501) 372-6175

HALE, QUINCY HAROLD, b. Spring Valley, Minn., Mar. 24, 1893; B.A., Univ. Minn., 1915, LL.B., 1918. Admitted to Minn. bar, 1918, Wis. bar, 1919; sr. partner firm Hale, Skemp, Hanson, Schnurrer & Skemp, LaCrosse, Wis., 1919—. Mem. bd. trustees LaCrosse County Tubercular Sanatorium, 1927-33; Pub. Library LaCrosse, 1951-76. Mem. Am., Wis. (past pres.), LaCrosse County (past pres.) bar assns. Home: 1603 Main St LaCrosse WI 54601 Office: 515 State Bank Building LaCrosse WI 54601 Tel (608) 784-3540

HALE, WILLIAM BRADLEY, b. Mobile, Ala., Oct. 30, 1933; A.B., U. Ala., 1954, LL.B., 1956; M.B.A., Harvard, 1958. Admitted to Ala. bar, 1956, Ga. bar, 1960; partner firm King & Spalding, Atlanta, 1961—; trustee So. Fed. Tax. Inst.; dir. Oxford Industries, Inc.; dir. Crawford & Co. Trustee, Canterbury Ct., Atlanta. Mem. Am. Coll. Probate Counsel, Am., Atlanta bar assns., Lawyers Club Atlanta.

HALES, PAUL RICHARD, b. Des Moines, Sept. 3, 1945; B.A., Wesleyan U., 1967; J.D., Columbia, 1973. Admitted to Mo. bar, 1973; U.S. Dist. Cts. Eastern and Western Dists. Mo. bars, 1973; since practiced in St. Louis, asso. firm Louis Gilden, 1973; partner Goldstein & Hales, 1974; individual practice law, 1975—; hearing officer St. Louis County Juvenile Ct., 1974. Chmn. Aid to Victims of Crimes, St. Louis, 1975-76; mem. bd. dirs. Utilities Consumer Council Mo., 1975-76; mem. legal panel ACLU, Eastern dist. Mo., 1974-76. Mem. St. Louis Met. Bar Assn., Bar Assn. State of Mo., Recipient Distinguished Service award, St. Louis Jaycees, 1975. Office: 3 S Newstead St Louis MO 63108 Tel (314) 652-2035

HALEY, JAMES OLIVER, b. Crystal Springs, Miss., June 17, 1912; student Howard Coll.; LL.B., Birmingham Sch. Law, 1938. Admitted to Ala. bar, 1936; asso. firm Lange, Simpson, Robinson & Somerville, 1936-68; judge, 1968—; mem. Ala. Supreme Ct. Adv. Com. Civil Rules of Procedure. Bd. dirs. Met. Birmingham (Ala.) YMCA, 1955-68. Fellow Am. Coll. Trial Lawyers; mem. Nat. Assn. Ins. Counsel, Am. Assn. R.R. Trial Lawyers, Birmingham Bar Assn. (pres. 1963). Contbr. articles to Ala. Lawyer. Home: 1405 Panorama Dr Birmingham AL 35216 Office: 312 Jefferson County Courthouse Birmingham AL 35203 Tel (205) 325-5635

HALEY, JOHNNIE MILLER, b. Memphis, Dec. 25, 1944; B.A., Miss. State Univ., 1966; J.D., U. Miss., 1973. Admitted to Miss. bar, 1973; law clk. Miss. Supreme Ct., Jackson, 1973-74; capt. JAGC, U.S. Army, 1974-76; partner firm Pogue, Pace & Haley, Aberdeen, Miss., 1976—. Mem. Amory C. of C., Miss., Monroe County bar assns., Miss. Trial Lawyers Assn. Contbr. articles in field to profl. jours. Office: PO Drawer E Aberdeen MS 39730 Tel (601) 369-4857

HALEY, NEDOM ANGIER, b. Atlanta, Nov. 19, 1943; B.S. in Indsl. Mgmt., Ga. Inst. Tech., 1965; J.D., Emory U., 1970; LL.M. in Taxation, Georgetown U., 1973. Admitted to Ga. bar, 1971, D.C. bar, 1973; trial atty. chief counsel's office IRS, Washington, 1971-74; mem. firm Bouhan, Williams & Levy, Savannah, Ga., 1974-76, Rock & Haley, Atlanta, 1976—; gen. counsel Better Bus. Bur. of Coastal Empire, Savannah, 1975-76. Mem. Am. Bar Assn. Office: 1500 Tower Pl 3340 Peachtree Rd NE Atlanta GA 30326 Tel (404) 231-1240

HALFERTY, JAMES BURKHARDT, b. Lancaster, Wis., Oct. 9, 1930; student Ripon Coll., 1948-49; B.A., U. Wis., 1952, LL.B., 1956. Admitted to Wis. bar, 1956; asso. firm I.E. Rasmus, Chippewa Falls, Wis., 1956-61; individual practice law, Lancaster, 1961—; dist. atty. Grant County (Wis.), 1962-72; city atty. City of Lancaster, 1975—, Village of Tennyson (Wis.), 1976—; instr. criminal justice U. Wis., Platteville, 1968—. Bd. dirs. Lancaster Municipal Hosp., 1975—. Mem. State Bar Wis. Home: 515 W Pine St Lancaster WI 53813 Office: 108 S Madison St Lancaster WI 53813 Tel (608) 723-4075

HALGREN, LEON ALDOUS, b. Ogden, Utah, May 17, 1918; B.A., Brigham Young U., 1949; J.D., U San Francisco, 1952. Admitted to Utah bar, 1953, Alaska bar, 1959; asso. firm Rich & Strong, Salt Lake City, 1955-58; commr. U.S. Cts., Anchorage, 1958-59; solicitor Dept. Interior, Salt Lake City, 1959-61; asst. atty. Salt Lake City Corp., 1961-68; asst. atty. gen. Dept. Hwys., Salt Lake City, 1969; acting atty. Salt Lake County, 1969-70; partner firm Ryberg, McCoy & Halgren, Salt Lake City, 1971—; asst. atty. gen. State of Utah, Salt Lake City, 1976—. Home: 2574 Sage Way Salt Lake City UT 84109 Office: Capitol Bldg Room 115 Salt Lake City UT 84114 Tel (801) 533-6684

HALL, ALFRED E., b. Haldeman, Ky., Oct. 25, 1928; B.E.E., Mont. State Coll., 1956; J.D., George Washington U., 1963. Admitted to Minn. bar, 1964; atty. UNIVAC, St. Paul, 1963-68; partner firm Foster & Hall, Burnsville, Minn., 1968-70, firm Happe, Happe, Hall & Chinnock, Burnsville, 1970-73, firm Hall & Sjoquist, Burnsville, 1973—; v.p. Dakota County Legal Aid Soc. Mayor, City of Burnsville, 1965-75. Mem. IEEE, Am., Ramsey County bar assns. Home: 505 Summit Ln Burnsville MN 55337 Office: 12904 Nicollet Ave Burnsville MN 55337 Tel (612) 894-1055

HALL, ALLAN JON, b. Krakow, Poland, Apr. 12, 1936; B.Bldg. Constrn., U. Fla., 1958, J.D., 1968. Constrn. engr. Robert L. Turchin, Miami Beach, Fla., then Allan J. Hall Constrn. Co., Orlando, Fla.; admitted to Fla. bar, 1968, Ga. bar, 1969; practiced in Atlanta, 1968—; asso. firms McCready Johnston, Atlanta, 1968-70, Troutman, Sander, Lockerman & Ashmore, Atlanta, 1970-72; partner firm Resnick, Lawson, Hall & Fishman, P.C., Atlanta, 1972-76, Hall & Fishman, P.C., 1976—; faculty U. Fla. Coll. Architecture, 1966-68. Task force leader Atlanta C. of C., 1973. Mem. Am., Ga., Fla. Atlanta bar assns., Nat. Assn. Home Builders, Nat. Bd. Realtors, Gargoyle. Office: Suite 1940 Tower Pl 3340 Peachtree Rd Atlanta GA 30328 Tel (404) 231-0900

HALL, DONALD ORELL, b. Waco, Tex., Nov. 11, 1926; LL.B., Baylor U., 1951, J.D., 1969. Admitted to Tex. bar, 1951, U.S. Dist. Ct., 1955, U.S. Circuit Ct. of Appeals bar, 1976; individual practice law, Waco, 1951-53; justice of the peace, Waco, 1954-55; asst. dist. atty. then first asst. dist. atty. then dist. atty. McLennan County, Tex., 1955-66; sr. partner firm Hall, Terrell & Kettler and predecessors, Waco, Tex., 1967—; mem. bd. dirs. Legal Aid Soc., 1973-75; speaker Adult Probation Dept. seminars on alcohol related offenses, 1967—; mem. 11th Tex. Congl. dist. grievance com., 1967-75. Pres., McLennan County Council on Alcoholism, 1970-71; unit dir. United Fund, 1967—. Mem. Am., Tex., Waco-McLennan County bar assns., Delta Theta Phi. Contbr. articles to legal jours. Home: 1217 Rambler Dr Waco TX 76710 Office: 504 Austin Ave Mall Waco TX 76701 Tel (817) 756-4471

HALL, EUGENE CHARLES, b. Kansas City, Mo., July 9, 1930; B.M., Kans. U., 1953; J.D., U. Mo., 1958. Admitted to Mo. bar, 1958; asst. sec. Hallmark Cards, Inc., 1960-70; sec., gen. counsel Crown Center Redevel. Corp., Kansas City, Mo., 1963-70; partner firm Gage & Tucker, Kansas City, 1970—. Pres. Downtown YMCA, 1971, St. Mary's Hosp., 1972-74; bd. dirs., sec. City of Fountains Found. Mem. Am., Mo., Kansas City bar assns., Lawyers Assn. Kansas City. Home: 833 W 53d St Kansas City MO 64112 Office: 2345 Grand Ave Kansas City MO 64108 Tel 474-6460

HALL, FRANK DAWSON, b. Fort Lauderdale, Fla., Oct. 14, 1927; B.A., Duke U., 1949; LL.B., U. Fla., 1951, J.D., 1967; diploma in comparative law City of London Coll., 1950. Admitted to Fla. bar, 1951; partner firm Hall & Hedrick, Miami, 1951—, Hall & Swann, Coral Gables, Fla., 1977—; gen. counsel Howard Johnson Co., N.Y.C., Boston and Miami, 1967-71; mem. adv. council Practicing Law Inst., 1970-71; mem. judicial nominating commn. Fla. Supreme Ct., 1975—. Bd. mgrs. Miami YMCA, 1964-67. Fellow Am. Bar Found.; mem. Am. (mem. exec. council gen. practice sect. 1972-76, chmn. real property trans. com. 1972—), Dade County, Inter-Am. bar assns., Fla. Bar (mem. exec. council, bd. dirs. real property div. 1958-62, vice chmn. internat. law com. 1971, 75, chmn. agri-bus. law com. 1976—), Fla. Bar Found., Am. Judicature Soc., U.S. C. of C. (mem. anti-trust com. 1970-71), World Assn. Lawyers, Phi Delta Phi. Editorial staff U. Fla. Law Rev., 1950; contbg. author Florida Real Property Practice, 1965, rev. edit., 1975; contbr. articles to legal jours. Home: 1119 Hardee Rd Coral Gables FL 33146 Office: 2801 Ponce de Leon St Coral Gables FL 33134 Tel (305) 445-1477 also 200 SE 1st St Miami FL 33131 Tel (305) 379-0755

HALL, JAMES DAVID, b. Warsaw, Ind., Mar. 10, 1936; B.S. in Mech. Engring., Purdue U., 1958; J.D., Ind. U., 1961; postgrad. George Washington U., 1966-67. Admitted to Ind. bar, 1961, U.S. Supreme Ct. bar, 1967, U.S. Patent Office bar, 1968; patent adviser AEC, Washington, 1965-67; patent atty. Oltsch & Knoblock, South Bend, Ind., 1967—. Dist. camping chmn. Boy Scouts Am., 1968-69, dist. activities chmn., 1969-71, dist. chmn., 1971-73, council commr., 1973; treas. Am. Cancer Soc., 1975—; pres. South Bend Rotary Club, 1976-77. Mem. Am., Ind., St. Joseph County bar assns., Bar Assn. 7th Fed. Circuit, Jr. C. of C. (bd. dirs. 1969-70). Named Dir. of Year, South Bend Jr. C. of C., 1970. Home: 53211 Kinglet Ln South Bend IN 46637 Office: 402 JMS Bldg South Bend IN 46601 Tel (219) 234-6091

HALL, JOHN HARRIS, b. N.Y.C., June 20, 1929; A.B. cum laude, Princeton, 1949; LL.B. magna cum laude, Harvard, 1957. Admitted to Calif. bar, 1958; asso. firm Latham & Watkins, Los Angeles, 1957-66, partner, 1966-72, 74—, chmn. tax and probate dept., 1975—; dep. asst. sec. for tax policy Dept. Treasury, Washington, 1972-74. Mem. State Bar Calif. (chmn. com. on taxation 1971-72), Los Angeles County (chmn. sect. taxes 1970-71), Am. (chmn. com. on sales exchanges 1970-72) bar assns. Contbr. articles to legal jours. Home: 2820 E California Blvd Pasadena CA 91107 Office: 555 S Flower St Los Angeles CA 90071 Tel (213) 485-1234

HALL, JOHN WESLEY, JR., b. Watertown, N.Y., Jan. 28, 1948; B.A., Hendrix Coll., 1970; J.D., U. Ark., 1973. Admitted to Ark. bar, 1973, D.C. bar, 1975, U.S. Supreme Ct. bar, 1976; dep. pros. atty. 6th Jud. Dist. Ark., Little Rock, 1973—; law clk. Ark. Supreme Ct., 1974; editor Ark. Prosecutor's Trial Manual, 1976—. Mem. Am., Ark. (mem. ho. of dels. 1976—), Pulaski County (Ark.) bar assns., Ark. Prosecuting Attys. Assn., Nat. Dist. Attys. Assn. Contbr. articles to law reviews. Home: 12920 Southridge Dr Little Rock AR 72212 Office: Room 304 Pulaski County Courthouse Little Rock AR 72203 Tel (501) 375-9143

HALL, KENNETH KELLER, b. Greenview, W.Va., Feb. 24, 1918; J.D., W. Va. U., 1948. Admitted to W.Va. bar, 1948; individual practice law, Madison, W.Va., 1948-53; judge 25th Jud. Circuit of W.Va., Madison, 1953-69, U.S. Dist. Ct. for So. Dist. W.Va., Charleston, 1971-76, U.S. Ct. Appeals for Fourth Circuit, Charleston, 1976—. Mem. Am., W.Va. bar assns., W.Va. Jud. Assn. Recipient Silver Beaver award Boy Scouts Am., 1962. Office: PO Box 2549 Charleston WV 25329 Tel (304) 346-3641

HALL, LARRY DEAN, b. Hastings, Nebr., Nov. 8, 1944; A.B., Kearney State Coll., 1964; J.D., U. Nebr., 1967. Admitted to Nebr. bar, 1967; partner firm Wright, Simmons, Hancock and Hall, Scottsbluff, Nebr., 1971; atty. Kans.-Nebr. Natural Gas Co., Inc., Hastings, 1971, atty., asst. treas., 1972-75, dir. regulatory affairs, 1975, v.p. regulatory affairs, 1976—. Deacon United Presbyterian Ch., 1968; bd. dirs. Scottsbluff United Way, 1970-71, 23 Club, Youth Baseball, 1971. Mem. Am. Nebr. bar assns., Fed. Power Bar. Home: Box 608 Hastings NE 68901 Office: 300 North St Joseph Ave Hastings NE 68901 Tel (402) 462-2141

HALL, LYNN ELLEN, b. Spanish Fork, Utah, Mar. 14, 1946; B.A. with distinction, Stanford, 1968; J.D., Yale, 1972. Admitted to Calif. bar, 1972; asso. firm Hill, Farrer & Burrill, Los Angeles, 1972—. Mem. Am., Los Angeles County bar assns., Women Lawyers Assn. Office: 445 S Figueroa St Los Angeles CA 90071 Tel (213) 620-0460

HALL, LYSLE GRIFFITH, JR., b. Jackson, Mich., Dec. 7, 1930; B.A., Albion Coll., 1952; J.D., Wayne State U., 1958; postgrad Nat. Coll. State Judiciary, U. Nev., 1971. Admitted to Mich. bar, 1958; individual practice law, Jackson, Mich., 1958-68; chief asst. pros. atty. Jackson County, Mich., 1959-64; justice of peace, Jackson, 1965-68; judge State Mich. Dist. Ct., 12th Dist., Jackson, 1969—; faculty mem. Spring Arbor (Mich.) Coll., 1975-76. Mem. Am., Mich., Jackson County bar assns., Am. Judicature Soc., Mich. Dist. Judges Assn. (sec.). Office: Jackson County Bldg 312 S Jackson St Jackson MI 49201 Tel (517) 788-4260

HALL, MARION HEYWOOD, b. Vidalia, Ga., Oct. 14, 1925; LL.B., Mercer U., 1951. Admitted to Ga. bar, 1951; with Crawford & Co., Atlanta, 1958-65; dir. claim tng. State Auto Ins. Group, Columbus, Ohio, 1965-68; v.p.-claims Volkswagen Ins. Co., St. Louis, 1968-73; nat. casualty-automobile mgr. Gen. Adjustment Bur., N.Y.C., 1973-76; v.p.-claims Ga. Casualty & Surety Co., Atlanta, 1976; asso. dir. tng. Farm Bur. Tech. div. So. Farm Bur. Ins. Co., Jackson, Miss., 1976—. Home: 1229 Woodfield Dr Jackson MS 39211

HALL, MILES LEWIS, JR., b. Ft. Lauderdale, Fla., Aug. 14, 1924; grad. Riverside Military Acad., Gainesville, Ga., 1942; A.B., Princeton, 1948; J.D., Harvard, 1950. Admitted to Fla. bar, 1951; asso. firm Hall & Hedrick, Miami, 1951-56, partner, 1956—; chmn. nominating commn. Dist. Ct. Appeal 3d Dist., Fla., 1972-75. Chmn. Dade County chpt. Am. Red Cross, 1963-64; pres. Orange Bowl Com., Miami, 1964-65; pres. Coral Gables (Fla.) War Meml. Youth Center Assn., 1969-72. Bd. visitors Fla. State U. Sch. Law, Tallahassee, 1975—. Mem. The Fla. Bar, Am. (chmn. membership com. sect. of corp. banking and bus. law 1972-76), Dade County (pres. 1967-68) bar assns., Am. Judicature Soc., Fla. Council Bar Pres. Home: 2907 Alhambra Circle Coral Gables FL 33134 Office: Suite 1104 Greater Miami Federal Bldg Miami FL 33134 Tel (305) 379-0755

HALL, NARRVEL ELWIN, b. Malta, Idaho, Jan. 30, 1940; B.S., Brigham Young U., 1964; J.D., U. Utah, 1967. Admitted to Utah bar, 1967, U.S. Tax Ct. bar, 1969; asso. firm Fabian & Clendenin, Salt Lake City, 1967-70, partner, 1971—; adj. instr. legal writing program Brigham Young U. Mem. Am., Utah, Salt Lake County bar assns., Estate Planning Council Salt Lake City, Mountain States Pension Conf. Contbr. articles to profl. jours. Office: Continental Bank Bldg Salt Lake City UT 84101 Tel (801) 531-8900

HALL, PETER ALFONZO, b. Prattville, Ala., Aug. 21, 1912; student Johnson C. Smith U., 1929-30, 30-31; LL.B., DePaul U., 1947, J.D., 1970; LL.D., Mary Holmes Coll., 1974. Admitted to Ala. bar, 1948; individual practice law, Birmingham, 1948-72; judge Birmingham Recorder's Ct., 1972—; asso. counsel NAACP Legal Def. Fund, 1950-72; mem. Ala. Constl. Commn.; mem. gen. assembly permanent jud. commn. United Presbyn. Ch. U.S.A. Bd. dirs. Operation New Birmingham. Mem. Am., Ala., Birmingham bar assns., Am. Judicature Soc., Am. Judges Assn. Home: #4 12th Ave N Birmingham AL 35204 Office: 102 City Hall Birmingham AL 35203 Tel (205) 254-2161

HALL, PHILO ITHAMAR, b. Brookings, S.D., Aug. 2, 1916; student S.D. State U., Brookings, 1934-36; LL.B., U. S.D., Vermillion, 1939. Admitted to S.D. bar, 1939; individual practice law, Brookings, 1939-40, Aberdeen, S.D., 1954-56; partner firms Scholosser & Hall, Brookings, 1940-41, Dwight Campbell & Philo Hall, Aberdeen, 1947-54; spl. agt. FBI, Newark, N.J., Providence, R.I., also Chgo., 1941-47; judge S.D. Circuit Ct., 5th Jud. Circuit, 1956—, presiding judge, 1974—; mem. faculty Nat. Coll. State Judiciary, 1966, 72. Mem. Judges Assn. S.D. (pres. 1965-66), Brown County (pres. 1948), Am. bar assns., State Bar S.D. (chmn. jury instruction project 1961-73), Soc. Former Spl. Agts. FBI. Home: 1403 S Main St Aberdeen SD 57401 Office: Courthouse 1 Court St Aberdeen SD 57401 Tel (605) 622-2265

HALL, RICHARD EDGAR, b. Boise, Idaho, Feb. 7, 1944; B.A., U. Idaho, 1966; J.D., Harvard U., 1969. Admitted to Idaho bar, 1970; asso. firm Moffatt, Thomas Barrett and Blanton, Boise, 1969-71, partner, 1971—; tchr. Idaho Bar Rev. Inc., 1973-76; lectr. Boise State U., 1977—. Chmn. div. lawyers United Way Campaign, Boise, 1976. Mem. Idaho State, Boise, Am. bar assns., Idaho Assn. Def. Counsel (panel), Pitts. Inst. Legal Medicine. Home: 3010 Hillway Dr Boise ID 83702 Office: PO Box 829 Boise ID 83701 Tel (208) 345-2334

HALL, RICHARD GORMAN, b. Mpls., June 3, 1923; student Wabash Coll., 1941-43, Moorhead State Coll., 1943-44; B.A., U. So. Calif., 1945; J.D., Loyola U., Los Angeles, 1949. Admitted to Calif. bar, 1949; asso. firm Joseph Scott, Los Angeles, 1949-52; partner firm Hall & Kent, Long Beach, Calif., 1952—. Bd. dirs. Long Beach YMCA, 1954—. Mem. Calif., Long Beach, Los Angeles bar assns., Artesia C. of C. (v.p. 1965-68). Home: 3230 Claremore Long Beach CA 90808 Office: 3815 Atlantic Ave Long Beach CA 90807

HALL, RICHARD WINSLOW, b. Salt Lake City, June 3, 1923; B.S., U. Ariz., 1945; J.D., John Marshall Law Sch., 1951. Admitted to Ill. bar, 1951; pvt. practice law, Park Forest, Ill., 1951—; instr. chemistry Chgo. Tech. Coll., 1951-55; community prof. Gov. State U., 1975-76; lectr. Northwestern U., 1972—. Village prosecutor, Park Forest, 1960—. Mem. Ill. Bar Assn. Kiwanian. Contbr. articles to profl. jours. Office: 274 Rich Rd Park Forest IL 60466

HALL, ROBERT HOWELL, b. Soperton, Ga., Nov. 28, 1921; B.S. in Commerce, U. Ga., 1941; LL.B., U. Va., 1948; LL.D., Emory U., 1973. Admitted to Ga. bar, 1948, U.S. Supreme Ct. bar, 1954; practiced in Atlanta, 1948-61; prof. law Emory U., 1948-61; asso. judge Ga. Ct. of Appeals, 1961-71, presiding judge, 1971-74; asso. justice Supreme Ct. Ga., 1974—; asst. atty. gen. Ga., 1953-61; head criminal div. State Law Dept., 1959-61; dir. Nat. Center State Cts., 1976—. Bd. dirs. YMCA, Atlanta, 1965-67; troop leader Boy Scouts Am., 1967. Mem. Am. (Ho. of Dels. 1971-73), Ga. bar assn. Am. Commn. on Inst. Justice (chmn. 1976-77), Am. Judicature Soc. (pres. 1971-73, Herbert Lincoln Harley award 1974), Jud. Council Ga. (chmn. 1973-74), Inst. Ct. Adminstrn. (trustee 1976—). Recipient Harvard Law Sch. Assn. Ga. award, 1967; Golden Citizenship award Grand Jurors Fulton County, Inc., 1975. Contbr. articles in field to legal jours. Home: 1630 E Clifton Rd NE Atlanta GA 30307 Office: Supreme Ct GA 40 Capitol Sq Atlanta GA 30334 Tel (404) 656-3472

HALL, ROBERT MALCOLM, b. Danville, Ill., Jan. 14, 1944; A.B., Ind. U., 1966, J.D., 1969. Admitted to Ind. bar, 1969; asso. firm Rex V. Keller, Covington, Ind., 1969-70; partner firm Keller & Hall, Covington, 1971-74; judge Circuit Ct. Warren County, Ind., Williamsport, 1974—; bd. dirs. region III Ind. Criminal Justice Planning Agency. Mem. Am., Ind., Warren County bar assns.; Fountain County Bar Assn. (pres. 1972-73), Am. Judicature Soc., Ind. Judges Assn., Nat., Ind. councils of juvenile ct. judges, Jaycees (pres. Covington 1972-73). Home: 520 N Monroe St Williamsport IN 47993 Office: Ct House Williamsport NY 47993 Tel (317) 762-3604

HALL, THOMAS GORDON, b. Fernandina, Fla., May 21, 1905; LL.B., U. Fla., 1935, J.D., 1967. Admitted to Fla. bar, 1935, U.S. Dist. Ct. bar, ICC bar, 1955; individual practice law, Fernandina Beach, 1936—; municipal judge City of Fernandina, 1941, municipal judge, city atty., 1952-54; pros. atty. Nassau County (Fla.), 1946-48, 63-71; atty. Bd. Pub. Instrn., Nassau County, 1948-53; city atty., Boulougne, 1962-63; county atty. Nassau County, 1971-73. Mem., counsel gen. Duncan Lamont Clinch Hist. Soc. of Amelia Island, 1964. Mem. Fla., Nassau County bar assns. Home: 114 S 17th St Fernandina Beach FL 32034 Office: 11 N 4th St PO Box 444 Fernandina Beach FL 32034 Tel (904) 261-4200

HALL, THOMAS LEAVITT, b. Kansas City, Mo., Nov. 9, 1907; B.A., U. Ariz., 1929; LL.B., U. Mich., 1931. Admitted to Ariz. bar, 1932, U.S. Dist. (Ariz) Ct., 1932; U.S. (9th Circuit) Ct. Appeals bar, 1933, U.S. Supreme Ct. bar, 1945; asso. firm Bird and Hall, Nogales, Ariz., 1932-40, partner, 1940-42, 49-57; col. JAGC, U.S. Army, 1942-47; adminstrv. asst. U.S. Senate, 1947-49; prof. law U. Ariz., 1957—; gen. counsel Ariz. Bd. Regents, 1962-74; dir. Pima County Legal Aid Soc., 1964-76. Pres., Border Intercollegiate Athletic Conf., 1960-61; chmn. Western Athletic Conf., 1964-65; alderman City of Nogales, 1938-40; trustee Nogales Sch Dist., 1950-52. Mem. State Bar Ariz., Pima County Bar Assn. (pres. 1966-67). Recipient Faculty Recognition award U. Ariz., 1967, Old Main award, 1974; Alumni Achievement award Ariz. Alumni Assn., 1975. Home: 5425 N Via Alcalde Tucson AZ 85718 Tel (602) 884-1907

HALL, VIC, b. Smackover, Ark., Feb. 4, 1926; J.D., Baylor U., 1953. Admitted to Tex. bar, 1953; individual practice law, Cleburne, Tex., 1953; asst. city atty., Waco, Tex., 1953-56; justice of the peace McLennan County (Tex.), 1956-59; judge McLennan County Ct., 1959-63; judge 54th Jud. Dist. Ct. Tex., Waco, 1963-69; asso. justice Ct. of Civil Appeals 10th Supreme Jud. Dist. Tex., Waco, 1969—. Mem. advisory bd. Salvation Army, Waco; bd. dirs. Heart O' Tex. Council Boy Scouts Am. Mem. Am., Tex., Waco-McLennan County bar assns. Recipient Silver Beaver award Boy Scouts Am., 1972. Office: PO Box 1606 Waco TX 76703 Tel (817) 753-7341

HALL, WALLACE CLARE, b. Harbor Beach, Mich., Apr. 12, 1894; A.B., U. Mich., 1916, LL.B., 1917, LL.M., 1921, J.D., 1921. Admitted to Mich. bar, 1920; staff firm Graves, Hatch & Rowley, Detroit, 1921-22; individual practice law, Detroit, 1922-68, Alpena, Mich., 1968—; prof. law Detroit Coll. Law, 1923-38. Mem. Mich. Bar Assn. Home: 6651 US Hwy 23 North Alpena MI 49707 Office: PO Box 492 Alpena MI 49707 Tel (517) 356-2545

HALL, WILLIAM GUION, JR., b. Memphis, Sept. 5, 1930; B.A., Washington and Lee U., 1952; J.D., Harvard, 1955, LL.M., 1963. Admitted to Tenn. bar, 1955, Mass. bar, 1959; asso. firm Herrick Smith Donald Farley & Ketchum, Boston, 1958-62; prof. law U. Md. Sch. Law, Balt., 1963—, asso. dean, 1968-72, pres. law sch. admission council, 1976—. Home: Route 2 Box 52 Hampstead MD 21074 Office: U Md Sch Law 500 W Baltimore St Baltimore MD 21201 Tel (301) 528-71S1

HALL, WILLIAM THOMAS, b. Port Arthur, Tex., May 20, 1936; B.A., Sam Houston State U., 1958; LL.B., U. Tex., 1967. Admitted to Tex. bar, 1967; staff counsel Gulf Oil Corp., Midland, Tex., 1968-69; individual practice law, Lubbock, Tex., 1970-71, Seguin, Tex., 1971-74; partner firm Stayton, Maloney, Hearne & Babb, Austin, Tex., 1974—. Mem. State Bar Tex., Tex., Am. assns. trial lawyers, Am. Bar Assn. Home: 4501 Balcones Dr Austin TX 78731 Office: 314 W 11th St Austin TX 78701 Tel (512) 472-8010

HALLE, ERNEST WARREN, b. Cheyenne, Wyo., Sept. 22, 1941; B.S., U. Wyo., 1963, J.D., 1969; Admitted to Wyo. State bar, 1969, U.S. Supreme Ct. bar, 1973; mng. atty. legal services Laramie County, Inc., Cheyenne, 1969-72; asso. firm Urbigkit, Halle, Mackay & Whitehead, Cheyenne, 1972-76; individual practice law, Cheyenne, 1976—; sr. judge Municipal Ct. City Cheyenne, 1973—. Mem. Assn. Trial Lawyers Am., Am. Bar Assn., Wyo. Trial Lawyers Assn., Am. Judicature Assn. Home: 1240 Madison St Cheyenne WY 82001 Office: 416 17th St Cheyenne WY 82001 Tel (307) 634-4111

HALLECK, ROGER ROY, b. Rockwell City, Iowa, Nov. 2, 1941; B.A., N.W. Mo. State U., 1963; J.D., Ind. U., 1966. Admitted to Iowa bar, 1966; asso. firm John L. Mowry, Marshalltown, Iowa, 1966-69; judge Municipal Ct., Marshalltown, Iowa, 1970-73; asso. judge 2d Dist. Iowa Dist. Ct., 1973—. Mem. Marshall County (Iowa) Republican Central Com., 1968; chmn. Marshall County Cancer Crusade, 1968. Mem. Marshall County, Iowa State bar assns., Phi Delta Phi, Alpha Kappa Lambda. Office: County Courthouse Marshalltown IA 50158 Tel (515) 752-7463

HALLER, ALBERT JOHN, b. N.Y.C., May 5, 1931; B.A., Washington U., St. Louis, 1953, J.D., 1958. Admitted to Mo. bar, 1958, Fed. Ct. bar, 1959, U.S. Supreme Ct. bar, 1966; partner firm Cupples, Cooper & Haller, Inc., St. Louis, 1962—; municipal judge City of Brentwood, 1963-69, pres. Municipal Judges Assn. Greater St. Louis, 1966-68, v.p. Mo. Municipal Judges Assn., 1968-69. Mem. Nat. Eagle Scout Assn., advisor Explorer post 517; bd. dirs. Children's Home Soc. Mo. Mem. Mo., St. Louis County (chmn. Pub. info. com. 1964-69) bar assns. Recipient Outstanding Citizen award Brentwood Jr. C. of C., 1963. Bus. mgr. Washington U. Law Quar., 1957-58. Home: 618 Spring Meadows Manchester MO 63011 Office: 7751 Carondelet Clayton MO 63105 Tel (314) 725-3070

HALLIBURTON, JACK LEWIS, b. Ripley, Tenn., Aug. 23, 1929; B.S., Memphis State U., 1953; J.D., U. Tenn., 1956. Admitted to Tenn. bar, 1957; partner firm Thomas, Halliburton & Ballin, Memphis, 1959—. Vice pres. Raleigh Civic Club, 1963. Mem. Am., Tenn., Memphis and Shelby County bar assns., Tenn. Trial Lawyers Assn. Home: 2051 Old Oak St Memphis TN 38138 Office: 81 Madison Bldg Memphis TN 38103 Tel (901) 526-7404

HALLIGAN, PATRICK DANIEL, b. Evanston, Ill., Oct. 1, 1942; A.B. with distinction Stanford, 1965, B.S., 1967; J.D., U. Chgo., 1968. Admitted to Ill. bar, 1968; with legal dept. Sears Roebuck & Co., Chgo., 1968-69; mem. firm Petit & Safeblade, Chgo., 1971—; panel hearing officers Ill. Office Edn., 1976—. Mem. Ill. State Bar Assn. (Lincoln Essay award 1976). Contbr. articles in field to profl. jours. Home: 437 Elm St Deerfield IL 60015 Office: 111 W Monroe St Chicago IL 60603 Tel (312) 726-1025

HALLISEY, JEREMIAH FRANCIS, b. Boston, Jan. 15, 1939; B.A., Boston Coll., 1960; M.A., Cornell U., 1962; LL.B., U. Calif., Berkeley, 1966. Admitted to Calif. bar, 1966; dep. dist. atty. Contra Costa County (Calif.), Martinez, 1966-68; trial atty. SEC, San Francisco, 1968-70; spl. counsel Alameda-Contra Costa Transit Dist., Oakland, Calif., 1970; partner firm O'Brien & Hallisey, San Francisco, 1971—. Mem. Democratic Nat. Fin. Council, 1975-76; Dem. nat. committeeman from Calif., 1976—. Mem. Am., Calif., San Francisco bar assns. Home: 1824 Piedras Circle Danville CA 94526 Office: One California St Suite 2245 San Francisco CA 94111 Tel (415) 433-5300

HALLMARK, WILLIAM LEWIS, b. St. Helens, Oreg., Apr. 15, 1939; B.A. in Polit. Sci., Stanford, 1961; J.D., U. Oreg., 1968. Admitted to Oreg. bar, 1968; law clk. Oreg. Supreme Ct., 1968-69; partner firm Jones, Lang, Klein Wolf & Smith, Portland, Oreg., 1969—; instr. ins. law Lewis and Clark Coll., 1976. Mem. Am., Oreg., Multnomah (chmn. law day program 1974) bar assns., Order of Coif. Contbr. article to legal jour. Home: 2665 SW Sherwood Dr Portland OR 97201 Office: 1 SW Columbia Portland OR 97258 Tel (503) 222-4422

HALLOCK, MAURINE MCINTOSH, b. Jamestown, Kans., Nov. 15, 1920; B.A., Washburn Coll., 1941, LL.B., 1943. Admitted to Kans. bar, 1943; asso. firm Roberts & Roberts, Winfield, Kans., 1943-47; asst. city atty. City and County of Denver, 1947-49; practiced in Denver, 1950-52, Walsenberg, Colo., 1953-55; investigator Colo. Bd. Standards Child Care, Denver, 1956—; judge Adams County (Colo.), 1965—. Mem. Colo., Adams County, Am. (chmn. membership Colo.) bar assns., Colo. Assn. County Judges (pres. 1968-69), Phi Delta Delta, Delta Gamma. Named Woman of Achievement Bus. and Profl. Women's Club, 1965. Home: 7040 Broadway Denver CO 80221 Office: 1931 E Bridge St Brighton CO 80601

HALLOCK, ROBERT WAYNE, b. Sterling, Ill., Jan. 13, 1944; A.B., Eureka Coll., 1966; J.D. with very highest honors, U. Ill., 1971. Admitted to Ill. bar, 1971; asso. firm Kirland & Ellis, Chgo., 1971—; lectr. in law Loyola U., Chgo., 1972-73, U. Ill. Law Sch., 1975-76. Mem. Am., Ill. State bar assns., Order of Coif. Home: 2129 St Johns Ave Highland Park IL 60035 Office: 200 E Randolph St Chicago IL 60601

HALLORAN, BERNARD THORPE, b. N.Y.C., May 27, 1931; A.B., U. So. Calif., 1953; LL.B., Columbia, 1959; LL.M., Georgetown U., 1963. Admitted to N.Y. bar, 1960, U.S. Supreme Ct. bar, 1964, D.C. bar, 1964, Pa. bar, 1967, Tex. bar, 1971; atty., advisor Office of Legal Adviser, U.S. Dept. of State, 1960-65; gen. counsel Hamilton Watch Co., 1965-69; v.p., gen. counsel UCC Internat., Inc., 1969-70; asst. gen. counsel Univ. Computing Co., 1970-72; sec., gen. counsel Reed Tool Co., Houston, 1973—, also gen. counsel Baker Oil Tools Groups, Baker Internat. Corp., Houston, 1976—; comml. arbitrator Am. Arbitration Assn., 1973—. Dir., legal counsel D.C. Jaycees, 1963-65; internat. com. chmn. U.S. Jaycees, 1964-65. Mem. Am., Tex. bar assns. Home: 13318 Alchester St Houston TX 77079 Office: 6501 Navigation Blvd PO Box 2119 Houston TX 77001 Tel (713) 926-3121

HALLORAN, MARIBETH, b. Mpls., Jan. 2, 1942; B.A., U. Minn., 1963; LL.B., 1966. Admitted to D.C. bar, 1967, Minn. bar, 1967, Calif. bar, 1972, U.S. Supreme Ct. bar, 1975; staff atty. Neighborhood Legal Services Program, Washington, 1966-71; partner firm Lorenz, Greene, Kelley & Halloran, San Francisco, 1973-77. Office: Box 62 Bowling Green OH 43402 Tel (419) 352-0582

HALLOWS, LEO CRAIG, b. St. Louis, Jan. 15, 1942; B.A., Ohio State U., 1963, J.D., 1966. Admitted to Ohio bar, 1966; spl. agent FBI, N.Y.C., 1966-69; asso. firm Gaier, Pratt & Freed, Piqua, Ohio, 1969-72; partner firm Gaier, Pratt, Freed & Hallows, Piqua, 1972-74, Turner, Hallows & King, 1974—; dir. law City of Piqua, 1972-76; pros. atty. Miami County (Ohio), 1977—. Pres. Miami County Big Brothers, 1970, Miami County Young Republicans, 1971. Mem. Am., Ohio State, Miami County bar assns. Home: 615 Broadway Piqua OH 45356 Office: 300 W High St Piqua OH 45356 Tel (513) 773-7347

HALPER, EMANUEL BARRY, b. Bronx, N.Y., June 24, 1933; B.A. with honors, City U. N.Y., 1954; J.D., Columbia, 1957. Admitted to N.Y. State bar, 1958; since practiced in N.Y.C., editorial asso. J. K. Lasser & Co., Bklyn., 1958; asst. gen. counsel Howard Stores Corp., Bklyn., 1960-61; asso. with Frederick Zissu, 1961-66; partner firm Zissu, Halper & Martin, 1966-72, Zissu, Lore, Halper & Robson, 1972-76, Zissu, Lore, Halper & Barron, 1976—; partner Canadian Pacific Realty Co.; mem. real estate com. Vornado, Inc.; dir. Gen. Microwave Corp.; mem. faculty N.Y. U. Real Estate Inst., adj. asso. prof., 1972—. Mem. World Assn. Lawyers (chmn. com. internat. real estate), Inst. Real Estate Studies (founder, vice chmn.), Am. Bar Assn. (certificate of merit 1976), Internat. Council Shopping Centers (law com. 1971-75). Author: The Wonderful World of Real Estate, 1976; contbr. articles to profl. jours. Office: 450 Park Ave New York City NY 10022 Tel (212) 371-3900

HALPERIN, JEROME ROGER, b. N.Y.C., Feb. 1, 1933; A.B., Columbia U., 1954, LL.B., 1956. Admitted to N.Y. bar, 1956; individual practice law, N.Y.C., 1956—. Office: 551 Fifth Ave New York City NY 10017

HALPERN, BARRY LEONARD, b. N.Y.C., Aug. 7, 1942; B.S. in Advt., U. Fla., 1965; J.D., U. Miami (Fla.), 1968. Admitted to Fla. bar, 1968, U.S. Supreme Ct. bar, 1971; since practiced in Miami, Fla.; asso. Halpern, Shenberg & Langer, and predecessors, 1968, jr. partner, 1969-71, partner, 1971-73, sr. partner, 1974—. Mem. Fla. State Coordinators Brown for Pres., 1976. Mem. Am. Bar Assn., Am. Judicature Soc., Fla. Trial Lawyers Assn., 1st Amendment Lawyers Assn., Phi Delta Phi. Office: 3000 Biscayne Blvd Miami FL 33137 Tel (305) 573-5240

HALPERN, ISIDORE, b. N.Y.C., July 1, 1901; LL.B., N.Y. U., 1923. Admitted to N.Y. State bar, 1923; sr. partner firm Halpern, Brown & Darienzo, Esquires, 1923—; chmn., organizer advanced med. course Practicing Law Inst.; lectr. Yale, Harvard, Columbia, numerous states. Fellow Am. Coll. Trial Lawyers, Internat. Acad. Trial Lawyers; mem. Ind. (life), Trial, Bklyn. (trustee, mem. joint bar grievance com.) bar assns. Recipient Wisdom award of Honor, 1970. Author: Attorneys Guide to Medical Terms, 1930; Trauma and Cancer. Contbr. articles to legal jours., law revs. Home: 128 Willow St Brooklyn NY 11201 Office: 26 Court St Brooklyn NY 11242 Tel (212) 875-8580

HALPERN, MARVIN JAY, b. Spokane, Wash., Dec. 19, 1945; B.A. in Econs., U. Wash., Seattle, 1968; J.D., U. Calif., Berkeley, 1971. Admitted to Calif. bar, 1972; asso. legal div. State of Calif. Franchise Tax Bd., Sacramento, 1971—. Mem. Phi Beta Kappa, Phi Eta Sigma, Omicron Delta Epsilon, Phi Delta Phi. Office: Aerojet Center Sacramento CA 95857 Tel (916) 355-0171

HALPERN, RALPH LAWRENCE, b. Buffalo, May 12, 1929; LL.B. cum laude, U. Buffalo, 1953. Admitted to N.Y. State bar, 1953; teaching asso. Northwestern U. Law Sch., 1953-54; served to capt. JAGC, 1954-57; asso. firm Jaeckle, Fleischmann, Kelly, Swart & Augspurger, Buffalo, 1957-59; asso. firm Raichle, Banning, Weiss & Halpern, and predecessors, 1958-59, partner, 1959—. Pres., Buffalo Council on World Affairs, 1972-74; chmn. Buffalo chpt. Am. Jewish Com.; bd. govs. United Jewish Fedn., 1972—. Mem. Am., N.Y. State (chmn. com. profl. ethics 1971-76), Erie County bar assns., Am. Judicature Soc., Am. Law Inst. Home: 84 New Amsterdam Ave Buffalo NY 14216 Office: 10 Lafayette Sq Buffalo NY 14203 Tel (716) 852-7587

HALSEY, EDWARD STEPHEN, b. Rock Springs, Wyo., May 4, 1922; J.D., U. Wyo., 1948. Admitted to Wyo. bar, 1948; asso. firm Thomas O. Miller, 1948-51, Halsey, Whitley & Linmos, 1958-68; individual practice law, Newcastle, Wyo., 1968—; mem. State Bd. Law Examiners, 1970. Mem. Wyo., Am. bar assns., Internat. Soc. Barristers. Home: Fountain View Condominium Newcastle WY 82701 Office: PO Box 427 Newcastle WY 82701 Tel (307) 746-2744

HALSTEAD, BILL GENE, b. Fairview, Okla., Oct. 18, 1938; B.E.E., Okla. State U., 1961; J.D., Okla. U., 1967. Admitted to Okla. bar, 1967; asso. firm Mitchell, Mitchell, DeClerck, Cox & Halstead, Enid, Okla., 1967-69, partner, 1969—; municipal judge Town of Ringwood (Okla.), 1973-74. Deacon Central Christian Ch., Enid, 1972-75, sec. bd. dirs., 1973-75; bd. dirs. YMCA, Enid, 1973—. Mem. Am., Okla., Garfield County bar assns. Recipient Service to Youth award YMCA, 1974. Home: 1210 Indian Dr Enid OK 73701 Office: Security National Bank Bldg Enid OK 73701 Tel (405) 234-5144

HALSTED, ABEL STEVENS, JR., b. Pasadena, Calif., Nov. 22, 1907; A.B., Stanford, 1929; LL.B., Harvard, 1932. Admitted to Calif. bar, 1932; practiced in Los Angeles, 1932—; mem. firm Macdonald, Halsted & Laybourne and predecessors, 1946—; lectr. U. So. Calif. Law Sch., 1952-57; pres. Harvard Law Sch. Assn. of So. Calif., 1958-60; bd. councilors So. Calif. Law Sch., 1970—. Pres. Town Hall of Los Angeles, 1953; trustee Scripps Coll., Hollenbeck Home. Mem. State Bar Calif. (gov. 1964-67, pres. 1967), Los Angeles County Bar (pres. 1961-62), Am. Bar Assn., Am. Judicature Soc., Phi Beta Kappa. Home: 360 W Bellevue Dr Pasadena CA 91105 Office: 1200 Wilshire Blvd Los Angeles CA 90017 Tel (213) 481-1200

HALVORSON, JAMES EARL, b. Mpls., July 21, 1949; B.A. U. Wis., 1971, J.D., 1974, M.S. in Indsl. Relations, 1974. Admitted to Wis. bar, 1974, Ct. of Mil. Appeals bar, 1975, Judge Adv. Gen. Corps, 1974; head Naval Legal Service Br. Office, Guantanamo Bay, Cuba, 1974-75, trial counsel Naval Legal Service Office, Treasure Island, San Francisco, 1975-76; legal officer aboard U.S.S. Enterprise CVN-65, 1976—. Mem. Am., Guantanamo Bay bar assns. Office: Legal Officer USS Enterprise CVN 65 FPO San Francisco CA 96601 Tel (415) 869-2064

HALVORSON, ROBERT MELVIN, b. Montevideo, Minn., Nov. 18, 1945; B.A., Concordia Coll., Moorhead, Minn., 1968; J.D., U. Iowa, 1971. Admitted to Iowa bar, 1971, Minn. bar, 1971, U.S. Dist. Ct. bar for Dist. Minn., 1971; asso. firm Gislason, Dosland, Malecki, Gislason & Halvorson and predecessor, New Ulm, Minn., 1972-74, partner, 1974—. Mem. Minn. Charities Rev. Council, 1975—; pres. United Way of New Ulm, 1976. Mem. Brown County (Minn.), Iowa State, Minn. State, Am. bar assns., Order of Coif, Omicron Delta Kappa. Mng. editor Iowa Law Rev., 1970-71. Home: 1833 Crestview Dr New Ulm MN 56073 Office: 1 S State St New Ulm MN 56073 Tel (507) 354-1111

HAM, WILLBURT DUNN, b. Ithaca, N.Y., Mar. 2, 1916; B.S. in Accounting, U. Ill., 1937, J.D., 1940; LL.M., Harvard, 1941. Admitted to Ill. bar, 1940, Ky. bar, 1951, U.S. Supreme Ct. bar, 1960; instr. Sch. Commerce, Bus. Adminstrn. U. Ala., Tuscaloosa, 1941-42; atty. Office Price Adminstrn., Springfield, Ill., 1942-46; asst. prof. law U. Cin., 1946-49; asso. prof. law U. Ky., Lexington, 1949-51, prof. law, 1951—, acting dean, summers 1953, 1959; sec. Ky. Securities Advisory Com., Frankfort, 1961-68; mem. adv. com. Ky. Corp. Law Revision, 1971-72. Bd. dirs. U. Ky. Research Found., Lexington, 1952-64. Mem. Am., Ky., Fayette County bar assns., Am. Judicature Soc., Assn. Am. Law Schs. (com. admissions to bar), Order of Coif. Contbr. articles to Ky. Law Jour. Home: 1227 Lakewood Dr Lexington KY 40502 Office: College Law University Kentucky Lexington KY 40506 Tel (606) 257-4698

HAMACK, KEITH HARTMOND, b. Seattle, Dec. 31, 1947; A.B., Coll. William Mary, 1969; J.D., Willamette U. Sch. Law, 1972. Admitted to Wash. bar, 1972; chief, claims, Office of Staff Judge Adv., U.S. Army, Ft. Riley, Kans., 1972; chmn. zoning planning commn. City of Milford (Kans.), 1974-75. Mem. Am., Washington bar assns. Office: Office Staff Judge Advocate Fort Riley KS 66442 Tel (913) 239-3830

HAMBLEN, LAPSLEY WALKER, JR., b. Chattanooga, Dec. 25, 1926; student Ga. Inst. Tech., 1944; B.A., U. Va., 1949, LL.B., 1953. Admitted to W.Va. bar, 1954, Ohio bar, 1955, Va. bar, 1957; asso. firm Smith, Schnacke & Compton, Dayton, Ohio, 1954-55, Spilman, Thomas, Battle & Klostermeyer, Charleston, W.Va., 1953-54; partner firm Caskie, Frost, Hobbs & Hamblen, and predecessors, Lynchburg, Va., 1957—; trial atty. Office Chief Counsel, IRS, Atlanta, 1955; atty. adviser Tax Ct. of U.S., 1956; past pres. Lynchburg Estate Planning Council; past chmn. Com. on Cooperation with C.P.A.'s, Va. State Bar; co-dir. Ann. Va. Conf. on Fed. Taxation, 1970—; trustee So. Fed. Tax Inst., Atlanta, 1971—. Counsel, past dir. Piedmont Heart Assn., Inc. Mem. Va. (past chmn. tax sect., bd. govs.), Am. bar assns., Am. Counsel Assn., Am. Judicature Soc., Newcomen Soc. N.Am., So. Pension Conf., Greater Lynchburg C. of C. (past pres., dir., mem. exec. com.), U. Va. Alumni Assn. (past pres. Lynchburg chpt.), Raven Soc., Order of Coif, Omicron Delta Kappa. Author: Split-Dollar Life Insurance and the Controlling Stockholder-Still Useful with Prudent Planning, 1975; contbg. author: Taxation of Deferred Employee and Executive Compensation, 1960. Home: 3708 Manton Dr Lynchburg VA 24505 Office: 2306 Atherholt Rd PO Box 1160 Lynchburg VA 24505 Tel (804) 846-2731

HAMBLETON, RICHARD NICOLAI, b. Balt., Nov. 16, 1923; B.A., U. Md., 1950, J.D., 1951. Admitted to Md. bar, 1954; atty. advisor C.E., U.S. Army, Balt., 1951-54; asso. firm Z. Townsend Parks, Balt., 1954-56, W. Gibbs McKenney, Balt., 1956-57; asst. solicitor Anne Arundel County (Md.), 1963-65, asst. state's atty., 1966-67; individual practice law, Annapolis, Md., 1967—; legal advisor police dept. Anne Arundel County, 1971-74. Mem. Am., Md. State, Anne Arundel bar assns., Exchange Club Annapolis (pres. 1971-72), Soc. of Cin. N.J., Mil. Order of World Wars (past comdr.). Home: 33 Southgate Ave Annapolis MD 21401 Office: 150 South St Annapolis MD 21401 Tel (301) 269-0255

HAMBRICK, JACKSON REID, b. Griffin, Ga., Nov. 14, 1917; A.B., Wofford Coll., 1938; LL.B., Duke, 1942. Admitted to N.Y. bar, 1943, D.C. bar, 1958; individual practice law, N.Y.C., 1942-47; atty. IRS, Treasury Dept., Washington, 1947-57; prof. law George Washington U., 1957—. Mem. Am., D.C. bar assns. Contbr. articles to law revs. Home: 6022 Oakdale Rd McLean VA 22101 Office: 720 20th St NW Washington DC 20006 Tel (202) 676-6747

HAMBURG, C. BRUCE, b. N.Y.C., June 30, 1939; B.Ch.E., Poly. Inst. Bklyn., 1960; J.D., George Washington U., 1964. Patent examiner U.S. Patent Office, Washington, 1960-63; admitted to N.Y. bar, 1964; patent atty. Celanese Corp. Am., N.Y.C., 1963-65; asso. firms Burns, Lobato & Zelnick, N.Y.C., 1965-67, Nolte & Nolte, N.Y.C., 1967-75; individual practice law, N.Y.C., 1976—. Mem. Am., Queens County (N.Y.), Bklyn., Bronx (N.Y.), Nassau County (N.Y.) bar assns., Am., N.Y. patent law assns., Queens C. of C., Licensing Execs. Soc., Phi Alpha Delta, Phi Lambda Upsilon, Omega Chi Epsilon, Tau Beta Pi. Recipient Superior Performance awards U.S. Patent Office, 1962, 63; author: Patent Fraud and Inequitable Conduct, 1972 and supplements, 1973—; asso. editor Patent Law Devels., 1965-70; columnist Patent and Trademark Rev., 1976—. Office: 535 Fifth Ave New York City NY 10017 Tel (212) 986-2340

HAMBURGER, SOL, b. N.Y.C., Nov. 5, 1930; B.S., Ariz. State U., 1957; J.D., U. Ariz., 1961. Admitted to Ariz. bar, 1961; dep. county atty. Maricopa County, Ariz., 1961-63; individual practice law, Phoenix, 1963—. Mem. Ariz. (com. on criminal justice), Maricopa County bar assns., Am. Assn. Trial Lawyers. Office: 1224 E Missouri St Phoenix AZ 85014

HAMBY, COLETTE DUSTHIMER, b. Atlanta, Sept. 5, 1924; student Ga. State U., 1960-62; LL.B., John Marshall U., 1952, LL.M., 1953. Admitted to Ga. bar, 1952, U.S. Supreme Ct. bar, 1955; claims atty. Ga. Dept. Vets. Services, Atlanta, 1952-61; legal counselor, prosecutor Atlanta Municipal Ct., 1961—; mem. women's adv. com. City of Atlanta, 1975—. Mem. State Bar Ga., Atlanta Bar Assn., Ga. Assn. Women Lawyers (past v.p., past sec.), Daus. Am. Legion, Am. Legion Aux., Iota Tau Tau. Office: 165 Decatur St SE Atlanta GA 30303 Tel (404) 658-6728

HAMEL, ALBERT HENRY, b. St. Louis, Oct. 30, 1928; A.B., Washington and Lee U., 1950; LL.B., Washington U., St. Louis, 1955. Admitted to Mo. bar, 1955; partner firm Kerth Thies, Schreiber, Hamel & Dee, Clayton, Mo., 1970-73, firm Lashly, Caruthers, Thies, Rava & Hamel, Clayton, 1973—; adminstrv. asst. to Congressman from Mo. during 85th Congress, 1958; exec. asst. to pros. atty. St. Louis County, 1967-68. Mem. Rep. Platform Steering Com., 1966; asst. U.S. Atty. Eastern Dist. Mo., 1960-61. Bd. dirs. Big Brothers Inc., 1965-71; chmn. Land Clearance Redevel. Authority St. Louis County, 1964-65; chmn. Human Relations Adv. Com. St. Louis County, 1963-64; chmn. Citizens Participation Com. Workable Program Community Improvement St. Louis County, 1963-66; mem. city Clayton Planning Commn.; sec. bd. dirs. St. Louis County Narcotics Commn., 1970-71. Mem. Mo. Bar Assn. (bd. govs. 1974-77), St. Louis County Bar Assn. (pres. 1967-68), Washington and Lee Alumni Assn. (pres. chpt. 1963). Home: 58 Conway Ln Ladue MO 63124 Office: 11 S Meramec St Clayton MO 63105 Tel (314) 727-8281

HAMEL, CHARLES, b. Los Angeles, July 27, 1926; Admitted to Calif. bar, 1957; prin. firm of Charles Hamel, Los Angeles, 1958—. Mem. Calif., Orange County trial lawyers assns., Criminal Ct. Bar Assn., Calif. Attys. for Criminal Justice Assn. Certified specialist in criminal law. Office: 304 S Broadway Los Angeles CA 90013 Tel (213) 626-0681

HAMEL, PAUL GERARD, b. New Bedford, Mass., Feb. 27, 1944; J.D., Boston Coll., 1967. Admitted to Mass. bar, 1968; legal clk. U.S. Marine Corps, 1968-70; individual practice law, New Bedford, 1970—. Mem. New Bedford City Council, 1971-75; mem. Mass. Gov.'s Council, 1973-74. Mem. Am. Judicature Soc., Am., Mass., Boston, New Bedford bar assns. Home: 3925 Acushnet Ave New Bedford MA 02745 Office: 179 William St New Bedford MA 02740 Tel (617) 997-6101

HAMES, LUTHER CLAUDE, JR., b. Marietta, Ga., Nov. 18, 1917; LL.B., Woodrow Wilson Coll. Law, 1939. Admitted to Ga. bar, 1939; individual practice law, Marietta, 1939-68; solicitor gen. Cobb Jud. Circuit, 1953-68, dist. atty. emeritus, 1968—; judge Cobb Superior Ct., 1968—; mayor pro tem City of Marietta; 1949, chmn. Com. Criminal Pattern Jury Instrn., 1973—; mem. Sentence Rev. Panel, 1975. Chmn. Marietta Housing Authority, 1950. Mem. State Bar Ga., Cobb Circuit Bar Assn. (pres. 1954), Dist. Atty. Assn. Ga. (pres. 1956), Council Superior Ct. Judges Ga. Home: 335 Old Trace Rd NW Marietta GA 30064 Office: 413 Jud Bldg Marietta GA 30060 Tel (404) 422-2320

HAMILTON, ANDREW JACKSON, b. Atlanta, Sept. 8, 1941; student Emory U., 1962; J.D., Mercer U., 1966. Admitted to Ga. bar, 1969; asso. firm Neely, Freeman & Hawkins, Atlanta, 1970-74, partner, 1974-76; partner firm Neely, Neely & Player, Atlanta, 1976—; mem. intern program Hartford Accident & Indemnity Co., Atlanta, 1966-69. Active Atlanta Heart Fund, United Way campaigns, 1974—. Mem. Am., Ga. bar assns., Lawyers Club of Atlanta, Nat. Assn. Railroad Trial Counsel, Defense Research Inst., Am. Judicature Soc., Atlanta Claims Assn., Jr. C. of C. Recipient Academic Achievement award West Pub. Co., 1965. Home: 40 Michelle Circle NW Atlanta GA 30342 Tel (404) 681-2600

HAMILTON, CHARLES ERNEST, b. Laramie, Wyo., Jan. 16, 1930; B.S., U. Wyo., 1951, J.D., 1960. Admitted to Wyo. bar, 1960, U.S. Supreme Ct. bar, 1974; sr. partner Hamilton & Harnsberger, Riverton, Wyo., 1969, Hamilton & Andrews, Riverton, 1970-72; sr. partner Hamilton, Hursh & Crofts, Riverton, 1974—; pres. Chemex Corp., Riverton, 1974—. Home: 204 Valley Circle Riverton WY 82501 Office: 105-107 S 6th St E Riverton WY 82501 Tel (307) 856-4157

HAMILTON, CLYDE HENRY, b. Edgefield, S.C., Feb. 8, 1934; B.S., Wofford Coll., 1956; J.D. with honors, George Washington U., 1961. Admitted to S.C. bar, 1961; reference asst. U.S. Senate Library, 1958-61; asso. firm J.R. Folk, Edgefield, S.C., 1961-63; partner firm Butler, Means, Evins & Browne, Spartanburg, S.C., 1966—. Pres., Spartanburg County Arts Council, 1971-73; mem. steering com. undergrad. merit fellowship program Converse Coll.; sustaining trustee Spartanburg Day Sch., chmn. bd., 1972-74; chmn. adminstrv. bd. Methodist Ch., 1969-73, chmn. fin. com., 1974-76. Mem. Am. Bar Assn., S.C. State Bar (jud. reform com.), Am. Judicature Soc. Mem. editorial staff Cumulative Index Congressional Com. Hearings, 1955-58, 59. Home: 106 Cameron Dr Spartanburg SC 29302 Office: 205 Magnolia St Spartanburg SC 29301 Tel (803) 582-5630

HAMILTON, DONALD JOHN, b. Great Falls, Mont., Apr. 26, 1941; A.B., Stanford, 1963; J.D., U. Mont., 1966. Admitted to Mont. bar, 1966; asso. firm Jardine, Stephenson, Blewett & Weaver, Great Falls, 1966-73, partner, 1974—. Commr. Great Falls Pub. Housing Authority, 1974—, chmn., 1976—. Mem. Cascade County (Mont.) sec. 1968), Mont., Am. bar assns. Home: 3004 Fox Farm Rd Great Falls MT 59404 Office: 700 1st Nat Bank Bldg Great Falls MT 59405 Tel (406) 727-5000

HAMILTON, FOWLER, b. Kansas City, Mo., May 7, 1911; B.A., B.C.L., M.A. (Rhodes scholar), Oxford U., 1934; B.A., U. Mo., 1935. Admitted to Mo. bar, 1935, D.C. bar, 1945, N.Y. bar, 1947; asso. firm Watson, Ess, Groner, Barnett & Whittaker, Kansas City, Mo., 1935-38; spl. asst. to atty. gen. U.S., 1938-42; dir. war frauds unit Dept. Justice, 1942; with econ. warfare div. Am. embassy, London, 1943, Fgn. Econ. Adminstrn., 1942-43; chief legal cons. Dept. Justice, 1945; partner firm Cleary, Gottlieb, Steen & Hamilton, N.Y.C., 1946-61, 63—; adminstr. AID, 1961-62; dir., mem. exec. com. New York Telephone Co.; trustee, mem. exec. com. Mut. Life Ins. Co. of New York. Mem. Am., N.Y. State, Inter-Am., Internat. bar assns., Assn. Bar City N.Y., New York County Lawyers Assn., Coll. Trial Lawyers, Am. Soc. Internat. Law, Fed. Bar Council. Home: 652 Riversville Rd Greenwich CT 06830 Office: One State St Plaza New York City NY 10004 Tel (212) 344-0600

HAMILTON, HERMAN LYNN, JR., b. Prescott, Ark., Feb. 20, 1934; B.A., U. Ark., 1955, J.D., 1957. Admitted to Ark. bar, 1957; partner firm Arnold, Hamilton & Streetman, Hamburg-Crossett, Ark., 1957-62; atty. City of Hamburg (Ark.), 1961-62; judge Hamburg Municipal Ct., 1962—; spl. asso. judge Ark. Supreme Ct., Hamburg, 1973, 77; chmn. Ark. Bd. Law Examiners, 1969-70, mem., 1966-71. Adminstrv. bd. Hamburg United Methodist Ch.; former pres. Hamburg PTA; bd. govs., vice chmn. Crossett (Ark.) Health Center; exec. council DeSoto Area council Boy Scouts Am. Mem. SE Ark. Legal Inst. Home: 503 S Cherry St Hamburg AR 71646 Office: 304 E Adams St Hamburg AR 71646 Tel (501) 853-5461

HAMILTON, JAY W., b. Dallas, July 30, 1927; B.S. Law, U. Wash., 1951, J.D., 1952. Admitted to Wash. State bar, 1952; examiner Puget Sound Title Co., Seattle, 1952-54; asso. firm Walthew, Oseran & Warner, Seattle, 1954-56; partner firm Niemeier & Hamilton, Poulsbo, Wash., 1956-70; judge Wash. State Superior Ct., 1970—; lectr. Wash. State Trial Judges Coll., 1973-75, dean., 1972, 73. Pres. bd. dirs. Harrison Meml. Hosp., Bremerton, Wash., 1965-66; v.p. bd. trustees Olympic Coll., 1969. Mem. Am. Judicature Soc., Am., Wash. State (hon.), Kitsap County (hon.) bar assns., Superior Ct. Judges Assn. (trustee 1975-77). Office: 614 Div Kitsap County Courthouse Port Orchard WA 98366 Tel (206) 876-7140

HAMILTON, JOHN LOUIS, b. Washington, Mar. 22, 1913; A.B., Princeton, 1935; LL.B., Georgetown U., 1938. Admitted to D.C. bar, 1938; partner firm Hamilton & Hamilton, Washington, 1938—; gen. counsel Met. D.C. Bd. Trade, 1971—. Chmn. bd. dirs., pres. Holton-Arms Sch., Washington; v.p., trustee St. John's Child Devel. Center, Washington; former trustee Hosp. Sick Children, Landon Sch., Canterbury Sch. Mem. Am., D.C. bar assns. Home: 4635 Dexter St Washington DC 20007 Office: 600 Union Trust Bldg 15th & H Sts NW Washington DC 20005 Tel (202) 347-2882

HAMILTON, MARY K., b. Denver, Aug. 3, 1926; B.S., Simmons Coll., 1948; J.D., U. Toledo, 1958. Admitted to Ohio bar, 1958; staff atty. Legal Aid Soc. Toledo, 1958-60, trustee, 1975—; asso. firm Cobourn, Smith, Rohrbacher & Gibson, Toledo, 1960-69; asst. trust officer Toledo Trust Co., 1969-70, trust officer, 1970-73, sr. trust officer, 1973—. Mem. budget com. Toledo Community Chest, 1975—. Mem. Toledo (1st v.p., 1976-77, pres. 1977-78), Ohio State (sect. bd. govs.), Am. bar assns. Home: 2647 Pemberton Dr Toledo OH 43606 Office: Toledo Trust Co 245 Summit St Toledo OH 43603 Tel (419) 259-8370

HAMILTON, PAT RAY, b. Oak Hill, W.Va., Feb. 14, 1923; LL.B., W.Va. U., 1949. Admitted to W.Va. bar, 1949; partner firm Hamilton, Mooney & Jackson, Oak Hill, Rainelle and Fayetteville, W.Va.; mem. W.Va. Senate, 1972—; mem. legis. com. W.Va. State Bar. Mem. Fay County Bar Assn. Home: 10 Arbuckle Rd Oak Hill WV 20901 Office: One Hamilton Place Oak Hill WV 20901 Tel (304) 409-2991

HAMILTON, ROBERT LEE, b. Minot, N.D., Jan. 10, 1940; B.B.A., U. N.D., 1962, J.D., 1964. Admitted to N.D. bar, 1964; individual practice law, Grand Forks, N.D., 1964—; asso. Grand Forks Abstract Co., 1964—; lectr. U. N.D., 1965-67; asst. city atty. City of Grand Forks, 1967-69; municipal judge City of Grand Forks, 1969-74. Mem. Agassiz Health Planning Council, 1972—, dir., 1973—, mem. exec. com., 1974—. Mem. N.D., Am. bar assns., N.Am. Judges Assn. (chmn. jud. ethics 1973), Order of Coif. Home: 2520 Olive St Grand Forks ND 58201 Office: 323 DeMers Ave Grand Forks ND 58201 Tel (701) 772-3484

HAMILTON, THOMAS MCPHERSON, b. Winfield, Kans., June 26, 1915; A.B., Southwestern Coll., Winfield, 1934; J.D., Stanford, 1937. Admitted to Calif. bar, 1937, U.S. Supreme Ct. bar, 1950; since practiced in San Diego, individual practice law, 1937-49; mem. firm McInnis & Hamilton, 1949-57; v.p. Cohu Electronics, 1957-59; mem. firm Luce, Forward, Hamilton & Scripps, 1959—; pres. Stanford Law Sch. Fund, 1970-72; trustee Pacific Legal Found., 1973—. Active County Hwy. Devel. Assn., County Republican Central Com., Greater San Diego Sports Assn.; mem. bd. visitors Stanford U., 1970-72; chmn. Calif. Gov's. Manpower Policy Task Force, 1972; trustee Scripps Clinic and Research Found., La Jolla. Mem. Am., San Diego County (past pres.) bar assns., Calif. State C. of C. (dir. 1973—), Calif. State Bar. Home: Box 82 Hagerman ID 83332 Office: 110 W A St Suite 1700 San Diego CA Tel (714) 236-1414

HAMLIN, H. WARD, JR., b. Buffalo, Dec. 22, 1946; A.B., Hamilton Coll., 1968; J.D., Albany (N.Y.) Law Sch., 1971. Admitted to N.Y. bar, 1972; trial atty. Travelers Indemnity Co., Albany, 1971—. Mem. N.Y. State, Albany County bar assns. Office: 80 Wolf Rd Albany NY 12205 Tel (518) 457-1551

HAMM, ROBERT PHILLIP, b. Madison, Wis., Apr. 12, 1916; Ph.B., Marquette U., 1939, J.D., 1941. Admitted to Wis. bar, 1941; with Sentry Ins., Stevens Point, Wis., 1944—, claims adjuster, Milw., 1944-45, claims examiner, Stevens Point, 1945-46, home office claims procedure mgr., Stevens Point, 1946-48, br. claims mgr., Madison, 1948-50, home office claims cons., Stevens Point, 1950-56, home office gen. claims mgr., Stevens Point, 1956-60, br. mgr., Boston, 1960-63, asso. counsel, Stevens Point, 1963-70, v.p., sec., Stevens Point, 1970—; dir. numerous cos. Mem. Am. Soc. Corp. Secs. Home: 2031 Indiana Ave Stevens Point WI 54481 Office: 1421 Strongs Ave Stevens Point WI 54481

HAMMA, ROY WILLIAM, b. Trenton, N.J., Oct. 3, 1944; B.S., U. Ala., 1966; J.D., Rutgers U., 1969. Admitted to N.J. bar, 1969, Calif. bar, 1971; individual practice law, Quincy, Calif., 1971-73, 1975—; partner firm Hamma & Flanagan, Qunicy, 1973-74; pub. defender Plumas County (Calif.), Quincy, 1976—. Office: POB M Quincy CA 95971 Tel (916) 283-2400

HAMMER, DAVID HARRY, b. Passaic, N.J., Mar. 7, 1909; LL.B., Fordham U., 1929. Admitted to N.J. bar, 1930, U.S. Supreme Ct. bar, 1958; sr. partner firm Hammer & Hammer, Passaic, 1930-72; individual practice law, Passaic, 1972—; magistrate Passaic Municipal Ct., 1960-63. Mem. Am. Arbitration Assn. Home: 152 Van Houten Ave Passaic NJ 07055 Office: 1 Howe Ave Passaic NJ 07055 Tel (201) 777-5400

HAMMER, FREDERIC EDWARD, b. N.Y.C., Apr. 7, 1909; LL.B., St. John's Coll., 1930. Admitted to N.Y. State bar, 1931; mem. firm Bernstein, Weiss Tomson, Hammer & Porter, N.Y.C., N.Y., 1931-67; mem. N.Y. State Senate, 1945-48; commr. N.Y. State Workmen's Compensation Bd., 1950-68; judge Civil Ct. N.Y.C., 1968-70; justice N.Y. State Supreme Ct., Jamaica, 1971—. Dir. Am. Cancer Commn., N.Y.; exec. mem. Boy Scouts Am., N.Y.; past pres. West End Temple, Rockaway, N.Y.; past pres. Rockaway Civic Club. Mem. Am., Queens County bar assns. Home: 360 Beach 148th St Neponsit NY 11694 Office: Supreme Ct 88-11 Sutphin Blvd Jamaica NY 11435 Tel (212) 520-3745

HAMMER, G. WILLIAM, b. Wyandotte, Mich., Dec. 5, 1922; A.B., Ball State U., Muncie, Ind., 1950; J.D., George Washington U., Washington, 1953. Admitted to D.C. bar, 1953, Va. bar, 1954; individual practice law, 1954-76; substitute judge 19th Jud. Dist., Fairfax, Va., 1974-76, judge, 1976—; asst. city atty., Falls Church, Va., 1959-61; substitute judge, Falls Church, 1969-76. Mem. Assn. Dist. Ct. judges Va., Am. Judges Assn., D.C. Bar Assn., Phi Delta Phi. Home: PO Box 242 Oakton VA 22124 Office: Fairfax County Courthouse Room 139 4000 Chain Bridge Rd Fairfax VA 22032 Tel (703) 691-2154

HAMMERMAN, MARY BELL, b. Bklyn., Nov. 30, 1917; B.S., Temple U., 1958, LL.B. (now J.D.), 1962. Admitted to Pa. Supreme Ct. bar, 1963, U.S. Supreme Ct. bar, 1967; clk. firm Peter P. Zion, Phila., 1962-64, firm Banks & Banks, Phila., 1964-65; individual practice law, Phila., 1965—; counsel Teen-Aid, Inc., 1968-76. Bd. dirs. Psychiatry unit St. Christopher's Hosp., Phila., Mem. Am., Pa., Phila. (asst. sec. 1973-75, sec. 1976—) bar assns., Am., Pa., Phila. (treas. 1975-77) trial lawyers assns. Contbr. articles in field to profl. jours. Office: 707 Land Title Bldg Philadelphia PA 19110 Tel (215) KI5-0566

HAMMOND, FRANK JOSEPH, b. Harvey, Ill., Dec. 9, 1919; B.A., Carleton Coll., 1941; LL.B., Harvard U., 1948. Admitted to Minn. bar, 1948; asso. firm Briggs and Morgan, St. Paul, 1948-54, partner 1954—; mem. faculty St. Paul Coll. Law, 1950-56; lectr. William Mitchell Coll. Law, St. Paul, 1962-67; lectr. extension div. U. Minn., 1967; bd. dirs. Legal Assistance of Ramsey County (Minn.), 1966-69. Pres. St. Paul Council Arts and Scis., 1958-60, Capitol Community Services, St. Paul, 1951-61; mem. bd. edn. City St. Paul, 1961-68; bd. dirs. Miller Meml. Found., Stillwater, Minn., 1967—, Carleton Coll., Northfield, Minn., 1962—, Wilder Found., St. Paul, 1976—, United Theol. Sem., New Brighton, Minn., 1976—. Mem. Am. Coll. Trial Lawyers, Am. Bd. Trial Advocates, Am., Minn. State, Ramsey County bar assns., Am. Judicature Soc. Home: 1366 Fairmount Ave St Paul MN 55105 Office: 1st Nat Bank Bldg St Paul MN 55101 Tel (612) 291-1215

HAMMOND, HARLAN Y., b. Salt Lake City, Aug. 5, 1927; A.B., U. Utah, 1949; LL.B., George Washington U., 1958. Admitted to Utah bar, 1960; dep. county atty., Utah, 1968-69; asst. atty. gen., Salt Lake City, 1970—; chief title examiner Dept. Hwys., 1961-65; atty. Attys'. Title Guaranty Fund, Inc., 1965-70, v.p., 1971-74; pres. Stewart Title of Utah, 1976—. Chmn. bd. Utah Heart Assn., 1976—. Mem. Assn. Utah Realtors, Home Builders Assn. Utah, Am., Utah bar assns. Office: 401 Commercial Security Bank Bldg Salt Lake City UT 84111 Tel (801) 532-8844

HAMMOND, JOE PHIL, b. Hugo, Okla., May 18, 1922; B.S., Okla. State U., 1943; LL.B., Columbia, 1948. Admitted to Okla. bar, 1949, Ill. bar, 1973; individual practice law, Enid, Okla., 1949-50; atty. Amoco Prodn. Co. (formerly Stanolind Oil & Gas Co. and Pan Am. Petroleum Corp.), subs. Standard Oil Co. (Ind.), Tulsa, 1952-61, gen. atty., 1961-70, gen. counsel, 1970-71; asst. gen. counsel Standard Oil Co. (Ind.), 1971-72, asso. gen. counsel, 1972-75, v.p. pub. and govt. affairs, 1975—. Mem. Am., Okla., Ill., Chgo. bar assns. Home: 1046 Cherokee Rd Wilmette IL 60091 Office: 200 E Randolph Dr Chicago IL 60601 Tel (312) 856-7945

HAMMOND, LOVEY JEWEL, b. Bryan, Tex., Apr. 17, 1927; Mus.B., Howard U., 1947; M.A., Case Western Res. U., 1951; J.D., Cleve. State U., 1960. Admitted to Tex. bar, 1971; tchr. Cleve. Pub. Schs., 1948-69; freelance legal research and writing, 1969-71; prof. Prairie View A. and M. U., 1971-72; individual practice law, Bryan, 1972—. Mem. AAUW, State Bar Tex., Am. Bar Assn. Columnist, Twin City Sentinel. Home: 900 N Randolph St Bryan TX 77801 Office: 208 W 21st St Bryan TX 77801 Tel (713) 822-9314

HAMMOND, SMITH CHRISTOPHER, b. N.Y.C., Nov. 6, 1938; A.B., Williams Coll., 1960; LL.B., Yale, 1963; Admitted to D.C. bar, 1964, Conn. bar, 1963, N.Y. bar, 1967; asso firm Whitman & Ransom, N.Y.C., 1966-70, partner, 1970-72, 76—; pres., chief exec. officer FAG Bearings Corp., Stamford, Conn., 1972-76, vice chmn. bd., sec., gen. counsel, 1976—; chmn. bd., chief exec. officer Barnes Engring. Co., Stamford, 1977—; fellow OAS, 1965-66. Home: 45 Westway Rd Southport CT 06490 Office: 522 Fifth Ave New York City NY 10036 Tel (212) 575-5000

HAMMOND, THOMAS WEST, b. Washington, June 5, 1942; B.B.A., George Washington U., 1966, J.D. with honors, 1969. Admitted to Maine bar, 1970; partner firm Eaton, Glass, Marsano & Hammond, Belfast, Maine, 1970-75; individual practice law, Belfast, 1975—; city solicitor, Belfast, 1970-72. Mem. Am., Waldo County bar assns. Home: Primrose Hill Belfast ME 04915 Office: Primrose Hill Belfast ME 04915 Tel (207) 338-1496

HAMNER, REGINALD TURNER, b. Tuscaloosa, Ala., June 4, 1939; B.S., U. Ala., 1961, LL.B., 1965, J.D., 1969. Admitted to Ala. bar, 1965, U.S. Supreme Ct. bar, 1968, U.S. Ct. Mil. Appeals bar, 1968; law clk. Ala. Supreme Ct., 1965; served with JAGC, USAF, 1966-68; dir. legal-legis. affairs Med. Assn. Ala., Montgomery, 1968-69; exec. dir. Ala. State Bar, Montgomery, 1969—. Bd. dirs. Montgomery County Mental Health Assn., 1969-70, Leukemia Soc., 1968-69; mem. advisory com. bd. trustees Ala. State U., 1976—. Mem. Am. Bar Assn. (ho. dels. 1972-76), Am. Judicature Soc., Am. Soc. Assn. Execs., Nat. Assn. Bar Execs. (treas. 1975-76, v.p. 1976-77, pres.-elect 1977-78). Home: 3407 Drexel Rd Montgomery AL 36106 Office: 415 Dexter Ave Montgomery AL 36104 Tel (205) 269-1515

HAMPE, RICHARD ALAN, b. Lynn, Mass., May 31, 1943; B.A., U. Mass., 1965; J.D. with honors, George Washington U., 1968. Admitted to N.H. bar, 1968; staff atty. N.H. Office Legis. Services, 1968-69, atty., Office Atty. Gen., 1969-70, asst. atty. gen. Chief Consumer Protection Div., 1970-72; individual practice law, Concord, N.H., 1972—; atty. Merrimack County (N.H.), 1973-76. Bd. dirs. Central N.H. Community Mental Health Services, Concord, 1974—; treas., bd. dirs. N.H. Welfare Council, Concord, 1969-71; pres. N.H. Medico-Legal Soc., Concord. Mem. Am., N.H., Merrimack County bar assns. Named Outstanding Young Man, 1973. Home: Garrison Ln Hopkinton NH 03301 Office: 91 N State St Concord NH 03301 Tel (603) 224-7411

HAMPERS, LAVONNE JOYCE, b. Mt. Vernon, Ind.; student Ind. U., 1956-59, Northwestern U., 1959-61; LL.B., Boston Coll., 1967; LL.M., Boston U., 1969. Admitted to Mass. bar, 1967; dir. ops. staff Research Assos., Inc., Chgo., 1959-64; asso. firm Wilson, Curran, Malkasian & Winward, Boston, 1968-74; individual practice law, Weston, Mass. 1974-75; asso. commr. Mass. Dept. Corps. and Taxation, Boston, 1975—; adviser Mass. Continuing Legal Edn. Assn. Mem. com. adminstrn. justice LWV, 1973—; trustee Meadowbrook Sch., Weston, 1976—. Mem. Boston Coll. Alumni Assn. Office: 100 Cambridge St Boston MA 02204 Tel (617) 727-4201

HAMPSEY, BERNARD JAMES, JR., b. Pitts., Oct. 11, 1937; B.S., Coll. Holy Cross, 1958; J.D., Duquesne U., 1961. Admitted to N.H. bar, 1961; staff atty. Manchester Savs. Bank, 1961-63; individual practice law, Jaffrey, N.H., 1963-66; partner firm Brighton, Fernald, Taft and Hampsey, Jaffrey, 1966—; spl. judge, asst. judge Jaffrey Dist. Ct., 1968, judge, 1968—. Com. chmn. local council Boy Scouts Am.; Republican chmn. Town of Jaffrey; v.p. Monadnock Communtiy Hosp. Mem. Am. Judges Assn., N.H. Dist. Ct. Assn., Am., N.H. bar assns. Home: Erin Ln Jaffrey NH 03452 Office: 42 Grove St Peterborough NH 03458 Tel (603) 924-3661

HAMPSON, THOMAS MEREDITH, b. Ann Arbor, Mich., Feb. 18, 1929; A.B., Cornell U., 1951, LL.B. with distinction, 1955. Admitted to N.Y. State bar, 1955, U.S. Dist. Ct. for Western Dist. N.Y. bar, 1955, U.S. Supreme Ct. bar, 1964, U.S. 2d Circuit Ct. Appeals bar, 1971; asso. firm Harris, Beach, Wilcox, Rubin and Levey and predecessor firms, Rochester, N.Y., 1955-62, partner, 1963—; instr. law, Cornell U., 1969-75. Pres. Friends of the Rochester Library, 1967-69; trustee Rochester Pub. Library, 1977—; mem. Monroe County Fair Campaign Practices Com., 1977—. Mem. Am., N.Y. State (vice-chmn. com. on legal edn. and admission to the bar 1976-77, chmn. 1977—), Monroe County bar assns., N.Y. Civil Liberties Union (dir. 1966-68), City Club Rochester (pres. 1963-64). Home: 83 Berkeley St Rochester NY 14607 Office: 2 State St Rochester NY 14614 Tel (716) 232-4440

HAMPTON, GORDON FRANCIS, b. Fullerton, Calif., July 14, 1912; A.B., Stanford, 1935; LL.B., Harvard, 1938. Admitted to Calif. bar, 1938, U.S. Supreme Ct. bar, 1946; asso. firm Mathes & Sheppard, Los Angeles, 1938-45; partner firm Sheppard, Mullin, Richter & Hampton, Los Angeles, 1945—; instr. Loyola U. Law Sch., Los Angeles, 1942-43; lectr. Calif. State Bar Continuing Edn. Program, 1950, 59. Vice chmn. Los Angeles County Republican Central Com., 1947-48; mem. Calif. Rep. Central Com., 1947-48; chmn. Fellows of Pasadena (Calif.) Art Mus., 1972-75; bd. dirs. Fellows of Contemporary Art, Los Angeles, 1975—. Fellow Am. Bar Found.; mem. Am. (chmn. Nat. Inst. on Antitrust Law 1967-71, mem. council antitrust law sect. 1971-75, budget officer antitrust law sect. 1975—), Internat., Calif., Los Angeles County (chmn. com. on legal ethics 1954, chmn. sect. on intellectual property and unfair competition 1967-68) bar assns. Editor Los Angeles Bar Bull., 1950-51; contbr. articles to legal jours. Home: 2665 Wallingford Rd San Marino CA 91108 Office: 333 S Hope St 48th floor Los Angeles CA 90071 Tel (213) 620-1780

HAMPTON, KENT BRONSON, b. Mattoon, Ill., June 3, 1920; A.B. in prelaw, Grinnell Coll., 1942; J.D., U. Mich., 1949. Admitted to Ill. bar, 1949, Ind. bar, 1952, Ohio bar, 1958, Wyo. bar, 1963, U.S. Supreme Ct. bar, 1960; partner firm Shuey & Hampton, Charleston, Ill., 1949-51; atty. Marathon Oil Co., Terre Haute, Ind. and Findlay, Ohio, 1951-60, div. atty. Terre Haute, 1960-62, Casper, Wyo., 1962-65, atty. internat. orgn., Findlay, 1965-67, sr. atty. prodn., 1967-72, asso. gen. counsel, 1972-74, gen. counsel, 1974—. Mem. Ill., Ohio, Findlay-Hancock County, Am. (vice chmn. oil com. natural resources sect. 1976-77) bar assns. Home: 605 Sutton Pl Findlay OH 45840 Office: 539 S Main St Findlay OH 45840 Tel (419) 422-2121

HAMPTON, WILLIAM PECK, b. Pontiac, Mich., Jan. 24, 1938; B.A., Mich. State U., 1960; J.D. with Honors, Wayne State U., 1963. Admitted to Mich. bar, 1964; partner firm Hampton & Hampton, Pontiac, 1963-70; mem. Mich. Ho. of Reps., 1964-70, majority leader, 1967-68, minority leader, 1969-70; judge Oakland County (Mich.) Circuit Ct., Pontiac, 1971-76; asso. firm Davidson, Gotshall et al, Farmington Hills, Mich., 1977—; mem. Mich. Comm. Criminal Justice, 1973-76. Mem. Am., Mich., Oakland County bar assns., Mich. Judges Assn. (officer, 1971-76). Named one of five outstanding young men of Mich., Mich. Jr. C. of C., 1970. Home: 4038 Nearbrook Rd Bloomfield Hills MI 48013 Office: 30840 Northwestern Hwy Farmington Hills MI 48024 Tel (313) 851-9500 Farmington Hills MI 48024 Tel (313) 851-9500 1200 N Telegraph Rd Pontiac MI 48053 Tel (313) 858-0365

HAMRICK, CLAUDE ARTHUR STUART, b. Tampa, Fla., Sept. 11, 1939; A.A., U. Fla., 1962, B.E.E., 1963; J.D., George Washington U., 1967. Admitted to U.S. Patent bar, 1965, Calif. bar, 1970, U.S. Supreme Ct. bar, 1976; examiner U.S. Patent Office, Washington, 1963-64; atty. patent law dept. Gen. Motors Corp., Washington, 1964-67, Varian Assos., Palo Alto, Calif., 1967-68; partner firm Lowhurst & Hamrick, Palo Alto, Calif., 1968-71, Schatzel & Hamrick, Santa Clara, Calif., 1972-76, Boone, Schatzel, Hamrick & Knudsen, Santa Clara and San Francisco, 1976—. Mem. Sunnyvale (Calif.) Bicentennial Commn., 1975-77; bd. dirs. Am. Lung Assn., Santa Clara County, 1972—. Mem. Am. (award young lawyers sect. 1974), Santa Clara County, Sunnyvale-Cupertino bar assns., Calif., Peninsula patent law assns., State Bar Calif. (certificate of appreciation 1975). Office: 1333 Lawrence Expy Suite 440 Santa Clara CA 95051 also 235 Montgomery St suite 420 San Francisco CA 94104

HAMRICK, FREDRICK DELMAR, JR., b. Shelby, N.C., June 5, 1908; student Davidson (N.C.) Coll., 1926-28; LL.B., U. N.C., Chapel Hill, 1932. Admitted to N.C. bar, 1931, U.S. Supreme Ct. bar, 1939; partner firm Hamrick and Hamrick, Rutherfordton, N.C., 1932-43, firm Hamrick and Jones, Rutherfordton, 1946-67; individual practice law, Rutherfordton, 1967-68; partner firm Hamrick and Bowen, Rutherfordton, 1968-73, firm Hamrick, Bowen & Nanney, Rutherfordton, 1973—. Pres. Piedmont Council Boy Scouts Am., Gastania, N.C., 1960-61. Fellow Am. Coll. Trial Lawyers; mem. Internat., Am., N.C. (exec. com. 1949-50), Rutherford County (pres. 1940) bar assns., Am. Judicature Soc., Am. Soc. Hosp. Atty., Delta Theta Phi. Mem. editorial bd. N.C. Law Rev., 1931-32. Home: 807 N Washington St Rutherfordton NC 28139 Office: 511 N Washington St Rutherfordton NC 28139 Tel (704) 286-9152

HAMSHER, FRANK COOLIDGE, b. St. Louis, Oct. 1, 1946; A.B., Princeton U., 1968; J.D., Yale, 1971. Admitted to Mo. bar, 1971, U.S. Dist. Ct. bar Eastern Dist. Mo., 1971, U.S. Ct. Appeals bar 8th Circuit, 1971; asso. firm Husch, Eppenberger, Donohue, Elson & Cornfeld, St. Louis, 1971-72, 73—. Mem. nat. staff McGovern for Pres., 1972; mem. Eastern Mo. bd. ACLU, 1974—; mem. youth services allocation com. United Way, 1975—. Mem. Am., Mo. bar assns., Bar Assn. Met. St. Louis. Home: 33 Waterman Pl Saint Louis MO 63112 Office: Boatmen's Tower 100 N Broadway Saint Louis MO 63102 Tel (314) 421-4800

HAMSTEAD, RICHARD ELBERT, b. Morgantown, W.Va., Jan. 27, 1931; A.B. in History and Polit. Sci., W.Va. U., 1952, J.D., 1957. Admitted to W.Va. bar, 1957, U.S. Supreme Ct. bar, 1965; partner firm Hamstead & Hamstead, Morgantown, 1957—; field investigator Workmen's Compensation Fund, 1957-60; asst. pros. atty. Monongalia County (W.Va.), 1968. Mem. W.Va., Monongalia bar assns., Practicing Law Inst., Phi Theta Kappa. Home: Route 7 Box 750 Morgantown WV 26505 Office: 717 Monongahela Bldg Morgantown WV 26505 Tel (304) 296-3636

HANCE, ELVIN DAVID, b. Creston, Iowa, May 22, 1947; B.S. in Elec. Engring., Gen. Motors Inst., 1969; M.S., Purdue U., 1970; M.B.A., U. Iowa, 1973, J.D., 1973. Admitted to Iowa bar, 1973; U.S. Dist. Ct. for So. Iowa bar, 1973, U.S. Dist. Ct. for No. Iowa bar, 1974, U.S. 8th Circuit Ct. Appeals bar, 1974, U.S. Supreme Ct. bar, 1976; counsel Iowa Crime Commn., Des Moines, 1973; asst. ct. adminstr. Iowa Supreme Ct., Des Moines, 1973-76; individual practice law, Altoona, Iowa, 1976—. Chmn. Iowa Runaway Service, Des Moines, 1976—; mem. Big Brother program, Des Moines, 1976—. Mem. Am., Iowa bar assns. Home: 4200 Grand Ave Apt A-19 Des Moines IA 50312 Office: 103 8th St SE Altoona IA 50009 Tel (515) 967-5984

HANCHEY, BEN RICHARD, b. Lake Charles, La., May 18, 1945; B.S., La. Tech. U., 1969; J.D., La. State U., 1970. Admitted to La. bar, 1970; partner firm Hudson, Potts & Bernsitin, Monroe, La., 1970—. Mem. La. State Bar Assn. (del. young lawyers sect.). Office: 1000 Ouachita Bank Bldg Monroe LA 71201

HANCOCK, JAMES, b. Chgo., Feb. 14, 1939; B.S., Ariz. State U., 1961; LL.B., U. Ariz., 1966. Admitted to Ariz. bar, 1966; city atty. Prescott (Ariz.), 1967-71; individual practice law, Prescott, 1968-73; judge Superior Ct. Yavapai County (Ariz.), Prescott, 1973—. Mem. Young Lawyers Ariz., Yavapai County Bar Assn. (pres.). Home: 583 Shalimar St Prescott AZ 86301 Office: Ct House Prescott AZ 86301 Tel (602) 445-7450

HANCOCK, JEROME CRAIG, b. Atchinson, Kans., June 12, 1912; A.B., Louisville Municipal Coll., 1935; LL.B., Howard U., 1939. Admitted to Ky. bar, 1940, D.C. bar, 1949; individual practice law, Louisville and Washington. Mem. Am., Nat. bar assns., Sigma Delta Tau, Alpha Phi Alpha. Home: 827 Thurman Ave Hyattsville MD 20783 Office: 4449 Benning Rd NE Washington DC 20019 Tel (202) 298-4050

HANCOCK, STEWART FREEMAN, JR., b. Syracuse, N.Y., Feb. 2, 1923; B.S., U.S. Naval Acad., 1945; LL.B., Cornell U., 1950. Admitted to N.Y. bar, 1950; partner firm Hancock, Estabrook, Ryan, Shove & Hust, Syracuse, 1951-62, 64-71; corp. counsel City of Syracuse, 1962-63; justice N.Y. Supreme Ct., 5th Jud. Dist., 1971—, adminstrv. justice, 1977—. Mem. Syracuse Bd. Edn., 1961; chmn. Onondaga County (N.Y.) Republican Com., 1964-66. Mem. N.Y. State, Onondaga County, Am. bar assns. Editorial bd. Cornell Law Quar., 1950. Home: 50 Presidential Plaza Syracuse NY 13202 Office: Onondaga County Courthouse Syracuse NY 13202 Tel (315) 425-2013

HANCOCK, WILLIAM FORRESTER, b. Waxahachie, Tex., Nov. 23, 1909; LL.B., U. Tex., 1933. Admitted to Tex. bar, 1934; atty. City of Waxahachie, 1934-37; criminal dist. atty. Ellis County (Tex.), 1939-42; individual practice law, Waxahachie, 1942—. Mem. Nat. Assn. Def. Counsel in Criminal Cases, Am. Judicature Soc., Tex. Criminal Def. Lawyers Assn., Am. Trial Lawyers Assn., Am., Tex., Ellis County, Dallas County, Dallas County Criminal bar assns. Home: F M Rd 878 7-H Bar Ranch Route 1 Box 64 Palmer TX 75152 Office: Hancock Bldg Waxahachie TX 75165 Tel (214) 937-2340

HAND, CHARLES CONNOR, b. Shubuta, Miss., Dec. 6, 1890; A.B., Millsaps Coll., 1909; student U. Va., 1910-12. Admitted to Miss. bar, 1912, Ala. bar, 1921; mem. firm Heidelberg & Hand, 1919-21, Armbrecht Hand & Meridith, Mobile, Ala., 1921-34; sr. mem. firm Hand Arendale Bedsole Greaves & Johnston, Mobile, 1940-77, of counsel, 1977—; dir. various investment cos. Pres., dir. Mitchell Found. Mem. Am., Ala., Mobile (past pres.) bar assns. Home: 1855 Dauphin St Mobile AL 36606 Office: First National Bank Bldg 30th Floor Mobile AL 36602 Tel (205) 432-5511

HANDEL, RICHARD CRAIG, b. Hamilton, Ohio, Aug. 11, 1945; A.B., U. Mich., 1967; M.A., Mich. State U., 1968; J.D., Ohio State U., 1974. Admitted to Ohio bar, 1974; asso. firm Smith & Schnacke, Dayton, Ohio, 1974—. Mem. Am., Ohio, Dayton bar assns., Order of Coif. Contbr. articles to legal jours. Home: 1F Rue Royale Dayton OH 45429 Office: 2000 Court House Plaza NE Dayton OH 45402 Tel (513) 226-6710

HANDLER, MILTON, b. N.Y.C., Oct. 8, 1903; A.B., Columbia, 1924, LL.B., 1926. Admitted to N.Y. bar, 1927; mem. faculty Columbia Law Sch., 1927-72, prof. emeritus law, 1972—; partner firm Kaye, Scholer, Fierman, Hays & Handler, N.Y.C., 1951—; pres. N.Y. Majestic Corp., 1937-48; gen. counsel Nat. Labor Bd., 1933-34; spl. asst. to gen. counsel U.S. Treasury Dept., 1938-40; asst. gen. counsel Lend Lease Adminstrn., 1942-43; spl. counsel Fgn. Econ. Adminstrn., 1943-44; Mitchell lectr. Buffalo Law Sch., 1956-57; lectr. U. Leyden (Netherlands), 1963; mem. Atty. Gen.'s nat. com. to study antitrust law, 1953-55. Hon. chmn. bd. dirs. Am. Friends Hebrew U., Jerusalem. Fellow Am. Coll. Trial Lawyers; mem. Am. Bar Found. (Fellows award for outstanding research in law and govt. 1977), Fed. Bar Council, Assn. Bar City N.Y., N.Y. County Lawyers Assn. Recipient bicentennial silver medallion Columbia, 1954, honor Milton Handler chair trade regulation Columbia Law Sch., 1974, alumni medal excellence, 1976, Scopus award Am. Friends of Hebrew U., 1963. Author: Antitrust in Perspective, 1957; Cases and Materials on Trade Regulations, 4th edit., 1967; Cases and Materials on Business Torts, 1972; Twenty-Five Years of Antitrust, 1973; (with others) Cases and Materials on Trade Regulation, 1975; contbr. articles to legal jours. Home: 625 Park Ave New York City NY 10021 Office: 425 Park Ave New York City NY 10022

HANDY, EDWARD OTIS, JR., b. Akron, Ohio, Jan. 9, 1929; A.B., Harvard U., 1951, LL.B., 1956. Admitted to R.I. bar, 1956; asso. firm Edwards & Angell, Providence, 1956-59; asst. sec. Textron Inc., Providence, asst. gen. counsel, asst. v.p., now gen. counsel. Trustee, R.I. Audubon Soc., Trnity Sq. Repertory Co., R.I. Zool. Assn.; pres., trustee Providence Atheneum. Mem. R.I. Bar Assn. Home: 18 James St Providence RI 02903 Office: 40 Westminster St Providence RI 02903 Tel (401) 421-2800

HANDY, FRANK HARLOW, JR., b. Boston, Oct. 25, 1928; B.S., U.S. Merchant Marine Acad., 1950; LL.B., Boston U., 1957. Admitted to Mass. bar, 1957, U.S. Dist. Ct., 1958, U.S. Circuit Ct. Appeals, 1961; partner firm Kneeland Kydd & Handy, Boston, 1970—. Mem. Scituate (Mass.) Historic Dist. Study Com., 1975; mem. Scituate Conservation Com., 1970. Mem. Maritime Law Assn., Plymouth County Bar Assn. Office: 1 State St Boston MA 02110

HANDY, GEORGE BROWN, b. Rigby, Idaho, Aug. 26, 1921; Asso. Sci., Weber State Coll., 1941; J.D., U. Utah, 1947. Admitted to Utah bar, 1949; mem. firm Handy, Judd & Sampson, Ogden, Utah; mem. Utah State Bd. Corrections, 1957-73, vice-chmn., 1968-73; chmn. Govt. Reorgn. Com., 1973-75. Chmn., Ogden Pioneer Days Com., 1975-76. Mem. Utah State, Weber County bar assns., Am. Trial Lawyers Assn. Home: 1310 Marilyn Dr Ogden UT 84403 Office: 2650 Washington Blvd Ogden UT 84401 Tel (801) 621-4015

HANES, JOHN GRIER, b. Cheyenne, Wyo., May 27, 1936; B.S. in Bus. Adminstrn., U. Wyo., 1958, J.D., 1960. Admitted to Wyo. bar, 1960, U.S. Supreme Ct. bar; dep. sec. State of Wyo., 1963-65; municipal judge, Cheyenne, 1965-68; individual practice law,

Cheyenne, 1965—; sec.-treas., dir. Discovery Oil, Ltd., DOL Resources, Inc.; senate atty. Wyo. Legis., 1967, 69; served with JACC, U.S. Army, 1960-62. Mem. C. of C., Sigma Nu. Home: 848 Creighton St Cheyenne WY 82001 Office: 1720 Carey Ave suite 600 Cheyenne WY 82001 Tel (307) 634-2731

HANEY, JAMES STUART, b. Amery, Wis., Jan. 10, 1945; B.A., U. Wis., 1967, J.D., 1972. Admitted to Wis. bar, 1972; asso. firm Smith & Schultz, Madison, Wis., 1972-74; pub. affairs dir. Bergstrom Paper Co., Neenah, Wis., 1974—, asst. sec., 1976—; instr. Madison Bus. Coll., 1972-74. Bd. Winnebago County Solid Waste Mgmt., 1975—; Citizens Adv. Com. to Senate Subcom. on Wis. Paper Industry, 1975—. Mem. Am., Wis., Winnebago County bar assns., Nat. Wildlife Fedn., Am. Paper Inst. (Wis. coordinator state and local govt. relations 1975—), Wis. Paper Council (chmn. govt. relations com.), Wis. Assn. Mfg. and Commerce (environ. com. 1974—), Wis. Alumni Assn., U. Wis. Union. Home: 1089 Eden Dr Neenah WI 54956 Office: Bergstrom Rd Neenah WI 54956 Tel (414) 725-3011

HANIFORD, DAVID WALLACE, b. Lafayette, Ind., Feb. 19, 1948; B.S. in Bus. Adminstrn., Ind. U., 1970, J.D., 1973. Admitted to Ind. bar, 1973; asso. firm Schultz, Ewan & Burns, Lafayette, 1973-75; dep. prosecutor Tippecanoe County, Lafayette, 1975-76. Mem. Am., Ind. State Bar assns., Assn. of Trial Lawyers of Am. Home: 811 S 12th St Lafayette IN 47905 Office: Room 22 133 N 4th St Lafayette IN 47901 Tel (317) 423-2651

HANKE, PAUL AUGUSTUS, b. Cleve., June 2, 1936; B.A., Coll. Wooster, 1958; J.D., U. Mich., 1961. Admitted to Ohio bar, 1961; served with JAGC, U.S. Army, 1961-65; asso. firm Porter, Stanley, Platt & Arthur, Columbus, Ohio, 1965-69, partner, 1970-77; partner firm Porter & Wright, Morris & Arthur, 1977—; lectr. Ohio Legal Center Inst., 1969; adj. prof. law Capital U., 1972-73. Mem. Am., Ohio, Columbus bar assns. Home: 1866 Fishinger Rd Columbus OH 43221 Office: 37 W Broad St Columbus OH 43215 Tel (614) 228-1511

HANKIN, ALBERT MARTIN, b. Phila., July 9, 1910; J.D., Dickinson Law Sch., 1931. Admitted to Pa. bar, 1931; individual practice law, Phila., 1931-47; partner firm Meyer, Lasch, Hankin & Poul, Phila., 1947—; mem. Com. of Censors, 1970-72, Pa. Supreme Ct. Disciplinary Bd., 1972—. Mem. Phila., Pa., Am. bar assns., Am. Judicature Soc., Assn. Trial Lawyers Am., Tau Epsilon Rho (nat. chancelor 1971; Distinguished Service award, 1956). Home: 504 Sabine Circle Wynnewood PA 19096 Office: 1 East Pennsylvania Sq Bldg Philadelphia PA 19107 Tel (215) LO 4-1040

HANKIN, BERNARD JACOB, b. Ewen, Mich., Apr. 6, 1913; A.B., U. Wis., 1934, LL.B., 1937. Admitted to Wis. bar, 1937; partner firm Kluwin, Dunphy, Hankin & McNulty, Milw., 1958—. Mem. Milw. Bar Assn.(pres. 1965-66), Fedn. Ins. Counsel, Internat. Acad. Trial Lawyers. Home: 5814 N Kent St Milwaukee WI 53217 Office: 1100 W Wells St Suite 700 Milwaukee WI 53233 Tel (414) 276-6464

HANLEY, ROBERT FRANCIS, b. Spokane, Wash., June 26, 1924; A.B., Northwestern U., 1948, J.D., 1950. Admitted to Ill. bar, 1950, U.S. Supreme Ct. bar, 1974; partner firm Isham, Leurolu & Beale, 1960-68, partner firm Jenner & Block, Chgo., 1969—; asst. atty. gen. State of Ill., 1952-54; lectr. Sch. Law, Northwestern U., 1960—; speaker Continuing Legal Edn. Insts., Ill., Mich. Pres. Legal Club Chgo., 1975—; mem. Law Club. Fellow Am. Coll. Trial Lawyers; mem. Chgo., Ill., Am. (chmn. sect. litigation, 1975-76, sect. del. to ho. of dels., 1976, speaker insts., 1970-76) bar assns. Contbr. articles to legal publs. Home: 2317 Central Park Ave Evanston IL 60201 Office: One IBM Plaza Chicago IL 60611 Tel (312) 222-9350

HANNA, FRANCIS M., b. Tulsa, Aug. 10, 1935; B.A., Chgo. State U., 1959; J.D., Northwestern U., 1962. Admitted to Mo. bar, 1962; asso. firm Stinson, May, Thomson, McEvers & Fizzell, Kansas City, Mo., 1962-67, partner, 1967—. Mem. Am., Mo. bar assns., Estate Planning Assn. Kansas City (treas. 1976, sec. 1977). Recipient Mo. Bar Smithson Essay award. Office: PO Box 19251 Kansas City MO 64141 Tel (816) 842-8600

HANNA, JOHN PAUL, b. N.Y.C., July 12, 1932; B.A., Stanford U., 1954, J.D., 1959. Admitted to Calif. bar, 1960; with firm Thoits, Lehman, Hanna & Love, and predecessors, Palo Alto, Calif., 1960—, partner, 1962—, v.p., 1975—. Trustee Castilleja Sch., Palo Alto, 1974—. Mem. Am. Bar Assn., Calif. State Bar, Palo Alto C. of C. (v.p. 1966). Author: The California Condominium Handbook, 1976; The Complete Layman's Guide to the Law, 1975; Teenagers and the Law, 1967; also articles. Office: 525 University Ave Palo Alto CA 94302 Tel (415) 327-4200

HANNA, LARRY LAVERNE, b. Florence, S.C., Aug. 13, 1947; B.S. in Chemistry, U. S.C., 1969, J.D., 1973. Tchr. Horry County, S.C., Schs., 1969-70; mem. staff S.C. Tax Commn. Columbia, 1972-73; admitted to S.C. bar, 1973; law clk. Clk of Ct. Richland County, S.C., 1972-73; asso. firm Charles L. Watson, Conway, S.C., 1973; individual practice law, Myrtle Beach, S.C., 1974—; agent So. Title Ins. Co., Myrtle Beach, 1975—. Mem. Am., S.C., Horry County (sec.-treas. 1974—), bar assns., Am. Judicature Soc., S.C. Trial Lawyers Assn. Co-editor: A Comparative Analysis of S.C. Income Tax Laws and the Internal Revenue Code, 1972. Home: 6206 Blynn Dr Myrtle Beach SC 29577 Office: Suite 405 16th Ave N and Oak St POB 1265 Myrtle Beach SC 29577 Tel (803) 448-1471

HANNA, THOMAS LEE, b. Hall Summitt, La., Sept. 25, 1938; B.A., Baylor U., 1961; LL.B., U. Tex., 1964. Admitted to Tex. bar, 1964; asst. dist. atty. Jefferson County (Tex.), 1964-66, criminal dist. atty., 1971—; practiced in Port Arthur, Tex., 1967-70; chmn. penal code com. New Tex. Penal Code, 1971-74. Mem. State Bar Tex. (chmn. sect. criminal law 1974-75), Jefferson County Bar Assn. (v.p. 1969), Tex. Dist. and County Attys. Assn. (pres. 1975), Nat. Dist. Attys. Assn. (dir. 1975—). Named Outstanding Young Lawyer of Jefferson County, 1974. Home: 1806 Franklin St Nederland TX 77627 Office: PO Box 2553 Beaumont TX 77704 Tel (713) 835-8550

HANNA, THOMAS MILES, b. Tulsa, Nov. 19, 1936; B.S., U. Tulsa, 1958, LL.B., 1960. Admitted to Okla. bar, 1960, Mo. bar, 1967; asso. firm Houston, Kline & Davidson, Tulsa, 1960-62; with NLRB, Ft. Worth, 1962-66; asso. firm McMahon, Berger, Breckenridge, Hanna, Linihan & Cody, St. Louis, 1966—; served to lt. JAG, USNR, 1965-71. Mem. Am. Bar Assn., Mo. Bar, Okla. Bar, Met. Bar Assn. St. Louis (chmn. labor law com. 1975-76). Home: 1632 Mason Valley Rd Saint Louis MO 63131 Office: 7701 Forsyth Blvd Suite 1153 Saint Louis MO 63105 Tel (314) 863-0355

HANNA, WARREN LEONARD, b. Defiance, Iowa, July 20, 1898; A.B., U. N.D., 1917, LL.D., 1970; J.D., U. Minn., 1923, M.A., 1924. Admitted to Minn. bar, 1923, Calif. bar, 1931; accountant So. Pacific Co., San Francisco, 1924-31; referee Calif. Indsl. Accident Commn., San Francisco, 1931-43; partner firm Hanna, Brophy, MacLean, McAleer & Jensen, San Francisco, 1943—; chmn. com. on workers' compensation State Bar Calif., 1965-66. Mem. Calif. Bar, Am. Bar Assn., Calif. C. of C. (chmn. com. on workers' compensation). Author: California Law of Employee Injuries, 1953; Montana's Many-Splendored Glacierland, 1976; The Grizzlies of Glacier; editor: Attorney General's Opinions of California, 1943-77; Workmen's Compensation Laws of California, 1937-77; California Compensation Cases, 1936-77; Standard Codes of California, 1949-77. Home: 154 Lawson Rd Kensington CA 94707 Office: 215 Market St San Francisco CA 94105 Tel (415) 982-6077

HANNAFORD, JOHN LIVINGSTON, b. St. Paul, Jan. 27, 1919; A.B., Yale, 1941, LL.B., 1948. Admitted to Minn. bar, 1948; asso. firm Doherty, Rumble & Butler, St. Paul, 1948-52, partner, 1953—. Sec., mem. exec. com. United Way of St. Paul Area; bd. dirs. Oakland Cemetery Assn. Mem. Ramsey County, Minn. State, Am. bar assns., Am. Coll. Probate Counsel. Office: 1500 First National Bank Bldg Saint Paul MN 55101 Tel (612) 291-9264

HANNAH, PAUL FRANCIS, b. Berlin, N.H., Nov. 11, 1905; B.S., Dartmouth Coll., 1927; J.D., George Washington U., 1933. Admitted to D.C. bar, 1931, U.S. Supreme Ct. bar, 1936, Mass. bar, 1946; asst. editor Nature Mag., Washington, 1928-32; asso. firm Morris, Kix Miller & Baar, Washington, 1932-36, jr. partner, 1936-41; gen. counsel Raytheon Co., Lexington, Mass., 1946-63, v.p., 1947-61, sec., 1947-61; partner firm Gadsby & Hannah, Boston and Washington, 1963-75, of counsel, 1976—; dir., mem. exec. council Waltham Fed. Savs. and Loan Assn. Fellow Am. Bar Found., Am. Law Inst.; mem. Am., Mass. bar assns., Assn. Gen. Counsel. Home: 44 Hubbard Rd Weston MA 02193 Office: 140 Federal St Boston MA 02110 Tel (617) 482-1700

HANNON, BARRY THOMAS, b. Boston, Nov. 21, 1935; B.S., Holy Cross Coll., 1958; LL.B., Boston U., 1961. Admitted to Mass. bar 1962; mem. Mass. Ho. of Reps. from Braintree, 1966-70; register of deeds Norfolk County, Dedham, Mass., 1970—. Bd. dirs. S. Shore Area Family Counseling and Guidance Centers Inc., 1970—, Cerebral Palsy of the S. Shore Area, 1976—. Mem. Bar Assn. of Norfolk County (pres. 1977), Mass. Bar Assn., Mass. Registers of Deeds Assn. Home: 305 West St Braintree MA 02184 Office: Norfolk County Registry of Deeds High St Dedham MA 02026

HANNON, EDWARD E., b. Omaha, Sept. 3, 1931; J.D., Creighton U., 1959. Admitted to Nebr. bar, 1959, U.S. Tax Ct. bar, 1971; partner firm Cronin & Hannon, O'Neill, Nebr., 1960—. Trustee St. Anthony's Hosp., O'Neill. Mem. Nebr. State, Am. bar assns., Am. Trial Lawyers Assn. Home: 912 E Londonderry Dr O'Neill NE 68763 Office: 103 S Fifth St O'Neill NE 68763 Tel (402) 336-1921

HANOFEE, EUGENE M., b. White Sulphur Springs, N.Y., July 14, 1922; B.A., William and Mary Coll., 1947; LL.B., Union U., 1950, J.D., 1968; postgrad. U. Richmond, Northwestern U. Admitted to N.Y. State bar; asso. firm James Dempsey, White Plains, N.Y., 1950-54, Peekskill, N.Y., 1950-54; individual practice law, Liberty, N.Y., 1954-58; partner firm Rothblatt, Hanofee & Friedman, 1958-77; judge Sullivan County Family Ct., Monticello, N.Y., 1977—; estate tax atty. County of Sullivan, 1975-77. Clk. Sullivan County Bd. Suprs., 1954-66; mem. Sullivan County Mental Health, Mental Retardation, and Alcoholism Services Bd.; v.p., bd. dirs. Sullivan County Council for Arts; pres., bd. dirs. Liberty Central Sch. Bd. Edn.; co-chmn. Sullivan County Narcotic Guidance Council; chmn. Liberty Narcotic Guidance Council; mem. exec. com. Catskill Regional Mental Health Planning Com.; pres., chmn. bd. dirs. Sullivan County Community Concert Assn.; bd. dirs. local chpt. ARC, Sullivan County Cancer Soc., Sullivan County Legal Aid Soc. Mem. N.Y. State Sullivan County (pres. bar assns., Sullivan County, N.Y. State, Nat. sch. bds. assns. Home: 43 Winslow Pl Liberty NY 12754 Office: Sullivan County Government Center Monticello NY 12701 Tel (914) 794-3000 extension 243

HANSARD, GEORGE HARVEY, b. Gorman, Tex., Oct. 1, 1926; B.A., Baylor U., 1949, LL.B., 1951. Admitted to Tex. bar, 1951; partner firm Clement & Hansard, Lamesa, Tex., 1951-71; judge Tex. Dist. Ct., 106th Jud. Dist., 1971—; county atty. Dawson County (Tex.), 1953-69; dist. atty. 106th Jud. Dist. Tex., 1969-70. Bd. dirs. Boy's Club. Mem. State Bar Tex. Home: 103 Juniper Dr Lamesa TX 79331 Office: Courthouse Lamesa TX 79331 Tel (806) 872-3740

HANSCOM, RICHARD JOHN, b. Chgo., Feb. 1, 1932; B.S., U. Wis., 1953; J.D., U. Calif., Los Angeles, 1958. Admitted to Calif. bar, 1959; with San Diego County (Calif.) Dist. Atty's. Office, 1959-72, chief dep. dist. atty., 1969-71, div. chief, 1971-72; judge Municipal Ct. San Diego Jud. Dist., 1972—. Bd. dirs. Girls Club of San Diego, Inc., 1967-70, 72-74, treas., 1968-70; mem. San Diego Community Relations Bd., 1975—; chmn. San Diego County Bench-Bar-Media Com., 1975—. Mem. Calif. Judges Assn. (exec. bd. 1976—). Contbr. articles to legal jours. Office: 220 W Broadway San Diego CA 92101 Tel (714) 236-3899

HANSEL, HELEN STEPHENS, b. Bklyn., Jan. 4, 1922; B.A., Adelphi U., 1942; postgrad. U. Kans., 1946; J.D., Stetson U., 1968. Admitted to Fla. bar, 1968; jr. engr. Signal Corps Engring. Labs., Fort Monmouth, N.J., 1942-46; asso. firm. Roney, Ulmer, Woodworth & Jacobs, and predecessors, St. Petersburg, Fla., 1968-69; individual practice law, St. Petersburg, 1969—. Mem. St. Petersburg Civil Service Bd., 1973—, vice chmn., 1974-76; candidate in Republican primary for U.S. senator from Fla., 1976; pres. Roslyn (N.Y.) LWV, 1952-54, bd. dirs. N.Y. State, 1957-60; mem. Sch. Bd., Central Sch. Dist. #1, Oyster Bea and Sea Cliff, N.Y., 1959-62. Mem. Am. (vice chmn. juvenile justice com. 1977—), St. Petersburg bar assns., Fla. Bar., Fla. Assn. Women Lawyers, Stetson Lawyers Assn. (dir.), Criminal Def. Lawyers Pinellas County, Am. Judicature Soc. Home: 1374 Monterey Blvd NE Saint Petersburg FL 33704 Office: 624 1st Ave S Saint Petersburg FL 33731 Tel (813) 822-5050

HANSEN, CONNOR THEODORE, b. Freeman, S.D., Nov. 1, 1913; B.Ed., Wis. State Tchrs. Coll., Eau Claire, 1934; LL.B., U. Wis., 1937. Admitted to Wis. bar, 1937; dist. atty. Eau Claire County, 1938-43; spl. agt. FBI, 1943-44; practiced in Eau Claire, 1945-58; judge Eau Claire County Ct., 1958-67; justice Wis. Supreme Ct., 1967—; circuit ct. commr. Eau Claire County, 1947-58; pres. Wis. Bd. Juvenile Ct. Judges, 1955-56; sec. Wis. Bd. County Judges. Mem. Camp Manito-wish com. North Central Area YMCA, 1937-77; bd. dirs. Wis. Welfare Council, 1968-71; Wis. chmn. NCCJ, 1969-70. Mem. Alumni Assn. of Wis. State U.-Eau Claire (pres. 1939), Jefferson County (Wis.), Eau Claire County (pres. 1953-54) bar assns., State Bar Wis., N.W. Peace Officers' Assn. (pres. 1942), Wis. Dist. Attys'. Assn. (pres. 1941, life). Recipient Distinguished award Eau Claire Jr. C. of C., 1941, Crime Prevention award Eau Claire Exchange Club, 1963, Distinguished Service award Alumni of U. of Wis.-Eau Claire, 1967, NCCJ, 1970. Home: 340 S Main St Lake Mills WI 53551 Office: Supreme Ct Chambers State Capitol Madison WI 53702 Tel (608) 266-1884

HANSEN, DAVID RASMUSSEN, b. Exira, Iowa, Mar. 16, 1938; B.A. with highest honors, Northwest Mo. State U., 1960; LL.B., J.D. with honors, George Washington U. Sch. Law, 1963. Admitted to Iowa bar, 1963, U.S. Court of Military Appeals bar, 1964, U.S. Supreme Court bar, 1967; judge advocate gen.'s corps U.S. Army, 1964-68; asso. firm Don W. Barker, Esq., Iowa Falls, Iowa, 1968-70; partner firm Barker and Hansen, 1970-73, partner firm Barker, Hansen and McNeal, 1973-76; judge Iowa Dist., Ct. from 2d Jud. Dist., 1976—; police court judge, City of Iowa Falls, 1969-73. Bd. dirs. Iowa Valley Community Coll., Marshalltown, 1971-76; chmn. Hardin County Rep. Central Com., 1975-76. Mem. Am., Iowa, Hardin County bar assns., Iowa Trial Lawyers Assn., Iowa Judges Assn., Phi Delta Phi. Home: RFD 4 PO Box 161 Iowa Falls IA 50126 Office: Hardin County Court House Eldora IA 50627 Tel (515) 858-3461

HANSEN, DONALD, b. Kent, Ohio, June 25, 1926; A.B., U. Ill., 1947; LL.B., Western Res. U., 1952. Admitted to Ohio bar, 1952, Oreg. bar, 1953; partner firm DeForest & Hansen, Medford, Oreg., 1954—; municipal judge, Medford, 1965-67. Mem. Medford City Council, 1955-63. Mem. Oreg. State Bar, Am. Bar Assn. Home: 1024 Winchester St Medford OR 97501 Office: 905 W 8th St Medford OR 97501 Tel (503) 773-5311

HANSEN, JAMES THOMAS, b. Holdrege, Nebr., May 29, 1943; B.A., Midland Coll., 1965; J.D., U. Kans., 1968. Admitted to Nebr. bar, 1968, Kans. bar, 1968; asst. pub. defender Scotts Bluff County (Nebr.), 1972-74, pub. defender, 1975—. Mem. Nebr. Bar Assn., Nat. Legal Aid and Defender Assn. Office: Box 471 10th St Gering NE 69341 Tel (308) 436-5661

HANSEN, JULIAN RIAL, b. Chgo., Aug. 7, 1927; J.D., U. Chgo., 1952. Admitted to Ill., Wis. bars, 1952, Calif. bar, 1954; asso. firm Fairchild, Foley & Sammond, 1952-55; partner firm Hansen & Hansen, Chgo., 1955-71; individual practice law, 1971—. Mem. Sch. Bd. Dist. #1, 1970-73; chmn. Barrington Hills, Ill., Zoning Bd. Appeals, 1974—; pres. Chgo. Council Navy League, 1975-76. Mem. Am., Calif., Wis., Ill., Chgo. bar assns., Order Coif. Home: 94 Hawthorne Rd Barrington Hills IL 60010 Office: 105 W Madison Chicago IL 60603 Tel (312) 346-9038

HANSEN, KENNETH D., b. Seattle, Mar. 26, 1947; B.S. in Psychology, U. Wash., 1969, J.D., 1972, M.D., 1976. Admitted to Wash. bar, 1972, Mich. bar, 1977; counsel Assn. Wash. Bus., Olympia, 1972-73; asst. atty. gen. State of Wash., Seattle, 1973-74; gen. counsel Wash. Med. Research Found., Seattle, 1974—; individual practice law, Seattle, 1973—; clin. instr. legal med. U. Wash., Seattle, 1976—; faculty depts. internal medicine and radiology U. Mich., 1977—. Mem. Am., Wash., Mich., Seattle-King County bar assns., Am., Mich., Wash. med. assns., King County, Washtenaw County (exec. bd. 1977) med. socs., Phi Delta Phi (recipient Award of Merit, 1972). Contbr. articles Wash. Law Review, asso. editor, 1971-72. Office: 18502 84th W Edmonds WA 98020 Tel (206) 778-7817

HANSEN, MILTON CHRISTIAN, b. Racine, Wis., Jan. 20, 1917; B.S., U. Wis., 1947; J.D., Loyola U., Chgo., 1953. Admitted to Ill. bar, 1953, U.S. Supreme Ct. bar, 1975; asst. patent counsel Great Lakes Carbon Corp., Morton Grove, Ill., 1953-55; asso. firm Marzall, Johnston, Cook & Root, Chgo., 1955-56; patent counsel Quaker Oats Co., Barrington, Ill., 1956—. Charter trustee Harper Coll., 1965-74, chmn., 1971-72. Mem. Ill. State, N.W. Suburban bar assns., Am. Patent Law Assn., Patent Law Assn. Chgo. Home: 661 S Elm St Palatine IL 60067 Office: 617 W Main St Barrington IL 60010 Tel (312) 381-1980

HANSEN, ROBERT BLAINE, b. Pocatello, Idaho, Aug. 13, 1925; B.S. in Elec. Engring., U. N.Mex., 1946; LL.B., Hastings Coll. Law, 1949; grad. Brookings Inst., 1972. Admitted to Utah bar, 1950, Calif. bar, 1950; practiced in Salt Lake City, 1950-68, Tooele, Utah, 1951-66; partner firm Hansen, Henriksen, Bradford & Young, Salt Lake City, 1953-58, Hansen, Madsen, Freebairn & Goodwill, Salt Lake City, 1964-68; dep. atty. gen. State of Utah, 1969-76, atty. gen., 1977—. Ward bishop Ch. of Jesus Christ of Latter-day Saints, 1958-62, state mission pres., 1969-72; bd. dirs. Youth Protection Com., Salt Lake City, 1968-72; Explorer Scout leader, 1972-74; state and county del. Republican Convs., 1964, 66, 76; mem. Rep. State Central Com., 1968-72, 77. Mem. Utah State Bar (mem. econs., family ct. coms. 1965-72), Order of Coif, Phi Kappa Phi. Home: 838 18th Ave Salt Lake City UT 84103 Office: State Capitol Bldg Salt Lake City UT 84114 Tel (801) 533-5261

HANSEN, THOMAS WERNER, b. Portland, Oreg., Mar. 19, 1918; J.D.S., Willamette U. Admitted to Oreg. bar, 1950, U.S. Supreme Ct. bar, 1955; dep. dist. atty. Marion County (Oreg.), 1955-60; judge, 1961—. Mem. Marion County, Oreg. State bars, Am. Judicature Soc. Office: Courthouse State and High Sts Salem OR 97301 Tel (503) 588-5024

HANSEN, WILLIAM ROGER, b. Alexandria, Minn., Mar. 11, 1946; B.A., Cal. State U., Long Beach, 1969; J.D., U. Chgo., 1973. Admitted to Md. bar, 1973; asso. firm Piper & Marbury, Balt., 1973—; mem. staff Peterson Commn. on Founds. and Pvt. Philanthropy, 1969-70. Mem. Md. State, Am. bar assns., Bar Assn. of Balt. City. Office: 2000 First Md Bldg 25 S Charles St Baltimore MD 21201 Tel (301) 539-2530

HANSHAW, A. ALAN, b. Kankakee, Ill., June 23, 1926; student U.S. Mcht. Marine Acad., 1944-46, Northwestern U., 1946, Beloit (Wis.) Coll., 1948-49; B.S. in Bus. Adminstrn., U. Ariz., 1951, LL.B., 1955. Admitted to Ariz. bar, 1955, U.S. Supreme Ct. bar, 1964; law clk. Ariz. Supreme Ct., 1955-56; asst. city atty., Tucson, 1956-58; partner firm Goddard, Gin, Hanshaw & Gianas, Tucson, 1958-69; individual practice law, Tucson, 1969-73; partner firm Waterfall, Economidis, Caldwell & Hanshaw, P.C., Tucson, 1973—. Bd. dirs. Sanitary Dist. No. 1, Tucson, 1961-64; pres. United Way, Tucson, 1977—. Fellow Am. Acad. Matrimonial Lawyers; mem. Fed., Am., Pima County (exec. com. 1970-76) bar assns., State Bar Ariz. (gov. 1975-76, disciplinary bd. 1976—), Phi Delta Phi, Beta Gamma Sigma. Office: 5151 E Broadway St Suite 1600 Tucson AZ 85711 Tel (602) 790-5828

HANSON, BURTON RANDALL, b. Benson, Minn., May 30, 1943; student So. Meth. U., 1961-62; B.A., U. Minn., 1964; J.D., Harvard, 1967. Admitted to D.C. bar, 1968, Minn. bar, 1969; spl. term law clk. Hennepin County (Minn.) Dist. Ct., 1969-70; law clk. to Justice C. Donald Peterson, Minn. Supreme Ct., 1970-72; ct. commr. Minn. Supreme Ct., 1972—. Mem. Hennepin County, Minn., Am. bar assns. Author: Recovery for Radiation Induced Genetic Damage, 1967. Home: 5111 Wooddale Ave S Edina MN 55424 Office: Minn State Capitol Saint Paul MN 55155 Tel (612) 296-6125

HANSON, DON JACKSON, b. Castlegate, Utah, Apr. 2, 1918; J.D., U. Utah, Salt Lake City, 1941. Admitted to Utah bar, 1947; with U.S. Dept. War, 1941-45, civilian employee JAG sect., 1945-46; atty. Utah State Tax Commn., 1949-52; individual practice law, Salt Lake City, 1946-49, 52-60; mem. firm Hanson & Garrett, Salt Lake City, 1960—; commr. Utah State Bar, 1951-54; state chmn. Def. Research Inst. Nat. dir. U.S. Jr. C. of C., 1954-55. Mem. Am., Utah State, Salt Lake County bar assns., Fedn. Ins. Counsel. Office: 520 Continental Bank Bldg Salt Lake City UT 84101 Tel (801) 328-4737

HANSON, EARL JOHN, b. Boise, Idaho, Feb. 23, 1941; B.S., Eastern Mont. Coll., 1963; J.D. with honors, U. Mont., 1968. Admitted to Mont. bar, 1968; asso. firm Luxan and Murfitt, Helena, Mont., 1968-70; partner firm Church, Harris, Johnson & Williams, Great Falls, Mont., 1970—. Pres., chmn. bd. Blue Cross Mont., 1972-75, trustee, 1971—. Mem. Am., Mont. State, Cascade County bar assns., Mont. Trial Lawyers Assn. Contbr. articles to legal jours. Home: 612 Doris Dr Great Falls MT 59403 Office: Box 1645 302 NW National Bank Bldg Great Falls MT 59401 Tel (406) 761-3000

HANSON, FRED BROWN, b. Alexandria, Va., Aug. 14, 1907; student DePauw U., 1924-26, Northwestern U., 1927-28; LL.B., Chgo-Kent Coll. Law, 1932. Admitted to Ill. bar, 1932; partner firms Ross Berchem & Hanson, Chgo., 1932-34, Hanson & Doyle, Chgo., 1946-52, Fred B. Hanson, Asso., Chgo., 1952—, Wilmette, Ill., 1975—; individual practice law, Chgo., 1934-36; house atty. Standard Oil Co. of Ind., Chgo., 1936-44, 45-46; police magistrate Village of Glenview (Ill.), 1945-49, village atty., 1949-53. Mem. Chgo., Ill., Am. bar assns. Contbr. numerous articles to legal jours. Home: 802 Normandy Ln Glenview IL 60025 Office: 135 S LaSalle St Chicago IL 60603 Tel (312) 236-2044 also 1000 Skokie Blvd Wilmette IL 60091

HANSON, JACK LLOYD, b. Balt., Feb. 11, 1947; A.A., U. Balt., 1967, J.D., 1970. Admitted to Md. bar, 1970; asso. firm Miles & Stockbridge, Balt., 1970; asst. state's atty. Balt., 1971-73; asst. pub. defender Md., Balt., 1973—. Mem. Lawyer Referral of Baltimore City. Home: 4050 Hunt Crest Rd Jarrettsville MD 21084 Office: 8903 Harford Rd Baltimore MD 21234

HANSON, JOHN FREDRIK, b. McCook, Nebr., Apr. 21, 1940; B.A. magna cum laude, Doane Coll., 1961; J.D. with distinction, U. Mich., 1964. Admitted to Nebr. bar, 1964; individual practice law, Indianola, Nebr., 1964-67; partner firm Hanson & Hanson, McCook, 1967—; county atty. Hayes County, Nebr., 1969-70, 72—; city atty. Indianola, 1964—; mem. Nat. Conf. Commrs. on Uniform State Laws, 1967-71. Mem. Am., Nebr. (ct. system study com.) bar assns., Am. Judicature Soc. Home: Indianola NE 69034 Office: 316 Norris Ave McCook NE 69001 Tel (308) 345-5120

HANSON, JON STEEN, b. Washington, Mar. 5, 1938; A.B., Stanford U., 1960; J.D., U. Mich., 1963. Admitted to Wis. bar, 1963; adminstrv. asst. to v.p. ins. ops. Northwestern Mut. Life Ins. Co., Milw., 1963-68; exec. sec., dir. research Nat. Assn. Ins. Commrs., Milw., 1968—. Mem. exec. com. YMCA Indian Guide program, 1971-72. Mem. Am. (vice chmn. com. on pub. regulation of ins. 1976-77), Wis. bar assns., Soc. Ins. Research. Author monographs, contbr. articles to legal jours. Home: 15340 Kata Dr Elm Grove WI 53122 Office: 633 W Wisconsin Ave Milwaukee WI 53203 Tel (414) 271-4464

HANSON, KENNETH HAMILTON, b. Chgo., Sept. 10, 1919; student North Park Coll., Chgo., 1939-40; B.S., Northwestern U., 1943, J.D., 1949. Admitted to Ill. bar, 1949; individual practice law, Chgo., 1949-53; atty. bus. devel. dept. First Nat. Bank of Chgo., 1953-61; trial atty. antitrust div. U.S. Dept. Justice, Chgo., 1961—. Mem. Am., Chgo. bar assns., Phi Delta Phi. Home: 955 Melody Rd Lake Forest IL 60045 Office: 219 S Dearborn St Chicago IL 60604 Tel (312) 353-7278

HANSON, RUDOLPH WILLIAM, b. Pickeral Lake Twp., Freeborn County, Minn., May 30, 1903; B.A., U. Minn., 1935, LL.B., 1937. Admitted to Minn. bar, 1937, since practiced in Albert Lea, Minn.; individual practice law, 1937-52; partner firm Hanson & Grinley, 1952-72; partner firm Hanson & Goodmanson, 1972-76, Peterson, Hanson, Goodmanson, Schlichting and Davies, 1976—; county atty. Freeborn County, Minn., 1946-54; mem. Minn. State Senate, 1954-70. Mem. Am., Minn. bar assns. Tel (507) 373-2405

HANSON, VICTOR G., b. Detroit, Oct. 26, 1923; LL.B., Wayne State U., 1949. Admitted to Mich. bar, 1949, U.S. Supreme Ct. bar, 1952; individual practice law, Detroit; mem. Bd. Immigration Appeals, U.S. Dept. Justice, 1954—. Mem. Mich. Gov.'s Spl. Fgn. Trade Expansion Commn., 1962—, Mich. Port Commn. Mem. Am., Mich., Detroit bar assns., Am. Judicature Soc., Am. Arbitration Assn. Tel (313) 532-1220

HANSON, WALTER DEAN, b. Oklahoma City, Oct. 16, 1904; LL.B., U. Okla., 1929. Admitted to Okla. bar, 1929, U.S. Supreme Ct. bar, 1950; asso. firm Rittenhouse, Lee, Webster & Rittenhouse, Oklahoma City; mem. firm Rittenhouse, Webster, Hanson & Rittenhouse, Oklahoma City, firm Hanson and Peterson, Oklahoma City, firm Hanson, Peterson & Tompkins, Inc., Oklahoma City. Mem. Fedn. Ins. Counsel, Internat. Assn. Ins. Counsel, Am. Bar Assn., Def. Research Inst., Okla. Assn. Def. Counsel. Contbr. articles to legal publs. Home: 3228 Wilshire Terr Oklahoma City OK 73116 Office: 401 N Hudson St Oklahoma City OK 73101 Tel (405) 232-8137

HANSON, WILLIAM C., b. 1909; B.A., LL.B., U. Iowa. Admitted to Iowa bar, 1935; judge U.S. Dist. Ct. So. Dist. Iowa, Ft. Dodge, 1962—, now chief judge. Mem. Am. Bar Assn. Address: PO Box 1157 Fort Dodge IA 50501*

HANZELIK, CARL HAROLD, b. Bklyn., May 5, 1945; A.B., Columbia Coll., 1967; J.D., U. Va., 1970. Admitted to Pa. bar, 1970; U.S. Supreme Ct. bar, 1974; asso. firm Dilworth, Paxson, Kalish & Levy, Phila., 1970-75, partner, 1975—. Mem. Am., Pa., Phila. bar assns. Office: 2600 The Fidelity Bldg Philadelphia PA 19109 Tel (215) 546-3000

HAPGOOD, CYRUS STOW, b. Lynn, Mass., Apr. 21, 1912; B.S., Mass. Inst. Tech., 1933; LL.D., Fordham U., 1936. Admitted to N.Y. bar, 1937; asso. firm Pennie, Davis, Mavin & Edmonds, N.Y.C., 1934-42; chief patent div. Bur. Ordinance, Dept. Navy, Washington, 1942-45; partner firm Davis, Hoxie, Faithful & Hapgood, N.Y.C., 1946—; dir. Mennen Co., Morristown, N.J., Allyn & Bacon Co., Boston. Mem. Am., N.Y. (pres. 1961-62) patent law assns. Home: Bobolink Ln Greenwich CT 06830 Office: 30 Broad St New York City NY 10004 Tel (212) 344-8450

HAPNER, JON CLARK, b. Hillsboro, Ohio, Nov. 10, 1934; B.A., Ohio State U., 1956, J.D., 1958. Admitted to Ohio bar, 1958; mem. firm Hapner & Hapner, Hillsboro, Ohio, 1958-76; judge Municipal Ct., Hillsboro, 1976—; solicitor, Hillsboro, 1965-68, legal advisor, 1972-75. Mem. Am., Ohio, Highland County bar assns. Home: 130 Willow St Hillsboro OH 45133 Office: 100 S High St Hillsboro OH 45133 Tel (513) 393-3487

HAPPEL, DAVID E., b. Vinton, Iowa, Apr. 18, 1939; B.A., Valparaiso (Ind.) U., 1961, LL.B., J.D., 1964. Admitted to Iowa bar, 1964; asso. firm Harold J. Swailes, Belle Plaine, Iowa, 1964-65; individual practice law, Vinton, 1965—; jud. magistrate 6th Jud. Dist. Iowa, 1974-75. Pres. Iowa AAU, 1970-72, treas., 1972—; sec. Vinton C. of C., 1966—. Mem. Am., Iowa, Benton County (pres. 1966-68) bar assns. Home: 703 W 17th St Vinton IA 52349 Office: 201 E 4th St Vinton IA 52349 Tel (319) 472-4300

HAPPY, JACK NELSON, b. Lawrence, Kans., Oct. 12, 1943; B.S., Syracuse U., 1964; J.D., Columbia, 1967. Admitted to Mo. bar, 1967, U.S. Supreme Ct. bar, 1975; mem. firm Dietrich, Davis, Dicus, Rowlands & Schmitt, Kansas City, Mo., 1967-76, Sildon, Happy, House & Cooling, Profl. Corp., Kansas City, 1977—. Chmn. Lewis-Clark council Boy Scouts Am., 1974—; mem. Kansas City Landmarks Commn., 1976—; bd. dirs. Hist. Kansas City Found.; bd. govs. Friends of Art, Nelson Gallery-Atkins Mus. Mem. Am., Mo., Kansas City bar assns., Kans. City Lawyers Assn., W. Mo. Def. Lawyers Assn. Contbr. articles to legal jours. Home: 4500 Rockhill Terr Kansas City MO 64110 Office: 16th Floor Ten Main Center Kansas City MO 64105 Tel (816) 474-0777

HARBIN, EDDIE RAY, b. Greenville County, S.C., July 24, 1938; B.A. in Polit. Sci., The Citadel, 1960; LL.B., U. S.C., 1963, J.D., 1970. Admitted to S.C. bar, 1963; asso. firm Waddell Byrd, Marion, S.C., 1963; with JAGC, USAF, 1964-66; individual practice law, Greenville, S.C., 1966—; USAF rep. Status of Forces Agreement Treaty negotiations with South Korea, 1965-66. Chmn. Greenville City Republican Party, 1971-75; del. Greenville County and S.C. Rep. convs., 1970, 72, 74, 76. Mem. S.C. Trial Lawyers Assn., S.C., Greenville County bar assns. Named Man of Year Wade Hampton club Civitan Internat., 1973. Office: POB 10384 Greenville SC 29603 Tel (803) 242-4112

HARBISON, STEPHEN FRANKLIN, b. Santa Monica, Calif., Dec. 28, 1943; B.A. in History, Stanford, 1965; LL.B., 1968. Admitted to Calif. bar, 1969; asso. firm Flint & MacKay, Los Angeles, 1968-72; partner firm Argue, Freston & Myers, Los Angeles, 1972—. Trustee Los Angeles Junior C. of C. Arts Found., 1974-77, First United Meth. Ch., Santa Monica, 1975—; chmn. ad hoc com. automotive repair facilities Los Angeles City Council. Mem. Am., Calif., Los Angeles County (vice-chmn. youth edn. com.) bar assns., Stanford Law Soc. of So. Calif. Home: 1130 Georgina Ave Santa Monica CA 90402 Office: 626 Wilshire Blvd 10th Floor Los Angeles CA 90017 Tel (213) 628-1291

HARBUS, RICHARD, b. N.Y.C., Sept. 15, 1940; A.B., Columbia, 1961; J.D., Yale, 1964. Admitted to N.Y. State bar, 1965; law clk. U.S. Ct. Appeals 2d circuit, N.Y.C., 1964-66; atty. Met. Life Ins. Co., N.Y.C., 1966-74; asst. prof. N.Y. Law Sch., N.Y.C., 1974—; arbitrator Small Claims div. N.Y. Civil Ct., 1976—. Mem. Am. Bar Assn. Am. Arbitration Assn. (panel), Am. Judges Assn. Office: 57 Worth St New York City NY 10013 Tel (212) 966-3500

HARD, LAWRENCE EDWARD, b. Detroit, Mar. 2, 1944; B.A., Amherst Coll., 1966; J.D., U. Mich., 1969. Admitted to Wash. bar, 1969; asso. firm LeSourd Patten Fleming & Hartung, Seattle, 1970-74, partner, 1975—; dep. city atty. Tukwila (Wash.), 1976—; spl. counsel Town of Index (Wash.), 1976—. Sec., Medic I, Emergency Med. Services Found., 1975—. Mem. Am., Wash., Seattle-King County bar assns. Home: 3707 NE 42d St Seattle WA 98105 Office: 1300 Seattle Tower Seattle WA 98101 Tel (206) 624-1040

HARDEE, DAVID WYATT, b. Greenville, N.C., Jan. 7, 1947; B.S. in Commerce, Washington & Lee U., 1969; J.D., Duke U., 1972. Admitted N.C. bar, 1972; since practiced in Charlotte, N.C., asso. firm Wardlow, Knox, Caudle & Knox, 1972-73, partner firm Caudle & Kinsey, 1973, Caudle, Underwood & Kinsey, 1973—. Mem. Am. Bar Assn. (mem. tax sect.), N.C. Bar Assn. Contbr. articles to profl. jours. Home: 1134 Lingamore Pl Charlotte NC 28203 Office: 900 Johnston Bldg Charlotte NC 28281 Tel (704) 333-9037

HARDEE, RICHARD BROOKS, b. Chandler, Tex., July 11, 1934; B.A., Tyler Jr. Coll., 1953; B.B.A., U. Tex., 1955, LL.B., 1957, J.D., 1957; certificate U. Va. Judge Advs. Gens. Sch., 1965. Admitted to Tex. bar, 1957, U.S. Ct. Mil. Appeals bar, 1958, U.S. Ct. Appeals bar, 1962, U.S. Supreme Ct. bar, 1963; served to capt. JAGC, U.S. Army, 1957-60; asst. U.S. atty. Eastern Dist. of Tex., Tyler, 1961-66, 1st asst. U.S. atty., 1966-68, U.S. atty., 1968-70; individual practice law, Tyler, 1970—; 3d U.S. Army legal assistance officer, 1961; spl. master U.S. Dist. Ct. Eastern Dist. Tex., 1973-74, mem. admissions to practice com., 1973—; dir. prosecution com. State Bar of Tex., 1974; lectr. in field. Mem. dist. Eagle rev. bd. Rose council Boy Scouts Am., 1965-66; chmn., diaconate Highland Presbyterian Ch., Tyler, 1968-69, ruling elder, 1971, 76; bd. dirs. Opportunities in Tyler, 1969-71; mem. com. NCCJ, Tyler, 1969-72; adv. group Tex. Constl. Revision Commn., Tyler, 1973-74; alt. commr. gen. assembly U.S. Presbyterian Ch., Tyler, 1974. Mem. Smith County, Tex. bar assns. Named Outstanding Citizen Rotary Club, 1951; recipient Quid Nunc award Quid Nunc Assn., 1953; citation U.S. Dept. Justice, 1968. Certified family law specialist, State Bar Tex., 1975. Home: 3714 Fry Ave Tyler TX 75701 Office: 2732 S Broadway St Tyler TX 75701 Tel (214) 597-1717

HARDESTY, ALONZO HOMER, b. Anderson, S.C., Nov. 6, 1944; B.A., Stetson U., 1967; J.D., 1971. Admitted to Fla. bar, 1971; asso. Howard S. Warner, Orange City, Fla., 1971-75; individual practice law, Orange City, 1975—; councilman Town of Orange City, 1974-76. Pres. bd. trustees United Meth. Ch., Orange City. Mem. Volusia County (Fla.) Bar Assn. Office: 2290 S Volusia Ave Orange City FL 32763 Tel (904) 775-3222

HARDESTY, DAVID CARTER, JR., b. Philadelphia, Miss., Sept. 20, 1945; B.A., W. Va. U., 1967; B.A. (Rhodes scholar), Oxford U., 1969; J.D., Harvard U., 1973. Admitted to W.Va. bar, 1973; partner firm Bowles, McDavid, Graff & Love, Charleston, W.Va., 1973—. Mem. W.Va. State Bar, W.Va. State, Am. bar assns. Home: 1251 Edgewood Dr Charleston WV 25302 Office: PO Box 1386 Charleston WV 25325 Tel (304) 344-9621

HARDESTY, MICHAEL JAMES, b. Columbus, Ohio, May 12, 1941; B.A., Harvard U., 1963; J.D., U. Cin., 1966. Admitted to Ohio bar, 1966; asso. firm Schottenstein, Garel, Swedlow & Zoy, Columbus, 1967-72; partner firm Hardesty & Callaro, Columbus, 1972-74, Hardesty & Gamble, Columbus, 1974-75; individual practice law, Columbus, 1975—. Trustee Christ Lutheran Ch., Worthington Hills Civic Assn. Mem. Am., Ohio, Columbus bar assns. lHome: 1394 Beechlake Dr Worthington OH 43085 Office: 246 E Sycamore St Columbus OH 43206 Tel (614) 221-0922

HARDESTY, RONALD J., b. Kansas City, Mo., Dec. 14, 1924; B.S.B.A., U. Denver, 1948, J.D., 1950. Admitted to Colo. bar, 1951, U.S. Supreme Ct. bar, 1962; spl. agt. FBI, Mpls. and Kansas City, Mo., 1951-53; asst. atty. gen., Denver, 1954-57; county atty. Jefferson County (Colo.), 1957-61; dist. atty. 1st Jud. Dist., Golden, Colo., 1961-65; practiced in Lakewood, Colo., 1957-65; dist. judge 1st Jud. Dist. Ct., Golden, 1965—. Home: 2436 S Hiwan Dr Evergreen CO 80439 Office: Hall of Justice Golden CO 80419 Tel (303) 279-0500

HARDESTY, WILLARD BENSON, b. Havre de Grace, Md., Aug. 8, 1946; B.S., U. Kans. Sch. Journalism and Pub. Info., 1968; J.D., U. Colo., 1971. Admitted to Colo. bar, 1971; partner firm Hardesty & Montgomery, Englewood, Colo., 1971-74; individual practice law, Lakewood, Colo., 1974—; bd. dirs. Denver Met. Legal Aid, 1975. Bd. dirs. Arvada Receiving Home for Girls (Colo.), 1971-72. Mem. Am., Colo., 1st Jud. Dist. (dir. young lawyers sect. 1976—), Arapahoe County (Colo.) bar assns., Phi Alpha Delta (Outstanding Scholastic Achievement award 1971, Outstanding Service award 1971). Live music critic Rocky Mountain News, Denver, 1975-77. Home: 3315 Moore St Wheat Ridge CO 80033 Office: 720 Kipling St Lakewood CO 80215 Tel (303) 234-1516

HARDIE, LESLIE GLENN, b. San Antonio, June 17, 1945; B.A., U. Calif., Los Angeles, 1967, J.D., 1970. Law clk. Superior Ct. of Los Angeles County, 1970-71; admitted to Calif. bar, 1971, U.S. 9th Circuit Ct. Appeals bar, 1971; asso. firm Nutter, Walter, Weinstock, Manion & King, Los Angeles, 1971-75, partner, 1975—; lectr. on paralegal tng. U. Calif., Los Angeles, U. So. Calif.; lectr. Ann. Legal Secs'. Program. Mem. Los Angeles County, Century City bar assns., Assn. Bus. Trial Lawyers. Office: 1888 Century Park E Los Angeles CA 90067 Tel (213) 879-4481

HARDIES, MELVIN ALBERT, b. Chgo., Apr. 20, 1912; Ph.B., U. Chgo., 1932; LL.B., Harvard, 1935. Admitted to Ill. bar, 1935; asso. firm Ross & Watts, Chgo., 1935-42; atty. No. Trust Co., 1946-50; partner firm Ross, Hardies, O'Keefe, Babcock & Parsons, Chgo., 1950—; asst. counsel Navy Price Adjustment Bd., Washington, 1943-45, counsel, 1945-46. Mem. Am., Ill., Chgo. bar assns., Law Club Chgo., Legal Club Chgo. Home: 505 N Exeter Pl Lake Forest IL 60045 Office: 1 IBM Plaza Chicago IL 60611 Tel (312) 467-9300

HARDIN, ADLAI STEVENSON, JR., b. Norwalk, Conn., Sept. 20, 1937; B.A., Princeton, 1959; LL.B., Columbia, 1962. Admitted to N.Y. bar, 1963, U.S. Supreme Ct. bar, 1967; asso. firm Milbank, Tweed, Hadley & McCloy, N.Y.C., 1963-70, partner, 1971—. Mem. N.Y. State, Am. bar assns., Assn. Bar City N.Y. (chmn. com. on profl. and jud. ethics 1970-73). Office: One Chase Manhattan Plaza New York City NY 10005 Tel (212) 422-2660

HARDIN, CHARLES LESLIE, b. Pocatello, Idaho, Aug. 19, 1938; B.S., U. Tenn., 1962, J.D., 1964; M.B.A. (hon.), U. Louisville, 1973. Admitted to Tenn. bar, 1965, Ky. bar, 1971; asso. firm Joyce, Anderson & Wood, Oak Ridge, 1965-66; atty. Fed. Land Bank of Louisville, 1966-75, gen. counsel, sec., 1975—. Mem. faculty team Ky. and Fourth Farm Credit Dist. Youth Conf.; chmn. bylaws com. Ky. Council for Co-ops. Mem. Ky., Tenn., Louisville bar assns. Home: 3410 Ascot Circle Louisville KY 40222 Office: 201 W Main St Louisville KY 40202 Tel (502) 587-9621

HARDIN, EDWARD JACKSON, b. Durham, N.C., Feb. 1, 1943; B.A., Wesleyan U., Middletown, Conn., 1965; J.D., Vanderbilt U., 1968. Admitted to N.Y. State bar, 1969, Ga. bar, 1972; asso. firm Milbank, Tweed, Hadley & McCloy, N.Y.C., 1968-71; asso. firm Powell, Goldstein, Frazer & Murphy, Atlanta, 1971-74, partner, 1975-76; partner firm Rogers & Hardin, Atlanta, 1976—. Trustee The Paideia Sch., Inc., 1973—, treas., 1974-76. Mem. Am., Ga., Atlanta bar assns., Assn. Bar City N.Y. (sec. com. profl. responsibility 1970-71), Order of Coif. Recipient Archie B. Martin Meml. medal Vanderbilt U., 1966, Jackson Meml. prize, 1967, Founders medal, 1968, Morgan prize, 1968; editor-in-chief Vanderbilt Law Rev., 1967-68. Home: 2925 Cedar Creek Pkwy Decatur GA 30033 Office: Suite 3200 101 Marietta Tower Atlanta GA 30303 Tel (404) 522-4700

HARDIN, RICHARD DEAN, b. Culver City, Calif., Nov. 20, 1943; student Calif. State U., Chico, 1961-66; J.D., U. Pacific, Sacramento, 1970. Admitted to Calif. bar, 1971, U.S. Supreme Ct. bar, 1976; dep. dist. atty. Alameda County (Calif.), 1971-72; partner firm Wies, Wies & Hardin, Hayward, Calif., 1972—. Mem. Calif. Attys. for Criminal Justice, Criminal Cts., Alameda County, So. Alameda County, Calif. bar assns. Office: 24301 Southland Dr 512 Hayward CA 94545 Tel (415) 785-1200

HARDING, FORREST ASHBY, b. Roanoke, Va., Nov. 4, 1913; A.A., San Angelo Coll., 1950; LL.B., Baylor U., 1953, J.D., 1953. Admitted to Tex. bar, 1953; city judge San Angelo Tex., 1953-57; individual practice law, San Angelo, 1953-77; mem. Tex. State Legislature, 1960-73. Mem. San Angelo Emergency Corp., Tex. Safety Assn., San Angelo Safety Assn. (v.p. 1956-58). Mem. Tex., Tom Green County bar assns., Am. Judicature Soc., Twin Mountain Gem and Mineral Soc. (pres. 1958-59), Tex. Gem and Mineral Soc., Tex., Concho Valley (pres. 1976-77) archeol. socs., Am. Realtors Assn., San Angelo Realtors, Phi Theta Kappa, Phi Delta Phi. Home: 1826 S Concho Dr San Angelo TX 76901 Office: 307 N Van Buren St San Angelo TX 76901 Tel (915) 653-2711

HARDING, MAJOR BEST, b. Charlotte, N.C., Oct. 13, 1935; B.S., Wake Forest U., 1957, LL.B., 1959. Admitted to N.C. bar, 1959, Fla. bar, 1960; asst. staff judge adv. U.S. Army Hdqrs., Ft. Gordon, Ga., 1960-62; asst. county solicitor Duval County (Fla.), 1962-63; practiced in Jacksonville, 1963-68; judge Duval County Juvenile Ct., 1968-70; judge Fla. Circuit Ct., 4th Jud. Circuit, 1970—, chief judge, 1974-77. Bd. dirs. Gateway Residence, Jacksonville, 1964-67, Young Life of Jacksonville, 1965-72, Family Consultation Jacksonville, 1970-75, Boy's Club of Jacksonville, 1970-76, Shawnee dist. Boy Scouts Am., 1974-75, Daniel Meml., Jacksonville, 1972—. Mem. Jacksonville Bar Assn. Office: 330 E Bay St Jacksonville FL 32202 Tel (904) 633-6840

HARDING, MARC STEVEN, b. Des Moines, Nov. 8, 1947; B.S., U. Iowa, 1970, J.D., 1973. Admitted to Iowa bar, 1973, U.S. Supreme Ct. bar, 1976; asso. firm George G. West, Des Moines, 1973-74; partner firm Harding & Stevens, Des Moines, 1974-75; individual practice law, Des Moines, 1975—. Mem. Am., Iowa, Polk County bar assns.,

Iowa Assn. Trial Lawyers. Home: RR 1 Elkhart IA 50073 Office: 1427 Army Post Suite 200 Des Moines IA 50315 Tel (515) 287-1454

HARDING, ROBERT BROOKS, b. Valparaiso, Ind., Feb. 10, 1942; A.B., DePauw U., 1964; J.D., U. Va., 1967. Admitted to Ind. bar, 1967, Va. bar, 1969, D.C. bar, 1972; legis. asst. Office of Minority Leader, U.S. Ho. of Reps., Washington, 1963-67; atty. SEC, Washington, 1967-68; partner firm Smith & Harrison, Arlington, Va., 1968-70; spl. asst. to Sec. HEW, Washington, 1970-71; counsel So. Calif. Edison Co., Washington, 1971-77; partner firm Groom and Nordberg, Washington, 1977—. Mem. Am., Ind., Va., D.C. bar assns. Named Congressional fellow Presdl. Classroom for Young Americans, 1971. Office: 1775 Pennsylvania Ave NW Washington DC 20006 Tel (202) 857-0620

HARDISTY, JAMES HERBERT, b. Edina, Minn., Feb. 23, 1941; A.B., Harvard, 1963, LL.B., 1966. Admitted to Ohio bar, 1966; asso. firm. Jones, Day, Cockley & Reavis, Cleve., 1966-69; asst. prof. law Washington U., St. Louis., 1969-70; asst. prof. law U. Wash., 1970-72, asso. prof., 1972-74, prof., 1974—. Contbr. articles in field to profl. jours. Home: 8424 SE 37th St Mercer Island WA 98040 Office: Law Sch Univ Wash Seattle WA 98195 Tel (206) 543-2261

HARDT, DANIEL REINHOLD, b. Medford, Wis., May 30, 1940; B.A., DePauw U., 1962; J.D., Ind. U., 1967. Admitted to Ind. bar, 1967, U.S. Tax Ct., 1973; staff atty. Marion County (Ind.) Dept. Pub. Welfare, Indpls., 1967-68; asso. firm Kitley, Schreckengast and Davis, Beech Grove, Ind., 1968-69; individual practice law, Speedway, Ind., 1970-74; partner firm Hardt & Haskett, Speedway, 1974—; dep. pros. atty. Marion County, 1971-74. Bd. dirs. United Pentecostal Ch. Ministers Retirement Fund, Inc., Hazelwood, Mo.; mem. Ind. dist. adv. council SBA, Indpls., 1971—. Mem. Ind., Indpls. bar assns. Home: 7699 Wyckford Ct Indianapolis IN 46224 Office: 5324 W 16th St Speedway IN 46224 Tel (317) 241-2891

HARDY, GEORGE PINCKNEY, JR., b. New Waverly, Tex., May 10, 1913; LL.B., U. Tex., 1936. Admitted to Tex. bar, 1936; city atty., Tex., 1938-46; county atty., Tex., 1947; judge, 1947—. Active Boy Scouts Am., ARC, Am. Heart Assn. Mem. Tex., Am. bar assns., Tex. State Bar. Home: 2401 Sims St Bay City TX 77414 Office: PO Box 627 Bay City TX 77414 Tel (713) 245-3150

HARDY, MICHAEL LYNN, b. St. Louis, Aug. 28, 1947; B.A. magna cum laude, John Carroll U., 1969; J.D. cum laude, U. Mich., 1972. Admitted to Ohio bar, 1972; partner firm Guren, Merritt, Sogg & Cohen, Cleve., 1977—. Mem. Ohio State, Am. bar assns. Contbr. articles to legal jours. Home: 3330 Dorchester Rd Shaker Heights OH 44120 Office: Guren Merritt et al 650 Terminal Tower Cleveland OH 44113 Tel (216) 696-8550

HARDY, RICHARD M., b. Portland, Ind., Oct. 11, 1938; B.S., Purdue U., 1960; J.D., Ind. U.-Indpls. Law Sch., 1971. Admitted to Ind. bar, 1971; house counsel Ind. Farm Bureau, 1971—; dep. prosecutor, Marion County, Ind., 1972-74; asso. firm Carvey, Watson & McNevin, Indpls., 1972-73; house counsel Ind. Farm Bur. Coop. Assn., Indpls.; engr. Allied Chem. Corp., N.Y.C., 1964-68. Mem. Am., Ind., Marion County bar assns. Address: 47 S Pennsylvania St Indianapolis IN 46204

HARGIS, DAVID MICHAEL, b. Warren, Ark., Feb. 10, 1948; B.S. with honors, U. Ark., 1970, J.D., 1973. Admitted to Ark. bar, 1973; mem. firm Williamson, Ball & Bird, Monticello, Ark., 1974-75; asst. U.S. atty., Little Rock, 1975-76; mem. firm House, Holmes & Jewell, Little Rock, 1976—. Mem. Am., Ark., Pulaski County bar assns., Beta Gamma Sigma, Omicron Delta Kappa. Editor in chief: Ark. Law Rev., 1972-73; recipient Appellate Advocacy award U. Ark. Home: 5228 R St Little Rock AR 72207 Office: 1550 Tower Bldg Little Rock AR 72201 Tel (501) 375-9151

HARGRAVES, GEORGE W., b. Pocatello, Idaho, May 4, 1918; B.S., U. Utah, 1940; J.D., U. Colo., 1948. Admitted to Idaho bar, 1948, U.S. Supreme Ct. bar, 1970; partner firm Gee & Hargraves, Pocatello, 1949-73; judge Idaho Dist. Ct., 6th Dist., Pocatello, 1974—; lectr. Idaho State U., 1966-73. Bd. dirs. ARC, Pocatello, Pocatello City Zoning Com.; pres. Central Council PTA, Pocatello; dir. Tendoy council Boy Scouts Am. Mem. Am. Bar Assn., Am. Judicature Soc., Am. Judges Assn., Am. Trial Lawyers Assn. Phi Delta Phi. Office: Bannock County Courthouse Box H Pocatello ID 83201 Tel (208) 232-2269

HARGROVE, EARL LEWIS, JR., b. Richmond, Va., May 11, 1929; B.S. in Bus. Adminstrn., Va. Poly. Inst. and State U., 1949; J.D., Washington and Lee U., 1954. Admitted to Va. bar, 1954; accountant Leach, Calkins & Scott, C.P.A.'s (merged with Coopers & Lybrand), Richmond, 1954-59; asst. treas., dir. taxes Robertshaw Controls Co., Richmond, 1959—. Mem. Va., Am. bar assns., Va., Am. insts. C.P.A.'s, Tax Execs. Inst. Home: 10504 Thames Dr Richmond VA 23233 Office: 1701 Byrd Ave Richmond VA 23261 Tel (804) 282-9561

HARGROVE, JOHN RAYMOND, b. Atlantic City, Oct. 25, 1923; student Morgan State Coll., 1941-43; B.A., Howard U., 1947; LL.B., U. Md., 1950. Admitted to Md. bar, 1950; individual practice law, Balt., 1950-55; asst. U.S. atty. for Dist. Md., Justice Dept., 1955-57, dep. U.S. atty., 1957-62; asso. judge People's Ct. of Balt., 1962-63; asso. firm Howard & Hargrove, 1963-68; asso. judge Municipal Ct., Balt., 1968-71; adminstrv. judge Md. Dist. Ct., Dist. 1, Balt., 1971-74; asso. judge Supreme Bench Balt., 1974—; mem. character com. Md. Ct. Appeals, com. on judiciary Md. Constl. Conv. Commn., Md. Adv. Bd. Correction, Parole and Probation; del. Md. Constl. Conv. Mem. adv. bd. trustees Sheppard Pratt Hosp.; trustee U. Md. Alumni Assn.-Internat. Mem. Balt. City, Md. State, Monumental City, Nat. bar assns. Home: 3524 Ellamont Rd Baltimore MD 21215 Office: Courthouse Calvert and Fayette Sts Baltimore MD 21202 Tel (301) 396-5052

HARGROVE, LAURIE ELIZABETH, b. Sumter County, Ga., Feb. 26, 1927; A.B., Tift Coll., 1946; LL.B., LaSalle Extension U., 1960. Admitted to Ga. bar, 1961; asso. firm Smith & Undercofler, Americus, Ga., 1961-66; partner firm Smith, Crisp & Hargrove, Americus, 1967-70, firm Smith & Hargrove, Americus, 1970-72; individual practice law, Americus, 1972—. Mem. vestry Calvary Episcopal Ch., 1969-70; bd. dirs. Sumter Players; sec. Am. Cancer Soc. Sumter Co., 1965-68; active Pilot Club. Mem. Americus (pres. 1965-66), Southwestern Circuit (sec. 1964-66, treas. 1971-74), Am. bar assns., State Bar Ga., Nat. (Ga. del. 1965-67), Ga. (3d v.p. 1965-66) assns. women lawyers. Composer song Georgia, 1965. Home: 208 Glenwood Rd Americus GA 31709 Office: PO Box 865 Americus GA 31709 Tel (912) 924-9046

HARGROVE, ROBERT CLYDE, b. Shreveport, La., Dec. 13, 1918; B.A., Rice U., 1939; LL.B., Yale U., 1942. Admitted to La. bar, 1946, D.C. bar, 1975; partner firm Hargrove, Guyton, Van Hook & Hargrove, 1946-56; asst. gen. counsel Tex. Eastern Transmission Corp., 1953-55; sec., counsel J.B. Beaird Co., 1954-56; partner Hargrove Oil & Gas Co., Shreveport, 1950—; v.p. Bechtel Internat. Corp., San Francisco, 1958-61; individual practice law, Shreveport, 1961—; of counsel firm Casey, Lane & Mittendorf, Washington, 1975—. Former trustee U. of the South; mem. nat. council Met. Opera Assn., Wolf Trap Found. for Performing Arts; Mem. Am., Fed. Power, D.C., La. bar assns., Nat. Lawyers Club. Office: Commercial Nat Bank Bldg Shreveport LA 71101 Tel (318) 221-8943

HARGROVE, WADE HAMPTON, b. Clinton, N.C., Mar. 6, 1940; A.B. with honors, U. N.C., 1962, J.D., 1965. Admitted to N.C. bar, 1965, D.C. bar, 1967; asso. firm Fletcher, Heald, Rowell, Kenehan & Hildreth, Washington, 1965-68, firm Maupin, Taylor & Ellis, Raleigh, N.C., 1968-70; partner firm Tharrington, Smith & Hargrove, Raleigh, 1970—; exec. dir., gen. counsel N.C. Assn. Broadcastors, 1970—; pres. dir. Century Communications, Inc., Wilson, N.C., 1976—; mem. N.C. Gov.'s Council on State Goals and Policy, 1974—; chmn. N.C. Security and Privacy Bd., 1976—; commr. N.C. Milk Commn., 1976—. Mem. N.C., FCC, D.C. bar assns. Recipient Distinguished Service award N.C. Assn. Broadcasters, 1973. Home: 6716 Jean Dr Raleigh NC 27612 Office: 300 BB & T Bldg Raleigh NC 27601 Tel (919) 821-4711

HARITON, IRA M., b. Bklyn., June 18, 1940; student Hunter Coll.; LL.B., J.D., Bklyn. Law Sch., 1964. Admitted to N.Y. State bar, 1964; now sr. partner Donner, Fagelson, Hariton & Berka, Bay Shore, N.Y.; counsel Suffolk Home for Emotionally Disturbed Children, Bay Shore. Mem. N.Y. State, Suffolk County, Queens County bar assns., Am. Arbitration Assn. Office: 2115 Union Blvd Bay Shore NY 11706 Tel (516) 666-7400

HARKAVY, IRA BAER, b. N.Y.C., Apr. 13, 1931; B.A., Bklyn. Coll., 1951; J.D., Columbia, 1954. Admitted to N.Y. bar, 1954, U.S. Supreme Ct. bar, 1960; partner firm Harkavy, Tell & Mendelson, N.Y.C., 1954-67; partner firm Harkavy & Tell, N.Y.C., 1967-70; partner firm Delson & Gordon, N.Y.C., 1970—; arbitrator Civil Ct., N.Y.C., 1964—, Am. Judges Assn., 1976. Pres., Bklyn. Coll. Alumni Assn., 1973—; sec. Bklyn. Coll. Found., 1958—; chmn. Community Bd. 14 of Bklyn., 1966—; mem. Bd., Borough of Bklyn., 1976—; trustee Bklyn. Pub. Library, 1975—; v.p. Madison Jewish Center. Mem. Am., N.Y., Bklyn. bar assns., N.Y. Trial Lawyers Assn. Recipient Presidential Medal of Honor, Bklyn. Coll., 1975, Bklyn. Bicentennial award, 1976, citation of merit Borough Bklyn., 1976. Home: 1784 E 29th St Brooklyn NY 11229 Office: 230 Park Ave New York City NY 10017 Tel (212) MU 6-8030

HARKINS, THOMAS IGNATIUS, b. Boston, Aug. 17, 1915; J.D., Suffolk U., 1939; postgrad. U. Md., 1951-52. Admitted to Mass. bar, 1939; communications officer, trial atty. AUS, PTO, 1941-46; negotiator Raymond Internat. Corp., N.Y.C., 1946-51; contracting officer U.S. Army, Washington, 1951-52; contract negotiator ITT, Nutley, N.J., 1952-54; chief contracts br. U.S. Air Force, Boston, 1954-60; contracts advisor, mgr. GTE Sylvania Corp., Waltham, Mass., 1960—. Mem. Am., Fed. bar assns., Electronic Industries Assn., Nat. Indsl. Security Assn. Home: 40 Cedar Hill Ln Waltham MA 02154 Office: Electronic Systems Group GTE Sylvania Inc 100 First Ave Waltham MA 02154 Tel (617) 890-9200

HARKNESS, HARVEY DAVE, b. Hollywood, Calif., Dec. 8, 1943; B.S. magna cum laude, N.Y. U., 1968; postgrad. in Econs. (Eahart fellow), U. N.C., 1968-69, J.D., 1971. Admitted to Ga. bar, 1972; asso. firm Powell, Goldstein, Frazer & Murphy, Atlanta, 1971—; adj. prof. econs. Ga. State U. Asso. counsel Republican Party of Fifth Congl. Dist., Atlanta; spl. conv. counsel Citizens for Reagan, summer 1976. Mem. Am., Atlanta bar assns., State Bar Ga. Recipient Founder's Day award N.Y. U., 1968. Home: 670 Creekwood Trail Marietta GA 30067 Office: 1100 C & S Nat Bank Bldg Atlanta GA 30303 Tel (404) 521-1900

HARKRADER, CARLETON ALLEN, b. Bristol, Va., Dec. 17, 1917; B.A., Va. Mil. Inst., 1940; LL.B., Yale, 1953. Admitted to D.C., Va. bars, 1953, U.S. Supreme Ct. bar, 1956; asso. firm Morison, Murphy, Clapp & Abrams, Washington, 1953-57; appellate atty., legal advisor FTC, Washington, 1957-61; partner firm Wald, Harkrader & Ross, and predecessors, Washington, 1961—. Mem. D.C. Bar, Va. Bar, Am., Fed., D.C. bar assns. Home: 905 Chinquapin Rd MacLean VA 22101 Office: 1320 19th St NW Washington DC 20036 Tel (202) 296-2121

HARLAN, THOMAS MICHAEL, b. Pasadena, Tex., Mar. 19, 1941; B.B.A., N. Tex. State U., 1965; J.D., S. Tex. State U., 1971. Admitted to Tex. bar, 1971; mem. firm Crouch, Crouch & Harlan, Alvin, Tex., 1971-74; individual practice law, Alvin, 1974—. Mem. Am., Tex., Brazoria County (dir. 1976-77) bar assns., Tex. Trial Lawyers Assn. Home: 1505 Martin Dr Alvin TX 77511 Office: PO Box 703 101 S Johnson St Alvin TX 77511 Tel (713) 331-6404

HARLAN, W. GLEN, b. Stuart, Iowa, Oct. 14, 1912; A.B., Simpson Coll., 1936; J.D., State U. Iowa, 1939. Admitted to Iowa bar, 1939, Ga. bar, 1942, N.Y. State bar, 1961; law clk. to Asso. Justice Wiley Rutledge U.S. Ct. Appeals, Washington, 1939-41; asso. firm Gambrell & White, Atlanta, 1941-47; partner firm Gambrell, Harlan, Russell & Moye, and predecessors, Atlanta, 1948-67; v.p. legal affairs Eastern Air Lines, Inc., N.Y.C. and Miami, 1967-69, sr. v.p., 1969—. Mem. Am. (ho. dels. 1956-58), Fed., Ga., N.Y., Atlanta, N.Y.C. bar assns., Am. Judicature Soc., Internat. Air Transport Assn. (legal com.), Order of Coif, Pi Kappa Delta. Contbr. articles to profl. jours. Home: 575 Bay Point Rd Miami FL 33137 Office: Eastern Air Lines Inc Miami International Airport Miami FL 33148 Tel (305) 873-3455

HARLESS, FRED STAPEL, b. Montgomery, Ala., July 9, 1919; LL.B., So. Meth. U., 1950. Admitted to Tex. bar, 1950; practiced in Dallas, 1950-70; judge Dallas County Dist. Ct., 1971—. Mem. State Bar Tex., Dallas Bar Assn., Delta Theta Phi (life).

HARMAN, ALLAN MIRANDA, b. Utica, Ohio, Aug. 7, 1909; J.D., U. Akron, 1934. Admitted to Ohio bar, 1934; legal staff mem. State Automobile Mut. Ins. Co., 1940-47; individual practice law, Shelby, Ohio, 1947—; mayor City of Shelby, 1953, dir. law, 1955. Mem. Ohio, Richland County bar assns., Am. Assn. Trial Lawyers. Home: 44 Harriette Dr Shelby OH 44875 Office: 41 E Main St Shelby OH 44875

HARMAN, DONALD JAMES, b. Milw., Oct. 12, 1930; B.A., U. Wis. at Madison, 1953, LL.D., 1960. Admitted to Wis. bar, 1960, U.S. Supreme Ct. bar, 1972; asso. firm Ven-Epps & Harman, Wis., 1960-62; mem. firm Johns, Flahery, Harman & Gillette, LaCrosse, Wis., 1962-75, firm Donald J. Harman, LaCrosse, 1975—; city atty. Weyauwega, Wis., 1961-62. Pres., St. Francis Hosp. Found., Inc.; mem. Lower W. Central Criminal Justice Planning Council; mem. LaCrosse County Bd. Suprs., 1966, 68, 70, 72, 74, 76. Home: 3033 S 29th Ct LaCrosse WI 54601 Office: 205 Hoeschler Exchange Bldg 205 5th Ave LaCrosse WI 54601 Tel (608) 782-7566

HARMAN, JAMES WILLIAM, JR., b. Richmond, Va., Sept. 29, 1922; B.S., Washington & Lee U., 1947, LL.B., 1949. Admitted to Va. bar, 1949; partner firm Harman & Harman, Tazewell, Va., 1949—; commonwealth's atty., Tazewell County, 1952-56; gen. counsel, sec.-treas. Coal Creek Coal Co., 1951—; gen. counsel SW Va. Nat. Bank, 1963-75; municipal atty. City of Tazewell, 1956-61; mem. 9th dist. commn. Va. State Bar, 1957-60, chmn., 1959-60. Mayor, Tazewell, 1961-67; pres. Tazewell Community Hosp., 1968-72. Mem. Tazewell County, Va., Am. bar assns., Va. Trial Lawyers Assn., Am. Judicature Soc., Phi Beta Kappa, Omicron Delta Kappa, Phi Delta Phi. Home: Sunset Hills Tazewell VA 24651 Office: 116 W Main St Tazewell VA 24651 Tel (703) 988-5538

HARMAN, WILLIAM BOYS, JR., b. Newport News, Va., June 5, 1930; A.B., Coll. William and Mary, 1951; J.D., 1956; LL.M., Georgetown U., 1960. Admitted to Va. bar, 1956, D.C. bar, 1961, U.S. Supreme Ct. bar, 1961, U.S. Tax Ct., 1961; tax atty. Gen. Motors Corp., Detroit, 1956-58; atty. office chief counsel IRS, Washington, 1958-59, Office of Tax Legis. Counsel, Dept. Treasury, Washington, 1959-61; atty. firm Cummings & Sellers, Washington, 1961-62; asso. gen. counsel Am. Life Conv., Washington, 1962-67, gen. counsel, 1968-72; v.p. law Am. Life Ins. Assn., Washington, 1973-74, exec. v.p., 1975; exec. v.p. Am. Council of Life Ins., Washington, 1976—. Mem. Am., Fed. bar assns., Va. State Bar, Bar Assn. D.C., Assn. Life Ins. Counsel, Am. Law Inst., SAR, William and Mary Law Sch. Assn., Phi Beta Kappa, Phi Alpha Delta, Sigma Alpha Epsilon. Home: 4905 N 35th Rd Arlington VA 22207 Office: 1730 Pennsylvania Ave NW Washington DC 20006 Tel (703) 536-7240 also (202) 393-1020

HARMON, BERT SNOW, b. N.Y.C., Jan. 22, 1906; B.A., Yale, 1927; M.A., Columbia, 1935; J.D., Harvard, 1930. Admitted to N.Y. bar, 1930, U.S. Dist. Ct. bar, 1936; partner firm Harmon-Hamburger, N.Y.C., 1933-53; individual practice law, N.Y.C., 1953—; pres. Harmon Realty Assos., N.Y.C., 1938—. Dep. dir. civil def. Village of Mamaroneck (N.Y.), 1960-63. Mem. Am., N.Y. State bar assns. Office: 60 E 42d St New York City NY 10017 Tel (212) 682-3254

HARMON, DAVID H., b. N.Y.C., Aug. 15, 1917; B.B.A., St. Johns U., 1943, LL.B., 1946, J.D., 1968. Admitted to N.Y. bar, 1946; individual practice law, N.Y.C., 1946—. Adv. com. Malverne (N.Y.) Bd. Edn., 1973. Mem. Am. Bar Assn., Am. Judicature Soc., N.Y. State Trial Lawyers Assn., N.Y. County Lawyers Assn., Delta Mu Delta. Home: 63 Tilrose Ave Malverne NY 11565 Office: 299 Broadway New York City NY 10007 Tel (212) 732-3665

HARMON, E(VERETT) GLENN, b. Port Orchard, Wash., Jan. 5, 1914; B.A. in English, Journalism, Wash. State U., 1940; LL.B., Gonzaga U., 1953. Admitted to Wash. State bar, 1953; law clk. Judge Charles T. Donworth, Wash. State Supreme Ct., 1954; bill drafter Wash. State Legislature, 1955; asso. firm Witherspoon, Kelley, Davenport & Toole, Spokane, 1955-59, partner, 1960—; instr. legal writing Gonzaga U., 1958-64; counsel Wash. Tax Control Council, Inc., 1961-66, Lake Coeur d' Alene (Idaho) Property Owners & Taxpayers Assn., Inc., 1964—. Pres. Spokane Municipal League, 1967. Mem. Am., Wash. (editor It's The Law Column, 1959-69), Spokane County bar assns. Home: E12124 21st Ave Spokane WA 99206 Office: Old National Bank Bldg Spokane WA 99201 Tel (509) 624-5265

HARMON, HENRY ANDREW, b. Fulton, Mo., Feb. 10, 1940; student Northwestern U., 1958-60; B.A., Drake U., 1962; J.D., U. Minn., 1965. Admitted to Iowa bar, 1965, U.S. Supreme Ct. bar, 1970; asso. firm Austin, Grefe, & Sidney, Des Moines, 1965-70; partner firm Grefe & Sidney, Des Moines, 1970—. Vice pres. Pub. Health Nursing Assn., Des Moines, 1968-72, pres., 1972-73; treas. Des Moines Art Center Mems. Council, 1968, Des Moines Center Sci. and Industry Action Council, 1974-75; bd. govs. Iowa Living History Farms, Inc., Des Moines, 1974—; vestryman St. Paul's Episcopal Ch., Des Moines, 1974—. Mem. Am., Iowa State (chmn. spl. com. on code and session law reform), Polk County (chmn. membership com.) bar assns., Iowa Assn. Def. Counsel. Home: 302 37th St Des Moines IA 50312 Office: 1980 Financial Center Des Moines IA 50309 Tel (515) 245-4300

HARMS, EDWARD CLAIR, JR., b. Roseburg, Oreg., Sept. 21, 1924; B.S., U. Oreg., 1947, J.D., 1949. Admitted to Oreg. bar, 1949, U.S. Supreme Ct. bar, 1965; individual practice law, Springfield, Oreg., 1949-68; sr. partner firm Harms & Harold, Springfield, 1968—; atty. City Springfield, 1964—; councilman City Springfield, 1950-52, mayor, 1952-61; lectr. Sch. Law Univ. Oreg., Eugene, 1958-75. Mem. Oreg. State Sanitary Authority, 1959-69; dir. League Oreg. Cities, Salem, 1955-61, v.p., 1956-58, pres., 1959-60; vice chmn. Oreg. Environ. Quality Commn., 1969-73; v.p. Oreg. State Bd. Higher Edn., 1976—. Mem. Am. Bar Assn., Phi Alpha Delta. Named Jr. First Citizen Springfield, Springfield Jaycees, 1956, Young Man of Yr., State Oreg., 1956, First Citizen Springfield, Oreg. Jaycees, 1957; recipient Spl. Community Citizenship award, City Springfield, 1960. Home: 845 Willacade Ct Springfield OR 97477 Office: Suite D 223 N A St Springfield OR 97477 Tel (503) 746-9621

HARNACK, DON STEGER, b. Milw., June 19, 1928; B.S., U. Wis., 1950; LL.B., Harvard, 1953. Admitted to Wis. bar, 1953, Ill. bar, 1961; lectr. econs. U. Ga., Columbus, 1954-55; atty. firm Quarles, Spence & Quarles, Milw., 1955-57; tax atty. chief counsel's office IRS, Chgo., 1957-61; asso. firm Dixon, Todhunter, Knouff & Holmes, Chgo., 1961-65; partner firm McDermott, Will & Emery, Chgo., 1965—; lectr. John Marshall Law Sch., 1962-69. Mem. Winnetka (Ill.) Zoning Bd. Appeals, 1971-76, Winnetka Planning Commn., 1974-76; gen. counsel, v.p. N.E. Ill. council Boy Scouts Am., 1974—; trustee Union League Boys' Club Found., 1975—. Mem. Am., Wis., Ill., Chgo. bar assns., Legal Aid Chgo. Contbr. articles to legal jours. Home: 459 Sheridan Rd Winnetka IL 60093 Office: 111 W Monroe St Chicago IL 60603 Tel (312) 372-2000

HARNETT, DANIEL JOSEPH, b. St. Paul, Aug. 1, 1930; B.S., Marquette U., 1951, J.D., 1953; certificate U. Calif., Los Angeles, 1967, Mass. Inst. Tech., 1968. Admitted to Wis. bar, 1953, Calif. bar, 1959, U.S. Supreme Ct. bar, 1962; with Northrop Corp., Beverly Hills, Calif., 1964-69; asst. adminstr. industry affairs and tech. utilization NASA, Washington, 1960-72, cons., 1972—; pres., chief operating officer, dir. Aerona, Inc., Torrance, Calif., 1972-76, also dir. subsidiaries; prin. Harnett & Assos., Los Angeles, 1976—. Mem. Sch. Bd., West Los Angeles, Calif., 1974; bd. consultors Marymount Schs. Fellow Nat. Contract Mgmt. Assn. (bd. advisers 1973—); mem. Am., Calif., Wis., Fed. bar assns., Reliability and Maintainability Symposiums (bd. advisers 1972—), Delta Theta Phi. Home: 127 N Cliffwood Ave Los Angeles CA 90049 Tel (213) 820-5651

HARNEY, NAOMI, b. Wayland, Ky.; B.A., U. Tex., 1948; J.D., U. Houston, 1957. Admitted to Tex. bar, 1957; city atty. City of Amarillo (Tex.), 1957-59, asst. dist. atty., 1959-60; county atty. Potter County (Tex.), Amarillo, 1961-74; judge County Ct. at Law, Amarillo, 1975—. Mem. Patter Randall County Citizens Com.; bd. dirs. Cath. Family Service; adv. bd. Parents without Partners. Mem. Amarillo Trial Lawyers Assn., Tex., Amarillo bar assns., Dist. and County Attys. Assn. Ky. col.; recipient 2d place award as most admired woman in Amarillo. Office: Court House Amarillo TX 79101 Tel (806) 373-9111

HARNSBERGER, RICHARD STEPHEN, b. Omaha, Dec. 14, 1921; B.S., U. Nebr., 1943, J.D. cum laude, 1949, M.A., 1951; S.J.D., U. Wis., 1959. Admitted to Nebr. bar, 1949; practiced in Lincoln, Nebr., 1949-55; mem. firm Stewart & Stewart, 1949-55; dep. county atty. Lancaster County, Nebr. 1956; asst. prof. law U. Nebr., 1956-59, asso. prof., 1960-63, prof., 1963—; trustee Rocky Mountain Mineral Law Found., 1965-68. Mem. City of Lincoln Mayor's Charter Revision Com., 1965. Mem. Nebr. State (vice chmn. exec. com. sect. on natural resources), Am. bar assns. Order of Coif. Recipient Distinguished Teaching award in humanities and social scis. U. Nebr. Found., 1966; author: (with others) Waters and Water Rights, 1970; contbr. numerous articles to legal jours. Home: 1919 S 48th St Lincoln NE 68506 Office: Coll of Law U of Nebr Lincoln NE 68583 Tel (402) 472-1245

HARNWOOD, STANLEY, b. N.Y.C., June 23, 1926; A.B., Columbia U., 1949, LL.B., 1952. Admitted N.Y. State bar, 1954, U.S. Supreme Ct. bar, 1958; asso. Benjamin Harwood, Bklyn., 1954-56; individual practice law, Levittown, N.Y., 1956-61; law sec. to justice N.Y. Supreme Ct., Mineola, N.Y., 1961-65; mem. firm Mishkin, Miner, Harnwood & Semel, Mineola, 1965-69, Shayne, Dachs, Weiss, Kolbrener, Stanisci & Harnwood, Mineola, 1969—; mem. N.Y. State Assembly, 1965-72; commr. elections Nassau County (N.Y.), 1976—. Chmn. Nassau Democratic County Com., 1973—. Mem. Nassau County, N.Y. State bar assns. Home: 711 Birchwood Dr Westbury NY 11590 Office: 1501 Franklin Ave Mineola NY 11501 Tel (516) 747-1100

HARONIAN, HOWARD RICHARD, b. Providence, Sept. 4, 1933; B.S., U. R.I., 1955; J.D., George Washington U., 1959. Admitted to R.I. bar, 1959; individual practice law, Providence, 1959-69; partner firm Haronian & Paquin, Inc., Warwick, R.I., 1969—; legal counsel R.I. Bd. Regents, 1973—; judge adv. R.I. Gov.'s Mil. Staff, 1973-77. City solicitor Warwick, 1967-72; chmn. Warwick Bd. Pub. Safety, 1977—. Mem. R.I. Bar Assn. Office: 1719 Warwick Ave Warwick RI 02889 Tel (401) 739-9330

HARP, WILLIAM RAY, b. Savannah, Ga., Mar. 25, 1931; student Emory U., 1949-51; J.D., U. Ga., 1954. Admitted to Ga. bar, 1953; partner firm Howard, Harp and Storey, Atlanta, 1954-60, Fryer, Harp & Turk, Atlanta, 1960-68, Arnall, Golden & Gregory, Atlanta, 1968—. Mem. Am., Atlanta bar assns., State Bar Ga., Lawyer's Club of Atlanta. Home: 1290 Mount Paran Rd Atlanta GA 30327 Office: 1000 Fulton Fed Bldg Atlanta GA 30303 Tel (404) 577-5100

HARPER, CARL HENRY, b. Greensboro, Ala., Dec. 15, 1912; B.A., Tex. Tech. Coll., 1935; LL.B., Yale, 1938; M.P.A., U. Ga., 1971. Admitted to Tex. bar, 1938, D.C. bar, 1940, Ga. bar, 1947; atty. Pub. Works Adminstrn., Ft. Worth, Tex., 1938-39, Fed. Security Agency, Washington, 1939-42, regional atty., Atlanta, 1943-53; regional atty. Dept. Health, Edn., Welfare, Atlanta, 1953—. Mem. Fed. Bar Assn. (pres. local chpt. 1958), Atlanta Lawyers Club. Author: Georgia Law of Evidence (with Prof. Thomas Green); contbr. articles to Ga. Bar Jour., Mercer Law Review. Home: 3194 Moss Oak Dr Doraville GA 30340 Office: Room 323 50 7th St NE Atlanta GA 30323 Tel (404) 526-5381

HARPER, DAVID WILBUR, b. Highland Park, Mich., Oct. 11, 1925; B.B.A., U. Oreg., 1952, J.D., 1952. Admitted to Mich. bar, 1952, Oreg. bar, 1953; asso. firm Vergeer & Samuels, Portland, Oreg., 1953-60; mem. firm Keane, Harper, Pearlman & Copeland, Portland, 1961—. Sec., Land Use Research Inst. Mem. Internat. Assn. Fin. Planners, Am. Trial Lawyers Assn., Am., Oreg., Multnomah County bar assns., Am. Adjudicator Soc., Delta Beta Phi. Home: 5344 SW Bancroft St Portland OR 97221 Office: 3500 First Nat Tower Portland OR 97201 Tel (503) 224-4100

HARPER, HOWARD WILSON, b. Wichita, Kans., Nov. 29, 1912; student U. Kans., 1934-35; student Washburn Coll., 1936-38, LL.B., 1940, J.D., 1970. Admitted to Kans. bar, 1940, U.S. Dist. Ct. bar, 1950, U.S. Ct. of Appeals bar, 1962, U.S. Supreme Ct. bar, 1965; county atty., Geary County (Kans.) 1942-46; individual practice law, Junction City, Kans., 1940—; chmn. jud. com. Kans. Jud. Council, 1959-64. Pres., Junction City USO Council, 1973-74, recipient Presdl. award, 1973-74; pres. Kans. Jr. C. of C., 1950; mem. Kans. Senate, 1959-64; bd. dirs. Kans. Heart Assn., 1965-67, recipient Gold medal award, 1974; bd. dirs. Am. Heart Assn., 1967-72. Fellow Internat. Acad. Trial Lawyers; mem. Internat. Soc. Barristers, Law Sci. Acad., Kans. Def. Attys., Ins. Attys. Assn. Fedn. Ins. Counsel, Kans. County Attys. Assn. (pres. 1944), Kans. (council 1968-75, pres. elect. 1976, Pres.'s Outstanding Service award 1973-74), Central Kans. (pres. 1958), Geary County (pres. 1948) bar assns., Junction City C. of C. (dir. 1959-64). Recipient Kans. Outstanding Young Man of Year award, 1945. Home: 300 W Vine St Junction City KS 66441 Office: 715 N Washington St Junction City KS 66441 Tel (913) 762-2100

HARPER, KENNETH A., b. Seymour, Mo., Sept. 1, 1933; B.A., U. Kans., 1957; LL.B., U. Denver, 1961; postgrad. Columbia, 1965. Admitted to Colo. bar, 1961, Ariz. bar, 1965; counsel Great Plains Fgn. Mktg. Assn., Bogota, Colombia, 1961-65; individual practice law, Phoenix, 1965—; sec. Ariz. World Trade Assn, Phoenix. Mem. Peruvian-Am. Found. Art and Edn. Mem. Nat. Planning Assn., Ariz. Bar Assn., Assn. Am. Trial Lawyers, Acad. Trial Advocacy. Rocky Mountain Mineral Law Found. grantee, 1961-62; contbr. articles to legal jours. Home: PO Box 13386 Phoenix AZ 85002 Office: 1455-B E Indian Sch Rd Phoenix AZ 85014 Tel (602) 279-6245

HARPER, ROBERT AUGUSTUS, JR., b. Crestview, Fla., Aug. 15, 1946; A.B. in Polit. Sci., U. Fla., 1968, U.D., 1970. Admitted to Fla. bar, 1970, U.S. Supreme Ct. bar, 1976; individual practice law, Gainesville and Tallahassee, Fla., 1970—. Mem. Alachua County Law Enforcement Com., Alachua County Community Crisis Center, Alachua County Safety Council. Mem. U. Fla. Law Center Assn., Am., Eighth Judicial (dir.) bar assns., Am. Judicature Soc. Contbr. articles to legal jours. Home: 735 E University Ave Gainesville FL 32601 Office: 735 E University Ave Gainesville FL 32602 Tel (904) 377-0735

HARPER, RONALD JAMES, lawyer; b. West Palm Beach, Fla., Dec. 20, 1945; B.A., Temple U., 1968, LL.B., 1971. Admitted to Pa. Supreme Ct., U.S. Dist. Ct. Eastern Pa., 1972; legal officer OIC of Am., Inc., Phila., 1971—. Mem. Barristers Assn. Phila (pres. 1977-78), Phila. (bar admissions and placement appointment com. 1974-76), Pa., Am., Nat. bar assns. Home: 336 Pelham Rd Philadelphia PA 19119 Office: 45 E Schoolhouse Ln Philadelphia PA 19144

HARPER, SARA JUANITA, b. Cleve., Aug. 10, 1926; B.S., Western Res. U., 1948, LL.B., 1952. Admitted to Ohio bar, 1952; individual practice law, Cleve., 1952-66; atty. Legal Aid Soc., Cleve., 1966-68; prosecutor Dept. Law, City of Cleve., 1968-69, asst. dir. law, 1969-70; judge Cleve. Municipal Ct., 1970—. Trustee E. End Neighborhood House, Inner City Parish. Mem. Nat. Council Negro Women (life), Nat. Bar Assn. (chmn. jud. council 1975-76). World Assn. Judges. Office: Cleveland City Hall 601 Lakeside Ave Cleveland OH 44114

HARPSTER, JAMES ERVING, b. Milw., Dec. 24, 1923; Ph.B., Marquette U., 1950, LL.B., 1952. Admitted to Wis. bar, 1952, Tenn. bar, 1953; asst. counsel to trustee IMC, Inc., 1965-66; partner firm Rickey, Shankman, Blanchard, Agee & Harpster, and Predecessors, Memphis, 1966—. Editor, asst. counsel Memphis and Shelby County Charter Commn., 1962; mem. Shelby County Election Commn., 1968-71; mem. Tenn. State Election Commn., 1971—, chmn., 1974. Mem. Am., Tenn., Shelby County, Memphis bar assns. Home: 3032 E Glengarry Rd Memphis TN 38128 Office: Suite 3500 100 N Main Bldg Memphis TN 38102 Tel (901) 523-2363

HARRAR, WILLIAM HUMISTON, b. N.Y.C., Oct. 19, 1911; student Princeton, 1929-32; LL.B., Columbia, 1937. Admitted to N.Y. bar, 1938; atty. advisor U.S. Bd. Tax Appeals, Washington, 1938-41; jr. asso. firm Davis, Polk, Wardwell, Sunderland & Kiendl, N.Y.C., 1941-43; sr. asso. firm Rathbone, Perry, Kelley & Drye, N.Y.C., 1944-49; v.p., gen. counsel Salmon Corp., N.Y.C., 1949—; dir. 500 Fifth Ave., Inc., Atlantic Leasing Co., Inc., Salmon Mgmt. Co., Inc. Mem. Assn. Bar City N.Y. Contbr. articles to legal jours. Office: 500 Fifth Ave New York City NY 10036 Tel (212) 221-6900

HARRELL, ALLEN WAYLAN, b. Bertie County, N.C., Dec. 24, 1922; B.S. in Bus. Adminstrn, U. N.C., Chapel Hill, 1950, J.D., 1953. Admitted to N.C. bar, 1953; asso. firm Allsbrook and Benton, Roanoke Rapids, N.C., 1953-55; individual practice law, Wilson, N.C., 1955-68; solicitor City Ct., Wilson, 1956-61, judge., 1961-68; judge N.C. Dist. Ct., 7th Jud. Dist., 1968—. Mem. N.C. State, 7th Jud. Dist. bar assns., Assn. N.C. Dist. Ct. Judges. Author: Splinters from My Gavel: Confessions of a Judge, 1970; (with Irene Harrell) The Opposite Sex., 1972; contbr. articles to N.C. Law Rev., religious publs. Home: 408 Pearson St Wilson NC 27893 Office: Courthouse Wilson NC 27893 Tel (919) 237-1591

HARRELL, MORRIS, b. Grandview, Tex., Apr. 16, 1920; B.B.A., LL.B., Baylor U., 1942. Admitted to Tex. bar, 1942; pvt. practice, Dallas, 1946-47; asst. U.S. atty. No. Dist. Tex., 1947-51; pvt. practice, Dallas, 1951-55; trial atty. firm Thompson, Knight, Wright & Simmons, Dallas, 1955-65; trial atty., partner Rain, Harrell & Emery, 1965—. Research fellow Southwestern Legal Found. Fellow Tex. Bar Found. (dir.); mem. Am., Dallas (pres. 1962) bar assns., State Bar Tex. (dir.). Home: 6629 Golf Dr Dallas TX 75205 Office: Republic Nat Bank Tower Dallas TX 75201 Tel (214) 742-1001*

HARRELSON, F. DANIEL, b. Wynne, Ark., Feb. 23, 1942; B.S. in Bus. Adminstrn., U. Ark., 1964, LL.B., 1967. Admitted to Ark. bar, 1967; clk. Ark. Supreme Ct., 1967-68; mem. firm Coleman, Gantt, Ramsay & Cox, Pine Bluff, Ark., 1968—. Chmn. budget com. Jefferson County (Ark.) United Way, 1973. Mem. Am., Ark., Jefferson County bar assns. Home: 108 Park Pl Pine Bluff AR 71601 Office: POB 8509 Pine Bluff AR 71611 Tel (501) 534-5221

HARREN, JOSEPH, b. Freeport, Minn., May 6, 1928; B.S. in Law, St. Paul Coll. Law, 1949, LL.B., 1951. Admitted to Minn. bar, 1951; individual practice law, Red Lake Falls, Minn., 1952-68; city atty. Red Lake Falls, 1952-65; judge Probate and Juvenile Cts. Red Lake County, 1965-69, Red Lake, Marshall County Dist., 1969-71; judge County Ct., Red Lake, Marshall, Pennington County Dist., 1971-74, chief judge, 1974—. Mem. Minn. Bar Assn., Minn. County Judges' Assn., Nat. Council Juvenile Judges. Tel (218) 681-4064

HARRIGAN, ARTHUR WASHINGTON, JR., b. N.Y.C., Mar. 16, 1944; B.A. cum laude, Harvard; LL.B. cum laude, Columbia. Admitted to N.Y. State bar, 1969, Wash. State bar; mem. firm Shearman & Sterling, N.Y.C., 1968; legal officer U.S. Coast Guard, 1968-71; mem. firm Lane, Powell, Moss & Miller, Seattle, 1971-74, partner, 1975—; counsel House Judiciary Com. Wash. State 1972 session; sr. counsel U.S. Senate select com. on intelligence activities (Church Com.), 1975-76. Mem. Wash. State Trial Lawyers Assn., Am., Wash. State bar assns. Recipient Am. Bar Assn. award for Profl. Merit, 1968; prin. author of Senate Select Com. Staff Report on IRS Intelligence Activities and Rights of Americans; contbr. articles to legal jours.; articles and book rev. editor Columbia Law Rev., 1967-68. Home: 736 37th Ave Seattle WA 78122 Office: 1700 Washington Bldg Seattle WA 98101 Tel (206) 223-7000

HARRIGAN, FREDERICK JOHN, b. Bethlehem, N.H., Feb. 21, 1920; A.B. magna cum laude, Harvard, U., 1942; LL.B., Georgetown U., 1947. Admitted to N.H. bar, 1947; individual practice law, Colebrook, N.H., 1947—; asso. judge Colebrook Municipal Ct., 1949; judge probate ct. Coos County, N.H., 1951—; served to lt. comdr. Judge Adv. Gen. USNR, 1942-46; pub. Colebrook News and Sentinel, 1960—. Moderator Colebrook Sch. Dist., 1948-68; mem. N.H. Commn. on Secondary Edn., 1974-76. Mem. Coos County, N.H. Am. bar assns., Am. Judicature Soc. Home: RTE 2 Box 172 S Hill Colebrook NH 03576 Office: 1 Bridge St Colebrook NH 03576 Tel (603) 237-4266

HARRINGTON, ANTHONY STEPHEN, b. Taylorsville, N.C., Mar. 9, 1941; A.B., U. N.C. at Chapel Hill, 1963; LL.B., Duke U., 1966. Admitted to N.C. bar, 1966, D.C. bar, 1968, U.S. Supreme Ct. bar, 1970; asst. dean Duke U. Sch. Law, 1966-68; asso. firm Hogan & Hartson, Washington, D.C., 1968-74, partner, 1974—; mem. staff Gov. state N.C., 1964. Mem. bd. dirs. Rosemount Center, Washington, 1972—, chmn., 1975—; counsel Democratic Party Charter Commn., 1973-74; mem. Duke U. Nat. Council, 1972-74. Mem. Am. Bar Assn., Bar Assn. D.C. Home: 3345 Runnymede Pl NW Washington DC 20015 Office: 815 Connecticut Ave Washington DC 20006 Tel (202) 331-4646

HARRINGTON, CATHRYN L., b. Alexandria, Ky., May 1, 1917; A.B., Western Coll., 1938; J.D., U. Cin., 1941; certificates, U. Colo., 1968, U. Nev., 1972. Admitted to Ky. bar, 1941, Ohio bar, 1941, U.S. Supreme Ct. bar, 1949; mem. firm Ebert, Coo & Burke, Newport, Ky., 1941-44, Harrington & Harrington, Van Wert, Ohio, 1946-58; judge Ct. of Common Pleas, Probate and Juvenile Div., Van Wert, 1958—; spl. asst. to atty. gen. of Ohio, 1956-58. Mem. Ohio State, Am. bar assns., Ohio, Nat. councils juvenile ct. judges, Ohio, Nat. assns. of probate ct. judges. Home: 239 N Jefferson St Van Wert OH 45891 Office: County Ct House Van Wert OH 45891 Tel (419) 238-0027

HARRINGTON, GEORGE WALTER, b. N.Y.C., Nov. 8, 1914; student Fordham U., 1931-33; LL.B., Bklyn. Law Sch., 1936. Admitted to N.Y. bar, 1940; mem. firms Hartsell & Harrington, N.Y.C., 1955-66, Wilson & Bave, Yonkers, N.Y., 1971—; mem. N.Y. Assembly, 1953, 54, 57-60, commr. arbitration, 1972-75, judge criminal ct., 1975—. Mem. N.Y. State, Bronx County bar assns. Home: 49 Schofield St Bronx NY 10464 Office: 100 Centre St New York City NY 10013 Tel (212) MO5-7500

HARRINGTON, JAMES CHARLES, b. Lansing, Mich., May 16, 1946; B.A., Pontifical Coll. Josephinum, 1968; M.A. in Philosophy, U. Detroit, 1970, J.D., 1973. Admitted to Tex. bar, 1973, U.S. Dist. Ct. So. Dist. Tex. bar, 1974, U.S. 5th Circuit Ct. Appeals bar, 1974, U.S. Supreme Ct. bar, 1977; staff atty. S. Tex. project ACLU Found., San Juan, 1973-75, dir., 1975—; instr. philosophy Wayne County Community Coll., Detroit, 1970-72; lectr. U. Detroit, 1970-73. U.S. rep. Overseas Devel. Council conf., Ecuador, 1976. Mem. Tex. Trial Lawyers Assn., Tex. Criminal Lawyers Def. Assn., Hildago County, FCC bar assns. Office: Box 1493 San Juan TX 78589 Tel (512) 787-8171

HARRINGTON, JAMES TIMOTHY, b. Chgo., Sept. 4, 1942; B.A., U. Notre Dame, 1964, J.D., 1967. Admitted to Ill. bar, 1967, Ind. bar, 1968, U.S. Ct. Appeals 7th Circuit bar, 1969; law clk. Hon. George N. Beamer U.S. Dist. Ct. No. Dist. Ind., 1967-69; asso. firm Rooks, Pitts, Fullagar and Poust, Chgo., 1969-76, partner, 1976—. Mem. Am., Ill., Ind., Chgo. bar assns. Office: 208 S LaSalle St Chicago IL 60604 Tel (312) 372-5600

HARRINGTON, JOHN CHARLES, b. Tulsa, Nov. 1, 1942; B.A., Tulane U., 1964, J.D., 1969. Admitted to Okla. bar, 1969; spl. dist. judge Okla., 1971-73; partner firm Harrington & Mann, Tulsa, 1969-71, 73—. Mem. Am. Judicature Soc., Tulsa Title and Probate Lawyers Assn. Office: 1108 Thompson Bldg Tulsa OK 74103 Tel (918) 587-6601

HARRINGTON, LOUIS ROBERT, b. Detroit, Nov. 30, 1904; J.D., U. Detroit, 1929; postgrad. U. Mich., 1930. Admitted to Mich. bar, 1929, U.S. Supreme Ct. bar, 1960; sec., dir. Commando Tool Co., Detroit, 1940—, McDonald Products, Detroit, 1970—, Sailmasters of Mich., 1972—. Mem. State Bar Mich. (chmn. probate and trust law sect. 1960-62), Mich. Conf. Bar Officers (chmn. 1970), Am. Coll. Probate Counsel, Advs. Club. Home: 494 N Foxx Hills Dr Bloomfield Hills MI 48013 Office: 1164 1st Nat Bldg Detroit MI 48226 Tel (313) 961-1621

HARRINGTON, ORVILLE GEORGE, b. Hollins, Ala., Nov. 12, 1908; student U. Ala., 1927-29, DePaul U., 1939-40; LL.B., Emory U., 1948, J.D., 1970. Admitted to Ga. bar, 1947; partner firm Covington & Harrington, Atlanta, 1949-69; individual practice law, Atlanta, 1969—. Mem. Ga., Atlanta bar assns., Phi Delta Phi, Sigma Phi Epsilon. Contbr. article to Ga. Bar Jour. Home: 1069 Cumberland Rd NE Atlanta GA 30306 Office: 401 Carnegie Bldg Atlanta GA 30303 Tel (404) 525-6335

HARRINGTON, ROBERT STUCKEY, b. Lathrop, Mo., Oct. 10, 1913; B.A., U. Mo., 1935; LL.B., U. Mich., 1938. Admitted to Mo. bar, 1938, Calif. bar, 1947; dist. atty. Clinton County (Mo.), 1939-43; spl. agt. FBI, 1942-44; judge adv. 9th Air Wing USMC, 1944-46; mem. firm Parker, Stanbury, Reese & McGee, Los Angeles, 1947-53; sr. partner firm Dryden, Harrington & Swartz, Los Angeles, 1953—; mem. Calif. State Bar Disciplinary Com.; lectr. in field. Diplomate Am. Bd. Trial Adv. Fellow Internat. Acad. Trial Lawyers, Am. Coll. Trial Lawyers; mem. Internat. Assn. Ins. Counsel, Am., Calif. trial lawyers assns., Def. Research Inst., Assn. Dist. Attys., Soc. Former Spl. Agts. FBI, Am. Judicature Soc., Law-Sci. Acad., Am. Los Angeles, Calif. bar assns. Author: (with others) California Book of Approved Jury Instructions, 1975-76; author trial techniques Calif. State Bar, U. Calif. Home: 3907 Durham Pl Pasadena CA 91103 Office: One Wilshire Bldg Suite 703 Los Angeles CA 90017 Tel (213) 628-2184

HARRINGTON, WILLIAM DAVID, b. N.Y.C., May 23, 1945; B.A. magna cum laude, Holy Cross Coll., 1966; M.B.A., Columbia U., 1970, J.D. cum laude, 1969. Admitted to N.Y. bar, 1970, U.S. Supreme Ct. bar, 1973; asso. firm Sullivan & Cromwell, N.Y.C., 1970-77; v.p., gen. counsel Copper div. Amax Inc., Greenwich, Conn., 1977—. Mem. Assn. Bar City N.Y., N.Y. State, Am. bar assns. Contbr. articles to legal jours. Home: 150 Greenway Terr Forest Hills NY 11375 Office: Amax Center Greenwich CT 06830 Tel (203) 622-3000

HARRINGTON, WILLIAM GEORGE, b. Marietta, Ohio, Nov. 21, 1931; A.B., Marietta Coll., 1953; M.A., Duke, 1955; J.D. Ohio State U., 1958. Admitted to Ohio bar, 1958, U.S. Supreme Ct. bar, 1972, Fla. bar, 1974; practiced in Marietta, 1958-62; counsel Ohio Sec. of State, Columbus, 1962-65; exec. v.p. Ohio Bar Automated Research and counsel Ohio State Bar Assn., Columbus, 1965-71; of counsel firm Stouffer, Wait & Ashbrook, Columbus, 1971—; cons. computer-assisted legal research Mead Data Central Co., N.Y.C., 1971—; mem. Ohio Select Com. on Criminal Code Revision, 1965-70. Adviser, Ohio Arts Council, 1971-75. Mem. Am., Ohio State, Fla. bar assns. Author novels, including: Trial, 1970; The Jupiter Crisis, 1971; Scorpio 5, 1975. Home: 987 Kenwood Ln Columbus OH 43220 Office: Suite 2830 50 W Broad St Columbus OH 43215 Tel (614) 221-4405

HARRINGTON, WILTON DANIEL, b. Moore County, N.C., June 7, 1926; student Middle Ga. Coll., 1947-49; LL.B., U. Ga., 1952. Admitted to Ga. bar, 1951, U.S. Dist. Ct. bar, 1952; individual practice law, Eastman, Ga., 1952-59; partner firm Smith & Harrington, Eastman, 1959—. Past pres. Eastman Jr. C. of C.; trustee Inst. Continuing Legal Edn.; bd. visitors Sch. Law, U. Ga., 1970-73. Mem. Am., Ga. (bd. govs. 1966—, exec. com. 1973—, pres. 1977—), Oconee Circuit (past pres.) bar assns. Student editor Ga. Bar Jour., 1950-52. Home: 800 8th Ave SW Eastman GA 31023 Office: PO Drawer 130 Eastman GA 31023 Tel (912) 374-3488

HARRIS, AARON, b. Washington, La., Oct. 8, 1935; B.S., So. U., 1957, M.Ed., 1962, J.D., 1971. Admitted to La. bar; tchr. high sch. St. Londry Parish, La., 1957-59, 61-68; asst. prof. law So. U., Baton Rouge, 1971-73, asso. dean sch. law, 1974—; individual practice law, La., 1972-74. Bd. suprs. elections St. Landry Parish, 1972-75, pres.; mem. St. Landry Parish Bi-Racial Com., 1972—. Mem. Am., La. (bd. govs.), bar assns., La. State Law Inst., Louis A. Martinet Legal Soc. Named Prof. of Year, So. U., Baton Rouge, 1972-73. Office: So U Law Sch Baton Rouge LA Tel (504) 771-3776

HARRIS, ALAN WAYNE, b. Balt., Oct. 22, 1947; B.A., Coppin State Coll., 1969, M.Ed., 1975; J.D., Tex. So. U., 1972. Law clk. firm Williams Lott and Peavy, Houston, 1971; intern States' Atty. Balt., 1971-72; staff Balt. Pub. Schl. System, 1974—; coordinator, asso. prof. Coppin State Coll., 1973—; pres. chmn. Sports Edn., Inc., Balt., 1976—; research aide Md. Constl. Conv. Commn., Balt., 1968-69. Mem. NAACP, AAUP, Md. Acad. Criminal Justice Profs., Phi Alpha Delta. Earl Warren Found. fellow, 1969-72. Office: Div Criminal Justice Coppin State Coll Baltimore MD 21216 Tel (301) 383-6531

HARRIS, BENJAMIN PEARCE, III, b. Providence, Oct. 12, 1936; A.B., Yale U., 1958; LL.B., Harvard U., 1961. Admitted to R.I. bar, 1962; asso. firm Edwards & Angell, Providence, 1962-69, partner, 1969—; dir. Providence Mut. Fire Ins. Co., Armbrust Chain Co., Providence. Bd. dirs. Community Workshops of R.I., Providence, 1967-77; trustee Women and Infants Hosp., Providence, 1969—; jr. warden Grace Ch., Providence, 1970-72. Mem. Am., R.I. bar assns. Office: Edwards & Angell 2700 Hospital Trust Tower Providence RI 02903 Tel (401) 274-9200

HARRIS, BURTON H., b. Richmond, Utah, Oct. 15, 1929; B.S., Utah State U., 1953; LL.B., J.D., U. Utah, 1958. Admitted to Utah bar, 1958, U.S. Supreme Ct. bar, 1971; partner firm Preston & Harris, Logan, Utah, 1958—; county atty. Cache County, Utah, 1961—. Mem. Am. Trial Lawyers Assn., Am. Bar Assn., Utah State Bar (pres. 1971), Cache C. of C. Home: 895 N 4th St E Logan UT 84321 Office: 31 Federal Ave Logan UT 84321 Tel (801) 752-3551

HARRIS, CARLETON, b. Pine Bluff, Ark., Dec. 31, 1909; student Union U., Jackson, Tenn., 1929-31; LL.B., Cumberland U., 1932; LL.D., Ouachita Bapt. Coll. Admitted to Ark. bar, 1932, U.S. Supreme Ct. bar, 1947; individual practice law, Pine Bluff, 1932-49; mem. Ark. Gen. Assembly, 1933-38; pros. atty. 11th Jud. Dist., Ark., 1947-48; chancery and probate judge 4th Chancery Dist., Ark., 1949-57; chief justice Ark. Supreme Ct., Little Rock, 1957—; chmn. State-Fed. Jud. Council Ark., 1971—; pres. State Judicial Council, 1954-55. Mem. at large nat. council Boy Scouts Am.; mem. exec. com. So. Bapt. Conv., 1967-75. Mem. Am., Ark. bar assns., Am. Judicature Soc., Phi Alpha Delta. Recipient Distinguished Alumnus Anniversary award Union U., 1975, Distinguished Alumni citation Cumberland Sch. Law, 1974, Outstanding Lawyer award Ark. Bar Assn. and Ark. Bar Found, 1973-74, Christian Citizenship award Pulaski County Bapt. Assn., Little Rock, 1976. Home: 2005 Laurel St Pine Bluff AR 71601 Office: Justice Bldg Little Rock AR 72201 Tel (501) 372-2315

HARRIS, CHARLES WILLIAM, b. Indpls., May 8, 1946; B.S. in Edn., Ball State U., 1968; J.D., Ind. U., Indpls., 1973. Admitted to Ind. bar, 1973; Admitted to Ind. bar, 1973; staff atty. Ind. Legis. Council, Indpls., 1973—; trust adminstr. 1st Bank & Trust Co., Speedway, Ind., 1971-73. Mem. Ind. Bar Assn. Home: 8420 Mandan Ct Indianapolis IN 46217 Office: Room 302 State House Indianapolis IN 46204 Tel (317) 269-3715

HARRIS, CLORIS LEO, b. Merkel, Tex., Feb. 24, 1908; student Tex. Technol. U., 1926-28, U. Tex., 1928-29; LL.B., U. Tex., 1939. Admitted to Tex. bar, 1940; individual practice, Lubbock, Tex., 1940—; mem. Tex. Ho. of Reps., 1937-41. Del., Dem. Nat. Conv., 1948. Mem. Am., Tex., Lubbock County bar assns., Am. Bus. Club. Home: 4832 45th St Lubbock TX 79414 Office: 416 Lubbock Nat Bank Bldg Lubbock TX 79401 Tel (806) 762-1696

HARRIS, DAVID, b. Pettigrew, Ark., Dec. 19, 1936; B.S. in Bus. Edn. and Bus. Adminstrn., Northeastern Okla. U., 1965; J.D., Okla. U., 1969. Admitted to Okla. bar, 1969, U.S. Dist. Ct. for Eastern Dist. Okla. bar, 1970, U.S. 10th Circuit Ct. Appeals bar, 1970; practiced in Stilwell, Okla., 1969—; individual practice law, 1969-71, 75—; asso. dist. judge Adair County, Okla., 1971-75. Mem. Am., Okla., Adair County bar assns., Stilwell Jaycees (pres. 1970). Home: 704 W Elm Stilwell OK 74960 Office: 219 W Division St Stilwell OK 74960 Tel (918) 774-7050

HARRIS, DAVID ALEXANDER, b. Canton, Miss, Dec. 12, 1933; B.A., Millsaps Coll., 1955; postgrad. U. Va., 1955-57, Tulane U., 1957-58; LL.B., U. Miss., 1959, J.D., 1968. Admitted to Miss. bar, 1959; practice law, Jackson, Miss., 1959—; sr. partner firm Harris & McLellan, Jackson, 1975—. Mem. Miss. Heart Assn. Recipient Outstanding Vol. Service certificate Miss. Heart Assn., 1976. Mem. Miss., State, Am., Hinds County bar assns., Am., Miss. trial lawyers assn., N.Jackson Lawyers Club (pres. 1974-75, v.p. 1975-77), SCV (camp adj. 1977, div. chmn. nat. com. on graves and monuments 1977, chmn. state mus. com. 1977). Home: 1000 E Northside Dr Jackson MS 39206 Office: 4541 Office Park Dr Jackson MS 39206 Tel (601) 982-0231

HARRIS, DE LONG, b. New Orleans, Dec. 9, 1922; LL.B., Terrell Law Sch., 1944. Admitted to D.C. bar, 1944, U.S. Supreme Ct. bar, 1952; individual practice law, Washington, 1944—. Pres., Motts Sch. PTA, 1958-59. Mem. Nat., Washington (pres. 1958-60, dir. 1958-73, Lawyer of Year award 1965) bar assns., Bar Assn. D.C., D.C. Bar Unified, Am. Judicature Soc. Office: 1816 11th St NW Washington DC 20001 Tel (202) 265-7000

HARRIS, DON VICTOR, JR., b. Nottingham Twp., Ind., Jan. 16, 1921; A.B., DePauw U., 1943; J.D., Harvard, 1945. Admitted to D.C. bar, 1947; law clk. to judge U.S. Ct. Appeals, 1945-46; asso. firm Covington & Burling, Washington, 1946-57, partner, 1957—; lectr. law George Washington U., 1963-64; mem. IRS Commr.'s Adv. Group, 1976. Mem. Am. Law Inst., Am. (chmn. sect. taxation 1976-77), D.C., Fed. bar assns., Phi Beta Kappa. Contbr. articles to legal jours. Home: 4525 Glebe Rd N Arlington VA 22207 Office: 888 16th St NW Washington DC 20006 Tel (202) 452-6188

HARRIS, DONALD RAY, b. Lake Preston, S.D., Apr. 21, 1938; B.A., U. Iowa, 1959, J.D., 1961. Admitted to Iowa bar, 1961, Ill. bar, 1963; asso. firm Jenner & Block, Chgo., 1963-70, partner, 1970—. Mem. Am., Ill., Iowa bar assns., Chgo. Legal Club. Office: 1 IBM Plaza Chicago IL 60611 Tel (312) 222-9350

HARRIS, EARL DOUGLAS, b. Athens, Ga., Apr. 9, 1947; B.S. in Agr. Engring., U. Ga., 1970, M.B.A., 1973, J.D., 1973. Admitted to Ga. bar, U.S. Dist. Ct. bar, 1973; individual practice law, Watkinsville, Ga., 1973-76; partner firm Harris & Rice, Watkinsville, 1976—; city atty., Bogart, Ga., 1974-75. Treas., Oconee County (Ga.) Democratic Com., 1976; bd. dirs. Am. Cancer Soc. of Oconee County. Mem. Oconee County C. of C. (dir. 1975—, sec.), Am., Ga., Western Circuit bar assns., Am., Ga. trial lawyers' assns., Assn. Am. Attys., Phi Alpha Delta, Omicron Delta Kappa, Sigma Iota Epsilon, Alpha Zeta, Blue Key. Home: POB 498 Watkinsville GA 30677 Office: POB 498 Watkinsville GA 30677 Tel (404) 769-7717

HARRIS, EDWARD, b. Rochester, N.Y., Sept. 24, 1912; A.B., Princeton U., 1935; LL.B., Cornell U., 1938. Admitted to N.Y. bar, 1939, D.C. bar, 1972. Asso. firm Hughes, Hubbard & Ewing, N.Y.C., 1938-39; asso. firm Harris, Beach, Wilcox, Rubin & Levey, 1939-45, partner, 1945—; trustee Rochester Savs. Bank; dir. Security Trust Co., Security N.Y. State Corp., Rochester. Mem. adv. bd. Cornell U. Law Sch.; bd. mgrs. Meml. Art Gallery U. Rochester; trustee U. Rochester, Springfield Coll. Mem. Am., N.Y. State, Monroe County bar assns. Office: 2 State St Rochester NY 14614

HARRIS, ELAINE JENSEN, b. Fresno, Calif., July 27, 1919; A.B., Fresno State Coll., 1940; J.D., U. Calif., 1973. Admitted to Calif. bar, 1973; staff atty. Fresno County Legal Services, Fresno, Calif., 1974-75; supr. atty. Legal Aid for Srs. Fresno County Legal Services, Inc., 1975—. Mem. Fresno County Bar Assn. Office: 1221 Fulton Mall Fresno CA 93721 Tel (209) 486-1830

HARRIS, FRANK CARLETON, b. Pine Bluff, Ark., Dec. 31, 1909; LL.B., Cumberland U., 1932. Admitted to Ark. bar, 1932, U.S. Supreme Ct. bar, 1947; individual practice law, Pine Bluff, Ark., 1943-49; mem. Ark. Gen. Assembly, 1933-38; prosecuting atty. 11th Jud. Dist., 1947-48; judge 4th Chancery Dist., 1949-57; chief justice Ark. Supreme Ct., Little Rock, 1957—; chmn. State-Fed. Jud. Council for Ark., 1976—. Mem. at Large Nat. Council of Boy Scouts Am. Mem. Jefferson County (pres. 1942), Ark. (Outstanding Lawyer award 1973-74), Am. bar assns., Am. Judicature Soc., Conf. Chief Justices (nat. chmn. 1966-67), Phi Alpha Delta. Recipient Distinguished Alumni Citation Cumberland Sch. Law, Samford U., 1974, Distinguished Alumnus Anniversary award Union U., 1975. Home: 2005 Laurel St Pine Bluff AR 71601 Office: Ark Supreme Ct Justice Bldg Little Rock AR 72201 Tel (501) 372-2315

HARRIS, FRED L., b. Los Angeles, May 31, 1930; B.A., Mich. State Coll., 1952; J.D., Wayne State U., 1963. Admitted to Mich. bar, 1964; asst. pros. atty. Wayne County (Mich.), Detroit, 1963-64; individual practice law, Southfield, Mich., 1964—; spl. asst. atty. gen. State Mich., 1975—. Mem. Oakland County Rd. Commn., 1971-76, chmn., 1975-76; pres. local union no. 58 Internat. Brotherhood Elec. Workers, 1967-75; bd. dirs. March of Dimes. Mem. State Bar Mich., Detroit, Oakland County bar assns., Cath. Lawyers Guild, Assn. Trial Lawyers Am., Mich., Detroit trial lawyers assns. Recipient writing award Am. Jurisprudence Soc., 1963. Office: 24700 Northwestern Hwy Suite 210 Southfield MI 48075 Tel (313) 352-0600

HARRIS, GEORGE ANDERSON, b. Los Angeles, Aug. 24, 1946; B.S. in Fin., U. So. Calif., 1968, J.D., 1971, M.B.A., 1973. Admitted to Calif. bar, 1972; law clk. Simon, Sheridan, Murphy, Thornton & Medven, 1970-71; asst. resident atty. Prudential Ins. Co. Am., 1973; asst. v.p., legal counsel Alison Mortgage Investment Trust, 1973-75; v.p., gen. mgr. BanCal Tri-State Mortgage Co., 1975-76; v.p. Umet Trust, Beverly Hills, Calif., 1976—. Mem. Am., Los Angeles County bar assns. Licensed real estate broker, Calif. Home: 1508 W Huntington Dr Alhambra CA 91801 Office: Suite 500 9595 Wilshire Blvd Beverly Hills CA 90212 Tel (213) 278-2101

HARRIS, GEORGE W., JR., b. Lynchburg, Va., Dec. 20, 1936; student U. Va., 1955-57; B.S. in Bus. Adminstrn., Va. Union U., 1963; J.D., N.C. Central U., 1967. Admitted to Va. bar, 1967; individual practice law, Roanoke, Va. Bd. dirs. Bur. Econ. Research and Devel., Va. State Coll., Hunton YMCA; Mem. Va. State Adv. Council, Nat. Legal Services Corp. Mem. Roanoke, Va., Am., Nat., bar assns. Home: 1802 Syracuse Ave NW Roanoke VA 24017 Office: 145 W Campbell Ave Suite 403 Roanoke VA 24011

HARRIS, GRACE SALZMAN, b. Pitts., July 12, 1929; B.A. in Edn., U. Pitts., 1951, J.D., 1968. Admitted to Pa. bar, 1968, U.S. Supreme Ct. bar, 1973; research asst., law clk. firm Baskin, Boreman, Sachs & Craig, Pitts., 1967; law clk. to chief judge U.S. Dist. Ct. for Western Pa., Pitts., 1968-69; asst. city solicitor City of Pitts. Dept. Law, 1970—, exec. asst. 1975—; chmn. Pitts. Bd. Water Assessors, 1971—; adj. instr. bus. law Allegheny Community Coll., 1970-71. Bd. dirs. Squirrel Hill Urban Coalition, Hebrew Inst., Beth Shalom Congregation. Mem. Am., Pa. (chmn. pub. records com.), Allegheny County (chmn. program com., vice-chmn., dir. taxation sect., dir. municipal and sch. solicitors' sect.) bar assns., Am. Judicature Soc., Pitts. Law Alumni Assn. (treas., gov.), Supreme Ct. Hist. Assn., ACLU (legal com.). Office: 313 City-County Bldg Grant St Pittsburgh PA 15219 Tel (412) 255-2014

HARRIS, H. REED, b. Chgo., Sept. 9, 1935; B.S., U. Colo., 1957; J.D., Northwestern U., 1960. Admitted to Ill. bar, 1960, U.S. Supreme Ct. bar, 1970; mem. firm Weisbard & Strauss, Chgo., 1960-62; individual practice law, Chgo., 1963—. Mem. Ill. State, Chgo. bar assns. Office: 39 S LaSalle St Chicago IL 60603 Tel (312) 346-4530

HARRIS, HAROLD ABRAHAM, b. N.Y.C., Sept. 27, 1912; LL.B., DePaul U., 1936, J.D., 1969. Admitted to Ill. bar, 1936; individual practice law, Chgo., 1936—. Mem. Chgo. Bar Assn., Decalogue Soc. Lawyers, Tech. Fund Assn. (past pres.). Home: 1055 Meadowbrook Ln Deerfield IL 60015 Office: 11 S LaSalle St Chicago IL 60603 Tel (312) 236-7587

HARRIS, HENRY, b. New London, Conn., Feb. 23, 1901; LL.B., Boston U., 1923, LL.M., 1927. Admitted to Conn. bar, 1923, Mass. bar, 1923; practice law, Pawcatuck, Conn.; dir. Washington Trust Co., Westerly Savs. Fund & Loan Assn. Mem. Conn., Am., London County bar assns. Home: 695 Pequot Ave New London CT 06320 Office: 6 Mechanic St Pawcatuck CT 06379 Tel (203) 599-5574

HARRIS, JAMES WITMER, b. Dodgeville, Wis., Nov. 7, 1944; B.S., U. Wis., 1966, J.D., 1974; M.A., U. Okla., 1971. Admitted to Wis. bar, 1974; clk. to judge Dane County (Wis.) Circuit Ct., 1973-74; individual practice law, Mineral Point, Wis., 1974—; counsel Mineral Point Unified Sch. Dist., 1974—, Meml. Hosp. of Iowa County (Wis.), 1974—, Mineral Point Twp., 1975—; city atty. City of Mineral Point, 1976—. Pres. council Hope Luth. Ch., Mineral Point, 1975-76; mem. Mineral Point Area Devel. Corp., 1976. Mem. Iowa County (pres. 1976—), Am. bar assns., State Bar Wis. Office: 249 High St Mineral Point WI 53565 Tel (608) 987-3351

HARRIS, JEAN LEONARD, b. San Diego, Mar. 15, 1939; B.S., San Diego State U., 1963; J.D., U. San Diego, 1970. Admitted to Calif. bar, 1971, U.S. Dist. Ct. for Calif. bar, 1971, U.S. Supreme Ct., 1977; dep. city atty. City of San Diego, 1971-73; sr. partner firm Harris, Daitch & Greenberg, San Diego, 1973-76; individual practice law, San Diego, 1976—. Pres. A St. Athletic Club, 1975-76; mem. Poway Planning and Devel. Commn., 1973-76. Mem. Am., Calif., San Diego bar assns., U. San Diego Alumni Assn. (dir. 1975-77), Phi Alpha Delta. Office: 233 A St Suite 204 San Diego CA 92101 Tel (714) 231-0646

HARRIS, JESSIE MOFFAT, b. Wheeling, W.Va., May 19, 1937; A.B., Duke U., 1959; J.D., Georgetown U., 1971. Admitted to D.C. bar, 1971; asso. firm Epstein, Friedman, Duncan & Medalie, Washington, 1971-74; individual practice law, Washington, 1974—; asso. with William B. Wolf, Jr., Washington, 1975—. Licensed real estate broker, D.C. Mem. D.C. Bar, Women's Bar Assn. D.C., Bar Assn. D.C. Home: 4401 W St NW Washington DC 20007 Office: 1001 Connecticut Ave NW Washington DC 20036 Tel (202) 296-3302

HARRIS, LYMAN HOWARD, b. Gadsden, Ala., Sept. 27, 1936; A.B., Presbyn. Coll., Clinton, S.C., 1958; J.D., Emory U., 1967. Claims rep. Liberty Mut. Ins. Co., Atlanta, 1960-62, Miami, Fla., 1962-63; claims rep. Am. Mut. Ins. Co., Atlanta, 1963-68, claims examiner, 1965-67; admitted to Ala. bar, 1967; asso. firm Lange, Simpson, Robinson & Somerville, Birmingham, Ala., 1967-70, partner, 1970—. Tchr. Sunday sch., elder Trinity Presbyn. Ch., Birmingham. Mem. Birmingham, Ala., Am. bar assns., Def. Lawyers Assn. Ala., Trial Attys. Am. Home: 906 Catherine St Birmingham AL 35215 Office: 1700 First Ala Bank Bldg Birmingham AL 35203 Tel (205) 252-9222

HARRIS, MICALYN SHAFER, b. Chgo., Oct. 31, 1941; A.B. (Coll. scholar), Wellesley Coll., 1963; J.D., U. Chgo., 1966. Admitted to Ill. bar, 1966, Mo. bar, 1967; law clk. to Judge James H. Meredith, U.S. Dist. Ct., Eastern Dist. Mo., 1967-68; atty. May Dept. Stores Co., St. Louis, 1968-70, Ralston Purina Co., St. Louis, 1970-72; asst. sec. Chromalloy Am. Corp., St. Louis, 1972-76; asso. firm Paul H. Schramm, St. Louis, 1976—. Mem. exec. bd., chmn. com. on status of women Am. Jewish Com., 1974—. Mem. Mo. (chmn. com. internat. law), Chgo. bar assns., Bar Assn. Met. St. Louis (co-chmn. TV com). Home: 15188 Isleview Dr Ballwin MO 63011 Office: 120 S Central Ave Saint Louis MO 63105 Tel (314) 721-5321

HARRIS, MICHAEL, b. London, Oct. 24, 1935; B.A., Stanford, 1956; J.D., U. Calif. at Los Angeles, 1959. Admitted to Calif. bar, 1960, U.S. Supreme Ct. bar, 1964; legal counsel The Mirisch Co., Los Angeles, 1960-63; mem. firm Rogers & Harris, Los Angeles, 1963—. Bd. dirs. Lake Sherwood Mutual Water; pres. Brentwood Homeowners Assn. Mem. Los Angeles, Beverly Hills, Hollywood bar assns., Copyright Soc. Contbr. articles to legal jours. Home: 635 Tuallitan Rd Los Angeles CA 90049 Office: 9200 Sunset Blvd Los Angeles CA 90049 Tel (213) 278-3142

HARRIS, MICHAEL ROBERT, b. Phila., Nov. 7, 1940; B.S. in Econs., U. Pa., 1962; J.D., Harvard, 1965; M.A., Villanova U., 1967; LL.M., N.Y. U., 1970. Admitted to Pa. bar, 1965, Fla. bar, 1973; asso. firm Mesirov, Gelman, Jaffe & Levin, Phila. 1965-67, Goodis, Greenfield, Narin & Mann, Phila., 1967-70; partner firm Krekstein, Yoalin, Wolfson & Harris, Phila., 1970-76; mem. firm Spencer Sherr & Moses, Norristown, Pa., 1976—. Mem. Am., Pa., Phila., Fla., Mont. County bar assns. Contbr. articles to legal jours. Home: 726 John Barry Dr Bryn Mawr PA 19010 Office: 107 E Main St Norristown PA 19401 Tel (215) 279-5300

HARRIS, MORTON ALLEN, b. Columbus, Ga., Mar. 13, 1934; B.B.A. summa cum laude, Emory U., 1956; LL.B., J.D., Harvard, 1959. Admitted to Ga. bar, 1959; mem. firm Page, Scrantom, Harris, McGlamry & Chapman, Columbus, 1961—; lectr. Great Plains Tax Inst., N.Mex. Tax Inst., N.Y. U. Inst. Fed. Taxation, Va. Conf. Fed. Taxation, Ga. Inst. Continuing Legal Edn., Ali-Aba Tax Seminars. Mem. exec. bd. NCCJ, Columbus, 1970—; bd. dirs. Bradley Center, Columbus, 1971—; mem. exec. com., bd. govs. Health Systems Agy. of Central Ga., 1976—; mem. Muscogee County (Ga.) Bd. Edn., 1972—, v.p., 1976-77; trustee Temple Israel, Columbus, 1966-68. Mem. Am. Bar Assn. (vice chmn. taxation sect. com. on profl. service corps.), State Bar Ga. (legis. com. fiduciary law sect.), Columbus Lawyers Club, Columbus Estate Planning Council, Am. Judicature Soc., So. Pension Conf., Beta Gamma Sigma. Editor Harvard Law Sch. Ann., 1958-59. Home: 2854 Cromwell Dr Columbus GA 31906 Office: 1043 3d Ave Columbus GA 31902 Tel (404) 324-0251

HARRIS, PATRICIA ROBERTS, b. Mattoon, Ill., May 31, 1924; A.B summa cum laude, Howard U., 1945; J.D. with honors, George Washington U., 1960; LL.D., Lindenwood Coll., 1967, Morgan State Coll., 1967, Russell Sage Coll., 1970, Tufts U., 1970, Dartmouth Coll., 1970, Johns Hopkins U., 1971, MacMurray Coll., 1971, U. Md., 1971, Williams Coll., 1971, Ripon Coll., 1972, Brown U., 1972, Wilberforce U., 1973, Aquinas Coll., 1973, Colby Coll., 1973, Brandeis U., 1973, No. Mich. U., 1973, U. Mich., 1973, Smith Coll., 1974, Wittenberg U., 1974, U. Mass., 1975, U. Portland, 1975, Chestnut Hill Coll., 1975, Coll. New Rochelle, 1975, Atlanta U., 1976, Adelphia U., 1976, Kent State U., 1976, Spelman Coll., 1977, Knox Coll., 1977; D.H.L., Miami U., Oxford, Ohio, 1967, Newton Coll. of Sacred Heart, 1972; D.C.L., Beaver Coll., 1968; P.Sc.D., Rollins Coll., 1974. Program dir. work with indsl. women YWCA, Chgo., 1946-49; asst. dir. Am. Council on Human Rights, Washington, 1949-53; exec. dir. Delta Sigma Theta, Washington, 1953-59; admitted to D.C. bar, U.S. Supreme Ct. bar, 1960; atty. sect. appeals and research, criminal div. Dept. Justice, Washington, 1960-61; asso. dean students, lectr. in law Howard U., 1961-63, asso. prof., 1963-65, prof. Sch. Law, 1967-69, dean, 1969; U.S. ambassador to Luxembourg, 1965-67; partner firm Fried, Frank, Harris, Shriver & Kampelman, Washington, 1970-77; sec. HUD, Washington, 1977—; former dir. 20th Century Fund, Scott Paper Co., IBM, Chase Manhattan Bank; mem. com. on grievances U.S. Dist. Ct. for D.C., 1971-77; chmn. D.C. Law Revision Commn., 1975-77. Mem. exec. bd. NAACP Legal Def. Fund, 1967-77; mem. Rockefeller U. Council, 1972-77; at-large mem. Democratic Nat. Com., 1973-77. Mem. Am., Fed. bar assns., Order of Coif, Phi Beta Kappa, Kappa Beta Pi, Delta Sigma Theta (Distinguished Service award 1963). Decorated Order of Oaken Crown Luxembourg Govt., 1967; recipient Centennial citation Wilson Coll., 1969; Emma V. Kelly award Daus. Elks, 1968; Distinguished Achievement award Women's Com. Yeshiva U., 1968; Distinguished Alumni award Howard U., 1966; Alumni Achievement award George Washington U., 1965; One Nation award Phila. Action br. NAACP, 1972; Achievement award in professions Black Enterprise, 1976; award in honor of women dirs. of corps. Catalyst, 1976; named Woman of Year Women's Aux. Jewish War Vets., 1968; Woman of Year in Bus. and Professions Ladies Home Jour. awards, 1974; medal of achievement Yale Women's Forum, 1976. Office: Dept Housing and Urban Devel Washington DC 20410

HARRIS, RICHARD BATES, b. Boston, Mar. 12, 1932; B.A., U. Rochester, 1954; J.D., New Eng. Sch. Law, 1964. Admitted to Mass. bar, 1964; individual practice law, Boston, 1964-69, Leominster, Mass., 1973—; asso. counsel No. Worcester County (Mass.) Legal Aid Soc., 1969-73; tchr. Centro Intercultural de Documentacion, Cuernavaca, Mexico, summers 1970-72; instr. law Mt. Wachusett Community Coll., 1972-73. Mass. Republican State committeeman, 1976—. Mem. Am., Worcester County, No. Worcester County, No. Middlesex bar assns., Am. Arbitration Assn. (panel), Assn. Trial

Lawyers Am. Office: 11 Park St Leominster MA 01453 Tel (617) 537-0653

HARRIS, RICHARD EUGENE VASSAU, b. Detroit, Mar. 16, 1945; B.A., Albion Coll., 1972; J.D., Harvard U., 1970; postgrad. Inst. Advanced Legal Studies, London 1970-71. Admitted to Calif. bar, 1972; asso. firm Orrick, Herrington, Rowley & Sutcliffe, San Francisco, 1972—. Mem. San Francisco Bar Assn., Barristers Club, Harvard Law Sch. Assn., Harvard Club of No. Calif., World Affairs Council of No. Calif. Home: 401 Hyde St San Francisco CA 94109 Office: 600 Montgomery St San Francisco CA 94111 Tel (415) 392-1122

HARRIS, RONALD EMMETT, b. Houston, Aug. 16, 1939; student Baylor U., Waco, Tex. 1957-58; B.S., J.D., U. Houston. Admitted to Tex. bar, 1963; partner firm Kessler, Nichols & Harris, Uvalde, Tex., 1967-76, firm Harris & Vaughan, Uvalde, 1976—. Mem. Uvalde Consol. Ind. Sch. Dist. Bd., 1971—; chmn. Uvalde County (Tex.) Bicentennial Com., 1976—. Mem. Am. Bar Assn., State Bar Tex. Home: 618 Farel Circle Uvalde TX 78801 Office: First State Bank Bldg Uvalde TX 78801 Tel (513) 278-2559

HARRIS, RUTH MORRISON, b. Chgo.; B.S., M.A., Northwestern U.; J.D., DePaul U.; postgrad. U. Chgo., Columbia. Admitted to Ill. bar, 1956; tchr. Chgo. Bd. Edn., 1949-77; individual practice law, Chgo., 1957-60, 65—; asso. firm Stratford, LaFontant and Fisher, Chgo., 1962-65; law clk. to U.S. atty., 1956-57; legal advisor clinic Ch. Fedn., Lawndale (Chgo.), 1966-69. Mem. Am., Chgo., Ill. State, Midwest, Fed. bar assns., Chgo. Council on Fgn. Relations. Home: 2626 Lakeview Ave Chicago IL 60614

HARRIS, SAMUEL WILLIAM, b. St. Petersburg, Fla., May 12, 1919; B.A., Vanderbilt U., 1941; LL.B., U. Fla., 1948, J.D., 1967. Admitted to Fla. bar, 1948; asso. firm Lincoln C. Bogue (now Harris & Brahm), St. Petersburg, 1948-49, partner, 1949—. Mem. St. Petersburg Civitan Club, 1950—, pres., 1956. Mem. Am., St. Petersburg (past pres.), Fla. bar assns. Office: Suite 205 300 West Bldg 3151 3d Ave N Saint Petersburg FL 33713 Tel (813) 821-4026

HARRIS, SAMUEL WILLIAM, b. Newark, July 10, 1905; LL.B., Rutgers U., 1926. Admitted to N.J. bar, 1927, Fla. bar, 1964; asso. firm Charles Hood, Newark, 1927-29; asso. Freund, Newark, 1929-31; partner firm Harris & Harris, Newark, 1931-42; practice law, Orlando, Fla., 1962—. Mem. N.J., Fla., Essex County, Orange County bar assns. Home: 3513 Wilder Ln Orlando FL 32804 Office: 100 S Orange Ave Orlando FL 32801 Tel (305) 423-2244

HARRIS, STEPHEN BATEMAN, b. Phila., Dec. 16, 1942; B.A., Lehigh U., 1964, B.S. in Chem. Engring., 1965; LL.B., Harvard, 1968. Admitted to Pa. bar, 1968, U.S. Supreme Ct. bar, 1972; with Bucks County Dist. Atty.'s Office, Doylestown, Pa., 1968—, 1st asst. dist. atty., 1972—; partner firm Harris & Harris, Warrington, Pa., 1971—. Mem. bd. dirs. Bucks County Dept. Child Welfare, 1970—, v.p., 1976—; mem. multi-disciplinary team for child abuse, Bucks County, 1976—. Mem. Bucks County (dir.), Pa. (zone del.), Am. bar assns., Am. Acad. Forensic Scis., Harvard Assos. Police Sci. Home: Box 116 R D #2 New Hope PA 18938 Office: 1760 Bristol Rd Box 160 Warrington PA 18976 Tel (215) 343-9000

HARRIS, STEPHEN HARRY, b. Richmond, Va., May 10, 1946; B.A. in History, U. Va., 1968; J.D., U. Ga., 1971. Admitted to Ga. bar, 1971, D.C. bar, 1972, U.S. Dist. Ct. bar, 1971; law clk. firm Falligant, Doremus, Karsman & Maurice, Savannah, Ga., 1969-71; asso. firm Falligant, Doremus, Karsman, Kent & Toporek, P.C., Savannah, 1971-74; partner firm Harris & Jackson, Savannah, 1974, pres., 1974-75, Stephen H. Harris, P.C., Savannah, 1974—; instr. John Marshall Law Sch., 1974. Mem. Am., Savannah, D.C. bar assns., State Bar of Ga., The Fed. Bar, Am. Trial Lawyers Assn., Ga. Trial Lawyers Assn., Assn. Criminal Def. Lawyers, Assn. Trial Lawyers Am., Savannah C. of C., NCCJ, Savannah Better Bus. Bur. Home: 412 E 53d St Savannah GA 31405 Office: POB 8998 Savannah GA 31402 Tel (912) 234-8051

HARRIS, STEPHEN JOHN, b. Pitts., Aug. 7, 1931; B.B.S., U. Pitts., 1953, LL.B., 1956. Admitted to Pa. bar, 1959; mem. firm Litman Litman Harris and Specter, Pitts., 1969—. Mem. Am., Allegheny County bar assns. Home: 1031 Washington Rd Pittsburgh PA 15228 Office: Grant Bldg 300 Grant St Pittsburgh PA 15219 Tel (412) 456-2000

HARRIS, WALTER BAKER, b. Jackson, Tenn., July 10, 1931; student Southwestern U., Memphis, 1949-51; LL.B., U. Tenn., 1954. Admitted to Tenn. bar, 1954; law specialist USN, 1955-58; asso. firm Schneider, Schneider & Harris, 1958-61; individual practice law, 1961-72; judge City Ct., Jackson, 1967-71, 71-72, Madison County (Tenn.) Ct., 1972—. Mem. Tenn. County Services Assn. (pres. 1975-76), Tenn., Nat. councils juvenile judges, Tenn. Commn. Children and Youth. Home: 319 Crescent St Jackson TN 38301 Office: Madison County Courthouse Jackson TN 38301 Tel (901) 427-9441

HARRIS, WAYNE MANLEY, b. Pittsford, N.Y., Dec. 28, 1925; LL.B., Albany Law Sch., 1951. Admitted to N.Y. State bar, 1952, U.S. Supreme Ct. bar, 1958; pres. Delta Labs., Inc., Rochester, N.Y., 1971—. Past pres Monroe County Conservation Council Inc. Mem. N.Y. State Bar Assn. Recipient Am. Motors award in Conservation, 1971. Home: Austin Rd Fairport NY 14450 Office: 220 Powers Bldg Main St Rochester NY 14614 Tel (716) 454-6950

HARRIS, WENDELL VARNER, b. Ringgold, Ga., Dec. 29, 1914; student Berry Coll., 1931-32, Ala. Poly. Inst., 1936; A.B., George Washington U., 1942; LL.B., U. Ga., 1948. Admitted to Ga. bar, 1947, Tenn. bar, 1948, Calif. bar, 1949; observer U.S. Weather Bur., Jacksonville, Fla., and Washington, 1936-40, officer in charge, Athens, Ga., 1946-48; economist WPB, Washington, 1941-42; individual practice law, Los Angeles, 1949-52, Fontana, Calif., 1953—; judge justice ct. Bloomington Jud. Dist., 1956-58. Mem. Am., Calif., San Bernardino County bar assns., Phi Alpha Delta. Home: 10973 Catawba Ave Fontana CA 92335 Office: 9461 Sierra Ave Fontana CA 92335 Tel (714) 822-3717

HARRIS, WILLIAM HENRY, b. Phila., Apr. 28, 1943; B.S., N.Mex. State U., 1966; M.B.A., Ariz. State U., 1970, J.D., 1972. Admitted to Ariz. bar, 1972, U.S. Supreme Ct. bar, 1976; individual practice law, Mesa, Ariz., 1974, Phoenix and Tempe, Ariz., 1974-75; partner firm Wiltbank, Peterson & Harris, Mesa, 1974; mem. firms Richard L. Basinger & Assos., Scottsdale, Ariz., 1975-76, Howard M. Klein, Phoenix, 1976—. Mem. State Bar Ariz., Maricopa County (Ariz.), Am. bar assns. Office: 237 E Virginia St Phoenix AZ 85004 Tel (602) 254-5311

HARRISON, BRUCE REMINGTON, b. Uniontown, Pa., Oct. 16, 1927; LL.B., Howard U., 1952. Admitted to D.C. bar, 1954, Md. bar, 1964; asso. firm Robertson & Roundtree, Washington, 1954-60; individual practice law, Washington, 1960-62; partner firm Harrison & Myrick, Washington, 1962-67; individual practice law, Seat Pleasant, Md., 1968—. Mem. Md. State, Prince George's County, Nat., Washington, D.C. bar assns. Office: 6819 George Palmer Hwy Seat Pleasant MD 20027 Tel (301) 336-3900

HARRISON, CHARLES JULIAN, b. Balt., Apr. 13, 1937; B.A., U. Md., 1960; J.D., U. Balt., 1964. Admitted to Md. bar, 1964; individual practice law, Balt., 1964—; chmn. Md. Home Improvement Commn., 1970—. Mem. Am., Md. State bar assns. Office: Suite 200 Everett Bldg 660 Kenilworth Dr Towson MD 21204 Tel (301) 821-9090

HARRISON, CHARLES MAURICE, b. Anderson, S.C., Aug. 30, 1927; A.B., Marshall U., 1949; J.D., W. Va. U., 1952; Admitted to W. Va. bar, 1952, D.C. bar, 1958, N.Y. bar, 1965, N.J. bar, 1972; legal asst. W. Va. Ins. Commn., 1952-54; dir. motor carrier div., hearing examiner Pub. Service Commn. W. Va., 1954-57; atty. Chesapeake and Potomac Tel. Cos. Group Headquarters, Washington, 1957-60; atty. Chesapeake and Potomac Tel. Co., Washington, 1960-63; atty. Chesapeake and Potomac Tel. Co. of W. Va., Charleston, 1963-64; tax. atty. mem. gen. attys. orgn., dir. Mfr.'s Junction Ry. subs. Western Electric, 1964-69; gen. atty., sec., treas. Bellcomm, Inc., Washington, 1969-71; asst. gen. counsel, asst. sec. Bell Tel. Labs., Murray Hill, N.J., 1971-75, gen. atty., sec., 1975-76, sec., gen. counsel corp. matters, 1976—. Mem. govt. relations com. Research and Devel. Council N.J., 1974; chmn. adminstrv. bd. Bridgewater United Meth. Ch., 1975—; mem. employment practices com. Bridgewater-Raritan Sch. Dist., 1977; trustee, chmn. pub. relations com. Family Counseling Service Somerset County, 1975—. Mem. W. Va., N.J., Am. bar assns., D.C. Bar, W. Va. State Bar, N.J. Assn. Corp. Counsel. Office: 600 Mountain Ave Murray Hill NJ 07974 Tel (201) 582-4948

HARRISON, EARL DAVID, b. Bryn Mawr, Pa., Aug. 25, 1932; B.A., Harvard, 1954; J.D., U. Pa., 1960. Admitted to D.C. bar, 1960; partner firm Marshall and Harrison, Washington, 1965-70; individual practice law, Washington, 1970—. Mem. Am., D.C. bar assns. Office: Suite 1030 1707 L St NW Washington DC 20036 Tel (202) 833-2353

HARRISON, EDWARD JAMES, b. Streator, Ill., June 21, 1926; B.S. in Law, U. Ill., Urbana, 1950, J.D., 1952. Admitted to Ill. bar, 1951, Tex. bar, 1974; asst. trade regulation counsel, bus. trainee Gen. Electric Co., N.Y.C. and Bridgeport, Conn., 1952-55; atty. antitrust div. Dept. Justice, Washington, 1955-60; internat. atty. Westinghouse Electric Corp., N.Y.C., 1960-66, chief counsel for internat. and East coast ops., 1966-69; v.p., sec., gen. counsel J.I. Case Co., Racine, Wis., 1969-74; sr. v.p., gen. counsel Tenneco, Inc., Houston, 1974-76; v.p., gen. counsel Esmark, Inc., Chgo., 1976—. Mem. Am., Fed., Tex., Ill., Chgo. bar assns. Home: 1119 N Sheridan Rd Lake Forest IL 60045 Office: 55 E Monroe St Chicago IL 60603 Tel (312) 431-3618

HARRISON, FRANK GIRARD, b. Washington, Feb. 2, 1940; A.B., King's Coll., 1961; LL.B., Harvard, 1964. Admitted to Pa. bar, 1965; individual practice, Wilkes-Barre, Pa., 1965-66; served with JAC, U.S. Air Force, 1966-69; asso. firm Rosenn, Jenkins & Greenwald, Wilkes-Barre, 1969-71, counsel, 1972—; lectr. govt. and politics King's Coll., Wilkes-Barre, 1969—. Bd. dirs. United Way Wyoming Valley, Luzerne County, Pa., 1973—, chmn. planning, allocations and resource devel. com. 1974-75, v.p., 1975—; bd. dirs. Commn. Economic Opportunity Luzerne County, 1972—; dir., Grit, Inc., Wilkes-Barre, 1972—, pres., 1972-74; dir. Osterhout Free Library, 1976—; chmn. Downtown Devel. Authority Wilkes-Barre City, 1976—; chmn. Luzerne Bicentennial Commn., 1975-76. Mem. Wilkes-Barre Law and Library Assn., Luzerne County Bar Assn. Recipient distinguished service award Wilkes-Barre Jaycees, 1976. Home: 120 W Ross St Wilkes-Barre PA 18702 Office: 1000 Blue Cross Bldg Wilkes-Barre PA 18711 Tel (717) 829-0511

HARRISON, GORDON FRANCIS, b. Providence, Sept. 20, 1914; Ph.B., Providence Coll., 1935; LL.B., Georgetown U., 1941; LL.M., George Washington U., 1952. Admitted to D.C. bar, 1940, U.S. Supreme Ct. bar, 1955; individual practice law, Washington, 1973—; trial atty. Dept. Justice, 1946-54; chief counsel, staff dir. U.S. Senate Com. Rules and Adminstr., 1955-72; capt. JAGC, USNR, ret. Mem. Am., Fed. bar assns., Am. Soc. Internat. Law. Editor: (with others) U.S. Senate Manual, 1957-71. Home: 6007 Softwood Trail McLean VA 22101 Office: 2101 L St NW Suite 203 Washington DC 20037 Tel (202) 785-1636

HARRISON, GRESHAM HUGHEL, b. Johnson County, Ga., June 19, 1924; LL.B., Mercer U., 1954, J.D., 1970. Admitted to Ga. bar, 1955, U.S. Supreme Ct. bar, 1961; asst. atty. gen. State of Ga., 1956-63; individual practice law, Lawrenceville, Ga., 1963—; judge recorders Ct. Gwinnett County (Ga.), 1972—. Mem. Am., Ga., Gwinnett County bar assns., Am. Judicature Soc. Office: POB 88 Lawrenceville GA 30246 Tel (404) 963-3421

HARRISON, JAMES THOMAS, b. Hankinson, N.D., Apr. 4, 1903; LL.B., St. Paul Coll. Law, 1926. Admitted to Minn. bar, 1927, N.D. bar, 1927, Mont. bar, 1930; practiced in Minot, N.D., 1927-28; ct. reporter Glasgow (Mont.) Dist. Ct., 1929-38; individual practice law, Malta, Mont., 1938-56; chief justice Mont. Supreme Ct., 1957-77; city atty. City of Malta, 1939-48; county atty. Phillips County (Mont.), 1948-54; chmn. Mont. Parole Bd., 1956-57. Mem. Am. Judicature Soc., State Bar Mont. Home: 1616 Highland St Helena MT 59601 Office: 2225 11th Ave Helena MT 59601 Tel (406) 442-6350

HARRISON, KARL CECIL, b. Columbiana, Ala., Dec. 29, 1907; student U. Ala., 1925-27; grad. Birmingham Sch. Law, 1934; grad. Am. Inst. Banking, 1930. Admitted to Ala. bar, 1934; individual practice law, Columbiana, 1936—; mem. Ala. State Senate, 1939-43, Ala. Ho. of Reps., 1947-55; chmn. bd. First Nat. Bank of Columbiana, also v.p.; dir. Peoples Bank of Pell City. Del., Democratic Nat. Conv., 1952. Mem. Ala., Shelby County bar assns. Home: Pine Hill St Columbiana AL 35051 Office: PO Box 557 Main St Columbiana AL 35051 Tel (205) 669-6701

HARRISON, LAWRENCE WADE, JR., b. Memphis, Oct. 6, 1938; B.S., Memphis State U., 1961; LL.B., 1963. Admitted to Tenn. bar, 1964; atty. Security Title Co., Memphis, 1970-75; partner firm Thompson & Harrison, Memphis, 1976—. Pres. Memphis Speakers Club. Mem. Memphis, Shelby County bar assns. Home: 2302 Lochlevin Memphis TN 38138 Office: 5575 Poplar #409 Memphis TN 38117 Tel (901) 682-8476

HARRISON, MARION EDWYN, b. Phila., Sept. 17, 1931; B.A., U. Va., 1951; LL.B., George Washington U., 1954, LL.M., 1959. Admitted to Va. bar, 1954, D.C. bar, 1958, U.S. Supreme Ct. bar, 1958; spl. asst. to gen. counsel Post Office Dept., 1958-60, asso. gen. counsel, 1960-61, mem. bd. contract appeals, 1958-61; partner firm Harrison, Lucey & Sagle and predecessors, Washington, 1961—. Mem. council Adminstrv. Conf. U.S., 1971—; mem. D.C. Law Revision Commn., 1975—. Bd. visitors JAG Sch., Charlottesville, Va., 1976—. Fellow Am. Bar Found.; mem. Am. (chmn. sect. adminstrv. law 1974-75), Fed., Inter-Am. bar assns., Bar Assn. D.C. (chmn. adminstrv. law sect. 1970-71, bd. dirs. 1971-72), George Washington U. Law Assn. (pres. 1974-77). Contbr. articles to profl. jours. Editor-in-chief Fed. Bar News, 1960-63. Home: 4526 N 41st St Arlington VA 22207 Office: 1701 Pennsylvania Ave NW Washington DC 20006 Tel (202) 298-9030

HARRISON, MARK I., b. Pitts., Oct. 17, 1934; A.B., Antioch Coll., 1957; LL.B., Harvard, 1960. Admitted to Ariz. bar, 1961, U.S. Supreme Ct. bar, 1968; law clk. to judge Ariz. Supreme Ct., 1960-61; partner firm Harrison, Myers & Singer, Phoenix, 1966—. Chmn. Phoenix Citizens Bond Adv. Com., 1976—. Mem. Am., Maricopa County (past pres.) bar assns., State Bar Ariz. (pres. 1975-76), Nat. Conf. Bar Pres.'s (pres. elect 1976-77, mem. exec. council 1971-73, 76—), Am. Trial Lawyers Assn., Def. Research Inst., Phoenix Assn. Def. Counsel, Am. Bd. Trial Advocates. Co-author: Arizona Appellate Practice, 1966. Office: 111 W Monroe Suite 1200 Phoenix AZ 85003 Tel (602) 252-7181

HARRISON, MARTIN LEIGH, b. Opelika, Ala., Apr. 4, 1907; A.B., U. Ala., 1927, LL.B., 1929, LL.D., 1959; LL.M., Harvard, 1935. Admitted to Ala. bar, 1929; individual practice law, Birmingham, Ala., 1929-34; instr. Law Sch. So. Methodist Univ., Dallas, 1935-38; asst. prof. law U. Ala., 1938-40, asso. prof., 1940-44, prof., 1944-66, dean, 1950-66, Warner prof., 1966—; research dir. Ala. Constl. Commn., 1970-75. Mem. Am., Ala. bar assns. Contbr. law rev. articles. Home: 29 Beech Hills Tuscaloosa AL 35401 Office: Law School University Alabama University AL 35486 Tel (205) 348-5930

HARRISON, ORVAL CHADWICK, b. Afton, Wyo., Jan. 15, 1940; B.S. in Civil Engring., U. Wyo., 1962; J.D., U. Mich., 1965. Admitted to Wyo. bar, 1965, Utah bar, 1966, Fed. bar, 1965, U.S. Ct. Claims bar, 1976; partner firm Fuller, Beesley & Harrison, Salt Lake City, Utah, 1966—; mem. Utah House Reps., 1977—. Mem. Am. Bar Assn. Contbr. articles to legal jours. Home: 1781 Hollywood Ave Salt Lake City UT 84108 Office: 15 E 4th S St Salt Lake City UT 84111 Tel (801) 328-0111

HARRISON, PATRICK WOODS, b. St. Louis, July 14, 1946; B.S., Ind. U., 1968, J.D., 1972. Admitted to Ind. bar, 1973, U.S. Dist. Ct. Ind., 1973; partner firm Goltra & Harrison, Columbus, Ind., 1974—. Mem. Am., Ind. bar assns., Ind. Trial Lawyers Assn., Am. Arbitration Assn. (arbitrator). Home: 4535 Woodcrest Dr Columbus IN 47201 Office: 415 Washington St Columbus IN 47201 Tel (812) 372-7897

HARRISON, REESE LENWOOD, JR., b. San Antonio, Jan. 5, 1938; B.B.A., Baylor U., 1959, M.S., 1965; J.D., So. Meth. U., 1962. Admitted to Tex. bar, 1962, U.S. Supreme Ct. bar, 1968, U.S. Ct. Customs and Patent Appeals, 1968, U.S. Ct. Claims, 1968, U.S. Tax Ct., 1972, U.S. Customs Ct. bar, 1973; chief asst. U.S. atty. U.S. Dept. Justice for Western Dist. Tex., 1964-72, spl. asst. U.S. atty., 1972-73; partner firm Oppenheimer, Rosenberg, Kelleher & Wheatley, San Antonio, 1972—; staff judge adv. Tex. Air N.G., 1963—; mil. judge, Tex., 1975—; mem. criminal justice com. Alamo Area Council Govts., 1966-71; cons. SSS, San Antonio, 1972-75. Vice pres. San Antonio Charity Horse Show, 1976, dir.; life dir. San Antonio Stock Show and Rodeo. Mem. Am., Fed. (pres. San Antonio chpt. 1971-72), Inter-Am., Internat., San Antonio bar assns., Nat. Dist. Attys. Assn., Judge Advs. Assn., Am. Judicature Soc., Assn. Trial Lawyers Am. Named Outstanding Young Man of San Antonio, San Antonio Jr. C. of C., 1973; contbr. articles to legal jours. Home: 11630 Sandman San Antonio TX 78205 Office: 711 Navarro St Suite 620 San Antonio TX 78205 Tel (512) 224-7581

HARRISON, WILLIAM K., b. Cin., Apr. 3, 1933; B.A., Vanderbilt U., 1954; J.D., U. Va., 1959. Admitted to Ohio bar, 1959, Ga. bar, 1965; asso. firm Frost & Jacobs, Cin., 1959-64; with law dept. Gulf Oil Corp., Atlanta, 1964-65; with legal dept. Merrell-Nat. Labs. div. Richardson-Merrell Inc., Cin., 1965—. Mem. Cin., Ohio State, Am. bar assns., Reading C. of C. (founder, pres. Ohio 1975—). Home: 8230 Hopewell Rd Cincinnati OH 45242 Office: 110 E Amity Rd Cincinnati OH 45215 Tel (513) 948-9111

HARRISON, WILLIAM OLIVER, JR., b. Corpus Christi, Tex., Oct. 16, 1945; B.A., Tex. Christian U., 1967; J.D., U. Tex., 1970. Admitted to Tex. bar, 1971; asso. firm Wood, Burney, Nesbitt & Ryan, Corpus Christi, 1971-75; individual practice law, Corpus Christi, 1975—. Mem. steering com. Goals for Corpus Christi, 1973-75; mem., 1st chmn. Leadership Corpus Christi; dir. Corpus Christi Area Conv. and Tourist Bur., 1977—. Mem. Am., Tex., Corpus Christi, Nueces County (sec. 1972) bar assns., Corpus Christi C. of C. (dir. 1973-75). Office: 5333 Everhart St Suite 125 Corpus Christi TX 78411 Tel (512) 855-3371

HARROD, SAMUEL GLENN, III, b. Peoria, Ill., May 10, 1940; B.A., Eureka Coll., 1962; J.D., U. Ill., 1964. Admitted to Ill. bar 1964, U.S. Supreme Ct. bar, 1976; partner firm Harrod & Harrod, Eureka, Ill., 1964-66; asso. judge 11th Circuit Ct. of Ill. Woodford County, Eureka, 1966-71, judge 1971—; vis. faculty Coll. Law U. Ill., 1970—; lectr. Eureka Coll., 1975. Past pres., past chmn. Central Ill. Youth Advisory Council; vice chmn., sec. Eureka Coll. Trustees; past sec., bd. mem., deacon Eureka Christian Ch. Mem. Ill. Judges Assn. (dir. 1970-71), Ill. State Bar Assn. (family law study com.), Woodford County Bar Assn., Am. Bar Assn. Recipient Order of the Arrow, Boy Scouts Am., 1955. Office: Woodford County Ct House Eureka IL 61530 Tel (309) 467-2131

HARROLD, BERNARD EUGENE, b. Wells County, Ind., Feb. 5, 1925; A.B., Ind. U., 1949, LL.B., 1951. Admitted to Ill. bar, 1951, U.S. Dist. Ct. bar, 1952, Circuit Ct. of Appeals bar, 1961, U.S. Supreme Ct. bar, 1971; asso., then partner firm Kirkland Ellis Hodson Chaffetz & Masters, Chgo., 1951-67; sr. partner firm Wildman, Harrold, Allen & Dixon, Chgo., 1967—. Mem. Winnetka Caucus Com., 1967. Mem. Am., Ill. State, Chgo., Internat., Inter-Am. bar assns., Law Club, Soc. of Trial Lawyers. Office: One IBM Plaza Chicago IL 60611 Tel (312) 222-0400

HARSHBARGER, LUTHER SCOTT, b. New Haven, Dec. 1, 1941; B.A., Harvard U., 1964, LL.B., 1968; postgrad. (Rockefeller fellow 1964-65) Union Theol. Sem., 1964-65. Admitted to Mass. bar, 1968; asso. firm Goodwin, Procter & Hoar, Boston, 1968-70; dir. Criminal Justice Project, Lawyer's Com. for Civil Rights, Boston, 1970-72; dep. chief counsel Mass. Defenders Com., Boston, 1972-75; chief pub. protection bur. dept. atty.-gen., Boston, 1975—; clin. asso. criminal trial advocacy Harvard Law Sch., 1972-73; supr. urban legal lab. Boston Coll. Law Sch., 1971. Bd. dirs. Justice Resources Inst., 1974—; mem. Boston Coordinating Council Drug Abuse, 1972—; treas.

Boston Lawyers Vietnam Com., 1969-72; bd. dirs. Greater Boston Legal Services, 1975—. Mem. Boston Bar Assn. Home: 14 Sacramento St Cambridge MA 02138 Office: One Ashburton Pl Boston MA 02108 Tel (617) 727-2207

HARSTAD, C. BLAINE, b. Harmony, Minn., Dec. 27, 1928; B.A. cum laude, Luther Coll., 1948; LL.B., U. Minn., 1956. Admitted to Minn. bar, 1956; now mem. firm Harstad & Rainbow, Mpls.; instr. U. Minn. Law Sch., 1960-65. Mem. Hennepin County (pres. 1977—), Minn. State, Am. bar assns., Order of Coif, Phi Delta Phi. Pres. bd. editors Minn. Law Rev., 1955-56. Office: 1038 Midland Bank Bldg Minneapolis MN 55401 Tel (612) 338-7811*

HART, BERNARD ELSHOFF, b. Medina, N.Y., Nov. 9, 1915; A.B., U. Rochester, 1936; LL.B., U. Mich., 1939. Admitted to N.Y. bar, 1939; individual practice law, Medina, 1946-49, 64-71; partner firm Skinner & Hart, Medina, 1949-64, firm Hart & Mack, Medina, 1971—; village justice Medina, 1946—. Mem. Orleans County (N.Y.) Bar Assn. Home: Erie St NE Medina NY 14103 Office: SA Cook Bldg Medina NY 14103 Tel (716) 798-1000

HART, B(UDDY) WARREN, b. Promise City, Iowa, Mar. 19, 1923; B.A., State U. Iowa, 1946; J.D., Harvard, 1950. Admitted to Minn. bar, 1951, U.S. Supreme Ct. Bar, 1971; law clk. to chief justice Minn. Supreme Ct., St. Paul, 1950; partner firm Moore, Costello & Hart, St. Paul, 1951—; city atty. City of West St. Paul, 1959-61; mem. ad hoc joint com. Fed. Judicial Conf. and Fed. Judicial Center, 1971; lectr., writer in field of constrn. industry litigation. Mem. exec. com. Indianhead council Boy Scouts Am., St. Paul, 1956-58; bd. dirs. St. Paul Community Chest, 1958-61, St. Croix Valley council Girl Scouts U.S.A., St. Paul, 1963-70; mem. St. Paul Mayor's Com. on Drug Abuse, 1969-70; elder House of Hope Presbyn. Ch., St. Paul, 1975—. Fellow Am. Coll. Trial Lawyers; mem. Am. Judicature Soc., Am. (nat. chmn. constrn. law com.; mem. fidelity and surety law com., pub. contract, litigation sects.), Minn., Ramsey County bar assns., Am. Arbitration Assn. (arbitrator 1960-64). Recipient Distinguished Service award St. Paul Jaycees, 1956. Home: 7455 S Robert Trail Inver Grove Heights MN 55075 Office: 1400 Northwestern National Bank Bldg 55 E 5th St Saint Paul MN 55101 Tel (612) 227-7683

HART, B(USTER) CLARENCE, b. Promise City, Iowa, Mar. 19, 1923; A.B., U. Iowa, 1947; J.D., Harvard, 1950. Admitted to Minn. bar, 1951, U.S. Ct. Mil. Appeals, 1956, U.S. Supreme Ct. bar, 1956; served to lt. col. JAGC U.S. Army, 1950-51; asso. and partner firm Briggs and Morgan, St. Paul, 1951—. Mem. bd. Lakewood Coll. Found., 1974-76; Minn. state pres., nat. v.p. Harvard Law Sch. Assn.; mem. Minn. Citizens Com. for Voyageurs Nat. Park, 1975—; pres. St. Paul Jr. C. of C., 1957-58; v.p. Downtown St. Paul, Inc., 1956-59; co-chmn. Neighborhood Div. United Fund, 1955, mem. bd. dirs. United Fund, 1958-61; mem. bd. St. Paul Athletic Club, 1969-70. Fellow Am. Coll. Trial Lawyers; mem. Am. (council ins. sect.), Minn. (chmn. ct. rules com.), Fed., Ramsey County bar assns., Internat. Assn. Ins. Counsel, Am. Trial Lawyers Assn., Am. Bd. Trial Advocates (advocate), Phi Beta Kappa. Named Outstanding Young Man of St. Paul, 1956. Contbr. articles to publs., papers, speeches to meetings. Office: W-2200 First Nat Bank Bldg Saint Paul MN 55101 Tel (612) 291-1215

HART, CHARLES EDWIN, 3D, b. Waterbury, Conn., Dec. 7, 1919; B.A., Yale, 1941; LL.B., Columbia, 1948. Admitted to N.Y. bar, 1948, Ohio bar, 1958, Calif. bar, 1961; asso. firm Chadbourne, Parke, Whiteside & Wolff, N.Y.C., 1948-51, 53-56; counsel Columbus (Ohio) div. North Am. Aviation, Inc., 1956-59, asst. gen. counsel, El Segundo, Calif., 1959-67; v.p. legal aerospace and systems group Rockwell Internat. Corp., El Segundo, 1967-71, staff v.p., asso. gen. counsel, 1971—. Sr. warden St. Matthew's Episcopal Ch., Pacific Palisades, Calif., 1964-65, 68-69; trustee Westlake Sch. for Girls, Los Angeles, 1973-76; mem. steering com. Los Angeles adv. council Episc. Ch. Found., 1976—. Mem. Am., Calif., Los Angeles County bar assns. Home: 563 Spoleto Dr Pacific Palisades CA 90272 Office: 2230 E Imperial Hwy El Segundo CA 90245 Tel (213) 647-5771

HART, FREDERICK MICHAEL, b. Flushing, N.Y., Dec. 5, 1929; B.S. in Math., Georgetown U., 1951, J.D., 1955; LL.M., N.Y. U., 1956; postgrad. (Peter Canisius fellow), U. Frankfurt (Germany), 1956-57. Admitted to D.C. bar, 1955, N.Y. bar, 1955, N. Mex. bar, 1970; instr. law N.Y. U., 1957-58, asst. prof., 1958-59, dir. food law program, 1957-59; prof. law Union U., 1959-61; asso. prof. law Boston Coll., 1961-62, prof., 1962-68; vis. prof. U. N.Mex., 1966-68, prof., 1968—; seminar leader Law Tchrs. Clinic. U. N.C., summer 1969; dir. indian law center U. N. Mex., 1968-70, dir. spl. scholarship program in law for Am. indians, 1967-72, dean sch. law, 1971—, pres. law sch. admissions council, 1974-76, chmn. research com., 1970-73, chmn. finance com., 1973-74. Mem. Assn. Am. Law Schs. (mem. govt. relations com. 1973; chmn. sect. on law sch. econs. 1973—), Am., N. Mex. State (chmn. supreme ct. com. on criminal law 1970—, Adminstrn. of Justice award 1972; Outstanding Service awards 1973, 74), Albuquerque Legal Aid Assn. (dir. 1970—), No. N. Mex. Legal Aid Soc. (dir. 1970-72), Better Bus. Bur. Consumer Arbitration Assn. (pres., chmn. 1971-73), N. Mex. Jud. Council. Author: Commercial Paper Under the Uniform Commercial Code, 1972; Collier on Bankruptcy, 1964; Drafting Techniques under the U.C.C., 1962; (with Willier) Forms and Procedures Under the Uniform Commercial Code, Vol. 1, 1963, vol. 2, 1969, Vol. 3, 1971; (with Willier and others) Uniform Commercial Code Reporter Digest, Vol. 1, 1965, Vol. 2, 1967, Vol. 3, 1968, Vol. 4, 1970, Vol. 5, 1972; (with Willier) Consumer Credit Handbook, 1969; contbr. articles and reviews to legal jours. Home: 1505 Cornell NE Albuquerque NM 87106 Office: Univ N Mex Sch Law Albuquerque NM 87131 Tel (505) 277-4700

HART, GEORGE MAXWELL, b. S.I., N.Y., Jan. 15, 1932; B.A., Wagner Coll., 1959; LL.B., N.Y. Law Sch., 1963, J.D., 1968. Admitted to N.Y. State bar, 1963, U.S. Supreme Ct. bar, 1967, U.S. Ct. Mil. Appeals bar, U.S. Tax Ct. bar, 1967; asso. firm Mitchell & Barker, N.Y.C., 1963-64; partner firm Hart & Gold, S.I., 1964-70, Tesnakis & Hart, S.I., 1970—; atty. Prudential Savs. & Loan Assn., 1969; counsel Serial Fed. Savs. & Loan Assn., N.Y.C., 1971—; local closing atty. Community Nat. Bank & Trust Co., N.Y.C., 1972—, East River Savs. Bank, 1973—; examining counsel U.S. Life Title Ins. Co., Chgo. Title Ins. Co., 1970—; counsel N.Y. State Senate, 1967-70. Republican candidate for dist. atty., S.I., 1971; law chmn. S.I. Republican County com., 1972, vice chmn., 1976. Mem. Richmond County (chmn. real estate com. 1967-68), N.Y. State bar assns. Mem. staff N.Y. Law Rev., 1962, articles editor, 1963; named Outstanding Young Man, Jaycees, 1968. Home: 190 Coverly Ave Staten Island NY 10301 Office: 25 Victory Blvd Staten Island NY 10301 Tel (212) 442-3600

HART, JAMES AUSTIN, b. Des Moines, Oct. 20, 1914; B.S. in Econs., Fordham U., 1936, M.A. in Econs., 1937, Ph.D. in Econs., 1940; J.D., Georgetown U., 1946. Admitted to Nebr. bar, 1946, Iowa bar, 1947, N.Y. State bar, 1955, D.C. bar, 1956, Ill. bar, 1969; individual practice law, Omaha, 1947-55, N.Y.C., 1955-58, Ill., 1968—; prof. fin. DePaul U., Chgo., 1958—, dean coll. commerce, 1958-71. Mem. Am. Bar Assn., Chgo. Assn. Commerce and Industry, Internat. Trade Club Chgo., Acad. Internat. Businesses, German-Am. C. of C. Contbr. articles to legal jours. Home: 294 Central St Highland Park IL 60035 Office: 7 S Dearborn Chicago IL 60603 Tel (312) 236-1586

HART, JAMES FREDERICK, b. Des Moines, Oct. 7, 1933; B.S., Henry's Coll.; LL.B., U. Ark., 1955. Admitted to Ark. bar, 1955, Tex. bar, 1963, N.Mex. bar, 1968; trial atty. IRS, Dallas, 1960-68; asso. firm, Clovis, N.Mex., 1968-74; individual practice law, Clovis, 1974—. Mem. Curry County (N.Mex.) Planning Commn. Mem. Am., N.Mex., Curry County bar assns. Home: 1415 Gidding St Clovis NM 88101 Office: 602 Mitchell St Clovis NM 88101 Tel (505) 762-7748

HART, JAMES POTTS, JR., b. Roanoke, Va., Oct. 18, 1907; B.C.E., Va. Mil. Inst., 1926; LL.B., U. Va., 1929. Admitted to Va. bar, 1929; partner firm Hart & Hart, Roanoke, 1929-34; atty. in charge loan service Memphis regional office Home Owners Loan Corp., 1934-39; partner firm Hart & Hart, Roanoke, 1946—; asst. gen. counsel U.S. Senate subcom. of com. on edn. and labor, Los Angeles office, 1939-40. Served as aide from Va. to Sec. of Army, 1967-69. Mem. Am. Bar Assn., Va. State Bar. Home: 1606 Persinger Rd SW Roanoke VA 24015 Office: 308 2nd St SW Roanoke VA 24011 Tel (703) 344-3278

HART, KARL VANCE, b. Mayo, Fla., June 25, 1937; B.S., Fla. State U., 1960; postgrad. U. N.C., 1960-61; LL.B., Harvard, 1964. Admitted to Fla. bar, 1964; law clk. U.S. Dist. Ct. Middle Dist. Fla., 1964-65; asso. firm Shutts & Bowen, Miami, Fla., 1965-68, partner, 1968—; atty. Dade County del. to Fla. Legis., 1967. Mem. Am., Fed., Dade County, Fla. bar assns. Editor in chief Harvard Jour. Legis., 1963-64. Home: 1133 N Greenway Dr Coral Gables FL 33134 Office: Southeast 1st National Bank Bldg Miami FL 33131 Tel (305) 358-6300

HART, MAURICE ARTHUR, b. N.Y.C., Dec. 22, 1927; B.S., U. So. Calif., 1950, J.D., 1963. Admitted to Calif. bar, 1963, U.S. Supreme Ct. bar, 1970; partner firm Neiter & Hart, Los Angeles, 1968-70, Hart Neiter & Leonard, Los Angeles, 1976—; pres. Dolman, Kaplan, Neiter & Hart, Los Angeles, 1970-76; judge protem Los Angeles Municipal Ct., 1975—. Mem. Beverly Hills, Am., Los Angeles County, Century City bar assns. Office: 1888 Century Park E Los Angeles CA 90067 Tel (213) 277-2236

HART, PHILIP BRENNAN, b. Pitts., Sept. 25, 1947; B.A., Ohio State U., 1970; J.D., Duquesne U., 1973. Admitted to Pa. bar, 1973; asst. dist. atty. Allegheny County (Pa.), 1973-74; asso. firm Meyer, Darragh, Buckler, Bebenek & Eck, Pitts., 1974—. Mem. Am., Pa., Allegheny County bar assns., Am. Trial Lawyers Assn. Home: 1000 Grandview Ave Pittsburgh PA 15211 Office: 2500 Grant Bldg Pittsburgh PA 15219 Tel (412) 261-6600

HART, RICHARD EVAN, b. Ottowa, Ill., Dec. 13, 1942; B.A. in Liberal Arts and Scis. with honors, U. Ill., 1964, J.D., 1967. Admitted to Ill. bar, 1967; asst. state's atty. Sangamon County (Ill.) 1967-68; partner firm Sorling, Northrup, Hanna, Cullen and Cochran, Springfield, Ill., 1967—; spl. asst. atty. gen. State of Ill., 1971—; mem. revision com. on Ill. Mechanic's Liens Handbook, Ill. Inst. Continuing Legal Edn. Pres. Boys' Farm Found., Buffalo, Ill., 1973, Sangamon County Hist. Soc., 1974. Editor Bicentennial Studies in Sangamon County History, 1975-76. Office: 820 Illinois Bldg 607 E Adams St Springfield IL 62701 Tel (207) 544-1144

HART, RONALD ALTON, b. Lewiston, Maine, July 11, 1932; J.D., U. Maine, 1958. Admitted to Maine bar, 1958; sr. mem. firm Hart, Stinson & Lupton, Bath, Maine, 1958-76; asso. judge Municipal Ct., Bath, 1959-62; county atty. Sagadahoc County (Maine), 1964-68; judge Sagadahoc County Probate Ct., 1968—; mem. Maine Jud. Council, Maine Probate Commn., 1974—. Bd. dirs. Bath YMCA, 1969-76, Maine SBA, 1967-68. Mem. Am., Maine (gov.) trial lawyers assns., Maine State (chmn. jr. bar. 1964-66), Am. bar assns. Home: 15 Judkins Ave Bath ME 04530 Office: 280 Front St Bath ME 04530 Tel (207) 442-8781

HART, RUSSELL HOLIDAY, b. Chgo., May 1, 1928; A.B., DePauw U., 1950; J.D., Ind. U., 1956. Admitted to Ind. bar, 1956, U.S. Ct. Appeals 7th Circuit bar, 1965, U.S. Supreme Ct. bar, 1973; partner firm Stuart, Branigin, Ricks & Schilling, Lafayette, Ind., 1961—. Fellow Am. Coll. Trial Lawyers; mem. Am., Ind., Tippecanoe County (past pres.) bar assns., Am. Judicature Soc., Ind. Defense Lawyers Assn., Order of the Coif. Sr. asso. editor Ind. Law Jour., 1955-56. Home: 228 Blueberry Ln West Lafayette IN 47906 Office: 801 Life Bldg Lafayette IN 47902 Tel (317) 423-1561

HARTE, HERBERT JEROME, b. N.Y.C., May 23, 1911; teaching certificate Fredonia State Tchrs. Coll., 1934; B.S., Columbia, 1944; J.D., N.Y. U., 1948. Admitted to N.Y. bar, 1951, U.S. Dist. Ct. for So. and Eastern Dists. N.Y. bars, 1957, U.S. Supreme Ct. bar, 1969; individual practice law; house counsel Consumer Carpet Workroom, New Hyde Park, N.Y. Mem. Nassau County (N.Y.), N.Y. State bar assns. Office: 1 Wildflower Ln Wantagh NY 11793 Tel (516) 796-3080

HARTER, ELMER ELLSWORTH, b. Muncy, Pa., June 5, 1905; B.A., U. Pitts., 1927, LL.B., 1930, J.D., 1968. Admitted to Pa. bar, 1930, U.S. Supreme Ct. bar, 1961; individual practice law, Harrisburg, Pa.; spokesman Ams. for Competitive Enterprise System; mem. Pa. Bd. Pub. Welfare. Mem. Am., Fed., Pa., Dauphin County (Pa.) bar assns., Am. Trial Lawyers Assn., Practicing Law Inst., Internat. Acad. Law Sci., Am. Judicature Soc., Pa. Trial Lawyers Assn., Selden Soc. London, Soc. Legal History, Pitts. Inst. Legal Medicine, Soc. Study Dem. Instns. Home: 3511 N 4th St Harrisburg PA 17110 Office: 105 N Front St Suite 400 Harrisburg PA Tel (717) 238-9555

HARTER, PHILIP JOSEPH, b. Columbus, Ohio, Apr. 14, 1942; A.B. with high honors, Kenyon Coll., 1964; M.A., U. Mich., 1966, J.D. magna cum laude, 1969. Admitted to U.S. Dist. Ct. bar for D.C., 1971, U.S. Ct. Appeals, D.C., 1971, Superior Ct. bar of D.C., 1972; atty. Gen. Counsel's Office, Dept. Transp., Washington, 1969-70; asso. firm Shea & Gardner, Washington, 1970-73; chief regulatory programs exptl. tech. incentives program Nat. Bur. Standards, Washington, 1973-75; sr. staff atty. adminstrv. Conf. of U.S., Washington, 1975—; adj. prof. Sch. Govt. and Pub. Adminstrn., Am. U., co-chmn. Pres.'s Task Force on Revision of Regulations of Occupational Safety and Health Adminstrn., 1976—; mem. Chmn.'s Task Force on Procedural Reform of NLRB, 1976—. Mem. D.C. Bar, Alumni Assn. Kenyon Coll. (exec. com. 1974—), Washington Area Kenyon Coll. Alumni Assn. (pres. 1971-73), Order of Coif. Mem. editorial bd. Mich. Law Rev., 1967-69. Home: 3028 Newark St NW Washington DC 20008 Office: Adminstrv Conf 2120 L St NW Washington DC 20037 Tel (202) 254-7065

HARTIG, ROBERT LEE, b. Marysville, Kans., Oct. 3, 1928; B.S., Kans. State U., 1953, M.S., 1955; J.D., Duquesne U., 1963. Admitted to D.C. bar, 1964, Wyo. bar, 1965, Alaska bar, 1969; with Mobil Oil Co., Oklahoma City, 1953-67; asst. atty. gen., State of Alaska, Anchorage, 1967-71; partner firm Cole, Hartig, Rhodes, Norman & Mahoney, Anchorage, 1971—; mem. Alaska Ho. of Reps., 1972-74. Mem. Alaska, Anchorage bar assns., Am. Assns. Petroleum Geologists, Anchorage C. of C. (pres. 1976-77). Certified petroleum geologist. Home: 3419 Fordham Dr Anchorage AK 99504 Office: 717 K St Anchorage AK 99501 Tel (907) 274-3576

HARTKE, JAN ALAN, b. Bloomington, Ind., Mar. 20, 1946; B.A., Brown U., 1968; J.D., U. Va., 1971. Admitted to N.Mex. bar, 1971; asso. firm Sutin, Thayer & Browne, Albuquerque, 1971-72, Marjon & Hartke, Albuquerque, 1972-73; asst. pub. defender, team leader N.Mex. Pub. Defender Dept., Albuquerque, 1973-76; chief pub. defender State of N.Mex., Albuquerque, 1976—. Pres. Bernalillo County (N.Mex.) Young Democrats, Albuquerque, 1973. Mem. N.Mex. Criminal Def. Lawyers Assn. (dir. 1975-76), N.Mex. State, Albuquerque bar assns., Nat. Legal Aid and Defender Assn., Western Regional Defenders Assn., Nat. Coll. Criminal Def. Lawyers and Pub. Defenders. Home: 6709 Harper Dr NE Albuquerque NM 87109 Office: 215 W San Francisco St Santa Fe NM 87501 Tel (505) 827-5344

HARTLEY, HOLLIS GIFFORD, b. Monrovia, Calif., Nov. 19, 1923; A.B., Stanford, 1948, J.D., 1950. Admitted to Calif. bar, 1951, U.S. Supreme Ct. bar, 1972; dep. dist. atty. San Bernardino (Calif.), 1951-55, chief dep. dist. atty., 1955-56, asst. dist. atty., 1956-58; mem. firm Gillespie, Hartley & Flory, San Bernardino, 1958-67; partner firm Hartley & Skousen, San Bernardino, 1967-74, pres., 1974—; adminstrv. hearing officer County San Bernardino, 1972—. Sr. warden St. Johns' Episcopal Ch., 1972; chmn. profl. div. Arrowhead United Way, 1974-75; chmn. Arrowhead dist. Boy Scouts Am., 1976—. Mem. Am., San Bernardino County County (pres. 1967) bar assns., Calif. State Bar, Am., Calif. trial lawyers assns., Estate Planning Council San Bernardino Valley, Am. Arbitration Assn. Home: 808 E Bernard Way San Bernardino CA 92404 Office: 505 N Arrowhead St San Bernardino CA 92401 Tel (714) 884-4867

HARTLEY, LYNN LEONARD, b. Jamestown, N.Y., Feb. 12, 1943; B.A., Allegheny Coll., 1964; J.D., Syracuse U., 1967. Admitted to N.Y. bar, 1967, U.S. Dist. Ct. Western Dist. N.Y., 1967; asso. Willard W. Cass, Jr., Jamestown, 1967-71; individual practice law, Jamestown, 1972-74; partner firm Hartley & Fessenden, Jamestown, 1975—; asst. pub. defender, Chautauqua County, N.Y., 1968-72; village atty. Village of Lakewood, N.Y., 1968—; atty. Jamestown Urban Renewal Agy., 1968-69, Town of Gerry, N.Y., 1972—, Village of Panama, N.Y., 1972. Bd. dirs. Jamestown Family Service, 1969-74. Mem. Am., N.Y. State, Jamestown (past pres.) bar assns., Am. Judicature Soc. Home: 342 W Summit Ave Lakewood NY 14750 Office: 400 Wellman Bldg Jamestown NY 14701 Tel (716) 484-7196

HARTLEY, MARVIN BUFORD, JR., b. Sandersville, Ga., Jan. 13, 1933; student Ga. Mil. Coll.; A.B. in Journalism, U. Ga., 1959, J.D., 1961. Admitted to Ga. bar, 1961; practice law, Sandersville, 1961-63; sr. partner firm Hartley & McNatt, Lyons, Ga., 1963—; judge Ga. State Ct. Toombs County, Ga., 1977—. Mem. State Bar Ga., Am. Bar Assn., Am. Judicature Soc. Home: 501 N Victory Dr Lyons GA 30436 Office: PO Box 660 Lyons GA 30436 Tel (912) 526-6435

HARTLEY, THOMAS ALLEN, b. Maben, Miss., Mar. 10, 1903; LL.B., Cumberland U., 1927; J.D. (hon.), Samford U., 1969. Admitted to Miss. bar, 1928, Mo. bar, 1968; individual practice law, Ackerman, Miss., 1928-29, Gulfport, Miss., 1929-30; partner firm Brown & Hartley, Starkville, Miss., 1930-36; individual practice law, Jackson, Miss., 1945-48, Kansas City, Mo., 1969—; IRS agt. St. Louis, 1936-45, estate tax examiner IRS, Kansas City, 1948-55, reviewer, 1955-60, supr. atty., 1960-68. Mem. Am., Fed., Mo., Kansas City bar assns. Recipient Albert Gallatin award U.S. Treasury Dept., 1968, Spl. Service award U.S. Treasury Dept., 1959; contbr. articles to legal jours. Home: 305 E 107th Terr Kansas City MO 64114 Office: 400 E Red Bridge Rd Suite 121 Kansas City MO 64131 Tel (816) 942-6045

HARTMAN, ALLEN, b. Chgo., July 1, 1927; B.S. in Law, Northwestern U., 1957, LL.B., 1959, J.D., 1972. Admitted to Ill. bar, 1959, U.S. Supreme Ct. bar, 1964; since practiced in Chgo., asst. corp. counsel City of Chgo., 1961-63, gen. counsel, 1965-70, 1st asst. corp. counsel, 1970-72, 73-74; judge Circuit Ct. Cook County, 1974—; individual practice law, 1963-64; exec. dir. Chgo. Home Rule Commn., 1971-72; chmn. seminars Ill. Jud. Conf. Mem. Am., Ill., Chgo. bar assns., Phi Alpha Delta. Contbr. articles to legal jours. Office: 2202 Daley Civic Center Court House Chicago IL 60602 Tel (312) 443-8068

HARTMAN, CHARLES EDWARD, II, b. Balt., Dec. 30, 1926; B.E.E., 1947; LL.B., Harvard, 1950. Admitted to Md. bar, 1950; asso. firm Fell & Hartman, 1950-56, partner, 1956-66; partner firm Hartman & Crain, Annapolis, Md., 1966—. Mem. Am., Md., Anne Arundel County bar assns. Office: 222 Severn Ave Annapolis MD 21403 Tel (301) 267-8166

HARTMAN, DON LEE, b. Baton Rouge, Feb. 13, 1935; A.B., U. N.Mex., 1963; J.D., Emory U., 1967. Admitted to Ga. bar, 1967, U.S. Supreme Ct. bar, 1971; asst. atty. gen. State Ga., Atlanta, 1968-69, spl. dep. asst. atty. gen., 1971—; dep. dir. Ga. State Bd. Workmen's Compensation, 1969-73; partner firm Brown, Harriss, Hartman & Ruskaup, Rossville, Ga., 1973-76; mem. Gov's. Adv. Council on Workmen's Compensation, 1974-76, Ga. Boundary Commn., 1968-69. Mem. Am., Ga., Lookout Mountain Circuit, Rossville bar assns., Ga. Trial Lawyers Assn., So. Assn. Workmen's Compensation Adminstrs. Home: 1322 Scenic Hwy Lookout Mountain GA 37350 Office: 210 McFarland Bldg Rossville GA 30741 Tel (404) 861-0203

HARTMAN, JAMES MATTHEW, b. N.Y.C., May 28, 1928; B.A., N.Y. U., 1950; LL.B., Columbia U., 1953. Admitted to N.Y. State bar, 1954, U.S. Supreme Ct. bar, 1964; asso. firm Cravath, Swaine & Moore, N.Y.C., 1954-55; individual practice law, N.Y.C., 1955-60; asso. firm Fellner & Rovins, N.Y.C., 1960-61; partner firm Harris, Beach, Wilcox, Rubin & Levey, Rochester, N.Y., 1962—; adj. asso. prof. Cornell U. Sch. Law, 1974—. Village trustee, Tarrytown, N.Y., 1959-60, counsel Tarrytown Municipal Housing Atty., 1955-58; counsel Greenburgh (N.Y.) Urban Renewal Commn., 1958-62; counsel N.Y. State Joint Legislative Com. State's Economy, 1961-64; mem. planning bd. town Penfield (N.Y.), 1970-74; mem. Monroe County Health Planning Council, 1972-74; mem. Human Resources Task Force, Rochester, N.Y., 1971-72; mem. pres.'s adv. bd. and bd. regents McQuaid Jesuit High Sch., 1972-76. Mem. Am., N.Y. State (chmn. trial lawyers sect. 1973-74) bar assns., Monroe County Bar Assn. (pres. 1975), Assn. Trial Lawyers Am. Home: 145 Clover Hills Dr Rochester NY 14618 Office: 2 State St Rochester NY 14614 Tel (716) 232-4440

HARTMAN, MORRIS N., b. Newark, July 10, 1907; LL.B., Rutgers U., 1928. Admitted to N.J. bar, 1929; judge County Ct., 1966-73, Superior Ct., 1973—; faculty Rutgers U. Law Sch. Mem. Am. Judicature Soc., Am. Bar Assn. (chmn. sect. family law), Essex County (N.J.), N.J. State bars. Contbr. articles to legal jours. Office: Hall of Records High St Newark NJ 07102 Tel (201) 961-7305

HARTMAN, RONALD FREDERICK, b. Cissna Park, Ill., May 9, 1933; B.S. in Indsl. Mgmt., U. Ill., 1953; postgrad. U. Tex., 1962; J.D., Capital U., 1967. Admitted to Ohio bar, 1967, U.S. Dist. Ct. So. Dist. Ohio, 1968, U.S. Supreme Ct. bar, 1970; gen. counsel, sec. Buckeye Internat., Inc., Columbus, Ohio, 1967-72; v.p., gen. counsel Summer & Co., Columbus, Ohio, 1972—, also dir. Mem. devel. bd. Children's Hosp., Columbus, 1971-73; pres. safety code steering com. State of Ohio Indsl. Commn., Columbus, 1972. Mem. Am., Ohio, Columbus bar assns., Ohio Corporate Counsels, Phi Alpha Delta, Am. Arbitration Assn., Mensa, Order of the Curia. Recipient Distinguished Service award U.S. Jr. C. of C. Home: 3801 Lakeview Dr Galena OH 43021 Office: 870 Michigan Ave Columbus OH 43215 Tel (614) 224-8191

HARTNETT, MAURICE A., III, b. Dover, Del., Jan. 20, 1927; B.S., U. Del., 1951, M.Ed., 1955; J.D., George Washington U., 1954. Admitted to Del. bar, 1955; individual practice law, Dover, 1955-76; vice chancellor Del. Ct. Chancery, 1976—; chmn. Del. State Tax Appeal Bd., 1973-76, Del. Commn. on Modernization of State Laws, 1962—; exec. dir. Del. Legis. Ref. Bur., 1961-69; master Del. Family Ct., 1959-60; mem. Nat. Conf. Commrs. on State Laws, 1962—, Del. Code Revision Commn., 1961-72, Del. Constn. Revision Commn., 1968-79. Commr., City of Rehoboth Beach, Del., 1972-76. Mem. Am. Bar Assn. Home: 144 Cooper Rd Dover DE 19901 Office: Court of Chancery 45 The Green Dover DE 19901

HARTSEL, NORMAN CLYDE, b. San Diego, Sept. 25, 1944; A.B., Kenyon Coll., 1967; J.D., Case Western Reserve U., 1970. Admitted to Ohio bar, 1970; asso. firm Shumaker, Loop & Kendrick, Toledo, Ohio, 1971-76, partner, 1977—; lectr. Ohio Legal Center Inst., 1973-75. Mem. Am., Ohio State, Toledo bar assns. Home: 113 Holly Ln Perrysburg OH 43551 Office: 811 Madison Ave Toledo OH 43624 Tel (419) 241-4201

HARTSFIELD, ARNETT LEE, JR., b. Bellingham, Wash., June 14, 1918; A.B. in Econs., U. So. Calif., 1951, LL.B., 1955. Admitted to Calif. bar, 1956; fireman City of Los Angeles, 1940-61; individual practice law, Los Angeles, 1956-64; asso. counsel Calif. Fair Employment Practices Commn., Los Angeles, 1964-65; exec. dir. Los Angeles Neighborhood Legal Services, 1965-67; chief mediator Los Angeles Community Mediation Center, 1967-69; asst. to dir. United Way Los Angeles, 1970-71; asst. prof. Calif. State U., Long Beach, 1972-74, asso. prof., 1974—; mem. Black Edn. Commn. Los Angeles Bd. Edn., 1970-72; mem. Los Angeles City CSC, 1973—, pres., 1973-74, 75-76. Mem. Nat. (dir. 1967-68), Calif. (pres. 1968-69) pub. defenders and legal aid assns. Recipient Spl. award Community Relations Conf. So. Calif., 1962; Citizen of Year award Omega Phi Psi; author: (with Billy Mills) The Old Stentorians: History of Black Firemen in the Los Angeles City Fire Department, 1973. Home: 8745 S Harvard Blvd Los Angeles CA 90047 Office: 6101 E 7th St Long Beach CA 90840 Tel (213) 753-5780

HARTVIG, DONALD HARRISON, b. San Francisco, May 19, 1920; A.A., Stockton Jr. Coll., 1941; J.D., U. Calif., San Francisco, 1949, Lewis and Clark Coll., 1970; postgrad. Harvard Bus. Sch., summer 1969. Vice pres. Chown Hardware & Machinery Co., Portland, Oreg., 1949—, house counsel, 1970—; admitted to Oreg. bar, 1970, Calif. bar, 1970; asso. firm Reeder & Rapp, Hillsboro, Oreg., 1976—; clk. U.S. Dist. Ct. for Oreg. Bankruptcy Ct., 1969. Mem. Lincoln County (Oreg.), Washington County (Oreg.) bar assns., Am. Trial Lawyers Assn. Home: 1235 SW Highland Rd Portland OR 97221 Office: 333 NW 16th Ave Portland OR 97209 Tel (503) 226-3601

HARTZELL, FRANKLIN MACVEAGH, b. Carthage, Ill., Aug. 24, 1923; B.S., U. Ill., 1948, LL.B., 1950. Admitted to Ill. bar, 1950, U.S. Tax Ct. bar, 1955; individual practice law, Carthage, 1950, 66; partner firm Hartzell, Glidden, Tucker & Neff, and predecessors, Carthage, 1956-65, 67—; city atty. Carthage, 1955-69. Bd. dirs. Meml. Hosp. Assos., Carthage, 1958—, Hancock County Nursing Home, 1967—. Mem. Am., Ill., Hancock County bar assns., Soc. Hosp. Attys., Phi Delta Phi. Home: 306 S Madison St Carthage IL 62321 Office: 608 Wabash St Carthage IL 62321 Tel (217) 357-3121

HARUM, ALBERT EDWARD, b. Bklyn., Feb. 7, 1911; B.B.A., U. Miami (Fla.), 1954, J.D., 1956; LL.M., N.Y. U., 1959, J.S.D., 1962. Admitted to Fla. bar, 1956, U.S. Supreme Ct. bar, 1965; prof. bus. law U. Miami, 1954—; city editor Bklyn. Eagle, 1939-41, Coral Gables (Fla.) Times, 1941-53; publisher Fla. Sun, 1949-51. Kenneson Found. fellow N.Y. U., 1958, Ford Found. fellow, 1959. Mem. Am., Fla., Coral Gables, Fed. bar assns. Contbr. articles to profl. jours. Home: 8860 SW 170th St Perrine FL 33157 Office: U Miami Coral Gables FL 33124 Tel (305) 284-4633

HARVEY, EDMUND LUKENS, b. Chester, Pa., July 21, 1915; B.S. in M.E., U. Pa., 1937, J.D., 1941. Admitted to Pa. Supreme Ct. bar, 1942, Delaware County (Pa.) Ct. bar, 1942, U.S. Supreme Ct. bar, 1969, Tax Ct. of U.S. bar, 1955, U.S. Dist. Ct. Eastern Dist. Pa. bar, 1961; individual practice law, Chester, Pa., 1946-70, Media, Pa., 1970—; dir., solicitor Security Savs. Assn., Chester, 1960—; solicitor Glenolden Savs. and Loan Assn., 1952—. Bd. dirs., solicitor J. Lewis Crozer Library, Chester, Pa., 1952—; bd. dirs. Lindsay Law Library, Chester, 1967—. Mem. Am., Pa., Delaware County bar assns. Home: Palmers Mill Rd Media PA 19063 Office: 105 W 3d St Media PA 19063 Tel (215) 565-0700

HARVEY, HAROLD LEE, b. Marshall, Mo., Sept. 29, 1905; A.B., Harvard, 1927, LL.B., 1932. Admitted to Mo. bar, 1932, U.S. Dist. Ct. bar, 1933, U.S. Ct. Appeals bar, 1954, U.S. Tax Ct. bar, 1972; asso. firm Thompson, Mitchell, Thompson & Young, 1932-39; partner firm Bellamy & Harvey, Marshall, 1940-52; gen. atty. Mo. Pacific R.R., 1952-70; individual practice law, St. Louis, 1970-72; legal advisor St. Louis County Police Dept., 1972-75; asst. St. Louis County counselor, Clayton, Mo., 1975—. Pres. Marshall C. of C., 1952. Mem. Mo., St. Louis bar assns., St. Louis Law Library Assn. (dir. 1966-69). Home: 79 Chafford Woods Saint Louis MO 63144 Office: 7900 Forsyth Blvd Clayton MO 63105 Tel (314) 889-2009

HARVEY, NORMAN LANSING, b. Canisteo, N.Y., Nov. 11, 1918; LL.B., Syracuse U., 1948. Admitted to N.Y. bar, 1948; partner firm Simpson, Morton & Harvey, Hornell, N.Y., 1948-51; legis. atty. office of Sec. of Air Force, 1951-56; partner firm Jerry, Lewis & Harvey, Plattsburgh, N.Y., 1956-68; justice N.Y. Supreme Ct., 4th Dist., Plattsburgh, 1968—; adminstrv. judge 4th Jud. Dist. of N.Y. 1975—; mayor Village of Canisteo, 1949-51. Mem. N.Y. Supreme Ct. Justices Assn. Home: 5 Cumberland Pl S Plattsburgh NY 12901 Office: Supreme Court Chambers Box 944 Plattsburgh NY 12901 Tel (518) 563-2620

HARVEY, NORMAN PAUL, b. Pottsville, Pa., Sept. 3, 1911; B.A. summa cum laude, LaSalle Coll., 1934; LL.B., U. Pa., 1937. Admitted to Pa. bar, 1941; U.S. Supreme Ct. bar, 1966; since practiced in Phila.; house counsel Kemper Ins. Co., 1941-54; counsel firm John J. McDevitt, III, 1954-64; partner firm Liebert, Harvey, Herting, Short and Lavin, 1964-70; sr. partner firm Harvey, Pennington, Herting & Renneisen, 1970—. Mem. Am., Pa., Phila. bar assns., Assn. Def. Counsel, Assn. Trial Lawyers Am., Am. Judicature Soc., Def. Research Inst., Pa. Trial Lawyers Assn. Home: 6114 Ensley Dr Flourtown PA 19031 Office: 7 Penn Center Plaza Philadelphia PA 19103 Tel (215) LO3-4470

HARVEY, ROBERT GORDON, b. Rochester, N.Y., Aug. 2, 1943; A.B., Hamilton Coll., 1965; J.D. cum laude, Boston U., 1968; grad. U.S. Naval Officers Candidates Sch., Newport, R.I., 1969. Admitted to N.Y. State bar, 1968; adminstrv. officer, legal assistance officer U.S. Naval Facility, Eleuthera, Bahamas, 1970-71; asso. firm Nixon, Hargrave, Devans & Doyle, Rochester, 1971—. Bd. dirs. Eastside Community Center of Rochester, Inc., 1975—. Mem. N.Y. State, Monroe County (N.Y.) bar assns. Recipient Am. Jurisprudence award Bancroft-Whitney Co. and Lawyers Co-op. Pub. Co., 1968; named Distinguished Naval Grad. U.S. Naval Officers Candidate Sch., 1969; asst. mng. editor Spectator, 1964-65; mem. jr. staff Boston U. Law Rev., 1966-67, sr. editor, 1967-68. Office: Nixon Hargrave Devans & Doyle Lincoln First Tower Rochester NY 14603 Tel (716) 546-8000

HARVEY, RUTH L., See CHARITY, Ruth Harvey.

HARVEY, ZOLA EMILE, b. Elizabethgrad, Russia, Jan. 6, 1906; came to U.S., 1906, naturalized 1912; LL.B., N.Y. U., 1928. Pres. Am. Legal Publs., Inc., N.Y.C., 1929—, Am. Book Exchange, Inc., 1926-39; founder Capitol Pub. Co., N.Y.C., 1941, pres., 1940-56; founder, pres. Harvey House, Irvington on the Hudson, N.Y., 1956—. Home: 12 Parkside Dr Great Neck NY 11023 Office: 5 S Buckhout St Irvington NY 10533*

HARVILLE, VERNON DALE, b. Leesville, La., Oct. 30, 1921; B.B.A., B.S., M.S., Tex. A. and I. U., 1948; J.D., U. Tex., 1955. Admitted to Tex. bar, 1954, U.S. Supreme Ct. bar, 1961; asst. city atty., city prosecutor, Corpus Christi, Tex., 1956-61; judge County Ct. Law No. 1, Nueces County, Tex., 1962-70, 105th Jud. Dist. Ct. of Tex., Corpus Christi, 1971—. Mem. Tex., Nueces County bar assns. Home: 537 Evergreen St Corpus Christi TX 78412 Office: Nueces County Ct House Corpus Christi TX 78401 Tel (512) 883-8521

HARWELL, DAVID WALKER, b. Florence, S.C., Jan. 8, 1932; LL.B., U. S.C., 1958, then J.D.; grad. Nat. Coll. for State Judiciary U. Nev., 1973, Am. Acad. Jud. Edn. U. Colo., 1976. Admitted to S.C. bar, 1958, U.S. Dist. Ct. bar for Dist. S.C., 1958, U.S. 4th Circuit Ct. Appeals bar, U.S. Supreme Ct. bar; partner firm Harwell & Harwell, Florence, S.C., 1958-73; judge S.C. Circuit Ct., 12th Jud. Circuit, 1973—; mem. S.C. Ho. of Reps., 1963-73. Chmn. S.C. Agr. Study Com. Mem. S.C., Am. bar assns., S.C., Am. trial Lawyers assns. Recipient Distinguished Service award Florence (S.C.) Jaycees. Home: 1034 Santee Dr Florence SC 29501 Tel (803) 665-3020

HARWOOD, RICHARD SOPER, b. Bloomington, Ill., June 9, 1946; A.B., Dartmouth Coll., 1968; J.D., Duke U., 1971. Admitted to Colo. bar, 1971; trust adminstr. 1st Nat. Bank of Colorado Springs, 1971-73, asst. trust officer, 1973-75, trust officer, 1975—. Active Colo. Springs Jaycees, 1971—. Mem. Am., Colo., El Paso County bar assns., Estate Planning Council Colorado Springs. Advanced estate planning certificate. Office: PO Box 1699 Colorado Springs CO 80942 Tel (303) 471-5122

HARWOOD, THOMAS PERKINS, JR., b. Green Bank, W.Va., Jan. 22, 1929; B.A., Va. Mil. Inst., 1950; J.D., U. Va., 1956. Admitted to Va. bar, 1956; asso. firm Lane Rogers & Paul, Richmond, Va., 1956-57, partner, 1958-60; dep. commr. Indsl. Commn. of Va., Richmond, 1960-64, commr., 1964-73; mem. Va. State Corp. Commn., Richmond, 1973—. Mem. Am., Va., Richmond bar assns., Va. State Bar. Home: 2736 Kenbury Rd Richmond VA 23225 Office: PO Box 1197 Richmond VA 23209 Tel (804) 786-3608

HARZENSTEIN, A.S., b. Phila., Nov. 18, 1899; LL.B., Temple U., 1924. Admitted to Pa. bar, 1924; mem. firm Stassen Kephart Sarkis & Kostos; individual practice law, Phila., 1924-30, 70—; field supr. enforcement U.S. Dept. Treasury, Phila. and Washington, 1931-47, adminstrv. law judge, 1947-70; head legal asst. to Gov. Pa., 1939; asst. chief counsel Ruth Commn., 1937-39. Mem. Phila., Fed. (nat. pres. 1970-71), Inter Am., Am. bar assns., World Assn. Lawyers. Home: 5623 Woodcrest Ave Philadelphia PA 19131 Office: 3d floor 1425 Walnut St Philadelphia PA 19102 Tel (215) GR 3-6081

HASENFLUE, OLIVER WENDELL, b. Geneva, Ohio, Jan. 17, 1919; A.B., Wooster Coll., 1940; J.D., Western Res. U., 1943. Admitted to Ohio bar, 1943, U.S. Supreme Ct. bar, 1963; mem. firm Spangenberg & Hasenflue, Cleve., 1943-72, Hasenflue & Drost, Cleve., 1974—. Trustee Grace Hosp., Cleve., 1969—; mem. Roscoe Pound Found. Mem. Greater Cleve., Cuyahoga County, Am. bar assns., Am., Ohio State, Cleve. trial lawyers assns., Am. Judicature Soc., Delta Theta Phi. Home: 516 Humiston Dr Bay Village OH 44140 Office: 433 Leader Bldg Cleveland OH 44114 Tel (216) 579-0388

HASKELL, NATHANIEL MERVIN, b. Pittsfield, Maine, Sept. 27, 1912; LL.B., Peabody Law Sch., 1934. Admitted to Maine bar, 1935; mem. firm Haskell & Keaney and predecessors, Portland, Maine, 1935—; judge probate ct., Cumberland County, Maine, 1953-73; mem. Commn. on Uniform Laws; speaker Maine Ho. of Reps., 1949-51; pres. Maine Senate, 1953. Mem. Am., Maine State bar assns., Nat. Coll. Probate Judges, Am. Judicature Soc. Home: 30 Higgins St Portland ME 04103 Office: 97A Exchange St Portland ME 04111 Tel (207) 773-4611

HASKETT, DAVID MAX, b. Elwood, Ind., Feb. 23, 1944; A.B., Ind. U., 1966, J.D., 1969. Asso. firm Locke, Reynolds, Boyd & Weisell, 1969-76, mem., 1976—. Mem. Am., Ind., Indpls. bar assns. Home: 11406 Lakeshore Dr W Carmel IN 46032 Office: One Indiana Sq Suite 2120 Indianapolis IN 46204 Tel (317) 639-5534

HASKINS, GEORGE LEE, b. Cambridge, Mass., Feb. 13, 1915; A.B. summa cum laude, Harvard, 1935, LL.B., 1942; postgrad. (Henry fellow) Merton Coll., Oxford U., 1935-36. Admitted to Mass. bar, 1943, Pa. bar, 1951, Maine bar, 1968, U.S. Supreme Ct. bar, 1952; asst. prof., asso. prof., prof. law U. Pa. Law Sch., Phila., 1946—, Algernon Sydney Biddle Prof. Law, 1974—; spl. atty., cons. counsel Pa. R.R., Penn-Central R.R., 1951—; permanent commn. O. W. Holmes Devise, 1957. Fellow Am. Soc. Legal History (hon.; pres. 1970-74, dir. 1977—); mem. Mass., Maine, Pa., Am., Phila. bar assns., Assn. Internationale pour l'Histoire du Droit (council 1975—), Third Circuit Jud. Conf., Am. Law Inst., Am. Judicature Soc., Order of Coif, Phi Beta Kappa. Author: The Statute of York, 1935; Pennsylvania Fiduciary Guide, 1957; Law and Authority in Early Massachusetts, 1968; (with others) American Law of Property, 1952; contbr. articles to legal jours. Office: 3400 Chestnut St Philadelphia PA 19104 Tel (215) 243-7497

HASKINS, JOHN FRANCIS, JR., b. Phila., Mar. 17, 1946; B.A., LaSalle Coll., 1967; J.D., Temple U., 1973. Admitted to Pa. bar, 1973; asso. firm Rosenstein & Kleitman, Norristown, Pa., 1973-76; atty. Montgomery County (Pa.) Legal Aid Soc., 1974—; spl. asst. pub. defender Montgomery County, 1975—; adj. prof. bus. law Phila. Coll. Textiles and Sci., 1974—. Mem. Collegeville (Pa.) Zoning Hearing Bd., 1976—; mem. exec. com. Dem. party Montgomery County, 1970-74. Mem. Pa., Montgomery County bar assns., Montgomery County Trial Lawyers Assn., Defenders Soc. Pa. Home: 359 E 9th Ave Collegeville PA 19428 Office: 409 Cherry St Norristown PA 19401 Tel (215) 279-3900

HASKINS, ROBERT LEE, b. Silverton, Oreg., Jan. 3, 1943; B.A. in History, U. Oreg., 1966; J.D., Harvard U., 1969. Admitted to Oreg. bar, 1969; asso. firm King, Miller, Anderson, Nash & Yerke, Portland, Oreg., 1969-71; asso. firm Morton H. Zalutsky, Portland, 1971; asst. atty. gen. Oreg. Dept. Justice, Portland, 1971—; speaker confs. environ. law. Mem. Oreg., Multnomah County (Oreg.) bar assns. Contbr. article to law rev. Home: 4223 SW 54th Pl Portland OR 97221 Office: Oregon Dept Justice 555 State Office Bldg 1400 SW 5th Ave Portland OR 97201 Tel (503) 229-5901

HASS, JEREMY DENNIS, b. Mpls., Mar. 24, 1936; B.A., Pomona Coll., 1959; student U. Calif. San Francisco Hastings Coll. Law, 1959-61; LL.B., Loyola U., Los Angeles, 1963. Admitted to Calif. bar, 1970; with Santa Barbara Title Co. (Calif.), 1966-68; partner firm Weldon & Hass, Santa Barbara, 1969—; inheritance tax referee State of Calif., 1976—. Pres. Santa Barbara chpt. SAR, 1974; dir. Santa Barbara Trust Hist. Preservation, 1970-76. Office: 211 E Anapamu St Santa Barbara CA 93101 Tel (805) 965-7014

HASS, WILLIAM RALPH, b. Springfield, Mo., Jan. 28, 1936; B.S. in Edn., SW Mo. State U., 1958; J.D., U. Ark., 1962. Admitted to Ark. bar, 1962, Mo. bar, 1969; partner firm Niblock & Hass, Fayetteville, Ark., 1964-66; asst. atty. gen. State of Ark., Little Rock, 1966-68; individual practice law, Thayer, Mo., 1969—; asst. pros. atty. Washington County (Ark.), Fayetteville, 1965-66; atty. City of Mammoth Spring (Ark.), 1970—, City of Thayer, 1970—. Mem. Mo., Ark. bar assns. Home: 320 10th St Thayer MO 65791 Office: 211 Chestnut St Thayer MO 65791 Tel (417) 264-7203

HASSELL, MORRIS WILLIAM, b. Jacksonville, Tex., Aug. 9, 1916; A.A., Lon Morris Coll., Jacksonville, 1936; LL.B., U. Tex., 1942. Admitted to Tex. bar, 1941, U.S. Supreme Ct. bar, 1973; atty. Cherokee County (Tex.), 1942-47; partner firm Norman, Hassell, Spiers, Holland & Thrall, and predecessors, Rusk, Tex., 1948—; dir. 1st State Bank, Rusk; v.p., dir. Citizens Indsl. Life Ins. Co.; mayor City of Rusk, 1959—. Chmn. exec. com. of bd. trustees Lon Morris Coll.; trustee Tex. conf. United Meth. Ch. Mem. State Bar Tex., Am., Cherokee County bar assns. Recipient Distinguished Alumnus award Lon Morris Coll., 1946. Home: 1300 Copeland St Rusk TX 75785 Office: 106 E 5th St Rusk TX 75785 Tel (214) 683-2227

HASSEMAN, DEAN MICHAEL, b. Abington, Pa., Mar. 15, 1946; B.A., Northeastern U., 1968; J.D., U. Va., 1971. Admitted to Pa. bar 1971; asst. defender Defender Assn. Phila., 1971-72; sr. atty. Sun Co., Inc., Phila., 1972—. Mem. Am., Pa., Phila. bar assns. Editorial bd. Va. Jour. Internat. Law, 1970-71. Home: 221 Hastings Ct Doylestown PA 18901 Office: 1608 Walnut St Philadelphia PA 19103 Tel (215) 972-4130

HASSETT, JOSEPH MARK, b. Buffalo, May 1, 1943; B.A. summa cum laude, Canisius Coll., 1964; LL.B. cum laude, Harvard U., 1967. Admitted to N.Y. State bar, 1967, D.C. bar, 1970, U.S. Supreme Ct. bar, 1976; asso. firm Hogan & Hartson, Washington, 1970-74, partner, 1974—. Mem. Am., D.C. bar assns. Home: 1940 35th St NW Washington DC 20007 Office: 815 Connecticut Ave NW Washington DC 20006 Tel (202) 331-4643

HASSON, CHARLES GIBBS, b. Johnstown, Pa., June 10, 1920; A.B., Notre Dame U., 1942, LL.B., 1947. Admitted to Pa. bar, 1947; U.S. Tax Ct., 1950; partner firm Hasson & Hasson, Ebenburg, Pa., 1947-52; individual practice law, Ebenburg, 1952—; asst. dist. atty. Cambria County, Pa., 1960-66; asst. atty. gen., Harrisburg, Pa., 1972. Mem. Pa. State Dem. Com., 1948-52. Mem. Cambria County, Pa. (sec. aeros. and space law sect.) bar assns. Office: Law Bldg Ebensburg PA 15931 Tel (814) 472-9290

HASSON, JAMES KEITH, JR., b. Knoxville, Tenn., Mar. 3, 1946; B.A., Duke U., 1967; J.D., 1970. Admitted to Ga. bar, 1971, D.C. bar, 1971; mem. firm Sutherland, Asbill & Brennan, Atlanta, 1970-75, partner firm, 1976—; adj. prof. law Emory Law Sch., Atlanta, 1975—. Asst. sec. Met. Atlanta Crime Commn., 1976—. Mem. Am., Atlanta bar assns., State Bar of Ga., Nat. Health Lawyers Assn., Nat. Assn. Coll. and Univ. Attys., Lawyers Club of Atlanta. Contbr. articles to profl. jours. Home: 224 Pineland Rd NW Atlanta GA 30342 Office: 3100 First Nat Bank Tower Atlanta GA 30303 Tel (404) 658-8805

HASTIE, JOHN D., b. Cuthrie, Okla., Dec. 9, 1939; B.A., U. Okla., 1961, LL.B., 1964. Admitted to Okla. bar, 1964; asso. firm Crowe, Dunlevy, Thweatt, Swinford, Johnson & Burdick, Oklahoma City, 1966-70; pres. Mgmt. Assos., Inc., Oklahoma City, 1970—, Investors Constrn. Corp., Oklahoma City, 1970-74; v.p. SW Constrn. Corp., 1970-74; dir. Firstbank of Marietta (Okla.), 1970—; partner firm Hastie & Kirschner, Oklahoma City, 1974—; lectr. profl. seminars. Mem. Am., Okla. bar assns., Bar Assn. City N.Y. Office: First National Center Suite 880C Oklahoma City OK 73102 Tel (405) 239-6404

HASTINGS, EDWIN HAMILTON, b. Yonkers, N.Y., Jan. 2, 1917; A.B., Amherst Coll., 1938; LL.B., Columbia, 1941. Admitted to N.Y. bar, 1941, R.I. bar, 1946, Mass. bar, 1951; asso. firm Larkin, Rathbone & Perry, N.Y.C., 1941-42; asso. firm Tillinghast, Collins & Graham, and predecessor firms, Providence, 1946-53, partner, 1953—; mem. Bd. Bar Examiners, State of R.I., 1966-74, chmn., 1972-74; chmn. Com. on Criminal Law of Future, R.I. Supreme Ct., 1973—. Mem. R.I., Am. bar assns., World Peace Through Law Center, World Assn. Lawyers. Home: 210 Payton Ave Warwick RI 02889 Office: 2000 Hospital Trust Tower Providence RI 02903 Tel (401) 274-3800

HASTINGS, ROBERT PUSEY, b. Los Angeles, May 23, 1910; B.A., Yale, 1933; LL.B., Harvard, 1936. Admitted to Calif. bar, 1936, since practiced in Los Angeles; counsel Motion Picture div. Office Coordinator Inter-Am. Affairs, 1942-43; partner firm Paul, Hastings, Janofsky & Walker, 1946—. Chmn., Calif. campaign USO, 1956-57; mem. Los Angeles-Mexico City Sister City Com.; pres., chmn. bd. Los Angeles Civic Light Opera Assn., 1959-65, now trustee; sec., trustee Music Center Operating Co., 1961-65; vice chmn. bd. Harvey Mudd Coll. Sci. and Engring., 1956—; chmn. Thacher Sch., 1965-70, trustee, 1938-42, 46-73; mem. bd. overseers, trustee Friends of Huntington Library and Art Gallery, 1971—; trustee Miss Porter's Sch., 1969-73, Winston Churchill Found. of U.S. 1964—; trustee Friends of Claremont Colls., 1970—, pres., 1973-75; chmn., trustee Harvard Law Sch. Assn. So. Calif., 1967-69. Mem. Am., Calif., Los Angeles County bar assns., Los Angeles Stock Exchange Club, Delta Kappa Epsilon. Decorated Order Brit. Empire. Office: 22d Floor 555 S Flower St Los Angeles CA 90071 Tel (213) 489-4000

HATCH, EDWIN BROWN, b. Pittsboro, N.C., Aug. 29, 1928; student The Citadel, 1944-46; A.B., U. N.C., 1950, LL.B., 1953. Admitted to N.C. bar, 1953, U.S. Tax Ct., 1962; asso. firm Pittman & Staton, Sanford, N.C., 1953-55; asso. firm Baucom & Adams, Raleigh, N.C., 1955-57; corp. counsel State of N.C., Raleigh, 1957-58; individual practice law, Pittsboro, 1958-66; chief trial atty. lands div. U.S. Dept. Justice, Washington, 1966-72; partner firm Purrington, Hatch & McNamara, Raleigh, 1973—. Mem. traffic and parking bd. City of Alexandria, Va., 1971-72; mem. Raleigh Historic Properties Commn., 1975—. Mem. Am., N.C., Wake County bar assns., Pittsboro C. of C. (pres. 1960-62), Phi Beta Kappa. Contbr. articles in field to profl. jours. Office: 605 Raleigh Bldg Raleigh NC 27602 Tel (919) 828-7214

HATCH, FARRELL MELTON, b. Dardanelle, Ark., July 4, 1935; student Southeastern State U., Okla., 1953-55; B.A., Hendrix Coll., 1960; B.D., Duke U., 1963; J.D., U. Okla., 1968. Admitted to Okla. bar, 1968; partner firm Spears, Hatch, Mickle & Wilhite, Durant, Okla., 1968—; judge Appellate div. Okla. Ct. on the Judiciary. Mem. Am., Oklahoma City (standards and goals com.), Bryan County (pres.) bar assns. Office: 400 W Main St Durant OK 74701

HATCH, STANLEY CRAIG, b. Logan, Utah, Jan. 16, 1934; B.S., Utah State U., 1955; J.D., Harvard U., 1958. Admitted to Calif. bar, 1959; dep. county counsel County of Santa Barbara (Calif.), 1960-64; partner firm Hatch, Parent & Abbott, Santa Barbara, 1968-71; pres. firm Hatch and Parent, Santa Barbara, 1973—. Mem. Santa Barbara County Bar Assn. (chmn. sect. environ. law 1974-75), State Bar Calif., Lawyer-Pilots Bar Assn., Barristers Club Santa Barbara (pres. 1970-71). Office: 21 E Carrillo St Santa Barbara CA 93101 Tel (805) 963-1971

HATCH, WILLIAM THOMAS, b. Raleigh, N.C., Apr. 1, 1905; LL.B., Wake Forest U., 1928, J.D., 1970. Admitted to N.C. bar, 1929, U.S. Supreme Ct. bar, 1961; individual practice law, 1929-59; mem. firm Hatch Little Bunn Jones Few & Berry, Raleigh, 1959—, sr. mem., 1969—; mem. N.C. Ho. of Reps., 1936-49; spl. judge N.C. Superior Ct., 1949-53. Mem. Wake County (N.C.) (pres. 1955), N.C., Am. bar assns. Home: 3300 Wake Forest Rd Raleigh NC 27609 Office: 327 Hillsborough St Raleigh NC 27602 Tel (919) 828-5952

HATCHELL, MICHAEL AUSTIN, b. Longview, Tex., Sept. 17, 1939; B.B.A., U. Tex., 1961, LL.B., 1964. Admitted to Tex. bar, U.S. Supreme Ct. bar; briefing atty., sr. asso. Justice Meade F. Griffin, Supreme Ct. Tex., 1964-65; partner firm Ramey, Flock, Hutchins, Grainger & Jeffus, Tyler, Tex., 1964—. Mem. Tyler Bd. Rev. for Juvenile Readers, 1969-70; trustee Carnegie Library, 1972—, chmn., 1975—; mem. acquisitions com. Tyler Mus. Art, 1976. Mem. Tex., Smith County bar assns., Tex. Assn. Def. Counsel. Home: 2920 Fry St Tyler TX 75701 Office: Box 629 Tyler TX 75701 Tel (214) 597-3301

HATCHER, RICHARD GORDON, b. Michigan City, Ind., July 10, 1933; B.S., Ind. U., 1956; J.D. with honors, Valparaiso U., 1959. Admitted to Ind. bar, 1959; asso. firm Walker & Walker, East Chicago, Ind., 1959-61; partner firm Shropshire & Hatcher, Gary, Ind., 1961-67; dep. prosecuting atty. Lake County Criminal Ct., Gary, Ind., 1961-63; councilman-at-large City of Gary, 1963-67, pres. council, 1964, mayor, 1967-77. Mem. Democratic Nat. Com., 1971-77, mem. exec. com. Nat. Urban Coalition, 1971-77; founder, Nat. Black Caucus of Locally Elected Ofcls.; mem. state central com. Ind. Dem. Party, 1974-77; v.p. Nat. Conf. Dem. Mayors, 1975-76; chmn. human resources com. Nat. League of Cities, 1974; bd. trustees U.S. Conf. of Mayors, 1974-77. Mem. Am. Bar Assn. Named One of 200 Most Outstanding Young Leaders, Time Mag., 1974, One of 100 Most Influential Black Americans, Ebony Mag., 1974-76; author: (with Barbara Milkulski) Mikulski Commission Report on Democratic Party Policy, 1974. Office: Office of Mayor City Hall 401 Broadway St Gary IN 46402

HATCHETT, JOSEPH WOODROW, b. Clearwater, Fla., Sept. 17, 1932; A.B., Fla. A & M U., 1954; LL.B., J.D., Howard U., 1959; certificate U.S. Naval Justice Sch., 1973. Admitted to Fla. bar, 1959; individual practice law, Daytona Beach, Fla., 1959-66; spl. asst. to atty. City Daytona Beach, 1964; asst. U.S. atty. Dept. Justice, Jacksonville, Fla., 1966-70; U.S. magistrate U.S. Cts., Jacksonville, 1971-75; justice Fla. Supreme Ct., Tallahassee, 1975—; cons., staff mem. Urban Renewal Dept., Daytona Beach, 1963-66. Vol. cooperating atty. NAACP Legal Def. Fund, Inc., Daytona Beach, 1960-66; mem. John T. Stocking Meml. Trust, med. sch. scholarships, Daytona Beach; bd. dirs., co-chmn. United Negro Coll. Fund, Daytona Beach. Mem. Am., Nat., Fla., Jacksonville, D.W. Perkins, Fed. bar assns., Am. Judicature Soc., Nat. Council Fed. Magistrates. Contbr. articles Fla. Bar Jour., Case and Comment, Seminars for U.S. Magistrates, Fed. Jud. Center cassette library. Office: Supreme Court Bldg Tallahassee FL 32304 Tel (904) 488-2281

HATFIELD, DOUGLAS SPENCER, JR., b. Plainfield, N.J., Oct. 29, 1935; A.B., Colby Coll., 1958; LL.B., Boston U., 1961. Admitted to N.H. bar, 1961; atty. firm Maurice Blodgett, Peterborough, N.H., 1961-62; atty., office mgr. firm Nelson, Winer & Lynch, Hillsborough, N.H., 1962-67; individual practice law, Hillsborough, 1967-76; partner firm Hatfield and Henderson, Hillsborough, 1976—; spl. justice Hillsborough Dist. Ct., 1969—; pres. N.H. Estate Planning Council, 1975. Mem. Planning Bd. Town of Hillsborough, 1963-69. Mem. Am., N.H. (chmn. com. on econs. of practice of law) bar assns., Hillsborough C. of C. Home: Shedd Jones Rd Hillsborough NH 03244 Office: Central Sq Hillsborough NH 03244 Tel (603) 464-5578

HATFIELD, PAUL GERHART, b. Great Falls, Mont., Apr. 29, 1928; LL.B., U. Mont., 1955. Admitted to Mont. bar, 1955; asso. firms Hoffman & Cure, Great Falls, Mont., 1955-56, Jardine, Stephenson, Blewett & Weaver, Great Falls, 1956-59; partner firm Hatfield & Hatfield, Great Falls, 1959-61; chief dep. county prosecutor Cascade County, Mont., 1959-61; judge Mont. Dist. Ct., 8th Jud. Dist., 1961-76; chief justice Mont. Supreme Ct., 1976—, chmn. div. sentence rev. Mont. Supreme Ct., 1970-75; mem. Mont. Youth Justice Advisory Council, Advisory Council Mont. Council on Criminal Justice Standards, Goals, Coll. Great Falls Pres's. Council; chmn. Cts. Task Force on Criminal Justice Standards, Goals. Mem. Mont., Am. (chmn. Mont. membership div. jud. adminstrn.) bar assns., Nat. Council Juvenile Ct. Judges, Nat. Assn. Probate Judges, Nat. Conf. State Trial Judges (Mont. del.). Home: 2308 5th Ave SW Great Falls MT 59405 Office: Capitol Bldg Helena MT 59601

HATHAWAY, GARY RAY, b. Liberal, Kans., July 5, 1942; B.A., Southwestern Coll., Winfield, Kans., 1964; J.D., Washburn U., 1969. Admitted to Kans. bar, 1969; partner firm Hathaway & Kimball, Ulysses, Kans., 1971—; county atty. Grant County (Kans.), 1971-73; city atty. City of Ulysses, 1971-75. Sec., Grant County Scholarship Assn., 1974—. Mem. Am., Kans., S.W. Kans., Grant County (sec.-treas. 1971—) bar assns. Home: PO Box 527 Ulysses KS 67880 Office: 123 N Glenn St Ulysses KS 67880 Tel (316) 356-3088

HATMAKER, DAVID JOY, b. Washington, Nov. 7, 1934; B.S. in Commerce, U. Va., 1956, LL.B., 1968. Admitted to Va. bar, 1968; asso. firm Aldhizer & Weaver, Harrisonburg, Va., 1968-71; individual practice law, Harrisonburg, 1971-74; partner firm Hatmaker, Dinsmore & Stables, Harrisonburg, 1974—; commr. in chancery, gen. reciever Circuit Ct. Rockingham County (Va.), 1971-76; spl. justice Rockingham Dist. Ct., 1975-76. Bd. dirs. Shenandoah Valley Choral Soc., Harrisonburg, 1970-76, Valley Community Concerts, Ltd., Harrisonburg, also pres.; bd. dirs. Shenandoah Valley Music Festival, Inc., Orkney Springs, Va. Mem. Va. State Bar, Va., Am. Harrisonburg-Rockingham bar assns. Home: 417 Monticello Ave Harrisonburg VA 22801 Office: 206 Virginia National Bank Bldg Harrisonburg VA 22801 Tel (703) 434-7306

HATT, DONALD GREGORY, b. Albany, N.Y., Sept. 18, 1917; B.A., Williams Coll., 1940; LL.B., Albany Law Sch., 1947. Admitted to N.Y. bar, 1947; asso. firm George J. Hatt, II, Albany, 1947-58; individual practice law, Albany, 1958-62, 75—; partner firm Olson, Sanford & Hatt, and predecessors, Albany, 1962-75; spl. lectr. bankruptcy law Albany Law Sch., 1963-71. Pres., Family and Children's Service, Albany, 1962-64; pres. NE N.Y. Speech Center, 1965-66, Council Community Services, 1972-74. Mem. Am., N.Y., Albany County bar assns., Am. Arbitration Assn. (panel arbitrators). Office: Donald G Hatt 90 State St Albany NY 12207 Tel (518) 463-1189

HAUBERG, ROBERT ENGELBRECHT, b. Brookhaven, Miss., Nov. 20, 1910; student Millsaps Coll., 1928-30; LL.B., Jackson Sch. Law, 1932. Admitted to Miss. bar, 1932; individual practice law, Jackson, 1932-54; prof. Jackson Sch. Law, 1933-64, registrar, 1933-44, vice dean, 1938-44, dean, 1944-64; asst. city pros. atty. Jackson (Miss.), 1932-37; asst. U.S. atty. So. Dist. Miss., 1944-54, U.S. atty., 1954—; mem. Miss. Senate, 1940-44. Trustee Hinds County chpt. ARC, 1937-45; bd. dirs. Miss. Assn. Crime and Delinquency, 1941; mem. Jackson Juvenile Council, Council Social Agys., 1939-43. Mem. Fed., Am., Miss., Hinds County bar assns., Alpha Omega, Sigma Delta Kappa. Recipient Boss of Year award Jackson Legal Sec. Assn., 1973-74; Distinguished Service award Miss. chpt. Fed. Bar Assn., 1976; Distinguished Service award Miss. Coll. Sch. Law, 1977. Home: 1045 Claiborne St Jackson MI 39209 Office: Box 2091 Jackson MI 30205 Tel (601) 969-4480

HAUDEK, WILLIAM E., b. Vienna, Austria, Mar. 24, 1905; J.D., U. Berlin, 1931; LL.B., Yale, 1938. Admitted to N.Y. bar, 1944, U.S. Supreme Ct. bar, 1952; law lectr. U. Berlin, 1926-33; asso. judge Dist. Ct., Berlin, Germany, 1932-33; mem. firm Pomerantz Levy Haudek & Block, N.Y.C., 1945—. Mem. Am. Bar Assn., N.Y. County Lawyers Assn., Assn. Bar City N.Y. Editor Yale Law Jour., 1938; author: The Intention of the Parties in the Conflict of Laws, 1931; contbr. articles to legal jours. Home: 1080 Fifth Ave New York City NY 10028 Office: 295 Madison Ave New York City NY 10017 Tel (212) 532-4800

HAUGEN, GENE MERVIN, b. Williston, N.D., Mar. 22, 1942; B.S., Kans. State U., 1965; J.D., Washburn U., 1971. Admitted to Kans. bar, 1971, N.D. bar, 1971; mem. firm McIntee & Whisenand, Williston, 1971—. Bd. dirs. Project Head Start, Williston, 1975—. Mem. Am., Kans., N.D. bar assns., Kans., Am. assns. trial lawyers. Home: 501 12th Ave W Williston ND 58801 Office: 113 E Broadway Williston ND 58801 Tel (701) 572-6781

HAUGEN, WILLIS GEORGE, b. Waterloo, Iowa, May 29, 1929; B.A., Iowa State Tchrs. Coll., 1951; M.A., U. Minn., 1953; LL.B., Harvard, 1959. Admitted to Ga. bar, 1959; partner firm Sanders, Mottola, Haugen, Wood & Goodson, Newnan, Ga., 1959—. Sec. Ga. Democratic Party, 1971-74; mem. Ga. Bd. Human Resource, 1974-76. Mem. Ga. State, Coweta County bar assns. Home: 14 Sherwood Dr Newnan GA 30263 Office: 11 Perry St Newnan GA 30263 Tel (404) 253-3880

HAUGH, JAMES T., b. Rutland, Vt., 1916; student U. Vt., 1934-37; LL.B., Boston U., 1940. Admitted to Vt. bar, 1941; now mem. firm Ryan, Smith & Carbine, Ltd., Rutland; city atty. City of Rutland, 1950-57. Fellow Am. Coll. Trial Lawyers; mem. Rutland County (pres. 1966-67), Vt. (jud. nominating bd. 1967—, pres. 1977-78), Am. bar assns., Internat. Assn. Ins. Counsel. Office: PO Box 310 Mead Bldg Rutland VT 05701 Tel (802) 773-3344*

HAUGHEY, JAMES MCCREA, b. Courtland, Kans., July 8, 1914; LL.B., U. Kans., 1939. Admitted to Kans. bar, 1939, Mont. bar, 1943; landman Carter Oil Co., various locations, 1939-43; asso. firm Crowley, Haughey, Hanson, Toole & Dietrich, and predecessors, Billings, Mont., 1943-50, partner, 1950—; mem. Mont. Ho. of Reps., 1960-64; mem. Mont. Senate, 1966-70, minority leader, 1969-70; pres. Rocky Mountain Mineral Law Found., 1957-58. Pres., Mont. Inst. Arts Found., 1965-67. Mem. Am., Mont., Yellowstone County (pres. 1960-61) bar assns., Am. Judicature Soc. Contbr. articles to legal jours. Home: 2205 Tree Ln Billings MT 59102 Office: 500 Electric Bldg Billings MT 59101 Tel (406) 252-3441

HAUGHT, WILLIAM DIXON, b. Kansas City, Kans., June 12, 1939; B.A., U. Kans., 1961; LL.B., 1964; LL.M., Georgetown U., 1968. Admitted to Kans. bar, 1964, Ark. bar, 1971, U.S. Supreme Ct. bar, 1968; with JAGC, U.S. Army, Korea and Washington, 1964-68; asso. firm Weeks, Thomas, Lysaught, Bingham & Johnston, Kansas City, 1968-70; partner firm Wright, Lindsey & Jennings, Little Rock, 1971—. Mem. Am. (vice chmn. bar related support activities com., sect. real property, probate and trust law), Ark., Pulaski County bar assns. Contbr. articles to legal jours. Office: 2200 Worthen Bank Bldg Little Rock AR 72201 Tel (501) 371-0808

HAUKOHL, ROBERT T., b. Milw., July 7, 1942; B.A., Lawrence Coll., 1964; J.D., U. Wis., 1967. Admitted to Wis. bar, 1967; dir. personnel, legal counsel Ken Cook Co., Milw., 1967-73, dir. purchases, personnel and legal counsel, 1973—. Mem. Am., Wis. bar assns., Am. Mgmt. Assn., Am. Purchasing Soc. Office: 9929 W Silver Spring Dr Milwaukee WI 53225 Tel (414) 466-6060

HAUPTMAN, HERBERT MORRIS, b. Chgo., May 26, 1907; diploma in commerce Northwestern U., 1931; LL.B., John Marshall Law Sch., 1934, J.D., 1970. Admitted to Ill. bar, 1936; office mgr. Lyons & Kennelly, Inc., Chgo., 1926-33; salesman Morris Fisheries, Inc., Chgo., 1933-34; comptroller Meadowmoor Dairies, Inc., Chgo., 1934-36; individual practice law, Chgo., 1936—; sr. partner firm Schur, Hauptman and Co., C.P.A.'s, 1937—. Bd. dirs. Temple, 1955—; mem. exec. bd. Nat. Fedn. Temple Men's Clubs, 1960—; v.p. Nat. Fedn. Temple Brotherhoods, 1966-72; exec. bd. Jewish Chautauqua Soc., 1962. Mem. Am., Ill. bar assns., Am. Judicature Soc. Home: 5000 Cornell Ave Chicago IL 60615 Office: 20 North Wacker Dr Chicago IL 60606 Tel (312) 782-6400

HAUSER, LAWRENCE LOUIS, b. Norwalk, Conn., Dec. 16, 1942; student Fribourg (Switzerland) U., 1963; A.B. in Philosophy, Georgetown U., 1964; J.D., George Washington U., 1967; postgrad. (Swiss Govt. grantee from Fulbright com.) U. Geneva, 1967. Admitted to Conn. bar, 1967, U.S. Supreme Ct. bar, 1971; legal research asst. Legal Advisors Office, Dept. State, Washington, 1967; partner firm Tierney, Zullo Flaherty & Hauser, Norwalk, Conn., 1967—. Chmn. UN and UNICEF, Norwalk, 1969-75; bd. dirs. Norwalk YMCA, 1970-76; trustee Soc. to Advance the Retarded, Fairfield County, Conn., 1973—. Mem. Norwalk-Wilton, Conn. (family law com.) bar assns. Named Young Man of Year Norwalk Jaycees, 1972. Home: Pine Hill Rd E Norwalk CT 06855 Office: 134 East Ave Norwalk CT 06852 Tel (203) 853-7000

HAUSER, ROGER ALEXANDER, b. Blauvelt, N.Y., July 3, 1940; A.B., Fordham U., 1961, J.D., 1964. Admitted to N.J. bar, 1965, U.S. Supreme Ct. bar, 1969; individual practice law, Hackensack, N.J., 1965-67; partner firm Hauser and Escala, Englewood, N.J., 1967-73, Hauser and Kahn, Englewood, 1974—; judge Northvale (N.J.) Municipal Ct., 1972—, Westwood (N.J.) Municipal Ct., 1976, Englewood Municipal Ct., 1975; counsel Bergenfield Bd. Adjustment, 1974, 75, Bergenfield Planning Bd., 1973, 77, Bergenfield Rent Levelling Bd., 1973, 77, Englewood Bd. Adjustment, 1971-72, Fine Arts Council Englewood, 1975-76. Pres., Art Center No. N.J. Mem. Am., N.J., Bergen County bar assns., Am. Judicature Soc., Atty's Soc. Bergen County (pres. 1971), Am. Judges' Assn. Office: 50 E Palisade Ave Englewood NJ 07631 Tel (201) 568-5353

HAUVER, ARTHUR RONALD, b. Frederick, Md., Sept. 1, 1938; B.A., Swarthmore Coll., 1960; J.D., U. Denver, 1968. Admitted to Colo. bar, 1968, U.S. Supreme Ct. bar, 1971, U.S. Ct. Appeals 10th Circuit bar, 1971, 7th Circuit bar, 1972, 6th Circuit bar, 1973, 8th Circuit bar, 1973, 9th Circuit bar, 1974, U.S. Dist. Ct. Colo. bar, 1968, U.S. Tax Ct. bar, 1969, D.C. Circuit bar, 1976; partner firm Jones, Meiklejohn, Kehl & Lyons, Denver, 1968—; lectr. Denver Coll. Law. Mem. Am., Colo., Denver, Arapahoe County bar assns., Motor Carriers Lawyers Assn, Assn. I.C.C. Practitioners. Contbr. articles in field to law jours. Home: 5825 Bell Flower Dr Littleton CO 80123 Office: 1600 Lincoln Center Bldg Denver CO 80264 Tel (303) 534-3245

HAVEL, RICHARD WILLIAM, b. Fairmont, Minn., Sept. 20, 1946; B.A., U. Notre Dame, 1968; J.D., U. Calif., Los Angeles, 1971. Admitted to Calif. bar, 1971; mem. firm Shutan & Trost, Los Angeles, 1971-77, partner, 1977—; adj. prof. Loyola Sch. Law, 1975-77. Mem. Am., Calif. State, Los Angeles County (asst. editor Comml. Law and Bankruptcy Digest, 1974-75) bar assns. Office: 1880 Century Park E Los Angeles CA 90067 Tel (213) 553-8100

HAVERLY, HARRY CALVERT, b. Omaha, July 13, 1930; B.S., U. Nebr., 1953, M.A., 1956, J.D., 1959; postgrad. U. Minn. Juvenile Justice Inst., 1969, U. Okla. Nat. Drug Edn. Seminar, 1973; grad. Nat. Coll. State Judiciary, 1970. Admitted to Nebr. bar, 1959; asso. firm W. H. Meier, Minden, Nebr., 1960-62; police judge City of Minden, 1961-62; dep. county atty. Adams County (Nebr.), 1962-63; judge Adams County Ct., 1963-72, 10th County Ct. Jud. Dist., 1973—; mem. Hastings (Nebr.) Youth Problems Council, 1963—, chmn., 1964-65; mem. Area 13 Youth Planning Commn., Crime Commn.; mem. adv. bd. on Juvenile Probation Laws and County Ct. Reorgn. for Nebr.; Nebr. del. at large White House Conf. on Children and Youth, 1970; mem. Gov.'s Task Force on Child Welfare, 1977—. Bd. dirs. Campus House for Girls, Kearney, Nebr., 1972—, chmn., 1972-73; bd. dirs. Foster Homes for Central Nebr.; mem. exec. com. Nebr. Com. for Children and Youth. Mem. Neb. 10th Jud. Dist., Adams County (pres. 1965-66) bar assns., Nebr. Juvenile Judges Assn. (pres. 1966-67), Nebr. County Judges Assn. (exec. bd., sec. 1973-74), Am. Judicature Soc., Nebr. Juvenile Justice Assn. (pres.-elect 1977), Nat. Council Juvenile Ct. Judges Assn., Nat. Coll. Probate Judges. Recipient Good Govt. award Hastings Jaycees, 1958. Home: 1130 Hastings Ave Hastings NE 68901 Office: POB 95 Courthouse Hastings NE 68901 Tel (402) 463-2491

HAVIGHURST, BRUCE JAMES, b. Cleve., Dec. 8, 1937; A.B. magna cum laude, Amherst Coll., 1959; J.D. magna cum laude, Harvard, 1963. Admitted to Ohio bar, 1964; law clk. to Judge William Hastie, Third Circuit Ct. Appeals, Phila., 1963-64; asso. firm Jones, Day, Reavis & Pogue, Cleve., 1964-68, 69—; asso. prof. Law Sch. U. Va., Charlottesville, 1968. Treas. Harvard Law Sch. Assn. Cleve., 1972—. Mem. Cleve. Bar Assn., Phi Beta Kappa (trustee Cleve. assn. 1974—, treas. 1975-77, v.p. 1977—). Home: 18432 Lynton Rd Shaker Heights OH 44122 Office: 1700 Union Commerce Bldg Cleveland OH 44115 Tel (216) 696-3939

HAVILAND, CAMILLA KLEIN, b. Dodge City, Kans., Sept. 13, 1926; A.A., Monticello Coll., 1946; A.B., Radcliffe Coll., 1948; LL.B., U. Kans., 1955, J.D., 1968. Admitted to Kans. bar, 1955, U.S. Dist. Ct., 1955; asso. firm Calvert & White, Wichita, 1955; individual practice law, Dodge City, 1956; probate, county and juvenile judge, Ford County, 1957-77; mem. Atty. Gen.'s Youth Com., 1962-66, probate law study com. Kans. Jud. Council, 1973-75, probate forms com., 1975—. Nat. committeewoman Young Democrats Kans., 1948-54; nat. v.p. Young Democrats Am., 1953-55; mem. adv. com. Kans. U. Sch. Relgion, 1968, Sch. Social Welfare, 1972—; mem. adv. bd. St. Mary of the Plains Coll., 1961-67, D.C. Corps, Salvation Army, 1956—. Mem. Am., S.W., Kans., Ford-Gray County bar assns., Order of Coif. Recipient Nathan Burkan Meml. award ASCAP, 1955, award of recognition Nat. Council Juvenile Ct. Judges, 1963; contbr. articles to profl. jours. Home: 2006 East Ln Dodge City KS 67801 Office: Box 17 Dodge City KS 67801 Tel (316) 225-5262

HAVRON, JAMES COWAN, b. Tullahoma, Tenn., Aug. 8, 1908; LL.B., Cumberland U., 1930, J.D., 1969. Admitted to Tenn. bar, 1931; mem. firm Callicott, Marshall & Havron, and predecessors, Nashville, 1931—; mem., sec. Humane and Juvenile Ct. Commn., Davidson County, Tenn., 1940-42; mem. Tenn. Ho. of Reps., 1935. Mem. Tenn., Nashville bar assns. Home: 334 Jocelyn Hollow Circle Nashville TN 37205 Office: 513 Nashville City Bank & Trust Bldg Nashville TN 37201 Tel (615) 242-6465

HAWES, DOUGLAS WESSON, b. West Orange, N.J., Nov. 17, 1932; B.A., Principia Coll., 1954; J.D., Columbia, 1957; M.B.A., N.Y. U., 1961. Admitted to N.Y. bar, 1958, U.S. Supreme Ct. bar, 1961; asso. firm LeBoeuf, Lamb, Leiby & MacRae, N.Y.C., 1958, now partner; adj. prof. law Vanderbilt U., 1972—, N.Y. U., 1976—; dir. Bradford Nat. Corp., Everfast, Inc., Hackensack Water Co. Mem. Am. (fed. securities law com.), N.Y. State bar assns., Bar Assn. City N.Y. (corp. law com.), Am. Law Inst. Contbr. articles to legal publs. Home: 755 Park Ave New York City NY 10021 Office: 140 Broadway New York City NY 10005 Tel (212) 269-1100

HAWGOOD, WILLIAM SHEPARD, II, b. Cleve., July 20, 1941; B.A., Duke U., 1963; J.D. with high distinction, U. Mich., 1966. Admitted to Ariz. bar, 1967; asso. firm Streich, Lang, Weeks, Cardon & French, Phoenix, 1967-70, mem., 1971—. Pres., chmn. bd. dirs. 7th Step Found., 1970—; pres. Ariz. Montessori Schs., 1972-74; chmn. inner city youtn programs com. YMCA, 1973—; bd. dirs. Phoenix Inner City Food Coop., 1973-74. Mem. Am., Maricopa County bar assns. Office: 2100 1st National Bank Plaza 100 W Washington Phoenix AZ 85003 Tel (602) 257-0999

HAWKINS, FRANCIS GLENN, b. Jamesville, Mo., May 31, 1917; A.B., S.W. Mo. State U., 1938; M.A., Okla. State U., 1941; J.D., U. Tulsa, 1955. Admitted to Okla. bar, 1955; with Bank of Okla., Tulsa, 1951—, v.p., 1957-66, sr. trust officer, after 1957, then sr. v.p., 1966—, now sr. v.p. adminstrn. Mem. Tulsa County, Okla. bar assns. Home: 4410 S Louisville St Tulsa OK 74135 Office: PO Box 2300 Tel (918) 588-6581

HAWKINS, HARMAN, b. Rockville Centre, N.Y., June 6, 1919; A.B., Amherst Coll., 1941; LL.B., Harvard U., 1947. Admitted to N.Y. State bar, 1947; mem. firm Duer, Strong & Whitehead, N.Y.C., 1950-68, firm DeForest & Duer, N.Y.C., 1968—; counsel Manhasset Union Free Sch. Dist., 1964—. Pres. Plandome (N.Y.) Assn., 1961—; trustee, water commr. Village of Plandome, 1966-73; bd. dirs. United Fund, Manhasset, 1966-71. Mem. Am., N.Y. bar assns., Assn. Bar City N.Y. Home: 22 Heights Rd Plandome NY 11030 Office: 20 Exchange Pl New York City NY 10005 Tel (212) 296-0230

HAWKINS, WILLIAM BLEDSOE, b. Lynchburg, Va., Aug. 27, 1912; A.B., Davidson Coll., 1932; LL.B., U. S.C., 1935. Admitted to S.C. bar, 1934, U.S. Dist. Ct. bar, 1954, U.S. Supreme Ct. bar, 1961; since practiced in Dillon, S.C.; partner firm Hawkins & Bethia, 1935-57; individual practice law, 1957-69; partner firm Hawkins and McInnis, 1969—; dir. First Citizens Bank & Trust Co.; mem. legislature, State of S.C., 1966-72. Chmn. Dillon County (S.C.) Devel. Bd., 1972—; trustee U. S.C.; bd. dirs. St. Eugene Community Hosp. Mem. Am., S.C. State, Dillon County (pres. 1968-70) bar assns., C. of C. (pres. 1966). Home: 310 Johnson Dr Dillon SC 29536 Office: 302 W Harrison St Dillon SC 29536 Tel (803) 774-8236

HAWLEY, PAUL FREDERICK, b. Cananea, Sonora, Mex., Apr. 26, 1910; B.E.E., U. Ariz., 1948; M.E.E., Calif. Inst. Tech., 1933, Ph.D., 1937; student Tulsa Law Sch., 1939-41; J.D., John Marshall Law Sch., 1943. Admitted to Ill. bar, 1943, Okla. bar, 1948; research engr. Wester Geoghys. Co., 1935-38; research physicist Standard Oil & Gas Co., 1938-41; patent agt. Standard Oil (Ind.), 1941-43; chief engr. Consol. Engring. Co., Pasadena, Calif., 1943-47; patent dir. Amoco Prodn. Co., Tulsa, 1947-75; prof. engring. Okla. State U., 1948-60; prof. engring. and law U. Tulsa, 1960—. Mem. Joint City/County Zoning Bd., Tulsa, 1950-70. Mem. Am. Bar Assn., Am. Patent Law Assn., Tau Beta Pi, Delta Theta Phi, Sigma Xi. Home: 5811 E 71st St Tulsa OK 74136 Office: 600 S College St Tulsa OK 74104 Tel (918) 492-9753

HAWORTH, BYRON ALLEN, b. Danville, Ind., June 27, 1907; A.B., Guilford Coll., 1928; LL.B., Duke, 1934. Admitted to N.C. bar, 1934; practiced in High Point, N.C., 1934-56; judge Municipal Ct., High Point, 1956-68, N.C. Dist. Ct., 18th Jud. Dist., 1968—; mem. N.C. Ho. of Reps., 1955-57. Trustee Guilford Coll. Home: 902 Fairway Dr High Point NC 27262 Office: 222 S Hamilton St High Point NC 27261 Tel (919) 886-8522

HAWSEY, LEMUEL EARL, JR., b. New Orleans, Aug. 13, 1923; B.S., La. State U., 1949, J.D., 1953. Admitted to La. bar, 1953; individual practice law, Baton Rouge, 1953-60; partner firm Baggett, Hawsey, McClain & Morgan, Lake Charles, La., 1960-76; judge 14th Jud. Dist. Calcasieu and Cameron parishes, La., 1976—. Bd. dirs. Family and Youth Counseling Agy., Inc. Mem. La., SW La., Am., bar assns., Am. Judicature Soc., La. Dist. Judges Assn. Home: 1117 LaFitte St Lake Charles LA 70601 Office: Calcasieu Parish Courthouse POB 3209 Lake Charles LA 70601 Tel (318) 436-3659

HAXBY, LEONARD JAMES, b. Whitehall, Mont., Oct. 30, 1938; LL.B., LaSalle U., 1962. Admitted to Mont. bar, 1964, U.S. Dist. Ct. bar, 1965, 9th Circuit Ct. Appeals bar, 1965; partner firm Holland, Holland & Haxby, 1965-74; asst. staff atty. Silver Bow County Legal Services, 1966-68; sr. counsel metall. div. Anaconda Mining Co., 1974-75; hearing officer Mont. Dept. Instns., Butte, 1975—; pub. defender, Silver Bow County, 1975-77. Pres. Silver Bow Humane Soc., 1969-72; bd. dirs. Big Bros. Am., 1966-67, United Givers, 1974-76. Mem. Am. Judicature Soc., Am., Mont., Silver Bow County (v.p. 1976-77), bar assns. Recipient certificate of achievement Law Day Presentation, 1969. Home: 2720 Wharton St Butte MT 59701 Office: 523 E Front St Butte MT 59701 Tel (406) 792-9222

HAY, JOHN LEONARD, b. Lawrence, Mass., Oct. 6, 1940; B.A. with distinction, Stanford, 1961; J.D., U. Colo., 1964. Admitted to Colo. bar, 1964, Ariz. bar, 1965, D.C. bar, 1971; asso. firm Lewis and Roca, Phoenix, 1964-69, partner, 1969—. Mem. Democratic Precinct Com., 1966—; mem. Ariz. Dem. Com., 1968—; chmn. Dem. Legis. Dist., 1971-74; mem. Maricopa County (Ariz.) Dem. Central Com., 1971-74; bd. dirs. Ariz. Civil Liberties Union, 1967—, pres., 1973—; bd. dirs. ACLU, 1972—. Mem. Am., Maricopa County (dir. 1971—) bar assns., State Bar Ariz. Home: 326 W Cypress St Phoenix AZ 85003 Office: 100 W Washington St 23d Floor Phoenix AZ 85003 Tel (602) 262-5331

HAYDEN, CARL THERAL, b. Saline, Mich., Apr. 1, 1941; A.B., Hamilton Coll., 1963; J.D., Cornell U., 1970. Admitted to N.Y. state bar, 1971; asso. firm Ziff, Weiermiller, Learned & Hayden, Elmira, N.Y., 1970-72, partner, 1972—. Chmn. Chemung County Charter Revision Commn., 1975-77; chmn. Chemung County chpt. ARC, 1975-77; pres. Chemung County Neighborhood Legal Services, 1974-75; mem. Finger Lakes Hosp. Planning Group, 1975-77. Mem. Am. Trial Lawyers Assn., N.Y. State, Chemung County bar assns. Recipient Good Neighbor award ARC, 1976; certificate appreciation Genessee Region Health Planning Council, 1976. Home: Watercure Hill Rd Elmira NY 14901 Office: 301 William St Elmira NY 14901 Tel (607) 734-1518

HAYDEN, CHARLES MICHAEL, JR., b. Batesville, Ark., Feb. 21, 1945; B.S. in Bus. Adminstrn., U. Ark., 1967; J.D., Emory U., 1973. Admitted to Ga. bar, 1973; law clk. firm George Montis, Decatur, Ga., 1972-74; asso. firm Henning, Chambers & Mabry, Atlanta, 1974—. Mem. Ga. Bar. Office: 2200 Century Pkwy Suite 825 Atlanta GA 30345 Tel (404) 325-4800

HAYDOCK, ROGER SILVE, b. Chgo., May 1, 1945; A.B., St. Mary's Coll., Minn., 1967; J.D., DePaul U., 1969. Admitted to Ill. bar, 1969, Minn. bar, 1970, U.S. Supreme Ct. bar, 1973; Reginald Heber Smith Community lawyer fellow Legal Assistance of Ramsey County (Minn.), 1969-71, chief counsel, 1972; asso. prof. law William Mitchell Coll. Law, St. Paul, 1972—; dir. William Mitchell Law Clinic, 1973—; cons. Legal Services Tng. Program, 1971—; lectr. Minn. Continuing Legal Edn. Program, 1973—; legal advisor Ramsey Action Programs Community Orgns., 1970-72. Mem. Minn. State, Ramsey County bar assns. Author: Consumer Rights Handbook; contbr. articles to legal jours. Home: 1934 Warbler Ln Saint Paul MN 55119 Office: 875 Summit St Saint Paul MN 55104 Tel (612) 227-7591

HAYES, DAVID EUGENE, b. New Castle, Ind., Feb. 27, 1922; A.B., Hiram Coll., 1946; LL.B., Western Reserve U., 1948. Admitted to Ind. bar, 1950; individual practice law, New Castle, 1951-67; judge Superior Ct., New Castle, Ind., 1968—. Mem. Ind. Juvenile Judges Assn., Ind. State Bar Assn., Ind. Judges Assn. Home: Rural Route 2 New Castle IN 47362 Office: Ct House Main St New Castle IN 47362 Tel (317) 529-6408

HAYES, DAVID JOHN ARTHUR, JR., b. Chgo., July 30, 1929; A.B., Harvard, 1952; LL.B., Ill. Inst. Tech., 1961. Admitted to Ill. bar, 1961; asst. trust officer, sec. First Nat. Bank Evanston (Ill.), 1961-63; gen. counsel Ill. State Bar Assn., 1963-66; asst. exec. dir. Am. Bar Assn., Chgo., 1966—. Mem. Am., Ill. bar assns., Nat. Conf. Bar Counsel, Naval Res. Lawyers Assn. Home: 1233 16th St Wilmette IL 60091 Office: 1155 E 60th St Chicago IL 60637 Tel (312) 947-4014

HAYES, EDWARD BEAN, b. Blue Hill, Maine, Dec. 30, 1896; A.B., U. Ill., 1918; LL.B., Harvard, 1921; LL.D., John Marshall Law Sch., 1949. Admitted to Ill. bar, 1921; partner firm Nortrup, Nortrup and Hayes, Havana, Ill., 1921-25; asst. atty. gen. State of Ill., 1924-25; asso. firm Scott, Bancroft, Martin & Macleish, Chgo., 1925-30, Cutting, Moore & Sidley, Chgo., 1930-32; partner firm Kremer, Branand & Hayes, Chgo., 1932-43; partner, of counsel Lord, Bissell & Brook, and predecessors, Chgo., 1943—; lectr. constnl. and maritime law; founder, 1st dir. admiralty and maritime law div. Grad. Inst. John Marshall Law Sch. Mem. Am., Ill., Chgo. (1st chmn. admiralty and maritime sect.), Inter-Am. bar assns., Maritime Law Assn., Phi Beta Kappa, Delta Upsilon. Home: 2323 Rue Adriane La Jolla CA 92037 Office: 115 S LaSalle St Chicago IL 60603

HAYES, FREDERICK CLAYTON, b. Pontiac, Mich., Dec. 27, 1930; B.A., Alma (Mich.) Coll., 1951; postgrad Columbia U., 1952-53, N.Y. Law Sch., 1953-57, Columbia Law Sch., 1957-58. Admitted to N.Y. bar, 1958; mem. firm Barron, Rice and Rockmore, N.Y.C., 1958-59, Harry H. Lipsig, N.Y.C., 1959-62; individual practice law, N.Y.C., 1962—; atty., legal counsel Harlem Preparatory Sch., N.Y.C., 1968—. Office: 250 W 57th St New York City NY 10019 Tel (212) 582-1265

HAYES, GEORGE NICHOLAS, b. Alliance, Ohio, Sept. 30, 1928; B.A., U. Akron, 1946; M.A., Western Res. U., 1953, LL.B., 1955. Admitted to Ohio bar, 1955, Alaska bar, 1959, Wash. bar, 1973; asst. pros. atty. Portage County (Ohio), Ravenna, 1955-57; asst. U.S. atty., Anchorage and Fairbanks, Alaska, 1957-59; dist. atty. Third Jud. Dist., Anchorage, 1960-62; atty. gen. State of Alaska, Anchorage, 1962-64; sr. mem. firm Delaney, Wiles, Moore, Hayes & Reitman, Inc., 1964—; spl. counsel to Gov. Alaska, 1964, also State of Alaska. Bd. dirs. Alaska State Housing Authority, Anchorage, 1964-66. Mem. Am., Ohio State, Alaska State, Wash. State bar assns. Home: 836 M St Apt 206 Anchorage AK 99501 Office: 1007 W Third Ave Anchorage AK 99501 Tel (907) 279-3581

HAYES, HARRY JOSEPH, b. Milw., Nov. 27, 1912; A.B., Marquette U., 1934, J.D., 1936. Admitted to Wis. bar, 1936; partner firms Hayes & Hayes, 1936-41, Burns Mehigan & Hayes, 1945-58, Mehigan & Hayes, 1958—; spl. agt. FBI, 1941-45; spl. investigator Milw. County Dist. Atty.'s Office, 1950-51; judge Whitefish Bay (Wis.) Municipal Ct., 1940-41, 48-50; atty. Village of Whitefish Bay, 1950-74; atty. Town of Manitowish Waters (Wis.), 1975-76. Mem. Wis., Oneida-Vilas County bar assns. Home and Office: Manitowish Waters WI 54545 Tel (715) 543-2270

HAYES, JOHN FRANCIS, b. Salina, Kans., Dec. 11, 1919; A.B., Washburn U., 1941; LL.B., 1946. Admitted to Kans. bar, 1946, U.S. Supreme Ct. bar, 1961; partner firm Gilliland, Hayes & Goering, Hutchinson, Kans.; mem. Kans. House Reps. 1953-55, 67—. Fellow Am. Coll. Trial Lawyers; mem. Kans., Am. bar assns., Internat. Assn. Insurance Counsel, Hutchinson C. of C. (pres.). Home: 106 Crescent Hutchinson KS 67501 Office: 330 W 1st St Hutchinson KS 67501 Tel (316) 662-0537

HAYES, JOHN LAURENCE, b. Attleboro, Mass., Feb. 25, 1934; B.A., U. R.I., 1957; J.D., U. Mich., 1968. Admitted to Conn. bar, 1968; asso. firm Robinson, Robinson & Cole, Hartford, Conn., 1968-70; partner firm Adinolfi, O'Brien & Hayes, Hartford, 1970—. Dir., Hist. Soc. Glastonbury (Conn.), 1975—. Mem. Am., Conn., Hartford County bar assns., Assn. Trial Lawyers Am. Contbr. articles to Conn. Bar Jour. Home: 86 Main St S Glastonbury CT 06073 Office: One Constitution Plaza Hartford CT 06103 Tel (203) 278-5080

HAYES, KYLE, b. Purlear, N.C., Oct. 4, 1905; LL.B., Wake Forest U., 1931, J.D., 1970. Admitted to N.C. bar, 1930, U.S. Supreme Ct. bar, 1946; individual practice law, North Wilkesboro, N.C., 1931-37; sr. partner firm Hayes and Hayes, North Wilkesboro, 1937—; pres. Northwestern Fin. Co., 1954-75; mem. N.C. Jud. Council, 1974—; mem. rules making com. U.S. Dist. Ct. for Middle Dist. N.C. Trustee Wilkes Community Coll., Wilkesboro, N.C.; mem. advisory bd. Gardner-Webb Coll., Boiling Springs, N.C.; deacon, Sunday Sch. tchr. Wilkesboro Baptist Ch.; Republican candidate for U.S. Congress, 1936, lt. gov., N.C., 1948, gov., N.C., 1956, U.S. Senate, 1960. Mem. Am., Fed., N.C. (bd. govs. 1970-73), Wilkes County (past pres.) bar assns., Am. Judicature Soc., Am. Trial Lawyers Assn., N.C. Trial Lawyers, Fed. Bar (asso.), Practicing Law Inst., Phi Alpha Delta. Home: 604 E Main St Wilkesboro NC 28697 Office: 309 9th St North Wilkesboro NC 28659 Tel (919) 838-5151

HAYES, MICHAEL SEAN, b. Seattle, July 3, 1947; B.A., Seattle U., 1970; J.D., U. Notre Dame, 1973. Admitted to Wash. State bar, 1973, U.S. Supreme Ct. bar, 1976; individual practice law, Seattle, 1973-76; asso. firm Jennings P. Felix, Inc., Seattle, 1976—. Mem. Am., Wash. State, Seattle-King County bar assns. Office: 3010 1st Ave Seattle WA 98121 Tel (206) 624-1290

HAYHURST, RICHARD ALLEN, b. Parkersburg, W.Va., Dec. 28, 1948; student Coll. William and Mary, 1965-66; A.B. in Econs., W.Va. U., 1969; J.D., U. Mich., 1972. Admitted to W.Va. bar, 1972; individual practice law, Parkersburg, 1972—; dep. commr. forfeited and delinquent lands, Wood County, W.Va., 1973-77; prosecuting atty. Ritchie County, W.Va., 1976—. Chmn. Wood County Republican exec. com., 1976-77; v.p., dir. Fine Arts Council Parkersburg, 1974—; trustee Gill I. Wilson Scholarship Fund, 1974—; dir. Actors' Guild Parkersburg, 1973—. Mem. W.Va. State, Am., Wood County, Third Judicial Circuit bar assns. Research asso. Charles Donahue, Jr. and Thomas E. Kauper in preparation Modern Property Law, 1971-72. Office: 209 1/2 4th St Parkersburg WV 26101 Tel (304) 485-7369

HAYNES, ALTON MYLES, b. Cliffside, N.C., May 17, 1927; A.B., U. N.C., 1949; LL.B., J.D., George Washington U., 1952. Admitted to N.C. bar, 1952, D.C. bar, 1953, U.S. Dist. Ct. for Western Dist. N.C. bar, 1959, U.S. Supreme Ct. bar, 1971, U.S. 4th Circuit Ct. Appeals bar, 1974; atty. Nationwide Ins. Co., 1953-59; mem. firm Kennedy, Covington, Lobdell & Hickman, 1953-59; mem. firm Kennedy, Covington, Lobdell & Hickman, 1959-61; partner firm Haynes, Baucom, Chandler & Claytor, Charlotte, N.C., 1961—. Chmn. Welfare Bd. Mecklenburg County (N.C.), 1961-63; chmn. Democratic Party Mecklenburg County, 1972-73; pres. Mecklenburg County Dem. Men's Club, 1960. Mem. N.C. State, 26th Jud. Dist. bar assns., Am. Judicature Soc., Internat. Assn. Ins. Counsel, Charlotte C. of C. (dir. 1972-73). Home: 3900 Stoney Ridge Trail Charlotte NC 28209 Office: 1512 E 4th St Charlotte NC 28204 Tel (704) 376-6527

HAYNES, SHELDON ELIAS, b. White Sulphur Springs, W.Va., Nov. 17, 1909; B.A., Duke, 1930; LL.B., W.Va. U., 1935. Admitted to W.Va. bar, 1935; individual practice law, Lewisburg, W.Va., 1935-42, 1946-54; mem. firm Holt & Haynes, Lewisburg, 1954-55, Haynes & Ford, 1955-74, Haynes, Ford and Guills, 1974—. Pres. Greenbrier County (W.Va.) Hist. Soc., 1974-76; mem. Lewisburg City Council, 1949-58; ruling elder Old Stone Presbyterian Ch., Lewisburg; commr. W.Va. Dept. Natural Resources, 1974—. Mem. Am., W.Va., Greenbrier County (past pres.) bar assns. Home: 211 Dwyer Ln Lewisburg WV 24901 Office: 203 W Randolph St Lewisburg WV 24901 Tel (304) 645-1858

HAYNSWORTH, CLEMENT FURMAN, JR., b. Greenville, S.C., Oct. 30, 1912; A.B. summa cum laude, Furman U., 1933, LL.D., 1964; LL.B., Harvard, 1936. Admitted to S.C. bar, 1936; asso. firm Haynsworth, Perry, Bryant, Marion & Johnstone, and predecessor, Greenville, 1936-40, partner, 1940-46, exec. partner, 1946-57; judge U.S. Ct. Appeals Ct., 4th Circuit, 1957—, chief judge, 1964—. Mem. adv. council Furman U. Mem. Am. Law Inst. (council), S.C., Am. bar assns., Am. Judicature Soc., Phi Beta Kappa, Phi Alpha Delta (hon.). Home: 111 Boxwood Ln Greenville SC 29601 Office: Fed Bldg E Washington St Greenville SC 29603 Tel (803) 235-8949

HAYNSWORTH, HARRY JAY, IV, b. Greensboro, N.C., Apr. 9, 193B; A.B., Duke, 1961, J.D., 1964; postgrad. U. Denver Law 0enter, 1972. Admitted to S.C. bar, 1965; partner firm Haynsworth, Perry, Bryant, Marion & Johnstone, Greenville, S.C., 1964-71; asso. prof. law. U. S.C., 1971-74, prof., 1974—, asso. dean, 1975-76, acting dean, 1976-77; mem. S.C. Legis. Com. to Continue Study of Uniform Consumer Credit Code, 1975—. Chmn. bd. S.C. Commn. for the Blind, 1973-75; bd. dirs. Greenville County (S.C.) Housing Commn., 1970-71; v.p., dir. United Speech and Hearing Center, Greenville, 1970-71; mem. legis. com. S.C. Mental Health Assn.; trustee Heathwood Hall, 1976—, Randolph-Macon Women's Coll., Lynchburg, Va., 1970-75. Mem. Am., S.C. (vice-chmn. consumer and comml. law com. 1975—, bd. govs. 1976-77, sec., mem. exec. com. 1972-75, exec. dir. 1971-72), Richland County bar assns., Am. Law Inst., 4th Circuit Jud. Conf. Author: Proposed Uniform Consumer Credit Code, a Comparative Analysis and Study of Existing S.C. Law, the U.C.C.C. and the Federal Truth in Lending Law, 1969; An Introduction to the Study of Article 9, 1973; Law Office Management, 1973; (with Webster Myers, Jr.) Partnership and Close Corporation Planning and Drafting, 1973; contbr. articles to law revs. and legal jours.; editorial bd. Am. Bar Assn. Jour., 1977—. Home: 1781 Roslyn Dr Columbia SC 29206 Office: Univ SC Sch Law Columbia SC 2920B Tel (803) 777-4155

HAYNSWORTH, KNOX LIVINGSTON, JR., b. Greenville, S.C., Jan. 10, 1934; student The Citadel, 1952-54; LL.B., U. S.C., 1959. Admitted to S.C. bar, 1959, D.C. bar, 1974; asso. firm Haynsworth, Perry, Bryant, Marion & Johnstone, Greenville, 1959-63; partner firm Thompson, Ogletree, Haynsworth & Deakins, Greenville, 1963-72, Haynsworth, Baldwin & Miles, 1972—; mem. 4th Circuit Jud. Conf. Mem. Am., S.C. (bd. govs. 1975, ho. dels. 1975-77, chmn. specialization com. 1975-77), D.C., Greenville County bar assns. Home: 20 Woodland Way Circle Greenville SC 29601 Office: PO Box 10005 Green Gate Park 25 Woods Lake Rd Suite 600 Greenville SC 29607 Tel (803) 271-7410

HAYS, DONALD CHAMBERLIN, b. N.Y.C., Apr. 30, 1911; B.A., U. Colo., 1932, LL.B., 1935. Admitted to N.Y. bar, 1937; law clk. firm Gifford, Woody, Carter & Hays, and predecessor, N.Y.C., 1935-42, partner, 1942—. Mem. Assn. Bar City N.Y., Am. Bar Assn., New York County Lawyers Assn., JAG Assn., Lawyers Club, Phi Delta Phi, Phi Delta Theta. Home: 501 E 79th St New York City NY 10021 Office: 14 Wall St New York City NY 10005 Tel (212) 349-7400

HAYS, JACK D. H., b. Lund, Nev., Feb. 17, 1917; B.S., So. Meth. U., 1939; LL.B., 1941. Admitted to Ariz. bar, 1946; individual practice law, Phoenix, 1946-49; asst. atty. City of Phoenix, 1949-52; U.S. atty Dist. Ariz., 1953-60; judge Maricopa County (Ariz.) Superior Ct., 1960-69, Maricopa County Juvenile Ct., 1964-66; justice Ariz. Supreme Ct., Phoenix, 1969—, chief justice, 1972-74; mem. Ariz. Ho. of Reps. 1952. Adv. bd. Roosevelt council Boy Scouts Am., Phoenix; bd. dirs. Salvation Army, Phoenix; pres. Maricopa County Jr. Coll. Found., 1965-66; bd. dirs. Maricopa County Legal Aid Soc., 1962-68. Mem. Am. Judicature Soc. (Herbert Lincoln Harley award 1974), Am., Ariz. bar assns., Ariz. Judges Assn. (past pres.), Phi Alpha Delta. Home: 1114 W Monte Vista Dr Phoenix AZ 85007 Office: State Capitol Room 221 Phoenix AZ 85007 Tel (602) 271-5789

HAYS, PAUL R., b. Des Moines, Apr. 2, 1903; A.B., Columbia, 1925, M.A., 1927, LL.B., 1933. Admitted to N.Y. State bar, 1933; asso. firm Cravath, deGersdorff, Swaine & Wood, N.Y.C., 1933-34, 35-36; counsel Nat. Recovery Adminstrn., Resettlement Adminstrn., Washington, 1934-35; asst. prof. Sch. Law, Columbia, N.Y.C., 1936-38, asso. prof., 1938-43, prof., 1943-57, 61-71, emeritus, 1971—; judge U.S. Circuit Ct., 2d circuit, N.Y.C., 1961—; mem. N.Y. State Bd. Mediation, 1940-44, U.S. Bd. Legal Examiners, 1941-44; legal cons. N.Y. State Banking Dept., 1936-37, N.Y. State Law Revision Com., 1937, 45, U.S. Dept. Justice, 1944, 45. Mem. N.Y.C. Bd. Health, 1954-60; presdl. elector, 1960. Mem. Am., N.Y. State bar assns., Assn. Bar City N.Y., N.Y. County Lawyers Assn., Phi Beta Kappa. Office: US Court House New York City NY 10007 Tel (212) 791-0913

HAYS, ROBERT DAVIES, b. Pitts., Apr. 12, 1927; B.S. in Bus. Adminstrn., Ohio State U., 1950, J.D., 1952. Admitted to Ohio bar, 1952; asso. firm Alexander, Ebinger and Wengar, Columbus, Ohio, 1952-56; asst. gen. counsel White Castle Systems, Inc., Columbus, 1956-77, asst. sec., 1964-72, sec., 1972—, gen. counsel, 1977—. Mem. Am., Columbus, Ohio bar assns., Nat., Ohio restaurant assns., Food Service and Lodging Inst., Ohio C. of C., Ohio State U. Alumni Assn. Recipient Distinguished Service award Columbus Jaycees, 1962. Office: PO Box 1498 555 W Goodale St Columbus OH 43216 Tel (614) 228-5781

HAYS, SAMUEL SPARTAN, b. Fairfield, Ala., Apr. 15, 1920; B.S., U. Ala., 1942, LL.B., 1952, J.D., 1952; M.S. in Govt. Mgmt., U. Denver, 1944. Admitted to Ala. bar, 1952; rep. Tax Assn. Md., 1944-45; research dir. Tax Assn. Mo., 1945-46; exec. dir. Tax Assn. Ark., 1946-50; cons. Tax Assn. Pa., summer 1952; partner firm Harsh, Glasser, Lankford & Hays, Birmingham, Ala., 1952-59; tax advisor Govt. of Iran, Tehran, 1959-65, Govt. of Jordan, Amman, 1965; individual practice law, Mountain Brook, Ala., 1966—. Bd. dirs. Jefferson County (Ala.) Jr. Achievement, 1957-59. Mem. Ala. State Bar Assn. (past chmn. tax com.). Editor Ala. Law Rev., 1952. Home: 3128 Ryecroft Rd Mountain Brook AL 35223 Office: 10 Office Park Circle Mountain Brook AL 35223 Tel (205) 879-9846

HAYS, STANLEY ROBERT, b. Denver, Dec. 4, 1923; B.B.S., Colo. U., 1948; LL.B., Westminster Law Sch., 1952. Admitted to Colo. bar, 1952; individual practice law, Denver, 1952-59; with securities div. State of Colo., Denver, 1959, securities commr., 1961—; ex-officio chmn. securities com. corp., banking and bus. law sect. Colo. Bar Assn., 1975. Mem. Midwest Securities Commrs. Assn. (v.p. 1968), N.Am. Securities Adminstrs. Assn. (pres. 1969). Office: State Office Bldg Denver CO 80203 Tel (303) 892-2607

HAYTON, CHARLES ANDREW, b. Charleston, Ill., Jan. 31, 1944; B.A., B.S., U. Ill., 1966, J.D., 1969. Admitted to Ill. bar, 1969; asso. firm Jacobs & Spencer, Villa Park, Ill, 1969-70, Carigan, Machay, Quetsch & O'Reily, 1971-72; asst. states atty. DuPage County (Ill.), 1972—. Mem. Ill., Dupage County (chmn. legal aid com., 1971-72) bar assns. Home: 506 Turf Ln Wheaton IL 60187 Office: 207 Reber St Wheaton IL 60167 Tel (312) 682-7605

HAYWARD, GEORGE JOHN, b. Kingston, Pa., Dec. 30, 1944; B.A., Kings Coll., 1966; J.D., Harvard, 1969. Admitted to Pa. bar, 1970; asso. firm Montgomery, McCracken, Walker & Rhoads, Phila., 1969-71, firm Wolf, Block, Schorr & Solis-Cohen, Phila., 1971-72; asso. counsel AAMCO Inc. Co., Inc., Bridgeport, Pa., 1973-74, gen. counsel, 1974—. Mem. Am., Pa., Phila., Montgomery County bar assns. Home: 1306 Lincoln Dr W Ambler PA 19002 Office: 408 E 4th St Bridgeport PA 19405 Tel (215) 277-4000

HAYWARD, THOMAS ZANDER, JR., b. Evanston, Ill., Apr. 21, 1940; B.A., Northwestern U., 1962, J.D., 1965; M.B.A., U. Chgo., 1970. Admitted to Ill. bar, 1966, Ohio bar, 1966; asso. firm Defrees & Fiske, Chgo., 1965-69, partner firm, 1969—. Mem. Ill., Chgo. (bd. mgrs. 1975-77), Am. (com. on ethics and profl. responsibility 1976-79) bar assns., Am. Judicature Soc., Northwestern U. Alumni Assn. (pres. 1977). Home: Rt 2 Box 8 Barrington Hills IL 60010 Office: Suite 1500 75 W Adams St Chicago IL 60603 Tel (312) 372-4000

HAZARD, GEOFFREY CORNELL, JR., b. Cleve., Sept. 18, 1929; B.A., Swarthmore Coll., 1953; LL.B., Columbia, 1954. Admitted to Oreg. bar, 1954, Calif. bar, 1960; asso. firm Davies, Biggs, Strayer, Stoel & Boley, Portland, Oreg., 1954-57; exec. sec. Oreg. Interim Com. on Jud. Adminstrn., 1957-58; asso. prof. law U. Calif., Berkeley, 1958-60, prof., 1960-64; exec. dir. Am. Bar Found., Chgo., also prof. law U. Chgo., 1964-70; prof. law Yale, 1970—, Garver prof. jurisprudence, 1976—; cons. in field. Mem. Am. Bar Assn. (reporter Commn. Standards Jud. Adminstrn. 1971-77), Calif. State Bar, Assn. Bar City N.Y., Law, Soc. Assn., Seldon Soc., Adminstrv. Conf. U.S. Author: (with D.W. Louisell) Practice and Procedure, 1962; 3d rev. edit. 1973; Research in Civil Procedure, 1963; editor: Law in a Changing America, 1968; (with T. Ehrlich) Going to Law School, 1975; contbr. articles to legal jours. Home: 207 Armory St New Haven CT 06511 Office: Yale Law Sch New Haven CT 06520 Tel (203) 436-8253

HAZARD, JOHN NEWBOLD, b. Syracuse, N.Y., Jan. 5, 1909; B.A., Yale, 1930; LL.B., Harvard, 1934; postgrad. (fellow) Inst. Current World Affairs, N.Y.C., 1934-39, Moscow Juridical Inst., 1935-37; J.S.D., U. Chgo., 1939. Admitted to N.Y. State bar, 1935, U.S. Supreme Ct. bar, 1945; asso. firm Baldwin, Todd & Young, N.Y.C., 1939-41; dept. dir. USSR br. Fgn. Econ. Adminstrn., Washington, 1941-46; prof. pub. law Columbia, 1946—. Corr. Fellow Brit. Acad.; mem. Am. Philos. Soc., Am. Acad. Arts and Scis., Am., N.Y. State bar assns., Assn. Bar City N.Y., Internat. Law Assn. (pres. Am. br. 1973—), Am. Fgn. Law Assn. (pres. 1973-76) Am. Soc. Internat. Law (hon. v.p. 1974—). Author: Soviet Housing Law, 1939; Law and Social Change in the USSR, 1953; Settling Disputes in Soviet Society, 1960; Communists and their Law, 1969. Home: 20 E 94th St New York City NY 10028 Office: Columbia U Law Sch New York City NY 10027 Tel (212) 280-2646

HAZELTINE, EARL HENRY, b. Janesville, Wis., Feb. 20, 1939; B.A., U. Wis., 1969, J.D., 1971. Admitted to Wis. bar, 1971; law clk. to justice Wis. Supreme Ct., 1971-72; asso. firm Bell, Blake & Metzner, Madison, Wis., 1972—. Mem. Am., Wis., Dane County bar assns. Mng. editor Wis. Law Rev., 1970-71. Home: 1117 Beech St Sun Prairie WI 53590 Office: 222 W Washington Ave Madison WI 53703 Tel (608) 257-3764

HAZELWOOD, HARRY, JR., b. Newark, Oct. 8, 1921; B.A., Rutgers U., 1943; LL.B., Cornell U., 1945. Admitted to N.J. bar, 1948; practiced in Newark, 1948-74; judge Municipal Ct., Newark, 1958-74, presiding judge, 1969-74; judge Essex County (N.J.) Ct., 1974—; asst. asst. prosecutor Essex County, 1956-58. Pres. Newark br. NAACP, 1949-50, 51-54; mem. Newark Charter Commn., 1954. Mem. Am., N.J. State, Nat., Essex County bar assns. Office: Essex County Cts Bldg Newark NJ 07102 Tel (201) 961-8090

HAZZARD, GERALD FRANCISCO, b. N.Y.C., Sept. 25, 1922; B.A., Coll. City N.Y., 1961. Admitted to N.Y. bar, U.S. Supreme Ct. bar, 1971; staff atty. Queens Legal Services Corp., Long Island City, N.Y. Mem. N.Y. County Lawyers Assn., N.Y. State Bar Assn. Home: 44 W 62d St New York City NY 10023 Office: 1B60 Broadway New York City NY 10023 Tel (212) 586-7761

HEACOCK, ROBERT DUSTIN, JR., b. Omaha, July 22, 1945; B.A. magna cum laude, U. Minn., 1967, J.D., 1970. Admitted to Minn. bar, 1970; prosecutor City of Bloomington (Minn.), asst. city atty., 1970-74; mem. firm Ince, Tischleder & Assos., Bloomington, 1974—. Mem. Youth Commn. Bloomington, 1975-78. Mem. Hennepin County (family law com.), Minn. State bar assns. Home: 7501 Landau Dr Bloomington MN 55438 Office: 8900 Penn Ave Suite 210 Minneapolis MN 55431 Tel (612) 888-8322

HEAD, JACK D., b. Fort Worth, June 18, 1915; LL.B., Washington and Lee U., 1939. Admitted to Tex. bar, 1939; asso. firm Vinson, Elkins, Weems & Francis, 1939-57; v.p., gen. counsel Tex. Eastern Transmission Corp., Houston, 1958-75, exec. v.p., gen. counsel, 1975—. Mem. Houston, Tex., Fed. Power, Am. bar assns., Am. Gas Assn., Phi Delta Phi. Home: 3652 Chevy Chase St Houston TX 77019 Office: PO Box 2521 Houston TX 77001 Tel (713) 651-0161

HEALEY, EDWARD VINCENT, JR., b. Providence, Nov. 23, 1922; A.B., Providence Coll., 1942; LL.B., Boston U., 1949. Admitted to R.I. bar, 1949; law clk., asso. firm Aram A. Arabian and Joseph Mainelli, R.I., 1949-50; asso. Christopher DelSesto, R.I., 1950-52, Healey & Mondlick, R.I., 1952-57, Coleman B. Zimmerman, 1956-59; asso. judge Juvenile Ct. R.I., 1960-61; asso. justice Family Ct. R.I., Providence, 1961—; exec. sec. to Gov. R.I., 1959-60; chmn. bd. trustees Nat. Juvenile Ct. Found., Inc., 1974-75; mem. bd. fellows Nat. Center for Juvenile Justice, 1973-75; faculty mem. Nat. Coll. Juvenile Justice; mem. adv. council Nat. Center for State Cts., 1971-76. Bd. dirs. Am. Parents Com., Inc., 1973—; mem. Juvenile Justice Adv. Com. R.I.; lectr. Providence Coll., U. R.I., R.I. Coll., Roger Williams Coll., High Sch. Seminars R.I.; mem. Commn. on Jud. Tenure and Discipline R.I., Judges Com. on Jud. Ethics R.I., Judges Com. on Family Ct. and Dist. Ct. Prosecutions R.I. Del., White House Conf. on Children, 1970; mem. Gov.'s Conf. on Children and Youth, Gov.'s Commn. to Revise Childrens Code, Gov.'s Task Force to Revise R.I. Criminal Laws, Gov.'s Adv. Com. on Mental Retardation, Gov.'s Adv. Com. on Developmental Disabilities; chpt. chmn. Nat. Found. March of Dimes; past v.p., mem. exec. com. Big Brothers R.I.; bd. dirs. Cranston (R.I.) Boys Club, R.I. League for Emotionally Disturbed Children, R.I. Assn. for Mental Health, Providence Child Guidance Clinic, Providence Youth Progress Bd., Inc., Sophia Little Home, R.I. Conf. Social Work. Mem. Nat. Council Juvenile Ct. Judges (pres. 1974-75, exec. com. 1968-71), R.I. Bar Assn., Internat. Assn. Youth Magistrates (hon. v.p.). Recipient Man of Year award Fraternal Order Eagles, 1969, Man of Year award Christian Brothers Boys Assn., 1973, award for jud. contbn. R.I. Assn. for Retarded Children, 1975. Home: 75 Massasoit Ave Cranston RI 02905 Office: 22 Hayes St Providence RI 02908 Tel (401) 277-3308

HEALEY, RICHARD F., b. Newark, Oct. 3, 1945; B.A., Seton Hall U., 1969, J.D., 1972. Admitted to N.J. bar, 1972; asst. to exec. v.p. Martindale-Hubbell, Inc., Summit, N.J., 1973—. Mem. Am., N.J. bar assns. Home: 105 New England Ave Summit NJ 07901

HEALY, NICHOLAS JOSEPH, lawyer; b. N.Y.C., Jan. 4, 1910; A.B., Coll. Holy Cross, 1931; J.D., Harvard, 1934. Admitted to N.Y. bar, 1935, U.S. Supreme Ct. bar, 1949; claims atty. Royal Indemnity Co., N.Y.C., 1934-36; asso. firm Crawford & Sprague, N.Y.C., 1936-40; pvt. practice law, N.Y.C., 1940-42; spl. asst. to Atty. Gen. U.S., N.Y.C., 1945-48; partner firm Healy & Baillie, and predecessors, N.Y.C., 1948—; instr. admiralty law N.Y. U. Sch. Law, 1947—, adj. prof. law, 1960—; dir. Victory Carriers, Inc. and affiliated cos., N.Y.C., 1968—; asso. editor American Maritime Cases, 1954—; mem. permanent adv. bd. Tulane Admiralty Inst., 1969—. Chmn., U.S. Coast Guard Adv. Panel on Rules of the Rd., 1966-72. Mem. Maritime Law Assn. U.S. (pres. 1964-66), Am. (mem. house dels. 1964-66), N.Y. State bar assns., Assn. Bar of City of N.Y., N.Y. County Lawyers Assn., Internat. Law Assn., Am. Soc. Internat. Law, Comite Maritime Internat. (mem. exec. council 1972—), Assn. of Average Adjusters of U.S. (chmn. 1960-61). Author: (with George C. Sprague) Cases on Admiralty, 1950; (with Brainerd Currie) Cases and Materials on Admiralty, 1965; (with David J. Sharpe) Cases and Materials on Admiralty, 1974. Home: 132 Tullamore Rd Garden City NY 11530 Office: 29 Broadway New York City NY 10006

HEALY, PATRICK FRANCIS, JR., b. Evergreen Park, Ill., Nov. 12, 1933; A.B., Loras Coll., 1957; J.D., Loyola U., Chgo., 1961. Admitted to Ill. bar, 1961; claims atty. Continental Casualty Co., Chgo., 1961-64; asso. firm Tim J. Harrington, Chgo., 1964-69; gen. atty. Ill. Central Gulf R.R., Chgo., 1969—. Mem. Ill. State, S.W. Side bars, Ill. Def. Council, Trial Lawyers Club. Home: 20400 Ithaca Rd Olympia Fields IL 60461 Office: 233 N Michigan Ave Chicago IL 60601 Tel (312) 565-1600

HEALY, WILLIAM TIMOTHY, b. Bayshore, N.Y., Sept. 13, 1932; B.S., Colgate U., 1954; J.D., U. Ariz., 1960. Admitted to Ariz. bar, 1961; atty. Pima County (Ariz.), Tucson, 1961-64, chief trial atty., 1964-66; partner Healy & Beal, Tucson, 1966—. Mem. Am., Pima County bar assns., State Bar Ariz., Am. Bd. Trial Advocates, Am. Trial Lawyers Assn. Home: 6171 Miramar Dr Tucson AZ 85715 Office: 504 Home Fed Tower Tucson AZ 85701 Tel (602) 624-5555

HEANEY, JAMES C., b. Buffalo, Jan. 8, 1924; student, Canisius Coll., 1943; LL.B., U. Buffalo, 1949. Admitted to N.Y. bar, 1950; lawyer Employers Liability Ins. Co., Buffalo, 1949-52; with firm Desmond & Drury, Buffalo, 1952-59; individual practice law, Buffalo, 1959—. Mem. Am. Bar Assn., Am. Arbitration Assn. Home: 387 Cornwall Ave Tonawanda NY 14150 Office: 514 Ellicott Sq Bldg Buffalo NY 14203 Tel (716) 852-2440

HEAP, FRANK KENNETH, b. Evanston, Ill., June 28, 1941; B.S., Northwestern U., 1963; J.D., U. Chgo., 1966. Admitted to Ill. bar, 1966; partner firm Bell, Boyd, Lloyd, Haddad & Burns, Chgo., 1973—. Mem. Fire and Police Commn., Winnetka, Ill., 1976—. Mem. Chgo. Bar Assn., Ill. Soc. CPA's, Am. Inst. CPA's, Am. Judicature Soc. Home: 3 Kent Rd Winnetka IL 60093 Office: 135 S LaSalle St Chicago IL 60603 Tel (312) 372-1121

HEAP, THEODORE HOWARD, b. Miami, Fla., June 8, 1944; B.A. in Accounting, Calif. State U., Fullerton, 1967; J.D., Willamette U., 1970. Admitted to Oreg. bar, 1970; of counsel firm Bauer, Murphy, Fundingsland, Bobbitt & Heap, Portland, Oreg., 1970-77; v.p. legal McCracken Bros. Motor Freight, 1977—; lectr. in field. Mem. com. world trade Portland C. of C. Mem. Oreg. State Bar, Assn. Trial Lawyers Am., Am. (Silver Key award div. law students 1969, gov. div. 1969-70), Multnomah County (Oreg.) bar assns., Oreg. Trial Lawyers Assn., Aircraft Owners and Pilots Assn. Editor-in-chief Willamette Lawyer, 1969-70. Home: 4 SW Touchstone St Lake Oswego OR 97034 Office: 3147 NW Front St Portland OR 97210 Tel (503) 636-8906

HEARD, OLIVER SAMUEL, JR., b. San Antonio, Dec. 18, 1943; B.A. in Govt., U. Tex., 1967, J.D. Admitted to Tex. bar, 1967, U.S. Supreme Ct. bar, 1973; individual practice law, San Antonio; mem. teaching faculty sociology dept. Trinity U., 1975—. Mem. San Antonio Young Lawyers Assn (pres.-elect), San Antonio Lawyers Assn., Tex. Criminal Def. Lawyers Assn., San Antonio Family Lawyers Assn., State Bar Tex., San Antonio Bar Assn. (chmn. continuing legal edn. com.). Home: 138 E Hollywood St San Antonio TX 78212 Office: 1019 Tower Life Bldg San Antonio TX 78205 Tel (512) 225-6763

HEARN, ETTA KAY, b. Clarksdale, Miss., Jan. 30, 1946; B.A. in Polit. Sci., So. U., 1966, J.D., 1969. Admitted to La. bar, 1970; asso. firm Bell, Hearn & McKee, 1970-71; partner firm Hearn & McKee, 1972-73, firm Etta Kay Hearn & Assos., Baton Rouge, 1973—; asst. parish atty. East Baton Rouge Parish; lectr. So. U. Law Sch., 1974—; legal counsel Scottlandville Area Adv. Council. Mem. Am., La. State bar assns., Legal Aid Soc. Louis A. Martinet Legal Soc. (pres.). Named Atty. of Year So. U. Law Sch. Alumni, 1974. Office: 1028 Swan St Baton Rouge LA 70807 Tel (504) 356-5252

HEARNE, WILLIAM MILBRA, b. Tomball, Tex., July 11, 1913; B.A., U. Tex., 1937, J.D., 1939. Admitted to Tex. bar, 1939; individual practice law, Teague, Tex., 1939-41; appeals officer, insp. CSC, Dallas, 1941-71, chief regional appeals office, 1971-72; individual practice law, Dallas, 1972—; arbitrator Fed. Mediation and Conciliation Service, 1972—. Mem. Tex. Bar Assn., Indsl. Relations Research Assn., Am. Legion. Recipient citation Tex. Gov.'s Com. for Employment of Handicapped, 1966; award Okla. VFW Handicapped Employment, 1964. Office: 3215 James St Dallas TX 75227 Tel (214) 381-1304

HEATH, CLAUDE ROBERT, b. Commerce, Tex., May 4, 1947; B.A., U. Tex., 1969, J.D., 1972. Admitted to Tex. bar, 1972; law clk. U.S. Dist. Judge, Western Dist. Tex., Austin, 1972-73; asst. atty. gen. Tex., Austin, 1973—, chmn. opinions div. office atty. gen., Austin, 1974—. Mem. Austin, Jr., Travis County bar assns. Home: 7625 Rockpoint St Austin TX 78731 Office: PO Box 12548 Austin TX 78711 Tel (512) 475-5445

HEATH, FRANK CRONMILLER, b. Weston, W.Va., Aug. 30, 1913; A.B. cum laude, Dartmouth Coll., 1934; J.D., Cornell U., 1937. Admitted to Ohio bar, 1938, U.S. Supreme Ct. bar, 1952, U.S. Circuit Ct. Appeals bar; asso. firm Tolles, Hogsett & Ginn, Cleve., 1937-38; asso. firm Jones, Day, Cockley & Reavis, Cleve., 1939-47; partner firm Jones, Day, Cockley & Reavis, Cleve., 1948-74; partner firm Jones, Day, Reavis & Pogue, Cleve., 1974—; dir. Lord Corp., Erie, Pa.; dir., sec. Erico Products, Inc., Cleve., 1960—. Mem. Cornell Law Sch. Adv. Council, 1958—, chmn., 1975—, chmn. Cornell U. Law Sch. Fund, 1965-69; dir., sec. Cuyahoga Unit Am. Cancer Soc., 1968-73, pres., 1973-75, trustee Ohio div. 1976—; sec. Inner City Protestant Parish, Cleve., 1954-58, chmn. bd. trustees, 1958-61, trustee 1954—. Mem. Am., Ohio, Greater Cleve. bar assns., Cornell Law Assn. (nat. pres. 1969-71), Order Coif, Delta Theta Phi (pres. Cornell Law Sch. chpt. 1937-38), Beta Theta Pi, Ct. Nisi Prius (clk. 1964-65). Editor, bus. mgr. Cornell Law Quar., 1936-37. Home: 22770 Canterbury Ln Shaker Heights OH 44122 Office: 1700 Union Commerce Bldg Cleveland OH 44115 Tel (216) 696-3939

HEATWOLE, MARION GROVE, b. Shenandoah Junction, W.Va., Sept. 1, 1919; B.S., Washington and Lee U., 1941, LL.B., 1946. Admitted to Pa. bar, 1947; atty. Carnegie-Ill. Steel Co., Pitts., 1946-52; gen. atty. U.S. Steel Corp., Pitts., 1952-67, sr. gen. atty., 1967-68, asst. gen. solicitor, 1968-70, asso. gen. counsel, 1970-71, gen. counsel, 1971—. Bd. dirs. Pitts.-Allegheny County chpt. A.R.C.; alumni bd. dirs. Washington and Lee U. Mem. Internat., Am., Pa., Allegheny County bar assns., Order of Coif, Phi Beta Kappa, Omicron Delta Kappa. Home: 2029 Murdstone Rd Pittsburgh PA 15241 Office: 600 Grant St Pittsburgh PA 15230*

HEAVRIN, HELEN HORTON, b. Louisville, Nov. 4, 1907; certificate Sch. Pub. Health, U. Louisville, 1926, student in arts and scis., part-time 1925—, J.D., 1954; LL.B., Jefferson Sch. Law, Louisville, 1928. Water and milk analyst Ky. Bd. Health, Louisville, 1926-28; admitted to Ky. bar, 1928; mgr. physician's lab., Louisville, 1928-38; med. technologist Louisville Bd. Edn., 1939; mgr. lab. Stovall Meml. Hosp., Grayson, Ky., 1950-51, King's Daus. Home, Louisville, 1966-73; individual practice law, Louisville, 1940—. Lectr. Bapt. Sunday Sch. Bd.; group capt., devotional chmn. adult class, sec. adult missionary circle Highland Bapt. Ch., Louisville, also tchr., supt. jr. dept. Sunday Sch. Mem. Am., Ky. bar assns., Ky. Hist. Soc., Am. Soc. Clin. Pathologists (affiliate). Home and office: 1925 Maplewood Pl Louisville KY 40205 Tel (502) 458-8462

HEBERT, DANIEL LEO, b. Salina, Kans., Oct. 17, 1944; B.A. magna cum laude, St. Benedicts Coll., Atchison, Kans., 1966; J.D., Notre Dame U., 1969. Admitted to Ill. bar, 1969, Kans. bar, 1973; asso. firm Seyfarth, Shaw, Fairweather & Geraldson, Chgo., 1969-73; individual practice law, Salina, Kans., 1973—; instr. bus. law Brown-Mackie Coll., 1975, Marymount Coll., 1976. Bd. dirs. Chgo. Vol. Legal Services, 1972-73. Mem. Am., Kans., Saline County bar assns. Home: 508 W Iron St Salina KS 67401 Office: Planters Bank Arcade Salina KS 67401 Tel (913) 825-5482

HECHT, ALAN JOHN, b. Cleve., Oct. 23, 1944; B.S., U. So. Calif., 1967, J.D., 1970. Admitted to Calif. bar, 1971; since practiced in San Diego, mem. firm Jenkins & Perry, 1970-73, McDonald & Riddle, 1973-74; partner firm McDonald, Riddle, Hecht & Worley, 1975—; instr. U. Calif. Extension, 1973—; lectr. Calif. Continuing Edn. for Bar, 1976. Mem. San Diego County, Calif. bar assns. Office: Suite 617 600 B St San Diego CA 92101 Tel (714) 239-3444

HECHT, ISAAC, b. Balt., Dec. 28, 1913; B.S. in Economics, Johns Hopkins, 1936; LL.B., U. Md., 1938. Admitted to Md. bar, 1938; U.S. Supreme Ct. bar, 1960; with firm Hecht and Hecht, Balt., 1973; mem. exec. com. Balt. Estate Planning Council, 1964-69, sec., 1964-66, v.p., 1966-67, pres., 1967-68. Fellow Am. Coll. Probate Counsel, Md. Bar Found.; mem. Assn. Life Ins. Counsel, Am. (com. estate gift taxes 1973—, mem. standing com. Clients security trust fund), Md. (chmn. com. unauthorized law practice) bar assns., Bar Assn. Balt. (exec. com. 1972-73). Home: 11 Slade Apt 307 Baltimore MD 21208 Office: Hecht & Hecht 1111 Fidelity Bldg Baltimore MD 21201

HECK, CHARLES HERMAN, b. Shreveport, La., Aug. 23, 1942; B.A., La. Poly. Inst., 1963; J.D., La. State U., 1970. Admitted to La. bar, 1970; law clk. to La. Ct. Appeal, 2d Circuit, 1970-71; partner firm Theus Grisham Davis & Leigh, Monroe, La., 1971—; asst. city atty. City of Monroe, 1972-76; mem. Judiciary Commn. La., 1975—. Mem. 4th Jud. Dist. (sec.-treas. 1974-76, v.p.-elect 1977), La., Am. bar assns., Phi Alpha Delta. Office: 1303 Bancroft Circle Monroe LA 71203 Tel (318) 388-0100

HECK, RONALD HENRY, b. Pitts., Aug. 11, 1942; A.B., Duquesne U., 1964, LL.B., 1967. Admitted to Pa. bar, 1967; partner firm Bagley, Weaver, Sydor & Heck, Pa., 1967-74; partner firm Doherty, Heck & Robb, Pitts., 1974—; solicitor Etna Borough Sch. Dist., 1969-71. Mem. Allegheny County, Pa. bar assns., Pa. Claimsmen Assn., Pa. Law Inst. (asso.). Home: 201 Hartle Rd Glenshaw PA 15166 Office: 404 Lawyers Bldg Pittsburgh PA 15219 Tel (412) 232-0110

HECKEMEYER, ANTHONY JOSEPH, b. Cape Girardeau, Mo., Jan. 20, 1939; B.S., Mo. U., 1961, J.D., 1972. Admitted to Mo. bar, 1973; individual practice law, Sikeston, Mo., 1973—; mem. Mo. Ho. of Reps., 1964-72, chmn. resolutions com., 1971-72. Vice-pres., Heritage House, Sikeston, 1976-77. Named Outstanding Legislator in Field of Conservation, Mo. Wildlife Fedn., 1970. Home: 108 Foust St Sikeston MO 63801 Office: 125 E Malone Sikeston MO 63801 Tel (314) 471-5299

HECKENKAMP, ROBERT GLENN, b. Quincy, Ill., June 29, 1923; B.S., Quincy Coll., 1947; J.D., DePaul U., 1949. Admitted to Ill. bar, 1949; law clk. U.S. Dist. Ct., So. Dist. Ill., 1949-50; asst. U.S. atty. So. Dist. Ill. Dept. Justice, 1951-53; mem. firm A. M. Fitzgerald, 1953-57; partner firm Heckenkamp & Fuiten, 1957—; lectr., writer Ill. Inst. Continuing Legal Edn. Mem. Sangamon County (Ill.), Ill. State (gov. 1976) bar assns., Ill. (1st v.p. 1976), Am. trial lawyers assns., Am. Coll. Trial Lawyers, Am. Judicature Soc. Home: 60 Yacht Club Rd Springfield IL 62707 Office: 522 E Monroe St Springfield IL 62701 Tel (217) 528-5627

HECKERLING, PHILIP EPHRAIM, b. N.Y.C., May 17, 1921; J.D., U. Fla., 1949; LL.M., U. Miami, 1963; LL.M., N.Y. U., 1964. Admitted to Fla. bar, 1949; practice law, Miami, 1949-67; counsel firm Greenberg, Traurig, Hoffman, Lipoff, Quentel & Wright, P.A., Miami, 1967—; prof. law U. Miami Law Sch., 1967—, dir. Inst. Estate Planning, 1967—, dir. grad. programs in estate planning and fed. taxation, 1973—; v.p., trust counsel Pan Am. Bank of Miami, 1967—; dir. Pan Am. Bank of Miami Beach. Fellow Am. Coll. Probate Counsel (mem. editorial bd. Probate Lawyer); mem. Am. Law Inst. Am. (taxation and real property com., probate and trust law com.), Fla. (exec. com. tax sect., chmn. estate and gift taxes in local law) bar assns. Co-author: Workbook for Florida Estate Planners, 1968; editor U. Miami Inst. Estate Planning, Vols. 1-11; contbr. numerous articles to profl. jours. Home: 6470 SW 116th St Miami FL 33156 Office: U Miami Law Sch Coral Gables FL 33124 Tel (305) 284-5567

HECKMAN, THOMAS PENROSE, b. Rochester, N.Y., Apr. 11, 1942; A.B., U. Rochester, 1964; J.D., U. Kans., 1969. Admitted to N.Y. bar, 1972; with Lincoln Rochester Trust Co., Rochester, 1964-66, Fiduciary Trust Co. N.Y., N.Y.C., 1969-72; asso. firm Kieffer & Hahn, N.Y.C., 1972-75; officer Irving Trust Co., N.Y.C., 1976—. Mem. Am., N.Y. State bar assns., N.Y. County Lawyers Assn. Recipient Am. Jurisprudence award. Home: 55 E End Ave New York City NY 10028 Office: Irving Trust Co 1 Wall St New York City NY 10015 Tel (212) 487-2326

HECKSCHER, MAURICE, b. Phila., May 24, 1907; A.B. cum laude, Harvard U., 1928, student Law Sch., 1928-30. Admitted to Pa. bar, 1932; mem. firm Duane, Morris & Heckscher, Phila., 1931-35, partner firm, 1935—; dir. Laurel Hill and W. Laurel Hill Cemetery Cos.; trustee Dolfinger-McMahon Found.; dir. Equitable Assurance Soc. of U.S., N.Y.C., Bd. dirs. Zool. Soc. of Phila.; former mem. vis. com. Harvard Divinity Sch.; former bd. dirs. Fund for Advancement of Edn., Ford Found. Mem. Phil. Bar Assn., Pa. Am. bar assns., Juristic Soc. of Phila. (past pres.), Am. Philos. Soc. (Phila.), Harvard Alumni Assn. (past v.p.), Asso. Harvard Clubs (past pres.). Home: 8400 Prospect Ave Philadelphia PA 19118 Office: 16th Floor 100 S Broad St Philadelphia PA 19110 Tel (215) 854-6317

HECOX, LAWRENCE ALLEN, b. Dallas, Feb. 15, 1932; B.A., Williams Coll., 1953; J.D., U. Colo., 1956. Admitted to Colo. bar, 1956, U.S. Supreme Ct. bar, 1965; practiced in Colorado Springs, Colo., 1956—; partner firm Cole, Hecox, Tolley, Edwards and Keene, and predecessors, 1959—. Commr., chmn. Colorado Springs Urban Renewal Authority, 1974-75; trustee Fountain Valley Sch., 1969—. Mem. Colo., Am. bar assns. Home: 70 Marland Rd Colorado Springs CO 80906 Office: 3 S Tejon St Colorado Springs CO 80903 Tel (303) 473-4444

HECTOR, LOUIS JULIUS, b. Ft. Lauderdale, Fla., Dec. 11, 1915; B.A., Williams Coll., 1938; postgrad. (Rhodes scholar) Oxford (Eng.) U., 1938-39; LL.B., Yale, 1942. Admitted to D.C. bar, 1942, Fla. bar, 1946; with Office of Asst. Solicitor Gen., Dept. Justice, Washington, 1942-43; asso. firm Anderson, Scott, McCarthy & Preston, Miami, Fla., 1946-48; partner firm Steel, Hector & Davis, and predecessors, Miami, Fla., 1955—; dir. S.E. Banking Corp., chmn. exec. com., 1968-74; dir. Nat. Airlines, Inc., S.E. Banks Trust Co.; mem. CAB, 1957-59; mem. advisory com. on FAA rule-making and enforcement procedures, 1961; mem. Pres.'s Com. on Equal Opportunity in Armed Forces, 1962-64; co-dir. Miami study team of Nat. Commn. on Causes and Prevention of Violence, 1968-69. Trustee Smith Coll.; trustee emeritus U. Miami; mem. Rockefeller U. Council; mem. Yale U. Council, 1971-73. Mem. Am., Dade County bar assns., Fla., D.C. bars, Am. Judicature Soc., Center for Adminstrv. Justice (dir.), Assn. of Bar City of N.Y., Yale Law Sch. Assn. (chmn. 1967-71). Contbr. articles to legal jours. Home: 3507 Saint Gaudens Rd Coconut Grove FL 33133 Office: 100 S Biscayne Blvd SE 1st Nat Bank Bldg Miami FL 33131 Tel (305) 577-2868

HEDA, RICHARD DANIEL, b. Chgo., Aug. 20, 1926; B.S., U. Ill., 1947; J.D., Northwestern U., 1950. Admitted to Ill. bar, 1951; individual practice law, Chgo., 1951—; pres. RDH Prodns. Former pres. Budlong Woods Civic Assn. Mem. Chgo. Bar Assn. (placement com.). Home: 2844 Catalpa Ave Chicago IL 60625 Tel (312) 784-2128

HEDDESHEIMER, WALTER JACOB, b. Arkon, Ohio, Nov. 11, 1910; A.B. magna cum laude, Ohio Wesleyan U., 1932; LL.B., Harvard, 1935. Admitted to Ohio bar, 1935, U.S. Supreme Ct. bar, 1960; asso. firm Musser, Kimber & Huffman, Akron, 1935-39; individual practice law, Wellington, Ohio, 1939-42; chief regional enforcement atty. Office Price Adminstrn., Cleve., 1942-47; atty. Central Nat. Bank, Cleve., 1947-56, v.p., head dept. law, 1956-72; counsel firm Baker, Hostetler & Patterson, Cleve., 1972—; mem. tech. advisory com. Controller of Currency Treasury Dept. Trustee Elyria (Ohio) Home, 1962—, Union Coll., Barbourville, Ky., 1963—. Mem. Cleve., Ohio State, Am. bar assns. Contbr. articles to Ohio State Bar Assn. jour. Home: 17668 Ridge Creek Dr Strongsville OH 44136 Office: 1956 Union Commerce Bldg Cleveland OH 44115 Tel (216) 621-0200

HEDEMAN, WILLIAM NORMAN, JR., b. Cin., Oct. 15, 1942; B.A., Gettysburg Coll., 1964; J.D., U. Md., 1968; LL.M. with highest honors, George Washington U., 1972. Admitted to Md. bar, 1968; asst. dist. counsel US Army C.E., Balt., 1968-72, counsel for regulatory programs, Washington, 1972—; profl. lectr. law George Washington U., 1974—. Mem. Fed. Bar Assn. Contbr. articles in field to profl. jours. Home: 1605 Crestline Rd Silver Spring MD 20904 Office: Office Chief of Engrs Forrestal Bldg 1000 Independence Ave Washington DC 20314 Tel (202) 693-6169

HEDERMAN, JOHN PETER, b. Bklyn., June 18, 1942; B.S. in Math., St. John's U., 1964, LL.B., 1967. Admitted to N.Y. bar, 1968, Fla. bar, 1973, D.C. bar, 1976, U.S. Supreme Ct. bar, 1974; served with JAGC, U.S. Marine Corps, 1967-70; asso. firm Mudge Rose Guthrie & Alexander, N.Y.C., 1970-76, partner, 1976—. Mem. Am., N.Y. State, Fla., D.C., N.Y.C. bar assns. Office: Mudge Rose Guthrie & Alexander 20 Broad St New York City NY 10005 Tel (212) 422-6767

HEDGER, CECIL RAYMOND, b. Tracy, Minn., Feb. 28, 1947; B.A., U. S.D., 1969; J.D., U. Nebr., 1972. Admitted to Calif. bar, 1972, Nebr. bar, 1973; asso. firm Nelson, Harding, Yeutter, Leonard & Tate, Lincoln, Nebr., now partner. Mem. Calif., Nebr., Am. bar assns. Home: 1865 High St Lincoln NE 68502 Office: 300 NSEA Bldg PO Box 82028 Lincoln NE 68501 Tel (402) 475-6761

HEDGES, ARTHUR JOSEPH, b. Iowa City, Nov. 10, 1914; B.A. in Econs., U. Iowa, 1938, M.A., 1946; J.D., Northwestern Coll. Law, 1954. Admitted to Oreg. bar, 1954; field examiner NLRB, Portland, Oreg., 1947-57, atty., 1957-70; labor arbitrator Fed. Mediation and Conciliation Service, Portland, 1970. Mem. Fed., Oreg. bar assns., Order of Artus. Office: 2929 SW Underwood Dr Portland OR 97225 Tel (503) 292-6113

HEDMAN, GEORGE WILLIAM, b. Chgo., Sept. 29, 1923; J.D., Chgo.-Kent Coll. Law, 1950. Admitted to Hawaii bar, 1951, Am. Samoa bar, 1953, Fla. bar, 1958; partner firm Hedman, Aluli, Scott & Kim, Honolulu, 1951-53; atty. gen. Am. Samoa, Pago Pago, 1953-55; exec. Edison Electric Inst., N.Y.C., 1956-62; partner Hedman & Cossaboom, Melbourne, Fla., 1962-77; individual practice law, Melbourne, 1977—. Mem. Brevard County (Fla.) Sch. Bd., 1968-72. Mem. Am., Hawaii, Fla. (exec. council family law div.) bar assns. Home: 3000 N A-1-A Indialantic FL 32903 Office: 1520 S Babcock St Melbourne FL 32901 Tel (305) 723-1616

HEDRICK, DAVID WARRINGTON, b. Jacksonville, Fla., Oct. 25, 1917; B.A. with honors, U. Fla., 1940, LL.B. with honors, 1947, J.D., 1967. Admitted to Fla. bar, 1947, U.S. Supreme Ct. bar, 1962; asso. firm LeRoy B. Giles, Orlando, Fla., 1947-53; partner firm Giles, Hedrick & Robinson, Orlando, 1953—; dir. First Fed. Savs. and Loan Assn. of Orlando; legal counsel, dir. Central Fla. council Boy Scouts Am., 1970—. Bd. dirs. Holiday Hosp., Orlando, 1966-69; pres. Orange County Human Services Planning Council, 1973-75; mem. Orlando Mayor's Interracial Adv. Com., 1967-70; dr. chmn. United Appeal of Orange County (Fla.), 1967, pres., 1970, chmn. bd. dirs., 1971, chmn. social planning com., 1973-76; chancellor Diocese of Central Fla., Winter Park, 1970—. Mem. Orange County, Fla., Am. bar assns., Am. Judicature Soc. Home: 1729 Reppard Rd Orlando FL 32803 Office: 109 E Church St PO Box 2631 Orlando FL 32801 Tel (305) 425-3591

HEEBE, FREDERICK JACOB REGAN, b. Gretna, La., Aug. 25, 1922; B.A., Tulane U., 1943, LL.B., 1949. Admitted to La. bar, 1949; practice in Gretna, 1949-60; dist. judge div. B, 24th Jud. Dist. Ct., Jefferson Parish, La., 1961-66; U.S. dist. judge Eastern Dist. La., 1966—, now chief judge. Charter mem. Community Welfare Council Jefferson Parish, 1957—; chmn. Jefferson Parish Bd. Pub. Welfare, 1953-55. Mem. Jefferson Parish Council, 1958-60, vice chmn., 1958-60. Bd. dirs. Social Welfare Planning Council New Orleans, New Orleans Regional Mental Center and Clinic, W. Bank Assn. for Retarded. Decorated Purple Heart, Bronze Star. Mem. Am., La., New Orleans, Fed. bar assns., Am. Judicature Soc., Phi Beta Kappa. Home: 1407 Whitney Ave Gretna LA 70053 Office: 400 Royal St New Orleans LA 70130*

HEEFNER, WILLIAM FREDERICK, b. Perkasie, Pa., July 8, 1922; A.B., Ursinus Coll., 1942, LL.D., 1975; LL.B., Temple U., 1949. Admitted to Pa. bar, 1951, U.S. Supreme Ct. bar, 1961; asso. firm Willard S. Curtin, Morrisville, Pa., 1951-53; partner firm Curtin & Heefner, Morrisville, 1953—; dir. William Penn Savs. & Loan Assn., Levittown, Pa., Morrisville Bank. Sec., Bedminster Twp. (Pa.) Planning Commn., 1961—; chmn. academic devel. com. Ursinus Coll., 1969-75; trustee Fonthill-Mercer Mus., Doylestown, Pa., 1973—. Mem. Am., Pa. (chmn. econs. of law practice com. 1972-74, mem. ho. of dels. 1972-75, gov. 1976—), Bucks County (pres. 1965-66) bar assns. Home: Old Bethlehem Rd Perkasie PA 18944 Office: 250 N Pennsylvania Ave Box 217 Morrisville PA 19067 Tel (215) 736-2521

HEELAN, JAMES RAYMOND, b. Chgo., June 28, 1934; J.D., DePaul U., 1962. Admitted to Ill. bar, 1963; asst. state's atty. Cook County (Ill.), 1963-71; asst. exec. dir. Nat. Dist. Attys. Assn., Chgo., 1971—. Mem. Ill. Bar Assn., Phi Alpha Delta. Office: 211 E Chicago Ave Suite 1515 Chicago IL 60611 Tel (312) 944-2577

HEERWAGEN, HERBERT ALFRED, b. Newark, Nov. 20, 1910; student Dickinson Coll., 1928-30; A.B., Cornell U., 1932, J.D., 1934. Admitted to N.Y. bar, 1934; asso. firm Davies, Hardy & Schenck and predecessors, N.Y.C., 1934-44, 46-57, partner, 1958-68, sr. partner firm Davies, Hardy, Ives & Lawther and predecessors, N.Y.C., 1968—. Mem. New Castle (N.Y.) Recreation Commn., 1957-69, vice chmn., 1962-65, chmn., 1965-67. Mem. Am., N.Y. State bar assns., Am. Judicature Soc., Nat. Council Juvenile Ct. Judges (asso.), Acad. Polit. Sci., Cornell Law Assn., Order of Coif, Phi Beta Kappa. Phi Kappa Phi. Recipient Boardman prize Cornell Law Sch., 1933, McKinney prize, 1934. Home: 133 Parker Ave Maplewood NJ 07040 Office: 2 Broadway New York City NY 10004 Tel (212) 422-1212

HEFFERAN, RICHARD PHELIM, b. Chgo., Dec. 16, 1933; B.A., Loyola U., Chgo., 1955, J.D., 1960. Admitted to Ill. bar, 1960; counsel Allied Van Lines, Broadview, Ill., 1961-70; asst. gen counsel Am. Mut. Ins. Alliance, Chgo., 1970—; mem. industry adv. com. Nat. Assn. Ins. Commrs., 1974—. Mem. Am. (past chmn. ins. com. tax sect.), Ill. bar assns. Recipient Merit award entry The Interpreter, 1976. Home: 604 Forestview St Park Ridge IL 60068 Office: 20 N Wacker Dr Chicago IL 60606 Tel (312) 346-5190

HEFFERNAN, NATHAN STEWART, b. Frederic, Wis., Aug. 6, 1920; B.A., U. Wis., 1942, LL.B., 1948; student Harvard Bus. Sch., 1943-44. Admitted to Wis. bar, 1948; asso. firm Schubring, Ryan, Peterson & Sutherland, Madison, 1948-49; practiced in Sheboygan, 1949-59; partner firm Buchen & Heffernan, 1951-59; counsel Wis. League Municipalities, 1949; research asst. to gov. Wis., 1949; asst. dist. atty., 1951-53; city atty., Sheboygan, 1953-59; atty. gen. State of Wis., 1954-62; U.S. atty., 1962-64; justice Wis. Supreme Ct., 1964—; lectr. municipal corps. U. Wis. Law Sch., 1961-64, lectr. appellate procedure and practice, 1971—; faculty Appellate Judges Seminar, N.Y. U., 1972—; chmn. Wis. Appellate Practice and Procedure Com., 1975-76. Wis. chmn. NCCJ, 1966-67, Distinguished Service award, 1968; gen. chmn. Wis. Democratic Conv., 1960, 61; bd. visitors U. Wis. Law Sch., 1970—, chmn., 1973-76; former corporate bd. Methodist Hosp.; curator Wis. Hist. Soc.; trustee Wis. Meml. Union, Wis. State Library; former mem. exec. bd. Four Lakes council Boy Scouts Am. Mem. Am. Law Inst., Inst. Jud. Adminstrn., Am. (former spl. com. on adminstrn. criminal justice, com. on fed.-state delineation of jurisdiction), Wis., Dane County, Sheboygan County (dir.) bar assns., Am. Judicature Soc., City Attys. Assn. (pres. 1958-59), Nat. Council State Ct. Reps. Nat. Center State Cts. (chmn.), Order of Coif, Iron Cross, Phi Kappa Phi, Phi Delta Phi. Home: 17 Thorstein Veblen Pl Madison WI 53705 Office: State Capitol Madison WI 53702 Tel (608) 266-1886

HEFLIN, HOWELL THOMAS, b. Poulan, Ga., June 19, 1921; A.B., Birmingham-So. Coll., 1942; LL.B., U. Ala., 1948. Admitted to Ala. bar, 1948; individual practice law, Tuscumbia, 1948-71; chief justice Supreme Ct. Ala., Montgomery, 1971-77; Tazewell Taylor vis. prof. law Coll. William and Mary, 1977—; lectr. U. Ala., 1946-48, Florence State U., 1949-52. Fellow Am. Coll. Trial Lawyers, Internat. Acad. Trial Lawyers, Internat. Soc. Barristers, Internat. Acad. Law and Sci.; mem. Am., Ala., Colbert County bar assns., Am. Judicature Soc. (Herbert Lincoln Harley award 1973), Ala. Law Sch. Alumni Assn. (pres.), Nat. Conf. Chief Justices (chmn. 1976), Ala. Plaintiff Lawyers Assn. (pres.), Omicron Delta Kappa, Phi Delta Phi. Tau Kappa Alpha, Lambda Chi Alpha. Recipient Daniel J. Meador award U. Ala. Law Sch., 1971, Distinguished Alumnus award U. Ala. and Birmingham-So. Coll., 1973, Am. Judges Assn. award, 1975; named Ala. Citizen of Year, Ala. Cable TV Assn., 1973, Ala. Broadcasters Assn., 1975. Home: 311 6th St Tuscumbia AL 35674 Office: 106 E 2d St Tuscumbia AL 35674

HEFTER, MARCIA ZIPSER, b. N.Y.C., Nov. 2, 1943; A.B., Boston U., 1964; LL.B., N.Y. U., 1966. Admitted to N.Y. bar, 1967, U.S. Dist. Ct. for Eastern and So. Dists. N.Y., U.S. Supreme Ct. Bar; partner firm Tooker, Tooker & Esseks, Riverhead, N.Y., 1966—. Mem. Suffolk County, N.Y. State bar assns., Internat. Fedn. Women Attys. Home: 39 Daly Ct Riverhead NY 11901 Office: 108 E Main St Riverhead NY 11901 Tel (516) 727-3277

HEFTMAN, RONALD NEIL, b. Chgo., Jan. 9, 1945; B.B.A., Washington U., 1967; J.D. cum laude, Northwestern U., 1971. Admitted to Ill. bar, 1971; partner firm Bellows & Bellows, Chgo. Mem. Ill. State, Chgo. bar assns. Home: 1286 Wendy Dr Northbrook IL 60062 Office: Bellows & Bellows One IBM Plaza Chicago IL 60611 Tel (312) 467-1750

HEGARTY, GERALD ROBERT, b. Springfield, Mass., Apr. 25, 1925; B.A., Yale, 1946; J.D., U. Mich., 1950. Admitted to Mass. bar, 1951, U.S. Dist Ct. Mass. bar, 1952, U.S. Dist. Ct. Conn. bar, 1969, U.S. Supreme Ct. bar, 1971, U.S. Circuit Ct. Appeals 1st Circuit bar, 1971; individual practice law, Springfield, Mass., 1951—. Bd. dirs., chmn. Hampden County chpt. Civil Liberties Union Mass., 1966-69; bd. dirs. Hampden Dist. Mental Health Clinic, Inc., 1956-62. Mem. Mass., Hampden County bar assns., Am. Soc. for Law and Medicine. Office: 1200 Main St Springfield MA 01103 Tel (413) 788-4563

HEGARTY, WILLIAM A., b. Phila., Apr. 5, 1926; B.A., Pa. State U., 1948; LL.B., U. Md., 1953, J.D., 1968. Admitted to Md. bar, 1953, U.S. Supreme Ct. bar, 1963; chief trial staff Transit Casualty Co., Balt., 1955-59; chief asst. city solicitor, Balt., 1959-62; partner firm Hegarty & McGarvey, Towson, Md., 1973—; mem. adv. bd. Pub. Defender System, Dist. #1, 1972—. Mem. Am., Md., Balt. bar assns., Internat. Assn. Ins. Counsel. Home: 223 Tunbridge Rd Baltimore MD 21212 Office: 701 Mercantile Towson Bldg Towson MD 21204

HEHL, LAMBERT LAWRENCE, b. Newport, Ky., July 22, 1924; J.D., Chase Coll. Law, No. Ky. U., 1952. Admitted to Ohio bar, 1952, Ky. bar, 1953; individual practice law, 1952-56; partner firm Benton, Luedeke, Rhoads & Hehl, Newport, Ky., 1956-62, Bischoff & Hehl, Newport, 1962-73; mem. Ky. Senate, 1960-63; city atty. Crestview (Ky.), 1956-63; dep. tax commr. Campbell County (Ky.), 1953-56, commr., 1963-73; county judge Campbell County, Newport, 1973—. Past pres. No. Ky. Area Planning Council, Ky. Magistrate and Commrs. Assn.; 2d v.p. No. Ky. Area Devel. Dist.; bd. dirs. Ohio-Ky.-Ind. Regional Council Govts., 1965—; mem. Ky. Democratic Exec. Com., 1966—. Mem. Ky., Campbell County bar assns., Ky. County Judges Assn. (1st v.p.). Home: 46 Maddonna Dr Fort Thomas KY 41075 Office: 412 Central Ave Newport KY 41071 Tel (606) 431-6626

HEHMEYER, ALEXANDER, b. N.Y.C., Oct. 20, 1910; B.S., Yale U., 1932; LL.B., Columbia U., 1935. Admitted to N.Y. State bar, 1936, Ill. bar, 1968; asso. firm Cravath, Swaine & Wood, N.Y.C., 1936-40, 1944-46; exec. Time, Inc., N.Y.C., 1940-43; legal, econ. cons. Fgn. Econ. Adminstrn., Washington, 1943-44; partner firm Paul, Weiss, Rifkind, Wharton & Garrison, N.Y.C., 1946-67; exec. v.p., gen. counsel Field Enterprises, Inc., Chgo., 1967-75; of counsel firm Isham, Lincoln & Beale, Chgo., 1976—. Fellow Am. Bar Assn.; mem. Chgo., Ill. State, N.Y. State bar assns., Assn. Bar City N.Y. Author: Time for Change-Proposal for a Second Constitutional Convention, 1943. Home: 20 W Burton Pl Chicago IL 60610 Office: One First Nat Plaza 42d Floor Chicago IL 60603 Tel (312) 786-7401

HEID, GEORGE JOSEPH, III, b. Ft. Devens, Mass., Feb. 9, 1945; B.A., Washington and Jefferson Coll., 1967; J.D., Ind. U., 1971. Admitted to Ind. bar, 1971; chief dep. pros. atty. Tippecanoe County (Ind.), 1973-74; with JAGC, Ind. N.G., 1975—. Bd. dirs. Lafayette (Ind.) YMCA, 1971—, Tippecanoe Ancient Fife and Drum Corps, 1974—; mem. fin. com. Sycamore Valley council Girl Scouts U.S.A., 1971—; pres. Tippecanoe County Young Republicans, 1974. Mem. Ind. State, Tippecanoe County (sec. 1974-75) bar assns., Bar Assn. 7th Fed. Circuit (vice chmn. com. on def. of indigents 1975—), Greater Lafayette C. of C. (chmn. com. law enforcement 1974—), Phi Alpha Delta. Home: 1528 Northstream Ave West Lafayette IN 47906 Office: 30 Lafayette Bank & Trust Bldg Lafayette IN 47901 Tel (317) 742-0158

HEIDENREICH, DOUGLAS ROBERT, b. St. Paul, Feb. 29, 1932; A.B., U. Minn., 1953; J.D., William Mitchell Coll. Law, 1961. Admitted to Minn. bar, 1961; asso. firm Erickson, Popham, Haik & Schnobrich, Mpls., 1961-63; asst. prof. law and asst. dean William Mitchell Coll. Law, St. Paul, 1963-64, prof. law and dean, 1964-75, prof. law, 1975—; spl. master in antibiotics anti-trust litigation, U.S. Dist. Ct., Dist. Minn., 1971—; exec. dir. Minn. Bd. Continuing Legal Edn., 1975—. Mem. Gov's. commn. on crime prevention and control, 1972-75; mem. state bd. human rights, 1972-75. Mem. Am., Minn. State bar assns., Am. Judicature Soc., Am. Law Inst., Selden Soc. Lectr., author for Minn. Continuing Legal Edn., Mich. Inst. Continuing Legal Edn. Home: 338 S Cleveland St Saint Paul MN 55105 Office: 875 Summit Ave Saint Paul MN 55105 Tel (612) 227-9171

HEIER, RONALD OMER, b. St. Louis, Feb. 17, 1940; B.S., St. Louis U., 1962, J.D., 1968. Admitted to Mo. bar, 1968; asso. county counselor St. Louis County, Mo., 1969-73; sec., counsel Nat. Marine Service Inc., St. Louis, 1973-75; atty. legal dept. Brown Group, Inc., St. Louis, 1975—; contract adminstr., engring. adminstr. McDonnell-Douglas Corp., St. Louis and Conductron-Mo. Corp., St. Charles, Mo., 1963-69. Alderman city Des Peres, Mo., 1975—, mem. planning and zoning commn., 1975—. Mem. Am., St. Louis County bar assns., Bar Assn. Met. St. Louis. Home: 2104 Pardoroyal Dr Des Peres MO 63131 Office: 8400 Maryland Ave St Louis MO 63105 Tel (314) 997-7500

HEIL, ROBERT J., b. Los Angeles, Nov. 14, 1943; B.A., Yale, 1965; postgrad. U. Munich (Ger.), 1965-66; J.D., U. Calif., Berkeley, 1969. Admitted to Calif. bar, 1970; asso. firm Musick, Peeler & Garrett, Los Angeles, 1969-73, firm Pettit, Evers & Martin, San Francisco, 1973-77, Ferguson, Hoffman, Henn & Mandel, San Francisco, 1977—. Mem. Am., San Francisco bar assns. Author: Wage-Price Control Manual, 1972; contbr. articles to profl. jours. Home: 6215 Ascot Dr Oakland CA 94611 Office: 1365 Columbus Ave San Francisco CA 94133 Tel (415) 673-8300

HEILMAN, WILLIAM OWENS, b. Harrisburg, Pa., June 26, 1906; M.S. in Chem. Engring., Lehigh U., 1929; LL.B., Rutgers U., 1935, J.D., 1970. Admitted to N.Y. bar, U.S. Supreme Ct. bar, U.S. Patent Office bar; atty. Esso Research & Engring. Co., Linden, N.J., 1929-71; admitted to N.Y. bar, 1935; partner firm Heilman & Heilman, N.Y.C., 1971-76; mayor Town of Millburn (N.J.), 1972-73. Mem. Millburn Bd. Edn., 1953-61, pres., 1957-61; mem. Millburn Town Council, 1961-73. Mem. N.Y. Patent Law Assn. Died May 18, 1976. Home: 76 Great Oak Dr Short Hills NJ 07078

HEIMAN, DAVID GILBERT, b. Cin., Apr. 12, 1945; B.B.A., U. Cin., 1967, J.D., 1970. Admitted to Ohio bar, 1971; mem. firm Hahn, Loeser, Freedheim Dean & Wellman, Cleve., 1970—. Chmn. legal issues com., trustee Cleve. chpt. Am. Jewish Com.; mem. cabinet met. div. and community relations com. Jewish Fedn. Cleve. Mem. Ohio State, Am. (exec. council young lawyers sect. 1976-77), Greater Cleve. (chmn. young lawyers sect. 1974-75, corporate bus. and banking coms. 1976-77) bar assns., Order of Coif. Article editor U. Cin. Law Review, 1969-70. Home: 3796 Elsmere Rd Shaker Heights OH 44120 Office: 800 Nat City E 6th Bldg Cleveland OH 44114 Tel (216) 621-0150

HEIMLICH, ROY A., b. N.Y.C., Mar. 14, 1943; B.A. magna cum laude, Washington Sq. Coll., N.Y. U., 1963; LL.B. cum laude, Harvard U., 1966. Admitted to N.Y. bar, 1967, N.J. bar, 1972; asso. firm Paul, Weiss, Rifkind, Wharton & Garrison, N.Y.C., 1966-72, Wilentz, Goldman & Spitzer, Perth Amboy, N.J., 1972-74; dep. atty. gen. State of N.J., 1974—. Office: State House Annex Bldg Trenton NJ 08625 Tel (609) 292-1962

HEIN, WILLIAM EUGENE, b. Loveland, Colo., July 22, 1942; B.S. in Elec. Engring., U. Colo., 1964, M.S. in Elec. Engring., 1965; J.D., U. Denver, 1970. Admitted to Colo. bar, 1970; electronic design engr., Hewlette-Packard Co., Loveland, Colo., 1965-71, patent atty., 1971—. Mem. Am., Colo. bar assns. Home: 1409 E 16th St Loveland CO 80537 Office: Box 335 Loveland CO 80537 Tel (303) 667-5000

HEINBECKER, PETER PAPIN, b. St. Louis, Feb. 25, 1939; A.B., U. Notre Dame, 1960; LL.B., Georgetown U., 1965; M.D., St. Louis U., 1974. Admitted to Mo. bar, 1965; asst. circuit atty. City of St. Louis, 1965-68; asso. firm Thompson, Mitchell, Douglas & Neil, St. Louis, 1968-69; resident in psychiatry St. Louis U. Hosp., 1974—. Mem. Mo. Bar Assn., Eastern Mo., Am. (Falk fellowship 1975-77) psychiat. assns. Recipient Sandoz award - psychiatry prize, 1973-74. Home: 2103 Lakeview Dr Crystal Lake Park MO 63131 Office: 1221 S Grand Blvd Saint Louis MO 63104 Tel (314) 432-8937

HEINE, H. EUGENE, JR., b. Phila., Apr. 29, 1925; B.S., St. Joseph's Coll., 1948; J.D., U. Pa., 1951; postgrad. Villanova U., Harvard U. Admitted to Pa. bar, 1952, U.S. Ct. Claims bar, 1955, U.S. Supreme Ct. bar, 1957, Ill. bar, 1977; individual practice, Phila., 1951-52; spl. asst. to atty. gen., Washington, 1952-59; counsel Nuclear Weapons div. Bendix Corp., Kansas City, Mo., 1959-62; dep. dir. Joint Com. Effective Adminstrn. Justice, Washington, 1962-64; dir. legal practice and edn. Am. Bar Assn., Chgo., 1964-70, dir. planning and devel., 1970-71, counsel, 1976—; dir. Fund for Pub. Edn., Chgo., 1972-76. Mem. Am., Pa., Ill. bar assns., Am. Judicature Soc., Am. Soc. Assn. Execs. Home: 706 S Ashland Ave LaGrange IL 60525 Office: 1155 E 60th St Chicago IL 60637 Tel (312) 947-3990

HEINE, NORMAN, b. Camden, N.J., Mar. 22, 1907. Admitted to N.J. bar, 1933, U.S. Supreme Ct. bar, 1953; partner firms Heine and Heine, Camden, 1933-63, Heine & Taylor, 1963-66; judge N.J. Superior Ct., 1966-77; county prosecutor Camden County (N.J.), 1958-66; atty. City of Camden, 1954-58; mem. N.J. County and Municipal Law Revision Commn., 1957-62. Mem. N.J. Air Pollution Control Commn., 1954-57; pres. Fedn. Jewish Charities, Camden County, 1956-58. Mem. N.J. Inst. Municipal Attys. (pres. 1960) N.J., Am., Camden bar assns. Recipient Cyrus Adler Community Service award Jewish Theol. Sem., 1967, Community Service award Camden County, 1969. Home: Towers of Windsor Park Toledo 6-S Cherry Hill NJ 08002 Office: 603 Courthouse Camden NJ 08102 Tel (609) 757-8100

HEINECKE, PHILIP STURTEVANT, b. Chgo., Jan. 10, 1934; A.B., Princeton, 1956; LL.B., Stanford, 1962. Admitted to Calif. bar, 1963; asso. firm Heller Enrman White & McAuliffe, San Francisco, 1963-68; v.p., gen. counsel Alec Inc. of Calif., Colma, 1968-71; sec., counsel Marcona Corp., San Francisco, 1972—; mem. San Anselmo (Calif.) Planning Commn., 1966-72, chmn., 1970-72. Mem. Am., Calif., San Francisco bar assns. Home: 97 Spring Grove Ave San Anselmo CA 94960 Office: 1 Maritime Plaza San Francisco CA 94111 Tel (415) 544-4026

HEINEMAN, FREDERIC W., b. Chgo., Aug. 10, 1908; A.B. with honors, U. Ill., 1929; J.D., U. Chgo., 1931. Admitted to Ill. bar, 1931, Ariz. bar, 1956; with firm Miller, Gorham & Wales, Chgo., 1931-42; individual practice law, Chgo., 1945-56, Phoenix, 1956-70; judge Superior Ct. Ariz. for Maricopa County, Phoenix, 1970—. Former pres. Community Consol. Sch. Dist. 6, DuPage County (Ill.). Mem. Am., Ariz., Maricopa County bar assns., Am. Judicature Soc., Am. Soc. Corporate Secs., Phi Beta Kappa, Alpha Delta Phi, Phi Delta Phi. Recipient certificate of appreciation Pres. U.S., 1942, Ill. State Council Def., 1943. Office: 101 W Jefferson St Phoenix AZ 85003 Tel (602) 262-3901

HEINEN, PAUL A., b. Teaneck, N.J., Jan. 9, 1930; B.B.A., U. Mich., 1954, J.D., 1956, M.B.A., 1957; S.M. (Sloan fellow), Mass. Inst. Tech., 1963. Admitted to Mich. bar; with Chrysler Corp., Detroit, 1957—, atty., 1957-62, 63-66, exec. asst. to v.p. legal affairs, 1966-68, asso. gen. counsel, 1968—, sec., 1969—, v.p., 1974—. Served to 1st lt. AUS, 1950-53. Mem. Am., Mich., Detroit bar assns., Am. Soc. Corporate Secs., Order of Coif, Beta Gamma Sigma, Phi Alpha Delta, Sigma Alpha Epsilon. Home: 31925 Cross Bow Ct Birmingham MI 48010 Office: 341 Massachusetts Ave Detroit MI 48231*

HEINER, SAMUEL PHILLIP, b. Roanoke, Va., Nov. 1, 1940; B.A. in Econs. with distinction, U. Va., 1962, LL.B., 1965. Admitted to Ga. bar, 1966; law clk. to chief judge U.S. Ct. Appeals 5th Circuit, Atlanta, 1965-66; partner firm Kilpatrick, Cody, Rogers, McClatchey & Regenstein, Atlanta, 1971-76, Long, Aldridge, Heiner, Stevens & Sumner, Atlanta, 1976—; exec. council State Bar Ga., 1972-73, dir., 1974-75, chmn. legal aid com., 1974-77; pres., chmn. exec. com. Ga. Legal Services Program, 1971-74, chmn. bd. dirs., 1975-77; chmn. Ga. adv. council Nat. Legal Services Corp., 1976-77. Trustee, chmn. St. Citizen Services of Met. Atlanta, 1976-77; mem. Leadership Atlanta; bd. dirs. Friends of the Atlanta Pub. Library, 1975-76. Mem. Am. Bar Assn., U. Va. Alumni Assn. (pres. Atlanta chpt. 1969-71). Home: 2691 W Wesley Rd Atlanta GA 30327 Office: 1900 Rhodes-Haverty Bldg 134 Peachtree St Atlanta GA 30303 Tel (404) 681-3000

HEININGER, ERWIN CARL, b. Ann Arbor, Mich., Apr. 9, 1921; A.B., U. Mich., 1943, J.D., 1952. Admitted to Mich. bar, 1953, Ill. bar, 1953, Fed. bar, 1954, U.S. Ct. Claims bar, 1957, U.S. Supreme Ct. bar, 1960; trial atty. antitrust div. U.S. Dept. Justice, Chgo., 1953-55; asso. firm Mayer, Friedlich, Spies, Tierney, Brown & Platt, Chgo., 1955-60; partner firm Mayer, Brown & Platt, 1960—. Mem. Am., Fed., Ill. State, Chgo. bar assns., Chgo. Council Lawyers, Law Club Chgo., Legal Club Chgo., Am. Trial Lawyers Assn., Maritime Law Assn. U.S., Phi Delta Phi. Contbr. articles to profl. jours. Office: 231 S LaSalle St Chicago IL 60604 Tel (312) 782-0600

HEINSMA, DAVID JOHN, b. Rock Rapids, Iowa, Mar. 11, 1940; A.B., Harvard, 1962; LL.B., U. Va., 1965. Admitted to Ga. bar, 1965; asso. firm Hull, Towill & Norman, Augusta, Ga., 1965-68; officer Alpha Fund, Inc., Alpha Investors Fund, Inc., Alpha Research Corp., Atlanta, 1968-74, pres., 1973-74; pres. Lundquist Heinsma Corp., Atlanta, 1975—, LHC Petroleum Corp., Atlanta, 1975—; mem. SEC rules com. Investment Co. Inst., 1973-74. Mem. Am., Ga. bar assns., Atlanta C. of C. (chmn. ambassadors com. 1974-75). Contbr. articles to legal jours. Home: 1480 Mount Paran Rd NW Atlanta GA 30327 Office: 2590 Tower Pl 3340 Peachtree Rd Atlanta GA 30326 Tel (404) 261-3927

HEINSZ, TIMOTHY, b. St. Charles, Mo., Aug. 28, 1947; A.B. magna cum laude, St. Louis U., 1969; J.D. with distinction, Cornell U., 1972. Admitted to Mo. bar, 1972; mem. firm Lewis, Rice, Tucker, Allen & Chubb, St. Louis, 1972-75; vis. asst. prof. law U. Toledo, 1975-76, asst. prof. law, 1976—. Mem. panel arbitrators Better Bus. Bur. Toledo, 1976, pub. mem. Toledo Labor-Mgmt. Citizens Com. 1976. Mem. Am., St. Louis bar assns., Am. Arbitration Assn., Phi Beta Kappa. Recipient Frazier award Cornell Law Sch., 1972. Home: 3210 E Lincolnshire St Toledo OH 43606 Office: U Toledo 2801 W Bancroft St Toledo OH 43606 Tel (419) 537-2874

HEINZ, JOHN PETER, b. Carlinville, Ill., Aug. 6, 1936; A.B., Washington U., 1958; LL.B., Yale, 1962. Admitted to D.C. bar, 1962, Ill. bar, 1966; instr. polit. sci. Washington U., 1960; asst. to Congressman P. Mack, Washington, 1958; atty., advisor Office of Sec. U.S. Air Force, Washington, 1962-65; White House social aide, Washington, 1964-65; asst. prof. law Northwestern U., 1965-68, asso. prof., 1968-71, prof., 1971—, dir. program in law and social scis., 1967-70; vis. scholar Am. Bar Found., 1975-77; vis. prof. U. Chgo., 1975-76. Bd. dirs. John Howard Assn. Ill., 1970—, pres. 1974-75; mem. exec. com. Project LEAP, 1974—; bd. dirs., mem. exec. com. Better Govt. Assn., 1973—. Mem. Chgo. Bar Assn., Commn. Adminstrn. of Criminal Justice In Cook County, Chgo. Council Lawyers, Am. Polit. Sci. Assn., Law and Society Assn. Contbr. articles to profl. jours. Home: 525 Judson Ave Evanston IL 60202 Office: 357 E Chicago Ave Chicago IL 60611 Tel (312) 649-8473

HEISER, RICHARD DONALD, b. N.Y.C., June 27, 1938; B.A., Northwestern U., 1960; J.D., U. Cin., 1963. Admitted to Ohio bar, 1963, Conn. bar, 1966; gen. atty. Procter & Gamble Co., Cin., 1963-66, Glendinning Cos., Westport, Conn., 1966-68; v.p., gen. counsel KDI Corp., Cin., 1968-77; partner firm Strauss Troy & Ruehlmann, Cin., 1977—. Mem. Am., Cin. bar assns. Home: 6606 Miami Dr Cincinnati OH 45227 Office: 5721 Dragonway Cincinnati OH 45227 Tel (513) 272-1421

HEISERMAN, JOHN EDWARD, b. Hawkeye, Iowa, July 18, 1905; B.A., U. Iowa, 1927. Admitted to Iowa bar, 1932; partner firm Doxsee, Doxsee & Heiserman, Monticello, Iowa, 1932-38; judge 18th Jud. Dist. Iowa, 1939-58; partner Remley & Hieserman, and predecessors, Anamosa, Iowa, 1959—; pres. Iowa Dist. Judges Assn., 1954; city atty. Anamosa, 1960-66; atty. Jones County, 1937-38. Mem. Am., Iowa, Jones County bar assns., Phi Alpha Delta. Home: 402 Cleveland St Anamosa IA 52205 Office: 121 1/2 E Main St Anamosa IA 52205 Tel (319) 462-3577

HEISLER, EDWIN AUGUST, b. New Britain, Conn., June 15, 1935; B.S., Tufts U., 1957; J.D., George Washington U., 1965. Admitted to D.C., Va. bars, 1965, Maine bar, 1971; asso. firm Miller & Chevalier, Washington, 1965-69; asso. prof. law U. Maine Sch. Law, Portland, 1969-71; partner firm Richardson, Hildreth, Tyler & Troubh, Portland, 1971—. Mem. Am., Maine, Cumberland County bar assns., Order of Coif. Office: 465 Congress St Portland ME 04111 Tel (207) 774-5821

HEISLER, QUENTIN GEORGE, JR., b. Jefferson City, Mo., June 30, 1943; A.B. magna cum laude, Harvard, 1965, J.D., 1968. Admitted to Ill. bar, 1968; staff atty. Office Minority Bus. Enterprise, Dept. Commerce, Washington, 1969-70; asso., McDermott, Will & Emery, Chgo., 1968-69, 1970-74, partner, 1974-76. Mem. bd. dirs. Jane Addams Center, Chgo., 1971-73. Mem. Chgo. Council Lawyers. Author: (with Karen K. Mackay) Discretionary Distribution, Trust Administration In Ill., 1976. Home: 529 Cedar Winnetka IL 60093 Office: 111 W Monroe Chicago IL 60603 Tel (312) 372-2000

HEKMAN, RANDALL JOHN, b. Grand Rapids, Mich., May 9, 1947; B.S. in Indsl. Mgmt., Mass. Inst. Tech., 1969; J.D., George Washington U., 1972. Admitted to Mich. bar, 1972; asst. pros. atty. Kent County (Mich.), 1972-74; judge Kent County Probate Ct., 1975—. Mem. Mich. Bar, Grand Rapids (Mich.) Bar Assn., Christian Legal Soc. Office: Kent County Juvenile Ct 1501 Cedar NE Grand Rapids MI 49503 Tel (616) 774-3700

HELAND, KENNETH VERNER, b. New Britain, Conn., Aug. 1, 1946; B.A., Yale U., 1968; J.D., U. Pa., 1971; Admitted to Ohio bar, 1971, Md. bar, 1976, U.S. Supreme Ct. bar, 1976; asso. firm Squire, Sanders & Dempsey, Cleve., 1971-72; partner Richardson, Rogan, Anderson & Heland, Salisbury, Md., 1972—. Mem. Am., Md., Wicomico County bar assns., Pi Sigma Alpha. Office: 130 E Main St Salisbury MD 21801 Tel (301) 742-8744

HELD, EDWARD, lawyer; b. Bklyn., Oct. 7, 1942; LL.B., N.Y. Law Sch., 1966, J.D., 1968. Admitted to N.Y. bar, 1966, U.S. Supreme Ct., 1976; pvt. practice law, Bklyn., 1966—. Chmn. bldg. fund Yeshiva of South Queens. Mem. N.Y. State Bar Assn., N.Y. State Trial Lawyers Assn. Recipient Am. Jurisprudence award, 1965. Office: 6403 Bay Pkwy Brooklyn NY 11204

HELD, JACK EUGENE, b. Talladega, Ala., Aug. 17, 1931; LL.B., U. Ala., 1955. Admitted to Ala. bar, 1957; legal asst. officer U.S. Army, Ft. Sam Houston, Tex., 1955-57; partner firm Sirote, Permutt, Friend, Friedman, Held & Applinsky, Birmingha, Ala., 1957—. Chmn. profl. div. Greater Birmingham United Appeal, 1973; pres. Birmingham Jewish Fedn., 1977; bd. govs. Downtown YMCA, 1966-70, Jewish Community Center, 1976—. Mem. Ala., Birmingham (exec. com. 1970-73) bar assns. Home: 3928 Knollwood Dr Birmingham AL 35243 Office: 2222 Arlington Ave S Birmingham AL 35205 Tel (205) 933-7111

HELDING, ROBERT NORRIS, b. Missoula, Mont., Feb. 26, 1925; J.D., U. Mont., 1951. Admitted to Mont. bar, 1951; casualty adjuster Gen. Adjustment Bur., Missoula, 1951-53; asst. county atty. Missoula County (Mont.), 1953-54; atty., mgr. pub. affairs J. Neils Lumber Co. div. St. Regis Paper Co., Libby, Mont., 1955-70; individual practice law, Missoula, 1970-75; exec. dir. Mont. Wood Products Assn., Missoula, 1975—. Pres., Mont. Taxpayers Assn., 1970-71, Keep Mont. Green Assn., 1969-70; mem. Mont. Adv. Council on Employment, 1956—, Mont. Pub. Land Law Rev. Commn., 1967-70; bd. dirs. Mont. Econ. Edn. Council, 1966-77. Mem. Am., Mont., Western Mont. bar assns., Phi Delta Phi. Recipient Pub. Service award Western Wood Products Assn., 1970, Nat. Foest Products Assn., 1964. Home: 2328 Cloverdale Dr Missoula MT 59801 Office: 316 Savings Center Bldg 110 E Broadway Missoula MT 59801 Tel (406) 728-3650

HELLER, FRANCIS HOWARD, b. Vienna, Austria, Aug. 24, 1917; J.D., U. Va., 1941, Ph.D. in Polit Sci., 1948. Asst. prof. U. Kans., 1948-51, asso. prof., 1951-56, prof. polit. sci., 1956—, vice-chancellor, dean faculties, 1967-72, Roy A. Roberts prof. law, 1972—; vis. prof. Inst. Advanced Studies, Vienna, 1965. Mem. vice-chmn. City Planning Commn. Lawrence, Kans., 1957-63; mem. com. on Revision of State Constn., 1957-61; bd. dirs. Truman Library Inst., 1958, v.p., 1962—; bd. dirs. Bendictine Coll., 1971—; chmn., 1973—. Mem. Supreme Ct. Hist. Soc., Am. Soc. for Legal History, Law and Soc. Assn., Douglas County Bar Assn., Order of Coif. Author: Introduction to American Constitutional Law, 1952; The Sixth Amendment, 1951; The Presidency, A Modern Perspective, 1960, contbr. articles to legal jours. Home: 1648 Stratford Rd Lawrence KS 66044 Office: Sch Law U Kans Lawrence KS 66045 Tel (913) 864-4550

HELLER, FREDERICK KEACH, JR., b. Lynchburg, Va., June 9, 1947; B.A., Yale, 1969, J.D., 1973. Admitted to Ga. bar, 1973; asso. firm Kilpatrick, Cody, Rogers, McClatchey & Regenstein, Atlanta, 1973—. Mem. State Bar Ga. Home: 247 Hillside Dr Atlanta GA 30342 Office: 3100 Equitable Bldg Atlanta GA 30303 Tel (404) 522-3100

HELLER, JACOB W., b. Bklyn., Dec. 6, 1934; B.A., B.R.E., Yeshiva U., 1956; LL.B., Yale, 1959. Admitted to N.Y. State bar, 1960, U.S. Supreme Ct. bar, 1969; law sec. judge Charles W. Froessel, N.Y. State Ct. Appeals, N.Y.C., 1959-61; asso. firm Reavis & McGrath, N.Y.C., 1961-63; individual practice law, N.Y.C., 1963-69; sr. partner firm Weiss, Rosenthal, Heller & Schwartzman, N.Y.C., 1969—. Pres., Hillel Sch., Lawrence, N.Y., 1971-74; liaison v.p. Nat. council Young Israel, N.Y.C., 1965-67; trustee Rabbi Isaac Elchanan Theol. Sem. Yeshiva Univ., N.Y.C. Mem. Am., N.Y., N.Y.C. bar assns., Order of Coif. Recipient Distinguished Community Service award, Yeshiva Univ. Alumni Assn., 1975; contbr. articles Yale Law Jour., editor, 1957-59. Office: 295 Madison Ave New York City NY 10017 Tel (212) 725-9200

HELLER, LAWRENCE HOWARD, b. Denver, Apr. 20, 1944; B.A., U. Colo., 1966, J.D., 1969; LL.M., N.Y.U., 1970. Admitted to Colo. bar, 1969, Calif. bar, 1971; asso. firm Meserve, Mumper & Hughes, Los Angeles, 1970-73, Gordon, Weinberg & Gordon, Los Angeles, 1973-75; partner firm Zipser, Heller & Romain, Los Angeles, 1975—; tch. law Valley U., North Hollywood, Calif., 1975. Mem. Am., Beverly Hills, Los Angeles County bar assns. Office: 10100 Santa Monica Blvd Suite 2500 Los Angeles CA 90067 Tel (213) 553-8200

HELLER, MARK L., b. Troy, N.Y., Feb. 14, 1934; A.B., Hamilton Coll., 1955; LL.B., Harvard, 1958. Admitted to N.Y. bar, 1958; asso. counsel Port of N.Y. Authority, N.Y.C., 1959-60; asso. firm Rein, Mound & Cotton, N.Y.C., 1960-62; Pennock & Roberts, N.Y.C., 1962-64; partner firm Nolan & Heller, Albany, N.Y., 1964—; town atty. Town of Berne (N.Y.), 1962—, Town of Westerlo (N.Y.), 1963—, Town of Rensselaerville (N.Y.), 1976—. Alderman, City of Albany, 1968-69. Mem. Am., N.Y. State bar assns., Fed. Bar Council. Home: 33 Aspinwall Rd Loudonville NY 12211 Office: 60 State St Albany NY 12207 Tel (518) 449-3100

HELLER, MICHAEL WILLIAM, b. Peoria, Ill., May 3, 1924; B.S., Northwestern U., 1947; J.D., Stanford U., 1950. Admitted to Calif. bar, 1951, Ill. bar, 1971; pres. W. Heller & Son, Inc., Peoria, 1951—. Mem. Am., Ill., Peoria County bar assns. Home: 687 E High Point Terr Peoria IL 61614 Office: Lawyers Bldg 311 Main St Peoria IL 61602 Tel (309) 676-5858

HELLER, MILTON, b. Washington, Aug. 11, 1929; B.S., George Washington U., 1950, J.D., 1957. Examiner in patents Dept. Commerce, Washington, 1954; admitted to D.C. bar, 1958, Md. bar, 1965, U.S. Supreme Ct. bar, 1962; clk. firm Covington and Burling,

Washington, 1958-59; individual practice law, Washington, 1959—; cons. Bur. Med. Devices and Diagnostic Products FDA. Bd. dirs. Arthritis and Rheumatism Assn. of Met. Washington. Mem. Bar Assn. D.C. (chmn. com. negligence law 1973-76), Am. Trial Lawyers Assn. (circuit gov. 1968-73), Jud. Conf. of D.C. Home: 4701 Willard Ave Irene Apts Chevy Chase MD 20015 Office: Suite 519 Investment Bldg 1511 K St NW Washington DC 20005 Tel (202) 737-4300

HELLERSTEIN, ALVIN KENNETH; b. N.Y.C., Dec. 28, 1933; A.B., Columbia U., 1954, LL.B., 1956. Admitted to N.Y. State bar, 1956, So. Dist. U.S. Dist. Ct., 1956, Eastern Dist., 1963; U.S. Ct. Appeals, 2d Circuit, 1960, U.S. Supreme Ct., 1964; partner firm Stroock & Stroock & Lavan, N.Y.C., 1960—; lectr. fed. practice and trial advocacy Columbia U., Practicing Law Inst. Vice-pres., mem. exec. com., chmn. publs. com. Bd. Jewish Edn., N.Y.C., 1971—. Mem. Assn. of the Bar of the City N.Y. (chmn. com. on Fed. Cts. 1972-75, com. on judiciary 1975—), Am., N.Y. State bar assns. Home: 115 W 86th St New York City NY 10024 Office: 61 Broadway New York City NY 10006

HELLERSTEIN, JEROME ROBERT, b. Denver, July 30, 1907; A.B., U. Denver, 1927; M.A., State U. Iowa, 1928; LL.B., Harvard, 1931. Admitted to N.Y. State bar, 1932; asst. corp. counsel, N.Y.C., 1938-40; partner firm Hellerstein, Rosier & Minkin, N.Y.C., 1946-75; partner firm Guggenheimer & Untermyer, N.Y.C., 1975—; faculty N.Y.U., 1946—, prof. law, 1959-71, adj. prof. law, 1971—. Author: State and Local Taxation - Cases and Materials, 3d edit., 1969; Taxes, Loopholes and Morals, 1963. Home: 285 Central Park W New York City NY 10024 Office: 80 Pine St New York City NY 10005 Tel (212) 344-2040

HELLMAN, JOSEPH S., b. N.Y.C., Sept. 12, 1930; A.B., Queens Coll., 1952; J.D., Columbia, 1954. Admitted to N.Y. bar, 1954, U.S. Supreme Ct. bar, 1964; asso. firm Botein, Hays, Sklar & Herzberg, N.Y.C., 1954-62; partner firm Kronish, Lieb, Shainswit, Weiner & Hellman, N.Y.C., 1963—; adj. prof. law N.Y. U., 1972—, mem. Securities Inst., 1976—. Mem. Am., N.Y. State bar assns., Assn. Bar City N.Y. Editorial bd. Columbia Law Rev., 1953-54. Office: 1345 Ave of Americas New York City NY 10019 Tel (212) 765-6000

HELLMAN, RONALD BARRY, b. N.Y.C., Feb. 29, 1936; B.A., Columbia U., 1957, J.D., 1960. Admitted to N.Y. State bar, 1963; individual practice law, Flushing, N.Y., 1965—; conference officer Family Court, Queens, N.Y., 1976—. Pres., Queens Council Arts; bd. dirs. Queens Community Theatre; mem. Gibson Theatre Workshop; treas. Flushing Jewish Center. Mem. Queens County Bar Assn. Home: 36 14 191st St Flushing NY 11358 Office: 39-15 Main St Flushing NY 11354 Tel (212) 939-9030

HELLMUTH, THEODORE HENNING, b. Detroit, Mich., Mar. 28, 1949; B.A., U. Pa., 1970; J.D. cum laude, U. Mo., 1974. Admitted to Mo. bar, 1974; asso. firm Armstrong, Teasdale, Kramer & Vaughan, St. Louis, Mo., 1974—. Mem. Am., Mo., Met. St. Louis bar assns., Order of Coif. Asso. editor-in-chief Mo. Law Rev., 1973-74. Home: 6 Sona Ln St Louis MO 63141 Office: 611 Olive St Suite 1950 St Louis MO 63101 Tel (314) 5070

HELLWEGE, PAUL EVERETT, b. Ogden, Iowa, July 3, 1912; B.A., Iowa U., 1936, J.D., 1938. Admitted to Iowa bar, 1938; individual practice law, Boone, Iowa, 1938-64; judge Iowa Dist. Ct., Boone, 1964—; atty. Boone County, 1943-48; city atty. Boone, 1953-58. Charter pres. United Fund, Boone, 1948. Mem. Am., Iowa, Boone County bar assns. Home: 203 S Cedar St Boone IA 50036 Office: Boone County Court House Boone IA 50036 Tel (515) 532-3210

HELM, HUGH BARNETT, b. Bowling Green, Ky., Dec. 27, 1914; B.A., Vanderbilt U., 1935, postgrad. Law Sch., 1936-37, 52-53; postgrad. Stanford, 1953-56, Nat. Coll. State Judiciary, 1976. Admitted to Ky. bar, 1938, Tenn. bar, 1938, U.S. Supreme Ct. bar, 1942; atty. Trade Practice Conf., FTC, Washinton, 1938-42; asso. counsel U.S. Internat. Prosecution Sect. G.H.Q., SCAP, Tokyo, Japan, 1946; practiced in Nashville, 1946-53; bond specialist Swett & Crawford, San Francisco, 1956-57; resident mgr. Totten & Co., San Francisco, 1958, v.p., gen. mgr., 1959-60; sr. trial atty. Bur. Restraint of Trade, FTC, Washington, 1961-66, chief div. of adv. opinions, 1966-71, dir. Bur. Industry Guidance, 1969-70; adminstrv. law judge Bur. Hearings and Appeals, Social Security Adminstrn., HEW, Chattanooga, 1971-73, adminstrv. law judge charge Western Ky. and So. Ill., Paducah, Ky., Central Ky., Louisville, 1973—; permanent mem. Social Security Jud. Council So. U.S., 1975—. Mem. Tenn. Gen. Assembly, 1949. Mem. Am. (com. civil service law 1961—, com. trade regulation 1968-69, com. adminstrv. law judges 1972, 76, 77), Ky., Tenn. bar assns., HEW Adminstrv. Law Judges Assn. (legis. com.), Fed. Conf. Adminstrv. Law Judges (legis. com.). Recipient Distinguished Service award FTC, 1969. Office: 1301 Broadway St Paducah KY 42001 Tel (502) 442-6817 also 600 Bank of Louisville Bldg Louisville KY 40202

HELM, RICHARD ALLAN, b. San Francisco, Nov. 27, 1945; A.B., U. Calif., Davis, 1967; J.D., Hastings Coll. Law, 1970. Admitted to Alaska bar, 1970, U.S. Dist. Ct. Alaska bar, 1970, 9th Ct. of Appeals U.S. bar, 1971; asso. firm Burr, Pease & Kurtz, Inc., Anchorage, Alaska, 1970-72, partner, 1972—; chmn. com. law examiners State of Alaska, 1974—. Mem. Am., Alaska, Anchorage bar assns., Am. Judicature Soc. Home: 2036 Cliffside Dr Anchorage AK 99501 Office: 825 8th Ave Anchorage AK 99501 Tel (907) 279-2411

HELMAN, ROBERT ALAN, b. Chgo., Jan. 27, 1934; B.S., Northwestern U., 1954, LL.B., 1956. Admitted to Ill. bar, 1956; asso. firm Isham, Lincoln & Beale, Chgo., 1956-64, partner, 1965-66; partner firm Mayer, Brown & Platt, Chgo., 1967—; chmn. citizens com. Juvenile Ct. of Cook County, 1969—; pres. Legal Assistance Found. Chgo., 1973-76. Mem. Am., Chgo. bar assns., Am. Law Inst., Chgo. Council Lawyers, Law Club Chgo., Legal Club Chgo., Order of Coif. Author: (with Wayne Whalen) Commentaries on the Illinois Constitution of 1970, 1971; contbr. articles to legal jours.; asso. editor Northwestern U. Law Rev., 1955-56. Home: 4940 S Kimbark Ave Chicago IL 60615 Office: 231 S LaSalle St Chicago IL 60604 Tel (312) 782-0600

HELMENSTINE, ROBERT ALAN, b. Viroqua, Wis., Oct. 2, 1939; B.M.E., U. Wis., 1962, B.B.A., 1963; J.D., Hastings Coll., San Francisco, 1967. Admitted to Calif. bar, 1968; asso. firm Erickson, Erickson, Lynch, Mackenroth & Arbuthnot, San Francisco, 1976—. Mem. Calif., San Francisco bar assns., Assn. Def. Counsel, Am. Arbitration Assn. Office: Pier 1 1/2 The Embarcadero San Francisco CA 94111 Tel (415) 362-7126

HELMER, DONALD JAMES, b. Biwabik, Minn., July 31, 1940; A.A., Va. (Minn.) Jr. Coll.; J.D., Calif. Western Coll. Law. Admitted to Calif. bar, 1966; asso. firm Sheela, Lightner, Hughes & Castro, San Diego, 1967-71; gen. counsel U.S. Financial, San Diego, 1971—; prof. Western State Coll. Law, San Diego, 1976—. Home: 4261 Alta Mira Dr La Mesa CA 92041 Office: 620 C St San Diego CA 92101

HELMETAG, CARL, JR., b. Phila., Dec. 2, 1913; B.S. in Econs., U. Pa., 1936, LL.B., 1939. Admitted to Pa. bar, 1939, U.S. Supreme Ct. bar, 1950; asst. solicitor Pa. R.R., Phila., 1939-49, asst. gen. solicitor, 1949-53, asst. gen. counsel, 1953-65, gen. atty., 1965-68; gen. atty. Penn Central Transp. Co., Phila., 1968-71, sr. gen. atty., 1971-73, gen. counsel reorganization, 1973-75, gen. counsel, 1975-76, v.p., gen. counsel, 1976—; guest lectr. U. Pa. Law Sch.; mem. drafting com. Pa. Criminal Code. Chmn. bd. Woodmere Art Gallery; bd. dirs. Chestnut Hill Community Assn., Met. YMCA, Meml. Hosp. Roxborough, Phila. Lyric Opera Co., Community Chest Phila. Mem. Am., Phila. bar assns., Juristic Soc. Phila. Contbr. articles to profl. jours. Home: 701 St Georges Rd Philadelphia PA 19119 Office: 3100 IVB Bldg 1700 Market St Philadelphia PA 19103 Tel (215) 972-3053

HELMHOLZ, RICHARD HENRY, b. Pasadena, Calif., July 1, 1940; A.B., Princeton, 1962; LL.B., Harvard, 1965; Ph.D., U. Calif., Berkeley, 1970. Admitted to Mo. bar, 1965; asso. firm Bryan, Cave, McPheeters & McRoberts, St. Louis, 1966—; prof. law and history Washington U., St. Louis, 1970—. Mem. Selden Soc., Bar Assn. St. Louis, Soc. Legal History. Author: Marriage Litigation in Medieval England, 1974. Home: 353 Westgate St St Louis MO 63130 Office: Sch of Law Washington U St Louis MO 63130 Tel (314) 863-0100

HELMS, JACK JEFFREY, b. Marshville, N.C., Oct. 22, 1928; A.A., Armstrong Coll., 1951; LL.B., U. Ga., 1954. Admitted to Ga. bar, 1954; dep. asst. atty gen., State of Ga., 1955-56; individual practice law, Homerville and Pearson, Ga., 1956—; judge county ct., Atkinson county, Ga., 1960-66; mem. Ga. Ho. of Reps., 1957-58. Mem. Ga. State Bar (chmn worker's compensation sect. 1976-77), Am., Ga. (pres. 1976-77) trial lawyers assns. Home: Fargo Rd Homerville GA 31634 Office: Municipal Bldg Homerville GA 31634 Tel (912) 487-5378

HELMS, WILLIAM RICHARD, b. Wilmington, Del., Mar. 4, 1929; B.S., Northwestern U., 1952, J.D., 1956; postgrad. U. Paris, 1952-53. Admitted to Ill. bar, 1956; asso. firm Jenner & Block, Chgo., 1956-63, partner firm 1963—. Mem. Chgo., Ill. State, Am. bar assns. Home: 1010 Walnut St Western Springs IL 60558 Office: One IBM Plaza Chicago IL 60611 Tel (312) 222-9350

HELSTAD, ORRIN L., b. Ettrick, Wis., Feb. 9, 1922; B.S., U. Wis., 1948, LL.B., 1950. Admitted to Wis. bar, 1950; research asso. State Legis. Council, Madison, Wis., 1950-61; asso. prof. U. Wis. Law Sch., Madison, 1961-65, prof., 1965—, asso. dean, 1972-75, acting dean, 1975-76, dean, 1976—; mem. Wis. Supreme Ct. Com. to Study the State Bar, 1977. Mem. Wis. State Bar, Am. (mem. council sect. local govt. law 1975-78), Dane County bar assns., Am. Judicature Soc., Bar Assn. 7th Fed. Circuit, AAUP. Editor, co-author: Wisconsin Uniform Commercial Code Handbook, 1965, 71; contbr. articles to legal jours. Home: 4134 Mandan Crescent Madison WI 53711 Office: University of Wis Law Sch Madison WI 53706 Tel (608) 262-0618

HELTON, JAMES CARTER, b. Pineville, Ky., May 16, 1927; LL.B., U. Ky., 1950. Admitted to Ky. bar, 1950; individual practice law, Pineville, Ky., 1950—. Mem. Bell County, Ky., Am. bar assns. Office: 2d floor Asher Bldg Pineville KY 40977 Tel (606) 337-3087

HELWEIL, ROBERT HERMAN, b. N.Y.C., Dec. 6, 1923; A.B., Bklyn. Coll., 1944; J.D., Columbia U., 1948. Admitted to N.Y. bar, 1948; partner firm Helweil & Crispino, N.Y.C., 1956—; lectr. N.Y.C. Community Coll., Bklyn., 1956-61. Mem. Nassau County, Bronx County bar assns. Home: 1 The Poplars Roslyn Estates NY 11576 Office: 79 Wall St New York City NY 10005 Tel (212) 344-0062

HEMANN, JOHN LAWRENCE, b. Salem, Oreg., Jan. 22, 1943; B.A., Willamette U., 1965, J.D., 1968. Admitted to Oreg. bar, 1968; with JAGC, USAF, 1968-72; partner firm Garrett Seideman & Hemann, 1972—, legal counsel Oreg. State Jaycees. Bd. dirs. Salem Boys' Club, March of Dimes. Mem. Am. Bar Assn., Oreg. Trial Lawyers. Home: 4770 20th Ave S Salem OR 97302 Office: 710 Capitol Tower Bldg PO Box 749 Salem OR 97308 Tel (503) 581-1501

HEMBEL, KENNETH JEFFREY, b. West Bend, Wis., Dec. 12, 1943; B.B.A., U. Wis., Madison, 1967, M.B.A., 1969, J.D. cum laude, 1972. Admitted to La. bar, 1973; tax staff Arthur Anderson & Co., New Orleans, 1972-74; tax coordinator La. Gen. Services, Inc., Harvey, La., 1974-75; tax supr. Ocean Drilling & Exploration Co., New Orleans, La., 1975—. C.P.A., La. Mem. C.P.A. socs.-La., New Orleans, Internat. Tax Group (Am. Jurisprudence award), Am., La. bar assns. Home: 5532 Willow St New Orleans LA 70118 Office: care Treasury Div 1600 Canal St New Orleans LA 70112 Tel (504) 561-2459

HEMBROW, WALTER EDWARD, b. Alexis, Ill., Aug. 26, 1899; student Coll. of Emporia, 1921-24; J.D., Washburn U., 1929. Admitted to Kans. bar, 1930; practiced in Council Grove, Kans., 1930-57; judge Kans. Dist. Ct., 8th Jud. Dist., 1957-71; individual practice law, Council Grove, 1971—. Pres. Morris County (Kans.) Hosp. Bd., 1952-57; trustee Coll. Emporia, 1965-73; mem. Council Grove Bd. Edn., 1946-48; lay leader Meth. Ch., Council Grove. Mem. Kans., Am. bar assns., Kans. Judges Assn., Morris County Bar. Office: 214 W Main St Council Grove KS 66846 Tel (316) 767-5112

HEMING, CHARLES E., b. N.Y.C., Mar. 1, 1926; A.B., Princeton, 1948; LL.B., Columbia, 1950. Admitted to N.Y. bar, 1950, U.S. Supreme Ct. bar, 1954; partner firm Dammann & Heming, N.Y.C., 1962—; sec., dir. U.S. Rubber Reclaiming Co., Inc.; dir. Sarco Internat. Corp. Trustee Village of Scarsdale (N.Y.), 1972-76. Fellow Am. Bar Found.; mem. Assn. Bar City N.Y. (sec. com. adminstrn. justice 1953-54, mem. com. taxation 1970-73, chmn. com. trusts, estates and surrogates cts. 1972-75, mem. com. lectures and continuing edn. 1975—), N.Y. State (chmn. estate and gift tax com. 1962-68, chmn. tax sect. 1971-72, exec. com. 1971-72, ho. of dels. 1972-73), Am. bar assns. Home: 30 Sage Terr Scarsdale NY 10583 Office: 380 Madison Ave New York City NY 10017 Tel (212) MU 7-0880

HEMINGWAY, RICHARD WILLIAM, b. Detroit, Nov. 24, 1927; B.S., U. Colo., 1950; J.D. magna cum laude, So. Methodist U., 1955; LL.M., U. Mich., 1969. Admitted to Texas bar, 1955; asso. firm Fulbright, Crooker & Jaworski, Houston, 1955-60; individual practice law, Waco, Tex., 1960-65, Dallas, 1966-68, Lubbock, 1969—; asso. prof. law Baylor Univ., Waco, Tex., 1960-65; vis. asso. prof. law, So. Meth. U., Dallas, 1966-68; Paul Horn prof. law Tex. Tech. Univ., Lubbock, 1969, acting dean, 1974-75. Mem. Tex., Lubbock bar assns., S. Plains Trial Lawyers, Scribes. Author: Law of Oil and Gas, 1971; Cases and Materials on Texas Land Titles; 1966; Cases and Materials on Real Property Transactions, 1972; mem. editorial bd. Oil and Gas Reporter, 1966—; contbr. articles in field to profl. jours. Home: 6804 Norfolk Lubbock TX 79413 Office: Texas Tech University School of Law Lubbock TX 79409 Tel (806) 742-6273

HEMINGWAY, RONALD LEE, b. Hamilton, Ohio, Jan. 29, 1935; B.S. in Chemistry, U. Cin., 1957; J.D., Salmon P. Chase Law Sch., 1968. Admitted to Ohio bar, 1968, U.S. Patent Office bar, 1969; patent atty. Procter & Gamble Co., Cin., 1968—. Mem. Montgomery (Ohio) Bd. Tax Appeals. Mem. Am. Bar Assn., Cin. Patent Law Assn. Home: 7405 Thumbelina Ln Montgomery OH 45242 Office: 11520 Reed Hartman Hwy Cincinnati OH 45241 Tel (513) 977-3713

HEMINGWAY, WHITLEY MAYNARD, b. Webster City, Iowa, Oct. 21, 1915; A.B., U. Iowa, 1936, J.D., 1938. Admitted to Iowa bar, 1938; partner firm Hemingway Myers & Bottorff, Webster City, 1938—; city atty. Webster City, 1946-57; dir. Farmers Nat. Bank, Webster City, 1956—, v.p., 1960—; commr. Jud. Dist. 2B, 1972-76. Treas., trustee Kendall Young Library, Webster City, 1960—. Mem. Hamilton County (Iowa), Iowa, Am. bar assns., Iowa, Am. trial lawyers assns. Home: 701 White Post Rd Webster City IA 50595 Office: 733 2d St Webster City IA 50595 Tel (515) 832-5342

HEMMERLING, GERALDINE S., b. Los Angeles, Oct. 4, 1928; B.S., U. Calif. at Los Angeles, 1949, J.D., 1952. Admitted to Calif. bar, 1953, U.S. Supreme Ct. bar, 1960; individual practice law, Los Angeles, 1953-59, 66-71; asso. firm Richards, Watson & Hemmerling, Los Angeles, 1960-65; mem. firm Abbott & Hemmerling, Los Angeles, 1971-76; of counsel firm Armstrong, Hendler & Barnet, Los Angeles, 1977—; lectr. various seminars. Mem. U. Calif. at Los Angeles Med. Center Human Subject Protection Com., 1976—. Fellow Am. Coll. Probate Counsel; mem. Am. Bar Assn. (chmn. com. on income taxation of estates and trusts, real property and trust sect. 1977—, Calif. State Bar (chmn. continuing edn. com. 1977—). Mem. editorial bd. Shepard's Citations, McGraw Hill Book Co., 1976—; author: (with John R. Cohan) Inter Vivos Trusts, 1975; Accumul.ation Trusts and Charitable Remainder Trusts; contbr. articles to profl. jours. Home: 369 Homewood Rd Los Angeles CA 90049 Office: 1888 Century Park E Los Angeles CA 90067 Tel (213) 553-0305

HEMMETT, GORDON M., JR., b. Rochester, N.Y., Aug. 5, 1940; B.A., Allegheny Coll., 1962; LL.B., Syracuse U., 1965. Admitted to N.Y. bar, 1965; individual practice law, Hudson Falls, N.Y.; law sec. Washington County (N.Y.) Judge, 1975—. Bd. dirs. Adirondack chpt. ARC, 1975. Mem. N.Y., Warren County, Washington County bar assns. Office: 214 Main St Hudson Falls NY 12839 Tel (518) 747-3596

HEMPHILL, DONALD JAMES, b. Spencer, Iowa, Mar. 19, 1948; B.A., U. Iowa, 1971, J.D., 1973. Admitted to Iowa bar, 1973, Circuit Ct. bar, 1976, U.S. Supreme Ct. bar, 1976; law clk. firm Meardon Sueppel, Downer and Hayes, Iowa City, Iowa, 1972-73; asso. firm Sackett and Sackett, Spencer, Iowa, 1973-75, partner firm Sackett, Sackett & Hemphill, Spencer, 1975—; city atty., Spencer, 1976—. Pres. Spencer United Way. Mem. Am., Iowa bar assns., Am. Trial Lawyers Assn., Iowa Assn. of Trial Lawyers, Phi Delta Phi. Home: 930 W 4th St Spencer IA 51301 Office: 1823 Highway Blvd Spencer IA 51301 Tel (712) 262-5564

HEMPHILL, ROBERT WITHERSPOON, b. Chester, S.C., May 10, 1915; A.B., U. S.C., 1936, LL.B., 1938. Admitted to S.C. bar, 1938; partner firm Hemphill & Hemphill, Chester, 1938-64; solicitor 6th S.C. Jud. Circuit, 1951-56; judge U.S. Dist. Ct., Dist. S.C., 1964—; mem. S.C. Ho. of Reps., 1947-48; mem. 79th Congress from 5th S.C. Dist. Chmn. Chester County Democratic Conv., 1947-49. Mem. S.C., Am. bar assns., Am. Law Inst., Am. Judicature Soc., Nat. Lawyers' Club. Recipient Algernon Sidney Sullivan award U. S.C., 1969, Jud. award of Merit, Am. Trial Lawyers Assn., 1973, Am. Legion Pub. Service award, 1976. Contbr. articles to Am. Legion Mag., S.C. Law Quar., The Transcript. Home: POB 187 167 York St Chester SC 29706 Office: 1100 Laurel St POB 867 Columbia SC 29201 Tel (803) 765-5136

HENDERSON, BUTLER THOMAS, b. Knoxville, Tenn., June 20, 1919; student Ark. A.M. and N. Coll., 1936-38; A.B., Morehouse Coll., 1944; M.A., N.Y. U., 1947, postgrad., 1955-57; LL.D., U. Ark., Pine Bluff, 1973. Chmn. dept. econs. and bus. Ark. A. M. and N. Coll., 1944-59; asst. to pres., asso. prof. econs. Morehouse Coll., 1960-68; asso. dir., dir. United Bd. for Coll. Devel., Atlanta, 1968-70; asst. dir. United Negro Coll. Fund, N.Y.C., 1970-72; exec. dir. Earl Warren Legal Tng. Program, Inc., N.Y.C., 1972—. Bd. dirs. Spence-Chapin Services to Families and Children; trustee Morristown (Tenn.) Coll. Mem. Am., So econ. assns., Omega Psi Phi, Sigma Pi Phi. Home: 69 Fifth Ave New York City NY 10003 Office: 10 Columbus Circle New York City NY 10019 Tel (212) 586-8397

HENDERSON, DANIEL ELI, JR., b. Houston, Mar. 16, 1921; A.B., Trinity U., 1950; M.A., George Washington U., 1962, LL.M., 1963; J.D., U. Tex., 1950. Admitted to Tex. bar, 1950, U.S. Supreme Ct. bar, 1956, Calif. bar, 1966; served as col. JAGC, USAF, 1950-66, ret. 1966; mem. firm Henderson & Merenbach, Santa Barbara, Calif., 1966-68, Cavalletto, Webster, Mullen & McCaughey, Santa Barbara, 1968-71, Henderson, Goodwin, Marking & Rogers, Santa Barbara, 1971-75, Henderson, Rogers, Sheffield & Henderson, Santa Barbara, 1975—. Mem. Arthritis Found. Santa Barbara, 1972—; pres. Legal Aid Found. Santa Barbara County, 1971-72. Mem. Am., Calif., Santa Barbara County bar assns., Assn. So. Calif. Def. Counsel, Phi Delta Phi, Phi Theta Kappa. Home: 1127 N Patterson Ave Santa Barbara CA 93111 Office: 1033 Santa Barbara St Santa Barbara CA 93111 Tel (805) 963-0484

HENDERSON, DAVID EARL, b. Canton, Ohio, Sept. 12, 1947; B.S., Ga. Inst. Tech., 1970; J.D., Mercer U., 1973. Admitted to Ga. bar, 1973; individual practice law, Macon, Ga., 1973; partner firm Marchman & Henderson, Macon, 1974, firm Marchman, Cueto & Henderson, Macon, 1974; individual practice law, Macon, 1974—. Mem. Ga., Am. bar assns., Ga. Jaycees. Home: 837 Laurel Ave Macon GA 31201 Office: 608 American Federal Bldg Macon GA 31201 Tel (912) 746-1216

HENDERSON, DOUGLAS BOYD, b. Pitts., Sept. 21, 1935; B.S., Pa. State U., 1957; J.D. with honors, George Washington U., 1963. Admitted to Va. bar, 1962, D.C. bar, 1963; mfr.'s agt. Arthur G. Henderson & Assos., Pitts., 1957-59; patent agt. Swift & Co., Washington, 1959-62; law clk. to Hon. Donald E. Lane, U.S. Ct. Claims, Washington, 1962-63; asso. firm Irons, Birch, Swindler & McKie, Washington, 1963-65; sr. partner firm Finnegan, Henderson, Farabow & Garrett and predecessors, Washington, 1965—. Mem. Am. Judicature Soc., Fed., Va., Am. (asst. sec. patent, trademark and copyright law sect. 1975—), D.C. (dir. 1975-76, chmn. sect. patent, trademark and copyright law 1974-75, chmn. ct. claims com. 1973-74) bar assns., Am. Patent Law Assn., Patent Office Soc., Phi Gamma

Delta, Delta Theta Phi. Home: 6715 Wemberly Way McLean VA 22101 Office: 1775 K St Washington DC 20006 Tel (202) 293-6850

HENDERSON, FREDERICK FOX, JR., b. Troy, Ala., Nov. 15, 1940; B.S., Washington and Lee U., 1963; J.D., U. Ala., 1968; LL.M., Harvard, 1969. Admitted to Ala. bar, 1968, Tenn. bar, 1974; asso. firm Bradley, Arant, Rose & White, Birmingham, Ala., 1968-71; asst. prof. law U. Ala. Sch. Law, Tuscaloosa, 1971-73; partner firm Ireland Reams Henderson & Chafetz, Memphis, 1974-76; v.p., sec., gen. counsel combined staff for Worthington Compressors, Inc., and Turbodyne Corp., Mpls., 1976—. Mem. Am., Ala., Tenn. bar assns., Order of Coif. Contbr. articles to legal jours.; editor Ala. Law Rev., 1966-68. Home: 4608 Moorland Ave Edina MN 55424 Office: 1612 First Nat Bank Bldg Minneapolis MN 55402 Tel (612) 378-8509

HENDERSON, GORDON DESMOND, lawyer; b. Oakland, Calif., May 25, 1930; A.B. magna cum laude, Harvard, 1951, J.D. magna cum laude, 1957. Admitted to D.C. bar, 1957, N.Y. bar, 1965; partner law firm Barrett Smith Schapiro Simon & Armstrong, N.Y.C., 1965—; spl. counsel to SEC, 1962-64. Mem. Scarsdale Planning Commn., 1975—; co-chmn. Advisory Com. to Bd. Edn. on Ednl. Planning, Scarsdale, N.Y., 1976-77; pres. Civic Assn. Hollin Hills, Alexandria, Va., 1962. Mem. Assn. of the Bar of City N.Y. (chmn. com. on corp. law, 1969-72), N.Y. State (sec. 1976, 2d vice chmn. tax sect. 1977), Am. bar assns., Am. Law Inst. Home: 35 Sage Terr Scarsdale NY 10583 Office: 26 Broadway New York City NY 10004

HENDERSON, HAROLD LAWRENCE, b. Wayne County, Iowa, Nov. 11, 1935; B.A., U. Chgo., 1962, J.D., 1964. Admitted to Ill. bar, 1966; asso. firm Cravath, Swaine & Moore, N.Y.C., 1964-66, firm Isham, Lincoln & Beale, Chgo., 1966-67, firm Mayer, Brown & Platt, Chgo., 1967-68; resource group counsel Gen. Dynamics Corp., Chgo., 1968-70; asst. counsel Firestone Tire & Rubber Co., Akron, Ohio, 1970—. Mem. adv. bd. Salvation Army, Akron, 1976—. Mem. Am., Chgo. bar assns. Home: 370 Wyoga Lake Blvd Stow OH 44224 Office: 1200 Firestone Pkwy Akron OH 44317 Tel (216) 379-6276

HENDERSON, STANLEY DALE, b. Monona, Iowa, June 17, 1935; A.B. magna cum laude, Coe Coll., 1957; postgrad. (Woodrow Wilson fellow) Cornell U., 1957-58; U. Chgo., 1958-59; J.D., U. Colo., 1961. Admitted to Colo bar, 1961, Va. bar, 1973; law clk. U.S. Dist. Ct. Colo., 1961-62; asso. firm Williams & Zook, Boulder, Colo., 1962-64; prof. law U. Wyo., 1964-70, U. Va., 1970—. Mem. Am. Arbitration Assn., Order Coif, Phi Beta Kappa, Phi Kappa Phi. Home: 1615 King Mountain Rd Charlottesville VA 22901 Office: Sch Law Univ VA Charlottesville VA 22901 Tel (804) 924-3522

HENDERSON, THOMAS WILLIAM, b. Washington, Pa., Nov. 29, 1939; A.B., Brown U., 1962; J.D., Duquesne U., 1966. Admitted to Pa. bar, 1967; partner firm McArdle, Henderson, Caroselli, Spagnolli & Beachler, Pitts., 1973—. Mem. Allegheny County, Pa., Am. bar assns., Am. Assn. Trial Lawyers. Home: 209 Hampton Rd Pittsburgh PA 15215 Office: 1100 Law & Finance Bldg Pittsburgh PA 15219 Tel (412) 391-9860

HENDON, ROBERT CARAWAY, JR., b. Des Moines, June 10, 1937; B.A., Princeton, 1959; certificate Woodrow Wilson Sch. for Pub. and Internat. Affairs, 1959; LL.B., Yale, 1964. Admitted to Tenn. bar, 1965; asso. firm Waller, Lansden, Dortch & Davis, Nashville, 1964-71, partner, 1971—. Chmn. Princeton Schs. Com. for Middle Tenn., 1969—. Mem. Princeton Alumni Assn. Middle Tenn. (pres. 1971-72). Office: 1200 Am Trust Bldg Nashville TN 37201 Tel (615) 244-6380

HENDRICKS, BENJAMIN EDGAR, JR., b. Miami, Fla., Mar. 12, 1941; B.A. with honors, U. Fla., 1963, J.D. with honors, 1966. Admitted to Fla. bar, 1966, U.S. Dist. Ct. bar, 1966; partner firm Hendricks and Hendricks, Miami and Coral Gables, Fla., 1966—. Mem. Dade County (Fla.) Bar Assn. (dir. 1968-70, 76-77, pres. 1973-74, 74-75), Nat. Council Bar Pres's., Am. Judicature Soc., Order of Coif, Phi Beta Kappa, Phi Kappa Phi, Phi Delta Phi. Office: 310 Alhambra Circle Coral Gables FL 33172 Tel (305) 445-3692

HENDRICKS, JOHN CHARLES, b. Sellersville, Pa., Oct. 26, 1941; A.B. in Polit. Sci. cum laude, Dickinson Coll., Carlisle, Pa., 1963; J.D., George Washington U., 1966, LL.M. in Taxation, 1973. Admitted to U.S. Dist. Ct. for D.C. bar, 1967, U.S. Ct. Appeals for D.C. bar, 1970, U.S. Tax Ct. bar, 1970, U.S. Ct. Claims bar, 1974, U.S. Supreme Ct. bar, 1973; partner firm Kurrus & Ash, Washington, 1969—; speaker profl. seminars. Bd. dirs. Lutheran Social Services of Met. Washington, 1975-77, pres., 1976. Mem. Am. (tax sect.), D.C. bar assns. Contbr. articles to profl. jours. Home: 129 N Irving St Arlington VA 22201 Office: 1055 Thomas Jefferson St #418 Washington DC 20007 Tel (202) 337-8848

HENDRICKS, STANLEY, b. N.Y.C., June 2, 1924; LL.B., Brooklyn Law Sch., 1949; LL.M., N.Y.U., 1953. Admitted to N.Y. State bar, 1950, U.S. Supreme Ct. bar, 1963, individual practice law, N.Y.C., 1950—; arbitrator N.Y.C. Small Claims Ct., 1966—. Mem. Am. Arbitration Assn. (panel of arbitrators), Assn. Arbitrators Small Claims Ct. (dir.), Am. Judges Assn. Office: 565 5th Ave New York City NY 10017 Tel (212) YU6-1888

HENDRICKS, THOMAS GRAHAM, b. Bremorton, Wash., Sept. 28, 1938; A.B., San Diego State Coll., 1960; J.D., Hastings Coll. Law, 1963. Admitted to Calif. bar, 1963, U.S. Dist. Ct. of Los Angeles and San Francisco bar, 1963, 9th Circuit bar, 1964; dep. counsel County of Imperial (Calif.), 1963-65; dep. counsel County of Marin (Calif.), San Rafael, 1965-75, asst. county counsel, 1975—; pres. Clearwater Ranch Inc., 1976—. Pres. Ross Valley Players, Ross Calif., 1968; chmn. Child Abuse Com., Marin County, 1974-75. Mem. Marin County Bar Assn. Office: Civic Center San Rafael CA 94903 Tel (415) 479-1100

HENDRICKSON, DAVID BURTON, b. St. Ansgar, Iowa, June 3, 1937; B.A., U. Iowa, 1961, J.D., 1963. Admitted to Iowa bar, 1963; partner firm Walker, Concannon & Hendrickson, Keokuk, Iowa, 1963-73; asst. atty. gen., Iowa, 1967-68; judge Dist. Ct. Iowa, Keokuk, 1973—. Mem. Iowa, Keokuk bar assns. Home: 1704 Grand Keokuk IA 52632 Office: 2nd Floor U S Post Office Bldg Keokuk IA 52632 Tel (319) 521-1711

HENDRICKSON, ROBERT AUGUSTUS, b. Indpls., Aug. 9, 1923; student Yale U., 1941-43; certificate U. Besancon (France), 1945; postgrad. Sorbonne, U. Paris, 1945-46; LL.B., Harvard U., 1948. Admitted to Ind. bar, 1948, N.Y. bar, 1949, Fla. bar, 1976, U.S. Supreme Ct. bar, 1959; asso. firm Lord Day & Lord, N.Y.C., 1948-52; law asst. surrogate's ct. N.Y. County, N.Y.C., 1952-54; asso. firm Breed Abbott & Morgan, N.Y.C., 1954-67; partner firm Lovejoy Wasson Lundgren & Ashton, N.Y.C., 1967-76; of counsel Coudert Bros., N.Y.C., 1977—. Mem. Am., N.Y. State, Ind., Fla. bar assns., Maritime Law Assn. U.S., Internat. Acad. Estate and Trust Law, Assn. Bar City N.Y., Am. Fgn. Law Assn., Consular Law Soc. Author: The Future of Money, 1970; The Cashless Society, 1972; Hamilton I, 1976; Hamilton II, 1976; contbr. articles to legal jours. Office: 200 Park Ave New York City NY 10017 Tel (212) 973-3223

HENDRICKSON, THOMAS ATHERTON, b. Indpls., May 12, 1927; B.A., Yale U., 1948; LL.B., Ind. U., 1952. Admitted to Ind. bar, 1952; asso. firm Buschman, Krieg, Deveult & Alexander, 1952-53; partner firm Purvis & Hendrickson, 1953-56; dep. prosecutor, Marion County, 1954-57; partner firm Royse & Travis, 1956-63; partner firm Royse, Travis, Hendrickson & Pantzer, Indpls., 1963—. Mem. planning com. Central Ind. Library Services Authority. Mem. Am., Ind. (chmn. group legal services com. 1976—, ho. of dels. mem. 1971—), Indpls. (v.p. 1972) bar assns. Home: 7979 Lantern Rd Indianapolis IN 46256 Office: 111 Monument Circle 500 Indianapolis IN 46204 Tel (317) 632-4417

HENDRIX, JACK HALL, b. Orleans, Nebr., Feb. 24, 1922; B.S. in Edn., U. Neb., 1947, J.D., 1948. Admitted to Nebr. bar, 1948; practiced in Culbertson, Nebr., 1948-49, Trenton, Nebr., 1950-69; judge 14th Jud. Dist. Ct. of Nebr., 1969—. Mem. Trenton (Nebr.) (pres. 1959), South Platte United (pres. 1965-66) chambers commerce, 14th Jud. Dist. Bar (pres.), Nebr., Am. bar assns., Phi Delta Phi. Home: 115 E A St Trenton NE 69044 Office: Courthouse Trenton NE 69044 Tel (308) 334-5270

HENDRY, EARL RONALD, b. Palm Beach County, Fla., May 11, 1934; student U. Fla., 1952-54, U. Miss., 1956-57; LL.B., U. Memphis and Memphis State U., 1964, J.D., 1964; grad. Am. Acad. Jud. Edn., 1972. Admitted to Tenn. bar, 1964, U.S. Supreme Ct. bar, 1971; practiced in Gatlinburg, Tenn., 1967-71; judge Tenn. Chancery Ct., 13th Div., 1971—; group leader, lectr. Nat. Coll. State Judiciary, 1973-74. Active Community Chest, Civic League; pres. Gatlinburg PTA, 1968-69; elder Gatlinburg Presbyterian Ch., 1974-76. Mem. Am., Tenn. (gov. 1971), Sevier County (Tenn.) bar assns., Am. Judicature Soc., Am., Tenn. trial lawyers assns., Tenn. Jud. Conf. Inst. Advanced Studies, Tenn. Trial Judges Assn. Author: Hendry's Manual On Tennessee Civil Procedure, 2 vols., 1974; Hendry's Handbook on Tennessee Discovery and Depositions, 1975; Handbook On Swimming Pool Liability, 1976; Swimming Pools and the Law, 1977. Home: Fox Trail Kings Ridge Gatlinburg-in-the-Smokies TN 37738 Office: POB 25 Gatlingburg TN 37738 Tel (615) 436-7230

HENDRY, ROBERT RYON, b. Jacksonville, Fla., Apr. 23, 1936; B.A. in Polit. Sci., U. Fla., 1958, J.D., 1963. Admitted to Fla. bar, 1963; asso. firm Harrell, Caro, Middlebrooks & Wiltshire, Pensacola, Fla., 1963-66; asso. firm Helliwell, Melrose & DeWolf, Orlando, Fla., 1966-67, shareholder, 1967-69; shareholder, pres. firm Hoffman, Hendry & Parker, Orlando, 1969-73, firm Hoffman, Hendry, Parker & Smith, Orlando, 1973—. Mem. Fla. Bar (vice chmn. internat. law com. 1974-75, chmn. 1976), Am., Orange County (treas. 1971-74) bar assns. Office: 200 E Robinson St Orlando FL 32801 Tel (305) 843-5880

HENEHAN, THOMAS PATRICK, b. New Orleans, Aug. 12, 1907; B.A., DePaul U., 1931, J.D., 19334; admitted to Ill. bar, 1934; partner firms Shipman, Barrett, Henehan & Abell, Chgo., 1934-42, Henehan, Barsotti & Stevenson, Chgo., 1942-50, Henehan & McInerney, Chgo., 1950-56; partner, pres. firm Henehan, Donovan & Isaacson, Ltd., Chgo. 1956—; mem. Ill. Gen Assembly, 1949-51. Mem. Am., Fed., Ill., Chgo. bar assns., Am. Judicature Soc. Home: 3801 Mission Hills Rd Northbrook IL 60062 Office: 135 S LaSalle St Chicago IL 60603 Tel (312) 346-5275

HENICAN, CASWELL ELLIS, b. New Orleans, Feb. 10, 1905; LL.B., Tulane U., 1926. Admitted to La. bar, 1926, U.S. Supreme Ct. bar; sr. mem. firm Henican, James & Cleveland, New Orleans, 1933—. Past pres. Mercy Hosp. Adv. Bd., Associated Cath. Charities, New Orleans Community Chest, 1940; bd. dirs. Family Service Soc., Bur. Govtl. Research. Mem. New Orleans Bar Assn. (pres. 1958), Soc. Hosp. Attys. (charter), Nat. Health Lawyers Assn., Serra Internat. (chpt. pres. 1960), Blue Key. Named Knight of St. Gregory, Knight of St. Louis King of France; Outstanding Man of Year, New Orleans Jr. C. of C., 1940; recipient F. Edward Hebert award Jesuit High Sch., 1960. Home: 1831 Octavia St New Orleans LA 70115 Office: One Shell Sq Suite 4440 New Orleans LA 70139 Tel (504) 581-7575

HENINGER, RALPH HUNTRESS, b. Iowa City, Mar. 7, 1933; B.A., U. Iowa, 1955, J.D., 1961. Admitted to Iowa bar, 1961; asso. firm Betty, Neuman, Heninger, & McMahon, Davenport, Iowa, 1961-66; partner firm Heninger and Heninger, Davenport, 1966—. Mem. Iowa Bar Assn. (environ. law com.), Am. Coll. Legal Medicine, Am. Soc. Hosp. Attys. Contbr. articles to legal rev. Office: Heninger & Heninger 401 1st National Bldg Davenport IA 52801 Tel (319) 324-0418

HENKE, DAN, b. San Antonio, Feb. 18, 1924; B.S., Georgetown U., 1943, J.D., 1951; LL.M., U. Wash., 1956. Bus. economist, office bus. econs. Dept. Commerce, Washington, 1948-51; admitted to Tex. bar, 1951, D.C. bar, 1951, Calif. bar, 1962, U.S. Supreme Ct. bar, 1959; asst. to law librarian U. Wash., 1955-56; head N.J. Bur. Law and Legis. Reference, Trenton, 1956-59; lectr. in law U. Calif., Berkeley, 1959-64, prof., 1965-70, law librarian, 1959-70; prof. law, dir. law library U. Calif. Hastings Coll. Law, San Francisco, 1970—; cons. Am. Bar Found., 1965-66, Fed. Jud. Center, 1976—. Mem. State Bar Calif. (chmn. com. on computers and the law 1975-76), Am. Bar Assn., Am. Judicature Soc., Am. Assn. Law Libraries, Am. Soc. Info. Sci., ALA, Assn. Am. Law Schs., Order of Coif, Beta Phi Mu. Author: (with Mortimer D. Schwartz) Anglo-American Law Collections, 1971; California Legal Research Handbook, 1971; California Law Guide, 1976; contbr. articles to legal jours. Office: Suite 316 198 McAllister St San Francisco CA 94102 Tel (415) 557-2259

HENKE, EDWARD WILLIAM, b. Charles City, Iowa, Nov. 9, 1921; student Cornell Coll., 1939-41; B.A., U. Iowa, 1946, J.D., 1947. Admitted to Iowa bar, 1947, Fed. bar, 1948, partner firm Henke & Henke, Charles City, 1947, Henke & Eggert, 1969-76, Henke, Eggert & Schroeder, 1977—; atty. Floyd County (Iowa), 1953-54, 67-72. Mem. Iowa State Rep. Central Com., 1959-61, chmn. Rep. State Judicial Conv., 1960. Mem. Floyd County, 2d Judicial Dist., Iowa bar assns., Iowa Trial Lawyers Assn. Home: Pin Oak Estates Rt 4 Charles City IA 50616 Office: 1000 S Grand Ave Charles City IA 50616 Tel (515) 228-6522

HENKE, MICHAEL JOHN, b. Evansville, Ind., Aug. 3, 1940; B.A., Baylor U., 1962, LL.B., 1965; LL.M., N.Y. U., 1966. Admitted to Tex. bar, 1965, D.C. bar, 1967; asso. firm Covington & Burling, Washington, 1966-73; asso. firm Vinson & Elkins, Washington, 1974-75, partner, 1976—. Mem. Am. Bar Assn., D.C. Bar. Contbr. articles to legal jours. Home: 4221 Wilton Woods Ln Alexandria VA 22310 Office: 1701 Pennsylvania Ave NW Washington DC 20006 Tel (202) 298-5550

HENKIN, LOUIS, b. Smolyan, Russia, Nov. 11, 1917; A.B. Yeshiva Coll., 1937; LL.B., Harvard, 1940; D.H.L., Yeshiva U., 1963. Admitted to N.Y. State bar, 1941, U.S. Supreme Ct. bar, 1947; law clk. Judge Learned Hand, U.S. Ct. Appeals, 1940-41; law clk. Justice Felix Frankfurter, U.S. Supreme Ct., 1946-47; cons. UN legal dept., N.Y.C., 1947-48; officer State Dept., Washington, 1945-46, 48-57; asso. dir. Legis. Drafting Research Fund, Columbia, 1956-57; prof. law U. Pa., 1957-62; prof. Columbia, 1962—, Hamilton Fish prof. internat. law and diplomacy, 1963—; pres. U.S. Inst. Human Rights, 1970—; mem. adv. Panel on Internat. Law, State Dept., 1967-69, 75—; adv. bd. internat. project Center for Law and Social Policy, 1972—; U.S. mem. Permanent Ct. Arbitration, 1963-69. Fellow Am. Acad. Arts and Scis.; mem. Council on Fgn. Relations, Am. Soc. Internat. Law (v.p. 1975-76), Internat. Law Assn. (v.p. Am. br. 1973—), Am. Soc. Polit. and Legal Philosophy, Am. Polit. Sci. Assn., Acad. Polit. Sci. Author: Arms Control and Inspection in American Law, 1958; How Nations Behave, Law and Foreign Policy, 1968; Law for the Sea's Mineral Resources, 1968; Foreign Affairs and the Constitution, 1972; bd. editors Am. Jour. Internat. Law, 1967—; editor: Arms Control: Issues for the Public, 1961; World Politics and the Jewish Condition, 1972; (with others) Transnational Law in a Changing Society, 1972; contbr. articles in field to profl. jours. Home: 460 Riverside Dr New York City NY 10027 Office: Columbia Univ Schl Law 435 W 116th St New York City NY 10027 Tel (212) 280-2634

HENLEY, MARY ANNA ANDERSON, b. Santa Monica, Calif., Feb. 5, 1944; student U. Oreg., 1961-63; B.A., Sacramento State Coll., 1964; J.D., U. Calif., San Francisco, 1971. Admitted to Calif. bar, 1972; atty. gen. State of Calif., 1972-73; pub. defender Los Angeles County, 1973—. Home: 2766 Santa Rosa St Altadena CA 91001 Office: 210 W Temple St Los Angeles CA Tel (213) 338-8461

HENLEY, WALTER BRUCE, b. Andalusia, Ala., Dec. 5, 1925; student Spring Hill Coll., Mobile, 1949; LL.B., U. Ala., 1952. Admitted to Ala. bar, 1952; individual practice law, 1952-63, 76; with firm Henley & Northington, 1963-75, asso. firm Henley & Clarke, Northport, Ala., 1976—; spl. asst. atty. gen. Hwy. Condemnaton, State of Ala., 1969; mem. advisory commn. Implementation of the Jud. Articles, 1974. Mem. Ala., Tuscaloosa County bar assns., Assn. Trial Lawyers Am., Ala. Trial Lawyers Assn. (exec. com., bd. govs.), Phi Delta Phi. Contbr. articles to law jours. Home: 545 35th St Tuscaloosa AL 35401 Office: 2101 Bridge Ave Northport AL 35466

HENN, HARRY GEORGE, b. New Rochelle, N.Y., Oct. 8, 1919; B.A. summa cum laude, N.Y. U., 1941; J.S.D., 1952; LL.B. with distinction, Cornell U., 1943. Admitted to N.Y. bar, 1944, U.S. Dist. Ct. for So. N.Y. bar, 1948, U.S. Supreme Ct. bar, 1950, U.S. Dist. Ct. for Western N.Y. bar, 1951, U.S. 2d Circuit Ct. Appeals bar, 1951, U.S. Dist. Ct. for Eastern N.Y. bar, 1953, U.S. Dist. Ct. for No. N.Y. bar, 1963; asso. firm Whitman, Ransom & Coulson, N.Y.C., 1943-53; asst. prof. law Cornell Law Sch., Ithaca, N.Y., 1953-56, asso. prof., 1956-57, prof., 1957—, Edward Cornell prof. law, 1970—, dir. Cornell Daily Sun, 1965-73, pres., 1971-73; mem. UNESCO Panel on Internat. Copyright, 1949-52; mem. Panel of Cons. on Gen. Revision of U.S. Copyright Law, 1954-61; cons. N.Y. State Law Revision Commn., 1954-57, Library of Congress, 1955-56, N.Y. State Joint Legis. Com. to Study Revision of Corp. Laws, 1959-60, Corp. Laws Annotated Project, Am. Bar Found., 1959-60, 65, 68-69. Acting justice Village of Cayuga Heights, N.Y., 1965-74; trustee S. Central Research Library Council, 1967-73, sec., 1971-73; pres. Ithaca Opera Assn., 1968-73. Mem. Am. (chmn. copyright subsect.), N.Y. State, Tompkins County bar assns., N.Y. County Lawyers Assn., AAUP, N.Y. State Assn. Magistrates, Copyright Soc. USA (pres. 1961-63, hon. life trustee), Scribes, Supreme Ct. Hist. Soc., Statler Club, Tower Club, Friends of Ithaca Coll., Ithaca Yacht Club Internationale Gesellschaft fur Urheberrecht E.V., Order of Coif, Phi Beta Kappa, Phi Kappa Phi, Delta Upsilon, Phi Delta Phi. Author: Handbook of the Law of Corporations and Other Business Enterprises, 2d edit., 1970; Agency-Partnership and Other Unincorporated Business Enterprises, 1972; Cases and Materials on the Laws of Corporations, 1974; contbr. articles to legal jours. and texts. Home: 130 Sunset Dr Ithaca NY 14850 Office: Myron Taylor Hall Ithaca NY 14853 Tel (607) 256-3416

HENNELLY, MARK M., b. 1916. Practice law, then judge, St. Louis, until 1957; with Mo. Pacific R.R. Co., 1957—. gen. solicitor, 1960-62, v.p., gen. counsel, 1962—, also dir.; v.p. law Texas & Pacific Ry. Co.; dir. Chgo. & Eastern Ill. R.R. Co. Office: Mo Pacific Railroad Mo Pacific Bldg Saint Louis MO 63103*

HENNENBERG, MICHAEL CLAIM, b. Weiden, W.Ger., Sept. 23, 1948; came to U.S., 1949; B.S., Ohio State U., 1970; J.D., Cleve. State U., 1974. Admitted to Ohio bar, 1974; mem. staff Pub. Defender's Office Cuyahoga County (Ohio), 1973-74; asso. firm Fink & Greene, Cleve., 1974—; staff atty. Cuyahoga County Juvenile Ct., Cleve., 1971-72. Mem. Nat. Assn. Criminal Trial Lawyers, Bar Assn. Greater Cleve., Cuyahoga County, Am., Ohio State, Cuyahoga County Criminal Cts. bar assns., Fraternal Order Police, Citizen's League Greater Cleve. Office: 901 Bond Ct Bldg Cleveland OH 44114 Tel (216) 687-0900

HENNESEY, JOHN JAMES, b. Port Deposit, Md., Mar. 10, 1946; B.S. cum laude, St. Peter's Coll., 1968; J.D., Rutgers U., 1971. Admitted to N.J. bar, 1971; Reginald Heber Smith fellow Somerset-Sussex Legal Services, Somerset, N.J., 1971-73; asso. law firm Krieger and Chodash, Esqs., Jersey City, N.J., 1973—. Mem. Middlesex County, Hudson County bar assns., Middlesex County Lawyer Referral Services. Editor: Rutgers Law Review, 1970-71. Home and office: 144 Carlton Av Piscataway NJ 08854 Office: 921 Bergen Jersey City NJ 07306

HENNESSEY, EDWARD F., b. 1919; B.S., Northeastern U.; LL.B., Boston U. Admitted to Mass. bar, 1949; now chief judge Supreme Jud. Ct. of Mass. Mem. Am. Bar Assn. Office: Supreme Jud Ct Pemberton Square Boston MA 02108*

HENNESSEY, GILBERT HALL, JR., b. El Paso, Ill., Nov. 30, 1916; B.S., U. Ill., 1938, J.D., 1940. Admitted to Ill. bar, 1940; asso. firm Jenner & Block, and predecessors, Chgo., 1940-42, 46-50, partner, 1950—. Trustee Lewis U., 1976—. Mem. Chgo., Ill., Fed., Am. bar assns., Legal Club Chgo. (pres. 1971-72), Law Club Chgo. Contbr. articles to legal jours. Home: 356 Cottage Ave Glen Ellyn IL 60137 Office: One IBM Plaza Suite 4200 Chicago IL 60611 Tel (312) 222-9350

HENNESSEY, JOSEPH FREDERICK, b. Boston, Apr. 5, 1932; A.B., Harvard, 1953; J.D., Georgetown U., 1959. Admitted to D.C. bar, 1960, Mass. bar, 1960, U.S. Supreme Ct. bar, 1964; partner firm Pittman, Lovett, Ford & Hennessey, Washington, 1968—. Mem.

judicial conf. U.S. Ct. Appeals D.C. Circuit, 1968-69. Mem. Am., D.C. bar assns., Bar Assn. D.C. (chmn. young lawyers sect. 1967-68), Am. Judicature Soc., Fed. Communications Bar Assn. Home: 3767 Oliver St NW Washington DC 20015 Office: 1819 H St NW Washington DC 20006

HENNESSEY, JOSEPH PAUL, b. Billings, Mont., Jan. 17, 1917; Mont. Tech. U., 1938-39, U. Wyo., 1941; B.A. in History and Polit. Sci., U. Mont., 1943, J.D., 1943. Admitted to Mont. Supreme Ct. bar, 1943, 9th Circuit U.S. Ct. Appeals bar, 1953, U.S. Supreme Ct. bar, 1961; mem. firms Mark J. Doepker, Butte, Mont., 1943-44, Hennessey & Hennessey, Billings, 1944-47; individual practice law, Billings, 1947—. Mem. Am., Mont., Yellowstone County (Mont.) bar assns., Am. Mont. trial lawyers assns., Am. Judicature Soc. Office: Suite 316 Transwestern Life Bldg Billings MT 59101 Tel (406) 259-5734

HENNESSEY, ROBERT JOHN, b. St. Paul, May 7, 1943; B.S. in Econs. with distinction, U. Minn., 1965, J.D., 1968. Admitted to Minn. bar, 1968; law clk. to Hon. Gerald W. Heaney, judge U.S. Ct. Appeals, 8th Circuit, 1968-69; partner firm Larkin, Hoffman, Daly & Lindgren, Ltd., Bloomington, Minn., 1969—. Mem. Hennepin County (Minn.), Minn. State bar assns. Home: 1186 Summit Ave Saint Paul MN 55105 Office: Suite 1500 Northwestern Financial Center 7900 Xerxes Ave S Bloomington MN 55431 Tel (612) 835-3800

HENNESSEY, TIMOTHY F., b. Pottstown, Pa., Nov. 4, 1947; B.S. in Mktg. and Mgmt., St. Joseph's Coll., Phila., 1969; J.D., Villanova U., 1972. Admitted to Pa. bar, 1972; chmn. Villanova Community Legal Services Project, 1971-72; asso. firm Binder, Binder, Yohn & Kalis, Pottstown, 1972-75; individual practice law Pottstown, 1975—; staff Montgomery County Pub. Defenders Office, 1973—. Bd. dirs. S.E. Pa. chpt. No. br. ARC, 1974-77. Mem. Montgomery, Pa. bar assns. Home: 1178 Foxview Rd Pottstown PA 19464 Office: Suite 301 1st Fed Bldg Pottstown PA 19464 Tel (215) 326-7700

HENNESSY, JOHN JOSEPH, b. Savannah, Ga., Dec. 20, 1905; A.B. magna cum laude, U. Ga.; postgrad. Harvard; J.D., Georgetown U.; LL.M. with highest distinction. Admitted to Ga. bar, 1931; individual practice law, Savannah, 1931-42, 1965—; partner firm Hennessy & Hennessy, Savannah, 1942-65; spl. hearing officer Dept. Justice, Savannah, 1948-67; speaker in field. Mem. Am., Ga., Savannah bar assns., Res. Officers Assn. (former state pres.), Navy, Coast Guard Leagues, SE Admiralty Law Inst., Maritime Law Assn. U.S., Harvard Law Sch. Assn., Georgetown U., Ga. alumni socs., Phi Beta Kappa, Delta Theta Phi. Editorial staff Georgetown Law Jour., 1930-31. Home: 233 E 52d St Savannah GA 31401 Office: Box 1114 Savannah GA 31402 Tel (912) 234-7292

HENNIGAN, J(AMES) DAVID, b. St. Louis, Dec. 5, 1920; B.S. in Jurisprudence, Washington U., St. Louis, 1942, J.D., 1943. Admitted to Mo. bar, 1942, Calif. bar, 1949; asso. firm McDonald, Bartlett & Muldoon, St. Louis, 1946-48; with Fed. Loyalty Bd., Civil Service Dept., San Francisco, 1949; mem. Calif. Bd. Bar Examiners, 1949; pub. defender Riverside County (Calif.), 1949-52; individual practice law, Riverside, 1952-53; partner firm Hennigan, Butterwick & Clepper, and predecessors, Riverside, 1953—; lectr. continuing edn.; panel speaker in field. Bd. dirs. Museum Assos., Children's Home Soc., Riverside Mental Health Assn., Riverside Art Center. Mem. Am., Riverside County (pres. 1966) bar assns., Am. Judicature Soc., Calif. Attys. for Criminal Justice (gov.). Home: 4660 Beacon Way Riverside CA 92501 Office: 4000 10th St Riverside CA 92501 Tel (714) 686-3092

HENNING, JOEL FRANK, b. Chgo., Sept. 15, 1939; A.B., Harvard U., 1961, J.D., 1964. Admitted to Ill. bar, 1965; asso. firm Sonnenschein, Levinson, Carlin, Nath & Rosenthal, Chgo., 1965-70; fellow, dir. program Adlai Stevenson Inst. Internat. Affairs, Chgo., 1970-73; nat. dir. Youth Edn. for Citizenship, 1972-75; dir. profl. edn. Am. Bar Assn., Chgo., 1975—; cons. on arts and humanities Carter-Mondale Transition Group; cons. Nat. Adv. Council on Adult Edn., U.S. Office Edn., Aspen Inst., Corporate Accountability Research Group; faculty Inst. on Law and Ethics, Council for Philos. Studies. Chmn., Gov.'s Commn. on Financing Arts in Ill., 1970-71; bd. dirs. Ill. Arts Council, 1971—, Hull House Theater Assn., 1969-70, U. Chgo. Project on Chgo. Humor; trustee Com. on Internat. Affairs, S.E. Chgo. Commn. Mem. Am., Chgo. bar assns., Chgo. Council Lawyers (co-founder). Author: Law-Related Education in America: Guidelines for the Future, 1975; contbr. articles to nat. mags. and legal publs. Home: 5723 S Blackstone Ave Chicago IL 60637 Office: 1155 E 60th St Chicago IL 60637 Tel (312) 947-3951

HENNING, R. BRUCE, b. Platteville, Wis., Sept. 4, 1907; B.A., U. Iowa, 1932, J.D., 1933. Admitted to Iowa bar, 1933, Nebr. bar, 1933; judge County Ct., Nebr., 1963-72, Dist. Ct., 1973—. Mem. Norfolk (Nebr.) Sch. Bd., 1941-50. Mem. Nebr. State Bar. Office: 112 E Norfolk Ave Norfolk NE 68701 Tel (402) 371-1115

HENRY, DAVID PATRICK, b. Searcy, Ark., Feb. 26, 1943; B.S., U. Ark., 1966, J.D., 1971. Admitted to Ark. bar, 1971; asst. atty. City of Little Rock; partner firm Kemp & Henry, Little Rock, 1971—. Mem. Am., Ark., Pulaski County bar assns. Home: 4020 Woodland Rd Little Rock AR 72212 Office: 1021 Pyramid Bldg Little Rock AR 72201 Tel (501) 372-7243

HENRY, E. L., b. Jonesboro, La., Feb. 10, 1936; B.A., Baylor U., 1958; LL.B., La. State U., 1961. Admitted to La. bar, 1961; mem. firm Emmons, Henry & Reeves, Jonesboro, 1962—; mem. La. Ho. of Reps., 1968—, speaker of house, 1972—; del. La. Constl. Conv., 1973-74, chmn., 1973-74. Mem. Jackson Parish (La.), La., Am. bar assns. Office: 415 Polk Ave Jonesboro LA 71251 Tel (318) 259-4164

HENRY, EDWARD ERNEST, b. Kansas City, Mo., Mar. 28, 1902; student Wash. State Nautical Sch., 1918-20, U. Wash., 1928-32; LL.B., George Washington U., 1935, J.D., 1935. Joined U.S. Merchant Marine, 1921, advanced through grades to chief mate, 1934; ret., 1935; admitted to Wash. bar, 1935; mem. staff U.S. Senator Homer Bone, 1933-35; dep. pros. atty., Seattle, 1935-40; spl. atty. Dept. Justice, U.S., 1940-41; mem. firm Houghton, Cluck, Coughlin & Henry, Seattle, 1943-60; judge Wash. Superior Ct., Seattle, 1960-77; mem. Wash. State House of Reps., 1937-41, 45-47, 51-53; dir., sec. Wakefield Fisheries, 1947-60. Bd. dirs. ACLU, Wash., 1931-60. Mem. Am. Bar Assn., Amnesty Internat., World Peace Through Law Center (charter), Am. Soc. Internat. Law, Internat. Commn. Jurists (asso.). Recipient Ralph Bunch award Seattle-King County Bar Assn. Contbr. articles of profl. jours. Home: 2105 E Interlaken Blvd Seattle WA 98112 Office: Judge Superior Ct Seattle WA 98104 Tel (206) 344-4064

HENRY, FREDERIC THOMAS, b. Canandaigua, N.Y., Mar. 16, 1897; LL.B., Cornell U., 1923. Admitted to N.Y. bar, 1924; asso. firm Dudley Stone & Sawyer, Buffalo, 1923-25; mng. atty. firm Eidlitz & Huise, N.Y.C., 1925-26; partner firm Knapp & Henry, Canandaigua, 1926-43; confidential clk. appellate div. N.Y. Supreme Ct., 1929-37, justice 7th dist., 1951-59, 4th dept. appellate div., 1960-73; counsel to atty. Frederic T. Henry, Jr., 1973—; surrogate Ontario County (N.Y.), 1943-50. Mem. Am., N.Y. State, Ontario County bar assns., Cornell Law Assn. Author: N.Y. Pattern Jury Instructions, Vol. 1, 1965, 2d edit., 1974, vol. 2, 1968; asso. editor Cornell Law Quar., 1922-23. Home: 93 Gorham St Canandaigua NY 14424 Office: 5 Court St Canandaigua NY 14424 Tel (716) 394-2068

HENRY, FREDERICK THOMAS, b. Arvada, Colo., Sept. 5, 1905; LL.B., U. Colo., 1929; individual practice law, Colorado Springs, Colo., 1935—; city atty. Colorado Springs, 1946-71; mem. Colo. Supreme Ct. Grievance Com., 1971-76. Mem. El Paso County (pres. 1949-50), Colo. (bd. govs.) bar assns. Home: 1413 Culebra Ave Colorado Springs CO 80907 Office: 513 Mining Exchange Bldg Colorado Springs CO 80903 Tel (303) 475-7090

HENRY, J. GORDON, b. Chgo., Nov. 21, 1916; A.B., cum laude, Washington and Jefferson Coll., 1938; J.D. cum laude, U. Chgo., 1941. Admitted to N.Y. State bar, 1942, Ill. bar, 1946; asso. firm Cravath, Swaine & Moore, N.Y.C., 1941-42, Rooks and Freeman, Chgo., 1942-52; atty. legal dept. No. Trust Co., Chgo., 1953-72, trust counsel, 1972—; dir. No. Trust Co. Ariz., Security Trust Co. (Cayman) Ltd., Nortrust Farm Mgmt., Inc.; prof. law Am. Inst. Banking, 1959-69, dean law faculty, 1964-69; mem. vis. com. U. Chgo. Law Sch., 1970-74; adv. council Ill. Inst. for Continuing Legal Edn., 1969-75, chmn., 1972-73. Fellow Am. Bar Found.; mem. U. Chgo. Law Sch. Alumni Assn. (dir. 1955-75, pres. 1972-74), Chgo. Bar Found. (dir. 1976—), Chgo. (bd. mgrs. 1968-70, chmn. com. on coms. 1971-72, 74-76), Ill. State (chmn. fed. taxation sect. 1968-69, chmn. long range planning com. 1976—), Am. (vice-chmn. com. on investments by fiduciaries 1973-76, chmn., 1976—) bar assns., Am. Bankers Assn. (trust counsel com. 1975—), Order of Coif, Phi Beta Kappa. Bd. editors Chgo. Bar Record, 1966—; recipient Law Club of Chgo. Pub. Service Citee award U. Chgo. Alumni Assn., 1976; Distinguished Service award Ill. Inst. for Continuing Legal Edn., 1975. Home: 1091 W Deerpath Lake Forest IL 60045 Office: 50 S LaSalle St Chicago IL 60675 Tel (312) 630-6000

HENRY, RICHARD VORN, JR., b. Chgo., July 14, 1915; B.A., U. Chgo., 1935; LL.B., Harvard, 1938. Admitted to Ill. bar, 1938; asso. firm Cameron & Heath, Chgo., 1938-41, Peterson, Rose, Rall, Barber & Seidel, Chgo., 1941-52, partner, 1952—. Mem. Flossmoor (Ill.) Planning Commn., 1956-58; mem. Flossmoor Park Dist., 1962-67, pres., 1966-67. Mem. Am., Ill. Chgo. bar assns. Home: 2404 Caddy St Flossmoor IL 60422 Office: 200 E Randolph Dr Suite 7300 Chicago IL 60601 Tel (312) 861-1400

HENRY, WILLIAM CHARLES ANTHONY, b. Phila., Dec. 29, 1902; B.S., Villanova U., 1925, LL.D., 1966; J.D., U. Pa., 1928. Admitted to Pa. bar, 1928; individual practice law, Phila.; chmn., prof. bus. law Villanova U. Mem. Am., Pa. Phila. bar assns. Home: 427 E Allens Ln Philadelphia PA 19119 Office: 1040 Philadelphia Savings Fund Bldg Philadelphia PA 19607 Tel (215) WA2-3222

HENSAL, C. DAVID, b. Wadsworth, Ohio, Mar. 22, 1938; A.B., Kent State U., 1965; J.D., Akron U., 1970. Admitted to Ohio bar, 1970; law reform dir. Summit County Legal Aid Soc., 1969-72; partner firm Hensal & Guldin, Wadsworth, 1972—; judge Medina County Ct. Wadsworth Dist., 1975—. Mem. Am., Ohio, Akron, Medina County bar assns., Am. Judicature Soc., Ohio Jud. Conf., Assn. Ohio County Ct. Judges. Office: 121 College St Wadsworth OH 44281 Tel (216) 335-2507

HENSLEY, WILLIAM WENDELL, II, b. Houston, Nov. 12, 1941; B.S., U. Houston, 1962, J.D., 1964. Admitted to Tex. bar, 1964, W.Va. bar, 1973; practice law, Houston, 1964-66, 71-72; corporate atty. Coastal States Gas Producing Co., Corpus Christi, Tex., 1967-71, Cabot Corp., Charleston, W.Va., 1972-75, Pampa, Tex., 1975—. Mem. Tex., Am. bar assns. Home: 3100 Crest Box 711 Pampa TX 79065 Office: Box 1101 Pampa TX 79065 Tel (806) 669-2581

HENSON, ROBERT FRANK, b. Ft. Smith, Ark., Apr. 10, 1925; B.S. Law, U. Minn., 1948, J.D., 1950. Admitted to Minn. Supreme Ct. bar, 1950, U.S. Dist. Ct. bar for Dist. Minn., 1950, U.S. Supreme Ct. bar, 1972; asso. firm Gray, Plant, Mooty & Anderson, Mpls., 1952-57, partner, 1958-66; sr. mem. firm Henson & Efron, Mpls., 1966—; chmn. Minn. Supreme Ct. Com. on Prepaid Legal Services, 1974. Trustee Mpls. Found., 1973—. Mem. Hennepin County, Minn., Am. bar assns. Home: 4509 Browndale Ave Minneapolis MN 55424 Office: 1200 Title Ins Bldg Minneapolis MN 55401 Tel (612) 339-2500

HENTEL, NAT HERBERT, b. N.Y.C., Mar. 29, 1919; B.S. in Social Sci., Coll. City N.Y., 1939; J.D., N.Y. U., 1946; grad. Nat. Coll. State Judiciary, U. Nev., Reno, 1971. Admitted to N.Y. bar, 1947, U.S. Supreme Ct. bar, 1956; asst. to dean N.Y. U. Sch. Law, 1946-48; law asst. to Surrogate Anthony P. Savarese, Queens County, N.Y., 1949-54; partner firm Karow & Hentel, N.Y.C., 1954-65; counsel firm Fields, Zimmerman & Segall, Jamaica, N.Y., 1967-69; judge N.Y.C. Civil Ct., Queens div., 1969—; acting judge N.Y.C. Criminal Ct., 1969-76; dist. atty. Queens County, 1966; bd. sponsors Inst. Trial Judges, Hunter Coll., City U. N.Y., 1973—; lectr. seminars Jud. Conf. State N.Y.., 1973—; mem. faculty Nat. Coll. State Judiciary, 1973—; pres. bd. judges N.Y.C. Civil Ct., 1974-76; adj. prof. adult collegiate program Sch. Gen. Studies, Queens Coll., City U. N.Y., 1976—, coordinator adv. bd. legal para—profl. program, 1976—. Vice pres. United Cerebral Palsy of Queens County, 1959—; bd. dirs. Queensborough Soc. for Prevention Cruelty to Children, 1966-69, 73—, v.p., 1968-69; chmn. bd. dirs. Brandeis Assn. of Queens, 1974-76. Mem. Am. (gavel awards com., cts. and the community com. jud. adminstrn. div. 1972—), N.Y. State (council jud. assns. jud. sect. 1974—), Queens County (editor bull. 1954-60, pres. 1963-64, vice chmn. com. centennial celebration 1973-76) bar assns., Nat. Conf. Bar Pres.'s, Nat. Conf. Spl. Ct. Judges (chmn. com. on cts. and community 1972-73), Assn. Bar City N.Y. (com. spl. requirements of cts. 1964—), Coll. City N.Y. Alumni Assn., N.Y. U. Law Alumni Assn. (pres. 1963); hon. mem. Phi Delta Phi, Assn. Asst. Dist. Attys. Queens County, Honor Legion of N.Y.C. Police Dept. Recipient numerous awards, including Alumni Meritorious Service medallion N.Y. U., 1953; past Pres.'s Honor award Queens Speech and Hearing Service Center, Queens U., 1962; Past Pres. Honor certificate N.Y. U. Alumni Fedn., 1964; Helping Hand award United Cerebral Palsy of Queens, 1966; Man of Year award South Queens Boys Club, Inc., 1966; Humanitarian award Queens County Council, Jewish War Vets., 1966; Torch of Liberty award Anti-Defamation League, Jamaica Div., B'nai B'rith, 1968. Editorial bd. N.Y. U. Law Quar. Rev., 1940-42; editor N.Y. U. Law Center Bull., 1947-51, alumni editor, 1953-58; editor newsletter Bd. Judges of Civil Ct. of City N.Y., 1974-76. Home: 215-18 85th Ave Hollis Hills NY 11427 Office: Civil Ct of NYC 120-55 Queens Blvd Kew Gardens New York City NY 11424 Tel (212) 520-3611

HENVEY, JOHN WILLIAM, b. Washington, Aug. 18, 1945; B.A. in Econs., Hardin-Simmons U., 1968; J.D., U. Tex., 1973. Admitted to Tex. bar, 1973, U.S. Ct. Appeals Fifth Circuit bar, 1976; individual practice law, Dallas, 1973—. Mem. Am., Dallas, Dallas Criminal bar assns. Home: 3612 Gillespie #C Dallas TX 75219 Office: 660 Dallas Fed Savings Tower Dallas TX 75225 Tel (214) 363-8394

HENZI, FREDRICK, b. Chgo., May 1, 1933; A.B., U. Chgo., 1961, J.D., 1964. Admitted to Ill. bar, 1964; asso. firm Clausen, Miller, Gorman, Caffrey & Witous, Chgo. and Glen Ellyn, Ill., 1964-66, 72-74; individual practice law, Glen Ellyn, 1966-72; asso. judge Ill. 18th Jud. Circuit Ct., 1975—. Mem. Am., DuPage County (Ill.) bar assns., Ill. State Bar. Home: 110 N Park Blvd Glen Ellyn IL 60137 Office: DuPage County Courthouse Wheaton IL 60187 Tel (312) 682-7292

HERALD, JOHN PATRICK, JR., b. Latrobe, Pa., Sept. 27, 1947; A.B., John Carroll U., 1969; J.D., U. Notre Dame, 1972. Admitted to Ill. bar, 1972; asso. firm Baker & McKenzie, Chgo., 1972—. Mem. Am., Ill., Chgo. bar assns., Trial Lawyers Club Chgo. (dir. 1975-77). Office: Suite 2700 Prudential Plaza Chicago IL 60601 Tel (312) 565-0025

HERBELIN, ALFRED FREDERICK, b. Waco, Tex., Aug. 26, 1911; B.A., Baylor U., 1932, LL.B., 1934, J.D., 1969. Admitted to Tex. bar, 1934, U.S. Supreme Ct. bar, 1955; individual practice law, Waco., 1934-37; asst. dist. atty. McLennan County (Tex.), 1937-41; asst. atty. gen. State of Tex., 1941-42; atty. VA, San Antonio, 1945-58, VA Central Office, Washington, 1958-61; regional atty. U.S. Dept. Agr., Washington, Dallas and Temple, Tex., 1961—. Mem. Tex., Bell County bar assns. Office: 102 S Main St Temple TX 76501 Tel (817) 773-1711

HERD, JAMES BRAXTON, b. St. Louis, Feb. 27, 1932; B.S., St. Louis U., 1954, LL.B., 1959. Admitted to Mo. bar, 1959, Ill. bar, 1959, U.S. Supreme Ct. bar, 1959; asso. firm Deeba, DeStefano, Sauter & Herd, St. Louis, 1961, partner, 1961—. Mem. Am., St. Louis, Mo. bar assns., Am. Trial Lawyers Assn., St. Louis Lawyers Assn. Home: 2016 Oak Timber Ct Kirkwood MO 63122 Office: 3411 Hampton Ave Saint Louis MO 63139 Tel (314) 781-3222

HERDER, ARTHUR EMILE, JR., b. St. Louis, 1929; J.D., St. Louis U., 1959. Admitted to Mo. bar, 1959; individual practice law, St. Louis, 1959-67; sr. partner firm Herder & Kearns, Mehlville, Mo., 1967—; asst. county supr. St. Louis County, 1960-61. Mem. Mo. Bar, St. Louis County Bar Assn. Home: 4448 Kinswood Ln Saint Louis MO 63129 Office: 88 South County Center Way Saint Louis MO 63129 Tel (314) 892-3400

HERIN, DAVID VANCE, b. Bemidji, Minn., Aug. 17, 1944; B.A., Baylor U., 1966, J.D., 1969. Admitted to Tex. bar, 1969; served as JAG, U.S. Air Force, 1969-73; asso. firm Fischer & Fischer, Corpus Christi, Tex., 1973—. Mem. State Bar Tex., Am., Fed., Nueces County bar assns., Soc. Labor Relation Profls., Phi Alpha Delta. Office: 1170 Bank and Trust Tower Corpus Christi TX 78477 Tel (512) 884-0477

HERIN, WILLIAM ABNER, b. Macon, Ga., May 14, 1908; A.B., U. Fla., 1930, J.D., 1933. Admitted to Fla. bar, 1933; adminstrv. asst. to Congressman J. Mark Wilcox of Fla., 1936-38; legis. counsel Dade County Delegation, Fla. Legislature, 1939-41; legal adviser office Fgn. Liquidation Commn., Dept. of State, Far East, 1946-47; asst. county atty., 1938-47; judge Circuit Ct., 11th Jud. Circuit, Miami, 1948—; bd. dirs. Nat. Conf. Met. Cts., pres., 1969-70; mem. vis. com. Inst. for Ct. Mgmt. bd. Founder, dirs. Boys Clubs Greater Miami; bd. dirs. Met. YMCA; mem. adv. bd. S.Fla. council Boy Scouts Am. Mem. Am., Fla. (chmn. pub. relations com. 1941), Dade County (v.p. 1941) bar assns., Am. Law Inst., Am. Judicature Soc., Phi Beta Kappa, Phi Kappa Phi, Phi Delta Phi. Author: Trial Jurors' Handbook, 1952—; Local Circuit Court Rules, 1957—; Standard Grand Jury Charge, 1958—; contbr. articles to legal jours. Home: 470 NE 51st St Miami FL 33137 Office: Dade County Courthouse Miami FL 33130 Tel (305) 579-5374

HERLIHY, THOMAS, III, b. Wilmington, Del., Aug. 29, 1936; B.A., Dartmouth Coll., 1957; LL.B., U. Va., 1960. Admitted to Del. bar, 1960, U.S. Supreme Ct. bar, 1964; partner firm Herlihy & Herlihy, Wilmington, 1974—; dep. atty. gen. State of Del., 1961-63, chief dep. atty. gen., 1964; practice law, Wilmington, 1964—. Chmn. Del. Alcoholic Beverage Control Commn., 1969-72; mem. planning council United Way of Del., 1975. Mem. Del., Am. bar assns., Am. Assn. Trial Lawyers. Home: 11 Aldrich Way Wilmington DE 19807 Office: 1100 King St Wilmington DE 19801 Tel (302) 654-3111

HERLOCKER, THOMAS DEAN, b. Winfield, Kans., Dec. 15, 1938; B.A., U. Kans., 1960, J.D., 1963. Admitted to Kans. bar, 1963; asso. firm Janicke, Herlocker & Bishop, Winfield, Kans. 1963-67; mem. firm Roberts & Herlocker, Winfield, 1970—; individual practice law, Winfield, 1967-70; county counselor Cowley County (Kans.), 1967-71; judge City Ct. of Winfield, 1971-77, Municipal Ct., Winfield, 1971—. Mem. Cowley County, Kans., Am. bar assns., Am. Judicature Soc., Kans. Spl. Ct. Judges Assn. Home: 721 E 10th St Winfield KS 67156 Office: 115 E 9th St Winfield KS 67156 Tel (316) 221-4600

HERMAN, LAWRENCE, b. Cin., May 13, 1929; A.B., U. Cin., 1951; LL.B., 1953; postgrad. Northwestern U. Sch. Law, 1953-54. Admitted to Ohio bar, 1953, U.S. Supreme Ct. bar, 1966, U.S. Ct. Mil. Appeals bar, 1955; teaching fellow Northwestern U. Sch. Law, 1953-54; served with Judge Adv. Gen's, Corps, Stuttgart, W.Ger., 1955-57; law clk. Fed. Dist. Judge J. J. Hoffman, Chgo., 1958-59; asst. prof. law Western Res. U., 1959-61; asst. prof. law Ohio State U., 1961-62, asso. prof., 1962-64, prof., 1964—; vis. prof. U. Mich., 1968; cons. Ohio Legislature Criminal Code Revision Project, 1964-68, Ohio Supreme Ct. Criminal Procedure Project, 1968-74. Bd. dirs. ACLU, 1968—. Mem. Internat. Assn. Penal Law, Order of Coif, Phi Beta Kappa. Author: The Right To Counsel In Misdemeanor Court, 1974; contbr. articles to legal jours. Office: 1659 N High St Columbus OH 43210 Tel (614) 422-2163

HERMAN, LEWIS, b. Budapest, Hungary, Mar. 2, 1905; student Cooper Union Inst., Columbia; LL.B., N.Y. U., 1931. Admitted to N.Y. bar, 1932; house counsel British-Am. Industries, N.Y.C., asso. firm Edward L. Corbett, N.Y.C., 1932-40; counsel Edifice Realty Corp., N.Y.C., 1948—. Chmn. New Hyde Park (N.Y.) Civic Orgn., 1948-49; officer Rep. Club, New Hyde Pk. 1949, 50. Mem. N.Y. State Defenders Assn. Home: 220-55 46th Ave Bayside NY 11361 Office: 154 Old Country Rd Hicksville NY 11803 Tel (516) 935-1355

HERMAN, ROBERT E., lawyer; b. N.Y.C., A.B., N.Y. U., 1939; LL.B., Columbia U., 1942. Admitted to N.Y. State bar, 1942, U.S. Supreme Ct., 1962; pvt. practice law, N.Y.C., 1942-43, 45; atty. U.S. OPA, 1946-49, rent adminstr., Queens, Nassau, Suffolk, Rent Adminstrn., State of N.Y., 1950-58, state rent adminstr., 1959—. Asso. village judge, Village of Thomaston, 1963-65; mem. N.Y. State Commn. to Study Rents, 1960-64; mem. Bd. Zoning Appeals, Village of Thomaston, 1960-64. Mem. N.Y. State, Nassau County bar assns. Home: 31 Remsen Rd Great Neck NY 11024 Office: 2 World Trade Center New York City NY 10045

HERMAN, WILLIAM CHARLES, b. N.Y.C., Nov. 6, 1935; B.A., City Coll. N.Y., 1958; LL.B., Columbia U., 1959. Admitted to N.Y. bar, 1960; partner firm Rosenthal & Herman, N.Y.C., 1960—. Mem. Am., N.Y. State Bar Assns., N.Y. County Lawyers Assn., Am. Acad. Matrimonial Law. Home: 95 Lord Kitchener Rd New Rochelle NY 10804 Office: 401 Broadway New York City NY 10013 Tel (212) 226-7971

HERMANN, RUSSELL ROYDEN, b. Seattle, May 18, 1924; B.A., Wash. State U., 1949; J.D., George Washington U., 1952. Admitted to D.C. bar, 1952, Calif. bar, 1961; U.S. atty., Nome, Alaska, 1953-60; asst. U.S. atty., Los Angeles, 1960-67; U.S. commr. Los Angeles, 1967-70; referee Superior Ct. Los Angeles County, 1970-71; commr. Los Angeles Superior Ct., 1971—. Home: 5146 Oakwood St La Canada CA 91011 Office: 300 E Walnut St Pasadena CA 91101 Tel (213) 796-9361

HERMELEE, BRUCE GRANT, b. N.Y.C., June 14, 1942; A.B., Princeton, 1963; LL.B., U. Pa., 1966, replaced by J.D., 1970. Admitted to N.Y. bar, 1967, Fla. bar, 1971; individual practice law, N.Y.C., 1967-70; asso. firm Pallot, Poppell, Goodman & Shapo, Miami, Fla., 1971-72; partner firm Hermelee & Neuman, S. Miami, 1972-73; partner firm Milledge Horn & Hermelee, Miami, 1974-76, Milledge & Hermelee, Miami, 1977—. Mem. Am., Dade County Bar Assns., Fla. Bar. Home: 6880 Maynada St Coral Gables FL 33146 Office: 2699 S Bayshore Dr Miami FL 33133 Tel (305) 858-5660

HERNANDEZ, BENIGNO CARLOS, b. Santa Fe, N.Mex., July 7, 1917; B.A., U. N.Mex., 1941; J.D., De Paul U., 1948. Admitted to N.Mex. bar, 1949; practiced in Albuquerque, 1949-67, 69-72; U.S. ambassador to Paraguay, 1967-69; judge N.Mex. Ct. Appeals, 1972—; spl. asst. U.S. atty., Albuquerque, 1951-52; mem. N.Mex. Jud. Standards Commn., 1972-73, N.Mex. Jud. Council, 1974—. Mem. nat. citizens adv. commn. on vocat. rehab. HEW, 1963-67; chmn. N.Mex. Bd. of Dept. Health and Social Services, 1971-72; mem. adv. com. Robert O. Anderson Sch. Bus. and Adminstrn. Sci., U. N.Mex., 1971—; mem. bd. visitors and govs. St. John's Coll., Annapolis, Md. and Santa Fe, 1975—; trustee Mus. of N.Mex. Found., 1975—. Mem. Am., N.Mex. bar assns., Alumni Assn. U. N.Mex. (pres. 1972-73, Rodey award 1963, award for inspiring leadership and devoted service 1973). Recipient certificate of recognition Fed. and Albuquerque bar assns., Albuquerque Lawyers Club, 1967, Grand Master of the Order of Nat. Merit award Republic of Paraguay, 1969, Brotherhood award NCCJ, 1971, Distinguished Alumni award De Paul U., 1975. Home: 600 Reynolds Ave SW Albuquerque NM 87104 Office: POB 2008 Santa Fe NM 87501 Tel (505) 827-2214

HERNANDEZ, MACK RAY, b. Austin, Tex., Sept. 8, 1944; B.A., U. Tex. at Austin, 1967, J.D., 1970. Admitted to Tex. bar, 1970; mem. Legal Aid and Defender Soc. Travis County (Tex.), 1970-71; individual practice law, Austin, 1971—. Mem. Assn. Trial Lawyers Am., Travis County, Tex. bar assns., Tex. Trial Lawyers Assn., Tex. Criminal Def. Lawyers Assn. Office: 1108 Lavaca St Suite 400 Austin TX 78701 Tel (512) 477-9433

HERNDON, ROBERT DUNLAP, b. Mesa, Ariz., June 17, 1944; B.S., U. Oreg., 1966, J.D., 1968. Admitted to Oreg. bar, 1968; asso. firm Ringle & Herndon, and predecessor, Gladstone, Oreg., 1968-71, partner, 1972—; city atty. City of Durham (Oreg.), 1975—; judge pro tempore Gladstone Municipal Ct. Chmn. Clachamon County (Oreg.) Explorers, Boy Scouts Am. Mem. Oreg., Clachamon County (1st v.p. 1975-76) bars, Oreg. Trial Lawyers Assn. Office: 405 W Arlington St Gladstone OR 97027 Tel (503) 656-0879

HEROLD, JOHN HENRY, b. Balt., Dec. 28, 1917; B.A., U. Va., 1939; J.D., Harvard U., 1942. Admitted to Md. bar, 1944, U.S. Supreme Ct. bar, 1950; law clk. to judge U.S. Dist. Ct. for Dist. Md., 1946-47; partner firms Hessey & Herold, Balt., 1947-61, Frank, Bernstein, Conaway & Goldman, Balt., 1961—; dir. Yeaton & Co., Inc., Balt., John O. Mitchell & Sons-Wiedefeld Home, Inc., Balt. Bd. dirs. Luth. Social Services of Md., Inc., 1962-65, Md. Bible Soc., 1967—. Fellow Am. Coll. Probate Counsel; mem. Am. (vice chmn. com. on investments by fiduciaries 1972-76), Md. State (chmn. sect. estate and trust law 1973-74), Balt. City (chmn. com. on profl. ethics 1976—) bar assns., Jud. Conf. 4th Circuit, Trial Table Law Club (pres. 1974-75), Barristers Club (pres. 1976-77). Author: (with others) How to Live and Die-With Maryland Probate, 2d edit., 1975. Home: 134 Homeland Ave Baltimore MD 21212 Office: 1300 Mercantile Bank & Trust Bldg 2 Hopkins Plaza Baltimore MD 21201 Tel (301) 547-0500

HEROLD, KARL GUENTER, b. Munich, Ger., Feb. 3, 1947; came to U.S., 1963, naturalized, 1969; B.A., Bowling Green State U., 1969; J.D., Case Western Res. U., 1972. Admitted to Ohio bar, 1972; asso. firm Jones, Day, Reavis & Pogue, Cleve., 1972—. Active Am. Cancer Soc., 1975—. Mem. Am., Cleve., Cuyahoga bar assns., Order of Coif. Home: 896 Englewood Rd Cleveland Heights OH 44121 Office: 1700 Union Commerce Bldg Cleveland OH 44115 Tel (216) 696-3939

HERRELL, STEPHEN BENNETT, b. Rochester, Minn., Oct. 25, 1938; B.A., Vanderbilt U., 1960; LL.B., Georgetown U., 1966. Admitted to Oreg. bar, 1966; since practiced in Portland, Oreg., asso. firm Black, Helterline, Beck & Rappleyea, 1966-70, asso. McMenamin, Joseph, Herrell & Paulson, and predecessors, 1970—, partner, 1973—. Mem. Tri-County Local Govt. Commn., 1976-77. Mem. Oreg. State, Am., Multnomah County bar assns., Comml. Law League. Home: 3205 NE US Grant Pl Portland OR 97212 Office: 729 SW Alder St Portland OR 97205 Tel (503) 226-6600

HERRICK, NEWTON JEHIEL, b. Canajoharie, N.Y., Jan. 24, 1905; A.B., Amherst Coll., 1926; LL.B., Albany Law Sch. 1931. Admitted to N.Y. bar, 1932; individual practice law Canajoharie, 1932-70, 75—; sr. atty. dept. law, real property bur. State of N.Y., 1971-75; U.S. Conciliation Commr., 1941-45; atty. Village of Canajoharie, 1940-56; counsel Canajoharie Central Sch. Dist., 1945-55; atty. Town of Root, N.Y., 1940-56. Mem. bd. edn., Canajoharie Central Sch. Dist., 1941-45, pres., 1944, 45. Mem. Montgomery County Bar Assn., Phi Delta Phi. Home and office: Seeber's Ln Canajoharie NY 13317 Tel (518) 673-2442

HERRIN, ELLIOTT CLAYTON, b. Shelby County, Ala., Jan. 19, 1930; B.S., Howard Coll. (now Stamford U.), 1952; LL.B., Birmingham Coll., 1963, J.D., 1968. Admitted to Ala. bar, 1963; partner firm Weaver and Herrin, Birmingham, 1964-71; individual practice law, Birmingham, 1971—; recorder City Irondale, Ala., 1967—. Mem. Am., Birmingham, Ala. State bar assns., Birmingham Plaintiff Lawyers, Ala. Trial Lawyers Assn., Ala. Municipal Judges Assn. Home: 1112 Bryan Dr Birmingham AL 35210 Office: 708 Frank Nelson Bldg Birmingham AL 35203 Tel (205) 324-3306

HERRIN, KENT, b. Chattanooga, May 4, 1919; B.S., East Tenn. State U., 1941; J.D., Vanderbilt U., 1948. Admitted to Tenn. bar, 1948; asso. firm Winston & Guinn, Johnson City, Tenn., 1948-51; partner firm Herrin & Sherwood, Johnson City, 1951—. Mem. Washington County (Tenn.) (pres. 1964), Tenn. bar assns., East Tenn. State U. Alumni Assn. (pres.), Res. Officers Assn., Tipton-Haynes Hist. Assn. (pres.). Decorated Legion of Merit, Silver Star, Bronze Star; decorated comdr. Order Brit. Empire. Home: Route 1 Johnson City TN 37601 Office: 805 E Watauga Ave Johnson City TN 37601 Tel (615) 929-7113

HERRING, CHARLES DAVID, b. Muncie, Ind., Mar. 18, 1943; B.A., Ind. U., 1965; J.D. cum laude, 1968. Admitted to Ind. bar, 1968, Calif. bar, 1971; research asso. Ind. U., 1965-68; intern prosecuting attys. office, Monroe County, Ind., 1967-68; served with JAGC, U.S. Army, 1968-72; mil. judge U.S. Army Judiciary, 1970-72; partner firm Herring & Stubel, San Diego, 1972—; prof. law Western State U., 1972—; Vice-chmn. Valle de Oro Planning Com., Spring Valley, Calif., 1972-75; chmn. Valle de Oro Citizens Exec. Com. for Community Planning, Spring Valley, 1975—. Mem. Ind., Calif., Am., San Diego County (mem. bench-media com.) bar assns., Conf. Spl. Ct. Judges, Calif. Trial Lawyers Assn., Order Coif. Recipient Nat. Best Brief award Am. Bar Assn., 1968. Author: (with Jim Wade) California Cases on Professional Responsibility, 1976. Home: 10325 Rancho Rd La Mesa CA 92041 Office: 1380 The Bank of California Plaza 110 W A St San Diego CA 92101 Tel (714) 234-6651

HERRING, GROVER CLEVELAND, b. Nocatee, Fla., Dec. 9, 1925; LL.B., U. Fla., 1950, J.D., 1967. Admitted to Fla. bar, 1950; mem. firm Haskins & Bryant, Sebring, Fla., 1950-52; partner firm Blakeslee, Herring & Bie, West Palm Beach, Fla., 1952-60; city atty., West Palm Beach, 1960-64; partner firm Herring, Fulton & Anderson and predecessors, West Palm Beach, 1964—; municipal judge West Palm Beach, 1954-55. Mem. Phi Delta Theta. Contbr. articles to legal jours. Home: 3515 Australian Ave West Palm Beach FL 33407 Office: Suite 904 Forum III Bldg 1665 Palm Beach Lakes Blvd West Palm Beach FL 33407 Tel (305) 689-3900

HERRING, NORMAN, b. Tonapah, Nev., Aug. 26, 1908; A.B., U. Ariz., 1930; LL.D., Duke, 1933. Admitted to Ariz. bar, 1934, Calif. bar, 1968; partner firms Gilmore & Herring, Douglas, Ariz., 1940-45, Richey & Herring, Douglas and Tucson, 1947-53; individual practice law, Tucson, 1953-60; mem. firm Langeman, Begam & Lewis, Phoenix, 1964-66; dep. county atty. Mariocopa County (Ariz.), 1937-38, Cochise County, 1942-46, Pima County, 1951-53; individual practice law, Phoenix, 1970-74, 75—. Mem. Am. Judicature Soc., Am. Trial Lawyers Assn., Ariz., Maricopa County, Calif. bar assns. Contbr. articles to legal jours. Home: 4542 N 18th Ave Phoenix AZ 85015 Office: 114 W Adams St Phoenix AZ 85003 Tel (602) 257-1630

HERRING, ROBERT HARKNESS, JR., b. Florence, S.C., May 23, 1948; B.A., Washington and Lee U., 1970; J.D., U. S.C., 1973; postgrad. Georgetown U. Admitted to S.C. bar, 1974, D.C. bar, 1975, Va. bar, 1976, U.S. Supreme Ct. bar, 1977; law clk. judiciary com. S.C. Ho. of Reps., Columbia, 1971-72; clk. to Senator Thomas E. Smith, Jr., Pamplico, S.C., 1972; appellate def. atty. U.S. Army Legal Services Agy., Falls Church, Va., 1974-77; asst. atty. gen. State of Va., 1977—. Mem. Am., Va. bar assns., Am. Judicature Soc., Judge Advs. Assn. Office: 930 Fidelity Bldg 830 E Main St Richmond VA 23219 Tel (804) 786-6563

HERRINGTON, GEORGE, b. Santa Clara, Calif., Aug. 2, 1895; A.B., U. Calif., 1918, J.D., 1920. Admitted to Calif. bar, 1919; former partner Orrick, Herrington, Rowley & Suteliffe, San Francisco, of counsel, 1976—. Home: 180 San Leandro Way San Francisco CA 94127 Office: 600 Montgomery St San Francisco CA 94111 Tel (415) 392-1122

HERRMANN, DANIEL LIONEL, b. N.Y.C., June 10, 1913; A.B., U. Del., 1935; LL.B., Georgetown U., 1939. Admitted to D.C. bar, 1938, Del. bar, 1940; practiced in Wilmington, 1940-51; asst. U.S. atty., 1948-51; asso. judge Superior Ct., Orphans Ct. Del., 1951-58; asso. justice Del. Supreme Ct., 1965—, chief justice, 1973—; sr. partner Herrmann, Bayard, Brill & Russell, 1958-65. Dir., mem. exec. com. Del. Power & Light Co., 1962-65. Chmn. State Goals Commn., 1960-64; mem. Wilmington Bd. Pub. Edn., 1961-65; chmn. State Planning Commn., 1962-64. Pres. Legal Aid Soc. Del.; pres., chmn. bd. Jewish Fedn. Del., 1956-58; former mem. bd. dirs., exec. com. United Community Fund, Children's Bur. Del., Welfare Council Del., Del-Mar-Va council Boy Scouts Am., Jewish Community Center, Kutz Home for Aging; trustee, v.p. U. Del.; trustee Wilmington Med. Center; bd. mgrs. Wilmington Inst. Free Library. Fellow Inst. Jud. Adminstrn.; mem. Am., Del. bar assns., Am. Judicature Soc. (dir.). Home: 705 E Matson Run Pkwy Wilmington DE 19802 Office: Court House Wilmington DE 19801*

HERRON, ELLEN PATRICIA, b. Auburn, N.Y., July 30, 1927; A.B. in English, Trinity Coll., 1949; M.A. in Am. History, Cath. U. Am., 1954; J.D., U. Calif., Berkeley, 1964. Admitted to Calif. bar, 1965, U.S. Supreme Ct. bar, 1970; asso. firm Knox & Kretzmer, Richmond, Calif., 1965; partner firm Knox, Herron & Masterson, and predecessor, Richmond, 1965-77; judge Superior Ct. Bench Contra Costa County (Calif.), 1977—; gen. partner Vanguard Investments, 1967—. Bd. dirs. Ronoh Sch., 1964-74, ARC, 1967-70, YWCA, 1967-71, 75—, bd. Richmond Meml. Youth Center, 1970-71, Neighborhood House, 1965-70; mem. Little Hoover Commn., Richmond, 1963-65. Mem. Am., Calif., Richmond, Contra Costa (exec. com. 1968-73) bar assns., Calif. Trial Lawyers Assn., Calif. Applicants Attys., Queens Bench, Nat., Calif. women lawyers. Home: 51 Western Dr Point Richmond CA 94801 Office: 2566 Macdonald Ave Richmond CA 94804 Tel (415) 237-0100

HERRON, MICHAEL JEFFREY, b. Chgo., Oct. 25, 1940; B.S.B.A., U. Fla., 1962; J.D., U. Miami, 1965. Admitted to Fla. bar, 1965; asso. firm Smith & Mandler, Miami Beach, Fla., 1965-67; asso. firm Kline, Moore, Klein & Herron, and predecessor, Miami Beach, 1967-69, partner, 1969—. Chmn. Miami Beach Charter Rev. Bd., 1971—. Mem. Fla. Bar, Miami Beach Bar Assn. Office: 407 Lincoln Rd Miami Beach FL 33139 Tel (305) 538-3771

HERRON, WILLIAM JOSEPH, b. Saranac Lake, N.Y., Dec. 31, 1904; B.S. in Commerce and Econs., U. Vt., 1926; LL.B., Fordham U., 1930. Admitted to N.Y. State bar, 1931; law clk. dept. investment law N.Y. Life Ins. Co., N.Y.C., 1928-30; mem. firm Herron, Lawler, Fischer & Hughes and predecessors, Malone, N.Y., 1932-74, of counsel, 1974—; mem. N.Y. State Temporary Commn. to Study Revision of N.Y. State Constn.; chmn. bd. Farmers Nat. Bank of Malone; mem. N.Y. State Appellate Div. 3d departmental com. for ct. adminstrn. Mem. acad. bd. Franklin Acad., Malone; mem. N.Y. State Cath. Welfare Com. Fellow Am. Coll. Trial Lawyers, Am. Bar Found.; mem. Franklin County (N.Y.) (pres. 1942-45), N.Y. State (sec. 1947-49), Am. bar assns., Scabbard and Blade. Decorated papal knight of St. Gregory; recipient plaque for service to community health care Alice Hyde Hosp., Malone, 1973, Alumni Distinguished Service award U. Vt., 1976. Home: 6 Porter Ave Malone NY 12953 Office: 130 E Main St Malone NY 12953 Tel (518) 483-1913

HERSCHER, DANIEL MOSES, b. Phila., July 13, 1927; B.S., U. Calif., Los Angeles, 1952; J.D., U. So. Calif., 1955. Admitted to Calif. bar, 1955; mem. firms Gold, Herscher & Taback, Beverly Hills, Calif., 1966-75; individual practice law, Beverly Hills, 1976—. Mem. Legion Lex, Order of Coif. Editorial bd. U. So. Calif. Law Rev., 1954-55. Office: 8500 Wilshire Blvd Beverly Hills CA 90211 Tel (213) 652-0490

HERSHCOPF, GERALD THEA, b. N.Y.C., Feb. 8, 1922; A.B., Columbia, 1943; certificate in French civilization U. Paris, 1945; J.D., Harvard, 1949. Admitted to N.Y. bar, 1949; asso. firm Marshall, Bratter, Greene, Allison & Tucker, N.Y.C., 1949-54; partner firms Starr & Hershcopf, N.Y.C., 1954-56, Hershcopf & Graham, N.Y.C., 1956—; chmn. bd. North Am. Planning Corp., 1968-71. Mem. Assn. Bar City N.Y., N.Y. State Bar Assn. Office: 230 Park Ave New York City NY 10017 Tel (212) MU 6-8992

HERSHEY, DALE, b. Pitts., Mar. 24, 1941; B.A., Yale, 1963; LL.B., Harvard, 1966. Admitted to Pa. bar, 1966; asso. firm Eckert, Seamans, Cherin & Mellott, Pitts., 1966-74, partner, 1975—. Bd. dirs. Neighborhood Legal Services; mem. fellows com. Carnegie Inst. Mus. Art, Pitts. History and Landmarks Found., Western Pa. Conservancy, Nat. Trust Historic Preservation. Mem. Am., Pa., Allegheny County (mem. pub. service com.) bar assns. Home: 102 Buckingham Rd Pittsburgh PA 15215 Office: 600 Grant St 42d Floor Pittsburgh PA 15219 Tel (412) 566-6000

HERSHMAN, HAROLD MARTIN, b. Bklyn., Aug. 9, 1931; B.A., N.Y. U., 1953, LL.B., 1956. Admitted to N.Y. bar, 1956, U.S. Supreme Ct. bar, 1965; asso. firm Guzik & Boukstein, N.Y.C., 1956-57; partner firm Hershman & Leicher, N.Y.C., 1959—; mem. malpractice panel 2d Jud. Dept. Mem. Queens County Bar Assn. (chmn. civil ct com. 1973—, com. municipal law 1971-73), N.Y. Trial Lawyers Assn., Brandeis Assn., Inc. (dir.). Home: 67 Lent Dr Plainview NY 11803 Office: 630 Third Ave New York City NY 10017 Tel (212) 687-1040

HERSHMAN, MENDES, b. Northampton, Pa., May 20, 1911; A.B., N.Y. U., 1929; LL.B., Harvard, 1932. Admitted to N.Y. bar, 1933; spl. counsel for housing New York Life Ins. Co., N.Y.C., 1946-62, asst. gen. counsel, 1962-64, asso. gen. counsel, 1964-69, v.p., gen. counsel, 1969-72, sr. v.p., gen. counsel, 1972—; chmn. Mayor's Com. on Judiciary, N.Y.C., 1972; mem. Moreland Act Commn., N.Y.C., 1975-76. Active N.Y.C. Pub. Devel. Corp., N.Y. Landmarks Conservancy; chmn. bd. Bronx-Lebanon Hosp. Center. Mem. Am., N.Y. State bar assns., Assn. Bar City N.Y., Am. Law Inst., Am. Council Life Ins., Phi Beta Kappa. Recipient certificate of outstanding pub. service N.Y. State, 1960; bd. editors New York Law Jour., 1976; contbr. articles to legal jours. Home: 200 E 66th St New York City NY 10021 Office: 51 Madison Ave New York City NY 10010 Tel (212) 576-6105

HERSHSON, MORRIS, b. Chorzele, Poland, Mar. 21, 1905; LL.B., St. Lawrence U., 1927. Admitted to N.Y. State bar, 1928, Tex. bar, 1935, U.S. Supreme Ct. bar, 1959; individual practice law, N.Y.C., 1928—; chief counsel iron and steel br. Office Price Adminstrn., Washington, 1943-45; pres., counsel Nat. Barrel and Drum Assn., Washington, 1948—. Mem. exec. com. Hazardous Materials Adv. Com., Washington. Mem. Packaging Assn. N.Y. Home: 215 W 78th St New York City NY 10024 Office: 370 Lexington Ave New York City NY 10017 Tel (212) 684-3708

HERSON, MORRIS A., b. N.Y.C., Dec. 11, 1909; B.A., Coll. City N.Y., 1930; M.A., Columbia U., 1932; J.D., Fordham U., 1933. Admitted to N.Y. bar, 1933; instr. Coll. City N.Y., 1930-40; individual practice law, Albany, N.Y., 1933—; gen. counsel West Side Iron Works, N.Y.C., 1939-48, Cindico, Inc., N.Y.C., 1950—. Mem. Am., N.Y. State, Albany County bar assns. Author: Egbert Benson, a Biography. Home: 13 Lake Shore Apts Watervliet NY 12189 Office: 11 N Pearl St Albany NY 12207 Tel (518) 465-2386

HERSRUD, LESLIE RAYMOND, b. Petrel, N.D., Apr. 6, 1914; B.A., St. Olaf Coll., 1935; J.D., U. Minn., 1938; postgrad. Nat. Coll. State Judiciary, 1968, 72, 74. Admitted to S.D. bar, 1938; individual practice law, Lemmon, S.D., 1940-55; atty. City of Lemmon, 1940-41; states atty. Perkins County (S.D.), 1947-51; judge S.D. Circuit Ct., 8th Circuit, 1955—; faculty advisor Nat. Coll. State Judiciary, Reno, 1971. Bd. dirs. Lutheran Hosps. and Homes Soc. Am., Fargo, N.D., 1950—, Five Counties Hosp., Lemmon, 1950—. Mem. Am. (exec. com. sect. jud. adminstrn.), S.D. bar assns. Editor, S.D. Bar Jour., 1951-52. Home: 304 3rd Ave W Lemmon SD 57638 Office: 14 4th St W Lemmon SD 57638 Tel (605) 374-3701

HERST, THEODORE JACOB, b. Chgo., June 18, 1924; A.B., U. Chgo., 1948, J.D., 1949. Admitted to Ill. bar, 1950, U.S. Dist. Ct. No. Dist. Ill., 1951, U.S. Ct. Appeals 7th Circuit, 1956, U.S. Ct. Mil. Appeals bar, 1954, U.S. Supreme Ct. bar, 1973; asso. firm Altheimer, Kabaker, Lipson & Naiburg, Chgo., 1950-56, Max W. Petacque, Chgo., 1956-61; mem. firm Petacque & Herst, Chgo., 1961-71; of counsel firm Altman, Kurlander & Weiss, Chgo., 1971-74, Lapin, Panichi & Levine, Chgo., 1976—; dir. Northbrook Savs. and Loan Assn. (Ill.), 1960. Sec., Forest Hosp., Des Plaines, Ill., 1957-75, trustee, 1957—; v.p., sec., trustee Ill. Sch. Profl. Psychology, Chgo., 1976—. Mem. Chgo., Ill., Am. bar assns. Office: 115 S LaSalle St Chicago IL 60603 Tel (312) 346-8111

HERTEL, THEODORE BERNHARD, JR., b. Milw., Jan. 23, 1947; student Freie Universitat Berlin, 1967-68; B.A., Carroll Coll., 1969; J.D., U. Wis., 1972. Admitted to Wis. bar, 1972, U.S. Dist. Ct. Eastern and Western Dist. Wis. bar, 1972; asso. firm Gaines & Saichek, Milw., 1972—. Mem. Am., Wis., Milw., Milw. Jr. bar assns., Am. Judicature Soc., Assn. Trial Lawyers Am., Wis. Acad. Trial Lawyers, Lectr. U. Wis., 1975—. Home: 4754 N Hollywood Whitefish Bay WI 53211 Office: 161 W Wisconsin Ave Milwaukee WI 53203 Tel (414) 271-1938

HERTZ, ERNEST WILLIAM, b. Menno, S.D., May 10, 1922; LL.B., Univ. Law Sch., Vermillion, S.D., 1948. Admitted to S.D. bar, 1948; state's atty., Hutchinson County, S.D., 1949-64; judge Circuit Ct., Olivet, S.D., 1970—; city atty., Menno, S.D. Mem. Menno Sch. Bd. Mem. S.D. Bar Assn., Am. Assn. Trial Lawyers. Home: 405 Pine St Menno SD 57045 Office: Olivet SD 57052 Tel (605) 387-5547

HERTZ, FREDERICK JACOB, b. St. Paul, Feb. 2, 1920; B.A., U. Wis., 1942, J.D., 1943. Admitted to Wis. bar, 1943, Ill. bar, 1946, U.S. Supreme Ct. bar, 1950; partner firm Hertz and Kallen and predecessors, Chgo., 1947-74; judge U.S. Bankruptcy Ct., U.S. Dist. Ct., No. Dist. Ill., 1974—; asst. gen. atty. Chgo. Park Dist., 1951-54. Mem. Chgo., Ill., Wis., Am. Fed. bar assns. Office: 219 S Dearborn St Chicago IL 60604 Tel (312) 435-5644

HERTZBERG, RICHARD JESSE, b. Toledo, Ohio, Nov. 23, 1933; B.S., U. Toledo, 1954; LL.B., U. Cin., 1958. Admitted to Ariz. bar, 1959, U.S. Supreme Ct. bar, 1971; individual practice law, Phoenix, 1959—. Mem. Ariz. Bar Assn., First Amendment Lawyers Assn. Mem. editorial bd. U. Cin. Law Rev., 1956-58. Home: 4922 N 46th St Phoenix AZ 85018 Office: 3003 N Central Ave Phoenix AZ 85012 Tel (602) 264-3281

HERTZBERG, ROBERT ARNOLD, b. Toledo, Mar. 7, 1938; B.A., Ohio State Univ., 1960; J.D., Western Reserve U., 1964. Admitted to Ariz. bar, 1964, U.S. Supreme Ct., 1971; deputy Maricopa County Atty.'s Office, Ariz., 1965-68; chief criminal deputy, 1968-69; individual practice law, 1969-71; dep. Maricopa County Public Defender's Office, 1971—. Office: 114 W Adams Phoenix AZ 85003 Tel (602) 258-7711

HERTZFELD, JEFFREY MARTIN, b. Phila., Mar. 26, 1942; B.A., U. Pa., 1963; LL.B., Harvard U., 1966. Admitted to Del. bar, 1966, N.Y. bar, 1969; law clk. Del. Supreme Ct., Wilmington, 1966-67; asso. firm Kaplan, Livingston, Goodwin & Berkowitz, Paris, 1967-69; faculty asso. U. Leiden (Netherlands) Law Sch., 1967-68; asso. firm Herzfeld & Rubin, N.Y.C., 1969-72; mem. firm Samuel Pisar, Paris, 1972—. Mem. Am., N.Y. bar assns., French Order Conseils Juridiques. Author articles, lectr. Office: Samuel Pisar 68 Blvd des Courcelles Paris 17 France

HERWITZ, CARLA BARRON, b. N.Y.C., June 1, 1932; A.B., Radcliffe Coll., 1955; LL.B., Harvard, 1955: Admitted to Mass bar, 1955, N.Y. bar, 1959; asso. firm Winthrop, Stimson, Putnam & Roberts, N.Y.C., 1957-60; asso. firm Choate, Hall & Stewart, Boston, 1960-71, partner, 1971—. Mem. town meeting, Swampscott, Mass., 1967—. Mem. Am., Boston bar assns.; contbr. articles to legal jours. Home: Litles Point Swampscott MA 01907 Office: 28 State St Boston MA 02109 Tel (617) 227-5020

HERWITZ, VICTOR JOSIAH, b. N.Y.C., Feb. 3, 1910; student Dartmouth Coll., 1927-28; LL.B., Bklyn. Law Sch., 1932; postgrad. N.Y. U. Law Sch., 1959-62. Admitted to N.Y. state bar, 1934, U.S. Supreme Ct. bar, 1962; legal asst. staff Investigation Dist. Atty. N.Y. County, 1931; legal asst. legislative investigation affairs city N.Y. 1931-32; law clk. to judge, 1932-33; asst. counsel Commr. Accounts, N.Y.C., 1934-35; deputy and asst. dist. atty., under Hon. Thomas E. Dewey, N.Y. County, 1935-42; spl. counsel N.Y. State Bd. Social Welfare, 1947-48; asst. corp. counsel City of New York, 1951-55; spl. counsel City of Hudson, N.Y., 1953; individual practice law, N.Y.C., 1955—. Pres. Met. Council United Synagogue Am., 1954-56; chmn. Speaker's Bur. Fed. Jewish Philanthopies, 1955-57; vice chmn. law com. Anti-Defamation League Am., 1976-77. Mem. N.Y. County, N.Y. State, Am. bar assns., Assn. Bar City N.Y. Home: 9 E 96th St New York City NY 10028 Office: 22 E 40th St New York City NY 10016 Tel (212) LE 2-9470

HERZ, CHARLES HENRY, b. Newark, Oct. 28, 1939; A.B., Princeton U., 1961; LL.B., Yale U., 1967. Admitted to D.C. bar, 1967; asso. firm Covington & Burling, Washington, 1967-76; gen. counsel NSF, Washington, 1976—; gen. counsel Planned Parenthood Washington. Pres. Bd. Planned Parenthood Assn. Met. Washington, 1973-75. Mem. Fed. Bar Assn. (dep. council chmn. Council Sci. Tech., and the Law, dep. chmn. Continuing Legal Edn. Com.). Home: 8319 Woodhaven Blvd Bethesda MD 20034 Office: 1800 G St NW Room 501 Washington DC 20550 Tel (202) 632-4386

HERZ, JOHN WILLIAM, b. N.Y.C., Nov. 10, 1914; A.B., Columbia, 1936, LL.B., 1938. Admitted to N.Y. bar, 1938; partner firm Wolf, Haldenstein, Adler, Freeman & Herz, N.Y.C., 1948—; dir. Barclay Industries, Inc., Coplay Cement Mfg. Co., H. Kohnstamm & Co., Inc., Whitehill Agy., Inc. Bd. dirs. Preventive Medicine Inst., 1963—; pres., chmn. New Rochelle (N.Y.) Guidance Center, 1965-67; chmn. Camp Madison-Felicia, Inc., 1970—. Mem. Am., N.Y. State bar assns., Bar Assn. City N.Y. Co-editor: Business Acquisitions, Planning and Practice, 1971. Home: 325 Weaver St Larchmont NY 10538 Office: 270 Madison Ave New York City NY 10016 Tel (212) 689-5300

HERZOG, PETER EMILIUS, b. Vienna, Austria, Dec. 25, 1925; B.A., Hobart Coll., 1952; J.D., Syracuse U., 1955; LL.M., Columbia, 1956. Admitted to N.Y. State bar, 1957; dep. asst. atty. gen. to asst. atty. gen. N.Y. State Dept. Law, Albany, 1956-58; asst. to asso. prof. law Syracuse (N.Y.) U., 1958-66, prof., 1966—; staff mem. Columbia project on internat. procedure, 1960-63, asso. dir. project on European Legal Instns., 1968; staff mem. N.Y. State Joint Legis. Com. on Met. Area Studies, 1958-60; vis. adj. prof. law Cornell U., 1976; vis. prof. U. Paris, 1976-77. Mem. Am. Soc. Internat. Law, Internat. Law Assn. (Am. br.), Onondaga County Bar Assn., Société de legislation comparée (France). Author: (with M. Weser) Civil Procedure in France; The Hague, 1967; (with F. G. Dawson and Ivan Head) International Law, National Tribunals and the Rights of Aliens, 1971; (with Hans Smit and others) The Law of the European Economic Community, 5 vols. Home: 112 Erregger Rd Syracuse NY 13224 Office: Coll Law Syracuse U Syracuse NY 13210 Tel (315) 423-4236

HERZSTEIN, MORTIMER HAMERSLOUGH, b. Trinidad, Colo., Dec. 20, 1925; B.A., U. Calif., Berkeley, 1947; LL.B., Stanford, 1950. Admitted to Calif. bar, 1951, U.S. Ct. Appeals 9th Circuit bar, 1951, U.S. Supreme Ct. bar, 1965; asso. firm Rogers & Clark, San Francisco, 1951-52; asso. firm Jaffa & Sumski, San Francisco, 1952-56; partner firm Herzstein & Maier, and predecessors, San Francisco, 1956—. Mem. State Bar Calif., Bar Assn. San Francisco, Am. Bar Assn. Home: 42 Digby St San Francisco CA 94131 Office: 500 Sansome St San Francisco CA 94111 Tel (415) 434-0610

HERZSTEIN, ROBERT ERWIN, b. Denver, Feb. 26, 1931; A.B. magna cum laude, Harvard U., 1952, LL.B. magna cum laude, 1955. Admitted to Colo. bar, 1955, D.C. bar, 1959, U.S. Supreme Ct. bar, 1959, U.S. Ct. Customs and Patent Appeals bar, 1976; asst. to gen. counsel Dept. Army, Washington, 1955-58; asso. firm Arnold & Porter, Washington, 1958-63, partner, 1963—. Bd. govs. Antioch Sch. Law, Washington; trustee Inst. for Internat. and Fgn. Trade Law, Georgetown U.; mem. overseers com. Harvard Law Sch., 1976—. Mem. Am. Bar Assn. (chmn. standing com. on customs law 1975, chmn. com. on tariffs, customs Internat. Law sect. 1975), Am. Soc. Internat. Law (vice chmn. study panel on internat. trade policy and institutions 1974-76, mem. bd. rev. and devel. 1977—). Home: 4962 Quebec St NW Washington DC 20016 Office: 1229 19th St NW Washington DC 20036 Tel (202) 872-6838

HESLET, JAMES HOLDEN, b. Kansas City, Mo., Mar. 9, 1941; B.B.A., Tex. Christian U., 1964; J.D., U. Tulsa, 1969. Admitted to Okla. bar, 1969; asst. dist. atty. Tulsa County, 1969-72; asso. firm Lassiter & Heslet, Tulsa, 1972—. Mem. Okla. State, Tulsa County bar assns., Okla. Trial Lawyers Assn., Okla. Criminal Defense Lawyers Assn. Office: 2601 Fourth Nat Bank Bldg Tulsa OK 74119 Tel (918) 587-1511

HESS, DAVID ROBERT, b. St. Louis, July 12, 1942; A.B., Washington U., St. Louis, 1967, J.D., 1967. Admitted to Mo. bar, 1967, Ill. bar, 1967; asst. staff mgr. Am. Tel. & Tel., Kansas City, Mo., 1967-68; asso. firms Evans and Dixon, St. Louis, 1968-69, Cook, Murphy, Lance and Mayer, St. Louis, 1970-71; asst. dir. Mo. Task Force On Organized Crime, St. Louis, 1969-70; individual practice law, Clayton, Mo., 1971—; sec., gen. counsel, dir. Hess Constrn. Co., St. Louis, 1971—. Mem. Clayton Twp. Democratic Com., 1972-75, Mo. Dem. Com., 1972-75; chmn. 2d Congl. Dist. Com. of Mo., 1974-75. Mem. Am., St. Louis County, Mo., Ill. bar assns., Met. Bar Assn. St. Louis. Home: 3 Dumbarton Dr Olivette MO 63132 Office: 130 S Bemiston St Clayton MO 63105 Tel (314) 727-8900

HESS, EMERSON GARFIELD, b. Pitts., Nov. 13, 1914; A.B., Bethany Coll., 1936; J.D., U. Pitts., 1939. Admitted to Pa. bar, 1940; sr. partner firm Hess, Humphrey & Lehman, Pitts., 1940—; solicitor Scott Twp. Sch. Bd., 1958-65; legal counsel Judiciary com. Pa. Ho. of Reps., 1967-69; solicitor Scott Twp., 1968-69, Crafton Borough, 1974—, Authority for Improvements in Municipalities of Allegheny County, 1977—. Bd. dirs. WQED Ednl. TV, Pitts., 1952-68, Golden Triangle YMCA, Pitts., 1945—; pres., dir. Civic Light Opera Assn., Pitts., 1967-68; mem. internat. com. YMCA World Service, N.Y.C., 1968—; chmn. Central Christian Ch., Pitts., 1962-63; pres. Anesthesia and Resuscitation Found., Pitts., 1964—, Pa. Med. Research Found., 1960—. Home: 43 Robin Hill Dr Pittsburgh PA 15136 Office: 908 Lawyers Bldg Pittsburgh PA 15219 Tel (412) 391-6533

HESS, GEORGE TAYLOR, b. Uniontown, Pa., July 23, 1925; A.B., Harvard, 1949; LL.B., U. Pa., 1953. Admitted to Pa. bar, 1954, Kans. bar, 1970, U.S. Supreme Ct. bar, 1967; individual practice law, Uniontown, 1954-60; dir., sec., gen. counsel Susquehanna Broadcasting Co., York, Pa., 1960-69; permanent mem. U.S. 3d Circuit Jud. Conf.; asst. gen. counsel United Telecommunications, Inc., Westwood, Kans., 1969-76, asst. gen. counsel, asst. sec., 1976—. Vice-pres. Kans. Girls Chorus, Inc., 1976-77. Mem. Am., Pa., Kans., Kansas City, Mo. bar assns. Home: 9815 Belinder Rd Leawood KS 66206 Office: 2330 Johnson Dr Westwood KS 66205 Tel (913) 384-7332

HESS, LAWRENCE EUGENE, JR., b. Phila., Aug. 18, 1923; grad. Princeton U., 1946; B.S., U.S. Naval Acad., 1947; J.D. with honors, George Washington U., 1954; postgrad. Temple U. Sch. Law, 1976. Admitted to Pa., D.C. bars, 1954, U.S. Supreme Ct. bar, 1963; with U.S. Navy, 1946-66; house counsel Nat. Liberty Life Ins. Co., Valley Forge, Pa., 1966-67, Standard Computers, Inc., Wynnewood, Pa., 1967-68; atty. Def. Personnel Support Center, Phila., 1968-69; counsel Am. Acceptance Corp., Phila., 1969-74. Pres. bd. trustees Glenside (Pa.) United Methodist Ch., 1973-76. Mem. Am., Fed., Pa., Phila., Montgomery County (Pa.) bar assns., Comml. Law League Am., Judge Advs. Assn., Naval Acad. Alumni Assn. Phila. (pres.). Editorial bd. George Washington U. Law Rev., 1952-53. Home and Office: 515 Dreshertown Rd Fort Washington PA 19034 Tel (215) MI 6-6956 or 643-0661

HESSBERGER, GEORGE LOUIS, b. Huntington, W.Va., July 29, 1947; B.S. in Accounting, DePaul U., 1969, J.D., 1972. Admitted to Ill. bar, 1972; asso. firm Wooster, Mugalian & Klingner, Chgo., 1972-73, offices Harold W. Klingner, Chgo., 1974—; asso. Chgo. Vol. Legal Services Found., Evanston, Ill. Chmn. Carey Blood Donation Campaign, DePaul U., 1971. Mem. Am., Chgo., Ill. bar assns. Author: Indian Title to Land: A Historical Perspective, 1972; Aircraft Hull Insurance, 1971. Office: 105 W Adams St 37th floor Chicago IL 60603 Tel (312) 372-0900

HESSE, HARRY RADER, b. Wheeling, W.Va., July 27, 1908; A.B., W.Va. U., 1931, J.D., 1932. Admitted to W.Va. bar, 1932; mem. firm Hesse and Petroplus, Wheeling, 1932-34; with Wheeling Steel Corp., 1934-64, sec., gen. counsel of corp. and subs's., 1958-64; mem. firm Petroplus, Bailey, Byrum and Hesse, Wheeling, 1964-72; individual practice law, Wheeling, 1972—. Mem. Ohio County (pres. 1971-72), W.Va., Am. bar assns., Am. Judicature Soc., Phi Alpha Delta. Home: 8 Lynwood Ave Wheeling WV 26003 Office: 8 Lynwood Ave Wheeling WV 26003 Tel (304) 242-6090

HESSE, ROBERT LOUIS, b. Chgo., Apr. 1930; A.B., Kenyon Coll., 1952; J.D., U. Pa., 1955. Admitted to Ill. bar, 1955, Fla. bar, 1970, U.S. Supreme Ct. bar, 1974; asso. firm Rooks, Pitts, Fullagar & Proust, Chgo., 1955-60, partner, 1960-68; partner firm Nelson, Hesse, Cyril & Weber, Sarasota, Fla., 1970—; faculty John Marshall Law Sch., Chgo., 1957-65; asst. sec. commerce state of Fla., 1969-70. Trustee Village of Palatine (Ill.), 1964-67; central committeeman Rep. party Cook County, Ill., 1965-67. Mem. Am., Fla., Sarasota bar assns. Home: 8100 Sanderling Rd Sarasota FL 33581 Office: 2070 Ringling Blvd Sarasota FL 33577 Tel (813) 366-7550

HESSER, CHARLES, b. Phila., Oct. 20, 1939; B.B.A., Temple U., 1961; J.D., Harvard, 1964. Admitted to Mass. bar, 1965; individual practice law, Boston, 1965—; pres. Social and Country Club Mgmt. and Cons. Co., Boston, 1974—. Mem. Am. Bar Assn., ACLU, Nat. Nudists Legal Rights Union (pres.), Delta Sigma Pi (Gold Key award 1971). Home: 25 Beacon St Apt 27 Somerville MA 02143 Office: Suite 1230 10 Post Office Sq Boston MA 02109 Tel (617) 482-4515

HESSERT, PETER LOUIS, b. Wausau, Wis., Jan. 1, 1947; B.S., Carroll Coll., 1969; J.D., U. Wis., 1973. Admitted to Wis. bar, 1973; asso. firm Tinkham, Smith, Bliss, Patterson & Richards, Wausau, 1973—. Bd. dirs. Half-Way House of Wausau, Inc., 1975—. Mem. Am., Marathon County (Wis.) bar assns., State Bar Wis. Office: 630 Fourth St Wausau WI 54401 Tel (715) 845-1151

HESSLEY, BERNARD JOSEPH, b. Warren, Pa., May 1, 1942; B.A., U. Notre Dame, 1964, J.D., Georgetown U., 1967. Admitted to Pa. bar, 1968; partner firm Wolfe & Hessley, Warren, 1968-70; individual practice law, Warren, 1970—; solicitor Deerfield Twp. Bd. dirs. Warren County (Pa.) Sch. Dist., 1975—. Mem. Am., Pa. trial lawyers assns., Am., Pa., Warren County bar assns., Pa. Assn. Twp. Solicitors, Am. Arbitration Assn. Home: 115 W Saint Clair St Warren PA 16365 Office: 602 Pennsylvania Bank and Trust Bldg Warren PA 16365 Tel (814) 723-6392

HESTER, JAMES DEVAUGH, b. Mize, Miss., Jan. 24, 1924; LL.B., U. Miss., 1950. Admitted to Miss. bar, 1950; individual practice law, Laurel, Miss., 1950-70; judge 18th Circuit Ct. Dist. Miss., Laurel, 1970—. Bd. trustees William Carey Coll., Hattiesburg, Miss. Mem. Miss., Jones County bar assns. Home: 3336 Audubon Dr Laurel MS 39440 Office: PO Box 794 Laurel MS 39440 Tel (601) 428-4572

HESTER, WORTH HUTCHINSON, b. Bladenboro, N.C., Apr. 6, 1923; B.S., Wake Forrest U., 1949, J.D., 1950. Admitted to N.C. bar, 1950, staff atty. N.C. Atty. Gen., Raleigh, 1954-55; partner firm Hester, Hester and Johnson and predecessor, Elizabethtown, N.C., 1955—. Chmn. Bladen County (N.C.) Bd. Social Services; vice chmn. bd. trustees Bladen County Hosp. Mem. N.C. Bar Assn., N.C. State Bar (council). Home: Hwy 87 E Elizabethtown NC 28337 Office: Courthouse Dr Elizabethtown NC 28337 Tel (919) 862-3191

HETHERWICK, GILBERT LEWIS, b. Winnsboro, La., Oct. 30, 1920; B.A. summa cum laude, Centenary Coll., 1942; J.D., Tulane U., 1949. Admitted to La. bar, 1949; atty. legal dept. Arkansas La. Gas Co., Shreveport, La., 1949-53; partner firm Blanchard, Walker, O'Quin & Roberts, Shreveport, 1953—. Mem. Shreveport City Charter Revision Com., 1955; mem. Shreveport Municipal Fire and Police Civil Service Bd., 1956—, vice chmn., 1957—. Mem. La., Am., Shreveport, Fed. Power bar assns., Order of Coif, Phi Delta Phi, Omicron Delta Kappa. Editor-in-chief Tulane Law Rev., 1948-49. Home: 4604 Fairfield Ave Shreveport LA 71106 Office: First Nat Bank Tower Shreveport LA 71163 Tel (318) 221-6858

HETKIN, ALFRED HENRY, b. N.Y.C., Jan. 26, 1907; B.A., Columbia U., 1927, LL.B., 1930; Admitted to N.Y. State bar, 1931; partner firm Hetkin, Barshay & Tuchman, and predecessors, Bklyn., 1930-33, N.Y.C., 1933—; dir. New Yorker mag., 1955. Mem. Assn. Bar City N.Y., N.Y. County Lawyers Assn. (chmn. real estate com. 1952-54), N.Y. State, Real Estate Tax Rev. (pres. 1963-64) bar assns. Office: 9 E 40th St New York City NY 10016 Tel (212) 689-1450

HETLAGE, ROBERT O., b. St. Louis, Jan. 9, 1931; A.B., Washington U., 1952, LL.B., 1954; LL.M., George Washington U., 1957. Admitted to Mo. bar, 1954; 1st lt. Office Judge Adv. Gen., Dept. Army, Washington, 1955-58; partner firm Hetlage and Hetlage, St. Louis, 1958-65, Peper, Martin, Jensen, Maichel and Hetlage, St. Louis, 1966—. Mem. Housing and Land Clearance Authorities of St. Louis County, 1966-74; pres. St. Louis Council on World Affairs, 1966-67. Mem. Mo. Bar (pres.), Bar Assn. Met. St. Louis (past pres.), Am. Bar Assn. (past mem. ho. dels.). Home: 7200 Creveling Dr University City MO 63105 Office: 720 Olive St St Louis MO 63101 Tel (314) 421-3850

HETLAND, JOHN ROBERT, b. Mpls., Mar. 12, 1930; B.S., U. Minn., 1952, J.D., 1956. Admitted to Minn. bar, 1956, Calif. bar, 1962; asso. firm Cant, Taylor, Haverstock, Beardsley & Grey, Mpls., 1956-59; asso. firm Hetland & Wilson, San Francisco, Berkeley, Calif., and Orinda Calif., 1959—; prof. law U. Calif., Berkeley, 1959—; vis. prof. Stanford, 1971, U. Singapore, 1972. Mem. Am., Minn., Calif. bar assns., Order of Coif. Author: California Real Estate Secured Transactions, 1970, Secured Real Estate Transactions, 1974, California Cases on Security Transactions in Land, 1975; Secured Real Estate Transactions, 1977. Contbr. articles to legal jours. Home: 20 Redcoach Ln Orinda CA 94563 Office: 366 Boalt Hall U California Berkeley CA 94720 Tel (415) 841-1403 also 2600 Warring St Berkeley CA 94704 Tel (415) 548-5900

HETRICK, PATRICK KIRK, b. Milw., Mar. 11, 1945; B.S., U. Wis., Milw., 1967; J.D. magna cum laude, Marquette U., 1971. Admitted to Wis. bar, 1971; asso. firm Whyte & Hirschboeck, Milw., 1971-72; asst. prof. law, asso. legal counsel Marquette U., 1972—. Mem. Wis., Milw. bar assns., Nat. Assn. Coll., Univ. Attys., Alpha Sigma Nu. Home: 2115 Glen Oaks Ln Mequon WI 53092 Office: 1103 W Wisconsin Ave Milwaukee WI 53233

HETSKO, CYRIL FRANCIS, b. Scranton, Pa., Oct. 4, 1911; B.A., Dickinson Coll., 1933; J.D. with distinction, U. Mich., 1936. Admitted to Pa. bar, 1937, N.Y. bar, 1938, U.S. Ct. Claims bar, 1955, U.S. Tax Ct., 1955, U.S. Supreme Ct. bar, 1965, U.S. Ct. Appeals 2d Circuit bar, 1967, other dist. cts.; asso. firm Chadbourne, Parke, Whitside & Wolff, N.Y.C., 1936-55, partner 1955-64; gen. counsel Am. Brands Inc. (formerly Am. Tobacco Co.), N.Y.C., 1964—, v.p., 1965-69, dir., 1965—, sr. v.p., 1969—; dir. Acme Visible Records, Inc., Crozet, Va., Acushnet Co., New Bedford, Mass.; Am. Brands Export Inc., Am. Tobacco Internat. Corp., Duffy-Mott Co., Inc., Sunshine Biscuits, Inc. (all N.Y.C.), James B. Beam Co., James B. Beam Distilling Internat Co., Wilson Jones Co. (all Chgo.), Gallaher Ltd., Gt. Britain, Andrew Jergens Co., Cin., Master Lock Co., Master Lock Export Inc. (both Milw.), Swingline Inc., Swingline Export Corp. (both L.I.). Mem. Am., Fed., N.Y. State bar assns., Assn. Bar City N.Y., Internat. C. of C., U.S. Trademark Assn. (dir. 1959-67, 68-72, 73-77, pres. 1965-66, hon. chmn. bd. 1966-67), Order of Coif, Phi Beta Kappa. Home: 714 Waverly Rd Ridgewood NJ 07450 Office: 245 Park Ave New York City NY 10017 Tel (212) 557-5050

HETTINGER, HARRY HOWARD, b. Hood River, Oreg., Mar. 26, 1922; B.S.L., U. Wash., 1948, LL.B./J.D., 1949. Admitted to Wash. bar, 1949; partner firm Tunstall & Hettinger, Yakima, Wash., 1949-73; judge Superior Ct. of Wash. State for Yakima County, 1973—. Chmn. Wash. State Aeros. Commn., 1969-73. Mem. Am., Lawyer-Pilots, Yakima County (pres. 1972-73), Wash. State bar assns., Am. Judicature Soc. Home: Route 6 PO Box 136-B Yakima WA 98908 Office: Yakima County Courthouse Yakima WA 98901 Tel (509) 575-4222

HETZEL, WILLIAM BARR, JR., b. Pitts., Sept. 18, 1933; A.B., Princeton, 1955; LL.B., Harvard, 1958. Admitted to Mass. bar, 1959; asso. firm Warner & Stackpole, Boston, 1959-65, partner, 1966—. Mem. Concord (Mass.) Bd. Appeals, 1972-74, chmn., 1975—. Mem. Am., Boston bar assns. Office: Warner & Stacpole 28 State St Boston MA 02109 Tel (617) 523-6250

HEUBACH, RANDOLPH E., b. Glen Ellyn, Ill., Sept. 6, 1942; B.A., U. Wis., 1967; J.D., U. Santa Clara, 1970. Admitted to Calif. bar, 1971; asso. firm Lopez, Kennedy & Srite, Redding, Calif., 1971, W.O. Weissich, San Rafael, Calif., 1971-74; v.p., sec. Weissich & Heubach, San Rafael, 1974—; of counsel Marin County Legal Aid Soc.; mem. Marin County Criminal Def. Panel, Marin County Lawyer Referral Service Panel. Mem. Calif., Marin County (asst. chmn. standing com.

on ct. rules 1974, mem. com. to revise criminal rules of procedure 1973) bar assns. Home: 61 Lincoln Park San Anselmo CA 94960 Office: 55 Professional Center Pkwy San Rafael CA 94903 Tel (415) 472-3300

HEUBLEIN, VINCENT WELLEY, b. Huntington Park, Calif., July 3, 1925; B.S., Columbia, 1944; LL.B., U. So. Calif., 1949; LL.D., Calif. Coll. Law, 1969. Admitted to Calif. bar, 1950; individual practice law, Los Angeles, 1950-52; city prosecutor, Pasadena, Calif., 1952-54; asst. city atty. Pasadena, 1954-57; commr., judge pro-tem Los Angeles Superior Ct., 1958-68; partner firm Kirtland & Packard, Los Angeles, 1968-72, Ruston & Nance, Fullerton, Calif., 1972-73, Ives, Kirwan & Dibble, 1973—; prof. law U. San Fernando Valley, La Verne Coll. Law, Calif. Coll. Law, U. Calif. Extension Sch.; legal advisor Pasadena Spastic League. Past pres. Pasadena Boys' Club, United Cerebral Palsy Assn. L.A., Narcotics Edn. Com., Pasadena Central Little League. Mem. Calif., Los Angeles County bar assns. Recipient Distinguished Service award Pasadena, 1959. Home: 1507 E Mountain St Pasadena CA 91104 Office: Suite 650 417 S Hill St Los Angeles CA 90013 Tel (213) 627-0113

HEUMANN, RONALD R., b. Bell Gardens, Calif., Mar. 6, 1937; B.A., Calif. State U. at Los Angeles, 1962; J.D., U. Calif., 1965. Admitted to Calif. bar, 1966; law clk. Superior Ct. Calif., Los Angeles, 1965-66; asso. firm Hennigan & Butterwick, Riverside, Calif., 1966-69; individual practice law, Riverside, 1969—; chmn. Calif. Continuation Edn. of the Bar Com., 1974, mem. governing bd., 1975—, chmn., 1976. Mem. Riverside County Air Pollution Control Dist. Hearing Bd., 1969-75. Mem. Riverside County, Internat., Barristers Riverside County (pres. 1969) bar assns. Home: 5631 Royal Hill Dr Riverside CA 92506 Office: Suite 200 4075 Main St Riverside CA 92501

HEUSER, E. WILLIAM, b. Chgo., Apr. 20, 1937; A.B., Gettysburg Coll., 1959. LL.B., Dickinson Sch. Law, 1962. Admitted to Pa. bar, 1963, asso. firm James E. Menneses, Norristown, Pa., 1962-66, asso. firm Torak, Heuser & Grant and predecessors, King of Prussia, Pa., 1966-68, partner, 1969-71, partner firm Myers & Heuser, Norristown, 1971—; asso. dist. atty., Montgomery County, Pa., 1970-71, asst. pub. defender, 1971-72. Mem. Pa., Montgomery County bar assns., Montgomery County Trial Lawyers Assn., Upper Merion Jaycees. Home: 254 Fox Run King of Prussia PA 19406 Tel (215) 275-1400

HEWES, GASTON HENDERSON, SR., b. Guflport, Miss., Mar. 19, 1903; LL.B., U. Miss., 1926; Admitted to Miss. bar, 1926; county pros. atty. Harrison County (Miss.), 1931-38; judge Harrison County, 1938—; individual practice law, Gulfport, 1926-38. Pres. Gulfport Recreational Center. Mem. Harrison County Bar Assn. (past pres.), Miss. State Bar Assn. Home: #15 55th St Gulfport MS 39501 Office: Ct House Gulfport MS 39501 also Ct House Biloxi MS 39533 Tel (601) 863-4598 or 864-5161 or 863-8983

HEWES, HARRY PRINGLE, b. Gulfport, Miss., Mar. 6, 1939; M.S., 1956; B.A., Vanderbilt U., 1971; LL.B., U. Miss., 1975. Admitted to Miss. bar; individual practice law, Gulfport, 1965—; municipal judge City of Gulfport, 1968-69; master in chancery Harrison County, 1968-72. Bd. deacons First Presbyterian Ch., Gulfport, chmn., 1975. Home: 900 2d St Gulfport MS 39501 Office: Hewes Bldg Suite 505 Gulfport MS 39501 Tel (601) 864-4525

HEWES, RICHARD DAVID, b. Biddeford, Maine, Aug. 16, 1926; B.A., Boston U., 1950, LL.B., 1953. Admitted to Maine bar, 1953, Mass. bar, 1954; asso. firms Clyfton Hewes, Saco, Maine, 1953, Meritt J. Aldrich, Boston, 1954-60; partner firms Robinson, Richardson, Leddy & Hewes, Portland, Maine, 1960-63, Woodman, Thompson, Chapman & Hewes, Portland, 1963-70, Hewes, Culley and Feehan, Portland, 1971—; mem. Maine Ho. of Reps., 1967-76, speaker, 1973-74; mem. Maine Senate, 1977—; gen. counsel NE Hist. R.R. Mem. exec. com. Maine YMCA, 2d v.p., 1977, bd. dirs., 1962-69, 70-75, treas., 1966-68; bd. dirs. Mercy Hosp., 1st Parish Ch. of the Art. Mem. Am., Maine, Cumberland County (Maine) bar assns., Fedn. Ins. Counsel, No. New Eng. Def. Counsel Assn. (pres. 1974). Home: 897 Shore Rd Cape Elizabeth ME 04107 Office: One Canal Plaza PO Box 7240 Portland ME 04112 Tel (207) 774-1486

HEWITT, BENJAMIN NIXON, b. Niagara Falls, N.Y., Feb. 16, 1919; B.A., Williams Coll., 1940; LL.B., Cornell U., 1949. Admitted to N.Y. bar, 1949; asso. firm Phelps, Gray, Mansour & Hewitt, and predecessor firm, Niagara Falls, 1949-55, partner, 1955—. Trustee Niagara Falls Meml. Med. Center, 1962—, DeVeaux Sch., Niagara Falls, 1970—. Fellow Am., N.Y. State (dir. 1975—) bar founds., Am. Coll. Trial Lawyers; mem. Am., Niagara Falls (pres. 1961), Niagara County (pres. 1960), N.Y. State (sec. 1974—) bar assn., Erie County Trial Lawyers Assn. Home: 920 Mohawk St Lewiston NY 14092 Office: POB 1095 Falls Station Niagara Falls NY 14303 Tel (716) 284-9901

HEWITT, NORMAN, b. N.Y.C., Jan. 4, 1928; B.S.S., City Coll. N.Y., 1948; LL.B., Harvard, 1951, J.D., 1968. Admitted to N.Y. bar, 1953, Conn. bar, 1956; atty., advisor FCC, Washington, 1953-54; mem. firm Otterbourg, Steindler, Houston & Rosen, N.Y.C., 1954-56; asso. firm Cohen & Wolf, Bridgeport, Conn., 1956-58; individual practice law, Bridgeport, 1958—; mem. Conn. State Senate, 1958-61. Chmn. adv. bd. Greater Bridgeport Mental Health Assn., 1974-77. Mem. Conn., Bridgeport bar assns. Named Fairfield (Conn.) Young Man of Yr., 1961; Bridgeport Young Man of Year, 1962; Outstanding Man of Year, B'nai B'rith, 1968; author: Desegretation of the South, 1962. Home: 126 Margemere Dr Fairfield CT 06604 Office: 177 State St Bridgeport CT 06430 Tel (203) 368-4277

HEYDINGER, THOMAS EUGENE, b. Plymouth, Ohio, Aug. 24, 1940; B.A., U. Dayton, 1964; J.D., Ohio No. U., 1967. Admitted to Ohio Supreme Ct. bar, 1967, U.S. Dist. Ct. bar for No. Dist. Ohio, 1971, U.S. Supreme Ct. bar, 1973; mil. lawyer Uniform Code Mil. Justice, U.S. Army, 1969-70; judge Crawford County (Ohio) Ct., 1971; asst. atty. gen. State of Ohio, Columbus, 1972-73; asst. prosecutor Huron County (Ohio) and partner firm Owens, Hauser and Heydinger, Norwalk, Ohio, 1974; judge juvenile and probate divs. Huron County Ct. of Common Pleas, 1975—. Chmn. advisory council Tiffin (Ohio), State Hosp. and Mental Retardation Center, mem. Huron County Bd. Mental Health and Mental Retardation. Mem. Huron County, Ohio State, Am. bar assns., Am. Judicature Soc., Nat. Assn. Juvenile Ct. Judges, Nat. Assn. Probate Ct. Judges. Home: 28 Stoutenburg Dr Norwalk OH 44857 Office: Juvenile Ct Norwalk OH 44857 Tel (419) 668-1616

HEYMAN, PHILIP JACOB, b. Bklyn., Mar. 6, 1939; A.B. summa cum laude, Yale, 1960; LL.B., Harvard U., 1963. Admitted to N.Y. bar, 1964, N.J. bar, 1976, U.S. Tax Ct. bar, 1977; mem. firm Friedman & Cherin, Newark. Trustee Young Israel 5th Ave., 1971-77. Mem. Am., N.Y. State, N.Y. City, N.J. State bar assns., Fed. Bar Assn. N.J. Office: 17 Academy St Newark NJ 07102 Tel (201) 623-3600

HIAASEN, CARL ANDREAS, b. Benson County, N.D., May 26, 1894; student State Teachers Coll., Valley City, N.D., 1914-17, U. Ill., 1919-20; J.D., U. N.D., 1922. Admitted to Fla. bar, 1923, U.S. Supreme Ct. bar, 1926, U.S. Ct. Claims, 1964; sr. mem. firm McCune, Hiaasen, Crum, Ferris & Gardner, Ft. Lauderdale, Fla., 1922—. Bd. dirs. Pitts. Theol. Sem., Com. for Chapel of Four Chaplains, Temple U. Life fellow Am. Bar Found.; mem. Am. Bar Assn., Bar Assn. City of N.Y., Order of Coif, Phi Delta Phi, Delta Sigma Rho. Contbr. articles to legal jours. Home: 2417 NE 27th Ave Fort Lauderdale FL 33305 Office: 25 S Andrews Ave 600 Century Nat Bank Bldg Box 14636 Fort Lauderdale FL 33302 Tel (305) 462-2000

HIATT, ROGER LAWRENCE, b. Spokane, Wash., Nov. 7, 1945; B.A. magna cum laude, Washburn U., 1967, LL.M. cum laude, 1971; diplôme étranger Centre Européen, U. Nancy (France), 1968; LL.M., U. Boston, 1973. Admitted to Kans. bar, 1971; clk. to judge U.S. 10th Circuit Ct. Appeals, 1971-72; partner firm Hiatt, Crockett, Hiatt & Carpenter, Topeka, 1973—; adj. asst. prof. law Washburn U., 1974—. Mem. Am., Kans. (editorial bd. jour. 1975—), Topeka bar assns., Phi Delta Theta. Home: 1612 Collins St Topeka KS 66604 Office: 207 Casson Bldg Topeka KS 66603 Tel (913) 232-7263

HIBBARD, EDWARD ANDREW, b. Toronto, Kans., Aug. 21, 1921; A.B., U. Kans., 1940, LL.B., 1941, J.D., 1968; certificate Am. Inst. Property and Casualty Underwriters, 1972. Admitted Kans. bar, 1941, U.S. Supreme Ct. bar, 1974; authorization officer rating bd. Va, 1945-51; owner, mgr. A-Ok Services, Eureka, Kans., 1951—. Home: 210 Village Ln Eureka KS 67045 Office: 406 N Main St Eureka KS 67045 Tel (316) 583-5506

HIBBS, LOYAL ROBERT, b. Des Moines, Dec. 24, 1925; B.A., U. Iowa, 1950, LL.B., 1952. Admitted to Iowa bar, 1952, Nev. bar, 1958, U.S. Supreme Ct. bar, 1971; partner firm Hibbs & Newton, Reno, 1972—. Mem. Am., Iowa, Nev. (bd. govs. 1968—, pres. 1977—), Washoe County (pres. 1967-68) bar assns., Phi Alpha Delta. Home: 3445 San Juan Dr Reno NV 89509 Office: 350 S Center St Reno NV 89501 Tel (702) 786-6868

HIBBS, REX F., b. Billings, Mont., Nov. 17, 1906; LL.B., U. Mont., 1935. Admitted to Mont. bar, 1935, since practiced in Billings; asso. firm Albert Anderson, 1935-37; individual practice law, 1937-40; county atty. Yellowstone County, 1940-43; partner firm Hibbs, Sweeney & Colberg, 1946—; mem. Mont. Senate, 1951-67. Mem. Am., Mont., Yellowstone County bar assns. Home: 1325 Yellowstone Ave Billings MT 59102 Office: First Northwestern Bank Center Billings MT 59101 Tel (406) 252-4101

HICKAM, HUBERT, b. Spencer, Ind., Apr. 19, 1892; LL.B., Ind. U., 1913. Admitted to Ind. bar, 1913; partner firm Hickam & Hickam, Spencer, 1913-19; mem. firm Barnes, Hickam, Pantzer & Boyd and predecessors, Indpls., 1923—. Chmn. Alien Enemy Hearing Bd. of Ind., 1941, Alumni Bd. Ind. U., Alumni Bd. Visitors Ind. U. Law Sch. Fellow Am. Coll. Trial Lawyers; mem. Am. Law Inst., Am., Ind., Indpls. (pres. 1935-36) bar assns., Bar Assn. 7th Fed. Circuit. Author: A Civil Action from Pleadings to Trial; (with others) Preparation for Trial. Home: 4000 N Meridian St Indianapolis IN 46208 Office: 1313 Merchants Bank Bldg Indianapolis IN 46204 Tel (317) 638-1313

HICKEL, GERARD FREDERICK, b. Pitts., Sept. 28, 1946; B.S., U. Dayton, 1968; J.D., U. Toledo, 1971. Admitted to Mich. bar, 1972, Pa. bar, 1973, U.S. Supreme Ct. bar, 1977; sr. atty. Duquesne Light Co., Pitts., 1972—. Mem. Am., Allegheny County bar assns. Home: Box 210 RD 7 Gibsonia PA 15044 Office: 435 Sixth Ave Pittsburgh PA 15219 Tel (412) 471-4300 X 6125

HICKERSON, JOSEPH ARTHUR, b. Bessemer, Ala., Oct. 31, 1922; A.B. in Bus. Adminstrn. Clark Coll., Atlanta, 1946; LL.D., New Eng. Law Sch., 1953. Admitted to Mass. bar, 1955, U.S. Supreme Ct. bar, 1960; individual practice law, Springfield, Mass., 1955-64, 70—; asst. exec. officer USIA, Washington, 1964-66, Bangkok, Thailand, 1966-68; chief atty., program dir. Neighborhood Legal Services, Springfield, 1968-70. Mem. sch. com. Springfield. Bd. Edn., 1960-62; chmn. com. legal redress Springfield br. NAACP, 1959-64; elder 1st Presbyn. Ch., Springfield, 1959—. Mem. Am., Hampden County (Mass.) bar assns., Mass. Black Lawyers Soc. (founder 1956, 1st pres. 1956-59). Recipient certificate of recognition Internat. Sch. Assn., Bangkok, 1967. Home: 606 Alden St Springfield MA 01109 Office: 292 Worthington St Springfield MA 01103 Tel (413) 732-4174

HICKEY, DANIEL WILLIAM, b. Dayton, Ohio, July 17, 1946; B.A. in Polit. Sci., Wright State U., 1968; J.D., Georgetown U., 1971. Admitted to Alaska bar, 1972; asst. atty. gen. State of Alaska, Juneau, 1971-73, chief prosecutor, 1975—; dist. atty., Juneau, 1973-75. Mem. Alaska, Juneau bar assns., Alaska Criminal Law Revision Commn. Office: Alaska Dept Law Criminal Div Pouch KC Juneau AK 99811 Tel (907) 465-3428

HICKEY, EDWARD HUTCHINS, b. Boston, July 22, 1912; A.B. cum laude, Harvard, 1933, LL.B., 1936. Admitted to Mass. bar, 1936, D.C. bar, 1946, Ill. bar, 1957; asso. firm Peabody & Arnold, Boston, 1936-38; spl. asst. to atty. gen. Dept. Justice, Washington, 1938-42, chief gen. litigation civil div., 1945-57; partner firm Bell, Boyd, Lloyd, Haddad & Burns, Chgo., 1957—; dir. 1st Nat. Bank of Winnetka (Ill.), Watson & Boaler, Inc. Trustee Village of Winnetka, 1971-72, pres., 1972-74; bd. dirs. United Charities of Chgo., 1969—; chmn. Winnetka Bicentennial Com., 1975-76. Mem. Am., Ill., Chgo. (chmn. coms. legal aid 1969, urban affairs 1970) bar assns., Bar Assn. 7th Fed. Circuit (pres. 1974-75), Nat. Legal Aid and Defender Assn., Am. Law Inst., Am. Judicature Soc., Supreme Ct. Hist. Soc., Law Club Chgo. Home: 823 Humboldt St Winnetka IL 60093 Office: 135 S LaSalle St Chicago IL 60603 Tel (312) 372-1121

HICKEY, EDWARD JAMES, b. Rochester, N.Y., Sept. 1, 1916; B.A., Georgetown U., 1938; LL.B., Yale U., 1941. Admitted to N.Y. State bar, 1942, U.S. Supreme Ct. bar, 1957; asso. firm Harris, Beach, Keating, Wilcox & Dale, Rochester, N.Y.C., 1945-51; asst. trust officer Union Trust Co., Rochester NY 1951-52; individual practice law, Rochester, N.Y., 1952-60; sr. partner firm Hickey, McHugh & Garlick, Rochester, N.Y., 1960—; lectr. in field. Chmn. Monroe County chpt. A.R.C.; bd. dirs. Birthright Rochester Inc., 1974, v.p., 1975; trustee Rochester Regional Research Library Council, 1970—, pres., 1974-76; mem. Friends Rochester Pub. Library, 1953—, pres. 1958-61; affiliated Rochester Area College, 1975—; bd. dirs. Rochester Gen. Hosp., 1964-70; bd. regents Am. Coll. Probate Counsel, 1976—; trustee, sec. bd. Nazareth Coll. Rochester, 1966—. Fellow N.Y. State, Am. bar founds.; mem. Am., N.Y. State (v.p. 1977—), Monroe County (pres. 1962) bar assns., Estate Planning Council Rochester (pres. 1960-61), Nat. Assn. Coll. Univ. Attys., Nat. Conf. Lawyers and Reps. Am. Bankers Assn. Home: 245 Edgemoor Rd Rochester NY 14618 Office: 850 Reynolds Arcade 16 Main St East Rochester NY 14614 Tel (716) 546-2434

HICKEY, KENNETH FRANCIS, b. Washington, July 21, 1942; B.S. in Accounting, Coll. Holy Cross, Worcester, Mass., 1963; J.D., Georgetown U., 1966. Admitted to D.C. bar, 1967; atty. Office of Investigations, Office JAG, U.S. Navy, 1966-68; partner firm Morgan, Lewis & Bockius, Washington, 1968—; mem. faculty Georgetown U. Law Center. Home: 20 Eton Overlook Rockville MD 20850 Office: 1800 M St NW Washington DC 20036 Tel (202) 872-5072

HICKEY, LAWRENCE PATRICK, b. Chgo., June 21, 1923; student Cornell Coll., Mt. Vernon, Iowa, 1941-42; B.A., U. Wis., 1948, postgrad. Sch. Law, 1949-50; J.D., DePaul U., 1951. Admitted to Ill. bar, 1951; since practiced in Chgo., asso. firm Pretzel, Stouffer and Nolan, 1951-57, partner, 1953-57, partner firm Young & Hickey, 1957-62, individual practice law, 1962—. Mem. Chgo., Ill. State, Am. bar assns., Am. Judicature Soc., Assn. Trial Lawyers Am., Ill. Trial Lawyers Assn., Roscoe Pound-Am. Trial Lawyers Found., Cath. Lawyers Guild Chgo. Home: 2440 N Lakeview St Chicago IL 60614 Office: 7 S Dearborn St Chicago IL 60614 Tel (312) 236-1660

HICKEY, WILLIAM JOHN, b. Washington, D.C., May 19, 1915; A.B., Brown U., 1937; LL.B., J.D., Georgetown U., 1948. Admitted to D.C. bar, 1947, Fed. bar, 1947, U.S. Supreme Ct. bar, 1953; asst. nat. bank examiner U.S. Dept. Treasury, Boston, 1937-39, Richmond, Va., 1940-41; bus. analyst Alien Property Custodian Washington, 1942-44; naval cost insp. U.S. Navy Dept., Silver Spring, Md., 1944-48; spl. asst. to atty. gen. U.S. Dept. Justice Adminstrv. Law Div., Washington, 1948-54; v.p., gen. counsel Am. Short Line R.R. Assn., Washington, 1954-63; partner firm Mulholland, Hickey, Lyman, McCormick, Fisher & Hickey and predecessor, Washington, 1964—. Mem. Am. Bar Assn., Bar Assn. D.C., Interstate Commerce Commn. Practioners Assn. Home: 9702 Hillridge Dr Kensington MD 20795 Office: 1125 15th St NW Suite 400 Washington DC 20005 Tel (202) 833-8855

HICKISCH, JOHN RICHARD, b. Denver, Aug. 28, 1917; A.B., U. Denver, 1942, LL.B., 1947. Admitted to Colo. bar, 1947; law clk. firm Weller, Friedrich, Hickisch & Hazlitt, and predecessors, Denver, 1942, 46-47, asso. firm, 1947-51, partner, 1952—; advisor SSS, 1948-76. Bd. dirs. Rude Park Community Nursery, 1950—, pres., 1955-57. Mem. Catholic Lawyers Guild Denver (pres. 1972-73, dir. 1970-74), Am., Colo., Denver bar assns., Internat. Assn. Ins. Counsel, Serra Internat. Home: 2285 S Jackson Denver CO 80210 Office: 900 Capitol Life Center Denver CO 80203 Tel (303) 861-8000

HICKMAN, PAUL MAJOR, b. Hillsboro, Ill., Apr. 3, 1914; LL.B., Chgo.-Kent Coll. Law, 1943. Admitted to Ill. bar, 1944; law clk. Judge Major, U.S. Ct. Appeals, Chgo., 1944-47; individual practice law, Hillsboro, Ill., 1947-50; partner firm Bullington, White & Hickman and predecessor, 1950-70; judge Circuit Ct. 4th Jud. Circuit Ill., 1970—. Pres. Hillsboro Sch. Bd. Mem. Montgomery County (Ill.), Ill. State bar assns. Home: 601 Fairmont St Hillsboro IL 62049 Office: Courthouse Hillsboro IL 62049 Tel (217) 532-5418

HICKMAN, T. ALEXANDER, b. 1925; LL.B., Dalhousie U., Halifax, N.S., Can. Called to Nfld. bar, 1947; now minister of justice and mem. Nfld. Ho. of Assembly from Grand Bank Dist. Mem. Canadian Bar Assn. Home: 62 Carpasian Rd Saint John's NF A1B 2R4 Canada Office: Confederation Bldg Saint John's NF A1C 5T7 Canada*

HICKMANN, CHARLES ANDREW, b. Bklyn., May 14, 1928; B.A., U. Notre Dame, 1950; J.D., Harvard, 1953. Admitted to N.Y. bar, 1954, Calif. bar, 1955, Fla. bar, 1971; asst. counsel to counsel U.S. Naval Tng. Device Center, Port Washington, N.Y., 1957-63; counsel Aerospace Systems div. RCA, Camden, N.J., and Van Nuys, Calif., 1963-64; asst. counsel Hazeltine Corp., Little Neck, N.Y., 1967-69; individual practice law, Huntington, N.Y., 1964-67, 70—; legal officer USNR, 1954-56. Treas., Elwood Sch. Dist., Huntington, 1959-62. Mem. Suffolk County Bar Assn. Home: 39 Colonial St East Northport NY 11731 Office: 43 Prospect St Huntington NY 11743 Tel (516) 549-9055

HICKS, CLARENCE FLIPPO, b. Fredericksburg, Va., Feb. 24, 1929; B.S. in Commerce, U. Va., 1950, LL.B., 1952. Admitted to Va. bar, 1952, U.S. Supreme Ct. bar, 1955; asst. atty. gen. State of Va., 1953-59; partner firm Martin, Hicks & Ingles, and predecessor, Gloucester, Va., 1959—; chief draftsman Potomac River Compact of 1958 for State of Va. Chmn. Va. Com. for Pub. Edn., 1964-66. Mem. 13th Jud. Circuit (past pres.), Va., Am. bar assns., Am. trial lawyers assns., Nat. Assn. Criminal Def. Lawyers. Home: Pinewold Gloucester VA 23061 Office: Martin Hicks & Ingles Ltd Court Circle Gloucester VA 23061 Tel (804) 693-2500

HICKS, CRAWFORD ELMER, b. Leitchfield, Ky., Feb. 10, 1921; LL.B., U. Louisville, 1960. Commd. 2d lt. USAF, 1942, advanced through grades to lt. col., 1967; ret., 1967; community services adviser HUD, Atlanta, 1969—; admitted to Ga. bar, 1972; partner firm Strother, Hicks & Wallace, Atlanta, 1972—. Mem. Ga., Atlanta, Am. bar assns. Home: 1748 Fort Valley Dr Atlanta GA 30311 Office: 1619 Norcross-Tucker Rd Norcross GA 30071 Tel (404) 448-5407

HICKS, GEORGE WASHINGTON, b. Portsmouth, Va., Nov. 16, 1901; B.S., Va. Union U., Richmond, 1924; LL.B., J.D., Boston U., 1928. Admitted to Mass. bar, 1928, N.Y. bar, 1931; individual practice law, N.Y.C.; lawyer Intercultural Ednl. Fund, Inc., N.Y.C., 1950—. Mem. Alpha Phi Alpha. Recipient U.S. Medal for Meritorious Service, 1945; Community Service award Vocat. Guidance and Workshop Center; Certificate of Achievement N.Y.C. Bd. Edn. Home: 480 Convent Ave New York City NY 10031 Office: 271 W 125th St New York City NY 10027 Tel (212) MO2-7200

HICKS, JAMES LOWERY, JR., b. Alma, Mich., Nov. 10, 1946; B.S., U. Mo., 1969; J.D., So. Meth. U., 1972. Admitted to Tex. bar, 1972, U.S. Supreme Ct. bar, 1975, U.S. Ct. Appeals 5th Circuit bar, 1972, D.C. bar, 1975; firm Mullinax, Wells, Mauzy & Baab, Inc., Dallas, 1972—. Mem. Am. Bar Assn. Home: Office: 8204 Elmbrook Dr Suite 200 Dallas TX 75247 Tel (214) 630-3672

HICKS, MARK C., JR., b. Sevierville, Tenn., Apr. 18, 1927; B.S., E. Tenn. State U., 1948; J.D., Vanderbilt U., 1951. Admitted to Tenn. bar, 1952; individual practice law, Jonesboro, Tenn., 1952-70; partner firm Hicks Arnold & Hayes, Jonesboro and Johnson City, Tenn., 1971—. Mem. Johnson City Power Bd., Tri City Airport Commn.; sec., gen. counsel Tenn. Republican Party, 1968—; Rep. nat. committeeman, 1976—. Mem. Am., Tenn., Washington County (past pres.) bar assns. Home: PO Box 206 Jonesboro TN 37659 Office: Courthouse Sq PO Box 206 Jonesboro TN 37659 Tel (615) 753-3201

HICKS, RALPH HARRIMAN, b. Jackson, Miss., Sept. 30, 1932; B.S., Ga. Inst. Tech., 1957; degree in Bus., Ga. State U., 1959; LL.B., Emory U., 1961. Admitted to Ga. bar, 1960, U.S. Supreme Ct. bar,

1975; partner firm Smith, Cohen, Ringel, Kohler & Martin, Atlanta, 1961—. Bd. dirs. Atlanta Legal Aid Soc., 1976—. Mem. Am., Atlanta (pres. elect 1977—), bar assns., Lawyers Club Atlanta. Home: 3435 Valley Rd NW Atlanta GA 30305 Office: 2400 1st Nat Bank Tower Atlanta GA 30303 Tel (404) 658-1200

HICKS, STEVE EDWIN, b. Clinton, Ky., Aug. 12, 1948; B.S., La. State U., 1970, J.D., 1973. Admitted to La. bar, 1973, D.C. bar, 1976; asso. firm McCollister, Belcher, McCleary, Fazaio, Mixon, Holliday & Jones, Baton Rouge, 1973-75, partner, 1976—; gen. counsel, com. on revenue and fiscal affairs La. State Senate, 1976—. Bd. dirs. Baton Rouge Legal Aid Soc. Mem. Am., La., Baton Rouge, D.C. bar assns., Municipal Fin. Officers Assn., Nat. Hosp. Lawyers Assn. Home: 1621 Blouin Ave Baton Rouge LA 70808 Office: One American Pl Suite 1800 Baton Rouge LA 70825 Tel (504) 387-5961

HIDDE, ORVAL LEROY, b. Marion, Wis.; B.A. in Biology, Wartburg Coll., 1952; D.C. cum laude, Nat. Coll. Chiropractic, Chgo., 1953; J.D., U. Wis., 1969. Admitted to Wis. bar, 1969; mem. faculty dept. physiology Nat. Coll. Chiropractic, Chgo., 1953-55; practice medicine specializing in chiropractics, Watertown, Wis., 1955—; sec. commn. on accreditation Am. Chiropractic Assn., 1962-72; chmn. accrediting commn. Council on Chiropractic Edn., 1972-77; co-chmn. legis. com. Soc. Wis. Chiropractors; pres. Orvin Corp., Watertown, 1968-77. Mem. Am., Wis. chiropractic assns., Alumni assns. Nat. Coll. Chiropractics, Wartburg Coll., U. Wis. Law Sch., Am., Wis., Jefferson bar assns., Beta Beta Beta. Named Wis. Chiropractor of the Year, 1957; recipient Pres. award, Wis. Chiropractic Assn., 1973, Outstanding Service award, 1974; Chiropractor of the Yr. award Am. Chiropractic Assn., 1975, Distinguished Service award, 1975; contbr. articles on chiropractics to profl. jours. Office: 1434 E Main St Watertown WI 53094 Tel (414) 261-9640

HIERS, JAMES BROUGHTON, JR., b. Atlanta, Nov. 5, 1927; student Northwestern U., 1947-48; A.B., Mercer U., 1950; J.D., Emory U., 1958. Admitted to Ga. bar, 1956; claims mgr. Am. Surety Co., Alexandria, La. and Memphis, 1951-55; v.p., sec. So. Gen. Ins. Co., Atlanta, 1955-59; partner firm Swift, Currie, McGhee & Hiers, and predecessors, Atlanta, 1959—, sr. partner, 1965—; co-legal counsel Atlanta Claims Assn. Mem. Druid Hills Civic Assn., Atlanta, pres., 1968-70, mem. North DeKalb Jr. C. of C., pres. 1962-63, named Outstanding Pres. 1963; elder, deacon Emory Presbyn. Ch.; mem. Atlanta area Mercer U. Alumni Assn., pres., 1965, 1966, nat. v.p., 1966. Mem. Fedn. Ins. Counsel (v.p. 1975-76, chmn. sect. workers compensation law), Am. (vice-chmn. com. workers compensation and employers' liability), Atlanta, Ga. bar assns., Lawyers Club Atlanta, Am. Judicature Soc., Old War Horse Lawyers Club., Law Sci. Acad. Home: 3872 Randall Ridge Rd NW Atlanta GA 30327 Office: 771 Spring St NW Atlanta GA 30308 Tel (404) 881-0844

HIESTER, TRAVIS DADE, b. Mission, Tex., Oct. 5, 1935; B.S., U. Tex., 1960; LL.B., St. Mary's U., 1963. Admitted to Tex. bar, 1963; partner firm Kelley, Looney & Alexander, Edinburg, Tex., 1963-75; partner firm Atlas, Hall, Schwarz, Mills, Gurwitz & Bland, McAllen, Tex., 1975—. Trustee Hidalgo County (Tex.) Mus. Soc., 1968—. Mem. Tex., Hidalgo County bar assns., Office: PO Box 3725 818 Pecan Ave McAllen TX 78501 Tel (512) 682-5501

HIETT, EDWARD EMERSON, b. Toledo, Nov. 24, 1922; B.B.A., U. Mich., 1946, M.B.A, LL.B., 1949. Admitted to Ohio bar, 1949; individual practice law, Toledo, 1949-52; atty. legal dept. Libbey-Owens-Ford Co., Toledo, 1952-63, sec., asst. gen. counsel, 1963-73, v.p., sec., gen. counsel, 1973—; lectr. in field. Mem. Am., Ohio, Toledo bar assns., Am. Soc. Corporate Secs., Assn. Gen. Counsels. Home: 3723 Brookside Rd Toledo OH 43606 Office: 811 Madison Ave Toledo OH 43695 Tel (419) 247-3756

HIGBEE, CHARLOTTE MARGARET, b. Milw., Jan. 19, 1921; B.S., U. Wis., 1941, LL.B., 1948. Admitted to Wis. bar, 1948; research asst. Office State Wis. Atty. Gen., Madison, 1948; partner firm Higbee & Higbee, Spring Valley, Wis., 1948-51; adminstrv. asst. Equal Rights div. State Wis., Milw., 1966-71; chief contractor employment compliance div. Dept. Def., Milw., 1971—. Mem. Wis. League Women Voters (mem. state bd. 1965-66), Wis. State Bar Assn., Fed. Ofcls. Assn., Center Pub. Representation, Wis. Law Alumni Assn., Order Coif, Phi Beta Kappa, Phi Kappa Phi, Delta Sigma Rho. Home: 9223 N 70th St Milwaukee WI 53223 Office: 744 N 4th St Milwaukee WI 53202 Tel (414) 272-8180 Ext 207

HIGDON, CARL M., JR., b. Ottumwa, Iowa, Aug. 9, 1924; B.A., State U. Iowa, 1948, J.D., 1949. Admitted to Iowa bar, 1949, Tex. bar, 1950; individual practice law, Elsa, Tex., 1950—. Mayor City of Elsa, 1965-69. Mem. State Bar of Tex., Hidalgo County Bar Assn. (pres. 1962-63). Office: 209 N Broadway St Elsa TX 78543 Tel (512) 262-1961

HIGER, DALE GORDON, b. Emmett, Idaho, June 23, 1941; B.A., U. Wash., 1963; J.D., Harvard, 1966. Admitted to Idaho bar, 1966, U.S. Dist. Ct. for Idaho bar, 1966, U.S. 9th Circuit Ct. Appeals bar, 1971, U.S. Supreme Ct. bar, 1971; chief dep. pros. atty's office Canyon County, Idaho, 1968-70; asso. firm Eberle, Berlin, Kading, Turnbow & Gillespie, Boise, Idaho, 1970-73, partner, 1974—; staff mem. Pres.'s Commn. on Campus Unrest, Washington, 1970; mem. Idaho Commn. on Women's Programs, 1971-74. Pres. Idaho Mental Health Assn., 1971-73; bd. dirs. Nat. Mental Health Assn., 1972-74; trustee Boise Gallery of Art, 1975—; mem. Boise City Planning and Zoning Commn., 1976—. Mem. Am. Bar Assn., Phi Beta Kappa. Home: 635 Warm Springs Ave Boise ID 83702 Office: PO Box 1368 Boise ID 83701 Tel (208) 334-8535

HIGGINBOTHAM, A. LEON, JR., b. Trenton, N.J., Feb. 25, 1928; student Purdue U., 1944-45; B.A., Antioch Coll., 1949; LL.B., Yale, 1952, M.A. (hon.); LL.D. (hon.), Allegheny Coll., Atlanta U., Drexel Inst. Tech., Haverford U., Lafayette Coll., LaSalle Coll., Lehigh U., Lincoln U., N.C. Coll. at Durham, Phila. Coll. Pharmacy and Sci., Rutgers U., Tougaloo Coll. (Miss.), U. Pa., Wilberforce U. (Ohio); J.S.D. (hon.), Villanova U. Admitted to Pa. bar, 1953; asst. dist. atty. Philadelphia County, 1953-54; spl. dep. atty. gen. Commonwealth of Pa., 1956-62; spl. hearing officer Dept. of Justice, 1960-62; commr. Pa. Human Relations Commn., 1961-62; partner firm Norris, Green, Harris & Higginbotham, Phila., 1954-62; commr. FTC, 1962-69; vis. prof. dept. sociology U. Hawaii, summers 1973-74; U.S. dist. judge Eastern Dist. Pa., 1964—; adj. prof. dept. sociology Wharton Grad. Sch., U. Pa., 1970—, lectr. in law Sch., 1971—; vis. lectr. Law Sch., U. Mich., 1976. Vice chmn. Nat. Commn. on Causes and Prevention of Violence; mem. Commn. on Reform Fed. Criminal Laws, Commn. on Correctional Facilities and Services; bd. dirs. Balch Inst., Greater Phila. Movement, Christian St. br. YMCA, Phila. Urban Coalition, Robin Hood Dell Concerts; trustee Thomas Jefferson U., U. Pa., Phila. Found., Phila. Awards; alumni fellow Yale; citizen regent Smithsonian Instn.; bd. advisers Inst. for Correctional Law, Villanova Sch. Law; life mem. NAACP. Fellow Am. Bar Found. Recipient Nat. Human Relations award NCCJ, 1968, William C. Menninger Meml. medallion Menninger Found., 1969, Samuel S. Fels award Sch. Dist. of Phila., 1969, Russwurm award Nat. Newspaper Pubs. Assn., 1969, Ann. Brotherhood award Congregation Rodeph Shalom of Phila., 1970, Citation of Merit award Yale Law Sch., 1975, Martin Luther King award Educators Roundtable, Phila., 1976; named One of Ten Most Outstanding Young Men in Am., U.S. C. of C., 1964, Outstanding Young Man of Year, Phila. C. of C., 1964, Outstanding Young Man in Govt., Nat. Arthur S. Fleming award, 1964, Outstanding Layman of Year, YMCA of Phila. and vicinity, 1970; contbr. articles to profl. jours. Office: US Court House 601 Market St Philadelphia PA 19106 Tel (215) 597-9157

HIGGINBOTTOM, DAVID BAINES, b. Landour, Mussoorie, India, June 5, 1919; A.B., Princeton, 1941; LL.B., U. Fla., 1948, J.D., 1948. Admitted to Fla. bar, 1948; individual practice law, Frostproof, Fla., 1948—; atty. City of Frostproof, 1957-70. Pres. Ridge League of Municipalities, 1961-62. Mem. Fla. Bar (exec. com. real property, probate and trust law sect. 1969-75), Am., 10th Jud. Circuit bar assns., Frostproof C. of C. (pres. 1960-62). Author: The Great Commandment and the Royal Law, 1963. Office: PO Box 697 Frostproof FL 33843 Tel (813) 635-4894

HIGGINS, HAROLD L., JR., b. Neptune, N.J., June 17, 1947; A.B., Brown U., 1969; J.D., Vanderbilt U., 1969. Admitted to Ariz. bar, 1972; dep. county atty. Pima County (Ariz.), 1972—. Active Big Bros. of Tucson, 1972-76. Office: 111 W Congress St Tucson AZ 85701 Tel (602) 792-8986

HIGGINS, JAMES CONWAY, b. Beckley, W.Va., Jan. 22, 1930; B.S.C., U. Notre Dame, 1952, J.D., 1955. Admitted to W.Va. bar, 1956; individual practice law, Beckley, 1956-58; mem. firm Higgins & Gorman, Beckley, 1958—; lectr. W.Va. Tax Inst., Parkersburg. Mem. Beckley Police CSC, 1962—; bd. dirs. YMCA, 1972-76; active local council Boy Scouts Am., 1968-76. Mem. Am., W.Va., Raleigh County bar assns. Home: 1400 Hakner Rd Beckley WV 25801 Office: 112 Professional Park Beckley WV 25801 Tel (304) 252-5321

HIGGINS, MICHAEL HAROLD, b. Bloomfield, N.J., July 20, 1898; M.B.A., Rutgers U., 1919; grad. Columbia Law Sch., 1922. Admitted to N.J. bar, 1922; mem. firm Higgins and Tailfello, Newark, 1926-28; pres. Bloomfield Savings Bank, 1946-73, chmn. bd., 1973—. Pres. bd. Bloomfield (N.J.) Pub. Library, 1930-40. Mem. Essex County Bar Assn. Home: 30 Heller Dr Upper Montclair NJ 07043 Office: 11 Broad St Bloomfield NJ 07003 Tel (201) 743-5000

HIGGINS, MICHAEL JOSEPH, b. Chgo., June 25, 1945; B.A., U. Notre Dame, 1967; J.D., John Marshall Law Sch., 1972. Admitted to Ill. bar, 1972; atty 0.S. Dept. Justice, Washington, 1973-74; atty. Office of U.S. Atty., Chgo., 1974-76; 1st. asst. states atty. DuPage County (Ill.), Wheaton, 1976—. Mem. Am., Ill., Chgo., DuPage County bar assns., Nat. Dist. Attys. Assn. Recipient Spl. Commendation award Dept. Justice, 1975. Office: 207 Reber St Wheaton IL 60187 Tel (312) 682-7050

HIGGINS, THOMAS JOSEPH, b. N.Y.C., Sept. 2, 1921; A.B., Fordham Coll., 1943, J.D., 1948. Admitted to N.Y. bar, 1957, U.S. Supreme Ct. bar, 1969; spl. agt. FBI, N.Y.C., 1946-48; v.p. Olympic Parking Service, N.Y.C., 1957—; counsel United Transp. Union, L.I. R.R.; lectr. Xavier Labor Inst. Mem. Nassau County Ethics Com., 1961—; commr. Boy Scouts Am., 1957-61. Mem. Am., N.Y. State, Nassau County bar assns., Fed. Bar Council, Delta Theta Phi. Home: 4 Fairview Ave East Williston NY 11596 Office: One Old Country Rd Carle Place NY 11514 Tel (516) 741-4455

HIGGINS, TIMOTHY RAYMOND, b. Evergreen Park, Ill., Nov. 30, 1941; B.B.S., Tulane U., 1967, J.D., 1972. Admitted to La. bar, 1972, Ga. bar, 1972; asso. firm James H. Morrison, Hammond, La., 1972-73; partner firm Morrison & Higgins, Hammond, 1973—; pub. defender 21st Jud. Dist. Ct., 1975-76; sr. intern La. Dept. Justice, New Orleans, 1971-72. Address: 106 N Cypress St Hammond LA 70401 Tel (504) 345-8300

HIGGS, A. JAMES, JR., b. Paducah, Ky., Apr. 17, 1936. J.D. with distinction, U. Ky., 1967. Admitted to Ky. bar, 1968; practiced in Frankfurt, Ky., 1968—; judge Frankfort City Ct., 1969, 74—; city atty. City of Frankfurt, 1972-74. Mem. Ky., Franklin County (Ky.) bar assns., Order of Coif, Omicron Delta Kappa. Office: 403 McClure Bldg Frankfort KY 40601 Tel (502) 227-2750

HIGHERS, ALAN EDWARD, b. Muskogee, Okla., July 5, 1937; A.A., Freed-Hardeman Coll., 1957; B.A., David Lipscomb Coll., 1963; J.D., Memphis State U., 1968. Admitted to Tenn. bar, 1968; asso. firm Gerber & Gerber, Memphis, 1968-71; asso. firm Neely, Green & Fargarson, Memphis, 1971-72; chief referee Memphis and Shelby County Juvenile Ct., 1972-76; judge Div. I 15th Jud. Circuit Tenn., 1977—; lectr. Memphis State U. Mem. Tenn., Nat. councils juvenile ct. judges. Recipient Distinguished Alumnus award Freed-Hardeman Coll., 1974. Office: Shelby County Courthouse 140 Adams St Memphis TN 38105 Tel (901) 528-3022

HIGHLAND, CECIL BLAINE, JR., b. New Martinsville, W.Va., Nov. 23, 1918; A.B., W.Va. U., 1939; J.D. magna cum laude, Harvard, 1949. Admitted to W.Va. bar, 1949; partner firm McWhorter, McNeer, Highland & McMunn, and predecessors, Clarksburg, W.Va., 1949—; asst. prof. law W.Va. U., 1949-55. Mem. Am., W.Va., Harrison County (W.Va.) bar assns., W.Va. State Bar. Office: Empire Nat Bank Bldg Clarksburg WV 26301 Tel (304) 622-0591

HIGHSAW, JAMES LEONARD, JR., b. Memphis, Tenn., Jan. 6, 1914; A.B., Princeton U.; J.D., Harvard U., 1941. Admitted to Tenn. bar, 1940, D.C. bar, 1954; atty. Fed. Home Loan Bank Bd., Washington, D.C., 1941-44; atty. Civil Aero. Bd., Washington, D.C., 1944-55; asso. firm Mulholland, Hickey, & Lyman, Washington, D.C., 1955-58, partner 1958-69; sr. partner firm Highsaw & Mahoney, 1970-76; sr. partner firm Highsaw, Mahoney & Friedman, Washington, D.C., 1976—; chief carrier relationship div. CAB, 1947-51, chief litigation and research, 1951-55. Chmn. city Drummond (Md.) City Govt., 1968-76. Mem. D.C., Fed., Am. bar assns., Phi Beta Kappa. Contbr. articles on transportation law and civil rights to legal jours. Home: 4601 Drummond Ave Chevy Chase MD 20015 Office: 1050 17th St NW Washington DC 20036 Tel (202) 296-8500

HIGHT, B. BOYD, b. Lumberton, N.C., Feb. 15, 1939; B.A., Duke U., 1960; LL.B., Yale U., 1966; diploma in comparative law, U. Stockholm, 1967. Admitted to Calif. bar, 1967; asso. firm O'Melveny & Myers, Los Angeles, 1966-74, partner 1974—; trustee Lawyers Com. for Civil Rights Under Law, 1976—. Exec. sec. Los Angeles Com. Fgn. Relations, 1969-74. Mem. Am. (adv. com. to standing com. on aero. law 1975), Calif. State, Los Angeles County bar assns. Home: 479 Mesa Rd Santa Monica CA 90402 Office: 611 W 6th St Los Angeles CA 90017 Tel (213) 620-1120

HIGINBOTHAM, GEORGE RANDALL, b. Somerset, Pa., Apr. 23, 1941; B.A., Tulane U., 1964, J.D., 1970. Admitted to W.Va. bar, 1970, La. bar, 1970; atty. New Orleans Legal Assistance Corp., 1970-72, Appalachian Research & Def. Fund, Inc., Charleston, W.Va., 1972-73; partner firm Higinbotham, Jones & Higinbotham, Fairmont, W.Va., 1973—; city atty. City of Fairmont, 1975-76. Bd. dirs. W.Va. Legal Service Plan Inc., N. Central Legal Aid Soc., Family Services of Marion and Harrison County, Inc., Marion County Sr. Aides program, Appalachian Research and Def. Fund Inc. Mem. Am., W.Va. bar assns. Home: 923 Farms Dr Fairmont WV 26554 Office: PO Box 567 Fairmont WV 26554 Tel (304) 366-2900

HILBORN, WALTER STERN, b. Boston, Sept. 11, 1879; A.B., Harvard U., 1901, J.D., 1903. Admitted to Mass. bar, 1903, N.Y. bar, 1906, Calif. bar, 1929; asso. firm Brandies, Dunbar & Nutter, and predecessors, Boston, 1903-05; partner firm Gallert, Hilborn & Raphael, N.Y.C., 1905-23; asso. firm Loeb & Loeb, Los Angeles, 1933-41, partner, 1941—. Pres., trustee, life mem. Jewish Fedn. Council Greater Los Angeles, 1931—; pres., life trustee Am. Jewish Com., 1943—; pres., hon. pres., life trustee Reiss-David Child Study Center, Los Angeles, 1950—; chmn., hon. chmn. Los Angeles chpt. Am. Jewish Com., 1950—. Mem. Bar Assn. City N.Y., Los Angeles County Bar Assn. Author: (with Gallert and May) Small Loan Legislation. Home: 716 N Alpine Dr Beverly Hills CA 90210 Office: Loeb & Loeb One Wilshire Bldg #1600 Los Angeles CA 90017 Tel (213) 629-0286

HILBRECHT, NORMAN TY, b. San Diego, Feb. 11, 1933; B.A., Northwestern U., 1956; J.D., Yale, 1959. Admitted to Nev. bar, 1959, U.S. Supreme Ct. bar, 1963; asso. firm Jones, Wiener & Jones, Las Vegas, Nev., 1959-61; asso. counsel Union Pacific R.R., Las Vegas, 1962; partner firm Ruymann, Hilbrecht & Jones, Las Vegas, 1963-66; pres. Hilbrecht, Jones, Schreck & Bybee, and predecessors, Las Vegas, 1966—; pres. Clark County Legal Aid, 1965; mem. Nev. State Assembly, 1966-73, minority leader, 1971; mem. Nev. Senate, 1974—. Pres. Clark County Law Library Bd., 1964-67. Mem. Am. Judicature Soc., Am., Nev., Clark County bar assns., Am. Trial Lawyers Assn. Contbr. articles to profl. jours. Home: 8601 S Mohawk St Las Vegas NV 89118 Office: 600 E Charleston Blvd Las Vegas NV 89104 Tel (702) 382-2101

HILBUN, BENJAMIN FRANKLIN, JR., b. Starkville, Miss., Aug. 20, 1934; B.S., Miss. State U., M.S., 1955; LL.B., U. Miss., 1960. Admitted to Miss. bar; individual practice law, Starkville; mem. Miss Senate, 1960-68. Mem. Miss. Bldg. Commn., 1960-66. Mem. Oktibbeha County (Miss.), Miss. State bar assns., Miss., Am. trial lawyers assns., C. of C. (dir.). Home and Office: PO Box 848 Starkville MS 39759 Tel (601) 323-3622

HILBURN, JAMES V., b. Dublin, Ga., Aug. 10, 1944; A.B., Fla. State U., 1966; J.D., Mercer U., 1969. Admitted to Ga. bar, 1969; partner firm Jones, Jones & Hilburn, Dublin; city atty. City of Dublin, 1973—; mem. legal adv. council Ga. State Bd. Workmen's Compensation. Mem. Am., Ga., Dublin bar assns., Ga. Trial Lawyers Assn. Office: 205 N Franklin St PO Box 218 Dublin GA 31021 Tel (912) 272-7933

HILBY, GERALD MAURICE, b. Spokane, Wash., Mar. 27, 1929; B.A., Wash. State U., 1952; J.D., Loyola U., Los Angeles, 1960. Admitted to Calif. bar, 1960; pub. defender Los Angeles County, 1960-61; asso. firm Cadoo & Tretheway, Inglewood, Calif., 1961; individual practice law, Redondo Beach, Calif., 1961—; judge pro tem Inglewood, S. Bay (Calif.) municipal cts., 1969—; dist. atty's. adv. council Los Angeles County, 1973—. Trustee El Camino Coll., Torrance, Calif., 1973—, S. Bay Union High Sch. Dist., 1971-73; mem. environ. control com. Los Angeles County, 1970-72, beach adv. com., 1973—; mem. planning commn. Manhattan Beach (Calif.), 1970-71, chmn. bd. zoning adjustment, 1972; coordinating council Redondo Beach, 1975—; bd. dirs. Alcoholism Council S. Bay, 1975—; bd. mgrs. S. Bay YMCA, 1971-72. Mem. Los Angeles County, S. Bay (dir.) bar assns., S.W. Criminal Bar Assn. (trustee), Redondo Beach C. of C. (pres. 1971-72). Home: 3504 The Strand St Manhattan Beach CA 90266 Office: 1611 S Pacific Coast Hwy Redondo Beach CA 90277 Tel (213) 540-1100

HILDEBRAND, DANIEL WALTER, b. Oshkosh, Wis., May 1, 1940; B.S., U. Wis., 1962, LL.B., 1964. Admitted to Wis. bar, 1964, N.Y. bar, 1965, U.S. Supreme Ct. bar, 1970; asso. firm Willkie Farr & Gallagher, N.Y.C., 1965-68; partner firm Ross & Stevens, Madison, Wis., 1968—; lectr. U. Wis. Law Sch. Pub. mem. Wis. Legis. Joint Survey Com. on Tax Exemptions, 1973—. Mem. State Bar Wis., N.Y. State Bar Assn. Home: 5725 Hempstead Rd Madison WI 53711 Office: 1 S Pinckney St Madison WI 53703 Tel (608) 257-5353

HILDER, FRAZER F., b. 1912; B.S., U. Mich., 1912; grad. George Washington U. Law Sch. With firm Kittelle, Sawyer & Lamb and successors, 1945-56; with Gen. Motors Corp., 1956—, asst. gen. counsel, 1967-73, asso. gen. counsel, 1973-74, v.p., gen. counsel, N.Y.C., 1974—. Office: Gen Motors Corp 767 Fifth Ave New York City NY 10022*

HILDRETH, RICHARD GEORGE, b. Hollywood Beach, Fla., Oct. 11, 1943; B.S.E. in Physics, U. Mich., 1965, J.D., 1968; diploma in law Oxford (Eng.) U., 1969, U. Stockholm, 1973. Admitted to Calif. bar, 1969; asso. firm Steinhart Law Firm, San Francisco, 1969-72; asso. prof. law U. San Diego, 1973—; mem. Calif. Bar Comml. Code Com., 1972-76; mem. Calif. Atty. Gen.'s Environ. Task Force for Orange and San Diego Counties, 1974—. Mem. Am. Bar Assn. Office: U of San Diego Sch of Law San Diego CA 92110 Tel (714) 291-6480

HILFIKER, HERMAN MAX, b. Piggott, Ark., Apr. 7, 1944; student U. Tex.; B.S., S.E. Mo. State Coll., 1971; J.D., S. Tex. Coll., 1974. Admitted to Mo. bar, 1974; asso. firm Edward F. O'Herin, Malden, Mo., 1974-75; individual practice law, Malden, 1975—; asst. pros. atty. Dunklin County (Mo.), 1975—. Mem. Am., Mo., Dunklin County bar assns., Mo. Pros. Attys. Assn. Home: 707 Dorothy Dr Malden MO 63863 Office: Box 266 Malden MO 63863 Tel (314) 276-2420

HILGENDORF, HOWARD WILLIAM, b. Juneau, Wis., Aug. 20, 1914; B.A., U. Wis., 1937, LL.B., 1938. Admitted to Wis. bar, 1938; practiced in Juneau, Wis., 1938-42; asst. U.S. atty. Eastern Dist. Wis., 1946-59; judge U.S. Bankruptcy Ct., Eastern Dist. Wis., 1959—. Mem. Nat. Conf. Bankruptcy Judges. Home: 5627 N Bay Ridge Ave Milwaukee WI 53217 Office: 517 E Wisconsin Ave Milwaukee WI 53202 Tel (414) 224-3291

HILL, ALFRED, b. N.Y.C., Nov. 7, 1917; B.S. in Social Sci., City Coll. N.Y., 1937; LL.B., Bklyn. Law Sch., 1941; S.J.D., Harvard, 1957. Admitted to N.Y. State bar, 1943, Ill. bar, 1958; various legal and adminstrv. positions with SEC, 1943-52; prof. law So. Meth. U., Dallas, 1953-56; prof. law Northwestern U., Chgo., 1956-62; prof. law Columbia, 1962—, Simon H. Rifkind, prof. law, 1975—. Mem. Am. Law Inst. Contbr. articles to profl. jours. Home: 152 Highwood Ave Tenafly NJ 07670 Office: Columbia Law Sch New York City NY 10027 Tel (212) 280-2620

HILL, ANDREW JUDSON, JR., b. Auburn, Ala., Aug. 8, 1926; student West Ga. Coll., 1946-47; J.D., U. Ga., 1950. Admitted to Ga. bar, 1951; asso. firm Crawford & Co., Atlanta, 1951-53; individual practice law, Lavonia, Ga., 1953—; atty. Franklin County (Ga.), 1958-68; city atty. City of Lavonia, 1964-74, 76—; Mem. No. Circuit (pres. 1966-67), Am. bar assns., State Bar Ga. (gov. 1964-68), Am., Ga. (v.p. 1974—) trial lawyers assns. Home: 119 Grogan St Lavonia GA 30553 Office: 110 Vickery St Lavonia GA 30553 Tel (404) 356-4010

HILL, BOBBY L., b. Athens, Ga.; B.S., Savannah State Coll., 1963; J.D., Howard U., 1966. Admitted to Ga. bar, 1967; sr. partner firm Hill, Jones & Farrington, Atlanta and Savannah; mem. Ga. Ho. of Reps., 1968—. Cooperating counsel NAACP Legal Def. Fund.; bd. dirs. Nat. Assembly Social Policy and Devel.; mem. Chatham County Citizens' Adv. Com. Community Improvement and Urban Renewal. Mem. Am., Ga., Savannah bar assns., Savannah C. of C., ACLU, Am. Trial Lawyers Assn. Office: 208 E 34th St Savannah GA 31401 Tel (912) 233-7728

HILL, EARL WESLEY, b. Mason City, Iowa, May 6, 1946; student Bob Jones U., 1964-66; B.A. in Polit. Sci., U. Mich., 1968; postgrad. Penn Valley Community Coll., 1969-70; J.D., Detroit Coll. Law, 1973. Admitted to Iowa bar, 1973; partner firm Buck & Hill, Britt, Iowa, 1973—; jud. magistrate Winnebago County (Iowa), 1973-74. Mem. Iowa, Am., Hancock County (Iowa) (pres. 1975—) bar assns. Home: 62 3d Ave SW Britt IA 50423 Office: 95 Main Ave S Britt IA 50423 Tel (515) 843-3873

HILL, EARL WHITE, b. Sylvania, Ga., Nov. 25, 1905; B. Ph., Emory U., 1927; J.D., George Washington U., 1938. Admitted to D.C. Bar, 1938, Ga., bar, 1945; dept. head Inter-Southern Life Ins. Co., Louisville, Ky., 1927-33; dept. head, asst. to gen. counsel Acacia Mutual Life Ins. Co. Washington, 1933-45; individual practice law, Sylvania, Ga., 1945—; solicitor City Ct. Sylvania, Ga., 1953-65; judge State Ct. Screven County, Ga., 1965-77. Mem. Am., Ga. Bar Assns. Rotary Club, Masons., Phi Delta Phi. Home: 202 Curtis Sylvania GA 30467 Office: PO Box 286 Sylvania GA 30467 Tel (912) 564-2631

HILL, GEORGE RICHARDS, b. Towanda, Pa., Oct. 2, 1920; A.A., George Washington U., 1947, LL.B., 1949, J.D., 1971. Admitted to D.C. bar, 1949, Pa. bar, 1951, Calif. bar, 1963, U.S. Supreme Ct. bar, 1971; atty., advisor U.S. Nat. Security Agy., Wash., D.C., 1950-56; subcontract advisor Hughes Aircraft Co., El Segundo, Calif., 1956-58, 65-68; contract adminstrn. Lockheed Aircraft Service, Inc., Ontario, Calif., 1958-60, Aerojet-Gen. Corp., Azusa, Calif., 1960-62, Autonetics div. N.Am. Aviation, Inc., 1962-64, Collins Radio Co., Newport Beach, Calif., 1964-65; asst. co. counsel McDonnel Douglas Corp., Long Beach, Calif., 1968—. Fellow Nat. Contract Mgmt. Assn. (former nat. mem. (sect. vice chmn.), dir. local chpt., pres.); mem. Fed. (pres. local chpt.), Calif., Internat. bar assns. Home: 6982 Church Circle Huntington Beach CA 92648 Office: 3855 Lakewood Blvd Long Beach CA 90846 Tel (213) 593-5118

HILL, GEORGE ROULAND, b. Globe, Ariz., Oct. 15, 1931; J.D., U. Ariz., Tucson, 1955. Admitted to Ariz. bar, 1955, Calif. bar, 1956; partner firm Shimmel, Hill, Bishop & Gruender, Phoenix, 1957—, mng. partner, 1963-70, pres., 1970-71, 73-74; spl. counsel Ariz. Legislature, 1965-66. Chmn. Phoenix Hist. Commn.; pres. Phoenix Legal Aid Soc. Mem. Am., Maricopa County bar assns., Ariz. State Bar (past chmn. com. on legis.). Home: 2932 W Manor Dr Phoenix AZ 85014 Office: 111 W Monroe St Phoenix AZ 85003 Tel (602) 257-5500

HILL, GEORGE RUSSELL, b. Ft. Knox, Ky., Jan. 14, 1947; B.A. in Econs., U. Tex., 1969, J.D., 1972. Admitted to Tex. bar, 1972; mem. firm Scott, Hulse, Marshall & Feuille, El Paso, Tex., 1972—; profl. commentator El Paso Estate Planning Council, 1976—. Mem. Am., Tex., El Paso County bar assns., Phi Beta Kappa, Phi Delta Phi. Home: 3960 Las Vegas St El Paso TX 79902 Office: El Paso National Bank Bldg El Paso TX 79901 Tel (915) 533-2493

HILL, HARRY GERALD, b. Bklyn., Dec. 26, 1900; B.M.E., N.Y. U., 1923; LL.B., St. John's U., 1928, LL.M., 1929, LL.D. (hon.), 1943. Admitted to N.Y. bar, 1930, U.S. Supreme Ct. bar, 1964; asso. firm Cullen and Dykman, Bklyn., 1929-40, partner, 1941—; gen. counsel Todd Shipyards Corp., N.Y.C., 1946-75, exec. v.p., 1953-75, also dir. Mem. Am., N.Y. State, Bklyn. bar assns., Am. Judicature Soc., N.Y. State Trial Lawyers Assn., Bklyn. Manhattan Trial Counsel Assn. Recipient Certificate of Commendation, U.S. Navy, 1947. Home: 175 Kensington Rd Garden City NY 11530 Office: 177 Montague St Brooklyn NY 11201 Tel (212) 855-9000

HILL, JEROME, IV, b. Jerome, Idaho, Feb. 15, 1937; B.S. in Commerce with honors, Washington and Lee U., 1957; LL.B., U. Tex., Austin, 1961, J.D., 1969; diploma Ruprecht Karl, Heidelberg, Germany, 1968. Admitted to Tex. bar, 1962; individual practice law, Austin, 1962-63, 67—; v.p. fiscal and legal affairs Student Travel, Inc., 1967-68, chief corp. counsel, U.S. and Western Europe, 1968-70. Speaker, James Stephen Hogg Soc., Austin, 1968-70. Mem. Tex. State Bar, Kappa Sigma, Phi Eta Sigma, Pi Sigma Alpha, Kappa Delta Pi. Contbr. articles to legal jours. Office: 1803 Sylvan Dr Austin TX 78741

HILL, JERRY MERL, b. Abilene, Kans., Nov. 5, 1942; B.A., Kan. State U., 1964; J.D., U. Mo., Columbia, 1966. Admitted to Calif. bar, 1967, U.S. Supreme Ct. bar, 1976; dep. dist. atty. County of Los Angeles, 1967-69; asso. firm Cox, Castle, Nicholson & Weekes and predecessor, Los Angeles, 1970-74, partner, 1974—; judge pro tem Beverly Hills (Calif.) Municipal Ct. Mem. Los Angeles County Central Democratic Com., 1968-70. Mem. Am., Los Angeles County, Beverly Hills, Century City bar assns., Assn. Bus. Trial Lawyers. Office: 2049 Century Park E 28th Floor Los Angeles CA 90067 Tel (213) 277-4222

HILL, JESSE WATSON, b. Americus, Ga., Apr. 21, 1948; A.B. in Econs., Duke U., 1970; J.D., Vanderbilt U., 1973. Admitted to Ga. bar, 1973; asso. firm Powell, Goldstein, Frazer & Murphy, Atlanta, 1973—. Mem. Am., Ga., Atlanta bar assns., Atlanta Council of Younger Lawyers (dir. 1976—). Office: 1100 C & S Nat Bank Bldg Atlanta GA 30303 Tel (404) 521-1900

HILL, JOHN EDWARD, b. Urbana, Ill., Nov. 23, 1940; A.B., U. Ill., 1962; J.D., U. Chgo., 1969. Admitted to Calif. bar, 1970; asso. firm Belli, Ashe, Ellison, Choulos and Lieff, San Francisco, 1969-73; individual practice law, San Francisco, 1974; partner firm Hill & Hansen, San Francisco, 1975—. Mem. Am., San Francisco bar assns., Calif., San Francisco, Am. assns. trial lawyers. Home: 171 Solano St Tiburon CA 94920 Office: 722 Montgomery St San Francisco CA 94111 Tel (415) 398-2434

HILL, JOHN LUKE, b. Breckenridge, Tex., Oct. 9, 1923; student Kilgore Jr. Coll.; LL.B., U. Tex. at Austin, 1947. Individual practice law; sec. state Tex., 1966-68; atty. gen. Tex., Austin, 1973—. Bd. dirs. Girlstown U.S.A., Young Life. Recipient Gold medal as U.S. lawyer contbg. most to law sci. movement Law Sch. Acad., 1960. Fellow Am. Coll. Trial Lawyers, Internat. Acad. Trial Lawyers, Tex. Bar Found.; mem. Nat. Coll. Dist. Attys. (bd. regents). Office: Office Attorney Gen Supreme Court Bldg Austin TX 78711*

HILL, JON HURD, b. Okolona, Miss., Jan. 5, 1940; B.S., Miss. State U., 1962; J.D., U. Miss., 1970. Admitted to Miss. bar, 1970; estate tax atty. IRS, Jackson, Miss., 1970-72; v.p., trust officer Security Bank, Corinth, Miss., 1972—. Mem. Akron County, Miss., Am. bar assns., Miss., Am. bankers assns., Corinth C. of C. Office: 601 Fillmore St Corinth MS 38834

HILL, LEO HOWARD, b. Greenville, S.C., May 26, 1927; B.A., Erskine Coll., 1949; J.D., U. S.C., 1952. Admitted to S.C. bar, 1952, since practiced in Greenville; partner firm Hill, Wyatt & Fayssoux; city atty. City of Greer (S.C.), 1963—; chmn. com. establishment Legal Aid Agy. in Greenville County, also Greenville County Pub. Defender Office; mem. S.C. Jud. Council, 1968. Mem. Greenville County, S.C. (pres. 1968-69), Am. (lawyers referral com. 1973-76) bar assns., Am. Trial Lawyers Assn., S.C. Assn. City Attys., Nat. Conf. Bar Pres.'s, Nat. Inst. Municipal Law Officers, S.C. Def. Lawyers Assn., Am. Judicature Soc., Jud. Conf. 4th Circuit Ct. Appeals, Phi Delta Phi. Home: 28 Montrose Dr Greenville SC 29607 Office: PO Box 2585 Greenville SC 29602 Tel (803) 242-5133

HILL, LOUIS G., b. Palm Beach, Fla., Mar. 10, 1924; B.S., Harvard U., 1944; LL.B., U. Pa., 1948. Admitted to Pa. bar, 1950; partner firm Dilworth, Paxson, Kalish & Levy, Phila., 1957—; mem. Pa. Senate, 1967—, chmn. judiciary com., 1970—. Mem. Pa. Bd. Pub. Welfare, 1968-70; bd. mgrs. St. Christopher's Hosp. for Children; bd. dirs. Pa. Pub. TV; trustee Episcopal Acad.; bd. mgrs. Overbrook Sch. for Blind. Mem. Phila., Am. bar assns. Home: 6610 Wissahickon Ave Philadelphia PA 19119 Office: 2600 Fidelity Bldg Philadelphia PA 19109 Tel (205) 546-3000

HILL, MILTON KING, b. Balt., Nov. 29, 1926; B.S., U. Md., 1950, LL.B., 1952. Admitted to Md. bar, 1952; asso. firm Smith, Somerville & Case, and predecessor, Balt., 1952-56, partner, 1956—; chmn. Md. Commrs. Uniform State Laws, 1959—; mem. Md. Trial Cts. Jud. Nominating Commn., 1974—. Bd. dirs. Union Meml. Hosp., Balt. Fellow Internat. Soc. Barristers, Am. Coll. Trial Lawyers; mem. Am. (vice chmn. automobile law 1971-76), Md. State (chmn. medico-legal com. 1975—) bar assns., Def. Research Inst. (chmn. legis. com.), Internat. Assn. Ins. Counsel, Nat. Conf. Commrs. on Uniform State Laws (exec. com. 1973-75), Assn. Def. Trial Counsel (pres. 1964-65). Office: 1700 One Charles Center Baltimore MD 21201 Tel (301) 727-1164

HILL, SHERMAN RUSSELL, b. Alexandria, S.D., Mar. 15, 1905; J.D., George Washington U., 1929. Admitted to Calif. bar, 1936; field atty. FTC, San Francisco, 1934-52, rev. atty., Washington, 1952-54, chief project atty., 1954-58, dir. Bur. Investigations, 1958-61, asst. to gen. counsel, 1961-63; dept. legal counsel Gen. Electric Co., Bridgeport, Conn., 1963-70. Bd. dirs., sec. 3d Laguna Hills Corp., Laguna Hills, Calif., 1976—. Mem. Phi Delta Phi. Recipient distinguished service award FTC, 1963. Home: 2203 A Via Mariposa E Laguna Hills CA 92653 Tel (714) 830-7757

HILL, THOMAS BOWEN, JR., b. Montgomery, Ala., Nov. 11, 1903; A.B., U. Ala., 1922. LL.B., 1924. Admitted to Ala. bar, 1924; asso. prof. German, U. Ala., 1923-24; sr. mem. firm Hill, Hill, Carter, Franco, Cole & Black, Montgomery, 1977—; chmn. bd. dirs. Union Bank & Trust Co., Montgomery, 1954-76. Chmn. ARC, Montgomery, 1945; bd. dirs. Children's Protective Home of Montgomery, 1954-56, Montgomery YMCA. Mem. Am. Judicature Soc., Am. Coll. Trial Lawyers, Internat. Acad. Trial Lawyers, Am. Bar Found., Farrah Law Soc., Am., Ala. bar assns., Ala. State Bar (v.p. 1951-52, pres. 1952-53, bd. commrs. 1953-77, chmn. com. on continuing legal edn., 1953-55), Montgomery County Bar Assn., Phi Beta Kappa, Phi Alpha Delta. Elected to Ala. Acad. of Honor, 1977. Office: Hill Bldg Montgomery AL 36101 Tel (205) 834-7600

HILL, THOMAS HOWARD, b. Austin, Tex., May 1, 1944; B.A., U. Tex., Austin, 1966, J.D., 1969. Admitted to Tex. bar, 1969, U.S. Dist. Ct. bar for So. Dist. Tex., 1970, U.S. Ct. Mil. Appeals bar, 1972; briefing atty. Tex. Supreme Ct., Austin, 1969-70; asso. firm Anderson, Smith, Null & Stofer, Victoria, Tex., 1970-76; hearing examiner Tex. R.R. Commn. gas utilities div., Austin, 1976—. Bd. dirs. Victoria Boys Club, 1972-76, v.p., 1975; bd. dirs. Youth Home of Victoria, 1972-76, pres., 1976; bd. dirs. Victoria County United Way, 1974-76; mem. Victoria Parks Commn., 1975-76; lay reader St. Matthews Episcopal Ch., Austin, 1976. Mem. State Bar Tex. Home: 7908 Ceberry Dr Austin TX 78759 Office: 326 Brown Bldg POB 12967 Austin TX 78711 Tel (512) 475-2747

HILL, WILLIAM CHARLES, b. Newark, May 10, 1917; A.B., N.Y. U., 1939, J.D., 1941; M.A., U. Vt., 1969. Admitted to N.Y. bar, 1942, Vt. bar, 1947; practiced in Burlington, Vt., 1946-58; judge Vt. Superior Ct., 1959—, chief judge, 1972—, asso. justice, 1976—, mem. Vt. Ho. of Reps., 1953, 57, 59. Mem. Am. Bar Assn., Am. Judicature Soc. Recipient Vt. Essay Contest prize Vt. Bar Assn., 1969; pub. Vt. Hist. Quar., 1971. Tel (802) 453-2839

HILL, WILLIAM EMMETT, b. New Orleans, Jan 25, 1950; B.A., Tulane U., 1970; J.D., Duke, 1973; LL.M., Georgetown U., 1974. Admitted to La. bar, 1973; asso. firm Schumacher, McGlinchey, Stafford & Mintz, New Orleans, 1974-75; asst. chief counsel for enforcement Food and Drug div. Office Gen. Counsel, HEW, Rockville, Md., 1975—. Mem. La. Bar Assn. Home: 2014 Baltimore Rd Rockville MD 20851 Office: 5600 Fishers Ln Rockville MD 20852

HILL, WILLIAM MURRAY, b. Montgomery, Ala., June 22, 1919; LL.B., Calif. Western U., 1950. Admitted to Calif. bar, 1952; individual practice law San Diego, 1952—; lectr. Western State U., 1971—. Recipient Literary Award, San Diego County Bar Assn. Tel (714) 297-0119

HILL, WILLIAM TEMPLE, JR., b. Denison, Tex., Aug. 11, 1942; B.B.A., So. Meth. U., 1964, J.D., 1967. Admitted to Tex. bar, 1967; asst. dist. atty., chief felony prosecutor, Dallas County (Tex.) Dist. Attys. Office, 1967-73; asso. firm Jordan, Ramsey, and Hill, Dallas, 1973—. Mem. Tex. Criminal Def. Lawyers Assn., Am., Tex., Dallas bar assns. Office: Jordan Ramsey Hill 2001 Bryan Tower Dallas TX 75201 Tel (214) 651-1919

HILL, WILMER BAILEY, b. Washington, May 18, 1928; A.B., Dartmouth, 1950; J.D., Georgetown U., 1953. Admitted to D.C. bar, 1956, U.S. Dist. Ct. bar, 1956, U.S. Ct. Claims bar, 1956, U.S. Supreme Ct. bar, 1973, U.S. Ct. Mil. Appeals bar, 1956; asso. firm Ames, Hill & Ames, Washington, 1956-59, partner, 1959-73, sec.-treas., 1973—. Vice pres. Brookdale Citizens Assn., Chevy Chase, Md., 1975-76. Mem. Am., D.C., Fed. bar assns., Motor Carrier Lawyers Assn., Delta Theta Phi. Home: 5016 Westport Rd Chevy Chase MD 20015 Office: 666 11th St NW Washington DC 20001 Tel (202) 628-9243

HILLER, MORTON BROWNE, b. Harlingen, Tex., June 22, 1931; B.A., Idaho State Coll., 1954; LL.B., U. Idaho, 1956. Admitted to Idaho bar, 1957; atty. govt. contracts dept. Westinghouse Electric Corp., Idaho Falls, Idaho, 1958-63; mem. firm St. Clair, St. Clair, Hiller, Benjamin & Wood, Chartered, Idaho Falls, 1963—; city atty. City of Arco (Idaho), 1957-58. Mem. 7th Jud. Dist. (past pres.), Am. bar assns., Idaho State Bar, Assn. Trial Lawyers Am., Idaho Assn. Def. Counsel (dir.), Bench and Bar. Office: 1st Security Bank Bldg POB 29 Idaho Falls ID 83401 Tel (203) 522-2350

HILLES, HENRY SMEDLEY, JR., b. Phila., July 25, 1939; B.A., Wesleyan U., Middletown, Conn., 1961; LL.B., U. Pa., 1964. Admitted to Pa. Supreme Ct. bar, 1965; asso. firm Drinker Biddle & Reath, Phila., 1964-70, partner, 1970—; sec. INA Investment Securities, Inc., Phila., 1973—; dir. Mary MacIntosh Services, Inc., Allentown, Pa., 1975—. Mem. Am., Pa., Phila. bar assns., Order of Coif, Phi Beta Kappa. Home: 219 W Allens Ln Philadelphia PA 19119 Office: 1100 Phila Nat Bank Bldg Philadelphia PA 19107 Tel (215) 491-7328

HILLIARD, DAVID CRAIG, b. Framingham, Mass., May 22, 1937; B.S., Tufts U., 1959; J.D., U. Chgo., 1962. Admitted to Ill. bar, 1962, U.S. Supreme Ct. bar 1966; served to lt. JAGC, USN, 1962-66; asso. firm Pattishall, McAuliffe & Hofstetter, Chgo., 1966-71, partner, 1971—; lectr. Northwestern U. Sch. Law, Chgo., 1971—. Pres., Chgo. Planned Parenthood Assn., 1975—; mem. aux. bd. Art Inst. Chgo., 1974—, Econ. Club Chgo., 1975—. Mem. Am., Ill., Chgo. (chmn. young lawyers sect. 1971-72, bd. mgrs. 1973—) bar assns., Am. Judicature Soc., Am., Chgo. (bd. mgrs. 1977—) patent law assns., Legal Club Chgo., Law Club Chgo., Phi Delta Phi. Recipient Maurice Weigle award for outstanding legal service Chgo. Bar Found., 1972. Author: (with Beverly W. Pattishall) Trademarks, Trade Identity and Unfair Trade Practices, 1974. Home: 1320 N State St Chicago IL 60610 Office: 3500 Prudential Plaza Chicago IL 60601 Tel (312) 642-9518

HILLIARD, EARL FREDERICK, b. Birmingham, Ala., Apr. 9, 1942; B.A. in Econs., Morehouse Coll., 1964; M.B.A., Atlanta U., 1970; J.D., Howard U., 1967. Admitted to Ala. bar, 1968; research asst. Howard U., 1965-67; instr. bus. Miles Coll., Birmingham, 1967-68; staff atty. Legal Aid Assn. Jefferson County (Ala.), 1970-72; partner firm Jackson Little & Stansel, Birmingham, 1972—. Mem. Ala. Black Lawyers Assn., Am., Ala. bar assns., Ala. Black Legis. Caucus (chmn.). Home: 1625 Castleberry Way Birmingham AL 35214 Office: PO Box 11385 Birmingham AL 35218 Tel (205) 322-3344

HILLIER, WILLIAM HERBERT, b. Chgo., Nov. 19, 1917; A.B., Washington and Lee U., 1938; J.D., U. Mich., 1941. Admitted to Mich. bar, 1941, Ill. bar, 1941; asso. firm Lord, Bissell & Kadyk, Chgo., 1940-51; partner firm Lord, Bissell & Brook, 1952—. Mem. Dist. 36 Bd. Edn., 1964-72, pres., 1966-72, mem. Dist. 200 Bd. Edn., 1972-74; bd. dirs. Central DuPage Hosp., 1976—; bd. dirs. Beverly Farm Found., Godfrey, Ill., 1964—, chmn., 1967-69, pres., 1973—. Mem. Am., Ill., Chgo. bar assns., Chgo. Law Club, Legal Club Chgo., Fed. Ins. Counsel. Home: 321 W Lincoln Ave Wheaton IL 60187 Office: 115 S LaSalle St Chicago IL 60603 Tel (312) 443-0363

HILLMAN, JORDAN JAY, b. Waukegan, Ill., July 8, 1924; M.A., U. Chgo., 1948, J.D., 1950; S.J.D., Northwestern U., 1965. Admitted to Ill. bar, 1950, U.S. Supreme Ct. bar, 1958; tech., legal advisor Ill. Commerce Commn., Chgo., 1950-53; atty. to v.p. law Chgo. & Northwestern Ry. Co., Chgo., 1954-67; prof. law Northwestern U., Chgo., 1967—; gen. counsel U.S. Ry. Assn., 1975-76, sr. legal cons., 1974-75, spl. counsel, 1976—; mem. Constitution Study Commn., State of Ill., 1965-67, 67-69. Mem. Evanston Zoning Amendment Com., 1963-68. Mem. Am., Chgo. bar assns., Phi Beta Kappa. Author: Competition and Railroad Price Discrimination, 1968; The Parliamentary Structuring of British Road-Rail Freight Coordination, 1973; contbr. articles in field to legal jours. Home: 1024 Lake Shore Blvd Evanston IL 60202 Office: 357 E Chicago Ave Chicago IL 60611 Tel (312) 649-8447

HILLMAN, PEGGY A., b. Evansville, Ind., Dec. 10, 1943; A.B. with honors, U. Mich., 1965; J.D., U. Chgo., 1968. Admitted to Ill. bar, 1968, Mont. bar, 1970; law clk. to Hon. Charles Levin, Mich. Supreme Ct., 1968-69; asso. firm Padgett, Greeley, Marumoto & Akinaka, Honolulu, 1969-70; individual practice law, Plains, Mont., 1970-71; partner firm Cotton, Watt, Jones, King & Bowlus, Chgo., 1972—. Mem. Chgo. Council Lawyers. Contbr. article to legal publ. Office: 1 IBM Plaza Suite 4750 Chicago IL 60611 Tel (312) 467-0590

HILLMAN, RICHARD LAZER, b. Annapolis, Md., Jan. 20, 1943; A.B., Johns Hopkins U., Balt., 1965; J.D., U. Md., 1968. Admitted to Md. bar, 1968, U.S. Supreme Ct. bar, 1974; partner firm Hillman & Hillman, Annapolis, 1970—, also dep. county solicitor Anne Arundel County Office of Law, Annapolis, 1975—; legal counsel Md. Jaycees, 1974-75. Pres. Annapolis Jaycees, 1974-75, regional state dir., 1976-77, senator internat.; mem. Annapolis Planning and Zoning Commn., 1975-76; trustee Annapolis Opera Co., 1974-75. Mem. Am., Md., Anne Arundel County bar assns. Named outstanding young Annapolitan Annapolis Jaycees, 1973. Home: 4 Randall Pl Annapolis MD 21401 Office: PO Box 668 Annapolis MD 21404 Tel (301) 263-3131

HILLMAN, WILLIAM CHERNICK, b. Providence, Oct. 15, 1935; J.D., Boston U., 1957, LL.M., 1968. Admitted to R.I. bar, 1957, U.S. Supreme Ct. bar, 1965; partner firm Strauss, Factor, Chernick & Hillman, and predecessors, Providence, 1957—; judge of probate, Barrington, R.I., 1975—. Mem. Am., R.I., Internat. bar assns., Scribes. Contbr. articles to legal jours. Office: 403 S Main St Providence RI 02903 Tel (401) 274-5440

HILLS, DAVID RUSSELL, b. Independence, Mo., Apr. 25, 1940; B.B.A., U. Mo., 1963, J.D., 1967. Admitted to Kans. bar, 1967; asso. firm Boddington, Brown and Unverferth, Kansas City, Kans., 1967-75; partner firm Harris and Hills, Kansas City, Kans., 1975—. Bd. govs. West Br. YMCA, Kansas City, Kans. Mem. Am., Kans., Wyandotte County bar assns., Kans. Trial Lawyers Assn. Home: 2 Navajo Lake Quivira Kansas City KS 66106 Office: 374 New Brotherhood Bldg 8th and State Ave Kansas City KS 66101 Tel (913) 371-5707

HILLS, GEORGE STROUGH, b. Winter Park, Fla., Nov. 1, 1900; A.B., Ind. U., 1922; LL.B., Harvard U., 1925. Admitted to N.Y. bar, 1926, U.S. Supreme Ct. bar, 1936; partner firm Menken, Ferguson & Hills, N.Y.C., 1930-37; partner firm Rogers, Hoge & Hills, N.Y.C., 1939—; dir. AMF Inc., 1941-72, dir. emeritus 1971—, gen. counsel, 1941-65; dir. Am. Viscose Corp., N.Y.C., 1946-69, gen. counsel, 1960-69; dir., gen. counsel, Bacardi Corp., San Juan, P.R., 1944-76, sec., 1944-74; dir., gen. counsel, Life Savers Corp., N.Y.C., 1950-56; dir. Raymond Internat. Inc., N.Y.C. and Houston, 1961-73; dir., gen. counsel Sterling Drug Inc., N.Y.C., 1940-73, adv. dir., 1973-75, sec., 1946-73, v. chmn., 1960-70. Mem. New Rochelle (N.Y.) Bd. Edn., 1967-70; mem. bd. govs. New Rochelle Hosp. Med. Center, 1959—, sec., 1960-74, pres., 1975-77. Mem. Assn. Bar City N.Y., Am., N.Y. state, Westchester bar assns., Am. Law Inst. Author: Law of Accounting and Financial Statements, 1957; Managing Corporate Meeting-A Legal and Procedural Guide, 1976; contbr. numerous articles to legal jours. Home: 396 Forest Ave New Rochelle NY 10804 Office: 90 Park Ave New York City NY 10016 Tel (212) 953-9204

HILLS, RODERICK M., b. Seattle, Mar. 9, 1931; A.B., Stanford, 1952, LL.B., 1955. Admitted to Calif. bar, 1957, U.S. Supreme Ct. bar, 1950; law clk. to Justice Stanley F. Reed, U.S. Supreme Ct., Washington, 1955-57; partner firm Munger, Tolles, Hills & Richerhauser, Los Angeles, 1962-75; counsel to Pres. U.S., Washington, 1975; chmn. SEC, Washington, 1975-77; lectr. law Stanford, 1960; vis. prof. law Harvard, 1969-70; chmn. bd. Republic Corp., Century City, 1971-75; chmn. research com. Am. Bar Found. Trustee Claremont U. Center. Mem. Am., Los Angeles County bar assns., Order of Coif, Phi Delta Phi. Bd. editors, comment editor Stanford Law Rev., 1953-55. Home: 3125 Chain Bridge Rd Washington DC 20016 Office: 500 N Capitol St Washington DC 20549 Tel (202) 755-1130

HILLS, THOMAS DERRILL, b. Atlanta, Aug. 21, 1944; B.A., Emory U., 1965, J.D., 1970; grad. Dartmouth Sch. Credit and Fin. Mgmt., 1972. Admitted to Ga. bar, 1971; v.p. corporate lending First Nat. Bank of Atlanta, 1965—. Active United Way, Atlanta, 1965, 72, 74-76; mem. exec. com. Atlanta Region Open Housing Coalition, 1971-75; bd. dirs. Atlanta Boy's Club, 1973-75; chmn. advisory council Atlanta Regional Commn., 1973-75. Mem. Atlanta Jr. C. of C. (dir. 1969-76), Atlanta C. of C. (dir. 1972-73), State Bar Ga., Atlanta, Am., Emory Student (v.p. 1969) bar assns., Phi Delta Phi. Home: 1797 Walthall Dr Atlanta GA 30318 Office: PO Box 4148 Atlanta GA 30302 Tel (404) 588-6744

HILLSBERG, RICHARD WARREN, b. N.Y.C., Nov. 26, 1941; B.S., U. Pa., 1963; J.D., Georgetown U., 1966. Admitted to D.C. bar, 1967, N.Y. bar, 1967, Ill. bar, 1971; served with Judge Adv. Gen. Corps, U.S. Army, Ft. Sheridan, Ill., 1967-71; partner firm Brown Fox and Blumberg, Chgo., 1974-76; gen. counsel FAI, Inc., Northfield, Ill., 1976—. Mem. Highland Park (Ill.) Lakefront Commn. Mem. Am., Ill., Chgo, N.Y. bar assns. Office: 480 Central Ave Northfield IL 60093 Tel (312) 441-6500

HILLYARD, LYLE WILLIAM, b. Logan, Utah, Sept. 25, 1940; B.S., Utah State U., 1965; J.D., U. Utah, 1967. Admitted to Utah bar, 1967; partner firm Hillyard, Gunnell & Low, Logan, 1967—; mem. adminstrn. bd. First Dist. Juvenile Ct., 1969-76; examiner Utah State Bar, 1976—. Mem. exec. bd. Cache Valley council Boy Scouts Am., 1969—; chmn. Cache County Republican Party, 1972-77. Mem. Cache County, Utah State, Am. bar assns., Assn. Trial Lawyers Am., Cache C. of C. (dir., pres. 1977). Recipient Distinguished Service award Logan Jaycees, 1972; named One of Three Outstanding Young Men Utah, Utah Jaycees, 1972. Home: 1584 E 1140 N Logan UT 84321 Office: 175 E 1st N Logan UT 84321 Tel (801) 752-2610

HILLYER, WILLIAM HUDSON, b. Dennison, Ohio, July 28, 1928; B.S. in Bus. Adminstrn., Ohio State U., 1950, J.D., 1952. Admitted to Ohio bar, 1953; pres., gen. mgr. Clay City Pipe Co., Uhrichsville, Ohio, 1956-76; partner firm Connolly, Hillyer & Lile, Uhrichsville, 1964—; chmn. Ohio Bd. Bar Examiners, 1976-77. Mem. Ohio Dept. Econ. Devel., 1956-58; chmn. Republican. Exec. Com. of Tuscarawas County, 1966-76; presidential elector, 1976. Mem. Ohio, Tuscarawas County bar assns. Office: 201 N Main St Uhrichsville OH 44683 Tel (614) 922-4161

HIMMEL, IRA KENNETH, b. Newark, Aug. 26, 1936; B.S. in Mgmt., Wilkes Coll., 1960; LL.B., U. Balt., 1965. Admitted to Md. bar, 1965, U.S. Supreme Ct. bar, 1976; asso. firm Hooper, Kiefer & Cornell, Balt., 1965-69, partner, 1969—; legal counsel Md. Jaycees, 1972, U.S. Jaycees Met. Conf., 1974. Pres., Balt. County Gen. Hosp. Found., 1974-76; trustee Efficiency and Economy Commn., 1972-74. Mem. Am., Md. (vice chmn. trusts and estates sect. 1974) bar assns. Home: 3618 Laguna Ct Randallstown MD 21133 Office: 343 N Charles St Baltimore MD 21201 Tel (301) 727-4700

HINCKLEY, HARRY GLENN, JR., b. Miami, Fla., Jan. 14, 1928; A.B., Stetson U., 1950; LL.B., U. Miami, 1955. Admitted to Fla. bar, 1955; partner firm Wicker, Smith, Blomqvist, Hinckley & Davant, Miami, 1955-65, Fischer & Hinckley, Ft. Lauderdale, Fla., 1965-72, Hinckley & Shores, Ft. Lauderdale, 1972—. Pres. Rio Vista Property Owners Assn., 1965-66. Mem. Am., Fla. (trial lawyers sect.), Broward County bar assns., Internat. Assn. Ins. Counsel, Phi Alpha Delta. Bus. mgr. Univ. Miami Law Sch. Jour., 1953-54. Office: 400 SE 6th St Ft Lauderdale FL 33301 Tel (305) 462-3623

HINCKS, JOHN WINSLOW, b. New Haven, Apr. 17, 1931; A.B., Yale, 1952, LL.B., 1959. Admitted to Conn. bar, 1959; asso. firm Robinson, Robinson & Cole, Hartford, Conn., 1959-65, partner, 1965—; dir. Middlesex Mut. Assurance Co., Hartford Stage Co., Hartford Dispensary; dir., mem. exec. com. Newington Children's Hosp., trustee Renbrook Sch., Nat. Rowing Course Found. Bd. dirs. Legal Aid Soc. Hartford County. Fellow Am. Coll. Probate Counsel; mem. Hartford County, Conn. (mem. ethics com.) bar assns. Office: 799 Main St Hartford CT 06103 Tel (203) 278-0700

HINDIN, MAURICE J., b. Los Angeles, Oct. 10, 1910; B.S., U. So. Calif., 1933, LL.D., 1935. Admitted to Calif. bar, 1935, U.S. Supreme Ct. bar, 1942; sr. partner firm Hindin McKittrick and Marsh, Los Angeles, 1935-72; judge Municipal Ct., Los Angeles Jud. Dist., 1972—. Mem. Am., Los Angeles County bar assns., Am. Judicature Soc., Conf. Calif. Judges. Office: County Courthouse Los Angeles CA 90012 Tel (213) 974-6221

HINDMAN, WILLIAM PARKHURST, JR., b. N.Y.C., Feb. 17, 1920; B.A., Pa. State U., 1941, B.S., 1942, J.D., Harvard, 1949. Admitted to N.Y. State bar, 1950, since practiced in N.Y.C.; asso. firm Winthrop, Stimson, Putnam & Roberts, 1949-52; asso. firm Townley, Updike, Carter & Rodgers, 1954-56, partner, 1957—; asst. chief counsel subcom. on adminstrn. internal revenue laws Com. Ways and Means, 83d Congress, Washington, 1953. Mem. Am. Bar Assn., Bar Assn. City N.Y. Home: 149 Highwood Ave Leonia NJ 07605 Office: 220 E 42d St New York City NY 10017 Tel (212) 682-4567

HINDS, RICHARD DECOURCY, b. Boston, Nov. 28, 1941; B.A., Tufts U., 1964; LL.B., Columbia, 1967. Admitted to N.Y. bar, 1967, D.C. bar, 1973; law clk. to judge 2d Circuit Ct. Appeals, 1967-68; asso. firm Sullivan & Cromwell, N.Y.C., 1968-71; asst. to asst. sec. U.S. Treasury, 1971-73; asso. firm Cleary Gottlieb Steen & Hamilton, Washington, 1973-76, partner, 1977—. Mem. Am. Bar Assn., D.C. Bar. Editor Columbia Law Rev., 1965-67. Office: 1250 Connecticut Ave NW Washington DC 20036 Tel (202) 223-2151

HINDS, WILLIAM LYLE, JR., b. Montgomery, Ala., Sept. 8, 1938; A.B. in English, The Citadel, 1960; LL.B., U. Va., 1965. Admitted to Ala. bar, 1965; asso. firm Bradley, Arant, Rose & White, Birmingham, Ala., 1965-72, partner, 1972—. Mem. Am., Ala., Birmingham bar assns. Home: 2509 Watkins Circle Birmingham AL 35223 Office: 1500 Brown Marx Bldg Birmingham AL 35203 Tel (205) 252-4500

HINDY, GEORGE VICTOR, b. Bklyn., Aug. 17, 1941; B.S. in Polit. Sci., Fordham U., 1963; J.D., St. John's U., 1966, M.B.A., 1973. Admitted to N.Y. bar, 1967; reader, title examiner Chicago Title Ins. Co., N.Y.C., 1966-67; claims examiner Aetna Casualty and Surety Co., N.Y.C., 1967; asso. firms Hargous & DeSantis, N.Y.C., 1967, Muscio, Camarda & Scibilia, Bklyn., 1967-68; asst. sec., legal officer Glore, Forgan, Staats, Inc., N.Y.C., 1968-70; asst. trust officer and legal adviser Am. Bank & Trust Co., N.Y.C., 1970-72; spl. counsel N.Y. Stock Exchange, N.Y.C., 1972-76; partner firm Adler, Greenberg, Hindy & Turner, N.Y.C., 1976—; small claims arbitrator N.Y.C. Civil Ct., 1976—. Mem. New York County Lawyers Assn., Bklyn. Bar Assn. Office: 150 E 58th St New York City NY 10001 Tel (212) 752-6610

HINES, JAMES PARKER, b. Toledo, Mar. 1, 1943; B.S. in Econs., U. Pa., 1965, M.S. in Accounting, 1966; J.D., U. Fla., 1969. Admitted to Fla. bar, 1970; atty.-adviser U.S. Tax Ct., Washington, 1969-71; asso. firm Mershon, Sawyer, Johnston, Dunwody & Cole, 1971-74, firm Trenam, Simmons, Kerker, Scharf & Barkin, 1974-75; individual practice law, Tampa, Fla., 1976--. Chmn. Congl. Action Council. Mem. Am., Fla., Hillsborough County (Fla.) bar assns. Recipient Pres's. award Greater Tampa C. of C., 1976. Home: 3601 Prunus Pl Tampa FL 33618 Office: 315 Hyde Park Ave Tampa FL 33606 Tel (813) 251-8659

HINES, NORMAN PETERS, JR., b. Wichita Falls, Tex., Sept. 26, 1928; B.B.A., So. Meth. U., 1950, J.D., 1960. Admitted to Tex. bar, 1959, U.S. Supreme Ct. bar, 1971; council for Producing Properties, Inc., Dallas, 1959-63; individual practice law, Dallas, 1963-72, 74—; asso. firm Weinberg, Sandoloski & Hines, Dallas, 1972-74. Mem. Am., Dallas (chmn. sole practitioners sect.) bar assns. Home: 3429 Amherst St Dallas TX 75225 Office: 310 Bank of Dallas Bldg 3635 Lemmon Ave Dallas TX 75219 Tel (214) 522-5530

HINES, ROBERT ALBERTO, b. Paducah, Ky., May 9, 1950; LL.B., U. Ky., 1950. Admitted to Ky. bar, 1950; city prosecutor City of Paducah, 1958-59; atty. Ky. State Alcoholic Beverage Control Dept., 1959-62; hearing officer Ky. Worker's Compensation Bd., 1970-76; asst. pub. defender McCracken County, Ky., 1974—. Mem. Am., Fed., Ky., McCracken County bar assns., Phi Alpha Delta. Home: 3721 Springdale Circle Paducah KY 42001 Office: 517 Broadway Paducah KY 42001 Tel (502) 443-5522

HINES, ROBERT LEWIS, b. Ft. Wayne, Ind., Mar. 22, 1923; B.S., Ind. U., 1947, J.D., 1949. Admitted to Ind. bar, U.S. Dist. Ct. bar, 1949; partner firm Leas, Hines & Snyder, and predecessors, Ft. Wayne, Ind., 1949-71; judge Allen County Superior Ct., Ft. Wayne, 1971—; asso. city atty., Ft. Wayne, 1960-63. Pres. Allen County Retarded Childrens' Soc., 1956-62. Mem. Am., Ind., Allen County bar assns. Home: 5110 Vance Ave Fort Wayne IN 46805 Office: Allen Superior Ct Fort Wayne IN 46802 Tel (219) 423-7118

HINKLE, CLARENCE EMMETT, b. Roswell, N.Mex., Oct. 5, 1901; student N.Mex. Mil. Inst., 1922; LL.D., Washington and Lee U., 1925. Admitted to N.Mex. bar, 1925; partner firm Hervey, Dow, Hill & Hinkle, Roswell, 1928-45; sr. partner firm Hinkle, Bondurant, Cox & Eaton, Roswell, 1963-76, firm Hinkle, Cox, Eaton, Coffield & Hensley, Roswell, 1977—; mem. N.Mex. Ho. of Reps., 1931-35, N.Mex. Senate, 1945-47. Pres. Roswell Municipal Sch. Bd., 1935-52; chmn. bd. regents N.Mex. Mil. Inst., 1952-58. Home: 407 N Washington St Roswell NM 88201 Office: 600 Hinkle Bldg Roswell NM 88201 Tel (505) 622-6510

HINKLE, JAMES ALLAN, b. Wichita Falls, Tex., Feb. 10, 1933; B.E.E., U. Va., 1956; LL.B., George Washington U., 1964. Admitted to Va. bar, 1964, D.C. bar, 1965, Ga. bar, 1969; asso. firm Mason, Fenwick & Lawrence, Washington, 1962-66; staff atty. Lockheed-Ga. Co., Marietta, Ga., 1966-70; partner firm Hinkle & Bianco, Stone Mountain, Ga., 1970—. Mem. Am. Bar Assn., Patent Office Soc., Am. Patent Lawyers Assn., Ga. Assn. Criminal Def. Lawyers. Office: 975 Main St Stone Mountain GA 30083 Tel (404) 469-3494

HINKLE, JOHN CHISHOLM, b. N.Y.C., Feb. 28, 1906; A.B., Harvard, 1927, LL.B., 1930, J.S.D., N.Y.U., 1935, LL.M., 1949. Admitted to N.Y. bar, 1931, U.S. Dist. Ct. So. Dist. and Eastern Dist. N.Y., 1937, U.S. Dist. Ct. No. Dist. N.Y. bar, 1956, U.S. Supreme Ct. bar, 1964; asso. firm Hunt, Hill & Betts, N.Y.C., 1931-34; asso. firm Alan R. Campbell, N.Y.C., 1935-36; asso. firm Chas. J. Katzenstein, N.Y.C., 1936-68, individual practice law, N.Y.C., 1938-42; atty. U.S. Civil Prod. Adminstrn., N.Y.C., 1946-48; atty. dept. audit and control, State of N.Y., Albany, N.Y., 1949-55; individual practice law, Hancock, N.Y., 1956—; capt. JAG, USAR, 1942-61; mayor Village of Hancock, 1959-61. Mem. Am., N.Y. State, Delaware County (pres. 1971-73) bar assns., Am. Legion (comdr. Hancock post 1961-62), 29th Div. Assn. (comdr. dept. N.Y. 1964-67). Office: 36 East Front St Hancock NY 13783 Tel (607) 637-3691

HINKLE, THOMAS L., b. Fresno, Calif., May 30, 1939; B.S., U. San Francisco, 1961; J.D., Hastings Coll. Law U. Calif., 1971. Admitted to Calif. bar, 1972; dep. dist. atty. County of Ventura (Calif.), 1972-74; asso. firm Heily, Blase, Ellison & Wellcome, Oxnard, Calif., 1974—; mem. Hastings Coll. Law Moot Ct. Bd. Mem. Calif., Ventura County bar assns. Office: Heily Blase Ellison Wellcome 220 S A St Oxnard CA 93030 Tel (805) 483-9563

HINRICHS, ROBERT MARBLE, b. Balt., Apr. 3, 1933; B.S., U.S. Mil. Acad., 1955; J.D., Stanford, 1965. Admitted to Calif. bar, 1965, U.S. Ct. Mil. Appeals, 1965, U.S. Supreme Ct., 1970; served with Judge Adv. Gen. Corps, U.S. Army, 1965-67; asso. firm Abramson, Church & Stave, and predecessors, Salinas, Calif., 1968-72, partner firm, 1972—. Dir., exec. v.p. Monterey County Symphony Assn., 1968-75. Mem. Calif., Am. bar assns., Monterey County Legal Aid Soc. (past pres.). Contbr. article to Mil. Law Rev. Office: 3d Floor Crocker Bank Bldg Salinas CA 93901 Tel (408) 758-2401

HINSEY, JOSEPH, IV, b. Palo Alto, Calif., Oct. 17, 1931; A.B., Cornell U., 1953, LL.B., 1955; M.B.A., Harvard, 1957. Admitted to N.Y. State bar, 1956; asso. firm White & Case, N.Y.C., 1957-65, partner, 1965—. Mem. Assn. Bar City N.Y., Am. (chmn. bus. mgmt. liability ins. com., chmn. audit inquiry responses com., mem. com. corp. law and accounting, corp., banking and bus. law sect.), N.Y. State (com. corporate laws) bar assns., Am. Law Inst. Home: 130 Old Army Rd Scarsdale NY 10583 Office: 14 Wall St New York City NY 10005 Tel (212) 732-1040

HINSON, THOMAS HARVEY, b. Macon, Ga., Jan. 24, 1948; B.A., U. Ga., 1970; J.D., Mercer U., 1973. Admitted to Ga. bar, 1973; asst. dist. atty. City of Macon, 1974-76, spl. crimes prosecutor, 1976—. Mem. Ga., Macon bar assns. Home: 3756 Berkley Dr Macon GA 31204 Office: 300 Bibb County Courthouse Macon GA 31201 Tel (912) 745-6871

HINTON, CHARLES FRANKLIN, b. Des Moines, June 30, 1932; B.A., U. Iowa, 1957, J.D., 1959. Admitted to Iowa bar, 1959; practiced in Waterloo, Iowa, 1959—; individual practice law, 1959-62; mem. firm Charles F. Hinton; asst. county atty. Black Hawk County, Iowa, 1960-64; asst. city solicitor City of Waterloo, 1966-68; spl. prosecutor, Black Hawk County, 1972—; atty. Heart Fund, 1966-70. Mem. Black Hawk County Republican Com., 1962-64. Mem. Am., Iowa, Black Hawk County (sec. 1966) bar assns., Am. Trial Lawyers Assn. Named Distinguished Club Pres. Sertoma Club, 1968. Home: 1815 Winterridge Rd Cedar Falls IA 50613 Office: 751 Progress Ave Waterloo IA 50701 Tel (319) 233-3301

HINTON, CHARLES MINOR, JR., b. San Diego, Aug. 14, 1943; B.A. in History, U. Tex., 1970; J.D., U. Ark., 1973. Admitted to Tex. bar, 1973, Ark. bar, 1973, U.S. Supreme Ct. bar, 1976; partner firm Reinberger, Eilbott & Smith, Pine Bluff, Ark., 1973—. Mem. Am., Tex., Ark., Jefferson County bar assns., Phi Alpha Delta. Recipient Am. Jurisprudence award, 1972. Home: 702 W 20th St Pine Bluff AR 71603 Office: 219 W 5th St Pine Bluff AR 71611 Tel (501) 534-3721

HINTZE, RAYMOND ANDERSON, b. Salt Lake City, Feb. 20, 1942; B.A., Brigham Young U., 1967; J.D., U. Utah, 1971. Admitted to Utah State bar, 1971; asso. firm Hunt-Walker, Salt Lake City, 1971-73; partner Walker, Hintze & Anderson, Inc., Salt Lake City, 1973—; labor contract negotiator Kerr McGee Corp., Trona, Calif., 1968. Mem. Am., Utah State, Salt Lake City County bar assns. Home: 444 Cumberland Rd Salt Lake City UT 84117 Office: Suite 202 Heritage Plaza 4685 Highland Dr Salt Lake City UT 84117 Tel (801) 278-4747

HINZ, EDWARD ARTHUR, JR., b. York, Nebr., May 26, 1933; A.B. with honors, U. Calif., Los Angeles, 1958; J.D., Hastings Coll. Law, 1961; grad. Calif. Trial Judges Coll., 1975. Admitted to Calif. bar, 1962, U.S. Supreme Ct. bar, 1966; dep. atty. gen. State of Calif., Sacramento, 1961-72, chief asst. atty. gen., Los Angeles, 1972-73; judge Municipal Ct., Los Angeles Jud. Dist., 1973-74, Los Angeles County Superior Ct., 1974—; mem. Calif. Gov's. Select Com. on Law Enforcement Problems, 1973, Calif. Gov.'s. Conf. on Criminal Justice, 1974; mem. advisory bd. to Calif. Joint Legis. Com. for Revision Penal Code. Mem. Los Angeles County, Los Angeles bar assns., Criminal Cts. Bar Assn., Conf. Calif. Judges, U. Calif. at Los Angeles, Hastings Coll. of Law alumni assns., Am. Judicature Soc., Peninsula Symphony Assn., Order of Coif, Phi Alpha Delta. Office: County Courthouse 111 N Hill St Los Angeles CA 90012 Tel (213) 974-1234

HIRSCH, ARTHUR SEYMOUR, b. Bklyn., Mar. 1, 1908; student Coll. City N.Y., 1926; LL.B., Bklyn. Law Sch., 1929; LL.M., St. Johns U., 1931. Admitted to N.Y. bar, 1931; asso. Edward E. Fay, U.S. commr. Eastern Dist. N.Y., 1931-34; individual practice, 1934-59; partner firm Hirsch & Wexner, N.Y.C., 1959-68; dir. adminstrn. of cts. for 2d Dept., 1968-71; justice Supreme Ct. N.Y., Bklyn., 1972—; dep. license commr. N.Y.C., 1937-45; counsel Joint Legis. Com. on Motor Vehicle Problems, 1947-54; counsel to majority leader N.Y. Senate, 1955-56; spl. counsel Joint Legis. Com. on Traffic Violations, 1957-59; dep. tax commr. N.Y., 1959-68; judge City Ct., 1962, Civil Ct. N.Y.C., 1966; adj. prof. John Jay Coll. Criminal Justice. Pres., Lawyers Club of United Jewish Appeal Fedn., Glenwood Community Civic League; v.p. Bklyn. Jewish Community Council; bd. dirs. Zionist Orgn., B'nai B'rith, Progressive Synagogue, Nat. Conf. Christians and Jews, East Flatbush Rugby YM-YWHA; legal adviser Tiny Heart Found. Mem. Am., N.Y., Bklyn. bar assns., Inst. Jud. Adminstrn. Home: 1415 E 49th St Brooklyn NY 11234 Office: Supreme Ct Civic Center Brooklyn NY 11201 Tel (212) 643-5884

HIRSCH, BARRY, b. N.Y.C., Mar. 19, 1933; B.S., U. Mo., 1954, B.A., 1954; LL.B., U. Mich., 1959; LL.M., N.Y. U., 1964. Admitted to N.Y. bar, 1960; asso., then partner firm Seligson & Morris, N.Y.C., 1960-69; v.p., sec., gen. counsel, dir. B.T.B. Corp., 1969-71; pres., dir. 1036 Park Corp., 1969-71; v.p., sec. gen. counsel Loews Corp., and subs., 1971—; dir. J.H. Snyder Co., Manhattan Fund, Liberty Fund, Hemisphere Fund, CNA Larwin Income Fund, Fundex, Inc.; lectr., panel mem. Practising Law Inst., Am. Bar Assn. Mem. Assn. Bar City N.Y., N.Y. State Bar Assn., Zeta Beta Tau, Phi Delta Phi. Home: 1010 Fifth Ave New York City NY 10028 Office: 666 Fifth Ave New York City NY 10019 Tel (212) 586-4400

HIRSCH, BURTON GENE, b. Chgo., Sept. 4, 1936; student U. Ill., 1954-55, Roosevelt U., 1957-58; LL.B., Chgo.-Kent Coll. Law Ill. Inst. Tech., 1961. Admitted to Ill. bar, 1962, Ariz. bar, 1966; practiced in Chgo., 1961-65; atty. Office Field Solicitor Dept. Interior, Phoenix, 1965-69; individual practice law, Phoenix, 1969—; judge pro tempore Phoenix Municipal Ct., 1973—. Mem. Ill. State, Ariz. State bar assns., Phi Delta Phi. Recipient Moot Ct. awards, 1959, 60; Am. Jurisprudence award Bancroft-Whitney Co., 1959-60; editor Chgo.-Kent Coll. Law Rev., 1960-61. Office: 111 W Monroe St Suite 711 Phoenix AZ 85003 Tel (602) 254-5044

HIRSCH, CHARLES SEYMOUR, b. Chgo., Aug. 17, 1904; Ph.B., U. Chgo., 1927, J.D., 1928. Admitted to Ill. bar, 1929; staff firm Frish & Frish, 1929-30; partner firm Alster & Hirsch, 1930-31; individual practice law, Chgo., 1931-42, 42-45, 48—; with Air Force

Intelligence, U.S. War Dept., 1945; spl. agt. intelligence div. Dept. Treasury, IRS, Chgo., 1945-48. Mem. Am., Chgo. bar assns. Office: 105 W Adams St Chicago IL 60603 Tel (312) 782-9101

HIRSCH, RICHARD GARY, b. Los Angeles, June 15, 1940; A.B. in Polit. Sci., U. Calif., Los Angeles, 1961; J.D., U. Calif., Berkeley, 1965. Admitted to Calif. bar, 1967, U.S. Supreme Ct. bar, 1972; aide Calif. State Legis., Sacramento, 1965-66; dep. dist. atty. Los Angeles County (Calif.), 1967-71; partner firm Nasatir, Sherman and Hirsch, Beverly Hills, Calif., 1971—; judge pro tem Beverly Hills Municipal Ct., 1975; lectr. in field. Bd. dirs. People Inc., Los Angeles, 1966-68; chmn. Univ. Camp Asso. Bd., Los Angeles, 1973-74; chmn. Greek Theatre Commn., Los Angeles, 1976—. Mem. Am. (chmn. So. Calif. young lawyers sect. prison reform com. 1973), Beverly Hills (chmn. criminal law com. 1975-76), Los Angeles County, Criminal Cts. bar assns., Nat. Assn. Criminal Def. Lawyers, First Amendment Lawyers Assn., Calif. Attys. Criminal Justice (dir.), ACLU. Office: 9911 W Pico Blvd Suite 1000 Los Angeles CA 90035 Tel (213) 277-3112

HIRSCH, ROBERT HOWARD, b. Chgo., Jan. 10, 1938; B.S., Drake U., 1959; J.D., DePaul U., 1962. Admitted to Ill. bar, 1962; individual practice law, Chgo., 1962-64, 69—; partner firm Chase & Hirsch, Chgo., 1964-69. Mem. Am., Ill. State. Chgo. bar assns., Decalogue Soc., Am. Acad. Matrimonial Lawyers. Office: 228 N LaSalle St Chicago IL 60601 Tel (312) 372-6560

HIRSH, HAROLD LESTER, b. Bklyn., Aug. 30, 1917; B.S., U. Md., 1938; M.D. cum laude, Georgetown U., 1942; J.D., Am. U., 1972. Intern, D.C. Gen Hosp., Washington, 1942-43, resident in medicine, 1943-44; fellow in medicine George Washington U., 1944-46; admitted to D.C. bar, 1973; clin. instr. medicine George Washington U., 1946-48; instr. Howard U., 1950-58, clin. asst. prof., 1958—, lectr. law and medicine, 1971—; examiner Nat. Bd. Med. Examiners, 1945-48, Am. Bd. Internal Medicine, 1950-58; profl. lectr. law George Washington U., 1972—, dept. health care adminstrn., 1972—; lectr. Am. U., 1972—, Cath. U., 1973; cons. in fields; mem. staffs. George Washington Univ. Hosp., 1945-47, D.C. Gen. Hosp., 1946—, Providence Hosp. Med. Clinic, 1949-55, Emergency Hosp. Med. Clinic, 1949-60, Sibley Meml. Hosp., 1958-67, Freedmen's Hosp., Hebrew Home of Greater Washington, 1953—, VA. Hosp., Washington, 1973—. Bd. dirs. Hebrew Home of Greater Washington, 1953—, chmn. med. service, 1953—; bd. dirs. Am. Jewish Soc. for Service, 1963—, Greater Washington Jewish Community Found., 1965—, United Jewish Appeal, 1965—, allied med. div. Bonds for Israel, 1960—, chmn., 1962. Mem. AMA, Med. Soc. D.C., Am. Fedn. Clin. Research, Jacobi Med. Soc., Am. Coll. Legal Medicine, Am., D.C. bar assns., Am. Hosp. Assn., Am., D.C. socs. internal medicine, Am. Soc. Law and Medicine, Bar Assn. D.C. Co-author: Penicillin; Medicine, Law and Public Policy; contbr. articles and chpts. to legal jours. and med. texts; certified Am. Bd. Internal Medicine; diplomate Nat. Bd. Med. Examiners. Home and Office: 2801 New Mexico Ave NW Washington DC 20007 Tel (202) 338-2363

HIRSHMAN, MELVIN, b. Washington, Sept. 24, 1931; A.A., Am. U., 1951, B.A. with high distinction, 1952, J.D. with high distinction, 1955. Admitted to D.C. bar, 1955, Md. bar, 1965, U.S. Supreme Ct. bar, 1959; individual practice law, Washington, also Langley Park, Md., 1956—; arbitrator Am. Arbitration Assn., 1970—. Bd. dirs. Adelphi (Md.) Boys Club, 1972; del. Md. State Republican Conv., 1966. Mem. Am., Md., D.C. Prince George's County bar assns., Am. Trial Lawyers Assn., Sigma Nu Phi. Home: 8405 20th Ave Adelphi MD 20783 Office: 7676 New Hampshire Ave Langley Park MD 20783 Tel (301) 434-4477

HITCHCOCK, BION EARL, b. Muscatine, Iowa, Oct. 9, 1942; B.E.E., Iowa State U., Ames, 1965; J.D., U. Iowa, 1968. Admitted to Iowa bar, 1968, Okla. bar, 1968; atty. Phillips Petroleum Co., Bartlesville, Okla., 1968-69, 73—; lt. JAGC, USN, 1970-73. Pres. Bartlesville Symphony Orch., 1975—; v.p., dir. Bartlesville Allied Arts and Humanities Council, 1976-77; precinct chmn., 1975-77; mem. Govt. and Fin. Goals for Bartlesville Coms., 1974-75. Mem. Am., Okla., Iowa, Washington County bar assns., Am. Patent Law Assn., Am. Judicature Soc., Eta Kappa Nu. Tel (918) 661-6963

HITCHCOCK, J. GARETH, b. Ft. Jennings, Ohio, June 10, 1914; LL.B., Ohio State U., 1939, J.D., 1969. Admitted to Ohio bar, 1939, U.S. Supreme Ct. bar, 1960; practiced in Paulding, Ohio, 1939-40, 59-60, Port Clinton, Ohio, 1946-51; spl. agt. FBI, Washington, 1940-41, Denver, 1941, Butte, Mont., 1941, San Juan, P.R., 1942; with JAG, AUS, 1944-46; protection chief Joseph Horne Co., dept. store, Pitts., 1951-57; investment counsel, salesman Federated Investors, Inc., Pitts., 1957-59; judge Paulding County Common Pleas Ct., 1960—. Mem. Ohio Common Pleas Judges Assn., Am. Judicature Soc., Judge Advs. Assn., Am. Security Council, Soc. Former Spl. Agts. FBI, Ohio State Bar Assn. (mem. spl. com. on pub. relations). Recipient Excellent Jud. Service awards Ohio Supreme Ct., 1973, 75, Outstanding Jud. Service award, 1974, 76. Home: 302 N Cherry St Paulding OH 45879 Office: Courthouse Paulding OH 45879 Tel (419) 399-2811

HITCHCOCK, VERNON THOMAS, b. Selma, Ind., Feb. 21, 1919; B.S. in Agri., Purdue U., 1940, J.D., Stanford U., 1953. Admitted to Calif. bar, 1954, U.S. Supreme Ct. bar, 1961; individual practice law, Healdsburg, Calif., 1954-56; dep. atty. gen. State Calif., Sacramento, 1956; dep. county counsel Sonoma County (Calif.), 1957-65; adminstrv. advisor Sonoma County Office Edn., 1968—; exec. dir. Libyan Aviation Co., Tripoli, Libya, 1966-67. Mem. Am., Sonoma County bar assns., Internat. Platform Assn., Reserve Officers Assn. (pres. local chpt., 1972-73). Home: 3411 Sidney Sq Santa Rosa CA 95405 Office: 2555 Mendolino Ave Santa Rosa CA 95401 Tel (707) 527-2429

HITE, ROBERT WESLEY, b. Fort Scott, Kans., Mar. 18, 1936; B.A. in Polit. Sci., Colo. Coll., 1958; student, Netherlands Coll., Breukelen, 1956-57; J.D., N.Y. U., 1961. Admitted to Colo. bar, 1961, U.S. Supreme Ct. bar, 1965; law specialist USN, Newport, R.I., 1962-65; asso. firm T. Raber Taylor, Denver, 1965-69; v.p. legal affairs and personnel, sec. Mr. Steak, Inc., Denver, 1969—. Bd. dirs. Met. Denver Sewage Disposal Dist. Mem. Am., Colo., Denver bar Assns., Colo. Assn. Corp. Counsel (pres. 1972-74), Denver Law Club, Internat. Franchise Assn. (legis. legal com. 1972-75). Office: 5100 Race Ct Denver CO 80216 Tel (303) 292-3070

HJELLUM, JOHN, b. Aurland, Sogn, Norway, Mar. 29, 1910 (parents Am. citizens); LL.B., U. N.D., 1934; Admitted to N.D. bar, 1934; asso. firm A.W. Aylmer, Jamestown, N.D., 1934-41; partner firm Hjellum, Weiss, Nerison, Jukkala & Vinje, and predecessors, Jamestown, 1941—; dir. Soo Line R.R. Co., Frederick, Inc., Smith Motors, Inc. Chmn. bd. trustees N.D. Ind. Coll. Fund, Jamestown, 1957-68, First United Meth. Ch., Jamestown, 1940-75; trustee Jamestown Coll., 1967-75. Fellow Internat. Acad. Trial Lawyers; mem. Am., Internat., N.D. (pres. 1957-58), Fourth Jud. Dist. (past pres.), Stutsman County (past pres.) bar assns., Order of Coif, Phi Delta Phi. Home: 916 NW 2d Ave Jamestown ND 58401 Office: Box 1560 Jamestown ND 58401 Tel (701) 252-2090

HJERPE, JOHN WILLFORD, b. Duluth, Minn., May 3, 1934; B. Geol. Engring., U. Minn., 1957; J.D., Loyola U., New Orleans, 1967. With Shell Oil Co., 1957—, sr. geol. engr., Houston, 1967-69, staff geol. engr. internat. region, 1976—; admitted to La. bar, 1967, Tex. bar, 1968. Mem. Tex. State Bar. Recipient Am. Jurisprudence prize Loyola U., New Orleans, 1965, 66, 67, award for best case note Loyola Law Rev., 1967, editorial bd., 1967. Office: PO Box 2099 Houston TX 77001 Tel (713) 220-1289

HJORTH, ROLAND L., b. Wisner, Nebr., Dec. 9, 1935; A.B., U. Nebr., 1957; postgrad. (Fulbright scholar) U. Heidelberg (Germany), 1958; LL.B., N.Y. U., 1961. Admitted to N.Y. bar, 1961, Wash. bar, 1971; asso. firm Paul, Weiss, Rifkind, Wharton & Garrison, N.Y.C., 1961-64; prof. law U. Wash., 1964—; vis. prof. law N.Y. U., 1969-70, U. Tex., 1976; of counsel Preston, Thorgrimson, Ellis, Holman and Fletcher, Seattle, 1976—. Contbr. articles, book revs. to legal jours. Office: Sch Law U Wash Seattle WA 98105

HLAVATY, MICHAEL CARL, b. Davenport, Iowa, July 15, 1942; B.S., Iowa State U., Ames, 1965; J.D., U. Iowa, Iowa City, 1972. Admitted to Iowa bar, 1973, Ill. bar, 1974, U.S. Patent Office, 1974; asso. firm Jungmann, Eldridge, Iowa, 1973-74; patent atty. Deere & Co., Moline, Ill., 1974—; asst. city atty. Bettendorf (Iowa), 1973; asst. county atty. Scott County (Iowa), 1973. Loaned exec. United Way Fund Dr., 1976; adviser Jr. Achievement, 1967-68. Mem. Ill., Iowa bar assns., Phi Alpha Delta. Home: 136 Forest Rd Davenport IA 52803 Office: John Deere Rd Moline IL 61265 Tel (309) 792-4232

HOADLEY, ROBERT REYNOLDS, JR., b. Cooperstown, N.Y., Apr. 6, 1937; A.B., Colgate U., 1959; LL.B., U. Denver, 1961. Admitted to Colo. bar, 1962; law specialist USN, 1962-67; dep. dist. atty., Denver, 1967-69; gen. counsel Mr. Steak, Inc., Denver, 1969—, also asst. sec. Mem. Am., Colo., Denver bar assns. Office: 5700 Race Ct Denver CO 80216 Tel (303) 292-3070

HOADLEY, THOMAS ALBERT, b. Bloomington, Ind., June 13, 1929; B.S., Ind. U., 1951, J.D., 1954. Admitted to Ind. bar, 1954, Fla. bar, 1965; dep. atty. gen. State of Ind., Indpls., 1956, state dep. pub. defender, 1957-61; pros. atty. Monroe County (Ind.), Bloomington, 1962-66; mem. firm Howell, Kirby, Montgomery, D'Aiuto & Dean, West Palm Beach, Fla., 1967-76; lectr. Ind. U., 1962-64. Mem. Am., Fla. bar assns., Fla. Trial Lawyers Assn. Home: 300 Tangier Ave Palm Beach FL 33480 Office: 1100 Harvey Bldg 224 Datura St West Palm Beach FL 33401 Tel (305) 833-1677

HOAGLAND, KENNETH WILLIAM, b. Bakersfield, Calif., Sept. 5, 1917; LL.B., J.D., U. Calif., Hastings, 1953. Admitted to Calif. bar, 1954; dist. atty., Kern County (Calif.), 1954-57; city atty., Bakersfield, 1957—. Mem. Am., Calif. bar assns., League Calif. Cities. Office: 1501 Truxtun Ave Bakersfield CA 93301 Tel (805) 861-2721

HOAR, LEONARD CLEMENT, JR., b. Bakersfield, Calif., Apr. 5, 1929; A.B., Stanford U., 1949; M.A. in Internat. Affairs, Johns Hopkins U., 1954; J.D., Humphreys Coll. Law, 1970. Admitted to Calif. bar, 1967, U.S. Supreme Ct. bar, 1974; field asso. J.D. Marsh & Assos., 1957-59; pvt. practice fin. planning, Washington, 1959, 63, Fresno, Calif., 1963-67; individual practice law, Fresno, 1967—. Mem. Am., Calif., Fresno trial lawyers assns., Am. Judicature Soc., Am., Fresno County, Inter-Am., Calif. bar assns., Acad. Law and Sci. Office: 5750 N Palm St Fresno CA 93704 Tel (209) 439-5503

HOBBS, CHARLES ALLEN, b. Cambridge, Mass., Sept. 9, 1928; B.A., Yale U., 1950; J.D. with honors, George Washington U., 1957. Admitted to D.C. bar, 1957, U.S. Supreme Ct. bar, 1961; law clk. Judge Warren E. Burger D.C. Circuit, 1957-58; asso. firm Wilkinson, Cragun & Barker, Washington, 1958-63, partner, 1963—; lectr. law George Washington Law Sch., 1961. Mem. Am., Fed., D.C. (chmn. ethics com. 1974-76) bar assns., D.C. Bar (bd. govs.). Editor in chief George Washington Law Rev., 1956-57; contbr. articles to legal jours. Home: 33 W Kirke St Chevy Chase MD 20015 Office: 1735 New York Ave Washington DC 20006 Tel (202) 833-9800

HOBBS, JOHN SALMON, b. San Diego, Feb. 11, 1928; B.A., U. Ariz., 1951, LL.B., 1958. Admitted to Ariz. bar, 1958; partner firm Jennings, Strouss & Salmon, Phoenix, 1958—. Bd. dir. Vis. Nurse Service, Phoenix, 1972-75; active Ariz. State Bd. Private Tech. and Bus. Schs., 1972-76. Mem. Am., Maricopa County bar assns., Am. Bd. Trial Advocates. Home: 7850 N 3d St Phoenix AZ 85020 Office: 111 W Monroe St Phoenix AZ 85003 Tel (602) 262-5808

HOBBY, WILLIAM MATTHEWS, III, b. Millen, Ga., Aug. 5, 1935; B. in Indsl. Engring., U. Fla., 1959; J.D., George Washington U., 1963. Admitted to D.C. bar, 1964, Fla. bar, 1967, U.S. Supreme Ct. bar, 1968; examiner U.S. Patent Office, Washington, 1963-65; asst. patent counsel Martin-Marietta Corp., Orlando, Fla., 1965-67; partner firm Duckworth, Hobby, Orman, Allen & Pettis, Orlando, 1967—. Dir. Fla. Conservation Found., Winter Park, 1976—. Mem. Am., Fla., Orange County (Fla.) bar assns., George Washington U. Fla. Alumni Assn. (v.p. 1972, pres. 1973, exec. council 1972-74), Am. Patent Law Assn., Phi Delta Phi. Recipient Spl. award, Mus. Store Assn., 1975. Home: 244 Sylvan Blvd Winter Park FL 32789 Office: 400 W Colonial Dr Orlando FL 32804 Tel (305) 841-2330

HOBELMAN, CARL DONALD, b. Hackensack, N.J., Dec. 26, 1931; B.C.E., Cornell U., 1954; J.D., Harvard, 1959. Admitted to N.Y. bar, 1960, U.S. Supreme Ct. bar, 1975; asso. firm LeBoeuf, Lamb, Leiby & MacRae, N.Y.C., 1960-64, partner, 1965—; sec. Empire State Electric Energy Research Corp., Northeast Power Coordinating Council. Mem. Am., N.Y., Fed. Power (exec. com. 1974—) bar assns., Assn. Bar City N.Y. (chmn. atomic energy com. 1970-73). Home: 480 Park Ave New York City NY 10022 Office: 140 Broadway New York City NY 10005 Tel (212) 269-1100

HOBERG, JOHN WILLIAM, b. Cleve., Apr. 12, 1943; B.A., Ohio Wesleyan U., 1965; J.D., U. Mich., 1968. Admitted to Ohio bar, 1968; mem. firm Vorys, Sater, Seymour and Pease, Columbus, Ohio, 1968—. Mem. environ. protection com. Interstate Oil Compact Commn., 1975—; committeeman Franklin County (Ohio) Republican Central Com., 1973-76. Mem. Am., Ohio, Columbus (chmn. environ. law com. 1974-76) bar assns. Home: 1953 Bluff Ave Columbus OH 43212 Office: 52 E Gay St Columbus OH 43215 Tel (614) 464-6213

HOBERMAN, OWEN O., b. Bklyn., Sept. 9, 1936; A.B., Brown U., 1958; LL.B., Columbia U., 1961. Admitted to N.Y. bar, 1962; asst. dist. atty. Kings County (N.Y.), 1965-68; counsel to mems. N.Y. State Assembly, 1966-67; individual practice law, Bklyn. Chmn. young lawyers div. United Jewish Appeal Kings County, 1970, 71. Mem. Bklyn., N.Y. State bar assns., N.Y. State Trial Lawyers Assn., Nat. Dist. Attys. Assn. Home: 7 Pickwick Terr Rockville Centre NY 11570 Office: 16 Court St Brooklyn NY 11241 Tel (212) 625-1100

HOBGOOD, JAMES ROBERT, b. Picayune, Miss., Apr. 5, 1939; J.D., Baylor U. Admitted to Tex. bar, 1971; asst. county atty., Harris County (Tex.). Home: 6739 Deer Ridge St Houston TX 77086 Office: 301 San Jacinto St Houston TX 77002 Tel (713) 228-8311

HOBLOCK, MICHAEL JOHN, JR., b. Troy, N.Y., July 4, 1942; B.B.A., Siena Coll., Newtonville, N.Y., 1964; LL.B. (now J.D.), Albany Law Sch., 1967. Admitted to N.Y. bar, 1967, U.S. Ct. Mil. Appeals bar, 1970; asst. atty. N.Y. State Dept. Edn., Albany, 1967; served as asst. staff judge advocate U.S. Marine Corps, 1968-71; asso. firm Zubres, D'Agostino and Hoblock, Albany, 1971—. Mem. Albany County, N.Y., Fed., Am. bar assns., Assn. Trial Lawyers Am., N.Y. Trial Lawyers Assn., Nat. Dist. Attys. Assn., Am. Judicature Soc. Home: 1 G Denise Dr Latham NY 12110 Office: 90 State St Albany NY 12207 Tel (518) 463-2251

HOBLOCK, WILLIAM J., b. Cohoes, N.Y., Aug. 1, 1934; B.S., Cornell U., 1957; LL.B., J.D., Albany Law Sch., 1960. Admitted to N.Y. bar, 1961; partner firm Zubres, D'Agostino & Hoblock, Albany, N.Y.; counsel Colonig (N.Y.) Planning Bd. Mem. Am., N.Y., Albany County bar assns. Home: 12 Strathmore Dr Londonville NY 12211 Office: 90 State St Albany NY 12207 Tel (518) 463-2251

HOBSON, DONALD LEWIS, b. Detroit, Jan. 11, 1935; B.S. in History, Eastern Mich. U., 1957; M.A., Mich. State U., 1960; postgrad. U. Mich., 1961-62, Hampton Inst., summer 1962; J.D., Detroit Coll. Law-Wayne, 1965. Tchr. social sci. Detroit Pub. Schs., 1957-64; coordinator Detroit Bd. Edn. Job Upgrading Program, 1964-65; admitted to Mich. bar, 1965, Wis. bar, 1965, D.C. bar, 1967, U.S. Supreme Ct. bar, U.S. Ct. of Appeals bar, 6th Circuit, U.S. Tax Ct. bar, U.S. Dist. Ct. bar Eastern Dist. Mich. and Eastern Dist. Wis.; asso.-partner firm Goodman, Eden, Millender, Goodman & Bedrosian, Detroit, 1965-72; judge Common Pleas Ct. City of Detroit, 1972—; asso. prof. Detroit Coll. Law; adj. lectr. law dept. Walsh Coll. Accountancy and Bus. Adminstrn.; vis. lectr. Shaw Coll. of Detroit; past mem. nat. bd. Council on Legal Ednl. Opportunities; past hearing referee Mich. Civil Rights Commn.; past sec. income tax rev. bd. City of Detroit; mem. spl. com. on landlord-tenant problems Mich. Supreme Ct. Co-chmn. Concerned Citizens for Mental Health, Detroit; bd. dirs. Mich. Youth Found., Police Athletic League; trustee Black Law Student Scholarship Fund; mem. exec. bd. Detroit chpt. NAACP. Mem. Am. Arbitration Assn. (Detroit regional adv. council), Nat. Lawyers Guild (exec. bd.), Am. Trial Lawyers Assn., Nat. (dir.), Mich. (counsel grievance bd.), Wolverine (pres., dir.) bar assns., Nat. (hon.), Mich. assns. criminal def. lawyers. Recipient Eastern Mich. U. Alumni Honors award, 1974. Home: 2136 Bryanston Crescent Detroit MI 48207 Office: City County Bldg 2 Woodward Ave Detroit MI 48226 Tel (313) 224-5442

HOBSON, ROBERT LOU, b. Gary, Ind., July 10, 1935; B.A., Wabash Coll., 1957; LL.B., U. Calif., San Francisco, 1964, J.D., 1964. Admitted to Calif. bar, 1965; tax atty. IRS, San Francisco, 1965-67; partner firm O'Brien, Hobson & McCrorey, Walnut Creek, Calif., 1967-71; gen. counsel IMA Assos., Menlo Park, Calif., 1971-72; v.p. Bank of Am., San Francisco, 1972—. Mem. Calif., San Francisco, Am. bar assns., Calif. Bankers Assn., Navy League of U.S. Office: 555 California St San Francisco CA 94104 Tel (405) 622-5100

HOCHBERG, STEPHEN, b. N.Y.C., June 9, 1945; B.A. magna cum laude in History, N.Y. U., 1967; J.D., Yale, 1970. Admitted to N.Y. State bar, 1971, D.C. bar, 1972, Fla. bar, 1974, U.S. Supreme Ct. bar, 1974; law clk. to judge U.S. Ct. Appeals for 3rd Circuit, Phila., 1970-71; gen. counsel Lefrak Orgn., Forest Hills, N.Y., 1971-73; prof. law N.Y. Law Sch., N.Y.C., 1973-76, cons. academic affairs, 1976—; cons. new drug regulation HEW, 1976—; adj. prof. law Baruch Coll., N.Y.C., 1976—; adj. prof. econs. City U. N.Y., 1974, Bloomfield (N.J.) Coll., 1976—. Class agt. Yale Law Sch. Fund, 1970—. Mem. Am. Bar Assn. (com. of young lawyers div., sect. real property 1974-75), Assn. Bar City N.Y., N.Y. County Lawyers Assn., Council N.Y. Law Assos., Fed. Bar Council, Mensa, Phi Beta Kappa. Recipient Founders' Day award N.Y. U., 1970. Contbr. articles to mags., newspapers and profl. jours.; editor Med. Law Letter, 1976—; editor, officer Yale Law Jour., 1968-70. Home: 30 Beekman Pl New York City NY 10022 Office: 30 Beekman Pl New York City NY 10022 Tel (212) 832-3543

HOCHHAUSER, STEPHEN, b. N.Y.C., Sept. 1, 1934; B.A., Harvard, 1956, LL.B., 1960. Admitted to N.Y. bar, 1961; asso. firm Saxe Bacon & O'Shea, N.Y.C., 1961-65; partner firm Steinhaus & Hochhauser, N.Y.C., 1965-76, Berg & Duffy, Lake Success, N.Y., 1976—. Mem. Am., N.Y. State, Nassau County, N.Y.C. bar assns. Office: Berg & Duffy 3000 Marcus Ave Lake Success NY 11040 Tel (516) 345-2500

HOCHMAN, WILLIAM S., b. Paterson, N.J., May 6, 1933; A.B., Ind. U., 1955; J.D. with honors, George Washington U., 1962. Admitted to D.C. bar, 1963, Calif. bar, 1964; asso. firm Pillsbury, Madison & Sutro, San Francisco, 1963-70; mem. firm Bagshaw, Martinelli Corrigan & Jordan, San Rafael, Calif., 1970—; dep. city atty. Sausalito and Mill Valley (Calif.), 1970—. Mem. Am., San Francisco, Marin County, Calif. bar assns., Phi Delta Phi. Editor George Washington Law Rev., 1961-62; recipient Am. Jurisprudence award, 1962. Home: 23 Corte Del Rey San Rafael CA 94903 Office: 950 Northgate Dr San Rafael CA 94903 Tel (415) 472-4500

HOCK, VINCENT MICHAEL, b Allentown, Pa., Jan. 21, 1942; A.B., Princeton, 1963; J.D., U. Pa., 1966. Admitted to Pa. bar, 1966; asso. firm Dower, Huston & Cahn, Allentown, 1966-68; staff atty. Lehigh Poortland Cement Co., Allentown, 1968-71, asst. sec., 1971—. Mem. Am., Pa., Lehigh County bar assns. Home: 3858 Lincoln Pkwy W Allentown PA 18104 Office: 718 Hamilton Mall Allentown PA 18105 Tel (215) 434-6171

HOCKENBURY, JAY DONALD, b. Wilmington, Del., Dec. 14, 1947; B.A., The Citadel, 1965-69; J.D., Wake Forest U., 1972. Admitted to N.C. bar, 1972; asso. firm W.K. Rhodes, Wilmington, 1972-75; individual practice law, Wilmington, N.C., 1975—; legal adviser Citizens for Decency through Law, 1976. Mem. Wilmington Community Devel. Com., 1974-76. Mem. New Hanover County (N.C.), N.C. bar assns. Home: 810 Midland Dr Wilmington DC 28401 Office: Suite 201 118 Princess St Wilmington NC 28401 Tel (919) 762-3383

HOCKLANDER, JOSEPH MONROE, b. Tuscaloosa, Ala., Nov. 23, 1926; J.D., U. Ala., 1950. Admitted to Ala. bar, 1950; practiced in Mobile, Ala., 1950-60; asso. judge Ala. Circuit Ct., 13th Jud.

Circuit, 1961—, presiding judge, 1969—; faculty adviser Nat. Coll. State Trial Judges. Pres. Greater Gulf State Fair; bd. dirs. Mobile Mental Health Center, ARC. Mem. Am. Bar Assn., Ala. State, Mobile County bars, Am. Judges Assn., Nat. Coll. State Trial Judges, Internat. Acad. Trial Judges (pres.-elect). Home: 255 S McGregor Ave Mobile AL 36608 Office: Mobile County Courthouse Mobile AL 36602 Tel (205) 438-3481

HODAN, THEODORE JAMES, b. Milw., Dec. 21, 1938; B.S. in Mech. Engring., Marquette U., 1960, LL.B., 1963, J.D., 1968. Admitted to Wis. bar, 1963, U.S. Supreme Ct. bar, 1966, U.S. Ct. Mil. Appeals, bar, 1966; partner firm Podell, Hodan & Podell, Milw., 1973—; instr. police sci. Milw. Area Tech. Coll., 1970—; lectr., sch. social welfare U. Wis., Milw., 1973; lectr. Police Dept. Tng. Sch., Milw., 1970-72; asst. dist. atty. Milwaukee County, Wis., 1967-73; co. commr. for Milw. County Ct., 1973—. Mem. Am., Wis. bar assns., Wis. Acad. Trial Lawyers, Nat. Assn. Criminal Def. Lawyers, Nat. Dist. Attys. Assn. Home: 8501 N Greenvale Rd Bayside WI 53217 Office: 625 N Milwaukee St Milwaukee WI 53202 Tel (414) 224-9494

HODES, ROBERT BERNARD, b. N.Y.C., Aug. 25, 1925; A.B., Dartmouth Coll., 1946; LL.B., Harvard U., 1949. Admitted to N.Y. bar, 1950; asso. firm Willkie Farr & Gallagher, N.Y.C., 1949-56, partner, 1956—. Mem. Am. Bar Assn., Am. Law Inst. Office: 1 Citicorp Center 153 E 53d St New York City NY 10022 Tel (212) 248-1000

HODES, SCOTT, b. Chgo., Aug. 14, 1937; A.B., U. Chgo., 1956; J.D., U. Mich., 1959; LL.M., Northwestern U., 1961. Admitted to Ill. bar, 1959, D.C. bar, 1963; partner firm Arvey, Hodes, Costello and Burman, Chgo., 1959-61, 64—; capt. JAGC, Dept. Army, Washington, 1962-64. Mem. Ill. Democratic State Central Com., 9th Congl. Dist., 1970—. Mem. Fed. Bar Found. (dir.), Am., Fed., Ill., Chgo. bar assns., Judge Adv. Assn. Recipient Cassandra Found. award, 1967; Fed. Bar Assn. Distinguished Service award, 1971, 73. Author: What Every Artist and Collector Should Know About the Law, 1974. Office: 180 N LaSalle St Chicago IL 60601 Tel (312) 855-5017

HODGE, JOHN ERNEST, JR., b. Charlotte, N.C., Dec. 3, 1944; B.S., U. N.C., 1967, J.D., 1972. Admitted to N.C. bar, 1972; mem. firm Tucker, Moon & Hodge, P.A., Charlotte. Mem. Order of the Coif, Beta Gamma Sigma. Mem. editorial bd. N.C. Law Review, 1971-72. Home: 1720-3 Delane Ave Charlotte NC 28202 Office: 2050 Southern Nat Center Charlotte NC 28202 Tel (704) 377-9714

HODGE, RICHARD ELSTON, b. Huntington Park, Calif., June 14, 1930; B.S., U. So. Calif., 1952, LL.B., 1955. Admitted to Calif. bar, 1956; partner, head firm Hodge & Hodges, and predecessors, Beverly Hills, Calif., 1956—. Mem. Beverly Hills, Los Angeles County, Am. bar assns., State Bar of Calif., Am. Arbitration Assn. (nat. panel arbitrators). Recipient Law Alumni award U. So. Calif., 1955. Mem. editorial bd. U. So. Calif. Law Review, 1953-54, asso. editor, 1954-55. Office: 1801 Century Park E Los Angeles CA 90067 Tel (213) 277-8300

HODGE, ROBERT LEROY, b. Crockett, Tex., Apr. 20, 1937; B.A. in Polit. Sci. and Sociology, Wiley Coll., 1959; J.D., Tex. So. U., 1972. Admitted to Tex. bar, 1972; mem. firm Bonner & Hodge, Houston, 1972-74, Anderson, Hodge, Jones & Hoyt, Houston, 1974—; tchr. govt. and civics, 1959-69; atty. Kendleton Sch. Bd., Brentwood Civic Club. Mem. Am., Nat. bar assns., Tex. Criminal Def. Lawyers Assn., Harris County Criminal Lawyers Assn., Houston Lawyers Assn., Phi Alpha Delta. Recipient Am. Jurisprudence award, 1972. Home: 4206 Worrell St Houston TX 77045 Office: 1802 Calumet St Houston TX 77004 Tel (713) 524-4651

HODGE, VERNE ANTONIO, b. St. Thomas, V.I., Nov. 16, 1933; B.S. magna cum laude, Hampton Inst., 1956; certificate in advanced income tax law for internal revenue agts. IRS, Pitts., 1960; J.D. cum laude, Howard U., 1969. Formerly internal auditor and internal revenue agt. tax div. V.I. Dept. Fin., comptroller Mannassah Bus Lines, Inc., St. Thomas, bus. mgr. and personnel dir, V.I. Dept. Pub. Works; admitted to D.C. bar, V.I. bar, U.S. Supreme Ct. bar; practiced law, 1969-73, then bacame atty. gen. V.I.; now chief justice Terr. Ct. of V.I. Mem. Eastern (past chmn.), Nat. assns. attys. gen., Nat. Assn. Securities Dealers (rep.). Registered pub. accountant. Address: Chief Justice Terr Ct of the V I Charlotte Amalie VI 00801*

HODGES, A(GIL) EARL, b. Brownwood, Tex., May 15, 1933; B.B.A., U. Tex., 1953, J.D., 1957. Admitted to Tex. bar, 1957, U.S. Supreme Ct. bar, 1973; atty. Continental Oil Co., Houston, 1958-67, counsel, 1967-74, asst. sec., 1961—, gen. atty. in charge corp. services div., 1974—. Bd. dirs. Houston Humane Soc., 1963-69. Mem. Houston, Am. bar assns., Phi Eta Sigma, Phi Delta Phi (exchequer local chpt. 1957). Office: 5 Greenway Plaza E Houston TX 77046 Tel (713) 965-1089

HODGES, GUS MACEY, b. Hoyt, Tex., Feb. 12, 1908; B.B.A., Univ. Tex., 1930, LL.B., 1932. Admitted to Tex. bar, 1932; asso. firm Leachman & Gardere, 1932-40; prof. U. Tex., Austin, 1932—. Mem. advisory com., Tex. Supreme Ct. Mem. Travis County Bar Assn. Author: Special Issue Submission in Texas, 1959, supplement, 1969; Cases Texas Procedure Prior to Trial, 1969; Cases Trial and Appellate Procedure in Texas, 1974. Home: 3714 Meredith St Austin TX 78703 Office: 2500 Red River St Austin TX 78705 Tel (512) 471-5151

HODGES, JACK DOUGLAS, b. Johnson City, Tenn., Jan. 12, 1933; B.S., East Tenn. State U., 1953; J.D., U. Tenn., 1955. Admitted to Tenn. bar, 1955; individual practice law, Johnson City, 1955—; magistrate Washington County (Tenn.) Ct., 1969—. Mem. Washington County (pres. 1974), Tenn., Am. bar assns., Tenn., Am. trial lawyers assns. Office: 205 W Walnut St Johnson City TN 37601 Tel (615) 926-3114

HODGES, JOHN ANDREWS, b. Pitts., Nov. 18, 1940; A.B., Harvard U., 1962; LL.B., Columbia U., 1968. Admitted to D.C. bar, also U.S. Supreme Ct. bar; law clk. to judge U.S. Dist. Ct., Wilmington, Del.; summer law clk. firm Patton, Blow, Verrill, Brand & Boggs, firm Patterson, Crawford, Arensberg & Dunn; asso. firm Covington & Burling, Washington; now partner firm Peabody, Rivlin, Lambert & Meyers, Washington. Mem. Am. Bar Assn. (vice chmn. com. emergency econ. controls sect. adminstrv. law). Home: 3036 Dent Place NW Washington DC 20007 Office: 1150 Connecticut Ave NW Washington DC 20036 Tel (202) 457-1043

HODGES, J(OHN) NORMAN, b. Silver City, N. Mex., Aug. 5, 1925; B.A., U. N. Mex., 1947, B.S., 1948, LL.B., 1951, J.D., 1966. Admitted to N. Mex. bar, 1951, U.S. Supreme Ct. bar, 1960; practiced in Silver City, N. Mex., 1951, Lordsburg, N. Mex., 1952-56; dist. atty. 6th Jud. Dist., 1957-63; judge N. Mex. Dist. Ct., 6th Jud. Dist., 1963—; with Judge Adv. Gen. Corps USNR, 1968. Pres. United Vets. Center, Silver City, 1963-75. Mem. Am., N. Mex. bar assns., Am. Judicature Soc., New M. Jud. Conf. Home: Pinos Altos Rd Silver City NM 88061 Office: POB 2339 Silver City NM 88061 Tel (505) 538-2975

HODGES, LEO CHARLES, b. Portland, Tenn., Jan. 31, 1946; B.A., Purdue U., 1968; J.D., Harvard, 1971. Admitted to Ind. bar, 1971; asso. firm Ice Miller Donadio & Ryan, Indpls., 1971-73, firm Savill & Hodges, Indpls., 1973; dir. Advanced Underwriting Service, Tax Companion and Estate Planner's Letter, R&R/Newkirk, Indpls., 1973-77. Active Sr. Citizens Center of Indpls., Noble Schs. & Industries for Retarded Children and Adults, Indpls., Cross-Roads Rehab. Center for Crippled Children and Adults, Indpls. Mem. Am., Ind. bar assns. Home: 523 E 60th St Indianapolis IN 46220 Office: PO Box 1727 Indianapolis IN 46206 Tel (317) 297-4360

HODGES, PAUL VINCENT, JR., b. Monroe, Wis., Feb. 4, 1913; A.B., Regis Coll., 1936; LL.B., U. Colo., 1939. Admitted to Colo. bar, 1939; spl. agt. FBI, Washington, 1939-46; partner firm Kay & Hodges, Denver, 1946-55; judge City and County of Denver Municipal Ct., 1955-59, Denver Superior Ct., 1960-65; mgr. Denver Dept. Welfare, 1959-60; hearing examiner, counselor Denver Pub. Utilities Commn., 1965-67; justice Colo. Supreme Ct., 1967—; mem. Colo. Ho. of Reps., 1952-54; election commr. City of Denver, 1947-52. Mem. Soc. Former FBI Agts., Denver, Colo. bar assns. Home: 2688 S Wadsworth Way Lakewood CO 80227 Office: 308 State Capitol Denver CO 80203 Tel (313) 892-2419

HODGES, THOMAS LUMPKIN, III, b. Atlanta, Apr. 20, 1948; B.A., Emory U., 1969; J.D. cum laude, U. Ga., 1972. Admitted to Ga. bar, 1972; asso. firm Coleman, Allen & Hodges, and predecessor, Augusta, Ga., 1972-73, partner, 1974-76; adminstr. Tenth Dist. Ct., 1976—. Mem. Am., Ga., Augusta bar assns. Home: 214 Simmons Pl Martinez GA 30907 Office: Suite 318 501 Greene St POB 195 Augusta GA 30903 Tel (404) 722-0731

HODGES, WILLIAM WHITLEY, b. Lumberton, N.C., Mar. 17, 1940; B.A. in Spanish, U. S.C., 1969, J.D., 1972. Admitted to S.C. bar, 1973, Fed. bar, 1976, U.S. Supreme Ct. bar, 1976, 4th Circuit Ct. Appeals bar, 1976; individual practice law, Columbia, S.C., 1973—; v.p., gen. counsel Central Warehouse Assos., Inc., Columbia, 1974—; instr. govt. Midlands Tech. Inst., Columbia, 1973—; certified arbitrator S.C. Dept. Labor, 1974—; exec. v.p. Lawyers Reporting Service, Columbia, 1976—; mem. comml. panel Am. Arbitration Assn., 1976—. Mem. Am., S.C. (columnist newsletter 1976—), Richland County bar assns., Assn. Trial Lawyers Am., Comml. Law League Am., S.C. Mental Health Assn., Phi Alpha Delta, Sigma Delta Pi. Recipient award for teaching Richland County (S.C.) Schs., 1968, award for excellence in torts, Am. Jurisprudence Soc., 1969. Office: 2d Floor 1316 Washington St Columbia SC 29201 Tel (803) 799-9985

HODGSON, DANIEL BLAKE, b. Athens, Ga., July 26, 1920; B.A., Yale, 1941; LL.B. summa cum laude, U. Ga., 1948. Admitted to Ga. bar, 1948, U.S. Supreme Ct. bar, 1975; partner firm Alston, Miller & Gaines, Atlanta, 1948—. Vestryman, All Saints Episcopal Ch., Atlanta, 1958-60, 62-64, 66-68, 73-75, sr. warden, 1967, 68; bd. sponsors Atlanta Symphony, 1972-75. Mem. State Bar Ga. (bd. govs. 1970—, trustee inst. continuing legal edn. 1971—, chmn. com. specialization and recertification 1974—) Am., Atlanta bar assns., Am. Law Inst., Lawyers Club Atlanta (pres. 1964-65), So. Council on Internat. and Pub. Affairs. Office: 12th Floor C&S Bank Bldg Atlanta GA 30303 Tel (404) 588-0300

HODSON, DARREL LEROY, b. Amboy, Ind., July 20, 1912; student Purdue U., 1929-30, U. Wis., 1931; B.S. in Bus. Adminstrn., Ind. U., 1935, J.D., 1937. Admitted to Ind. bar, 1937, U.S. Supreme Ct. bar, 1943, U.S. Ct. Mil. Appeals, 1953; asso. firm Overson & Manning, Kokomo, Ind., 1937-38; served with U.S. Army, 1942-46; civilian employee U.S. Army, Europe, 1946-47; partner firm Hodson, Lucas & Hillis, Kokomo, 1938-40, firm Winslow & Hodson, Kokomo, 1940-42; dir. U.S. Claims Commns. Europe, 1946-47, dep. chief claims Europe, 1946-47; individual practice law, Kokomo, 1948-62; partner firm Hodson & Osborn, Kokomo, 1962—; city judge Kokomo, 1938, pros. atty., 1941-42, 55-58; county atty. Howard County (Ind.), 1950-52. Mem. Howard County, Am., Ind. bar assns., Judge Advs. Assn. Home: 1217 W Sycamore St Kokomo IN 46901 Office: 216 E Walnut St Kokomo IN 46901 Tel (317) 457-7264

HOEFFEL, HARRY PETER, b. Appleton, Wis., Apr. 10, 1904; B.A., U. Wis., 1929, LL.B., 1930. Admitted to Wis. bar; practice law, Appleton; city atty. Appleton, 1936-54. Mem. Am., Wis., Outagamie County bar assns., Am. Coll. Trial Lawyers. Home: 331 W 6th St Appleton WI 54911 Office: 206 S Memorial Dr Appleton WI 54911 Tel (414) 734-4567

HOEGEN, PETER JOSEPH, JR., b. St. Louis, Oct. 8, 1937; A.B., U. Md., 1965; J.D., U. Notre Dame, 1971. Admitted to Pa. bar, 1971; spl. agt. U.S. Army Intelligence Corps, 1961-65, FBI, Phila., Monterey, Calif., and N.Y.C., 1965-68; asso. firm Rosenn, Jenkins & Greenwald, Wilkes-Barre, Pa., 1971-75, Fahey & Casper, Wilkes-Barre, 1975—. Mem. Am., Pa., Fed. bar assns., Wilkes-Barre Law and Library Assn. Home: 78 Lathrop St Kingston PA 18704 Office: Fahey & Casper 930 United Penn Bank Bldg Wilkes-Barre PA 18701 Tel (717) 824-5711

HOEHN, CHARLES, III, b. San Francisco, Feb. 19, 1944; A.B., U. Calif., Berkeley, 1965; J.D., Hastings Coll. Law., 1968. Admitted to Calif. bar, 1969; dep. pub. defender Contra Costa County (Calif.), 1969-74; individual practice law, Richmond, Calif., 1974—. Mem. Alameda, Calif., Richmond (law day chmn. 1975) bar assns. Office: 3707 Bissell Ave Richmond CA 94805 Tel (415) 232-5184

HOEHN, ROBERT EDMUND, b. Cleve., Sept. 10, 1942; A.B., Allegheny Coll., 1964; J.D., Vanderbilt U., 1967. Admitted to Ohio bar, 1967, Tenn. bar, 1969; asso. firm Roemisch & Wright, Cleve., 1967-68; clk. firm Hooker, Hooker & Willis, Nashville, 1968; mem. firm Taylor & Schlater, Nashville, 1970-73; partner firm Quilkn, Wilson, Nimmo & Hoehn, Nashville, 1973—. Mem. Am., Tenn., Nashville (chmn. moral fixtures com. 1976—) bar assns. Home: 1200 Cliftee Dr Brentwood TN 37027 Office: 95 White Bridge Rd Suite 308 Nashville TN 37205 Tel (615) 356-1580

HOEPER, PETER JOHN, b. Salem, Oreg., Mar. 24, 1947; J.D., U. Wis., 1972. Admitted to Wis. bar, 1972; partner firm Hooker & Hoeper, Waupun, Wis., 1972—. Mem. Waupun City Adminstrn. Planning Com., 1974. Mem. Wis., Fond du Lac County, Dodge County (chmn. Project Inquiry 1974-76, sec.-treas. 1976-77) bar assns. Home: 6 1/2 Fond du Lac St Waupun WI 53963 Office: 512 E Main St Waupun WI 53963 Tel (414) 324-2121

HOEQUIST, CHARLES ERNEST, b. Orlando, Fla., Mar. 18, 1929; B.S. in Bus. Adminstrn., U. Fla., 1953, LL.B., 1959. Admitted to Fla. bar, 1959; asso. firm Baker & Baker, Clearwater, Fla., 1959; partner firm Edwards & Hoequist, Orlando, 1959-63; individual practice law, Orlando, 1963-64; partner firm Hoequist & McLarry, Orlando, 1964—. Mem. The Fla. Bar, Orange County, Am. Bar Assns. Home: 4318 Irentonian Court Orlando FL 32806 Office: 3319 Maguire Blvd Suite 135 Orlando FL 32803 Tel (305) 894-7911

HOERNER, ROBERT JACK, b. Fairfield, Iowa, Oct. 12, 1931; B.A., Cornell Coll., 1953; J.D., U. Mich., 1958. Admitted to Ohio bar, 1960, U.S. Supreme Ct. bar, 1964; law clk. Chief Justice Earl Warren, U.S. Supreme Ct., Washington, 1958-59; chief evaluation sect. antitrust div. Dept. Justice, Washington, 1963-65; partner firm Jones, Day, Reavis & Pogue, Cleve., 1967—. Mem. Am., Ohio, Cleve. bar assns. Editor-in-chief U. Mich. Law Rev., 1957-58; contbr. articles to legal jours. Home: 1700K E 13th St Apt 22A Cleveland OH 44114 Office: 1700 Union Commerce Bldg Cleveland OH 44115 Tel (216) 696-3939

HOERTEL, WILLIAM WADSWORTH, b. St. Louis, Mar. 7, 1930; student Mo. Sch. Mines and Metallurgy, 1948-50; J.D., U. Mo., 1959. Admitted to Mo. bar, 1959, U.S. Supreme Ct. bar, 1975; individual practice law, Rolla, Mo., 1959-75; partner firm Hoertel & Wiggins, Rolla, 1975—; juvenile officer Phelps County (Mo.), 1961-75, pros. atty., 1961-67. Trustee, State Fed. Soldiers Home, St. James, Mo., 1972. Mem. Phelps County Bar (past pres.), Phi Alpha Delta. Home: 612 Salem Ave Rolla MO 65401 Office: 207 Scott Bldg Rolla MO 65401 Tel (314) 364-4103

HOESLY, BERTA SOWA, b. Milw., Feb. 1, 1949; B.A., U. Wis., 1970, J.D., 1974. Admitted to Wis. bar, 1974; asst. city atty. Janesville (Wis.), 1974—. Mem. Wis., Rock County bar assns. Office: 18 N Jackson St Janesville WI 53545 Tel (608) 754-2811

HOFER, WALTER, b. Vienna, Austria, July 28, 1929; B.S. in Bus. Adminstrn., N.Y. U., 1952; LL.B., Bklyn. Law Sch., 1955. Admitted to N.Y. bar, 1956, since practiced in N.Y.C.; lectr. Mem. Am., N.Y. State bar assns. Contbr. articles profl. jours. Office: 221 W 57th St New York City NY 10019 Tel (212) 582-5030

HOFF, JOHN SEABURY, b. Balt., Aug. 12, 1940; A.B. magna cum laude, Harvard U., 1962, LL.B. cum laude, 1965. Admitted to D.C. bar, 1966, U.S. Supreme Ct. bar, 1971; law clk. to judge U.S. Ct. Appeals, D.C. Circuit, 1965-67; asso. firm Leva, Hawes, Symington, Martin & Oppenheimer, Washington, 1967-72, partner, 1973—. Home: 4624 Chesapeake St NW Washington DC 20016 Office: 815 Connecticut Ave NW Washington DC 20006 Tel (202) 298-8020

HOFF, TIMOTHY, b. Freeport, Ill., Feb. 27, 1941; A.B., Tulane U., 1963, J.D., 1966; LL.M., Harvard, 1970. Admitted to Fla. bar, 1967, Ala. bar, 1973; asso. firm Williams, Parker, Harrison, Dietz & Getzen, Sarasota, Fla., 1966-69; prof. law U. Ala., University, 1970—; cons. in field. Bd. dirs. Tuscaloosa County Humane Soc., 1975—, Tuscaloosa County Preservation Soc., 1972—. Mem. AAUP, Internat. Assn. for Philosophy of Law and Social Philosophy, Order of Coif, Phi Beta Kappa. Home: Battle-Friedman House 1010 Greensboro Ave Tuscaloosa AL 35401 Office: Law School University Alabama University AL 35486 Tel (205) 348-5930

HOFFER, PHILIP, b. Bklyn., Oct. 17, 1911; student Coll. City N.Y., 1928-30; LL.B., cum laude, Bklyn. Law Sch., 1933, J.D., 1970. Admitted to N.Y. State Supreme Ct. bar, 1934, U.S. Supreme Ct. bar, 1960; partner firm Hoffer & Hoffer, N.Y.C., 1954—, pres. 1973—; v.p., gen. counsel, dir. Empire Mut. Ins. Co., N.Y.C., 1958—, Allcity Ins. Co., N.Y.C., 1963—; pres. Empal Agy. Inc.; dir. Surplus Lines Inc. Mem. Alumni Assn. Bklyn. Law Sch. (pres. 1963-70), Am., N.Y. State, Bronx County (N.Y.), Queens County (N.Y.) bar assns., Assn. Bar City N.Y., Bklyn.-Manhattan Trial Lawyers Assn. Recipient Distinguished Alumni award Bklyn. Law Sch., 1970, seminar room named name in his honor, 1977; contbr. articles to legal jours. Office: 1965 Broadway New York City NY 10023 Tel (212) 870-8424

HOFFER, ROSE LIEBMAN, b. N.Y.C., June 14, 1911; student N.Y. U. Sch. of Journalism, 1930-33; LL.B., Bklyn. Law Sch., 1954. Admitted to U.S. Supreme Ct. bar, 1955, U.S. Customs Ct. bar, 1969, U.S. Ct. Appeals 2d Circuit bar, 1973; partner firm Hoffer & Hoffer, N.Y.C., 1955—; gen. counsel Empire Mut. Ins. Co., N.Y.C., 1958, also dir.; gen. counsel Allcity Ins. Co., N.Y.C., 1963. Master civil ct. City of N.Y., 1966-68; hearing officer N.Y.C. Parking Violations Bur., 1970—. Mem. Am., N.Y., Bronx Women's bar assns., Nat. Assn. Women Lawyers, Internat. Fedn. Women Lawyers, Am. Arbitration Assn. (arbitrator). Recipient Distinguished Alumna award Bklyn. Law Sch., 1973. Office: 1965 Broadway St New York City NY 10023 Tel (212) CI5-3060

HOFFIUS, RICHARD STUART, b. Grand Rapids, Mich., July 14, 1914; student Colgate U.; LL.B., U. Mich. Admitted to Mich. bar, 1939; spl. agt. FBI, 1942-45; practiced in Grand Rapids; pros. atty. Kent County (Mich.), 1954-59; judge Mich. Circuit Ct., 1960—; commr. State Bar Mich., 1973—; mem. Mich. Commn. on Criminal Justice. Pres. Family Service Assn., 1952-54, United Fund and Community Services, 1966-68, Grand Rapids Art Mus., 1969-71, West Mich. Health Systems Agy. Fellow Am. Bar Found.; mem. Mich. Judges Assn. (pres. 1971-72). Office: 333 Monroe St NW Grand Rapids MI 49502 Tel (606) 774-3650

HOFFMAN, ABRAHAM, b. Phila., Feb. 22, 1908; B.A., U. Del., 1928. Admitted to Del. bar, 1932; partner firm Hoffman & Hoffman, Wilmington, 1932-43, 46-50; individual practice law, Wilmington, 1950—; lectr. in field.; chief dep. sheriff, sheriff's atty. New Castle County, Del., 1936-37; chief atty. New Castle County, 1948-49. Chief dep. treas. New Castle County, 1941-42. Mem. Am., Del. bar assns., Am. Trial Lawyers Assn. Office: 6 E 13th St POB 2012 Wilmington DE 19899 Tel (302) 655-8839

HOFFMAN, ALLAN L., b. Coffeyville, Kans., Mar. 8, 1943; B.M.E., U. Fla., 1964, J.D., 1970. Admitted to Fla. bar, 1971; practice law, Palm Beach Fla. Office: 509 N Dixie St W Palm Beach FL 33401 Tel (305) 659-7666

HOFFMAN, CHRISTIAN MATTHEW, b. N.Y.C., Apr. 17, 1944; B.A., Boston Coll., 1966; J.D., Harvard, 1969. Admitted to Mass. bar, 1969; asso. firm Foley, Hoag & Eliot, Boston, 1969-73, partner, 1974—. Bd. dirs. Wellesley Children's Community Center, 1974—. Mem. Am., Mass., Boston bar assns. Home: 53 Audubon Rd Wellesley Hills MA 02181 Office: 10 Post Office Sq Boston MA 02109 Tel (617) 482-1390

HOFFMAN, DANIEL STEVEN, b. N.Y.C., May 4, 1931; B.A., U. Colo., 1951; LL.B. magna cum laude, U. Denver, 1958. Admitted to Colo. bar, 1959, U.S. Dist. Ct. bar, 1960; sr. partner firm Hoffman, McDermott & Hoffman, Denver, 1970—. Mgr. safety and excise Mayor's Cabinet fort City and County of Denver, 1963-65. Fellow Am. Coll. Trial Lawyers (state chmn. 1975-76); mem. Internat. Soc. Barristers, Colo. Bar Assn. (pres. 1976-77, award of merit for outstanding young lawyer of year 1965), Colo. Trial Lawyers Assn. (pres. 1961). Office: Suite 675 50 S Steele St Denver CO 80209 Tel (303) 399-6037

HOFFMAN, EDWARD B., b. Elmira, N.Y., Apr. 3, 1931; B.A., Cornell U., 1953, J.D., 1955. Admitted to N.Y. bar, 1955; asso. firm Sayles, Evans, Brayton, Palmer & Tifft, Elmira, 1955-62, partner, 1962—. Sec., So. Tier Econ. Growth, 1968-74, pres., 1974-76; bd. mgrs. Arnot Ogden Hosp., 1969—. Mem. Chemung County (N.Y.), N.Y. State, Am. bar assns., Am. Coll. Trial Lawyers. Home: Woodslane Elmira NY 14905 Office: 415 E Water St Elmira NY 14902 Tel (607) 734-2271

HOFFMAN, ELLIOT LEE, b. Bklyn., June 29, 1930; A.B. magna cum laude, Harvard, 1951; LL.B. with honors, Yale, 1954. Admitted to N.Y. bar, 1955, U.S. Ct. Appeals bar, 1956, U.S. Supreme Ct. bar, 1973; law asst. asso. judge Charles W. Froessel, N.Y. Ct. Appeals, Albany and N.Y.C., 1954-56; asst. U.S. atty. So. dist. N.Y., N.Y.C., 1956-58; individual practice law, N.Y.C., 1958-60, 60—; counsel N.Y. State Com. of Investigation, 1960-61; partner firm Beldock, Levine & Hoffman, 1965—; lectr. Temple U., 1976, New Sch. Social Research, 1977, Harvard U., 1977, N.Y. U., 1977. Mem. community council Town of Kent, Carmel, N.Y., 1974—; trustee Newport Folk Found., N.Y. Studio Sch. Spl. counsel Town of Kent Planning Bd. Mem. N.Y. State Bar Assn., N.Y. State Dist. Attys. Assn., Harvard Alumni Assn., Am. Arbitration Assn., Phi Beta Kappa. Editor: Yale Law Jour., 1954. Home: 72 Bank St New York City NY 10014 Office: 565 Fifth Ave New York City NY 10017 Tel (212) 490-0400

HOFFMAN, ELMO ROGERS, b. Salisbury, N.C., July 7, 1935; B.S., U. S.C., 1957; J.D., Stetson U., 1966. Admitted to Fla. bar, 1966; asso. firm Howell, Kirby, Montgomery, Sands & D'aiuto, Jacksonville, Fla., 1966-69; partner firm Hoffman, Hendry, Parker & Smith, Orlando, Fla., 1969—. Mem. Orange County, Am. bar assns., Fla. Bar, Am. Judicature Soc., Fla. Def. Lawyers Assn., Def. Research Inst., Inc. Office: 200 E Robinson St Orlando FL 32801 Tel (305) 843-5880

HOFFMAN, HAROLD M., b. N.Y.C., Sept. 13, 1929; B.B.S., City Coll. N.Y., 1949; M.A., Columbia, 1950; LL.B., Yale, 1952. Admitted to N.Y. bar, 1952, since practiced in N.Y.C.; partner firm Putney, Twombly, Hall & Hirson, 1958-68, Kronish, Lieb, Shainswit, Weiner & Hellman, 1968—; police judge Village of Great Neck Estates, 1971—. Mem. N.Y. State Bar Assn. Author: (with Jerome Frank) Not Guilty, 1957; contbr. articles to legal jours. Home: 11 South Dr Great Neck NY 11021 Office: 1345 Ave of Americas New York City NY 10019 Tel (212) 765-6000

HOFFMAN, HARRY, b. Ottawa, Ont., Can., Sept. 14, 1892; LL.B., N.Y. U., 1915. Admitted to N.Y. bar, 1915, U.S. Supreme Ct. bar, 1934; partner firm Guggenheimer & Untermyer, N.Y.C., 1944—; sec. to police commr. N.Y.C., 1917. Mem. Am., N.Y. State bar assns., N.Y. County Lawyers Assn., Assn. Bar City N.Y., Am. Soc. Internat. Law, Am. Judicature Soc. Office: 80 Pine St New York City NY 10005 Tel (212) 344-2040

HOFFMAN, JOSEPH ANTHONY, b. N.Y.C., June 20, 1933; B.A., Seton Hall U., 1955, J.D., 1961. Admitted to N.J. bar, 1962, U.S. Supreme Ct. bar, 1967; asst. atty. gen., chief of litigation State of N.J., 1965-66, chief, criminal investigation, 1967-68, 1st. asst. atty. gen., 1968-69, commr. dept. labor industry, 1973-76; corporate atty. N.J. Bell Telephone Co., Newark, 1969-73; partner firm Lum, Biunno & Tompkins, Newark, 1976—. Chmn. N.J. Econ. Devel. Authority, 1973-76; exec. dir. N.J. Democratic Com., 1969. Mem. N.J. Bar Assn. (Outstanding Young Lawyer 1968, chmn. corporate law sect. 1973-74). Recipient Alumni of Year award Seton Hall U. Law Sch., 1975. Office: Lum Biunno & Tompkins 550 Broad St Newark NJ 07102 Tel (201) 622-2300

HOFFMAN, LEONARD, b. Dwight, Ill., Apr. 18, 1918; A.B., U. Chgo., 1938, J.D., 1940. Admitted to Ill. Supreme Ct. bar, 1940, U.S. Supreme Ct. bar, 1949; practiced in Morris, Ill., 1945-57; city atty. City of Morris, 1949-50; judge Grundy County (Ill.) Ct., 1950-57, Ill. Circuit Ct., 13th Jud. Circuit, 1957-59; justice Ill. Appellate Ct., 4th Dist., 1959-63; judge 13th Ill. Jud. Circuit Ct., 1963—; mem. Ill. Pattern Jury Instrns. Com. Pres. Rainbow council Boy Scouts Am., 1963-65; ruling elder Morris Presbyterian Ch. Mem. Ill. Circuit and Superior Judges Assn. (v.p. 1959). Named Outstanding Citizen of Morris, 1967; bd. editors U. Chgo. Law Rev., 1939-40. Home: 424 Vine St Morris IL 60450 Office: Courthouse Ottawa IL 61350 Tel (815) 434-6492

HOFFMAN, LEWIS ACKLEY, b. Kittanning, Pa., July 18, 1943; A.B., Dartmouth, 1965; J.D., Syracuse U., 1968. Admitted to N.Y. bar, 1968; corp. atty. Oneida Ltd. (N.Y.), 1968-71; individual practice law, Oneida, 1971—. Mem. Madison County (N.Y.), N.Y. State, Am. bar assns. Home and Office: 3851 Prospect St Oneida NY 13421 Tel (315) 363-8843

HOFFMAN, LOUIS LAMONTE, b. Litchfield, Minn., Jan. 16, 1927; B.B.A., U. Minn., 1949; B.S., William Mitchell Coll., St. Paul, 1955, LL.B., 1957. Admitted to Minn. bar, 1957; individual practice law, Princeton, Minn., 1958—; atty. City of Princeton, 1961—. Mem. Minn. State Bar Assn. Home: 302 S 7th Ave Princeton MN 55371 Office: 106 S 5th Ave Princeton MN 55371 Tel (612) 389-1551

HOFFMAN, PAUL GORDON, b. Lafayette, Ind., Apr. 12, 1922; B.S., Purdue U., 1947; J.D., U. Mich., 1950. Admitted to Minn. bar, 1950; individual practice law, St. Cloud, Minn., 1950-68; spl. judge Municipal Ct., St. Cloud, 1960-68; judge Minn. 7th Jud. Dist., St. Cloud, 1968—. Pres. ARC Stearns County, St. Cloud; mem. Campfire Girls Council; chmn. Stearns County Republicans. Mem. Am., Minn. bar assns., Am. Judicature Soc. Home: 33 Highbanks Pl St Cloud MN 56301 Office: Ct House St Cloud MN 56301 Tel (612) 251-3613

HOFFMAN, ROBERT JAMES, b. Indpls., Sept. 29, 1945; B.A., Ind. U., 1968; J.D. Summa cum laude, Indpls. U., 1974. Admitted to Ind. bar, 1974; asso. firm Lowe, Linder, Gray, Steele & Wiles, Indpls.; law clk. Ind. Ct. Appeals, 1973-74; lectr. Indpls. Law Sch., 1975-76. Mem. Am., Ind., Indpls. bar assns. Office: 1 Indiana Sq Suite 3130 Indianapolis IN 46204 Tel (317) 635-8020

HOFFMAN, STANLEY, b. N.Y.C., June 15, 1928; LL.B., Bklyn. Law Sch., 1958. Admitted to N.Y. bar, 1959, U.S. Supreme Ct. bar, 1964; transp. counsel Union Carbide Corp., N.Y.C., 1960—; instr. transp. law and practice Acad. Advanced Traffic, N.Y.C., 1968—. Mem. Zoning Bd. Appeals, Mamaroneck, N.Y., Mem. N.Y. Bar Assn., ICC Practitioners Assn., Maritime Law Assn. Author: Model Legal Forms for Shippers, 1970; contbr. articles to profl. jours. Office: 270 Park Ave New York City NY 10017 Tel (212) 551-5836

HOFFMAN, WALTER EDWARD, b. Jersey City, July 18, 1907; B.S. in Econs., U. Pa., 1928; LL.B., Washington and Lee U., 1931, LL.D., 1970. Admitted to Va. bar, 1929; since practiced in Norfolk, Va., asso. firm Rumble & Rumble, 1931-35; partner firm Breeden & Hoffman, 1935-54; judge U.S. Dist. Ct., Eastern Dist. Va., 1954—; dir. Fed. Jud. Center, Washington, 1974—. Pres., Norfolk YMCA, 1948-52; active Norfolk Community Fund, 1953-55; v.p. Salvation Army, 1944-50; bd. dirs. Mental Hygiene Center, Muscular Dystrophy Assn.; trustee Randolph-Macon Coll., 1953-74. Mem. Am. Bar Assn., Nat. Inst. Corrections (adv. bd.), Nat. Conf. Fed. Trial Judges, Order of Coif. Author: Sentencing Philosophy, 1969. Office: US Dist Ct Court House Norfolk VA 23510 Tel (804) 625-7076

HOFFMANN, CHARLES RICHARD, b. N.Y.C., Dec. 14, 1938; B.S. in Mgmt. Engring., Rensselaer Polytech. Inst., 1960; LL.B., N.Y. U., 1965. Admitted to N.Y. bar, 1966, Patent bar, 1967; mem. firm Kane, Dalsimer, Kane, Sullivan & Kurucz, N.Y.C., 1965-69, partner, 1969—. Mem. Assn. Bar City N.Y., Am, N.Y. patent law assns., Am., N.Y. State bar assns. Home: 5 Wood Ct Bayville NY 11709 Office: 420 Lexington Ave New York City NY 10017 Tel (212) 532-9400

HOFFMANN, MALCOLM ARTHUR, b. N.Y.C., Nov. 26, 1912; A.B. magna cum laude, Harvard U., 1934, J.D., 1937. Admitted to N.Y. bar, 1938, U.S. Supreme Ct. bar, 1943; sr. atty. NLRB, Washington, 1939-43; spl. atty. appellate sect. criminal div. Dept. Justice, 1943, spl. asst. to atty. gen. anti-trust div., 1944-55; asso. firm Rosenman, Goldmark, Colin and Kaye, N.Y.C., 1955-59; of counsel firm Greenbaum, Wolff & Ernst, N.Y.C., 1959-60; sr. partner firm Malcolm A. Hoffmann, 1960—; lectr. Practising Law Inst., 1957—; mem. faculty Joint Com. on Continuing Legal Edn., Am. Law Inst., Am. Bar Assn., 1966; lectr. trade problems Am. Mgmt. Assn., 1967-71; lectr. antitrust sect. meeting Am. Bar Assn., Honolulu, 1967, litigation sect. meeting, 1976. Chmn. Talk Club, 1955—, Hoffmann Sch., Inc. Mem. World Assn. Lawyers, Am. Judicature Soc., Am. (vice-chmn. com.), Internat., Fed. (former editor jour., past sec. trade regulation com.), N.Y. State (past chmn. com., mem. exec. com.) bar assns., Assn. Bar City N.Y. (past chmn. subcom.), Fed. Bar Council, Nat. Lawyers Club. Author: Government Lawyer, 1955; (with Morris Ernst) On Saving the Union, 1968; Back and Forth, 1966; editor: Hoffmann's Antitrust Law and Techniques, 1963; contbr. articles to law jours. and reviews. Home: 5440 Independence Ave Riverdale NY 10471 Office: 12 E 41st St New York City NY 10017 Tel (212) MU5-0535

HOFFMANN, ROBERT ANDREW, b. Memphis, Aug. 8, 1911; B.S., Georgetown U., 1932; J.D., Cath. U. Am., 1934. Admitted to Tenn. bar, 1934; individual practice law, Memphis, 1934-41; judge Gen. Sessions Ct., Memphis, 1949-58; chancellor Chancery Ct. of Tenn., Memphis, 1958—; dean Law Sch., U. Memphis, 1952-62. Mem. Am., Tenn., Shelby County, Memphis bar assns., Delta Theta Phi. Home: 291 Stonewall St Memphis TN 38112 Office: 309 Shelby County Courthouse Memphis TN 38103 Tel (901) 528-3000

HOFFMEYER, WILLIAM FREDERICK, b. York, Pa., Dec. 20, 1936; A.B., Franklin and Marshall Coll., 1958; J.D., Dickinson Coll., 1961. Admitted to Pa. bar, 1962; individual practice law, York, 1962—; pres. York Abstracting Co. Mem. Am., York County, Pa. bar assns. Home: R D 11 York PA 17406 Office: 30 N George St York PA 17401 Tel (717) 846-8846

HOFNAGEL, WENDY, b. Milw., Oct. 6, 1949; B.A., Marquette U., 1971, J.D., 1974. Admitted to Wis. bar, 1974; asst. dist. atty. Milwaukee County, Milw., 1974—. Mem. Wauwatosa (Wis.) Drug Info. and Counseling Commn., 1974—. Mem. Wis. Bar Assn. Office: 821 W State St Milwaukee WI 53233 Tel (414) 278-4646

HOFSTETTER, W. THOMAS, b. Virginia, Ill., June 7, 1928; LL.B., Vanderbilt U., 1952. Admitted to Ill. bar, 1952, D.C. bar, 1974; partner firm Pattishall, McAuliffe & Hofstetter, Chgo., 1955—; adj. prof. John Marshall Law Sch., Chgo., 1962—. Mem. Am., Chgo., Ill. bar assns., Am., Chgo. patent law assns., Bar Assn. D.C., Legal Club Chgo., Law Club Chgo. Home: 1111 Ashland Ave Wilmette IL 60691 Office: 3500 Prudential Plaza Chicago IL 60601 Tel (312) 642-9518

HOGAN, ROSCOE BENJAMIN, JR., b. Birmingham, Ala., Sept. 5, 1921; A.B., Samford U., 1947; LL.B., U. Ala., 1950. Admitted to Ala. bar, 1950, U.S. Supreme Ct. bar, 1965; practiced in Birmingham, 1950—. Mem. Am., Ala., Birmingham bar assns., Ala. Plaintiff's Lawyers Assn. (pres. 1961-62), Am. (bd. govs. 1961, 63, 65-69 nat. chmn. environ. law sect. 1970-72), Ala. (past pres.) trial lawyers assns., Roscoe Pound Research Found. (trustee 1964-68). Office: 1201 City Federal Bldg Birmingham AL 35203 Tel (205) 324-5635

HOGAN, TIMOTHY SYLVESTER, b. Wellston, Ohio, Sept. 23, 1909; A.B., Xavier U., Cin., 1930, LL.D. (hon.), 1976; J.D., U. Cin., 1931. Admitted to Ohio bar, 1931, U.S. Supreme Ct. bar, 1941; partner firm Cohen, Baron, Druffel & Hogan, Cin., 1931-66; judge U.S. Dist. Ct., Cin., 1966—; spl. counsel atty. gen. Ohio, 1936-41, 46-50. Mem. Clermont County (Ohio) Planning Commn., 1956-62. Mem. Ohio, Clermont County, Cin. bar assns. Home: 3810 Eileen Dr Cincinnati OH 45209 Office: 801 US Post Office and Courthouse Cincinnati OH 45202 Tel (513) 684-2968

HOGAN, WILLIAM EDWARD, b. Bridgeport, Conn., Mar. 31, 1928; A.B., Boston, Coll., 1949, LL.B., 1952; S.J.D., Harvard, 1962. Admitted to Mass. bar, 1952, N.Y. State bar, 1973; asst. prof. law Boston Coll., 1955-58, asso. prof. 1958-60; J. duPratt White Prof. Law, Cornell U., 1960—; vis. prof. law., Columbia, 1962, Harvard, 1964-65, U. Minn., 1969-70; commr. Uniform State Laws Commn., N.Y., 1974—; mem. permanent editorial bd. Uniform Comml. Code, 1974—. Mem. Am. Bar Assn. (chmn. sec. on corp. bus. and banking law in Am.), Am. Law Inst., Nat. Bankruptcy Conf. Author: (with Coogan and Vagts) Secured Transactions under the U.C.C., 1963; (with Warren) Cases and Materials on Debtor-Creditor Law, 1974; (with Warren) Cases and Materials on Comml. and Consumer Law, 1972.

HOGG, STANLEY ROE, b. Lexington, Ky., May 14, 1930; B.S. in Commerce, U. Ky., 1952, LL.B., J.D., 1954. Admitted to Ky. bar, 1954, U.S. Supreme Ct. bar, 1974; law clk. Ky. Ct. Appeals, 1954-55; served to 1st lt. JAGC, USAR, 1955-58; trial atty. NLRB, Los Angeles and Cin., 1958-60; individual practice law, Whitesburg, Ky., 1960-65; trial atty. Ky. Dept. Hwys., 1966-67; partner firm Creech & Hogg, Ashland, Ky., 1967—; county atty. Letcher County (Ky.), 1962-65. Mem. Am., Ky. bar assns., Am., Ky. trial lawyers assns. Home: 2109 Woodland St Ashland KY 41101 Office: 2d National Bank Bldg Ashland KY 41101 Tel (606) 324-7122

HOGGETT, PIERCE ALEXANDER, b. Junction, Tex., Feb. 14, 1934; B.S., SW Tex. U., 1956; LL.B., U. Tex., 1965; postgrad SW Grad. Sch. Banking, 1975-77. Admitted to Tex. bar, 1965; partner firm Stevenson & Hoggett, Junction, 1965-68; chief bus. devel. Frost Nat. Bank, San Antonio, 1968-73; head trust dept. San Angelo Nat. Bank (Tex.), 1973—. Dir. W. Tex. Boys Ranch; capt. United Way Dr.; mem. Tex. Bankers Pub. Relations Com., 1976. Mem. Tom Green County Estate Planners Council (pres. 1975), Tex., Tom Green County Jr., Sr., bar assns., Tex. Sheep and Goat Raisers Assn. (past dir.). Guest speaker seminars sponsored by farm bur. extension service, estate planning councils, 1975-76. Home: 2713 Southland San Angelo TX 76901 Office: Beauregard St San Angelo TX 76901 Tel (915) 653-1491

HOGOBOOM, WILLIAM PERRY, b. Pasadena, Calif., Oct. 31, 1918; A.B., Occidental Coll., 1939; M.S., U. So. Calif., 1941; J.D., 1949. Admitted to Calif. bar, 1949, U.S. Supreme Ct. bar, 1967; partner firm Iverson & Hogoboom, Los Angeles, 1950-68; judge Calif. Superior Ct. for Los Angeles County, 1968—, asst. presiding judge, 1975-76, presiding judge, 1977—; presiding judge Los Angeles County Juvenile Ct., 1973-74. Bd. dirs. Los Angeles YMCA; mem. exec. bd. Los Angeles Area Council Boy Scouts Am.; trustee Occidental Coll. Mem. Am., Los Angeles County bar assns. Office: 111 N Hill St Los Angeles CA 90012 Tel (213) 974-5562

HOGUE, LOUIS LYNN, b. Little Rock, Jan. 8, 1944; A.B., William Jewell Coll., 1966; M.A., U. Tenn., Knoxville, 1968, Ph.D., 1972; J.D., Duke, 1974. Instr. English, N.C. State U., Raleigh, 1969-71; admitted to N.C. bar, 1974; asst. prof. pub. law and govt. Inst. Govt., U. N.C., Chapel Hill, 1974-76; vis. asst. prof. U. Detroit Law Sch., 1977—. Mem. Am. Pub. Health Assn. (steering com. of com. health law), Am. Soc. Legal History, Am. Studies Assn., N.C. Bar Assn., Poe Studies Assn., South Atlantic Modern Lang. Assn. Home: 1200 Willow Dr Chapel Hill NC 27514 Tel (919) 929-7482

HOHN, EDWARD LEWIS, b. Winslow, Ariz., Aug. 11, 1933; B.S. Admitted to Ala. bar, 1965, Ariz. bar, 1965, U.S. 9th Circuit Ct. Appeals bar, 1971, U.S. Supreme Ct. bar, 1971; individual practice law; pres. Hohn Enterprises Mem. Phoenix Mens Art Council; bd. dirs. Antique Aircraft Assn. Mem. Ala. State Bar, Ariz. State Bar (pres. sect. trial practice 1975-76), Ariz., Am. trial lawyers assns. Office: 3520 E Indian Sch St Phoenix AZ 85018 Tel (602) 956-2300

HOKKANEN, JOEL ERNEST, b. Sauk Centre, Minn., Jan. 26, 1943; B.A., Carleton Coll., 1965; J.D., U. Maine, 1973. Admitted to Maine bar, 1973; asso. firm Collins & Crandall, Rockland, Maine, 1973-75; individual practice law, Rockland, 1975—. Mem. Maine, Knox County bar assns. Office: 419 Main St Rockland ME 04841 Tel (207) 594-2971

HOLBROOK, DONALD EARL, b. Clare, Mich., Aug. 20, 1909; LL.B., Detroit Coll. Law, 1931. Admitted to Mich. bar, 1931; pros. atty. Clare County, 1937-42; atty. City of Clare, 1936-43; judge 21st Jud. Circuit Ct. Mich., 1948-65, Mich. Ct. of Appeals, Dist. 3, Clare, 1965—. Del. Gen. Conf. United Methodist Ch., 1956, 64, 68, 72, mem. Commn. on Christian Higher Edn., 1956-60; pres. Community Council; mem. Clare Bd. Edn., 1947-48; trustee Albion Coll., Dillard U. Mem. Mich. Judges Assn. (past pres.), Am., Mich., Tri-County, Clare County bar assns., Am. Judicature Soc., Inst. Jud. Adminstrn., Clare C. of C. (past pres.). Recipient Hon. Legion of Honor, DeMolay, 1950, Silver Beaver award Boy Scouts Am., 1959. Home: 4230 E Colonville Rd Clare MI 48617 Office: 501 N Hemlock St Clare MI 48617 Tel (517) 386-7735

HOLBROOK, RAYMOND BRIMHALL, b. Raymond, Alta., Can., Mar. 16, 1902; B.S., Brigham Young U., 1927; LL.B., Stanford U., 1931. Admitted to Utah bar, 1931; city atty., Provo, Utah, 1933-36; asst. to v.p. and gen. mgr. Western ops. U.S. Smelting, Refining & Mining Co., 1938-41, atty., 1941-54, counsel, 1954-70; mem. firm Senior & Senior, Salt Lake City, 1970—. Chmn. pub. lands com. Am. Mining Congress, 1953-57; former chmn. adv. council Salt Lake Area C. of C. Mem. Am. (ho. of dels. 1958-59), Utah, Salt Lake County bar assns. Author: Legal Obstacles to Uranium Development, 1955. Home: 711 S 13th St E Salt Lake City UT 84102 Office: 36 S State St Salt Lake City UT 84111 Tel (801) 521-1900

HOLCOMB, LYLE DONALD, JR., b. Miami, Fla., Feb. 3, 1929; B.A., U. Mich., 1951; J.D., U. Fla., 1954. Admitted to Fla. bar, 1955, U.S. Supreme Ct. bar, 1966; partner firm Holcomb & Holcomb, Miami, Fla., 1955-72; asso. firm Copeland, Therrel, Baisden & Peterson, Miami Beach, Fla., 1972-75; partner firm Therrel, Baisden, Stanton, Stillman, Brown & Wood, Miami Beach, 1976—; mem. organizing bd. Econ. Opportunity Legal Services Program (now Legal Services of Greater Miami, Inc.), 1965-75; pres. S. Florida Migrant Legal Services Program, Inc. (now Fla. Rural Legal Services), 1966-68. Mem. exec. bd. S. Fla. council Boy Scouts Am., 1958—; pres. Inter-Faith Agy. for Social Justice, 1968-69. Mem. Soc. Mayflower Descendants (Brewster colony), SAR (past chpt. pres.), Am., Dade County (sec. 1963-71), Miami Beach (treas. 1976, v.p. 1977) bar assns., Am. Judicature Soc. Recipient Silver Beaver award S. Fla. council Boy Scouts Am., 1966; author of titles Fla. Law & Practice, 1956; author: The Watson Family in Barry County, Michigan, 1966. Home: 700 Malaga Ave Coral Gables FL 33134 Office: Suite 600 1111 Lincoln Rd Mall PO Box 390558 Miami Beach FL 33139 Tel (305) 672-1921

HOLCOMB, MARY CATHERINE TIPTON, b. Lafayette, Ind., July 25, 1938; A.B., Ind. U., 1960; B.C.L., Coll. William and Mary, 1965. Admitted to Va. bar, 1965, Ky. bar, 1966, N.C. bar, 1972; atty. Ky. Dept. Revenue, Frankfort, Ky., 1966-68; partner firm Coffman & Holcomb, Virginia Beach, Va., 1968; annotator Ky. Statutes, 1969-71; tchr. bus. law N.C. State U., Raleigh, 1972—. Bd. dirs. N.C. Equal Rights Amendment United, 1974-76. Mem. Am. Bus. Law Assn., Ky., Va. bar assns., AAUW (county pres., state legis. chmn.). Contbg. author: Real Estate Transactions in North Carolina, 1976. Home: 509 Carriage Lane Cary NC 27511 Office: NC State U 3111 D H Hill Library Raleigh NC 27607 Tel (919) 737-2472

HOLCOMB, WELDON GLENN, b. Tyler, Tex., Aug. 24, 1925; B.B.A., U. Tex., 1949. Admitted to Tex. bar, 1952, U.S. Ct. Appeals 5th Circuit bar, 1965, U.S. Supreme Ct. bar, 1967; asst. atty. gen. State of Tex., 1952-53; asst. dist. atty. Smith County, Tyler, 1953-58, criminal dist. atty., 1959-62; sr. partner firm Holcomb & Horwood, Tyler, 1963—. Mem. State Bar Tex., Smith County Bar Assn., Am. Judicature Soc., Nat. Assn. Criminal Def. Lawyers, Tex. Criminal Def. Laweyrs Assn. (dir., 1st v.p. 1974, pres. 1976). Office: 111 B N Spring St Tyler TX 74701 Tel (214) 597-5595

HOLCOMB, WILLIAM A., b. Lockhart, Tex., Oct. 31, 1926; B.B.A., U. Tex., 1949; J.D., U. Houston, 1963. Accounting supr. Firemen's Fund-Am. Ins. Cos., Houston, 1950-51; with Transcontinental Gas Pipe Line Corp., Houston, 1951-74, asst. mgr. ins. and pensions, 1972, asst. treas., asst. sec., 1972-74; corp. sec. Transo Cos., Inc. and subs.'s, Houston, 1974—; dir. Gen. Assurance Services, Ltd. Mem. Tex. Assn. Bus. (life), Am., Southeastern gas assns., Ind. Natural Gas Assn. Am., Am. Mgmt. Assn., Am. Soc. Corporate Secs., Ex-Students Assn. U. Tex., Houston Soc. Risk Mgmt. (past pres.). Office: PO Box 1396 Houston TX 77001 Tel (713) 626-8100

HOLCOMBE, KENNETH HENRY, b. Plattsburgh, N.Y., Feb. 22, 1927; B.N.S., Coll. Holy Cross, 1946; J.D., Harvard, 1951. Admitted to N.Y. bar, 1951; mem. firm Tierney & Holcombe, Plattsburgh, 1951-52; partner firm Robinson & Holcombe, Plattsburgh, 1953-67; prin. firm K.H. Holcombe, Plattsburgh, 1967-69; partner firm Holcombe & Dame, Plattsburgh, 1970—; adminstr. Clinton County (N.Y.) Assigned Counsel Plan, 1966-74. Chmn. Clinton County Draft Bd., 1966-76. Mem. Fedn. Bar Assns. (pres. 4th judicial dist. 1959-61), Am., N.Y. State (ho. of dels. 1969-76, v.p. 1974-76), Clinton County (pres. 1968-69) bar assns. Office: 62 Brinkerhoff St Plattsburgh NY 14873 Tel (518) 561-2130

HOLDEN, JAMES STUART, b. Bennington, Vt., Jan. 29, 1914; A.B., Dartmouth U., 1935; LL.B., Union U., 1938. Admitted to Vt. bar, 1938, Fed. bar, 1938; state's atty. Bennington County, Vt., 1947-48; chmn. Vt. Pub. Service Commn., Montpelier, 1948-49; judge Superior Ct. Vt., 1948-56; asso. justice Vt. Supreme Ct., 1956-63, chief justice, 1963-72; chief judge U.S. Dist. Ct. for Vt., Rutland, 1972—; chmn. Nat. Conf. State Chief Justices, 1971-72. Mem. Bennington County, Vt., Am. bar assns., Am. Judicature Soc., Inst. Jud. Adminstrn., Am. Law Inst. Home: Overlea Rd North Bennington VT 05257 Office: US Courthouse Rutland VT 05701 Tel (802) 775-2001

HOLDEN, JOHN FRANCIS, JR., b. White Plains, N.Y., Jan. 5, 1927; B.S., Fordham Coll., 1950; J.D., Columbia, 1953. Admitted to N.Y. bar, 1954, U.S. Ct. Appeals 2d Circuit bar, 1956, U.S. Supreme Ct. bar, 1971; atty. Gen. Atty. Office N.Y. Central R.R. Co., N.Y.C., 1955-61; law sec. to Westchester County (N.Y.) judge, 1961; sec. to justice N.Y. State Supreme Ct., White Plains; dep. corp. counsel City of White Plains, 1962-68, corp. counsel, 1969-75; of counsel firm Rogers, Hoge & Hills, White Plains and N.Y.C.; village atty. Village of Scarsdale, N.Y., 1975—. Mem. Am., N.Y. State, Westchester County, White Plains, bar assns. Home: 90 Smith Ave White Plains NY 10605 Office: 1 N Broadway St White Plains NY 10601 Tel (914) 761-0500

HOLDEN, LAWRENCE THOMAS, JR., b. Boston, May 14, 1939; A.B., Dartmouth, 1961; LL.B., Boston U., 1966; LL.M., Harvard, 1969. Admitted to Mass. bar, 1966; asso. firm Goodwin, Procter & Hoar, Boston, 1966-68; spl. asst. solicitors office U.S. Dept. Labor, Washington, 1969-70; chmn. Mass. Bd. Conciliation and Arbitration, Boston, 1972-75; labor arbitrator, Lincoln, Mass., 1975—. Mem. Am. Bar Assn., Nat. Acad. Arbitrators, Mediation Adv. Bd., Am. Arbitration Assn., Assn. Labor Mediation Agys. (exec. bd. 1973-75), Indsl. Relations Research Assn. (pres. Boston chpt. 1975-76). Home and Office: Weston Rd Lincoln MA 01773 Tel (617) 259-0530

HOLDEN, STEPHEN, III, b. White Plains, N.Y., Feb. 27, 1939; B.A., Hamilton Coll., 1961; J.D. Cornell U., 1964. Admitted to N.Y. bar, 1965; partner firm Holden Bros., Esquires, White Plains, 1965—. Mem. N.Y., West County, White Plains (past pres.) bar assns. Office: 124 Court St White Plains NY 10601 Tel (914) 949-7940

HOLDERNESS, RICHARD ALBERT, b. Carlisle, Pa., Feb. 27, 1944; A.B., U. Calif., Los Angeles, 1966; J.D., U. San Francisco, 1973. Admitted to Calif. bar, 1973; law clk. San Francisco Superior Ct., 1972, Calif. Supreme Ct., 1972-73; asso. firm Dingus, Haley & Boring, San Francisco, 1973—; teaching asst. U. San Francisco Law Sch., 1972-73. Mem. Calif. State Bar, Bar Assn. San Francisco, Barrister Club San Francisco. Office: One California St San Francisco CA 94111 Tel (415) 391-0405

HOLDMANN, LEE F., b. Milw., July 6, 1937; B.A., Marquette U., 1959; LL.B., Georgetown U., 1962, LL.M. in Tax and Estate Planning, 1968. Admitted to Md. bar, 1963, D.C. bar, 1968; asso. firm Mudd & Mudd, La Plata, Md., 1963-67; atty. advisor U.S. Tax Ct., Washington, 1967-68; asso., then partner Mercier Sanders Baker & Schnabel, Washington, 1972-74; practice law as Lee F. Holdmann, P.A., Bethesda, Md., 1974—; instr. wills and estates Montgomery Coll., 1971—. Mem. Am., Md. D.C., Montgomery County (Md.) bar assns. Author tax mgmt. portfolios Bur. Nat. Affairs. Office: 7315 Wisconsin Ave Suite 502E Bethesda MD 20014 Tel (301) 656-8022

HOLDYCH, THOMAS JAMES, b. Rockford, Ill., Dec. 17, 1944; B.A., Rockford, Coll., 1966; J.D., U. Ill., 1970. Admitted to Calif. bar, 1971; law clk. Calif. Supreme Ct., San Francisco, 1970-71; asso. firm O'Melveny and Myers, Los Angeles, 1971-72; asst. prof. law U. Puget Sound, Tacoma, 1972-74; asso. prof., 1974—. Mem. Am. Bar Assn., Order of Coif., Phi Beta Kappa. Office: 8811 S Tacoma Way Tacoma WA 98499 Tel (206) 757-3327

HOLLADAY, ROBERT LAWSON, b. Greenwood, Miss., Jan. 28, 1948; B.S., Delta State U., 1970; J.D., U. Miss., 1973. Admitted to Miss. bar, 1973; partner firm Townsend, McWilliams & Holladay, Drew, Miss., 1973—. Mem. Am., Miss. State, Sunflower County bar assns., Assn. Trial Lawyers Am., Miss. Trial Lawyers Assn. (gov. 1976—), Phi Alpha Delta. Home: 365 N Ruby Ave Ruleville MS 38771 Office: 111 S Main St Drew MS 38737 Tel (601) 745-8517

HOLLAND, ANN, b. Gebo, Wyo., May 24, 1933; A.B. cum laude, Barnard Coll., 1955; J.D. cum laude, Harvard, 1958. Admitted to Mass. bar, 1959, D.C. bar, 1959, Calif. bar, 1971; atty. SEC, Washington, 1958-60; asso. firm Herrick & Smith, Boston, 1960-70; partner firm Kindel & Anderson, Los Angeles, 1972—. Mem. Am., Los Angeles County bar assns. Office: 555 S Flower St Los Angeles CA 90071 Tel (213) 680-2222

HOLLAND, GEORGE, b. Shreveport, La., Mar. 31, 1941; A.A., City Coll. San Francisco, 1963; B.A., San Francisco State Coll., 1965; J.D., Golden Gate U., 1972. Admitted to Calif. bar, 1973; dep. pub. defender City and County of San Francisco, 1976—. Mem. Charles Houston, Nat. (dir. western region) bar assns. Office: 1515 Vallejo St San Francisco CA 94109 Tel (415) 673-3113

HOLLAND, JERRY HOLMAN, b. Oklahoma City, Oct. 11, 1927; B.S., U. Okla., 1955; J.D., Oklahoma City Sch. Law, 1965. Admitted to Okla. bar, 1965; individual practice law, Tulsa, 1968—; house counsel U.S. Fidelity & Guaranty Co., 1966-67; asst. atty. gen. State of Okla., 1967-68; partner firm Sanders, McElroy & Carpenter, Tulsa, 1968—; lectr. univs. Mem. Okla. Bar Assn., Phi Alpha Delta. Contbr. articles to legal jours. Home: 1844 E 58th St Tulsa OK 74105 Office: 624 S Denver St Tulsa OK 74119 Tel (918) 582-5181

HOLLAND, LOUIS TODD, b. Bonita, Tex., Sept. 25, 1906; B.A., Tex. Christian U., 1931; LL.B., Cumberland U., 1933. Admitted to Tex. bar, 1933; individual practice law, Nocona, Tex., 1933-36; county dist. atty., Montague County, Tex., 1937-42; judge Montague County (Tex.), 1942-43, 45-46; judge Dist. Ct., Tex., 1946-62; judge 8th Adminstrv. Jud. Dist. of Tex., Montague, 1963—. Bd. dirs. North Tex. Easter Seals Rehab. Center for Crippled Children, Wichita Falls. Mem. Tex. Bar Assn., Tex. Jud. Council (bd. dirs.), Law Enforcement Officers Assn. Tex. (pres.). Home: Box 57 Montague TX 76251 Office: Ct House Montague TX 76251 Tel (817) 894-2077

HOLLAND, LYMAN FAITH, JR., b. Mobile, Ala., June 17, 1931; B.S. in Bus. Adminstrn., U. Ala., 1953, LL.B., 1957. Admitted to Ala. bar, 1957; asso. firm Hand, Arendall, Bedsole, Greaves & Johnston, Mobile, 1957-62, partner, 1963—. Mem. Mobile Historic Devel. Commn., 1965-69, v.p., 1967-68; bd. dirs. Mobile chpt. ARC, 1960—, vice chmn. bd., 1975—; bd. dirs. Mobile Azalea Trail, 1963-68, chmn. bd., 1963-65; bd. dirs. Mobile Mental Health Center, 1969—, pres., 1973; bd. dirs. Greater Mobile Mental Health-Mental Retardation Bd., 1975—, pres., 1975-77; bd. dirs. Deep South council Girl Scouts U.S.A., 1965-71, Gordon Smith Center, 1973, Bay Area Council on Alcoholism, 1973-76. Mem. Am., Ala. bar assns., Am. Coll. Probate Counsel, Farrah Law Soc., Phi Delta Phi. Co-author: Legal Aspects of Real Estate Transactions, 1971. Home: 717 Westmoreland Dr West Mobile AL 36609 Office: PO Box 123 Mobile AL 36601 Tel (205) 432-5511

HOLLAND, NORMAN NORWOOD, b. Princess Anne, Md., Feb. 19, 1896; B.E., Johns Hopkins, 1920; LL.B., Fordham U., 1923; postgrad. Columbia, 1923. Admitted to N.Y. bar, 1924; sr. partner firm Holland Armstrong, Wilkie & Previto, and predecessors, 1926—; lectr. cons. Practising Law Inst., 1956-67. Mem. Am. Bar Assn. (chmn. sect. patent trademark copyright law 1951, mem. council 1946-49, 51-54), Bar. City N.Y. (chmn. patent com. 1959-61), Am. (bd. mgrs. 1955-58), N.Y. (pres. 1954-55) patent law assns., Internat. Patent and Trademark Assn. (sec. 1949-52, exec. com. 1960-68), Johns Hopkins Alumni Assn., Tau Beta Pi, Omicron Delta Kappa. Home: 880 Fifth Ave New York City NY 10021 Office: 225 Broadway New York City NY 10007 Tel (212) 962-7337

HOLLAND, PAUL DELEVAL, b. Los Angeles, Feb. 1, 1910; student U. Calif., Los Angeles, 1928-31; A.B., U. So. Calif., 1932, J.D., 1934. Admitted to Calif. bar, 1934; individual practice law, Los Angeles, 1934-42, 70—, Beverly Hills, Calif., 1945-70. Pres. Calif. Epilepsy Soc., 1966-71; pres. Epilepsy Found. Am., 1973-75, chmn. bd. dirs., 1975—. Mem. State Bar Calif., Los Angeles County, Century City, Am. bar assns., Am. Judicature Soc. Home: 12023 Monogram Ave Granada Hills CA 91344 Office: 1880 Century Park E Suite 213 Los Angeles CA 90067 Tel (213) 553-5689

HOLLAND, RANDY JAMES, b. Elizabeth, N.J., Jan. 27, 1947; B.A. in Econs., Swarthmore Coll., 1969; J.D. cum laude, U. Pa., 1972. Admitted to Del. bar, 1972, U.S. Supreme Ct. bar, 1976; with Dunlap, Holland & Eberly, and predecessors, Georgetown, Del., asso., 1973, partner, 1973—; solicitor City of Milford (Del.). Bd. dirs. Sussex County Arts Council, Sr. Citizens Assn. Mem. Am., Del., Sussex County bar assns., Am. Trial Lawyers Assn. Recipient Henry C. Loughlin prize U. Pa., 1972. Office: 8 W Market St Georgetown DE 19947 Tel (302) 856-6366

HOLLAND, SAMUEL CLIFFORD, b. Rochester, Pa., Oct. 2, 1924; A.B., Pa. State U., 1948; LL.B., Dickinson Sch. Law, 1951. Admitted to Pa. bar, 1952; individual practice law, Beaver, Pa., 1952-65; mem. firm Panner, Holland and Autenreith, Beaver, 1966—; spl. asst. atty. gen. State of Pa., 1965-70. Bd. dirs. pres. Beaver County br. Pa. Assn. for Blind, 1967—; bd. dirs. Beaver County Mental Health Soc. Mem. Am., Pa., Beaver County bar assns., Am. Judicature Soc. Home: 395 Dutch Ridge Rd Beaver PA 15009 Office: 345 Commerce St Beaver PA 15009 Tel (412) 775-8500

HOLLAND, WARNER LAMOINE, b. San Antonio, Mar. 8, 1933; B.S., Rice U., 1955; J.D., St. Mary's U. Admitted to Tex. bar, 1963; individual practice law, San Antonio, 1963—; mem. Tex. Ho. of Reps., 1967-70. Mem. San Antonio Bar Assn. Home: 508 Garraty Rd San Antonio TX 78209 Office: 1010 Main Plaza Bldg San Antonio TX 78205 Tel (512) 225-6151

HOLLAND, WILLIAM MEREDITH, b. Live Oak, Fla., Feb. 2, 1922; A.B., Fla. A. and M. U., 1947; B.A., Boston U., 1951, J.D., 1951. Admitted to Fla. bar, 1951, U.S. Supreme Ct. bar, 1956; mem. firm Holland & Smith, W. Palm Beach, 1954—; judge City of Riviera Beach (Fla.), 1972—. Mem. Fla. Bar, Am., Palm Beach County bar assns., Am. Judicature Soc., Fla. Municipal Judges Assn. (dir.). Home: 611 W Kalmia Dr Lake Park FL 33403 Office: 605 Clematis St West Palm Beach FL 33402 Tel (305) 833-3770

HOLLANDER, BRIAN L., b. New London, Conn., Feb. 10, 1940; A.B., Brandeis U., 1962; LL.B., N.Y. U., 1965. Admitted to Conn. bar, 1966; law clk. for U.S. Dist. judge, Hartford, Conn., 1965-66; staff mem. Neighborhood Legal Services, Hartford, 1966-67; asso. firm Day, Berry & Howard, Hartford, 1967-70; pres. Hartford Inst. Criminal and Social Justice, Inc., 1970—; mem. Conn. Alternate Sentencing Commn. Bd. dirs. Hartford Dispensary; mem. Conn. Pub. Defender Services Commn.; bd. dirs. Community Resources for Justice, Inc., San Juan Center, Conn. Jr. Republic, Community Energy Corp. Chmn., Greater Hartford chpt. Am. Jewish Com. Home: Juniper Rd Bloomfield CT 06002 Office: 15 Lewis St Hartford CT 06103 Tel (203) 527-1866

HOLLANDER, CARL ROBERT, b. N.Y.C., July 2, 1943; B.A. cum laude, Cornell U., 1965, J.D., 1968. Admitted to N.Y. state bar, 1968; asso. firm Davies, Hardy, Ives & Lawther, N.Y.C., 1968-72; asso. firm Lovejoy, Wasson, Lundgren & Ashton, N.Y.C., 1972-75, mem., 1976—; dir. Nielsen, Wurster & Assos., Inc., N.Y.C., Substral Am., Inc., Ohio, Clay Basin Storage Co., Utah. Trustee Bar Harbor (Maine) Festival Soc., 1970-72. Mem. Assn. Bar City N.Y., N.Y. State (chmn. com. fed. legislation) Am. bar assns. Home: 30 Beekman Pl New York City NY 10022 Office: 250 Park Ave New York City NY 10017 Tel (212) 697-4100

HOLLANDER, GEORGE MITCHELL, b. Chgo., Mar. 21, 1934; B.S. in Bus. Adminstrn., Northwestern U., 1955, J.D., 1958. Admitted to Ill. bar, 1958; atty. Chgo. and North Western Transp. Co. (formerly Chgo. and North Western Ry. Co.), Chgo., 1958-64, gen. atty., 1964-66, asst. gen. counsel, 1967-74, gen. solicitor, 1975—; counsel tax com. Ill. R.R. Assn., 1962-64, 1974—; rep. Ill. Multistate Tax Compact Adv. Com., 1968; mem. Joint Com. on Ill. Revenue Article, chmn. excise tax subcom., mem. real estate tax subcom., 1968-69. Mem. Ill. State (state tax council 1962-69, chmn. 1967-69), Chgo. (fed. tax com., chmn. consol. regulations subcom. 1965-69), Am. bar assns., Assn. Am. R.R.'s (various coms. 1962—), R.R. Income Tax Adminstrs. Conf. (chmn. Ill. r.r. property tax litigation com. 1975—), Nat. Assn. Ry. Tax Commrs., Chgo. Tax Club, Order of Coif, Beta Alpha Psi, Beta Gamma Sigma. Home: 1856 Ivy Ln Northbrook IL 60062 Office: 400 W Madison St Chicago IL 60606 Tel (312) 454-6510

HOLLANDER, PATRICIA ANN, b. St. Louis, Feb. 17, 1928; B.S., St. Louis U., 1949, J.D., 1952; postgrad. in Labor Law, Harvard, 1969-70. Admitted to Mo. bar, 1952, N.Y. bar, 1964; regional atty. central states region Internat. Ladies' Garment Workers' Union, St. Louis, 1952-60; asso. firm David F. Mix, Buffalo, 1965-67; lectr. in indsl. relations Sch. Mgmt., asst. to dean div. continuing edn. State U. N.Y., Buffalo, 1967-73, lectr. Sch. Law, 1973—, admissions officer, 1975-76, dir. program law and social sci. Survey Research Center, adj. asst. prof., faculty Social Scis. and Adminstrn., 1976—; gen. counsel Am. Assn. Univ. Adminstrs., Buffalo, 1972—; lectr. in field. Bd. dirs. Camp Fire Girls of Buffalo and Erie County (N.Y.), 1972-74. Mem. Am., Mo., N.Y., Erie County, St. Louis bar assns., Nat. Assn. Coll. and Univ. Attys., Am. Assn. Univ. Adminstrs. (chmn. com. constn. and by-laws 1971-72), AAUP, St. Louis U., Harvard Law Sch. alumni assns. Author: Legal Liabilities of Adminstrators-Civil Rights Law and Actions in Tort, 1975; The Simulated Law Firm and Other Contemporary Law Simulations, 1977; Legal Handbook for Educators, 1978. Home: 30 Foxcroft Ln Williamsville NY 14221 Tel (716) 632-6422

HOLLANDER, SHERMAN SCHILLER, b. Cleve., Mar. 7, 1920; A.B., Western Res. U., 1941, LL.B., 1946. Admitted to Ohio bar, 1946; title officer Hollander Abstract Co., Cleve., 1946-68, pres., 1954-68; chief title officer, pres., Ohio Title Corp., Cleve., 1968-72; partner firm Terrell, Williams & Salim, Cleve., 1972—. Mem. Bd. Edn., Beachwood, Ohio, pres., 1960-72. Mem. Am., Ohio, Greater Cleve., Cuyahoga County (trustee) bar assns. Recipient Beachwood Civic League Citizenship award, 1973. Home: 23902 Woodway Rd Beachwood OH 44122 Office: 1620 Standard Bldg Cleveland OH 44113 Tel (216) 621-6784

HOLLBERG, WILLIAM BEALER, b. Atlanta, Apr. 27, 1947; B.A., Wheaton Coll., 1968; J.D., U. Ga., 1971. Admitted to Ga. bar, 1971, Fla. bar, 1971; legis. asst. U.S. Senator David H. Gambrell, 1972; asso. firm Fine and Block, Atlanta, 1973—. Mem. steering com. Va. Highland Civic Assn., 1975-77, chmn. zoning enforcement com., 1976-77; vol. atty., Common Cause Ga., 1973-77, legis. coordinator, 1974-77, chmn., 1976-77, co-chmn., 1977-78; counsel Childbirth Edn. Assn. Atlanta, Inc., 1975—. Home: 744 Elkmont Dr NE Atlanta GA 30306 Office: 100 Colony Sq Suite 1905 Atlanta GA 30361 Tel (404) 892-7160

HOLLER, JAMES EDWARD, b. Bluefield, W.Va., Jan. 23, 1940; B.S., U. S.C., 1963, J.D., 1969. Admitted to S.C. bar, 1969; atty. firm Belser, Belser & Baker, Columbia, S.C., 1969-70; atty. firm Hyatt & Holler, Columbia, 1970-74, firm Holler, Gregory & McKellar, Columbia, 1974—; asst. solicitor 5th Jud. Circuit, Columbia, 1972-74. Vice chmn. Muscular Sclerosis Dr., Columbia. Mem. Richland County, S.C., Am. bar assns., S.C., Am. trial lawyers assns., Phi Delta Phi, Sigma Chi. Home: 4500 Ivy Hall Dr Columbia SC 29206 Office: 1804 Bull St PO Box 11006 Columbia SC 29211 Tel (803) 765-2968

HOLLETT, BYRON P., b. Indpls., Sept. 28, 1914; B.A., Wabash Coll., 1936, LL.D., 1974; J.D., Harvard, 1939. Admitted to Ind. bar, 1939; asso. firm Hollett, Lafuze & Hollett, 1939-51; partner firm Baker & Daniels, Indpls., 1951—. Bd. dirs. United Way Greater Indpls.; mem. Mayor's Greater Indpls. Task Force, 1973-75; mem. bus. and profl. friends com. for Nat. Center for State Cts. Mem. Am., Ind., Indpls. bar assns., Indpls. Lawyers Club, Am. Judicature Soc., Nat. Legal Aid and Defenders Assn. Decorated Bronze Star. Home: 3802 Springfield Overlook Indianapolis IN 46234 Office: 800 Fletcher Trust Bldg Indianapolis IN 46204 Tel (317) 636-4535

HOLLIDAY, JAMES SIDNEY, JR., b. Baton Rouge, Mar. 6, 1941; B.S. La. A. and M. Coll., 1962, J.D., 1965. Admitted to La. bar, 1965; asso. firm McCollister, Belcher, McCleary, Fazio, Mixon, Holliday and Jones, Baton Rouge, 1965-66, partner, 1967—. Active United Givers Assn., Baton Rouge, 1967-70. Mem. Am., La. (bd. govs.), Baton Rouge bar assns., Maritime Law Assn. U.S. Contbr. article to law jours. Home: 1459 Oakley Dr Baton Rouge LA 70806 Office: PO Box 2706 Baton Rouge LA 70821

HOLLIN, SHELBY WHITE, b. Varilla, Ky., July 29, 1925; B.B.A., St. Mary's U., 1965, J.D., 1970. Admitted to Tex. bar, 1969, U.S. Supreme Ct. bar, 1974; individual practice law, San Antonio, 1969—. Mem. Am., Tex., San Antonio bar assns. San Antonio Trial Lawyers Assn., Res. Officers Assn., West San Antonio C. of C. (sec.-treas. 1974—), Delta Theta Phi. Home and office: 7710 Stagecoach San Antonio TX 78227 Tel (512) 674-2584

HOLLINGSWORTH, CYRIL, b. Little Rock, Oct. 10, 1942; B.A., Southwestern U., 1964; J.D., U. Va., 1967. Admitted to Ark. bar, 1967, U.S. Supreme Ct. bar, 1972; partner firm David, Plastiras & Horne, Little Rock, 1967—. Mem. Am., Ark., Pulaski County bar assns. Office: PO Box 3363 Little Rock AR 72203

HOLLINGSWORTH, DONALD MICHAEL, b. Little Rock, Jan. 12, 1945; B.A. in History with distinction, Southwestern at Memphis, 1967; J.D., Vanderbilt U., 1972. Admitted to Tenn. bar, 1972; staff atty. Memphis and Shelby County Legal Services Assn., Memphis, 1972—, mng. atty. N. Memphis Office, 1975—. Mem. Joint Legis. Com. on Sch. Fin. in Tenn.; bd. dirs. Memphis Planned Parenthood, 1975—. Mem. Memphis-Shelby County, Tenn. bar assns., ACLU. Recipient Spl. Service award Tenn. Assn. for Children with Learning Disabilities, 1977. Home: 1977 #4 Peabody St Memphis TN 38104 Office: 325 Dermon Bldg Memphis TN 38103 Tel (901) 526-8210

HOLLINGSWORTH, JAY ALAN, b. Cleve., June 6, 1930; B.S., Kent State U., 1953; LL.B., Western Res. U., 1956. Admitted to Ohio bar, 1956, U.S. Supreme Ct. bar, 1964; partner firm Hollingsworth and Hollingsworth, Cleve., 1957—. Mem. bd. zoning appeals, Chester Twp. (Ohio), 1975-76. Mem. Ohio, Greater Cleve., Cuyahoga County, Geauga County bar assns. Office: 1414 Superior Bldg Cleveland OH 44144 Tel (216) 781-2626

HOLLINGSWORTH, JERRY RAY, b. Amarillo, Tex., Jan. 23, 1934; LL.B., Baylor U., 1958. Admitted to Tex. bar, 1958; individual practice law, Amarillo, 1958—. Bd. dirs. Amarillo Hist. Preservation Found., Amarillo Sr. Citizens' Assn., Panhandle Plains Hist. Soc.; chmn. Potter County Hist. Commn. Mem. State Bar Tex. (com.

history and traditions). Home: 1912 Tyler St Amarillo TX 79109 Office: PO Box 148 Amarillo TX 79105 Tel (806) 372-3444

HOLLINGSWORTH, PERLESTA ARTHUR, b. Little Rock, Apr. 12, 1936; A.B., Talladega Coll., 1958; J.D., U. Ark., 1969. Admitted to Ark. bar, 1969; asso. firm Walker, Rotenberry, Kaplan & Lavey, Little Rock, 1969-70; legal adviser gov's. office State of Ark., Little Rock, 1970; dep. prosecuting atty., Pulaski County, Ark., 1971; dist. counsel SBA, Little Rock, 1972-74; sr. partner firm Hollingsworth, Bilheimer & Crutcher, Little Rock, 1976—; mem. bd. dirs. City of Little Rock, 1972-76, asst. mayor, 1974-76. Herbert Lehman fellow. Office: Hollingsworth Bilheimer & Crutcher 500 Tower Bldg Little Rock AR 72201

HOLLINS, EUGENE THOMPSON, JR., b. Nashville, May 29, 1903; LL.B., Vanderbilt U. Admitted to Tenn. bar, 1927; individual practice law, Nashville, 1927—. Mem. Nashville Bar Assn. (past sec.-treas.). Home: 1506 Clayton Ave Nashville TN 37212 Office: 903 Stahlman Bldg Union St Nashville TN 37201 Tel (615) 256-2260

HOLLIS, EVERETT LOFTUS, b. Wilkes-Barre, Pa., Dec. 6, 1914; B.S., U. Ill., 1936; LL.B., Harvard, 1939. Admitted to Mass. bar, 1939, N.Y. bar, 1954, Ill. bar, 1966, D.C. bar, 1970; law clk. to justice Mass. Supreme Jud. Ct., 1940; practiced in Boston, 1941; atty. Office Price Adminstrn., Washington, 1941-43; with AEC, Washington, 1947-52, gen. counsel, 1951-52; gen. corp. counsel Gen. Electric Co., N.Y.C., 1952-65; partner firm Mayer, Brown & Platt, Chgo. and Washington, 1965—, sr. partner, 1976—; mem. Pres's. Commn. on Contract Compliance, 1952; exec. dir. Commn. on Founds. and Pvt. Philanthropy; mem. Nat. Commn. on Med. Profl. Liability. Bd. dirs. Chgo. Better Bus. Bur. Mem. Internat., Fed., Am., Chgo., N.Y.C., Ill., D.C. bar assns., Am. Law Inst., Acad. Politics and Soc. Sci., Chgo. Council Fgn. Relations, English-Speaking Union, Beta Gamma Sigma. Contbg. author: Federal Conflict of Interest Laws, 1960; Congress and the Public Trust, 1970. Home: 3400 N Lake Shore Dr Chicago IL 60657 Office: 231 S La Salle St Suite 1955 Chicago IL 60604 Tel (312) 782-0600 also 888 17th St NW Washington DC Tel (202) 785-4443

HOLLIS, HOWELL, b. Columbus, Ga., Dec. 8, 1919; B.S. in Commerce, U. Ga., 1940. Admitted to Ga. bar, 1941; practice law, Columbus, 1945—; partner firm Hatcher, Stubbs, Land, Hollis & Rothschild, 1969—; gen. counsel Ga. Commn. Edn., 1960; chmn. bd. Nat. Bank & Trust Co. of Columbus; v.p., dir. Illges Realty Co.; dir. G s Light Co. Columbus, Golden Foundry & Machine Co., Lummus Industries, Inc. Pres. Columbus Coll. Found.; mem. bd. visitors U. Ga. Law Sch., 1963-69; rep. Ga. Legislature, 1948-54, 59-60; mem. Ga. Senate, 1955-56; mem. Ga. Ports Authority, 1959-67; chmn. bd. St. Francis Hosp., 1950—; former pres. Columbus Mus. Arts; trustee Berry Schs., U. Ga. Found. Fellow Am. Coll. Trial Lawyers, Am. Bar Found.; mem. Columbus Lawyers Club (pres. 1968), Ga. Bar Assn. (pres. 1956-57), U.S. 5th Circuit Jud. Conf. Home: 844 Overlook Ave Columbus GA 31906 Office: 500 Ralston Center PO Box 2707 Columbus GA 31902 Tel (404) 324-0201

HOLLISTER, CHARLES AMMON, b. Newport, Nebr., June 15, 1918; B.A., Nebr. State Coll., 1940; M.A., U. Ariz., 1945; Ph.D. in Pub. Law, U. Pa., 1957. Law clk. to presiding judge 17th Pa. Jud. Dist., researcher Anderson Law Office, 1974-75; clk., researcher Ronald L. Tulin, 1975; researcher State's Atty.'s Office, Coles County, Ill., Charleston, 1976—; pre-legal adviser, prof. pub. law, Eastern Ill. U., Charleston, 1967—. Chmn. Charleston Mayor's Advisory Com., 1972—; chmn. Union County (Ill.) Democratic Party, 1963-67. Mem. Am. Bar Assn. Contbr. articles to profl. jours. Home: 2515 S 4th St Charleston IL 61920 Office: 214 Coleman Hall Eastern Ill Univ Charleston IL 61920 Tel (217) 581-2523

HOLLMAN, TELFORD FRANCIS, b. Chgo., Sept. 14, 1912; Ph.B., U. Chgo., 1933, J.D., 1935; LL.M., John Marshall Law Sch., 1964; M.B.A., DePaul U., 1968. Admitted to Ill. bar, 1935, Iowa bar, 1969; atty. Massen and Whitney, Chgo., 1935-37; v.p., chief counsel Checker Cleaners, Inc., Chgo., 1937-68; prof. law U. No. Iowa, 1968—. Mem. Cedar Falls (Iowa) Cable TV Commn., 1973-76. Mem. Am., Iowa State, Black Hawk County bar assns., Am. Bus. Law Assn., Nat. Assn. Bus. Law Tchrs., Delta Mu Delta. Contbr. articles to legal jours. Home: 2519 Rownd St Cedar Falls IA 50613 Office: Sch Bus U No Iowa 23rd and College Sts Cedar Falls IA 50613 Tel (319) 273-6070

HOLLORAN, JAMES PATRICK, b. St. Louis, Dec. 14, 1943; B.S. in Indsl. Engring., St. Louis U., 1965, J.D., 1968. Admitted to Mo. bar, 1968; partner firm Sommers & Holloran, St. Louis, 1970—. Mem. Lawyers Assn. St. Louis (v.p. 1976), Bar Assn. Met. St. Louis (exec. council young lawyers sect. 1972-76), Am., Mo. (young lawyers council 1970-76) bar assns., Mo. Assn. Trial Attys., Am. Trial Lawyers Assn. Recipient Lon O. Hocker Meml. Trial Lawyer award, 1974. Home: 831 S Gore St Saint Louis MO 63119 Office: 818 Olive St Saint Louis MO 63101 Tel (314) 436-2088

HOLLORAN, MICHAEL JOSEPH, b. Washington, June 12, 1944; B.A., George Washington U., 1966; J.D., 1969. Admitted to D.C. bar, 1970, Colo. bar, 1970, U.S. Dist. Ct. bar Colo., 1970; asso. firm Van Cise, Freeman, Tooley & McClearn, Denver, 1970-72; partner firm Grassby & Holloran, Steamboat Springs, Colo., 1972—; judge municipal ct. City of Steamboat Springs, 1974-76. Pres. East Routt Meml. Library Dist., Steamboat Springs, 1975-76; sec. Steamboat Springs Council for the Arts and Humanities, 1972-74. Mem. Am., Colo., NW Colo. (v.p. 1973-74), Routt County (pres. 1972-74) bar assns., Colo. Trial Lawyers Assn. Home and office: POB AP Steamboat Springs CO 80477 Tel (303) 879-2410

HOLLOWAY, CARL LEROY, JR., b. Greenwood, S.C., Dec. 27, 1945; B.A. in Pol. Sci., The Citadel, 1968; J.D., U. S.C., 1971. Admitted to S.C. bar, 1971, U.S. 4th Circuit Ct. Appeals bar, 1974, U.S. Dist. Ct. for S.C. bar, 1974; Served with JAGC, USAF, 1971-72; with legal affairs dept. S.C. Dept. Edn., 1972-73; asso. firm Lumpkin, Lafaye and Bowman, Columbia, S.C., 1973-75; individual practice law, Columbia, 1975—; city atty., Forest Acres, S.C., 1976—. Vice chmn. fund drive Am. Cancer Soc., Columbia, 1974. Mem. Am., S.C., Richland County bar assns., Am. Judicature Soc., Columbia Young Lawyers Club. Home: 4104 Blossom St Columbia SC 29205 Office: 1 Minckton Blvd Suite 201 Columbia SC 29206 Tel (803) 782-0235

HOLLOWAY, EDWARD, JR., b. Bklyn., Nov. 19, 1918; A.B., Princeton U., 1940; J.D., Yale U., 1947. Admitted to N.Y. bar, 1947; since practiced in N.Y.C., asso. firm Armitage & Holloway, 1947-49, firm Bannister, Stitt, Holloway & Krause, 1949-53, partner, 1953-71; partner firm Eaton, VanWinkle, Greenspoon & Grutman, and predecessor, 1971—. Mem. Am., N.Y. State bar assns., Assn. Bar City N.Y., Soc. Med. Jurisprudence. Home: 205 W 89th St New York City NY 10024 Office: 600 3rd Ave New York City NY 10016 Tel (212) 867-0606

HOLLOWAY, HILIARY HAMILTON, b. Durham, N.C., Mar. 7, 1928; B.S. in Bus. Adminstrn., N.C. Central U., 1949; Ed.M. in Bus. Edn., Temple U., 1956, J.D., 1964. Admitted to Pa. bar, 1965; asso. firm Hazell & Bowser, Phila., 1965-68; asst. counsel, Fed. Res. Bank of Phila., 1968-73, v.p., gen. counsel, 1973—; bus. mgr. St. Augustine's Coll., Raleigh, N.C., 1950-53; nat. exec. dir. Kappa Alpha Psi frat., 1953-65. Bd. dirs. N.C. Central Univ. Found., United Negro Coll. Fund, Mt. Olivet Village Corp., housing for elderly. Mem. Am., Fed., Pa., Phila. bar assns. Recipient Distinguished Service award Kappa Alpha Psi, 1972, Distinguished Philadelphian award Alpha Kappa Alpha, 1973, Distinguished Citizens award St. Matthews Ch., 1974, citation for outstanding community service Chapel of Four Chaplains. Home: 2293 Bryn Mawr Ave Philadelphia PA 19131 Office: 100 N 6th St Philadelphia PA 19105 Tel (215) 574-6390

HOLLOWAY, ROBERT LEE, JR., b. Buffalo, July 19, 1946; B.A., Amherst Coll., 1968; J.D., Boston U., 1973. Admitted to Mass. bar, 1973; asso. firm Ardiff, Ardiff & Morse, Danvers, Mass., 1973-76, partner, 1977—; mem. legal panel Mass. Civil Liberties Union, 1975—. Lectr. Endicott Coll., 1977. Mem. exec. com. Danvers Hist. Soc., 1973-76, chmn. mgmt. com., 1974—. Mem. Assn. Trial Lawyers Am., Am., Mass., Boston bar assns. Home: 47 Locust St Danvers MA 01923 Office: 32 Maple St Danvers MA 01923 Tel (617) 774-7121

HOLLOWAY, WILEY JACKSON, b. Smyrna, Tenn., June 6, 1920; B.S., Middle Tenn. State U., 1940; J.D., U. Tenn., 1946. Admitted to Tenn. bar, 1946; practiced in Murfreesboro, Tenn., 1946-62; dist. atty. State of Tenn., 1962-69; judge Circuit Ct. 8th Circuit, 1969—. Mem. Rutherford County (pres. 1962-64), Tenn. (dir. 1976—), Am. bar assns., Nat. Conf. State Trial Judges Assn., Tenn. Dist. Atty. Conf. (sec. 1966-67), Tenn. Jud. Conf. (pres. 1976—). Editorial bd. U. Tenn. Law Rev., 1946. Home: Riverview Dr Murfreesboro TN 37130 Office: Courthouse Murfreesboro TN 37130 Tel (615) 893-3949

HOLM, KENNETH EUGENE, b. Hays, Kans., Mar. 1944; B.A., U. Kans., 1966, J.D., 1969. Admitted to Kans. bar, 1969; atty. Urban Renewal Agy., Kansas City, Kans., 1969-73; asso. firm Finnigan, Poizner & Tucker, Kansas City, 1973-74, Boddington, Brown & Unverferth, Kansas City, 1974—; atty. Pub. Bldg. Commn. Kansas City. Mem. Kansas City Civic Arts Council, 1972. Mem. Am., Kans., Wyandotte County bar assns., Kans. Trial Lawyers Assn. Home: 5535 Suwanee St Fairway KS 66205 Office: 465 New Brotherhood Bldg Kansas City KS 66101 Tel (913) 371-1272

HOLM, RICHARD VERNON, b. Superior, Wis., Feb. 2, 1943; B.S. in Secondary Edn., U. Wis., Superior, 1966, J.D., Madison, 1971. Tchr. English, high schs., Bruce, Wis., 1965-68; admitted to Wis. bar, 1971; asso. firm Hansen, Eggers, Berres & Kelley, Beloit, Wis., 1971—. Cub scout leader Sinnissippi council Boy Scouts Am. Mem. Wis. Alumni Assn. (dir., pres. Beloit chpt. 1975), Beloit (pres. 1975), Rock County bar assns. Home: 3723 Oak Lane Dr Beloit WI 53511 Tel (608) 365-4401

HOLMAN, JAMES ALLEN, b. Seattle, July 8, 1932; B.A., U. Wash., 1957; postgrad. Middlebury Coll., 1956; LL.B., Harvard, 1961. Admitted to Wash. bar, 1963, U.S. Tax Ct. bar, 1965; asso. firm Elliott, Lee, Carney, Thomas & Smart, and predecessor, Seattle, 1961-65, partner, 1965-68; prin. Holman Law Offices, Seattle, 1969—; spl. asst. atty. gen. State of Wash., 1965. Mem. Am., Wash. State, Seattle-King County bar assns. Home: 1608 Federal Ave E Seattle WA 98102 Office: 1224 Denny Bldg Seattle WA 98121 Tel (206) 623-6536

HOLMAN, JOHN CLARKE, b. Milw., Apr. 19, 1938; B.S. in Metallurgy, U. Wis., 1961; J.D., Am. U., 1965; postgrad. Holborn Coll. Law, London, 1965-67. Patent examiner U.S. Patent Office, Washington, 1961-65; admitted to D.C. bar, 1966, U.S. Supreme Ct. bar, 1972; Am. patent law expert Marks & Clerk, London, 1965-67; sr. partner Holman & Stern, Washington, 1967—. Mem. Am. Patent Law Assn., Am. Bar Assn., Am. Inst. Mining, Metall., and Petroleum Engrs., Am. Soc. Metals, Internat. Assn. Protection Indsl. Property, Delta Theta Phi. Recipient Am. Jurisprudence award, 1964; contbr. articles in field to legal jours.; staff editor Am. U. Law Rev., 1964-65. Office: 2401 15th St NW Washington DC 20009 Tel (202) 483-2234

HOLMBERG, ARTHUR ROLAND, b. Chgo., Aug. 27, 1908; J.D., John Marshall Law Sch., Chgo., 1936. Admitted to Ill. bar, 1938, Iowa bar, 1973; corporate personnel dir. Penick & Ford, Ltd., Cedar Rapids, Iowa, 1952-73; mem. firm Ford, Tepstra & Wilkinson, Cedar Rapids, 1973-75; asst. city atty. Cedar Rapids, 1975—, collective bargaining rep., 1975—. Mem. Iowa, Linn County bar assns. Home: 312 Trailridge Rd Cedar Rapids IA 52403 Office: City Hall Cedar Rapids IA 52401 Tel (319) 398-5008

HOLMES, ALLEN CORNELIUS, b. Bethel, Ohio, May 27, 1920; A.B., U. Cin., 1941; J.D., U. Mich., 1944. Admitted to Ohio bar, 1944, U.S. Supreme Ct. bar, 1964; asso. firm Jones, Day, Reavis & Pogue, Cleve., 1944-54, partner, 1954-74, mng. partner, 1974—. Campaign chmn. United Torch, 1976; trustee Cleve. Inst. Music, 1966—; trustee, exec. com. Case Western Res. U., 1971—; bd. dirs., exec. com. Greater Cleve. Growth Assn., 1972—. Mem. Am. (past chmn. FTC com. antitrust sect., mem. sect. council, sect. del. to ho. dels.), Ohio, Cleve. bar assns., Assn. Bar City N.Y., Am. Law Inst. Contbr. articles to profl. publs. Home: 1 Bratenahl Pl Bratenahl OH 44108 Office: 1700 Union Commerce Bldg Cleveland OH 44115 Tel (216) 696-3939

HOLMES, DALLAS SCOTT, b. Los Angeles, Dec. 2, 1940; B.A. cum laude, Pomona Coll., 1962; M.Sc., London Sch. Econs., 1964; J.D., Boalt Hall, U. Calif., 1967. Admitted to Calif. bar, 1968; asso. firm Best, Best & Krieger, Riverside, Calif., 1968-74, partner firm, 1974—; exec. asst. to majority floor leader Calif. State Assembly, Sacramento, 1969-70; adj. prof. U. Calif. at Riverside. Pres. Easter Seal Soc. Riverside and Imperial counties, 1972-74; v.p. World Affairs Council Inland So. Calif., 1974—. Mem. Am., Internat., Riverside County (exec. com.) bar assns., Am. Judicature Soc., State Bar Calif. Named one of Young Men of Year Riverside Jr. C. of C., 1962, Man of Year Riverside Press-Enterprise, 1972; recipient Tileston Physics prize, 1961, Joseph Story award, 1962, Am. Jurisprudence awards, 1966-67; contbr. articles to profl. jours. Office: 4200 Orange St Riverside CA 92501 Tel (714) 686-1450

HOLMES, DAVID EDWARD, b. Miami, Aug. 6, 1943; A.B., Univ. So. Calif., 1966, J.D., 1969. Admitted to Calif. bar, 1970; asso. counsel So. Calif. Edison Co., Los Angeles, 1969-71; asst. gen. counsel Cordura Corp., Los Angeles, 1971-74; asso. firm Collins, Gregory & Rutter, Los Angeles, 1974-76; asso. gen. counsel IHOP Corp., N. Hollywood, Calif., 1976—. Mem. Manhattan Beach Environmental Commn., 1975. Mem. Am., Calif., Los Angeles, Beverly Hills bar assns. Home: 13633 Doty Ave #38 Hawthorne CA 90250 Office: 6837 Lankershim Blvd N Hollywood CA 91605 Tel (213) 982-2620

HOLMES, JAMES RICHARD, JR., b. Southington, Conn., Sept. 9, 1944; B.S. in Econs., Wharton Sch. Fin., U. Pa.; J.D., U. Fla. Admitted to Fla. bar, 1970; mng. atty. Fla. Rural Legal Services, Pompano Beach, 1970-73; judge Broward County (Fla.) Ct., 1973—. Bd. dirs. Broward County Health Planning Council, Urban League of Broward County, Spectrum House Drug Programs, Fla. Mem. Fla., Broward County bar assns. Recipient Recognition of Merit, Nat. Safety Council and Ex-Offender Program. Office: Broward County Courthouse Fort Lauderdale FL 33301 Tel (305) 765-4765

HOLMES, JOHN WILLARD, b. Alma, Mich., Nov. 5, 1904; A.B., U. Mich., 1926, LL.B., 1928. Admitted to Calif. bar, 1929, U.S. Supreme Ct. bar, 1952; atty. legal dept. City of Pasadena (Calif.), 1929-36, City of Los Angeles, 1936-38; asso. firm Lawler, Felix & Hall, Los Angeles, 1938-40; individual practice law, Pasadena, Los Angeles, 1940-68; judge Superior Ct., Los Angeles, 1968—. Mem. Am., Los Angeles, Pasadena bar assns. Contbr. numerous articles to legal publs. including Mich., Calif. law revs. Home: 1010 Laguna Rd Pasadena CA 91105 Office: 111 N Hill St Los Angeles CA 90012 Tel (213) 974-5707

HOLMES, KENNETH HOWARD, b. St. Paul, June 13, 1936; B.S. in Law, U. Minn., 1958, LL.B. magna cum laude, 1960. Admitted to Minn. bar, 1960, N.Y. bar, 1962, U.S. Supreme Ct. bar, 1969; asso. firm Dewey, Ballantine, Bushby, Palmer & Wood, N.Y.C., 1961-69, partner, 1969—. Mem. Am., N.Y. bar assns., Assn. Bar City N.Y., Order of Coif. Home: 864 Hillside Ave Westfield NJ 07092 Office: 140 Broadway New York City NY 10005 Tel (212) 344-8000

HOLMES, MARION HERRON, JR., b. Trenton, Tenn., Mar. 21, 1914; student West Tenn. State Tchrs. Coll. (now changed to Memphis State U.), Memphis Coll. Law, 1941. Admitted to Tenn. bar, 1941; practiced in Trenton, 1946-67; judge Gibson County (Tenn.) Gen. Sessions Ct., 1967—; city atty. City of Trenton, 1966-76. Elder 1st Presbyn. Ch., Trenton. Mem. Gibson County, Tenn. bar assns., Tenn. Gen. Session Judges Conf. (v.p. 1974). Home: 711 High St Trenton TN 38332 Office: Gibson County Courthouse Trenton TN 38382 Tel (901) 855-1971

HOLMES, NORMAN LEONARD, b. N.Y.C., Mar. 15, 1928; B.S., U. Wis., 1949; LL.B., Columbia, 1957; LL.M., Georgetown U., 1960. Admitted to N.Y. bar, 1958, Pa., 1972; atty. Fed. Trade Commn., Washington, 1961-65; counsel Bank & Currency Com. U.S. Ho. Reps., Washington, 1965-68; asst. to Hon. Hubert H. Humphrey, Vice Pres. of the U.S., 1967-69; partner firm Blank, Rome, Klaus & Comisky, Phila., 1971—; pres. Internat. Study Project, Washington, 1969-70. Mem. Pa., Phila. bar assns. Recipient Lawyers Co-op. Publ. Co. award, 1957, F.T.C. certificate of commendation, 1963; F.T.C. Superior Service award, 1963; contbr. ABA sect. antitrust law Merger Case Digest, 1964-65. Home: 308 Echo Valley Ln Newtown Sq PA 19073 Office: 4 Penn Center Plaza Philadelphia PA 19103 Tel (215) 569-3700

HOLMQUIST, DAVID KELTY, b Massillon, Ohio, Sept. 29, 1936; B.S. in B.A., Ohio State U., 1958, J.D., 1961. Admitted to Ohio bar, 1961; mem. gen. hearing bd. Ohio Dept. Taxation, Columbus, 1961-63; asst. counsel Albee Homes, Inc., Niles, Ohio, 1963-67; house counsel Ajax Magnethermic Corp., Warren, Ohio, 1967-69, house counsel, indsl. relations mgr., 1969-73, asst. sec., house counsel, indsl. relations mgr., 1973—. Chmn. corporate counsel inst. Salt Fork Lodge, Cambridge, Ohio, 1974. Capt. United Appeal drives, 1972, 73, Youngstown Playhouse membership campaign, 1977. Mem. Ohio (bd. govs. corporate counsel sect.), Mahoning County bar assns. Office: 1745 Overland Ave Warren OH 44482 Tel (216) 372-7808

HOLROYD, DONALD DEAN, b. Tulsa, July 7, 1929; B.A., Ariz. State U., 1951, M.A., 1954; LL.B., U. Ariz., 1958. Admitted to Ariz. bar, 1958; tchr. Mesa High Sch., 1954-55; partner firm Shelley & Holroyd, 1959-61, firm Jestila & Holroyd, 1964-74, firm Burke & Holroyd, Phoenix, 1974—. Bd. dirs. Small Bus. Devel. Center, 1965, Ariz. Indian Centers, 1976, pres., bd. dirs. Phoenix Indian Center, 1974. Mem. Maricopa County, Ariz. bar assns., Am. Trial Lawyers Assn. Recipient Community Service awards Met. Indian Coalition, Phoenix Indian Center. Home: 13013 N Surrey Circle Phoenix AZ 85029 Office: 512 Luhrs Tower Phoenix AZ 85003 Tel (602) 252-6836

HOLSCHUH, JOHN DAVID, b. Ironton, Ohio, Oct. 12, 1926; A.B., Miami U., Oxford, Ohio, 1948; J.D., U. Cin., 1951. Admitted to Ohio bar, 1951, U.S. Ct. of Appeals bar, 1952, U.S. Dist. Ct. bar, 1952, U.S. Supreme Ct. bar, 1956; law clk. to Hon. Mel. G. Underwood, U.S. Dist. Ct., So. Dist. Ohio, 1952-54; partner firm Alexander, Ebinger, Holschuh, Fisher & McAlister, Columbus, Ohio, 1954—; adj. prof. med.-legal problems Coll. of Law, Ohio State U., 1970-76; spl. asst. atty. gen. of Ohio, 1972-76; mem. bd. commrs. on character and fitness and com. on uniform rules of evidence Supreme Ct. of Ohio. Sec. bd. of trustees United Way of Franklin County, Ohio, 1971-73. Fellow Am. Coll. Trial Lawyers; mem. Am., Ohio State, Columbus bar assns., Nat. Assn. of R.R. Trial Counsel (exec. com. 1969-72), Sixth Circuit Judicial Conf. Home: 2630 Charing Rd Columbus OH 43221 Office: 17 S High St Columbus OH 43215 Tel (614) 221-6345

HOLST, DALE LAWSON, b. Cedar Rapids, Iowa, Oct. 21, 1929; B.S. in Commerce, State U. Iowa, 1950; LL.B., U. Denver, 1955. Admitted to Colo. bar, 1956; individual practice law, Colorado Springs, Colo., 1956—. Chmn. 20th Rep. Dist., Republican Com., 1976-77. Mem. Am., Colo. (bd. govs. 1974—), El Paso County (past pres.) bar assns., Estate Planning Council Colorado Springs, Am. Judicature Soc. Home: 17 Crescent Ln Colorado Springs CO 80904 Office: 228 N Cascade St Colorado Springs CO 80903

HOLSTEDT, ROBERT E., b. Sheridan, Wyo., Mar. 7, 1920; J.D., U. Wyo., 1949. Admitted to Wyo. bar, 1949, since practiced in Sheridan; municipal ct. judge, Sheridan, 1950-51, city atty., 1953-55; mem. Wyo. Ho. of Reps., 1951-54; county and pros. atty. Sheridan County, 1963-66; U.S. magistrate, 1971-72. Mem. Wyo. Community Coll. Commn., 1956-77, Sheridan Planning Commn., 1969-75. Mem. Am., Wyo. (grievance com. 1973-77), Sheridan County bar assns. Home: 322 1st West Pkwy Sheridan WY 82801 Office: 113 W Brundage St Sheridan WY 82801 Tel (307) 674-7479

HOLSTEIN, JOHN CHARLES, b. Springfield, Mo., Jan. 10, 1945; B.A., SW Mo. State U., 1967; J.D., U. Mo., 1976. Admitted to Mo. bar, 1970; asso. firm Moore & Brill, 1970-75; probate judge Howell County (Mo.), W. Plains, 1975—; instr. bus. law SW Mo. State U. Chmn. Howell County chpt. ARC, 1975-76. Mem. C. of C., Mo., Howell County bar assns. Home: Route 3 Box 619 West Plains MO 65775 Office: Howell County Courthouse West Plains MO 65775

HOLT, CLYDE, III, b. Beaver, Pa., Sept. 16, 1947; B.A., Northwestern U., 1969; J.D., U. N.C., 1972. Admitted to N.C. bar, 1972; asso. city atty., Raleigh, N.C., 1972-76; partner law firm Baggett & Holt, Raleigh, N.C., 1976—. Mem., Raleigh Library Bd., 1977—. Mem. Am., N.C., Wake County bar assns., Brentwood Exchange Club. Home: 3604 Ingram Dr Raleigh NC 27604 Office: 5 W Hargett St Raleigh NC 27602

HOLT, EDWARD BREWSTER, b. Champaign, Ill., June 8, 1926; B.M.E., U. Mich., 1947; J.D., George Washington U., 1951. Admitted to Ill. bar, 1952; asso. firm Carlson, Pitzner, Hubbard & Wolfe, Rockford, Ill., 1952-56; mem. firm Leydig, Voit, Osann, Mayer & Holt, and predecessors, Rockford, 1956—; dir. Winnebago County Bar Found., 1973—, pres., 1975-76. Bd. dirs. Winnebago County Mental Health Assn., 1962-73, pres., 1965-67. Mem. Am., Winnebago County bar assns., Patent Law Assn. Chgo. Home: 1636 National Ave Rockford IL 61103 Office: 815 N Church St Rockford IL 61103 Tel (815) 963-7661

HOLT, GEORGE EREKSON, b. Salt Lake City, Dec. 20, 1936; J.D., U. Utah, 1964. Admitted to Nev. bar, 1964; partner firm Jones & Holt, Las Vegas, Nev., 1965-74; pros. atty. Las Vegas, 1968-69, 70, dist. atty., 1975—; chief dep. pub. defender Las Vegas, 1973; mem. Nev. State Crime Commn., 1975—. Scoutmaster, Boulder Dam council Boy Scouts Am., 1973-75; mem. adv. bd. Salvation Army, Las Vegas, 1971—. Mem. Nev., Clark County bar assns., Nat. (dir.), Nev. dist. attys. assns., Delta Theta Phi. Recipient Superior Law Enforcement Service award Las Vegas C. of C., 1975. Home: 1013 Ironwood Dr Las Vegas NV 89101 Office:

HOLT, IVAN LEE, JR., b. Marshall, Mo., May 4, 1913; student Princeton, 1931-34; A.B., U. Chgo., 1935, J.D., 1937. Admitted to Mo. bar, 1937; asso. firm Marion C. Early, St. Louis, 1937-40; asst. circuit atty. City of St. Louis, 1940-42; asso. firm Jones, Hocker, Gladney and Grand, St. Louis, 1948-49; judge Mo. Circuit Ct., 22d Jud. Circuit, 1949—; asst. prof. law Washington U., St. Louis, 1947-48; mem. council judges Nat. Council on Crime and Delinquency, 1953-75, chmn., 1972-75; mem. Mo. Commn. on Retirement, Removal and Discipline, 1972—. Bd. dirs. Barnes Hosp., St. Louis, Goodwill industries, St. Louis, Meth. Children's Services of Mo., St. Louis. Mem. Am. Bar Assn. (chmn. div. jud. adminstrn. 1962-63), Mo. Bar, Bar Assn. Met. St. Louis (Pub. Service citation 1963), Am. Law Inst., Inst. Jud. Adminstrn., Am. Judicature Soc. Recipient Pub. Service citation U. Chgo. Alumni Assn., 1955. Contbr. articles to legal publs. Home: 4910 W Pine Blvd Saint Louis MO 63112 Office: Civil Cts Bldg 10 N 12th St Saint Louis MO 63101 Tel (314) 453-4421

HOLT, JOHN THOMAS, b. Lebanon, Mo., Sept. 4, 1902; LL.B., U. Colo., 1929; postgrad. Oxford (Eng.) U., 1974. Admitted to Calif. bar, 1930; chief trial dep. San Diego County Office Dist. Atty., 1930-36; practice law, San Diego, 1936—; mem. firm Hervey & Holt, 1936-42, Holt, Macomber & Baugh, 1942-50, Holt & Baugh, 1950-76, Holt, Baugh, Geitner & MacCartee, 1976—; sr. partner Holt, Rhoades & Hollywood, 1970—. Mem. San Diego (pres. 1936, honored at Blackstone Ball 1976), Am., Internat., San Diego County bar assns., Am. Bd. Trial Advs., Am. Coll. Trial Lawyers (a founder, charter), Am. Judicature Soc., Calif., San Diego trial lawyers assns., San Diego County Barristers Club, State Bar Calif. Home: 6929 Fairway Rd La Jolla CA 92037 Office: 530 Broadway Suite 1114 San Diego CA 92101 Tel (714) 232-7441

HOLT, MARJORIE SEWELL, b. Birmingham, Ala., Sept. 17, 1920; student Jacksonville Jr. Coll., 1941; J.D., U. Fla., 1949. Admitted to Md. Bar, 1949; individual practice, Severna Park, Md., 1962-66; mem. 93d-95th Congresses from 4th Md. Dist.; mem. Armed Services Com., Budget Com.; dir. Office Technol. Assessment, 1975-76, vice chmn., 1977. Chmn. Republican Study Commn., 1975-76; supr. elections Anne Arundel County, Md., 1963-65; clk. Circuit Ct. Annapolis, Md., 1966-72; del. Rep. Nat. Conv., 1967, 76. Mem. Am., Md., Anne Arundel County bar assns., Md. Court Clks. Assn., Phi Kappa Phi, Phi Delta Delta. Editor: The Case Against Reckless Congress, 1976. Office: 1510 Longworth House Office Bldg Washington DC 20515 Tel (202) 225-8090

HOLTAN, HARVEY ALFRED, b. Zumbrota, Minn., Feb. 2, 1920; student U.S. Mil. Acad., 1938-42, St. Olaf Coll., 1944-45, U. Iowa, 1945-46; B.S. in Law, U. Minn., 1947, J.D., 1949; grad. Nat. Coll. State Trial Judges, 1968, 71. Admitted to Minn. bar, 1949; practiced in Lakefield and Jackson, Minn.; county atty. Jackson County, Minn., 1951-63; legal officer Minn. Civil Def., 1953—; dir. 1st State Bank of Lakefield (Minn.), 1965—; asso. St. Olaf Coll., 1964—; judge 5th Minn. Jud. Dist. Ct., 1967—; mem. Minn. Select Com. on State Jud. System, 1974—; mem. faculty Nat. Coll. State Judiciary, 1975. Chmn. Jackson County Republican. Com., 1952-62; pres. Jackson County Library Assn., 1959-62; bd. dirs. Southwestern Minn. Mental Health Center, Luverne, Minn. Mem. Minn. Dist., Minn., Jackson County, Am. bar assns., Nat. Assn. State Trial Judges, Nat. Assn. Dist. Prosecuting Attys., Am. Judicature Soc. Home: 301 5th Ave Lakefield MN 56150 Office: Courthouse Windom MN 56101 Tel (507) 831-2358

HOLT-HARRIS, JOHN EVAN, JR., b. Stapleton, N.Y., Feb. 10, 1917; A.B., Cornell U., 1937, LL.B., 1939, J.D., 1969. Admitted to N.Y. bar, 1939; asso. firm Milbank, Tweed, Hope & Webb, N.Y.C., 1939-40, firm Brown & Gallagher, Albany, N.Y., 1940-41; asso. firm DeGraff & Foy, Albany, 1945-51, partner, 1951—; lectr. Albany Law Sch., 1951-70; judge Recorders Ct., Albany, 1952—; mem. N.Y. State Bd. Law Examiners, 1969—. Trustee Albany Med. Center Hosp., 1952—, Albany Acad. for Boys, 1952—; bd. dirs. Mid-Hudson Library Assn., 1956—; mem. Bd. Edn. Albany, 1952-70. Mem. Am., N.Y., Albany County bar assns., Nat. Conf. Bar Examiners, Am. Jud. Soc., Nat. Conf. State Trial Judges. Recipient Page One award Newspaper Guild N.Y., 1959. Home: Waverly Pl Albany NY 12203 Office: 90 State St Albany NY 12207 Tel (518) 462-5301

HOLTORF, HANS JOHN, JR., b. Wahoo, Nebr., Oct. 10, 1914; student Luther Coll., Wahoo, 1933-35; A.B., U. Nebr., 1937, LL.B., 1939, J.D., 1969. Admitted to Nebr. bar, 1939; individual practice law, Gering, 1939-42; partner firm Holtorf, Hansen, Kovarik & Nuttleman and predecessors, 1946—; city atty. City of Gering, 1947-52, 64-73; county atty. Scotts Bluff County, Nebr., 1953-55. Vice pres. Scotts Bluff-Gering Indsl. Found., 1964-66; sec. Gering Indsl. Found. Fellow Internat. Assn. Barristers; mem. Scotts Bluff County (pres. 1952-53), Western Nebr. (pres. 1963-64), Nebr. State (ho. of dels. 1954-57, 74-75), Am. (chmn. com. on worker compensation, 1972-74) bar assns., Assn. Ins. Attys. (pres. 1969-70), Internat. Assn. Ins. Counsel (com. on advocacy), Fedn. Ins. Counsel (v.p. 1976—), Scribes. Contbr. articles to profl. jours.; asso. editor Forum for Work Compensation Matters, 1965-70. Office: 1715 11th St Gering NE 69341 Tel (309) 436-2137

HOLTZ, DAVID, b. Tucson, Jan. 18, 1926; B.S., Los Angeles State Coll., 1955; J.D., Southwestern U., Los Angeles, 1964. Admitted to Calif. bar, 1964; individual practice law, El Monte, Calif., 1964—; prof. law Orange U. (now Pepperdine Coll. Law), Santa Ana, Calif., 1964-66, Beverly Law Sch., Whittier Coll., Los Angeles, 1966-76. Office: 11401 Valley Blvd El Monte CA 91731 Tel (213) 442-4418

HOLTZ, EDGAR WOLFE, b. Clarksburg, W.Va., Jan. 18, 1922; B.A., Denison U., 1943; J.D., U. Cin., 1949. Admitted to Ohio bar, 1949, U.S. Supreme Ct. bar, 1957, D.C. bar, 1961; asso. firm Matthews & Matthews, Cin., 1949-53, partner, 1953-55; asst. dean Chase Law Sch., Cin., 1952-55; asst. city solicitor Cin., 1950-55; asst. chief, office of opinions & rev. FCC, Washington, 1955-56, dep. gen. counsel, 1956-60; mem. firm Hogan & Hartson, Washington, 1960—. Trustee, Denison U., Granville, Ohio, 1970—. Mem. Am., Ohio, D.C., FCC (pres. 1977) bar assns., Am. Judicature Soc. Home: 3400 O St NW Washington DC 20007 Office: 815 Connecticut Ave NW Washington DC 20006 Tel (202) 331-4520

HOLTZMAN, ALEXANDER, b. Newark, Oct. 20, 1924; A.B., U. Ariz., 1949; LL.B., Cornell U., 1952. Admitted to N.Y. bar, 1952; partner firm Conboy, Hewitt, O'Brien & Boardman, N.Y.C., 1960-67; asst. gen. counsel, Phillip Morris Inc., N.Y.C., 1968-74, asso. gen. counsel, 1974—. Mem. N.Y. State Bar Assn., Assn. of the Bar of City N.Y. Office: 100 Park Ave New York City NY 10017 Tel (212) 679-1800

HOLZ, MARVIN CHRISTIAN, b. Milw., May 19, 1917; LL.D., U. Wis., 1942; postgrad. Nat. Coll. State Judges, 1975. Admitted to Wis. bar, 1942; fellow in law U. Wis., Madison, 1942-43; asst. dir. disputes Nat. War Labor Bd., Chgo., 1943-46; practiced in Milw., 1946-66; judge Milwaukee County Ct., 1962-66, Milwaukee County 2d Circuit Ct., 1966—; presiding judge Milwaukee County Family Ct., 1972—; faculty adviser Nat. Coll. State Judges; dean Wis. Jud. Coll., 1974—. Bd. dirs. United Community Services, Milw., 1968-74, Family Service Inc., Milw., 1970—, Children's Service Soc., Milw., 1974—, Multiple Sclerosis Soc., Milw., 1970-73. Mem. Am. Bar Assn., Wis. State Bar, Nat. Conf. State Trial Judges, Assn. Family Conciliation Cts. (dir.). Contbr. articles to legal jours. Home: 2117 W Apple Tree Rd Milwaukee WI 53205 Office: Milwaukee County Courthouse Milwaukee WI 53233 Tel (414) 278-4484

HOLZ, MICHAEL HAROLD, b. Dayton, Ohio, Apr. 10, 1942; A.B., Wittenberg U., 1964; J.D., U. Cin., 1967. Admitted to Ohio bar, 1968; legal aid Butler County (Ohio), 1968; legal dep. Montgomery County (Ohio) Probate Ct., 1971-73; asst. pros. atty., Greene County, Ohio, 1973; individual practice law, Centerville, Ohio, 1974—; instr. in field. Precinct committeeman Democratic Party, Dayton, Mem. Ohio, Dayton bar assns., Oakwood Community Jaycees (charter), Phi Alpha Delta. Home: 606 Acorn Dr Dayton OH 45419 Office: 9356 Lebanon Pike enterville OH 45459 Tel (513) 433-4993

HOLZER, HENRY MARK, b. N.Y.C., Oct. 31, 1933; B.A., N.Y.U., 1954, J.D., 1959. Admitted to N.Y. State bar, 1959, U.S. Supreme Ct. bar, 1963, U.S. Ct. Mil. Appeals bar, 1972; individual practice law, N.Y.C., 1959-72; asst. prof. law Bklyn. Law Sch., 1972-73, asso. prof., 1973-76, prof., 1976—. Mem. legal adv. bd. Soc. for Animal Rights, 1972—, bd. dirs., 1975—. Mem. N.Y. State Bar Assn. Contbr. articles to newspapers, mags. and legal jours. Office: Brooklyn Law Sch 250 Joralemon St Brooklyn NY 11201 Tel (212) 625-2200

HOLZER, SIDNEY, b. N.Y.C., Jan. 5, 1927; A.B., Bklyn. Coll., 1947, J.D., 1950. Admitted to N.Y. bar, 1950, U.S. Supreme Ct. bar, 1964; asso. firm Finke, Jacobs & Tirsch, N.Y.C., 1950-54, firm Reich, Peller, Cuadagno & Caine, N.Y.C., 1954-56; individual practice law, N.Y.C., 1956-66; mem. firm Holzer & Nappi, Huntington, N.Y., 1970—. Counsel to Nassau County Children's Center, Mineola, N.Y. Mem. Assn. Bar City of N.Y., N.Y. County Lawyers Assn., Nassau County, Suffolk County bar assns. Office: 425 New York Ave Huntington NY 11793 Tel (516) 271-0505

HOLZMAN, SHERIDAN VERNE, b. Detroit, Jan. 22, 1930; B.A., Wayne State U., 1954, J.D., 1955. Admitted to Mich. bar, 1955; practice law, Detroit; lectr. law U. Mich., 1969-70, Wayne State U., 1970. Chmn. Southfield Democratic Club, 1967-68; mem. Oakland County Dem. Com., 1967—; mem. 17th dist. Dem. exec. com., 1975—. Mem. State Bar Mich., Am. Trial Lawyers Assn., Am. Judicature Soc., ACLU (vice chmn. 1972-75, gen. counsel 1975—). Home: 30485 Old Stream Cricle Southfield MI 48076 Office: 1926 1st Nat Bldg Detroit MI 48226 Tel (313) 963-5643

HOMANS, WILLIAM VALMOND, b. Warsaw, Poland, June 25, 1907; LL.B., St. John's U., 1929. Admitted to N.Y. State bar, 1931, U.S. Supreme Ct. bar, 1960; individual practice law, N.Y.C., 1931—; small claims arbitrator Civil Ct. City N.Y., 1955—. Mem. U.S. Army Fgn. Claims Commn., 1946. Mem. Am., N.Y. State, Bronx County bar assns., Assn. Bar City N.Y., Assn. Trial Lawyers Am., Am. Arbitration Assn. (arbitrator 1972—). Office: 122 E 42d St New York City NY 10017 Tel (212) 687-1595

HOMBERG, JAMES JOHN, b. Sioux City, Iowa, Sept. 17, 1928; B.S.C., Creighton U., 1951, J.D., 1954. Admitted to Nebr. bar, 1954, U.S. Supreme Ct. bar, 1963; asso. firm Cropper & Cropper, Omaha, 1954-56; contract adminstr. Dale Electronics, Inc., Columbus, Nebr., 1956-57, sec., gen. counsel, 1958-63, v.p., 1963--. Adv. council Nebr. Dept. Labor, 1968-75; mem. Platte County (Nebr.) Joint Planning Commn., 1973-75; bd. dirs. Big Bros. Columbus, 1972—. Mem. Am., Nebr., Platte County bar assns., Columbus Area C. of C. (past pres.). Home: 4809 Country Club Dr Columbus NE 68601 Office: PO Box 609 1356 28th Ave Columbus NE 68601 Tel (402) 564-3131

HOMER, LLOYD WILLIAM, b. San Francisco, Nov. 7, 1933; B.S. in Bus. Adminstrn., U. Calif., Berkeley, 1957; J.D., U. San Francisco, 1964. Admitted to Calif. bar, 1965; accountant San Francisco, 1959-64; mem. firm Robidoux & Homer, P.C., Campbell, Calif., 1965—; instr. in field U. Santa Clara, 1965-67. Bd. dirs. Episcopal Homes Found., 1969-71; active Am. Cancer Soc., 1967. C.P.A., Calif. Mem. Am., Calif., Santa Clara County bar assns., Am. Inst. C.P.A.'s, Calif. Soc. C.P.A.'s Office: 1999 S Bascom Av #1010 Campbell CA 95008 Tel (408) 377-3901

HOMNACK, PETER A., b. Donora, Pa., B.S., U. Pitts., 1947, M.Litt., 1949; J.D., Duquesne U., 1954. Admitted to U.S. Dist. Ct. bar, 1957, Pa. Supreme Ct. bar, 1957; individual practice law, 1957—. Mem. Pa., Beaver County (sec. 1967-72), Allegheny County bar assns. Office: 13th St and Merchant St Ambridge PA 15003 Tel (412) 266-7030

HONEYMAN, ROBERT WAYNE, b. Norristown, Pa., Feb. 11, 1918; B.A., U. Pa., 1939, LL.B., 1942. Admitted to Pa. bar, 1942; mem. firm Duffy, McElhone & Honeyman, Norristown, Pa., 1946-48; mem. firm Fox, Differ & Honeyman, Norristown, 1948-59; judge Ct. of Common Pleas 38th Jud. Dist. Montgomery County (Pa.), 1960-70, 1970—. Chmn. bd. consultors Villanova U. Sch. Law, Villanova, Pa. Mem. Am. (jud. adminstrn. sec.), Pa. bar assns., Montgomery County Assn. (former dir.), Pa. Conf. of Trial Judges (former pres.). Recipient Citizen of Year W. Norriton Twp., Montgomery County, 1966. Home: 905 Cherry Circle Bethel Grant Lansdale PA 19446 Office: Court House Norristown PA 19404 Tel (215) 275-5000

HONIG, EMANUEL A., b. Franklin, N.J., Oct. 5, 1909; A.B., Lehigh U., 1931; J.D., Columbia U., 1934. Admitted to N.Y. bar, 1935, N.J. bar, 1936; now partner firm Honig & Honig, Franklin; sec. to pres. N.J. State Senate, 1951; municipal atty., 1958-75. Mem. panel arbitrators Am. Arbitration Assn.; chmn. bd. dirs. Alexander Linn Hosp., 1968—. Mem. Sussex County (pres. 1964-65), N.J. State (pres. 1977—), Am. bar assns. Office: 83 Main St Franklin NJ 07416*

HONIGSBERG, IRVING, b. N.Y.C., Sept. 3, 1907; B.A., N.Y. U., 1929, LL.B., 1930. Admitted to N.Y. bar, 1930, U.S. Fed. Cts. Eastern and So. Dists. N.Y. bar, 1937, U.S. Supreme Ct. bar, 1961; individual practice law, Bklyn., 1930—. Mem. Bklyn. Bar Assn. Office: 16 Court St Brooklyn NY 11241 Tel (212) 625-1084

HONNOLD, JOHN OTIS, b. Kansas, Ill., Dec. 5, 1915; A.B., U. Ill., 1936; J.D., Harvard, 1939. Admitted to N.Y. bar, 1940, U.S. Supreme Ct. bar, 1946, Pa. bar, 1953; asso. firm Wright, Gordon, Zachry & Parlin, N.Y.C., 1939-41; atty. SEC, Washington, 1941; chief ct. rev. Office of Price Adminstrn., Washington, 1942-46; prof. law U. Pa., Phila., 1946-71, 75—; chief Internat. Trade Law UN, N.Y.C., 1969-75; U.S. del. internat. legal confs.; chief counsel Miss. Office Lawyers Com. Civil Rights Under Law, 1965; bd. dirs. Am. Friends Service Com., 1968-70. Guggenheim fellow, 1958; Fulbright Research scholar U. Paris, 1958; author: Life of the Law, 1964; Unification of Law Governing International Sale of Goods, 1966; Sales & Sales Financing, 4th edit., 1976; Credit Transactions and Consumer Protection, 1976; Commercial Law, 3d edit., 1976, Constitutional Law, 3d edit., 1968; contbr. articles in field to legal jours.; bd. editors Am. Jour. Comparative Law, 1975—. Office: 3400 Chestnut St Philadelphia PA 19104 Tel (215) 243-7674

HOOD, DAVID ROBINSON, b. Tacoma, June 14, 1935; B.A. in Econs. magna cum laude, Gonzaga U., 1960; J.D., Harvard U., 1963. Admitted to Wash. bar, 1964, Mich. bar, 1970; asso. firm MacDonald, Hoague & Bayless, Seattle, 1964-66, partner, 1966-70; asso. prof. law Wayne State U., 1970-73; dean prof. law U. Hawaii, 1973-76; dir. Commonwealth program Carnegie Corp. N.Y., N.Y.C., 1976—; mem. Washington State advisory com. to the U.S. Commn. on Civil Rights, 1965-70; bd. dirs. Fund for Equal Justice, 1970-71; mem. Nat. Advisory Council Center for the Adminstrn. Justice, 1970-71; Nat. Commn. on Uniform State Laws, 1974-75. Mem. Am. Bar Assn. Author: (with B. Bell) In-migration as a Component of Hawaii Population Growth, the Constitutional Principles, 1973. Office: Carnegie Corp of New York 437 Madison Ave New York City NY 10022 Tel (212) 371-3200

HOOD, DONALD CURTIS, b. Beaumont, Tex., Oct. 29, 1944; Sc.B., Lamar U., 1967; J.D., U. Tex., Austin, 1970. Admitted to Tex. bar, 1970, U.S. Dist. Ct. bar for No. Dist. Tex., 1970, U.S. Ct. Appeals bar, 5th Circuit, 1971; com. clk. spl. called session Tex. Ho. of Reps., 1968, regular session, 1969; asso. firm Wilson, Berry, Jorgenson & Johnson, Dallas, 1970-75; individual practice law, Dallas, 1976—; instr. in para-legalism El Centro Coll.; mem. exec. com. Moot Ct. Bd. U. Tex. at Austin. Fellow Internat. Acad. Forensic Psychology; mem. Teaching Quizmaster Assn., Dallas Bar Assn., State Bar Tex., Tex., Dallas trial lawyers assns., Am. Soc. Internat. Law, Order of Barristers, Delta Theta Phi, Sigma Phi Epsilon (adviser for alumni ops. in Tex.). Home: 7139 Shook Ave Dallas TX 75214 Office: 3614 Oak Grove St Suite 214 Dallas TX 75204 Tel (214) 521-0120

HOOD, HAROLD, b. Detroit, Jan. 14, 1931; A.B., U. Mich., 1952; J.D. with distinction, Wayne State U., 1959. Admitted to Mich. bar, 1960, U.S. Supreme Ct. bar, 1966; prin. asst. corp. counsel City of Detroit, 1961-69; chief asst. U.S. atty. East Detroit, 1969-73; judge Wayne County (Mich.) Ct. Common Pleas, Detroit, 1973—; dir. Wayne County Neighborhood Legal Services, Detroit, 1973-77; judge Recorders' Ct., 1977—. Bd. dirs. Kirwood Gen. Hosp., Detroit, 1973—, Nat. Council Alcoholism, Detroit, 1976—; commr. Detroit Area council Boy Scouts Am., 1966-69. Mem. Nat. (jud. council), Am., Mich., Wolverine, Fed. bar assns., Am. Judicature Soc., Am., Mich. judges assns. Recipient Service award City of Ecorse, 1976, Theodore R. Owens Service award Kappa Alpha Psi, 1971. Home: 2233 Webb St Detroit MI 48202 Office: 604 Frank Murphy Hall of Justice 1441 Saint Antoine St Detroit MI 48226 Tel (313) 224-2491

HOOD, JACK BRIAN, b. Clarksville, Ga., Jan. 22, 1948; A.B., U. Ga., 1969, J.D., 1971; diploma internat. law U. Cambridge (Eng.), 1972. Admitted to Ga. bar, 1971, D.C. bar, 1976, C.Z. bar, 1976; legis. intern Ga. Ho. of Reps., 1971; judge adv. JAGC, U.S. Air Force, 1972-76; individual practice law, C.Z., 1976—; instr. Fla. State U., 1973—. Mem. Ga., C.Z., Inter-Am. bar assns., World Peace Through Law, Am. Soc. Internat. Law. Contbr. articles to legal jours. Home: PO Box 1754 Albrook AFS CZ Office: Box 503 Balboa CZ Tel (CZ) 52-6659

HOOD, JAMES CALTON, b. Ft. Gulick, Panama, C.Z., Oct. 29, 1947; B.A., U. N.H., 1969; J.D., Georgetown U., 1972. Admitted to N.H. bar, 1972; asso. firm McLane, Graf, Greene, Raulerson & Middleton, Manchester, N.H., 1972—. Bd. dirs. Manchester YMCA. Mem. Am., N.H., Manchester bar assns., Phi Beta Kappa, Phi Kappa Phi. Home: 65 Ray St Manchester NH 03101 Office: 40 Stark St Manchester NH 03105 Tel (603) 625-6464

HOOD, JAMES MICHAEL, b. Des Moines, Mar. 27, 1945; B.A., Drake U., 1967, J.D., 1970. Admitted to Iowa bar, 1970; asso. firm Beving Swanson & Forrest, Des Moines, 1972-73, Dircks & Saylor, Davenport, Iowa, 1973-74, firm Peart Wells & McNally, Davenport, 1974-75; partner firm Peart & Hood, Davenport, 1975—. Mem. Am., Iowa, Scott County bar assns., Am., Iowa acads. trial lawyers. Home: 2213 Fairhaven Rd Davenport IA 52803 Office: 315 Union Arcade Davenport IA 52801 Tel (319) 322-0978

HOOD, JOHN THOMAS, JR., b. Hazlehurst, Miss., Aug. 16, 1909; B.A., La. State U., 1931, LL.B., J.D., 1933. Admitted La. bar, 1933; practiced in Jennings, 1933-46; sec. Police Jury Jefferson Davis Parish, 1936-40; judge 14th Jud. Dist. Ct. La., 1946-60; judge 3d Circuit Ct. of Appeals, 1960—, chief judge, 1975—; served to maj. J.A.G. Dept., AUS, 1942-46; vis. prof. law La. State U. Law Sch., 1973; mem. jud. ethics com. La. Supreme Ct.; Past pres. Lake Charles YMCA; past vice chmn. Bayou Dist. Calcasieu Area council Boy Scouts Am.; past chmn. joint alumni and bd. suprs. com. La. State U.; adv. counsel La. Outdoor Drama Assn.; Lake Charles Power Squadron; Lake Charles Golf and Country Club. Mem. Am. (mem.

Appellate Judges Conf.), La. (past chmn. sect. jud. adminstrn.), S.W. La. bar assns., Am. Judicature Soc., Inst. Jud. Adminstrn., La. Conf. Ct. Appeal Judges (chmn.), La. Law Inst. (chmn. liaison com. on judiciary 1958-60), La. Dist Judges Assn. (past pres.), La. Jud. Council, Scribes, Am. Legion, VFW, La. State U. Alumni Fedn. (past pres., Alumni Service award 1970), La. State U. Law Sch. Alumni Assn. (past pres.), Greater Lake Charles C. of C. (Civic Service award 1970), Order of Coif, Order DeMoley (Legion of Honor 1973), Omicron Delta Kappa, Alumnus Lambda Chi Alpha. Recipient Citizens award Salvation Army, 1966, K.C. Outstanding Pub. Servant award, 1974; contbr. articles to legal jours. Home: 1008 8th St Lake Charles LA 70601 Office: POB 3000 Lake Charles LA 70601 Tel (318) 433-9403

HOOK, THOMAS WESLEY, b. Waterville, N.Y., Mar. 15, 1881; Ph.B., Syracuse U., 1904; postgrad. So. Meth. U., 1923-32. Admitted to N.Y. bar, 1907, Tex. bar, 1908; partner firm Hook Law Office, Falfurrias and Kingsville, Tex., 1907-18; partner firm Martin and Hook, Weatherford, Tex., 1920-32; individual practice law, Alvarado, Tex., 1933—. Active Boy Scouts Am., recipient Silver Beaver award. Mem. Tex. State, Johnson County bar assns. Died Feb. 20, 1977. Home: 400 S Spear Alvarado TX 76009

HOOKER, ARTHUR BOWLES, b. Cleve., May 28, 1925; B.A., Yale U., 1950, LL.B., 1953. Admitted to N.Y. bar, 1954; asso. firm Lord, Day & Lord, N.Y.C., 1953-60, partner, 1960—; dir. Alfred T. White Community Center, Bklyn., pres. 1966-69. Mem. Am., N.Y. State bar assns., Assn. Bar City N.Y. (ethics com. 1974-77). Office: Lord Day & Lord 25 Broadway New York City NY 10004 Tel (212) 344-8480

HOOKER, EDWARD WIGHT, b. Waupun, Wis., Mar. 31, 1899; B.S., Amherst Coll., 1921; LL.B., U. Wis., 1924. Admitted to Wis. bar, 1924; partner firm Hooker & Hoeper, Waupun, 1974; dir. Nat. Bank of Waupun, 1928-77, pres., 1941-68, chmn. bd., 1968-77; atty. City of Waupun, 1927-33. Mem. Wis., Dodge County, Fond du Lac County bar assns. Home: 200 S Watertown St Waupun WI 53963 Office: 512 E Main St Waupun WI 53963 Tel (414) 324-2121

HOOKER, JOHN DILLARD, b. Stuart, Va., May 24, 1909; B.S., U. Richmond, 1930; LL.B., U. Va., 1933. Admitted to Va. bar, 1933; partner firm Hooker and Hooker, Stuart, 1933-40; judge Patrick County (Va.) Ct., 1934-42, 46-48; atty., 1948-51; judge Circuit Ct., Stuart, 1951—. Pres. Patrick County Meml Hosp.; chmn. Library Bd.; trustee Patrick Henry Community Coll. Mem. Va. State Bar Assn., Va. Jud. Conf. Recipient Silver Beaver award Boy Scouts Am. Home: Sunset Dr Stuart VA 24171 Office: Courthouse Bldg Main St Stuart VA 24171 Tel (702) 694-3775

HOOPER, CHARLES NEWTON, b. Atlanta, June 14, 1933; B.S., Davidson Coll., 1955; LL.B./J.D., Emory U., 1961. Admitted to Ga. bar, 1960; law asst. Ct. Appeals of Ga., Atlanta, 1961-69, 72-77, Supreme Ct. Ga., 1969-72, 77—. Home: 6465 Scott Valley Rd NW Atlanta GA 30328 Office: State Judicial Bldg Atlanta GA 30334

HOOPER, GEORGE GETMAN, b. Tulsa, Sept. 17, 1943; B.B.A., Tex. Christian U., 1965; J.D., U. Tulsa, 1972. Admitted to Okla. bar, 1972; mem. firm Boyd & Parks, Tulsa, 1971—; with Tulsa County Legal Aid, 1971. Mem. Am., Okla., Tulsa County (econ. status com., Explorer Scout com.) bar assns. Office: 217 W 5th St Tulsa OK 74103 Tel (918) 582-3222

HOOPER, GEORGE ROBERT, b. Oak Park, Ill., Mar. 16, 1924; A.B., Harvard, 1947, J.D., 1949. Admitted to D.C. bar, 1949, Ill. bar, 1950; asso. firm Pritchard, Heath, Montgomery & Pennington, Chgo., 1949-53, partner, 1953-57; gen. counsel Booz-Allen & Hamilton, Chgo., 1957-60; partner firm Chadwell, Kayser, Ruggles, McGee & Hastings, Chgo., 1961—; commr. Uniform State Laws Commn., 1969-73. Mem. Am., Chgo., Ill. State bar assns., Legal Club Chgo., Law Club Chgo., Am. Judicature Soc. Home: 650 S Edgewood St La Grange IL 60525 Office: 8500 Sears Tower Chicago IL 60603 Tel (312) 876-2130

HOOPER, JAMES R. L., b. Robbinsville, N.C., Aug. 21, 1928; student Western Carolina Coll., 1945-46, Atlantic Union Coll., 1948-49, U. of Pacific, 1952-53, LL.B., U. San Francisco, 1953, J.D., 1957. Admitted to Calif. bar, 1957; individual practice law, Crescent City, Calif., 1957-60, 60—; atty. City of Crescent City, 1958-64, spl. counsel, 1964—; gen. counsel Crescent City Redevel. Agy., 1964—. Mem. western regional adv. bd. Nat. Park Service, San Francisco, 1973-74; chmn. Del Norte County (Calif.) Republican Central Com., 1966. Mem. Am., Del Norte County, Humboldt County bar assns., Nat. Area Devel. Inst. Council, Del Norte County C. of C. (1st v.p.), Am. Judicature Soc., State Bar Calif. Recipient Distinguished Service award City of Crescent City, 1970, County of Del Norte, 1970, Crescent City Harbor Dist., 1969, Humboldt Bay Municipal Water Dist., 1970, Coll. of the Redwoods, 1976. Contbr. to legal handbook, 1964. Home: 288 W 7th St Crescent City CA 95531 Office: 686 G St Hooper Bldg Crescent City CA 95531 Tel (707) 464-3124

HOOPER, PERRY, b. Birmingham, Ala., Apr. 8, 1925; B.S., U. Ala., 1949, LL.B., 1953. Admitted to Ala. bar, 1953; since practiced in Montgomery, Ala.; law clk. Ala. Supreme Ct., 1954-55; partner firm Hooper & Waller, 1956-64; judge Probate Ct. Montgomery County, 1964-74, 15th Jud. Circuit Ct., 1975—. Mem. Am., Ala., Montgomery bar assns., Ala. Circuit Judges' Assn. (pres. 1974). Contbr. articles in field to legal jours. Home: 3221 Warrenton Rd Montgomery AL 36111 Office: Montgomery County Court House Montgomery AL 36101 Tel (205) 265-8889

HOOSE, HARNED PETTUS, b. Kuling, China, June 2, 1920; B.A., U. So. Calif., Los Angeles, 1942, LL.B., 1948. Admitted to Calif. bar, 1949; clk. Calif. Supreme Ct., San Francisco, 1949-50; asso. firm O'Melveny & Myers, Los Angeles, 1950-54; sr. partner firm Harned Pettus Hoose, Los Angeles, 1957—; lectr. Calif. Bar Continuing Edn. Program; bd. govs. Beverly Hills Bar; lectr. law Hastings Coll. Law, U. Calif., U. So. Calif.; cons. prof. internat. bus. Grad. Sch. Bus. Adminstrn., U. So. Calif. Trustee, fellow L.S.B. Leakey Found., Isotope Found.; mem. Bleitz Wildlife Found.; chmn. bd. trustees United Methodist Ch. Mem. Am., Calif., Los Angeles bar assns., Am. Judicature Soc., Los Angeles C. of C., Los Angeles Fgn. Affairs Council, Los Angeles Philanthropic Found., World Peace Through Law Assn., Beverly Hills Bar Assn. Author: Peking Pigeons and Pigeon Flutes, 1938; contbr. articles to legal jours. Tel (213) 472-2828

HOOVER, JAMES CHARLES, b. Manchester, Conn., July 4, 1934; A.B., U. Fla., 1959, LL.B., 1962. Admitted to Fla. bar, 1962, Ga. bar, 1964, since practiced in Atlanta; partner firm Costangy & Prowell, 1964-71, Paul & Hoover, 1971-75, Elarbee, Clark & Paul, 1975—. Mem. Am., Ga., Fla., Atlanta bar assns., Order of Coif. Editor Fla. Law Rev., 1962. Office: 800 Peachtree Cain Tower Atlanta GA 30303 Tel (404) 659-6700

HOOVER, JUDSON REXFORD, b. Elmira, N.Y., Mar. 11, 1898; LL.B., U. Buffalo, 1925. Admitted to N.Y. bar, 1926, U.S. Dist. Ct. bar for Western Dist. N.Y., 1926, for No. Dist. N.Y., 1964, U.S. Ct. Appeals bar, 2d Circuit, 1958; asso. firm Wilmot E. Knapp, Elmira, 1925-26, individual practice law, Elmira, 1927-39, 40-47, 52-56, 64-71, mem. firm Casson, Hoover & Stein, Elmira, 1939-40, Hoover & Ziff, Elmira, 1947-52, Hoover & Peterson, Elmira, 1957-64, Hoover & Balok, Elmira, 1972—; former acting judge Elmira City Ct. Mem. N.Y. State, Chemung County (pres. 1968) bar assns., Am. Judicature Soc., Assn. Trial Lawyers Am. Home: RD 1 Millport NY 14864 Office: 216 William St Elmira NY 14901 Tel (607) 734-8193

HOOVER, RUSSELL JAMES, b. Evanston, Ill., Apr. 27, 1940; A.B., U. Notre Dame, 1962; J.D., Georgetown U., 1965. Admitted to Ill. bar, 1965; asso. firm Jenner & Block, Chgo., 1968-75, partner, 1975—. Mem. Am., Ill. State bar assns., Chgo. Council Lawyers. Home: 32 N Portwine Rd Roselle IL 60172 Office: One IBM Plaza Suite 4300 Chicago IL 60611 Tel (312) 222-9350

HOPE, GARLAND H., b. Payne, Okla., July 18, 1911; B.S. in Bus. Adminstrn., U. Okla., 1937, LL.B., 1942, J.D., 1970; postgrad. Nat. Coll. Judiciary, 1970, 72. Admitted to Okla. bar, 1942, U.S. Supreme Ct. bar, 1962; practice law, Oklahoma City and Maysville, Okla., 1946-53, Maysville, 1957-59; county judge Garvin County (Okla.), Pauls Valley, 1953-69; dist. judge Garfield County, Enid, 1969-74; city atty., Wayne, Okla., 1975—; individual practice law, Pauls Valley, Okla., 1975—; pres. County Judges Assn., 1961-62, County Officers Assn. Okla., 1967. Mem. Am., Okla., Garfield County bar assns., Juvenile Judges Assn. Address: RFD 3 Box 4 Pauls Valley OK 73075 Tel (405) 238-6223

HOPFL, CHARLES ERNEST, b. N.Y.C., Feb. 16, 1936; B.S., N.Y. U., 1957, J.D., 1960, LL.M., 1961, M.B.A., 1966. Admitted to N.Y. bar, 1960, Tenn. bar, 1972; atty. FTC, N.Y.C., 1960-61; corp. counsel Gen. Time Corp., N.Y.C., 1961-64; gen. counsel Ward Foods, Inc., N.Y.C., 1964-69, Cinecom Corp., N.Y.C., 1969-71, Am. Recreation Services, Inc., N.Y. and Tenn., 1971-74; spl. cons. HUD, Washington, 1974-75; individual practice law, N.Y.C., 1975—. Mem. N.Y.C. planning bd. No. 7, 1965-69, 77—. Mem. Assn. Bar City N.Y., N.Y. State, Am., Tenn. bar assns. Contbr. articles to real estate and legal jours. Home: 390 West End Ave New York City NY 10024 Office: 500 Fifth Ave New York City NY 10036 Tel (212) 730-1096

HOPKINS, ALBERT LAFAYETTE, b. Hickory, Miss., Apr. 27, 1886; student Millsaps Coll., 1900-01, U. Miss., 1901-02; A.B., U. Chgo., 1905; J.D., Harvard U., 1908, LL.B., 1909. Admitted to Ill. bar, 1908; partner firm Hopkins, Sutter, Milroy, Davis & Cromartie, Chgo.; asst. U.S. atty. No. Dist. Ill., 1913-17; asst. counsel ICC, Washington, 1917-19; spl. atty. IRS, 1919. Mem. Chgo. Bar Assn. Author: Autobiography of a Lawyer; Save Our Country. Home: 1308 E 58th St Chicago IL 60637 Office: One 1st Nat Plaza Suite 5200 Chicago IL 60603 Tel (312) 786-6727

HOPKINS, BRUCE RICHARD, b. Sault Ste. Marie, Mich., Apr. 25, 1941; B.A., U. Mich., 1964; J.D., George Washington U., 1967, LL.M., 1971. Admitted to D.C. bar, 1969; partner firm Williams, Myers and Quiggle, Washington, 1969-76, Baer Marks and Upham, Washington, 1976—; lectr. in law George Washington U., 1973—. Pres. Fox Hills West Citizens Assn., Potomac, Md., 1975, dir. 1974, 75. Mem. Am., D.C. bar assns., Nat. Assn. Coll. and Univ. Attys. Author: The Law of Tax-Exempt Organizations, 2d edit., 1977. contbr. articles to legal jours. Home: 9113 Willow Pond Ln Potomac MD 20854 Office: 1150 17th St NW Suite 607 Washington DC 20036 Tel (202) 467-5712

HOPKINS, GEORGE MATHEWS MARKS, b. Houston, June 9, 1923; B.S. in Chem. Engring., Ala. Polytech. Inst., 1944; J.D., U. Ala., 1949. Admitted to Ala. bar, 1949, Ga. bar 1954, U.S. Patent Office bar, 1953, Can. Patent Office bar, 1954, U.S. Ct. Customs and Patent Appeals bar, 1956, U.S. Supreme Ct. bar, 1961, U.S. Ct. Mil. Appeals bar, 1964; partner firm Newton, Hopkins & Ormsby, Atlanta, 1961-67, firm Newton, Hopkins, Jones & Ormsby, Atlanta, Ga., 1967—; instr. math. U. Ala., 1946-49; asst. dir. research Auburn Research Found., 1954-55. Registered profl. engr., Ga. Mem. Ga. (chmn. patent trademark and copyright sect. 1970-71), Ala., Am. bar assns., Am. Patent Law Assn., Phoenix Soc., Submarine Vets. World War II (pres. Ga. chpt. 1977-78), Nat. Lawyers Club, Phi Delta Phi, Sigma Alpha Epsilon. Home: 765 Old Post Rd NW Atlanta GA 30328 Office: 1010 Equitable Bldg Atlanta GA 30303 Tel (404) 688-1788

HOPKINS, H. LOWELL, b. Hollywood, Fla., Feb. 10, 1931; student Emory U., 1949-51, J.D., 1953. Admitted to Ga. bar, 1953; ins. adjustor U.S. Fidelity & Guaranty Co., 1954-59; asso. firm Howard & Harp, 1959-61; partner firm O'Kelley, Hopkins & VanGerpen, 1961-70; sr. partner firm Hopkins, Gresham & Whitley, Atlanta, 1970—. Mem. Am., Ga., Atlanta, Decatur-DeKalb bar assns., Ga. Def. Lawyers Assn. Home: 3298 Henderson Creek Rd Atlanta GA 30341 Office: 101 Marietta Tower Atlanta GA 30303 Tel (404) 688-0033

HOPKINS, W. DEAN, b. Richland County, Ohio, Nov. 10, 1909; B.S., Coll. Wooster, 1930; LL.B., Harvard U., 1933. Admitted to Ohio bar, 1933; asso. firm Fackler, Dye & Hopkins and predecessor, Cleve., 1933-46; partner, then mem. firm McDonald, Hopkins & Hardy, Cleve., 1946—. Trustee Coll. Wooster, 1940—; mem. Lakewood Bd. Edn., 1957-70. Mem. Am., Ohio State, Cleve., Cuyahoga County bar assns. Contbr. articles to profl. jours. Home: 18144 Clifton Rd Lakewood OH 44107 Office: 1105 E Ohio Bldg Cleveland OH 44114 Tel (216) 621-3480

HOPKINS, WILLIAM HAYES, b. Moscow, Idaho, Aug. 5, 1943; B.A., Yale, 1965; J.D., Vanderbilt U., 1968. Admitted to Conn. bar, 1968, N.H. bar, 1969; asso. firm Wakefield & Ray, Plymouth, N.H., 1969-75; partner firm Ray & Hopkins, Plymouth, 1975--; dir., legal counsel Pemigewasset Devel. Center, 1970-75; instr. Plymouth State Coll., 1972—. Health officer Town of Plymouth, 1971-77. Mem. Am., N.H., Grafton County (dir. 1975—) bar assns. Office: 85 Main St PO Box 270 Plymouth NH 03264 Tel (603) 536-1737

HOPKINS, WILLIAM PAUL, JR., b. Chgo., Oct. 4, 1921; B.S.C., De Paul U., 1949; M.B.A., U. Chgo., 1953; J.D., U. So. Calif., 1967. Admitted to Calif. bar, 1967, U.S. Supreme Ct. bar, 1971; city atty. City of Anaheim, Calif., 1976—. Mem. Orange County, Los Angeles County, SE, Criminal Cts. Bar Assns., Bar of Supreme Ct. of U.S., Legion Lex, Phi Alpha Delta. Office: 106 N Claudina St Anaheim CA 92805 Tel (714) 533-5361

HOPP, KENNETH HARVEY, b. Tacoma, July 27, 1923; B.S., U. Wash., 1948; J.D., 1949; LL.M., Georgetown U., 1961. Admitted to Wash. bar, 1950, Md. bar, 1958, D.C. bar, 1959, Tex. bar, 1963, Calif. bar, 1965; individual practice law, Bridgeport, Wash., 1954-58, Adelphi, Md., 1958-62, San Bernadino, Calif., 1967-71, Redlands, Calif., 1971—; prof. SW Union Coll., Keene, Tex., 1962-64; gen. counsel Loma Linda (Calif.) U., 1964-67; city atty. Bridgeport. Mem. Wash., Calif., San Bernadino County bar assns., Assn. of Seventh Adventist Lawyers, Bridgeport C. of Co. (sec. 1965-68). Home: 36265 Panorama Dr Yucaipa CA 92399 Office: 306 E State St Redlands CA 92373 Tel (714) 793-2668

HOPP, WALTER JAMES, b. Longmont, Colo., Jan. 17, 1945; B.A., U. Colo., 1967, J.D., 1970. Admitted to Colo. bar, 1970; clk. to judge U.S. Dist. Ct., Denver, 1970-71; asso. firm Schey & Schey, Longmont, 1971-73, partner, 1973—. Bd. dirs. Longmont Info. and Vol. Center, 1972-74; chmn. Longmont Profl. Dr., Am. Cancer Soc., 1976. Mem. Am., Colo., Boulder County (chmn. juvenile, family law com. 1973-75, trustee 1975—, bd. dirs. legal services corp. 1975) bar assns., Colo., Am. trial lawyers assn. Home: 1249 Brookfield Dr Longmont CO 80501 Office: Box 267 Longmont CO 80501

HOPPER, EDWARD BERNARD, II, b. Stamford, Conn., May 7, 1939; B.A., Vanderbilt U., 1961, J.D., 1964. Admitted to Tenn. bar, 1964, Ind. bar, 1967, U.S. Supreme Ct. bar, 1970; asso. firm Bamberger & Felbleman, Indpls., 1967-72, partner, 1973-76; partner firm Hopper & Opperman, Indpls., 1977—. Vestryman, St. Albans Episcopal Ch., 1968-71. Home: 4205 Manning Rd Indianapolis IN 46208 Office: 414 Union Federal Bldg Indianapolis IN 46204 Tel (317) 635-8000

HOPPER, GEORGE ANDREW, b. Omaha, Dec. 8, 1921; A.B., San Jose State Coll., 1942, postgrad., 1942; postgrad. U. Calif., Berkeley, 1942, Carnegie Inst. Tech., 1943-44; J.D., Stanford, 1949; postgrad. Nat. Coll. State Judiciary, 1968, 70, 71, 72. Admitted to Calif. bar, 1949; individual practice law, Orange Cove, Calif., 1949-63; city atty. Orange Cove, 1949-63, McFarland (Calif.), 1957-63, Arvin (Calif.), 1961-63; atty McFarland San. Dist., 1957-60, Cutler Pub. Utility Dist., 1961-63; judge Municipal Ct., Fresno, 1963-77; asso. justice Calif. Ct. Appeal, 5th Dist., Fresno, 1977—; elections examiner NLRB, 1947; instr. law Reedley (Calif.) Coll., 1956-63; lectr. criminal law and procedure Calif. State U., Fresno, 1971-75. Chmn. Fresno County Democratic Central Com., 1958-63; first chmn. Fresno County Econ. Opportunities Commn., 1965. Mem. Calif. Judges Assn., Am. Bar Assn., Am. Judicature Soc., Am. Fgn. Law Assn., Law and Soc. Assn., Western Govtl. Assn., Am. Soc. for Pub. Adminstrn., Internat., Am., Western polit. sci. assns., Am. Soc. for Legal History, Acad. Polit. Sci. Contbr. articles and book revs. to legal jours. Home: 1053 N College St Fresno CA 93728 Office: 5077 State Bldg 2550 Mariposa St Fresno CA 93721 Tel (209) 488-5161

HOPPER, ROBERT LUTHER, III, b. Boston, May 20, 1946; B.A., U. Ala., 1968, J.D., 1971. Admitted to Colo. bar, 1971; atty. Colo. Rural Legal Services, Boulder, 1971-72; individual practice law, Grand Junction, Colo., 1972; mem. firm Hopper & Hober, Grand Junction, 1972-76, Hopper, Hober & Witt, Grand Junction, 1976, Hopper & Witt, Grand Junction, 1976—; trustee U.S. Dist. Ct., bankruptcy div., Denver. Bd. dirs. Colo. West Community Action Program, chmn., Grand Junction. Mem. Colo., Am., Mesa County bar assns. Home: 112 Epps Dr Grand Junction CO 81501 Office: 131 S 6th St Grand Junction CO 81501 Tel (303) 245-4758

HOPPIN, CHARLES SWORDS, b. N.Y.C., Sept. 4, 1931; A.B., Harvard U., 1953; LL.B., Columbia U., 1959. Admitted to Calif. bar, 1960, N.Y. State bar, 1964; law clk. justice Supreme Ct. Calif., 1959-60; asso. firm Cooley, Crowley, Gaither, Godward, Castro & Huddleson, San Francisco, 1960-73; asso. firm Davis Polk & Wardwell, N.Y.C., 1963-68, partner, 1968—. Mem. N.Y. State Bar Assn., Bar Assn. City N.Y. Office: One Chase Manhattan Plaza New York NY 10005 Tel (212) 422-3400

HOPPING, WADE LEE, b. Dayton, Ohio, Aug. 12, 1931; B.A., Ohio State U., 1953, LL.B., 1955, J.D., 1967. Admitted to Ohio bar, 1955, Fla. bar, 1958; partner firm Adams and Hopping, Columbus, Ohio, 1957-58; research asst. Justice T. Frank Hobson Supreme Ct. Fla., 1958-59; asso. firm M.F. Baugher, W. Palm Beach, Fla., 1960-61; asst. to Chief Justice Glenn Terrell Supreme Ct. Fla., 1962-64; dir. continuing legal edn. The Fla. Bar, Tallahassee, 1964-67; legis. asst., constitutional law advisor to Fla. Gov. Claude R. Kirk, Jr., 1967-68; justice Supreme Ct. Fla., 1968-69; partner firm Mahoney, Hadlow & Adams, Tallahassee, Fla., 1969—. Fellow Am. Bar Found.; mem. The Fla. Bar, Am. Bar Assn. Office: PO Box 5716 Tallahassee FL 32301 Tel (904) 222-7500

HOPPS, SIDNEY BRYCE, b. Yale, Mich., May 10, 1934; B.A., U. Mich., 1957, J.D., 1960. Admitted to Ohio bar, 1960; partner firm Squire, Sanders & Dempsey, Cleve., 1960—. Mem. Ohio State, Greater Cleve. bar assns., Phi Beta Kappa, Phi Kappa Phi. Editorial bd. U. Mich. Law Rev., 1959-60. Home: 5540 Sleepy Hollow Rd Valley City OH 44280 Office: 1800 Union Commerce Bldg Cleveland OH 44115 Tel (216) 696-9200

HORAN, CHARLES PATRICK, b. Chgo., May 6, 1900; LL.B., J.D., DePaul U., 1933. Admitted to Ill. Supreme Ct. bar, 1933, U.S. Dist. Ct. bar, for No. Dist. Ill., 1933, U.S. Supreme Ct. bar, 1970; asso. corporate counsel, City of Chgo., 1933-50; asst. corp. counsel, chief div. gen. counsel City of Chgo., 1950-54, chief div. torts, 1955-62; judge Municipal Ct., Chgo., 1962-64; asso. judge Cook County (Ill.) Ct., 1964-71; judge Ill. Circuit Ct., Circuit of Cook County, 1971-76; presiding judge First Municipal Dist. Circuit Ct. Cook County, 1976—. Mem. Ill. State, Chgo., Am. bar assns., Celic Legal Soc. of Chgo. (Man of Year award 1975), Cath. Lawyers Guild of Chgo., Ill. Judges Assn. (award 1971, pres.), Recipient award Young Mems. Sect. Chgo. Bar Assn., 1976, Outstanding Jud. Services award Ill. Trial Laweyrs Assn., 1974, Distinguished Service award Trial Bar Assn. of Cook County, 1973. Office: Chicago Civic Center Randolph and Clark Sts Chicago IL 60602 Tel (312) 443-8050

HORAN, ROBERT, b. Bklyn., Apr. 22, 1928; B.B.A., City Coll. N.Y., 1950; J.D., St. John's U., 1953; LL.M., N.Y. U., 1958. Admitted to N.Y. bar, 1953; asso firm Hamlin, Hubbell & Davis, N.Y.C., 1953-58, firm Kadel, Wilson & Potts, N.Y.C., 1958-66, firm Phillips, Nizer, Benjamin, Krim & Ballon, N.Y.C., 1966-70, partner, 1970—. Mem. N.Y.C. Bar Assn. Home: 18 Beacon Hill Rd Ardsley NY 10502 Office: 40 W 57th St New York City NY 10019 Tel (212) 977-9700

HORBALY, JAN, b. Cleve., Oct. 5, 1944; A.B., Case Western Res. U., 1966, J.D., 1969; LL.M., U. Va., 1976. Admitted to Ohio bar, 1969, U.S. Supreme Ct. bar, 1973; asso. firm Will G. Horbaly & Assos., Cleve., 1969-70; served with JAGC, U.S. Army, def. counsel Ft. Knox, Ky., 1970-71, prosecutor Hdqrs., Vietnam, 1971-72, chief mil. justice, Vietnam, 1972, faculty advisor Nat. Coll. Dist. Attys.,

Houston, 1972, asso. prof. JAG Sch., Charlottesville, Va., 1972-76; spl. adv. com. on mil. justice to Judge Adv. Gen. of U.S. Army, 1973-76; curriculum com. Nat. Coll. Dist. Attys., 1972. Mem. Ohio State Bar Assn., Nat. Dist. Attys. Assn., Omicron Delta Kappa. Home: 771 Madison Ave Charlottesville VA 22903 Tel (804) 977-4728

HORDE, GAITHER WILSON, JR., b. Fresno, Calif., July 5, 1926; J.D., Vanderbilt U., 1951. Admitted to Tenn. bar, 1952, U.S. Supreme Ct. bar, 1959; individual practice law, Nashville, 1953-56; partner firm Stone Bozeman & Horde, Knoxville, Tenn., 1956-63; 1st asst. U.S. Atty.'s Office, Knoxville, 1963-67; div. counsel, dir. law dept. Union Carbide Corp., Oak Ridge, 1967—. Mem. 6th Circuit Jud. Conf. (life), Am., Tenn., Knoxville, Anderson County, Fed. bar assns., Nat. Security Indsl. Assn., Am., Tenn. trial lawyers assns., Delta Theta Phi. Home: 9409 Needles Dr Knoxville TN 37919 Office: Union Carbide Corp PO Box Y Oak Ridge TN 37830 Tel (615) 483-8611

HORKA, RUPERT FRANCIS, b. Shreveport, La., May 16, 1941; student U. Notre Dame, 1959-60; B.A., U. Tex., 1964; J.D., St. Mary's U., San Antonio, 1968. Admitted to Tex. bar, 1968, U.S. Supreme Ct. bar, 1972; partner firm Horka & Robinson, Silsbee, Tex., 1968-69; asst. dist. atty. Jefferson County (Tex.), Beaumont, 1969-76, chief misdemeanor prosecutor, 1969-73, maj. crimes prosecutor, 1973-76; county atty. Hardin County (Tex.), Kountze, 1977—. Pres., Silsbee (Tex.) Little Dribblers Basketball League, 1975, Silsbee Little League, 1976. Mem. Tex. Bar Assn., Tex. County and Dist. Attys. Assn., Delta Theta Phi. Home: 312 Willow Oak Ln Silsbee TX 77656 Office: Hardin County Courthouse Kountze TX 77625 Tel (713) 246-3361

HORKAN, GEORGE ARTHUR, JR., b. Moultrie, Ga., Mar. 9, 1926; A.B., Mercer U., 1950; J.D., U. Ga., 1952. Admitted to Ga. bar, 1952; partner firm Horkan & Peters, Moultrie, 1952-69; judge Moultrie Municipal Ct., 1957-69; dist. Atty. So. Jud. Circuit Ga., Moultrie, 1969-72; judge Ga. Superior Ct., So. Jud. Circuit, Moultrie, 1972—; mem. Ga. Criminal Justice Council, 1975-76. Adult advisor Moultrie Youth Center. Mem. Ga. Council Superior Ct. Judges. Author: Pre-Trial Motions in Criminal Cases in Ga., 1975; editor Ga. Bar Jour., 1952. Home: 20 17th Ave Se SE Moultrie GA 31768 Office: Courthouse Moultrie GA 31768 Tel (912) 985-1598

HORKAN, THOMAS ANTHONY, JR., b. Miami, Fla., Nov. 10, 1927; A.B., U. Miami, Coral Gables, Fla., 1948, LL.B., 1950. Admitted to Fla. bar, 1950; practiced in Miami, 1951-69; exec. dir. Fla. Cath. Conf., Tallahassee, 1969—. Mem. Am. Bar Assn., Fla. Assn. Acad. Nonpub. Schs. (founding dir., pres. emeritus), Nat. Assn. State Cath. Conf. Dirs. (v.p.), Cath. Lawyers Guild. Home: 2344 Limerick Dr Tallahassee FL 32303 Office: POB 1571 Tallahassee FL 32302 Tel (904) 222-3803

HORLBECK, JOHN MILES, b. Charleston, S.C., Jan. 29, 1925; A.B., Yale Coll., 1947; LL.B., U. Va., 1950. Admitted to S.C. bar, 1950; partner firm Cornish & Horlbeck, Charleston, 1953-75; individual practice law, Charleston, 1975—. Mem. S.C. House Reps., 1955-58. Mem. Charleston, S.C. bar assns. Office: PO Box 297 Charleston SC 29402 Tel (803) 722-7678

HORN, ALLWIN E., III, b. Birmingham, Ala., Apr. 7, 1944; LL.B., U. Ala., 1968. Admitted to Ala. bar, 1968; asso. firm Spain Gillon Riley Tate & Etheredge, Birmingham, 1969-75, partner, 1975—. Mem. Ala., Birmingham bar assns., Ala. Def. Lawyers Assn. Home: 139 Euclid Ave Birmingham AL 35213 Office: Spain Gillon et al 800 John Hand Bldg Birmingham AL 35203 Tel (205) 328-4100

HORN, CARL LEWIS, b. Highland Park, Mich., Aug. 18, 1928; A.B., U. Mich., 1950, J.D., 1952. Admitted to Mich. bar, 1952, U.S. Dist. Ct. bar for Eastern Dist. Mich., 1952; asso. firm Harty, Austin & Dingell, Detroit, Southfield, Mich., 1956-59; individual practice law, Standish, Mich., 1959-72; judge 34th Jud. Circuit, 1972—; prosecutor Arenac County (Mich.), 1960-72; city atty. City of Standish, 1960-72, City of Omer (Mich.), 1960-72; pub. adminstr. Arenac County, 1960-72. Chmn. bd. Standish Community Methodist Ch., 1963; chmn. Arenac County Republican Com., 1968-72. Mem. State Bar Mich., Am. Bar Assn., Mich. Judge's Assn., Am. Judicature Soc., Delta Theta Phi. Home: 617 Orchard St Standish MI 48658 Office: POB 749 Courthouse Standish MI 48658 Tel ((517) 846-6131

HORN, JOHN HAROLD, b. Eugene, Oreg., Mar. 4, 1927; B.S. in Polit. Sci., U. Oreg., 1949, LL.D., 1951. Admitted to Oreg. bar, 1951; mem. firm Horn & Slocum, Roseburg, Oreg., 1952-65, Horn, Slocum & Washburn, Roseburg, 1966-69, Riddlesbarger, Pederson, Young & Horn, Eugene, Oreg., 1970-74, Young, Horn, Cass & Scott, Eugene, 1975—. Chmn. bd. dirs. ARC, 1968. Mem. Oreg. State (service award 1970), Am., Douglas County (pres. 1960) bar assns., Am. Arbitration Assn. (panel), Lane County Estate Planning Council, Full Gospel Bus. Men's Fellowship Internat. (sec.), Pi Kappa Delta, Phi Delta Phi, Kappa Mu Epsilon. Home: 40 Elwood Ct Eugene OR 97401 Office: 101 E Broadway St suite 200 Eugene OR 97401 Tel (503) 687-1515

HORN, SYDNEY IRA, b. Lake Charles, La., July 31, 1939; J.D., Tulane U., 1964. Admitted to La. bar, 1964; individual practice law, Lake Charles, 1964—; pres. Renba Inc., Lake Charles, 1972-76, Abner Horn Investment Co., Lake Charles, 1974-76. Mem. Southwest La., La. State bar assns. Author: Louisiana Notarial Handbook and Study Guide. Office: 343 Broad St Lake Charles LA 70601 Tel (318) 439-4579

HORNBECK, DAVID BRUCE, b. Springfield, Ohio, Aug. 24, 1939; B.A., Ohio Wesleyan U., 1962; J.D., Ohio State U., 1969. Admitted to Ohio bar, 1970; partner firm Carnes & Hornbeck; asso. firm Hertlein, Brown & Carnes; partner firm Reibel, Reinhard, Carnes, Mackin & Hornbeck, firm Mackin, Hornbeck DiRosario, Precario & Portman, Columbus, Ohio. Mem. Ohio, Columbus bar assns. Home: 847 Gatehouse Ln Worthington OH 43085 Office: 150 E Mound St Suite 302 Columbus OH 43215 Tel (614) 224-7883

HORNBERGER, ROBERT EVANS, b. Milw., Sept. 3, 1947; B.S. in Bus. Adminstrn., U. Ark., 1969; J.D., 1972. Admitted to Ark. bar, 1972; partner firm Shaw and Ledbetter, Ft. Smith, Ark., 1972—. Mem. Ft. Smith Bicentennial Commn., 1976. Mem. Ark. Bar Found., Ark. Trial Lawyers Assn., Am., Ark., Sebastian County (sec. treas. 1976—) bar assns. Office: S 7th St and Parker St Fort Smith AR 72901 Tel (501) 782-7294

HORNBY, DAVID BROCK, b. Brandon, Man., Can., Apr. 21, 1944; B.A. with honors, U. Western Ont., 1965; J.D. cum laude, Harvard, 1969. Admitted to Va. bar, 1973, Maine bar, 1974; law clk. U.S. Ct. Appeals, New Orleans, 1969-70; asst. prof. law U. Va., 1970-73, asso. prof., 1973-74; asso. firm Perkins, Thompson, Hinckley & Keddy, Portland, Maine, 1974-75, partner, 1976—. Trustee, sec. Portland (Maine) Soc. Art, 1975-76, trustee, 1st v.p., 1976—; mem. Maine com. Skowhegan Sch. Painting and Sculpture, 1974—. Mem. Am., Maine bar assns. Contbr. articles in field to legal jours. Home: 635 Shore Rd Cape Elizabeth ME 04107 Office: One Canal Plaza POB 426 Portland ME 04112 Tel (207) 774-2635

HORNE, FOY SUMMERLIN, JR., b. Columbus, Ga., Jan. 2, 1943; A.A., Columbus Coll., 1963; A.B., U. Ga., 1968, LL.B., 1967. Admitted to Ga. bar, 1967; individual practice, Athens, Ga., 1968—. Mem. Am., Athens (past pres.) bar assns., Am., Ga. trial lawyers assns. Home: 486 Highland Ave Athens GA 30606 Office: PO Box 102 Athens GA 30603 Tel (404) 549-6376

HORNE, MICHAEL STEWART, b. Mpls., May 10, 1938; B.A., U. Minn., 1959; L.L.B., Harvard, 1962. Admitted to U.S. Supreme Ct. bar, 1968; asso. firm Covington & Burling, Washington, 1964-71, mem., 1971—. Mem. D.C., Am., FCC bar assns. Editor Harvard Law Rev., 1960-62, devels. editor, 1961-62. Home: 9008 Le Velle Dr Chevy Chase MD 20015 Office: 888 16th St NW Washington DC 20006

HORNE, THOMAS CHARLES, b. Montreal, Que., Can., Mar. 28, 1945; came to U.S., 1950, naturalized, 1959; B.A. in Govt. magna cum laude, Harvard, 1967, J.D., cum laude, 1970. Admitted to Mass. bar, 1970, Ariz. bar, 1972, U.S. Supreme Ct. bar, 1974; asso. firm Donovan, Leisure, Newton & Irvine, N.Y.C., 1971; Lewis and Roca, Phoenix, 1971-75, partner, 1975—. Mem., Ariz. State Air Pollution Control Hearing Bd., 1976—, vice chmn., 1977—; pres. Phoenix Young Democrats, 1972-74; research co-chmn. Castro for Ariz. Gov. Campaign Com., 1974. Mem. Am. (chmn. constrn. law div.), Ariz., Mass., Maricopa County bar assns. Home: 2824 E Mission Ln Phoenix AZ 85028 Office: 100 W Washington St Phoenix AZ 85003 Tel (602) 262-5738

HORNIG, THOMAS STONE, b. Wisconsin Rapids, Wis., July 1, 1947; B.B.A., U. Wis., 1969, J.D., 1972. Admitted to Wis. bar, 1972; mem. firm Brennan, Steil, Ryan, Basting & MacDougall, Janesville, Wis., 1972—. Trustee Cargill United Meth. Ch., Janesville, 1976—. Mem. Am., Wis., Rock County (sec. 1977-78) bar assns., U. Wis. Alumni Club (pres. local chpt. 1975), Order of Coif, Beta Gamma Sigma, Phi Kappa Phi. Home: 2037 Williamsburg Pl Janesville WI 53545 Office: PO Box 1148 Janesville WI 53545 Tel (608) 756-4141

HORNING, HUBERT, b. Stewartsville, Mo., Jan. 26, 1897; A.B., U. Kans., 1923, LL.B., 1925. Admitted to Kans. bar, 1925; individual practice law, Fort Scott, Kans., 1925-26, Howard, Kans., 1927—; asso. firm. Stephens, Dresia, & Horning, Columbus, Kans., 1926-27; county atty. Elk County, Kans., 1929-63. Mem. Kans., SE Kans. bar assns., Howard C. of C. Office: 117 S Wabash St Howard KS 67349 Tel (316) 374-2430

HORNING, JOHN CHARLES, JR., b. Pitts., May 20, 1934; B.A., Stanford, 1955, LL.B., 1961. Admitted to Calif. bar, 1962; asso. firm Moerdyke, Anderson & Joyce, Palo Alto, Calif., 1962-65; dep. pub. defender Office of Pub. Defender, San Jose, Calif., 1965—. Mem. Calif. State, Santa Clara County bar assns. Office: 70 W Hedding St San Jose CA 95110 Tel (408) 998-5121

HORNSBY, JAMES RUSSELL, b. Manchester, Ky., July 3, 1924; student Center Coll., 1946-47; LL.B., John B. Stetson U., 1950. Admitted to Fla. bar, 1940, U.S. Supreme Ct. bar, 1959; individual practice law, Orlando, Fla., 1950—. Mem. Am., Fla., Orange County bar assns., Acad. Fla. Trial Lawyers, Internat. Acad. Law and Sci. Home: 480 S Lake Sybelia Dr Maitland FL 32751 Office: 311 N Rosalind Ave Orlando FL 32801 Tel (305) 843-9690

HORNSTEIN, GEORGE DAVID, b. N.Y.C., Mar. 29, 1904; A.B., Coll. City N.Y., 1924; J.D., Columbia 1926. Admitted to N.Y. bar, 1926, U.S. Supreme Ct. bar, 1940; individual practice law, N.Y.C., 1927-63; prof. N.Y.U. Sch. Law, 1963-69, Murry and Ida Becker prof. law, 1969—; mem. Joint Conf. Legal Edn. State N.Y., 1961-67, chmn. Selective Adv. Bd. N.Y.C. 1940-45. Pres., Soc. Libraries N.Y.U. 1970-72. Mem. Am. Law Inst., Am. Bar Assn., N.Y. County Lawyers Assn., Am. Arbitration Assn. (nat. panel arbitrators 1940—). Recipient N.Y.U. Presdl. citation, 1974, N.Y. U. Great Tchr. award, 1977, Congressional certificate merit, 1946; author: Corporation Law and Practice, 1959; contbr. articles to profl. jours. Home: 37 Washington Sq W New York City NY 10011 Office: 40 Washington Sq S New York City NY 10012 Tel (212) 598-2578

HOROWITZ, DONALD J., b. Bklyn., Jan. 13, 1936; B.A., Columbia, 1956; LL.B., Yale, 1959. Admitted to N.Y. bar, 1959, Wash. bar, 1960; law clk. Judge Harry E. Foster, Supreme Ct. Wash., 1959-60; individual practice law, Olympia, 1961-63; partner firm Farris, Bangs & Horowitz, Seattle, 1963-69; sr. asst. atty. gen. Wash., chief social and health services div., 1970-73; dep. sec. Wash. Dept. Social and Health Services, 1973; judge Superior Ct. Wash. for King County, 1974-77; partner firm Levinson, Friedman, Vhugen, Duggan, Bland & Horowitz, Seattle, 1977—; cons. Gov.'s Task Force on Decision Making in Corrections, 1972-74, Gov.'s Task Force on Jails and Detention Facilities, 1972-73; mem. King County Criminal Justice Coordinating Council, 1974-75; participant Nat. Conf. on Capital Punishment, N.Y.C., 1968; instr. Pacific Lutheran U., 1971, Olympia Adult Evening Sch., 1961-63; guest lectr. U. Wash., Seattle U., Seattle Pacific Coll.; adj. prof. U. Puget Sound Law Sch., 1977—; producer, co-moderator TV series With Justice for All? KCTS-TV, Seattle, 1969, numerous other television appearances. Hearing officer conscientious objector cases Dept. of Justice, 1965-67; active Wash. Urban Affairs Council, 1969-72, Wash. Commn. for Humanities, 1972—, Wash. Assn. Mental Health Task Force on Childhood Mental Illness, 1972-73; co-chmn. Conf. on Rights of Mentally Handicapped, San Francisco, 1972; del. Nat. Conf. on Criminal Justice, Washington, 1973; cons. Wash. Fedn. State Employees (AFL-CIO), 1973, John F. Kennedy U. (Calif.), 1973, Conf. N.W. Assn. Rehab. Industries-Focus-1980, 1973; mem. Gov.'s Adv. Council for Drug Abuse Prevention, 1975-76; founder, bd. dirs. United Inner City Devel. Found., 1968-69; founder, pres., trustee Central Area Mental Health Center, 1967-70; bd. dirs. Wash. chpt. Nat. Fedn. Concerned Drug Abuse Workers, 1974-76; mem. adv. com. U. Wash. Sch. Communications, 1973—, Inst. on Alcoholism and Drug Abuse, 1974, Soc. and Justice Program, 1975—; bd. dirs. Solo Center; trustee Bush Sch., Seattle, Puget Sound Big Sisters. Fellow Internat. Acad. Law and Sci.; mem. Am. (adv. bd. Center on Correctional Econs. 1974—), Wash., Thurston-Mason County (treas. 1962), Seattle-King County (chmn. spl. TV subcom. 1968-69) bar assns., Am. Judicature Soc., Am. Trial Lawyers Assn., Wash. Superior Ct. Judges Assn., Govtl. Lawyers Assn., Correctional Industries Assn. Contbr. articles to legal jours. Home: 2536 Lake Park Dr S Seattle WA 98144 Office: 1600 Seattle Tower House Seattle WA 98101 Tel (206) 624-8844

HOROWITZ, PAMELA SUE, b. Mpls., Mar. 31, 1946; A.B., in Econs., Macalester Coll., 1967; J.D., Boston U., 1973. Admitted to Ala. bar, 1974, D.C. bar, 1976; personnel adminstr. Control Data Corp., Mpls., 1967-70; exec. dir. Operation New Prichard, Prichard, Ala., 1973-74; staff atty. So. Poverty Law Center, Montgomery, Ala., 1974—. Mem. Ala. advisory com. to U.S. Commn. on Civil Rights, 1975—. Mem. Ala. Bar Assn. Recipient Am. Jurisprudence award, 1973. Home: 20 Howard St Montgomery AL 36104 Office: 1001 S Hull St Montgomery AL 36104 Tel (205) 264-0286

HOROWITZ, ROBERT MARC, b. N.Y.C., Jan. 22, 1944; B.A., Columbia, 1964, M.A. in Philosophy, 1970; J.D., Harvard, 1967. Admitted to N.Y. State bar, 1967, Wis. bar, 1972; asso. firm Rubin, Wachtel, Baum & Levin, N.Y.C., 1969-71; asso. firm Stafford, Rosenbaum, Rieser & Hansen, Madison, Wis., 1971-73, partner, 1974—; lectr. Wis. State Bar Seminars, 1975-76. Mem. Am., Wis., Dane County bar assns. Contbr. articles in field to profl. jours. Home: 6 S Prospect Ave Madison WI 53705 Office: 131 W Wilson St Suite 1200 POB 1784 Madison WI 53701 Tel (608) 256-0226

HORRIGAN, ALBERT PATRICK, b. Flint, Mich., Apr. 6, 1937; B.A., Sacred Heart Sem., Detroit, 1959; J.D., U. Mich., 1962. Admitted to Mich. bar, 1962; practiced in Flint, 1962-69; judge Mich. 68th Jud. Dist., 1969—; jud. adviser Wayne State U. Center for Adminstrn. Justice; mem. Mich. Supreme Ct. Advisory Com. on Ct. Statis. Reporting; mem. Mich. Gov.'s. Invitation Conf. on Traffic Law Reform; mem. exec. com. Mich. Conf. on Problem Driver and Traffic Safety; mem. Genesee County (Mich.) Traffic Safety Commn. Mem. State Bar Mich., Mich. Dist. Judges Assn. (v.p.), Am. Judges Assn., Am. Judicature Soc. Office: 120 E Fifth St Municipal Center Flint MI 48502 Tel (313) 766-7489

HORSEY, ALONZO REVEL, b. Merion, Pa., Jan. 16, 1929; A.B. cum laude, Princeton, 1950; J.D., Dickinson Sch. Law., 1955. Admitted to Pa. bar, 1956; law clk. Montgomery County Orphans' Ct., 1955-60; partner firm Henderson, Wetherill, O'Hey & Horsey, Norristown, Pa., 1960—; solicitor Twp. Lower Merion (Pa.), 1970—. Mem. Am., Pa., Montgomery County bar assns., Am. Coll. Probate Counsel, Nat. Assn. Estate Planning Councils (past pres.). Home: 1228 Arwyn Ln Gladwyne PA 19035 Office: 530 DeKalb St Norristown PA 19404 Tel (215) 279-3370

HORSKY, CHARLES ANTONE, b. Helena, Mont., Mar. 22, 1910; A.B., U. Wash., 1931; LL.B., Harvard, 1934. Admitted to N.Y. bar, 1935, D.C. bar, 1938; clk. to judge Augustus N. Hand, 1934-35; with office solicitor gen. Dept. Justice, 1935-37, 38-39; partner firm Covington & Burling, Washington, 1939-62, 67—; advisor to Pres. of U.S., 1962-67. Bd. dirs. Eugene and Agnes E. Meyer Found., Washington, 1969—, pres., 1970-73, chmn. bd., 1973—; chmn. D.C. Bd. Higher Edn., 1967-70. Mem. Am., D.C., Fed. bar assns., Am. Coll. Trial Lawyers, D.C. bar (dir. 1972—). Author: The Washington Lawyer, 1952. Home: 1227 Pinecrest Circle Silver Spring MD 20910 Office: 888 16th St NW Washington DC 20006 Tel (202) 452-6076

HORTON, EARLE CICERO, b. Tampa, Fla., Mar. 8, 1943; B.A., Fisk U., 1964; J.D., Western Res. U.-Cleve. State U., 1968. Admitted to Ohio bar, 1969; individual practice law, Cleve., 1969-70; partner firm Rogers, Horton & Forbes, Cleve., 1970—; spl. counsel, atty. gen. Ohio, 1972—; chmn. Cuyahoga County (Ohio) Pub. Defender Commn. Trustee NAACP, Central Service Corp., Cleve. Mem. Am. (regional dir.), Ohio, Cleve., Cuyahoga County bar assns., Nat. Bar Assn. (regional dir.), John M. Harlan Law Club (pres. 1975—). Home: 2472 Overlook Dr Cleveland Heights OH 44106 Office: 616 Marion Bldg 1276 W 3d St Cleveland OH 44113 Tel (216) 696-7170

HORTON, JAMES WRIGHT, b. Belton, S.C., Dec. 24, 1919; B.A., Furman U., 1942; J.D., Harvard, 1948. Admitted to S.C. bar, 1948; mem. firm Nettles & Horton, Greenville, S.C., 1948-52; partner firm Reiney, Fant & Horton, Greenville, 1952-70; pres. firm Horton, Drawdy, Marchbanks, Ashmore, Chapman & Brown, Greenville, 1970—. Bd. dirs. Greenville Family and Childrens Service, 1953-36, pres., 1954-55, 68-70; trustee Greenville County Sch. Dist., 1964-60; vice chmn. Greenville County Sch. Bd., 1969; pres. United Fund Greenville County, 1959; bd. dirs. Greenville Mental Health Clinic, 1956-59, Carolinas United Salvation Army, 1970—. Mem. Am., S.C. bar assns., Furman Alumni Assn. Decorated Silver Star. Home: 2 Osceola Dr Greenville SC 29605 Office: 307 Pettigru St Greenville SC 29602

HORTON, PAUL BRADFIELD, b. Dallas, Oct. 19, 1920; B.A., U. Tex., 1943, postgrad. Law Sch., 1941-43; LL.B., So. Meth. U., 1947. Admitted to Tex. bar, 1946; asso. firm Jackson Walker Winstead Cantwell & Miller, Dallas, 1947-48; partner firm McCall Parkhurst & Horton, Dallas, 1948—. Mem. Gov.'s Com. for Tex. Edn. Code, 1967-69. Mem. Am., Dallas bar assns., Nat. Water Resources Assn., Tex. Water Conservation Assn., Municipal Fin. Officers Assn., Delta Theta Phi. Contbr. articles to legal jours. Home: 5039 Seneca Dr Dallas TX 75209 Office: 1400 Mercantile Bank Bldg Dallas TX 75201 Tel (214) 748-9501

HORTON, STEPHEN BERNARD, b. Hartford, Conn., Nov. 27, 1936; B.S. magna cum laude, U. Hartford, 1968; J.D. with honors, U. Conn., 1972. Admitted to Conn. bar, 1972, U.S. Supreme Ct. bar, 1975; asso. firm Cardwell & Cardwell, Hartford, 1973, partner, 1974-76; individual practice law, Hartford, 1977—. Mem. Assn. Immigration and Nationality Lawyers (chmn. Conn. chpt. 1976—). Home: 44 Betty Rd Enfield CT 06082 Office: 60 Washington St Suite 610 Hartford CT 06106

HORTON, WILLIAM STEPHEN, b. McAlester, Okla., May 6, 1903; LL.B., U. Okla., 1928. Admitted to Okla. bar, 1928; since practiced in McAlester, partner firm Horton & Horton, 1971-51, individual practice law, 1951—; chmn. Okla. Bd. Bar Examiners, 1946-66; U.S. Commr., McAlester, 1940-75. Mem. administrv. bd. Grand Ave. Meth. Ch., McAlester. Mem., Am., Okla., Pittsburgh County bar assns. Home: 527 E Adams St McAlester OK 74501 Office: 124 1/2 Choctaw St McAlester OK 74501 Tel (405) 423-5128

HORWITZ, DAVID MAXWELL, b. Los Angeles, Apr. 25, 1943; B.A., U. Calif., Berkeley, 1964; LL.B., U. Calif., Los Angeles, 1967, J.D., 1967. Admitted to Calif. bar, 1968; asst. house counsel United Fruit Co., Burbank, Calif., 1969; asst. city atty., criminal div. City of Santa Monica (Calif.), 1969-72; partner firm Horwitz & Genser, Santa Monica, 1972—. Bd. dirs. Legal Aid Soc., Greater Santa Monica Bay Area, 1974-76. Mem. Los Angeles County Bar Assn. (exec. com. criminal law and procedures sect.), Los Angeles County Juvenile Cts. Bar Assn. (pres. 1975—), State Bar Calif. Home: 861 Greentree Rd Pacific Palisades CA 92072 Office: 606 Wilshire Blvd #702 Santa Monica CA 90401 Tel (213) 393-0239

HORWITZ, JULIAN VICTOR, b. El Paso, Tex., Dec. 4, 1931; B.A., U. Tex., Austin, 1954, J.D., 1961. Admitted to Tex. bar, 1961; individual practice law, El Paso, 1961—. Chmn. Jewish Family Service, El Paso, 1975—. Mem. Tex. Trial Lawyers Assn., Tex. Bar

Assn., Am. Judicature Soc. Home: 6419 Los Robles El Paso TX 79912 Office: 710 Bassett Tower El Paso TX 79901 Tel (915) 542-1905

HORWITZ, MAYER, b. Phila., Aug. 11, 1939; B.B.A., Pa. State U., 1961; J.D., Temple U., 1964. Admitted to Pa. bar, 1965, U.S. Supreme Ct. bar, 1970; asso. firm Donsky Katz & Levin, Phila., 1964-66; asso. firm Tabas Smith & Furlong, Phila., 1966-73, partner, 1973—. Pres., William Portner lodge B'nai B'rith, 1972, men's club Temple Adath Israel, Merion, Pa., 1974-76. Mem. Am. Judicature Soc. (faculty), Am., Pa., Phila. (chmn. compulsory arbitration com.) bar assns., Tau Epsilon Rho. Home: 138 Colwyn Ln Bala Cynwyd PA 19004 Office: One East Penn Sq Bldg Suite 512 Philadelphia PA 19107 Tel (215) LO 4-3333

HOSE, RALPH LORENZ, b. Cleve., Aug. 24, 1924; B.A., Bowling Green State U., 1949; M. of Govt. Adminstrn., U. Pa., 1951; J.D., Temple U., 1961. Admitted to Pa. Supreme Ct. bar, 1962, U.S. Ct. Appeals bar, 1962; resident in hosp. adminstrn. Phila. Gen. Hosp., 1951-52; adminstr. Tyler Meml. Hosp., Meshappen, Pa., 1952-54; asst. dir. Pontiac Gen. Hosp., Pontiac, Mich., 1954-57; asst. controller Einstein Med. Center, Phila., 1957-61; asso. firm Katz, Slifkin & Greenberg, Phila., 1961-62; counsel Security Ins. Group, Phila., 1962-64; v.p., mem. firm Haws, & Burke, Ardmore, Pa., 1964—. Bd. dirs. Gulph Mill Civic Assn., Gulph Mills, Pa., 1960—; bd. dirs. Wolfson Meml. Library, Upper Merion Twp., Pa., 1965-72. Mem. Am., Pa., Montgomery bar assns., Am., Pa., Montgomery trial lawyers assns., Pa., Research def. insts. Home: 955 Longview Rd Gulph Mills PA 19406 Tel (215) MI 9-5200

HOSEMANN, CHARLES DELBERT, JR., b. New Orleans, June 30, 1947; B.B.A., U. Notre Dame, 1969; J.D., U. Miss., 1972; LL.M., N.Y. U., 1973. Admitted to Miss. bar, 1972; asso. firm Dossett, Magruder & Montgomery, Jackson, Miss., 1973—. Team capt. profl. div. United Givers Fund, 1974; trustee Miss. Regional Blook Center, 1974—, sec. bd., 1974—. Mem. Am., Miss. State, Hinds County bar assns., Miss. Bar Legal Services, Miss. Art Assn., Jackson Young Lawyers Assn. (pres.-elect 1977), Miss. Law Inst. (dir. 1975—), U. Notre Dame Alumni Assn., Delta Theta Phi. Home: 5415 Melwood Dr Jackson MS 39211 Office: 1800 Deposit Guaranty Plaza Jackson MS 39201 Tel (601) 354-5504

HOSENBALL, S. NEIL, b. N.Y.C., May 23, 1925; B.S., U. Mich., 1948; LL.B., Harvard, 1951. Admitted to Fla. bar, 1951, Ohio bar, 1951, U.S. Supreme Ct. bar, 1965; individual practice law, Cleve., 1951-61; atty. NASA, Washington, 1961-63, chief counsel, 1963-66, asst. gen. counsel Lewis Research Center, Cleve., 1966-67, dep. gen. counsel, 1967-75, gen. counsel, Washington, 1975—; U.S. rep. to UN Com. on Peaceful Uses of Outer Space, 1970—; mem. Adminstrv. Conf. of U.S., 1960—. Mem. Fla. Bar Assn. Recipient NASA Exceptional Service and Distinguished Service medals; contbr. articles to profl. jours. Home: 4605 30th St NW Washington DC 20008 Office: 400 Maryland Ave SW Washington DC 20545 Tel (202) 755-3875

HOSKINS, EDWARD EVANS, b. Tonganoxie, Kans., Sept. 9, 1917; A.B., U. Kans., 1939; LL.B., So. Law U., 1949; M.B.A., Memphis State U., 1965, LL.B. endorsement, 1967; Ph.D. in Finance, U. Miss., 1976. Admitted to Tenn. bar, 1950; practiced law, Memphis, 1950-65; prof. bus. law Coll. Bus., Memphis State U., 1965—. Mem. Am., Memphis and Shelby County bar assns. Contbr. articles to profl. publs. Home: 4340 Powell Ave Memphis TN 38122 Office: 403 100 N Main Bldg Memphis TN 38103 Tel (901) 526-2256 also (901) 683-9870

HOSSNER, WILLIAM LYNN, b. Ashton, Idaho, Dec. 16, 1939; B.A., U. Idaho, 1963; J.D., George Washington U., 1965. Admitted to D.C. bar, 1965, Idaho bar, 1965; individual practice law, St. Anthony, Idaho, 1965—; pros. atty. Fremont County (Idaho), 1967—. Mem. Idaho Bar Assn., Idaho Trial Lawyers Assn., Nat. Dist. Attys. Assn., Idaho Pros. Attys. Assn. Home: Box 704 Ashton ID 83420 Office: Courthouse Saint Anthony ID 83445 Tel (208) 624-3782

HOSTER, CRAIG WILLIAM, b. Fort Worth, Tex., Apr. 11, 1946; B.B.A., Okla. U., 1971, J.D., 1973. Admitted to Okla. bar, 1973; asso. firm Conner, Winters, Ballaine, Barry & McGowen, Tulsa, Okla., 1973—. Mem. Am., Tulsa, Okla. bar assn., Order of Coif, Phi Delta Phi. Editor: U. Okla. Law Rev., 1972-73. Home: 2255 S Rockford Tulsa OK 74114 Office: 2400 Ft National Tower Tulsa OK 74103 Tel (918) 586-5685

HOSTERMAN, JOHN WILLIAM, b. Columbus, Ohio, Jan. 20, 1949; A.B., Dartmouth, 1971; J.D., Ohio State U., 1974. Admitted to Ohio bar, 1974; asso. firm Margulis, Gussler, Hall and Hosterman, Circleville, Ohio, 1974-76, partner, 1977—. Mem. Ohio State, Franklin County, Pickaway County bar assns. Home: PO Box 227 Circleville OH 43113 Office: 126 S Court St Circleville OH 43113 Tel (614) 474-6084

HOSTETTLER, HOMER ELMER, b. Henryville, Ind., Oct. 24, 1898; LL.B., U. Louisville, 1926. Admitted to Ind. bar, 1926; individual practice law, Henryville, 1926—. Office: Bank Bldg Henryville IN 47126 Tel (812) 294-1415

HOTCHKISS, RAY CALVIN, b. Vicksburg, Mich., June 2, 1929; B.A. with honors, Albion Coll., 1951; grad. U.S. Army Counter Intelligence Sch., Balt., 1952; M.A., Mich. State U., 1953; J.D. with distinction, Wayne State U., 1959. Tchr. elementary pub. schs., Lansing, Mich., 1951-54; grad. asst. debate coach, Mich. State U., 1952-53; instr. U. Md. overseas program, Nurenberg, Germany, 1955-56; admitted to Mich. bar, 1959; practiced in Lansing, 1959-66; juvenile judge Ingham County (Mich.) Probate Ct., 1961-66; probate and juvenile judge, 1966-70; judge Mich. Circuit Ct., 30th Jud. Dist., 1970—; conf. lectr. and cons.; sr. instr. in law Lansing Community Coll., 1960-72; asso. prof. criminal justice Mich. State U. Sch. Social Scis., 1972-77. Mem. Nat. Crime, Delinquency Council, Tri-County Law Enforcement Council, Am. Judicature Assn., Mich. Council Children, Youth, Nat. Juvenile Ct. Judges Assn., Vols. in Ct. Assn. Mng. editor Wayne Law Rev., 1958-59. Home: 721 Linden St East Lansing MI 48823 Office: City Hall Lansing MI 48933 Tel (517) 482-5548

HOTTLE, DARRELL RIZER, b. Hillsboro, Ohio, Sept. 13, 1918; B.A., Ohio State U., 1940; LL.B., Western Res. U., 1947. Admitted to Ohio bar, 1947; practiced in Hillsboro, 1947-55; solicitor City of Hillsboro, 1949; pros. atty. Highland County (Ohio), 1949-52; judge Highland County Common Pleas Ct., 1955—. Lay leader West Ohio United Meth. Conf., 1971. Mem. Am. Judicature Soc., Ohio Common Pleas Judges Assn., Ohio State (exec. com. 1967-70), Am., Highland County (pres. 1974) bar assns., Ohio Jud. Conf. Recipient Silver Beaver award Boy Scouts Am., 1967. Home: 335 W Walnut St Hillsboro OH 45133 Office: Courthouse Hillsboro OH 45133 Tel (513) 393-2422

HOTZ, HARTMAN, b. Fayetteville, Ark., July 30, 1928; B.A., U. Ark., 1948; J.D., Yale, 1951. Admitted to Ark. bar, 1951, Tex. bar, 1952, U.S. Supreme Ct. bar, 1971; asso. firm Leake & Henry, Dallas, 1951-53; judge adv. gen. USAF, 1953-55; instr. U. Ark. Sch. Law, 1967-69; clerk Eastern Dist. Ark., 1969-70; individual practice law, Fayetteville, Ark., 1970—; mem. Ark. Fed. Legis. & Procedures Com. Mem. Washington County, Ark., Am. bar assns., Phi Beta Kappa, Omicron Delta Kappa. Contbr. articles to legal jours. Home: 533 N Razorback Rd Fayetteville AR 72701 Office: 30 E Spring St Fayetteville AR 72701 Tel (501) 442-8301

HOUCHARD, JOHN EMIL, b. Plain City, Ohio, June 19, 1934; B.S. in Bus. Adminstrn., Ohio State U., 1959, J.D., 1961. Admitted to Calif. bar, 1962, Ohio bar, 1964; individual practice law, Plain City, Ohio, 1964—. Home: 424 S Chillicothe St Plain City OH 43064 Office: 128 W Main St Plain City OH 43064 Tel (614) 873-4911

HOUCHIN, LARRY KENNETH, b. Los Angeles, Jan. 18, 1939; B.S. in History, Portland State U., 1960; J.D., U. Oreg., 1963. Admitted to Oreg. bar, 1963, U.S. Dist. Ct. bar for Dist. Oreg., 1967; with Judge Adv. Gen. Corps USN, 1963-67; partner firm Wilshire & Houchin, Lebanon, Oreg., 1967; dep. dist. atty. Linn County (Oreg.) Dist. Atty's. Office, Albany, Oreg., 1967—, chief dep., 1968—; instr. Linn-Benton Community Coll., Oreg. Police Acad. Mem. Oreg., Linn County (Oreg.) (pres. 1975—) bar assns. Office: PO Box 100 Linn County Courthouse Albany OR 97321 Tel (503) 967-3836

HOUGH, STEVEN HEDGES, b. Cleve., May 24, 1938; B.S. in Bus. Adminstrn., Chico State Coll., 1961; J.D. Hastings Coll., 1964. Admitted to Calif. bar, 1966, U.S. Supreme Ct. bar, 1972; dep. pub. defender Los Angeles County, Long Beach, Calif., 1966—, acting head dep., 1977—. Bd. dirs. Am. Youth Soccer Assn., Westminster, Calif., 1975—. Mem. Am., Long Beach bar assns., Am. Judicature Soc., Calif., Los Angeles County pub. defenders assns., Los Angeles County Criminal Cts. Bar Assn. (dir. 1975—), Calif. Attys. Criminal Justice. Office: Suite 600 415 W Ocean Blvd Long Beach CA 90802 Tel (213) 432-0411

HOUGHTALING, EARLE HANNUM, JR., b. Newburgh, N.Y., Mar. 14, 1918; A.B., Rutgers U., 1939; LL.B., Cornell U., 1942, J.D., 1969. Admitted to N.Y. State bar, 1942, U.S. Supreme Ct. bar, 1958; asso. firm Hunt, Hill & Betts, N.Y.C., 1942-44; asso. counsel Com. to Investigate Adminstrn. Workmen's Compensation Law, N.Y.C., 1944-45; individual practice law, Walden, N.Y., 1945—; judge Ct. of Spl. Sessions, Walden, 1946—. Pres. U.S. Flag Found., 1975—; chmn. bd. trustees St. Mary's Sch., Peekskill, N.Y., 1974-76; chmn. Zoning Commn. Walden, 1954-56. Fellow Internat. Bar Assn.; mem. Am., N.Y. State bar assns., Assn. Bar City of N.Y., World Peace Through Law Center, Law Soc. London (fellow), UN Assn. N.Y. (dir. 1974—). Home: 150 Ulster Ave Walden NY 12586 Office: 3 Bank St PO Box 284 Walden NY 12586 Tel (914) 778-5509

HOUGHTON, JAMES PRICKETT, b. Indpls., Aug. 25, 1948; A.B. magna cum laude, Ind. U., 1970; J.D., U. Va., 1973. Admitted to N.Mex. bar, 1973; asso. firm Modrall, Sperling, Roehl, Harris & Sisk, Albuquerque, 1973—; mem. N.Mex. Ct. Reporters Bd. Mem. Am. Bar Assn., Albuquerque Lawyers Club. Office: 4th & Silver SW Public Service Bldg Albuquerque NM 87103 Tel (505) 243-4511

HOUGHTON, WOODSON PLYER, b. Washington, Apr. 19, 1893; B.A., Washington and Lee U., 1915; LL.B., Georgetown U., 1918. Admitted to D.C. bar, 1918; mem. firm Ellis, Houghton & Ellis, Washington, 1919-68, sr. partner, 1948-68; individual practice law, Washington, 1968—; prof. law Nat. U., 1923-26. Pres. Family Service Assn.; bd. dirs. Family Welfare Assn. Am., Community Chest D.C.; pres. Dupont Circle Citizens Assn. Mem. The Barristers, Phi Delta Phi. Home: 2337 California St NW Washington DC 20008 Office: 815 Connecticut Ave NW Washington DC 20006 Tel (202) 298-8290

HOUGLAND, GERALD LEE, b. Olathe, Kans., Mar. 19, 1932; B.A., Washburn U., 1958, J.D., 1959. Admitted to Kans. bar, 1959, U.S. Dist. Ct. bar, 1959; individual practice law, Olathe, 1959—; asst. pros. atty. Johnson County (Kans.), 1960-67; sch. dist. atty., Olathe, 1960-69; state rep. Kans. Legislature, 1969-72; housing authority atty. HUD, 1969-75; asso. dist. judge, Olathe, 1977—. Troop com. chmn. Boy Scouts Am., 1965-70; judge adv., bd. dirs. Navy League, 1969-74. Mem. Am., Kans., Johnson County bar assns. Home: 603 S Troost St Olathe KS 66061 Office: Johnson County Courthouse Olathe KS 66061 Tel (913) 782-5000

HOUGLAND, WHAYNE MILLER, b. Owensboro, Ky., June 30, 1940; B.S., Western Ky. U., 1964; J.D., U. Ky., 1967. Admitted to Ky. bar, 1968; asst. commr. and legal counsel Ky. Dept. Banking and Securities, Frankfort, 1968-70; partner firm Harkins & Hougland, Lexington, Ky., 1970-73, firm Stites, McElwain & Fowler, Frankfort, 1973—. Chmn. Woodford County Bd. Recreation, 1973—. Mem. Am., Ky., Franklin County, Woodford (pres.) bar assns. Office: 500 McClure Bldg Frankfort KY 40601 Tel (502) 223-3477

HOUK, GARETH WESLEY, b. Visalia, Calif., Dec. 12, 1903; J.D., Southwestern U., Los Angeles, 1930. Admitted to Calif. bar, 1931; individual practice law, Visalia, Calif., 1932-69; partner firm Houk & Houk, Visalia, 1969—; justice of peace Visalia Twp., 1934-48; police judge City of Visalia, 1934-48. Mem. Calif. Recreation Commn., 1947-61; chmn. Visalia Park Playground and Recreation Commn.; pres. bd. dirs. Tulare County (Calif.) YMCA; active Visalia chpt. ARC. Mem. Calif., Tulare County bar assns. Office: 1441 S Mooney Blvd Visalia CA 93277 Tel (209) 732-2293

HOURIGAN, ANDREW, JR., b. Wilkes-Barre, Pa., July 14, 1915; B.A., Princeton, 1937; LL.B., U. Pa., 1940. Admitted to Pa. bar, 1940; individual practice law, 1940-42, 45-48; partner firm White, Rowlands, Aston & Hourigan, 1948-56, firm Hourigan, Kluger & Spohrer, Wilkes-Barre, 1972—; chmn. merit selection panel Pa. Gov.'s Adv. Commn. on Jud. Qualifications, 1968; dir. United Penn Bank, Bertels Metal Ware Co., Motor Twins, Inc. Bd. dirs. Wyoming Valley Community Chest, 1953-58; bd. dirs. Wyoming Valley United Fund, 1955—, chmn. planning council 1955-58, pres., 1958-60; bd. dirs. Community Services Pa., 1966-73, v.p., 1970-73; adv. bd. Nat. Community Funds and Councils Am., 1959-69, vice chmn., 1962-65; bd. dirs. Blue Cross Northeastern Pa., 1959, v.p., 1963—; trustee Wilkes Coll., 1962—. Mem. Am. Bar Assn. (chmn. com. unauthorized practice law 1966-67, chmn. com. nat. conf. groups 1970-73, mem. ho. dels. 1967-68, 71—, state del. 1971-74, bd. govs. 1973-76), Pa. Bar Assn. (chmn. com. unauthorized practice law 1954-62, gov. 1966-69, v.p. 1967, pres, 1968), Am. Judicature Soc. (dir. 1969-73), Nat. Inst. Justice (commn. mem. 1976—), Nat. Legal Aid and Defender Assn. (exec. com. 1971-75), Jud. Conf. 3d Circuit Ct. Appeals (permanent), Law Alumni Soc. U. Pa. (gov. 1958-64), Greater Wilkes-Barre C. of C. (dir. 1955-58, 61—, pres. 1961-62). Home: 1720 Wyoming Ave Forty Fort PA 18704 Office: 700 United Penn Bank Bldg Wilkes-Barre PA 18701 Tel (717) 825-9401

HOUSE, CHARLES STAVER, b. Manchester, Conn., Apr. 24, 1908; A.B., Harvard U., 1930, LL.B., 1933; LL.D., Suffolk U., 1975. Admitted to Conn. bar, 1933; mem. firm Day, Berry & Howard, Hartford, Conn., 1933-53; judge Conn. Superior Ct., 1953-65; justice Conn. Supreme Ct., 1965—, chief justice, 1971—; vice chmn. Nat. Adv. Com. on Criminal Justice Standards and Goals, 1975-76; mem. Conn. Ho. of Reps., 1941; mem. Conn. Senate, 1947, 49, minority leader, 1949, chmn. legis. council, 1949; asst. state's atty. Hartford County, 1942-46; chmn. Conf. Chief Justices, 1975-76; vice-chmn. Nat. Com. Adminstrn. of Criminal Justice, 1975-76. Fellow Am. Bar Foundl; mem. Am., Conn., Hartford County bar assns. Home: Manchester CT Office: Drawer N Sta A Hartford CT 06106 Tel (203) 566-4469

HOUSE, ROLAND LEE, b. Fisher County, Tex., Oct. 1, 1899; B.A., Hardin-Simmons U., 1923; J.D., U. Tex., Austin, 1929. Prin., Roby (Tex.) High Sch., 1923-24, Ward High Sch., Ballinger, Tex., 1924-25; head dept. math., coach Abilene (Tex.) High Sch., 1925-26; admitted to Tex. bar, 1929, U.S. Supreme Ct. bar, 1955; sr. partner firm House, Mercer, House, Brock & Wilson, San Antonio, 1929—. Chmn. bd. trustees, mem. bd. deacons 1st Bapt. Ch., San Antonio, 1948—; trustee Bapt. Meml. Hosp., San Antonio, 1952-63, chmn. bd. trustees, 1957-62; trustee Hardin-Simmons U., 1958—, chmn. bd. trustees, 1973-74. Mem. San Antonio, Am. bar assns., State Bar Tex. Home: 201 Wildwood Dr E San Antonio TX 78212 Office: 1007 Nat Bank of Commerce Bldg San Antonio TX 78205 Tel (512) 226-9211

HOUSE, WILLIAM MICHAEL, b. Birmingham, Ala., Dec. 19, 1945; B.S., Auburn U., 1968; J.D., U. Ala., 1971. Admitted to Ala. bar, 1971; legis. asst. James M. Collins, 1971-72; adminstrv. asst. to Ala. Supreme Ct. Chief Justice Howell Heflin, 1972-75; dir. Permanent Study Commn. on Ala. State Cts., 1975-76; asso. firm Odom, Argo & Enslen, Montgomery, Ala., 1976—; v. chmn. Montgomery Criminal Justice Com. Mem. Am. Judicature Soc., Am., Fed. bar assns., Ala. Bar (mem. discipline, correction, indigent defense, state constn., legis., jud. office coms.), Ala. Young Lawyers (pres. 1976-77), Farrah Law Sch., Bench and Bar Honor Soc., U.S. Jaycees (outstanding state chmn. 1975, dist. pres. 1976), Ala. Jaycees (state external v.p. 1976-77), Omicron Delta Kappa, Omicron Delta Epsilon, Pi Kappa Alpha. Office: 1318 Woodward St Montgomery AL 36106 Tel (205) 834-2460

HOUSEHOLTER, FRANCIS J., b. Kress, Tex., Feb. 22, 1913; student Wichita State U.; LL.B., Valparaiso U., 1937. Admitted to Ill. bar, 1937; asst. atty. gen. State of Ill., 1960-61, spl. asst. atty. gen., 1969-75; now mem. firm Householter & Householter, Kankakee, Ill.; pres. Ill. Bar Officers Conf., 1964-65. Mem. Chgo., Kankakee County (pres. 1961-66), Ill. State (gov. 1967—, pres. 1976-77), Am. (ho. of dels. 1974—) bar assns., Assn. Trial Lawyers Am., Am. Judicature Soc., Fedn. Local Bar Execs. (pres. 3d dist. eastern div. 1963-64). Office: City Nat Bank Bldg Suite 609 Kankakee IL 60901 Tel (815) 932-2831*

HOUSEMAN, ALAN WILLIAM, b. Colo. Springs, Colo., Apr. 23, 1942; B.A., Oberlin Coll., 1965; J.d. (Field fellow), N.Y. U., 1968. Admitted to Mich. bar, 1968; Reginald Heber Smith fellow Wayne County (Mich.) Neighborhood Legal Services, 1968-69; dir. Mich. Legal Services, Detroit, 1969-76, dir. Research Inst. Legal Assistance, Legal Services Corp., Washington, 1976—, adj. prof. Sch. Law Wayne State Univ., Detroit, 1969—; lectr. Law Sch. U. Mich., Ann Arbor, 1973-75; chmn. Orgn. Legal Services Back-up Centers, 1973-74, vice chmn. Project Advisory Group, 1973-75; co-chmn. Mayor Coleman Young's Lawyers Com., Detroit, Mem. Am. Bar Assn., Am. Judicature Soc., Nat. Legal Aid and Defender Assn. (chmn. civil com., 1975—, dir., mem. exec. com. 1975—, recipient Spl. award, 1974), Soc. Am. Law Tchrs. Home: 3316 Mount Pleasant St NW Washington DC 20010 Office: 733 15th St NW Washington DC 20005

HOUSTON, CHARLES IRVIN, b. Butler, Pa., June 3, 1905; B.A., Westminster Coll., 1926; LL.B., Duquesne U., 1929. Admitted to Pa. bar, 1929; individual practice law, St. Mary's, Pa., 1932-62; partner firm Houston & Daghir, St. Mary's, 1962—; solicitor St. Mary's Area Schs., 1935—. Mem. Pa., Elk County bar assns. Office: Farmers & Merchants Bank Bldg St Mary's PA 15857 Tel (814) 834-3619

HOUSTON, FREDERIC PRIBER, b. N.Y.C., Apr. 19, 1910; A.B., Williams Coll., 1931; J.D., Harvard, 1934. Admitted to N.Y. bar, 1934, U.S. Supreme Ct. bar, 1956; asso. firm Alger, Peck, & Grafton, N.Y.C., 1934-35; asso. and partner firm Otterbourg, Steindler, Houston & Rosen, N.Y.C., 1936—; gen. counsel Textile Fabrics Assn., 1952-62; asso. and gen counsel v.p. N.Y. Bd. Trade, 1963—. Mem. Am., N.Y. State, N.Y.C. bar assns., N.Y. County Lawyers' Assn. Office: 230 Park Ave New York NY 10017 Tel (212) 679-1200

HOUTCHENS, BARNARD, b. Johnstown, Colo., Aug. 5, 1911; A.B., U. Nebr., 1933, LL.B., 1935; LL.D., U. No. Colo., 1963. Admitted to Colo. bar, 1935; city atty. City of Greeley (Colo.), 1941-47, 49-50; pres. bd. dirs. United Bank of Greeley; dir. Geriatrics, Inc., Meroco Broadcasting Co., Noffsinger Mfg. Co., Inc., Miner & Miner Cons. Engrs. Inc. (all Greeley). Chmn. Bar Com., Bd. Law Examiners, 1948—; trustee State Colls. in Colo., 1948-65, pres. bd., 1964-65; nat. sec. Assn. Governing Bds. State Univs. and Allied Insts., 1960-62; bd. dirs., v.p. U. No. Colo. Found. Fellow Am. Coll. Trial Lawyers; mem. Am., Colo., Weld County (pres. 1946-47) bar assns. Home: 1020 48th Ave Greeley CO 80631 Office: 1007 9th Ave Greeley CO 80631 Tel (303) 353-9195

HOVAN, JOHN JOSEPH, b. Newark, May 13, 1945; A.B. in English, U. Scranton, 1967; J.D., Duquesne U., 1970. Admitted to Pa. bar, 1970; asso. firm Hobbs, Morgan & DeWitt, Tunkhannock, Pa., 1970-71; individual practice law, Tunkhannock, 1971—; asso. firm David P. Posatko, Tunkhannock, 1975—; pub. defender Wyoming County (Pa.), 1972-74; solicitor Wyoming County Housing and Redevel. Authority, 1973—. Mem. Am., Pa., Wyoming-Sullivan County bar assns. Office: 154 Warren St Tunkhannock PA 18657 Tel (717) 836-3121

HOVANESIAN, ARCHIBALD, JR., b. Hartford, Conn., Apr. 5, 1941; A.B. cum laude, Princeton, 1962; J.D. with honors, U. Conn., 1970; A.M., Center for Middle Eastern Studies Harvard, 1974. Admitted to Conn. bar, 1970; asso. firm S.E. Perakos, New Britain, Conn., 1970-72; sr. staff analyst Arthur D. Little Inc., Cambridge, Mass. (work location, Ministry of Petroleum, Riyadh, Saudi Arabia), 1972-75; faculty Sch. Law U. Conn., 1970-73; cons., individual practice law and cons. service, Cambridge and Boston, 1975—; justice peace, Conn., 1972-74. Mem. Harvard Augmented Long Planning Council, 1973-74. Mem. Conn., Am., Hartford County, New Britain bar assns., Conn. ACLU. Contbr. articles to profl. jours.; editor Law Review, 1968-70. Home: 10 Greenwood St New Britain CT 06051 also Box 385 (School St) Edgartown MA 02539 Office: 89 Franklin St Suite 200 Boston MA 02110 Tel (617) 482-8971

HOVIS, JAMES B., b. Yakima, Wash., Dec. 15, 1922; B.S., U. Wash., 1949, J.D., 1950. Admitted to Wash. bar, 1950, U.S. Supreme Ct. bar, 1956; since practiced in Yakima, asso. firm Velikanje & Velikanje, 1950-52; partner firm Hovis, Cockrill & Roy, 1952—; town atty. Zillah (Wash.), 1950-61, Granger (Wash.), 1950-59; tribal atty. Yakima Indian Nation, 1954—. Mem. Wash. State Parks and Recreation Commn., 1961-66, chmn., 1962-65. Mem. Am., Wash. State, Yakima County (pres. 1972) bar assns. Home: 2 S 28th Ave Yakima WA 98902 Tel (509) 453-3165

HOVIS, RAYMOND LEADER, b. Phoenixville, Pa., Jan. 13, 1934; B.S. in Econs., U. Pa., 1955, J.D., 1958. Admitted to Pa. bar, 1959; asso. firm Stock and Leader, York, Pa., 1959-66, partner, 1966—; mem. Pa. Ho. of Reps., 1969-72. Pres. York County (Pa.) Govt. Study Commn., 1973-74; bd. dirs., mem. exec. com. Pa. affiliate Am. Heart Assn., 1974-75. Mem. York County (dir. 1976—), Pa., Am. bar assns., Assn. Trial Lawyers Am. Recipient Charles E. Rohlfing Citizenship award U. Pa., 1955. Home: RD 2 Wrightsville PA 17368 Office: 35 S Duke St York PA 17401 Tel (717) 843-8871

HOWALD, JOHN KENT, b. Waynesville, Mo., Jan. 9, 1950; B.S. in Bus. Adminstrn., William Jewell Coll., 1971; J.D., U. Mo., Kansas City, 1974. Admitted to Mo. bar, 1974; asso. firm Beckham, Hale & Howald, Steelville, Mo., 1974—. Mem. Am., 42d Jud. bar assns., Pi Gamma Mu, Delta Mu Delta. Asso. editor U. Mo. Kansas City Law Rev., 1973-74. Home: Steelville MO 65565 Office: PO Box B Courthouse Sq Steelville MO 65565 Tel (314) 775-2141

HOWARD, ARTHUR ELLSWORTH DICK, b. Richmond, Va., July 5, 1933; B.A., U. Richmond, 1954; B.A., Oxford (Eng.) U., 1960, M.A., 1965; LL.B., U. Va., 1961. Admitted to Va. bar, 1961, D.C. bar, 1961; asso. firm Covington & Burling, Washington, 1961-62; law clk. to Justice Hugo L. Black, U.S. Supreme Ct., 1962-64; asso. prof. law U. Va., 1964-67, prof., 1967-76, White Burkett Miller prof., 1976—; exec. dir. Va. Commn. on Constl. Revision, 1968-69; fellow Woodrow Wilson Internat. Center for Scholars, Washington, 1974-75, 76-77; counsel Va. Gen. Assembly, 1969, 70; cons. to Senate Judiciary Com. subcom. on constl. rights, 1974—. Mem. Va. Independence Bicentennial Commn., 1966—; Va. sec. Rhodes Scholarship Trust. Mem. Va. Bar (v.p.). Author: The Road from Runnymede: Magna Carta and Constitutionalism in America, 1968; Commentaries on the Constitution of Virginia, 2 vols., 1974; State Aid to Private Higher Education, 1977; bd. editors Am. Oxonian, 1964—. Home: 627 Park St Charlottesville VA 22901 Office: Sch of Law U of VA Charlottesville VA 22901 Tel (804) 924-7354

HOWARD, CALVIN MARVIN, b. Savannah, Tenn., Aug. 19, 1937; B.E.E., Auburn U., 1960; J.D., Cumberland U., 1969. Admitted to Ala. bar, 1969; distbn. engr. Ala. Power Co., Birmingham, 1960-69; individual practice law, Birmingham, 1969-75; asst. prof. Cumberland U. Sch. Law, 1975—. Mem. Am., Ala., Birmingham bar assns. Registered prof. engr., Ala. Home: 531 Currie Way Birmingham AL 35209 Office: Cumberland Sch Law Birmingham AL 35209 Tel (205) 870-2701

HOWARD, DAGGETT HORTON, b. N.Y.C., Mar. 20, 1917; B.A. in Econs. magna cum laude, Yale, 1938, J.D., 1941. Admitted to N.Y. bar, 1942, D.C. bar, 1961, U.S. Supreme Ct. bar, 1962; legal staff Root, Clark, Buckner and Ballantine, N.Y.C., 1941-43, Lend-Lease Adminstrn. and Fgn. Econ. Adminstrn., Washington, 1943-44; exec. asst. to spl. counsel to Pres., Washington, 1945; legal adviser Fgn. Econ. Adminstrn. and Dept. State, Washington, 1945-47, Internat. and Rules div. CAB, Washington; asso. gen. counsel Dept. Air Force, Washington, 1952-56, dep. gen. counsel, 1956-58; gen. counsel FAA, Washington, 1958-62; partner firm Cox, Langford and Brown, Washington, 1962-66; sr. partner firm Howard, Poe and Bastian, Washington, 1966—; mem. policy com. Daniel and Florence Guggenheim Aviation Safety Center, 1963-68. Mem. ann. corp. bd. Children's Hosp. Nat. Med. Center, Washington, 1968—. Mem. Am., Fed. bar assns., Yale Law Sch. Assn. Washington, Phi Beta Kappa. Recipient Exceptional Civilian Service award Dept. Air Force, 1958, Distinguished Service award FAA, 1962; mem. bd. editors Yale Law Jour. Home: 4554 Klingle St NW Washington DC 20016 Office: 1701 Pennsylvania Ave NW Washington DC 20006 Tel (202) 298-8333

HOWARD, DOROTHY YANCY, b. Malvern, Ark., Mar. 7, 1917; student Little Rock Jr. Coll., 1936; LL.B., LaSalle U., 1947. Admitted to Ark. bar, 1947, U.S. Dist. Ct. for Eastern Dist. Ark. bar, 1947, U.S. Supreme Ct. bar, 1950; partner firm Howard and Yancy, Little Rock, 1947-67; standing master in chancery Pulaski County (Ark.) Chancery Ct., 1965—; partner firm Howard, Howard, & Howard, Little Rock, 1967—. Mem. Am., Ark., Pulaski County bar assns., Nat., Ark. assns. women lawyers, Internat. Fedn. Women Lawyers, Phi Alpha Delta. Recipient Nat. Service Achievement award Nat. Assn. Women Lawyers, 1964; editor Nat. Assn. Women Lawyers Jour., 1956-57, mem. edit. bd., 1968-63. Home: 1215 Skyline Dr North Little Rock AR 72116 Office: Master in Chancery Pulaski County Ct House Little Rock AR 72201 Tel (501) 374-7360

HOWARD, EDWARD O'NEAL, b. Boston, Nov. 17, 1935; B.S., Boston U., 1960; M.A., N.Y. U., 1961, LL.B. cum laude, 1964. Admitted to N.Y. bar, 1964, U.S. Ct. Appeals 2nd Circuit bar, 1965, U.S. Supreme Ct. bar, 1976; mng. partner firm Howard & Hagood, N.Y.C., 1969-71, Covington, Howard, Hagood & Holland, N.Y.C., 1971—. Trustee N.Y.C. Pub. Edn. Assn., 1975—. Mem. Assn. of Bar of City N.Y., N.Y. State Bar Assn. Office: 15 Columbus Circle New York City NY 10023 Tel (212) 265-3340

HOWARD, GILBERT POSTON, b. Dallas, Dec. 29, 1908; A.B., U. Tex., 1930, LL.B., So. Methodist U., 1933. Admitted to Tex. bar, 1933, since practiced in Dallas; mem. firm Bell, Goode & Howard, 1933-38; asso. J.L. Goggans, 1938-39; atty. Lawyers Title Co. of Tex., 1939-40; asso. firm Hamilton, Harrell, Hamilton & Turner, 1940-42; served to capt., def. counsel, asst. staff judge adv. USAAF, 1942-45; regional atty. OPA, 1945-46; mem. firm Turner, Atwood, Howard, McLane & Francis and predecessors, 1946-51, Howard & Jones, 1951-52; individual practice law, 1951-64, 74—; atty. Lone Star Gas Co., 1964-74. Mem. Dallas, Am. bar assns., Southwestern Legal Found. (charter mem.). Home: 5841 Williamstown Rd Dallas TX 75230 Office: Suite 500 North Dallas Bank Tower 12900 Preston Rd at LBJ Dallas TX 75230 Tel (214) 233-7255

HOWARD, HOYT DICKEY, b. Oluster, Okla., Nov. 21, 1916; B.S., Southwestern State U., 1940; J.D., So. Meth. U., 1950. Admitted to Tex. bar, 1950; individual practice law, San Angelo, Tex., 1950-53; atty. City of San Angelo, 1953-58, city mgr., 1958—. Mem. Tom Green, Tex. bar assns., Tex., Nat. city mgmt. assns. Home: 2621 Vista del Arroyo San Angelo TX 71901 Office: Box 1751 City Hall San Angelo TX 76901 Tel (915) 655-9121

HOWARD, JOHN ROBERT, b. Lubbock, Tex., May 27, 1947; B.A., U. Tex., 1969, J.D., 1972. Admitted to Tex. bar, 1972; asso. firm Simons, Cunningham, Coleman, Nelson & Howard, Austin, Tex., now partner. Mem. Tex., Travis County bar assns. Office: 501 W 12th St Austin TX 78701 Tel (512) 478-9332

HOWARD, LAWRENCE, b. Sioux City, Iowa, Apr. 11, 1931; LL.B., U. Ariz., 1957. Admitted to Ariz. bar, 1957; practiced law, Tucson, 1954-64, 64-66; magistrate City of Tucson, 1964; spl. asst. Ariz. Atty. Gen., 1964-66; judge Superior Ct. Ariz., 1967-69, Juvenile Ct. Tucson, 1969, Ariz. State Ct. Appeals, Div. II, 1969—. Pres. Tucson Awareness House, 1972-73, Tucson Metropolitan Youth, 1972-73. Mem. Am. Bar Assn., Am. Judicature Soc., Ariz. State, Pima County (Ariz.) bars, Ariz. Judges Assn. (pres. 1973-74), Western Correction Assn. (sec. 1972-73, chief judge div. II 1975-76). Author Ariz. Hwy. Dept. publ.; Arizona Law of Eminent Domain, 1966. Office: 45 W Congress St Tucson AZ 85701 Tel (602) 882-5506

HOWARD, LOWELL BENNETT, b. New Boston, Ohio, Feb. 12, 1925; B.A., Bowling Green State U., 1947; LL.B., Ohio State U., 1949, M.A., 1954, J.D., 1967, Ph.D., 1975. Admitted to Ohio bar, 1950, U.S. Supreme Ct. bar, 1968; individual practice law, Wellston, Ohio, 1950-51; sr. partner Howard and Gilliland, Wellston, 1954-56; individual practice law, Athens, Ohio, 1955-71; city solicitor Wellston, 1954-56; asst. prof. law Ohio U., Athens, 1955-59, asso. prof., 1959-65, prof., 1955-73, adj. prof. govt. and criminal justice, 1976—; judge Ct. of Common Pleas, Athens County, Ohio, 1971—. Chmn. Athens Charter Commn., 1969-70; mem., sec. Bd. Zoning Appeals Athens, 1964-66. Mem. Am., Ohio, Athens County bar assns., Am. Econ. Assn., Am. Polit. Sci. Assn., Am. Judicature Soc., Am. Judges Assn., AAUP. Author: Business Law, An Introduction, 1965; co-author: College Business Law, 1960; contbr. articles to legal jours.; recipient awards for jud. service. Home: 68 Briarwood Dr Athens OH 45701 Office: Ct House Athens OH 45701 Tel (614) 592-2077

HOWARD, MALCOLM JONES, b. Kinston, N.C., June 24, 1939; B.S., U.S. Mil. Acad., 1962; J.D., Wake Forest U., 1970. Admitted to N.C. bar, 1970, U.S. Ct. Appeals 4th Circuit bar, 1973; sec. Judge Adv. Gen. Sch., Charlottesville, Va., 1970-71; legis. counsel to sec. Army, Washington, 1971-72; asst. U.S. atty. Eastern Dist. N.C., Raleigh, 1972-73; dep. spl. counsel to Pres. U.S., Washington, 1974; sr. partner firm Howard, Vincent & Duffus, Greenville, N.C., 1974—. Standing trustee in bankruptcy U.S. Dist. Ct. for Eastern N.C., 1976. Mem. N.C., Am. bar assns., Greenville C. of C. (chmn. polit. action com. 1976—). Home: 212 Chowan Rd Greenville NC 27834 Office: 301 Evans St PO Box 859 Greenville NC 27834 Tel (919) 758-1403

HOWARD, WILLIAM BARTON, b. Jonesboro, Ark., Nov. 25, 1920; student Ark. State U., George Washington U., Cleve. Coll., Western Res. U.; LL.B., Cumberland U., 1947, J.D., 1969. Admitted to Ark. bar, 1947; individual practice law, Jonesboro, 1947—; atty. City of Jonesboro, 1948-50; mem. Ark. State Claims Commn., 1953-55. Mem. Am., Ark. trial lawyers assns., Am. Judicature Soc., Craighead County, Ark., Am. bar assns. Home: 509 E Thomas St Jonesboro AR 72401 Office: 807 Jefferson St Jonesboro AR 72401 Tel (501) 932-3599

HOWARTH, DON, b. Providence, Mar. 9, 1946; B.A. magna cum laude, Harvard, 1968, J.D. cum laude, 1972. Admitted to Calif. bar, 1972; law clk. to judge U.S. Ct. Appeals for 9th Circuit, Los Angeles, 1972-73; asso. firm Gibson, Dunn & Crutcher, Los Angeles, 1973—; instr. Constl. Rights Found.; bd. councilors U. So. Calif. Law Sch., 1974—. Mem. bd. editors Nat. Jour. Christian Legal Soc. Office: 515 S Flower St Los Angeles CA 90071 Tel (213) 488-7312

HOWARTH, WALTER ORBIN, b. Allegheny County, Pa., Nov. 29, 1920; B.S. in Mech. Engring., U. Pitts., 1941, LL.B., 1948. Admitted to Pa. bar, 1949, U.S. Dist. ct. bar Western Dist. Pa., 1949; asso. firm Mahlon E. Lewis, Pitts., 1948-51, McCrady & Nicklas, Pitts., 1952-58, Gregg & Price, Pitts., 1958-62; atty. to gen. atty. Aluminum Co. Am., Pitts., 1962—. Mem. Am., Pa., Allegheny County bar assns. Home: 448 Winthrop Dr Pittsburgh PA 15237 Office: Alcoa Bldg Pittsburgh PA 15219 Tel (412) 553-4784

HOWE, BARBARA KERR, b. Balt., Dec. 25, 1938; A.A., Greenbrier Coll., 1956; A.B., Randolph-Macon Woman's Coll., 1959; J.D., U. Md., 1969. Admitted to Md. bar, 1969; asso. firm Kerr, Kerr and Howe, and predecessor, Towson, Md., 1969-74, partner, 1975—; asst. zoning hearing examiner Harford County (Md.), Bel Air, 1975—. Pres. Kingsville (Md.) Coordinating Council, 1973. Mem. Am., Md. State, Baltimore County bar assns., AAUW, Assn. Trial Lawyers Am., U. Md. Law Sch. Alumni Assn. (exec. council 1974—). Home: 11714 Silver Spruce Terr Kingsville MD 21087 Office: 210 W Pennsylvania Ave Towson MD 21203 Tel (301) 823-3414

HOWE, JONATHAN THOMAS, b. Evanston, Ill., Dec. 16, 1940; B.A. with honors, Northwestern U., 1963; J.D. with distinction, Duke, 1966. Admitted to Ill. bar, 1966, U.S. Supreme Ct. bar, 1970, D.C. bar, 1975; partner firm Jenner & Block, Chgo., 1966—; lectr. in field; mem. lawyers council Am. Soc. Assn. Execs., 1964—. Mem. Ill. Dist. 27 Bd. Edn., Northbrook, 1969—, sec., 1969-72, pres., 1973—; mem. Ill. Commn. on Children, 1972-74; pres. Ill. Assn. Sch. Bds., 1977—; deacon Village Presbyn. Ch. of Northbrook, 1975—. Mem. Am. (chmn. membership com. sect. young lawyers of Ill. 1967—, mem. council for ednl. programs 1974-75), Ill. State (co-editor Antitrust Newsletter 1968-70), Chgo. (chmn. judiciary and bench bar relations com. 1971-72, mem. exec. com. sect. young lawyers 1971-72), D.C. bar assns., Duke U. (decade program mem. 1975-77), Northwestern U. (alumni fraternity bd. 1973—) alumni assns., Phi Alpha Delta (Outstanding Scholastic Achievement award 1966). Author: (with Thomas P. Sullivan) Injunctions, Civil Practice Before Trial, 2d edit., 1973; (with Philip W. Tone) Briefs, Illinois Appellate Practice, 2d edit., 1976; Real Estate Sales People in the United States—Independent Contractor or Employee, 1977; contbr. articles to profl. pubs.; contbg. editor Ill. Inst. Continuing Legal Edn., 1973—. Home: 3845 Normandy Ln Northbrook IL 60062 Office: Jenner & Block One IBM Plaza Chicago IL 60611 Tel (312) 222-9350

HOWE, LAWRENCE, b. Evanston, Ill., Nov. 16, 1921; A.B., Harvard U., 1942; J.D., U. Chgo., 1948. Admitted to Ill. bar, 1948; asso. firm Pope & Ballard, Chgo., 1948-52; asso. firm Vedder, Price, Kaufman & Kammholz, Chgo., 1952-54, partner 1954-66, 74-75; v.p. Bell & Howell Co., Chgo., 1966-74; exec. v.p., gen. counsel Jewel Cos., Inc., Chgo., 1975—. Pres. village Winnetka, Ill., 1964-68. Mem. Am., Chgo. bar assns. Home: 175 Chestnut St Winnetka IL 60093 Office: 10th Floor 5725 E River Rd Chicago IL 60631 Tel (312) 693-6000

HOWE, RICHARD RAY, b. Decatur, Ill., Aug. 23, 1932; A.B., U. Mo., 1954, J.D., 1959. Admitted to Mo. bar, 1959; individual practice law Canton, Mo., 1959—; pros. atty. Lewis County, Mo., 1968-72. Mem. Canton Bd. Edn., 1962-68; commr., chmn. Commn. to Reapportion Mo. Legislature, 1971; mem. Mo. Commn. on Human Rights, 1974-76; bd. trustees Canton Pub. Library, 1961-70. Mem. Am. Bar Assn., Mo. Bar Integrated, Assn. Trial Lawyers Am. Home: Route 2 Canton MO 63435 Office: 436 Lewis St Canton MO 63435 Tel (314) 288-3212

HOWE, SHIRLEY MAE DAVIS, b. Beloit, Wis., Sept. 11, 1935; J.D., Loyola U., Chgo., 1964. Admitted to Ill. bar, 1964, Calif. bar, 1976; asso. firm Riordan and Malone, Chgo., 1965-70; individual practice law, Chgo., 1970—; prof. Loyola U., 1976—. Mem. State Bar Calif., Ill., Chgo. bar assns. Editor: Mertens Law of Federal Income Taxation, 1965-70. Home: 2434 N Orchard St Chicago IL 60614 Office: 41 E Pearson St Chicago IL 60611 Tel (312) 670-2927

HOWELL, ALAN PETER, b. Honolulu, Aug. 1, 1927; B.A., Yale U., 1950; LL.B., Cornell U., 1953. Admitted to Hawaii bar, 1954; law clk. to chief justice Ter. of Hawaii Supreme Ct., 1953-54; asst. pub. prosecutor City and County of Honolulu, 1954-58; partner firm Hogan, Howell, Rother & Grimes, and predecessor, Honolulu, 1958-71, firm Howell & Gerson, Honolulu, 1973-74; individual practice law, Honolulu, 1971-73, 74—; 6th dist. magistrate for Dist. Honolulu, 1963-67; sec., gen. counsel Schuman Carriage Co., Ltd., 1976—. Chmn. exec. bd. 1st Ch. of Christ Scientist, Honolulu, 1966-68, 70-72; pres. chpt. 184 Exptl. Aircraft Assn. Mem. Am., Hawaii (chmn. law day com. 1964) bar assns., Am. Judicature Soc., Aircraft Owners and Pilots Assn., Am. Arbitration Assn. (nat. panel arbitrators 1963—). Home: 76 Kailuana Pl Kailua HI 96734 Office: Suite 301 735 Bishop St Honolulu HI 96813 Tel (808) 524-2225

HOWELL, ARTHUR, b. Atlanta, Aug. 24, 1918; A.B., Princeton, 1939; LL.B., Harvard, 1942, J.D., 1969; LL.D., Oglethorpe U., 1973. Admitted to Ga. bar, 1943; asso. firm F.M. Bird, Atlanta, 1942-45; partner firm Jones, Bird & Howell and predecessor, Atlanta, 1945—, sr. partner, 1957—; asst. atty. gen. bd. regents Univ. System of Ga., 1948-55; spl. counsel Ga. Edn. Authority, 1951-67, Ga. Ports Authority, 1952-65, Ga. Prison and Rehab. Authority, 1953-67. Pres. Atlanta United Fund, 1956, Atlanta Community Council, 1962; chmn. Atlanta Adv. Com. on Parks, 1958-73. Fellow Am. Coll. Probate Counsel; mem. Am., Ga., Atlanta bar assns., Am. Law Inst., Lawyers Club Atlanta (pres. 1955-56), Atlanta Legal Aid Soc. (pres. 1953), Am. Judicature Soc. (spl. com. on Ga. corp. code 1967—), Phi Beta Kappa. Named Hon. Alumnus Ga. Inst. Tech., 1967. Home: 3290 Ridgewood Rd NW Atlanta GA 30327 Office: Haas-Howell Bldg Atlanta GA 30303 Tel (404) 522-2508

HOWELL, BAXTER CANNON, JR., b. Milford, Conn., Sept. 3, 1946; A.B. in Bus. Adminstrn., U. Ga., 1967, J.D., 1970. Admitted to Ala. bar, 1970, Ga. bar, 1971; asso. firm Beauchamp & Howell, Albany, Ga., 1972-76; partner firm Zeese & Howell, Albany, 1976—; served to 1st lt. JAGC, U.S. Army, 1971-72. Mem. N.G. Assn. Ga. and U.S.A., Ga., Atlanta bar assns., Ga. Trial Lawyers Assn. Home: 1723 Lowell Ln Albany GA 31707 Office: 420 Pine Ave Albany GA 31701 Tel (912) 883-2218 or 883-2219

HOWELL, FLAVIUS JOSEPHUS, JR., b. Little Rock, June 22, 1929; B.S., U. Ark., 1957, LL.B., 1957, S.J.D., 1969. Admitted to Ark. bar, 1957; asso. firm Howell, Price & Worsham, Little Rock, 1957; dep. pros. atty. Pulaski County (Ark.), 1957-58; partner firm Howell, Price, Howell & Barron, Little Rock, 1958—. Mem. Am., Ark., Pulaski County bar assns. Office: 211 Spring Little Rock AR 72201 Tel (501) 372-4144

HOWELL, JOHN STEPHEN, b. San Francisco, Sept. 4, 1917; A.B., Stanford, U. 1938, LL.B., 1941. Admitted to Calif. bar, 1941; asst. dist. atty. City and County of San Francisco, 1945-48; asso. firm Sedgwick, Detert, Moran & Arnold, San Francisco, 1949-57, partner, 1957—; prof. law San Francisco Law Sch., 1947-49; pres. Jr. Bar Calif., 1953. Fellow Am. Coll. Trial Lawyers; mem. Am., Calif., San Francisco bar assns. Home: 2842 Filbert St San Francisco CA 94123 Office: suite 1100 111 Pine St San Francisco CA 94123 Tel (415) 982-0303

HOWELL, LOUIS P., b. Orangeburg, S.C., Sept. 12, 1932; B.S., U. S.C., 1954, LL.B., 1958. Admitted to S.C. bar, 1958; now mem. firm Ward, Howell, Barnes, Long, Hudgens & Adams, Spartanburg, S.C. Mem. Am., Spartanburg County bar assns., S.C. Bar (pres. 1976-77), Def. Research Inst., Inc., Phi Delta Phi. Office: 200 Library St Office Bldg PO Box 5663 Spartanburg SC 29304 Tel (803) 582-5683*

HOWELL, RONALD WOOD, b. Newdale, N.C., June 28, 1946; A.B. in Polit. Sci., U. N.C., J.D. with honors, 1966. Admitted to N.C. bar; with JAGC, USAF, 1966-70; practiced in N.C., 1970-76; resident judge N.C. Superior Ct., 24th Jud. Dist., 1976—. Tel (704) 649-3651

HOWER, WARD EDWARD, b. Cowley, Wyo., June 18, 1921; A.B., Stanford, 1947, J.D., 1949. Admitted to Iowa bar, 1949, Tex. bar, 1954, Idaho bar, 1958; individual practice law, Sioux City, Iowa, 1949-52; title analyst Shell Oil Co., Midland, Tex., 1952-55; tchr., Seattle, 1955-56; lectr. Boise (Idaho) Jr. Coll., 1956-57; legis. asst. to Senator Frank Church, Washington, 1957-61, adminstrv. asst., 1961-64; dep. dir. Peace Corps., Brazil, 1964-66, dir., Guyana, 1966-68; dep. dir. office of evaluation, Washington, 1968-70; pros. atty. Valley County (Idaho), 1971-73, pub. defender, 1973—. Mem. Idaho State Bar. Home and office: Box 799 Cascade ID 83611 Tel (208) 382-4546

HOWERTON, JAMES WILLIAM, b. Paducah, Ky., Oct. 22, 1931; B.S. in Commerce, U. Ky., 1953, J.D., 1961. Admitted to Ky. bar, 1961; pros. atty. City of Paducah, 1961-66, corp. counsel, 1967-72, city mgr., asso. counsel, 1972-76; judge Ky. Ct. Appeals Dist. I, Paducah, 1976—; gen. counsel Paducah Bank & Trust Co., 1970-76. Pres. Greater Paducah Indsl. Devel. Assn., 1973; lifetime trustee Paducah Jr. Coll., 1975—. Mem. Am., Ky., McCracken County (Ky.) (v.p. 1972-73) bar assns., Greater Paducah C. of C. (v.p. 1974). Home: 3954 Primrose Pl Paducah KY 42001 Office: 1532 Lone Oak Rd PO Box 194 Paducah KY 42001 Tel (502) 443-8227

HOWLAND, WILLIAM LARSEN, b. Hastings, Nebr., Mar. 2, 1942; B.A., Hastings Coll., 1964; J.D., U. Nebr., 1967. Admitted to Nebr. bar, 1967; practiced in Lincoln, Nebr., 1967; asst. city atty. City of Grand Island (Nebr.), 1969-70; dep. county atty. Hall County (Nebr.), 1971-72, Scotts Bluff County (Nebr.), 1972; partner firm Bump & Howland, Chadron, Nebr., 1973—. Mem. Am., Nebr. bar assns., Nebr. Trial Attys., Nat. Dist. Attys. Assn. Office: PO Box 1140 Chadron NE 69337 Tel (308) 432-4411

HOWLEY, LEE CHRISTOPHER, b. Cleve., June 16, 1910; B.A., Wittenberg U., 1932; LL.B., Case Western Res. U., 1935. Admitted to Ohio bar, 1935; asso. Ray T. Miller, Cleve., 1935-39; asst. U.S. dist. atty. for Ohio, 1939-45; law dir. City of Cleve., 1945-51; asst. gen. counsel Cleve. Electric Illuminating Co., 1951, gen. counsel, v.p.,

1952-75; partner firm Weston Hurd Fallon Paisley & Howley, Cleve., 1975—. Pres., Govtl. Research Inst., Cleve. Conv. Bur.; past pres. Cath. Charities Corp.; trustee St. Vincent Charity Hosp., chmn. bd. trustees Kaiser Community Health Fund; pres. Govtl. Research Inst. Office: 2500 Terminal Tower Cleveland OH 44113 Tel (216) 241-6602

HOWREY, EDWARD FREELAND, b. Waterloo, Iowa, Sept. 6, 1903; A.B., U. Iowa, 1925; J.D. with honors, George Washington U., 1927. Admitted to Iowa bar, 1927, D.C. bar, 1927, Va. bar, 1938; with U.S. Dept. Justice, Washington, 1927-29; asso. firm Sanders, Childs, Bobb & Mescott, Washington, 1929-37; partner firm Sanders, Gravelle, Whitlock & Howrey and predecessors, Washington, 1937-53; chmn. FTC, Washington, 1953-55; partner firm Howrey & Simon, Washington, 1955—. Fellow Am. Coll. Trial Lawyers, Am. Bar Found.; mem. Am. Soc. Internat. Law, Internat. Bar Assn., Am. Judicature Soc., Acad. Polit. Sci., English Speaking Union, Am. Bar Assn., Phi Kappa Psi, Phi Delta Phi, Order Coif. Contbr. articles to legal jours. Home: St Brides Farm Upperville VA 22176 Office: 1730 Pennsylvania Ave NW Washington DC 20006 Tel (202) 872-8800

HOY, MARION ALSWORTH, b. Farmington, Mo., Nov. 15, 1906; A.B., U. Mo., 1930; J.D., John Marshall Law Sch., 1939, LL.M., 1941. Admitted to Ill. bar, 1941; researcher Am. Can Co., Maywood, Ill., 1930-48; mem. firm Duday & Hoy, Oak Park, Ill., 1949-70, Hoy, Oddo & Kucia, Oak Park, 1970—; instr. food and drug law Lawyers' Inst. of John Marshall Law Sch., Chgo., 1958-76; guest lectr. on food and drug law Purdue U., 1958, 61, Rutgers U., 1958, 61, U. Wis., Madison, 1961, U. Mo., Columbia, 1968; dir., sec. Ave.-Lake Plaza Assn., Champagne Music Corp., Cunningham-Reilly, Inc., N.Am. Machinery Co. Pres. W. Suburban Homemakers Assn., 1974; bd. dirs. Child and Family Services, Chgo.; elder First Presbyterian Ch. of River Forest; violinist Macdowell Artists Assn., Civic Symphony of Oak Park and River Forest. Mem. Am., Ill., Chgo., Du Page County bar assns., Bar Assn. of 7th Fed. Circuit, Am. Chem Soc., Am. Judicature Soc., Inst. Food Technologists, Delta Theta Phi, Alpha Kappa Delta, Acacia. Recipient Distinguished Service award John Marshall Law Sch. Alumni Assn., 1972. Contbr. articles to profl. jours. Home: 243 Ashland Ave River Forest IL 60305 Office: 104 N Oak Park Ave IL 60301 Tel (312) 383-3000

HOYLE, WILLIAM SIDNEY, b. Durham, N.C., May 17, 1940; A.B., N.C. Wesleyan Coll., 1965; J.D., U. N.C., 1968. Admitted to N.C. bar, 1968; asso. firm Dill, Exum, Fountain & Hoyle, and predecessors, Rocky Mount, N.C., 1968-71, partner, 1971—; vol. counsel Nash and Edgecombe County (N.C.) Legal Aid Services, 1972-73; legal counsel Rocky Mount Zoning Bd. Adjustment, 1975—. Mem. adminstrv. bd. 1st United Meth. Ch., 1971-72, 74-75; mem. Rocky Mount Housing Bd. Appeals, 1972-75. Mem. Am., N.C. Nash-Edgecombe County bar assns., Rocky Mount C. of C. (life mem., v.p. 1974), Phi Alpha Theta, Delta Theta Phi. Named Holderness Moot Ct. Competition winner U. N.C. Sch. Law, 1965; recipient Personal Property Book award Lawyers Co-op Pub. Co., 1965. Office: 330 Sunset Ave Rocky Mount NC 27801 Tel (919) 446-0041

HOYT, MERLYN H., b. Ely, Nev., June 13, 1933; B.S. in Bus. Adminstrn., U. Nev., 1957; J.D., Am. U., 1963. Admitted to D.C. bar, Nev. bar, 1963; gen. atty. Solicitor's Office Dept. of Interior, Washington, 1963-65; asst. U.S. atty. Nev., Reno, 1965-67; dist. atty. White Pine County (Nev.), 1967-74; judge 7th Jud. Dist. State of Nev., Ely, 1974—. Mem. Am., Nev. bar assns. Home: 479 Cedar St Ely NV 89301 Office: Court House Compton St Ely NV 89301 Tel (702) 289-4813

HOYT, WADE COTHRAN, III, b. Rome, Ga., July 20, 1946; A.B., U. Ga., 1968, J.D., 1971. Admitted to Ga. bar, 1971; partner firm Rogers, Magruder & Hoyt, Rome, 1971-77, Patton & Hoyt, Rome, 1977—; mem. Ga. Bar Exam Rev. Com., 1974—; chmn. Floyd County Legal Ethics Rev. Bd., 1974—. Bd. dirs. Rome Salvation Army, 1975—, Rome Better Bus. Bur., 1975—. Mem. Am., Ga. bar assns., Criminal Def. Lawyers Assn. Ga. Home: 207 Saddle Mountain Rd Rome GA 30161 Office: 408 E 1st St Rome GA 30161 Tel (404) 291-9620

HRDLICKA, ALBERT FRANK, b. Saugerties, N.Y., Jan. 7, 1944; B.E.E., Union Coll., Albany, N.Y., 1967, J.D., 1970. Admitted to N.Y. bar, 1971; clk. firm Carnright & Schirmer, Saugerties, 1970-71; partner firm Carnright Schirmer & Hrdlicka, Saugerties, 1971-73, Schirmer & Hrdlicka, Saugerties, 1973—; asst. dist. atty. Ulster County (N.Y.), 1971—. Mem. N.Y., Ulster County bar assns. Home: 4480 Rt 32 Saugerties NY 12477 Office: 3 Lafayette St Saugerties NY 12477 Tel (914) 246-9697

HRONES, STEPHEN BAYLIS, b. Boston, Jan. 20, 1942; B.A., Harvard U., 1964; postgrad. (Fulbright fellow), Sorbonne U., 1964-65; J.D., U. Mich., 1968. Admitted to Iowa bar, 1969, Mass. bar, 1972; individual practice law, Heidelberg, W. Ger., 1970-72, Boston, 1973—; clin. asso. Suffolk Law Sch., 1976—. Mem. Boston, Mass. bar assns., Mass. Assn. Criminal Defense Lawyers. Fulbright fellow, France, 1968-69. Home: 14 Peck Ave Arlington MA 02174 Office: 27 State St Boston MA 02109 Tel (617) 742-5261

HRUSOFF, RONALD REX, b. Oakland, Calif., Jan. 20, 1935; B.A., U. Calif., 1957; LL.B., Georgetown U., 1963, LL.M., 1965. Admitted to Va. bar, 1963, D.C. bar, 1965, Calif. bar, 1966, U.S. Supreme Ct. bar, 1971; asso. firm Hewitt, Klitgaard & McMahon, San Diego, 1966-67, firm Hillyer & Irvin, San Diego, 1967-69; partner firm Augustine, Delafield & Hrusoff, San Diego, 1969-75, firm Gramm & Hrusoff, San Diego, 1975—; adj. instr. legal asst. program U. San Diego. Mem. Am. Bar Assn. Contbr. articles to legal jours. Home: 2913 Arnoldson Ave San Diego CA 92112 Office: Suite 202 1501 6th Ave San Diego CA 92101 Tel (714) 236-1937

HUBBARD, CARROLL, b. Murray, Ky., July 7, 1937; B.S., Georgetown Coll., 1959; J.D., U. Ky., 1962. Admitted to Ky. bar, 1962; partner firm Hubbard, Null & West, Mayfield, Ky., 1962-74; mem. U.S. Ho. of Reps., 1975—. Mem. Democratic Study Group, 94th Dem. Caucus. Mem. Am., Ky. bar assns. Names Outstanding Young Man of Mayfield-Graves County, Mayfield Jaycees, 1966, 67, 68; Outstanding Young Dem. Legislator, Ky. Young Dems', 1972. Home: 410 Macedonia Rd PO Box 462 Mayfield KY 42066 Office: 204 Cannon House Office Bldg Washington DC 20515 Tel (202) 225-3115

HUBBARD, PERRY, b. Tarrant City, Ala., Mar. 17, 1921; B.S. in Commerce and Bus. Adminstrn., U. Ala., 1943, LL.B., 1945. Admitted to Ala. bar, 1945; asso. firm Spain, Gillon, Grooms & Young, Birmingham, 1945-48; individual practice law, Tuscaloosa, 1949-53; asso. firm LeMaistre, Clement & Gewin, Tuscaloosa, 1953-61; partner firm Hubbard and Waldrop, Tuscaloosa, 1961—; adj. prof. law U. Ala., 1948—; council Ala. Law Inst.; mem. advisory coms. on appellate rules to Supreme Ct. Ala. and U.S. Ct. Appeals 5th Circuit. Bd. dirs. Met. YMCA, pres. 1971-73; mem. selective service local bd. Mem. Tuscaloosa County, Ala., Am. Bar Assns., Am. Coll. Trial Lawyers, Am. Judicature Soc. Office: Post Office Box 2427 Tuscaloosa AL 35401 Tel (205) 752-3506

HUBER, GERALD PATRICK, b. Hillsboro, Ill., Aug. 28, 1943; B.S. in Psychology, St. Louis U., 1966; J.D., U. San Francisco, 1972. Admitted to Ill. bar, 1973, Calif. bar, 1973; asso. firm George E. Ginos, Hillsboro, 1974-75; individual practice law, Raymond, Ill., 1975—. Hillsboro chmn. Montgomery County (Ill.) Right-to-Life Orgn.; precinct committeeman Republican Party, Hillsboro. Mem. Am., Ill., Montgomery County (pres.) bar assns. Home: 317 E Summer St Hillsboro IL 62049 Office: 318 E Broad St Raymond IL 62560 Tel (217) 229-4425

HUBER, WILLIAM EVAN, II, b. Celina, Ohio, Mar. 10, 1943; B.S. in Edn., Ohio No. U., 1965, J.D., 1968. Admitted to Ohio bar, 1968, U.S. Dist. Ct. bar, 1972, U.S. Supreme Ct. bar, 1972; partner firm Kemp & Huber, St. Marys, Ohio, 1969—; asst. pros. atty. Auglaize County, 1969-76. Chmn. St. Marys Recreation Adv. Bd., 1976—; pres. Little League Baseball, 1971—, St. Marys Jaycees, 1969-70; state v.p. Ohio Jaycees, 1971-72; chmn. United Fund Drive, 1970; trustee Community Improvement Corp., 1969—; chmn. St. Marys Medic-Search, Inc., 1977. Mem. Auglaize County Bar Assn. (pres. 1975), Comml. Law League, C. of C. (v.p. 1977). Named St. Marys outstanding Jaycee, 1971. Office: Box 302 Home Bank Bldg Saint Marys OH 45885 Tel (419) 394-3341

HUCK, RALPH FRANCIS, b. Quincy, Ill., Mar. 8, 1903; student U. Ill., 1921-23; LL.B., U. Mich., 1926. Admitted to Ill. bar, 1926; asso. firm Chapman & Cutler, Chgo., 1926—, partner, 1943—; dir. Harris Trust & Savs. Bank, 1960-73. Trustee, Quincy (Ill.) Coll. Mem. Am. (chmn. com. on banking sect. of corp., banking and bus. law 1965-67), Ill., Chgo. bar assns., Am. Judicature Soc. Contbr. articles to profl. jours. Home: 1630 Sheridan Rd Wilmette IL 60091 Office: 111 W Monroe St Chicago IL 60603 Tel (312) 726-6130

HUCKABY, GARY CARLTON, b. Lanett, Ala., July 12, 1938; B.A., U. Ala., 1960, J.D., 1962. Admitted to Ala. bar, 1962; law clk. to Chief Justice Ala. Supreme Ct., 1962; asst. to U.S. Senator Lister Hill, Washington, 1963; served to capt. JAGC, USAF, 1963-66; partner firm Smith, Huckaby & Graves, Huntsville, Ala., 1966—. Dir. Tenn. Valley council Boy Scouts Am., 1975—, Huntsville-Madison County Mental Health Bd., 1974—, Madison County Assn. Mental Health, 1970—. Mem. Am. Bar Assn. (chmn. spl. com. delivery legal services), Ala. Trial Lawyers Assn., Farrah Law Soc. (chmn.). Home: 1200 Kennamer Dr SE Huntsville AL 35801 Office: Central Bank Bldg Huntsville AL 35801 Tel (205) 533-5040

HUCKABY, HILRY, III, b. Shreveport, La., June 27, 1944; B.A., So. U., 1966, J.D., 1969. Admitted to La. bar, 1972; staff Equal Employment Opportunity Commn., New Orleans, 1969-72; asso. firm Huckaby, Piper and Brown, Shreveport, 1972—, sr. partner, 1976—; village atty., South Mansfield, La., 1975—. Chmn. bd. Blacks United for Lasting Leadership. Mem. Am., Nat., Shreveport bar assns., ACLU, NAACP. Home: 2114 Utah Dr Shreveport LA 71101 Office: 2600 Jewella Ave Shreveport LA 71109 Tel (318) 636-2950

HUDDLESTON, JOSEPH RUSSELL, b. Glasgow, Ky., Feb. 5, 1937; A.B., Princeton, 1959; J.D., U. Va., 1962. Admitted to Ky. bar, 1962, U.S. Supreme Ct. bar, 1970; partner firm Huddleston Bros., Bowling Green, Ky., 1962—; 1st asst. Commonwealth's atty. 8th Jud. Dist. Ky., Bowling Green, 1970; mem. exec. com. Ky. Crime Commn., 1972—, mem. adv. com. for criminal law revision, 1969-71. Mem. Am., Ky. (ho. of dels. 1970—), Bowling Green (past pres.) bar assns., Am., Ky. (dir., v.p., sec.) trial lawyers assns., Phi Alpha Delta. Home: 2626 Smallhouse Rd Bowling Green KY 42101 Office: 1032 College St POB 2130 Bowling Green KY 42101 Tel (502) 842-1659

HUDGINS, ERNEST NEWTON, b. Norfolk, Va., Jan. 22, 1902; LL.B., Cath. U. Am., 1936, LL.M., M.P.L., 1937; A.B., Nat. U., 1938; S.J.D., George Washington U., 1939. Admitted to Va. bar, 1935, D.C. bar, 1936; individual practice law, Fairfax, Va., 1935-61, Mathews, Va., 1961—; substitute judge Trial Justice Ct. and Juvenile-Domestic Relations Ct., Fairfax County, Va., 1948-58; spl. justice Fairfax County Ct., 1948-58, 9th Jud. Circuit Ct. Va., 1967—; commr. in chancery Circuit Ct., Fairfax, 1948-61, Mathews, 1961—. Mem. George Washington U. Law Assn., Middle Peninsula Bar Assn., Sigma Delta Kappa. Office: Box 516 Mathews Courthouse Mathews VA 23109 Tel (804) 725-2801

HUDSON, HERMAN EMERSON, b. Rusk, Tex., Jan. 6, 1926; B.A. in History and Govt., U. Tex., 1949, J.D., 1950. Admitted to Tex. bar, 1949; asso. firm Burford, Ryburn, Hincks & Ford, Dallas, 1951-52; individual practice law, Dallas and Odessa, Tex., 1952-55; asst. dist. atty. Dallas, 1955-57; individual practice law, Dallas, 1957-58; atty. Vets. Land Bd., Austin, Tex., 1958, Domestic Relations Office, Austin, 1959, Tex. State Dept. Hwys. and Pub. Transp., Austin, 1962-76. Mem. Tex. Bar Assn. Home: 7002 Rufus Dr Austin TX 78752 Office: 307 E 14th St Austin TX 78761 Tel (512) 453-3656

HUDSON, JACK HARLAN, b. Tarentum, Pa., Dec. 25, 1929; B.S. in Pharmacy, U. Pitts., 1952; J.D., Cleve. State Marshall Coll. Law, 1961. Admitted to Ohio bar, 1968; asst. county prosecutor Cuyahoga County, Ohio; instr. Def. Edn. Act Seminars, 1973; instr. pharmacology Cuyahoga Community Coll., Cleve., 1973. Chmn. Bd. Zoning Appeals, Lakewood, Ohio, 1965-70. Mem. Am., Ohio, Cuyahoga County bar assns., Ohio State Pharm. Assn., Cleve. Acad. Pharmacy. Contbr. article to Law Rev. Cleve. Marshall Law Sch. Home: 13511 Detroit Ave Lakewood OH 44107 Tel (216) 623-7748

HUDSPETH, STEPHEN MASON, b. Pitts., Jan. 22, 1947; B.A., Yale, 1968, M.A., 1968, J.D., 1971. Admitted to N.Y., Pa., Mass. bars; asso. firm Lord, Day & Lord, N.Y.C., 1971—; adj. prof. Wagner Coll., 1973—. Mem. Am., N.Y. bar assns., Assn. Bar City N.Y., Phi Beta Kappa. Home: 1000 Arden Ave Staten Island NY 10312 Office: 25 Broadway New York City NY 10004 Tel (212) 344-4880

HUENERGARDT, DARREL J., b. Holdrege, Nebr., June 20, 1943; B.S., Union Coll., 1965; J.D., U. Nebr., 1968. Admitted to Nebr. bar, 1968, U.S. Supreme Ct. bar, 1975; dep. county atty. Gage County (Nebr.), 1968-70; partner firm O'Brien & Huenergardt, Kimball, Nebr., 1970—; city atty. City of Kimball, 1974—. Chmn. Kimball County Bicentennial Com., 1974-77; v.p. Kimball Community Concerts, 1976. Mem. Am., Tri-county bar assns., Nat. Inst. Municipal Law Officers, Kimball County Jaycees (pres. 1972). Office: 109 S Walnut St Kimball NE 69145 Tel (308) 235-3617

HUERTA, JOHN EDMUND, b. Portland, Oreg., Apr. 25, 1943; B.A., Calif. State U., 1965; J.D., U. Calif., Berkeley, 1968, postgrad. (Overseas Service fellow) Internat. Legal Center, Lima, Peru, 1970. Admitted to Calif. bar, 1970; asso. atty. Calif. Rural Legal Assistance, Santa Maria, 1970-71; staff atty. Defenders Program of San Diego, Inc., 1972-73; acting prof. law U. Calif. Davis, 1973—; instr. Escuela Libre de Derecho, Mexico City, summer, 1975; instr. cons. Council on Legal Edn. Opportunities Inst., 1970-74. Fellow law and humanities Harvard, 1976-77. Mem. Calif. Bar Assn., La Raza Nat. Lawyers Assn., Order of the Coif. Contbr. articles in field to profl. jours. Home: 217 E 8th St Davis CA 95616 Office: Law Sch Univ Calif Davis CA 95616 Tel (916) 752-2586

HUETTEMAN, WILLIAM FRANCIS, b. Grosse Pointe Farms, Mich., Oct. 27,; J.D., U. Detroit, 1955. Admitted to Mich. bar, 1959, U.S. 6th Circuit Ct. Appeals bar, 1970, U.S. Supreme Ct. bar, 1974; v.p. trust dept. Detroit Bank & Trust Co., 1959-69; individual practice law, Detroit, 1969—. Mem. council Grosse Pointe Woods, Mich., 1966-69, trustee, bd. edn., 1969—, pres. Grosse Pointe War Meml., 1967. Mem. Am., Detroit bar assns., Office: 2612 Buhl Bldg Detroit MI 48226 Tel (313) 963-5343

HUEY, JOHN W., b. Washington, Sept. 14, 1947; B.S., U. Kans., 1969, J.D., 1972. Admitted to Kans. bar, 1972; asso. firm Glenn, Cornish and Leuenberger, Topeka, 1972-76; atty. corp. law dept. Borden, Inc., Columbus, Ohio, 1976—. Bd. dirs. N.E. Kans. chpt. March of Dimes, Topeka, 1976; mem. exec. com. Central Ohio chpt. Nat. Found. March of Dimes, Columbus. Mem. Am., Kans. bar assns. Home: 1033 Autumn Crest Ct Westerville OH 43081 Office: 180 E Broad St Columbus OH 43215 Tel (614) 225-4123

HUFF, BERNARD, b. Columbus, Ga.; J.D., Ind. U., 1964. Admitted to Ind. bar, 1964; dep. atty. gen. State of Ind., Indpls., 1964-66; mng. atty. Legal Services Orgn., Indpls., 1966-69; atty. Allison div. Gen. Motors Corp., Speedway, Ind., 1969-73; dist. counsel Indpls. dist. office Equal Employment Opportunity Council, Indpls., 1973—. Mem. Hoosier, Nat., Ind., Marion County bar assns. Contbr. articles to legal jours. Tel (317) 269-7597

HUFF, JEWETT EUGENE, b. Altus, Okla., Oct. 1, 1932; B.A., U. Okla., 1954; postgrad. Harvard Law Sch., 1954-55; LL.B., U. Tex., 1961. Admitted to Tex. bar, 1961; asso. firm Simpson, Adkins, Fullingim & Hankins, Amarillo, Tex., 1961-69; mem. firm Gibson, Ochsner, Adkins, Harlan & Hankins, Amarillo, 1969—. Bd. dirs. Better Bus. Bur. Amarillo, 1971—. Mem. State Bar Tex., Amarillo Bar Assn. (pres. 1974-75), Tex. Assn. Bank Counsel (pres. 1976-76), Phi Beta Kappa, Order of Coif. Editorial bd. Tex. Law Rev. Home: 2810 Teckla St Amarillo TX 79106 Office: 500 1st Nat Bank Bldg 8th and Taylor Sts Amarillo TX 79101 Tel (806) 372-4271

HUFF, JOSEPH BASCOM, b. Mars Hill, N.C., Apr. 8, 1919; student Mars Hill Coll., 1938; LL.B., Wake Forest U., 1942. Admitted to N.C. bar, 1942, U.S. Dist. Ct. for western dist. N.C., 1948, U.S. Dist. Ct. for middle dist. Ky., 1956, U.S. 4th Circuit Ct. Appeals bar, 1976; individual practice law, Asheville, N.C., 1946-53; asso. firm Harkins, Van Winkle, Walton & Buck, Asheville, 1953-55; partner firm Mashburn & Huff, Marshall, N.C., 1955-72, individual practice law, 1972—; atty. Town of Mars Hill, 1956. Mem. Am., N.C. (mem. bar candidate com., 1968—; com. on cts. and jud. procedure, 1973-78; bd. govs. 1976-78), Madison County (pres.) bar assns., 24th Dist. (pres. 1969) bar assns., N.C. State Bar, Am. Trial Lawyers Assn. Home: POB 366 Mars Hill NC 28754 Office: POB 8 Marshall NC 28753 Tel (704) 649-2851

HUFF, MARTIN VANBUREN, b. Brady, Mont., Aug. 19, 1917; B.S. in Bus., U. Idaho, 1940, LL.B., 1946, J.D., 1969. Admitted to Idaho bar, 1947; individual practice law, Moscow, Idaho, 1947-63; Mountain Home, Idaho, 1971; Lewiston, 1972-73; mem. legal div. Idaho State Highway Dept., 1963; dept. pros. atty., Ada County, Idaho, 1963-64; pros. atty., 1964-66; clk. Idaho Supreme Ct., 1966-70; counsel Idaho State Tax Commn., 1970-71; dir. Lewis-Clark Legal Services, Lewiston, Idaho, 1971-72; magistrate 2d Jud. Dist. Nez Perce County, Idaho, 1973—. Mem. Idaho State Bar Assn. Home: 420 21st Ave Lewiston ID 83501 Office: Courthouse Lewiston ID 83501 Tel (208) 746-1331

HUFF, WILLIAM STERLING, b. Texarkana, Ark., Oct. 24, 1934; B.S., U. Ark., 1957, J.D., 1957; Rhodes Scholar, Oxford U. (Eng.), 1957; LL.M., Harvard U., 1962. Admitted to Ark. bar, 1957, Colo. bar, 1962; since practiced in Denver; asso. firm Davis, Graham & Stubbs, 1962-65; prof. law U. Denver, 1965—; vis. prof. Cornell U., 1973; cons. Am. Nat. Bank, Denver, 1969-73; spl. counsel firm Holme Roberts & Owen, 1973-76, partner, 1976—; lectr. various colls. and insts. Bd. dirs. Denver Met. Legal Aid Soc., 1968-73. Fellow Am. Coll. Probate Counsel; mem. Am., Denver, Colo. bar assns., Denver Estate Planning Council. Contbr. articles in field to law jours.; recipient Outstanding Prof. award U. Denver, 1973. Home: 3055 Ohm Way Denver CO 80209 Office: 200 W 4th St Denver CO 80204 also 1700 Broadway Denver CO 80290 Tel (303) 573-8000

HUFFAKER, JOHN BOSTON, b. Nashville, Nov. 1, 1925; B.S., Yale, 1946; LL.B., U. Va., 1948. Admitted to Va. bar, 1948, D.C. bar, 1949, Pa. bar, 1967; asso. firm Cummings, Stanley, Truitt & Cross, Washington, 1949-51; staff atty. Joint Com. Internal Revenue Taxation U.S. Ho. of Reps., Washington, 1953-56; asso. firm Duane, Morris & Heckscher, Phila., 1956-61; mem. firm Rawle & Henderson, Phila. and Washington, 1961-66, Pepper Hamilton & Scheetz, Phila. and Washington, 1966—. Trustee Baldwin Sch., Bryn Mawr, Pa., 1972—, Welcome House, Inc., Doylestown, Pa., 1974—; bd. govs. Pa. Economy League, 1974—. Mem. Am. (chmn. subcom. tax sect.), Fed., Pa., Phila. bar assns. Co-author: Tax Problems of Fiduciaries; contbr. articles to legal jours. Home: 229 Pennswood Rd Bryn Mawr PA 19010 Office: 1776 F St NW Suite 200 Washington DC 20006 also 2001 Fidelity Bldg Philadelphia PA 19010

HUFFER, JOHN CARNES, b. Toledo, Ohio, Jan. 30, 1932; B.A., Miami U., Ohio, 1953; LL.B. cum laude, U. Toledo, 1957. Admitted to Ohio bar, 1958, Okla. bar, 1974; partner firm Millward & Huffer, Toledo, 1958-72; asst. dir. law City of Toledo; counsel Toledo Urban Renewal Agy., 1966-72; Fulbright prof. law, Kabul, Afghanistan, 1972-74; asst. prof. law Oklahoma City U., dir. Community Legal Services Center, 1974—. Mem. Am., Okla. trial lawyers' assns., Am., Okla. State, Okla. County bar assns., Assn. Am. Law Schs., ACLU. Home: 6321 Brentford Pl Oklahoma City OK 73132 Office: 1539 NW 25th St Oklahoma City OK 73106 Tel (405) 525-5875

HUFFMAN, ELRIDGE CARPER, b. Maggie, Va., Apr. 12, 1920; B.A., The Citadel, 1947; LL.B., U. Miss., 1951, J.D., 1968. Admitted to Miss. bar, 1951, Tenn. bar, 1956, S.C. bar, 1954, Va. bar, 1956; individual practice law, Myrtle Beach, S.C., 1956-63; New Castle Va., 1964—. Pres., S.C. div. Travelers Proctective Assn. Am., 1962-63.

Mem. Va. Bar Assn. Home: 504 Salem Ave New Castle VA 24127 Office: 414 Main St New Castle VA 24127 Tel (703) 864-5323

HUFFMAN, HARRY DALE, b. Rolfe, Iowa, July 7, 1943; B.S., Iowa State U., 1969; J.D., Drake U., 1970. Admitted to Iowa bar, 1970; asso. Fitzgibbons Law Office, Estherville, Iowa, 1970-72; jud. magistrate Pocahontas County (Iowa), 1972-73, county atty., 1973—, chmn. crime commn., 1975—. Chmn. Republican party Pocahontas County, 1976—. Mem. Iowa Bar Assn. Home: Rural Route Pocahontas IA 50574 Office: 15 3d Ave NW Pocahontas IA 50574 Tel (712) 335-3265

HUFFMAN, RANDALL AVERY, b. Corpus Christi, Tex., Jan. 5, 1946; A.B. with highest honors, U. Okla., 1967, M.A., 1968; J.D., Yale, 1971. Admitted to Conn. bar, 1971, N.Y. bar, 1973; asso. firm Willkie Farr and Gallagher (Sykes, Galloway and Dikeman), N.Y.C., 1973—. Mem. Am., N.Y. State bar assns., Phi Beta Kappa. Home: 20 Woods End Lane Hartsdale NY 10530 Office: 120 Broadway New York City NY 10005 Tel (212) 248-1000

HUFFMAN, YALE BRYANT, b. Lincoln, Nebr., Apr. 6, 1916; student George Washington U., 1932-36; grad. FBI Acad., Quantico, Va., 1939; J.D., U. Denver, 1960. Dir. pub. safety, Colonial Williamsburg, Va., 1940-42; dist. mgr. Am. Tobacco Co., 1946-52, sales mgmt., Denver, 1952-58; mem. Colo. Ho. of Reps., 1958-60; admitted to Colo. bar, 1961; asst. U.S. atty. for Colo. Dept. Justice, 1961-62; chief dep. dist. atty. for Denver, 1973-75; individual practice law, Denver, 1962-72; asso. prof. criminal law Met. State Coll., Denver, 1975—; counsel Sobriety House, Denver, 1968—; cons. U.S. Dept. Justice, Univ. Research Corp., Washington, 1976—. Mem. Denver, Colo. bar assns. Recipient Recognition award Colo. Trial Lawyers' Assn., 1972; author Denver Post series, 1975. Home: 699 E 9th Ave Denver CO 80203 Office: Box 10 Metro State Coll Auraria Denver CO 80204 Tel (303) 832-2220

HUFFSTETLER, LESLIE ROBERT (BOB), JR., b. Umatilla, Fla., Jan. 18, 1935; B.S. in Bus. Adminstrn., Stetson U., 1956; J.D., U. Fla., 1963; postgrad. Rollins Coll. Admitted to Fla. bar; practiced in Eustis, Fla., 1965-71; county judge Lake County (Fla.), 1969-73; judge Fla. Circuit Ct., 5th Jud. Circuit, 1973—; city prosecutor City of Eustis, 1966-69; pros. atty. Lake County, 1967-69; founder Lake County Crisis Intervention Center, 1971. Mem. Lake County Farm Bur., Lake County Conservation Council, Withlacoochee Regional Planning Council, Citrus County, Fla.; deacon 1st Presbyn. Ch., Eustis, 1972-74. Mem. U. Fla. Alumni Assn. (v.p. Lake County chpt. 1970, pres. 1971), U. Fla. Law Center Assn., Fla. Conf. Circuit Ct. Judges, Nat. Council Juvenile Ct. Judges, Internat., Nat. assns. probate judges, Fla., Lake-Sumter, Tri-county bar assns., Pi Kappa Phi, Delta Theta Phi. Recipient Lucky Norris Safety award, 1970. Home: Route 3 PO Box 233 B Crystal River FL 32629 Office: Courthouse Brooksville FL 33512 Tel (904) 796-2114

HUFSTEDLER, SETH MARTIN, b. Dewar, Okla., Sept. 20, 1922; B.A., U. So. Calif., 1944; LL.B., Stanford, 1949. Admitted to Calif. bar, 1950; mem. firm Lillick, Geary & McHose, Los Angeles, 1950-51; asso. Charles E. Beardsley, Los Angeles, 1951-53; partner firm Beardsley, Hufstedler & Kemble, Los Angeles, 1953—. Co-chmn. pub. commn. on county govt., Los Angeles, 1975-76; mem. Calif. Citizens Commn. on Tort Reform, 1976—, Calif. Jud. Council, 1977—; mem. planning council United Way, Los Angeles, 1971—. Fellow Am. Bar Found. (trustee 1975—), Am. Coll. Trial Lawyers; mem. Am. Law Inst., Am. Judicature Soc., State Bar Calif. (bd. gov. 1971-74, pres. 1973-74), Am., Los Angeles County (pres. 1969-70, Shattuck Price Memorial award 1976) bar assns., Order Coif. Legislation editor Stanford Law Rev., Vol. I. Home: 720 Inverness Dr Flintridge CA 91103 Office: 611 W 6th St Los Angeles CA 90017 Tel (213) 626-0671

HUG, PROCTER RALPH, JR., b. Reno, Mar. 11, 1931; B.S., U. Nev., 1953; LL.B., Stanford U., 1958. Admitted to Nev. bar, 1958; mem. firm Woodburn, Wedge, Blakey, Folsom and Hug, Reno, 1963—. Bd. regents U. Nev., 1962-71, chmn., 1969-71; pres. Young Democrats of Washoe County, 1961-62; v.p. Young Dems. of Nev., 1962-63. Mem. Nev. State, Washoe County, Am. (Nev. del. ho. of dels., bd. govs. 1976—) bar assns., Am. Judicature Soc. (dir. 1975—), Am. Law Inst., Nat. Assn. Coll. and Univ. Attys. (dir. 1964-66, 75-76), U. Nev. Alumni Assn. (pres. 1960-61, Outstanding Alumni award 1967). Home: 2125 Pheasant Ln Reno NV 89509 Office: One E First St PO Box 2311 Reno NV 89501 Tel (702) 329-6131

HUGGARD, VICTOR ARTHUR, JR., b. Jamaica, N.Y., Sept. 24, 1936; B.S. in Civil Engring., Valparaiso U., 1962; J.D., Bklyn. Law Sch., 1967. Admitted to N.Y. bar, 1969; jr. civil engr. N.Y.C. Housing Authority, 1962-64, asst. civil engr., 1964-67; bldg. insp., asst. dir. devel. City of Schenectady, 1967-70; partner Cons. for Action, Schenectady, 1969-72; commr. engring. and pub. works County of Schenectady, 1970-72; chief bldg. constrn. contacts adminstr. State of N.Y., 1972—. Bd. dirs. Schenectady Community Action Program, 1969-72; pres. First English Lutheran Ch. Schenectady, 1972. Mem. ASCE, Am. Soc. Pub. Adminstrn., Am., N.Y., Schenectady County bar assns. Home: 1055 Morningside Ave Schenectady NY 12309 Office: Office of General Services Tower Bldg Empire State Plaza Albany NY 12242 Tel (518) 474-0201

HUGGINS, LUELLA ALICE, b. Springfield, Ohio; LL.B., Nat. U., 1923, LL.M., 1924, M.P.L., 1924; postgrad. Am. U., 1921-24. Secretarial staff Chinese ambassador to U.S., Washington, 1921-22; office staff Ohio legislature, Columbus, 1925; examiner U.S. Pension Bur., Washington, 1924; social and welfare work Fresno County (Calif.) Welfare Dept., Merced County (Calif.) Welfare Dept. and Asso. Charities, Oakland, 1930-32; relief and welfare work Columbus (Ohio) Welfare Dept., 1934, Franklin County Welfare Dept., 1935, U.S. Dept. Pub. Welfare, 1936; admitted to D.C. bar, 1924, Ohio bar, 1925, Calif. bar, 1930, also U.S. Supreme Ct. bar; spl. prosecutor, juvenile ct. Columbus, 1927-28; individual practice law, Washington, 1924, Columbus, 1927-28, Kerman, Calif., 1940—. Founder Found., Research in Field Human Behavior, 1959. Mem. Am., Ohio bar assns., State Bar Calif., Bar Assn. D.C., Nat. Assn. Women Lawyers, Internat. Fedn. Women Lawyers. Fellow Edward MacDowell Found., Peterborough, N.H., 1941. Author: Behavior and the Law, 1959, Behavior Problems in the Making, 1959. Home: 508 E Mendocino St Altadena CA 91001

HUGGINS, ROLLIN CHARLES, JR., b. Berwyn, Ill., Oct. 11, 1931; A.B., Knox Coll., 1953; LL.B., Harvard, 1958. Admitted to Ill. bar, 1958, U.S. Tax Ct. bar, 1959; partner firm Bell, Boyd, Lloyd, Haddad & Burns, Chgo., 1958—; lectr. Ill. Inst. Continuing Legal Edn., 1972-76. Pres. Wilmette (Ill.) Vis. Nurse Assn., 1976. Mem. Am., Ill. State, Chgo. bar assns., Am. Coll. Probate Counsel, Phi Beta Kappa; Beta Theta Pi, Chgo. Law Club, Chgo. Legal Club. Author: Estate Planning for the Corporate Executive, 1975. Home: 700 Greenwood Ave Wilmette IL 60091 Office: 135 S LaSalle St Chicago IL 60603 Tel (312) 372-1121

HUGGLER, DAVID HORTON, b. Bryn Mawr, Pa., July 30, 1944; B.S. in Bus. Adminstrn., U. N.C., 1966; J.D., Villanova U., 1969. Admitted to Pa. Bar, 1970; asso. firm Pepper, Hamilton & Scheetz, Phila., 1969—. Mem. Am., Pa., Phila. bar assns. Comment and project editor Villanova Law Rev., 1968-69. Office: 123 S Broad St Philadelphia PA 19109 Tel (215) 545-1234

HUGHES, ANDREW LAWRENCE, b. N.Y.C., Aug. 10, 1922; student Bklyn. Coll., 1940-42, 46; LL.B., St. John's U., 1948. Admitted to N.Y. bar, 1949, U.S. Supreme Ct. bar, 1961; asso. firm Townley Updike Carter & Rodgers, N.Y.C., 1949-61, partner, 1961—. Mem. N.Y. State Bar Assn. Editor-in-chief St. John's Law Rev., 1948. Home: 1 Sawmill Rd Huntington NY 11743 Office: 220 E 42d St New York City NY 10017 Tel (212) 682-4567

HUGHES, BRUCE RICHARD, b. Sioux City, Iowa, June 11, 1926; B.A., U. Iowa, 1948, J.D., 1951. Admitted to Iowa bar, 1951, Calif. bar, 1957; partner firm Reed, Beers, Beers & Hughes, Waterloo, Iowa, 1951-57; partner firm Severson, Zang, Werson, Berke & Larson, San Francisco, 1957-66, firm Miller, Van Dorn, Hughes & O'Connor, San Francisco, 1966-69; legal counsel Central Banking Systems, Oakland, Calif., 1969-73; v.p., asso. counsel Union Bank, San Francisco, 1973—. Mem. State Bar Calif., Am., San Francisco bar assns., Bay Area Bank Counsel, Phi Beta Kappa, Order of Coif. Home: 18 Salt Landing Tiburon CA 94920 Office: 50 California St suite 3400 PO Box 45500 San Francisco CA 94145 Tel (415) 445-6218

HUGHES, CARSON MC CLAIN, b. Charleston, Miss., May 1947; B.B.A., U. Miss., 1969, J.D., 1971. Admitted to Miss. bar, 1971, U.S. Supreme Ct. bar, 1974; asso. firm Overstreet & Kuykendall, Jackson, Miss., 1971—. Pres. Capital City Kiwanis Club. Mem. Jackson Young Lawyers Assn., Hinds County, Miss. bar assns. Home: 5837 Kinder Jackson MS 39211 Office: 1529 Deposit Guaranty Bldg Jackson MS 39201 Tel (601) 948-3014

HUGHES, CHARLES JOSEPH, b. Conshohocken, Pa., Apr. 23, 1907; B.A., U. Mo., 1932, LL.B., 1933. Admitted to Mo. bar, 1942; foreclosure atty. Fed. Land Bank, St. Louis, 1933-37; spl. asst. U.S. Atty., St. Louis, 1937-41; judge adv. U.S. Air Force, 1941-45, 50-66; spl. asst. U.S. Atty., 1946-50; U.S. Commr., St. Louis, 1967-69. Address: 6628 Widoda Ave Saint Louis MO 63109 Tel (314) 781-6628

HUGHES, CHARLES JOSEPH ARTHUR, b. Fredericton, N.B., Can., Mar. 2, 1909; B.A., U. N.B., 1930; LL.D., St. Thomas U., 1972; read law with Hon, Mr. Justice P. J. Hughes. Called to N.B. bar, 1933, created queen's counsel, 1952; now chief justice N.B. Supreme Ct. Home: 186 Waterloo Row Fredericton NB E3B 1Z2 Canada Office: NB Supreme Ct Legis Bldg Fredericton NB Canada*

HUGHES, DAN SIDNEY, b. Colorado Springs, Colo., Sept. 1, 1940; B.S., U. Colo., 1962, LL.B., 1967. Admitted to Colo. bar, U.S. Dist. Ct. bar, 1967, U.S. Supreme Ct. bar, 1975; partner firm Trott, Kunstle & Hughes, and predecessors, Colorado Springs, 1967—. Mem. Am., Colo., El Paso County bar assns. Home: 304 Crystal Hills Blvd Manitou Springs CO 80829 Office: 321 1st Nat Bank Bldg Colorado Springs CO 80903 Tel (303) 636-5123

HUGHES, HARRY ROE, b. Easton, Md., Nov. 13, 1926; B.S., U. Md., 1949; LL.B., George Washington U., 1952. Admitted to Md. bar, 1952; partner firm Everngam & Hughes, Denton, Md., 1952-58; individual practice law, Denton, 1959-73; sec. transp. State of Md., 1971—; mem. Md. Ho. of Dels., 1955-58, Md. Senate, 1959-70. Mem. Md. Bar Assn. Home: 20 Bouton Green St Baltimore MD 21210 Office: PO Box 8755 Airport MD 21240 Tel (301) 768-9520

HUGHES, HENRY LESTER, b. Natchitoches, La., July 26, 1892; student Holy Cross Coll., New Orleans; B.A., La. State U.; postgrad. Harvard; J.D., Tulane U. Admitted to La. bar, 1919; individual practice law, La., 1919-27, Natchitoches, 1929—; partner firm Phanor Breaeale, 1927-29; dist. atty. Natchitoches and Red River parishes, 1936-60; mem. La. Senate. Mem. La. State Democratic Com., mem. La. Tax Commn. Home: 416 Jefferson St Natchitoches LA 71457 Office: 704 3d St Natchitoches LA 71457 Tel (318) 352-2831

HUGHES, JAMES ELLIOTT, b. Clayton, Mo., May 6, 1913; A.B., Columbia, 1933, LL.B., 1935. Admitted to N.Y. State bar, 1936; asso. firm Coudert Bros., N.Y.C., 1935-44, partner, 1945—. Mem. Am., N.Y. State, N.Y.C. bar assns. Office: Coudert Bros 200 Park Ave New York City NY 10017 Tel (212) 973-4742

HUGHES, JAMES LEWIS, JR., b. Birmingham, Ala., Sept. 16, 1915; A.B., Birmingham So. Coll., 1936; LL.B., U. Va., 1940, J.D., 1940; diploma in internat. law U.S. Naval War Coll., 1956. Admitted to Ala. bar, 1940, C.Z. bar, 1947; individual practice law, Birmingham, 1940-43; commr. Judge Advocate Gen. Dept., U.S. Navy, 1943-64; prof. law Samford U., Birmingham, 1964—; bar examiner Ala., 1968, 69. Mem. Am., Ala., Birmingham bar assns., Phi Alpha Delta. Home: 3840 Glencoe Dr Birmingham AL 35213 Office: Cumberland Sch Law Samford U 800 Lakeshore Dr Birmingham AL 35209 Tel (205) 870-2701

HUGHES, JOHN LLOYD, b. Jefferson County, Wis., Dec. 11, 1919; LL.B., John B. Stetson U. Admitted to Fla. bar, 1949, Ill. bar, 1955; since practiced in Waukegan, Ill., police magistrate, 1959-64; magistrate Circuit Ct., 1964-70; asso. judge Circuit Ct., 1970-74, judge, 1974—. Bd. dirs. Jack Benny Center for Arts, 1972—; mem. Lake County Symphony Com., 1973—. Mem. Am., Ill., Lake County bar assns., Am. Judicature Soc. Office: Lake County Court House 18 N County St Waukegan IL 60085 Tel (312) 689-6386

HUGHES, LYNN NETTLETON, b. Houston, Sept. 9, 1941; B.A., U. Ala., 1963; J.D., U. Tex., 1968. Admitted to Tex. bar, 1966, U.S. Supreme Ct. bar, 1971; individual practice law, Houston, 1966-73; partner firm Howard & Hughes, and predecessor, Houston, 1973—; adj. prof. S. Tex. Coll. Law, 1973—. Mem. Am., Houston bar Assns., Am. Soc. Legal History, Am. Judicature Soc., Am. Anthrop. Assn. Home: 609 Saddlewood St Houston TX 77024 Office: 4605 Post Oak Pl Suite 210 Houston TX 77027 Tel (713) 629-9100

HUGHES, MARK F., b. Bklyn., Dec. 11, 1904; A.B., Yale, 1925; LL.B., Columbia, 1928. Admitted to N.Y. bar, 1928, U.S. Supreme Ct. bar; partner firm Willkie Farr & Gallagher, N.Y.C., 1943-74; vice chmn. com. on character and fitness, mem. com. judiciary relations 1st Jud. Dept. N.Y. State. Mem. Am., N.Y. State bar assns., New York County Lawyers Assn., Assn. Bar City N.Y., Fed. Bar Counsel, Am. Judicature Soc., Am. Coll. Trial Lawyers, Am. Bar Found. Home: 4 Garfield Rd Elberon NJ 07740 Office: 1 Chase Manhattan Plaza New York City NY 10005 Tel (212) 248-1000

HUGHES, MICHAEL JOHN, b. Glendive, Mont., Nov. 18, 1922; B.B.A., U. Mont., 1947, B.A., 1947, J.D., 1949. Admitted to Mont. bar, 1949, U.S. Supreme Ct. bar, 1962; law clk. U.S. Ct. Appeals, San Francisco, 1949-51; partner firm Hughes, Bennett & Cain, and predecessors, Helena, Mont., 1951—; mem. Gov.'s Commn. to Revise Mont. Corp. Codes, 1965-66; mem. Mont. Bd. Bar Examiners, 1973—. Mem. State Bar Mont., Am. 1st Dist. bar assns., Am. Judicature Soc., Am. Coll. Probate Counsel. Home: 1014 Stuart St Helena MT 59601 Office: 406 Fuller Ave Helena MT 59601 Tel (406) 442-3690

HUGHES, RICHARD JOSEPH, b. Florence, N.J., Aug. 10, 1909; student St. Cahrles Coll., 1926-28, St. Joseph's Coll., 1928; LL.B., N.J. Law Sch., 1931. Admitted to N.J. bar, 1932; asst. U.S. atty. Dist N.J., 1939-45; partner firm Lord & Hughes, Trenton, 1945-48; judge Mercer County (N.J.) Ct., 1948-52; judge Superior Ct. N.J., 1952-59, also assignment jusge Union County; gov. N.J., 1961-70; partner firm Hughes, McElroy, Connell, Foley & Geiser, Newark, 1970—; now chief justice N.J. Supreme Ct., Trenton. Mem. Am. (chmn. commn. on correctional facilities and services), N.J., Mercer County (pres. 1953-54), Essex County bar assns. Home: 90 Wescott Rd Princeton NJ 08540 Office: Supreme Ct NJ State House Annex Trenton NJ 08625*

HUGHES, ROBERT HIGGINS, b. Dallas, Nov. 25, 1925; S.J.D., So. Meth. U. Admitted to Tex. bar, 1949, U.S. Supreme Ct. bar, 1954; partner firms Hughes & Monroe, 1950-54, Hughes & Hughes, 1954-56, Hughes Douosky McChochen & Hunt, 1956-63, Rogers Hughes & Herman, Austin, Tex., 1969—; asst. atty. gen. State of Tex.; judge Tex. Dist. Ct.; mem. Tex. Ho. of Reps., 1957-63; city atty. City of West Lake Hills (Tex.). Mem. Tex., Am. Dallas, Travis County (Tex.) bar assns. Home: 9 Hull Circle Austin TX 78746 Office: 1200 SW Tower Bldg Austin TX 78746 Tel (512) 474-6381

HUGHES, ROBERT LOUIS, b. Visalia, Calif., Feb. 2, 1926; B.A., U. Calif., Berkeley, 1948, LL.B., Hastings Coll. Law, San Francisco, 1957. Reporter, editor San Francisco Chronicle, 1948-59; admitted to Calif. bar, 1958; individual practice law, Oakland, Calif., 1958-68; judge U.S. Bankruptcy Ct., Oakland, 1968—; lectr. U. San Francisco Sch. Law, 1973-74; mem. faculty Seminars for Bankruptcy Judges, 1975-77. Office: PO Box 2070 Oakland CA 94604 Tel (415) 451-7687

HUGHES, WILLIAM AUGUSTUS, JR., b. Decatur, Tex., June 29, 1920; B.S., North Tex. State Tchrs. Coll., 1942; LL.B., Baylor U., 1948, J.D., 1971. Admitted to Tex. bar, 1948; practiced in Gainesville, Tex., 1948-50, Decatur, Tex., 1950-57; county and dist. atty. Wise County (Tex.), 1951-53; judge Tex. Dist. Ct., 43d Jud. Dist., 1957-71, 235th Jud. Dist., 1971-76; asso. justice Ct. Civil Appeals 2d Supreme Jud. Dist., Fort Worth, 1976—; atty. Wise Electric Coop., Decatur Bapt. Coll., VA. Bd. dirs. Baylor U. Ex-Students Assn. Mem. State Bar Tex., Am. Judicature Soc., Wise County Bar Assn., Recipient Silver Beaver award Boy Scouts Am., 1968. Office: Wise County Courthouse PO Box 456 Decatur TX 76234 Tel (817) 627-3200

HUGHSTON, THOMAS LESLIE, JR., b. Spartanburg, S.C., July 25, 1943; B.A., The Citadel, 1965; J.D., U. S.C., 1968. Admitted to S.C. bar, 1968; U.S. Dist. Ct. for S.C. Bar, 1968; U.S. 4th Circuit Ct. Appeals bar, 1974; asso. firm Nicholson & Nicholson, Greenwood, S.C., 1968-72; partner firm Mays, Bishop & Hughston, Greenwood, 1972—; judge municipal ct., City Greenwood, 1972-74; pub. defender, Greenwood and Abbeville counties, S.C., 1974-76; mem. S.C. Ho. Reps. Chmn. Democratic Party, Greenwood, 1968-72. Mem. S.C. State Bar, S.C. Trial Lawyers Assn., S.C. Pub. Defenders Assn. Home: 215 Stanley Ave Greenwood SC 29646 Office: PO Box 457 Greenwood SC 29646 Tel (803) 223-8511

HUGILL, ELBERT ABRAM, JR., b. Berkeley, Calif., June 7, 1908; A.B., U. Calif., 1930, J.D., 1933. Admitted to Calif. bar, 1933, N.Y. bar, 1950; atty. Shell Oil Co., N.Y.C., 1933-59; gen. atty. Shell N.Y., N.Y.C., 1955-59; v.p., sec. Shell Oil, N.Y.C., 1959-68; individual practice law, San Francisco, 1971-75, San Diego, 1976—; partner firm Brown Wood, Fuller, Caldwell and Ivey, San Francisco, 1971-76. Trustee City of Bronxville (N.Y.), 1955-65, mayor, 1959-65. Mem. State Bar Calif. Address: 12370 Greens E Rd San Diego CA 92128 Tel (714) 485-5488

HUGIN, ADOLPH CHARLES, b. Washington, Mar. 28, 1907; B.S. in Elec. Engring., George Washington U., 1928; M.S. in Elec. Engring., Mass. Inst. Tech., 1930; J.D., certificate in patent law and practice Georgetown U., 1934; certificate in radio communication, Union Coll., 1944; LL.M., Harvard U., 1947; S.J.D., Cath. U. Am., 1949. Admitted to D.C. bar, 1933, U.S. Supreme Ct. bar, 1945, Mass. bar, 1947, U.S. Ct. Customs Patent Appeals bar, 1934, U.S. Ct. Claims bar, 1953, U.S. Patent and Trademark Office bar, 1933; examiner U.S. Patent Office, 1928; engr. Gen. Elec. Co., Lynn, Mass., 1928-30, in charge gas-electric drive devel. lab., Lynn, 1929-30, patent investigator, Washington, 1930-33, patent lawyer, Washington, 1933-34, patent lawyer, Schenectady, N.Y., 1934-46, engr. in charge sect. aeros. and marine engring. div., Schenectady, 1942-45; individual practice law, Cambridge and Arlington, Mass., 1946-47; vis. prof. law Catholic U. Am. Law Sch., 1949-55; individual practice law, Washington, D.C., 1947—, also cons. engr. Mem. Am. Bar Assn., Am. Patent Law Assn., Delta Theta Phi. Author: Private International Trade Regulatory Arrangements and the Antitrust Laws, 1949; editor-in-chief Am. Patent Law Assn. Bull., 1948-54; contbr. articles to profl. jours. Home: 7602 Boulder St North Springfield VA 22151 Office: Nat Press Bldg Washington DC 20045 Tel (202) 638-1147

HUIE, ROBERT BURKS, b. Birmingham, Ala., July 5, 1942; B.S. U. Ala., 1964, LL.B., 1966. Admitted to Ala. bar, 1967; asso. firm Huie, Fernam-Bucq, Stewart & Smith, Birmingham, 1967-74, partner, 1975—. Pres. Hoover Valley Lions Club, 1975—; cabinet sec. Lions Club Dist. 34C, 1974-75. Mem. Am., Ala., Birmingham bar assns. Home: 1804 Glendmer Dr Birmingham AL 35216 Office: 825 1st Ala Bank Bldg Birmingham AL 35203 Tel (205) 251-1193

HUIE, WILLIAM ORR, b. Arkadelphia, Ark., Sept. 15, 1911; A.B., Henderson State U., 1932; LL.B., U. Tex., 1935; S.J.D., Harvard, 1953. Admitted to Tex. bar, 1935; asso. firm Greenwood, Moody and Robertson, Austin, Tex., 1935-36; asst. prof. law, U. Tex., 1936-39, asso. prof., 1939-46, prof. law, 1946-65, asst. dean sch. law, 1946-48, Sylvan Lang prof. law, 1965—; vis. prof. law, Harvard, 1961-62. Mem. Tex. State Bar, Travis County Bar Assn. Author: Texas Cases on Marital Property Rights, 1966; (with M.K. Woodward and E.E. Smith III) Cases on Oil and Gas, 2d edition, 1972; contbr. articles to legal jours. Home: 3401 Barranca Circle Austin TX 78731 Office: 2500 Red River St Austin TX 78705 Tel (512) 471-5151

HUIE, WILLIAM STELL, b. College Park, Ga., Dec. 23, 1930; LL.B., Emory U., 1953. Admitted to Ga. bar, 1953; practice law, Atlanta, 1953—, partner firm Huie, Ware, Sterne, Brown & Ide, and predecessors, 1959—; lectr. Emory U. Law Sch., Atlanta, 1957-60, Emory U. Dental Sch., 1959-68. Chmn., Atlanta Fund Appeals Rev. Bd., 1969-71; trustee Westminster Schs., 1966—; pres. State YMCA of Ga., 1967-70, bd. dirs., 1965—. Fellow Am. Bar Found.; mem. Am., Atlanta (pres. 1968-69) bar assns., Atlanta Lawyers Found., State Bar Ga. (pres. 1975-76), Am. Judicature Soc., Bryan Soc. Home: 363 Manor Ridge Dr NW Atlanta GA 30305 Office: 1200 Standard Fed Bldg Atlanta GA 30303 Tel (404) 522-8700

HULETT, CHARLES WILBUR, b. Indpls., July 27, 1917; LL.B., Ind. U., 1947. Admitted to Ind. bar, 1947; asst. ops. mgr. Aero Mayflower Transit Co., Inc., Indpls., 1947-55, ops. mgr., 1955-57, v.p.-ops., 1957-70, exec. v.p., 1970-77, exec. v.p., gen. mgr., 1977—; group v.p. Mayflower Corp. Bd. dirs. Indpls. Conv. and Visitors Bur., Crossroads Rehab. Center; bd. dirs., mem. exec. com. Am. Movers Conf. Mem. Ind., Indpls. bar assns. Home: 7950 Meridian Hills Ln Indianapolis IN 46240 Office: PO Box 107B Indianapolis IN 46206 Tel (317) 299-1191

HULKOWER, M. WALTER, b. N.Y.C., Nov. 16, 1934; B.A., Yeshiva U., 1955; LL.B., N.Y. Law Sch., 1958, LL.M., 1961. Admitted to N.Y. bar, 1959, Calif. bar, 1962; asso. firm Curran, Maloney Cohn & Stim, N.Y.C., 1959-61; individual practice law, N.Y.C., 1961, Sherman Oaks, Calif., 1962—; dep. city atty. City of Burbank (Calif.), 1961. Mem. Calif., Los Angeles trial lawyers assns., Los Angeles County, San Fernando Valley bar assns. Recipient ASCAP award, 1961. Office: 15300 Ventura Blvd Sherman Oaks CA 91403 Tel (213) 990-9151

HULL, DANIEL TALMADGE, JR., b. Birmingham, Ala., Sept. 3, 1942; B.S. in Chem. Engring. with honors, U. Ala., 1964; J.D., Samford U., 1972. Staff engr. Rust Engring. Co., Birmingham, 1967-68, 69-72, atty., 1972-73, asst. gen. counsel, 1973-75; process licensing liaison Coppee-Rust S.A., Brussels, 1968-69; admitted to Ala. bar, 1973. Mem. Am., Birmingham bar assns., Am. Inst. Chem Engrs., Phi Alpha Delta. Registered profl. engr., Ala. Office: First Ala Bank Bldg Suite 1515 417 N Twentieth St Birmingham AL 35203 Tel (205) 251-2094

HULL, HARRY ROURKE, JR., b. New Orleans, Apr. 28, 1937; A.A., St. Joseph Sem., St. Benedict, La., 1957; LL.B., Loyola U., New Orleans, 1963. Admitted to La. bar, 1963; legal officer USMC, 1963-67; asst. dist. atty. New Orleans, 1967-71, chief asst. dist. atty. juvenile div., 1975—; asst. U.S. atty. Dept. Justice, New Orleans, 1971-73; partner firm Brown & Hull, Metairie, La., 1973-75. Mem. La., Fed. bar assns., La. Dist. Attys. Assn., Marine Corps Res. Officers Assn., New Orleans Right To Life Assn. First editor Legal Rag, 1960-61. Home: 4222 Eden St New Orleans LA 70125 Office: Room 101 421 Loyola Ave New Orleans LA 70112 Tel (504) 586-0880

HULL, J(AMES) RICHARD, b. Keokuk, Iowa, Dec. 5, 1933; B.A., Ill. Wesleyan U., 1955; J.D., Northwestern U., 1958. Admitted to Ill. bar, 1958; with Honeggers & Co., Inc., Fairbury, Ill., 1959-65, v.p. adminstrn., 1962-65, corp. sec., 1960-65, gen. counsel, 1960-65; corp. sec., corp. counsel, head corp. legal div. Am. Hosp. Supply Corp., Evanston, Ill., 1965—. Mem. Am., Ill., Chgo. bar assns., Legal Club Chgo., Am. Soc. Corp. Secs., Am. Soc. Hosp. Attys. Home: 2603 Oak Ave Northbrook IL 60062 Office: 1740 Ridge Ave Evanston IL 60201 Tel (312) 869-2580

HULL, THOMAS JOSEPH, b. Kingston, N.Y., Dec. 8, 1940; A.B., U. Notre Dame, 1963, LL.B., 1966. Admitted to N.Y. State bar, 1967; asso. firm Rappaport, Kaman & Hull, Binghamton, N.Y., 1966-75; partner firm Kaman & Hull, Binghamton, 1976—. Bd. dirs. Binghamton Police Athletic League, 1967—, pres., 1972-73. Mem. N.Y. State, Broome County bar assns. Home: 31 Davis St Binghamton NY 13905 Office: 66 Hawley St Binghamton NY 13902 Tel (607) 723-5406

HULSE, FRED BERKLEY, b. New London, Mo., Feb. 19, 1899; LL.B., Washington U., St. Louis, 1926. Admitted to Mo. bar, 1926; partner firm Hulse & Hulse, 1926-36; city atty., Hannibal, Mo., 1929-35; asst. atty. Mo. Hwy. Commn., Jefferson City, 1936-40; gen. chmn. Mo. Bar Adminstrn., Sedalia, 1940-72. Mem. Am. Bar Assn., Nat. Conf. Bar Council, Am. Legion. Home: 7565 Parkdale Ave Clayton MO 63105

HULSE, RALPH RAYMOND, b. Fillmore, Mo., Jan. 21, 1901; student Mo. Wesleyan Coll., 1926; A.B., Baker U., 1927; LL.B., Mich. Law Sch., 1931, J.D., 1945. Admitted to Mo. bar, 1931; mem. firm Mitchell & Hulse, St. Joseph, Mo., 1933-71; counselor firm Dale, Flynn, Baumann & Liles, St. Joseph, 1971-77; tchr. and coach schs. Mo., Kans., Mich., 1920-30; trustee Baker U., Baldwin, Kans. Pres. Sertoma Club, St. Joseph, 1945-46; Sunday Sch. tchr. First United Meth. Ch., St. Joseph. Mem. Am., Mo. (sr. counselor), bar assns. Profl. golfer, Mich. Home: 1905 Lovers Ln Saint Joseph MO 64503 Office: 1205 Jules St Saint Joseph MO 64501 Tel (816) 232-7788

HULSTRAND, GEORGE EUGENE, b. Cannon Falls, Minn., Aug. 3, 1918; B.A., Gustavus Adolphus Coll., 1943; J.D., Yale, 1946. Admitted to Minn. bar, 1947; asso. with Roy A. Hendrickson, Willmar, Minn., 1947-53; partner firm Hulstrand, Anderson, & Larson, Willmar, 1953—; asst. atty. Kandiyohi County (Minn.), 1947-50. Mem. Willmar City Council, 1953-56, chmn. Willmar Planning Commn., 1957-67, 74—. Mem. Kandiyohi County, Minn., Am. bar assns., Am. Judicature Soc. Recipient Willmar Jaycees Distinguished Service award, 1952. Home: 325 N 7th St Willmar MN 56201 Office: Willmar Bldg PO Box 130 Willmar MN 56201 Tel (612) 235-4313

HULTIN, JERRY MACARTHUR, b. Lansing, Mich., May 17, 1942; B.A., Ohio State U., 1964; J.D., Yale, 1972. Admitted to Ohio bar, 1972, U.S. Dist. and Circuit Ct. Appeals bar, 1973; asso. firm Clayman & Jaffy & Taylor, Columbus, Ohio, 1972; partner firms Taylor, Hultin & Ludwig, Columbus, 1973-75, Moots, Hultin, Weinberger & Cope, Columbus, 1976—; staff counsel Joint Select Com. on Workmen's Compensation Gen. Assembly of Ohio, 1975-76. Mem. Columbus Cable TV Task Force, 1975; mem. Columbus Area Cable TV Advisory Com., 1976. Mem. Am., Ohio, Columbus bar assns. Editor Yale Review of Law and Social Action, vol. 2, 1971-72; contbr. article to Yale Rev. Law and Social Action. Office: Suite 721 21 E State St Columbus OH 43215 Tel (614) 221-3121

HUMER, JAMES RAMSAY, b. Carlisle, Pa., Sept. 15, 1919; A.B., Dickinson Coll., 1941, LL.B., 1947. Admitted to Cumberland County bar, 1949; Pa. Supreme Ct. bar, 1951, Pa. Superior Ct. bar, 1951; individual practice law, Carlisle, 1949-53; partner firm Weary, Hess & Humer, Carlisle, 1954-65; individual practice law, Carlisle, 1965—; pub. defender, Carlisle, 1969-72. Mem. Am., Pa. Cumberland County (pres. 1974) bar assns., Am. Assn. Trial Lawyers. Home: 230 S College St Carlisle PA 17013 Office: 1 W High St Carlisle PA 17013 Tel (717) 243-3831

HUML, LODY, b. Prague, Czechoslovakia, May 4, 1895; naturalized, 1917; LL.B., Cleve.-Marshall, 1924. Admitted to Ohio bar, 1924; individual practice law, Cleve., 1924-76; senator Ohio Legislature, Columbus, 1935-49. Mem. Cuyahoga County Bar Assn. Contbr. Cleve. Plain Dealer & Press. Address: care Malcolm Huml 514 Lincoln Way E Mishawaka IN 46544

HUMPHREY, CURRUN CLEVELAND, b. Santa Fe, Tenn., Feb. 25, 1930; B.S. in Engring., Tenn. Tech. U., 1958; J.D., Cumberland U., 1952; Admitted to Tenn. bar, 1952, Ala. bar, 1959; capt. JAGC, U.S. Army, 1953-56; engr. Thiokol Chem. Corp., Redstone Arsenal, Ala., 1958-59; since practiced law in Huntsville, Ala., mem. firm Ramey & Humphrey, 1959-60, Humphrey & Lutz, 1960-61, Humphrey, Lutz & Smith, 1961-73, Humphrey & Smith, 1973—. Chmn. Madison County Cancer Crusade, 1962. Mem. Fed. Bar Assn., Assn. Trial Lawyers Am., Ala. Trial Lawyers Assn. Home: Rt 2 Box 461 Harvest AL 35749 Office: 509 Madison St Huntsville AL 35801 Tel (205) 533-1116

HUMPHREY, STEVEN ROY, b. Mineola, N.Y., June 4, 1941; B.A., Conn. Wesleyan U., 1966; J.D., Vanderbilt U., 1966. Admitted to Mass. bar, 1966, Conn. bar, 1967; asso. firm Robinson, Robinson & Cole, Hartford, Conn., 1966-71, partner, 1972—; adj. prof. bus. law U. Hartford, 1970-74. Selectman, Town of W. Hartford, 1972. Mem. Am., Mass., Conn., Hartford County bar assns. Home: 10 Jensen Rd West Hartford CT 06117 Office: 799 Main St Hartford CT 06103 Tel (203) 278-0700

HUMPHREYS, DOUGLAS DAVID, JR., b. Cumberland Furnace, Tenn., Aug. 25, 1907; ed. U. Tenn.; LL.B., Cumberland U. Admitted to Tenn. bar, 1928; mem. firm Boyd & Humphreys, Waynesboro, Tenn., 1928-32; individual practice law, Hohenwald, Tenn., 1932-69; mem. firm Humphreys, Townsend & Doyle, Hohenwald, Linden, Tenn., 1969-74; judge Gen. Sessions, Lewis County, Tenn., Hohenwald, 1950—. Active Civic Club, 1955—. Home and office: Ct House Hohenwald TN 38462 Tel (615) 796-2926

HUMPHRIES, JAMES DONALD, III, b. Newark, Ohio, Sept. 27, 1944; B.S. in Commerce, Washington and Lee U., 1966, J.D. cum laude, 1969. Admitted to Ga. bar, 1970; asso. firm Kilpatrick, Cody, Rogers, McClatchey & Regenstein, Atlanta, 1969-73; partner firm Harland, Cashin, Chambers & Parker, Atlanta, 1973-75, firm Morton, Humphries & Payne, Atlanta, 1976—. Mem. Am., Ga., Atlanta bar assns., Lawyers Club Atlanta (exec. com. 1976—). Contbr. articles to law jours. Home: 1951 Greystone Rd Atlanta GA 30318 Office: 2950 101 Marietta Tower Atlanta GA 30303 Tel (404) 522-2950

HUMPHRIES, LEWIS LEE, b. Rupert, Idaho, Aug. 27, 1920; B.E.E., Iowa State U., 1946; J.D., U. Utah, 1949; LL.M., U. So. Calif., 1964. Admitted to Utah bar, 1949, Calif. bar, 1955; patent atty. Rockwell Internat., Anaheim, Calif., 1952-69, corporate patent counsel, 1969—. Mem. Long Beach Bar Assn. Home: 7821 Tibana St Long Beach CA 90808 Office: 2230 E Imperial Hwy El Segundo CA 90245 Tel (213) 647-5787

HUNDLEY, SEYMOUR, JR., b. Munich, Ger., Nov. 4, 1947; B.A. in Polit Sci., Va. State Coll., 1969; J.D., Howard U., 1972. Admitted to N.J. bar, 1974, D.C. bar, 1976; complaint investigator Neighborhood Consumer Info. Center, Washington, 1970-72; law clk. to judge, Trenton, N.J., 1972; staff atty., acting dir. affirmative action officer State Office Legal Services, Trenton, 1972-75; individual practice law, Trenton, 1976—; vol. Parole Program. Active Nat. Democratic Orgn., Ewing Twp. Dem. Club; treas. Mercer County Adv. Com.; bd. dirs. Central N.J. Health Planning Council, Inc., Ewing Twp. YMCA. Mem. NAACP (exec. com. Trenton), Am., N.J., Nat., Garden State, D.C. bar assns., Assn. Trial Lawyers Am., Civil Affairs Assn., Phi Alpha Delta. Office: 140 Spring St Trenton NJ 08618 Tel (609) 393-6878

HUNGATE, JOSEPH WYNE, b. Oberlin, Ohio, June 15, 1938; A.B., Princeton U., 1960; J.D., U. Calif., 1966. Admitted to Ohio bar, 1966; asso. firm Squire, Saunders & Dempsey, Cleve., 1966-72; atty. TRW, Inc., Cleve., 1972—. Mem. Am., Ohio, Cleve. bar assns. Office: 23555 Euclid Ave Cleveland OH 44117 Tel (216) 383-3410

HUNKER, CHESTER A., b. Las Vegas, N.M., Oct. 31, 1913; A.B., Highlands U., 1934; J.D., U. Mo., 1969. Admitted to N.M. Supreme Ct., 1942; city atty., Las Vegas, N.M., 1943-46; atty. N.M. Bur. Revenue, Santa Fe, N.M., 1947-51; pvt. practice law, Clovis, N.M., 1951—.

HUNKER, GEORGE HENRY, JR., b. Las Vegas, N.Mex., Sept. 1, 1914; student N.Mex. Highlands U., Las Vegas, 1932-33, U. Mo., 1933-36; LL.B., U. Colo., 1939, J.D., 1970. Admitted to N.Mex. bar, 1939, Kans. bar, 1939, U.S. Supreme Ct. bar, 1944; asst. atty. gen. State of N.Mex., 1940-42; mem. firm Hervey, Dow & Hinkle, Roswell, N.Mex., 1946-63; individual practice law, Roswell, 1964-71; partner firm Hunker-Fedric, Roswell, 1971—. Mem. Roswell City Sch. Bd., 1964-65; mem. interim bd. Roswell Ind. Sch. Dist., 1965-66; commr. Roswell Housing Authority, 1971-76. Mem. Am., N.Mex., Chaves County bar assns., N.Mex. Oil and Gas Assn. Office: PO Box 1837 Roswell NM 88201 Tel (505) 622-2700

HUNKINS, RAYMOND BREEDLOVE, J.D., U. Wyo., 1968. Admitted to Wyo. bar, 1969; partner firm Jones, Jones, Vines & Hunkins, Wheatland, Wyo., 1969—; mem., sec. Wyo. Gov.'s Crime Commn., 1969-74, chmn. exec. com., and sub com. on edn. and tng., 1970-74; mem. adv. bd. Wyo. State Police Officers' Tng. Acad., 1970-74. Chmn., Platte County March of Dimes, 1969-72, Platte County Republican Central Com., 1973-75. Home: Route 1 Box 183 Wheatland WY 82201 Office: PO Box 189 Wheatland WY 82201 Tel (307) 822-2883

HUNSAKER, WILLIAM J., b. Los Angeles, Dec. 16, 1937; B.B.A., Wichita (Kans.) State U., 1959; J.D., Washburn U., Topeka, 1965. Admitted to Kans. bar, 1965, Colo. bar, 1966; atty. U.S. Dept. Justice, Washington, 1965-66; law clk. U.S. Ct. Appeals, 10th Circuit, Denver, 1966-67; mem. firm. Johnson, Makris & Hunsaker, Denver, 1967—; editor-in-chief Washburn U. Law Jour., 1964-65. Mem. Colo., Denver, Lawyer-Pilots bar assns. Home: 6119 Newcombe St Aruada CO 80004 Office: 555 Capitol Life Center Denver CO 80203 Tel (303) 292-2960

HUNSICKER, OSCAR AARON, b. Wooster, Ohio, Jan. 30, 1898; A.B., U. Akron, 1919, LL.D. (hon.), 1965; LL.B., Case Western Res. U., 1922; LL.M. (hon.), Cleve. Marshall Law Sch., 1954. Admitted to Ohio bar, 1922; city solicitor, Kenmore (Ohio), 1923-26; pros. atty. Summit County (Ohio), 1927-28; judge Common Pleas Ct., Summit County Juvenile Div., Akron, Ohio, 1930-46; judge Ct. Appeals of Ohio, Akron, 1946-71, spl. assignment, 1971—; dean Akron Law Sch., 1941-59. Pres. Ohio Welfare Conf., 1942, Better Akron Fedn., 1931-32, Akron Community Chest, 1932-40, United Fund Summit County, 1941-44; trustee Archbishop Hoban High Sch., 1962-74. Mem. Akron (chmn. law way com. 1965-71), Ohio State (rules com., criminal div. 1969-71), Am. bar assns. Home: 900 W Market St Akron OH 44313 Office: Ct Appeals Courthouse 209 S High St Akron OH 44308 Tel (216) 379-5750

HUNSUCKER, JOHN THOMAS, b. Loma Linda, Calif., Sept. 15, 1946; B.B.A., George Washington U., 1970; J.D., U. Calif., Los Angeles, 1973. Admitted to Calif. bar, 1973; asso. firm Schell & Delamer, Los Angeles, 1973—. Mem. Am., Los Angeles County bar assns., State Bar Calif., Def. Research Inst., So. Calif. Def. Counsel. Office: 1200 Wilshire Blvd Los Angeles CA 90017 Tel (213) 481-1140

HUNT, FREDERICK MONROE, b. Geneva, N.Y., Oct. 2, 1917; A.B., Syracuse U., 1938, LL.B., 1940. Admitted to N.Y. bar, 1940; individual practice law, Dundee, N.Y., 1946—; dist. atty. Yates County (N.Y.), 1966-72; counsel N.Y. State Senate Com. on Taxation, 1958-66. Mem. N.Y. State, Yates County bar assns. Home: 46 Main St Dundee NY 14837 Office: 9 Main St Dundee NY 14837 Tel (607) 243-5416

HUNT, GORDON, b. Los Angeles, Oct. 26, 1934; B.A., U. Calif., Los Angeles, 1956; J.D., U. So. Calif., 1959. Admitted to Calif. bar, 1960; clk. appellate dept. Los Angeles County Superior Ct., 1959-60; asso. firm Behymer, Hoffman & Hunt and predecessors, Los Angeles, 1960-65, partner, 1965-68; partner firm Munns, Kofford, Hoffman, Hunt & Throckmorton, Pasadena, Calif., 1969—; lectr. Continuing Edn. of Bar, 1971, 77. Mem. Am., Calif. (conv. del. 1964-69), Los Angeles County (spl. advisor 1966-67, co-chmn. continuing edn. com. 1969-71, exec. com. real property sec. 1970-72, sec. 1972-73, vice chmn. 1972-76, chmn. 1976—) bar assns. Contbr articles to law jours. Home: 10506 Casanes St Downey CA 90240 Office: 199 N Lake Ave Pasadena CA 91101 Tel (213) 795-9733

HUNT, MERRILL ROBERTS, b. Portland, Maine, Jan. 23, 1939; B.A., Trinity Coll., 1962; J.D., U. Maine, 1969. Admitted to Maine bar, 1969; asso. firm Mahoney, Robinson, Mahoney & Norman and predecessors, Portland, 1969-70, partner, 1971-75; partner firm Robinson, Hunt & Kriger, Portland, 1976—. Chmn. Falmouth (Maine) Sewer Bd. Appeals, 1972-73; mem. Falmouth Bd. Zoning Appeals, 1974—, chmn., 1976—. Mem. Am., Maine, Cumberland County bar assns., Am. Judicature Soc., Def. Research Inst. Office: 4 Canal Plaza Portland ME 04111 Tel (207) 775-6191

HUNT, PETER, b. Butte, Mont., Jan. 10, 1928; A.B., U. Calif., Berkeley, 1948, J.D., 1952. Admitted to Calif. bar, 1953; since practiced in San Francisco, asso. firm Thelen, Marrin, Johnson & Bridges, 1952-54, Shapro & Rothchild, 1955-56; individual practice law, 1956-62; partner Kelso, Hunt, Ashford & Ludwig, and predecessors, 1962—; lectr. real property law U. Calif., Berkeley, 1963-66; Calif. Continuing Edn. of the Bar, 1967. Chmn. Democratic Council, Berkeley, 1952-54; chmn. Cath. Bd. Edn., Berkeley, 1971-72. Mem. Am., Calif., San Francisco bar assns., Am. Judicature Soc., Alpha Delta Phi (alumni counsellor Berkeley 1960-62). Home: 924 Oxford St Berkeley CA 94707 Office: 111 Pine St Suite 1800 San Francisco CA 94111 Tel (415) 788-7200

HUNT, RICHARD HOWARD, JR., b. Miami, Fla., Mar. 24, 1937; B.A., Yale, 1959; LL.B., U. Fla., 1962, J.D., 1967; LL.M., N.Y. U., 1963. Admitted to Fla. bar, 1962, D.C. bar, 1976; asso. firm Smathers & Thompson, Miami, 1963-69, partner, 1969—; instr. law U. Miami, 1968-70, adj. asst. prof., 1970-73. Trustee Dade County Law Library, 1968—. Mem. Am., Dade County (dir. 1967-70) bar assns., Fla. Bar (exec. council tax sect. 1972—). Office: 1301 Alfred I DuPont Bldg Miami FL 33131

HUNT, ROGER DAVIS, b. Colorado Springs, Colo., Mar. 25, 1932; A.B., U. Colo., 1954, LL.B., 1960, J.D., 1968. Admitted to Colo. bar, 1960; partner firm Foard, Foutch & Hunt, 1964-70, firm Haney Howbert & Akers, 1970-75; asst. city atty. Colorado Springs, 1966-68. Mem. Am., Colo., El Paso County bar assns. Office: 401 Mining Exchange Bldg Colorado Springs CO 80903 Tel (303) 633-3815

HUNT, WILLIAM DONALD, b. Independence, Kans., Feb. 24, 1946; B.A., U. Tulsa, 1968, J.D., 1971. Admitted to Okla. bar, 1971, also 10th Circuit U.S. Ct. Appeals; mem. firm Rucker, McBride, & Hopkins, Tulsa, 1972-76, Schuman, Milsten & Jackson, 1976—; prof. bus. law Tulsa Jr. Coll., 1974—. Mem. Am. Bar Assn. Home: 6004 E 62d St Tulsa OK 74136 Office: Philtower Bldg Tulsa OK 74103 Tel (918) 583-7575

HUNTER, CHARLTON LEE, b. Coral Gables, Fla., Oct. 3, 1949; student U. N.C., 1967-69; B.B.A., U. Miami, 1971, J.D., 1974. Admitted to Fla. bar, 1974; asso. firm Smathers & Thompson, Miami, 1974—. Mem. Am., Dade County bar assns., Order of Barristers, Soc. Bar and Gavel, Delta Theta Phi. Home: 1210 Capri St Coral Gables FL 33134 Office: 1301 Alfred I DuPont Bldg Miami FL 33131 Tel (305) 379-6523

HUNTER, DANNYE LEE, b. Morton, Miss., Nov. 20, 1940; B.A., U. Miss., 1962, J.D., 1965. Admitted to Miss. bar, 1965, U.S. Supreme Ct. bar, 1976; individual practice law, Forest, Miss., 1965—; county youth ct. referee Scott County, Miss., 1975; county atty., 1976—; commr. Miss. State Bar, 1969. Mem. Miss. Bar, Miss (bd. govs. 1977-78), Am. trial lawyers assns., Miss. Prosecutors Assn., Miss. Def. Lawyers Assn., Phi Alpha Delta. Home: 1101 Melwood Dr Forest MS 39074 Office: 222 E Main St Forest MS 39074 Tel (601) 469-2682

HUNTER, DONALD FORREST, b. Mpls., Jan. 30, 1934; B.A., U. Minn., 1961, LL.B., 1963. Admitted to Minn. bar, 1963; since practiced in New Ulm, Minn.; asso. firm Gislason, Dosland, Hunter & Malecki, and predecessors, 1963-66, partner, 1967-76; gen. counsel, corp. sec., dir. Med. Investment Corp., Shipstads & Johnson Ice Follies, Inc., Holiday on Ice, 1975—, exec. v.p., 1976—; gen. counsel, corp. sec., dir. Blaine Thompson Co., Inc., 1975—. Mem. Am., Minn., 9th Dist. bar assns., Minn. Def. Lawyers Assn. Home: 1440 Louisiana Ave N Minneapolis MN 55427 Office: 1600 Dain Tower Minneapolis MN 55402

HUNTER, ELMO BOLTON, b. St. Louis, Oct. 23, 1915; A.B., U. Mo., 1936, LL.B., 1938; postgrad. U. Mich., 1941. Admitted to Mo. bar, 1938, U.S. Supreme Ct. bar, 1942; law clk. Judge K. Stone 8th Circuit Ct. Appeals, asst. counsel City Kansas City, 1938-41; partner firm Sebree, Shook, Hardy & Hunter, Kansas City, 1945-51; judge Jackson County (Mo.) Circuit Ct., 1951-57, Kansas City Ct. Appeals, 1957-65; U.S. Dist. Ct., Kansas City, 1965—; lectr., tchr. Law Sch. Univ. Mo., Kansas City. Trustee U. Mo. at Kansas City, Sch. Ozarks, Point Lookout, Mo.; elder Ward Parkway Presbyterian Ch., Kansas City. Fellow Am. Bar Assn.; mem. Am. Judicature Soc., Am. Bar Assn., Lawyers Assn. Kansas City, Phi Beta Kappa. Fellow William Rockhill Nelson Gallery Art. Contbr. numerous opinions, reviews, articles to legal publications. Office: 613 US Courthouse Kansas City MO 64106 Tel (816) 421-7077

HUNTER, EMMETT MARSHALL, b. Denver, Aug. 18, 1913; LL.B., So. Meth. U., 1936. Admitted to Tex. bar, 1936; asso. firm Vaughan & Work, Dallas, 1936, Thorton & Montgomery, Dallas, 1937, Frank J. Winslow, Houston, 1938-42; served with JAGC, USNR, 1942-45, mem. Res., 1945-55; with Humble Oil & Refining Co. and successor firm Exxon Co. U.S.A., Tyler, Tex., 1945-77. Registrar, mem. bd. mgrs. SAR. Mem. Tex. Bar Assn. Office: Tel (214) 592-4331

HUNTER, HOWARD OWEN, b. Brunswick, Ga., Oct. 14, 1946; B.A., Yale, 1968, J.D., 1971. Admitted to Ga. bar, 1971; asso. firm Hogan & Hartson, Washington, 1971-72; Hansell, Post, Brandon & Dorsey, Atlanta, 1972-76; asst. prof. law Emory U., 1976—. Sec., dir. Ga. Vol. Lawyers for the Arts; sec. Atlanta Contemporary Dance Co.; mem. Atlanta Com. Fgn. Relations, mem. speakers council, 1976-77. Mem. Am., Atlanta bar assns., State Bar Ga., ACLU; contbr. articles to legal jours. Office: Emory U Sch of Law Atlanta GA 30322 Tel (404) 329-6507

HUNTER, JACK DUVAL, b. Elkhart, Ind., Jan. 14, 1937; B.B.A., U. Mich., 1959, LL.B., 1961. Admitted to Mich. bar, 1961, Ind. bar, 1962; atty. law dept. Lincoln Nat. Life Ins. Co., Ft. Wayne, Ind., 1961-64, asst. counsel, 1964-68, v.p., gen. counsel, 1975—, asst. gen. counsel, asst. sec. parent co. Lincoln Nat. Corp., Ft. Wayne, 1968-71, gen. counsel, 1971-72, v.p., gen. counsel, 1972—. Mem. Allen County (Ind.), Ind. State, Mich. State, Am. bar assns., Assn. Life Ins. Counsel. Named Boss of Year Ft. Wayne Legal Secs. Assn., 1975. Office: 1301 S Harrison St Fort Wayne IN 46801 Tel (219) 742-5421

HUNTER, JERRY L., b. Mt. Holly, N.C., Sept. 1, 1942; B.S., N.C. Agrl. and Tech. U., 1964; J.D., Howard U., 1967. Admitted to D.C. bar, 1968, U.S. Supreme Ct. bar, 1971; partner firm Roundtree, Knox, Hunter & Parker, Washington, 1970—. Mem. community adv. com. Howard U. Cancer Research Center, Washington. Mem. Am., Nat., D.C. bar assns., Assn. Plaintiffs Trial Attys. Recipient Am. Jurisprudence award, 1965. Office: 1822 11th St NW Washington DC 20001 Tel (202) 234-1723

HUNTER, MACKIELL JAMES, b. Montezuma, Ga., Feb. 7, 1946; B.A., Ft. Valley State Coll., 1968; J.D., Howard U., 1973. Admitted to Ga., Iowa bars, 1973; trial atty. Atlanta regional office of gen. counsel Equal Employment Opportunity Commn., 1973—, decision writer, 1971-73. Co-chairperson Com. of Civil Rights Lawyers to Assist the Regional Office of NAACP. Mem. Am., Nat., Gate City, Iowa bar assns., State Bar Ga., Phi Alpha Delta. Contbr. articles to legal jours. Home: 3479 Rolling Green Ridge SW Atlanta GA 30331 Office: 1389 Peachtree St NE Suite 200 Atlanta GA 30331 Tel (404) 526-2176

HUNTER, WILLIAM MORGAN, b. Fort Worth, Mar. 9, 1923; B.B.A., U. Tex. at Austin, 1943, LL.B., 1948. Admitted to Tex. bar, 1948, U.S. Supreme Ct. bar, 1955; accountant Arthur Andersen & Co., Houston, 1943-46; lectr. U. Tex., at Austin, 1946-48; trial atty. Chief Counsel, Bur. Internal Revenue, Phila., 1949-51; asso. firm McGinnis, Lochridge & Kilgore, Austin, 1951-57, partner, 1957—. C.P.A., Tex. Mem. State Bar Tex., Tex. Bar Found., Am., Travis County bar assns. Home: 3500 Mount Bonnell Rd Austin TX 78731 Office: 5th Floor Tex State Bank Bldg Austin TX 78701 Tel (512) 476-6982

HUNTER, WILLIAM SPURDGEON, b. Bell, Calif., Mar. 29, 1944; B.A., Chapman Coll., 1966; J.D., U. Calif. at San Francisco, 1969; LL.M., Harvard U., 1970. Admitted to Calif. bar, 1970; partner firm Duryea, Randolph, Malolm & Daly, Newport Beach, Calif., 1974—; instr. Western State U. Coll. Law, Fullerton, Calif. Mem. Am., Calif. bar assns. Home: 20112 Kline Dr Santa Ana CA 92707 Office: Duryea Randolph et al 4301 MacArthur Blvd Newport Beach CA 92660 Tel (714) 833-0730

HUNTLEY, ROBERT EDWARD ROYALL, b. Winston-Salem, N.C., June 13, 1929; B.A. in English, Washington and Lee U., 1950, LL.B. summa cum laude, 1957; LL.M., Harvard, 1962; LL.D., Wake Forest U., 1971, Randolph-Macon Coll., 1971, Coll. Charlston, 1976. Admitted to Va. bar, 1957; asso. firm Booth, Dudley, Koontz & Booth, Alexandria, Va., 1957-58; prof. law Washington and Lee U., 1958-68, dean Sch. Law, 1967-68, pres., 1968—; dir. Best Products, Inc., Shenandoah Life Ins. Co., Central Tele. & Utilities Corp., Philip Morris, Inc. Mem. Va. State Bd. Edn., 1970-74; pres. Va. Found. for Ind. Colls., 1974-76; trustee Salem Coll., 1975—; trustee George C. Marshall Research Found 1968—. Mem. Am., Va., Va. State Bar Assns., Phi Beta Kappa, Omicron Delta Kappa, Order of the Coif, Phi Delta Phi, Delta Tau Delta. Home: 601 Ross Rd Lexington VA 24450 Office: Washington Hall Washington and Lee Univ Lexington VA 24450 Tel (703) 463-9111

HUNTSMAN, CLAIR LENHART, b. Leipsic, Ohio, Aug. 22, 1931; J.D., Ohio No. U., 1954. Admitted to Ohio bar, 1954; individual practice law, Leipsic, 1954—; county judge Putnam County, Ohio, 1963—. Mayor City of Leipsic, 1960-63. Mem. Ohio, N.W. Ohio, Putnam County (sec.-treas. 1959—) bar assns., Ohio Assn. County Ct. Judges (pres. 1969-73). Home: 635 Prospect St Leipsic OH 45856 Office: 116 E Main St Leipsic OH 45856 Tel (419) 943-3107

HUPF, PAUL MICHAEL, b. Buffalo, Dec. 21, 1921; A.B., Canisius Coll., 1943; J.D. cum laude, U. San Francisco, 1948. Admitted to Calif. bar, 1949; mem. firms Hupf & Etcheverry, Daly City, Calif., 1957-66, Hupf, Etcheverry & Blum, Daly City, 1969-75; individual practice law, San Francisco, 1949-57; sr. partner firm Paul M. Hupf & Frank B. Blum, Jr., and predecessor, Daly City, 1957—; judge San Mateo County Municipal Ct., No. Jud. Dist., 1966-69; mem. Daly City Council, 1956, 57, 72-76; city atty. Daly City, 1957-66. Pres. San Francisco Archdiocesan Council of Cath. Men., 1966-68; chmn. bd. trustees Dominican Coll., San Rafael, Calif., 1969-74. Mem. San Francisco, San Mateo County bar assns., State Bar Calif. (disciplinary bd.), Daly City C. of C. (pres. 1972-73, dir.). Recipient St. Thomas More award Nat. Council Cath. Men, Washington, 1968. Office: 7316 Mission St Daly City CA 94014 Tel (415) 756-5500

HUPY, MICHAEL FREDERICK, b. Milw., Oct. 11, 1946; B.A., Marquette U., 1968, J.D., 1972. Admitted to Wis. bar, 1972, U.S. Supreme Ct. bar, 1976; since practiced in Milw. partner firm Hupy & Glasschroeder, 1972-76, Hausmann, McNally & Hupy, 1976—. Mem. Wis., Milw., Milw. Jr., Am. bar assns., Assn. Trial Lawyers Am. Home: 872 W Laramie Ln Bayside WI 53217 Office: 633 W Wisconsin Ave Suite 1815 Milwaukee WI 53203 Tel (414) 271-5300

HURLEY, JAMES HENRY, JR., b. Washington, Oct. 6, 1940; B.A., U. Calif., Berkeley, 1962; LL.B., U. Calif., San Francisco, 1965. Admitted to Calif. bar, 1966; mem. firm Price, Postell & Parma, Santa Barbara, Calif., 1966—. Mem. Santa Barbara County, Calif., Am. bar assns. Office: 200 E Carrillo St Santa Barbara CA 93102 Tel (805) 962-0011

HURLEY, JOHN MICHAEL, JR., b. Cambridge, Mass., May 2, 1943; B.S. in Civil Engring., U. Mass. at Amherst, 1965; J.D., Boston Coll. Law Sch., 1971. Admitted to Mass. bar, 1972, Vt. bar, 1974, N.H. bar, 1976; legal asst. Project Place, Boston, 1971-72; adviser Medfield-Norfolk Prison Project, Medfield, Mass., 1973-74; asso. with Robert O'Donnell, Woodstock, Vt., 1974-76; partner firm Ingram & Hurley, Canaan, Vt., 1975—. Mem. Citizens Participatory Politics, Boston, 1970-73; active Ams. for Democratic Action, Vietnam Vets. Against War. Mem. Am., Mass., Vt., N.H. bar assns. Tel (617) 256-8695

HURLEY, MICHAEL EDWARD, b. Pontiac, Mich., Mar. 29, 1941; B.A. cum laude, Carroll Coll., 1963; LL.B., U. San Francisco, 1966. Admitted to Ariz. bar, 1966; atty. Maricopa County, Ariz., 1966-68; city prosecutor, Scottsdale, Ariz., 1968-69; individual practice law, Phoenix, 1969—. Pres., Phoenix Boys Club 1977—. Mem. Maricopa, Ariz. bar assns. Home: 14820 N Skokie Ct Phoenix AZ 85022 Office: 91 E Monte Vista Rd Phoenix AZ 85004 Tel (602) 257-8011

HURLEY, PATRICK WEEMS, b. Amarillo, Tex., May 23, 1937; B.M.E., Stanford U., 1960; M.M.E., U. N.Mex., 1963, J.D., 1968. Admitted to N.Mex. bar, 1968; mem. firm Keleher & McLeod, Albuquerque, 1968—. Mem. Am. Bar Assn. Contbr. articles to Natural Resources Jour. Office: PO Drawer AA Albuquerque NM 87103 Tel (505) 842-6262

HURLEY, THOMAS MICHAEL, JR., b. Washington, Aug. 16, 1945; B.S., St. Joseph's Coll., Phila., 1967; J.D., Vanderbilt U., 1972. Admitted to Ga. bar, 1972; asso. firm Smith, Cohen, Ringel, Kohler & Martin, Atlanta, 1972—. Asso. mng. editor Vanderbilt Law Rev., 1971-72. Home: 1185 Collier Rd NW Atlanta GA 30318 Office: 2400 1st Nat Bank Tower Atlanta GA 30303 Tel (404) 658-1200

HURLEY, TROY CLINTON, b. Lubbock, Tex., Feb. 25, 1944; B.A. in Govt., Tex. Tech. U., 1967, J.D., 1970. Admitted to Tex. bar, 1970; asst. dist. atty. Lubbock County (Tex.), 1970-72, Bell County (Tex.), 1973-76; partner firm Odom & Hurley, Killeen, Tex., 1976—; instr. Temple (Tex.) Jr. Coll., 1974—. Mem. Bell-Lampasas-Mills Bar Assn., Tex. Dist. and County Atty. Assn., Tex. Narcotics Officers Assn., Central Tex. Peace Officers Assn., Killeen C. of C. Home: 4609 Spanish Oak St Temple TX 76501 Office: 303 W Rancier St Killeen TX 76541 Tel (817) 634-2621

HURSH, JOHN RAY, b. Scottsbluff, Nebr., Feb. 16, 1943; B.A., U. Wyo., 1965, J.D., 1968. Admitted to Wyo. bar, 1968, U.S. Supreme Ct. bar, 1974; with Judge Adv. Gen. Corps, USMC, 1968-72; asso. Paul B. Godfrey, Cheyenne, Wyo., 1972; individual practice law, Riverton, Wyo., 1973-74; mem. firm Hamilton, Hursh & Crofts, P.C., Riverton, Wyo., 1974—; mem. Wyo. Ho. of Reps., 1974—, mem. legis. judiciary com.; pres. Hursh Agy., Inc., Riverton, dir. 1st Guarantee Savs. & Loan, Riverton. Mem. Wyo., Am. bar assns., Wyo. State Bar, Wyo. State, Am. trial lawyers assns. Home: West of Riverton WY 82501 Office: 105-107 S 6th St E Riverton WY 82501 Tel (307) 856-4157

HURST, JAMES WILLARD, b. Rockford, Ill. Oct. 6, 1910; B.A., Williams Coll., 1932; LL.B., Harvard, 1935; M.A., Cambridge (Eng.) U., 1967. Admitted to Ill. bar, 1936, Wis. bar, 1950; Mem. faculty Law Sch., U. Wis., Madison, 1937—, prof., 1946—, Vilas prof., 1962—; vis. prof. Northwestern U., 1939, Stanford, 1950, 62, U. Utah, 1956; Pitt prof. Am. history and instns. Cambridge U., 1967-68. Mem. Wis. Bar Assn., Am. Philos. Soc., Am. Acad. Arts and Scis. Social Sci. Research Council (past bd. dirs.). Author numerous books including: The Growth of American Law, 1950; Law and the Conditions of Freedom in the 19th Century United States, 1956; Law and Social Process in United States History, 1960; Law and Economic Growth, 1964; The Legitimacy of the Business Corporation, 1970; A Legal History of Money in the United States, 1973; contbr. articles to profl. jours. Home: 3972 Plymouth Circle Madison WI 53705 Office: Law School University of Wisconsin Madison WI 53706

HURST, QUINCY BYRUM, JR., b. Hot Springs, Ark., Mar. 14, 1949; B.S., U. Ark., 1971, J.D., 1974. Admitted to Ark. bar, 1974, since practiced in Hot Springs. Mem. Garland County (Ark.) Democratic Central Com. Mem. Ark., Garland County, Am. bar assns., Am. Trial Lawyers Assn. Home: 1 Circle Dr Hot Springs AR 71901 Office: 201 Woodbine St Hot Springs AR 71901 Tel (501) 623-2565

HURT, WILLIAM EWING, b. Cheyenne, Wyo., Mar. 29, 1945; B.A., U. Kans., 1967; postgrad. U. London, 1967; J.D., Cumberland Sch. Law, 1972. Admitted to Mo. bar, 1972; clk. firm Denaburg, Schoel & Meyerson, Birmingham, Ala., 1971; clk. Mo. Ct. Appeals, Kansas City, 1971-72; asst. counsel Mo. Div. Welfare, Jefferson City, 1973-74; asst. dir. continuing legal edn. Mo. Bar Center, Jefferson City, 1974—. Active Legal Aid Soc., Birmingham, 1970, Jefferson City Bicentennial Ensemble, 1976—; bd. dirs. Jefferson City Meth. Ch., 1975—. Mem. Am. Bar Assn., Smithsonian Assos., Nat. Dist. Attys. Assn., Assn. Continuing Legal Edn. Adminstrs., Nat. Assn. Pros. Coordinators, Mo. Pros. Attys. Assn. (staff coordinator 1974—), Cordell Hall Internat. Law Soc., U. Kans. Alumni Assn. Home: 320 Washington St Jefferson City MO 65101 Office: 326 Monroe St Jefferson City MO 65101 Tel (314) 635-4128

HURWITZ, DAVID LYMAN, b. N.Y.C., Feb. 22, 1928; A.B., Bucknell U., 1947; J.D., Columbia, 1950. Admitted to N.Y. bar, 1951, U.S. Dist. Ct. So. Dist. N.Y. bar, 1957, U.S. Dist. Ct. Eastern Dist. N.Y. bar, 1957, U.S. Supreme Ct. bar, 1975, U.S. Ct. Appeals 2d Circuit bar, 1975; since practiced in N.Y.C., asso. firm Blumberg, Miller, Aberman & Singer, 1950-51; spl. dist. atty. gen., N.Y. State, 1951-54; asso. firm Tretter & Stern, 1954-57; partner firm Hurwitz & Vail, 1957—; pres. The Algonquin Press, Inc., 1965—; pres. Corp. Adminstrn., Inc., 1966—; lectr. Practising Law Inst. 1971-72. Trustee Broadcasting Found. Am., 1966-71, Bucknell U., 1975—; chmn. Nat. Wills and Bequests Com. NCCJ, 1974—; chmn. Bequest Com., Dowling Coll., 1974—. Mem. N.Y. State Bar Assn., Phi Beta Kappa. Home: Hickory Kingdom Rd Bedford NY 10506 Office: 122 E 42d St New York City NY 10017 Tel (212) OX7-3140

HURWITZ, ISADORE BERNARD, b. N.Y.C., Oct. 2, 1914; LL.B., Bklyn. Law Sch., 1937. Admitted to N.Y. State bar, 1938, U.S. Supreme Ct. bar, 1964; individual practice law, N.Y.C. Mem. N.Y. County Lawyers Assn. Office: 10 E 40 St New York City NY 10016 Tel (212) 889-1880

HURWITZ, STEPHEN AVRAM, b. New Bedford, Mass., June 5, 1943; A.B., Cornell U., 1965, J.D., 1968. Admitted to Mass. bar, 1968; asso. firm Gaston, Snow, Motley & Holt, Boston, 1969-73; partner firm Testa, Hurwitz & Thibeault, Boston, 1973—; v.p. Cornell Legal Aid Clinic, 1967-68. Mem. Am., Boston bar assns., Am. Arbitration Assn. (mem. comml. panel 1976—). Office: 100 Federal St Boston MA 02110 Tel (617) 956-4500

HUSTED, ELDON LYNN, b. St. Louis, Sept. 9, 1933; B.S., Millikin U., 1955; J.D., U. Wis., 1958. Admitted to Wis. bar, 1958, Ariz. bar, 1974; practice law, Madison, Wis., 1958; asst. exec. dir. State Bar Wis., 1960-64; exec. dir. State Bar Ariz., Phoenix, 1964—. Mem. Joint Conf. Merit Selection of Judges, 1973-74; rep. Ariz. Council of Professions, 1968-74. Mem. Am. (council bar activities sect. 1969-72), Maricopa County bar assns., Nat. Assn. Bar Execs. (pres. 1975-76), Western States Bar Conf. (sec. 1970-72), Phoenix Lawyers Club (dir. 1972—), State Bar Wis., State Bar Ariz., Phi Delta Phi, Delta Sigma Phi. Home: 3623 E Colter St Phoenix AZ 85018 Office: 234 N Central St Phoenix AZ 85004 Tel (602) 252-4804*

HUSTON, CRAIG, b. Phila., Aug. 16, 1904; A.B., Princeton, 1926; LL.B., Temple U., 1936. Admitted to Pa. bar, 1938, U.S. Tax Ct., bar, 1966; individual practice law, Phila., 1937—. Mem. Am., Phila., bar assns., Shakespearean Authorship Soc. London, Shakespeare Oxford Soc. Washington. Author: The Shakespeare Authorship Question, Evidence for Edward de Vere, 17th Earl of Oxford, 1971. Home: The Studio Lehman Ln Philadelphia PA 19144 Office: 1400 Philadelphia Bank Bldg Philadelphia PA 19107 Tel (215) LO3-1536

HUSTON, ROBERT KLINE, b. Akron, Ohio, Nov. 27, 1916; B.S. in Commerce and B.A., U. Ala., 1940, J.D., 1942. Admitted to Ohio bar, 1946; asst. to dean of men U. Ala., 1940-42; spl. agt. Ohio Bell Telephone Co., Cleve., 1945-51, atty., 1951-61, gen. atty., 1961-64, gen. solicitor, 1964—; dir. Chillicothe Telephone Co. (Ohio). Mem. Ohio Constnl. Revision Commn., 1974—. Mem. Am., Ohio, Cuyahoga County, Cleve. bar assns. Home: 2359 Mirmar Blvd University Heights OH 44118 Office: 100 Erieview Plaza Cleveland OH 44114 Tel (216) 822-4723

HUSZAGH, ELENIE KOSTOPOULOS, b. Portland, Oreg., May 1, 1937; A.B., U. Chgo., 1957; J.D., John Marshall Law Sch., 1963. Admitted to Ill. bar, 1963, U.S. Dist. Ct. bar for No. Dist. Ill., 1965; house counsel Liberty Loan Corp., Chgo., 1963-64; asso. firm A.J. Geo-Karis, Zion, Ill., 1964-65; partner firm Huszagh & Huszagh, Glenview, Ill., 1965-70; pres. firm Miller & Huszagh, Ltd., Glenview, 1970—. Mem. council Greek Orthodox Archdioces of North and South Am., 1975—. Mem. Chgo., Women's, Hellenic bar assns. Named Woman of Month, Lerner Press, Apr. 1975. Home: River Ridge Northbrook IL 60062 Office: 800 Waukegan Rd Glenview IL 60025 Tel (312) 729-3320

HUTCHESON, ELWOOD, b. Montesano, Wash., Apr. 24, 1902; A.B., U. Wash., 1922, LL.B. cum laude, 1925. Admitted to Wash. bar, 1925; asso. firm Skeel, Seattle, 1925-29; partner firm Cheney & Hutcheson, Yakima, Wash., 1929-47; individual practice law, Yakima, 1947—; mem. State Bd. Examiners, 1946-52; city atty. Yakima, 1953-56. Mem. Am., Wash., Yakima County bar assns., Am. Judicature Soc. Home: 316 N 42d Ave Yakima WA 98908 Office: 314 Miller Bldg Yakima WA 98901 Tel (509) 248-3550

HUTCHESON, HOMER ALBERS, b. Patterson, N.J., Apr. 11, 1907; student Alfred U., 1925; B.S., Hobart Coll., 1929; J.D., Cornell U., 1931. Law clk. firm Andrew Edward Krieger, Salamanca, N.Y., 1931-34; admitted to N.Y. bar, 1935, U.S. Supreme Ct. bar; individual practice law, Salamanca, 1936—; acting judge Salamanca Municipal Ct., 1938-70; corp. counsel City of Salamanca, 1964-68. Mem. Am., N.Y. State, Cattaraugus County (N.Y.) bar assns. Home: 60 Summit St Salamanca NY 14779 Office: 111 Main St Salamanca NY 14779 Tel (716) 945-3247

HUTCHESON, JON SCOTT, b. Springfield, Mo., July 18, 1949; B.A., U. Mo., 1971, J.D., 1973. Admitted to Mo. bar, 1974; partner firm Couert and Hutcheson, Houston, Mo., 1974—; pros. atty. Texas County (Mo.), 1975—. Mem. Texas County Mental Health Commn. Mem. Am., Mo., Tex. County (past pres.) bar assns., Houston C. of C., Phi Alpha Delta, Sigma Nu. Home: PO Box 42 Houston MO 65483 Office: 109 N Grand St Houston MO 65483 Tel (417) 967-4178

HUTCHINGS, JOHN A., b. Chgo., July 12, 1922; LL.B., Northwestern U., 1949. Admitted to Ill. bar, 1949; asso. firm Taylor, Miller, Busch & Magner, Chgo., 1949-55, partner, 1955-62; partner firm Taylor, Miller, Magner, Sprowl & Hutchings, Chgo., 1962—. Fellow Am. Coll. Trial Lawyers, Soc. Trial Lawyers; mem. Am., Ill., Chgo. bar assns. Home: 1260 Carol Ln Deerfield IL 60015 Office: 120 S LaSalle St Chicago IL 60603 Tel (312) 782-6070

HUTCHINSON, EVERETT, b. Hempstead, Tex., Jan. 2, 1915; B.B.A., U. Tex., 1939; LL.B., J.D., 1940. Admitted to Tex. bar, 1939, D.C. bar, 1963; individual practice law, Hempstead and Austin, Tex., 1940-55; partner firm Fulbright & Jaworski, Washington, 1968—; mem. Tex. Legis., 1941-45; served to capt. JAG USN, 1942-45; mem. ICC, 1955-65, chmn., 1961; dep. sec. U.S. Dept. Transp., Washington, 1966-68. Mem. State Bar Tex., Am., Fed., D.C. bar assns., Motor Carrier Lawyers Assn., ICC Practitioners Assn., Nat. Def. Transp. Assn. (pres. 1975-77), Tex. Breakfast Club (pres. 1970), Tex. State Soc. of D.C. (pres. 1964-65), U. Tex. Ex-Students (pres. D.C. chpt. 1958-59). Contbr. articles to legal jours. Home: 5401 Albemarle St Washington DC 20016 Office: 1150 Connecticut Ave NW Suite 400 Washington DC 20036 Tel (202) 452-6844

HUTCHINSON, JAMES DANIEL, b. Wilkes-Barre, Pa., June 17, 1944; B.A., Dickinson Coll., 1965; J.D., Villanova U., 1968. Admitted to Pa. bar, 1969, D.C. bar, 1971; adminstr. pension and welfare benefit programs U.S. Dept. Labor, Washington, 1975-76; partner firm Steptoe & Johnson, Washington, 1976—; asso. dep. atty. gen. U.S. Dept. Justice, 1974-75. Mem. Am., D.C., Pa. bar assns. Mem. adv. bd. BNA Pension Reporter; contbr. articles to profl. jours. Office: 1250 Connecticut Ave NW Washington DC 20036 Tel (202) 862-2087

HUTCHINSON, PETER JAMES, b. Roseburg, Oreg., Oct. 7, 1946; B.S., U. Idaho, 1968, J.D., 1973. Admitted to Idaho bar, 1973; partner firm Mosley & Hutchinson, St. Maries, Idaho, 1973-75; pros. atty. Benewah County (Idaho), St. Maries, 1974—, City of St. Maries, 1974—. Home: Route 1 Box 285A Saint Maries ID 83861 Office: Courthouse Saint Maries ID 83861 Tel (208) 245-2596

HUTCHISON, ROBERT NICHOLAS, b. Chgo., Dec. 16, 1939; J.D., DePaul U., 1963. Admitted to Ill. bar, 1963, Fla. bar, 1972; asst. state's atty. Cook County (Ill.), 1963-67, 70-71; individual practice law, Chgo., 1969; partner firm Sheridan Hutchison & Sheridan, Chgo., 1967-69; project dir. Ill. Law Enforcement Commn., Chgo., 1969-70; exec. dir. Ill. State's Attys. Assn., Hinsdale, 1971-75, Ill. Prosecutors' Adv. Council, Chgo., 1975—. Pres., Riverside (Ill.) Community Fund, 1975; mem. Riverside Bd. Edn., 1976—. Mem. Am., Ill. bar assns., Nat. Dist. Attys. Assn., Ill. State's Attys. Assn. Home: 319 Gatesby Rd Riverside IL 60546 Office: 100 N LaSalle St suite 1812 Chicago IL 60602 Tel (312) 793-3830

HUTCHISON, STANLEY PHILIP, b. Joliet, Ill., Nov. 22, 1923; B.S., Northwestern U., 1947; LL.B., Chgo-Kent Coll. Law, 1951. Admitted to Ill. bar, 1951; with Washington Nat. Ins. Co., Evanston, Ill., 1947—, gen. counsel, 1960-70, v.p., 1963-66, exec. v.p., 1966-67, sec., 1967-70, chmn. exec. com., 1970-74, vice chmn. bd., 1974-76, chmn. bd., chief exec. officer, 1976—; exec. v.p., gen. counsel, sec., mem. exec. com. Washington Nat. Corp., Evanston, 1968-70, pres., 1970—, mem. exec. com., 1970-74, chmn. exec. com., 1974—, also dir.; dir. Anchor Corp., Elizabeth, N.J., Anchor Funds, Elizabeth, Anchor Nat. Life Ins. Co., Phoenix, Anchor Nat. Fin. Services, Inc., Phoenix, Washington Nat. Devel. Co., Evanston, Washington Nat. Life Ins. Co. of N.Y., N.Y.C. Pub. mem. Ill. Bd. Vocat. Edn. and Rehab., 1971-72. Mem. Am., Ill. bar assns., Am. Mgmt. Assn., Assn. Life Ins. Counsel (hon.), Am. Council Life Ins. (v.p. Ill. chpt. 1970—), Evanston C. of C. (pres. 1973-74). Phi Delta Phi, Phi Gamma Delta. Home: 3001 Indian Wood Rd Wilmette IL 60091 Office: 1630 Chicago Ave Evanston IL 60201 Tel (312) 866-3000

HUTT, PETER BARTON, b. Buffalo, Nov. 16, 1934; A.B., Yale, 1956; LL.B., Harvard, 1959; LL.M., N.Y. U., 1960. Admitted to N.Y. State bar, 1959, D.C. bar, 1961, U.S. Supreme Ct. bar, 1967; asso. firm Covington & Burling, Washington, 1960-68, partner, 1968-71, 75—; chief counsel FDA, Washington, 1971-75; dir. Legal Action Center, N.Y.C., Am. Sterilizer Corp., Erie, Pa.; advisory panel regulatory reform U.S. Senate Com. Govt. Ops.; mem. Washington Lawyers Commn. for Civil Rights Under Law. Bd. dirs. Sidwell Friends Sch., Washington. Mem. Inst. Med., Nat. Acad. Scis. Recipient Arthur S. Flemming award, 1974, Award Merit, FDA, 1973, 75, Distinguished Service award, HEW, 1974. Home: 5325 Chamberlin Ave Chevy Chase MD 20015 Office: 888 16th St NW Washington DC 20006 Tel (202) 452-6300

HUTTASH, ROBERT ALEXANDER, b. Jacksonville, Tex., Sept. 4, 1941; B.A., Baylor U., 1962; J.D., U. Tex., 1965. Admitted to Tex. bar, 1965, U.S. Supreme Ct. bar, 1970; asst. dist. atty. Travis County (Tex.), 1965-71; asst. state pros. atty. Tex. Ct. Criminal Appeals, Austin, 1971-73, asst. adminstrn., 1971, 1973—. Mem. Travis County Bar Assn., Am. Judicature Soc. Home: 8202 Millway Dr Austin TX 78758 Office: Box 12308 Capitol Station Austin TX 78711 Tel (512) 475-5936

HUTTENBRAUCK, DANIEL R., b. N.Y.C., July 9, 1912; B.S., Fordham U., 1937, LL.B., 1941, J.D., 1968. Admitted to N.Y. bar, 1942, U.S. Dist. Ct. bar So. Dist. N.Y., 1944, Eastern Dist. N.Y., 1951, Western Dist. N.Y., 1967, U.S. Customs Ct. bar, 1968, Supreme Ct. U.S. bar, 1953; dist. atty. N.Y. County, N.Y.C., 1941-46; sr. partner firm Mendes & Mount, N.Y.C., 1946—. Mem. adv. bd. Tulane U. Admiralty Law Inst. Mem. Am., N.Y. State bar assns., Maritime Law Assn., Internat. Assn. Ins. Counsel, The Scribes, Copyright Soc. Contbr. to Jour. Internat. Assn. Ins. Counsel. Home: 535 E 86th St New York City NY 10028 Office: 27 William St New York City NY 10005 Tel (212) 344-7100

HUTTON, JAMES LAWRENCE, b. Marion, Va., June 29, 1932; B.A., Emory and Henry Coll., 1957; LL.B., U. Richmond, 1965. Admitted to Va. bar, 1965; mem. firm Gilmer, Sadler, Ingram, Sutherland and Hutton, Blacksburg, Va., 1965—; judge Blacksburg Municipal Ct., 1968-73; substitute judge Montgomery County and Blacksburg Dist. Ct., 1969-74. Mem. Blacksburg C. of C., Am., Va., Pulaski County, Montgomery-Floyd-Radford bar assns., Phi Delta Phi. Home: 305 Hemlock Dr Blacksburg VA 24060 Office: PO Box 908 Blacksburg VA 24060 Tel (703) 552-1061

HUYCK, WILLIAM THOMAS, b. Des Moines, Apr. 10, 1938; B.A., Dartmouth, 1960; J.D., U. Chgo., 1963. Admitted to Ill. bar, 1963; trial atty. antitrust div. Dept. Justice, Chgo., 1963-68; asst. U.S. atty. No. Dist. Ill., 1968-73; partner firm Ross, Hardies, O'Keffe, Babcock & Parsons, Chgo., 1973—. Mem. Am., Chgo. bar assns., Chgo. Council of Lawyers. Home: 1718 E 55th St Chicago IL 60615 Office: One IBM Plaza Chicago IL 60611 Tel (312) 467-9300

HVASS, CHARLES T., b. N.Y.C., Apr. 9, 1922; LL.B. with honors, U. Tex., 1946. Admitted to Tex. bar, 1946, Minn. bar, 1947, U.S. Supreme Ct. bar, 1961; now mem. firm Hvass, Weisman & King, Mpls.; trustee Roscoe-Pound-Am. Trial Lawyers Assn. Found., 1964-71; mem. Minn. Bd. Profl. Responsibility, 1973—. Fellow Internat. Soc. Barristers (pres. bd. govs. 1971), Internat. Acad. Trial Lawyers, Am. Coll. Trial Lawyers; mem. Hennepin County (pres. 1976-77), Minn. State (gov. 1973-75), Am. bar assns., Assn. Trial Lawyers Am. (nat. appellate com. 1956—, chmn. ins. com. 1966-72), Am. Judicature Soc., Law Sci. Acad. Am., Am. Bd. Trail Advs. (diplomate), Chancellors, Phi Delta Phi. Bd. editors Tex. Law Rev., 1945-46. Office: 715 Cargill Bldg North Star Center Minneapolis MN 55402 Tel (612) 333-0201*

HYAMS, MILTON MARK, b. Ross, Calif., Jan. 27, 1943; B.A., U. San Francisco, 1964, J.D., 1967. Admitted to Calif. bar, 1968; individual practice law, San Rafael, Calif., 1969; dep. dist. atty. Marin County (Calif.), 1970—, chief Family Support div., 1971—; mem. Calif. Food Stamp Fraud Task Force, 1973, Calif. Child Stealing Task Force, 1974-75, Calif. Family Support Council, also past pres. Mem. Calif. Dist. Attys. Assn., Calif., Marin County bar assns., Nat. Reciprocal and Family Support Enforcement Assn., Phi Alpha Delta. Office: Hall of Justice San Rafael CA 94903 Tel (415) 479-1100

HYDE, DAVID ROWLEY, b. Norwalk, Conn., Aug. 21, 1929; A.B., Yale, 1951, LL.B., 1954. Admitted to Conn. bar, 1954, N.Y. bar, 1956, U.S. Supreme Ct. bar, 1969; asso. firm Cahill Gordon & Reindel, N.Y.C., 1954-59, 64-65, partner, 1966—; asst. U.S. atty. So. Dist. N.Y., 1959-63, chief civil div. U.S. Atty.'s Office, 1961-63. Editor in chief: Yale Law Jour., 1953-54. Home: 35 W 12th St New York City NY 10011 Office: 80 Pine St New York City NY 10005 Tel (212) 825-0100

HYDE, DEWITT STEPHEN, b. Washington, Mar. 21, 1909; J.D., George Washington U., 1935. Admitted to D.C. bar, 1935, M.D. bar, 1952; with Farm Credit Adminstrn., Washington, 1933-38; individual practice law, Washington and Bethesda, Md., 1938-59; instr. law Benjamin Franklin U., 1946-52, 60-71; asso. judge Municipal Ct. D.C., 1959-70; asso. judge D.C. Ct. of Gen. Sessions (now Superior Ct. D.C.), 1970—; mem. Md. Ho. of Dels., 1947-50, Md. Senate, 1950-51; mem. 83d-85th Congresses from 6th Md. Dist. Mem. The Barristers, Am. Bar Assn., Bar Assn. D.C., Lawyers Club. Home: 5606 McLean Dr Bethesda MD 20014 Office: 4th and E Sts NW room 316 Washington DC 20001 Tel (202) 727-1080

HYDE, JOHN GARY, b. Abilene, Tex., May 30, 1942; B.A., Hardin Simmons U., 1964; J.D., U. Tex., 1967. Admitted to Tex. bar, 1967; asst. city atty. Midland (Tex.), 1970-75; partner firm Freeman & Hyde, Midland, 1975—. Mem. Tex., Midland County, Midland County Jr. (pres. 1975-76), Am. bar assns. Named Midland Legal Secs. Boss of Year, 1973-74. Home: 2610 Terrace Ave Midland TX 79701 Office: 133 Western United Life Bldg Midland TX 79701 Tel (915) 683-6141

HYDE, ROBERT CUNNINGHAM, b. Sharon, Pa., Sept. 15, 1903; grad. Mercersburg Acad., 1921; student Kenyon Coll., 1925; LL.B., City Coll. Law and Fin., St. Louis, 1937. Admitted to Mo. bar, 1937; individual practice law, Poplar Bluff, Mo., 1937—. Pres. SE Mo. Council Boy Scouts Am., Cape Girardeau, Mo., 1955-58; pres. Poplar Bluff and Butler County (Mo.) United Fund, Poplar Bluff Sch. Bd., 1957-68. Mem. Am. (tax com.), Mo. (tax com.) bar assns. Contbr. articles to profl. publs. Home: 544 N 11th St Poplar Bluff MO 63901 Office: Commerce Bank Bldg Poplar Bluff MO 63901 Tel (314) 686-4141

HYDEN, JAMES WARREN, b. Ft. Smith, Ark., July 12, 1944; B.S. in Bus. Adminstrn., U. Ark., 1967, J.D., 1972; LL.M., Coll. William and Mary, 1973. Admitted to Ark. bar, 1972; counsel Dow Badische Co., Williamsburg, Va., 1973-74; asso. firm Coleman, Gantt, Ramsay & Cox, Pine Bluff, Ark., 1974—. Mem. Jefferson County, Ark., Am. bar assns. Home: 3401 Linden St Pine Bluff AR 71603 Office: Box 8509 Pine Bluff AR 71611 Tel (501) 534-5221

HYDER, ROBERT LEE, b. Howell County, Mo., Feb. 26, 1910. Admitted to Tex. bar, 1933, Mo. bar, 1934; first asst. atty. gen. State of Mo., 1938-41; asst. atty. gen. U.S., 1941-42; chief counsel Mo. Highway Commn., Jefferson City, 1951-74; atty. City of West Plains (Mo.), Willow Springs (Mo.), Mt. View (Mo.), Thayer (Mo.). Mayor of Jefferson City, 1975—. Mem. Mo., Cole County bar assns. Contbr. articles to legal jours. Registered profl. engr., Mo. Office: 202A E High St Jefferson City MO 65101 Tel (314) 634-3234

HYER, WILLIAM HENRY, b. Olathe, Kans., Oct. 3, 1920; B.S.B., U. Kans., 1942; J.D., U. So. Calif., 1948. Admitted to Calif. bar, 1949; mem. firm Hyer & Graeber, San Bernardino, Calif., 1949-64; bankruptcy judge U.S. Dist. Ct., San Bernardino, 1964—. Deacon Judson Baptist Ch., San Bernardino. Mem. Barristers of Calif. (pres.). Home: 3700 N Mountain St San Bernardino CA 92404 Office: 141 N Arrowhead St San Bernardino CA 92408 Tel (714) 383-5739

HYLAND, NATHANIEL E., b. Radcliffe, Iowa, Feb. 24, 1910; B.A., Iowa State Tchrs. Coll., 1938; LL.B., Drake U., 1953. Admitted to Iowa bar, 1954; tchr. rural schs., elementary and high sch., 1928-42, supt. Butler County Schs., 1942-51; dep. sheriff, chief civil div., Dept. Commn. of Safety, legal advisor Iowa State Dept. Pub Instruction, 1955-58; exec. sec. Des Moines Edn. Assn., 1958-60; individual practice law, Des Moines, 1961—. Home: 6600 SW 48th Ave Des Moines IA 50321 Office: 550 39th St Des Moines IA 50312 Tel (515) 255-3370

HYLAND, TIMOTHY JEROME, b. Monroe, Wis., Mar. 30, 1947; B.B.A., U. Wis., Whitewater, 1970; J.D., U. Houston, 1973. Admitted to Wis. bar, 1974; served with JAGC, U.S. Army, Ft. Campbell, Ky., 1975—. Mem. Am., Wis. bar assns. Home: E-106 2190 Memorial Dr Clarksville TN 37040 Office: Office of the Staff Judge Advocate Fort Campbell KY 42223 Tel (502) 798-6161

HYLAND, WILLIAM FRANCIS, b. Burlington, N.J., July 30, 1923; B.S. in Econs., U. Pa., 1944, LL.B., 1949. Admitted to N.J. bar, 1949, U.S. Supreme Ct. bar, 1960; mem. firm Hyland, Davis and Reberkenny, Cherry Hill, N.J., 1949-74; atty. gen. N.J., 1974—. Mem. N.J. Gen. Assembly from Camden County, 1954-61, speaker of house, 1958; acting gov. N.J., 1958; pres. N.J. Bd. Pub. Utility Commrs., also mem. cabinet Gov. Meyner and Gov. Hughes, 1961-68; chmn. N.J. Atomic Energy Council, 1968-69; chmn. N.J. Commn. Investigation, 1969-71; co-chmn. Reapportionment Commn. Chmn. Brazilian Mission Com., 1962-65. Del.-at-large Dem. Nat. Conv., 1964, del., 1968. Asso. trustee U. Pa. Decorated knight Order of St. Gregory (Pope Paul VI), 1964; recipient Outstanding Young Man in Govt. N.J. award N.J. Jaycees, 1958; Distinguished Service award Camden County Jaycees, 1954. Mem. Camden County Bar Assn. (pres. 1959), Nat. Assn. R.R. and Utilities Commrs. (exec. com. 1965-68), Phi Kappa Psi. Home: 201 Horse Shoe Ct Cherry Hill NJ 08034 Office: State House Annex Dept Law and Pub Safety Trenton NJ 08625*

HYMAN, ALLAN, b. N.Y.C., Jan. 24, 1907; B.S. in Econs., U. Pa., 1927; LL.B., St. John's U., N.Y.C., 1935. Admitted to N.Y. State bar, 1936, U.S. Supreme Ct. bar, 1958; individual practice law, N.Y.C., 1936-50, Freeport, N.Y., 1950-55; partner firm Kelly, Hyman & Deeley, Freeport, 1955-60, Kelly, Warburton, Hyman Deeley & Connolly, Mineola, N.Y., 1960-62, Warburton, Hyman, Deeley & Connolly, Mineola, 1960-66, Hyman & Deeley, Mineola, 1966-70; chmn. bd. firm Koeppel Hyman Sommer Lesnick & Ross, Mineola, 1970-72; pres. firm Hyman & Hyman, Mineola, 1972—. Mem. Nassau County (N.Y.), N.Y. State bar assns., Nassau Lawyers Assn. Office: 220 Old Country Rd Mineola NY 11501 Tel (516) 747-6301

HYMAN, JACOB DAVID, b. Boston, Dec. 6, 1909; A.B., Harvard, 1931, LL.B., 1934. Admitted to N.Y. State bar, 1935, U.S. Supreme Ct. bar, 1941; asso. firm Samuel Blumberg, N.Y.C., 1934-39; chief appellate sect., wage-hour div. Office of Solicitor, Dept. Labor, 1939-42; atty., chief ct. rev. div. Office of Price Adminstrn., Washington, 1942-46; asso. gen. counsel, 1945-46; prof. law State U.N.Y., Buffalo, 1946—, dean Sch. of Law, 1953-64. Chmn. charter revision com. City of Buffalo, 1956-59. Mem. Am., N.Y. State, Erie County bar assns., Nat. Acad. Arbitrators, Fed. Mediation and Conciliation Services, N.Y. State Mediation Bd., Am. Arbitration Assn. Contbr. articles to legal jours. Office: 410 O'Brian Hall State U New York North Campus Buffalo NY 14260 Tel (716) 636-2071

HYMAN, JEROME ELLIOT, b. Rosedale, Miss., Dec. 26, 1923; A.B., Coll. William and Mary, 1944; LL.B. magna cum laude, Harvard U., 1947. Admitted to N.Y. State bar, 1949, D.C. bar, 1960; mem. fgn. funds control staff Dept. Treasury, U.S. Mil. Govt., Frankfurt and Berlin, Germany, 1945-46; law clk. to judge, U.S. Ct. Appeals, Boston, 1947-48; asso. firm Cleary, Gottlieb, Steen & Hamilton, N.Y.C., 1948-58, partner, 1959—; bd. dirs., mem. exec. com. Practicing Law Inst., N.Y.C., 1972—. Pres., Lexington Democratic Club, N.Y.C., 1956-58. Mem. Am. Bar Assn., Assn. Bar N.Y.C., Am. Law Inst., Phi Beta Kappa. Bd. editors Harvard Law Rev., 1945-47. Home: 1125 Park Ave New York City NY 10028 Office: Cleary Gottlieb Steen & Hamilton 1 State St Plaza New York City NY 10004 Tel (212) 344-0600

HYMAN, MARSHAL JAY, b. Wilkes-Barre, Pa., Dec. 15, 1945; B.S., Temple U., 1967; J.D. magna cum laude, U. Pitts., 1972. Admitted to Pa. bar, 1972; sr. tax accountant Arthur Young & Co., Pitts., 1972-75; asst. tax mgr. Dynalectron Corp., McLean, Va., 1975—; tax instr. C.P.A. rev. course, Washington, 1975—. Vice-pres. Action for a Cleaner Environment, Pits., 1973-75. Mem. Am. Bar Assn., Am., D.C. insts. C.P.A.'s, Beta Gamma Sigma, Order of Coif. Home: 19 Honey Brook Ln Gaithersburg MD 20760 Office: 1313 Dolly Madison Blvd McLean VA 22101 Tel (703) 356-0480

HYMAN, MILTON BERNARD, b. Los Angeles, Nov. 19, 1941; B.A., U. Calif., 1963; J.D. (Sheldon Travelling fellow), Harvard, 1966. Admitted to Calif. bar, 1967; asst. to gen. counsel Office Sec. of the Army, Washington, 1967-70; asso. firm Irell & Manella, Los Angeles, 1971-73, partner, 1973—; lectr. in field. Bd. dirs. Camp Ramah, Los Angeles, 1974—, v.p., 1976. Mem. Am. Bar Assn. Office: 1800 Ave of the Stars Los Angeles CA 90067 Tel (213) 277-1010

HYMAN, MONTAGUE ALLAN, b. N.Y.C., Apr. 19, 1941; LL.B., St. John's U., 1965. Admitted to N.Y. State bar, 1965, U.S. Supreme Ct. bar, 1973; mem. firm Hyman & Deeley, Mineola, N.Y., 1966-69, Koeppel, Hyman, Sommer, Lesnick & Ross, P.C., Mineola, 1969-73, Hyman & Hyman, profl. corp., Mineola, 1973—; lectr. in field. Mem. Nassau County Bar Assn., Nassau Lawyers Assn. Contbr. articles to legal publs. Home: 21 Bondsburry Ln Melville NY 11746 Office: 220 Old Country Rd Mineola NY 11501 Tel (516) 747-6301

HYMAN, PETER DEWITT, b. Florence, S.C., July 11, 1927; LL.B., U. S.C., 1954; LL.M., Harvard, 1970. Admitted to S.C. bar, 1953, U.S. Supreme Ct. bar, 1961; partner firm Hyman, Morgan & Brown, Florence, 1974—; gen. counsel Peoples Bank of S.C.; magistrate Florence County, 1955-59; mem. S.C. Ho. of Reps., 1960-69, chmn. sub-com. on higher edn., 1974—. Mem. S.C., Am. bar assns., Am., S.C. trial lawyers assns. Home: 439 Whitman Ave Florence SC 29501 Office: 170 Courthouse Sq PO Box 1770 Florence SC 29503 Tel (803) 662-6321

HYMERS, GEORGE WILLIAM, JR., b. Jones County, Miss., Apr. 22, 1913; LL.B., Cumberland U., Lebanon, Tenn., 1938. Admitted to Miss. bar, 1939, Tenn. bar, 1972; spl. agt. FBI, 1940-65; dir. personnel, in charge security Jackson-Madison County (Tenn.) Gen. Hosp., 1966-74; dist. atty. gen. Tenn. 12th Jud. Dist., 1974—. Mem. Miss. State, Tenn. State, Jackson-Madison County bar assns. Tel (901) 424-8632

HYNDMAN, EDWARD ANTHONY, JR., b. New Orleans, Nov. 27, 1945; B.S. cum laude, Spring Hill Coll., 1965; J.D., Tulane U., 1967; LL.M. in Taxation, N.Y. U., 1968. Admitted to Ala., La. bars, 1967; partner firm Hand, Arendall, Bedsole, Greaves & Johnston, Mobile, Ala., 1974—. Mem. Am., La., Ala. bar assns., Order of Coif, Phi Alpha Delta. Home: 5962 N Chalet Dr Mobile AL 36608 Office: First National Bank Bldg Mobile AL 36601 Tel (205) 432-5511

HYNES, JOHN DENNIS, b. Billings, Mont., Sept. 9, 1936; B.A., U. Colo., 1958, LL.B., 1960. Admitted to Colo. bar, 1960, N.Y. State bar, 1961. Teaching fellow Columbia Law Sch., N.Y.C., 1960-61; asso. firm Shearman & Sterling, N.Y.C., 1961-64; prof. law U. Colo., Boulder, 1964—. Mem. Colo. Bar Assn. Author: Agency-Partnership, Cases, Materials and Problems, 1974. Home: 830 20th St Apt 302 Boulder CO 80302 Office: Sch Law U Colo Boulder CO 80309 Tel (303) 492-7013

IANNONE, ELEANOR, b. Endicott, N.Y., Oct. 25, 1925; A.B., Houghton Coll., 1947; LL.B., Albany Law Sch., 1950. Admitted to N.Y. bar, 1951; mem. firm Chernin and Gold, Binghamton, N.Y.; counsel to N.Y. State Senate Majority Leader, 1975—. Mem. Am., N.Y., Broome County bar assns., Nat. Assn. Women Lawyers (pres. 1976-77). Office: 71 State St Binghamton NY 13902*

IANNUZZI, JOHN NICHOLAS, b. N.Y.C., May 31, 1935; B.S., Fordham Coll., 1956; J.D., N.Y. Law Sch., 1962. Admitted to N.Y. bar 1962, U.S. Supreme Ct. bar, 1971; asso. firm Broder and Levine, N.Y.C., 1962-63; partner firm Iannuzzi and Iannuzzi, N.Y.C., 1963—; asst. counsel to N.Y. Gov.'s Com. to Revise Drug Laws. Mem. Fed., Am., N.Y. State bar assns., Assn Bar City N.Y., New York County Lawyers Assn., Columbian Lawyers Assn. Author: (novels) What's Happening, 1963; Part 35, 1970; Sicilian Defense, 1973; Courthouse, 1975. Office: 233 Broadway New York City NY 10007 Tel (212) BA7-9595

I'ANSON, LAWRENCE WARREN, b. Portsmouth, Va., Apr. 21, 1907; A.B., Coll. William and Mary, 1928, LL.D., 1964; LL.B., U. Va., 1931. Admitted to Va. bar, 1931; practiced in Portsmouth, 1931-41; commonwealth's atty., Portsmouth, 1938-41; judge Ct. of Hustings, 1941-58; justice Supreme Ct. Va., 1958—, now chief justice; Mem. jud. council, 1948-70; chmn. com. that prepared Handbook for Jurors used in all cts. of record in Va. Mem. Council of Higher Edn. of Va., 1956-59. Pres. Beazley Found., Inc., Found. Boys Acad.; mem. exec. council Conf. Chief Justices. Trustee Eastern Va. Med. Sch. Found., Frederick Mil. Acad. Named First Citizen Portsmouth, 1946; recipient William and Mary Alumni medallion; U. Va. Sesquicentennial award; Lincoln Harley award Am. Judicature Soc.; Distinguished Service award Va. Trial Lawyers. Mem. Va. Bar Assn. (chmn. jud. sect. 1949), Phi Beta Kappa, Order of Coif, Pi Kappa Alpha, Omicrom Delta Kappa, Phi Alpha Delta. Home: 214 West Rd Portsmouth VA 23707 Office: Va Fed Bldg Penthouse Suite B Portsmouth VA 23704 also Supreme Court Bldg Richmond VA 23219*

IAVARONE, NICHOLAS PETER, b. Chgo., Nov. 20, 1940; B.A., No. Ill. U., 1966; J.D., Chgo.-Kent Coll. Law, 1974. Admitted to Ill. bar, 1974; with Cook County (Ill.) States Atty. Office, Chgo., 1974—, supr. Organized Crime div., 1975—. Mem. Am., Ill. bar assns., Nat. Dist. Atty. Assn. Office: 2600 S California St Chicago IL 60608 Tel (312) 542-2910

IBLER, STANLEY ALBERT, JR., b. Freeport, Ill., May 23, 1937; A.B., Stanford, 1959; J.D. with honors, Golden Gate U., 1965. Asso. firm Boccardo, Blum, Lull, Niland & Bell, San Jose, Calif., 1965-76, jr. partner, 1976—; admitted to Calif. bar, 1966, U.S. Ct. of Appeals

9th Circuit Ct. bar, 1966, U.S. Dist. Ct. for No. Dist. Calif. bar, 1966, U.S. Supreme Ct. bar, 1973. Mem. Calif., St. Clara (Calif.) bar assns. Office: 111 W Saint John St San Jose CA 95113 Tel (408) 298-5678

ICE, HARRY TREESE, b. Paulding, Ohio, Oct. 17, 1904; A.B., Butler U., 1926; LL.B., Harvard U., 1929; LL.D. (hon.), Ind. Central U., 1966. Admitted to Ind. bar, 1929, U.S. Supreme Ct. bar, 1936; asso. firm Ice Miller Donadio & Ryan, Indpls., 1929-32, partner, 1932—; dir. Am. United Life Ins. Co., Fairbanks Broadcasting Co., Union City Body Co., Inc. Bd. dirs. Community Hosp. Found., Indpls.; dir., past pres. bd. Crossroads council Boy Scouts Am., Indpls.; dir., v.p., exec. com. Greater Indpls. Progress Com.; bd. dirs., past pres. United Way of Greater Indpls. Fellow Ind. Acad.; mem. Am., Ind., Indpls. bar assns., Harvard Law Sch. Assn., Indpls. C. of C. (past v.p., dir.), Ind. State C. of C. (past v.p., dir.). Recipient Butler medal, 1969; Distinguished Eagle Scout award, Nat. Ct. Honor Boy Scouts Am., 1970; Silver Beaver award Crossroads council Boy Scouts Am., 1958. Home: 6370 Spring Mill Rd Indianapolis IN 46260 Office: 111 Monument Circle Indianapolis IN 46204 Tel (317) 635-1213

ICHIDA, WESLEY WAYNE, b. Honolulu, May 6, 1946; B.A., U. Mich., 1968; J.D., U. Colo., 1971. Admitted to Hawaii bar, 1971, U.S. Dist. Ct. for Dist. Hawaii bar, 1971, 9th Circuit Ct. Appeals bar, 1971; asso. firm Case, Kay, Clause & Lynch, Honolulu, 1971-74, partner, 1975—. Bd. dirs. Legal Aid Soc. Hawaii, Salvation Army. Mem. Hawaii State (pres. sect. young lawyers 1976), Am. bar assns., Am. Trial Lawyers Assn. Home: 836 Pomahina Pl Kailua Honolulu HI 96734 Office: 1100 1st Hawaiian Bank Bldg 165 S King St Honolulu HI 96813 Tel (808) 536-7261

IDAR, EDWARD, JR., b. Laredo, Tex., Dec. 28, 1920; B.J., U. Tex., 1949, J.D., 1956. Admitted to Tex. bar, 1956, U.S. Supreme Ct. bar, 1972; mem. firm Sanchez & Idar, McAllen, Tex., 1956-62; individual practice law, San Angelo, Tex., 1962-68; insp. Office of Inspection, OEO, Austin, Tex., 1968-70; dir. San Antonio office Mexican-Am. Legal Def. Fund, 1970-73; asst. atty. gen. State of Tex., Austin, 1973—. State chmn., exec. sec. Am. GI Forum of Tex., 1950-66. Mem. Am. Judicature Soc. Home: 8110 Shenandoah St Austin TX 78753 Office: Supreme Court Bldg Austin TX 78711 Tel (512) 475-3281

IDE, ROY WILLIAM, b. Geneva, Ill., Apr. 23, 1940; B.A. cum laude, Washington and Lee U., 1962; LL.B., U. Va., 1965; M.B.A., Ga. State U., 1972. Admitted to Ga. bar, 1966; law clk. to judge U.S. Ct. Appeals, 5th Circuit, 1965-66; asso. firm King & Spalding, Atlanta, 1966-71; partner firm Huie, Ware, Sterne, Brown & Ide, and predecessors, Atlanta, 1971—; co-founder, pres. Ga. Indigent Legal Services, 1970, dir., 1970-77. Mem. Am. (chmn. sect. young lawyers 1975-76), Atlanta bar assns., State Bar Ga. (pres. sect. younger lawyers 1974-75, gov. 1976-77), Ga. Criminal Justice Council (chmn. 1976-77), Nat. Legal Aid and Defender Assn. (dir. 1974-77, Arthur Van Briesen award 1974), Am. Judicature Soc. (dir. 1976—), Nat., Atlanta lawyers clubs. Recipient Atlanta's 5 Outstanding Young Men of Year award Atlanta Jaycees, 1976. Home: 2222 Mount Paran Rd Atlanta GA 30327 Office: 1200 Standard Fed Savings Bldg Atlanta GA 30303 Tel (404) 522-8700

IFERT, JAMES RICHARD, b. Punxsutawney, Pa., Dec. 21, 1921; B.S., Pa. State U., 1942; J.D., Dickinson Sch. Law, 1948. Admitted to Pa. bar, 1949, U.S. Dist. Ct. bar, 1957; staff counsel Aluminum Co. Am., Pitts., 1956-57; asso. firm Edwin L. Snyder, Punxsutawney, 1969-71; partner firm Ifert & Lukehart, Punxsutawney, 1972—. Solicitor, Borough of Punxsutawney, 1970—. Mem. Am., Pa., Jefferson County bar assns. Home: 515 N Main St Punxsutawney PA 15767 Office: 200 S Findley St Punxsutawney PA 15767 Tel (814) 938-8110

IGLEHART, RICHARD BRANDITZ, b. Oswego, N.Y., Aug. 20, 1942; B.S., U. Calif., Berkeley, 1964; J.D., U. Santa Clara, 1969. Admitted to Calif. bar, 1970; cons. Criminal Justice Com., Calif. State Assembly, Sacramento, 1969-70; sr. trial dep. Alameda County Dist. Atty's. Office, Oakland, Calif., 1970—. Mem. Calif. Peace Officers Assn. (legis. rep. 1973-76), State Bar Calif., Alameda County Bar Assn. (criminal justice com., legal aid com.), Alameda County Criminal Cts. Bar Assn., Calif. Dist. Attys. Assn. (legis. rep. 1973-76). Recipient award Merit, Calif. Peace Officers Assn., 1975; Spl. Achievement award Woman's Peace Officers Assn., 1976. Author: Summary of California Legislation, 4th edit., 1976. Home: 11 La Fond Ln Orinda CA 94563 Office: 12th St and Fallon St Oakland CA 94612 Tel (415) 874-6565

IGLESKI, THOMAS ROBERT, b. Chgo., June 16, 1934; B.B.A., U. Notre Dame, 1955; J.D., De Paul U., 1962. Admitted to Ill. bar, 1962, U.S. Supreme Ct. bar, 1971; corporate sec., asst. gen. counsel CNA Fin. Corp., CNA Ins. Cos., Chgo. Mem. Am., Ill. State, Chgo. bar assns., Am. Soc. Corporate Secs. Home: 19110 Pierce St Homewood IL 60430 Office: CNA Plaza Chicago IL 60685 Tel (312) 822-5698

IGO, LOUIS DANIEL, b. Boston, Sept. 21, 1939; B.S. in Econs. and Accounting, Mo. Valley Coll., 1963; J.D., U. Tulsa, 1967. Accountant, Lipoff, Sharlip, Pesman & Co., Kansas City, Mo., 1963-64; asst. to sales mgr. Lynn Ins. Group, Kansas City, 1965-66; cost accountant Gulf Oil Corp., Kansas City, 1966; admitted to Okla. bar, 1967, Calif. bar, 1973, U.S. Supreme Ct. bar, 1973; U.S. Tax Ct. bar, 1973; contracts and real estate specialist Texaco, Inc., Tulsa, 1969-70; accountant, taxman Arthur Young and Co., Long Beach, Calif., 1970-71; asso. prof. law and accounting Los Angeles, Community Coll. Dist.; asso. firm R.E. Harper, Los Angeles, 1973—, Gilbert Gilbert & Moustakous, Beverly Hills, 1974—; with JAGC, U.S. Army, 1964-67, USN, 1967—; arbitrator Am. Arbitration Assn.; moderator, lectr. Law for The 70's, ednl. TV series; chmn. sect. civil rights Community Town Hall Project, Los Angeles, 1975-76. Mem. Naval Res. Lawyers' Assn. Lawyers' Club Los Angeles, Los Angeles County Bar Assn. Recipient Instructional TV award, 1976; reviser; The Time-Life Family Guide, 1976; Law for the 70's Syllabus, 1976. Office: 855 N Vermont St Los Angeles CA 90029 Tel (213) 663-9141

IKARD, FRANK NEVILLE, JR., b. Wichita Falls, Tex., June 26, 1942; student U. of South, 1962-63; B.A., U. Tex., 1965, LL.B., 1968. Admitted to Tex. bar, 1968; asso. firm, Clark, Thomas, Winters & Shapiro, Austin, Tex., 1968-75, partner, 1975—. Mem. State Bar Tex., Jr. Bar Tex., Am. Bar Assn., Travis County Jr. Bar. Home: 1610 Watchhill Rd Austin TX 78703 Office: PO Box 1148 Austin TX 78767 Tel (512) 472-8442

IKARD, JAMES ASA, b. Oklahoma City, May 31, 1947; B.A. in Polit. Sci., Kans. State U., 1969; J.D., U. Okla., 1972. Admitted to Okla. bar, 1972; individual practice law, Oklahoma City, 1972—; spl. cons. joint interim com. on pub. service cos. Okla. Legislature, 1976. Mem. Okla. Bar Assn. Named Conservationist of Year, Okla. Wildlife Fedn., 1975. Office: 1329 Classen Dr Oklahoma City OK 73103 Tel (405) 239-2379

IKAZAKI, HERBERT T., b. Honolulu, May 13, 1927; B.A., U. Hawaii, 1949; M.B.A., N.Y. U., 1951; J.D., DePaul U., 1959. Admitted to Ill. bar, 1959, U.S. Supreme Ct. bar, 1962, Calif. bar, 1965, Hawaii bar, 1968; with Office of Chief Counsel, IRS, Washington, 1959-61, Office of Regional Counsel, Los Angeles, 1961-65; pvt. practice law, Honolulu, 1965—. Mem. Am., Calif., Los Angeles County, Hawaii bar assns., Hawaii Soc. C.P.A.'s. C.P.A., Hawaii, 1960. Home: 1218 Aloha Oe Kailua HI Office: 1412 Amfac Bldg 700 Bishop St Honolulu HI 96813 Tel (808) 521-1456

IKLE, RICHARD ADOLPH, b. Mineola, N.Y., Mar. 25, 1930; B.A., Amherst Coll., 1953; LL.B., Columbis U., 1960, J.D., 1969. Admitted to N.Y. bar, 1961, U.S. Supreme Ct. bar, 1967, Fla. bar, 1975; asso. firm Thacher, Proffitt & Wood and predecessors, N.Y.C., 1960-68, partner, 1969—; dir. City Title Ins. Co., 1975—; adjunct asst. prof. real estate N.Y. U., 1976—. Deacon The Community Reformed Ch. of Manhasset (N.Y.), 1975—. Mem. N.Y., Fla., Am. bar assns., Assn. of Bar of City N.Y. (mem. real property law com.), Theta Delta Chi., Phi Delta Phi. Office: 40 Wall St New York City NY 10005 Tel (212) 483-5936

ILARDO, ANTHONY C., b. Buffalo, Sept. 22, 1926; B.A., U. Buffalo, 1949, LL.B., 1960, J.D., 1968. Admitted to N.Y. bar, 1950; sr. mem. firm Ilardo, Ilardo, Ilardo & Nichols, Hanburg, N.Y., 1950—. Mem. Erie County Bar Assn., Comml. Law League Am. Office: 20 Buffalo St Hamburg NY 14075 Tel (716) 649-2880

ILLIG, CARL, b. Houston, Sept. 10, 1909; B.A., Rice U., 1930; J.D., U. Tex., 1933; postgrad. Harvard, 1959. Admitted to Tex. bar, 1933, U.S. Supreme Ct. bar, 1955, U.S. Ct. Appeals 5th Circuit bar, 1955, Washington Circuit bar, 1966; atty. Humble Oil and Refining Co., Houston, 1934-61, asso. gen. counsel, 1961-67; individual practice law, Houston, 1967—; chmn. corp. banking and bus. law sect. State Bar of Tex., 1961—; law mem. Tex. Water Devel. Bd., 1971-76. Bd. dirs. Lighthouse for the Blind, Houston, 1974—; bd. govs. Rice U., 1970-74. Mem. Houston C. of C. (chmn. water com. 1968-69), Houston Community Council (chmn. 1960), Am. (ho. of dels. 1967-68), Houston bar assns., Harvard Bus. Sch. Alumni Council. Contbr. articles to legal jours. Home: 5327 Doliver Houston TX 77056 Office: 3636 Westheimer Houston TX 77027 Tel (713) 622-0699

ILVEDSON, ROY A., b. Minot, N.D., Feb. 17, 1910; student Minot State Coll. Clk., apprentice law firm; admitted to N.D. bar, 1934; sr. partner firm Ilvedson, Pringle, Herigstad & Meschke, 1952-63; judge Dist. Ct., 5th Dist., Minot, 1963—. Mem. N.D. Bar Assn., Minot C. of C. (past pres.). Home: 315 2d St SE Minot ND 58701 Office: Courthouse Minot ND 58701 Tel (701) 838-9524

IMBESI, JOSEPH ANTHONY, b. Balt., Oct. 22, 1940; J.D., U. Balt., 1964. Admitted to Md. bar, 1965; spl. asst. atty. gen. toll facilities State of Md., Balt. Office: 1005 Fell St Baltimore MD 21231 Tel (301) 342-3992

IMIG, WILLIAM GRAFF, b. Omaha, Aug. 13, 1941. Admitted to Colo. bar, 1965, U.S. Supreme Ct. bar, 1969, U.S. Ct. Mil. Appeals, 1967, U.S. Ct. Appeals, 1965; partner firm Ireland, Stapleton, Pryor & Holmes, Denver, 1970—. Mem. Am., Colo. (bd. govs.), Denver bar assns. Mem. editorial bd. Cornell Law Rev., 1964-65. Home: 1758 Cherry St Denver CO 80220 Office: 1700 Broadway Suite 2017 Denver CO 80290 Tel (303) 825-4400

IMMEL, VINCENT CLARE, b. Gibsonburg, Ohio, Mar. 15, 1920; student U. Toledo, 1937-38; B.S. in Edn. magna cum laude, Bowling Green State U., 1941; J.D. with distinction, U. Mich., 1948. Admitted to Ohio bar, 1949, Mo. bar, 1961, U.S. Supreme Ct. bar, 1960; asst. prof. to prof. law Ohio No. U. Sch. Law, Ada, 1948-58; asso. prof. law St. Louis U., 1958-60, prof. law, 1960—, asst. dean, 1959-62, dean, 1962-69. Bd. dirs. Little Symphony Soc., St. Louis, Legal Aid Soc. of City and County of St. Louis, St. Louis Symphony Soc. Mem. Am., Ohio State, Mo. bar assns., Am. Judicature Soc., Am. Law Inst., Phi Alpha Delta. Contbr. articles to legal jours. Home: 4475 W Pine Blvd Saint Louis MO 63108 Office: 3642 Lindell Blvd Saint Louis MO 63108 Tel (314) 535-3300

IMPERATO, JOSEPH P., b. Bklyn., Sept. 2, 1907; student Coll. City N.Y.; LL.B., St. John's U., 1932; LL.D., Shaw U., 1976. Admitted to N.Y. State bar, 1932; individual practice law, Bklyn., 1932-64; counsel to majority leader N.Y.C. Council, 1964-70; judge Civil Ct., N.Y.C., 1970—; instr. St. Francis Coll., Bklyn., 1965. Chmn. local draft bd. SSS, 1942-72, adviser dir. N.Y.C. SSS, 1972—. Recipient certificate of Merit SSS, 1971. Office: Civil Ct 141 Livingston St Brooklyn NY 11201 Tel (212) 643-2865

INDEN, ARTHUR, b. Phila., Jan. 8, 1941; B.A. in Psychology, U. Del., 1962; LL.B., Dickinson Sch. Law, Carlisle, Pa., 1965. Admitted to Pa. bar, 1965, Del. bar, 1966; mem. firm Freedman Borowski & Lorry, Phila., 1965-66, Aerenson & Balick, Wilmington, Del., 1966-67; partner firm Young Conaway Stargatt & Taylor, Wilmington, 1967—; prof. real estate law Brandywine Coll., Wilmington, 1969-72. Mem. com. United Fund and Council of Del., 1970-72, chmn. gen. bus. unit, 1973. Mem. Am., Del. bar assns. Office: 1401 Market Tower Wilmington DE 19801 Tel (302) 571-6637

ING, LAWRENCE NYUK CHOON, b. Honolulu, Aug. 4, 1941; B.A., U. Hawaii, 1963; J.D., U. Calif., 1966. Admitted to Hawaii bar, 1966; dep. corp. counsel City and County of Honolulu, 1966-67; individual practice law, Honolulu, 1967, dep. county atty. Maui, 1967-68; partner firm Ueoka, Vail, Luna & Ing, Wailuku, Hawaii, 1969-72; individual practice, Wailuku, 1972—; instr. law Dept. Edn., State of Hawaii, Maui Community Coll., 1974—. Bd. dirs. Big Bros. of Maui, Inc., Maui Assn. to Help Retarded Citizens. Mem. Maui County Bar Assn. (officer), Maui C. of C. Home: 567 Waikala St Kahului HI 96732 Office: Suite 419 2180 Main St Wailuku HI 96793 Tel (808) 244-7975

INGALLS, JOHN M., b. Albany, N.Y., Dec. 19, 1944; B.A., St. Michael's Coll., Winooski, Vt., 1966; J.D., Albany Law Sch., 1969. Admitted to N.Y. bar, 1969; asst. county atty. Warren County (N.Y.), 1971-74; partner firm Lawson & Ingalls, Glens Falls, N.Y., 1974-76, firm Ingalls & Mathias, Glens Falls, 1976—; asst. dist. atty. Warren County, 1974—. Mem. Am., N.Y., Warren County bar assns. Home: 43 Coolidge Ave Glens Falls NY 12801 Office: 124 Bay St Glens Falls NY 12801 Tel (518) 798-1736

INGERSOLL, DONALD MCKEE, b. Olympia, Wash., Aug. 20, 1945; B.A., U. Wash., 1966, J.D., 1969. Admitted to Wash. bar, 1969; partner firm Ingersoll & Ingersoll, Olympia, 1969—; town atty. Town of Rainier (Wash.). Mem. Am. Bar Assn., Am. Trial Lawyers Assn. Home: 1713 11th Ct SW Olympia WA 98502 Office: 701A Evergreen Plaza Olympia WA 98501 Tel (206) 357-4333

INGMIRE, GARY DEAN, b. Orlando, Okla., Nov. 2, 1943; B.A., Central State U. Okla., 1966; J.D., Oklahoma City U., 1971. Admitted to Okla. bar, 1971, U.S. Dist. Ct. for Western dist. Okla. bar, 1971; asso. counsel Okla. Dept. Pub. Safety, Oklahoma City, 1971; asst. dist. atty. Okla. County, 1971—. Mem. Am., Okla. bar assns., Dist. Attys. Assn. Home: 3600 NW 65 Oklahoma City OK 73116 Office: 518 County Office Bldg Oklahoma City OK 73102 Tel (405) 236-2727

INGRAHAM, FRANK CALVIN, b. Nashville, Mar. 26, 1929; B.A. cum laude, Baylor U., 1951; J.D., Vanderbilt U., 1954; grad. Profl. Trial Lawyers Inst. Admitted to Tenn. bar, 1954, U.S. Supreme Ct. bar, 1971; sr. partner firm Ingraham, Young & Corbett, Nashville and Franklin, Tenn.; capt. JAGC USAF. Chmn. beef devel. task force Tenn. Livestock Assn. Mem. Am., Tenn. (past v.p. jr. bar), Nashville, Williamson County bar assns., Nashville Area (past dir.), Williamson County chambers commerce, Tenn. Hist. Soc. Am. Trial Lawyers Assn., Am. Trial Lawyers Found. (founder), Scribes. Contbr. articles to religious publs.; editor Vanderbilt Law Rev., 1952-53. Home: Tap Root Farm Clovercroft Rd Franklin TN 37064 Office: 1720 Parkway Towers Nashville TN 37219 Tel (615) 244-6632 also Main St Franklin TN Tel (615) 794-3506

INGRAM, DENNY OUZTS, b. Kirbyville, Tex., Mar. 23, 1929; B.A., U. Tex., 1955, J.D., 1957. Editor, The Kirbyville Banner, 1949-50; mem. Tex. Ho. of Reps., 1951-52; admitted to Tex. bar, 1956, N.Mex. bar, 1967, Utah bar, 1969; asso. firm Graves, Dougherty & Gee, Austin, Tex., 1957, 59-60, partner, 1961-66; asst. prof. law U. Tex., 1957-59; asso. prof. law U. N.Mex., 1966-67; prof. law U. Utah, 1968-77; partner firm McGinnis, Lochridge & Kilgore, Austin, 1977—; vis. prof. law U. Calif. at Davis, 1973-74, U. Tex., summer 1968, 75; cons. N.Mex. Constl. Revision Commn., 1966; research dir. Utah Constl. Revision Commn., 1969-71, 73-74; cons. Humble Oil & Refining Corp., Houston, summer 1972; faculty Pacific Coast Banking Sch., 1973-77, Southwestern Legal Found., 1975-77. Mem. Am. Law Inst., Utah, Tex., N.Mex., Am. bar assns., Order of Coif, Phi Delta Phi. Contbr. articles and monographs to law jours. Home: 2885 Live Oak Circle Salt Lake City UT 84117 Office: 5th floor Tex State Bank Bldg 900 Congress Ave Austin TX 78701 Tel (512) 476-6982

INGRAM, JOHN DWIGHT, b. Chgo., Mar. 10, 1929; A.B., Harvard, 1950; C.L.U., Am. Coll. Life Underwriters, 1957; J.D., John Marshall Law Sch., 1966. Admitted to Ill. bar, 1966; ins. broker Griffin, Ingram & Pfaff, Chgo., 1950-70, pres., 1967-70; partner firm Simon & Ingram, Chgo., 1966-73; prof. John Marshall Law Sch., Chgo., 1966—. Vestryman Christ Ch., Winnetka, Ill., 1971-75; pres. Winnetka Park Dist., 1975-77. Mem. Chgo., Am. bar assns. Contbr. articles to legal jours. Home: 1264 Forest Glen N Winnetka IL 60093 Office: 315 S Plymouth Ct Chicago IL 60604 Tel (312) 427-2737

INGRAM, JOHN GERARD, b. N.Y.C., June 14, 1943; B.S. in Marine Transp., State U. of N.Y. Maritime Coll., 1964; J.D., St. John's U., 1969. Admitted to N.Y. State bar, 1969, U.S. Supreme Ct. bar, 1975; asso. firm Burlingham, Underwood & Lord, N.Y.C., 1969-75, partner, 1975—; adj. asst. prof. law N.Y. Law Sch., 1975—; mem. Bd. Fire Suprs., 1973-76; counsel Point Breeze Vol. Fire Dept., 1969—. Mem. Am. Bar Assn., Maritime Law Assn. U.S., Maritimes Assos. City N.Y. (bd. govs. 1975—, v.p. 1977—), N.Y. State Maritime Coll. Alumni Assn. (pres. 1975—), Naval Res. Assn., Militia Officers Assn., U.S. Naval Inst., Am. Legion. Office: 1 Battery Park Plaza New York City NY 10004 Tel (212) 422-7585

INGRAM, ROBERT BRUCE, b. Des Moines, July 19, 1940; B.A., Drake U., 1962; J.D., Coll. William and Mary 1970. Admitted to Calif. bar, 1971, U.S. Supreme Ct. bar, 1974; counsel Human Resources Devel. Agy., State of Calif., Sacramento, 1970-71; asso. firm Belli & Choulos, San Francisco, 1971—. Bd. dirs. Marin County (Calif.) chpt. Am. Heart Assn., 1975—. Mem. Am., San Francisco, bar assns., Assn. Trial Lawyers Am., Calif., San Francisco (bd. dirs.) trial lawyers assns. Current decisions editor William and Mary Law Rev., 1969-70, also article. Office: 722 Montgomery St San Francisco CA 94111 Tel (415) 981-1849

INGRAM, VERNER MERRITT, b. Potsdam, N.Y., Aug. 27, 1911; A.B., Cornell U., 1933; LL.B., J.D., Union U., 1936. Admitted to N.Y. State bar, 1937, U.S. Dist. Ct. for No. Dist. N.Y. bar, 1937, U.S. 2d Circuit Ct. Appeals bar, 1968; individual practice law, Potsdam, 1937-70; partner firm Ingram & Ingram, Potsdam, 1970—; spl. surrogate St. Lawrence County; justice of the peace, 1940-56; mem. N.Y. State Assembly, 1957-66; dir. North County Savs. Bank, Marine Midland Bank. Mem. Am., N.Y. State, St. Lawrence County bar assns., Am., N.Y. State Trial Lawyers Assns. Co-author: Pastor's Legal Advisor. Office: 19 Market St Potsdam NY 13676 Tel (315) 265-8680

INGRAM, WILLIAM THETFORD, b. Columbus, Ga., June 22, 1927; B.B.A., U. Ga., 1953; LL.B., Atlanta Law Sch., 1974. Credit analyst 1st Nat. Bank, Atlanta, 1953-55; credit investigator Dun & Bradstreet, Inc., Atlanta, 1956-57; realty officer VA, Jacksonville, Fla., 1962-64, HUD Atlanta, 1966-74; real estate broker Ingram Realty Co., Columbus, 1959—, Wm. Ingram Real Estate, Sandy Springs, Ga.; admitted to Ga. bar, 1974; individual practice law, Sandy Springs, 1974—; counseling mem. Lawyer-To-Lawyer Consultation Panel. Mem. Am. Soc. Appraisers (sr.). Author: American Dilemma-Then and Now, 1976. Office: Suite 206 1st Fed Bldg 6160 Roswell Rd NW Sandy Springs GA 30328 Tel (404) 255-1852

INMAN, ROBERT DALE, b. Mitchell, Ind., Feb. 6, 1920; B.A., U. Colo., 1941, LL.B., 1947. Admitted to Colo. bar, 1947; clk. Boulder County (Colo.) Ct., asst. U.S. Atty. for Colo., 1953-56; asst. atty.-gen. Colo., 1956-60; mem. firm Inman, Flynn and Coffee, Denver, 1961—. Office: 1040 Capitol Life Center Denver CO 80401 Tel (303) 861-8147

INOUYE, DANIEL KEN, b. Honolulu, Sept. 7, 1924; B.A. in Govt. and Econs., U. Hawaii, 1950; J.D., George Washington U., 1952. Admitted to Hawaii bar, 1953; asst. prosecutor City of Honolulu, 1953; mem., majority leader Hawaii Territorial House, 1954-58; mem. Hawaii Territorial Senate, 1958; mem. U.S. Ho. Reps., 1959-62; mem. U.S. Senate, 1962—; mem. Senate Appropriations Com., 1971; chmn. Fgn. Ops. Subcom., 1973; mem. Senate Commerce Com., 1969—; chmn. Mcht. Marine and Tourism Subcom., 1971—; mem. Select Com. Presdl. Campaign Activities, 1973-74; chmn. Senate Select Com. on Intelligence, 1976—; mem. Senate Dist. Columbia Com., Asst. Majority Whip, U.S. Senate, 1965-76; sec. Senate Dem. Conf., 1977—. Mem. Am., Hawaii bar assns. Author: Journey to Washington, 1967; keynoter, temp. chmn. 1968 Democratic Nat. Conv.; recipient Thomas A. Dooley Found Splendid Am. award 1967; George Washington U. Alumnus of Yr. award, 1961; George Washington Law Assn. Distinguished Alumnus award, 1973; Am. Acad. Achievement Golden Plate award, 1968, Am. Legion Nat. Commdr's Award, 1973; named one of 10 Outstanding Young Men of Yr., U.S. Jr. C. of C., 1960. Home: 469 Ena Rd Honolulu HI 96815

Office: 442 Russell Senate Office Bldg Washington DC 20510 Tel (202) 224-3934

INTERDONATO, ANTHONY PAUL, b. Washington, Jan. 8, 1949; student Gonzaga Coll., 1966; A.B., Xavier U., 1970; J.D., Cath. U. Am., 1973. Admitted to Md. bar, 1973, D.C. bar, 1974; law clk. firm Interdonato, Lombard, Reilly & Comstock, Washington, 1971-73, Superior Ct. D.C., 1973-74; asst. state's atty. Prince George's County, Upper Marlboro, Md., 1974—. Mem. Am., D.C., Md. State, Prince George's County bar assns, Delta Theta Phi. Home: 12301 Hatton Point Rd Oxon Hill MD 20022 Office: Court House Upper Marlboro MD 20870 Tel (301) 952-3540

IOVENKO, MICHAEL, b. N.Y.C., Jan. 19, 1930; B.A., Dartmouth, 1951; J.D., Columbia, 1954. Admitted to N.Y. bar, 1959; partner firm Putney, Twombly, Hall & Hirson, N.Y.C., 1959-71; dep. supt., counsel N.Y. Dept. Banking, N.Y.C., 1971-72; partner firm LeBoeuf, Lamb, Leiby & MacRae, N.Y.C., 1972—; alt. U.S. Rep. 5th spl. session gen. assembly UN, 1967. Bd. dirs., pres. Berkshire Farm Center and Services Youth, Canaan, N.Y. Mem. Am., N.Y. State, N.Y. County Lawyers bar assns. Home: 26 E 93rd St New York City NY 10028 Office: 140 Broadway St New York City NY 10005 Tel (212) 269-1100

IPPOLITO, HENRY RUSSELL, b. Dunkirk, N.Y., Oct. 7, 1942; A.B., Syracuse U., 1960-64; J.D., Cornell U., 1967. Admitted to N.Y. bar, 1967; asso. firm Chamberlain, D'Amanda, Bauman, Chatman & Oppenheimer, Rochester, N.Y., 1971-75, partner, 1975—; instr. Cornell U., 1973-75. Mem. Am., N.Y., Monroe County bar assns., Order of Coif, Phi Beta Kappa, Phi Kappa Phi. Home: 43 Colonial Dr Penfield NY 14526 Office: 1100 Crossroads Office Bldg Rochester NY 14614 Tel (716) 232-3730

IRELAND, MARILYN JEAN, b. Mariemont, Ohio, Mar. 4, 1943; student U. Va., 1964-66; B.A., Miami U., Oxford, Ohio, 1966; J.D. (Mecham scholar), U. Chgo., 1969. Admitted to Ill. bar, 1969, Mo. bar, 1976; asso. firm Friedman & Kover, Chgo., 1969-72; asst. prof. law Washington U., St. Louis, 1972—, asso. dean Sch. Law, 1973-75. Parliamentarian Ill. Young Republican Fedn., 1968. Mem. Am., Ill. bar assns., Am. Judicature Soc., Order of Coif, Phi Beta Kappa. Editorial bd. U. Chgo. Law Rev., 1968-69. Home: 8016 Walinca St Clayton MO 63105 Office: Washington U Saint Louis MO 63130 Tel (314) 863-0100

IRION, JAMES RAGUET, III, b. Wichita Falls, Tex., Feb. 3, 1932; B.A., Tex. Christian U., 1955; J.D., U. Tex., 1958. Admitted to Tex. bar, 1958; asst. atty. gen. State of Tex., Austin, 1958-60; staff atty. Phillips Petroleum Co., Austin, 1961; asso. firm Brewster, Pannell, Dean & Kerry, Ft. Worth, 1961-65, Simon, Crowley, Wright, Ratliff & Miller, Ft. Worth, 1965-66; atty. for liquidator-receiver State Bd. of Ins., Austin, 1966—. Mem. State Bar Tex., Travis County (Tex.) Bar Assn. Home: 5600 Ridge Oak Dr Austin TX 78731 Office: 211 E 11th St Austin TX 78701 Tel (512) 475-4508

IRION, MORTIMER RAGUET, b. Overton, Tex., July 26, 1904; student U. Tex., 1922-5; postgrad. U. Colo. Law Sch., summer 1930; LL.B., So. Meth. U., 1931. Admitted to Tex. bar, 1931, U.S. Supreme Ct. bar, 1940; partner firm Irion, Cain, Magee and Davis, Dallas, 1938—; asst. atty. gen. State of Tex., 1939; dir. Tex-Lite, Inc. Bd. dirs. Dallas Mental Health Assn., Dean Meml. Home. Mem. Am., Dallas bar assns., State Bar Tex. Home: 10215 Daria Pl Dallas TX 75229 Office: 830 Mercantile Bank Bldg Dallas TX 75201 Tel (214) 747-3567

IRION, VALENTINE EGAN, b. Benton, La., Nov. 4, 1899; LL.B., Tulane U., 1926, J.D., 1969; postgrad. Harvard Law Sch., 1946. Admitted to La. bar, 1926, U.S. Supreme Ct. bar, 1943; asso. firm Monroe & Lemann, New Orleans, 1926-27, firm Liskow & Irion, Lake Charles, La., 1927-28, firm Kaufman & Irion, New Orleans, 1928-30, firm Irion & Switzer, Shreveport, La., 1930-50, firm Lunn, Irion, Switzer, Trichel & Johnson, Shreveport, 1950-60, firm Lunn, Irion, Switzer, Johnson & Salley, Shreveport, 1960—; mem. La. Bd. Tax Appeals, 1940. Chmn. Shreveport City Planning Commn., 1935-40; mem. Shreveport Charter Commn., 1948-49; chmn. Tax Inst. Ark., La., Tex. 1947-48. Mem. Shreveport, La. Am. bar assns., Am. Judicature Soc. Contbr. articles to legal jours. Home: 569 Unadilla St Shreveport LA 71106 Office: 500 Slattery Bldg Shreveport LA 71101 Tel (318) 222-0665

IRISH, LEON EUGENE, b. Superior, Wis., June 19, 1938; B.A., Stanford U., 1960; J.D., U. Mich., 1964; D.Phil., Oxford (Eng.) U., 1973. Admitted to Calif. bar, 1965, D.C. bar, 1969; law clk. to Asso. Justice Byron R. White, U.S. Supreme Ct., 1967-68; cons. Office Fgn. Direct Investments, 1968-69; asso. firm Caplin & Drysdale, Washington, 1969-72, partner, 1973—; chmn. com. on fed. appellate ct. system D.C. Bar; professorial lectr. law George Washington U., 1975-76; adj. prof. Georgetown U. Law Sch. 1977—. Sec., bd. dirs., chmn. exec. com. Vols. in Tech. Assistance, Mt. Ranier, Md. Mem. Am. Bar Assn. (tax sect.). Home: 3301 Highland Pl NW Washington DC 20008 Office: 1101 17th St NW Washington DC 20036 Tel (202) 862-5075

IRONS, DAVID LESTER, b. St. Louis, Sept. 3, 1936; A.B., Northwestern U., 1958; LL.B., Stanford, 1964. Admitted to Calif. bar, 1964, Hawaii bar, 1965; asso. firm Carlsmith, Carlsmith, Wichman & Case, Honolulu, 1964-69, partner, 1969—. Mem. Am., Hawaii bar assns., Honolulu Jaycees (bd. dirs. 1966-68). Home: 253 Lumahai Pl Honolulu HI 96825 Office: 2200 Pacific Trade Center Box 656 Honolulu HI 96813 Tel (808) 524-5112

IRONS, FRED R., b. Granville, N.D., May 31, 1911; LL.B., U. Omaha, 1939. Admitted to Nebr. bar, 1939; partner firm Conway & Irons, Hastings, Nebr., until 1971; judge 10th Jud. Dist. Ct., Hastings, 1971—. Chmn. Hastings chpt. ARC, 1955; mem. Hastings Pub. Sch. Bd., 1957-63, v.p., 1956. Mem. Am., Nebr. (ho. of dels. 1960-63, exec. com. 1964-69), 10th Jud. Dist. bar assns., Nebr. Dist. Judges Assn. (past pres.). Home: 3226 Park Ln Dr Hastings NE 68901 Office: Courthouse Hastings NE 68901 Tel (402) 463-2491

IRONS, LESTER, b. Sullivan County, Ind., May 14, 1908; A.B., Ind. State U., 1929; J.D., U. Mich., 1935. Admitted to Mo. bar, 1935, Ind. bar, 1936, N.Y. State bar, 1940; mem. staff law dept. Gen. Am. Life Ins. Co., St. Louis, 1935-38, Shell Oil Co., N.Y.C., 1940-46; partner firm Barnes, Hickam, Pantzer & Boyd, Indpls., 1942—. Mem. Indpls., Ind., Am. bar assns. Home: 8403 Overlook St Indianapolis IN 46260 Office: 1313 Merchants Bank Bldg Indianapolis IN 46204 Tel (317) 638-1313

IRONS, SPENCER ERNEST, b. Chgo., Sept. 15, 1917; A.B., U. Chgo., 1938; J.D., U. Mich., 1941. Admitted to Ill. bar 1941, U.S. Supreme Ct. bar 1962; asso. firm Holmes, Dixon, Knouff & Potter, Chgo., 1946-49; asso. firm McKinney, Carlson, Leaton, & Smalley, Chgo., 1950-54, partner, 1955-58; sr. atty. Brunswick Corp., Skokie, Ill., 1959—; served to lt. col. JAG, AUS, 1961-62; chmn. com. on Character and Fitness 1st Judicial Dist. Ill., 1969-70. Mem. Chgo. Crime Commn., 1954—, asst. sec., 1956-57, sec., 1962-63; mem. Flossmoor (Ill.) Village Library Bd., 1959-61. Mem. Am., Chgo. (bd. mgrs. 1954-56) bar assns., Law Club, Legal Club. Bd. editors, Mich. Law Review, 1939-41. Home: 1760 Western Ave Flossmoor IL 60422 Office: One Brunswick Plaza Skokie IL 60076 Tel (312) 982-6000

IRONS, WILLIAM LEE, b. Birmingham, Ala., June 9, 1941; B.A., U. Va., 1963; J.D., Samford U., 1966. Admitted to Ala. bar, 1966; law clk. firm Speir, Robertson & Jackson, Birmingham, Ala., 1964-65; asso. firm James L. Shores, Jr., 1965-66; asst. judge advocate Whiteman AFB, Mo., 1966-67, Gunter AFB, 1967-68; dir. mil. justice, Maxwell AFB, Ala., 1968-69; partner firm Speir, Robertson, Jackson & Irons, Birmingham, 1970-71; partner firm Spier and Irons, 1971-72; partner firm William L. Irons, Birmingham, 1972—. Candidate, Ala. Ho. Reps., 1966. Mem. Am., Birmingham bar assns., Am. Trial Lawyers Assn., Nat. Assn. Certified Judge Advocates, Fed. Bar Assn., Nat. Assn. Judge Advocates, Nat. Res. Officers Assn., Nat. Lawyers Club, Sigma Delta Kappa. Home: 316 Gran Ave Birmingham AL 36203 Office: 1227 City Fed Bldg Birmingham AL 35203 Tel (205) 328-5150

IRVIN, ROBERT ANDREW, b. Atlanta, Sept. 9, 1948; J.D., Emory U., 1973; A.B., Coll. William and Mary, 1970. Admitted to Ga. bar, 1974; asso. firm Zusmann, Sikes, Pritchard & Cohen, Atlanta, 1974—; mem. Ga. Gen. Assembly, 1973—. Mem. Am., Atlanta bar assns. Home: 150 S Atlanta St Roswell GA 30015 Office: 1795 Peachtree Rd NE Atlanta GA 30309 Tel (404) 897-7088

IRVINE, LOUIS JAMES, b. Clyde, Kans., Oct. 5, 1915; B.S.L., St. Paul Coll. Law, 1942, LL.B., 1947. Admitted to Minn. bar, 1948; practiced in St. Paul, 1948-50, Wells, Minn., 1950-55; judge Dist. Ct., Fairmont, Minn., 1955—. Mem. Minn. State, Am. bar assns., State Dist. Judges Assn. (pres. 1975-76). Office: Courthouse Fairmont MN 56031 Tel (507) 235-5269

IRVINE, PERRY ARMSTRONG, b. N.Y.C., May 7, 1941; B.A., Syracuse U., 1962; J.D., Georgetown U., 1966. Admitted to Calif. bar, 1966; asso. firm Quentin L. Kopp, San Francisco, 1966-67, Morgan, Beauzay & Hammer, San Jose, Calif., 1967-71; partner firm Jarvis, Irvine & Bialson, Palo Alto, Calif., 1971—. Pres. Epilepsy Soc. of Santa Clara County, Inc.; San Jose, 1973-76; mem. Early Childhood Edn. com. Palo Alto Unified Sch. Dist., Mem. Am., Santa Clara County, Palo Alto Area bar assns., Calif., Am. trial lawyers assns., Am. Arbitration Assn. Home: 847 Greenwich Pl Palo Alto CA 94303 Office: 2600 El Camino Real Suite 500 Palo Alto CA 94306 Tel (415) 326-4535

IRVING, JOHN F.X., b. Jersey City, Jan. 10, 1928; A.B., St. Peter's Coll., Jersey City, 1950; J.D., Fordham U., 1956; LL.M., N.Y. U., 1962. Admitted to N.J. bar, 1956, Ill. bar, 1963; field atty. Nat. Legal Aid and Defender Assn., Am. Bar Assn., 1962-65; exec. dir. Nat. Council Juvenile Ct. Judges, 1965-69; chmn. Ill. Law Enforcement Commn., Chgo., 1969-71; dean Sch. Law, Seton Hall U., Newark, 1971—; cons. U.S. Dept. Justice, 1972-77, U.S. Office Edn., 1973—; adv. bd. U.S. commr. edn., 1973—; chmn. Nat. Coll. Criminal Def. Lawyers, Houston, 1975. Mem. Am., N.J. bar assns. Recipient plaque for contbns. to Am. juvenile cts. Nat. Council Juvenile Ct. Judges, 1969; Arthur von Briesen award Nat. Legal Aid and Defender Assn., 1975; Ben Gurian award State of Israel, 1976; named hon. pub. defender Ill. Pub. Defender Project, 1973. Home: 24 Apple Tree Ln Basking Ridge NJ 07920 Office: Seton Hall Law Center 1111 Raymond Blvd Newark NJ 07079 Tel (201) 642-8500

IRWIN, CLAUDE KARL, b. Meadows, Idaho, July 15, 1912; B.A., Wash. State U., 1934; J.D., U. Wash., 1937; postgrad. in taxation law Harvard, 1957. Admitted to Wash. bar, 1937, U.S. Dist. Ct. bar, 1939; partner firm Jamar & Irwin, Pullman, Wash., 1938-43, Irwin & Kimball, Colfax, Wash., 1943-47; partner firm Irwin, Friel & Myklebust and predecessors, Pullman, 1947—; pros. atty., Whitman County, Wash., 1943-47. Mem. Am. Bar Assn., Pullman C. of C. (pres. 1965). Home: SE 550 Derby Pullman WA 99163 Office: POB 604 226 Old Nat Bank Bldg Pullman WA 99163 Tel (509) 564-1178

IRWIN, DALE KENNETH, b. Russelville, Mo., Oct. 1, 1948; B.A. in Polit. Sci., U. Mo., 1971, J.D., 1973. Admitted to Mo. bar, 1973; atty. Legal Aid and Defender Soc. of Greater Kansas City (Mo.), 1973—. Mem. Am., Mo. bar assns. Home: 3534 Campbell St Kansas City MO 64109 Office: 3200 Wayne St Kansas City MO 64109 Tel (816) 861-9388

IRWIN, DAVID MEREDITH, b. Rochester, N.Y., May 13, 1940; B.A., Wesleyan U., 1962; LL.B., Harvard, 1965. Admitted to N.Y. bar, 1965; law clk. to judge U.S. Dist. Ct. N.Y., 1965-66; served as lt. JAGC, U.S. Navy, 1966-69; asso. firm Dewey, Ballantine, Bushby, Palmer & Wood, N.Y.C., 1969-75, partner, 1975—. Mem. Am., N.Y. State, N.Y.C. bar assns. Home: 401 E 89th St New York City NY 10028 Office: 140 Broadway Dewey Ballantine Bushby Palmer & Wood New York City NY 10005 Tel (212) 344-8000

IRWIN, JAMES LEE, b. Austin, Tex., May 24, 1949; B.A., U. Tex. at Austin, 1971, J.D., 1973. Admitted to Tex. bar, 1973; since practiced in Dallas. Mem. State Bar Tex., Am., Dallas Jr. bar assns. Home: 3834 Constitution St Dallas TX 75229

IRWIN, MICHAEL EDWARD, b. Heber Springs, Ark., Aug. 11, 1948; B.S. in Bus. Adminstrn., U. Ark., 1970, J.D., 1973. Admitted to Ark. bar, 1973; partner firm Thomas, Irwin & Giles, Heber Springs, 1973—; dep. pros. atty. 14th Jud. Dist., Heber Springs, 1974—. Mem. planning and zoning commn., Heber Springs-Cleburn County, 1974-77; chmn. fin. com. 1st United Meth. Ch., Heber Springs, 1974-76. Mem. Am., Ark. bar assns., Ark. Prosecuting Atty. Assn., Heber Springs Rotary (2d v.p.), Cleburne County Bar Assn. (sec. 1973-74). Home: Route 4 Box 168 Heber Springs AR 72543 Office: 405 W Searcy St Heber Springs AR 72543 Tel (501) 362-5871

IRWIN, PAT, b. Leedey, Okla., June 12, 1921; LL.B., U. Okla., 1949, J.D., 1970. Admitted to Okla. bar, 1949; atty. Dewey County, Taloga, Okla., 1949-50; mem. Okla. Senate, 1951-54; sec., commr. Okla. Land Office, Oklahoma City, 1954-58; justice Okla. Supreme Ct., Oklahoma City, 1959—, chief justice, 1969-70. Home: Leedey OK Office: State Capitol Oklahoma City OK 73105 Tel (405) 521-3841

ISAAC, ALLEN HAROLD, b. Dec. 15, 1933; B.A., City Coll. N.Y., 1951; LL.B., Bklyn. Law Sch., 1957, J.D., 1967. Admitted to N.Y. bar, 1958; sr. partner firm Gladstein & Isaac, N.Y.C.; mem. N.Y. state Med. Malpractice Mediation Panel, 1976. Mem. N.Y. State Workman's Compensation (past sec.), Am., Bklyn., N.Y. State bar assns., Am. Arbitration Assn., Nassau County Lawyers Assn., N.Y. State Trial Lawyers Assn., Trial Lawyers Assn. Am., Def. Research Inst., Met. Trial Lawyers N.Y.C. Office: 127 John St New York City NY 10038 Tel (212) 952-1111

ISAAC, ROBERT MICHAEL, b. Colorado Springs, Colo., Jan. 27, 1928; student U. Colo., 1945-46; B.S., U.S. Mil. Acad., 1951; J.D., U. So. Calif., 1962. Admitted to Calif. bar, 1962, Colo. bar, 1962; individual practice law, Colorado Springs, 1962-65; mem. firm Trott, Kunstle, Isaac & Hughes, Colorado Springs, 1969-72, firm Isaac & Walsh, Colorado Springs, 1972-73, firm Isaac, Walsh & Johnson, Colorado Springs, 1973-77, Isaac, Johnson & Alpern, 1977—; asst. city atty. Colorado Springs, 1962-65; asst. dist. atty. 4th Jud. Dist., El Paso County (Colo.), 1965-66; municipal judge, Colorado Springs, 1966-69. Gen. chmn. $3 million YW-YMCA-USO Devel. Program, 1971; mem. nat. council USO, 1971; bd. dirs. YMCA, 1964-68; pres. Pikes Peak Y, 1969-71, El Paso County Soc. for Crippled Children and Adults, 1965-68, W. Point Soc. Pikes Peak Region, 1975; vice chmn. Nat. Council on Alcoholism, Pikes Peak Region, 1969; mem. City Council Colorado Springs, 1975—; chmn. Pikes Peak Area Council Govts., 1976—. Home: 3916 N Midsummer Ln Colorado Springs CO 80917 Office: 550 United Bank Bldg Colorado Springs CO 80903 Tel (303) 471-7955

ISAACS, JULIUS, b. N.Y.C., Dec. 31, 1896; B.A. cum laude, Coll. City N.Y., 1917; J.D., N.Y. U., 1924. Tchr. English and citizenship N.Y.C. Night Schs., 1921-26; admitted to N.Y. Supreme Ct. bar, 1925; practiced in N.Y.C., 1925-33, 47—; asst. corp. counsel City of N.Y., 1934-38, acting corp. counsel in charge real estate and condemnation, 1938-45; magistrate City of N.Y., assigned to ct. spl. sessions, 1945-47; spl. counsel Village of Suffern (N.Y.), 1955; examiner N.Y.C. Dept. Personnel, 1961; lectr. in field; mem. N.Y.C. Citizens Union Com. on Ct. Reorgn. and Selection of Judges, 1962—; mem. Mayor John V. Lindsay's Com. on Cts., 1962-72. Chmn. citizens' advisory com. Operation Bowery, N.Y.C. Dept. Pub. Welfare, 1963-73; v.p. Laymen's Nat. Bible Com., 1964—; chmn. legislation for aging Community Service Soc. N.Y.C., 1961-76; completed mission for Nat. Found. Arts and Humanities in Samoa, 1966. Mem. N.Y. State Bar Assn. (com. pub. health), Assn. Bar City N.Y. (chmn. com. med. jurisprudence 1952-56, mem. com. cts. superior jurisdiction, com. criminal cts., municipal affairs com.), New York County Lawyers Assn. (dir. 1957-63, ethics com., med. jurisdication com., uniform laws com.), PEN (treas. Am. Center, v.p., del. Six World Congresses Writers 1959—), Phi Beta Kappa (chmn. com. admissions Gamma chpt. 1975—). Author: Oath of Devotion, 1949; contbr. articles to HEW reports, to legal jours. Home: 21 E 10th St New York NY 10003 Office: 292 Madison Ave New York City NY 10017 Tel (212) MU-6-5226

ISAACSON, DAVID, b. N.Y.C., Dec. 16, 1929; student Bklyn. Coll., 1947-49; LL.B., Bklyn. Law Sch., 1952; postgrad. Coll. City N.Y., 1955-56. Admitted to N.Y. bar, 1953, U.S. Supreme Ct. bar, 1964, U.S. Ct. Mil. Appeals bar, 1964, U.S. Ct. Claims bar, 1964; asso. firm Singer & Weiss, N.Y.C., 1955, William H. Ross, N.Y.C., 1955-56; individual practice law, N.Y.C., 1956—. Mem. N.Y. State, Bronx County Criminal Cts. bar assns. Office: 170 E 161st St Bronx NY 10451 Tel (212) 993-1900

ISAACSON, MARC RICHARD, b. Chgo., May 24, 1945; B.A., U. Chgo., 1965, M.B.A., 1967, J.D., 1971. Admitted to Calif. bar, 1972; asso. firm Gibson, Dunn, & Crutcher, Los Angeles, 1971—. Mem. Am., Los Angeles County bar assns. Home: 5251 W 9th St Los Angeles CA 90036 Office: 515 S Flower St Los Angeles CA 90071 Tel (213) 488-7285

ISAAK, G. EUGENE, b. Bismarck, N.D., Nov. 23, 1937; B.S. in Bus. Adminstrn., U. N.D., 1959, J.D., 1961; LL.M. in Taxation, N.Y. U., 1962. Admitted to N.D. bar, 1961, Ariz. bar, 1963; mem. firm Dunseath Stubbs & Burch, Tucson, 1963-73, Miller Pitt & Feldman, Tucson, 1973—. Comdr., Ariz. Wing CAP, 1971-76, dep. comdr. S.W. region, 1976—; bd. dirs. Tucson Planned Parenthood Center, 1963-69. Mem. Am., Ariz., Pima County bar assns., So. Ariz. Estate Planning Council. Home: 425 E Yvon Dr Tucson AZ 85704 Office: 111 S Church Ave Tucson AZ 85701 Tel (602) 792-3836

ISBELL, DAVID BRADFORD, b. New Haven, Feb. 18, 1929; B.A., Yale U., 1949, J.D., 1956. Admitted to Conn. bar, 1956, D.C. bar, 1957; asso. firm Covington & Burling, Washington, 1957-59, 61-65, partner, 1965—; asst. staff dir. U.S. Commn. Civil Rights, 1959-61; lectr. U. Va. Law Sch., 1962—. Bd. dirs. S.E. Neighborhood House, Washington, 1965-69. Mem. Am. Bar Assn., Bar Assn. D.C., Yale Law Sch. Assn. (pres. 1964-65), ACLU (dir. Nat. Capital area 1962—, chmn. 1972-74; nat. dir. 1963—, vice chmn. 1968-74). Contbr. articles to legal jours. Home: 3709 Bradley Ln Chevy Chase MD 20015 Office 888 16th St NW Washington DC 20006 Tel (202) 452-6044

ISHAM, RICHARD BASIL, b. San Diego, Aug. 8, 1939; B.A., Occidental Coll., 1961; LL.B., U. Calif., Berkeley, 1965. Admitted to Calif. bar, 1966; estate tax examiner IRS, San Francisco, 1965; dist. atty. Tulare County (Calif.), Visalia, 1966-67; asso. firm Frederic H. Jacobus, Visalia, 1967-70; partner firm Jacobus, Isham & Humpal, Visalia, 1970-73; individual practice law, Visalia, Calif., 1973—; atty. City of Visalia, 1972—. Mem. Am., Calif., Tulare County bar assns., Am. Judicature Soc. Office: 1441 S Mooney Blvd Suite D Visalia CA 93277 Tel (209) 733-2257

ISHMAEL, RANDALL W., b. Jonesboro, Ark., Oct. 7, 1937; B.S., Ark. State U., 1963; LL.B., George Washington U., 1966. Admitted to Ark. bar, 1966, U.S. Tax Ct. bar; since practiced in Jonesboro, asso. firm Barrett, Wheatley, Smith & Deacon, 1966-68, partner, 1969-76; individual practice law, 1976—. Bd. dirs. Craighead County ARC, 1966-74, Jonesboro YMCA 1968-69. Mem. Ark., Am. bar assns., Ark. Bar Found., NE Ark., Craighead County bar assns. C.P.A., Ark. Home: 1202 Tony Dr Jonesboro AR 72401 Office: McAdams Trust Bldg PO Box 4096 Jonesboro AR 72401 Tel (501) 972-1400

ISHMAEL, SAMUEL THOMPSON, b. Kiowa, Kans., Dec. 18, 1931; B.S. Law, U. Wyo., 1962, J.D., 1964. Admitted to Wyo. bar, 1964, Kans. bar, 1970, Ariz. bar, 1971; individual practice law, Rawlins, Wyo., 1964-68, Overland Park, Kans., 1970; dir. of liaison Citizens for Justice with Order, N.Y.C., 1968-70; partner firms Stanfield, McCarville Coxon & Ishmael, Casa Grande, Ariz., 1971-74, Karman & Ishmael, P.C., Casa Grande, 1975—; judge Rawlins Municipal Ct., 1965-66; city atty. Eloy, Ariz., 1971—; mem. disciplinary bd. State Bar Ariz. mem. exec. com. U.S. Jaycees, 1968-69; senator Jr. C. of C. Internat., 1968—. Mem. Wyo., Ariz., Am., Pinal County (Ariz.) (pres. 1974) bar assns., Casa Grande C. of C. (pres. 1976). Recipient Clayton Frost award U.S. Jaycees, 1968. Home: 1220 E Rodeo Rd Casa Grande AZ 85222 Tel (602) 836-8222

ISRAEL, JEROLD HARVEY, b. Cleve., June 14, 1934; B.B.A., Western Reserve U., 1956; LL.B., Yale, 1959. Admitted to Ohio bar, 1959, Mich. bar, 1967; law clerk Justice Potter Stewart, U.S. Supreme Ct., 1959-61; asst. prof. law U. Mich., 1961-64, asso. prof., 1964-67, prof., 1967—; vis. prof. Stanford Law Sch., 1966, U. Fla. Law Sch., 1974; exec. sec. Mich. Law Revision Commn., 1974—. Mem. State Bar Mich. Author: (with others) Modern Criminal Procedure, 1974, Criminal Procedure in a Nutshell: Constitutional Limitations, 1975. Home: 2037 Winsted St Ann Arbor MI 48103 Office: 341 Hutchins Hall Ann Arbor MI 48109 Tel (313) 764-9353

ISRAEL, MARTIN ANDREW, b. Phila., Mar. 19, 1920; A.B., U. Ala., 1942; J.D., N.Y. U., 1948. Admitted to N.Y. bar, 1949, N.J. bar, 1970, U.S. Supreme Ct. bar, 1959; with firm Gair Gair & Conason, N.Y.C., 1948—; with JAGC USAR. Mem. Am., N.Y. State trial lawyers assns., Fed., N.J., Monmouth County (N.J.) bar assns. Home: 21 Adele Ct River Plaza NJ 07701 Office: 84 William St New York City NY 10038 Tel (212) 943-1090

ISRAEL, ROBERT LEON, b. Seattle, May 22, 1944; B.A. in History magna cum laude, U. Wash., 1966; J.D., Harvard, 1969. Admitted to Wash. bar, 1969; asso. firm Lane, Powell, Moss & Miller, Seattle, 1969-74, partner, 1975—. Mem. Am., Wash., Seattle-King County bar assns., Wash. State Trial Lawyers Assn., Wash. Assn. Def. Counsel, Phi Beta Kappa. Contbr. articles to legal jour. Home: 8304 SE 62nd Mercer Island WA 98040 Office: 1700 Washington Bldg Seattle WA 98101 Tel (206) 223-7000

ISSELBACHER, RHODA SOLIN, b. Springfield, Mass., June 12, 1932; B.A., Cornell U., 1954; LL.B., J.D., Harvard, 1959. Admitted to Mass. bar, 1960; asso. Irving Fanger, Boston, 1960-65, firm Rudman & Pollock, Boston, 1965-70; of counsel Epstein, Salloway & Kaplan, Boston, 1970—. Alderman, Woods Hole, Mass., 1970-72; trustee Beaver Country Day Sch., Brookline, Mass., 1974—. Mem. Mass. Bar Assn. Designer patient adv. program Mass. Gen. Hosp., Boston, 1971-73; co-author: Science. Home: 20 Nobscot Rd Newton Center MA 02159 Office: 131 State St Boston MA Tel (617) 742-5400

ISSLER, HARRY, b. Cologne, Germany, Nov. 14, 1935; B.S. in Psychology, U. Wis., 1955; LL.B., Cornell U., 1958, J.D., 1969. Admitted to N.Y. bar, 1958, U.S. Supreme Ct. bar, 1962, U.S. Ct. Mil. Appeals bar, 1967; asso. firm Wing & Wing, N.Y.C., 1958-60, Fuchsberg & Fuchsberg, N.Y.C., 1960-62; partner firm Issler & Fein, N.Y.C., 1962-68, Shaw, Issler & Rosenberg, N.Y.C., 1968-70; individual practice law, N.Y.C., 1971—; JA 42d inf. div. N.Y. Army N.G., 1964—. Mem. N.Y. State Bar Assn., Am., N.Y. State trial lawyers assns. Office: 110 E 59th St New York City NY 10022 Tel (212) PL8-1600

ITSKOWITZ, HERMAN, b. N.Y.C., July 4, 1911; B.S., N.Y. U., 1931, J.D., 1934. Admitted to N.Y. bar, 1934; individual practice law, N.Y.C., 1935—; counsel to comptroller N.Y.C., 1948-53. Vice-chmn. bd. govs. Young Israel Concourse; pres. Men's Club; mem. Anti-Defamation League; chmn. B'nai Brith. Mem. N.Y. County Lawyers Assn., N.Y. State Plaintiffs Trial Lawyers Assn., Assn. Arbitrators City N.Y., Am. Arbitration Assn. Home: 601 E 20th St New York City NY 10010 Office: 305 Broadway New York City NY 10007 Tel (212) CO7-2268

ITTENBACH, JOHN FRANK, b. Indpls., Mar. 30, 1944; B.S., Ball State U., 1966; J.D. magna cum laude, Ind. U., Indpls., 1973. Admitted to Ind. bar, 1973; quality control engr., Chrysler Corp., 1966-69; systems analyst, Ind. Nat. Bank, 1969-70; law clk. to asso. justice Ind. Ct. Appeals, 1971-73; trial dep. Marion County (Ind.) Prosecutor's Office, 1973-76, supr. Career Criminal Programs Trial Sect., 1975-76; pub. defender, Indpls., 1976—; asso. law firm, 1973—; asso. prof. law, Butler U. Mem. Profl. Soc. Quality Control Engrs. Office: 1014 Circle Tower Bldg Indianapolis IN 46204 Tel (317) 639-9501

IVERSEN, ROLAND EDMUND, b. Paso Robles, Calif., Oct. 8, 1928; B.A., U. Calif., Berkeley, 1952, LL.B., J.D., 1955. Admitted to Calif. bar, 1952; individual practice law, Paso Robles, 1956-57; dep. dist. atty., San Luis Obispo County (Calif.), 1958-66, Placer County (Calif.), 1970-76. Mem. Republican Central Com., San Luis Obispo County. Mem. Calif. Bar Assn., Calif. Dist. Attys. Assn. Office: Court House Auburn CA 95603 Tel (916) 823-4451

IVES, ANDREW MCCORMACK, JR., b. Chgo., July 22, 1944; A.B., Dartmouth Coll., 1967; J.D., U. Calif., 1972. Admitted to N.Mex. bar, 1973; U.S. Supreme Ct. bar, 1976; asso. firm Bigbee, Stephenson, Carpenter & Crout, Santa Fe, N.Mex., 1973-76, partner, 1976—. Mem. Am., N.Mex. bar assns. Office: Suite 200 Bokum Bldg Santa Fe NM 87501 Tel (505) 982-4611

IVES, STEPHEN BRADSHAW, JR., b. N.Y.C., Oct. 6, 1924; A.B., Harvard U., 1948, LL.B., Yale U., 1951. Admitted to R.I. bar, 1952, D.C. bar, 1970, U.S. Supreme Ct. bar, 1960; practice law, Providence, 1952-61; asso. firm Hinckley, Allen, Salisbury & Parsons, 1952-57, partner, 1957-61; exec. asst. to adminstr. AID, Washington, 1961-62, dir. Office Korea Affairs, 1962-64, dir. Office E. Asian Affairs, 1964-66, asso. asst. adminstr. Far East, 1966-67, dep. asst. adminstr. E. Asia, 1967-68, gen. counsel, 1968-70; partner firm Wald, Harkrader and Ross, Washington, 1970—; mem. R.I. Mechanics Lein Law Commn., R.I. Commn. Interstate Coop. Bd. dirs. Providence Community Fund, Children's Friend and Service R.I. Mem. Am., D.C., R.I. (past mem. exec. com.), Fed. bar assns., Washington Fgn. Law Soc. (past pres.), Am. Soc. Internat. Law, Am. Arbitration Assn. (panel), Order of Coif, Phi Beta Kappa. Home: 3508 Macomb St NW Washington DC 20016 Office: 1320 19th St NW Washington DC 20036 Tel (202) 296-2121

IVESTER, JOHN HERMANN, b. New Orleans, July 15, 1941; B.E.E., U. Ark., 1964, J.D., 1972; M.E.E., So. Meth. U., 1968. Admitted to Ark. bar, 1972; mem. firm Friday, Eldredge & Clark, Little Rock, 1972—. Mem. Am., Ark., Pulaski County bar assns. Home: 5 Leslie Circle Little Rock AR 72205 Office: 20th floor First Nat Bldg Little Rock AR 72201 Tel (501) 376-2011

IVEY, JOHN COURTNEY, b. Dillon, S.C., Aug. 12, 1903; B.S., Yale, 1928, LL.B., 1929. Admitted to N.Y. State bar, 1932; partner firm Brown, Wood, Ivey Mitchell & Petty, N.Y.C., 1942—. Mem. Am., N.Y. State bar assns., Bar Assn. City N.Y., Down Town Assn. Home: 10 Brooklands Bronxville NY 10708 Office: One Liberty Plaza New York City NY 10006 Tel (212) 349-7500

IVEY, ROBERT LUTHER, b. Americus, Ga., May 11, 1941; B.A., Davidson (N.C.) Coll., 1964; LL.B., U. Va., 1967. Admitted to Va. bar, 1967, Calif. bar, 1970; law clk. Foley & Lardner, Milw., 1966; asso. firm Pettit, Evers & Martin, San Francisco, 1970-75; partner firm Levine and Krom, Beverly Hills, Calif., 1975—. Mem. Am., Los Angeles County, Beverly Hills bar assns. Notes editor: Va. Jour. of Internat. Law, 1966-67. Office: 404 N Roxbury Dr Beverly Hills CA 90210 Tel (213) 273-3555

IVEY, WILLIAM JAMES, b. DeLand, Fla., Aug. 8, 1930; B.A., Yale, 1952, LL.B., Harvard, 1955. Admitted to D.C. bar, 1955, N.Y. bar, 1957; asso. firm Sullivan & Cromwell, N.Y.C., 1955-62, partner firm, 1963—. Mem. Am., N.Y. bar assns., Assn. Bar City N.Y., N.Y. County Lawyers Assn. Home: 26 Saratoga Way Short Hills NJ 07078 Office: 125 Broad St New York City NY 10004 Tel (212) 952-8014

IVINS, JAMES ELBERT, b. Chgo., Oct. 8, 1912; Ph.B., U. Wis., 1935, J.D., 1938. Admitted to Wis. bar, 1938, Mo. bar, 1941, Ill. bar, 1946, Tex. bar, 1950, Md. bar, 1969; atty. SEC, Chgo., 1939-40, St. Louis, 1940-42; asso. firm Pam, Hurd & Reichmnann, Chgo., 1945-49; atty. Tenn. Gas Transmission Co. (name changed to Tenneco Inc.), Houston, 1949-52, corp. sec., 1952-58, v.p., sr. atty., 1960-65, v.p., gen. counsel, 1965-68; pres. Tenneco Corp., Wilmington, Del., 1968-74; individual practice law, Easton, Md., 1968—. Mem. Tex., Wis., Am., Md., Talbot County bar assns., Kappa Sigma (nat. pres. 1959-61). Home and Office: Box 538 Route 5 Easton MD 21601 Tel (301) 822-3395

IVONE, MICHAEL THOMAS, b. Bronx, N.Y., May 11, 1926; B.A., Bklyn. Coll., 1956; LL.B., N.Y. U., 1960. Admitted to N.Y. bar, 1961; asso. firm Dwyer & Lawler, Bklyn., 1960-61; trial atty. firm Cymrot, Wolin & Simon, N.Y.C., 1961-63, firm Bower, O'Connor, & Taylor, N.Y.C., 1963-68; partner firm Morris, Duffy, Ivone & Jensen, N.Y.C., 1968—. Mem. Am., N.Y., Suffolk County, bar assns., Nassa-Suffolk, Met. trial lawyers assns., Columbian Lawyers Assn. Office: 233 Broadway Ave New York City NY 10007 Tel (212) 766-1888

IZARD, JOHN, b. Hartford, Conn., Mar. 4, 1923; B.S., Yale, 1945; LL.B., U. Va., 1949. Admitted to Ga. bar, 1950; mem. firm King & Spalding, Atlanta, 1949—. Pres. Atlanta Legal Aid Soc., 1960; chmn. St. Citizens Services of Met. Atlanta, 1964-65; trustee Ga. Conservancy, 1970—; trustee U. Va. Law Sch. Found., 1974—. Mem. Am. Bar Assn. (chmn. sec. antitrust law 1974-75), Atlanta Bar Assn., State Bar Ga., Lawyers Club of Atlanta. Editor-in-chief Va. Law Review, 1948-49. Home: 4061 Glen Devon Dr Atlanta GA 30327 Office: 2500 Trust Co Tower Atlanta GA 30303 Tel (404) 572-4600

JABLON, ARNOLD E., b. N.Y.C., Oct. 17, 1943; B.A., State U. N.Y. at Albany, 1965; M.A., U. Md., 1971, J.D., 1968. Admitted to Md. bar, 1969, D.C. bar, 1973; mem. firm Jablon & Jablon, Balt., 1969—; lectr. U. Md. Mem. Am., Md., Balt., D.C. bar assns. Home: 3674 Forest Hill Rd Baltimore MD 21207 Office: 1018 Mondawmin St Baltimore MD 21215 Tel (301) 523-2122

JABLON, SAUL, b. Queens, N.Y., Oct. 8, 1938; B.A. in Social Scis., U. Md., 1962, LL.B., 1966. Admitted to Md. bar, 1966; sr. asst. state's atty., Balt., 1968-71; individual practice law, Balt., 1966—. Mem. Am., Md. State., Balt. City bar assns. Home: 3915 N Charles St Baltimore MD 21218 Office: 1018 Mondawmin Concourse Baltimore MD 21215 Tel (301) 523-2122

JABLONSKI, JOSEPH ZBIGNIEW, b. Ostrzeszow, Poland, Mar. 8, 1906; Magister Juris, U. Poznan (Poland), 1928; LL.B., Bklyn. Law Sch., 1954, J.D., 1967. Admitted to N.Y. State bar, 1956; individual practice law N.Y.C. 1956—; county judge, Poland, 1935-39. Chmn. Brit.-Polish War Pensions Appeal Tribunal, London, 1944-45. Mem. Polish Juridical Soc. in U.S. (sec. 1970—). Office: 276 Fifth Ave New York City NY 10001 Tel (212) 679-4737

JACHIMCZYK, JOSEPH ALEXANDER, b. Bridgeport, Conn., Sept. 15, 1923; M.D., U. Tenn., 1948; J.D., Boston Coll., 1958. Admitted to Tex. bar, 1959; intern Queen's Hosp., Honolulu, 1948-49; resident in pathology Hamot Hosp., Erie, Pa., 1949, Norwalk (Conn.) Hosp., 1949-50, Cleve. City Hosp., 1950-53; asst. med. examiner State of Md., Balt., 1953; staff USPHS Hosp., Brighton, Mass., 1954-56; teaching fellow dept. legal medicine Harvard U., 1954-57; forensic pathologist Office Med. Examiner Harris County (Tex.), Houston, 1957-60, chief med. examiner, 1960—; clin. prof. pathology U. Tex. Postgrad. Sch. Biomed. Scis.; asso. clin. prof. pathology Baylor U. Med. Sch.; instr. law enforcement La. State U.; guest lectr. Nat. Dist. Attys. Coll., U. Houston Law Sch.; sr. cons. pathology M.D. Anderson Tumor Inst., Houston. Diplomate Am. Bd. Pathology, Nat. Assn. Med. Examiners. Fellow Coll. Am. Pathologists, Am. Soc. Clin. Pathologists; mem. Am., Houston bar assns., Law Sci. Acad. Am., Nat. Advs. Soc., Law Enforcement Officers Assn. Tex., So., Tex. med assns., Harris County Med. Soc., Assn. Am. Physicians and Surgeons, Nat. Med. and Dental Assn., Soc. Nuclear Medicine, Tex. Soc. Pathologists, Houston Soc. Clin. Pathologists. Contbr. articles in field to profl. jours.; editorial bd. The Book of Health, 3d edit., 1973. Office: Room 209 301 San Jacinto St Houston TX 77002 Tel (713) 221-5250

JACK, ROBERT GEORGE, b. Nelsonville, Ohio, July 15, 1924; B.S. in Commerce, Ohio U., 1948; J.D., Duke, 1951. Admitted to Ohio bar, 1951, U.S. Supreme Ct. bar, 1964; agt. FBI, 1951-54; individual practice law, Columbus, Ohio, 1954—; mem. firm Jack & Merwin, Columbus, 1958—. Mem. Columbus Bd. Zoning Appeals, 1973—. Mem. Ohio, Columbus bar assns. Home: 184 Ceramic Dr Columbus OH 43214 Office: 85 E Gay St Columbus OH 43215 Tel (614) 224-3161

JACK, WILLIAM HARRY, b. Kaufman, Tex., Dec. 13, 1899; J.D., U. Tex., 1922, B.A., 1923. Admitted to Tex. bar, 1922, U.S. Supreme Ct. bar, 1950; partner firm Jack & Jack, Corsicana, Tex. 1923-26; partner firm Saner, Jack, Sallinger Nichols, Dallas, 1926—; dir. Booth, Inc., Carrollton, Tex. Pres., Blanche Mary Taxis Found., Dallas, 1958—; bd. dirs. Dallas Child Guidance Clinic, 1956-58. Fellow Am. Bar Found., SW Legal Found. (trustee 1966—, vice chmn. 1970-75); mem. Am. Coll. Probate Counsel (dir. 1959-63, pres. 1963-64), Am. (ho. dels. 1957-59, 68-70), Dallas (pres. 1951) bar assns., State Bar Tex. dir., v.p. 1962-63), Phi Beta Kappa, Phi Delta Phi. Home: 4349 Potomac Ave Dallas TX 75205 Office: 1200 Republic Bank Bldg Dallas TX 75201 Tel (214) 742-5464

JACKETT, WILBUR ROY, b. Tompkins, Sask., Can., June 27, 1912; B.A., U. Sask., 1931, LL.B., 1933; B.A. in Jurisprudence (Rhodes scholar) Oxford (Eng.) U., 1936, B.C.L., 1937, M.A., 1949. Admitted to Sask. bar, 1938, Ont. bar, 1952, Que. bar, 1960, B.C., 1964; Queen's counsel, 1949; asso. with G.H. Yule, Saskatoon, 1937-38; with Canadian Dept. Justice, 1939-60, dep. minister justice, dep. atty. gen. Can., 1957-60; gen. counsel C.P. Ry., 1960-64; pres. Exchequer Ct. of Can., 1964-71; chief justice Fed. Ct. Can., 1971—. Hon. lectr. Osgoode Hall Law Sch., Toronto, 1954. Contbr. legal articles to profl. jours. Home: Tiffany Apts 150 Driveway Ottawa ON Canada Office: Supreme and Exchequer Ct Bldg Ottawa ON Canada*

JACKSON, ALPHONSO ROY, b. Marshall, Tex., Sept. 9, 1946; B.S., NE Mo. State U., 1968, M.A., 1969; J.D., Washington U., 1973. Asst. prof. criminal justice dept. U. Mo., St. Louis, 1973—; dir. dept. pub. safety City of St. Louis, 1977—; asst. vis. prof. Washington U., 1976; vis. lectr. U. Lagos (Nigeria), 1974; legal clk. IRS, St. Louis, 1973. Vice-pres., mem. exec. com. Drug and Substance Council of Met. St. Louis, 1975-77. Mem. Am. Soc. Criminology, Nat. Conf. Black Lawyers, St. Louis Council on World Affairs, U.S. Sister Cities Internat., Law and Soc. Assn., ACLU Eastern Mo. (trustee 1976—). Kellog fellow, 1969-70; contbr. articles to legal jours. Office: 8001 Natural Bridge Rd Saint Louis MO 63121

JACKSON, CECIL CAIRNES, JR., b. Asheville, N.C., Aug. 16, 1934; B.A., Wake Forest U., 1956, LL.B., 1959. Admitted to N.C. bar, 1960; spl. agt. FBI, 1960-62; individual practice law, Asheville, 1962—. Mem. Buncombe County Bar Assn., N.C. State Bar, Am. Trial Lawyers Assn. Office: 18 S Pack Sq Asheville NC 28801 Tel (704) 252-1562

JACKSON, CHARLES GORDON, JR., b. Dallas, May 4, 1927; B.B.A., U. Tex., 1950; J.D., So. Meth. U., 1960. Admitted to Tex. bar, 1960; individual practice law, Dallas, 1960—; pres. Gordon Jackson Co., Realtors, Dallas, 1950—, Gordon Jackson Realty Co., property mgmt., Dallas, 1950—, Gordon Jackson Real Estate Counselors, Dallas, 1960—; lectr. Sch. Bus., So. Meth. U., Dallas Coll., El Centro Jr. Coll., Massey Bus. Coll., Chmn., real estate div. Dallas County Cancer Soc., 1973. Mem. Nat., Tex. (lectr., dir. 1974—) assns. realtors, Inst. Real Estate Mgmt. (pres. Dallas-Ft. Worth area 1954-56), Greater Dallas Bd. Realtors (pres. 1973-74), Tex. Bar Assn. Office: 4505 N Central Expy Dallas TX 75205 Tel (214) 521-9941

JACKSON, DAVID DICKARD, b. Dallas, Sept. 30, 1942; B.A., So. Methodist U., 1964, LL.B., 1967. Admitted to Tex. bar, 1967; mem. firm Luna & Jackson, Dallas, 1967-73; judge Probate Ct. #2 Dallas County (Tex.), Dallas, 1973—. Mem. Dallas, Am., Tex. (mem. admissions com.) bar assns., Phi Alpha Delta. Office: Probate Ct #2 Records Bldg Dallas TX 75201 Tel (214) 749-8138

JACKSON, EDWARD NATHAN, b. San Francisco, Feb. 15, 1902; A.B., U. Calif., Berkeley, 1923; J.D., Hastings Coll. Law, U. Calif., 1926. Admitted to Calif. bar, 1927, U.S. Supreme Ct. bar, 1949; individual practice law, San Francisco, 1927—. Past v.p., bd. dirs. Legal Aid Soc. San Francisco. Mem. Am., San Francisco bar assns., Lawyers Club San Francisco (past pres.), Hastings Coll. Law Alumni Assn. (past pres.). Author: California Debt Collection Practice. Office: 1255 Post St Suite 946 San Francisco CA 94109 Tel (415) 776-7677

JACKSON, FRANCIS CLARK, b. Phila., June 26, 1941; B.A., Regis Coll., 1964; grad. Denver U. Law Sch., 1967. Admitted to Colo. bar, 1968; individual practice law, 1968-69; dep. dist. atty. 1969-74; dist. ct. referee City of Golden (Colo.), 1974—. Mem. Juvenile Judges Council for Colo. Home: 8794 Chase Dr Arvada CO 80003 Office: Hall of Justice Golden CO 80401 Tel (303) 279-6511

JACKSON, FRANK BROWNLOW, b. Hendersonville, N.C., May 26, 1947; A.B., U. N.C., 1969, J.D., 1971. Admitted to N.C. bar, 1972; asso. firm Manning, Allen & Hudson, Chapel Hill, N.C., 1972-73; partner firm Cabe & Jackson, Franklin, N.C., 1973-74, Graham, Manning, Cheshire & Jackson, Chapel Hill, 1974-77, firm Manning, Jackson, Osborn & Frankstone, P.A., 1977—. Mem. Am., N.C., Orange County bar assns., N.C. Acad. Trial Lawyers, Profl. Trial Lawyers Inst. Recipient Am. Jurisprudence award, 1971. Office: Suite 308 NML Bldg E Chapel Hill NC 27514 Tel (919) 968-4413

JACKSON, GARY MONROE, b. Denver, Nov. 10, 1945; B.A., U. Colo., 1967, J.D., 1970. Admitted to Colo. bar, 1971; with Denver Dist. Attys. office, 1970-74, U.S. Attys. Office, Dist. Colo., 1974-76; asso. firm DiManna, Eklund & Ciancio, Denver, 1976—; prof. Webster Coll., Denver, 1976; vis. prof. U. Colo., Denver, 1976; mem. adv. com Legis. Com. on Judiciary; mem. state adv. com. U.S. Civil Rights Commn. Bd. dirs. Urban League Colo. Mem. Am., Colo., Sam Cary bar assns., Nat. Conf. Black Lawyers. Recipient spl. commendation U.S. Atty. Gen. Home: 655 Pearl St Denver CO 80203 Office: 50 S Steele St Denver CO 80209 Tel (303) 320-4848

JACKSON, GEORGE TERRY, b. Rutherfordton, N.C., Oct. 27, 1943; B.A., Atlantic Christian Coll., 1966; J.D., U. Ga., 1971. Admitted to Ga. bar, 1971; gen. atty. Office Gen. Counsel, VA, Washington, 1971-73; asso. firm O.B. Langford, Winder, Ga., 1974; mem. firm Harris & Jackson, Savannah, Ga., 1974-75; individual practice law, Savannah, 1975—. Bd. dirs. Isle of Hope Methodist Ch., Savannah, YMCA Indian Guide, Savannah, Bethesda Home for Boys, Savannah. Mem. Am., Ga., Savannah bar assn., Am., Ga. trial lawyers assns., Ga. Criminal Def. Lawyers Assn., Sigma Phi Epsilon. Home: 13 Pinewood Ave Savannah GA 31406 Office: Suite 302 31 W Congress S POB 9417 Savannah GA 31402 Tel (912) 234-6350

JACKSON, GEORGE WINFIELD, b. Belhaven, N.C., Nov. 17, 1937; A.B., U. N.C., 1960, J.D., 1966. Admitted to N.C. bar, 1966; since practiced in Roxboro, N.C., partner firm Jackson & Hicks, and predecessors, 1966—; N.C. commr. Nat. Conf. Commrs. on Uniform State Laws, 1974—; mem. Butner municipal adv. com. N.C. Dept. Human Resources, 1973—, Gov. N.C.'s Com. on Law and Order, 1975; city atty. Roxboro, 1969-71; mem. prof. adv. com. Person-Orange Mental Health Authorities, 1969-70; mayor, Roxboro, 1971-76. Mem. Person County Bd. Health, 1971—; mem. Roxboro Jaycees, v.p., 1969, dir., 1968, 69, 71; pres. Santa's Helpers, 1970, dir., 1970-74; sec. Person County United Fund, 1968, dir., 1969; chmn. Person County Cancer Crusade, 1969. Mem. Roxboro C. of C., Am., N.C. State, Person County, 9th Jud. Dist. bar assns., Delta Beta Phi. Home: 612 Hillhaven Terr Roxboro NC 27573 Office: POB 490 Roxboro NC 27573 Tel (919) 599-0211

JACKSON, JAMES A., b. Providence, Dec. 10, 1929; B.A. magna cum laude, Providence Coll., 1952; J.D., Georgetown U., 1955. Admitted to D.C. bar, 1955, R.I. bar, 1956; legal specialist USNR, 1956-59; asso. firm Tillinghast, Collins & Graham, and predecessors, Providence, 1959-65, partner, 1965—; town solicitor Barrington (R.I.), 1962-73. Mem. Republican town com., Barrington, 1960—. Mem. Am., R.I. bar assns. Bd. editors Georgetown Law Jour., 1955. Home: 22 Robbins Dr Barrington RI 02806 Office: 2000 Hospital Trust Tower Providence RI 02903 Tel (401) 274-3800

JACKSON, JAMES KINSEY, b. Savoy, Tex., Sept. 12, 1940; B.B.A., So. Meth. U., 1963; LL.B., U. Tex., 1966. Admitted to Tex. bar, 1966, D.C. bar, 1970; with Office of Chief Counsel, IRS, Washington, 1966-70, asst. br. chief; asso. firm Steptoe & Johnson, Washington, 1970-75; partner firm Pepper, Hamilton & Scheets, Washington, 1976—. Mem. Tex., D.C., Am. bar assns. Contbr. articles to legal jours. Home: 902 Hurley Ave Rockville MD 20850 Office: 1776 F St NW Washington DC 20006 Tel (202) 467-6500

JACKSON, JERRY W., b. Haleyville, Ala., Dec. 3, 1939; A.S., Walker Coll., Jasper, Ala., 1965; B.S., Florence (Ala.) State Coll., 1966; J.D., Samford U., 1969. Admitted to Ala. bar, 1969, U.S. Dist. Ct. No. Dist. Ala. bar, 1970; individual practice law, Haleyville, Ala., 1969—; city judge City of Haleyville, 1972—. Pres. Haleyville Area C. of C., 1973-74, Haleyville Civitan Club, 1973-74. Mem. Assn. Trial Lawyers Am., Am., Ala., Winston County bar assns., Am. Judicature Soc., Ala. Trial Lawyers Assn. Home: Route 1 Haleyville AL 35565 Office: 914 19th St PO Box 819 Haleyville AL 35565 Tel (205) 486-3618

JACKSON, JOHN HOWARD, b. Kansas City, Mo., Apr. 6, 1932; A.B., Princeton, 1954; J.D., U. Mich., 1959. Admitted to Mich. bar, 1970, Mo. bar, 1959, Wis. bar, 1959, Calif. bar, 1965; asso. firm Foley, Sammond & Lardner, Milw., 1959-61; asso. prof. to prof. law U. Calif., Berkeley, 1961-66; vis. prof. law U. Mich., 1964; research scholar Hdqrs. Gen. Agreement on Tariffs and Trade, Geneva, 1965; prof. law U. Mich., 1966—; vis. prof., Rockefeller fellow, Brussels, 1975-76; vis. prof. law U. Delhi (India), 1968-69; gen. counsel Office of the Spl. Trade Rep., U.S. Exec. Office of the Pres., Washington, 1973-74. Mem. Am. Bar Assn., Council on Fgn. Relations, Am. Soc. Internat. Law. Author: World Trade and the Law of GATT, 1969; Contract Law in Modern Society - Cases and Materials, 1973; Legal Problems of International Economic Relations, 1977; editorial bd. Jour. World Trade Law, 1967, Jour. Law and Policy in Internat. Bus., 1969. Home: 1 Heatheridge St Ann Arbor MI 48104 Office: 965 Legal Research Bldg Univ Michigan Law School Ann Arbor MI 48109 Tel (313) 764-2359

JACKSON, JOSEPH ELMER, b. Fillmore, Utah, Nov. 7, 1935; B.S. in Banking and Fin., U. Utah, 1958, S.J.D., 1961. Admitted to Utah bar, 1961; congressional asst. Congressman Sherman Lloyd, Utah, 1961-63; partner firm Cline & Jackson, 1963-65, firm Clint, Jackson & McCoy, 1965-68, firm Cline, Jackson & Jackson, 1968-72, firm Cline, Jackson, Mayer & Benson, Cedar City, Utah, 1971—. Mem. Utah Bar Commn., 1970-76. Bd. dirs. Little League Baseball, 1971-75, Jr. League Football, 1971-75. Mem. Am., Utah, So. Utah (pres. 1966-68) bar assns. Home: 293 S 450 W Cedar City UT 84720 Office: 110 N Main St North F Cedar City UT 84720 Tel (801) 586-6532

JACKSON, LENWOOD A., b. Concord, Ga., Jan. 11, 1944; B.A., Morris Brown Coll., 1966; J.D., Emory U., 1969. Admitted to Ga. bar, 1970; law clk. OEO, summer 1967, firm Johnson & Jordan, Atlanta, 1968-69; legal asst. Emory U. Neighborhood Law Office, Atlanta, 1969; atty. Region 21, NLRB, Los Angeles, 1969-70; asso. firm Latimer, Haddon & Stanfield, Atlanta, 1971-72; partner firm Patterson, Parks, Jackson & Howell, Atlanta, 1972—; asso. atty. Atlanta Bd. Edn., 1971—; instr. Atlanta U., 1973. Mem. Am., Nat., Gate City, Ga., Atlanta bar assns., Nat. Orgn. on Legal Problems of Edn., Nat. Council Sch. Attys. (exec. com.), Phi Delta Phi. Home: 1691 Laurens Dr SW Atlanta GA 30311 Office: 101 Marietta St NW Suite 2222 Atlanta GA 30303 Tel (404) 577-5900

JACKSON, MAYNARD HOLBROOK, b. Dallas, Mar. 23, 1938; B.A. in Polit. Sci. (Ford Found. Early Admission scholar 1952-56, Glancy fellow 1954-56), Morehouse Coll., 1956; J.D. cum laude, N.C. Central U., 1964. Claims examiner Main Cleve. office Ohio Bur. Unemployment Compensation, 1957-58; admitted to Ga. bar, 1965; gen. atty. NLRB, Atlanta, 1964-67; atty. Emory U. Community Legal Services Center, Atlanta, 1967-68; mng. atty., dir. community relations Emory U. Neighborhood Law Offices, Atlanta, 1968-69; sr. partner firm Jackson, Patterson & Parks, Atlanta, 1970-73; vice mayor, pres. bd. aldermen City of Atlanta, 1970-74, mayor, 1974—. Democratic candidate U.S. Senate, 1968. Mem. Am., Ga., Atlanta bar assns., Atlanta Legal Aid Soc. Tel (404) 658-6100

JACKSON, MORTON BARROWS, b. Devil's Lake, N.D., July 17, 1921; student Harvard U.; J.D., U. So. Calif., 1948. Admitted to Calif. bar, 1949, U.S. Supreme Ct. bar, 1968; asso. firm Dana, Bledsoe & Smith, San Francisco, 1948-51; v.p. Far East ops. Intercontinental Engring. Corp. of San Francisco, Bangkok, Thailand, 1951-54; exec. asst. to dir. Intergovtl. Com. for European Migration, Geneva, 1954-58; regional commr. immigration for Southeastern U.S. and Carribean area Immigration and Naturalization Service, Dept. Justice, Richmond, Va., 1958-59; asso. firm Hill, Farrer & Burrill, Los Angeles, 1959-64, partner, 1964-68; partner firm Jackson & Goodstein, Los Angeles, 1968—; analyst, commentator, polit. editor Radio Sta. KMPC, Los Angeles, 1960—; counsel Am. Youth Symphony. Founding dir. Los Angeles Chamber Orch.; chmn. bd. Thomas Jefferson Research Center, Pasadena, Calif.; bd. dirs. Inst. Advanced Musical Studies. Mem. Am. Arbitration Assn. (panelist) Los Angeles County, Fed. (pres. Los Angeles chpt. 1968-70), Am. (Gavel awards, 1965, 66) bar assns., Am. Judicature Soc., State Bar Calif., Bus. Trial Lawyers Assn., U. So. Calif. Alumni Assn., Legion Lex (dir. 1967-70), Order of Coif, Phi Delta Phi. Recipient medal for broadcast material Freedoms Found., 1966; editorial bd. U. So. Calif. Law Rev., 1946-48. Office: 1901 Ave of the Stars Suite 1600 Los Angeles CA 90067 Tel (213) 277-0200

JACKSON, RANDALL CALVIN, b. Baird, Tex., Mar. 21, 1919; B.B.A., U. Tex., Austin, 1941, J.D., 1946; postgrad. Harvard Practicing Law Inst., 1961, 67, 76. Admitted to Tex. bar, 1946, U.S. Supreme Ct. bar, 1964; practiced in Baird, 1947-62, Abilene, Tex., 1962—, individual practice law, Baird, 1947-49; partner firm Jackson & Jackson, 1949—; lectr. continuing legal edn. Mem. Tex. Securities Bd.; chmn. Sears Meth. Retirement Center, Abilene; pres. West Tex. Hereford Assn.; bd. dirs. Sweetwater Hereford Assn.; chmn. bd. trustees Abilene dist. United Meth. Ch. Fellow Am. Coll. Probate Counsel; mem. State Bar Tex., Am., Taylor County (1st v.p.) bar assns., Tex. Bar Found. (charter), Am. Judicature Soc., Southwestern Legal Found. Home: Route 2 POB 703 Abilene TX 79601 Office: 210 Bank of Commerce Bldg Abilene TX 79605 Tel (915) 698-9280

JACKSON, RANDOLPH, b. Bklyn., Oct. 10, 1943; B.A., N.Y. U., 1965; J.D., Bklyn. Law Sch., 1969. Admitted to N.Y. bar, 1970, U.S. Supreme Ct. bar, 1976; asso. firm Mudge, Rose, Guthrie & Alexander, N.Y.C., 1969-70; individual practice law, Bklyn., 1971-73; partner firm Jackson Kupperman & Clarke and predecessor, Bklyn., 1973—. Bd. dirs. Concord Nursing Home, Inc. Mem. Bedford-Stuyvesant Lawyers Assn. (pres. 1974—), Nat., N.Y. State, Bklyn. bar assns. Office: 189 Montague St Brooklyn NY 11201 Tel (212) 858-2890

JACKSON, RAYMOND SIDNEY, JR., b. Bklyn., Sept. 17, 1938; B.A., Williams Coll., 1960; J.D., Harvard, 1966. Admitted to N.Y. bar, 1967; partner firm Thacher, Proffitt & Wood, N.Y.C., 1966—. Mem. Am. Bar Assn., Maritime Law Assn. U.S. Office: 40 Wall St New York City NY 10005 Tel (212) 483-5809

JACKSON, RICHARD LYNN, b. Bay City, Tex., Oct. 31, 1944; student U. Tex., Austin, 1963-65, North Tex. State U., 1965-67; J.D., Baylor U., 1970. Admitted to Tex. bar, 1970, U.S. Supreme Ct. bar, 1974; partner firm Johnson, Bromberg, Leeds & Riggs, Dallas, 1975-76; individual practice law, Dallas, 1976—. Mem. Tex., Dallas bar assns. Contbr. articles to Baylor Law Rev., editor-in-chief, 1969-70. Home: 3500 Lexington Ave Dallas TX 75205 Office: 1240 1st Nat Bank Bldg Dallas TX 75202 Tel (214) 742-1701

JACKSON, ROBERT HOWARD, b. Cleve., Dec. 12, 1936; A.B., U. Ill., 1958; J.D., Case Western Res. U., 1961. Admitted to Ohio bar, 1961; atty. SEC, Cleve., 1961-66; partner firm Kohrman & Jackson, 1969—; lectr. on securities; chmn. subcom. proxy solicitations shareholders proposals Fed. Securities Commn., 1969-73. Dir. Mor-Flo Industries, Inc., Budget Inns of Am., Inc. Mem. Am., Fed., Internat., Cleve. bar assns., Fed. Securities Commn. (chmn. Cleve. chpt.). Contbr. articles to profl law jours. Home: 3661 Traver Rd Shaker Heights OH 44122 Office: 1600 Central Nat Bank Bldg Cleveland OH 44114 Tel (216) 696-8700

JACKSON, SELWYN CHARLES, b. Boston, Oct. 11, 1912; LL.B., Boston Coll., 1938; LL.M., George Washington U., 1951. Admitted to Mass. bar, 1939, Ohio bar, 1949; individual practice law, Boston, 1939-42; chief claims sect. Wright-Patterson AFB, 1949-55; individual practice law, Dayton, Ohio, 1955—. Mem. Dayton Bar Assn. Home: 815 Hallworth St Trotwood OH 45426 Office: 2253 N Gettysburg St Dayton OH 45406 Tel (513) 277-8931

JACKSON, THEODORE RICHARD, b. N.Y.C., Apr. 20, 1923; A.B., Columbia, 1944, LL.B., 1948. Admitted to N.Y. State bar, 1949, U.S. Supreme Ct. bar, 1955; asso. firm Gilbert & Gilbert, N.Y.C., 1949-57, partner, 1958—. Mem. Am., New Rochelle bar assns., Fed. Bar Council (past pres.), Copyright Soc. U.S.A. (former trustee), Assn. Bar City N.Y. Home: 335 Beechmont Dr New Rochelle NY 10804 Office: 10 E 40th St New York City NY 10016 Tel (212) 532-3140

JACKSON, THOMAS, b. Saginaw, Mich., Oct. 2, 1930; B.A., U. Idaho, 1953; J.D., U. So. Calif., 1959; Admitted to Calif. bar, 1960; individual practice law, Redondo Beach, Calif., 1960-62; atty. Mangla Dam contractors Guy F. Atkinson, South San Francisco, Calif., 1962-65; asst. staff counsel San Francisco Bay Area Rapid Transit Dist., Oakland, Calif., 1966-69, asso. gen. counsel, 1969—; lectr. law Golden Gate U. Law Sch., eves. 1970-71. Home: 59 Wildomar St Mill Valley CA 94941 Office: 800 Madison St Oakland CA 94607 Tel (415) 465-4100

JACKSON, THOMAS SEARING, b. Washington, Dec. 1, 1909; A.B., George Washington U., 1933, LL.B., 1935. Admitted to D.C. bar, 1935, Md. bar, 1941, U.S. Supreme Ct. bar, 1949; asso. firm Brandenburg & Brandenburg, Washington, 1935-57; partner firm Jackson, Campbell & Parkinson, and predecessors, Washington, 1957—; gen. counsel Am. Land Title Assn., Restaurant Assn. Met. Washington; dir. Eastern-Liberty Fed. Savs. & Loan Assn. Mem. Montgomery County (Md.) Bd. Edn., 1958-59, chmn., 1959. Fellow Am. Coll. Trial Lawyers (bd. regents 1964-68, sec. 1968, pres. found. 1969-75), Am. Bar Found.; mem. Internat. Assn. Ins. Counsel, Am. Bar Assn., Am. Judicature Soc. (past dir.), Bar Assn. D.C. (pres. 1962-63), Nat. Inst. Trial Advocacy (bd. dirs.), The Barristers (past pres.), Lawyers Club Washington (pres. 1975-77). Recipient Alumni Achievement award George Washington U., 1975. Home: 4545 MacArthur Blvd NW Washington DC 20007 Office: 1828 L St NW Suite 1111 Washington DC 20036 Tel (202) 457-1620

JACKSON, TRAVIS MOORE, b. Harrisburg, Ark., June 17, 1930; B.S. in Econs. and Bus., Wheaton Coll., 1956; J.D., U. Calif., Berkeley, 1960. Admitted to Calif. bar, 1961; mem. firm Truce, Veal, Jackson & Taylor, San Carlos, Calif., 1961—. Mem. San Carlos C. of C., Christian Legal Soc., Christian Estate Planners Calif. Recipient Wall St. Jour. Scholastic Achievement award Wheaton Coll., 1956. Office: 1710 Industrial St San Carlos CA 94070 Tel (415) 593-1871

JACKSON, WILLIAM ARTHUR, b. Cuba City, Wis., Apr. 14, 1920; Ph.B., U. Wis., 1942, J.D., 1948. Admitted to Wis. bar, 1948, Supreme Ct. U.S. bar, 1975; pub. accountant Ronald Mattox & Assos., Madison, Wis., 1941-43, 46-48; individual practice law, Portage, Wis., 1948-51; asso. Harvey Peters, Milw., 1951-69; gen. counsel, sec. Plastics Engring. Co., Sheboygan, Wis., 1969—. Mem. Am., Wis. bar assns., Wis. Soc. C.P.A.'s, Am. Inst. C.P.A.'s, Phi Alpha Delta, Delta Chi. C.P.A., Wis. Home: 1727 Ridge Rd Sheboygan WI 53081 Office: PO Box 551 Sheboygan WI 53081

JACKSON, ZALPH BOONE, b. Humansville, Mo., July 5, 1910; student Draughons-Springfield (Mo.) Bus. U., 1927-29, George Washington U., 1931-33; LL.B., J.D., Golden Gate Coll., 1947. Admitted to Calif. bar, 1947; sr. partner firm Jackson & Hertogs, San Francisco, 1948-75, of counsel, 1975—; chmn., dir. Bank of Trade of San Francisco, 1961—. Mem. Calif., San Francisco bar assns., Immigration and Nationality Lawyers Assn. Contbr. articles to legal jours. Office: 580 Washington St San Francisco CA 94111 Tel (415) 986-4559

JACO, LYSTON GAINES, JR., b. Normandy, Tenn., June 13, 1921; B.S., U. Tenn., 1941; grad. meteorologist Mass. Inst. Tech., 1942; J.D., U. Mich., 1949. Admitted to Calif. bar, 1950; with United Calif. Bank, Los Angeles, 1949—; v.p., 1955—, trust counsel, 1972—. Mem. Am., Calif., Los Angeles County bar assns., Los Angeles Life Ins. and Trust Counsel (past pres.), So. Calif. Trust Officers Assn. (pres. 1974-75), Calif. Bankers Assn., Los Angeles C. of C. Home: 4184 Chevy Chase Dr Flintridge CA 91011 Office: 707 Wilshire Blvd Los Angeles CA 90017 Tel (213) 614-3337

JACOB, WILLIAM ANDREW, b. Detroit, Oct. 27, 1926; B.S. in Indsl. Engring., Syracuse U., 1946; J.D., U. Fla., 1966. Admitted to Fla. bar, 1966; asso. firm J. Russell Hornsby, Orlando, Fla., 1966-67; individual practice law, Orlando, 1967-71, 76—; partner firm Jacob & Benson, Orlando, 1971-76. Mem. Am., Orange County bar assns., Fla. Bar (chmn. lawyer referral com. 1973, 76). Home: 2179 Whitehall Dr Winter Park FL 32792 Office: Suite 950 Hartford Bldg Orlando FL 32801 Tel (305) 849-0670

JACOBI, ROBERT BENNETT, b. Washington, May 19, 1930; LL.B., Washington and Lee U., 1954; A.B., Am. U., 1958; LL.M., Georgetown U., 1962. Admitted to Va. bar, 1954, D.C. bar, 1958; with FCC, Washington, 1958-61, 63-65; asso. firm Cohn and Marks, Washington, 1965-71, partner, 1972—. Mem. Va., DC., Fed. Communications bar assns. Office: 1920 L St NW Washington DC 20036 Tel (202) 293-3860

JACOBS, ALAN LAWRENCE, b. N.Y.C., Jan. 10, 1942; B.A., Franklin and Marshall Coll., 1963; J.D., Columbia, 1966. Admitted to N.Y. state bar, 1967, Mass. bar, 1969, Fed. bar, 1968; asso. firm Parker, Chapin, Flattau & Klimpl, N.Y.C., 1963-68; asso. firm Rudman, Pollock & Katz, Boston, 1968-70; partner firm Pollock, O'Connor & Jacobs, Boston and Waltham, Mass., 1970—; dir. New Boston Bank Co., 1969-76, Am. Program Bur., Inc., Chestnut Hill, Mass., 1970-76, DataCon Cos., Inc., Woburn, Mass., 1973—, Gemini Artists Mgmt. N.Y.C., 1975—. Chmn. Lawyers Div. Boston Chpt. Am. Friends Hebrew U. Jerusalem, 1974-75; mem. group services subcom. social planning and allocations com. Combined Jewish Philanthropies Greater Boston, 1976—; mem. leadership cabinet United Jewish Appeal, 1975-76. Mem. Am., Mass., Boston, N.Y. State bar assns., Assn. Bar City N.Y. (mem. arbitration com.). Home: 10 Emerson Place Boston MA 02114 Office: 470 Totten Pond Rd Waltham MA 02154 Tel (617) 890-0500

JACOBS, ALBERT LIONEL, b. Boston, Sept. 30, 1899; B.S., Harvard, 1922; LL.B., Georgetown, 1923-26; admitted to D.C. bar, 1926, U.S. Supreme Ct. bar, 1931; asso. Commr. Patents James T. Newton, Washington, 1926-27; patent advisor U.S. Dept. Navy, Washington, 1928; asso. firm Green & McCallister, Pitts., 1929-41, partner, 1936-41; head dept. patents Sterling Drug, Inc., N.Y.C., 1941-47; founder, sr. mem. firm Jacobs & Jacobs, P.C., N.Y.C., 1947—; lectr. in field. Fellow Am. Inst. Chemists; mem. D.C., Am., Fed. bar assns., Fed. Bar Council, N.Y. Patent Law Assn., Am. Judicature Soc., Am. Chem. Soc., AAAS, Licensing Execs. Soc., Internat. Assn. Protection Intellectual Property. Author: Patent Forms, 1957, supplement, 1961; Patent & Trademark Forms, 1967, rev. edit. (with Albert L. Jacobs, Jr.) 1976; contbr. articles to profl. jours.; patentee in field. Home: 325 E 41st St New York City NY 10017 Office: 521 Fifth Ave New York City NY 10017 Tel (212) 687-1636

JACOBS, ARNOLD STEPHEN, b. N.Y.C., Feb. 26, 1940; B.M.E., Cornell U., 1961, M.B.A., 1963, LL.B., 1964. Admitted to N.Y. bar, 1964; asso. firm Hughes, Hubbard & Reed, N.Y.C., 1964-71, Shea, Gould, Climenko & Casey, N.Y.C., 1971—; lectr. in field. Mem. N.Y. State, N.Y.C. bar assns. Author: The Impact of Rule 106-5, vol. 1, 1974, vol. 2, 1976; contbr. articles to legal jours. Home: 108 E 82d St New York City NY 10028 Office: Shea Gould Climenko & Casey 330 Madison Ave New York City NY 10017 Tel (212) 661-3200

JACOBS, DAVID HAROLD, b. N.Y.C., Oct. 9, 1909; A.B., Clark U., 1930; LL.B., Yale, 1934. Admitted to Conn. bar, 1934, Mass. bar, 1940; partner firm Jacobs & Jacobs, Meriden, Conn., 1934-59; judge U.S. Circuit Ct. of Appeals of Conn., 1959-73, chief judge, 1973-75; judge Ct. of Common Pleas, Meriden, 1975—; vis. prof. law U. Ghana, Accra, 1972. Mem. Hartford (Conn.) Commn. on Adult Probation, 1971-73, Conn. Jud. Rev. Council, Hartford, 1973-75. Mem. Conn. Safety Council, 1973-75. Mem. Meriden-Southington-Wallingford, Conn. (editor in chief jour. 1946-53, pres. 1955-56), Am. bar assns., Phi Beta Kappa. Contbr. articles, book revs. to legal publs. Home: 127 Lambert Ave Meriden CT 06450 Office: 165 Miller St Meriden CT 06450 Tel (203) 237-6765

JACOBS, DOUGLAS PERRI, b. N.Y.C., Mar. 19, 1948; B.A., Bklyn. Coll., 1968; J.D., Boston U., 1971. Admitted to N.Y. state bar, 1972, Fla. bar, 1972; asso. firm Aranow, Brodsky, Bohlinger, Benetar, Einhorn & Dann, N.Y.C., 1971-72; staff atty. SEC, N.Y. regional office, N.Y.C., 1972-76, chief atty. br. enforcement, 1976—. Mem. N.Y. State Bar Assn., Fla. Bar. Office: 26 Federal Plaza New York City NY 10007 Tel (212) 264-1600

JACOBS, HAROLD WEINBERG, b. Kingstree, S.C., June 5, 1923; B.S., U.S. Naval Acad., 1945; LL.B., U. S.C., 1960. Admitted to S.C. bar, 1960; partner firm Nexsen, Pruet, Jacobs & Pollard, Columbia, 1962—; chmn. com. character and fitness S.C. Supreme Ct., 1974-77. Sr. warden St. Michaels and All Angels Episcopal Ch., Columbia, 1974-75. Mem. Am., S.C. (chmn. com. jud. reform 1968—, award for services in area of jud. reform 1973, pres. 1972-73), Richland County (S.C.) (chmn. grievance com. 1965-68) bar assns., Am. Judicature Soc. (Herbert Lincoln Harley award 1974, dir. 1974—), Fedn. Ins. Counsel, Conf. Bar Pres's., S.C. Def. Attys. Assn. (pres. 1970-71). Home: 5 Northlake Rd Columbia SC 29204 Office: 1st Nat Bank Bldg Main St Washington Sts Columbia SC 29201 Tel (803) 771-8900

JACOBS, HERBERT SAMUEL, b. Atlantic City, Feb. 15, 1933; A.B., Dartmouth Coll., 1954; J.D., N.Y. U., 1957. Admitted to N.J. bar, 1958; practiced in Atlantic City, 1959-61; asst. U.S. atty. Dist. N.J., 1961-64; judge Atlantic County (N.J.) Dist. Ct., 1964—. Office: 1201 Bacharach Blvd Atlantic City NJ 08401 Tel (609) 344-0393

JACOBS, JACK BERNARD, b. Houston, July 23, 1942; A.B., U. Chgo., 1964; LL.B., Harvard, 1967. Admitted to Del. bar, 1968, U.S. Ct. Appeals 3d Circuit bar, 1968, U.S. Ct. Appeals 3d Circuit bar, 1968, U.S. Supreme Ct. bar, 1975; law clerk Del. Superior and Chancery Cts., Wilmington, 1967-68; asso. firm Young, Conaway, Stargatt & Taylor, Wilmington, 1968-71, partner, 1971—. Vice pres., dir. Mental Health Assn. Del., Wilmington, 1971-73; dir. Congregation Beth Shalom, Wilmington, 1973-76, v.p., 1976—. Mem. Am., Del. bar assn., Phi Beta Kappa. Home: 105 Hitching Post Dr Wilmington DE 19803 Office: 1401 Market Tower Wilmington DE 19801 Tel (302) 571-6634

JACOBS, JOHN CLAYTON, JR., b. Guymon, Okla., June 27, 1917; B.S. in Chem. Engring., Ga. Inst. Tech., 1939; LL.B./J.D., Yale, 1948. Admitted to Tex. bar, 1949, U.S. Supreme Ct. bar, 1952; asso. firm Heldt & O'Boyle, Dallas, 1948-52; individual practice law, Dallas, 1952-54; with Tex. Eastern Corp., Houston, 1954—, exec. v.p., 1975—. Bd. dirs. English Speaking Union, Tex. Bill of Rights Found. Mem. Am. Bar Assn. Author: (with others) The Dynamic Natural Gas Industry, 1963. Address: PO Box 2521 Houston TX 77001

JACOBS, JOHN HOWZE, b. Wynne, Ark., Dec. 26, 1938; B.S., U. Ark., 1963, J.D., 1969. Admitted to Ark. bar, 1969; atty.-advisor Interstate Commerce Commn., 1969-70; dep. prosecuting atty. 6th Jud. Dist., Ark., 1970-72; asso. firm Fulk, Lovett & Mayes, Little Rock, 1972-74; partner Hoover, Jacobs & Storey, Little Rock, 1974—. Mem. Ark. Gov.'s Commn. on Crime and Law Enforcement. Mem. Am., Ark., Pulaski County bar assns., Little Rock C. of C. (chmn. com. on crime prevention and adjudication 1975). Office: Suite 210 Comml Nat Bank Little Rock AR 72201 Tel (501) 372-4125

JACOBS, JOSEPH CLAYTON, b. Albany, Ga., Mar. 1, 1923; B.S., Stetson U., 1946; LL.B., 1950. Admitted to Fla. bar, 1950; U.S. Ct. Appeals 5th Circuit bar, 1952, U.S. Supreme Ct. bar, 1959; pros. atty. Suwannee County (Fla.), 1952-55; asst. atty. gen. State of Fla., Tallahassee, 1957-63, 1st asst. atty. gen., chief trial counsel, 1963-64; partner firm Ervin, Varn, Jacobs, Odom & Kitchen, Tallahassee, 1965—; atty. Suwannee County Sch. Bd., 1956-57; mem. Fla. Constitutional Revision Commn., 1965-67. Mem. Fla. House of Rep., 1951-52. Mem. The Fla. Bar, Am., Tallahassee bar assns. Home: 1205 Hemlock St Tallahassee FL 32301 Office: 305 S Gadsden St Tallahassee FL 32302 Tel (904) 224-9135

JACOBS, LESLIE WILLIAM, b. Akron, Ohio, Dec. 5, 1944; B.S., Northwestern U., 1965; J.D., Harvard, 1968. Admitted to Ohio bar, 1968, U.S. Supreme Ct. bar, 1971; law clk. to chief justice Ohio Supreme Ct., 1968-69; asso. firm Thompson, Hine & Flory, Cleve., 1968-76, partner, 1976—. Chmn. jud. candidates com. Citizens League Greater Cleve., 1971, trustee, 1972—; vice chmn. Shaker Heights (Ohio) Recreation Bd., 1974—; vice chmn., mem. exec. com. Citizens Adv. Bd., Cuyahoga County Juvenile Ct., 1975—; mem. exec. com. Shaker Heights Republican Club, 1972—; mem. Shaker Heights Citizens Com., 1975—; deacon Fairmont Presbyn. Ch., 1975—. Fellow Ohio State Bar Found.; mem. Am., Ohio (chmn. com. on jud. adminstrn. and legal reform 1976—, chmn. spl. com. on substantive changes in tort law 1976—, council of dels. 1977—), Cleve. bar assns. Contbr. articles to legal jours. Office: 1100 Nat City Bank Bldg Cleveland OH 44114 Tel (216) 241-1880

JACOBS, MARSHALL ALAN, b. Toledo, May 17, 1919; A.B., U. Ariz., 1940; LL.B., Harvard, 1943. Admitted to N.Y. State bar, 1944; asso. firm Simpson, Thacher & Bartlett, N.Y.C., 1943-54; mem. firm Jacobs, Persinger & Parker, N.Y.C., 1954—; mem. task force on orgn. of exec. br., 1968. Mem. Assn. Bar City N.Y. Home: 45 E 72nd St New York City NY 10021 Office: 70 Pine St New York City NY 10005 Tel (212) 344-1866

JACOBS, RICHARD JOSEPH, b. Cin., Nov. 28, 1948; B.A., Miami U., Oxford, Ohio, 1970; J.D., U. Colo., 1972. Admitted to Colo. bar, 1973; asso. firm Smith & McClure, Alamosa, Colo., 1973-74, John C. McClure, Alamosa, 1974-75; partner firm McClure & Jacobs, Alamosa, 1975—. Mem. Am., Colo., San Luis Valley bar assns., Colo. Trial Lawyers Assn. Home: 307 West Ave Alamosa CO 81101 Office: 915 4th St Alamosa CO 81101 Tel (303) 589-6603

JACOBS, ROBERT, b. Bklyn., June 21, 1941; B.S. in Chem. Engring., City U. N.Y., 1963; J.D., Temple U., 1968. Admitted to D.C. bar, 1968, Del. bar, 1969; legal dept. Atlas Chem. Industries, Wilmington, Del., 1967-70; asso. firm Bader, Dorsey & Kreshtool, Wilmington, 1971-74, partner, 1975—; with Westinghouse Labs., West Mifflin, Pa., 1963-74. Bd. dirs. Del. State PTA, 1975—; mem. citizens adv. com. Alfred I. duPont Sch. Dist., 1974-76; mem. Alfred I. duPont Task Force on Desegregation, 1975-76; bd. dirs. Beth Shalom Synagogue, Wilmington, 1976—. Mem. Am. Trial Lawyers Assn., Am. bar Assn. Home: 624 Wilson Rd Wilmington DE 19803 Office: Bader Dorsey & Kreshtool 1102 West St Wilmington DE 19801 Tel (302) 655-7421

JACOBS, ROBERT ALAN, b. Waco, Tex., June 23, 1937; B.B.A., U. Tex., 1957; LL.B., N.Y. U., 1960, LL.M. in Taxation, 1963. Admitted to N.Y. state bar, 1961; mem. staff office chief counsel IRS, Washington, D.C., 1963-67; asso. firm Paul, Weiss, Rifkind, Wharton & Garrison, N.Y.C., 1967-69; mem. firm Milgrim Thomajan & Jacobs, P.C., N.Y.C., 1969—; spl. counsel to Sec. Treasury, 1966-67; vis. prof. law, U. Calif., Davis, Sch. Law, 1977; mem. adj. faculty N.Y. U. Sch. Law, 1976—. Vice chmn. Scarsdale Dem. Town Com., 1975-76. Mem. Am., N.Y. State, bar assns., N.Y. County Lawyers Assn. Contbr. articles on taxation to legal jours. Office: 25 Broadway New York City NY 10004 Tel (212) 952-9292

JACOBS, ROBERT SAMUEL, b. Chgo., Mar. 16, 1931; Ph.B., U. Chgo., 1950; LL.B., Harvard, 1954. Admitted to Ill. bar, 1954, D.C. bar, 1954; asso. law firm Friedman & Koven, Chgo., 1957-63, partner, 1963—. Mem. Ill. Spl. Events Commn., 1977, Glencoe (Ill.) Plan Commn., 1977—; mem. nat. bd. govs., chmn. Chgo. chpt. Am. Jewish Com., 1977—. Mem. Am., Ill., Chgo., D.C. bar assns., Am. Judicature Soc., Am. Soc. Hosp. Attys. Home: 580 Longwood Ave Glencoe IL 60022 Office: Friedman & Koven 208 S LaSalle St Chicago IL 60604

JACOBS, RUTH ZERLINA, b. N.Y.C., Feb. 5, 1918; LL.B., Southwestern U., Los Angeles, 1953. Admitted to Calif. bar, 1955, U.S. Supreme Ct. bar, 1958; individual practice law, Los Angeles, 1955-58, San Francisco, 1958-77; mem. firm Hadfield, von Beroldingen, Jacobs, Jorgensen, Graubert, Pressman & Pressman, San Francisco, 1977—. Pres., San Francisco chpt. ACLU, 1974—, v.p. No. Calif. affiliate, 1976—. Mem. Calif. Women Lawyers, San Francisco Lawyers Club, San Francisco Queen's Bench. Office: 4th floor 900 N Point St San Francisco CA 94109 Tel (415) 441-1211

JACOBS, WILLIAM, b. Marshall, Tex., July 25, 1943; B.A., Tex. So. U., 1965, J.D., 1971; M.A., N. Tex. State U., 1967. Admitted to Tex. bar, 1971; individual practice law, Dallas, 1972—; stock broker I.D.S., Houston, 1971-72; v.p., sec. via Pride Products Inc. Mem. Tex. Bar Assn., Dallas Criminal Bar, J. L. Turner Legal Soc., Kappa Alpha Psi. Office: 3101 Forest Ave Dallas TX 75215 Tel (214) 428-0709

JACOBS, WILLIAM LESTER, b. Parkersburg, W.Va., Mar. 24, 1923; J.D., W.Va., U., 1949. Admitted to W.Va. bar, 1949, U.S. Supreme Ct. bar, 1955; asso. firm William Bruce Hoff, Parkersburg, 1949-55; partner firm Jacobs, Ronning & Bailey, Parkersburg, 1955-57; individual practice law, Parkersburg, 1957—. Chmn. Toys for Tots, Parkersburg; chmn. Wood County (W.Va.) Democratic Exec. Com. Mem. Am. (W.Va. chmn. sect. jr. bar 1955-56), Wood County (pres. 1955-56), W.Va. State bar assns., Am., W.Va. (treas. 1962) trial lawyers assns. Home: 2810 Riverview Dr Parkersburg WV 26101 Office: Citizens Bank Bldg POB 185 Parkersburg WV 26101 Tel (304) 485-7528

JACOBS, WILLIAM RUSSELL, II; b. Chgo., Oct. 26, 1927; B.S., Northwestern U., 1951, LL.B., 1953, J.D., 1970. Admitted to Ill. bar, 1953, Dist. Ct. No. Ill., 1958, U.S. Supreme Ct., 1977; claims adjuster Kemper Ins. Co., Chgo., 1953-54; examiner, trial atty. Continental Casualty Co., Chgo., 1954-58; asso. law firm Horwitz and Anesi, Chgo., 1958-62; individual practice law, Chgo. and Des Plaines, Ill., 1962-70; partner firm Mells and Jacobs, Ltd., Chgo. and Des Plaines, 1970; prin., William R. Jacobs & and Assos., Chgo. and Des Plaines, 1970-75; partner law firm Jacobs, Camodeca and Timpone, Chgo., 1975—. Alderman, Des Plaines, Ill., 1953-54. Mem. Am., Ill., Chgo., Northwest Suburban bar assns., Am., Ill. trial lawyers assn., Am. Acad. Matrimonial Lawyers. Office: 7 S Dearborn St Chicago IL 60602 also 601 Lee St Des Plaines IL

JACOBSEN, EDWARD FREDERICK, b. St. Paul, Dec. 8, 1907; LL.B., St. Paul Coll. Law, 1933. Admitted to Minn. bar, 1933, Fed. bar, 1938; title atty. Fed. Land Bank, St. Paul, 1933-35; city atty. Litchfield (Minn.), 1962-68; county atty. Meeker County (Minn.), 1954-58; city atty. Eden Valley (Minn.), 1936-55; individual practice law, Litchfield, 1955—. Mem. St. Olaf Coll. Assos., Northfield, Minn. Mem. Minn. Bar Assn. Tel (612) 693-3463

JACOBSEN, ISAAC, b. Trondhjem, Norway, Jan. 19, 1920; B.S. in Law, U. Ill., 1948; J.D., John Marshall Law Sch., 1950. Admitted to Ill. bar, 1950. Mem. Am., Ill., Lake County bar assns. Home: 419 Park Ave Round Lake IL 60073 Office: 305 E Rollins Rd Round Lake IL 60073 Tel (312) 546-4666

JACOBSEN, W.A., b. Minot, N.D., Aug. 31, 1901; B.A., U. N.D., 1924, B.S., 1925, LL.B., 1926. Admitted to N.D. bar, 1926; individual practice law, Watford City, N.D., 1926—; atty. Ideal Sch. Dist., 1928-42; city atty., Watford City, 1928-42; state's atty. McKenzie County (N.D.), 1932-42; U.S. judge for Germany, 1946-52; alt. judge Flea Circus Ct. Mem. N.D. Bar Assn. (recipient award 1977). Office: 108 N Main St Watford St ND 58854 Tel (701) 842-2568

JACOBSON, EINO MATTI, b. Globe, Ariz., Jan. 18, 1933; LL.B., U. Ariz., 1957. Admitted to Ariz. bar, 1957, U.S. Dist. Ct. bar Ariz., 1957; asso. firm Favor & Quail, Prescott, 1957-59; partner firm Kingsbury & Jacobson, Prescott, 1959-63; individual practice law, Prescott, 1963-69; judge Ct. of Appeals, Div. 1, Phoenix, 1969—, chief judge, 1973-74; county atty. Yavapai County, 1964-68; co-chmn. Ariz. Appellate Project, 1974—. Chmn. March of Dimes, Prescott, 1962, Cancer Crusade, Prescott, 1963; pres. Prescott Jr. C. of C., 1962; bd. dirs. Prescott YMCA. Mem. Am., Ariz., Yavapai (pres. 1960-61) bar assns., Ariz. Judges Assn. (pres. 1974-75), Am. Law Inst. Contbr. articles to legal jours. Home: 505 Highland St Prescott AZ 86301 Office: State Capitol Bldg 1700 W Washington St Phoenix AZ 85007 Tel (602) 271-5304

JACOBSON, FRUMAN, b. Chgo., Oct. 11, 1948; B.A., U. Ill., 1970; J.D., Northwestern U., 1973. Admitted to Ill. bar, 1973; mem. firm Sonnenschein, Carlin, Nath & Rosenthal, Chgo., 1973—. Mem. Am., Ill., Chgo. bar assns., Chgo. Council of Lawyers. Home: 1640 E 50th St Apt 4B Chicago IL 60615 Office: 8000 Sears Tower Chicago IL 60606 Tel (312) 876-8123

JACOBSON, HOWARD HAHN, b. Toledo, Apr. 1, 1902; S.B., Harvard, 1924, J.D., 1927. Admitted to Ohio bar, 1927, N.Y. bar, 1948; div. counsel Doehler-Jarvis div. NL Industries, Inc., 1946-72. Mem. Am., Ohio, Toledo (exec. com. 1968-71) bar assns. Contbr. articles to legal jours. Home: 2914 Pembroke Rd Toledo OH 43606 Office: 937 Spitzer Bldg Toledo OH 43604 Tel (419) 243-2265

JACOBSON, IRVING, b. Dayton, June 22, 1926; B.A., Harvard, 1948, J.D., 1952. Admitted to N.Y. State bar, 1953; mem. law dept. RCA Corp., N.Y.C., 1952-53; asso. firm Szold & Brandwen, N.Y.C., 1953-58; asso. firm Shea Gould Climenko & Casey, N.Y.C., 1958-61, partner, 1961—. Mem. Am., N.Y. bar assns., Assn. Bar of N.Y.C., Phi Beta Kappa. Editor Harvard Law Review, 1950-52. Home: 251 Fox Meadow Rd Scarsdale NY 10583 Office: 330 Madison Ave New York City NY 10017 Tel (212) 661-3200

JACOBSON, MARSHALL S., b. Clearfield, Pa., June 5, 1937; B.S., Pa. State U., 1959; LL.B., Dickinson U., 1962. Admitted to Pa. bar, 1964, D.C. bar, 1964, U.S. Supreme Ct. bar, 1967; tax law specialist IRS, Washington, 1963-67; asso. firm Rosenn Jenkins & Greenwald, Wilkes-Barre, Pa., 1968-73, partner, 1973—. Mem. United Cerebral Palsy of Wyoming Valley (Pa.), 1973—, pres., 1974-76; treas. Congregation B'nai B'rith of Wilkes-Barre, 1974-76, v.p., 1976—. Mem. Am., Pa. bar assns., Wilkes-Barre Law and Library Assn. Home: 15 Pinetree Rd Mountaintop PA 18707 Office: 1000 Blue Cross Bldg Wilkes-Barre PA 18711 Tel (717) 829-0511

JACOBSON, MYRON GERALD, b. Lynbrook, N.Y., Jan. 17, 1943; B.S., Cornell U., 1965; J.D., Bklyn. Law Sch., 1968. Admitted to N.Y. State bar, 1969; individual practice, Lynbrook, 1969—; spl. counsel Village of Lynbrook (N.Y.), 1971—. Mem. Nassau, N.Y. State bar assns. Office: 377 Sunrise Hwy Lynbrook NY 11563 Tel (516) 599-0888

JACOBSON, ROBERT STANLEY, b. Morgantown, W.Va., Oct. 30, 1924; B.S. in Chem. Engring., W.Va. U., 1945, J.D., 1955. Admitted to W.Va. Supreme Ct. Appeals bar, 1955, U.S. Supreme Ct. bar, 1967; individual practice law, W.Va., 1960—; prosecuting atty. Pocahontas County, W.Va., 1960-64, 68-72; dir. Bank of Marlinton. Bd. dirs. Pocahontas County chpt. ARC, Pearl S. Buck Birthplace Found., Hillsboro, W.Va., Greenbrier Valley Mental Health Bd., Lewisburg, W.Va.; mem. Greenbrier County (W.Va.) Library and Museum Commn.; chmn. mus. com.; pres. Greenbrier County unit Am. Cancer Soc., 1971-73, dir., 1971—; chmn. bd. rev. Lewisburg troop council Boy Scouts Am. Mem. W.Va. State Bar (gov. 1961-64), W.Va. Bar Assn. Recipient Distinguished Service award W.Va. U., 1968, award of Honor for Outstanding Achievement in Community Beautification W.Va. Garden Club, 1972. Home: 201 Preston St Lewisburg WV 24901 Office: 215 N Court St Lewisburg WV 24901 Tel (304) 645-2011

JACOBSON, SANDRA WEINSTEIN, b. Bklyn., Feb. 1, 1930; B.A., Vassar Coll., 1951; J.D., Yale, 1954. Admitted to N.Y. bar, 1955, U.S. Supreme Ct. bar, 1960, U.S. Dist. Ct. for So. Dist. N.Y. bar, 1972, U.S. Ct. Appeals for 2d Circuit bar, 1975; partner firm Mulligan & Jacobson, N.Y.C. Mem. Assn. Bar City N.Y., N.Y. Women's, Westchester bar assns. Office: 36 W 44th St New York City NY 10036 Tel (212) MU7-0096

JACOBSON, STEPHEN WAYNE, b. Girard, Kans., June 26, 1947; B.A., Northwestern U., 1969; postgrad. U. Mo., Kansas City, 1969-71; J.D. with honors, U. Md., 1973. Admitted to Mo. bar, 1973; law clk. chief judge U.S. Ct. Appeals, 8th Circuit, Kansas City, Mo., 1973-75; asso. firm Lathrop, Koontz, Righter, Clagett, Parker, & Norquist, Kansas City, 1975—. Mem. Am., Kansas City bar assns., Lawyers Assn. Kansas City. Home: 501 E 89th Terr Kansas City MO 64131 Office: 1500 Ten Main Center Kansas City MO 64105 Tel (816) 842-0820

JACOWITZ, BURTON JOSEPH, b. Bklyn., July 29, 1937; B.A., Hobart Coll., 1959; J.D., LL.B., Columbia, 1962. Admitted to N.Y. State bar, 1962, U.S. Supreme Ct. bar, 1968, N.J. bar, 1970; atty. Consol. Mut. Ins. Co., N.Y.C., 1962-65; asso. firm Michael Jacowitz, N.Y.C., 1965-70; partner firm Jacowitz & Severance, P.C., N.Y.C., 1970—. Mem. bd. ethics Old Bridge Twp., 1975—. Mem. N.Y. State, N.J., Bklyn. bar assns., N.Y. State Workmen's Compensation Bar Assn.

JACZUN, VICTOR STEVEN, b. Phila., Jan. 13, 1939; B.S. in Econs., Villanova U., 1960; LL.B., Temple U., 1963. Admitted to Pa. bar, 1964, U.S. Supreme Ct. bar, 1973; pub. defender Phila., 1964-69; asso. firm Power, Bowen & Valimont, 1969-72, firm Smith, Mountenay & Wilson, 1972-74; partner firm Jaczun & Grabowski, Perkasie, Pa., 1974—. Pres., Pennridge Republican Club. Mem. Am., Pa., Phila., Bucks County bar assns., Pa. Def. Inst. on Med. Malpractice. Home: 728 E Creamery Rd Perkasie PA 18944 Office: 1 S 5th St Perkasie PA 18944 Tel (215) 257-8066

JAFFE, HOWARD M(ARTIN), b. Phila., Feb. 25, 1936; B.S. in Econs., U. Pa., 1958, LL.B., 1961; LL.M., N.Y. U., 1969. Admitted to N.J. bar, 1961, N.Y. bar, 1963, U.S. Supreme Ct. bar, 1965, Calif. bar, 1972; law sec. to chief justice, N.J. Supreme Ct., 1961-62; asso. firm Chester C. Davis, N.Y.C., 1962-66; partner firm Davis & Cox, N.Y.C., 1966—; corporate sec. Summa Corp., Las Vegas, 1972—; corporate sec. Hughes Air Corp., San Francisco, 1973—. Mem. State Bar Calif., Am. Bar Assn., Am. Judicature Soc., Fed. Bar Council, Order of the Coif. Case editor U. Pa. Law Review, 1959-61. Office: 1 State St Plaza New York NY 10004 Tel (212) 425-0500

JAFFE, HOWARD STEPHEN, b. Bklyn., May 18, 1944; B.A., Bklyn. Coll., 1966; J.D., 1969. Admitted to N.Y. bar, 1970; staff atty. Legal Aid Soc., N.Y.C., 1970-73; partner firm Gotlin and Jaffe, N.Y.C., 1973—. Mem. Am., N.Y. bar assns., Bklyn. Law Sch. Alumni Assn. Home: 50-18 Concord Ave Great Neck NY 11020 Office: 401 Broadway New York City NY 10013 Tel (212) 966-5897

JAFFE, MARK M., b. Paterson, N.J., Sept. 18, 1941; B.S., U. Pa., 1962; J.D., Columbia, 1965; postgrad N.Y. U., 1965. Admitted to N.J. bar, 1965, La. bar, 1968, N.Y. bar, 1970; asso. firm Hill, Betts & Nash, N.Y.C., 1969-72, partner, 1972—; sec. Dart Containerline, N.Y.C.; sec., dir. Tower Cranes of Am., Inc., Fairfield, N.J. Mem. Am., N.J., La. bar assns., Am. Judicature Soc., Maritime Law Assn., N.Y. Law Inst. Office: Suite 5215 1 World Trade Center New York City NY 10048 Tel (212) 466-4900

JAFFERY, SHELDON RONALD, b. Cleve., Apr. 22, 1934; B.A., Ohio State U., 1957; B.S., Kent State U., 1959; J.D., Case Western Res. U., 1964. Admitted to Ohio bar, 1964, U.S. Supreme Ct. bar, 1970; practiced in Cleve., 1964—; asso. firm Ascherman, Barrisch, Kreinberg & Wurzman, 1964-67, Jerome Silver, 1967-68; asso. firm Zellmer & Gruber, 1968-71, partner, 1971—; spl. counsel Office of Atty. Gen., State of Ohio, 1971-74. Mem. Vol. Lawyers for the Arts, 1974—; mem. Beachwood Arts Council, 1976—; trustee Hebrew Free Loan Assn. Mem. Ohio, Greater Cleve. (past chmn. fine arts com. 1974-76) bar assns., Am., Ohio trial lawyers assns. Home: 23834 Wendover Dr Beachwood OH 44122 Office: 1400 Leader Bldg Cleveland OH 44114 Tel (216) 771-7155

JAFFIN, CHARLES LEONARD, b. N.Y.C., Feb. 17, 1928; A.B., Princeton, 1948; J.D., Columbia, 1951. Admitted to N.Y. State bar, 1951; partner firm Battle, Fowler, Lidstone, Jaffin, Pierce & Kheel, and predecessor, 1959—. Mem. N.Y.C., Am. bar assns.

JAFFY, STEWART RALPH, b. Lorain, Ohio, July 22, 1930; B.A., Ohio U., 1953, J.D. summa cum laude, 1958. Admitted to Ohio bar, 1959, U.S. Supreme Ct. bar, 1963; individual practice law, Columbus, Ohio, 1959-68; partner firm Clayman & Jaffy, Columbus, 1968—. Former treas. Alvis House, trustee. Mem. Am. Arbitration Assn. (mem. nat. panel arbitrators), Fed. (nat. v.p. 6th dist. 1963, nat. council 1963—), Columbus (chmn. com. on judiciary 1971-73), Am., Ohio bar assns., Am. Assn. Trial Lawyers, Ohio State U. Law Alumni Assn. (treas. 1974-76), Order of Coif, Omicron Delta Kappa. Author: Workmen's Compensation Manual; editor-in-chief Ohio State Law Jour., 1958. Office: 71 E State St Suite 401-5 Columbus OH 43215 Tel (614) 228-6148

JAHN, LEROY MORGAN (MRS. LEROY MORGAN JAHN), b. San Tome, Venezuela, May 21, 1943; B.B.A., U. Tex., Austin, 1964, J.D., 1968. Admitted to Tex. bar, 1968; litigation atty. Dept. Labor, Washington, 1968-72; practiced in San Antonio, 1972-75; asst. U.S. Atty., chief appellate sect. Western Dist. Tex., 1976—. Bd. dirs. Children's Service Bur., San Antonio, San Antonio Jr. Forum. Mem. San Antonio Bar Assn. Home: 916 Garraty Rd San Antonio TX 78209 Office: 655 E Durango Blvd Suite G-13 San Antonio TX 78206 Tel (512) 229-6532

JAHNS, JEFFREY, b. Chgo., July 6, 1946; A.B., Villanova U., 1968; J.D., U. Chgo., 1971; Admitted to Ill. bar, 1971, U.S. Supreme Ct. bar, 1976; asso. firm Roan & Grossman, 1971-76, partner, 1977—. Mem. Am., Chgo. bar assns., Chgo. Council Lawyers. Contbr. articles in field to law jours. Home: 1129 Drummond Pl Chicago IL 60614 Office: 120 S LaSalle St Chicago IL 60603 Tel (312) 263-3600

JAHR, ALFRED DAVID, b. Ottynia, Austria, Oct. 10, 1896; B.S., Coll. City N.Y., 1918; M.A., Columbia, 1920; LL.B., N.Y. Law Sch., 1926, J.D., 1968. Admitted to N.Y. State bar, 1926, U.S. Supreme Ct. bar, 1959, Customs Ct. bar, 1972; individual practice law, N.Y.C., 1926-30; asst. corp. counsel City of N.Y., 1930-48; individual practice law, N.Y.C., 1948—; counsel N.Y.C. Tunnel Authority, 1932-45; lectr. in field of eminent domain. Bd. dirs. N.Y. Law Sch. Alumni Found. Mem. Am. Bar Assn., N.Y. County Lawyers Assn. Home: 19 Oakstwain Rd Scarsdale NY 10583 Office: 258 Broadway St New York City NY 10007 Tel (212) 267-2624

JALOVEC, RICHARD STANLEY, b. Berwyn, Ill., May 12, 1940; B.A. in History, U. Notre Dame, 1962; J.D., Northwestern U., 1965. Admitted to Ill. bar, 1965; law clk. to judge Ill. Appellate Ct., 1965-66; asst. U.S. atty. No. Dist. Ill., 1966-68; asst. states atty. Cook County (Ill.), 1968-72; chief spl. prosecutions unit State's Atty. of Cook County, 1969-70; individual practice law, Chgo., 1972—; atty. Village of Justice (Ill.), 1975—; atty. Roberts Park Fire Protection Dist., Justice, 1972—. Mem. Am., Ill., Chgo. bar assns. Home: 143 Post Rd Burr Ridge IL 60521 Office: 150 N Wacker Dr Chicago IL 60606 Tel (312) 726-2725

JAMES, DRAYTON NOBLES, b. Selma, Ala., Jan. 5, 1938; B.S., Auburn U., 1961; J.D., U. Ala., 1969. Admitted to Ala. State bar, 1969; mem. firm Beddow, Embry & Beddow, Birmingham 1969-72; individual practice law, Birmingham, 1973; partner firm Clark & James, Birmingham, 1974—. Bd. dirs. The Red Mountain Sch., Birmingham. Mem. Ala. State, Birmingham bar assns., Ala. Trial Lawyers Assn. Office: Suite 817 Frank Nelson Bldg Birmingham AL 35203 Tel (205) 322-3636

JAMES, ERICH WILLIAM, b. Memphis, Mar. 25, 1931; B.A., Vanderbilt U., 1953, J.D., 1960. Admitted to Tenn. bar, 1960; asso. firm Tual, Allan, Keltner & Lee, Memphis, 1960-61; partner firm Lee, James, & Hall, Memphis, 1961-63; asso. firm Waring, Cox, James, Sklar & Allen, and predecessors, Memphis, 1963-65, partner, 1965—. Mem. Memphis-Shelby County (v.p. sect. young lawyers 1963-64), Tenn., Am. bar assns., Tenn. Def. Lawyers, Am. Trial Lawyers Assn., Am. Judicature Soc., Def. Research Inst. Asso. editor Vanderbilt Law Rev., 1959-60. Office: 2000 Sterick Bldg Memphis TN 38103 Tel (901) 525-2431

JAMES, GEORGE EDWARD, b. Madison, Ind., Nov. 24, 1943; B.A., Eastern Ky. U., 1968; J.D., U. Ky., 1971. Admitted to Ind. bar, 1971, Ky. bar, 1972; individual practice law, Vevay, Ind., 1971-72; asst. atty. gen. Commonwealth of Ky., Frankfort, 1972-74; asst., acting dir. Ky. Workmen's Compensation Bd., Frankfort, 1974-75; judge County Ct., Vevay, Ind., 1976—. Chmn., Switzerland County (Ind.) Democratic Central Com., 1975. Mem. Ind., Ky. bar assns., Ind. Judges' Assn. Home: 221 W Main St Vevay IN 47043 Office: Court House Vevay IN 47043 Tel (812) 427-3410

JAMES, GRACEMARY BOOTH, b. Mineola, N.Y., Aug. 24, 1939; A.B., Bryn Mawr Coll., 1961; J.D., Fordham, 1967; postgrad. Pacific Coast Banking Sch., 1975. Admitted to N.Y. bar, 1967, Colo. bar, 1972; individual practice law, N.Y.C., 1967-68; trust adminstr. Chase Manhattan Bank, N.Y.C., 1968-71; personal trust officer United Bank Denver, 1972—. Mem. Am., Colo., Denver bar assns., Altrusa Internat., Bus. & Profl. Women's Assn., Nat. Assn. Bank Women. Fulbright fellow 1961-62, Woodrow Wilson fellow 1961-62. Office: 1740 Broadway Denver CO 80217 Tel (303) 861-8811

JAMES, IRVING ARTHUR, b. N.Y.C., Feb. 20, 1922; B.S., Coll. City N.Y., 1941; J.D., N.Y.U., 1947. Admitted to N.Y. bar, 1948; partner firm Sommerfield & James, N.Y.C. and Jericho, N.Y., 1957—; adj. lectr. polit. sci. C.W. Post Coll., L.I., N.Y., 1968; dir. Photronics Corp., Hicksville, N.Y., Vynamics Corp., N.Y.C., Dale Systems, Garden City, N.Y., Pickwick Orgn., Deer Park, N.Y., Oyster Bay (N.Y.) Indsl. Devel. Corp. Pres., Jericho (N.Y.) Pub. Library, 1970, trustee, 1965-70; commr. Commerce, Industry & Labor, Oyster Bay, 1966—; vice chmn. state law com. liberal party; 1st vice chmn. Nassau County Liberal Party, 1967—. Mem. Nassau County Bar Assn., Tau Delta Phi. Home: 130 Bounty Ln Jericho NY 11753 Office: 366 N Broadway Jericho NY 11753 Tel (516) 433-0986

JAMES, JERIN TIMOTHY RAY, b. Los Angeles, Mar. 21, 1942; B.A., Tex., Christian U., 1963; J.D., U. Houston, 1967. Admitted to Tex. bar, 1966; asst. atty. gen. Atty. Gen.'s Office, Houston, 1967; individual practice law, Houston, 1968; partolman Houston Police Dept., 1968; staff legal asst. to Atty. Gen., agt. in charge organized crime div., State Tex., Austin, 1973—; lectr. in field. Mem. Am. Bar Asssn., Tex. Narcotics Officers Assn., Internat. Assn. Chiefs Police (rep. Tex. com. law enforcement officer standards, edn., exec. com.), Tex. Law Enforcement Intelligence Units Assn. Named Rookie of Yr., Houston Police Dept., 1968. Office: Box 12548 Capitol Station Austin TX 78711 Tel (512) 475-3636

JAMES, RITA G., b. Erie, Pa., Feb. 16, 1947; A.B., U. Ga., 1968, J.D., 1970. Admitted to Ga. bar, 1970, Utah bar, 1972; staff atty. U. Ga. Sch. Law Legal Aid and Defender Soc., Athens, 1970; individual practice law, Ogden, Utah, 1971—; judge pro tem Ogden City Ct., 1973—. Utah coordinator Nat. Orgn. for Reform of Marijuana Laws; trustee Weber County Legal Services, Ogden, 1975-76, We Care Alcohol Rehab. Center, Ogden. Mem. Utah, Weber County bar assns. Home: 1074 24th St Ogden UT 84401 Office: 818 26th St Ogden UT 84401 Tel (801) 399-9291

JAMES, ROBERT BLEAKLEY, JR., b. Washington, June 17, 1927; student Washington and Lee U., 1945-48, Sch. Law, 1948-50; LL.B. Cath. U. Am., 1951, J.D., 1970. Admitted to Va. bar, 1951, D.C. bar, 1951; real estate atty. So. Ry. Co., Washington, 1952-56; trial atty. Office of Gen. Counsel, Post Office Dept., Washington, 1959-70; mem. bd. contract appeals GSA, Washington, 1970-73, chief adminstrv. judge bd. contract appeals, 1973—. Vice pres. N.W. Annandale (Va.) Civic Assn. 1965-66, 69-70. Mem. Am., Va., Fed. bar assns., Nat. Conf. Bd. Contract Appeals Mems. Home: 7411 Galanis Dr Annandale VA 22003 Office: GSA Bd of Contract Appeals Room 7004 18th and F Sts NW Washington DC 20405 Tel (202) 566-0720

JAMES, ROBERT TATOM, b. N. Platte, Nebr., Feb. 21, 1923; B.S., U. Denver, 1949, LL.B., 1950, J.D., 1970. Admitted to Colo. State bar, 1950, Okla. bar, 1957; asso. firm Hamm, Johnson & Shinn, Lamar, Colo., 1950-51; served with JAG, U.S. Air Force, 1951-53; individual practice law, Fowler, Colo., 1953-56; Colorado Springs, Colo., 1960—; staff atty. Amerada Petroleum Corp., Tulsa, 1956-60. Mem. Am., Colo., El Paso County bar assns. Home: 1983 N Academy Blvd Colorado Springs CO 80909 Office: 1515 N Academy Blvd Colorado Springs CO 80909 Tel (303) 597-9400

JAMES, THOMAS WILLIAM, b. Evanston, Ill., May 18, 1925; A.B., Harvard, 1947; LL.B., U. Mich., 1951. Admitted to Ill. bar, 1952; judge U.S. Bankruptcy Dist. Ct., No. Dist. of Ill., Chgo., 1972—. Office: 219 S Dearborn St Chicago IL 60604 Tel (312) 435-5550

JAMESON, PAUL, b. Newton, Mass., July 30, 1922; A.B., Fordham U., 1944; LL.B. (Distinguished Academic Achievement award), Northeastern U., 1953. Admitted to Mass. bar, 1953, U.S. Supreme Ct. bar, 1959, U.S. Tax Ct. bar, 1971; partner Hurst, Jameson, Pezella & Goldberg, Boston, 1953-55, Dempsey, Jameson & Locke, Wellesley, Mass., 1955-61, Jameson, Locke & Fullerton, Wellesley, 1961—. Moderator, Town of Wellesley, 1963-68; chmn. Mass. Gov.'s Commn. Civil and Legal Rights of Developmentally Disabled, 1974-76; v. dir. Mass. Assn. Retarded Persons, Inc., 1970-76. Mem. Am., Mass., Boston, Norfolk County bar assns. Home: 58 Ridge Hill Farm Rd Wellesley MA 02181 Office: 8 Grove St Wellesley MA 02181 Tel (617) 235-7000

JAMESON, WILLIAM JAMES, b. Butte, Mont., Aug. 8, 1898; A.B., U. Mont., 1919, J.D., 1922, LL.D., 1952; LL.D., U. Man., 1954, Rocky Mt. Coll., 1969, McGeorge Coll. Law, 1965. Admitted to Mont. bar, 1922; since practiced in Billings; asso. firm Coleman, Jameson & Lamey, and predecessors, 1922-29, mem. firm, 1929-57; judge U.S. Dist. Ct. Mont., 1957-69, sr. judge, 1969—; mem. Mont. Ho. of Reps., 1927-30. Mem. bd. sch. trustees, Billings, 1930-32; chmn. Yellowstone County chpt. ARC, 1931-45; past bd. dirs. Deaconess Hosp., Billings; trustee Rocky Mountain Coll. Mem. Am. (pres. 1953-54, Gold medal 1973), Mont. (pres. 1936-37) bar assns., Am. Judicature Soc. (pres. 1956-58, Herbert Harley award 1974), Am. Law Inst. (council 1956—), Billings C. of C. (pres. 1946-47). Home: 1008 Poly Dr Billings MT 59102 Office: POB 2115 Billings MT 59103 Tel (406) 657-6551

JAMISON, FRANCIS WESLEY, b. Denver, Mar. 26, 1929; B.A., U. Denver, 1951, LL.B., 1956. Admitted to Colo. bar, 1956; individual practice law, Denver, 1956-65; judge Jefferson County Colo., 1965-70; prof. law U. Denver, 1970—; faculty Nat. Coll State Judiciary, Reno, 1972—; Am. Acad. Jud. Edn., Washington, 1972—; mem. commn. on ct. backlog Colo. Supreme Ct., 1968. Mem. Lakewood (Colo.) Liquor Authority, 1973-76. Mem. Am., Colo. bar assns., Am. Judicature Soc. Office: 200 W 14th Ave Denver CO 80204 Tel (303) 753-2655

JAMISON, JOHN AMBLER, b. Florence, S.C., May 14, 1916; J.D., Samford U., 1941; postgrad. George Washington U., 1943-44. Admitted to S.C. bar, 1941, Va. bar, 1942, U.S. Supreme Ct. bar, 1945; atty. Va. Div. Motor Vehicles, 1947-54; individual practice law,

Fredericksburg, Va., 1954-72; judge 15th Jud. Circuit Va., Fredericksburg, 1972—, chief judge, 1976—; dir., counsel Nat. Bank Fredericksburg, 1968-73. Hon. chmn. Fredericksburg Bicentennial Commn., 1976; charter mem. Thomas Jefferson Inst. Religious Freedom, 1975—; mem. adv. bd. Va. Govs. Hwy. Safety Commn., 1956-58; naval aide to govs. Va., 1954-72; pres. Fredericksburg Rescue Squad, 1960-62, now hon. life mem.; chmn. bd. Fredericksburg Area Mental Hygiene Clinic, 1962-63; dir Rappahannock Area Devel. Commn., 1960-66. Mem. Am., Va., S.C., 15th Jud. Circuit (pres. 1959-60, 69-70) bar assns., Am. Judicature Soc., Jud. Conf. Va., Cumberland Order Jurisprudence, Cumberland Law Sch. Alumni Assn. (pres.-elect), Sigma Delta Kappa, Blue Key. Office: 2d Floor Circuit Courthouse Fredericksburg VA 22401 Tel (703) 373-3796

JAMISON, ROBERT EDGAR, b. New Castle, Pa., Aug. 24, 1916; A.B., Westminster Coll., 1938; J.D., U. Mich., 1941. Admitted to Pa. bar, 1942, U.S. Supreme Ct. bar, 1960; asso. firm Jamison & Jamison, New Castle, 1942-51, Jamison & Jones, New Castle, 1951-75, Jamison, Seltzer & Harper, New Castle, 1975—; asst. city solicitor, City of New Castle, 1947-60; solicitor Redevel. Authority New Castle, 1950-60, Union Sewer and Disposal Authority, 1956—; mayor of New Castle, 1968. Sec. bd. dirs. YMCA; bd. dirs. Human Services of New Castle; elder Clen-Moore United Presbyn. Ch., New Castle; bd. dirs. Westminster Coll., 1964—. Mem. Am., Pa., Lawrence County (pres. 1974) bar assns. Home: 310 Sumner Ave New Castle PA 16105 Office: 506 First Federal Plaza New Castle PA 16101 Tel (412) 652-9231

JAMRA, JAMILLE G., b. Toledo, Sept. 24, 1917; B.A., Northwestern U., 1939; J.D., U. Mich., 1941. Admitted to Ohio bar, 1941; now with firm Eastman, Stichter, Smith & Bergman, Toledo. Mem. Toledo (pres. 1961-62), Ohio State (pres. 1976-77), Am. bar assns., Assn. Ins. Attys. Office: 700 United Savs Bldg 240 Huron St Toledo OH 43604 Tel (419) 241-6152*

JANATA, RUDOLPH, b. Pitts., May 19, 1920; A.B., U. Pitts., 1941; J.D., Harvard, 1948. Admitted to Ohio bar, 1949; asso. firm Wright, Harlor, Morris & Arnold, Columbus, Ohio, 1948-54, partner, 1954—. Pres. Columbus Area Council Chs., 1958-60; trustee Nat. Council on Crime and Delinquency, N.Y.C., 1962-65; mem. exec. com. Ohio Citizens Council, 1963-68; pres. Columbus Met. YMCA, 1973-76; trustee Heidelberg Coll., 1965-75, vice chmn., 1967-74. Mem. Am., Ohio (pres. 1972-73), Columbus bar assns., Def. Research Inst. (pres. 1974, chmn. bd. 1975), Internat. Assn. Ins. Counsel, Am. Arbitration Assn., Am. Judicature Soc. Recipient U.S. Jr. C. of C. Distinguished Service award, 1953. Home: 6976 Clark State Rd Blacklick OH 43004 Office: 37 W Broad St Columbus OH 43215 Tel (614) 224-4125

JANDER, KLAUS HEINRICH, b. Glogau, Germany, May 17, 1940; came to U.S., 1952; B.A., City U. N.Y., 1961; LL.D., Cornell U., 1964; postgrad. U. of the Saar, Saarburcken, Germany, 1966-67. Admitted to N.Y. State bar, 1964, U.S. Supreme Ct. bar, 1968; asso. firm Carter Ledyard & Milburn, N.Y.C., 1964-65; served with JAGC, U.S. Air Force, 1965-68; asso. firm Alexander & Green, N.Y.C., 1968-72, partner, 1972—; dir. Delden Fabrics, Inc., Raxon Fabrics, Inc., Berthold of N.Am., Inc. Mem. Assn. Bar City N.Y. (com. fgn. and comparative law), N.Y. County Lawyers Assn. (com. internat. law, com. mil. justice), N.Y. State Bar Assn. Contbr. articles to German legal jours. Home: 35 Shady Ln Greenwich CT 06830 Office: 299 Park Ave New York City NY 10017 Tel (212) 758-6900

JANDERA, JOHN E., b. Morrowville, Kans., Apr. 29, 1925; B.A., Washburn U., 1949, J.D., 1951. Admitted to Kans. bar, 1951; asst. gen. counsel Kans. Corp. Commn., 1952-53; asst. city atty. Topeka, 1954-55; practiced in Topeka, 1955—; mem. subcom. Jud. Council, 1972—. Pres. Motor Carrier Lawyers Assn., 1969-70. Contbr. articles to legal jours. Home: 2220 W 32d St Topeka KS 66611 Office: 641 Harrison St Topeka KS 66603 Tel (913) 234-0565

JANDT, ELIZABETH CARRIE, b. Deguin, Tex., Oct. 30, 1939; LL.B., St. Mary's Law Sch., San Antonio, 1963. Admitted to Tex. bar, 1963; mem. firm Jandt & Jandt, Seguin, 1963-68; county atty., Seguin, 1968—. Home: 1720 W Court St Seguin TX 78155 Office: Courthouse Seguin TX 78155 Tel (512) 379-6095

JANGER, RICHARD K., b. Chgo., Oct. 21, 1936; B.S., Northwestern U., 1958, J.D., 1961. Admitted to Ill. bar; asso. firm McDermott, Will & Emery, Chgo., 1962-64; partner firm Levenfeld, Kanter, Baskes & Lippitz, Chgo., 1964—. Mem. Am., Ill., Chgo. bar assns. C.P.A. (Ill.); contbr. articles to legal jours. Office: 10 S LaSalle St Chicago IL 60603 Tel (312) 346-8380

JANICKE, PAUL MARTIN, b. N.Y.C., Dec. 20, 1940; B.E.E., Manhattan Coll., 1961; LL.B., N.Y. U., 1964; LL.M., George Washington U., 1971. Admitted to N.Y. bar, 1964, Tex. bar, 1972; patent advisor AEC, 1968-69, U.S. Ct. Customs and Patent Appeals, 1969-71; asso. firm Arnold, White & Durkee, Houston, 1971—. Sec. Briar Park Community Improvement Assn., Houston, 1973-74. Mem. Am. Bar Assn., Am., Houston patent law assns. Contbr. articles in English and Japanese to legal jours.; editor: (with others) Court Review of Patent Office Decision, 1972. Office: 2100 Transco Tower Houston TX 77056 Tel (713) 621-9100

JANKLOW, WILLIAM JOHN, b. Chgo., Sept. 13, 1939; B.S. in Bus. Adminstrn., U. S.D., 1964, J.D., 1966. Admitted to S.D. bar, 1966, U.S. Supreme Ct. bar, 1970; staff atty. S.D. Legal Services, 1966-67, directing atty., chief officer, 1967-72; chief trial atty. S.D. Atty. Gen.'s Office, Pierre, 1973-74, atty. gen., 1975—. Bd. dirs. Legal Services Corp., 1975—. Mem. Am., S.D. bar assns., Am., S.D. trial lawyers assns., Am. Judicature Soc. Office: Atty Gen Capitol Bldg Pierre SD 57501 Tel (605) 224-3215

JANNONE, RAPHAEL P., b. Bklyn., Apr. 16, 1936; B.A., St. John's U., 1957; LL.B., Bklyn. Law Sch., 1963. Admitted to N.Y. bar, 1963; asso. firm Connolly, Frey, Eschmann & LaPasta, Queens Village, N.Y., 1964-66, Cullen & Dykman, Bklyn., 1966-68, Hawkins, Delafield, & Wood, N.Y.C., 1968-70; dep. mortgage officer, legal supr. Bowery Savs. Bank, N.Y.C., 1970—. Mem. N.Y., Bklyn. bar assns., N.Y. County Lawyers Assn. Office: 110 E 42d St New York City NY 10017 Tel (212) 953-8532

JANOFSKY, LEONARD S., b. Los Angeles, Oct. 13, 1909; A.B., Occidental Coll., 1931; LL.B., Harvard U., 1934. Admitted to Calif. bar, 1934; since practiced in Los Angeles, asso. firm Faries & McDowell, 1934-42; sr. regional atty. NLRB, So. Calif. and Ariz., 1935-36; asso. firm Bodkin, Breslin & Luddy, 1945-51; spl. trial counsel eminent domain proc. Housing Authority City of Los Angeles, 1950-54; partner firm Paul, Hastings, Janofsky & Walker, 1951—; Dept. State del. ILO Conf., Geneva, 1969-70; pres. Nat. Conf. Bar Pres.'s, 1974-75. Chmn. bd. trustees Occidental Coll.,

1969-72; mem. overseers com. Harvard Law Sch., 1969-74; bd. visitors Stanford Law Sch., 1972-75. Fellow Am. Coll. Trial Lawyers, Am. Bar Found.; Am. Law Inst.; mem. Am. (ho. of dels. 1975—, chmn. sect. labor relations law 1975-76), Calif. (pres. 1972-73, gov. 1970-73), Los Angeles County (Shattuck-Price award 1977; trustee 1967-70, pres. 1968-69) bar assns., Nat. Legal Aid and Defender Assn. (dir.). Recipient Medallion award St. Thomas More Law Honor Soc., 1977. Office: 555 S Flower St Los Angeles CA 90071 Tel (213) 489-4000

JANSMA, ARTHUR BEREND, b. Washington, Pa., Sept. 27, 1936; B.A., U. Miss., J.D., 1972. Admitted to Miss. bar, 1972; practice law, Greenville, Miss. Office: 1024 Washington St Greenville MS 38701 Tel (601) 378-9257

JANUS, MURRAY JOSEPH, b. Richmond, Va., July 8, 1938; A.B., Dartmouth, 1960; LL.B., U. Va., 1963. Admitted to Va. bar, 1963, U.S. Supreme Ct. bar, 1972; partner firm Bremner, Baber & Janus, and predecessors, Richmond, 1963—; with JAGC, U.S. Air N.G.; guest lectr. U. Richmond Law Sch., U. Va. Law Sch., Nat. Coll. Criminal Def. Lawyers, Houston and Richmond police depts. Bd. dirs. Jewish Community Center, Richmond, 1970-72. Mem. Va. State Bar (Meritorious Service award sect. criminal law 1974, chmn. bail bond study commn., 1974), Va., Richmond, Am. bar assns., Richmond Criminal Bar Assn. (pres. 1971-73), Nat. Assn. Criminal Def. Attys. Home: 300 Tarrytown Dr Richmond VA 23229 Office: Suite 1500 701 E Franklin St Richmond VA 23219 Tel (804) 644-0721

JANVEY, RICHARD L., b. Rockville Center, N.Y., Sept. 22, 1945; A.B., U. Wis., 1970; J.D., U. Chgo., 1970. Admitted to N.Y. bar, 1971, Calif. bar, 1972; law clerk to Hon. David N. Edelstein chief judge U.S. Dist. Ct. So. Dist. N.Y., 1970-72; asso. firm Debevoise, Plimpton, Lyons & Gates, N.Y.C., 1972—. Mem. N.Y.C. Bar Assn., Fed. Bar Council (trustee). Fellow, summer 1969. Home: 67 E 11th St New York City NY 10003 Office: 299 Park Ave New York City NY 10017 Tel (212) 752-6400

JARET, FREDERICA A., b. N.Y.C., June 13, 1945; A.B., Cornell U., 1966; J.D., N.Y. U., 1969; atty. in charge Litigation Unit Corp. Counsel, N.Y.C., 1969-74; asso. mem. firm Sage Gray Todd & Sims, N.Y.C., 1974-76; counsel French and Polyclinic Med. Sch. and Health Center, N.Y.C., 1976—; mem. Cornell Secondary Sch. Com., 1973-75; jr. bd. govs. Jewish Assn. Services to Aged, Council N.Y. Law Assos. Mem. N.Y. State Bar Assn. (mem. com. on arrangements, young lawyers sect. 1973-75). Home: 370 E 76th St New York City NY 10021 Office: 330 W 30th St New York City NY

JARNICKI, HAROLD, b. Germany, July 10, 1949; B.A. in Polit. Sci., U. Cin., 1967; J.D., Ohio No. Coll., 1974. Admitted to Ohio bar, 1974; asso. firm Jack M. Marshall, Lebanon, Ohio, 1974-75; partner firm Marshall & Jarnicki, Lebanon, 1975—; asst. pros. atty., Warren County, Ohio, 1974—; arbitration panelist Hamilton County Common Pleas Ct., Cin., 1975—; bankruptcy trustee Fed. Dist. Ct., Dayton, Ohio, 1975—. Bd. dirs. Lebanon Kiwanis Club, 1975—, v.p., 1976—. Mem. Am., Ohio State, Warren County bar assns., Delta Theta Phi. Office: 27 N East St Lebanon OH 45036 Tel (513) 932-5792

JAROS, MURRAY MARCUS, b. Poland, Dec. 1, 1933; B.A., Siena Coll., 1955; LL.B., Albany Law Sch., 1957. Admitted to N.Y. bar, U.S. Supreme Ct. bar; asso. firm Norman S. Weiss, Albany, N.Y., 1959-60; atty. N.Y. State Bd. Equalization and Assessment, Albany, 1960-66; atty. State U. N.Y., Albany, 1966; asso. counsel law div. N.Y. State Office for Local Govt., Albany, 1967-73, dir. div., 1973-74; counsel Assn. Towns of State N.Y., Albany, 1975—; lectr. in field. Del.-at-large Jewish Community Council, Schenectady, 1974—. Mem. N.Y. State Bar Assn. (exec. com. municipal law sect. 1971—, chmn. exec. com. 1976—, ho. of dels. 1974-76). Contbr. articles to profl. jours. Office: 90 State St Albany NY 12207 Tel (518) 465-7933

JARRETT, CHARLES B., JR., b. 1927; B.A., Williams Coll., 1949; J.D., U. Pitts., 1954; postgrad. Loyola U. Sch. Law. Atty., Gulf Oil Corp., 1956-68, asst. corp. sec., 1968-73; v.p., counsel Mellon Nat. Corp., Pitts., 1973—. Office: Mellon Nat Corp Mellon Square Pittsburgh PA 15230*

JARVIS, BILLY BRITT, b. Amarillo, Tex., Jan. 9, 1943; B.S., Tex. A. and M. U., 1965; J.D., So. Meth. U., 1968. Admitted to Tex. bar, 1968; asst. county atty. Hutchinson County (Tex.), 1968-69; individual practice law, Spearman, Tex., 1971—. Mem. Am., Northeastern Panhandle (pres. 1974-75) bar assns., Tex. Criminal Def. Lawyers Assn., State Bar Tex., State Bar Council of Bar Pres.'s. Address: 124 W Kenneth St PO Box 515 Spearman TX 79081 Tel (806) 659-3517

JARVIS, GLENN, b. San Benito, Tex., Jan. 20, 1938; B.A., Rice U., 1960; J.D., U. Tex., 1963. Admitted to Tex. bar, 1963, U.S. Supreme Ct. bar, 1973; with firm Ewers, Toothaker, Ewers, Abbott, Talbot, Hamilton & Jarvis, McAllen, Tex., 1963—, partner, 1967—. McAllen city chmn. Hidalgo County chpt. Nat. Found., March of Dimes, 1964-65, county vice chmn., 1965-66, advisor to bd. dirs., 1966-67; past pres., bd. dirs. McAllen Boys Club, 1965-76; bd. dirs. McAllen United Fund, 1972-75; bd. dirs. McAllen Trade Zone, Inc., 1973-76, v.p., gen. counsel, 1975-76; trustee, sec. bd. McAllen Ind. Sch. Dist., 1973-75, 76—; former mem. McAllen Traffic Commn.; former mem. ofcl. bd. 1st United Methodist Ch., McAllen. Certified specialist labor law. Mem. State Bar Tex. (dir. 1969-70, mem. pub. affairs com., exec. council labor law sect.), Tex. Bar Found. (dir. 1969-70), McAllen C. of C. (past chmn. civic affairs com.), Phi Delta Phi. Asso. editor Tex. Law Rev., 1962-63; mem. editorial bd. Texas Lawyers Practice Guide, 1967. Home: N Ware Rd McAllen TX 78501 Office: 1630 N 10th St PO Box 3670 McAllen TX 78501 Tel (512) 686-3771

JARVIS, ROBERT ANTHONY, b. Pitts., June 13, 1911; A.B., U. Pitts., 1933, J.D., 1936. Admitted to Pa. bar, 1936, U.S. Supreme Ct. bar, 1960; partner firm Beck, McGinnis & Jarvis, Pitts., 1936—; pres. 1st Nat. Bank Point Marion, Pa., 1953; mem. Grievance Com. U.S. Dist. Ct., 1950—; spl. asst. to atty. Gen. U.S., 1953-55; permanent mem. 3d Circuit Judicial Conf. Mem. Allegheny County, Pa., Am. bar assns., Trial Lawyers Assn. Am., Acad. Trial Lawyers Allegheny County. Home: Chatham Center Apartment Tower Pittsburgh PA 15219 Office: 800 Porter Bldg Pittsburgh PA 15219 Tel (412) 281-2738

JASCOURT, HUGH DONALD, b. Phila., Mar. 25, 1935; A.B. with honors, U. Pa., 1956; J.D., Wayne State U., 1960. Admitted to Mich. bar, 1961, U.S. Supreme Ct. bar, 1964, D.C. bar, 1967; atty.-advisor NLRB, 1964-66; exec. dir. Fed. Bar Assn., Washington, 1966-67; head counsel, dir. legal services Am. Fedn. State, County and Municipal Employers AFL-CIO, Washington, 1967-69; labor relations counsel Fed. Res. Bd., Washington, 1969-72; dir. Pub.

Employment Relations Research Inst., Washington, 1972—; labor relations counsel Dept. Interior, 1974—; prof. law George Washington U., 1971—; chmn. panel unfair labor practice Prince George's County (Md.) Pub. Employment Relations Bd., 1973—; speaker in field. Bd. dirs. Nat. Jogging Assn.; mem. Greenbelt (Md.) Employee Relations Bd., 1977—. Mem. Am. (co-chmn. subcom. pub. sector labor law), D.C. bar assns., Soc. Profl. Dispute Resolution, Soc. Fed. Labor Relations Profs., Indsl. Relations Research Assn., Am. Arbitration Assn. (panel), Am. Soc. Pub. Adminstrn., Internat. Personnel Mgmt. Assn., Soc. Am. Law Tchrs. Named Outstanding Md. Phys. Fitness Leader, Md. Jaycees, 1965, Outstanding Md. Recreation Vol. Md. Park and Recreation Assn., 1966, an Outstanding Young Man of Md., Md. Jaycees, 1969, Outstanding Com. Chmn., Fed. Bar Assn., 1974; recipient citation of merit City of Greenbelt, 1973, Spl. award Practising Law Inst., 1975, Am. Jurisprudence award Wayne State Law Sch., 1960. Author: Trends in Public Sector Labor Relations, 1975; Public Sector Labor Relations: Trends and Developments, 1975. Founder, Run For Your Life program, 1963. Labor relations editor Jour. Law and Edn., 1972—. Home: 7 Maplewood Ct Greenbelt MD 20770 Tel (202) 343-6331

JASEN, MATTHEW JOSEPH, b. Buffalo, Dec. 13, 1915; student Canisius Coll.; LL.B., U. Buffalo, 1939; postgrad. Harvard, 1944. Admitted to N.Y. State bar, 1940; individual practice law, Buffalo, 1940-43; judge U.S. Mil. Ct., Heidelberg, Ger., 1946-49; partner firm Jasen, Manz, Johnson & Bayger, Buffalo, 1949-57; justice N.Y. Supreme Ct. 8th Jud. Dist., 1957-67; asso. judge N.Y. State Ct. Appeals, Albany, 1968—. Mem. council U. Buffalo, 1963-66; trustee Chair of Polish Culture, Canisius Coll., Nottingham Acad. (now part of Nichols Sch.); mem. Bishop's Bd. Govs. Buffalo Diocese. Mem. Nat. Conf. Appellate Judges, Am., N.Y. State, Erie County bar assns., Am. Judicature Soc., Profl. and Businessmen's Assn. Western N.Y. (pres. 1952), Nat. Advocates Club, U. Buffalo Law Sch. Alumni Assn. (dir. 1962-65, pres. 1965-66), Phi Alpha Delta, Di Gamma. Recipient Distinguished Alumni awards U. Buffalo Sch. Law, 1969, State U. N.Y., 1976, Distinguished Jud. Service award Erie County Trial Lawyers Assn., 1967; Law Day award N.Y. State Trial Lawyers Assn., 1968; fellow Hilbert Coll., 1972. Home: 26 Pine Terr Orchard Park NY 14127 Office: Ct Appeals Hall Albany NY 12207 also Erie County Hall Buffalo NY 14202 Tel (518) 474-2188 and (716) 852-1291

JASKIEWICZ, LEONARD ALBERT, b. Norwich, Conn., Aug. 25, 1927; A.B., U. Conn., 1949; M.A., Syracuse U., 1950; J.D., George Washington U., 1959. Admitted to D.C. bar, 1954, U.S. Supreme Ct. bar, 1961; fiscal mgmt. ofcl. U.S. Navy Dept., Washington, 1950-53; asso. firm Dow Lohnes & Albertson, Washington, 1953-64; partner firm Grove, Jaskiewicz, Gilliam & Cobert, Washington, 1964—. Mem. Am., D.C. bar assns., Motor Carrier Lawyers Assn., Assn. ICC Practitioners. Home: 4879 Old Dominion Dr Arlington VA 22207 Office: 1730 M St NW Washington DC 20036 Tel (202) 296-2900

JASPER, BRUCE ROBERT, b. Nashua, N.H., Apr. 10, 1947; B.A., U. N.H., 1970; J.D., U. Tulsa, 1972. Admitted to N.H. bar, 1973; asso. firm Edes & Elliott, Newport, N.H., 1973-76; asso. Louie Elliott, Newport, 1976-77; partner firm Elliott & Jasper, Newport, 1977—. Mem. Am., N.H. bar assns., Phi Alpha Delta. Home: Rural Route 1 Box 155 Newport NH 03773 Office: 35B Main St Newport NH 03773 Tel (603) 863-4105

JASPER, EZEKIEL, b. N.Y.C., Sept. 26, 1904; LL.B., Fordham U., 1925. Admitted to N.Y. State bar, 1925, U.S. Dist. Ct. So. Dist. N.Y. bar, 1927, U.S. Dist. Ct. Eastern Dist. N.Y. bar, 1930; practiced in N.Y.C., 1925—; individual practice law, 1925-55; partner firm Jasper & Jasper, 1957—. Mem. N.Y. Trial Lawyers Assn., N.Y. County Lawyers Assn. Home: 515 Ave I Brooklyn NY 11230 Office: 253 Broadway New York City NY 10007 Tel (212) RE2-2292

JASPER, SEYMOUR, b. N.Y.C., May 15, 1919; B.S., N.Y. U., 1939; J.D., Columbia, 1956. Admitted to N.Y. State bar, 1956; research asst. to Prof. Richard R. Powell, Columbia Law Sch., 1954-56; asso. firm Young, Kaplan & Edelstein, N.Y.C., 1956-59; partner firm Jasper, Sandler & Lipsay, N.Y.C., 1959-62; individual practice law, N.Y.C., 1962—; arbitrator N.Y. Civil Ct., 1966—; panelist Am. Arbitration Assn., 1970—. Mem. Bar Assn. City of N.Y., N.Y. State, Am. bar assns. Home: 115 E 87th St New York City NY 10028 Office: 1270 Ave of the Americas New York City NY 10020 Tel (212) 757-8880

JASTROCH, LEONARD ANDREW, b. Milw., Dec. 31, 1948; J.D., Marquette U., 1972. Admitted to Wis. bar, 1973, U.S. Supreme Ct. bar, 1976; individual practice law, Waukesha, Wis., 1973—, Milw., 1973—. Mem. panel com. on Legal Assistance to Vietnamese Refugees. Mem. Wis., Waukesha County, Milw. County, Am. bar assns. Home: 7950 Manitoba St W Allis WI 53219 Office: 507 N Grand Ave PO Box 1226 Waukesha WI 53186 also 1125 W Oklahoma Ave Milwaukee WI 53215 Tel (414) 547-6144

JAVITCH, VICTOR MARTIN, b. Cleve., July 4, 1937; B.A., U. Mich., 1959; LL.B., Case Western Res. U., 1962. Admitted to Ohio bar, 1962, N.Y. bar, 1974; asso. firm Gardner Spilka & Weltman, Cleve., 1962-64; individual practice law, Cleve., 1964-68; partner Javitch & Greenwald, Cleve., 1968—; lectr. in field. Mem. Am., Cleve., Ohio, Cuyahoga County bar assns., Tau Epsilon Rho. Office: 1331 Terminal Tower Cleveland OH 44113 Tel (216) 241-6774

JAVITS, ERIC M., b. N.Y.C., May 24, 1931; B.A., Columbia, 1952, J.D., 1955. Admitted to N.Y. bar, 1955, U.S. Supreme Ct. bar, 1959; asso. firm Javits & Javits, N.Y.C., 1955-58, mem., 1958—; dir. various public and pvt. cos.; cons. Office of Def. Mobilization, Washington, 1951; charter mem. World Peace Through Law Center, Washington, 1964; counsel N.Y. Senate Com. on Affairs of N.Y.C., 1959. Mem. Am., N.Y. bar assns., N.Y. County Lawyers Assn., Assn. Bar City N.Y., Am. Judicature Soc., Nat. Inst. Social Sci., Phi Beta Kappa, Phi Alpha Delta. Author: SOS New York, 1961. Office: 1345 Ave of the Americas New York City NY 10019 Tel (212) 586-4050

JAWORSKI, LEON, b. Waco, Tex., Sept. 19, 1905; LL.B., Baylor U., 1925, LL.D., 1960; LL.M., George Washington U., 1926; numerous hon. degrees. Admitted to Tex. bar, 1925; sr. partner firm Fulbright & Jaworski, Houston, 1951—; spl. asst. U.S. atty. gen., 1962-65; spl. counsel atty. gen. Tex., 1963-65, 72-73; dir. Office Watergate Spl. Prosecution Force, 1973-74; dir., chmn. exec. com. Bank of Southwest; dir. Southwest Bancshares Inc.; Houston, Anderson Clayton & Co., Houston, Regent Nat. Coll. Dist. Attys. Mem. Pres.'s Commn. on Law Enforcement and Adminstrn. of Justice; U.S. mem. Permanent (Internat.) of Arbitration, The Hague; mem. Commn. on Marine Sci., Engring. and Resources, Pres.'s Commn. on Causes and Prevention of Violence; chmn. gov's Com. on Pub. Sch. Edn. Bd. dirs. A.R.C., chpt. chmn., 1954-55; trustee United Fund, 1958—; chmn. trustees, mem. exec. com. Southwestern Legal Found; trustee Tex. Med. Center, Baylor Coll. Medicine; pres. Baylor Med. Found., M.D. Anderson Found. Served as col. AUS, 1942-46, chief war crimes trial sect. judge Adv. Gen. Dept.; ETO. Fellow Am. Coll. of Trial Lawyers (regent 1958-66, also pres. 1961-62), Am. Bar Found., Am. Law Inst.; mem. State Bar Tex. (pres. 1962-63), Am. (pres. 1971-72), Canadian (hon.), Houston (pres. 1949) bar assns., Tex. Civil Jud. Council (pres. 1950-52), C. of C. (pres. 1960), Order of Coif, Phi Delta Phi. Author: After Fifteen Years, 1961. Contbr. articles to legal jours. Home: 3665 Ella Lee Lane Houston TX 77027 Office: Bank of Southwest Bldg Travis and Walker Houston TX 77002*

JAY, JOHN BURNS, b. Washington, Sept. 21, 1945; A.B., Washington and Lee U., 1968; J.D., Emory U., 1972. Admitted to Ga. bar, 1973; adminstrv. asst. trust dept. Trust Co. Ga., 1973; asso. William R. Bassett, Atlanta, 1974-75; asso. firm Deming & Oxendine, Norcross, Ga., 1975-77; partner firm Oxendine, Jay & Cook, Norcross, 1977—. Mem. Am. Bar Assn., State Bar Ga. Office: 5430 Jimmy Carter Blvd Suite 112 Norcross GA 30093 Tel (404) 449-8686

JAYCOX, JACK STEWART, b. McKeesport, Pa., Jan. 29, 1947; B.A., Geneva Coll., 1969; J.D., U. Minn., 1972. Admitted to Minn. bar, 1972; mem. firm Douglas, Jaycox, Trawick, McManus & Lippert, Mpls., 1976—; former chmn. Hennepin County Family Law Com.; Family Ct. referee, summer 1975. Mem. Hennepin County, Minn. State, Am. bar assns. Home: 5029 Wooddale Ln Minneapolis MN 55424 Office: 247 Third Ave S Minneapolis MN 55415 Tel (612) 339-4946

JEANSONNE, VERNON JOSEPH, b. Marksville, La., July 26, 1924; LL.B., La. State U., 1951, J.D., 1968. Admitted to La. bar, 1951; exec. dir. Housing Authority, Lake Arthur, La., 1951-71; city atty. Town of Lake Arthur, 1951-71; 74-76. Counsellor, Calcasieu Area council Boy Scouts Am., Lake Charles, 1956—; bd. dirs. Jennings (La.) Am. Legion Hosp., 1958-62; coach Little League, Lake Arthur, 1966—. Mem. La. State, Jefferson Davis Parish bar assns. Home: 193 Grand Ave Lake Arthur LA 70549 Office: 104 Arthur Ave Lake Arthur LA 70549 Tel (318) 774-2611 mailing address PO Drawer AR Lake Charles LA 70549

JEDEIKIN, JOSEPH, b. Kobe, Japan, Jan. 4, 1927; A.A., U. Calif., 1948, LL.B., 1951. Admitted to Calif. bar, 1954; with Ins. Co. N.Am., San Francisco, 1953-54; partner firm Jedeikin & Connor, San Francisco, 1976—. Mem. Am. Bar Assn., Lawyers Club San Francisco, Assn. Def. Counsel No. Calif. Office: 1225 Hearst Bldg San Francisco CA 94103 Tel (415) 781-7050

JEFFERIES, JACK P., b. Radford, Va., Dec. 5, 1928; B.S. in Commerce, U. Va., 1949, J.D., 1951, LL.M., 1952; J.S.D., Yale U., 1954. Admitted to N.Y. State bar, 1959, Va. bar, 1953, aslo Fed. bar, U.S. Supreme Ct. bar; served with JAGC, U.S. Army, 1954-57; with firm Lord, Day & Lord, N.Y.C., 1958—, now partner. Mem. White House Conf. Equality To Fulfill These Rights, 1966; trustee Policy Sci. Center; sec. Downtown-Lower Manhattan Assn., Inc.; mem. Historic Areas Rev. Bd., Historic Tappan and Palisades (N.Y.); bd. dirs. Pakistan-Am. Internat. Inc.; pres. Fund for Peace, 1967-68; trustee Am. Waterways Wind Orch. Mem. Assn. Bar City N.Y., Am. Bar Assn. Contbr. articles to legal jours. Home: Lawrence Ln Sneden's Landing Palisades NY 10964 Tel (212) 344-8480

JEFFERIES, ROBERT AARON, JR., b. Richmond, Ind., June 30, 1941; A.B. in Polit. Sci. with departmental honors, Earlham Coll., 1963; J.D. with distinction, Ind. U., 1966. Admitted to Ind. bar, 1966, Ohio bar, 1966, Mo. bar, 1970, Ill. bar, 1970; asso. firm Shumaker, Loop & Kendrick, Toledo, Ohio, 1966-69; staff atty. May Dept. Stores, St. Louis, 1969-72, gen. counsel, 1972-77; v.p., gen. counsel, sec. Leggett & Platt Inc., Carthage, Mo., 1977—. Mem. Am., Mo., Ill., Ohio, Ind., St. Louis bar assns., Order of Coif. Contbr. articles to legal jours. Office: 600 W Mound St Carthage MO 64836 Tel (417) 358-8131

JEFFERS, FRED HARDS, b. Montrose, Pa., Apr. 19, 1899; B.S. in Econs., U. Pa., 1922; LL.D., Cornell U., 1926. Admitted to N.Y. bar, 1926; asso. firm Stanchfield, Collin, Lovell & Sayles, Elmira, N.Y., 1926-29; mem. firm Mandeville, Waxman, Buck, Teeter & Harpending, Elmira, 1929-39; individual practice law, Binghamton, N.Y., 1939-56, Windsor, N.Y., 1956—. Chmn. Broome County Vets. Adv. Council, 1947; pres. Broome County Sch. Bds. Assn., 1947-48, N.Y. State Poultry Assn., 1954-57; chmn. Delahanna dist. Boy Scouts Am., 1949-50. Mem. Broome County Bar Assn. Author: Jeffers Motion Practice, 1938; A Selection of Old Poultry Books, 1954. Home and office: 1 Church St Windsor NY 13865 Tel (607) 655-1151

JEFFERSON, ANDREW L., JR., b. Dallas, Aug. 19, 1934; B.A., Tex. So. U., 1956; J.D., U. Tex., 1959. Admitted to Tex. bar, 1959, U.S. Supreme Ct. bar; partner firm Washington & Jefferson, Houston, 1960-61; asst. dist. atty. Bexar County (Tex.), San Antonio, 1961-62; asst. U.S. atty. Western Dist. Tex., 1962-66, chief asst., 1966-68; trial counsel, labor relations counsel Humble Oil & Refining Co., 1968-71; capt. JAGC, U.S. Army Res.; judge Ct. Domestic Relations, Harris County, 1971-74, 208th Dist. Ct., Harris County, 1974-75; individual practice law, Houston, 1975—; past dir. Standard Savs. & Loan Assn., Nav. Bank; mem. adv. com. Ct. Vol. Services, Harris County. Vice chmn. jud. com. Tex. Constl. Revision Commn.; bd. dirs. Houston Council Human Relations, pres., 1974-75; bd. dirs. Houston Legal Found., treas., 1973, 1st v.p., 1974-75; bd. dirs., mem. exec. com. United Fund of Houston and Harris County; bd. dirs. Model Sch. of Houston, Inc., Houston Citizens for Good Schs., San Antonio Community Welfare Council, San Antonio Family Welfare Assn., San Antonio Heart Assn., NCCJ, Met. San Antonio YMCA, Rice U. Center for Community Design and Research, Sickle Cell Disease Research Found. Tex., Big Bros. Houston, Houston Area Urban League, Houston Bus. Growth Corp., Gov.'s Drug Abuse Council; bd. regents Tex. So. U.; trustee Ecumenical Center for Religion and Health; adv. bd. San Antonio Med. Found. Mem. Am. (com. chmn. 1974-75), Nat., Fed., Tex., Houston bar assns., Houston Lawyers Assn. (v.p. 1969-70), Alpha Phi Alpha, Phi Alpha Delta. Recipient Nat. Torch of Liberty award Anti-Defamation League, 1974, Community Services award LaRaza, 1974, Forward Times Community Service award, 1975, Charles A. George Community Service award, 1975, Nat. Community Service award League United Latin Am. Citizens, 1975. Office: 2260 Two Shell Plaza Houston TX 77002 Tel (713) 224-8900

JEFFERSON, RUFUS OLNEY, b. Tampa, Fla., Sept. 3, 1925; student Corpus Christi Tex. Jr. Coll., 1945-46; B.S., Fla. State U., 1949; LL.B., U. Fla., 1952, J.D., 1967. Admitted to Fla. bar, 1952; asst. atty. gen. City of Tallahassee, 1952; individual practice law, Tallahassee, 1952-54, 72—; asso. firm Meginnis, Thompson & Morrison, Tallahassee, 1954-55; legal adviser to Gov. of Fla., Tallahassee, 1955-57; judge Leon County (Fla.) Juvenile Ct., 1957-72; chmn. Juvenile Ct. Rules Com. of Fla., 1975-76. Pres., North Central div. Children's Home Soc., Tallahassee, 1965-66, Visually Handicapped Children, Tallahassee, 1973-74. Mem. Fla. Bar, Tallahassee Bar Assn., Nat., Fla. (pres. 1966-67) councils juvenile ct. judges. Recipient Redfearn award U. Fla. Law Sch., 1952, Distinguished Service award Tallahassee Jr. C. of C., 1960; author: Flordia Juvenile Law, 1971. Home: 2401 Nancy Dr Tallahassee FL 32301 Office: 103 N Gadsden St Tallahassee FL 32302 Tel (904) 224-6325

JEFFREYS, ALBERT LEONIDAS, b. Chase City, Va., May 26, 1923; B.A., Fla. So. Coll., Lakeland, 1949; J.D., So. Meth. U., 1968. Admitted to Tex. bar, 1971; engring. writer Radio Corp. Am., Camden, N.J., 1955-59, Collins Radio Co., Dallas, 1959-61, LTV Electrosystems, 1961-71; corporate atty. Earth Resources Co., Dallas, 1971-73; gen. counsel Liquid Paper Corp., Dallas, 1973—. Mem. Am., Tex. bar assns., World Assn. Lawyers. Home: 328 Huffhines St Richardson TX 75081 Office: 9130 Marksville Dr Dallas TX 75231 Tel (214) 234-3211

JEFFRIES, MCCHESNEY HILL, b. Norfolk, Va., Jan. 3, 1922; A.B. cum laude, Davidson Coll., 1947; LL.B. cum laude, Harvard, 1950. Admitted to Ga. bar, 1950; asso. firm Moise, Post & Gardner, Atlanta, 1950-58, partner, 1958-62; partner firm Hansell, Post, Brandon & Dorsey, Atlanta, 1962—; dir. R & R Mfg. Co., Octagon Properties, Inc. Trustee Presbyn. Home, Inc., Atlanta Speech Sch., Inc., Hillside Cottages, Inc., Atlanta Lawyers Found., Inc. Mem. Am. Law Inst., Am., Ga., Atlanta bar assns., Lawyers Club Atlanta (pres. 1955-56), Phi Beta Kappa, Omicron Delta Kappa. Home: 3051 Habersham Rd NW Atlanta GA 30305 Office: 3300 First Nat Bank Bldg Atlanta GA 30303 Tel (404) 581-8033

JEFFS, M(ELVIN) DAYLE, b. Provo, Utah, Mar. 7, 1930; student Brigham Young U., 1948-52, 54; J.D., U. Utah, 1957. Admitted to Utah bar, 1957; mem. firm Jeffs & Jeffs, Provo, 1959—; individual practice law, Provo, 1957-59; county atty. Utah County, 1966-70. Chmn. Provo Freedom Festival, 1966. Mem. Utah County, Utah State, Am. bar assns. Home: 160 E 4320 N Provo UT 84601 Office: 90 N 100 E PO Box 683 Provo UT 84601 Tel (801) 373-8848

JEGEN, WILLIAM EDWARD, b. Indpls., May 13, 1944; B.S. in Mech. Engring. with distinction, Purdue U., 1966; J.D., John Marshall Law Sch., 1970. Patent agt. Link Belt Co., Chgo., 1966-68; patent agt. firm Hill, Sherman, Meroni, Gross & Simpson, Chgo., 1968-70, asso., 1970-71; admitted to Ill. bar, 1970; asso. firm Demling & Jegen and predecessor, Glen Ellyn, Ill., 1971-75, partner, 1975—. Mem. DuPage County (Ill.) Republican Central Com. Mem. Ill. State Bar Assn. Office: 493 Duane St Glen Ellyn IL 60137 Tel (312) 858-3130

JEKEL, LOUIS GLANZ, b. Denver, June 2, 1941; A.B., Occidental Coll., 1963; J.D., U. Ariz., 1966. Admitted to Ariz. bar, 1966; predecessors, Scottsdale, Ariz., 1966-75; individual practice law, Scottsdale, 1976—. Bd. mgrs. Scottsdale br. YMCA, 1970-75; mem. adv. bd. Camelback Hosp. Mental Health Center, Scottsdale, 1971-76. Mem. Scottsdale (pres. 1977—), Maricopa County, Am. bar assns., Am. Assn. Trial Lawyers, Scottsdale C. of C. (dir. 1977—). Office: 4323 N Brown Ave Suite E Scottsdale AZ 85251 Tel (602) 994-5588

JENKINS, DAVID LYNN, b. Madison, Wis., Feb. 9, 1943; J.D., U. Wis., 1972. Admitted to Wis. bar, 1972; mem. firm Richard D. Endicott & Assos., Hillsboro, Wis., 1972-76, Jenkins & Stittleberg, Viroqua, Wis., 1977—; city atty. City of Viroqua. asst. dist. atty. Vernon County (Wis.), 1976—. Mem. Am., Vernon County (treas.) bar assns., State Bar Wis., Viroqua Area C. of C. (dir. 1977). Home and Office: 418 S Main St Viroqua WI 54665 Tel (608) 637-7064

JENKINS, MARTHA MILLS, b. East Lansing, Mich., May 11, 1941; B.A., Macalester Coll., 1964; J.D., U. Minn., 1965. Admitted to N.Y. bar, 1966, Miss. bar, 1968, Ill. bar, 1970, U.S. Supreme Ct. bar, 1970; asso. firm White & Case, N.Y.C., 1965-67; atty., Lawyers Com. for Civil Rights Under Law, Jackson, Miss., 1967-69, chief counsel, Cairo, Ill., 1969-71; city atty., Fayette, Miss., 1969; asso. firm Schiff, Hardin & Waite, Chgo., 1971-75, individual practice law, Chgo., 1976—; prof. law (part-time) Ill. Inst. Tech., 1976—. Mem. Chgo. Council Lawyers (bd. govs.), Am. Bar Assn. (chmn. litigation sect. individual small firm practice com.), Chgo. Bar Assn. Contbr. article to law jour. Home: 6315 N Magnolia St Chicago IL 60660 Office: 77 W Washington St Chicago IL 60602 Tel (312) 726-3360

JENKINS, PETER CORNELIUS, b. Los Angeles, July 23, 1943; B.S. in Mgmt. Engring., Rensselaer Polytechnic Inst., 1965; LL.B., U. Va., 1968; LL.M. (Barrett E. Prettyman fellow), Georgetown U., 1970. Admitted to Va., D.C. bars, 1968, Idaho bar, 1971; asso. firm Eberle, Berlin, Kading, Turnbow & Gillespie, Boise, Idaho, 1970-75; individual practice law, Boise, 1976—. Instr. Transcendental Meditation program World Plan Exec. Council, Pacific Palisades, Calif., 1976—. Mem. Am., Idaho bar assns., Order of Coif. Home and Office: 1601 N 8th Boise ID 83702 Tel (208) 336-2769

JENKINS, THOMAS ARTHUR, b. Gallatin, Tenn., Dec. 7, 1919; LL.B., Cumberland U., 1947. Admitted to Tenn. bar, 1946; individual practice law, Manchester, Tenn. Mem. Tenn. Bar Assn., Am. Trial Lawyers Assn. Home: 311 Rickenbacker St Tullahoma TN 37388 Office: Public Sq Manchester TN 37355 Tel (615) 728-2414

JENKINS, WALLACE ALFRED, b. Cleve., Aug. 23, 1928; A.B., Ohio No. U., 1950; LL.B., Cleve. Marshall Law Sch., 1956, J.D., 1969, LL.M., 1960. Admitted to Ohio bar, 1957, U.S. Supreme Ct. bar, 1971; claims atty. Nationwide Ins. Co., Canton, Ohio, 1956-64; asso. firm Payne & Payne, Cleve., 1964—. Mem. Ohio, Cuyahoga County (chmn. grievance com. 1973-76), Greater Cleve. bar assns., Ohio Def. Assn. Home: 8455 N Akins Rd North Royalton OH 44133 Office: 2130 Illuminating Bldg Cleveland OH 44113 Tel (216) 241-5900

JENKINS, WARWICK HOXIE, b. Waco, Tex., Dec. 4, 1921; B.A., LL.B., Baylor U., 1948. Admitted to Tex. bar, 1948; since practiced in Waxahachie, Tex., individual practice law, 1948-56, 58-62, 66-70; partner firm Jenkins & Allen, 1956-58, Jenkins & Jones, 1962-66, Jenkins & Johnson, 1970-72, Jenkins & Jenkins, 1973—. Trustee, Sims Library, Waxahachie, 1969—. Mem. Am., Ellis County (pres. 1951-54) bar assns., Am. Judicature Soc., Am., Tex. trial lawyers assns., Tex. Criminal Defense Lawyers Assn., Waxahachie C. of C. (pres. 1962-63). Home: Lakeshore Dr Waxahachie TX 75165 Office: 516 W Main St Waxahachie TX 75165 Tel (214) 937-5710

JENKS, GEORGE MILAN, b. Dickinson, N.D., Feb. 26, 1933; A.S., C.E., Multnomah Coll., 1958; B.S. in Edn., U. Oreg., 1960, M.Ed. in Counseling, 1961; J.D., Lewis and Clark Coll., 1971. Tchr. Aberdeen (Wash.) Sch. Dist., 1960-62, David Douglas Sch. Dist., Portland, Oreg., 1963-72; admitted to Oreg. bar, 1972; individual practice law, Portland, 1972-75; partner firm Jenks & Weinstein, P.C., Portland, Oreg., 1975—. Treas. Troop 143 Columbia Pacific council Boy Scouts Am., 1968-74; bd. dirs. Milwaukie (Oreg.) Lutheran Meml. Found.,

1975—; sec.-treas. Milwaukie Luth. Ch. Found., 1975—. Mem. Oreg. State, Am. bar assns., Oreg. Trial Lawyers' Assn. Home: 14223 SE Vista Ln Milwaukie OR 97222 Office: 1724 NE 42nd Ave Portland OR 97213 Tel (503) 288-5087

JENKS, MICHAEL RONALD, b. Valdosta, Ga., Jan. 21, 1945; B.A., Fla. Atlantic U., 1967; J.D., U. Miami, 1970. Admitted to Fla. bar, 1970, U.S. Ct. of Appeals bar, 1971, U.S. Supreme Ct. bar, 1974; atty. firm Walton, Lantaff, Schroeder & Carson, Miami, Fla., 1970—. Mem. Am., Dade County bar assns., Am. Arbitration Assn. Address: 900 Alfred I DuPont Bldg Miami FL 33131

JENNER, ALBERT ERNEST, JR., b. Chgo., June 20, 1907; J.D., U. Ill., 1930; LL.D., John Marshall Law Sch., 1962, Columbia Coll., 1974, U. Notre Dame, 1975, Northwestern U., 1975, William Mitchell Law Sch., 1975, U. Mich., 1976. Admitted to Ill. bar, 1930; practiced in Chgo. 1930—, partner firm Jenner & Block, and predecessors, 1933—, sr. partner, 1949—; prof. Northwestern U., 1952-53; chmn. Ill. Commn. on Uniform State Laws, 1952—; mem. Nat. Conf. Commrs. Uniform State Laws, 1952—, pres., 1969-71; spl. asst. atty. gen. State of Ill., 1956-65; mem. adv. com. on fed. rules of civil procedures U.S. Supreme Ct., 1960-70, chmn. adv. com. on fed. rules of evidence, 1965-75; sr. counsel Presdl. Commn. to Investigate Assassination of Pres. Kennedy (Warren Commn.), 1963-64; chief spl. counsel to Minority, Ho. of Reps. Judiciary Com. that conducted impeachment inquiry of Pres. Richard M. Nixon, 1973-74; mem. Pres.'s. Nat. Commn. on Causes and Prevention of Violence in U.S., 1968-69. Trustee Fund for the Republic. Fellow Am. Coll. Trial Lawyers (regent 1953-60, pres. 1958-59), Internat. Acad. Trial Lawyers; mem. Ill. Soc. Trial Lawyers, Nat. Assn. Def. Lawyers in Criminal Cases, Am. (ho. of dels. 1948—, mem. standing com. on fed. judiciary 1964-68, mem. council sect. on legal edn. and admission to bar 1971-76, chmn. sect. individual rights and responsibilities 1973-74, bd. govs. 1977—), Ill. (pres. 1949-50), Chgo. (bd. mgrs. 1944-49, sec. 1947-49) bar assns., Assn. Bar City N.Y., Am. Judicature Soc. (pres. 1958), Am. Inst. Jud. Adminstrn., Nat. Lawyers Com. for Civil Rights Under Law (dir., nat. co-chmn. 1975-77), Bar Assn. U.S. Ct. Appeals 7th Circuit (gov. 1955-60), Am. Law Inst., Fund For Republic, Inc. (Robert Maynard Hutchins Distinguished Service award 1976), Chgo. Council Lawyers, Center For Study Democratic Instns. (dir. 1975—), NAACP Legal Def. Fund, Nat. Conf. Bar Assn. Pres.'s. U.S. (pres. 1952-53), Order of Coif, Alpha Chi Rho, Phi Delta Phi. Recipient Distinguished Alumni award U. Ill., 1962; Distinguished Civic Achievement award Am. Jewish Com., 1973; Distinguished Citizen's award N.Y. U., 1975, others; named Chicagoan of Year, Chgo. Press Club, 1975. Author: Illinois Civil Practice Act Annotated, 1933; Smith-Hurd Illinois Annotated Statutes, 7 edits., 1935-76; contbr. articles to legal publs.; permanent editorial bd. Uniform Comml. Code, 1961—. Home: 119 Tudor Pl Kenilworth IL 60043 Office: Jenner & Block One IBM Plaza Chicago IL 60611 Tel (312) 222-9350

JENNINGS, ALSTON, b. W. Helena, Ark., Oct. 30, 1917; B.A., Columbia, 1938; J.D., Northwestern U., 1941. Admitted to Ark. bar, 1941, U.S. Supreme Ct. bar, 1955; spl. agt. Intelligence Unit, Treasury Dept., Little Rock, 1946; individual practice law, Little Rock, 1947-49; asso. firm Wright, Lindsey & Jennings, and predecessors, Little Rock, 1949-51, partner, 1951—; dep. pros. atty. Pulaski and Perry Counties (Ark.), 1947-49. Adv. bd. Salvation Army Pulaski County. Fellow Am. Coll. Trial Lawyers (bd. regents 1975—); mem. Am., Ark., Pulaski County (former pres.) bar assns., Internat. Assn. Ins. Counsel (pres. 1972-73). Named Outstanding Lawyer, Ark. Bar Assn. and Found., 1973. Home: 5300 Sherwood Rd Little Rock AR 72207 Office: 2200 Worthen Bank Bldg Little Rock AR 72201 Tel (501) 375-6481

JENNINGS, DENNIS WAYNE, b. Cheyenne, Wyo., June 17, 1947; B.A., U. Mo., 1969, J.D., 1972. Admitted to Mo. bar, 1973; asso. firm William J. Cason, Clinton, Mo., 1973-76, Lilleston & Roberts, Clinton, 1976—. Chmn. Henry County (Mo.) Cancer Crusade, Clinton, 1973; pres. Henry County Cancer Unit, 1975, chmn. bus. and profl. cancer crusade, 1977. Mem. Am., Henry County bar assns. Home: 414 S 2d St Clinton MO 64735 Office: 104 W Jefferson St Clinton MO 64735 Tel (816) 885-6161

JENNINGS, JAMES TRAYNOR; b. Tucumcari, N.Mex., Apr. 8, 1914; A.B., U. Notre Dame, 1935; LL.B., U. Tex., 1938. Admitted to Tex. bar, 1938, N.Mex. bar, 1938; individual practice law, Roswell, N.Mex., 1938-66; mem. firm Jennings & Copple, Roswell, 1966-70, Jennings, Christy & Copple, Roswell, 1970—. Mem. N.Mex. (pres. 1960-61), Tex., Am. (state del.) bar assns. Home: 1208 Avenida del Sumbre Roswell NM 88201 Office: Box 1180 Roswell NM 88201 Tel (505) 622-8432

JENNINGS, JEFFREY HOWELLS, b. Pitts., Feb. 16, 1919; A.B., Columbia, 1941, LL.B., 1944, J.D., 1968; student N.Y. U. Sch. Edn. Admitted to N.Y. bar, 1944; asso. to counsel Columbia U., N.Y.C., 1944-55; asst. U.S. atty. Eastern dist. N.Y., Bklyn., 1961-66; librarian Old Mill Sch., N.Y.C., 1973. Pres. Smithtown C. of C., 1959-60; prin. clk. Smithtown Hwy. Dept., 1961. Mem. Am. Arbitration Assn. Recipient Cross of Honor, Order DeMolay, 1972. Home: 641 Meadow Rd Smithtown NY 11787 Office: 146 Rider Ave Patchogue NY 11772 Tel (516) GR5-3640

JENNINGS, RICHARD W., b. Bois D'Arc, Mo., Oct. 19, 1907; A.B., Park Coll., 1972, LL.D. (hon.), 1975; A.M., U. Pa., 1934; J.D., U. Calif., Berkeley, 1939. Admitted to Calif. bar, 1939; asso. firm Jesse H. Steinhart, San Francisco, 1939-45, mem., 1945-47; lectr. law U. Calif., 1940-42, prof., 1947-55, Corffroth prof., 1955—; vis. prof. Stanford U., 1953, vis. Fulbright prof. Tokyo U., 1961; vis. prof. U. Mich., 1963, U. Cologne, 1972; lectr. Salzburg Seminar of Am. Studies, 1972; cons. SEC, 1962. Mem. Am. Law Inst., Am. Bar Found., Am. Bar Assn. Author: (with Marsh) Securities Regulation—Cases and Materials, 1977; (with Marsh) Selected Statutes, Rules and Forms Under the Federal Securities Law, 1977; (with Lattin and Buxbaum) Cases and Materials on Corporations, 1968. Home: 425 Vassar Ave Berkeley CA 94708 Office: Sch Law U Calif Berkeley CA 94720 Tel (415) 642-1731

JENNINGS, WILLIAM HOWARD, b. San Diego, Jan. 20, 1899; student U. Calif., Berkeley, 1921; J.D., Los Angeles Coll. Law, 1930. Admitted to Calif. bar, 1930; with Calif. Legis. Counsel Bur., 1930-31; individual practice law, La Mesa, Calif., 1931; mem. firm Jennings, Engstrand and Henrikson, San Diego, and predecessor, 1948—; city atty., La Mesa, 1934-52, El Cajon, 1937-38; gen. counsel Helix Irrigation Dist., 1936-69; legal cons. Internat. Boundary and Water Commn., U.S., Mexico, 1952; tech. cons. Colo. River Bd., 1946; gen. counsel San Diego County Water Authority, 1944. Bd. dirs. Calif. Water Commn., 1958-74. Home: 3421 Park Blvd San Diego CA 92103 Office: 2297 Camino Del Rio S San Diego CA 92108 Tel 291-0840

JENSEN, CARL ARTHUR, b. Sleepy Eye, Minn., Dec. 11, 1920; B.S.L., U. Minn., 1948, LL.B., 1949. Admitted to Minn. bar, 1949, U.S. Dist. Ct. bar, 1950; individual practice law, Sleepy Eye, 1949—; mem. Minn. Ho. of Reps., 1950-60, State Senate, 1966—; atty. City of Sleepy Eye, 1961—; atty. Minn. State Assn. Twp. Officers, 1963-67; atty. Minn. Bankers Assn., 1963-64. Pres. Sleepy Eye PTA, 1959-60. Mem. Am., Minn., Brown County, Dist. bar assns., Sleepy Eye Lions, Sleepy Eye Golf Club, Am. Legion, C. of C., Ish-Tak-Ha-Ba. Home: 209 1st Ave S Sleepy Eye MN 56085 Office: 127 E Main St Sleepy Eye MN 56085 Tel (507) 794-5471

JENSEN, CHRISTOPHER WILLIAM, b. Long Island, N.Y., Apr. 25, 1948; B.S., State U. N.Y., 1970; J.D., U. Ariz., 1973. Admitted to Ariz. bar, 1973; asso. firm Leek, Oehler and Martin, Kingman, Ariz., 1973-74; partner firm Pope and Jensen, Bullhead City, Ariz., 1974; individual practice law, Prescott, Ariz., 1974-76; partner firm Jensen and Sult, Prescott, 1976—. Democratic precinct committeeman, Bullhead City, 1974. Mem. Am. Bar Assn., State Bar of Ariz., Phi Alpha Delta. Asso. editor: Ariz. Advocate, 1972-73. Home: 1205 Doka Dr Prescott AZ 86301 Office: POB 1948 Prescott AZ 86301 Tel (602) 778-2660

JENSEN, DIANE LYNNE, b. N.Y.C., May 19, 1948; B.A., U. Mich., 1969, J.D., 1972. Admitted to Fla. bar, 1972; clk. firm Carrel, Pustina & Zelinski, Thunder Bay, Ont., Can., 1972-73; asso. firm Pavese, Shields, Garner, Harverfield & Kluttz, Ft. Myers, Fla., 1973—; dir. Lee County Legal Aid Soc., 1976—, treas., 1977—. Legacy chmn. Lee County div. Am. Cancer Soc., 1974—, sec., 1976—; mem. legacy com. Fla. div., 1976—. Mem. Am., Fla., Lee County bar assns., Lee County Estate Planning Soc., Phi Beta Kappa. Office: 1833 Hendry St Fort Myers FL 33901 Tel (813) 334-2195

JENSEN, GEORGE ALBERT, b. St. Louis, June 27, 1929; A.B., Washington U., 1952, J.D., 1954. Admitted to Mo. bar, 1954; mem. firm Peper, Martin, Jensen, Maichel and Hetlage, and predecessors, St. Louis, 1954-58, partner, 1958—; dir., gen. counsel Commerce Bank of Mound City; dir. Nat. Aviation Underwriters, Inc., Nat. Gen. Ins. Co., A.G. Edwards & Sons, Inc.; lectr. in field. Bd. dirs., pres. Tower Village, Inc., St. Louis; trustee St. Louis Soc. for Blind, Nat. Urban League, N.Y.C. Mem. Mo., Am. bar assns., Bar Assn. Met. St. Louis, Order of Coif, Phi Beta Kappa, Phi Delta Chi. Contbr. articles to legal jours. Home: 6 Forest Ridge St Clayton MO 63105 Office: 720 Olive St Saint Louis MO 63101 Tel (314) 421-3850

JENSEN, HOWARD FRANCIS, b. Breckenridge, Tex., Oct. 31, 1921; student Tex. A. and M. U., 1938-40; LL.B., U. Tex., 1943. Admitted to Tex. bar, 1943; law clk. Supreme Ct. Tex., Austin, 1943-44; asso. firm Burford, Ryburn & Ford, Dallas, 1944-45, partner, 1945-59; v.p., gen. counsel, sec. Lone Star Steel Co., Dallas, 1960—; mem. Dallas Park Bd., 1955-57. Mem. N.A.M. (dir. 1973—), Am. Soc. Corporate Secs. Office: PO Box 35888 Dallas TX 75235 Tel (214) 352-3981

JENSEN, ROBERT TRYGVE, b. Chgo., Sept. 16, 1922; student U. N.C., 1943; B.S., Northwestern U., 1949, LL.B., 1949, J.D., 1970; LL.M., U. So. Calif., 1955. Admitted to Calif. bar, 1950, U.S. Supreme Ct. bar, 1954; asst. counsel Douglas Aircraft Co., Inc., Santa Monica, Calif., 1950-52, 58-60, counsel El Segundo (Calif.) div., 1952-58; gen. counsel Aerospace Corp., El Segundo, 1960—, asst. sec., 1961-67, sec., 1967—. Mem. Am., Beverly Hills bar assns., Am. Arbitration Assn. (nat. panel arbitrators), World Assn. Lawyers of World Peace Through Law Center, Alpha Delta Phi, Phi Delta Phi. Certified specialist taxation law Calif. Bd. Legal Specialization. Home: 10610 Ashton Ave Los Angeles CA 90024 Office: 2350 E El Segundo Blvd El Segundo CA 90245 Tel (213) 648-6702

JENSEN, WILLIAM NEALE, b. Billings, Mont., Dec. 13, 1939; B.S. in Edn., Eastern Mont. Coll., 1964; J.D., U. Mont., 1970. Admitted to Mont. bar, 1970; staff atty. Mont. Legal Services Assn., Billings, 1970-71, dep. dir., Helena, Mont., 1971-72; asst. atty. gen. Mont., Helena, 1972-73; partner firm Hibbs, Sweeney & Colberg, Billings, 1973—; trustee Mont. Legal Services Assn., 1974—; mem. legal services com. State Bar Mont., 1975—. Mem. Am. Bar Assn. Home: 1029 N Broadway Billings MT 59101 Office: First Northwestern Bank Center Billings MT 59101 Tel (406) 252-4101

JENTZ, GAYLORD ADAIR, b. Beloit, Wis., Aug. 7, 1931; B.A., U. Wis., 1953, J.D., 1957, M.B.A., 1958. Admitted to Wis. bar, 1957; individual practice law, Madison, Wis., 1957-58; asst. prof. U. Okla., Norman, 1958-59, asso. prof., 1959-65; asso. prof. to prof. U. Tex., Austin, 1965—; vis. instr., vis. prof. U. Wis., 1957-65. Active Anderson High Sch. Band Parents, Booster Club, Heritage Soc., N.W. Little League, N.W. Pony/Colt League. Mem. Am. Judicature Soc., Am. Bus. Law Assn., Am. Arbitration Assn., Wis. State Bar Assn., Tex. Assn. Coll. Tchrs., Southwestern Social Sci. Assn., Omicron Delta Kappa, Phi Kappa Phi. Recipient Teaching Excellence awards Coll. Bus. Adminstrn., 1967, 71. Co-author bus. law text; contbr. articles to bus. edn. publs. Home: 4106 North Hills Dr Austin TX 78731 Office: BEB 615 U Texas Austin TX 78712 Tel (512) 471-3322

JERCHOWER, DAVID, b. Newark, Nov. 18, 1933; B.A., Rutgers U., 1955, LL.B., 1958. Admitted to N.J. bar, 1959, U.S. Supreme Ct. bar, 1965; individual practice law, Irvington, N.J., 1964—. Vice-pres., chmn. personnel com. Boonton (N.J.) Twp. Bd. Edn.; pres. Temple Beth Sholom, Boonton, 1972-74. Mem. N.J., Essex County, Morris County, Irvington (pres. 1971-75) bar assns. Home: R D 3 Powerville Rd Boonton NJ 07005 Office: 1064 Clinton Ave Irvington NJ 07111 Tel (201) 371-7676

JEREN, JOHN ANTHONY, JR., b. Youngstown, Ohio, Feb. 23, 1946; B.B.A., Ohio State U., 1968; J.D., Ohio No. U., 1973. Admitted to Ohio bar, 1973; atty. Thomas Peter Wellman Co., Youngstown, 1973—; mem. nat. moot ct. bd. Ohio No. U., Ada, 1972-73. Mem. Am., Ohio, Mahoning County bar assns. Named to Willis Soc., Ohio No. U., 1974. Home: 4241 Wedgewood Dr Youngstown OH 44511 Office: 5212 Mahoning Ave Suite 305 Youngstown OH 44515 Tel (216) 792-2336

JERNIGAN, JOHN LEE, b. Atlanta, May 29, 1942; A.B., Davidson Coll., 1964; J.D., U. N.C., 1967. Admitted to N.C. bar, 1967; partner firm Smith, Anderson, Blownt & Mitchell, Raleigh, N.C., 1969—. Mem. Wake County (N.C.) (exec. com.), N.C. bars, Am. Bar Assn. Home: 3225 Laudr Rd Raleigh NC 27609 Office: PO Box 750 Raleigh NC 27609 Tel (919) 821-1220

JERUE, JAMES MICHAEL, b. Providence, Nov. 7, 1936; B.S. in Indsl. Engring., U. R.I., 1958; LL.B. cum laude, Boston U., 1963. Admitted to R.I. bar, 1963; law clk. to chief judge U.S. Dist. Ct., R.I., 1963-64; partner firm Beals, Jerue & DiFiure, Providence, 1964-74; exec. counsel to gov. State of R.I., 1972-74; dir. adminstrn. State of R.I., 1974-76; legal counsel Labor Relations Bd., 1968-72; pres. town council Town of E. Greenwich (R.I.), 1970-72. Home: 20 Teakwood Ct East Greenwich RI 02818 Office: 144 Westminster St Providence RI 02903 Tel (401) 272-2770

JESKE, ARNOLD CARL, b. Priddy, Tex., Oct. 12, 1915; B.S., Daniel Baker Coll., 1939; LL.B., Baylor U., 1948. Admitted to Tex. bar, 1948; owner Jeske Homes and Constrn., Bryan, Tex., 1948—; v.p. Farmers & Merchants Bank Uninc, Priddy, 1969—. Mem. State Bar of Tex. Home and Office: 112 Royall St Bryan TX 77801 Tel (713) 846-2307

JESSEE, C. JAMES, JR., b. Norton, Va., Dec. 19, 1924; B.A. in Econs., U. Va., 1949, J.D., 1954. Admitted to Va. bar, 1952, Tenn. bar, 1954, Ga. bar, 1959; sr. mem. firm Jessee, Ritchie & Duncan, P.C., Atlanta. Chmn., Community Planning Council of Sandy Springs, 1967-75; pres. Sandy Springs Businessmen's Assn., 1964; mem. Bd. Zoning Appeals, Fulton County, Ga. Mem. Am., Atlanta bar assns., Fedn. Ins. Counsel, Ga. Def. Lawyers Assn., Am., Ga. trial lawyers assns., Am. Judicature Soc., Lawyers Club Atlanta. Home: 780 Douglas Rd NE Atlanta GA 30342 Office: 620 Northside Tower 6065 Roswell Rd NE Atlanta GA 30328 Tel (404) 256-0991

JESSEE, GARY DAVID, b. Dayton, Ohio, Feb. 27, 1941; A.B., Union Coll., Barbourville, Ky., 1962; J.D., Ohio State U., 1967. Admitted to Ohio bar, 1967; payroll clk. Inland Mfg. Co., Dayton, Ohio, 1962-64; asso. firm Kimmel & Martin, Fairborn, Ohio, 1967-68; partner firm Kimmel, Martin & Jessee, Fairborn, 1969-75; individual practice law, Fairborn, 1975—. Tchr. Am. Savings and Loan Inst., 1969, 70. Trustee Fairborn Neighborhood Services; trustee Greene County Opportunities Industrialization Center, Greene County, Ohio, 1970-71. Mem. Am., Ohio, Greene County bar assns., Am. Judicature Soc. Home: 2145 Rockdell Dr Fairborn OH 45324 Office: 717 W Xenia Dr Fairborn OH 45324 Tel (513) 879-3200

JESSER, STEVEN H., b. Chgo., Feb. 29, 1948; B.A., Northwestern U., 1970; J.D., Chgo.-Kent Coll. Law, 1974. Admitted to Ill. bar, 1974, D.C. bar, 1975; asst. state's atty. Cook County, Chgo., 1974—; lectr. Ill. State's Attys. Assn. Mem. Am., Ill. State, Chgo. bar assns. Author continuing legal edn. column Chgo. Daily Law Bull., 1975—; contbr. Law Enforcement Legal Def. Manual. Office: 2600 S California Ave Chicago IL 60608 Tel (312) 542-2900

JESSUP, STEPHEN MILLS, b. Kokomo, Ind., Feb. 3, 1944; B.A., Hanover (Ind.) Coll., 1966; J.D., Ind. U., 1969. Admitted to Ind. bar, 1969; asso. firm Lacey, Angel & Good, Kokomo, 1969-71, partner, 1972—; research analyst Jud. Study Commn. State of Ind., 1967-69. Bd. dirs. Howard County unit Am. Cancer Soc., 1972-76, United Way of Howard County, 1974-76. Mem. Am., Ind., Howard County (pres. 1976) bar assns. Home: 507 Devonshire Dr Kokomo IN 46901 Office: POB 805 Kokomo IN 46901

JESSUP, WARREN T., b. Eureka, Calif., Aug. 1, 1916; B.S., U. So. Calif., 1937; J.D., George Washington U., 1942. Admitted to D.C. bar, Calif. bar, U.S. Supreme Ct. bar; engr. Gen. Electric Co., 1937-38, patent dept., 1938-42; mem. patent div. USN, 1944-46; patent counsel 11th Naval Dist., 1946-50; mem. firm Huebner, Beehler, Worrel & Herzig, 1950-56; partner firms Herzig and Jessup, 1957-59, Jessup & Beecher, Sherman Oaks, Calif., 1968—; individual practice law, 1959-68; instr. patent law and legal problems in engring. U. Calif. Extension, U. So. Calif. Bd. dirs. Ventura County (Calif.) Cultural Heritage; mem. Ventura County Mental Health Adv. Bd.; mem. Santa Monica Mountains Citizens Adv. Com. Mem. Calif. Soc. Profl. Engrs., Patent Law Assn. Los Angeles (pres. 1974), Order of Coif, Conejo Valley Hist. Soc. (dir.), Phi Delta Phi, Tau Beta Pi, Eta Kappa Nu. Author: Patent Guide for Navy Inventors, 1950. Home: 1697 W Potrero Rd Thousand Oaks CA 91360 Office: 15233 Ventura Blvd Sherman Oaks CA 91403

JESTER, TOM D., JR., b. Texarkana, Ark., Feb. 2, 1940; B.S. in Bus. Adminstrn., U. Ark., 1962; J.D., So. Meth. U., 1967. Admitted to Tex. bar, 1967; asso. firm Minor & Knight, Denton, Tex., 1967-75; partner firm Minor, Jester & Davidge, Denton, 1975—; spl. instr. bus. law Tex. Womans U., Denton, 1976; municipal judge, Denton, 1969-70, mem. city council, 1972-76, mayor pro tem, 1973-75, mayor, 1975-76. Mem. ins. com. 1st Baptist Ch., Denton. Mem. Tex., N. Tex., Denton County (pres. 1974-75) bar assns. Home: 1101 Ridgecrest St Denton TX 76201 Office: 116 W McKinney St PO Box 280 Denton TX 76201 Tel (817) 387-7585

JETER, KATHERINE LESLIE BRASH, b. Gulfport, Miss., July 24, 1921; B.A., Tulane U., 1943, J.D., 1945. Admitted to La. bar, 1945; asso. firm Montgomery, Fenner & Brown, New Orleans, La., 1945-46, firm Tucker, Martin, Holder, Jeter & Jackson and predecessors, Shreveport, La., 1947—. Pres., League of Women Voters, 1950-51, YWCA, 1963, Little Theatre of Shreveport, 1966-67, Shreveport Art Guild, 1974-75; treas., Am. Nat. Theatre and Acad., Shreveport, 1963. Mem. Am., La., Shreveport bar assns., Nat. Assn. of Women Lawyers, La. State Law Inst. (advisory com. on revision of civil code book III), Order of the Coif; Phi Beta Kappa. Editor: Tulane Law Review, 1945; contbr. articles to legal jours. Home: 3959 Maryland St Shreveport LA 71106 Office: 1300 Beck Bldg Travis St Shreveport LA 71101 Tel (318) 425-7764

JETER, ROBERT MCLEAN, JR., b. Shreveport, La., Aug. 18, 1918; B.S., Washington and Lee U., 1941; LL.B., Tulane U., 1944. Admitted to La. bar, 1944; partner firm Tucker, Martin, Holder, Jeter & Jackson, and predecessors, Shreveport, 1945—. Pres., Shreveport Family and Children's Service Agy., 1953, Shreveport Goodwill Industries, 1954, Community Council of Caddo and Bossier Parishes, 1955-56, Shreveport Little Theatre, 1960; bd. dirs. Shreveport Community Chest, 1954-56, 58-60; bd. dirs. United Fund of Caddo and Bossier Parishes, 1967-69, treas., 1968; bd. dirs. Shreveport-Bossier Found., 1961—, sec., 1961-69, chmn., 1969-75. Mem. Am., La., Shreveport (past pres.) bar assns., Am. Judicature Soc., Order of Coif. Editor-in-chief: Tulane Law Rev., 1944. Home: 3959 Maryland Ave Shreveport LA 71106 Office: 1300 Beck Bldg Shreveport LA 71101 Tel (318) 425-7764

JEWELL, ALLEN LEE, b. Kansas City, Mo., July 31, 1929; A.B., Vanderbilt U., 1951, LL.B., 1956. Admitted to Tenn. bar, 1956, Alaska bar, 1961; mem. first staff state atty. gen's. office pursuant to statehood, Anchorage, 1959; partner firm Hahn, Jewell & Stanfill, Anchorage, 1964—; chmn. Anchorage Bd. Examiners and Appeals, 1969. Chmn. Chugach dist. Boy Scouts Am., 1968-69; pres. Anchorage World Affairs Council, 1970, Anchorage Symphony Bd., 1974-76. Mem. Alaska, Anchorage, Am. bar assns., Am. Trial Lawyers Assn. Home: 837 N St Anchorage AK 99501 Office: 542 W 2d Ave Anchorage AK 99501 Tel (907) 279-1544 also Homer AK 235-8709

JEWELL, WILLIAM HORACE, b. Hope, Ark., Dec. 16, 1919; LL.B., U. Ark., 1944. Admitted to Ark. bar, 1944; partner firm House, Holmes & Jewell, Little Rock, 1944—. Mem. Pulaski County, Ark., Am. bar assns. Home: 306 Fairfax St Little Rock AR 72205 Office: 1550 Tower Bldg Little Rock AR 72201 Tel (501) 375-9151

JIGANTI, MEL RICHARD, b. Chgo., July 16, 1932; B.S., U. Notre Dame, 1954; LL.B., DePaul U., 1956. Admitted to Ill. bar, 1956; trial atty. Chgo. Transit Authority, 1959-61; asso. firm Petit, Olin, Overmyer & Fazio, Chgo., 1962; judge Oak Lawn (Ill.) Village Ct., 1963, Cook County (Ill.) Circuit Ct., 1964-75, Ill. Appellate Ct., 1976—. Mem. Chgo., Ill., Am. bar assns., Am. Judicature Soc. Office: Civic Center Chicago IL 60602 Tel (312) 793-5432

JILLSON, ROBERT LYMAN, b. Detroit, May 18, 1936; A.B. in English with high honors, U. Mich., 1958; J.D., 1961. Admitted to Ohio bar, 1962, D.C. bar, 1974; asso. firm Lepaulle, Jeantet et L'Eleu, Paris, 1961-62; asso. firm Squire, Sanders & Dempsey, Cleve., 1962-71, gen. partner, 1971—. Mem. Am., Ohio, Cleve., D.C. bar assns., Order of Coif, Phi Beta Kappa. Articles editor Mich. Law Rev., 1960-61. Home: 2875 Broxton Rd Shaker Heights OH 44120 Office: 1800 Union Commerce Bldg Cleveland OH 44115 Tel (216) 696-9200

JIMENEZ, BALDEMAR ARELLANO, b. San Antonio, Oct. 5, 1937; B.A., U. Tex., 1960; LL.B., St. Mary's U., San Antonio, 1963, J.D., 1967. Admitted to Tex. bar, 1962; title examiner Alamo Title Co., 1961-64; tax atty. City of San Antonio, 1964-67, chief prosecutor municipal ct., 1967-71, civil trial atty., 1971-72, chief prosecutor, 1972—; instr. law enforcement San Antonio Coll., 1972-73. Mem. Tex. Bar Assn. Office: 302 S Laredo St San Antonio TX 78285 Tel (512) 225-7641

JOANIS, JOHN WESTON, b. Hopewell, Va., June 13, 1918; LL.B., U. Wis., 1942; postgrad. Harvard Grad. Sch. Bus. Adminstrn., 1950. Admitted to Wis. bar, 1943; atty. Thompson & Guenewold, Oshkosh, Wis., 1945-47; atty. Hartware Mutuals, 1947-48, asst. sec., 1948-52; sec., gen. counsel Hardware Mutuals and Sentry Life Ins. Co., 1952-53, v.p., gen. counsel, 1954-62, exec. v.p., 1962-64; exec. v.p. Sentry Ins., 1964-66, pres., chief exec. officer, 1966-72, chmn. bd., chief exec. officer, 1972—; chmn. bd., chief exec. officer, dir. Sentry Ins.-A Mut. Co., Sentry Life Ins. Co.; chmn. bd., pres., chief exec. officer, dir. The Sentry Corp.; chmn. bd.; dir. Middlesex Ins. Co., Patriot Gen. Ins. Co., Dairyland Ins. Co., Great Southwest Fire Ins. Co.; dir. Patriot Gen. Life Ins. Co., Hardware Mutual Casualty Co., Sentry Life Ins. Co. N.Y., Sentry Found., Inc., Sentry Indemnity Co., Dairyland Found., Inc., Hardware Dealers Mutual Fire Ins. Co., Sentry Investment Mgmt., Inc., Manor Ins. Co., Ltd. (Bermuda), Cloverleaf Ins. Co., Sentry Ins. Mgmt., Ltd., Sentry Ins. (Australasia), Ltd., Sydney, Sentry Holdings, Ltd., Sydney, Comml. Life Assurance Ltd., Sydney, City of Westminister Assurance Co., Ltd., London, Sentry Capital, Ltd., Sentry Fin., Ltd., Sentry Ins. Group (U.K.) Ltd., Australian Casualty Co., Ltd., Sentry United Kingdom Ins. Co., Ltd., Sentry Holdings (PTC) Ltd., Sentry Life Assurance, Consolidated European Reins. Co., Ltd. (Eng.), Sentry Holdings (Asia), Ltd., Employee Benefit Plan Pty., Ltd., Sydney, Gaudery Ltd., North Bridge Corp., Concord, 1st Nat. Bank, Stevens Point, Wis., A.E. Staley Mft. Co., Decatur. Mem. Wis. Gov.'s Council Econ. Devel., Portage County Econ. Devel. Task Force; pres. bd. trustees YMCA; bd. govs. Internat. Ins. Seminars, Inc.; bd. dirs. River Pines Adv. Bd., Stevens Point, U. Wis., Stevens Point Found.; Stevens Point Area Health Found., Inc., Property and Casulaty Ins. Counsel, Ins. Inst. Am., Am. Inst. Property and Liability Underwriters; bd. dirs., mem. exec. and fin. coms. Am. Mut. Ins. Alliance; chmn. bd. trustees Northland Coll., Ashland, Wis. Mem. Health Ins. Assn. Am. (dir.), Am., Portage County bar assns., Internat. Assn. Ins. Counsel, Wis. Assn. Mfrs. and Commerce (dir.). Office: 1800 North Point Dr Stevens Point WI 54481 Tel (715) 344-2345

JOBLIN, MICHAEL, b. Bklyn., Jan. 28, 1944; A.B., Harvard, 1965, J.D., 1968. Admitted to Calif. bar, 1969, Mass. bar, 1971; programmer Cambridge Computer Assos., Inc. (Mass.), 1965-68, exec. v.p., 1968—, treas., 1971—, also dir. Mem. Calif. Bar Assn. Home: 68 Locust Ave Lexington MA 02173 Office: 222 Alewife Brook Pkwy Cambridge MA 02138 Tel (617) 868-1111

JOCKISCH, WESLEY CHRISTIAN, b. Balt., Dec. 18, 1938; A.B., U. Md., 1961, LL.B., 1964; LL.M. with highest honors (Water Resources Law fellow), George Washington U., 1971. Admitted to Md. bar, 1965; bailiff Md. Circuit Ct. of Balt., 1964-65; atty. adviser Balt. dist. C.E., 1965-71, dep. div. counsel Ohio River Div., Cin., 1971-73, div. counsel, 1973—. Home: 10037 Windzag Ln Cincinnati OH 45242 Office: 550 Main St Cincinnati OH 45201 Tel (513) 684-3083

JOEL, DAVID JOSEPH, b. Pitts., Dec. 18, 1939; B.S. in Bus. Adminstrn., W.Va. U., 1961, J.D., 1965. Admitted to W.Va. bar, 1965; partner firm Stanley Preiser, Charleston, W.Va., 1965-69, firm Riley & Yahn, Wheeling, W.Va., 1969-72, firm John, Joel & Robinson, Wheeling, 1972-74; individual practice law, 1974-76; partner firm Joel, Petroplus & Thompson, Wheeling, 1976—; exec. dir. Legal Aid for Ohio County (W.Va.), 1971-73; spl. asst. pros. atty. Ohio County, 1973-74; mem. spl. task force Am. Trial Lawyers, 1972-74. Mem. W.Va., Ohio County bar assns., Am., W.Va. assns. trial lawyers. Home: 44 Heiskell Ave Wheeling WV 26005 Office: 586 National Rd Wheeling WV 26003 Tel (304) 233-7440

JOEL, RICHARD AEDAN, b. Jersey City, Aug. 4, 1935; B.M.E., Stevens Inst. Tech., 1956; M.B.A., N.Y. U., 1959, J.D., 1964, LL.M., 1967. Admitted to N.J. bar, 1965, D.C. bar, 1965, N.Y. bar, 1966; engr. Esso Research, 1956-59; atty. Western Electric Corp., 1959-67, AMF, Inc., 1967-68; counsel Gen. Time Co. 1968-69, Timex Corp., 1969-74; partner firm Irons, Sears & Spellman, 1974-75, firm Spellman & Joel, White Plains, N.Y., 1975—. Mem. Bd. Edn. Oradell (N.J.), 1969—; candidate for 7th Congressional Dist., 1975. Mem. Am., N.Y. State, N.J. State, Bergen County, Weschester County, White Plains bar assns., Am., N.Y., N.J. patent law assns. Home: 594 Blauvelt Dr Oradell NJ 07649 Office: 34 S Broadway White Plains NY 10601

JOFFE, ROBERT DAVID, b. N.Y.C., May 26, 1943; A.B., Harvard, 1964, J.D., 1967. Admitted to N.Y. bar, 1970, U.S. Supreme Ct. bar, 1973; Ford Found. Africa Pub. Service fellow, Republic Malawi, Africa, 1967-69, successively as asst. to commnr. law revision, 1967-68, local cts. commnr., 1968, state counsel, 1968-69; asso. firm Cravath, Swaine & Moore, 1969-75, partner, 1975—. Mem. Am., N.Y., N.Y.C. bar assns. Home: Apt 7-B 440 W End Ave New York City NY 10024 Office: One Chase Manhattan Plaza New York City NY 10005 Tel (212) 422-3000

JOH, ERIK EDWARD, b. Binghamton, N.Y., Mar. 28, 1945; A.B., Dartmouth, 1967; J.D., Albany Law Sch., 1970. Admitted to N.Y. State bar, 1971; asso. firm Hinman Howard & Kattell, Binghamton, N.Y., 1970—. Chmn. Broome County (N.Y.) chpt. ARC, 1975-76; pres. Assn. N.Y. State Young Republican Clubs, 1976—. Mem. Am., N.Y. State, Broome County bar assns. Home: 7 Vine St Binghamton NY 13903 Office: 724 Security Mutual Bldg Binghamton NY 13901 Tel (607) 723-5341

JOHNS, COURTNEY ROLFE, b. Astoria, Oreg., Aug. 24, 1910; J.D., Willamette U., 1937; grad. Nat. Coll. State Judiciary. Admitted to Oreg. bar, 1937; practiced in Portland, Oreg., 1937-42; served with JAGC, 1942-46; partner firm Goode & Johns, Albany, Oreg., 1946-50; dist. atty. Linn County (Oreg.), 1950-68; judge. Mem. Am. Bar Assn., Oreg. State Bar, Nat. Council Juvenile Judges. Home: 3230 S Park Terr Albany OR 97321 Office: PO Box 100 Albany OR 97321 Tel (503) 926-7962

JOHNS, HORACE EDWARD, b. Murfreesboro, Tenn., Mar. 26, 1945; B.A., Vanderbilt U., 1967, J.D., 1970; M.A., Peabody Coll., 1976. Admitted to Tenn. bar, 1970; asso. firm Haynes, Hull & Ray, Tullahoma, Tenn., 1970-72; staff atty. Tenn. Treasury Dept., Nashville, 1972-74; atty. Life Casualty Ins. Co. Tenn., Nashville, 1976—; adminstrv. asst. majority leader Tenn. H. of Reps., 1975-76. Mem. Tenn., AM. bar assns. Home: Murfreesboro Rd Eagleville TN 37060 Office: 27th floor Life & Casualty Tower Nashville TN 37219 Tel (615) 254-1511

JOHNS, MITCHEL BRADY, b. Walsenburg, Colo., Dec. 8, 1913; LL.B., U. Colo., 1943, B.A., 1949. Admitted to Colo. bar, 1946; judge Colo. Superior Ct., Denver, 1953-54; asst. city atty., Denver, 1951-53; judge Colo. Municipal Ct., Denver, 1953-54; judge Dist. Ct., Denver, 1961—. Bd. dirs. March of Dimes, Denver, Colo. Cystic Fibrosis Assn., Colo. Boys Ranch, La Junta, Colo.; v.p. Colo. Prison Assn., bd. dirs., 1976—. Mem. Denver, Colo., Am. bar assns., Nat. Conf. Trial Judges. Recipient Man of Year Am. Legion Post No. 1, Denver, 1965; certificate of service award Colo. Med. Soc., 1965. Home: 901 S Columbine St Denver CO 80209 Office: Room 306 City & County Bldg Denver CO 80202 Tel (303) 297-2681

JOHNS, WALTER SCOTT, III, b. Akron, Ohio, Jan. 18, 1926; B.E.E., Lehigh U., 1949; J.D., U. Pa., 1955. Admitted to Pa. bar, 1956, U.S. Supreme Ct. bar, 1960; student engr. Phila. Electric Co., 1948; jr. engr. Atlantic Refining Co., Phila., 1949-52; sr. mem. firm W. Scott Johns, III, Wayne, Pa., 1955—; mem. panel arbitrators Am. Arbitration Assn. Mem. alumni council Mercersburg (Pa.) Acad., 1961-67, 71—, v.p., 1972-74, pres., 1974-76, bd. regents, 1977—. Mem. Am., Pa., Delaware County (dir., chmn. mastership list com. 1971—) bar assns., Am. Judicature Soc., IEEE. Home: 573 Tory Hill Rd Devon PA 19333 Office: 130 W Lancaster Ave Wayne PA 19087 Tel (215) 688-5426

JOHNSON, ALAN BOND, b. Cheyenne, Wyo., Jan. 14, 1939; B.A., Vanderbilt U., 1961; J.D., U. Wyo., 1964. Admitted to Wyo. bar, 1964; judge adv. USAF, Eglin AFB, Fla., 1964-67; asso. Paul B. Godfrey, Cheyenne, 1968-71, firm Hanes, Carmichael, Johnson, Gage & Speight, Cheyenne, 1971-75; magistrate U.S. Dist. Ct. Wyo., Cheyenne, 1975—. Vice pres. Laramie County unit Am. Cancer Soc., 1968-70; treas. Cheyenne Symphony and Choral Soc., 1973; chmn. Cheyenne Police Civil Service Commn., 1973-75; bd. dirs. Cheyenne Little Theatre, 1971-72; trustee Laramie County Council for the Arts, 1973-75. Mem. Am., Wyo., Laramie County (sec.-treas. 1968-70) bar assns., Wyo. Jud. Conf. (sec.). Office: City and County Bldg Cheyenne WY 82001 Tel (307) 634-4301

JOHNSON, ALAN GLENN, b. Chgo., July 16, 1934; B.S. in Fin., U. Ill., 1957, M.S. in Fin., 1958; J.D., St. Louis U., 1966. Admitted to Mo. bar, 1966; v.p., treas. Scherck, Stein & Franc, Inc., St. Louis, 1960-70; pres. The Fisher Corp., St. Louis, 1970-74; partner firm Susman, Stern, Agatstein, Heifetz & Gallop, St. Louis, 1974-76, Gallop, Johnson, Godiner, Morganstern & Crebs, St. Louis, 1976—; lectr. law St. Louis U. Law Sch., 1966—; dir. Tiffany Industries, Inc., 1972—, KV Pharm. Co., 1976—, Landmark Central Bank & Trust Co., 1976—, Midwest Stock Exchange, 1970-75. Bd. dirs. Narcotics Service Council, Inc., 1966—. Mem. Mo., Am. bar assns., Bar Assn. Met. St. Louis, Inst. Chartered Fin. Analysts, St. Louis Soc. Fin. Analysts. Home: 12801 Coulange Ct Saint Louis MO 63141 Office: 7733 Forsyth Blvd suite 1800 Saint Louis MO 63105 Tel (314) 862-1200

JOHNSON, ALFRED ALLAN, b. Laramie, Wyo., Dec. 27, 1930; B.S., U. Wyo., 1956; LL.B., U. Colo., 1963. Admitted to Colo. bar, 1963; individual practice law, Ft. Collins, Colo., 1963—. Home: 1700 N Overland Trail Fort Collins CO 80521 Office: PO Box 2225 Fort Collins CO 80522 Tel (303) 484-7474

JOHNSON, ALMETA ANN, b. Rockingham County, N.C., Mar. 11, 1947; A.B., Johnson C. Smith U., 1968; J.D., Ohio State U., 1971. Admitted to Ohio bar, 1971; law clk. firm Metzenbaum, Gaines, Finley & Stern, Cleve., 1970; research asst. Ohio State U., Columbus, 1970-71; asso. firm Benesch, Friedlander, Mendelson & Coplan, Cleve., 1971-75; chief police prosecutor city Cleve., 1975—. Chmn. East. Cleve. Citizen Adv. Com., 1973-75; chmn. East Cleve. Charter Review Commn., 1976-77. Mem. Ohio State, Am. bar assns., Bar Assn. Greater Cleve., Black Women Lawyers Assn. Recipient Lett Civil Liberties award, Ohio State U. Coll. Law, 1971; outstanding young citizen award Cleve. Jaycees, 1976; outstanding achievement award Negro Bus. and Profl. Women's Club, 1975; outstanding achievement award Nat. Council Negro Women, 1975.

JOHNSON, ANDREW LEE, JR., b. Youngstown, Ohio, Oct. 4, 1931; B.S., Northwestern U., 1953; J.D., Cleve. State U., 1959. Admitted to Ohio bar, 1960; individual practice law, Cleve., 1960—; acting judge Shaker Heights (Ohio) Municipal Ct., 1970—; pres. Home Owners Title Corp., Cleve., 1970-74. Chmn. bd. trustees Forest City Hosp., Cleve., 1970—. Mem. Bar Assn. Greater Cleve. (meritorious service award 1970). Home: 3083 N Park Blvd Cleveland Heights OH 44118 Office: Suite 513 33 Public Sq Cleveland OH 44113 Tel (216) 621-3550

JOHNSON, ARNOLD CALE, b. Iowa Falls, Iowa, July 6, 1925; B.A., Tufts Coll., 1949; LL.B., Harvard U., 1952. Admitted to Mass. bar, 1953, D.C. bar, 1959; atty. legal advisory staff U.S. Treasury Dept., Washington, 1954-56, atty., staff of the Joint Com. on Internal Revenue Taxation, 1956-59; mem. firm Hogan & Hartson, Washington, 1959—; lectr. law Northeastern U., Boston, evening sch., 1954. Mem. Am., Fed. (hon.), D.C. bar assns. Contbr. articles to legal jours. Office: 815 Connecticut Ave NW Washington DC 20006 Tel (202) 331-4615

JOHNSON, BENJAMIN FRANKLIN, III, b. Atlanta, Aug. 20, 1943; B.A., Emory U., 1965; J.D., Harvard, 1968. Admitted to Ga. bar, 1968; law clk. to Hon. Griffin B. Bell of U.S. Ct. Appeals, Atlanta, 1968-69; asso. firm Alston, Miller & Gaines, Atlanta, 1971-76, partner, 1976—. Mem. governing bd. Woodward Acad., Atlanta; bd. sponsors Alliance Theatre, Atlanta. Mem. Atlanta Bar Assn. (mem. crime task force), Phi Beta Kappa, Omicron Delta Kappa. Contbr. articles in field to legal jours. Home: 687 E Pelham Rd Atlanta GA 30324 Office: 1200 Citizens & So Nat Bank Bldg Atlanta GA 30303 Tel (404) 588-0300

JOHNSON, BRUCE K., b. Brookline, Mass., Oct. 22, 1934; B.S., U. N.H., 1959; LL.B., Suffolk U., 1966. Admitted to Mass. bar, 1967, N.H. bar, 1972; asso. firm Robinson, Kasilowski & Robinson, Lowell, Mass., 1967-68; staff atty. N.H. Legal Assistance, Dover and Portsmouth, 1968-72; partner firm McManus & Johnson, Dover, 1972—; asst. county atty. Strafford County (N.H.), 1977—. Bd. dirs. Strafford County (N.H.) Homemaker Home Health Aide Assn., Dover, 1975—. Mem. Am., N.H., Mass., Strafford County bar assns. Office: 52 Old Rochester Rd Dover NH 03820 Tel (603) 742-7916

JOHNSON, CARL LOWELL, b. Harris, Minn., Aug. 18, 1938; B.S., U. Minn., 1960, M. Aero. Engring., 1962; J.D., William Mitchell Coll. Law, 1966. Admitted to Minn. bar, 1966, U.S. Patent Office bar, 1967; patent atty. Honeywell Co., Mpls., 1966-68; partner firm Jacobson & Johnson, St. Paul, 1968—. Mem. Minn. Patent Law Assn., Minn. State Bar, Am. Bar Assn., Sigma Gamma Tau. Office: 200 S Robert St Saint Paul MN 55107 Tel (612) 222-3775

JOHNSON, CARL ROBERT, b. Columbus, Ohio, Mar. 25, 1912; B.A., Ohio State U., 1936, LL.B., 1936, J.D., 1964. Admitted to Ohio bar, 1936; with Ohio Dept. Taxation, 1936-48; individual practice law, Columbus, 1945-55; dep. insp. municipal audits Ohio State Auditor's Office, 1955-63; chmn. Ohio Pub. Utilities Commn., Columbus, 1963-71, commr., 1971-75, sr. adviser, 1975—. Mem. Gt. Lakes Conf. Pub. Utilities Commrs. (pres. 1969-70), Ohio Bar Assn. Home: 429 Central College Rd Westerville OH 45081 Office: 180 E Broad St Columbus OH 43215 Tel (614) 882-4513

JOHNSON, CARL TRAVIS, b. Braden, Tenn., Jan. 21, 1942; B.B.A., U. Tex., 1963, J.D., 1965. Admitted to Tex. bar, 1967; asst. prof. La. Tech. U., Ruston, 1968-70; asso. firm Richard Yetter, El Paso, 1970-72, dir. firm Johnson, Allen & Aycock, El Paso, 1972—; instr. bus. law U. Tex., 1970-73. Trustee Lydia Patterson Inst., 1976-79, Trinity United Meth. Ch., 1975-77, Landsun Homes, Inc., 1976—. Mem. El Paso, Am. bar assns., Young Lawyers Assn. State Bar Tex. (grievance com.), Am. Bus. Law Assn., Phi Alpha Delta, Delta Sigma Pi. Home: 8404 Basil Ct El Paso TX 79925 Office: 5959 Gateway W Suite 542 El Paso TX 79925 Tel (915) 779-3571

JOHNSON, CHARLES FREDERIC, JR., b. Sinton, Tex., July 23, 1923; student John Tarleton Agrl. Coll., 1942; J.D., U. Tex., 1950. Admitted to Tex. bar, 1950, U.S. Dist. Ct. for So. Tex., 1954, U.S. 5th Circuit Ct. Appeals bar, 1964; individual practice law, Sinton, Tex., 1950—. Mem. Am., Tex., San Patricio County bar assns., Nueces County Trial Lawyers Assn., AAAS, Am. Inst. Planners (asso.). Home: 4 Northwood Rd Sinton TX 78387 Office: 111 N Odem St Sinton TX 78387 Tel (512) 364-3338

JOHNSON, CHARLES JOHN, JR, b. Jersey City, N.J., Jan. 23, 1932; B.A., Yale U., 1953; LL.B., Harvard U., 1956. Admitted to N.Y. State bar, 1957, Conn. bar, 1970; asso. firm Brown, Wood, Ivey, Mitchell & Petty, N.Y.C., 1957-67, partner 1967—. Dir. Darien (Conn.) United Way and Community Council, also pres. Mem. Am. Bar Assn., Assn. Bar City N.Y. Home: 223 Old Kings Hwy S Darien CT 06820 Office: One Liberty Plaza New York City NY 10006 Tel (202) 349-7500

JOHNSON, CHARLES SIMONS, b. Topeka, Dec. 8, 1940; B.S., U. Kans., 1962; J.D., U. Va., 1965. Admitted to Mo. bar, 1965; partner Stinson, Mag, Thomson, McEvers & Fizzell, Kansas City, Mo., 1968-76; v.p. corp. devel. Price Condy Co., Kansas City, Mo., 1976—; exec. v.p., sec. Medicalodges, Inc., 1969-74; dir. Host Internat. Inc., 1969-70, 72-73. Bd. dirs. Kansas City chpt. Boys Club, 1974—. Mem. Am. (chmn. young lawyers sect. corp. law com. 1976, dir. and mem. exec. council Young Lawyers sect. 1975-76; mem. task force bar services and activities 1976—), Kansas City bar assns., Lawyers Assn. of Kansas City. Home: 9600 W 106th St Overland Park KS 66212 Office: One W Armour Blvd Kansas City MO 64111 Tel (816) 931-4422

JOHNSON, CHRIS T., b. Bartlett Damn, Ariz., June 11, 1938; B.A., LL.B., U. Ariz. Admitted to Ariz. bar, 1963; atty. State Compensation Fund, 1963-64; individual practice law, Phoenix, 1965—. Mem. Ariz. Ho. of Reps., 1964-66; mem. Ariz. State Senate, 1966-70, majority whip, 1968-70; chmn. State Bar Workmen's Compensation, 1973. Office: 934 W McDowell Rd Phoenix AZ 85007 Tel (602) 254-6461

JOHNSON, DAVID EDWIN, b. Bradford, Pa., Oct. 26, 1929; B.S. in Econs., U. Pa., 1951, LL.B., 1954. Admitted to Pa. bar, 1954; asso. firm Reed, Smith, Shaw & McClay, Pitts., 1957-62; partner firm Ruffin, Hazlett, Perry & Lonergan, Pitts., 1962—. Mem. Allegheny County (Pa.), Pa., Am. bar assns. Home: 200 Hunt Rd Pittsburgh PA 15215 Office: 2323 Grant Bldg Pittsburgh PA 15219 Tel (412) 471-9300

JOHNSON, DAVID REYNOLD, b. Binghamton, N.Y., Aug. 8, 1945; B.A., Yale U., 1967, J.D., 1972; postgrad. Univ. Coll., Oxford, Eng., 1967-68. Admitted to D.C. bar, 1973; law clk. U.S. Ct. Appeals for D.C., 1972-73; asso. firm Wilmer, Cutler & Pickering, Washington, 1973—. Home: 4607 Van Ness St NW Washington DC 20016 Office: 1666 K St NW Washington DC 20006 Tel (202) 872-6274

JOHNSON, DAVID WESLEY, b. Rochester, N.Y., Mar. 13, 1933; B.A. in Govt., U. Rochester, 1954; LL.B., Columbia, 1959. Admitted to N.Y. bar, 1961; counsel, sec., v.p. Textile Banking Co., Inc., N.Y.C., 1959-68; legis. counsel C.I.T. Fin. Corp., N.Y.C., 1968-70; partner firm Otterbourg, Steindler, Houston and Rosen, N.Y.C., 1970-71; partner firm Palmer and Johnson, Tupper Lake, N.Y., 1971-74; individual practice law, Tupper Lake, 1974—. Bd. trustees N. Country Community Coll., Saranac Lake, N.Y., 1973—, chmn., 1977—. Mem. N.Y., Franklin County (treas. 1971—) bar assns. Home and Office: 51 Lake St Tupper Lake NY 12986 Tel (518) 359-3394

JOHNSON, DEAN, b. Sheridan, Wyo., Dec. 9, 1911; A.B., U. Denver, 1935, LL.B., 1937. Admitted to Colo. bar, 1937; asst. atty. gen. State Colo., Denver, 1940-41; atty. Office Price Adminstrn., Denver, 1942-45; spl. atty. antitrust div. U.S. Dept. Justice, Denver, 1945-48; individual practice law, Burlington, Colo., 1948-70; dep. dist. atty. Kit Carson County, 1949-56, 1968-70; atty. City Burlington, 1949-52, 1959-70; judge Kit Carson County (Colo.) County Ct.,

1957-65; Colo. Dist. Ct., 13th Dist., Ft. Morgan, 1971—. Mem. Am., Colo., Morgan County bar assns. Home: 717 Nancy St Ft Morgan CO 89701 Office: Courthouse Ft Morgan CO 80701 Tel (303) 867-8266

JOHNSON, DEANE FRANK, b. Des Moines, Sept. 2, 1918; A.B., Stanford, 1939, J.D., 1942. Admitted to Calif. bar, 1942, U.S. Supreme Ct. bar, 1946; asso. firm O'Melveny & Myers, Los Angeles, 1942-49, partner, 1950—; chmn. bd. visitors Stanford Law Sch., 1964-66. Vice-chmn., trustee Calif. Inst. Tech.; trustee Am. Film Inst., Up with People. Mem. Am. Bar Assn., Am. Judicature Soc., Los Angeles Copyright Assn., Order of Coif. Office: 1800 Century Park E Los Angeles CA 90067 Tel (213) 553-6700

JOHNSON, DONALD CLAY, b. Lafayette, Ind., Apr. 17, 1944; B.S., Ind. State U., 1966. Admitted to Ind. bar, 1969; spl. agt. FBI, 1969-72; dep. pros. atty. Tippecanoe County (Ind.), 1972-73; partner firm Gothard & Johnson, Lafayette, 1973—. Mem. Lafayette City Council, 1975-76. Mem. Am., Ind., Tippecanoe County bar assns. Home: 116 Reba Dr West Lafayette IN 47906 Office: 2d and Columbia Sts Lafayette IN 47901 Tel (317) 423-5676

JOHNSON, DONALD DEANE, b. Racine, Wis., Apr. 25, 1935; B.S., U. Wis., 1959, LL.D., 1961. Admitted to Wis. bar, 1962, U.S. Tax Ct. bar, 1969, U.S. Supreme Ct. bar, 1971; asso. firm Melli, Smith & Shiels, 1962-65; partner firm Lee, Johnson & Kilkelly, Madison, Wis., 1965—; vis. prof. law U. Wis., 1973-75. Active lawyers div. United Way, Madison, 1972. Mem. Dane County (exec. com. 1968-74), Wis., Am. bar assns., Madison Estate Council (dir. 1969-74). Home: 4235 Wanda Pl Madison WI 53711 Office: One W Main St Madison WI 53703 Tel (608) 256-9046

JOHNSON, ELLIOTT AMOS, b. Soldier, Iowa, Feb. 21, 1907; Ph.B., U. Chgo., 1928, J.D., 1931; LL.B., S. Tex. Coll., 1937. Admitted to Ill. bar, 1931, Tex. bar, 1937; gen. counsel, v.p. fin. Schlumberger Corps., Houston, 1936-68; sr. partner firm Johnson & Milligan, Houston, 1968—. Home: 1831 Post Oak Park Dr Houston TX 77027 Office: 2200 S Post Oak Rd Suite 707 Houston TX 77056 Tel (713) 627-2440

JOHNSON, ELLSWORTH TREFRY, b. Gloucester, Mass., Aug. 18, 1926; A.A., Harvard U., 1972, A.B., 1973; J.D., Suffolk Law Sch., 1955. Admitted to Mass. bar, 1975; docket clk. Superior Ct., Salem, Mass., 1955-57; individual practice law, Gloucester, 1957-67; counsel Mass. Labor Relations Commn., Boston, 1967-70; gen. counsel Water Resources Commn. Div. Water Pollution Control, Boston, 1970—; gen. counsel Dept. Environ. Quality Engring., Boston, 1975—. Mem. Gloucester, Essex, Mass. bar assns. Tel (617) 727-3855

JOHNSON, FOLGER, b. Portland, Oreg., Nov. 4, 1914; B.A., Pomona Coll., 1937; LL.B., Northwestern Coll., 1941. Admitted to Oreg. bar, 1941; mem. firm Flegel, Vosburg, Joss & Hedlund, Portland, 1946-50; dep. city atty. City Portland, 1950-55; referee and bankruptcy judge U.S. Cts., Portland, 1955—. Mem. Am., Internat. bar assns., Am. Judicature Soc., Delta Theta Phi. Office: 313 Pioneer Courthouse 520 SW Morrison St Portland OR 97204 Tel (503) 221-2231

JOHNSON, FRANCES ELIZABETH, lawyer; b. Pike Road, Ala., Aug. 16, 1908; B.S., Auburn U., 1941; LL.B., Jones Law Sch., 1956. Admitted to State Bar Ala., 1956; claims examiner VA Regional Office, Montgomery, Ala., 1946-59; legis. analyst Legis. Reference Service, State of Ala., Montgomery, 1959-73; pvt. practice law, Pike Road, Ala., 1973—. Mem. State Bar of Ala., Ala. Women Lawyers Assn. Home and Office: PO Box 115 Pike Road AL 36064

JOHNSON, FRANK MINIS, JR., b. Winston County, Ala., Oct. 30, 1918; grad. Gulf Coast Mil. Acad., 1935, Massey Bus. Coll., 1937; LL.B., U. Ala., 1943; LL.D. (hon.), U. Notre Dame, 1973, Princeton U., 1974; J.D. (hon.), St. Michael's Coll., Winooski, Vt., 1975. Admitted to Ala. bar, 1946; mem. firm Curtis, Maddox and Johnson, Jasper, Ala., 1946-53; U.S. atty. No. Dist. Ala., 1953-55; judge U.S. Dist. Ct., Middle Dist. Ala., 1955—, now chief judge; mem. Jud. Conf. Rev. Com., 1969—; mem. Spl. Com. on Habeas Corpus, 1971—; mem. Joint Com. on Code of Jud. Conduct for Fed. Judges, 1972—, Temporary Emergency Ct. Appeals of U.S., 1972—. Home: 118 N Haardt Dr Montgomery AL 36105 Tel (205) 263-1978

JOHNSON, FREDERIC AUGUSTUS, b. Cin., Dec. 27, 1894; A.B., Yale, 1917; LL.B., Harvard, 1924. Admitted to Pa. bar, 1924, N.Y. bar, 1926; spl. counsel, div. water supply N.Y.C. Office Corp. Counsel, 1929-30; justice's clk. N.Y. State Supreme Ct., N.Y., 1930-43, N.Y. County Supreme Ct., N.Y.C., 1943; asso. firm Parker & Duryee, N.Y.C., 1943-45; house counsel Sta. WINS-Radio, N.Y.C., 1954-60; prof. law Bklyn. Law Sch., 1939-46; contbg. editor N.Y. Law Jour., 1969—. Mem. Am. Bar Assn., Assn. Bar City N.Y. Home: San Carlos Hotel 150 E 50th St New York City NY 10022 Office: 233 Broadway New York City NY 10007 Tel (212) 964-2581

JOHNSON, GARY CHARLES, b. Pikeville, Ky., Nov. 2, 1946; B.A., Berea Coll., 1969; J.D., U. Ky., 1972. Admitted to Ky. bar, 1973; individual practice law, Pikeville, 1973—. Chmn., Ky. Young Lawyers Disaster Relief Program for Pike County, 1974. Mem. Ky., Pike County, Am. bar assns., Am. Trial Lawyers Assn. Home: Box 231 Pikeville KY 41501 Office: Box 231 107 Grace Ave Pikeville KY 41501 Tel (606) 437-4001

JOHNSON, GARY GEORGE, b. Chgo., Mar. 29, 1946; B.S., Roosevelt Univ., 1968; J.D., DePaul, 1973. Admitted to Ill. bar, 1973; staff atty. Legal Assistance Found., Chgo., 1973-75; dir. Student's Legal Services, Ill. State U., Normal, 1975-76, asst. prof. bus. law 1975-76; legal founds., 1976—. Bd. dirs. McLean County Legal Aid Corp., 1976—, Project OZ, 1975—. Mem. Ill., McLean County bar assns., ACLU. Asso. editor: DePaul Law Review, 1973; contbr. articles in field to profl. jours. Home: 1114 West Ave Normal IL 61761 Office: 4 Citizen's Sq Normal IL 61761 Tel (309) 452-4541

JOHNSON, GENE DERWOOD, b. Cranfills Gap, Tex., July 22, 1929; B.B.A., Baylor U., 1951, J.D., 1955; grad. Nat. Coll. State Judiciary, 1969, postgrad, 1971; student U. Edinburgh (Scotland), 1955. Admitted to Tex. bar, 1955; asso. firm Harold Clark, Waco, Tex., 1956-60; justice of peace McLennan County (Tex.), 1961-62; judge McLennan County Ct., 1963-67, McLennan County Dist. Ct., 74th Dist., 1968—. Pres. First Lutheran Ch., Waco, 1968-72, Heart of Tex. Goodwill Industries, Waco, 1970-71; bd. dirs. Norwegian-Am. Historical Assn., Northfield, Minn., 1961—. Mem. Waco-McLennan County Bar Assn., Am. Judicature Soc. Recipient Medal Merit, State Tex., 1975; contbr. articles Tex. Bar Jour., Norwegian-Am. Studies. Home: 1425 Hilltop Dr Waco TX 76710 Office: Courthouse Waco TX 76701

JOHNSON, GLEN HERMAN, b. Sioux Falls, S.D., Mar. 31, 1947; B.S. in Accounting, U. S.D., 1969, J.D. with honors, 1972. Admitted to S.D. bar, 1972; law clk. to judge U.S. Dist. Ct., S.D., 1972-73; asso. firm Gunderson, Farrar, Aldrich, Warder, DeMersseman & Johnson, and predecessors, Rapid City, S.D., 1973-75, partner, 1975—. Mem. Am., S.D., Pennington County bar assns., S.D. Trial Lawyers Assn. Mng. editor S.D. Law Rev. 1971-72. Home: 4312 Circle Dr Rapid City SD 57701 Office: 516 5th St Rapid City SD 57701 Tel (605) 342-2814

JOHNSON, GLENN T., b. Washington, Ark., July 19, 1917; B.S., Wilberforce U., 1941; J.D., John Marshall Law Sch., 1949, LL.M., 1950; postgrad. Nat. Coll. State Trial Judges, Reno, Nev., 1971. Admitted to Ill. bar, 1950, U.S. Supreme Ct. bar, 1958; asst. atty. gen. of Ill., 1957-63; sr. atty. Met. Sanitary Dist. of Greater Chicago, 1963-66; asso. judge Circuit Ct. of Cook County (Ill.), Chgo., 1966-68, judge, 1968-73; justice Appellate Ct. of Ill., Chgo., 1973—. Active YMCA, NACCP, Urban League, Woodlawn Boys Club; trustee Woodlawn African Methodist Episcopalian Ch., 1960—. Mem. Nat., Am., Ill., Chgo., Cook County bar assns., World Assn. of Judges, World Peace Through Law, Am. Judicature Soc., Conf. of Conciliation Cts., Am. Acad. Matrimonial Lawyers. Recipient bar assn. awards; Citation of Merit John Marshall Law Sch., 1970. Home: 6133 Evans Ave Chicago IL 60637 Office: Chicago Civic Center Chicago IL 60602 Tel (312) 793-5431

JOHNSON, HANS WALDEMAR, b. Hawley, Minn., Aug. 5, 1927; B.S., U. Minn., 1950, J.D., 1952. Admitted to Minn. bar, 1952, Colo. bar, 1953; asst. city atty., Denver, 1953-62; partner firm Johnson, Makris & Hunsaker, Denver, 1962—. Bd. regents Augustana Coll., Sioux Falls, S.D. Mem. Am., Colo., Denver bar assns. Home: 3246 S Newport St Denver CO 80224 Office: 555 Capital Life Center 16th St and Grant St Denver CO 80203 Tel (203) 292-2960

JOHNSON, HERMEL, b. Jackson, Miss., Aug. 27, 1946; B.A., Jackson State U., 1967; postgrad. Harvard U., 1966; J.D., U. Miss., 1970. Admitted to Miss. bar, 1970; partner firm Hall, Abram, Tucker & Johnson, 1970-73, Johnson & Walker, 1973-76; individual practice law, Jackson, 1976—; case analyst Equal Employment Opportunity Commn., 1968-70. Mem. Hinds County Bar Assn., Jackson Young Lawyers Assn. Home: 1081 Alta Vista Blvd Jackson MS 39202 Office: Suite 972 Deposit Guaranty Plaza Jackson MS 39201 Tel (601) 948-4579

JOHNSON, HOWARD DUSTON, b. Chgo., Aug. 5, 1942; B.A., Brown U., 1964; J.D., Georgetown U., 1968. Admitted to Ill. bar, 1970; law clk. to judge U.S. Dist. Ct., Chgo., 1968-69; asso. firm Martin, Craig, Chester & Sonnenschein, Chgo., 1970-75, partner, 1976—; village prosecutor Village of La Grange Park (Ill.), 1975—. Mem. Am., Ill., Chgo. bar assns. Home: 1960 N Lincoln Park W Chicago IL 60614 Office: 135 S LaSalle St Chicago IL 60603 Tel (312) 236-2400

JOHNSON, I.S. LEEVY, b. Columbia, S.C., May 16, 1942; Asso. Mortuary Sci., U. Mont., 1962; B.S., Benedict Coll., 1965; J.D., U. S.C., 1968. Admitted to S.C. bar, 1968; law clk. firm Jenkins, Perry & Pride, 1966-67; partner firm Johnson & Mance, 1972-74, firm Johnson, Toal & Battiste, Columbia, 1974—; mem. S.C. Ho. of Reps., 1970-72, 1974-76. Mem. Am., S.C., Richland County bar assns., S.C. Trial Lawyers Assn. Home: 3134 Windwood Pl Columbia SC Office: 1108 Blanding St Columbia SC Tel (803) 252-9700

JOHNSON, INGE PRYTZ, b. Svendborg, Denmark, Dec. 19, 1945; Candidatur Juris, U. Copenhagen, 1969; M. Comparative Law, U. Ala., 1970, J.D., 1973. Admitted to Denmark bar, 1969, Ala. bar, 1973; asso. firm Dragsted, Kromann, Norregaard & Friis, Vognmagergade, Copenhagen, 1970-71; partner firm Johnson & Johnson, Tuscumbia, Ala., 1973—. Mem. Am., Ala., Colbert County bar assns. Office: Suite 204 Avalon Plaza 801 E Avalon Ave Muscle Shoals AL 35660 Tel (205) 383-5082

JOHNSON, JACK, b. Etowah, Tenn., Dec. 19, 1923; B.A., Lincoln Meml. Coll., 1943; J.D., U. Va., 1948. Admitted to Va., Tenn. bars, 1948; individual practice law, Athens, Tenn.; county atty. McMin County (Tenn.), 1950-64, gen. session judge, 1958-74. Mem. Am., Tenn. bar assns. Home: 1209 Woodward Park Athens TN 37303 Office: 118 1/2 N White St Athens TN 27203 Tel (615) 745-0633

JOHNSON, JAMES EVERETTE, b. Cash, Ark., Nov. 15, 1913; student Ark. State Coll., 1931-34; LL.B., U. Ark., 1937, J.D., 1971. Admitted to Ark. bar, 1937, Nev. bar, 1969; individual practice law, Jonesboro, Ark., 1937-41; served with U.S. Army, 1941-67, with JAGC, 1948-67; staff, faculty JAG Sch., Charlottesville, Va., 1958-63, staff judge adv., Japan, 1963-66; asso. dean Nat. Coll. State Judiciary U. Nev., Reno, 1967—. Mem. Am., Ark., Nev., Washoe County (Nev.) bar assns. Decorated Legion of Merit U.S. Army, 1967. Home: 2355 Audubon Way Reno NV 89509 Office: Nat Coll of State Judiciary U of Nev Reno NV 89557 Tel (702) 784-6747

JOHNSON, JAMES FORD, 4TH, b. Washington, Sept. 6, 1941; B.A. magna cum laude, Yale, 1963, LL.B., 1966. Admitted to N.Y. bar, 1967; asso. firm LeBoeuf, Lamb, Leiby & MacRae, N.Y.C., 1966-75, partner, 1975—. Trustee Coop. Nursery Center, Summit, N.J., 1973-77; bd. dirs. Clear Pool Camp, Carmel, N.Y., 1973—, sec., 1973—. Mem. Am. Bar Assn. Office: 140 Broadway New York City NY 10005 Tel (212) 269-1100

JOHNSON, JAMES MCDADE, b. Shreveport, La., Dec. 5, 1939; B.A., La. State U., 1962, J.D.S., 1964. Admitted to La. bar, 1964; partner firm Campbell, Campbell & Johnson, Minden, La., 1966—; 1st asst. dist. atty. Bossier-Webster Parishes, 1975. Chmn. Minden Democratic Exec. Com., 1964-74. Mem. Am., La., Webster Parish bar assns., Am., La. trial lawyers assns. Home: Route 1 Box 127 E Minden LA 71055 Office: PO Box 834 Minden LA 71055 Tel (318) 377-4974

JOHNSON, JAMES NOEL, b. Stevens Point, Wis., Oct. 7, 1919; Ph.B., Marquette U., 1941; LL.B., Cornell U., 1943; LL.D. (honoris causa), Coll. Racine, 1973. Admitted to Wis. bar, 1943; asso. firm Olwell & Brady, Milw., 1943-46; asso. of James D. Porter, Milw., 1946-50; partner firm Porter, Johnson, Quale & Porter, Milw., 1950-61; sec., gen. counsel A. O. Smith Corp., Milw., 1961-67, v.p., sec., gen. counsel, 1967—; proctor Marquette U. Law Sch., 1957-61. Pres. Health Service Data, Wis., Milw., 1966-68; chmn. Milw. Med. Resources Study Com., 1965-68. Chmn. bd. govs. Coll. Racine, 1968-74. Mem. Am. Soc. Corp. Secs., Am., Internat., Inter-Am., Wis., Milw. bar assns. Contbr. articles to legal jours. Home: 13550 Wrayburn Rd Elm Grove WI 53122 Office: 3533 N 27th St Milwaukee WI 53201 Tel (414) 447-4087

JOHNSON, JAMES THOMAS, b. St. Joseph, Mich., May 19, 1932; B.A., U. Mich., 1954, LL.B., 1960. Admitted to Calif. bar, 1961, Mich. bar, 1963; sr. trial atty. special legal div. Calif. Dept. Transp., San Francisco, 1961-72; partner firm Fitzgerald, Johnson, Berg & Edgar, San Francisco, 1972-76; sr. mem. firm Dobbs, Doyle & Nielsen, San Francisco, 1977—. Mem. Bar Assn. San Francisco, State Bar of Calif. Office: 1 Maritime Plaza Suite 2500 San Francisco CA 94111 Tel (415) 362-1940

JOHNSON, JENNINGS BRYAN, SR., b. Whitley County, Ky., Apr. 10, 1897; grad. Eastern Ky. U., 1924; J.D., U. Ky., 1926. Admitted to Ky. bar, 1926; individual practice law, Williamsburg, Ky., 1926-36, 64—, Harlan, Ky., 1952-57; city atty. Williamsburg, 1926-35; commonwealth atty. 34th Jud. Dist., 1936-45, circuit judge, 1945-52, 58-64. Mem. Ky., Whitley County bar assns. Contbr. weekly column Old Time Country Customs to Corbin Times, Whitley Republican (winner 1st prize Ky. Press Assn. 1976). Home: Williamsburg KY 40769 Office: 325 Main St Williamsburg KY 40769 Tel (606) 549-3585

JOHNSON, JIM, b. Crossett, Ark., Aug. 20, 1924; LL.B., Cumberland U., 1947. Admitted to Tenn. bar, 1947, Ark. bar, 1948, U.S. Supreme Ct. bar, 1953; individual practice law, Crossett, Ark., 1948-59, Little Rock, 1966—; asso. justice Ark. Supreme Ct., Little Rock, 1959-66. Mem. Ark. State Senate, 1951-55. Mem. Ark. Bar Assn. Home: Route 3 Box 458 Conway AR 72032 Office: 601 Union Life Bldg Little Rock AR 72201 Tel (501) FR2-6711

JOHNSON, JOHN WILLIAM, JR., b. Langdale, Ala., July 19, 1920; B.S., U. Ala., 1942, LL.B., 1947. Admitted to Ala. bar, 1947; individual practice law, Lanett, Ala., 1947—; mem. Ala. Senate, 1951-55. Trustee Chambers County Library, Chattahoochee Valley Hosp. Soc. Mem. Am., Ala., Chambers County bar assns. Home: 6105 26th Ave Langdale AL 36864 Office: 201 Johnson Bldg Lanett AL 36863 Tel (205) 644-1171

JOHNSON, JUSTIN MORRIS, b. Wilkinsburg, Pa., Aug. 19, 1933; B.A., U. Chgo., 1954, J.D., 1962. Admitted to Pa. bar, 1962, U.S. Dist. Ct. for Western Dist. Pa. bar, 1962, U.S. Supreme bar, 1968; partner firm Johnson & Johnson and predecessor, Pitts., 1962-72, sr. partner, 1973—; asst. solicitor Pitts. Bd. Pub. Edn., 1964-70, solicitor, asst. sec., 1970—; mem. Pa. Bd. Law Examiners, 1968—, vice-chmn. 1975—; bd. dirs. Neighborhood Legal Services Assn., Pitts., 1966-71, pres. 1969-70; bd. dirs. Blue Cross Western Pa., Community Chest Allegheny County (Pa.), 1968-70; mem. bd. mgmt. Homewood-Bruston YMCA, Pitts., 1967-76; trustee Mercy Hosp. Pitts., 1976—. Mem. Pa., Allegheny County bar assns., Assn. Municipal and Sch. Solicitors. Home: 4136 Bigelow Blvd Pittsburgh PA 15213 Office: 1919 Frick Bldg Pittsburgh PA 15219 Tel (412) 281-8330

JOHNSON, KENNETH HOWELL, b. Houston, Feb. 19, 1936; B.S. in Chemistry, U. Tex., 1957; J.D., 1963. Admitted to Tex. bar, 1963; counsel Sun Oil Co., Phila., 1964-70, Petro-Tex Chem. Corp., Houston, 1970-72; individual practice law, Houston, 1972-76; asso. firm Johnson & Dry, Houston, 1977—; patent examiner U.S. Patent Office Washington, 1963-64. Mem. Tex. Bar Assn., Houston Patent Law Assn. Office: 1333 W Loop S Suite 1010 Houston TX 77027 Tel (713) 626-4680

JOHNSON, KENNETH T., JR., b. Kansas City, Mo., Feb. 24, 1947; B.A., Knox Coll., 1969; J.D., U. Mich., 1972. Admitted to Colo. bar, 1972; asso. firm Manter Marks & Wasko, Denver, 1972-74; individual practice law, Glenwood Springs, Colo., 1974—; asst. county atty. Garfield County, Colo., 1974—; dep. dist. atty. 9th Jud. Dist. Colo., Glenwood, Springs, 1972-73. Vestryman, St. Barnabas Episc. Ch., 1975—. Mem. Colo., 9th Jud. Dist. bar assns. (past pres.). Home: 501 10th St Glenwood Springs CO 81601 Office: POB 1055 Glenwood Springs CO 81601 Tel (303) 945-6552

JOHNSON, KENNETH THEODORE, b. Jamestown, N.Y., May 28, 1912; A.B., Allegheny Coll., 1934; J.D., U. Mich., 1937. Admitted to N.Y. bar, 1938, ICC bar, 1941, U.S. Supreme Ct. bar, 1956, U.S. Tax Ct. bar, 1961; asso. firm Lombardo & Pickard, Jamestown, N.Y., 1937-39, firm Clive L. Wright, Jamestown, N.Y., 1939-40; individual practice law, Jamestown, 1940-43, 46-52; partner firm Johnson and Peterson (now Johnson, Peterson, Tener & Anderson), Jamestown, 1952-56, mng. partner, 1956—. Mem. Am., N.Y. bar assns., Motor Carrier Lawyers Assn., Assn. ICC Practitioners. Home: Waldheim W E Jamestown NY 14701 Office: Bankers Trust Bldg Jamestown NY 14701 Tel (716) 664-5210

JOHNSON, LANCE BARRY, b. Corpus Christi, Tex., June 2, 1944; B.A., Boston U., 1966, J.D., 1969. Admitted to Ohio bar, 1969; partner firm Arter & Hadden, Cleve., 1969—; instr. Case Western Res. U. Law Sch.; guest lectr. Duke Law Sch. Forum; trustee, counsel Florence Crittenton Services of Cleve., legal adviser Greater Cleve. Growth Assn. Council Smaller Enterprises. Mem. Cleve., Ohio, Am. bar assns. Office: 1144 Union Commerce Bldg Cleveland OH 44115 Tel (216) 696-1144

JOHNSON, LARRY DEAN, b. Rockford, Ill., July 29, 1939; B.A., U. Minn., 1962; J.D., Loyola U., 1971. Admitted to Ill. bar, 1971; dir. personnel Perkin-Elmer Corp., Oak Brook, Ill., 1969-72; v.p., labor atty. Employers Assn. Greater Chgo., 1972-77; asso. counsel Marshall Field & Co., Chgo., 1977—. Mem. Am., Ill. State, Chgo. bar assns. Home: 1227 Belleforte Oak Park IL 60302 Office: Marshall Field & Co Corporate Offices Law Dept 25 E Washington St Chicago IL 60690 Tel (312) 236-7272

JOHNSON, LEE, b. Oreg., Sept. 8, 1930; A.B., Princeton, 1953; LL.B., Stanford, 1959. Anti-trust atty. U.S. Dept. Justice, Washington, 1959-61; mem. firm Mautz, Souther, Spaulding, Kinsey & Williamson, Portland, Oreg., 1961-68; atty. gen. State of Oreg., 1968—. Mem. Oreg. Ho. of Reps., 1964-68. Office: 100 State Office Bldg Salem OR 97310*

JOHNSON, LOIS STRAIGHT, b. Bradford, Pa., Jan. 26, 1907; A.B. U. Kans., 1929; LL.B., U. Okla., 1935. Admitted to Okla. bar, 1935; since practiced in Bartlesville, Okla.; atty. Cities Service Oil Co., 1936-64; partner firm Johnson and Johnson, 1964—; dir. Bartlesville YWCA, 1974—. Mem. Okla. Assn. Women Lawyers (past pres.), Washington County Bar Assn. (past pres.), Nat. Soc. Colonial Dames Am., Tulsa Shakespeare Club. Home: 2801 N Sheridan Rd Bartlesville OK 74003 Office: 215-1/2 Foster Bldg Bartlesville OK 74003 Tel (918) 336-3214

JOHNSON, LYNN CUTLER, b. Berwind, W.Va., Jan. 22, 1923; A.B., W.Va. U., 1948, J.D., 1950. Admitted to (W.Va.) bar, 1950; asso. firm Strother and Christie, Welch, W.Va., 1950-55; asst. land agt. Pocahontas Land Corp., Bluefield, W.Va., 1955—, land agt., real estate atty. Chmn., Bluefield Housing Authority, 1966-75. Mem. W.Va., Mercer County (W.Va.) bar assns., Phi Alpha Delta. Home: 504 Monterey Hill Bluefield WV 24701 Office: POB 1517 Bluefield WV 24701 Tel (304) 327-8101

JOHNSON, MARK H., b. Boston, Jan. 1, 1911; B.S.S., City Coll. N.Y., 1932; J.D., N.Y. U., 1935. Admitted to N.Y. bar, 1936; partner firm Rabkin & Johnson, N.Y.C., 1942-66; counsel firm Roberts & Holland, N.Y.C., 1966—; lectr. Sch. Law, N.Y. U., 1943-48. Mem. adv. group on partnership taxation Ways and Means Com., U.S. Ho. of Reps., 1957-58. Mem. Am. (council, sect. on taxation), N.Y. State Bar Assns., Bar Assn. City of N.Y., Am. Law Inst. (spl. adviser on taxation). Author: (with Jacob Rabkin) Federal Income, Gift and Estate Taxation, 16 vols., 1942-66, Current Legal Forms, 22 vols., 1948-66. Home: 6909 Veronese St Coral Gables FL 33146 Office: 1301 Ave of the Americas New York City NY 10019 Tel (212) 586-5200

JOHNSON, MORDECAI CHRISTOPHER, b. Florence County, S.C., Oct. 29, 1931; B.A., S.C. State Coll., Orangeburg, 1951; LL.B., Howard U., 1959, J.D., 1975; LL.M., Georgetown U., 1961. Admitted to S.C. bar, 1960, D.C. bar, 1960; practiced in Washington, 1960-62, Florence, 1969—; mem. firms Davis & Johnson, Washington, 1960-62; atty.-adviser HEW, Washington, 1962-65, U.S. Commn. on Civil Rights, Washington, 1965-66; dir. TEAM, Greenville, S.C., 1967-68; individual practice law, 1969—; lectr. U. S.C., 1972-73. Pres. S.C. Council on Human Relations, 1971-72; bd. dirs. So. Regional Council, 1972—. Mem. S.C. Bar, S.C. Black Lawyers Assn. Recipient Superior Performance award HEW, 1965, Office: POB 1804 Florence SC 29503 Tel (803) 669-1891

JOHNSON, MYRON ALFRED, b. Oakland, Calif., Aug. 21, 1921; B.A., U. Calif., Berkeley, 1949, J.D., 1951. Admitted to Calif. bar, 1952; asso. firm Norman Johnson, Fort Bragg, Calif., 1951-54, firm Miller, Kroloff and Brown, Stockton, Calif., 1954-55; research atty. Calif. Ct. Appeal, 3d Dist., Sacramento, 1955; asst. city atty. City of Hayward (Calif.), 1955—; individual practice law, Hayward, 1955—. Mem. Calif., Alameda County, So. Alameda County (pres. 1972) bar assns., Phi Delta Phi. Home: 527 Fairway St Hayward CA 94544 Office: 22300 Foothill Blvd Room 1135 Hayward CA 94541 Tel (415) 581-2345

JOHNSON, NEWTON ALBERT, b. Mpls., Sept. 5, 1918; student Gustavus Adolphus Coll., 1936-38; B.S., William Mitchell Coll. Law, 1940, LL.B., 1942. Admitted to Minn. bar, 1942; spl. agt. FBI, 1942-48; practice law, Fairmont, Minn., 1948—; sr. partner firm Johnson, Berens & Wilson, 1972; city atty. City of Fairmont, 1971—. Rep. Minn. Legislature, 1967-71; Martin County Republican chmn., 1963-67; former pres. Grace Lutheran Ch. Mem. Am. Trial Lawyers Assn., Minn., Martin County (past pres.), 17th Jud. Dist. (state gov. 1971-73) bar assns. Home: 514 Day St Fairmont MN 56031 Office: 201 E 3d St Fairmont MN 56031 Tel (507) 235-5544

JOHNSON, NORMA HOLLOWAY, b. Lake Charles, La.; B.S., D.C. Tchrs. Coll., 1955; J.D., Georgetown U., 1962. Admitted to D.C. bar, 1962, U.S. Supreme Ct. bar, 1967; practiced in Washington, 1963; atty. Dept. Justice, Washington, 1963-67; asst. corp. counsel D.C., 1967-70; judge D.C. Superior Ct., 1970—. Bd. dirs. Columbia Heights Youth Club, Washington, Operation Sisters United, Washington, Big Sisters, Met. Washington. Mem. Am., Nat., Washington bar assns., Nat. Council Juvenile Ct. Judges, Am. Judicature Soc. Office: 223 Pension Bldg 440 G St NW Washington DC 20001 Tel (202) 727-1088

JOHNSON, NORMAN PIKE, JR., b. Olean, N.Y., Dec. 25, 1937; A.B., Princeton, 1959; LL.B., Columbia, 1962. Admitted to Ariz. bar, 1964, U.S. Supreme Ct. bar, 1968; partner firm Johnson & Douglas, Phoenix, 1964-66, Carmichael, Johnson & Stephens, Phoenix, 1966-69; individual practice law, Phoenix, 1969-73; judge Municipal Ct., Phoenix, 1973—. Mem. Ariz. Municipal Judges Assn., Maricopa County Bar Assn. (dir.). Home: 201 E Portland #5 Phoenix AZ 85004 Office: 12 N 4th Ave Phoenix AZ 85003 Tel (602) 262-6681

JOHNSON, NORMAN STANLEY, b. Boise, Idaho, Sept. 28, 1930; student San Jose State Coll., 1948-49, Brigham Young U., 1949-50, 54; J.D., U. Utah, 1959. Admitted to Utah bar, 1959, 10th Circuit Ct. Appeals bar, 1971, U.S. Supreme Ct. bar, 1972, D.C. Circuit Ct. Appeals bar, 1976; law clk. Utah Supreme Ct., 1959; asst. atty. gen. State of Utah, Salt Lake City, 1959-64; trial atty. div. trading and markets U.S. SEC, Salt Lake City and Los Angeles, 1965-67; chief counsel Utah State Tax Commn., 1961; asso. firm Christensen & Jensen, 1967-68; partner firm Gardiner & Johnson, 1968-71, firm Johnson, Parsons & Kruse, 1971-74, firm Johnson & Spackman, Salt Lake City, 1974—. Mem. Am. (securities litigation com., chmn. securities proc. subcom. 1976), Fed., Utah (pres. corporate, banking and bus. law sect. 1973-74, now council), Salt Lake County bar assns., Delta Theta Phi. Contbr. articles to profl. jours. Home: 3444 Monte Verde Dr Salt Lake City UT 84109 Office: 1320 Continental Bank Bldg Salt Lake City UT 84101 Tel (801) 322-5614

JOHNSON, OWEN KENNETH, b. Taylor, Tex., Sept. 18, 1920; B.B.A., U. Tex., 1947, LL.B., 1948. Admitted to Tex. bar, 1948, U.S. Supreme Ct. bar, 1961; partner firms Rogers & Johnson, Wichita Falls, Tex., Allen, Crompton, Johnson & Purcell, Wichita Falls, Johnson & Browning, Wichita Falls, Johnson & Balch, Wichita Falls; spl. dist. judge Wichita County, 1958. Mayor City of Wichita Falls, 1960-62. Mem. Am., Tex. trial lawyers assns., Am. Bar Assn., Tex. State Bar, Wichita County Bar (pres. 1956). Home: 3512 Junifer Ln Wichita Falls TX 76307 Office: 625 Oil and Gas Bldg Wichita Falls TX 76301 Tel (817) 723-0934

JOHNSON, PAUL HENRY, b. Boston, Oct. 21, 1937; B.S. in Economics, Loyola U., Los Angeles, 1959; LL.B., Southwestern U., 1965. Admitted to Calif. bar, 1966; dep. city atty. Los Angeles City Atty's. Office, 1966-68; asst. counsel legal dept. Bank Am., Los Angeles, 1968-72; asso. counsel law div. Union Bank, Los Angeles, 1972—; counsel to Estonian Consulate, Los Angeles. Mem. Lawyers Club, Fin. Lawyers Conf., Am. Judicature Soc., Lawyer-Pilots Bar Assn. Office: 445 S Figueroa St Los Angeles CA 90071 Tel (213) 687-6290

JOHNSON, PAUL HOUSTON, b. Tulsa, Aug. 19, 1926; B.S.E.E., Okla. State U., 1959; J.D., U. Tulsa, 1957. Admitted to Okla. bar, 1957; partner firm Head, Johnson & Chafin, Tulsa, 1959—. Chmn. Tulsa Housing Authority, 1973-77; past pres. Gilcrease Museum Assn. Mem. Am., Okla., Tulsa Bar Assn. Contbr. articles to legal jours. Home: 2526 W Newton Tulsa OK 74127 Office: 212 Beacon Bldg Tulsa OK 74103 Tel (918) 584-4187

JOHNSON, PERRY H., b. Lebanon, Tenn., July 15, 1918; student Peabody Coll., U. Tenn.; LL.B., Cumberland U., 1954; J.D., Samford U., 1969. Admitted to Tenn. bar, 1954; individual practice law, Lebanon, Tenn.; clk. Circuit Ct.; clk., master Chancery Ct., Wilson County, Tenn. Mem. Am., Tenn., Wilson County bar assns. Home: 706 Westwood St Lebanon TN 37087

JOHNSON, PHILIP FREDERICK, b. Springfield, Ohio, June 18, 1938; A.B. with honors, Ind. U., 1959; LL.B., Yale, 1962. Admitted to Ill. bar, 1962; partner firm Kirkland & Ellis, Chgo., 1962—. Mem. Am. Bar Assn. (chmn. com. on commodities regulation). Mng. editor Yale Law Jour., 1962; contbr. articles in field to legal jours. Office: 200 E Randolph Dr Chicago IL 60601 Tel (312) 861-2240

JOHNSON, PHILLIP ALLEN, b. Davenport, Iowa, Sept. 19, 1943; B.A., Grinnell Coll., 1965; J.D. cum laude, Harvard, 1968. Admitted to Iowa Supreme Ct. bar, 1968; commd. 2d lt. USAF, 1965; advanced through grades to maj., 1976; asst. staff judge adv. Hdqrs. 4th Air Force, Hamilton AFB, Calif., 1969; asst. staff judge adv. Hdqrs. 1st Air Force, Stewart AFB, N.Y., 1969; chief civil law 4600 Air Base Wing, Ent AFB, Colo., 1969-71; chief military justice Cam Ranh Air Base, Republic Vietnam, 1971-72; instr. to asso. profl. law USAF Acad., 1972—. Mem. Am., Iowa bar assns., Am. Soc. Internat. Law. Home: 13475 Holmes Rd Colorado Springs CO 80908 Office: Dept Law US Air Force Academy CO 80840 Tel (303) 472-3680

JOHNSON, PRESTON LAWRENCE, b. Walla Walla, Wash., Aug. 1, 1936; A.B., Whitman Coll., 1959; J.D., U. Wash., 1970. Admitted to Wash. bar, 1970; asso. Malcolm L. Edwards, Seattle, 1969-71; atty. Burlington No., Seattle, 1971-72; individual practice law, Seattle and Federal Way, Wash., 1972—; judge pro-tem Federal Way Dist. Ct., 1975—; tchr. transp. law Highline Community Coll., Midway, Wash., 1973; supervising atty. legal internship program U. Wash. Legal Aid Soc., Seattle, 1973—; legal counsel S. King County Community Planning Bd., Federal Way, 1971—. Mem. Met. Citizens Transit Adv. Comm., 1973—; mem. Federal Way Community Council, 1971—, chmn., 1974-75; pres. Federal Way Republican Club, 1975-76; sr. v.p. Eddie Wagner's Boys' Town NW, Seattle, 1976—. Mem. Am. Bar Assn., Christian Legal Soc. Home: 28414 15th Ave S Federal Way WA 98003 Office: 181 S 333d St Suite 108 Federal Way WA 98003 Tel (206) 838-3454

JOHNSON, R. EDGAR, b. Caldwell, Kans., July 28, 1935; B.S., Kans. State U., 19S7; J.D., Washburn U., 1959. Admitted to Kans. bar, 1959, U.S. Dist. Ct. Kans. bar, 1959, U.S. Ct. Mil. Appeals, 1962, U.S. Ct. Appeals 10th Circuit bar, 1969; staff JAGC, USAF, 1959-62; partner firm Deam & Johnson, Junction City, Kans., 1962-65; county atty. Geary County (Kans.), 1965-67; U.S. commr. Kans., Junction City, 1967-68; individual practice law, Junction City, Kans., 1968-71; partner firm Johnson & Bengtson, Junction City, 1971-72; pres. firm Johnson, Bengtson, Waters & Thompson, Junction City, 1972—. Mem. Am., Kans., Central Kans., Geary County bar assns., Am., Kans. trial lawyers assns. Home: 1328 Shamrock St Junction City KS 66441 Office: 1206 W 8th St PO Box 848 Junction City KS 66441 Tel (913) 762-2901

JOHNSON, RAYMOND CHARLES, b. Chgo., Aug. 20, 1936; B.S., U. Wis. at Eau Claire, 1958; J.D., George Washington U., 1965. Admitted to Va. bar, 1965, Wis. bar, 1965, U.S. Supreme Ct. bar, 1976; asso. firm Donnelly & Johnson, Eau Claire, 1965-68; mem. firm Adler, LaFave & Johnson, Eau Claire, 1968—; mem. Wis. State Senate, 1967-75, majority leader, 1973-75. Mem. Va., Wis., Eau Claire County, Am. bar assns., Wis. Acad. Trial Lawyers, Am. Assn. Trial Lawyers. Office: 415 S Farwell St Eau Claire WI 54701 Tel (715) 832-1983

JOHNSON, RICHARD BENNION, b. Salt Lake City, Oct. 19, 1940; B.S., Utah State U., 1964; J.D., U. Utah, 1967. Admitted to Ariz. bar, 1968; law clk. U.S. Dist. Ct. for Dist. of Utah, 1967; law clk. Ariz. Supreme Ct., 1967-68; partner firm Shimmel, Hill, Bishop & Gruender, Phoenix, 1968—. Mem. Am., Ariz., Maricopa bar assns. Home: 1229 Commodore Pl Tempe AZ 85283 Office: 111 W Monroe St Phoenix AZ 85003 Tel (602) 257-5500

JOHNSON, RICHARD TENNEY, b. Evanston, Ill., Mar. 24, 1930; A.B., U. Rochester, 1951; postgrad. Trinity Coll., Dublin, 1955; LL.B., Harvard, 1958. Admitted to D.C. bar, 1959; atty. Office Sec. Def., Washington, 1959-63; dep. gen. counsel Dept. Army, 1963-67, Dept. Transp., 1967-70; gen. counsel CAB, 1970-73, NASA, 1973-75, ERDA, 1975-76; mem. CAB, Washington, 1976—; cons. U.S. Commn. on Fed. Procurement, 1971-72; chmn. U.S. side Joint Working Group on Intellectual Property, U.S./USSR Coop. Agreement on Sci. and Tech., 1974—; chief legal del. U.S. Mission to Internat. Civil Aviation Orgn. Triennial Meeting, 1971. Pres., Carderock Springs Citizens Assn. Mem. Fed., D.C. bar assns. Recipient Exceptional Civilian Service award Dept. Army, 1967, Meritorious Achievement award Dept. Transp., 1968, Distinguished Service award Energy Research and Devel. Adminstrn., 1976; contbr. articles to profl. jours. Home: 8424 Magruder Mill Ct Bethesda MD 20034 Office: 1825 Connecticut Ave NW Washington DC 20428 Tel (202) 673-5222

JOHNSON, ROBERT ELLIS, b. Dallas, Jan. 11, 1929; B.B.A., So. Meth. U., 1949, LL.B., 1955. Admitted to Tex. bar, 1954; partner firm Speck, Johnson & Alexander, Dallas, 1955-63; exec. dir. Tex. Legis. Council, Austin, 1963—; mem. Tex. Ho. of Reps., 1956-63, parliamentarian, 1965—. Mem. Dallas C. of C., Delta Theta Phi. Home: 5205 Tortuga Trail Austin TX 78731 Office: Box 12128 Capitol Station Austin TX 78711 Tel (512) 475-2736

JOHNSON, ROBERT LELAND, b. Denver, May 1, 1933; student Yale, 1955; J.D., U. Denver, 1958, A.B., 1962. Admitted to C Colo. bar, 1959, U.S. Supreme Ct. bar, 1971; law clk. to justice Colo. Supreme Ct., 1958; asst. regional counsel U.S. GSA Region 8, Denver, 1959-61; individual practice law, Denver, 1961—. Mem. SAR (v.p. gen. 1975-76), Nat. Soc. Sons Am. Colonists (nat. chancellor), Colo. Yale Assn., Mil. Order of Loyal Legion U.S. (Phila.), Hist. Soc. Pa. (Phila.), Colo. Council for the Experiment in Internat. Living (Denver), Internat. Platform Assn., Am., Colo., Denver, Adams County bar assns., Colo. Trial Lawyers Assn., Am. Judicature Soc. Recipient Patriot's medal Colo. Soc. SAR, 1976, certificate of merit U. Denver Coll. Law, 1958; named Community Leader Am., 1969, 72; author: A Genealogical Excursion Through Historic Philadelphia, 1976; Colorado Mechanics' Liens, 1971; Matrimonial Practice in Colorado Courts, 1969; Trial Handbook for Colorado Torts Lawyers, 1967; Statute Annotations, 1968-75; The American Heritage of James Norman Hall, 1970; Newspaper Accounts of B.F. Wright, Esq., and Others of Louisa County, Iowa, 1967. Home: 9751 Melody Dr Northglenn CO 80204 Office: 705 W 8th Ave Denver CO 80204 Tel (303) 893-5062

JOHNSON, ROBERT MAURICE, b. Detorit, Sept. 12, 1938; B.A., Amherst Coll., 1960; M.A. in Econs., LL.B., Yale, 1965. Admitted to Tenn. bar, 1965, U.S. Dist. Ct. bar, 1965, U.S. Ct. of Appeals bar, 1965; since practiced in Memphis; law clk. to Chief Judge Bailey Brown, 1965; trial atty. FTC, 1966; asso. firm Canada, Russell & Turner, 1967-72, partner, 1973—. Bd. dirs. Memphis House Drug Treatment Center, 1970—, pres., 1974; bd. dirs. Family Service of Memphis, 1972—, treas., 1976. Mem. Am., Tenn., Shelby County, Memphis bar assns. Home: 200 Waring Rd Memphis TN 38117 Office: 12th Floor Union Planters' Bank Bldg 67 Madison Ave Memphis TN 38103 Tel (901) 521-1111

JOHNSON, ROBERT VEILING, II, b. Laconia, N.H., Apr. 29, 1939; A.B., Boston U., 1961, J.D., 1967; diploma Internat. Grad. Sch., Stockholm, Sweden, 1963; M.S., U. Stockholm, Sweden, 1964. Admitted to N.H. bar, 1967, U.S. Supreme Ct. bar, asso. firm Upton, Sanders & Smith, Concord, N.H., 1967-71; asst. atty. gen. State of N.H., Concord, 1971—. Chmn., Concord Conservation Commn., 1970—; bd. dirs. N.H. Assn. Conservation Commns., 1976—. Mem. Am., N.H., Merrimack County bar assns. Home: RFD 6 Oak Hill Rd Concord NH 03301 Office: Office Atty Gen State House Annex Concord NH 03301 Tel (603) 271-3671

JOHNSON, RONALD BRUCE, b. Wheeling, W.Va., Sept. 28, 1943; B.S., West Liberty State Coll., 1970; J.D., W.Va. U., 1973. Admitted to W.Va. bar, 1973; asso. firm Schrader, Miller, Stamp & Recht, Wheeling, 1973-76, partner, 1976—. Mem. Am., W.Va. bar assns., W.Va. State Bar, Order of Coif. Bd. editors W.Va. Law Rev., 1972-73. Home: 8 Laurelwood Estates Wheeling WV 26003 Office: 816 Central Union Bldg Wheeling WV 26003 Tel (304) 233-3390

JOHNSON, RONALD E., b. Chgo., Mar. 11, 1939; B.Engring Sci., Rensselaer Poly. Inst., 1966; J.D., Union U., 1969. Admitted to N.Y. State bar, 1969, U.S. Tax Ct. bar, 1976; asso. firm Johnson & Johnson, and predecessors, Nyack, N.Y., 1969-71, partner, 1971—; asso. firm Schwartz, Kobb, Scheinert & Hamerman, Spring Valley, N.Y., 1972-74, partner, 1975—; asst. city atty. Grand-View-on-Hudson (N.Y.), 1970-71, atty., 1971-74. Mem. Am., N.Y. State, Rockland County bar assns. Contbr. articles in field to law revs. Office: 7 S Madison Ave PO Box 299 Spring Valley NY 10977 Tel (914) 352-5100

JOHNSON, RONALD F., b. Hallock, Minn., July 20, 1938; B.A., U. Minn., 1961; J.D., Wm. Mitchell Coll. Law, 1965. Admitted to Minn. bar, 1965; mem. firm Quinlivan Williams Johnson & Quinlivan, St. Cloud, Minn., 1965-74, firm Schmitt & Johnson, St. Cloud, 1974—; bd. dirs. St. Cloud Legal Services, Inc. Mem. Am., Minn. State, Stearns-Benton-Sherburne-Mille Lacs bar assns. Home: 918 Riverside Dr SE Saint Cloud MN 56301 Office: 400 E St Germain St Saint Cloud MN 56301 Tel (612) 251-9500

JOHNSON, RONALD LEE, b. Burbank, Calif., Aug. 12, 1937; B.A., U. Redlands, 1959; LL.B., U. Calif., Berkeley, 1963. Admitted to Calif. bar, 1964; asso. firm Best, Best & Krieger, Riverside, Calif., 1965-66, State of Calif. Dept. Transp., Los Angeles, 1966-70; chief dep. city atty. City of San Diego, 1971—. Mem. San Diego, Los Angeles trial lawyers assns., Calif. State Bar Assn. Home: 1559 Santa Elena Ct Solona Beach CA 92075 Office: 202 C St San Diego CA 92101 Tel (714) 236-6220

JOHNSON, RONALD PAUL, b. Quincy, Mass., Feb. 13, 1936; A.B., Stonehill Coll., 1958; M.S., Boston U. Sch. Pub. Communication, 1960; J.D., New Eng. Law Sch., 1972. Admitted to Mass. bar, 1972, U.S. Dist. Ct. bar for Dist. Mass., 1973, U.S. Tax Ct., 1976; dir. informational services Boston Sch. Dept., 1965-76; individual practice law, Boston, 1976—. Mem. Am., Mass., Boston bar assns., Mass. Sch. Pub. Relations Assn. Home: 28 Hilltop St Quincy MA 02169 Office: Suite 948 141 Milk St Boston MA 02109 Tel (617) 426-6897

JOHNSON, RUFUS WINFIELD, b. Montgomery County, Md., May 1, 1911; student Howard U., 1930-34, B.A., 1936, LL.B., 1939. Admitted to Washington Ct. Appeals bar, 1944, U.S. Supreme Ct. bar, 1948, Republic S. Korea Supreme Ct. bar, 1952, Calif. bar, 1952; law clk. firm Earl C. Broady, Sr., Los Angeles, 1948-50, asso., 1953-54; served with Judge Adv. Gen. Corps U.S. Army, 1952-53; individual practice law, San Bernardino, Calif., 1954—, Santa Barbara, Calif., 1956-58. Mem. State Bar Calif., San Bernardino County Bar Assn., Judge Advs. Assn., San Bernardino County Criminal Def. Attys. Assn., Am. Judicature Soc., Am. Acad. Polit. and Social Sci. Home: 3168 N Sierra Way San Bernardino CA 92405 Office: 1145 W Base Line San Bernardino CA 92411 Tel (714) 885-0625

JOHNSON, SAM D., b. Hubbard, Tex., Nov. 17, 1920; B.B.A., Baylor U., 1946; LL.B., U. Tex., 1949. Admitted to Tex. bar, 1949; individual practice law, Hillsboro, Tex., 1949-52; county atty. Hill County, Tex., 1953-54; dist. atty. 66th Jud. Dist., Hillsboro, Tex., 1955-58; judge Dist. Dist. Ct., 66th Jud. Dist., Hillsboro, 1959-65; exec. dir. Houston Legal Found., 1965-66; asso. justice Tex. Ct. Civil Appeals, 14th Dist., Houston, 1967-72; justice Tex. Supreme Ct., Austin, 1973—. Bd. dirs. Presbyterian Children's Home and Service Agency. Mem. Appellate Judges Conf. (chmn.), Am. Bar Assn., Nat. Legal Aid and Defender Assn. (exec. com.), Baylor Univ. Ex-students Assn. (former pres.). Home: 1811 Exposition St Austin TX 78703 Office: Supreme Court Bldg Austin TX 78711 Tel (512) 475-4615

JOHNSON, SANDER LEROY, b. Grand Forks, N.D., Jan. 24, 1921; B.S., U. N.D., 1941; LL.B., Harvard, 1944. Admitted to Calif. bar, 1948; asst. U.S. atty. Central Dist. Calif., Los Angeles, 1948-50; individual practice law So. Calif., 1951-72; partner firm Long & Levit, Los Angeles, 1972—. Mem. Am., Los Angeles County, Beverly Hills bar assns. Office: 1900 Ave of the Stars #1800 Los Angeles CA 90067 Tel (213) 879-1222

JOHNSON, SEARCY LEE, b. Dallas, Aug. 30, 1908; B.A., Williams Coll., 1929; LL.B., U. Tex., 1932. Admitted to Tex. bar, 1933, D.C. bar, 1938; spl. prosecutor, Dallas, 1938, asso. firm Johnson, Guthrie, Nash & Shanklin, Dallas; sr. partner, founder firm Johnson, Guthrie, White & Stanfield; legal adviser to Gen. Hershey on vets. re-employment, Washington, 1944-45; spl. asst. to U.S. Atty. Gen., Dept. Justice, Washington, 1945-47. Mem. Nat. Press Club, Am. Judicature Soc., Am. Soc. Authors and Composers, Dallas Ins. Club; fellow Tex. Bar, Dallas Hist. Soc., English Speaking Union. Contbr. articles to legal jours. Composer songs, including Sweet Bird of Youth, 1964; Votive Offering, 1964; also The Ballad of the Thresher. Home: 3901 Gillon Ave Dallas TX 75205 Office: 1410 Republic Nat Bank Bldg Dallas TX 75201 Tel (214) 741-2464

JOHNSON, SETH MARK, b. Hungington, Utah, June 6, 1930; B.S.L., U. Utah, 1956, J.D., 1957. Admitted to Utah bar, 1957; individual practice law, Bountiful, Utah, 1957-70; judge city ct.,

Bountiful, 1970—; law clk. to justice Supreme Ct. Utah, 1957-58; dep. atty. Davis County, Utah, 1961-67; mem. Utah State Jud. Council, 1974—; mem. Utah State Council on Criminal Justice Adminstrn., 1975—. Mem. Am. Bar Assn., Nat. Conf. Spl. Ct. Judges, Am. Judicature Soc., Utah Assn. City Ct. Judges (past pres.), Davis County Bar Assn. (past pres.). Home: 1359 Millbrook Way Bountiful UT 84010 Office: 745 S Main St Bountiful UT 84010 Tel (801) 295-2301

JOHNSON, SOLOMON ELIHU, b. Atlanta, Sept. 25, 1920; A.B., Morehouse Coll., 1946; J.D., Howard U., 1949. Admitted to Calif. bar, 1955; accountant J.B. Blayton & Co., C.P.A., Atlanta, 1944-46; agt. U.S. Dept. Treasury, San Francisco, 1951-52; dep. collector Dept. Internal Revenue, San Francisco, 1952-55; individual practice law, San Francisco, 1955—. Housing commr. City and County of San Francisco, 1961-64; vice chmn. United Negro Coll. Fund, 1963; exec. bd. NAACP, 1962-64; mem. Citizens Charter Revision Commn., City and County of San Francisco, 1972-74; mem. state adv. com. to Gov. Reagan, 1970-71. Mem. Calif. (bd. govs. 1975), San Francisco (bd. govs. 1973-74) trial lawyers assns., State Bar of Calif., Charles O. Houston Bar Assn. Office: 785 Market St Suite 1500 San Francisco CA 94103 Tel (415) 392-7818

JOHNSON, STUART FISK, b. Suffern, N.Y., June 19, 1943; B.A., Williams Coll., 1965; LL.B., U. Va., 1968. Admitted to Vt. bar, 1968, D.C. bar, 1971, U.S. Supreme Ct. bar, 1976; asst. U.S. atty. Dept. Justice, Rutland, Vt., 1969; atty. advisor Office Gen. Counsel, U.S. Bur. Prisons, Washington, 1969-70; individual practice law, Washington, 1971—. Mem. Bar Assn. D.C., D.C. Bar, Superior Ct. D.C. Trial Lawyers Assn. Home: 1004 Butterworth Ln Upper Marlboro MD 20870 Office: 475 H St NW Washington DC 20001 Tel (202) 628-0059

JOHNSON, TED E.G., b. Cortland, Ohio, July 6, 1925; LL.B., Youngstown U., 1952, J.D., 1969. Admitted to Ohio bar, 1952; individual practice law, Warren, Ohio, 1952—. Chmn. Trumbull County (Ohio) Republican Party, 1966-76, Trumbull County Bd. Elections, 1968—; del. Rep. Nat. Conv., 1972, 76; city law dir. Newton Falls (Ohio), 1967-71. Mem. Ohio State, Trumbull County bar assns., Ohio Assn. Election Ofcls. Home: 139 Hyde Ave Niles OH 44446 Office: 501-2 Union Savings and Trust Bldg Warren OH 44481 Tel (216) 395-4433

JOHNSON, TERRY JAY, b. Lake Charles, La., Feb. 9, 1948; B.A., McNeese State U., 1970; J.D., La. State U., 1973. Admitted to La. bar, 1973; mem. SW La. Legal Aid Soc., Inc., Oakdale, La., 1973-75; individual practice law, Oakdale, 1975—; asst. dist. atty. 33d Jud. Dist., Allen Parish, La., 1976—. Pres. Oakdale Jaycees, 1975-76. Mem. Am., La. State bar assns., La. Dist. Attys. Assn. Home: 303 W Dixie St PO Box 548 Oakdale LA 71463 Office: 109 S 11th St Oakdale LA 71463 Tel (318) 335-1605

JOHNSON, THOMAS STUART, b. Rockford, Ill., May 2, 1942; B.A., Rockford Coll., 1964; LL.B., Harvard, 1967. Admitted to Ill. bar, 1967; partner firm Williams, McCarthy, Kinley, Rudy & Picha, Rockford, 1974—. Fellow Am. Bar Found., mem. Am. (chmn. consortium on legal services and the public 1976—), Ill. (bd. govs. 1976—), Winnebago bar assns. Home: 913 N Main St Rockford IL 61103 Office: Williams McCarthy Kinley Rudy & Picha 400 Talcott Bldg Rockford IL 61101 Tel (815) 987-8900

JOHNSON, TIMOTHY AUGUSTIN, JR., b. Clearwater, Fla., Dec. 17, 1945; B.A., U. Fla., 1966, J.D. with honors, 1969. Admitted to Fla. bar, 1969; asso. firm Carlton, Fields, Ward, Emmanuel, Smith, & Cutler, Profl. Assn., Tampa, Fla., 1969-73; stockholder firm Johnson, Blakely, Pope & Bokor, Profl. Assn., Clearwater, 1973—. Treas. Clearwater Concert Soc. Assn., Mem. Am., Clearwater bar assns., Fla. Bar (gov. sect. young lawyers 1972-73, 76—), Am. Judicature Soc., Pinellas County (Fla.) Trial Lawyers Assn., U. Fla. Law Rev. Alumni Assn., Order of Coif, Phi Kappa Phi. Exec. editor: U. Fla. Law Rev., 1968-69. Home: 410 Magnolia Dr Clearwater FL 33516 Office: POB 1368 Clearwater FL 33517 Tel (813) 441-2440

JOHNSON, TIMOTHY VINCENT, b. Champaign, Ill., July 23, 1946; B.A. with highest honors (James scholar), U. Ill., 1969, J.D. (Herrick scholar), 1972. Admitted to Ill. bar; asso. firm Finfrock & Johnson, and predecessor, Urbana, Ill., 1972-75, partner, 1975; partner firm Johnson, Frank & Frederick, Urbana, 1975—; instr. Coll. of Commerce U. Ill., 1971-72, Coll. Law U. Ill., 1972-73, Parkland Jr. Coll., 1973—. Active, Urbana Assn. Commerce and Industry, Com. on State Govt. Affairs; chmn. Urbana lawyers sect. Am. Cancer Soc., Multiple Sclerosis Dr.; participant Law Day local high sch.; mem. Urbana Human Relations Commn., 1970-71, Urbana City Council, 1971-75; precinct committeeman Republican Party, 1968—, vice chmn. Cunningham Twp. Rep. Central Com., 1968-74; del. to Ill. State Conv.; chmn. Champaign County Com. to Re-elect the Pres., 1972; vice chmn. Champaign County Rep. Central Com., 1974—. Mem. Am., Ill., Champaign County bar assns., Bronze Tablet, Order of Coif, Phi Beta Kappa, Phi Kappa Phi, Phi Alpha Theta. Named Outstanding History Undergrad. U. Ill., 1969. Home: 103 N Race St Urbana IL 61801 Office: 207 W Elm St Urbana IL 61801 Tel (217) 367-6092

JOHNSON, TOM, b. Lake Worth, Fla., Dec. 16, 1927; LL.B., U. Miami (Fla.), 1953. Admitted to Fla. bar, 1953; partner firm Johnson, Ackerman & Bakst, and predecessors, W. Palm Beach, Fla., 1953-74; asst. county solicitor Palm Beach County (Fla.), 1955-57; municipal judge, Riviera Beach, Palm Beach Shores, Fla., 1958-64; states atty. 15th jud. circuit Fla., 1964-68; city atty. Riviera Beach, 1968-70; judge 15th Jud. Circuit Ct. Fla., 1977—; mem. Fla. State Senate, 1970-74. Mem. Am., Fla. bar assns. Home: 1272 Yacht Harbor Dr Riviera Beach FL 33404 Office: 2139 Palm Beach Lakes Rd West Palm Beach FL 33402 Tel (305) 686-8600

JOHNSON, WALKER PITTS, JR., b. Newnan, Ga., Feb. 23, 1937; B.A., Emory U., 1959, LL.B., 1962. Admitted to Ga. bar, 1961; trial atty. Ga. Atty. Gen's. Office, Atlanta, 1962; asso. firm Sanders Mottola and Haugen, Newnan, Ga., 1963-65; trial atty. civil rights div. Dept. Justice, Wash., D.C., 1965-66; asst. U.S. Atty., Middle Dist. Ga., Macon, 1966-70; interim U.S. Atty., Macon, 1969-70; asso. firm Anderson, Walker and Reichert, Macon, 1970-71; asst. dist. atty. Macon Judicial Circuit, 1971-76, interim dist. atty., 1972-73, 76-77, dist. atty., 1977—; dir. prosecutorial clinic Mercer U. Sch. Law, Macon, 1974-77. Mem. Federal, Ga., Macon Bar Assns., Am. Judicature Soc. Contbr. to Mercer Law Jour. Home: 5752 Kentucky Downs Dr Macon GA 31210 Office: Room 300 Bibb County Courthouse Macon GA 31201 Tel (912) 745-6871

JOHNSON, WAYNE GORDON, b. Ortonville, Minn., July 8, 1921; student Mich. Mining & Tech. Inst., 1943, N.D. State U., 1946-48; B.S., U. Minn., 1950; LL.B., Mpls. Coll. Law, 1952. Admitted to Minn. bar, 1952, U.S. Supreme Ct. bar, 1974; mem. firm Johnson & Thomas, Silver Bay, Minn.; atty. City of Beaver Bay, 1953—, City of Silver Bay, 1956—, spl. county atty. Cook County (Minn.), 1965, Lake County (Minn.), 1968; dir. LSM Corp. Minn. Mem. Am., Minn. bar assns., Am. Trial Lawyers Assn., Lawyer-Pilots Assn., Arrowhead Gen. Aviation Assn. (past pres.), Assn. Flying Sportsmen (past pres.). Named Mr. Aviation Minn., Minn. Dept Aeros., 1969. Home: Beaver Bay MN 55614 Office: Norshor Bldg Silver Bay MN 55614 Tel (218) 226-3790

JOHNSON, WILLIAM ANDREW, b. Mpls., Nov. 29, 1945; B.A. with high honors, Mich. State U., 1967; J.D. cum laude, Harvard, 1972. Admitted to Minn. bar, 1972; law clk. Minn. Supreme Ct., 1972-73; partner firm Schmitz & Johnson, Northfield, Minn., 1973-76; judge Rice County (Minn.) Ct., Faribault, 1976—; mem. Minn. Supreme Ct. Adv. Com. on Rules of Evidence, 1974—. Mem. Am., Minn., 5th Dist., Rice County bar assns. Contbr. article to law rev. Office: Rice County Courthouse Faribault MN 55021 Tel (507) 334-3906

JOHNSON, WILLIAM ARCHIBALD, b. Lillington, N.C., Sept. 1, 1920; A.B., U. N.C., 1941, J.D., 1944. Admitted to N.C. bar, 1944; staff atty. Reynolds Metals Corp., Richmond, Va., 1944; individual practice law, Lillington, 1945-61, 67—; county atty. Harnett County (N.C.), 1948-58; city atty. City of Lillington, 1947-60; commr. revenue State of N.C., 1961-64, resident superior ct. judge 11th Jud. Dist. N.C., 1964-66. Mem. exec. bd. Occoneechee council Boy Scouts Am., Raleigh, N.C., 1957-60; vice chmn. bd. trustees Campbell Coll., 1952-53; trustee U. N.C., 1961-72, bd. govs., 1972—, chmn., 1976—. Mem. 11th Jud. Dist. (pres. 1968-69), N.C., Am. bar assns., Am. Judicature Soc., Order of Coif. Editor-in-chief N.C. Law Rev., 1943-44. Home: 211 E Front St Lillington NC 27546 Office: 31 E Harnett St Lillington NC 27546 Tel (919) 893-5107

JOHNSON, WILLIAM EMMERSON, b. Chgo., Oct. 6, 1928; B.A., Grinnell Coll., 1951; LL.B., U. Wis., 1956, LL.D., 1966. Admitted to Wis. bar, 1956, U.S. Supreme Ct. bar, 1969; asso. firm Swinger Stern & Lenahan, Madison, Wis., 1956-61; individual practice law, Madison, 1963-70; partner firm Oldenburg Manzer & Johnson, Madison, 1962-63, Johnson Bieber & Swingen, Madison, 1970—; lectr., acting prof. U. Wis., Madison, 1974-76. Fund raising com. Am. Cancer Soc.; bd. dirs. Wis. Ballet Co., 1968-72. Mem. Am., Wis., Dane County bar assns., Am. Trial Lawyers Assn., Wis. Acad. Trial Lawyers (dir.), Phi Alpha Delta. Office: 411 W Main St Madison WI 53703 Tel (608) 257-4715

JOHNSON, WILLIAM HARRIS, b. Binghamton, N.Y., Apr. 16, 1921; A.B., Hamilton Coll., Clinton, N.Y., 1943; LL.B., Cornell U., 1949. Admitted to N.Y. bar, 1949; asso. firm Twining & Fischer, Binghamton, 1949-51, partner, 1952-65; partner firm Travis & Johnson, Binghamton, 1965-70; individual practice law, Binghamton, 1970—; asst. corp. counsel City of Binghamton, 1951, spl. and city judge, 1959-62. Mem. Binghamton Housing Authority, 1955-73. Mem. Am., N.Y. State, Broome County bar assns., Am. Assn. Trial Lawyers. Home: 22 Edgecomb Rd Binghamton NY 13905 Office: 200 Security Mutual Bldg Binghamton NY 13901 Tel (607) 723-5441

JOHNSON, WILLIAM MARTIN, b. Alhambra, Calif., June 13, 1931; B.A., Calif. State U., Los Angeles, 1959; LL.B., Southwestern U., 1964. Admitted to Calif. bar, 1968, U.S. Dist. Ct. bar for Dist. San Diego, 1971; staff Imperial County (Calif.) Dist. Atty's. Office, 1968-71; dep. dist. atty. Imperial County Pub. Defenders Office, 1971—; sr. partner firm Johnson & McDonough, El Centro, Calif., 1971—. Mem. Calif. State, Imperial County (treas. 1971, 75—) bars. Office: 229 S 8th St El Centro CA 92243 Tel (714) 352-4593

JOHNSTON, ALAN ERIC, b. St. Louis, Jan. 22, 1948; A.S., Marion (Ala.) Inst., 1968; B.A., U. Ala., 1970; J.D., Samford U., 1972. Admitted to Ala. bar, 1973; asso. Donald L. Collins, Birmingham, Ala., 1973-74; partner firm Collins & Johnston, Birmingham, 1974-75; individual practice law, Birmingham, 1975—; clk. Ala. State Dept. Ct. Mgmt., Montgomery, 1972. Mem. Am., Ala., Birmingham bar assns., Am. Judicature Soc., Sigma Delta Kappa. Office: 2010 City Fed Bldg Birmingham AL 35203 Tel (205) 328-9000

JOHNSTON, ALBERT CALDWELL, b. Chattanooga, Dec. 7, 1909; A.B., George Washington U., 1930, J.D., 1934. Admitted to D.C. bar, 1933, N.Y. bar, 1936, U.S. Supreme Ct. bar, 1958; examiner U.S. Patent Office, Washington, 1930-35; asst. atty. Nat. Recovery Adminstrn., Washington, 1935-36; asso. Hammond & Littell, N.Y.C., 1936-40, partner, 1940-49; partner firm Pollard & Johnston, N.Y.C., 1949-59, Keith, Johnston & Isner, N.Y.C., 1964-71; individual practice law, N.Y.C., 1959-64, 71—. Mem. Darien (Conn.) Bd. Edn., 1949-56, chmn., 1954-56; mem. Darien Bd. Selectmen, 1960-64; chmn. Darien Priorities Com., 1969-70. Mem. Am. Bar Assn., Am., N.Y. (pres. 1967) patent law assns., Assn. of Bar City of N.Y. (chmn. patent com. 1972-75), Am. Judicature Soc., U.S. Trademark Assn., N.Y. Chemists Club, Phi Delta Phi, Order of Coif. Author: (with F.A. Fitch) Design Piracy - the Problem and Its Treatment under N.R.A. Codes, 1936. Home: 25 Outlook Dr Darien CT 06820 Office: 230 Park Ave New York City NY 10017 Tel (212) 889-3393

JOHNSTON, BRUCE, b. Los Angeles, Nov. 30, 1919; B.A., U. Calif. at Los Angeles, 1941; J.D., U. So. Calif., 1948. Admitted to Calif. bar, 1949; individual practice law, Ventura, Calif., 1949—. Mem. Ventura City Council, 1953-55, Ventura Sch. Bd., 1957-66; pres. Ventura Boys' Club, 1969, Ventura Concert Series Assn., 1951; sec. Big. Bros. Ventura County, 1975—. Mem. Am., Ventura County (pres.) bar assns., State Bar Calif. Recipient Distinguished Service award Ventura Jr. C. of C., 1950. Home: 2179 Foster Ave Ventura CA 93003 Office: POB 1475 Ventura CA 93001 Tel (805) 643-8685

JOHNSTON, EDWARD ALLAN, b. Balt., Sept. 25, 1921; B.B.A., U. Balt., 1942, B.S., 1947, LL.B., 1949, LL.M., 1957. Admitted to Md. bar, 1949; partner Johnston and Co., CPA's, Balt., 1946-62; partner firm Whiteford, Taylor, Preston, Trimble & Johnston, Balt., 1954—. Trustee Contact Balt. Inc., 1974—, chmn., 1977—; chmn. ofcl. bd. Mt. Vernon Pl. United Methodist Ch., 1965-69. Mem. Md. State Golf Assn. (pres. 1968), U. Balt. Alumni Assn. (pres. 1975-77), Am., Md. State, Balt. City bar assns. Home: 2449 Pickwick Rd Baltimore MD 21207 Office: Floor IBM Bldg 100 E Pratt St Baltimore MD 21202 Tel (302) 752-0987

JOHNSTON, GEORGE W., III, b. Dallas, Oct. 3, 1945; A.B. in Polit. Sci. cum laude with honors, Kenyon Coll., 1968; J.D., U. Va., 1971. Admitted to Va. bar, 1971, Ohio bar, 1971; law clk. firm Stephenson, Stephenson & Cunningham, New Philadelphia, Ohio, 1969-70; asso. firm Kuykendall, Whiting, Costello & Hanes, Winchester, Va., 1971—; counsel Winchester/Frederick County Big Bros.-Big Sisters. Treas. Winchester City Republican Com. Mem. Va., Va. State, Am. bar assns. Home: 439 Handley Ave Winchester VA 22601 Office: 20 S Cameron St Winchester VA 22601 Tel (703) 667-4640

JOHNSTON, JAY JAMES, b. Peoria, Ill., July 28, 1942; B.S., Marquette U., 1964; LL.B., U. Notre Dame, 1967. Admitted to Ill. bar, 1967; partner firm Hall, Meyer, Fisher, Holmberg & Snook, Waukegan, Ill., 1967—. Mem. Am., Ill., Chgo., Lake County bar assns. Home: 751 Oak Spring Rd Libertyville IL 60048 Office: 25 N County St Waukegan IL 60085 Tel (312) 244-0600

JOHNSTON, JOHN DEVEREAUX, JR., b. Asheville, N.C., Oct. 1, 1932; A.B., Duke, 1954, LL.B., 1956. Admitted to N.C. bar, 1956, U.S. 4th Circuit Ct. of Appeals, 1969, U.S. Supreme Ct. bar, 1969; asso. J.P. Morgan & Co., N.Y.C., 1956-58; asso. firm Wright & Shuford, Asheville, N.C., 1959-62; asst. dean Duke Law Sch., 1962-63, asst. prof., 1963-65, asso. prof., 1965-67; vis. asso. prof. law N.Y. U., 1967-68, prof., 1969—; vis. prof. Vanderbilt U., 1972, U. Calif., Los Angeles, 1975. Mem. Am. Bar Assn., Soc. Am. Law Tchrs. Author: (with George Johnson) Land Use Control, 3 vols., 1973-74; contbr. articles to legal jours.; editor Jour. Legal Edn., 1964-66. Home: 1 Shoal Point Ln Riverside CT 06878 Office: NY U Sch of Law 40 Washington Square S New York City NY 10012 Tel (212) 598-2558

JOHNSTON, JOSEPH FORNEY, b. Birmingham, Ala., July 31, 1906; A.B., Princeton, 1927; LL.B., Harvard, 1930. Admitted to Ala. bar, 1929, Va. bar, 1939; asso. firm Cabaniss, Johnston, Gardner, Dumas & O'Neal, Birmingham, 1930-38, partner, 1946—; gen. solicitor Seaboard AirLine R.R. Co., Norfolk, Va., 1938-42; lt. col., staff Legal Br., Office of Dir. Materiel, Hdqrs. Army Service Forces, Washington, 1942-46; mem. Ala. Constl. Commn.; chmn. com. on Jud. Articles, 1970-76; chmn. Ala. Adv. Commn. on Jud. Article Implementation, 1975; chmn. adv. com. Rules of Jud. Adminstrn., 1976. Trustee Birmingham Mus. Art, 1955—; chmn. bd. trustees Birmingham YWCA, 1970—. Mem. Va., Ala., Birmingham bar assns., Am. Law Inst. (council). Recipient Herbert Harley award for promoting effective adminstrn. of justice, 1977. Home: 2825 Overton Rd Birmingham AL 35223 Office: 1900 First National Southern Natural Bldg Birmingham AL 35203 Tel (205) 252-8800

JOHNSTON, LAWRENCE VINCENT, b. Portsmouth, Va., June 12, 1947; B.A. in Polit. Sci., Fla. Atlantic U., 1969; J.D., U. Fla., 1972. Admitted to Fla. bar, 1972; asst. state's atty. Brevard County (Fla.), 1972-75; judge Cocoa (Fla.) City Ct., 1975-76, Rockledge (Fla.) City Ct., 1975-76; mem. firm Meadows & Johnston, Cocoa, 1975—. Home: 3 S Hardee Circle Rockledge FL 32955 Office: PO Box 1907 Cocoa FL 32922 Tel (303) 636-4953

JOHNSTON, PAUL, b. Birmingham, Ala., Feb. 6, 1908; A.B., Harvard, 1930; LL.B., Yale, 1933. Admitted to Ala. bar, 1933; mem. legal dept. RFC, Washington, 1933-35; asso. firm Cabaniss, Johnston, Gardner & Clark, and predecessors, Birmingham, 1935-41, partner, 1941-65; partner firm Johnston & Shores, Birmingham, 1966—. Mem. Am., Ala., Birmingham bar assns., Am. Law Inst. Named Man of Year, City of Birmingham, 1958; recipient William Crawford Gorgas award Med. Assn. Ala., 1960. Home: 32 Ridge Dr Birmingham AL 35213 Office: 1101 1st Nat-So Natural Bldg Birmingham AL 35203 Tel (205) 251-1261

JOHNSTON, PETER R., b. Detroit, June 7, 1931; A.B., U. Mich., 1953; J.D., Wayne State U., 1958. Admitted to Mich. bar, 1958, U.S. Dist. Ct. bar, 1959; partner law firm Kurth, Bonfiglio & Johnston, Detroit, 1960-67; pvt. practice law, Dearborn, Mich., 1967—. Mem. Mich., Detroit, Dearborn bar assns. Office: 6550 Schaefer Rd Dearborn MI 48126 Tel (313) 846-6777

JOHNSTON, RICHARD LEITER, b. Hagerstown, Md., June 2, 1907; B.S. in Chemistry, Johns Hopkins, 1929; LL.B., George Washington U., 1936. Admitted to D.C. bar, 1935, Ill. bar, 1937; patent asst. E.I. DuPont & Co., Wilmington, Del. and Washington, 1929-31, patent atty., 1932-36; partner firm Johnston, Keil, Thompson & Shurtleff, and predecessors, Chgo., 1936-76; instr. law Northwestern U., Chgo., 1939-42. Mem. Elementary Sch. Bd., Arlington Heights, Ill., 1952-58, pres., 1957-58. Mem. Am., Ill. bar assns., Am., Chgo. (bd. mgrs. 1959-60) patent law assns. Mem. bd. editors George Washington Law Rev., 1935-36. Home: 532 Banbury Rd Arlington Heights IL 60005 Office: 135 S LaSalle St Chicago IL 60603 Tel (312) 236-2953

JOHNSTON, ROBERT GILBERT, b. Walpahu, Hawaii, Nov. 28, 1931; B.A., U. Chgo., 1957, J.D., 1960. Admitted to Ill. bar, 1960, Hawaii bar, 1970; asso. firm Herbert Caplan, Chgo., 1960-64; prof. John Marshall Law Sch., 1965-69, 75—; exec. dir. Legal Aid Soc., Honolulu, 1970-72; individual practice law, Honolulu, 1973-75; reporter Hawaii Penal Procedures Com., 1972-73. Contbr. articles to profl. jours. Office: 315 S Plymouth Ct Chicago IL 60604 Tel (312) 427-2737

JOHNSTON, ROBERT MURRAY, b. Corning, N.Y., Jan. 11, 1941; B.A., Notre Dame, 1963; J.D., Tulane U., 1966. Admitted to La. bar, 1966; asso. firm Beard, Blue, Schmitt & Treen, New Orleans, 1966-72; partner firm Beard, Blue, Schmitt & Maethes, New Orleans, 1973-76, Johnston & Duplass, New Orleans, 1976—. Mem. Am., La. bar assns., Internat. Assn. Ins. Counsel, La., New Orleans assns. defense counsel. Office: 1330 Saratoga Bldg 212 Loyola Ave New Orleans LA 70112 Tel (504) 561-8991

JOHNSTON, ROY EDENS, b. Lufkin, Tex., July 20, 1932; B.B.A., U. Tex., 1954, LL.B., 1955. Admitted to Tex. bar, 1955; individual practice law, San Antonio, 1958—. Mem. Phi Alpha Delta. Home: 259 Geneseo St San Antonio TX 78209 Office: Ar105 Petroleum Center San Antonio TX 78209 Tel (512) 824-9505

JOHNSTON, SHEPHERD DAVIS, b. Miami, Fla., Sept. 17, 1947; B.A., Davidson Coll., 1969; J.D., U. Fla., 1972. Admitted to Fla. bar, 1972; asso. firm Smathers & Thompson, Miami, 1972—. Mem. Dade County, Am. bar assns., Phi Delta Phi. Home: 6401 Snapper Creek Dr Miami FL 33143 Office: 1301 Alfred I DuPont Bldg Miami FL 33131 Tel (305) 379-6523

JOHNSTON, STUART GOODLOE, JR., b. San Antonio, Tex., Sept. 8, 1930; student U. Tex.; J.D. with highest honors, St. Mary's U., 1956. Admitted to Tex. bar, 1956, Okla. bar, 1965; mem. firm Kelso, Locke & King, San Antonio, 1956-59, Stubbeman, McRae, Sealy & Laughlin, Midland, Tex., 1964-68; legal adviser to gen. mgr. Standard Oil of Ohio, Oklahoma City, 1964-68; v.p., gen. counsel Elcor Corp., Midland, 1968-70; individual practice law, Dallas, 1970—. Mem. Am., Tex., Okla., Dallas bar assns. Recipient Lawyer's Title award Lawyers Title Ins. Co., 1956. Home: 12011 Shirestone Ln Dallas TX 75234 Office: 3303 Lee Pkwy Suite 406 Dallas TX 75219 Tel (214) 521-0901

JOHNSTONE, JAMES MCCLURE, b. Denver, July 24, 1934; B.A., Yale, 1955, LL.B., 1960. Admitted to D.C. bar, 1960, U.S. Supreme Ct. bar, 1969; trial atty. antitrust div. Dept. Justice,

Washington, 1960-62; asso. firm Kirkland, Ellis & Rowe, and predecessors, Washington, 1962-65, partner, 1965—. Mem. Am. Bar Assn. Home: 3637 Fulton St NW Washington DC 20007 Office: 1776 K St NW Washington DC 20007 Tel (202) 862-5060

JOHNSTONE, QUINTIN, b. Chgo., Mar. 29, 1915; A.B., U. Chgo., 1936, J.D., 1938; LL.M., Cornell U., 1941; J.S.D., Yale, 1951. Admitted to Ill. bar, 1939, Oreg. bar, 1948; individual practice, Chgo., 1939-40; atty. U.S. Office of Price Adminstrn., 1941-47; mem. faculty Willamette U., 1947-49, U. Kans., 1950-55; dean, prof. law Haile Sellassie I. U., Ethiopia, 1967-69; mem. faculty Yale Law Sch., 1955—, Justus S. Hotchkiss prof. law, 1969—. Mem. Am., Conn. bar assns. Home: 22 Morris St Hamden CT 06517 Office: Law School Yale U New Haven CT 06520 Tel (203) 436-8711

JOHNTZ, JOHN HOFFMAN, JR., b. Alva, Okla., Apr. 26, 1937; A.B., Harvard, 1959; J.D., U. Kans., 1965. Admitted to Kans. bar, 1965, U.S. Dist. Ct. bar for Dist. Kans., 1965, U.S. Supreme Ct. bar, 1971; partner firm Payne & Jones, Chartered, Olathe, Kans., 1965—. Chmn. Bacchus Cultural and Ednl. Found., Kansas City, Mo.; pres. Town and Country Homes Assn., Prairie View, Kans., Harvard-Radcliffe Club of Kansas City. Mem. Johnson County (Kans.), Kans., Am. bar assns., U. Kans. Law Alumni Assn. of Greater Kansas City (pres.), Phi Beta Kappa. Named Internat. Grad. of Year Phi Delta Phi; bd. editors Kans. Bar Jour.; contbr. articles to U. Kans. Law Rev. Home: 4424 W 84th St Shawnee Mission KS 66207 Office: The Tower Bldg PO Box 151 Olathe KS 66061 Tel (913) 782-2500

JOKELSON, NEIL ERIC, b. N.Y.C., May 21, 1944; B.S. in Econs., Wharton Sch. Fin. and Commerce, 1965; J.D. cum laude, Harvard, 1968. Admitted to Pa. bar, 1968; law clk. to Superior Ct. of Pa., 1968-69, sr. law clk., 1971; asso. firm Goodis, Greenfield, Narin & Mann, Phila., 1969-71; mem. firm Jokelson & Rosen, Phila., 1971—; lectr. U. Pa., 1969-72, Baldwin Sch., 1971—. Bd. dirs. Beth Tikvah B'nai Jeshuran Synagogue, 1975. Mem. Phila. Bar Assn., Lawyers Club of Phila. Author: History of the Philomathean Soc. 1813-1968, 1967. Office: 215 S Broad St 7th Floor Philadelphia PA 19107 Tel (215) 735-7556

JOLLES, BERNARD, b. Bklyn., Oct. 5, 1928; B.A., N.Y. U., 1951; LL.B., Lewis and Clark Coll., 1961. Admitted to Oreg. bar, 1963; asso. firm Anderson, Franklin, Jones & Olson, Portland, Oreg., 1963-65; partner firm Franklin, Bennett, Ofert & Jolles, Portland, 1966—; instr. law Lewis and Clark Coll., 1970—. Mem. Am. Bar Assn., Am., Oreg. trial lawyers assns. Home: 2820 NE 18th Ave Portland OR 97212 Office: 3232 1st Nat Bank Tower Portland OR 97201 Tel (503) 225-0870

JOLLES, IRA HERVEY, b. N.Y.C., Dec. 12, 1938; A.B., Columbia Coll., 1959; J.D., Harvard U., 1962. Admitted to N.Y. state bar, 1963; asso. firm Breed, Abbott & Morgan, N.Y.C., 1963-66; dir. N.Y.C. Income Tax Bur., 1966-68; asso. firm Berlack, Israels & Liberman, N.Y.C., 1968-70, partner 1970—. Dir. Forest Hills Community House, N.Y.C., 1975—; mem. nat. exec. council Am. Jewish Com., 1975—. Mem. Am. Bar Assn., Assn. Bar City N.Y. Home: 610 W End Ave New York City NY 10024 Office: 26 Broadway St New York City NY 10004 Tel (212) 248-6900

JOLLY, RAYMOND ALONZO, JR., b. Anderson, S.C., Feb. 23, 1936; B.A. in English, U. N.C., 1958, J.D., 1961. Admitted to N.C. bar, 1961; served with JAGC, USAF, 1961-64; asso. firm Ruff; Perry; Bond, Cobb Wade, Charlotte, N.C., 1964-67; partner, 1968-70, partner firm Hedrick McKnight, Parham, Helms, Warley & Holly, Charlotte, 1971-72; asso. gen. counsel Duke Power Co., Charlotte, 1972—; instr. real estate law Central Piedmont Community Coll., 1970-72. Mem. Am., N.C. bar assn., N.C. State Bar, 26th Jud. Dist. Bar (sec. 1970-71), Phi Beta Kappa. Home: 1509 Scotland Ave Charlotte NC 28207 Office: 422 S Church St POB 2178 Charlotte NC 28242 Tel (704) 373-8018

JOLY, CYRIL MATTHEW, JR., b. Waterville, Maine, May 22, 1925; B.A., Colby Coll., 1948; J.D., Boston U., 1951. Admitted to Maine bar, 1951; mem. firms Joly & Marden, Waterville, 1951-61, Joly & Joly, 1961—; spl. asst. to Sec. HEW, 1955-56; dir. pub. affairs NAM, N.Y.C., 1957-60; mayor City of Waterville, 1962-65; mem. Maine Senate, 1973-74. Rep. state chmn., Maine, 1967-70; Rep. nat. committeeman, 1973—. Mem. Maine, Kennebec County, Waterville bar assns. Home: 63 Mayflower Hill Dr Waterville ME 04901 Office: 222 Main St Waterville ME 04901 Tel (207) 872-5568

JONAS, ALAN LESTER, b. Bklyn., Oct. 7, 1931; LL.B., DePaul U., 1954. Admitted to Ill. bar, 1954; asso. firm Epton, Scott, McCarthy & Epton, Chgo., 1954-58, George M. Schatz, Chgo., 1958-63; individual practice law, Chgo., 1963-67; partner firm Jonas, Schey & Assos., Chgo., 1967—. Mem. Am., Chgo., Ill. bar assns., Def. Research Inst., Decalogue Soc. Lawyers, Trial Lawyers Club Chgo. Office: 188 W Randolph St Chicago IL 60601 Tel (312) 263-0057

JONAS, JOHN, b. Chgo., June 21, 1922; student Western Mich. U., 1941-43; B.B.A., U. Mich., 1947, M.B.A., 1948; LL.B., Wayne State U., 1951. Admitted to Mich. bar, 1952, Ind. bar, 1973; tax accountant Ernst & Ernst, Detroit, 1951-53; tax analyst Gen. Motors Corp., Detroit 1953-55; tax analyst Gen. Motors Corp., Detroit, 1953-55; tax adminstr. Isenberg Newman & Co., Detroit, 1955-58; chief tax counsel Burroughs Corp.; Detroit, 1958-67; tax atty., treas. CTS Corp., Elkhart, Ind., 1967-72; individual practice law, Elkhart, 1972—. Mem. Am., Ind. bar assns., Am. Inst. C.P.A.'s. C.P.A., Mich., Ind. Home: 1520 Ash Dr E Elkhart IN 46514 Office: 219 S 3d St Elkhart IN 46514 Tel (219) 293-7751

JONES, ALBERT PEARSON, b. Dallas, July 19, 1907; B.A., U. Tex., 1927, M.A., 1927, LL.B., 1930. Admitted to Tex. bar, 1930, U.S. Supreme Ct. bar, 1950; asso. firm Baker & Botts, Houston, 1930-43; partner firm Helm & Jones, 1943-62; Joseph C. Hutcheson prof. law U. Tex., Austin, 1962—; 1st asst. atty. gen. Tex., 1963; pres. Texas Law Rev. Publs., Inc. 1971-74, State Bar Tex., 1950-51. Fellow Am. Coll. Trial Lawyers; mem. Am., Tex. bar assns., Am. Law Inst., Am. Judicature Soc., Nat. Legal Aid and Defender Assn., Phi Beta Kappa, Phi Delta Phi. Co-author: Texas Trial and Appellate Procedure, 1974; The Judicial Process in Texas Prior to Trial, 2d edit., 1977; author: Cases and Materials on Employees' Rights, 1970; contbr. articles to law jours. Home: 4 Niles Rd Austin TX 78703 Office: 2500 Red River Austin TX 78705 Tel (512) 471-5151

JONES, ALEXANDER GRAY, b. Princess Anne, Md., Mar. 25, 1927; B.A., Washington Coll., 1951; postgrad. (Fulbright scholar), U. Sheffield (Eng.), 1951-52; J.D., U. Md., 1955. Admitted to Md. bar, 1955; partner firm Jones & Jones, Princess Anne, 1955-74, pres., 1974—. Mem. standing com. on rules of practice and procedure Ct. of Appeals of Md., 1969—; bd. visitors, bd. govs. Washington Coll., 1967—. Mem. Am., Md. (gov. 1967-68, 74-75), Somerset County bar assns. Home: Linden Ave Princess Anne MD 21853 Office: 311 S Somerset Ave Princess Anne MD 21853 Tel (301) 651-2747

JONES, BENJAMIN ROWLAND, b. Wilkes-Barre, Pa., May 29, 1906; student Wyoming Sem., Kington, Pa., 1923; A.B., Princeton, 1927; LL.B., U. Pa., 1930. Admitted to Pa. bar, 1930; partner Bedford, Waller, Jones & Darling, Wilkes-Barre, 1930-51; pres. judge Orphans' Ct. of Luzerne County, 1952-57; justice Pa. Supreme Ct., 1957-72, chief justice, 1972—. Trustee Wyoming Sem. Mem. Am., Pa. bar assns., Wilkes-Barre Law and Library Assn. (past pres.). Home: RD 2 Benton PA 17814 Office: 464 City Hall Philadelphia PA 19107*

JONES, C. PAUL, b. Grand Forks, N.D., Jan. 7, 1927; B.B.A., U. Minn., 1950, J.D., 1950; LL.M., William Mitchell Coll. Law, 1955. Admitted to Minn. bar, 1951, U.S. Supreme Ct. bar, 1960; asso. firm Lewis, Hammer, Heaney, Weyl & Halverson, Duluth, Minn., 1950-51, Maun & Hazel, St. Paul, 1960-61; asst. to county atty. Hennepin County (Minn.), 1952-55, chief dep. asst., 1955-58; asst. U.S. atty. Minn. dist., 1959-60; partner firm Dorfman, Rudquist, Jones, & Ramstead, Mpls., 1961-65; state pub. defender State of Minn., Mpls., 1966—; prof. William Mitchell Coll. Law, 1970—; adj. prof. law U. Minn., 1970—; mem. Minn. Supreme Ct. Adv. Com. on Rules of Criminal Procedure; mem. Minn. Supreme Ct. Jud. Council Select Com. on Structure and Financing of Minn. Ct. System; mem. Minn. Gov's Crime Commn. Active Minn. Fair Trial-Free Press Assn., Citizens' League, Mpls.-St. Paul. Mem. Am., Minn. State, Hennepin County, Ramsey County (Minn.) bar assns., Am. Judicature Soc., Nat. Legal Aid Defender Assn., Nat. Dist. Attys. Assn., Am. Trial Lawyers Assn. Organizer Legal Assistance to Minn. Prisoners, 1972, Legal Assistance of Minn., 1974. Home: 4617 Edina Blvd Minneapolis MN 55424 Office: Law Sch U of Minn Minneapolis MN 55455 Tel (612) 373-5725

JONES, C. RANDALL, JR., b. Pineville, Miss., Aug. 20, 1919; B.S.C., U. Miss., 1942; LL.B., U. Va., 1948, J.D., 1970. Admitted to Miss. bar, 1948; individual practice law, Pass Christian, Miss., 1948—; chmn. Harrison County (Miss.) Law Library, 1966—. Mem. Am., Harrison County (pres. 1971), Miss. State bar assns., Pass Christian C. of C. (pres. 1958). Home: 11 Wisteria Dr Pass Christian MS 39571 Office: 115 E Beach St Heritage Bldg Pass Christian MS 39571 Tel (601) 452-4154

JONES, CARLETON SHAW, b. N.Y.C., Sept. 8, 1942; B.A., Denison U., 1964; LL.B., Yale, 1967. Admitted to Ohio bar, 1967, Fla. bar, 1971, D.C. bar, 1973; law clk. U.S. Ct. Appeals 6th Circuit, 1967; dep. gen. counsel Price Commn., Exec. Office of the Pres., Washington, 1971-73; asso. firm Shaw, Pittman, Potts & Trowbridge, Washington, 1973—. Mem. Am., D.C. bar assns., Phi Beta Kappa. Office: 1800 M St NW Washington DC 20036 Tel (202) 331-4100

JONES, CHARLES EDWIN, b. McLeansboro, Ill., Sept. 14, 1924; B.S., U. Ill., 1948, J.D., 1950. Admitted to Ill. bar, 1950; practiced in McLeansboro, 1950-54; judge Hamilton County (Ill.) Ct., 1954-58; asso. judge Hamilton County Circuit Ct., 1962-64; judge Ill. 2d Jud. Circuit Ct., 1962-74, Ill. Appellate Ct., 1974—. Trustee Wesley Found., U. Ill. Mem. Ill. Bar Assn., U. Ill. Alumni Assn. (dir.), VFW. Decorated Air medal. Home: W Randolph St McLeansboro IL 62859 Office: POB 40 McLeansboro IL 62859 Tel (618) 643-2822

JONES, CHESTER LLOYD, b. Orange, N.J., Dec. 21, 1921; student Yale, 1943; LL.B., U. Mich., 1948. Admitted to Colo. bar, 1949, Mont. bar, 1951; with Phillips Petroleum Co., Denver, 1948-50; individual practice law, Virginia City, Mont., 1951—; atty. Madison County (Mont.), 1955—. Mem. Am., Mont. bar assns., Mont. County Attys. Assn. Home: Box 176 Ennis MT 59729 Office: Box 347 Virginia City MT 59755 Tel (406) 843-5413

JONES, CHESTER S., b. Upton, Wyo., Dec. 11, 1920; B.A., U. Wyo., 1942, LL.B., 1947. Admitted to Wyo bar, 1947; partner firm Wakeman & Jones, Newcastle, Wyo., 1947-50; individual practice law, Newcastle, 1950-52; partner firm Jones & Dumbrill, Newcastle, 1952—; county, atty. Weston County, Wyo., 1949-59, dist. ct. commr. Weston County, Wyo. 1960—, commr. Wyo. State Bar. Pres., mem. bd. Weston County Hosp. 1972—. Mem. A.B.A., Weston County, Wyo. State Bars, Trial Lawyers Assn. Home: 118 Donielson Dr Newcastle WY 82701 Office: 18 W Main Newcastle WY 82701 Tel (307) 746-2926

JONES, CHRISTIAN TREVOR, b. Chgo., Apr. 6, 1943; B.A., Occidental Coll., Los Angeles, 1965; J.D., Northwestern U., 1968. Admitted to Ill. bar, 1968; gen. atty. Household Fin. Corp., Chgo., 1969—. Mem. Am., Ill., Chgo. bar assns. Editor: Comsumer Finance Law Bull. 1976—; author: (with Roger S. Barrett) Summary of State Consumer Credit Laws and Rates, 5th edit., 1976. Office: Suite 3200 Prudential Plaza Chicago IL 60601 Tel (312) 944-7174

JONES, CLARENCE ROLAND, JR., b. Spartanburg, S.C., Apr. 4, 1945; A.B., Wofford Coll., 1967; postgrad. U. N.C., 1967-68; J.D., U. S.C., 1972. Admitted to S.C. bar, 1972; teaching asso. U. S.C. Law Center, 1972-74; clk. U.S. Dist. Ct. for S.C. dist., 1974-75; asst. solicitor for 7th Jud. Circuit, Spartanburg, S.C., 1975—. Mem. S.C., Spartanburg County bar assns. Author: History of the Magistrate System in South Carolina, 1971. Home: 33 Lucille Ct Spartanburg SC 29302 Office: Spartanburg County Ct House Spartanburg SC 29301 Tel (804) 585-4811

JONES, DENNIS LEE, b. Cheyenne, Wyo., July 21, 1941; A.A., George Washington U., 1963, B.A., 1964; J.D., U. Maine, 1969. Admitted to Maine bar, 1969; asso. firm Clark and Jones; and predecessor, Gardiner, Maine, 1969-71, partner, 1972—. Mem. Bowdoinham (Maine) Zoning Bd., 1973. Mem. Maine, Am. bar assns., Maine, Am. trial lawyer assns. Home: RFD 2 Richmond ME 04357 Office: 2 Church St Gardiner ME 04345 Tel (207) 582-6550

JONES, DWAIN LEON, b. Lincoln, Nebr., Jan. 4, 1927; B.A., Nebr. Wesleyan U., 1950; LL.B., U. Nebr., 1958. Admitted to Nebr. bar 1958, Minn. bar 1962, Ohio bar 1966, Ill. bar 1969; asst. atty. gen. State of Nebr., Lincoln, 1960-62; gen. counsel Western Life Ins. Co., St. Paul, 1962-66; sr. counsel Western & So. Life Ins. Co., St. Paul, 1966-69; sr. v.p. and gen. counsel Benefit Trust Life Ins. Co., Chgo., 1969—, dir., 1971—. Mem. Am., Ill., Nebr., Chgo. bar assns., Assn. of Life Ins. Counsel. Office: 1771 Howard St Chicago IL 60676 Tel (312) 274-8100

JONES, ERIC LANCE, b. Washington, Nov. 28, 1938; B.B.A., U. Ga., 1961, LL.B. cum laude, 1963. Admitted to Ga. bar, 1963; mem. firm Jones, Jones & Hilburn, Dublin, Ga., 1963—. Mem. Am., Georgia bar assns., Phi Delta Phi. Home: 1506 Camellia Dr Dublin GA 31021 Office: 205 N Franklin St Dublin GA 31021 Tel (912) 272-1260

JONES, FORREST LEE, b. Houston, Nov. 25, 1939; B.B.A., So. Meth. U., 1962, LL.B., 1965. Admitted to Tex. bar, 1965; individual practice law, Donna, Tex., 1965—; partner firms Rankin, Kern, Martinez & Jones, Donna and McAllen, Tex., 1975-76, Smith, McIlheran, Lauderpole & Jones, Weslaco, Tex., 1977—. Mem. Hidalgo County (Tex.) (dir.), Am. bar assns. Recipient Outstanding Young Lawyer State of Tex. award Tex. Jr. Bar Assn., 1972. Home: 1603 Scobey St Donna TX 78537 Office: 123 S 8th St Donna TX 78537 Tel (512) 464-3552

JONES, GLOWER WHITEHEAD, b. Atlanta, May 4, 1936; A.B., Dartmouth, 1958; J.D. with distinction, Emory U., 1963. Admitted to Ga. bar, 1962, Ga. Supreme Ct. bar; asso. firm Smith, Currie & Hancock, Atlanta, 1963-67, partner, 1967—. Bd. dirs. Met. Atlanta Boys Clubs, 1965—, asst. sec., 1973—; charter mem., bd. dirs., sec., v.p. Decatur-DeKalb Boys Club; bd. dirs. Samuel L. Jones Boys Club, So. region Boys Clubs Am., Child Services and Family Counselling, Carrie-Steele Pitts Home; bd. dirs., asst. treas. Gate City Day Nursery Assn.; trustee, pres. Atlanta Florence Crittenton Services, 1971-73. Mem. Am., Fed., Ga. (com. mem.), Atlanta (chmn. prepaid legal com. 1976-77) bar assns., Am. Judicature Soc., Trial Attys. Am., Am. Assn. Trial Lawyers, Atlanta Lawyers Club. Mem. editorial bd. Ga. State Bar Jour., 1976; recipient Golden Boy award Boys Clubs Am., 1971. Home: 997 Viscount Ct Avondale Estates GA 30002 Office: 2600 Harris Tower Peachtree Center Complex 233 Peachtree St NE Atlanta GA 30303 Tel (404) 521-3800

JONES, GRANVILLE PHILIP, b. Johnson County, Ill., Apr. 10, 1925; student So. Ill. U., Carbondale, 1947-49, Meridian Jr. Coll., 1964, Jackson Sch. Law, 1953. Admitted to Miss. bar, 1953; individual practice law, Meridian, Miss., 1953-76; sr. partner firm Jones, Shields and Woodall, Meridian, 1976—. Mem. Lauderdale County (Miss.), Miss. State, Am. bar assns. Home: Knob Hill Route 1 PO Box 55 B Collinsville MS 39325 Office: 102 Shields Bldg PO Box 1562 Meridian MS 39301 Tel (601) 693-1343

JONES, HARRIS WEBSTER, b. Meridian, Miss., Jan. 7, 1945; B.B.A., U. Miss., 1967, J.D., 1972. Admitted to Miss. bar, 1972; individual practice law, Meridian, 1972—. Mem. Am., Lauderdale County, Miss. bar assns. Home: 1616 11th Ave Meridian MS 39301 Office: Suite 1012 Great Miss Life Bldg Meridian MS 39301 Tel (601) 693-2683

JONES, HARTWELL KELLEY, JR., b. Columbia, S.C., Mar. 4, 1941; B.J., U. S.C., 1963, M.A. in Internat. Studies, 1966, J.D., 1970. Reporter, Columbia Record, 1961-64; press sec. to S.C. Rep. A.W. Watson, 1964-67; reporter govt. affairs, night city editor The State Newspaper, Columbia, 1967-70; admitted to S.C. bar, 1970, U.S. Supreme Ct. bar, 1976; legal asst., press sec. to Gov. S.C., 1970-74; gen. counsel S.C. Dept. Ins., Columbia, 1974—. Mem. Am., S.C. bar assns., Nat., S.C. wildlife fedns., Bass Anglers Sportsman Soc., Am. Bass Fishermen, Bass Fishing Club Am. Home: 2609 Riverland Dr Cayce SC 29033 Office: 2711 Middleburg Dr Columbia SC 29204 Tel (803) 758-2861

JONES, HELEN HART, b. Lakewood, Ohio, July 30, 1921; A.B., Miami U., Oxford, Ohio, 1943; LL.B., Western Res. U., 1945; LL.M., Northwestern U., 1950. Admitted to Ohio bar, 1943, Ill. bar, 1952; atty. NLRB, Washington, 1946-47; asso. gen. counsel Chgo. Housing Authority, 1947-49; asso. firm Cotton, Watt, Jones, King and Bowlus, Chgo., 1954-59, partner, 1959—; lectr. Northwestern U. Sch. Law, 1974—. Bd. dirs. Ill. div. ACLU, 1976—. Mem. Chgo. Council Lawyers (dir. 1974-76), Chgo., Ill. bar assns., Women's Bar Assn. of Ill. (pres. 1967-68). Home: 4820 S Kenwood Ave Chicago IL 60615 Office: Suite 4750 One IBM Plaza Chicago IL 60611 Tel (312) 467-0590

JONES, HERBERT JOHN, b. Titusville, Pa., Jan. 10, 1926; A.B., Coll. Wooster, 1950; J.D., U. Fla., 1955. Admitted to Fla. bar, 1955; individual practice law, Gainesville, Fla., 1955—. Mem. Am., Eighth Jud. Circuit bar assns., Fla. Bar. Contbr. articles to legal publs. Office: 515 N Main St Gainesville FL 32602 Tel (904) 377-1778

JONES, HUGH RICHARD, b. New Hartford, N.Y., Mar. 19, 1914; B.A., Hamilton Coll., 1935, LL.D., 1974; J.D., Harvard U., 1939. Admitted to N.Y. bar, 1940, U.S. Supreme Ct. bar; asso. firm Burke & Burke, N.Y.C., 1939-42; partner firm Evans, Burdick, Severn & Jones and predecessor firms, Utica, 1949-72; asso. judge N.Y. Ct. of Appeals, 1973—. Chancellor, Episcopal Diocese Central N.Y., 1957—, lay dep. Gen. Conv., 1952, 58, 61, 64, 67, 70, 73, 76, Spl. Gen. Conv. II, 1969; del. Anglican Congress, Toronto, 1963; chmn. Alumni Fund, Hamilton Coll., 1957-58, Alumni Council, 1962-63, trustee, 1967—; chmn. N.Y. State Select Com. on Correctional Instns. and Programs, 1971-72; co-chmn. N.Y. State Citizens Com. for Revenue Sharing, 1971-72; chmn. N.Y. State Bd. Social Welfare, 1964-69; pres. N.Y. State Assn. Councils and Chests, 1950-52, Family Service Assn. Am., 1955-57, N.Y. State Welfare Conf., 1959; bd. dirs. Am. Pub. Welfare Assn., 1967; mem. exec. com. Nat. Social Welfare Conf., 1958-61; trustee State U. N.Y., 1969-72. Fellow Am. Coll. Probate Council, Am. Bar Found.; mem. Am. Law Inst., Am., N.Y. State (pres. 1971-72, chmn. exec. com. 1970-71, chmn. com. on profl. ethics 1959-63, chmn. tax sect. 1967), Oneida County (pres. 1962) bar assns., Assn. Bar City of New York, Am. Judicature Soc. Recipient Humanitarian award for services to Spanish Speaking Community N.Y., 1969, Civic award Colgate U., 1970, William R. Hopkins Bronze medal St. Davids Soc. N.Y., 1974. Home: 111 Paris Rd New Hartford NY 13413 Office: Oneida County Court House Utica NY 13501 Tel (315) 798-5909

JONES, J. MAYNARD, b. Utica, N.Y., Dec. 7, 1909; B.S., Hamilton Coll., 1932. Admitted to N.Y. bar, 1937; law clk. firm Miles W. Jones, Utica, N.Y., 1932-37; with firm Judson & Jones, and predecessor, Utica, N.Y., asso., 1937-41, partner, 1941-49; surrogate judge Oneida County (N.Y.), Utica, 1949—; asst. dist. atty. Oneida County, 1939-49. Mem. N.Y. State, Oneida County bar assns., N.Y. State Surrogates Assn. Office: Ct House Utica NY 13501 Tel (315) 798-5866

JONES, JAMES REESE, b. Brenham, Tex., July 1, 1949; B.B.A., Tex. Christian U., 1971; J.D., Baylor U., 1973. Admitted to Tex. bar, 1973; mem. firm Hollon & Marion, Boerne, Tex., 1974-76; individual practice law, Brenham, Tex., 1976—. Mem. Am. Bar Assn., State Bar Tex. Editorial bd. Baylor Law Rev. Home: 407 Tison St Brenham TX 77833 Office: 205 E Vulcan St Brenham TX 77833 Tel (713) 836-4679

JONES, JERALD ELTON, b. Ripley, W.Va., Dec. 1, 1932; A.B., Marshall U., 1954; LL.B., W.Va. U., 1959. Admitted to W.Va. bar, 1959; asso. firm Deem & Marstiller, Clarksburg, W.Va., 1959-66, partner, 1966-68; partner firm Jones, Williams, West & Jones, Clarksburg, 1969—. Chmn. Harrison County (W.Va.) Republican Exec. Com., 1962-65; mem. W.Va. Rep. Exec. Com., 1968-70; mem. Clarksburg Policemen's CSC, 1972—; dir. Central Dist. Mental

Health Center. Mem. W.Va., Am. bar assns., W.Va. State Bar, W.Va. Trial Lawyers Assn. Recipient Patrick Duffy Koontz Scholarship award; editor W.Va. Law Rev., 1956-59. Home: 611 Joseph St Clarksburg WV 26301 Office: Union Bank Bldg Clarksburg WV 26301 Tel (304) 624-5501

JONES, JERRY P., b. Bovina, Tex., Nov. 15, 1931; B.S., W. Tex. State Coll., 1953; LL.B., U. Tex., 1959. Admitted to Tex. bar; mem. firm Thompson, Knight, Simmons & Bullion, Dallas, 1959—. Mem. Am. Arbitration Assn., Tex., Dallas Assns. def. counsel, Am. Bar Assn., Am. Bd. Trial Advs. Home: 7220 Meadow Rd Dallas TX 75230 Office: 2300 Republic Nat Bank Bldg Dallas TX 75201 Tel (214) 655-7527

JONES, JERRY SEBERT, b. Johnson City, Tenn., Feb. 9, 1944; B.S., E. Tenn. State U., 1968; J.D., U. Tenn., 1973. Admitted to Tenn. bar, 1974; law clerk, asso. firm Alfred W. Taylor, Milligan Coll., Tenn., 1973-74; individual practice law, Johnson City, 1974—; judge City of Watauga, Tenn., 1975—; tchr. law Steed Coll., 1975—. Bd. dirs. Juvenile Home, Johnson City. Mem. Am., Tenn., Washington County bar assns., Am. Trial Lawyers Assn., Johnson City C. of C., E. Tenn. U. Alumni Assn., U. Tenn. Alumni Assn. Office: 802 Buffalo St Johnson City TN 37601 Tel (615) 929-8821

JONES, JOHN BAILEY, b. Mitchell, S.D., Mar. 30, 1927; B.B.A., U. S.D., 1951, LL.B., 1953. Admitted to S.D. bar, 1953; judge County Lyman, S.D., 1953-56; individual practice law, Presho, S.D., 1953-67; judge Circuit Ct. S.D., Kennebec, 1967—; mem. S.D. Jud. Qualifications Commn., 1973—; mem. S.D. Ho. of Reps., 1957-61. Mem. S.D. Bar Assn., S.D. Judges Assn. (pres.). Home: Box 287 Presho SD 57568 Office: Court House Kennebec SD 57544 Tel (605) 869-2275

JONES, JOHN FRANK, b. Carrington, N.D., Feb. 24, 1922; B.S., U. N.D., 1946; M.S. in Organic Chemistry, U. Wis., 1953; J.D., U. Akron, 1956. Admitted to Ohio bar, 1956; patent atty. B.F. Goodrich Co., Akron, Ohio, 1956-62; sr. patent atty. Standard Oil Co., Cleve., 1962-70, patent counsel, 1970—; food and drug atty. Vistron Corp. subs. Standard Oil Co., Cleve., 1968—. Mem. Am., Ohio bar assns., Am., Cleve. patent law assns., Am. Chem. Soc. Patentee in field of polymer chemistry. Contbr. articles to chem. jours. Home: 2724 Cedar Hill Rd Cuyahoga Falls OH 44223 Office: Midland Bldg Cleveland OH 44115 Tel (216) 575-5616

JONES, JOHN MELVIN, b. Detroit, June 30, 1944; B.A. in History, Howard U., 1967; J.D., 1970, M.B.A., U. Pa., 1972. Admitted to Pa. bar, 1973, U.S. Supreme Ct. bar, 1976; cons. firm Johnson & Higgins, Phila., 1971-73; pension dept. head Rittenhouse Assos., Phila., 1973-74; asso. prof. law and ins. Pa. State U., 1974—; asst. rep. U.S. Commn. on Civil Rights, Washington, 1967-68; law clk. U.S. Indian Claims Commn., Washington, 1970. Mem. edn. com. NAACP, Harrisburg, Pa., 1974-75; vols. in probation, Harrisburg, 1975-77. Mem. Am., Pa., Dauphin County, Phila. bar assns., Am. Bus. Law Assn., (treas. NE region), Harrisburg Jaycees. Contbr. articles to legal jours. Office: 2 N Market Sq Harrisburg PA 17101 Tel (717) 236-4241

JONES, JOSEPH ALVA, b. Needham, Ind., June 28, 1936; B.S. in Chem. Engring., Purdue U., 1958, J.D. (Dedication scholar, Faculty award), Ind. U., 1972. Admitted to Ind. bar, 1972; chem. engr. Procter & Gamble Co., Cin., 1958-59; chem. engr. Eli Lilly & Co., Indpls., 1959-70; liaison, Greenfield, Ind., 1970-73; patent atty., Greenfield, 1973-76, Indpls., 1976—. Active Boy Scouts Am., Indpls., 1967—. Mem. Ind. Bar Assn. (sec.-treas. patent, trademark and copyright sect. 1976-77), Am. Patent Law Assn. Editor, Ind. Legal Forum, 1970, editor-in-chief, 1971. Office: 307 E McCarty St Indianapolis IN 46206 Tel (317) 261-3474

JONES, KEITH ALDEN, b. Tulsa, July 11, 1941; B.A., Harvard, 1963, LL.B., 1966. Admitted to Mass. bar, 1966, U.S. Supreme Ct. bar, 1972; asst. prof. law Boston U., 1966-67; lectr. in law Harvard, 1967-68; asso. firm Ropes & Gray, Boston, 1968-70; minority counsel U.S. Senate Select Com. on Small Bus., Washington, 1970-72; asst. to solicitor gen. of U.S., Dept. Justice, Washington, 1972-75, dep. solicitor gen., 1975—. Mem. Harvard Law Sch. Assn. Home: 3111 34th St NW Washington DC 20008 Office: Dept of Justice Washington DC 20530 Tel (202) 739-4281

JONES, LAMRA, b. Newport, N.C.; A.B., U. N.C., 1950, J.D., 1952. Admitted to N.C. bar, 1953; individual practice law, Kinston, N.C., 1953—. Mem. N.C., Lenoir County bar assns., Comml. Law League, N.C. Acad. Trial Lawyers. Home: 1203 Greenbriar Rd Kinston NC 28501 Office: 111 S Queen St Kinston NC 28501 Tel (919) 523-8121

JONES, LAURENCE MONTGOMERY, b. Clear Lake, Iowa, Sept. 29, 1908; A.B., U. Iowa, 1930, J.D., 1932; LL.M., Harvard, 1933, S.J.D., 1934. Admitted to Iowa bar, 1932; asso. with Ira W. Jones, Clear Lake, 1932-35; asst. prof. law Emory U., Atlanta, 1935-39, asso. prof., 1939-41; vis. asso. prof. law, U. Mo., Columbia, 1941-42, U. Md., Balt., 1942-46, prof., 1946—. Mem. Md. State Bar Assn. Contbr. articles to legal publs. Home: 100 W Cold Spring Ln Baltimore MD 21210 Office: Univ Maryland Sch Law 500 W Baltimore St Baltimore MD 21201 Tel (301) 528-7194

JONES, LEWIS E., b. Anderson, Ind., May 2, 1928; B.S. in Bus., Ind. U., 1950; LL.B., Boston Coll., 1952. Admitted to Ind. bar, 1953; partner firm Jones, Withers, Ketner & Adair, Anderson, 1953—; house atty. Ind. Ho. Reps., 1955-63; asst. city atty. Anderson, 1964-66, 70-72; probate commr. Madison County Superior Ct., 1967-70; atty. Madison County Planning and Zoning Commn., 1974-76. Mem. Ind. State, Madison County bar assns. Home: 5106 Kingswood Ln Anderson IN 46011 Office: 813 Meridian St PO Box 1036 Anderson IN 46016 Tel (317) 649-3551

JONES, LIGON LEE, b. Hopewell, Va., Dec. 29, 1916; B.S., Randolph-Macon Coll., 1939; LL.B., U. Richmond, 1942. Admitted to Va. bar, 1941; practiced in Hopewell, 1942-62; mem. Va. Ho. of Dels., 1948-50; commonwealth atty. City of Hopewell, 1950-62; judge Va. Circuit Ct., 3d Jud. Circuit, 1962—. Mem. Phi Beta Kappa. Recipient Murray Proficiency medal Randolph-Macon Coll., 1936, Smithey Math. medal, 1939, Murray Scholarship medal, 1939; named Best Grad. U. Richmond Law Sch., 1942. Home: 600 Riverside St Hopewell VA 23860 Office: POB 269 Municipal Bldg Hopewell VA 23860 Tel (804) 458-1281

JONES, LOUIS BUCKNER, JR., b. Memphis, Aug. 12, 1946; B.A. in History and Polit. Sci., Hendrix Coll., Conway, Ark., 1968; J.D. U. Ark., 1972. Admitted to Ark. bar, 1972; asso. firm Butler and Hicky, Forrest City, Ark., 1972-74; partner Butler, Hicky & Jones, 1975—; treas. St. Francis County Abstract Co., Inc., 1974-76, pres., 1976—. Deacon First Baptist Ch., Forrest City; bd. dirs., pres. St. Francis County (Ark.) Center for Exceptional Children, 1973-76; pres. East Ark. Community Concert Assn., 1974-76. Mem. Forrest City C. of C. (dir.), Am., Ark. (mem. exec. council young lawyers sec. 1976—), St. Francis County bar assns., Hendrix Coll. Alumni Assn. (sec. 1975—), Phi Alpha Delta. Office: POB 830 First Natonal Bank Bldg Forrest City AR 72335 Tel (501) 633-4611

JONES, MARK E., b. Indpls., Oct. 15, 1920; B.A., Roosevelt U., 1948; J.D., Loyola U., Chgo., 1950. Admitted to Ill. bar, 1950; asst. states atty. Cook County, Ill., 1951-57; mem. firm McCoy, Ming & Leighton, Chgo., 1958-62; partner firm Tate & Jones, Chgo., 1962-63; judge Cook County Circuit Ct., Chgo., 1963—. Trustee, Roosevelt Univ., Chgo., 1967-71; bd. dir. NAACP, Chgo., 1960-68, Better Boys Found., Chgo., 1960—. Mem. Nat. (treas., charter mem. Jud. Council), Am., Cook County bar assns. Recipient Eleanor Roosevelt Key award, Roosevelt U. Alumni; contbr. to law rev. publs. Office: Chicago Civic Center Chicago IL 60602 Tel (312) 443-8290

JONES, MARVIN ENNIS, b. Bernie, Mo., June 8, 1921; student SE Mo. State U., 1939-41; J.D., U. Mo., 1950. Admitted to Mo. bar, 1950; atty. MFA Mutual Ins. Co., Dexter, Mo., 1951-58; partner firm Powell & Jones (then Powell, Jones & Ringer), Dexter, 1958-67; commr. Mo. Pub. Service Comm., Jefferson City, 1967-71, chmn., 1971-73; adminstrv. law judge U.S. EPA, Kansas City, Mo., 1973—. Chmn., Stoddard County (Mo.) Welfare Comm., 1951-65; mem. Dexter Library Bd., 1961-67; chmn. Dexter United Fund, 1959; chmn., bd. dir. First Baptist Ch. Dexter, 1962-63. Mem. Mo. (adminstrv. law com.), Am., Fed., Stoddard County (former pres.) bar assns., Midwest Assn. RR and Utility Commr's. (former pres.), Am. Judicature Soc. Contbr. articles Jour. Mo. Bar, Pub. Utilities Fortnightly. Home: 608 W 50th St Kansas City MO 64112 Office: 1735 Baltimore St Kansas City MO 64108 Tel (816) 374-5495

JONES, MARY GARDINER, b. N.Y.C., Dec. 10, 1920; B.A., Wellesley Coll., 1943; J.D., Yale U., 1948; LL.D., N.Y. Law Sch., 1976. Admitted to N.Y. state bar, 1948, also U.S. Supreme Ct. bar, D.C. bar; asso. firm Donovan, Leisure, Newton & Irvine, N.Y.C., 1948-53; trial atty. antitrust div. U.S. Dept. Justice, N.Y.C., 1953-60; asso. firm Webster, Sheffield, Fleischmann, Hitchcock & Chrystie, N.Y.C., 1960-64; mem. FTC, Washington, 1964-73; prof. U. Ill., Champaign, 1974-75, adj. prof. 1975—; v.p. consumer affairs dept. Western Union Telegraph Co., Washington, 1975; dir. MCA, Inc., Los Angeles, Safeway Stores, San Francisco, Alcen Labs.; cons. in field. Trustee Wellesley Coll., 1971—, Colgate U., 1972—, N.Y. U. Law Sch., 1976—. Mem. Council Econ. Priorities, Am. Soc. Info. Sci., Nat. Consumers League (pres.), Nat. Assn. Women Lawyers, AAUW, D.C. Bar Assn., Am. Bar Assn., Am. Home Economics Assn. (hon.). Editor: (with David Gardner) Consumerism, 1976; contbr. articles to profl. jours. Home: 1631 Suter's Ln NW Washington DC 20007 Office: 1828 L St NW Washington DC 20036 Tel (202) 624-0117

JONES, MICHAEL RIDGWAY, SR., b. Royston, Ga., May 20, 1942; B.B.A., U. Ga., 1964; postgrad. Ga. State U., 1969-72; J.D., Woodrow Wilson Coll. Law, Atlanta, 1973. Admitted to Ga. bar, 1973; individual practice law, Monroe, Ga., 1973, Loganville, Ga., 1973—; judge City of Loganville, 1973-74; atty., 1975—. Mem. Monroe Housing Authority, 1975—, Loganville City Council, 1976—, Walton County Mental Health Commn., 1976—; mem. Walton County Democratic Exec. Com., 1972—; deacon Corinth Christian Ch., Walton County, 1975—. Mem. Am., Walton County (v.p.) bar assns. Home: Covington St Loganville GA 30249 Office: 112 N Broad St Monroe GA 30655 Tel (404) 267-6832

JONES, NORMAN DAVIS, b. Corpus Christi, Mar. 20, 1946; B.S. in Psychology, U. Houston, 1969; J.D., South Tex. Coll. Law, 1972. Admitted to Tex. bar, 1972, U.S. Dist. Ct. bar for So. Dist. Tex., 1973; trial atty. Houston Legal Found., 1973; asst. criminal dist. atty., Victoria County, Tex., 1973—; lectr. Victoria Police Acad., Victoria County Sheriffs Acad., clubs, civic groups; asso. justice Honor Ct. South Tex. Coll. Law, 1972. Chmn. Victoria Sesquicentennial Com., 1973. Mem. Victoria County Bar Assn. (sec.-treas.), Tex. Dist. and County Attys. Assn., Victoria County Peace Officers Assn., Alumni Assn. South Tex. Coll. Law. Home: 407 W Commercial St Victoria TX 77901 Office: Room 241 Victoria County Courthouse Victoria TX 77901 Tel (512) 575-0468

JONES, NORMAN PEARCE, b. Tulsa, June 17, 1944; B.S., Okla. U., 1967; J.D., U. Okla., 1970; postgrad. Cameron U. Admitted to Okla. bar, 1970; legal research asst. firm Hines, Klaus & Wilsey, Oklahoma City, 1968-69, legal intern, 1970-71, asso., 1971; atty. JAGC, U.S. Army, 1972-73; partner firm Sullivan, Sullivan & Jones, Duncan, Okla., 1973—. Bd. dirs. Duncan Okla., Jr. Achievement, 1976—, Stephens County (Okla.) Mental Health Assn., 1975—; bd. dirs. Duncan United Way, 2d v.p., 1974-75, 1st v.p., 1975-76, pres., 1975-76; bd. dirs. Duncan Boys' Club, 1973—. Mem. Am., Okla., Stephens County bar assns. Home: 1810 Country Club Rd Duncan OK 73533 Office: 15 N 9th St Duncan OK 73533 Tel (405) 255-1111

JONES, ORTON ALAN, b. Spencer, W. Va.,Jan. 24, 1938; student Glenville State Coll., 1955-58; J.D., W. Va. U., 1961. Admitted to W. Va. bar, 1961; prosecuting atty. Roane County, W. Va., 1965-68; mem. W. Va. Ho. of Dels., 1968-72, W.Va. Senate, 1972—. Mem. Am. W. Va. bar assns., Roane County C. of C., W. Va., Upper Vandalia hist. socs., Am. Legion, Phi Delta Phi, Kappa Sigma Kappa. Named one of W. Va.'s 5 Outstanding Young Men, W. Va. Jaycees, 1970. Home: Ridgemont Rd Spencer WV 25276 Office: PO Box 16 Spencer WV 25276 Tel (304) 927-3790

JONES, RALPH LORNE, b. Haileyville, Okla., July 12, 1915; B.A., Okla. U., 1937; LL.B., U. Okla., 1940. Admitted to Okla. bar, 1940, N.Y. State bar, 1946; asso. firm Brown, Wood, Ivey, Mitchell & Petty, N.Y.C., 1945-54, mem., 1954—. Mem. Assn. Bar City N.Y., N.Y. Bar Assn., Order of Coif, Phi Delta Phi. Contbr. articles in field to profl. jours. Office: 1 Liberty Plaza New York City NY 10006 Tel (212) 349-7500

JONES, RAYMOND DEAN, b. Pueblo, Colo., Nov. 30, 1945; B.A., Colo. Coll., 1967; J.D., Harvard, 1971. Admitted to Colo. bar, 1971; law clk. to chief justice Colo. Supreme Ct., 1971-72; asso. firm Holme, Roberts & Owen, Denver, 1972-74; chief counsel Met. Denver Dist. Atty. Consumer Office, Denver, 1974-77; judge Denver County Ct., 1977—; hearing officer Colo. Supreme Ct. hearings on bar exam. petitions, 1975-77; mem. State Bd. Law Examiners, 1972—. Chmn. Colo. Black Caucus, 1973; sec. Colo. Democratic Party, 1975—; bd. dirs. Denver Opportunity, Inc., 1974—, New Dance Theatre, Inc., 1973—; mem. citizens adv. bd. Denver Election Commn., 1976—. Mem. Denver, Sam Gary (sec.), Colo., Am., Nat. bar assns., Am. Arbitration Assn. (arbitrator). Recipient Barney Ford Community award for Law and Justice, 1977. Home: 787 Garfield St Denver CO 80206 Office: Courtroom C Denver County Ct City and County Bldg Denver CO 80202 Tel (303) 297-5103

JONES, RICHARD CYRUS, b. Oak Park, Ill., Oct. 20, 1928; Ph.B., DePaul U., 1960, J.D., 1963. Admitted to Ill. bar, 1963; title examiner, customer relations rep., dept. mgr. Chgo. Title and Trust Co., 1947-64; mem. firm Sachnoff, Schrager Jones & Weaver, Ltd., and predecessor firms, 1964—. Mem. Am. (real property com.), Ill. (real estate law com.), Chgo. (real property com.) bar assns., Am. Judicature Soc., Chgo. Mortgage Attys., Delta Theta Phi. Home: 1044 Forest Ave River Forest IL 60305 Office: One IBM Plaza Suite 4700 Chicago IL 60611 Tel (312) 644-2400

JONES, RICHARD OWENS, b. Brewton, Ala., Mar. 2, 1946; B.S., U. Ala., 1968, J.D., 1970. Admitted to Ala. bar, 1970; adminstrv. asst. Ala. Defender Program U. Ala., 1968-70, research asst. Clinton McGee, 1968-70; law clk. firm Phelps, Owens & Jones, and predecessors, Tuscaloosa, Ala., 1969-70, asso., 1970-73, partner, 1974-76; individual practice law, Tuscaloosa, 1976—. Bd. dirs. Tuscaloosa County Day Care and Child Services, 1974—; active com. for restoration Tuscaloosa County Hist. Preservation Authority, 1976—. Mem. Am., Ala., Tuscaloosa County (sec.-treas. 1971-73, v.p. 1974-75, pres. 1975-76) bar assns., Am. Judicature Soc., Tuscaloosa County Home Builders Assn., Farrah Order Jurisprudence, Phi Alpha Delta. Named Outstanding Young Man, U.S. Jaycees, 1976. Home: 20 Oakwood Ct Tuscaloosa AL 35401 Office: 2524 8th St Tuscaloosa AL 35401 Tel (205) 349-2353

JONES, ROBERT CORDWELL, b. St. Louis, Sept. 14, 1933; A.B., Washington U., St. Louis, 1957, J.D., 1957. Admitted to Mo. bar, 1957, U.S. Dist. Ct. bar Eastern Dist. Mo., 1957, Supreme Ct. U.S. bar, 1976; asso. firm Cook, Murphy, Lance & English, St. Louis, 1957-60; partner firm Jones & Steiner, Clayton, Mo., 1961, Ziercher, Hocker, Tzinberg, Human & Michenfelder, Clayton, 1961—; municipal judge City of Ballwin (Mo.), 1963-65; city atty. City of Sunset Hills (Mo.), 1957-69. Mayor City of Ballwin, 1965-71. Mem. Am., Mo., St. Louis County bar assns., Met. Bar Assn. St. Louis. Home: 404 Nottingham Dr Ballwin MO 63011 Office: 130 S Bemiston Ave Suite 405 Clayton MO 63105 Tel (314) 727-5822

JONES, ROBERT HANCOCK, b. Atlanta, Apr. 5, 1904; B.A., U. Tex., 1927; LL.B., Washington and Lee U., 1927. Admitted to Tex. bar, 1927; practice law, Dallas. Mem. Tex. Bar Assn. Office: 3330 Republic National Bank Bldg Dallas TX 75201 Tel (214) 742-4092

JONES, ROBERT L., b. 1932; LL.B., U. Tex., 1956. Practiced law, Corpus Christi and Houston, 1958-63; resident counsel Gulf & Western Industries, Inc., N.Y.C., 1963-65, asst. sec., resident counsel, 1965-68, v.p., resident counsel, 1968—. Office: Gulf & Western Industries 1 Gulf and Western Plaza New York City NY 10023*

JONES, ROBERT LLOYD, JR., b. St. Louis, June 20, 1947; B.A., U. of the Pacific; J.D., U. Calif., Davis. Admitted to Calif. bar, 1972; asso. firm Richardson and Gaskill, Fresno, Calif., 1972—; mem. Fed. Indigent Panel; vol. atty. Fresno County Legal Services. Mem. State Bar Calif., Am., Fresno County bar assns., Fresno County Barristers Assn. Office: 1230 M St Fresno CA 93721 Tel (209) 486-6680

JONES, ROGER WESLEY, JR., b. Seattle, May 16, 1944; A.B., Princeton, 1966; LL.B., Univ. Wash., 1972. Admitted to Wash. bar, 1972; asso. firm Macbride, Sax & MacIver, Seattle, 1972—; prof. Seattle City Coll., 1975-77. Mem. Wash., Seattle, King County bar assns., Estate Planning Council of Seattle, S.R. (sec. Wash. chpt.). Contbr. articles in field to profl. jours. Home: 852 E Gwinn Place Seattle WA 98102 Office: 1415 5th Ave #1900 Seattle WA 98171 Tel (206) 344-2160

JONES, RONALD DAVID, b. Oneida, N.Y., Jan. 2, 1930; B.S., Yale, 1951; LL.B. cum laude, Harvard, 1958. Admitted to N.Y. State bar, 1958; asso. firm LeBoeuf, Lamb, Leiby & MacRae, N.Y.C., 1958-65, partner, 1965—. Mem. Am. (chmn. electricity com. pub. utilities sect. 1971-73, 76—, mem. counsel 1973-76), Fed. Power (chmn. tax devel. com. 1973—), N.Y. State (vice-chmn. pub. utility law com. 1973—) bar assns. Contbr. articles to legal jours. Home: 64 Somerstown Rd Ossining NY 10562 Office: 140 Broadway New York City NY 10005 Tel (212) 269-1100

JONES, RUSSELL DEAN, b. Los Angeles, Aug. 17, 1933; B.B.A., Loyola U. (Calif.), 1954, J.D., 1957. Admitted to Calif. bar, 1960; asst. city adminstr., Culver City, Calif., 1954-60; sr. asst. to city mgr., Santa Monica, Calif., 1960-64; city adminstr., Placentia, Calif., 1964-67; asst. dir. Calif. Dept. Housing and Community Devel., Sacramento, Calif., 1967-68; legal counsel R.A. Watt Co., Inc. (predecessor of Boise Cascade Bldg Co.), Los Angeles, 1968-69; v.p., dir. adminstrn. Boise Cascade Bldg Co., Los Angeles, 1969-72, So. Calif. regional mgr., 1973—; real estate devel. cons., developer, Los Angeles, 1972—. Mem. Gov.'s Advisory Com. on Factory Built Housing, 1969-72; mem. subdiv. advisory com. Calif. Dept. of Real Estate, 1968-71. Mem. Western Govtl. Research Assn., Internat. City Mgmt. Assn., Bldg. Industry Assn. (v.p. 1971-72), Phi Alpha Delta, Alpha Delta Gamma (nat. pres. 1956-57). Certificate Advanced Law Studies, U. So. Calif., 1959. Home: 16 Surrey Ln Rancho Palos Verdes CA 90274 Office: 5959 W Century Blvd Suite 1100 Los Angeles CA 90045 Tel (213) 641-3300

JONES, SAMUEL BEAUCHAMP THOMAS, III, b. Gulfport, Miss., Sept. 26, 1949; B.S., Miss. State U., 1971; J.D., U. Miss., 1974. Admitted to Miss. bar, 1974; asso. firm Singley, Minniece, Hamilton, Neville & Hamill, Meridian, Miss., 1974-77; asso. firm Joe Clay Hamilton, 1977—; instr. bus. law, Meridian Jr. Coll., 1975—. Mem. Miss. State, Lauderdale County bar assns., Lauderdale County Claim Assn. Home: 1821 25th Ave Meridian MS 39301 Office: PO Box 2146 Meridian MS 39301 Tel (601) 693-5548

JONES, SCRANTON, b. Ft. Worth, Tex., July 29, 1921; A.B., U. Tex., Austin, 1942, J.D., 1942. Admitted to Tex. bar, 1947; asst. dist. atty. Tarrant County, Ft. Worth, 1947-49; asso. firm Jones & Morris, Ft. Worth, 1950-67; adj. prof. bus. law Tex. Christian U., Ft. Worth, 1968-76; mem. firm Rattikin, Newman & Jones, Ft. Worth, 1976—; asst. atty. gen. Tex., Austin, 1962-63. Mayor pro tempore and city councilman, Ft. Worth, 1963-67. Mem. State Bar Tex., Ft. Worth, Tarrant County bar assns. Author: The Legal Environment of Business, 1972. Home: 5817 El Campo Terr Fort Worth TX 76107 Office: 5144 Trail Lake Dr Fort Worth TX 76133 Tel (817) 294-0010

JONES, SEABORN GUSTAVUS, b. Macon, Ga., Aug. 27, 1910; student Mercer U., 1931-32; LL.B., Maynard Sch. Law, 1931. Admitted to Ga. bar, 1931; individual practice law, Macon, 1932—. Mem. Macon (pres. 1957), Am. bar assns., Ga. Assn. Trial Lawyers (pres. 1962-64, bd. govs. 1962—), State Bar Ga. (bd. govs. 1964—), Am. Judicature Soc., Am. Soc. Internat. Law, Internat. Acad. Trial Lawyers. Home: 2855 Sheffield Rd Macon GA 31204 Office: 582 Walnut St Macon GA 31201

JONES, SHELDON ATWELL, b. Melrose, Mass., Apr. 20, 1938; B.A., Yale, 1959; LL.B., Harvard, 1965. Admitted to Mass. bar, 1965; asso. firm Gaston, Snow, Motley & Holt, Boston, 1965-72; partner firm Gaston Snow & Ely Bartlett and predecessor, Boston, 1972—. Mem. Am., Boston bar assns. Office: One Federal St Boston MA 02110 Tel (617) 426-4600

JONES, STANLEY RAY, b. Culver City, Calif., Aug. 9, 1939; B.A., Pomona Coll., 1961; LL.B., U. Calif. at Los Angeles, 1965. Admitted to Calif. bar, 1965, U.S. Supreme Ct. bar, 1970; asso. firm Latham & Watkins, Los Angeles, 1965-66; dep. dist. atty. Orange County (Calif.), 1966-67; partner firm Jones & Williams, Santa Ana, Calif., 1968-70, firm Jensen & Jones, Santa Ana, 1970-75; individual practice law, Santa Ana, 1975; partner firm Layman, Hanson & Jones, Newport Beach, Calif., 1975—. Bd. dirs. Youth Problem Center, Costa Mesa, Calif., 1971-72; judge pro tempore Orange County Superior Ct., 1975—; judge pro tempore Orange County Municipal Ct., 1974—. Mem. Orange County Bar Assn., Orange County Trial Lawyers Assn., Assn. Bus. Trial Lawyers, Order of Coif, Phi Delta Phi. Asso. editor U. Calif. Los Angeles Law Rev., 1964-65. Home: 8 Encore Ct Newport Beach CA 92663 Office: 500 Newport Center Dr #945 Newport Beach CA 92660 Tel (714) 640-5650

JONES, STEPHEN LESLIE, b. Lafayette, La., July 1, 1940; student U. Tex., 1959-63; LL.B., U. Okla., 1966. Admitted to Okla. bar, 1966, U.S. Ct. Appeals 10th Circuit bar, 1969, U.S. Supreme Ct. bar, 1970, U.S. Ct. Appeals D.C. bar, 1974, U.S. Ct. Appeals 8th Circuit bar, 1974, U.S. Ct. Appeals 2d Circuit bar, 1975; personal asst. to Richard M. Nixon, N.Y.C., 1964; adminstrv. asst. to Congressman Paul Findley, Washington, 1966-67; legal counsel to Gov. of Okla., Oklahoma City, 1967; legal asst. to Congressman Don Rumsfeld, Washington, 1968; partner firm Otjen, Carter & Jones, Enid, Okla., 1969-70, firm Jones, Gungoll, and Pranter, Enid, 1977—; spl. prosecutor State of Okla., 1977; gen. counsel ACLU. Mem. Okla. Adv. Com. to U.S. Civil Rights Commn.; Republican nominee atty. gen. Okla., 1974. Mem. Am., Okla., Garfield County bar assns., Criminal Def. Attys. Assn., Phi Alpha Delta. Contbr. articles to legal jours. Home: 1315 Vinita St Enid OK 73701 Office: 317 W Cherokee St Enid OK 73701 Tel (405) 233-4321

JONES, STEPHEN WILSON, b. Hackensack, N.J., May 10, 1942; B.A., Franklin and Marshall Coll., 1964; J.D., U. Calif., San Francisco, 1967. Admitted to Calif. bar, 1967; law clk. Calif. Ct. Appeal for 1st Appellate Dist., 1968; partner firm Sedgwick, Detert, Moran & Arnold, San Francisco, 1968—. Mem. sch. com. Oakland Master Plan, 1973—. Mem. Calif., San Francisco bar assns., Barristers Club, Order of Coif. Office: 111 Pine St San Francisco CA 94111 Tel (415) 982-0303

JONES, THOMAS C., JR., b. Cannon, Ga., June 6, 1936; B.S., N. Ga. Coll., Dahlonega, 1957; LL.B., Atlanta Law Sch., 1966. Admitted to Ga. bar, 1976; partner firm Schwall & Heuett, Atlanta, 1966-69; individual practice law, Atlanta, 1969—. Mem. Am., Atlanta bar assns., Am. Judicature Soc. Home: 2417 Sagamore Hills Dr Decatur GA 30033 Office: 148 Cain St NE Suite 540 Atlanta GA 30303 Tel (404) 588-0241

JONES, THOMAS WILLIAM, b. Sylva, N.C., Aug. 29, 1943; B.A., Mars Hill Coll., 1965; J.D., Wake Forest U., 1968. Admitted to N.C. bar, 1968; asso. firm Monteith, Coward and Coward, Sylva, 1968-72; partner firm Coward, Coward & Jones, Sylva, 1972-74, firm Coward, Coward, Jones & Dillard, Sylva, 1974-76; individual practices, Sylva, 1977—. Mem. N.C., 30th Dist. (sec.-treas. 1977) bar assns., Jackson County Jaycees (pres. 1972). Home: Route 1 Box 33A Sylva NC 28779 Office: 297-1 E Main St Sylva NC 28779 Tel (704) 586-5589

JONES, WILLIAM BLAKELY, b. Cedar Rapids, Iowa, Mar. 20, 1907; A.B., Notre Dame U., 1929, LL.B., 1931. Admitted to Mont. bar, 1931, D.C. bar, 1945, Md. bar, 1954; practiced in Mont., 1931-37; atty. Dept. Justice, Washington, 1937-43, Office Price Adminstrn., Washington, 1943; exec. asst. to Am. chmn. Joint Brit.-Am. Patent Interchange Com., Washington, 1943-46; mem. firm Hamilton and Hamilton, Washington, 1946-62; judge U.S. Dist. Ct., D.C., 1962—, chief judge, 1975-77. Fellow Am. Coll. Trial Lawyers (jud.), Am. Bar Found.; mem. D.C., Am. (chmn. div. jud. adminstrn. 1972-73) bar assns., Lawyers Club of Washington. Home: 5516 Grove St Chevy Chase MD 20015 Office: US Courthouse Washington DC 20001 Tel (202) 426-7335

JONES, WILLIAM KENNETH, b. N.Y.C., Sept. 1, 1930; A.B., Columbia U., 1952, LL.B., 1954. Admitted to N.Y. state bar, 1955, Ohio bar, 1958; law clk. Justice U.S. Supreme Ct., 1954-55; atty. U.S. Air Force, 1955-56; atty. firm Jones, Day, Cockley & Reavis, Cleve., 1956-59; mem. faculty Columbia U. Law Sch., 1959—, now prof. law; pub. service commr. State N.Y., 1970-74. Author: Regulated Industries, 1967, 76; Electronic Mass Media, 1976. Home: 20 Creston Ave Tenafly NJ 07670 Office: 4135 W 116 St New York City NY 10027

JONES, WOODROW WILSON, b. nr. Rutherfordton, N.C., Jan. 26, 1914; A.A., Mars Hill Coll., 1934; LL.B., Wake Forest U., 1937. Admitted to N.C. bar, 1937, U.S. Supreme Ct. bar, 1955; mem. firm Hamrick & Jones, Rutherfordton, 1945-67; judge U.S. Dist. Ct., Western Dist. N.C., 1967—, chief judge, 1968—. Mem. N.C., Rutherford County (N.C.) (pres. 1946), Am. bar assns. Recipient Outstanding Service award Rutherfordton Lions Club, 1956, Spl. citation for outstanding service Gardner-Webb Coll., 1968. Home: 1018 N Main St Rutherfordton NC 28139 Office: Rutherford County Courthouse Rutherfordton NC 28139 Tel (704) 287-4356

JONJAK, PAUL LEON, b. Radisson, Wis., Mar. 30, 1941; B.S. in Mech. Engring., U. Wis., 1963; J.D., Harvard, 1971. Engr., NW Paper Co., Cloquet, Minn., 1963-65; mgr. Daymaker Cranberries, Inc., Gordon, Wis., 1965-68; admitted to Wis. bar, 1971; clk. to justice Wis. Supreme Ct., 1971-72; partner firm Ebbeson & Jonjak, Sturgeon Bay, Wis., 1972-75; individual practice law, Sturgeon Bay, 1975-76; partner firm Jonjak, Havens & Kase, Sturgeon Bay, 1976—. Pres. Bayview Terr., Inc., non-profit housing for elderly, Sturgeon Bay, 1973-76; mem. Door County (Wis.) Commn. on Aging, 1975-76; mem. Door County Econ. Devel. Com., 1976—. Mem. Am., Wis., Door-Kewaunee County (Wis.) bar assns. Recipient Distinguished Service award Door County Jaycees, 1974. Office: 306 S 3d Ave Sturgeon Bay WI 54235 Tel (414) 743-9221

JONSSON, JON MARVIN, b. Seattle, Mar. 22, 1928; B.A. in Econs. and Bus. Adminstrn., U. Wash., 1952, J.D., 1954. Admitted to Wash. bar, 1954, U.S. Supreme Ct. bar, 1967; individual practice law, Seattle, 1954—; consul for Iceland at Seattle, 1968—; mem. Wash. Ho. of Reps., 1958-60. Mem. Wash. State, King County bar assns. Office: 5610 20th NW Seattle WA 98107 Tel (206) 783-4100

JORDAN, ALEXANDER JOSEPH, JR., b. New London, Conn., Oct. 11, 1938; B.S., U.S. Naval Acad., 1960; J.D., Harvard, 1968. Admitted to Mass. bar, 1968; asso. firm Gaston Snow & Ely Bartlett, and predecessor, Boston, 1968-74, partner, 1974—. Mem. Boston Bar Assn., Harvard Law Sch. Alumni Assn., Naval Res. Assn., U.S. Naval Acad. Alumni Assn. Office: One Federal St Boston MA 02110 Tel (617) 426-4600

JORDAN, BILLY JENKINS, b. Columbus, Miss., July 26, 1937; student Delta State U., 1955-56; B.S., Miss. State U., 1958, postgrad., 1958-59; postgrad. La. State U., 1959-60; J.D., U. Miss., 1963. Admitted to Miss. bar, 1963, U.S. Supreme Ct. bar, 1970; individual practice law, Columbus, 1963—. Cooperating trial counsel, dir. ACLU of Miss. Chmn., life mem. Lowndes County (Miss.) Cancer Dr. Mem. Am., Fed. bar assns., Am. Trial Lawyers Assn., Nat. Coll. Criminal Def. Attys., Nat. Defenders Assn. Home: Forrest Glenn Rd Columbus MS 39701 Office: POB 295 Columbus MS 39701 Tel (601) 328-2222

JORDAN, EDMUND ANDREW, b. Spokane, Wash., Jan. 16, 1913; student Oreg. State U., 1930-32; J.D., Northwestern Coll. Law Lewis and Clark Coll., 1957. Salesman, Tidewater Asso. Oil Co., Portland, Oreg., 1936-47; owner, operator Paramount Oil Co., Portland, 1947-57; admitted to Oreg. bar, 1957; individual practice law, Portland, 1957-64; judge Municipal Ct., Portland, 1964-71, Oreg. Dist. Ct., Multnomah County, 1971—. Mem. Portland Sch. Dist. 1 Bd. Edn., 1960-64, chmn., 1963. Mem. Oreg. State Bar, Multnomah County (Oreg.) Bar Assn., Am. Judges Assn. (v.p. 1974-75, pres.-elect 1976—), Delta Theta Phi. Home: 2408 SW Chelmsford St Portland OR 97201 Office: 1021 SW 4th Ave Portland OR 97204 Tel (503) 248-3986

JORDAN, G. MCGREGOR, JR., b. Macon, Ga., Feb. 3, 1944; B.S., U. Wash.; J.D., Mercer U. Admitted to Ga. bar, 1973; law asst. Ga. Supreme Ct., 1973-74; asso. firm Harris, Watkins, Taylor & Davis, Macon, 1974—. Mem. Ga. State Bar. Editorial bd. Mercer U. Law Rev., 1970-73. Home: 2532 Vineville Ave Macon GA 31204 Office: PO Box 246 Macon GA 31202 Tel (912) 745-1181

JORDAN, GARY LEO, b. Florence, Kans., Jan. 26, 1943; B.A. cum laude, Washburn U., 1965, J.D., 1968. Admitted to Kans. bar, 1968, U.S. Dist. Ct. bar, 1968; asso. firm Gleason & Pinet, Ottawa, Kans., 1968-69; partner firm Gleason, Pinet and Jordan Chartered, Ottawa, 1969-70; individual practice law, Ottawa, 1970—; spl. workmen's compensation examiner, 1968-69. Blood program chmn. Franklin County chpt. ARC, 1969—. Mem. Kans. (dir. young lawyers sect. 1969-72), Franklin County (sec. 1975, v.p. 1976) bar assns., Kans. Trial Lawyers Assn. Home: Box 202 Ottawa KS 66067 Office: 313 S Hickory St Box 202 Ottawa KS 66067 Tel (913) 242-5566

JORDAN, JAMES FLOYD, b. Wilkes County, N.C., May 24, 1891; LL.B., Wake Forest Coll., Wilkesboro, N.C., 1922. Admitted to N.C. bar, 1922; individual practice law, Wilkesboro, 1922—. Home: 601 E M St Wilkesboro NC 28697 Tel (919) 838-5572

JORDAN, JOHN RICHARD, JR., b. Winton, N.C., Jan. 16, 1921; B.A., U. N.C., 1942, LL.D., 1948. Admitted to N.C. bar, 1948; mem. staff atty. gen. N.C., 1948-51; individual practice law, Raleigh, 1951—. Chmn. bd. dirs. N.C. div. Am. Cancer Soc., 1959, pres., 1960; pres. Wake County Cancer Soc., 1950, Wake County Hist. Soc., 1961, Wake County chpt. Arthritis Found., 1966, Friends of Library, N.C. State U., 1966; mem. Gov.'s Cancer Commn., 1962-64; N.C. chmn. Nat. Soc. for Crippled Children and Adults, 1963, ARC, 1966; pres. N.C. Arthritis Found., 1966-70; mem. Adv. Council on Tchr. Edn. and Profl. Standards, 1961-62; mem. Gov.'s Coordinating Com. on Traffic Safety, 1961-62, Gov.'s Commn. on Edn. Beyond High Sch., 1961-62; N.C. rep. Nat. Com. for Support Pub. Schs., 1962—; chmn. Commn. on Med. Aid for Aged in N.C., 1962-63; N.C. del. Legis. Confs. So. Regional Edn. Bd., 1962, 64; mem. N.C. Commn. on Higher Edn. Facilities, 1964—, N.C. Bd. Higher Edn., 1964; chmn. N.C. Bd. Social Services, 1969-73; vice chmn. N.C. Commn. on Internat. Cooperation, 1970—; mem. N.C. Senate, 1959, 61, 63; permanent chmn. N.C. Democratic Conv., 1974; bd. dirs. English Speaking Union; trustee Ravenscroft Found., N.C. Cancer Inst., 1961-63; bd. govs. U. N.C. System, 1971—. Mem. Am., Internat., N.C., Wake County (chmn. exec. com. 1955) bar assns., Am. Judicature Soc., N.C. Acad. Trial Lawyers, Pi Kappa Alpha, Phi Delta Phi. Recipient Distinguished Service award as Raleigh's Young Man of Year, 1955, Distinguished Service award N.C. Pub. Health Assn., 1964, Gold medal award Am. Cancer Soc., 1963; named Tar Heal of Week, 1955. Bd. editors N.C. Law Rev., 1947-48. Home: 808 Westwood Dr Raleigh NC 27607 Office: 1414 Branch Banking and Trust Bldg Raleigh NC 27607 Tel (919) 828-2501

JORDAN, KENNETH JAMES, b. Beaumont, Tex., July 24, 1944; B.S., U. San Diego, 1968; J.D., U. Denver, 1971. Admitted to Colo. bar, 1971, Nev. bar, 1973; law clk. firm Rose, Norwood & Edwards, Las Vegas, 1971-72; law clk.-investigator Carson City (Nev.) Dist. Atty.'s Office, 1973, dep., 1973-75; individual practice law, Carson City, 1976—; atty. Carson-Tahoe Hosps. Women's Aux. Bd. dirs. Big Bros., Big Sisters of Carson City, Mem. Am., Colo., Nev. bar assns., Am. Trial Lawyers Assn., Am. Judicature Soc., Phi Alpha Delta. Home: 910 Angus St Carson City NV 89701 Office: 208 N Curry St Carson City NV 89701 Tel (702) 883-5858

JORDAN, LEWIS HENRY, b. Spencer, Iowa, Apr. 12, 1930; B.A., State U. Iowa, 1957, J.D., 1958. Admitted to Iowa bar, 1958, U.S. Dist. Ct. So. dist. Iowa, 1962; asso. firm Webster, Jordan, Oliver & Walters, and predecessors, Winterset, Iowa, 1958-60; partner, 1960—; atty. Madison County Dem. Central Com., 1972—. Mem. Am., Iowa, Madison County bar assns., Am. Judicature Soc., Iowa Acad. Trial Lawyers, Am. Trial Lawyers Assn. Home: 605 W Jefferson Winterset IA 50273 Office: Farmers & Merchants Bldg Winterset IA 50273 Tel (515) 462-3731

JORDAN, MALCOLM STEWART, b. Chgo., Dec. 31, 1941; A.B., U. Calif., Los Angeles, 1963; M.A., Calif. State U., Los Angeles, 1966; J.D., Calif. Coll. Law, 1968; Ph.D., U. So. Calif., 1975. Admitted to Calif. bar, 1969, U.S. Supreme Ct. bar, 1975; dep. dist. atty. Los Angeles County, 1969—; teaching asst. in Constl. law and internat. law U. So. Calif., Los Angeles, 1968-71, instr., 1971-72, sr. lectr., 1972—. Mem. Adv. Council Korean Assn. So. Calif., 1975; pres. Los Angeles Met. Republican Club, 1976—; asso. mem. Rep. State Central Com. Calif., 1976—. Mem. Calif. Bar Assn., Am., Western polit. sci. assns., Sigma Tau Sigma, Pi Sigma Alpha. Author: The Contempt Powers Clash Between the Court and the Advocate, 1975. Office: Dist Atty 210 W Temple St Los Angeles CA 90012 Tel (213) 672-9111 ext 291

JORDAN, OSCAR ROBERT, b. Biloxi, Miss., Mar. 7, 1935; student U. So. Miss., 1953-55; B.B.A., U. Miss., 1957, LL.B., 1963, J.D., 1968. Admitted to Miss. bar, 1963; individual practice law, Ocean Springs, Miss., 1963—; atty. City of Ocean Springs, 1964—, police justice, 1967-75. Mem. Am., Miss., Jackson County bar assns., Am. Judicature Soc., Ocean Springs C. of C. (past. dir.). Recipient Distinguished Service award Ocean Springs Jaycees, 1966. Home: 1213 Iola Ocean Springs MS 39564 Office: 914 Washington Ocean Springs MS 39564 Tel (601) 875-5400

JORDAN, PAUL SIDNEY, b. Severy, Kans., Mar. 31, 1903; A.B., U. Calif., Berkeley, 1925, J.D., 1927; LL.D., Golden Gate U., 1973. Admitted to Calif. bar, 1927, since practiced in San Francisco; partner firm Byrne, Lamson & Jordan, 1932-51, Lamson, Jordan & Walsh, 1951-64, Lamson, Jordan, Walsh & Lawrence, 1964-76, Jordan, Walsh, Lawrence, Dawson & Carbone, 1976—; mem. faculty Sch. Law, Golden Gate U., 1933-44, dean, 1944-59. Fellow Am. Bar Found.; mem. Am., San Francisco (pres. 1960) bar assns., Am. Judicature Soc. Home: 990 Chestnut St San Francisco CA 94109 Office: 235 Montgomery St suite 1249 San Francisco CA 94104 Tel (415) 392-4142

JORDAN, ROBERT ELIJAH, III, b. South Boston, Va., June 20, 1936; S.B., Mass. Inst. Tech., 1958; J.D. magna cum laude, Harvard U., 1961. Admitted to D.C. bar, 1962, Va. bar, 1964, U.S. Supreme Ct. bar, 1967; spl. asst. for civil rights Office Sec. Def., Washington, 1963-64; asst. U.S. atty., Washington, 1964-65; exec. asst. for enforcement Office Sec. Treasury, Washington, 1965-67; gen. counsel Dept. Army, also spl. asst. to Sec. Army, 1967-71; partner firm Steptoe & Johnson, Washington, 1971—. Mem. Am. Bar Assn., D.C. Bar, Va. State Bar. Contbr. articles, chpts. to legal jours., books. Home: 6963 Duncraig Ct McLean VA 22101 Office: 1250 Connecticut Ave NW Washington DC 20036 Tel (202) 862-2641

JORDAN, ROBERT HENRY, b. Talbotton, Ga., Feb. 6, 1916; J.D., U. Ga., 1941. Admitted to Ga. bar, 1940, U.S. Supreme Ct. bar, 1954; practiced in Talbotton, 1945-60; judge Ga. Ct. Appeals, 1960-72; justice Ga. Supreme Ct., 1972—; mem. Ga. Senate, 1953-54, 59-60, pres. pro tem, 1959-60. Chmn. Talbot County (Ga.) Bd. Edn., 1952-56; mem. Franklin D. Roosevelt Meml. Commn., Warm Springs, Ga., 1960—. Mem. Ga. Bar Assn. (v.p. 1956), State Bar Ga., Am. Judicature Soc. Author: History of Court of Appeals, 1961; There was a Land, 1971. Home: Macon Rd Talbotton GA 31827 Office: 541 State Jud Bldg Atlanta GA 30334 Tel (404) 656-3471

JORDAN, SUSAN B., b. Chgo., June 21, 1941; A.B., U. Mich., 1963; M.S., Yeshiva U., 1965; J.D. (Urban Law fellow 1969, Reginald Heber Smith Community Lawyer fellow 1970), Northwestern U., 1970. Admitted to Ill. bar, 1970, Calif. bar, 1971; asso. firm Cunningham, Deutsch, Haas, Radish & Stang, Chgo., 1971-72; partner firm Cumings and Jordan, San Francisco, 1973—; student instr. Northwestern U. Sch. Law, 1969, New Coll. of Calif. Law Sch., San Francisco, 1975; mem. fed. defender appt. panel No. Dist. Calif.; appt. panel 9th Circuit Ct. Appeals, City and County of San Francisco; speaker in field. Mem. Criminal Trial Lawyers Assn. (dir.), Calif. Attys. for Criminal Justice. Office: 96 Jessie St San Francisco CA 94105 Tel (415) 495-4495

JORDAN, THOMAS DAVID, b. Richmond, Va., Oct. 2, 1916; B.A., U. Richmond, 1949; LL.B., Smithdeal-Massey Coll. Law, 1952. Admitted to Va. bar, 1956; legal officer Va. Med. Examiner System, Richmond, 1956—; asso. prof. legal medicine Med. Coll. Va., Va. Commonwelath U., Richmond, 1962—. Mem. Va. Bar Assn., Va. State Bar, Am. Soc. Law and Medicine, Am. Soc. Hosp. Attys. Contbg. author Modern Concepts of Hospital Administration, 1962; editor (with G.T. Mann) Personal Injury Problems, 1963. Office: 9 N 14th St Richmond VA 23219 Tel (804) 786-3174

JORDAN, THOMAS JAMES, b. N.Y.C., Jan. 16, 1928; B.B.A., U. Miami, 1951, J.D., 1953. Admitted to Fla. bar, 1953; tchr. bus. law Dade County Schs., 1953-56; individual practice law, Miami, Fla., 1957—. Democratic committeeman; mem. Dade County steering com. Dem. Party, 1949-76; parlimentarian Dade County Dem. Exec. Com., 1962-66; mem. U. Miami Endowment Com., 1972-77. Mem. Am. Judicature Soc., Dade County Bar Assn., Fla. Bar (crimes and juvenile delinquency com. 1960-68, probate com. 1976-78), Fla. State Juvenile Officers Assn., Pi Kappa Alpha. Home: 100 NE 123d St N Miami FL 33161 Office: 302 Roper Bldg 20 SE 3d Ave Miami FL 33131 Tel (305) 373-3663

JORDAN, VERNON MURRAY, b. Floresville, Tex., Feb. 9, 1935; B.B.A., U. Tex., 1957, LL.B., 1959. Admitted to Tex. bar, 1959, U.S. Supreme Ct. bar, 1962; judge adv. U.S. Navy, 1959-62; asst. atty. gen. State of Tex., 1963-64; county atty. McCulloch County (Tex.), 1965-70; dist. atty. 198th Jud. Dist. Tex., Brady, 1970—. Chmn. bd. First Christian Ch., Brady, 1975. Mem. Tex., Hill Country bar assns. Office: 107 E Main St Brady TX 76825 Tel (915) 597-2134

JORDAN, WALTER ELLSWORTH, b. Pitts., July 25, 1918; B.A., U. Okla., 1942; LL.B., U. Tex., 1947. Admitted to Tex. bar, 1947; asso. firm Stone, Agerton, Parker & Kerr, Ft. Worth, 1951-56, M. Henricks Brown, Ft. Worth, 1956-59; partner firm Hudson, Keltner, Jordan & Smith, Ft. Worth, 1959-63; judge Tex. Dist. Ct., 48th Dist., Ft. Worth, 1963—. Mem. Ft. Worth-Tarrant County Bar Assn. Author: Trial Handbook for Texas Lawyers, 1971; Modern Texas Discovery, 1974; Texas Pattern Jury Charges, 1970. Home: 6804 Dwight St Fort Worth TX 76116 Office: Civil Courts Bldg Fort Worth TX 76102 Tel (817) 334-1461

JORDAN, WILLIAM HUGHES, b. Charleston, S.C., Nov. 12, 1948; B.A., Bapt. Coll., Charleston, 1970; J.D., U. S.C., 1973. Admitted to S.C. bar, 1973; mem. firm Furman, Jenkins & Brist, North Charleston, S.C., 1973—; served as 1st lt. JAGC, USAF, 1974-76. Mem. Am., S.C., Charleston County bar assns., Rotary Internat. (chmn. fellowship com. 1976-77). Home: 127 Beaufain St Charleston SC 29401 Office: Suite 201 6296 Rivers Ave North Charleston SC 29405 Tel (803) 554-6000

JORGENSEN, ERIK HOLGER, b. Copenhagen, July 19, 1916; J.D., San Francisco Law Sch., 1960. Admitted to Calif. bar, 1961; individual practice law, San Francisco, 1961-70; partner firm Hersh, Hadfield, Jorgensen & Fried, San Francisco, 1970-76; mem. firm Hadfield, von Beroldingen, Jacobs, Jorgensen, Graubart, Pressman & Pressman, 1976—; pres. Viking Mortgage Co., San Francisco. Pres., Aldersly Danish Retirement Home, San Rafael, Calif., 1974, Bay Area chpt. Rebild Park Soc., 1974. Fellow Scandinavian Am. Found. (hon.); mem. Am. Bar Assn., Am. Trial Lawyers Assn., San Francisco Lawyers Club (gov.), Bar Assn. San Francisco, Calif. Assn. Realtors (hon. life dir.). Author: Master Forms Guide for Successful Real Estate Agreements, 1970; Successful Real Estate Sales Agreements, 1976; mem. editorial and curriculum bd. Calif. Dept. Real Estate, 1975. Office: 900 Northpoint St San Francisco CA 94109 Tel (415) 441-1211

JORGENSEN, ROBERT NORMAN, b. Reno, Feb. 1, 1932; B.A., U. Utah, 1954; J.D., U. Calif. at Berkeley, 1967. Admitted to Calif. bar, 1968; dep. dist. atty., organized crime div. Los Angeles County; practice law, Los Angeles; Los Angeles County rep. Commn. on Rev. of Nat. Policy Towards Gambling, 1976. Mem. State Bar Calif. (hearing examiner Los Angeles 1972). Office: 210 W Temple St Los Angeles CA 90012 Tel (213) 974-3900

JORGENSON, DONALD ROGER, b. Eau Claire, Wis., Mar. 3, 1946; B.A. in Econs., Hamline U., 1968; J.D., U. Minn., 1972. Admitted to Minn. bar, 1972; partner firm Isaacs & Jorgenson, Ltd., St. Paul, 1975—. Co-chmn. Minn. Crime Watch Commn. for West Saint Paul, Minn., 1973-75; active Boy Scouts Am. Mem. Am., Minn. State, Ramsey County bar assns. Recipient St. Paul Area Distinguished Service award Boy Scouts Am., 1965, Nat. Distinguished Service award, 1969. Home: 1141 Ivy Hill Dr Mendota Heights MN 55118 Office: 222 Degree of Honor Bldg Saint Paul MN 55101 Tel (612) 224-2362

JORLING, THOMAS CASH, b. Cin., June 25, 1940; B.S. in Biology, U. Notre Dame, 1962; LL.B., Boston Coll., 1966; M.S. in Ecology, Wash. State U., 1969. Admitted to D.C. bar, 1966, Mass. bar, 1973; atty. U.S. Dept. Interior, Washington, 1966-67; asst. gen. counsel Smithsonian Inst., Washington, 1967-68; minority council com. on pub. works U.S. Senate, Washington, 1968-72, cons., 1972—; dir. center for environ. studies, asso. prof. Williams Coll., 1972—. Mem. planning bd. Town of Williamstown, Ma., 1975—. Mem. AAAS, Ecol. Soc. Am., D.C. Bar Assn. Contbr. articles in field to profl. jours. Office: Center for Environ Studies Williams Coll Williamstown MA 01267 Tel (413) 597-2346

JOSCELYN, KENT BUCKLEY, b. Binghamton, N.Y., Dec. 18, 1936; B.S. in Physics, Union Coll., Schenectady, 1957; LL.B., Albany Law Sch., 1960, J.D., 1968. Admitted to N.Y. bar, 1961, U.S. Ct. Mil. Appeals bar, 1962, D.C. bar, 1967; practiced in Deposit, N.Y., 1961, 64-65; with JAGC, USAF, 1961-64; atty.-adviser USAF, Washington, 1965-67; asso. prof. forensic studies Ind. U., 1967-75; research scientist, atty., head div. pub. factors Hwy. Safety Research Inst. U. Mich., 1976—; regional dir. Ind. Criminal Justice Planning Agy., Bloomington, 1969-72; vice chmn. Ind. Organized Crime Prevention Council, Indpls., 1969-72; dir. Inst. for Research in Pub. Safety, Bloomington, 1970-75; mem. automobile assessment advisory panel Office Tech. Assessment, U.S. Congress, 1976—. Commr. of pub. safety City of Bloomington, 1974-76. Mem. Am., N.Y. bar assns., Acad. Criminal Justice Scis., Am. Soc. Pub. Adminstrn., AAAS, Am. Soc. Criminology, Soc. Automotive Engrs., Sigma Xi. Editor: Internat. Jour. Criminal Justice, 1971—; research in traffic law and ct. system, hwy. safety. Home: 2255 Blueberry Ln Ann Arbor MI 48103 Office: Hwy Safety Research Inst U Mich Huron Pkwy at Baxter Rd Ann Arbor MI 48109 Tel (313) 763-1276

JOSEM, ERNEST L., b. N.Y.C., Oct. 3, 1911; B.A., Wesleyan U., 1931; J.D., Harvard, 1936. Admitted to Conn. bar, 1936; partner firm Josem & Josem, Norwalk, Conn., 1936—; chmn. Norwalk Charter Revision Commn. Mem. Norwalk Bd. Edn., 1960-66, chmn., 1964. Mem. Conn., Norwalk-Wilton bar assns. Office: 111 East Ave Room 333 Norwalk CT 06851 Tel (203) 838-2311

JOSEPH, ALAN HARVEY, b. Bklyn., Jan. 24, 1940; B.A., Adelphi Coll., 1962; J.D., N.Y. Law Sch., 1965. Admitted to N.Y. bar, 1966, U.S. Supreme Ct. bar, 1970; asso. firm Breitbart & Breitbart, 1965-67; asso. firm Wolinsky & Wolinsky, 1968-70; partner firm Mastropieri & Joseph, Glendale, N.Y., 1971—. Mem. Community Sch. Dist. 28 N.Y.C. Bd. Edn., 1970-72; supt. task force Plainview (N.Y.)—Old Bethpage Sch. Dist., 1974. Mem. Blackstone Assn. of Ridgewood, N.Y. State, Queens County Am. bar assns. Mem. N.Y. Law Rev., Contbr. articles to legal jours. Office: 6740 Myrtle Ave Ridgewood NY 11227 Tel (212) 821-2210

JOSEPH, ALLAN JAY, b. Chgo., Feb. 4, 1938; B.B.A., U. Wis., 1959, J.D. with honors, 1962. Admitted to Wis. bar, 1962, Calif. bar, 1964; with Judge Adv. Gen. Corps, U.S. Army, 1962-65; asso. firm Pettit, Evers & Martin, San Francisco, 1965-70, partner, 1970—. Mem. Am. Bar Assn. (chmn. pub. contracts sect. 1977-78), State Bar Calif., State Bar Wis., Order of Coif. Home: 240 Cascade St Mill Valley CA 94941 Office: 600 Montgomery St San Francisco CA 94111 Tel (415) 434-4000

JOSEPH, LEONARD, b. Phila., June 8, 1919; B.A., U. Pa., 1941; J.D., Harvard, 1947. Admitted to N.Y. bar, 1949, U.S. Supreme Ct. bar, 1956; asso. firm Dewey, Ballantine, Bushby, Palmer & Wood, N.Y.C., 1948-57, partner, 1957—. Fellow Am. Bar Found., Am. Coll. Trial Lawyers; mem. Am., N.Y. State bar assns., Assn. Bar City N.Y., Am. Judicature Soc., Harvard Law Sch. Assn. N.Y.C. (trustee 1965-68). Office: 140 Broadway New York City NY 10005 Tel (212) 344-8000

JOSEPHSON, EDWIN IRA, b. Chgo., Feb. 21, 1944; B.S. in Accounting, Roosevelt U., 1965; J.D., DePaul U., 1968. Admitted to Ill. bar, 1968; partner firm Mass., Miller & Josephson, Chgo., 1968—. Vice pres., dir. Northgate Civic Assn., Arlington Heights, Ill., 1972-75. Mem. Am., Chgo. bar assns. C.P.A. Home: 3129 N Windsor Dr Arlington Heights IL 60004 Office: 221 N LaSalle St Chicago IL 60601 Tel (312) 726-3666

JOSEPHSON, JOSEPH PAUL, b. Trenton, N.J., June 3, 1933; B.A. in Polit. Sci., U. Chgo., 1953; J.D., Cath. U. Am., 1960. Admitted to Alaska bar, 1961; individual practice law, Anchorage, 1961—; chmn. Alaska adv. com. U.S. Commn. on Civil Rights, 1961-62; mem. Alaska Ho. of Reps., 1963-67; city councilman City of Anchorage, 1966-68, mayor pro tem, 1967-68; borough assemblyman Greater Anchorage Area Borough, 1967-68, pres. pro tem, 1967-68; mem. Alaska State Senate, 1969-72, minority leader, 1971-72; state co-chmn. Joint Fed.-State Land Use Planning Commn. for Alaska, 1972-74; lectr. U. Alaska and Alaska Meth. U., 1975—; vice chmn. mayor's ad hoc com. on status of Anchorage, 1976. Bd. dirs. South-Central Alaska chpt. ARC, 1964-65; mem. steering com. Operation Breakthrough, 1969; bd. dirs. Alaska Pub. TV, 1974; hon. chmn. fund dr. Alaska Center for Environment, 1974. Mem. Anchorage Bar Assn. (chmn. legal aid com. 1962 mem. com. on family law 1973-74, 76-77), Am. Arbitration Assn. (arbitrator 1976—), Alaska World Affairs Council (dir. 1961-63). Mem. staff Law Rev. Cath. U. Am. Home: 1526 F St Anchorage AK 99501 Office: Suite 930 425 G St Anchorage AK 99501 Tel (907) 276-7133

JOSEPHSON, WILLIAM HOWARD, b. Newark, Mar. 22, 1934; A.B., U. Chgo., 1952; J.D., Columbia, 1955. Admitted to N.Y. State bar, 1956, D.C. bar, 1966, U.S. Supreme Ct. bar, 1959; asso. firm Paul, Weiss, Rifkind, Wharton & Garrison, N.Y.C., 1955-58, firm Joseph L. Rauh, Jr., Washington, 1959; regional counsel Far East, ICA, Washington, 1959-61; spl. asst. to dir. Peace Corps, Washington, 1961-62, dep. gen. counsel, 1961-63, gen. counsel, 1963-66; asso. firm Fried, Frank, Harris, Shriver & Jacobson, N.Y.C., 1966-67, partner, 1968—; spl. counsel N.Y.C. Human Resources Adminstrn., 1966-67, N.Y.C. Bd. Edn., 1968-71. Nat. coordinator Democratic vice presdl. campaign, 1972. Mem. Assn. Bar City N.Y. (spl. com. on Congl. ethics 1968-70), Council on Fgn. Relations. Recipient William A. Jump award for achievement pub. adminstrn., 1965; mem. bd. editors Columbia Law Rev., 1953-55. Home: 58 S Oxford St Brooklyn NY 11217 Office: 120 Broadway New York City NY 10005 Tel (212) 964-6500

JOSIAS, STEVEN LEE, b. N.Y.C., Aug. 8, 1949; B.A. in History, The Citadel, 1970; J.D., Notre Dame, 1973. Admitted to Fla. bar, 1973, U.S. Tax Ct. bar, 1973; law clk. firm Globensky, Bleich & Peterson, St. Joseph, Mich., 1972-73; asso. firm Zeiher & Brinkley, Ft. Lauderdale, Fla., 1973-74; partner firm Josias & Shulmister, Ft. Lauderdale, 1974—; city atty. Pembroke Pines (Fla.), 1976—. Chmn. new leadership State Israel Bonds, 1975—. Mem. Am., Broward bar assns., Fla. Bar, Young Lawyers Assn., South Fla. Citadel Club (pres., dir.), Assn. Citadel Men, U.S. Jaycees, Ft. Lauderdale C. of C. (sub-task force and task force mem. 1976—). Home: 1713 NW 36th Court Fort Lauderdale FL 33309 Office: Suite 602 3101 N Federal Hwy Fort Lauderdale FL 33306 Tel (305) 563-1123

JOSLIN, ALFRED HAHN, b. Providence, Jan. 29, 1914; A.B. magna cum laude, Brown U., 1935; LL.B., cum laude, Harvard, 1938; L.H.D. (hon.), Bryant Coll., 1975. Admitted to R.I. bar, 1938, U.S. Dist. Ct. for R.I., 1939, U.S. Supreme Ct. bar, 1945; mem. firm Aisenberg & Joslin, Providence, 1946-63; asso. justice Supreme Ct. R.I., 1963—. Trustee Brown U., 1963-69, vice-chancellor, 1968-69, fellow, 1969—, sec., 1972—. Pres. Providence Community Fund, 1955-57; v.p., chmn. budget com. United Fund. R.I., 1952-57; v.p. R.I. Health Facilities Planning Council, 1965-70; bd. dirs. Greater Providence YMCA, R.I. Legal Aid Soc.; mem. Narragansett Council Boy Scouts Am.; trustee Temple Emanual, Providence, 1946; trustee, pres. emeritus Butler Hospital, Providence, 1956—; sec., hon. trustee Miriam Hosp., 1947—. Mem. Am., R.I. bar assns. Named Man of Yr., Univ. Club, 1974; Big Brother of Year, 1957. Home: 4 Mulberry Rd Bristol RI 02809 Office: 250 Benefit St Providence RI 20903 Tel (401) 277-3290

JOSLIN, GEORGE STANLEY, b. Sextonville, Wis., July 20, 1911; B.A., Cornell Coll., 1934; LL.B., U. Wis., 1939; J.D., 1968; LL.M., U. Mich., 1952; Ford Found. grantee, Eng., 1963-64. Admitted to Wis. bar, 1939, Ga. bar, 1955; individual practice law, Portage, Wis., 1939-42; instr. law U. Ky., 1947; prof. Emory U., Atlanta, 1947—, Charles Howard Candler prof., 1960—, acting dean law sch., 1960-61; interim judge Ga. Ct. Appeals, 1967; research asst. Ga. Ct. Appeals, 1960; legal counsel Atlanta-Fulton Sch. Study Commn., 1954-55; mem. adv. com. on bankruptcy rules U.S. Supreme Ct., 1962-76. Mem. DeKalb County Republican Exec. Com., 1958. Mem. Nat. Assn. Law Schs., Am. Assn. Law Schs. (chmn. council on securities regulation 1959-60, chmn. creditors' rights com. 1960, mem. fgn. exchange law faculties com. 1970-72), Am. Bar Assn., Euthanasia Soc. Am., Tau Kappa Alpha, Phi Delta Phi. Author: The Minister's Law Handbook, 1962; Law for the High School, 1968; Everyman's Law, 1968. Contbr. articles to legal jours. Home: 822 Houston Mill Rd NE Atlanta GA 30329 Office: Sch of Law Emory U Atlanta GA 30322 Tel (404) 329-6835

JOSLIN, ROGER SCOTT, b. Bloomington, Ill., June 21, 1936; B.S. in Bus., Miami U., Oxford, Ohio, 1958; J.D., U. Ill., 1961. Admitted to Ill. bar, 1961; asso. firm Davis, Morgan & Witherell, Peoria, Ill., 1961-63; controller Union Ins. Group, Bloomington, 1963-64; asst. v.p. State Farm Mut. Automboile Ins. Co., Bloomington 1964-69, v.p., controller, 1969—. Chmn. McLean County (Ill.) Republican Central Com., 1966-76; del. Rep. Nat. Conv., 1968, 76. Mem. Am., Ill., McLean County bar assns., Ill. Soc. C.P.A.'s, Soc. C.P.C.U.'s, Soc. C.L.U.'s, McLean County Assn. Commerce and Industry (dir.), Order of Coif, Phi Beta Kappa, Omicron Delta Kappa. Home: 2001 E Cloud St Bloomington IL 61701 Office: 1 State Farm Plaza Bloomington IL 61701 Tel (309) 662-2934

JOYCE, BERNARD F., b. N.Y.C., July 7, 1930; B.S., Fordham Coll., 1952, LL.D., 1958; LL.M., N.Y. U., 1961. Admitted to N.Y. State bar, 1958; jr. accountant Arthur Young & Co., N.Y.C., 1954-56; asso. firm Emmet, Marvin & Martin, N.Y.C., 1956-62, partner, 1962—. Mem. Am., N.Y., N.Y.C. bar assns. Home: Bacon Hill Rd Pleasantville NY 10570 Office: 48 Wall St New York City NY 10005 Tel (212) 422-2974

JOYCE, DOUGLAS DEE, b. Logansport, Ind., Apr. 25, 1944; B.A., DePauw U., 1966; J.D., Ind. U., 1969. Admitted to Mo. bar, 1970; exec. v.p., counsel Warranty Service Co., St. Louis, 1969-72; pres., chief counsel Physicians Placement Group, Inc., St. Louis, 1972—. Mem. Mo. Bar Assn., DePauw U., Ind. U. Sch. Law alumni assns., Phi Alpha Delta. Office: 970 Executive Pkwy St Louis MO 63141 Tel (314) 727-1213

JOYCE, JOHN CLELAND, b. Portland, Oreg., June 13, 1940; B.A., Columbia, 1962; J.D., Georgetown U., 1965. Admitted to Md. bar, 1965, Dist. of Columbia, 1966; partner firm Duckett, Orem, Christie & Beckett, Hyattsville, Md., 1965—. Mem. Am., Md., D.C., Prince George's County bar assns. Home: 309 Soapstone Ln Silver Spring MD 20904 Office: 6401 New Hampshire Ave Hyattsville MD 20783 Tel (301) 270-2800

JOYCE, JOHN FRANCIS, b. Chgo., Oct. 29, 1947; B.A. in Bus. Adminstrn., Coll. St. Thomas, St. Paul, 1969; J.D., Loyola U., Chgo., 1973. Admitted to Ill. bar, 1973; asso. firm John A. Leemon, Mt. Carroll, Ill., 1973-76; individual practice law, Mt. Carroll, 1976—. Mem. Am., Ill. bar assns., Comml. Law League, Delta Theta Phi. Home: 206 E Market St Mount Carroll IL 61053 Office: 106 E Market St Mount Carroll IL 61053 Tel (815) 244-2895

JOYCE, JOSEPH BENEDICT, b. Council Bluffs, Iowa, July 18, 1932; A.B., U. Notre Dame, 1955, LL.B., 1956. Admitted to Iowa bar, 1956; mem. firm Holliday Miller & Stewart, and predecessor, Des Moines, 1956-74; asso. firm Adler Brennan Joyce & Steger, Des Moines, 1974—. Mem. Des Moines Bd. Adjustment, 1976—; bd. dirs. Goodwill Industries Des Moines, Cath. Council of Social Concern. Mem. Am., Iowa assns. trial lawyers, Am., Iowa, Polk County (past pres. jr. bar assn., chmn. family law com.) bar assns. Home: 4610 Wakonda Pkwy Des Moines IA 50315 Office: 707 Central Nat Bank Bldg Des Moines IA 50309 Tel (515) 244-1391

JOYNER, SAMUEL ANDREW, III, b. Lawton, Okla., Nov. 3, 1941; B.S., George Washington U., 1963; J.D. with honors, U. Okla., 1966. Admitted to Okla. bar, 1966; partner firm Godlove, Joyner, Godlove, Garrett and Meyers, Inc., Lawton, 1966—; magistrate Western Dist. Okla., 1976—. Treas. Lawton YMCA, 1969-70, pres., 1970-71; bd. dirs. Lawton Indsl. Found. Mem. Am., Okla., Comanche County (Okla.) bar assns., Order of Coif, Phi Delta Phi (pres. 1965-66). Named Outstanding Young Man of Lawton, Lawton Jaycees, 1971. Home: 809 NW 51st St Lawton OK 73501 Office: 802 C Ave POB 1488 Lawton OK 73501 Tel (405) 353-6700

JOYNT, FRANCIS WILLIAM, b. Rome, N.Y., Dec. 25, 1938; B.A., Niagara U., 1961; J.D., St. John's U., 1964, LL.M., N.Y. U., 1970. Admitted to N.Y. State bar, 1965; asst. prof. law U.S. Mil. Acad., West Point, N.Y., 1965-70; v.p., sec. Ayco Corp., Albany, N.Y., 1970—. Home: 55 S Manning Blvd Albany NY 12203 Tel (518) 459-7910

JOYNT, JOHN HOWARD, b. Birmingham, Ala., Feb. 6, 1903; B.S., Carnegie Inst. Tech., 1925; M.S., Mass. Inst. Tech., 1929; LL.B., George Washington U., 1931. Admitted to D.C. bar, 1931, U.S. Supreme Ct. bar, 1943; asso. firm Janney, Blair & Curtis, N.Y.C., 1931-32; individual practice law, Washington, 1932-70, Alexandria, Va., 1970—; examiner U.S. Patent Office, Washington, 1928-31. Mem. Am. Bar Assn., Am. Patent Law Assn., Am. Judicature Soc., Bar Assn. D.C. Contbr. articles to profl. jours. Home: 601 Duke St Alexandria VA 22314 Office: 1007 King St Alexandria VA 22314 Tel (703) 548-8010

JUDGE, CHARLES ROGERS, b. St. Louis, Oct. 31, 1906; LL.B., Washington U., St. Louis, 1929. Admitted to Mo. bar, 1929, U.S. Supreme Ct. bar, 1951; asso. firm Dubail, Judge, Kilker, Maier, and predecessors, St. Louis, 1932—, now partner. Alderman City of Clayton (Mo.), 1967-75. Mem. St. Louis, Mo., Am. bar assns. Home: 6454 Cecil Ave Clayton MO 63105 Office: 1 Mercantile Center Saint Louis MO 63101 Tel (314) 241-4261

JUDGE, WILLIAM CAMPBELL, b. San Francisco, Feb. 26, 1941; B.A., U. Calif., Berkeley, 1962, LL.B., 1965. Admitted to Calif. bar, 1966; asso. firm Donahue, Richards & Gallagher, Oakland, Calif., 1965-66; asso. firm Sedwick, Detert, Moran & Arnold, San Francisco, 1966-73, partner, 1974—. Mem. Calif. Bar Assn., Assn. Def. Counsel. Office: 111 Pine St San Francisco CA 94111 Tel (415) 982-0303

JUDSON, SOL S., b. Kansas City, Mo., July 21, 1921; A.A., Kansas City Jr. Coll., 1940; B.A., U. Kansas City, 1942; J.D., U. Mo., 1948. Admitted to Mo. bar, 1948, Calif. bar, 1949; individual practice law, Pittsburg, Calif., 1949—. Mem. Am., Calif., Contra Costa County, Alameda County bar assns., Alameda-Contra Costa Counties, Calif. trial lawyers assns., Assn. Trial Lawyers Am., Am. Legion, Pittsburg C. of C. Home: 101 Fernwood Dr Moraga CA 94556 Office: 3846 Railroad Ave Pittsburg CA 04565 Tel (415) 439-9181

JUDSON, WILFRED, b. Eng., 1902; student Osgoode Hall, Toronto, Ont., Can. Called to Ont. bar, 1932; apptd. justice Supreme Ct. of Ont., 1951; puisne judge Supreme Ct. Can., 1958—. Office: Supreme Ct of Can Wellington St Ottawa ON K1A 0J1 Canada*

JUDY, FREDERICK A., b. N.Y.C., June 4, 1933; B.S., Denison U., 1955; LL.B., Cornell U., 1958. Admitted to N.Y. State bar, 1958; asso. firm Neale & Wilson, Scarsdale, N.Y., 1958-61, firm Smith, Ranscht, Pollock & Barnes, White Plains, N.Y., 1961-67; partner firm Judy & Miller, Scarsdale, 1967—; village atty. Scarsdale, 1969-72. Bd. dirs. White Plains YMCA, 1969-75; mem. village bd. and sch. bd. nominating coms., 1968, 74-75. Mem. N.Y. State (exec. com. municipal law sect.), Westchester County bar assns. Office: Harwood Bldg Scarsdale NY 10583 Tel (914) 725-0300

JUERGENS, STEPHEN JOSEPH, b. Dubuque, Iowa, Mar. 6, 1947; B.A., Loras Coll., 1969; J.D., State U. Iowa, 1973. Admitted to Iowa bar, 1973; partner firm Fuerste, Carew & Coyle, Juergens & Sudmeier, Dubuque, 1976—. Sec., Dubuque Parent and Childbirth Assn. Mem. Am., Iowa, Dubuque County bar assns. Home: 1806 Lori St Dubuque IA 52001 Office: 900 Dubuque Bldg Dubuque IA 52001 Tel (319) 556-4011

JUERGENS, WILLIAM GEORGE, b. Steeleville, Ill., Sept. 7, 1904; A.B., Carthage Coll., 1925, LL.D., 1970; J.D., U. Mich., 1928. Admitted to Ill. bar, 1928; since practiced in Chester, Ill.; individual practice law, 1928-38; judge Randolph County, 1938-50; judge 3d Jud. Circuit Ct. Ill., 1951-56, U.S. Dist. Ct., Eastern Dist. Ill., 1956—, chief judge, 1965-72, sr. judge, 1972—. Mem. Fed., Ill., Randolph County, 7th Jud. Circuit bar assns. Recipient 1st Annual Alumnus award Carthage Coll., 1961. Home: 1836 Swanwick St Chester IL 62233 Office: 1st Nat Bank Bldg Chester IL 62233 Tel (618) 826-4421

JUERGENSMEYER, JULIAN CONRAD, b. Paintsville, Ky., Aug. 24, 1938; A.B. summa cum laude, Duke, 1959, J.D. with honors, 1963; Certificat des Etudes Politiques, U. Bordeaux (France), 1960; Diplomas I and II, Internat. Faculty of Comparative Law, Strasburg, France, 1968, 69. Admitted to Ohio bar, 1963; asso. firm Squire, Sanders & Dempsey, Cleve., 1963-65; asso. prof. law Ind. U., 1965-68, Haile Sellassie I U., Addis Ababa, Ethiopia, 1969-70; asso. prof. law Tulane U., 1970-73; prof., dir. Cuban Am. lawyers program, dir. Cambridge Warsaw internat. trade law program U. Fla., 1973—; land commr. Fed. Dist. Ct. for So. Dist. Ind., 1965-67; mem. Ind. Trust Code Study Commn., 1966-68; hearing commr. Fla. Dept. Adminstrn., 1974—. Mem. World Peace Through Law Center, Internat. Water Law Assn., African Law Assn., Instituto Cultural Mexicano Etiope (hon.). Author: Comparative Materials on Natural Resources and Environment Law, 1974; (with J. Wadley) Water Law in Eastern Africa, 1975; Florida Land Use Restrictions, 1976. Home: 2721 SW 7th Pl Gainesville FL 32607 Office: Holland Law Center U of Fla Gainesville FL 32611 Tel (904) 392-2211

JULIA, PERCY LAVON, JR., b. Chgo., Aug. 21, 1940; B.A., Oberlin Coll., 1962; J.D., U. Wis., 1966. Admitted to Wis. bar, 1966, U.S. Supreme Ct. bar, 1970, also U.S. Ct. Appeals bars; since practiced in Madison, Wis.; sr. partner firm Julian & Assos. S.C., 1966—; lectr. U. Wis., 1969-70, 1974; vice chmn., sec. Wis. State Personnel Bd., 1972-75, chmn., 1975-76; chmn. Wis. State Com. U.S. Commn. on Civil Rights, 1971—; mem. Gov's. Citizens Study Com. on Jud. Orgn., 1972-73; Madison Legal Aid Soc., 1963-65; Wis. Employment Relations Study Commn., 1975—. Mem. Madison Urban League (dir. 1975—). Mem. NAACP, ACLU, Am., Dane County bar assns., Nat. Assn. Criminal Def. Lawyers, Bar Assn. 7th Fed. Circuit, Internat. Personnel Mgmt. Assn., Delta Sigma Rho. Contbr. articles in field to profl. jours.; named Member of the Year, Wis. Civil Liberties Union, 1972. Office: 330 E Wilson St Madison WI 53703 Tel (608) 255-6400

JULIAN, DAVID HOPKINS, b. Chgo., Nov. 23, 1941; B.A., Cornell U., J.D., U. Mich. Admitted to Ill. bar, 1966, Tax Ct. bar, 1967; tax atty. Office of Regional Counsel, Buffalo, N.Y., 1967-69; gen. counsel Bankers United Mgmt. Corps., Oakbrook, Ill., 1969-73; pres., IDC Asset Mgmt. Corp., Chgo., 1973-74, exec. v.p., 1975—; partner cons. Mgmt. Corp. Mem. Ill. State, Chgo. bar assns. Office: 550 Frontage Rd Suite 388 Northfield IL 60093 Tel (312) 441-6648

JULIANO, JOHN LOUIS, b. Queens, N.Y., Oct. 21, 1944; B.B.A., St. John's U., 1966; J.D., Bklyn. Law Sch., 1969. Admitted to N.Y. bar, 1970; asso. firm Juliano Karlsson and Weisberg, Suffolk, N.Y., 1970-72; individual practice law, East Northport, N.Y., 1972—. Mem. Suffolk County Budget Com. Mem. Assn. ICC Practitioners, Am. Trial Lawyers Assn., N.Y. State, Suffolk County bar assns., Columbian Lawyers Assn. (pres. 1974-75). Home: 129 Grissom Way Hauppauge NY 11787 Office: 39 Doyle Ct East Northport NY 11731 Tel (516) 864-9300

JULIUS, BAYER ARTHUR, JR., b. Monterey, Calif., June 8, 1945; B.A., U. Nev., 1968; J.D., Am. U., 1971. Admitted to Nev. bar, 1971; dep. atty. gen. State of Nev., Carson City, 1971-72; individual practice law, Carson City, 1972—. Mem. Am. Trial Lawyers Assn., Am. Bar Assn. Office: 412 N Curry St Carson City NV 89701 Tel (702) 883-4404

JUNGROTH, JAMES RALPH, b. Jamestown, N.D., Sept. 10, 1925; student Presbyn. Coll. S.C., 1944, Jamestown Coll., 1946-47; Ph.B., U. N.D., 1950, LL.B., 1950, J.D., 1970. Admitted to N.D. bar, 1950; adjustor Nat. Farmers Union Property and Casualty Co., Jamestown, 1950-51, N.D. claims mgr., 1951-52; partner firm Mackenzie & Jungroth, Jamestown, 1952—; state's atty. Stutsman County (N.D.), 1960-62; mem. N.D. State Legislature, 1965-67. Mem. N.D. Water Commn., 1967-75, N.D. Water Pollution Control Bd., 1967-68. Mem. Stutsman County, Am. bar assns., Am. Trial Lawyers Assn. Home: 910 8th Ave NW Jamestown ND 58401 Office: 404 2d ST SE POB 1367 Jamestown ND 58401 Tel (701) 252-3460

JUNKERMAN, WILLIAM JOSEPH, b. N.Y.C., May 5, 1904; A.B., N.Y. U., 1925; LL.B., Fordham U., 1928. Admitted to N.Y. bar, 1929, U.S. Supreme Ct. bar, 1947; asst. counsel L.I. State Park Commn., 1929-32; asso. firm Milbank Tweed Hope & Webb, N.Y.C., 1933-41, 46-47; regional atty. CAA Pacific N.W., Seattle, 1947-48; asso. firm Haight, Gardner, Poor & Havens, N.Y.C., 1948—, partner 1950—. Fellow Am. Coll. Trial Lawyers; mem. Am., N.Y. State bar assns., N.Y. County Lawyers Assn., Maritime Law Assn., U.S., Nat. Pilots Assn., Am. Legion, Mil. Order World Wars, Navy League U.S., Internat. Assn. Ins. Counsel. Contbr. articles to profl. jours. Home: 311 W 245th St Fieldston NY 10471 Office: 1 State St Plaza New York City NY 10004

JUPINKO, GEORGE STEPHAN, b. Pitts., Oct. 10, 1942; B.S., Duquesne U., 1965; J.D., Capital U., 1972. Admitted to Ohio bar, 1972, Fla. bar, 1973; title officer Am. Realty Title Co., Columbus, Ohio, 1972-74; individual practice law, Columbus, 1974-75; chief legal counsel Ohio Dept. Hwy. Safety, Columbus, 1975—. Mem. Am., Ohio, Fla. bar assns. Home: 2633-B Petzinger Rd Columbus OH 43209 Office: 240 Parsons Ave Columbus OH 43215 Tel (614) 466-2550

JURCO, STEPHEN, b. Vrbove, Czechoslovakia, Dec. 13, 1913; J.D., DePaul U., 1935. Admitted to Ill. bar, 1935; individual practice law, Chgo., 1935-42, 46-60; sr. partner firm Jurco Damisch & Sinson, Chgo., 1960-70, Jurco & Collins, Chgo., 1970-73; pres. Querrey Naurow Gulanick Kennedy Ltd., Chgo., 1973—; village atty. Arlington Heights (Ill.), 1956-60. Chmn. bd. dirs. N.W. Suburban YMCA, Des Plaines, Ill. Mem. Am., Ill., Chgo., N.W. Suburban bar assns., Nat. Counter Intelligence Corps Assn. (pres. 1974-75, dir. 1947—), Am. Judicature Soc. Office: 135 S LaSalle St Chicago IL 60603 Tel (312) 236-9850

JUROW, GEORGE LAURENCE, b. N.Y.C., Feb. 3, 1943; B.S., U. Pa., 1963; J.D., Yale U., 1966; Ph.D., Adelphi U., 1971. Admitted to N.Y. State bar, 1968; asst. prof. U. City N.Y., 1970-72; 1st dep. commr. N.Y. City Dept. Mental Health and Mental Retardation Services, N.Y.C., 1973—. Mem. Am. Psychol. Assn. Contbr. articles to profl. jours. Home: 139 E 18th St New York City NY 10003 Office: 93 Worth St New York City NY 10013 Tel (212) 566-3950

JUROW, LUCIE SCHUMER, b. N.Y.C., Feb. 27, 1908; B.A., Adelphi Coll., 1928; LL.B., Bklyn. Law Sch., 1930, J.D., 1931. Admitted to N.Y. bar, 1932; law librarian Bklyn. Law Sch., 1950-73; law book broker, Bklyn., 1973—. Mem. Am., Greater N.Y. (life), Upper N.Y. State (life) law librarians assns., Bklyn. Bar Assn. (trustee). Address: 100 Remsen St Brooklyn NY 11201 Tel (212) 522-1888

JUST, DAVID LINCOLN, b. Quincy, Mass., Dec. 20, 1942; B.S. in Chemistry, Pace Coll., 1965; LL.D., Fordham U., 1969. Chemist, Mallory Battery, Tarrytown, N.Y., and Petro Chems. Co., N.Y.C., 1965-69; asso. firm Eyre, Mann, Lucas & Just and predecessor, N.Y.C., 1969-75, partner, 1976—; admitted to N.Y. bar, 1970. Mem. N.Y. State, Am. bar assns., N.Y. Patent Law Assn., Chemists Club of N.Y. Home: 216 Manhattan Ave Tuckahoe NY 10707 Office: 155 E 44th St New York City NY 10017 Tel (212) 682-4980

JUSTICE, JACK BURTON, b. Hardy, Ky., Aug. 2, 1931; A.B., W. Va. Univ. 1952; B.A. in Jurisprudence, Oxford (Eng.) U., 1954, M.A., 1960. Admitted to Pa. bar, 1956; asso. firm Drinker, Biddle & Reath, Phila., 1956-62, partner, 1962—. Bd. dirs. ACLU; chmn. SE Pa. chpt. Am. for Democratic Action, 1968-70; bus. mgr. The Am. Oxonian, 1967—. Mem. Am., Pa., Phila. N.Y.C. bar assns., Am. Law Inst., Assn. Am. Rhodes Scholars (sec. 1967—). Contbr. articles in field to profl. jours. Home: 3805 The Oak Rd Philadelphia PA 19129 Office: 1345 Chestnut St Philadelphia PA 19107 Tel (215) 491-7225

JUSTICE, JOHN B., b. Attleboro, Mass., May 8, 1911; LL.B., Union U. Admitted to N.Y. bar, 1952, U.S. Supreme Ct. bar, 1970; asso. firm Donohue & Koheman, Albany, 1952-56; partner firm Justice and Justice, and predecessors, Albany, 1956—; counsel N.Y. State Legis. Bill Drafting Commn., 1971-72, commr., 1972-73. Mem. Am., N.Y. State, Albany County bar assns., Capital Dist. Trial Lawyers Assn., Am. Arbitration Assn. Home: 34 Bancker St Albany NY 12208 Office: 90 State St Albany NY 12207 Tel (518) 436-0702

JUZA, WILLIAM JOSEPH, b. Salem, Oreg., Jan. 7, 1927; B.B.A., U. Oreg., 1950; J.D., Willamette U., 1956. Admitted to Oreg. bar, 1956; individual practice law, Salem, 1957-63; atty. City of Salem, 1964—. Mem. Oreg. State Bar (chmn. local govt. com. 1968), Am., Marion County (pres. 1969) bar assns., Nat. Inst. Municipal Law Officers (state chmn.). Home: 2590 Sunrise Ave Salem OR 97302 Office: 555 Liberty St SE Salem OR 97301 Tel (503) 588-6085

KABATCHNICK, NEIL BERNARD, b. Scranton, Pa., Dec. 23, 1926; B.S., U. Scranton, 1950; J.D., George Washington U. 1954. Admitted to D.C. bar, 1955, U.S. Ct. Claims bar, 1957, U.S. Ct. Mil. Appeals bar, 1957, U.S. Supreme Ct. bar, 1959; staff mem. Army Bd. for Correction of Mil. Records, Washington, 1955-56; individual practice law, Washington, 1956—. Mem. Judge Advs. Assn. (sect. adminstrv. law), Bar, Am. Bar Assn. (council 1971-74, chmn. adv. mil. law commn. 1970-73, 75—, chmn. vets. com. 1974-76, chmn. civil service law com. 1967-69, vice-chmn. adminstrv. law judges com. 1974—, vice-chmn. mil. lawyers com. gen. practice sect. 1977—), Bar Assn. of D.C. (chmn. mil. law com. 1968-71, 74—, certificate of appreciation 1976-77, chmn. civil service law com. 1966-68). Home: 904 Loxford Terr Silver Spring MD 20901 Office: 1800 M St NW Washington DC 20036 Tel (202) 872-1051

KABATZNICK, MAX, b. Wilno, Russia, Feb. 28, 1894; came to U.S., about 1900, naturalized, 1918; LL.B. (J.D.), Boston U., 1918; Adj. Arts, Harvard, 1944. Admitted to Mass. bar, 1918; U.S. Supreme Ct. bar, 1932; sr. mem. firm Kabatznick, Stern and Cooper, Boston, 1940—. Trustee, Maimonides Sch., Brookline, Mass., Jewish Community Council Met. Boston; hon. v.p. Zionist Orgn. Am., Jewish Nat. Fund N.Y., Jewish Nat. Fund New Eng.; mem. mens assos., Hebrew Rehab. Center, Jewish Meml. Hosp. Boston. Mem. Am., Mass., Boston bar assns., Am. Trial Lawyers Assn. Home: 50 Longwood Ave Brookline MA 02146 Office: 131 State St Boston MA 02109 Tel (617) 523-8181

KABB, KENNETH SAMUEL, b. Cleve., Apr 21, 1939; B.S.M.E., Ohio U., 1964; J.D., Cleve. State Law Sch., 1969. Admitted to Ohio bar, 1969; mech. engr. IBM Corp., Endicott, N.Y., 1964-65; bio-med. engr. Mt. Sinai Hosp., Cleve., 1965-69; asso. firm Brannon, Ticktin, Baron & Mancini, Cleve., 1969-74; partner firm Ticktin, Baron, Kabb & Valore, Cleve., 1974—. Mem. temple bd. Mayfield-Hillcrest Synagogue, 1973—, v.p., 1974-75; mem. urban affairs com. and del. assembly, chmn. criminal justice com. Jewish Community Fedn.; legal services program atty. Am. Jewish Congress; mem. Zionist Orgn. Am., Cleve. Lawyers for Justice to Soviet Jews; sec.-treas. Mid Day Lodge B'nai B'rith; mem. legal com. ACLU; skipper Heights Y Ship 5601 Sea Explorers council Boy Scouts Am. Mem. Am., Ohio, Cleve., Cuyahoga County (exec. com. workmen's compensation sec.) bar assns., Am., Ohio trial lawyers assns., Cleve. Acad. Trial Lawyers, ASME, Am. Soc. Artificial Internal Organs, Tau Beta Pi. Contbr. articles to legal and sci. publs.; sailing instr. USCG Aux. Office: 930 Keith Bldg 1621 Euclid Ave Cleveland OH 44115 Tel (216) 781-3858

KACIR, BARBARA BRATTIN, b. Buffalo, July 19, 1941; B.A., Wellesley Coll., 1963; J.D., U. Mich., 1967. Admitted to Ohio bar, 1967; asso. firm Arter & Hadden, Cleve., 1967-74, partner, 1974—; lectr. Franklin Backus Sch. Law Case Western Res. U., 1975—; mem. regional bd. Am. Arbitration Assn., 1973—. Mem. Am., Ohio (counsel of dels. 1972—), Greater Cleve. (trustee 1973—) bar assns. Home: 3280 Ingleside Rd Shaker Heights OH 44122 Office: 1144 Union Commerce Bldg Cleveland OH 44115 Tel (216) 696-1144

KADISH, AARON, b. Bklyn., July 9, 1940; B.S. in Pharmacy, U. Md., 1963, LL.B., 1968, J.D., 1969. Admitted to Md. bar, 1969; asso. firm Gomborov, Steinberg & Schlachman, Balt., 1969-71; individual practice law, Balt., 1971—. Pres. Beth Jacob Hebrew Sch. P.T.A., Balt., 1976—. Mem. Am. Pharm. Assn., Am., Md. (chmn. membership com. young lawyers sect. 1975-77, chmn. membership com., 1976—, mem. sect. council young lawyers sect. 1975-77) bar assns., Bar Assn. Balt. City. Office: 200 Blaustein Bldg Baltimore MD 21201 Tel (301) 385-1177

KADISH, SANFORD HAROLD, b. N.Y.C., Sept. 7, 1921; B.S.S., Coll. City N.Y., 1942; LL.B., Columbia, 1948. Admitted to N.Y. bar, 1948, Utah bar, 1954; practice law, N.Y.C., 1948-51; prof. law U. Utah, 1951-60, U. Mich., 1961-64; prof. law U. Calif. at Berkeley, 1964-75, dean, Morris vis. prof. Harvard, 1960-61, Freiburg U., 1967, Stanford, 1970; lectr. Salzburg Seminar Am. Studies 1965; Fulbright distinguished lectr. Kyoto (Japan) U., 1975; vis. fellow Inst. Criminology, Cambridge (Eng.) U., winter 1968. Reporter, Cal. Legislative Penal Code Project, 1964-68; public mem. Wage Stblzn. Bd., region XII, 1951-53; cons. Pres.'s Commn. on Law Enforcement, 1966; mem. Calif. Council Criminal Justice, 1968-69. Fulbright lectr. Melbourne (Australia) U., 1956; fellow Center Advanced Study Behavioral Scis., 1967-68, Guggenheim fellow Oxford, 1974-75. Fellow Am. Acad. Arts and Sci.; mem. A.A.U.P. (nat. pres. 1970-72), Nat. Acad. Arbitrators, Am. Soc. Legal and Polit. Philosophy, Am. Assn. Law Sch. (exec. com. 1960), Phi Beta Kappa, Order of Coif (exec. com. 1966-67, 74-75. Author: (with M.G. Paulsen) Criminal Law and Its Processes, 3d edit., 1975; (with M.R. Kadish) Discretion to Disobey—A Study of Lawful Departures from Legal Rules, 1973; also articles. Home: 774 Hilldale St Berkeley CA 94708*

KAESS, FREDERICK WILLIAM, b. Detroit, Dec. 1, 1910; student U. Mich., 1926-28; LL.B., Detroit Coll. Law, 1932, LL.D., 1961. Admitted to Mich. bar, 1932; justice of the peace City of St. Clair Shore (Mich.), 1932-33; atty., claims mgr. Mich. Mut. Liability Co., Lansing, 1933-45; partner firm Davidson, Kaess, Gotschall & Kelly, Detroit, 1945-53; U.S. atty. for Eastern Dist. Mich. Justice Dept., Detroit, 1953-60; judge U.S. Dist. Ct., Eastern Dist. Mich., 1960—, chief judge, 1972-75, sr. judge, 1975—; dept. commr. State Workmen's Compensation Commn., 1939-40. Trustee Brighton (Mich.) Hosp., 1975—. Mem. State Bar Mich., Am., Fed. bar assns., Am. Judicature Soc., Internat. Assn. Ins. Counsel. Named Outstanding Fed. Adminstr. of 1959, City of Detroit; recipient Outstanding Achievement award Crisis Club, 1960. Office, 707 Fed Bldg 231 W Lafayette St Detroit MI 48226 Tel (313) 226-6066

KAGAN, RICHARD LEE, b. Chgo., July 1, 1946; B.A., U. Ill., 1967; J.D., DePaul U., 1973. Admitted to Ill. bar, 1973; asst. state's atty. Cook County (Ill.), 1973-76; partner firm Belmonte, Kagan & Hibbler, Chgo., 1976—. Mem. Am., Ill., Chgo. bar assns., Decalogue Soc. Lawyers. Home: 2754 Summit St Highland Park IL 60035 Office: 33 N LaSalle St Suite 3800 Chicago IL 60602 Tel (312) 236-0360

KAHL, RICHARD CHARLES, b. Vandergrift, Pa., Apr. 19, 1924; A.B., Allegheny Coll., 1948; LL.B., J.D., U. Buffalo, 1953. Admitted to N.Y. bar, 1954; individual practice law, Niagara Falls, N.Y., 1954—; counsel Lewiston-Porter Sch. Dist., 1967—; atty. Village of Youngstown, 1970—. Mem. Village of Lewiston Planning Commn., 1956-57; mem. Lewiston Porter Central Sch. Dist. Bd. Edn., 1965-68, pres. 1968. Mem. Niagara County, Niagara Falls bar assns. Home: 920 Mohawk St Lewiston NY 14092 Office: 911 United Office Bldg Niagara Falls NY 14303 Tel (716) 285-5729

KAHLENBECK, HOWARD, JR., b. Ft. Wayne, Ind., Dec. 7, 1929; B.S. with distinction, Ind. U., 1952; LL.B., U. Mich., 1957. Admitted to Ind. bar, 1957; partner firm Krieg, DeVault, Alexander & Capehart, Indpls., 1957—; sec., dir. Buehler Corp., Indpls., 1971—, Am. Monitor Corp., Indpls., 1971—, Am. Underwriters, Inc., Indpls., 1973—, Am. Interstate Ins. Co. of Ga., Atlanta, 1973—, Am. Interstate Ins. Corp. of Wis., Milw., 1973—. Mem. Am., Ind., Indpls. bar assns., Beta Gamma Sigma, Alpha Kappa Psi, Delta Theta Phi, Delta Upsilon (sec., dir. 1971—). Home: 6320 Old Orchard Rd Indianapolis IN 46226 Office: 2860 Ind Nat Bank Tower Indianapolis IN 46204 Tel (317) 636-4341

KAHN, ANTHONY C., b. Aylesbury, Eng., May 18, 1942; B.A., Cornell U., 1963; J.D. magna cum laude, Harvard, 1966. Admitted to N.Y. State bar, 1967, U.S. 2d Circuit Ct. Appeals bar, 1967; practiced in N.Y.C., 1967—; law clk. U.S. Dist. Ct., 1966-67; asso. firm Cleary, Gottlieb, Steen & Hamilton, 1967-73, Paris, 1969-72; asso. firm Coudert Brothers, 1973-74, partner, 1975—. Mem. Am., N.Y. State bar assns., Assn. Bar City N.Y., Internat. Law Assn. Office: 200 Park Ave New York City NY 10017 Tel (212) 973-3060

KAHN, DAVID MILLER, b. Port Chester, N.Y., Apr. 21, 1925; B.A., U. Ky., 1947; LL.B. cum laude, N.Y. Law Sch., 1950. Admitted to N.Y. State bar, 1951, Fed. Dist. Ct. bar for Eastern and So. Dists. N.Y., 1953, U.S. Supreme Ct. bar, 1958; individual practice law, White Plains, N.Y., 1951-60; partner firm Kahn & Rubin, White Plains, 1960-66; partner firm Kahn & Goldman, White Plains, 1967—; spl. counsel Village of Port Chester, N.Y., 1960-63; commr. appraisal Westchester County Supreme Ct., 1973-77. Founder, chmn. bd. dirs. Port Chester-Rye Town Vol. Ambulance Corps, 1968-77; chmn. Westchester County Citizens for Eisenhower, 1950-52; pres. Westchester County Young Republican Clubs, 1958-60. Fellow Am. Acad. Matrimonial Lawyers (bd. govs. N.Y. chpt. 1976-79); mem. Am., N.Y. State, Westchester County, White Plains bar assns. Home: 6 Mark Dr Port Chester NY 10573 Office: 175 Main St White Plains NY 10601 Tel (914) 761-1800

KAHN, DAVID VICTOR, b. Oak Park, Ill., June 17, 1930; A.B., U. Chgo., 1949, J.D., 1952. Admitted to Ill. bar, 1952, U.S. Supreme Ct. bar, 1965, U.S. Ct. Claims, 1976, U.S. Tax Ct., 1970; teaching asso. Northwestern U. Sch. Law, Evanston, Ill., 1952-53; asst. staff judge adv. USAF, 1953-57; asso. firm Antonow & Weissbourd, Chgo., 1958; asso. firm Altheimer & Gray, and predecessors, Chgo., 1959-62, partner, 1962—. Treas., sec. Am. Jewish Congress Midwest Region, 1970—; trustee Anshe Emet Synagogue, Chgo., 1974—, v.p., 1977. Mem. Am., Fed., Ill. State, Chgo. (chmn. various real property law subcoms. 1971-75) bar assns. Author chpt. Ill. State Bar Assn. Handbook, 1966, 71. Home: 3400 N Lake Shore Dr Chicago IL 60657 Office: One IBM Plaza Suite 3700 Chicago IL 60611 Tel (312) 467-9600

KAHN, DOUGLAS ALLEN, b. Spartanberg, S.C., Nov. 7, 1934; B.A., U. N.C., 1955; J.D., George Washington U., 1958. Admitted to D.C. bar, 1958, Mich. bar, 1965; trial atty. Dept. Justice, Washington, 1958-62; asso. firm Sachs and Jacobs, Washington, 1962-64; asst. prof. law U. Mich., 1964-67, asso. prof., 1967-69, prof., 1969—. Mem. Am., Mich. bar assns. Recipient Emil Brown Fund prize for best leading article written in 1969 in preventive law; author: Basic Corporate Taxation, 2d edit., 1973; Federal Income Tax, 1975; (with Earl Colson) Federal Taxation of Estates, Gifts and Trusts, 2d edit., 1975; (with Lawrence Waggoner) Federal Taxation of Gifts, Trusts and Estates, 1977; contbr. articles to profl. publs. Home: 3465 Wexford Ct Ann Arbor MI 48104 Office: U Mich Law Sch Ann Arbor MI 48109 Tel (313) 764-9326

KAHN, GORDON BARRY, b. Mobile, Ala., Dec. 3, 1931; B.A., U. Ala., 1953, LL.B., 1958; LL.B., N.Y. U., 1959. Admitted to Ala. bar, 1959; partner firm Lyons, Pipes & Cook, Mobile, 1958-74; bankruptcy judge U.S. Dist. Ct. So. Dist. Ala., Mobile, 1974—. Mem. Am., Ala., Mobile bar assns. Home: 230 S McGregor Ave Mobile AL 36608 Office: 331 United States Court House Mobile AL 36602 Tel (215) 690-2391

KAHN, HERBERT, b. N.Y.C., Dec. 30, 1927; B.A., N.Y. U., 1949; LL.B., Bklyn. Law Sch., 1952. Admitted to N.Y. bar, 1952; individual practice law, N.Y.C., 1952-68; asso. firm Phillips, Nizer, Benjamin Krim & Ballon, N.Y.C., 1968—; Pres. Temple Beth Am, Queens, N.Y., 1968-70, pres. Queens Council for Better Housing and Community Devel., Rockville Centre, N.Y., 1968-73, Com. for Better Edn., 1975—. Mem. Bklyn. Law Sch. Alumni Assn. Home: 371 Woodbridge Rd Rockville Centre NY 11570 Office: 40 W 57th St New York City NY 10019 Tel (212) 977-9700

KAHN, LAWRENCE EDWIN, b. Troy, N.Y., Dec. 8, 1937; A.B., Union Coll., Schenectady, 1959; J.D., Harvard, 1962; law certificate Oxford (Eng.) U., 1963. Admitted to N.Y. State bar, 1963; practiced in Albany, N.Y., 1963-73; judge Albany County (N.Y.) Surrogate Ct., 1974—; lectr. Jr. Coll. Albany, Maria Coll. Author: (with Robert W. Kahn) Divorce Lawyers Casebook, 1972. Office: Albany County Courthouse Albany NY 12207 Tel (518) 445-7616

KAHN, RICHARD DREYFUS, b. N.Y.C., Apr. 25, 1931; A.B., Harvard, 1952, J.D., 1955. Admitted to N.Y. State bar, 1955; asso. firm Debevoise, Plimpton, Lyons & Gates, N.Y.C., 1955-62, partner, 1963—. Bd. dirs. Found. for Child Devel., 1970—; trustee Am. Soc. for Psychical Research, 1966—. Mem. Assn. Bar City N.Y., Am., N.Y. State bar assns. Office: 299 Park Ave New York City NY 10017 Tel (212) PL 2-6400

KAHN, RONALD LEE, b. Chgo., Nov. 4, 1930; B.S., U. Ill.; J.D., U. So. Calif., 1957. Admitted to Calif. bar; partner firm Kahn & Goldstein, Century City, Calif., 1960-75; practice law, Los Angeles, 1975—. Mem. Am., Los Angeles, Beverly Hills, Century City (past mem. bd. govs.) bar assns., Am., Calif., Los Angeles trial lawyers assns. Home: 428 S Bedford St Beverly Hills CA Office: 1888 Century Park E 6th Floor Los Angeles CA 90067 Tel (213) 277-2236

KAISER, HENRY, b. Bklyn., Oct. 6, 1911; B.A., Coll. City N.Y., 1932; LL.B., U. Wis., 1937. Admitted to Wis. bar, 1938, U.S. Supreme Ct. bar, 1945, D.C. bar, 1947, U.S. (D.C.) Circuit Ct. Appeals bar, 1948; mem. faculty U. Wis., 1936-38; asso. gen. counsel AFL, Washington, 1938-47; chief legal sect. labor branch Office of Gen. Purchasing Agent, ETO, 1943-45; sr. partner firm VanArkel, Kaiser, Gressman, Rosenberg & Driesen, Washington, 1947—. Mem. Internat. (patron), Am., D.C. bar assns., Assn. Bar D.C. Contbr. articles to legal jours. Office: 1828 L St NW Suite 701 Washington DC 20036 Tel (202) 466-8400

KAISER, JAMES STEWART, b. Huntington, W.Va., Oct. 31, 1936; B.S. in Indsl. Mgmt., Ga. Inst. Tech., 1960; J.D., Ohio State U., 1963. Admitted to Ohio Supreme Ct. bar, 1964, U.S. Dist. Ct. bar, So. Dist. Ohio, 1967, U.S. Supreme Ct. bar, 1973, U.S. 4th Circuit Ct. Appeals bar, 1973; spl. agt. FBI, 1963-67; partner firm Ater & Kaiser, Chesapeake, Ohio, 1967-70; individual practice law, Chesapeake, 1970-73; partner firm Kaiser & Burd, Chesapeake, 1973—; judge Lawrence County Ct., Chesapeake, Ohio, 1973—; spl. counsel Ohio Atty. Gen., Chesapeake, 1971-73. Pres. Planned Parenthood S.E. Ohio, 1972-74. Mem. Ohio State, Lawrence County (Ohio) bar assns., Am. Judicature Soc. Recipient Outstanding Jud. Service award Ohio Supreme Ct., 1975. Office: 411 Rockwood Ave Chesapeake OH 45619 Tel (614) 867-3159

KAKLIS, VASILIOS WILLIAM, b. Kittanning, Pa., Nov. 16, 1942; B.B.A., U. Miami, 1964; J.D., U. Fla., 1968. Admitted to Fla. bar, 1969; asso. firm Miller, Gallen, Kaklis & Venable, and predecessors, Bradenton, Fla., 1969-73, partner, 1973—. Councilman, City of Palmetto (Fla.), 1972—; v.p. Palmetto Br. Boys' Club, 1976—. Mem. Am., Fla., Manatee County bar assns. Office: 701 W 11th St Bradenton FL 33505 Tel (813) 746-4121

KALAFUT, ROBERT JOSEPH, b. Youngstown, Ohio, Apr. 14, 1929; B.B.A., Youngstown State U., 1951; LL.B., Case Western Res. U., 1954. Admitted to Ohio bar, 1954; individual practice law, Youngstown, 1956—; city solicitor Struthers (Ohio), 1961-63, municipal judge, 1964—; judge adv. VFW post, 1958-64. Mem. Ohio, Mahoning County bar assns. Recipient Spl. awards Ohio Supreme Ct., 1976. Home: 35 Lakeshore Dr Youngstown OH 44471 Office: 206 Legal Arts Centre Youngstown OH 44503 Tel (216) 746-6591

KALBFLEISCH, GIRARD EDWARD, b. Piqua, Ohio, Aug. 3, 1899; LL.B., Ohio No. U., 1923, LL.D., 1960. Admitted to Ohio bar, 1924; practices in Mansfield, Ohio; pros. atty. Richland County (Ohio), 1929-33; judge Municipal Ct., Mansfield, 1936-42, Richland County Common Pleas Ct., 1942-59, U.S. Dist. Ct., No. Dist. Ohio, 1959—, sr. judge, 1970—. Bd. dirs. Mansfield Civilian Def., 1941-46. Fellow Ohio Bar Found.; mem. Richland County, Ohio State, Am., Fed. bar assns., Soc. Benchers. Home: 545 Stewart Ln Mansfield OH 44907 Office: US Dist Ct Cleveland OH 44114 Tel (216) 522-4359

KALBRUNNER, ROGER JOHN, b. Cleve., Nov. 20, 1948; A.B., Kenyon Coll., 1970; J.D., Case Western Reserve U., 1973. Admitted to Ohio bar, 1973, Fed. bar, 1975; individual practice law, Cleve., 1973-74; staff atty. Cleve. Dept. Pub. Utilities, 1974—. Mem. Citizens League, 1973, Cuyahoga Valley Assn., 1973, Cleve. Playhouse, 1974. Mem. Am., Cuyahoga, Greater Cleve. bar assns. Home: 6209 Dellbank Dr Cleveland OH 44144 Office: 1201 Lakeside Ave Cleveland OH 44114 Tel (216) 694-3328

KALEMKARIAN, STEPHEN ALBERT, b. Medford, N.J., June 18, 1931; B.A., Fresno State U., 1954; J.D., U. Calif. Berkeley, 1966. Admitted to Calif. bar, 1968; individual practice law, Fresno, Calif., 1968-72; partner firm Kelso & Kalemkarian, and predecessors, Fresno, 1972—; judge pro tempore Fresno County (Calif.) Superior Ct., 1976—. Mem. Calif. Trial Lawyers Assn., Calif., Fresno County (domestic relations com.) bar assns. Office: 1616 W Shaw St Fresno CA 93711 Tel (209) 224-5050

KALILL, PAUL MICHAEL, b. Pittsfield, Mass., Feb. 27, 1943; A.B., Norwich U., 1965; J.D., Suffolk U., 1968. Admitted to Mass. bar, 1968; partner firm Nassar Hunter Howes & Kalill, Springfield, Mass., 1971-75; individual practice law, Springfield, 1975—; mem. Springfield City Council, 1973—. Mem. Western Mass. Health Planning Council, Springfield, 1975—. Mem. Hampden County (Mass.), Mass., Am. bar assns., Mass. Conveyancers Assn. Home: 145 Chapin Terr Springfield MA 01107 Office: 95 State St Springfield MA 01163 Tel (413) 781-1240

KALISH, HARRY ALEXANDER, b. Phila., Nov. 30, 1907; grad. Dickinson Law Sch., 1928. Admitted to Pa. bar, 1930; founder firm Dilworth, Paxson, Kalish & Levy, Phila., 1933—, now sr. partner. Chmn. Phila. chpt. Weizmann Inst. Sci., also dir.; trustee Phila. Community Found., Inc. Mem. Am., Pa., Phila. bar assns., Tau Epsilon Rho. Home: 250 S 17th St Philadelphia PA 19103 Office: 2600 Fidelity Bldg Philadelphia PA 19109 Tel (215) 546-3000

KALISH, MYRON, b. N.Y.C., Dec. 3, 1919; B.S. in Social Sci., Coll. City N.Y., 1940; LL.B. cum laude, Harvard, 1943. Admitted to N.Y. bar, 1944; asso. firm Arthur, Dry & Dole, N.Y.C., 1946-61, partner, 1955-61; sr. partner Arthur, Dry & Kalish, P.C., and predecessor, N.Y.C., 1961—; gen. counsel U.S. Rubber Co. (now Uniroyal, Inc.), 1961—; dir. Paul B. Mulligan & Co., Inc., Scarsdale, N.Y. Adv. bd. Southwestern Legal Found.; mem. lawyers adv. com. to gen. counsel Nat. Assn. Mfrs. Adv. bd. Southwestern Legal Found.; mem. lawyers adv. com. to gen. counsel Nat. Assn. Mfrs. Mem. Am., N.Y. State bar assns., Assn. Bar City N.Y., Internat. and Comparative Law Center. Home: 430 Bryant Ave Roslyn Harbor NY 11576 Office: 1230 Ave of the Americas New York City NY 10020 Tel (212) 489-4575

KALLEN, EDWARD PAUL, b. Bklyn., N.Y., Feb. 6, 1946; B.S., Pa. State U., 1967; J.D., Bklyn. Law Sch., 1971. Admitted to N.Y. State bar, 1972, also U.S. Supreme Ct. bar, U.S. Ct. Appeals for 2d Circuit bar, U.S. Dist. Ct. bars for So. and Eastern Dists. N.Y.; asso. firm Granik, Garson, Silverman & Nowicki, New City, N.Y., 1972-74; individual practice law, New City, N.Y., 1974-77; asso. firm Brent, Phillips, Dranoff & Davis, P.C., Nanuet, N.Y., 1977—; law sec. to judge N.Y. State Family Ct., 1974-77; adj. prof. bus. law Rockland Community Coll., Suffern, N.Y., 1974—; arbitrator Better Bus. Bur. of Bergen, Passaic, Rockland Counties Inc., 1976—. Asst. counsel Ramapo (N.Y.) Democratic Com., 1974-75, mem. exec. bd. Clarktown Young Dems., 1976—; legal asst. Fortune Soc., 1970-72, Legal Aid Soc. City N.Y., 1968; mem. exec. bd. Rockland County chpt. N.Y. Civil Liberties Union. Mem. N.Y. State, Rockland County bar assns. Home: 47 Johnson's Ln New City NY 10956 Office: 20 Old Turnpike Rd Nanuet NY 10954 Tel (914) 623-2800

KALLICK, DAVID ARIN, b. Chgo., Nov. 7, 1945; A.B., Princeton, 1967; J.D., Northwestern U., 1971. Admitted to Calif. bar, 1972, Ill. bar, 1971; law clk. Ill. Appellate Ct., Chgo., 1971-72; asso. firm McCutchen, Doyle, Brown & Enersen, San Francisco, 1972-74; asst. dean U. So. Calif. Law Center, Los Angeles, 1974-76, also instr.; instr., asst. dean Chgo.-Kent Coll. Law, Ill. Inst. Tech., Chgo., 1976—. Nat. law career advisor Peace Corps, VISTA Vols., Mem. Am., Calif., Ill. bar assns. Home: 1841 Berkeley Rd Highland Park IL 60035 Office: Chgo-Kent Coll Law 77 S Wacker Dr Chicago IL 60606 Tel (312) 567-5010

KALLMAN, JAMES THEODORE, b. Bronx, N.Y., Oct. 27, 1927; A.B., U. Mich., 1949; grad. Wayne State U. Law Sch., 1957. Admitted to Mich. bar, 1957; claims adjuster USF&G, Lansing, 1957-60; commr. Ingham County Circuit Ct., 1960-62; individual practice law, Lansing, 1958-63; judge Ingham County Probate Ct., 1963-73, Ingham County Circuit Ct., 1973—; tchr. Mich. State U., Lansing, summer 1974; mem. Jud. Tenure Commn. Mich., 1968-72. Deacon, trustee, treas., Sunday Sch. tchr., asst. Sunday Sch. supt. Baptist chs., deacon Williamston Bapt. Ch.; chmn. Greater Lansing Child Evangelism Fellowship; mem. Mich. Gov.'s Crime Commn.; coach jr. basketball teams YMCA Basketball League; past bd. dirs. YMCA, Downtown Coaches Club. Mem. Am., Mich., bar assn., Am. Judicature Soc., Christian Legal Soc., Wayne State Alumni Club (pres. 1969—). Office: City Hall Lansing MI 48933 Tel (517) 482-1213

KALMA, FREDERICK JULIUS, b. Neptune, N.J., July 18, 1944; B.A., Monmouth Coll., 1967; J.D., Seton Hall Coll., 1970. Admitted to N.J. bar, 1970; 1972; asst. county prosecutor Monmouth County (N.J.), 1971-73; asso. Samuel S. Sagotsky, Freehold, N.J., 1973-74; individual practice law, Matawan, N.J., 1974—; instr. constl. law Middlesex County Community Coll., 1973-74; instr. Monmouth County Police Acad., 1971-73; lectr. bus. law Brookdale Community Coll., 1972-73. Mem. Am., N.J., Monmouth County bar assns., Manalapan Twp. Jaycees. Office: 128 Main St Matawan NJ 07747 Tel (201) 583-3400

KALODNER, HOWARD ISAIAH, b. Phila., Dec. 16, 1933; B.A., Haverford Coll., 1954; LL.B., Harvard U., 1957. Admitted to Pa. bar, 1958; law clk. U.S. Supreme Ct., 1958-59; asso. firm Schnader, Harrison, Segold & Lewis, Phila., 1960; legal advisor U.S. Dept. State, Washington, 1961-62; solicitor U.S. Dept. Labor, Washington, 1962-64; prof. law N.Y. U., 1964-77; dean Western New Eng. Coll. Law, 1977—; bd. dirs. MFY Legal Services Corp., N.Y.C.; dir. Inst. Jud. Adminstrn., 1976—. Home: PO Box 161 Monterey MA 01245

KALUZNY, EUGENE LEWIS, b. Milw., Sept. 27, 1937; B.S. in Pharmacy, U. Wis., 1959; J.D., Marquette U., 1963. Admitted to Wis. bar, 1963; individual practice law, Milw., 1965—. Mem. Am. Bar Assn., State Bar Wis. Author: Pharmacy Law Digest, 1965—. Office: 924 W Oklahoma Ave Milwaukee WI 53215 Tel (414) 481-7207

KAMAN, ROBERT BARTON, b. Albany, N.Y., May 24, 1926; B.A., U. Rochester, 1947; LL.B., Cornell U., 1950. Admitted to N.Y. bar, 1950; asso. firm Charles J. Bellew, Johnson City, N.Y., 1951-55; partner firm Rappaport, Kaman & Hull, Binghamton, N.Y., 1955-75, Kaman & Hull, Binghamton, 1976—. Mem. N.Y. State, Broome County bar assns. Home: 21 Avon Rd Binghamton NY 13905 Office: 66 Hawley St Box 1965 Binghamton NY 13902 Tel (607) 723-5406

KAMB, BOYNTON, b. Mt. Vernon, Wash., June 7, 1913; B.A., U. Wash., 1935, J.D., 1938. Admitted to Wash. State bar, 1938, U.S. Dist. Ct. bar, 1954, Republic of Philippines bar, 1948, U.S. Ct. of Claims bar, 1950; served as 1st lt. JAG, U.S. Army, 1946-48; mem. U.S. Claims Commn., Philippines, 1948-49; dep. atty. Skagit County, Wash., 1938-39; individual practice law, Mt. Vernon, 1950-76; city atty., Mt. Vernon, 1972-74. Mem. Am., Skagit County bar assns., Am. Trial Lawyers Assn. Recipient commendation from Pres. of Philippines, 1948. Office: 815 Cleveland St Mount Vernon WA 98273 Tel (206) 336-3030

KAMENSKY, MARVIN, b. Chgo., Aug. 16, 1939; B.S., U. Ill., 1961; J.D., DePaul U., 1966. Admitted to Ill. bar, 1966, U.S. Tax Ct. bar, 1966, No. Dist. Ill. bar, 1966; agt. IRS, U.S. Treasury Dept., 1961-67; mem. firm Altman, Kurlander & Weiss, Chgo., 1967-69, partner; 1970; partner firm Carlins & Kamensky, Chgo., 1970—. Mem. Northfield Twp. Sch. Dist. 31 Bd. Edn., Northbrook, Ill., 1975—. Mem. Am., Ill. Chgo. bar assns., Ill. Soc. C.P.A.'s, Am. Lawyers Assn. (adv. bd.). C.P.A., Ill. Home: 2101 Valley Rd Northbrook IL 60062 Office: 120 S LaSalle St Chicago IL 60603 Tel (312) 368-1666

KAMINE, BERNARD SAMUEL, b. Oklahoma City, Dec. 5, 1943; B.A., U. Denver, 1965; J.D., Harvard U., 1968. Admitted to Calif., Colo. bars, 1969, U.S. Supreme Ct. bar, 1973; dep. atty. gen. Calif. Dept. Justice, Los Angeles, 1969-72; asst. atty. gen. Colo. Dept. Law, Denver, 1972-74; asso. firm Shapiro & Maguire, Beverly Hills, Calif., 1974-76, individual practice law, Los Angeles, 1976—; instr. Glendale (Calif.) U. Coll. Law, 1971-72; judge pro-tem Beverly Hills Municipal Ct., 1974-77, Los Angeles Municipal Ct., 1977—; panel of arbitrators Am. Arbitration Assn., 1976—. Pres., Pheasant Run Homeowners' Assn., Aurora, Colo., 1973-74; trustee Colo. Centennial-Bicentennial Found., 1973-74. Mem. Am., Calif. State, Los Angeles County (vice chmn. Superior Cts. com. 1975—, del. State Bar conf. dels. 1977) Beverly Hills, Glendale bar assns., Bus., Los Angeles trial lawyers assns. Contbr. articles to legal jours. Office: Suite 250 World Trade Center 350 S Figueroa St Los Angeles CA 90071 Tel (213) 972-0119

KAMINSKY, JAMES RAYMOND, b. Milw., Nov. 12, 1945; B.A., Ohio Weselyn U., 1968; postgrad. Ohio State U., 1969; J.D., U. Cin., 1973. Admitted to Ohio bar, 1973, U.S. Ct. Appeals, 1974; partner firm Tidwell and Kaminsky, Columbus, Ohio, 1974—. Mem. Am., Ohio, Columbus, Cin. bar assns., Am., Ohio trial lawyers assns. Home: 2676 York Rd Columbus OH 43221 Office: 155 N High St Columbus OH 43215 Tel (614) 228-2721

KAMISAR, YALE, b. N.Y.C., Aug. 29, 1929; A.B., N.Y. U., 1950; LL.B., Columbia U., 1954. Admitted to D.C. bar, 1955; research asso. Am. Law Inst., N.Y.C., 1953; asso. firm Covington & Burling, Washington, 1955-57; asso. prof. U. Minn. Law Sch., Mpls., 1957-59, prof., 1959-64; vis. prof. Harvard U. Law Sch., 1964-65; prof. law U. Mich., Ann Arbor, 1965—; adviser Am. Law Inst. Model Code of Pre-Arraignment Procedure, 1965-75; mem. law sch. and coll. dept. editorial and adv. bd. West Pub. Co., 1968—; co-reporter uniform rules criminal procedure Nat. Conf. Commrs. on Uniform State Laws, 1971-73; cons. Nat. Adv. Commn. on Civil Disorders, 1967—, Nat. Commn. Causes Prevention Violence, 1968—. Mem. Am. Bar Assn. (chmn. com. on rights of accused, individual rights and liberties 1965—), Am. Judicature Soc., Am. Law Inst., Nat. Dist. Attys. Assn. (asso.), Nat. Legal Aid and Defender Assn. (asso.), Phi Beta Kappa. Author: (with F. Inbau and T. Arnold) Criminal Justice in Our Times, 1965; (with W. LaFave and J. Israel) Modern Criminal Procedure, 1974; (with W. Lockhart and J. Choper) Constitutional Law: Cases, Comments and Questions and The American Constitution, 1975. Bd. editors: Columbia Law Rev., 1953-54; mem. editorial adv. bd. Criminal Law Bull., 1970-77. Contbr. articles to profl. jours. Home: 2 Londonderry Circle Ann Arbor MI 48104 Office: 333 Hutchins Hall U Mich Law Sch Ann Arbor MI 48109 Tel (313) 764-9340

KAMLOWSKY, JOHN HENRY, b. Kansas City, Mo., Aug. 10, 1925; B.S., Xavier U., 1950; J.D., W.Va. U., 19S5. Admitted to W.Va. bar, 1955; individual practice law, Wheeling, W.Va., 1955-61; asst. U.S. atty. No. Dist. W.Va., 1961-64, U.S. atty., 1964-69; bankruptcy judge No. Dist. W.Va., Wheeling, 1969—. Mem. W.Va. Bar Assn. Home: 126 Elm St Wheeling WV 26003 Office: PO Box 70 Wheeling WV 26003 Tel (304) 233-1655

KAMMER, ALFRED CHARLES, II, b. New Orleans, June 19, 1945; B.A. summa cum laude, Spring Hill Coll., 1969; J.D., Yale U., 1972; M. Div. magna cum laude, Loyola U., Chgo., 1977. Admitted to Ga. bar, 1972, Fed. bar, 1972, Ill. bar, 1974, U.S. Supreme Ct. bar, 1976; mem. Atlanta Legal Aid Soc., 1972-73, 77, summers 74, 75, 76; mem. Chgo. Lawyers Com. Civil Rights Under Law, 1974-77; vis. asst. prof. Fla. State U. Sch. Law, Tallahassee, summer 1976; mem. S.J. Mem. Am., Atlanta bar assns., State Bar Ga. Office: 800 Fulton Fed Bldg 11 Pryor St SW Atlanta GA 30303 Tel (404) 524-5811

KAMPELMAN, MAX M., b. N.Y.C., Nov. 7, 1920; A.B., N.Y. U., 1940, J.D., 1945; M.A. in Polit. Sci., U. Minn., 1946, Ph.D., 1951. Admitted to N.Y. bar, 1947, D.C. bar, 1950, Md. bar, 1956; partner firm Fried Frank Harris Shriver & Kampelman, Washington, N.Y.C. and London, 1955—; vis. prof. polit. sci. Claremont (Calif.) Colls., summer 1963; vis. professorial lectr., dept. govt. Howard U., Washington, 1954-56; instr. polit. sci. U. Minn., 1946-48; prof. Bennington Coll., 1948-53; legis. counsel to U.S. Senator Hubert Humphrey, 1949-55; sr. adviser U.S. del. UN, 1966-67; moderator Washington Week in Rev. TV program, Eastern Edn. Network, 1967-70. Pres., Am. Friends of Hebrew U., 1975—; mem. v.p. study commn. Nat. Dem. Com., 1973-74; bd. dirs. Greater Washington Ednl. Telecommunications Assn., 1963—, chmn., 1963-70; bd. dirs. Mt. Vernon Coll., 1972—, Am. Peace Soc., 1973—, Arena Stage, 1974—, Am.-Israel Cultural Found., 1974—, Atlantic Council of U.S., 1965-70, Nat. Tng. Labs., 1966-68; trustee Hebrew U. Jerusalem, 1973—, Inst. Am. Univs., Aix-en-Provence, France, 1959—, Am. Histadrut Cultural Exchange Inst., 1968-72, Fed. City Council, 1965-75; bd. overseers Coll. of V.I., 1963—; v.p. Helen Dwight Reid Ednl. Found., 1959—; mem. nat. commn. Anti-Defamation League, 1973—; hon. pres. Friends of the Nat. Zoo, 1958—. Mem. Am., Fed., D.C. (chmn. police relations 1969-71) bar assns., Am. Polit. Sci. Assn. (past nat. treas., past chpt. pres.). Author: The Communist Party vs. The C.I.O.: A Study in Power Politics, 1957; (with others) The Strategy of Deception, 1963; (with others) The Job of the Congressman, 1970; also articles. Address: 600 New Hampshire Ave NW Washington DC 20037 Tel (202) 965-9400

KANAGA, LAWRENCE WESLEY, b. Chgo., Dec. 25, 1940; B.A., Williams Coll., 1962; LL.B., Harvard, 1965. Admitted to Conn. bar, 1965, Dist. Ct. for Dist. Conn. bar, 1965, U.S. Ct. Appeals 2d Circuit bar, 1968; asso. firm Goldstein & Peck, Bridgeport, Conn., 1965-71; partner firm Zeldes, Needle & Cooper, Bridgeport, 1971—. Mem. Am., Conn., Greater Bridgeport bar assns. Home: 62 Lyons Plains Rd Westport CT 06880 Office: 333 State St Bridgeport CT 06604 Tel (203) 333-9441

KANAK, JOSEPH ROBERT, b. Dayton, Ohio, Feb. 14, 1947; B.A., U. Dayton, 1969; J.D., U. Cin., 1974. Admitted to Ohio bar, 1974, Fed. Dist. Ct. bar for So. Dist. Ohio, 1977; asso. firm Jack E. Staley, Dayton, 1974—. Mem. Am., Ohio, Dayton bar assns. Home: 1301 Lamar St Dayton OH 45404 Office: Grammer's Sq 101 Pine St Dayton OH 45402 Tel (513) 222-4273

KANAK, MARVIN REEVES, b. El Campo, Tex., Jan. 13, 1928; B.B.A., U. Tex., 1952; J.D., S.Tex. Sch. Law, Houston, 1963. Admitted to Tex. bar, 1963; individual practice law, Needville, Tex.; city atty. Needville, 1964-76, Mem. Needville C. of C. (pres.). Home: 9035 Antonia St Needville TX 77461 Office: POB 392 Needville TX 77461 Tel (713) 793-6321

KANALEY, JOHN COLLINS, b. Syracuse, N.Y., May 24, 1942; B.B.A., U. Notre Dame, 1964; J.D., Syracuse U., 1968. Admitted to N.Y. State bar, 1968, U.S. Supreme Ct. bar, 1972; mem. firm J.C. Kanaley, Atty. at Law, Syracuse, 1971—; county legislator, Onondaga County (N.Y.) 1976—. Mem. senate U. Notre Dame. Mem. Am., N.Y. State (com. taxation 1970—), Onondaga County bar assns. Home: 5050 Majors Dr Onondage NY 13215 Office: Box 96 Syraucse NY 13215 Tel (315) 478-1824

KANAR, STEPHEN PATRICK, b. Abbeville, S.C., Feb. 2, 1944; student Emory U., 1962-63; B.A., U. Fla., 1966; J.D., Duke U., 1969. Admitted to Fla. bar, 1969, U.S. Supreme Ct. bar, 1972; partner firm Fishback, Davis, Dominick & Simonet, Orlando, Fla., 1969—. Mem. Am. Bar Assn., Am. Trial Lawyers Assn. Office: 170 E Washington St Orlando FL 32801 Tel (305) 425-2786

KANAREK, HERBERT KARL, b. N.Y.C., June 8, 1930; B.S., Coll. City N.Y., 1951; LL.B., Harvard, 1954; postgrad. Columbia, 1960. Admitted to N.Y. bar, 1955; clk. firm Edward W. Willing, Mt. Vernon, N.Y., 1956; asst. counsel Waterfront Crime Commn., N.Y.C., 1957-58; partner firms Kanarek, Nocca, Shalof and Florio, and predecessor, Yonkers, N.Y., 1958-69, Kanarek and Pardes, Scarsdale, N.Y., 1969-72, Campbell, Hyman and Kanarek, New Rochelle, N.Y., 1972—; mem. Yonkers Mayor Citizens' Com. Investigating Juvenile Crime. Chmn. bd. Taxpayers' Orgn. N.E. Yonkers; mem. exec. bd. Washington Irving Council, Westchester, N.Y. Mem. Am., N.Y. State, New Rochelle, Westchester County (N.Y.) (chmn. com. consumer affairs) bar assns., Am. Trial Lawyers Assn., N.Y. State Trial Lawyers Assn., Yonkers Lawyers Assn. Home: 50 Brookdale Dr Yonkers NY 10710 Office: 2 Hamilton Ave New Rochelle NY 10801 Tel (914) 632-4030

KANBARA, BERTRAM TERUO, b. Honolulu, Jan. 7, 1926; B.A., U. Hawaii, 1950; J.D., Harvard, 1953. Admitted to Hawaii bar, 1953; U.S. Supreme Ct. bar, 1960; dep. corp. counsel City and County Honolulu, 1954-62; dept. atty. gen. State of Hawaii, 1963-68, asst. gen., 1968-69, atty. gen., 1969-71; individual practice law, Honolulu, 1971-76, judge Hawaii Dist. Ct., 1976—. Mem. Am., Hawaii bar assns., Am. Arbitration Assn., Indsl. Relations Research Assn. Home: 1332 Alewa Dr Honolulu HI 96817 Office: Dist Ct 915 Fort St Honolulu HI 96813 Tel (808) 548-2860

KANDARAS, HOMER MICHAEL, b. Aberdeen, S.D., Aug. 23, 1929; J.D., U. S.D., 1954, postgrad. polit. sci., 1956-58. Admitted to S.D. bar, 1954; individual practice law, Rapid City, S.D., 1958—; mem. S.D. Senate, 1971-76, chmn. judiciary com., 1973-76, chmn. spl. study com. reform probate laws, 1973-74, mem. spl. study com. criminal laws, 1975, mem. spl. study com. criminal procedure, 1976; mem. S.D. Code Commn., 1971-76. Home and office: PO Box 589 Rapid City SD 57709 Tel (504) 348-2465

KANDEL, NELSON ROBERT, b. Balt., Sept. 15, 1929; B.A., U. Md., 1951, LL.B., 1954. Admitted to Md. bar, 1954; individual practice law, Balt., 1957—; legal panel ACLU. Trustee Richmond Fellowship Halfway House, Balt., Methadone Maintenance Program, Balt. Mem. Am., Md., Balt. bar assns. Office: 215 Blaustein Bldg Baltimore MD 21201 Tel (301) VE 7-0646

KANE, CHARLES JAY, b. Phila., Aug. 27, 1940; B.S. in Econs., U. Pa., 1962; J.D., U. Miami, 1965; LL.M., N.Y. U., 1966. Admitted to Fla. bar, 1965, U.S. Supreme Ct. bar, 1975; with JAGC, U.S. Army, 1966-70; asso. firm Broad & Cassel, Miami Beach, 1971; partner firm Green & Kane, Miami Beach, 1972—. Mem. Am. Bar Assn., Fla. Bar. Recipient Nat. Def. Service medal. Home: 10004 SW 78th Ct Miami FL 33156 Office: 627 71st St Miami Beach FL 33141 Tel (305) 865-4311

KANE, CHRISTOPHER EDWARD, b. Detroit, June 22, 1942; B.S., Marquette Univ., 1968; J.D., Detroit Coll., 1971. Admitted to Mich. bar, 1971; individual practice law, Detroit, 1971-75; counsel firm

Cherf & Greenup, Detroit, 1975—; pres. Panacom, Ltd., Detroit, 1974—. Mem. Am., NW (officer), Detroit bar assns. Home: 16545 Edinborough Detroit MI 48219 Office: 19640 Grand River Detroit MI 48223 Tel (313) 255-2820

KANE, DAVID NORMAN, b. Bethesda, Md., Feb. 5, 1945; B.A., Haverford Coll., 1966; J.D., Georgetown U., 1971; certificate U. Geneva, 1967; C.L.U., Am. Coll. Life Underwriters, Bryn Mawr, Pa., 1976. Admitted to Md. bar, 1971, D.C. bar, 1971, Calif. bar, 1973; asst. counsel Bankers Security Life Ins. Soc., Washington, 1971-72; 2d v.p., asst. counsel United Services Life Ins. Co., Washington, 1973-76; asst. to pres. Equitable Gen. Corp., McLean, Va., 1976—. Co-chmn. United Way. Mem. Md., D.C., Calif. bar assns. Home: 10401 Grosvenor Pl Rockville MD 20852 Office: 1700 Old Meadow Rd McLean VA 22101 Tel (703) 821-3900

KANE, JAMES BERNARD, b. Buffalo, July 21, 1924; B.B.A., Canisius Coll., 1948; LL.B., Georgetown U., 1951. Admitted to D.C. bar, 1951, N.Y. bar, 1952; practiced in Buffalo, 1952-67; judge City Ct., Buffalo, 1967-69, N.Y. State Family Ct., Erie County, 1969-75; justice N.Y. State Supreme Ct., Buffalo, 1976—; chmn. City of Buffalo Bd. Assessors, 1960-67. Bd. dirs. Southtowns Community Services, East Aurora, N.Y., Corp. V.-Mental Health, West Seneca, N.Y. Mem. N.Y. State Supreme Ct. Justices Assn., Erie County (N.Y.) Bar Assn. Decorated D.F.C., Air medal with 5 oak leaf clusters. Home: 68 Fox Meadow Ln Orchard Park NY 14127 Office: Erie County Hall 95 Franklin St Buffalo NY 14202 Tel (716) 852-1291

KANE, KEVIN PETER, b. Floral Park, N.Y., Mar. 24, 1946; B.A. in English, Providence Coll., 1967; J.D., Harvard, 1970. Asso. firm Kindel & Anderson, Los Angeles, 1970—; admitted to Calif. Supreme Ct. bar, 1971; prof. law San Fernando Valley Coll. Law, 1972-73, Beverly Sch. Law, 1974-75, Southwestern U., 1975—; guest speaker People's Forum TV show. Active ACLU, 1973-75. Mem. Am., Los Angeles County bar assns., Am. Judicature Soc., Constl. Rights Found. (certificates of merit 1974, 75), Lawyers' Club of Los Angeles County, Center for Law in Pub. Interest. Home: 375 Mesa Rd Santa Monica CA 90402 Office: 555 S Flower St Los Angeles CA 90071 Tel (213) 680-2222

KANE, RICHARD, b. Bartlesville, Okla., Oct. 15, 1917; B.A., U. Kans., 1939; J.D., U. Mich., 1946. Admitted to Okla. bar, 1941, since practiced in Bartlesville; partner firm Kane, Kane and Roark and predecessors, 1946—; spl. justice Supreme Ct. Okla., 1967. Pres. local chpt. YMCA, chmn. SW area council, mem. nat. bd., v.p. nat. council, mem. pres.'s com., exec. com., chmn. standing com. World Alliance YMCA's. Mem. Am., Okla., Washington County bar assns., Bartlesville C. of C. (pres. 1972). Recipient Distinguished Services awards, Jr. C. of C., 1952, Southwest Area Council YMCA, 1961; Nat. Council YMCA, 1975. Office: 400 Profl Bldg Bartlesville OK 74003 Tel (918) 336-2310

KANE, ROBERT PATRICK, b. York, Pa., July 10, 1930; B.A., Dickinson Coll., 1952, LL.B., 1955. Corporate taxing officer Pa. Dept. Revenue, 1956-57, asst. dir. bur. county collections, 1957-58, acting dir. bur., 1958-59; adminstrv. asst. to Congressman N. Craley, Jr., Washington, 1965-66; dep. chmn. Pa. Democratic State Com., 1959-64; sec. revenue Commonwealth of Pa., 1971-74; atty. gen. Pa., 1975—; admitted to Pa. bar, 1959; practiced in York, 1959—. Active gubernatorial campaigns. Home: 182 Highland Rd York PA 17403 Office: Office of Attorney Gen Harrisburg PA 17127*

KANE, THOMAS PATRICK, b. Washington, Nov. 13, 1942; B.A., U. Minn., 1964; J.D., William Mitchell Coll., 1968. Admitted to Minn. bar, 1968, U.S. Supreme Ct. bar, 1973; asso. firm Oppenheimer, Wolff, Foster, Shepard and Donnelly, St. Paul, 1968-73, partner, 1973—. Pres. Community Devel. Corp. of Greater St. Paul, 1972—. Mem. Minn. State (pres. sect. young lawyers 1973, gov. 1974), Am. bar assns., Am. Trial Lawyers Assn. Home: 865 Fairmount St Saint Paul MN 55105 Office: 1700 First Nat Bank Bldg Saint Paul MN 55101 Tel (612) 227-7271

KANEY, FRANK NATHANIEL, b. Tampa, Fla., Feb. 4, 1937; B.S. in Speech, Fla. State U., 1958; LL.B., U. Miami, 1965. Admitted to Fla. bar, 1965; asso. firm Maguire, Voorhis & Wells, Orlando, Fla., 1965-68; atty. County Solicitor's Office, Orange County, Fla., 1968; individual practice law, Orlando, 1968-72; judge Orange County (Fla.) Ct., Orlando, 1972-76, Circuit Ct. Ninth Circuit of Fla., 1977—. Bd. dirs. Fla. Symphony Orch. Mem. Orange County Bar Assn., Am. Judicature Soc., Conf. County Ct. Judges, Am. Hist. Soc. Home: 2510 Shoreham Rd Orlando FL 32803 Office: 2000 E Michigan Ave Orlando FL 32806 Tel (305) 420-3810

KANNE, MICHAEL STEPHEN, b. Rensselaer, Ind., Dec. 21, 1938; B.S., Ind. U., 1962, J.D., 1968. Admitted to Ind. bar, 1968; since practiced in Rensselaer, individual practice law, 1968-72; city atty. Rensselaer, 1972; acting judge 30th Jud. Circuit Ct., Ind., 1972, judge, 1972—; lectr. in law St. Joseph's Coll., 1975-76; mem. com. on character and fitness State Bd. Law Examiners, 1976—. Bd. dirs. Am. Lung Assn. N.W. Ind., 1976—. Mem. Am., Ind., Jasper County bar assns., Am. Judicature Soc., Ind. Judges Assn. (bd. mgrs.), Am. Acad. Jud. Edn. (faculty), Ind. Jud. Center (faculty). Recipient Service award St. Joseph's Coll. Alumni Assn., 1973. Home: 605 Milroy Ave Rensselaer IN 47978 Office: 30th Jud Circuit Ct Court House Rensselaer IN 47978 Tel (219) 866-7766

KANNER, FREDERICK WILKINSON, b. N.Y.C., Apr. 25, 1943; B.A., U. Va., 1965; J.D., Georgetown U., 1968. Admitted to N.Y. bar, 1969; asso. firm Dewey, Ballantine, Bushby, Palmer & Wood, N.Y.C., 1968-76, partner, 1976—. Mem. Am., N.Y. bar assns., Assn. Bar City N.Y. Office: Dewey Ballantine Bushby Palmer & Wood 140 Broadway New York City NY 10005 Tel (212) 344-8000

KANT, HAROLD SANFORD, b. N.Y.C., July 29, 1931; B.A. in Sociology, U. Wash., 1951; M.S. in Clin. Psychology, Pa. State U., 1953; J.D. with honors, Harvard, 1958. Admitted to Calif. bar, 1959, U.S. Supreme Ct. bar, 1971; law clk. to Sr. Judge William E. Orr, U.S. Ct. Appeals, 9th Circuit, 1958-59; practiced in Los Angeles, 1959—, asso. firm Schwab & Sears, 1959-60, partner firm Schwab & Kant, 1961-63, partner firm Kant, Gordon & Meyers and predecessor, 1964-70, individual practice law, 1970—; exec. dir. Legal and Behavioral Inst., Beverly Hills Calif. Mem. Beverly Hills, Los Angeles County, Calif. State bar assns., Am. Psychol. Assn., Am. Sociol. Assn., Soc. for Sci. Study of Sex, Am. psychology-Law Soc., Authors Guild, Authors League Am. Author: (with M. J. Goldstein and J. J. Hartman) Pornography and Sexual Deviance, 1973; contbr. articles on behavioral sci. to profl. jours. Office: 8601 Wilshire Blvd Suite 501 Beverly Hills CA 90211 Tel (213) 652-6670

KANTER, ALAN NORMAN, b. Balt., Dec. 15, 1942; B.S., U. Md., 1965; J.D., Am. U., 1969. Admitted to Md. bar, 1969, U.S. Supreme Ct. bar, 1972; tax law specialist, pension trust br. IRS, Washington, 1969-71; pres. Alan N. Kanter & Assos., Inc., Balt., 1972—; asso. prof. accounting U. Balt., 1976—; lectr. paralegal program Villa Julie Coll. Chmn. com. pension and profit sharing Israel Bonds, 1974—. Mem. Am., Fed. (pres. Balt. chpt. 1977—), Md. State, Balt. City bar assns., Balt. Assn. Tax Counsel, Am. Soc. Pension Actuaries (asso.). Contbr. articles to tax jours. Office: Vermont Fed Bldg Suite 701 25 W Fayette St Baltimore MD 21201 Tel (301) 332-8111

KANTER, BENJAMIN J., b. Chgo., May 13, 1904; A.A., Ill. Inst. Tech., 1924; LL.B., John Marshall Law Sch., 1937, J.D., 1970. Admitted to Ill. bar, 1937, U.S. Supreme Ct. bar, 1963; practiced in Chgo., 1937-64; magistrate Ill. Circuit Ct. of Cook County, 1964-71, asso. judge, 1971—. Mem. Chgo., Ill. State, Am. bar assns., Judicature Soc. Lawyers, Decalogue Soc. Lawyers. Office: Chgo Civic Center Randolph and Clark Sts Chicago IL 60602 Tel (312) 443-8306

KANTER, BURTON WALLACE, b. Jersey City, Aug. 12, 1930; B.A., U. Chgo., 1951, J.D., 1952. Admitted to Ill. bar, 1952; instr. Law Sch. U. Ind., Bloomington, 1952-54; atty.-adviser Tax Ct. U.S., Washington, 1954-56; partner firm Levenfeld, Kanter, Baskes & Lippitz, and predecessors, Chgo., 1956—; spl. cons. U.S. Treasury Dept., Washington, 1959-61; dir. Hyatt Corp., Lincoln Am. Corp. Bd. dirs. U. Chgo. Sch. Biol. Scis., Pritzker Sch. Medicine, Chgo. Internat. Film Festival; adv. com. Columbia Coll. Mem. Am., Fed., Ill., Chgo. bar assns. Contbr. articles to tax law jours. Office: 10 S LaSalle St Chicago IL 60603 Tel (312) 346-8380

KANTOR, HAL HALPERIN, b. Chgo., Apr. 4, 1945; B.B.A., Tulane U., 1967; M.B.A., U. Calif., Berkeley, 1969; J.D., U. Fla., 1972. Admitted to Fla. bar, 1972; asst. prof. Coll. Law U. Fla., 1971-72, asst. prof. bus. law Coll. Bus. Adminstrn., 1971-72; asso. firm Lowndes, Peirsol, Drosdick & Doster, Orlando, Fla., 1972—. Mem. Orlando Mayor's Mgmt. and Efficiency Study Commn. task force com., 1975—. Mem. Fla. Bar (editorial staff jour. 1973-75), Orange County (Fla.) (sec. 1974—, editor-in-chief The Briefs 1975—), Am. bar assns., Scribes, Orlando Jaycees, Omicron Delta Kappa, Zeta Beta Tau, Phi Delta Phi. Editor-in-chief U. Fla. Law Rev., 1971-72. Home: 175 Lake Destiny Trail Maitland FL 32751 Office: Suite 433 First Fed Bldg Orlando FL 32802 Tel (305) 843-4600

KANTOR, STANLEY, b. Balt., Jan. 9, 1933; A.B., Johns Hopkins, 1953; LL.B., U. Md., 1957. Admitted to Md. bar, 1957; partner firm Glaser, Kantor & Winegrad, Balt., 1960—. Mem. Am., Md., Balt. City bar assns. Home: 3213 Midfield Rd Baltimore MD 21208 Office: 1504 Arlington Fed Bldg Baltimore MD 21201 Tel (301) 685-7666

KANTOROWICZ, RICHARD JOHN, b. Mpls., Jan. 21, 1930; B.S. in Law, U. Minn., 1952, LL.B., 1954. Admitted to Minn. bar, 1954; spl. asst. atty. gen. Mpls., 1957-61; judge Hennepin (Minn.) Municipal Ct., 1965-73, Minn. Dist. Ct., Mpls., 1973—. Pres., Mpls. Park Bd., 1957-58; mem. Mpls. City Council, 1961-65, Indsl. Devel. Commn. Mpls., 1965-77. Home: 309 France Ave N Golden Valley MN 55422 Office: 1659 Govt Center Minneapolis MN 55487 Tel (612) 348-2868

KANTROWITZ, BENJAMIN EARL, b. N.Y.C., Sept. 14, 1922; B.S., City Coll. N.Y., 1942; M.A., Columbia, 1943; J.D. (Scholar), N.Y. U., 1948. Admitted to N.Y. bar, 1948, U.S. Supreme Ct. bar, 1957; individual practice law, N.Y.C., 1948—. Research fellow N.Y. U. Sch. Law, 1949-50, teaching fellow, 1950. Mem. Am. Bar Assn., N.Y. Civil Liberties Union (bd. dirs., 1973—). Contbr. articles to profl. jours. Home: Rt 45 Pomona NY 10970 Office: 4879 Broadway New York City NY 10034 Tel (212) 569-3262

KAPLAN, ALAN HIRSH, b. N.Y.C., Apr. 26, 1930; A.B., N.Y. U., 1951, LL.M., 1957; J.D., Harvard, 1954. Admitted to N.Y. State bar, 1954, D.C. bar, 1960, U.S. Supreme Ct. bar, 1968; gen. counsel office HEW, FDA div., Washington, 1957-60; partner firm Kleinfeld, Kaplan & Becker, Washington, 1960—; professorial lectr. George Washington U., 1961—. Mem. Am., Fed., D.C. bar assns., Am. Judicature Soc. Contbr. articles in field to profl. jours.; co-editor Cases Under Federal Food, Drug, Cosmetic Act, 4 vols., 1958-74. Home: 5310 Edgemoor Ln Bethesda MD 20014 Office: 1200 17th St NW Washington DC 20036 Tel (202) 659-2155

KAPLAN, ALLEN J., b. Bklyn., Dec. 16, 1925; LL.B., St. Johns U., 1948. Admitted to N.Y. State bar, 1949, U.S. Supreme Ct. bar, 1960; sr. partner firm Goldsmith, Fravitz, Siken, Kaplan & Robson, 1955-65, firm Kaplan & Mandel, Jericho, N.Y., 1969—; arbitrator Am. Arbitration Assn., 1964—. Pres. Jericho B'nai B'rith, 1958; chmn. bd. Jericho Jewish Center, 1964; vice-chmn. Nassau County Bridge Authority, 1970-73. Mem. Nassau County Bar Assn., Am. Trial Lawyers Assn., Assn. Med. Jurisprudence. Office: 410 Jericho Turnpike Jericho NY 11753 Tel (516) 681-4120

KAPLAN, CARL E., b. N.Y.C., Apr. 17, 1939; A.B. Columbia Coll., 1959; LL.B., Columbia U., 1962. Admitted to N.Y. bar, 1963, U.S. Supreme Ct. bar, 1970; asso. firm Reavis & McGrath, N.Y.C., 1963-69, partner, 1969—. Mem. Am., N.Y. State bar assns., Assn. Bar City N.Y. Home: 180 East End Ave New York City NY 10028 Office: 345 Park Ave New York City NY 10022 Tel (212) 752-6830

KAPLAN, EDWARD ALAN, b. Marshal, Tex., Sept. 10, 1941; B.S., La. State U., 1964, J.D., 1969. Admitted to La. bar, 1969; individual practice law, Alexandria, La., 1970—. Chmn. adv. bd. Salvation Army of Rapides Parish, La., 1976-77. Home: 4827 Westgarden Blvd Alexandria LA 71301 Office: 720 Murray St Alexandria LA 71301 Tel (318) 448-0831

KAPLAN, JARED, b. Chgo., Dec. 28, 1938; A.B., U. Calif., Los Angeles, 1960; LL.B., Harvard, 1963. Admitted to Ill. bar, 1963; since practiced in Chgo., asso. firm Ross, Hardies, O'Keefe, Babcock & Parsons, 1963-69, partner, 1970; partner firm Roan & Grossman, 1970—. Trustee Erikson Inst. Early Edn., Chgo., 1973—; nat. pres. Ripon Soc., 1975-76; bd. dirs. Donors' Forum Chgo., 1976—. Mem. Am., Ill., Chgo. bar assns. (chmn. various coms. nat., local assns.). Contbr. articles in field to legal jours. Office: 120 S LaSalle St Chicago IL 60603 Tel (312) 263-3600

KAPLAN, JOHN, b. N.Y.C., July 9, 1929; A.B. in Physics, Harvard U., 1951, LL.B., 1954. Admitted to N.Y., Calif., D.C. bars; law clk. to U.S. Supreme Ct. Justice Tom C. Clark, 1954-55; spl. atty. U.S. Dept. Justice, 1957-58; asst. U.S. atty. No. Dist. Calif., 1958-61; asso. prof. law Northwestern U., 1964-65; prof. law Stanford U., 1955—. Author: (with Jon R. Waltz) The Trial of Jack Ruby, 1965; (with David Louisell and Jon R. Waltz) Cases and Materials on Evidence, 1968, Principles of Evidence and Proof, 1960; Marijuana—the New Prohibition, 1970; (with William Cohen) The Bill of Rights, 1976. Office: Stanford U Stanford CA 94305

KAPLAN, LOUIS MARVIN, b. Bklyn., Nov. 19, 1930; B.A., Western Res. U., 1951; L.L.B., Harvard U., 1954. Admitted to D.C. bar, 1957, N.Y. State bar, 1955, U.S. Supreme Ct. bar, 1961; atty. office Gen. Counsel CAB, Washington, 1954-56; law clk. U.S. Ct. Appeals D.C. Circuit, 1957-58; asst. U.S. atty., Washington, 1958-60; sr. v.p., gen. counsel Psychiat. Insts. Am., Washington, 1969—; sr. partner firm Bonner, Thompson, Kaplan, O'Connell, Washington, 1960—; adj. prof. law Georgeton U., 1973-76; chmn. bd. Community Fed. Savings & Loan Assn., Washington, 1974—. Mem. Soc. Hosp. Attys., Health Lawyers Assn.

KAPLAN, MARK NORMAN, b. N.Y.C., Mar. 7, 1930; A.B., Columbia U., 1951, J.D., 1953. Admitted to N.Y. bar, 1953; since practiced in N.Y.C., law clk., U.S. Dist. Ct. for So. Dist. N.Y., 1953-54; asso. firm Wickes, Riddell, Bloomer, Jacobi & McGuire, 1955-59; asso. firm Marshall, Bratter, Greene, Allison & Tucker, 1959-60, partner, 1960-67, sr. partner, 1967-70; sr. partner firm Burnham and Co., 1970—; pres., chief exec. officer Drexel Burnham Lambert Inc., 1976—; dir. Elgin Nat. Industries, Inc., Grey Advt., Inc., Neonex Internat. Ltd., The Harvey Group, Inc., Refac Tech. Devel. Corp., Utilities and Industries Corp, White Chem. Corp., Unishops, Inc., Marvin Josephson Assos., Inc., The Unimax Corp., Inc.; exchange ofcl. Am. Stock Exchange, N.Y.C., 1974—, gov., 1975, vice-chmn., 1976. Mem. Center for Nat. Policy Rev.; bd. dirs. Am. Place Theatre, 1974—. Home: 146 Central Park W New York City NY 10023 Office: 60 Broad St New York City NY 10004 Tel (212) 480-7007

KAPLAN, MARSHALL, b. Chgo., June 20, 1931; B.C.S., DePaul U., 1953, J.D. summa cum laude, 1956. Admitted to Ill. bar, 1956, U.S. Ct. Mil. Appeals bar, 1957, U.S. Supreme Ct. bar, 1961; served to capt. JAGC, U.S. Army, 1957-60; partner firm Kaplan and Kaplan, Chgo., 1960—. Active boys baseball and basketball, Skokie, Ill. Mem. Am., Ill., Chgo. bar assns. assns., Dealogue Soc., Am., Ill. trial lawyers assns. Recipient Phi Alpha Beta Freshman Law Student award, 1956. Home: 8447 N Drake Ave Skokie IL 60076 Office: 188 W Randolph St Chicago IL 60601 Tel (312) 236-2540

KAPLAN, MELVIN JAMES, b. Chgo., Dec. 29, 1931; B.A., Roosevelt U., 1958; B.Law, Chgo-Kent Coll. Law, 1958, J.D., 1969. Admitted to Ill. bar, 1958; individual practice law, Chgo., 1959—. Mem. World Assn. Lawyers, Am. Judicature Soc., Am., Ill., Chgo. bar assns., Chgo. Council Lawyers. Author: Out Of Debt Through Chapter 13, 1972; How To Get Completely Out of Debt Through Chapter 13, 1975. Office: 105 W Adams St Chicago IL 60603 Tel (312) 372-8890

KAPLAN, MICHAEL A., b. N.Y.C., May 16, 1942; B.A., Alfred U., 1964; LL.B., Union U., 1967, J.D., 1968. Admitted to N.Y. State bar, 1968, Calif. bar, 1970; individual practice law, N.Y.C., 1968; asst. gen. counsel Fotomat Corp., La Jolla, Calif., 1971—. Mem. Am., N.Y. State, Calif., San Diego bar assns. Decorated Bronze Star, U.S. Army. Home: 5904 Tulane St San Diego CA 92122 Office: Suite 505 7590 Fay Ave La Jolla CA 92037 Tel (714) 459-1340 or 459-7552

KAPLAN, MILTON, b. Binghamton, N.Y., Dec. 20, 1915; A.B., Hamilton Coll., 1937; LL.B., Harvard, 1940. Admitted to N.Y. State bar; asso. firms of William G. Mulligan, N.Y.C., 1941, 53-57; asst. atty. gen. N.Y. State, 1941-42, 59-62, asso. counsel Dept. Audit and Control, 1956-57; 1st asst. counsel to gov. N.Y. State, 1957-58; corp. counsel Cortland (N.Y.), 1950-52; prof. law State U. N.Y., Buffalo, 1965—; cons. in field. Contbg. author: American Assembly, Ombudsman for American Government?; contbr. articles to legal jours. Home: 130 Brooklane Dr Buffalo NY 14221 Office: O'Brian Hall State U NY Amherst Campus Buffalo NY 14260 Tel (716) 636-2071

KAPLAN, NATHAN JOSEPH, b. Chgo., June 29, 1910; LL.B., Chgo. Law Sch., 1934. Admitted to Ill. bar, 1935; practiced in Chgo., 1935-66; partner firm Kaplan & Sparberg, 1945-63; mem. Ill. Ho. of Reps., 1957-63; alderman, City of Chgo., 1963-66; judge 1st Dist. Ill. Circuit Ct. for Cook County, 1966—. Pres. Peterson Park Improvement Assn., 1947-50. Home: 3434 W Glenlake Ave Chicago IL 60659 Office: 2171 Civic Center Chicago IL 60603 Tel (312) 443-8472

KAPLAN, WILLIAM LEON, b. Brockton, Mass., Nov. 20, 1939; B.A., Am. U., 1963; J.D., Washington Coll. Law, 1966. Admitted to D.C. bar, 1967, Md. bar, 1967, U.S. Supreme Ct. bar, 1970; sr. partner firm Kaplan, Smith, Joseph, Greenwald & Laake, Langley Park, Md., 1975—. Mem. Am., D.C., Md. State, Montgomery County (Md.), Prince Georges County (Md.) bar assns. Office: 1345 University Boulevard E Langley Park MD 20783 Tel (301) 439-3900

KAPLOWITZ, BERNARD, b. Nyack, N.Y., Feb. 23, 1937; A.B., U. Pa., 1959; J.D., Albany Law Sch., Union U., 1962. Admitted to N.Y. bar, 1962; partner firm Bernard & Kaplowitz, Albany, N.Y., 1970-76; asso. firm Walworth Harding & Welt, Delmar, N.Y., 1976—. Pres., Bethlehem Republican Com., 1976—; mem. Albany County Legislature from 35th Dist., 1974—. Mem. Bethlehem C. of C., Am., N.Y. State, Albany County bar assns. Home: 46 Linda Ct Delmar NY 12054 Office: 425 Kenwood Ave Delmar NY 12054 Tel (518) 439-9324

KAPNER, LEWIS, b. West Palm Beach, Fla., May 21, 1937; B.A., U. Fla., 1958; student Harvard, 1956; postgrad. George Washington U. Law Sch., 1961; J.D., Stetson Law Sch., 1962; postgrad. Fla. Atlantic U., 1970-73; grad. Nat. Coll. State Judiciary, 1970, 73, 74. Admitted to Fla. bar, 1962, U.S. Supreme Ct. bar, 1965; asst. county solicitor Palm Beach County (Fla.), 1962-65; partner firm Kapner & Kapner, West Palm Beach, Fla., 1965-67; judge Palm Beach County Juvenile and Domestic Relations Ct., 1967-73, Palm Beach County Circuit Ct., 1973—; gen. counsel Palm Beach County Legis. Del., 1967; city prosecutor City of West Palm Beach, 1965-66; regional chmn. Gov.'s. Task Force on Juvenile Delinquency, 1969-71; del. White House Conf. on Children, 1970. Pres. Internat. Found. for Gifted, 1972-74, Palm Beach County Assn. for Gifted, 1973-74. Mem. Am., Fla. (chmn. editorial bd. Fla. Bar Jour. 1973-74), Palm Beach County bar assns., Conf. Circuit Ct. Judges, Forum Club, Mensa. Named 1 of 5 Outstanding Young Men in Fla., Fla. Jaycees, 1972. Office: County Courthouse West Palm Beach FL 33401 Tel (305) 837-2593

KAPNER, NORMAN JOSEPH, b. Newport, R.I., July 18, 1934; B.S.B.A., U. Fla., 1956, J.D., 1959. Admitted to Fla. bar, 1959, U.S. Supreme Ct. bar, 1966; partner firm Anderson, Hope & Kapner, Palm Beach, Fla., 1960-64, firm Kapner & Kapner, West Palm Beach, Fla., 1964-68, firm Campbell, Colbath Kapner & Fine, West Palm Beach, 1968—; asst. pub. defender Palm Beach County (Fla.), 1968-72, chief appellate div., 1968-72; judge ad litem Town of Lantana (Fla.), 1968—, City of Lake Worth (Fla.), 1972—. Mem. Fla., Palm Beach County bar assns. Home: 509 26th St West Palm Beach FL 33407

Office: 1920 Palm Beach Lakes Blvd 202 West Palm Beach FL 33409 Tel (305) 683-3322

KAPPEL, JOHN C., b. St. Louis, Oct. 9, 1903; J.D., St. Louis U., 1927. Admitted to Mo. bar, 1927; sr. partner firm Kappel, Neill, Staed & Wolff, St. Louis, 1940—. Mem. Am., Mo. bar assns., Met. Bar Assn. St. Louis, Lawyers Assn. St. Louis. Office: 706 Chestnut St Suite 518 Saint Louis MO 63101 Tel (314) 241-3355

KAPS, WARREN JAY, b. Bklyn., June 4, 1930; B.A., Rutgers U., 1952, LL.B. (scholar), 1954; LL.M. (Sterling fellow), Yale, 1955. Admitted to N.J. bar, 1955, D.C. bar, 1955, U.S. Ct. Mil. Appeals bar, 1957, U.S. Tax Ct. bar, 1962, N.Y. bar, 1964; asst. prof. law U. Ark., 1955-56, U. Md. Sch. Law, 1959-60; served to 1st lt. JAGC, U.S. Army, 1956-59; asso. firm Stein, Rosen & Ohrenstein, N.Y.C., 1960-64, partner, 1964-75; individual practice law, N.Y.C. and Hackensack, N.J., 1975—; lectr. in field. Mem. N.J. State, Bergen County, N.Y. State bar assns., Assn. Bar City N.Y. Editor Rutgers Law Rev., 1952-54; co-author: Moore's Federal Practice, 1960; contbr. articles to legal jours. Office: 39 Hudson St Hackensack NJ 07601 Tel (201) 487-5323

KARAHALIOS, JAMES N., b. Chgo., Nov. 30, 1945; J.D., De Paul U., 1970. Admitted to Ill. bar, 1970, Fla. bar, 1975, Calif. bar, 1976; asst. state's atty. Cook County (Ill.), Chgo., 1970—; instr., lectr. Cook County Sheriff's Police Tng. Acad., 1974-75. Mem. Chgo., Ill., Fla., Calif., Am. bar assns., Hellenic Bar Assn. Ill. (dir.). Office: 500 Richard J Daley Center Chicago IL 60602 Tel (312) 443-8914

KARASIK, HOWARD, b. Bklyn., Apr. 1, 1937; B.A., Bklyn. Coll., 1958; J.D., Harvard, 1961. Admitted to N.Y. bar, 1962, D.C. Bar, 1963, U.S. Supreme Ct. bar, 1968; partner firm Sherman & Citron, N.Y.C., 1972—. Mem. Assn. Bar City N.Y., N.Y. State, Bankruptcy bar assns. Home: 1349 Lexington Ave New York City NY 10028 Office: 1290 Ave of Americas New York City NY 10019 Tel (212) 581-8500

KARCAZES, GEORGE DEMETRIOS, b. Chgo., Aug. 11, 1938; B.A., U. Chgo., 1957, LL.D., 1960. Admitted to Ill. bar, 1960, partner firm Martin, Drucker, Karcazes & Kite, and predecessors, Chgo., 1964—; spl. asst. atty. gen. State of Ill., 1973—. Past pres. Hellenic Found.; Midwest regional chmn. United Hellenic Am. Congress. Mem. Am., Ill., Chgo., Hellenic bar assns., Am. Judicature Soc., Hellenic Profl. Soc. Ill. (past pres.), Phi Delta Phi. Office: 10 S LaSalle St Chicago IL 60603 Tel (312) 332-4550

KAREKEN, FRANCIS A., b. Buffalo, Mar. 30, 1930; B.A. magna cum laude, U. Buffalo, 1954; J.D., U. Chgo., 1958. Admitted to D.C. bar, 1959, N.Y. bar, 1961, Wash. bar, 1968; law clk. to judge 2d Circuit U.S. Ct. of Appeals, N.Y.C., 1958-59; with Antitrust div. Dept. Justice, Washington, 1959-61; asso. firm Hughes, Hubbard & Reed, N.Y.C., 1961-68; atty. Weyerhaeuser Co., Tacoma, 1968-72, asst. gen. counsel, 1972-75, v.p., gen. counsel, 1975—. Mem. Am., Wash. bar assns., Order of Coif, Phi Beta Kappa. Mng. editor U. Chgo. Law Rev., 1957-58. Office: Weyerhaeuser Co Tacoma WA 98401 Tel (206) 924-2162 Tel (206) 924-2162

KARESS, MARTIN JAY, b. Bronx, N.Y., Feb. 6, 1939; B.A., Pa. Mil. Coll., 1960; J.D., Temple U., 1963. Admitted to Pa. bar, 1964, Pa. Supreme Ct. bar, 1964, U.S. Dist. Ct. Eastern Pa. bar. Partner firm Walker, Thomas, Karess, Lipson & Zieger, Allentown, Pa., 1966-76; individual practice law, Allentown, 1976—; solicitor Borough of Catasauqua, 1970-77. Bd. dirs. Allentown Boys Club, 1969—, Lehigh County unit Am. Cancer Soc. Mem. Am., Pa., Lehigh County (chmn. ins. com., 1st v.p., pres. elect) bar assns. Home: 3636 Highland St Allentown PA 18104 Office: 215 N 9th St Allentown PA 18102 Tel (215) 435-3530

KARGER, ARTHUR, b. N.Y.C., Apr. 17, 1914; A.B., Coll. City N.Y., 1932; J.D., Columbia U., 1935. Admitted to N.Y. bar, 1935, U.S. Supreme Ct. bar, 1960; now individual practice law, N.Y.C.; law sec. to Chief Judge Irving Lehman, N.Y. Ct. Appeals, 1943-44; confidential law sec. N.Y. Ct. Appeals, 1944-48; adj. asso. prof. law N.Y. U., 1953-67; mem. N.Y. State Bd. Law Examiners, 1967—, chmn., 1969—; chmn. Nat. Conf. Bar Examiners, 1976—. Mem. Bronx County, N.Y. State, Am. bar assns., Assn. Bar City N.Y., New York County Lawyers' Assn., Am. Law Inst., Phi Beta Kappa. Author: (with Cohen) The Powers of the New York Court of Appeals, 1952; Titles of Actions and Special Proceedings, 1957; editor Columbia Law Rev., 1933-35. Office: 600 Madison Ave New York City NY 10022 Tel (212) 371-3330*

KARGMAN, MARIE WITKIN, b. Chgo., Aug. 28, 1914; A.A., Crane Jr. Coll., 1932; J.D., DePaul U., 1936; A.M., Harvard, 1951. Admitted to Ill. bar, 1936, Mass. bar, 1954; partner firm Kargman & Kargman, Chgo., 1936-45; pub. defender Boys' Ct., Chgo., 1936; individual practice marriage counselor, Boston, 1951—; lectr. Boston U., 1965-68; ct. investigator, Boston, 1970—; chmn. Mass. Gov's. Adv. Council Home and Family, 1966—. Active Mass. Commn. Status of Women, 1975-76. Mem. Mass. Bar Assn., Mass. Assn. Women Laweyrs, Internat. Fedn. Women Lawyers, Nat. Council Family Relations. Contbr. articles to legal jours. Home: 115 Rutledge Rd Belmont MA 02178 Office: 151 Tremont St Boston MA 02111 Tel (617) 423-4958

KARL, FREDERICK BRENNAN, b. Daytona Beach, Fla., May 14, 1924; student U. Fla., 1942; LL.B., Stetson U., 1949. Admitted to Fla. bar, 1950, U.S. Supreme Ct. bar, 1965; asso. David L. Black, Daytona Beach, 1950-53; partner firm Raymond, Wilson, Karl, Conway & Barr, Daytona Beach, 1953-74, Karl, Harris, McConnaughhay & Weidner, Tallahassee, 1976; city atty. Ormond Beach, 1960-65, Daytona Beach, 1965-68; atty. Volusia County Bd. Pub. Instrn., 1962, Volusia County Dist, # 3 Zoning Bd., 1965-68, Fla. Bd. Optometry, 1973—; pub. counsel, 1974-75; counsel House Select Com. on Jud. Impeachment, 1975; justice Fla. Supreme Ct., Tallahassee, 1976—. State chmn. Am. Cancer Soc. Crusade, 1967-68; past chmn. M.S. Campaign; past pres. Volusia County Hearing Soc.; past chmn. legis. adv. council So. Regional Edn. Bd.; mem. Fla. Ho. of Reps., 1956-64; mem. Fla. Senate, 68-72; mem. State Bd. Ind. Colls. and Univs., 1974—; bd. dirs. Mental Health Assn. Fla., Volusia County Mental Health Soc., YMCA, Family Welfare Assn., Goodwill Industries; trustee St. Leo Coll., Ormond Beach Meml. Hosp. Mem. Am., Fla. (past com. chmn.), Tallahassee bar assns. Recipient Distinguished Service award, 1962, Good Govt. award, 1963 both from Daytona Beach Jr. C. of C.; Good Govt. award Fla. Jr. C. of C., 1963; Hon. State Farmer degree Fla. chpt. Future Farmers Am., 1962; Sch. Bell award Fla. Edn. Assn., 1962; co-author: A Manual of Practice and Procedure on Executive Suspensions in the Florida Senate, 1974. Home: 2510 Killarney Way Tallahassee FL 32303 Office: Supreme Ct Fla Tallahassee FL 32304 Tel (904) 488-0357

KARL, JOHN F., JR., b. Covington, Ky., Feb. 26, 1943; B.S. in Elec. Engring., U. Cin., 1966, J.D., 1969. Admitted to Ohio bar, 1969, Ky. bar, 1970; individual practice law, Covington, 1969—; hearing officer Ky. Workmen's Compensation, 1975-77. Mem. Covington Sch. Bd., 1973-74. Mem. Ky. Bar Assn. Office: 107 Park Pl Covington KY 41011 Tel (606) 491-1844

KARL, MELVIN B., b. Bklyn., June 17, 1931; B.A., Bklyn. Coll., 1949-52; J.D., L.I. U., 1954-56; J.D., Bklyn. Law Sch., 1959. Admitted to N.Y. State bar, Fla. bar; staff Screen Actors Guild, 1959—, asst. nat. exec. sec., S.E. regional dir. Screen Actors Guild, Coral Gables, Fla., 1970—. Active Big Brothers Am.; bd. dirs. Variety Childrens Hosp., Miami, Fla. Mem. N.Y., Fla. bar assns., Am. Arbitration Assn., Footlighters, Nat. Acad. TV Arts and Scis., Fla. Motion Picture and TV Assn. Office: 3226 Ponce de Leon Blvd Coral Gables FL 33134 Tel (305) 444-7670

KARL, NELSON GEORGE, b. Cleve., Aug. 1, 1926; B.A., Western Res. U., 1949; LL.B., Cleve.-Marshall Law Sch., 1953, J.D., 1968. Admitted to Ohio Supreme Ct. bar, 1953, U.S. Dist. Ct. bar for No. Dist. Ohio, 1955, U.S. Ct. Appeals bar, 6th Dist., 1955, U.S. Supreme Ct. bar, 1973; individual practice law, Cleve., 1953-71; mem. firm Rudd, Karl, Sheerer, Lybarger & Campbell Co., Cleve., 1971—; instr. bus. law Cuyhahoga Community Coll., 1963-69; arbitrator Am. Arbitration Assn. Gen. counsel Ohio Civil Liberties Union, 1974—; chmn. ACLU of Greater Cleve., 1976. Mem. Ohio, Cleve. bar assns. Home: 3631 Concord St Beachwood OH 44122 Office: 33 Pub Square Suite 210 Cleveland OH 44113 Tel (216) 241-3646

KARLEN, DELMAR, b. Chgo., Jan. 6, 1912; B.A., U. Wis., 1934; LL.B., Columbia, 1937. Admitted to N.Y. State bar, 1937, Wis. bar, 1945; asso. firm Simpson, Thacher & Bartlett, N.Y.C., 1937-53; asst. to prof. law U. Wis., 1945-53; prof. law N.Y. U., 1953—; dir. Inst. Jud. Adminstrn., N.Y.C., 1963-72; vis. prof. univs. Chgo., Ankara, Sydney, Soochow and So. Calif. and Fla. Recipient Warren E. Burger award Inst. Ct. Mgmt., 1976. Mem. Am. Law Inst., Middle Temple (hon.), Order of Coif. Author: Judicial Administraton: The American Experience, 1970; others. Contbr. articles to legal jours. Home: POB 12 Garrison NY 10524 Office: 40 Washington Sq W New York City NY 10012 Tel (212) 598-7143

KARLL, STEPHEN PAUL, b. Brookline, Mass., Aug. 18, 1946; B.S. in Edn., Boston State Coll., 1968; J.D., Suffolk U., 1971. Admitted to Mass. bar, 1971; individual practice law, Chelsea, Mass. and Braintree, Mass., 1971—; counsel, sr. research asst. to joint legis. com. on state adminstrn. Mass. Legislature, 1971—. Mem. Mass., Chelsea-Revere bar assns., Norfolk County bar Assn. Home: 7 Poulos Rd Braintree MA 02184 Office: 375 Broadway St Chelsea MA 02150 Tel (617) 884-0573

KARLSSON, KENT, b. N.Y.C., Aug. 22, 1945; B.A., Coll. City N.Y., 1966; J.D., Bklyn. Law Sch., 1969. Admitted to N.Y. State bar, 1969; staff atty. Legal Aid Soc., N.Y.C., 1969-71; dir. litigation Bedford Stuyvesant Legal Services, Bklyn., 1971-72; partner firm Cammer & Karlsson, Bklyn., 1972—. Mem. N.Y. State, Am., Bklyn. bar assns., N.Y. County Lawyers Assn., Nat. Lawyers Guild. Author: (manual) Summary Proceedings in Landlord-Tenant Law for Poverty Attorneys, 1971; New York City Housing Court Manual, 1976. Home: 508 E 78th St New York City NY 10021 Office: 50 Court St Brooklyn NY 11201 Tel (212) 875-6578

KARMEL, ROBERTA SEGAL, b. Chgo., May 4, 1937; B.A., cum laude, Radcliffe Coll., 1959; LL.B. cum laude, N.Y. U., 1962. Admitted to N.Y. bar, 1962, U.S. Supreme Ct. bar, 1968; atty., asst. regional adminstr., atty. br. chief SEC, N.Y.C., 1962-69; asso. firm Willkie, Farr & Gallagher, N.Y.C., 1969-72; partner firm Rogers & Wells, N.Y.C., 1972—; adj. prof. Bklyn. Law Sch., 1973—. Trustee Temple Beth Shalom, Hastings-on-Hudson, N.Y., 1971-74. Mem. Am. Bar Assn., Assn. Bar City N.Y., Am. Judicature Soc. Contbr. articles in field to profl. jours. Home: 26 Hopke Ave Hastings-on-Hudson NY 10706 Office: 200 Park Ave New York City NY 10017 Tel (212) 972-5393

KARNOPP, DENNIS CHARLES, b. Lincoln, Nebr., July 9, 1942; B.A., U. Nebr., 1965, J.D., 1967. Admitted to Nebr. bar, 1967, Oreg. bar, 1967; asso. firm Panner, Johnson, Marceau, Karnopp & Kennedy, Bend, Oreg., 1967-69, partner, 1970—. Chmn., Deschutes County Republican Central Com., 1973-74; pres. Central Oreg. Community Coll. Found., 1974-75. Mem. Am., Nebr., Oreg., Central Oreg. (pres. 1973-74, mem. com. natural resources 1972-74, mem. com. on unauthorized practice 1974—, chmn. 1976-77, vice chmn. gen. practice sect. 1977—) bar assns., Phi Delta Phi. Contbr. articles to legal jours. Home: 1610 NW Vicksburg Ave Bend OR 97701 Office: 1026 NW Bond St Bend OR 97701 Tel (503) 382-3011

KAROL, JEFFREY WARREN, b. Newton, Mass., Sept. 29, 1945; A.B. magna cum laude, Amherst Coll., 1967; M.S. in Econs., London Sch. Econs. and Polit. Sci., 1968; J.D. cum laude, Harvard, 1971. Admitted to Mass. bar, 1971; asso. firm Foley, Hoag & Eliot, Boston, 1971—; mem. Community Legal Assistance Office, Cambridge, Mass., 1969-70; firm rep. Boston Bus. Resource Center, 1975—. Mem. Expt. in Internat. Living, 1963—. Mem. Am., Boston (mem. bankruptcy law com.) bar assns., Phi Beta Kappa. Home: 57 Mt Vernon St Boston MA 02108 Office: 10 Post Office Sq Boston MA 02109 Tel (617) 482-1390

KAROW, JOSEPH, b. N.Y.C., Feb. 25, 1912; A.B., N.Y. U., 1933, J.D., 1935, M.A., 1948. Admitted to N.Y. bar, 1936, U.S. Supreme Ct. bar, 1956; individual practice law, N.Y.C., 1936-42; asso. firm Goldstone & Wolff, N.Y.C., 1946-54; partner firm with Nat H. Hentel, N.Y.C., 1954-66; individual practice law, N.Y.C., 1966-71; partner with Stanely Hagendorf, N.Y.C., 1971-76; individual practice, 1976—; guest lectr. Law Sch. N.Y. U., 1960-61; mem. nat. panel arbitrators, Am. Arbitrator Assn., state panel arbitrators, N.Y. State Mediation Bd.; panel mediators and fact finders, N.Y. State Pub. Employment Relations Bd.; panel arbitrators Fed. Mediation and Conciliation Service. Mem. bd. trustees Little Red Sch. House, 1967-73; mem., chmn. bd. Selective Service System, 1958-71; dir. N.Y. U. Law Alumni Assn., 1962-67; bd. dirs. Queen's Speech and Hearing Center, Queen's Coll., 1960-63. Mem. Am., N.Y. State Bar Assns., N.Y. County Lawyers Assn. Home: 140 E 83d St New York City NY 10028 Office: 711 3d Ave New York City NY 10017 Tel (212) 687-8990

KARP, BARRY ARNOLD, b. Atlanta, Dec. 14, 1938; B.A. in Law, Emory U., 1960, LL.B., 1962, J.D. 1968. Admitted to Ga. bar, 1962; trial atty. NLRB, Houston and Atlanta, 1962-65; partner firms Clein, Babush & Karp, Atlanta, 1968-73, Karp & Karp, Atlanta, 1973—; prof. law John Marshall U., 1972—. Vice pres. Zionists Am., Atlanta, 1970-71; pres. Young Ams. for Israel, 1970-71. Mem. Am., Atlanta bar assns., State Bar Ga., Trial Lawyers Am., Ga. Trial Lawyers, Am. Judicature Soc. Office: 1517 William Oliver Bldg Atlanta GA 30303 Tel (404) 522-6900

KARP, MARVIN DAVID, b. N.Y.C., Aug. 7, 1930; B.A., Bklyn. Coll., 1952; LL.B., Bklyn. Law Sch., 1955, J.D., 1974. Admitted to N.Y. State bar, 1955; asso. firm Finke, Jacobs & Hirsch, N.Y.C., 1956; individual practice law, N.Y.C., 1957—; arbitrator Am. Arbitration Assn., N.Y.C., 1970—. Mem. Nassau County (N.Y.) Bd. Assessment Rev., 1974—. Mem. New York County Lawyers Assn., N.Y. State Bar Assn. Book rev. editor Bklyn. Law Sch. Law Rev., 1953-55. Home: 2743 Shore Dr Merrick NY 11566 Office: 3020 Empire State Bldg New York City NY 10001 Tel (212) 239-0045

KARP, SELWYN, b. N.Y.C., Sept. 22, 1932; B.B.A. cum laude, Baruch Sch. City Coll. N.Y., 1953; J.D., N.Y. U., 1955. Admitted to N.Y. bar, 1956; individual practice law, Far Rockaway, N.Y., 1956—; small claim arbitrator, civil ct. Vice pres., Sh'or Yoshuv Inst., Far Rockaway, N.Y., Young Israel Woodmere (N.Y.). Mem. Am. Arbitration Assn. Office: 1600 Central Ave Far Rockaway NY 11691 Tel (212) 327-1130

KARPEL, JEFFREY ELIOT, b. Jamaica, N.Y., May 4, 1942; A.A., Valley Coll., 1963; B.A., U. San Fernando Valley, 1965, J.D., 1968. Admitted to Calif. bar, 1968, U.S. Supreme Ct. bar, 1973; individual practice law, Century City, Calif., 1968-74; mem. firm Karpel and Melby, 1974—, Bd. dirs. Impact, Drug House. Mem. Los Angeles, Century City bars, Am. Bar Assn., Trial Lawyers Assn. Am. Office: 1901 Ave of the Stars Suite 500 Century City CA 90067 Tel (213) 553-4435

KARPOOK, RUSSELL DAVID, b. Balt., Sept. 10, 1947; B.A., U. Md., 1969, J.D., 1972. Admitted to Md. bar, 1972, U.S. Supreme Ct. bar, 1976; asso. firm George W. McManus, Jr., Balt., 1972-73; asso. firm Power & Mosner, Towson, Md., 1973-76, partner, 1977—. Mem. Am., Md. State (3rd circuit rep. exec. council young lawyers sect.), Balt. County bar assns., Omicron Delta Kappa. Office: 21 W Susquehanna Ave Towson MD 21204 Tel (301) 823-1250

KARR, LLOYD, b. Monticello, Iowa, May 19, 1912. Admitted to Iowa bar, 1937, U.S. Supreme Ct. bar, 1957; since practiced in Webster City, Iowa; county atty. Hamilton County (Iowa), 1940-48; pub. Webster City (Iowa) Daily Freeman Jour., 1952-55, Winter Park (Fla.) Sun-Herald, 1959-63. Fellow Am. Coll. Probate Counsel, Iowa Acad. Trial Lawyers; mem. Am., Iowa (bd. govs. 1956-61, pres. 1962-63; award of merit), 11th Jud. Dist., Hamilton County (pres. 1951) bar assns., Am. Judicature Soc., Sigma Delta Chi. Home: 1420 Wilson Ave Webster City IA 50595 Office: 711 2d St Webster City IA 50595 Tel (515) 832-3204

KARR, MARGARET PHELAN, b. Fort Dodge, Iowa, June 13, 1918. Admitted to Iowa bar, 1943, U.S. Supreme Ct. bar, 1957; partner firm Phelan, Karr & Karr, Webster City, Iowa, 1943-64, Karr, Karr & Karr, Webster City, 1964—; county atty. Hamilton County (Iowa), 1943-46. Fellow Am. Coll. Probate Counsel; mem. Hamilton County Bar Assn. (pres. 1954), Iowa State, Am. bar assns., Iowa Trial Lawyers Assn. Home: 1420 Willson Ave Webster City IA 50595 Office: 711 Second St Webster City IA 50595 Tel (515) 832-3204

KARR, STEPHEN WILLIAM, b. Samos, Greece, June 20, 1919; B.A., U. Mich., 1941, J.D., 1947. Admitted to Mich. bar, 1947; partner firm Luyendyk, Hainer, Karr & Edens, Grand Rapids, Mich., 1950-73; U.S. magistrate U.S. Dist. Ct., Grand Rapids, 1973—; with JAGC, USAR, 1958-72, U.S. commr., 1950-71. Mem. Am., Mich., Grand Rapids bar assns., Nat. Council U.S. Magistrates. Office: 666 Federal Bldg Grand Rapids MI 49502 Tel (616) 456-2309

KARRE, ALBERT MICHAEL, b. Crowley, La., July 9, 1918; B.A., La. State U., 1940; J.D., Loyola U., 1954. Admitted to La. bar, 1954; individual practice law, Lafayette, La., 1954—; asst. city atty., city prosecutor Lafayette, 1956-62, 72—. Mem. Am., La., Lafayette Parish bar assns., Am. Judicature Soc., Am., La. trial lawyers assns., St. Thomas More Law Club. Office: 208 W Main St Lafayette LA 70502 Tel (318) 235-5704

KASPER, DANIEL MATHEW, b. St. Joseph, Mo., Apr. 23, 1945; A.B., Kans. U., 1967; J.D., U. Chgo., 1970, M.B.A., 1971. Admitted to Ill. bar, 1970, Calif. bar, 1972; lectr., asst. prof. grad. sch. bus. U. So. Calif., Los Angeles, 1971-76; asst. prof. grad. sch. bus. adminstr. Harvard, Cambridge, Mass., 1976—. Mem. Am., Calif. bar assns., Am. Bus. Law Assn., Acad. Mgmt. Contbr. articles to legal jours. Home: 90 Abbott Rd Wellesley MA 02181 Office: Grad Sch Business Soldiers Field Boston MA 02163 Tel (617) 495-6200

KASPERS, WILLIAM FREEMAN, b. Sterling, Ill., July 13, 1948; A.B., Princeton U., 1970; J.D., U. Mich., 1973. Admitted to Ga. bar, 1973, Mich. bar, 1973; law clk. firm Dykema, Gossett, Spencer, Goodnow & Trigg, Detroit, summer 1972; asso. atty. firm Fisher & Phillips, Atlanta, 1973—. Mem. State Bar Ga., State Bar Mich., Atlanta, Am. bar assns., Phi Beta Kappa. Home: 1165 Churchill Downs Rd Atlanta GA 30319 Office: 3500 1st Nat Bank Tower Atlanta GA 30303

KASS, ARTHUR, b. N.Y.C., Mar. 23, 1931; B.A., Coll. City N.Y., 1952; J.D., Columbia, 1955. Admitted to N.Y. bar, 1955; asst. counsel N.Y. State Temporary Housing Rent Commn., 1955-62; asst. counsel, dep. chief litigation atty. N.Y. City Dept. of Rent and Housing, 1962-76; spl. asst. atty. planning and zoning Town of Yorktown (N.Y.), 1976; spl. counsel Town of N. Salem (N.Y.), 1976—, town atty., 1974-76; counsel N. Salem Citizens Com., 1973-74. Mem. Civil Service Bar Assn. (dir. 1975-76). Home: Hillside Ave Croton Falls NY 10519 Office: Croton Falls NY 10519 Tel (914) 277-8597

KASS, BENNY L., b. Chgo., Aug. 20, 1936; B.S. in Journalism, Northwestern U., 1957; LL.B., U. Mich., 1960; LL.M., George Washington U., 1967. Admitted to D.C. bar, 1960; with Maritime Adminstrn., 1960-62, House Govt. Info. Subcom., 1963-65, Senate Subcom. on Adminstrv. Practice, 1965-69; individual practice law, Washington, 1969—. Commr. Uniform State Laws, 1969—. Mem. Am., Fed. bar assns., Sigma Delta Chi. Contbr. articles to profl. jours.; columnist Washington Post. Home: 3642 Jocelyn St NW Washington DC 20015 Office: 1225 19th St NW Washington DC 20036 Tel (202) 659-3436

KASS, FREDERIC CHARLES, b. Phila., July 14, 1948; A.B., Cornell U., 1974; J.D., N.Y. U., 1973. Admitted to N.Y. bar, 1974; asso. firm Rogers and Wells, N.Y.C., 1974, Washington, 1977—; clk. to Thomas J. Downey, Washington, 1975-76. Mem. Am. Bar Assn. City N.Y., Council N.Y. Law Assos., Am. Bar Assn. Contbr. Capitol Comment, bi-monthly column for N.Y. Law Jour., articles to legal publs. Home: 724A 9th St SE Washington DC 20003 Office: 1666 K St NW Washington DC 20006 Tel (202) 331-7760

KASSAL, BENTLEY, b. N.Y.C., Feb. 28, 1917; B.A., U. Pa., 1937; LL.B., Harvard, 1940, J.D., 1969. Admitted to N.Y. State bar, 1940; asso. firms Hartman, Sheridan & Tekulsky, N.Y.C., 1940-41, Weisman, Celler, Quinn, Allan & Spett, N.Y.C., 1941-42; partner firm Kassal & Kapelman, N.Y.C., 1945-50; individual practice law, N.Y.C., 1950-69; judge Civic Ct., N.Y.C., 1970-75; justice N.Y. Supreme Ct., N.Y.C., 1976—; mem. N.Y. State Assembly, 1957-62. Trustee at large Fedn. Jewish Philanthropies. Mem. Assn. Bar City N.Y., Am. Bar Assn. Recipient Man of Year award Comml. Law League, 1975. Home: 5 W 86th St New York City NY 10024 Office: Supreme Ct 60 Centre St New York City NY 10007 Tel (212) 374-4744

KASSOFF, EDWIN, b. Bklyn., July 15, 1924; B.B.A., City Coll. N.Y., 1947; J.D., Bklyn. Law Sch., 1953. Admitted to N.Y. bar, 1953, U.S. Dist. Ct. for So. and Eastern Dists. N.Y. bars, 1957, U.S. Supreme Ct. bar, 1963; individual practice law, N.Y.C., 1953-71; instr. law, Queens Coll., 1956-63; asso. prof. law Pace U., 1964-74, prof., 1974—; judge civil ct. N.Y.C., 1971-73; Justice supreme ct., State of N.Y., Jamaica, 1974—; vis. prof. law Columbia U., 1966-67; vis. lectr. law N.Y. Med. Coll., 1975—; mem. faculty Nat. Coll. of the State Judiciary, Reno, Nev., 1975—; mem. N.Y. State Temporary State Commn. on Causes of Campus Unrest, 1970; asst. counsel to Joint Legis. Com. on Mass Transp., 1969; co-counsel to the legis. com. of the N.Y. State Constitutional Conv., 1967; research counsel to the majority party of the N.Y. State Assembly, 1968. Mem. Assn. Supreme Ct. Justices of N.Y. State, Assn. Supreme Ct. Justices City N.Y., Am. Business Law Assn. (pres. 1972), Am., Queens County bar assns., Author: Business Law Text, 1964; Sales and Bailment Text, 1972; Am. Comml. Law Text., 1975; Advanced Am. Comml. Law Text, 1976. Office: Supreme Ct Queens County 88-11 Sutphin Blvd Jamaica NY 11435 Tel (212) 520-3798

KASTANTIN, MATTHEW JOSEPH, b. Brockton, Mass., Feb. 20, 1943; B.A., St. Vincent Coll., 1965; J.D., Catholic U. of Md., 1969. Admitted to Md. bar, 1970, D.C. bar, 1971; asso. firm Galiher, Clarke, Martell & Donnelly, Washington, 1969-75; individual practice law, Rockville, Md., 1975—. Mem. Bar Assn. Montgomery County (sec. 1974-75, exec. com. 1975-76), Md., D.C. bar assns., Assn. Trial Lawyers Am. Office: 17 W Jefferson St Rockville MD 20850 Tel (301) 424-9010

KASTEL, HOWARD LESLIE, b. Chgo., June 11, 1932; A.B., Harvard, 1954; J.D. cum laude, Loyola U., Chgo., 1960. News reporter, corr. Boston Post, 1951-53; personnel dir. Chgo. Roto Print Co., 1953-56; asst. to chmn. spl. standing com. on labor relations Am. Newspaper Pubs. Assn., Chgo., 1956-60; admitted to Ill. bar, 1960; asso. firm Aaron, Aaron, Schimberg & Hess, Chgo., 1961-62; asso. firm Altheimer & Gray, Chgo., 1962-66, partner, 1966—. Mem. Am. Judicature Soc., Chgo. Council Lawyers, Am., Ill. (chmn. sub-com. 1967-69) bar assns., Phi Alpha Delta. Home: 180 E Pearson St Chicago IL 60611 Office: suite 3700 One IBM Plaza Chicago IL 60611 Tel (312) 467-9600

KATAYAMA, ARTHUR SHOJI, b. Los Angeles, June 10, 1927; A.B., Morningside Coll., 1951; LL.B., Pacific Coast U., 1956. With intelligence div. U.S. Treasury Dept., Los Angeles, 1953-58; with N. Am. Aviation, Los Angeles, 1958-59; admitted to Calif. bar, 1959, U.S. Supreme Ct. bar, 1971; practiced in Los Angeles, 1959-60; partner firm Mori & Katayama, Los Angeles, 1960-77; mem. advisory bd. Sumitomo Bank Calif., Los Angeles. Mem. Calif. Democratic State Central Com., 1958-60. Mem. Am., Los Angeles County bar assns., Am. Trial Lawyers Assn. Home: 2212 Racquet Hill Santa Ana CA 92705 Office: 4040 MacArthur Blvd Suite 320 Newport Beach CA 92660 Tel (714) 833-0882

KATCHER, MONROE IRVINE, II, b. Bklyn., Dec. 13, 1908; A.B., Columbia, 1929; J.D., St. John's U., 1931. Admitted to N.Y. State bar, 1933, U.S. Supreme Ct. bar, 1944; atty. N.Y. State Liquor Authority, 1934-44; individual practice law, N.Y.C., 1945—; lectr. Practising Law Inst., 1963-64. Mem. N.Y. State (chmn. adminstrv. law com.), Westchester County bar assns., Assn. Bar. City N.Y., N.Y. County Lawyers Assn. Contbr. articles to legal jours. Home: 2 Dunbow Dr Chappaqua NY 10514 Office: 475 Fifth Ave New York City NY 10017 Tel (212) 685-2958

KATES, HARVEY EUGENE, b. N.Y.C., Sept. 6, 1921; B.S.S., City Coll. N.Y., 1944; LL.B., Columbia, 1946. Admitted to N.Y. bar, 1946; asso. firm A. Alan Reich, N.Y.C., 1947-48; asso. firm James Brooks, Sheepshead Bay, N.Y. and Bklyn., 1948-50; individual practice law, Bronx, N.Y., 1950-62; partner firm Platt & Kates, Bronx and N.Y.C., 1962-73; individual practice law, Farmingdale, N.Y., 1973—. Mem. N.Y. State Bar Assn. Home: 208 Martin Dr Syosset NY 11791 Office: 132 S Front St Farmingdale NY 11735 Tel (516) 420-1128

KATSH, SALEM MICHAEL, b. N.Y.C., May 5, 1948; B.A., N.Y. U., 1970; J.D., 1972. Admitted to N.Y. State bar, 1973; asso. firm Weil, Gotshal & Manges, N.Y.C., 1972—. Mem. N.Y. State, Am. bar assns., C. C. U.S., Order of Coif. Home: 180 West End Ave New York City NY 10023 Office: 767 5th Ave New York City NY 10022 Tel (212) 758-7800

KATSKEE, MELVIN ROBERT, b. Omaha, Nov. 19, 1945; B.A. cum laude, Creighton U., 1967; J.D., U. Nebr., 1970. Admitted to Nebr. bar, 1970, U.S. Supreme Ct. bar, 1975; law clk. U.S. Dist. Ct., 1970-71; asso. firm White, Lipp, Simon & Powers, 1971-73; gen. atty. Omaha Nat. Corp., 1973—; adj. prof. law Creighton U., 1972—. Mem. Am., Nebr. (com. on judiciary) bar assns., Am. Judicature Soc., Am. Acad. Polit. and Social Scientists, Phi Alpha Theta. Contbr. articles to law jours. Home: 613 S 68th St Omaha NE 68106 Office: 945 Woodmen Tower 1700 Farnam St Omaha NE 68102 Tel (402) 348-7907

KATSKY, RONALD L., b. Los Angeles, Nov. 10, 1938; A.B., Princeton, 1960; J.D., U. Calif., 1964. Admitted to Calif. bar, 1964; since practiced in Los Angeles, partner firm Hagenbaugh & Murphy, 1965-70; partner firm Kruse & Katsky, 1970-76, Stroock & Stroock & Lavan, 1976—; dep. commn. corps., state Calif., 1965; arbitrator Am. Arbitration Assn. Mem. Calif., Los Angeles County Bar Assns. Home: 644 Hanley Ave Los Angeles CA 90049 Office: 707 Wilshire Blvd Suite 605 Los Angeles CA 90017 Tel (213) 629-2400

KATZ, ALAN HARVEY, b. Cambridge, Mass., Mar. 19, 1946; B.S. in Bus. Adminstrn., Boston U., 1967, J.D., 1970. Admitted to Mass. bar, 1970, U.S. Dist. Ct. bar, 1975; asso. firm Shapiro & Rome, Framingham, Mass., 1970-72; individual practice law, Arlington, Mass., 1972-73; partner firm Katz & Grannan, Arlington, 1973—. Mem. Local Growth Policy Com., Arlington, Mass.; incorporator Arlington Boys' Club; dir. Community Chest, United Way; incorporator Symmes Hosp., Arlington, Mass. Mem. Mass., Middlesex bar assns. Home: 10 Apache Trial Arlington MA 02174 Office: 1173 Massachusetts Ave Arlington MA 02174 Tel (617) 646-2900

KATZ, ALLAN JACK, b. St. Louis, Apr. 30, 1947; B.A. in History, U. Mo.-Kansas City, 1969; J.D., Am. U., 1974. Admitted to Mo. bar, 1974; exec. dir. Jackson County Youth Commn., 1971-72; legis. counsel Congressman Bill Gunter, Dem., Fla., Washington, 1973-74; legis. dir. Congressman David Obey, Dem., Wis., Washington, 1975-76; gen. counsel Commn. on Adminstrv. Rev. of U.S. Ho. of Reps., 1976—. Mem. Am., Mo. bar assns. Recipient award Western Mo. chpt. ACLU, 1969. Home: 3405 Prospect St NW Washington DC 20007 Office: SW-1 Rayburn House Office Bldg Washington DC 20515 Tel (202) 225-3543

KATZ, ASCHER, b. N.Y.C., Apr. 16, 1927; B.E.E., Coll. City N.Y.; J.D., Harvard U., 1951. Admitted to N.Y. State bar, 1952; pvt. practice law, N.Y.C., 1955—, White Plains, N.Y., 1976—; N.Y.C. and White Plains, N.Y., 1955—; law asst. office N.Y. City Corp. Counsel, 1954-55; staff atty. civil br. Legal Aid Soc. N.Y., 1952-54; justice Town of Greenburgh (N.Y.), Westchester County, 1976—; small claims night ct. arbitrator Civil Ct. City N.Y., 1970-75, culpulsory arbitrator, 1972-75. Mem. Am., N.Y. State, Westchester County bar assns., Assn. Trial Lawyers Am., Am. Judges Assn., Am. Judicature Soc., N.Y. State Assn. Magistrates, Westchester County Magistrates Assn. Columnist: Legal Plain Talk, White Plains Reporter Dispatch, 1971. Home: 24 Primrose Ave W White Plains NY 10607 Office: 14 Mamaroneck Ave White Plains NY 10601 Tel (914) 428-1400 also 60 E 42 St New York City NY Tel (212) 490-0670

KATZ, AVRUM SIDNEY, b. Melrose Park, Ill., Oct. 10, 1939; B.S. in Elec. Engring., Ill. Inst. Tech., 1962; J.D., George Washington U., 1966. Admitted to Ill. bar, 1966, U.S. Patent bar, 1967; examiner U.S. Patent Office, Washington, 1962-65; law clerk firm Hurvitz & Rose, Washington, 1965-66; asso. firm Leonard G. Nierman, Chgo., 1966-67, Fitch, Even, Tabin & Luedeka and predecessor, Chgo., 1967-70, partner, 1971—; bd. dirs. The Lase Co., Chgo., 1970—. Mem. Am., Chgo. bar assns., Am. Patent Law Assn., Patent Law Assn. Chgo., IEEE, Tau Beta Pi, Eta Kappa Nu. Home: 88 E Niles St Lake Forest IL 60045 Office: 135 S LaSalle St Suite 900 Chicago IL 60603 Tel (312) FR2-7842

KATZ, BERTRAM, b. N.Y.C., Jan. 19, 1930; LL.B., Bklyn. Law Sch., 1952. Admitted to N.Y. State bar, 1952, U.S. Supreme Ct. bar, 1957; individual practice law, Bronx, N.Y., 1952—; asst. dist. atty. Bronx County, 1964-66; arbitrator compulsory arbitration Bronx Civil Ct., 1971; tax commr. City of N.Y., 1974—. Arbitrator small claims N.Y.C. Civil Ct., 1956—; counsel Hellenic Orthodox Community of Bronx, 1969—. Mem. Bronx County, N.Y. State bar assns., Bronx County Criminal Bar Assn., Fed. Bar Council, N.Y. State, Nat. dist. attys. assns., Internat. Assn. Assessing Officers. Recipient certificate of appreciation Mayor City of N.Y., 1964. Office: 2744 E Tremont Ave New York City NY 10461 Tel (212) 823-6500

KATZ, BRUCE MARTIN, b. Chgo., May 15, 1942; B.S. Roosevelt U., 1965; J.D., De Paul U., 1968. Admitted to Ill. bar, 1968, asso. Leonard M. Groupe, Chgo., 1974—. Mem. Chgo., Ill. State, Am. bar assns. Contbr. chpt. to Bankruptcy Practice, 1975. Office: 30 W Washington Chicago IL 60602 Tel (312) 236-4290

KATZ, DAVID ALLAN, b. Toledo, Nov. 1, 1933; B.Sc. in Bus. Adminstrn., Ohio State U., 1955, J.D. summa cum laude, 1957. Admitted to Ohio bar, 1957; asso. firm Spengler, Nathanson, Heyman, McCarthy & Durfee, Toledo, 1957-62, partner, 1962—. Pres., Jewish Welfare Fedn. of Toledo, Temple Bnai Israel, Toledo, 1967-70; mem. nat. council Ohio State U. Law Alumni Assn., 1976—. Mem. Am., Ohio, Toledo (sec. 1975—, exec. com. 1975—) bar assns. Home: 4231 Merriweather St Toledo OH 43623 Office: Nat Bank Bldg Toledo OH 43604 Tel (419) 241-2201

KATZ, DAVID LAWRENCE, b. Balt., May 2, 1947; B.A., Franklin and Marshall Coll., 1969; J.D., U. Md., 1973. Admitted to Md. bar, 1973; asst. state's atty. City of Balt., 1973—. Mem. Md. Bar Assn., Md. State's Atty. Assn. Home: 1518 Park Ave Baltimore MD 21217 Office: 204 Courthouse Bldg Baltimore MD 21202 Tel (301) 396-4726

KATZ, ELI, b. Bklyn., Oct. 10, 1912; B.S. N.Y.U., 1933; LL.B., Columbia, 1936; LL.M., N.Y.U., 1950. Admitted to N.Y. State bar 1936, U.S. Dist. Ct. So. Dist. N.Y. bar, 1939, U.S. Supreme Ct. bar, 1969; individual practice law, N.Y.C., 1937-43, Jamaica, N.Y., 1946-64, Great Neck, N.Y., 1964-71, Roslyn Heights, N.Y., 1971—. Trustee Village of Thomaston (N.Y.), 1962-65, mayor, 1965-67. Mem. Nassau County, Queens County, N.Y. State bar assns., B'nai B'rith (pres. 1947, membership chmn. for Queens and Nassau counties 1950-52, chmn. Citizen of Yr. award com. Great Neck Lodge 1954-57). Office: 99 Powerhouse Rd Roslyn Heights NY 11577 Tel (516) 484-5900

KATZ, FREDERICK, b. N.Y.C., Nov. 5, 1898; student N.Y. U., 1917; LL.B., N.Y. Law Sch., 1921. Admitted to N.Y. bar, 1922; mem. firm Katz & Leibowitz, N.Y.C., 1922-30, firm Katz & Spector, N.Y.C., 1930-44, firm Katz, Samuelsohn & Sapir, N.Y.C., 1944-62; individual practice law, N.Y.C., 1962—; dir. Nat. Safety Bank and Trust Co., N.Y.C.; dir., chmn. exec. com. Marine View Savs. and Loan Assn., Middletown, N.J.; dir., sec. Checkmaster Plan, Inc.; dir., mem. exec. com. Security Mut. Ins. Co.; dir. Modern Life Ins. Co.; mem. adv. bd. Chem. Bank, N.Y.C.; spl. asst. atty. gen. State of N.Y. 1947; mem. com. character and fitness 1st Jud. Dept. State N.Y., 1977—. Mem. Assn. Bar City N.Y., N.Y. County Lawyers, Bronx County Bar Assn. Home: 340 E 64th St New York City NY 10021 Office: 36 W 44th St New York City NY 10036 Tel (212) 869-1200

KATZ, GEORGE ALAN, b. N.Y.C., Oct. 30, 1931; B.A., Coll. City N.Y., 1952, LL.B., N.Y. U., 1954, LL.M., 1959. Admitted to N.Y. State bar, 1954, U.S. Supreme Ct. bar, 1961; practiced in N.Y.C., 1954—; asso. firm Becker, Ross & Stone, 1956-63; partner firm Seligson & Morris, 1963-64; founding partner firm Wachtell, Lipton, Rosen & Katz, 1965—; lectr. N.Y. U., 1970-75, panelist Am. Arbitration Assn. Trustee Jewish Inst. for Geriatric Care, New Hyde Park, N.Y., 1975—; bd. govs. Hebrew U. Jerusalem, 1974—; chmn. Greater N.Y. Lawyers div. Am. Friends of Hebrew U., 1970-75. Mem. Assn. Bar City N.Y., Am., N.Y. State bar assns., Gallatin Assn. N.Y. U., Vanderbilt Assn. N.Y. U. Contbr. articles in field to law jours. Home: 2 Grenwolde Dr Kings Point NY 11024 Office: 299 Park Ave New York City NY 10017 Tel (212) 371-9200

KATZ, HANNA, b. Berlin, came to U.S., 1941, naturalized, 1946; J.D., Friedrich Wilhelm U., Berlin, 1921; LL.B., St. John's U., 1944. Admitted to Berlin bar, 1930, N.Y. bar, 1946, West Berlin bar, 1954, U.S. Supreme Ct. bar, 1960; individual practice law, Berlin, 1930-41, N.Y.C., 1948—; asso. firm Klein, Alexander & Pohl, N.Y.C., 1946-47; asso. firm Sullivan & Cromwell, N.Y.C., 1948; asso. firm Ruge Gerlach Ruge Leisberg, West Berlin, 1962—. Interpreter Berlin Ct. Appeals, 1932-38; sec. World Trade Mark Soc., 1927-38, 1959—. Mem. Assn. Bar City N.Y., Am. Bar Assn., Internat. Law Assn. (sec. trademarks com. 1926-52). Contbr. articles to law reviews; author: Lucken im Arbeitsvertrage, 19—. Office: 88 Morningside Dr New York City NY 10027 Tel (212) 663-3300 also Fasanenstrasse 5 D-1000 Berlin 12 Germany

KATZ, HAROLD AMBROSE, b. Shelbyville, Tenn., Nov. 2, 1921; B.A., Vanderbilt U., 1943; J.D., U. Chgo., 1948, M.A., 1958. Admitted to Ill. bar, 1948; partner firm Katz & Friedman, Chgo., 1948—; mem. Ill. Ho. of Reps., 1965—, chmn. judiciary com., 1975—, co-chmn. rules com., 1975—; lectr. Univ. Coll. U. Chgo., 1959-64; master-in-chancery Ill. Circuit Ct. of Cook County, 1963-67; chmn. Ill. Commn. on Orgn. of Gen. Assembly, 1966—. Mem. Am., Ill., Chgo. bar assns., Chgo. Council Lawyers, Am. Trial Lawyers Assn. (chmn. sect. workman's compensation 1963-64). Author: (with Charles O. Gregory) Labor Law: Cases, Materials and Comments, 1948; contbr. articles to legal publs.; editor: Improving the State Legislature: A Report of the Illinois Commission on the Organization of the General Assembly, 1967. Home: 1180 Terrace Ct Glencoe IL 60022 Office: 7 S Dearborn St Chicago IL 60603 Tel (312) 263-6330

KATZ, JOSEPH ABBOTT, b. Mpls., Nov. 18, 1919; B.S.L., U. Minn., 1942, J.D., 1947; grad. Nat. Coll. State Trial Judges, 1967. Admitted to Minn. bar, 1947, Calif. bar, 1948; partner firm Spears & Katz, San Bernardino, Calif., 1948-54; individual practice law, San Bernardino, 1954-66; judge San Bernardino Municipal Ct., 1966, San Bernardino County Superior Ct., 1966—; chmn. San Bernardino County Air Pollution Hearing Bd., 1959-66; mem. San Bernardino Police Commn., 1965-66. Bd. dirs. Family Service Agy., San Bernardino, 1974—. Mem. Calif. Judges Assn., Nat. Coll. Probate Judges, Nat. Assn. Family Conciliation Cts. Home: 13624 Westwood Dr Victorville CA 92392 Office: County Courthouse Arrowhead Ave San Bernardino CA 92415 Tel (714) 245-1050

KATZ, LEON ARNOLD, b. N.Y.C., Dec. 10, 1931; B.S., LL.B., N.Y. U. Admitted to N.Y. State bar, 1967; individual practice law, N.Y.C. Mem. N.Y. City Council, 1969—. Mem. Bklyn. Bar Assn. Contbr. articles to newspapers. Home: 3531 Bedford Ave Brooklyn NY 11210 Office: 26 Court St Brooklyn NY 11242 Tel (212) 834-9300

KATZ, LEON W., b. N.Y.C., Mar. 23, 1916; A.A. in Police Sci., Coll. City N.Y., B.B.A.; J.D., N.Y. Law Sch. Admitted to N.Y. bar; partner firm Katz & Katz, Hartsdale, N.Y.; cons. N.Y.C. Police Dept.; insp. gen. N.Y.C. Correctional Insts.; cons. U.S. Econ. Devel. Corps., Correction Insts. Chmn., vol. exec. dir. Children's Free Clinics N.Y., 1946-71; scoutmaster Boy Scouts Am.; bd. dirs. Young Israel of Scarsdale (N.Y.); vol. atty. Jewish Def. League, Lord Whelan Youth Center. Mem. Am., N.Y. State, Westchester County bar assns. (chmn. correctional affairs com. county assn.). Recipient N.Y.C. Mayor's award for aid to underprivileged children, 1953, 65. Office: 141 Central Park Ave S Hartsdale NY 10530 Tel (914) 428-4464

KATZ, LOUIS SAMUEL, b. Indpls., Nov. 2, 1923; B.A., San Francisco State U., 1949; J.D., Hastings Coll. Law, 1953. Admitted to Calif. bar, 1954, U.S. Supreme Ct. bar, 1972; partner firm Rowell & Katz, Redwood City, Calif., 1954-55; individual practice law, San Francisco, 1955-57; partner firm Gostin & Katz, Inc., San Diego, 1957—; mem. faculty U. San Diego Law Sch., 1974-76, Nat. Coll. Criminal Def. Lawyers, Houston, 1974-76. Pres. San Diego County Democratic Clubs, 1967-68; chmn. Lawyers Against Death Penalty, 1972-73. Mem. ACLU (panel 1957—), NAACP (legal panel 1957-67), Calif. Attys. Criminal Justice (dir. 1974-76, pres. 1977), San Diego County Bar Assn. (dir. 1971-74, v.p. 1973-74), Calif. Trial Lawyers Assn. (pres. 1975-76), San Diego Criminal Def. Lawyers Club (past pres.). Recipient award outstanding contbn. legal redress to San Diego Community, NAACP, 1974. Office: 2550 Fifth Ave suite 731 San Diego CA 92103 Tel (714) 233-7705

KATZ, MARCEL, b. As, Czechoslovakia, Feb. 25, 1947; B.A., Ind. U., 1969, J.D., 1972. Admitted to Ind. bar, 1972; atty. Legal Aid Soc., Lafayette, Ind., 1972-74; dep. pros. atty. Tippecanoe County (Ind.), 1974-76; individual practice law, Lafayette, 1974—. Pres., Legal Aid Corp. of Tippecanoe County; v.p., dir. Tippecanoe Sr. Center; bd. dirs., v.p. Crisis Center, Lafayette; bd. dirs. Hebrew Free Loan Soc., Lafayette; v.p. local chpt. B'nai B'rith; bd. dirs. Head Start. Mem. Am., Ind. State, Tippecanoe bar assns. Home: 1114 Berkley Rd Lafayette IN 47904 Office: 22 Lafayette Bank & Trust Lafayette IN 47901 Tel (317) 423-2651

KATZ, MAURICE HARRY, b. N.Y.C., Jan. 18, 1937; A.B. cum laude, Columbia, 1958; J.D., Harvard, 1961. Admitted to N.Y. State bar, 1962, Calif. bar, 1963; mem. firm Loeb & Loeb, Los Angeles, 1962-64, firm Freshman, Marantz & Comsky, Beverly Hills, 1964-66, firm Grobe, Reinstein, Freid & Katz, Los Angeles, 1967-76, firm Katz & Weisman, 1976—; prof. law U. San Fernando Sch. Law, Sepulveda, Calif., 1966-76, U. West Los Angeles Sch. of Law, 1976—; hearing examiner Los Angeles County Civil Service Commn., 1976—; judge pro tem, Los Angeles, 1975-76, Beverly Hills, 1973-74; cons. publ. Calif. Continuing Edn. of Bar, 1972-73. Mem. Los Angeles County, Beverly Hills, Century City bar assns. Home: 315 N McCadden Pl Los Angeles CA 90004 Office: 1880 Century Park E Suite 615 Los Angeles CA 90067 Tel (213) 553-4500

KATZ, MELVIN SEYMOUR, b. Hartford, June 1, 1915; B.A., Yale, 1937, LL.B., 1940. Admitted to Conn. bar, 1940; since practiced in Hartford, mem. firm Levine & Katz, 1940-41, 1946-76, Schatz & Schatz, 1976—; served with U.S. Army Judge Adv. Gen., 1941-46. Mem. Am. Judicature Soc. (dir.), Assn. Trial Lawyers Am. (gov.), Conn. Trial Lawyers Assn. (gov., past pres.), Am., Conn. (fed. bench-bar com., chmn. civil justice com.), Hartford County bar assns. Home: 40 Wiltshire Ln West Hartford CT 06117 Office: Schatz & Schatz One Financial Plaza Hartford CT 06103 Tel (203) 522-3234

KATZ, MILTON, b. N.Y.C., Nov. 29, 1907; A.B., Harvard, 1927, J.D., 1931. Admitted to N.Y. bar, 1932, Mass. bar, 1959, U.S. Supreme Ct. bar, 1936; law. clk. to Judge Julian W. Mack of U.S. Circuit Ct. Appeals for 2d Circuit, 1931-32; asst. counsel RFC, Washington, 1932-33; asst. counsel Nat. Recovery Adminstrn., Washington, 1933-35; exec. asst. to chmn. and spl. counsel SEC, Washington, 1935-38; spl. asst. to U.S. atty. gen. antitrust div., U.S. Dept. Justice, Washington, 1938-39; lectr. law Harvard Law Sch., 1939-40, prof., 1940-41, Byrne prof. adminstrv. law, 1948-50, Henry L. Stimson prof. law, dir. internat. legal studies, 1954—; solicitor WPB, Washington, 1941-43; U.S. exec. officer Combined Prodn. Bd., U.S.A.-U.K., Can., Washington, 1942-43; gen. counsel European Hdqrs., ECA, Paris, 1948-49; U.S. spl. rep. in Europe (chief Marshall Plan, Paris, 1950-51; U.S. rep. to Econ. Commn. Europe, Geneva, 1950-51; chmn. fin. and econ. com. NATO, Paris, 1950-51; v.p. Ford

Found., Pasadena, Calif. and N.Y.C., 1951-54; chmn. energy adv. com. Office Tech. Assessment, U.S. Congress, Washington, 1973—; mem. adv. bd. Mass. Inst. Tech. Energy Lab., Cambridge, 1973—. Chmn. bd. Carnegie Endowment Internat. Peace, 1969—; chmn. bd. Internat. Legal Center, N.Y.C., 1969—; pres. Citizens Research Found., Princeton, N.J., 1970—; trustee, exec. com. World Peace Found., 1956—; trustee Brandeis U., 1965—, Case Western Res. U., 1968—; chmn. com. manpower White House Conf. Internat. Cooperation, 1965; chmn. Com. Life Scis. and Social Policy Nat. Acad. Scis.-NRC, 1968-75; mem. Panel Tech. Assessment, Nat. Acad. Scis., 1968-69. Fellow Am. Acad. Arts and Scis.; mem. Am., Mass., Cambridge-Belmont-Arlington bar assns., Nat. Conf. Sci. and Law, Am. Law Inst., Am. Soc. Internat. Law. Author: Cases and Materials in Adminstrative Law, 1947; (with others) Government Under Law and the Individual, 1957; (with K. Brewster, Jr.) Law of International Transactions and Relations, 1960; The Things that Are Caesar's, 1966; The Relevance of International Adjudication, 1968; The Modern Foundation: Its Dual Nature, Public and Private, 1968; (with others) Man's Impact on the Global Environment, 1970; editor Federal Regulation of Campaign Finance: Some Constitutional Questions, 1972. Home: 6 Berkeley St Cambridge MA 02138 Office: Harvard Law Sch Cambridge MA 02138 Tel (617) 495-3115

KATZ, RALPH PAUL, b. N.Y.C., Jan. 1, 1928; B.A. magna cum laude, Harvard, 1948; LL.B., 1951. Admitted to N.Y. state bar, 1952, U.S. Supreme Ct. bar, 1962; asso. firm Sargoy & Stein, N.Y.C., 1951-52; legal asst. to bd. mem. NLRB, Washington, 1952-53; asso., then partner firm Miller & Seegar, N.Y.C., 1953, 55-60; atty. Judge Adv. Gen. Corps, U.S. Army, 1953-55; individual practice law, N.Y.C., 1960-63; asso., gen. partner firm Delson & Gordon, N.Y.C., 1963—; lectr. in field; judge, N.Y. Law Sch. Robert F. Wagner Ann. Nat. Labor Law Competition. Pres. Bklyn. Young Democrats, 1958-59, N.Y. Young Dem. Club, Inc., 1959-60; bd. dirs. Mid-Manhattan br. NAACP. Mem., Fed. Bar Council, N.Y. State (chmn. com. on jud. adminstrn. 1973-75), Am. (trustee 1962-65) bar assns., Am. Arbitration Assn., Phi Beta Kappa. Recipient prize Fed. Communications Bar Assn. Law Journal, 1952. Home: 17 Lakeside Dr New Rochelle NY 10801 Office: 230 Park Ave New York City NY 10017 Tel (212) 686-8030

KATZ, RICHARD ALAN, b. Meriden, Conn., Oct. 15, 1946; B.A., U. Conn., 1968; J.D., U. Miami (Fla.), 1971. Admitted to Fla. bar, 1971; sr. partner firm Katz & Rosen, Coconut Grove, Fla., 1971—. Home: 1 Palm Bay Ct Miami Fl 33138 Office: 2951 S Bayshore Dr Coconut Grove FL 33133 Tel (305) 446-5943

KATZ, SANFORD NOAH, b. Holyoke, Mass., Dec. 23, 1933; A.B., Boston U., 1955; J.D., U. Chgo., 1958; postgrad. (USPHS fellow) Yale Law Sch., 1963-64. Law clk. Marvin Jones judge U.S. Ct. of Claims, Washington 1958-59; admitted to D.C. bar, 1959, U.S. Supreme Ct. bar, 1963, Mass. bar, 1970; asso. prof. law Cath. U. Am., 1959-63; prof. law U. Fla., 1964-68, Boston Coll., 1968; asso. Clare Hall Cambridge (Eng.) U., 1973. Mem. Mass. Gov.'s Adv. Council on Marriage and Family; mem. Mass. Atty. Gen.'s Spl. Com. Mem. Am. (exec. council sec. family law), Mass. bar assn., Internat. Family Law Soc. (council). Author: When Parents Fail: The Laws Response to Family Breakdown, 1971; The Youngest Minority: Lawyers In Defense of Children, 1974; Child Neglect Laws In America, 1976—editor: Creativity In Social Work: Selected Writing of Lydia Rapoport, 1975; editor-in-chief Family Law Quar., 1970—. Office: 885 Centre St Newton Centre MA 02159 Tel (617) 969-0100

KATZ, SAUL SIMON, b. N.Y.C., June 22, 1926; A.B., Bklyn. Coll., 1950; LL.B., Harvard, 1953. Admitted to Calif. bar, 1954, N.Y. state bar, 1955; legal aid referee sect. N.Y. State Dept. Labor, N.Y.C., 1958-59; jr. atty. N.Y. State Rent Commn., N.Y.C., 1959-60; atty. N.Y. State Liquor Authority, N.Y.C., 1960-67; sr. atty. N.Y. State Office Crime Control Planning, N.Y.C., 1967-60, N.Y. State Div. Housing & Community Renewal, Great Neck, 1970—. Nat. v.p. Am. Youth Hostels, pres. local council, 1961-64. Mem. N.Y. State Bar Assn., N.Y. County Lawyers Assn. Home and office: 71 Hicks Ln Great Neck NY 11024 Tel (516) 466-6436

KATZ, S(EYMOUR) EDWARD, b. N.Y.C., Feb. 2, 1939; B.A., Hofstra Coll., 1960; J.D., N.Y. U., 1963. Admitted to N.Y. bar, 1964; individual practice law, N.Y.C., 1966—. Office: 1350 Ave of Americas New York City NY 10019 Tel (212) 765-6090

KATZAN, STEPHAN Z., b. Kovel, Poland, Oct. 5, 1931; B.A. in Econs., Reed Coll., 1953; J.D., U. Chgo., 1956. Admitted to Oreg. bar, 1957, Calif. bar, 1965; individual practice law, Portland, Oreg., 1958-63, Los Angeles, 1965—; with Estate and Gift Tax Sect., IRS, Los Angeles, 1963-64. Mem. Am., Oreg., Calif., Los Angeles County, Beverly Hills bar assns., Lawyers Club Los Angeles. Editor The Lawyer's Newsletter, 1971—. Home: 1521 S Oakhurst Dr Los Angeles CA 90035 Office: 1180 S Beverly Dr Los Angeles CA 90035 Tel (213) 553-9980

KATZEN, SALLY, b. Pitts., Nov. 22, 1942; B.A. magna cum laude, Smith Coll., 1964; J.D. magna cum laude, U. Mich., 1967. Admitted to D.C. bar, 1968, U.S. Supreme Ct. bar, 1971; law clk. U.S. Ct. Appeals D.C. Circuit, 1967-68; asso. firm Wilmer, Cutler, Pickering, Washington, 1968-75, partner, 1975—. Pres. Women's Legal Def. Fund, Washington, 1976—. Mem. Am., D.C., FCC bar assns., Washington Council Lawyers, Order of Coif. Editor in chief U. Mich. Law Rev., 1966-67. Office: 1666 K St N W Washington DC 20006 Tel (202) 872-6156

KATZENBACH, NICHOLAS DEBELLEVILLE, b. Phila., Jan. 7, 1922; B.A., Princeton, 1945; LL.B., Yale, 1947; postgrad. (Rhodes scholar) Balliol Coll. Oxford (Eng.) U., 1947-49. Admitted to N.J. bar, 1950, Conn. bar, 1955, N.Y. State bar, 1972; asso. firm Katzenbach, Gildea & Rudner, Trenton, N.J., 1950; atty., adviser office gen. counsel USAF, Washington, 1950-52, cons., 1952-56; asso. prof. law Yale, 1952-56; prof. U. Chgo., 1956-60; asst. atty. gen. Dept. Justice, Washington, 1961-62, dep. atty. gen., 1962-64, acting atty. gen., 1964, atty. gen., 1965-66; under sec. of state Dept. State, Washington, 1966-69; v.p., gen. counsel IBM, Armonk, N.Y., 1969—, also dir. Ford Found. fellow, 1960-61. Mem. Am. Law Inst., Am. Bar Assn., Am. Judicature Soc. Decorated Air medal with 3 oak leaf clusters; author: (with Morton A. Kaplan) The Political Foundations of International Law, 1961; contbr. articles to legal jours; editor-in-chief Yale Law Jour., 1947. Home: 5225 Sycamore Ave Riverdale NY 10471 Office: IBM Corp Armonk NY 10504 Tel (914) 765-4810

KAUFER, ALVIN S., b. Wilkes-Barre, Pa., Aug. 12, 1932; A.B., Wesleyan U., 1954; J.D., U. Mich., 1959. Admitted to Calif. bar, 1960; asso. firm Nossaman, Krueger & Marsh, Los Angeles, 1960-66, partner, 1966—, mng. partner, 1975—; asso. mem. faculty Law Sch. U. Calif., Berkeley, 1959-60; mem. faculty Law Sch. U. San Fernando Valley, 1964-65. Trustee Center for Law in the Pub. Interest, Multiple Sclerosis Soc., Am. Jewish Com. Mem. Am., Calif., Los Angeles County bar assns., Chancery Club, Assn. Bus. Trial Lawyers. Asso. editor Los Angeles County Bar Bull., 1963-67, editor, 1967-69; contbr. articles to legal jours.; lectr. seminars. Home: 774 Ranch Ln Pacific Palisades CA 90272 Office: 445 S Figueroa St Los Angeles CA 90071 Tel (213) 628-5221

KAUFF, JEROME BERNARD, b. Bklyn., Mar. 12, 1938; B.A. cum laude, Bklyn. Coll., 1958; LL.B., N.Y. U., 1961, LL.M., 1965. Admitted to N.Y. bar, 1962; atty. Internat. Ladies' Garment Workers Union, N.Y.C., 1962-65, asst. gen. counsel, 1965-67; asso. firm Phillips, Nizer, Benjamin, Krim & Ballon, N.Y.C., 1967-70, partner, 1970-72; partner Dretzin & Kauff, N.Y.C., 1972—. Mem. Am. Bar Assn., Assn. Bar City N.Y. Contbg. editor Morris, The Developing Labor Law, 1971. Office: 123 E 62d St New York City NY 10021 Tel (212) 832-2001

KAUFFMAN, BRUCE WILLIAM, b. Atlantic City, Dec. 1, 1934; B.A., U. Pa., 1956; LL.B., Yale, 1959. Admitted to Pa. bar, 1961, N.J. bar, 1960, U.S. Supreme Ct. bar, 1965; asso. firm Dilworth, Paxson, Kalish & Levy, Phila., 1960-65, partner, 1965—, chmn. litigation dept., 1975—; chmn. Montgomery County (Pa.) Govt. Study Commn., 1973-74; mem. com. of censors U.S. Dist. Ct. Eastern Pa., 1966-68; del. Pa. Constl. Conv., 1969. Mem. Am. Judicature Soc., Am. Juristic Soc., Am., Pa., Phila. bar assns., Pa. Soc., Phila. Lawyers Club, Phi Beta Kappa. Office: 2600 Fidelity Bldg 123 S Broad St Philadelphia PA 19109 Tel (215) KI-6-3000

KAUFFMAN, DAVID LIN, b. Mohrsville, Pa., June 13, 1930; B.A., Albright Coll., 1958; LL.B., U. Md., 1964. Admitted to Md. bar, 1965, U.S. Supreme Ct. bar, 1976; accountant Easco Corp., Balt., 1958-64, legal asst., 1964-68, asst. sec., 1968-71, corp. counsel, 1970—, sec., 1971—. Mem. Am., Md., Baltimore City, Harford County (Md.) bar assns., Md. Assn. C.P.A.'s, Am. Assn. Attys-C.P.A.'s, Am. Soc. Corp. Secs. Home: 405 Mountain Rd Fallston MD 21047 Office: 201 N Charles St Baltimore MD 21201 Tel (301) 837-9550

KAUFFMAN, JAY GUY, b. Jonesville, Va., Apr. 6, 1927; B.S., U. Va., 1949, J.D., 1952. Admitted to Va. bar, 1952; partner firm Emroch, Cowan, Kauffman & Emroch, Richmond, Va., 1967-72; prin. Jay G. Kauffman & Assos., Richmond, 1972—. Mem. Chesterfield, Va. bar assns., Va. Trial Lawyers Assn. (dir.). Home: 11940 Buckingham Rd Midlothian VA 23113 Office: 1909 Huguenot Rd Richmond VA 23235 Tel (804) 272-7559

KAUFMAN, CHARLES RUDOLPH, b. Chgo., Dec. 25, 1908; B.A., U. Mich., 1930; J.D., Harvard U., 1933. Admitted to D.C. bar, Ill. bar, 1938, U.S. Supreme Ct. bar, 1947; legal sec. Judge Learned Hand, U.S. Ct. of Appeals, 1933-34; supervising atty. SEC, Washington, 1934-37; mem. firm Pope & Ballard, Chgo., 1937-52; partner firm Vedder, Price, Kaufman & Kammholz, Chgo., 1952—. Mem. Am., Ill., Chgo. bar assns., Chgo. Law Club. Legis. editor Harvard Law Rev., 1932-33. Home: 170 Westview Rd Winnetka IL 60093 Office: 115 S La Salle St Chicago IL 60603 Tel (312) 781-2222

KAUFMAN, COLIN KELLY, b. Tucson, Dec. 4, 1946; B.A., U. Tex., 1967; J.D., Harvard, 1970, LL.M., 1976. Admitted to Tex. bar, 1970, Kans. bar, 1976; asso. firm Kleberg, Mobley, Lockett & Weil, Corpus Christi, Tex., 1970, 72-74; teaching fellow Harvard, 1974-76; asst. prof. law Washburn U., Topeka, 1976—; capt. JAGC, USAF, 1970-72. Mem. Am., Tex., Kans. bar assns., Assn. Am. Law Sch., Air Force Assn., Common Cause. Contbr. articles to law jours. Home: 3806 Illinois Ave Topeka KS 66609 Office: Washburn Univ Sch Law Topeka KS 66621 Tel (913) 295-6660

KAUFMAN, DEAN STEWART, b. Vallejo, Calif., Mar. 7, 1945; A.B., U. Calif., Los Angeles, 1966; J.D., U. Oreg., 1969. Admitted to Oreg. bar, 1969, Am. Samoa bar, 1969; vol. VISTA, Pago Pago, Am. Samoa, 1969-70; staff atty. Lane County Legal Aid, Eugene, Oreg., 1970-72; partner firm Bennett & Kaufman, Eugene, 1972—. Mem. Lane County, Oreg. State bar assns., Phi Beta Kappa. Editor Am. Samoa Reporter & Digest, 1974—. Office: 1590 High St Eugene OR 97401 Tel (503) 344-4277

KAUFMAN, IRA GLADSTONE, b. N.Y.C., Dec. 13, 1909; B.S., Washington Sq. Coll., 1933; J.D., N.Y. U., 1936; D.B.A. (hon.), Cleary Coll., Ypsilanti, Mich., 1976. Admitted to Mich. bar, 1937; individual practice law, Detroit, 1938-59; judge Probate Ct., Wayne County (Mich.), 1959—, presiding judge, 1973-74, 77—; lectr. Inst. Continuing Legal Edn., 1960-68, U. Detroit Law Sch., 1966-74, Moot Ct. judge, 1966—. Life pres. Adat Shalom Synagogue; chmn. ad hoc com. on alcoholism Detroit United Community Services, 1967-68; chmn. Greater Detroit Council on Alcoholism, 1967-68, Detroit Com. on Fgn. Relations, 1974-75; mem. Gov.'s Com. on Mental Health Statute Rev. Commn., 1970-72; bd. dirs. Hebrew Free Loan Soc., Detroit Jewish Nat. Fund, Midrasha Bd.; v.p. United Hebrew Sch., Detroit, 1948-60, Mich. Soc. Mental Health, 1960—, Childrens Charter Mich., 1965; chmn. bd., pres. Met. Soc. for Blind, Detroit, 1966-70; trustee Park Community Hosp., 1965-71; trustee, exec. bd. Detroit Inst. Tech., 1962—; mem. exec. bd. League for Handicapped-Goodwill, 1970—; bd. overseers Dropsie U., Phila., 1973-75. Mem. Mich. Probate and Juvenile Ct. Assn. (exec. bd. 1969-72, chmn. mental health com. 1960-70, pres. 1970-71), Am., Mich., Fed., Detroit bar assns. Author: Vol. 4, Wills and Estates, 1960. Home: 18701 Pennington St Detroit MI 48221 Office: City-County Bldg Detroit MI 48226 Tel (313) 224-5672

KAUFMAN, IRVING ROBERT, b. N.Y.C., June 24, 1910; LL.B., Fordham U., 1931; LL.D., Jewish Sem. Am., Fordham U., Oklahoma City U.; D.C.L., N.Y. U. Admitted to N.Y. bar, 1932; spl. asst. to U.S. atty. So. Dist. N.Y.; asst. U.S. atty., spl. asst. to atty. gen. U.S. charge of lobbying investigation; set up permanent lobbying unit for Dept. Justice, served as head; pvt. practice law, N.Y.C.; partner firm Noonan, Kaufman & Eagan; spl. asst. to atty. gen. U.S., 1947-48; U.S. dist. judge So. Dist. N.Y., 1949-61; circuit judge U.S. Ct. Appeals, 2d circuit, 1961-73, chief judge, 1973—. U.S. del. 2d UN Congress Prevention Crime and Treatment Offenders, Conf. Anglo-Am. Adminstrv. Law Exchange, London, Eng., 1969. Trustee emeritus Riverdale Country Sch. Recipient Achievement in Law award Fordham Coll. Alumni Assn., Fordham Coll. Encaenia award, medal Fordham Law Sch. Alumni. Office: US Courthouse New York City NY 10007*

KAUFMAN, JACK IRWIN, b. Bklyn., Sept. 24, 1917; B.A., Bklyn. Coll., 1940; J.D. cum laude, St. John's U., 1939. Admitted to N.Y. bar, 1940, Pa. bar, 1954; asst. city solicitor City of Allentown, Pa., 1960-66, 70—; solicitor Allentown Human Relations Commn., 1970—; mem. panel arbitrators Am. Arbitration Assn.; mem. Pa. Bur. Mediation, 1972—, N.J. Bur. Mediation, 1973—. Mem. Am., Pa., Lehigh County (dir. 1963-66) bar assns., Assn. Trial Lawyers Am., Nat. Inst. Municipal Law Officers. Home: 132 N Arch St Allentown PA 18104 Office: Hotel Traylor 1444 Hamilton St Allentown PA 18105 Tel (215) 439-0211

KAUFMAN, JERRY JACK, b. Cleve., Sept. 3, 1935; B.S. in Engring., U. Ariz., 1957; J.D., Calif. Western U., 1965; grad. Nat. Coll. Judiciary, 1976. Admitted to Nev. bar, 1966, U.S. Supreme Ct. bar; with firm Jones, Jones, Bell, LeBaron, Close, Bilbry & Kaufman, 1967-74; individual practice law, Las Vegas, 1974—; alt. judge municipal bench, Las Vegas, 1973-76. South Nev. chmn. March of Dimes, 1973-74; pres. Nev. State Easter Seal Soc., 1974; chmn. state Nev. March of Dimes, 1975-77. Mem. Phi Alpha Delta. Office: 500 S 4th St Las Vegas NV 89101 Tel (702) 384-9971

KAUFMAN, LEONARD, b. N.Y.C., Apr. 30, 1913; student City Coll. N.Y., 1929-31; LL.B., Fordham U., 1936. Admitted to N.Y. bar, 1937, U.S. Supreme Ct. bar, 1959; asso. firm Nathan Burkan, N.Y.C., 1933-36; asso. firm Schwartz & Frohlich, N.Y.C., 1936-49; mem. legal dept. Paramount Pictures Corp., N.Y.C., 1949-64, gen. counsel, 1964-67; partner firm Kaufman & Kaufman, N.Y.C., 1969-75; partner firm Kommel, Rogers, Kaufman, Lorber & Shenkman, N.Y.C., 1975—. Mem. Am., N.Y. State bar assns., Assn. Bar City N.Y. (mem. antitrust and copyright coms.), Copyright Soc. U.S.A. (past trustee), B'nai B'rith (v.p. cinema unit). Home: 400 Orienta Ave Mamaroneck NY 10543 Office: 380 Madison Ave New York City NY 10017 Tel (212) 986-9779

KAUFMAN, PAUL, b. N.Y.C., Nov. 16, 1947; B.A., U. Wis., 1970; J.D., N.Y. Law Sch., 1973. Admitted to N.Y. bar, 1974, N.J. bar, 1974; law sec. to judge Superior Ct. N.J., 1973-74; staff atty. Adminstrv. Office of the Cts., Trenton, N.J., 1974; asso. firm Weitz, Gutfleish, Wurtzel & Sterling, Englewood, N.J., 1975; partner firm Kaufman & Rosen, Fort Lee, N.J., 1975—; atty. Fort Lee Rent Leveling Bd., 1977, Fort Lee Consumer Protection Bd., 1976; spl. counsel Fort Lee Zoning Bd. Adjustment, 1976. Mem. Am., N.J., Bergen County bar assns. Office: 2175 Lemoline Ave Fort Lee NJ 07024

KAUFMAN, PAUL JOSEPH, b. Charleston, W.Va., Mar. 16; A.B., W.Va. U., 1942; J.D., U. Va., 1948. Admitted to W.Va. bar, 1948; partner firm Kaufman & Boiarsky, Charleston, 1949-59, Kaufman & Browning, Charleston, 1959-61, Kaufman, Ghiz, Vealey & Sergent, Charleston, 1963-69, Kaufman & Ratliff, Charleston, 1973—; mem. W.Va. Senate, 1960-68; dir. Appalachian Research & Def. Fund, Charleston, 1970-73. Commr., Charleston Police Civil Service, 1955-59. Mem. Am., W.Va., Kanawha County bar assns. Home: 410 Sheridan St Charleston WV 25314 Office: 701 Stanley Bldg Charleston WV 25314 Tel (304) 344-2437

KAUFMAN, ROGER WAYNE, b. Elizabeth, N.J., Aug. 27, 1938; A.B., Cornell U., 1960; LL.B., Harvard, 1963. Admitted to Ariz. bar, 1964; asso. firm Lewis & Roca, Phoenix, 1963-68, partner, 1968—. Mem. Am., Ariz., Maricopa bar assns., Am. Soc. Hosp. Attys., Ariz. Assn. Hosp. Attys. (pres. 1974—), State Bar Ariz. (chmn. com. on civil practice and procedure 1974-76). Author: Arizona Courtroom Handbook, 2d edit., 1970. Office: 100 W Washington Phoenix AZ 85003 Tel (602) 262-5311

KAUFMAN, SIDNEY BERNARD, b. Jersey City, July 21, 1927; B.A., Upsala Coll., 1951; J.D., Seton Hall U., 1955. Admitted to N.J. bar, 1955, U.S. Supreme Ct. bar, 1964; judge Roselle (N.J.) Municipal Ct., 1958; municipal atty. Boro of Roselle, 1959-63; individual practice law, Perth Amboy, N.J., 1955—. Mem. N.J., Middlesex County bar assns., Am. Trial Lawyers Assn. Home: 18 Plymouth Rd Westfield NJ 07090 Office: 214 Smith St Perth Amboy NJ 08861 Tel (201) 442-0212

KAUFMANN, ANTHONY STEVEN, b. N.Y.C., Mar. 19, 1942; B.A., Dartmouth, 1964; B.Litt. in Social Anthropology, Oxford (Eng.) U., 1965-67; J.D., U. Pa., 1970. Admitted to N.Y. bar, 1971; asso. firm Mudge, Rose, Guthrie & Alexander, N.Y.C., 1970-73, Botein, Hays, Sklar & Herzberg, N.Y.C., 1973—. Mem. Assn. Bar City N.Y., Council N.Y. Law Assos. Co-editor, contbg. author Practicing Law in New York City, 1975. Home: 351 E 84th St New York City NY 10028 Office: 200 Park Ave New York City NY 10017 Tel (212) 867-5500

KAUFMANN, BASIL LIONEL, b. Apr. 29, 1897. Admitted to Mo. bar, 1918, U.S. Supreme Ct. bar; sr. mem. firm Culver Phillip Kaufmann and Smith; of counsel firm Utz Litvak Thackery Utz and Taylor, St. Joseph, Mo.; pres. Arcade Investment Corp., Basil L. Kaufmann Found. Inc.; dir. Am. Investment Corp., St. Louis, Commerce Bank St. Joseph, Hirsch Brother Dry Goods Co., Sta. KRES. Home and Office: 1208 Corby Bldg Saint Joseph MO 64501 Tel (816) 232-6037

KAUFMANN, DAN, b. Mpls., May 13, 1918; A.B., U. So. Calif., 1939, LL.B., 1946, LL.M., 1955. Admitted to Calif. bar, 1946; dep. atty. gen., to then asst. atty. gen., 1966; judge Los Angeles Municipal Ct., 1966-76, Los Angeles Superior Ct., 1976—. Office: 6230 Sylmar Ave Van Nuys CA 91401 Tel (203) 787-3350

KAUFMANN, ELSA RAICHELSON, b. Springfield, Mass., Jan. 21, 1931; B.A., Wellesley Coll., 1952; J.D. with honors, George Washington U., 1965. Admitted to D.C. bar, 1966, Md. bar, 1967, U.S. Supreme Ct. bar, 1970; partner firm Pasternak and Kaufmann, Washington, 1968—. Mem. D.C. Women's Bar Assn. (pres. 1973-74), Chevy Chase Bus. and Profl. Women's Club, Nat. Assn. Women Laywers. (Md.) Home: 4701 Willard Ave Chevy Chase MD 20015 Office: 4400 Jenifer St Washington DC 20015 Tel (202) 362-4060

KAUFMANN, KENNETH K., JR., b. 1930; B.A., U. Calif., Los Angeles, 1952; J.D., U. So. Calif., 1957. Atty., State of Calif., 1957-62; v.p., asst. sec. law United Calif. Bank, Los Angeles, 1962-70, v.p., mgr. div. law, San Francisco, 1970-73; v.p., asst. sec. Western Bancorp., Los Angeles, 1973-74, v.p., sec., gen. counsel, 1974—. Office: 707 Wilshire Blvd Los Angeles CA 90017*

KAUFMANN, NORMAN, b. Md., May 13, 1902; LL.B., U. Md., 1925, J.D. Admitted to Md. bar, 1926, U.S. Supreme Ct. bar, 1948; practice law, Md., 1926—; legal officer USN; hon. consul Honduras, Central Am.; real property assessor; asst. atty. gen. Am. Samoa. Author: Divorce in Maryland, 1938. Home: 9 Auburndale Terr Portland ME 04103

KAUFMANN, STEPHEN HANS, b. Mannheim, Germany, May 3, 1922; A.A., U. Calif., Berkeley, 1944, B.S., 1946; J.D., Hastings Coll. Law U. Calif., San Francisco, 1960. Mfr's rep., San Francisco, 1948-60; admitted to Calif. bar, 1961; individual practice law, San Rafael, Calif., 1961—; gen. counsel Strawberry Recreation Dist., Marin County, Calif., 1961—. Bd. dirs. Legal Aid Soc. of Marin County, 1970—, chmn. bd., 1975—. Mem. State Bar Calif., Marin County Bar Assn. (dir. 1968-71, 75—). Office: 1005 A St San Rafael CA 94901 Tel (415) 454-4824

KAUL, DONALD ALLEN, b. Phila., Apr. 21, 1935; B.M.E., Ohio State U., 1958; J.D., George Washington U., 1962. Admitted to D.C. bar, 1962, U.S. Supreme Ct. bar, 1967; partner firm Jacobi, Davidson and Jacobi, Washington, 1964-67; partner firm Roylance, Abrams, Berdo and Kaul, and predecessors, Washington, 1967—. Mem. Bar Assn. D.C. (chmn. patent sect. 1976-77), Am., Internat. bar assns., Am. Patent Law Assn. Office: 1225 Connecticut Ave NW Washington DC 20036 Tel (202) 659-9076

KAUS, OTTO M., b. Vienna, Austria, Jan. 7, 1920; came to U.S., 1939, naturalized, 1942; B.A., U. Calif., Los Angeles, 1942; LL.B., Loyola U., Los Angeles, 1949. Admitted to Calif. bar, 1949; asso. firm Chase, Rotchford, Downen & Drukker, Los Angeles, 1949-61; justice Ct. of Appeals, Second Appellate Dist. Calif., Los Angeles, 1965—. Mem. Am. Law Inst., Am. Bar Assn. Office: 3580 Wilshire Blvd Los Angeles CA 90010 Tel (213) 736-2641

KAVALER, THOMAS J., b. N.Y.C., Dec. 10, 1948; B.A., Coll. City N.Y., 1969; J.D., Fordham U., 1972; LL.M., N.Y. U., 1975. Admitted to N.Y. bar, 1973, U.S. Supreme Ct. bar, 1976; law clk. to judge U.S. Dist. Ct. for So. N.Y., 1972-74; asso. firm Cravath, Swaine & Moore, N.Y.C., 1974-75, firm Cahill, Gordon & Reindel, N.Y.C., 1975—. Mem. Am., Fed., N.Y. State bar assns., Assn. Bar City N.Y., New County Lawyers Assn., Am. Trial Lawyers Assn., Council of N.Y. Law Assos. Office: 80 Pine St New York City NY 10005 Tel (212) 825-0100

KAVANAGH, THOMAS MATTHEW, b. Carson City, Mich., Aug. 4, 1909; LL.B., U. Detroit, 1932. Admitted to Mich. bar, 1932; practice law, Detroit, 1932-35, Carson City, 1935-55; city atty. Carson City and Perrington, Mich., 1943-54; village clk. Carson City, 1943-54; atty. gen. Mich., 1954-57; justice Mich. Supreme Ct., Lansing, 1957-64, chief justice, 1964—. Chmn. Gt. Lakes Commn. Mem. Ionia-Montcalm Bar Assn. (pres.). Home: 3934 Barton Rd Lansing MI 48917 Office: Capitol Bldg Lansing MI 48933*

KAVANAUGH, GERARD P., b. 1916; A.B., Allegheny Coll.; J.D., Georgetown U. Admitted to Del. bar, 1941; now asso. gen. counsel Hercules, Inc. Mem. Del. State Bar (pres. 1977—). Office: Delaware Trade Bldg Wilmington DE 19899*

KAVOUKLIS, MICHAEL NICHOLAS, b. Tarpon Springs, Fla., Nov. 5, 1935. B.S., Fla. State U., 1958; J.D., Stetson Coll. Law, 1962. Admitted to Fla. bar, 1962; atty., adminstrv. asst. Fla. Milk Commn., Tallahassee, 1962-63; asst. atty. gen. State of Fla., Tallahassee, 1963-64, 69-70; research asst. to Justice Richard W. Ervin, Jr., Fla. Supreme Ct., 1964-66; asst. state atty. Fla. 6th Jud. Circuit, 1966; practiced in Clearwater, Fla., 1966-68, Tampa, Fla., 1969-70, 72; judge Oldsmar (Fla.) Municipal Ct., 1967-69; asst. state atty. Fla. 13th Jud. Circuit, 1968-69; asst. county solicitor Hillsborough County (Fla.), 1970-72; judge Hillsborough County Ct., 1972—; instr. Hillsborough Community Coll. Mem. Am., Fla., Tampa bar assns., Am. Judicature Soc., Conf. County Ct. Judges Fla. (pres. 1974-75). Office: Courthouse Annex Room 115 Tampa FL 33602 Tel (813) 229-0572

KAWAKAMI, NORITO, b. Eleele, Kauai, Hawaii, Jan. 1, 1912; LL.B., U. Colo., 1952. Admitted to Hawaii bar, 1953; practiced in Honolulu, 1952, Lihue Kauai, 1952-56; judge Hawaii Dist. Ct., Kauai, 1956-70, 1st Circuit Ct., Honolulu, 1971—. Mem. Hawaii Bar Assn. (hon.). Office: Room 222 Lihue Shopping Center Honolulu HI 96809 Tel (808) 245-3870

KAY, HERMA HILL, b. Orangeburg, S.C., Aug. 18, 1934; B.A., So. Meth. U., 1956; J.D., U. Chgo., 1959. Admitted to Calif. bar, 1960; law clk. Justice Roger Traynor, Calif. Supreme Ct., 1959-60; prof. law U. Calif., Berkeley, 1960—, chairperson Berkeley div. Acad. Senate, 1973-74; vis. prof. law Harvard U., fall 1976; co-reporter Uniform Marriage and Divorce Act, Commrs. on Uniform State Laws, Chgo., 1968-70. Chairperson bd. dirs. Equal Rights Advocates, Inc., San Francisco; trustee Russell Sage Found. Mem. Calif. Bar Assn., Calif. Women Lawyers (bd. govs. 1975—), Order of Coif. Author: (with K. Davidson and R.B. Ginsburg) Cases and Materials on Sex-Based Discrimination, 1974; (with R. Cranton and D. Currie) Conflict of Laws: Cases-Comments-Questions, 1975; contbr. articles to legal publs. Office: Sch Law Boalt Hall U Calif Berkeley CA 94720 Tel (415) 642-0259

KAY, JOHN FRANKLIN, JR., b. Charleston, W.Va., Nov. 11, 1929; B.A., Washington & Lee U., 1951, LL.B., 1955. Admitted to Va. bar, 1955; partner firm Allen & Kay, Waynesboro, Va., 1955-57; partner firm Mays, Valentine, Davenport & Moore, Richmond, Va., 1957—. Bd. trustees The Collegiate Schs., Richmond, 1969—, chmn., 1972-74. Fellow Am. Coll. Trial Lawyers, Internat. Soc. Barristers; mem. Va. State Bar, Richmond, Va., Am. bar assns., Am. Judicature Soc., Nat. Assn. Railroad Trial Counsel, Order Coif, Phi Beta Kappa, Omicron Delta Kappa. Editor: Washington & Lee Law Review, 1954-55. Home: 4 S Wilton Rd Richmond VA 23226 Office: PO Box 1122 Richmond VA 23208 Tel (804) 644-6011

KAY, JOHN ROSS, b. DeLeon, Tex., July 10, 1925; B.B.A., Baylor U., 1949; LL.B., Bates Coll., 1961. Admitted to Tex. Supreme Ct. bar, 1961; v.p., trust officer First Hutchings-Sealy Nat. Bank, Galveston, Tex., 1965-69; v.p., trust officer Lufkin (Tex.) Nat. Bank, 1969-72; partner firm McFarland & Kay, Lufkin, 1972-75; individual practice law, Lufkin, 1975—. Mem. Deep E. Tex. Estate Planning Council. Office: 206 E Lufkin Ave Lufkin TX 75901 Tel (713) 632-6695

KAY, MICHAEL BOYCE, b. Memphis, Jan. 27, 1944; B.S., Memphis State U., 1966, J.D., 1968. Admitted to Tenn. bar, 1968, U.S. Supreme Ct. bar, 1974; asso. firm Ratner, Sugarmon, Lucas, Salky & Henderson, Memphis, 1968-77; individual practice law, Memphis, 1977—. Mem. Tenn. Bar Assn., Am. Judicature Soc., Delta Theta Phi. Asso. editor Memphis State U. Law Rev., 1966-68. Home: 1768 S Trezevant St Memphis TN 38114 Office: 414 Commerce Title Bldg Memphis TN 38103 Tel (901) 523-8174

KAY, MITCHELL N., b. N.Y.C., July 12, 1936; B.S., Long Island U., 1958; LL.B., Brooklyn Coll., 1962, J.D., 1967. Admitted to N.Y. bar, 1962, U.S. Dist. Ct. bar Eastern Dist. N.Y., 1964, U.S. Dist. Ct. bar So. Dist. N.Y., 1964, U.S. Ct. Appeal bar 2d Circuit, 1966, U.S. Ct. Mil. Appeals, 1966, U.S. Supreme Ct., 1966, D.C. bar, 1973, U.S. Ct. Appeals bar D.C. Circuit, 1974; legal clk. firm Philips, Nizer, Benjamin, Krim & Ballon, N.Y.C., 1960-61, firm Tell, Cheser, Werner & Britbart, N.Y.C., 1961-62; individual practice law, Mineola, N.Y., 1962—. Mem. N.Y.S., Bar Assn., Bar Assn. Nassau County, N.Y. State Trial Lawyers Assn., Nat. Assn. Def. Lawyers in Criminal Cases. Office: 1565 Franklin Ave Mineola NY 11501 Tel (516) 248-9380 also 38 W 32d St New York City NY 10001 Tel (212) 695-8155

KAY, ROBERT A., b. Milw., Aug. 28, 1944; B.S., U. Wis., 1966, J.D., 1969. Admitted to Wis. bar, 1969; individual practice law, Madison, Wis., 1969—. Supr. Dane County (Wis.) Bd., 1969-70, mem. agr. com.; adv. bd. Family Planning, Madison. Office: 222 S Hamilton St Madison WI 53703 (608) 251-0761

KAY, ROBERT HENRY CHRISTOPHER, b. Royal, W.Va., Mar. 7, 1896; B.S., Marshall Coll. (now Marshall U.), 1916; LL.D., W.Va., U., 1923. Admitted to W.Va. bar, 1923, U.S. Supreme Ct. bar, 1957; individual practice law, 1923-30; partner firm Kay, Casto & Chaney, and predecessor, Charleston, W.Va., 1934—. Chmn. W.Va. Republican State Exec. Com., 1938-44. Fellow Am. Coll. Trial Lawyers, Internat. Acad. Trial Lawyers; mem. Nat. Assn. R.R. Trial Counsel, Am. Judicature Soc., Am., W.Va. (v.p. 1936), W.Va. State, Kanawha County (W.Va.) (pres. 1935) bar assns., W.Va. U. Alumni Assn. (pres. 1947-48). Home: 1021 Circle Rd Charleston WV 25314 Office: 1616 Charleston Nat Plaza POB 2031 Charleston WV 25327 Tel (304) 343-4831

KAY, WENDELL PALMER, b. Watseka, Ill., Aug. 17, 1913; A.B., DePauw U., 1935; J.D., Northwestern U., 1938. Admitted to Ill. bar, 1938, Alaska bar, 1948; regional atty. Bur. Land Mgmt., Portland, 1945-46; individual practice law, Anchorage, 1948-75; partner firm Kay, Christie, Fuld & Saville, Anchorage, 1975—; vis. prof. law Ariz. State U., 1973-77; mem. Alaska Legislature, 1951, 53, 55, 70, speaker, 1955. Exec. dir. Alaska Housing Authority, Anchorage, 1946-47. Mem. Am. Bar Assn., Am. Trial Lawyers Assn. Contbr. articles to legal jours. Office: 2600 Denali St Anchorage AK 99501 Tel (907) 276-4335

KAYE, HARVEY, b. N.Y.C., Oct. 19, 1934; B.S. in Engring., Lowell U., 1956; J.D., George Washington U., 1960. Admitted to Va. bar, 1960, D.C. bar, 1961; patent examiner U.S. Patent Office, Washington, 1956-57; individual practice law, Washington, 1961-62; partner firm Spencer & Kaye, Washington, 1962—. Mem. Am., Fed. bar assns., Am. Patent Law Assn., D.C. Bar (chairperson customs com. div. 14 1975—). Contbr. articles in field to profl. jours. Office: 1920 L St NW Washington DC 20036 Tel (202) 659-9720

KAYE, JUDITH SMITH, b. Monticello, N.Y., Aug. 4, 1938; B.A., Barnard Coll., 1958; LL.B. cum laude, N.Y. U., 1962. Admitted to N.Y. State bar, 1963; asso. firm Sullivan & Cromwell, N.Y.C., 1962-64; staff atty. IBM, N.Y.C., 1964-65; mem. firm Olwine, Connelly, Chase, O'Donnell & Weyher, N.Y.C., 1969—. Mem. N.Y. State Bar Assn., Assn. Bar City N.Y. Home: 101 Central Park W New York City NY 10023 Office: 299 Park Ave New York City NY 10017 Tel (212) 688-0400

KAYE, ROBERT PAUL, b. Rockville Centre, L.I., N.Y., Mar. 4, 1929; B.A., U. Fla., 1950; J.D., U. Miami, 1957. Admitted to Fla. bar, 1957; mem. firm Walters, Moore & Costanzo, Miami, Fla., 1957-58; asst. state atty. 11th Jud. Circuit, Dade County, Fla., from 1970, later div. chief several cts., with maj. crimes div., from 1973, dep. div. chief Career Criminal Div., 1976—, project dir. Career Criminal Div., 1977—; news dir. WQAM Radio, Miami, 1958-68, WIOD Radio, 1968-69, WINZ Radio, 1969-70. Mem. Fla. Bar Assn., Fla., Nat. prosecutors assns. Home: 16130 SW 102 Ct Miami FL 33157 Office: 1351 NW 12 St Miami FL 33153 Tel (305) 547-7107

KAYE, STEPHEN RACKOW, b. Nyack, N.Y., May 4, 1931; A.B., Cornell U., 1952, LL.B. with honors, 1956. Admitted to N.Y. State bar, 1956, U.S. Supreme Ct. bar, 1961; asso. firm Sullivan & Cromwell, N.Y.C., 1956-63; asso. firm Proskauer Rose Goetz & Mendelsohn, N.Y.C., 1964-68, partner, 1968—. Mem. Am., N.Y. State bar assns., Assn. Bar City N.Y., New York County Lawyers Assn., Order of Coif, Phi Kappa Phi. Mng. editor Cornell Law Quar., 1955-56. Office: 300 Park Ave New York City NY 10022 Tel (212) 593-9308

KAYE, WILLIAM HERBERT, b. Detroit, Mar. 10, 1947; B.A., Pa. State U., 1969; J.D., Am. U., 1972. Admitted to Pa. bar, 1972, U.S. Supreme Ct. bar, 1976; individual practice law, Chambersburg, Pa., 1972—. Mem. Am., Pa. bar assns. Home: 187 Harvest Ln Chambersburg PA 17201 Office: 221 Professional Arts Bldg Chambersburg PA 17201 Tel (717) 264-3290

KAYLOR, HAL MICHAEL, b. Hickory, N.C., Apr. 13, 1948; B.A., Clemson U., 1970; J.D., U. S.C., 1973. Admitted to S.C. bar, 1973, U.S. Supreme Ct. bar, 1976; asso. firm Brooks and Hartman, Columbia, S.C., 1973-75; partner firm Brooks and Kaylor, Columbia, 1975—; lectr. Midlands Coll., Columbia, 1975—. Mem. S.C., Am. trial lawyers assns., Am., Richland County, S.C. bar assns., Richland Def. Lawyers Assn. Recipient citation for outstanding community service in youth work Optimist Clubs S.C., 1976. Home: 1614 S Beltline Dr Columbia SC 29205 Office: 2126 Devine St Columbia SC 29205 Tel (803) 799-5400

KAYMAN, PHILIP MARVIN, b. Chgo., Dec. 6, 1941; B.B.A. with distinction, U. Mich., 1963; J.D. cum laude, Northwestern U., 1967. Admitted to Ill. bar, 1967, U.S. Supreme Ct. bar, 1970; asso.-in-law U. Cal. Sch. of Law (Boalt Hall), Berkeley, 1967-68; mem. firm Friedman & Koven, Chgo., 1968-73, partner firm, 1973—. Mem. Am., Ill., Chgo. bar assns., Chgo. Council Lawyers, Order of Coif. Asso. editor Northwestern U. Law Rev., 1966-67. Home: 1034 N Marion St Oak Park IL 60302 Office: 208 S LaSalle St Chicago IL 60604 Tel (312) 346-8500

KAYSON, DAVID, b. Washington, Sept. 4, 1921; LL.B., George Washington U., 1950. Admitted to D.C. bar, 1952, Md. bar, 1970, U.S. Supreme Ct. bar, 1973; individual practice law, Washington, 1952-70, Kensington, Md., 1970—. Mem. Bar Assn. D.C., Md. State, Montgomery County bar assns., Assn. Trial Lawyers Am. (gov. 1974-77), Assn. Plaintiff's Trial Attys. Met. Washington (pres. 1973-74), Md. Trial Lawyers Assn. (v.p. Montgomery County 1972-75). Office: 10400 Connecticut Ave Kensington MD 20795 Tel (301) 949-1556

KEADY, GEORGE CREGAN, JR., b. Bklyn., June 16, 1924; B.S., Fordham U., 1949; J.D., Columbia, 1950. Admitted to Mass. bar, 1950; since practiced in Springfield; asso. firm Ganley & Crook, 1950-53; mem. firm Peter D. Wilson, 1953-57; partner firm Wilson, Keady & Ratner, 1958—; spl. justice Dist. Ct. of Springfield, 1972—; dean Western New Eng. Coll. Law Sch., 1970-73. Pub. adminstr. Hampden County, 1956—; trustee Baystate Med. Center; selectman Town of Longmeadow (Mass.), 1957-67, moderator, 1967-73. Mem. Hampden County Bar Assn. (pres. 1965-67). Home: 470 Pinewood Dr Longmeadow MA 01106 Office: Suite 2512 1500 Main St Springfield MA 01115 Tel (413) 732-7478

KEADY, WILLIAM C., b. Greenville, Miss., Apr. 2, 1913; LL.B., Washington U., St. Louis, 1936. Admitted to Miss. bar, practiced in Greenville; judge U.S. Dist. Ct. No. Miss., 1968—, now chief judge. Mem. Miss. Ho. of Reps., 1940-43; mem. Miss. Seante, 1944-45, chmn. judiciary com. Mem. Am., Miss. bar assns. Address: US Dist Ct PO Box 190 Greenville MS 38701*

KEAN, JOHN VAUGHAN, b. Providence, Mar. 12, 1917; A.B. cum laude, Harvard, 1938, J.D., 1941. Admitted to R.I. bar, 1942; asso. firm Edwards & Angell, Providence, 1941-54, partner, 1954—. Bd. dirs. Greater Providence YMCA. Mem. Am., R.I. bar assns., N.G. Assn., Assn. U.S. Army, Harvard Club of R.I. Decorated Legion of Merit. Home: 2 Angell St Providence RI 02903 Office: 2700 Hosp Trust Tower Providence RI 02903 Tel (401) 274-9200

KEANE, EDWARD WEBB, b. Detroit, Sept. 18, 1930; A.B., Harvard, 1952, J.D., 1957. Admitted to D.C. bar, 1957, N.Y. bar, 1960, U.S. Supreme Ct. bar, 1965; law clk. Justice William J. Brennan, Jr., U.S. Supreme Ct., 1957-58; asso. firm Sullivan & Cromwell, N.Y.C., 1958-65, partner, 1966—. Mem. Am., N.Y. bar assns., Assn. Bar City N.Y., Am. Judicature Soc. Home: 1 Lexington Ave New York City NY 10010 Office: 48 Wall St New York City NY 10005 Tel (212) 952-8272

KEANE, GERALD BRIAN, b. N.Y.C., Oct. 10, 1945; B.S. in Mech. Engring., Manhattan Coll., 1967; J.D., U. Fla., 1972. Admitted to Fla. bar, 1973; asso. firm Wilson, Wilson & O'Connell, Chartered, Sarasota, Fla., 1973-76, jr. partner, 1976-77; individual practice, 1977—. Mem. Am. Bar Assn. Home: 5104 San Jose Dr Sarasota FL 33580 Office: 2067 Main St Sarasota FL 33580 Tel (813) 366-7255

KEANE, WILLIAM TIMOTHY, b. Cin., Dec. 28, 1939; B.S. in Chemistry, U. Cin., 1961, M.S. in Indsl. Hygiene, 1965, D.Sc. in Environ. Health, 1967; J.D., U. Ariz., 1972. Admitted to Ariz. bar, 1972; asso. firm Langerman, Begam, Lewis, Leonard & Marks, Phoenix, 1972-75; individual practice law, Phoenix, 1975—. Mem. Am., Phoenix trial lawyers assns., Am., Maricopa County bar assns., Air Pollution Control Assn., AAAS, Am. Indsl. Hygiene Assn. (pres. area sect.), Drug Info. Assn., N.Y. Acad. Sci., Soc. Toxicology. Contbr. articles to environ. and legal jours. Office: Suite 611 Ave Security Bldg 234 N Central Phoenix AZ 85004 Tel (602) 257-1323

KEARNEY, FRANK PATRICK, b. Stamford, Conn., Sept. 27, 1916; B.A., Mt. St. Mary's Coll., Emmitsburg, Md., 1937; LL.B., Georgetown U., 1941. Admitted to Calif. bar, 1948; asst. dist. atty. County Santa Barbara (Calif.), 1948-53; judge Municipal Ct., Santa Barbara, 1953-76. Office: 118 E Figuerua St Santa Barbara CA 93104 Tel (805) 963-6604

KEARNEY, JOHN LEE, b. Pastoria, Ark., Jan. 12, 1944; B.A., Agrl., Mech. and Normal Coll., Pine Bluff, Ark., 1965; J.D., U. Ark., 1974. Admitted to Ark. bar, 1974; tchr. Dollarway Sch. Dist., Pine Bluff, 1965-71; counselor Jefferson County OEO, Pine Bluff, summers 1970, 71; adminstrv. asst. U. Ark., Pine Bluff, 1974-76, asst. prof., 1976-77; asso. firm Hunt & Kearney, Pine Bluff, 1974-75; partner Hunt, Jamison & Kearney, Pine Bluff, 1976; pvt. practice, 1976—; bd. dirs. Legal Aid Bur. Central Ark. Instl. chmn. United Way Fund, Pine Bluff, 1974, 75; bd. dirs. Pine Bluff and Jefferson County Econ. Opportunity Commn., 1976; Child Care Inc., Jefferson County; 3d v.p. Pine Bluff br. NAACP, 1977. Mem. Am., Ark., Jefferson County bar assns., U.S. Jaycees (Pine Bluff br.), Phi Alpha Delta. Home: 1715 Hickory St Pine Bluff AR 71603 Office: 1001 Missouri St Pine Bluff AR 71601 Tel (501) 536-1056

KEARNS, THOMAS CHARLES, b. Chgo., Aug. 10, 1933; B.S., Loyola U., Chgo., 1955, J.D., 1961. Admitted to Ill. bar, 1961; asso. firm Hinshaw, Culbertson, Moelmann & Hoban, Chgo., 1962-66; partner firm Edlin & Kearns, Chgo., 1966-68; individual practice law, Wheeling, Ill., 1968-71; partner firm Stitt, Moore, Kearns & Szala, Arlington Heights, Ill., 1971-76; individual practice law, Arlington Heights, 1976—; asst. corp. counsel John Nuveen & Co., Chgo., 1966. Trustee, Village of Palatine (Ill.), 1965-69; mem. bd. edn. St. Thomas Villanove Sch., Palatine, 1974—. Mem. Am., Chgo., Ill., Northwest Suburban bar assns., Comml. Law League Am., Phi Alpha Delta. Office: 210 Campus Dr Arlington Heights IL 60004 Tel (312) 255-5650

KEATING, FRANCIS ANTHONY, II, b. St. Louis, Feb. 10, 1944; B.A., Georgetown U., 1966; J.D., U. Okla., 1969. Admitted to Okla. bar, 1969; mem. firm Blackstock, Joyce, Pollard, Blackstock & Montgomery, Tulsa, 1972—; mem. Okla. Ho. of Reps., 1972-74, Okla. Senate, 1974—; asst. dist. atty., Tulsa County, Okla., 1971-72. Mem. Am., Okla., Tulsa County bar assns. Home: 2423 E 31st St Tulsa OK 74105 Office: 300 Petroleum Bldg Tulsa OK 74119 Tel (918) 585-2751

KEATING, WILLIAM FRANCIS, b. Elizabeth, N.J., Aug. 14, 1946; B.S., St. Peter's Coll., 1968; J.D., Fordham U., 1971; LL.M. in taxation, George Washington U., 1978. Admitted to N.J. bar, 1971, Ga. bar, 1976, U.S. Supreme Ct. bar, 1976, U.S. Tax Ct. bar 1976; law clk. to judge, Superior Ct. N.J., Newark, 1971-72; asso. firm Schumann, Hession, Kennelly & Dormant, Jersey City, N.J., 1972-73; chief defense counsel U.S. Army Judge Adv. Corps, Ft. Gordon, Ga., 1973-75; asst. gen. counsel Nat. Security Agy., Fort Meade, Md., 1975—. Mem. Ga. State, N.J., Hudson County bar assns. Office: Nat Security Agy Savage Rd Fort Meade MD 20755 Tel (301) 677-7703

KEATON, HARRY JOSEPH, b. Prague, Czechoslovakia, June 8, 1925; student San Francisco City Coll., 1947-48; B.A. in Econs., U. Calif. at Berkeley, 1950, J.D., 1953. Admitted to Calif. bar, 1954, U.S. Supreme Ct. bar, 1963; law clk., atty. U.S. Dept. Justice, Washington, 1953-55; asso. firm Loeb & Loeb, Los Angeles, 1955-60, partner, 1960-66; partner firm Rutan & Tucker, Los Angeles and Santa Ana, Calif., 1966-72; partner firm Mitchell, Silberberg & Knupp, Los Angeles, 1972—; dir. Los Angeles Legal Services Soc., Inc., 1968-71. Sponsor Atlantic Council U.S., 1963—; treas., mem. exec. com. Atlantic Assn. Young Polit. Leaders, 1963-65. Mem. Am., Calif., Los Angeles County (past trustee, past chmn. labor law com.) bar assns., Am. Hosp. Assn. (ad hoc labor relations com.), Am. Judicature Soc., Order of Coif, Phi Beta Kappa, Phi Alpha Delta. Author: Congress and the Faithful Execution of Laws-Should Legislators Supervise Administrators?, 1953; asso. editor The Developing Labor Law, 1975—; contbr. articles in field to legal jours. Home: 1131 Angelo Dr Beverly Hills CA 90210 Office: 1800 Century Park E Los Angeles CA 90067 Tel (213) 553-5000

KEATON, WALTER BOHANNON, b. Rushville, Ind., Feb. 14, 1912; A.B., Ind. U., 1935, LL.B., 1937. Admitted to Ind. bar, 1937, U.S. Supreme Ct. bar, 1946; individual practice law, Rushville, Ind., 1937—; partner firm Keaton & Keaton, Rushville, 1971—; city atty., 1968-69. Mem. Am., Ind. State, Indpls. bar assns., Fedn. Ins. Counsel, Internat. Assn. Ins. Counsel, Defense Research Inst. Contbr. articles to legal jours. Home: RR 6 Rushville IN 46173 Office: 126 W 2d St Rushville IN 46173 Tel (317) 932-3947

KEATS, ROBERT WILLIAM, b. Chgo., May 23, 1946; B.A., U. Louisville, 1969, J.D., 1972. Admitted to Ky. bar, 1972, U.S. Tax Ct. bar, 1973, U.S. Ct. Customs and Patent Appeals bar, 1974, U.S. Supreme Ct. bar, 1975; asst. counsel Louisville and Jefferson County (Ky.) Met. Sewer Dist., 1972-73, legal counsel, 1973—; partner firm Keats & Lambert, Louisville, 1974—. Mem. Ky., Am., Louisville, Fed. (sec. Louisville chpt.) bar assns. Home: 3226 Murray Hill Pike Louisville KY 40222 Office: POB 332 Louisville KY 40201 Tel (502) 587-0591

KEBERLE, RONALD DOUGLAS, b. Milw., Sept. 2, 1927; B.A., U. Wis., 1951, LL.B., 1951. Admitted to Wis. bar, 1951; atty. City of Wausau (Wis.), 1951-55; dist. atty. Marathon County, 1955-62; judge Marathon County Ct., 1962-70, Wis. Circuit Ct., 16th Circuit, Wausau, 1970—. Bd. dirs. Wausau YMCA, 1971-74. Mem. Am., Wis. bar assns., Am. Judicature Soc., Bd. Circuit Judges, Wis. Jud. Conf., Wausau C. of C. (dir. 1967-70). Named Outstanding Young Man, City Wausau, 1956, State Wis., 1957. Home: 830 Brown St Wausau WI 54401 Office: Courthouse Wausau WI 54401 Tel (715) 842-2141

KECK, ROBERT CLIFTON, b. Sioux City, Iowa, May 28, 1914; A.B., Ind. U., 1936; J.D., U. Mich., 1939; L.H.D., Nat. Coll. Edn., 1974. Admitted to Ill. bar, 1939; asso. firm Keck, Cushman, Mahin & Cate and predecessors, Chgo., 1939-45, partner 1946—; dir. Am. Hosp. Supply Corp., Chgo., 1st Ill. Corp., Chgo., Methode Electronics Inc., Chgo., Rust-Oleum Corp., Chgo., Schwinn Bicycle Co., Chgo., Signode Corp., Chgo., Union Spl. Corp., Chgo., U.S. Gypsum Co., Chgo. Pres. bd. trustees Nat. Coll. Edn., Evanston, Ill., 1964—; bd. dirs. Sears-Roebuck Found., Chgo., 1976. Mem. Am., Ill., Chgo., Fed. bar assns., Bar Assn. 7th Fed. Circuit (pres. 1976—). Home: 1043 Seneca Rd Wilmette IL 60091 Office: 8300 Sears Tower 233 S Wacker Dr Chicago IL 60606 Tel (312) 876-3411

KEDERSHA, GEORGE BESHAR, b. Union City, N.J., Aug. 28, 1902; LL.B., N.Y. Law Sch., 1926. Admitted to N.J. bar, 1934; individual practice law, Union City, N.J., 1934—. Mem. N.J., Hudson County bar assns., North Hudson Lawyers Club. Home: 61 Regent St Bergenfield NJ 07621 Office: 4800 Kennedy Blvd Union City NY 07087 Tel (201) 863-7677

KEEDY, CHRISTIAN DAVID, b. Worchester, Mass., Jan. 9, 1945; B.B.A., Tulane U., 1967, J.D., 1972. Admitted to Fla. bar, 1972; asso. firm Smathers & Thompson, Miami, 1972—. Mem. Dade County, Am., Fla. bar assns., Maritime Law Assn. U.S., Phi Alpha Delta. Office: 1301 Alfred I DuPont Bldg 169 E Flagler St Miami FL 33131

KEEDY, THOMAS JOHN, b. Elmhurst, Ill., June 16, 1950; B.S. in Agrl. Econs., U. Mo., Columbia, 1972, J.D., 1974. Admitted to Mo. bar, 1974; pros. atty. Putnam County, Mo., 1974—. Chmn. Region XI, Mo. Council on Criminal Justice, 1975-76; chmn. Unionville Community Betterment, 1975-76. Mem. Mo. Bar Assn. Office: PO Box 349 Unionville MO 63565 Tel (816) 947-3723

KEEFE, JOHN WILLIAM, b. Cin., Apr. 24, 1915; B.A., U. Cin., 1936, LL.B., 1939. Admitted to Ohio bar, 1940; judge Ohio 1st Appellate Dist. Ct. Appeals, Cin., 1975—. Home: 3662 Kendall Ave Cincinnati OH 45208 Office: Hamilton County Ct House Cincinnati OH 45202 Tel (513) 632-8437

KEEFER, NEIL SEWARD, b. Billings, Mont., Jan. 7, 1930; B.A., George Washington U., 1954; B.A., Mont. State U., 1955, J.D., 1957. Admitted to Mont. bar, 1957; asso. firm Dewey, Ballantine, Bushby, Palmer & Wood, N.Y.C., 1957; practiced in Billings, 1958—; individual practice law, 1958-69; mem. firm Keefer & Roybal, 1970—; mem. Mont. Gov.'s Adv. Commn. on Worker's Compensation, 1969-73; lectr. in field; atty. Billings-Yellowstone County Planning Bd., 1963-67. Mem. Am., Mont., Yellowstone County bar assns., Def. Research Inst., Am. Trial Lawyers Assn., Internat. Assn. Indsl. Accident Bds. and Commns. Author: Montana Workers Compensation Practice Manual, 1976; contbr. articles to Mont. Law Rev., Def. Research Inst. Jour. Home: 2902 Ramada Dr Billings MT 59102 Office: 412 Hart Albin Bldg Billings MT 59101 Tel (406) 259-4548

KEEGAN, THOMAS WILLIAM, b. Albany, N.Y., Oct. 14, 1940; B.A. cum laude, Siena Coll., 1962; J.D., Villanova U., 1965. Admitted to N.Y. State bar, 1966, U.S. Supreme Ct. bar, 1970. Law asst. N.Y. State Dept. Commerce, Albany, 1965-66; asst. corp. counsel City of Albany, 1966-71, exec. dep. corp. counsel, 1971-72; justice Albany Police Ct., 1972—; individual practice law, Albany, 1966—. Mem. sch. bd. Acad. Holy Names; bd. dirs. Project Equinox drug treatment program, Am. Nat. Red Cross, Albany chpt. Cystic Fibrosis Soc., Albany chpt. Multiple Sclerosis, Albany City and County Youth Bur., Albany County Traffic Safety Bd. Mem. Am., N.Y. State, Albany County bar assns. Office: 40 Steuben St Albany NY 12207 Tel (518) 434-1147

KEEL, CLARENCE JOSEPH, JR., b. Peoria, Ill., Oct. 30, 1928; student Bradley U., 1948-49; J.D., U. Miami, 1953. Admitted to Fla. bar, 1953; personal injury specialist State Farm Ins., Tampa, Fla., 1957-58; casualty adjustor Western Adjustment and Inspection Co., Peoria, 1953-57; sr. partner firm Yade, Keel, Nelson, Casper, Bergmann & Newcomer, profl. assn., Tampa, Fla., 1959—. Mem. Fla., Tampa, Hillsborough, Am. bar assns., Am., Fla. trial lawyers assns., Am. Arbitration Assn. Home: 4208 Cleveland St Tampa FL 33609 Office: Suite 603 4950 W Kennedy Blvd Tampa FL 33609 Tel (813) 870-2660

KEELE, HAROLD MARQUISS, b. Monticello, Ill., Aug. 26, 1901; A.B. cum laude, U. Ill., 1923, LL.B., 1927. Admitted to Ill. bar, 1928; asst. U.S. atty. No. Dist. Ill., 1928-29; asst. state's atty. Cook County, 1929-32; asso. firm Greenberg, Keele, Lunn & Aronberg, and predecessors, Chgo., 1932-38, partner, 1938—; mem. English faculty U. Ill., 1924-25, U. Mont., 1925-26; gen. counsel Select Com. to Investigate Tax Exempt Founds., 82d Congress, 1952. Mem. Am., Ill. bar assns., Phi Beta Kappa, Phi Delta Phi, Zeta Psi, Alpha Alpha Alpha, Delta Sigma Rho. Contbr. articles to legal jours. Home: 200 E Pearson St Chicago IL 60611 Office: One IBM Plaza Suite 4500 Chicago IL 60611 Tel (312) 828-9600

KEELE, HAROLD OLEN, b. Dysart, Iowa, June 28, 1911; A.B., Cornell, 1933; J.D., U. Iowa, 1936. Admitted to Iowa bar, 1936, U.S. Supreme Ct. bar, 1946; individual practice law, W. Liberty, Iowa, 1936-73; partner firm Keele & Keele, W. Liberty, 1973—. Mayor, City of W. Liberty, 1946-56. Mem. Am., Iowa bar assns. Home: 201 W Maxson Ave West Liberty IA 52776 Office: 104 E 3d St West Liberty IA 52776 Tel (319) 627-2216

KEELE, JAMES ROBERT, b. Iowa City, Dec. 5, 1947; B.A., Cornell U., 1970; J.D., U. Iowa, 1972, M.A., 1973. Admitted to Iowa bar, 1973; partner firm Keele & Keele, W. Liberty, Iowa, 1973—. Mem. Am., Iowa bar assns., Assn. Trial Lawyers Iowa. Office: 104 E 3d St West Liberty IA 52776 Tel (319) 627-2216

KEELER, CHARLES ADDISON, b. Binhamton, N.Y., Apr. 11, 1897; A.B., Hamilton Coll., 1920. Admitted to N.Y. bar, 1924; partner firm Hinman, Howard & Kattell, Binghamton, 1926—. Active Binghamton Community Chest, Broome County (N.Y.) United Fund; chmn. bd. trustees Susquehanna Presbytery, 1960-69; pres. bd. visitors Binghamton State Hosp., 1949-76; mem. nat. council and nat. exec. council YMCA, pres. Binghamton chpt., 1925-26; chmn. bd. trustees Link Found., 1953-75; chmn. Broome County Council Commn. Against Discrimination, 1945-55. Fellow Am. Coll. Trial Lawyers, Am. Bar Found.; mem. Am. Bar Assn. (ho. of dels. 1966), Broome County (pres. 1942-44), N.Y. State (pres. 1959-60) bar assns. Home: 14 Campbell Rd Ct Binghamton NY 13905 Office: Security Mutual Bldg Binghamton NY 13901 Tel (607) 723-5341

KEELER, HENRY ALLAN, b. N.Y.C., Nov. 13, 1920; student Columbia, 1939-40, Rutgers U., 1943-44, Pace Coll., 1946. A.B., U. Mo., Kansas City, 1963, J.D., 1963; grad. Mo. Coll. Trial Judges, 1975. Adminstrv. asst. Am. Machine & Metals, Inc., N.Y.C., 1946; exec. asst. Lazard Freres & Co., N.Y.C., 1946-49; sr. intelligence officer CIA, Washington, 1950-51; salesman Thomas A. Edison, Inc., N.Y.C., 1951-52, Butterick Co., N.Y.C., 1952-55, E. I. duPont de Nemours & Co., N.Y.C., 1955-59; admitted to Mo. bar, 1963; practiced in Sedalia, 1963-73; pros. atty. Pettis County, 1966-70; city att. City of Sedalia, 1971; judge California (Mo.) Probate, Magistrate and Small Claims Ct., 1973—. Mem. Mo., Moniteau County (Mo.), South Central Mo., Pettis County (pres. 1965) bar assns., Am. Judicature Soc., Nat. Coll. Probate Judges, Mo. Probate and Magistrate Judges Assn., Phi Delta Phi. Home: Sharon Ln California MO 65018 Office: Moniteau County Courthouse California MO 65018 Tel (314) 796-4671

KEELER, WILLIAM JOSEPH, SR., b. Buffalo, Apr. 21, 1916; student Washington and Lee U., 1937-41; J.D., U. Buffalo, 1946; B.A., St. Mary's U., 1960; LL.M., Temple U., 1965. Admitted to N.Y. bar, 1946, U.S. Ct. Mil. Appeals bar, 1951, U.S. Supreme Ct. bar, 1964, Calif. bar, 1969; asso. firm Gold, Speranza & Keeler, and predecessors, Lockport, N.Y., 1946-47, partner, 1947-49; served to lt. col. JAGC, U.S. Air Force, 1949-66; asst. prof. U. Md., 1960-62; asso. prof. U. Ark., 1966-67; trust officer Bank of Am., Santa Ana, Calif., 1967-69; partner firm Gunderson & Keeler, Laguna Hills, Calif., 1969-73; individual practice law, Laguna Hills, 1973-74; pres., treas. firm Keeler & Keeler, Laguna Hills, 1974—. Mem. Rotary Internat., 1964—; N.J. Civilian Mil. Adv. Council, 1965-66, Def. Transp. Bd., 1961-72; mem. adv. council Cath. Soc. Welfare Bd. Orange County (Calif.), 1972—. Mem. Calif., Am., Orange County, So. Orange County bar assns., Lawyer to Lawyer Consultation Panel, Kappa Phi Kappa. Contbr. articles to legal jours. Home: 25391 Classic Dr Mission Viejo CA 92675 Office: 23521 Paseo de Valencia Laguna Hills CA 92653 Tel (714) 586-9070

KEEN, PAUL RODNEY, b. Hazard, Ky., Aug. 26, 1949; B.A. cum laude, Lincoln Meml. U., 1971; J.D. with distinction, U. Ky., 1973. Admitted to Ky. bar, 1974; atty. Ashland Oil, Inc., 1974-76; counsel TRW Inc., Cleve., 1976—. Mem. Ky. Bar Assn., Lincoln Meml. U. Alumni Assn. (pres. 1974-75). Home: 18408 Winslow Rd Shaker Heights OH 44122 Office: 23555 Euclid Ave Cleveland OH 44117 Tel (216) 383-2227

KEENAN, PATRICK ALOYSIUS, b. Detroit, July 22, 1945; B.A., U. Detroit, 1966; J.D., U. Chgo., 1969; postgrad. fellow U. Aix-Marseille, (France), 1969-70. Admitted to Mich. bar, 1970, Ill. bar, 1969, U.S. Dist. Ct. for No. Ill., 1970, 7th Circuit bar, 1970, U.S. Supreme Ct. bar, 1973, U.S. Dist. Ct. for Eastern Dist. Mich. bar, 1976, 6th Circuit bar, 1976; staff atty. Cook County (Ill.) Legal Asst. Found., Inc., Brookfield, 1970-72, law clinic dir., 1972; spl. investigator Dept. Children and Family Services, State of Ill., Chgo., 1973; asso. prof. law DePaul U., Chgo., 1972—; asso. prof. law U. Detroit, 1976—. Mem. Chgo. Council Lawyers, Mich. Bar Assn., Fed. Bar Assn., ACLU. Author: An Illinois Tragedy, an Analysis of the placement of Illinois Wards in the State of Texas, 1973; contbr. articles to legal jours. Home: 19390 Canterbury Rd Detroit MI 48221 Office: Univ Detroit Sch Law 651 E Jefferson Detroit MI 48226 Tel (313) 927-1545

KEENAN, WILLIAM QUIGLEY, b. Cleve., Apr. 27, 1921; A.B., Georgetown U., 1947; LL.B., Harvard, 1949. Law clk. to U.S. Dist. Judge, Boston, 1949-50; commerce counsel New Haven R.R., 1950-60; admitted to Mass. bar, 1951, N.Y. State bar, 1961, U.S. Supreme Ct. bar, 1956; gen. solicitor REA Express Co., N.Y.C., 1960-68; partner firm Arsham & Keenan, N.Y.C., 1968—. Chmn. Wallingford (Conn.) Bd. Finance, 1958-60; mem. White Plains (N.Y.) Bd. Edn., 1965-70; N.Y. State 24th Dist. del. to Democratic Nat. Conv., 1968, alt. del., 1976. Mem. Assn. Bar City N.Y. (chmn. com. adminstrv. law 1967-68), White Plains Bar Assn., Motor Carrier Lawyers Assn., ICC Practitioners Assn. Home: 62 Greenridge Ave White Plains NY 10605 Office: 277 Park Ave New York City NY 10017 Tel (212) 759-1000

KEENE, JOHN CLARK, b. Phila., Aug. 17, 1931; B.A., Yale, 1953; J.D., Harvard, 1959; M. City Planning, U. Pa., 1966. Admitted to Pa., 1960, U.S. Supreme Ct. bar, 1976; asso. firm Pepper, Hamilton & Scheetz, Phila., 1959-64; asst. prof. city and regional planning U. Pa., 1966-68, asso. prof., 1968—; prof. in residence Urban Land Inst., Washington, 1975-76. Mem. Am., Pa., Phila. bar assns., Am. Inst. Planners (chmn. dept. planning and law 1976—). Author: Untaxing Open Space, 1976. Office: 3400 Walnut St Philadelphia PA 19174 Tel (215) 243-7880

KEENE, KENNETH PAUL, b. Torrington, Wyo., Oct. 29, 1940; student Miami U., Oxford, Ohio, 1958-61; B.S., U. Nebr., 1962, J.D. cum laude, 1965. Admitted to Nebr. bar, 1965, Colo. bar, 1968; served with JAGC, U.S. Army, 1965-69; partner firm Cole, Hecox, Tolley, Edwards & Keene, P.C., Colorado Springs, Colo., 1970—. Mem. allocations com. Colorado Springs chpt. United Way, 1971-73; bd. dirs. Silver Key Sr. Services, Inc., Colorado Springs, 1974—, chmn., 1977. Mem. Colorado Springs Estate Planning Council. Home: 506 Orion Dr Colorado Springs CO 80906 Office: Suite 400 3 S Tejon St Colorado Springs CO 80903 Tel (313) 473-4444

KEENE, RICHARD CLINTON, b. Balt., Dec. 19, 1938; A.B., Loyola Coll., Balt., 1960; LL.B., J.D., U. Md., 1967. Admitted to Md. bar, 1967, U.S. Tax Ct. bar, 1969, U.S. Circuit Ct. bar 4th Circuit, 1975, U.S. Supreme Ct. bar, 1975, U.S. Dist. Ct. bar Md., 1968; asso. firm O'Connor & Preston, Balt., 1968-70; individual practice law, 1970-75; partner firm Keene, Eichhorn & Plitt, Balt., 1975-77; asst. gen. atty. Chessie System Law Dept., Balt., 1975—; asst. prof. bus. law and real estate Essex Community Coll., 1969-75. Pres. Hawthorne Civic Assn., Balt. County, 1971-72, 74-76. Mem. Am., Md. bar assns. Office: Room 321 2 N Charles St Baltimore MD 21201 Tel (301) 237-3121

KEENEN, ROMAN THOMAS, b. Cleve., Dec. 31, 1918; A.B., Miami U., 1941; M.A. in History, U. Okla., 1942; J.D., Yale, 1948; M.A. in Law, Case-Western Reserve Law Sch., 1968. Admitted to Ohio bar, 1948, Ill. bar, 1957; partner firm Ray, Robinson, Keenen & Hanninen, Cleve., 1948—; spl. lectr. in admiralty, Cleve.-Marshall Law Sch., Cleve. State U., 1967—; served in Admiralty Sect., JAG USN, 1950-53. Sec., treas. Internat. Ship Masters Assn., 1948—. Mem. Greater Cleve., Am., Fed. Bar Assns., Internat. Assn. Ins. Counsel, Maritime Law Assn. U.S., Am. Adjudicature Soc., Am. Assn. Average Adjusters, Phi Beta Kappa. Home: 1801 E 12th St Cleveland OH 44114 Office: 1500 Union Commerce Bldg Cleveland OH 44115 Tel (216) 861-4533

KEET, JAMES HOLLAND, JR., b. Springfield, Mo., July 6, 1914; A.B., Princeton, 1936; LL.B., Harvard, 1939. Admitted to Mo. bar, 1939; asso. law offices Irving Schwab and William R. Collinson, Springfield, 1939-41; individual practice law, Springfield, 1941-61; partner firm Lincoln, Haseltine, Keet, Forehand & Springer, Springfield, 1961-65; judge 31st Jud. Circuit Mo., Springfield, 1965—; spl. judge Mo. Supreme Ct. and Mo. Ct. of Appeals, St. Louis Dist., 1973, Springfield Dist., 1974; lectr. Am. Jud. Conf. Mo.; mem. com. on rules Mo. Supreme Ct., 1969—. Mem. Mo. Ho. of Reps., 1941-42; vestryman Christ Episcopal Ch. Diplomate Nat. Conf. on Juvenile Justice. Mem. Mo., Greene County bar assns. Contbr. articles to legal jours. Home: 1455 Meadowmere St Springfield MO 65804 Office: Greene County Courthouse Springfield MO 65802 Tel (417) 869-3581

KEETON, ROBERT ERNEST, b. Clarksville, Tex., Dec. 16, 1919; B.B.A., U. Tex., 1940, LL.B., 1941; S.J.D., Harvard, 1956. Admitted to Tex. bar, 1941, Mass. bar, 1955; asso. firm Baker & Botts, Houston, 1941-42, 45-51; asso. prof. law So. Meth. U., 1951-54; asst. prof. Harvard, 1954-56, prof., 1956—, Langdell prof. law, 1973—, asso. dean Sch. Law, 1975—; Mass. commr. Uniform State Laws, 1971—; dir. Nat. Inst. Trial Advocacy, 1973-76. Fellow Am. Bar Found.; mem. Am. Law Inst., Am., Mass. bar assns., State Bar Tex., Am. Risk and Ins. Assn. Author: Trial Tactics and Methods, 1954, rev. edit., 1973; Legal Cause in the Law of Torts, 1963; Venturing To Do Justice, 1969; Basic Text On Insurance Law, 1971; (with O'Connell) Basic Protection for the Traffic Victim, 1965, After Cars Crash—The Need for Legal and Insurance Reform, 1967; editor casebooks torts and ins. law, contbr. articles to legal jours. Home: 25 Avon St Cambridge MA 02138 Office: Harvard Law Sch Cambridge MA 02138 Tel (617) 495-4634

KEETON, WERDNER PAGE, b. Clarksville, Tex., Aug. 22, 1919; B.A., U. Tex., Austin, 1931, LL.B., 1931; S.J.D., Harvard, 1936. Admitted to Tex. bar, 1931; instr. U. Tex. Law Sch., 1932-42, asst. dean, 1940-42; counsel petroleum adminstrn for war Office Price Adminstrn, Washington, 1942-45; dean U. Okla. Law Sch., 1946-49; dean U. Tex Sch. Law, 1949-74, prof. law, 1974-77; mem. Tex. Constitutional Revision Commn., 1973-74; chmn. state bar advisory com. on reformation of Tex. penal code, 1965-70; chmn. Med. Profl. Liability Study Commn., 1975-76. Bd. dirs. Wesley Found., chmn. 1972—; mem. com. on Higher Edn. SW Tex. Conf. Meth. Ch., 1971-74; mem. advisory bd. Brackenridge Hosp., 1955-65. Mem. Am., Tex. bar assns., Assn. Am. Law Schls., Am. Law Inst., Philos. Soc. Tex., Order of the Coif, Phi Beta Kappa. Editorial bd. The Found. Pres., 1966-76; author: (with Seavy, Warren A. and Thurston, Edward S.) Cases on Torts, 1950; Cases and Materials on Fraud and Mistake, 1954; (with Warren A. Seavey and Robert E. Keeton) Cases and Materials on the Law of Torts, 1957, 2d ed. 1964; (with Shapo) Products and the Consumer, Defective and Dangerous Products, 1970; (with Robert E. Keeton) Cases and Materials on the Law of Torts, 1971; (with Marshall Shapo) Products and the Consumer, Deceptive Practices, 1972; (with Robert E. Keeton) 1974 Supplement to Cases and Materials on Law of Torts, 1974; recipient Am. Bar Assn. award of Excellence, 1975; teaching excellence award U. Tex. Yearbook, 1970. Home: 5316 Western Hills Austin TX 78731 Office: 2500 Red River Austin TX 78705 Tel (512) 471-5151

KEEZEL, ROY, b. Washington, Feb. 3, 1941; B.S. in Pharmacy, U. Houston, 1964, J.D., 1970. Admitted to Tex. bar, 1970; sr. atty. Treasury Dept. Office Regional Counsel, Atlanta, 1970-73; atty. Mitchell Energy and Devel. Corp., Houston, 1974-76; mem. firm Parks, Keezel & Tradd, Bellaire, Tex., 1976—; counsel Am. Buddhist Assn. Mem. Tex., Am. (chmn. subcom. com. on liens, levies and limitations), Fed., Houston bar assns., Am. Judicature Soc. Recipient St. John Garwood award U. Houston Bates Coll. Law, 1969. Achievement award Treasury Dept., 1971. Home: 1955 University Blvd Houston TX 77030 Office: 5909 W Loop S room 250 Bellaire TX 77401 Tel (713) 661-4844

KEFAUVER, JAMES MURDOCH, b. Frederick, Md., July 12, 1940; B.A., Am. U., 1962; LL.B., U. Mich., 1965. Admitted to D.C. bar, 1966, U.S. Supreme Ct. bar, 1969; staff atty. FTC, Washington, 1965-67; asso. firm Glassie, Pewett, Beebe & Shanks, Washington, 1967-73, mem. firm, 1973—. Mem. D.C., Am., Fed. bar assns. Contbr. article to legal jour. Home: 4831 Park Ave Bethesda MD 20016 Office: 1737 H St NW Washington DC 20006 Tel (202) 466-4310

KEHL, WILLIAM WADDINGHAM, b. Watertown, N.Y., Apr. 12, 1937; B.A., Harvard U., 1959; LL.B., U. Va., 1965. Admitted to S.C. bar, 1966; partner firm Wyche, Burgess, Freeman & Parham, Greenville, SC., 1970—. Mem. S.C., Am. bar assns. Home: 7 Seven Oaks Dr Greenville SC 29605 Office: 44 E Camperdown Way Greenville SC 29603 Tel (803) 242-3131

KEHOE, LEO PAUL, b. Carthage, N.Y., May 21, 1938; B.S., Syracuse U., 1959, LL.D., 1962. Admitted to N.Y. bar, 1962, U.S. Supreme Ct. bar, 1967; asso. firm Sconlon, Wright, Willmott & Aylward, Watertown, N.Y., 1962-66; partner firm Brandt, Kehoe & Parenti, Lyons, N.Y., 1966—; dist. atty. Wayne County (N.Y.), 1967-71. Mem. North Rose-Wolcott (N.Y.) Central Sch. Bd. Edn., 1974—. Mem. Wayne County, N.Y. State, Am. bar assns. Home: W Port Bay Rd Wolcott NY 14590 Office: One Montezuma St Lyons NY 14489 Tel (315) 946-6512

KEHOE, RICHARD LAWRENCE, JR., b. Yonkers, N.Y., Sept. 5, 1945; B.S., Manchester Coll., 1968; J.D., U. Notre Dame, 1973. Admitted to Ind. bar, 1973; individual practice law, Rochester, Ind., 1976—; city atty. City of Rochester. Mem. Fulton County (Ind.) (sec.-treas.), Ind. State, Am. bar assns. Home: PO Box 327 Rochester IN 46975 Office: Suite 202 100 W Ninth St Rochester IN 46975 Tel (219) 223-4124

KEHOE, WILLIAM FRANCIS, b. Stoneham, Mass., Dec. 3, 1933; A.B., Dartmouth, 1955; M.A. in English, Yale, 1956; postgrad. (Fulbright scholar) Trinity Coll., Dublin, Ireland, 1959-60; LL.B.,

Harvard, 1963. Admitted to Mass. bar, 1963, Fed. Dist. Ct. Mass. bar, 1964; asso. firm Gaston, Snow & Ely Bartlett, Boston, 1963-70, partner, 1970—. Bd. dirs., treas. Eire Soc. Boston, 1973—, corp. mem. Frederick E. Weber Charities Corp., Boston, 1974—. Mem. Mass., Boston bar assns., Phi Beta Kappa. Author: Enjoying Ireland, 1966; contbr. articles profl. jours. Office: 82 Devonshire St Boston MA 02109 Tel (617) 426-4600

KEIL, CHARLES K., b. Wilmington, Del., Sept. 14, 1933; B.S. in Econs., U. Pa., 1955, J.D., 1961. Admitted to Del. bar, 1961; partner firm Bayard, Brill & Handelman, P.A., Wilmington, 1961—; mem. Del. Ho. of Reps., 1965-66; adminstrv. asst. to gov. Del., 1963-65. Mem. Del. Constn. Revision Com., 1968-70; vice chmn. Del. Gov.'s Com. on Exec. Departmental Reorgn., 1969-71; trustee Del. Dept. Mental Health. Mem. Del. (asst. sec. 1969-71), Am. bar assns., Am. Judicature Soc., Fedn. Ins. Counsel. Home: 204 Hitching Post Dr Wilmington DE 19803 Office: 300 Market Tower POB 1271 Wilmington DE 19899 Tel (302) 575-0130

KEILBACH, JOHN JOSEPH, b. Pueblo, Colo., Nov. 2, 1942; B.S. in Commerce, St. Louis U., 1964, J.D., 1967. Admitted to Mo. bar, 1967, Colo. bar, 1967; asso. firm Deeba, DeStefano, Sauter & Herd, St. Louis, 1967-68, 70-72; asso. firm Preston, Altman & Parlapiano, Pueblo, 1972-74, partner, 1975—. Leader law explorer post Boy Scouts Am., 1974-75; bd. dirs. Friends of Library, Pueblo, 1975—, pres., 1976—. Mem. Am., Mo., Colo., Pueblo County, Met. St. Louis bar assns., Assn. Trial Lawyers Am., Colo. Trial Lawyers Assn., Am. Judicature Soc., Beta Gamma Sigma. Mem. staff St. Louis U. Law Jour., 1965-66, mem. editorial bd., 1966-67. Office: POB 333 Pueblo CO 81003 Tel (303) 545-7325

KEIM, DONALD D., b. Lincoln, Nebr., June 11, 1902; J.D., LL.B., U. Colo., 1925. Admitted to Wash. State bar, 1925, Colo. bar, 1926; asst. atty. Denver Tramway Co., 1928-30; gen. counsel Denver C. of C., 1930-35; gen. counsel Colo. State C. of C., 1935-55; individual practice law Denver, 1955. Pres. Denver Area Council Boy Scouts Am., 1948-49; candidate for dist. atty. 9th Jud. Dist. Colo., 1976. Mem. Colo. Bar Assn., Phi Delta Phi. Home and office: 1950 Hwy 133 Carbondale CO 81623 Tel (303) 963-3255

KEIM, EARL STUART, b. Youngwood, Pa., Aug. 14, 1913; A.B., Duquesne U., 1936, LL.B., 1942. Admitted to Pa. bar, 1943; individual practice law, Greensburg, Pa., 1945-51; asst. dist. atty. Westmoreland County, 1950-58, dist. atty., 1958; judge Ct. Common Pleas. 1958-62, 62—; justice Supreme Ct. Pa., 1962; judge adv. 31st Dist., Pa. Am. Legion, 1952-58, Post 446, Mt. Pleasant, 1958; justice Supreme Forum, Loyal Order Moose, 1969, chief justice, 1972-73, prelate, pres. Western Pa. Assn., 1972-73, also mem. Supreme Council. Life mem. Carbon Vol. Fire Dept.; trustee Jeannette Dist. Meml. Hosp. Mem. Pa., Westmoreland County bar assn., Westmoreland County Law Enforcement Officers Assn., Pa. Conf. State Trial Judges (exec. com. Zone 6), Sons of Columbus of Am. (hon.), 40 and 8, U.S. Power Squadron, United Comml. Travelers, Western Pa. (hon.), Westmoreland County firemens assns., U.S. Naval Inst. Recipient citations VFW, 1965, DAV, 1974, Rillton Vets. Fgn. Wars, 1972, Western Pa. Firemens Assn., 1965, Carbon Vol Fire Dept., 1967, Sons of Columbus of Am., 1957. Home: 808 Depot St Youngwood PA 15697 Office: Court House 3d Floor Greensburg PA 15601 Tel (412) 834-2191

KEISER, HENRY BRUCE, b. N.Y.C., Oct. 26, 1927; B.A. in Econs. with honors, U. Mich., 1947; J.D. cum laude, Harvard U., 1950. Admitted to N.Y. bar, 1950, D.C. bar, 1955, Fla. bar, 1956, U.S. Supreme Ct. bar, 1954; trial atty. CAB, Washington, 1950-51; head counsel alcoholic beverages sect. OPS, 1951-52; legal asst. to judge Tax Ct. U.S., Washington, 1953-56; prin. firm Henry B. Keiser, Washington, 1956—; pres., chmn. bd. Fed. Pubs., Inc., 1959—; chmn. bd. Gene Galasso Assos., Inc., Washington, 1963—; mem. adv. cabinet Southeastern U., 1965—; cons. AEC, 1965-74; profl. lectr. Dept. Agr., 1960—, George Washington U., 1961—, U. San Francisco, 1965—, Coll. William and Mary, 1966-75, Calif. Inst. Tech., 1967-72, U. So. Calif., 1973-74, U. Santa Clara, 1975—, U. Denver, 1975—, Air Force Inst. Tech., 1976. Fellow Nat. Contract Mgmt. Assn.; mem. Am. (council pub. contract law sect. 1972-75), Fed. (nat. council 1966-76), N.Y. State, Fla., D.C. (dir. 1965-66, chmn. adminstrv. law sect. 1964-65) bar assns. Contbr. articles to legal jours. Home: 6009 Plainview Rd Bethesda MD 20034 Office: 1725 K St NW Washington DC 20006 Tel (202) 337-7000

KEISER, LARRY STEPHEN, b. Phila., Jan. 8, 1947; B.A., Pa. State U., 1968; J.D. (Sylvan Balder Meml. scholar), Temple U., 1971. Admitted to Pa. bar, 1971, U.S. Supreme Ct. bar, 1976; asso. firm Becker, Fryman and Ervais, Phila., 1971—. Mem. Am., Pa., Phila. (treas. young lawyers sect., certificate of achievement 1976, asso. editor The Retainer) bar assns., ICC Practitioners Assn., Am. Arbitration Assn., Lawyers Club Phila. Mem. Temple Law Quar. Home: 141 Cedarbrook Rd Ardmore PA 19003 Office: 12 South 12th Street Suite 2520 Philadelphia PA 19107 Tel (215) WA 3-8300

KEITH, DAMON JEROME, b. Detroit, July 4, 1922; B.A., W.Va. State Coll., 1943, LL.D. (hon.), 1965; LL.B., Howard U., 1949, LL.D. (hon.), 1974; LL.M., Wayne State U., 1956, LL.D. (hon.), 1973; LL.D. (hon.), Lincoln U., 1975, U. Detroit, 1975, Atlanta U., 1975, U. Mich., 1974. Admitted to Mich. bar, 1950; sr. partner firm Keith Conyers Anderson Brown & Wahls, Detroit, 1963-67; chief judge U.S. Dist. Ct., Eastern Dist. Mich., Detroit, 1967—; commr. State Bar Mich., chmn. bail and criminal justice com., 1965; rep. 6th Circuit, Jud. Conf. U.S., 1975; guest lectr. Howard U. and Fed. Jud. Center; mem. legal staff Detroit Bd. Edn. Mem. Wayne County Bd. Suprs., 1958-63; chmn. Mich. Civil Rights Commn., 1967; chmn. subcom. adminstrn. and orgn. Citizens Adv. Com. on Equal Ednl. Opportunities; pres. Detroit Housing Commn., 1958-67; co-chmn. United Negro Coll. Fund; mem. Mayor's Health Adv. Com.; active Detroit YMCA, Detroit Area council Boy Scouts Am.; trustee Med. Center Corp., Cranbrook Sch., Interlochen Arts Acad., Mercy Coll., Detroit Arts Commn.; bd. visitors Wayne State U. Law Sch. Mem. Am., Nat. (Jud. award 1971), Wolverine, Mich., Detroit bar assns., Am. Arbitration Assn. Recipient Outstanding Citizen awards Mich. Chronicle, 1960, 64, 74, Emancipation Freedom award Windsor, Ont., 1961; Outstanding Community Service award Detoit Urban League Guild; Layman of Year award Detroit Council Chs., 1963; Citizen of Year award Detroit Med. Soc., 1966; Russwurm award for Distinguished Jud. Services, Nat. Newspaper Pubs., 1974; Distinguished Citizen award Mich. State U., 1974; Spingarn medal NAACP, 1974; Fed. Judge of Year award Black Law Sch. Students, 1974; Nat. Social Workers award, 1974. Home: 3130 W Outer Dr Detroit MI 48221 Office: US Dist Ct Fed Bldg Detroit MI 48226 Tel (313) 226-6890

KEITH, MARTIN LANGHORNE, b. Washington, Nov. 4, 1936; B.A., U. Va., 1958, J.D., 1970. Admitted to Va. bar, 1970, D.C. bar, 1971; asso. firm Hogan & Hartson, Washington, 1970-72; county atty. Fairfax County (Va.), 1972-73; asso. firm Hogan & Hartson, Washington, 1973-76, partner, 1977—. Mem. Am., Va., Fairfax bar assns. Office: 815 Connecticut Ave Washington DC 20006 Tel (202) 331-4736

KEITH, SAMUEL PALMER, JR., b. Bessmer, Ala., Jan. 14, 1913; student U. Va., 1930-31, U. Ala., 1932; LL.B., Birmingham Sch. Law, 1936. Admitted to Ala. bar, 1936; gen. counsel United Security Life Ins. Co., 1962-66; Ala. rep. Guarantee Trust Life Ins., Chgo. Mem. Birmingham Bar Assn., State Bar Ala., Pi Kappa Alpha (Outstanding Alumni U. Ala. chpt.). Named Hon. Dep. Sheriff Thomasville, Ga. Home: 317 Windsor Dr Birmingham AL 35209 Office: 723 Frank Nelson Bldg Birmingham AL 35209 Tel (205) 254-3155

KEITH, THOMAS JEFFERY, b. Passaic, N.J., June 9, 1944; A.B., U. N.C., Chapel Hill, 1967; J.D., Wake Forest Sch. Law, 1970. Admitted to N.C. bar; asst. dist. atty. Forsyth County (N.C.), 1971-72; asso. firm Moore and Green, Winston-Salem, N.C., 1972-76; partner firm Moore and Keith, Winston-Salem, 1976—; instr. on criminal law Forsyth Tech. Inst., winters 1972-75; juvenile pub. defender Forsyth County, 1975-76. Trustee Alcoholism Residential Care Authority, Inc., 1972-76; chmn. Forsyth County Bd. Elections, 1974-76. Mem. Forsyth County Jr. Bar Assn. Home: PO Box 328 Lewisville NC 27023 Office: 405 1st Center Bldg 2000 W First St Winston-Salem NC 27104 Tel (919) 723-0355

KEKER, JOHN WATKINS, b. Winston-Salem, N.C., Jan. 4, 1944; A.B. cum laude, Princeton, 1965; LL.B., Yale, 1970. Admitted to Calif. bar. 1971, law clk. to Ret. Chief Justice Earl Warren, 1970-71; staff atty. Nat. Resources Def. Council, Washington, 1971; asst. fed. pub. defender No. Dist. Calif., San Francisco, 1971-73; partner firm Kipperman, Shawn & Keker, San Francisco, 1972—. Office: 407 Sansome St San Francisco CA 94111 Tel (415) 788-2200

KELEHER, MICHAEL LAWRENCE, b. Albuquerque, Sept. 21, 1934; B.A., U. N.Mex., 1956; M.A., N.Y. U., 1958; LL.B., U. Miss., 1962. Admitted to Miss. bar, 1962, N.Mex. bar, 1962; partner firm Keleher & McLeod, Albuquerque, 1962—. Mem.-at-large Old Lincoln County (N.Mex.) Meml. Commn., 1970—; trustee U. Albuquerque, 1971—, sec., 1974—; mem. Albuquerque City Planning Commn., 1973-75. Mem. Am., Albuquerque bar assns., Miss. State Bar, State Bar N.Mex. Home: 1400 Morningside Dr NE Albuquerque NM 87110 Office: PO Drawer AA Albuquerque NM 87103 Tel (505) 842-6262

KELLAHIN, JASON, b. Roswell, N.Mex., Dec. 26, 1909; A.B., U. N.Mex., 1929; J.D., U. Denver, 1951. Admitted to N.Mex. bar, 1951, U.S. Supreme Ct. bar, 1971; atty. N.Mex. Oil Conservation Commn., Santa Fe, 1951-52, State Corp. Commn., Santa Fe, 1952; partner firm Kellahin & Fox, Santa Fe, 1952—; mem. legal com. Interstate Oil Compact Commn., 1951—. Mem. advisory bd. Southwestern Law Enforcement Inst., Dallas, 1963—; mem. bd. mgrs. Sch. Am. Research, Santa Fe, 1965—; mem. N.Mex. State Police Bd., 1952-54. Mem. N.Mex., First Judicial Dist. bar assns. Home: 112 Malaga Rd Santa Fe NM 87501 Office: 500 Don Gaspar St Box 1769 Santa Fe NM 87501 Tel (505) 982-4315

KELLAM, RICHARD B., b. 1909. Admitted to Va. bar, 1934; chief judge U.S. Dist. Ct. Va., Norfolk. Office: Room 316 US Courthouse Norfolk VA 23510*

KELLEHER, DANIEL F., b. Wilmington, Del., May 8, 1935; A.B., St. Mary's Seminary & U., 1958; LL.B., Georgetown U., 1961. Admitted to D.C. bar, 1962, Del. bar, 1962; partenr firm Theisen, Lank & Kelleher, Wilmington, 1962-72; asso. judge Family Ct. State Del., 1972—. Pres. Beechwood Sch.; v.p. Del. Alcoholism Council; bd. dirs. YMCA. Mem. Del. Bar Assn., Nat. Council Juvenile Ct. Judges, Am. Judicature Soc. Home: 45 Old Guyencourt Rd Greenville DE 19807 Office: 600 Market St Wilmington DE 19899 Tel (302) 571-2230

KELLEHER, HERBERT DAVID, b. Camden, N.J., Mar. 12, 1931; B.A., Conn. Wesleyan U., 1953; LL.B., N.Y. U., 1956. Admitted to N.J. bar, 1957, Tex. bar, 1962, U.S. Supreme Ct. bar, 1970; clk. Supreme Ct. N.J., Newark, 1957-59; asso. firm Lum Biunno & Tompkins, Newark, 1959-61; partner firm Matthews, Nowlin, Macfarlane & Barrett, San Antonio, 1961-69; sr. partner firm Oppenheimer, Rosenberg, Kelleher & Wheatley, San Antonio, 1969—. Pres., San Antonio Travelers' Aid Soc., 1964-66, St. Mary's Hall, San Antonio, 1970-73; chmn. State Senatorial Dist. 19, 1968, 70; del. Democratic Nat. Conv., 1964, 68; campaign coordinator Connally for Gov., 1961-65, Bentsen for Sen., 1970-76. Mem. Am., Tex., San Antonio bar assns., Phi Delta Phi. Root-Tilden scholar, 1953-56. Home: 144 Thelma Dr San Antonio TX 78212 Office: Suite 620 711 Navarro St San Antonio TX 78205 Tel (512) 224-7581

KELLEHER, JOSEPH THOMAS, b. St. Louis, Sept. 22, 1928; J.D., St. Louis U., 1953. Admitted to Ill. bar, 1953, Mo. bar, 1953, U.S. Supreme Ct. bar, 1968; atty. Madison County Abstract & Title Co., 1953-60, Chgo. Title & Trust Co., 1961-63; magistrate Ill. Circuit Ct., 1964-71; individual practice law, Edwardsville, Ill., 1972—; hearing officer Ill. Pollution Control Bd., 1972—; asst. prof. div. chmn. Lewis & Clark Community Coll., Godfrey Ill., 1972; instr. Maryville Coll. of Sacred Heart, Creve Coeur, Mo., 1973, Ill. Bd. Realtors. Mem. Ill. Bar Assn., Ill. Circuit Ct. Magistrates Assn. (pres. 1968-70). Home: 532 Sunset St Edwardsville IL 62025 Office: POB 224 Edwardsville IL 62025 Tel (618) 656-4118

KELLER, BERTWIN JULE, b. Oxford, Ohio, May 19, 1927; A.B., Miami U., Oxford, 1950, LL.B., U. Cin., 1953. Admitted to Ohio bar, 1953, Ind. bar, 1953; pros. atty. Wayne County (Ind.), 1955-58; city atty. Richmond (Ind.), 1966-68; individual practice law, Richmond, 1968—. Mem. Am., Ind. State (sec. 1975), Wayne County bar assns., Def. Research Inst., Am. Trial Lawyers Assn. Home: 2 Parkway Ln Richmond IN 47374 Office: Suite 400 First Nat Bank Bldg Richmond IN 47374 Tel (317) 962-7527

KELLER, DAVID, b. Mt. Vernon, N.Y., Dec. 28, 1927; B.S. in Social Sci., Coll. City N.Y., 1946; LL.B., Columbia, 1948; LL.M. in Taxation, N.Y. U., 1952; postgrad. Adelphi U., 1976—. Admitted to N.Y. bar, 1949; partner firm Keller & Jamin, N.Y.C., 1953-68, firm Hesterberg & Keller, N.Y.C., 1968—; counsel Pub. Adminstr. Kings County (N.Y.). Mem. Am., Bklyn. bar assns. Office: 32 Court St Brooklyn NY 11201 also 60 E 42d St New York City NY 10017 also 33 Ridge Dr E Great Neck NY 11021 Tel (212) 875-7450

KELLER, GUSTAVE JOSEPH, b. Appleton, Wis., Mar. 23, 1898; LL.B., U. Wis., 1922. Admitted to Wis. bar, 1922; partner firm Keller & Keller, Appleton, 1922-30, Keller, Keller & O'Leary, Appleton and Neenah, Wis., 1930-36, Gustave Keller & Ormond Capener, Appleton, 1936-40; individual practice law, Appleton, 1940-61; municipal and county judge br. 2 Outagamie County (Wis.), 1961-68, res. county judge, 1968-76. Mem. Appleton Bd. Edn., 1949-53; chmn. Outagamie County Condemnation Commn., 1958-61; panel mem. Wis. State Personnel Com. Mem. Wis., Outagamie (past pres.) bar assns. Recipient citation Wis. Legislature, numerous civic awards and citations. Home and Office: 1311 Greengrove Rd Appleton WI 54911 Tel (414) 733-5497

KELLER, JOHN E., b. Terre Haute, Ind., Mar. 23, 1930; B.S.Bus. in Mktg., Ind. U., 1955, J.D., 1963. With DX Sunray Oil Co., 1955-59; claims rep. Am. States Ins. Co., 1960-63; admitted to Ind. Supreme Ct. bar, 1963; mem. firms Stephenson, Kendall & Stephenson, Danville, Ind., 1963-66; individual practice law, 1966—; adj. asso. prof. polit. sci. Ind. State U., 1969-71; dep. prosecuting atty. Vigo County, Ind., 1966-70. Bd. dirs. Big Bros.-Sisters, Terre Haute, Ind., 1967-75, pres., 1974. Office: 70 Meadows Center Terre Haute IN 47803 Tel (812) 234-0833

KELLER, JOHN WILLIAM, b. Waynesboro, Pa., Mar. 15, 1927; B.A., Gettysburg Coll., 1948; J.D., Dickinson Sch. Law, 1951. Admitted to Pa. Supreme Ct. bar, 1952, U.S. Supreme Ct. bar, 1958; partner firm Keller & Keller, Waynesboro, Pa., 1952-68; judge Pa. Ct. of Common Pleas 39th Jud. Dist., 1968—; borough atty. Borough of Waynesboro, 1953-68; solicitor Franklin County (Pa.), 1960-68; solicitor Borough Waynesboro Planning Commn., Franklin County Planning Commn., 1960's; del. Pa. Constl. Conv., 1967-68. Mem. Am., Pa., Franklin County bar assns., Pa. Assn. State Trial Judges, Am. Judicature Soc. Home: 221 E 3d St Waynesboro PA 17268 Office: Courthouse Annex Chambersburg PA 17201 Tel (717) 264-4125

KELLER, JOSEPH EUGENE, b. Dayton, Ohio, Apr. 9, 1907; A.B., U. Dayton, 1928, LL.B., 1930; LL.M., Georgetown U., 1935. Admitted to Ohio bar, 1930, D.C. bar, 1936, U.S. Supreme Ct. bar, 1938; judge appellate ct., Dayton, 1934; prin. atty. FCC, Washington, 1934-36; partner firm Dow, Lohnes, & Abertson, Washington, 1937-62; prof. law, 1950-75; partner firm Keller & Heckman, Washington, 1962—. Served to maj. AUS, 1942-44. Mem. Am., D.C. bar assns. Contbr. articles to legal jours. Home: 4525 Macomb St NW Washington DC 20016 Office: 1150-17th St NW Washington DC 20016 Tel (202) 457-1100

KELLER, MICHAEL BOYD, b. Martinsburg, W.Va., Aug. 8, 1944; B.S. in Accounting, W.Va. U., 1966, J.D., 1973. Admitted to W.Va. bar, 1973; mem. firm Rice, Hannis & Douglas, Martinsburg, 1973—; municipal judge, Martinsburg, 1975—; mental hygiene commr. Berkeley County (W.Va.), 1975—. Former mem. Martinsburg Planning Commn.; bd. dirs. Berkeley County War Meml. Park. Mem. W.Va., Berkeley County (past pres.) bar assns., Order of Coif. Asso. editor W.Va. U. Law Rev., 1972-73. Home: 200 N Georgia Ave Martinsburg WV 25401 Office: Old National Bank Bldg Martinsburg WV 25401 Tel (304) 263-0836

KELLER, RICHARD OVERTON, b. Washington, Dec. 10, 1942; A.B., Emory U., 1964, J.D., 1967. Admitted to Ga. bar, 1967, Calif. bar, 1967, U.S. Supreme Ct. bar. 1971; judge adv. U.S. Air Force, 1967-72; asso. firm Brown, Norris, King, Graaskamp & Snell, Fremont, Calif., 1972-74; partner firm Brown, Norris, King, Snell & Keller, Fremont, Calif., 1974—; instr. European div. City Colls. Chgo., Wiesbaden, Germany, 1971-72. Trustee Fremont-Newark Community Coll. Dist., 1976—; finance chmn. Mission Peak Dist. council Boy Scouts Am., 1975-76; bd. advisors young mother's program Fremont Unified Sch. Dist., 1973—. Mem. State Bar Ga., State Bar Calif., Alameda County, Wash. Twp. (dir. 1976—, sec.-treas. 1975-76) bar assns. Office: 2000 Peralta Blvd Fremont CA 94536 Tel (415) 793-4343

KELLER, STANLEY, b. N.Y.C., Aug. 16, 1938; B.A., Columbia Coll., 1959; LL.B. magna cum laude, Harvard, 1962. Admitted to Mass. bar, 1962; asso. firm Palmer & Dodge, Boston, 1962-68, partner, 1969—; lectr. Boston U. Law Sch. Mem. Am., Mass., Boston bar assns. Home: 25 Rivard Rd Needham MA 02192 Office: 1 Beacon St Boston MA 02108 Tel (617) 227-4400

KELLER, WILLIAM WOODBURY, b. Laconia, N.H., May 19, 1912; A.B., Harvard, 1933, LL.B., 1936. Admitted to N.H. bar, 1936; individual practice law, 1936-57; asso. justice N.H. Superior Ct., 1957-71, chief justice, 1971—; atty., Belknap County, 1947-53. Mem. Laconia City Council, 1939-41; city solicitor, Laconia, 1941-43, 46; mem. Laconia Planning Bd., 1948-53, chmn., 1948-50. Mem. Am., N.H. bar assns., Am. Judges Assn. Home: RFD 2 Meredith NH 03253 Office: 613 Main St Laconia NH 03246 Tel (603) 524-5013

KELLEY, COLIN CAMPBELL, b. Riverside, Calif., Apr. 17, 1920; B.A., Stanford, 1942, postgrad. Law Sch., 1946-49; LL.B., San Francisco Law Sch., 1950, also J.D. Admitted to Calif. bar, 1951; asso. firms Treadwell & Laughlin, San Francisco, 1951-54, John Moran, San Mateo, Calif., 1954-56, Nichols, Williams, Morgan & Digardi, Oakland, Calif., 1956-58; individual practice law, Oakland, 1958—; referee Am. Arbitration Assn., Oakland, 1969—; mem. Alameda County (Calif.) Lawyers' and Judges' Liaison Com., 1970—; speaker in field. Mem. Republican Central Com., San Mateo County, 1952-55, vice. chmn., Alameda County, 1964-66; mem. Calif. Rep. Central Com., 1952, 66; Rep. candidate for Calif. Senate, 1966. Mem. Am., Alameda County bar assns., Am. Judicature Assn., Am., Calif. trial lawyers assns., Am. Arbitration Assn., Phi Alpha Delta. Decorated Bronze Star, Purple Heart; contbr. articles to Am. Bar Jour. Office: 11 Embarcadero St W Oakland CA 94607 Tel (415) 444-1776

KELLEY, DAVID ERWIN, b. Mankato, Minn., Mar. 10, 1942; B.A., Mankato State U., 1969; J.D., U. Minn., 1969. Admitted to Minn. bar, 1969; individual practice law, Lake Crystal, Minn., 1969-71, Mankato, 1971-76. Sec., Eagle Lake Planning Commn., 1976; legal counsel Mankato Area Jaycees, 1976. Mem. Am., Minn., Blue Earth County bar assns. Home: 224 Blace St Eagle Lake MN 56024 Office: Suite 107 510 Long St Mankato MN 56001 Tel (507) 387-4352

KELLEY, DONALD ELMER, b. McCook, Nebr., Jan. 19, 1908; LL.B., U. Nebr., 1930. Admitted to Nebr. bar, 1930, Colo. bar, 1945; partner firm Kelley & Kelley, McCook, 1930-38; asst. atty. gen., Lincoln, Nebr., 1939-41; county atty., Red Willow County, Nebr., 1942-44; individual practice law, Denver, 1945-53; U.S. atty., Dist. of Colo., 1953-59; city atty., Denver, 1959-61; sr. partner firm Kelley, Inman, Flynn & Coffee, 1962-67; judge Colo. Supreme Co., 1967—; mem. Colo. State Senate, 1963-67. Chmn. exec. com. Colo. div. Am. Cancer Soc., 1963-65, now hon. life mem. Mem. Am., Colo., Denver bar assns., Am. Law Inst., Am. Judicature Soc. (dir. 1970-74), Phi Delta Phi, Delta Upsilon. Contbr. articles in field to profl. jours.; named hon. life mem. Am. Cancer Soc. Home: 3144 S Columbine St Denver CO 80210 Office: 250 State Capitol Bldg Denver CO 80203 Tel (303) 892-2024

KELLEY, DONALD HAYDEN, b. Denver, May 27, 1929; B.Sc. in Law, U. Nebr., 1950, LL.B., 1952. Admitted to Nebr. bar, 1952, Fla. bar, 1967; trial atty. U.S. Dept. Justice, Washington, 1955; tax trial atty. IRS, Office of Regional Council, Dallas, 1956; pvt. practice, North Platte, Nebr., 1956—; partner firm Kelley and Wallace, P.C., North Platte, 1967—; lectr. in field. Mem. Nebr. (chmn. sect. on real estate probate and trust law 1973-75), Fla., Am. bar assns., Am. Judicature Soc., Nebr. Assn. Trial Attys., Am. Coll. Probate Counsel, Internat. Acad. Estate and Trust Law, Am. Law Inst. Comment editor: Nebr. Law Rev., 1951-52. Contbr. articles in field to profl. jours. Home: 2002 Sunset Dr North Platte NE 69101 Office: 202 W 2d St North Platte NE 69101 Tel (308) 532-7110

KELLEY, FRANK JOSEPH, b. Detroit, Dec. 31, 1924; pre-law certificate U. Detroit, 1948, J.D., 1951. Admitted to Mich. bar, 1952; gen. practice law, Detroit, 1952-54, Alpena, 1954-61; atty. gen. Mich., Lansing, 1962—. Instr. econs. Alpena Community Coll., 1955-56; instr. pub. adminstrn. Alpena County, 1956; atty. city real estate law U. Mich. Extension, 1957-61. Mem. Alpena County Bd. Suprs., 1958-61; pres. Alpena Community Services Council, 1956; chmn. Gt. Lakes Commn., 1971. Founding dir., 1st sec. Alpena United Fund, 1955; founding dir., 1st pres. Northeastern Mich. Child Guidance Clinic, 1958; pres., bd. dirs. Northeastern Mich. Cath. Family Service, 1959. Mem. Am., 26th Jud. Circuit (pres. 1956) bar assns., State Bar Mich., Nat. Assn. Attys. Gen. (pres. 1967), Internat. Movement Atlantic Union, Alpha Kappa Psi. Home: 4267 Mar-Moor Dr Lansing MI 48917 Office: Law Bldg Capitol Complex Lansing MI 48913*

KELLEY, JAMES PEARCE, b. LeMars, Iowa, Apr. 25, 1910; B.A., U. Iowa, 1931; J.D., State U. Iowa, 1934; L.H.D., Westmar Coll., 1965. Admitted to Iowa bar, 1934; individual practice law, LeMars, 1934-62; solicitor City of LeMars, 1962; judge Iowa Dist. Ct., 3d Dist., LeMars, 1962-71, chief judge, 1971—. Pres. Easter Seal Soc. Crippled Children and Adults Iowa, Inc., Des Moines, 1972-74. Mem. Am., Iowa, Plymouth County, Woodbury County bar assns., Am. Judicature Soc. Home: 920 Plymouth St LeMars IA 51031 Office: Plymouth County Courthouse LeMars IA 51031 Tel (712) 546-5827

KELLEY, JAMES THOMAS, b. Louisville, Nov. 21, 1945; B.A., Western Ky. U., 1967; J.D., U. Ky., 1970. Admitted to Ky. bar, 1970; individual practice law, Elizabethtown, Ky., 1970-75; partner firm Kelley & Meredith, Elizabethtown, 1975—. Mem. Elizabethtown Bd. Adjustments, 1973; trustee Hardin Meml. Hosp., 1974. Mem. Ky., Hardin County bar assns., Hardin County Soc. Indigent Criminal Def. (pres. 1974). Home: 108 Lakeview Dr Elizabethtown KY 42701 Office: 6 Public Sq Elizabethtown KY 42701 Tel (502) 769-2368

KELLEY, JOHN PATRICK, b. Phila., Apr. 24, 1937; B.A., Villanova U., 1959; J.D., U. Pa., 1962. Admitted to Pa. bar, 1963; asso. firm Beasley & Ornsteen, Phila., 1963; asst. U.S. atty. Eastern dist. Pa., 1964-66; spl. hearing officer U.S. Dept. Justice, Washington, 1967-70; partner firm Krusen, Evans & Byrne, Phila., 1966—; capt. JAGC, USAR, 1963-69. Mem. Democratic exec. com. Philadelphia County, 1958-66. Mem. Am., Pa., Fed., Phila. bar assns., Lawyer's Club Phila. Home: 3428 Warden Dr Philadelphia PA 19129 Office: 21 S 12th St Philadelphia PA 19107 Tel (215) 568-3800

KELLEY, JOSEPH H., b. Colfax, Ill., July 22, 1943; B.S., Ill. State U., 1967; J.D., Coll. William and Mary, 1970. Admitted to Ill. bar, 1970; asso. firm Arnold & Gesell, 1970-74; asso. judge U.S. Ct. Appeals, 1974—. Mem. Ill. State, McLean County (Ill.) bar assns. Home: Rural Route 4 Bloomington IL 61701 Office: McLean County Courthouse Bloomington IL 61701 Tel (309) 829-5341

KELLEY, PETER STEPHEN, b. Houlton, Maine, Dec. 3, 1940; B.A., Harvard, 1963; J.D., Am. U., 1966. Admitted to Maine bar, 1966, U.S. Dist. Ct. bar for Dist. Maine, 1968; individual practice law, Caribou, Maine, 1968—; staff personnel dept. IRS, Washington, summer 1963; mem. Maine Ho. of Reps., 1971-72, Maine Senate, 1973—; mem. Caribou City County, 1967-70; dep. mayor City of Caribou, 1969; dir. Washburn Trust Co. Chmn. Maine Mining Commn., 1968; mem. citizen advisory com. Maine Dept. Health and Welfare; chmn. Aroostook County (Maine) March of Dimes, 1967-68; chmn. Citizens for Cheaper Elec. Rates, Augusta, Maine, 1973. Mem. Aroostook County Am. bar assns. Named 1 of 2 Outstanding Legislators in 105th Legislature Eagleton Inst., 1972. Home: 16 Teague St Caribou ME 04736 Office: Downtown Mall PO Box 66 Caribou ME 04736 Tel (207) 498-2581

KELLEY, RALPH HOUSTON, b. Chattanooga, Sept. 23, 1928; student U. Md., 1948-49; B.A., U. Chattanooga, 1951; LL.B., Vanderbilt U., 1954. Admitted to Tenn. bar, 1954; partner firm Kelley, Dirisio & Shattuck, Chattanooga, 1954-69; mayor City of Chattanooga, 1963-69; bankruptcy judge U.S. Dist. Ct. for Eastern Dist. Tenn., Chattanooga, 1969—; faculty English and speech dept. U. Chattanooga Evening Coll., 1954-58. Pres., Hamilton County Young Democratic Club, 1956-60; mem. Tenn. Ho. of Reps., 1959-61. Mem. Am., Tenn., Chattanooga bar assns., Am. Judicature Soc., Lambda Chi Alpha. Home: 18 Sweetbriar Ave Chattanooga TN 37411 Office: Federal Bldg Chattanooga TN 37401 Tel (615) 266-2126

KELLEY, THOMAS JOSEPH, b. Los Angeles, Dec. 9, 1936; B.S. in History, U. Santa Clara, 1958; J.D., Loyola U., Los Angeles, 1966. Admitted to Calif. bar, 1966, U.S. Supreme Ct. bar, 1970; asso. firm Schell & Delamer, Los Angeles, 1966-73; asso. firm Musick, Peeler & Garrett, Los Angeles, 1973-75, partner, 1975—; judge pro tem Los Angeles Municipal Ct., 1970—. Mem. Am., Los Angeles County bar assns., State Bar Calif., Assn. So. Calif. Def. Counsel, Assn. Bus. Trial Lawyers, Loyola Law Sch. Alumni Assn. Office: Suite 2000 1 Wilshire Bldg Los Angeles CA 90017 Tel (213) 629-3322

KELLEY, WILLIAM MICHAEL, b. Pasadena, Calif., Aug. 19, 1947; B.A., Occidental Coll., Los Angeles, 1969; J.D., Ariz. State U., 1972. Admitted to Ariz. bar, 1974; dean of students Prescott (Ariz.) Coll., 1972-74; dep. county atty. (Ariz.), Prescott, 1974-77; prof. law, environ. law and consumer protection law Prescott Coll. and Yavapai Coll., Prescott, 1975-77; asso. firm Garbarind & Lee, Flagstaff, Ariz., 1977—. Mem. Ariz. State Bar Assn., Nat. Dist. Attys. Assn., Ariz. Acad. Author: Arizon Rule of Criminal Procedure 28.2, 1973. Home: 3725 S Yagui Dr Flagstaff AZ 86001 Office: PO Box M Flagstaff AZ 86002 Tel (602) 774-1881

KELLIHER, FRANCIS, b. Albany, N.Y., Jan. 12, 1902; B.A., Yale, 1922; LL.B., Albany Law Sch., 1926. Admitted to N.Y. State bar, 1926; asso. firm Whalen, Murphy, McNamee & Creble, Albany, 1926-30; individual practice law, Albany, 1930-44; sr. atty. N.Y. State Dept. Taxation and Fin., 1944-49, asso. atty., 1949-60, prin. atty., 1960-68; lectr. Albany Law Sch., 1927-45; dir. N.Y. State Joint Legis. Com. Real Property Tax Exemptions, 1969-70. Mem. Albany County Bar Assn. Editor: American Bankruptcy Reports, 1935-44. Home: 6 Homestead Ave Albany NY 12203 Tel (518) 482-7090

KELLISON, JAMES BRUCE, b. Richmond, Va., June 18, 1922; B.A., U. Richmond, 1943; J.D., George Washington U., 1948. Admitted to D.C. bar, 1948, Supreme Ct. U.S. bar, 1952; mem. trust dept. Union Trust Co. D.C., Washington, 1948-50; atty. bd. govs. Fed. Res. System, Washington, 1950; asso. law office Frederick M. Bradley, Washington, 1950-54; partner firm Hogan & Hartson, Washington, 1954-73, Altmann & Kellison, Washington, 1973—; mem. adv. com. on rules of probate procedure Superior Ct. D.C., 1972—. Pres. bd. trustees Louise Home, Washington, 1971—; trustee Columbia Lighthouse for Blind, Washington, 1969-76, Audubon Naturalist Soc., 1968-71. Fellow Am. Coll. Probate Counsel; mem. Am., D.C. (mem. steering com. probate and trust law) bar assns., D.C. Estate Planning Council, Omicron Delta Kappa. Home: 4518 Klingle St NW Washington DC 20016 Office: 1616 H St NW Washington DC 20006 Tel (202) 628-5093

KELLOGG, JOHN GOERES, b. Appleton, Wis., Mar. 25, 1940; B.A., U. Wis., 1964, J.D., 1965. Admitted to Wis. bar, 1965; summer apprentice firm Sidley, Austin, Burgess & Smith, Chgo., 1963, Robins, Davis & Lyons, Mpls., 1964; mem. firm McKenzie, Hebbe, Downey & Kellogg, and predecessors, Appleton, 1965—. Adv. bd. Salvation Army, 1966-71, chmn. 1970-71; mem. Appleton Pub. Library Bd., 1971—, pres., 1974-76; bd. suprs. Outagamie County, 1972—; mem. Outagamie County Welfare Bd., 1972-76, sec., 1974-75, vice-chmn., 1975-76; chmn. Outagamie County Health Com., 1974—; mem. Outagamie County Bd. Ethics Com., 1974; mem. Community Health Services Bd., 1974—, chmn. mental health subcom., 1976—; vice-chmn. Outagamie County Bd. Human Services Com., 1976-77, chmn., 1977—; chmn. Appleton Pub. Library Cons. Selection Com., 1976; mem. Outagamie County Bd. Ad Hoc Health Center Com., 1976. Mem. Outagamie County Bar Assn. Home: 8 Brokaw Pl Appleton WI 54911 Office: 230 N Morrison St Appleton WI 54911 Tel (414) 734-1826

KELLOGG, MARK EDWARD, b. Ocala, Fla., Dec. 15, 1947; B.A., in Polit. Sci., U. Fla., 1969, J.D., 1972. Admitted to Fla. bar, 1972; atty. estate tax IRS, Orlando, Fla., 1972-76, sr. atty. estate tax, Washington, 1976—. Mem. Fla. Bar, Am. Bar Assn. Recipient High Quality award IRS, 1975. Home: 204 Glen Ave SW Vienna VA 22180 Office: Suite 1015 1201 E St NW Washington DC 20226 Tel (202) 376-0109

KELLOGG, THEODORE, b. Rock Creek, Ohio, Aug. 18, 1904; LL.B., U. N.D., 1930. Admitted to N.D. bar, 1930; mem. firm Mackoff, Kellogg, Kirby & Kloster, and predecessors, Dickinson, N.D., 1933-70, of counsel, 1970—; state's atty. Stark County (N.D.), 1933-37; asst. atty. gen. State of N.D., 1951, 57-58. Fellow Am. Coll. Trial Lawyers, Internat. Acad. Trial Lawyers, Am. Bar Found.; mem. Am., N.D. (past pres.) bar assns., Bar of No. Plains and Mountains (founding), Dickinson C. of C. (past pres.). Home: 538 2d Ave W Dickinson ND 58601 Office: 100 Liberty Nat Bank Dickinson ND 58601 Tel (701) 225-8143

KELLOGG, THOMAS RICHARDS, b. Bryn Mawr, Pa., Jan. 20, 1937; B.A., Williams Coll., 1958; J.D., Harvard, 1962. Admitted to Pa. bar, 1963; asso. firm Dilworth, Paxson, Kalish, Kohn & Dilks, Phila., 1963-64; atty. Community Legal Services, Phila., 1966-68; asso. firm MacElree, Platt & Harvey, West Chester, Pa., 1968-73; atty. SmithKline Corp., Phila., 1973—; solicitor Pocopson Twp., Chester County, Pa., 1970-73. Mem. Am., Pa., Phila., Chester County bar assns., Phi Beta Kappa. Home: RD 3 Box 30 Yellow Springs Rd Malvern PA 19355 Office: 1500 Spring Garden St Philadelphia PA 19101 Tel (215) 854-5060

KELLOGG, WENDELL WALTER, b. Stockton, Kans., July 1, 1941; B.A., Kansas State U., 1963, J.D., U. Kans., 1966. Admitted to Kans. bar, 1966; partner firm Marietta & Kellogg, Salina, Kans., 1966—; served with JAGC, U.S. Army, 1968-70. Mem. Am., Kans., Salina County bar assns., Civitan. Home: 2268 Roach Salina KS 67401 Office: 148 S 7th Salina KS 67401 Tel (913) 825-5403

KELLY, AGNES ALOYSIA, b. Pitts., June 21, 1906; B.B.A., Case Western Res. U., 1956, LL.B., 1958. Admitted to Ohio bar, 1958; partner firm Kelly & Kelly, Cleve., 1958—. Mem. Ohio, Greater Cleve. bar assns., Phi Alpha Delta. Home: 22350 Hilliard Blvd Rocky River OH 44116 Office: 13604 Lorain Ave Cleveland OH 44111 Tel (216) 941-7760

KELLY, BAXTER BURRELL, III, b. Florence, S.C., Apr. 23, 1943; A.B., U. S.C., 1966, J.D., 1969. Admitted to Supreme Ct. S.C., 1969, U.S. Dist. Ct. S.C., 1969, U.S. Ct. Appeals, 1973, U.S. Supreme Ct., 1974; pvt. practice law, Mt. Pleasant, S.C., 1969-76; partner law firm Kelly & Bell, Mt. Pleasant, S.C., 1977—. Pres., East Cooper Civic Council, 1971-75. Mem. Am., S.C., Charleston County bar assns., Am. Judicature Soc., Charleston Lawyers Club. Clubs: Exchange of Mt. Pleasant (v.p. 1972-73), Optimist of East Cooper (pres. 1971-72, Outstanding Leadership award 1971-72), Patriots Point Lions (pres. 1976-77). Home: 1043 Royalist Rd Mt Pleasant SC 29464 Office: 409 Coleman Blvd Mt Pleasant SC 29464

KELLY, CHARLES ARTHUR, b. Evanston, Ill., Mar. 2, 1932; B.A. cum laude, Amherst Coll., 1953; LL.B., Harvard U., 1956. Admitted to Ill. bar, 1956, D.C. bar, 1956; asso. firm Hubacheck, Kelly, Rauch & Kirby, Chgo., 1956-70, partner, 1970—; served to col. JACC, USAFR. Trustee Gads Hill Center, 1961—, pres., 1971-74; trustee Lakeland Found., 1968—, Quetico Superior Found., 1961—. Mem. Am. Coll. Probate Counsel, Ill. State, Chgo., Am., Fed. bar assns. Home: 140 Robsart Pl Kenilworth IL 60043 Office: 3100 Prudential Plaza Chicago IL 60601 Tel (312) 944-2400

KELLY, EDWARD JAMES, b. Des Moines, July 18, 1947; B.A., Coll. of St. Thomas, 1969; J.D., Creighton U., 1973. Admitted to Iowa bar, 1973, Nebr. bar, 1973; mem. firm Whitfield, Musgrave, Selvy, Kelly & Eddy, Des Moines, 1973—. Bd. dirs. Des Moines Jr. C. of C., 1976, Des Moines Boys Club, 1977. Del., Rep. State Conv., 1976. Mem. Am., Iowa, Nebr. bar assns., Def. Research Inst. Home: 5309 Harwood Dr Des Moines IA 50312 Office: 1400 Central Nat Bank Bldg Des Moines IA 50309 Tel (515) 288-6041

KELLY, EDWARD SPENCE, b. Atlanta, Aug. 8, 1903; LL.B., 1935. Admitted to Ga. bar, 1935, D.C. bar, 1948; asso. firm Smith, Cohen, Ringel, Kohler & Martin, Atlanta, 1968—; claims atty. Royal Globe Ins. Cos., 1936-68, Gen. Adjustment Bur., Inc., 1949-68. Mem. Atlanta Bar Assn., Ga. Def. Lawyers Assn. Home: 2734 Peachtree Rd NE Apt A-204 Atlanta GA 30305 Office: 2400 First National Bank Tower Atlanta GA 30303 Tel (404) 658-1200

KELLY, HUBERT E., b. Worthington, Ind., Apr. 23, 1927; B.A., Ind. State U., 1949; J.D., Ind. U., 1953. Admitted to Ind. bar, 1953, Ariz. bar, 1965; sr. trial atty. Office Chief Counsel IRS, SE and Central regional offices, 1953-60; individual practice law, Terre Haute, Ind., 1960-64, Phoenix, 1964—. Mem. Am., Ind., Ariz., Maricopa County bar assns. Office: 222 N Central Ave Phoenix AZ 85004 Tel (602) 257-0979

KELLY, JAMES THOMAS, JR., b. San Jose, Calif., Nov. 26, 1929; B.S. in Accounting, U. Santa Clara, 1951, J.D., 1954. Admitted to Calif. bar, 1955, U.S. Supreme Ct. bar, 1965; partner firm Kelly, Leal & Olimpia, and predecessor, Sunnyvale, Calif., 1957—; chmn. Santa Clara County Probate & Trust Com., 1972-74, Santa Clara County Ins. Com., 1966; arbitrator Am. Arbitration Assn. Vice chmn. Santa Clara Urban Renewal Agy., 1963-66. Mem. Calif., Santa Clara County, Sunnyvale bar assns. Office: 697 E Remington Dr Sunnyvale CA 94086 Tel (408) 735-8530

KELLY, JOHN MARTIN, b. Oshkosh, Wis., Dec. 13, 1948; B.A. in Econs., U. Wis., Madison, 1971; J.D., Georgetown U., 1974; postgrad. in Bus. Adminstrn., Harvard. Admitted to Wis. bar, 1974, D.C. bar, 1975; trial atty. Office of Chief Counsel, IRS, Washington, 1974-76, consultant, 1976—. Mem. D.C., Wis. bar assns. Office: 2 Crawford St Apt 1 Cambridge MA 02139 Tel (617) 547-2766

KELLY, JOHN P., b. 1933; A.A., Boston U.; B.A., U. Mich.; LL.B., Boston Coll. Asso. firm Hoberg, Finger, Brown & Abramson, San Francisco, 1963-68; asst. gen. atty. Consol. Freightways, Inc., San Francisco, 1968-74, atty., then gen. counsel, 1974-75, v.p., gen. counsel, 1975—. Office: Consol Freightways Inc Internat Bldg San Francisco CA 94108*

KELLY, KENNETH B., b. Wells County, Ind., Oct. 5, 1905; pvt. law office study with Albert S. Hinds, Shelby, Mich., 1924-29. Admitted to Mich. bar, 1929; partner firm Hinds & Kelly, Shelby, 1929-33; prosecuting atty. Oceana County (Mich.), 1933-35; individual practice law, Hart, Mich., 1935-37, Kalamazoo, 1937-42, Owosso, Mich., 1942—; city atty., Corunna, Mich., 1958-75; Perry, Mich., 1957—. Chmn., Republican Party, Shiawassee County, Mich., 1958-63. Mem. Mich. Bar Assn. Home: 901 Ada St Owosso MI 48867 Office: 511 W Main St Owosso MI 48867 Tel (517) 723-5127

KELLY, KEVIN DONAL, b. Ferris, Ill., Sept. 24, 1912; student Quincy Coll., 1931-32, Carthage Coll., 1935-36; LL.B., John Marshall Law Sch., Chgo., 1942. Admitted to Ill. bar, 1942; individual practice law, La Salle, Ill., 1946—. Mem. La Salle County, La Salle-Peru-Oglesby (pres.) bar assns. Home: Point Lookout Oglesby IL 61348 Office: 208 Marquette St La Salle IL 61301 Tel (815) 223-3051

KELLY, LAWRENCE VINCENT, b. N.Y.C., Aug. 15, 1940; A.B., Columbia, 1962; LL.B., Fordham U., 1965; LL.M., N.Y. U., 1966. Admitted to N.Y. bar, 1965, N.J. bar, 1968; law sec. to judge N.Y.C. Civil Ct., 1965-67; law asst. to justices N.Y. State Supreme Ct., 1st Jud. Dept., N.Y.C., 1967-68, law sec. to justice, 1968; asso. prof. law Fordham U., N.Y.C., 1968-72; sr. asso. firm Curtis Mallet-Prevost Colt & Mosle, N.Y.C., 1972-76, partner, 1976—. Mem. N.Y. County Democratic Com., 1965-68. Mem. Am., N.Y. State, N.J. State, Hudson County bar assns. Office: Curtis Mallet-Prevost Colt & Mosle 100 Wall St New York City NY 10005 also 243 Cleveland Ave Hasbrouck Heights NJ 07604 Tel (212) 248-8111

KELLY, MICHAEL JOSEPH, b. New London, Wis., Apr. 14, 1941; B.A. in Philosophy and Psychology, St. Marys Coll. Calif., 1963; postgrad. aerospace ops. mgmt. U. So. Calif., 1967-68, govt. contracts adminstrn. U. Calif., 1967; LL.D., McGeorge Sch. Law U. Pacific, 1972. Admitted to Calif. bar, 1972; asso. firm Kinkle, Rodiger, Graf, Dewberry & Spriggs, Ventura, Calif., 1973; partner firm Kelly & Bleuel, Ventura, 1973—; sales engr. Lockheed Aircraft Service Co., Ontario, Calif., 1965-69; guest lectr. businessmen seminars Ventura C. of C. Mem. State Bar Calif. Mem. staff Pacific Law Jour., 1970-72. Office: Kelly & Bleuel 455 E Main St Suites 7 and 8 Ventura CA 93001 Tel (805) 643-2251

KELLY, PATRICK BANNERMAN, b. Albany, N.Y., July 8, 1941; B.A., Russell Sage Coll., 1968; J.D., Western State U., Anaheim, Calif., 1972. Admitted to Calif. bar, 1973; mem. firm Kelly, Sink's Wright, Vista, Calif., 1973—. Mem. Am., San Diego County bar assns., Lawyer-Pilot's Bar Assn. Home: 2155 Subida al Cielo Vista CA 92083 Office: 702 Escondido Ave Vista CA 92083 Tel (714) 724-0531

KELLY, PHILLIP, b. Oberlin, Kans., Apr. 17, 1934; B.A., Los Angeles State Coll., 1956; LL.B., U. So. Calif., 1959. Admitted to Calif. bar, 1959; sr. partner firm Kelly & Graham, Torrance, Calif., 1967—; gen. counsel Vacation Industries; dir. Torrance Nat. Bank, 4 Jay Investments Inc. Mem. Calif. State, South Bay bar assns. Recipient Pub. Service commendation City of El Segundo, Calif., 1972. Home: 8 Hackamore Rd Rolling Hills CA Office: 21515 Hawthorne Blvd Torrance CA 90503 Tel (213) 371-3535

KELLY, RICHARD LEO, b. Tyler, Minn., July 25, 1928; B.A., St. John's U., Minn., 1952; LL.B., William Mitchell Coll. Law, 1957. Admitted to Minn. bar, 1957; asso. firm Douglass Bell & Donlin, St. Paul, 1957-67; individual practice law, Springfield, Minn., 1967-72; partner firm Kelly & O'Leary, Springfield, 1972—; city atty. City of Springfield, 1968—; dir. F & M Bank, Springfield, 1974—. Trustee St. Raphael's Ch., Springfield, 1971-76. Mem. Minn. Bar Assn. Office: 103 N Marshall St Springfield MN 56087 Tel (507) 723-4755

KELLY, RICHARD SMITH, b. Chgo., Jan. 18, 1925; B.A., U. Mich., 1948; J.D., Northwestern U., 1951. Admitted to Ill. bar, 1951; partner firm Springer, Bergstrom & Crowe, Chgo., 1951-55; asso. firm McDermott, Will & Emery, Chgo., 1955-60; atty. Container Corp. Am., Chgo., 1960-67, asst. gen. counsel, 1967-69, gen. counsel, 1969-71, v.p., gen. counsel, 1971-77, dir., 1975—, sr. v.p., gen. counsel, 1977—; asst. gen. counsel Marcor Inc., Chgo., 1968-71, sec., 1968—, gen. counsel, 1971—, dir., 1976—. Mem. Am., Ill., Chgo. bar assns., Am. Soc. Corporate Secs. Home: 423 Laurel Ave Wilmette IL 60091 Office: One Montgomery Ward Plaza Chicago IL 60671 Tel (312) 786-5456

KELLY, ROBERT QUAINE, b. Chgo., Apr. 3, 1922; B.A., St. Mary of the Lake U., 1945; M.A. in L.S., Rosary Coll., 1950; J.D., DePaul U., 1957. Admitted to Ill. bar, 1957, Nebr. bar, 1975; librarian DePaul U. Coll. Law, 1950-73; prof. law Creighton U., 1973—, dir. law library, 1973—. Mem. bd. trustees, N. Riverside, Ill., 1969-72. Mem. Am. Bar Assn., Am. Assn. Law Libraries (treas. 1964-66), Bibliog. Soc. Am. Contbg. editor: Legal Reference Books, 1975. Home: 717 Sunset Trail Omaha NE 68132 Office: 2500 California St Omaha NE 68178 Tel (402) 536-2875

KELLY, ROGER EMMET, b. Winnepeg, Man., Can., Jan. 23, 1916; B.A., Loyola U., Los Angeles, 1936, LL.B., 1939. Admitted to Calif. bar, 1939; asso. firm Kenneth J. Murphy, Los Angeles, 1939-41, firm

Nourse & Jones, Los Angeles, 1941-42, 45; partner firm Jones, Thompson & Kelly and predecessor, Los Angeles, 1946-48, firm Gilbert, Bauder, Thompson & Kelly and predecessor, Los Angeles, 1948-67, firm Gilbert, Kelly, Crowley & Jennett, Los Angeles, 1967—. Fellow Am. Coll. Trial Laweyrs; mem. Am. Bd. Trial Advocates (hon., Trial Lawyer of Yr. 1960), Internat. Acad. Trial Attys. Office: 1541 Wilshire Blvd Suite 500 Los Angeles CA 90017 Tel (213) 484-2330

KELLY, THOMAS LAWSON, JR., b. Denver, Jan. 28, 1946; B.A., So. Meth. U., 1968, J.D., 1971. Admitted to Tex. bar, 1971, U.S. Supreme Ct. bar, 1975; asso. firm Patterson, Lamberty & Kelly, and predecessor, Dallas, 1971-76, partner, 1976—. Active United Way Dallas, 1975. Mem. State Bar Tex., Dallas Bar Assn., Dallas Jr. Bar Assn., Comml. Law League Am. Home: 6661 Lakewood Blvd Dallas TX 75214 Office: 2011 Cedar Springs Dallas TX 75201 Tel (214) 742-1156

KELLY, THOMAS MICHAEL, b. Mpls., Aug. 9, 1941; B.A., U. Minn., 1963, J.D., 1968. Admitted to Minn. bar, 1968, U.S. 8th Circuit Ct. Appeals bar, 1968, U.S. Dist. Ct. for Minn. bar, 1968; individual practice law, Mpls., 1968—; fed. community defender, Mpls., 1976—. Mem. Am., Minn. State, Hennepin County bar assns., Am., Minn. trial lawyers assns., Am. Arbitration Assn. Home: 1801 Emerson Ave S Minneapolis MN 55403 Office: 2210 IDS Center 80 S 8th St Minneapolis MN 55402 Tel (612) 339-5055

KELLY, WALTER MYNATT, b. McAllen, Tex., May 24, 1931; B.B.A., Baylor U., 1954, J.D., 1956. Admitted to Tex. bar, 1956; asst. criminal dist. atty. Hidalgo County (Tex.), 1957-60; with firm Barnes, Kelly & Ornelas, McAllen, 1960-69; judge Hidalgo County Ct., Edinburg, Tex., 1969-76; house counsel McAllen State Bank. Chmn. McAllen Housing Authority, 1965. Mem. State Bar Tex., Hidalgo County Bar Assn. (past pres.), Am. Judicature Soc., Phi Alpha Delta. Office: 2 S Broadway St McAllen TX 78501 Tel (512) 686-1733

KELLY, WILLIAM DONALD, JR., b. Stamps, Ark., Dec. 23, 1940; B.S. in Bus. Adminstrn., U. Ark., Fayetteville, 1962, J.D., Little Rock, 1974. Accountant, R.M. Brown, C.P.A., Little Rock, 1964-65, Mercing & Thomas, C.P.A.'s, Little Rock, 1965-67; auditor HEW, Little Rock, 1967-73; pub. accountant Lovett, Baer & Kelly, C.P.A.'s, Little Rock, 1970-74; admitted to Ark. bar, 1973; individual practice law, Little Rock, 1973—; human services advocate Ark. Dept. Human Services, Little Rock, 1976—. Mem. Am., Ark., Pulaski County (Ark.) bar assns., Central Ark. C.P.A's., Ark. Soc. C.P.A's., Am. Inst. C.P.A's. Office: 406 Nat Old Line Bldg Little Rock AR 72201 Tel (501) 371-1001

KELLY, WILLIAM PALMER, b. Pensacola, Fla., Oct. 24, 1943; B.A. in Biology, U. of South, 1966; M.B.A., Am. U., 1968; J.D., George Washington U., 1972. Admitted to Tex. bar, 1972; spl. asst. to chief staff, polit. liaison, marine sci. USCG Hdqrs., Washington, 1968-70; asst. U.S. Atty., Civil Div., Houston, 1973-74, chief lands natural resources div., 1974—. Mem. Fed. Bar Assn., Tex., Houston Jr. bar assns. Office: US Attorneys Office Lands Natural Resources Div 515 Rusk St Houston TX 77007 Tel (713) 226-4762

KELNER, ROBERT STEVEN, b. N.Y.C., Dec. 13, 1946; B.A., Franklin and Marshall Coll., 1968; J.D., Columbia, 1971. Admitted to N.Y. State bar, 1971, U.S. Dist. Ct. for So. and Eastern Dists. N.Y. bars, 1972; partner firm Kelner, Stellies & Glotzer, N.Y.C., 1974—; lectr., author in field. Mem. N.Y. State Trial Lawyers Assn.

KELSEY, ROGER DENHAM, b. Wilmington, Del., Apr. 26, 1940; B.A., U. Del., 1962; LL.B., Washington and Lee U., 1965, J.D., 1969. Admitted to Del. bar, 1965, Fed. bar, 1965; clk. Judge W.J. Storey, Del. Superior Ct., summers 1964-65; asso. firm Schmittinger & Rodriguez, Dover, 1965-66; U.S. commr., 1966-67; individual practice law, Dover, 1966-68; house atty. 123d Del. Gen. Assembly Session, 1967-68; judge Family Ct. Del., Dover, 1969—. Dist. vice chmn. Mid-Del. Dist., Delmarva council Boy Scouts Am., 1969-71, dist. commr., 1971-72, dist. chmn., 1972, dist. vice chmn., 1973, dist. chmn., 1974, Order of Merit, 1975, dist. vice chmn., council mem. at large, 1976; mem. adv. bd. Dover chpt. Big Bros., Inc., 1969-73; founding mem. Dover Heritage Trail, 1973—. Mem. Am., Del. bar assns., Nat. Conf. Spl. Ct. Judges, Am. Judicature Soc. Home: 146 Crescent Dr Dover DE 19901 Office: 11 North St Arden Bldg Dover DE 19901 Tel (302) 674-0210

KELTNER, CECIL GREEN, b. Ripley, Tenn., Nov. 10, 1919; student U. Tenn., 1941-43; B.S., Memphis State U., 1946, LL.B., 1951. Admitted to Tenn. bar, 1951, Ct. Mil. Appeals, 1956; partner firm Tual, Keltner, Allan & Lee, Memphis, 1959-69; asso. firm Riley Hinds & Keltner, Memphis, 1969—; instr. lt. col. JAGC, USAR, 1969-72. Mem. Res. Officers Assn., Memphis, Tenn., Shelby County bar assns. Named Distinguished Instr. JAGC Command and Gen. Staff Sch., U.S. Army, 1973; recipient Actors award Union Ave. Bapt. Ch., 1968; author: Sam D. Tail, 1948. Office: 1001-100 N Main Bldg Memphis TN 38103 Tel (901) 523-7178

KELTNER, GARY GRAYSON, b. Phoenix, Apr. 18, 1936; B.A., U. Ariz., 1958, J.D., 1960. Admitted to Ariz. bar, 1960, U.S. Supreme Ct. bar, 1963, U.S. Ct. Mil. Appeal, 1961; with def. appellate div. JAGC, U.S. Army, Washington, 1961-63; with firm Jennings Strouss & Salmon, Phoenix, 1964—, partner, 1967—. Vice chmn. profl. div. Greater Maricopa County United Way, 1973; bd. dirs. Villa Montessori, Inc., Phoenix, 1975—. Mem. State Bar of Ariz., Am., Maricopa County bar assns., Am. Judicature Soc., Ariz. State U. Law Soc. (dir. 1971—). Office: 111 W Monroe St Phoenix AZ 85003

KELTON, JOHN TREMAIN, b. Bay City, Mich., Mar. 12, 1909; B.S. in Chem. Engring., Mass. Inst. Tech., 1932; LL.B., Harvard, 1935. Admitted to N.Y. bar, 1936; asso. firm Watson, Bristol, Johnson & Leavenworth, N.Y.C., 1935-40, 46-49; mem. firm Watson, Leavenworth, Kelton & Taggart, and predecessor, N.Y.C., 1950—. Mem. Am., N.Y. State bar assns., Assn. Bar City N.Y., Am. (pres. 1973-74), N.Y. (pres. 1967) patent law assns. Home: 6 Nutmeg Ln Westport CT 06880 Office: Watson Leavenworth et al 100 Park Ave New York City NY 10017 Tel (212) 683-4221

KEMMER, ALBERT T., b. Beaverton, Oreg., Feb. 7, 1903; LL.B., Northwestern Coll. Law, 1929. Buyer purchasing dept. Union Pacific Co.; admitted to Oreg. bar; practice law, Beaverton. Active Boy Scouts Am.; com. chmn. Democratic Central Com.; mem. Washington County (Oreg.) Dem. Central Com.; pres. Young Dem. Clubs Oreg. Mem. Washington County, Multnomah County (Oreg.) bars, Am. Bar Assn. Home: Route 1 PO Box 1118 Beaverton OR 97005 Office: 12270 SW 2d St Beaverton OR 97005 Tel (503) 644-6645

KEMP, CARROLL ABRAMS, b. Hazlehurst, Miss., Nov. 27, 1908; LL.B., U. Miss., 1931. Admitted to Miss. bar, 1931; abstractor U.S. Dept. Agr., Washington, 1935; individual practice law, Hazlehurst, 1937—; atty. City of Hazlehurst, 1938-61; chancery judge, 1961-62. Home: 255 N Ragsdale Ave Hazlehurst MS 39083 Office: 113 Downing St Hazlehurst MS 39083

KEMP, JAMES LAURENCE, b. Millport, Pa., Mar. 20, 1933; A.A., Hershey Jr. Coll., 1956; student U. Md., 1957; law office study, 1964-70. Admitted to N.Y. bar, 1970; individual practice law, Rochester, N.Y., 1970—; law officer N.Y. CAP. Mem. Am., N.Y. State, Monroe County, Fed. Bar assns., Am. Judicature Soc. Home: 144 Lakeshire Rd Rochester NY 14612 Office: 260 S Plymouth Ave Rochester NY 14614 Tel (716) 546-8442

KEMP, MARGARET JEAN, b. Chgo., Sept. 3, 1944; B.S. in Edn., U. Ill., Urbana, 1965; M.A. in Polit. Sci., U. Calif., Berkeley, 1966, J.D., 1971. Admitted to Calif. bar, 1972; dep. dist. atty. San Mateo County, Calif., 1972-76; partner firm Thirkell, Pierpoint & Kemp, San Mateo, Calif., 1976—. Mem. Calif., San Mateo County bar assns. Office: 181 2d Ave San Mateo CA 94401 Tel (415) 348-1016

KEMP, WILLIAM FRANKLIN, b. Austin, Tex., Nov. 7, 1932; B.B.A. with honors, U. Tex., 1954, J.D., 1959. Admitted to Tex. bar 1959, U.S. Supreme Ct. bar, 1967; partner firm Kemp & Prud'homme, Austin, 1960-74, firm Kemp & Spiller, Austin, 1974—; lectr. Austin Community Coll., 1972-74. Chmn. Travis County Lawyer Referral Service, 1973—; legal counsel Austin Symphony Orch. Soc., 1969-77. Mem. State Bar Assn. Tex., Am. Trial Lawyers Assn., Austin C. of C., Knights of the Symphony (Tex. lord chancellor 1971), West Austin Rotary. Recipient Spl. Achievement award Austin Symphony Orch. Soc., 1973. Home: 2909 Greenlee Dr Austin TX 78703 Office: 1900 Am Bank Tower Austin TX 78701 Tel (512) 474-5757

KEMPER, ALBERT STRAYER, JR., b. Port Republic, Va., Mar. 20, 1901; LL.B., U. Va., 1927. Admitted to Va. bar, 1925, W.Va. bar, 1927; mem. firm Richardson, Kemper & Hancock and predecessor, Bluefield, W.Va., 1929-50, 70-75, counsel, 1971—; house counsel, officer Tierney Interests, Bluefield, 1950-69; mem. W.Va. Commn. on Constl. Revision, 1958-64; mem. advisory bd. W.Va. Dept. Commerce, 1961-68. Chmn. fund dr. ARC, Bluefield, 1950. Mem. Mercer County (pres. 1940), W.Va. (pres. 1947), Va. State (hon.), Am. bar assns., W.Va., Va. state bars. Named Man of Year Greater Bluefield Jaycees, 1961; asso. editor Va. Law Rev., 1925-26. Home: 805 Groveland Dr Bluefield WV 24701 Office: 602 Law & Commerce Bldg Bluefield WV 24701 Tel (304) 327-7158

KEMPER, EDWARD CRAWFORD, III, b. Seattle, Dec. 7, 1942; B.A., George Washington U., 1965, J.D. with honors, 1968. Admitted to Hawaii bar, 1969; asso. firm Cades, Schutte, Fleming & Wright, Honolulu, 1969-71; partner firm Mattoch, Kemper & Brown, Honolulu, 1971-74, firm Kemper & Watts, 1975—; editor-in-chief Hawaii Bar Jour., 1972—; dir. Kokua Kalihi Valley. Bd. dirs. Sunshine Festival, Honolulu, 1973. Mem. Hawaii Bar Assn. (dir.). Contbr. articles to law revs. Home: 1307 Onaona Pl Kailua HI 96734 Office: 130 Merchant St Honolulu HI 96813 Tel (808) 524-0330

KEMPER, GERALD T., b. Frankfort, Ky., Oct. 4, 1942; A.B., Eastern Ky. U., 1964; J.D., U. Ky., 1967. Admitted to Ky. bar, 1967; individual practice law, Owenton, Ky. Mem. Kay. Bar Assn. Home: Route 3 Owenton KY 40359 Office: 125 W Seminary St Owenton KY 40359 Tel (502) 484-2790

KEMPF, DONALD G(EORGE), JR., b. Chgo., July 4, 1937; A.B., Villanova U., 1959; LL.B., Harvard U., 1965; M.B.A., U. Chgo., 1976. Admitted to Ill. bar, 1965; asso. firm Kirkland & Ellis, Chgo., 1965-70, partner, 1971—. Home: 2225 Beechwood Ave Wilmette IL 60091 Office: 200 E Randolph Dr Chicago IL 60601 Tel (312) 861-2264

KENDALL, DAVID MATTHEW, b. N.Y.C., May 11, 1923; B.A., Queen's Coll., City U. N.Y., 1948; LL.B., Yale, 1951. Admitted to Tex. bar, 1952, U.S. Supreme Ct. bar, 1974; asso. firm Thompson, Knight, Simmons & Bullion, Dallas, 1951-62; partner firm Woodruff, Kendall & Smith, Dallas, 1962-72; with Office Atty. Gen. State Tex., Austin, chmn. opinion com., 1973-74, exec. asst. atty. gen., 1974, 1st asst. atty. gen., 1974—. Fellow Tex. Bar Found. (life); mem. Order of Coif. Home: 1403 Westbury Trail Austin TX 78758 Office: 708 Supreme Court Bldg Austin TX 78711 Tel (512) 475-5861

KENDALL, PHILLIP ALAN, b. Lamar, Colo., July 20, 1942; B.S. in Engring., Stanford, 1964; postgrad. U. Freiburg (Germany), 1965; J.D., U. Colo., 1969. Admitted to Colo. bar, 1969; since practiced in Colorado Springs, Colo., asso. firm Asher, Kraemer, Kendall & Felt, 1969-72, partner, 1972—; mem. Colorado Springs Estate Planning Council, 1972—; pres. Pikes Peak Legal Services, 1974, dir., 1972—. Pres. bd. dirs. Colorado Springs Symphony, 1975—. Mem. Am., Colo., El Paso County (trustee) bar assns. Named Outstanding Young Lawyer by bd. trustees El Paso County Bar Assn., 1976. Home: 4313 Ridgecrest Dr Colorado Springs CO 80907 Office: 430 N Tejon Colorado Springs CO 80903 Tel (303) 471-3690

KENDALL, WILLIAM GEORGE, b. Lima, Ohio, Feb. 28, 1945; B.A., Ohio No. U., 1968, J.D., 1973. Admitted to Ohio bar, 1973; asso. firm Robenalt, Daley, Balyeat & Balyeat, Lima. Mem. Ohio, Allen County bar assns. Home: 1743 Northlea Dr Lima OH 45801 Office: 110-112 N Elizabeth St Lima OH 45801 Tel (419) 227-5006

KENDRICK, HERBERT SPENCER, JR., b. Brownfield, Tex., Nov. 16, 1934; B.B.A., So. Meth. U., 1957, LL.B., 1960; LL.M., Harvard, 1961. Admitted to Tex. bar, 1960, U.S. Supreme Ct. bar, 1963; trial atty. tax div. Dept. Justice, 1961-65; since practiced in Dallas, partner firm Kendrick & Kendrick, 1965-69, Turner, Rodgers, Winn, Scurlock & Sailers, 1969-71, Kendrick, Kendrick & Bradley, 1971-76, Jenkens & Gilchrist, 1976—; dir. Capital Bank, Dallas; lectr. tax law So. Meth. U., 1966—. Mem. Am., Tex., Dallas bar assns., Phi Alpha Delta. Co-author: Texas Transaction Guide (10 vols.), 1972, 73. Home: 4421 Larchmont St Dallas TX 75205 Office: 2200 First Nat Bank Bldg Dallas TX 75202 Tel (214) 741-1131

KENDRICK, JOHN JESSE, JR., b. Brownfield, Tex., Nov. 22, 1943; B.B.A., So. Meth. U., 1965, J.D., 1968. Admitted to Calif. bar, 1969, Tex. bar, 1970; auditor Peat, Marwick, Mitchell & Co., 1965; asso. firm Nossaman, Waters, Scott, Krueger & Riordan, Los Angeles, 1968-69; asso. Bache & Co., Inc., N.Y.C., 1969-70; partner firm Jenkens & Gilchrist, and predecessors, Dallas, 1970—; dir. Capital Bank, Dallas. Mem. Dallas Jr. (treas. 1973), Dallas bar assns. Contbr. articles in field to profl. Jours.; co-author: Texas Transaction Guide, 1972. Home: 4800 Drexel Dr Dallas TX 75205 Office: First Nat Bank Bldg Dallas TX 75202 Tel (214) 741-1131

KENISON, FRANK ROWE, b. Conway, N.H., Nov. 1, 1907; A.B., Dartmouth, 1929, LL.D., 1954; LL.B., Boston U., 1932, LL.D., 1955; LL.D., U. N.H., 1966, Franklin Pierce Coll., 1966; S.J.D., Suffolk U., 1959; L.H.D., Franklin Pierce Law Center, 1977. Admitted to N.H. bar, 1932; solicitor Carroll County (N.H.), 1935-37; asst. atty. gen. State of N.H., 1937-40, atty. gen., 1940-42, 45-46; asso. justice N.H. Supreme Ct., Concord, 1946-52, chief justice, 1952—. Mem. Am., N.H. assns., Am. Law Inst., Am. Judicature Soc. Home: 176 Centre St Concord NH 03301 Office: Supreme Court Bldg Concord NH 03301 Tel (603) 271-3415

KENLINE, ROBERT HENRY, b. Dubuque, Iowa, Nov. 6, 1910; B.A., Loras Coll., 1932; LL.B., Notre Dame U., 1935, J.D., 1969. Admitted to Iowa bar, 1935; partner firm Reynolds, Kenline, Breitbach, McCarthy, Clemens & McKay, Dubuque, 1977—. Bd. dirs. Dubuque Boy's Club, 1939-64, pres., 1956. Mem. Dubuque County, Iowa, Am. bar assns., Internat. Assn. Ins. Counsel. Home: 142 S Grandview Ave Dubuque IA 52001 Office: 222 Fischer Bldg Dubuque IA 52001 Tel (319) 583-1768

KENN, EDWARD JOHN, b. N.Y.C., June 1, 1918; B.S. in Social Studies, City Coll. N.Y., 1939; LL.B., Columbia, 1942. Admitted to N.Y. State bar, 1942, Ill. bar, 1961; asso. firm White & Case, N.Y.C., 1942-60; v.p., sec., gen. counsel Packaging Corp. of Am., Evanston, Ill., 1960—. Mem. Am., Ill., Chgo. bar assns., Phi Beta Kappa Assos. Office: Box 1408 Evanston IL 60204

KENNEDY, BERNARD JOSEPH, b. Niagara Falls, N.Y., Aug. 16, 1931; B.A., Niagara Univ., 1953; LL.B., Univ. Mich., 1958. Admitted to N.Y. bar, 1960; legal asst. Iroquois Gas Corp., Buffalo, 1958-63, gen. atty., 1963-67, sec., 1967-71, dir., 1971-74; sec. Nat. Fuel Gas Corp., Buffalo, 1974-75, v.p., gen. counsel, 1975—, exec. v.p., 1976—; dir. GAS, Ltd. Bd. dirs. ARC, Blue Cross Western N.Y.; chmn. bd. advisers Erie County Dept. Soc. Welfare; adv. bd. Canisius Coll. Bus. Sch. Mem. Buffalo C of C, Fed. Power, Am. (vice chmn. gas com. pub. utility law sect.), N.Y. (past chmn. pub. utility com.), Erie County bar assns. Home: 33 Ruskin Rd Eggertsville NY 14226 Office: 10 Lafayette Square Buffalo NY 14203 Tel (716) 854-4360

KENNEDY, CHARLES ALLEN, b. Maysville, Ky., Dec. 11, 1940; A.B., Morehead (Ky.) Coll., 1965, M.A. in Edn., 1968; J.D., U. Akron, 1969; LL.M., George Washington U., 1974. Admitted to Ohio bar, 1969; mem. fgn. agr. and spl. programs div. Office of Gen. Counsel, U.S. Dept. Agr., Washington, 1969-71; partner firm Kauffman, Eberhart, Ciconetti & Kennedy Co., and predecessors, Wooster, Ohio, 1972—; asst. city solicitor City of Wooster, 1972. Mem. Am., Fed., Ohio, Wayne County bar assns., Assn. Am. Trial Lawyers, Ohio Trial Acad. Recipient A.Y. Lloyd award in pub. adminstrn., 1965. Office: 517 N Market St Wooster OH 44691 Tel (216) 246-9622

KENNEDY, DANIEL LENNON, b. Joliet, Ill., Dec. 7, 1932; A.B., U. Notre Dame, 1954; J.D., U. Chgo., 1956. Admitted to Ill. bar, 1956; atty. JAGC, USAF, 1957-60; partner firm Dunn, Stefanich, McGarry & Kennedy, Joliet, 1960—. Trustee Joliet Jr. Coll., 1968—, now chmn. Mem. Am., Ill., Will County bar assns. Home: Rollingwood Ct Joliet IL 60435 Office: 81 N Chicago St Joliet IL 60431 Tel (815) 726-4774

KENNEDY, DAVID BOYD, b. Ann Arbor, Mich., Sept. 2, 1933; A.B., Ind. U., 1958; LL.B., U. Mich., 1963. Admitted to Mich. bar, 1964, Wyo. bar, 1965; asso. firm Henry A. Burgess, Sheridan, Wyo., 1964-70; partner firm Burgess, Kennedy & Davis, Sheridan, 1970-73, Kennedy, Connor & Healy, Sheridan, 1977—; atty. gen. State of Wyo., 1974-75. Chmn., Wyo. Republican Party, 1971-73; mem. Rep. Nat. Com. for Wyo., 1976—. Mem. Am., Wyo., Sheridan County bar assns. Home: 510 S Jefferson St Sheridan WY 82801 Office: 40 S Main St Sheridan WY 82801 Tel (307) 672-2295

KENNEDY, DOROTHY, b. Hamersville, Ohio, Jan. 14, 1919; teacher's degree Wilmington Coll., 1938; LL.B., Salmon P. Chase Coll. Law, Cin., 1948, J.D., 1960. Admitted to Ohio bar, 1948; pros. atty. Brown County, Ohio, 1949-57. Pres. Women's Democratic Club of Brown County (Ohio), 1960-62; historian criminal law com. Ohio State Bar, until 1962; pres. Brown County Bar Assn., 1960-62, also past sec. Contbr. articles to profl. jours. Home and Office: 525 Laura Dr Bethel OH 45106 Tel (513) 734-4519

KENNEDY, EDWIN J., b. Red Bank, N.J., Apr. 12, 1912; A.B., U. Notre Dame, 1932; LL.D., Georgetown U., 1939. Admitted to D.C. bar, 1940, N.J. bar, 1941, Fla. bar, 1946; individual practice law, Sarasota, Fla. Mem. D.C., N.J., Fla. bars. Home: 1208 Northport Dr Sarasota FL 33581 Office: 2620 Bee Ridge Rd Sarasota FL 35579 Tel (813) 922-1433

KENNEDY, FRANK ROBERT, b. Strafford, Mo., July 27, 1914; A.B., S.W. Mo. State Coll., 1935; LL.B., Washington U., St. Louis, 1939; J.S.D., Yale U., 1953. Admitted to Mo. bar, 1939, Iowa bar, 1961; instr. law State U. Iowa, 1940-41; asst. prof. law U. Mich., 1941-46, asso. prof., 1946-49, prof., 1961—; exec. dir. Commn. on Bankruptcy Laws, Washington, 1971-73; acting chief counsel indsl. user unit, rationing div. OPA, Washington, 1942-43; reporter for adv. com. on bankruptcy rules Jud. Conf. U.S., 1960-76. Mem. Am. Bar Assn., Am. Law Inst., Nat. Bankruptcy Conf. Author: (with L. P. King) Collier on Bankruptcy, vols. 4 and 4A, 14th edit., 1959; recipient Distinguished Faculty Achievement award U. Mich., 1971. Home: 2515 Manchester Ann Arbor MI 48104 Office: 926 Legal Research Bldg U Mich Ann Arbor MI 48109 Tel (313) 764-9354

KENNEDY, GEORGE CURTIS, b. Aiken, S.C., Apr. 29, 1912; student Aiken Inst., 1925-28, Mercer U., 1929-30; LL.B., Walter F. George Sch. Law, 1933; partner firm Hammond, Kennedy & Kennedy, Augusta, Ga., 1933-36; partner firm Neely and Kennedy, Manchester, Ga., 1936-39; asst. dir. Ga. Dept. Pub. Welfare, Atlanta, 1939-41; pres. Ga. Fla. Lumber Co., Manchester, Ga., 1943-49; individual practice law, Manchester, 1949—. Mem. State Bar Ga., Am., Coweta Circuit, Meriwether County bar assns., Am. Judicature Soc., Am. Trial Lawyers Assn. Home: 514 Webster Dr Manchester GA 31816 Office: 105 Broad St Manchester GA 31816 Tel (404) 846-3156

KENNEDY, HAYES, b. Joliet, Ill., Sept. 10, 1898; Ph.B., U. Chgo., 1922, J.D., 1924. Admitted to Ill. bar, 1925; mem. firm Ryan, Condon & Livingston, Chgo., 1924-48; gen. claims atty., asst. gen. counsel, Greyhound Corp., Chgo., 1948-64; mem. firm Ryan, Condon & Livingston, Chgo., 1964-67; pres., counsel Ill. Comml. Mens' Assn., Chgo., 1967—; tchr. Loyola U. Sch. Law, Chgo., 1926-37; dir., counsel Brach Candy Co., Chgo., 1931-66. Trustee Lewis U., Lockport, Ill., 1962-74, St. Francis Coll., Joliet, 1954-62; founder Am. Legion Boys' State in Ill., 1935, pres., 1935-63; chmn. police and fire bd., Joliet, 1951-56; mem. planning and zoning commn., Joliet,

1963-74. Mem. Will County, Ill. State, Am. bar assns., Internat. Assn. Ins. Counsel. Recipient Distinguished Service citation U. Chgo. Alumni Assn., 1961; citation Am. Legion Nat. Dept., 1964. Home: 309 N William St Joliet IL 60435 Office: One W Harris St LaGrange IL 60525 Tel (312) 352-7100

KENNEDY, JAMES LORNE, b. Gary, Ind., Jan. 18, 1941; B.S. in Bus. Adminstrn., Ind. U. at Bloomington, 1963, J.D., 1968; grad. Nat. FBI Acad., 1976. Admitted to Ind. bar, 1968; asso. firm Schroer, Eichhorn & Morrow, Hammond, Ind., 1968-71; adminstr. Region I, Ind. Criminal Justice Planning Agy., 1969-70; dep. prosecutor Lake County (Ind.), 1971; div. dir. Ind. U. Police Dept., 1971—; asso. faculty mem. Ind. U. Sch. Criminal Justice Edn., Bloomington, 1972—; lectr. Ind. Law Enforcement Acad., 1972—; chief dep. investigator Lake County Coroner's Office, 1968-71. Mem. Ind. Assn. Police Legal Advisors (past pres.), Internat., Ind. assns. chiefs of police. Contbr. articles to legal jours. Home: 1916 Sussex St Bloomington IN 47401 Office: 400 E 7th St Bloomington IN 47401 Tel (812) 337-7603

KENNEDY, JAMES MADISON, b. San Francisco, May 10, 1938; B.A., U. Calif., Berkeley, 1958, J.D., 1962. Admitted to Calif. bar, 1963, 9th Circuit Fed. Ct. and Dist. Ct., 1963; individual practice law, San Rafael, Calif., 1965—. Mem. Am., Calif. Marin County bar assns., Calif. Trial Lawyers Assn., Am. Arbitration Assn. (arbitrator), Calif. Atty. Gen. Vol. Adv. Council. Office: 30 N San Pedro Rd POB Z San Rafael CA 94903 Tel (415) 479-7375

KENNEDY, JOHN LLOYD, b. Holly Springs, Miss., Mar. 24, 1931; student Miss. State U., 1949-50, U.S. Naval Acad., 1950-53, San Francisco State Coll., 1954-55; B.A., U. Miss., 1956, LL.B., J.D., 1959. Admitted to Miss. bar, 1959; individual practice law, Holly Springs, 1959—; real estate broker, Holly Springs, 1959—; chmn. Miss. Real Estate Commn.; del. Nat. Conf. on Law and Poverty, 1966. Del. Nat. Democratic Conv., 1968, 72; del., co-chmn. Miss. del. Dem. Conv., Kansas City, 1974; trustee Rust Coll., Holly Springs; chmn. Marshall County (Miss.) Mental Health Dr. Mem. Miss. Econ. Council, Miss. Edn. Assn., Marshall County Tchrs. Assn., Miss. State, U. Miss. alumni assns. Home: 320 Chulahoma Ave Holly Springs MS 38635 Office: 111 College Ave Holly Springs MS 38635 Tel (601) 252-2824

KENNEDY, JOHN PAUL, b. Mpls., Dec. 18, 1941; A.B. cum Laude, Harvard, 1963; J.D., Stanford, 1966. Admitted to Ill. bar, 1966, Utah bar, 1972, U.S. Supreme Ct. bar, 1972; asso. firm Seyfarth, Shaw, Fairweather, & Geraldson, Chgo., 1966-72; partner firm Boyden, Kennedy, Romney & Howard, Salt Lake City, 1972—. Active Boy Scouts Am. Mem. Utah, Salt Lake City bar assns. Mem. Stanford Law Rev., 1964-66. Home: 1385 Yale Ave Salt Lake City UT 84105 Office: 1000 Kennecott Bldg 10 East South Temple Salt Lake City UT 84133 Tel (801) 521-0800

KENNEDY, ORIAN RAY, lawyer; b. Boyer, W.Va., Dec. 31, 1913; LL.B., Nat. U. Law Sch., 1942. Admitted to D.C. bar, 1942, Fla. bar, 1965; agt. FBI, Washington, Miami, Fla. and New Orleans, 1939-65; partner firm McCutcheon, Fleece & Kennedy, St. Petersburg, Fla., 1965-68; v.p., trust officer Sun Bank & Trust Co., St. Petersburg, 1968—. Mem. St. Petersburg Bar Assn. Home: 507 39th Ave Saint Petersburg Beach FL 33706 Office: 301 4th St N Saint Petersburg FL 33701

KENNEDY, PETER LAWSON, b. N.Y.C., Apr. 21, 1933; A.B., Harvard, 1955; LL.B., Columbia, 1961. Admitted to R.I. bar, 1962, U.S. Supreme Ct. bar, 1974; asso. firm Adler, Pollock & Sheehan, Inc., Providence, 1962-68, partner, 1968—; asst. city solicitor, prosecutor City of Cranston (R.I.), 1964-69. Mem. R.I. Bar Assn., Am. Arbitration Assn., Am. Trial Lawyers Assn. Home: 35 Westchester Way Warwick RI 02886 Office: 1 Hospital Trust Plaza Providence RI 02903 Tel (401) 274-7200

KENNEDY, RICHARD R., b. Lafayette, La., Oct. 18, 1941; B.A., U. Southwestern La., 1962; LL.B., Tulane U., 1965. Admitted to La. bar, 1965, U.S. Supreme Ct. bar, 1971; law clk. Western Dist. La., 1966-67; individual practice law, Lafayette, 1967—. Mem. Am., La., Lafayette Parish bar assns., La., Am. trial lawyers assns., Maritime Law Assn. U.S. Office: 311 E Main St PO Box 3892 Lafayette LA 70502 Tel (318) 232-1934

KENNEDY, RONALD EUGENE, b. Chgo., July 1, 1942; B.A., U. Ill., 1965, J.D., Northwestern U., 1973. Admitted to Ill. bar, 1973, U.S. Dist. Ct. for No. Dist. Ill., bar, 1973; asso. firm Sidley & Austin, Chgo., 1973-74; asso. prof. law Northwestern U., 1974—. Mem. Am. (mem. hous. dels.), Cook County bar assns., Chgo. Council Lawyers (mem. bd. govs.), Assn. Am. Law Schs. (exec. com. minorities sect. 1976—), Order Coif. Recipient Jr. Counselor award Cook County Bar Assn., 1976. Home: 601 Groveland Park Chicago IL 60611 Office: 357 E Chicago Ave Chicago IL 60611 Tel (312) 649-8374

KENNEDY, THOMAS JOHN, b. Milw., July 29, 1947; B.A., U. Wis., 1969, J.D. cum laude, 1972. Admitted to Wis. bar, 1972, U.S. Dist. Ct. for Western Dist. Wis., 1972, for Eastern Dist. Wis., 1972; asso. firm Goldberg, Previaux & Nelmen, Milw., 1972—. Mem. State Bar Wis., Am. Bar Assn. Editorial bd. U. Wis. Law Rev., 1971-72. Home: 500 W Bradley St C-330 Milwaukee WI 53217 Office: 788 N Jefferson St Milwaukee WI 53202 Tel (414) 271-4500

KENNEDY, VICTOR NEAL, b. Ida Grove, Iowa, Apr. 27, 1931; B.S., Northwestern U., 1955, J.D., 1958. Admitted to Iowa bar, 1958; partner firm Scholz & Kennedy, Oskaloosa, Iowa, 1958-61, Fulton, Frerichs, Nutting & Kennedy, Waterloo, Iowa, 1968-74; individual practice, Waterloo, 1961-68, 74—; asst. county atty. Mahaska County (Iowa), Oskaloosa, 1958-60; city atty. Elk Run Heights (Iowa), 1962—; 1st asst. city atty. Waterloo, 1974—. Pres., Broadway Theatre League NE Iowa, 1967-69, Waterloo Symphony Orch. Assn., 1970-72; chmn. Oskaloosa CSC, 1960-61. Mem. Iowa, Black Hawk County (pres. real estate, probate and trust sect. 1969), 1-B Jud. Dist. (pres. 1973) bar assns., Iowa Trial Lawyers Assn. Home: 857 Sunrise Blvd Waterloo IA 50701 Office: Suite 400 First Nat Bldg PO Box 2621 Waterloo IA 50705 Tel (319) 235-7975

KENNEDY, WILLIAM JOSEPH, b. New Hampton, Iowa, June 16, 1911; student Drake U., 1930; J.D., Notre Dame U., 1935. Admitted to Iowa bar, 1935; county atty. Chickasaw County (Iowa), 1937-40; city atty. New Hampton (Iowa), 1956-59, Lawler (Iowa), 1960-68; individual practice law, New Hampton, 1935—; sr. partner firm Kennedy and Kennedy, New Hampton, 1968—. Chmn. adv. bd. St. Joseph's Hosp., gen. chmn. fin. campaign, 1965. Mem. Iowa, Chickasaw County (pres. 1945), 13th Jud. Dist. (pres. 1948), Am. bar assns., Cath. Lawyers Guild for Archdiocese of Dubuque (pres. 1957). Office: Kennedy Law Bldg 12 E Main St New Hampton IA 50659 Tel (515) 394-2245

KENNEDY, WILLIAM MONROE, b. Texarkana, Tex., May 15, 1924; B.B.A., U. Tex., 1951, LL.B., 1950. Admitted to Texas bar, 1950; oil scout, Monsanto Co., Houston, 1951-53, landman, 1953-54, dist. landman, 1954-62, regional landman, 1962-76, land mgr., 1976-77; land mgr. ADA Resources, Inc., 1977—. Mem. Am. Assn. Petroleum Landmen (dir. 1975-76), Houston Assn. Petroleum Landmen (past pres.). Home: 5442 Imogene Houston TX 77096 Office: 6910 Fannin Houston TX 77001 Tel (713) 797-9966

KENNELLY, CLYDE BROWN, b. Brown, Tex., June 26, 1916; student Stanford U., 1943-44; B.A., U. Tex., 1938, LL.B., 1938; postgrad Baylor U., 1946. Admitted to Tex. bar, 1938; atty. Ft. Bend County (Tex.), 1941-42; asst. atty. gen. State of Tex., 1947-53, 58; judge Ft. Bend County, 1959-66; individual practice law, Richmond, Tex., 1967—; probate judge Ft. Bend County, 1959-66, juvenile judge, 1959-66; instr. bus. law Alvin Jr. Coll., 1957. Chmn. Fort Bend County chpt. ARC, 1955-62, Fort Bend County March of Dimes, 1959-66; mem. exec. bd. Baptist Gen. Conv. Tex., 1959-64; dist. chmn. local council Boy Scouts Am.; trustee Houston Baptist U. Mem. Tex., Ft. Bend County bar assns. Editor U. Tex. Law Rev., 1936-38. Home: 1027 Timberlane St Rosenberg TX 77471 Office: 512 6th St Richmond TX 77469 Tel (713) 342-4992

KENNER, HARRIS PALMER, b. Brinsmade, N.D., June 5, 1927; J.D., U.N.D., 1972. Admitted to N.D. bar, 1952; partner firm Waldron, Kenner & Halvorson, Minot, N.D., 1952—. Chmn. Fifth Dist. Republicans, First Lutheran Found. Mem. State Bar Assn. N.D., Am. Bar Assn., Am. Judicature Soc., Assn. Trial Lawyers Am. Office: 615 S Broadway Box 36 Minot ND 58701 Tel (701) 852-4118

KENNERSON, PAUL ROBERT, b. Rochester, N.Y., Apr. 26, 1941; B.A. summa cum laude, Georgetown U., 1963; LL.B., Yale, 1966. Admitted to N.Y. bar, 1966, Calif. bar, 1970, U.S. Supreme Ct. bar, 1972; legal officer, Miramar Naval Air Sta. USN, San Diego, 1967-69; asso. firm Welsh & Gibson (now Gibson & Kennerson), San Diego, 1969-72, partner, 1972—; asso. prof. U.S. Internat. Div., San Diego, 1969; lectr. legal malpractice; dir. Fed. State Appellate Defenders, 1973—. Author: Preventing Legal Malpractice: Katie, Bar the Door, or How to Keep the Wolf Away. Office: Gibson & Kennerson 1212 Home Tower 707 Broadway San Diego CA 92101 Tel (714) 236-1255

KENNETT, JOHN HOLLIDAY, JR., b. Atlanta, June 28, 1929; B.S. in Accounting, Va. Poly. Inst., 1951; LL.B., U. Va., 1954. Admitted to Va. bar, 1953; asso. firm Holman Willis, Roanoke, Va., 1954-60; individual practice law, Roanoke, 1961—. Mem. Am., Va., Roanoke bar assns., Roanoke Estate Planning Council (pres. 1961-62). Office: 133 Kirk Ave SW PO Box 255 Roanoke VA 24002 Tel (703) 345-0946

KENNEY, JAMES ALBERT, III, b. Salisbury, Md., Mar. 26, 1937; B.A., Dickinson Coll., 1959; postgrad. Yale Law Sch., 1959-60; J.D., George Washington U., 1963. Admitted to Md. bar, 1963, D.C. bar, 1964; law clk. Covington & Burlington, Washington, 1960-63; asso. firm Barco, Cook & Patton, Washington, 1963-64; individual practice law, Lexington Park, Md., 1964-66; partner firm Briscoe, Kenney & Kaminetz, and predecessors, Lexington Park, Leonardtown, Md., 1966—; asst. states atty. Md., 1964-67; vis. prof. law St. Marys Coll. Md., 1964—. Pres., St. Marys Bd. Library Trustees (Md.), 1966-77. Mem. Md. Bar Assn. (v.p. 1969-70), St. Marys County Bar Assn. (pres. 1967-68). Office: 1 Willows Circle Lexington Park MD 20653 Tel (301) 863-7054

KENNEY, JAMES FRANCIS, b. Bridgeport, Conn., June 29, 1921; A.B., Cath. U. Am., 1942; J.D., Georgetown U., 1949. Admitted to D.C. bar, 1949, Conn. bar, 1949, U.S. Supreme Ct. bar, 1953; sr. partner firm Clancy, Kenney & Scofield, Bridgeport, 1949—; welfare atty. City of Bridgeport, 1950-52, trial atty., 1952-58; mem. Jud. Council of Conn., 1957-73. Mem. Bridgeport Charter Revision Commn., 1966. Mem. Bridgeport, Am., Conn. bar assns., Internat. Assn. Ins. Counsel, Fedn. Ins. Counsel, Trial Attys. Am. Author: Guide for Medico-Legal Relations, 1957. Home: 27 Far Horizons Dr Easton CT 06612 Office: 955 Main St Bridgeport CT 06604 Tel (203) 366-5661

KENNEY, JAMES LEO, b. Brookline, Mass., June 5, 1916; A.B., Boston Coll., 1937, LL.B., 1940. Admitted to Mass. bar, 1941; individual practice law, Boston, 1941-66, Oak Bluffs, Mass., 1969—. Mem. Mass., Duke County (past pres.) bar assns., Boston Coll. Law Sch. Alumni Assn. (pres. 1951-52). Address: 45 Tuckernuck Ave Oak Bluffs MA 02557 Tel (617) 693-2161

KENNEY, RAYMOND JOSEPH, JR., b. Boston, Aug. 3, 1932; A.B cum laude, Boston Coll., 1953, J.D., 1958. Admitted to Mass. bar, 1958, U.S. Dist. Ct. bar, 1959, 1st Circuit Ct. of Appeals bar, 1969; mem. firm Martin, Magnuson, McCarthy & Kenney and predecessor firm, Boston, 1958—; instr. law Mass. Dept. Edn., Univ. Extension, 1958-60, Boston U., 1961-66. Mem. Winchester (Mass.) Fin. Com., 1967-70, chmn., 1970-71; moderator Town of Winchester, 1972-77; chmn. Mass. Jud. Nominating Commn., 1975-77; bd. dirs. Winchester chpt. ARC, 1968-71; corporator Winchester Savs. Bank, 1973—. Fellow Am. Coll. Trial Lawyers, Am., Mass. bar founds.; mem. Am., Mass. (pres. 1977-78), Middlesex, Lowell bar assns., Internat. Assn. Ins. Counsel. Author: Automobile Law, Mass. Practice Series (West). Asso. editor Mass. Law Quar., 1965-72, editor-in-chief, 1973-76. Home: 5 Sailsbury St Winchester MA 01890 Office: 73 Tremont St Boston MA 02108 Tel (617) 227-3240

KENNEY, SAMUEL FREELAND, b. Balt., Dec. 15, 1928; B.S., Mt. St. Mary's Coll., Emmitsburg, Md., 1951; LL.B., U. Md., 1957. Admitted to Md. bar, 1957; asso. firm Thomas F. Dempsey, Balt., 1961-65, firm Callanan, Goff, Moring & Callanan, Balt., 1966-69, firm Ehrhart & Kenney, Towson, Md., 1969-72; individual practice law, Towson, 1972—; trial magistrate Baltimore County, 1967-69. Mem. Baltimore County Bar Assn., Am. Arbitration Assn., Soc. Am. Mil. Engrs. Home: 24 Overbrook Rd Catonsville MD 21228 Office: 31 Allegheny Ave Towson MD 21204 Tel (301) 823-5500

KENNEY, THOMAS JAMES, b. Thompsonville, Conn., July 1, 1926; A.B., St. Michael's Coll., Vt., 1950; LL.B., Fordham U., 1954. Admitted to N.Y. bar, 1955, Vt. bar, 1959; asst. to pres. St. Michael's Coll., 1955-60, trustee, 1967—; individual practice law, Burlington, Vt., 1961—; sec. civil and mil. affairs, adminstrv. asst. to gov. State of Vt., 1963-66. Mem. Vt. Legis. Apportionment Bd., 1972-74. Mem. Am., Vt., Chittenden County bar assns., Nat. Assn. Coll. and Univ. Attys. Home: Main St Richmond VT 05477 Office: 200 Main St Burlington VT 05401 Tel (802) 864-5716

KENNEY, WILLIAM JOHN, b. Oklahoma City, June 16, 1904; A.B., Stanford, 1926; LL.B., Harvard U., 1929. Admitted to Calif. bar, 1929, D.C. bar, 1969; asso. firm Orrick, Palmer & Dahlquist, San Francisco, 1929-36; chief oil and gas unit SEC, Washington, 1936-38; indivdual practice law, Los Angeles, 1938-40; asst. gen. counsel U.S. Dept. Navy, Washington, 1941-44, gen. counsel, 1944-45; partner firm Sullivan, Shea & Kenney, Washington, 1952-70; partner firm Cox, Langford & Brown, Washington, 1970—; vice chief office procurement and material U.S. Dept. Navy, Washington, 1945-46, asst. sec. of Navy, 1946-47, undersec., 1947-49; minister-in-charge Marshall Plan Mission to U.K., 1949-51, dep. dir. mut. security, adminstr. Mut. Security Agy., Washington, 1952. Chmn. D.C. chpt. ARC, 1968-71; trustee, mem. exec. com. George C. Marshall Research Found., 1970—; mem. adv. council John Hopkins Sch. Advanced Internat. Studies. Mem. Am., D.C., Calif. bar assns. Home: 78 Kalorama Circle Washington DC 20008 Office: 21 Dupont Circle Washington DC 20036 Tel (202) 785-0200

KENNEY, WILLIAM RICHARDSON, b. Mineola, N.Y., Sept. 17, 1922; student U. Cin., 1941-43; LL.B. cum laude, U. Balt., 1950; grad. Air Command and Staff Coll., 1951, Nat. Coll. State Trial Judges, 1970. Admitted to Md. bar, 1950; legal officer USAF, 1950-73; pres. Fed. Bar Assn., 1975-76; chmn. bd. dirs. Potomac Sch. Law, 1975—; v.p. Mil. Law Inst., 1970—. Bd. dirs. Friendly Citizens Assn., 1975—. Mem. Am., Fed. (pres. St. Louis 1958-59, The Pentagon 1964-65, Anchorage, Alaska 1965-66, nat. exec. com. 1970—) bar assns., Nat. Conf. Fed. Trial Judges (chmn. com. mil. judges 1971-72), Judge Advocates Assn. (dir. 1962—), Air Force Assn., Nat. Lawyers Club. Editor legal jours. Home: 9207 Doris Dr Oxon Hill MD 20022 Office: 1815 H St NW Washington DC 20006 Tel (202) 638-0252

KENNON, WILLIAM REAMY, b. Douglas, Ariz., Oct. 11, 1948; A.B. in Polit. Sci., U. So. Calif., 1970, J.D., 1973. Admitted to Calif. bar, 1973; mem. firm Ingram, Baker & Griffiths, Covina, Calif., 1973—. Asso., Town Hall Calif., Los Angeles World Affairs Council. Mem. Am., Citrus County, Los Angeles County bar assns., Los Angeles Trial Lawyers Assn., Phi Alpha Delta.

KENRICK, CHARLES WILLIAM, b. Chgo., June 16, 1946; A.B. cum laude, Kenyon Coll., Gambier, Ohio, 1968; J.D., Duquesne U., Pitts., 1972. Admitted to Pa. bar, 1972; partner firm Dickie, McCamey & Chilcote, Pitts., 1977—. Mem. Am., Pa., Allegheny County bar assns. Office: 3180 US Steel Bldg Pittsburgh PA 15219 Tel (412) 281-7272

KENT, BRUCE WARD, b. Lincoln, Nebr., Dec. 15, 1943; B.S., Kans. State U., 1967; J.D., Washburn U., 1970; LL.M., U. Miami, 1973. Admitted to Kans. bar, 1970; prin., v.p., partner firm Ryan, Kent and Wichman, Hays, Kans., 1970—. Mem. Am., Kans. (exec. com. tax sect.) bar assns., Kans. Trial Lawyers Assn. (bd. govs'., exec. com.), Am. Judicature Soc. Contbr. articles to Washburn Jour., Kans. Trial Lawyers Jour., Kans. Bar Jour. Home: 224 Northridge Dr Hays KS 67601 Office: 201 W 11th St Hays KS 67601 Tel (913) 625-6519

KENT, ROBERT CUNNINGHAM, b. Jacksonville, Fla., Jan. 31, 1941; B.S. in Advt., U. Fla., 1962, B.S. in Journalism, 1963, J.D., 1967. Admitted to Fla. bar, 1968; asso. firm Clark & Franson, Jacksonville, Fla., 1968-70, Bryant, Dickens, Rumph, Franson & Miller, Jacksonville, 1970-72; prin. Robert C. Kent, P.A., Jacksonville, 1972—. Mem. alumni bd. dirs. U. Fla., 1967-73; v.p., mem. bd. dirs. Jacksonville Adult Devel. Centers Project, 1975—. Mem. Am., Fla., Jacksonville bar assns. Home: 1528 Cornell Rd Jacksonville FL 32207 Office: 1532 Atlantic Blvd Jacksonville FL 32207 Tel (904) 396-6623

KENYON, ARNOLD OAKLEY, JR., b. Ord, Nebr., June 29, 1926; student Grinnell Coll., 1943-44, Central Coll., Fayette, Mo., 1944-45, U. Notre Dame, 1945-46, U. Iowa Law Sch., 1948-50; LL.B., Drake U., 1949. Admitted to Iowa bar, 1950; asst. county atty. Union County, Iowa, 1951, county atty., 1952-55; individual practice law, Creston, Iowa, 1955—. Chmn. central com. Union County Republican Party, 1965-70; bd. dirs. Creston C. of C. Mem. Iowa Trial Lawyers Assn., Am., Union County (pres. 1974), State of Iowa bar assns. Home: 1209 N Oak St Creston IA 50801 Office: 100 E Montgomery St Creston IA 50801 Tel (515) 782-7064

KENYON, THOMAS GENE, b. Okmulgee, Okla., Feb. 7, 1927; LL.B., So. Meth. U., 1951. Admitted to Tex. bar, 1951; atty. City of Clute (Tex.), 1958-62; judge City of Freeport (Tex.), 1959-62, Domestic Relations Ct. Brazoria County (Tex.), Angleton, 1973—; dist. atty., 1963-66. Pres. bd. dirs. Brazoria County Youth Homes, Inc., 1967-75. Mem. Brazoria County Bar Assn. (pres. 1968), State Bar Tex. Home: Route 2 Box 35 Freeport TX 77541 Office: Brazoria County Courthouse Angleton TX 77515 Tel (713) 849-5001

KENYON, WILLIAM RANDALL, b. Rochester, N.Y., July 30, 1943; B.A., U. Rochester, 1965; LL.B., Syracuse U., 1967. Admitted to N.Y. bar, 1967; since practiced in Rochester, asso. firm Culley, Marks, Corbett, Jordan, Tenenbaum & Reifsteck, 1967-68; asso. firm Forsyth, Howe, O'Dwyer & Kenyon, and predecessor, 1968-72, partner, 1972—. Pres., Sr. Adult Housing and Recreation in Ogden, Presbyn. Ch., 1970-71, ruling elder, 1975-76. Mem. N.Y. State, Monroe County bar assns., Justinian Hon. Law Soc., Spencerport Jaycees (pres. 1968-69). Home: 59 Morningside Dr Spencerport NY 14559 Office: 950 Midtown Tower Rochester NY 14604 Tel (716) 325-7515

KEPLINGER, MICHAEL SCOTT, b. Martinsburg, W.Va., July 26, 1940; B.S. in Chemistry, W.Va. U., 1963; J.D., Georgetown U., 1971. Admitted to Md. bar, 1972; computer specialist Nat. Bur. Standards, Inst. for Computer Scis. and Tech., Washington, 1967-76; asst. exec. dir., sr. atty. Nat. Commn. on New Tech. Uses of Copyrighted Works, Washington, 1976—; research advisor com. on automation opportunities in service areas Fed. Council on Sci. and Tech., Office Sci. and Tech., Washington, 1971-74; mem. coms. Nat. Standards Inst., 1970-77. Mem. Am. Soc. Info. Sci. (chmn. com. on proprietary use and rights 1973-74), Am., Md. bar assns., Computer Law Assn. (bd. dirs. 1973-76). Contbr. articles to profl. jours. Home: 5905 Wilmett Rd Bethesda MD 20034 Office: Nat Commn New Tech Uses of Copyrighted Works Washington DC 20558 Tel (202) 557-0996

KEPPELER, H(ERBERT) K(ARL) BRUSS, b. Honolulu, Jan. 13, 1937; B.A., U. Wash., 1959, J.D., 1966. Admitted to Hawaii bar, 1966, U.S. Supreme Ct. bar, 1972; dep. atty. gen. State of Hawaii, Honolulu, 1966-69, asst. hwy. safety coordinator, 1969-71; atty. Dillingham Corp., Honolulu, 1971-75; v.p., counsel, sec. Hawaii Corp., Honolulu, 1975-76; individual practice law, Honolulu, 1976—; bd. dirs. Legal Aid Soc. Hawaii, 1971-72; vice chmn. Hawaii Pub. Defender Council, 1976—. Bd. dirs. Hawaiian Scholars Program, 1974—, Moanalua Gardens Found., Inc., Honolulu, 1975—, Aloha Week Hawaii, Inc., 1977—. Mem. Hawaii State, Am. bar assns., Hawaiian Businessmen's Assn., Phi Delta Phi. Home: 307 Elelupe Rd Honolulu HI 96821 Office: 33 S King St Suite 223 Honolulu HI 96813 Tel (808) 533-6294

KEPPLER, ERNEST CARL, b. Sheboygan, Wis., Apr. 5, 1918; B.A. in Politics and Govt., U. Wis., Madison, 1949, J.D., 1950. Admitted to Wis. bar, 1950; individual practice law, Sheboygan, 1950—; asst. dist. atty., Sheboygan, 1953-54. Scoutmaster, explorer adviser Kettle Moraine council Boy Scouts Am., 1930—; dir. Civil Defense, Sheboygan County, Wis., 1956-61; alderman City of Sheboygan, 1941-45, 51-53; mem. Wis. State Assembly, 1943-45; mem. Wis. Senate, 1961—, senate majority leader, 1969-73, v.p. senate, 1973-75. Recipient Eagle Scout award Boy Scouts Am., 1935, Silver Beaver award, 1960, Distinguished Eagle Scout award, 1969. Home and Office: 909 New York Ave Sheboygan WI 53081 Tel (414) 457-7794

KERBY, JAMES BILLY, b. Dew, Tex., Feb. 4, 1932; B.A. in Govt., N. Tex. State Coll., 1957, postgrad. So. Meth. U. Law Sch., 1963-67. Admitted to Tex. bar, 1967; claims adjuster Tex. Employers Ins., Fort, 1957-59, Pacific Employers Ins. Co., Dallas, 1960; claims examiner Nat. Auto and Casualty Ins. Co., Dallas, 1961-62; claims examiner Argonaut Ins. Co., Dallas, 1963-68. Mem. Tex., Garland bar assns. Office: 1530 W Kingsley Garland TX 75041 Tel (214) 278-7655

KERIAN, JON ROBERT, b. Grafton, N.D., Oct. 23, 1927; Ph.B., U. N.D., 1955, J.D., 1957. Admitted to N.D. bar, 1957, U.S. Supreme Ct. bar, 1963; individual practice law, Grand Forks, N.D., 1958-61; asst. atty. gen. State of N.D., 1961-67; partner firm Bosard, McCutcheon, Kerian, Schmidt & Holum, Ltd., Minot, N.D., 1968—; instr. Bismarck Jr. Coll., 1965-67; asst. city atty. City of Minot, 1968-76; atty. Minot Planning Commn., 1968-76. Mem. N.D. (exec. com. 1975), 5th Jud. Dist. (pres. 1975) bar assns. Contbr. articles to profl. jours. Home: 1800 8th St SW Minot ND 58701 Office: 200 Heritage Pl Minot ND 58701 Tel (701) 852-3578

KERIG, DWAN VINCENT, b. Balt., Sept. 10, 1924; student Tex. A. and M. U., 1942-43, 46-48; LL.B., U. Tex., 1950; M.A., Fletcher Sch., Tufts U., 1961. Admitted to Tex. bar, 1950; commd. 1st lt. JAGC, U.S. Army, 1950, advanced through grades to lt. col., 1965; ret., 1967; prof. law U. San Diego, 1967—. Named Most Outstanding Prof., U. San Diego Law Sch., 1970, 71, U. San Diego, 1976. Office: U San Diego Law Sch Alcala Park San Diego CA 92110 Tel (714) 291-6480 X 346

KERLIN, GILBERT, b. Camden, N.J., Oct. 10, 1909; student Grenoble (France) U., 1929; B.A., Harvard, 1933, LL.B., 1936; postgrad. Trinity Coll., Cambridge, Eng., 1933. Admitted to N.Y. bar, 1938, U.S. Supreme Ct. bar, 1945; asso. firm Shearman & Sterling, N.Y.C., 1936-42, 46-51, partner, 1951—; dir., officer numerous cos. Mem. French C. of C. in the U.S. (councillor), Riverdale Community Planning Assn. (dir.), Wave Hill Inc. (chmn., dir.), Expt. in Internat. Living (counsel). Home: 700 W 247th St Riverdale NY 10471 Office: 53 Wall St New York City NY 10005 Tel (212) 483-1000

KERN, WILLIAM FRANCIS, b. Springfield, Mass., July 17, 1940; B.A., St. Michael's Coll., Vt., 1961; J.D., Western New Eng. Law Sch., 1969. Admitted to Mass. bar, 1972, Fed. Dist. Ct. Mass. bar, 1972; dean of men, lectr. bus. law St. Michael's Coll., 1969-70; supr. drug edn. Mass. Dept. Edn., 1971-77; individual practice law, Springfield, 1972—. Pres. Group Homes, Inc., Springfield, 1967-69; mem. Springfield Juvenile Delinquency Commn., 1965-69. Mem. Am., Mass., Hampden County bar assns. Home: 60 Lake Dr PO Box 305 Indian Orchard Springfield MA 01151 Office: 31 Elm St Springfield MA 01103 Tel (413) 732-5802

KERNOCHAN, JOHN MARSHALL, b. N.Y.C., Aug. 3, 1919; A.B., Harvard, 1942; J.D., Columbia, 1948. Admitted to N.Y. bar, 1949, U.S. Dist. Ct. So. N.Y. bar, 1950; asst. dir. Legis. Drafting Research Fund Columbia, 1950-51, acting dir., 1951-52, dir., 1952-69, lectr. law, 1951-52, asso. prof., 1952-55, prof., 1955—; exec. dir. Council for Atomic Age Studies, Columbia, 1956-59, co-chmn., 1960-62; chmn. bd. Galaxy Music Corp. Mem. civil and polit. rights com. Pres.'s Commn. on Status Women, 1962-63; con. Temporary State Commn. to study Organizational Structure Govt. N.Y.C., 1953. Bd. dirs. Vol. Lawyers for the Arts. Mem. Assn. Bar City of N.Y. Contbr. articles in field to profl. jours. and textbooks. Home: 16 Highgate Rd Riverside CT 06878 Office: Columbia Univ 435 W 116th St New York City NY 10027 Tel (212) 280-3146

KERR, ANDREW PHILIP, b. Fresno, Calif., May 4, 1944; A.B., Dartmouth, 1966; J.D., Willamette U., 1969. Admitted to Oreg. bar, 1969; asso. firm White, Sutherland & Gilbertson, Portland, Oreg., 1969-72; partner firm Gilbertson, Brownstein, Sweeney & Kerr, Portland, 1973—. Mem. adv. commn. Pittock Mansion, Portland, 1970-76, chmn., 1974-76; bd. dirs. Portland Civic Theatre, 1974-76, Urban League Portland, 1974—. Mem. Am., Multnomah County bar assns., Oreg. Securities Law Assn. Contbg. author: Land Use, 1976. Office: 522 S W 5th St Portland OR 97204 Tel (503) 221-1772

KERR, DAVID KENNETH, b. Wichita, Kans., June 6, 1942; A.B., Knox Coll., 1964; J.D., U. Denver, 1967. Admitted to Colo. bar, 1967; asso. Weller, Friedrich, Hickisch & Hazlitt, 1967-73, partner, 1974—. Mem. Denver, Colo., Am. bar assns. Recipient Order of St. Ives, 1967. Home: 641 S Monroe Way Denver CO 80209 Office: 900 Capitol Life Center Denver CO 80203 Tel (303) 861-8000

KERR, EDMUND HUGH, b. Pitts., Nov. 27, 1924; A.B., Stanford, 1949, LL.B., 1951. Admitted to N.Y. bar, 1952, U.S. Dist. Ct. for So. Dist. N.Y. bar, 1954, U.S. Ct. Appeals for 2d Circuit bar, 1954, U.S. Supreme Ct. bar, 1975, U.S. Tax Ct. bar, 1976; asso. firm Cleary, Gottlieb, Steen & Hamilton, N.Y.C., 1951-62, partner, 1962—; dir. Franklin Custodian Funds, Inc., San Mateo, Calif. Mem. Am., N.Y., Fed. bar assns., N.Y. County Lawyers Assn., Assn. Bar City N.Y., Order of Coif. Contbr. articles to legal jours. Home: Cedar Hill Greenwich CT 06830 Office: 1 State St Plaza New York City NY 10004 Tel (212) 344-0600

KERR, HAWLEY COE, b. Tulsa, Nov. 12, 1901; A.B., Tulsa U., 1922; LL.B., Okla. U., 1925. Admitted to Okla. bar, 1925, U.S. Ct. Appeals 10th Circuit bar, 1944, U.S. Supreme Ct. bar, 1949; practiced in Tulsa, 1925—; individual practice law, 1925-37, staff Skelly Oil Co., 1937-51, gen. atty., 1951-60, gen. counsel, corp. sec., 1960-66, cons., 1967-69; asso. firm Ungerman, Grabel & Ungerman. Mem. Am., Okla., Tulsa County bar assns. Lectr. law Tulsa U., 1937-42. Home: 3153 S Utica Tulsa OK 74105 Office: 6th Floor Wright Bldg Tulsa OK 74103 Tel (918) 584-6101

KERR, JOHN GRINHAM, b. N.Y.C., Nov. 15, 1931; A.B. cum laude, Harvard, 1952; J.D., U. Calif., Los Angeles, 1969. Admitted to Calif. bar, 1970; research clk. firms O'Melveny & Myers, Los Angeles, 1967, Munger, Tolles, Hills & Rickershauser, Los Angeles, 1968-70; asso. firm Tyre & Kammins, Los Angeles, 1970-72; individual practice law, Los Angeles, 1972—; of counsel firms Richard P. Nahrwold, Los Angeles, 1973—, Axelrad, Sevilla and Ross, Los Angeles, 1973—; dir. Screen Actors Guild, 1977—. Mem. Order of Coif. Office: 606 S Olive St Suite 1414 Los Angeles CA 90014 Tel (213) 627-2131

KERR, MARY BROCK, b. Atlanta, Aug. 28, 1943; A.B. in Econs., U. Miami (Fla.), 1964; J.D., Emory U., 1967. Admitted to Ga. bar, 1968; asso. firm Gary Bach Kerr & Norman, Mableton, Ga., 1970—; mem. staff, records land div. U.S. Forest Service, 1967, 68. Mem. Am., Ga., Cobb County (Ga.) bar assns., Ga. Women Lawyers Assn., Ga. Trial Lawyers Assn. Recipient litigation award Emory U., 1967. Home: 1780 Ridgewood Dr NE Atlanta GA 30307 Office: 511 Bankhead Hwy Mableton GA 30059 Tel (404) 941-8890

KERR, THOMAS ROCKWELL, b. Pasadena, Calif., Mar. 10, 1929; A.B., U. N.C., 1951; LL.B., Yale, 1954. Admitted to Calif. bar, 1955; asso. firm Derby Cook Quinby & Tweedt, San Francisco, 1959-64; partner firm Silver Rosen & Kerr, San Francisco, 1964-68; asst. prof. rhetoric U. Calif., Berkeley, 1968-72; asso. prof. law Hastings Coll. Law, 1972—. Mem. Calif. State Bar. Home: 3332 Las Huertas Rd Lafayette CA 94549 Office: 198 McAllister St San Francisco CA 94102 Tel (415) 557-3004

KERSCHNER, ELLEN JAY, b. Chgo., June 7, 1947; B.A., U. Ill., 1968, J.D., 1971. Admitted to Ill. bar, 1971, U.S. Supreme Ct. bar, 1974; law clk. Ill. Appellate Ct., Chgo., 1971-73; asso. firm Peterson, Ross, Rall, Barber & Seidel, Chgo., 1973—. Mem. Ill., Chgo. bar assns., Bar Assn. 7th Fed. Circuit. Home: 9422 Harding Evanston IL 60203 Office: 135 S LaSalle St Chicago IL 60603 Tel (312) 263-7300

KERSEY, GEORGE EUCLID, b. Pueblo, Colo., Apr. 3, 1927; LL.B., Harvard, 1959; B.S., U. Colo., 1952; M.S., Mass. Inst. Tech., 1956. Admitted to N.Y. bar, 1960, N.J. bar, 1963, U.S. Supreme Ct. bar, 1964, Mass. bar, 1966; patent atty. Bell Telephone Labs., Inc., 1959-66; with firm Porzio, Bromberg & Newman, Morristown, N.J., 1964-66, Dike, Thompson & Bronstein, Boston, 1966-68; patent contract and internat. patent atty. Western Electric Co., Inc., N.Y.C., 1968-72; with firm Woodward, Kersey & Kojima, N.Y.C., 1972-73; indsl. property cons. Kersey & Assos., Annandale, N.J., 1973—. Mem. Am., N.Y. State, N.J. bar assns., N.Y., Boston patent law assns., N.Y. County Lawyers Assn. Rotary Found. fellow, 1952-53; Tripos honors in Mech. Scis., Cambridge (Eng.) U., 1953; patentee in elec. field. Home: Allerton Rd Annandale NJ 08801 Office: PO Box 126 Annandale NJ 08801 Tel (201) 735-4470

KERSHNER, WILLIAM FRANKLIN, b. Allentown, Pa., May 14, 1939; B.A., Pa. State U., 1961; J.D., U. S.C., 1968. Admitted to Pa. bar, 1969; labor atty. Bethlehem Steel Corp. (Pa.), 1968-71; mem. firm Morgan, Lewis & Bockius, Phila. and Harrisburg, Pa., 1971—. Mem. Am., Pa., Lehigh County, Phila., Dauphin County bar assns. Home: 1556 Temple Dr Maple Glen PA 19109 Office: 123 S Broad St Philadelphia PA 19109 Tel (215) 491-9373 also 800 N 3d St Harrisburg PA 17102 Tel (717) 238-1780

KERSKER, PETER WHEELER, b. St. Petersburg, Fla., Dec. 27, 1942; B.A., Johns Hopkins U., 1965; J.D., Tulane U., 1968. Admitted to Fla. bar, 1969, U.S. Supreme Ct. bar, 1973; individual practice law, St. Petersburg, 1970—; owner Bucs Weekly football newspaper, Tampa, Fla.; dir. Peter's Place café, St. Petersburg. Bd. dirs. Fla. Gulf Coast Symphony, St. Petersburg, 1973-74, St. Petersburg Opera Co., 1976—, San Carlo Opera, St. Petersburg. Mem. Fla. Bar, St. Petersburg Bar Assn. Office: 210 Beach Dr NE Saint Petersburg FL 33701 Tel (813) 898-1543

KERSTEN, JOHN CHARLES, b. Richmond, Va., Dec. 14, 1940; B.A., U. Miami, 1962, J.D., 1965. Admitted to Fla. bar, 1965, U.S. Supreme Ct. bar, 1971; partner firm Sheffey & Kersten, Ft. Lauderdale, Fla., 1965-67, firm Duffy, Sladon & Kersten, 1968-70, Friedrich, Kersten, Blackwell & Mikos, 1971—; asst. city atty. Ft. Lauderdale, 1967. Bd. dirs. Opera Guild of Ft. Lauderdale, 1974—. Mem. Am., Fla., Broward County bar assns., Am., Broward County trial lawyers assns., Acad. Fla. Trial Lawyers. Office: 2851 E Oakland Park Blvd Fort Lauderdale FL 33306

KERXTON, ALAN SMITH, b. Balt., Mar. 19, 1938; B.A., Ohio State U., 1960, J.D., 1962. Admitted to Ohio bar, 1962, D.C. bar, 1964, Md. bar, 1966; atty., br. corporate reorgn. SEC, 1963-66; prin. firm Greenbaum & Kerxton, Washington, 1966-76, firm Levitan, Ezrin, Cramer, West & Weinstein, Washington, 1976—; lectr. creditors rights and bankruptcy law Cath. U., 1973. Mem. D.C., Am., Montgomery County bar assns. Office: Suite 1400 5454 Wisconsin Ave Washington DC 20015 Tel (301) 656-0915

KESLER, JOHN A., b. Marshall, Ill., Apr. 25, 1923; A.B., Ind. U., 1948, J.D., 1951. Admitted to Ind. bar, 1951, Ill. bar, 1951; individual practice law, Marshall and Terre Haute, Ind., 1951—; chief dep. prosecutor Vigo County (Ind.), 1954-58; probate commr. Vigo Circuit Ct., 1971-74; mem. Ind. Ho. of Reps., 1969-73. Bd. dirs. West Vigo Community Center. Mem. Am., Ind. State, Terre Haute bar assns., Am. Trial Lawyers Assn. Recipient Good govt. award Terre Haute Jaycees, 1957, West Vigo Jaycees, 1971. Home: Rural Route 15 PO Box 177 West Terre Haute IN 47885 Office: 505 Ohio St Terre Haute IN 47807 Tel (812) 235-1255

KESLER, MORTON ALLEN, b. Balt., Apr. 29, 1935; LL.B., U. Md., 1959, B.S., Loyola Coll., Balt., 1956. Admitted to Md. bar, 1959, Fla. bar, 1965; estate tax atty. IRS, Balt., 1959-64; law clk. to chief judge U.S. Dist. Ct., Middle Dist. Fla., 1964-65; asst. state atty., Duval County, Fla., 1965-68, judge county ct., 1973—; partner firm Gutman & Kesler, Jacksonville, Fla., 1969-72. Chmn. Air Pollution Control Bd. Jacksonville, Fla., 1969-72; chmn. Fla. Council Clean Air, 1973—; mem. bd. dirs. Fla. Lung Assn., 1972—. Mem. Jacksonville, Fla. bar assns. Home: 9920 Cove View Dr E Jacksonville FL 32217 Office: 332 Duval County Courthouse Jacksonville FL 32202 Tel (904) 633-2574

KESSEL, OLIVER DENNIS, b. Ripley, W.Va., Jan. 12, 1901; A.B., W.Va. U., 1924, J.D., 1928. Admitted to W.Va. bar, 1928; individual practice law, Ripley, 1928-29, 32-52, 53-56, 72—; pros. atty. Jackson County, W.Va., 1929-32; judge Circuit Ct., 5th Jud. Circuit, W.Va., 1956-71; justice Supreme Ct. Appeals W.Va., 1972; mayor City of Ripley, 1952-53; participant Gov's Com. Crime, Delinquency and Correction, Active Jackson County Devel. Assn., Jackson County Bldg Commn., Mid-Ohio Valley Assn. Mem. W.Va. Jud. Assn. (pres. 1967-68). Home: 213 Charleston Dr Ripley WV 25271 Office: 220 W Main St Ripley WV 25271 Tel (304) 372-3872

KESSLER, ALAN BURTON, b. Mineola, N.Y., Dec. 1, 1925; J.D., U. Miami (Fla.), 1949. Admitted to Fla. bar, 1949; partner firm Wienkle and Kessler, Miami, 1949-66, Coral Gables, Fla., 1966—. Pres. Temple Beth Am., Miami, 1966-68. Mem. Union Am. Hebrew Congregations (pres. SE council 1972-76, nat. bd. trustees 1968—, exec. com. 1968—, pres. South Fla. Fedn. 1968-72), B'nai Brith. Recipient Hall of Fame award Hospitality Mag., 1968; Tower of David award State of Israel Bonds, 1969; Distinguished Jewish Service award Hebrew Union Coll., 1976. Home: 6747 SW 122 Dr Miami FL 33156 Office: 299 Alhambra Circle Suite 518 Coral Gables FL 33134 Tel (305) 445-8881

KESSLER, DOUGLAS WILSON, b. Atlanta, Jan. 10, 1948; B.A., cum laude, Harvard, 1970; J.D. cum laude, N.Y.U., 1973. Admitted to Ga. bar, 1973; asso. firm Swift, Currie, McGhee & Hiers, Atlanta, 1973—. Mem. Am., Atlanta bar assns. Home: 3201 Rilman Rd Atlanta GA 30327 Office: 771 Spring St NW Atlanta GA 30308 Tel (404) 881-0844

KESSLER, EVA DIANNE, b. Urbana, Ohio, June 15, 1948; B.A. in Bus. Adminstrn., Bowling Green State U., 1970; J.D., U. Cin., 1973. Admitted to Ohio bar, 1973; mgmt. trainee Gen. Electric Co., Cin., 1973-75; individual practice law, Hamilton, Ohio, 1975—; instr. econs. and bus. law So. Ohio Coll., 1976—. Mem. Ohio, Butler County, Hamilton County bar assns. Home: 2904 Pleasant Ave Hamilton OH 45015 Office: 220 High St Hamilton OH 45011 Tel (513) 868-3988

KESSLER, FREDERICK PHILLIP, b. Milw., Jan. 11, 1940; B.S., U. Wis., 1962, LL.B., 1966. Admitted to Wis. bar, 1966; individual practice law, Milw., 1966-72; judge Milw. County Ct., 1972—; mem. Wis. Assembly, 1960-62, 64-72, chmn. elections com., 1971. Bd. dirs. Wis. Civil Liberties Union, 1969-72, Milw. chpt. ACLU, 1969-72, Neighborhood House Milw., 1969—; Wis. Council on Alcoholism, Milw., 1974—. Wis. Correctional Assn., Milw., 1972-75. Mem. Am. (exec. bd. conf. spl. ct. judges, com. on alcoholism and drug abuse), Wis., Milw. Jr. bar assns. Contbr. article to Wis. Bar Bull. Home: 2913 N Sheppard St Milwaukee WI 53211 Office: Courthouse Room 409 Milwaukee WI 53233 Tel (414) 278-4554

KESSLER, HENRY CHARLES, b. York, Pa., June 20, 1914; A.B., Cath. U. Am., 1935, J.D., 1937. Admitted to Pa. bar, 1941, Pa. Supreme Ct. and Pa. Superior Ct. bars, 1941, U.S. Supreme Ct. bar, 1952, also Fed. Dist. ct., U.S. Circuit Ct. Appeals; individual practice law, York, 1941—; v.p., sec., dir., gen. counsel Candy Mfg. Corp., York, 1941-64; asso. prof. law York Coll. of Pa., 1968—, asso. prof. dept. bus. adminstrn., 1968—; law librarian York County, 1939-42; legal counsel York County Recorder of Deeds, 1951-54, county controller, 1958-65. Chmn., York Mayor's Inter-Racial Commn., 1942; 1st chmn. fund raising dr. Cerebral Palsy, 1948; pres., v.p., bd. dirs. York Community Baseball Club, 1942-65; gen. chmn. Armed Forces Observance, York, 1950-56. Mem. Pa., York County (past sec.) bar assns., Am. Soc. Bus. Law Profs., Cath. U. Law Sch. Alumni Assn. (nat. v.p. 1950). Author: Barrister at Ease, 1966; Life and Love of Judge Mooney, 1976. Contbr. articles to legal jours. Office: 101 E Philadelphia St York PA 17401 Tel (717) 854-5594

KESSLER, HENRY MICHAEL, b. N.Y.C., June 2, 1910; B.B.A., St. John's U., 1934, LL.B., 1936, J.S.D., 1937. Admitted to N.Y. bar, 1938; partner firm Zahler & Kessler, C.P.A.'s, N.Y.C., 1970—. Mem. Am., N.Y. socs. C.P.A.'s. Office: 450 7th Ave New York City NY 10001 Tel (212) PE6-2220

KESSLER, MURIEL SELMA, b. Bklyn., July 31, 1925; A.B., Hunter Coll., 1945; LL.B., Cornell U., 1948. Admitted to N.Y. bar, 1948; partner firm Kessler & Kessler, N.Y.C., 1949—; instr. in adult edn. law Bronx Community Coll., 1975; hearing officer N.Y.C. Dept. Motor Vehicles; adjudicator State of N.Y. Dept. Motor Vehicles Appeals Board; arbitrator Bronx Civil Ct. Compulsory Arbitration Program. Co-pres. sisterhood Riverdale Jewish Center, Bronx, N.Y.; mem. exec. com. Riverdale Democratic Club; mem. exec. bd. United Jewish Appeal of Greater N.Y., Inc. Mem. Bronx Women's Bar Assn. (pres. 1971-73), Bronx County (dir.), N.Y. State bar assns., New York County Lawyers (chmn. joint bar assn. screening com. for parking violations bur. N.Y.C.). Recipient Silver Jubilee award United Jewish Appeal Bronx Lawyers' Div., 1973. Tel (212) 986-0960

KESSLER, WILLIAM EDMOND, b. Jacksonville, Fla., Aug. 24, 1929; B.A., Ohio State U., 1957, LL.B., 1959, J.D., 1959. Admitted to Ohio bar, 1959; practice in Tipp City, Ohio, 1959-73, 75; judge Miami County (Ohio) Common Pleas Ct., 1973-74, Municipal Ct., Troy, Ohio, 1976—; prosecutor Miami County, 1965-69. Office: Courthouse W Main St Troy OH 45373 Tel (513) 335-8341

KESTER, RANDALL BLAIR, b. Vale, Oreg., Oct. 20, 1916; A.B., Willamette U., 1937; J.D., Columbia, 1940. Admitted to Oreg. bar, 1940, U.S. Supreme Ct. bar, 1960; asso. firm Maguire, Shields and Morrison, Portland, Oreg., 1940-51, partner Maguire, Shields, Morrison and Bailey, 1951-56, Maguire, Shields, Morrison, Bailey and Kester, 1958-65, Maguire, Kester and Cosgrave, 1966-71, Cosgrave and Kester, 1972—; asso. justice Oreg. Supreme Ct., 1957-58; gen. solicitor Union Pacific R.R. Co., 1958—; instr. Northwestern Coll. Law, 1947-56; mem. legis. interim com. on jud. adminstrn., 1957-58, Jud. Council Oreg., 1970-71. Pres. Portland C. of C., 1973, chmn. bd., 1974. Mem. Multnomah (pres. 1956), Am. bar assns., Oreg. State Bar (treas. 1965-66), Am. Law Inst., Inst. Jud. Adminstrn., Nat. Assn. R.R. Trial Counsel. Recipient Silver Beaver award Boy Scouts Am., 1956; contbr. articles to legal jours. Home: 10075 S W Hawthorne Ln Portland OR 97225 Office: 628 Pittock Block Portland OR 97205 Tel (503) 288-8221

KETCHAM, CHESTER SAWYER, b. Salisbury, Vt., Dec. 6, 1927; B.A., U. Vt., 1951; LL.B., Yale U., 1954. Admitted to Vt. bar, 1954, U.S. Supreme Ct. bar, 1964; law clk. to judge U.S. Dist. Ct., 1954-55; asso. firm Edmond Austin Wick, 1955-62; dep. atty. gen. State of Vt., 1963-65; partner firm Lynch, Ketcham and Foley, and predecessor, Middlebury, Vt., 1966-76; individual practice law, Middlebury, 1976—; mem. Vt. Gen. Assembly, 1974—. Mem. Am., Vt. (bd. mgrs. 1972—) bar assns. Home: Painter Hill Rd Middlebury VT 05753 Office: Box 724 70 Court St Middlebury VT 05753 Tel (802) 388-6353

KETCHAM, ORMAN WESTON, b. Bklyn., Oct. 1, 1918; B.A., Princeton, 1940; LL.B., Yale, 1947, J.D., 1971. Admitted to D.C. bar, 1948, U.S. Supreme Ct. bar, 1952; asso. firm Covington & Burling, Washington, 1947-52; Washington rep. Fund for the Republic, 1953; asst. gen. counsel FOA, Washington, 1953-55; trial atty. antitrust div. Dept. Justice, Washington, 1955-57; judge Juvenile Ct. of D.C., 1957-71, Superior Ct. of D.C., 1971—; adj. prof. law Georgetown U., 1963-67, U. Va., 1970—; faculty Salzburg (Austria) Seminar in Am. Legal Studies, 1976; U.S. del. UN Congress on Crime, Stockholm, 1965, Geneva, 1975; exec. com., bd. dirs. Nat. Council on Crime and Delinquency. Mem. Am. Bar Assn., D.C. Bar, Bar Assn. D.C., Am. Law Inst., Am. Judicature Soc., Nat. Council Juvenile Ct. Judges (pres. 1965-66), Internat. Assn. Youth Magistrates (exec. v.p. 1966-74). Recipient Distinguished Community Service award Princeton Club of Washington, 1972; author: (with others) Justice for the Child, 1962; (With M. Paulsen) Juvenile Court Cases & Materials, 1967. Home: Two E Melrose St Chevy Chase MD 20015 Office:

Superior Ct of DC 410 E St NW Washington DC 20001 Tel (202) 727-1090

KETTLER, CHARLES JOSEPH, JR., b. Luverne, Ala., July 15, 1933; B.A., U. Ala., 1954, LL.B., 1958. Admitted to Ala. bar, 1958, U.S. Supreme Ct. bar, 1973; partner firm Turner & Kettler, Luverne, 1959-63, partner firm Kettler & Kettler, Luverne, 1964-66; individual practice law, Luverne, 1967—; city recorder Luverne, 1965-74; judge Equity Ct. Crenshaw County (Ala.), 1974—. Vice pres. Ala. Pvt. Sch. Assn., 1973—. Mem. Ala., Crenshaw County bar assns. Home: 501 E First St Luverne AL 36049 Office: Glenwood & 4th Sts Luverne AL 36049 Tel (205) 335-3262

KEVAN, JAMES LAWRENCE, b. Twin Falls, Idaho, Sept. 21, 1947; B.S., U. Idaho, 1969, J.D., 1972. Admitted to Idaho bar, 1973; dep. pros. atty. Elmore County (Idaho), Mountain Home, 1972-73; partner firm Hicks & Kevan, Mountain Home, 1973—. Mem. Idaho, Boise, Elmore bar assns. Office: 220 American Legion Blvd Mountain Home ID 83647 Tel (208) 587-3376

KEYES, GEORGE PETER, b. Bklyn., Jan. 18, 1936; A.B., U. Notre Dame, 1957; J.D., Columbia, 1960. Admitted to N.Y. State bar, 1962; since practiced in Binghamton, N.Y.; asso. firm Coughlin, Dermody & Guy, 1962, Levene, Gouldin & Thompson, 1962-67, partner firm, 1967—; lectr. assns., citizens' groups. Mem. N.Y. State (ins. negligence and compensation law sec., com. on legis.), Broome County bar assns. Home: 46 Matthews St Binghamton NY 13905 Office: 902 Press Bldg Binghamton NY 13902 Tel (607) 772-9200

KEYES, HENRY WILDER, b. Haverhill, N.H., Mar. 22, 1905; A.B., Harvard, 1926, LL.B., J.D., 1930; postgrad. Episcopal Theol. Sch., Cambridge, Mass., 1962-63. Admitted to Mass. bar, 1930, N.H. bar, 1933, U.S. Supreme Ct. bar, 1935; asso. Boston Legal Aid Soc., 1929, firm Sherburne, Powers & Needham, Boston, 1930-50; asso. firm Spencer & Stone and predecessor, Boston, 1950-59, partner, 1960—; v.p. Woodsville Nat. Bank (N.H.), 1939-58, 75—, pres. 1959-75; v.p., dir. Lafayette Nat. Bank, 1975-77, emeritus, 1977—; v.p. Mass. Title Ins. Co., 1953-65, pres., 1965—, also dir.; asst. sec. First Am. Title Ins. Co. N.Y., 1976—. Mem. Newton (Mass.) Sch. Com., 1950-57, chmn., 1954-57. Mem. Mass., N.H., Boston (exec. sec. 1946, council 1955-58) bar assns., Mass. Conveyancers Assn., Am., New Eng. (pres. 1972) land title assns., New Eng. Law Inst. Contbr. articles to profl. jours. Home: 40 Puddingstone Ln Newton Center MA 02159 Office: 50 Beacon St Boston MA 02108 Tel (617) 227-3410

KEYES, LEONARD JOHN, b. Mpls., June 4, 1922; B.A., U. Minn., 1942; J.D., Harvard, 1948. Admitted to Minn. bar, 1948; asso. firm Otis, Fariey & Burger, St. Paul, 1948-53; partner firm Allen, Courtney & Keyes, St. Paul, 1954-57; municipal judge City of St. Paul, 1957-61; dist. judge Minn., 1961-70; partner firm Briggs & Morgan, St. Paul, 1970—; chmn. Minn. Gov's. Com. on Crime Prevention Control, 1972-75, Minn. Gov's. Com. on Prison Security, 1972. Fellow Am. Bar Found.; mem. Am. (ho. of dels.), Ramsey County (past pres.) bar assns., Phi Beta Kappa. Home: 1869 Eagle Ridge Dr Saint Paul MN 55118 Office: W-2200 1st Nat Bank Bldg Saint Paul MN 55101 Tel (612) 291-1215

KEYES, MICHAEL FRANCIS, b. Butte, Mont., May 16, 1943; B.A. with honors, Gonzaga U., 1965, M.S., 1968, J.D., 1969. Admitted to Wash. bar, 1969; law clk. Wash. State Ct. Appeals, Spokane, 1969-72; partner firm Woods & Keyes, Spokane, 1972-74; ct. commr. Wash. State Ct. Appeals, Spokane, 1974—; exec. editor Constrn. Liens and Claims, 1969—; adj. prof. law Gonzaga U., 1973—; sec.-membership chmn., nat. com. appellate staff counsel Appellate Judges Conf. Mem. Am. Bar Assn. (litigation sec.), Pi Mu Epsilon. Author: The Construction Lien Practice and Procedure Manual for the State of Washington, 1976; The Retainage Lien and Bond Claim Practice and Procedure Manual for the State of Washington, 1976; The Miller Act Practice and Procedure Manual, 1977; contbr. articles to legal jours. Home: N 8512 Jefferson Spokane WA 99208 Office: Suite 301 Broadway Centre Bldg Spokane WA 99201 Tel (509) 456-3095

KEYES, WILLIAM ALFRED, JR., b. Patterson, N.J., June 24, 1947; B.S., Western Ky. U., 1969; J.D. with honors, U. Fla., 1972. Admitted to Fla. bar, 1972; partner firm Stewart, Stewart, Jackson & Keyes, Ft. Myers, Fla., 1972—; hearing examiner Lee County (Fla.) Sch. Bd. Bd. dirs. Lee County Legal Aid Assn., Ft. Myers. Mem. Am., Lee County bar assns., Assn. Trial Lawyers Am., Fla. Acad. Trial Lawyers. Home: 1512 Cranville Sq Fort Myers FL 33901 Office: 1534 Hendry St Fort Myers FL 33901 Mailing Address: PO Drawer 790 Fort Myers FL 33902 Tel (803) 334-7477

KEYES, WILLIAM HOWARD, b. Sidney, Ohio, Jan. 17, 1928; B.S., Ind. U., 1950, LL.B., 1952. Admitted to Ind. bar, 1952, So. Dist. Fed. bar, 1952; pvt. practice law, Mt. Vernon, Ind., 1952-55; with Nat. Homes Corp. and subsidiaries, Lafayette, Ind., 1955-67, sec., corp. counsel, v.p. and land subsidiaries, 1965-67; referee Ind. Employment Security Div., Indpls., 1967-69; asso. prof. Ferris State Coll., 1969-71; Ind. state counsel Lawyers Title Ins. Corp., Indpls., 1972-76; atty. Abstract Co. of St. Joseph County, South Bend, Ind., 1976—; chmn. Bus. Law Curriculum Com., Sch. Bus., Ferris State Coll., 1970. Mem. Ind. State, St. Joseph County bar assns., Ind. Land Title Assn. (chmn. legislative com. 1976). Home: 2615 Lance Ct Bldg 26 South Bend IN 46628 Office: 211 JMS Bldg South Bend IN 46601

KEYSA, STANLEY JAY, b. Buffalo, Dec. 9, 1943; B.A. in History, Canisius Coll., 1964; LL.B., Cornell U., 1967. Admitted to N.Y. State bar, 1967; mem. firm Keysa and Keysa, Lancaster, N.Y., 1967, 1970—; legal assistance officer 7th Transp. Commd., Ft. Eustis, Va., U.S. Army, 1968, served with JAG, 1969-70; village justice, Lancaster, 1971-75, town supr., 1976—. Mem. Erie County (chmn. law day program 1976), N.Y. State, Am. bar assns. Home: 65 Court St Lancaster NY 14086 Office: 5455 Broadway Lancaster NY 14086

KEYT, DOUGLAS STEPHEN, b. Piqua, Ohio, Jan. 10, 1940; B.A., Denison U., 1961; J.D., Ohio State U., 1964. Admitted to Ohio bar, 1964, Ill. bar, 1965; with No. Trust Co., Chgo., 1964—, trust officer, 1967-70, 2d v.p., 1970-76, v.p., 1976—. Mem. Ill., Chgo. (fed. taxation com., trust law com.) bar assns., Am. Bankers Assn. (trust and probate com.), Corporate Fiduciary Assn. Ill. (tax com.), Phi Delta Phi. Home: 341 Oakdale Ave Lake Forest IL 60045 Office: No Trust Co 50 S LaSalle St Chicago IL 60690 Tel (312) 630-6000 X 7155

KFOURY, PAUL ROBERT, b. Lawrence, Mass., Oct. 9, 1943; A.B., U. N.H., 1965; J.D., Suffolk U., 1968. Admitted to Mass. bar, 1969, N.H. bar, 1969; asso. firm Howard J. Nedved, Nashua, N.H., 1969-70; sr. partner firm Kfoury & Williams, Manchester, N.H., 1970—; asso. justice Hooksett (N.H.) Dist. Ct., 1972—; instr. in law Notre Dame Coll., Manchester, 1970—; dir. Bedford (N.H.) Bank, 1973—. Manchester chmn. St. Jude's Children's Hosp., 1968-70. Mem. Manchester (pres. 1975-76), N.H. (chmn. spl. com. on prepaid legal service plans 1973-75) bar assns. Recipient Am. Jurisprudence award, 1968. Home: Castle Dr Hooksett NH 03104 Office: 814 Elm St Manchester NH 03101 Tel (603) 668-3444

KHARASCH, ROBERT NELSON, b. Washington, Dec. 13, 1926; Ph.B., U. Chgo., 1946, B.S., 1948, J.D., 1951. Admitted to D.C. bar, 1952, U.S. Supreme Ct. bar, 1957; partner firm Galland, Kharasch, Calkins & Short, Washington, 1955—; cons. U.S. Dept. Transp., 1967-68; mem. Maritime Transp. Research Bd., 1975—; dir. Computer Ops., Inc., 1974—. Mem. Am., D.C., Maritime Adminstrv. bar assns., Maritime Law Assn. U.S. Author: The Institutional Imperative, 1973; inventor The Teachall Teaching Machine, 1961. Home: 2914 Fessenden St NW Washington DC 20008 Office: 1054 31st St NW Washington DC 20007 Tel (202) 333-2200

KHOURY, ALVIN GEORGE, b. Longview, Tex., Oct. 15, 1936; B.A., So. Meth. U., 1957, LL.B., 1959. Admitted to Tex. bar, 1959; asso. firm R. L. Whitehead, Sr., 1959-65; individual practice law, 1965-72; chief felony prosecutor Gregg County (Tex.) Dist. Atty's Office, 1972—. Mem. Tex. State Bar, Gregg County Bar Assn., Longview Jr. C. of C. (pres. 1967-68). Named Jaycee of Month Longview Jaycees; recipient Sparkplug award. Office: PO Box 2403 Gregg County Courthouse Longview TX 75601 Tel (214) 758-6181

KIDD, JOHN EDWARD, b. Syracuse, N.Y., Jan. 17, 1936; B.S. in Physics, Le Moyne Coll., Syracuse, 1957; LL.B., Georgetown U., 1961. Admitted to Va. bar, 1961, N.Y. bar, 1968; trial atty. civil div. U.S. Dept. Justice, Washington, 1963-67, spl. counsel to dept., 1967; asso. firm Kenyon & Kenyon, N.Y.C., 1967-70; partner firm Pennie & Edmonds, N.Y.C., 1971—; lectr. Practising Law Inst., N.Y.C., 1967; referee N.Y. Supreme Ct. 9th Jud. Dist., 1968-69. Cub Scout master Westchester-Putnam council Boy Scouts Am., Bronxville, N.Y., 1972-76; residential chmn. United Fund, Bronxville, 1976, bd. dirs. Bronxville-Eastchester-Tuckahoe, 1977—. Mem. Am. Bar Assn., Assn. Bar City N.Y., N.Y. Patent Law Assn. Home: 24 Tanglewylde Ave Bronxville NY 10708 Office: 330 Madison Ave New York City NY 10017 Tel (212) 986-8686

KIDDER, FRED D., b. Cleve., May 22, 1922; student Coll. William and Mary, 1943-44; B.B.A. with distinction, U. Akron, 1948; LL.B./J.D., Case Western Res. U., 1950. Admitted to Ohio bar, 1950; partner firm Arter & Hadden, and predecessors, Cleve., 1950—. Chmn., Shaker Heights (Ohio) Recreation Bd.; mem. Citizens League; trustee Shaker Charitable Trust. Mem. Am., Ohio, Greater Cleve. bar assns., Cleve. Estate Planning Council, Cleve. Tax Club, Phi Delta Phi, Phi Beta Sigma, Beta Delta Psi, Phi Sigma Alpha, Order of Coif. Home: 13415 Shaker Blvd Cleveland OH 44120 Office: 1144 Union Commerce Bldg Cleveland OH 44115 Tel (216) 696-1144

KIDWELL, WAYNE LEROY, b. Council, Idaho, June 15, 1938; B.A., U. Idaho, 1960, J.D., 1964. Admitted to Idaho bar, 1964, U.S. Supreme Ct. bar, 1971; asso. firm Moffatt, Thomas, Barrett & Blanton, Boise, Idaho, 1965; pros. atty. Ada County (Idaho), 1966-68; individual practice law, Boise, 1968-74; atty. gen. State of Idaho, Boise, 1975—; mem. Idaho Senate, 1969-72, majority leader, 1971-72; legal dir. Am. Legion Boys' State; legal adviser Columbian Club. Bd. dirs. Boise Art Gallery, Boise Philharmonic Assn.; chmn. Idaho Citizens for Reagan, 1975-76; co-chmn. Idaho Pres. Ford Com., Boise, 1976. Mem. Am. Trial Lawyers Assn., Am. Judicature Soc., Nat. Dist. Attys. Assn., Western Conf. Attys. Gen. (v.p.), Phi Alpha Delta. Named Outstanding Young Man of Boise, Boise Jr. C. of C., 1967. Home: 1479 Rimrock Ct Boise ID 83702 Office: Room 210 Statehouse Boise ID 83720 Tel (208) 384-2400

KIEF, PAUL ALLAN, b. Montevideo, Minn., Mar. 22, 1934; B.A., U. Minn., 1957, LL.B., 1957. Admitted to Minn. bar, 1957; individual practice law, Bemidji, Minn., 1959—; asst. atty. Beltrami County (Minn.), 1959-63; asst. pub. defender 9th Jud. Dist., 1966-67, pub. defender, 1968—. Vice-chmn. Beltrami County Planning Adv. Commn.; chmn. Region A adv. council Gov.'s Crime Commn., 1971—. Mem. Beltrami County (past pres.), Am., Minn. State, 15th Dist. bar assns., Am., Minn. trial lawyers assns., Nat. Coll. Criminal Def. Lawyers and Pub. Defenders, Lawyer-Pilots Bar Assn., Minn. Pub. Defenders Assn. (v.p.). Home: Box 212 Bemidji MN 56601 Office: Box 844 207 Fourth St Bemidji MN 56601 Tel (218) 751-2221

KIEFFER, MARVIN LEWIS, b. Weiner, Ark., Mar. 11, 1923; B.S., U. Ark., 1950, LL.B., 1951. Admitted to Ark. bar, 1951, U.S. Supreme Ct. bar, 1960; examining agt. IRS, Little Rock and Jonesboro, Ark., 1951-59; individual practice law, Jonesboro, Ark., 1959—. Mem. Craighead County (Ark.) (pres. 1971-72), Ark., Am. bar assns., Ark. Bar Found. (treas. 1976-77), N.E. Ark. Estate Council (pres. 1976-77), Jonesboro C. of C. (dir.). Office: McAdams Trust Bldg Jonesboro AR 72401 Tel (501) 932-1120

KIEL, EDWARD ROWLAND, b. Phila., Aug. 10, 1944; B.A., U. Conn., 1966; J.D. cum laude, 1971. Admitted to Conn. bar, 1971, Vt. bar, 1972, U.S. Supreme Ct. bar, 1975; dep. state's atty., Franklin County, Vt., 1971; asso. firm Whitcomb, Clark & Moeser, Springfield, Vt., 1972-74; individual practice law, Springfield, Vt., 1974—. Mem. Am., Vt. (profl. responsibility com. 1976—), Windsor County (pres. 1976—) bar assns., Assn. Trial Lawyers Am. Contbr. article to law jour. Office: 20 Park St Springfield VT 05156 Tel (802) 885-2141

KIELY, MICHAEL JOSEPH, b. N.Y.C., March 19, 1903; B.A., Coll. City N.Y., 1925; LL.B., Fordham Law Sch., 1929. Admitted to N.Y. State bar, 1930; partner firm Wormser, Kiely, Alessandroni & McCann, and predecessors, N.Y.C., 1940—. Mem. N.Y.C., N.Y. State bar assns. Home: 2391 Webb Ave New York City NY 10468 Office: 100 Park Ave New York City NY 10017 Tel (212) 889-8480

KIENER, JOHN LESLIE, b. Ft. Madison, Iowa, June 21, 1940; B.A. cum laude, Loras Coll., Dubuque, Iowa, 1962; J.D., Drake U., Des Moines, 1965. Admitted to Iowa bar, 1965, Tenn. bar, 1972, U.S. Supreme Ct. bar, 1974; individual practice law, Decorah, Iowa, 1965-68; asst. atty. gen. State of Iowa, 1968-72; partner firm Cantor, Kiener, Johnson City, Tenn., 1972—; city judge Johnson City, 1975—; continuing edn. tchr. bus. law E. Tenn. State U., 1975—. Mem. Am., Tenn., Iowa, Washington County bar assns., Tenn. Trial Lawyers Assn. Home: 2403 Camelot Circle Johnson City TN 37601 Office: 126 Spring St Johnson City TN 37601 Tel (615) 926-5112

KIEPURA, THOMAS ANDREW, b. Chgo., June 25, 1945; B.A., U. Ill., 1967, M.A., 1968, J.D., 1971. Admitted to Ill. bar, 1971; with Continental Ill. Nat. Bank & Trust Co., Chgo., 1971-72; asso. firm Kralovec, Sweeney, Marquard & Doyle, Chgo., 1972-77, firm Haskell & Perrin, Chgo., 1977—. Mem. Am., Ill. State, Chgo. bar assns. Office: 208 S La Salle St Chicago IL 60604 Tel (312) 236-5801

KIES, SAUL, b. Kreslavka, Russia, Aug. 17, 1907; student Coll. City N.Y.; LL.B., Bklyn. Law Sch., 1933. Admitted to N.Y. bar, 1934, U.S. Supreme Ct. bar, 1960; presiding insp. N.Y. Immigration and Naturalization Service, 1941-46; individual practice law, N.Y.C., 1946—. Bd. dirs. Jewish Nat. Fund; mem. exec. com. Jewish Labor Com. Mem. N.Y. County Lawyers Assn., N.Y. Bar Assn., Assn. Immigration and Nationality Lawyers (bd. govs.), Am. Immigration and Citizenship Conf. (dir.). Home: 25 Central Park W New York NY 10023 Office: 350 Fifth Ave New York NY 10001 Tel (212) 564-8254

KIESEL, MICHAEL THOMAS, b. N.Y.C., Dec. 13, 1946; A.B. cum laude, Princeton, 1969; J.D., U. Pa., 1972; postgrad. N.Y. U. Admitted to N.Y. State bar, 1973; asso. firm Whitman & Ransom, N.Y.C., 1972—. Mem. Am., N.Y. State bar assns. (mem. tax sect.). Home: 35 E 35th St New York City NY 10016 Office: 522 Fifth Ave New York City NY 10036 Tel (212) 575-5800

KIESLING, NORMAN LOUIS, b. Logansport, Ind., Jan. 31, 1912; J.D., Valparaiso U., 1935; grad. Coll. State Trial Judges U. Nev., 1971. Admitted to Ind. bar, 1935; practiced in Logansport, 1935-59; judge Ind. Circuit Ct. of Cass County, 1959—; pros. atty. Cass County, 1937-38; mem. Ind. Ho. of Reps. 1949-50. Pres. Three Rivers council Boy Scouts Am., 1971-72, v.p. Sagamore council, 1973-74; active ARC. Mem. Cass County Bar Assn., Am. Judicature Soc. Home: 1118 Kiesling Rd Logansport IN 46947 Office: Cass Circuit Ct Courthouse Logansport IN 46947 Tel (219) 753-3944

KIFER, JAMES ELDON, b. Ada, Okla., Sept. 2, 1950; B.A., E. Central Okla. State U., 1971; J.D., U. Tulsa, 1973. Admitted to Okla. bar, 1974; asso. firm R. Burl Harris, Ada, 1974; atty. Kerr-McGee Corp., Oklahoma City, 1974-77, Mustang Fuel Corp., Oklahoma City, 1977—. Mem. Am., Okla. bar assns. Office: Suite 1166 E First Nat Center Oklahoma City OK 73125 Tel (405) 272-9471

KIGHT, BENNETT LEXON, b. Waycross, Ga., Aug. 13, 1940; A.B., Emory U., 1963, LL.B., 1966. Admitted to Ga. bar, 1966, D.C. bar, 1967, U.S. Supreme Ct. bar, 1971; law clk. to chief judge Elbert P. Tuttle, U.S. 5th Circuit Ct. Appeals, 1966-67; asso. firm Sutherland, Asbill & Brennan, Atlanta, 1967-72, partner, 1972—; counsel to com. on crime and poverty Met. Atlanta Commn. on Crime and Juvenile Delinquency, 1967-68. Mem. Am. (com. on corp.-stockholder relationship, tax sec. 1971—), Ga., Atlanta bar assns., Bar Assn. D.C. Home: 56 Westminster Dr NE Atlanta GA 30309 Office: 3100 1st Nat Bank Tower Atlanta GA 30303 Tel (404) 658-8745

KIGHT, PAULA THRUN, b. Crawfordsville, Ind., May 28, 1948; B.A., Butler U., 1970; J.D., Ind. U., 1973. Admitted to Ind. bar, 1973; individual practice law, Indpls., 1973—. Mem. Am., Ind. State, Indpls. bar assns., Indpls. Lawyers Assn., Phi Alpha Delta. Office: 1101 Inland Bldg 156 E Market St Indianapolis IN 46204 Tel (317) 639-4126

KIHLE, DONALD ARTHUR, b. Noonan, N.D., Apr. 4, 1934; B.S. in Indsl. Engring., U. N.D., 1957; J.D., U. Okla., 1967. Admitted to Okla. bar, 1967, U.S. Supreme Ct. bar, 1971; engr. trainee Continental Pipe Line, Ponca City, Okla., 1957, staff engr., 1958-61, sr. staff engr., 1964-65; sr. project engr. Oasis Oil Co., Tripoli, Libya, 1961-62; asso. firm Huffman, Arrington, Scheurich & Kincaid, Tulsa, 1967-71; partner firm Huffman, Arrington, Scheurich & Kihle, 1971—. Trustee Undercroft Montessori Sch., 1974—, pres., 1976—; commr. Tulsa Minor Hockey League, 1976—. Mem. Am., Okla., Tulsa County bar assns., Phi Delta Phi. Bd. editors Okla. Law Rev., 1965-67. Home: 4717 S Lewis Ct Tulsa OK 74105 Office: 510 Oklahoma Natural Bldg Tulsa OK 74119 Tel (918) 585-8141

KILBANE, JAMES PATRICK, b. Cleve., Apr. 25, 1923; B.S.Sci., John Carroll U., 1948; LL.B., Western Res. U., 1951, J.D., Case-Western Res. U., 1968. Admitted to Ohio bar, 1952; sr. partner firm Kilbane, McDonnell & Sweeney, Cleve., 1952-73; judge Cuyahoga County (Ohio) Common Pleas Ct., 1973—; mem. Ohio Ho. of Reps., 1955-63, Ohio Senate, 1963-65; asst. atty. gen., spl. counsel State of Ohio, 1959-65; lectr. polit. sci. Pres. Irish Civic Assn., Cuyahoga County, 1969-71; chmn. Emerald Charity Ball, Westlake, Ohio, 1971-75; trustee Leukemia Soc., Cuyahoga County, 1971—. Mem. Am., Cleve., Ohio, Cuyahoga County bar assns., Trial Lawyers Assn., Am. Judicature Soc. Recipient Outstanding Jud. Service award Ohio Supreme Ct., 1973, 74, 75, 76, Good Fellow award Jolly Bros., 1971, Service award Gaelic Athletic League, 1976. Home: 31569 Center Ridge Rd Westlake OH 44145 Office: Common Pleas Ct Justice Center Cleveland OH 44113 Tel (216) 621-5800

KILBANE, THOMAS JAMES, b. Cleve., Aug. 19, 1937; A.B., Case Western Res. U., 1960; J.D., Capital U., 1967. Admitted to Ohio bar, 1968; mgr. Williams & Co., Inc., Columbus, Ohio and Charleston, W.Va., 1960-70; referee Franklin County (Ohio) Probate Ct., 1970-73; asso. firm Bessey & Kilbane, Columbus, 1973-74; individual practice law, Columbus, 1974—; lectr. Ohio Legal Center Inst., 1975-76. Bd. dirs. Columbus Area Council on Alcoholism, 1970-73, Columbus Birthright, Inc., 1972-74. Mem. Am., Ohio, Columbus (probate com. 1970—) bar assns., Columbus Lawyers Club. Home: 2718 Camden Rd Columbus OH 43221 Office: 338 S High St Columbus OH 43215

KILBANE, THOMAS STANTON, b. Cleve., Mar. 7, 1941; B.A. magna cum laude, John Carroll U., 1963; J.D., Northwestern U., 1966. Admitted to Ohio bar, 1966, Fed. bar, 1967, U.S. Supreme Ct. bar, 1975; asso. firm Squire, Sanders, & Dempsey, Cleve., 1966-67, 69-76, partner, 1976—. Mem. Democratic Precinct Com., Rocky River, Ohio, 1972-76; mem. Rocky River (Ohio) City Sch. Dist. Study Commn., 1976. Mem. Am., Ohio, Greater Cleve. bar assns., Def. Research Inst., Am. Right of Way Assn., Greater Cleve. Growth Assn. Decorated Bronze Star; named 1 of 10 Outstanding Young Men Cleve. Jaycees, 1972; editorial bd. Northwestern Law Rev., 1965-66. Home: 20702 Beachwood Dr Rocky River OH 44116 Office: 1800 Union Commerce Bldg Cleveland OH 44115 Tel (216) 696-9200

KILBERG, WILLIAM JEFFREY, b. Bklyn., June 12, 1946; B.S., Cornell U., 1966; J.D., Harvard, 1969. Admitted to N.Y. bar, 1970, D.C. bar, 1972, U.S. Supreme Ct. bar, 1976; asso. firm Mudge, Rose, Guthrie & Alexander, N.Y.C., 1968; White House fellow, 1969-70; gen. counsel Fed. Mediation and Conciliation Service, Washington, 1970-71; asso. solicitor U.S. Dept. Labor, Washington, 1971-73, solicitor labor, 1973-76; partner firm Breed, Abbott & Morgan, Washington, 1977—. Mem. N.Y., D.C., Fed., Am. bar assns., Counsel on Fgn. Relations, Am. Judicature Soc., Cornell, Harvard alumni assns. Recipient award for Outstanding Service to Spanish Speaking, League of United Latin Am. Citizens, 1973; Arthur S. Fleming award D.C. C. of C., 1975. Contbr. articles to legal jours. Home: 821 Clinton Pl McLean VA 22101 Office: 815 Connecticut Ave NW Washington DC 20006 Tel (202) 785-5230

KILBOURNE, GEORGE WILLIAM, b. Berea, Ky., Mar. 29, 1924; B.S. in Mech. Engring., U. Mich., 1946; J.D., U. Calif., Berkeley, 1951. Admitted to Calif. bar, 1952, Ind. bar, 1958; individual practice law, Berkeley, 1952-57; mem. firm Hays & Hays, Sullivan, Ind., 1957-59, Boyle & Kilbourne, Sullivan, 1960-63; mem. firm Bernal, Rigney & Kilbourne, Berkeley, 1963-68; individual practice law, Pleasant Hill, Calif., 1968—; lectr. John F. Kennedy U., 1975-76. Mem. Am., Mt. Diable, Contra Costa bar assns., Calif. Trial Lawyers, Am. Judicature Soc. Home: 241 Christie Dr Martinez CA 94553 Office: 70 Doray Dr 20 Pleasant Hill CA 94523 Tel (415) 798-7525

KILCARR, JOHN EDWARD, b. Bronx, N.Y., July 5, 1933; B.B.A., Manhattan Coll., 1955; LL.B., Am. U., 1962. Admitted to Va. bar, 1964, D.C. bar, 1964; dep. clk. Circuit Ct., Arlington, Va., 1962-64, dep. sheriff, 1960-62; asst. Commonwealth atty. Va., 1964-66; individual practice law, 1966-70, 72—; partner firm Elson Kilcarr Perrin & Waters, 1970-72. Mem. Va. Bar Assn., Am., Va. trial lawyers assns. Home: 3166 N 20th St Arlington VA 22201 Office: 2330 Wilson Blvd Arlington VA 22201 Tel (703) 525-9335

KILEY, THOMAS DANIEL, b. Braddock, Pa., Apr. 29, 1943; B.S. in Chem. Engring., Pa. State U., 1965; J.D., George Washington U., 1969. Admitted to Calif. bar, 1970, U.S. Ct. Customs and Patent Appeals, 1972; examiner U.S. Patent Office, 1965-67; patent agt. legal dept. E. I. du Pont de Nemours & Co. Inc., Arlington, Va., 1967-69; asso. firm Lyon & Lyon, Los Angeles, 1969-74, partner, 1975—. Mem. Am. Bar Assn., Am., Calif., Los Angeles (chmn. ann. seminar, chmn. legis. com. 1975) patent law assns., Order of Coif. Editorial staff George Washington Law Rev., 1969; contbr. articles to legal jours. Home: 26836 Westvale Dr Palos Verdes Peninsula CA 90274 Office: Lyon & Lyon Inc 800 Wilshire Blvd Los Angeles CA 90017 Tel (213) 489-1600

KILEY, THOMAS FRANCIS, b. Lynn, Mass., July 21, 1925; B.S. in Civil Engring., Cornell U., 1948; J.D., Boston Coll., 1951. Admitted to Mass. bar, 1951; individual practice law, Lynn, 1953—; spl. town counsel, Swampscott, Mass., 1974—. Mem. Lynn Planning Bd., 1956-66; chmn. town Swampscott Bldg Code Bd. Appeals, 1976, mem. high sch. bldg. adv. com. 1976; clk. Lynn Indsl. Devel. Corp., 1976—. Mem. Lynn, Essex County, Mass., Am. bar assns. Home: 12 Phillips Beach Ave Swampscott MA 01907 Office: 140 Union St Lynn MA 01901 Tel (617) 592-7460

KILGANNON, FRANK X., b. Rockville Centre, N.Y., Oct. 6, 1938; B.B.A., St. John's U., 1960; LL.B., N.Y. U., 1964. Admitted to N.Y. State bar, 1965; partner firm Fine & Kilgannon, Mineola, N.Y., 1968—; adj. asso. prof. Nassau Community Coll., 1963—. Mem. sch. bd. St. Thomas Sch., West Hempstead, N.Y., 1967-70, pres., 1969-70. Mem. Cath. Lawyers Guild (pres. 1975—), N.Y. State, Nassau County bar assns. Home: 504 Kent Place West Hempstead NY 11552 Office: 1551 Kellum Place Mineola NY 11501 Tel (516) 746-5530

KILGANNON, WILLIAM, b. N.Y.C., Sept. 4, 1927; B.S., Fordham U., 1950; LL.B., St. John's U., 1956. Admitted to N.Y. State bar, 1956, U.S. Supreme Ct. bar, 1958; asso. firm Davis, Hoxie, Faithfull & Hapgood, N.Y.C., 1957-62, partner firm, 1962—; research chemist Evans Research and Devel. Corp., N.Y.C., 1950-55; patent agt. FMC Corp., N.Y.C., 1956-57. Mem. N.Y. Patent Law Assn. (gov.), Assn. Bar City N.Y. (patent com.). Home: 29 Carver Terr Yonkers NY 10710 Office: 45 Rockefeller Center New York City NY 10020 Tel (212) 344-8450

KILGORE, JOE MADISON, b. Brown County, Tex., Dec. 10, 1918; student Westmoorland Coll., 1935-36; student pre-law U. Tex., 1936-37, 38-39, law, 1939-41, 45-46. Admitted to Tex. bar, 1946; mem. firm Rankin, Kilgore & Cherry, Edinburg, Tex., 1946-55; partner firm McGinnis, Lochridge & Kilgore, Austin, Tex., 1965—; mem. Tex. Ho. of Reps., 1947-55, U.S. Ho. of Reps., 1955-65. Fellow Tex., Am. bar founds.; mem. Tex., Am. bar assns. Adminstrv. Conf. U.S. (council 1968-71). Home: 3311 River Rd Austin TX 78703 Office: 5th Floor Tex State Bank Bldg Austin TX 78701

KILLEEN, JOSEPH A., b. Lowell, Mass., June 13, 1917; J.D., New Eng. Sch. Law, 1970. Admitted to Mass. bar, 1971, Fed. bar, 1972; instr. Middlesex County Tng. Sch., Chelmsford, Mass., 1962-72; ct. and crime reporter Lowell (Mass.) Sun Publishing Co., 1941-48, night city editor, 1948-54, 1954-62; individual practice law, Tewksbury, Mass. 1971—. Sec. Tewksbury Indsl. Commn., 1955-60; chmn. Tewksbury Bd. Registars, 1965—; mem. Municipal Band Concert Commn., 1950-54. Mem. Am., Mass. bar assns., Mass. Acad. Trial Attys., Mental Health Legal Advs. Com. Mass. Supreme Judicial Ct. Recipient lawyers coop. book prize for Criminal Procedure, 1970, writing awards in publishing field. Office: 778 Main St Tewksbury MA 01876 Tel (617) 851-7467

KILLEEN, MARY ANN, b. Buffalo, May 23, 1927; B.A., Trinity Coll., Washington, 1948; LL.D., State U. N.Y., Buffalo, 1952. Admitted to N.Y. State bar, 1952; asso. firm Kenefick, Bass, Letchworth, Baldy & Phillips, Buffalo, 1958-68; judge Family Ct. of County of Erie (N.Y.), 1968—; lectr. law and family problems Canisius Coll., State U. N.Y., Buffalo. Mem. Am., N.Y. State, Erie County (treas. 1957-58) bar assns., Women Lawyers Assn. of Western N.Y. (pres. 1954-56), Cath. Lawyers Guild, Kappa Beta Pi. Recipient Woman of Yr. award Inter-Club Council of Western N.Y., 1973, Bus. and Profl. Women of Buffalo, 1975; certificate of recognition NCCJ, 1967. Office: 25 Delaware Ave Buffalo NY 14202 Tel (716) 846-8181

KILLIAN, JOHN DORAN, b. Woodhaven, N.Y., Nov. 5, 1928; A.B., Hofstra U., 1950; J.D., Cornell U., 1953; LL.M., 1954. Admitted to N.Y. bar, 1954, Pa. bar, 1958, U.S. Supreme Ct. bar, 1958; dep. atty. gen. State of Pa., 1957-64; sr. partner firm Killian & Gephart, Harrisburg, Pa., 1964—. Pres. Presbyterian Homes, Inc., Harrisburg, 1967-72, Pa. Council Chs., Harrisburg, 1970-72, Dauphin County (Pa.) Library System, 1972—; chmn. Council on Adminstrv. Services, United Presbyn. Ch. N.Y.C., 1974—; chmn. Pa. Pub. Sch. Employees Retirement Bd., 1971—; former trustee Lancaster (Pa.) Theol. Sem. Mem. Am., Pa. Dauphin County bar assns., Am. Judicature Soc., Am., Pa. trial lawyers assns. Contbr. articles in field to profl. jours. Home: 3737 Maple St Harrisburg PA 17109 Office: 216-218 Pine St Harrisburg PA 17101 Tel (717) 232-1851

KILPATRICK, ANDREW JONES, II, b. Boca Raton, Fla., Mar. 11, 1944; A.B.J., U. Ga., 1966; J.D., Mercer U., 1969. Admitted to Ga. bar, 1969; partner firm Maguire & Kilpatrick, Augusta, Ga., 1971-74; individual practice law, Augusta, 1974-76; partner firm Kilpatrick & Paine, Augusta, 1976—; asst. city atty. Augusta, 1971-74. Mem. Am. Bar Assn. Office: 457 Greene St Augusta GA 30901 Tel (404) 724-5607

KILPATRICK, J. THOMAS, b. Atlanta, Aug. 12, 1943; B.S., U. Tenn., 1965, J.D., 1968. Admitted to Tenn. bar, 1968, Ga. bar, 1969; asso. firm Smith, Currie & Hancock, Atlanta, 1968-71, partner, 1971—. Mem. Am., Ga., Tenn. bar assns. Contbr. articles to legal jours. Home: 5666 Woodsong Dr Dunwoody GA 30338 Office: 1400 Fulton Nat Bank Bldg Atlanta GA 30303 Tel (404) 521-3800

KILPATRICK, ROY, b. Salem, Oreg., Jan. 29, 1914; J.D., U. Oreg., 1935. Admitted to Oreg. bar, 1955; individual practice law, Grant County, Oreg., 1935—. Fellow Am. Coll. Trial Lawyers; mem. Am. Bar Assn., Am. Trial Lawyers Assn., Am. Bd. Trial Advs. (named Trial Lawyer of Year, Oreg. chpt. 1972). Home: Mount Vernon St Hot Springs OR 97865 Office: Box A Mount Vernon OR 97865 Tel (503) 932-4455

KIM, BEN HYUN, b. Pusan, Korea; LL.B., Seoul Nat. U., 1955; M.S., M.A. in Polit. Sci., U. Mo., 1959; J.D., John Marshall Law Sch., 1969. Admitted to Ill. bar, 1969; individual practice law, Chgo., 1969—; legal advisor Korean Pharm. Assn. of Chgo., Korean Med. Soc. Chgo. Bd. dirs. Korean Am. Community Service, 1976—; advisor Korean Karate Assn. Midwest, 1976—; bd. govs. Korean Assn. Chgo., 1974. Mem. Am., Ill., Chgo., Fed., NW Suburban bar assns., Am. Judicature Soc., World Peace Through Law Center, Phi Alpha Delta. Contbr. articles to legal jours. Home: 1560 N Sandburg Terr Chicago IL 60614 Office: 120 S LaSalle St suite 648 Chicago IL 60603 Tel (312) 368-1656

KIMBALL, DANIEL P., b. Springfield, La., Oct. 10, 1915; B.A., La. State U., 1938, LL.B., 1947. Admitted to La. bar, 1947, 18th Dist. bar, 1947; practiced in Port Allen, La., 1947-61; judge La. Dist. Ct., 18th Jud. Dist., div. A, 1961—; mem. jud. council La. Supreme Ct., 1967-69; mem. advisory com. for preparation of juvenile code, 1971-72. Bd. dirs. Donaldsonville (La.) Mental Health Clinic, 1967-73, West Baton Rouge Assn. for Retarded, 1968-70; dist. advancement chmn., vice chmn. dist. exec. com. Boy Scouts Am. Mem. La. State Bar Assn. (ho. of dels. 1957-59), La. Council Juvenile Ct. Judges (pres. 1968), Blue Ridge Inst., for So. Juvenile Ct. Judges (pres. 1969). Home: 521 Ave E Port Allen LA 70767 Office: Courthouse Port Allen LA 70767 Tel (504) 343-9758

KIMBALL, GEORGE ALLEN, b. Clio, La., Sept. 28, 1903; LL.B., La. State U., 1928, J.D., 1968. Admitted to La. bar, 1928; partner firm Kimball & Smith, Monroe, La., 1929-32; individual practice law, Monroe, 1932-35; asso. firm Sholars & Gunby, Monroe, La., 1933-44; partner firm Jones & Kimball, and successors, Lake Charles, 1944-76, firm Kimball, McLeod & Dow, Lake Charles, 1976—; v.p., dir. Tidelands Life Ins. Co., Bunkie, La., 1956-72, Tidelands Capital Corp., 1966-76; dir. Am. Tidelands Life Ins. Co., Birmingham, Ala., 1972-76; mem. La. Gov.'s Com. Intergovtl. Relations, 1966-70, Gov.'s Pub. Ethics Com., 1968; mem. La. Ins. Commn., 1941-48, chmn., 1945-48. Dir., sec. Second Univ. Homesites, Inc., 1950—; v.p. La. Civil Service League, 1973—; trustee U. of South, Sewanee, Tenn., 1952-62, bd. regents, 1961-67, chmn. bd., 1965-67. Fellow Am. Coll. Trial Lawyers; mem. Am., La., S.W. bar assns., La. C. of C. (dir. 1960-75, pres. 1965, 66), Phi Delta Phi. Home: 117 Pithon St Lake Charles LA 70601 Office: Magnolia Life Bldg Lake Charles LA 70601 Tel (318) 439-5726

KIMBALL, PAUL CLARK, JR., b. Detroit, June 5, 1943; B.A., Williams Coll., 1965; J.D., Northwestern U., 1968. Admitted to Ill. bar, 1968; law clk. Judge Robert E. English of Ill. Appellate Ct., 1st Dist., 1968-69; asso. firm Peterson, Ross, Rall Barber & Seidel, Chgo., 1969-72; partner firm Spindell, Kemp & Kimmons, Chgo., 1972—; lectr. Ill. Inst. Continuing Legal Edn. Trustee Lawrence Hall Sch. For Boys, Chgo., 1970—, v.p., 1975—. Mem. Am. (bd. editors Barrister 1975-77), Ill. State, Chgo. (chmn. young lawyers sect. 1977-78) bar assns. Office: 135 S LaSalle St Chicago IL 60603 Tel (312) 372-2900

KIMBERLIN, SAM OWEN, JR., b. Wichita Falls, Tex., Feb. 4, 1928; B.B.A., U. Tex., 1951, LL.B., 1953; grad. with highest honors Stonier Grad. Sch. Banking, Rutgers U., 1972. Admitted to Tex. bar, 1953; 1st asst. dist. atty. Travis County (Tex.), Austin, 1953-54; asst. atty. gen. State of Tex., Austin, 1955-56; gen. counsel Tex. Dept. Banking, Austin, 1956-62; gen. counsel, exec. dir. Assn. State Chartered Banks in Tex., Austin, 1962-64; exec. v.p. Tex. Bankers Assn., Austin, 1964—. Mem. Tex. (banking laws com.), Travis County bar assns., Am., Tex. socs. assn. execs., Tex. Assn. Bank Counsel, Am. Bankers Assn. (chmn. elect state div. 1976-77), Conf. So. Bankers Assn. Execs. (pres. 1967-68), Phi Alpha Delta. Contbr. articles to profl. publs. Home: 3503 Scenic Hills Dr Austin TX 78703 Office: 203 W 10th St Austin TX 78701 Tel (512) 472-8388

KIMBERLIN, WILLIAM MORLAN, b. Garden City, Mo., Nov. 20, 1915; LL.B., U. Mo., 1939, J.D., 1969. Admitted to Mo. bar, 1939; prosecuting atty. Cass County (Mo.), 1947-51; mayor City of Harrisonville, Mo., 1951-53; judge 17th Jud. Circuit Ct. (Mo.), Harrisonville, 1954—. Mem. Mo. Bar Assn. Home: 201 Stella St Harrisonville MO 64701 Office: Ct House Harrisonville MO 64701 Tel (816) 884-4462

KIMBERLING, JOHN FARRELL, b. Shelbyville, Ind., Nov. 15, 1926; A.B., Ind. U., 1947, J.D., 1950. Admitted to Ind. bar, 1950, Calif. bar, 1954, U.S. Supreme Ct. bar, 1976; asso. firm Bracken, Gray, DeFur & Voran, Muncie, Ind., 1950-51; asso. firm Lillick, McHose & Charles, Los Angeles, 1953-62, partner 1963—; dir. Mitsui Bank Calif., 1974—. Bd. dirs. Los Angeles Ballet, 1973—, v.p., 1973. Fellow Am. Coll. Trial Lawyers; mem. Maritime Law Assn. U.S., Los Angeles County, Calif., Am. bar assns., Los Angeles Jr. C. of C. (pres. 1961). Home: 2101 Castilian Dr Los Angeles CA 90068 Office: 707 Wilshire Blvd Los Angeles CA 90017 Tel (213) 620-9000

KIMBRELL, HORACE WARREN, b. Lee's Summit, Mo., Apr. 19, 1916; A.B., U. Kansas City, 1936, J.D., 1939. Admitted to Mo. bar, 1936, U.S. Dist. Ct. for Western Mo. bar, 1939, U.S. Supreme Ct. bar, 1951, U.S. 8th Circuit Ct. Appeals bar, 1953; individual practice law, Kansas City, Mo., 1939-42, 46-53; asst. U.S. atty., Western Dist. Mo., 1953-57, 1st asst., 1957-61; asst. gen. counsel Kansas City Life Ins. Co. (Mo.), 1961-71, exec. adminstr. pub. affairs, 1971-76, asso. dir. pub. relations, 1976—. Pres. Goodwill Industries, Am., Inc., 1961-66, chmn., 1966-68. Mem. Am., Kansas City, Mo., Fed. (pres. Kansas City chpt. 1958; nat. v.p., 1964-66; mem. nat. council, 1966—) bar assns., Fed. Bar Found., Kansas City Lawyers Assn., Am. Judicature Soc., Am. Soc. Internat. Law, Inter-Am. Bar Assn., Internat. Bar Assn., World Assn. Lawyers, U. Mo-Kans Sch. Law Found., Bench and Robe Soc. (hon.). Home: 5900 E 129th St Grandview MO 64030 Office: Kansas City Life Ins Co 3520 Broadway Kansas City MO 64111 Tel (816) 753-7000

KIMBROUGH, ARTHUR RICHARD, b. Denver, Aug. 10, 1912; A.B., U. Calif., 1934, LL.B. (now J.D.), 1937. Admitted to Calif. bar, 1937; asso. firm Latham & Watkins, Los Angeles, 1937-48, partner, 1949—; lectr. in field. Trustee John Stauffer Charitable Trust, Los Angeles, Henry B. Allen Family Found. Mem. State Bar Calif. (chmn. com. to confer with life underwriters 1968-69), Am. (bd. govs. 1969-72, v.p. 1972), Los Angeles County (chmn. club quarters com. 1968-69, trustee 1960-62, chmn. com. on probate law and procedure 1951-55) bar assns., U. Calif. Law Sch. Alumni Assn. (pres. 1966-67). Asso. editor Calif. Law Rev., 1935-37. Office: 555 S Flower St Los Angeles CA 90071 Tel (213) 485-1234

KIMEL, LARRY SAMUEL, b. Raleigh, N.C., May 6, 1947; A.B., U. Ga., 1969, J.D., 1972. Admitted to N.C. bar, 1972, asst. clk. Buncombe County (N.C.) Superior Ct., 1968; asso. firm Haynes, Baucom & Chandler, Charlotte, N.C., 1972-74; individual practice law, Asheville, N.C., 1974-75; partner firm Gray, Kimel & Connolly, Asheville, 1975—. Mem. N.C. (practical skills com.; disaster relief com. young lawyers sect.), 28th Jud. Dist., Buncombe County, Am. (charter mem. litigation sect.) bar assns., Am. Trial Lawyers Assn., Buncombe County Young Lawyers Club (past pres.), N.C. Acad. Trial Lawyers. Home: 15 Red Oak Rd Asheville NC 28801 Office: POB 7235 Asheville NC 28807 Tel (704) 254-2348

KIMMEL, MELVIN, b. N.Y.C., May 26, 1930; B.A., Bklyn. Coll., 1959; J.D., N.Y. U., 1957. Admitted to N.Y. bar, 1958; individual practice law, Bklyn., 1958—; lectr. Author med.-legal textbooks. Home: 227 Corbin Pl Brooklyn NY 11235 Office: 16 Court St Brooklyn NY 11241 Tel (212) 648-2161

KIMURA, GEORGE YOICHI, b. Honolulu, Mar. 28, 1933; B.A., Tulane U., 1955, LL.B., 1959. Admitted to Hawaii bar, 1962, La. bar, 1959; law clk. to chief justice Hawaii Supreme Ct., Honolulu, 1961-62, to chief judge U.S. Dist. Ct. for Dist. Hawaii, 1962; dep. corp. counsel City and County of Honolulu, 1962-63, dep. pros. atty., 1963-66; jr. partner firm Cobb & Gould, Honolulu, 1966-69; partner firm Conklin & Kimura, Honolulu, 1969-74; individual practice law, Honolulu, 1974—. Mem. Honolulu div. Selective Service Bd., 1973-75. Mem. Hawaii, La., Am. bar assns., Am., Calif. trial lawyers assns. Home: 4340 Pahoa Ave 7D Honolulu HI 96816 Office: 333 Queen St Suite 604 Honolulu HI 96813 Tel (808) 531-6561

KIMZEY, HERBERT BENNETT, b. Dougherty County, Ga., May 18, 1909; student North Ga. Coll., 1926-27, U.S. Mil. Acad., 1927-28; LL.B., U. Ga., 1931. Admitted to Ga. bar, 1931, U.S. Supreme Ct. bar, 1973; individual practice law, Toccoa, Ga., 1931-32; mem. firm Hamilton & Herbert B. Kimzey, Cornelia, Ga., 1932-43; law asst. Ga. Ct. Appeals, Atlanta, 1943-44, 46; mem. firm Kimzey & Kimzey, Cornelia, 1946-69; solicitor City Ct. of Habersham County (Ga.), 1956-60; solicitor gen. Mountain Jud. Circuit of Ga., 1965-68; dist. atty. Mountain Jud. Circuit, 1968-72; judge Mountain Jud. Circuit Superior Ct., 1972; individual practice law, Cornelia, 1973-76; mem. firm Kimzey, Kimzey & Carter, Cornelia, 1976—; mem. Ga. Com. to Aid in Preparation of Rule of Procedure, 1963; city atty. City of Cornelia, 1950-60, Town of Alto (Ga.), 1960-68; county atty. Banks County, Ga., 1955-65. Mem. Mountain Jud. Circuit Bar, State Bar Ga., Am. Bar Assn. Home: 400 Grandview Circle Cornelia GA 30531 Office: 117 S Main St Cornelia GA 30531 Tel (404) 778-6823

KINARD, JOHN MAJOR, b. N.Y.C., June 17, 1944; B.B.A., U. Miss., 1966; J.D., 1970. Admitted to Miss. bar, 1970; spl. asst. atty. gen. Miss., Jackson, 1970-72; individual practice law, Pascagoula, Miss., 1972—. Mem. Am., Miss., Jackson County (treas. 1975) bar assns., Hinds County Young Lawyers, Delta Theta Phi. Home: 1106 Martin St Pascagoula MS 39567 Office: 3112 Canty Pascagoula MS 39567 Tel (601) 762-2271

KINARD, MILAM MICHAEL, b. Waldo, Ark., July 13, 1939; student So. State Coll., 1957-60; LL.B., Ark. Law Sch., 1966. Admitted to Ark. bar, 1966, U.S. Supreme Ct. bar, 1971; partner firm Woodward & Kinard, Magnolia, Ark., 1966—; atty. City of Waldo, 1966-76; dep. pros. atty. 13th Jud. Dist. Ark., 1966-73, pros. atty., 1977—. Bd. dirs. Magnolia-Columbia County C. of C., 1968-69; pres. Columbia County Wildlife Assn., 1975—; dir. Ark. State Wildlife Assn., 1975-76. Mem. Am., Ark. (ho. of dels. 1975—), Columbia County bar assns., Ark. Trial Lawyers Assn. (dir. 1973—), Ark. Pros. Attys. Assn. (dir. 1977—), Assn. Trial Lawyers Am., Magnolia Jaycees (pres. 1968-69). Recipient Leadership in Action award, 1970, Distinguished Service award Magnolia Jaycees, 1971. Home: 1318 N Jackson St Magnolia AR 71753 Office: PO Box 727 Magnolia AR 71753 Tel (501) 234-4727

KINCAID, EUGENE DAVIS, III, b. Uvalde, Tex., Mar. 7, 1941; B.A., Baylor U., 1962; J.D., U. Tex., 1966. Admitted to Tex. bar, 1966; briefing atty. Tex. Ct. Criminal Appeals, 1968; asst. city atty. City of San Antonio, 1969; atty. Tex. Water Rights Commn., Austin; individual practice law, Uvalde, 1971—; commr. Uvalde Housing Authority, 1972—. Mem. Border Dist., Uvalde (past pres.), Tex. bar assns. Office: 243 N Getty St Uvalde TX 78801 Tel (512) 278-6922

KINCAID, HUGH REID, b. Fayetteville, Ark., Sept. 30, 1934; B.B.A., U. Ark., 1956, J.D., 1959. Admitted to Ark. bar, 1959, U.S. Supreme Ct. bar, 1963; with JAGC, U.S. Army, 1959-61; trial atty. ct. of claims sect. Dept. Justice Civil Div., Washington, 1961-63; individual practice law, Fayetteville, 1963-67; partner firm Kincaid, Horne & Trumbo, and predecessor, Fayetteville, 1967—; city atty. Fayetteville, 1965-69; mem. Ark. Ho. of Reps., 1971-75; lectr. in bus. law U. Ark. Coll. Bus. Adminstrn., 1963—. Mem. Fayetteville Sch. Bd., 1969-72, 76—; bd. dirs. North Ark. Symphony Soc. Mem. Am., Ark., Washington County (Ark.) (pres. 1969-70) bar assns., Am., Ark. trial lawyers assns., Fayetteville C. of C. (dir. 1973-76). Home: 310 Baxter Ln Fayetteville AR 72701 Office: suite 202 Kincaid Horne & Trumbo First Nat Bank Bldg Fayetteville AR 72701 Tel (501) 521-7050

KINCAID, JAMES LEWIS, b. Carthage, Mo., Oct. 3, 1936; A.B., Harvard, 1958, LL.B., 1961. Admitted to Okla. bar, 1961; asso. firm Huffman, Arrington, Scheurich & Kincaid, and predecessors, Tulsa, 1961-66, partner, 1966-71; sr. partner firm Conner, Winters, Ballaine, Barry & McGowen, Tulsa, 1971—. Vice pres. Tulsa Minor Hockey Assn.; bd. dirs. Margaret Hudson Program for Sch.-Age Parents, Tulsa. Mem. Am., Okla., Tulsa County bar assns., Harvard Law Sch. Assn., Harvard U. Assn. Author: Techniques of Successful Debating, 1961. Home: 1346 E 26th St Tulsa OK 74114 Office: 2400 First National Tower Tulsa OK 74103 Tel (918) 586-5680

KINDRED, MICHAEL JON, b. Decorah, Iowa, June 26, 1938; B.A., U. Chgo., 1960, J.D., 1962, M. Comparative Law., 1964. Admitted to Iowa bar, 1962; asst. prof. civil law Haile Sellassie I U., Addis Ababa, Ethiopia, 1964-69, asst. dean, 1966-68; asso. prof. law Ohio State U., 1969-71, prof., 1971—, asso. dean Coll. Law, 1975—; chmn. com. legal advocacy United Cerebral Palsy Assns., Inc.; cons. Pres.'s Com. on Mental Retardation. Mem. com. for ethical rev. of research proposals Ohio Dept. Mental Health and Mental Retardation, 1974-76, chmn., 1975-76; chmn. Franklin County (Ohio) Children Services Citizens Adv. Com.; chmn. bd. dirs. Assn.

Developmentally Disabled, Columbus. Mem. Ohio State, Am. (chmn. subsect. on mental retardation and law) bar assns., Am. Orthopsychiat. Assn., Am. Assn. Mental Deficiency. Recipient Outstanding Service to Mentally Retarded recognition Ohio Assn. Retarded Children, 1974, commendation for dedication and service to mentally ill and mentally retarded citizens of Ohio, Ohio Senate, 1976; prin. editor, contbg. author: The Mentally Retarded Citizen and the Law, 1976. Home: 984A Chatham Village Columbus OH 43221 Office: 1659 N High St Columbus OH 43210 Tel (614) 422-2631

KING, ARTHUR JAMES, b. Astoria, N.Y., Apr. 27, 1943; B.S., Villanova U., 1965; postgrad. Temple U., 1966, J.D., 1970. Admitted to Pa. Supreme Ct. bar, 1970, U.S. Supreme Ct. bar, 1975; labor relations asst. SKF Industries, Phila., 1966-67; personnel asst. Shell Chem. Co., Princeton, N.J., 1967-69; partner firm McCarthy and King, Norristown, Pa., 1971-73; partner firm McCarthy, King, Narducci & Signore, Norristown, 1973-76; individual practice law, Norristown, 1976—. Alumni rep. Villanova U. Planning Com., 1971-72; bd. dirs. Meridian Youth Service Bur., 1975-76; chmn. PRO; mem. Perkiomen Twp. Republican Com. Mem. Am., Pa., Montgomery County bar assns., Montgomery County Trial Lawyers Assn. Recipient Kessler award, 1968; Ginsburg award, 1968. Office: 516 DeKalb St Norristown PA 19401 Tel (215) 275-0600

KING, BENJAMIN CHAMBERLIN, b. New Iberia, La., May 14, 1915; B.A., Tulane U., 1935, J.D., 1938. Admitted to La. bar, 1940; individual practice law, Iberia, La., 1940-41; sr. partner firm Cook, Clark, Egan, Yancey & King, Shreveport, 1946—. Mem. Am., La., Shreveport (pres. 1974) bar assns. Home: 4524 Fairfield Ave Shreveport LA 71106 Office: 600 Commercial National Bank Bldg Shreveport LA 71101 Tel (318) 221-6277

KING, BILLY D., JR., b. Lismore, La., Oct. 10, 1939; B.A., St. Mary's U., 1963, J.D., 1966. Admitted to Tex. bar; atty. Aetna Casualty & Surety Co., San Antonio, 1966-68; asso. firm T. W. Proctor & Assos., Houston, 1968-69; partner firm Nesheim & King, Houston, 1969-71; house counsel St. Paul Ins. Co., Houston, 1971-73; with IMCO Services Co., Houston, 1973—. Mem. Am., Tex., Harris County (Tex.) bar assns., Delta Theta Phi. Home: 206 Houghton St Katy TX 77450 Office: PO Box 22605 Houston TX 77027 Tel (713) 622-5555

KING, CECIL GAMMILL, b. Clarksville, Ark., May 28, 1918; B.A., Coll. of the Ozarks, 1941; LL.B., Columbia, 1948, LL.M., 1950, J.D., 1969. Admitted to Ark. bar, 1949, Mass. bar, 1953, Mo. bar, 1956, Ohio bar, 1958; atty. State Mut. Life Assurance Co., Worcester, Mass., 1950-55; gen. atty. Life Ins. Co. of Mo., St. Louis, 1955-57; group counsel Nationwide Ins. Cos., Columbus, Ohio, 1957—. Treas. Upper Arlington (Ohio) Civic Orch., 1971-73. Mem. Am. (life ins. com. sect. ins., negligence and compensation law), Ohio State, Columbus bar assns., Assn. Life Ins. Counsel. Contbr. articles to profl. jours. Home: 3925 Bickley Pl Columbus OH 43220 Office: One Nationwide Plaza PO Box 2399 Columbus OH 43216 Tel (614) 227-8375

KING, CLARENCE LEROY, JR., b. Salina, Kans., Apr. 5, 1932; B.S., Kans. Wesleyan U., 1954; J.D., Washburn U., 1957. Admitted to Kans. bar, 1957, U.S. Supreme Ct. bar, 1972; individual practice law, Salina, 1957-58; partner, pres. firm King, Stokes, Knudson & Nitz, and predecessor firms, Salina, 1958—; hwy. commr. State of Kans., 1974-75. Bd. dirs. chmn. Children's Spl. Edn. Center, Salina, 1966-67, Central Kans. Mental Health Center, Salina, 1964-65; sec. youth com. Salinas YMCA; pres. Grace Stewart PTA, Salinas, 1966-67, also life mem.; founder, hon. bd. dirs. Big Brothers, Big Sisters Salina, Salina Youth Care Home Found., Inc.; chmn. Salinas County Democrats, 1966-74, del. nat. conv., 1968, state platform com., 1968, 1970, 1976. Mem. Am., Kans., N.W. Kans., Saline County (pres. 1973) bar assns., Kans. (v.p. 1959, pres. 1964), Saline County (pres. 1964) young lawyers assns., Am., Kans. trial lawyers assns., Defense Research Inst., Kans. Coll. Ofcls. Assn. (bd. dirs. 1959-60), Kans. Wesleyan Univ. Alumni Assn. (pres. 1959-60). Named Outstanding Young Man Salina, C. of C., 1961, Outstanding Young Alumnus, Kans. Wesleyan Univ., 1965; recipient St. Francis Distinguished Service to Youth award St. Francis Boys Homes, Kans. and N.Y., 1971. Home: Rural Route 1 Smolan KS 67479 Office: Box 942 Salina KS 67401 Tel (913) 825-1606

KING, CYRUS ARTHUR, II, b. Lake Charles, La., Nov. 20, 1936; B.A., La. State U., 1957, LL.B., 1960; LL.M., N.Y. U., 1962. Admitted to La. bar, 1960; asso. firm Hall Raggio & Farrar, 1962-63; individual practice law, 1963-75; partner firm King & Ricketts, Lake Charles, 1975—; mem. com. on bar admissions La. Supreme Ct. Pres., Lake Charles Civic Symphony, Calcasieu Hist. Preservation Soc.; chmn. dept. academic instns. Episcopal Diocese of La. Mem. Am., La., S.W. La. bar assns. Home: 624 Ford St Lake Charles LA 70601 Office: 612 Weber Bldg Lake Charles LA 70601 Tel (318) 436-0558

KING, DONALD BARNETT, b. Corvallis, Oreg., July 11, 1932; B.S. in Psychology with honors, Wash. State U., 1954; J.D., Harvard, 1957; LL.M., N.Y. U., 1963. Admitted to Wash. bar, 1958, U.S. Supreme Ct. bar, 1963, Mo. bar, 1970; instr. U. Wash., 1957-58; atty. dept. land transactions Weyerhauser Co., Tacoma, 1958-59; individual practice law, Tacoma, 1958-59; asst. prof. Dickinson Sch. Law, 1959-62; asso. prof. Wayne State U., 1962-64; prof. St. Louis U., 1965—; vis. prof. U. Cin., 1965, Stetson Law Sch., 1974; adj. prof. social work Washington U., St. Louis, 1975-77; dir. Juvenile Delinquency Law Forum-Clinic, St. Louis, 1967-69, Nat. Juvenile Law Center, 1970-71; mem. adv. bd. St. Louis City Juvenile Ct., 1968-70; del. White House Conf. on Children, 1970, White House Conf. on Youth, 1971; mem. adv. bd. St. Louis U. Sch. Social Work, 1970-72, U. Mo. Sch. Social Work, 1976—. Mem. Am. Law Inst., AAUP (pres. chpt. 1970-72), Assn. Am. Law Schs. (chmn. sects. 1968-69, 76), Phi Beta Kappa (pres. chpt. 1976). Author books, including: Law Reform: A Modern Perspective, 1969; 100 Injustices to the Juvenile, 1971; (with others) Commercial Transactions Casebook, 1968, 2d edit., 1974; Consumer Protection Experiments in Sweden, 1974; contbr. numerous articles to legal jours.; editor Internat. Legal Edn. Newsletter, 1963—. Home: 7414 Chamberlain Ave University City MO 63130 Office: 3642 Lindell Blvd Saint Louis MO 63108 Tel (314) 535-3300

KING, DONALD BRUCE, b. San Francisco, Feb. 24, 1931; B.S., U. San Francisco, 1952, J.D., 1958. Admitted to Calif. bar, 1959, U.S. Supreme Ct. bar, 1965; partner firm King & Sullivan, San Francisco, 1959-76; judge San Francisco Superior Ct., 1976—. Office: City Hall 480 San Francisco CA 94102 Tel (415) 558-3261

KING, DONALD EDWARD, b. Atlantic City, Mar. 24, 1934; A.B., Lafayette Coll., 1956; LL.B., St. John's U., 1960, J.D., 1964. Admitted to N.J. bar, 1960; formal referee div. workmen's compensation N.J. Dept. Labor and Industry, 1960-61; partner firm Zashin & King, East Orange, N.J., 1962-70; asst. corp. counsel City of Newark, 1970-73, corp. counsel, 1973-74; judge Juvenile & Domestic Relations Ct., Essex County, N.J., 1974—; mem. Essex County Ethics Com.; instr. Rutgers Inst. for Continuing Legal Edn. Mem. Essex County, Am., Nat. Garden State bar assns., Nat., N.J. councils of juvenile ct. judges, NAACP, Urban League. Office: Juvenile & Domestic Relations Ct 470 High St Newark NJ 07102 Tel (201) 961-7311-12

KING, FLOYD R., b. Salt Lake City, July 1, 1934; B.S., U. Utah, 1958; J.D., U. Wyo., 1961. Admitted to Wyo. bar, 1961; asso. firm Yonkee & Yonkee, Thermopolis, Wyo., 1961; individual practice law, Jackson, Wyo., 1962—; pros. atty. Teton County (Wyo.), 1963-67; atty. City of Jackson, 1962-71; U.S. commr., magistrate, 1968-75. Mem. Am., Wyo. bar assns., Am. Trial Lawyers Assn., C. of C. (pres. 1970). Bd. editors Wyo. Law Rev., 1960-61. Office: 140 S Cache St Jackson WY 83001 Tel (307) 733-2904

KING, HENRY SPENCER, b. Charlotte, N.C., Feb. 7, 1941; B.A., Furman U., 1963; J.D. cum laude, U. S.C., 1968. Admitted to S.C. bar, 1968; partner firm Butler, Means, Evins & Browne, Spartanburg, S.C., 1968; prosecutor City of Spartanburg, 1970-72. Mem. Am., S.C., Spartanburg bar assns., Def. Research Inst., S.C. Def. Attys. Assn. (exec. com.). Contbr. articles and notes S.C. Law Rev. Home: 140 Shoreham Rd Spartanburg SC 29302 Office: PO Drawer 451 Spartanburg SC 29304 Tel (803) 582-5630

KING, HOWARD DEAN, b. Sterling, Ohio, Dec. 11, 1905; B.S., Ohio State U., 1929; LL.B., Cleve. Law Sch., 1934. Admitted to Ohio bar, 1934; practiced in Wooster, Ohio, 1945—; judge Wooster Municipal Ct., 1952-64. Home: 2857 Tuckahoe Circle Wooster OH 44691 Office: 505 N Market St Wooster OH 44691 Tel (216) 262-8171

KING, JACK ALAN, b. Lafayette, Ind., July 29, 1936; B.S. in Fin., Ind. U., 1958, J.D., 1961. Admitted to Ind. bar, 1961; partner firm Ball, Eggleston, King & Bumbleberg, Lafayette, 1961-70; judge Superior Ct. #2, Tippecanoe County, Ind., 1970—; spl. counsel City of Lafayette, 1968; hearing officer Ind. Appellate Ct., 1970, Supreme Ct. Ind., 1973. Mem. Lafayette Bd. Zoning Appeals, 1964-69. Mem. Am., Ind. State, Tippecanoe County bar assns., Ind. Judges Assn., Ind. Jud. Conf. Office: Tippecanoe County Courthouse Lafayette IN 47901 Tel (317) 742-4075

KING, JAMES NEDWED, b. Chgo., July 9, 1947; B.B.A., U. Notre Dame, 1969; J.D., U. N.Mex., 1972. Admitted to N.Mex. bar, 1972; v.p. adminstrn. and ops. Bradbury & Stamm Constrn. Co., Inc., Albuquerque, 1972—. Mem. Associated Gen. Contractors. Home: 1205 Los Arboles St NW Albuquerque NM 87107 Office: POB 25027 Albuquerque NM 87125 Tel (505) 765-1200

KING, JANET LENORA (JAN. L.), b. Gainesville, Fla., May 16, 1937; student U. Fla., 1955-57, b. Gainesville, Fla. So. Coll., 1958-60; LL.B., Stetson U., 1963. Admitted to Fla. bar, 1963, U.S. Dist. Ct. bar, 1966, U.S. Supreme Ct. bar, 1970; individual practice law, Lakeland, Fla., 1963-69, 75—; partner firm Carver & King, Lakeland, 1969-75; asst. city judge, Lakeland. Mem. 10th Judicial Circuit Permanent Bench-Bar Com. on Probate and Guardianship; bd. dirs. Greater Lakeland chpt. ARC; trustee Southside Baptist Ch. Endowment Fund, Lakeland. Mem. Lakeland Bus. & Profl. Women's Club (pres. 1968-69), Am., Lakeland (pres. 976-77) bar assn., Am. Judicature Soc., Assn. Trial Lawyers Am., Acad. Fla. Trial Lawyers; Polk County Trial Lawyers Assn. Home: 987 Lake Hollingsworth Dr Lakeland FL 33803 Office: The King Bldg 107 Morningside Dr Lakeland FL 33803 Tel (813) 683-7491

KING, JOHN FRANCIS, b. Waynesboro, Pa., Apr. 24, 1925; A.B., Dickinson Coll., 1949; LL.B., Georgetown U., 1952. Admitted to Md. bar, 1952; asso. firm Anderson & Barnes, Balt., 1952-54, firm Anderson, Barnes & Coe, Balt., 1955-59; mem. firm Anderson, Coe & King, Balt., 1960—; mem. faculty Johns Hopkins U., 1955-73. Mem. Md. Conf. for Social Concerns 1968—, chmn., 1970. Fellow Am. Coll. Trial Lawyers; mem. Am., Md. State bar assns., Am. Judicature Soc., Bar Assn. Balt. City. Contbr. articles to med. and legal publs. Office: 800 Fidelity Bldg Baltimore MD 21201 Tel (301) 752-1630

KING, JOHN PAUL, b. St. Clair, Mo., Feb. 27, 1937; LL.B., St. Louis U., 1960. Admitted to Mo. bar, 1960; since practiced in St. Louis, asso. firm Leo Lyng, 1960-62; individual practice law, 1962-65; asso. Thomas, Bussee et al., 1965-67; partner firm King, Yusman & Buechner, 1967—; judge, Webster Groves, Mo.; dir. First No. Co., Bank & Trust Co. Pres., 13th Ward Republican Club; mem. Rep. State Com., No. State Rep. Fin. Com. Home: 626 Sherwood Dr Webster Groves MO 63119 Office: 1600 S Hanley Rd Saint Louis MO 63144 Tel (314) 781-0700

KING, LAWRENCE PHILIP, b. Schenectady, Jan. 16, 1929; B.S.S., Coll. City N.Y., 1950; LL.B., N.Y. U., 1953; LL.M., U. Mich., 1957. Admitted to N.Y. State bar, 1954, U.S. Supreme Ct. bar; atty. Paramount Pictures Corp., N.Y.C., 1955-56; asst. prof. law Wayne State U., 1957-59; asst. prof. N.Y. U., 1959-61, asso. prof., 1961-63, prof., 1963—, asso. dean Sch. Law, 1973—; asso. reporter adv. com. on bankruptcy rules U.S. Jud. Conf., 1968-76. Mem. Nat. Bankruptcy Conf., Am. Law Inst., Am., N.Y. State bar assns., Assn. Bar City N.Y., Am. Judicature Soc., Comml. Law League Am. (Man of Year award 2d Dist. 1969). Author: (with R. Duesenberg) Sales and Bulk Transfers under the U.C.C., 1966; contbr. articles, book revs. to legal jours.; editor-in-chief Collier On Bankruptcy, 1964—. Office: NY U Sch of Law 40 Washington Square S New York City NY 10012 Tel (212) 598-7748

KING, MICHAEL HOWARD, b. Bklyn., Oct. 15, 1940; B.A. cum laude, Columbia, 1961, LL.B. summa cum laude, 1964. Admitted to N.Y. State bar, 1964; since practiced in N.Y.C.; asso. firm Botein, Hays, Sklar, & Herzberg, 1964-72, partner, 1973—. Mem. Paramus (N.J.) Charter Study Commn., 1974—. Mem. N.Y. State Bar Assn., Assn. Bar City N.Y. Contbr. articles in field to law jours. Home: 23 Brown Circle Paramus NJ 07652 Office: 200 Park Ave New York City NY 10017 Tel (212) 867-5500

KING, PATRICK CLEBURNE, JR., b. Ft. Gaines, Ga., Oct. 10, 1911; A.B., Mercer U., 1933, LL.B., 1934. Admitted to Ga. bar, 1934; individual practice law, Ft. Gaines, 1934-40; asso. firm Jones, Jones & Sparks, Macon, Ga., 1941-42, firm T. Elton Drake, Atlanta, Ga., 1949-50, firm Reuben A. Garland, Atlanta, 1950-52; individual practice law, Dawson, Ga., 1952-59, Atlanta, 1959-69, Ft. Gaines, 1969—; solicitor City Ct., Ft. Gaines, 1935-39; adjudicator, VA, Atlanta, 1946-47. Pres. Ft. Gaines Hist. Soc., 1969-76. Mem. Pataula Bar Assn. Author: Fort Gaines and Environs, 1976; Kings, Ball, Strozier and Related Families, 1976; The Towns Family of Ga., 1976. Home and Office: 308 E Jefferson St Fort Gaines GA 31751 Tel (912) 768-2416

KING, PETER THOMAS, b. N.Y.C., Apr. 5, 1944; B.A., St. Francis Coll., Bklyn., 1965; J.D., U. Notre Dame, South Bend, Ind., 1968. Admitted to N.Y. bar, 1969, U.S. Dist. Ct. bars for So. and Eastern Dists. N.Y., 1977; asso. firms Saxe, Bacon & Bolan, N.Y.C., 1968-70, Max E. Greenberg, Trayman, Harris, Cantor, Reiss & Blasky, N.Y.C., 1970-72; dep. atty. Nassau County (N.Y.), Mineola, 1972-74, exec. asst. to chief Dep. Exec., 1974-76, chief dep. atty., 1976-77; gen. counsel Nassau Off-Track Betting Corp., 1977—. Mem. Nassau County Republican Com., 1971, 73—; exec. leader Seaford (N.Y.) Rep. Committeemen's Council, 1975—; mem. Nassau County Rep. Exec. Com., 1975—. Mem. N.Y. State, Am., Nassau County bar assns. Home: 1442 Roth Rd Seaford NY 11783 Office: 220 Fulton Ave Hempstead NY 11550 Tel (516) 292-8300

KING, ROBERT LEE, b. Vincennes, Ind., June 19, 1946; student U. Denver, 1964-66; B.S., Ind. U., 1968; J.D., Harvard U., 1972. Admitted to Fla. bar, 1973, Ind. bar, 1973; law clk. firm McGuire, Woods & Battle, Richmond, Va., 1971; asso. firm English, McCaughan & O'Bryan, Ft. Lauderdale, Fla., 1973-76; individual practice law, Fort Lauderdale, 1976—; dir. The Chord Properties, Inc., Ft. Lauderdale, 1975—. Mem. Ind. Assn. CPA's (asso.), Ind. U. Alumni Assn. Broward County, Fla. (v.p. 1976—), Beta Gamma Sigma, Beta Alpha Psi. Home: 3500 Galt Ocean Dr Apt 302 Fort Lauderdale FL 33308 Office: 19 Southeast 3d Ave Fort Lauderdale FL 33301 Tel (305) 764-7117

KING, ROBERT WATKINS, JR., b. Wilson, N.C., Apr. 28, 1930; B.S., Hampden-Sydney Coll., 1952; J.D. with honors, U. N.C., 1959. Admitted to N.C. bar, 1959; mem. firm Moore & Van Allen, Charlotte, N.C., 1959—. Central br. bd. mgrs. YMCA, Charlotte; bd. dirs. Charlotte-Mecklenburg Heart Assn. Mem. Am., N.C., 26th Jud. Dist. bar assns. Asso. editor N.C. Law Rev., 1958-59. Home: 2154 Norton Rd Charlotte NC 28207 Office: 3000 NCNB Plaza Charlotte NC 28280 Tel (204) 374-1300

KING, ROBERT WILSON, b. Durant, Miss., Sept. 30, 1926; B.A., Cumberland U., 1948, J.D. (Delta Theta Phi scholar), 1950. Admitted to Miss. bar, 1950; individual practice law, Jackson, Miss., 1950—; lectr. in field. Chmn. Jackson Municipal Library Bd., 1970-74; bd. dirs. Jackson Symphony, 1971-75, Bapt. Children's Village, 1968—, Miss. Opera Assn., 1970—. Mem. Am., Miss., Hinds County bar assns., Am. Judicature Soc. Contbr. articles Miss. Law Inst., Miss. Bankers Publs. Home: 3671 Woodward Pl Jackson MS 39216 Office: 429 Tombigbee PO Box 123 St Jackson MS 39205 Tel (601) 948-1547

KING, RUFUS, b. Seattle, Mar. 25, 1917; student U. Wash., 1934-35; A.B., Princeton, 1938; student Stanford U. Law Sch., 1940-41; J.D., Yale, 1943. Admitted to N.Y. bar, 1944, D.C. bar, 1949, Md. bar, 1954; atty. Air Transport Assn., 1944-46; individual practice law, Washington, 1947—; counsel Senate Crime Com., 1951-52; partner firm Rice & King, 1953-60. Chmn. Washington Bd. Trade Coms. Mem. Am. Bar Assn. (ho. of dels. 1960-62, 68-70), Am. Law Inst., Am. Judicature Soc., Inst. Jud. Adminstrn., D.C. Bar Assn., Bar Assn. City N.Y., Scribes. Author: The Drug Hang-Up, 1973; Gambling and Organized Crime, 1969; contbr. articles to profl. jours. Home: 3524 Williamsburg Ln NW Washington DC 20008 Office: 808 Woodward Bldg Washington DC 20005 Tel (202) 638-4117

KING, RUFUS GUNN, III, b. New Haven, Conn., June 16, 1942; A.B., Princeton U., 1966; J.D. Georgetown U., 1971. Admitted to Dist. Columbia bar, 1971; since practiced in Washington, D.C.; asso. firm Karr & Greensfelder, 1971-73, Rollinson, Stein & Halpert, 1973; individual practice law, 1973—; staff counsel Automobile Owners Action Council. Mem. Bar Assn. D.C., Am. Bar Assn., Phi Alpha Delta. Home: 1323 E Capitol St SE Washington DC 20003 Office: 808 Woodward Bldg Washington DC 20005 Tel (202) 638-4117

KING, SAMUEL PAILTHORPE, b. Hankow, China, Apr. 13, 1916 (parents Am. citizens); B.S., Yale, 1937, LL.B., 1940. Admitted to D.C. bar, 1940, Hawaii bar, 1940; practiced in Honolulu, 1941-42, 46-61, 70-72, Washington, 1942; mem. firm King & McGregor, 1947-53, King & Myhre, 1957-61; judge 1st Circuit Ct. Hawaii, 1961-70, Family Ct., 1966-70; judge U.S. Dist. Ct. for Hawaii, 1972—, chief judge, 1974; faculty Nat. Coll. State Judiciary, 1968-73. Chmn. Hawaii Central Com., Republican Party, 1953-55, Nat. Com., 1971-72. Fellow Am. Bar Found.; mem. Am., Hawaii (pres. 1953) bar assns., Order of Coif. Co-translator, co-editor: The Theory and Practice of Go (O. Korschelt), 1965. Home: 1717 Mott-Smith Dr Honolulu HI 96822 Office: Federal Bldg Honolulu HI 96813 Tel (808) 546-7132

KING, THOMAS HENRY, b. Washington, Jan. 17, 1904; J.D., Am. U., 1925. Admitted to N.C. bar, 1927, D.C. bar, 1933, U.S. Supreme Ct. bar, 1948; individual practice law, Sparta, N.C., 1930-33, Washington, 1947—; house counsel Liberty Mut. Ins. Co., Balt., 1936-68; v.p., asso. counsel Nat. Lloyds, Balt., 1938-41; served with JAGC, U.S. Army, 1941-47. nat. judge adv. Res. Officers Assn., 1948-50, nat. pres., 1953-54, ret. as brig. gen. Res., 1964; pres. Judge Advs. Assn., 1955; gen. counsel Armed Forces Communication Assn., 1953-73, chmn. ct. claims com., 1975-76. Mem. D.C. Bar Assn. Decorated Legion of Merit, Bronze Star. Office: 805 15th St NW Suite 524 Washington DC 20005 Tel (202) 347-6144

KING, TUNNEY LEE, b. Columbus, Ohio, Oct. 19, 1949; B.A. cum laude, Ohio State U., 1971, J.D. summa cum laude, 1974. Admitted to Ohio bar, 1974; individual practice law, Columbus, 1974—. Mem. Ohio State, Columbus bar assns., Am. Trial Lawyers Assn., Ohio Acad. Trial Lawyers. Contbr. article to law review. Home: 215 S Roosevelt Bexley OH 43209 Office: 88 E Broad St Columbus OH 43215 Tel (614) 224-0933

KING, WILLARD LEROY, b. Batavia, Ill., Dec. 9, 1893; student Knox Coll., 1912-14; Ph.B., U. Chgo., 1916, J.D., 1917; D.C.L. (hon.), Bowdoin Coll., 1951; LL.D., Knox Coll., 1954. Admitted to Ill. bar, 1917, U.S. Supreme Ct. bar, 1950; asso. firm King, Robin, Gale & Pillinger, and predecessor firms, 1920-26, partner, 1926—; mem. loyalty review bd. Civil Service Commn., 1951-53; mem. Ill. Gov's Mental Health Commn., 1964-68. Trustee Museum Sci. and Industry, 1949—; Chgo. Hist. Soc., 1949—; Menninger Found., 1950—. Mem. Chgo. Law Inst. (pres. 1938, Law Club Chgo. (pres. 1953-54), Am., Ill., Chgo. (gov. 1929-38) bar assns., Order of Coif. Co-Author: Opinion Evidence in Illinois, 1942; author: Melville Weston Fuller, Chief Justice of United States, 1888-1910, 2d edit. 1967; Lincoln's Manager David Davis, 2d edit., 1976; articles to profl. jours. Home: 5801 Dorchester Chicago IL 60637 Office: 135 S LaSalle St Chicago IL 60603 Tel (312) CE6-4280

KING, WILLIAM BRUCE, b. Boston, June 3, 1932; A.B., Harvard, 1954, LL.B., 1959. Admitted to Mass. bar, 1959; asso. firm Goodwin, Procter & Hoar, Boston, 1959-67, partner, 1968—; trustee Cambridge Savs. Bank (Mass.), 1965—, mem. bd. investment, 1974—; chmn. greater Boston com. Harvard Law Sch. Fund, 1975—. Trustee

Buckingham Browne & Nichols Sch., Cambridge, 1970-76, sec., 1970-73, vice chmn. bd., 1974-76; vice chmn. Cambridge Hist. Commn., 1973—. Mem. Boston, Cambridge-Arlington-Belmont (pres. 1974-75) bar assns. Home: 25 Hurlbut St Cambridge MA 02138 Office: 28 State St Boston MA 02109 Tel (617) 523-5700

KING, WILLIAM DAVIS, b. Anniston, Ala., Nov. 27, 1939; A.B., Duke U., 1963, LL.B., 1965. Admitted to Fla. bar, 1965; asso. firm Mahnoey Hadlow & Adams, Jacksonville, Fla., 1965-69, mem. firm, 1969—. Mem. Fla. Bar, Jacksonville, Am. bar assns., Am. Judicature Soc., Jacksonville C. of C. (com. of 100 1974—). Office: 100 Laura St Jacksonville FL 32202 Tel (904) 354-1100

KING, WILLIAM HAVEN, b. Huntington, W.Va., Oct. 15, 1911; A.B., Dartmouth, 1933; LL.B., U. Richmond, 1936. Admitted to Va. bar, 1935, U.S. Supreme Ct. bar, 1955; partner firm McGuire, Woods & Battle, and predecessors, Richmond, Va., 1942—; mem. Va. Bd. Bar Examiners, 1951—; mem. bd. mgrs. Nat. Conf. Bar Examiners, 1962-68, chmn., 1966-67. Chmn. parking bd. City of Richmond, 1958-64; pres. Richmond chpt. ARC, 1956-58, bd. dirs. Richmond YMCA, 1957-64; pres. Va. League Planned Parenthood, 1955-56; mem. gov's. adv. com. on Medicare and Medicaid, 1969—; gen. counsel Blue Cross of Va., Blue Shield of Va., 1950—, Citizens Home Ins. Co., 1956—; Fellow Am. Bar Found. (Va. chmn.), Am. Coll. Trial Lawyers; mem. Am. (ho. of dels. 1967-68), Va. State (pres. 1960-61, chmn. com. legal ethics 1958-60, chmn. com. on judiciary 1970-71), Richmond (pres. 1957-58) bar assns. Home: 6126 Saint Andrews Circle Richmond VA 23226 Office: McGuire Woods & Battle 1400 Ross Bldg Richmond VA 23219 Tel (804) 644-4131

KING, WILLIAM THEODORE, b. Detroit, Feb. 3, 1933; B.A. cum laude, Principia Coll., 1954; J.D., Harvard, 1957. Admitted to U.S. Supreme Ct. bar, 1964, Calif. Supreme Ct. bar, 1958, U.S. Dist. Ct. bar for So. Dist. Calif., 1958, U.S. Tax Ct. bar, 1970; asso. firm Lovell, King & Case, Los Angeles, 1958-60, partner, 1961—. Pres. Los Angeles Bd. Traffic Commrs., 1973-75; commr. Los Angeles Dept. Water and Power, 1975-76. Mem. Am., Calif. State, Los Angeles County bar assns., State Bar Calif., Calif. Trial Lawyers Assn. Home: 339 N Palm Dr Apt 101 Beverly Hills CA 90212 Office: 550 S Flower St Suite 910 Los Angeles CA 90071 Tel (213) 626-4481

KINGSBURY, BURTON ALEXANDER, b. Burlington, Kans., Dec. 27, 1908; A.B., U. Kans., 1929, LL.B., 1933. Admitted to Kans. bar, 1933, Wash. bar, 1939; individual practice law, Burlington, 1933-38; partner firms Livesey Kingsbury & Livesey, and predecessor, Bellingham, Wash., 1939-42, 44-73, Kingsbury & Ludwigson, Bellingham, 1973-74, McCush, Kingsbury, O'Connor, Ludwigson, Thompson & Hages, Bellingham, 1974—; city atty. City of Burlington, 1933-38; county atty. Coffey County (Kans.), 1934-38. Trustee Western Wash. State Coll., 1949-57, 65-71, chmn., 1950-57, 69-71. Mem. Whatiom County (pres. 1947), Wash. State (bd. govs. 1962-65), Am. bar assns. Home: 233 Middlefield Rd Bellingham WA 98225 Office: 220 W Prospect St Bellingham WA 98225 Tel (206) 734-2000

KINGSBURY, HAROLD NELSON, b. Ashland, Wis., Jan. 17, 1943; B.S. in Math., U. Wis., 1965, M.S., 1967, J.D., 1973. Admitted to Wis. bar, 1974; systems analyst, programmer Oscar Mayer Co., Madison Wis., 1968-70; partner firm Pressentin & Kingsbury, Monona, Wis., 1975—. Mem. Assn. Computing Machinery, ACLU, Am., Dane County, Wis. bar assns. Home: 3445 Portland Ave Minneapolis MN 55407 Office: 7400 Metro Blvd Edina MN 55413 Tel (612) 824-0998

KINGSLEY, JAMES RANDOLPH, b. Lorain, Ohio, Feb. 8, 1947; B.A., Muskingum Coll., 1969; J.D., U. Toledo, 1972. Admitted to Ohio bar, 1972, Fed. bar, 1974; mem. firm Gerhardt and Kingsley, Circleville, Ohio, 1972-75; individual practice of law, 1975—, Circleville, 1975—; asst. prosecuting atty. Pickaway County, 1972-75, pros. atty., 1977—; instr. Ohio Peace Officers Tng. Counsel, 1974-75. Bd. dirs. ARC, 1975-76; legal counsel Community Fund, 1975-76. Mem. Am., Ohio State, Pickaway County bar assns. Note and comment editor U. Toledo Law Review, 1972. Home: 623 Beverly Rd Circleville OH 43113 Office: 157 W Main St Circleville OH 43113 Tel (614) 474-4911

KINKEAD, SIDNEY CLAY, JR., b. Lexington, Ky., July 21, 1933; B.B.A., U. Va., 1955; LL.B., U. Ky., 1964, J.D., 1970. Admitted to Ky. bar, 1965; partner firm Harbison, Kessinger, Lisle & Bush, Lexington, 1972—. Chmn. Lexington-Fayette Urban County Govt. Civil Service Commn.; pres. Lexington Humane Soc. Mem. Fayette County, Ky., Am. bar assns., Order of Coif. Editorial bd. U. Ky. Law Jour. Home: 1222 Richmond Rd Lexington KY 40502 Office: 101 E Vine St Lexington KY 40507 Tel (606) 252-3591

KINLEY, JOHN ROBERT, b. Rockford, Ill., Nov. 25, 1915; B.A., Beloit (Wis.) Coll., 1937; J.D. Northwestern U., Evanston, Ill., 1940. Admitted to Ill. bar, 1940; asso. firm Williams, McCarthy, Kinley, Rudy & Picha, Rockford, 1946—; lectr. Chmn. Rockford Fair Housing Bd., 1969-74; trustee Beloit Coll., 1968-71. Mem. Am., Ill., Winnebago County (pres. 1969-70) bar assns. Contbr. articles profl. jours. Home: 821 Parkwood St Rockford IL 61107 Office: Talcott Bldg 321 W State St Rockford IL 61101 Tel (815) 987-8900

KINNEY, STEVENS PARK, II, b. Boulder, Colo., Jan. 24, 1933; B.A., U. Colo., 1956, LL.B., 1958. Admitted to Colo. bar, 1960, Mil. Ct. Appeals bar, 1967, U.S. Supreme Ct. bar, 1967; mem. firm Vivian, Sherman & Kinney, Denver, 1960-63; individual practice law, Denver, 1963-73; mem. firm Torgan, Hall & Kinney, Denver, 1973—; municipal judge City of Arvada (Colo.), 1969—. Trustee Denver Lions Found. Mem. Am., Colo., Denver bar assns., Colo. Trial Lawyers Assn., Colo. Municipal Judges Assn., Am. Judges Assn., Am. Judicature Soc. Home: 12465 W 66th Ave Arvada CO 80004 Office: 1728 Lincoln Center Bldg Denver CO 80203 Tel (303) 893-1776

KINSELLA, JAMES HALL, b. Hartford, Conn., July 12, 1924; A.B., Trinity Coll., Hartford, 1947; LL.B., U. Nebr., 1952. Admitted to Nebr. bar, 1952, Conn. bar, 1953; asso. firm Kinsella & Goldfarb, 1953-60; judge Probate Ct., Dist. of Hartford, 1960—; partner firm Kinsella & Krass, Hartford, 1970—; pres. Conn. Probate Assembly, 1973-75; mem. Hartford City Council, 1953-60; dep. mayor City of Hartford, 1953-55, mayor, 1957-60. Mem. Hartford County, Conn., Am. (vice chmn. pre-paid legal service sub-com. div. real estate and probate bar assns. Office: 1 Lewis St Hartford CT 06103 Tel (203) 522-3265

KINSELLA, JOHN DEGAN, b. Syracuse, N.Y., Mar. 6, 1941; B.S. in Accounting, Syracuse U., 1965, J.D., 1970. Admitted to N.Y. State bar, 1971; asst. regional counsel SBA, Syracuse, 1971-73; asst. dist. atty. Onondaga County (N.Y.), 1973—; legis. counsel N.Y. State Assembly, 1971-73; auditor Gen. Telephone & Electronics, Syracuse, 1965-67. Mem. Fed. (pres. Upstate N.Y. chpt. 1973-77), Am., N.Y. State, bar assns., Phi Alpha Delta, Nat. Dist. Attys. Assn. Home: 111 Lathrop Rd Syracuse NY 13219 Office: 505 E Washington St Syracuse NY 13202 Tel (315) 488-5031

KINSER, HENRY EUGENE, b. Grayson County, Ky., Jan. 17, 1946; B.A. in History and Govt., Western Ky. U., 1968; J.D., 1973. Admitted to Ky. bar, 1974; individual practice law, Lexington, Ky., 1974-75; asso. firm Kincaid, Wilson, Schaeffer & Hembree, Lexington, 1975—. Mem. Central Ky. Criminal Def. Lawyers Assn. Office: 400 Central Bank Bldg Lexington KY 40507 Tel (606) 254-9371

KINSEY, ROBERT STANLEIGH, III, b. Highland Park, Ill., Dec. 31, 1944; B.A., Grinnell Coll., 1967; J.D., U. Iowa, 1973; student Albert Schweitzer Coll., Switzerland, 1965-66. Admitted to Iowa bar, 1973; mem. firm Brown, Kinsey & Funkhouser, Mason City, Iowa, 1973—. Bd. dirs. HOPE Enterprises, ARC, YMCA, United Way, Legal Aid Corp. Mem. Am., Cerro Gordo County (sec.), Iowa bar assns. Home: 915 N Delaware St Mason City IA 50401 Office: 19 1/2 E State St POB 1282 Mason City IA 50401 Tel (515) 423-6223

KINSEY, RONALD CLARKE, b. Washington, June 28, 1942; A.B., Dartmouth Coll., 1964; J.D., U. Wash., 1967. Admitted to Wash. bar, 1970; since practiced in Seattle, dep. pros. atty. King County, 1970-71; legal cons. Municipal Research & Services Center Wash., 1971—. Mem. Wash. State Bar Assn., Am. Soc. Pub. Adminstn., Delta Theta Phi. Contbr. articles to legal jours. Home: 4346 NE 58th Seattle WA 98105 Office: 4719 Brooklyn Ave NE Seattle WA 98105 Tel (206) 543-9050

KINTNER, EARL WILSON, b. Corydon, Ind., Nov. 6, 1912; A.B., DePauw U., 1936; J.D., Ind. U., 1938; LL.D., DePauw U., 1970. Admitted to Ind. bar, 1938, D.C. bar, 1950; prosecuting atty. Princeton, Ind., 1938-44; trial atty. FTC, Washington, 1948-53, gen. counsel, 1953-59, chmn., 1959-61; individual practice law, Princeton, Ind., 1938-44; sr. partner firm Arent, Fox, Kintner, Plotkin & Kahn, Washington, 1961—. Mem. Am., Fed. bar assns. Author: The Hadamar Trial, 1947, History of the United Nations War Crimes Commission and the Development of the Law of War, 1949; Federal Trade Commission's Manual for Attorneys, 1951; Equal Justice Under Law, 1965; An Antitrust Primer, 1970; A Robinson-Patman Primer, 1970; A Primer on Deceptive Business Practices, 1971; A Primer on the Law of Mergers, 1973; An International Antitrust Primer, 1974; An Antitrust Primer, 1975; An Intellectual Property Primer, 1975; A Legislative History of the Antitrust Laws of the United States, 1978; Kintner on the Antitrust Laws of the United States, 1978; contbr. articles to profl. jours. Office: 1815 H St NW Washington DC 20006 Tel (202) 857-6040

KINTNER, JANET IDE, b. Dayton, Ohio, Feb. 25, 1944; B.A., U. Ariz., 1966, J.D., 1968. Admitted to Ariz. bar, 1968, Calif. bar, 1969; civil atty. Legal Aid Soc., San Diego, 1969-70; dep. city atty. City of San Diego, 1971-74; individual practice law, San Diego, 1974-76; municipal ct. judge San Diego Jud. Dist., 1976—; tchr. law for laymen San Diego Coll., 1973-75, San Diego State U., 1974. Mem. Calif. Atty.' Gen.'s Consumer Task Force, 1972-76; So. Calif. Consumer Protection Com., 1972-73, ad hoc consumer edn. com. San Diego City Schs., 1974-75. Mem. San Diego County Municipal Ct. Judges Assn., Calif. Judges Assn., San Diego County Bar Assn. (dir. 1973-75, v.p. 1976). Office: 220 W Broadway San Diego County Courthouse San Diego CA 92101 Tel (714) 236-2121

KINZIE, RAYMOND WYANT, b. Chgo., Oct. 20, 1930; B.A., Carleton Coll., 1952; LL.B., Yale, 1955, J.D., 1967. Admitted to Ill. Supreme Ct. bar, 1956, U.S. Supreme Ct. bar, 1964; asso. firm McBride & Baker, Chgo., 1955-56; asso. trust counsel Continental Ill. Nat. Bank and Trust Co., Chgo., 1956-59; asst. trust officer Lake View Trust and Savings Bank, Chgo., 1959-65, asst. v.p., comml. loan officer, head credit dept., 1965-71, v.p., trust officer, head trust dept., 1971—. Mem. Leadership Council Ravenswood Hosp. Med. Center, Chgo., bd. dirs. hosp. and med. center, 1975—. Mem. Chgo. Bar Assn., Land Trust Council of Ill. Home: 1027 N Marion St Oak Park IL 60302 Office: 3201 N Ashland Ave Chicago IL 60657 Tel (312) 525-2180

KIPLE, CHARLES MURRAY, b. Ottumwa, Iowa, Nov. 11, 1939; B.B.A., U. Iowa, 1961, J.D., 1968. Admitted to Iowa bar, 1968; asso. firm Barnes & Schlegel, Ottumwa, 1968-69; partner firm Kiple & Kiple, Ottumwa, 1969—; alt. judge Ottumwa Municipal Ct., 1970-74; jud. magistrate Wapello County, Iowa, 1974-75. Mem. Ottumwa Planning and Zoning Commn., 1971-75. Mem. Wapello County, 8th Jud. Dist. Iowa, Iowa, Am. bar assns., Iowa Assn. Trial Lawyers. Articles editor Iowa Law Rev., 1967-68. Home: Route 6 Oakridge Farm Ottumwa IA 52501 Office: 106 N Market St Ottumwa IA 52501 Tel (515) 683-1626

KIPLE, JAMES LEON, b. Ottumwa, Iowa, Aug. 15, 1942; B.S., State U. Iowa, 1964, J.D. with distinction, 1966. Admitted to Iowa bar, 1966; asso. firm Barnes & Schlegel, Ottumwa, 1966-69; partner firm Kiple & Kiple, Ottumwa, 1969—; jud. hospitalization referee Wapello County (Iowa), 1976—. Mem. Ottawa bd. Iowa Community Sch. Dist. Bd. Edn., 1968-71; trustee Ottumwa Area Devel. Corp., 1971—. Mem. Am., Iowa State, 8th Jud. Dist., Wapello County (pres. 1973-74) bar assns. Comments editor Iowa Law Rev., 1965-66; contbr. articles to legal jours. Home: 127 E Pennsylvania St Ottumwa IA 52501 Office: 106 N Market St Ottumwa IA 52501 Tel (515) 683-1626

KIPP, CARMAN E., b. Salt Lake City, Dec. 16, 1927; J.D., U. Utah, 1950. Admitted to Utah bar; partner firm Kipp & Christian, Salt Lake City; mem. Utah Bar Commn., 1975—. Active ARC, Cancer Soc., United Fund, Presbyn. Ch. Mem. Am., Utah State, Salt Lake County bar assns., Am. Trial Lawyers Assn., Am. Bd. Trial Assos. Recipient Distinguished Service award Utah Jaycees, 1958, Outstanding Nat. Chmn. award U.S. Jaycees, 1959, Nat. Outstanding Alumnus award Phi Delta Theta, 1968. Office: 600 Comml Club Bldg 32 Exchange Pl Salt Lake City UT 84111 Tel (801) 521-3773

KIRBO, CHARLES HUGHES, b. Bainbridge, Ga., Mar. 5, 1927; LL.B., U. Ga., 1939. Admitted to Ga. bar; partner firm King & Spalding, Atlanta, 1960—. Chmn. Ga. Democratic Party, 1970-74. Mem. Am. Coll. Trial Lawyers, Am. Judicature Soc. Home: 10705 Stroup Rd Roswell GA 30075 Office: 2500 Trust Co Tower Atlanta GA 30303 Tel (404) 572-4600

KIRBY, JAMES CORDELL, JR., b. Macon County, Tenn., June 19, 1928; B.A., Vanderbilt U., 1950; J.D., LL.M., N.Y. U., 1954. Admitted to Tenn. bar, 1954, Ill. bar, 1966, Ohio bar, 1971, N.Y. State bar, 1975; asso. firm Waller, Davis and Lansden, Nashville, 1954, 57-61; served to 1st lt. JAGC, U.S. Army, 1954-57; chief counsel U.S. Senate Judiciary Subcom. on Constl. Amendments, Washington, 1961-63; asso. prof. law Vanderbilt U., Nashville, 1963-64, prof., 1964-65; prof. law Northwestern U., Chgo., 1965-68; prof. law N.Y. U., N.Y.C., 1968-70, 74—, v.p., gen. counsel, 1974-75, also dir. appellate judges seminars, 1976—; dean, prof. law Ohio State U., Columbus, 1970-74. Mem. Am., N.Y.C. (exec. dir. spl. com. 1967-70) bar assns. Author: (with others) Congress and the Public Trust, 1970; Rights of Americans, 1970; contbr. articles to law revs. Home: 33 Washington Sq W New York City NY 10011 Office: 40 Washington Sq S New York City NY 10012 Tel (212) 598-2571

KIRBY, JEFFERSON DAVIS, III, b. Shubuta, Miss., Aug. 28, 1940; B.A., U. Va., 1961, LL.B., 1964; LL.M., Georgetown U., 1965. Admitted to Va. bar, 1964, D.C. bar, 1965, Ga. bar, 1968; asso. firm Fisher & Phillips, Atlanta, 1967-68, Hansell, Post, Brandon & Dorsey, Atlanta, 1968—. Mem. Am., Ga., Va., Atlanta bar assns., Phi Beta Kappa. Home: 3687 Windy Ct Tucker GA 30084 Office: 3300 1st Nat Bank Tower Atlanta GA 30303 Tel (404) 581-8162

KIRBY, JEROME W., b. Goldthwaite, Tex., Aug. 15, 1922; B.B.A., U. Tex., Austin, 1950, LL.B., J.D., 1956. Admitted to Tex. bar, 1956; sr. partner firm Kirby, Ratliff & Sansom, Littlefield, Tex., 1956—; dir. First Fed. Savs. and Loan Assn., Littlefield. Mem. Tex. State Bar Assn., Order of Coif. Contbr. article to legal jour. Home: 136 E 23rd St Littlefield TX 79339 Office: Box 888 Littlefield TX 79330 Tel (806) 385-3455

KIRBY, JERRY ARNOLD, b. Monroe, La., Mar. 19, 1941; B.A. in History, Northeast State Coll., Monroe, 1966; J.D., Loyola U., 1969. Admitted to La. bar, 1969, Fed. bar, 1969, U.S. Supreme Ct bar, 1973; partner firm Bruscato & Kirby, Monroe, 1969-70; partner firm Kirby & McLeod, Monroe, 1972-74; asst. dist. atty. Monroe, 1975; individual practice law, 1975—. Mem. Counsel on Alcoholism and Drug Abuse, Ouachita Parish, Monroe, 1971—. Mem. La. Assn. Trial Lawyers. Recipient Am. Jurisprudence Award, 1968. Mem. Loyola Law Review, 1967-69. Home: 3719 Caddo St Monroe LA 71201 Office: PO Box 3151 Monroe LA 71201 Tel (318) 388-3701

KIRBY, JOHN JOSEPH, JR., b. Washington, Oct. 22, 1939; A.B., Fordham U., 1961; B.A. (Rhodes scholar), Oxford U., 1964; LL.B., U. Va., 1966. Admitted to Va. bar, 1966, N.Y. bar, 1969, D.C. bar, 1972; dep. dir. Pres.'s Commn. Campus Unrest, 1970; spl. asst. Civil Rights div. U.S. Dept. Justice, Washington, 1967-68; asst. prof. law U. Va. Law Sch., Charlottesville, 1966-67; asso. firm Mudge, Rose, Guthrie & Alexander, N.Y.C., 1969-70, partner, 1971—. Bd. dirs. Georgetown U. Mem. Assn. Bar City N.Y., Am., Va., D.C. bar assns., Lawyers Club. Home: 417 Park Ave New York City NY 10022 Office: 20 Broad St New York City NY 10005 Tel (212) 422-6767

KIRBY, LE GRAND CARNEY, III, b. Dallas, Feb. 25, 1941; B.B.A., So. Meth. U., 1963, LL.B., 1965. Admitted to Tex. bar, 1965; mem. firm Arthur Young & Co., Dallas, 1967—. Mem. Dallas Jr. Bar, Dallas C.P.A.'s, Tex. Soc. C.P.A.'s. Home: 5520 Swiss Ave Dallas TX 75214 Office: 2900 Republic Bank Bldg Dallas TX 75214 Tel (214) 742-2333

KIRBY, MICHAEL EDWARD, b. Port Sulphur, La., Apr. 6, 1948; J.D., La. State U., 1973. Admitted to La. bar, 1974, U.S. Ct. Appeals 5th Circuit bar, 1975, U.S. Dist. Ct. Eastern Dist. La. bar, 1975; individual practice law, Port Sulphur, 1974-75; mem. firm Kirby & Ragusa, Port Sulphur, 1976—. Mem. Am., La. State bar assns. Home: POB 5 Port Sulphur LA 70083 Office: POB 901 Port Sulphur LA 70083 Tel (504) 564-2587

KIRBY, STEVEN EVANS, b. Burbank, Calif., Oct. 9, 1945; B.S., U. Ore., 1967; J.D. cum laude, U. San Francisco, 1971. Admitted to Calif. bar, 1972; asso. firm O'Melveny & Myers, Los Angeles, 1971-73, firm Hollister & Brace, Santa Barbara, Calif., 1973—, prin., 1976. Bd. dirs. Legal Aid Found., Santa Barbara, 1976—. Mem. Am., Los Angeles County, Santa Barbara County bar assns., McAuliffe Honor Soc. Editor in chief U. San Francisco Law Rev., 1970-71. Office: 1126 Santa Barbara St Santa Barbara CA 93101 Tel (805) 963-6711

KIRBY, WILLIAM ROY, b. Concordia, Kans., Sept. 6, 1914; A.B., U. Kans., 1937, LL.B., 1939. Admitted to Kans. bar, 1939; asso. firm Yancey & Douglass, Oklahoma City, 1939-40; partner firm Hildreth & Kirby, Coffeyville, Kans., 1940-41; individual practice law, Coffeyville, 1945-71; partner firm Hall, Kirby & Levy, Coffeyville, 1971-75; individual practice law, Coffeyville, 1975—; asst. county atty. Montgomery County, Kans., 1947-48, county atty., 1949-52; city atty. City of Coffeyville, 1975; mem. subcoms. Kans. Jud. Council. Pres. Coffeyville C. of C., 1974; Republican candidate Kans. Legislature, 1976. Mem. Am., Kans., Okla., Montgomery County bar assns., Order of Coif, Phi Delta Phi. Home: 1209 W 4th St Coffeyville KS 67337 Office: PO Box 236 Coffeyville KS 67337 Tel (316) 251-5500

KIRK, HUGH ADAM, b. Toledo, Ohio, Aug. 15, 1916; B.S., U. Toledo; B. Comml. Sci., Benjamin Franklin U.; LL.B., M.P.L., S.J.D., Nat. U. Admitted to D.C. bar, 1939, Ohio bar, 1954, also U.S. Supreme Ct. bar; mem. patent dept. Electric Autolite Co., 1935-36; mem. examining corps U.S. Patent Office, 1936-41; mem. patent dept. Shell Devel. Co., San Francisco, 1941-45; mem. patent dept. Internat. Tel. & Tel., N.Y.C. and Antwerp, Belgium, 1945-47; individual practice law, Antwerp, 1947-50, Little Rock, 1950-51, Toledo, Ohio, 1951—. Mem. Am. Chem. Soc., AAAS, Am., Toledo patent law assns., Am., Toledo, Lucas County bar assns. Home: 4120 Tantara Dr Toledo OH 43623 Office: 4210 W Central Ave Toledo OH 43606 Tel (419) 531-1467

KIRK, JOHN JOSEPH, b. Pitts., Oct. 6, 1933; B.A. summa cum laude, U. Pitts., 1958; J.D. summa cum laude, Duquesne U., 1962. Admitted to Pa. bar, 1962, Fla. bar, 1974, U.S. Supreme Ct. bar, 1964; staff counsel Alcoa, 1962-65; asst. dist. atty. Allegheny County, 1965-67; individual practice law, Pitts., 1967—; dir. Landmark Inc. Pitts., 1965—, solicitor Steelhaulers Health Care & Pension Fund, 1970—. Com. chmn. City of McCandless, 1969-73; mem. N. Allegheny Sch. Bd. 1972-74; v.p. Big Bros. Allegheny City, 1973—. Mem. Am., Pa., Allegheny City, Fla., Nat. bar assns., Am., Pa., N.Y. State trial lawyers assns., Am. Acad. Law and Sci., Am. Arbitration Assn., Am. Judicature Soc., Pitts. Med.-Legal Inst., Am. Lawyers Assn. Author: (with Matthew Bender) What I Know of the Practice of Law, 1970; Sine Qua Non, Revisited, 1972; The Role of the Minor

Judiciary in Criminal Cases, 1974. Home: 1921 Brandywine Dr Allison Park PA 15101 Office: 1902 Law and Finance Bldg Pittsburgh PA 15219 Tel (412) 391-7575

KIRK, RAYMOND DOUGLAS, b. Warfield, Ky., Jan. 8, 1949; B.A., Morehead State U., 1970; J.D., U. Ky., 1972; M.S., Marshall U., 1974. Admitted to Ky. bar, 1973; asso. firm Knight & Kirk, Inez, Ky., 1973-75; individual practice law, Inez, 1975—; pub. defender, Martin County, Ky., 1973-76. Mem. Am., Ky., Martin County bar assns., Am. Soc. Criminology, Acad. Criminal Justice, Ky. Pub. Defenders Assn., Nat. Legal Aid Defenders Assn., NEA, Ky. Edn. Assn. Home: Box 9 Saltwell Rd Inez KY 41224 Office: Main St Inez KY 41224 Tel (606) 298-3056

KIRK, WILLIAM OLIVER, JR., b. Tuscaloosa, Ala., Mar. 21, 1939; B.S., U. Ala., 1961, LL.B., 1964, J.D., 1969. Admitted to Ala. bar, 1964; mem. firm Gaillard, Wilkins & Smith, Mobile, Ala., 1964; mem. firm Curry & Kirk, Carrollton, Ala., 1969—; mem. Ala. Bd. Bar Commrs. Pres. Pirkery County Heart Unit, 1971-72, fund chmn., 1976; bd. dirs. Pickery County Hosp. Mem. Am., Ala. bar assns., 24th Judicial Circuit of Ala. Bar Assn., Bench & Bar, Sigma Delta Kappa. Mem. editorial bd. Ala. Law Review, 1964—. Home: PO Drawer A-B Carrollton AL 35447 Office: Phoenix Ave Carrollton AL 35447 Tel (205) 367-8125

KIRKLAND, ARTHUR CHARLES, JR., b. Detroit, Oct. 24, 1947; B.S. in Bus. Adminstrn., Wayne State U., 1969; J.D., Harvard U., 1972. Admitted to N.Y. State bar, 1973; mem. auditing staff Plante & Moran, C.P.A.'s, Southfield, Mich., 1968-69, tax dept. staff, 1970; asso. firm Milbank Tweed Hadley & McCloy, N.Y.C., 1971-77, firm Honigman Miller Schwartz & Cohn, Detroit, 1977—; counselor Cambridge (Mass.) Community Legal Assistance Office; adviser, incorporator South End Tenants Mgmt. Firm. Mem. Am., N.Y. State, N.Y. County, Nat., Queens County bar assns., Bedford-Stuyvesant Lawyers Assn., Macon B. Allen Black Bar Assn., Beta Gamma. Office: 2290 First Nat Bldg Detroit MI 48226 Tel (313) 962-6708

KIRKLAND, TALLEY, b. Nicholls, Ga., Mar. 15, 1901; LL.B., Mercer U., 1922. Admitted to Ga. bar, 1922; law clk. Ga. Ct. Appeals, 1926; individual practice law, Atlanta, 1922—. Mem. Atlanta, Ga. bar assns. Home: 2638 Parkside Dr NE Atlanta GA 30305 Office: 709 Walton Bldg Atlanta GA 30303 Tel (404) 521-1531

KIRKLAND, WILLIAM DAVID, b. Danville, Ky., June 30, 1942; B.A., Centre Coll., 1964; LL.B., Vanderbilt U., 1967. Admitted to Ky. bar, 1967; asst. U.S. Atty. U.S. Dept. Justice, 1970-75; asso. firm Tarrant, Combs, Bullitt and McBrayer, Lexington, Ky., 1975—; instr. Ky. Law Enforcement Council, 1971, Atty. Gens. Sch. Trial Advocacy, Washington, 1973-75. Pres. Frankfort (Ky.) Community Chorus, 1976; deacon S. Frankfort Presbyterian Ch. Mem. Am., Ky., Fayette County bar assns. Home: 1203 Pradero St Frankfort KY 40601 Office: 1212 First Security Plaza Lexington KY 40601 Tel (606) 255-6824

KIRKMAN, MONROE WAKEFIELD, b. Sacramento, June 24, 1924; student Ind. U., 1946-48; A.B., Stanford, 1949, J.D., 1952. Admitted to Calif. bar, 1953; asso. firm Luce, Forward, Kunzel & Scripps, San Diego, 1953-58, firm Reed, Vaughn & Brockway, San Diego, 1958-60; individual practice law, San Diego, 1960—. Lawyer del. Ninth Circuit Judicial Conf., 1972-77, Mem. Calif. State, San Diego County Bar Assns., Am. Arbitration Assn. Home: 7667 Hillside Dr La Jolla CA 92037 Office: Suite 1921 1010 Second Ave San Diego CA 92101 Tel (714) 239-2061

KIRKPATRICK, ANDREW BOOTH, JR., b. Asheville, N.C., Jan. 16, 1929; B.S. cum laude, Davidson Coll., 1949; LL.B. magna cum laude, Harvard, 1954. Admitted to Del. bar, 1954, Fla. bar, 1955, U.S. Supreme Ct. bar, 1958; clk. to chief judge U.S. Ct. Appeals, Phila., 1954-55; atty. Morris, Nichols, Arsht & Tunnell, Wilmington, Del., 1955-58, partner, 1958—; chmn. censor com. Del. Supreme Ct., 1970—. Pres. Kennett Pike Assn., Wilmington, 1967-68; chmn. Del. Gov.'s Commn. Organized Crime, 1972-73; trustee Tatnall Sch., Wilmington, 1973—; pres. Young Republican Club, New Castle County, Del., 1957-58; trustee Unidel Found., 1977—. Mem. Am., Del. (pres. elect 1977-78) bar assns., Phi Beta Kappa, Beta Theta Phi. Home: 9 Barley Mill Dr Wilmington DE 19807 Office: 12th and Market Sts Wilmington DE 19801 Tel (302) 658-9200

KIRKPATRICK, C. RODNEY, b. Newberg, Oreg., July 6, 1942; B.A., Portland State U., 1965; J.D., Willamette U., 1968. Admitted to Oreg. bar, 1968; since practiced in Portland, Oreg.; asso. firm Galton & Poppick, 1968-72, firm Wilson & Erickson, 1972; individual practice law, 1972-76; partner firm Kirkpatrick & Howe, 1976—. Mem. Multnomah County Bar Assn., Am., Oreg. (past mem. bd. govs., various coms., trial lawyers assns. state Home: 3803 NE 142d St Portland OR 97230 Office: 1937 NE 122d St Portland OR 97230 Tel (503) 256-0780

KIRKPATRICK, JACK REID, b. Urbana, Ill., Nov. 18, 1914; A.B., U. Ill., 1938, LL.B., 1942. Admitted to Ill. bar, 1946, atty. claims div. State Farm Ins. Co., Mattoon, Ill., 1946-50, Chgo. Motor Club., 1950-56; asst. state's atty. Knox County (Ill.), Galesburg, 1956-64; asso. judge 9th Jud. Circuit Ct., Galesburg, 1964—. Mem. Knox County Bar Assn., Ill. Magistrates Assn. (pres. 1964). Office: Court House Galesburg IL 61401 Tel (309) 343-3121

KIRKPATRICK, JOHN EVERETT, b. Meadville, Pa., Aug. 20, 1929; A.B. magna cum laude, Amherst Coll., 1951; LL.B., Harvard U., 1954. Admitted to Ohio bar, 1955, Ill. bar, 1962; asso. firm Squire, Sanders & Dempsey, Cleve., 1954-61; partner firm Kirkland & Ellis, Chgo., 1962—. Chmn. fund dr. Central DuPage Hosp., 1973-75; Republican precinct committeeman, Shaker Heights, Ohio, 1958-61. Mem. Am., Ill., Chgo. bar assns. Home: 1617 Wadsworth Rd Wheaton IL 60187 Office: 200 E Randolph Dr Chicago IL 60601 Tel (312) 861-2060

KIRKPATRICK, WILLIAM MARTIN, JR., b. Evanston, Ill. Sept. 3, 1942; B.A., Gonzaga U., 1964; J.D., U. Mont., 1968. Admitted to Mont. bar, 1968; atty. Silver Bow County (Mont.) Legal Services, 1968-69; law clk. to judge U.S. Dist. Ct., Butte, Mont., 1969-72; dep. atty. Silver Bow County, 1972-74; individual practice law, Butte, 1974—. Mem. Am., Mont., Silver Bow County bar assns. Home: 1325 W Quartz St Apt 103 Butte MT 59701 Office: 211 W Park St Butte MT 59701 Tel (406) 792-4636

KIRN, JOHN JOSEPH, b. Cleve., Oct. 28, 1941; A.B., Western Res. U., 1964; J.D., Cleve. State U., 1970. Admitted to Ohio bar, 1971, U.S. Dist. Ct. bar N.E. Ohio, 1972, U.S. Supreme Ct. bar, 1975; law clk. Cuyahoga County Ct. Common Pleas, Cleve., 1971-72; asst. corporate counsel Island Coal Co., Cleve., 1972-73; asst. sec. Oglebay Norton Co., Cleve., 1973—. Mem. Ohio, Cleve. bar assns., Cleve. Law Library Assn. Office: 1200 Hanna Bldg Cleveland OH 44115 Tel (216) 861-3300

KIRP, DAVID LESLIE, b. N.Y.C., Apr. 15, 1944; B.A. cum laude, Amherst Coll., 1965; LL.B. cum laude, Harvard, 1968. Admitted to N.Y. State bar, 1968; instr., asst. to dean Harvard Grad. Sch. Edn., 1968-69, dir. Center for Law and Edn., asst. prof., 1969-71; acting and asso. prof. grad. sch. pub. policy U. Calif. at Berkeley, 1971—, research scholar childhood and govt. project, 1974; cons. in field; columnist Christian Sci. Monitor, 1972-75. Mem. nat. adv. bd. Center for Study of Families and Children, Vanderbilt U., 1975—; trustee Amherst Coll., 1971-74. Mem. Phi Beta Kappa. Author: (with Mark Yudof) Educational Policy and the Law, 1974; also articles; named Spencer fellow Nat. Acad. Edn., 1976; Van Leer Jerusalem fellow, 1977; Ford Found. Travel-Study fellow, 1977. Home: 471 Vassar St Berkeley CA 94708 Office: Sch Law U Calif Berkeley CA 94720 Tel (415) 642-4670

KIRSCH, FLORENCE WEITZ, b. Bklyn., Feb. 16, 1922; B.B.A., City Coll. N.Y., 1943; LL.B., Bklyn. Law Sch., 1945. Admitted to N.Y. State bar, 1945, Mass. bar, 1965; individual practice law, Marblehead, Mass., 1965—; part-time probate atty., Boston, 1971-75. Pres. Neighborhood Legal Services, Inc., 1975-77, bd. dirs., 1967-77. C.P.A. Mem. Mass., Boston bar assns., Mass. Assn. Women Lawyers, Boston Estate Planning Council (dir.), Mass. Soc. C.P.A.'s, Am. Inst. C.P.A.'s. Home: 20 Homestead Rd Marblehead MA 01945 Tel (617) 631-9593

KIRSH, BENJAMIN SOLLOW, b. N.Y.C., Mar. 15, 1898; A.B., Columbia, 1918, postgrad. law sch., 1918-1919; LL.B., N.Y. Law Sch., 1920. Admitted to N.Y. bar, 1920, U.S. Supreme Ct. bar, 1923; spl. asst. in prosecution of Sherman Anti-Trust case U.S. Atty., N.Y.C., 1921-23; individual practice law, N.Y.C., 1920—; mem. firm Kirsh, Rosenman & Brandeis, 1922-24; chmn. trucking commn., mem. wage adjustment bd. in bldg. trades Nat. War Labor Bd., Washington, 1943-46. Chmn. Class of 1920 Columbia Law Sch., 1965-77. Author: Trade Associations: The Legal Aspects, 1928; National Industrial Recovery Act, 1933; Trade Associations IN Law and Business, 1938; The Anti-trust Laws and Labor, 1941; Automation and Collective Bargaining, 1964; editor: Columbia Law Rev., 1918-20; contbr. articles to profl. jours. Home: 505 West End Ave New York City NY 10024 Office: 253 Broadway New York NY 10007 Tel (212) 962-1021

KIRSHENBAUM, ISIDORE, b. Providence, July 7, 1911; LL.B., N. Eastern U., Boston, 1933. Admitted to R.I. bar, 1933; individual practice law, Providence, 1933-35; partner firm Kirshenbaum & Kirshenbaum, Providence, 1935-73, pres., 1973—. Mem. R.I. Bar Assn. (chmn. domestic relations com. 1974). Home: 56 Wingate Rd Providence RI 02906 Office: 86 Weybosset St Providence RI 02903 Tel (401) 421-9439

KIRWAN, RALPH DEWITT, b. Albany, Calif., Aug. 30, 1942; A.B in Econs. with honors, U. Calif., Berkeley, 1966; J.D., U. San Francisco, 1969. Admitted to Calif. bar, 1970; asso. firm Schell & Delamer, Los Angeles, 1971-73, Lillick McHose & Charles, Los Angeles, 1973—. Mem. Los Angeles County, Am., Calif. bar assns. Home: 312 S Grand St Pasadena CA 91105 Office: 707 Wilshire Blvd 45th Floor Los Angeles CA 90017 Tel (213) 620-9000

KISER, JACK DARREL, b. Grassey Creek, Ky., Oct. 26, 1942; B.A., U. Ky., 1968, J.D., 1972. Admitted to Ky. bar, 1972. With Ball Homes, Inc., Lexington, Ky., 1968-72; area counsel St. Paul Title Ins. Co., 1977—; individual practice law, Lexington, 1972—. Mem. Am., Ky. bar assns. Home: 129 McDowell Rd Lexington KY 40502 Office: 865 Sparta Ct Lexington KY 40504

KISER, TERRY BEAUFORD, b. Phoenix, Aug. 22, 1943; B.S., Ariz. State U.; J.D., U. Utah. Admitted to Ariz. bar, 1971; asso. firm Wilson, McConnel & Moroney, Phoenix, 1971-72; mem. firm Hash, Cantor & Tomanek, Phoenix, 1972—. Mem. Am. Bar Assn., Phi Alpha Delta, Gamma Theta Epsilon. Home: 2937 E Sylvia St Phoenix AZ 85032 Office: 111 W Monroe St Phoenix AZ 85003 Tel (602) 254-4187

KISSEL, LESTER, b. Hartford, Wis., June 14, 1903; B.A., U. Wis., 1925; postgrad. U. Geneva, 1925-26; J.D., Harvard U., 1931. Admitted to N.Y. bar, 1933; asso. firm Shearman & Sterling, N.Y.C., 1931-47; partner firm Seward & Kissel, and predecessors, N.Y.C., now of counsel; gen. partner A.W. Jones Co., investment firm, N.Y.C., 1955—. Fellow Am. Bar Found.; mem. Assn. Bar City N.Y., N.Y. State, Am. bar assns. Home: 1170 Fifth Ave New York City NY 10029 Office: 63 Wall St New York City NY 10005 Tel (212) 248-2800

KISSEL, RICHARD JOHN, b. Chgo., Nov. 27, 1936; B.A., Northwestern U., 1958, J.D., 1961. Admitted to Ill. bar, 1961; asso. firm Peterson, Lowry, Rall, Barber & Ross, Chgo., 1961-65; div. counsel Abbott Labs., North Chicago, Ill., 1965-70; mem. Ill. Pollution Control Bd., Chgo., 1970-72; spl. asst. to dir. Ill. Dept. Local Govt. Affairs, 1972-73; partner firms Burditt and Calkins, Chgo., 1973-74, Martin Craig, Chester & Sonnenschein, Chgo., 1974—; lectr. environ. law Chgo. Kent Coll. Law, Ill. Inst. Continuing Legal Edn.; chmn. com. environ. affairs Ill. C. of C., 1973-76; mem. adj. faculty, dept. environ. health scis. U. Ill. Sch. Pub. Health. Office: 115 S LaSalle St Chicago IL 60603 Tel (312) 368-9700

KISSELL, ADOLPH JOHN, b. Nashua, N.H., Sept. 11, 1920. B.S., Boston Coll., 1942, J.D., 1949. Underwriter surety claims Mass. Bonding & Ins. Co., Boston, 1949-55; admitted to Mass. bar, 1955; individual practice law, Boston, 1955—; asso. firm Avery Dooley Post & Avery, Boston, 1960-65. Mem. Nashua Airport Commn., 1946-52; campaign mgr. for Mayor John B. Hynes, Boston, 1955-56. Decorated Air medal with five oak leaf clusters, D.F.C. Home: 40 Virginia St Boston MA 02125 Office: 112 Water St Boston MA 02109 Tel (617) 523-0815

KISSELL, FRANCES CIFRINO, b. Boston, Dec. 15, 1922; A.B., Radcliffe Coll., 1943; J.D., Boston Coll., 1948. Admitted to Mass. bar, 1948, U.S. Supreme Ct. bar, 1969, numerous others including U.S. Circuit Ct. Appeals 1st and 2 circuits, U.S. Dist. Cts. for Mass., Vt., Conn.; individual practice law, Boston, 1948-61; asst. U.S. atty. Mass. Dist., Dept. Justice, Boston, 1961-67; litigation atty. SBA, Boston, 1967—. Legal adviser Friends of Boston City Hosp., 1955—; 1st v.p., editor bull., 1955-61. Mem. Fed. Bar Assn. Home: 59 Prospect St RFD #3 Buzzards Bay MA 02532 Tel (617) 223-5835

KISSELOFF, SAMUEL J., b. N.Y.C., Apr. 27, 1927; LL.B., St. John's U., 1948. Admitted to N.Y. bar, 1948; partner firm Trause, Kisseloff, Lesser & Peulman, N.Y.C., 1948-57, Haber & Kisseloff, Bronx, N.Y., 1957-60, Chananau, Haber & Kisseloff, N.Y.C., 1960-61, Buckley & Kisseloff, N.Y.C., 1961-73, Abrams, Kisseloff & Kissin, N.Y.C., 1973—; small claims arbitrator N.Y.C. Civil Ct., 1960—; panel arbitrator Bronx Civil Ct., 1970—; guest lectr. Real Estate Inst. N.Y. U. Mem. N.Y. County Lawyers Assn., Am. (savs. and loan assn. panel), Bronx County (chmn. grievance com. 1975—) bar assns. Office: 1350 Ave of Americas New York City NY 10019 Tel (212) 581-8600

KISTLER, HERBERT DONALD, b. Butte, Mont., Mar. 15, 1908; B.A., Princeton U., 1930; LL.B., Stanford U., 1934. Admitted to Calif. bar, 1934, D.C. bar, 1935, U.S. Supreme Ct. bar, 1938; practiced in Washington, 1934—; asso. firm Kremer & Bingham, 1934-46; partner firm Robb, Porter, Kistler & Parkinson and predecessors, 1946-69, Jackson, Campbell & Parkinson and predecessors, 1969—; chmn. law and legislation com. Met. Washington Bd. Trade, 1959-60. Mem. bd. mgrs. Chevy Chase Village, 1958-72, chmn., 1969-72; bd. dirs. Washington Rotary Club, 1971-74. Fellow Am. Bar Found., Am. Coll. Probate Counsel; mem. Am., D.C. bar assns. Home: 4016 Oliver St Chevy Chase MD 20015 Office: 1828 L St Washington DC 20036 Tel (202) 457-1636

KISTLER, ROBERT KING, b. State College, Pa., Nov. 17, 1925; B.S., Webb Inst. Naval Architecture, 1946; J.D., Stanford, 1950. Admitted to Calif. bar, 1951, Pa. bar, 1955; dep. dist. atty. Merced County (Calif.), 1951-53; mem. firm Winton & Kistler, Merced, Calif., 1953-55; individual practice law, State College, 1955-56; partner firm Miller, Kistler & Campbell, Inc., and predecessors, State College, 1956—; borough solicitor State College, 1957—. Bus. chmn. Cancer Soc., 1960-70. Mem. Pa., Am. Calif., Centre County bar assns. Home: 200 Tall Oaks Dr State College PA 16801 Office: 1500 S Atherton St State College PA 16801 Tel (814) 234-1500

KITCH, EDMUND WELLS, b. Wichita, Kans., Nov. 3, 1939; B.A., Yale U., 1961; J.D., U. Chgo., 1964. Admitted to Kans. bar, 1964, Ill. bar, 1966, U.S. Supreme Ct. bar, 1973; asst. prof. law Ind. U., 1964-65; asst. prof. law U. Chgo., 1965-68, asso. prof., 1968-71, prof., 1971—; spl. asst. solicitor gen. U.S. Dept. Justice, 1973-74; exec. dir. adv. com. on procedural reform CAB, 1975-76; adj. scholar Am. Enterprise Inst., 1975—; reporter com. on pattern Jury instrns. Ill. Supreme Ct., 1966-69. Mem. Am. Bar Assn., Phi Beta Kappa. Author: (with Harvey Permon) Legal Regulation of the Competitive Process, 1972; contbr. articles to legal jours. Office: 1111 E 60th St Chicago IL 60637 Tel (312) 753-2446

KITCHEN, CHARLES WILLIAM, b. Cleve., July 17, 1926; B.A., Western Res. U., 1948; J.D., 1950. Admitted to Ohio bar, 1950; partner firm Kitchen, Messner & Deery, Cleve., 1954—; pres. Cleve. Def. Atty.'s Group, 1971-72. Mem. Greater Cleve. Growth Assn., Citizens League; sec. Alcoholism Services of Cleve., Inc. Mem. Am., Ohio bar assns., Ohio Def. Assn. (pres. 1975-76), Internat. Assn. Ins. Counsel, Am. Arbitration Assn. (arbitrator), Am. Legion. Home: 28949 Turnbridge Rd Bay Village OH 44140 Office: 1305 Superior Bldg Cleveland OH 44114

KITCHEN, JOHN MILTON, b. Indpls., Apr. 15, 1912; A.B., Wabash Coll., 1934; J.D., Harvard, 1937. Admitted to Ind. bar, 1936, U.S. Supreme Ct. bar, 1950; since practiced in Indpls., partner firm Rauch, Chase & Kitchen, 1946-72, of counsel firm Dutton Kappes & Overman, 1972—; pres. John M. Kitchen Agy., Inc., 1955—; gen. counsel, dir. Permanent Magnet Co., 1970—. Gen. counsel Indpls. Sesquicentennial Commn., 1970-72; chmn. Gov.'s Commn. for Jud. Reform, 1969-70; chmn. Ind. Conf. Bankers and Lawyers, 1975—. Fellow Am. Bar Found.; mem. Indpls. (pres. 1969-70), Am. (ho. of dels.), Ind. (ho. of dels.) bar assns., Indpls. Bar Found. (pres. 1969-72), Phi Beta Kappa. Contbr. articles to legal publs. Office: 710 Guaranty Bldg Indianapolis IN 46204 Tel (317) 635-5395

KITCHEN, MARGARET APPLEGATE, b. Noblesville, Ind., Nov. 24, 1922; A.B., U. Mich., 1944, M.S., 1946; J.D., U. Toledo, 1952; postgrad. So. Meth. U., 1960. Admitted to Ohio bar, 1953, U.S. Supreme Ct. bar, 1957; petroleum geologist Mich. exploration Sun Oil Co., 1946-60; partner firm Kitchen & Kitchen, Toledo, 1960-74; sec. firm Kitchen & Rosenberger Co. L.P.A., Toledo, 1974-75, also dir. firm Kitchen, Hamilton & Mitzger Co. L.P.A., Toledo, 1975-76; sec., dir. Kitchen, Kitchen & Assos. C.P.A.'s, Toledo, 1976—; adj. asst. prof. geology U. Toledo, 1960—. Mem. Toledo, Lucas County, Ohio bar assns., Am. Assn. Petroleum Geologists, Geol. Soc. Am., Mich., Ohio geol. socs., Ohio Oil and Gas Assn. Home: 3788 Hillandale Rd Toledo OH 43606 Office: Suite 200 Baristers Bldg 335 N Superior St Toledo OH 43604 Tel (419) 243-6234

KITCHENS, JOHN BROWN, JR., b. Newman, Ga., Sept. 20, 1943; B.S., U. Ala., 1965, J.D., 1968; LL.M., Emory U., 1975. Admitted to Ala. bar, 1968, Ga. bar, 1971; adminstrv. asst. Birmingham (Ala.) Trust Nat. Bank, 1969-70; legal editor The Harrison Co., Atlanta, 1970-71; asso. firm Ware, Sterne, & Griffin, Atlanta, 1971-75; fin. advisor FSC Adv. Corp., Atlanta, 1975—. Sec., treas., adminstrv. v.p. Toastmasters, 1970-74. Mem. Ga., Ala., Am. bar assns. Home: 97 Peachtree Park Dr Apts S-1 Atlanta GA 30309 Office: 148 Cain St Atlanta GA 30303 Tel (404) 351-4853

KITCHENS, PAUL EDWARD, b. Minden, La., Dec. 11, 1945; B.A., La. State U., 1967, J.D., 1971. Admitted to La. bar, 1971, U.S. Dist. Ct. Western Dist. La., 1971, Ct. Mil. Appeals bar, 1971; capt. Judge Advocates Office, Ft. Benning, Ga., 1971-74, sr. trial atty., 1974, chief of criminal justice, 1974; partner firm Kitchens, Benton & Kitchens, Minden, La., 1975—. Vice pres. Minden Jaycees, 1976; bd. dirs. Minden C. of C., 1976. Mem. Am., La., Webster Parish bar assns., Assn. Trial Lawyers Am., Phi Delta Phi. Named Outstanding Young Man of Minden, 1976. Home: 320 Pennsylvania St Minden LA 71055 Office: PO Box 740 Minden LA 71055 Tel (318) 377-5331

KITE, RICHARD LLOYD, b. Chgo., Jan. 26, 1934; B.S. with highest honors, U. Calif., Los Angeles, 1955, LL.B., 1958, J.D., 1958. Admitted to Calif. bar, 1958, Wis. bar, 1964; practiced in Beverly Hills, Calif., 1959-64; gen. house legal counsel Marcus Corp., Milw., 1964—, now v.p., dir.; pres. Marcus Theatres Corp.; v.p., sec., dir. Marcus Hotel Corp., Marc's Big Boy Corps.; dir. Mid-Am. Bank, Milw., Wis. No-Fault Ins. Co., Guardian State Bank, Milw. Bd. dirs. Milw. Jewish Fedn., Milw. Jewish Community Center; mem. joint distbn. com., young leadership cabinet United Jewish Appeal, N.Y.C.. Mem. Nat. Assn. Theatre Owners (dir. Wis. chpt., mem. Pres.'s advisory com.), Young Pres.'s. Orgn., state bars Wis., Calif., Order of Coif, Phi Beta Kappa, Phi Eta Sigma, Beta Gamma Sigma. Recipient Outstanding Accounting Student award Controller's Inst. Am., 1955, William Nickoll Young Leadership award Milw. Jewish Fedn., 1972. Office: 212 W Wisconsin Ave Milwaukee WI 53203 Tel (414) 272-6020

KITE, STEVEN B., b. Chgo., May 30, 1949; B.A., U. Ill., 1971; J.D., Harvard, 1974. Admitted to Ga. bar, 1974; asso. firm Huie, Ware, Sterne, Browne & Ide, Atlanta, 1974—. Mem. adv. bd. dirs. Atlanta Legal Aid Soc., 1976—. Mem. Am., Atlanta Bar Assn., State Bar Ga.,

Phi Eta Sigma, Phi Beta Kappa. Office: 1200 Standard Federal Savings Bldg Atlanta GA 30303 Tel (404) 522-8700

KITTELSEN, RODNEY OLIN, b. Albany Twp., Wis., Mar. 11, 1917; Ph.B., U. Wis., 1939, LL.B., 1940. Admitted to Wis. bar, 1940, D.C. bar, 1945, U.S. Supreme Ct. bar, 1945; asso. firm Coleman, McCauley & Becker, Milw., 1940; spl. agt. FBI, 1940-45; sr. mem. firm Kittelsen, Barry & Ross, Monroe, 1946—; vis. lectr. U. Wis. Law Sch., 1973-74; dist. atty. Green County, 1947-53; chmn. Dist. 12 Grievance Com., 1974-75. Chmn., Monroe Police and Fire Commn., 1948—; mem. Monroe Sch. Bd. Edn., 1947-72, pres., 1960-72; bd. dirs. Wis. Assn. Sch. Bds., 1968-72. Mem. Am., Wis. (bd. govs. 1969-73, pres. 1976—), Green County bar assns. Recipient Outstanding Sr. Citizen award Monroe C. of C., 1977; named U. Wis. Outstanding Alumnus, Green County Alumni Assn., 1974; contbr. to Wis. Sch. Bd. News and Wis. Bar Bull. Home: 708 26th Ave Monroe WI 53566 Office: 916 17th Ave Monroe WI 53566 Tel (608) 325-2191

KITTLESON, HENRY MARSHALL, b. Tampa, Fla., May 13, 1929; B.S. in Bus. Adminstrn., U. Fla., 1951, LL.B., 1953. Admitted to Fla. bar, 1953; partner firm Holland & Knight, and predecessors, Bartow, Fla., and Lakeland, Fla., 1953—. Fellow Am. Bar Found.; mem. Fla., Am. bar assns., Am. Law Inst., Fla. Law Revision Council (vice-chmn. 1969-71). Home: 5334 Woodhaven Dr Lakeland FL 33803 Office: 92 Lake Wire Dr Lakeland FL 33802 Tel (813) 682-1161

KITTNER, JOSEPH MORDECAI, b. Weldon, N.C., May 10, 1917; B.C.S., U. N.C., 1937, J.D., 1939. Admitted to N.C. bar, 1940, D.C. bar, 1962, U.S. Supreme Ct. bar, 1945; with FCC, Washington, 1941-55, asst. to gen. counsel, 1951, asst. chief broadcast safety and spl. radio services burs., 1951-56; mem. firm McKenna, Wilkinson & Kittner, Washington, 1956—. Mem. Am., Fed., FCC bar assns. Home: 4200 Massachusetts Ave NW Washington DC 20016 Office: 1150 17th St NW Washington DC 20036 Tel (202) 296-1600

KITZMAN, OLIVER STANLEY, b. near Pattison, Tex., Aug. 21, 1934; B.B.A., Tex. A. and M. U., 1959; J.D., S. Tex. Coll. Law, 1965. Admitted to Tex. bar, 1965; individual practice law, Brookshire, Tex., 1965—; dist. atty. 155th Jud. Dist. Tex., 1967—. Pres., San Jacinto (Tex.) Lung Assn., 1974. Mem. Tex. (council criminal law sect.), Tex. Aggie, Tri-County bar assns., Houston-Galveston Area Council (chmn. criminal justice adv. com.), Nat. (v.p.), Tex. (pres. 1974) dist. attys. assns. Home: 3502 5th St Brookshire TX 77423 Office: Box 336 Brookshire TX 77423 Tel (713) 371-0204

KIVETT, AUSTIN WARREN, b. Stilesville, Ind., Dec. 18, 1898; Ph.B., U. Chgo., 1924, J.D., 1927. Admitted to Ind. bar, 1925, Ill. bar, 1928, Wis. bar, 1935; asso. firm Smith, Rowe, Dunn & Howe, Chgo., 1928-34; mem. firm Dougherty, Arnold & Kivett, Milw., 1935-41; mem. firm Kivett & Kasdorf, Milw., 1945—. Mem. Wis. Republican State Exec. Com., Wis., 1960-64. Fellow Am. Coll. Trial Lawyers. Home: 555 Elmspring Ave Wauwatosa WI 53226 Office: 2051 W Wisconsin Ave Milwaukee WI 53233 Tel (414) 342-4400

KIZER, BERNICE LICHTY, b. Ft. Smith, Ark., Aug. 15, 1915; student Stephens Coll., 1937-38; LL.B., U. Ark., 1947, J.D., 1969. Admitted to Ark. bar, 1947; partner firm Rose & Kizer, Ft. Smith, 1957-63; mem. Ark. Ho. of Reps., 1961-74; mem. Gov's. Commn. Status Women, 1964—; joint budget com. Ark. Legis. Council, 1964-74, vice chmn., 1973—; judge Crawford, Franklin and Sebastian counties, 1977—; dir. City Nat. Bank, Ft. Smith, 1976. Bd. dirs. Cottey Coll., Nevada, Mo., 1975-76, Western Ark. Planning and Devel. Assn., Ft. Smith, 1974, Western Ark. Counseling and Guidance Assn., Ft. Smith, 1975; chancellor 10th Chancery Dist. State of Ark., 1975—; active Van Buren YMCA. Mem. Am. Bar Assn., LWV, AAUW, Bus. and Profl. Womens Clubs. Home: 221 May Ave Fort Smith AR 72901 Office: Crawford County Courthouse Van Buren AR 72956

KLAFTER, CARY IRA, b. Chgo., Sept. 15, 1948; B.A. magna cum laude, Mich. State U., 1968, M.S., 1971; J.D., U. Chgo., 1972. Admitted to Calif. bar, 1972; asso. firm Morrison & Foerster, San Francisco, 1972—. Mem. Bar Assn. San Francisco, State Bar Calif., Am. Bar Assn., Ill. Acad. Criminology, Order of Coif, Phi Eta Sigma, Phi Kappa Phi, Phi Delta Phi. Asso. editor U. Chgo. Law Rev., 1971-72. Home: 2743 Baker St San Francisco CA 94123 Office: 1 Market Plaza San Francisco CA 94105 Tel (415) 777-6000

KLAFTER, MELVIN LESLIE, b. Chgo., June 29, 1914; A.B., DePaul U., 1936, J.D., 1938. Admitted to Ill. bar, 1938, U.S. Dist. Ct. No. Dist. bar, 1938, 7th Circuit bar, 1948, U.S. Supreme Ct. bar, 1965; with Hearst Papers, 1935-38; individual practice law, Chgo., 1939-40; asst. U.S. atty. No. Dist. Ill., Chgo., 1948-54; partner firm Nathan & Klafter, Chgo., 1954—; col. JAGC, AUS; instr. 5th U.S. Army Judge Adv. Gen. Sch., Northwestern U., 1951-52, comdt., 1953-54. Vice pres. USO, Chgo., 1969—; pres. Lawyers Shrine Club; trustee Ill. Masonic Med. Center, St. Xavier's Coll. Mem. Am., Fed., Chgo. bar assns., Am. Judicature Soc., Judge Adv. Assn., Delta Theta Phi. Recipient Distinguished service award USO, 1971. Home: 219 E Lake Shore Dr Chicago IL 60611 Office: 39 S LaSalle St Chicago IL 60603 Tel (312) 726-7855

KLAMPE, MICHAEL DAN, b. Rochester, Minn., Jan. 19, 1947; J.D., U. Kans., 1972. Admitted to Minn. bar, 1972; partner firm Brown Bins & Klampe, Rochester, 1972—. Mem. Minn. Bar Assn., Minn. Trial Lawyers Assn. Home: 1918 26th Ave NW Rochester MN 55901 Office: 217 100 First Ave Bldg Rochester MN 55901 Tel (507) 288-7402

KLAPHEKE, WILLIAM THOMAS, II, b. Louisville, Feb. 18, 1948; B.A. in Psychology, U. Louisville, 1970, J.D., 1972. Admitted to Ky. bar, 1973; partner firm Berry & Klapheke, Glasgow, Ky., 1973—; Barren County atty., 1978-82. Bd. dirs. Jr. Achievement Glasgow-Barren County Inc., 1976—; chmn. Barren County chpt. ARC, 1974-76; chmn. Barren county chpt. Am. Cancer Soc., 1975-76. Mem. Comml. Law League Am., Barren County Bar Assn. (sec.-treas. 1973-74). Rotary Internat. Group Study Exchange fellow, Ireland, 1976. Home: 115 St Mary's Ct Glasgow KY 42141 Office: 117 E Washington St Glasgow KY 42141 Tel (502) 651-6191

KLAPINSKY, RAYMOND JOSEPH, b. Beaver Meadows, Pa., Dec. 7, 1938; B.A., U. Del., 1960; J.D., George Washington U., 1967. Admitted to D.C. bar, 1967, Pa. bar, 1970; law clk. firm Sidley, Austin, Burgess and Smith, Washington, 1965-67; trial atty. SEC, 1967-69; asso. counsel Wellington Mgmt. Co., 1969-75; v.p., sec. Vanguard Group of Investment Cos., Valley Forge, Pa., 1975—. Mem. Am., Pa., D.C., Fed. bar assns., Am. Arbitration Assn. Bus. editor George Washington Law Rev. Home: 180 Woodhill Ln Media PA 19063 Office: 1250 Drummers Ln PO Box 876 Valley Forge PA 19482 Tel (215) 293-1100

KLASS, MARVIN JOSEPH, b. Sioux City, Iowa, Nov. 6, 1913; B.A., Morningside Coll., Sioux City, 1936; LL.B., Harvard U., 1939. Admitted to Iowa bar, 1939; with firm Stewart, Hatfield, Klass & Whicher, Sioux City, 1946—, sr. partner, 1966—; tchr. bus. law Morningside Coll., 1946-49; commr. Client Security and Atty. Disciplinary Commn., 1973—. Mem. Sioux City CSC, 1966-68. Mem. Am., Iowa, Woodbury (pres. 1969-70) bar assns. Home: 3937 Douglas St Sioux City IA 51104 Office: Suite 830 Frances Bldg Sioux City IA 51101 Tel (712) 252-1866

KLAYMAN, ROBERT ALAN, b. Cin., Apr. 5, 1929; B.S., W.Va. U., 1951, LL.B., 1954. Admitted to W.Va. bar, 1954, D.C. bar, 1964; atty. Office Chief Counsel, IRS, Washington, 1957-60; atty. Office Tax Legis. Counsel U.S. Treasury Dept., Washington, 1960-62, asst. tax legis. counsel, 1962-64, asso. tax legis. counsel, 1964; asso. firm Caplin & Drysdale, Washington, 1964-65, partner 1966—; asso. profl. lectr. George Washington U. Coll. Law, 1965-72. Bd. govs. Beauvoir Sch., Washington, 1976—. Mem. Am. Bar Assn., Washington Council Lawyers, Phi Beta Kappa. Contbr. articles on taxation to legal jours. Office: 1101 17th St NW Washington DC 20036 Tel (202) 862-5020

KLEIGER, S. STUART, b. Jersey City, May 15, 1911; B.S., Ohio U., 1932; LL.B., St. Lawrence U., 1936. Admitted to N.Y., U.S. Supreme Ct. bars; partner firm Kleiger & Kleiger, N.Y.C., 1941—. Mem. N.Y. County Lawyers Assn., N.Y. Trial Lawyers Assn. Home: 250 East 73d St New York City NY 10021 Office: 250 Broadway New York City NY 10007

KLEIMAN, BERNARD, lawyer; b. Chgo., Jan. 26, 1928; B.S., Purdue U., 1951; J.D., Northwestern U., 1954. Admitted to Ill. bar, 1954; practice law in assn. with Abraham W. Brussell, 1957-60; dist. counsel United Steel Workers Am., 1960-65, gen. counsel, 1965—; partner Kleiman, Cornfield & Feldman, Chgo., 1960; individual practice law, 1960—; mem. collective bargaining coms. for nat. labor negotiations in basic steel, aluminum and can mfg. industries. Served with AUS, 1946-48. Mem. Am., Ill., Chgo., Allegheny County bar assns. Contbr. articles to legal jours. Office: Suite 1910 United of Am Bldg 1 E Wacker Dr Chicago IL 60601*

KLEIMAN, DAVID H., b. Kendallville, Ind., Apr. 2, 1934; B.S., Purdue U., 1956; J.D., Northwestern U., 1959. Admitted to Ind. bar, 1959; mem. editorial bd. Northwestern Legal Publs., 1957-59, editor-in-chief Jour. Air law, Commerce, 1958-59; dep. pros. atty., 1961-62; now partner firm Dann Pecar Newman Talesnick & Kleiman, Indpls.; counsel Met. Devel. Commn., Indpls., 1965—. Mem. Indpls., Ind. State, Am. bar assns., Assn. Trial Lawyers Am. Phi Delta Phi. Office: 1600 Market Square Center 151 Delaware St Indianapolis IN 46204*

KLEIN, ALFRED, b. Stuttgart, Germany, Oct. 22, 1946; came to U.S., 1947, naturalized, 1953; B.A. (NSF scholar), U. Mich., 1968; J.D., U. Calif., Berkeley, 1971. Admitted to Calif. bar, 1972; field atty. NLRB region 31, W. Los Angeles, 1971-72, region 20, San Francisco, 1972-73; mem. firm Musick, Peeler & Garrett, Los Angeles, 1973-75; atty. Atlantic Richfield Co., Los Angeles, 1975—; instr. U. Calif., Hastings Sch. Law, San Francisco, 1973-74. Mem. Town Hall Calif., Los Angeles, 1973—. Mem. Am., Calif., Los Angeles County bar assns. Contbr. to Jour. of Am. Hosp. Assn. Office: 515 S Flower St Los Angeles CA 90071 Tel (213) 486-1520

KLEIN, ALLAN WINSTON, b. St. Paul, Aug. 6, 1945; A.B., Princeton, 1968; J.D., U. Minn., 1971. Admitted to Minn. bar, 1972; securities examiner Minn. Securities Div., St. Paul, 1971-72, sr. securities examiner, 1972-73, staff atty., 1973-75, dep. commr., 1975-76; individual practice law, St. Paul, 1976—. Mem. Am., Minn., Ramsey County bar assns., Midwest Securities Commrs. Assn. (vice chmn. enforcement com. 1975-76). Home and Office: 742 Fairmount Ave Saint Paul MN 55105

KLEIN, ALVIN FRANK, b. Akron, Ohio, Oct. 2, 1911; B.S., N.Y. U., 1932; J.D., Harvard, 1935. Admitted to N.Y. bar, 1935; individual practice law, N.Y.C., 1937-63; judge Civil Ct., N.Y.C., 1963-72; justice Supreme Ct. State of N.Y., 1st Jud. Dist., N.Y.C., 1972—; adminstrv. asst. to Hon. Charles A. Buckley, chmn. house pub. works com. U.S. Congress, 1949-63. Vice pres. Bronx div. Am. Jewish Congress. Mem. N.Y. County Lawyers Assn., Bronx County Bar Assn. Home: 300 E 56th St New York City NY 10022 Office: 100 Centre St New York City NY 10013 Tel (212) 374-6298

KLEIN, ARTHUR, b. N.Y.C., Jan. 24, 1919; B.S. in Accounting, L.I. U., 1947; LL.B., Bklyn. Law Sch., 1951. Admitted to N.Y. bar, 1951, U.S. Supreme Ct. bar, 1967; individual practice law, Suffern, N.Y., 1951-72; partner firm Klein & Klein, Suffern, 1972—. Mem. N.Y. State, Rockland County (N.Y.) bar assns., N.Y. State Soc. C.P.A.'s. Office: 144 Route 59 Suffern NY 10901 Tel (914) 357-7900

KLEIN, ARTHUR LOUIS, b. Harrisburg, Pa., Sept. 21, 1943; B.S., U. Pa., 1964, LL.B., 1967; LL.M., N.Y. U., 1968. Admitted to Pa. bar, 1969; asso. firm Morgan, Lewis & Bockius, Phila., 1968—; lectr. law Temple U., Phila., 1975—. Mem. Am. (chmn. sect. taxation com. 1977—), Pa., Phila. bar assns. Office: 123 S Broad St 2100 Fidelity Bldg Philadelphia PA 19109 Tel (215) 491-9444

KLEIN, CHARLES, b. Atlantic City, Sept. 16, 1900; LL.B., Temple U., 1921, LL.D., 1949; postgrad. Villanova U., 1922; LL.D., Franklin and Marshall Coll., 1959, U. Pa., 1967, LaSalle Coll., 1968; L.H.D., Dickinson Coll., 1960; J.D., St. Joseph's Coll., 1961; D.C.L., Bucknell U., 1963. Admitted to Pa. bar, 1921; practiced in Phila., 1921-27; spl. counsel Pa. Dept. Banking, 1927-31; spl. dep. Pa. Atty. Gen., 1931-34; judge Phila. Orphans' Ct., 1934—, presiding judge, 1952-69, adminstrv. judge Orphans' Ct. div., 1970-75, sr. judge, 1976—; acting dean Temple U. Sch. of Law, 1941-42. Home: A1121 Presidential Apts City Line Philadelphia PA 19131 Office: 542 City Hall Philadelphia PA 19107 Tel (215) MU 6-2200

KLEIN, DAVID MALCOLM, b. Bronx, N.Y., May 9, 1947; B.A., State U. N.Y., Albany, 1969, J.D., Facility of Law and Jurisprudence, Buffalo, 1972. Admitted to N.Y. bar, 1973, U.S. Dist. Ct. bar for So. and Eastern Dists. N.Y., 1974, U.S. Ct. Appeals bar, 2d Circuit, 1975; partner firm Klein & Klein, Suffern, N.Y., 1973—; atty. Spring Valley chpt. NAACP, 1975—. Chmn. bd. Meals on Wheels of Rockland County (N.Y.), 1974—; mem. Ramapo (N.Y.) Commn. on Environ. Quality, 1974—. Mem. N.Y. State, Rockland County bar assns. Home: 29 Somerset Dr Suffern NY 10901 Office: 144 Route 59 Suffern NY 10901 Tel (914) 357-7900

KLEIN, FREDERICK SIDNEY, b. Chgo., Apr. 26, 1946; B.A., U. Ill., 1968; J.D., U. Ariz., 1972. Admitted to Ariz. bar, 1972, D.C. bar, 1973; law clk. to justice Supreme Ct. Ariz., Phoenix, 1972-73; asst. pub. defender Pima County, 1973-75; dir. Neighborhood Law Offices, Tucson, 1975-76; partner firm Klein & Klein, Tucson, 1976—. Mem. Pima County, Fed., Am. bar assns., State Bar Ariz., D.C. Bar, Assn. Trial Lawyers Am., Nat. Assn. Criminal Def. Lawyers, Am. Judicature Soc., Nat. Legal Aid and Defender Assn. Office: Suite 306 100 N Stone Ave Tucson AZ 85701 Tel (602) 623-3436

KLEIN, GERALD STANLEY, b. Washington, Aug. 27, 1941; A.A., U. Balt., 1960, LL.B., 1963; LL.M., U. Chgo., 1965. Admitted to Md. bar, 1963, U.S. Supreme Ct. bar, 1972; atty. Singer Co., N.Y.C., 1966; asst. city solicitor City of Balt., 1967-75; individual practice, Balt., 1967—. Mem. Am., Md., Balt. bar assns. Home: 3515 Overbrook Rd Pikesville MD 21208 Office: 2502 One N Charles St Baltimore MD 21201 Tel (301) 752-7651

KLEIN, HERMAN FRED, b. Akron, Ohio, May 13, 1913; B.S. in Edn., U. Akron, 1935, M.S. in Edn., 1940, J.D., 1947; postgrad. Harvard U., U. Calif., Ohio Wesleyan U., Ohio State U. Admitted to Ohio bar, 1953; mem. faculty Armstrong Coll., 1947-51; high sch. tchr., Ohio, 1935-47, 52-60; atty. examiner State of Ohio Dept. Hwys., 1960-63, Pub. Utilities Commn. Ohio and Bd. Tax Appeals Ohio, 1969-71; individual practice law, Groveport, Ohio, 1953—; pres. Madrid Real Estate Co., Inc., Columbus, Ohio. Mem. vol. staff Mt. Carmel Med. Center. Mem. Ohio State Bar Assn., Columbus Bd. Realtors. Home: 1283 Piedmont Rd South Venice FL 33585 Office: 530 Main St Groveport OH 43125 Tel (614) 836-5948

KLEIN, JAMES MARTIN, b. Toledo, Ohio, June 14, 1944; A.B., U. Mich., 1966; J.D. Case Western Res. U., 1969. Admitted to Ohio bar, 1969, Calif. bar, 1970, U.S. Supreme Ct. bar; Reginald Heber Smith fellow Contra Costa Legal Services Found., Richmond, Calif., 1969-71; asso. prof. law U. Toledo, 1971—, co-dir. Civil Law Clinic, 1971—; hearing examiner Ohio Civil Rights Commn.; cons. in field. Vice pres. bd. dirs. Advocates for Basic Legal Equality, Inc., Toledo; bd. dirs. N.W. Ohio chpt. Multiple Sclerosis Soc., Toledo. Mem. Calif., Toledo, U.S. Supreme Ct. bar assns. Author: (with H. First) Ohio Municipal Judges Deskbook, 1974. Mem. editorial bd. Case Western Res. Law Rev., 1968-69. Home: 2524 Orchard Rd Toledo OH 43606 Office: University of Toledo College of Law Toledo OH 43606 Tel (419) 537-2948

KLEIN, JEROME ALLEN, b. Cleve., Feb. 11, 1922; B.S. in Econs., U. Pa., 1943; LL.B., Harvard, 1948. Admitted to Supreme Ct. Ohio bar, 1949, U.S. Supreme Ct. bar, 1966; asso. firm Howard M. Metzenbaum, Cleve., 1948-52; atty. anti trust div. U.S. Dept. Justice, Cleve., 1952-53; partner firm Klein & Klein, Cleve., 1955—; municipal judge City of S. Euclid (Ohio), 1960—. Pres. S. Euclid chpt. Greater Cleve. Safety Council, 1960-64. Mem. Greater Cleve., Cuyahoga County, War Veterans (pres. 1959-60) bar assns., Nat. Acad. Arbitrators, Am. Arbitration Assn. (mem. nat. panel). Home: 4605 Birchwold Rd South Euclid OH 44121 Office: 1700 Investment Plaza Cleveland OH 44114 Tel (216) 241-0244

KLEIN, JOEL HARVEY, b. San Antonio, July 1, 1943; B.B.A., U. Tex., 1965, J.D., 1967. Admitted to Tex. bar, 1967, U.S. Supreme Ct. bar, 1971; mem. firm Lester L. Klein & Joel H. Klein, San Antonio, 1967-71, partner, 1971—. Pres. San Antonio Dist. of Zionist Organization of Am., 1972-74; dir. San Antonio Jewish Social Service Fedn., 1973-76; commr. San Antonio Fiesta, 1974-76; pres. Congregation Agudas Achim, San Antonio, 1976—. Mem. San Antonio, Tex. bar assns., San Antonio Young Lawyers Assn., Comml. Law League Am. Home: 3310 Scenic Ln San Antonio TX 78230 Office: 1004 Milam Bldg San Antonio TX 78205 Tel (512) 227-8253

KLEIN, JOSEPH, b. Weehawken, N.J., May 21, 1936; B.A., Rutgers U., 1960, LL.B., Newark, 1962. Admitted to N.J. bar, 1963; law clk. firm Soriano, Henkel & Klein and predecessors, Newark, 1961-63, asso., 1963-65, partner, 1965-73; asso. firm Skoloff & Wolfe, Newark, 1973-74; individual practice law, Union, N.J., 1974—. Mem. Essex County (N.J.) Republican Com., 1966-67; mem. Millburn-Short Hills Police Aux. Millburn, N.J., 1974; trustee N.J. Shakespeare Festival. Fellow Am. Acad. Matrimonial Lawyers; mem. Am., N.J., Essex County bar assns., Union Lawyers Club. Home: 806 Morris Turnpike Short Hills NJ 07078 Office: 1460 Morris Ave Union NJ 07083 Tel (201) 686-2272

KLEIN, KEITH EDWARD, b. San Antonio, Aug. 18, 1939; B.A., U. Tex., 1961, LL.B., 1963. Admitted to Tex. bar, 1963; asso. A. J. Klein, San Antonio, 1963—. Trustee Northside Ind. Sch. Dist., San Antonio, 1970-73. Mem. State Bar Tex., Am., San Antonio bar assns., Am. Judicature Soc., Am. Am. Trial Lawyers Assn. Home: 10806 Teton Ln San Antonio TX 78230 Office: 504 Milam Bldg San Antonio TX 78205 Tel (512) 227-8391

KLEIN, LEON, b. Garfield, N.J., Nov. 21, 1925; B.S., Rutgers U., 1948; J.D., N.Y. U., 1951. Admitted to N.J. bar, 1952, U.S. Supreme Ct. bar, 1955; individual practice law, Clifton, N.J., 1952—; 1st legal asst. law dept. City of Clifton, 1972—. Mem. N.J., Passaic County bar assns. Office: 1126 Clifton Ave Clifton NJ 07013 Tel (201) 777-2844

KLEIN, LEONARD, b. N.Y.C., May 22, 1941; B.A., U. Buffalo, 1963; LL.B., Union U., 1966, J.D., 1968. Admitted to N.Y. State bar, 1966, U.S. Dist. Ct. for So. Dist. N.Y. bar, 1969, U.S. Supreme Ct. bar, 1976; asso. firm Grandeau and Dahowski, Poughkeepsie, N.Y., 1966-68; individual practice law, Poughkeepsie, 1968-70; partner firm Cutler and Klein, Poughkeepsie, 1970—; tchr. Arlington Sch. Dist., Poughkeepsie, 1967-68; asst. pub. defender Dutchess County (N.Y.), Poughkeepsie, 1968-69; lectr. matrimonial law. Publicity chmn. local council Cub Scouts Am., Poughkeepsie, 1974-75; mgr. United Way, Lagrange, N.Y., 1975; bd. dirs. Community Hebrew Sch., Poughkeepsie, 1976—. Mem. Am., N.Y. State, Dutchess County bar assns. Mem. Albany Law Sch. Law Rev. Bd., 1964-66. Home: Clover Hill Poughkeepsie NY 12603 Office: 309 Mill St Poughkeepsie NY 12601 Tel (914) 452-2420

KLEIN, LESTER LOUIS, b. Pitts., Oct. 13, 1914; B.A., U. Tex., 1941, J.D., 1941. Admitted to Tex. bar, 1941, U.S. Dist. Ct. bar, 1950; city tax atty., 1946-50; individual practice, 1950-66; partner Lester L. Klein and Joel H. Klein, 1966—. Mem. San Antonio Bar Assn. (estate planners council). Office: 1004 Milam Bldg San Antonio TX 78205 Tel (512) 227-8253

KLEIN, MICHAEL ROGER, b. N.Y.C., Apr. 10, 1942; B.B.A., U. Miami, 1963, J.D., 1966; LL.M., Harvard, 1967. Admitted to Fla. bar, 1967, D.C. bar, 1969; asst. prof. law La. State U., 1967-69; asso. firm Wilmer, Cutler & Pickering, Washington, 1969-73, partner, 1974—; adj. faculty U. Va. Law Sch., 1969-71; lectr. Geo. Washington U. Law Sch., 1974-77. Mem. Fla., Am., D.C. bar assns. Contbr. articles to legal jours. Home: 1280 21st St NW 901 Washington DC 20036 Office: 1666 K St NW Washington DC 20006 Tel (202) 872-6000

KLEIN, PAUL EDWARD, b. N.Y.C., Oct. 2, 1938; B.S. in Accounting, Queens Coll., 1959; LL.B., N.Y.U., 1962. Admitted to N.Y. bar, 1962, U.S. Supreme Ct. bar, 1975; atty. NLRB, N.Y.C., 1962-65; labor atty. firm Simpson, Thacher & Bartlett, N.Y.C., 1965-67; dir. pub. employment practices and representation N.Y. State Pub. Employment Relations Bd., Albany, 1967-76; gen. counsel N.Y. Educators Assn., Albany, 1976—. Mem. Am., Fed. N.Y. bar assns., Am. Arbitration Assn., Soc. Profls. in Dispute Resolution. Recipient Am. Jurisprudence award for excellence in procedure N.Y.U., 1962. Asso. editor N.Y. U. Law Rev., 1960-62. Contbr. articles to profl. jours. Home: 63-6 Woodlake Rd N Albany NY 12203 Office: 50 Wolf Rd Albany NY 12205 Tel (518) 459-7840

KLEIN, PAUL L., b. N.Y.C., Jan. 24, 1925; B.A., Cornell U., 1945; J.D., Columbia, 1948. Admitted to N.Y. bar, 1958, U.S. Supreme Ct. bar, 1962, U.S. Ct. Appeals bar 2d Circuit, 1963, U.S. Dist. Ct. bar So. and Eastern Dists. N.Y., 1960; individual practice law, 1958-70; successively asst. atty. in charge Civil Appeals Bur., atty. in charge Chelsea Neighborhood office, asst. atty. in charge Civil Div., Legal Aid Soc., N.Y.C., 1970—. Trustee Municipal Employees Legal Services Fund, Inc. Mem. Assn. Bar City N.Y. (mem. ethics com.), N.Y. County, Westchester, Putnam County bar assns. Home: RFD 1 Lane Gate Rd Cold Spring NY 10516 Office: Legal Aid Society 11 Park Pl New York City NY 10007 Tel (212) 227-2237

KLEIN, RICHARD L., b. Dallas, Sept. 14, 1941; B.A. in History and Econs., U. N.Mex., 1965, J.D., 1971. Admitted to N.Mex. bar, 1972; individual practice law, Albuquerque, 1972—; owner, mgr. Land and Home Enterprises, Albuquerque; gen. partner CAP Co., Albuquerque. Office: 8338 D Comanche St NE Albuquerque NM 87110 Tel (505) 294-5666

KLEIN, RONALD PLATT, b. San Francisco, Nov. 28, 1927; A.B. in Psychology, Stanford, 1949; LL.B., Harvard, 1952. Admitted to Calif. bar, 1953, Ariz. bar, 1959; law clk. Judge William E. Orr, U.S. Ct. of Appeals, 9th Jud. Circuit, San Francisco, 1952-53; individual practice law, San Francisco, 1953-58; with Del E. Webb Corp., Phoenix, 1958-66, dir. legal dept., 1961-64, v.p., gen. counsel, 1964-66, v.p., sec., gen. counsel, 1966; v.p., gen. counsel Hunt Foods and Industries, Fullerton, Calif., 1966-68; v.p., gen. counsel Occidental Petroleum Corp., Los Angeles, 1968—. Mem. Am., Ariz., Calif., Los Angeles bar assns. Home: 401 N Carmelina Ave Los Angeles CA 90049 Office: 10889 Wilshire Blvd Los Angeles CA 90024 Tel (213) 879-1700

KLEIN, THEODORE, b. Czechoslovakia, Mar. 3, 1940; B.B.A., U. Miami (Fla.), 1961; J.D., 1964; LLM., Yale, 1967. Admitted to Fla. bar, 1967; asso. firm Knight, Underwood & Peters, 1964-66; asst. U.S. atty., 1967-70; asso. firm Fine, Jacobson, Block, Goldberg & Semet, Miami, 1970—; adj. prof. law U. Miami, 1970—. Mem. Fed. (dir., v.p. 1977), Dade County bar assns., Am. Judicature Soc., U. Miami Law Alumni Assn. (treas. 1976; sec. 1977), Phi Kappa Phi, Omicron Delta Kappa. Contbr. articles to law jours. Home: 11625 SW 103d St Miami FL 33176 Office: 2401 Douglas Rd Miami FL 33145 Tel (305) 443-1571

KLEINBERG, JOEL WILLIAM HARRIS, b. Madison, Wis., Apr. 8, 1943; B.A., Yale, 1964, J.D., 1967. Admitted to D.C. bar, Calif. bar, 1968, U.S. Supreme Ct. bar, 1975; asso. firm Rose, Klein & Marias, Los Angeles, 1968-70; individual practice law, Los Angeles, 1970—; prof. La Verne (Calif.) Coll. Law Center, 1971—. Mem. Am., Calif., Los Angeles County, Orange County bar assns., Calif., Los Angeles trial lawyers assns. Office: One Wilshire Blvd Los Angeles CA 90017 Tel (213) 624-1990

KLEINFELD, ANDREW JAY, b. N.Y.C., June 12, 1945; B.A., Wesleyan U., Middletown, Conn., 1966; J.D., Harvard, 1969. Admitted to Alaska bar, 1970, Mass. bar, 1973, U.S. Supreme Ct. bar, 1974; law clk. to justice Alaska Supreme Ct., 1969-71; individual practice law, Fairbanks, Alaska, 1971—; dir. Alaska Legal Services Corp., 1971-72. Pres. Fairbanks Estate Planning Council, 1974-75, Birthright of Fairbanks, 1974-75. Mem. Am., Alaska, Tanana Valley (sec. 1971-73, treas. 1973-74, v.p. 1974-76, pres. 1976—) bar assns. Contbr. articles in field to profl. jours. Home: Star Route Box 40014 Fairbanks AK 99701 Office: 216 Nerland Bldg Fairbanks AK 99701 Tel (907) 452-1305

KLEINMAN, BENNET, b. Cleve., May 25, 1919; B.B.A., Cleve. State U., 1940, LL.B., 1947. Admitted to Ohio bar, 1947; agt. IRS, Cleve., 1946-48; individual practice law, Cleve., 1948-62; partner firm Kahn, Kleinman, Yanowitz & Arnson, Cleve., 1962—; lectr. in field, 1947—. Pres. Temple Emanu El, Cleve., 1972-73, Coll. Jewish Studies, 1964-76; bd. dirs. Jewish Community Fedn. Cleve., 1950—, Citizens League, 1970—. Mem. Cleve., Ohio State, Cuyahoga County bar assns. Named Cleve. Man of Year, Orgn. for Rehab. and Tng., 1974; Israel Bond honoree, 1969, Jewish Nat. Fund honoree, 1972. Home: 24675 Hilltop Dr Beachwood OH 44122 Office: 1300 Bond Ct Bldg Cleveland OH 44114 Tel (216) 696-3311

KLEINMAN, SEYMOUR, b. N.Y.C., Oct. 22, 1918; B.A. magna cum laude, Bklyn. Coll., 1938; J.D. cum laude, Harvard, 1941. Admitted to N.Y. bar, 1941, U.S. Supreme Ct. bar, 1948; mem. staff gen. counsel's office SEC, 1941-42, 45-46; asso. firm Issers, Myers & Verdon, 1946-47; asst. gen. counsel C.I.T. Fin. Corp., 1947-57; partner firm Golenbock and Barell, N.Y.C., 1957—, now sr. partner; adj. prof. law Columbia U., 1971—. Pres. Karen Horney Clinic; gov., trustee Am. Friends of Hebrew U. Mem. N.Y.C. Bar Assn., Am. Bar Assn., County Lawyers Assn. Author: (with Rudolf Callmann) Unfair Competition, Trade Marks and Monopolies; Fundamentals of Business Law, 1973; Business Law, 1976. Home: 7 N Clover Dr Great Neck Estates Long Island NY 11022 Office: 645 Fifth Ave New York City NY 10022 Tel (212) 935-9800

KLENK, WILLIAM GEORGE, II, b. Phila., May 9, 1933; B.A., U. Pa., 1955, LL.B., 1958. Admitted to Pa. bar, 1960; asst. solicitor City of Phila., 1963-65; asst. dist. atty. City of Phila., 1965-66; partner firm Sidkoff, Pincus, Greenberg & Golden, Phila., 1972-76; asso. firm Brobyn & Forceno, Phila., 1976—; controller City of Phila., 1974—. Chmn. Phila. Gas Commn.; mem. Mid Atlantic Intergovernmental Audit Forum, 1974—, chmn., 1976—; mem. Sinking Fund Commn., City of Phila. 1974—, mem. bd. Pensions and Retirement City of Phila., 1974—. Home: 300 W Springfield Ave Philadelphia PA 19118 Office: 1230 Municipal Services Bldg Philadelphia PA 19107 Tel (215) 686-6680

KLEPAK, HENRY, b. N.Y.C., Jan. 14, 1912; student Dixie U., 1929-31; LL.B., Somerville Law Sch., 1933. Admitted to Tex. bar, 1933, U.S. Supreme Ct. bar, 1945, ICC bar, 1940; individual practice law, Dallas, 1933—. Bd. dirs. Dallas Civic Opera, Dallas Civic Ballet, Dallas Symphony Orch., Shakespeare Soc., Dallas Mus. Fine Arts; chmn. bd. U.S. Reclamation Div. Tex.; instr. USAAF. Mem. Am., Tex., Dallas bar assns., Am. Judicature Soc., Am. Trial Lawyers Assn. Home: 11234 Shelterwood Circle Dallas TX 75229 Office: Mercantile Commerce Bldg 22d Floor Dallas TX 75201 Tel (214) 747-9992

KLETT, EDWIN LEE, b. Clearfield, Pa., Dec. 8, 1935; B.S. in Commerce and Fin., Bucknell U., 1957; J.D., Dickinson Sch. Law, 1962. Admitted to Pa. bar, 1962; asso. firm Eckert, Seamans, Cherin & Mellott, Pitts., 1962-69, partner, 1969—. Mem. Am., Pa., Allegheny County bar assns. Office: 42d floor 600 Grant St Pittsburgh PA 15219 Tel (412) 566-6031

KLIGFELD, STANLEY, b. N.Y.C., May 22, 1926; A.B., Trinity Coll., Hartford, Conn., 1946; M.A. in Econs., Columbia U., 1948; LL.B., Bklyn. Law Sch., 1953. Staff writer Wall St. Jour., N.Y.C., 1946-53; admitted to N.Y. bar, 1954; practiced in N.Y.C., 1954-75; asso. prof. law Del. Law Sch. Widener Coll., 1974-75, prof., 1975—. Mem. Am. Bar Assn. (vice chmn. com. on securities sect. adminstrv. law 1972—). Recipient Am. Heritage Found. award, 1952; author: The SEC's New Rule 144, 1972. Office: Del Law Sch Widener Coll 2001 Washington St Wilmington DE 19802 Tel (302) 648-8042

KLINE, JAMES EDWARD, b. Fremont, Ohio, Aug. 3, 1941; B.S., John Carroll U., 1963; J.D., Ohio State U., 1966. Admitted to Ohio bar, 1966; asso. law firm Eastman, Stichter, Smith & Bergman, Toledo, Ohio, 1966-70, partner, 1970—. Trustee, Kidney Found. Northwestern Ohio, Inc.; trustee, vice-pres. Crosby Park Bd. Mem. Am., Ohio (vice-chmn. corporate law com.), Toledo bar assns. Home: 5958 Swan Creek Dr Toledo OH 43614 Office: 700 United Savings Bldg Toledo OH 43604

KLINE, MICHAEL JOSEPH, b. Phila., Nov. 5, 1944; B.S. in Economics summa cum laude, U. Pa., 1966, J.D. cum laude, 1969. Admitted to Pa. bar, 1969, N.J. bar, 1976; asso. firm Pasco-L. Schiavo, Hazleton, Pa., 1969-70; asso. firm Cohen, Shapiro, Polisher, Shiekman and Cohen, Phila., 1970-76; mem. firm, 1977—. Sec. Deborah Heart and Lung Center, Browns Mills, N.J., Deborah Hosp. Found., Browns Mills. Mem. Am., Pa., Phila. bar assns. Home: 14 Blossom Ct Cherry Hill NJ 08003 Office: 12 S 12th St Philadelphia PA 19107 Tel (215) 922-1300

KLINE, ROBERT EDWARD, b. Hazleton, Pa., Sept. 22, 1916; A.B., Harvard, 1938, LL.B., 1941. Admitted to Pa. bar, 1942; asso. firm Baker, Watts & Woods, Pitts., 1960-62; partner firm Kline and Smith, Pitts., 1963—. Home: 1012 Gilchrest Dr Pittsburgh PA 15235 Office: 1320 Grant Bldg Pittsburgh PA 15219 Tel (412) 471-1011

KLINE, SIDNEY DELONG, b. West Reading, Pa., June 15, 1902; A.B., Dickinson Coll., 1924, M.A., 1926, J.D., 1926, LL.D., 1963; LL.D., Albright Coll., 1955. Admitted to Pa. bar, 1926; trust clk. Mut. Trust of Phila., 1926-27; asst. trust officer Union Bank & Trust Co., Phila., 1927-28, Corn Exchange Bank & Trust Co., Phila., 1928-29; trust officer Colonial Trust Co. of Reading, Pa. (merged with Berks County Trust Co.), 1929-33, v.p., trust officer Berks County Trust Co., Reading, 1933-44, pres., 1944-60, pres., chmn. bd., 1960-64; pres., chmn. bd. Am. Bank & Trust Co. of Pa. (formerly Berks County Trust Co.), Reading, 1964-68, chmn. bd., chief exec. officer, 1968-72, chmn. bd., 1972—; chmn. bd., dir. Berks Title Ins. Co., Reading. Pres. Community Chest of Berks County, 1952; metro chmn. jobs program Nat. Alliance Businessmen, 1969-70; mem. Berks County Planning Commn., 1958-75, chmn., 1976—. Mem. Am., Pa., Berks County bar assns., Pa. Bankers Assn. (chmn. trust div. 1947-48, pres. 1954-55). Home: 62 Grandview Blvd Wyomissing Hills Reading PA 19609 Office: 35 N 6th St Reading PA 19601 Tel (215) 375-5151

KLINE, SIDNEY DELONG, JR., b. West Reading, Pa., Mar. 25, 1932; A.B., Dickinson Coll., 1954, LL.B. with honors 1956. Admitted to Pa. bar, 1956, U.S. Supreme Ct. bar, 1967. Asso. firm Stevens & Lee, Reading, Pa., 1956-63, partner, 1963—; dir. Wyomissing New Home Fed. Savs. and Loan Assn., Am. Bus. Credit Corp., Am. Venture Capital Corp. Bd. dirs. United Way Berks County (Pa.), 1968—, pres., 1972-74; chmn. planning div. United Community Services, 1968-70; bd. dirs. Berks County chpt. ARC, 1959-66, chmn., 1964-66; bd. dirs. Reading-Berks Tuberculosis and Health Assn., 1959-65; mem. advisory com. Berks County Children's Services, 1968-76; chmn. Berks County Young Republican Com., 1963, 64, 66; deacon St. James United Ch. Christ, West Reading, 1964-67; mem. Berks County advisory com. Pa. State U., 1967-72; bd. mgrs. Reading Hosp. and Med. Center, 197; dir. Chit Chat Found., 1974—. Fellow Am. Coll. Probate Counsel; mem. Am., Pa. (mem. hos. delegates), Berks County bar assns. Named Outstanding Young Republican, Berks County Young Republicans., 1965; contbr. articles to law reviews. Home: 21 Merrymount Rd Wyomissing Hills PA 19609 Office: PO Box 679 Reading PA 19603 Tel (215) 376-9781

KLINE, STANLEY JAY, b. Memphis, Aug. 25, 1942; B.S., Memphis State U., 1965, J.D., 1967. Admitted to Tenn. bar, 1967; individual practice law, Memphis, 1967—. Mem. Memphis and Shelby County, Tenn., Am. bar assns. Home: 3015 Woodstone Manor Memphis TN 38138 Office: Suite 2516 100 N Main Bldg Memphis TN 38103 Tel (901) 526-0812

KLING, CARL CHRISTOPHER, b. Evansville, Ind., June 14, 1930; A.B., U. Evansville, 1952; J.D., Ind. U., 1957; LL.M., Georgetown U., 1958. Admitted to D.C. bar, 1958, N.Y. bar, 1960. Pres. United Way of No. Westchester, 1974-75. Mem. Am., N.Y. State bar assns., Am. Patent Law Assn. Office: 22 Annadale St Armonk NY 10504 Tel (914) 273-9274

KLINGBERG, DOUGLAS JOHN, b. Beloit, Wis., Feb. 25, 1941; B.S., Carroll Coll., 1963; M.S., Kent State U., 1965; J.D., U. Wis., 1968. Admitted to Wis. bar, 1968, Fed. bar, 1968; mem. firm Terwilliger, Wakeen, Diehler, Conway & & Klingberg, Wausau, Wis., 1968—. Bd. dirs. United Way, 1975—, Halfway House, 1969-71. Mem. Am., Wis. State, Marathon County bar assns. Office: 401 4th St Wausau WI 54401 Tel (715) 845-2121

KLINGENSMITH, H. JACK, b. DuBois, Pa., July 21, 1937; B.A., De Pauw U., 1959; J.D., Northwestern U., 1962. Admitted to Ill. bar, 1963, Fla. bar, 1965, U.S. Supreme Ct. bar, 1969. Asst. staff JAG, USAF, Spokane, Wash., 1963-65; mem. firm Kuvin, Klingensmith & Lewis, Miami, Fla., 1972—, firm Carey, Dwyer, Austin, Cole & Selwood, Miami, 1965-72. Mem. Fla., Dade County bar assns., Fla., Dade County (sec., exec. com.) def. bar assns., Def. Research Inst., Phi Beta Kappa, Phi Delta Phi. Recipient Am. Jurisprudence award, 1961; contbr. articles to profl. jours.; asso. editor Northwestern U. Law Rev., 1961-62. Office: 2951 S Bayshore Dr Suite E-6 POB 330739 Miami FL 33133 Tel (305) 446-8671

KLINGER, NORMAN ASHTON, b. Cairo, Egypt, Nov. 15, 1937; B.S., Drexel Inst. Tech., 1959; J.D., U. Pa., 1963. Admitted to Pa. bar, 1964; clk. to judge U.S. Dist. Ct., Eastern Dist. Pa., Phila., 1964; sr. counsel Norman Ashton Klinger and Assos., Phila., Norristown, Pa., 1964—; lectr. Phila. Coll. Textiles, 1967-70; speaker in field; conducted study Scotland Yard, Brit. Juvenile Ct. System, 1969. Chmn. spl. gifts Am. Cancer Soc., Phila., 1972-73; vice chmn. Montgomery County Cancer Crusade, 1976, chmn. residential crusade tng. program, 1977; bd. dirs. Suburban Gen. Hosp., Norristown, 1973—; trustee United Way, Phila., 1976; mem. exec. bd. Valley Forge Council Boy Scouts Am., 1975; commr.-at-large Plymouth Twp., Pa., 1970-74, pres. bd. commrs., 1972-74. Mem. Am. (chmn. drug abuse edn. local area), Pa., Montgomery County, Phila. bar assns. Guest columnist Today's Post. Home: Gawain Rd Plymouth Meeting PA 19462 Office: 612 Swede St Norristown PA 19401 Tel (215) 275-1112

KLINGER, RICHARD DAVID, b. Jersey City, Nov. 15, 1936; B.A., Harvard, 1958; LL.B., Columbia U., 1963. Admitted to N.Y. bar, 1964, Mont. bar, 1973; dir. bus. affairs CBS Records, Hollywood, Calif., 1968-69; profl. mgr. April-Blackwood Music, Hollywood, 1969-71; staff counsel Mont. Environ. Quality Council, Helena, 1973-74; environ. affairs legal officer Mont. Dept. Health and Environ. Scis., Helena; individual practice law, Bigfork, Mont., 1976—; asst. prof. journalism Calif. State U., 1970-73; bd. dirs. Alternative Energy Research Orgn. Mem. Helena Citizen's Adv. Council, 1974-76; chmn. Community Devel. Com., Helena, 1975. Mem. Mont. Bar Assn. Home: Route 1 Bigfork MT 59911 Office: PO Box 397 Bigfork MT 59911 Tel (406) 837-6952

KLINGNER, HAROLD WILLIAM, b. Chgo., May 3, 1920; J.D., Chgo. Kent Coll. Law, 1950. Admitted to Ill. bar, 1950; asso. firm Guilford R. Windes, Chgo., 1950-59; partner firm Windes, Thomas & Klingner, Chgo., 1959-66, Wooster, Mugalian, Thomas & Klingner, Chgo., 1966-69, Wooster, Mugalian & Klingner, Chgo., 1969-72; individual practice law, Chgo., 1972—. Mem. Arlington Heights (Ill.) Bd. Local Improvements. Mem. Am., Ill. State, Fed., Chgo. (lectr. fed. income tax subjects) bar assns. Home: 1123 N Belmont Ave Arlington Heights IL 60004 Office: 105 W Adams St 37th Floor Chicago IL 60603 Tel (312) 372-0900

KLINK, FREDRIC J., b. N.Y.C., Oct. 4, 1933; A.B., Columbia, 1955, LL.B., 1960. Admitted to N.Y. State bar, 1960; asso. firm Hughes, Hubbard, Blair & Reed, N.Y.C., 1960-68; mem. firm Shea, Gould, Climenko, Kramer & Casey, N.Y.C., 1968-75, firm Walter, Conston, Schurtman & Gumpel, N.Y.C., 1975—. Mem. Am., N.Y. State, N.Y. C., Internat. bar assns. Home: 120 Leeuwarden Rd Darien CT 06820 Office: 280 Park Ave New York City NY 10017 Tel (212) 682-2323

KLITGAARD, ROBERT JOSEPH, b. San Francisco, June 29, 1916; A.B., U. Calif., 1937; LL.B., Stanford U., 1940. Admitted to Calif. bar, 1940; practice in San Diego, 1947—; sr. partner firm Klitgaard and Jones, San Diego, 1969—; dep. dist. atty. San Diego County, 1946. Mem. Am. Bar Assn. Home: 939 Coast Blvd La Jolla CA 92037 Office: 530 B St San Diego CA 92101 Tel (714) 232-6491

KLITZKE, RAMON ARTHUR, b. Chgo., June 7, 1928; B.S. in Engring., Ill. Inst. Tech., 1950; J.D., Ind. U., 1957; LL.M., N.Y.U., 1958. Admitted to N.Y. bar, 1959, Tex. bar, 1960, Wis. bar, 1966, U.S. Supreme Ct. bar, 1966; patent atty. Union Carbide Corp., N.Y.C., 1957-59; asso. prof. law Tex. So. U., Houston, 1959-66, Marquette U., Milw., 1966—; dir. Inst. Poverty and the Law, 1966-70; bd. dirs. Milw. Legal Services. Mem. adv. bd. Milw. County Project Turnaround. Mem. Am., Wis., Tex., Milw., Waukesha bar assns., Am. Patent Law Assn., Assn. Am. Law Schs. (chmn. local govt. law sect.). Editor: Legal Counseling for the Indigent, 1968; contbr. articles to legal jours. Home: 1935 Sunnyside Dr Waukesha WI 53186 Office: Marquette U Law Sch 1103 W Wisconsin Ave Milwaukee WI 53233 Tel (414) 224-7094

KLOCK, GEORGE EDWIN, b. Fredonia, Kans., Apr. 9, 1919; B.B.A., U. Tex., 1941, J.D., 1961; M.B.A., U. Chgo., 1946. Admitted to Tex. bar, 1961, Calif. bar, 1963, Ark. bar, 1968, U.S. Supreme Ct. bar, 1975; dep. dist. atty. County of Riverside, Calif., 1963-68; economist, stock market analyst, pvt. trader, Ft. Smith, Ark., 1968—; bus. analyst Dept. of Army Far East Command, 1947-53. Mem. Ark., Tex., Calif. bar assns. Office: 2500 S M St Fort Smith AR 72901 Tel (501) 783-6918

KLOCKAU, WALTER JOHN, JR., b. Rock Island, Ill., July 24, 1913; A.B., U. Ill., 1938; J.D., Harvard, 1942. Admitted to Ill. bar, 1942, U.S. Supreme Ct. bar, 1945, Ariz. bar, 1970; law clk. firm Webster & Garside, N.Y.C., 1942; asso. firm Bell, Boyd & Marshall, Chgo., 1942-44; partner firm Crampton & Klockau, Moline, Ill., 1944-48; individual practice law Moline and East Moline, Ill., 1948-69; legal sec. to Ill. Supreme Ct. justices, Moline, East Moline and Springfield, Ill., 1948-69. Mem. State Bar Ariz. Contbr. articles to legal jours. Home: 616 Camino Esplendido Tubac AZ 85640 Tel (602) 398-2770

KLOESS, LAWRENCE HERMAN, JR., lawyer; b. Mamaroneck, N.Y., Jan. 30, 1927; A.B., U. Ala., 1954, J.D., 1956. Admitted to Ala. bar, 1956, U.S. Dist. Ct. Ala., 1956, U.S. Ct. Appeals, 1957, U.S. Supreme Ct., 1971, U.S. Ct. Mil. Appeals, 1971; pvt. practice law, Birmingham, Ala., 1956-60; corp. counsel Bankers Fire & Marine Ins. Co., Birmingham, 1960-62; pvt. practice law, Birmingham, 1962-66; dist. counsel U.S. VA, Montgomery, Ala., 1966—; lt. col. JAG, USAFR. Mem. exec. com. Citizens Conf. on Ala. Cts., Inc.; mem. staff Citizens Conf. on Criminal and Juvenile Justice, 1975. Mem. Birmingham, Montgomery County (law day chmn. 1972, chmn. state bar liaison com. 1975, chmn. bd. dirs. 1977), Fed. (pres. 1973), Ala. State (law day chmn. 1973, chmn. citizenship edn. com. 1974, character and fitness com. 1976) bar assns., Farrah Law Soc., Res. Officers Assn. U.S. (judge adv., dept. of Ala. 1977—). Mem. editorial adv. bd. com. The Alabama Lawyer, 1970—, chmn., 1975—. Home: 3174 Highfield Dr Montgomery AL 36111 Office: Suite 234 Aronov Bldg 474 S Court St Montgomery AL 36104

KLONOWSKI, STEPHEN MICHAEL, b. Canton, Ohio, Jan. 20, 1946; B.S. in Bus. Adminstrn., Bowling Green State U., 1969; J.D., U. Toledo, 1974. Admitted to Ohio bar, 1974; since practiced in Cleve., asso. firm Merkle, Campbell, Dill & Zetzer, 1974-75, individual practice law, 1975-76, asso. firm Bartunek, Bennett, Garofoli & Hill, 1976—; asst. dir. law City of Solon (Ohio), 1976—. Exec. com. Cuyahoga County Democratic Party, 1976—. Mem. Ohio State, Greater Cleve., Cuyahoga County bar assns. Home: 606 Trevitt Circle W Cleveland OH 44143 Office: 1003 Bond Ct Bldg Cleveland OH 44114 Tel (216) 623-1400

KLOS, JEROME JOHN, b. LaCrosse, Wis., Jan. 17, 1927; B.S., U. Wis., 1948, J.D., 1950. Admitted to Wis. bar, 1950; asso. firm Fairchild, Foley & Sammond, Milw., 1950-53; partner firm Steele, Smyth, Klos & Flynn, LaCrosse, 1953—; pub. adminstr. LaCrosse County, 1962-73; spl. trial counsel for condemnations Wis. Atty. Gen.'s Office, 1962-72. Past pres. LaCrosse Indsl. Devel. Council; past vice chmn. LaCrosse County Bd., LaCrosse County Indsl. and Comml. Devel.; bd. dirs. LaCrosse County Devel., LaCrosse Area Growth, West Salem (Wis.) Area Growth. Fellow Am. Coll. Probate Counsel; mem. Am., Wis., LaCrosse County (pres. 1963-64) bar assns., Order of Coif. Exec. editor Wis. Law Rev., 1950. Home: 346 N Leonard St West Salem WI 54669 Office: 800 Lynne Tower Bldg LaCrosse WI 54601 Tel (608) 784-8600

KLOSE, WOODY NICHOLAS, b. St. Louis, Dec. 6, 1938; B.A., Cornell U., 1960; J.D., Albany U., 1971. Admitted to N.Y. State bar, 1972; asso. firm Aldrich & Mac Donald, Poughkeepsie, N.Y., 1971-73; individual practice law, Red Hook, N.Y., 1973—; dept. pub. defender Dutchess County (N.Y.), 1973—; atty. Village of Tivoli (N.Y.), 1975—; asst. counsel N.Y. State Senate Standing Com. on Banks, 1977. Mem. Am., N.Y., Dutchess County bar assns. Home: 15 North Rd Tivoli NY 12583 Office: 35 E Market St Red Hook NY 12571 Tel (914) 758-8871

KLOTTER, JOHN CHARLES, b. Louisville, Nov. 6, 1918; A.B. in Sociology and Econs., Western Ky. U., 1941; J.D., U. Ky., 1948. Admitted to Ky. bar, 1948, U.S. Supreme Ct. bar, 1967; tchr. Louisville Pub. Schs., 1941-42; spl. agt. FBI, 1948-50; legal officer Ky. State Police, Frankfort, 1951-52; dir. Ky. div. Probation and Parole, 1952-56; prof. law U. Louisville, 1957—; dean sch. police adminstrn., 1971—; mem. Louisville-Jefferson County (Ky.) Crime Commn., 1967—, vice-chmn., 1967-74; mem. Ky. Crime Commn., 1972-76, Ky. Law Enforcement Council, 1971—; mem. Louisville Regional Criminal Justice Commn., 1974—, chmn., 1975—; mem. Atty. Gen's. Prosecutor's Adv. Commn., 1973—; pvt. security task force to Nat. Adv. Com. on Criminal Justice Standards and Goals, 1975-76. Mem. Ky., Louisville bar assns., Internat. Assn. Chiefs Police, Res. Officers Assn. Co-Author: Constitutional Law for Police, 1968; Criminal Evidence for Police, 1971; contbr. articles in field to profl. jours. Home: 11905 Cedardale Rd Anchorage KY 40223 Office: U Louisville 3d St and Eastern Pkwy Louisville KY 40208 Tel (502) 588-6561

KLOVSKY, SIDNEY BRYAN, b. Phila., Oct. 29, 1922; B.S., Temple U., 1945, J.D., 1948. Admitted to Pa. bar, 1949; partner firm Klovsky, Kuby & Harris, Phila., 1955—. Trustee, OEO Community Legal Services Bd., 1969—. Mem. Am., Pa., Phila. (chmn. coms.) bar assns., Am., Pa., Phila. (past pres.) trial lawyers assns. Recipient Sigma Pi Monroe award, 1945. Home: 306 Penbree Circle Cynwyd PA 19004 Office: 13th Floor Packard Bldg 15th & Chestnut Sts Philadelphia PA 19102 Tel (215) 568-1919

KLUCK, J. JEROME, b. West St. Paul, Minn., July 13, 1920; LL.B., St. Paul Coll. Law, 1949. Admitted to Minn. bar, 1950; practiced in Minn., 1950-61; judge Municipal Ct., West St. Paul, 1951-61, 1st Jud. Dist. Ct., 1973—; county atty. Dakota County (Minn.), 1961-73. Mem. Dakota County, 1st Dist., 8th Dist., Minn. State bar assns., Dist. Judges Assn., Minn. County Attys. Assn. (pres. 1967-68). Home: 412 E Haskell St West Saint Paul MN 55118 Office: Courthouse Glencoe MN Tel (612) 437-3191

KLUTTZ, GEORGE O., b. Jacksonville, Fla., Nov. 2, 1935; B.B.A., U. Fla., 1960, LL.B., 1962. Admitted to Fla. bar, 1962, U.S. Supreme Ct. bar, 1974; partner firms Ward & Ward, Miami, Fla., 1968, Alderman, Johnson, Pack & Kluttz, Ft. Myers, Fla., 1968-71, Pavese, Shields, Garner, Haverfield & Kluttz, Ft. Myers, 1971—. Bd. dirs. S.W. Fla. Mental Health Dist. Bd. 19, Canterbury Sch., Inc. Mem. Fla. Bar (dir. sect. gen. practice), Fla. Acad. Trial Lawyers, Am. Bar Assn. Home: 1357 Wales Dr Fort Myers FL 33901 Office: 1833 Hendry St Fort Myers FL 33901 Tel (813) 334-2195

KLUWIN, JOHN ANDREW, b. Oshkosh, Wis., Sept. 16, 1907; LL.B., Marquette U., 1930, J.D., 1971. Admitted to Wis. bar, 1930; sr. partner firm Kluwin, Dunphy, Hankin & McNulty, Milw., 1961—. Mem. Am. (state del. 1965-76, bd. govs. 1976—), Wis. (pres. 1962-63), Milw. (pres. 1955-56) bar assns., Internat. Assn. Ins. Counsel (pres. 1956-57), Am. Coll. Trial Lawyers (regent 1964-68), Am., Wis. bar founds., Am. Judicature Soc., Am. Law Inst., Marquette U. Alumni Assn. (pres. 1964-65). Home: 9325 Hickory Dr Kewaskum WI 53040 Office: 1100 W Wells St Milwaukee WI 53233 Tel (414) 276-6464

KNAG, PAUL EVERETT, b. Flushing, N.Y., Feb. 26, 1948; B.A. magna cum laude, Queens Coll., 1967; J.D. cum laude, Harvard, 1970. Admitted to N.Y. bar, 1971, Conn. bar, 1971, U.S. Supreme Ct. bar, 1974; clk. judge Leonard P. Moore U.S. Circuit Ct., N.Y.C., 1970-71; asso. firm Cummings & Lockwood, Stamford, Ct., 1971—. Mem. Am., Stamford (chmn. by-laws com., 1975—), Conn. bar assns., Phi Beta Kappa. Contbr. articles to profl. pubis. Office: One Atlantic St Stamford CT 06904 Tel (203) 327-1700

KNAPP, CHARLES LINCOLN, b. Zanesville, Ohio, Oct. 22, 1935; B.A., Denison U., 1956; postgrad. U. Sydney (Australia), 1957; J.D., N.Y. U., 1960. Admitted to N.Y. State bar, 1961; asso. firm Paul, Weiss, Rifkind, Wharton & Garrison, N.Y.C., 1960-64; asst. prof. law N.Y. U., 1964-67, asso. prof., 1967-70, prof., 1970—; vis. prof. U. Ariz., 1973, Harvard, 1974-75. Author: Problems in Contract Law—Cases and Materials, 1976. Home: 12 Washington Mews New York City NY 10003 Office: NY U Law Sch 40 Washington Square S New York City NY 10012 Tel (212) 598-2581

KNAPP, CLEMENT BERNARD, JR., b. Hammond, Ind., Jan. 29, 1942; A.B. in Govt., Georgetown U., 1963; J.D., Ind. U., 1968. Admitted to Ind. bar, 1969; sec. Am. Savs. & Loan Assn., Munster, Ind., 1969-71, exec. v.p., 1971-77, pres., 1977—, also dir. Mem. Am., Ind., Hammond bar assns. Home: 7220 Forest Ave Hammond IN 46324 Office: 8230 Hohman Ave Munster IN 46321 Tel (219) 836-5870

KNAPP, DENNIS RAYMOND, b. Putnam County, W.Va., May 13, 1912; B.A., W.Va. Inst. Tech., 1932; M.A., W.Va. U., 1934, LL.B., 1940. Supt. schs. Putnam County, 1935-37; admitted to W.Va. bar, 1940; individual practice law, Nitro, W.Va., 1940-56; atty. City of Nitro, 1946-56; judge Ct. of Common Pleas, Kanawha County, W.Va., 1956-70; judge U.S. Dist. Ct. for So. Dist. W.Va., 1970-73, chief judge, 1973—. Mem. pres.'s adv. com. Marshall U. Mem. Am. Bar Assn., W.Va. State Bar, W.Va. Judicial Assn. Office: 500 Quarrier St Charleston WV 25301 Tel (304) 342-8712

KNAPP, JAMES LINCOLN, b. Marion, Ohio, Dec. 21, 1905; A.B., Denison U., 1925; J.D., Ohio State U., 1928. Admitted to Ohio bar, 1928; judge Zanesville Municipal Ct., Zanesville, Ohio, 1934-41; city solicitor City of Zanesville, 1942-53; judge Muskingum County Pleas Ct., 1963—. Pres. United Way, Zanesville, 1952. Mem. Ohio State Bar Assn., Ohio Common Pleas Judges Assn. Office: Courthouse Main St Zanesville OH 43701 Tel (614) 454-1231

KNAUER, JAMES A., b. Terre Haute, Ind., Sept. 18, 1946; A.B., Ind. U., 1968, J.D., 1971. Admitted to Ind. bar, 1971; partner firm Kroger Gardis and Regas, Indpls., 1972—; asst. to Mayor Richard G. Lugar, Indpls., 1969-72. Mem. Indpls., Ind., Am. bar assns., Comml. Law League Am. Contbr. articles to legal publs. and seminars. Home: 1104 W 72d St Indianapolis IN 46260 Office: 414 Guaranty Bldg Indianapolis IN 46204 Tel (317) 634-6328

KNAUER, LEON THOMAS, b. N.Y.C., July 16, 1932; B.S. in Math., Fordham U., 1954; J.D., Georgetown U., 1961. Admitted to Conn. bar, 1961, D.C. bar, 1961; law clk. to judge U.S. Dist. Ct. D.C., 1961-62; asso. firm Wilkinson, Cragun & Barker, Washington, 1962-68, partner 1968—; instr. Georgetown U. Law Center, Washington, 1964-68. Pres. Catholic Apostolate Mass Media, 1977. Mem. Am., D.C., Conn. bar assns. Recipient NAACP award outstanding legal services, Paterson, N.J., 1973. Office: 1735 New York Ave NW Washington DC 20006 Tel (202) 833-9800

KNAUF, HAROLD LOUIS, b. Rochester, N.Y., Aug. 24, 1918; ed. U. Iowa, 1939-41, U. Chgo., 1943; LL.B., St. John's U., Bklyn., 1948. Admitted to N.Y. bar, 1948; mem. firms Castle Fitch Swan & Jefferson, 1948-50; individual practice law, Rochester, 1950—; counsel Emil Miller Constrn. Co., Inc., 1954-60; supr. Town of Trondequoit (N.Y.), 1960-66, 68-69; mem. Monroe County (N.Y.) Bd. Suprs., 1960-67, Monroe County Legislature, 1970-75, Monroe County Charter Commn., 1969. Mem. Monroe County Bar Assn., N.Y. State Assn. Towns (exec. com.). Home: 30 Barons Rd Rochester NY 14617 Office: 745 Titus Ave Rochester NY 14617 Tel (716) 544-1340

KNEECE, ROBERT EDWARD, b. Columbia, S.C., Dec. 20, 1933; grad. U. S.C., 1956, LL.B., 1958. Admitted to S.C. bar, 1958; partner firm Kneece and Lewis, 1958-63, firm Kneece, Kneece & Freeman, Columbia, 1963—; mem. S.C. Ho. of Reps., 1967—, past chmn. judiciary com.; chmn., bd. dirs. S.C. Dept. Social Services. Mem. Am., S.C. State (chmn. criminal laws sect.) bar assns., S.C. Trial Lawyers Assn., Am. Judicature Soc. Home: 4110 Parkman Dr Columbia SC 29206 Office: 1338 Pickens St Columbia SC 29201 Tel (803) 799-9393

KNEISEL, EDMUND MOORE, b. Atlanta, Feb. 21, 1946; A.B., Duke U., 1968; J.D., U. Ga., 1974. Admitted to Ga. bar, 1974; clk. judge R.C. Freeman, U.S. Dist. Ct. Ga., No. Dist., Atlanta, 1974-76; asso. firm Kilpatrick, Cody, Rogers, McClatchey & Regenstein, Atlanta, 1976—. Mem. Am., Ga., Atlanta bar assns. Contbr. note Ga. Law Review. Office: 3100 Equitable Bldg Atlanta GA 30303 Tel (404) 522-3100

KNEPPER, WILLIAM EDWARD, b. Tiffin, Ohio, Oct. 25, 1909; A.B., Ohio State U., 1931; student Columbus Coll. Law, 1932. Admitted to Ohio bar, 1933; partner firm Knepper, White, Richards & Miller, Columbus, Ohio, 1933—; adj. prof. law Ohio State U., 1972—; lectr. in law U. Mich., 1973; mem. bar exam. com. Supreme Ct. Ohio, 1945-50, chmn., 1949-50. Pres., United Appeal Franklin County (Ohio), 1969. Fellow Am. Coll. Trial Lawyers; mem. Am., Ohio (exec. com. 1951-54), Columbus (pres. 1947-48) bar assns., Am. Judicature Soc., Def. Research Inst. (pres. 1965-66, chmn. 1966-67), Internat. Assn. Ins. Counsel (pres. 1962-63). Author: Liability of Corporate Officers and Directors, 1969, 2d edit., 1973; Ohio Civil Practice, 1970; co-author: Ohio Manual of General Practice, 1956; Judicial Conveyances and Eminent Domain, 1960; Ohio Eminent Domain Practice, 1976; contbr. articles to legal jours.; editor Ins. Counsel Jour., 1955-61. Home: 3135 Herrick Rd Columbus OH 43221 Office: 180 E Broad St Columbus OH 43215 Tel (614) 221-3155

KNICKERBOCKER, DANIEL CANDEE, JR., b. Glen Ridge, N.J., Apr. 16, 1919; A.B., Syracuse U., 1940; postgrad. Harvard U. Grad. Sch. Arts and Sci., 1940-41; J.D. with distinction, Cornell U., 1950. Admitted to N.Y. bar, 1951, Mass. bar, 1964; accounting dept. Bethlehem Steel Co., 1942-47; asso. with various law firms, N.Y.C., 1950-63; tax counsel John Hancock Mut. Life Ins. Co., Boston, 1963-66, counsel, 1966-70, v.p., counsel, 1970—; mem. tax mgmt. adv. bd. on estates, trusts and gifts, 1972—. Bd. dirs. Family Counselling and Guidance Centers, Boston, 1974—, chmn. fin. and budget com., 1974—. Mem. Am. Bar Assn. (vice chmn. com. on pension and profit sharing trusts sect. of real property, probate and trust law 1970—), Assn. Bar City N.Y., Am. Law Inst., Assn. Life Ins. Counsel, Am. Council on Life Ins. (chmn. subcom. on fed. taxes 1977—). Contbr. articles in field to profl. jours. Home: 55 Frost St Cambridge MA 02140 Office: John Hancock Pl Boston MA 02117 Tel (617) 421-6174

KNICKERBOCKER, GEORGE BURTON, b. Chgo., Sept. 28, 1946; B.A., DePauw U., 1968; J.D., U. Ill., 1971. Admitted to Ill. bar, 1972; asso. firm Hofert & Samelson, Des Plaines, Ill., 1971-75, partner firm, 1975-76; partner firm Samelson & Knickerbocker, Des Plaines, 1976—; village atty. Elk Grove Village (Ill.), 1976; village atty. Sleepy Hollow (Ill.), 1976. Mem. Ill., N.W. Suburban bar assns. Home: 508 E Wilson St Palatine IL 60067 Office: 780 Lee St Des Plaines IL 60016 Tel (312) 827-5117

KNIERIM, GLENN EDWARD, b. Schenectady, N.Y., May 19, 1930; B.S., Cornell U., 1952; LL.B., U. Conn., 1960. Admitted to Conn. bar, 1960; partner firm Joseloff, August, Sudarsky & Knierim, Hartford, Conn., 1960-73; judge Conn. Probate Ct., Dist. Simsbury, 1967—; adminstr. Conn. Probate Ct., Hartford, 1973—; mem. Conn. Gov's. Adoption Law Task Force, 1971-73; mem. Conn. Commn. to Reorganize and Unify Cts., 1973-76; mem. Conn. Jud. Council, 1973-75; mem. services advisory com. Conn. Dept. Social Services, 1976; mem. Conn. Council on Adoption, 1976. Chmn. Simsbury Charter Revision Commn., 1971-73; chmn. Simsbury Republican Bicentennial Com., 1976. Mem. Conn. (exec. com. sect. estates and probate), Am., Hartford County bar assns., Nat. Assn. Ct. Adminstrn., Am. Judicature Soc., Conn. Probate Assembly, Nat. Coll. Probate Judges (exec. com.). Editor Nat. Coll. Probate Judges Newsletter, 1975—. Office: 75 Lafayette St Hartford CT 07106 Tel (203) 522-1136

KNIGHT, ALFRED CONWAY, b. Newburyport, Mass., Jan. 14, 1907; B.S., Mass. Inst. Tech., 1928; LL.B., Boston Coll., 1936. Admitted to Mass. bar, 1937; served to lt. col. U.S. Army, 1940-52; register Probate Ct. Mass., 1953-66, judge, 1967—. Mem. Mass. Bar Assn. Home: 24 Popponesset Rd Cotuit MA 02635 Office: Courthouse Barnstable MA 02630 Tel (617) 362-2511

KNIGHT, ANDREW HENDRIX, b. Columbus, Ga., Sept. 18, 1904; B.A., Samford U., 1926; J.D., Harvard, 1930. Admitted to Ala. bar, 1930; since practiced in Birmingham, Ala., partner firm Thompson & Knight, 1930-41; sr. gen. atty. south U.S. Steel Corp., 1941-69; of counsel firm Balch, Bingham, Baker Hawthorne & Williams, 1971-72; individual practice law, 1973—. Mem. Jefferson (Ala.) County Bd. Edn., 1940-51, pres., 1944-45, 49-50; gen. co-chmn. Jefferson County United Appeal, 1960; pres. Birmingham Area council Boy Scouts Am., 1966-68, Birmingham Symphony Assn., 1972-73; chmn. Ala. Motorist Assn., 1974—; trustee Judson Coll., 1966-69; corporator Perkins Sch. for Blind, Watertown, Mass., 1961—; pres. Birmingham Execs. Club, 1944-45, English-Speaking Union-Birmingham br., 1976—. Mem. Am., Ala., Birmingham bar assns., Omicron Delta Kappa. Named Distinguished Alumnus of Year Samford U., 1967; contbr. articles to legal jours. Home and Office: 1412 Avon Circle Birmingham AL 35213 Tel (205) 324-8030

KNIGHT, GEORGE FREDERICK, b. Manchester, N.H., Dec. 11, 1943; A.B., St. Anselm's Coll., 1965; J.D., Cath. U., 1968. Admitted to Va. bar, 1971; editor criminal law reporter Bur. Nat. Affairs, Inc., Washington, 1959—, editor Law Officers Bull., 1976—; mem. firm Crouch, Morse & Knight, Arlington, Va., 1973-75. Mem. Am., Va. State bar assns., Phi Alpha Delta. Contbg. editor The Criminal Law Revolution and Its Aftermath, 1960-76. Office: 1231 25th St NW Washington DC 20037 Tel (202) 452-4356

KNIGHT, H. GARY, b. St. Joseph, Mo., Dec. 8, 1939; A.B., Stanford, 1961; J.D., So. Meth. U., 1964. Admitted to Calif. bar, 1965; asso. firm Nossaman, Waters, Scott, Krueger & Riordan, Los Angeles, 1964-68; asst. prof. law and marine scis., La. State U., Baton Rouge, 1968-71, asso. prof., 1971-75, prof., 1975—, Campanile prof. marine resources law, 1971—; mem. adv. com. on law of sea NSC, 1972—; U.S. del. UN Law of Sea Conf., 1974; cons. State Dept., 1974-75; chmn. sci. and statis. com. Gulf Region Fishery Mgmt. Council, 1977—. Mem. Am. Bar Assn., Law of the Sea Inst. (exec. bd. 1972—), Am. Soc. Internat. Law (bd. rev. and devel. 1975—), Internat. Law Assn., Beta Theta Pi, Phi Alpha Delta. Contbr. articles to legal jours.; author: Law of the Sea; Cases, Documents and Readings, 1976; The Future of International Fisheries Management, 1975; Managing the Sea's Living Resources, 1977. Home: 1152 Ingleside Dr Baton Rouge LA 70806 Office: Law Center La State U Baton Rouge LA 70803 Tel (504) 388-8701

KNIGHT, JAMES, b. Henderson, Ky., May 30, 1919; B.S., Ind. U., 1942; LL.B., U. Mich., 1949. Admitted to Fla. bar, 1950; partner firm Walton, Lantaff, Schroeder & Carson, Miami, Fla., 1952—. Mem. Am., Fla. bar assns. Home: 9300 SW 181st St Miami FL 33154 Office: 900 A I DuPont Bldg Miami FL 33131 Tel (305) 379-6411

KNIGHT, KENNETH EDWIN, b. Crown Point, Ind., Jan. 1, 1921; A.B., DePauw U., 1942; J.D., Ind. U., 1944. Admitted to Ind. bar, 1944; practiced in Crown Point, 1944—; partner firms Knight & Knight, 1944-50, Knight & Stanton, 1970—; individual practice law, 1950-70; atty., dir. Crown Point Savs. and Loan Assn., 1950-72, Griffith Fed. Savs. and Loan Assn., 1950—. Mem. Crown Point Sch. Bd., 1952-68; pres. Ind. Sch. Bds. Assn., 1962. Mem. Ind. State, South Lake County (Ind.), Am. bar assns. Home: 385 Ellendale Pkwy Crown Point IN 46307 Office: 310 E Joliet St Crown Point IN 46307 Tel (219) 663-1368

KNIGHT, RICHARD FINLEY, b. Bogalusa, La., Feb. 14, 1933; B.S., La. State U., 1955, J.D., 19S8. Admitted to La. bar, 1958, U.S. Supreme Ct. bar, 1964; jud. adminstr. Supreme Ct. La., New Orleans, 1958-60; partner firm Talley, Anthony, Hughes & Knight, 1960—; chmn. Indigent Defender Bd. La. 22d Jud. Dist. Ct.; mem. permanent rules com. La. Supreme Ct. Mem. Democratic Nat. Platform Com., Dem. State Central Com., La., Bogalusa Charter Commn.; 1st v.p. La. Pub. Affairs Research Council. Mem. Am., La. bar assns., Am. Judicature Soc., Inst. Judicial Adminstrn., Omicron Delta Kappa, Phi Delta Phi. Home: 1404 Charwood Dr Bogalusa LA 70427 Office: 322 Columbia St Bogalusa LA 70427 Tel (504) 732-7151

KNIGHT, RONALD THOMAS, b. Charleston, S.C., Mar. 26, 1937; A.B., U. Ga., 1959; B.D., Christian Theol. Sem., 1962; J.D., Emory U., 1969. Admitted to Ga. bar, 1969; asst. U.S. atty. Middle Dist. Ga., Macon, 1970-74, U.S. atty., 1974-76; mem. firm Almand, Grice and Knight, 1977—. Mem. Fed., Ga., Macon (v.p. 1977) bar assns. Home: 5650 Kentucky Downs Macon GA 31204 Office: Suite 909 American Federal Bldg Macon GA 31201 Tel (912) 742-0965

KNISELY, GARY THEODORE, b. Harrisburg, Pa., Sept. 11, 1948; A.B. in Polit. Sci., Albright Coll., 1973; J.D., Dickinson Sch. Law, 1973. Admitted to Pa. bar; asso. firm Alexander, Alexander & Tucker, York, Pa. Bd. dirs. York Twinning Assn., 1975—; mem. council St. Paul's Luth. Ch., York, 1976—; sec. Environ. Info. Services, Mechanicsburg, Pa. Mem. Pa. (sec. com. on environ., natural and mineral resources), Am. bar assns. Editor Enviroguide. Office: 46 S Duke St York PA 17401 Tel (717) 848-3625

KNOBLAUCH, LEO NATHAN, b. Reading, Pa., July 4, 1917; B.S., U. Pa., 1938; LL.B., John Marshall Law Sch., 1941. Admitted to N.J. bar, 1942, U.S. Supreme Ct. bar, 1955; mem. N.J. State Assembly, 1952-58; asst. prosecutor Hudson County (N.J.), 1959-63, asst. county counsel, 1963-73; individual practice law, Jersey City, 1973—. Mem. Hudson County, N.J. State bar assns. Home: 138 Jewett Ave Jersey City NJ 07304 Office: 26 Journal Sq Jersey City NJ 07306 Tel (201) 656-4720

KNOEPP, TERRY JAY, b. Pitts., Jan. 31, 1938; B.A., U. Calif., Berkeley, 1960, LL.B., 1963. Admitted to Calif. bar, 1965, U.S. Supreme Ct. bar, 1972; dep. city atty., San Diego, 1965; individual practice law, San Diego, 1965-66; dep. dist. atty. for San Diego, 1966-75; U.S. atty. So. Dist. Calif., San Diego, 1975—; del. State Bar Conv., 1973, 74. Mem. Calif., San Diego County (chmn. criminal law sect. 1973) bar assns. Office: 940 Front St Room 5-N-19 San Diego CA 92189 Tel (714) 293-5690

KNOLL, DAVID DENYS, b. Hugo, Okla., Aug. 1, 1943; student Georgetown U., 1961-62; B.A., Gannon Coll., 1965; J.D., Villanova U., 1968. Admitted to Pa. bar, 1968, D.C. bar, 1973, Tex. bar, 1975; practiced in Phila., 1968-69; with JAGC, U.S. Army, 1969-72; appellate def. counsel U.S. Army, Falls Church, Va., 1971-72; gen. atty. Hoffmann-LaRoche, Inc., Nutley, N.J., 1972-73; atty. Am. Gen. Ins. Co., Houston, 1973-74, asst. counsel, 1974-76, 2d v.p., asso. counsel, 1976; v.p., gen. counsel, sec. Variable Annuity Life Ins. Co., Houston, 1976—; adj. prof. law Georgetown U. Law Center, 1970-72. Mem. Am. Bar Assn., Am. Coll. Legal Medicine, Am. Acad. Forensic Scis. Home: 12443 Stafford Springs Dr Houston TX 77077 Office: 2777 Allen Pkwy Houston TX 77019 Tel (713) 526-5251

KNOLL, JOHN PHILIP, b. Lafayette, Ind., Jan. 11, 1941; B.A., Ind. U., 1962, LL.B., 1965. Admitted to Ind. bar, 1965, Calif. bar, 1970; served with JAG, USN, 1965-69; individual practice law, San Diego, 1970—, partner firm Knoll & Corr, 1973—; comdg. officer Naval Reserve Law Co., 1972-75. Head San Diego County Speakers Bur. Jimmy Carter campaign. Mem. Am., San Diego County bar assns.,

San Diego Trial Lawyers Assn. Contbr. articles to legal jours. Office: Suite 1300 110 W C St San Diego CA 92101 Tel (714) 239-2201

KNOLL, RAYMOND, b. Economy, Ind., Aug. 3, 1924; B.S., Ind. U., 1949, LL.B., 1951. Admitted to Ind. bar, 1951; asso. firm Pell and Good, Shelbyville, Ind., 1952-53; partner firm Knoll, Kolger and Sowers, Richmond, Ind., 1953—; city judge, Shelbyville, 1952-53; dep. pros. atty. Wayne County (Ind.), 1957-58. Mem. Wayne County, Ind., Am. bar assns. Home: 4380 South C St Richmond IN 47374 Office: 111 S 7th St Richmond IN 47374 Tel (317) 966-2683

KNOPP, ALBERT JOSEPH, b. Cleve., Dec. 31, 1924; B.A., Ohio Wesleyan U., 1947; J.D., Cleve. State U., 1961. Admitted to Ohio bar, 1961; asso. firm Baker, Hostetler & Patterson, Cleve., 1961-67, partner, 1967—; councilman City of Berea (Ohio), 1965-73. Mem. Am., Ohio, Greater Cleve. bar assns., Internat. Assn. Ins. Counsel. Home: 547 Race St Berea OH 44017 Office: 1956 Union Commerce Bldg Cleveland OH 44115 Tel (216) 621-0200

KNOSHAUG, DEWAYNE ALLAN, b. Stanley, N.D., Aug. 21, 1937; B.S., Iowa State U., 1959; LL.B., Drake U., 1963. Admitted to Iowa bar, 1963; asso. firm Maddocks & Knoshaug, Clarion, Iowa, 1963-65; individual practice law, Clarion, 1965—; county atty. Wright County (Iowa), 1965-72. Mem. Iowa, Wright County bar assns. Home: 119 4th Ave NW Clarion IA 50525 Office: 118 Central Ave E Clarion IA 50525 Tel (515) 532-3194

KNOTT, JOHN CHARLES, b. Tallahassee, July 28, 1900; B.A. in Bus. Adminstrn., Eastman Coll., 1928; LL.B., U. Fla., 1950. Admitted to Fla. bar, 1951; sales rep. John B. Stetson Co., Melbourne, Australia, 1921-25; ins. examiner Fla. State Ins. Comm., 1929-33; dep. Motor Vehicle Commn., State of Fla., Tallahassee, 1933-50, gen. counsel, 1950-74; legal cons. Dept. Hwy. Safety and Motor Vehicles, State of Fla., 1974—. Mem. Tallahassee C. of C., Kappa Alpha, Phi Delta Phi. Home and office: 301 E Park Ave Tallahassee FL 32301 Tel (904) 222-2220

KNOTTS, MARCUS MILLS, b. Independence, Kans., Apr. 19, 1907; student Coffeyville (Kans.) Jr. Coll., 1924-26; J.D., Washburn Law Sch., 1930. Admitted to Kans. bar, 1930, Calif. bar, 1938; individual practice law, Coffeyville, 1930-36, Santa Monica, Calif., 1938—. Mem. Santa Monica Bar Assn. Home: 16001 Pacific Coast Hwy Pacific Palisades CA 90272 Office: 111 Santa Monica Blvd Santa Monica CA 90401 Tel (213) 394-1754

KNOWLES, JOSEPH FRANK, b. New Bedford, Mass., Apr. 25, 1914; A.B. magna cum laude, Harvard, 1936, J.D., 1939. Admitted to Mass bar., 1939; asso. firm Goodwin Procter & Hoar, Boston, 1939-55, partner, 1955—. Mem. corp., trustee Babson Coll. Mem. Boston, Mass., Am. bar assns., Am. Coll. Probate Counsel. Home: 135 Great Plain Ave Wellesley MA 02181 Office: 28 State St Boston MA 02109 Tel (617) 523-5700

KNOWLES, MARJORIE FINE, b. Bklyn., July 4, 1939; B.A., Smith Coll., 1960; LL.B., Harvard, 1965. Admitted to N.Y. bar, 1966, Ala. bar, 1975; asst. U.S. atty., N.Y.C., 1966-67, asst. dist. atty., 1967-70; exec. dir. Joint Found. Support, N.Y.C., 1970-72; asso. prof. law U. Ala., 1972-75, prof., 1975—; chmn. adv. com. Women's Rights Project ACLU, N.Y.C., 1976—; mem. adv. bd. Women's Rights Project, Center for Law and Social Policy, Washington, 1974—; mem. bd. Ms. Found. for Women, N.Y.C., 1975—. Mem. exec. com. So. Regional Council, Atlanta, 1974—; mem. task force on equal rights for women in edn. Edn. Commn. of the States, Denver, 1974—. Mem. Ala. Bar Assn., Soc. Am. Law Tchrs. Home: 301 Caplewood Dr Tuscaloosa AL 35401 Office: Box 1435 Law Sch U Ala University AL 35486 Tel (205) 348-5930

KNOWLES, ROBERTA PADGETT, b. Lake Butler, Fla., Oct. 5, 1920; student U. Fla., summer 1940; B.J., Fla. State Coll. Women, 1941; J.D., Stetson U., 1962. Tchr. pub. schs., Fla., 1941-48; tchr. info. specialist War Assets Adminstrn., Washington, 1946-47; mng. editor post newspaper Buckingham Army Air Field, Ft. Myers, Fla., 1943-45; civilian tng. ccordinator Sarasota (Fla.) AFB, 1945-46; legal sec. firm Knowles & Kirk, Bradenton, Fla., 1950-53; admitted to Fla. bar, 1962; asso. firm Goodrich & Hampton, Bradenton, 1962-68; individual practice law, Bradenton, 1968-72; judge Manatee County (Fla.) Ct., 1973—. Mem. Fla. Democratic Com., 1950-54, 66-72; bd. dirs. Bradenton United Fund, 1969-72. Mem. Manatee County, Fla., Am. bar assns., Bus. and Profl. Women's Club. Home: 410 N 31st St W Bradenton FL 33505 Tel (813) 747-6212

KNOX, ALAN ANTHONY, b. Orange, Calif., Dec. 27, 1940; A.B., U. Redlands, 1962; J.D., Pepperdine U., 1970. Admitted to Calif. bar, 1972; title cons. 1st Am. Title Ins. Co., Santa Ana, Calif., 1964-70; mem. debenture div. Perpetual Trustee Co., Ltd., Sydney, Australia, 1971; mem. firm Mitchell, Hart & Brisco, Santa Ana, 1972-74, individual practice law, Santa Ana, 1974—. Mem. Orange County, Los Angeles County bar assns., Calif., Orange County trial lawyers assns. Contbr. articles to legal jours. Home: 1517 E Portola Ave Santa Ana CA 92701 Office: Suite 905 888 N Main St Santa Ana CA 92701 Tel (714) 835-0202

KNOX, ENOS PHILLIPS, b. Champaign, Ill., Apr. 23, 1946; B.S., Miami U., Oxford, Ohio, 1968; J.D., U. Ill., 1971. Admitted to Ill. bar, 1971, U.S. Supreme Ct. bar, 1975; asso. firm Phillips, Phebus, Tummelson & Bryan, Urbana, Ill., 1971, partner, 1972—; dir. Busey First Nat. Bank, Urbana, 1972—. Trustee Champaign County Hist. Mus., 1974—, v.p., 1976—. Mem. Urbana C. of C. (chmn. legis. com. 1973-74), Am., Ill., Champaign County bar assns., Am. Judicature Soc., Delta Sigma Pi, Phi Eta Sigma, Omicron Delta Kappa. Home: 2005 Vawter St Urbana IL 61801 Office: 136 W Main St Urbana IL 61801 Tel (217) 367-1144

KNOX, MICHAEL ROBBINS, b. Ft. Worth, Feb. 16, 1943; B.A., Baylor U., 1965, LL.B., 1967, J.D., 1970. Admitted to Tex. bar, 1967; asst. staff judge adv. U.S. Air Force, 1968-70; staff judge adv., Sawyer AFB, Mich., 1970-73; asso. firm Thompson Coe Cousins & Irons, Dallas, 1973—; instr. bus. law No. Mich. U., Marquette, 1971-73. Mem. Am. (mem. property ins. law com.), Dallas bar assns., State Bar Tex., Dallas Jr. Bar Assn. (constl. revision com. 1974), Dallas Assn. Def. Counsel. Home: 645 Lewis Dr Hurst TX 76053 Office: Thompson Coe et al 2001 Bryan Tower suite 1000 Dallas TX 75201 Tel (214) 742-8621

KNUCK, THEODORE, b. Elkhart, Ind., Sept. 27, 1948; A.B., U. Notre Dame, 1970; J.D. cum laude, St. Louis U., 1973. Admitted to Ariz. bar, 1973; asso. firm Laber, Lovallo & Colarich, Tucson, 1973-75; partner firm Beaman, Knuck & Gallup, Tucson, 1975—. Mem. Am., Pima County bar assns. Home: 7611 Dido Pl Tucson AZ 85704 Office: 507 Pioneer Plaza 100 N Stone St Tucson AZ 85701 Tel (602) 884-9030

KNUDSEN, DEREK THOMAS, b. Oakland, Calif., Sept. 5, 1943; A.B., Dartmouth, 1965, M.B.A., 1966; J.D., Harvard, 1969. Admitted to Calif. bar, 1970; asso. firm Brookes, Maier & Wilson, 1970-74; asso. firm Winokur, Schoenberg, Maier, Hammerman & Knudsen, San Francisco, 1974-75, mem., 1975—; asst. prof. law U. Calif., San Francisco, 1975—. Bd. dirs. Conrad House, 1971-74. Mem. Am., San Francisco bar assns. Office: 1 California St San Francisco CA 94111 Tel (415) 392-8308

KNUDSEN, RICHARD A., b. Omaha, June 21, 1924; A.B., U. Nebr., 1948, LL.B., 1950. Admitted to Nebr. bar, 1950; now partner firm Knudsen, Berkheimer, Endacott & Beam, Lincoln, Nebr. Fellow Am. Coll. Trial Lawyers, Am. Bar Found.; mem. Lincoln (pres. 1971), Nebr. State (pres. 1976-77), Am. bar assns., Internat. Assn. Ins. Counsel, Nat. Assn. R.R. Trial Counsel, Am. Judicature Soc., Am. Law Inst., Phi Delta Phi. Office: 1000 NBC Center Lincoln NE 68508 Tel (402) 475-7011*

KNUPP, LARRY SHELDON, b. Whittier, Calif., Apr. 7, 1940; B.A., Pomona Coll., 1961; J.D., U. Calif., Berkeley, 1964. Admitted to Calif. bar, 1965; mem. firm Knupp Knupp & Smith, Whittier, 1965-75; commr. Whittier Municipal Ct., 1975—. Mem. Calif., Los Angeles County, Whittier Bar assns. Office: 7339 S Painter Ave Whittier CA 90602 Tel (213) 698-6251

KNUST, JAC EDWARD, b. Balt., Feb. 5, 1948; B.S. in Indsl. Mgmt., Clemson U., 1969; J.D., U. Balt., 1973. Admitted to Md. bar, 1972, U.S. Dist. Ct. bar Md., 1972, U.S. Ct. Appeals bar for 4th Circuit, 1974, U.S. Supreme Ct. bar, 1976; individual practice law, Columbia, Md., 1972—; asst. state's atty. Howard County (Md.), 1973; instr. bus. law Catonsville Community Coll., 1973—. Mem. Am., Md., Howard County bar assns. Office: 300 Teachers Bldg Columbia MD 21044 Tel (301) 730-6277

KNUTSON, DAVID HARRY, b. St. Paul, Dec. 17, 1934; A.B., Harvard, 1956, LL.B., 1961; postgrad. (Fulbright grantee) U. Copenhagen, 1961-62. Admitted to Minn. bar, 1962, N.Y. bar, 1963; asso. firm Lord, Day & Lord, N.Y.C., 1962-69; staff atty. Freeport Minerals Co., N.Y.C., 1969—, asst. sec. 1970, sec. 1975. Mem. Assn. Bar City N.Y., Am. Bar Assn. Home: 201 E 79th St New York City NY 10021 Office: 200 Park Ave New York City NY 10017 Tel (212) 687-8100

KNUTSON, JAMES ELLING, b. St. Paul, Mar. 16, 1935; B.A., U. Minn., 1959; LL.B., William Mitchell Coll. Law, 1963. Admitted to Minn. bar, 1963; partner firm Peterson, Popovich, Knutson & Flynn, St. Paul, 1963—. Mem. Minn., Ramsey County bar assns., Minn. Council Sch. Attys. Home: 13805 High Dr Burnsville MN 55337 Office: 314 Minnesota Bldg St Paul MN 55101 Tel (612) 222-5515

KNUTSON, OCIE LEE, b. Richland Springs, Tex., Aug. 29, 1924; B.B.A., S.W. Texas U., 1951, J.D., U. Ark., 1971. Admitted to Tex. bar, 1969; mem. claims dept. Am. Gen. Ins. Co., Houston, Balt., San Francisco, Little Rock, 1955-71, counsel, Houston, 1971—. Mem. Am., Tex., Harris County bar assns. Home: 5005 Georgia Ln 115 Houston TX 77092 Office: 2777 Allen Pkwy Houston TX 77019 Tel (713) 526-9185

KOBAYASHI, BERT TAKAAKI, b. Honolulu, July 8, 1916; A.B., Gettysburg Coll., 1938; J.D., (hon.), 1966; J.D., Harvard, 1943. Admitted to Hawaii bar, 1946; law clk. atty. gen. Hawaii, 1945; dept. atty. City and County of Honolulu, 1946; dept. pub. prosecutor, 1947-48; individual practice law, Honolulu, 1948-62; atty. gen. State of Hawaii, 1962-69; asso. justice Supreme Ct. Hawaii, 1969—; magistrate, Waialua Ct., Hawaii, 1952-59; mem. subersive activities commn., State of Hawaii, 1958-62; mediator-arbitrator, 1963-75. Mem. advisory bd. coll. advocacy Hastings Law Sch., 1975—. Mem. Am., Hawaii bar assns. Office: Judiciary Bldg Honolulu HI 96813 Tel (808) 537-3047

KOBER, DALE PHILIP, b. West Bend, Wis., Mar. 14, 1939; B.S., U. Wis., Madison, 1961, LL.B., 1964. Admitted to Wis. bar, 1964, Ill. bar, 1966; title officer Chgo. Title Ins. Co., Waukegan, Ill. Trustee Bethany Ch., Highland Park, Ill. Mem. Wis., Ill. (mem. assembly 19th Jud. Circuit), Lake County (bd. govs.) bar assns. Home: 991 Bob o Link Rd Highland Park IL 60035 Office: 15 S County St Waukegan IL 60085 Tel (312) 662-8000

KOBLEGARDE, BENJAMIN RUPERT, b. Forest Grove, Oreg., Oct. 26, 1937; B.S., Portland State U., 1964, C.P.A. certificate, Oreg., 1966; J.D., Northwestern Sch. of Law of Lewis and Clark, 1970. Admitted to Oreg. bar, 1970; staff accountant Peat Marwick Mitchell & Co., Portland, Oreg., 1964-65; instr. Multnomah Jr. Coll., Portland Community Coll., Northwestern Sch. of Law, 1966-70; individual practice law, C.P.A., Portland, 1970—. Bd. dirs. Evangel Coll., Springfield, Mo., 1969-71. Mem. Oreg. Soc. of C.P.A.s, Am. Inst. of C.P.A.s, Am. Bar Assn. Recipient Am. Jurisprudence awards, 1966-70. Home: 4254 SW Washouga Ave Portland OR 97201 Office: 310 Mayer Bldg 1130 S W Morrison St Portland OR 97205 Tel (503) 227-1411

KOBLENZ, A. ABBA, b. Albany, N.Y., Oct. 10, 1922; B.S., State U. N.Y., 1947; LL.B., Albany Law Sch., 1950, J.D., 1968. Admitted to N.Y. State bar, 1950, U.S. Tax Ct. bar, 1970; partner firm Koblenz and Koblenz, Albany, 1950—; confdl. law clk. to justice N.Y. State Supreme Ct., Albany, 1967-70; law sec. to judge N.Y. Ct. of Claims, Albany, 1970—. Pres. Temple Israel, Albany, 1961-63, Jewish Community Center, Albany, 1970-72, Jewish Community Council, Albany, 1967-69; bd. dirs., v.p. Daus. of Sarah Nursing Home, Albany. Mem. Albany County, N.Y. State bar assns. Home: 140 Milner Ave Albany NY 12208 Office: 90 State St Albany NY 12207 Tel (518) 462-4242

KOCH, THEODORE MORGAN, b. Scranton, Pa., Feb. 15, 1938; B.A., Ind. Central Coll., 1962; J.D., Ind. U., 1966. Admitted to Ind., Wis. bars, 1966; partner firm Slocum & Koch, Indpls., 1967-71, Burton & Koch, Indpls., 1971-76, Crapo, Koch & Sherron, 1976—; dep. prosecutor, Marion County, Ind., 1969-71. Mem. Indpls. Bar Assn., Indpls. Trial Lawyers' Assn. Office: 3035 S Keystone Ave Indianapolis IN 46227 Tel (317) 783-7769

KOCH, THOMAS F(REDERICK), b. Hackensack, N.J., Nov. 24, 1942; A.B., Middlebury Coll., 1964; J.D., U. Chgo., 1967. Admitted to Vt. bar, 1967, asso. firm Free & Bernasconi, Barre, Vt., 1970-74; partner firm Bernasconi & Koch, Barre, 1974—; mem. Vt. Gen. Assembly, 1977—. Mem. Am., Vt. (chmn. com. on unauthorized practice of law), Washington County (Vt.) bar assns. Home: RR 2 Lowery Rd Barre VT 05641 Office: POB 892 25 Keith Ave Barre VT 05641 Tel (802) 476-4141

KOCKRITZ, FRANK JOSEPH, b. Berkeley, Calif., May 16, 1912; A.B., U. Calif., 1933; J.D., Harvard, 1936. Admitted to Calif. bar, 1936, U.S. Supreme Ct. bar, 1950; asso. firm Pillsbury, Madison & Sutro, San Francisco, 1936-42, 46; asso. firm Gray, Cary, Ames & Frye, San Diego, 1947-49, partner, 1949—, presiding partner, 1973-75; lectr. in field. Trustee, sec. Scripps Clinic and Research Found., La Jolla, Calif.; pres., trustee Fine Arts Soc. of San Diego; trustee Combined Arts and Edn. Council, San Diego. Mem. Calif., Am., San Diego County bar assns., Barristers Club of San Francisco (pres. 1941), Am. Judicature Soc. Home: 1921 Hypatia Way La Jolla CA 92037 Office: 2100 Union Bank Bldg San Diego CA 92101 Tel (714) 236-1661

KOEGEL, WILLIAM FISHER, b. Wash., D.C., Aug. 18, 1923; B.A., Williams Coll., 1944; LL.B., U. Va., 1949. Admitted to N.Y. bar, 1950, U.S. Supreme Ct. bar, 1957; asso. firm Dwight, Royall, Harris, Koegel & Caskey (now Rogers & Wells), N.Y.C., 1949-58, partner, 1958-68, sr. partner, 1968—. Mem. Am., N.Y., N.Y.C. bar assns., Order of Coif. Editor, contbr. articles to Va. Law Rev., 1947-49. Home: 7 Chesterfield Rd Scarsdale NY 10583 Office: 200 Park Ave New York City NY 10017 Tel (212) 972-5380

KOEGLER, WALTER ALBERT, b. Pitts., Aug. 22, 1917; B.A., U. Pitts., 1939, LL.B., 1942. Admitted to Pa. bar, 1943; individual practice law, Pitts., 1945-70; sr. partner firm Koegler & Tomlinson, Pitts., 1970—; Pitts. counsel Office Gen. Counsel, USN, 1945; judge Ct. Common Pleas, Allegheny County, Pa., 1965-66. Former pres. Greater Pitts. Guild for Blind. Mem. Pa., Allegheny County bar assns., Lawyer's Club Allegheny County, Acad. Trial Lawyers. Home: 620 Arden Ln Pittsburgh PA 15243 Office: 502 Frick Bldg Pittsburgh PA 15219 Tel (412) 281-1555

KOEHLER, HENRY JAMES, IV, b. Akron, Ohio, Jan. 8, 1935; A.B., Princeton U., 1956; J.D., U. Mich., 1965. Admitted to Ohio bar, 1965, Calif. bar, 1972; asso. firm Alpeter, Diefenbach & Davies, Akron, 1964-65; trustee-in-bankruptcy U.S. Bankruptcy Ct., Akron, 1964-66; asst. dir. law City of Akron, 1966-67; asso. firm Henry James Koehler, Westminster, Calif., 1972—; counsel 1st Fin. Funding Corp. Am., Beverly Hills, Calif., 1969; owner N.J. Koehler & Co., Beverly Hills. Trustee Westminster Civic Center Authority, 1972—; mem. privacy and control bd. Orange County (Calif.), 1974-75, commr. scenic hwys. adv. bd., 1975—. Mem. Orange County Trial Lawyers Assn. Author: Total Security. Home: 7091 Bestel Ave Westminster CA 92683 Office: 6531 Westminster Ave Westminster CA 92683 Tel (714) 897-2161

KOEHN, JAMES HOWARD, b. Auburn, Ala., Aug. 19, 1941; B.A., U. Tex., 1963, LL.B., 1968. Admitted to Tex. bar, 1968; asso. firm Funderburk, Murray & Ramsey, Houston, 1968-70; atty. Tex. Bd. Ins., Austin, 1970-73; mem. firm Flahive & Ogden, Austin, 1973-76; partner firm Leonard, Koehn & Rose, Austin, 1976—. Mem. Am., Travis County, Travis County Jr. bar assns. Home: 2603 Tip Cove Austin TX 78704 Office: 1408 Capital National Bank Bldg Austin TX 78701 Tel (512) 476-0237

KOELBL, CHRISTIAN GERARD, III, b. Buffalo, Feb. 10, 1945; A.B., Hamilton Coll., 1967; J.D., Yale, 1971. Admitted to N.Y. bar, 1972; law clk. to U.S. Dist. judge, Buffalo, 1971-73; asso. firm Hodgson, Russ, Andrews, Woods & Goodyear, Buffalo, 1973-75, mem. firm, 1976—. Mem. Am., N.Y. State, Erie County bar assns. Home: 13054 Main St Alden NY 14004 Office: 1800 One M & T Plaza Buffalo NY 14203 Tel (716) 856-4000

KOEMPEL, ALICE TRAEGER, b. Sumner, Iowa, Oct. 21, 1925; B.A., State U. Iowa, 1946, J.D. with distinction, 1948. Admitted to Iowa bar, 1948; partner firm Traeger & Koempel, W. Union, Iowa, 1948—; city atty., West Union, 1967—. Mem. Iowa State, 1st Jud. Dist., Fayette County bar assns., Iowa Municipal Attys. Assn. (regional v.p. 1975—), Phi Beta Kappa, Kappa Beta Pi. Home: 103 Lincoln Dr West Union IA 52175 Office: 103 N Vine St West Union IA 52175 Tel (319) 422-3859

KOENIGSBERG, MARVIN LEE, B.S.L., Northwestern U., 1942, J.D., 1942. Admitted to Ill. bar, 1942; partner law firm Friedman & Koven (and predecessor firms), Chgo., 1951—; dir., Marshall Internat. Trading Co., Skokie, Ill. Bd. dirs. Jewish Home for Aged. Mem., Chgo., Ill., Am. bar assns. Home: 5630 N Sheridan Rd Chicago IL 60660 Office: 208 S LaSalle St Chicago IL 60604

KOEPPEN, BART, b. Pendleton, Oreg., Nov. 12, 1933; student Columbia, 1951-52; B.A., U. Oreg., 1956; LL.B., Stanford U., 1962. Admitted to Calif. bar, 1962; law clk. 9th Circuit Ct. Appeals, San Francisco, 1962-63; asso. firm Brobeck, Phleger & Harrison, San Francisco, 1963-68; asso. prof. law U. Minn., Mpls., 1968-72, prof., 1972—. Mem. Am., Calif. bar assns., Order of Coif, Phi Beta Kappa. Office: Law School University Minnesota Minneapolis MN 55455 Tel (612) 373-2733

KOERBER, JANET PEARL, b. Milw., Nov. 22, 1933; B.A., Marquette U., 1964, J.D., 1966. Admitted to Wis. bar, 1966, U.S. Supreme Ct. bar, 1972; individual practice law, Milw., 1966—, Fox Point, Wis., 1976—, dir. Design & Print Shop, Inc., Bay-Point Pharmacy, Ozaukee Apothecary, Energy Savers, Inc., Melody Ranch; legal adviser Am. Saddle Horse Breeders Futurity of Wis., Inc. Mem. Am., Milw. bar assns., Nat. Police Officers Assn., Am. Law Enforcement Officers Assn., Nat. Radio Posse, Kappa Beta Phi. Home: N 29 W 6323 Lincoln Blvd Cedarburg WI 53012 Office: POB 17468 400 W Silver Spring St Milwaukee WI 53217

KOERNER, JAMES ALOYSIUS, b. Tallahassee, Dec. 11, 1943; B.A., Catholic U. Am., 1965; J.D., Georgetown U., 1969. Admitted to Md. bar, 1969, D.C. bar, 1970; asso. firm Putbrebe & Fletcher, Washington, 1969-70, Stambler & Shrinsky, P.C., 1970-74; mem. firm Stambler & Shrinsky, P.C., 1974-76, Baraff, Koerner & Olender, P.C., 1976—. Treas., Recreation Council, Cheverly, Md., 1971-72. Mem. Bar Assn. D.C., D.C. Bar Unified, Md., Fed. Communications bar assns. Home: 7020 Richard Dr Bethesda MD 20034 Office: 2033 M St NW Washington DC 20036 Tel (202) 452-8200

KOFFORD, CREE-L., b. Santaquin, Utah, July 11, 1933; B.S., U. Utah, 1955; J.D., U. So. Calif., 1961. Admitted to Calif. bar, 1962; asso. firm Munns, Kofford, Hoffman, Hunt & Throckmorton, and predecessors, Pasadena, Calif., 1962-69, partner, 1962—; mem. faculty U. So. Calif. Grad. Sch., 1975-76; lectr. in field. Bd. dirs. San Gabriel Valley council Boy Scouts Am., 1973—. Mem. Los Angeles, Calif. State bar assns., Am. Arbitration Assn. (arbitrator 1971). Contbr. articles to profl. jours., mags. Home: 1330 Rodeo Rd Arcadia CA 91006 Office: 199 N Lake Ave Suite 300 Pasadena CA 91101 Tel (213) 795-9733

KOGA, GEORGE, b. Honolulu, Mar. 19, 1928; B.A., U. Hawaii, 1950; J.D., Georgetown U., 1956. Admitted to D.C. bar, 1956, Hawaii bar, 1956; chief counsel Legal Aid Soc. Hawaii, Honolulu, 1957-58; partner firm Wong, Lo & Koga, Honolulu, 1958-64; individual practice law, Honolulu, 1964—; mem. Hawaii Ho. Reps., 1959-64; mem. Honolulu City Council, 1964—, chmn. 1971-75. Mem. Am., Hawaii (sec. 1959) bar assns. Home: 1254 Center St Honolulu HI 96816 Office: 700 Bishop St Honolulu HI 96813 Tel (808) 537-1763

KOHL, DONALD PHILLIP, b. Springfield, Ohio, Sept. 11, 1933; B.A. in Polit. Sci., Ohio State U., 1955; J.D., George Washington U., 1959. Admitted to Va. bar, 1960, Fla. bar, 1962, U.S. Supreme Ct. bar, 1970; individual practice law, W. Palm Beach, Fla., 1962-67; judge Small Claims Magistrate Ct., Palm Beach County, 1967-72; sr. partner firm Kohl, Springer & Springer, W. Palm Beach, 1973—; mem. traffic ct. adv. com. Supreme Ct. Fla., 1970-72; municipal judge Mangonia Park, Fla., 1973-76. Councilman, Palm Springs, 1961-63. Mem. Fla., Va. bar assns., Am. Trial Lawyers Assn., Am. Judicature Soc. Recipient Distinguished Service award Palm Springs Jaycees, 1964, Good Govt. award, 1971; named Cog of Year S.W. Palm Beach Exchange Club, 1972. Home: 260 Ohio Rd Lake Worth FL 33463 Office: 3003 S Congress Ave Palm Springs FL 33461 Tel (305) 968-1600

KOHL, TIMOTHY ORIN, b. Hartford, Wis., Mar. 15, 1942; B.S., U. Wis., 1964, J.D., 1967. Admitted to Wis. bar, 1969; atty. Chgo. Title and Trust Co., 1967-69, Wis. Dept. Transp., Madison, 1969-74, Oscar Mayer & Co., Inc., Madison, 1974—. Mem. Nat. Trust for Historic Preservation; bd. dirs. Vis. Nurse Service, Madison, 1976—. Mem. Am., Dane County bar assns., State Bar Wis. Home: 2110 Bascom St Madison WI 53705 Office: 910 Mayer Ave Madison WI 53704 Tel (608) 238-7068

KOHLER, WILLIAM ROBERT, b. N.Y.C., Oct. 12, 1940; B.S., Fordham Coll., 1962, J.D., 1965; LL.M., N.Y.U., 1971. Admitted to N.Y. State bar, 1966; served to capt. JAGC, U.S. Army, 1966-69; counsel, asst. sec. Burns Internat. Security Services, Inc., 1969-70; v.p., gen. counsel Rockwood Nat. Corp., Elmsford, N.Y., 1970—; atty. Village of Cold Spring, N.Y., 1972—. Mem. Am., Fed., N.Y. State bar assns., Cold Springs Lions Club (v.p.). Home: Bear Mountain Bridge Rd Garrison NY 10524 Office: 33 W Tarrytown Rd Elmsford NY 10523 Tel (914) 593-3100

KOHLMAN, JEFFREY WOLFE, b. Kokomo, Ind., Jan. 7, 1944; B.A., Grinnell Coll., 1966; grad. Villanova Law Sch., 1969. Admitted to D.C. bar, 1969, Ga. bar, 1973; atty. ICC, Washington, 1969-72; atty.-adviser firm Heyman & Sizemore, Atlanta, 1972-74; asso. firm Born and May, Atlanta, 1974-76; mem. firm Born, May, Kohlman & Sawyer, Atlanta, 1976—. Mem. Am. Bar Assn., ICC Practitioners Assn. Home: 2447 Terrace Trail Decatur GA 30035 Office: 1447 Peachtree St NE Atlanta GA 30309 Tel (404) 892-8020

KOHLS, BILLY EDWIN, b. Keavenworth, Wash., July 2, 1924; LL.B., U. Gonzaga, 1953, J.D., 1970; grad. State Trial Judges Coll., 1973. Admitted to Wash. bar, 1954; individual practice law, Grandview, Wash., 1953, Omak, Wash., 1954-61; partner firm Hancock & Kohls, Omak, 1961-70; pros. atty. Okanogan County (Wash.), 1971-73; judge Superior Ct. Okanagan and Ferry Counties, Wash., 1973—. Mem. Wash. Bar Assn., Wash. State Judges Assn. Home: Route 2 Box 99C Omak WA 98841 Office: Box 112 Okanogan WA 99840 Tel (509) 422-3980

KOHN, ALAN CHARLES, b. St. Louis, Feb. 14, 1932; A.B., Washington U., St. Louis, 1953, LL.B., 1955. Admitted to Mo. bar, 1955, U.S. Supreme Ct. bar, 1958; law clk. U.S. Supreme Ct. Justice Charles E. Whittaker, 1957-58; asso. firm William Kohn, 1958-59; asso. firm Coburn, Croft & Kohn, 1959-62, partner, 1962-70; partner firm Kohn, Shands, Elbert, Gianoulakis & Giljum, St. Louis, 1970—; mem. Mo. Bd. Law Examiners, 1969—, pres., 1975—. Chmn. Mo. Housing Devel. Commn., 1975—; treas. University City (Mo.) Bd. Edn., 1970-71. Mem. Am., Mo. bar assns., Bar Assn. St. Louis, Order of Coif, Omicron Delta Kappa, Phi Beta Kappa. Editor in chief Washington U Law Quar. Office: 411 N 7th St St Louis MO 63101 Tel (314) 241-3963

KOHN, JOHN PETER, JR., b. Montgomery, Ala., Dec. 27, 1902; LL.B., U. Ala., 1925. Admitted to Ala. bar, 1925; former atty. Montgomery County (Ala.); interim judge Supreme Ct. Ala., 1968; practice law, Montgomery. Mem. Am., Montgomery (pres. 1931) bar assns. Author: The Cradle-Anatomy of a Town, 1968. Home: 2542 Woodley Rd Montgomery AL 36111 Office: Suite 924 First Ala Bank Bldg 8 Commerce St Montgomery AL 36104 Tel (205) 263-7505

KOHN, VILMA LAVETTI, b. Buffalo, Jan. 21, 1927; B.A., U. Buffalo, 1948, M.A., 1950; Ph.D., U. Mich., 1956; J.D., Case Western Res. U., 1971. Admitted to Ohio bar, 1971; law clk. Ohio Eighth Dist. Ct. Appeals, Cleve., 1971-73, ct. adminstr., 1973—; asso. firm Squire Sanders & Dempsey, Cleve., 1973-76. Bd. dirs. Women Space; vis. com. Case Western Res. U. Law Sch. Mem. Am., Ohio, Greater Cleve. bar assns. Home: 2060 S Belvoir Blvd South Euclid OH 44121 Tel (216) 621-3285

KOINES, NILES PETER, b. West Newton, Mass., Aug. 31, 1932; A.B., Yale U., 1954; LL.B., Harvard U., 1957. Admitted to Mass. bar, 1957, Calif. bar, 1962; atty. div. corporate fin. SEC, Washington, 1958-61; asso. firm Older, Hahn, Cazier & Hoegh, Los Angeles, 1961-65; atty. law dept. Sears, Roebuck & Co., Los Angeles, 1965-68; corporate counsel Petrolane, Inc., Long Beach, Calif., 1969; atty. Santa Fe R.R. Co., Los Angeles, 1970; asst. gen. counsel Pacific Mut. Life Ins. Co., Newport Beach, Calif., 1971-77; gen. counsel Beneficial Standard Properties, Inc. and Beneficial Standard Mortgage Co., Los Angeles, 1977—. Bd. dirs. East Arroyo Assn., Pasadena, Calif., 1963-72, pres., 1964-69; bd. dirs. Montessori Schs., Pasadena, 1965-70, chmn. bd., 1969. Mem. Am., Orange County bar assns., Fin. Lawyers Conf. Los Angeles, Calif. Mortgage Bankers Assn. (legis. com.). Home: 18022 Weston Pl Tustin CA 92680 Office: 700 Newport Center Dr Newport Beach CA 92663

KOIVUNEN, REINO SOLOMON, b. South Range, Mich., Nov. 7, 1907; B.S., No. Mich. U., 1930; J.D., U. Mich., 1938. Tchr., secondary schs., Norway, Mich., 1930-35; admitted to Mich. bar, 1938; individual practice law, Calumet, Mich., 1938-70; judge Probate Ct. Houghton County (Mich.), Houghton, 1971—; pros. atty, Keweenaw County, Mich., 1939-57; village atty., Laurium, Mich., 1956-76. Mem. Calumet Sch. Bd., 1960-65. Mem. Am., Mich., Copper Country bar assns. Home: 340 Florida St Laurium MI 49913 Office: 401 Houghton Ave Houghton MI 49931 Tel (906) 482-3120

KOKULIS, PAUL NICHOLAS, b. Goffstown, N.H., Mar. 30, 1924; B.S. in Chem. Engring., Worcester Poly. Inst., 1945; LL.B., George Washington U., 1950. Engr., Naval Research Lab., Washington, 1945-46; research asso./law clk. firm Cushman, Darby & Cushman, Washington, 1946-50, asso., 1950-54, partner, 1954—; admitted to D.C. bar, 1950. Elder 4th Presbyn. Ch., Bethesda, Md., 1957—. Mem. Am., D.C. bar assns., Am. Patent Law Assn. Home: 9409 Falls Rd Potomac MD 20854 Office: 1801 K St NW Washington DC 20006 Tel (202) 833-3000

KOLA, ARTHUR ANTHONY, b. New Brunswick, N.J., Feb. 16, 1939; A.B., Dartmouth, 1961; LL.B., Duke, 1964. Admitted to Ohio bar, 1964, U.S. Supreme Ct. bar, 1972; asso. firm Squire, Sanders & Dempsey, Cleve., 1964-65, 68-74, partner, 1974—; asst. prof. law Ind. U., 1967-68; instr. Case Western Res. U. Sch. Law, 1976. Mem. Greater Cleve., Ohio, Am. bar assns. Office: 1800 Union Commerce Bldg Cleveland OH 41115 Tel (216) 696-9200

KOLB, ALAN FOSTER, b. New Orleans, Feb. 2, 1944; B.A. in Polit. Sci., Mich. State U., 1965, M.A., 1968; J.D., Ind. U., 1971. Admitted to Ind. bar, 1972; personnel interviewer St. Lawrence Hosp., Lansing, Mich., 1967; tchr. Laingsburg (Mich.) Community Schs., 1967-68; market research analyst Blue Cross, Indpls., 1968-69; field rep. Sch. Bldgs., Inc., Indpls., 1969-73, v.p., 1973—, gen. counsel, 1973—. Mem. Am., Ind., Indpls. bar assns., Phi Delta Phi. Home: 3029 Lehigh Ct Indianapolis IN 46268 Office: 50 W Market St Suite 404 Indianapolis IN 46204 Tel (317) 637-1549

KOLB, DAVID LEE, b. Charleston, W.Va., Feb. 5, 1939; B.S. in Chem. Engring., W.Va. U., 1961; M. Commerce, U. Richmond, 1967; J.D., Fordham U., 1973. Admitted to N.J. bar, 1973; designer engr. fibers div. Allied Chem. Corp., Hopewell, Va., 1961-64, supr. engr., 1965-69, mgr. fin. services, 1969-70, asst. controller, 1970-72, controller, 1973-74, v.p. tech., 1975, v.p. home furnishing, 1976—. Active Va. United Givers Fund, 1975-76, U.S. Savs. Bond Dr. Petersburg, Va., 1975-76; deacon, treas. Somerset (N.J.) Presbyterian Ch. 1973-76. Mem. N.J. State Bar Assn., Va. Soc. Profl. Engrs. Registered profl. engr., Va. Recipient Am. Jurisprudence award, 1971. Home: 19 Layne Rd Somerset NJ 08873 Office: 1411 Broadway New York City NY 10036 Tel (212) 391-5041

KOLBA, GERALD WILFRED, b. Spring Valley, N.Y., Dec. 18, 1908; B.A., Rutgers U., 1929, LL.B., 1932, J.D., 1970. Admitted to N.J. bar, 1932; individual practice law, Union, N.J. Mem. Fed., N.J., Essex County bar assns., Union Twp. Lawyers Club, Nat. Council Juvenile Ct. Judges, Am. Judicature Soc., Rutgers, Rutgers Law Sch. alumni assns. Home: 28 Sommer Ave Maplewood NJ 07040 Office: 2424 Morris Ave Union NJ 07083 Tel (201) 964-8844

KOLESAR, MICHAEL PAUL, b. Cleve., Jan. 7, 1944; B.A., Cleve. State U., 1968, J.D., 1972. Admitted to Ohio bar, 1972; asso. firm Speck Wilbur Senn, Parma, Ohio, 1974-76; asst. county prosecutor Cuyahoga County (Ohio), 1973—. Mem. Am., Parma, Ohio, Cuyahoga County, Greater Cleve. bar assns., Am. Trial Lawyers Assn. Home: 8023 Deerfield Dr Parma OH 44129 Office: 5700 Pearl Rd Parma OH 44129 Tel (216) 886-0206

KOLTNOW, H. ROBERT, b. Atlantic City, Aug. 19, 1929; student Dickinson Coll., 1947-50; J.D., U. Miami, 1953. Admitted to Fla. bar, 1953; individual practice law, Miami, Fla., 1953—. Mem. Am., Fla., Dade County bar assns. Home: 13575 SW 72 Ave Miami FL 33156 Office: 3000 Biscayne Blvd Suite 306 Miami FL 33137 Tel (305) 371-8852

KOLTS, RAYMOND GREELY, b. Los Angeles, June 20, 1940; student Calif. State U., Los Angeles, J.D., Loyola U., Los Angeles, 1967. Admitted to Calif. bar, 1967; asso. firm Harry Hunt & Assos., Los Angeles, 1967-69; partner firm Dryden, Harrington & Swartz, Los Angeles, 1969—. Mem. Republican Central Com. Los Angeles, 1972-76. Rep. State Central Com. Calif., 1972-74. Mem. Calif., Los Angeles County bar assns. Office: One Wilshire Bldg suite 703 Los Angeles CA 90017 Tel (213) 628-2184

KONDRACKI, EDWARD JOHN, b. Elizabeth, N.J., Sept. 27, 1932; B.S.E.E., Newark Coll., 1959; J.D. with honors, George Washington U., 1963. Admitted to D.C. bar, 1964, Va. bar, 1964, U.S. Ct. Customs, 1968, Ct. of Claims, 1976; patent atty. Gen. Electric Co., Washington, 1959-63; partner firm Cameron, Kerkam, Sutton, Stowell & Stowell, Arlington, Va., 1963—. Mem. adv. bd. St. Ambrose Ch., Annandale, Va., 1963-74. Mem. Am., Va. bar assns., Am. Patent Lawyers Assn., Bar Assn. D.C., D.C. Bar Office: 2341 Jefferson Davis Hwy Arlington VA 22202 Tel (703) 920-8980

KONECKY, JOHN PHILLIP, b. Moline, Ill., May 7, 1946; B.S. with distinction, Ind. U., 1968; J.D., U. Mich., 1971. Admitted to Ill. bar, 1971; asst. pub. defender City of Rock Island, Ill., 1971-72; instr. bus. law Blackhawk Coll., Rock Island, 1972-75; asst. state's atty., Rock Island, 1975; asso. firm Potter Gillman Galvin Collinson Konecky & Keesee, Rock Island, 1971—. Chmn., Rock Island Youth Service Bur., 1976—. Mem. Ill., Rock Island bar assns., Beta Gamma Sigma, Sigma Iota Epsilon. Office: 311 Safety Bldg Rock Island IL 61201 Tel (309) 793-1304

KONOVE, ROBERT, b. Ho-Ho-Kus, N.J., July 18, 1919; B.A., Syracuse U., 1939; LL.B., Columbia U., 1942. Admitted to N.Y. bar, 1945; since practiced in N.Y.C., asso. firm William Gold, 1946-51, partner firm McHugh, Gottlieb & Konove, 1951-61, Gottlieb, Kanove & Zeck, 1961-64; individual practice law, 1964—; ednl. cons. to mayor N.Y.C. Chmn. exec. council, v.p. United Parents Assn. Mem. N.Y. State Bar Assn., Assn. Bar City N.Y., N.Y. County Lawyers Assn. Home: 2 Stuyvesant Oval New York City NY 10009 Office: 60 E 42d St New York City NY 10017 Tel (212) 682-1727

KONOWE, MILTON MARLOWE, b. N.Y.C., May 16, 1922; student U. Rochester, 1945, L.I. U., 1947; LL.B., Bklyn. Law Sch., 1949; postgrad. in labor law N.Y. U. Grad. Sch. Law, 1951. Admitted to N.Y. bar, 1949, U.S. Supreme Ct. bar, 1955; individual practice law, N.Y.C., 1958—; spl. asst. atty. gen. for election frauds State of N.Y., 1959. Mem. New York County Lawyers Assn. Home: 120 Riverside Dr New York City NY 10024 Office: 360 Lexington Ave 12th floor New York City NY 10017 Tel (212) 867-9162

KONZ, GERALD KEITH, b. Racine, Wis., Apr. 3, 1932; B.S., U. Wis., Madison, 1957, LL.B., 1960. Admitted to Wis. bar, 1960; dir. corporate taxes S.C. Johnson & Son, Inc., Racine, 1960-76; mem. adv. com. Wis. Dept. Revenue, 1970—. Mem. Tax Execs. Inst. (past pres. Wis. chpt.), Am., Wis., Racine County bar assns. Home: 3515 Taylor Ave Racine WI 53405 Office: 1525 Howe St Racine WI 53405 Tel (414) 554-2473

KOONZ, JOSEPH HAYES, JR., b. Cornwall, N.Y., Nov. 27, 1934; B.A., St. Anselm's Coll., 1956; J.D., Georgetown U., 1959. Admitted to D.C. bar, 1960; asso. firm Ashcraft, Gerel & Koonz, and predecessors, Washington, 1960-66, partner, 1966-70, sr. partner, mng. partner, 1970—. Pres. Wyngate Citizens Assn., Bethesda, Md., 1961-62, Walnut Woods Citizens Assn., Rockville, Md., 1970-71. Mem. Am., D.C. (chmn. workmen's compensation com., 1971, chmn. prepaid legal services com., 1976) bar assns. Contbr. articles to law jours. Home: 5510 Chamberlin Ave Chevy Chase MD 20015 Office: 2101 L St NW Washington DC 20037 Tel (202) 783-6400

KOOTA, AARON EDWARD, b. N.Y.C., Nov. 10, 1905; LL.B., Bklyn. Law Sch., 1927, LL.M., 1928. Admitted to N.Y. State bar, 1927, U.S. Supreme Ct. bar, 1945; asst. dist. atty. Kings County, N.Y., 1950-68, chief asst. atty., 1963-64, dist. atty., 1964-68; justice N.Y. State Supreme Ct., 1969-75. Chmn. Israel Bonds, 1964-68. Mem. Bklyn. (William W. Liebman award, 1968), N.Y. State, Kings County Criminal bar assn. Home: 1801 Dorchester Rd Brooklyn NY 11226 Office: 186 Joralemon St Brooklyn NY 11201 Tel (212) 855-1111

KOPELMAN, LEONARD, b. Cambridge, Mass., Aug. 2, 1940; B.A., Harvard, 1962, J.D., 1965. Admitted to Mass. bar, 1966, U.S. Supreme Ct. bar, 1970; atty. SEC, 1965; asso. firm Warner & Stackpole, Boston, 1966-73; sr. partner firm Kopelman & Soltz, Boston, 1973—; lectr. Harvard, 1966—; counsel Town of Brookline (Mass.), 1967-75; permanent master Mass. Superior Ct., Mass., 1972—; counsel Republic of Finland, 1975—, Town of Stoughton (Mass.), 1976—; asso. counsel AAUP. Trustee Faulkner Hosp., 1975—; sr. pre-law adviser Harvard U., 1975—. Mem. Am. (editor law notes 1974—), Mass., Boston bar assns., Am. Judges Assn., Mass. C. of C. (pres. 1973—). Nat. Endowment Humanities grantee, 1975; author Rent Control. Home: 60 Beech Rd Brookline MA 02146 Office: 10 Post Office Square Boston MA 02109 Tel (617) 482-4515

KOPP, CHARLES LEO, b. Los Angeles, Jan. 10, 1922; A.A., Los Angeles City Coll., 1943; student U. Redlands, 1943-45; J.D., U. So. Calif., 1949. Admitted to Calif. bar, 1950; practiced in Los Angeles, 1950-68, San Francisco, 1968—; asso. counsel Pacific Mut. Life Ins. Co., Los Angeles, 1950-58; asst. gen. counsel Pacific Finance Corp., 1958-64; v.p., head law dept. United Calif. Bank, 1964-68; corp. sec. Indsl. Indemnity Co., San Francisco, 1968-69; gen. counsel, sec. West Coast Life Ins. Co., San Francisco, 1970—; faculty U. So. Calif. extension div., 1954-57. Mem. Am., San Francisco, Calif. bar assns., Calif. C. of C., Phi Alpha Delta. Author: Life Insurance in Divorce Cases, 1956. Home: 190 Via Lerida Greenbrae CA 94904 Office: 50 California St San Francisco CA 94111

KOPPEL, RICHARD ULRICH, b. Dortmund, Germany, June 8, 1922; Bachelor, Wycliffe Coll., Eng., 1938; B.A., Coll. City N.Y.; LL.B., N.Y. U., 1948, LL.M., 1950. Admitted to N.Y. State bar, 1948; partner firm Joseph & Koppel, N.Y.C., 1954—. Mem. N.Y.C. Bar Assn. (com. internat. law). Contbr. articles to legal jours.; mem. editorial bd. N.Y. U. Law Rev., 1947-48. Home: 37 Elm St Great Neck NY 11021 Office: 60 E 42d St New York City NY 10017 Tel (212) 687-1466

KOPSKY, PAUL WILLIAM, b. St. Louis, Mar. 3, 1939; B.B.A., Creighton U., 1960; LL.B., Washington U., St. Louis, 1962. Admitted to Mo. bar, 1963, U.S. Supreme Ct. bar, 1970; asso. firm Bernard Baer, Lee, Timm & McDonale, and predecessors, St. Louis, 1965-67, partner, 1967-74; partner firm Mastorakos & Kopsky, Chesterfield, Mo., 1974—; lectr. Meramac Jr. Coll., St. Louis. Mem. Am., Mo., St. Louis bar assns. Home: Route 1 Box 638 Glencoe MO 63038 Office: PO Box 8 Chesterfield MO 63017 Tel (314) 532-3434

KORDUS, ARTHUR CHARLES, b. Kronenwetter, Wis., Dec. 17, 1929; student Salvatorian Sem., 1946-50; B.A., St. Paul Sem., 1952, postgrad. in Theology, 1952-55; M.A., U. Minn., 1958; J.D., U. Wis., 1962. Admitted to Wis. bar, 1962; asso. firm Hoffman, Trembath & Gullickson, Wausau, Wis., 1962-64; individual practice law, Schofield, Wis., 1964—; atty. Town of Kronenwetter, 1966-71. Mem. Am., Marathon County, Wis. State bar assns., Schofield Businessmen (pres. 1964, dir., 1963-65), S. Area Businessmen's Assn. (pres. 1967, dir. 1965-67), Am. Judicature Soc. Home: Rt 2 Box 44 Mosinee WI 54455 Office: 1328 Schofield Ave Schofield WI 54476 Tel (715) 359-3750

KORETZ, ROBERT FRANKLIN, b. Syracuse, N.Y., July 6, 1912; A.B., Syracuse U., 1933, J.D., 1938; LL.M., Harvard, 1939. Admitted to N.Y. State bar, 1938; mem. staff NLRB, Washington, 1939-46; asst. prof. Syracuse U., 1946-47, asso. prof., 1948-54, prof., 1954—; vis. asso. prof. N.Y. U., 1953; mem. enforcement com. WSB, 1951-52; adv. council N.Y. Labor and Mgmt. Practices Act, 1959-70; labor arbitrator, 1949—. Mem. Human Rights Com. Syracuse-Onondaga County, 1960-66. Mem. Am., N.Y. State bar assns., Nat. Acad. Arbitrators. Author: Statutory History of U.S. Labor Organization, 1970; contbr. articles in field to legal jours. Home: 119 Windsor Pl Syracuse NY 13210 Office: Syracuse U Coll of Law Syracuse NY 13210 Tel (315) 423-2533

KORMAN, JAMES WILLIAM, b. Washington, Apr. 29, 1943; B.A., Coll. of William & Mary, 1965; J.D., George Washington U., 1968. Admitted to Va. bar, 1968, D.C. bar, 1970; asso. firm Kinney, Smith & Korman, Arlington, Va., 1968-72, partner, 1973—; adv. bd. Bank of Arlington; served with JAGC, USAR, 1968-74. Chmn. exploring team Nat. Capital Area council Boy Scouts Am., 1971-73, group advisor, 1973-75; bd. dirs. Glebe Commons Homeowners Assn., Arlington, 1969-75, Temple Rodef Shalom, Falls Church Va., 1975-76. Mem. Am., Va. State, Washington, Arlington (exec. bd.) bar assns., Assn. Trial Lawyers Am., Va. Trial Lawyers Assn., No. Va. Young Lawyers Assn., Falls Church Jaycees (pres. 1975-76, chmn. 1976—). Recipient Meritorious Service award Legal Aid Bur., 1968, Exploring award Nat. Capital Area Council Boy Scouts Am., 1972. Home: 3852 N 26th St Arlington VA 22207 Office: 2007 N 15th St Arlington VA 22216 Tel (703) 525-4000

KORMAN, MILTON DANIEL, b. Washington, Oct. 22, 1904; LL.B., Georgetown U., 1925, J.D., 1925; postgrad. George Washington U., 1926. Admitted to D.C. bar, 1925, U.S. Supreme Ct. bar, 1940; practiced in Washington, 1925-37; asst. corp. counsel D.C., 1937-56, chief criminal div., 1941-43, chief civil litigation div., 1951-56, prin. asst. corp. counsel, 1956-65, acting corp. counsel, 1965-66; atty. for D.C. in sch. desegregation cases U.S. Supreme Ct., 1951-54; judge D.C. Superior Ct., 1967—; adj. prof. law Southeastern U., 1964-67; mem. Jud. Conf. D.C. and U.S. D.C. Circuit. Gen. counsel Nat. Capital Area council Boy Scouts Am., 1957-67, exec. bd., 1957—; v.p. Nat. Children's Center, Washington, 1971—; bd. dirs. Hebrew Home of Greater Washington, 1971—, Jewish Hist. Soc., 1974—. Mem. Am., D.C., Fed. (nat. council 1969-74) bar assns., Am. Judicature Soc., Delta Theta Phi. Recipient Silver Beaver award Boy Scouts Am., 1960, Distinguished Pub. Service award Nat. Inst. Municipal Law Officers, 1965, Alumni Achievement award Georgetown U. Law Center, 1967; named Hon. Fire Chief D.C. Fire Dept., 1974. Home: 4201 Cathedral Ave NW Washington DC 20016 Office: care Superior Ct of DC 500 Indiana Ave NW Washington DC 20001 Tel (202) 727-1411

KORNBLUM, GUY ORVILLE, b. Indpls., Oct. 29, 1939; A.B., Ind. U., 1961; J.D., U. Calif., 1966. Admitted to Ind. bar, 1966, Calif. bar, 1966, U.S. Supreme Ct. bar, 1971; atty. firm Ice, Miller, Donadio & Ryan, Indpls., 1966-67, Bledsoe, Smith, Cathcart, Johnson & Rogers, San Francisco, 1967-70; asso. prof. law Hastings Coll., 1970—, asst. dean, 1970-72; partner firm Pettit, Evers and Martin, San Francisco, 1972—; dir. Coll. Advocacy, Hastings Coll., 1970-72; bd. dirs., mem. exec. com. Hastings Center for Trial and Appellate Advocacy, Hastings Coll., 1972—. Bd. dirs. San Francisco Neighborhood Legal Assistance Found., 1970-72; trustee San Francisco Consortia, 1970-72. Mem. Fed., Am., Ind., Calif., San Francisco bar assns., Fedn. Ins. Counsel, Internat. Assn. Ins. Counsel, Order of Coif, Phi Delta Phi, Phi Eta Sigma. Mem. editorial bd. Hastings Law Jour., 1965-67. Contbr. articles to profl. jours. Office: 600 Montgomery St San Francisco CA 94111 Tel (415) 434-4000

KORNER, JULES GILMER, III, b. Washington, July 27, 1922; B.A., U. Va., 1943, LL.B., 1947, J.D., 1970. Admitted to Va. bar, 1947, D.C. bar, 1948, U.S. Supreme Ct. bar, 1951, Md. bar, 1953; asso. firm Korner, Doyle, Worth & Crampton, Washington, 1947-51, partner, 1951-70; partner firm Pope, Ballard & Loos, Washington, 1970—; adj. prof. law Georgetown U. Law Sch., 1961-65. Mem. Internat., Am., D.C., Va., Inter-Am. bar assns. Contbr. articles to legal jours. Office: 888 17th St NW Washington DC 20006 Tel (202) 298-8600

KORNFEIN, WILLIAM, b. Zurich, Switzerland, Mar. 9, 1947; B.S. in Edn., U. Kans., 1969; J.D., U. Mo., 1972. Admitted to Mo. bar, 1972; asst. counselor City of St. Louis, 1972-75; atty., advisor Bur. Hearings and Appeals Social Security Adminstrn., St. Louis, 1975—. Mem. Am., Mo. bar assns., Phi Alpha Delta. Home: 894 Oklahoma Ave Manchester MO 63011 Office: 210 N 12th St Room 1427 Saint Louis MO 63101 Tel (314) 425-4881

KORNMANN, CHARLES BRUNO, b. Watertown, S.D., Sept. 14, 1937; B.A. in Polit. Sci., Coll. St. Thomas, 1959; LL.B., Georgetown U., 1962. Admitted to S.D. bar, 1962; legis. aide Senator George McGovern of S.D., 1963; exec. sec. S.D. Democratic Party, 1963-65; asso. firm Richardson, Groseclose, Kornmann & Wyly, and predecessors, Aberdeen, S.D., 1965-68, partner, 1968—; mem. S.D. Citizens Commn. on Exec. Reorgn., 1970-71, S.D. Constl. Revision Commn., 1973-76. Mem. S.D. Bd. Charities and Corrections, 1972—, pres., 1976—; bd. dirs. Aberdeen Boys' Club, 1971—; chmn. S.D. Dem. Conv., 1968. Mem. Am., S.D. (pub. relations com.), Brown County bar assns. Home: RR1 Aberdeen SD 57401 Office: Milwaukee Station Bldg Box 489 Aberdeen SD 57401 Tel (605) 225-6310

KOROSEC, KENNETH DAVID, b. Cleve., Oct. 15, 1943; B.A. cum laude, Case Western Res. U., 1963; J.D. cum laude, Cleve. State U., 1967. Admitted to Ohio bar, 1967, U.S. Dist. Ct. for No. Ohio bar, 1976; individual practice law, Cleveland, 1967-71, Chesterland, Ohio, 1971—; comml. rep. Ohio Bell Telephone Co., Cleve., 1963-64; Premier Indsl. Corp., Cleve., 1964-66; staff atty. Cleve.-Seven County Transp.-Land Use Study, 1967-69; community services officer NE Ohio Areawide Coordinating Agency, Cleve., 1969-71; Geauga County Adminstr., Chardon, Ohio, 1971-75. Exec. v.p. Community Improvement Corp., Geauga County Ohio, 1971—. Mem. Am., Ohio State, Geauga County bar assns., West Geauga Fathers Club, Am. Field Service, Geauga County YMCA, Chesterland C. of C., Delta Theta Phi Alumni Club, Delta Upsilon Alumni Club. Recipient Delta Theta Phi Scholarship award, 1966, 67; Central Nat. Bank award, 1967; Banks-Baldwin Publishing Co. awards of excellence, 1966, 67. Home: 11919 Caves Rd Chesterland OH 44026 Office: Shenandoah Bldg 8491 Mayfield Rd Chesterland OH 44026 Tel (216) 729-1414

KOROTKI, ABRAHAM PAUL, b. Florence, Italy, Mar. 3, 1946; came to U.S., 1950, naturalized 1956; A.A., U. Balt., 1965, J.D., 1970; LL.B., Mt. Vernon Sch. Law, 1968. Admitted to Md. bar, 1971; individual practice law, Towson, Md., 1971—. Mem. Baltimore County, Baltimore City bar assns. Address: 516 W Allegheny Ave Towson MD 21204 Tel (301) 828-8822

KORP, WILLIAM ROBERT, b. Lima, Ohio, Nov. 29, 1932; student U. Fla.; LL.B., Stetson U., 1962. Admitted to Fla. bar, 1962; partner firm Korp, Wheeler & McGill, Venice, Fla.; prosecutor City of Venice, 1965-66; judge Venice City Ct., 1966-67; U.S. commr., 1972. Mem. Sarasota County (Fla.), Am. bar assns., Fla. Bar. Home: 1208 N Casey Key Rd Osprey FL 33559 Office: 609 S Tamiami Tr Venice FL 33595 Tel (813) 485-5486

KORZENIK, ARMAND ALEXANDER, b. Hartford, Conn., Oct. 31, 1927; A.B., magna cum laude, Harvard, 1951, J.D., 1951; LL.M., Yale, 1952. Admitted to Conn. bar, 1951, U.S. Supreme Ct. bar, 1959; individual practice law, Hartford; mem. staff Judge Adv. Conn. Air N.G., 1953—; now col.; justice of peace, Hartford, 1960-73; counsel Redevel. Agy., 1966-68, Hartford Bd. Edn., 1968-72. Mem. Hartford County (editor Barfly 1975—, chmn. publs. com. 1975—, chmn., family relations com. 1975-77, now chmn pub. relations com.), Conn. (editor jour. del. Ho. of Dels.) bar assn., Judge Adv. Assn., Comml. Law League Am., Nat. Inst. Municipal Law Officers. Phi Beta Kappa. Author: The Discovery of Discovery, 1956; A Visit to the Doctor, 1956; The Interpretation of Following Closely, 1959; Coping with Teachers Strike, 1971. Home: 120 Terry Rd Hartford CT 06105 Office: 37 Lewis St Hartford CT 06103 Tel (203) 278-2800

KORZENIK, HAROLD, b. N.Y.C., Oct. 2, 1903; B.A., Columbia, 1925, LL.B., J.D., 1927. Admitted to N.Y. State bar, 1928, U.S. Supreme Ct. bar, 1936; partner firm Lhowe & Obstfield, N.Y.C., 1930-35; sr. partner firm Rothstein & Korzenik N.Y.C., 1935—; asso. counsel Kings County Ambulance Chasing Investigation, 1928-29; spl. asst. Atty. Gen. State of N.Y.; counsel indsl. union pension funds; lectr. Practicing Law Inst. of N.Y., Wharton Sch., U. Pa. Trustee, v.p., pres. Bklyn. region YM-WHA of Greater N.Y.; trustee ILGWU Retirement Fund; Am. counsel, internat. bd. govs. Shenkar Coll., Ramat Gan, Israel. Mem. Assn. of Bar of City of N.Y. (mem. com. on arbitration, labor law), Nat. Panel Arbitrators, Am. Arbitration Assn. (mem. comml. law com.), Bklyn. Bar Assn. (chmn. com. on labor law, com. on profl. ethics, com. on coordination of law bar). Contbr. articles to profl. jours. Home: 2705 Ave J Brooklyn NY 11210 Office: 51 Chambers St New York City NY 10007 Tel (212) 962-1185

KOSENE, MILTON, b. N.Y.C., July 13, 1918; student Middlesex Jr. Coll., 1936-39, U. Newark (now Rutgers U.), 1940, N.J. Law Sch. (now Rutgers U.), 1942-45. Admitted to N.J. bar, 1945; individual practice law, Fair Haven, N.J., 1945—; mayor Borough of Fair Haven, 1962. Mem. N.J., Monmouth County bar assns. Author: Evidence Law in New Jersey, 1954. Home: 411 River Rd Fair Haven NJ 07701 Office: 596 River Rd Fair Haven NJ 07701 Tel (201) 747-2819

KOSHALEK, JOHN ALLEN, b. Wausau, Wis., Oct. 23, 1940; B.A., U. Wis., Madison, 1963, J.D., 1966. Admitted to Wis. bar, 1966; asso. firm Riley, Pierce, Lynch & Garner, Madison, 1966-71; partner firm Riley & Koshalek, Madison, 1971-76, firm Dewa, Koshalek, Heim & Brush, Madison, 1976-77, firm Koshalek, Heim & Brush, Madison, 1977—. Mem. State Bar Wis., Dane County (Wis.) Bar Assn. Home: 116 E Gilman St Madison WI 53703 Office: 25 W Main St Madison WI 53703 Tel (608) 257-5520

KOSHIBA, JAMES EDMUND TAKEO, b. Wailuku, Maui, Hawaii, Nov. 22, 1941; B.A., U. Hawaii, 1963; J.D., Drake U., 1967; LL.M., Northwestern U., 1969. Admitted to Iowa bar, 1967, Ill. bar, 1967, Hawaii bar, 1968; partner firm Kobayashi, Hoshiba & Watanabe, Honolulu, 1968—. Mem. Hawaii State, Iowa, Am. bar assns., Am. Bd. Trial Lawyers, Calif. Trial Lawyers Assn. Contbr. articles to legal jours. Office: 745 Fort St Honolulu HI 96813 Tel (808) 524-5700

KOSKO, GEORGE CARTER, b. Tampa, Fla., Apr. 14, 1944; B.S. in Econs., U. S.C., 1966, J.D., 1971; grad. Nat. Inst. Trial Advocacy, 1973. Admitted to S.C. bar, 1971; U.S. Supreme Ct. bar, 1976; individual practice law, Columbia, S.C., 1971-75; partner firm Kosko, Coffas & Hostetter, and predecessor, Columbia, 1975—; solicitor Richland County Family Ct., 1971-72; asst. solicitor Fifth Jud. Circuit, 1972-75; legal officer CAP. Mem. Lawyers-Pilot Bar Assn., Am., S.C., Richland County bar assns., Am., S.C. trial lawyers assns., Nat. Dist. Attys. Assn. Home: 9 Sims Alley Columbia SC 29205 Office: 1303 Elmwood Ave Columbia SC 29201 Tel (803) 771-6565

KOSMERL, WAYNE THOMAS, b. Reading, Pa., Dec. 23, 1947; B.A., Gettysburg Coll., 1969; J.D., U. Md., 1972. Admitted to Md. bar, 1973; asso. firm Hartman and Crain, Annapolis, Md., 1973—. Mem. Anne Arundel County (Md.), Am. bar assns. Home: 124 Prince George St Annapolis MD 21401 Office: 222 Severn Ave POB 3323 Annapolis MD 21403 Tel (301) 267-8166

KOSTER, JOHN CHARLES, b. Muskegon, Mich., July 17, 1941; B.A., Notre Dame U., 1963; J.D., U. Mich. Law Sch., 1968. Admitted to State N.Y. bar, 1969; naval officer USN, 1963-65; asso. firm Healy and Baillie, N.Y.C., 1969-73, partner, 1973—. Mem. Am. Bar Assn., Maritime Law Assn. Contbr. articles to Il Diritto Marittimo, Jour. Maritime Law and Commerce. Home: 19 E 65th St New York NY 10021 Office: 29 Broadway St New York NY 10006 Tel (212) 943-3980

KOSTNER, JOSEPH OTTOKAR, b. Chgo., Nov. 15, 1923; B.A. in Polit. Sci., Yale U., 1947; postgrad. Northwestern U. Law Sch., 1947-49; J.D., Kent Coll., 1954. Admitted to Ill. bar, 1954, U.S. Supreme Ct. bar, 1963; mem. firm Quinn, Jacobs, Barry & Latchford, Chgo., 1955-66; individual practice law, Chgo., 1966-67; sr. partner firm Frankel, McKay, Orlikoff, Denten & Kostner, Chgo., 1967—; dir. Lawndale Trust & Savs. Bank, 1969-77, Water Tower Trust & Savs. Bank; pres. Water Tower Financial Group, Inc., 1974—. Mem. Am. (merit award com. bar activities sect.), Fed., Ill. (assembly del. chmn. finance com. 1972-74), Chgo., Internat. (sec. on bus. law, 1972—) bar assns., Ill. Assn. Registered Bank Holding Cos. (v.p., gen. counsel, dir.). Decorated Bronze Star, Purple Heart with two oak leaf clusters. Home: 49 E Cedar St Chicago IL 60610 Office: 208 S LaSalle St Chicago IL 60604 Tel (312) 263-4040

KOTARBA, RICHARD G., b. Allison, Pa., July 5, 1941; B.A., John Carroll U., Cleve., 1963; LL.B., Boston U. Admitted to Pa. bar, 1966, Supreme Ct. U.S. bar, 1971; partner firm Meyer, Unkovic & Scott, Pitts., 1966—. Trustee LaRoche Coll., Pitts., 1973—. Mem. Am., Pa., Allegheny County bar assns., Order of Coif. Office: Frick Bldg Pittsburgh PA 15219 Tel (412) 281-5700

KOTHE, HOWARD KLINTWORTH, b. N.Y.C., Dec. 19, 1925; B.S. in Chem. Engring., Mass. Inst. Tech., 1949; LL.B., St. Lawrence U., 1953; postgrad. N.Y. U., 1955. Admitted to N.Y. bar, 1953; mem. legal dept. Cities Service Oil Co., N.Y.C., 1950-53; atty. Union Carbide Corp, N.Y.C., 1954-58, div. atty., 1959-60; asso. firm Watson, Leavenworth et al, N.Y.C., 1961-64, partner, 1965—; v.p., dir. Artfiber Corp., N.Y.C., 1964, Actmedia, Inc., N.Y.C., 1973-75, Beekman Terr. Inc., 1974—. Mem. Am., N.Y. patent law assns., Am. Bar Assn., Assn. Bar City N.Y. Home: 455 E 51st St New York City NY 10022 Office: 100 Park Ave New York City NY 10017 Tel (212) MU3-4221

KOTOUC, THOMAS OTTO, b. Lincoln, Nebr., May 4, 1942; B.A., U. Nebr., 1964; J.D., Harvard, 1967. Admitted to Nebr. bar, 1967, Ga. bar, 1972, N.C. bar, 1973; gen. counsel Kotouc and Fankhauser, Humboldt, Nebr., 1967—; atty. Lawyer's Title Ins. Co., Atlanta, 1972; individual practice law, Atlanta and Charleston, S.C., 1972—; area rep. The Navigators, Charleston, 1974—. Tchr., Ref. Presbyterian Ch., Charleston, 1973—. Mem. Am. Bar Assn., Christian Legal Soc. Home and Office: Box 1932 Amman Jordan

KOTTKAMP, JOHN HARLAN, b. Portland, Oreg., Oct. 19, 1930; B.S., U. Oreg., 1952, J.D., 1957. Admitted to Oreg. bar, 1957; asso. firm Kilkenny & Fabre, Pendleton, Oreg., 1957-59; partner firm Fabre, Collins & Kottkamp, Pendleton, 1959-61; Kottkamp & O'Rourke, Pendleton, 1964—; disciplinary rev. bd. Oreg. State Bar, 1975—. Fellow Am. Bar Found.; mem. Am. Bd. Trial Advs., Pendleton C. of C. (former dir.). Home: 910 NW 12th St Pendleton OR 97801 Office: 331 SE 2nd St Pendleton OR 97801 Tel (503) 276-2141

KOURY, JOHN A., JR., b. Pottsville, Pa., May 28, 1943; B.S., U. Pitts., 1965; J.D., Duquesne U., 1968. Admitted to Pa. bar, 1969; asso. firm Prince & Prince, Pottstown, Pa. 1969-72; partner firm O'Donnell, Weiss, Mattei, Koury & Suchoza, Pottstown, 1972—; municipal solicitor, Borough of Pottstown, 1972—, East Coventry Twp., Pa., 1972—, Borough of Elverson, Pa., 1972—. Mem. Am. Bar Assn., Pa. Trial Lawyers Assn., C. of C., Vis. Nurse Assn. Home: Rural Delivery #1 Box 378 Pottstown PA 19464 Office: 41 High St Pottstown PA 19464 Tel (215) 323-2800

KOVACEVICH, ROBERT EUGENE, b. Des Moines, Nov. 9, 1933; grad. St. Martins Coll., 1955; J.D., Gonzaga U., 1959; LL.M., N.Y. U., 1960. Admitted to Wash. bar, 1959; asso. firm Kizer, Gaiser, Stoeve, Layman & Powell, Spokane, Wash., 1960-63; partner firm Kovacevich and Algeo, Spokane, 1963—; lectr. tax policy and procedure Gonzaga U., 1973—. Pres. Spokane Estate Planning Council, 1974. Mem. Am., Wash., Spokane County bar assns. Home: South 4603 Pittsburg St Spokane WA 99203 Office: Suite 703 Lincoln Bldg Spokane WA 99201 Tel (509) 747-2104

KOVACS, PAUL EUGENE, b. Newark, June 26, 1944; A.A., Monmouth Coll., 1964, B.S., 1966; J.D., U. Mo., 1969. Admitted to Mo. bar, 1969; asso. firm Carter, Brinker & Doyen, Clayton, Mo., 1969-73, partner, 1974—. Bd. dirs. Lawyers Reference Service 1974—. Mem. Am., Mo., St. Louis County (chmn. speakers and pub. relations com. 1972-75), Met. St. Louis (grievance com. 1971-73) bar assns., Assn. Def. Counsel (treas. 1975, sec. 1976), Phi Alpha Delta. Home: 65 Fair Oaks St Louis MO 63124 Office: 130 S Bemiston Clayton MO 63105 Tel (314) 863-6311

KOZAK, JOHN W., b. Chgo., July 25, 1943; B.S. in Elec. Engring., U. Notre Dame, 1965; J.D., Georgetown U., 1968. Admitted to Ill. bar, 1968, D.C. bar, 1968; atty. Dept. Navy, Corona, Calif., 1968-69; asso. firm Wolfe, Hubbard, Leydig, Voit & Osann, Ltd., Chgo., 1969-74; partner firm Leydig, Voit, Osann, Mayer & Holt, Chgo., 1974—. Bd. dirs. Willow Walk Inc., 1974-77, pres., 1975. Mem. Am., Chgo. bar assns., Chgo. Patent Law Assn. Office: 1 IBM Plaza Suite 4600 Chicago IL 60611 Tel (312) 822-9666

KOZELKA, FRANK JOSEPH, III, b. Cleve., Nov. 2, 1945; A.B. in Sociology, John Carroll U., 1967; J.D., Cleve. Marshall Law Sch., 1970. Admitted to Ohio, Fla. bars, 1971; clk. Cuyahoga County (Ohio) Common Pleas Ct., 1971-73; asst. pros. atty. Cuyahoga County, 1973—. Active Broadview Heights (Ohio) Democratic Club, 1974—. Mem. Nat. Dist. Atty's. Assn., Fla., Ohio, Cleve., Cuyahoga County bar assns., Assn. U.S. Army. Home: 2207 E Wallings Rd Brecksville OH 44141 Office: 1200 Ontario Ave 9th floor Justice Towers Cleveland OH 44113 Tel (216) 623-7854

KOZOLCHYK, BORIS, b. Havana, Cuba, Dec. 6, 1934; D.C.L., U. Havana, 1956; LL.B. cum laude, U. Miami (Fla.), 1959; LL.M., U. Mich., 1960, S.J.D., 1966. Admitted to Cuba bar, 1956, Ariz. bar, 1972; asso. firm Ammerman and Landy, Miami, Fla., 1959; asst. prof. law So. Meth. U., Dallas, 1960-64; cons. Rand Corp., Santa Monica, Calif., 1964-67; cons. dir. law project USAID, San Jose, Costa Rica, 1967-69; prof. law U. Ariz., 1969—; vis. lectr. Universidad Catolica de Santo Tomas de Villanueva, Havana, 1963, Facultad de Ciencias Juridicas y Sociales, U. Santiago (Chile), 1969; vis. prof. law. Nat. U. Mexico, 1961, Nat. U. Chile, Santiago, 1962. Pres. Ariz. Friends of Music, 1975-76. Author: Commercial Letter of Credit in the Americas, a Comparative Study, 1966; Law and the Credit Structure in Latin America, 1966; The Political Biographies of Three Castro Officials, 1966; Guide to the Law and Legal Literature of Colombia in Matters of Interest to Economists and Political Scientists, 1966; Legal Foundations of Military Life in Colombia, 1967; Legal Aspects of the Acquisition of Major Weapons by Six Latin American Countries, 1967; Jurisprudencia Mercantil, 1967; Curso de Derecho Mercantil, Texto y Material de Estudio, 1967; El Credito Documentario en el Derecho Americano, 1974; translator: The Mexican Civil Code of 1932, 1963; contbr. articles to legal jours. NSF research grantee, 1973-75. Home: 7401 N Skyline Dr Tucson AZ 85718 Tel (602) 884-1801

KOZYRIS, PHAEDON JOHN, b. Thessaloniki, Greece, Jan. 2, 1932; Law Diploma summa cum laude Thessaloniki Law Sch., 1954; M.Comparative Law, U. Chgo., 1955; J.D. with distinction, Cornell U., 1960. Asso. firm Cahill, Gordon, Reindel & Ohl, N.Y.C., 1960-69; admitted to N.Y. bar, 1961, Ohio bar, 1973; prof. law Ohio State U., 1969—; vis. prof. Duke, 1971-72, Thessaloniki Law Sch., 1974-75. Mem. Am. Soc. Internat. Law, Am. Assn. Law Schs., Am. Bar Assn. Contbr. articles to legal jours. Home: 2377 Edington Rd Columbus OH 43221 Office: 1659 N High St Columbus OH 43210 Tel (614) 422-0701

KRACKE, ROBERT RUSSELL, b. Decatur, Ga., Feb. 27, 1938; A.B. Birmingham So. Coll, Samford U., 1962; J.D., Cumberland Law Sch., 1965. Admitted to Ala. bar, 1965, U.S. Supreme Ct. bar, 1971, U.S. Tax Ct. bar, 1971; partner firm Kracke, Caddis, Gwin, Bashinsky & Woodward, Birmingham, 1967—. Mem. Am., Ala., Birmingham bar assns., Sigma Alpha Epsilon. Contbr. articles to law jours. Home: 4410 Briarglen Dr Birmingham AL 35243 Office: City Federal Bldg Birmingham AL 35203 Tel (205) 328-3904

KRAEGE, RICHARD CARTER, b. Orange, N.J., Nov. 20, 1947; B.A., DePauw U., Greencastle, Ind., 1970; J.D., Washington U., St. Louis, 1973. Admitted to Ind. bar, 1973; clk. Ind. Atty. Gen., 1973; asso. firm Ecklund & Frutkin, Indpls., 1973-76, Harrison, Moberly & Gaston, 1976—; mem. asso. faculty Ind. U.-Purdue U., Indpls., 1974-77. Mem. Am., Ind., Indpls. bar assns. Comment editor of Urban Law Annual, 1973. Office: 777 Chamber of Commerce Bldg Indianapolis IN Tel (317) 639-4511

KRAEMER, DONALD JACK, b. Milw., July 9, 1938; B.S. in Bus. Adminstrn., Marquette U., 1960, LL.B., 1962. Admitted to Wis. bar, 1962; since practiced in Milw., asst. gen. counsel Milw. Ins. Co., 1965-68; asso. Habush, Gillick, Habush, Davis & Murphy, 1968-70, partner, 1971—. Mem. Brookfield (Wis.) Sch. Bd., 1969—, pres., 1973-74; mem. Brookfield Park and Recreation Bd., 1971-74. Mem. Am., Wis., Milw., Jr., Waukesha bar assns., Am. Trial Lawyers Assn. Office: 212 W Wisconsin St Milwaukee WI 53203 Tel (414) 271-0900

KRAEMER, KENNETH, b. Portland, Oreg., May 25, 1918; B.A., Harvard, 1939, J.D., 1942. Admitted to Oreg. bar, 1946; asso. firm Chamberlain Thomas & Kraemer, Portland, 1946-51; individual practice law, Portland, 1951—; mem. Oreg. State Legislature, 1951-53. Office: 410 American Bank Bldg Portland OR 97205 Tel (503) 228-9408

KRAEMER, MICHAEL FREDERICK, b. N.Y.C., Jan. 21, 1947; B.A., Amherst Coll., 1969; J.D., U. Pa., 1972. Admitted to Pa. bar, 1972, N.J. bar, 1973; asso. firm Kleinbard, Bell & Brecker, Phila., 1976—. Mem. Center City Residents Assn., 1975-77. Mem. ACLU, Am., Pa., Phila. bar assns. J. Woodruff Simpson fellow, 1969-71. Home: 2419 Pine St Philadelphia PA 19103 Office: Kleinbard Bell & Brecker 123 S Broad St Philadelphia PA 19109 Tel (215) 985-1000

KRAEMER, SANDY FREDERICK, b. Chgo., May 10, 1937; B.S. in Engring., Stanford, 1959; J.D., U. Colo., 1963. Admitted to Colo. bar, 1963; individual practice law, Denver, 1963-64; mem. firm Kraemer & Kendall, Colorado Springs, 1976—; dep. county atty. El Paso County (Colo.), 1972-74; panel trustee U.S. Dist. Ct. for Colo., 1964-68; chmn. White House Conf. on Children and Youth, El Paso County, 1970; pres., nat. dir. USO, 1968; commr. Colo. Springs Charter Rev. Commn., 1975. Bd. regents U. Colo., 1977—. Mem. Am., Colo., El Paso County bar assns., Estate Planning Council Colorado Springs (pres. 1974-75), Rocky Mountain Stanford Alumni Club (pres. 1968-69). Named Colo. Conservationist of Year, 1967; Outstanding Young Man, Colorado Springs Jaycees, 1968; contbr. articles to legal jours.; inventor games and toys. Home: 2402 Ceresa Ln Colorado Springs CO 80909 Office: 430 N Tejon Colorado Springs CO 80903 Tel (303) 471-3690

KRAFT, C. WILLIAM, JR., b. Phila., Dec. 14, 1903; B.A., U. Pa., 1924, LL.B., 1927. Admitted to Pa. bar, 1927; asso. firm Robert W. Beatty, Media, Pa., 1927-37; asst. dist. atty. County of Delaware (Pa.), 1928-37, dist. atty., 1944-52; sr. partner firm Kraft, Lippicott & Donaldson, Media, 1954-55; judge U.S. Dist. Ct., Eastern Dist. Pa., 1955—, sr. judge, 1970—. Mem. Delaware County, Phila. lawyers clubs, Delaware County, Am., Pa. bar assns., Am. Judicature Soc., Socialegal Club, Jr. Legal Club. Home: Brickhouse Farm Middletown Rd PO Box 239 RD Glen Mills PA 19342 Office: 5613 US Courthouse 601 Market St Philadelphia PA 19106 Tel (215) WA2-1737

KRAFT, C. WILLIAM, III, b. Upper Darby, Pa., Apr. 10, 1943; B.A., U. Pa., 1965; J.D., Villanova U., 1968. Admitted to Pa. bar, 1968; clk. to judge U.S. Ct. Appeals 3d Dist., 1968-69; asso. firm Beasley, Hewson & Casey, 1969-71, Beasley, Hewson, Casey, Kraft & Colleran, 1971-76, Kraft & Beebe, Media, Pa., 1976—. Bd. dirs. Camp Sunshine, Delaware County, Pa., 1973-74. Mem. Trial Lawyers Assn. Am. (dir. 1974-76), Pa. Trial Lawyers Assn., Am., Pa., Delaware County bar assns. Bd. editors Villanova Law Rev., 1967-68; contbr. articles to legal jours. Home: Box 235 Rural Delivery 1 Glen Mills PA 19342 Office: 1 Olive St Media PA 19063

KRAFT, MELVIN D., b. N.Y.C., Jan. 12, 1926; student N.Y. U., 1942-43; B.S., Ohio State U., 1948; J.D., Harvard, 1953. Admitted to Conn. bar 1953, N.Y. State bar, 1956, U.S. Supreme Ct. bar, 1961; practice law, Conn., 1953-56, N.Y.C., 1956—; program chmn., lectr. contract litigation Practicing Law Inst., 1968—. Mem. Com. on Cts. of Citizens Union, 1971-72. Mem. Am., N.Y. State bar assns., Am. Arbitration Assn. (panel arbitrators), Assn. of the Bar of the City of N.Y. Author: The Presentation of Evidence in Arbitration, 1969; editor: Using Experts in Civil Cases, 1977; contbr. articles to legal jours. Office: 522 Fifth Ave New York City NY 10036 Tel (212) 575-7800

KRAG, DONALD O., b. Alexander, Iowa, Aug. 4, 1903; J.D., Southwestern U., 1933. Admitted to Calif. bar, 1933, U.S. Supreme Ct. bar, 1950; partner firm Krag & Krag, Alhambra, Calif.; trustee, sec. Ingleside Mental Health Center, 1950—. Trustee, Alhambra Community Hosp., 1967-73, pres., 1968-70. Mem. Am., San Gabriel Valley (past pres.), Los Angeles County (past trustee) bar assns., Am. Judicature Soc., State Bar Calif., Am. Soc. Hosp. Attys. Home: 639 Arbolada Dr Arcadia CA 91006 Office: 100 S 1st St Alhambra CA 91802 Tel (213) 282-1164

KRAGEN, ADRIAN ALBERT, b. San Francisco, June 3, 1907; A.B., U. Calif., Berkeley, 1931, J.D., 1934. Admitted to Calif. bar, 1934, U.S. Supreme Ct. bar, 1941; individual practice law, Oakland, Calif., 1934-39; dep. atty. gen. Calif., San Francisco, 1940-44; partner firm Loeb & Loeb, Los Angeles, 1944-52; Shannon Cecil Turner Prof. law U. Calif., Berkeley, 1952-73, emeritus, 1973—; counsel Steinbart, Feigenbaum, Goldberg & Lader, San Francisco, 1973-75; prof. U. Calif. Hastings Coll. Law, San Francisco, 1975—; vice chancellor U. Calif. at Berkeley, 1960-64. Trustee Alta Bates Hosp., Berkeley, 1960—; pres. Guardian Health Found., Berkeley, 1976—; unemployment ins. adv. bd. Calif., 1950-64. Mem. Am., Calif. bar assns., Internat. Fiscal Assn. Author: (with John McNulty) Cases and Materials on Federal Income Taxation, 1974; contbr. articles to legal jours. Home: 1141 Arlington Blvd El Cerrito CA 94530 Office: 452 Hastings Coll Law San Francisco CA 94102 Tel (415) 557-1650

KRAHMER, JOHANNES ROBERT, b. Mannheim, Germany, Feb. 29, 1932; A.B. magna cum laude, Dartmouth, 1953; J.D. cum laude, Harvard, 1959. Admitted to D.C. bar, 1959, Del. bar, 1965; asso. firm Ivins, Philips & Barker, Washington, 1959-62; atty. Office Tax Legis. Counsel, U.S. Dept. Treasury, Washington, 1962-64; asso. firm Morris, Nichols, Arsht & Tunnell, Wilmington, Del., 1964-65, partner, 1966—. Mem. estate and gift tax adv. bd. Princeton Theol. Sem., 1972—, trustee tax mgmt. Mem. Am. (chmn. subcom. estate liquidity sect. taxation), Del. (taxation com.) bar assns. Contbr. articles to legal publs. Office: 1105 N Market St Wilmington DE 19801 Tel (302) 658-9200

KRAHULIK, JON DAVID, b. Indpls., Dec. 31, 1944; A.B., Ind. U., 1965, J.D. cum laude, 1969. Admitted to Ind. bar, 1969; since practiced in Indpls., asso. firm Baker & Daniels, 1969-71, Bingham, Summers, Welsh & Spilman, 1971-74, partner firm, 1974—. Bd. dirs. Ind. Lawyers Commn., 1973—. Mem. Indpls., Ind. State, Am. bar assns., Ind. Legal Forum. Home: 6295 N Olney Indianapolis IN 46220 Office: 2700 Ind Tower Indianapolis IN 46204 Tel (317) 635-8900

KRAIG, JERRY B., b. Cleve., Aug. 20, 1937; B.A., Kent State U., 1959; J.D., Cleve-Marshall Law Sch., 1963. Admitted to Ohio bar, 1963; partner firm Dunn & Kraig, Cleve., 1972—. Mem. Ohio State, Cleve. bar assns. Editorial bd. Cleve-Marshall Law Rev. Home: 3324 Somerset Dr Shaker Heights OH 44122 Office: 1111-33 Public Square Bldg Cleveland OH 44113 Tel (216) 696-4000

KRAL, JOSEPH ANTHONY, b. Cleve., Oct. 19, 1948; A.B., St. Louis U., 1970; J.D., So. Meth. U., 1973. Admitted to Mo. bar, 1973, Ill. bar, 1975; asso. firm Coburn, Croft, Shepherd & Herzog, St. Louis, 1973—. Mem. Am., Mo., Ill., St. Louis bar assns. Contbr. articles to legal jours. Office: One Mercantile Center Suite 2900 Saint Louis MO 63101 Tel (314) 621-8575

KRAMER, DANIEL CALEB, b. Chgo., Sept. 23, 1934; B.A., Kenyon Coll., 1955; LL.B., Harvard, 1959; Ph.D., U. Pa., 1964. Admitted to Pa. bar, 1959, Md. bar, 1960; atty. Old Age and Survivors Ins. div. Gen. Counsel Office, HEW, 1959-60; asst. prof. polit. sci. U. Ill., 1964-67; asst. to asso. prof. polit. sci. Richmond Coll., S.I., N.Y., 1967—. Mem. Law and Soc. Assn., Am. Polit. Sci. Assn. Author: Participatory Democracy, 1972; contbr. articles to legal jours. Home: 54 Rokeby Pl Staten Island NY 10310 Office: 130 Stuyvesant Pl Staten Island NY 10301 Tel (212) 720-3103

KRAMER, DENNIS RALPH, b. Hammond, Ind., July 9, 1942; B.S. in Indsl. Mgmt., Purdue U., 1966; J.D., U. Houston, 1970. Indsl. engr. Union Tank Car Co., Whiting, Ind., 1966, Electronics Communications Co., St. Petersburg, Fla., 1968; admitted to Ind. bar, 1971; dep. prosecutor Lake County (Ind.), 1972; individual practice law, Crown Point, Ind., 1972—; judge Lake County Div. 3, 1976—. Mem. South Lake County (pres. 1975-76), Ind. (v.p., sec.), Am. bar assns., Trial Lawyers Assn., Am. Judicature Soc. Recipient Pollack award U. Houston Law Sch., 1969; 1st editor Legal Research Service U. Houston Law Sch., 1969-70. Office: 224 S Court St Crown Point IN 46307 Tel (219) 663-0300

KRAMER, EUGENE LEO, b. Barberton, Ohio, Nov. 7, 1939; A.B., John Carroll U., 1961; J.D., U. Notre Dame, 1964. Admitted to Ohio bar, 1964, U.S. Ct. Appeals bar, 7th Circuit, 1964; law clk. to Judge Roger J. Kiley, U.S. Ct. Appeals, 7th Circuit, 1964-65; asso. firm Squire, Sanders & Dempsey, Cleve., 1965-74, partner, 1974—; dir. of law City of Willowick (Ohio), 1968. Mem. Am., Ohio State bar assns., Bar Assn. Greater Cleve., Nat. Municipal League, Greater Cleve. Growth Assn. Home: 13945 Lake Ave Lakewood OH 44107 Office: 1800 Union Commerce Bldg Cleveland OH 44115 Tel (216) 696-9200

KRAMER, FLOYD W., b. Stroudsburg, Pa., Dec. 23, 1906; J.D., U. Denver, 1949. Admitted to Colo. bar, 1951; individual practice law, Denver, 1950-64, 1967—; of counsel McNichols, Wallace, Nigro & Johnson, Denver, 1964-67; spl. chmn. Colo. Banking Bd., 1963-65, mem., 1957-65. Contbr. articles law jours. Office: 821 Grape St Denver CO 80220 Tel (303) 322-6496

KRAMER, FRANKLIN DAVID, b. Liberty, N.Y., Nov. 13, 1945; B.A. cum laude, Yale, 1967; J.D. magna cum laude, Harvard, 1971. Admitted to N.Y. bar, 1972, D.C. bar, 1972, U.S. Supreme Ct. bar, 1975; law clk. to Hon. J. Edward Lumbard, U.S. Ct. Appeals, 2d Circuit, 1971-72; asso. firm Shea & Gardner, Washington, 1972—. Mem. Am. Bar Assn., D.C. Bar (chmn. com. on appellate advocacy 1976—), Washington Council Lawyers, Harvard Law Sch. Assn. Contbr. articles to legal jours., newspapers; exec. editor Harvard Law Rev., 1970-71. Home: 6209 Goldsboro Rd Bethesda MD 20034 Office: 734 15th St Washington DC 20005 Tel (202) 737-1255

KRAMER, HARRY A., b. Pitts., July 4, 1924; A.B., U. Pitts., 1948, J.D., 1950. Admitted to Pa. bar, 1950; asso. firm Rahauser, Van der Voort, Royston, Robb & Leonard, Pitts., 1950-52; atty., asst. sec. Columbia Gas System, Inc., 1952-59; sr. partner firm Kramer, Livingston & Miller, Pitts., 1959-65; judge Orphans Ct. div. Ct. of Common Pleas Allegheny County (Pa.), 1965-69; judge Commonwealth Ct. Pa., Pitts., 1969—. Chmn. Diocesan Human Relations Commn.; ch. committeeman St. Pauls Cathedral; pres. Pitts. Council Pub. Edn.; mem. Citizens Adv. Com. to Pitts. Sch. Bd.; mem. Pa. Ho. of Reps., 1960-64; mem. adv. bd. St. Francis Coll., LaRoche Coll.; trustee U. Pitts. Mem. Am., Pa., Allegheny bar assns., Am. Judicature Soc., Gen. Alumni Assn. U. Pitts. (exec. bd.), Coll. Arts and Scis. Alumni Assn. U. Pitts. (exec. bd.). Home: 4739 Bayard St Pittsburgh PA 15213 Office: City-County Bldg Pittsburgh PA 15219 also PO Box 1136 Harrisburg PA 17108 Tel (412) 355-4641

KRAMER, HOWARD A., b. Alexandria, La., May 11, 1944; B.S. in Agr., U. Wis., Madison, 1966; J.D., U. N.C., 1969. Admitted to N.Y. bar, 1971, N.C. bar, 1972; asst. v.p. savs. banks Life Ins. Fund, N.Y.C., 1970-72; asst. atty. gen. N.C. Dept. Justice, Raleigh, 1972-74, dep. atty. gen. for legal affairs, 1974—. Mem. Democratic Nat. Platform Com., 1976; trustee Beth-El Synagogue, Durham. Mem. Durham Young Lawyers Assn., Am. (Consumer protection com. 1974—), N.C. bar assns. Patentee seat belt device for infants and children Office: POB 629 Raleigh NC 27602 Tel (919) 733-3377

KRAMER, KENNETH STEPHEN, b. Washington, Oct. 5, 1941; B.S. with high honors, U. Wis., 1963; J.D. cum laude, Harvard U., 1966. Admitted to D.C. bar, 1967, U.S. Ct. Claims bar, 1967, U.S. Ct. Appeals bar, 1967, U.S. Supreme Ct. bar, 1976, U.S. Ct. Mil. Appeals bar, 1967; law clk. to chief judge Wilson Cowen, U.S. Ct. Claims, 1966-67; capt. JAGC, U.S. Army, 1967-70; asso. law firm Fried, Frank, Harris, Shriver & Kampelman, Washington, 1970-75, partner, 1975—. Mem. D.C. Bar Assn. Editorial cons. Fed. Contracts Report, Bur. Nat. Affairs, 1968-74. Office: Suite 1000 600 New Hampshire Ave NW Washington DC 20037

KRAMER, PAUL ROSS, b. Balt., June 6, 1936; B.A., Am. U., 1959, J.D., 1961. Admitted to Md. bar, 1961, D.C. bar, 1962, U.S. Supreme Ct. bar, 1965; law clk. firm Covington & Burling, Washington, 1959-62; staff atty., dep. dir. Legal Aid Agy., D.C. Fed. Pub. Defender's Office, Washington, 1962-63; asst. U.S. Atty. Dist. Md., 1963-69; 1st asst. U.S. Atty. Md., Balt., 1969—; instr. U. Md. Sch. Law, 1975—; asso. prof. law Villa Julie Coll., 1976—. Mem. exec. bd. Balt. Area council Boy Scouts Am., 1975—. Mem. Fed. (nat. circuit v.p. 1973—, permanent mem. 4th circuit conf., pres. Balt. chpt. 1973-74), Am. bar assns. Home: 6804 Hunt Court Baltimore MD 21209 Office: US Courthouse 101 W Lombard St Baltimore MD 21202 Tel (301) 539-2940

KRAMER, ROBERT, b. Davenport, Iowa, Aug. 17, 1913; A.B. cum laude, Harvard, 1935, LL.B. magna cum laude, 1938. Admitted to D.C. bar, 1938, N.Y. State bar, 1947; atty. NLRB, Washington, 1938-40, antitrust div. Dept. Justice, Washington, 1941-42; asso. firm Paul, Weiss, Wharton & Garrison, N.Y.C., 1946-47; prof. law Duke U., Durham, N.C., 1947-59; vis. prof. law Stanford (Calif.), 1950, U. Wis., Madison, 1956, U.N.C., Chapel Hill, 1957, N.Y.U., N.Y.C., 1958, Northwestern U., Evanston, Ill., 1959; asst. atty. gen. Office Legal Counsel, Washington, 1959-61; dean Nat. Law Center George Washington U., Washington, 1961—. Mem. Am. Bar Assn., Am. Law Inst., Assn. Am. Law Schs. (exec. com. 1959). Author: (with C.L.B. Lowndes) Federal Estate & Gift Taxes, 1974; editor Jour. Law and Contemporary Problems, 1947-56, Jour. Legal Edn., 1948-55, Bus. Law Rev., 1952-55. Home: 4326 36th St NW Washington DC 20008 Office: 720 20th St NW Washington DC 20052 Tel (202) 676-6288

KRAMER, RUSSELL ARNOLD, b. Maryville, Tenn., Dec. 13, 1918; B.A., Maryville Coll., 1940; postgrad. U. Tex. Law Sch., 1941; J.D., U. Mich., 1946. Admitted to Tenn. bar, 1942; practiced in Knoxville, Tenn., 1946—; mem. firm Kramer, Dye, Greenwood, Johnson, Rayson & McVeigh and predecessor firm, 1947-74; v.p., dir., gen. counsel Aluminum Co. Am., Pitts., 1974—. Bd. dirs. Maryville Coll. Mem. Am., Tenn., Knoxville bar assns. Home: 1411 Grandview Ave Pittsburgh PA 15211 Office: Alcoa Bldg Pittsburgh PA 15219*

KRAMER, TIMOTHY EUGENE, b. Cleve., Mar. 21, 1943; B.A., John Carroll U., 1965; J.D., Case Western Reserve U., 1968. Admitted to Ohio bar, 1969; law clerk Cuyahoga County Common Pleas Ct., Cleve., 1970-72, chief law clerk, 1972-73; asst. counsel Jacobs, Visconsi & Jacobs, Cleve., 1973—. Mem. Ohio State Bar Assn. Home: 1151 Brentwood Rd Cleveland Heights OH 44121 Office: 25425 Center Ridge Rd Westlake OH 44145 Tel (216) 871-4800

KRAMER, VICTOR HORSLEY, b. Cin., Feb. 8, 1913; A.B., Harvard, 1935; LL.B., Yale, 1938. Admitted to Ohio bar, 1938, D.C. bar, 1947; spl. atty., antitrust div. U.S. Dept. Justice, Washington, 1938-57; partner firm Arnold & Porter, Washington, 1958-70; atty. Center for Law and Social Policy, Washington, 1970-71; dir. Inst. for Pub. Interest Representation, Georgetown U., 1971—, prof. law, 1971—; pub. mem. Adminstrv. Conf. of U.S., 1972—; mem. bd. govs. D.C. bar, 1973-76. Author: The National Institutes of Health, a Study in Public Adminstration, 1937; (with James M. Graham) Appointments to the Regulatory Agencies, 1976; contbr. articles to profl. jours. Office: 600 New Jersey Ave NW Washington DC 20001 Tel (202) 624-8390

KRAMER, WILLIAM JOSEPH, b. Rockville Centre, N.Y., Mar. 21, 1939; B.S., Fairfield U., 1960; LL.B., Fordham U., 1963. Admitted to N.Y. State bar, 1963, D.C. bar, 1976; legal officer U.S. Marine Corps, 1964-67; asso. firm Mudge, Rose, Guthrie & Alexander, N.Y.C., 1963, 67-74, partner, 1974—; dep. village atty. Village of Massapequa Park (N.Y.), 1969-70. Mem. sch. bd. St. Joseph Sch., Garden City, N.Y., 1973-76. Mem. N.Y., D.C., Nassau County bar assns. Comments editor: Fordham Law Rev., 1962-63. Home: 15 Kensington Rd Garden City NY 11530 Office: 20 Broad St New York City NY 10005 Tel (212) 422-6767

KRAMON, JAMES MARSHALL, b. N.Y.C., Jan. 23, 1944; B.S. in Math., Carnegie-Mellon U., 1966; J.D. with honors, George Washington U., 1969; LL.M., Harvard, 1970; M.L.A., Johns Hopkins, 1976. Admitted to D.C. bar, 1969, Md. bar, 1969, U.S. Supreme Ct. bar, 1974; law clk., trial atty. tax div. Dept. Justice, Washington, 1968-69; research asso. George Washington U., 1968, cons. program of policy studies in sci. and tech., 1971; law clk. to judge U.S. Ct. Appeals, 7th Circuit, Chgo., 1970-71; asst. U.S. atty. for Dist. Md., 1971-75; partner firm Kramon & Graham, Balt., 1975—; lectr. U. Md. Sch. Law, 1977—. Mem. Am. (sect. natural resources law), Fed. (pres. elect Balt. chpt.), Md. State bar assns., Bar Assn. D.C., Bar Assn. Balt. City (com. on profl. ethics and grievances). Contbr. articles to legal jours. Home: 2014 Geist Rd Baltimore County MD 21071 Office: Kramon & Graham Sun Life Bldg Charles Center Baltimore MD 21201 Tel (301) 752-6030

KRANZ, HARRY, b. N.Y.C., Dec. 25, 1923; B.Litt., Rutgers U., 1944; J.D., Am. U., 1962, Ph.D., 1974. Admitted to Md. bar, 1962, D.C. bar, 1963, U.S. Supreme Ct. bar, 1970; reporter, editor various newspapers, N.J., 1944-47; dir. legis. and pub. relations N.J. State CIO, 1947-57; asst. to pres. UAW Internat., Detroit, 1957-59; dep. dir. Fgn. Trade Union Tng. Program, Am. U., 1959-61; asst. to asso. dir. Peace Corps, 1961-62; dir. recruitment, selection and tng. Pres.'s Study Group, Nat. Service Corps., 1962-63; adminstr. U.S. Dept. Labor, Washington, 1963—. Chmn. 3rd Ward Democratic Assn., E. Orange, N.J., 1953-57; mem. fed. adv. council Bur. Employment Security, Dept. Labor, 1951-57; recipient various gubernatorial appointments, 1949-57. Mem. D.C., Am., Md. bar assns., ACLU, Am. Soc. Pub. Adminstrn., Am. Polit. Sci. Assn., Internat. Personnel Mgmt. Assn., Indsl. Relations Research Assn., Am. Fedn. Govt. Employees, Nat. Civil Service League. Co-winner Leonard White award Am. Polit. Sci. Assn., 1975; author: The Participatory Bureaucracy: Women and Minorities in a More Representative Public Service, 1976; contbr. articles to legal jours. Home: 6527 Elgin Ln Bethesda MD 20034 Office: 601 D St NW Washington DC 20213 Tel (202) 376-6532

KRASHES, BERTRAM PHILIP, b. Haverstraw, N.Y., Mar. 29, 1931; J.D., St. John's U., N.Y.C., 1955. Admitted to N.Y. State bar, 1956, U.S. Supreme Ct. bar, 1963; individual practice law, partner firm Krashes, Ross & Gess, Spring Valley, N.Y., 1972—; dir. Spring Valley Savs. and Loan Assn., 1973—. Bd. dirs. Ramapo Indsl. Devel. Corp., Rockland County, N.Y. Mem. Rockland County (N.Y.) (pres. 1976), N.Y. State (ho. of dels.), Am. bar assns. Home: 12 Balmoral Dr New City NY 10956 Office: 52 S Main St Spring Valley NY 10977 Tel (914) 356-7080

KRASNICKI, ROGER CHARLES, b. St. Louis, Mar. 14, 1942; B.S. in Commerce, St. Louis U., 1964, J.D., 1967. Admitted to Mo. bar, 1968, U.S. Supreme Ct. bar, 1976, U.S. Tax Ct., 1976; mem. legal staff St. Louis Union Trust Co., 1967-69, asst. v.p. tax dept., 1976—; atty. IRS, from 1969 also sr. reviewing atty., group mgr., to 1975, appellate conferee, 1976. Mem. local parochial Sch. Bd., 1973-74. Mem. Mo. Bar, St. Louis Met. Bar Assn. Recipient Regional Commr's. commendation IRS, 1975, commendation U.S. Atty. of Eastern Dist. Mo., 1975. Home: 6 Crabtree Ln Lakewood Hills Pacific MO 63069 Office: 510 Locust St Saint Louis MO 63101 Tel (314) 231-9300

KRASNIEWSKI, WALTER JACOB, b. Toledo, July 22, 1929; B.S., Xavier U., Cin., 1951; J.D., U. Toledo, 1955. Admitted to Ohio bar, 1955; asst. atty. gen. State of Ohio, Toledo, 1959-63; asst. U.S. atty., Toledo, 1963-65; U.S. bankruptcy judge, Toledo, 1965—. Mem. Ohio, Lucas County, Fed., Toledo bar assns., Comml. Law League, Nat. Conf. Bankruptcy Judges. Office: 113 US Court House Toledo OH 43624 Tel (419) 259-6440

KRASNOW, C. HAROLD, b. Boston, Jan. 20, 1934; M.A., U. Scranton, 1962; J.D., Suffolk U., 1966. Admitted to Mass. bar, 1969; asso. firm Wasserman & Salter, Boston, 1969-72, Brown, Rudnick, Freed & Gesner, Boston, 1972-75; individual practice law, Boston, 1975—; ordained rabbi, 1957; rabbi, Hebrew sch. prin., 1957-69, spiritual leader Montefiroe Synagogue, Lowell, Mass., 1960-63. Mem. Brookline (Mass.) Town Meeting, 1972-75. Mem. Boston Bar Assn. Home: 77 Salisbury Rd Brookline MA 02146 Office: 15 Court Sq Boston MA 02108 Tel (617) 227-8368

KRASTIN, KARL, b. Toledo, June 29, 1910; A.B., Western Reserve U., 1931, LL.B., 1934; S.J.D., Yale, 1955. Admitted to Ohio bar, 1934; partner firm Walder and Krastin, Cleve., 1934-41; asst. prof. law, U. Fla., Gainesville, 1948-51, asso. prof., 1951-54, prof., 1954-63; dean, prof. law Univ. Toledo, 1963-76; prof. law Center for Study Law Nova U., Ft. Lauderdale, 1976—. Bd. dirs. Toledo Legal Aid Soc., 1971-76, v.p., 1975-76; bd. dirs. Ct. Diagnostic and Treatment Center, Toledo, 1971-76, Advocates for Basic Legal Equality, Toledo, 1963-76, bd. dirs. Community Relations, Toledo, 1964-68. Mem. Toledo, Ohio bar assns., Order of Coif, Soc. Benchers. Contbr. numerous articles to legal jours. Office: Center for Study Law Nova University College Ave Fort Lauderdale FL 33314 Tel (305) 587-6660

KRATCHMAN, JACK, b. N.Y.C., Oct. 12, 1926; B.S., City Coll. N.Y., 1948; M.S., N.Y. U., 1953; J.D., George Washington U., 1964. Admitted to Md. bar, 1965; asso. profl. lectr. Nat. Law Center, George Washington U., Washington, 1966-75; dep. dir. office congressional and pub. affairs NSF, 1975-77; mem. staff ERDA, Washington, 1977—. Home: 11612 Greelane Dr Potomac MD 20854 Office: US Energy Devel Adminstrn Washington DC 20545 Tel (301) 353-4493

KRATHEN, DAVID HOWARD, b. Phila., Nov. 17, 1946; B.B.A., U. Miami, 1969, J.D., 1972. Admitted to Fla. bar, 1972, D.C. bar, 1972, U.S. Supreme Ct. bar, 1976; atty., advisor ICC, Washington, 1972-73; asst. pub. defender Ft. Lauderdale (Fla.), 1973-74; partner firm Glass, Krathen, Rastatter Stark & Tarlowe, profl. assn., Ft. Lauderdale, 1974—. Mem. Fed., Am. bar assns., Assn. Trial Lawyers Am., Fla. Bar (workmen's compensation and rules coms.), Fla. Acad. Trial Lawyers, Soc. Bar and Gavel, Delta Theta Phi. Office: 524 S Andrews Ave Fort Lauderdale FL 33301 Tel (305) 463-2965

KRATOCHVIL, OTTO, b. Cicero, Ill., Apr. 10, 1919; J.D., La. State U., 1950; LL.M., George Washington U., 1959. Admitted to La. bar, 1950, Kans. bar, 1970; research atty. La. State U., Baton Rouge, 1950-51; judge advocate USAF, 1951-69; prof. law Washburn U., Topeka, 1969—; asst. prof. law USAF Acad., 1960-64; lectr. mil. law Air Command and Staff Coll., Maxwell AFB, Ala., 1965-68. Council chmn. Boy Scouts Am., 1956-60; mem. Montgomery (Ala.) Sch. Bd., bd. dirs. Consumer Credit Counseling Service, Montgomery. Mem. Am., Fed., Kans. bar assns., Phi Delta Phi. Contbr. articles to profl. jours. Home: 1616 Mac Vicar Topeka KS 66604 Office: Sch Law Washburn U Topeka KS 66621 Tel (913) 925-6660

KRATT, PETER GEORGE, b. Lorain, Ohio, Mar. 7, 1940; B.A., Miami U., Oxford, Ohio, 1962; J.D., Case Western Res. U., 1966. Admitted to Ohio bar, 1966; atty., asso. counsel Cleve. Trust Co., Cleve., 1966—. Mem. Cleve. Bar Assn. Home: 31760 Schwartz Rd Avon OH 44011 Office: Cleveland Trust Company Cleveland OH 44101 Tel (216) 687-5517

KRAUSE, CHARLES FREDRICK, b. Chgo., Aug. 28, 1931; B.A., Valparaiso U., 1957; LL.B., Rutgers U., 1960. Admitted to N.Y. bar, 1961, D.C. bar, 1970, U.S. Supreme Ct. bar, 1970; mem. firm Speiser & Krause, N.Y.C., 1961—; dir., sec. Hydrophilics Internat.; dir. Columbian Mut. Life Ins. Co. Mem. Fed., N.Y., Am. (chmn. aviation com. 1974-76), D.C. bar assns. Mem. editorial bd. N.Y. State Bar Journal, 1973—. Office: 200 Park Ave New York City NY 10017 Tel (212) 661-0011

KRAUT, ROSE BAUM, b. N.Y.C., Dec. 31, 1908; B.S., N.Y. U., 1931; J.D., 1936. Admitted to N.Y. bar, 1936, U.S. Supreme Ct. bar, 1963; individual practice, N.Y.C., 1936-40; editor tax dept. Research Inst. Am., N.Y.C., 1936-40; individual practice law, Poughkeepsie, N.Y., 1950—; organizer, vol. gen. counsel Dutchess County Legal Aid Soc., 1954-60. Pres., N.Y. State Tb Assn., 1965-69, Vassar Temple Sisterhood, 1954-58; v.p. Dutchess County League Women Voters, 1960-62; bd. dirs. Vassar Hosp. Women's Aux., 1967-75, Jewish Center Aux., 1950-52. Mem. Am. (legal aid and referrel coms.), N.Y. State (mem. legal aid, referral and admission to bar coms.), N.Y.C., Dutchess County bar assns., Internat. Fedn. Women Lawyers, Lung Assn. N.Y. State. Recipient award for Outstanding Service in Def. of Civil Liberties, N.Y. State Bar Assn., Assn. Bar of N.Y.C. and N.Y. County Lawyers Assn., 1961. Home: 6 Wilbur Ct Poughkeepsie NY 12601 Office: 256 Main Mall Poughkeepsie NY 12601 Tel (914) 454-3210

KRAVETS, LEONARD, b. Chgo., Dec. 25, 1929; B.S., U. Ill., 1951; J.D., U. Mich., 1954. Admitted to Ill. bar, 1954; partner firm Crane & Kravets, Chgo., 1954—; town atty. Town of Norwood Park (Ill.), 1975—. Mem. Chgo., Ill. bar assns., Delta Theta Phi. Office: 100 W Monroe St Chicago IL 60603

KRAVITCH, PHYLLIS, b. Savannah, Ga., Aug. 23, 1920; A.B., Goucher Coll., 1941; LL.B., U. Pa., 1943. Admitted to Ga. bar, 1944, Fed. bar, 1944, U.S. Supreme Ct. bar, 1948; individual practice law, Chatham County, Ga., 1944—; judge superior ct. Eastern Judicial Circuit Ga., Savannah, 1977—; mem. Chatham County Sch. Bd., 1949-55. Mem. Savannah (pres. 1975), Am. bar assns., State Bar Ga., Am. Judicature Soc., Assn. Trial Lawyers Am. Home: 30 E 53d St Savannah GA 31405 Office: Chatham County Ct House Savannah GA 31402 Tel (912) 234-5326

KRAVITT, JASON HARRIS PAPERNO, b. Chgo., Jan. 19, 1948; A.B., Johns Hopkins, 1969; J.D., Harvard, 1972; diploma in comparative legal studies Cambridge (Eng.) U., 1973. Admitted to Ill. bar, 1973; asso. firm Mayer, Brown & Platt, Chgo., 1973—. Mem. men's council Mus. Contemporary Art, Chgo. Mem. Chgo. Council Lawyers. Contbr. article to legal jour. Home: 2143 N Hudson St Chicago IL 60614 Office: 231 S LaSalle St Chicago IL 60604 Tel (312) 782-0600

KRAWOOD, BENJAMIN, b. Detroit, Mar. 8, 1918; B.S. in Accounting, Wayne State U., 1946, J.D., 1960, LL.M. in Taxation, 1964. Accountant, Price-Waterhouse & Co., Detroit, 1945-46, Charles K. Harris & Co., Detroit 1947-50; pvt. practice accounting, Detroit, 1951-60; admitted to Mich. bar, 1961; individual practice law, taxation and accounting, 1961—; instr. Wayne State U., 1964-74; lectr. Eastern Mich. U., 1975—. Mem. Mich. State Bar Assn., Mich. Assn. C.P.A.'s. C.P.A., Mich. Contbr. articles on taxation to profl. jours. Office: 1515 E Eleven Mile Rd Royal Oak MI 48067 Tel (313) 545-6030

KREAGER, DAVID JAY, JR., b. Tulsa, Apr. 28, 1929; B.A., Tex. A. and M. U., 1950; J.D., U. Tex., 1953. Admitted to Tex. bar, 1953, U.S. Supreme Ct. bar, 1972; partner firm Orgain, Bell & Tucker, Beaumont, Tex., 1953—; dir. State Bar Tex., 1973-76, vice chmn. Tex. Bar Found., 1975-76. Dir. Beaumont Civil Service Commn., 1962-70. Mem. Fedn. Ins. Counsel, Internat. Assn. Ins. Counsel, Tex. Assn. Ins. Counsel, Trial Attys. Am., Am. Bar Assn. Home: 1245 Nottingham Lane Beaumont TX 77706 Office: 4th Floor Beaumont Savings Bldg Beaumont TX 77701 Tel (713) 838-6412

KREAMER, ROBERT ALBERT, b. Jackson, Miss., July 26, 1945; B.A. in Philosophy, Washington Coll., 1968; J.D., Suffolk U., 1971. Admitted to Mass. bar, 1971, Md. bar, 1972; asst. county atty. Harford County (Md.), 1973-74, dep. county atty., 1974—; partner firm Boutin Landbeck & Kreamer, Aberdeen, Md., 1976—. Mem. Am., Md., Mass. bar assns. Home: 701 Beards Hill Rd Aberdeen MD 21001 Office: 105 W Belair Ave Aberdeen MD 21001 Tel (301) 274-6636

KREBS, SCHUYLER ASHER, b. Los Angeles, Apr. 5, 1947; A.A., Los Angeles Valley Coll., 1967; B.A., U. Calif., Los Angeles, 1969; J.D., U. Calif., Davis, 1972. Admitted to Calif. bar, 1972; law clk. to judge U.S. Ct. Appeals, 1972-73; lt. JAGC, U.S. Navy, 1974-77; mem. firm McCutchen, Doyle, Brown & Enersen, San Francisco, 1977—. Mem. Assn. Am. Trial Lawyers, Order of Coif. Recipient Am. Jurisprudence award, 1971. Home: 639 B Santa Clara Ave Alameda CA 94501 Office: San Francisco CA

KREBS, WILLIAM DOUGLAS, b. Milw., May 28, 1917; A.B., Ripon Coll., 1938, B.B.A., U. Wis., 1947, J.D., 1947. Admitted to Wis. bar, 1947, N.Y. bar, 1948; asso. firm Howard R. Sanford, Potsdam, N.Y., 1947-48; partner firm Sanford & Krebs, Potsdam, 1948-49; individual practice law, Potsdam, 1949-74; partner firm William D. Krebs P.C., and predecessors, Potsdam, 1974—. Mem. St. Lawrence County Magistrates Assn. (pres. 1971-72). Recipient St. Lawrence County Council Boy Scouts Am. Silver Beaver award, 1963. Home: 15 Hillcrest Dr Potsdam NY 13676 Office: 75 Market St Potsdam NY 13676 Tel (315) 265-9040

KREIMER, HILLARD, b. Pitts., Dec. 28, 1921; B.S., U. Pitts., 1942; LL.B., Yale, 1949. Admitted to Pa. bar, 1950; partner firm McCrady, Kreimer, Ravick & Bonistalli and predecessors, Pitts., 1953—; labor arbitrator, 1960—. Trustee Am. Jewish Com., Pitts., 1965—; chmn. law explorer post Boy Scouts Am., 1967-72; chmn. Pitts. Jewish Community Relations Com., 1967-69; v.p., Squirrel Hill Urban Coalition, 1972—. Mem. Am., Pa., Allegheny County bar assns., Am. Judicature Soc, Nat. Acad. of Arbitrators, Am. Arbitration Assn., Fed., Pa. Mediation Service (arbitration panel). Home: 115 Lang Ct Pittsburgh PA 15208 Office: 1617 Frick Bldg 437 Grant St Pittsburgh PA 15219 Tel (412) 261-2640

KREINDLER, DONALD L., b. N.Y.C., Jan. 28, 1931; A.B., Bklyn. Coll., 1952; LL.B., Columbia U., 1952. Admitted to N.Y. bar, 1956, U.S. Supreme Ct. bar, 1975; asso. firm Otterbourg, Steindler, Houston & Rosen, N.Y.C., 1956-70, firm Kreindler, Relkin & Goldberg, N.Y.C., 1970—. Bd. govs. textile sect. N.Y. Bd. Trade, 1976—. Mem. Lawyers Assn. Textile Industry (bd. govs. 1966—), Am., N.Y. State bar assns., N.Y. County Lawyers Assn., Am. Arbitration Assn. (arbitrator 1966—). Contbr. articles to legal jours. Office: 500 Fifth Ave New York City NY 10036 Tel (212) 594-9600

KREINDLER, HARRY E., b. Krakow, Austria, Nov. 3, 1896; A.B., N.Y. U., 1918, LL.B., 1918. Admitted to N.Y. State bar, 1920; partner firm Kreindler & Kreindler, N.Y.C. Mem. N.Y. State Bar Assn., N.Y. County Lawyers Assn., N.Y. State Met. trial lawyers assns. Home: 75 Central Park W New York City NY 10023 Office: 99 Park Ave New York City NY 10016 Tel (212) 687-8181

KREINDLER, LEE STANLEY, b. N.Y.C., Mar. 11, 1924; A.B., Dartmouth Coll., 1945; LL.B., Harvard U., 1949. Admitted to N.Y. bar, 1949; partner firm Kreindler & Kreindler, N.Y.C., 1949—. Mem. Am. (chmn. aviation and space law com.), N.Y., Fed. bar assns., Assn. Bar City N.Y., World Assn. Lawyers, Am., Met. trial lawyers assns., N.Y. County Lawyers Assn., Internat. Acad. Trial Lawyers (pres. 1976-77). Author: Aviation Accident Law, 1963. Contbr. monthly column to profl. jours. Home: 25 McKesson Hill Rd Chappaqua NY 10514 Office: 99 Park Ave New York City NY 10016 Tel (212) 687-8181

KREINDLER, ROBERT STANTON, b. N.Y.C., Mar. 28, 1927; student Bklyn. Coll., 1944-47-48; LL.B., Bklyn. Law Sch., 1950. Admitted to N.Y. bar, 1951, U.S. Supreme Ct. bar, 1955; partner firm Kreindler & Winant, N.Y.C., 1951-57; asst. U.S. atty. Eastern Dist. N.Y., 1957-61, chief sect. organized crime and racketeering, 1959-60, chief criminal div., 1961; individual practice law, N.Y.C., 1962-66, 66-68; partner firm Kreindler & Komissaroff, N.Y.C., 1962-66; judge N.Y.C. Civil Ct., 1966, N.Y.C. Criminal Ct., 1969—; acting justice N.Y. Supreme Ct. in Kings County, 1973—; arbitrator Nat. Arbitration Assn., 1966-68. Mem. Am., Bklyn. bar assns. Home: 820 Ocean Pkwy Brooklyn NY 11230 Office: Supreme Ct Justices Chambers Civic Centre Brooklyn NY 11201 Tel (212) 643-3187

KREKSTEIN, MICHAEL HARRY, b. Phila., Mar. 29, 1945; B.S., U. Pa., 1968; J.D., Temple U., 1971. Admitted to Pa. bar, 1971, Fla. bar, 1976; mem. firm Krekstein, Shapiro, Bressler & Wolfson, Phila., 1971—. Mem. Phila., Pa., Am., Fla. bar assns. Editor: Temple Law Quar., 1970-71. Office: 1845 Walnut St Philadelphia PA 19103 Tel (215) 561-6400

KRELL, BRUCE EDWARD, b. N.Y.C., Apr. 28, 1943; A.B., Fla. State U., 1965; J.D., John Marshall Sch. Law, 1971. Admitted to Iowa bar, 1971, Calif. bar, 1972; instr. bus. law Chgo. Career Coll., 1970; law clk. to Hon. U.S. Schwartz, Ill. Appellate Ct., Chgo., 1971-72; asso. firm Belli, Ashe, Ellison & Choulos, San Francisco, 1972; individual practice law, San Francisco, 1972—; asso. prof. law Lincoln U., San Francisco, 1972—. Bd. dirs. ACLU, San Francisco, 1973-74, San Francisco Neighborhood Legal Assistance Found., 1972—. Mem. San Francisco, Calif., Iowa bar assns., Lawyers Club San Francisco, Lawyers Guild, Gavel Soc. Author: Evidence Through Video Tape at Trial, 1971; editor: John Marshall Law Rev., 1971. Home: 187 San Marcos Ave San Francisco CA 94116 Office: 345 Grove St San Francisco CA 94102 Tel (415) 861-4414

KRENGEL, HERBERT BERNHARDT, b. St. Paul, Aug. 31, 1912; B.A., U. Minn., 1934; LL.B., St. Paul Coll. Law, 1942. Admitted to Minn. bar, 1942; with law dept. No. Pacific Ry. Co., 1945-48, atty. to gen. solicitor, 1948-70; asst. v.p., gen. solicitor Burlington No., Inc., St. Paul, 1970-74, gen. counsel, 1974—. Mem. Am., Minn., Ramsey County bar assns. Home: 246 W Marie Ave West Saint Paul MN 55118 Office: 176 E 5th St Saint Paul MN 55101 Tel (612) 298-3279

KRENTS, HAROLD ELIOT, b. N.Y.C., Nov. 5, 1944; B.A. cum laude, Harvard, 1967, J.D., 1970; diploma in law Oxford (Eng.) U., 1974. Admitted to N.Y. bar, 1970, D.C. bar, 1972; atty. bus. affairs br. legal dept. ABC, 1970-71; asso. firm Surrey, Karasik and Morse, Washington, 1971—; legal counsel Mainstream, Inc., 1975—. Mem. Am., D.C. bar assns. Author: To Race the Wind, 1972. Office: 1156 15th St NW Washington DC 20005 Tel (202) 331-4077

KRENZLER, ALVIN I., b. Chgo., Apr. 8, 1921; A.B., Case Western Res. U., 1946, LL.B., 1948; LL.M., Georgetown U., 1963. Admitted to Ohio bar, 1948; practiced in Cleve., 1948-68; judge Cuyahoga County (Ohio) Ct. Common Pleas, 1968-70, Ohio Ct. Appeals, Cleve., 1970—; counsel, dir. Ohio Narcotics Investigation, 1953-55; asst. atty. gen. State of Ohio, 1951-56; trial atty. office chief counsel IRS, Washington, 1960-63. Chmn., Cuyahoga County Bd. Mental Retardation, 1967-70; trustee Cleve. State U., 1967-70, Mt. Sinai Hosp., Cleve., 1973—; chmn. Ohio Criminal Justice Supervisory Commn., 1975—. Mem. Am., Greater Cleve., Cuyahoga County, Fed. bar assns. Home: 24550 Meldon Blvd Beachwood OH 44122 Office: 1 Lakeside Ave Cleveland OH 44113 Tel (216) 621-3285

KRESS, JACK MANUEL, b. N.Y.C., July 5, 1943; A.B., Columbia U., 1965, J.D., 1968; D. Criminology (Ford Found. fellow), Cambridge (Eng.) U., 1969. Admitted to N.Y. State bar, 1969; contract aide AEC, N.Y.C., 1964-65; asst. dist. atty. N.Y. County, 1969-73; asst. prof. law grad sch. criminal justice State U. N.Y., Albany, 1973—; dir. Sentencing Guidelines Research Project, 1974—; sec. Criminal Justice Research Center, 1975—; cons. in field. Mem. Am. Bar Assn., Am. Judicature Soc., Nat. Dist. Attys. Assn. Contbr. articles in field to profl. jours. and texts. Home: 301 Parkview Dr Schenectady NY 12303 Office: 1400 Washington Ave Albany NY 12222 Tel (518) 457-8261

KRESS, RALPH HERBERT, b. N.Y.C., Jan. 27, 1933; B.A., N.Y. U., 1953, J.D., 1956, LL.M., 1957. Admitted to N.Y. bar, 1957, U.S. Supreme Ct. bar, 1961; legal asst. atty. advisor to Solicitor for the Port of N.Y., U.S. Treasury Dept., 1956-57; spl. counsel U.S. Ho. Reps., 1964-73; individual practice law, Long Island City, N.Y., 1957—; referee, arbitrator N.Y.C. Civil Ct., 1964—; conf. officer N.Y.C. Family Ct., 1976—; co-chmn. State N.Y. Com. for Presl. Candidate. Pres., dir. Queensboro Soc. for the Prevention of Cruelty to Children; nat. v.p. Muscular Dystrophy Assns. Am., 1975—; dirs. United Cerebral Palsy, 1973-75; mem. Met. Mus. of Art, Mus. Natural History, UN Assn. Mem. Inst. Jud. Adminstrn., Am. Judges Assn., Nat. Council Juvenile Ct. Judges, Am., N.Y. State, Queens County bar assns., Assn. Bar City N.Y., Am. Judicature Soc., N.Y. State Trial Lawyers Assn., Long Island City Lawyers Club, m. Arbitration Assn. Office: 37-09 30th Ave Long Island City NY 11103 Tel (212) 721-8700

KRETCHMER, JEROME, b. N.Y.C., Sept. 15, 1934; B.A., N.Y. U., 1955; LL.B., Columbia U., 1958. Admitted to N.Y. bar, 1959; asso. Ralph Bernstein, 1959-64; partner firm Olshan, Grundman, Frome & Kretchmer, N.Y.C., 1965-75; of counsel firm Gates & Laber, N.Y.C., 1976—; mem. assembly State of N.Y., 1963-70; environ. protection adminstr. City of N.Y., 1970-73; counsel minority N.Y. State Senate, 1975—. Mem. Bar Assn. State N.Y. Home: 262 Central Park W St New York City NY 10024 Office: 1345 Ave of Americas New York City NY 10019 Tel (212) 757-7220

KRETZER, ALAN R., b. Youngstown, Ohio, July 28, 1947; A.B., Ohio U., 1965; J.D., Case Western Res. U., 1968. Admitted to Ohio bar, 1968; asst. to dean Ohio U., 1968-69; asso. firm Green, Schiavani, Murphy & Haines, Youngstown, 1970-73; prin. firm Alan R. Kretzer Co. and partner firm Burdman, Gilliland, Fleck & Mostov, Youngstown, 1973—; chmn. Ohio Com. on Crime and Delinquency, Columbus, 1973-76; pres. bd. dirs. Mahoning County (Ohio) Pub. Defender, 1973-76. Mem. exec. bd., policy bd. Ohio Citizens Council, Columbus, 1973-76; mem. Gov. Ohio Adv. Com. on Corrections and Rehab. in Ohio, 1974-75; mem. exec. com., precinct committeeman Mahoning County Democratic Party. Mem. Ohio, Mahoning County, Am. bar assns., Mahoning County Community Corrections Assn. Home: 2121 Elm St Youngstown OH 44505 Office: 1200 Wick St Youngstown OH 44503 Tel (216) 747-8621

KRETZER, IRWIN I., b. Bobroisk, Russia, Aug. 15, 1909; LL.B., Youngstown State U., 1934, J.D., 1934. Admitted to Ohio bar, 1935, referee Ct. of Common Pleas, 1961—; chief prosecutor City of Youngstown (Ohio). Pres. Temple Emanu-El, Youngstown, pres. Youngstown Zionist Dist. and Mahoning Lodge B'nai B'rith. Mem. Ohio State, Mahoning County bar assns. Home: 465 Redondo Rd Youngstown OH 44504 Office: 711 Union Nat Bank Bldg Youngstown OH 44503

KREUTZ, WILLIAM LEWIS, b. Cin., Jan. 12, 1923; student Syracuse U., 1942-43, U. Mexico, 1947; B.S., Northwestern U., 1948; LL.B., Case-Western Res. U., Cleve., 1951. Admitted to Ohio bar, 1951; asso. firm Fuller, Harrington & Seney, Toledo, 1953-59; labor counsel Owens-Corning Fiberglas Corp., Toledo, 1959-63, dir. labor relations, 1963-68, sr. counsel, 1969, spl. counsel, 1970—. Pres. Vol. Bur. Toledo, 1964-66, Community Planning Council Northwestern Ohio, 1968-72; bd. dirs. Community Chest Northwestern Ohio, 1970-73. Mem. Am., Toledo bar assns. Home: 3904 W Bancroft St Toledo OH 43606 Office: Fiberglas Tower Toledo OH 43659 Tel (419) 248-8220

KRIEG, GARELD FREDERICK, b. Billings, Mont., Sept. 28, 1930; B.A., Stanford, 1952; J.D., U. Mont., 1957. Admitted to Mont. bar, 1957; asso. firm Crowley, Haughey, Hanson, Toole & Dietrich, Billings, 1957-67, partner, 1967—. Chmn. Billings Bd. Adjustment, 1965-76. Mem. Am., Mont., Yellowstone County (Mont.) bar assns. Office: 500 Electric Bldg Billings MT 59102 Tel (406) 252-3441

KRIER, ALAN RALPH, b. Bklyn., Feb. 24, 1943; B.A., Pa. State U., 1964; J.D., Dickinson Sch. Law, 1967. Admitted to Pa. bar, 1967; partner firm Jubelirer, Carothers, Krier & Halpern, and predecessors, Altoona, Pa., 1967—; solicitor Bellwood-Antis Sch. Dist., Bellwood, Pa., 1969—, Borough of Bellwood (Pa.), 1969—. Mem. Am., Pa. trial lawyers assns., Pa. Borough Solicitors Assn. Bd. editors Dickinson Law Rev., 1965-67. Home: 3300 W Chestnut Ave Altoona PA 16601 Office: 221 Central Trust Bldg Altoona PA 16601 Tel (814) 943-1149

KRIGBAUM, MARY KATHRYN, b. Ithaca, N.Y., Jan. 11, 1950; B.A., Northwestern U., 1971, J.D., 1974; student U. Munich, W. Ger., 1969-70. Admitted to Ill. bar, 1974; asso. firm Aaron, Aaron, Schimberg & Hess, Chog., 1974—. Mem. Am., Ill., Chgo. bar assns. Office: 1 1st National Plaza Chicago IL 60603 Tel (312) 787-2860

KRINSKY, MARK PETER, b. St. Paul, Apr. 2, 1942; B.A., Yale, 1964; J.D., U. Calif., 1967; LL.M., N.Y. U., 1968. Admitted to Calif. bar, 1968, N.Y. bar, 1969; asso. firm Breed, Abbott & Morgan, N.Y.C., 1968-70, Cooley, Godward, Castro, Huddleson & Tatum, San Francisco, 1970-73; partner firm Burden, Reis, Aiken & Krinsky, San Francisco, 1974—. Mem. Calif., San Francisco bar assns., San Francisco Barristers Club. Home: 47 Telegraph Pl San Francisco CA 94133 Office: 451 Jackson St San Francisco CA 94111 Tel (415) 421-0404

KRISHER, RALPH EDWARD, JR., b. Dayton, Ohio, Jan. 7, 1938; Mech. Engr., U. Cin., 1962; J.D., George Washington U., 1966. Admitted to D.C. bar, 1966, Ind. bar, 1968; patent examiner U.S. Patent Office, Washington, 1962-66; patent counsel Gen. Electric Co., Ft. Wayne, Ind., 1966-67, 69—; patent counsel C.T.S. Corp., Elkhart, Ind., 1967-69. Mem. D.C., Ind. State bar assns. Office: 1635 Broadway St Fort Wayne IN 46804 Tel (219) 743-7431 ext 3540

KRISLOV, MOSES, b. Cleve., July 14, 1924; A.B., Adelbert Coll. Western Res. U., 1948, LL.B., Case Western Res. U., 1950, J.D., 1968. Admitted to Ohio bar, 1950, U.S. Supreme Ct. bar, 1963, Ky. bar, 1969, U.S. Ct. Appeals, U.S. Dist. Ct.; individual practice law, Cleve., 1950—; instr. law Cleve. Marshall Law Sch., 1952; law dir. City of Brunswick, 1972; govt. appeal agt. Selective Service System, 1954-69; state chmn. Am. Vets. Com., Ohio, 1962; chmn. New London Hosp., 1974-77. Mem. Am., Ohio State, Cleve., Cuyahoga bar assns. Home: 3741 Lily Ct Brunswick OH 44201 Office: 800 Engrs Bldg Cleveland OH 44114 Tel (216) 621-3532

KRISS, RONALD A., b. N.Y.C., Oct. 11, 1946; B.S., Wharton Sch., 1968; J.D., U. Pa., 1971. Admitted to N.Y. bar, 1972; asso. firm Dewey, Ballantine, Bushby, Palmer & Wood, N.Y.C., 1971—. Mem. Am. Bar Assn. Home: 21 Quintree Ln Melville NY 11746 Office: 140 Broadway New York City NY 10005 Tel (212) 344-8000

KRIVOSHIA, ELI, JR., b. Midland, Pa., Apr. 20, 1935; B.A., U. Pitts., 1957; LL.B., Harvard, 1960. Admitted to Pa. bar, 1961; asso. firm Thorp, Reed & Armstrong, Pitts., 1960-69, partner, 1970—; dir. Delray Connecting R.R. Mem. Allegheny County, Pa., Am. bar assns. Office: 2900 Grant Bldg Pittsburgh PA 15219 Tel (412) 288-7751

KROEGER, HARRY WILLIAM, b. St. Louis, Dec. 10, 1897; A.B., Washington U., 1919, LL.B., 1922; LL.M., Columbia, 1923. Admitted to Mo. bar, 1922; asso. firm Nagel and Kirby, 1923-38, partner firm, 1938-45; partner firm Shepley, Kroeger, Fisse & Ingamells, St. Louis, 1945-71; individual practice law, St. Louis, 1971—; dir. Mallinckrodt, Inc., St. Louis. Mem. Am., Law Inst., Am. Bar Assn., Mo. Bar, Bar Assn. Met. St. Louis. Contbr. articles in field to profl. jours. Home: 6315 Alexander Dr Clayton MO 63105 Office: 720 Olive St Saint Louis MO 63101 Tel (314) 231-4255

KROEMER, JOHN ALBERT, b. Macon, Ga., Nov. 13, 1943; B.Indsl. Engring., Ga. Inst. Tech., 1966; J.D. with honors, U. Conn., 1970. Admitted to Conn. bar, 1970, Ga. bar, 1971; trial atty. Atlanta field office, antitrust div. Dept. Justice, 1970-75, Dallas field office, 1975—; lectr. in law Ga. State U., 1971-74, So. Meth. U., 1976—. Mem. Am., Ga. bar assns. Office: 1100 Commerce St Dallas TX 75242 Tel (214) 749-7059

KROGSTAD, L. KENNETH, b. Huntington Park, Calif., Apr. 14, 1945; B.B.A., U. Miss., 1967, J.D., 1971. Admitted to Miss. bar, 1971; since practiced in Jackson and Gulfport, Miss., asso. firm Daniel, Coker, Horton, Bell & Dukes, 1971-74, partner firm Eaton, Cottrell, Galloway & Lang, 1974-76, partner firm Bryant & Stennis, 1976—; lectr. Lutheran Theological Seminary, Columbus Ohio. Bd. dirs. ARC, Jackson, Miss. 1972; area chmn. United Way Gulfport 1974; pres. Bethel Lutheran Church Biloxi, Miss., 1974. Mem. Gulf Coast Law Inst. (chmn. 1976—), Am. (resolutions com. 1976—), Miss. State, Harrison County (pres. 1976—) bar assns., Phi Delta Phi. Home: 211 Southern Circle Gulfport MS 39501 Office: 2510 16th St Gulfport MS 39501 Tel (601) 863-6101

KROLL, MARTIN NEIL, b. N.Y.C., Nov. 30, 1937; B.A., Cornell U., 1959; J.D., U. Pa., 1963. Admitted to N.Y. bar, 1964; asso. firm Antuso & Kroll, 1963-67; partner firm Moss, Rose & Kroll, N.Y.C., 1967-69; sr. partner firm Kroll, Levy, Baron & Feinstein, P.C., N.Y.C., 1969—; receiver Chrysler Bldg. and Chrysler Bldg. East, N.Y.C., 1975—. Pres. Solomon Schechter Day Sch. of Nassau County (N.Y.), 1970-73; mem. Nassau County Republican Com., 1974—. Mem. Am. N.Y. State bar assns., Assn. Bar Nassau County, Jewish Lawyers Assn. Office: 600 Fifth Ave New York City NY 10020 Tel (212) 489-6220

KROLL, MILTON PAUL, b. Paterson, N.J., Feb. 6, 1914; B.A., W.Va. U., 1934; J.D., Harvard U., 1937. Admitted to N.J. bar, 1938, D.C. bar, 1948, U.S. Supreme Ct. bar, 1973; mem. legal staff SEC, 1938-39, asst. gen. counsel, Washington, 1948-52, asso. gen. counsel, 1952-53; individual practice law, Washington, 1953-61; partner firm Freedman, Levy, Kroll & Simonds, Washington, 1961—; lectr. law George Washington U., 1952-59; cons. fed. securities code project Am. Law Inst., 1969—. Mem. Am., D.C., Fed. bar assns., Am. Law Assn., Phi Beta Kappa. Contbr. articles to legal jours. Home: 3411 Woolsey Dr Chevy Chase MD 20015 Office: 1730 K St NW Washington DC 20006 Tel (202) 331-8550

KROLL, SAMUEL ROBERT, b. Bklyn., June 4, 1934; B.A., Hofstra Coll., 1955; LL.B., Bklyn. Law Sch., 1958. Admitted to N.Y. State bar, 1958, U.S. Supreme Ct. bar, 1963; individual practice law, Merrick, N.Y., 1968—; partner firm Medowar & Kroll, Merrick, 1970. Pres. Merrick Jewish Centre, 1974-76; bd. dirs. Rapport of Merricks and Bellmores, 1969-73. Mem. Bar Assn. Nassau County, N.Y. State Assn. Trial Lawyers, Jewish Lawyers Assn., Lawyers Square Club, Nassau-Suffolk Trial Lawyers Assn., Nassau Lawyers Assn., Merrick C. of C. Home: 2077 Illona Ln Merrick NY 11566 Office: 1808 W Merrick Rd Merrick NY 11566 Tel (516) 378-3051

KROM, DAVID B., b. Marshfield, Wis., Apr. 25, 1931; B.S. in Polit. Sci., U. Wis., 1961; LL.B., U. Ariz., 1965; LL.M. in Internat. Law, So. Meth. U., 1971. Admitted to Ariz. bar, 1965; dep. county atty. Maricopa County (Ariz.), Phoenix, 1965-66, 72—; partner firm Wolfram & Krom, Phoenix, 1967-69; asso. firm Stewart & Florence, Phoenix, 1971-72; mem. Ariz. Appellate Handbook Project. Treas., Ariz. Young Audiences, Phoenix, 1972-73. Mem. State Bar Ariz., Maricopa County, Am., Inter-Am. bar assns., Am. Soc. Internat. Law, Am. Soc. Pub. Adminstrn. Contbr. articles to legal jours. Home: 5536 N Homestead Ln Paradise Valley AZ 85253 Office: 400 Superior Court Bldg 101 W Jefferson St Phoenix AZ 85003 Tel (602) 262-3431

KRONFELD, EDWIN, b. N.Y.C., June 28, 1931; LL.B., Harvard U., 1958; LL.M., Georgetown U., 1962. Admitted to N.Y. State bar, 1958, D.C. bar, 1961; partner firm Morgan, Lewis & Bockius, Washington, 1969—; adj. prof. law Georgetown U. Law Center, D.C., 1969—. Mem. Am. (fed. regulation of securities com., sec. on corp. banking and bus. law, utility fin. com. sec. on pub. utility law, part-time tchr. com. sec. on legal edn. and admissions to bar), Fed. (exec. council, securities law com.), D.C. bar assns. Home: 6108 Kennedy Dr Chevy Chase MD 20015 Office: 1800 M St NW Washington DC 20036 Tel (202) 872-5020

KRONINGER, ROBERT HENRY, b. Whittier, Calif., Oct. 29, 1923; A.B. in Psychology, U. Calif., Berkeley, 1944. B.S. in Bus. Adminstrn., 1945, J.D., Boalt Hall, 1948. Psychologist War Dept., Oakland, Calif., 1945-46; admitted to Calif. bar, 1948; law clk. to Chief Justice Calif. Supreme Ct., 1948-50; practiced in Oakland, 1950-59; judge Oakland (Calif.) Municipal Ct., 1959-63, Calif. Superior Ct., 1963—; lectr. Boalt Hall U. Calif.; speaker on law, Calif. history, pub. and private welfare. Past pres. Calif. Assn. Health and Welfare, Alameda County Family Service Bur; bd. dirs. Oakland Museums Assn. Author: Sarah and the Senator (Calif. award Commonwealth Club, 1st prize State Bar Calif.) 1964; contbg. author legal texts, including: California Appellate Practice, 1964, California Civil Procedure Before Trial, others. Named Citizen of Year AFL-CIO. Office: 1225 Fallon St Oakland CA 94612 Tel (415) 874-6586

KRONMILLER, BERT WILSON, b. Mt. Erie, Ill., Jan. 6, 1904; J.D., Creighton U., 1931. Admitted to Nebr. bar, 1931, Mont. bar, 1931; city atty., Hardin, Mont., 1933-38, county atty., Big Horn County, Mont., 1939-54; pvt. practice law, Hardin, Mont., 1931—. Spl. asst. atty. gen., Mont., 1945-46. Home: 618 W 2d St Hardin MT 59034 Office: 314 N Custer St Hardin MT 59034

KROPITZER, HAROLD, b. N.Y.C., Aug. 26, 1923; B.S., Coll. City N.Y., 1943; LL.B., Boston U., 1949. Admitted to Oreg. bar, 1950, U.S. Supreme Ct. bar, 1971; with Bonneville Power Adminstrn., Dept. Interior, 1949—, contracts counsel, 1962-64, asst. to power mgr., 1964-67, exec. asst. to adminstr., Portland, Oreg., 1967—. Mem. Oreg. State Bar, Fed. Bar Assn., Electric Club of Oreg. Recipient Outstanding Performance award Bonneville Power Adminstrn.; author: Handbook of Power Sales and Service Policy, 1951; Annotations of the Columbia River Treaty and Related Documents, 1965; The Hanford Project: A Legislative History, 1967. Home: 3025 NW Monte Vista Terr Portland OR 97210 Office: PO Box 3621 Portland OR 97208 Tel (503) 234-3361

KROSTUE, SIGURD WINFIELD, b. Farmington, Wis., Feb. 14, 1915; LL.B., U. Wis., 1939. Admitted to Wis. bar, 1940; asso. with Wendell McHenry, Waupaca, Wis., 1940-41; individual practice law New London, Wis., 1946—; pres. New London Nat. Bank, 1972-75, dir., 1963-75. Mayor, New London, 1968-72, city atty., 1948-68. Mem. Waupaca County, Wis. bar assns. Recipient Distinguished Service award U.S. Jaycees, 1967, New London Outstanding Citizen award, 1977. Home: 412 W Beacon Ave New London WI 54961 Office: 120 1/2 N Water St New London WI 54961 Tel (414) 982-3344

KRUEGER, EVERETT HEATH, b. Cleve., Apr. 19, 1919; A.B., Yale U., 1941; J.D., Case Western Res. U., 1947. Admitted to Ohio bar, 1948; U.S. Dist. Ct. for No. Dist. Ohio bar, 1949, U.S. Dist. Ct. for So. Dist. Ohio bar, 1951, U.S. Supreme Ct. bar, 1954; asso. firm Krueger, Gorman & Davis, 1948-51; asst. atty. Office Atty. Gen. of Ohio, 1951-57, 1st asst., 1955-57, exec. sec. to Gov. of Ohio, Columbus, 1957; mem. Ohio Pub. Utilities Commn., Columbus, 1957-62, chmn., 1957-60; sr. v.p., gen. counsel, sec. City Nat. Bank & Trust Co., Columbus, 1962—. Mem. Columbus Met. Park Bd., 1970—, chmn., 1977; mem. exec. com. Columbus Arts Council, 1972—; treas. Hearing and Speech Center of Central Ohio, 1969—, pres., 1975—; trustee Columbus Symphony Orch., 1965, pres., 1971-73; mem. bd. trustees Vets. Meml., 1963—; bd. dirs. Grant Hosp., Columbus, 1976—; trustee Ohio Dominican Coll., 1971—, Central Ohio Heart Chpt., 1976—. Mem. Am., Ohio, Columbus, Cleve. bar assns., Am., Ohio bankers assns., Ohio, Columbus chambers commerce. Home: 3503 Rue De Fleur Columbus OH 43221 Office: 100 E Broad St Columbus OH 43215 Tel (614) 461-8940

KRUEGER, ROBERT BLAIR, b. Minot, N.D., Dec. 9, 1928; A.B., U. Kans., 1949; J.D., U. Mich., 1952; postgrad. U. So. Calif., 1960-65. Admitted to Kans. bar, 1952, Calif. bar, 1955; practiced in Los Angeles, 1955—; asso. firm O'Melveny & Myers, 1955-59; partner firm Blair & Krueger, 1959-61; partner firm Nossaman, Krueger & Marsh and predecessors, 1961—; adj. prof. U. So. Calif., 1973-74, 77, bd. councilors Law Center, 1972—; lectr. in field. Mem. Calif. Gov.'s Adv. Commn. on Ocean Resources, 1966-68, Adv. Council, Inst. Marine Resources, U. Calif., 1966-74, Calif. Adv. Com. on Marine and Coastal Resources, 1968-73, chmn., 1970-73; mem. Nat. Security Council Adv. Com. on Law of Sea, 1972—, chmn. subcom. internat. law and relations, 1972—; adviser U.S. Delegation to UN Seabeds Com., 1973; del. 3d UN Law of Sea Conf., 1974—; mem. com. visitors U. Mich. Law Sch., 1967-71, nat. com. of Law Sch., 1970—. Fellow Am. Bar Found.; mem. Am. (past com. chmn., Council sect. real property probate and trust law 1973—), Internat., Inter-am. (com. deep sea resources), Los Angeles County (chmn. real property sect. 1961-65, mem. delegation Calif. Bar Conf. 1961-69, trustee 1972—) bar assns., Am. Soc. Internat. Law (panel on law of sea), Internat. Law Assn., Brit. Inst. Internat. and Comparative Law, World Assn. Lawyers, Barristers Club, Tau Kappa Epsilon, Phi Alpha Delta. Asst. editor Mich. Law Rev., 1951-52; editor Los Angeles Bar Bull., 1961-63; bd. editors Calif. Bar Jour., 1963-66, 69-74; project dir., editor Study Outer Continental Shelf Lands of the United States, 1968; contbr. numerous articles on coastal and offshore devel. to profl. publs. Home: 501 Vallombrosa Dr Pasadena CA 91107 also 9828 La Jolla Farms Rd La Jolla CA 92037 Office: 445 S Figueroa St 30th Floor Los Angeles CA 90071 Tel (213) 628-5221

KRUGER, LEWIS, b. N.Y.C., Nov. 14, 1935; A.B. in Econs. cum laude, Harvard, 1956; LL.B., Columbia, 1959. Admitted to N.Y. bar, 1959; with Judge Adv. Gen. Corps USAR, 1959-65; asso. firm Krause, Hirsch & Gross, N.Y.C., 1962-68, partner, 1968—; spl. counsel to Gov. N.Y. State, 1975, to U.S. Senate Subcom. on Antitrust and Monopoly, 1975-76; lectr. in law Columbia, 1972—. Vice chmn. Manhattan Community Planning Bd. 8, 1968-70, 1st vice chmn. 7, 1972-74; chmn. bd. dirs. Citizens for Clean Air, Inc. Mem. Assn. Bar City N.Y. Author Practicing Law Inst. course handbooks: Bankruptcy Practice and Procedure, 1974, Creditor Representation in Bankruptcy, 1975. Office: 41 E 42d St New York City NY 10017 Tel (212) 986-1122

KRUMME, ROBERT DARRELL, b. St. Joseph, Mo., Oct. 13, 1938; B.S., U. Nebr., 1960; J.D. with honors, George Washington U., 1963. Admitted to N.Y. State bar, 1964, U.S. Supreme Ct. bar, 68; asso. firm Covington & Burling, Washington, 1962-63; asso. firm Sullivan & Cromwell, N.Y.C., 1963-69; gen. counsel, corp. sec. Cluett, Peabody & Co., Inc., N.Y.C., 1969—. Mem. Am. (com. on corp. law depts.), N.Y. State bar assns., Assn. Bar City N.Y., Am. Soc. Corp. Secs., Phi Delta Phi. Contbr. articles to profl. jours. Home: 98 Larchmont Ave Larchmont NY 10538 Office: 510 Fifth Ave New York City NY 10036 Tel (212) 697-6100

KRUPANSKY, BLANCHE ETHEL, b. Cleve., Dec. 10, 1925; A.B., FLora Stone Mather Coll., 1947; J.D., Case Western Res. U., 1948, LL.M., 1966. Admitted to Ohio bar, 1949; practiced in Cleve., 1949-51; asst. atty. gen. State of Ohio, 1952-56; asst. chief counsel Bur. of Workmen's Compensation of Ohio, Cleve. and Columbus, 1957-59; judge Cleve. Municipal Ct., 1961-69, Cuyahoga County (Ohio) Common Pleas Ct., 1969—. Mem. vis. com. Case Western Res. U. Sch. Law, 1974, 75, bd. govs., 1975. Mem. Ohio State, Cleve., Cuyahoga County bar assns., Nat. Assn. Women Lawyers, Cleve. Women Lawyers, Common Pleas Judges Assn., Ohio Assn. Attys. Gen., John Harlan Law Club. Named Woman of Achievement Inter-Club Council, Cleve., 1969; recipient Outstanding Jud. Service awards Ohio Supreme Ct., 1973, 74, 75. Office: Cuyahoga County Common Pleas Courthouse 1 Lakeside Ave Cleveland OH 44113 Tel (216) 621-5800

KRUPNICK, MARSHALL P., b. Boston, Sept. 3, 1937; B.S. in Physics, Worcester Poly. Inst., 1959; J.D., Seton Hall U., 1968. Admitted to N.J. bar, 1969, Fla. bar, 1971; trust officer Century Nat. Bank, Ft. Lauderdale, Fla., 1971-73; asso. firm Leonard Grand, profl. assn., Hallandale, Fla., 1973-75; partner firm Grand & Krupnick, profl. assn., Hallandale, Fla., 1975—. Mem. Am., Fla., N.J., Broward County, S. Broward bar assns. Home: 1701 NW 87th Way Pembroke Pines FL 33024 Office: Suite 711 2500 E Hallandale Beach Blvd Hallandale FL 33009 Tel (305) 456-7111

KRUSE, ROLAND ROBERT, b. Wapakoneta, Ohio, Apr. 7, 1917; A.B., Miami U., 1937; J.D., U. Mich., 1940. Admitted to Ohio bar, 1940, Ariz. bar, 1951; individual practice law, Wapakoneta, Ohio, 1940-41, St. Mary's, Ohio, 1941-42; ins. adjuster, Ariz. Adjustment Agency, Phoenix, 1947-52; asso. firm Snell & Wilmer, Phoenix, 1952-66, partner, 1966—; buyer B.F. Goodrich Co., Akron, Ohio, 1946-47. Pres. N. Congregational Homes, Phoenix, 1964-71; dist. dir. Campfire Girls, Phoenix, 1958-60. Mem. Am., Maricopa County bar assns., State Bar Ariz. (chmn. real property, probate and trust sect. 1968-74, 75—), Am. Judicature Soc., Am. Coll. Probate Counsel (state chmn. 1968-75). Contbr. articles to legal publs. Home: Villa 46 1500 N Markdale St Mesa AZ 85201 Office: 3100 Valley Center Phoenix AZ 85073 Tel (602) 257-7221

KRUSE, SCOTT AUGUST, b. N.Y.C., July 15, 1947; A.B., Princeton, 1969; J.D., Harvard, 1972. Admitted to Calif. bar, 1972; asso. firm Gibson, Dunn, & Crutcher, Los Angeles, 1972-77; gen. counsel Fed. Mediation and Conciliation Service, Washington, 1977—. Exec. sec. Citizens Task Force, Los Angeles County Collective Bargaining Ordinance, 1974; adviser on pub. employee legis. Office of Gov. Calif., 1975; mem. labor com. Calif. Dem. Party Platform Commn., 1976. Mem. Calif., Am. bar assns., Indsl. Relations Research Assn. Office: Fed Madiation and Conciliation Service 2100 K St Washington DC 20427

KRUSEN, LESLIE CONRAD, b. Phila., May 7, 1897; B.S., U. Pa., LL.B., 1922. Admitted to Pa. bar, 1922, U.S. Supreme Ct. bar, 1939; asso. firm Biddle, Paul, Dawson & Yocum, Phila., 1922-30; partner firm Krusen Evans and Byrne, Phila., 1930—. Vice pres., dir. Burlington County (N.J.) Community Fund; solicitor Phila. Maritime Exchange, 1933—; mem. Delaware River Ports Council for Emergency Ops., 1975—. Mem. Am., Pa., Phila. bar assns., Maritime Law Assn. (exec. com. 1944-47, 53-56). Office: 21 S 12th St Philadelphia PA 19107 Tel (215) 568-3800

KRUTECK, LAURENCE R., b. N.Y.C., Dec. 11, 1936; B.A., Dartmouth, 1958; LL.B., U. Va., 1961. Admitted to Va. bar, 1961, N.Y. State bar, 1962, U.S. Ct. Mil. Appeals bar, 1962, Fed. Dist. Ct. bar S.D., also Eastern Dist. N.Y., 1963; asso. firm Arthur, Dry, Kalish, Taylor & Wood, N.Y.C., 1963-66; asso. firm Cohn and Glickstein, N.Y.C., 1966-70; partner firm Cohn, Glickstein, Lurie, Ostrin & Lubell, 1970—; asst. sec., dir. Shenandoah Corp., 1968—; asst. sec. San Juan Racing Assn., Inc., 1968—, v.p. corporate affairs, 1975—; arbitrator Am. Arbitration Assn., 1974—; asst. sec. SJR Communications, Inc., 1968—, v.p., 1975—; lectr. mil. law Coll. City N.Y., Fordham U., 1964-73; served to capt. JAGC, U.S. Army, 1961-63, now lt. col. Res. Bd. dirs. Little League; asst. sec. Washington Diplomats Profl. Soccer Club, 1975—. Mem. Am., N.Y. State, Va. bar assns., Assn. Bar City N.Y., Judge Adv.'s Assn. Office: 1370 Ave of Americas New York City NY 10019 also El Commandante Race Track Canovanas PR 00938 Tel (212) 757-4000

KRYDER, PATRICIA PORTER, b. Akron, Ohio, Jan. 11, 1949; B.A. magna cum laude, Denison U., 1970; J.D., Vanderbilt U., 1973. Admitted to Fla. bar, 1973, Tenn. bar, 1974; atty. Advanced Fin. Planning Corp., Nashville, 1973-74, Fidelity Mut. Ins. Co., Nashville, 1973-74; asso. corp. counsel Hosp. Affiliates Internat., Nashville, 1974-76; asso. firm Little, Thrailkill & Owen, Nashville, 1976—; mem. Joint Commn. on Accreditation of Hosps., 1975-76. Mem. Am., Tenn., Fla., Nashville bar assns., Nat. Health Lawyers Assns., Tenn. Hosp. Attys. Home: Cedarcrest 6806 Charlotte Pike Nashville TN 37209 Office: 25th Floor 1st American Center Nashville TN 37238 Tel (615) 259-3456

KUBINSKI, CHARLES ALBERT, b. Nanticoke, Pa., Sept. 25, 1935; B.B.A., St. John's U., 1960; J.D., George Washington U., 1966. Admitted to D.C. bar, 1968; individual practice law, Washington, 1969—. Mem. D.C. Bar (com. on delivery of services to indigents), Superior Ct. Trial Lawyers Assn. Home: 1509 Foxhall Rd NW Washington DC Office: 2603 P St NW Washington DC 20007

KUBOTA, ERNEST HISAO, b. Hilo, Hawaii, Sept. 21, 1931; B.A., U. Hawaii, 1953; LL.D., U. Wash., 1958. Admitted to Hawaii bar, 1958; partner firm Kushi & Kubota, Hilo, Hawaii, 1959-71; dist. judge 3rd Jud. Circuit Ct., Hilo, 1972-74; circuit judge, Hilo, 1974—; dist. magistrate County Hawaii, 1961-71. Office: Box 1007 Hilo HI 96720 Tel (808) 961-7300

KUCHINSKI, JOHN JOSEPH, b. Cleve., Oct. 18, 1939; B.S. in Pharmacy, U. Toledo, 1962; J.D., Cleve. State U., 1970. Admitted to N.Y. bar, 1970, Fla. bar, 1972; staff atty. firm Morton-Nornich, Inc., Norwich, N.Y., 1970-71; v.p., sec., counsel Roux Lab., Inc., Jacksonville, Fla., 1971—. Trustee Oxford N.Y., 1971; pres. Right to Life, Norwich, 1971. Mem. Am., N.Y. State, Fla. bar assns., Nat. Assn. Retail Druggists. Registered pharmacist, Ohio, N.Y. Home: 4125 Howalt Ct Jacksonville FL 32211 Office: 3733 University Blvd W Jacksonville FL 32217 Tel (904) 731-3050

KUDER, ARMIN ULRICH, b. Phila., Nov. 14, 1935; A.B., Lafayette Coll., 1956; LL.B., Harvard, 1959. Admitted to D.C. bar, 1959, U.S. Ct. Appeals bar D.C., 1959, U.S. Ct. Mil. Appeals bar, 1962; atty. Office of Judge Adv. Gen., U.S. Navy, 1960-63; asso. firm Coles & Goertner, Washington, 1963-65, firm Mehler, Smollar & Buschmann, Washington, 1965-67; partner firm Smollar, Kuder & Sherman, Washington, 1967-68, firm Kuder, Sherman, Fox, Meehan & Curtin, P.C., Washington, 1968—. Pres. Arthritis and Rheumatism Assn., Washington, 1972-75; trustee Arthritis Found., 1975—, recipient nat. vol. service citation, 1976; chmn. nat. health agencies Nat. Capitol Area Council, 1977; sec. Washington Combined Health Appeal, 1976—. Mem. Am., D.C. (domestic relations com. 1968—) bar assns. Home: 5426 MacArthur Blvd Washington DC 20016 Office: 1900 M St NW Washington DC 20036 Tel (202) 331-7120

KUECHENMEISTER, FREDERICK WILLIAM, b. Carlstadt, N.J., Sept. 5, 1926; A.A., Fairleigh Dickinson U., 1949; LL.B., Baylor U., 1952, J.D., 1969; postgrad. Hague (Netherlands) Acad. Internat. Law, 1972. Admitted to Tex. bar, 1952, N.J. bar, 1954, U.S. Supreme Ct. bar, 1969; trial atty. Allstate Ins. Co., Saddle Brook, N.J., 1954-55; asst. gen. counsel Mack Trucks Inc., South Plainfield, N.J., 1955-56; practiced law in Hackensack, N.J., 1956-70; judge Bergen County (N.J.) Dist. Ct., 1970—, presiding judge, 1973—; mem. Carlstadt (N.J.) City Council, 1960-62, pres., 1961-62; undersheriff Bergen County, 1965-70. Mem. Tex., Bergen County bar assns., Lawyers Club Bergen County, Assn. Attenders and Alumni of The Hague Acad. Internat. Law. Home: 16 Berkeley Pl Fair Lawn NJ 07410 Office: Bergen County Courthouse Hackensack NJ 07601 Tel (201) 646-2440

KUEHN, OSCAR RAYMOND, b. E. St. Louis, Ill., Oct. 13, 1912; B.S., U. Ill., Urbana, 1934; J.D., St. Louis U., 1937. Admitted to Mo. bar, 1937, Ill. bar, 1937; practice law, Chgo. Mem. Am., Ill. State bar assns., Phi Delta Phi, Tau Kappa Epsilon. Home: 6147 N Legett Ave Chicago IL 60646 Office: 20 N Wacker Dr Chicago IL 60606 Tel (312) 236-6989

KUEHN, ROGER WILLIAM, b. Stillwater, Minn., Dec. 27, 1927; B.B.A., Hamiline U., 1952; LL.B., U. Minn., 1955, J.D., 1972. Admitted to Minn. bar, 1955; pres. Kuehn Law Firm, St. Paul. Mem. Minn. Bar Assn., Am., Minn. trial lawyers assns. Home: 55 Western Ave N Saint Paul MN 55102 Office: 912 Commerce Bldg Saint Paul MN 55101 Tel (612) 222-2586

KUEHNLE, KENTON LEE, b. Chgo., Nov. 10, 1945; B.A., Augustana Coll., 1967; J.D., Duke U., 1970. Admitted to Ohio bar, 1970; asso. firm Dunbar, Kienzle, & Murphey, Columbus, 1970—; asst. legal counsel Ohio Jaycees, 1976—. Mem. Columbus (chmn. real property com. 1976—, chmn. spl. subcom. drafting revised condominium statue Ohio), Ohio, Am. bar assns. Mem. exec. bd. Duke Law Jour., 1969-70. Home: Box 316 Rt 2 Orient OH 43146 Office: 250 E Broad St Columbus OH 43215 Tel (614) 228-4371

KUHL, PAUL BEACH, b. Elizabeth, N.J., July 15, 1935; B.A., Cornell U., 1957; LL.B., Stanford U., 1960. Admitted to Calif. bar, 1961; asso. Walter C. Kohn, San Francisco, 1961-63; asso., partner Sedgwick, Detert, Moran & Arnold, San Francisco, 1963—; lectr. in field. Mem. Am., San Francisco bar assns., Am. Judicature Soc., No. Calif. Assn. Def. Counsel, Def. Research Inst. Home: PO Box 574 Ross CA 94957 Office: 111 Pine St #1100 San Francisco CA 94111

KUHLMEY, WALTER T., b. Chgo., Apr. 11, 1918; B.A., Yale, 1940, J.D., 1947. Admitted to Ill. bar, 1948; asso. firm Kirkland & Ellis and predecessors, Chgo., 1947-54, partner, 1954—. Mem. Chgo., Am., 7th Fed. Circuit Bar Assns., Law Club Chgo., Legal Club Chgo. Home: 1840A Wildberry Dr Glenview IL 60025 Office: 200 E Randolph Dr Chicago IL 60601 Tel (312) 861-2234

KUHN, JAMES EDWARD, b. Hammond, La., Oct. 31, 1946; A.B., Southeastern La. U., 1968; J.D., Loyola U. of the South, 1972. Admitted to La. bar, 1973; asso. firm Pittman & Matheny, Hammond, 1973-75; partner firm Fayard, Morrison, Fayard & Kuhn, Denham Springs, La., 1975—. Atty. for Tangipahoa Assn. for Retarded, Sigma Tau Gamma of Southeastern La. U. Mem. New Orleans Fed., La., 21st Judicial Dist., Livingston Parish bar assns., La. Trial Laweyrs Assn., Delta Theta Phi. Home: Route 4 Box 44AC Hammond LA 70401 Office: 519 Florida Blvd W Denham Springs LA 70726 Tel (504) 664-4193

KUHN, PERLA M., b. Cordoba, Argentina, July 21, 1940; grad. U. Cordoba Law Sch., 1959; LL.M., Tulane U., 1961; postgrad. U. Pa., 1962; LL.B., N.Y. U., 1967. Admitted to practice of law Argentina, 1959, N.Y. State bar, 1968; atty. asst. chief counsel's office Dept. Treasury, N.Y.C., 1968-72; asso. firm Busby, Rivkin, Sherman, Levy & Rehm, N.Y.C., 1972-75; counsel Hartz Mountain Corp., Harrison, N.J., 1975—. Mem. N.Y. State Bar Assn. Home: 50 Edstone Dr Staten Island NY 10301 Office: 700 S 4th St Harrison NJ 07029 Tel (201) 481-4800

KUHN, RICHARD IRWIN, b. E. Cleveland, Ohio, Mar. 5, 1919; student Ohio State U., 1937-39; J.D., Cleve. Law Sch., 1943. Admitted to Ohio bar, 1943; atty. U.S. Ordnance Dept., 1943-45; law clk. to judge U.S. Ct. Appeals 6th Circuit, 1945-47, to judge U.S. Dist. Ct., Cleve., 1947-49; asso. firm Shumaker, Loop & Kendrick, Toledo, 1952-54; asst. sec., house counsel Affiliated Gas Equipment Inc., Cleve., 1949-52; counsel Central Nat. Bank of Cleve., 1954-61, now sr. v.p., asst. to chmn. bd. Councilman City of Rocky River (Ohio), 1955-61. Mem. Ohio Bar Assn., Bar Assn. Greater Cleve. (treas.), Ohio C. of C. (dir.). Home: 17804 Lake Rd Lakewood OH 44107 Office: PO Box 6179 Cleveland OH 44172 Tel (216) 861-7800

KUHR, JOHN B., b. Havre, Mont., Dec. 26, 1931; B.S., U. Utah, 1953; J.D., U. Mich., 1956. Admitted to Mont. bar, 1956; partner firm Weber, Bosch, Kuhr, Dugdale, Warner & Martin, Havre, 1959—. Trustee No. Mont. Hosp., 1970—, pres. of assn., chmn. bd., 1971—; trustee Blue Cross of Mont. Mem. Mont., Am. bar assns. Home: 5 Lila Dr Havre MT 59501 Office: 4th Ave at 4th St Havre MT 59501 Tel (406) 265-6706

KUHSE, HAROLD HENRY, b. Sac County, Iowa, Dec. 7, 1921; B.S. in Engring., Iowa State U., 1949; J.D., U. Iowa, 1951. Admitted to Iowa bar, 1951, Ariz. bar, 1954; asst. dir. indsl. relations Oliver Corp., Chgo., 1951-53; dir. collections State of Wash., Olympia, 1953-54; city prosecutor City of Mesa (Ariz.), 1954-64; asso. firm Kuhse Petrie & Reynolds, Mesa, 1958—. Mem. Ariz. Bar Assn., Mesa C. of C. (dir.). Home: 514 W Fairway Circle Mesa AZ 85201 Office: 500 Valley Nat Bank Bldg Mesa AZ 85201 Tel (602) 969-2246

KUKLIN, ANTHONY BENNETT, b. N.Y.C., Oct. 9, 1929; A.B., Harvard, 1950; LL.B., Columbia U., 1953. Admitted to N.Y. bar, 1953, D.C. bar, 1970; asso. firm Dwight, Royall, Harris, Koegel & Caskey, N.Y.C., 1955-61, Paul, Weiss, Rifkind, Wharton and Garrison, N.Y.C., 1961-68, partner, 1969—. Mem. Am., N.Y. State bar assns., Assn. Bar City N.Y. Contbr. articles to legal jours. Home: 13 Ervilla Dr Larchmont NY 10538 Office: 345 Park Ave New York City NY 10022 Tel (212) 644-8730

KULLER, HENRY MICHAEL, b. Allentown, Pa., Apr. 18, 1946; B.A. in Econs., U. Pa., 1968; J.D. Temple U., 1971. Admitted to Pa. bar, 1971, U.S. Dist. Ct. bar, 1972, U.S. Tax Ct. bar, 1972; partner firm Wright Thistle & Gibbons, Phila., 1971—; lectr. Law, Temple U., 1973—. Councilman Borough Jenkintown (Pa.), 1976—. Mem. Am., Pa., Phila. bar assns., Am. Trial Lawyers Assn., Phila. Lawyers Club. Home: 222 Runnymede Ave Jenkintown PA 19046 Office: 1718 Locust St Philadelphia PA 19103 Tel (215) 732-4710

KULLMAN, THOMAS MAXSON, b. Decatur, Ala., May 11, 1941; B.S., U.S. Mil. Acad., 1964; J.D., U. Ala., 1973. Admitted to Ala. bar, 1973, U.S. Supreme Ct. bar, 1976; defense counsel, trial counsel, chief mil. justice JAGC, U.S. Army, Ft. Knox, Ky., 1973-76; detailed to JAG Sch., Charlottesville, Va., 1976-77; assigned Office JAG, Washington, 1977—. Scoutmaster Boy Scouts Am., Fort Knox 1974-76. Mem. Ala., Am. bar assns., Dist. Attys. Assn., Phi Alpha Delta. Home: 6804 Galax Ct Springfield VA 22151 Office: Office of Judge Adv Gen US Army Washington DC Tel (703) 695-6433

KULP, VICTOR KRAMER, b. Chgo., May 5, 1943; B.S. in Bus. Adminstrn., U. Tulsa, 1967, J.D., 1968; LL.M. in Taxation, N.Y. U., 1973. Admitted to Okla. bar, 1968; with JAGC, U.S. Army, 1968-72; tax atty. legal div. Cities Service Co., Tulsa, 1973—. Mem. Okla., Tulsa County, Am. bar assns., Phi Delta Phi. Tel (918) 586-4392

KUMMEL, R. D., b. 1921; B.S., LL.B., U. Wis. With J.I. Case Co., 1948-52; with Carnation Co., Los Angeles, 1953—, v.p. research and new products planning, 1965-69, v.p. legal, research and new products planning, 1969-70, sr. v.p. legal, research and devel., gen. counsel, 1970—, also dir. Office: 5045 Wilshire Blvd Los Angeles CA 90036*

KUMPE, PETER GRAY, b. Little Rock, Apr. 8, 1947; student Duke, 1965-67; B.A., Little Rock U., 1969; J.D., U. Tex., 1972. Admitted to Tex., Ark. bars, 1972; staff atty. gen. State Ark., Little Rock, 1972; law clk. to Judge U.S. Dist. Ct., Eastern Dist. Ark., 1972-74; asso. firm Wright, Lindsey & Jennings, Little Rock, 1974—. Mem. Am., Ark., Tex. bar assns., Order of Coif. Mng. editor Tex. Law Review, 1971-72. Home: 441 Midland St Little Rock AR 72205 Office: 2200 Worthen Bank Bldg Little Rock AR 72201 Tel (501) 371-0808

KUN, ALBERT MIKLOS, b. Budapest, Hungary, Dec. 5, 1938; B.A., Duke, 1962; J.D., Golden Gate U., 1971. Admitted to Calif. bar, 1973; with Kaiser Industries, Oakland, Calif., 1973; individual practice law, San Francisco, 1973—. Pres. Pacific div. Am. Hungarian Fedn., 1975—; v.p. Hungarian House of San Francisco, 1973—. Mem. Calif., San Francisco bar assns. Author: St. Stephen's Crown—the Source of Hungarian Law, 1973. Home: 112 Crescent Ave Sausalito CA 94965 Office: 556 Commercial St San Francisco CA 94111 Tel (415) 362-4000

KUNC, CLARENCE CHARLES, b. Crab Orchard, Nebr., July 6, 1911; A.B., U. Nebr., 1939, LL.B. cum laude, 1941; LL.M., U. Mich., 1942. Admitted to Nebr. bar, U.S. Dist. Ct. bar, 1941; since practiced in Wilber, Nebr.; individual practice law, 1947-72; judge County Ct. 7th Dist. Nebr., 1973—; city atty., Wilber, 1948-62, Dewitt, Clatonia, Swanton, 1956-72; atty. Wilber Sch. Bd. and Ednl. Service, 1960-72. Bd. dirs. Wilber Nursing Home, 1965-76; mem. Wilber Bd. Edn., 1956-62; bd. dirs. Saline County Bd. Mental Health, 1950-72. Mem. Am., Nebr. bar assns., Am. Judicature Soc., Order of Coif., Phi Beta Kappa. Editor Nebr. Law Rev., 1940-41. Home: 314 W 3d St Wilber NE 68465 Office: Saline County Court House Wilber NE 68465 Tel (402) 821-2131

KUNES, GEORGE GERALD JOSEPH, JR., b. Tifton, Ga., Oct. 23, 1947; B.A. in Polit. Sci., U. Ga., 1969; J.D., 1972. Admitted to Ga. bar, 1972, Fla. bar, 1973; partner firm Kunes, Kunes and Flemming, Tifton, 1972—. Mem. Am., Ga., Fla., Tifton bar assns., Ga. Trial Lawyers Assn., Profl. Golfers Assn., Phi Delta Phi. Recipient Student Govt. award Abraham Baldwin Agrl. Coll., 1975. Home: 105 Melanna Dr Tifton GA 31794 Office: 236 E 2d St Tifton GA 31974 Tel (912) 382-2303

KUNIK, ISAAC JORDAN, b. Hartford, Conn., Nov. 10, 1912; A.B. in Chemistry, Wesleyan U., 1934; J.D., Harvard, 1937. Admitted to Conn. bar, 1938, N.Y. State bar, 1949; individual practice law, Hartford, 1938-48, N.Y.C., 1948—. Fellow, AAAS, Am. Inst. Chemists, Radio Club Am., Internat. Acad. Law and Sci.; mem. Am., Fed. bar assns., Assn. Bar City N.Y. (patent com. 1969-72), Am., N.Y., Conn. patent law assns., Am. Judicature Soc., Am. Chem. Soc., IEEE, Am. Soc. for Metals, N.Y. Acad. Scis., Licensing Execs. Soc., Authors Guild. Author: Controversy on Patents, 1960; contbr. articles to profl. jours. Home: 215 E 80th St New York City NY 10021 Office: 521 Fifth Ave New York City NY 10017 Tel (212) 687-3480

KUNKEL, DAVID NELSON, b. Rochester, N.Y., Apr. 5, 1943; B.A., U. Va., 1965; LL.B., U. Pa., 1968. Admitted to Pa. bar, 1969, N.Y. bar, 1972, U.S. Supreme Ct. Bar, 1972; asso. firm Montgomery, McCracken, Walker & Rhoads, Phila., 1968; asso. firm Nixon, Hargrave, Devans & Doyle, Rochester, N.Y., 1971—; legal officer, USNR, 1969-71; chmn. Standardized Nuclear Unit Power Plant System Legal Com., 1974-75. Mem. Am., N.Y., Monroe County bar assns. Home: 14 Smallwood Dr Pittsford NY 14534 Office: Lincoln First Tower Rochester NY 14603 Tel (716) 546-8000

KUNKLE, JOHN HENRY, JR., b. Pitts., July 7, 1927; B.B.A., U. Mich., 1949, J.D., 1952. Admitted to Pa. bar, 1953; partner firm Lewis & Drew, Pitts., 1953-58; pres. Union Title Guaranty Co., Pitts., 1958-76, Pa. Land Title Assn., Phila., 1976—; vice-chmn. bd. Commonwealth Land Title Ins. Co., Phila., 1969—; gov. Am. Land Title Assn., Washington, 1959. Bd. dirs. Pitts. YMCA. Mem. Young Pres.'s Orgn., Am., Pa. bar assns. Home: 2333 Engelwood Dr Pittsburgh PA 15241 Office: 210 Grant St Pittsburgh PA 15219 Tel (412) 471-1492

KUNSTLER, WILLIAM MOSES, b. N.Y.C., July 7, 1919; B.A., Yale, 1941; LL.B., Columbia U., 1948. Admitted to N.Y. bar, 1948, D.C. bar, 1957; partner firm Kunstler & Kunstler, N.Y.C., 1949-76; v.p., vol. staff atty. Center Constitutional Rights, N.Y.C., 1966—; asst. prof. law N.Y. Law Sch., 1949-61; adj. asst. prof. law Pace Coll., N.Y.C., 1952-64; lectr. New Sch. Social Research, N.Y.C., 1967, 70; lectr. English, Columbia U., 1949-51. Mem. Assn. Bar City N.Y., ACLU, Phi Beta Kappa, Phi Delta Phi. Author: The Law of Accidents, 1956; And Justice for All, 1961; The Case for Courage, 1963; The Minister and the Choir Singer, 1964; Deep in My Heart, 1966; First Degree, 1960; Our Pleasant Vices, 1941; Corporate Tax Summary, 1954; Beyond a Reasonable Doubt, 1961. Recipient Civil Rights award N.Y. State Bar Assn., 1963; press award, 1958, numerous radio and TV awards. Office: 853 Broadway New York City NY 10003 Tel (212) 674-3303

KUNTZ, EUGENE OSCAR, b. Corpus Christi, Tex., Oct. 8, 1913; A.B. cum laude, Baylor U., 1940, J.D. cum laude, 1946; LL.M., Harvard, 1947. Admitted to Tex. bar, 1938, Okla. bar, 1956; asso. firm Sanders & Scott, Amarillo, Tex., 1940-41; asst. prof. law U. Wyo., 1947-50, asso. prof., 1950-52; prof. U. Okla., 1952-71, George Lynn Cross research prof. law, 1971—, dean Sch. Law, 1965-70, dean emeritus, 1970—; partner firm McAfee, Taft, Cates, Kuntz & Mark, Oklahoma City, 1958-65, of counsel, 1971—; chmn. bd. dirs. Norman Bank of Commerce. Chmn. bd. trustees Washita Presbytery. Mem. Okla. (asso. editor jour. 1970—), Am. bar assns. Recipient Gerald B. Klien award Okla. Bar Found., 1970. Author: Newspaper Laws of Wyoming, 1951; Thornton, Oil & Gas, pocket part supplements, 1956, cumulative supplement, 1960; Kuntz on Oil & Gas, vols. 1-4, 1962-72, supplemental pocket parts, 1971; contbr. articles to legal jours. Okla. editor Oil and Gas Reporter, 1955—. Home: 2504 Walnut Rd Norman OK 73069 Office: 100 Park Ave Bldg Oklahoma City OK 73102 Tel (405) 235-9621

KUNTZ, RAYMOND GEORGE, b. Mt. Vernon, N.Y., Apr. 6, 1937; B.S. in Econs., Fordham Coll., 1959, LL.D., 1962. Admitted to U.S. Dist. Ct. So. Dist. N.Y., 1963; U.S. 2d Circuit Ct. Appeals, 1965; asso. firm Perell, Neilson & Stevens, N.Y.C., 1963; asso. firm Mendes & Mount, N.Y.C., 1963-65; partner firm Miller, Ouimette, Moran & Kuntz, Poughkeepsie, N.Y., 1965-69; partner firm Kuntz & Donohue, Poughkeepsie, 1969-72; individual practice law, Poughkeepsie, 1972-75; pres. Raymond G. Kuntz, P.C., 1975—; atty. for schs. in Poughkeepsie, Arlington, Carmel, Dobbs Ferry, Hendrick Hudson, Mahopac, Little Falls, North Salem, Oneonta and Wiltyck, Yonkers; pres. Legal Services Bur., Poughkeepsie, 1967-72. Mem. Am., N.Y. State (1st vice chmn. municipal law sect.), Dutchess County, Westchester County bar assns., Fed. Bar Council, N.Y. State Assn. Sch. Attys. (pres. 1974). Contbr. articles to law jours. Home: Saddle Ridge Rd Pound Ridge NY 10576 Office: 19 Davis Ave Poughkeepsie NY 12603 Tel (914) 454-5030

KUNTZ, WALTER NICHOLS, III, b. Waco, Tex., Aug. 25, 1941; B.A., So. Meth. U., 1963; LL.B., U. Tex., 1966. Admitted to Tex. bar, 1966; partner firm Akin, Gump, Strauss, Hauer & Feld, Dallas, 1970—. Mem. Am., Tex. bar assns. Office: Republic National Bank Bldg Dallas TX 75201 Tel (214) 655-2723

KUNZE, WILLIAM E., b. Charter Oak, Iowa, Sept. 16, 1924; J.D., U. S.D., 1946. Admitted to S.D. bar, 1946, Iowa bar, 1958; claim rep. Travelers Ins. Co., Sioux Falls, S.D., 1946-58; partner firm Gleysteen, Harper, Kunze, Eidsmoe and Heidman, Sioux City, Iowa, 1959—. Mem. Siouxland Health Planning Council, Sioux City, 1968-76; pres. Siouxland United Way, Sioux City, 1974; mem. Iowa Health Coordinating Council, 1976; pres. Iowa Health Coordinating Council, 1976; pres. Iowa Health Systems Agy., 1976; bd. dirs. U. S.D. Dakota Dome Corp.; trustee St. Joseph Mercy Hosp., Sioux City, Briar Cliff Coll. Fellow Am. Coll. Trial Lawyers, Iowa Acad. Trial Lawyers; mem. Internat. Soc. Barristers, Internat. Assn. Ins. Counsel, Iowa Bar Assn. (gov. 1972-76), Iowa Def. Counsel (dir.). Home: 5000 Country Club Blvd Sioux City IA 51104 Office: 200 Home Federal Bldg Sioux City IA 51101 Tel (712) 255-8838

KUPERS, EDWARD CARLTON, b. Phila., Mar. 24, 1909; B.A., George Washington U., 1930, M.D., 1934; J.D., U. Calif. at Los Angeles, 1965. Intern, Albert Einstein Med. Center, 1934-36; resident Stark Gen. Hosp., Charleston, S.C., 1943-44; mem. staff, Cedars-Sinai Med. Center, Los Angeles, 1970—, Sunset Blvd. Hosp. Los Angeles, 1968—; admitted to Calif. bar, 1966; individual practice law, Los Angeles, 1966—; mem. nat. panel arbitrators Am. Arbitration Assn. Mem. com. on wills, bequests and gifts Shriners Hosp. Fellow Am. Coll. Legal Medicine; mem. AMA, Calif., Los Angeles County, Pan Am. (councillor in forensic medicine), World (U.S. com.) med. assns., Am. Bar Assn., Am. Heart Assn., Am. Rheumatism Assn., Am. Soc. Internal Medicine, A.C.P., Med. Research Assn. Calif., Arthritis Found., Geriatric Soc., Lung Assn. Cancer Control, others. Contbr. numerous articles to med. and legal jours. Office: Suite 101 5255 Sunset Blvd Los Angeles CA 90027 Tel (213) 463-6884

KURLAND, PHILIP B., b. N.Y.C., Oct. 22, 1921; A.B., U. Pa., 1942; LL.B., Harvard, 1944. Admitted to N.Y. bar, 1945, Ill. bar, 1972, also U.S. Supreme Ct.; law sec. to Judge Jerome N. Frank, 1944-45, Supreme Ct. Justice Felix Frankfurter, 1945-46; atty. Dept. Justice, 1946-47; mem. firm Kurland & Wolfson, N.Y.C., 1947-50; asst. prof. law Northwestern U. Law Sch., 1950-53; mem. faculty U. Chgo., 1953—, prof. law, 1956—, William R. Kenan Jr. prof., 1973—; counsel firm Rothschild, Barry & Myers, Chgo., 1972—; cons. Econ. Stblzn. Agy., 1951-52; chief cons., subcom. on separation of powers U.S. Senate Judiciary Com., 1967—; mem. Oliver Wendell Holmes Devise Com., 1975—. Guggenheim fellow, 1950-51, 54-55. Fellow Am. Acad. Arts and Scis.; mem. Am., Chgo. bar assns., Am. Law Inst., Chgo. Council Lawyers, New Brougham Soc. Author: Jurisdiction of Supreme Court of U.S., 1950; Mr. Justice, 1964; Religion and the Law, 1962; Frankfurter: Of Law and Life, 1965; The Supreme Court and the Constitution, 1965; The Great Charter, 1965; Moore's Manual, 1964-70, Felix Frankfurter on the Supreme Court, 1970; Politics, The Constitution and the Warren Court, 1970; Mr. Justice Frankfurter and the Constitution, 1971; Landmark Briefs and Arguments of the Supreme Court of the United States, vols. 77-80, 1975. Editor: Supreme Court Rev., 1960—. Home: 4840 Woodlawn Av Chicago IL 60615*

KURLAND, SHELDON CONRAD, b. Bklyn., June 10, 1936; B.B.A., U. Miami, 1957, J.D., 1970, LL.M., 1972. Admitted to Fla. bar, 1970; agt. IRS, Fort Lauderdale, Fla., 1961-70; partner firm Davis & Kurland, Miami, Fla., 1970-71; individual practice law, Ft. Lauderdale, 1972-75; partner firm Kurland & Ross, Ft. Lauderdale, 1976—; adj. prof. taxation and accounting masters program Fla. Atlantic U., Boca Raton; lectr. U. Miami. Mem. Am., Fla., Broward County bar assns., Am. Inst. C.P.A.'s, Fla. Inst. C.P.A.'s, Mensa. Home: 4400 SW 95th Ave Davie FL 33328 Office: 504 Courthouse Square Bldg 200 SE 6th St Fort Lauderdale FL 33301

KURLANDER, CLYDE, b. Bklyn., July 15, 1945; B.A., Bklyn. Coll., 1966; J.D., Northwestern U., 1969. Admitted to Ill. bar, 1969, Fed. Ct. No. Dist. Ill., 1969; partner firm Springer, Carstedt & Kurlander, Chgo., 1969—. Mem. Am., Ill. (chmn. newsletter editor pub. utilities and transp. law sect.), Chgo. bar assns. Contbr. column to Chgo. Daily Law Bull. Home: 615 Lake Ave Crystal Lake IL 60014 Office: 39 S LaSalle St Chicago IL 60603 Tel (312) 236-6200

KURLANDER, LAWRENCE THEODORE, b. Bklyn., July 26, 1939; B.A., Alfred U., 1961; J.D., Cornell U., 1964. Admitted to N.Y. bar, 1964, U.S. Supreme Ct. bar, 1975; asso. firm Fix, Spindelman & Turk, Rochester, N.Y., 1964-67; partner firm Philippone, Kurlander, Grossman & Horton, Rochester, 1967-69; partner firm Salamone, Kurlander & Aloi, Rochester, 1969-75; dist. atty. Monroe County (N.Y.), Rochester, 1975—. Mem. Am., N.Y. State, Monroe County bar assns., Am. Judicature Soc., Am., N.Y. State trial lawyers assns., Nat. Dist. Attys. Assn. (exec. com. 1976—), Am. Arbitration Assn. (arbitrator 1967-75). Home: 80 Coral Way Rochester NY 14618 Office: 201 Hall of Justice Rochester NY 14614 Tel (716) 428-2334

KURNIT, PHILIP SHELDON, b. Bklyn., Feb. 4, 1936; B.A., Queens Coll., 1957; LL.B., Columbia U., 1960. Admitted to N.Y. bar, 1961, N.J. bar, 1971, Calif. bar, 1972; asso. atty. ABC, N.Y.C., 1963-66; mem. firm Tabak, Kurnit and Ruden, and successors, N.Y.C., 1968-72, Kurnit and Adler, 1974-75; individual practice law, N.Y.C., 1972—. Mem. N.Y. State, N.J., Bergen County, Beverly Hills bar assns., State Bar Calif. Office: 488 Madison Ave New York City NY 10022 Tel (212) 752-3033

KURTH, SIDNEY PEARCE, b. Ft. Benton, Mont., Dec. 2, 1919; B.A. in Bus. Adminstrn., U. Mont., Missoula, 1943, J.D., 1949; postgrad. U. Calif., Berkeley, 1946; LL.M. in Taxation, N.Y. U., 1950. Admitted to Mont. bar, 1949; mem. staff tax sect. U.S. Steel Corp., N.Y.C., 1950-54; partner firm Kurth, Felt, Speare & Lalonde, P.C., Billings, Mont., 1954—; lectr. U. Mont. Tax Inst. Mont. del. to Western States Water Council, 1960-64; trustee Agriservices Found., Clovis, Calif., 1970—. Office: 450 Hart Albin Bldg Billings MT 59101 Tel (406) 248-1111

KURTZ, ARTHUR BERNARD, b. N.Y.C., Jan. 7, 1921; B.B.A., Coll. City N.Y., 1941; LL.B., Bklyn. Law Sch., 1957, J.D., 1967. Admitted to N.Y. State bar, 1958; partner firm Lesser, Rutman & Kurtz, N.Y.C., 1959—; counsel Associated Millinery Women, Inc., 1960—. Mem. adv. com. Great Neck Sch. Bd., 1966——; mayor Village of Russell Gardens (N.Y.), 1976—, trustee, 1971-76; pres. Russell Gardens Assn., 1970-71. Mem. N.Y. County Lawyers, N.Y. State Soc. C.P.A.'s, Am. Arbitration Assn. (panel). Home: 21 Wensley Dr Great Neck NY 11021 Office: 475 Fifth Ave New York City NY 10017 Tel (212) 685-7908

KURTZ, CHARLES JEWETT, III, b. Columbus, Ohio, May 13, 1940; B.A., Williams Coll., 1962; J.D., Ohio State U., 1965. Admitted to Ohio bar, 1965; law clk. to justice Ohio Supreme Ct., 1965-67; partner firm Porter, Stanley, Platt & Arthur, Columbus, 1967—. Mem. Columbus, Ohio, Am. bar assns., Def. Research Inst., Columbus (pres. 1976-77), Ohio def. assns. Home: 47 N Stannood Rd Columbus OH 43209 Office: 37 W Broad St Columbus OH 43215 Tel (614) 228-1511

KURTZ, HERMAN WILLIAM, b. Newark, July 10, 1905; LL.B., Rutgers U., 1927. Admitted to N.J. bar, 1928; asst. town atty. Irvington (N.J.), 1943-75, ret., 1975. Mem. Essex County Bar Assn. Home and Office: 47 Webster St Irvington NJ 07111 Tel (201) 372-5553

KURTZ, LLOYD SHERER, JR., b. Toledo, Feb. 23, 1934; A.B. cum laude, Princeton, 1956; grad. Stanford U. Sch. Law, 1959. Admitted to Alaska bar, 1961; instr. real estate law, bus. law and econs. U. Alaska, 1959-63; law clk. to chief justice Alaska Supreme Ct., 1959-60; asso. firm McNealy, Merdes & Camarot, Fairbanks, 1961-62; atty. Alaska State Housing Authority, Anchorage, 1962-63; asso. firm Burr, Boney & Pease, Anchorage, 1964-67; partner firm Burr, Pease & Kurtz, Inc., Anchorage, 1967—. Mem. Am., Alaska (bd. govs. 1970-74, pres. 1973-74, chmn. higher edn. com. 1974-76), Anchorage bar assns., Am. Judicature Soc. Mng. editor Stanford Law Rev., 1958-59. Office: 825 W 8th Ave Anchorage AK 99501 Tel (907) 279-2411

KURTZ, SHELDON FRANCIS, b. Syracuse, N.Y., May 18, 1943; A.B., Syracuse U., 1964, LL.B., 1967. Admitted to N.Y. State bar, 1967, Iowa bar, 1973; asso. firm Mudge, Rose, Guthrie & Alexander, N.Y.C., 1967-69, Cleary, Gottlieb, Steen & Hamilton, N.Y.C., 1969-72; asso. prof. law U. Iowa, Iowa City, 1973-76, prof., 1976—. Mem. Iowa, N.Y. State bar assns. Author: (with Robert Reimer) Iowa Estates: Taxation and Adminstration, 1975; Income and Estate Taxation of Decedents and Their Estates, 1977. Home: 3123 Alpine Ct Iowa City IA 52240 Office: College of Law U Iowa Iowa City IA 52240 Tel (319) 353-6787

KURTZ, WILLIAM ALBERT, b. Cleve., Jan. 27, 1947; B.A., U. Notre Dame, 1969; J.D., Ohio State U., 1971. Admitted to Ohio bar, 1972; staff atty. Legal Aid Soc. of Cleve., 1972-74; asst. legal dir. Cuyahoga County Juvenile Ct., Cleve., 1974—; mem. Cuyahoga County Pub. Defenders Task Force, 1976. Mem. Ohio Bar Assn. Contbr. to Merrick-Rippner Ohio Probate Law. Home: 2527 Derbyshire Rd Cleveland Heights OH 44106 Office: 2163 E 22d St Cleveland OH 44115 Tel (216) 771-8400

KURY, ELIZABETH HERZLETT, b. Pitts., Mar. 20, 1939; B.A., Cornell U., 1960, J.D., U. Pitts., 1963; LL.M. N.Y. U. Admitted to Pa. bar, 1964; partner firm Kury & Kury, Sunbury, Pa., 1964—. Pres. bd. dirs. Danville State Hosp., 1975—. Mem. Pa., Am., County bar assns. Home: Box 284 C R D 1 Sunbury PA 17801 Office: 800 N 4th St Sunbury PA 17801

KURY, FRANKLIN LEO, b. Sunbury, Pa., Oct. 15, 1936; B.A., Trinity Coll., 1958; LL.B., U. Pa., 1962. Admitted to Pa. bar, 1962; law clk. Atty. Gen. Office, Dept. Justice, Harrisburg, Pa., 1962-62, dep. atty. gen., 1962; mem. Pa. Ho. of Reps. from 108th dist., 1966-72, Pa. Senate from 27th dist., 1972—; partner firm Kury & Kury, Sunbury, 1963—. Home: R D 1 Box 284C Sunbury PA 17801 Office: 800 N 4th St Sunbury PA 17801 Tel (717) 286-5866

KURZER, MARTIN JOEL, b. Milw., May 6, 1938; B.B.A., U. Wis., Milw., 1960; J.D., Marquette U., 1968; LL.M., U. Miami, 1971. Admitted to Wis., Fla. bars, 1968; asso. firm Blackwell, Walker, Gray, Powers, Flick & Hoehl, Miami, Fla., 1968-72, mem., 1973—; adj. prof. U. Miami Law Sch., 1976—. Mem. Fla. Bar, Wis. Bar, Fed., Dade County bar assns., Fla. (v.p. 1975—), Am. assns. atty.-C.P.A.'s, Am. Inst. C.P.A.'s, Am. Soc. Hosp. Attys., Greater Miami Tax Inst. Contbr. articles to legal revs. Home: 1532 NE 104th St Miami Shores FL 33138 Office: 2400 First Federal Bldg One SE 3rd St Miami FL 33131 Tel (305) 358-8880

KURZET, CHESTER SZCZSENY, b. Przemysl, Poland, Apr. 7, 1927; came to U.S., 1940, naturalized, 1946; B.A. cum laude, Princeton, 1945; LL.B., Yale, 1950. Admitted to N.Y. State bar, 1950, Oreg. bar, 1954, U.S. Supreme Ct. bar, 1970; asso. firm Chadbourne, Hunt, Jaeckel & Brown, N.Y.C., 1950-53; sr. atty. U.S. Dept. Treasury, Portland, Oreg., 1953—; spl. asst. atty. gen. elections, N.Y.C., 1952. Mem. Equal Employment Opportunity Commn., Portland, 1970; troop treas. Columbia Pacific council Boy Scouts Am., 1966-67. Mem. N.Y. State, Oreg., Fed. bar assns. Home: 1265 S W Cardinell Dr Portland OR 97201 Office: 1220 S W 3d Ave Portland OR 97204 Tel (503) 221-3131

KUSHNER, ERVAN FREDERICK, b. Paterson, N.J., Sept. 21, 1915; B.S., Fordham U., 1936, J.D., 1939. Admitted to N.J. bar, 1940, U.S. Supreme Ct. bar, 1958; individual practice law, Paterson, 1946-52; pros. atty. Paterson, 1952-54, city atty., 1954-57; presiding judge Municipal Ct. Paterson, 1967—. Mem. Passaic County Bar Assn. Col. AUS Ret.; decorated Bronze Star with oak leaf cluster, Legion of Merit, Army Commendation medal. Author: A Guide to Mineral Collecting in Ouray, Colorado, 1972, 74; A Guide to Mineral Collecting at Franklin and Sterling Hill, New Jersey, 1970, 73, 75; A Manual of Abbreviated Criminal Complaints for Use in Municipal Courts, 1969, 74. Home: 609 E 26th St Paterson NJ 07504 Office: 5 Colt St Paterson NJ 07505 Tel (201) 742-8532 also 684-9126

KUSHNER, LOUIS BERNARD, b. Pitts., Mar. 22, 1942; B.S., Pa. State U., 1964; LL.B., U. Pitts., 1967. Admitted to Pa. bar, 1968; partner firm Rothman, Gordon, Foreman and Groudine, Pitts., 1971—. Bd. dirs. Greater Pitts. Anti-Defamation League, Y-IKC East End Center. Mem. Am., Pa., Allegheny bar assns., ACLU (dir. chpt., vice chmn. prepaid legal services com.). Home: 13 Dunmoyle Pl Pittsburgh PA 15217 Office: 300 Grant Bldg Pittsburgh PA 15219 Tel (412) 281-0705

KUSHNICK, JERROLD H., b. Mar. 8, 1931; B.A., Bklyn. Coll., 1952, LL.B., 1954. Admitted to N.Y. bar, 1956; partner firm Beldock & Kushnick, and predecessors, N.Y.C., 1965-71; individual practice law, N.Y.C., 1971—; pres. Mgmt. Cons. Co., N.Y.C., 1973—. Chmn., Morton S. Kramer Scholarship Fund, N.Y. U., 1971—; counsel Pub. Sch. 49 PTA, N.Y.C., 1971-73. Mem. AFTRA, Screen Actors Guild. Office: 720 Fifth Ave New York City NY 10019 Tel (212) 246-9600

KUSHNICK, MARTIN JAY, b. Bklyn., Sept. 29, 1928; LL.B., Bklyn. Law Sch., 1955. Admitted to N.Y. bar, 1956; partner firm Gordon, Kotler & Kushnick, Huntington, N.Y., 1971—. Mem. N.Y., Suffolk County bar assns., Am., N.Y., Suffolk-Nassau trial lawyers assns., Am. Arbitration Assn. Home: 3 Rosemont Ct Greenlawn NY 11740 Office: 780 New York Ave Huntington NY 11743 Tel (516) 427-4545

KUSHNICK, MICHAEL GORDON, b. N.Y.C., Apr. 18, 1933; B.A., Colgate U., 1955; LL.B., Columbia, 1958. Admitted to D.C. bar, 1958, U.S. Supreme Ct. bar, 1966; asst. to commnr. FTC, Washington, 1961-66; asso. firm Zuckert, Scott & Rasenberger, Washington, 1966-68; partner firm Bebchick, Sher & Kushnick, Washington, 1968-73; partner firm Rose & Kushnick, Washington, 1973-77, Rose, Schmidt & Dixon, Washington and Pitts., 1977—; lectr. adminstrv. law Am. U., 1970-71. Mem. Am., Fed. bar assns. Co-editor: Omnibus Copyright Revision, Am. Soc. Info. Services. Home: 107 Pommander Walk Alexandria VA 22314 Office: 818 Connecticut Ave NW Suite 300 Washington DC 20006 Tel (202) 296-5950

KUSMER, TOBY HAROLD, b. St. Louis, July 4, 1944; B.S. in Elec. Engring., Washington U., 1966; J.D., Am. U., 1970. Admitted to Va. bar, 1970, U.S. Patent bar, 1972, Mass. bar, 1973; patent examiner U.S. Patent Office, 1966-72; asso. firm Schiller & Pandiscio, Waltham, Mass., 1972—. Mem. Am., Boston bar assns. Home: 16 Pinckney St Boston MA 02114 Office: 60 Hickory Dr Waltham MA 02154 Tel (617) 890-5610

KUSTELL, CARL BARNARD, b. Buffalo, Sept. 22, 1939; B.A., U. Buffalo, 1963; J.D., State U. N.Y. at Buffalo, 1965. Admitted to N.Y. State Bar, 1965; asso. firm Williams, Williams, Volgenau & Tisdall, Buffalo, 1965-69, partner, 1969-73; partner firm Ellis, Kustell & Mullenhoff, Buffalo, 1973—. Mem. adv. com. Clarence Sch. Bd., 1976, 77. Mem. Erie County (chmn. young lawyers com. 1968-69), N.Y. State, Am. bar assns., N.Y. State, Erie County trial lawyers assns. Home: 5370 Shimerville Rd Clarence NY 14031 Office: 1660 Kensington Ave Buffalo NY 14215 Tel (716) 837-1515

KUSTER, LLOYD JOHN, b. Grand Forks, N.D., Mar. 5, 1915; grad. Mayville State Coll., 1935; LL.U., Lincoln U., San Francisco, 1966. Admitted to Calif bar, 1966; individual practice law, San Francisco, 1968—. Office: 225 W Portal Ave San Francisco CA 94127 Tel (415) 661-9019

KUSTER, RICHARD JAY, b. Bloomington, Ind., May 21, 1947; B.S., Ind. U., 1969, J.D., 1972. Admitted to Ind. bar, 1972; mem. firm Kuster & Kuster, Ligonier, Ind., 1972—. Mem. Noble County, Am. bar assns. Office: 309 S Cavin St Ligonier IN 46767 Tel (219) 894-3156

KUSZYNSKI, JOSEPH PETER, b. Buffalo, Mar. 5, 1921; student Canisius Coll., 1939-42, LL.B., U. Buffalo, 1944; L.H.D., Alliance Coll., 1975. Admitted to N.Y. bar, 1944; practiced in Buffalo, 1944-58; judge City Ct., Buffalo, 1958-65; justice N.Y. State Supreme Ct., trial Div., assigned to Western N.Y., Buffalo, 1965—; asst. county atty. Erie County (N.Y.), 1954-58. Trustee Alliance Coll., 1947-51; bd. mgrs. Buffalo and Erie County Hist. Soc., 1965—. Mem. N.Y. State, Erie County bar assns., Lawyers Club, Buffalo Advocates Assn. Home: 98 Dana Rd Buffalo NY 14216 Office: Erie County Hall 92 Franklin St Buffalo NY 14202 Tel (716) 852-1291

KUTNER, MAURICE JAY, b. Far Rockaway, N.Y., May 19, 1940; B.B.A., 1962, J.D., 1965. Admitted to Fla. bar, 1965, U.S. Ct. Mil. Appeals bar, 1965; appellate govt. counsel U.S. Army, Washington, 1965-67, chief prosecutor Ft. Benning, Ga., 1967-68; asst. pub. defender Dade County (Fla.), 1968-70; spl. asst. atty. gen. State of Fla., 1965; practice law, Miami, Fla., 1965—. Mem. Am. Bar Assn., Nat. Assn. Def. Lawyers, Assn. Trial Lawyers Am., Fla. Trial Lawyers. Home: 1141 S W 69th Terr Miami FL 33144 Office: 28 W Flagler St Miami FL Tel (305) 377-9411

KUTSCHE, ARTHUR JOHN, b. Mpls., Aug. 28, 1940; B.S. in Bus. Adminstrn., U. Fla., 1962, J.D., 1965. Admitted to Fla. bar, 1965; chief asst. solicitor Brevard County (Fla.), 1966-70; asst. city atty., prosecutor City of Titusville (Fla.), 1966-70; asst. state atty. 18 Jud. Circuit, Brevard County, 1970-74, asst. pub. defender, 1974-76; mem. firm Lovering, Pound & Lober, Rockledge, Fla., 1974-76; partner firm Studstill & Kutsche, Titusville, 1976—. Mem. Fla. Bar, Brevard County Bar Assn., Nat. Assn. Dist. Attys., Fla. Pros. Attys. Assn., Acad. Fla. Trial Lawyers, Phi Delta Phi. Home: 1428 Gleneagles Way Rockledge FL 32955 Office: 503 Palm Ave Titusville FL 32780 Tel (305) 269-0666

KUVIN, LAWRENCE PHILIP, b. Newark, Oct. 11, 1933; B.S. in Econs., U. Pa., 1955; J.D., U. Miami, 1958. Admitted to Fla. bar, 1958; mem. firm Carey, Dwyer, Austin, Cole & Selwood, Miami, Fla., 1960-72, firm Kuvin, Klingensmith & Lewis, Miami, 1972—. Mem. Fla. (chmn. no-fault com.), Dade County bar assns., Fedn. Ins. Counsel, Am. Arbitration Assn., Dade County Def. Bar Assn. (pres. 1970-72). Home: 611 San Antonio St Coral Gables FL 33146 Office: POB 330739 Coconut Grove Miami FL 33133 Tel (305) 446-8671

KUYKENDALL, JOHN MCCLAIN, JR., b. Charleston, Miss., Sept. 14, 1915; B.A., U. Miss., 1938, LL.B., 1940. Admitted to Miss. bar, 1940, U.S. Supreme Ct. bar, 1956; spl. agt. FBI, 1940-43; asst. atty. gen. State of Miss., 1947-51; mem. firms Overstreet & Kuykendall and predecessors, 1951—. Mem. Hinds County (Miss.), Miss. State, Am., Fed., Fed. Power bar assns. Office: PO Box 961 Jackson MS 39205 Tel (601) 948-3014

KUZMIER, DAVID XENOPHON, b. Huntington, N.Y., Jan. 3, 1927; M.B.A., St. John's U., 1970. J.D., 1972. Admitted to N.Y. State bar, 1954; asso. firm Kuzmier, McKeon, Zweibel & Schmitt, N.Y.C., 1953-55; asso. firm Rothbard, McCalley & Schullman, N.Y.C., 1955-58; v.p. Mason Supply Corp., Huntington, 1960-69; chief trial counsel Legal Aid Soc. Suffolk County, 1970-73; law sec. surrogate Suffolk County, 1973-75; dep. chief clk. Surrogates Ct. Suffolk County 1975-77; chief clk. County Ct. Suffolk County, 1977—; asso. adj. prof. bus. adminstrn. Suffolk County Community Coll., 1970—; instr. estate planning C.W. Post Coll., Greenvale, N.Y., 1975—. Bd. dirs. Legal Aid Soc. Suffolk County 1973—. Mem. N.Y. State, Suffolk County bar assns. Office: County Ct Criminal Cts Bldg Center Dr S Riverhead NY 11901 Tel (516) 727-4700

KUZMIER, DIRK BELL, b. Huntington, N.Y., Sept. 12, 1926; B.A., Dartmouth, 1948; J.D., N.Y. U., 1950. Admitted to N.Y. bar, 1951, U.S. Dist. Ct. for So. and Eastern N.Y. bars, 1956, U.S. Supreme Ct. bar, 1960, U.S. 2d Circuit Ct. Appeals bar, 1962; partner firm Kuzmier, MeKeon, Carrion & Siskind, N.Y.C., 1951—; spl. pretrial master Civil Ct., N.Y.C., 1965-66. Bd. dirs. Amagansett Villiage Improvement Soc. Mem. Am. Bar Assn., Assn. Trial Lawyers Am., N.Y. State Trial Lawyers Assn., Met. Trial Lawyers Assn. (mem. exec. com., dir. 1966—), Bklyn.-Manhattan Trial Council Assn. (pres. 1977), Am. Arbitration Assn., Assn. Bar City N.Y. (sec. med. juris. com. 1963-66), N.Y. State Bar Assn. (dir. trial lawyers sect. 1964-67). Home: 205 S Broadway Irvington NY 10533 Office: 12 E 41st St New York City NY 10017 Tel (212) MU6-5835

KWALWASSER, HAROLD JOSEPH, b. N.Y.C., Jan. 1, 1947; B.A., Swarthmore Coll., 1968; J.D., Yale, 1971. Admitted to Calif. bar, 1972; law clk. Judge Max Rosenn, U.S. Ct. Appeals for 3d Circuit, Phila., 1971-72; mem. firm Tuttle and Taylor, Los Angeles, 1972—; chmn. City Attys. Citizen Rev. Commn., Los Angeles, 1973-74. Mem. Am. Bar Assn. Bd. editors Yale Law Jour., 1969-71. Home: 9947 1/2 Young Dr Beverly Hills CA 90212 Office: 609 S Grand Ave Los Angeles CA 90017 Tel (213) 683-0600

KWASS, SIDNEY JACK, b. Pocahontas, Va., Nov. 11, 1908; J.D., W.Va. U., 1931. Admitted to W.Va. bar, 1931, ICC bar, 1934, FCC bar, 1934, IRS bar, 1935; individual practice law, Bluefield, W.Va., 1931-46; partner firm Kwass Stone McGhee & Feuchtenberger, Bluefield, 1946—; city atty. Bluefield, 1933-37; commr. Mercer County (W.Va.) Circuit Ct., 1938-46; referee in bankruptcy U.S. Dist. Ct. So. W.Va., 1942-46; mem. W.Va. Workmen's Compensation Appeals Bd., 1959-69, chmn., 1961-69; adj. prof. cts. and jud. processes Bluefield State Coll., 1976. Founding mem., 1st sec. Bluefield Community Chest, 1936; bd. dirs., past pres. Bluefield-Princeton Jewish Congregation. Mem. 4th Jud. Circuit Conf., W.Va. State Bar (standing com. on jurisprudence and law reform, past mem. bd. govs.), Mercer County Bar Assn. (past pres.). Home: 1208 Hilltop Ln Bluefield WV 24701 Office: Law and Commerce Bldg Suite 305 Bluefield WV 24701 Tel (304) 327-8193

KYHOS, WAYNE CHARLES, b. Washington, Jan. 23, 1944; B.A., DePauw U., 1966; J.D., U. Akron, 1969. Admitted to Ohio bar, 1969, Ga. bar, 1973; estate tax atty. IRS, Cleve., 1969-70; served as capt. JAG U.S. Army, 1970-73; asso. firm Amerman, Burt & Jones, Canton, Massillon, Ohio, 1973—. Mem. Ohio, Stark County, Ga., Am. bar assns., Massillon (Ohio) Lawyers (v.p. 1975-76, pres. 1976-77). Home: 3942 Darlington Ave NW Canton OH 44708 Office: 1972 Wales Rd NE Massillon OH 44646 Tel (216) 837-4666

KYLE, CHARLES DERRICK, b. Wayneburg, Pa., Sept. 16, 1904; A.B., Amherst Coll., 1925, LL.B., Harvard, 1928. Admitted to N.Y. bar, 1929; asso. firm Milbank, Tweed, Hadley & McCloy, and predecessors, N.Y.C., 1928-37, partner, 1937—. Mem. Am., N.Y. State N.Y.C. bar assns. Home: Windover Lumberville PA 18933 Office: 1 Chase Manhattan Plaza New York City NY 10005 Tel (212) 422-2660

KYLER, WILLIAM ALEXANDER, b. Jeromesville, Ohio, June 25, 1938; B.A., Ohio Wesleyan U., 1960; LL.B. (Citizenship Clearinghouse fellow; Africa/Asia Pub. Service fellow), Duke U., 1964. Admitted to Ohio bar, U.S. Dist. Ct. bar, 1964; asso. firm Arter & Hadden, Cleve., 1964-67; partner firm Smith Renner, Hanhart, Miller & Kyler, New Philadelphia, Ohio, 1967—. Pres., bd. dirs. United Way, Tuscarawas County, Ohio, 1974; pres. Kent State U. Found. Tuscarawas County, 1975; pres., bd. dirs. Tuscarawas County YMCA, 1976. Mem. Am., Ohio, Tuscarawas County bar assns. (pres. county chpt. 1971). Recipient Distinguished Service award New Philadelphia Jaycees, 1975. Office: PO Box 668 New Philadelphia OH 44663 Tel (216) 343-5585

LABADIE, DWIGHT DANIEL, b. Farmington, Mich., Dec. 16, 1940; A.B., Kalamazoo Coll., 1963; J.D. cum laude, Wayne State U., 1971. Admitted to Mich. bar, 1971; claims rep. Aetna Casualty and Surety Co., Detroit, 1964-68; workmen's compensation rep. Chrysler Corp., Highland Park, Mich., 1968-71; asso. firm Davidson, Gotshall, Kohl, Secrest, Wardle, Lynch and Clark, Farmington Hills, Mich., 1971—. Mem. Mich. Bar Assn.

LABATON, EDWARD, b. Bklyn., Jan. 6, 1932; B.B.A., Coll. City N.Y., 1952; LL.B., Yale, 1955. Admitted to N.Y. State bar, 1957, U.S. Supreme Ct., 1975; since practiced in N.Y.C., asso. firm Rosston, Hort & Brussel, 1958-61, asso. firm Kramer & Lans, 1961-64, partner firm Kramer, Bandler & Labaton, 1964-70, partner firm Shatzkin, Cooper, Labaton, Rudoff & Bandler, 1970—. Mem. Am. Bar Assn., Assn. of Bar of City of N.Y., Fed. Bar Council, N.Y. County Lawyers Assn. Home: 75 Merrall Dr Lawrence NY 11559 Office: 235 E 42d St New York City NY 10017 Tel (212) 687-8800

LABE, LOUIS JAY, b. New Orleans, Oct. 7, 1945; B.A. in History, U. Colo., 1967, J.D., 1970. Law clk. to judge Denver Dist. Ct., 1968-69, to judge Colo. Ct. of Appeals, Denver, 1971-72; admitted to Colo. bar, 1971, U.S. Ct. Claims bar, 1974; partner firm Tilly and Graves, Denver, 1972—. Mem. Am., Colo. bar assns., Am. Judicature Soc. Asso. editor U. Colo. Law Rev., 1970. Office: 50 S Steele St Suite 800 Denver CO 80209 Tel (303) 321-8811

LABES, LEON MARTIN, b. N.Y.C., Aug. 7, 1913; B.A., Bklyn. Coll., 1933; LL.B., Bklyn. Law Sch., 1936, J.S.D. cum laude, 1937. Admitted to N.Y. State bar, 1937; since practiced in N.Y.C., mem. firm Bainbridge Colby, Brown and Pollack, 1938-42, Hartman, Sheridan, Tekulsky & Pecora, 1942-52, Alderman & Labes, 1952-55, individual practice law, 1955-70, mem. firm Auerbach & Labes, 1970—; cons. U.S. War Prodn. Bd., 1942-45; exec. dir., counsel Electronic Mfrs. Assn., N.Y.C., 1962-74; moderator Labor Relations Forum, WEVD, N.Y.C., 1962-65; lectr. labor law Columbia, Coll. City N.Y., N.Y. U.; dir. Manpower Edn. Inst., N.Y.C., 1968-76, N.Y. Urban League, Manhattan div., 1970—; mem. panel on med. malpractice N.Y. appellate div. First Dept., spl. master Supreme Ct. County of N.Y. Mem. Am., N.Y. State (mem. Attica Relief Com.) bar assns., N.Y. County Lawyers (mem. labor com.), N.Y. State Trial Lawyers Assn. Author: A Fresh Approach to the Problem of Strikes, 1968; contbr. numerous articles to profl. jours. Home: 1010 Fifth Ave New York City NY 10028 Office: 605 3d Ave Suite 1501 New York City NY 10016 Tel (212) 972-1100

LABRANCHE, FRANS JOSEPH, JR., b. New Orleans, June 17, 1934; A.A., St. Joseph's Sem., 1955; J.D., Loyola U., New Orleans, 1960. Admitted to La. bar, 1960; individual practice law, New Orleans, 1960; capt. Judge Adv. Gen.'s Corps, U.S. Air Force, 1961-63; partner firm Connolly, Labranche & Lagarde, New Orleans, 1964—; lectr. bus. law Loyola U., 1964-73; adj. asso. prof. legal medicine Tulane U. Med. Sch., 1970—. Coordinator, Easter Seals Walkathon, 1975; active Boy Scouts Am. Mem. Am. (com. on medicine and law 1973—), La., New Orleans bar assns., Am. Judicature Soc., Am. Trial Lawyers Assn., St. Thomas More Cath. Lawyers Assn. (past v.p.). Contbr. articles to med. jours. Home: 935 Picheloup Pl New Orleans LA 70119 Office: 3914 Canal St New Orleans LA 70119 Tel (504) 482-5785

LACEY, MICHAEL CHARLES, b. Anderson, Ind., Sept. 18, 1948; B.A., Western Mich. U., 1970; J.D., Ind. U., 1973. Admitted to Ind. bar, 1973; mem. firm Davisson, Davisson & Davisson, Anderson, 1973—. Treas., Madison County Republican Central Com., 1974—. Mem. Ind. (com. group legal services), Am. bar assns. Home: 106 N Shore Blvd Anderson IN 46011 Office: PO Box 847 Anderson IN 46015

LACEY, WILLIAM CHARLES, b. Sioux Falls, S.D., Mar. 25, 1907; LL.B. magna cum laude, U. S.D., 1929. Admitted to S.D. bar, 1929, U.S. Supreme Ct. bar, 1963; individual practice law, Sioux Falls, 1929-46; partner firm Lacey & Perry, Sioux Falls, 1946-53, Lacey & Parliman, Sioux Falls, 1953-61, Lacey & Lacey, Sioux Falls, 1969—; chmn. com. jud., uniform laws S.D. Ho. of Reps., 1949-50, 55-58, 63-70. Active S.D. Constl. Revision Commn., 1970-73. Home and Office: 1004 E 35th St Sioux Falls SD 57105 Tel (605) 334-9322

LA CHANCE, JAMES MARTIN, b. Gardner, Mass., Nov. 16, 1947; A.B. in English Lit., Middlebury Coll., 1969; J.D., Boston Coll., 1972. Admitted to Mass. bar, 1972; atty. Cambridge (Mass.) & Somerville

Legal Services, Inc., 1972—. Mem. Mass., Boston bar assns. Home: 103 Pinckney St Boston MA 02114 Office: 24 Thorndike St Cambridge MA 02141 Tel (617) 492-5520

LACHIATTO, ALEXANDER MICHAEL, b. Concord, N.H., Nov. 5, 1938; B.A., Providence Coll., 1960; J.D., Suffolk U., 1963. Admitted to N.H. bar, 1963; partner firm Daniell & Lachiatto, Franklin, N.H., 1963-72; individual practice law, Franklin, 1972—; judge Franklin Dist. Ct., 1974—; city solicitor, Franklin, 1970-73. Mem. Franklin City Council, 1966-69; trustee Franklin Hosp. Mem. Am., Merrimack County bar assns. Office: Nat Bank Bldg Franklin St Franklin NH 03235 Tel (603) 934-2110

LACINA, LOUIS JOHN, JR., b. Brenham, Tex., Nov. 14, 1949; B.B.A., Baylor U., 1972, J.D., 1972. Admitted to Tex. bar, 1972; partner firm Hodde & Lacina, Brenham, 1972—; county atty. Washington County, Tex., 1974—. Mem. Washington County Bicentennial Com., 1976; leader Sam Houston Council Boy Scouts Am., Brenham, 1973—. Mem. Am., Tex., Washington County (pres. 1974-75) bar assns. Home: 701 3rd Brenham TX 77833 Office: PO Box 557 Brenham TX 77633 Tel (713) 836-5288

LACKLAND, JOHN, b. Parma, Idaho, Aug. 29, 1939; B.A., Stanford U., 1962; J.D., U. Wash., 1964. Admitted to Wash. bar, 1965, U.S. Ct. Appeals 9th Circuit bar, 1965, U.S. Supreme Ct. bar, 1973; asso. firm Lane, Powell, Moss & Miller, Seattle, 1965-69; asst. atty. gen. State of Wash., Seattle, 1969-72, asst. chief U. Wash. div., 1969-72; v.p., sec., gen. counsel Western Farmers Assn., Seattle, 1972-76, Fotomat Corp., Stamford, Conn., 1976—. Bd. dirs. Mercer Island (Wash.) United Ch., 1967-70, pres. bd. dirs., 1970; mem. Land Use Plan Steering com. City of Mercer Island, 1970-72; dir. Mercer Island Sch. Dist., 1970-73, v.p. bd. dirs., 1972, pres., 1973. Mem. Am., Wash. State bar assns. Office: 1200 High Ridge Rd Stamford CT 06905 Tel (203) 329-8831

LACKMEYER, MICHAEL ROY, b. Kilgore, Tex., Dec. 4, 1945; B.A., So. Methodist U., 1966; J.D., Baylor U., 1970. Admitted to Tex. bar, 1970; asst. city atty. City of Waco (Tex.), 1970-71; asst. dist. atty. 27th Jud. Dist., Bell County, Tex., 1971-72; individual practice law, Killeen, Tex., 1972—; speaker State Bar Inst., 1976. Mem. Bell County Child Welfare Bd.; bd. dirs. C. R. Clements' Boys' Club, Killeen. Office: 210 E Ave C Killeen TX 76541 Tel (817) 526-8381

LA COUR, LOUIS BERNARD, b. Columbus, Ohio, Aug. 12, 1926; B.A., Ohio State U., 1951; LL.B., Franklin U., 1961; J.D., Capital U., 1967. Right of way agt. Ohio State Hwy. Dept., 1957-59; property acquisition supr., Columbus, 1959-60, land acquisition officer, 1960-62; admitted to Ohio bar, 1963; individual practice law, Columbus, 1963—; adj. prof. Capital U. Law Sch.; village solicitor Urbancrest (Ohio), 1968-71; rep. various community orgns.; cons. to civic orgns. Trustee Columbus Symphony; adv. bd. Bishop Hartley High Sch.; mem. steering com. Devel. Com. for Greater Columbus; past vice-chmn. Columbus Civic Center Commn.; mem. Selective Service Appeals Bd.; past chmn. Columbus Leadership Conf.; past v.p. Columbus Area Internat. program; past sec. Mid-Ohio Regional Planning Commn.; past pres. Columbus Urban League; past v.p. United Community Council. Mem. Columbus Bar Assn. Home: 2349 N Cassady Ave Columbus OH 43219 Office: 48 E Gay St Columbus OH 43215 Tel (614) 224-2101

LACOUR, VANUE BARTHOLOMEW, b. Natchez, La., Sept. 10, 1915; B.A., Xavier U., 1938; J.D., Howard U., 1941. Admitted to Mo. bar, 1942, La. bar, 1949; individual practice law, Kansas City, Mo., 1942-47; prof. So. U. Law Sch., Baton Rouge, 1947-70, dean, 1970-71; partner firm Lacour & Calloway, Baton Rouge, 1971—. Mem. Am., La., Baton Rouge bar assns. Home: 2578 79th Ave Baton Rouge LA 70807 Office: PO Box 73588 8050 Scenic Hwy Baton Rouge LA 70807 Tel (504) 775-6297

LACY, ALEXANDER SHELTON, b. S. Boston, Va., Aug. 18, 1921; B.S., U. Ala., 1943; LL.B., U. Va., 1949. Admitted to Ala. bar, 1949; assoc. firm Bradley, Arant, Rose & White, Birmingham, Ala., 1949-54; v.p. atty. Ala. Gas Corp., Birmingham, 1954—. Chmn. Birmingham-Jefferson Civic Center Authority, 1965-71; pres. chmn. Birmingham Symphony Assn., 1964-67; v.p. Nat. Municipal League, 1970-77. Mem. Am., Fed., Ala., Birmingham bar assns., Fed. Power Bar Assn., Am. Judicature Soc. Home: 3730 Montrose Rd Birmingham AL 33213 Office: 1918 1st Ave N Birmingham AL 35295 Tel (205) 323-4611

LACY, JOHN FORD, b. Dallas, Sept. 11, 1944; B.A., Baylor U., 1965; J.D., Harvard, 1968. Admitted to Tex. bar, 1968; asso. firm Akin, Gump, Strauss, Hauer & Feld, Dallas, 1968-72, partner, 1973—; dir. Dallas Legal Services Found., Inc., 1975—. Trustee Dallas County Heritage Soc., Inc., 1975—. Mem. Am., Tex., Dallas bar assns. Office: 2800 Republic Nat Bank Bldg Dallas TX 75201 Tel (214) 655-2724

LADAS, PAUL MICHAEL, b. Muskegon, Mich., Oct. 28, 1934; A.B., U. Mich., 1956, J.D., 1959. Admitted to Mich. bar, 1960; asst. pros. atty. Muskegon County (Mich.), 1960-63, chief asst. pros. atty., 1963-64, pros. atty., 1965-72; asst. atty. gen. State of Mich., Lansing, 1964; atty. Twp. of Fruitland (Mich.), 1973—; individual practice law, Muskegon, Mich., 1973—; mem. regional bd. Law Enforcement Assistance Adminstrn., 1972. Bd. dirs. Muskegon Community Action Against Poverty, 1969. Mem. Am., Mich., Muskegon County bar assns., Am. Judicature Soc., Am., Mich. trial lawyers assns. Recipient Reverence for Law award Eagles, 1973. Home: 2877 Scenic Dr Muskegon MI 49445 Office: 435 Whitehall Rd Muskegon MI 49445 Tel (616) 744-6218

LADD, DAVID LOWELL, b. Nauvoo, Ohio, Sept. 18, 1926; student, Kenyon Coll., 1944; B.A., U. Chgo., 1949, J.D., 1953. Admitted to Ill. Bar, 1953, Ohio bar, 1970; practiced in Chgo., 1953-61, 63-70; U.S. Commr. Patents, 1961-63; of counsel Biebel, French & Nauman, Dayton, Ohio, 1969—; U.S. observer Com. Patent Experts, Council Europe, 1962; adj. prof. law Ohio State U., 1970—; U.S. Rep. to Consultative Com. Internat. Bur. for Protection of Indsl. Property, Geneva, 1961-62; founder Com. for Internat. Coop. in Info. Retrieval among Examining Patent Offices; vis. prof. U. Miami (Fla.), 1975—; adv. bd. Assn. for the Advancement of Sci. and Innovation, 1971—. Mem. Dayton, Chicago, Am. (spl. com. to study patent system 1965-66) patent law assns., Am., Chgo. bar assns. Patent Office Soc. (hon.). Home: 7802 William Penn Ln Dayton OH 45459 Office: 2500 Winters Bank Tower Dayton OH 45402 Tel (513) 461-4543

LADD, ROBERT POWELL, b. Detroit, Apr. 16, 1949; B.A. with honors, Mich. State U., 1971; J.D., Ind. U., 1974. Admitted to Mich. bar, 1974; asso. firm Best, Arnold, Gleeson & Best, Jackson, Mich., 1975—; dir. Jackson County Legal Aid Soc. Mem. Mich., Jackson County bar assns., Assn. Trial Lawyers Am., So. Mich. Claims Assn. Office: 410 S Jackson St Jackson MI 49204 Tel (517) 787-2620

LADEN, LARRY R., b. Mt. Pleasant, Tex., Jan. 26, 1947; B.B.A., J.D., U. Tex. Admitted to Tex. bar, 1972; asst. dist. atty. Travis County (Tex.), Austin, 1st trial asst., then 1st asst. dist. atty.; now with firm Hall & Laden, Assos., Austin. Home: 2210 Del Curto Austin TX 78704 Office: 314 W 11th St Suite 302 Austin TX 78701 Tel (512) 472-8010

LADER, PHILIP, b. Jackson Heights, N.Y., Mar. 17, 1946; B.A., Duke, 1966; M.A., Oxford (Eng.) U., 1968; J.D., Harvard, 1971. Admitted to Fla. bar, 1972, D.C. bar, 1973; asso. firm Sullivan & Cromwell, N.Y.C., 1972; law clk. to U.S. circuit judge, 1973; v.p. Sea Pines Assos., Hilton Head Island, S.C., 1973-76; partner firm Hartzog, Lader, & Richards, Washington, 1974—; counsel Secretariat for Tourism Integration of Central Am. Mem. Am. Bar Assn. (vice chmn. young lawyers sect. environ. quality com.), Phi Beta Kappa. Home: 5680 Grove St S Saint Petersburg FL 33705 Tel (803) 785-2984

LADNER, OSCAR BUREN, b. Presntiss, Miss., Sept. 4, 1924; B.S., Miss. State U., 1949; LL.B., U. Miss., 1961. Admitted to Miss. bar, 1961; partner firm Ladner & Emil, Gulfport, Miss., 1973—. Mem. Am. Trial Lawyers Assn., Am. Judicature Soc. Home: 176 Allan Dr Gulfport MS 39501 Office: 2301 14th St Gulfport MS 39501 Tel (601) 864-3926

LA FACE, RONALD C., b. Pitts., July 4, 1940; B.S., U. Fla., 1963, J.D., 1966. Admitted to Fla. bar, 1966; asso. firm Walton Lantaff Schroeder & Carson, Miami, Fla., 1966-69; asst. atty. gen. State of Fla., Tallahassee, 1969-70; partner firm LaFace & Baggett, Tallahassee, 1972—. Mem. Am. Bar Assn., Am. Judicature Soc., Fla. Bar (chmn. adminstrv. law sect.), Tallahassee C. of C. Office: 101 E College Ave Tallahassee FL 32302 Tel (904) 222-6891

LA FARGUE, JERON JAMES, b. Sulphur, La., Sept. 13, 1934; J.D., Tulane U., 1958. Admitted to La. bar, 1958, U.S. Dist. Ct. bar, 1961; individual practice law, Sulphur, 1958-76, Lake Charles, La., 1976—. Pres. La. Assn. Fairs and Festivals, 1974-75; mem. Sulphur Democratic Exec. Com., 1961—. Mem. La., Southwest La. bar assns. Home: 920 Lilliput Ln Sulphur LA 70663 Office: 710 W Prien Lake Rd Lake Charles LA 70601 Tel (318) 478-5366

LAFAVE, ARTHUR JOSEPH, b. Cleve., Mar. 28, 1933; B.A., Williams Coll., 1955; LL.B., Yale, 1958. Admitted to Oreg. bar, 1958, Ohio bar, 1960; asso. firm Black & Apicella, Portland, Oreg., 1958-60, firm Arter, Hadden, Wykoff & Van Duzer, Cleve., 1960-65; sr. v.p., dir. Internat. Mgmt. Group, Cleve., 1965—. Tel (216) 522-1200

LAFF, CHARLES ALAN, b. Chgo., Feb. 17, 1934; B.S. in Chem. Engring., Purdue U., 1955; J.D., Harvard, 1958. Admitted to Ill. bar, 1959, Fla. bar, 1961, U.S. Supreme Ct. bar, 1972; asso. firm Neuman, Williams, Anderson & Olson, Chgo., 1957-58, asso., 1959-65, partner, 1966-72; partner firms Alter, Weiss, Whitesel & Laff, Chgo., 1972-74, Laff, Whitesel & Rockman, Chgo., 1974—; lectr. Loyola U. Sch. Law, Chgo., 1974-76. Mem. Am., Chgo., Ill., Fla., 7th Circuit bar assns., Am., Chgo. patent law assns., Chgo. Council Lawyers, U.S. Trademark Assn., Assn. Internat. Indsl. Property Inst. Contbr. article to legal jour. Home: 431 A Grant Pl Chicago IL 60614 Office: Laff Whitesel & Rockman John Hancock Center Suite 2460 875 N Michigan Ave Chicago IL 60611 Tel (312) 649-0200

LA FOLLETTE, BRONSON CUTTING, b. Washington, Feb. 2, 1936; B.A., U. Wis., 1958, J.D., 1960. Admitted to Wis. bar, 1960, U.S. Supreme Ct. bar, 1966; asst. U.S. atty. Western Dist. Wis., 1962-64; atty. gen. State of Wis., Madison, 1964—; individual practice law, Madison, 1968-74; mem. Bd. Commrs. Pub. Lands, Bd. State Canvassers, Jud. Council, Council on Drug Abuse, Controlled Substances Bd., Group Ins. Bd., Council on Criminal Justice, Gt. Lakes Compact Com. Chmn., Pres.'s Consumer Adv. Council, 1966-68; pres. Wis. Consumers League, 1969; bd. dirs. Consumers Union, 1968-77; trustee State Library. Mem. Nat. Assn. Attys. Gen. Am. Specialists Abroad Program grantee, 1965. Office: 114 E State Capitol Madison WI 53702 Tel (608) 266-1221

LA FOND, JOHN QUINN, b. Chgo., Oct. 9, 1943; B.A., Yale, 1965, LL.B., 1968. Admitted to N.Y. State bar, 1969; asso. firm Debevoise, Plimpton, Lyons & Gates, N.Y.C., 1971-73; vis. asso. prof. law U. Colo., 1973-74; asso. prof. U. Puget Sound, 1974—. Mem. N.Y. State, Am. bar assns. Home: 8910 49th St W Tacoma WA 98467 Office: 8811 S Tacoma Way Tacoma WA 98499 Tel (206) 756-3327

LA FORCE, A.H. JOHN, II, b. San Pedro, Calif., July 4, 1932; B.S., U. Mo., 1962, J.D., 1960; LL.M., Georgetown U., 1967; Admitted to Mo. bar, 1960, U.S. Supreme Ct. bar, 1964, Tex. bar, 1970; asso. firm Clark & Becker, Columbia, Mo., 1960-62; atty. tax div. Dept. Justice, Washington, 1962-68; with Panhandle Eastern Pipe Line Co., Houston, 1968—, gen. atty., 1976—. Mem. State Bar Tex., Am., Mo., Houston bar assns., Phi Delta Phi, Order of Coif. Office: 3000 Bissonnet St Houston TX 77005 Tel (713) 664-3401

LAGUEUX, RONALD RENE, b. Lewiston, Maine, June 30, 1931; A.B., Bowdoin Coll., 1953; LL.B., Harvard U., 1956. Admitted to R.I. bar, 1957, Fed. bar, 1958, U.S. Ct. Appeals bar, 1960, U.S. Supreme Ct. bar, 1967; asso. firm Edwards & Angell, Providence, 1956-63; exec. counsel to Gov. R.I., 1963-65; partner firm Edwards & Angell, Providence, 1965-68; asso. justice R.I. Superior Ct., Providence, 1968—. Office: 250 Benefit St Providence RI 02903 Tel (401) 277-3250

LAHEY, EDWARD VINCENT, JR., b. Boston, Mar. 11, 1939; A.B., Holy Cross Coll., 1960; J.D., Georgetown U., 1964; postgrad Bus. Sch. Columbia U., 1969-70. Admitted to D.C. bar, 1964, N.Y. bar, 1966; mem. firm Hester, Owen & Crowder, Washington, 1964-65; atty. PepsiCo, Inc., Purchase, N.Y., 1965-68, asst. gen. counsel, 1969-73, sec., 1970—, v.p., gen. counsel, 1973—. Trustee Village of Tuckahoe, N.Y., 1970. Mem. Am., D.C. bar assns., Am. Soc. Corporate Secs. Home: 4 Willow Ave Larchmont NY 10538 Office: PepsiCo Inc Purchase NY 10577

LA HOOD, MICHAEL THOMAS, b. San Antonio, Jan. 18, 1937; B.B.A., St. Mary's U., 1959, J.D., 1967. Admitted to Tex. bar, 1967; asso. firm Jack Leon, San Antonio, Tex., 1967-68; individual practice law, San Antonio, 1969—. Mem. San Antonio, Tex., Fed. bar assns., Tex., San Antonio, Am. trial lawyers assns., Am. Judicature Soc., Law Sci. Acad., Tex. Criminal Def. Lawyers Assn. Office: Villita Sq Bldg 120 Villita San Antonio TX 78205 Tel (512) 227-8236

LAHR, JACK LEROY, b. Toledo, Ohio, Aug. 5, 1934; B.S. in Mech. Engring., U. Toledo, 1956; J.D. with honors, George Washington U., 1963. Admitted to D.C. bar, 1963, Va. bar, 1963; partner firm Arent, Fox, Kintner, Plotkin & Kahn, Washington, 1963—. Mem. Am. Bar Assn., Nat. Lawyers Club. Author: (with Kintner) An Intellectual Property Law Primer, 1975; contbr. articles to legal jours. Office: 1815 H St NW Washington DC 20006 Tel (202) 857-6080

LAIRD, EVALYN WALSH, b. Chgo., Feb. 6, 1902; J.D., De Paul U., 1926. Admitted to Ill. bar, 1926; U.S. Supreme Ct. bar, 1958; individual practice law, Chgo., 1926—; spl. agt. Prudential Ins. Co., Chgo., 1951-60; mgr. Edward J. Walsh Reporting Services, Chgo., 1960—. Pres. 7 dist. Vicariate 11 Council of Cath. Women, 1973-76; personnel com. Girl Scouts U.S.A., Chgo., 1974—; co-chmn. women's com. Esther Saperstein for Senator, Rogers Park, Ill.; pub. relations Girl Scouts U.S.A., 1969-76; del Rogers Park Community Council, 1976-77. Mem. Chgo. (com. subcoms. on tax), Ill. State, Women's (law day com.) bar assns. Home: 19295 Pine Ave Grand Beach New Buffalo MI 49117 Office: 127 N Dearborn St Suite 1541 Chicago IL 60602

LAIRD, MARTIN LUTHER, III, b. Alexandria, La., May 22, 1936; B.S., La. State U., 1958, J.D., 1961. Admitted to La. bar; asst. dist. atty. Rapides Parish (La.), Alexandria, 1969-72; judge Dist. Ct., 9th Jud. Dist., Alexandria, 1972—. Home: 1312 McNutt Dr Alexandria LA 71301 Office: Rapides Parish Court House Alexandria LA 71301 Tel (318) 448-3291

LAIST, JAMES WALLACE, b. Anaconda, Mont., Aug. 20, 1910; student Mont. State Coll., 1928-29; B.S., Harvard, 1932; M.S., Columbia, 1933; LL.B., Fordham U., 1936. Admitted to N.Y. bar, 1936, D.C. bar, 1953; law clk. firm Pennie, Davis, Marvin & Edmonds, N.Y.C., 1933-36, asso., 1936-42, 45-48; mem. firm Pennie & Edmonds, and predecessors, N.Y.C., 1948—; prodn. mgr., treas. Electrons, Inc., Newark, 1942-45; dir. Specialty Composites Corp. Chmn. Montclair (N.J.) Planning Bd., 1955-64; Montclair rep. Joint Council for Solid Waste Disposal, 1965-66; commr. Montclair Redevel. Agy., 1966—. Mem. Am., D.C. bar assns., Assn Bar City of N.Y., Am., N.Y.C. patent law assns. Author: Copper, Silver and Gold, 1954. Home: 14 Glenside Terr Upper Montclair NJ 07043 Office: 330 Madison Ave New York City NY 10017 Tel (212) 986-8686

LAISY, ALBERT WADE, b. Berea, Ohio, Feb. 22, 1932; B.A., Yale, 1954; LL.B., U. Pa., 1959. Admitted to Pa. bar, 1960, Md. bar, 1960, Ohio bar, 1976; asso. firm Reilly, Wood & Fogwell, W. Chester, Pa., 1959-60; atty. B&O R.R. Co., Balt., 1960-64, asst. gen. atty., 1964-72; commerce counsel Chessie System, Balt., 1972-76, gen. atty., Cleve., 1976—. Mem. Am., Md. bar assns., Cleve. bar assn., Engring. Soc. Balt. Home: 2886 Glengary Rd Shaker Heights OH 44120 Office: Chessie System PO Box 6419 Terminal Tower Cleveland OH 44101 Tel (216) 623-2481

LAKE, DAVID ALAN, b. El Campo, Tex., Jan. 15, 1938; B.A., Baylor U., 1960; B.Div., Southwestern Sem., 1963; J.D., So. Meth. U., 1966. Admitted to Tex. bar, 1966; partner firm Nickerson & Lake, Pittsburg, Tex., 1967-69; individual practice law, Tyler, Tex., 1969—; gen. partner Colonial Manor, Tyler, 1968—, Golden Manor, Pittsburg, 1969—; pres., Gardendale, Inc., Jacksonville, Tex., 1973—; sec. dir. Sunset Care-Center, Inc., Jacksonville, 1973—; dir., Cypress Savs. and Loan Assn., Pittsburg, 1976—. Bd. dirs. Way of Life, Inc., 1972-75, Smith County Heart Assn., 1974-75; vice-chmn., dir. Smith County Red Cross, 1972-76, chmn., 1976-77. Mem. Tex., Smith County bar assns., Tex. Nursing Home Assn. (v.p., dir.). Recipient Area 5 Speak-Up award, Jaycees, 1966. Home: 815 Pinedale St Tyler TX 75701 Office: PO Box 6776 700 Southwest Loop 323 Tyler TX 75701 Tel (214) 561-5050

LAKE, ELLEN, b. N.Y.C., Nov. 11, 1944; B.A., Radcliffe Coll., 1966; J.D., Case Western Res. U., 1970. Admitted to Calif. bar, 1971; law clk. to asso. justice Calif. Supreme Ct., San Francisco, 1970-71; staff atty. Legal Aid Soc. Alameda County, Oakland, Calif., 1971-73, United Farm Workers Am., Calif., 1973-74; atty. ACLU of No. Calif., San Francisco, 1974-75; atty. Calif. Agrl. Labor Relations Bd., Sacramento, 1975—. Mem. Calif. Bar Assn. Home: 2320 Prince St Berkeley CA 94705 Office: 915 Capitol Mall Sacramento CA 95813 Tel (916) 322-7024

LAKE, JOHN HAROLD, b. Fulton, Mo., Aug. 17, 1946; B.B.A., N.E. Mo. State U., 1968; J.D., U. Mo., 1972. Admitted to Mo. bar, 1973; mem. firm Goller & Hedrick, Jefferson City, Mo., 1973—. Reader gen. assembly Mo. Senate, 1974-76. Mem. Am., Mo., Cole County bar assns., Jefferson City Football Ofcls. Assn. Recipient Outstanding Citizen award Cole County Human Devel. Corp., 1975. Home: Route 5 Jefferson City MO 65101 Office: Goller & Hedrick 131 E High St Jefferson City MO 65101 Tel (314) 635-6181

LAKEY, ROBERT FRANKLIN, JR., b. New Orleans, Mar. 13, 1948; J.D., Tulane U., 1973. Admitted to La. bar, 1974; law clk. to judge La. 24th Jud. Dist. Ct., 1973-77; dep. Jefferson Parish Sheriff's Dept., Jefferson Parish, La., 1973-77; individual practice law, New Orleans. Mem. La., Jefferson Parish bar assns., Jefferson Parish Criminal Bar Assn. Home: 4632 Hastings St Metairie LA 70002 Tel (504) 888-2334

LAKIN, LEONARD, b. N.Y.C., July 9, 1931; B.B.A. cum laude, Coll. City N.Y., 1953; J.D., N.Y. U., 1956. Admitted to N.Y. State bar, 1956, Hawaii bar, 1958; asso. firm Levinson & Cobb, Honolulu, 1957-58, partner, 1959-60; asst. gen. counsel Walter E. Heller & Co., Inc., N.Y.C., 1960-62; asso. gen. counsel A. J. Armstrong Co., Inc., N.Y.C., 1962-64; gen. counsel, sec. Nat. Car Rental System, Inc., N.Y., 1964-65; individual practice law, N.Y.C., 1965—; asso. prof. law Bernard M. Baruch Coll., U. City N.Y., 1967—; cons. bd. examiners Am. Inst. C.P.A.'s., N.Y. State Regents univ. baccalaureate degree in bus., also pubs. legal asst. N.Y. State Bd. Law Examiners; lectr. N. Y. County Lawyers Assn., N.Y. State Soc. C.P.A. Candidates; guest lectr. U. Hawaii Grad. Sch. Social Work; chmn. Commn. on Uniform State Laws of N.Y. State. Mem. City Coll. Alumni Assn. (dir. 1969-72), Beta Gamma Sigma (pres 1974-76, bd. govs. alumni in N.Y.C. 1966-69). Author: (with Howard J. Berger) Guide to Secured Transactions, 1970, CPA Business Law Examination Review, 1972; (with M. Stansky) Cases and Materials in the Law of Business Contracts, 1973. Editor: (with others) Multistate Bar Examination Rev., 1973; also articles. Home: 77 Holly Pl Briarcliff Manor NY 10510 Office: Baruch Coll U City NY 17 Lexington Ave New York City NY 10010 Tel (212) 725-3373

LA LANNE, THOMAS JOHN, b. San Francisco, Oct. 17, 1947; B.A., U. Calif., Santa Barbara, 1969; J.D., U. Calif., San Francisco, 1972. Admitted to Calif. bar, 1973; asso. firm Dunn & McDonald, San Francisco, 1973-76, partner, 1976; pvt. practice, 1977—. Chmn. Mt. Olympus Def. Com., San Francisco, 1974-76. Mem. San Francisco Med Soc. (mem. advisory bd. 1975-76), Am. Arbitration Assn.

(arbitrator), San Francisco, Am. bar assns., Calif. Bar, No. Calif. Assn. Def. Counsel. Recipient Edward Strong Merrill III award Sigma Pi, 1976. Office: 473 Jackson St San Francisco CA 94111 Tel (415) 434-1122

LA LUMERE, LOUIS CHUCK, b. Phila., May 26, 1941; A.A., Millersville State Coll., 1960; B.A., St. Joseph's Coll., 1963; M.Ed., 1964; J.D., Duquesne U., 1969. Admitted to Pa. bar, 1970; atty. Bail div. Office Pub. Defender, Pitts., 1967-68; atty., trial div. Evans, Ivory & Evans, Pitts., 1968-70; mem. firm Watzman, Levenson & Snyder, Pitts., 1970-74; individual practice law, Pitts., 1974—. Mem. adv. bd. Carnegie Salvation Army; pres. bd. trustees Crafton Masonic Hall Assn.; exec. bd. Boys' Club of Carnegie (Pa.). Mem. Am., Pa., Allegheny County bar assns., Am., Pa. trial lawyers assns. Home: 26 Winthrop Rd Rosslyn Farms Carnegie PA 15106 Office: 3624 Mellon Bank Bldg Pittsburgh PA 15219 Tel (412) 232-0332 also 411 E Main St Carnegie PA 15106 Tel (412) 276-2365

LAMAR, ROBERT STANDRING, JR., b. Montezuma, Ga., Nov. 8, 1941; A.B., U. Ala., 1963, LL.B., 1966. Admitted to Ala. bar, 1966, U.S. Supreme Ct. bar, 1974; mem. firm Ball, Ball, Duke & Matthews, Montgomery, Ala., 1966—, partner, 1970—; instr. Jones Law Sch., 1968-72; asst. staff judge adv. Ala. Army N.G., 1969-73; spl. asst. atty. gen. State of Ala., 1969—. Mem. Am., Ala., Montgomery County bar assns., Ala. Def. Lawyers Assn. (dir. 1975). Home: 3373 Southview Ave Montgomery AL 36111 Office: One Court Sq Montgomery AL 36104 Tel (205) 834-7680

LAMB, COLIN DOUGLAS, b. Portland, Oreg., Dec. 9, 1944; B.A. in Polit. Sci., Willamette U., 1966, J.D., 1969. Admitted to Oreg. bar, 1969; asso. firm C.E. Hodges, Jr., Portland, 1969-71; individual practice law, Portland, 1971-73; partner firm Erwin, Lamb & Erwin, Portland, 1973—; counsel for Oreg. State bar disciplinary matter, 1976. Mem. Am., Oreg. (com. disciplinary rules and procedure 1975—), Multnomah County bar assns. Home: 3285 SE Ankeny St Portland OR 97214 Office: 3323 SW Harbor Dr Portland OR 97201 Tel (503) 226-4525

LAMB, JOHN JOSEPH, b. Phila., Dec. 11, 1928; B.S. in Psychology, St. Joseph's Coll., Phila., 1950; LL.B., Temple U., 1953. Admitted to Pa. bar, 1954; asso. firm Zink, Shinehouse & Homes, Phila., 1954-56, firm Frank H. Gelman Esq., Phila., 1959-60; asso. firm Mesirov, Gelman, Jaffe & Cramer, Phila., 1960-63, partner, 1963—; atty. sales and use Tax Dept. Commonwealth of Pa., 1956-62. Mem. Am., Pa., Phila. bar assns. Home: 934 Tookany Creek Pkwy Cheltenham PA 19012 Office: 1510 Fidelity Bldg Philadelphia PA 19109 Tel (215) 893-5026

LAMB, LOMAX BENJAMIN, JR., b. Batesville, Miss., June 25, 1917; B.A., Yale, 1938, LL.B., 1942. Admitted to Tenn. bar, 1942, Ala. bar, 1946, Miss. bar, 1949; asso. firm Root, Clark, Buckner & Ballantine, N.Y.C., 1942, White, Bradley, Arant & All, Birmingham, Ala., 1946-49; individual practice, Marks, Miss., 1949—; of counsel firm Rickey, Shankman, Blanchard, Agee & Harpster, Memphis, 1972—. Mem. Marks City Beautification Commn., 1971—. Mem. Am., Miss. (commr. 1971-72), Quitman County (past pres.) bar assns. Home: 601 Riverside Dr Marks MS 38646 Office: 315 Locust St Marks MS 38646 Tel (601) 326-6141

LAMB, MARGARET WELDON, b. Arlington, Mass.; student Wellesley Coll., 1953-56; B.A., U. Denver, 1959, postgrad. in Law, 1959-62; LL.B., Boston Coll., 1964. Admitted to Mass. bar, 1964, N. Mex. bar, 1969; asso. firm Hill & Barlow, Boston, 1964-65; asst. atty. gen. State of Mass., Boston, 1965-67, State of N. Mex., Santa Fe, 1969-71; hearing officer Commonwealth of Mass., Boston, 1967-68; chief pilot, counsel Air Health Care, Denver and Taos, N. Mex., 1971-74; individual practice law, Taos, 1972-74, 75-76; partner, chief pilot Sangre de Cristo Aviation, Inc., Taos, 1972-74; pub. defender N. Mex. 8th Jud. Dist., 1973-74, 75-76, N. Mex. 2d Jud. Dist., 1974-75; asst. dist. atty. 8th Jud. Dist., 1977—; mem. Albuquerque Met. Criminal Justice Coordinating Council, 1974-75. Mem. Taos Airport Commn., 1973-75, chmn., 1976—. Mem. Lawyer-Pilots Bar Assn., Mass. Bar Assn., State Bar N. Mex. Author: Colorado High County, 1964; contbr. monthly aviation law column to N. Mex. Flying Rev., 1974—, articles to profl. jours. Home: 918 Stagecoach Rd Santa Fe NM 87501 Office: PO Drawer OO Taos NM 87571 Tel (505) 758-2005

LAMB, PAUL ALLISON, b. Yates Center, Kans., Mar. 22, 1901; LL.B., U. Kans. Admitted to Kans. bar; individual practice law, Caney, Kans., 1924-55; partner firm Lamb & Shaw, and predecessor, Coffeyville, Kans., 1955—; city atty. Caney, 1958-60; mem. Kans. State Senate, 1960-64; mem. Caney Planning Commn., 1960—. Mem. Am., Kans., Montgomery County, Coffeyville bar assns., Phi Alpha Delta. Home: 107 N Hooker St Caney KS 67333 Office: 103 Dale Bldg Coffeyville KS 67337 Tel (316) 251-2540

LAMB, WILLIAM ROBERT, b. Water Valley, Miss., Nov. 29, 1930; B.B.A., U. Miss., 1956, LL.B., 1959, J.D., 1968. Admitted to Miss. bar, 1959; individual practice law, Oxford, Miss., 1959-75; circuit judge Third Dist. Miss., 1975—; pros. atty. Lafayette County, 1960-68; judge City of Oxford, 1971-75. Mem. Am., Oxford (pres. 1967), Miss. bar assns. Recipient Distinguished Service award Jaycees, 1962. Home and Office: PO Box 349 Oxford MS 38655 Tel (601) 234-4951

LAMBERD, LUTHER SENTMAN, b. Balt., Sept. 22, 1901; LL.B., U. Md., 1924. Admitted to Md. bar, 1925; dept. mgr. Md. Casualty Co., Balt., 1926-69. Home and Office: 3821 Beech Ave Baltimore MD 21211 Tel (301) 243-0822

LAMBERT, DAVID M.F., b. Hartford, Conn., Mar. 30, 1925; B.A., Trinity Coll., 1948; LL.B., Cornell U., 1951. Admitted to U.S. Dist. Ct. bar, 1955, U.S. Ct. Appeals bar, 1955, U.S. Supreme Ct. bar, 1958, U.S. Ct. Claims bar, 1975; spl. agt. FBI, Washington, 1951-55; legis. atty. Gen. Accounting Office, Washington, 1955-58; with Hughes Aircraft Co., 1958-60; dir. contracts dept. Hughes Tool Co., Culver City, Calif., 1960-63; dir. contract adminstrn. Rockwell Internat. Corp., Los Angeles, 1963-69; dir. small bus. and econ. utilization policy Office Sec. Def., Washington, 1969-71; dir. Office Domestic Bus. Policy, U.S. Dept. Commerce, Washington, 1971-72; dep. dir. Office Rev., Renegotiation Bd., Washington, 1972-73, gen. counsel, 1973-76; gen. counsel SBA, Washington, 1976—. Chmn. small bus. com. Nat. Contract Mgmt. Assn. Fellow Nat. Contract Mgmt. Assn.; mem. Am., Fed. bar assn., Adminstrs. Conf. U.S. Founding editor Nat. Contract Mgmt. Jour., also mem. editorial bd.

LAMBERT, EDMUND GEORGE, b. Altoona, Pa., June 4, 1942; B.S., Clarion (Pa.) Coll., 1966; J.D., Villanova (Pa.) U., 1972. Admitted to Colo. bar, 1972; dep. city atty. City of Lakewood (Colo.), 1972-74; individual practice law, Denver, 1974—; municipal prosecutor City of Wheat Ridge (Colo.), 1974-75; instr. Community Coll. Denver, 1975; real estate broker; panel trustee U.S. Dist. Bankruptcy Ct.; legal advisor Lakewood Liquor Authority, 1974; adminstrv. hearing officer Bldg. Code Violations, Wheat Ridge. Mem. Am., Colo., 1st Jud. bar assns., Am., Colo. trial lawyers assns., Jefferson County Bd. Realtors. Home: 4856 Juniper Ln Evergreen CO 80439 Office: 1485 Holland St Lakewood CO 80215 Tel (303) 237-9508

LAMBERT, GEORGE ROBERT, b. Muncie, Ind., Feb. 21, 1933; B.S., Ind. U., 1955; J.D., Chgo.-Kent Coll. Law, 1962. With Washington Nat. Ins. Co., Evanston, Ill., 1958—, asst. gen. counsel, 1964-68, asso. gen. counsel, 1968-70, gen. counsel, sec., 1970—, also v.p., 1975—; admitted to Ill. bar, 1962. Mem. Lake Bluff (Ill.) Sch. Caucus, 1967-69, chmn., 1968-69; mem. Lake Bluff Elementary Sch. Bd., 1970-71; bd. dirs. Chgo.-Kent Coll. Law. Mem. Am. Council Life Ins. (legal sect.), Assn. Life Ins. Counsel, Am., Ill. State, Chgo. bar assns., Am. Judicature Soc., Chgo. Estate Planning Council. Home: 1525 Judson Ave Evanston IL 60201 Office: 1630 Chicago Ave Evanston IL 60201 Tel (312) 866-3070

LAMBERT, JEREMIAH DANIEL, b. N.Y.C., Sept. 11, 1934; A.B., Princeton, 1955; postgrad. (Fulbright scholar), U. Copenhagen, 1955-56; LL.B., Yale, 1959. Admitted to N.Y. bar, 1960, D.C. bar, 1964, U.S. Supreme Ct. bar, 1971; asso. firm Cravath, Swaine & Moore, N.Y.C., 1959-63; mem. firm Peabody, Rivlin, Lambert & Meyers, Washington, 1969—; treas. Gas Employees Polit. Action Com., 1972; advisor, vis. faculty mem. Georgetown Inst. Fgn. Trade and Investment, 1971—; lectr. Advanced Mgmt. Research Seminars on Constrn. Mgmt., 1971-74. Active Cleve. Park Citizens Assn., 1971—. Mem. Bar Assn. City N.Y., D.C., Am. bar assns., Am. Soc. Internat. Law. Contbr. articles to legal publs. Home: 3400 Newark St NW Washington DC 20016 Office: 1150 Connecticut Ave NW Washington DC 20036 Tel (202) 457-1000

LAMBERT, RICHARD GORDON, b. Marion, Ill., Mar. 9, 1935; B.S., So. Ill. U., 1958; LL.B., U. Ill., 1963. Admitted to Ill. bar, 1963; partner firm Harris & Lambert, Marion, 1964—; mem. com. on rules of evidence Ill. Supreme Ct. Mem. Am., Ill., Williamson County bar assns., Am., Ill. trial lawyers assns. Home: 519 S Market St Marion IL 62959 Office: 300 W Main St Marion IL 62959 Tel (618) 993-2616

LAMBERTON, JAMES WILSON, b. Winona, Minn., Jan. 26, 1925; A.B. magna cum laude, Carleton Coll., 1949; LL.B., Yale U., 1952. Admitted to D.C. bar, 1953, N.Y. bar, 1960; since practiced in N.Y.C., asso. firm Cleary, Gottleib, Steen & Hamilton, 1953-62, partner, 1963—; Bd. dirs. S.I. Mental Health Soc., 1965-73, Community Action for Legal Services, N.Y.C., 1968-74. Mem. Am., N.Y. State bar assns., N.Y. County Lawyers Assn. (dir. 1973—, v.p. 1977—), Assn. Bar City N.Y., Phi Beta Kappa. Home: 207 Congress St Brooklyn NY 11201 Office: 1 State St Plaza New York City NY 10004 Tel (212) 344-0600

LAMBETH, HARRY JOSEPH, b. Chgo., Dec. 23, 1918; B.S. in Journalism, U. Ill., 1940; LL.B., Georgetown U., 1950. Admitted to Ill. bar, 1951, D.C. bar, 1954, Md. bar, 1970; reporter City News Bur., Chgo., 1940-41, 45-46, Honolulu Star-Bull., also Honolulu Advertiser, 1946-48; instr. journalism U. Md., College Park, 1949-50; editor Bethesda (Md.) Tribune, 1950; atty. Armour & Co., Chgo., 1952-53, AMA, Washington, 1954, C. of C. U.S., Washington, 1955-65; partner firm Barton & Lambeth, Washington and Chevy Chase, Md., 1965—; hearing examiner Montgomery County Bd. Edn., Rockville, Md., 1974—. Mem. Am., Md., Montgomery County, D.C. bar assns. Contbr. articles, book reviews to legal jours. Home: 5605 Grosvenor Ln Bethesda MD 20014 Office: 725 15th St NW Washington DC 20005 Tel (202) 638-0555 also 6935 Wisconsin Ave Chevy Chase MD 20015

LAMBRIGHT, STEPHEN KIRK, b. Kansas City, Mo., Dec. 3, 1942; B.S. in Accounting, U. Mo., 1965; J.D. cum laude, St. Louis U., 1968. Admitted to Mo. bar, 1968; asso. firm Lashly, Caruthers, Thies, Rava & Hamel, St. Louis, 1970-71, partner, 1972-75, officer, dir., 1976—; faculty Law Sch. St. Louis U., Meramec (Mo.) Community Coll. Bd. dirs. St. Louis Vocat. Counseling and Rehab. Services, Inc., 1974—. Mem. Am., Mo., St. Louis, St. Louis County bar assns., St. Louis Estate Planning Council, Phi Delta Phi. C.P.A., Mo.; contbr. St. Louis Law Jour. Office: 11 S Meramec St Saint Louis MO 63105 Tel (314) 727-8281

LAMBROS, LAMBROS J., Now v.p., gen. counsel Amerada Hess Corp., N.Y.C. Office: 1185 Ave of Americas New York City NY 10036*

LAMENDOLA, JOHN JOSEPH, b. N.Y.C., Apr. 5, 1946; A.B., Fordham U., 1967; J.D., Bklyn. Law Sch., 1971. Admitted to N.Y. bar, 1972, N.J. bar, 1972; law sec. to presiding justice Extraordinary and Spl. Trial Term State N.Y., N.Y.C., 1976—. Mem. Civil Ct. Law Secs. Assn. (sec.-treas. 1973-75), Supreme Ct. Law Secs. Assn., Am., N.J. State bar assns. Office: 100 Centre St New York City NY 10013 Tel (212) 374-4783

LAMENSDORF, ROLLAND G., b. N.Y.C., Sept. 21, 1911; B.S. in Econ., U. Pa., 1932; J.D., Georgetown U., 1937. Admitted to D.C. bar, 1936, Miss. bar, 1936; individual practice law, Washington, 1937—. Pres., Forrest Hills Citizens Assn., 1958-59, Ft. Reno Community Council, 1960; del. Fedn. of Citizens' Assns., 1960. Fellow Am. Acad. Matrimonial Lawyers; mem. Am. (family law sect. council 1966-77), D.C. (chmn. domestic relations com. 1965-67, dir. 1969-71) bar assns. Contbr. articles to legal jours. Decorated Bronze Star. Home: 5123 Linnean Ave NW Washington DC 20008 Office: 1815 H St NW Suite 408 Washington DC 20006 Tel (202) 393-1565

LAMIA, THOMAS ROGER, b. Santa Monica, Calif., May 31, 1938; B.S., U. So. Calif., 1961; J.D., Harvard, 1964. Admitted to Calif. bar, 1965; asso. firm McCutchen, Black, Verleger & Shea, Los Angeles, 1964-66; asso. firm Paul, Hastings & Janofsky, Los Angeles, 1968-72, partner, 1972—; lectr. law U. Ife, Ile-Ife, Nigeria, 1966-67, U. Zambia, Lusaka, 1967-68. Mem. Calif. State, Am., Los Angeles County, Internat. bar assns., Harvard Law Sch. Assn. So. Calif. (council 1971—), Lawyers Adv. Council Constl. Rights Found. (exec. com. 1975—). Office: 555 S Flower St 22nd floor Los Angeles CA 90071 Tel (213) 489-4000

LAMM, CHARLES CADMUS, JR., b. Wilson, N.C., Nov. 10, 1944; B.A., Wake Forest U., 1966, J.D., 1969. Admitted to N.C. bar, 1969; partner firm Holshouser & Lamm, Boone, N.C., 1969—; atty. Watauga County (N.C.), 1972-74. Mem. N.C., Watauga County, 24th Jud. Dist. bar assns. Home: Route 4 Boone NC 28607 Office: 103 N Depot St Boone NC 28607 Tel (704) 264-8800

LAMM, RICHARD DOUGLAS, b. Madison, Wis., Aug. 3, 1935; B.B.A., U. Wis., 1957; LL.B., U. Calif., 1961. Admitted to Calif. bar, 1962, Colo. bar, 1962; accountant Ernst & Ernst, 1961-62; counsel Colo. Antidiscrimination Commn., Denver, 1962-63; asso. firm Jones, Meiklejohn, Kilroy, Kehl & Lyons, Denver, 1963-65; individual practice law, Denver, 1965-74; asso. prof. law U. Denver, 1969-74; gov. State of Colo., 1975—; mem. natural resource and environ. mgmt. com. Nat. Govs. Conf., also chmn. energy impact assistance subcom. Mem. Colo. Ho. of Reps., 1966-74; pres. Denver Young Democrats, 1963; v.p. Colo. Young Dems., 1964; mem. Conservation Found., Denver Center for Performing Arts Center for Growth Alternatives, Central City Opera House Assn. Named An Outstanding Young Leader in Am., Time mag., 1974; C.P.A., Colo.

LAMOREAUX, JOHN RAWLING, b. Hoquiam, Wash., Jan. 13, 1922; LL.B., U. Calif., Berkeley, 1949. Admitted to Calif. bar, 1950; individual practice law, Salinas, Calif., 1954—; atty. Guarantee Ins. Co., Los Angeles, 1949-54. Mem. Calif. State, Monterey County bar assns., Assn. Ins. Attys., Assn. Def. Counsel. Office: Lamoreaux Bldg 1263 Padre Dr Salinas CA 93901 Tel (408) 424-0591

LAMP, JOHN ERNEST, b. Spokane, Wash., Jan. 17, 1943; B.A., Wash. State U., 1965; J.D., Willamette U., Salem, Oreg., 1968. Admitted to Wash. bar, 1968; asst. atty. gen. State of Wash., Olympia, 1968-69; sr. asst. atty. gen. chief Spokane and Eastern Wash. br. Washington State Atty. Gen's. Office, 1971—. Pres. Citizens Against S. Expressways, Spokane, 1975-76. Mem. Wash. Bar Assn., Nat. Assn. Coll. and Univ. Attys. Home: E 2105 Southeast Blvd Spokane WA 99203 Office: 1305 Old Nat Bank Bldg Spokane WA 99201 Tel (509) 456-3123

LAMPE, WILLIAM NEATHERY, b. Amarillo, Tex., July 24, 1926; student Amarillo Coll., 1946-48; J.D., U. Tex. Admitted to Tex. bar, 1951; city tax atty. Amarillo, 1952-54; asst. dist. atty. 47th Jud. Dist. Tex., 1955-56; atty. Pioneer Corp., Amarillo, 1956-62, asst. sec. and atty., 1962-67, sec. and gen. atty., 1967-68, sec. and gen. atty., 1968-70, v.p. and sec., 1970—. Bd. dirs. YMCA; mem. budget com. United Way; legal counsel Crises Intervention; rep. Salvation Army and Travelers Aid. Mem. Tex., Amarillo, Am., Fed. Power bar assns., So. Gas Assn. Home: 3409 Carlton Dr Amarillo TX 79109 Office: PO Box 511 Amarillo TX 79163 Tel (806) 376-4841

LAMPL, ROBERT CHARLES, b. Cleve., Mar. 24, 1944; B.A., Ohio State U., 1967; J.D., Chase Law Sch., Cin., 1971. Admitted to Ohio bar, 1971; atty. Licking County (Ohio) Legal Aid Soc., Inc., Newark, 1971—. Bd. dirs. Family Service, Newark, 1971—, sec., 1973. Mem. Ohio State, Licking County bar assns. Home: 964 Crossley Rd Newark OH 43055 Office: 38 S 3d St Newark OH 43055 Tel (614) 345-0850

LAMPRON, EDWARD JOHN, b. Nashua, N.H., Aug. 23, 1909; A.B., Assumption Coll., Worcester, Mass., 1931, LL.D., 1954; J.D., Harvard, 1934. Admitted to N.H. bar, 1935; city solicitor City of Nashua, 1936-46; asso. justice N.H. Superior Ct., 1947-49, N.H. Supreme Ct., 1949—. Trustee Nashua Pub. Library, 1950—; mem. adv. bd. St. Joseph Hosp., Nashua, 1955—. Mem. Nashua, Am. bar assns. Named Outstanding Catholic Layman, N.H. Cath. War Vets., 1957; recipient Citizen of Year award Nashua C. of C., 1965. Home: 27 Wood St Nashua NH 03060 Office: 115 Main St Nashua NH 03060 Tel (603) 889-9411

LAMPROPLOS, GEORGE WILLIAM, b. Demitsana, Greece, June 24, 1915 (parents Am. citizens); A.B., Wooster Coll., 1938; LL.B., U. Cin., 1941. Admitted to Ohio bar, 1941, Pa. bar, 1942, Fed. bar, 1946; served as capt. JAGC, U.S. Army, 1941-46; individual practice law Greensburg, Pa., 1946-48; partner firm Cassidy & Lamproplos, Greensburg, 1948—; county solicitor Westmoreland County, 1965-68. Trustee Westmoreland Hosp., 1967—, pres. 1975—; chmn. Westmoreland Mental Health Mental Retardation Commn., 1965-69; bd. dirs. Am. Cancer Soc., 1955-65; trustee Greensburg Library Bd., 1960-77. Mem. Westmoreland (pres. 1964-65), Pa., Am. bar assns., Am. Judicature Soc., Westmoreland Acad. Trial Lawyers (pres. 1973-74). Office: 121 N Main St Greensburg PA 15601 Tel (412) 824-6450

LAMPROPLOS, MILTON WILLIAM, b. Johnstown, Pa., Sept. 24, 1910; A.B., Dartmouth, 1932; LL.B., Pitts. Coll., 1941. Admitted to Pa. bar, 1942, U.S. Supreme Ct. bar, 1952; law clk. to judge U.S. Ct. Appeals 3d Circuit, 1941-42; asso. firm Smith, Buchanan, Ingersoll, Rudewall & Eckert, Pitts., 1942-51, partner, 1952-57; partner firm Eckert, Seamans, Cherin & Mellott, Pitts., 1958-75, of counsel, 1975—. Fellow Am. Coll. Trial Lawyers; mem. Am., Pa., Allegheny County bar assns., Acad. Trial Lawyers Allegheny County. Home: 19 Scenery Rd Pittsburgh PA 15221 Office: 4200 US Steel Bldg Pittsburgh PA 15219 Tel (412) 566-6009

LANAHAN, DANIEL JOSEPH, b. Bklyn., Jan. 13, 1940; J.D., San Francisco Law Sch., 1969. Claims mgr. Consol. Ins. Cos., San Francisco, 1963-68, Eldorado Ins. Co., Palo Alto, Calif., 1968-70; admitted to Calif. bar, 1970; asso. firm Ropers, Majeski, Kohn, Bentley & Wagner, Redwood City, Calif., 1970-76, partner, 1976—; instr. law San Mateo Jr. Colls., 1972-76. Dir., Res. Police, Menlo Park, Calif., 1970—. Mem. Am., Calif., San Francisco, San Mateo bar assns. Author: (with Brickley) Search and Seizure, Laws of Arrest and Firearms, 1976. Tel (415) 364-8200

LANCASTER, HAROLD MARTIN, b. Wayne County, N.C., Mar. 24, 1943; B.A., U. N.C., Chapel Hill, 1965, J.D., 1967. Admitted to N.C. bar, 1967, U.S. Ct. Mil. Appeals, 1968, U.S. Supreme Ct. bar, 1970; asst. staff judge adv. 12th Naval Dist., San Francisco, 1968; staff judge adv. USS Hancock, 1968-70, asst. staff judge adv. Naval Dist., Washington, 1970; partner firm Baddour and Lancaster, 1970—; U.S. Magistrate, Goldsboro, N.C., 1973-75. Bd. dirs. Wayne County Cancer Soc., 1971—; chmn. Wayne County chpt. ARC, 1976—; deacon 1st. Presbyn. Ch., Goldsboro, 1972-75; chmn. Goldsboro/Wayne County Bicentinnial Commn., 1974-76; pres. Goldsboro Community Arts Council, 1975-76, Wayne Community Concert Assn., 1974-75; trustee Wayne County Pub. Library, 1973—; dir. Wayne Agy. for Economic Solvency, 1972—. Mem. Am., N.C., 8th Jud. Dist., Wayne County bar assns., Am. Trial Lawyers Assn., Wayne County Hist. Soc., U. N.C. Law Alumni Assn (dir.), Phi Alpha Theta, Phi Alpha Delta. Recipient Distinguished Service award Jaycees, 1976. Home: 607 E Beech St Goldsboro NC 27530 Office: 208 S William St Goldsboro NC 27530 Tel (919) 735-7275

LANCASTER, RALPH IVAN, JR., b. Bangor, Maine, May 9, 1930; A.B., Coll. Holy Cross, 1952; LL.B., Harvard, 1955. Admitted to Mass. and Maine bars, 1955; law clk. to dist. judge U.S. Dist. Ct. for Maine, 1957-59; partner firm Pierce, Atwood, Scribner, Allen & McKusick, Portland, Maine, 1959—. Mem. Internat. Soc. Barristers, Am., Maine, Cumberland bar assns., Am. Coll. Trial Lawyers, Nat. Assn. R.R. Trial Counsel, Def. Research Inst., Assn. Trial Lawyers

Am., Nat. Assn. Hosp. Attys., Maine Trial Lawyers Assn. Home: 111 West St Portland ME 04102 Office: 1 Monument Sq Portland ME 04111 Tel (207) 773-6411

LANCASTER, WILLIAM JAMES, b. Lexington, N.C., Feb. 16, 1907; B.S. in Edn., Duquesne U., 1936, LL.B., 1939. Admitted to Pa. bar, 1941; individual practice law, Pitts., 1941—, also of counsel firm Lancaster, Mentzer, Coyne and Duffy, Pitts. Mem. Allegheny County (Pa.), Pa., Am. bar assns. Home: 11 Newport Rd Pittsburgh PA 15221 Office: 608 Grant Bldg Pittsburgh PA 15219 Tel (412) 471-4530

LANCE, (DOWE) JEFF, b. Oregon County, Mo., May 25, 1916; J.D., U. Mo., 1948. Admitted to Mo. bar, 1948, U.S. Supreme Ct. bar, 1962; partner firms Maus & Lance, Monett, Mo., 1948-50, Cook Murphy Lance & Mayer, St. Louis, 1956-60, 63-77, firm Armstrong, Teasdale, Kramer & Vaughan, St. Louis, 1977—; examiner Mo. Pub. Service Commn., Jefferson City, 1950-51; legal sec. to Gov. Mo., Jefferson City, 1951-52; atty. S.W. Bell Co., St. Louis, 1952-56; U.S. atty. Eastern Dist. Mo., St. Louis, 1960-63. Mem. St. Louis County Bd. Police Commrs., 1972-76. Fellow Am. Coll. Trial Lawyers, Am. Bar Found.; mem. Am. Bar Assn. Mo. Bar, Bar Assn. St. Louis, U. Mo. Alumni (pres. 1959-63), Am. Arbitration Assn., Order of Coif. Named Distinguished Alumni, Alumni Assn. of U. Mo., 1975. Home: 450 W Adams St Kirkwood MO 63122 Office: 611 Olive St Saint Louis MO 63101 Tel (314) 621-1462

LANCIONE, BERNARD GABE, b. Bellaire, Ohio, Feb. 2, 1939; B.C.S., Ohio U., Athens, 1960; J.D., Capital U., Columbus, Ohio, 1965. Admitted to Ohio bar, 1965, U.S. Supreme Ct. bar, 1969; asso. firm Nelson Lancione, Columbus, 1964-65; partner firm Lancione, Lancione, Lancione & Hanson, Bellaire, 1965—; city solicitor Bellaire, 1968-72; asst. prosecutor Belmont County, 1969-72. Mem. Ohio, Belmont County (pres.) bar assns., Ohio Acad. Trial Lawyers. Recipient award of merit Acad. Trial Lawyers, 1972. Home: 1425 National Rd Lansing OH 43934 Office: 38th and Jefferson Sts Bellaire OH 43906 Tel (614) 676-2034

LANCIONE, NELSON, b. Bellaire, Ohio, July 10, 1918; B.S., Ohio State U., 1941, LL.B., 1943, J.D., 1967. Admitted to Ohio bar, 1943, U.S. Supreme Ct. bar, 1963; with Office Gen. Counsel, Treasury Dept., 1943-49, treasury rep., Manila, Philippines, 1945-47, acting treasury attache Am. embassy, Manila, 1946-47; asst. atty. gen. State of Ohio, 1949-50; individual practice law, Columbus, Ohio, 1951—; spl. counsel Ohio Atty. Gen., 1958- 62; sec., gen. counsel NAM Equitable Life Assurance Co., 1959-68. Chmn., Franklin County Bd. Elections, 1973—. Mem. Columbus, Ohio, Am., Inter-Am. bar assns., Am. Judicature Soc., Assn. Trial Lawyers Am., Am. Soc. Internat. Law. Office: 42 E Gay St Suite 1312 Columbus OH 43215 Tel (614) 228-6626

LAND, JOSEPH HAROLD, b. Krebs, Okla., Apr. 1, 1913; B.S., Okla. State U., 1935; LL.B., Southeastern U., Washington, 1941. Investigator U.S. GAO, 1935-47; admitted to Okla. bar, 1947; partner firm Gill and Land, Oklahoma City, 1953-72; asso. municipal judge, Oklahoma City, 1972-76; individual practice law, Oklahoma City, 1976—; asst. county atty Oklahoma County, 1956; pres. AAA, Okla. Motor Club, 1949-57. Bd. dirs. SSS, Oklahoma City, 1970-76; dist. commr. Dan Beard dist. Last Frontier council Boy Scouts Am., 1967-76; supr. young people tchr. Nichols Hills Bapt. Ch., 1949-59; mem. Oklahoma City Beautiful Com., 1974-76. Fellow Harry Truman Library Inst.; mem. Okla., Am. bar assns., Am. Jurisprudence Soc., Am. Judges Assn. Recipient Certificate Appreciation Award Pres. United States, 1976. Home: 8204 N May Ave Oklahoma City OK 73120 Tel (405) 843-3768

LAND, MARVIN JACK, b. Balt., Aug. 11, 1936; A.A., U. Balt., 1955, LL.B., 1958. Admitted to Md. bar, 1958; asso. firm Mason, Kruger, Kremer and Myerberg, Balt., 1958-64; partner firm Miller, Rosenthal & Land, Balt., 1964-71; individual practice law, Towson, Md., 1971; judge Md. Dist. Ct., for Baltimore County, 1971-75, Circuit Ct. for Baltimore County 3d Jud. Circuit, 1975—. Office: County Courts Bldg 401 Bosley Ave Towson MD 21204 Tel (301) 494-3206

LAND, STUART JAY, b. Chgo., May 18, 1930; B.A., Syracuse U., 1951; LL.B., Harvard U., 1954. Admitted to D.C. bar, 1954, U.S. Supreme Ct. bar, 1960; asso. firm Arnold & Porter, and predecessor, Washington, 1958-62, partner, 1962-70, sr. partner, 1971—. Co-chmn. Washington Lawyers Against the War, 1970-72, Washington Lawyers Com. for Civil Rights Under Law, 1976—. Mem. Am., Fed. bar assns., Phi Beta Kappa. Contbr. articles to legal jours. Home: 3024 Cortland Pl NW Washington DC 20008 Office: 1229 19th St NW Washington DC 20036 Tel (202) 872-6886

LANDA, HOWARD M., b. Bklyn., Oct. 12, 1943; B.A., Bklyn. Coll., 1964; J.D., U. Chgo., 1967. Admitted to N.Y. State bar, 1968; asso. firm Edward Garfield, N.Y.C., 1968-69, firm Szold, Brandwen, Meyers & Altman, 1969-74; dir., sec., gen. counsel IPCO Hosp. Supply Corp., White Plains, N.Y., 1974—. Mem. Am. Mgmt. Assn., Westchester-Fairfield County Corp. Counsel Assn., N.Y. County Lawyers Assn., Health Industry Mgrs. Assn., Risk and Ins. Mgmt. Soc. Office: 1025 Westchester Ave White Plains NY 10604 Tel (914) 682-4533

LANDAN, HENRY SINCLAIR, b. Chgo., Aug. 4, 1943; B.S., DePaul U., 1965, J.D., 1969; LL.M. in Taxation, N.Y. U., 1970. Admitted to Ill. bar, 1969, N.Y. State bar, 1971, U.S. Supreme Ct. bar, 1976; asso. firms Altman, Kurlander & Weiss, Chgo., 1969-70, Roberts & Holland, N.Y.C., 1970-71; partner firm Carlins & Kamensky, Chgo., 1971—; counsel Caribbean Hotel Assn., Santurce, P.R., 1975—; sec., dir. Howard Ecker & Co., Chgo., 1975—; sec. Columbus Dental Assos., Chgo., 1975—. Mem. exec. com., dir. Young Men's Jewish Council, Chgo., 1972—. Mem. Am., Ill. State, Chgo. bar assns. Contbr. articles to profl. jours. Home: 1560 N Sandburg Terr Chicago IL 60610 Office: 120 S LaSalle St Chicago IL 60603 Tel (312) 368-1666

LANDAU, BROOKSLEY ELIZABETH, b. San Francisco, Aug. 27, 1940; A.B., Stanford, 1961, J.D., 1964. Admitted to Calif. bar, 1965, D.C. bar, 1966; asso. firm Arnold & Porter, Washington, 1965-73, partner, 1974—; clk. to judge U.S. Ct. Appeals for D.C. Circuit, 1964-65; adj. prof. law Georgetown U. Law Center, 1972-73; lectr. law Cath. U., 1972-74; bd. dirs. Nat. Legal Aid and Defenders Assn.; chmn. Women's Rights Project, Center for Law and Social Policy, Am. Indian Lawyers Tng. Project; bd. govs. D.C. Bar, sec., 1975-76. Mem. Order of Coif, Am. Bar Assn. (chmn. sect. individual rights 1977-78, mem. standing com. on fed. judiciary 1977—). Recipient Stanford Law Sch. Outstanding Grad. award 1964; pres. Stanford Law Rev., 1963-64. Home: 3506 Pinetree Terr Falls Church VA 22041 Office: 1229 19th St NW Washington DC 20036 Tel (202) 872-6832

LANDAU, SYBIL HARRIET, b. N.Y.C., Nov. 26, 1937; B.A., Hunter Coll., 1958; LL.B., Columbia, 1961; B.C.L., U. Oxford (Eng.), 1963. Admitted barrister-at-law, U.K., 1965, N.Y. State bar, 1965, U.S. Supreme Ct. bar, 1970; asst. prof. law Bristol (Eng.) U., 1963-65; asst. dist. atty. N.Y. County, 1965-72; asso. prof. Hofstra U., Hempstead, N.Y., 1972-74; cons., reporter N.Y. State Family Ct., 1974—; asso. prof. Benjamin N. Cardozo Sch. of Law, N.Y.C., 1975—, asst. dean, 1975—; adj. vis. asso. prof. Bklyn. Law Sch., fall 1975. Bd. dirs. Hunter Coll. Alumna Assn., 1975—. Mem. Am. Law Inst., N.Y. City Bar Assn. Office: 55 Fifth Ave New York City NY 10003 Tel (212) 255-5600

LANDERS, JOSEPH WHEELER, JR., b. Chattanooga, Sept. 13, 1942; B.A., Stetson U., 1964, J.D., 1970. Admitted to Fla. bar, 1970; asst. dir. admission Stetson U., 1966-68; adminstrv. asst. to Fla. Sec. of State, 1970; govt. asst. Fla. Gov. Reubin Askew, Tallahassee, 1971-74; exec. dir. Internat. Improvement Trust Fund, Tallahassee, 1974-75; sec. Fla. Dept. Environ. Regulation, Tallahassee, 1975—. Mem. Fla. Bar. Home: 211 N Meridian St Tallahassee FL 32301 Tel (904) 488-4807

LANDERS, ROBERT TIMOTHY, b. Youngstown, Ohio, Feb. 18, 1944; B.B.A., Youngstown U.; M.B.A., Coll. William and Mary; J.D., Akron U. Admitted to Ohio bar, 1970; partner firm Keating & Landers, 1970-72, Landers & Urban, Warren, Ohio, 1972—; village solicitor West Farmington (Ohio), 1972-75, Orwell (Ohio), 1976—, Lordstow (Ohio), 1976—. Mem. Ohio, Trumbull County bar assns., Comml. Law League. Home: PO Box 28 North Bloomfield OH 44450 Office: 434 High St NE Warren OH 44481 Tel (216) 392-7543

LANDIS, EDWARD BROWDY, b. Slutsk, Russia, Dec. 2, 1898; student Amherst Coll., 1918; B.S., U. Mass., 1921; LL.B., Yale U., 1928. Admitted to Mass. bar, 1928, U.S. Fed. Cts. bar, 1931; practiced in Springfield, Mass., 1928—; mem. firm Leary Cummings & Leary, 1928-39; individual practice law, 1939—; master, auditor Mass. Superior and Probate Cts. Mem. Mayor's Council Aging. Mem. Mass., Hampden County bar assns. Home: 46 Bronson Terr Springfield MA 01108 Office: 31 Elm St Springfield MA 01103 Tel (413) 733-9161

LANDIS, ROBERT M., b. Fleetwood, Pa., 1920; A.B., Franklin and Marshall Coll., 1941; J.D., U. Pa., 1947. Admitted to Pa. bar, 1947; now with firm Dechert Price & Rhoads, Phila.; past pres. Nat. Conf. Bar Presidents. Fellow Am. Coll. Trial Lawyers; mem. Phila. Bar Assn. (chancellor 1970—). Office: 3400 Centre Square W 1500 Market St Philadelphia PA 19102 Tel (215) 972-3400*

LANDMAN, GEORGINA BARBARA, b. Miami Beach, Fla., Feb. 16, 1938; certificate in advanced French, U. Sorbonne (Paris), 1966; B.A., Trinity U., 1967; certificate in criminology U. Montreal (Can.), 1967; J.D., U. Denver, 1970; M.A., St. Louis U., 1972; LL.M., U. Mo., Kansas City, 1973. Admitted to Okla. bar, 1975; law clk. U.S. 8th Circuit Ct. Appeals, St. Louis, 1970; legal staff, urban intern HUD, St. Louis, 1971-72; spl. asst. to regional adminstr. U.S. Dept. Justice, Kansas City, Kans., 1972-73; teaching fellow U. Mo., Kansas City, 1972-73; asst. prof. law U. Tulsa, 1973-75, asst. dean, 1975-76, asso. prof., 1976—; asso. firm Rogers and Bell, Tulsa, 1976-77; law editor Shepard's Citations, Colorado Springs, 1968, 69; cons. Community Relations Commn., Tulsa, 1974-76; mem. flood-plain tech. adv. com. Tulsa Met. Area Planning Commn., 1975-77. Mem. Am., Okla., Tulsa County bar assns., Am. Assn. Law Schs. Phi Alpha Delta. Contbr. articles to profl. jours.; grad. editor Urban Lawyer, 1972-73. Home: 3241 S Troost Tulsa OK 74105 Office: PO Box 3209 Tulsa OK 74101 Tel (918) 582-5201

LANDMEIER, ALLEN LEE, b. Elmhurst, Ill., Nov. 24, 1942; B.S. in Elec. Engring., Valparaiso U., 1964, J.D., 1967. Admitted to Ill. bar, 1967, U.S. Patent Office bar, 1973, Fed. Ct. Eastern Dist. Wis. bar, 1976, U.S. Supreme Ct. bar, 1977; served with Judge Adv. Gen. Corps. USNR, 1968-70; asso. firm Muehler and Aichele, Chgo., 1970-72, Smith, McCracken & Landmeier and predecessor, Geneva, Ill., 1972—; city atty. St. Charles, Ill., 1977; park dist. atty. Geneva Park Dist., 1975—; instr. real estate law Fox Valley chpt. Inst. Fin. Planning, 1975—. Chmn., St. Mark's Luth. Ch., 1977. Mem. Am., Ill. (mem. council state Taxation sect. 1977—), Kane County (sec.) bar assns., Patent Law Assn. of Chgo., Tau Beta Pi. Notes editor Valpariso U. Law Review, 1966-67. Office: 15 N 2nd St Geneva IL 60134 Tel (312) 232-2880

LANDON, JAMES HENRY, b. Atlanta, Oct. 24, 1945; B.A., Vanderbilt U., 1967; J.D., Harvard, 1970. Admitted to Ga. bar, 1971, U.S. Supreme Ct. bar, 1976; asso. firm White & Case, N.Y.C., 1970; asso. firm Hansell, Post, Brandon & Dorsey, Atlanta, 1971-76, partner 1976—. Mem. Am., Ga., Atlanta bar assns. Contbr. articles to legal jours. Home: 3990 N Stratford Rd NE Atlanta GA 30342 Office: 3300 1st Nat Bank Tower Atlanta GA 30303 Tel (404) 581-8000

LANDON, ROBERT DONALD WIKE, II, b. Binghamton, N.Y., June 17, 1940; B.A. cum laude, Amherst Coll., 1962; LL.B., Harvard U., 1965. Admitted to N.Y. bar, 1965, N.J. bar, 1971, Fla. bar, 1973; mem. firm Simpson, Thacher, & Bartlett, N.Y.C., 1967-72; mem. firm Smathers & Thompson, Miami, Fla., 1973-77, partner, 1977—; adj. prof. law U. Miami Sch. Law, 1976—. Mem. Dade County (chmn. probate legis. com. 1975-76), Am., N.J., N.Y. State, Fla. bar assns., Assn. Bar City N.Y. Office: 1301 Alfred I DuPont Bldg Miami FL 33131 Tel (305) 379-6523

LANDRITH, THOMAS ARCH, JR., b. Buffalo, Kans., Sept. 17, 1917; J.D., U. Okla., 1941. Admitted to Okla. bar, 1941; individual practice law, Tulsa, 1941-54, 56—; atty., head legal dept. City of Tulsa, 1954-56; lectr. Sch. Law U. Tulsa, 1960-65. Bd. dirs. Thomas Gilcrease Mus. Natural History and Art, Tulsa, 1956; 1st. v.p., bd. dirs. Tulsa Civic Music Assn., 1961; trustee All Souls Unitarian Ch., Tulsa. Mem. Tulsa County, Okla., Am. bar assns., Okla. Trial Lawyers Assn. Home: 2632 E 57th Pl Tulsa OK 74105 Office: Suite 200 Granada Bldg 3336 E 32d St Tulsa OK 74135 Tel (918) 743-8831

LANDRY, ROBERT WATSON, b. Madison, Wis., June 22, 1922; A.B., U. Chgo., 1946; LL.B., U. Wis., 1949. Admitted to Wis. bar, 1949, U.S. Supreme Ct. bar, 1956, U.S. Ct. Mil. Appeals, 1956; mem. firm Landry & Landry Milw., 1949-54; mem. Wis. Ho. of Reps. from 1st Dist., Milw., 1951-54; judge Civil Ct. of Milw., 1954-59; judge Circuit Ct. of Wis., Milw., 1959—; capt. JAG, USNR; instr. Nat. Coll. Trial Judges; chmn. State Bd. Circuit Judges. Mem. Wis., Milw. bar assns., State Bd. of Judges. Recipient B'nai B'rith Human Rights award, 1971; contbr. articles to profl. jours. Home: 3554 N Summit Ave Milwaukee WI 53211 Office: Milwaukee County Ct House Milwaukee WI 53233 Tel (414) 278-4488

LANDRY, WALTER JOSEPH, b. Jefferson Parish, La., Jan. 23, 1931; B.S. in Mech. Engring., U. Notre Dame, 1952; postgrad. George Washington U., 1955-57; J.D., Tulane U., 1958; M.A. in Internat. Relations, Am. U., 1969, Ph.D. in Govt., 1975. Admitted to La. bar, 1958, U.S. Supreme Ct. bar, 1961; with Gen. Electric Co., 1954-55; patent examiner U.S. Commerce Dept., Washington, 1955-56; legis. asst. to senator from La., Washington, 1956-57; individual practice law, New Orleans, 1958-61; fgn. service officer U.S. Dept. State, Washington, 1961-70, 3d sec. embassy, Paraguay, 1962-64, vice consul, Spain, 1964-66, asso. ops. officer, editor Exec. Secretariat Dept., 1967-68, adviser to U.S. Mission to OAS, 1968-70; sr. researcher La. Constl. Conv., 1973-74; asst. prof. polit. sci. U. Southwestern La., 1970-74, 76—; partner firm Landry, Poteet and Landry, Lafayette, 1974—. Mem. Lafayette Parish Democratic Exec. Com., 1975, chmn., 1976—; chmn. Carter-Mondale Campaign Lafayette Parish, 1976; active Cub Scouts, Lafayette, 1975—; mem. La. Dem. Central Com., 1977—; pres. La. Assn. Dem. Exec. Coms., 1977-78. Mem. La. State Bar Assn. Contbr. articles to profl. publs. Home: 501 Tulane Ave Lafayette LA 70503 Office: 215 W Main St Lafayette LA 70501

LANDY, BURTON AARON, b. Chgo., Aug. 16, 1929; B.S., Northwestern U., 1950; J.D., U. Miami, 1952; student Nat. U. Mexico, 1948; scholar U. Havana (Cuba), 1951; fellow Inter-Am. Acad. Comparative Law (Havana), 1955-56. Admitted to Fla. bar, 1952; individual practice law, Miami, Fla., 1955-57; partner firm Ammerman & Landy, Miami, 1957-63, Paul, Landy, Beiley and Yacos, Miami, 1964—; lectr. Latin-Am. bus. law Law Sch. U., Miami, 1972—; lectr. Internat. Law Confs.; mem. U.S. Dept. Commerce Regional Export Expansion Council, 1969-74. Bd. dirs. Inter-Am. Bar Legal Found. Mem. Inter-Am. (asst. sec.-gen. 1957-59, treas. 11th conf. 1959, mem. council 1969—, exec. com. 1975—), Am. (chmn. com. arrangements internat. and comparative law sect. 1964-65), Spanish-Am., Fla. (chmn. aero. law com. 1968-69), Dade County (former com. chmn.) bar assns., Am. Foreign Law Assn. (former local pres.), Miami Jr. C. of C., Phi Alpha Delta. Contbg. editor Econ. Devel. Lawyer of Am., 1969-74; contbr. articles to legal jours. Home: 6255 Old Cutler Rd Miami FL 33156 Office: Penthouse Greater Miami Federal Bldg Miami FL 33131 Tel (305) 358-9300

LANDY, SAMUEL HENRY, b. Phila., Mar. 1, 1909; B.S. Lehigh U., 1931; J.D., Temple U., 1935. Admitted to Pa. bar, 1934, Pa. Supreme Ct. bar, 1944, U.S. Dist. Ct. bar, 1944, U.S. Supreme Ct. bar, 1945; since practiced in Phila., assoc. firm Landy & Sutton, 1935-44; Freedman, Landy & Lorry, 1944-64, Cohen, Shapiro, Polisher, Skeikman & Cohen, 1964—. Mem. Internat., Am., Pa., Phila. Bar Assns., Trial Lawyers Assn., Am. Arbitration Assn. Home: 1919 Chestnut St Philadelphia PA 19103 Office: 2200 PSF Bldg Philadelphia PA 19107 Tel (215) 922-1300

LANE, ARTHUR LEE, b. Goldsboro, N.C., Dec. 20, 1920; B.A., Howard U., 1948, J.D., 1951. Admitted to N.C. bar, 1952, D.C. bar, 1952; partner firm Minnis, Lane & Cooper, Washington, 1952-56; individual practice law, Fayetteville, N.C., 1956—; atty. F.B.C. Corp., Fayetteville, Mechs. and Farmers Bank, McDuffie Village, Inc.; cooperating atty. NAACP. Bd. dirs. Fuller Sch. for Exceptional Children, 1960—, Day Care Center for Retarded Children, 1970—; pres. Fayetteville State U. Found. Mem. Am., Nat. bar assns., N.C. State Bar. Office: 273 Gillespie St PO Box 675 Fayetteville NC 28302 Tel (919) 484-8139

LANE, ARTHUR STEPHEN, b. Arlington, Mass., Dec. 26, 1910; grad. Phillips Exeter Acad., 1930; B.A., Princeton, 1934; LL.B., Harvard, 1937. Admitted to N.J. bar, 1939; law sec. to N.J. vice chancellor, 1937-39; asst. pros. atty. Mercer County, N.J., 1946-56; partner firm Minton, Dinsmore & Lane, Trenton, 1946-56; judge Mercer County Ct., 1956-60, U.S. Dist. Ct., N.J., 1960-67; v.p., gen. counsel, dir. Johnson & Johnson, New Brunswick, N.J., 1967-76; partner firm Smith, Stratton, Wise & Heher, Princeton, N.J., 1976—; dir. Trenton Times Newspapers, 1961-67. Candidate N.J. Senate, 1953; pres. George Washington council Boy Scouts Am., 1955-67, mem. regional exec. com., 1966-67; chmn. exec. com. Nat. Council on Crime and Delinquency, 1971-76; trustee Princeton U., 1968-72. Mem. Am., N.J., Mercer County bar assns., Alumni Assn. Exeter Acad. (exec. com. 1960-70), Assn. Gen. Counsel. Named mem. Sport's Illus Silver Anniversary Football Team, 1959; recipient Silver Beaver award Boy Scouts Am., 1956, Silver Antelope award, 1960. Home: Pleasant Valley Rd Titusville NJ 08560 Office: 1 Palmer Sq Princeton NJ 08540 Tel (609) 924-6000

LANE, CHARLES RAY, b. Oklahoma City, Feb. 11, 1944; B.A. in Psychology, U. Okla., 1966, J.D., 1972, M.B.A., 1974. Admitted to Okla. bar, 1972, U.S. Supreme Ct. bar, 1975; clk. firm Leroy Powers, Oklahoma City, 1966-67; legal intern firm Barefoot, Moler & Claro, Oklahoma City, 1971-72; sr. atty. Halliburton Services div. Halliburton Co., Duncan, Okla., 1973—; adj. prof. Sch. Social Work, U. Okla., Norman, 1973—. Coach youth wrestling team Duncan YMCA; deacon, ofcl. bd. First Christian Ch., Duncan. Mem. Am., Okla. (chmn. subcom. ct.-appointed counsel), Stephens County (chmn. com. law focused curriculum pub. schs.) bar assns., Am., Okla. trial lawyers assns., Okla. Def. Attys. Assn., Maritime Law Assn. U.S. Home: 2201 Country Club Rd Duncan OK 73533 Office: Box 1431 Duncan OK 73533 Tel (405) 251-3228

LANE, GARY M., b. Fairfield, Iowa, Oct. 12, 1944; B.A., U. Iowa, 1967, J.D. with distinction, 1969. Admitted to Iowa bar, 1969; asst. atty. Scott County (Iowa), Davenport, 1969—; instr. criminal law and procedure Eastern Iowa Community Coll., 1969-72, lectr. in field.; pres. bd. dirs. HELP Legal Services Corp., 1976—. Mem. exec. com., dir. Legal Services Corp. of Iowa, 1977—. Fellow Iowa Acad. Trial Lawyers; mem. Iowa State, Scott County (exec. council) bar assns. Office: 206 Kahl Bldg Davenport IA 52801 Tel (319) 323-9360

LANE, JEREMY, b. Yonkers, N.Y., Apr. 22, 1944; B.A., U. Notre Dame, 1965; J.D., Fordham U., 1968. Admitted to N.Y. bar, 1969, Minn. bar, 1970; asso. firm Vaughn & Lyons, N.Y.C., 1968-69; staff atty. Queens Legal Services, N.Y.C., 1969-70; staff atty. Mpls. Legal Aid Soc., 1970—, mng. atty., 1976—. Bd. dirs. East Calhoun Community Orgn., 1973—, pres., 1976. Home: 3141 James Ave S Minneapolis MN 55408 Office: 501 Park Ave Minneapolis MN 55415 Tel (612) 332-1441

LANE, MARC JAY, b. Chgo., Aug. 30, 1946; B.A. with high distinction, U. Ill., 1967; J.D., Northwestern U., 1971. Admitted to Ill. bar, 1971, U.S. Tax Ct. bar, 1974; pres. firm Marc. J. Lane, Chgo., 1971—; pres. Medico-Legal Inst., Chgo.; lectr. profl. assns.; coordinator optometric jurisprudence curriculum Ill. Coll. Optometry, 1973—. Mem. Chgo. Council Lawyers (past chmn. com. on corp. responsibility), Am., Ill. State (Lincoln award 1973, 74), Chgo. bar assns. Author: The Doctor's Lawyer: A Legal Handbook for Doctors, 1974; (with others) 32nd Annual Federal Tax Course, 1975; The Legal Handbook for Small Business, 1977; contbr. articles to legal jours. Home: 6625 N Kostner Ave Lincolnwood IL 60646 Office: 180

N LaSalle St Chicago IL 60601 Tel (312) 372-1040 also 77 Wimpole St London England also 170 Phillip St Sydney Australia Tel 01-935 0151

LANE, MARK, b. N.Y.C., Feb. 24, 1927; LL.B., Bklyn. Law Sch., 1951. Admitted to N.Y. bar, 1951; practiced in N.Y.C., 1952-62; founder Mid-Harlem Community Parish Narcotics Clinic, 1953, East Harlem Reform Democratic Club, 1959; prof. law Catholic U., Washington, 1975—. Dir. Citizens Commn. Inquiry, 1975—; founder Wounded Knee Legal Def.-Offense Com., 1973; founder The Covered Wagon, Mountain Home, Idaho, 1971; mem. N.Y. State Assembly, 1960-62. Author: Rush to Judgment, 1966; A Citizens Dissent, 1968; Chicago Eye-Witness, 1969; Arcadia, 1970; Conversations with Americans, 1970; Executive Action, 1973. Producer firm (with Emile de Antonio) Rush to Judgment, 1967. Founder publs. Citizens Quar., 1975. Helping Hand, 1971. Home: 105 2d NE Washington DC 20002 Office: 103 2d St NE Washington DC 20002*

LANE, MILLS, III, b. Savannah, Ga., Nov. 12, 1937; B.S. in Bus. Adminstrn., U. Nev., 1963; J.D., U. Utah, 1970. Admitted to Nev. bar, 1970; asso. firm Sanford, Sanford, Fahrenkopf & Mousel, Reno, 1970-74; dep. dist. atty. Washoe County (Nev.), 1971-74, chief dep. dist. atty., criminal div., 1974—; speaker Drug Enforcement Adminstrn., Nat. Dist. Attys. Assn.; participant, homicide investigators seminar Sacramento Police Dept., 1974. Mem. Am., Nev., Washoe County bar assns., Nev. Dist. Attys. Assn. (v.p. 1974). Office: PO Box 11130 Reno NV 89510 Tel (702) 785-4240

LANE, MORGAN E., b. N.Y.C., Sept. 9, 1907; LL.B., St. John's Coll., Bklyn., 1929. Admitted to N.Y. State bar, 1930, U.S. Dist. Ct. bar for Eastern Dist. N.Y., 1934, So. Dist. N.Y., 1948, U.S. Supreme Ct. bar, 1963; practiced in Bklyn., 1930-50; asst. dist. atty. Kings County (N.Y.), 1950-64; justice Civil Ct., N.Y.C., 1964—. Mem. Bklyn., Kings County Criminal bar assns. Home: 250 E 63d St New York City NY 10021 Office: 141 Livingston St New York City NY 11201 Tel (212) 643-3312

LANE, NORMAN DOW, b. Portland, Tenn., Nov. 20, 1935; A.B., Western Ky. U., 1959; LL.B., U. Tenn., 1960. Admitted to Tenn. bar, 1960, U.S. Supreme Ct. bar, 1964; legal advisor to comptroller State of Tenn., 1960-61; served to capt. JAGC, U.S. Army, 1961-63; asst. U.S. atty., Middle Dist. Tenn., 1963-64; individual practice law, Nashville, 1964—. Mem. Am., Tenn. trial lawyers assns. Home: Route 2 Box 137 Cottontown TN 37048 Office: 214 3rd Ave N Nashville TN 37201 Tel (615) 244-2070

LANE, RICHARD SYDNEY, b. Boston, July 7, 1919; A.B. magna cum laude, Harvard, 1941, LL.B. cum laude, 1947. Admitted to N.Y. State bar, 1948; law sec. Charles Wyzanski, Jr., fed. dist. judge, Boston, Mass., 1947-48; asst. dist. atty. N. Y. County, 1948-50; asso. firms Paul, Weiss, Rifkind, Wharton & Garrison, N.Y.C., 1950-53, Skadden Arpst Slate, N.Y.C., 1953-55; partner firm Shadlen & Lane, N.Y.C., 1955-61; individual practice law, N.Y.C., 1961-69; judge N.Y.C. Civil Ct., 1969—; arbitrator N.Y.C. Small Claims Ct., 1957-69, Am. Arbitration Assn., 1962-69; chief counsel joint legis. com. N.Y. State Legis., 1965-66. Bd. dirs. Henry Kaufmann Campgrounds, Pearl River, Rockland County N.Y., 1952—, v.p., 1975—; v.p. Nat. Council to Combat Blindness, 1958—; mem. N.Y.C. Borough Pres's. Community Planning Bd., 1961-69; dist. leader N.Y.C. Democratic Party, 1961-69; mem. N.Y. State Dem. Platform Com., 1962, 66. Mem. Am., N.Y. State bar assns., Assn. Bar City N.Y. (chmn. com. on uniform state laws 1972-75). Home: 120 E 81st St New York NY 10028 Office: 111 Centre St New York NY 10013 Tel (212) 374-8458

LANE, TOM LEE, JR., b. Clarksville, Tenn., July 25, 1944; B.B.A., U. Ga., 1966, J.D., 1970. Admitted to Ga. bar, 1970; asso. firm Ware, Sterne & Griffin, Atlanta, 1971-74; partner firm Lane & Wilson, Atlanta, 1974-76, firm Sellers, Lane, Wilson & Atkinson, Atlanta, 1976—. Office: 1900 The Exchange Suite 326 Atlanta GA 30339 Tel (404) 433-1586

LANER, RICHARD WARREN, b. Chgo., July 12, 1933; student U. Ill., 1951-54; B.S., Northwestern U., 1955, LL.B., 1956. Admitted to Ill. bar, 1956; asso. firm Dorfman, De Koven, Cohen & Laner and predecessor, Chgo., 1956-62, partner, 1962—. Mem. Chgo. (chmn. com. labor law 1972-73), Am. bar assns., Chgo. Assn. Commerce and Industry, Adminstrv. Mgmt. Soc., Order of Coif. Contbr. articles to profl. jours.; editorial bd. Northwestern Law Rev., 1954-56. Home: 1590 Little John Ct Highland Park IL 60035 Office: One IBM Plaza Suite 3301 Chicago IL 60611 Tel (312) 467-9800

LANEY, JOHN MALCOLM, JR., b. Tuscaloosa, Ala., July 17, 1946; B.S., U. Ala.; J.D., Stanford U. Admitted to Ala. bar, 1971; mem. firm London, Yancey, Clark & Allen, Birmingham, Ala. Mem. Am., Ala., Birmingham bar assns., Ala. Def. Lawyers Assn. Office: 2100 First Nat So Nat Bldg Birmingham AL 35203 Tel (205) 251-2531

LANG, DOUGLAS STEWARD, b. St. Louis, July 25, 1947; B.S. in Bus. Adminstrn., Drake U., 1969; J.D., U. Mo., 1972. Admitted to Mo. bar, 1972, Tex. bar, 1973; law clk. to judge Mo. Supreme Ct., 1972-73; asso. firm Weber, Baker & Allums, Dallas, 1973-77; partner firm Weber, Baker, Allums & Lang, 1977—; dir. Jr. Bar Tex., 1976—. Mem. State Bar Tex., Dallas Assn. Young Lawyers (pres. 1977), Dallas, Tex., Mo. bar assns. Office: 917 Republic Nat Bank Tower Dallas TX 75201 Tel (214) 744-4023

LANG, HOWARD BURTON, b. Fulton, Mo., Aug. 7, 1912; A.B. in Polit. Sci. with distinction, U. Mo., 1934, J.D., 1936, M.A. in Govt., 1937. Admitted to Mo. bar, 1936; govt. economist, 1936-37; partner firm Clark, Boggs, Peterson & Becker, Columbia, Mo., 1937-47; pros. atty. Boone County (Mo.), 1947-49; chief claims atty. MFA Ins. Cos., Columbia, 1949-53, v.p. charge claims, 1953-64, sr. v.p., 1964—. Mem. adv. council U. Mo. Arthritis Center; mayor City of Columbia, 1953-57; mem. bd. curators Stephens Coll., chmn. bd. trustees, 1958-70. Mem. Nat. Assn. Mut. Ins. Cos. (past pres., dir.), Conf. Casualty Ins. Cos. (past pres., dir.), Mo., Boone County bar assns., Columbia C. of C. (v.p.). Home: 407 Russell Blvd Columbia MO 65201 Office: 1817 W Broadway Columbia MO 65201 Tel (314) 445-8441

LANG, JAMES CLAY, b. Tulsa, Nov. 10, 1940; B.A., U. Tulsa, 1962, M.A., 1970, J.D., 1964. Admitted to Okla. bar, 1964, U.S. Supreme Ct. bar, 1969; spl. agt. FBI, Phila., 1966-69; asst. dist. atty. Tulsa County (Okla.), 1969-71; partner firm Sneed, Lang, Trotter, Adams, Hamilton and Downie, Tulsa, 1971—; mem. adv. com. to dept. police sci. Tulsa Jr. Coll., 1969—. Mem. Am., Okla., Tulsa County bar assns. Home: 2441 E 25th Pl Tulsa OK 74114 Office: 411 Thurston Nat Bldg Tulsa OK 74103 Tel (918) 583-3145

LANG, RICHARD JOHN, b. Chgo., Apr. 21, 1945; B.S., Loyola U., 1967; J.D. cum laude, Northwestern U., 1970. Admitted to Ill. bar, 1970; asst. prof. DePaul Coll. Law, Chgo., 1976—. Mem. Wilmette (Ill.) Plan Commn., 1975—. Mem. Am., Ill., Chgo. bar assns. Office: 25 E Jackson St Chicago IL 60603 Tel (312) 321-7700

LANGBEIN, JOHN HARRISS, b. Washington, Nov. 17, 1941; A.B., Columbia, 1964; LL.B., Harvard, 1968; LL.B., Cambridge (Eng.), 1969, Ph.D., 1971. Admitted to D.C. bar, 1969, Inner Temple Barrister at Law, Eng., 1970, Fla. bar, 1971; prof. law U. Chgo., 1971—. Mem. Am. bar Assn., Am. Hist. Assn., Am. Soc. for Legal History, Selden Soc. Contbr. articles and monographs to legal jours. Office: 1111 E 60th St Chicago IL 60637 Tel (312) 753-2447

LANGDON, DONALD ANTHONY, b. Council Bluffs, Iowa, Nov. 20, 1921; J.D., Creighton U. Admitted to Nebr. bar, 1950; asst. gen. counsel Mut. of Omaha Ins. Co., Omaha, 1950—. Mem. Nebr. Bar Assn. Home: 707 Grandview Ave Council Bluffs IA 51501 Office: 3316 Farnam St Omaha NE 68131 Tel (402) 342-7600

LANGDON, JIM C., b. Stephenville, Tex., Dec. 14, 1914; student John Tarleton Coll., 1932-33; J.D., U. Tex., 1940. Admitted to Tex. bar, 1939; spl. agt. FBI, 1940-43; practiced in McCamey, Tex., 1946-54; judge Tex. Dist. Ct., 112th Jud. Dist., 1954-59; chief justice Tex. Ct. Civil Appeals, El Paso, 1959-63; mem. R.R. Commn. Tex., Austin, 1963—; chmn. legal com. Interstate Oil Compact Commn., supply-demand com. Tex. Gov's. Energy Adv. Council. Bd. dirs. West Tex. Boys' Ranch. Fellow Tex. Bar Found. (charter); mem. State Bar Tex., Nat. Assn. Regulatory Utility Commrs. Recipient Hat's Off award Tex. Ind. Producers and Royalty Owners Assn., 1968; named Distinguished Displaced West Texan, West Tex. C. of C. Home: 5828 Trailridge St Austin TX 78731 Office: PO Drawer 12967 Austin TX 78711 Tel (512) 475-3365

LANGDON, ROBERT LEE, b. Ottawa, Kans., Jan. 11, 1948; B.S., U. Mo., 1970, J.D., 1972. Admitted to Mo. bar, 1973, Fed. Western Dist. Mo. bar, 1973; asso. firm Bradley, Skelton & Schelp, Lexington, Mo., 1973—. Dir. Lexington Bicentennial Com. Mem. Mo., Kansas City, Lafayette County (pres. 1974) bar assns. Office: 10 S 10th St PO Box 130 Lexington MO 64067 Tel (816) 259-221

LANGE, GARY HENRY, b. St. Louis, Nov. 27, 1929; B.A., Washington U., St. Louis, 1952, J.D., 1959. Admitted to Mo., Ill. bars, 1959; individual practice law, St. Louis, 1959-65; partner firm Mills & Lange, St. Louis, 1965-72; partner firm Baxtley, Goffstein, Bollato & Lange, St. Louis and Clayton, Mo., 1972—; asst. chief staff for air Mo. Air N.G. Mem. Mo., Ill., St. Louis, St. Louis County bar assns., Assn. Trial Lawyers, Inst. Navigation. Home: 3748 Cranberry Ct Florissant MO 63033 Office: Suite 604 130 S Bemiston St Clayton MO 63105 Tel (314) 727-0922

LANGE, MORTON KEEFER, b. St. Louis, Dec. 12, 1906; LL.B., Washington U., St. Louis, 1932. Admitted to Mo. bar, 1932, U.S. Cts. for Allied High Commn. in Germany, 1949; asso. firm Wilbur C. Schwartz, St. Louis, 1932-43; legal officer and advisor Mil. Govt. Bavaria, Germany, 1946-49; judge 8th Jud. Circuit U.S. Cts. in Germany, 1946-49; individual practice law, Germany, 1949-63, St. Louis and Cuba, Mo., 1963—; magistrate judge Probate Ct. Crawford County (Mo.), 1964-67, pros. atty., 1967-69, 73-77; atty. City of Glendale (Mo.), 1937-43. Mem. Am., Mo., St. Louis, 42d Jud. Circuit, Southwestern Mo. bar assns., Assn. Am. Lawyers in Europe (sec. 1954-55). Contbr. articles to legal jours. Home: 1204 DuBois Ct Kirkwood MO 63122 Office: 205 W Washington St Cuba MO 65453 Tel (314) 885-7725

LANGENKAMP, ROBERT DOBIE, b. Tulsa, Aug. 14, 1936; B.A. in Polit. Sci. magna cum laude, Stanford, 1958; LL.B., Harvard, 1961. Admitted to Okla. bar, 1964, U.S. Supreme Ct. bar, 1970; asso. firm Collier, Shannon, Rill & Edwards, Washington, 1962-64; asso. firm Doerner, Stuart, Saunders, Daniel & Langenkamp, and predecessor, Tulsa, 1962-64, partner, 1966—; owner, mgr. cattle and grain farm, Mayes County, Okla. Mem. Tulsa Com. on Fgn. Relations; chmn. police task force Gov's. Adv. Commn. on Criminal Justice, Goals and Standards of Okla., 1976—; bd. dirs. Tulsa County Legal Aid Soc.; vestryman Trinity Episcopal Ch.; chmn., dir. Tulsa County OEO; del. Democratic Nat. Conv., 1976. Mem. Okla., Tulsa (exec. com.) bar assns. Named Outstanding Young Lawyer Tulsa Bar Assn., 1971. Home: 2445 E 27th Pl Tulsa OK 74114 Office: 1200 Atlas Life Bldg Tulsa OK 74103 Tel (918) 585-5541

LANGFORD, CHARLES DOUGLAS, b. Montgomery, Ala., Dec. 9, 1922; B.S., Tenn. State U., 1948; LL.B., Catholic U. Am., 1952, J.D., 1967. Admitted to Ala. bar, 1953; partner firm Gray, Seay & Langford, Montgomery and Tuskegee, Ala., 1968—; legal advisor Ala. State Assn. Elks. Mem. Nat., Am., Ala. State bar assns. Home: 918 E Grove St Montgomery AL 36104 Office: 352 Dexter Ave Montgomery AL 36104 also PO Box 239 Tuskegee AL 36083 Tel (205) 269-2563

LANGLAS, THOMAS WILLIAM, b. Waterloo, Iowa, Jan. 31, 1943; B.A., Coll. St. Thomas, St. Paul, 1964; J.D., U. Iowa, 1967. Admitted to Iowa bar, 1967; asso. firm Kildee, Keith, Gallagher, Lybbert & Martin, Waterloo, 1967-70; gen. partner firm Gallagher, Martin, Keith & Langlas, Waterloo, 1970—; asst. city atty. Waterloo, 1968-76. Pres. bd. dirs. Waterloo Jaycees, 1970-71, Waterloo Community Playhouse, 1972-73, Boys' Club Waterloo, 1975—; pres. Black Hawk County chpt. Am. Cancer Soc., 1975-76. Mem. Am., Iowa, Black Hawk County bar assns., Am., Iowa assns. trial lawyers. Recipient Distinguished Service award Waterloo Jaycees, 1976. Office: 405 E 5th St PO Box 2615 Waterloo IA 50705 Tel (319) 233-6163

LANGROCK, PETER FORBES, b. N.Y.C., Feb. 2, 1938; A.B., U. Chgo., 1958, J.D., 1960. Admitted to Vt. bar, 1960; state's atty. of Addison County (Vt.), 1960-65; individual practice law Middlebury, 1965-69; partner firm Langrock and Sperry, Middlebury, 1969—; participant The Advocates, ednl. TV series, 1973; lectr. schs.; participant TV panel discussions. Mem. Am. Bar Assn. (council on individual rights and responsibilities 1973—), Nat. Conf. Commrs. on Uniform State Laws (exec. com. 1975—). Contbr. articles to profl. jours. Office: 15 S Pleasant St Middlebury VT 05753 Tel (802) 388-7979

LANGSDORF, J(ESSE) GUTHRIE, b. Salmon, Idaho, Feb. 28, 1911; B.A., U. Wash., 1933, J.D., 1935; grad. Nat. Juvenile Ct. Judges Sch., 1956. Admitted to Wash. State bar, 1935; partner firm Wilkinson & Langsdorf, Vancouver, Wash., 1935-55; judge Clark County (Wash.) Superior Ct., dept. 1, 1955-76; mem. Wash. State Jud. Council, 1965-74; judge pro tempore Wash. Supreme Ct., 1965-66, fall, 1973. Chmn. Clark County Republican Central Com., 1946-54; elder Presbyn. Ch., Vancouver. Mem. Clark County Bar Assn. (pres. 1948), Wash. Superior Ct. Judges' Assn. (pres. 1974-75), Wash. State Judges Assn. (v.p. 1973-74). Decorated Bronze Star. Home and office: 8317 NW Bacon Rd Vancouver WA 98665 Tel (206) 693-1706

LANGSLET, JOHN LORING, b. Portland, Oreg., July 16, 1944; B.S., Portland State U., 1966; J.D., U. Calif. at Berkeley, 1972. Admitted to Oreg. bar, 1972; with firm Martin, Bischoff, Templeton & Biggs, Portland, 1972—, partner, 1976—; grad. research asst. Center for Study Law and Soc., Berkeley, 1970-71. Mem. Am., Multnomah County bar assns., Oreg. State Bar, Am. Trial Lawyers Assn., Am. Judicature Soc., Order of Coif. Home: 1228 SW Texas St Portland OR 97219 Office: 2908 1st Nat Bank Tower Portland OR 97201 Tel (503) 224-3113

LANGSTON, JOHN WADE, b. Little Rock, June 19; J.D., U. Ark., 1966. Admitted to Ark. bar; v.p. firm Langston & Langston, Ltd., Little Rock, 1966—. Mem. Pulaski County (Ark.), Ark., Am. bar assns. Home: 2904 Painted Valley Dr Little Rock AR 72216 Office: Suite 400 Am Foundation Life Bldg Little Rock AR 72201 Tel (501) 374-8203

LANGSTON, LEROY, b. Greenville, S.C., June 20, 1931; LL.B., U. Ga. Admitted to Ga. bar, 1958; individual practice law, Atlanta, 1959—. Mem. Am., Ga. bar assns., Am., Ga. trial lawyers assns. Home: 2148 Melante Dr NE Atlanta GA 30324 Office: 2301 Nat Bank of Ga Bldg Atlanta GA 30303 Tel (404) 524-2878

LANGUM, DAVID JOHN, b. Oakland, Calif., Oct. 24, 1940; A.B., Dartmouth, 1962; J.D., Stanford, 1965; M.A. in History, San Jose State U., 1976. Admitted to Calif. bar, 1966, U.S. Supreme Ct. bar, 1972; research clk. Ct. Appeals, San Francisco, 1965-66; asso. firm Dunne, Phelps & Mills, San Francisco, 1966-68; partner firm Christenson, Hedemark, Langum & O'Keefe, San Jose, Calif., 1968—; prof. law Lincoln U., 1968—. Mem. Calif., Santa Clara bar assns., Am. Soc. Legal History, Western History Assn. Contbr. articles to legal and profl. jours. Home: 1161 Chapman St San Jose CA 95126 Office: 111 W St John St #700 San Jose CA 95113 Tel (408) 292-8780

LANHAM, JOHN CALHOUN, b. Summerton, S.C., Dec. 6, 1924; LL., U. S.C., 1949. Admitted to S.C. bar, 1949, Hawaii bar, 1955; individual practice law, Wahiawa, Hawaii, 1955-70; judge advocate gen.'s corps, U.S. Army, 1950-55; mem. Ho. of Reps., Hawaii, 1958-66; mem. Senate Hawaii Legis., 1966-70; judge 1st Circuit Ct. of Hawaii, Honolulu, 1970—. Mem. Am. Bar Assn., Am. Judicature Soc. Home: 1533 Kamole St Honolulu HI 96821 Office: Judiciary Bldg Honolulu HI 96809 Tel 548-2441

LANHAM, R. RHODES, b. Evanston, Ill., Mar. 7, 1936; B.A., Northwestern U., 1959, J.D., 1963. Admitted to Ill. bar, 1964. Atty. N.Y. Central RR, Chgo., 1964-69; atty. Security Mut. Casualty Co., Chgo., 1969-71, sec., gen. counsel, 1972—; asso. firm Burditt & Calkins, Chgo., 1971-72. Mem. Am., Ill. State, Chgo. bar assns. Office: 222 S Riverside Plaza Chicago IL 60606 Tel (312) 648-4581

LANIER, ROBERT ALLISON, b. Memphis, Nov. 2, 1938; B.S., Memphis State U., 1960; LL.B., U. Miss., 1962, J.D., 1968. Admitted to Miss. bar, 1962, Tenn. bar, 1963, U.S. Supreme Ct. bar, 1974; asso. firm Armstrong McAdden, Allen, Braden & Goodman, Memphis, 1964-68; partner firm Farris, Hancock Gilman Branan & Lanier, Memphis, 1968—; spl. judge city and gen. sessions cts. Mem. Shelby County (Tenn.) Republican Exec. Com., 1970-72; pres. Memphis Humane Soc., 1974, chmn. bd., 1976; dir. Memphis Heritage Inc. Mem. Miss. State Bar, Tenn., Am., Memphis-Shelby County (editor Syllabus 1975—) bar assns., Maritime Law Assn. Contbr. to Memphis State U. Law Rev., Ins. Law Jour. Home: 635 West Dr Memphis TN 38112 Office: 1620 1st Nat Bank Bldg Memphis TN 38112 Tel (901) 523-8080

LANIER, RUSSELL JARVIS, JR., b. N.C., July 20, 1944; B.S., Campbell Coll., 1965; J.D., U. N.C., 1968. Admitted to N.C. bar, 1968; partner firm Lanier & Lanier, Jacksonville and Kenansville, N.C.; town atty. Town of Beulaville (N.C.). Mem. N.C. Bar Assn., Am. Trial Lawyers Assn., N.C. Acad. Trial Lawyers. Home: PO Box 461 Buelaville NC 28518 Office: PO Box 87 Kenansville NC 28349 Tel (919) 296-5781

LANK, AUBREY BIDDLE, b. Davenport, Iowa, June 14, 1925; B.A., U. Del., 1949; J.D., Georgetown U., 1951. Admitted to D.C. bar, 1951, Del. bar, 1952; law clk. to judge U.S. Dist. Ct., Dist. Del., 1951-52; asso. firm Logan, Marvel, Boggs and Theisen, Wilmington, Del., 1953-60; partner firm Theisen, Lank & Mulford and predecessor, Wilmington, 1960—. Mem. Del. Hwy. Commn., 1961-65; chmn. Del. Authority of Regional Transit, 1968-71; spl. counsel Del. Dept. Natural Resources and Environ. Control, 1972—. Mem. Am. Judicature Soc., Am. Assn. Trial Lawyers, Am., Del. (pres. 1976—) bar assns. Office: 1118 Wilmington Trust Bldg PO Box 1470 Wilmington DE 19899 Tel (302) 656-7712

LANNEAU, FRANK BLISS, III, b. Macon, Ga., Apr. 19, 1943; A.B. magna cum laude, Mercer U., 1965, LL.B., 1968. Admitted to Ga. bar, 1970; asso. firm Westmoreland & Patterson, Macon, Ga., 1970-71; individual practice law, Macon, 1971—; with installment loan dept. Citizens & So. Nat. Bank, Macon, 1969. Mem. Ga., Macon bar assns. Home: 1008 Birch St Macon GA 31204 Office: 309 Am Fed Bldg Macon GA 31201 Tel (912) 745-7606

LANSDALE, ARLYNE, b. Denver, July 14, 1905; B.S., Wilson's Coll., 1922; LL.B., Southwestern U., 1931. Admitted to Calif. bar, 1934, U.S. Supreme Ct. bar, others. Mem. Los Angeles, Orange County bar assns., Iota Tau Tau. Office: 8331 Westminster Ave Westminster CA 92683 Tel (714) 893-2306

LANZO, JAMES RUDOLPH, b. Youngstown, Ohio, Dec. 23, 1944; B.S. in Edn., Youngstown U., 1966, J.D., 1971. Admitted to Ohio bar, 1972; partner firm Clemente & Lanzo, Struthers, Ohio, 1973-75; individual practice law, Struthers, 1976—; solicitor City of Struthers, 1976—. Mem. Ohio State, Am., Mahoning County bar assns., Struthers Businessman's Assn. (v.p. 1976). Home: 604 Maplewood St Struthers OH 44471 Office: 32 State St Suite 103 Struthers OH 44471 Tel (216) 750-1371

LAPADULA, PASCHAL ROBERT, b. N.Y.C., Mar. 5, 1924; B.S., Georgetown Coll., 1947, J.D., 1950. Admitted to D.C. bar, 1950, Md. bar, 1956; lawyer Office of Sec. Defense, Gen. Counsel's Office, Washington, 1951-54; pvt. practice law, Bethesda, Md., 1954—. Mem. D.C., Md. bar assns., Comml. Law League Am. Editor: Fed. Bar Jour., 1953. Office: 4400 East-West Hwy Bethesda MD 20014

LAPIC, JEFFREY ROBERT, b. Mpls., Dec. 28, 1941; A.B., Dartmouth, 1963; J.D., Duke, 1970. Admitted to Calif. bar, 1971; asso. firm Orrick, Herrington, Rowley & Sutcliffe, San Francisco,

1970-75; counsel Bank of America NT & SA legal dept., San Francisco, 1975-76, sr. counsel, 1976—; asst. prof. Armstrong Coll. Sch. of Law, Berkeley, Calif., 1975—. Participant San Francisco Lawyers Com. for Urban Affairs Legal Services Project, 1973-75. Mem. Am. Bar Assn., Order of Coif. Research editor Duke Law Jour., 1969-70. Home: 69 Edison Ave Corte Madera CA 94925 Office: 555 California St San Francisco CA 94104 Tel (415) 622-2189

LAPIDUS, ALLAN ELLIOT, b. N.Y.C., Jan. 24, 1943; B.S., U. Wis., 1964; J.D., U. Mich., 1967. Admitted to Ill. bar, 1967; lawyer FCC, Washington, 1967-69; asst. U.S. atty., Chgo., 1969-73; mem. firm Vedder, Price, Kaufman & Kammholz, Chgo., 1973—. Mem. Chgo. Bar Assn., Chgo. Council Lawyers. Home: 2337 N Commonwealth Ave Chicago IL 60614 Office: 115 S LaSalle St Chicago IL 60603 Tel (312) 781-2242

LAPIN, HARVEY IRWIN, b. St. Louis, Nov. 23, 1937; B.S. in Accounting, Northwestern U., 1960, J.D., 1963; LL.M. in Taxation, Georgetown U., 1967. Admitted to Ill. bar, 1963, U.S. Tax Ct. bar, 1964, U.S. Supreme Ct. bar, 1967; trial atty. Office of Chief Counsel, IRS Washington, 1963-68; asso. firm Fiffer & D'Angelo, Chgo., 1968-72, partner, 1972-75; pres. firm Lapin, Panichi & Levine, Ltd., Chgo., 1975—; instr. Tax Inst., John Marshall Law Sch., Chgo., 1969—; dir. Lawyers Asst. program Roosevelt U., Chgo., 1974—. Mem. cemetery advisory bd. Comptroller State of Ill., 1973—. Mem. Am., Ill., Chgo. bar assns. Editor: Cemetery Business and Legal Guide, 1973—. Office: 115 S La Salle St Chicago IL 60603 Tel (312) 346-8111

LAPORTA, ALFRED, b. N.Y.C., June 5, 1933; B.A., City Coll. City N.Y., 1955; J.D., N.Y. U., 1959. Admitted to N.Y. bar, 1960; partner firm LaPorta & LaPorta, Bronx, N.Y., 1961—; arbitrator State of N.Y. 1st Jud. Dept. Compulsory Arbitration Service, 1972—. Mem. Bronx County Bar Assn., Columbia Lawyers Assn. Home: 11 Pine Ave Pelham NY 10803 Office: 483 Willis Ave Bronx NY 10455 Tel (212) LU5-2658

LAPORTA, EDWARD, b. N.Y.C., Sept. 8, 1930; B.B.A., City Coll. N.Y., 1953; J.D., N.Y. U., 1959. Admitted to N.Y. bar, 1959; partner firm LaPorta & LaPorta, Bronx, N.Y., 1961—; arbitrator N.Y. State 1st Jud. Dept. Compulsory Arbitration Service, 1972—. Trustee sr. council Sch. No. 5, Yonkers, N.Y., 1972-76. Mem. Bronx County Bar Assn., Columbia Law Assn. Home: 25 Fenimore Ave Yonkers NY 10701 Office: 483 Willis Ave Bronx NY 10455 Tel (212) LU5-2658

LAPORTE, EWING, b. Normandy, France, Oct. 16, 1894; LLB., George Washington U., 1916; student Yale, 1917-18; A.B., U. Pitts., 19—. Admitted to D.C. bar, 1917, U.S. Supreme Ct. bar, 1926, Pa. bar, 1955; dep. stg. at arms, U.S. Senate, 1913-16; connected with IRS, war risk ins. and customs burs., U.S. Treasury Dept., 1916-20, apptd. asst. sec. Treasury, by President Wilson, 1920, reapptd. by President Harding, 1921, resigned, 1921; fin. sec. U. Pitts., 1921-22; individual practice law, Washington, 1923-33; Pa. state mgr. Home Owners Loan Corp., 1934; regional mgr., N.Y., N.J., and Conn., 1935; individual practice law, Washington, 1936—. Exec. sec. Dem. Nat. Conv., 1932, exec. sec. arrangements Com., 1932. Mem. D.C., Pa. bar assns. Home: 3139 Oliver St NW Washington DC 20015 Office: Nat Press Bldg Washington DC 20045 Tel (202) DI7-6631

LAPP, RICHARD NELSON, b. Phila., Mar. 21, 1944; B.A. in Econs. and Social Scis., So. Meth. U., 1966, M.B.A. in Fin., 1969, J.D., 1970. Admitted to Tex. bar, 1971; account exec. E. F. Hutton & Co., Dallas, 1971-73, co-founder, v.p. E. F. Hutton Real Estate Corp. of Tex., Dallas, 1973-76; partner EM Properties, Inc., Dallas, 1976—; guest lectr. Costa Sch. Mortgage Banking, So. Meth. U. Mem. Assn. M.B.A. Execs. Home: 6424 Mimosa Ln Dallas TX 75230 Office: 407 Carillon Tower W 13601 Preston Rd Dallas TX 75240 Tel (214) 387-4575

LAPPIN, FRANCIS LEO, b. Lowell, Mass., Jan. 13, 1915; LL.B., Northeastern U., 1937. Admitted to Mass. bar, 1938; practiced in Lowell, 1938-62; justice Mass. Superior Ct., 1962—, presiding justice appellate div., 1972—; legis. counsel Gov. Mass., 1961-62; town counsel Town of Dracut (Mass.), 1946-61; mem. Mass. Senate, 1959-60. Mem. Lowell, Mass., Boston, bar assns., New Eng. Trial Judges. Home: 36 Chapman St Dracut MA 01826 Office: Superior Ct Boston MA 02108 Tel (617) 442-2040

LAPPIN, ROBERT SIDNEY, b. Boston, Oct. 6, 1928; B.A., Norwich U., 1951; M.B.A., Boston U., 1955; LL.B., Boston Coll., 1959. Admitted to Mass. bar, 1959; mem. tax staff Lybrand, Ross Bros. & Montgomery, Boston, 1955-61; individual practice law, Boston, 1962-70; partner firm Lappin, Rosen, Goldberg, Slavet, Levenson & Wekstein, Boston, 1970—; mem. faculty Bentley Coll., 1964-65, Boston U., 1960-63, Boston Coll. Law Sch., 1966-68. Mem. Boston Bar Assn., Norwich U. Alumni Assn. (pres. bd. dirs. 1976-78). Home: 180 Beacon St Boston MA 02116 Office: 35th Floor One Boston Pl Boston MA 02108 Tel (617) 261-1000

LARAMEY, THOMAS AVRIETT, JR., b. Temple, Tex., Sept. 16, 1945; B.B.A., Tex. A. and M. U., 1967; J.D., U. Tex., 1971. Admitted to Tex. bar, 1971; legal counsel Tex. Office Econ. Opportunity, Austin, 1972-73; cons. Tex. Edn. Agy., Austin, 1973-74; gen. counsel Tex. Dept. Community Affairs, Austin, 1974—; advisor 62d Tex. Legis., Austin, 1972. Mem. Am., Tex., Travis County, Austin Jr. bar assns., Austin Soc. Pub. Adminstrn. Contbr. articles to legal jours. Office: 210 Barton Springs Rd Austin TX 78704 Tel (512) 475-6903

LAREAU, RICHARD GEORGE, b. Woonsocket, R.I., June 11, 1928; B.A., St. Michaels Coll., Vt., 1949; J.D., U. Minn., 1952. Admitted to Minn. bar, 1952; served to lt. JAGC, USAF, 1952-56; asso. firm Oppenheimer, Wolff, Foster, Shepard and Donnelly, Mpls., 1956-60, partner, 1960—; sec. Control Data Corp., Mpls., 1966-71, dir., 1971—. Mem. Am., Minn. (chmn. corp., banking and bus. law sect. 1976-77), Hennepin County bar assns. Home: 2150 Angell Rd West Saint Paul MN 55118 Office: 4008 IDS Center 80 S 8th St Minneapolis MN 55402 Tel (612) 332-6451

LAREY, BERT BETHEL, b. Texarkana, Ark., Feb. 23, 1896; student Ark. State Tchrs. Coll., 1915-18; LL.B., Vanderbilt U., 1925, J.D., 1969; prin. Taylor (Ark.) High Sch., 1920-21; supt. schs., Benton, Ark., 1921-23; admitted to Ark. bar, 1923, Tenn. bar, 1925, U.S. Supreme Ct. bar, 1960; individual practice law, El Dorado, Ark., 1925-32, Texarkana, Ark., 1932—; municipal judge, Texarkana and Miller County, Ark., 1967-74; mem. bar exam. com. 8th Jud. Dist. Ark., 1934-35, Fed. Bar Exam. Com. Western Dist. Ark., 1935—; govt. appeal agt. Miller County (Ark.), 1940-46. Trustee Ark. State Tchrs. Coll., 1939-42; Democratic Presdl. elector, 1944. Mem. Am., Ark., Miller-Bowie Counties, SW Ark. bar assns., Trial Lawyers Assn. Home: 2600 Locust Texarkana AR 75501 Office: Box 8001 Texarkana AR 75501 Tel (501) 772-4431

LARGAY, TIMOTHY LEO, b. Boston, June 12, 1943; A.B. Georgetown U., 1965, J.D., 1969. Admitted to Conn. bar, 1969; since practiced in Hartford, Conn.; asso. firm Murtha, Cullina, Richter & Pinney, 1969-74, partner, 1974—; dir. Buell Industries, Inc., 1976—. Mem. Am., Conn., Hartford County bar assns. Home: 7 Highwood Circle Avon CT 06001 Office: 101 Pearl St Hartford CT 06103 Tel (203) 549-4500

LARGE, EDWARD WILSON, b. Collingswood, N.J., Mar. 9, 1930; B.A., Marshall U., 1952; LL.B., U. Va., 1955. Admitted to Va. bar, 1955, N.Y. State bar, 1956, Conn. bar, 1961; asso. firm Shearman & Sterling, N.Y.C., 1955-60; staff atty. United Technologies Corp., Hartford, Conn., 1960-64, asst. gen. counsel, 1964-69, gen. counsel, 1969-70, v.p., gen. counsel, 1970—; trustee, mem. exec. com. Soc. for Savs., Hartford. Mem. Am., Conn. bar assns. Home: 5 Orchard Rd West Hartford CT 06117 Office: United Technolgies Bldg Hartford CT 06101 Tel (203) 728-7000

LARGEN, GERALD, b. Emory Gap, Tenn., Oct. 6, 1935; LL.B., U. Tenn., 1958. Admitted to Tenn. bar, 1959; individual practice law, Roane County, Tenn., 1959—. Office: Court House Sq Kingston TN 37763 Tel (615) 376-5316

LARGEN, WILLIAM ANDREW, b. Fayetteville, Tenn., Sept. 30, 1935; LL.B., Vanderbilt U., 1961, J.D., 1969. Admitted to Tenn. bar, 1961; asso. firm Strawbridge, Herron, Dresden, Tenn., 1965; individual practice law, Dresden, 1966—; instr. Bus. and Real Estate law, U. Tenn., Martin, 1975-76. Pres. Rotary Club, 1972-73; treas. Dresden Sesquicentennial Corp., 1975; v.p. Dresden Jaycees, 1966. Mem. Weakley County (pres. 1967-68), Am., Tenn. bar assns. Home: Meadowlawn Dr Dresden TN 38225 Office: S Side Court Square Dresden TN 38226 Tel (901) 364-2933

LARKIN, JOHN JOSEPH, b. Boston, Dec. 8, 1913; A.B., Boston Coll., 1936, M.S.W., 1938; LL.B., George Washington U., 1952. Admitted to U.S. Dist. Ct. bar for D.C., 1952, U.S. Circuit Ct. Appeals, D.C. Circuit, 1952; probation officer D.C. Juvenile Ct., 1938-43, chief probation officer, 1945-54, dir. social work, 1954-64, hearing commr., 1964-71; hearing commr. D.C. Superior Ct., 1971—. Mem. Bar Assn. D.C. Home: 3803 W St NW Washington DC 20007 Office: 410 E St NW Washington DC 20001 Tel (202) 727-1797

LARKIN, LEO A., b. 1911; A.B., Fordham U., 1932, LL.B., 1935; postgrad. in Law and Bus., N.Y.U. Practiced law, N.Y.C., 1935-54; corp. counsel Corp. Counsel Office N.Y.C., 1954-66; v.p., sec., gen. counsel W.R. Grace and Co., N.Y.C., 1966—. Office: 1114 Ave of Americas New York City NY 10036*

LARKIN, MURL ALTON, b. Lebo, Kans., Feb. 18, 1917; LL.B., Southeastern U., 1939; postgrad. Naval War Coll., 1963. Admitted to D.C. bar, 1938, U.S. Supreme Ct. bar, 1952, Tex. bar, 1969; commd. lt. JAG U.S. Navy, 1941, advanced through grades to capt., 1959; asst. judge advocate gen., 1967-68; prof. law Tex. Tech U., Lubbock, 1968—, prof. Franklin Pierce Law Center, 1974; sec., v.p. Ct. Practice Inst., Chgo.; cons. in field. Mem. Am. Bar Assn., Ret. Officers Assn., Order of Coif, Phi Kappa Phi. Decorated Legion of Merit; author: (with Joe H Munster) Military Evidence, 1961, biennial supplements, 1963, 65, 67, 69, 71, 73, 75, 2d edit., 1977; contbr. articles in field to profl. jours. Home: 6011 Vernon Ave Lubbock TX 79412 Office: Sch Law Tex Tech U Lubbock TX 79409 Tel (806) 742-3785

LARKINS, JOHN DAVIS, JR., b. Morristown, Tenn., June 8, 1909; B.A., Wake Forest U., 1929, student law 1930. Admitted to N.C. bar, 1930; U.S. Conciliation Commr., Trenton, N.C., 1934-36; state senator N.C., 1936-55, pres. pro tempore, 1941-42; legis. counsel to gov. of N.C., 1955-56; judge U.S. Dist. Ct., Trenton, N.C., 1961-75, chief judge, 1975—. Chmn. N.C. Democratic Party, 1954-58; mem. Dem. Nat. Com., 1958-60; del. Dem. Nat. Conv., 1936, 40, 44, 48, 52, 56, 60. Office: Federal Bldg Trenton NC 28585 Tel (919) 448-2521

LARNER, SAMUEL ARA, b. Burlington, Vt., May 31, 1909; A.B., Univ. Heights Coll. N.Y. U., 1930; LL.B., Columbia, 1933. Admitted to N.J. bar, 1934, U.S. Supreme Ct. bar, 1950; partner firm Budd & Larner, Newark, 1934-66; judge N.J. Superior Ct., Newark, 1966—, appellate div., 1975—; assignment judge Hudson County (N.J.), 1970-75; spl. counsel to N.J. Gov., 1945; apptd. to investigate City of Jersey City, 1952-54; chmn. Supreme Ct. Com. on Civil Practice. Mem. Am., N.J., Essex County (N.J.), Hudson County bar assns. Home: 2 Hobson Dr Livingston NJ 07039 Office: 520 Broad St Newark NJ 07102 Tel (201) 648-2833

LARRAZOLO, PAUL FREDERICK, b. Albuquerque, Dec. 2, 1910; student U. N.Mex., 1929-32; LL.B., Georgetown U., 1937. Admitted to D.C. bar, 1937, N.Mex. bar, 1940; U.S. atty. N. Mex., Albuquerque, 1953-57; dist. judge 2d Jud. Dist., Albuquerque, 1961-74; individual practice law, Albuquerque, 1957-61, 74—. Pres. bd. regents U. N.Mex., Albuquerque, 1951-54; trustee Coll. Santa Fe (N. Mex.), 1960-62. Tel (505) 268-5163

LARRICK, JOHN FREDERICK, b. Balt., Oct. 1, 1917; B.S. in Chemistry, Va. Mil. Inst., 1940; J.D., U. Va., 1948. Admitted to Va. bar, 1947; practiced in Winchester, Va. 1949—; partner firms Larrick and Larrick, 1949-50, firm Harrison, Benham and Thoma, 1950-61; individual practice law, 1961-64; partner firm Larrick & White, 1964-77, Larrick, White and Rabun, 1977—; dir. F & M Nat. Corp., Farmers and Merchants Nat. Bank, 1st Fed. Savs. & Loan Assn. of Front Royal (Va.). Mem. Handley Bd. Trustees, Winchester; mem. Va. Supreme Ct. Com. for Preparation of Pattern Jury Instructions. Mem. Winchester-Frederick County, Va. (v.p. Valley chpt. 1971-72), Am. (ho. of dels. 1973—) bar assns., Va. State Bar (council 1967-73, exec. com. 1972-73), Internat. Assn. Ins. Counsel, Va. Trial Lawyers Assn., Assn. Trial Lawyers Am. Home: 514 Tennyson Ave Winchester VA 22601 Office: 29 N Braddock St PO Box 764 Winchester VA 22601 Tel (703) 662-2507

LARRIMER, JOHN B., b. Hannibal, Mo., Jan. 16, 1941; B.S., S.W. Mo. State U., 1968; M.B.A., Ark. U., 1970; J.D., U. Mo., 1974. Admitted to Mo. bar, 1974; prof. Stephens Coll., Columbia, Mo., 1969-74, instr. law and medicine, 1975—; partner firm Larrimer & O'Donnell, Columbia, 1974—. Chmn. Columbia Bd. Health; mem. Columbia Environ. and Nat. Resources Commn. Mem. Am., Mo., Boone County bar assns., Am. Soc. Trial Lawyers, ACLU. Office: 915 W Broadway Columbia MO 65201 Tel (314) 442-8355

LARSEN, DAVID CLAIR, b. Salt Lake City, Nov. 24, 1946; student Johns Hopkins, 1965-66, Brigham Young U., 1969-71; J.D., U. Utah, 1973. Admitted to Calif. bar, 1973; asso. firm Rutan & Tucker, Santa Ana, Calif., 1973—; gen. counsel Huntington Beach Union High Sch. Dist., 1976—; dep. city atty. Irvine, Cypress, Lynwood, La Palma, and Yorba Linda (Calif.), 1974—. Alt. mem. high council Newport Beach Stake, Ch. Jesus Christ Latter Day Saints, 1976—. Mem. Orange County Bar Assn., Order of Coif. Mng. editor Utah Law Rev., 1972-73. Home: 24601 Via Tequila El Toro CA 92630 Office: 401 Civic Center Dr W Santa Ana CA 92702 Tel (714) 835-2200

LARSEN, WILLIAM W., b. San Diego, July 20, 1940; B.S., Fresno State U., 1962; J.D., Hastings Coll. of Law, 1965. Police officer City of Madera (Calif.), 1961-62; asst. to city atty. City of San Francisco, 1965-66; admitted to Calif. bar, 1966; dep. dist. atty. Office Dist. Atty. San Mateo County (Calif.), Redwood City, 1966-72, asst. dist. atty., 1972—. Mem. Eagle bd. of rev. Boy Scouts Am., Redwood City, 1971-72. Mem. Calif., San Mateo County bar assns., Calif. Peace Officers Assn. Author: Manual of Policies, Procedures and Forms San Mateo County District Attorney's Office, 1974; co-author: Continuing Education of the Bar Criminal Law II Supplement on Extradition, 1976. Office: Hall of Justice Redwood City CA 94063 Tel (415) 364-5600

LARSON, ARTHUR, b. Sioux Falls, S.D., July 4, 1910; A.B., Augustana Coll., 1931; B.A. in Jurisprudence, Oxford U., 1935, B.C.L., 1957, D.C.L., 1957. Admitted to Wis. bar, 1936; asso. firm Quarles, Spence & Quarles, Milw., 1935-39; prof. law, Cornell U., Ithaca, N.Y., 1945-53; dean U. Pitt. Law Sch., Pitts., 1953-54; under-sec. labor, Washington, 1954-57; dir. USIA, D.C., 1957-58; spl. asst. to pres., Washington, 1958-59, spl. cons., 1959-61, cons. to Pres. Johnson internat. affairs, 1964-68; James B. Duke Prof. law Duke U., Durham, N.C., 1958—; mem. 2 Social Security Advisory Councils; cons. to Council of Econ. Advisors. Vice pres. Nat. Council of Chs., 1965-70. Mem. Am. Bar Assn., Am. Soc. of Internat. Law. Author: (with Stevens) Cases on Corporations, 1947; The Law of Workmen's Compensation (8 vols.), 1952-76; The Law of Employment Discrimination (2 vols.), 1975; Industrial Injuries and Death (2 vols.), 1972; Sovereignty Within the Law, 1965; (with Whitton) Propaganda, 1964; (with Lee) Population and Law, 1971. Home: One Learned Pl Durham NC 27705 Office: Duke Univ Law Sch Durham NC 27706 Tel (919) 684-3518

LARSON, BYRON GARDNER, b. Muskegon, Mich., Oct. 12, 1923; B.A., LL.B., U. Colo. Admitted to Kans. bar, 1951; city atty. Dodge City, Kans., 1953-61; practice law, Dodge City. Mem. Am., Kans. bar assns. Home: 115 Plaza St Dodge City KS 67801 Office: 617 2d Ave Dodge City KS 67801 Tel 225-4168

LARSON, DEAN MARTIN, b. Omaha, Oct. 10, 1942; B.S., U. Denver, 1963; J.D., Northwestern U., 1966; M.S., U. Wyo., 1967; Ph.D., Am. U., 1972. Admitted to Colo. bar, 1966, Wyo. bar, 1967; law clk. to v.p. and gen. counsel Nat. Tea Co., Chgo., 1964-66; prof. econs. and politics Sheridan (Wyo.) Coll., 1967-69; prof. econs. and bus. Frederick (Md.) Coll., 1969-72; partner firm Larson & Larson, Riverton, Wyo., 1972—. Pres., founder Wyomingites Against Communism, Inc., Riverton, 1975—. Mem. Am., Fremont County, Wyo. bar assns. Home: 224 W Sunset St Riverton WY 82501 Office: 513 E Main St Riverton WY 82501

LARSON, E. LEIGH, b. Miami, Ariz., Jan. 17, 1934; LL.B., U. Ariz., 1961. Admitted to Ariz. bar, 1961; individual practice law, Nogales, Ariz., 1961—; atty. Santa Cruz County, Ariz., 1964—, City of Nogales, 1974—. Mem. Ariz., Santa Cruz County bar assns. Named County Atty. of Year, Ariz. County Attys. and Sheriffs Assn., 1971. Home: 2150 Old Patagonia Rd Nogales AZ 85621 Office: 750 Grand Ave Nogales AZ 85621 Tel (602) 287-3670

LARSON, EARL RICHARD, b. Mpls., Dec. 18, 1911; B.A., U. Minn., 1933, LL.B., 1935. Admitted to Minn. bar, 1935; partner firm Wattson & Larson, Mpls., 1937-40; asst. U.S. atty., St. Paul, 1940-42; partner firm Larson, Loevinger, Lindquist, Freeman & Fraser, Mpls., 1946-61; judge U.S. Dist. Ct., Mpls., 1961—. Chmn., Gov.'s Commn. on Human Rights, 1955-60. Mem. Am. Bar Assn. Home: 2036 Kenwood Pkwy Minneapolis MN 55405 Office: 669 US Court House Minneapolis MN 55401 Tel (612) 725-2577

LARSON, JOHN DAVID, b. Madison, Wis., July 6, 1941; B.B.A., U. Wis., 1964; J.D., 1965, M.B.A., 1966. Admitted to Wis. bar, 1965; C.P.A., Wis. 1969; asst. to pres. Nat. Guardian Life Ins. Co., Madison, 1969-71, treas., 1970-74, v.p., 1971-73, exec. v.p., 1973, pres., 1974—, dir., 1974—; dir. 1st Wis. Nat. Bank of Madison, 1975—. Treas., ARC, 1971-74, chmn., 1974-75, bd. dirs., 1969-75; v.p. campaign United Way of Dane County, 1973, pres., 1975, bd. dirs., 1973-76. Mem. Am., Wis. bar assns., Wis. Inst. of C.P.A.'s, Am. Soc. of CLUs, Madison C. of C. (bd. dirs. 1976-77). Home: 309 Laurel Ln Madison WI 53704 Office: PO Box 1191 Madison WI 53701 Tel (608) 257-5611

LARSON, MYRUS BAXTER, b. Cut Bank, Mont., Aug. 16, 1918; student U. Minn., 1936-39; LL.B., U. Mont., 1941. Admitted to Mont. bar, 1941, U.S. Tax Ct. bar, 1971; asso. firm Maury & Shone, Butte, Mont., 1941-43; asst. atty. gen. State of Mont., Helena, 1946-48; partner firm Dougherty & Larson, Helena, 1949-51; individual practice law, Wolf Point, Mont., 1953—; served to 2d lt. JAGC, AUS, 1943-46; chmn. Mont. Indsl. Accident Bd., 1951-52; mem. Commn. on Practice, Supreme Ct. Mont., 1973—. Mem. Mont. Hwy. Commn., 1975—, Dist. 45 Sch. Bd., Wolf Point, 1954-60. Mem. Mont. Bar Assn. Home: 308 Edgar St Wolf Point MT 59201 Office: 321 Main St PO Box 859 Wolf Point MT 59201 Tel (406) 543-1721

LARSON, RICHARD DUNCAN, b. Chgo., Nov. 6, 1944; B.A., U. Ill., 1966, J.D., 1969. Admitted to Ill. bar, 1969; asst. prof. bus. and labor law No. Ill. U., DeKalb, 1969-72; individual practice law, DeKalb, 1972-75; partner firm Larson & Donnelly, DeKalb, 1975—; asst. pub. defender DeKalb County, 1972-76, pub. defender, 1976—. Mem. DeKalb County Tb Sanitarium Bd., 1972-76, pres., 1976—; mem. DeKalb County Bd. Health, 1976—. Mem. Am., Ill., Chgo. bar assns., Ill. Trial Lawyers Assn., Ill. Pub. Defender Assn. Office: 317 E Locust St DeKalb IL 60115 Tel (815) 758-6626

LARSON, STEPHEN PER, b. Mpls., Aug. 16, 1947; B.A., U. Minn., 1969, J.D. cum laude, 1972. Admitted to Minn. bar, 1972, Fed. dist. Minn. bar, 1976; law clk. Anoka County Atty., Anoka, Minn., 1970-71; law clk. firm Richards, Montgomery, Cobb & Bassford, Mpls., 1971-72; partner firm Flora, Johnston & Larson, Long Prairie, Minn., 1972—; asst. pub. defender 7th Jud. Dist., 1972—. Mem. Community Corrections Adv. Bd. Todd and Wadena Counties, Minn., 1974—. Mem. Am., Minn., 7th Dist. bar assns. Office: 274 Central Ave Long Prairie MN 56347 Tel (612) 732-2191

LARSON, STEPHEN RICHARD, b. Oshkosh, Wis., Nov. 11, 1946; A.B., Coll. William and Mary, 1968; J.D., Columbia, 1971. Admitted to Va. bar, 1971; asso. firm Christian, Barton, Epps, Brent & Chappell, Richmond, Va., 1971—; adj. asso. prof. T.C. William Sch. Law U. Richmond, 1974—. Mem. Am. (mem. fed. securities law com.), Va.,

Richmond bar assns. Contbr. articles to legal jours. Office: 1200 Mutual Bldg Richmond VA 23219 Tel (804) 644-7851

LARSON, W(ALTER) LOUIS, b. Augusta, Ga., Nov. 29, 1943; B.S., Portland State U., 1966; J.D., Willamette U., 1969. Admitted to Oreg. bar, 1969; VISTA vol. atty. OEO, Portland, 1969-70; legal aid atty. Multnomah County (Oreg.) Bar Assn. Legal Aid Service, 1970; asst. county counsel Washington County (Oreg.), 1970-74, county counsel, 1974-75; county counsel Clatsop County (Oreg.), 1975—. Mem. Am., Oreg. State bar assns. Home: 1179 Harrison St Astoria OR 97103 Office: Clatsop County Courthouse Astoria OR 97103 Tel (503) 325-7441

LARUE, PAUL HUBERT, b. Somerville, Mass., Nov. 16, 1922; Ph.B., U. Wis., 1947, J.D., 1949. Admitted to Wis. bar, 1949, Ill. bar, 1955; staff Office Atty. Gen., State of Wis., 1949-50; atty. FTC, Washington, 1951-55; partner firm Chadwell, Kayser, Ruggles, McGee & Hastings, Chgo., 1958—; mem. adv. bd. The Antitrust Bulletin, 1967—; pub. mem. Ill. Conflict of Interest Laws Commn., 1965-67; Ill. Com. for a Constl. Conv., 1968, Com. for Modern Cts. in Ill., 1964. Mem. Am. (chmn. Robinson-Patman Act com. sect. antitrust law 1975—), Fed., Ill. State, Wis., Chgo. (chmn. antitrust law com. 1970-71) bar assns. Contbr. articles to legal jours. Home: 250 Cuttriss Pl Park Ridge IL 60068 Office: 8500 Sears Tower 233 S Wacker Dr Chicago IL 60606 Tel (312) 876-2167

LARY, CAMM CARRINGTON, JR., b. Johnson City, Tex., Nov. 26, 1941; B.A. in Econs., Tex. A. and M. U., 1964; LL.B., U. Tex., 1967. Admitted to Tex. bar, 1967; atty. Tex. Water Rights Commn., Austin, 1968; asst. atty. gen. Tex. Atty. Gen.'s Office, Austin, 1968-70; individual practice law, Burnet, Tex., 1970—; mem. Tex. Ho. of Reps., 1972-76. Home and Office: PO Box 456 Burnet TX 78611 Tel (512) 756-2156

LARY, EUGENE, b. Denver, Nov. 28, 1906; student U. Tex., Austin, 1925, Ft. Worth Sch. Law, 1926-27, So. Meth. U., 1943; LL.D., Universidad Autónoma de Puebla, Mexico, 1964, El Ilustre Colegio de Puebla, 1964; Académico and LL.D., Academia Mexicana de Derecho Internacional, 1964. Admitted to Tex. bar, 1927, Republic of Mexico bar, 1944, U.S. Supreme Ct. bar, 1944; asso. firm Phillips, Trammell, Chizum, Price & Estes, Ft. Worth, 1927-36; individual practice law, Dallas, 1937-70, San Antonio, 1971—; atty., counsellor Mexican Consulate, Dallas, 1944-68; judge Municipal Ct., City of University Park, 1950-60. Mem. Interam., Tex. bar assns., Kappa Alpha. Decorated Order Aztec Eagle (Mexico), La Cruz Laureada, La Orden Mexicana del Derecho y La Cultura; recipient Homenaje de Simpatía award La Asociación Nacional de Abogados, 1944, Nat. award Am. Bar Assn., 1957. Home and Office: 7039 San Pedro #905 San Antonio TX 78216 Tel (512) 342-7994

LA SALLE, RICHARD NORMAN, b. Somerset, Mass., Mar. 17, 1936; B.A. in Journalism and Polit. Sci., Marquette U., 1957; J.D., New England Sch. of Law, 1961. Admitted to Mass. bar, 1962, U.S. Dist. Ct. bar, 1963, U.S. Tax Ct. bar, 1967, U.S. Supreme Ct. bar, 1968, U.S. Ct. of Appeals bar, 1973; asst. news dir. Sta. WALE, Fall River, Mass., 1957-58; editor, New England Hotel and Restaurant News, Boston, 1958-59; dir. pub. relations N.E. Inst. of Tech., Boston, 1961-65; gen. counsel Mass. Assn. of Plumbing-Heating and Cooling Contractors, Boston, 1961-65; individual practice law, Fall River, Mass., 1962—; gen. counsel Somerset Housing Authority, 1963-74, Seekonk Housing Authority, 1973—; town solicitor, Rehoboth, Mass., 1974—; spl. asst. atty. gen. Commonwealth of Mass., 1975—. Founder and sec. Kiwanis Club of Somerset-Swansea, 1963-67; vice-chmn. Somerset Housing Authority, 1964-66; judge advocate Knights of Columbus, Bishop Cassidy Council, Swansea, Mass., 1970-76; chmn. United Fund Drive, 1967 (United Fund citation). Mem. Am., Fed., Mass., Bristol County, Fall River bar assns., Am., Mass. trial lawyers assns., Am. Judicature Soc., Nat. Lawyers Club, Greater Fall River Trial Lawyers Assn. (dir.). Recipient Benefactor award, St. Annes Hosp. Century Club, Inc., Fall River, 1973-74. Home: 866 County St Somerset MA 02726 Office: 657 Highland Ave Fall River MA 02720 Tel (617) 674-4664

LASCELL, DAVID MICHAEL, b. Medina, N.Y., Apr. 11, 1941; A.B., Hamilton Coll., 1963; LL.B., Cornell U., 1966. Admitted to N.Y. bar, 1966; partner firm Nixon, Hargrave, Devans & Doyle, Rochester, N.Y., Washington and Palm Beach, Fla., 1966—. Trustee, Wells Coll., Aurora, N.Y., 1974—. Mem. Am., N.Y. State, Monroe County bar assns. Home: 330 Allens Creek Rd Rochester NY 14618 Office: 2200 Lincoln First Tower Rochester NY 14603 Tel (716) 546-8000

LASCHER, EDWARD LEONARD, b. Evanston, Ill., Jan. 19, 1928; B.A., DePauw U., 1951; J.D., U. Mich., 1953. Admitted to Ind. bar, 1953, Calif. bar, 1955; asso. firm Slaymaker, Locke and Reynolds, Indpls., 1953-54; mem. law dep. NBC, Inc and Radio Corp. Am., Los Angeles, 1954-57; practiced in Van Nuys, Calif., 1958-70, Ventura, Calif., 1967—; Fellow Am. Bar Found.; mem. Calif. Acad. Appellate Lawyers (pres. 1974-75), Am., Los Angeles County, Ventura County bar assns., Bar Assn. San Francisco, State Bar Calif. (gov. 1975—, v.p. 1976—), Lawyers Club of Los Angeles, Scribes, Sigma Delta Chi. Author Lascher at Large, column Calif. State Bar Jour., 1972—; contbr. articles to legal. jours.; editor Calif. State Bar Jour., 1974-75. Home: 1848 Hillcrest Dr Ventura CA 93003 Office: 605 Poli St Ventura CA 93001 Tel (805) 648-3228

LASHNITS, GEORGE ROBERT, b. N.Y.C., Mar. 4, 1911; B.A., Yale, 1932, J.D., 1935. Admitted to Conn. bar, 1935, N.Y. bar, 1938; asso. firm Chadbourne, Hunt, Jaeckel & Brown, N.Y.C., 1936-44; partner firm Lashnits & Lundgren, Ansonia, Conn., 1935-36; partner firm Brown, Wood, Ivey, Mitchell & Petty, and predecessor firms, N.Y.C., 1944—; village atty., Pelham Manor, N.Y., 1960-67. Mem. Assn. Bar City N.Y., Am., N.Y. State bar assns., N.Y. County Lawyers Assn. Home: 2 Cliff Pl Pelham Manor NY 10803 Office: 1 Liberty Plaza New York City NY 10006 Tel (212) 349-7500

LASKI, FRANK JOSEPH, b. Bklyn., May 1, 1929; B.S. in Econs., Coll. of Holy Cross, 1951; LL.B., J.D., Buffalo Law Sch., 1954. Admitted to N.Y. bar, 1954, U.S. Supreme Ct. bar, 1957; partner firm Phillips, Lytle, Hitchcock, Blaine & Huber, Buffalo, 1957-73; gen. counsel, sec. Marine Midland Banks, Inc., Buffalo, 1973—, Marine Midland Bank, 1976—; legal officer U.S. Naval Tng. Center, San Diego, 1955-56; instr. U.S. Naval Justice Sch., Newport, R.I., 1957. Mem. Am., N.Y. State (chmn. banking law com. 1969-72, banking, corporate and bus. law sect. 1972-73), Erie County bar assns., Am. Soc. Corporate Secs., Assn. Bank Holding Cos. (mem. lawyers com., chmn. securities com. 1976—). Editor-in-chief Buffalo Law Rev., 1954-55. Office: 2400 Marine Midland Center Buffalo NY 14203 Tel (716) 843-2865

LASKIN, BORA, b. Ft. William, Ont., Can., Oct. 5, 1912; B.A., U. Toronto (Ont.), 1933, M.A., 1935, LL.B., 1936, LL.D., 1968; postgrad. Osgoode Hall Law Sch., Toronto; LL.M., Harvard U., 1937; LL.D., Queen's U., Kingston, Ont., 1965, Edinburgh U., 1966, Trent U., 1967, Dalhousie U., Halifax, N.S., Cana., 1970, Law Soc. of Upper Can., 1970; D.C.L., N.B. (Can.) U., Fredericton, 1968, Windsor U., 1969. Called to Ont. bar, 1937, created queen's counsel, 1956; lectr. in law U. Toronto, 1940-43, asst. prof., 1943-45, prof., 1949-65; lectr. Osgoode Hall Law Sch., 1945-49; justice Ct. of Appeal of Ont., 1965-70; puisne judge Supreme Ct. of Can., 1970-73, chief justice, 1973—; bd. govs. Carleton U.; chmn. bd. govs. Ont. Inst. for Studies Edn., 1965-69; read law with W.C. Davidson. Mem. Assn. Canadian Law Tchrs. (pres. 1953-54), Canadian Assn. Univ. Tchrs. (pres. 1964-65, 1st Milner award 1971), Nat. Acad. Arbitrators. Named Hon. Bencher, Lincoln's Inn; author: Canadian Constitutional Law, 3d edit., 1966; Cases and Notes on Land Law, new edit., 1964; contbr. articles to legal jours.; asso. editor Dominion Law Reports and Canadian Criminal Cases, 1942-65. Home: 200 Rideau Terr Apt 1405 Ottawa ON Canada Office: Supreme Ct of Canada Wellington St Ottawa ON K1A 0J1 Canada*

LASKIN, LEE BERNARD, b. Atlantic City, June 30, 1936; student Am. U., 1954-56, Temple U., 1958; LL.B., Rutgers U., 1961, J.D., 1968. Admitted to N.J. bar, 1962, U.S. Supreme Ct. bar, 1966; law clk. to U.S. Congressman W. T. Cahill, 1958-61; individual practice law, Haddonfield, N.J., 1966—; asst. city atty. City of Camden (N.J.), 1962-63; asst. U.S. dist. atty. State of N.J., 1964-66; founder, dir. Glendale Nat. Bank N.J., Voorhees, 1972-75, chmn. bd., 1972-75. Chmn. Camden County Republican Orgn., 1976-77; mem. N.J. Gen. Assembly, 1967-69; mem. Camden County Bd. Chosen Freeholders, 1969-72; commr. Camden County Mosquito Commn., 1971-72; mem. N.J. Bd. Pub. Welfare, 1972-74; bd. dirs. S. Camden YMCA, 1967-71, LWV, 1967-71. Mem. Am., N.J., Camden County bar assns., N.J. Inst. Municipal Attys., Am. Arbitration Assn. Named Man of Year B'rith Sholom Lodge No. 41, 1969. Home: Pams Path Cherry Hill NJ 08034 Office: 36 Tanner St Haddonfield NJ 08033 Tel (609) 795-1500

LASKOWSKI, EDWARD J., b. Wilkes-Barre, Pa., Aug. 25, 1925; B.A., King's Coll., Wilkes-Barre, 1950; J.D., Cath. U. Am., 1954. Admitted to Nebr. bar, 1972; petroleum land cons., 1966-72. Mem. Am., Nebr. bar assns., Am., Denver assns. petroleum landmen, Gamma Eta Gamma. Office: PO Box 164 Mitchell NE 69357

LASKY, TERRY ANN, b. St. Louis, Jan. 27, 1938; B.A. in Philosophy, Boston U., 1970; J.D., Suffolk U., 1973. Admitted to Mass. bar, 1973; atty. Henry Wynn, Boston, 1973, Robert Gollins, Cambridge, Mass., 1974; individual practice law, Boston, 1974—. Mem. Mass. Bar Assn., Mass. Assn. Women Lawyers. Office: 33 Newbury St Boston MA 02114 Tel (617) 353-0275

LASSETER, JACK HUBERT, b. Detroit, Jan. 27, 1943; B.S., U. Ariz., 1965, J.D., 1967. Admitted to Ariz. bar, 1967, U.S. Supreme Ct. bar, 1971; with JAGC, USAF, 1967-71; asso. firm Feldman, Wolin & Lahr, P.C., Tucson, 1972-74, partner, 1974-76; individual practice law, Tucson, 1976—; instr. bus. law Pima Community Coll., 1975—. Mem. Am., Ariz., Pima County bar assns., Am. Judicature Soc. Office: 1535 E Broadway Tucson AZ 85719 Tel (602) 792-0430

LASSITER, JAMES MADISON, b. Murray, Ky., July 31, 1919; B.S., Murray (Ky.) State U., 1946; J.D., U. Ky., 1949. Admitted to Ky. bar, 1949; individual practice law, Murray, Ky., 1949-52; mem. Ky. State Senate, 1952-54; atty. Commonwealth of Ky., 1954-67; circuit judge, Murray, 1967—. Mem. Am., Ky. bar assns. Home: 1313 Wells Blvd Murray KY 42071 Office: Court House Murray KY 42071 Tel (502) 753-4324

LASSWELL, HAROLD DWIGHT, b. Donnellson, Ill., Feb. 13, 1902; Ph.B., U. Chgo., 1922, Ph.D., 1926; postgrad. univs. London, Geneva, Paris, Berlin, 1923-24, 25; D.Litt., Jewish Theol. Sem., N.Y.C.; LL.D., U. Ill. Asst. dept. polit. sci. U. Chgo., 1922-24, instr., 1924-27, asst. prof., 1927-32, asso. prof., 1932-38; polit. scientist Washington Sch. Psychiatry, 1938-39; dir. war communications research Library Congress, Washington, 1939-45; prof. law Yale, 1946—, prof. law and polit. sci., 1952-61, Edward J. Phelps prof. law and polit. sci., 1961-71, Ford Found. prof. law and social sci. emeritus, emeritus fellow Bradford Coll.; prof. John Jay Coll. Criminal Justice, N.Y.C., 1970-73, Temple U., 1973-74, 75—, Policy Scis. Center, N.Y.C. Vixs. prof. Syracuse (N.Y.) U., 1926, Western Res. U., Cleve., 1929, U. Cal., 1935, Yenching U., 1937, Tokyo, 1955; vis. Sterling lectr. Sch. Law, New Haven, 1938-45; lectr. New Sch. for Social Research, N.Y., 1939-46; vis. prof. U. Patna (India), U. Santiago (Chile); fellow Center for Advanced Study in Behavioral Scis., Stanford, Cal., 1954, Social Sci. Research Council, 1928-29. Mem. research adv. bd. Com. for Econ. Devel.; Commn. on Freedom of Press (auspices U. Chgo.). Recipient prize Am. Council Learned Socs., 1960. Fellow World Acad. Art and Sci.; mem. Am. Soc. Internat. Law, Am. Econ. Assn., Am. Acad. Arts and Scis., Am. Polit. Sci. Assn. (pres. 1955-56), Am. Sociol. Soc. Phi Beta Kappa, Delta Sigma Rho, Tau Kappa Epsilon. Author books including: Propaganda Technique in the World War, 1927; Psychopathology and Politics, 1930; World Politics and Personal Insecurity, 1935; Politics: Who Gets What, When, How, 1936; Democracy Through Public Opinion, 1941; Politics Faces Economics, 1946; The Analysis of Political Behaviour, 1948; Power and Personality, 1948 (the Salmon Meml. Lectures, N.Y. Acad. Med.); (with N. Leites, assos.) Language of Politics: Studies in Quantitative Semantics, 1949; (with A. Kaplan) Power and Society: A Framework for Political Inquiry, 1950; World Revolution of Our Time, 1951; (with D. Lerner) The Policy Sciences: Recent Developments in Scope and Method, 1951; World Revolutionary Elites: Studies in Coercive Ideological Movements, 1966; (with R. Arens) In Defense of Public Order, 1961; The Future of Political Science, 1963; (with M.S. McDougal, I. Vlasic) The Public Order of Space, 1963; (with A. Rogow) Power, Corruption and Rectitude, 1963; (with R. Rubenstein) The Sharing of Power in A Psychiatric Hospital, 1966; Propaganda Technique in World War I, 1971; Pre-View of Policy Sciences, 1973; Adv. editor Ethics, Inquiry (Oslo). Address: Dept Law Yale U New Haven CT 06520*

LATCHUM, JAMES LEVIN, b. Milford, Del., Dec. 23, 1918; A.B., Princeton, 1940; LL.B., U. Va., 1946. Admitted to Va. bar, 1942, Del. bar, 1947; asso. firm Southerland, Berl & Potter, Wilmington, 1946-51; partner firm Berl, Potter & Anderson, Wilmington, 1951-67, Potter, Anderson & Corroon, 1967-68; judge U.S. Dist. Ct., Wilmington, 1968—, chief judge, 1973—; atty. Del. Hwy. Dept., New Castle County, 1949-51; asst. U.S. atty., 1951-53; atty. Del. Interstate Hwy. Div., 1955-63, Delaware River and Bay Authority, 1963-68. Mem. Wilmington Park Trust Fund Com., 1963-67; chmn. Charter Revision Com. for Wilmington, 1961-62, Del. Constl. Revision Commn., 1968. Mem. Am., Va., Del. bar assns., Nat. Conf. Trial Judges (steering com.). Home: 2209 Baynard Blvd Wilmington DE 19802 Office: US Courthouse Lockbox 20 844 King St Wilmington DE 19801 Tel (302) 571-6167

LATHAM, PATRICIA HORAN, b. Hoboken, N.J., Sept. 5, 1941; B.A., Swarthmore Coll., 1963; J.D., U. Chgo., 1966. Admitted to D.C. bar, 1967, U.S. Supreme Ct. bar, 1970; asso. firm Fried, Frank, Harris, Shriver & Kampelman, Washington, 1966-69; atty. Office of Gen. Counsel, SEC, Washington, 1969-71; partner firm Martin, Whitfield, Thaler & Bebchick, Washington, 1971—. Mem. Bar Assn. D.C., Am., Fed., D.C. bar assns. Home: 10529 Mac Arthur Blvd Potomac MD 20854 Office: 1701 Pennsylvania Ave NW Washington DC 20006 Tel (202) 298-6350

LATHAM, WELDON HURD, b. Bklyn., Jan. 2, 1947; B.A., Howard U., 1968; J.D., Georgetown U., 1971. Admitted to D.C. bar, 1972, U.S. Ct. Mil. Appeals, 1974, U.S. Ct. Claims, 1975, U.S. Supreme Ct. bar, 1975; asso. firm Covington & Burling, Washington, 1971-73; capt., honors program Gen. Counsel's Office, U.S. Air Force, The Pentagon, 1973-74; sr. atty. Fed. Energy Adminstrn., Washington, 1974; asst. gen. counsel Office Mgmt. and Budget, Exec. Office of Pres., 1974-76; asso. firm Hogan & Hartson, Washington, 1976—; adj. prof. Howard U. Sch. Law, 1972-76; guest prof. U. Va. Law Sch., 1976—. Mem. Washington steering com. NAACP Legal Def. Fund, 1975—. Mem. Washington Council Lawyers (dir. 1973), Am., Nat., Fed. bar assns., Bar Assn. D.C. Home: 3901 Woodlawn Rd Chevy Chase MD 20015 Office: 815 Connecticut Ave NW Washington DC 20006 Tel (202) 331-4713

LATHROP, MITCHELL LEE, b. Los Angeles, Dec. 15, 1937; B.S., U.S. Naval Acad., 1959; J.D., U. So. Calif., 1966. Admitted to Calif. bar, 1966, D.C. bar, 1966, U.S. Ct. Mil. Appeals bar, 1968, U.S. Supreme Ct. bar, 1969; dep. counsel County of Los Angeles, 1966-68; asso. firm Brill, Hunt, De Buys & Burby, Los Angeles, 1968-70, partner, 1970-71; partner firm Macdonald, Halsted & Laybourne, Los Angeles, 1971—; lectr. in field; spl. advisor Los Angeles County Delinquency & Crime Commn., 1968-75. Western regional chmn. Met. Opera Nat. Council, 1971—; dir., sec. Music Center Opera Assn., Los Angeles, 1972—; trustee Honnold Library of Claremont Colls., The Thacher Sch., Ojai, Calif. Mem. Am., Fed., Calif., D.C., Los Angeles County bar assns., The Judge Adv. Assn. Contbr. articles in field to profl. jours. Office: 1200 Wilshire Blvd Los Angeles CA 90017 Tel (213) 481-1200

LATIMER, GEORGE W., b. Draper, Utah, Nov. 28, 1900; J.D., U. Utah, 1924. Admitted to Utah bar, 1925, U.S. Supreme Ct. bar, 1924, Md. bar, 1951; individual practice law, Salt Lake City, 1925-40, 45-46; 61—; justice Utah Supreme Ct., 1947-51; mem. U.S. Ct. Mil. Appeals, 1951-61; chmn. Utah Bd. Pardons, 1965—. Bd. dirs. Salvation Army, Salt Lake City. Mem. Am. (past chmn. spl. com. on mil. justice), Utah bar assns., Delta Theta Phi, Sigma Pi. Office: 79 S State St PO Box 11898 Salt Lake City UT 84147 Tel (801) 532-1234

LATIMER, HUGH, b. N.Y.C., Mar. 23, 1933; A.B., Harvard, 1955, J.D., 1958. Admitted to D.C. bar, 1959; asso. firm Bergson, Borkland, Margolis & Adler, D.C., 1960-65, mem., 1965—. Bd. dirs. Met. Washington Planning and Housing Assn., 1971-74; bd. dirs., treas. Lincoln-Westmoreland Housing, Inc., 1970-75. Mem. D.C. (treas. jr. bar sect. 1964-65), Am. bar assns. Co-editor Am. Bar Assn. Merger Case Digest, 1971. Home: 9228 Farnsworth Dr Potomac MD 20854 Office: 11 DuPont Circle Washington DC 20036 Tel (202) 462-5930

LATIMER, JOHN THOMAS, b. Hamilton, Ohio, May 25, 1922; B.S. U. Pa., 1944, J.D., U. Cin., 1947. Admitted to Ohio bar, 1947; partner firm Millikin & Fitton, Hamilton, Ohio, 1947-73, asst. prof. Miami U., Oxford, Ohio, 1973—. Bd. dirs. United Appeals, 1952—; ARC, 1952-72; Am. Cancer Assn., 1962-70. Mem. Am., Ohio bar assns., Am. Bus. Law Assn., Phi Delta Phi. Author: History of Butler County (Ohio) Bar, 1972. Home: 100 Glencross Hamilton OH 45013 Office: Laws Hall Oxford OH 45056 Tel (513) 529-3634

LATIMER, KENNETH ALAN, b. Chgo., Oct. 26, 1943; B.S. with honors, U. Wis., 1966; J.D. with honors, George Washington U., 1969. Admitted to D.C. bar, 1969, Ill. bar, 1970; staff atty. office gen. counsel Comptroller Gen. U.S., Washington, 1969-70; asso. firm Berger Newmark & Fenchel, Chgo., 1970-74, partner, 1975—. Mem. Chgo., Ill., Am. bar assns., Chgo. Estate Planning Council. Office: 180 N La Salle St Chicago IL 60601 Tel (312) 782-5050

LATIMER, STEPHEN MARK, b. Bklyn., July 15, 1939; A.B., Tufts U., 1961; J.D., N.Y. U., 1968. Admitted to N.Y. State bar, 1968, Fed. bar, 1970, U.S. Supreme Ct. bar, 1975; asso. firm Halpern, Shivitz, Scholer & Steingut, N.Y.C., 1969-71; dir. Supervised release project N.Y. Lawyers Com. for Civil Rights under Law, N.Y.C., 1972-73; dir. community devel. and law reform, Bronx Legal Services, N.Y.C., 1973—; lectr. in law Rutgers U. Law Sch., 1975—. Mem. bd. dirs. Citizens Inquiry on Parole and Criminal Justice, Inc., N.Y.C., 1974—. Mem. Assn. Bar City N.Y., Nat. Lawyers Guild. Home: 8 Bosko Dr East Brunswick NJ 08816 Office: 579 Courtlandt Ave Bronx NY 10451 Tel (212) 993-6250

LATIMER, WILLIAM HARRISON, JR., b. Pitts., June 16, 1921; A.B., Harvard, 1943, LL.B., 1948. Admitted to Pa. bar, 1949; individual practice law, Pitts., 1948-49; with trust dept. Mellon Bank, Pitts., 1949—, v.p., 1961—; chmn. trust div. Pa. Bankers Assn., 1973-74. Pres. Children's Hosp. Pitts., 1973-76; mem. investment com. Shriners Hosps. for Crippled Children, 1962—. Mem. Pa. (treas. probate sect. 1976—), Allegheny County bar assns. Office: Mellon Bank N A Mellon Sq Pittsburgh PA 15230 Tel (412) 232-5465

LATIN, OSCAR BECKMAN, b. Phila., Mar. 9, 1923; B.S., U. Wis., 1949, J.D., 1951; M.A., U. Pa., 1954. Admitted to Wis. bar, 1951, Ohio bar, 1954; dir. claims and real estate Toledo Edison Co., 1956-74; adminstrv. law judge Ohio Power Siting Commn., Columbus, 1975-76; atty. Borden, Inc., Columbus, 1976—; lectr. in history Bowling Green State U.; arbitrator Am. Arbitration Assn. Mem. Ohio, Wis. bar assns., Am. Right of Way Assn. (sr.). Contbr. articles to Am. Right of Way Jour. Office: Borden Inc Law Dept 27th floor 180 E Broad St Columbus OH 43215 Tel (614) 225-4447

LATRONE, ROBERT ALBERT, b. Camden, N.J., July 7, 1931; B.A. cum laude, Temple U., 1952, LL.B., 1956, LL.D., 1959. Admitted to Pa. bar, 1957; practiced in Philadelphia County, 1957-67; asst. city solicitor City of Phila., 1960-67; magistrate City of Phila., 1968-69, judge Municipal Ct. of Phila., 1969-71; judge Ct. of Common Pleas of Phila., 1st Jud. Dist. of Pa., 1972—. Mem. Am. Arbitration Assn., Nat. Polit. Sci. Soc., Temple Law Alumni, N. Am. Judges Assn., Phila. Bar Assn., Justinian Soc., Conf. State Trial Judges, Nat. Coll. State Judiciary. Office: 481 City Hall Philadelphia PA 19107 Tel (215) Mu-6-7908

LATTANZI, RICHARD EMIL, b. Balt., Mar. 1, 1943; B.S. in Bus. Adminstrn., Loyola Coll., Balt., 1964; LL.B., U. Balt., 1967. Admitted to Md. bar, 1968; house counsel Equitable Trust Co., Balt., 1968-77; partner firm Rohe and Lattanzi, Balt., 1977—. Mem. Md. State, Am.

bar assns. Home: 8 Lagan Ct Baltimore MD 21236 Office: 9105 Belair Rd Baltimore MD 21236 Tel (301) 256-3783

LATTIN, WARD ELGIN, b. Hesperia, Mich., July 30, 1905; A.B., Wayne State U., 1927; LL.B., Georgetown U., 1932, J.D., 1934. Admitted to D.C. bar, 1934; law clk. Justice James McReynolds, U.S. Supreme Ct., 1934; sr. atty. GAO, Washington, 1935-42; partner firm Gardner, Morrison, Sheriff & Beddow, Washington, 1947—; asst. sec. to Senator Vandenberg, 1928-34. Contbr. articles to legal jours. Home: 8525 Thornden Terr Bethesda MD 20034 Office: 1126 Woodward Bldg Washington DC 20005 Tel (202) 783-6800

LATTO, LAWRENCE J., b. Bklyn., Sept. 23, 1920; B.S., Coll. City N.Y., 1941; LL.B., Columbia U., 1948. Admitted to N.Y. bar, 1948, D.C. bar, 1949, Va. bar, 1954; asso. firm Shea & Gardner, Washington, 1948-54, mem., 1954—. Mem. Am., D.C., Va. bar assns., Am. Law Inst., Center Law and Social Policy (trustee). Editor in chief Columbia Law Rev. Home: 928 S 26th St Arlington VA 22202 Office: 734 15th St NW Washington DC 20005 Tel (202) 737-1255

LATTON, HOWARD WILLIAM, b. Medford, Wis., Apr. 27, 1916; B.A., U. Wis., 1938, LL.B., 1941, J.D., 1966. Admitted to Wis. bar, 1941; individual practice law, Portage, Wis., 1941-73; judge 25th Jud. Circuit, Portage, 1973—; dist. atty. Columbia County (Wis.), 1953-58. Mem. Am., Marquette-Waushara, Sauk County, Columbia County bar assns. Home: 809 W Edgewater St Portage WI 53901 Office: Adminstrn Bldg Portage WI 53901 Tel (608) 742-2195

LAUBENGAYER, ROBERT EDWARD, b. Great Bend, Kans., Feb. 8, 1941; B.S., Phillips U., 1967; J.D., St. Thomas More Coll., 1972. Admitted to Calif. bar, 1972, Kans. bar, 1973; asso. firm Miner, Aylward & Svaty, 1973; partner firm Aylward, Svaty & Laubengayer, Ellsworth, Kans., 1974—; atty. Ellsworth County, 1975-76, City of Wilson (Kans.), City of Holyrood (Kans.). Cub scout leader local council Boy Scouts Am. Mem. Am., Kans., Calif. bar assns., Am., Kans. trial lawyers assns., Nat. Dist. Attys. Assn. Home: Star Route Ellsworth KS 67439 Office: 126 N Douglas Box 83 Ellsworth KS 67439 Tel (913) 472-3186

LAUCHENGCO, JOSE YUJUICO, JR., b. Manila, Philippines, Dec. 6, 1936; A.B., U. Philippines, Quezon City, 1959; M.B.A., U. So. Calif., 1964; J.D., Loyola U., Los Angeles, 1971. Comml. loan officer United Calif. Bank, Los Angeles, 1968-71; admitted to Calif. bar, 1972, U.S. Supreme Ct. bar, 1975; asso. firm Demler, Perona, Langer Bergkvist, Lauchengco & Manzella, and predecessor, Long Beach, Calif., 1972-73, partner, 1973—. Mem. Am., Los Angeles County, Orange County (Calif.) bar assns., Calif. Trial Lawyers Assn., Criminal Cts. Bar Assn., Confrat. of Christian Doctrine, St. Thomas More Law Honor Soc. Recipient Degree of Distinction, Nat. Forensic League, 1955, Leadership medal U. Philippines, 1959. Office: 4201 Long Beach Blvd Suite 101 Long Beach CA 90807 Tel (213) 426-6155

LAUCKS, SAMUEL SECHRIST, JR., b. York Twp., Pa., July 15, 1917; A.B., Ursinus Coll., Collegeville, Pa., 1939; LL.B., J.D., U. Pa., 1942. Admitted to Pa. bar, 1942; partner firm Laucks & Laucks, York, 1942-55; sr. partner firm Laucks & Monroe, York, 1955—; solicitor York County, 1950-51. Mem. Am., Pa., York County bar assns. Office: 139 E Market St York PA 17401 Tel (717) 845-8602

LAUER, THEODORE E., b. Beloit, Wis., Feb. 4, 1931; B.A., Millikin U., 1953; LL.B., Washington U., St. Louis, 1956; S.J.D., U. Mich., 1958. Admitted to Mo. bar, 1956, N.Mex. bar, 1974; legis. analyst U. Mich. Law Sch., 1956-58; partner firms Cave & Lauer, Fulton, Mo., 1958-62, Lauer & Lauer, Santa Fe, N. Mex., 1974—; asst. prof. law U. Mo., Columbia, 1962-65, asso. prof., 1965-69, prof., 1969-70; vis. prof. law St. Louis U., 1970-74, dep. dir. Nat. Juvenile Law Center, 1970-71, dir., 1971-74; pros. atty. Callaway County, Mo., 1961-62. Mem. Am. Bar Assn., Mo. Bar, State Bar N.Mex., N.Mex. Criminal Def. Lawyers Assn. (pres. 1976—), Order of Coif. Author: (with Dominic B. King and Wilbert L. Ziegler) Water Resources And The Law, 1958; (with Donald B. King, Calvin A. Kuenzel, Neil O. Littlefield and Bradford Stone) Commercial Transactions Under the Uniform Commercial Code, 1968, rev. edit., 1974; contbr. articles to legal jours. Home: 13 Calle de Valle Santa Fe NM 87501 Office: 302 E Palace Ave Santa Fe NM 87501 Tel (505) 988-8044

LAUGHLIN, EVERETT EUGENE, b. Hannibal, Mo., Sept. 2, 1915; B.A., Cornell Coll., Mt. Vernon, Iowa, 1937; LL.B., U. Ill., 1939. Admitted to Ill. bar, 1939; partner firm Laughlin & Laughlin, Freeport, Ill., 1939-73; judge Ill. Circuit Ct. for 15th Jud. Circuit, 1973—; Mem. Ill. Senate, 1961-72; state's atty. Stephenson County, 1952-56. Pres. Freeport Bd. Edn., 1948-52. Mem. Am., Ill. State, Stephenson County bar assns. Office: Stephenson County Courthouse Freeport IL 61032 Tel (815) 235-8620

LAUGHLIN, JOHN ROYER, b. Phila., Mar. 9, 1944; A.B. cum laude, Princeton, 1966; fellow Athens (Greece) Coll., 1967; J.D. cum laude, U. Mich., 1970. Admitted to Calif. bar, 1971, Md. bar, 1972; asso. firm Pillsbury Madison & Sutro, San Francisco, 1970-71, Rosenstock & McSherry, Frederick, Md., 1971-72; individual practice law, Frederick, 1972—; lectr. Hood Coll., Frederick, 1974-76; pres. Digital Systems Corp., Walkersville, Md., 1974—. Bd. dirs. Frederick Planned Parenthood Assn., 1973—, Frederick County Hist. Soc., 1975—. Mem. Calif., Md., Frederick County bar assns. Fulbright fellow, 1970-71; Ford Found. fellow, 1971; CRB fellow, 1970. Home: October Farm Route 2 Box 75A Union Bridge MD 21791 Office: care Digital Systems Corp N Main St Walkersville MD 21793 Tel (301) 845-4141

LAUGHLIN, R. GORDON, b. San Diego, Apr. 14, 1932; A.B., San Diego State Coll., 1950; J.D., U. So. Calif., 1956. Admitted to Calif. bar, 1956; individual practice law, Santa Monica Calif.; commr. Santa Monica. Mem. Am., Los Angeles, Santa Monica bar assns., Los Angeles Trial Lawyers Assn., Am. Arbitration Assn. (arbitrator). Office: 2415 Wilshire Blvd Santa Monica CA 90403 Tel (213) 828-5678

LAUGHLIN, STANLEY IRA, b. N.Y.C., Oct. 2, 1924; B.E.E., Pratt Inst., 1949; M.S., Poly. Inst. Bklyn., 1963; J.D., N.Y. Law Sch., 1970. Admitted to N.Y. State bar, 1971; dist. operator LILCO Co., Hicksville, N.Y., 1949-57; engr. Sperry Gyroscope Co., Lake Success, N.Y., 1957-61, patent specialist, 1961-64; patent engr. AIL div. Cutler-Hammer Corp., Deer Park, N.Y., 1964-70; patent agt. U.S. Philips Corp., Briarcliffe Manor, N.Y., 1970-73; individual practice law, North Babylon, N.Y., 1973—; asst. county atty. Suffolk County, N.Y., 1974—. Pres. Magro Park Civic Assn. of North Babylon, 1953; scoutmaster Suffolk County council Boy Scouts Am.; active Great Scout Bay council Girls U.S.; Republican committeeman 36th electoral dist., Suffolk County, 1974—. Mem. Am., N.Y., Suffolk County bar assns. Registered profl. engr., N.Y. Home and office: 11 Frankie Ln North Babylon NY 11703 Tel (516) 669-1999

LAUNDRY, MELBURN EDWARD, b. Oak Park, Ill., Feb. 8, 1931; B.S., U.S. Mil. Acad., 1953; J.D., Chgo-Kent Coll. Law-Ill. Inst. Tech., 1964; M. Comparative Law, U. Chgo. and U. Frankfurt (Germany), 1967. Admitted to Ill. bar, 1964; patent atty. Internat. Harvester Co., Chgo., 1964-65; asso. firm Baker, McKenzie & Hightower, Zurich, Switzerland, 1966; atty. Coudert Frere's, Paris, 1967, Gulf Oil Co., Chgo., 1967-68; internat. counsel Motorola, Inc., Chgo., 1968-70; gen. counsel United Devel. Co., home bldg. subs. Aetna Ins. Co., Chgo., 1970-73; sr. partner firm Laundry & Assos., Ltd., Chgo., 1970—; asst. prof. bus. law Loyola U. of Chgo., 1971—. Mem. condominium com. Homebuilders Assn. of Greater Chgo. Mem. Am., Chgo. bar assns., AAUP. Contbr. articles to real estate and legal jours. Home: 505 Berkely Rd Riverside IL 60546 Tel (312) 321-3996

LAUR, G(EORGE) DAVID, b. Hudson, Mich., May 29, 1947; B.A., Ohio State U., 1969, J.D., 1972. Admitted to Ind. bar, 1972; individual practice law, Albion, Ind., 1972-75; partner firm Finley, Finley, Rowe, Laur, & Spindler, Albion, 1976—; pros. atty. Noble County (Ind.), 1975—. Mem. Noble County, Am. bar assns., Ind. Pros. Attys. Assn. Named Officer of Year Noble County, 1976. Home: Route 1 N Liberty St Albion IN 46701 Office: 107 W Jefferson St Albion IN 46701 Tel (219) 636-7776

LAURICELLA, JOHN ETTORE, b. San Francisco, Aug. 11; A.B., Calif. State U., Sacramento, 1958; J.D., U. Calif., San Francisco, 1961. Admitted to Calif. bar, 1962; partner firm Roach & Lauricella, Woodland, Calif., 1962—. Office: 189 1st St Woodland CA 95695 Tel (916) 662-7396

LAURIE, CHARLES R., JR., b. Cleve., Aug. 25, 1949; B.A., U. Dayton, 1971; J.D., Cleve. State U., 1974. Admitted to Ohio bar, 1974, Fla. bar, 1974; partner firm Laurie, Laurie, Hull & Steely, Cleve., 1974—. Chief examiner Westlake (Ohio) Civil Service Commn., 1974-76; pres. Westlake Democratic Club, 1975-76. Mem. Am., Ohio, Fla., Cleve., Cuyahoga County bar assns., Comml. Law League, Am. Arbitration Assn. Office: 124 Engineers Bldg Cleveland OH 44114

LAUSCH, EUGENE WILBUR, b. Indpls., Aug. 24, 1938; A.B., Ind. Central U., 1960; J.D., U. Mich., 1964. Admitted to Ind. bar, 1966; research asst., law clk. Ind. Supreme Ct., Indpls., 1964-66; lectr. bus. law Ind. Central U., Indpls., 1965-69; dep. prosecutor Marion County Prosecutor's Office, Indpls., 1966-68; asso. firm Dulberger & Heeter, Indpls., 1966-68; enforcement atty. div. planning and zoning Indpls. Dept. Met. Devel., 1968-70, adminstr. div. code enforcement, 1970-72, dep. dir., 1972—. Mem. bd. dirs. YMCA Greater Indpls., 1976—; trustee Ind. Central U., 1974—; mem. adv. bd. Atkins Boys Club, 1976—. Mem. Ind., Indpls. bar assns. Home: 4248 Washington Blvd Indianapolis IN 46205 Office: 1860 City-County Bldg Indianapolis IN 46204 Tel (317) 633-3198

LAUTEN, HERMAN GEORGE, b. Washington, Nov. 30, 1902; student Sch. Law, Georgetown U., 1921-24. Admitted to D.C. bar, 1924, U.S. Supreme Ct. bar, 1930; v.p., trust officer Nat. Savs. and Trust Co., Washington, 1929-72; asso. firm Jackson, Campbell and Parkinson, and predecessor, Washington, 1972—. Mem. Am., D.C. bar assns. Home: 4444 Brandywine St NW Washington DC 20016 Office: Suite 1111 1828 L St NW Washington DC 20036 Tel (202) 457-1600

LAUTERBACH, LEON A., b. Yonkers, N.Y., Feb. 26, 1927; B.A., N.Y. U., 1948, LL.B., 1950, LL.M., 1955. Admitted to N.Y. bar, 1950, Fla. bar, 1973; asso. firm Edward Lauterbach, Yonkers, 1950-51; asst. corp. counsel City of Yonkers, 1951-52; partner firm Lauterbach and Lauterbach, Yonkers, 1953—. Vol. counsel Yonkers Hebrew Relief Assn., 1959—; sec. Yonkers Parking Authority, 1964-70. Mem. Westchester County, N.Y. State, Am. bar assns., Yonkers Lawyers. Home: 171 Kneeland Ave Yonkers NY 10705 Office: 20 S Broadway Yonkers NY 10705

LAVELLE, BRIAN FRANCIS DAVID, b. Cleve., Aug. 16, 1941; B.A., U. Va., 1963; LL.B., Vanderbilt U., 1966; LL.M. in Taxation, N.Y. U., 1969. Admitted to N.C. bar, 1966, Ohio bar, 1968. Served with Judge Adv. Corps, USAF, Moody AFB, Ga., 1966-67; mem. firm Van Winkle, Buck, Wall, Starnes, Hyde & Davis, P.A., Asheville, N.C., 1968-74, partner, 1974—. Vice chmn. Buncombe County, N.C. Indsl. Facilities and Pollution Control Financing Authority, 1976—. Mem. Am., N.C., Buncombe County bar assns. Home: 45 Brookside Rd Asheville NC 28803 Office: 18 Church St PO Box 7376 Asheville NC 28807 Tel (704) 258-2991

LAVENDER, GEORGE WILLIAM, b. Texarkana, Tex., Dec. 28, 1938; B.S. in Edn., U. Ark., 1962, J.D., 1971. Admitted to Ark. bar, 1971, U.S. Supreme Ct. bar, 1974; asso. firm Arnold & Arnold, Texarkana, 1971-73; partner firm Arnold, Arnold & Lavender, Texarkana, 1973-77, Arnold, Arnold, Lavender & Rochelle, Texarkana, 1977—. Chmn. Texarkana Planning Commn., 1973-75; mem. Texarkana Airport Authority, 1977—. Mem. Am., SW Ark. (pres.), Texarkana (past treas.) bar assns. Tel (501) 773-3187

LAVERGHETTA, JOSEPH CHARLES, b. Balt., Dec. 7, 1944; B.S. in History, Mt. St. Mary's Coll.; J.D., U. Balt. Admitted to Md. bar, 1972; law clk. Circuit Ct. Baltimore County, 1971-72; asst. state's atty. Baltimore County, 1972-75; asso. firm Henry W. Klemkowski, P.A., Balt., 1977—. Home: 904 Coteswood Circle Cockeysville MD 21030 Office: 1028 Munsey Bldg Baltimore MD 21202 Tel (303) 752-5539

LAVERY, HARRY D., b. Jacksonville, Ill., Dec. 8, 1922; A.B. cum laude, U. Notre Dame, 1943; LL.B., Columbia, 1948. Admitted to Ill. bar, 1948, U.S. Supreme Ct. bar, 1963; partner firm Berger, Newmark & Fenchel, Chgo.; Ill. Gen. Assembly, 1955-56. Mem. Chgo. Bar Assn. (fed. civil procedure com., judiciary com.). Office: Berger Newmark & Fenchel 180 N LaSalle St Chicago IL 60601 Tel (312) 782-5050

LAVEY, STEWART EVAN, b. Newark, July 24, 1945; A.B., Syracuse U., 1967; J.D., Fordham U., 1970. Admitted to N.Y. State bar, 1971; asso. firm Kelley Drye & Warren, N.Y.C., 1970-71, Emil, Kobrin, Klein & Garbus, N.Y.C., 1971-72, Zimet, Haines, Moss, & Goodkind, N.Y.C., 1972-75; asst. sec., asst. gen. counsel Norlin Corp., N.Y.C., 1975—; adj. asso. prof. law Fordham U., N.Y.C., 1976—. Mem. Am., N.Y., N.Y.C. bar assns. Mem. Fordham Law Rev., 1968-70. Office: 200 Park Ave Suite 1702 New York City NY 10017 Tel (212) 986-8900

LA VINE, KENNETH NETTLETON, b. N.Y.C., July 1, 1911; B.A., Dartmouth, 1932; LL.B., Yale, 1935. Admitted to N.Y. bar, 1936; asso. firm Curtis, Mallet-Prevost, Colt & Mosle, N.Y.C., 1935-50, partner, 1950; with JAGC, U.S. Army, 1942-45; dir. Carlisle Corp., Cin., 1971—, Dover Corp., N.Y.C., 1972—, Leach Corp., Los Angeles, 1953—. Office: 100 Wall St New York City NY 10005 Tel (212) 248-8111

LA VINE, ROBERT LEON, b. San Francisco, Dec. 24, 1929; B.S., U. Calif., 1952, J.D., 1959. Admitted to Calif. bar, 1960. Mem. Calif., San Francisco bar assns., Calif. Soc. C.P.A.'s. Home: 170 San Felipe Way San Francisco CA 94127 Office: Suite 415 Hearst Bldg San Francisco CA 94103 Tel (415) 981-6677

LAVINSKI, JOSEPH MICHAEL, b. Allentown, Pa., July 25, 1943; J.D., St. Louis U., 1967. Admitted to Mass. bar, 1968, U.S. Dist. Ct. bar for Dist. Mass., 1970; individual practice law, Springfield, Mass., 1970—. Mem. advisory bd. Salvation Army, Springfield, 1975—. Mem. Hampden County (Mass.), Boston, Westfield (Mass.), Mass. bar assns. Home: 8 White Oaks Dr Feeding Hills MA 01030 Office: 115 State St Springfield MA 01103 Tel (413) 739-9702

LAVNER, MAURICE, b. Bklyn.; LL.B., St. Johns U. Admitted to N.Y. bar; individual practice law, Bklyn.; spl. dep. atty. gen. Election Frauds Bur., 1952; arbitrator N.Y.C. Civil Ct., 1957. Mem. Bklyn. Bar Assn., Kings County Criminal Bar Assn. Home: 531 N Terrace Ave Mt Vernon NY 10552 Office: 26 Court St Brooklyn NY 11201 Tel (212) UL8-9041

LAVORATO, LOUIS ANTHONY, b. Des Moines, Sept. 29, 1934; B.S. in Bus. Adminstrn., Drake U., 1959, J.D., 1962. Admitted to Iowa bar, 1962, U.S. Supreme Ct. bar, 1976; mem. firm Williams, Hart, Lavorato & Kirtley, West Des Moines, 1965—; legis. counsel Iowa Ho. of Reps., 1965. Mem. Polk County (Iowa), Iowa State, Am. bar assns., Am., Iowa (co-chmn. com. med. malpractice and products liability 1976) assns. trial lawyers, Acad. Iowa Trial Lawyers, Phi Eta Sigma, Beta Gamma Sigma, Phi Alpha Delta, Delta Sigma Pi, Order of Coif. Asst. editor Drake U. Law Rev., 1962; contbr. articles to legal jours. Home: 1123 SW Rose St Des Moines IA 50315 Office: 700 W Towers 1200 35th St West Des Moines IA 50265 Tel (515) 225-1125

LAW, FRED HERMAN, JR., b. Niles, Ohio, Dec. 1, 1922; B.A., Cornell U., 1943; M.B.A., U. Pa., 1946, LL.B., 1949. Admitted to Pa. bar, 1950, Ohio bar, 1950, Ill. bar, 1952, U.S. Supreme Ct. bar, 1960; asso. firm Busser & Bendiner, Phila., 1950-51; atty examiner FTC, Chgo. Dist. Office, 1951-53; asso. firm Gatenbey, Spuller & Law, and predecessor, Chgo., 1953-65, partner, 1965—. Mem. Am., Ill. State bar assns. Contbr. articles to legal jours. Home: 663 Hillcrest Ave Elmhurst IL 60126 Office: 111 W Washington St Chicago IL 60602 Tel (312) 726-1940

LAW, THEODORE WANNAMAKER, JR., b. Bishopville, S.C., Feb. 7, 1907; A.B., Wofford Coll., 1927; LL.B., U. S.C., 1951. Admitted to S.C. bar, 1951, U.S. Supreme Ct. bar; asso. firm Kirkland, Aaron & Alley, Columbia, S.C., 1971; individual practice law, Columbia, S.C., 1971—. Mem. Am., S.C., Richland County bar assns. Home and office: 1311 Cambridge Ln Columbia SC 29204 Tel (803) 256-6457

LAWLER, EDWARD JAMES, b. Chgo., Sept. 15, 1908; Ph.B., U. Chgo., 1930; J.D., Harvard, 1933. Admitted to Ill. bar, 1933, Tenn. bar, 1941; atty.-auditor income tax sect., office of collector IRS, Chgo., 1933-34, spl. atty. office of gen. counsel, 1935-36; individual practice law, Chgo., 1937-38; atty. SEC, Chgo., 1939-41; individual practice law, Memphis, 1941—; mem. advisory panel on internat. law U.S. Dept. State, Washington, 1967—. Fellow Am. Bar Found.; mem. Internat., Am., Chgo., Tenn., Memphis bar assns., Am. Soc. Internat. Law, Am. Law Inst., Am. Judicature Soc., Phi Beta Kappa. Decorated Bronze Star. Home: 644 S Belvedere Blvd Memphis TN 38104 Office: Suite 1500 First Tennessee Bldg Memphis TN 38103 Tel (901) 523-8088

LAWLER, JAMES FRANCIS, b. Phila., Oct. 9, 1922; student St. Josephs Coll.; J.D. cum laude, U. Pa., 1951. Admitted to Pa. bar, 1952; law clk. Ct. of Common Pleas of Philadelphia County, 1952; asso., partner firm Ostroff & Lawler, Phila., 1952—; asst. city solicitor Phila., 1956-58. Founder, active Little League baseball, football, basketball. Mem. Am., Pa., Phila. bar assns., Order of Coif. Home: 627 Renz St Philadelphia PA 19128 Office: 37 S 20th St Philadelphia PA 19103 Tel (215) 665-9455

LAWRANCE, HAROLD IRVIN, b. Greenville, Mich., Nov. 24, 1930; A.B., U. Mich., 1952, LL.B., 1956; grad. Nat. Trust Sch., Northwestern U., 1960, Pacific Coast Banking Sch., U. Wash., 1967. Admitted to Mich. bar, 1956, Ill. bar, 1958, Calif. bar, 1965, U.S. Supreme Ct. bar, 1974; research atty. Am. Bar Found., Chgo., 1957-58; trust adminstr. Continental Ill. Nat. Bank and Trust Co., Chgo., 1958-62; with Security Pacific Nat. Bank, Los Angeles, 1962—, v.p. and trust counsel, 1968-73, sr. v.p. trust dept., 1973—; sec. Bunker Hill Income Securities, Inc., Los Angeles, 1973—. Mem. adv. bd. St. Anne's Maternity Hosp., Los Angeles, 1967-72; mem. legal adv. com. Music Center, Los Angeles, 1971. Mem. Am., Calif., Los Angeles County bar assns., Am., Calif bankers assns., Internat. Acad. Estate and Trust Law, Chancery Club, Los Angeles Area C. of C. Contbr. articles to legal jours. Home: 561 LaLoma Rd Pasadena CA 91105 Office: 333 S Hope St Los Angeles CA 90071 Tel (213) 613-7005

LAWRENCE, ALEXANDER ATKINSON, b. Savannah, Ga., Dec. 28, 1906; A.B. magna cum laude, U. Ga., 1929. Admitted to Ga. bar; partner firm Bouhan, Williams, Lawrence and Levy, Savannah, 1930-68; judge U.S. Dist. Ct., So. Dist. Ga., 1968—; mem. Ga. Bd. Bar Examiners, 1951-58. Pres. Ga. Hist. Soc., 1945-50, 66-68; mem. Ga. Hist. Commn., 1951-67. Mem. Ga. Bar Assn. (pres. 1949-50), Phi Beta Kappa. Author: James Moore Wayne, Southern Unionist, 1945; Storm Over Savannah, 1951; James Johnston, Georgia's First Printer, 1956; A Present for Mr. Lincoln, 1961; Johnny Leber and the Confederate Major, 1962. Home: 401 E 44th St Savannah GA 31404 Office: PO Box 9029 Savannah GA 31402 Tel (912) 234-1273

LAWRENCE, ANTHONY A., b. Dunmore, Pa., May 29, 1916; B.A., U. Scranton, 1939; J.D., Georgetown U., 1945. Admitted to D.C. bar, 1945, Pa. bar, 1949; mem. firm Ligi and Lawrence, and predecessors, Scranton, 1947—; solicitor for Prothonotary's Office, Lackawanna County, Pa., 1949—; former solicitor Borough of Dunmore, Dunmore Sch. Dist. Chmn. Democratic party, Dunmore. Mem. Pa., Lackawanna bar assns., Am. Trial Lawyers Assn. Home: 1624 Monroe Ave Dunmore PA 18512 Office: 202 Mears Bldg Scranton PA 18503 Tel (717) 347-3315

LAWRENCE, BILL, b. Santa Monica, Calif., Sept. 4, 1946; B.A., Brigham Young U., 1969; J.D., U. Calif., Los Angeles, 1973. Admitted to Alaska bar, 1973; asso. firm Hughes, Thorsness, Lowe, Gantz & Powell, Anchorage, 1973-75; partner firm Hoge, Lekisch, Cardwell, Marquez & Lawrence, Anchorage, 1975—. Bd. dirs. Blood Bank of Alaska, Inc., 1976—. Mem. Am. Bar Assn., Anchorage Estate

Planning Council (past sec.). Office: Suite 706 3201 C St Anchorage AK 99503 Tel (907) 274-5511

LAWRENCE, CHARLES B., b. Bklyn., Jan. 12, 1920; B.S.S., Coll. City N.Y., 1941; LL.B. cum laude, Bklyn. Law Sch., 1950. Admitted to N.Y. bar, 1951; practiced in N.Y.C., 1951-70; judge N.Y.C. Civil Ct., 1971—; gen. counsel Carver Fed. Savs. & Loan Assn., 1968-70. Mem. Harlem, Bedford-Stuyvesant lawyers assns., N.Y. Trial Lawyers Assn. Office: 141 Livingston St Brooklyn NY 11201 Tel (212) 643-5922

LAWRENCE, GEORGE DURWOOD, b. Wilkinson County, Ga., Sept. 28, 1924; B.S.A., U. Ga., 1945, LL.B., 1946. Admitted to Ga. bar, 1946, also U.S. Supreme Ct. bar; individual practice law, Eatonton, Ga., 1946-52; solicitor gen. Ocmulgee Jud. Circuit of Ga., 1953-71, dist. atty. emeritus, 1971—; mem. firm Lawrence, Rice & Lawrence, Eatonton, 1972—; mem. Gov.'s Commn. on Jud. Processes, Ct. Orgn. and Structure. Mem. Dist. Attys. Assn. of Ga. (exec. dir. 1971-72), Solicitors Gen. Assn. of Ga. (past pres.), Am., Ga. State, Ocmulgee Jud. Circuit bar assns. Home: 118 Windsor Dr Eatonton GA 31024 Office: 106 E Marion St Eatonton GA 31024 Tel (404) 485-3111

LAWRENCE, JACK WILSON, b. Greenwood, S.C., Sept. 6, 1943; A.B., Wofford Coll., 1965; J.D., U. S.C., 1968. Admitted to S.C. bar, 1969; asso. firm Butler, Chapman, Parler & Morgan, Spartanburg, S.C., 1970-71; asso. firm Butler, Means, Evins & Browne, Spartanburg, 1971-74, partner, 1974-76; individual practice law, Spartanburg, 1976—. Pres. Legal Aid Soc., Spartanburg County, S.C., 1975-77; mem. bd. dirs. Charles Lea Center for Mentally and Emotionally Handicapped, Spartanburg, 1974-76, v.p. bd. dirs., 1975, pres. bd. dirs., 1976; asst. community campaign div. head United Way, Spartanburg, 1976. Mem. Am., S.C. Bar Assns., Defense Lawyers Assn. S.C. Office: 207 Magnolia St Box 5722 Spartanburg SC 29304 Tel (803) 585-2562

LAWRENCE, KELVYN HAROLD, b. Chgo., June 18, 1935; B.A., Yale, 1957; LL.B., Duke, 1961. Admitted to Ill. bar, 1961; partner Wilson & McIlvaine, Chgo., 1961—. Mem. Chgo. Bar Assn. Author: Choosing A Form of Business Organization, 1963. Home: 175 E Delaware Pl Chicago IL 60611 Office: 135 S LaSalle St Chicago IL 60603 Tel (312) 263-1212

LAWRENCE, PAUL SANFORD, b. N.Y.C., Mar. 23, 1915; B.S., L.I. U., 1938; LL.B., St. John's U., Bklyn., 1947, J.D., 1962. Admitted to N.Y. bar, 1947; individual practice law, N.Y.C. and Mineola, N.Y.; partner firm Lawrence & Atkins, Mineola, 1953-70; sr. partner law dept. Nassau County (N.Y.) Dist. Ct., 1959, chief clk., 1960-70; judge Nassau County Dist. Ct., 1971-76; acting judge Nassau County Ct., 1976; mem. judiciary relations com. 9th and 10th Jud. Dists. Bd. dirs. Nassau County Health and Welfare Council, L.I. region Anti-Defamation League B'nai B'rith, Am. Com. Italian Migration; bd. dirs., mem. exec. com., sec. and chmn. speakers bur. Nat. Conf. Christians and Jews; mem. advisory bd. of ct. adminstrn. Adelphi U.; mem. advisory council on alcoholism South Oaks Hosp., Amityville, N.Y. Mem. St. John's Law Rev. Alumni Assn., N.Y. State, Nassau County bar assns., Jewish Lawyers of Nassau County (pres. 1971-72, chmn. bd. 1972-73). Named Man of Year L.I. State Pkwy. Police Assn., 1970; recipient Man of Year award Nassau Lawyers Assn., 1973, Americanism award Am. Legion, 1976; editorial bd. St. John's Law Rev., 1941-42. Office: Nassau County Ct 262 Old Country Rd Mineola NY 11501 Tel (516) 535-3948

LAWRENCE, RAYBURN WAYNE, b. Logan, Tex., Nov. 3, 1920; A.A., Coll. of Marshall, 1939; B.A., U. Tex., 1941; LL.B., Baylor U., 1952. Admitted to Tex. bar, 1952, U.S. Dist. Ct. bar for Eastern Dist. Tex., 1964; practiced in Teague, Tex., 1952-53, Palestine, Tex., 1953-64; judge Anderson County (Tex.) Ct., 1962-64, Tex. Dist. Ct., 3d Jud. Dist., 1965—; mem. Tex. Criminal Justice Div. Adv. Bd., 1975—. Active Anderson County div. Am. Heart Assn.; mem. service unit com. Salvation Army, Palestine, Tex.; mem. Baylor U. Council for Instl. Devel. Mem. State Bar Tex., Phi Delta Phi. Home: 54 Rambling Rd Palestine TX 75801 Office: Courthouse Palestine TX 75801 Tel (214) 729-0161

LAWS, VICTOR H., b. Salisbury, Md., May 8, 1919; student Salisbury State Coll.; A.B., U. Md., 1939, LL.B., 1941. Admitted to Md. bar, 1941, U.S. Supreme Ct. bar, 1974; asso. firm Levin, Claude and Bailey, Salisbury, 1941; asso. firm Miles, Walsh, O'Brien & Morris, Balt., 1942-50, partner, 1950-57; partner firm Adkins, Potts & Laws, Salisbury, 1957-63; individual practice law, Salisbury, 1963-72; partner firm Long, Laws, Hughes & Bahen, Salisbury, 1974—; solicitor City of Salisbury, 1960-66. Chmn. Wicomico County (Md.) Urban Services Commn., 1959-60, Wicomico County Democratic State Central Com., 1962-66; mem. Wicomico County Council, 1974—. Mem. Am., Md. (v.p. 1967-68), Wicomico County (pres. 1962) bar assns. Home: 610 Hunting Park Dr Salisbury MD 21801 Office: 124 E Main St Salisbury MD 21801 Tel (301) 749-2356

LAWSON, EUGENE EDWARD, b. Cleveland, Tenn., July 30, 1937; A.B., U. Chattanooga, 1960; J.D., Woodrow Wilson Coll. Law, 1971. Admitted to Ga. bar, 1971; prosecutor Juvenile Ct. of Clayton County, Ga., 1974—. Mem. Citizens Adv. Com. on Child Abuse, 1976. Mem. Am., Clayton County bar assns. Home: 2778 Lake Jodeco Dr Jonesboro GA 30236 Office: 6 Courthouse Way Jonesboro GA 30237 Tel (404) 478-8894

LAWSON, FRANK CHESTER, b. London, Ont., Can., Nov. 22, 1912; came to U.S., 1936, naturalized, 1940; B.A., U. Western Ont., 1934; J.D., Detroit Coll. Law, 1948; LL.M., Wayne State U., 1963. Admitted to Mich. bar, 1948, Fla. bar, 1972, U.S. Supreme Ct. bar, 1957; prof. Detroit Coll. Law, 1962-68. Mem. Am., Mich., Fla. bar assns. Home: 244 Bal Bay Dr Bal Harbor FL 33154 Office: PO Box 521 Big Pine Key FL 33043 Tel (305) 872-2929

LAWSON, ROBERT WILLIAM, JR., b. Gainsville, Ga., Oct. 12, 1942; A.B., U. Ga., 1964, J.D., 1967. Admitted to Ga. bar, 19641964; partner Palmour, Palmour & Lawson, Gainesville, 1972-76, Lawson & Brown, Gainsville, 1976—; asst. dist. atty. N.E. Jud. Circuit, 1970-72; solicitor City of Gainesville, 1969. Chmn. Hall County (Ga.) Heart Fund, Hall County Easter Seals Dr. Mem. Am. Bar Assn., Ga. Trial Lawyers Assn. Home: 660 Fulton Dr Gainesville GA 30501 Office: 454 Green St Gainesville GA 30501 Tel (404) 536-2304

LAWSON, WILLIAM HENRY, b. Rogersville, Tenn., Nov. 20, 1939; B.S. in Finance cum laude, Eastern Tenn. State U., 1964; M.B.A. in Finance, Ga. State U., 1968; J.D. cum laude, U. Ga., 1971. Research asso. Inst. Law and Govt. U. Ga., 1968-71; admitted to Ga. bar, 1971; asso. firm Stack & O'Brien, Atlanta, 1971-74, partner, 1974-76; partner firm Lawson and Davis, Atlanta, 1976—. Mem. Am., Ga., Atlanta bar assns., Lawyers Club Atlanta, Nat. Judicature Soc., Phi Alpha Delta, Beta Gamma Sigma, Phi Kappa Phi. Home: 220 Skyland Dr Roswell GA 30075 Office: 2000 Cain Tower Atlanta GA 30303 Tel (404) 588-0505

LAWTON, LARRY DAVID, b. Cheyenne, Wyo., June 12, 1942; B.A., U. Wyo., 1967; J.D., Duke, 1970. Admitted to Calif. bar, 1971, Wyo. bar, 1973; law clk. Dist. Atty. Los Angeles County, Los Angeles, 1970-71; dep. dist. atty., 1971-73; asso. firm Guy, Williams & White, Cheyenne, 1973—. Mem. Laramie County, Wyo., Am. bar assns. Home: 5046 Seminole Rd Cheyenne WY 82001 Office: 1600 Van Lennen Ave PO Box 568 Cheyenne WY 82001 Tel (307) 634-2184

LAWYER, JAMES, b. Indianola, Iowa, Aug. 24, 1925; J.D., Drake U., 1950. Admitted to Iowa bar, 1950; partner firm Lawyer, Lawyer & Jackson, Des Moines, 1955—. Mem. Am., Iowa, Polk County bar assns., Assn. Trial Lawyers Am. (state committeeman 1964-66, 73-75, now gov.), Assn. Trial Lawyers Iowa (pres. 1973-74, gov. 1973—). Home: Rural Route Cummings IA 50061 Office: 427 Fleming Bldg Des Moines IA 50309 Tel (515) 288-2213

LAWYER, VERNE, b. Indianola, Iowa, May 9, 1923; J.D., Drake U., 1949. Admitted to Iowa bar, 1949, U.S. Supreme Ct. bar, 1957; mem. firm Lawyer, Lawyer & Jackson, Des Moines, 1949—; spl. asst. atty. gen. for trial of antitrust litigation, Iowa, 1966, Alaska, 1967. Mem. Iowa Aeros. Commn., 1973-79. Fellow Am. Trial Lawyers Roscoe Pound Found., Am. Bar Found., Internat. Soc. Barristers; mem. Polk County, Iowa State (rules com. 1965, spl. com. on fed. practice 1971—, spl. automobile reparations com. 1972—, chmn. rules of civil procedure com. 1968-69), Am. (com. on trial techniques 1969-70, state chmn. membership com. 1970—) bar assns., Lawyer-Pilots Bar Assn., Des Moines, Iowa, Am. (v.p. for Iowa 1956-57, membership chmn. for Iowa 1972-74, bd. govs. 1962-63, co-chmn. tort sect. 1962-63, aviation sect. 1971—, automobile accident reparations com. 1971—, internat. aviation com. 1973—, trial advs. scholarship com. 1973—, nat. sec. 1963-64, 67-68, nat. seminar chmn. 1964-65, 66-67, chmn. nat. speakers bur., 1964-65, criminal law sect., 1965-66), Am. Judicature Soc., Iowa (sec., treas., 1962—), Internat. (chmn. aviation and space law com., 1970, mem. Am. Bar Assn. ad hoc com. to study ct. congestion, 1973) Acads. Trial Lawyers, Law Sci. Acad. Am., World Peace Through Law Center, World Assn. Lawyers (founding), Phi Alpha Delta. Author: Trial By Notebook, 1964; co-author: The Art of Persuasion in Litigation, 1966, How to Defend a Criminal Case from Arrest to Verdict, 1967; speaker Am. Mil. Trial Lawyers Assn. conv., Germany, 1969; editor: Iowa Acad. Trial Lawyers Newsbulletin, 1962—, Weekly Verdict Summary, 1970—. Home: 5831 N Waterbury Rd Des Moines IA 50312 Office: 427 Fleming Bldg Des Moines IA 50309 Tel (515) 288-2213

LAY, KENNETH SWIFT, b. St. Louis, July 18, 1921; LL.B., George Washington U., 1949. Admitted to Mo. bar, 1949, D.C. bar, 1950; spl. agt. FBI, 1949-52; practice law, St. Louis, 1952—; now partner firm Tremayne Lay Carr & Bauer, St. Louis; municipal judge City of Glendale (Mo.), 1955—. Troop com. chmn. Pioneer dist. Boy Scouts Am., St. Louis, 1962-69, commr., 1969—. Mem. Mo. Bar, Bar Assn. Met. St. Louis, St. Louis County (pres. 1964), Am. bar assns., Assn. Trial Lawyers Am., Municipal Judges Assn. Greater St. Louis (pres. 1959). Home: 1165 Glenway Glendale MO 63122 Office: 222 S Central Ave Saint Louis MO 63105 (314) 863-4151

LAY, S. HOUSTON, b. Virden, Ill., Jan. 31, 1912; A.A., Blackburn Coll., 1932; A.B., U. Ill., 1936, J.D., 1937; LL.M., Columbia, 1938. Admitted to Ill. bar, 1937, U.S. Supreme Ct. bar, 1950, D.C. bar, 1952; sr. atty. Office of Gen. Counsel, REA, Dept. Agr., 1938-42; dep. asst. legal adviser adminstrn. and fgn. services Dept. State, 1946-50; chief adminstrv. law sect. Office of Gen. Counsel, Office of the U.S. High Commr. Germany, Frankfort and Bonn, 1950-51, dir. law com. and legis. affairs div., 1951-53, asst. gen. counsel, 1953-54; dep. dir. then acting dir. Office of Spl. Consular Services, Dept. State, 1954-55; counsel mut. security affairs, NATO officer Am. embassy, Athens, Greece, then sr. insp. Fgn. Service Inspection Corps, Dept. State, 1955-58; head team to survey ops. Visa Office, Dept. State, 1961-62; dir. internat. affairs and legal profession program Am. Bar Found., 1962-67; partner firm Rose, Stansbury, Albright, Mason and Lay, Chgo. and Washington, 1964-67; prof. Calif. Western Sch. Law, San Diego, 1967—, dir. Inst. for Study of Internat. Law, 1974—. Mem. Inter-Am., Am., Fed., Ill., Chgo., San Diego (chmn. internat. law sect.) bar assns., Am. Soc. Internat. Law, Fgn. Law Assn., Am. Inst. Aeros. and Astronautics, World Peace Through Law Center, Chgo. Council Fgn. Relations, Am. Fgn. Service Assn., Assn. Am. Law Schs. (chmn. internat. law sect.), UN Assn. (chmn. San Diego chpt.), Am. Acad. Polit. and Social Sci. Author: (with Howard Taubenfeld) The Law of Activity in Space, 1970; New Dimensions on Law of the Sea, 1973, Vol. 5, 1977; contbr. articles in field to profl. jours. Home: 3882 Liggett Dr San Diego CA 92106 Office: Calif Western Sch Law 350 Cedar St San Diego CA 92101 Tel (714) 239-0391

LAYDEN, JOHN JOSEPH, b. Whitehall, N.Y., May 21, 1924; A.B., Holy Cross Coll., 1947; LL.B., Harvard, 1950. Admitted to N.Y. State bar, 1950, U.S. Supreme Ct. bar, 1961; individual practice law, Whitehall, N.Y., 1950—. Mem. Am., N.Y. State, Washington County bar assns. Home: 54 Williams St Whitehall NY 12887 Office: 134 Main St Whitehall NY 12887 Tel (518) 499-1255

LAYLIN, EDWARD HAGERMAN, b. Columbus, Ohio, Aug. 14, 1910; A.B., Ohio Wesleyan U., 1931; LL.B., Harvard, 1934. Admitted to Ohio bar, 1934, U.S. Supreme Ct. bar, 1956; practiced in Columbus, 1934—; partner firms Eagleson & Laylin, 1934-59, Laylin & Laylin, 1959-61, Laylin, McConnaughey & Stradley, 1961-67, Laylin and Shawan, 1967—; instr. Ohio State U. Coll. Law, 1948. Bd. dirs. Meth. Union, Columbus, 1937-74, pres., 1956-66; mem. Met. Area Ch. Bd., Columbus, 1966—, pres., 1970-71; mem. Ohio Council Chs., 1968—, pres., 1975—; area rep. Am. Field Service Internat. Scholarships, 1963—. Mem. Columbus, Ohio State bar assns., Am. Law Inst. (life). Home: 2541 Lane Rd Columbus OH 43220 Office: 50 W Broad St 4230 Columbus OH 43215 Tel (614) 228-6171

LAYLIN, JOHN GALLUP, b. Norwalk, Ohio, Aug. 9, 1902; A.B., Cornell U., 1925; J.D., Harvard, 1928. Admitted to N.Y. bar, 1932, D.C. bar, 1937; jr. legal adviser to Ambassador Dwight Morrow, Mexico, 1928; asso. firm Sullivan & Cromwell, N.Y.C., 1928-33; internat. law work, Argentina, Chile, Uruguay, 1929-30, Cuba, 1932; spl. asst. to under sec. Dept. Treasury, also asst. gen. counsel, 1933-35; mem. firm Covington & Burling, Washington, 1935—; legal adviser to various Latin Am., European, Middle Eastern, S.Asian govts. problems, UN and its specialized agys. Hon. trustee Deep Springs Jr. Coll.; mem. exec. com. Citizens Assn., Gt. Falls, Va. Mem. Internat. Law Assn. (exec. com. Am. br.), Am. Law Inst., Am., Inter-Am. bar assns., Am. Soc. Internat. Law, Middle East Inst., Washington Inst. Fgn. Affairs (v.p., exec. com.). Decorated comdr. Order of Lion (Finland), comdr. Order of Dannebrog (Denmark), Sitara-I (Pakistan), comendador Order San Carlos (Colombia); author: The Uses of the Waters of International Rivers, 1956; contbr. numerous articles to legal jours.; author numerous monographs including: Principles of Law Governing Use of International Rivers, Development of the Law of State Responsibility-Equality of Treatment and the International Standard, Allocating Water on International Streams, Legal Climate for Private Enterprise Under the Alliance for Progress, Renegotiation of Concession Agreements, Past, Present and Future Development of the Customary International Law of the Sea and Deep Seabed. Home: 438 River Bend Rd Great Falls VA 22066 Office: 888 16th St NW Washington DC 20006 Tel (202) 452-6132

LAZAR, CHARLES STEVEN, b. N.Y.C., May 12, 1943; B.A. in Govt., Am. U., 1965, J.D., 1968. Admitted to Md. bar, 1972; asso. firm Staley, Prescott & Ballman, Kensington, Md., 1973-76; asso. firm Sheeskin & Hillman, Rockville, Md., 1976—. Mem. Am. Bar Assn. Office: 6110 Executive Blvd Rockville MD 20852 Tel (301) 770-6730

LAZAROV, SIDNEY, b. Memphis, Oct. 27, 1917; LL.B., Memphis State U., 1938. Admitted to Tenn. bar, 1938; individual practice law, Memphis, 1938-60; partner firm Hurley, Lazarov & Royal, Memphis, 1960—. Mem. Am., Tenn. bar assns. Home: 5450 Pecan Grove Ln Memphis TN 38117 Office: 2803 Clark Tower Bldg 5100 Poplar Memphis TN 38137 Tel (901) 767-2034

LAZAROW, MARTIN SIDNEY, b. Schenectady, July 10, 1937; B.S. cum laude, State U. of N.Y. at Albany, 1968, M.S., 1969; LL.B., Albany Law Sch., 1966. Admitted to N.Y. State bar, 1966, Fed. Dist. Ct. bar, 1966, U.S. Tax Ct. bar, 1967; mem. firm Nathan M. Goldberg, Albany, N.Y., 1966-67; counsel to commn. on taxation, N.Y. State Senate, 1976; counsel to Zoning Bd. of Appeals, Clifton Pk., N.Y., 1976; prof. accounting and law State U. of N.Y. at Albany. Mem. N.Y. State, Saratoga County, Schenectady County bar assns., Am. Inst. of CPA's, N.Y. State Soc. of CPA's. C.P.A., N.Y. Home: 4 Mountain View Ballston Lake NY 12019 Office: PO Box 284 Barney Road Clubhouse Clifton Park NY 12065 Tel (518) 371-9250

LAZARUS, ARTHUR, JR., b. Bklyn., Aug. 30, 1926; B.A. cum laude, Columbia, 1946; J.D., Yale, 1949. Admitted to N.Y. State bar, 1951, D.C. bar, 1952, U.S. Supreme Ct. bar, 1954; asso. firm Fried, Frank, Harris, Shriver & Kampelman, Washington, 1950-57, partner, 1957—; vis. prof. law Yale, New Haven, 1973-74, 75-76; dir. Am. Indian Lawyers Tng. Program, Inc., Oakland, Calif., 1974—. Trustee Georgetown Day Sch., Inc., Washington, 1961-70. Mem. Am., Fed., D.C. bar assns. Home: 3201 Fessenden St NW Washington DC 20008 Office: 600 New Hampshire Ave NW Suite 1000 Washington DC 20037 Tel (202) 965-9400

LAZARUS, HERBERT BENEDICT, b. Bayonne, N.J., June 8, 1907; Ph.B., Yale, 1927, LL.B., 1929. Admitted to N.Y. State bar, 1930, U.S. Supreme Ct. bar, 1945; v.p., sec., gen. counsel Am. Broadcasting Paramount Theatres, Inc., N.Y.C., 1956-57; pres. Parmelee Transp. Co., N.Y.C., 1958-69; v.p., gen. counsel Checker Motors Corp., N.Y.C., 1969-77. Mem. Assn. Bar City N.Y., Am., N.Y. State bar assns., Judge Advocates Assn. Home: 56 Grace Ln Ossining NY 10562 Tel (914) 941-6066

LAZARUS, HERMAN, b. Phila., Apr. 21, 1910; B.S. in Edn., Temple U., 1933, LL.B., 1937; LL.M., U. Pa., 1941. Admitted to Pa. bar, 1938, D.C. bar, 1941; atty. NLRB, 1942-46, asst. to gen. counsel, 1946-47; head labor mgmt. sect. Pub. Affair Inst., 1947-49; counsel U.S. Senate Com. on Labor and Pub. Welfare, 1949-51; pub. mem. rev. and appeals com. Wage Stblzn. Bd., Washington, 1951-53, pub. mem. and vice chmn., 1952-53; sr. partner firm Cohen, Shapior, Polisher, Shiekman & Cohen, Phila., 1972—. Mem. Am., Pa., Phila. bar assns., Jewish Employment and Vocat. Soc. (hon. pres.). Home: William Penn House 1919 Chestnut St Philadelphia PA 19107 Office: 12 S 12th St Philadelphia PA 19107 Tel (215) 922-1300

LAZEROW, HERBERT IRVIN, b. Balt., Apr. 12, 1939; A.B., U. Pa., 1960; J.D., Harvard, 1963; LL.M. (teaching fellow), George Washington U., 1964. Admitted to D.C. bar, 1964, Ky. bar, 1966, Calif. bar, 1969; lawyer, chief counsel's legislation and regulations div., IRS, Washington, 1964-66; asst. prof. law, U. Louisville, 1966-67; asso. prof. law U. San Diego, 1967-70, prof., 1970—, asso. dean for academics, dir. Inst. Internat. and Comparative Law, 1972—; cons. in field; chmn. San Diego Legal Panel Am. Civil Liberties Union, 1968-70; instr. Calif. Bar review course, 1970-71. Mem. San Diego Mayor's Social Sci. Adv. Com., 1968-71 (chmn., 1970-71), San Diego County Employee Relations Panel, 1971-73; moderator San Diego Open Forum, 1971-72; mem. contemporary arts com. San Diego Fine Arts Gallery, 1970-73. Mem. Calif., San Diego County bar assns., Soc. Am. Law Tchrs. Recipient Fed. Bar Assn. essay prize; author: Organization for Economic Cooperation and Development Draft Influence on United States Income Tax Treaties, 1976; contbr. articles in field to profl. jours. Home: 8601 Kilbourn Dr La Jolla CA 92037 Office: School of Law University San Diego Alcala Park San Diego CA 92110 Tel (714) 291-6480 ext 378

LAZERUS, GILBERT, b. N.Y.C., June 24, 1912; Ph.B., Yale, 1931; J.D., Columbia, 1934. Admitted to N.Y. bar, 1934; asso. with Joseph V. McKee, 1935-45; partner firm Stroock & Stroock & Lavan, N.Y.C., 1945—. Home: 1175 York Ave New York City NY 10021 Office: 61 Broadway New York City NY 10006 Tel (212) 425-5200

LAZO, LEO MICHAEL, b. Boston, Apr. 2, 1927; B.S., Northeastern U., 1951; J.D., Boston U., 1958. Admitted to Mass. bar, 1958, Fed. bar, 1958, U.S. Supreme Ct. bar, 1974; sr. partner firm Badger, Sullivan, Kelley & Cole, Boston, 1958—; notary pub., Boston, 1958—. Mem. Mass., Norfolk bar assns., Mass. Trial Lawyers Assn., Am. Arbitration Assn. (arbitrator Nat. Panel Arbitrators 1968—), Mass. Dept. Reserve Officers Assn. U.S. (pres.), Eastern Council Navy League of U.S. (dir. 1970—), Delta Theta Phi. Home: 49 Martin St W Roxbury MA 02132 Office: 84 State St Boston MA 02109 Tel (617) 523-3400

LEA, LOLA STENDIG, b. N.Y.C., Sept. 20, 1934; B.A. cum laude, N.Y. U., 1954; LL.B., Yale, 1957. Admitted to N.Y. State bar, 1958, U.S. Supreme Ct. bar, 1963; law clk. to judge U.S. Dist. Ct. for So. Dist. N.Y., 1957-59; asst. U.S. atty. So. Dist. N.Y., 1959-61; asso. firm Chester C. Davis, N.Y.C., 1961-67; mem. firm Davis & Cox, N.Y.C., 1967-71, firm Lea, Goldberg & Spellun, N.Y.C., 1971—, also firm Trubin, Sillcocks, Edelman & Knapp, N.Y.C., 1977—; spl. counsel Joint Interprofl. Com. Drs. and Lawyers, 1972—; mem. deptl. coms. for ct. adminstrn. of appellate divs., 1st, 2d depts.; lectr. Practising Law Inst., 1969-70, 74. Fellow Am. Bar Found.; mem. Am., N.Y. State (ho. of dels. 1972—, exec. com. 1976—), N.Y.C. (chairperson com. medicine and law 1969-71, com. on new mems. 1971-74; mem. com. on judiciary 1971-74, com. on grievances 1974—) bar assns. Contbr. articles to legal jours. Office: 375 Park Ave New York City NY 10022 Tel (212) 759-5400

LEA, STEPHEN RICHARD, b. Elgin, Ill., Dec. 16, 1941; B.A., U. Mich., 1963; J.D., Wayne Law Sch., 1969. Admitted to Ariz. bar, 1970; law clk. judge Phoenix, 1969-70; asso. firm Gorodezky, Marron & Diamond, Phoenix, 1970-71; partner firm Hadley & Lea, Phoenix, 1971—; ct. commr., 1972-76; spl. master, Phoenix, 1973. Mem. Maricopa County, Ariz. bar assns., Am. Trial Lawyers Assn. Author: Tax Aspects of Redemptions. Office: 3001 W Indian Sch Rd Phoenix AZ 85017 Tel (602) 264-7692

LEACH, DAVID GEORGE, b. Detroit, Aug. 25, 1935; B.A., Wayne U., 1957; J.D., Detroit Coll., 1960. Admitted to Mich. bar, 1960, Calif. bar, 1963, U.S. Supreme Ct. bar, 1967; claims supr. Chareus, Dargan & Co., 1960-63; house counsel Sayre & Toso, Inc., 1964; asso. firm Eliassea & Postel, 1964-67; partner firm Tamba, Hill, Schneider, Leach & D'Andre, San Francisco, 1968—. Mem. No. Calif., San Francisco bar assns. Office: 989-3222 1000 Hearts Bldg 5-3d St San Francisco CA 94103 Tel (415) 989-3222

LEACH, JOHN WYLY, b. Memphis, Apr. 12, 1948; B.A., Vanderbilt U., 1970; J.D., Memphis State U., 1973. Admitted to Tenn. bar, 1974; clk. firm Ireland, Reams, Henderson & Chafetz, Memphis, 1973-74; asso. firm Kirkpatrick & Lucas, 1974-75, Nelson, Norvell, Wilson, McRae, Ivy & Sevier, 1975—, Memphis. Mem. Tenn., Memphis-Shelby County bar assns. Recipient Am. Jurisprudence award, Bancroft-Whitney Co., 1973; contbr. article Memphis State Univ. Law Rev. Office: 3130 100 N Main St Memphis TN 38103 Tel (901) 523-2364

LEACH, PARKER O'NEAL, b. Pacific, Mo., July 16, 1935; B.S., Calif. State U., Los Angeles, 1963, J.D., 1966. Admitted to Calif. Supreme Ct. bar, 1967, U.S. Supreme Ct. bar, 1974, U.S. Tax Ct. bar, 1974; Dep. County Counsel San Diego County Counsel's Office, 1967-69; dep. city atty. City of San Bernardino City Atty.'s Office, 1974-75; individual practice law, Escondido, Calif., 1969-73, Yreka, Calif., 1974, Solana Beach, Calif., 1975—; vis. prof. Pepperdine U. Vista Center for Para-Legal Program, 1976. Mem. San Diego County, North County (Calif.), San Bernardinto County (Calif.), Siskiyou County (Calif.) bar assns. Home: 200 Cerco Rosado San Marcos CA 92069 Office: Suite 101 200 N Ash St Escondido CA 92027 Tel (714) 741-8585

LEADER, HENRY BOYER, b. York, Pa., Jan. 7, 1922; A.B. with honors, Swarthmore Coll., 1942; LL.B., Yale, 1947. Admitted to Pa. bar, 1948; asso. firm McClean Stock, York, 1948-52, partner, 1952—; legis. sec. to Gov. Pa., 1955-59; mem. reorgn. commn. Commonwealth of Pa., 1955-56. Chmn. redevel. authority City of York, 1957-62, 70—, chmn. housing authority, 1957-68. Mem. Am., Pa., York County bar assns. Mem. editorial bd. Yale Law Jour., 1946-47. Home: 448 Linden Ave York PA 17404 Office: 35 S Duke St York PA 17401 Tel (717) 843-8871

LEANZA, ANTHONY VICTOR, b. Cleve., Dec. 21, 1921; A.B., Adelbert Coll., Western Res. U., 1947; LL.B., Western U., 1949. Admitted to Ohio bar, 1949, U.S. Supreme Ct. bar, 1964; individual practice law, Cleve., 1949-59; asst. law dir. City of Cleve., 1959-69; U.S. adminstrv. law judge, Cleve., 1970—. Home: 5811 Alberta Dr Lyndhurst OH 44124 Office: 814 Superior Ave Suite 1919 Cleveland OH 44114 Tel (216) 522-7065

LEAPHART, WALTER WILLIAM, b. Butte, Mont., Dec. 3, 1946; B.A., U. Mont., 1969, J.D., 1972. Admitted to Mont. bar, 1972, U.S. Supreme Ct. bar, 1975; law clk. to judge U.S. Fed. Dist., Butte, 1972-74; asso. firm Leaphart, Helena, Mont., 1974—; pub. defender, 1974-75. Mem. Mont. Bar Assn., Mont. Criminal Def. Lawyers Assn. Asso. editor Mont. Law Rev., 1971-72. Contbr. articles to legal jours. Office: 1 N Last Chance Gulch Helena MT 59601 Tel (406) 442-4930

LEARNARD, JOHN NORRIS, b. San Diego, Aug. 15, 1940; B.S. in Ins., San Diego State U., 1965; J.D., U. San Diego, 1970. Admitted to Calif. bar, 1971; individual practice law, San Diego, 1971-76; partner firm Learnard & Geile, San Diego, 1976—; instr. torts Western State U. Sch. Law, San Diego, 1976—. Mem. Am. Bar Assn., Am., Calif., San Diego trial lawyers assns. Office: 1010 2d Ave Suite 2200 San Diego CA 92101 Tel (714) 231-4990

LEARNED, JAMES ROY, b. Kenosha, Wis., Aug. 25, 1920; B.A., U. Wyo., 1947, J.D., 1948. Admitted to Wyo. bar, 1949, U.S. Dist. Ct. for Wyo. bar, 1959, U.S. Ct. Appeals bar, 1967; atty. Husky Oil Co., Cody, Wyo., 1949-51, div. atty., 1951-53, gen. atty., 1953-56, mgr. land and exploration, 1956-59; v.p. Argus Exploration Corp., Guatemala City, Guatemala, 1956-59; practice in Cheyenne, 1959—; petroleum cons., 1959—. Mem. Am., Wyo., Laramie County bar assns., Am. Assn. Petroleum Geologists, Rocky Mountain Assn. Petroleum Geologists, Wyo., Mont. geol. assns., Rocky Mountain Oil and Gas Assn. Home: 415 W 3d Ave Cheyenne WY 82001 Office: 222 E 21st St Cheyenne WY 82001 Tel (307) 638-9806

LEARNED, PHILIP CARLTON, b. Elmira, N.Y., June 30, 1932; B.A., Colgate U., 1954; LL.B., U. Va., 1957, J.D., 1960. Mem. N.Y. bar, 1961; asso. firm Sayles Evans Bryaton Palmer & Tifft, Elmira, 1960-61; partner firm Ziff Weiermiller Learned & Hayden, Elmira, 1961—; atty. LeValley McLeod Inc., 1964—. Bd. dirs., atty. Chemung County (N.Y.) Soc. for Prevention of Cruelty to Animals, 1975-76; bd. dirs. Chemung County Council on Alcoholism, 1965—, pres., 1969-72; atty. City Rescue Mission, Inc., 1965—. Mem. N.Y. State, Chemung County bar assns. Home: 925 Oak Hill Dr Elmira NY 14905 Office: 301 William St Elmira NY 14902 Tel (607) 734-1518

LEARY, JOHN EDWARD, JR., lawyer; b. New Haven, Conn., Sept. 6, 1938; B.S., Fairfield U., 1962; LL.B., U. Conn., 1967. Admitted to Conn. bar, 1967, U.S. Dist. Ct., 1969; partner firm Selzman, Cantor and Leary, New Haven, Conn., 1968-70; partner firm Heffernan, Leary and Gibson, West Haven, Conn., 1970—. Town atty., East Haven, Conn., 1975—; chmn. East Haven Bicentennial Commn., 1974-75; mem. Charter Revision Commn., East Haven, Conn., 1974. Mem. Conn., New Haven County bar assns. Home: 12 Maynard Rd East Haven CT 06513 Office: 420 Campbell Ave West Haven CT 06516

LEARY, LEO WILLIAM, b. Gratiot, Wis., Aug. 5, 1919; B.A., U. Wis., 1940, LL.B., 1946; S.J.D., U. Mich., 1953. Admitted to Wis. bar, 1946; asso. prof. law U. Tex., Austin, 1946-48; asso. prof. Marquette U., 1948-58, prof., 1958—; research reporter com. property revision State Bar Wis., 1968-71, 76—. Mem. Am. (Wis. reporter com. on significant current legislation, probate and trust div. sect. real property probate and trust law), Wis., Milw. bar assns. Home: 13335 Watertown Plank Rd Elm Grove WI 53122 Office: 1103 W Wisconsin Ave Milwaukee WI 53233 Tel (414) 224-7094

LEATHERMAN, JOHN B., JR., b. Muncie, Ind., Dec. 1, 1939; B.C.E., Cornell U., 1962; J.D., Ind. U., 1969. Admitted to Ohio bar, 1970, Ind. bar, 1969; patent atty. Procter & Gamble, Cin., 1969-71; pres. McLain Trucking, Inc., Anderson, Ind., 1977—. Mem. Ohio Bar Assn., Ind. Motor Truck Assn. (sec.), Am. Trucking Assn. Office: 2425 Walton St Box 2159 Anderson IN 46011 Tel (317) 643-3376

LEATON, JAMES CULVER, b. Taylorville, Ill., Oct. 10, 1898; LL.B., Webster Coll. Law (now Kent Coll. Law), 1915. Admitted to Ill. bar, 1921, U.S. Supreme Ct. bar, 1929; asst. U.S. Atty. No. Dist. Ill., Chgo., 1929-34, spl. asst. U.S. Atty. Gen., Chgo., 1934-35; master in chancery Cook County (Ill.) Circuit Ct., 1942-67; mem. firms McConnel & Leaton, 1940-42, West, Leaton & West, 1943-55, McKinney, Leaton & Smallex, Chgo., 1955-60; individual practice law, Chgo., 1960—; pres. Chgo. Crime Commn., 1955-57. Mem. Am., Ill., Chgo. (bd. mgrs. 1954-56) bar assns. Author: Manual for Grand Juries, 1948. Home: 722 Washington Ave Wilmette IL 60091 Office: Suite 2126 135 S LaSalle St Chicago IL 60603 Tel (312) 332-3202

LEAVELL, JEROME FONTAINE, b. Blue Mountain, Miss., Feb. 14, 1928; B.A., U. Miss., 1951, LL.B., 1951, J.D., 1969; LL.M. (Sterling fellow), Yale, 1964; postgrad. (Ford Found. fellow) Balliol Coll. Oxford (Eng.) U., 1969; J.S.D., Yale, 1972. Admitted to Miss. bar, 1951, N.Y. State bar, 1957, Ga. bar, 1965, Ark. bar, 1972, U.S. Supreme Ct. bar, 1965; atty. FTC, Washington, 1951-52; law clk. to Judge Edwin R. Holmes, U.S. Ct. Appeals, 5th Circuit, 1952; asso. firm Brewer & Brewer, Clarksdale, Miss., 1953-54, Cadwalader, Wickersham & Taft, N.Y.C., 1955-57; atty. Chase Manhattan Bank, N.Y.C., 1958-62; individual practice law, N.Y.C., 1962-63, Atlanta, 1965, Little Rock, Williamsburg and Jackson, Miss., 1966-76, Clinton, Miss., 1977—; atty. Merrill, Lynch, Pierce, Fenner & Smith, N.Y.C., 1963-64; asst. prof. U. Ark., 1966-67, asso. prof., 1967-72; vis. prof. La. State U., 1972; asso. prof. Marshall-Wythe Sch. Law Coll. William and Mary, 1972-75; prof. Miss. Coll., 1975—; Distinguished vis. prof. in communications law U. Ark., Little Rock, 1972; mem. nat. panel cons. Nat. Commn. Protection Human Subjects of Biomed. and Behavioral Research, 1976. Mem. Am., Hinds County (Miss.), Miss., Pulaski County (Ark.), Fed., Va. bar assns., Am. Assn. Law Schs., Oxford Law Soc., Am. Judicature Soc., Soc. Legal History, Soc. Internat. Law, Delta Theta Phi (hon., Outstanding Prof. award 1971), Phi Alpha Delta, Sigma Alpha Epsilon. Recipient Cannon prize Chase Manhattan Bank, 1959, Outstanding Tchr. award Phi Alpha Delta-Student Bar Assn., 1971; certificate merit William and Mary Law Sch., 1975; hon. barrister at law Inner Temple (Inn of Ct.), London, 1969; author: Treatise on Law and Ethics of Organ Transplants, 1972; contbr. articles to legal jours.; case editor Ark. Lawyers' Assn. Brief mag., 1966-69. Home: 401 W Madison St Clinton MS 39056 Office: 401 W Madison St Clinton MS also Miss Coll Sch of Law POB 4008 Clinton MS 39058 Tel (601) 924-7720 also 924-5131

LEAVY, ZAD, b. Los Angeles, June 16, 1930; B.S., U. Calif., Los Angeles, 1952, LL.B., 1958; LL.M., U. So. Calif., 1965. Admitted to Calif. bar, 1959, U.S. Supreme Ct. bar, 1966; dep. dist. atty., Los Angeles County, 1959-62; partner firm Beilenson & Leavy, Beverly Hills, Calif., 1964-68, Levinson, Rowen & Leavy, Beverly Hills, 1959-74; of counsel firm Levinson, Rowen, Miller, Jacobs & Kabrins, Beverly Hills, 1974—. Chmn. exec. com. Anti-Defamation League, Los Angeles, 1972-74, bd. dirs., 1963—, also mem. Nat. Civil Rights Commn.; bd. dirs. Calif. Com. Therapeutic Abortion, 1965-74; mem. Calif. Coastal Commn., 1977—. Mem. Am., Calif., Los Angeles, Beverly Hills bar assns. Contbr. articles to legal jours. Home: Coast Ridge Rd Big Sur CA 93920 Office: 8601 Wilshire Blvd 8th Floor Beverly Hills CA 90211 Tel (408) 667-2545

LEBAN, MARK KING, b. Miami, Fla., Apr. 3, 1947; B.A., Boston U., 1969; J.D., U. Miami, 1972. Admitted to Fla. bar, 1972, D.C. bar, 1973, U.S. Supreme Ct. bar, 1975; asst. pub. defender Appellate Div., Miami, 1972-76; individual practice law, Miami, 1976—; moot court judge U. Miami, 1976. Mem. Fla., D.C., Dade County bar assns. Conducts lectures throughout Fla. in appellate practice for continuing edn. Office: 66 W Flagler St 808 Concord Bldg Miami FL 33130 Tel (305) 374-5500

LEBEDOFF, DAVID MICHAEL, b. Mpls., Apr. 29, 1938; B.A., U. Minn., 1960; LL.B., Harvard, 1963. Admitted to Minn. bar, 1963; spl. asst. atty. gen. State of Minn., 1963-65; spl. asst. to Senator Walter F. Mondale, Washington, 1966; individual practice law, Mpls., 1967—. Commr. Minn. Higher Edn. Coordinating Bd., 1975—; trustee Mpls. Soc. Fine Arts, 1975—; mem. Minn. Gov.'s Commn. on Arts, 1975—; treas. Minn. Democratic Farmer-Labor Party, 1976—. Mem. Am., Minn., Hennepin County (Minn.) bar assns., Minn. Phi Beta Kappa Assn. (pres. 1975—). Author: The 21st Ballot, 1969; Ward Number Six, 1972; contbr. articles to nat. mags. Home: 17 S 1st St apt 1702A Minneapolis MN 55401 Office: 619 Midland Bank Bldg Minneapolis MN 55401 Tel (612) 339-2141

LEBEDOFF, JONATHAN GALANTER, b. Mpls., Apr. 29, 1938; B.A. cum laude, U. Minn., 1960, LL.B., 1963. Admitted to Minn. bar, 1963; individual practice law, Mpls., 1963-66; partner firm Gitis & Lebedoff, Mpls., 1966-71; judge Hennepin County (Minn.) Municipal Ct., 1971-74, Minn. State Dist. Ct., 4th Jud. Dist., Mpls., 1974—; mem. Gov's. Commn. Crime Prevention and Control, 1971-76. Active Citizens League, Mpls. Mem. State Dist. Ct. Judges Assn., Minn., Hennepin County, Am. bar assns. Home: 17 S First St Minneapolis MN 55402 Office: 1759 Courts Tower Hennepin County Government Center Minneapolis MN 55487 Tel (612) 348-6324

LEBENSOLD, LINDA R., b. N.Y.C., Nov. 24, 1944; A.B. cum laude, Barnard Coll., 1965; LL.B., Columbia, 1968. Admitted to N.Y. bar, 1968; atty. Mut. Life Ins. Co. N.Y., N.Y.C., 1968-70, asst. counsel, 1970-73, asso. counsel, 1973-76, counsel, 1976—; pres., dir. River Point Towers Coop., Inc., 1975—. Mem. Am., N.Y. State bar assns., Harlan Fiske Stone Fellowship Columbia Law Sch., Columbia Law Sch. Alumni Assn. Home: 555 Kappock St Riverdale NY 10463 Office: 1740 Broadway New York City NY 10019 Tel (212) 586-4000

LE BEY, BARBARA SYDELL, b. Newark, Feb. 28, 1939; student Sarah Lawrence Coll., 1955-58; A.B., Montclair State Coll., 1959; J.D., Emory U., 1970. Admitted to Ga. bar, 1970; staff atty. Atlanta Legal Aid Soc., 1970-71; asso. firm Arnall, Golden & Gregory, Atlanta, 1971-73; adminstrv. law judge State Bd. Workmen's Compensation, Atlanta, 1974—. Vice chmn. Ga. State Personnel Bd., 1971-74. Mem. State Bar Assn. Ga., Am., Atlanta bar assns. Named Atlanta Woman of Year in Law, 1974. Home: 1922 Cedar Canyon Dr Atlanta GA 30345 Office: 684 State Labor Bldg Atlanta GA 30334 Tel (404) 656-6682

LEBHERZ, GEORGE HENRY, JR., b. Worcester, Mass., Oct. 17, 1929; LL.D., Boston U., 1958. Admitted to Mass. bar, 1958; asso. firm Talamo & Talamo, Worcester, 1958-60; partner firm Munson Lebherz & Ament, Falmouth, Mass., 1960—. Mem. Falmouth Sch. Com., 1965-71, chmn., 1971; pres. Falmouth Taxpayers Assn., 1961-62, Falmouth Youth Hockey, Inc., 1976-77; bd. dirs. Legal Services of Cape Cod, 1975-77. Mem. Fed., Mass., Barnstable County (v.p.) bar assns., Am. Trial Lawyers Assn. Sr. editor Boston U. Law Rev., 1957-58. David Stoneman scholar, 1957-58. Home: 328 Elm Rd Falmouth MA 02540 Office: PO Box 546 Old Bailey Ct Falmouth MA 02541 Tel (617) 548-6600

LEBIT, EDWARD ALAN, b. Chgo., Oct. 23, 1936; A.B., Western Res. U., 1958; J.D., Cleve.-Marshall Law Sch., 1965. Admitted to Ohio bar, 1965; asso. firm McCarthy & Greenwald Co., Cleve., 1965-70, partner, 1970—; lectr. in field. Mem. Am., Fed., Ohio State, Cleve., Cuyahoga County bar assns. Asso. editor: Merrick-Rippner Ohio Probate Code, 1966. Home: 1902 Camberly Dr Lyndhurst OH 44124 Office: 962 Illuminating Bldg Cleveland OH 44113 Tel (216) 696-1422

LE BLANC, STEVE, b. Donaldsonville, La., Mar. 28, 1946; B.A. in Psychology, La. State U., 1970, J.D., 1973. Admitted to La. bar, 1973; individual practice law, Baton Rouge, 1973—. Mem. La., Am., Baton Rouge bar assns. Home: 1468 Ross Ave Baton Rouge LA 70808 Office: 1746 Scenic Hwy PO Box 3295 Baton Rouge LA 70821 Tel (504) 355-0341

LEBOWITZ, WALTER BERNARD, b. Newark, May 7, 1930; B.B.A., U. Miami, J.D., 1954. Admitted to Fla. bar, 1954; individual practice law, Miami Beach, Fla., 1954—; house counsel Aeronaves Del Peru S.A. 1957-63, city atty. Sweetwater Fla. 1965-66, municipal judge Sweetwater, Fla. 1965-67, public defender Miami Beach, 1967-71, v.p. corp. sec., house counsel Alarmtec Internat. Corp., gen. counsel Alarm Cos. Fla. 1970-72; instr. Bus. Law Ft. Lauderdale Coll., 1976—, U. Miami, 1976—. Democratic committeeman Miami Beach, mem. Dade county Exec. Com. 1956-64, atty. Democratic com. Dade County 1956-58. Mem. Fla. bar Assn., Fla. Municipal Judges Assn. Contbr. articles to legal jours. Home: 4550 No Bay Rd Miami Beach FL 33140 Office: 350 Lincoln Rd Miami Beach FL 33139 Tel (305) 672-0666

LEBRUN, GENE NOE, b. Langdon, N.D., July 4, 1939; B.A., St. John's U., 1961; J.D., U. N.D., 1964. Admitted to N.D. bar, 1964, S.D. bar, 1964; partner firm Lynn, Jackson, Shultz, Ireland & Lebrun, Rapid City, S.D., 1964—; mem. S.D. State Legislature, 1971-74, speaker of the house, 1973-74. Mem. Rapid City C. of C. (dir. 1975—), S.D., N.D., Am. bar assns., S.D. Jud. Council (chmn. 1977—), S.D. Trial Lawyers Assn. Recipient R.A. Pier Meml. award Rapid City Jaycees, 1973. Home: 2806 Arrowhead Dr Rapid City SD 57701 Office: 724 Saint Joe St PO Box 1377 Rapid City SD 57709 Tel (605) 342-2592

LEBUS, BETTY VIRGINIA, b. Bremerton, Wash., May 8, 1923; B.S., U. Wash., Seattle, 1947, LL.B., 1948, B.A. in Law Librarianship, 1949. Admitted to Wash. State bar, 1948; asst. law librarian U. Wash., Seattle, 1948-50; law librarian Ind. U., Bloomington, 1950—. Mem. Am. Assn. Law Libraries, Ind. Library Assn. (pres. 1961-62), Wash. State Bar Assn. Home: 413 S Henderson Apt 22 Bloomington IN 47401 Office: Law Library Indiana University School Law Bloomington IN 47401

LECHNER, BERNARD JOHN, b. Evanston, Ill., Apr. 24, 1934; J.D., Loyola U., Chgo., 1960. Admitted to Ill. bar, 1960, Fla. bar, 1965; sec., v.p. fin. Sportcraft Homes, Clearwater, Fla., 1963-68; sec.-treas. Allen Homes, Clearwater, 1968—. Mem. Am., Ill. bar assns., Fla. Bar, Am. Assn. Atty.-C.P.A.'s, Am. Inst. C.P.A.'s, Ill. Soc. C.P.A.'s. Home: 2039 Brendla Rd Clearwater FL 33515 Office: 1991 Drew St Clearwater FL 33515 Tel (813) 446-1547

LECHNER, EDWARD JAMES, b. Pensacola, Fla., June 18, 1945; B.A., U. Minn., 1967, J.D., 1971. Admitted to Minn. bar, 1971; pres. firm E. J. Lechner, J.D., Ltd., Edina, Minn.; v.p. Centre Investment Group, Inc.; chmn. Hennepin County (Minn.) Unauthorized Practice of Law Com. Mem. Minn. (unauthorized practice of law com. 1973-77), Hennepin County, Am. bar assns., Assn. Fin. Planners. Office: 3101 W 69th St Edina MN 55435 Tel (612) 925-2089

LECHNER, IRA MARK, b. N.Y.C., May 5, 1934; B.A., Randolph-Macon Coll., 1955; LL.B., Yale, 1958. Admitted to N.Y. bar, 1958, Va. bar, 1967, D.C. bar, 1968; served with JAG, U.S. Army, 1960-64; atty. NLRB, Washington, 1964-66; individual practice law, Washington and Va., 1968-76; partner firm Roman, Davenport, Lechner, Seifman & Sando, Vienna, Va., Washington, 1976—. Mem. Va. Gen. Assembly, 1973—; Arlington (Va.) Hos. & Nursing Home Commn., 1974—. Mem. Am., Va. bar assns. Home: 2812 N Kensington St Arlington VA 22207 Office: 8320 Old Courthouse Rd Vienna VA 22180 Tel (703) 790-1262

LECKIE, BERNARD ARTHUR, b. Los Angeles, Dec. 10, 1932; B.S., U. So. Calif., 1957, LL.B. (Law Week award), 1959. Admitted to Calif. bar, 1960; with Office Dist. Atty. Los Angeles, 1960-61; asso. firm Betts Ely & Loomis, Los Angeles, 1961-63, firm Ely Kadison & Quinn, Los Angeles, 1963-65; individual practice law, Los Angeles, 1965—. Examiner for Calif. bar, 1967-68. Mem. Am. Arbitration Assn. (nat. panel), Am., Los Angeles County bar assns., State Bar Calif. (chmn. disciplinary com. 1972-73), Calif., Los Angeles trial lawyers assns., Am. Judicature Soc., Assn. Dep. Dist. Attys. Los Angeles County, Assn. Trial Lawyers Am., Phi Delta Phi. Office: One Wilshire Blvd Suite 2323 Los Angeles CA 90017 Tel (213) 628-6183

LEDDY, ALBERT MURRAY, b. Pasadena, Calif.; B.A., U. Calif., Berkeley, 1947, J.D., 1949. Admitted to Calif. bar, 1950; partner firms Leddy & Reddy, Bakersfield, Calif., 1950-51, Bradley Wazy Barker Hislap & Gibbons, Bakersfield, 1965-70; dep. dist. atty. Kern County, Calif., 1952-62, asst. dist. atty., 1962-65, dist. atty., 1971—; adviser U. Calif. Continuing Edn. of Bar, 1972—. Mem. Calif., Am., Kern County bar assns., Calif. Dist. Attys. Assn. (dir. 1974—). Home: 2501 Dracena St Bakersfield CA 93304 Office: 1415 Truxtun Ave Bakersfield CA 93301 Tel (805) 861-2421

LEDDY, DANIEL DAVID, JR., b. Bklyn., Oct. 1, 1940; B.A., Fordham U., 1962, J.D., 1966. Admitted to N.Y. bar, 1966, U.S. Supreme Ct. bar, 1972; individual practice law, S.I., N.Y., 1967—. Mem. Am., N.Y., Richmond County bar assns., Guild of Catholic Lawyers, Fordham Law Alumni. Office: 15 Beach St Staten Island NY 10304 Tel (212) 442-3343

LEDERER, EUGENE WILLIAM, b. State College, Pa., Aug. 5, 1920; B.S., Pa. State U., 1942; J.D., U. Pa., 1948. Admitted to Pa. bar, 1949, U.S. Supreme Ct. bar, 1953, U.S. Dist. Ct. bar for D.C., 1960; individual practice law, Bellefonte, Pa., 1949-51, State College, 1949-60; mem. staff gen. counsel's office FCC, Washington, 1960-61; partner firm Gill, Lederer, Rayback & Price, State College, 1961—; vis. lectr. Pa. State U., 1962-65. Mem. State College Borough Planning

Commn., 1954-60; bd. viewers Centre County (Pa.), 1954-60. Mem. Am., Pa. bar assns. Home: PO Box 195 State College PA 16801 Office: 102 E College Ave State College PA 16801 Tel (814) 238-3053

LEDERMAN, IRVING, b. London, Dec. 4, 1904; LL.B., Fordham U., 1926. Admitted to N.Y. bar, 1927; individual practice law, N.Y.C.; housing judge N.Y.C. Civil Ct., 1973-76; mem. firm Dreyer & Traub, N.Y.C., 1976, Rosenberg & Rosenberg, N.Y.C., 1976—. Appeal agt. SSS, Bklyn., 1941-75. Mem. Bklyn. Bar Assn. Home: 750 Lido Blvd Lido Beach NY 11561 Office: 16 Court St Brooklyn NY 11241

LEDFORD, LEE BRADLEY, b. Smith, Ky., Aug. 3, 1918; B.S., U.S. Mil. Acad., 1941; J.D., Harvard, 1950. Commd. lt. U.S. Army, 1941, advanced through grades to col., 1960; instr. polit. sci. U.S. Mil. Acad.; staff JAC, Korean Communication Zone; chief procurement law Dept. Army; ret., 1961; admitted to Ky. bar, 1950, N.Y. bar, 1976; v.p. adminstrn. Kollsman Instrument Corp., Syosset, N.Y., 1961-68; v.p., gen. counsel, sec. Universal Container Corp., Louisville, 1968-73; pub. defender Southeastern Ky., 1973-74; gen. counsel, sec., Am. Export Industries Inc., N.Y.C., 1975—. Mem. Am., N.Y., Ky. bar assns. Home: 570 Park Ave New York City NY 10021 Office: 26 Broadway New York City NY 10004 Tel (212) 482-4909

LEDGERWOOD, THOMAS PHIL, b. Indpls., Feb. 3, 1943; B.A., Ind. Central U., 1964; J.D., Ind. U., 1969. Admitted to Ind. bar, 1969; asso. firm Rocap, Rocap, Reese & Young, Indpls., 1969-76, partner, 1976—; clk. Ind. Supreme Ct., 1967, chief justice, 1969; sheriff, 1966. Dir., Greater Indpls. Progress Com., 1977. Mem. Am., Ind., Indpls. bar assns. Office: 45 N Pennsylvania St Indianapolis IN 46204 Tel (317) 639-6281

LE DUC, DON RAYMOND, b. Milw., Apr. 7, 1933; B.A., U. Wis., 1959, Ph.D. (Ford fellow), 1970; J.D., Marquette U., 1962. Admitted to Wis. bar, 1962, U.S. Supreme Ct. bar, 1969; asso. firm Arnold, Murray & O'Neill, Milw., 1962-63; asso. Kaftan Law Firm, Green Bay, Wis., 1964-67; chief counsel Wis. Dept. Ins., Madison, 1967-69; prof. communication law U. Md., 1970-71, Ohio State U., 1971-73, U. Wis., 1973—; mem. cable TV adv. com. FCC, 1972—; dir. Comparative Telecommunications Research Center, 1975—. Mem. Wis. Bar Assn., Internat. Broadcast Inst., Broadcast Edn. Assn. (chmn. broadcast regulation com. 1972-74). Author: Cable Television and the FCC, 1973 Issues in Broadcast Regulation, 1974; editor Client, 1972—; contbr. articles to legal jours. Home: 305 Cheyenne Trail Madison WI 53705 Office: Dept Communication Arts Vilas Hall University of Wisconsin Madison WI 53705 Tel (608) 238-9785

LEDWITH, JAMES ROBB, b. Bryn Mawr, Pa., Feb. 14, 1936; A.B., Princeton, 1958; LL.B., U. Pa., 1963. Admitted to Pa. bar, 1964; asso. firm Pepper, Hamilton & Scheetz, Phila., 1963-71, partner, 1971—. Bd. dirs. Bryn Mawr Civic Assn., Buck Lane Meml. Day Care Center, Haverford, Pa.; pres. Coll. Settlement of Phila.; elder Bryn Mawr Presbyterian Ch., 1972-75. Fellow Am. Coll. Probate Counsel; mem. Am., Pa., Phila. (officer probate sect.) bar assns., Pa. Bar Inst. (dir.), Phila. Estate Planning Council (officer). Office: 2001 Fidelity Bldg Philadelphia PA 19109 Tel (215) KI 5-1234

LEDWITH, PETER KEVIN, b. Bklyn., May 14, 1940; A.B., Providence Coll., 1962; LL.B., Fordham U., 1966, J.D., 1968. Admitted to N.Y. State bar, 1967, U.S. Dist. Ct. for So. and Eastern dists. N.Y. bar, 1967, U.S. Supreme Ct. bar, 1976, 2d Circuit Ct. Appeals bar, 1976; asso. firm Francis J. Heneghan, N.Y.C., 1967-69, Joseph F. Waldorf, Great Neck, N.Y., 1969-74; mem. firm Waldorf, Ledwith & McGrane, Great Neck, 1974-76, Lynn, Perlman & Ledwith, Garden City, N.Y., 1977—; pros. atty. Village of Lynbrook (N.Y.), 1969—. Mem. Am., N.Y. State, Nassau County (N.Y.) bar assns., Nassau-Suffolk Trial Lawyers Assn., Def. Assn. N.Y., Am. Arbitration Assn. Home: 37 Pearsall Ave Lynbrook NY 11563 Office: 585 Stewart Ave Garden City NY 11530 Tel (516) 222-0620

LEDYARD, ROBINS HEARD, b. Nashville, Oct. 14, 1939; B.A., Vanderbilt U., 1965, LL.B., 1966. Admitted to Tenn. bar, 1966, U.S. Dist. Ct. bar, 1967, U.S. Ct. of Appeals bar, 1968, U.S. Supreme Ct. bar, 1975, U.S. Tax Ct. bar, 1977, U.S. Ct. Claims bar, 1977; atty. Nat. Life & Accident Ins. Co., Nashville, 1966-68, asst. counsel, 1968, asso. counsel, 1969-71, counsel, 1971, asso. gen. counsel, 1972-75, gen. counsel, 1975—; sec.-treas. Atlic, 1973-74, v.p., 1974-75, pres., 1975-76. Vice chmn. United Diocesan Givers, 1970-72; active Girl Scouts U.S.A., Boy Scouts Am., United Way. Mem. Nashville Bar Assn., Assn. Life Ins. Counsel, Am. Council Life Ins., Assn. Tenn. Life Ins. Cos., Order of Coif. Recipient Bennett Douglas Bell Meml. prize, 1966; author: Employment Discrimination, An Overview and Compliance Primer, 1972; asst. editor Vanderbilt Law Rev., 1965-66. Home: 1215 Chickering Rd Nashville TN 37215 Office: 2540 Nat Life Center Nashville TN 37250 Tel (615) 749-1592

LEE, DANIEL MCKINNON, b. Forrest County, Miss., Apr. 19, 1926; student U. So. Miss., 1946-47; LL.B., J.D., Jackson Sch. Law, 1949; grad. Nat. Coll. State Judiciary, 1975, Miss. Jud. Coll., 1974. Admitted to Miss. bar, 1948, Ky. bar, 1955, Ark. bar, 1957; mem. firm Franklin & Lee, Jackson, Miss., 1948-54; partner firm Lee, Moore & Countiss, Jackson, 1954-71; county judge Hinds County, Miss., 1971—; mem. Miss. Oil and Gas Bd., 1968-71, Interstate Oil Compact Commn., 1968-71. Mem. Am. Bar Assn., Miss. State, Hinds County bars, Am. Judicature Soc., Nat. Assn. Trial Judges, Miss. Jud. Conf., Aircraft Owners and Pilots Assn. Home: 1615 Myrtle Heights Jackson MS 39202 Office: PO Box 327 Jackson MS 39205 Tel (601) 354-3787

LEE, EDWARD BROWN, III, b. Tarentum, Pa., Sept. 19, 1941; B.C.E., N. Mex. State U., 1965; J.D., U. Pitts., 1971. Admitted to Pa. bar, 1972, U.S. Patent bar, 1974, U.S. Supreme Ct. bar, 1976; asso. firm Lindsay McGinnis Mclandless & McCabe, Pitts., 1972—. Mem. Allegheny County (Pa.) Bar Assn. Registered profl. engr., Pa., N. Mex., Vt. Home: 1015 Jefferson Heights Dr Pittsburgh PA 15235 Office: 930 Grant Bldg Pittsburgh PA 15219 Tel (412) 471-2420

LEE, GENE BAXTER, b. Rensselaer, Ind., Nov. 6, 1923; B.S. in Bus. Adminstr., Ind. U., LL.B., 1946, J.D., 1967. Admitted to Ind. bar, 1946, since practiced in Warsaw; mem. firm Brubaker, Rockhill & Lee, from 1946, successively Rockhill & Lee, Rockhill, Vandeveer, Rowdabaugh & Lee, Rockhill, Vandeveer, Kennedy & Lee, until 1962; city atty., Warsaw, 1948; pros. atty. Kosciusko County, Ind., 1949-52; judge Kosciusko Circuit Ct., 1963—. Bd. dirs., officer Five County Mental Health Clinic, 1962-70; active Bakers Boys Club; mem. Kosciusko County Election Commn., 1962-70. Mem. Ind. State, Kosciusko County bar assns., Ind. Judges Assn. Home: Rural Route 7 Valley Springs Warsaw IN 46580 Office: PO Box 727 Warsaw IN 46580 Tel (219) 267-5582

LEE, HAROLD KENNETH, b. Asheville, N.C., Aug. 23, 1905; A.B., Lehigh U.; LL.B., U. N.C. Admitted to N.C. bar, 1928; individual practice law, Asheville, 1928—. Mem. Am., N.C., Buncombe County bar assns., N.C. State Bar (pres. 1971-72). Home: 85 Edwin Pl Asheville NC 28801 Office: 600 Gennett Bldg Box 7586 Asheville NC 28807 Tel (704) 253-5397

LEE, JAMES GARDNER, b. Dancy, Ala., Mar. 1, 1935; B.S., Auburn U., 1957; LL.B., U. Ala., 1966. Admitted to Ala. bar, 1966; asso. firm Zeanah & Donald, Tuscaloosa, 1966-70; partner firm Zeanah, Donald & Lee, Tuscaloosa, 1970-75; individual practice law, Tuscaloosa, 1976—; mem. Ala. Ho. of Reps., 1974—, vice chmn. constn. and elections com. Mem. Am., Ala., Tuscaloosa bar assns., Am., Ala. trial lawyers assns. Home: 2 Wood Manor Tuscaloosa AL 35401 Office: 2600 6th St Tuscaloosa AL 35401 Tel (205) 345-8643

LEE, JESSIE CAIL, b. Sylvania, Ga., Dec. 2, 1924; B.S. in Bus. Adminstrn., U. Fla., 1949; J.D., U. Miami (Fla.), 1953; grad. Nat. Coll. Judiciary U. Nev., 1968. Admitted to Fla. bar, 1953; practiced in Fort Lauderdale, 1953-66, 69-71; atty. Ft. Lauderdale (Fla.) Housing Authority, 1958-61; city prosecutor City of Oakland Park (Fla.), 1963-64; asso. judge Oakland Park City Ct., 1964-65; judge Broward County (Fla.) Ct. of Record, 1966-69, 72; asso. judge Fla. Dist. Ct. Appeal, for 4th Dist., 1973; judge Fla. Circuit Ct., 17th Jud. Circuit, 1973—; temporary justice Fla. Supreme Ct., 1974, 75; chmn. com. jud. selection and tenure Circuit Ct. Judges Conf., 1975. Mem. Fla. (chmn. com. jud. adminstrn. 1970-71), Broward County bars, Am. Bar Assn., Am. Judicature Soc., Fla. Blue Key, Phi Eta Sigma, Phi Kappa Phi, Kappa Sigma. Office: Broward County Courthouse Fort Lauderdale FL 33301 Tel (305) 765-4703

LEE, JOHN DAVIS, b. Tellico Plains, Tenn., May 3, 1929; B.S., E. Tenn. State U., 1951; J.D., U. Tenn., 1954. Admitted to Tenn. bar, 1954, U.S. Supreme Ct. bar, 1957; dir., founder, pres. Citizens Legal Clinic, Inc.; clk., master Monroe Chancery Ct., 1954-59; mem. Tenn. Supreme Ct. Bar Unification Commn., 1975—. Sec. Tenn. Conservation Commn.; del. Tenn. Constl. Conv., 1953, 77; chmn. Monroe County Democratic Exec. Com., 1954. Mem. Am. (pres. 1972-73), Tenn. (pres.) trial lawyers assns., Internat. Acad. Trial Lawyers, Internat., Am., Knoxville, Tenn., Monroe County (pres.) bar assns., Internat. Soc. Barristers, Inner Circle Advs., Ky. Assn. Trial Lawyers (hon.). Author: Testament of Intent; contbr. articles to legal jours. Home: Oak Grove Rd Madisonville TN 37354 Office: 1214 Hwy 411 N Madisonville TN 37354 Tel (615) 442-2497

LEE, JOHN MICHAEL, b. Okla. City, Okla., June 15, 1930; B.A., Baylor U., 1952, J.D., 1954. Admitted to Tex. bar, 1954; partner firm McMahon, Smart, Wilson, Surovik & Suttle, Abilene, Tex., 1959-75, Fillmore, Camp & Lee, Ft. Worth, 1975—. Mem. Tex. Assn. Defense Counsel (dir. 1966-68, 72—), Assn. Ins. Atty's. Home: 1263 Roaring Springs Rd Ft Worth TX 76114 Office: 1325 Electric Service Bldg Ft Worth TX 76102 Tel (817) 338-4881

LEE, JOHN PETER, b. San Francisco, Aug. 6, 1926; B.A., U. Nev., 1955; J.D., U. San Francisco, 1954. Admitted to Calif. bar, 1954, Nev. bar, 1955; asso. firm G. William Coulthard, Las Vegas, Nev., 1955-67; individual practice law, Las Vegas, 1967-73; pres. John Peter Lee, Ltd., Las Vegas, 1973—. Chmn. Clark County (Nev.) chpt. Nat. Found. Infantile Paralysis, 1960, Clark County chpt. Tb Assn., 1961; chmn., trustee Clark County Legal Aid, 1961-62. Mem. Clark County, Am. bar assns., state bars Nev., Calif. 89106 Office: 300 S 4th St Suite 1501 Las Vegas NV 89101 Tel (702) 382-4044

LEE, LAWRENCE J., b. St. Louis, Nov. 4, 1932; B.S., St. Louis U., 1954, J.D., 1956. Admitted to Mo. bar, 1957; mem. firm Morris A. Shenker, 1956-64; pros. atty. St. Louis, 1964-66; individual practice law, St. Louis, 1966—; mem. Mo. State Senate, 1966—. Mem. Am., Mo. bar assns., Bar Assn. Met. St. Louis. Recipient award for Meritorious Pub. Service St. Louis Globe Democrat. Home: 9 Arundel Pl Saint Louis MO 63105 Office: 506 Olive St Saint Louis MO 63101 Tel (314) 621-2333

LEE, PAUL ROBERT, b. Lonaconing, Md., July 5, 1944; B.A., U. Md., 1966; J.D., U. Balt., 1972. Admitted to Md. bar, 1972, U.S. Supreme Ct. bar, 1976; asso. firm Irvine B. Schaffer, Balt., 1973; estate tax atty. IRS, Balt., 1973—. Mem. Am., Md. (co-chmn. bar exam. subcom.) bar assns. Address: 1205 Fairfield Ave Baltimore MD 21209 Tel (301) 377-0245

LEE, PETER MARK, b. Bridgeport, Conn., Aug. 7, 1941; B.S. in Econs., U. Pa., 1963; LL.B., N.Y. U., 1966. Admitted to Conn. bar, 1966, Ill. bar, 1969, Minn. bar, 1971; atty. Burlington No. Inc., St. Paul, 1969—. Mem. Ramsey County, Minn. State bar assns., ICC Practitioners Assn. Home: 2465 Londin Ln Apt 407 Maplewood MN 55119 Office: 176 E 5th St St Paul MN 55101

LEE, RALEIGH BRADFORD, b. Aurora, N.C., May 17, 1898; A.B., U. N.C., 1922, LL.B., 1922, J.D., 1967. Admitted to N.C. bar, 1922; mem. firm Harding & Lee, Greenville, N.C., 1928-51; city atty. city of Greenville (N.C.), 1935-65; individual practice law, 1965—. Mem. Pitt County, N.C. bar assns. Home: Falkland Hwy Greenville NC 27834 Office: Skinner Bldg Third and Washington Sts Greenville NC 27834 Tel (919) 752-3337

LEE, RANDY HALE, b. Balt., Nov. 27, 1944; B.A., Washington and Lee U., 1966, J.D. summa cum laude, 1969. Admitted to Md. bar, 1969; asso. firm Semmes-Bowen & Semmes, Balt., 1969-72; asst. atty. gen. State of Md., 1973-75; gen. counsel Md. Port Authority, Balt., 1973-75; asst. prof. law U. N.D., Grand Forks, 1975—; trustee Bar Assns. Ins. Trust, Balt., 1974-75; reporter for Speedy Trial Act, Dist. N.D. Mem. Am. (chmn. com. uniform rules, adminstrv. law sect.), Md., Inter-Am. bar assns., Am. Judicature Soc., Phi Beta Kappa, Omicron Delta Kappa, Order of Coif, Mu Beta Psi. Home: 3725 University Ave apt 304 Grand Forks ND 58201 Office: Sch Law Univ ND Grand Forks ND 58202 Tel (701) 777-2961

LEE, REX EDWIN, b. Los Angeles, Feb. 27, 1935; B.A., Brigham Young U., 1960; J.D., U. Chgo., 1963. Admitted to Ariz. bar, 1963, D.C. bar, 1966, Utah bar, 1972; law clk. to Justice Byron R. White, U.S. Supreme Ct., 1963-64; asso. firm Jennings, Strouss & Salmon, Phoenix, 1964-66, partner, 1967-72; dean J. Reuben Clark Law Sch., Brigham Young U. 1972-75; asst. atty. gen. civil div. Dept. Justice, Washington, 1975—. Bd. dirs. Theodore Roosevelt council Boy Scouts Am., Ariz. region Salvation Army, Utah Endowment for the Humanities. Home: 2840 Iroquois Dr Provo UT 84601 Office: Dept Justice Civil Div Washington DC 20530 Tel (202) 739-3301

LEE, RICHARD STEWART, b. Bklyn., May 23, 1945; B.A. (Regent's scholar), N.Y. U., 1967; J.D., Bklyn. Law Sch., 1970. Admitted to N.Y. State bar, 1971; intern Kings County Dist. Atty.'s Office, N.Y., 1969; asso. firm Roth & Winograd, N.Y.C., 1969-72; asso. house counsel, dir. officer corporate subs. Bedford Stuyvesant Restoration Corp., Bklyn., 1972—; spl. asst. State Senator Donald Halperin, 1970-73. Office: 1368 Fulton St Brooklyn NY 11216 Tel (212) 636-3345

LEE, RICHARD VINCENT, b. Norwood, Mass., July 24, 1932; B.A., San Diego State U., 1959; J.D., U. San Diego, 1969. Admitted to Calif. bar, 1970; partner firm Shuford & Lee, Indio, Calif., 1970—. Pres., Coachella Valley (Calif.) Boys' Club, 1976. Mem. Desert Bar Assn. Home: 77-170 Florida Ave Palm Desert CA 92260 Office: 81-730 Hwy 111 Indio CA 92201 Tel (714) 347-0731

LEE, ROBERT EARL, b. Kinston, N.C., Oct. 9, 1906; B.S., Wake Forest U., 1928, LL.B., 1928; M.A. in Pub. Law, Columbia, 1929; LL.M., Duke U., 1935, J.D., 1941. Admitted to N.C. bar, 1927; prof. law Temple U., Phila., 1929-45, U.S. Army U., Shrivenham, England, 1945-46; prof. law Wake Forest U., Winston-Salem, N.C., 1946—, dean, 1946-50; chief counsel U.S. Office Price Stabilization, Region Four, Richmond, Va., 1951-52; chmn. trusts drafting com. N.C. Gen. Statutes Commn., Raleigh. Pres., Phila. PTA, 1942-44; gen. counsel Lone Scouts Found., New London, N.C., 1936—. Mem. N.C. (v.p. 1960-61), Forsyth County (pres. 1958-59) bar assns., Internat. Family Law Soc., Scribes. Author law books, numerous legal articles; legal columnist for newspapers. Home: 2180 Faculty Dr Winston-Salem NC 27106 Office: School Law Wake Forest University Winston-Salem NC 27109 Tel (919) 761-5000

LEE, ROBERT EDWARD, b. Woodhaven, N.Y., Apr. 21, 1927; B.B.A., St. John's U., 1950, J.D., 1952. Admitted to N.Y. bar, 1953; atty. Home Title Guaranty Co., Mineola, N.Y., 1952-53; asso. firm David Holman, Mineola, 1953-56; partner firm S.M. & D.E. Meeker, Bklyn., 1956—; mem. title adv. bd. Security Title & Guaranty Co., 1970—. Mem. Am., N.Y. bar Assns., Savs. Banks Lawyers Assn. Bklyn. Home: 30 Hofstra Dr Plainview NY 11803 Office: 1 Hanson Pl Brooklyn NY 11243 Tel (212) 783-3340

LEE, ROBERT EDWARD, JR., b. Miley, S.C., May 20, 1922; LL.B., John B. Stetson U., 1949. Admitted to Fla. bar, 1950; individual practice law, Jacksonville and DeLand, 1950-64; judge Juvenile Ct., Volusia County, Fla., 1964-73; judge Circuit Ct., Daytona Beach, Fla., 1973—. Mem. Am., Volusia County, Fla. bar assns. Home: 2100 N Thorpe Ave Orange City FL 32763 Office: Volusia County Court House Daytona Beach FL 32018 Tel (904) 258-7000

LEE, ROBERT EVENSEN, b. Watertown, S.D., Sept. 3, 1926; J.D., Tulane U., 1960. Admitted to La. bar, 1960; individual practice law, Gretna, La., 1960—; asst. dist. atty. Parish of Orleans, 1967-68. Mem. Am., La. bar assns., Am. Trial Lawyers Assn., Navy League U.S. Home and Office: 384 Westmeade Dr Gretna LA 70053 Tel (504) 362-2823

LEE, ROBERT EWELL, b. Pontotoc, Miss., Oct. 31, 1922; LL.B., Cumberland U., Lebanon, Tenn., 1947; B.S., Union U., Jackson, Tenn., 1948; J.D., U. Mo., Kansas City, 1957. Admitted to Tenn. bar, 1957; individual practice law, Lebanon, 1958—; asst. U.S. atty. Middle Dist. Tenn., 1966; city prosecutor City of Lebanon, 1969. Mem. Am., Tenn., Lebanon bar assns., Am. Judicature Soc., Tenn., Am. trial lawyers assns., Tenn. Criminal Lawyers Assn. Recipient award for outstanding service U.S. Courthouse Credit Union, Nashville, 1971. Home: 1722 Cherokee Dr Lebanon TN 37087 Office: 202 E Gay St Lebanon TN 37087 Tel (615) 444-3900

LEE, ROBERT MALONE, b. Alpine, Tex., Apr. 8, 1941; B.A., U. Colo., 1963; J.D., U. Mo., 1966. Admitted to Mo. bar, 1966; gen. counsel, sec. Commonwealth Life & Accident Ins. Co., St. Louis, 1969-76, 77—; pres., chief exec. officer Ind. Mut. Fire Ins. Co., St. Louis, 1976-77; dir. Exchange Mgmt. Services, Inc., Ind. Mut. Ins. Cos. St. Louis, Houston, Ill., Ind. Mem. Am., Mo., Met. St. Louis (Outstanding Achievement award 1976) bar assns. Office: 3500 Lindell Blvd Saint Louis MO 63103 Tel (314) 652-3883

LEE, STEPHEN ELMER, b. Hutchinson, Minn., July 24, 1938; B.A., U. Minn., 1960; LL.B., 1963. Admitted to Minn. bar, 1964, Calif. bar, 1965, Ariz. bar, 1974; law clk. to Chief Justice Traynor, Calif. Supreme Ct., San Francisco, 1963-64; asso. firm Faegre & Benson, Mpls., 1964-69; prof. law Ariz. State U., Tempe, 1969—, vis. prof. Cornell U., Ithaca, N.Y., 1971-72; dir. summer insts. Council on Legal Edn. Opportunity, 1970, 73. Mem. Am. Law Inst., AAUP, Am. Bar Assn., Soc. Am. Law Tchrs., Ariz., Maricopa County bar assns., Assn. Am. Law Schs. Pres. Minn. Law Rev., 1962-63. Home: 5615 N 45th St Phoenix AZ 85018 Office: College of Law Arizona State U Tempe AZ 85281

LEE, THOMAS HOWERTON, b. Durham, N.C., Oct. 20, 1934; A.B., Davidson Coll., 1957; LL.B., Duke U., 1960. Admitted to N.C. bar, 1960; individual practice law, Durham, 1960-63; asst. solicitor N.C. Superior Ct., Durham, 1963-66, resident judge 14th Jud. Dist., 1975—; judge N.C. Dist. Ct., 14th Jud. Dist., 1966-74. Mem. N.C. Bar Assn., N.C. Conf. Superior Ct. Judges. Home: 3518 Barcelona Ave Durham NC 27707 Office: Durham County Courthouse Durham NC 27701

LEE, WILLIAM FRANCIS, JR., b. Newnan, Ga., Feb. 13, 1943; B.A., U.Ga., 1965, LL.B., 1967. Admitted to Ga. bar, 1967; law clk. U.S. Circuit Ct., Atlanta, 1968-69; assoc. firm Latimer, Haddon and Stanfield, Atlanta, 1969-72; individual practice law Newnan, Ga., 1972-75; dist. atty., Newnan, 1975—. Mem. Newnan Bar Assn., Dist. Attys Assn. Ga. Home: 16 Waverly Circle Newnan GA 30263 Office: 21 Spring St Newnan GA 30263 Tel (404) 253-8175

LEE, WILLIAM MARSHALL, b. N.Y.C., Feb. 23, 1922; student U. Wis., 1939-40; B.S. in Aero. Engring., U. Chgo., 1942; postgrad. U. Cal. at Los Angeles, 1946-48; J.D., Loyola U. (Chgo.), 1952. Admitted to Ill. bar, 1952; thermodynamicist Northrop Aircraft Co., Hawthorne, Calif., 1947-49; patent agt. Hill, Sherman, Meroni, Gross & Simpson, Chgo., 1949-51, Borg-Warner Corp., Chgo., 1951-53; partner firm Hume, Clement, Hume & Lee, Chgo., 1953-72; individual practice law, Chgo., 1973-74; sr. partner firm Lee & Smith, Chgo., 1974—. Pres. Glenview (Ill.) Citizens Sch. Com., 1953-57; v.p. Glenbrook High Sch. Bd., 1957-63. Mem. Am. (mem. patent sec., chmn. patent div. 1974-75, dir. budget and fin. 1976—, chmn. various coms. 1968—), Ill. State, Chgo., 7th Fed. Circuit bar assns., Internat., Am., Chgo. patent law assns., Licensing Exec. Soc. (trustee 1973-75, v.p. 1975—), Phi Alpha Delta. Author speaker legal subjects. Home: 84 Otis Barrington IL 60010 Office: 10 S Riverside Plaza Chicago IL 60606 Tel (312) 726-1982

LEE, WILLIAM SWAIN, b. Phila., Dec. 18, 1935; A.B., Duke, 1957; LL.B., U. Pa., 1960. Admitted to D.C. bar, 1961, Del. bar, 1964; dep. atty. gen. State Del., and Sussex County, Del., 1965-70; partner firm Betts and Lee, Georgetown, Del., 1970—; gen. counsel Sussex County

Legal Entitlement Program, 1966-69; soliciter, Sussex County, 1970-72; gen. counsel Republican State Com., 1968-72. Chmn., Sussex County Republican Party, 1973—. Mem. Am., Del., Sussex County bar assns., Am. Judicature Soc. Home: 12 Park Ave Rehoboth Beach DE 19971 Office: 15 S Race St Georgetown DE 19947 Tel (302) 856-7755

LEECH, NOYES ELWOOD, b. Ambler, Pa., Aug. 1, 1921; A.B., U. Pa., 1943, J.D., 1948. Admitted to Pa. bar, 1949; asso. firm Dechert, Price & Rhoads, and predecessors, Phila., 1948-49, 1951-53; instr. U. Pa. Law Sch., Phila., 1949-56, prof. law, 1957—. Mem. AAUP, Am. Soc. Internat. Law., Order of Coif, Phi Beta Kappa. Co-author: The International Legal System, 1973. Home: 162 W Queen Ln Philadelphia PA 19144 Office: 3400 Chestnut St Philadelphia PA 19104 Tel (215) 243-6790

LEECH, WILLIAM MCMILLAN, JR., b. Charlotte, Tenn., Nov. 5, 1935; B.S., Tenn. Tech. Inst., 1958; J.D., U. Tenn., 1966. Admitted to Tenn. bar, 1967; asst. dist. atty. 11th Jud. Circuit, Columbia, Tenn., 1967-69; city judge, Columbia, 1970-71; mem. firm Leech, Hardin & Knolton, Columbia, 1975—; mem. nominating commn. Tenn. Appellate Ct., 1973-77; pres. Ltd. Constl. Conv. Tenn., 1971; del. elect Constl. Conv. Tenn., 1977. Drive chmn. Maury County United Givers Fund, 1971, pres., 1972. Mem. Am., Tenn. (pres., gov. young lawyers conf. 1970-71), Maury County (pres. 1974) bar assns., Am. Judicature Soc. (mem. bd.), Maury County C. of C. (pres. 1973). Home: Columbia Hwy Santa Fe TN 38482 Office: 805 S Garden St Columbia TN 38401 Tel (615) 388-4022

LEEDY, RICHARD J., b. Nov. 18, 1942; B.S., U. Utah, 1965; LL.B./J.D., 1966. Admitted to Utah bar, 1966, U.S. Supreme Ct. bar, 1976; partner firm Leedy, Oberhansley & O'Connell, 1969-72, firm Bottom & Leedy, 1972-74; individual practice law, Salt Lake City, 1974—. Mem. Utah, Salt Lake County bar assns. Contbr. articles to legal jours. Home and Office: 2795 Comanche Dr Salt Lake City UT 84108 Tel (801) 583-1467

LEEDY, WILLIAM HUDSON, b. Kansas City, Mo., May 18, 1928; A.B., Washington and Lee U., 1949; LL.B., U. Mo., 1952; LL.M. in Taxation, N.Y. U., 1957. Admitted to Mo. bar, 1952; asso. firm Lathrop, Koontz, Righter, Clagett, Parker & Norquist and predecessor, Kansas City, 1954-62, 69—; gen. counsel Fed. Res. Bank of Kansas City, 1962-64; mem. firm Gage & Tucker, Kansas City, 1964-69; bd. govs. Mo. Bar, 1967-73; mem. Appellate Jud. Commn. of Mo., 1974—. Mem. Bd. Police Commrs., Kansas City, 1961-62. Mem. Am., Kansas City bar assns., Am. Law Inst., Am. Judicature Soc., Lawyers Assn. Kansas City. Home: 814 Westover Rd Kansas City MO 64113 Office: 1500 Ten Main Center Kansas City MO 64105 Tel (816) 842-0820

LEEGER, LUTHER LINDSEY, b. Union City, N.J., Jan. 8, 1923; student Dartmouth, 1942-43, Columbia, 1943-44, U. Pa., 1945-46; LL.B., Harvard, 1950. Admitted to Calif. bar, 1951; dep. dist. atty. San Diego County (Calif.), 1953-56; individual practice law, San Diego, 1957-64; partner firm Mizeur & Leeger, San Diego, 1964—; lectr. in law U. San Diego, Calif. Western Law Sch.; city atty. City of Del Mar (Calif.), 1959-61. Mem. State Bar Calif., San Diego County Bar Assn., Christian Legal Soc. San Diego County (chmn.). Office: suite 1909 Crocker Nat Bank 1010 Second Ave San Diego CA 92101 Tel (714) 233-8941

LEEK, TERRENCE STARR, b. Great Bend, Kans., Apr. 18, 1939; A.B., Washburn U., 1962, J.D., 1965. Admitted to Kans. bar, 1965, Ariz. bar, 1968; partner firm Markor & Leek, Topeka, 1965-67; partner firm Leek & Oehler, Bullhead, Ariz., 1968—; dir. The State Bank, Ariz., 1976—. Mem. Ariz., Mohave County, Am. bar assns. Office: Box 687 Bullhead City AZ 86432 Tel (602) 758-3988

LEEMHUIS, JOHN PETER, b. Erie, Pa., Aug. 5, 1930; B.S., Holy Cross Coll., 1952; J.D., U. Pa. at Phila., 1958. Admitted to Pa. bar, 1959, U.S. Supreme Ct. bar, 1973; partner firm Quinn, Gent, Buseck, and Leemhius, Erie, 1958—. Mem. Erie County, Pa., Am. bar assns., Am. Arbitration Assn. Home: 370 W Arlington Rd Erie PA 16509 Office: 1400 G Daniel Baldwin Bldg Erie PA 16501 Tel (814) 456-6261

LEEMON, JOHN ALLEN, b. Hoopeston, Ill., Jan. 12, 1928; B.S., U. Ill., 1950, LL.B., 1952. Admitted to Ill. bar, 1952; individual practice law, Savanna, Ill., 1952-54; mem. firm Eaton & Leemon, Mt. Carroll, Ill., 1954-66; mem. firm Eaton, Leemon & Rapp, Mt. Carroll, 1966-69; individual practice, Mt. Carroll, 1969—; spl. asst. atty. gen., 1969—. Mem. Am., Ill. State Mem. negligence council 1961-66, grievance com. 1967-70), Carroll County bar assns. Home: East St Mount Carroll IL 61053 Office: 102 1/2 Market St Mount Carroll IL 61053 Tel (815) 244-3422

LEEN, WALTER VICTOR, b. Chgo., Jan. 13, 1911; student U. Mich., 1928-31; Ph.B., U. Chgo., 1933, J.D., 1934. Admitted to Ill. bar, 1934; asso. S.J. & A. Wolf, 1934-39; atty. Ill. Dept. Revenue, 1939-41; mem. legal dept. Golan Wine Inc., Los Angeles, 1942, individual practice law, 1946-47; staff asst. Law Sch. U. Chgo., 1947, atty. spl. constrn. staff, 1948-50, mem. legal dept., 1950-53, asso. legal counsel, 1953-62, gen. counsel, sec. bd. trustees, 1962-77, spl. asst. to pres., 1977—; gen. counsel, officer, dir. Univ. Interstate Corp., also Country Home for Convalescent Children, 1962—. Trustee Chgo. Sinai Congregation, 1976—. Mem. Am., Fed., Ill., Chgo. bar assns., Nat. Assn. Coll. and Univ. Attys. (charter). Home: 1243 E 50th St Chicago IL 60615 Office: 5801 S Ellis Ave Chicago IL 60637 Tel (312) 753-4004

LEEPSON, PETER LAWRENCE, b. N.Y.C., July 2, 1941; B.A., Brandeis U., 1963; LL.D., Fordham U., 1966. Admitted to N.Y. bar, 1966; asso. firm DeForest Elder & Mulreany, N.Y.C., 1966-68; asso. atty. CBS, N.Y.C., 1968-69; asso. firm Leepson, Rubman & Ross, N.Y.C., 1969—. Mem. N.Y. Bar Assn. (com. real estate trusts estates). Recipient Am. Jurisprudence prize Estate Planning Excellence, 1966. Home: 24 Canal Rd Westport CT 06880 Office: 230 Park Ave New York City NY Tel (212) 661-2929

LEES, MATTHEW NELSON, b. Phila., May 1, 1940; A.B., Ind. U., 1964, J.D., 1967. Admitted to Ind. bar, 1967, Calif. bar, 1971; served to capt. JAGC, U.S. Army, 1967-72; trial atty. Fed. Defender Orgn. of San Diego, 1972-73; individual practice law, San Diego, 1973—; asso. prof. Western State Coll. Law, 1972—. Mem. Am., Calif., San Diego County trial lawyers assns., Calif., San Diego bar assns., San Diego Def. Bar Assn. Decorated Bronze Star; recipient Valley Forge Freedom Found. award 1969. Office: 916 Union St San Diego CA 92101 Tel (714) 232-1122

LEFF, ARTHUR ALLEN, b. N.Y.C., Jan. 6, 1935; B.A., Amherst Coll., 1956; LL.B., Harvard, 1959; M.A. (hon.), Yale, 1971. Admitted to N.Y. bar, 1960, U.S. Supreme Ct. bar, 1968; clk. Honorable Irving R. Kaufman, Chief Judge 2d Circuit U.S. Ct. Appeals, 1959-60; asso. firm Fried, Frank, Harris, Shriver, Jacobson, N.Y.C., 1960-64; asst. prof. Washington U., St. Louis, 1964-67, asso. prof., 1967-68; asso. prof. law Yale, 1968-71, prof., 1971—. Mem. Am. Econ. Assn. Nat. Endowment for Humanities fellow, 1972-73; Guggenheim Memorial Found. grantee, 1976; author: Swindling and Selling, 1976. Office: Yale Law School New Haven CT 06520 Tel (203) 436-4707

LEFFLER, RAYMOND G., b. Bklyn., June 1, 1932; B.A., U. City N.Y., 1954; J.D., Columbia, 1957. Admitted to N.Y. State bar, 1958, U.S. Supreme Ct. bar, 1970; former partner firm Leffler and Landau, 1976; prof. law Baruch Coll., 1976—; individual practice law, N.Y.C., 1976—; judge Yonkers, N.Y., 1964. Mem. Arbitration Assn. Author: The Fundamentals of Partnership Law in Modern Business, 1976. Office: 21 E 40th St New York City NY 10016 Tel (212) 889-1922

LEFKOWITZ, EUGENE EDWARD, b. N.Y.C., June 29, 1910; student N.Y. Law Sch., 1933. Admitted to N.Y. State Appellate Div. 2d Dept. bar, 1935; mng. atty., asso. George L. Madden, N.Y.C., 1935-42; individual practice law, N.Y.C., 1945—; arbitrator Small Claims div. N.Y. City Civil Ct. Trustee Temple Beth Sholom, Flushing, N.Y., 1973-75, v.p., 1975-77. Mem. Am. Judges Assn., Am. Judicature Soc., Queens County Bar Assn., Fedn. Jewish Philanthropies. Home: 45-54 166th St Flushing NY 11358 Office: 366 Broadway New York City NY 10013 Tel (212) 732-7268

LEFKOWITZ, LAWRENCE, b. N.Y.C., Feb. 5, 1938; A.B., Franklin and Marshall Coll., 1959; J.D., Columbia, 1962. Admitted to N.Y. bar, 1962; atty.-examiner U.S. Securities and Exchange Commn., Washington, 1962-64; asso. firm Guzik and Boukstein, N.Y.C., 1964-69, partner, 1969-73; partner firm Reavis & McGrath, N.Y.C., 1973—. Chmn. Hartsdale (N.Y.) Pub. Parking Dist., 1973—. Mem. Am. Bar Assn. Office: 1 Chase Manhattan Plaza New York City NY 10005 Tel (212) 269-7600

LEFKOWITZ, LOUIS J., b. N.Y.C., July 3, 1904; LL.B. cum laude, Fordham U., 1925. Admitted to N.Y. bar, 1926; pvt. practice law, N.Y.C.; justice Municipal Ct., N.Y.C., 1935, City Ct., 1954; atty. gen. N.Y.; Albany, 1957—. Mem. N.Y. Assembly, 1928-30; del. Republican Nat. Conv., 1944, 48, alt. del., 1956. Active numerous civic activities, Bd. dirs. Florence Crittenton League. Mem. Assn. Bar. City N.Y., N.Y. County Lawyers Assn., Fed., Am. bar assns., Nat. Assn. Attys. Gen. (pres.), Assn. Lawyers Criminal Cts. Manhattan, Grand St. Boys Assn., Am. Jewish Congress. Home: 575 Park Ave New York City NY 10021 Office: 80 Centre St New York City NY 10013 also The Capitol Albany NY 12201*

LEFLAR, ROBERT ALLEN, b. Siloam Springs, Ark., Mar. 22, 1901; B.A., U. Ark., 1922; LL.B., Harvard, 1927; S.J.D., 1932. Admitted to Ark. bar, 1928, U.S. Supreme Ct. bar, 1942; with U. Ark., Fayetteville, 1927—, distinguished prof. law, 1956—, dean law sch., 1942-54; prof. law N.Y. U., 1954—; vis. prof. law U. Kans., Lawrence, 1932-33, U. Mo., Columbia, 1936-37, U. Colo., Boulder, 1952, U. Okla., Norman, 1972, 73-74, Vanderbilt U., Nashville, 1972-73; asso. justice Ark. Supreme Ct., 1949-51; chmn. Ark. Statute Revision Commn., 1947-54; pres. Ark. State Constl. Conv., 1968-70; commr. on Uniform State Laws, 1945—. Mem. Am., Ark., Washington County bar assns., Nat. Conf. Commrs. on Uniform State Laws. Author: Arkansas Law of Conflict of Laws, 1938; American Conflicts Law, 1968; The First 100 Years: Centennial History of University of Arkansas, 1972; Appellate Judicial Opinions, 1975; Internal Operating Procedures of Appellate Courts, 1976; contbr. articles to legal jours. Home: 1717 W Center St Fayetteville AR 72701 Office: Sch Law U Ark Fayetteville AR 72701

LEFRAK, JOSEPH SAUL, b. N.Y.C., Sept. 23, 1930; B.S., N.Y. U., 1952; LL.B., Bklyn. Law Sch., 1955, J.D., 1955. Admitted to N.Y. State bar, 1955, U.S. Supreme Ct. bar, 1960; partner firm Winter & Lefrak, C.P.A.'s., N.Y.C., 1959-66, Blackman Lefrak & Blackman, C.P.A.'s, N.Y.C., 1966-72; partner firms Blackman Lefrak Feld & Fischer, N.Y.C., 1966-76, Lefrak Fischer Myersch & Mandell, N.Y.C., 1976—. Bd. dirs. Asso. Camps, N.Y.C., Reece Sch., N.Y.C.; trustee, v.p. Congregation Rodeph Sholom, N.Y.C. Mem. Assn. Bar City N.Y., Am. Bar Assn., N.Y. State, Am. assns. attys.-C.P.A.'s., Am. Inst. C.P.A.'s., Young Men's Philanthropic League. C.P.A., N.Y. Home: 983 Park Ave New York City NY 10028 Office: 424 Madison Ave New York City NY 10017 Tel (212) 421-7633

LEFSTEIN, STUART RONALD, b. Rock Island, Ill., Jan. 7, 1934; A.B., Augustana Coll., Rock Island, 1955; LL.B., U. Mich., 1958. Admitted to Ill. bar, 1958, U.S. Supreme Ct. bar, 1973; asst. state's atty. Rock Island County, Ill., 1958-59; partner firms Ferguson & Lefstein, Rock Island, 1959-64, Katz, McAndrews, Durkee & Telleen, Rock Island, 1964—; hearing officer Ill. Fair Employment Practices Commn., 1971-75; instr. Augustana Coll. Bus. Law, 1976-77. Trustee Black Hawk Jr. Coll., 1970-74. Mem. Rock Island County, Ill. State, Am. bar assns., Am. Judicature Soc., Nat. Legal Aid and Defender Assn., Appellate Lawyers Assn. Ill., Ill. Def. Counsel. Author monograph: Wrongful Death: More Than Survivors Survive, 1975. Home: 3312 34th Ave Ct Rock Island IL 61201 Office: 200 Cleaveland Bldg Rock Island IL 61201 Tel (309) 788-5661

LEGENDRE, JOHN PETER, b. St. Louis, Jan. 23, 1938; B.S., U. Ill., 1961; J.D., U. Tex. Austin, 1967; LL.M., So. Meth. U., 1974. Admitted to Tex. bar, 1967; asso. firm Humphrey, Gibson and Darden, Wichita Falls, Tex., 1967-70; atty. Texas and Pacific R.R. Co., Dallas, 1970-76; commerce counsel Mo. Pacific R.R. Co., Dallas, 1976—. Mem. Am., Tex., Dallas bar assns., Dallas Internat. Law Assn. Contbr. articles to profl. jours. Home: 5831 Caladium St Dallas TX 75230 Office: 505 N Industrial Blvd Dallas TX 75207 Tel (214) 748-8181

LEGG, REAGAN HOUSTON, b. Kaufman, Tex., Nov. 18, 1924; B.B.A., U. Tex., 1947, LL.B., 1948. Admitted to Tex. bar, 1948, U.S. Supreme Ct. bar, 1961, U.S. Dist. Cts., Tex., 5th Circuit Ct. Appeals. Individual practice law, Midland, Tex., 1949-51; county atty., Midland County, Tex., 1951-55; partner law firm Legg, Saxe & Baskin, and predecessor firm, Midland, 1959—. Mem. bd. regents Permian Jr. Coll. System, 1970-73; mem. Permian Basin Regional Planning Commn., 1977—; chmn. Permian Basin Multiple Sclerosis Soc., 1968-71, others. Pres. bd. trustees Midland Coll.; pres. bd. govs. Midland Community Theater. Mem. Am., Midland County bar assns., Tex. Trial Lawyers Assn., Am. Jurisprudence Soc., Midland C. of C. (pres. bd. dirs. 1969-71). Home: 902 Country Club Dr Midland TX 79701 Office: PO Box 107 1000 Midland Savs Bldg Midland TX 79701

LEGG, ROGER ELLIOTT, b. Glen Ridge, N.J., Aug. 12, 1937; A.B., DePauw U., 1959; J.D., U. Mich., 1962; M.B.A., U. Pa., 1964. Admitted to N.J. bar, 1962, Pa. bar, 1972; asso. firm Stryker, Tams & Dill, Newark, 1964-66; labor relations counsel Sinclair Oil Corp., Chgo., 1966-69, Atlantic Richfield Co., Phila., 1969-72; partner firm Gawthrop & Greenwood, West Chester, Pa., 1972—. Mem. Pa., N.J. bar assns. Home: Highland Eyrie Coatesville PA 19320 Office: 409 W Lincoln Hwy Exton PA 19341 Tel (215) 363-1717

LEGG, WILBUR STEPHEN, b. Bloomington, Ind., May 26, 1922; A.B., Ind. U., 1944; LL.B., Harvard, 1949. Admitted to Ind. bar, 1949, Ill. bar, 1950; mem. staff Ill. Commerce Commn., 1949-52; asso. firm Lord, Bissell & Brook, Chgo., 1953-57, partner, 1958—. Mem. village council Village of Winnetka, Ill., 1975—. Mem. Am., Ill. (del. assembly 1974—), Chgo. bar assns., Law Club Chgo., Univ. Club. Home: 765 Sheridan Rd Winnetka IL 60093 Office: 115 S LaSalle St Suite 3400 Chicago IL 60603

LEGGE, WINSTON VAUGHAN, JR., b. Athens, Ala., July 4, 1939; B.S., U. Ala., 1962; J.D. cum laude, Samford U., 1969. Admitted to Ala. bar, 1969, U.S. Supreme Ct. bar, 1973; partner firm Patton Latham & Legge, Athens, Ala., 1971—. Mem. Limestone County Democratic exec. com., Athens-Limestone Devel. Com.; commr. Tennessee Valley council Boy Scouts Am. Mem. Limestone County (pres. 1973-75), Am. bar assns., Curia Honoris, Athens-Limestone C. of C. Contbr. articles to legal jours. Home: 307 S Beaty St Athens AL 35611 Office: 315 W Market St Athens AL 35611 Tel (205) 232-2010

LEGLER, MITCHELL WOOTEN, b. Alexandria, Va., June 3, 1942; B.A. in Polit. Sci. with honors, U. N.C., 1964; J.D., U. Va., 1967. Admitted to Va. bar, 1967, Fla. bar, 1967; partner firm Commander & Legler, Jacksonville, Fla., 1976—; chmn. Fla. Bar Consumer Protection Law Com. Chmn. sch. bd. St. Andrews Episcopal Day Sch., Jacksonville. Mem. bar assns. Va., Fla. (lectr. continuing legal edn.), Order of Coif, Phi Beta Kappa, Phi Eta Sigma, Delta Upsilon, Delta Theta Phi. Editorial bd. Va. Law Rev., 1966-67. Office: Suite 2000 Independent Sq Jacksonville FL 32202 Tel (904) 354-0424

LEGRAND, CLAY, b. St. Louis, Feb. 26, 1911; LL.B., Cath. U. Am., 1934. Admitted to Iowa bar, 1934; practice law, Davenport, Iowa, 1934-57; judge Dist. Ct., 1957-67; justice Iowa Supreme Ct., 1967—; lectr. St. Ambrose Coll., 1957-67. Mem. law alumni council Cath. U. Am. Law Sch. Recipient award for Outstanding Achievement in field of law and cts. Cath. U. Am., 1969; award for Profl. Achievement, St. Ambrose Coll., 1976. Mem. Am., Iowa, Scott County bar assns., Am. Judicature Soc. Inst. Jud. Adminstrn. Home: Rural Route LeClaire IA 52753 Office: State House Des Moines IA 50319 Tel (515) 281-5174

LEHMAN, STANLEY ALLEN, b. Abilene, Kans., Apr. 29, 1938; B.A., Kans. U., 1960, postgrad. U. Kans., 1960-61; J.D., U. Ariz., 1963; intern pub. affairs, Coro Found. Los Angeles, 1963-64. Admitted to Ariz. bar, 1963, Calif. bar, 1965; intern job devel. div. East Los Angeles Youth Tng. and Employment, 1964-65; mem. firm Gorey & Ely, Phoenix, Ariz., 1965-66; asso. firm Gerald Machmer, Phoenix, 1966-67; partner firm Machmer & Lehman, Phoenix, 1968-71; asso. firm Locklear & Wolfinger, Prescott, Ariz., 1971-73; individual practice law Prescott and Cottonwood, Ariz., 1973—; law clk. U.S. Atty.'s Office, Tucson, 1962-63; legal cons. OEO, Legal Services Div., Seattle, 1970. Pres. Yavapai Easter Seal Soc., 1974-75; chmn. bd. dirs. Yavapai Community Hosp., 1975-76; v.p. bd. dirs. Ariz. Christian Conf. Youth and Adult Problems, 1967. Mem. Young Lawyers Maricopa County (pres. 1965-66), Young Lawyers Ariz. (pres. 1971-72), Yavapai County, (pres. 1975-76), Los Angeles County, Am. bar assns., Omicron Delta Kappa. Home: 53 Hassayampa Country Club Prescott AZ 86301 Office: 106 N Cortez St Prescott AZ 86301 Tel (602) 445-9370

LEHMER, MARY CONDAS, b. Salt Lake City, Jan. 5, 1919; LL.B., U. Utah, 1940, J.D., 1968. Admitted to Utah bar, 1941; individual practice law, Salt Lake City, 1941—; atty. NLRB, Washington, 1942-43; city atty. Park City (Utah), 1968-70; mem. city council Park City, 1972-76. Trustee YWCA, Salt Lake City, 1968-74; commr. Park City Fire Protection Dist., 1976-77. Mem. Utah State Bar Assn., Bus. and Profl. Women of Utah, AAUW. Recipient Woman of Year award Bus. and Profl. Women Assn. Utah, 1952. Home: Box 626 Deer Valley Rd Park City UT 84060 Office: 4528 S 2070 East Salt Lake City UT 84117 Tel (801) 278-9687

LEHNARDT, DETLEF GUNTER, b. Berlin, May 7, 1941; B.A., U. Pa., 1966, J.D., 1969. Admitted to N.Y. bar, 1970, Utah bar, 1972; asso. firms Reid & Priest, N.Y.C., 1969-70, Kirton, McConkie, Boyer & Boyle, Salt Lake City, 1971-72; prosecutor U.S. Army, Ft. Ord, Calif., 1970, chief cts. and bds., 1971; asso. firm Walter, Conston, Schurtman & Gumpel, N.Y.C., 1973-75, mem., 1975—. Mem. ednl. com. Town Club, Scarsdale, N.Y., 1975—. Mem. Assn. Bar City N.Y. Contbr. to U. Pa. Law Rev. Home: 8 Elm Rd Scarsdale NY 10583 Office: 280 Park Ave New York City NY 10017 Tel (212) 682-2323

LEHNER, ROBERT JOSEPH, b. N.Y.C., Sept. 1, 1936; B.A., Columbia, 1957, LL.B., 1961. Admitted to N.Y. State bar, 1961; asst. dist. atty. New York County, N.Y.C., 1961—, bur. chief, homicide bur., 1973-76, sr. trial counsel, 1976; dep. chief counsel Ho. of Reps. Com. Assassinations, Washington, 1976—. Mem. N.Y. State Dist. Attys. Assn. (mem. legis. coms. 1974—). Home: 560 N St SW Apt N914 Washington DC 20024 Office: Ho of Reps Com Assassinations Washington DC 20515

LEHRKINDER, DONALD WILLIAM, b. Union City, N.J., July 16, 1923; A.B., Muhlenberg Coll., Allentown, Pa., 1946; J.D., Temple U., 1949. Admitted to Pa. bar, 1950, U.S. Supreme Ct. bar, 1960; asso. with Edward D. McLaughlin, Chester, Pa., 1950-57; partner firm Lehrkinder & Gillingham, Media, Pa., 1957—. Bd. dirs. Delaware County Legal Assistance, Springfield Symphony Soc., 1965-70. Mem. Pa., Delaware County bar assns., Am. Judicature Soc., Am. Arbitration Assn. Home: 165 Hart Ln Springfield PA 19064 Office: 217 N Olive St Media PA 19063 Tel (215) LO6-7333

LEHRMAN, JAY JACOB, b. N.Y.C., June 26, 1902; LL.B., N.Y. Law Sch., 1927. Admitted to N.Y. bar, 1928; individual practice law, N.Y.C., 1935—, Bklyn., 1928-35; mem. indigent defendant's legal panel, appellate div. 1st Jud. dept. Mem. N.Y. County Lawyers Assn., N.Y. Law Sch. Alumni Assn. Office: 11 Park Pl New York City NY 10007 Tel (212) 227-3080

LEHRMAN, STEPHEN JAY, b. N.Y.C., June 22, 1945; B.A., Boston U., 1966; J.D., Bklyn. Law Sch., 1969. Admitted to N.Y. bar, 1970; asso. firm Heiko & Bush, N.Y.C., 1971-73; sr. asso. firm Myron Marcus, White Plains, N.Y., 1973-75; asso. firm Fink, Weinberger, Fredman & Charney, White Plains, 1975—. Mem. Am., N.Y., Westchester County, White Plains bar assns. Office: 235 Main St White Plains NY 10601 Tel (914) 761-7550

LEIBOLD, ARTHUR WILLIAM, b. Ottawa, Ill., June 13, 1931; A.B., Haverford Coll., 1953; J.D., U. Pa., 1956. Admitted to Pa. bar, 1957, D.C. bar, 1972; asso. firm Dechert Price & Rhoads, Phila., 1956-65, partner, 1965-69, Washington, 1972—; gen. counsel Fed. Home Loan Bank Bd. and Fed. Savs. & Loan Ins. Corp., Washington, 1969-72, Fed. Home Loan Mortgage Corp., Washington, 1970-72; mem. Pres's. Lawyers Com. on Civil Rights, 1963. Mem. Phila. Com. of 70, 1965-74; mem. Adminstrv. Conf. U.S., 1969-72. Mem. Am. (ho. of dels. 1967-69), Fed. (nat. council 1971—), Phila., D.C. bar assns., Juristic Soc., Order of Coif, Phi Beta Kappa. Contbr. numerous articles to profl. publs. Office: 888 17th St NW Washington DC 20006 Tel (202) 872-8600

LEIBOWITT, S. DAVID, b. N.Y.C., Feb. 18, 1912; B.A., Lehigh U., 1933; J.D., Harvard, 1936. Admitted to N.Y. bar, 1937, Conn. bar, 1971; individual practice law, N.Y.C., 1937—, Stamford, Conn., 1971—; sec., dir. Behavioral Research Lab., Inc. (Calif.); pres., dir. Apco Capital Corp. Pres., Am. Soc. Technion UN, Conn., 1970—, also dir.; mem. nat. com. Anti-Defamation League, 1974—; nat. v.p. Union Orthodox Congregations of Am., 1969-73. Mem. Am., N.Y. State bar assns., Assn. Bar City N.Y., Am. Arbitration Assn. (panel), Phi Beta Kappa. Recipient human relations award Anti-Defamation League, 1969, spl. award, 1971. Home: 2 Fanton Hill Weston CT 06883 Office: 300 Broad St Stamford CT 06901 Tel (203) 325-3828

LEIBOWITZ, EPHRAIM KING, b. N.Y.C., June 28, 1929; A.B., Bklyn. Coll., 1951; LL.B., N.Y. U., 1954. Admitted to N.Y. bar, 1956, U.S. Supreme Ct. bar, 1957; partner firm Leibowitz, Platzer & Fineberg, N.Y.C., 1961—. Mem. N.Y. County Lawyers Assn. Author: New Bankruptcy Guide for Petition, Schedules and Statement of Affairs, 1976; contbr. monthly column to legal jour. Office: 1500 Broadway St New York City NY 10036 Tel (212) 730-1144

LEIBOWITZ, LEONARD, b. Bklyn., Dec. 15, 1938; B.A., Bucknell U., 1960; J.D., Bklyn. Law Sch., 1965. Admitted to N.Y. bar, 1965; mem. firm Cohn & Glickstein, N.Y.C., 1965-69, firm Leder, Bogen & Leibowitz, Flushing, N.Y., 1969-71; partner firm Sipser, Weinstock, Harper, Dorn & Leibowitz, N.Y.C., 1971—. Home: 120 W 86th St New York City NY 10024 Office: 380 Madison Ave New York City NY 10017

LEIBOWITZ, SAUL RUBEN, b. Chgo., July 7, 1943; B.S. in English, Loyola U., Chgo., 1966; J.D., Northwestern U., 1969. Admitted to Ill. bar, 1969, U.S. Supreme Ct. bar, 1973; vice-pres. Wis. Iron & Metal Co., Chgo., 1964-70, pres., 1970—; individual practice law, Chgo., 1970—. Mem. Am., Ill., Chgo. (chmn. defense of prisoners com.) bar assns., Chgo. Council of Lawyers, Appellate Lawyers Assn., Am. Judicature Soc., Bar Assn. 7th Fed. Circuit, Decalogue Soc. of Lawyers. Office: 7 S Dearborn St Suite 1012 Chicago IL 60603 Tel (312) 641-7170

LEIDERMAN, ROBERT JOSEPH, b. Chattanooga, Oct. 21, 1942; B.S., U. Chattanooga, 1968; J.D., U. Tenn., 1969. Admitted to Tenn. bar, 1969, U.S. Dist. Ct. bar, 1970; asst. city atty. Chattanooga, 1969-70; asso. firm Collins & Seal, Chattanooga, 1969-70; partner firm Kelly, Leiderman & Kelly, Jasper, Tenn., 1970—; asst. dist. atty gen. State of Tenn., 1970-75; city atty., Jasper, 1973—; county atty., Marion County, 1970—; city atty., Kimball, Tenn., 1976. Sec.-treas. Marion County Speech and Hearing Clinic, 1973-75; bd. dirs. Moccasin Bend Mental Health Center, Chattanooga, 1974—; sec.-treas. Marion County Democratic Party, 1972-75. Mem. Am., Tenn., Marion County Hamilton County bar assns., Am., Tenn. trial lawyers assns. Recipient Outstanding Community Service award as legal counsel Jasper Jaycees, 1975-76. Office: Betsy Pack Dr Jasper TN 37347 Tel (615) 942-3495

LEIDNER, NELSON J., b. Phila., Apr. 6, 1912; B.S. in Econs., U. Pa., 1933, LL.B., 1936; LL.M., U. N.Z., 1943. Admitted to Pa. bar, 1936; partner firm Leidner & Leidner, Phila., 1936-41, 46-47; v.p. Rosenau Bros., Inc., Phila., 1953-59, exec. v.p., 1959-67; v.p. 1st Pa. Bank N.A., Phila., 1967-77. Chmn. womens and childrens apparel div. United Fund, Phila., 1952-54; city del. Community Chest, 1956-58; chmn. deferred gift and bequest program U. Pa., 1960; trustee United Campaign Fund, 1963-66, Phila. Orch. Assn., Acad. Music; mem. mens fund raising com. Abington Meml. Hosp.; treas., bd. dirs. Prisoners Family Welfare Assn., Spl. award, 1977; cons. United Way Southeastern Pa., 1976-77. Mem. Am., Pa., Phila. bar assns., Lawyers Club Phila. Decorated Order Brit. Empire. Home: 1425 Grasshopper Rd Huntingdon Valley PA 19006 Office: 1300 Two Penn Center Plaza Philadelphia PA 19102 Tel (215) 241-8160

LEIFER, LARRY LEWIS, b. Newark, Aug. 15, 1941; B.S., Coll. Pharmacy, Rutgers U., 1963; J.D., Seton Hall U., 1969. Admitted to N.J. bar, 1969, Fla. bar, 1976; atty. with John W. Taylor, E. Orange, N.J., 1969; asso. firm Friedman & D'Alessandro, E. Orange, 1970-74; individual practice law, E. Orange, 1974-76, Maplewood, N.J., 1977—; lectr. Rutgers U. Coll. Pharmacy, 1977. Mem. Am., N.J. State, Essex County bar assns., Am., N.J. trial lawyers assns. Home: 30 Connel Dr West Orange NJ 07052 Office: 7 Highland Pl Maplewood NJ 07040 Tel (201) 763-8555

LEIGH, MONROE, b. South Boston, Va., July 15, 1919; B.A., Hampden-Sydney Coll., 1940; LL.B., U. Va., 1947. Admitted to Va. bar, 1947, D.C. bar, 1948, U.S. Supreme Ct. bar, 1950; asso. firm Covington, Burling, Rublee, Acheson & Shorb and successors, Washington, 1947-51; mem. UN Mission to North Atlantic Council, London, 1951-52, Paris, 1953-53; dep. asst. gen. counsel for internat. affairs Office Sec. of Def., Washington, 1953-55, asst. gen. counsel for internat. affairs, 1955-59; asso. firm Steptoe & Johnson, Washington, 1959-61, partner, 1961-75, 77—; legal adviser Dept. State, Washington, 1975-77; mem. U.S. Nat. Group on Permanent Court Arbitration, The Hague, 1975—; lectr. U. Va. Law Sch., 1964-75; mem. advisory com. Parker Sch. Fgn. Law Columbia U., Procedural Aspects of Internat. Law Inst.; mem. advisory bd. Internat. and Comparative Law Center Southwestern Legal Found. Mem. Am. Bar Assn., Am. Law Inst., Am. Soc. Internat. Law (hon. v.p.), Internat. Law Assn. (bd. editors Am. Jour. Internat. Law 1974-75, 77—), Council Fgn. Relations, Washington Inst. Fgn. Affairs, Order of Coif. Contbr. articles to legal jours.; decisions editor Va. Law Rev., 1946, editor-in-chief, 1946-47; bd. advisers George Washington U. Jour. Internat. Law and Econs., 1975—; adv. bd. Va. Jour. Internat. Law, 1976—. Home: 5205 Westwood Dr Washington DC 20016 Office: 1250 Connecticut Ave Washington DC 20036 Tel (202) 862-2072 also Internat Ct Justice Peace Palace The Hague 2012 Netherlands

LEIGH, THOMAS WATKINS, b. Winnsboro, La., Apr. 8, 1903; LL.B., La. State U., 1924. Admitted to La. bar, 1924, U.S. Supreme Ct. bar, 1948; individual practice law, Monroe, La., 1924-27; asso. firm Theus, Grisham Davis & Leigh and predecessor, Monroe, 1927-29, partner, 1929—; del. La. Constnl. Conv., 1973. Bd. suprs. La. State U., 1940-60, chmn., 1950-52; chmn. La. Mineral Bd., 1966-72; bd. dirs. Council for a Better La., 1973—. Fellow Am. Bar Found.; mem. La. State (pres. 1954-55), Am. (ho. of dels. 1958—, gov. 1975—) bar assns., Am. Coll. Trial Lawyers, Am. Coll. Probate Counsel, Am. Judicature Soc., Order of Coif. Home: 1401 S Grand St Monroe LA 71202 Office: 1303 Bancroft Circle Monroe LA 71203 Tel (318) 388-0100

LEIGHNER, WILLIAM HUESTON, b. Pitts., Dec. 8, 1929; B.S., Northwestern U., 1952; J.D., U. Mich., 1958. Admitted to Ohio bar, 1958; asso. and partner firm Bricker, Evatt, Barton & Eckler, Columbus, Ohio, 1958—. Mem. Columbus, Ohio, Am. bar assns. Home: 1110 Regency Dr Columbus OH 43220 Office: 100 E Broad St Columbus OH 43215 Tel (614) 221-6651

LEIGHTON, RICHARD JOSEPH, b. N.Y.C., Oct. 16, 1939; B.A., Pa. State U., 1962; J.D., Am. U., 1970. Admitted to Md. bar, 1971, D.C. bar, 1971, U.S. Ct. Appeals bar, 1973, U.S. Supreme Ct. bar, 1975; resident Washington counsel firm Vorys, Sater, Seymour & Pease, 1975-77; mng. partner firm Leighton & Conklin, Washington, 1977—. Mem. Md. State, Fed., Am. bar assns. Contbr. articles to profl. jours. Office: 2033 M St NW Washington DC 20036 Tel (202) 785-4800

LEINENWEBER, HARRY DANIEL, b. Joliet, Ill., June 3, 1937; A.B., U. Notre Dame, 1959; J.D., U. Chgo., 1962. Admitted to Ill. bar, 1962; atty. City of Joliet, 1964-68; spl. prosecutor Will County (Ill.) Circuit Ct., 1968-70; mem. Ill. Ho. of Reps., 1973—, minority spokesman, judiciary com., 1977—. Mem. Ill., Will County bar assns. Home: 613 Catherine St Joliet IL 60435 Office: 81 N Chicago St Joliet IL 60431 Tel (815) 726-4776

LEISTER, CRAIG DOUGLAS, b. Alliance, Ohio, Dec. 25, 1949; B.S. in Bus. Adminstrn., Bowling Green State U., 1971; J.D., Duke U., 1974. Admitted to Ohio bar, 1974, U.S. Ct. Appeals bar, 1975, U.S. Dist. Ct. for So. Dist. Ohio bar, 1975; mem. firm Means, Bichimer, Burkholder & Baker, Columbus, Ohio, 1975—, atty. Judge Adv. Gen. USN, 1974. Mem. Columbus, Ohio State bar assns., Phi Kappa Phi, Beta Gamma Sigma. Office: 50 W Broad St Columbus OH 43215 Tel (614) 221-3135

LEISURE, PETER KEETON, b. N.Y.C., Mar. 21, 1929; B.A., Yale U., 1952; LL.B., U. Va., 1958. Admitted to N.Y. bar, 1959, U.S. Supreme Ct. bar, 1966; since practiced in N.Y.C., asso. firm Breed Abbott & Morgan, 1958-61; asst. U.S. atty. So. Dist. N.Y., 1962-66; partner firm Curtis Mallet-Prevost Colt & Mosle, 1967—; lectr. Practicing Law Inst., 1968-70. Bd. dirs. Retarded Infants Services, 1968—, pres., 1971-75; bd. dirs. Community Council of Greater N.Y., 1972—, Youth Consultation Services, 1971—; trustee Ch. Club of N.Y., 1973—. Fellow Am. Bar Found., Am. Coll. Trial Lawyers, Am. Law Inst.; mem. Am., N.Y. State, City of N.Y. bar assns., Fed. Bar Council (trustee, v.p. 1973—, mem. com. 2d circuit cts. 1974—). Contbr. articles to legal jours. Home: 1185 Park Ave New York City NY 10028 Office: 100 Wall St New York City NY 10028 Tel (212) 248-8111

LEITCH, JOHN DAVID, JR., b. Norfolk, Va., Sept. 30, 1917; student U. Grenoble (France), 1934, Coll. William and Mary, 1936; B.A., U. Va., 1940, J.D., 1942. Admitted to Va. bar, 1941; individual practice law, Norfolk, 1946—; commr. in chancery City of Virginia Beach (Va.), 1949-76; asst. trial justice Princess Anne County (Va.), 1951-56. Mem. Va. State Bar, Norfolk-Portsmouth Bar Assn. Home: 4184 N Witchduck Rd Virginia Beach VA 23455 Office: 504 Law Bldg Norfolk VA 23510 Tel (804) 625-2972

LEITH, JEFFREY BRIAN, b. San Francisco, Mar. 16, 1943; B.A., U. San Francisco, 1964, J.D., 1967. Admitted to Calif. bar, 1970; with Operating Engrs. Local Union 3, San Francisco, 1971-72; individual practice law, San Francisco, 1972—. Mem. San Francisco Mayor's Com. for Civic Planning, 1972. Mem. San Francisco Bar Assn. Home: 2814 Pine St San Francisco CA 94115 Tel (415) 921-1727

LEITMAN, EDDIE, b. Birmingham, Ala., May 15, 1941; B.S. in Bus. Adminstrn., U. Ala., 1963, LL.B., 1966. Admitted to Ala. bar, 1966; since practiced in Birmingham, asso. firm Berkowitz, Lefkovits & Patrick, 1968-70, partner, 1970-76. Vice-pres. Temple Emanuel Men's Group, 1976; dir. Birmingham Jewish Fedn., 1974; mem. Birmingham Jewish Com. Counsel, 1974; dir. Anti-Defamation League, 1973; chmn. St. Vincent's Hosp. Gala. Mem. Ala., Am., Birmingham bar assns., Ala. Trial Lawyers Assn., Birmingham C. of C. Home: 3588 Spring Hill Rd Birmingham AL 35223 Office: 1400 City Nat Bank Bldg Birmingham AL 35203 Tel (205) 328-0480

LEJNIEKS, JOHN HARRY, b. Detmold, Germany, May 17, 1946; came to U.S., 1951, naturalized, 1957; A.B., Calif. State U., Long Beach, 1969; J.D., Hastings Coll. Law, 1973. Admitted to Calif. bar, 1973; asso. law offices Paul Kennedy, Jr., Irvine, Calif., 1973—. Mem. Am., Orange County bar assns., Orange County Barristers Club. Office: 18662 MacArthur Blvd #106 Irvine CA 92715 Tel (714) 833-8486

LELONEK, RICHARD LOUIS, b. Canonsburg, Pa., Mar. 9, 1926; A.A., U. Balt., J.D., 1953. Admitted to Md. bar, 1957; adminstr. budget controls B. & O. R.R.; supr. budgets and personnel, dept. mdse. traffic C. & O. R.R., Balt. Vice pres. Belair-Edison Improvement Assn., 1955-65, pres. 1965-75, pres. emeritus, 1975—; mem. mayor's adv. com. on criminal justice, 1974—; mem. city planning commn., 1976—. Mem. Md. Bar Assn. Home: 4026 Elmora Ave Baltimore MD 21213 Tel (301) 237-3542

LEMANN, ARTHUR ANTHONY, III, b. Augusta, Ga., May 14, 1942; B.A., Tulane U.; LL.B., Loyola U. of South, New Orleans, 1967; LL.M., George Washington U., 1968. Admitted to La. bar, 1967; asso. firm Polack, Rosenberg & Rittenberg, New Orleans, 1968-69; of counsel firm Marullo & Mora, New Orleans, 1970-71; asst. prof. law Loyola U. of South, 1970-73, asso. prof., 1974—, dir. law clinic, 1970—; research supr. La. Constl. Conv., 1973; commr. La. Commn. on Law Enforcement and Adminstrn. Criminal Justice, 1974—; mem. New Orleans Criminal Justice Coordinating Council, 1976. Pres. Young Democrats, New Orleans, 1971, pres. La., 1971-73, nat. committeeman, 1973-74; bd. dirs. Community Service Center, New Orleans, 1975-76. Mem. Am., La. (bd. govs. 1973-75), New Orleans Criminal bar assns., Am., La. trial lawyers assns., Nat. Assn. Criminal Def. Lawyers. Editor-in-chief Loyola Law Rev., 1966-67. Home: 6301 Constance St New Orleans LA 70118 Office: PO Box 49 6363 St Charles Ave New Orleans LA 70118 Tel (504) 865-3130

LEMAY, PAULETTE MARIE, b. Paterson, N.J., Sept. 17, 1940; A.B., Vassar Coll., 1962; LL.B., U. Pa., 1965. Admitted to N.J. bar, 1965; law clk. to judge Superior Ct. Middlesex County (N.J.), 1965-66; asso. firm Cole, Berman & Belsky, Paterson, 1966-69; individual practice law, Paterson, 1969; sr. editor Prentice-Hall, Inc., Englewood Cliffs, N.J., 1969-73; asso. gen. counsel Unishops, Inc., Jersey City, 1973—. Sec., Paterson Mayor's Charter Study Commn., 1969. Mem. Am., N.J. bar assns. Fellow Hague Acad. Internat. Law, The Hague, Netherlands, 1964. Office: 21 Caven Point Ave Jersey City NJ 07305 Tel (201) 433-0100

LEMEN, WILLIAM LAURENCE, b. San Juan, Tex., Apr. 19, 1926; B.A., U. Tex., 1948, LL.B., 1950. Admitted to Tex. bar, 1950, since practiced in San Juan; partner firm Alamia, Perkin & Lemen, 1958-62; individual practice law, 1950-58, 62—; mayor City of San Juan, 1960-71. Mem. Am., Tex., Hidalgo County bar assns., Phi Delta Phi. Home: 118 E 8th St San Juan TX 78589 Office: PO Box 54 511 Standard Ave San Juan TX 78589 Tel (512) 787-3393 also (512) 787-9441

LEMLECH, BERNARD, b. Los Angeles, Jan. 26, 1924; B.S. in Accounting, U. Calif., Los Angeles, 1950, J.D., 1958. Accountant, Irving Klubok & Co., C.P.A.'s., Los Angeles, 1950-53; accountant Kenneth Leventhal & Co., C.P.A.'s., Los Angeles, 1958-67, partner, 1967—; admitted to Calif. bar, 1959. Mem. Calif. State Soc. C.P.A's., Am. Inst. C.P.A's., Beverly Hills (Calif.), Los Angeles County bar assns., Calif. State Bar. Office: 2049 Century Park E 17th floor Los Angeles CA 90067 Tel (213) 277-0880

LEMPERT, DENNIS ALAN, b. Bronx, N.Y., Mar. 18, 1943; B.S., N.Y. U., 1963; LL.B. (now J.D.), Bklyn. Coll., 1966. Admitted to N.Y. bar, 1966, Calif. bar, 1968; atty. IRS, San Francisco, 1966-68; supervising dep. dist. atty., consumer fraud Santa Clara County (Calif.), San Jose, 1968-76. Mem. Calif. Dist. Attys. Assn. (dir.), Santa Clara County Bar Assn. Office: suite 204 4000 Moorpark Ave San Jose CA 95117 Tel (408) 249-5152

LEMPERT, RICHARD A., b. 1932; B.A., Columbia U., 1953, LL.B., 1955. Asso. firm Haight, Gardner, Poor & Haven, 1958-63; atty. Am. Airlines, Inc., N.Y.C., 1963-70, asst. v.p., asst. gen. counsel, 1970-72, v.p., chief counsel, 1972—. Office: 633 3d Ave New York City NY 10017*

LEMPERT, RICHARD OWEN, b. Hartford, Conn., June 2, 1942; A.B. in Govt. magna cum laude with highest honors, Oberlin Coll., 1964; J.D. summa cum laude, U. Mich., 1968, Ph.D. in Sociology, 1971. Asst. prof. law U. Mich., 1968-72, asso. prof., 1972-74, prof., 1974—; adv. panel law and social scis. NSF, 1976—, subcom. legal indicators Social Sci. Research Council, 1976—. Mem. Am. Sociol. Assn., Law and Soc. Assn., Soc. Am. Law Tchrs., Order Coif, Phi Beta Kappa, Phi Kappa Phi, Tau Beta Alpha. Author: (with Stephen Saltzburg) A Modern Approach to Evidence, 1977. Contbr. numerous articles to legal and sociol. jours.; editorial bd. Law and Soc. Rev., 1972—. Office: Hutchins Hall U of Mich Law Sch Ann Arbor MI 48109 Tel (313) 763-0106

LENEFSKY, SELIG, b. Grodna, Russia, May 1, 1907; LL.B., St. Lawrence U., LL.M., 1929; LL.M., N.Y. U., 1956. Admitted to N.Y. bar, 1930, U.S. Supreme Ct. bar, 1956; individual practice law, N.Y.C., 1930-72; partner firm Lenefsky, Galina, Maas, Berne & Hoffman, N.Y.C., 1972-76, firm Lenefsky & Lenefsky, 1976—. Mem. Queens, N.Y. County bar assns. Home: 93-54 Queens Blvd New York City NY 11374 Office: 477 Madison Ave New York City NY 10018 Tel (212) 962-7200

LENGA, ROBERT ALLEN, b. Cleve., Jan. 2, 1938; B.A., Bowling Green State U., 1960; J.D., Case Western Res. U., 1964. Admitted to Ohio bar, 1965; asso. firm Harrington, Huxley & Smith, Youngstown, Ohio, 1966-69, partner, 1969—. Mem. Am., Ohio State, Mahoning County bar assns., Ohio Def. Assn. (dist. dir.). Office: 1200 Mahoning Bank Bldg Youngstown OH 44503 Tel (216) 744-1111

LENGYEL, LINDA BRENNER, b. Trenton, N.J., Jan. 11, 1938; B.A., Ursinus Coll., 1959; J.D., Temple U., 1962. Admitted to N.J. bar, 1963; individual practice law, Trenton, 1963—; asst. city atty. Trenton, 1964-68; asst. prof. dept. criminal justice Trenton State Coll., 1970—. Mem. aux. bd. Community Guidance Center; teaching staff Trinity Episcopal Cathedral, Trenton. Mem. N.J., Mercer County bar assns. Home: 5 Mountainview Rd Trenton NJ 08626 Office: 31 S Market St Trenton NJ 08628 Tel (609) 393-2444

LENIHAN, F. THOMAS, b. Westerly, R.I., Feb. 17, 1939; B.S. and A.B., Boston U., 1962; LL.B., Suffolk U., 1966. Admitted to Mass. bar, 1966, R.I. bar, 1966; asso. firm Gillogly, Beals, Tiernan & Sweeney, Providence, 1966-68; individual practice law, Westerly, 1968-70; mem. firm Longolucco, Parrilla & Lenihan, Westerly, 1970—; probate judge Town of Westerly, 1967-69, 72-73; asst. town solicitor Westerly, 1972-74. Mem. Westerly Charter Revision Com., 1967-68. Mem. R.I., Am. bar assns., Am. Trial Lawyers Assn. Home: Wagner Rd Shelter Harbor RI 02891 Office: 43 Broad St Westerly RI 02891 Tel (401) 596-0151

LENNON, WILLIAM FRANCIS, b. Chgo., Mar. 28, 1921; Ph.B., John Carroll U., 1942; J.D., DePaul U., 1949. Admitted to Ill. bar, 1949; individual practice law, Chgo., 1949—; pres. Local 4 Jewelry Workers Union AFL-CIO, 1951, internat. v.p., 1952. Del., Ill. Constl. Conv., 1969-70. Mem. Chgo. Bar Assn. Office: 22 W Monroe St Chicago IL 60603 Tel (312) 263-1515

LENNOX, THOMAS ARTHUR, b. Bklyn., Mar. 4, 1935; B.S. in Chem. Engring., U. Del., 1957; J.D., Temple U., 1967. Admitted to Pa. bar, 1967, U.S. Patent bar, 1969, N.J. bar, 1970; chemist, tech. service, Rohm & Haas, Phila., 1957-62, tech. advisor staff plastics color, 1962-64, engr., asst. product mgr., 1964-66, patent atty., legal div., Phila., 1967-69; with legal div. ESB div. Internat. Nickel Co., Phila., 1969-71; individual practice law, tri-county area Camden County, Berlin, N.J., 1971—; solicitor Cherry Hill Planning Bd.; real estate atty. Atco Nat. Bank; legal counsel for civic assn. and charitable corp., trustee charitable corp. Chmn. Cherry Hill Civic Fedn., 1971; Acolyte Guild Advisor, mem. church council, Lutheran Ch., 1975; scoutmaster South Jersey council Boy Scouts Am., 1971; pres. Cherry Hill Rotary Club., 1976; alumni fund chmn. U. Del., 1968. Mem. Camden County, N.J., Pa., Am. Bar Assns., Phila., Pa. Patent Bar Assns. Recipient Leadership award, Omicron Kappa Delta, U. Del., 1957. Home: 5 Robin Lake Dr Cherry Hill NJ 08003 Office: 47 State Highway 73 Box 127 Berlin NJ 08009 Tel (609) 767-6767

LENSSEN, JOHN L., b. Norwalk, Conn., July 19, 1936; A.B., Dartmouth Coll., 1958; LL.B., Stanford U., 1964. Admitted to Calif. bar, 1965, N.Mex. bar, 1973; practice law, Santa Fe. Office: PO Box 1904 Santa Fe NM 87501 Tel (505) 983-6373

LENT, BERKELEY, b. Los Angeles, Sept. 22, 1921; student Reed Coll., 1947; J.D., Willamette U., 1950. Admitted to Oreg. bar, 1950; asso. editor Bancroft-Whitney Law Pub. Co., San Francisco, 1950; since practiced in Portland, Oreg.; atty. Bonneville Power Adminstrn.,

1951-53; asso. firm Peterson & Pozzi, 1953-56; partner firm Lent, York, Paulson & Bullock, and predecessors, 1957-70; individual practice law, 1970-71; judge Oreg. Circuit Ct., 1971-76; justice Oreg. Supreme Ct., 1976—; mem. Oreg. House of Reps., 1957-67, Oreg. State Senate, 1967-71. Mem. Oreg., Multnomah bar assns. Home: 13955 SW Barlow Pl Beaverton OR 97005 Office: 1 Supreme Ct Bldg Salem OR 97310 Tel (503) 378-6022

LENTZ, ROBERT HENRY, b. Lake Huntington, N.Y., Dec. 9, 1924; B.E.E. magna cum laude, Poly. Inst. Bklyn.; J.D., Loyola U., Los Angeles, 1956. Admitted to Calif. bar, 1956; patent counsel Litton Industries, Inc., Beverly Hills, 1959-66, gen. staff atty., 1966-67, v.p., chief counsel, 1967—. Office: 360 N Crescent Dr Beverly Hills CA 90201 Tel (213) 273-7860

LENTZ, ROBERT WESLEY, b. Washington, Mar. 16, 1934; A.B., Lafayette Coll., 1955; J.D., U. Pa., 1959. Admitted to Pa. bar, 1958, U.S. Supreme Ct. bar, 1970; partner firm Lentz, Riley, Cantor, Kilgore & Massey, Paoli, Pa., 1969; mem. Trial Ct. Nominating Commn., 1976, Chester County rules com. Common Pleas and Orphans Ct., 1970; chmn. minor ct. civil procedural rules com. Pa. Supreme Ct., 1975—, chmn. hearing com., disciplinary bd. Treas., Good Will Underwater Recovery Unit; chmn. West Chester Human Relations Council, 1965, Chester County Drug Com., 1972, law adv. com. West Chester Area Sch. Dist., 1967-69; pres. West Chester Civic Assn., 1970, West Chester Opportunities Bd., 1971, Open Door Drug Center, 1972; bd. dirs. Chester County Assn. Retarded Children, Citizens for Better Housing. Mem. Pa., Chester County (sec. 1963-72, v.p. 1973, pres. 1974) bar assns. Home: 2083 Welsh Valley Rd Valley Forge PA 19481 Office: 30 Darby Rd Paoli PA 19301 Tel (215) 647-3310

LENWEAVER, THOMAS EDWIN, b. Syracuse, N.Y., July 22, 1940; B. Chem. Engring., Rensselaer Poly. Inst., 1962; J.D., Am. U., 1968. Admitted to N.Y. State bar, 1969; chem. engr. Goodrich Gulf Chem. Co., Cleve., 1965-68; with firm Houghton & Pappas, Rochester, N.Y., 1968—. Councilman City of Irondequoit (N.Y.), 1973-77. Office: 17 Main St E Rochester NY 14614 Tel (716) 232-1292

LENZ, EDWARD ARNOLD, b. White Plains, N.Y., Sept. 28, 1942; A.B., Bucknell U., 1964; J.D., Boston Coll., 1967; LL.M., N.Y. U., 1968. Admitted to N.Y. bar, 1968, D.C. bar, 1973; atty. Civil div. U.S. Dept. Justice, Washington, 1970-72; asso. gen. counsel Cost of Living Council, Washington, 1973; asso. firm Miller & Chevalier, Washington, 1973—. Mem. Bar Assn. D.C., N.Y., Fed., Am. bar assns., Nat. Polit. Sci. Honor Soc. Home: 4429 Fessenden St NW Washington DC 20016 Office: 1700 Pennsylvania Ave NW Washington DC 20006

LENZ, FRANCIS LAWRENCE, b. Beaver Dam, Wis., July 9, 1925; LL.B., U. Notre Dame, 1949; LL.M., U. Wis., 1950. Admitted to Wis. bar, 1950, Ill. bar, 1962; state claim mgr. London & Lancashire Group Ins. Co., Madison, Wis., 1950-60; claims atty. Gen. Casualty Ins. Co. of Wis., Freeport, Ill., 1960-66, asst. gen. counsel, 1966-69; asst. state's atty., Stephenson County, Freeport, 1969-71, state's atty., 1971-73; judge 15th Jud. Circuit, Ogle County, Oregon, Ill., 1973—. Chmn., Stephenson County Cancer Crusade, Am. Cancer Soc., 1965. Mem. Am. Judicature Soc., Am., Ill., Wis., Ogle County bar assns., Nat. Council Juvenile Ct. Judges. Home: 417 Bruce Ln Mount Morris IL 61054 Office: Courthouse Oregon IL 61061 Tel (815) 732-6661

LEO, ROBERT GEORGE, JR., b. Des Moines, May 8, 1948; B.S., U. Colo., 1970, J.D., 1973. Admitted to Colo. bar, 1973, U.S. Dist. Ct. bar for Dist. Colo., 1973; asso. firm Pacheco and Auer, P.C., Denver, 1973—. Mem. City and County of Denver Bd. Examiners, 1973-75; bd. dirs. Metropolitan Denver Sewage Disposal Dist. 1, 1976—. Home: 1035 S Clayton Way Denver CO 80209 Office: suite 777 Capitol Life Center 225 E 16th Ave Denver CO 80203 Tel (303) 892-5700

LEON, PHILLIP, b. Wichita, Kans., May 26, 1931; B.A., Wichita State U., 1955; J.D., Washburn U., 1958. Admitted to Kans. bar, 1958; individual practice law, Wichita, 1958—; judge pro tempre Wichita, 1967—. Examiner, Kans. Civil Rights Commn., 1973—; mem. Kans. Arts Comm., 1970—. Mem. Pan Am. Golf Assn. (nat. pres.). Moderator, Sta. KARD-TV, 1976-77. Home: 3140 N Sedgwick St Wichita KS 67204 Office: 1540 N Broadway Wichita KS 67214 Tel (316) 265-7869

LEONARD, CHARLES JEROME, JR., b. N.Y.C., June 2, 1936; A.B., U. N.C., 1960, J.D., 1966. Admitted to N.C. bar, 1966, U.S. Supreme Ct. bar, 1971; partner firm Leonard & Austin, Charlotte, N.C., 1973—; instr. U. N.C., Charlotte, 1971-73. Mem. N.C., N.C. State, Am. bar assns. Home: 1640 Maryland Ave Charlotte NC 28209 Office: Suite 1009 Cameron Brown Bldg Charlotte NC 28204 Tel (704) 377-6909

LEONARD, DAVID JEFFREY, b. N.Y.C., July 6, 1940; B.A., U. Ariz., 1962, LL.B., 1964. Admitted to Ariz., Calif. bars, 1964; atty. antitrust div. U.S. Dept. Justice, Washington, 1964-66; partner firm Miller, Pitt & Feldman, Tucson, 1966-76, Schorr & Leonard, Tucson, 1976—. Pres., Tucson Hebrew Acad., 1972-76, chmn. bd. dirs., 1976—. Mem. Ariz. Bar Assn. (mem. civil practice com.), Am. Trial Lawyers Assn., Phi Beta Kappa. Recipient Ariz. Atty. Gen. prize, 1964. Home: 6211 Paseo Tierra Alta Tucson AZ 85715 Office: 155 W Council St Tucson AZ 85701 Tel (602) 622-7733

LEONARD, GEORGE ADAMS, b. Clinton, Iowa, June 16, 1924; student Western Res. U., 1942-43; A.B., U. Mich., 1948, J.D., 1951. Admitted to Mich. bar, 1951, Ohio bar, 1956; asso. firm Slyfield, Hartman, Reitz & Tait, Detroit, 1951-56; asst. sec. Kroger Co., Cin., 1958-66, gen. counsel, 1966—, v.p., sec., 1970—; dir. Gleaner Lite Ins. Soc. Chmn., North Star dist. Boy Scouts Am., Cin., 1966. Bd. dirs., mem. exec. com. Cin. chpt. A.R.C., Legal Aid Soc., Cin. Decorated D.F.C., Air medal with four oak leaf clusters. Mem. Am., Ohio, Cin. bar assns., State Bar Mich. Home: 10477 Adventure Lane Cincinnati OH 45242 Office: 1014 Vine St Cincinnati OH 45201*

LEONARD, HENRY KENNEDY, b. St. Paul, Jan. 6, 1915; B.A., U. Wis., 1937; J.D. magna cum laude, U. Toledo, 1948. Admitted to Ohio bar, 1948; partner firm Marshall, Marshall & Leonard, Toledo, 1948-50, Owen & Owen, 1950-73, Wilson, Leonard & Clemens, 1974-76; counsel firm Wilson, Fraser, Raptes & Clemens, Toledo, 1977—; pres. Toledo Mental Hygiene Clinic, 1976. Mem. Am., Toledo bar assns., Am., Toledo (pres., 1950-51) patent law assns., Mensa, Phi Kappa Phi. Author: Patent Fundamentals for Engineers, 1954. Office: 316 N Michigan Toledo OH 43624 Tel (419) 241-3344

LEONARD, JAMES M., b. N.Y.C., July 21, 1928; A.B., Fordham U., 1948, J.D., 1951. Admitted to N.Y. bar, 1952, U.S. Supreme Ct. bar; asso. firm Macklin, Speer, Hanan & McKerman, N.Y.C., 1956-62; partner firm McHugh & Leonard, N.Y.C., 1962-70, McHugh, Heckman, Smith & Leonard, N.Y.C., 1970—. Trustee Elwood Sch. Bd., Huntington, N.Y., 1969-75, v.p., 1972-75. Mem. Am., N.Y. State, Maritime bar assns. Home: 9 Olympia Pl East Northport NY 11731 Office: 80 Pine St New York City NY 10005 Tel (212) 422-0222

LEONARD, JAMES MICHAEL, b. Los Angeles, Dec. 13, 1946; B.A., U. Calif., Berkeley, 1967; J.D., U. Calif., Los Angeles, 1970. Admitted to Calif. bar, 1971, U.S. Supreme Ct. bar, 1974; mem. firm David Henry Simon, Los Angeles, 1971-72, Dolman, Kaplan, Neiter & Hart, Los Angeles, 1972-76; partner firm Hart, Neit & Leonard, 1976—; law clk. to Ralph M. Holman, Justice Supreme Ct. of Oreg., 1970-71; judge pro tem Beverly Hills (Calif.) Municipal Ct., 1976—. Bd. dirs. Camp JCA, Los Angeles, 1971—. Mem. Los Angeles, Beverly Hills, Am. bar assns., Calif. Trial Lawyers Assn., Order of Coif. Home: 2707 Midvale Ave Los Angeles CA 90064 Office: 1888 Century Park E 6th Floor Los Angeles CA 90067 Tel (213) 277-2236

LEONARD, JOHN CLARENCE, JR., b. Columbia, Tenn., Oct. 29, 1938; B.A., Vanderbilt U., 1960; J.D., YMCA Law Sch., 1967. Admitted to Tenn. bar, 1968; individual practice law, Lewisburg, Tenn., 1968—. Chmn., Lewisburg Zoning Appeals Bd.; elder Cumberland Presbyn. Ch., Lewisburg, 1972-75, 1976—. Mem. Am., Tenn., Marshall County (sec. 1976—) bar assns., Am., Tenn. trial lawyers assns. Home: 1060 Ellington Pkwy S Lewisburg TN 37091 Office: 115 W Commerce St Lewisburg TN 37091 Tel (615) 359-1365

LEONARD, LARRY DALE, b. Horton, Kans., Jan. 7, 1948; B.S. in Edn., U. Kans., 1971, J.D., 1974. Admitted to Okla. bar, 1974, Kans. bar, 1974; dep. dist. atty. Wyandotte County, Kans., summer 1973; asso. firm Blackstock, Joyce, Pollard, Blackstock & Montgomery, Tulsa, 1974-77, partner, 1977—. Mem. Am., Okla., Tulsa County, Kans. bar assns., Okla. Trial Lawyers Assn. Home: 1223 E 20th St Tulsa OK 74120 Office: 300 Petroleum Club Bldg Tulsa OK 74119 Tel (918) 585-2751

LEONARD, RICHARD C., b. N.Y.C., Mar. 21, 1946; B.A., U. Calif., Los Angeles, 1967; J.D., U. Calif., Berkeley, 1970. Admitted to Calif. bar, 1971; asso. firm Simon, Sheridan, Murphy Thornton and Medvene and predecessors, Los Angeles, 1971-75; individual practice law, Los Angeles, 1976—; prof. law U. San Fernando Valley, 1973; lectr. Constitutional Rights Found. Mem. Am., Los Angeles Bar Assns., Assn. of Bus. Trial Lawyers. Office: 433 N Camden Dr Suite 1200 Los Angeles CA 90210 Tel (213) 278-9750

LEONARD, STEPHEN, b. Kendallville, Ind., Sept. 11, 1918; student Washington and Lee U., 1936-38; B.S. in Bus. Adminstrn., Ind. U., 1940, J.D., 1942. Admitted to Ind. bar, 1942, D.C. bar, 1952, Md. bar, 1968; individual practice law, Anderson, Ind., 1942-53; asst. U.S. Atty. So. Dist. Ind., 1953-56; asso. gen. counsel NLRB, 1956-58; legis. counsel U.S. Senate, 1958-61. Mem. Am., Fed., Ind., Md., D.C. bar assns. Home and Office: 700 New Hampshire Ave NW Washington DC 20037 Tel (202) 333-0660

LEONARD, TERRENCE EUGENE, b. Evanston, Ill., Dec. 9, 1939; B.A., U. Notre Dame, 1961; M.A. in Teaching, Northwestern U., 1962; J.D., Loyola U., 1967. Admitted to Ill. bar, 1967; asso. firm McCarthy, Scheurich, Duffy and McCarthy, Chgo., 1967-70, firm Pretzel, Stouffer, Nolan & Rooney, Chgo., 1970-74; partner firm Karr & Leonard, Chgo., 1974—. Mem. Ill., NW Suburban bar assns., Am., Ill. trial lawyers assns. Home: 130 N Gibbons Ave Arlington Heights IL 60004 Office: 33 N Dearborn St Chicago IL 60602 Tel (312) 263-4604

LEONARD, WILLIAM F., b. Quincy, Fla., Sept. 4, 1926; student Fla. State U., 1947-49; LL.B., U. Fla., 1951, J.D., 1967. Admitted to Fla. bar, 1951, U.S. Dist. Ct. bar, 1953; asso. firm Stephen C. O'Connell, Ft. Lauderdale, Fla., 1953-55; partner firm Coleman, Leonard & Morrison and predecessor firm, Ft. Lauderdale, 1955—; mem. bd. govs. Nova Law Center, Ft. Lauderdale, 1973—; legal counsel, dir. Ft. Lauderdale C. of C., 1973-75; dir. Inverrary Classic Found., Inc., Ft. Lauderdale, 1974—; dir. Southeast Everglades Bank; Southeast Bank Broward (Fla.), Lauderdale Abstract & Title Co. Trustee Holy Cross Hosp., Ft. Lauderdale, 1976—. Mem. Fla. Bar (bd. govs. 1975—), Broward County Bar Assn. (pres. 1974), U. Fla. Alumni Assn. (pres. Broward County chpt. 1958-59), Pi Kappa Alpha, Phi Delta Phi. Home: 4311 NE 25th Ave Fort Lauderdale FL 33306 Office: 2810 E Oakland Park Blvd Fort Lauderdale FL 33306 Tel (305) 563-2671

LEONARDI, JOHN FRANCIS, JR., b. Highland Park, Ill., July 18, 1938; B.S. in Bus. Adminstrn., Marquette U., 1960; J.D., John Marshall Law Sch., 1968. Propr., Leonardi Real Estate, Highwood, Ill., 1960-68; admitted to Ill. bar, 1968; with Pioneer Nat. Title Ins. Co., Waukegan, Ill., 1968-73; v.p., co-owner Mid America Title Co., Waukegan, 1973—; mem. govs. adv. council State of Ill., 1968-72. Bd. dirs. Lake Forest (Ill.) Montessori Sch., 1965-67. Mem. Lake County, McHenry County bds. realtors, Lake County, Ill., McHenry County bar assns., Lake County Home Builders Assn. Home: 1880 Clifton Ave Highland Park IL 60055 Office: 222 N County St Waukegan IL 60085 Tel (312) 249-1200

LEONARDO, JOHN STEPHEN, b. Des Moines, Jan. 4, 1947; B.A., Notre Dame U., 1969; J.D., George Washington U., 1972. Admitted to Md. bar, 1972, Ind. bar, 1972, Fed. No. Dist. Ind. bar, 1973, 7th Circuit Ct. Appeals bar, 1974; asst. state atty. Upper Marlboro, Md., 1972-73; asst. U.S. atty. No. Dist. Ind., South Bend, 1973—. Mem. St. Joseph County Bar Assn. Home: 51270 Lilac Rd South Bend IN 46628 Office: 204 S Main St South Bend IN 46601 Tel (219) 232-3086

LEONHARD, ALBERT EDWARD, b. New Orleans, Sept. 11, 1905; LL.B., Loyola U., New Orleans, 1930. Admitted to La. bar, 1930; atty., sec., treas. Auto Painting & Repairing Co., Inc., New Orleans, 1930—. Mem. La. State Bar Assn. Home: 4300 General Pershing St New Orleans LA 70125 Office: 1725 Dufossat St New Orleans LA 70115 Tel (504) 895-4801

LEOPOLD, ARTHUR FREDRIC, b. Woodmere, N.Y., Nov. 10, 1919; A.B. magna cum laude, Dartmouth, 1941; J.D., Columbia, 1948. Admitted to N.Y. bar, 1948, Calif. bar, 1951; asso. firm Cravath, Swaine & Moore, N.Y.C., 1948-50; partner firm Youngman, Hungate & Leopold, Los Angeles, 1954—; mem. Beverly Hills (Calif.) City Council, 1964-72; mayor City of Beverly Hills, 1967-68, 71-72. Del. Democratic Nat. Conv., 1968. Mem. Beverly Hills, Los Angeles County bar assns., State Bar Calif., State Bar N.Y., Los Angeles Copyright Soc. (trustee 1975—). Editor Columbia Law Review. Home: 616 N Alpine Dr Beverly Hills CA 90210 Office: 1801 Century Park E Suite 1101 Los Angeles CA 90067 Tel (213) 277-3333

LEOPOLD, FREDERICK ORRIN, b. Springfield, Mass., Feb. 25, 1934; A.B. in Human Relations and Psychology, U. Miami, 1955, J.D., 1965; postgrad Syracuse U., 1955-56. Admitted to Fla. bar, 1965; asso. firm Thomas A. Thomas, Hollywood, Fla., 1965-68; partner firm Thomas, Sturrup, Della, Donna and Davie, Fla., 1970—; city prosecutor, Hollywood, 1966; asst. city atty., Hollywood, 1967-68; municipal judge Hacienda Village (Fla.), 1974-77; arbitrator Am. Arbitration Assn. Miami, Fla., 1967—. Mem. Fla., South Broward Bar Assn., Fla. Assn. Realtors (chmn. local bd. atty. panel, Orlando, 1973—). Home: 1520 Jackson St Hollywood FL 33020 Office: 7200 Griffin Rd Davie FL 33314 Tel (305) 583-5484

LE PAGE, CLIFFORD BENNETT, JR., b. Reading, Pa., May 17, 1944; B.A. in Classics magna cum laude, Brown U., 1966; J.D., U. Pa., 1969. Admitted to Pa. bar, 1969; partner firm Austin, Speicher, Boland, Connor & Giorgi, Reading, 1975—. Bd. dirs. Family Guidance Reading. Mem. Berks County, Pa. (workmen's compensation com.) bar assns., Pa. Trial Lawyers Assn., Phi Beta Kappa. Home: 1144 Belmont Ave Wyomissing PA 19610 Office: 44 N 6th St Reading PA 19610 Tel (215) 374-8211

LEPGOLD, BERNARD JOSEPH, b. Milw., Nov. 11, 1915; Ph.B., Marquette U., 1941, LL.B., 1945, J.D., 1968. Admitted to Wis. bar, 1945, Ill. bar, 1964, U.S. Supreme Ct. bar, 1954; individual practice law, Milw., 1945—; commr. Milw. County Ct., 1975. Mem. Milw., Wis. bar assns., Am. Acad. Matrimonial Lawyers. Office: 536 W Wisconsin Ave Suite 610 Milwaukee WI 53203 Tel (414) 272-3791

LEPOME, ROBERT CHARLES, b. Buffalo, May 23, 1943; B.A. in Biology, State U. N.Y. at Buffalo, 1965, J.D., 1968. Admitted to N.Y. bar, 1968, Nev. bar, 1970, U.S. Supreme Ct. bar, 1974; partner firm LePome & Gorman, Las Vegas, 1975—. Mem. Am., Fed. (pres. Nev. chpt.), Nev., Clark County bar assns., Las Vegas C. of C. Recipient Am. Jurisprudence award, 1968. Home: 2617 Yardley St Las Vegas NV 89102 Office: 417 S Bridger St Las Vegas NV 89101 Tel (702) 382-3360

LEPP, GERALD PETER, b. Milw., Sept. 26, 1932; B.A., U. Wis., 1954; J.D., Harvard, 1959; LL.M., N.Y. U., 1973. Admitted to Wis. bar, 1959, D.C. bar, 1961, N.Y. bar, 1962; gen. atty. Gen. Services Adminstrn., Washington, 1959-61; asso. firm Choate, Mitchell, Baker and Nelson, N.Y.C., 1961-63; asst. counsel M & T Chems., Inc., N.Y.C., 1964-65; chief counsel Photo and Bldg. Products div. GAF Corp., N.Y.C., 1966-69; asso. counsel, asst. sec. Continental Grain Co., N.Y.C., 1969—. Mem. Am. Fgn. Law Assn., Inc. (sec. 1973—), Am. Bar Assn. (chmn. far east com. internat. sect. 1975—), Assn. Bar City N.Y. Home: 30 Hilltop Dr Chappaqua NY 10514 Office: 277 Park Ave New York City NY 10017 Tel (212) 826-5457

LERBLANCE, WILLIAM PENN, III, b. Dallas, Apr. 7, 1942; B.A., Oklahoma City U., 1961; M.A., U. Okla., 1963; J.D., 1966. Admitted to Okla. bar, 1966, U.S. 10th Circuit Ct. Appeals bar, 1966, U.S. Dist. Ct. eastern and western dist. Okla. bar, 1967; asst. atty. gen. Okla., 1966-68; referee Okla. Ct. Criminal Appeals, 1968-73; asst. prof. law, Oklahoma City U., 1973-76, asso. prof., 1976—, asst. dean, 1976—. Mem. Am., Oklahoma County, Okla. bar assns., Assn. Central Okla. Govts. (mem. criminal justice planning council), Am. Judicature Soc. Contbr. articles to law jours. Office: Sch Law Oklahoma City U Oklahoma City OK 73106 Tel (405) 525-5411

LERMAN, MARVIN STEPHEN, b. N.Y.C., June 17, 1940; B.S., U. Pa., 1962; LL.B., N.Y. U., 1965, LL.M., 1970. Admitted to N.Y. bar, 1967, U.S. Dist. Ct. for So. dist. N.Y., 1970, U.S. Ct. Appeals, 1976; asso. firm Tenzer, Greenblat, Fallow & Kaplan, N.Y.C., 1967-68; asso. firm Richenthal, Abrams & Moss., N.Y.C., 1968-73; individual practice law, N.Y.C., 1973-76; partner firm Rosenbaum, Lerman & Katz, N.Y.C., 1976—. Pres. Ned D. Frank Philanthropic League, N.Y.C., 1974—; trustee Temple Israel, N.Y.C., 1977—. Mem. N.Y. County Lawyers Assn. Decorated Bronze Star. Office: 300 Madison Ave New York City NY 10017 Tel (212) 986-5515

LERNER, ALAN BURTON, b. N.Y.C., Nov. 17, 1930; B.B.A., Coll. City N.Y., 1951; LL.B., Yale, 1954. Admitted to N.Y. bar, 1954, D.C. bar, 1973; asso. firm Chadbourne, Parke, Whiteside & Wolff, N.Y.C., 1956-60; mem. legal dept. C.I.T. Fin. Corp., N.Y.C., 1960—, gen. counsel, sec., 1976—, v.p., 1977—; cons. Fed. Res. Bd., 1973, Nat. Conf. Commrs. on Uniform State Laws, 1966-68. Mem. Am., D.C. bar assns., Assn. Bar City N.Y., Nat. Consumer Fin. Assn. (chmn. Law Forum 1970-71), Assn. Comml. Fin. Attys. Home: Greenwich CT 06830 Office: 650 Madison Ave New York City NY 10022 Tel (212) 572-6224

LERNER, EUGENE MICHAEL, b. Annapolis, Md., Dec. 18, 1931; grad. U. Balt. Sch. Law, 1954. Admitted to Md. bar, 1954, U.S. Supreme Ct. bar, 1960; individual practice law, Annapolis, 1956—; city atty. City of Annapolis, 1969—; alderman, 1961-65, trial magistrate, 1958-59, mem. planning and zoning commn., 1961-63. Mem. Md. State, Am., Anne Arundel County (pres. 1976-77) bar assns., Am. Judicature Soc. Home: 317 Halsey Rd Annapolis MD 21401 Office: 155 Duke of Gloucester St Annapolis MD 21401 Tel (301) 263-3901

LERNER, HARRY, b. Easton, Pa., Jan. 24, 1939; B.A. in Math., Cornell U., 1960; J.D., N.Y.U., 1963. Admitted to N.Y. bar, 1963, N.J. bar, 1966; asso. firm Otterbourg, Steindler, Houston & Rosen, N.Y.C., 1964-65; asso. firm Robert Greenberg, West New York, N.J., 1965-67; asst. house counsel Ronson Corp., Bridgewater, N.J., 1967-71, asst. to gen. counsel, 1971-75, sec., corp. counsel, 1975—. Mem. N.J. Bar Assn., Am. Soc. Corp. Secs. Office: One Ronson Rd Bridgewater NJ 08807

LEROY, LEIGHTON NEIL, b. Boston, Apr. 8, 1932; A.B. summa cum laude, Lafayette Coll., 1953; J.D. cum laude, Harvard, 1956. Admitted to N.Y. bar, 1957, Mass. bar, 1963, R.I. bar, 1967; asso. firm Willkie, Farr & Gallagher, N.Y.C., 1956-62; div. counsel Sylvania Electric Products Inc., Waltham and Danvers, Mass., 1962-67; partner firm Tobin, LeRoy & Silverstein, Providence and Woonsocket, R.I., 1967—; dir. corps.; corporator Woonsocket Instn. for Savings, 1973—. Corporator Woonsocket Hosp., 1975—. Mem. Am., R.I., Boston, Woonsocket bar assns., Phi Beta Kappa. Home: Luther Dr Cumberland RI 02864 Office: Indsl Bank Bldg Providence RI 02903 Tel (401) 274-6300

LERRIGO, FRANK CHARLES, b. Topeka, May 23, 1906; student Deep Springs Coll., 1923-24; B.A., Stanford, 1928, LL.B., 1931. Admitted to Calif. bar, 1931; legal advisor to commr. Calif. Div. Corps., San Francisco, 1931-32; atty. Regional Agrl. Credit Corp., San Francisco, 1932-33, Fed. Intermediate Credit Bank, Berkeley, Calif.,

1933-34; individual practice law, Fresno, Calif., 1935-55; partner firm Lerrigo, Thuesen, Walters, Nibler & Hedrick, Fresno, 1955—; U.S. commr., 1936-70; U.S. magistrate, 1970-76. Bd. advisers Fresno Community Hosp. Mem. Fresno County (sec.), Calif., Am., Los Angeles County bar assns., Calif. Bankers Assn. (chmn. legal seminar on agrl. financing). Recipient Silver Beaver award Boy Scouts Am., 1975. Home: 1831 S Claremont St Fresno CA 93727 Office: 8th Floor Security Bank Bldg 1060 Fulton Mall Fresno CA 93721 Tel (209) 485-4010

LESCH, SOLOMON ISADORE, b. N.Y.C., Nov. 25, 1940; B.A., City Coll. N.Y., 1962; J.D., N.Y. U., 1965. Admitted to N.Y. bar, 1966; individual practice law, Bronx, N.Y., 1966—; counsel Mid-Queens Boys Club, 1976—. Mem. Queens-Nassau Civic Assn., 1967-72; trustee Hollis Hills Jewish Center, 1971—. Mem. N.Y. State, Bronx bar assns., Order of Coif, Phi Beta Kappa. Office: 860 Grand Concourse Bronx NY 10451 Tel (212) 292-1131

LESHY, JOHN DAVID, b. Winchester, Ohio, Oct. 7, 1944; A.B., Harvard, 1966, J.D., 1969. Admitted to Ohio bar, 1969, Calif. bar, 1972; trial atty. Civil Rights Div., U.S. Dept. Justice, Washington, 1969-72; staff atty. Natural Resources Def. Council, Western Office, Palo Alto, Calif., 1972-77; asso. solicitor U.S. Dept. Interior, Washington, 1977—. Contbr. articles to legal jours. Office: Dept of Interior Washington DC

LESINSKI, T. JOHN, b. Detroit, Apr. 28, 1925; J.D., U. Detroit, 1950; LL.D., Detroit Coll. Law, 1972. Admitted to Mich. bar, 1951, U.S. 6th Circuit Ct. Appeals bar, 1951, U.S. Supreme Ct. bar, 1975, U.S. 7th Circuit Ct. Appeals bar, 1976; partner firm Lesinski & Paruk, Hamtramck, Mich., 1951-64; judge Mich. Ct. Appeals, 1965-76, chief judge, 1965-76; mem. firm Schlussel, Lifton, Simon, Rands, Kaufman & Lesinski, Southfield, Mich., 1976—; mem. Mich. Ho. of Reps., 1951-60; lt. gov. State of Mich., 1961-64; vice chmn. Nat. Lt. Gov.'s Conf., 1964; fgn. trade adviser Mich. Senate, 1967; mem. adv. council Nat. Center for State Cts., 1972—; appt. spl. judicial adminstr. to manage Recorders Ct. Detroit, 1977—; lectr. in field, 1968—. U.S. rep. Internat. Trade Fair, Poznan, Poland, 1963; mem. Interstate Coop. Commn., 1957-64. Mem. Am. (chmn. nat. conf. appellate judges 1972-73), Advocates bar assns., Inst. Jud. Adminstrn., Appellate Judges Conf. Home: 60 Willow Tree Pl Grosse Pointe Shores MI 48036 Office: 500 NBS Financial Center 29201 Telegraph St Southfield MI 48034 Tel (313) 353-9500

LESKOVYANSKY, JOHN JOSEPH, b. Senecaville, Ohio, Mar. 28, 1925; LL.B., Youngstown U., 1953, J.D., 1969; postgrad. Western Res. U., U. Ala. Admitted to Ohio bar, 1953; asst. city prosecutor, Youngstown, Ohio, 1954-59; law dir., Youngstown, 1959-61; judge Municipal Ct. of Youngstown, 1961-72; judge Ct. of Common Pleas div. domestic relations Mahoning County (Ohio), Youngstown, 1972—; individual practice law, Youngstown, 1954-61. Adviser Camp Fire Girls, Boy Scouts Am., Buckeye Elks; councilman Catholic Slovak Union Ch.; commentator Ch. of St. Matthias; founder Mahoning Valley Civic and Cultural Soc. Mem. Ohio, Mahoning County bar assns., Ohio Juvenile and Probate, Ohio Common Pleas judges assns. Recipient St. George award Cath. Boy Scouts Am., Silver Beaver award Mahoning Valley council Boy Scouts Am. Home: 2714 Shirley Rd Youngstown OH 44502 Office: 120 Market St Mahoning County Ct House Youngstown OH 44503 Tel (216) 747-2092

LESLIE, RICHARD MCLAUGHLIN, b. Chgo., Oct. 31, 1936; A.B., U. Fla., 1958; J.D., U. Mich., 1961. Admitted to Fla. bar, 1962, Ill. bar, 1961; sr. partner firm Shutts & Bowen, Miami, Fla., 1964—. Mem. Fedn. Ins. Counsel, Maritime Law Assn., Am. Fla., Ill., Dade County bar assns., Dade County, Fla. def. bar assns., Def. Research Inst. Home: 4500 University Dr Coral Gables FL 33146 Office: 1000 First Nat Bank Bldg Miami FL 33131 Tel (305) 358-6300

LESLIE, RICHARD STEPHEN, b. N.Y.C., July 15, 1940; B.A. in English, U. N.C., 1963; J.D., Bklyn. Law Sch., 1968. Admitted to N.Y. bar, 1968, Calif. bar, 1973; mem. criminal def. div. Legal Aid Soc. N.Y., 1970-72; asst. dist. atty. Orange County (N.Y.), 1972; law and justice officer San Diego County (Calif.) Human Relations Commn., 1973-77; mem. faculty Southwestern Coll., Bonita, Calif., 1975-76, San Diego State U., 1974. Bd. dirs. Beach Area Community Clinic, San Diego, 1975—; mem. project community adv. group San Diego Police Dept., 1973-74; mem. community relations and adminstrn. of justice com. NCCJ, 1974. Mem. N.Y. State, San Diego County bar assns. Named Civil Libertarian of Year San Diego br. ACLU, 1975. Home: 1068 Hornblend St San Diego CA 92109 Office: 836 Prospect St LaJolla CA 92037 Tel (714) 459-0234

LESLIE, RONALD LEE, b. Goodland, Kans., Aug. 19, 1940; B.S. in Bus., U. Kans., 1962; J.D., 1965. Admitted to Kans. bar, 1965; staff atty. Judge Adv.'s Office, Edgewood Arsenal, Md., 1966-67; asso. firm Branine & Chalfant, Hutchinson, Kans., 1967-68; partner firm Hess, Leslie, Berkley, and Granger, Hutchinson, 1968—; judge S. Hutchinson Municipal Ct., 1969—; atty. City of Nickerson (Kans.), 1975—. Former pres. Big Bros. Hutchinson, Reno County (Kans.) Halfway House, Inc., also bd. dirs.; bd. dirs. Reno County YMCA, Reno County United Way; chmn. Reno County Republican Party, 1972-74, exec. com., 1972—; mem. Kans. State Rep. Com., 1972—. Mem. Am., Kans., S.W. Kans., Reno County bar assns., Hutchinson C. of C. (chmn. pub. affairs com. 1976—), Phi Delta Phi. Contbr. article Kans. Law Rev. Home: 2703 Pama Lou St Hutchinson KS 67501 Office: 10 E 5th St Hutchinson KS 67501 Tel (316) 663-2171

LE SOURD, FRANCIS ANCIL, b. Seattle, June 22, 1908; LL.B., U. Wash., 1932. Admitted to Wash. bar, 1932; asso. firm Chadwick, Chadwick & Mills, Seattle, 1932-33; atty. PWA, Wash., 1933-34; spl. asst. to atty. gen. tax div. Dept. Justice, Wash., 1934-37; asso. firm William Stanley, Wash., 1937-38; individual practice law, Seattle, regional atty. lands div. Dept. Justice, Seattle, 1938-40; partner firm LeSourd, Patten, Fleming & Hartung, and predecessors, Seattle, 1941—; lectr. taxation and constl. law U. Wash., Washington Coll. Law; chmn., dir. Crystal Mountain, Inc.; sec., dir. Bryant Corp., Seattle. Former state rep. nat. adv. bd. Council Pub. Lands; mem. Seattle Municipal Civil Service Commn., 1945-50; commr. Housing Authority, Seattle, 1939-41; ednl. dir. Wash. Democratic Central Com., 1954; mem. Wash. Dem. Fin. Com., 1955-56; past pres. Seattle Opera Assn. Mem. Am., Wash., Seattle bar assns., Order of Coif, Phi Beta Kappa. Home: 3143 W Laurelhurst Dr NE Seattle WA 98105 Office: 1300 Seattle Tower Seattle WA 98101 Tel (206) 624-1040

LESPERANCE, TIMOTHY JOHN, b. Two Rivers, Wis., Sept. 6, 1944; B.S. in Econs., U. Wis., Madison, 1971, J.D., 1974, M.S. in Indsl. Relations, 1974. Admitted to Wis. bar, 1974; partner Kissling Law Offices, Lake Mills, Wis., 1974—. Mem. Jefferson County, Wis. bar assns., Res. Officers Assn. U.S. Office: 140 E Lake St Lake Mills WI 53551 Tel (414) 648-2512

LESSER, JOAN L., b. Los Angeles, Apr. 12, 1947; B.A., Brandeis U., 1969; J.D., U. So. Calif., 1973. Admitted to Calif. bar, 1973; asso. firm Irell & Manella, Los Angeles, 1973—. Mem. Am., Los Angeles County bar assns., Order of Coif. Exec. editor So. Calif. Law Rev., 1972-73. Office: 1000 Ave of Stars #900 Los Angeles CA 90067 Tel (213) 277-1010

LESSER, SAUL, b. Newark, May 4, 1922; LL.B., N.Y. U., 1946, LL.M. in Taxation, 1966. Admitted to N.Y. State bar, 1946, Fla. bar, 1972, U.S. Supreme Ct. bar, 1961; tax editor Prentice-Hall, N.Y.C., 1946-48; asso. gen. counsel, sec., v.p., sr. officer U.S. Life Ins. Co., N.Y.C., 1948-71; lectr. N.Y. U., 1968-69, instr. Coll. Ins., 1953-59; adj. lectr. Nova U. Law Sch., 1976—. Mem. N.Y. County Lawyers Assn., Fla. Bar Assn., Assn. Life Ins. Counsel, Am. Life Conv. Contbr. articles to legal jours. Home and office: 2100 S Ocean Ln Apt 2210 Fort Lauderdale FL 33316 Tel (305) 524-6315

LESSLER, ARTHUR LAWRENCE, b. Bronx, Nov. 5, 1937; B.E.E., Cooper Union Coll., 1959; M.S. in Elec. Engring., Poly. Inst. of Bklyn., 1962; LL.B., J.D., Bklyn. Law Sch., 1965. Admitted to N.Y. State bar, N.J. bar, D.C. bar; electronics and system devel. engr. Grumman Aircraft Engring. Corp., 1969-73; transistor circuit design engr. Sperry Gyroscope Co., adminstr., tech. asst. ITT, individual practice law, 1973—; mem. U.S. patent prosecution staff RCA, also patent counsel; gen. counsel Van Dyk Research Corp., 1972-73. Active Boy Scouts Am., 1975—. Mem. Trial Lawyers of N.J., N.J. State, Middlesex County Bar assns., N.J. Patent Law Assn., Nat. Assn. of Immigration and Nationality Lawyers.

LESSLER, STANLEY MICHAEL, b. Bridgeport, Conn., Aug. 29, 1937; B.A., Tufts U., 1959; LL.B., U. Conn., 1962. Admitted to Conn. bar, 1962, U.S. Supreme Ct. bar, 1963; individual practice law, Trumbull, Conn., 1962—; clk. Bridgeport Superior Ct., 1962; organizer, dir. Bank of Trumbull, 1973; counsel, 1976—; asst. prof. Housatonic Community Coll., 1965-71. Bd. dirs. Bridgeport Ballet. Mem. Conn., Bridgeport, Am. bar assns. Office: 935 White Plains Rd Trumbull CT 06611 Tel (203) 261-9811

LESSY, ROY PAUL, b. Chester, Pa., Mar. 14, 1906; B.S. in Economics, Franklin and Marshall Coll., 1927; LL.B., Temple U., 1931. Admitted to Pa. bar, 1931, U.S. Supreme Ct. bar, 1960; solicitor Ridley Twp., Pa., 1937—; atty. Pa. Dept. Justice, 1939-55; atty. Sec. Banking, State Pa., 1941; asst. dist. atty. Delaware County, Pa., 1942-52; solicitor Chester Twp. Pa., 1945-47; atty. Brandywine Battlefield Park Commn., 1948-49; solicitor Chester (Pa.) Housing Authority, 1950-55; solicitor controller Delaware County, 1955-60; bd. viewers Delaware County, 1972—; solicitor Pa. Assn. First Class Twps., 1945—; sol. Delaware County Twp. Commrs., 1945—. Past chmn. Delaware County ARC; past pres. Furness Free Library, 1973; mem. Pa. Municipal Retirement Bd., 1974—. Mem. Pa., Delaware County (dir. 1961-64) bar assns. Recipient Selective Service medal U.S. Govt., 1949; Gold medal Service Award, Pa. Assn. Twp. Commrs, 1962; Outstanding Service award, Delaware County Assn. Twp. Commrs., 1969; citation Pa. Ho. Rep. for Municipal Law Activities., 1975. Home: 108 Westminster Dr Wallingford PA 19086 Office: 507 Welsh St Chester PA 19013 Tel (215) TR2-5414

LESTER, JOHN ROBERT, b. Rocky Mount, N.C., June 5, 1942; B.A., U. S.C., 1964, J.D., 1967. Admitted to S.C. bar, 1967; with JAGC, USAF, 1967-72; partner firm Lester & Lester, Columbia, S.C., 1972-76, Beale & Lester, Columbia, 1977—. Mem. Am., S.C., Richland County (S.C.) bar assns., S.C. Trial Lawyers Assn. Home: 5012 Circle Dr Columbia SC 29206 Office: 1413 Calhoun St Columbia SC 29201 Tel (803) 779-5920

LESTER, RICHARD ALLAN, b. Kansas City, Kans., Jan. 31, 1947; B.S. in B.A., Kans. State U., 1969; J.D., Kans. U., 1972. Admitted to Kans. bar, 1972; partner firm Scott, Daily, Vasos & Lester, Kansas City, Kans., 1972—; instr. bus. law Kansas City Community Jr. Coll., 1974—. Mem. Kansas City Citizens Adv. Com., 1973. Mem. Am., Kans., Wyandotte County bar assns., Am., Kans. trial lawyers assns. Home: 6211 W 76th Pl Prairie Village KS 66208 Office: 811 N 9th St Kansas City KS 66101 Tel (913) 321-9600

LETA, JOSEPH, JR., b. Campofelice, Sicily, Italy, Mar. 25, 1900; A.B., U. Mich., 1923, LL.B., 1925, LL.D. Admitted to Pa. bar, 1927; individual practice law, New Castle, Pa. Pres. Circolo Italiano; bd. dirs. T.B. Soc., New Castle, Pa.; first pres. Nat. Assn. of The Wolves, New Castle, 1951. Mem. Lawrence County Bar Assn. Home and Office: 938 Winslow Ave New Castle PA 16101 Tel (412) 654-0882

LETSON, WILLIAM N., b. 1930; B.A., Harvard U., 1952, J.D., 1955. With firm Shearman & Sterling, 1955-62; sr. partner firm Letson, Letson, Griffith & Knightlinger 1962-71; gen. counsel Dept. Commerce, 1971-73; v.p., sec., gen. counsel Dept. Commerce, 1971-73; v.p., sec., gen. counsel Westinghouse Electric Corp., Pitts., 1973—. Office: Westinghouse Bldg Gateway Center Pittsburgh PA 15222*

LETTEAU, ROBERT MASON, b. San Francisco, May 17, 1942; B.A., Stanford, 1964; J.D., U. Calif., San Francisco, 1967. Admitted to Calif. bar, 1967; partner firm Ross, Pierson & Letteau, Inglewood, Calif., 1968—. Councilman, City of Inglewood, 1971-77. Home: 723 N Roxbury Dr Beverly Hills CA 90210 Office: 12301 Wilshire Blvd Los Angeles CA 90025 Tel (213) 826-8335

LETVIN, DAVID JAY, b. Detroit, Feb. 20, 1948; B.A., Oakland U., 1970; J.D., Wash. U., 1973. Admitted to Ill. bar, 1973, Mo. bar, 1975; law clk. Ill. Supreme Ct., East St. Louis and Springfield, 1973-75; mem. firm Cohn, Carr, Korein, Kunin and Brennan, E. St. Louis, 1975—. Office: 412 Missouri Ave E St Louis IL 62201 Tel (618) 274-0434

LEUBSDORF, JOHN DAVID, b. N.Y.C., Feb. 11, 1942; B.A., Harvard, 1963, J.D., 1967; M.A., Stanford, 1964. Admitted to Mass. bar, 1968; U.S. Ct. Appeals 1st Circuit bar, 1968, U.S. Dist. Ct. for Dist. Mass. bar, 1968. Law clk. Hon. Bailey Aldrich, Boston, 1967-68; asso. firm Foley, Hoag & Eliot, Boston, 1968-73, partner, 1974-75; asso. prof. law Boston U., 1975—. Mem. Boston Bar Assn. Contbr. articles to profl. publs. Home: 8 Fairfield St Boston MA 02116 Office: 765 Commonwealth Ave Boston MA 02215 Tel (617) 353-4420

LEUENBERGER, JAN WESLEY, b. Topeka, Kans., Oct. 5, 1936; B.B.A., Washburn U., 1958, J.D., 1961. Admitted to Kans. bar, 1961; partner firm Glenn, Cornish & Leuenberger, Topeka, 1964—; lectr. bus. law Washburn U., 1961-75; paralegal edn., 1975-76. Pres. March of Dimes, 1965-66; bd. dirs., treas. YMCA, Topeka, 1973—; trustee, sec. YMCA Found., Topeka, 1976—; bd. dirs. Topeka Day Care Assn., 1973-76; judge adv. Elks Club, 1967-69. Mem. Kans. (bd. govs. 1975—), Am. trial lawyers assns., Am., Kans., Topeka bar assns., Comml. Law League, Delta Theta Phi, Sagamore Honor Soc. Home: 3516 Oak Pkwy Topeka KS 66614 Office: 610 1st Nat Bank Tower Topeka KS 66603 Tel (913) 232-0545

LEUKART, RICHARD HENRY, II, b. Detroit, Mar. 15, 1942; A.B., Dartmouth, 1964, postgrad. in Bus. Adminstrn., 1963-64; JD., U. Mich., 1967. Admitted to Ohio bar, 1967; asso. firm Baker, Hostetler & Patterson, Cleve., 1967-75, partner, 1976—. Deacon, Fairmount Presbyterian Ch., Cleveland Heights, Ohio, 1968-71, chmn., 1970-71. Mem. Am., Ohio, Cleve. (chmn. fringe benefits com. 1972) bar assns. Home: 13302 Cormere Ave Cleveland OH 44120 Office: 1956 Union Commerce Bldg Cleveland OH 44115 Tel (216) 621-0200

LEVA, MARX, b. Selma, Ala., Apr. 4, 1915; B.S. in Bus. Adminstrn., U. Ala., 1937; LL.B. magna cum laude, Harvard, 1940. Admitted to Ala. bar, 1940, U.S. Supreme Ct. bar, 1946, D.C. bar, 1950; law clk. to Justice Hugo L. Black, 1940-41; gen. counsel Dept. Def., 1947-49; asst. sec. def., legal and legis., 1949-51; partner firm Leva, Hawes, Symington, Martin & Oppenheimer and predecessors, Washington, 1951—. Mem. Am., Fed., D.C. bar assns. Home: 7115 Bradley Blvd Bethesda MD 20034 Office: 815 Connecticut Ave Washington DC 20006 Tel (202) 298-8020

LEVANT, S. ROBERT, b. West Chester, Pa., Dec. 28, 1926; LL.B., Temple U., 1951. Admitted to Pa. bar, 1953; with firm Markovitz, Stern & Shusterman, Phila., 1953-60; partner firm Ehrenreich, Sidkoff, Edelstein & Shusterman, Phila., 1961-69; asso. firm Bennett, Bricklin & Saltzburg, Phila., 1969-70; partner firm Richter, Syken, Ross & Levant, Phila., 1970—; instr. Temple U., Phila., 1954—. Mem. Pa., Phila. bar assns., Am., Pa. trial lawyers assns., Lawyers Club Phila. Home: 1030 Lakeside Ave Philadelphia PA 19126 Office: 835 Land Title Bldg Philadelphia PA 19110 Tel (215) 564-3700

LEVBARG, MARK Z., b. Neptune, N.J., Aug. 11, 1943; B.A., Rutgers U., 1964; LL.B., U. Tex., 1967. Admitted to Tex. bar, 1967; partner firm Levbarg, Weeks & Chapman, Austin, Tex., 1968—. Chmn. Tex. Civil Liberties Found., 1972-73. Mem. Tex. Trial Lawyers Assn., Am. Bar Assn. Contbr. book revs. to Tex. Internat. Law Jour. Home: 1157 The High Rd Austin TX 78746 Office: 807 Rio Grande St Austin TX 78701 Tel (512) 976-6096

LEVEL, EDWARD ELDRIDGE, b. Paradise, Mont., Dec. 4, 1919; B.A., U. Wash., 1942, J.D., 1948. Admitted to Wash. bar, 1949; asst. atty. gen. State of Wash., 1954-64; mem. firm Miles & Level, Olympia, Wash., 1964-68; mem. firm Bell, Ingram, Johnson & Level, Everett, Wash., 1968-75, mem. firm John & Level, Everett, 1975—; mem. Wash. Supreme Ct. Com. on Uniform Jury Instructions, 1963-72; chmn. court rules and procedures com., 1973-74; justice of peace, 1950-54. Mem. Wash., Am. bar assns. (mem. bar exam. com. Wash. 1974—). Home: 1914 Bailey Ave Everett WA 98203 Office: 420 First Nat Bank Bldg Everett WA 98201 Tel (206) 258-3596

LEVEN, DAVID C., b. Rochester, N.Y., Apr. 27, 1943; A.B., U. Rochester, 1965; J.D., Syracuse U., 1968. Admitted to N.Y. bar, 1969; law clk. Falk, Schoenwald, Klafter & Ange, Rochester, 1968-69; staff atty. Monroe County Legal Assistance Corp., Rochester, 1969-71, dep. dir., 1971-73, exec. dir., 1973—; mem. Counsel for Indigents Task Force Monroe County Family Ct. Mem. guardianship com. Monroe County chpt. N.Y. State Assn. Retarded Children, 1973-74; mem. project adv. group Nat. Legal Services Program, 1975; enabler task force on corrections jud. process com. Genessee Ecumenical Ministries, 1973—; mem. correction adv. com. on minimum standards for local correctional facilities N.Y. State Commn. on Correction, 1975-76; mem. policy com. N.Y. State Coalition for Criminal Justice, 1975—; chmn. Rochester Action Coalition, 1976-77; bd. dirs. Vols. in Partnership, Rochester, 1973—, v.p., 1974; bd. dirs. Genessee Valley chpt. N.Y. Civil Liberties Union, 1975-76. Mem. Am., N.Y. State, Monroe County (coordinator study on minimum jail standards) bar assns., Nat. Legal and Defenders Assn. Home: 195 San Gabriel Dr Rochester NY 14610 Office: 80 W Main St Rochester NY 14614 Tel (716) 325-2520

LEVEN, STANLEY, b. Logan, Utah, Jan. 28, 1919; B.A. cum laude, Harvard, 1941; LL.B., Yale, 1947. Admitted to Conn. bar, 1947; individual practice law, Hartford, Conn., 1947—; sec., dir. H.P. Kopplemann, Inc., Gerber Sci. Instrument Co.; v.p. Gerber Sci.-Europe, S.A., Brussels, Beta Engring. and Devel., Ltd., Beer Sheva, Israel; sec. Gerber Scientific-U.K. Ltd., London, Gerber Sci. Instruments GmbH, Munich. Mem. West Hartford (Conn.) Town Council, 1959-61, Capitol Region Planning Agy., 1962-72; research asso. Conn. Constl. Conv., 1965. Mem. Am., Conn., Hartford County bar assns. Home: 777 Prospect Ave West Hartford CT 06105 Office: 111 Pearl St Hartford CT 06103 Tel (203) 278-2802

LEVENFELD, MILTON ARTHUR, b. Chgo., Mar. 18, 1927; Ph.B., U. Chgo., 1947; J.D., 1950. Admitted to Ill. bar, 1950, U.S. Tax Ct. bar, 1959, U.S. Supreme Ct. bar, 1970; with firm Levenfeld, Kanter, Baskes & Lippitz, and predecessors, Chgo., asso., 1951-60, partner, 1961—. Trustee, Spertus Coll. Judaica; bd. dirs. Council for Jewish Elderly; bd. dirs. Jewish Fedn. Met. Chgo.; co. gen. chmn. Chgo. Jewish United Fund, 1977. Mem. Am., Ill., Chgo. bar assns., Lawyers' Com. for Civil Rights Under Law. Home: 866 Stonegate Dr Highland Park IL 60035 Office: 10 S LaSalle St Chicago IL 60603 Tel (312) 346-8380

LEVENSOHN, JAMES, b. Worcester, Mass., June 3, 1909; A.B., Harvard, 1930, J.D., 1933. Admitted to Mass. bar, 1933; individual practice, Boston, 1933; asso. firms Mapplebeck, Alberts & Sugarman, 1934-37, Ritvo & Levensohn, 1937-61, Levensohn and Zahka, 1961-71; of counsel firm Weiss, Zimmerman and Angoff, Boston, 1973—; served with Judge Adv. div. U.S. Army, 1943-45; commr. civil service Commonwealth Mass., 1961-64, spl. asst. atty. gen., 1975—; land ct. examiner Mass. Conveyancers Assn. Named master Superior Ct. Mass. Mem. Brookline (Mass.) Town Meeting; treas., v.p. Community Center. Mem. Mass., Boston, Norfolk County bar assns. Home: 269 Clark Rd Brookline MA 02146 Office: 50 Congress St Boston MA 02109 Tel (617) 742-3840

LEVENSON, ALAN JOEL, b. Portland, Maine, July 11, 1934; A.B., Brown U., 1956; LL.B., Portland U., 1959. Admitted to Maine bar, 1959, U.S. Supreme Ct. bar, 1962; partner firm Levenson & Levenson, Portland, 1959—. Pres. Jewish Home for Aged, Portland, 1970-72, Jewish Fedn. of So. Maine, 1973-74. Mem. Am., Maine, Cumberland County (Maine) bar assns., Am. Judicature Soc. Office: 187 Middle St Portland ME 04111 Tel (207) 774-7841

LEVENSON, ELI HAROLD, b. Denver, Dec. 26, 1908; A.B., U. So. Calif., 1931, J.D., 1934; grad. Nat. Coll. State Trial Judges U. Nev., 1968. Admitted to Calif. bar, 1934, U.S. Supreme Ct. bar, 1953; practiced in Los Angeles, 1934-36, San Diego, 1936-59; judge Superior Ct. Calif., 1959—, presiding judge, 1975, 76, presiding judge criminal div., 1967-68; mem. faculty Calif. Center for Jud. Edn. and

Research, Berkeley, 1973-74. Bd. dirs. Travelers' Aid Soc., Bd. Pub. Welfare, San Diego, Children's Home Soc., San Diego; v.p. Community Chest, San Diego. Mem. Am. Bar Assn., Am. Judicature Soc. Office: 220 W Broadway San Diego CA 92101 Tel (714) 236-2121

LEVENSON, HARVEY STUART, b. N.Y.C., May 1, 1940; B.A., Drake U., 1962, J.D., 1963; LL.M., Georgetown U., 1966. Admitted to Iowa bar, 1963, N.Y. bar, 1964, Conn. bar, 1968; atty. IRS, Washington, 1964-68; atty. firm Murtha, Cullina, Richter & Pinney, Hartford, Conn., 1968—, partner, 1970—; lectr. law U. Conn. Sch. Law, Hartford, 1970-74; Yale U., 1971-74; Tax Inst., 1975. Mem. Am., N.Y. State, Iowa, Conn. (chmn. tax sect. 1974), Hartford County bar assns. Office: 101 Pearl St Hartford CT 06103 Tel (203) 549-4500

LEVENTHAL, HAROLD, b. N.Y.C., Jan. 5, 1915; A.B., Columbia, 1934, LL.B., 1936. Admitted to N.Y. State bar, 1936, D.C. bar, 1946; law clk. to Justice Harlan F. Stone, U.S. Supreme Ct., 1936-37, to Justice Stanley Reed, 1938; mem. staff Office Solicitor Gen. Washington, 1938-39; chief of litigation div. bituminous coal Dept. Interior, Washington, 1939-40; asst. gen. counsel Office Price Adminstrn., Washington, 1940-43; mem. staff Justice Jackson, Nuremberg Trials, Germany, 1945-46; exec. officer task force on ind. regulatory commns. Hoover Commn., 1948; chief counsel Office Price Stblzn., Washington, 1951-52; mem. firm Ginsburg & Leventhal and successors, Washington, 1946-65; judge U.S. Ct. Appeals, D.C. Circuit, 1965—; gen. counsel Democratic Nat. Com., 1952-65; vis. lectr. Yale Law Sch., 1957-62; Regents lectr. U. Calif., Los Angeles, 1974; Mooers lectr. Am. U., 1975; Sulzbacher lectr. Columbua, 1976. Mem. Fed. (nat. council 1951-52), Am., D.C. bar assns., Phi Beta Kappa. Recipient Green prize Columbia, 1934, Toppan prize, Ordronaux prize, 1936; author: The Role of the Price Lawyer, 1947; contbr. articles to legal publs. Home: 2406 44th St Washington DC 20007 Office: US Ct of Appeals Washington DC 20001

LEVENTHAL, NORMAN PERRY, b. Washington, Sept. 7, 1943; B.A. with honors, U. Md., 1965; LL.B., Yale, 1968. Admitted to D.C. bar, 1968, U.S. Supreme Ct. bar, 1972; asso. firm McKenna, Wilkinson & Kittner, Washington, 1968-73, partner, 1973—. Mem. Am., D.C., FCC bar assns. Home: 12817 Lamp Post Ln Potomac MD 20854 Office: 1150 17th St Washington DC 20036 Tel (202) 296-1600

LEVENTON, LAWRENCE F., b. Pitts., Aug. 15, 1944; B.A., Kenyon Coll., 1966; J.D., U. Pitts., 1969. Admitted to Pa. bar, 1969; law clk. Allegheny County (Pa.) Ct. Common Pleas, Pitts., 1969-70; partner firm Leventon & Leventon, Pitts., 1973—. Mem. Allegheny County Bar Assn. Office: 101 Lawyers Bldg Pittsburgh PA 15219 Tel (412) 281-1740

LEVESQUE, GERARD D., b. Port Daniel, Que., Can., 1926; LL.B., McGill U. Called to Que. bar, 1949; partner firm Sheehan & Levesque, New Carlisle, Que., until 1960; mem. Que. Legislature for Bonaventure, 1956-60; minister game and fisheries Province of Que., Quebec City, 1960-62, minister industry and commerce, 1962-66, 70-72, mem. Que. Parliament, 1966-70; minister intergovtl. affairs, 1970-71, 72—, vice prime minister and minister of justice, 1972—; partner firm Levesque & Arsenault 1966-73, Levesque & Landry, 1973—. Mem. Quebec Assn. Automobile Dealers, Gaspe Peninsula C. of C. Home: Sillery PQ Canada Office: Parliament Bldgs PQ Canada*

LEVEY, HAROLD LAWRENCE, b. Cleve., Feb. 27, 1944; B.S. in Bus. Adminstrn., Miami U., Oxford, Ohio, 1965; J.D., Northwestern U., 1968. Admitted to Ohio Supreme Ct. bar, 1968, U.S. Dist. Ct. for No. Dist. of Ohio eastern div. bar, 1972, U.S. Supreme Ct. bar, 1975; staff counsel community devel. Cleve. Legal Aid Soc., 1969-71; asso. firm Berkman, Gordon, and Kancelbaum, Cleve., 1971-75; individual practice law, Cleve., 1975—; vol. atty. VISTA, 1968-69. Mem. Am., Cleve., Ohio bar assns. Home: 2319 Halcyon Rd Beachwood OH 44122 Office: 830 Leader Bldg Cleveland OH 44114 Tel (216) 781-7879

LEVI, DEMPSEY MEYER, b. New Orleans, Nov. 29, 1941; B.S. in Chemistry, Millsaps Coll., 1963; B.S. in Pharmacy, U. Miss., 1965, J.D., 1969. Admitted to Miss. bar; individual practice law, Pascagoula, Miss., 1969-73; partner firm Levi, Wilson & Denham, Pascagoula and Ocean Springs, Miss., 1973—; dir., gen. mgr. Sav-Rex Pharmacies, Controllex Enterprises, 1969—; mem. Miss. Ho. of Reps., 1976—. Mem. Miss. State, Jackson County pharm. assns., Miss. State, Jackson County, Am. bar assns., Am. Soc. Pharmacy Law (charter). Tel (601) 769-2563

LEVI, EDWARD HIRSCH, b. Chgo., June 26, 1911; Ph.B., U. Chgo., 1932, J.D., 1935; J.S.D. (Sterling fellow 1935-36), Yale U., 1938; numerous hon. degrees. Admitted to Ill. bar, 1936; asst. prof. law U. Chgo., 1936-40, prof., 1945-75, dean 1950-62, provost 1962-68, pres. 1968-75, pres. emeritus 1975—, Karl Llewellyn distinguished service prof., 1975—; spl. asst. to atty. gen. U.S., Washington, 1940-45; 1st. asst. war div. U.S. Dept. Justice, 1943, 1st. asst. antitrust div., 1944-45; chmn. interdepartmental com. monopolies and cartels, 1944; counsel Fed. Atomic Scientists with Respect to Atomic Energy Act, 1946; counsel Subcom. Monopoly Power, Jud. Com. 81st Congress, 1950; guest prof. U. Colo., summer 1960; Benjamin N. Cardozo lectr., also Randolph Tucker lectr.; atty. gen. U.S., Washington, D.C., 1975-76. Trustee Urban Inst., 1968-75, Internat. Legal Center, 1966-75, Mus. Sci. and Industry, 1971-75, Russell Sage Found., 1971-75, Aspen Inst. Humanist Studies, 1970-75, Inst. Internat. Edn., 1969, Woodrow Wilson Nat. Fellowship Found., 1972-75, Inst. Psychoanalysis Chgo., 1961-75; mem. research adv. bd. Com. Econ. Devel., 1951-54; bd. dirs. Social Sci. Research Council, 1959-62, Commn. on Founds. and Pvt. Philanthropy, 1969-70; mem. Citizens Commn. on Grad. Med. Edn., 1963-66; mem. White House Task Force on Edn., 1966-67; mem. Pres.'s Task Force on Priorities in Higher Edn., 1969-70; mem. Sloan Commn. Cable Communications, 1970-71; mem. Nat. Commn. Productivity, 1970-75; mem. White House Central Group Domestic Affairs, 1964; mem. Nat. Council on the Humanities, 1974-75. Fellow Am. Bar Found., Am. Acad. Arts and Scis.; mem. Am., Ill., Chgo. bar assns., Am. Law Inst., Am. Judicature Soc., Phi Beta Kappa, Order of Coif. Author: Introduction to Legal Reasoning, 1949; Four Talks on Legal Education, 1952; Point of View, 1969; The Crisis in the Nature of Law, 1969; (with Roscoe Steffen) Elements of the Law, 1950; (with James W. Moore) Gilbert's Collier on Bankruptcy, 1936; mem. editorial bd. Jour. Legal Edn., 1956-58; asso. editor Nat. Law Forum 1956-68; bd. editors Encyclopedia Britannica, 1968-75. Recipient distinguished citizen award, Ill. St. Andrews Soc., 1975; centennial award, Chgo. Bar Assn., 1975; award Fed. Bar Assn., 1975; Herbert H. Lehman Ethics medal, Jewish Theol. Sem. Miami, 1976; Learned Hand Medal for Excellance in Fed. Jurisprudence, Fed. Bar Council, N.Y.C., 1976; Wallace award, Am. Scottish Found., 1976; Morris J. Kaplun Meml. prize, 1976. Office: President Emeritus U Chgo 5801 S Ellis Ave Chicago IL 60637

LEVI, JAMES HENRY, b. Stevens Point, Wis., July 16, 1913; student U. Wis., Stevens Point, 1931-33; LL.B., U. Notre Dame, 1937. Admitted to Wis. bar, 1937; br. office claims mgr. Sentry Ins. Co., Stevens Point, 1937-42; mem. firm Cashin, Dunn, Bablitch & Levi, Stevens Point, 1945-51; judge Portage County (Wis.) Ct., Stevens Point, 1951-68, 7th Jud. Circuit Ct. Wis., 1969—; dist. atty. Portage County, 1948-51; pres. Wis. Bd. Juvenile Ct. Judges, 1957; mem. Bd. Circuit Judges, 1969—. Mem. Stevens Point Bd. Health, 1950-66; bd. dirs. St. Michael's Hosp. Stevens Point, 1958—, pres., 1965. Mem. Portage County Bar Assn., Wis. State Bar. Recipient Distinguished Citizen award for Stevens Point Stevens Point Jaycees, 1968; named Papal Honor Knight of the Holy Sepulchre, 1969. Home: 1516 Wisconsin St Stevens Point WI 54481 Office: County-City Bldg Stevens Point WI 54481 Tel (715) 346-2071

LEVI, PETER STEVEN, b. Washington, June 3, 1944; B.A., Northwestern U., 1966; J.D., U. Mo., Kansas City, 1969, LL.M., 1971, Carnegie-Mellon U. fellow, 1975. Admitted to Mo. bar, 1969; dep. exec. dir., gen. counsel Mid-Am. Regional Council, Kansas City, Mo., 1969—; lectr. Sch. Law U. Mo., Kansas City, 1972-76. Mem. Am., Mo., Kansas City bar assns., Am. Soc. Pub. Adminstrn. Author: Model-Subdivision Regulations, 1975; contbr. Midwest Rev. Pub. Adminstrn., U. Mo. Law Rev., The Urban Lawyer. Home: 9630 Chadwick St Overland Park KS 66206 Office: Suite 200 20 W 9th St Kansas City MO 64105 Tel (816) 474-4240

LEVIE, HOWARD SIDNEY, b. Wolverine, Mich., Dec. 19, 1907; A.B., Cornell U., 1928, J.D., 1930; LL.M., George Washington U., 1957. Admitted to N.Y. bar, 1931, Mo. bar, 1965, U.S. Supreme Ct. bar, 1947; assoc. firm Weit & Goldman, N.Y.C., 1933-42; served to col. JAGC, 1942-63; prof. law St. Louis U., 1963—; Charles H. Stockton Chair Internat. Law, Naval War Coll., Newport, R.I., 1971-72. Trustee St. Louis Council on World Affairs, 1968-76, v.p., 1971-73. Mem. Am., St. Louis bar assns., Am. Soc. Internat. Law. Legal adviser UN Command Korean Armistice Del., 1951-52; contbr. articles to legal jours. Home: 4905 Lindell Blvd St Louis MO 63108 Office: 3700 Lindell Blvd St Louis MO 63108 Tel (314) 535-3300

LEVIE, JOSEPH HENRY, b. N.Y.C., Jan. 19, 1929; A.B., Columbia, 1949, LL.B., 1951. Admitted to N.Y. State bar, 1951, U.S. Supreme Ct. bar, 1959; Bigelow fellow U. Chgo. Law Sch., 1951-52; asso. firm Laporte & Meyers, N.Y.C., 1953-58; asso. gen. counsel Loew's Theatres & Hotels, N.Y.C., 1958-63; mem. firm Rathheim Hoffman Kassel & Silverman, N.Y.C., 1963-67, partner, 1967—. Mem. Assn. Bar City N.Y., N.Y. County Lawyers Assn., Assn. Comml. Fin. Attys., Practicing Law Inst. (chmn. programs 1976, 77, participant equipment leasing program). Contbr. articles to legal jours. Home: 131 Riverside Dr New York City NY 10024 Office: 61 Broadway New York City NY 10006 Tel (212) 943-3100

LEVIN, A. LEO, b. N.Y.C., Jan. 1, 1919; B.A., Yeshiva Coll., 1939; J.D., U. Pa., 1942. Admitted to N.Y. bar, 1947; Univ. fellow Columbia, N.Y.C., 1946-47; instr. to asst. prof. law U. Iowa, Iowa City, 1947-49; asst. to asso. prof. law U. Pa., Phila., 1949-53, prof., 1953—, vice provost, 1965-68; v.p. academic affairs Yeshiva U., N.Y.C., N.Y., 1969-70; dir. Nat. Inst. Trial Advocacy, 1971-73; bd. dirs. Council on Legal Edn. for Profl. Responsibility, 1973—; exec. dir. Commn. on Revision of Fed. Ct. Appellate System, 1973-75. Chmn., Pa. Legis. Reapportionment Commn., 1971-73; pres. Jewish Publ. Soc. Am., 1975—. Mem. Am., Phila. bar assns., Am. Law Inst., Order of the Coif (nat. pres. 1967-70). Author: (with E. Woolley) Dispatch and Delay: A Field Study of Judicial Adminstrn. in Pa., 1961; (with H. Cramer) Problems on Trial Advocacy, 1968; (with J. Chadbourn and P. Shuchman) Cases on Civil Procedure, 2d edit., 1974. Home: 2207 Delancey Pl Philadelphia PA 19103 Office: 3400 Chestnut St Philadelphia PA 19104 Tel (215) 243-7486

LEVIN, ARNOLD SAMPSON, b. Lorain, Ohio, Dec. 10, 1909; J.D., Ohio State U. Admitted to Ohio bar, 1934, U.S. Supreme Ct. bar, 1958, U.S. Ct. Claims bar, 1949; mem. firm Levin & Levin, Lorain, 1934-42, 46-64, Levin & Durfee, Lorain, 1965—. Mem. Am., Ohio State, Lorain County bar assns., Assn. Trial Lawyers Am., Ohio Acad. Trial Lawyers. Home: 5555 Lake Rd Sheffield Lake OH 44054 Office: 216 7th St Lorain OH 44052 Tel (216) 245-6979

LEVIN, CARL, b. Detroit, June 28, 1934; B.A., Swarthmore Coll., 1956; LL.B., Harvard, 1959. Admitted to Mich. bar, 1959; mem. firm Grossman, Hyman & Grossman, Detroit, 1959-64; asst. atty. gen., Mich., 1964-67; gen. counsel Mich. Civil Rights Commn., 1964-67; head appellate div. Defender's Office, Detroit, 1968-69; councilman, City of Detroit, 1970—, pres., 1974—; former instr. U. Detroit Law Sch., Wayne U. Law Sch. (Detroit). mem. defense servies com. Mich. Supreme Ct.; exec. com. Southeastern Mich. Council of Govts. Advisory bd. United Found. Mem. Mich., Detroit, Am. bar assns. Recipient Detroit ACLU Bill Rights Award, 1964; Detroit Audubon Soc. Honors Award, 1972; Harriett Ross Tubman Award, 1974; Ethnic of Year Award, 1976. Home: 20044 Renfrew St Detroit MI 48221 Office: City-County Bldg Detroit MI 48226 Tel (313) 224-4500

LEVIN, CHARLES LEONARD, b. Detroit, Apr. 28, 1926; B.A., U. Mich., 1946, LL.B., 1947. Admitted to Mich. bar, 1947, N.Y. State bar, 1949, D.C. bar, 1954; partner firm Levin, Levin, Garvett & Dill, Detroit, 1950-66; judge Mich. Ct. of Appeals, 1966-72; justice Mich. Supreme Ct., 1973—; mem. Mich. Law Revision Commn., 1966. Mem. Am. Law Inst. Home: 18280 Fairway Dr Detroit MI 48221 Office: 1008 Travelers Tower 26555 Evergreen Rd Southfield MI 48076 Tel (313) 444-8484

LEVIN, DAVID HAROLD, b. Pensacola, Fla., Nov. 19, 1928; A.B., Duke, 1949; J.D., U. Fla., 1952. Admitted to Fla. bar, 1952; asst. county solicitor Escambia County, Fla., 1952; sr. partner firm Levin, Warfield, Middlebrooks, Graff, Mabie, Rosenbloum & Magie, Pensacola, Fla.; chmn. 1st Jud. Circuit Fla. Nominating Commn., 1976—; chmn. Fla. Pollution Control Bd., 1971-74. Chmn., Escambia County Cancer Crusade, 1963-65; pres. Escambia County unit Am. Cancer Soc., 1964-65; bd. dirs. W. Fla. Heart Assn., 1966-69; chmn. United Jewish Appeal Escambia County, 1967-68. Mem. Fla. Alumni Assn. (pres. Escambia County chpt. 1960), U. Fla. Alumni Assn. (dist. v.p. 1961-62). Recipient Good Govt. Pensacola Jaycees, 1972. Home: 3632 Menendez Dr Pensacola FL 32503 Office: 226 S Palafox St Pensacola FL 32501 Tel (904) 432-1461

LEVIN, DAVID LAWRENCE, b. Galveston, Tex., Jan. 14, 1947; B.A., U. Houston, 1970, J.D., 1973. Admitted to Tex. bar, 1973; asso. firm Nussbaum & Redmond, Galveston, 1973-74; sr. analyst Exxon Co. U.S.A., Houston, 1974-75; staff atty. Amoco Prodn. Co., Houston, 1975—. Mem. Am. Bar Assn., Alpha Phi Omega, Delta Theta Phi, U. Houston Alumni Assn. Recipient Am. Jurisprudence award Acad. Excellence Legal Studies, 1972; editor Houston Law Rev., 1972-73. Office: PO Box 3092 Houston TX 77001 Tel (713) 652-5402

LEVIN, EDWARD M., JR., b. Chgo., Oct. 16, 1934; B.S., U. Ill., 1955; LL.B., Harvard, 1958. Admitted to Ill. bar, 1958, U.S. Supreme Ct. bar, 1968; mem. firm Ancel, Stonesifer, Glink & Levin, and predecessors, Chgo., 1958, 61-68; draftsman Ill. Legis. Reference Bur., Springfield, 1961; spl. asst. to regional adminstr. HUD, Chgo., 1968-71, asst. regional adminstr. for community planning and mgmt., 1971-73; asst. dir. Ill. Dept. Local Govt. Affairs, Chgo., 1973-77; of counsel firm Holleb, Gerstein & Glass, Ltd., Chgo., 1977—; lectr. U. Ill. Inst. Govt. and Pub. Affairs, 1972-73; adj. asso. prof. urban scis. U. Ill., 1973—; lectr. Loyola U., 1976—. Mem. Ill. Nature Preserves Commn., 1963-68, Northeastern Ill. Planning Commn., 1974—, Ill. Ind. Bi-State Commn., 1974—. Mem. Ill. Bar Assn. (Lincoln award 1977), Chgo. Council of Lawyers, Am. Soc. Planning Ofcls., Urban Land Inst., ACLU (dir. Ill. div.). Contbr. articles to profl. jours. Home: 5445 S Hyde Park Blvd Chicago IL 60615 Office: One IBM Plaza Chicago IL 60611 Tel (312) 822-9060

LEVIN, FREDRIC GERSON, b. Pensacola, Fla., Mar. 29, 1937; B.S.B.A., U. Fla., 1958, LL.B., 1961. Admitted to Fla. bar, 1961; partner firm Levin, Warfield, Middlebrooks, Graff, Mabie, Rosenbloum & Magie, and predecessors, Pensacola, 1961—. Fellow Acad. Fla. Trial Lawyers; mem. Soc. of Bar 1st Jud. Circuit (exec. com. 1966), Fla. Bar, Am. Bar Assn., Ala. Trial Lawyers Assn., Assn. Trial Lawyers Am., Order of Coif, Phi Kappa Phi. Recipient Harrison Top Freshman award U. Fla., 1959, Brick Legal Writing award, 1960. Home: 3600 Menendez Dr Pensacola FL 32503 Office: 9th floor Seville Tower 226 S Palafox St Pensacola FL 32501 Tel (904) 432-1461

LEVIN, GEORGE, b. Erie, Pa., Oct. 15, 1925; B.A., U. Pitts., 1948, LL.B., 1950. Asso. firm Jess S. Jiuliante, Erie, 1950-59; admitted to Pa. Supreme Ct. bar, 1951, U.S. Dist. Ct. bar, 3d Circuit Ct. U.S., others; mem. firm Clinton Shamp, Erie, 1959-64; partner firm Shamp, Levin, Arduini & Hain, Erie, 1964-72, 73—; judge Ct. Common Pleas of Erie County of 6th Jud. Dist. of Pa., 1972-73; lectr. Behrend Campus Pa. State U., Erie, 1950-60, Mercyhurst Coll., Erie, 1974—. Mem. Pa. N.W. Regional Justice Commn. Mem. Erie County Bar, Pa., Am. bar assns., Pi Gamma Mu. Home: 311 Arlington Rd Erie PA 16509 Office: 329 W 6th St Erie PA 16512 Tel (814) 452-3151

LEVIN, MAX, b. Russia, Nov. 15, 1900; A.B., Brown U., 1923; J.D., Harvard, 1926. Admitted to R.I. bar, 1926; practice law, Providence; mem. R.I. Ho. of Reps., 1951-52. Mem. Am. Acad. Matrimonial Lawyers, R.I. (lectr. continuing legal edn. 1971), Am. bar assns. Home: 1 Jackson Walkway Providence RI 02903 Office: 401 Turks Head Bldg Providence RI 02903 Tel (401) 831-6968

LEVIN, MORRIS JACOB, b. St. Louis, Aug. 30, 1909; J.D., Washington U., St. Louis, 1930. Admitted to Mo. bar, 1931, U.S. Supreme Ct. bar, 1938; asso. Victor Packman, St. Louis, 1931-50; sr. partner firm Levin & Weinhaus, St. Louis, 1959—; chmn. labor law com. Mo. Bar Integrated, 1973. Mem. Am., Mo., St. Louis (past chmn. labor law com.) bar assns. Home: 55 Clermont Ln Ladue MO 63124 Office: 1602 Executive Bldg 515 Olive St Saint Louis MO 63101 Tel (314) 621-3863

LEVIN, MURRAY SIMON, b. Phila., Feb. 8, 1943; B.A., Haverford Coll., 1964; M.A., Harvard, 1968, LL.B., 1968; Root-Tilden Law fellow N.Y. U. Law Sch., 1964; certificate Hague Internat. Acad. Law, 1967. Admitted to Pa. bar, 1968; instr. English, Harvard, 1965-68; law clk. to judge U.S. Dist. Ct. for Eastern Pa., 1968-70; instr. govt. Haverford (Pa.) Coll., 1970-71; partner firm Pepper, Hamilton & Scheetz, Phila., 1970—; producer, interviewer radio program Sta. WUHY-FM, Phila., 1971—. Pres. Phila. Council Expt. Internat. Living, 1967-70; mem. Phila. Urban Coalition Housing Task Force, 1968—; chmn. coll. div. Allied Jewish Appeal, 1968-70; pres. Central Phila. Reform Democrats, 1973-74. Mem. Phi Beta Kappa. Contbr. revs. to legal jours. Office: Pepper Hamilton & Scheetz 123 S Broad St Philadelphia PA 19109 Tel (215) 545-1234

LEVIN, NORMAN LEWIS, b. Lewistown, Pa. Dec. 11, 1924; B.A., Dickinson Coll., 1948, J.D., 1950. Admitted to Pa. bar, 1950, U.S. Supreme Ct. bar, 1960; partner firm Stuckenrath & Levin, Lewistown, 1951-54; individual practice law, Lewistown, 1954-67; partner firm Brugler & Levin, Lewistown, 1967—. Mem. Am., Pa., Mifflin County (sec.-treas. 1963-65, pres. 1965-67) bar assns., Assn. Trial Lawyers Am., Am. Jurisprudence Soc., Pa. Sch. Bd. Solicitors Assn. (pres. 1967). Home: 624 S Wayne St Lewistown PA 17044 Office: 10 S Wayne St Lewistown PA 17044 Tel (717) 248-4971

LEVIN, ROBERT DANIEL, b. N.Y.C., Feb. 27, 1930; B.A., Rutgers U., 1951; J.D., Columbia, 1954. Admitted to N.Y. bar, 1954; partner firm Demov, Morris, Levin & Shein, N.Y.C., 1954-63, sr. partner, 1963—. Mem. N.Y. State Bar Assn., Bar Assn. City N.Y. (state legislation and real property law com.), Phi Beta Kappa, Phi Alpha Delta. Asso. editor N.Y. Law Jour. Realty Law Digest, 1970—. Home: 12 Varian Ln Scarsdale NY 10583 Office: 40 W 57th St New York City NY 10019 Tel (212) 757-5050

LEVIN, ROGER MICHAEL, b. N.Y.C., Oct. 20, 1942; B.A. in Polit. Sci., U. Chgo., 1964; Fulbright scholar, U. Sri Lanka, 1964-65; M.A. with distinction in Polit. Sci. (Woodrow Wilson fellow), U. Calif., Berkeley, 1966; J.D., N.Y. U., 1969. Admitted to N.Y. bar, 1970, U.S. Ct. Appeals for 2d Circuit bar, 1971, U.S. Dist. Ct. So. Dist. N.Y., 1971, U.S. Dist. Ct. Eastern N.Y., 1971, U.S. Customs Ct. bar, 1974, U.S. Ct. of Customs and Patent Appeals bar, 1974, U.S. Supreme Ct. bar, 1974; personal asst. to U.S. rep. Dept. State, Quang Nam Province, S.Vietnam, 1966; asst. to dir. Nr. East/S. Asia Bur., Office Internat. Security Affairs, Office Sec. Def., Washington, 1967; asso. firm Wien, Lane & Malkin, N.Y.C., 1969-70; partner firm Levin & Weissman, N.Y.C., 1975—. Mem. Am., N.Y. State bar assns., Assn. Bar City N.Y., Am. Soc. Internat. Law Inst. Internat. Edn., Woodrow Wilson Nat. Fellowship Found., Asia Soc. Named Best Oralist, Jessup Internat. Law Moot Ct. Regional Competition, N.Y. U., 1969. Research editor N.Y. U. Jour. Internat. Law and Politics. Office: 122 E 42d St New York City NY 10017 Tel (212) 867-7070

LEVIN, STUART IRWIN, b. Bridgeport, Conn., May 2, 1930; B.S., U. Conn., 1952; J.D., Boston U., 1955. Admitted to Conn. bar, 1955, U.S. Supreme Ct. bar, 1959; sr. partner firm Levin and Charmoy, Bridgeport, 1965—; mem. panel of arbitrators Am. Arbitration Assn. Bd. dirs. Easton (Conn.) Babe Ruth League, 1973-76. Mem. Am., Conn., Bridgeport bar assns., Comml. Law League Am. Office: 1188 Main St Bridgeport CT 06604 Tel (203) 336-4444

LEVIN, SUZANNE, b. Balt., Jan. 2, 1935; A.B., Goucher Coll., 1956; J.D., Am. U., 1973. Admitted to Md. bar, 1973; asst. county atty., Montgomery County, Rockville, Md., 1974—. Mem. Am., Md., Montgomery County Bar Assns. Office: 100 Maryland Ave Rockville MD 20850 Tel: (301) 279-1346

LEVINE, BARRY JAY, b. Bklyn., June 6, 1945; A.B., Syracuse U., 1967; J.D., Bklyn. Law Sch., 1970. Admitted to N.Y. State bar, 1971, U.S. Supreme Ct. bar, 1974; asst. dist. atty. Nassau County (N.Y.), 1971-74; individual practice law, Valley Stream, N.Y., 1974-76; partner firm Ansell and Levine, Mineola, N.Y., 1977—; prosecutor Village of Bayville (N.Y.), 1975—. Mem. Nassau County Bar Assn. Office: 274 Old Country Rd Mineola NY 11501 Tel (516) 741-0222

LEVINE, BERNARD DAVID, b. Buffalo, Dec. 10, 1939; A.B., Syracuse U., 1961; LLB., U. Buffalo, 1964, J.D., 1968. Admitted to N.Y. State bar, 1964; partner firm Rosenbaum, Agnello, Agnello & Levine, Rochester, N.Y., 1968-73; individual practice law, Rochester, 1973—, confidential clk., N.Y. Supreme Ct., 1970-73. Trustee Temple Sinai, Rochester, 1976—. Mem. N.Y. State, Monroe County bar assns., Am. Arbitration Assn. Office: 1000 Reynolds Arcade Bldg Rochester NY 14614 Tel (716) 454-5382

LEVINE, BERNARD LEON, lawyer; b. Hurleyville, N.Y., May 26, 1921; student St. John's U., 1938-39, student N.Y. U., 1940-42, 46-47; LL.B., Bklyn. Law Sch., 1949. Admitted to N.Y. bar, 1949; sr. mem. law firm Levine & Levine, Liberty, N.Y., 1949-76. Mem. Sullivan County (sec. 1950-52, pres. 1974-75), Am., N.Y. State bar assns. Trustee, Community Gen. Hosp. of Sullivan County. Home: Liberty NY 12754

LEVINE, DAVID NORMAN, b. Bklyn., Jan. 17, 1944; B.A., Bklyn. Coll., 1964; J.D., N.Y. U., 1968. Admitted to N.Y. State bar, 1968, U.S. Ct. Appeals bar, 1972, U.S. Supreme Ct. bar, 1972; v.p., atty. Charles Goodman, Nassau, Hirsch, Inc., Elmsford, N.Y., 1968—; partner firm Goodman & Levine, profl. corp., Elmsford, 1974—. Contbr. articles to legal jours. Home: 516 Bellwood Ave North Tarrytown NY 10571 Office: 570 Taxter Rd Elmsford NY 10523 Tel (914) 592-3333

LEVINE, EDWARD LESLIE, b. Sheboygan, Wis., June 11, 1927; B.A., U. Wis., 1950, LL.B., 1952. Admitted to Wis. bar, 1952, N.Y. bar, 1957; counsel Comptroller of the Currency, Dept. Treasury, Washington, 1952-56; asso. firm Cole & Deitz, N.Y.C., 1956-62, partner, 1962—. Mem. devel. council C.W. Post Center of L.I. U., 1970—. Mem. Am., N.Y. State bar assns., State Bar Wis. Home: 157 Hemlock Rd Manhasset NY 11030 Office: 40 Wall St New York City NY 10005 Tel (212) 269-2500

LEVINE, HOWARD ARNOLD, b. Mar. 4, 1932; B.A., Yale, 1953, LL.B., 1956. Admitted to N.Y. bar, 1956; asst. in instruction, research asso. in criminal law Yale Law Sch., 1956-57; asso. firm Hughes, Hubbard, Blair, Reed, N.Y.C., 1957-59; practiced in Schenectady, 1959-70; asst. dist. atty. Schenectady County (N.Y.), 1961-66, dist. atty., 1967-70; judge Schenectady County Family Ct., 1971—; acting judge Schenectady County Ct., 1971—; vis. lectr. Albany Law Sch.; mem. N.Y. Gov.'s. Panel on Juvenile Violence; mem. N.Y. State Temporary Commn. on Child Welfare, N.Y. State Juvenile Justice Advisory Bd. Bd. dirs. Schenectady County Child Guidance Center, Carver Community Center Freedom Forum of Schenectady. Mem. Am. Law Inst., Assn. Family Ct. Judges of State N.Y. (treas.). Home: 1312 Rowe Rd Schenectady NY 12309 Office: County Bldg 620 State St Schenectady NY 12307 Tel (518) 382-3306

LEVINE, IRVING A., b. Washington, July 10, 1924; LL.B., George Washington U., 1949. Admitted to D.C. bar, 1950, Md. bar, 1955; individual practice law, Washington, 1950-66, Montgomery County, Md., 1950-66; judge Md. Tax Ct., 1965-67; asso. judge 6th Jud. Circuit of Md., 1967-72, Md. Ct. Appeals, Rockville, 1972—. Mem. Am., Md. State, Montgomery County bar assns., Nat. Conf. of Appellate Judges, Am. Judicature Soc. Recipient Distinguished Alumnus award George Washington U. Law Sch., 1974. Home: 9805 Inglemere Dr Bethesda MD 20034 Office: PO Box 226 Ct House Station Rockville MD 20850 Tel (301) 340-2424

LEVINE, LAWRENCE EDWARD, b. N.Y.C., Feb. 19, 1936; B.A., U. Mich., 1956, J.D., 1959. Admitted to N.Y. bar, 1960, Tenn. bar, 1961; individual practice law, Nashville, 1961-71; partner firm Levine & Rosenblum, Nashville, 1971—. Mem. Am., Tenn., Nashville bar assns. Recipient Bloomfield prize U. Mich. Law Sch., 1957. Office: 18th floor Life & Casualty Tower Nashville TN 37219 Tel (615) 244-4944

LEVINE, LAWRENCE STEVEN, b. N.Y.C., Mar. 30, 1934; A.B., Colgate U., 1955; LL.B., Yale, 1958. Admitted to N.Y. bar, 1958, U.S. Supreme Ct. bar, 1973; asst. U.S. atty. Dept. Justice Eastern Dist. N.Y., 1958-62; asso. firm Kronish & Leib, N.Y.C., 1962-63; partner firm Beldock, Levine & Hoffman, N.Y.C., 1964—; co-operating counsel N.Y. Civil Liberties Union; counsel Gotham Community Services, N.Y.C. Trustee Harry Levine Meml. Found., 1958—. Mem. Fed Bar Assn., N.Y. County Lawyers Assn., N.Y. Dist. Attys. Assn., Yale Law Sch. Alumni Assn. Home: 122 E 76th St New York City NY 10021 Office: 565 Fifth Ave New York City NY 10017 Tel (212) 490-0400

LEVINE, MARTIN, b. N.Y.C., June 1, 1939; A.B. summa cum laude, Brandeis U., 1960; J.D. with honors, Yale U., 1963; postgrad. Los Angeles Psychoanalytic Inst., 1972—. Admitted to D.C. bar, 1964, Calif. bar, U.S. Supreme Ct. bar; law clk. to U.S. Circuit Ct. judge, Washington, 1963-64, firm Gallop, Climenko & Gould, N.Y.C., 1963; prof. law U. So. Calif., Los Angeles, 1964—, spl. asst. to v.p., 1973; vis. prof. law U. Calif., San Diego, 1967, 71, Columbia U., N.Y.C., 1968-69; sr. dep. fed. pub. defender, Los Angeles, 1971-72, spl. dep., 1972-73; spl. counsel firm Ball, Hunt, Hart, Brown & Baerwitz, 1975-76; gen. counsel U.S. Senate Com. on Judiciary, Subcom. on Constl. Rights, Washington, 1976—; chmn. bd. Western Center on Law and Poverty, Los Angeles; v.p. Nat. Sr. Citizens Law Center, Los Angeles, 1977—. Mem. Calif., D.C., Los Angeles County bars, Am. Psychoanalytic Assn. (affiliate), Am. Psychology-Law Assn. Author: The Current Status of Juvenile Law, 1972; editor Yale Law Jours.; contbr. articles to legal jours. Office: Law Center U So Calif University Park Los Angeles CA 90007 also 102 B Old Senate Office Bldg Washington DC 20510 Tel (213) 746-2106

LEVINE, MELVIN CHARLES, b. Bklyn., Nov. 12, 1930; B.C.S., N.Y. U., 1952; LL.B., Harvard, 1955. Admitted to N.Y. bar, 1956, U.S. Supreme Ct bar, 1964; asso. firm Kriger & Haber, Bklyn., 1956-58; asso. firm Black, Varian & Simon, N.Y.C., 1958-59; individual practice law, N.Y.C., 1959—. Mem. New York County Lawyers Assn. Home: 146 Waverly Pl New York City NY 10014 Office: 475 Fifth Ave New York City NY 10007 Tel (212) MU5-6958

LEVINE, MICHAEL ELIAS, b. N.Y.C., Apr. 8, 1941; B.A. in Philosophy, Reed Coll., 1962; LL.B., Yale, 1965; postgrad., 1965-66; postgrad. (law and econs. fellow), U. Chgo., 1967-68. Asst. prof. law U. So. Calif., 1968-70, asso. prof., 1970-72, prof., 1972—; Luce prof. law and social change in the technol. society Calif. Inst. Tech., 1973—; atty. U.S. Civil Aero. Bd., 1965-66; spl. asst. Task Force on Econ. Growth and Opportunity, U.S. C. of C., 1966-67; vis. prof. law Duke, 1972-73; cons. in field. Trustee Center for Law in the Pub. Interest, 1970-76. Contbr. articles to law revs. Home: 1550 Arroyo View Dr Pasadena CA 91103 Office: Law Center Univ So Calif Los Angeles CA 90007 Tel (213) 741-2390

LEVINE, PHILIP J., b. Toronto, Ont., Can., Feb. 1, 1914; B.A., Coll. City N.Y., 1935; J.D., Columbia U., 1938. Admitted to N.Y. bar, 1938; individual practice law, 1938-55, S.I., N.Y., 1972—; partner Costantino, Levine & Napolitano, and predecessor, 1955-71; arbitrator small claims N.Y.C. Civil Ct. Mem. N.Y. State, Richmond County bar assns. Office: 30 Bay St Staten Island NY 10301 Tel (212) 273-4800

LEVINE, RICHARD LAWRENCE, b. Fall River, Mass., Aug. 7, 1941; A.B., Harvard U., 1963, LL.B., 1966. Admitted to Mass. bar, 1966, D.C. bar, U.S. Supreme Ct. bar, 1972; dep. asst. and asst. atty. gen. Mass., 1968-69; exec. asst. to the adminstr. Law Enforcement Assistance Adminstrn., Washington, D.C., 1969-70; asso. firm Hale & Dorr, Boston, 1970—, partner 1976—; law clk. U.S. Dist. Ct., Conn., 1966-67; instr. Met. Coll. of Boston U., 1972-73; Toor lectr. legal studies Brandeis U., 1977. Mem. Mass. Gov.'s Com. Criminal Justice, Boston, 1970-74. Mem. Boston (co-chmn. criminal law com. 1976), Mass., Am. bar assns. Recipient spl. achievement award, U.S. Dept. Justice, 1970. Home: 11 Bay State Rd Boston MA 02215 Office: 28 State St Boston MA 02109 Tel (617) 742-9100

LEVINE, RICHARD STEVEN, b. DuBois, Pa., Aug. 16, 1946; B.A., Pa. State U., 1968; J.D., Dickinson Coll., 1971; LL.M., U. Wis., 1973. Admitted to Pa. bar, 1971; mem. legal staff Neighborhood Legal Services, Pitts., 1971-72; staff atty. Dane County (Wis.) Legal Services, Madison, 1972-73; asst. atty. gen. Pa. Human Relations Commn., Pitts., 1973; legal counsel Nat. Center for Juvenile Justice, U. Pitts. Law Sch., 1973-75; instr. child advocacy U. Pitts., 1975—; bd. dirs. Children's Lobby of Western Pa., 1975—; chairperson juvenile rights com. ACLU of Pitts., 1976—. Mem. Am., Allegheny County, Pa. bar assns., Am. Orthopsychiat. Assn., Child Welfare League Am. Contbr. articles in field to profl. jours. Home: 37 East West Dr Pittsburgh PA 15237 Office: 517 Frick Bldg Pittsburgh PA 15219 Tel (412) 765-2517

LEVINE, SOLOMON L., b. N.Y.C., Aug. 7, 1923; B.B.A., Coll. City N.Y., 1948; J.D., N.Y. Law Sch., 1953. Admitted to N.Y. bar, 1954; individual practice law, Flushing, N.Y., 1954—; instr. bus. law Adelphi U., 1972; dir. United Vets. Mutual Housing Co., Inc., 1957-60. Pres. Manhasset Hills Estates Civic Assn., 1963-65. Mem. Am., Queens County bar assns., Flushing Lawyers Club, N.Y. Trial Lawyers Assn., Am. Arbitration Assn. Office: 39-01 Main St Flushing NY 11354 Tel (212) 463-6200

LEVINS, WILLIAM FRANCIS, b. N.Y.C., May 19, 1921; B.B.A., Coll. City N.Y., 1942; J.D., U. Calif., San Francisco, 1949. Jr. accountant firm Peat, Marwick & Mitchell, CPA's, N.Y.C., 1946; admitted to Calif. bar, 1950, since practiced in Oakland, Calif.; asso. firm Dieden & Moran, 1949-52, Schofield & Cunningham, 1952-65; judge Municipal Ct. Oakland-Piedmont-Emeryville (Ca.), 1965—. Trustee, Oakland Zoo, 1971-76. Mem. Conf. Calif. Judges, Alameda County Bar Assn., Alameda County Municipal Ct. Judges' Assn. Home: 12 Shetland Ct Oakland CA 94605 Office: 600 Washington St Oakland CA 94607 Tel (415) 874-6381

LEVINSON, BERNARD HIRSH, b. Austin, Tex., Sept. 2, 1907; B.A. with high honors, U. Cin., 1929; J.D., Harvard, 1932. Admitted to Wash. bar, 1933, Hawaii bar, 1946, U.S. Supreme Ct. bar, 1937; practice law, Seattle, 1933-39; atty. U.S. Dept. Justice, Washington, 1939-42; atty. Office Solicitor, U.S. Dept. Interior, Washington, 1942-45, Surplus Property Office, Honolulu, 1945-47; dep. atty. gen. Ter. Hawaii, 1947; practice law, Honolulu, 1947-65; judge 1st Circuit Ct., Honolulu, 1966-67; asso. justice Supreme Ct. Hawaii, 1967-74; individual practice law, Honolulu, 1974-77; partner firm Levinson & Levinson, Honolulu, 1977—; vis. prof. law U. Hawaii, 1975-76. Mem. Am., Hawaii bar assns. Recipient Allan F. Saunders award Hawaii chpt. ACLU, 1974. Home: Hilton Lagoon Apts Apt 11J Honolulu HI 96815 Office: 904 Castle & Cook Bldg 130 Merchant St Honolulu HI 96807 Tel (808) 536-7315

LEVIS, ROBERT JOHN, b. Detroit, July 17, 1932; B.S. in Econs., Villanova U., 1954, LL.B., 1959. Admitted to Pa. bar, 1960, U.S. Supreme Ct. bar, 1965; partner firm Levis Connors & Swanick, Media, Pa., 1968—. Mem. Pa., Delco (jour. editor, 1970-71) bar assns. Home: 1005 Richmond Rd Broomall PA 19008 Office: 211 N Olive St Media PA 19063 Tel (215) LO 6-5600

LEVISS, SIDNEY, b. N.Y.C., July 21, 1917; LL.B., N.Y. U., 1941. Admitted to N.Y. bar, 1942; asst. dist. atty. Queens County (N.Y.), 1955; individual practice law, 1946-55, 56-58; asst. commnr. borough works Queens County, 1958-62, dep. borough pres., 1963-68, borough pres., 1969-71; justice Supreme Ct. N.Y., Jamaica, 1972—. Bd. dirs. Flushing (N.Y.) YMCA, YWCA, Queensboro Council Social Welfare, N. Shore Boys' Club, NCCJ, Bowne House Hist. Soc., Flushing; chmn. Queens UN Day; exec. bd. Queens council Boy Scouts Am.; borough coordinator Queens Civilian Def.; active ARC, March of Dimes, United Jewish Appeal, Fedn. Jewish Philanthropies, United Hosp. Appeal, Greater N.Y. Fund, Queens Lighthouse, Nat. Democratic Club; chmn. bd. advisors Queens Art and Cultural Center. Mem. N.Y., Queens County bar assns., Assn. Justices Supreme Ct. State N.Y., Flushing Mchts. Assn., Flushing C. of C. (dir.), N.Y. U. Law Alumni Assn. (adv. council). Office: 88-11 Sutphin Blvd Jamaica NY 11435 Tel (212) 520-3159

LEVIT, JAY JOSEPH, b. Phila., Feb. 20, 1934; A.B., Case Western Res. U., 1955; J.D., U. Richmond, 1958; LL.M., Harvard, 1959. Admitted to Va. bar, 1958, D.C. bar, 1961, U.S. Supreme Ct. bar, 1961; individual practice law, Richmond, Va., 1959-60; trial atty. U.S. Dept. Justice, Washington, 1960-64; sr. atty. electronics div. Gen. Dynamics Corp., Rochester, N.Y., 1965-67; partner firm Stallard & Levit, Richmond, 1967—; instr. U. Mich., 1964-65; adj. asso. prof. law U. Richmond, 1974—. Mem. Am. (mem. labor law com. 1974—), Fed., Va. bar assns., Phi Alpha Delta. Home: 1608 Harborough Rd Richmond VA 23233 Office: 2120 Central Nat Bank Bldg Richmond VA 23219 Tel (804) 644-5453

LEVIT, VICTOR BERT, b. Singapore, Apr. 21, 1930; A.B. with great distinction, Stanford, 1950, J.D. with highest honors, 1953. Admitted to Calif. bar, 1953; asso. firm Long & Levit, San Francisco and Los Angeles, 1953-55, partner, 1955—, mng. partner, 1974—; mem. Los Angeles Consular Corps, 1971—; mem. San Francisco Consular Corps, 1971—, hon. vice dean, 1975-77; guest lectr. Stanford Law Sch., 1958—, Haile Selassie I U. Law Sch. (Ethiopia), 1972—; grader Calif. State Bar Exams., 1956-61; hon. consul Ethiopia, 1971—; chmn. panels on legal malpractice Continuing Edn. of the Bar, 1973, 74; mem. exec. com. San Francisco Lawyers Com. for Urban Affairs, 1975—. Pres. San Francisco Lung Assn., 1966-68, San Francisco Assn. Mental Health, 1968-71; bd. visitors Stanford Law Sch., 1969-75. Mem. Am. (vice chmn. ins. com. of econs. law sect.), San Francisco (chmn. ins., travel coms.) bar assns., World Assn. Lawyers (chmn. com. on rules of parliamentary procedure 1976—), Consular Law Soc., U.S. (gen. counsel, mem. exec. com. 1959-61), San Francisco (pres. 1958) jr. chambers commerce, Phi Beta Kappa, Order of Coif. Named Outstanding Young Man of San Francisco, 1970, one of five Outstanding Young Men of Calif., 1961; author: California Legal Malpractice, 1974; note editor: Stanford Law Review, vol. 5, 1953; legal editor: Underwriters' Report, 1962—; contbr. articles to legal jours. Home: 45 Beach Rd Belvedere CA 94920 Office: 465 California St San Francisco CA 94104 Tel (415) 397-2222

LEVITAN, DAVID M(AURICE), b. Tver, Lithuania, Dec. 25, 1915 (parents Am. citizens); B.S., Northwestern U., 1936, M.A., 1937; Ph.D., U. Chgo., 1940; J.D., Columbia, 1948. Admitted to N.Y. bar, 1948, U.S. Supreme Ct. bar, 1953; individual practice law, N.Y.C., 1948-66; partner firm Hahn Hessen Margolis & Ryan, N.Y.C., 1966—; adj. prof. pub. law Columbia, 1946-63, Johhn Jay Coll. Criminal Justice, City U. N.Y., 1966-75; adj. prof. polit. sci. Post Coll., 1964-66. Mem. Nassau County (N.Y.) Welfare Bd., 1965-69. Mem. Am. N.Y. State bar assns., Assn. Bar City N.Y., Am. Polit. Sci. Assn., Am. Soc. Internat. Law. Contbr. articles to legal jours. Home: 250 Scudders Ln Roslyn Heights NY 11526 Office: Hahn Hessen et al 350 Fifth Ave New York City NY 10001 Tel (212) 736-1000

LEVITAN, KATHERINE, b. Vienna, Austria, July 8, 1933; B.A. cum laude, N.Y. U., 1954, J.D. cum laude, 1955, postgrad., 1971—. Admitted to N.Y. bar, 1956, U.S. Supreme Ct. bar, 1974; instr. N.Y. Inst. Tech., Old Westbury, 1969; asso. firm Malone & Dorfman, Freeport, N.Y., 1970-71, Corso & Engleberg, Jericho, N.Y., 1971—; counsel temple Emanuel, New Hyde Park, N.Y., 1974—. Bd. dirs. N.Y. Civil Liberties Union, Nassau County, 1974—; adv. bd. Mid-Island YM & YWHA, Wantagh, N.Y., 1970-73; Democratic committeewoman 15th Assembly Dist. New Hyde Park, 1969—; mem. Nat. Council Jewish Women, 1973—. Fellow Am. Acad. Matrimonial Lawyers; mem. Am., N.Y., Nassau, Nassau-Suffolk Women's (v.p.) bar assns. Recipient Florence Allen award N.Y. U., 1955, Certificate Merit, Nassau County, 1975. Contbr. articles to legal jours. Office: 350 Jericho Turnpike Jericho NY 11753 Tel (516) 822-6383

LEVITON, EUGENE, b. N.Y.C., Dec. 17, 1934; B.A., U. Calif., Los Angeles, 1956, LL.B., 1959, J.D., 1959. Admitted to Calif. bar, 1960; asso. firm Horowitz & Howard, Los Angeles, 1960; individual practice law, Long Beach, Calif., 1960-61; asso., partner firm Levy & VanBourg, and predecessors, Los Angeles, 1961-72; mem. firm Banks & Leviton, Inc., Santa Ana, Calif., 1972—. Mem. Orange County Democratic Central Com., 1968—. Mem. Am., Los Angeles County, Orange County, Calif. (chmn. workers' compensation com. 1975-76) bar assns., Calif. Applicants Attys. Assn. (bd. govs. 1972—, treas., 1975—). Office: 1600 N Broadway Suite 640 Santa Ana CA 92702 Tel (714) 835-1404

LEVITT, EUGENE JONATHAN, b. Hicksville, N.Y., Feb. 13, 1927; B.A., Hofstra Coll., 1949; LL.B., N.Y. U., 1952. Admitted to N.Y. bar, 1953, U.S. Supreme Ct. bar, 1960; partner firm Salee & Levitt, Huntington, N.Y., 1957-67; individual practice law, Huntington, 1967—. Bd. dirs. Huntington Twp. United Fund, 1967-72, Huntington Hosp., 1969—; trustee Harborfields Pub. Library, Greenlawn, N.Y., 1970-74. Mem. N.Y., Suffolk County (award of recognition 1976) bar assns. Home: 6 Gina Dr Centerport NY 11721 Office: 23 Carver St E Huntington NY 11743 Tel (516) 427-8780

LEVITT, SIDNEY BERNARD, b. Bklyn., Mar. 23, 1920; B.A., Bklyn. Coll., 1942; LL.B., Bklyn. Law Sch., 1948, J.D., 1967; LL.M. in Labor Law, N.Y. U., 1953. Admitted to N.Y. bar, 1949, U.S. Supreme Ct. bar, 1956; mem. firms Haller & Levitt, Bklyn., 1950-56, Cardile, Levitt & Canadé, Bklyn., 1969-71; individual practice law, Bklyn., 1949-50, 56-69, 71—; arbitrator N.Y.C.-Kings County Civil Ct. Trustee YMHA, Rugby-E. Flatbush, Bklyn.; mem. N.Y.C. Local Planning Bd.; com. chmn. Bklyn. council Boy Scouts Am.; active Republican Party of Kings County. Mem. Bklyn. Bar Assn. Home: 9114 Ave A Brooklyn NY 11236 Office: 16 Court St Brooklyn NY 11241 Tel (212) MA 4 4333

LEVY, ABRAHAM D., b. N.Y.C., Aug. 13, 1904; LL.B., N.Y. Law Sch., 1925; student Columbia, 1923-25. Admitted to N.Y. bar, 1927; partner firm Paley, Levy & Fino, and predecessors, N.Y.C.; asso. atty. State Tax Comm., N.Y.C., 1943-45, prin. atty., 1954-55, 1959-60; ofcl. referee Appellate Div. Supreme Ct., 1956-59; justice Supreme Ct. 1st dept., 1959; judge County Ct. Bronx County, 1960; pub. adminstr. Bronx County, 1966—. Mem. Am., Bronx, N.Y. State bar assns., Assn. Custom Bar. Home: 271-26 L Grand Central Pkwy Floral Park NY 11005 Office: 851 Grand Concourse Bronx NY 10451 Tel (212) 293-7660

LEVY, ANDREW HARRIS, b. Washington, Mar. 20, 1944; B.A., Harvard U., 1966, J.D., 1969. Admitted to D.C. bar, 1969, Calif. bar, 1971; asso. firm Arent, Fox, Kintner, Plotkin & Kahn, Washington, 1969-70, 71-76, partner, 1977—; with Nat. Gen. Corp., 1970-71. Mem. Am., Fed. bar assns. Contbr. articles periodicals. Office: 1815 H St NW Washington DC 20006 Tel (202) 857-6164

LEVY, CARL DEVEROUX, b. Macon, Ga., Aug. 24, 1911; LL.B., U. Ga., 1936, J.D., 1969. Admitted to Ga. bar, 1936, Tex. bar, 1946, U.S. Supreme Ct. bar, 1947; trial counsel JAGC, 12th Air Force War Crimes Investigation Commn., Italy, 1945; sr. partner firm Smith, Levy & Fisher, Beaumont, Tex., 1945-54; pres., gen. counsel Jefferson Amusement Co., also Tex. TV Co., Beaumont, 1954-69; individual practice law, Beaumont, 1969—. Chmn., Beaumont Housing Authority, 1950—; founder, hon. chmn. bd. Beaumont Cerebral Palsy Found., 1950—; founder, pres. United Fund, Beaumont, 1955-56; pres., chmn. bd. dirs. Beaumont Community Found., 1957—. Mem. Am., Tex., Jefferson County bar assns. Co-author: Guide to Military Justice, 1945; also articles in field. Office: 309 Goodhue Bldg Beaumont TX 77701 Tel (713) 835-3492

LEVY, EDWIN M., b. Bklyn., Oct. 20, 1929; B.S., L.I. U., 1950; LL.B., Bklyn. Law Sch., 1953, J.S.D., 1956. Admitted to N.Y. State bar, 1954; individual practice law, N.Y.C., 1954—. Office: 529 Fifth Ave New York City NY 10017 Tel (212) 986-8345

LEVY, ELI BENNETT, b. N.Y.C., Sept. 22, 1909; B.S., N.Y. U., 1929, J.D., 1932. Admitted to N.Y. bar, 1933, U.S. Supreme Ct. bar, 1940; mem. firm Goldstein & Goldstein, N.Y.C., 1931-68; individual practice law, N.Y.C., 1968—; dep. asst. atty. gen. State of N.Y., 1934. Mem. Am. Bar Assn., New York County Lawyers Assn. Home: 2 Sutton Pl S New York City NY 10022 Office: 250 Broadway New York City NY 10007 Tel (212) 732-3443

LEVY, HERBERT MONTE, b. N.Y.C., Jan. 14, 1923; A.B., Columbia, 1943, LL.B., 1946. Admitted to N.Y. bar, 1946, U.S. Supreme Ct. bar, 1951; asso. firm Rosenman Goldmark Colin & Kaye, N.Y.C., 1946-47, Javits & Javits, N.Y.C., 1947-48; staff counsel ACLU, N.Y.C., 1949-56; individual practice law, N.Y.C., 1956-65, 69—; partner firm Hofheimer, Gartlir, Hofheimer, Gottlieb & Gross and predecessor, N.Y.C., 1965-69; lectr. Practising Law Inst. Mem. N.Y. State Democratic Com., 1954-62, 64-66. Mem. Assn. Bar City N.Y., New York County Lawyers Assn. (co-chmn. course on appellate practice 1976), Am. Bar Assn., Fed. Bar Council (chmn. com. on Bill of Rights 1965-74). Author: How to Handle an Appeal, Justice-After Trial; editor: Columbia Law Rev., 1945-46. Home: 285 Central Park W New York City NY 10024 Office: 9 E 40th St New York City NY 10017 Tel (212) 725-5959

LEVY, JACK, b. N.Y.C., Aug. 14, 1937; B.B.A., Adelphi Coll., 1960; J.D., U. So. Calif. 1967. Admitted to Calif. bar, 1967. Mem. Los Angeles County, Beverly Hills bar assns. Office: 8601 Wilshire Blvd Suite 1100 Beverly Hills CA 90211 Tel (213) 652-3911

LEVY, JACK I., b. Brownsville, Pa., Aug. 22, 1910; A.B., U. Mich., 1931, J.D., 1934. Admitted to D.C. bar, 1935, Ill. bar, 1935; Exec. v.p. GATX Corp., Chgo., 1971—, also dir. Home: 1335 N Astor St Chicago IL 60610 Office: 120 S Riverside Dr Chicago IL 60606 Tel (312) 621-6208

LEVY, JOEL H., b. Bklyn., June 25, 1935; A.B., Dartmouth Coll., 1957; LL.B., Harvard U., 1960. Admitted to N.Y. State bar, 1960, D.C. bar, 1963; atty. FCC, Washington, 1960-65; partner firm Cohn and Marks, Washington, 1965—. Nat. v.p. Am. Jewish Congress, 1976—, pres. Nat. Capitol chpt., 1970-76. Mem. Am., Fed. Communications bar assns. Office: 1920 L St NW Washington DC 20036 Tel (202) 293-3860

LEVY, JOSEPH, b. N.Y.C., June 9, 1928; B.B.A. cum laude, Coll. City N.Y., 1950; J.D. cum laude, N.Y. U., 1954. Admitted to N.Y. bar, 1955; asso. firm Parker, Chapin and Flattau, N.Y.C., 1954-62; partner firm Busby, Rivkin, Sherman, Levy and Rehm and predecessors, N.Y.C., 1962—; sec. Savin Bus. Machines Corp., 1961—; sec. On Line Systems Inc., 1967-75, dir., 1976—; sec. Programming Methods, Inc., 1969-72. Mem. N.Y. State, Am. bar assns. Recipient Benjamin F. Butler award N.Y. U. Sch. Law, 1954; contbr. articles to N.Y. U. Law Rev. Home: 254 University Way Paramus NJ 07652 Office: 750 3d Ave New York City NY 10017 Tel (212) YU6-5220

LEVY, JULES ELLIOT, b. Bklyn., May 13, 1939; B.B.A., Coll. City N.Y., 1961; J.D., Cornell U., 1964; LL.M., N.Y. U., 1970. Admitted to N.Y. bar, 1965; asso. firm Hofheimer, Gartlir, Gottlieb & Gross, N.Y.C., 1964-69; partner, 1970—; mem. N.Y. Atty. Gen.'s Advisory Com. for Condominium and Coop. Legislation, 1973-74. Mem. N.Y. State Bar Assn., Assn. Bar City N.Y. Home: 10 Winthrop Dr Woodbury NY 11797 Office: 100 Park Ave New York City NY 10017 Tel (212) 725-0400

LEVY, JULIUS, b. Bklyn., Feb. 15, 1913; B.A., U. Mo., 1934; LL.B., Columbia, 1936. Admitted to N.Y. State bar, 1937, U.S. Dist. Ct. bar, 1942, U.S. Supreme Ct. bar, 1946; partner firm Pomerantz, Levy, Haudek & Block, N.Y.C. Bd. dirs. Univ. Settlement House. Mem. N.Y.C. Bar Assn. (asso.), N.Y. County Lawyers Assn., Zeta Beta Tau. Office: 295 Madison Ave New York City NY 10017 Tel (212) 532-4800

LEVY, KENNETH JORDAN, b. Oakland, Calif., May 26, 1931; A.B. in Philosophy, U. Calif. at Berkeley, 1953; M.A. in Lang. Arts, Calif. State U. at San Francisco, 1956; J.D., San Francisco Law Sch., 1961. Admitted to Calif. bar, 1962; cons. editor Bancroft Whitney Co., San Francisco, 1962-64; asso. firm Schuman, Payne & Clancy, San Francisco, 1964-65; partner firm Payne & Levy, San Francisco, 1965-66; counsel Title Ins. & Trust Co., San Francisco, 1966; asst. editor-in-chief Matthew Bender & Co., San Francisco, 1967—; instr. San Francisco Unified Sch. Dist., 1956-61. Bd. dirs. Temple Rodef Sholom, San Rafael, Calif. Mem. State Bar Calif. Home: 9 Coast Oak Way San Rafael CA 94903 Office: PO Box 2329 San Francisco CA 94126 Tel (415) 433-0656

LEVY, LEWIS MARK, b. N.Y.C., Jan. 20, 1945; student Coll. of Charleston, 1963-64; A.B., U. S.C., 1967, J.D., 1971. Admitted to S.C. bar, 1971; asso. firm Belser, Baker, Belser, Barwick & Toal, Columbia, S.C., 1971—. Trustee Clariosophic Found., Columbia, 1971—, chmn., 1975—. Mem. Am., Richland County (S.C.) bar assns., S.C. Bar, S.C. Def. Attys. Assn., Order of Wig and Robe, Phi Alpha Delta. Editorial bd. S.C. Law Rev., 1971. Home: I 101 Suffolk Dr Huntington Columbia SC 29206 Office: 1213 Lady St PO Box 11848 Columbia SC 29211 Tel (803) 799-9091

LEVY, MARVIN JAY, b. LaCrosse, Wis., May 26, 1946; B.S., U. Wis., 1968, J.D., 1971. Admitted to Wis. bar, 1971; law. clk. U.S. Dist. Ct., Memphis, 1971-72; v.p. Ed. Phillips & Sons, Madison, Wis., 1972—; dir. Telephone & Data Systems Data, Inc., 1976—. Bd. dirs. Greater Madison Conv. and Visitor Bur., 1973-76, pres., 1975. Mem. Am., Wis. bar assns. Home: 921 Farwell Dr Madison WI 53704 Office: 2620 Royal Ave Madison WI 53713 Tel (608) 222-9177

LEVY, MICHAEL RICHARD, b. Dallas, May 17, 1946; B.S., U. Pa., 1968, J.D., U. Tex., 1972. Admitted to Tex. bar, 1972; pub. Texas Monthly Mag., Austin, 1972—; pres. Mediatex Communications Corp., Austin, 1972—. Mem. Tex. Bar Assn., Mag. Pubs. Assn., Headliners Club. Home: PO Box 146 Austin TX 78767 Office: PO Box 1569 Austin TX 78767 Tel (512) 476-7085

LEVY, MORRIS JAY, b. N.Y.C., Apr. 24, 1913; B.A., Coll. City N.Y., 1934; LL.B., N.Y. U., 1937. Admitted to N.Y. bar, 1938, U.S. Supreme Ct. bar, 1949; individual practice law, N.Y.C., 1938-76; sr. partner firm Levy & Levy, N.Y.C., 1976—. Group leader Boy Scouts Am., Flushing, N.Y., 1962-65. Mem. N.Y. State Bar Assn., N.Y. County Lawyers Assn. Home: 67-35 179th St Flushing NY 11365 Office: 233 Broadway New York City NY 10007 Tel (212) 962-1559

LEVY, RICHARD ALAN, b. N.Y.C., Aug. 27, 1942; B.S., Cornell U., 1964; J.D., N.Y. U., 1968. Admitted to N.Y. bar, 1968; asso. appellate counsel, criminal appeals bur., Legal Aid Soc., N.Y.C., 1968-71; partner firm Eisner Levy Steel & Bellman, N.Y.C., 1971—; adj. prof. State U. N.Y. Coll. at Old Westbury, 1976—; faculty Practicing Law Inst., 1977. Mem. N.Y. County Lawyers Assn., Assn. Bar of City of N.Y., Nat. Lawyers Guild. Contbr. article to legal publ. Office: 351 Broadway New York City NY 10013 Tel (212) 966-9620

LEVY, ROBERT JOSEPH, b. Phila., June 27, 1931; B.A., Kenyon Coll.; J.D., U. Pa. Admitted to D.C. bar, 1957, Minn. bar, 1966; trial atty. Dept. Justice, Washington, 1957-59; prof. law U. Minn., Mpls., 1959—. Author: (with Caleb Foote and Frank Sander) Cases and Materials on Family Law, 1st edit., 1966, 2d edit., 1976; (with Thomas Lewis and Peter Martin) Cases on Social Welfare and the Individual, 1970. Office: Law Sch U Minn Minneapolis MN 55422 Tel (612) 373-2731

LEVY, ROBERT MORTON, b. Huntington, W.Va., Feb. 12, 1926; student Purdue U., Marshall U.; J.D., W.Va. U., 1951. Admitted to W.Va. bar, 1951; individual practice law, Huntington, 1951-56; sr. partner firm Levy & Patton, Huntington, 1956—. Pres. Huntington Galleries, Huntington Pediatric Clinic, Ohev Sholom Temple, Huntington; pres. Cabell County (W.Va.) Library Friends. Mem. Am., W.Va., Cabell County bar assns. Author Model Med. Examiners Act. Home: 699 13th Ave Huntington WV 25701 Office: Suite 200 401 Bldg Huntington WV 25701 Tel (304) 525-8133

LEVY, ROBERT STANLEY, b. Scranton, Pa., June 27, 1933; A.B., U. Pa., 1955; LL.B., Harvard, 1958. Admitted to Fla. bar, 1958, also Pa. bar; individual practice law, West Palm Beach, Fla., 1958—. Active United Fund, West Palm Beach, Assn. for the Gifted; past pres. Jewish Fedn. Palm Beach County; past gen. chmn. Combined Jewish Appeal; past v.p. Palm Beach chpt. Am. Jewish Com.; past pres. B'nai B'rith; past chmn. bd. Temple Beth El of West Palm Beach; past vice chmn. Nat. Young Leadership Cabinet, United Jewish Appeal; mem. Lawyers Title Guaranty Fund. Mem. Am., Fla., Palm Beach County bar assns. Home: 842 Lakeside Dr North Palm Beach FL 33408 Office: 302 Citizens Bldg West Palm Beach FL 33401 Tel (305) 655-8166

LEVY, RONALD WARREN, b. N.Y.C., Jan. 28, 1936; B.A., Adelphi U., 1957; J.D., Bklyn. Coll. Law, 1960. Admitted to N.Y. bar, 1961; clk. Am. Arbitration Assn., N.Y.C., 1960-62; atty. civil div. Legal Aid Soc., N.Y.C., 1962-64; individual practice law, N.Y.C., 1964—; ct. conf. officer Family Ct. Queens County, N.Y. Mem. Am., Queens County bar assns., N.Y. State, N.Y. County lawyers assns. Home: 345 E 80th St New York City NY 10021 Office: 20 Vesey St New York City NY 10007 Tel (212) 732-7881

LEVY, SAMUEL ROBERT, b. Bklyn., Nov. 25, 1931; B.A., N.Y. U., 1953, LL.B., 1954, J.D., 1968. Admitted to N.Y. bar, 1954; partner firm Levy & Levy, Bklyn., 1957-58; individual practice law, 1959—. Mem. N.Y. State Bar Assn. Home: 1845 Ocean Ave Brooklyn NY 11230 Office: 66 Court St Brooklyn NY 11201 Tel (212) MA4-2362

LEVY, SAMUEL SANFORD, b. Bastrop, La., Jan. 27, 1902; LL.B., Loyola U., New Orleans, 1922, J.D., 1970. Admitted to La. bar, 1922; exec. v.p. Union Indemnity Co., Lawyers Title Ins. Co., 1922-28, Ins. Securities Co. Inc., New Orleans, 1928-33; practiced in New Orleans, 1933-64; judge 1st City Ct., New Orleans, 1964-65; judge Parish of Orleans (La.) Civil Dist. Ct., 1965—, chief judge, 1974—; judge ad hoc La. Supreme Ct., 1970. Mem. Am., La. State, New Orleans bar assns., Judicature Soc., Nat. Coll. Probate Judges, Nat. Coll. State Trial Judges. Home: 832 St Louis St New Orleans LA 70112 Office: 828 St Louis St New Orleans LA 70112 also Civil Ct Bldg Poydras and Loyola Sts New Orleans LA 70112 Tel (504) 525-7153

LEVY, SHELDON S., b. Bklyn., July 27, 1927; B.A., Columbia, 1948; LL.B., Yale, 1951. Admitted to N.Y. State bar, 1951; asst. counsel N.Y.-N.J. Waterfront Commn. and N.Y. State Crime Commn., 1951-53; asst. dist. atty. N.Y. County, 1953-60; legal asst. N.Y. State Supreme Ct. 1st Jud. Dist., 1960-69; spl. referee N.Y. State Supreme Ct. 1st Jud. Dist., 1970-72; judge Civil Ct. of N.Y.C., 1973—; acting justice of Supreme Ct. of N.Y. State, 1974—. Home: 250 W 94th St New York City NY 10025 Office: 111 Centre St New York City NY 10013 Tel (212) 374-8454

LEVY, STANLEY HERBERT, b. Phila., Apr. 11, 1922; B.A., Cornell U., 1943; LL.B., J.D., Harvard, 1949. Admitted to N.Y. State bar, 1949, also U.S. Supreme Ct. bar, So. and Eastern dists. U.S. Dist. Ct. bars, others, since practiced in N.Y.C. Mem. Bar Assn. City of N.Y. Home: 7 Leatherstocking Ln Scarsdale NY 10583 Office: 645 Fifth Ave New York City NY 10022 Tel (212) MU3-4917

LEVY, WILLIAM BYRON, b. New Orleans, Feb. 15, 1946; B.S., La. State U., 1967; J.D., 1969. Admitted to La. bar, 1969, Calif. bar, 1973; capt. JAGC, U.S. Army; asso. firm Ropers, Majeski, Kohn, Bentley & Wagner, Redwood City, Calif. Mem. Calif., San Mateo County bar assns., Phi Kappa Phi. Home: 545 W Hillsdale Blvd San Mateo CA 94403 Office: 425 Marshall St Redwood City CA 94063 Tel (415) 364-8200

LEWANDOWSKI, ALEX M., b. St. Louis, Nov. 16, 1946; B.A. in Bus., Central Meth. Coll., 1968; J.D., U. Mo.-Kansas City, 1972, LL.M., 1976. Admitted to Mo. bar, 1973; asso. firm Reeder, Griffin, Dysart, Taylor & Penner, Kansas City, Mo.; gen. counsel Alpha Phi Omega, 1975—. Mem. Am., Mo., Kansas City bar assns., Lawyers Assn. Kansas City. Office: 1221 Baltimore St Kansas City MO 64105 Tel (816) 221-1464

LEWANE, CONRAD CHARLES, b. Irvington, N.J., Aug. 26, 1937; B.S., U. Richmond, 1960, J.D., 1962. Admitted to Va. bar, 1962, Ga. bar, 1964; capt. UAGC, U.S. Army, 1963-66; asso. firm White Cabell, Paris & Lowenstein, Richmond, 1966-70, partner, 1970-76; individual practice law, Richmond, 1976—. Pres., Mayberry Elementary Sch. PTA, 1973. Mem. Am., Fed., Va., Henrico County, Richmond bar assns., Va., Richmond (v.p. 1977) trial lawyers assns., Richmond Criminal Bar Assn. Home: 9401 Treetop Ln Richmond VA 23229 Office: 1910 Byrd Ave Richmond VA 23230 Tel (804) 288-7245

LEWENSOHN, LEONARD J., b. Milw., Dec. 13, 1933; B.S., U. Wis., 1958, LL.B., 1960, J.D., 1970. Admitted to Wis. bar, 1960; individual practice law, Milw., 1960-65; v.p.-ops. Checker Express Co., Milw., 1965-68, pres., 1968—; v.p. Check-Air, Inc., Milw., 1975—. Trustee Mt. Sinai Hosp., Milw. Mem. Am., Wis. bar assns., Wis. Trucking Commn., Young Pres.'s Orgn. Address: 235 W Dean St Milwaukee WI 53217

LEWIN, TRAVIS HERBERT DUMAS, b. Long Beach, Calif., Aug. 24, 1933; B.A., S.D. U., 1958, LL.B., 1958; S.J.D., U. Mich., 1967. Admitted to S.D. bar, 1958, Fed. Dist. Ct. bar, 1958, N.Y. State bar, 1972; clk. U.S. Dist. Ct., Sioux Falls, S.D., 1958-59; asso. firm Woods, Fuller, Schultz & Smith, Sioux Falls, S.D., 1959-61; asst. U.S. atty. Dist. S.D., 1961-65; asst. prof. law, Syracuse U., 1967-70, asso. prof., 1970-72, prof., 1972—; cons. Mich. Dept. Mental Health, 1967; legal advisor Police Dept., Syracuse, N.Y., 1970-71; dir. symposium on Law and The Aging, Syracuse, N.Y., 1971, 73; dir. Psychiat. Def. Center, Syracuse N.Y., 1969—; founder, past dir. Law and Gerontology Center; dir. Syracuse U. Gerontology Center, 1971-72, 75-76. Vice-pres. Community Theater, Sioux Falls, 1964-65. Mem. Am. Bar Assn., Am. Assn. Law Schs., AAUP, ACLU, Am. Psychology and Law Assn., Am. Assn. Against Involuntary Hospitalization, Law Tchrs. Assn. Recipient Cook fellowship, 1965-67; co-author: Psychiatric Evaluations in Criminal Cases, 1967; The Aged and Property Management; contbr. articles in field to profl. jours. Home: 102 Stonecrest Dr Dewitt NY 13214 Office: U Syracuse Coll Law Syracuse NY 13210 Tel (315) 423-2531

LE WINTER, WILLIAM JACOB, b. Pitts., July 13, 1929; student Mugganutten Military Acad., Woodstock Va., 1947; A.B., U. Pitts., 1951, LL.B., 1954, J.D., 1968. Admitted to D.C. bar, 1954, Pa. bar, 1955; individual practice law, Pitts., 1954-60, 1975—; mem. firm Lipsitz, Nassau & LeWinter, 1960-65, partner, 1966; mem. firm Krimsly & LeWinter, Pitts., 1966-74; mem. firm Neely, Krimsly, Stockdale & Le Winter, Pitts., 1974-75; hearing examiner Pa. Labor Relations Bd., 1973—; arbitrator Fed. Mediation and Conciliation Service, Pa. Mediation Bd., Am. Arbitration Assn.; lectr. labor studies Pa. State U., 1971—. Bd. dirs. Rodef Shalom Congregation, Pitts., 1962-63; pres. Rodef Shalom Jr. Congregation, 1962-63; bd. dirs. Jewish Cultural Center, Pitts., 1971-72. Mem. Am., Allegheny County (bd. gov. labor sect. 1973) bar assns., Phi Alpha Delta. Home: 7 Allegheny Center Apt 917 Pittsburgh PA 15212 Office: 502 Frick Bldg Pittsburgh PA 15219 Tel (412) 261-3344

LEWIS, ALBERT LANIER, b. Ellisville, Miss., June 11, 1922; LL.B., U. Fla., 1950, J.D., 1957. Admitted to Fla. bar, 1950, U.S. Supreme Ct. bar, 1954; partner firm Beardall, Lewis Blankner and LeCotte, and predecessor, Orlando, Fla., 1954—. Pres. Open Door Mission of Orlando, 1970-77; chmn. bd. deacons Faith Bapt. Ch., Orlando, 1974-75; bd. dirs. State of Fla. Child Evangelism, 1975-77. Mem. Orlando County, Fla. bar assns. Home: 2022 Montana St Orlando FL 32803 Office: 60 N Court Ave Orlando FL 32802 Tel (305) 425-1626

LEWIS, ALFRED JACKSON, b. Phila., Jan. 27, 1935; A.B., Temple U., 1962, J.D., 1965; A.M. in L.S., U. Mich., 1967. Admitted to Pa. bar, 1965; chief readers's services librarian, law library U. Mich., 1965-68; asst. law librarian, lectr. law U. Calif. at Davis, 1968—. Mem. Am. Assn. Law Librarians, Assn. Am. Law Schs. Author: Using Law Books, 1976; contbr. articles in field to profl. jours. Home: 1615 Orange Ln Davis CA 95616 Office: Law Library Univ Calif Davis CA 95616 Tel (916) 752-3325

LEWIS, ALYIN BOWER, JR., b. Pitts., Apr. 24, 1932; B.A., Lehigh U., 1954; LL.B., Dickinson U., 1957. Admitted to Pa. bar, 1957; partner firm Lewis, Brubaker and Christianson, Hershey, Pa., also Lebanon and Palmyra, Pa., 1957—; dist. atty. Lebanon County, Pa., 1961-68; pres. Pa. Dist. Attys. Assn., 1967-68; chmn. Pa. Crime Commn., South Central Council, 1969-72; chmn. Southcentral Council Gov's. Justice Commn. Pa., 1972-74; chmn. Lancaster County (Pa.) crime hearings, 1974, Lebanon County (Pa.) crime hearings, 1974. Active ARC, Boy Scouts Am., Salvation Army; mem. Community Library bd. Mem. Am., Lebanon County (pres.) bar assns., Lebanon Valley C. of C. Home: 1126 S Green St Palmyra PA 17078 Office: 418 Chestnut St Lebanon PA 17042 Tel (717) 273-1651 and 101 W Cherry St Palmyra PA 17078 Tel (717) 838-1321

LEWIS, ARTHUR M., b. Hartford, Conn., Dec. 27, 1923; B.S. in Bus. Adminstrn., Boston U., 1949, LL.B., 1951. Admitted to Conn. bar, 1951, Mass. bar, 1951, U.S. Supreme Ct. bar, 1975; partner firm Danaher, Lewis & Tamoney, Hartford, 1958—; asso. mem. Nat. Conf. Commrs. Uniform State Laws, 1959-76; vice chmn. Conn. Jud. Council, 1967-68. Bd. visitors Boston U., 1967-76; chmn. Conn. Gov's. Teen-age Alcohol Use Study Commn., 1961-67; pres. Trinity Coll. Parents Assn. Fellow Comml. Law League Am., Am. Bar Found.; mem. Am. (consortium legal services and publs.), Conn. (pres. 1967-68), bar assns. Recipient Conn. Centennial award Boston U. Sch. Law, 1973. Home: 135 Mohegan Dr West Hartford CT 06117 Office: Danaher Lewis & Tamoney 39 Russ St Hartford CT 06106 Tel (203) 278-2300

LEWIS, CYRUS ROYS, b. Tuskegee, Ala., Feb. 8, 1915; A.B., U. Ala., 1937, LL.B., 1939. Admitted to Ala. bar, 1939, U.S. Supreme Ct. bar, 1967; individual practice law, Dothan, Ala., 1939-74; partner firm Lewis & Hornsby, 1975—; atty. City of Dothan, 1946-69. Mem. Ala. Trial Lawyers Assn., Assn. Trial Lawyers Am., Houston County Bar Assn. (pres. 1952, 72-73). Home: 1604 W Newton St Dothan AL 36301 Office: 114 S Oates St Dothan AL 36301 Tel (205) 792-5157

LEWIS, DAVID THOMAS, b. Salt Lake City, Apr. 25, 1912; B.A., U. Utah, 1934, LL.B., 1937; LL.D., 1971. Admitted to Utah bar, 1938; practiced Salt Lake City, 1938-50; state dist. judge, 1950-56; U.S. circuit judge 10th Circuit 1956—, chief judge, 1970—. Chmn. Circuit Chief Judges Conf., 1974-75. Mem. Utah Legislature, 1947-48. Mem. Am., Fed., Utah bar assns., Martime Law Assn., Order of Coif, Phi Delta Phi. Home: 1333 Emigration Circle Salt Lake City UT 84109 Office: Fed Bldg Salt Lake City UT 84138*

LEWIS, DICKIE DARVIN, b. Athens, Tex., Oct. 3, 1942; B.A., U. Mont., 1965, J.D., 1968. Admitted to Colo. bar, 1969, Mont. bar, 1968; clerk Mont. Supreme Ct., 1968-69, Colo. Supreme Ct., 1969-70; public defender Grand Junction, Colo., 1970-74, individual practice law, 1974—. Mem. Colo., Mesa County bar assns. Office: 435 No 8th St Grand Junction CO 81501 Tel (303) 243-7335

LEWIS, DUDLEY CUSHMAN, b. Honolulu, Mar. 26, 1909; A.B., Harvard, 1930, LL.B., 1934. Admitted to Hawaii bar, 1935, U.S. Supreme Ct. bar, 1954; dep. atty. gen. Hawaii, 1935-36; since practiced in Honolulu, asso. firm Robertson, Castle & Anthony, 1936-41; partner firm Lewis, Saunders and Key and predecessors, 1947-73; of counsel Damon, Shicekane, Key & Char, 1974—; dir. C. Brewer & Co., Ltd., 1st Hawaiian Bank, 1st Hawaiian Inc., Hawaiian Elec. Co., Inc., Hawaii Thrift and Loan; dept. atty. gen., 1946-47. Mem. Am., Hawaii bar assns. Home: Office: PO Box 3117 Honolulu HI 96802 Tel (808) 531-8031

LEWIS, EDWARD GREY, b. Atlantic City, N.J., Sept. 27, 1937; A.B., Princeton U., 1959; LL.B., U. Pa., 1963. Admitted to Pa. bar, 1964, D.C. bar, 1964; staff atty. Pub. Defender Service, Washington, 1964-65; asst. U.S. atty. for D.C., 1965-68; dept. asst. atty. gen. Civil div., Dept. Justice, 1971-73; gen. counsel Dept. Navy, Washington, 1973—. Mem. D.C., Pa. bar assns. Home: 408 Duke St Alexandria VA 22314 Office: Office of Gen Counsel Dept Navy Washington DC 20360 Tel (202) 692-7328

LEWIS, FRANKLIN CHARLES, b. Cleve., Sept. 10, 1939; B.A., Case-Western Res. U., 1960; J.D., Ohio State Coll. Law, 1963. Admitted to Ohio bar, 1963; served to capt. JAGC, USAF, 1964-67; atty. Cleve. Trust Co., 1967-69; asso. firm Daus, Schwenger & Kottler, Cleve., 1969-72; asst. sec., sr. atty. East Ohio Gas Co., Cleve., 1972—.

Mem. corporate solicitation com. Cleve. Orch. Soc., 1973. Mem. Ohio State, Greater Cleve. bar assns. Contbr. articles to legal jours. Home: 3666 Rawnsdale Rd Shaker Heights OH 44122 Office: PO Box 5759 Cleveland OH 44101 Tel (216) 623-4852

LEWIS, FREDRIC, b. N.Y.C., Mar. 14, 1931; B.S., N.Y. U.; J.D., Bklyn. Law Sch., 1954. Admitted to N.Y. bar, 1955, U.S. Supreme Ct. bar, 1964, U.S. Ct. of Claims bar, 1964; partner firm Lewis, Robbins, Zaslav & Auerbach, N.Y.C., 1965—; arbitrator Civil Ct., N.Y.C., 1975—, Am. Arbitration Assn., N.Y.C., 1975—. Mem. Bronx County Bar Assn., N.Y. Trial Lawyers Assn. Contbr. articles in field to legal jours. Office: 30 Vesey St New York City NY 10007 Tel (212) 349-7300

LEWIS, GEORGE TOLBERT, JR., b. Bells, Tenn., Mar. 6, 1914; J.D., U. Tenn., Knoxville, 1936. Admitted to Tenn. bar, 1936, U.S. Supreme Ct. bar, 1959; since practiced in Memphis, partner firm Waring, Walker, Cox and Lewis, 1936-72, firm Watson, Lewis and Knolton, 1972-75, firm Lewis, McKee and Hall, 1976—; chancellor 10th Chancery Div. of Tenn., 1977—; v.p., asso. gen. counsel World Service Life Ins. Co. of Fort Worth, 1966—, also dir. Active March of Dimes, past state dir.; mem. Shelby United Neighbors; mem. Memphis-Shelby County Mental Health Soc., also past pres.; deacon Second Presbyn. Ch. Memphis; chmn. bd. trustees Tenn. Dept. Mental Health, 1953-74. Mem. Am., Tenn., Memphis and Shelby County bar assns. Recipient Jr. C. of C. Distinguished Service award City of Memphis, 1948; named Jr. C. of C. Outstanding Young Man of Tenn., 1948. Home: 694 East Dr Hein Park Memphis TN 38112 Office: Room 312 Shelby County Courthouse Memphis TN 38103 Tel (901) 525-8161

LEWIS, GRANT STEPHEN, b. N.Y.C., Apr. 27, 1942; B.A., Bates Coll., 1962; J.D., Harvard, 1965. Admitted to N.Y. State bar, 1966; asso. firm Le Boeuf, Lamb, Leiby & Macrae, N.Y.C., 1965-73, mem. firm, 1973—. Mem. Assn. Bar City N.Y., Am. Bar Assn. Contbr. articles to profl. jours. Home: 2 Fifth Ave New York City NY 10011 Office: 140 Broadway Ave New York City NY 10005 Tel (212) 269-1100

LEWIS, HERBERT JAMES, JR., b. Birmingham, Ala., July 12, 1918; A.B., Birmingham So. Coll., 1942; LL.B., U. Ala., 1942; postgrad. Harvard Law Sch., 1942. Admitted to Ala. bar, 1942; asst. chief atty. VA, Montgomery, Ala., 1949-58, chief atty., 1958-73, dist. counsel, 1973—; coordinator, dir. Regional Conf. Med. Malpractice Med. Jurisprudence, 1970. Editorial adv. bd. Ala. Lawyer, 1975—, also contbr.; recipient Adminstr's. Spl. Achievement award VA, 1970, Superior Performance award, 1973; Meritorious Service award Probate Judges Assn. Ala., 1972. Mem. Fed., Ala., Montgomery County (Ala.) bar assns. Home: 2185 Campbell Rd Montgomery AL 36111 Office: Vets Adminstrn 474 S Court St Montgomery AL 36104 Tel (205) 832-7046

LEWIS, J.D. (JEFF), b. Stamford, Tex., Feb. 10, 1945; B.B.A., McMury Coll., 1967; J.D., Tex. Tech. U., 1970. Admitted to Tex. bar, 1970; staff city atty.'s office Abilene, Tex., 1970-72, dist. atty.'s office, Abilene, 1972-73; individual practice law, Abilene, 1973—. Bd. dirs. Child Welfare Assn. Mem. Abilene Jr. Bar Assn. (pres.). Named Outstanding Young Man Am., 1975. Home: 3817 Brookhollow St Abilene TX 79605 Office: 212 First State Bank Bldg Abilene TX 79602 Tel (915) 673-8384

LEWIS, JACK MEDLIN, b. Pangburn, Ark., Sept. 14, 1933; B.A., U. Ark., 1959; Admitted to Ark. bar, 1962; individual practice law, Clinton, Ark., 1966—; judge Van Buren County, Ark., 1967-74. Office: 1 Boykin St Clinton AR 72031 Tel (501) 745-2408

LEWIS, JAMES RAY, b. Tyler, Tex.; student U. Ky., 1945-46, No. Tex. State U., 1946-47. Sales rep. Prescott-Wright-Snyder Co., Ft. Worth, 1925-31; exec. sec. West Central Tex. Refinery Assn., Abilene, 1932-33; with Dept. Interior, 1933-53, spl. agt. div. investigations, Tyler, 1933, examiner Fed. Tender Bd. (name later Fed. Petroleum Bd.), Kilgore, Tex., also Houston, 1934-45, mem., Fed. Petroleum Bd., Kilgore 1946-48, chmn., 1948-53; admitted to Tex. bar, 1951; individual practice law, Tyler, 1953—. Mem. Tex. State Bar, Smith County Bar Assn. (v.p. 1973). Recipient spl. commendation Sec. Interior, 1937, U.S. Atty. Gen., 1937. Home: Route 4 Box 710 Tyler TX 75703 Office: 806 Fair Found Bldg Tyler TX 75702 Tel (214) 592-0101

LEWIS, JAMES WILLIAM, b. Mobile, Ala., July 20, 1941; A.B. magna cum laude, Spring Hill Coll., 1965; LL.B. U. Va., 1968. Admitted to Ala. bar, 1969; law clk. U.S. 5th Circuit Ct. Appeals, 1968-69; partner firm Bradley, Arant, Rose & White, Birmingham, Ala., 1974—; lectr. U. Ala. Sch. Law, 1971, 73; chmn. Ala. Continuing Legal Edn. Tax Seminar Planning Com., 1975-76; trustee Ala. Inst. Fed. Taxation, 1976—; cons. Tax Mgmt., Inc. Mem. Am., Ala. bar assns. Contbr. articles in field to law jours.; mem. editorial bd. Va. Law Rev., 1966-68. Home: 3649 Kingshill Rd Mountain Brook AL 35223 Office: 1500 Brown-Marx Bldg Birmingham AL 35203 Tel (205) 252-4500

LEWIS, JAMES WOODROW, b. Darlington County, S.C., Mar. 8, 1912; A.B., U.S.C., 1932. Admitted to S.C. bar, 1935; mem. S.C. Hwy. Commn., 1936-40; mem. S.C. Ho. of Reps. from Darlington County, 1935-36, 43-45; judge 4th Jud. Circuit S.C., 1945-61; asso. justice Supreme Ct. S.C., 1961-75, chief justice, 1975—. Address: PO Box 53 Darlington SC 29532*

LEWIS, JEFFREY EDWARD, b. Tillamook, Oreg., Sep. 23, 1944; A.B., Duke U., 1966, J.D., 1969. Admitted to Ohio bar, 1969; asst. prof. law U. Akron, 1970-72; asso. prof. Law U. Fla., Gainesville, 1972-77, prof., 1977—; sec. U. Fla. Law Center Assn., Fla. Civil Rules Com., Fla. Appellate Rules Com. Mem. Citizens Adv. Com. for Community Devel., Gainesville. Mem. Am. Bar Assn. Home: 2026 NW 19th Ave Gainesville FL 32605 Office: Coll Law U Fla Gainesville FL 32601 Tel (904) 342-2211

LEWIS, JEROME JACK, b. N.Y.C., Sept. 10, 1937; B.B.A. in Accounting, Coll. City N.Y., 1959, J.D., Bklyn. Law Sch., 1975. Admitted to N.Y. State bar, 1976, D.C. Ct. Appeals bar, 1975; auditor David Berdon & Co., N.Y.C., 1959-62; controller Ivan Obolensky Inc., N.Y.C., 1962-63; controller, sales mgr. George Braziller, Inc., N.Y.C., 1963-74; gen. mgr. Assn. Am. Univ. Presses, Inc., 1974—; mng. dir. Am. Univ. Press Services, Inc., N.Y.C., 1974—. Mem. Am. Inst. C.P.A.'s, N.Y. Soc. C.P.A.'s, Am., N.Y. State, D.C. bar assns. Contbr. articles to profl. jours. Home: 10 Bellingham Ln Great Neck NY 11023 Office: 1 Park Ave New York City NY 10016 Tel (212) 889-3510

LEWIS, JOHN FRANCIS, b. Oberlin, Ohio, Oct. 25, 1932; exchange scholar Eastbourne Coll., Sussex, Eng., 1951-52; B.A. cum laude, Amherst Coll., 1955; J.D., U. Mich., 1958. Admitted to Ohio bar, 1958, U.S. Supreme Ct. bar, 1974; asso. firm Squire, Sanders & Dempsey, Cleve., 1958-67; partner firm, 1967—. Active Playhouse Sq. Assn., 1974-76; trustee Hawkins Sch., Playhouse Sq. Found., 1976—, Shaker Lakes Nature Center, 1972-76. Mem. Am., Ohio State, Cuyahoga bar assns., Cleve. Bar Assn. (vice-chmn. grievance com.), Nat. Assn. Coll. & Univ. Attys., Ohio Council Sch. Bd. Attys. (pres.), Nat. Sch. Bd. Assn. Home: 2001 Chestnut Hills Dr Cleveland Heights OH 44106 Office: 1800 Union Commerce Bldge Cleveland OH 44115 Tel (216) 696-9200

LEWIS, JON MARK, b. Pitts., Mar. 5, 1946; B.S. in Engring., U. Pitts., 1968, J.D., 1972. Admitted to Pa. bar, 1972; asso. firm Mahady & Mahady, Greensburg, Pa., 1972-74; individual practice law, Greensburg, 1974—. Mem. Westmoreland County, Pa., Am. bar assns., Pa., Am. trial lawyers assns., Pitts., Am. patent law assns. Home: 25 Waverly Dr Greensburg PA 15601 Office: 205 Coulter Bldg Greensburg PA 15601 Tel (412) 836-4730

LEWIS, JOSEPH H., b. Mass., Aug. 14, 1899; LL.B., Suffolk Law Sch., 1924. Admitted to Mass. bar, 1924; individual practice law, Framingham, Mass., 1930—; town counsel Town of Framingham. Office: 100 Concord St Room 4 Framingham MA 01701 Tel (617) 872-3104

LEWIS, JOSEPH WILLIAM, b. St. Louis, July 3, 1912; A.B., Princeton, 1934; LL.B., Harvard, 1937. Admitted to Mo. bar, 1937, U.S. Supreme Ct. bar, 1957; partner firm Lewis, Rice, Tucker, Allen and Chubb, St. Louis, 1937—; dep. mil. gov. W.Ger., ETO; judge Municipal Ct. City of Ladue (Mo.), 1966-70; chmn. Mobar Research, Inc. Mem. St. Louis (former chmn. probate and trust sect.), Am. (sec. sect. sci. and tech.), Fed. bar assns. Contbr. articles to legal jours. Home: 919 Tirrill Farms Rd Saint Louis MO 63124 Office: 611 Olive St Suite 1400 Saint Louis MO 63101 Tel (614) 231-5833

LEWIS, LEONARD JOHN, b. Rexburg, Idaho, Jan. 10, 1923; B.A., U. Utah, 1947; J.D., Stanford U., 1950. Admitted to Utah bar, 1950; asso. firm VanCott, Bagley, Cornwall & McCarthy, Salt Lake City, 1950-64, mgn. partner, 1964-75, pres., 1975—; dir., counsel Fed. Resources Corp., Centennial Devel. Company, Monroc, Inc. Bd. visitors Law Sch. Stanford Univ., Palo Alto, Calif. Mem. Am. Trial Lawyers Assn., Am., Internat. bar assns. Home: 1173 Alton Way St Salt Lake City UT 84108 Office: 141 E 1st S St Salt Lake City UT 84111 Tel (801) 532-3333

LEWIS, LORAN LODOWICK, b. Pitts., Nov. 23, 1901; A.B., Adrian Coll., 1925; LL.B., Cornell U., 1928. Admitted to Pa. bar, 1928; practiced in Pitts., 1928-43, 46-52; asst. city solicitor Pitts., 1934-38; presiding judge Am. Mil. Govt. Cts., Land Baden, Germany, 1945-46; mil. gov. Mannheim, Germany, 1945-46; asst. dist. atty. Allegheny County, Pa., 1948-52; judge Allegheny County Ct. Common Pleas, 1952—; chief counsel Office Price Adminstrn. of Western Pa., 1942-43; chmn. Pa. Supreme Ct. Com. on Criminal Pattern Jury Instructions, 1972—. Bd. dirs. Port Authority of Allegheny County, 1960-72, chmn., 1962-68; pres. bd. trustees Adrian Coll., 1967—; mem. Pa. Transp. Commn., 1970-74; bd. dirs. George Jr. Republic, Grove City, Pa., 1965—. Mem. Allegheny County, Pa. bar assns. Home: 1400 Ashtola Rd Pittsburgh PA 15204 Office: 314 Courthouse Grant St Pittsburgh PA 15219 Tel (412) 355-5434

LEWIS, MARION MCLEAN, b. Beeville, Tex., Sept. 25, 1927; LL.B., U. Tex., 1950. Admitted to Tex. bar, 1950; individual practice law, Sinton, Tex., 1950-51, Goliad, Tex., 1951-65; mgr. Goliad County Abstract Co. (Tex.), 1954-64; partner firm Guittard & Henderson, and predecessor, Victoria, Tex., 1965—, sr. partner, 1975—; mem. city council, mayor pro tempore City of Victoria, 1971-73; county atty. Goliad County, 1955-65; city atty. City of Goliad, 1956-65. Trustee Goliad Ind. Sch. Dist., 1964-65. Mem. State Bar Tex., Am., Victoria County bar assns., Tex. Assn. Bank Counsel, Phi Alpha Delta. Office: 209 First Victoria Nat Bank Bldg Victoria TX 77901 Tel (512) 573-4344

LEWIS, MARSHALL AARON, b. Chgo., Oct. 2, 1934; A.A., U. Calif., Los Angeles, 1955, B.A., 1957, J.D., 1963. Admitted to N.Y. State bar, 1964, Calif. bar, 1964; asso. firm Cravath, Swaine & Moore, N.Y.C., 1963-71, Paris, France, 1969-71; mem. firm Fredman, Silverberg & Lewis, Inc., San Diego, 1971—. Counsel, coordinator local issues San Diego Common Cause; bd. dirs. San Diego Civic Youth Orch. Mem. Assn. Bar City N.Y., State Bar Calif., San Diego County Bar Assn., Order of Coif. Mng. editor U. Law Rev., 1962-63. Office: 3252 Fifth Ave San Diego CA 92103 Tel (714) 291-3434

LEWIS, NONALD JACK, b. Detroit, Aug. 10, 1925; B.S., Northwestern U., 1949, LL.B., 1950. Admitted to Wis. bar, 1950, U.S. Supreme Ct. bar, 1963, U.S. Ct. Appeal, 1972; collection mgr. Time Ins. Co., Milw., 1950-51; asst. claims mgr. Standard Oil Co., Milw., 1951-52; individual practice law, Waukesha, Wis., 1952-53; asso. firm Kivett & Kasdorf, Milw., 1953-63; partner firm Kasdorf, Dall, Lewis & Swietlik, Milw., 1964—. Mem. lay com. sch. dist. consolidation Sch. Dist. 21 Dixon Sch. PTA, Brookfield, Wis., 1962; mem. Brookfield (Wis.) Bd. Zoning Appeals, 1969; mem. Fire and Police Commn., Brookfield, 1970—. Mem. Waukesha County, Am. bar assns., Defense Research Inst., Bar Assn. of 7th Fed. Circuit, Ins. Trial Counsel of Wis., Am. Arbitration Assn. (John Wigmore certificate). Tel ((414) 342-4400

LEWIS, ORME, b. Phoenix, Jan. 7, 1903; LL.B., George Washington U., 1926. Admitted to Ariz. bar, 1926, Calif. bar, 1931, U.S. Supreme Ct. bar, 1955, D.C. bar, 1969; practiced in Phoenix, 1926—; now mem. firm Lewis and Roca; asst. sec. Dept. Interior, Washington, 1953-55. U.S. rep. GATT meetings, Geneva, 1955; mem. legal com. Ariz. Oil and Conservation Commn.; mem. Interstate Oil Compact Commn. Fellow Am. Bar Found.; mem. Am., Fed., Ariz. (past gov.), Calif., Maricopa County (past dir.) bar assns., Am. Judicature Soc. (past dir.), Lawyers Club Phoenix (past pres.), Law Soc. State U. (past pres.). Home: 97 Mountain Shadows W Scottsdale AZ 85253 Office: 100 W Washington Phoenix AZ 85003 Tel (602) 262-5311

LEWIS, PAUL M., b. Earlington, Ky., July 22, 1923; J.D., U. Ky. Admitted to Ky. bar, 1949; partner firm Lewis, Bland & Preston, Elizabethtown, Ky.; sec. 9th Jud. Dist. Mem. Ky. Bar Assn. (del., bd. govs.). Office: 30 Public Sq Elizabethtown KY 42701 Tel (502) 765-7106

LEWIS, RHODA VALENTINE, b. Chgo., Aug. 31, 1906; A.B., Stanford, 1927, J.D., 1929. Admitted to Calif. bar, 1929, N.Y. State bar, 1933, Hawaii bar, 1937, U.S. Supreme Ct. bar, 1950; asso. firm Falk, Siemer, Glick, Tuppen & Maloney, and predecessors, Buffalo, 1933-36; mem. pub. prosecutor's office Honolulu, 1936, dep. or asst. atty. gen., Honolulu, 1937-59; asso. justice Supreme Ct. Hawaii, 1959-67, ret. judge, service in assigned cases, 1974-76; sec., com. bar examiners State Bar Calif., San Francisco, 1929-32; del., Constl. Conv. Hawaii, 1968; mem. disciplinary bd. Hawaii Supreme Ct., 1974. Mem. Bar Assn. Hawaii, Am. Bar Assn., Inst. Jud. Adminstrn., Am. Judicature Soc., World Peace Through Law Center, Order Coif, Phi Beta Kappa. Home: 2943 Kalakaua Ave Apt 806 Honolulu HI 96815

LEWIS, RICHARD HAYES, b. Hopkinsville, Ky., Dec. 3, 1937; B.S., Murray State U., 1960; J.D., U. Ky., 1965. Admitted to Ky. bar, 1965; partner firm Lovett, Lewis, Johnson & Shapiro, Benton, Ky., 1965-70; mem. Ky. Ho. of Reps., 1970-75; chief exec. officer Gov. Ky., 1975-76; mem. Ky. Workmen's Compensation Bd., Benton, 1976—. Mem. Am., Ky., Marshall County (Ky.) bar assns., Murray State U. Alumni (pres. 1976—), Phi Alpha Delta. Recipient Ray M. Moreland Service award Ky. Coll. Law, 1965; named Outstanding Freshman Ky. Gen. Assembly, 1970. Home: Route 8 Merrywood Dr Benton KY 42025 Office: 1100 1/2 Main St PO Box 186 Benton KY 42025 Tel (502) 527-1343

LEWIS, ROBERT JOHN, JR., b. Grand Rapids, Mich., July 17, 1941; A.B., U. Mich., 1963, J.D., 1970. Admitted to Mich. bar, 1971; legis. asst. to U.S. Senator Robert Griffin, Washington, 1970-71; staff asst. to Pres. U.S., Washington, 1972; asst. to chmn. FTC, Washington, 1973-74, gen. counsel, 1975—. Mem. Am. Bar Assn. Home: 2508 Paxton St Woodbridge VA 22192 Office: FTC Pennsylvania Ave at 6th St Washington DC 20580 Tel (202) 523-3613

LEWIS, TEAIRL W., b. San Saba, Tex., July 8, 1908; B.B.A., U. Tex., 1930, LL.B., 1934. Admitted to Tex. bar, 1934; asso. firm Morriss, Boatwright, Lewis & Davis, San Antonio, Tex., 1945-50, partner, 1950—. Mem. adv. com. to San Antonio city council on purchase of expressway right-of-way, 1954-56; trustee San Antonio Pub. Library, 1955-61, v.p., 1958-61; bd. dirs. San Antonio Research and Planning Council, 1955-61, 64-67, sec., 1960; bd. dirs. Tex. Lions Camp Crippled Children, 1959-62, sec., 1968-72; active Boy Scouts Am. Mem. Am. Judicature Soc., Am., Tex., San Antonio bar assns. Office: 1215 National Bank Commerce Bldg San Antonio TX 78205 Tel (512) 227-8304

LEWIS, WILLIAM CLEATON, JR., b. Pitts., Sept. 17, 1938; B.B.A., Emory U., 1960, LL.B., 1963. Admitted to Fla. bar, 1963, Ga. bar, 1962; asso. firm Kilpatrick Codey Rogers McClathey & Regenstein, Atlanta, 1963-64; partner firm Smathers & Thompson, Miami, Fla., 1965—. Mem. Ga., Fla. bar assns., Phi Delta Phi, Omicron Delta Kappa. Co-editor-in-chief Emory Jour. Pub. Law, 1963. Home: 4320 Santa Maria St Coral Gables FL 33146 Office: 1301 Alfred I DuPont Bldg Miami FL 33131 Tel (305) 379-6523

LEWIS, WILLIAM OUREN, b. Harlan, Iowa, Oct. 6, 1921; B.S., Northwestern U., 1943; J.D., U. Iowa, 1948; Admitted to Iowa bar, 1948; mem. firm Hines, Sawin, Lewis & Salvo, Harlan; county atty. Shelby County, Harlan, 1952-58. Mem. Shelby County Extension Council. Mem. Am., Iowa bar assns., Comml. Law League. Home: RTE 4 Box 49 Harlan IA 51537 Office: Hines Sawin Lewis & Salvo 711 Court St Harlan IA 51537 Tel (712) 755-3141

LEWISS, MATTHEW LOEB, b. Westerly, R.I., July 6, 1939; B.A., Tufts U., 1961; J.D., Boston U., 1965. Admitted to R.I. bar, 1965, Fed. bar, 1968; individual practice law Westerly, 1965—. Mem. Westerly Citizens Adv. Com., 1966—; dir. Center for the Arts, Inc., Westerly, 1974—. Mem. Am., R.I. (mem. house dels. 1972—), Wash. County (treas. 1971—) bar assns., Am. Judicature Soc. Home: Avondale Hills Westerly RI 02891 Office: 2 Elm St Westerly RI 02891 Tel (401) 596-1009

LEWYN, THOMAS MARK, b. N.Y.C., July 2, 1930; B.A., Stanford U., 1952, postgrad., 1952-54; LL.B., Columbia U., 1955. Admitted to N.Y. bar, 1957; asso. firm Simpson, Thacher & Barlett, N.Y.C., 1957-64, partner, 1965-75, sr. partner, 1976—; counsel Gulf & Western Industries, Inc., N.Y.C.; sec., dir. Paramount Pictures Corp., N.Y.C., dir. Kreisler Group, N.Y.C.; dir. Cinema Internat. Corp. Mem. Am., N.Y. bar assns., Assn. Bar City N.Y. Home: 911 Park Ave New York City NY 10021 Office: 1 Battery Park Plaza New York City NY 10004 Tel (212) 483-9000

LEXA, ROBERT C., b. Cleve., Jan. 9, 1925; B.B.A., Cleve. State U., 1950, J.D., 1954; Admitted to Ohio bar, 1954; with Clevite Corp., Cleve., 1955-69, tax accountant, 1957-61, budget dir., 1961-67, European controller, 1967-68, chief accountant, 1968-69, asst. sec., 1968-69, asst. treas., 1968-69; v.p., sec. Mogul Corp., Chagrin Falls, Ohio, 1969—. Office: Mogul Corp PO Box 200 Chagrin Falls OH 44022 Tel (216) 247-5000

LEYDEN, ROBERT G., b. Springfield, Mass., Sept. 21, 1939; student Holy Cross Coll., 1961; LL.B., Union U., 1964. Admitted to N.Y. State bar, 1964; asso. firm Cooper, Erving & Savage, Albany, N.Y., 1964—. Mem. Albany County Legislature, 1970—. Mem. Am., N.Y. State, Albany County bar assns. Home: 571 Providence St Albany NY 12208 Office: 35 State St Albany NY 12207 Tel (518) 434-8131

LEYDIG, CARL FREDERICK, b. Denver, Jan. 24, 1925; B.S. in Chem. Engring., Ill. Inst. Tech., 1945; J.D., DePaul U., 1950. Admitted to Ill. bar, 1950, U.S. Supreme Ct. bar, 1971; patent atty. Standard Oil Co. (Ind.), 1946-54; partner firm Leydig, Voit, Osann, Mayer & Holt, Ltd., and predecessors, Chgo., 1954—. Mem. Am., Chgo. bar assns., Am., Chgo. patent law assns., Chgo. Law Club. Office: 1 IBM Plaza Suite 4600 Chicago IL 60611 Tel (312) 822-9666

LEZAK, SIDNEY IRVING, b. Chgo., Nov. 8, 1924; student Northwestern U., 1941-42; Ph.B., U. Chgo., 1946, J.D., 1949. Admitted to Oreg. bar, 1949; individual practice law, Portland, 1949-61; partner firm Bailey, Lezak, Swink & Gates, Portland, 1954-61; U.S. atty. Dist. Oreg., 1961—. Mem. cabinet U. Chgo.; bd. govs. World Affairs Council Oreg.; bd. overseers Lewis and Clark Coll. Mem. Am., Fed. (pres. Oreg. br. 1962-63), Oreg., Multnomah County bar assns., Am. Judicature Soc. Contbr. articles to legal publs. Home: 1811 SW Boundary St Portland OR 97201 Office: PO Box 71 US Courthouse Portland OR 97207 Tel (503) 221-2765

LI, VICTOR H., b. 1941; B.A., Columbia U., 1961, LL.B., 1964; LL.M., Harvard U., 1965, S.J.D., 1971. Admitted to N.Y. bar, 1965; vis. asst. prof. law U. Mich., 1967-69; asst. prof. law Columbia U., 1969-72; asso. prof. Stanford U., 1972-74, Lewis Talbot and Nadine Hearn Shelton prof. internat. legal studies, 1974—; vis. prof. U. Hawaii, spring 1977. Office: Stanford Law Sch Stanford CA 94305 Tel (415) 497-1931*

LIBER, THOMAS CHARLES, b. Alliance, Ohio, Nov. 18, 1945; B.S., Bowling Green State U., 1967; J.D., Case Western Res. U., 1970. Admitted to Ohio bar, 1970; asso. firm Kelley, McCann & Livingstone, Cleve., 1970-76; partner, 1977—; mem. Cuyahoga County Commr.'s Pub. Defender Task Force, Cleve., 1976; Trustee Citizens' League Greater Cleve., 1975—. Mem. Am., Ohio (pres. bd. trustees 1977—) bar assns., Bowling Green State U. Alumni Assn. Contbr. to articles to legal jours. Home: 30611 Winston Dr Bay Village OH 44140 Office: 1519 Nat City Bank Bldg Cleveland OH 44114 Tel (216) 241-3141

LIBERACE, GERALD CARL, b. Darby, Pa., Apr. 25, 1941; B.S. in Chemistry, Phila. Coll. Textiles and Sci., 1963; J.D., Villanova U., 1967. Admitted to Pa. bar, 1967, U.S. Supreme Ct. bar, 1975; partner firm Liberace and DeLiberty, Broomall, Pa., 1974—; dist. justice, Havertown, Pa., 1976—. Mem. Pa., Delaware County bar assns., Ct. Initial Jurisdiction. Recipient Bur. Nat. Affairs award, 1967; editor Delaware County Legal Jour., 1972. Home: 10 Strathmore Rd Havertown PA 19083 Office: 2701 W Chester Pike Broomall PA 19008 also Bldg O Manoa Shopping Center Havertown PA 19083 Tel (215) 353-0322 also HI 9-1177

LIBSACK, LAURENCE, b. Odessa, Wash., Sept. 2, 1929; B.A., Gonzaga U., 1951, J.D., 1954. Admitted to Wash. bar, 1954; individual practice law, Odessa, 1956—. Sec. Lincoln-Adams County (Wash.) Fire Protection Dist. 3, 1974—. Mem. Am., Wash., Lincoln County bar assns. Home: 103 W 6th Ave Odessa WA 99159 Office: 9 E 1st Ave Odessa WA 99159 Tel (509) 982-2672

LICCIARDI, JOHN LOUIS, b. Rochester, N.Y., Feb. 24, 1947; B.S. in Anthropology with honors, Colgate U.; J.D., Cornell Law Sch. Admitted to N.Y. State bar, 1973; now sr. asso. firm Liebschutz, Sutton, De Leeuw, Rochester, N.Y.; chief justice High Sch. UN Conf., 1974. Mem. Am., Monroe County (golf champion 1974, 75), N.Y. State bar assns. Home: 618 Eastbrooke Ln Rochester NY 14618 Office: 31 E Main St Rochester NY 14614 Tel (716) 546-8990

LICHT, DAVID EMANUEL, b. N.Y.C., June 14, 1927; B.S., Columbia U., 1951, J.D., 1953; individual practice law, N.Y.C., 1955—. Pres. Jewish Center Jackson Heights, 1972-75; pres. Jackson Heights-Elmhurst Kehilla, 1974-75. Mem. N.Y. County Lawyers Assn., Air Pollution Control Assn. Address: 280 Madison Ave New York City NY 10016 Tel (212) 725-4998

LICHTEN, EARL BARTON, b. Chgo., Feb. 2, 1923; B.S. in Mech. Engring., Ill. Inst. Tech., 1944; J.D., Loyola U., 1958. Admitted to Ill. bar, 1958; cons. mech. engr. for building trades, Ill., 1944-58; individual practice law, Chgo., 1958-70; asso. firm Berger, Newmark & Fenchel, Chgo., 1970—. Pres., Riverwoods (Ill.) Residents' Assn., 1964; chmn. Riverwoods Zoning Bd. Appeals, 1965—. Mem. Chgo. Bar Assn. Registered profl. engr., Ill. Home: 1800 Trillium Ln Riverwoods IL 60015 Office: 10 S LaSalle St Chicago IL 60603 Tel (312) 782-5050

LICHTMAN, ARTHUR, b. Bayonne, N.J., Nov. 26, 1932; LL.B., Tulane U., 1957; Admitted to La. bar, 1957, N.Y. bar, 1962; partner firm Capriano & Lichtman, P.C., N.Y.C., 1968—. Office: 80 Wall St New York City NY 10005 Tel (212) 269-3444

LICHTMAN, PAUL ALAN, b. N.Y.C., Aug. 13, 1944; B.S. in Agr., Ohio State U., 1966; B.S. in Pharmacy, U. L.I., 1970; J.D., Cleve. State U., 1973. Admitted to Ohio bar, 1973; partner firm Lichtman, Finneran, Hayek, Jacobs and Lorenzen, Euclid, Ohio, 1973—. Mem. mayor's adv. com., Mayfield Heights, Ohio, 1976—; mem. Mayfield Heights Bicentennial Com., 1976—; Mayfield Heights Democratic Com., 1976—. Mem. Ohio State, Cuyahoga County, Cleve. bar assns. Home: 1450 Golden Gate Mayfield Heights OH 44124 Office: 333 Babbitt Rd Euclid OH 44123 Tel (216) 732-8300

LICKE, W(ALLACE) JOHN, b. Bemidji, Minn., Jan. 23, 1945; student Bemidji State U., 1963-65; B.A. in Polit. Sci. and Sociology, U. Minn., 1967, M.A. in Indsl. Relations, 1970, J.D. cum laude, 1973. Instr. in bus. Itasca Community Coll., 1968-70; law clk. firm Helgesen, Peterson, Engberg & Spector, Mpls., 1972-73; admitted to Minn. bar, 1973; asso. firm Peterson, Engberg & Peterson, Mpls., 1973-75; gen. counsel Blandin Paper Co., Grand Rapids, Minn., 1975—. Mem. Itasca County (Minn.), Minn., Am. bar assns., Phi Beta Kappa. Bd. editors Minn. Law Rev., 1972-73. Home: Rural Route 4 PO Box 30 Grand Rapids MN 55744 Office: 115 1st St SW Grand Rapids MN 55744 Tel (218) 326-8531

LICKSON, CHARLES PETER, b. N.Y.C., May 16, 1939; B.A., Johns Hopkins, 1961; J.D., Georgetown U., 1964. Admitted to Conn. bar, 1968; asst. sec., asst. gen. atty. Bunker-Ramo Corp., Stamford, Conn., 1967-68; individual practice law, Stamford and Darien, Conn., 1968—; lectr. Mercy Coll., 1976—. Dep. dir. Stamford Emergency Service, 1973-75, Darien Civil Preparedness Office, 1975—; chief Stamford Aux. Police Corps, 1973-75; dir., founder State Opera, Inc., Stamford, Pink Tent Festival of Arts, Inc., Stamford. Mem. Am., Conn., Stamford bar assns., Am. Arbitration Assn. (panel of arbitrators). Contbr. articles to legal jours. Office: PO Box 1151 Darien CT 06820 Tel (203) 655-9432

LIDSCHIN, MARK R., b. Chgo., Mar. 7, 1931; A.B., Carleton Coll., 1952; J.D., U. Mich., 1955. Admitted to Ill. bar, 1955, U.S. Supreme Ct. bar, 1959; asst. state's atty. Lake County, Ill., 1958-60; asso. firm Lidschin & Pucin, 1960-74; partner firm Lidschin & Lidschin, Waukegan, Ill., 1974—; arbitrator Am. Arbitration Assn. Mem. Waukegan Pub. Library Bd., 1970-76, v.p., 1974-76. Mem. Am., Ill., Lake County bar assns., ALA, Ill. Library Assn. Home: 708 Chandler Rd Gurnee IL 60031 Office: 4 S Genesee St Waukegan IL 60085 Tel (312) MA 3-2255

LIEB, CHARLES HERMAN, b. N.Y.C., July 21, 1907; B.S., U. Pa., 1927; LL.B., Fordham Coll., 1930. Admitted to N.Y. bar, 1931, Conn. bar, 1959; mem. firm Paskus, Gordon & Hyman, N.Y.C., 1939—. Mem. Am. Bar Assn. (copyright div. chmn. 1971-72), Copyright Soc. U.S. (trustee 1972-75). Adv. bd. BNA Patent, Trademark and Copyright Jour. Home: Redding Rd Easton CT 06883 Office: 733 3d Ave New York City NY 10017 Tel (212) 557-9300

LIEB, MORTON, b. N.Y.C., Mar. 29, 1934; A.B., N.Y. U., 1955; LL.B., Bklyn. Law Sch., 1958. Admitted to N.Y. bar, 1959; individual practice law, N.Y.C. and Orangeburg, N.Y., 1959—; arbitrator Am. Arbitration Assn., 1967—. Mem. N.Y. County, Rockland County lawyers assns., Alpha Epsilon Pi. Home: 112 Constitution Dr Orangeburg NY 10962 Office: 229 Broadway New York City NY 10007 Tel (212) 285-1616 also 112 Constitution Dr Orangeburg NY 10962 Tel (914) 359-7979

LIEBELER, WESLEY JAMES, b. Langdon, N.D., May 9, 1931; B.A., Macalester Coll., 1953; J.D. cum laude, U. Chgo., 1957. Admitted to N.Y. State bar, 1958; asso. firm Carter, Ledyard & Milburn, N.Y.C., 1957-64; asst. counsel Pres.'s Commn. to Investigate Assassination of Pres. Kennedy, 1964; prof. law U. Calif., Los Angeles, 1964—; dir. Office Policy Planning and Evaluation, Fed. Trade Commn., 1974-75; cons. U.S. Price Commn., 1972, Fed. Trade Commn., 1976. Articles editor U. Chgo. Law Rev.; contbr. articles on antitrust, trade regulation and law to profl. jours. Home: 30373 Morning View Dr Malibu CA 90265 Office: University of California Law School 405 Hilgard Ave Los Angeles CA 90024 Tel (213) 825-1994

LIEBERMAN, GEORGE ERIC, b. N.Y.C., Sept. 1, 1942; B.A., Coll. City N.Y., 1964; J.D., Northwestern U., 1967. Admitted to Calif. bar, 1968, Pa. bar, 1969; research asst. Northwestern U. Sch. Law, 1966; asso. firm Morgan, Lewis & Bockius, Phila., 1968—; judge regional competition Nat. Mock Trial Competition; vol. observer primary and gen. elections Com. of 70; arbitrator Common Pleas Ct. Philadelphia County; preceptor Am. Found. for Negro Affairs. Mem. Am. (fed. procedure, trial practice coms. sect. on litigation; trial techniques com. sect. on ins., negligence and compensation law), Pa., Phila. (medico-legal com., jury trial com.), Calif. bar assns., Nat. Assn. R.R. Trial Counsel (program chmn., nat. sec., lectr.), Pa. Def. Inst., Omicron Chi Epsilon. Contbr. articles to The Chronicle. Home: Salem Harbour 247 A-1 High Rd Andalusia PA 19020 Office: 2200 The Fidelity Bldg Philadelphia PA 19109 Tel (215) 491-9200

LIEBERMAN, JOSEPH, b. N.Y.C., Feb. 24, 1906; B.S., N.Y. U., 1926, LL.B., 1927. Admitted to N.J. bar, 1928, N.Y. State bar, 1934; individual practice law, N.Y.C., 1934—. Mem. N.Y. County Lawyers Assn. Tel (212) 891-2372

LIEBESNY, HERBERT JOSEPH, b. Vienna, Mar. 6, 1911; LL.D., U. Vienna, 1935. Research fellow Columbia, 1939, U. Pa., 1939-42; lectr. in law of Near East U. Pa., 1942-43; analyst Office Strategic Services, Washington, 1943-46; dep. dir. Found. Fgn. Affairs, Washington, 1946-48; spl. legal adviser Am. Ind. Oil Co., Washington, 1946-50; mem. staff Near East research office Dept. State, Washington, 1950-72, dep. dir., 1965; professorial lectr. George Washington U. Nat. Law Center, 1955—, coordinator Afghan Legal Tng. Program, 1973—. Mem. Washington Fgn. Law Soc. (co-founder; v.p. 1958-59), Am. Fgn. Law Assn., Am. Soc. Internat. Law, Middle East Inst., Middle East Studies Assn. Recipient Meritorious honor award Dept. State, 1964, Superior Honor award, 1967; author: (with others) Zenon Papyri, vol. 2, 1940; The Government of French North Africa, 1943; The Law of the Near and Middle East: Readings, Cases and Materials, 1975; Materials on Comparative Law, 1977; editor: (with Majid Khadduri) Law in the Middle East, 1955; bd. advisory editors Middle East Jour., 1946—; contbr. articles, revs. to profl. jours. Home: 4250 S 35th St Arlington VA 22206 Office: Afghan Legal Tng Program Nat Law Center George Washington U suite 120 2025 Eye St NW Washington DC 20006

LIEBHAFSKY, DOUGLAS SMALL, b. Schenectady, Apr. 5, 1941; A.B., Harvard, 1961; LL.B. (Root-Tilden scholar), N.Y. U., 1964. Admitted to N.Y. bar, 1965, U.S. Ct. Appeals bar, 1966, U.S. Dist. Ct. bar, 1968, U.S. Supreme Ct. bar, 1973; law clk. to Hon. Warren E. Burger, U.S. Ct. Appeals, Washington, 1964-65; asst. U.S. Atty., So. Dist. N.Y., 1965-68, asst. chief appellate atty., 1968-69; asso. firm Wachtell, Lipton, Rosen & Katz, N.Y.C., 1969-71, partner, 1971—. Mem. Am., N.Y. State, N.Y.C. bar assns., Fed. Bar Council. Editor-in-chief: N.Y. U. Law Review, 1963-64. Home: 61 E 75th St New York City NY 10021 Office: 299 Park Ave New York City NY 10017 Tel (212) 371-9200

LIEBMAN, HERBERT DAVID, b. N.Y.C., May 1, 1926; B.A., U. Richmond (Va.), 1948; LL.B., U. Ky., 1951. Admitted to Ky. bar, 1951, Fla. bar, 1964; individual practice law, Frankfort, Ky., 1951—; judge City of Frankfort, 1955-60. Chmn. Franklin County Bd. Edn.; dir. Ky. Sch. Bds. Assn., 1974-76. Mem. Am., Ky., Franklin County (pres. 1974-75) bar assns. Home: 453 Blackfoot Trail Frankfort KY 40601 Office: PO Box 815 Frankfort KY 40601 Tel (502) 223-1176

LIEBMANN, FELIX G., b. Germany, Dec. 25, 1923; B.S. cum laude in Soc. Sci., Coll. City N.Y., 1948; J.D. with distinction, Cornell U., 1951. Admitted to N.Y. state bar, 1951, U.S. Supreme Ct. bar, 1960; asso. firm Davis, Polk, Wardwell, Sunderland & Kiendl, N.Y.C., 1951-56; tax. supr. Arabian Am. Oil Co., N.Y.C., 1956-58; tax counsel Carrier Corp., Syracuse, N.Y., 1958-61; asso. firm Harris, Beach, Wilcox, Rubin, & Levey, Rochester, N.Y., 1961-63, partner 1963—; dir., exec. com. Superba Cravats, Inc., Rochester, 1966—, Caldwell Mfg. Co., Rochester, 1972—. Bd. dirs. Hillside Children's Center, Rochester, 1970—, pres., 1976—. Mem. N.Y. State, Monroe County, (chmn. sect. banking, corps. and bus. law 1974) bar assns., Am. Judicature Soc., Acad. Polit. Sci., Am. Hist. Soc., N.Y. State Conservation Council, Order Coif, Phi Beta Kappa, Phi Kappa Phi. Editor-in-chief Cornell Law Quar., 1950-51. Office: 2 State St Rochester NY 14614 Tel (716) 232-4440

LIEBMANN, JACK S., b. New Haven, Jan. 29, 1921; B.S., U. Tampa, 1942; J.D., U. Miami, 1953. Admitted to Fla. bar, 1953, since practiced in Miami Beach; pres. Jack S. Liebmann & Assos. Mem. Fla., Miami Beach bar assns., ASCAP. Office: 420 Lincoln Rd Suite 206 Miami Beach FL 33139 Tel (305) 531-7673

LIEBOLT, FREDERICK LEE, JR., b. N.Y.C., June 30, 1941; B.A., U. Pa., 1963; LL.B., U. N.C., 1966. Admitted to N.Y. State bar, 1968; asso. firm Brown, Wood, Ivey, Mitchell & Petty, N.Y.C., 1967-75, partner firm, 1976—. Mem. Am., N.Y. State bar assns., Assn. Bar City of N.Y. Home: 115 E 90th St New York City NY 10028 Office: One Liberty Plaza New York City NY 10006 Tel (212) 349-7500

LIEBOWITZ, SIDNEY I., b. N.Y.C., Apr. 22, 1924; B.A., Yale, 1944; LL.B., Columbia, 1946. Admitted to N.Y. bar, 1947; partner firm Cowan, Liebowitz & Latman, N.Y.C., 1959—; arbitrator Am. Arbitration Assn. Mem. N.Y. State Bar Assn., Assn. Bar City N.Y. Editor-in-chief Columbia Law Rev., 1945-46. Home: Tripp St Mount Kisco NY 10549 Tel (212) YU 6-6272

LIENBERGER, WILLIAM MEREDITH, b. Columbus, Ind., Aug. 6, 1916; A.B., Ind. U., 1938, J.D., 1941. Admitted to Ind. bar, 1941; partner firm Shinn & Lienberger, Columbus, Ind., 1941-43; individual practice law, Columbus, 1946, 51-56; pros. atty. Bartholomew County (Ind.), 1942-43, 47-50; judge Bartholomew County Circuit Ct., 9th Jud. Circuit, 1956—. Mem. Bartholomew County, Ind. State bar assns., Am. Judicature Soc., Ind. Judges Assn., Nat., Ind. councils juvenile ct. judges. Recipient Good Govt. award Columbus Jr. C. of C., 1957. Home: 2205 Franklin St Columbus IN 47201 Office: Bartholomew Circuit Ct Courthouse Third and Washington Sts Columbus IN 47201 Tel (812) 372-2511

LIFE, GREG A., b. Oskaloosa, Iowa, June 16, 1948; B.S. in Edn., Northeast Mo. State Coll., 1970; J.D., Drake U., 1973. Admitted to Iowa bar, 1974; mem. firm Life, Davis & Life, Oskaloosa, Iowa, 1974—. Sec. Oskaloosa Airport Commn., 1975—. Mem. Iowa State, Mahasko County (v.p.) bar assns. Office: 124 1st Ave W Oskaloosa IA 52577 Tel (515) 673-8365

LIFLAND, WILLIAM THOMAS, b. Jersey City, Nov. 15, 1928; B.S., Yale, 1949; LL.B., Harvard, 1952. Admitted to D.C. bar, 1952, N.Y. bar, 1956, N.J. bar, 1965; with Office Gen. Counsel, USAF, 1952-54; law clk. to Justice Harlan, U.S. Supreme Ct., Washington, 1955; asso. firm Cahill Gordon & Reindel, N.Y.C., 1955—, partner, 1965—, asso. Paris office, 1958-60. Mem. Am. Bar Assn. (chmn. civil practice and procedure com. antitrust law sect. 1970-72, mem. sect. council 1975—, mem. commn. on law and economy 1975—), N.Y. State Bar Assn. (chmn. antitrust law sect. 1973-74). Pres., Harvard Law Rev., 1951-52; contbr. articles to profl. publs.; author monthly column N.Y. Law Jour. Home: 138 Wilson Rd Princeton NJ 08540 Office: 80 Pine St New York City NY 10005 Tel (212) 825-0100

LIFLANDER, E. PHILIP, b. N.Y.C., Apr. 2, 1907; B.A., Columbia, 1928, LL.B., 1930. Admitted to N.Y. State bar, 1931, U.S. Dist. Ct. for So. and Eastern Dist. bars, 1935; practiced in N.Y.C., 1931—; asso. firm Saul S. Myers, 1930-31; partner firm Liflander & Levin and predecessors, 1932-64; individual practice law, 1964—. Mem. N.Y. State Trial Lawyers Assn. Office: 60 E 42nd St New York City NY 10017 Tel (212) 697-6612

LIFSET, HARVEY MERVIN, b. Schenectady, Mar. 6, 1916; A.B., Union Coll., 1937, J.D., 1940. Admitted to N.Y. State bar, 1940, U.S. Supreme Ct. bar, 1954; asst. atty. Legal Aid Soc. Albany, Inc. 1950-56; mem. N.Y. State Gen. Assembly, 1957-68, chmn. ways and means com., 1966-68. Mem. N.Y. State, Albany County bar assns. Home: 380 Albany Shaker Rd Loudonville NY 12211 Office: 112 State St Albany NY 12207 Tel (518) 434-0114

LIFSHITZ, HARRIS T., b. Middletown, Conn., Mar. 22, 1946; A.B., Boston U., 1967; M.S., Wayne State U., 1970; J.D., U. Conn., 1971. Admitted to Conn. bar, 1971, Mich. bar, 1974; asso. firm Ritter & Berman, Hartford, 1971-73, R.D. Tulisano, Rocky Hill, Conn., 1973—; chmn. Rocky Hill Charter Revision Commn., 1974-75; justice of peace, Rocky Hill, 1977—. Mem. Conn., Mich., Am. bar assns., Am. Chem. Soc. Contbr. articles to profl. jours. Home: Trinity Ridge Rocky Hill CT 06067 Office: 2606 Main St Rocky Hill CT 06067 Tel (203) 563-9305

LIFSON, CARL KALMON, b. Capulia, Russia, Aug. 10, 1904; B.A., U. Minn., 1926; J.D., Harvard, 1929. Admitted to Minn. bar, 1930; since practiced in Mpls., asso. firm Brill & Maslon, 1930-35; mem. firm Schwartz & Lifson, 1935-38; individual practice law, 1939-62; mem. firm Lifson, Kelber, Abrahamson, Breuning & Weinstein, and predecessors, 1962—. Former bd. dirs. United Fund of Greater Mpls.; past pres. Talmud Torah of Mpls., Jewish Family and Children's Service of Greater Mpls.; former sec. Oak Park Home for Orphans, Mpls. Mem. Minn., Hennepin County bar assns. Home: 30 Russell Ct Minneapolis MN 55410 Office: 850 Shelard Plaza Minneapolis MN 55426 Tel (612) 544-1521

LIFTON, FRED BERNARD, b. Detroit, Sept. 24, 1928; A.B., Wayne State U., 1959, J.D., 1951. Admitted to Mich. bar, 1952, Ill. bar, 1959; partner firm Lifton & Lifton, Detroit, 1952-57; legis. coordinator Boating Industry Assn., 1957-64, exec. dir., 1964-69; sr. partner firm Robbins, Schwartz, Nicholas & Lifton, Ltd., Chgo., 1971—; exec. dir. Mich. State Waterways Commn., 1954-56. Mem. bds. edn. Niles (Ill.) High Sch. Dist. 219, 1967-70, Skokie Sch. Dist. 68, 1960-67; mem. Skokie Fine Arts Commn., 1966-70. Mem. Am., Ill., Mich., Chgo. bar assns. Recipient Distinguished Prof. award Nat. Acad. Sch. Execs., 1976; co-author: Contract Analyzer, 1972, supplement, 1975; Analysis of Iowa School Negotiations Proposals; contbr. practice handbooks for Ill. State Bar Assn., 1975, 76. Home: 9300 Kilbourn St Skokie IL 60076 Office: 29 S LaSalle St Chicago IL 60603 Tel (312) 332-7760

LIGDA, PAUL CHARLES, b. Oakland, Calif., July 13, 1934; A.B., San Jose State Coll., 1956; J.D. cum laude, Golden Gate Coll., 1961. Admitted to D.C. bar, 1961, Calif. bar, 1962, U.S. Supreme Ct. bar, 1967; atty. FTC, San Francisco, 1962-63; dep. dist. atty. Santa Clara County (Calif.), 1963-65; pub. defender El Dorado County (Calif.), 1965-68; Solano County (Calif.), 1968—; lectr. adminstrv. law Golden Gate U., 1973—. Mem. Calif. Pub. Defenders Assn (dir., past pres.), Nat. Legal Aid and Defender Assn. (dir., mem. exec. com.), Calif. Bar Assn. (com. on profl. ethics). Contbr. articles to legal jours. Home: 1129 Valle Vista Vallejo CA 94590 Office: Hall of Justice 550 Union Ave Fairfield CA 94533 Tel (707) 429-6254

LIGGIO, CARL DONALD, b. N.Y.C., Sept. 5, 1943; A.B., Georgetown U., 1963; J.D., N.Y. U., 1967. Admitted to N.Y. State bar, 1967, D.C. bar, 1967; cons. firm Arent, Fox, Kintner, Plotkin & Kahn, Washington, 1968-69; asso. firm White & Case, N.Y.C., 1969-72; gen. counsel Arthur Young & Co., N.Y.C., 1972—. Mem. Am., N.Y. State, D.C. bar assns., Assn. Bar City N.Y. Contbr. articles to legal and bus. jours. Home: 11 E 86th St New York City NY 10028 Office: 277 Park Ave New York City NY 10017 Tel (212) 922-2465

LIGHT, DONALD EUGENE, b. Springfield, Mo., Mar. 7, 1933; student San Diego State U., 1955-56; J.D., U. Mo., 1962. Admitted to Mo. bar, 1963, Tenn. bar, 1970; subrogation supr. MFA Ins. Co., Columbia, Mo., 1962-64, litigation supr., Kansas City, Mo., also Ky. and Tenn., 1964-66, regional claims dir., Ind., Ky., Tenn., and Miss., 1966—. Loaned exec. Columbia United Givers Fund, 1964, div. chmn., 1969. Mem. Mo. Bar. Home: 405 Vaden Dr Brentwood TN 37027 Office: Box 40506 Nashville TN 37204 Tel (615) 383-5449

LIGHT, FRANK NELSON, b. Rustburg, Va., Aug. 25, 1924; J.D., Washington and Lee U., 1952. Admitted to Va. bar, 1952; partner firm Light & Light, Chatham, Va., 1952-55; individual practice, Chatham, 1955-73; judge Cts. Not-of-Record of Pittsylvania County (Va.), 1955—. Mem. Va. State Bar, Va. Bar Assn., Am. Judicature Soc., N.Am. Judges Assn., Jud. Conf. Dist. Cts. Va., Va. Dist. Cts. Judges Assn. Home: Route 2 Box 49A Cherrystone Rd Chatham VA 24531 Office: 107 Moses Bldg 21 N Main St Chatham VA 24531 Tel (804) 432-2041 X214

LIGHT, IVAN HUBER, b. Normal, Ill., Mar. 10, 1906; A.B., Harvard, 1927, LL.B., 1930. Admitted to Ill. bar, 1930, Mo. bar, 1934, Wis. bar, 1948; asso. Light & Light, Bloomington, Ill., 1930-32, Thompson, Mitchell, Thompson & Young, St. Louis, 1932-40; individual practice law, St. Louis, 1941-54, Bloomington and Normal, Ill., 1954—; magistrate McLean County (Ill.) Circuit Ct., 1964-65; atty. for trustees St.L.& S.F. Ry. Co., 1935-42. Twp. committeeman Republican Party, 1958-68; pres. McLean County Civil War

Roundtable, 1962, Decatur (Ill.) Civil War Roundtable, 1976. Author: Blooming Town, 1956; contbr. articles to profl. publs. Address: Rt 1 Shirley IL 61772 Tel (309) 828-3400

LIGHTFOOT, WARREN BRICKEN, b. Montgomery, Ala., Aug. 21, 1938; B.A., U. Ala., 1960, LL.B., 1964. Admitted to Ala. bar, 1964; asso. firm Bradley, Arant, Rose & White, Birmingham, Ala., 1964-71, mem., 1971—. Elder, Ind. Presbyn. Ch., 1975—. Mem. Birmingham (past pres. young lawyers sect., past mem. exec. com.), Ala., Am. bar assns., Ala. Def. Lawyers Assn. Contbr. articles to legal jours. Home: 3364 Faring Rd Birmingham AL 35223 Office: Bradley Arant Rose & White 1500 Brown Marx Bldg Birmingham AL 35203 Tel (205) 252-4500

LIGNELL, STEG J., b. Grand Rapids, Mich., Sept. 25, 1909; A.B., U. Mich., 1932, J.D., 1934. Admitted to Mich. bar, 1934, individual practice law, Grand Rapids, 1934-38; gen. counsel Preferred Ins. Co., Grand Rapids, 1938-58; with legal dept. Transamerica Ins. Co., Battle Creek, Mich., 1958-69; judge 4th Jud. Dist. of Mich., Cassopolis, 1969—. Bd. dirs. Big Bros. of Am. Mem. Am., Mich. State, Cass County bar assns., Am. Judicature Soc., Am., Mich. judges assns. Home: Route 7 Dutch Settlement St Dowagiac MI 49047 Office: Ct House Cassopolis MI 40031 Tel (616) 445-8621

LIIVAK, ARNO, b. Tallinn, Estonia, Oct. 8, 1942; B.A., Rutgers U., 1965, M.L.S., 1966, J.D., 1969. Admitted to N.J. bar, 1969; asst. prof. law, law librarian Rutgers U. Sch. Law, Camden, N.J., 1969-72, asso. prof., law librarian, 1972-73, prof., law librarian, 1973—; mem. N.J. Supreme Ct. Com. on Ct. Opinions, 1974—; cons. W.S. Hein Co., 1975. Mem. Assn. Am. Law Schs., Am. (fgn. law com. 1976—), Internat. assns. law librarians. Contbr. articles to law jours. Home: 316 Pleasant Valley Ave Moorestown NJ 08057 Office: Rutgers Univ Sch Law 5th and Penn Sts Camden NJ 08102 Tel (609) 757-6173

LILES, JOSEPH ROBERT, b. Nacogdoches, Tex., Apr. 19, 1909; LL.B., Cumberland U., 1930. Admitted to Tex. bar, 1930, U.S. Supreme Ct. bar, 1961; asso. firm Strode & Pitts, Conroe, Tex., 1930-31, firm Pitts & Liles, Conroe, 1931-55, firm Phelps, Davis, Liles & Gray, Houston, 1961-64; individual practice law, Conroe, Tex., 1964—; judge 9th Dist. Ct. Tex., 1957-60. Mem. Tex., Montgomery County bar assns. Office: W Bldg Conroe TX 77301 Tel (713) 756-0057

LILIAN, ERIC LLOYD, b. Klagenfurt, Austria, June 20, 1930; B.S., Temple U., 1952, M.S., 1960, J.D., 1964. Admitted to Pa. bar, 1965; individual practice law, Phila., 1965—; trial counsel Phila. Legal Aid Soc., 1965-75; instr. Temple U. Sch. Law, 1972. Asso. editor-in-chief Temple Law Quar., 1963-64; pub. Phila. Med. Examiner. Home: 424 Hendrix St Philadelphia PA 19116 Office: 22 S 22d St Philadelphia PA 19103 Tel (215) LO-4-1711

LILLARD, ROBERT EMMITT, b. Nashville, Mar. 23, 1907; student Biggins Comml. Coll.; LL.B., Kent Coll. Admitted to Tenn. bar, 1966; partner firm Lillard & Vincent, Nashville, 1936—. Bd. dirs. United Givers Fund, March of Dimes, Am. Cancer Soc., ARC, local council Boy Scouts Am. Mem. Am., Tenn., Nashville, Nat. bar assns., Am. Judicature Soc. Home: 35050 Kings Ln Nashville TN 37218 Office: 1031 Stahlman Bldg 211 Union St Nashville TN 37201 Tel (615) 254-6489

LILLARD, ROSS W., b. South Bend, Ind., Sept. 20, 1931; A.B., U. Mo., 1952, LL.B., 1954. Admitted to Mo. bar, 1954; asso. firm Hogsett, Houts, James, Randall & Hogsett, Kansas City, Mo., 1957-59; partner firm McKenzie, Williams, Merrick, Beamer & Stubbs, Kansas City, Mo., 1959-61; partner firm Stinson, Mag, Thomson, McEvers & Fizzell, Kansas City, Mo., 1961—; lectr. in field. Bd. dirs. Internat. Relations Council, Kansas City, Mo., Wornall House Com., Kansas City, Mo. Mem. Mo. Bar (chmn. com. on pensions and retirement, past chmn. com. on taxation), Am., Kansas City bar assns., Lawyers Assn. of Kansas City. Contbr. articles to legal jours. Home: 1000 W 57th St Kansas City MO 64113 Office: 2100 Ten Main Center Kansas City MO 64105 Tel (816) 842-8600

LILLESTON, GEORGE RANDALL, b. Clinton, Mo., July 31, 1940; B.S., Central Mo. State U., 1967; J.D., U. Mo., 1971. Admitted to Mo. bar, 1971; taxation specialist, auditor Lybrand Ross Bros. & Montgomery, 1968-71; trust officer United Mo. Bank, 1972; partner firm Lilleston & Roberts, Clinton, Mo., 1972—. Sec. Clinton Meml. Airport. Mem. Mo. Bar Assn. Home: 504 S 2d St Clinton MO 64735 Office: 104 W Jefferson St Clinton MO 64735 Tel (816) 885-6161

LILLEY, JUDSON MERRILL, b. San Antonio, Dec. 4, 1909; B.A., U. of West, 1931; LL.B., Los Angeles, 1934. Admitted to Calif. bar, 1934; individual practice law, Long Beach, Calif., 1934-61; judge Municipal Ct., Long Beach, 1961—. Office: 415 W Ocean St Long Beach CA 90802 Tel (213) 432-0411

LILLICH, RICHARD BONNOT, b. Amherst, Ohio, Jan. 22, 1933; A.B., Oberlin Coll., 1954; LL.B., Cornell U., 1957; LL.M., J.S.D. in Internat. Law, N.Y. U., 1960. Admitted to N.Y. State bar, 1957; individual practice law, N.Y.C., 1957-60; teaching fellow N.Y. U. Law Sch., 1958-60; vis. asst. prof. Ind. U. Law Sch., 1960; asst. prof. Syracuse (N.Y.) U. Coll. Law, 1960-63, asso. prof., Ford Found. fellow, London and Cambridge, Eng., 1963-67; prof., Guggenheim fellow, London, 1966-67, 1967-69; Charles H. Stockton Chair of Internat. Law, U.S. Naval War Coll., 1968-69; prof. U. Va. Sch. Law, Charlottesville, 1969—; NEH fellow, Cambridge, Eng., 1974-75. Mem. Am. Soc. Internat. Law, Assn. Bar City N.Y., Brit. Inst. Internat. and Comparative Law, Internat. Law Assn., Procedural Aspects of Internat. Law Inst. (pres.), U.S. Inst. of Human Rights. Author: International Claims: Their Settlement by Lump Sum Agreements, 1975, other books; editor Am. Jour. Internat. Law, 1969—; editor Procedural Aspects of Internat. Law Series, 1964-77. Home: Locust Mountain Farm Charlottesville VA 22901 Office: Univ Va Sch Law Charlottesville VA 22901

LILLIE, MARGARET ELIZABETH, b. Bennington, Vt., Jan. 2, 1924; B.A., U. Vt., 1944; J.D., Boston Coll., 1953. Admitted to Vt. bar, 1953; pros. atty. Bennington County (Vt.), 1955-61; judge of probate Dist. Bennington, 1961-74; partner firm Clark & Lillie, Bennington, 1974—. Trustee, So. Vt. Coll., Bennington, 1972-76. Mem. Am., Vt., Bennington County bar assns. Home: Office: 204 Union St Bennington VT 05201 Tel (802) 447-7824

LILLIE, SUSAN JANE, b. Seattle, July 19, 1922; LL.B., George Washington U., 1950, B.B.A. in Accounting, 1966, LL.M., 1970. Admitted to Md. bar, 1950, D.C. bar, 1950; individual practice law, Rockville, Md., 1950-56; atty.-adviser Pub. Housing Adminstrn., Washington, 1956-59; asst. reporter U.S. Tax Ct., Washington, 1962-66; tax law specialist IRS, Washington, 1966-75; supr. internat. tax group Touche Ross & Co., N.Y.C., 1975-76; partner firm Robert Feinschreiber & Assos., N.Y.C., 1976-77; asso. firm Mudge, Rose, Guthrie & Alexander, 1977—. speaker World Trade Inst. seminars, 1975—. Del. Md. Republican State Conv., 1950. Mem. D.C. Integrated Bar, Fed. Bar Assn. (chmn. fgn. visitors subcom. com. internat. law 1963-65, vice chmn. taxation com. 1966-67, agy. rep. 1962-70). Home: 155 W 68th St Apt 1728 New York City NY 10023 Office: 20 Broad St New York City NY 10005 Tel (212) 734-3119

LILLY, THOMAS GERALD, b. Belzoni, Miss., Sept. 17, 1933; B.B.A., Tulane U., 1955; LL.B., U. Miss., 1960, J.D., 1968. Admitted to Miss. bar, 1960; asso. firm Stovall & Price, Corinth, Miss., 1960-62; asst. U.S. atty. No. Dist. Miss., 1962-66; asso. firm Wise Carter Child Steen & Caraway and predecessor, Jackson, Miss., 1966-67, partner, 1967—. Mem. Miss. State Bar, Hinds County (Miss.) Bar, Fed. (pres. Miss. chpt. 1969-70, rec. sec. 1975-76, gen. sec. 1976-77), Am. bar assns., Phi Delta Phi, Omicron Delta Kappa. Home: 4408 Deer Creek Dr Jackson MS 39211 Office: PO Box 651 925 Electric Bldg Jackson MS 39205 Tel (601) 354-2385

LILLY, THOMAS JOSEPH, b. Bklyn., Feb. 17, 1931; B.A., St. Johns Coll., 1953; J.D., Fordham U., 1961; LL.M., N.Y. U., 1967. Admitted to N.Y. bar, 1961; dir. research Office and Profl. Employees Internat. Union, AFL-CIO, N.Y.C., 1960-62; asst. U.S. atty. Eastern Dist. N.Y., Bklyn., 1962-66; partner firm Doran, Colleran, O'Hara, Pollio & Dunne, N.Y.C., 1966—; arbitrator N.Y. State Mediation Bd., 1967—; mediator, fact finder N.Y. State Pub. Employment Relations Bd., 1971—. Mem. N.Y., N.Y.C., Nassau County bar assns., Am. Arbitration Assn. (labor panel). Home: 136 8th Ave Sea Cliff NY 11579 Office: 1140 Ave of Americas New York City NY 10036 Tel (212) 986-3737

LIMA, SALVATORE ANTONIO, b. San Francisco, Feb. 6, 1937; J.D., U. San Francisco, 1968; LL.M. in Taxation, N.Y. U., 1971. Admitted to Calif. bar, 1969, U.S. Tax Ct., 1974, U.S. Dist. Ct. No. Dist. Calif., 1974, U.S. Ct. Claims, 1974; mem. tax dept. Coopers & Lybrand, N.Y.C., 1969-73; individual practice law, San Francisco, 1974—; of counsel firm Frolik, Filley & Schey, San Francisco; adj. prof. taxation Golden Gate U., 1973—. Mem. Am., San Francisco bar assns., San Francisco Jr. C. of C. (dir. 1963). C.P.A., Calif., N.Y. Recipient Outstanding Tax Faculty award Graduate Sch. Taxation Golden Gate U., 1975. Office: 22 Battery St Suite 1100 San Francisco CA 94111 Tel (415) 956-5700

LIMBACH, KARL AVERELL, b. Cleve., Apr. 2, 1932; A.B., Middlebury Coll., 1954; J.D., Western Res. U., 1957. Admitted to Ohio bar, 1957, Calif. bar, 1958; partner firm Limbach Limbach & Sutton, San Francisco, 1968—. Mem. Am., San Francisco bar assns., Am. Patent Assn., State Bar Calif. (pres. patent trademark and copyright sect. 1976), San Francisco Patent Law Assn. (pres., 1970). Office: 2000 Ferry Bldg San Francisco CA 94111 Tel (415) 433-4150

LIMMER, STEPHEN GENE, b. Pensacola, Fla., Jan. 3, 1945; B.B.A., Hofstra U., 1967; J.D., St. John's U., 1971. Admitted to N.Y. bar, 1972; confidential law clk. N.Y. Supreme Ct. Appellate Div., Rochester, 1971-73; mem. firm Schiffmacher, Cullen & Farrell, Great Neck, N.Y., 1973—; mem. law services dept. OEO, Glen Cove, N.Y., 1969-70; asst. dist. atty. Village Cts., Village of Great Neck, Kings Point, N.Y., 1973—. Asso. trustee Temple Beth-El of Great Neck, 1976—. Mem. N.Y. State, Nassau County bar assns., Great Neck Lawyers Assn. Home: 2 Devonshire Ln Great Neck NY 11023 Office: 98 Cutter Mill Rd Great Neck NY 11021 Tel (516) 482-7600

LINCOLN, ARTHUR FREDERICK, JR., b. Phila., Feb. 5, 1943; B.S., U.S. Mil. Acad., 1966; J.D., Boston Coll., 1971. Admitted to Maine bar, 1971, Mass. bar, 1971, U.S. Supreme Ct. bar, 1975, U.S. Ct. Mil. Appeals bar, 1971, U.S. Army Ct. Mil. Rev., 1971; commd. 2d lt. JAGC, U.S. Army, 1971, advanced through grades to capt., 1968; asst. prof., atty. U.S. Mil. Acad., 1973-76; house counsel Acton Corp. (Mass.), 1976—. Mem. Am., Maine bar assns. Recipient Lawyer of Year award N.Y.C. Criminal and Civil Bar Assn., 1976. Home: Duffy Rd Boylston MA 01505 Office: Acton Corp Acton MA 01720 Tel (617) 293-7711

LINCOLN, FRANKLIN BENJAMIN, JR., b. Bklyn., Jan. 18, 1908; A.B., Colgate U., 1931, LL.D. (hon.), 1960; J.D., Columbia, 1934. Admitted to N.Y. bar, 1934, U.S. Supreme Ct. bar, 1944, D.C. bar, 1960; asso. firm Sullivan & Cromwell, N.Y.C., 1934-41; partner firm Lundgren, Lincoln & McDaniel, N.Y.C., 1941-59, Seward & Kissel, N.Y.C., 1964-66; sr. partner Mudge, Rose, Guthrie & Alexander, N.Y.C., 1966—; asst. sec. def., 1959-61; Nixon rep. presdl. transition, Wash., D.C., 1968-69; mem. Pres.'s Fgn. Intelligence Adv. Bd., 1969-73; v.p., dir. Cypress Communications Corp., 1965-69; dir. Pacific Tin Consol., N.Y.C., 1969—, ITEL Corp., N.Y.C., 1970—, World Bd. Trade, 1973-75; chmn. Fed. Home Loan Bank N.Y., 1974-77, dir., 1977—. Trustee Colgate U., Hamilton, N.Y., 1967-74, chmn., 1975—. Mem. Am., N.Y., D.C. bar assns., Assn. Bar City N.Y. Recipient Distinguished Pub. Service medal Dept. Defense, 1961; author: Presidential Transition, 1969. Home: 22 Roland Dr Short Hills NJ 07078 Office: 20 Broad St New York City NY 10005 Tel (212) 422-6767

LIND, DENNIS EARL, b. Hardin, Mont., July 7, 1947; B.A. in Econs., History and Polit. Sci., U. Mont., 1970, J.D., 1973. Admitted to Mont. bar, 1973; chief civil dep. Mont. Atty. Gen., Helena, 1973-74; chief civil dep. Missoula County (Mont.) Attys. Office, 1974-76; asso. firm Datsopoulos & Macdonald, Missoula, 1976—. Mem. Am., Mont., Western Mont. bar assns., Missoula Young Lawyers Assn. Office: suite A Century Plaza Missoula MT 59801 Tel (406) 728-0810

LIND, THOMAS OTTO, b. New Orleans, Apr. 24, 1937; B.M.E., Tulane U., 1959, LL.B., 1965. Admitted to La. bar, 1965; clk. firm Terriberry, Rault, Carroll, Yancey & Farrell, New Orleans, 1963-64; asso. firm Jones, Walker, Waechter, Poitevant, Carrere & Denegre, New Orleans, 1965-66; counsel Ingram Corp., New Orleans, 1966—, corporate sec., 1967—. Sect. leader United Fund, New Orleans, 1970, New Orleans Symphony Fund, 1972; vestryman, chmn. Every Mem. Canvass, Trinity Episcopal Ch., 1975—. Mem. La. State (council sect. corp. law, 1970-72), Am., New Orleans bar assns., Notaries Assn. New Orleans. Home: 1126 Octavia St New Orleans LA 70115 Office: 4100 One Shell Sq New Orleans LA 70139 Tel (504) 588-2400

LINDAUER, ERIC B., b. Red Bluff, Calif., Oct. 20, 1938; B.S., Oreg. State U., 1963; J.D., Willamette Coll., 1966. Admitted to Oreg. bar; exec. asst. to Senator Mark O. Hatfield, Washington, 1966-69; partner firm Clark, Marsh & Lindauer, Salem, Oreg., 1971—; pro tem judge Oreg. Dist. Ct.; mem. panel of arbitrators Fed. Mediation and Conciliation Service. Bd. dirs. United Way, Salem Art Assn., Vol. Bur. Salem Area Srs., Westminster United Presbyterian Ch. Mem. Merion County (dir.), Am., Oreg. State bar assns. Office: 880 Liberty St NE Salem OR 97301 Tel (503) 581-1542

LINDE, FLORENCE, b. Lynn, Mass.; A.B. magna cum laude, Radcliffe Coll.; LL.B. magna cum laude, New England Sch. Law. Admitted to Mass. bar; mem. law dept. Boston Ordnance Dist.; now asso. firm Nutter, McClennen & Fish, Boston. Mem. Am., Mass., Boston bar assns., Mass. Assn. Women Lawyers. Home: 36 Cherry St Lynn MA 01902 Office: 75 Federal St Boston MA 02110 Tel (617) 423-7011

LINDE, LLEWELLYN HERBERT, b. Cyrus, Minn., May 11, 1928; B.A., Concordia Coll., Moorhead, Minn., 1953; M.A., Ind. U., 1957; J.D., William Mitchell Coll. Law, 1960. Admitted to Minn. bar, 1960; gen. counsel Correctional Service of Minn., St. Paul, 1960-66; supr. foster care and adoption Minn. Dept. Pub. Welfare, St. Paul, 1967-70; chmn. adult corrections commn. Minn. Dept. Corrections, St. Paul, 1971-74, exec. officer juvenile releases, 1974—; lectr. continuing edn. in social work U. Minn. Pres. Hastings (Minn.) Family Service, 1973, 76. Mem. Minn. State, Dakota County (Minn.) bar assns. Contbr. articles on social work and law to profl. jours. Home: 1610 Tyler St Hastings MN 55033 Office: 238 Metro Square Bldg Saint Paul MN 55101 Tel (612) 296-3560

LINDEEN, GORDON R., b. Spokane, Wash., Jan. 23, 1930; B.A., Yale U., 1952; J.D., Stanford U., 1955. Admitted to Calif. bar, 1956; contract adminstr. N.Am. Aviation, Inc., Rocketdyne divs., Canoga Park, Calif., 1958-61; individual practice law, Simi Valley, Calif., 1958—; atty. Simi Valley Recreation and Park Dist., 1961—, Arroyo Tapo Protection Dist., 1962-68. Personnel commr. Simi Valley Unified Sch. Dist., 1968—, chmn., 1971—; bd. dirs., v.p. Ventura County chpt. ARC; bd. dirs. Simi Valley Pub. Cemetery Dist.; trustee United Methodist Ch., Simi Valley. Mem. Ventura County Bar Assn. Office: 4220 Los Angeles Ave Suite 204 Simi Valley CA 93063 Tel (805) 526-2586

LINDEN, JEFFREY L., b. Los Angeles, Nov. 1, 1942; A.B., U. Calif., Los Angeles, 1964, J.D., 1967. Admitted to Calif. bar, 1968; atty., SEC, Los Angeles, 1967-68; mem. firm Dolman, Wolf & Linden, Los Angeles, 1968—; judge pro tem Los Angeles Municipal Ct., 1975, 76; lectr. U. Calif. extension, Los Angeles. Mem. adv. council Sherman Oaks (Calif.) Elementary Sch., 1975—. Mem. Am., Los Angeles County, Beverly Hills, Century City (bd. govs., treas.) bar assns. Office: 1888 Century Park E Los Angeles CA 90067 Tel (213) 277-2236

LINDEN, STEPHEN, b. Detroit, July 24, 1948; B.A., U. Mich., 1970; J.D., Wayne State U., 1972. Admitted to Mich. bar, 1973; asso. firm Bielfield, Becker & Zipser, 1972-73, Rosin & Kobel, 1973; mem. firm Linden & Schwartz, P.C., Southfield, Mich., 1974—; active legal aid clincs RICCOD, Hearing Aid, Oakland County Legal Aid, Gateway Crisis Center. Mem. Fed., Mich., Oakland County, Detroit, Southfield bar assns., Am. Arbitration Assn. Office: 30215 Southfield Rd Suite 204 Southfield MI 48076 Tel (313) 646-0120

LINDENBAUM, ABRAHAM M., b. N.Y.C., Mar. 12, 1909; B.A., N.Y. U., 1927; LL.B., Bklyn. U., 1930; LL.D., Bklyn. Law Sch., 1969. Admitted to N.Y. bar, 1930; partner firm Lindenbaum & Young, Bklyn., 1949—; commr. N.Y.C. Housing Authority, 1957-59, N.Y.C. Planning Commn., 1959-62. Mem. Fed., N.Y. State, Bklyn. bar assns. Recipient Met. award Yeshiva U., 1971, Louis Marshal award Jewish Theol. Sem., 1970. Home: 9 Prospect Park W Brooklyn NY 11215 Office: 16 Court St Brooklyn NY 11241 Tel (212) 875-8000

LINDENMUTH, NOEL CHARLES, b. Chgo., Nov. 27, 1940; J.D., Loyola U., Chgo., 1970. Admitted to Ill. bar, 1970; asso. firm Horwitz, Anesi, Ozmon & Assos., Chgo., 1970—. Mem. Chgo., Ill., Am. bar assns., Chgo., Ill. trial lawyers assns., Assn. Am. Trial Lawyers. Home: 4901 W Montrose Ave Chicago IL 60641 Office: 188 W Randolph St Chicago IL 60601 Tel (312) 372-3822

LINDER, ROBERT DUANE, b. Oelwein, Iowa, Jan. 10, 1932; B.A., U. Iowa, 1954, J.D., 1959; M.B.A., Harvard U., 1961; LL.M., George Washington U., 1969. Admitted to Iowa bar, 1959, Va. bar, 1969, U.S. Supreme Ct. bar, 1969; analyst Bur. of Budget, Office of Mgmt. and Budget, Washington, 1961-73; chief exec. clk. The White House, Washington, 1973—. Mem. Iowa, Va., Am. bar assns. Office: The White House Washington DC 20500 Tel (202) 456-2954

LINDERMAN, RICHARD DONALD, b. Reading, Pa., Mar. 27, 1939; B.A., Ursinus Coll., 1969; J.D., Duquesne U., 1973. Admitted to Pa. bar, 1973, U.S. Dist. Ct. for Eastern Dist. Pa. bar, 1973; asso. firm O'Donnell, Weiss, Mattei, Koury & Suchoza, Pottstown, Pa., 1973—. Bd. dirs. Bicentennial Com. for Lower Pottsgrove, Pa., 1976. Mem. Am., Pa., Montgomery County bar assns., Pa., Montgomery County trial lawyers assns. Contbr. articles to law reviews. Home: 1123 Rambler Ave Pottstown PA 19464 Office: 41 High St Pottstown PA 19464 Tel (215) 323-2800

LINDH, ALFRED JOHN, b. Wilmington, Del., July 8, 1936; B.A., U. Del., 1958; J.D., Georgetown U., 1961. Admitted to D.C. bar, 1961, Del. bar, 1962; research asst. Inst. for Internat. and Fgn. Trade Law, Frankfort, W. Ger., 1961-62; individual practice law, Wilmington, Del., 1962-63, 65—; asst. U.S. atty., Del., 1964-65. Mem. human rights subcom. clin. research and publs. com. Wilmington Med. Center. Mem. Del. Bar Assn. Author drug abuse law, Del., 1973. Home: 2211-A Prior Rd Wilmington DE 19809 Office: 512 Market Tower Wilmington DE 19801 Tel (302) 652-1196

LINDHEIM, WILLIAM SETH, b. N.Y.C., Apr. 1, 1945; A.B., U. Calif., Los Angeles, 1966; J.D., U. San Diego, 1969. Admitted to Calif. bar, 1970; asso. firm Rose, Klein & Marias, Los Angeles, 1970-75, Richman & Garrett, Los Angeles, 1975—. Mem. Constl. Rights Found. Mem. Los Angeles County, Mexican-Am. bar assns. Office: 1336 Wilshire Blvd Los Angeles CA 90017 Tel (213) 483-7400

LINDHOLM, DWIGHT HENRY, b. Blackduck, Minn., May 27, 1930; student Macalester Coll., 1948-49; B.B.A., U. Minn., 1951, LL.B., 1954; postgrad. Mexico City Coll. (now U. Ams.), 1956-57. Admitted to Minn. bar, 1954, Calif. bar, 1958; with JAGC, USAF, 1954-56; individual practice law, Los Angeles, 1976—; partner firm Lindholm & Johnson, and predecessor, Los Angeles, 1965-76. Mem. Republican Central Com. of Calif., 1962-63, of Los Angeles County, 1962-66; bd. dirs. Family Service Los Angeles, 1964-70, v.p., 1968-70; bd. dirs. Wilshire YMCA and Los Angeles Met. YMCA, 1976—; elder, dir. Hollywood (Calif.) Presbyn. Ch. Mem. Los Angeles County Bar Assn., Lawyers Club Los Angeles, Los Angeles Trial Lawyers Assn., State Bar Calif., Delta Sigma Pi, Delta Sigma Rho, Delta Theta Phi (state chancellor 1972-73). Recipient Presdl. award Los Angeles Jr. C. of C., 1959. Home: 255 S Rossmore Ave Los Angeles CA 90004 Office: 3701 Wilshire Blvd Suite 700 Los Angeles CA 90010 Tel (213) 487-1334

LINDOVER, DONALD, b. Aug. 15, 1941; B.A., Coll. City N.Y., 1964; LL.B., J.D., Syracuse U., 1966. Admitted to N.Y. State bar, 1967; mem. firm Wallman, Kramer, Paley, Roemer & Duben, N.Y.C., 1967-71; individual practice law, N.Y.C., 1971—. Mem. Assn. Immigration and Nationality Lawyers (sec. N.Y. chpt.). Home: 55 W 11th St New York City NY 10011 Office: 233 Broadway Suite 760 New York City NY 10007 Tel (212) 349-5550

LINDROOTH, CHARLES HUTCHINSON, b. Chgo., Sept. 12, 1932; B.S. in Gen. Engring., U. Ill., 1956; J.D., George Washington U., 1962. Admitted to Va. bar, 1962, Pa. bar, 1963; examiner U.S. Patent Office, Washington, 1958-62; asso. firm Synnestvedt & Lechner, Phila., 1962-68, partner, 1968—; dir. Am. Bioculture, Inc. Sec. Bryn Athyn Borough Authority, 1973-75, councilman, 1975—; mem. Bryn Athyn Civil Service Commn., 1964—, Home Rule Study Commn., 1976—. Mem. Am., Phila. bar assns., Am., Phila. patent law assns. Office: 12 S 12th St Philadelphia PA 19107 Tel (215) WA3-4466

LINDSAY, DENNIS JOHN, b. Winnipeg, Man., Can., Mar. 22, 1918; B.A., Oberlin Coll., 1938; J.D., U. Mich., 1941. Admitted to Mich. bar, 1941, N.Y. State bar, 1945, Oreg. bar, 1948; atty. Dept. Interior, 1941-43; asso. firm Cahill, Gordon, Zachery & Reindel, N.Y.C., 1943-48; dep. dist. atty. County of Multnomah, Oreg., 1948-50; sr. partner firm Lindsay, Nahstoll, Hart & Krause, Portland, 1950—. Mem., pres. Port of Portland Commn., 1957-69; pres. Portland Devel. Commn., 1974—. Mem. Am., Multnomah County bar assns., Oreg. State Bar, Maritime Law Assn., Am. Assn. Average Adjusters Am. Judicature Soc. Home: 11050 SW Riverside Dr Portland OR 97219 Office: 1331 SW Broadway Portland OR 97201 Tel (503) 226-1191

LINDSAY, GEORGE NELSON, b. N.Y.C., Oct. 20, 1919; B.A., Yale, 1941, LL.B., 1947. Admitted to N.Y. State bar, 1947; asso. firm Debevoise, Plimpton, Lyons & Gates, N.Y.C., 1947-54, partner, 1955—; dir. Ogilvy & Mather Internat., Inc.; mem. advisory council on Africa, Dept. State, 1964-68; mem. exec. com. Lawyers Com. for Civil Rights Under Law, 1969—, co-chmn., 1969-71; bd. dirs. Am. Fund for Free Jurists, 1961-67, Am. Assn. for Internat. Commn. of Jurists, 1968—. Mem. Urban Design Council of City N.Y., 1969-75; vice chmn., dir. African-Am. Inst., 1969—; mem. Yale U. Council, 1974—; bd. dirs. Planned Parenthood-World Population, 1964-68, chmn., 1965-68. Fellow Am. Bar Found.; mem. Am. Judicature Soc., Am., N.Y. State bar assns., Assn. Bar City N.Y. (mem. exec. com., 1973-77, chmn. exec. com. 1976-77, v.p. 1977). Home: 16 Sutton Pl New York City NY 10022 Office: 299 Park Ave New York City NY 10017 Tel (212) 752-6400

LINDSEY, HENDERSON CROCKETT, b. Gulfport, Miss., Jan. 11, 1946; B.A., U. Miss., 1968, J.D., 1970. Admitted to Miss. bar, 1970, U.S. Ct. Appeals 5th Circuit bar, 1973—; individual practice law, Gulfport, 1970—; municipal ct. judge City of Gulfport, 1975—. Mem. Am., Miss. bar assns., Assn. Trial Lawyers Am., Miss Trial Lawyers Assn. Home: 504 Kahler St Gulfport MS 39501 Office: 1119 31st Ave Gulfport MS 39501 Tel (601) 863-4798

LINDSEY, ROBERT SOURS, b. Dixon, S.D., May 1, 1913; A.B., Washington U., St. Louis, 1936, LL.B., 1936. Admitted to Mo. bar, 1936, Ark. bar, 1943; individual practice law, St. Louis, 1936-43, Little Rock, 1943-45; partner firm Wright, Lindsey & Jennings, Little Rock, 1946—; sec., dir. Ferncliff, Inc., 1945-66. Bd. dirs. Presbyn. Village, Inc., 1962-66, 70-76, pres., 1972-74; bd. dirs. Met. YMCA, 1962-68, pres., 1965-66, bd. dirs. Ark. Assn. Mental Health, 1960-69, treas., 1963-65; bd. dirs. Presbyn. Found. Ark., Inc., 1962-71, pres., 1966-67; mem. Ark. Merit System Council, 1967-76, chmn., 1968-69; trustee Ark. Law Sch., Austin Presbyn. Theol. Sem., 1971-77, Ark. Found. Associated Colls., 1975—. Fellow Am. Bar Found.; mem. Ark. (chmn. exec. com. 1965-66, Outstanding Lawyer award 1969, chmn. exec. council 1976-77), Am., Pulaski County (pres. 1972-73) bar assns., Internat. Assn. Ins. Counsel, Am. Judicature Soc., Am. Counsel Assn., Phi Delta Phi. Home: 20 E Palisades Dr Little Rock AR 72207 Office: Worthen Bank Bldg Little Rock AR 72201 Tel (501) 371-0808

LINER, DAVID VERNON, b. High Point, N.C., May 29, 1941; B.S., Wake Forest U., 1963, J.D., 1969. Admitted to N.C. bar, 1969; partner firm Drum and Liner, Winston-Salem, N.C., 1969-76; partner firm Liner & Habegger, Winston-Salem, 1976—. Mem. N.C., Forsyth Jr., Am. bar assns., N.C. Acad. Trial Lawyers. Home: 2301 Bryan Terrace Clemmons NC 27012 Office: 206 W 4th St PO Box 2840 Winston-Salem NC 27102 Tel (919) 725-9235

LINES, FARRELL LAVAR, b. Lordsburg, N. Mex., Sept. 16, 1937; A.B., Eastern Ariz. Jr. Coll., 1957; B.S., Brigham Young U., 1963; J.D., George Washington U., 1968. Admitted to D.C. bar, 1969, N.Mex. bar, 1968; legis. asst. U.S. Senator Clinton P. Anderson, 1968-70; asso. firm Modrall, Sperling, Roehl, Harris & Sisk, Albuquerque, 1970-73; partner firm Lamb, Metzgar, Franklin & Lines, Profl. Assn., Albuquerque, 1974—. Chmn. N.Mex. Juvenile Reform Com., 1976—. Mem. Am., N.Mex., Albuquerque (dir. 1976—) bar assns. Home: 13201 Cedarbrook St NE Albuquerque NM 87111 Office: 1010 Bank of New Mexico Bldg Albuquerque NM 87101 Tel (505) 247-0107

LINKLATER, WILLIAM JOSEPH, b. Chgo., June 3, 1942; A.B., U. Notre Dame, 1964; J.D., Loyola U., 1968. Admitted to Ill. bar, 1968, U.S. Supreme Ct. bar, 1968; partner firm Baker & McKenzie, Chgo., 1968—. Dir. Notre Dame Alumni Assn. Chgo., 1971-74, sec., 1974-76, dir. scholarship found., 1973-76. Mem. Am., Ill., Chgo. bar assns., Trial Lawyers' Club, Alpha Sigma Nu. Contbr. articles to legal publs. Office: 2700 Prudential Plaza Chicago IL 60601 Tel (312) 565-0025

LINLEY, CHESTERMAN CAIN, b. Lincoln, Nebr., May 16, 1912; A.B., Kans. U., 1934, LL.B., 1936. Admitted to Kans. bar, 1936; individual practice law, Cimarron, Kans., 1937-57; asst. atty. gen., chief atty. Kans. Alcohol Beverage Control, 1955; gen. counsel Kans. Corp. Commn., 1956, dir. oil and gas conservation div., 1957; legal staff Panhandle Eastern Pipe Line, Liberal, Kans., 1957-77; asso. firm Smith Greenleaf & Brooks, Liberal, 1977—; atty. Gray County (Kans.), 1937-41, 43-47; atty. City of Cimarron, 1937-54; mem. legal com. Interstate Oil Compact Commn., 1956-57, 65-77. Mayor City of Cimarron, 1953-54. Mem. Kans., S.W. Kans., Seward County bar assns. Home: 1226 N Calhoun St Liberal KS 67901 Office: PO Box 296 Liberal KS 67901 Tel (316) 624-6266

LINN, DAVID, b. Augustow, Poland, Mar. 20, 1917; A.B., U. Chgo., 1938, J.D., 1940. Admitted to Ill. bar, 1940; practice law, Chgo., 1940—; asso. judge Circuit Ct. of Cook County, 1971-76; justice Appellate Ct. of Ill., 1976—; instr. U.S. Judge Adv. Gen. Dept.; lectr. profl. socs. Mem. Ill. Commn. Human Relations, 1966-68; mem. Constl. Conv. Ill., 1969-70; treas., bd. dirs. SE Community Orgn. Fellow Internat. Acad. Law and Sci., Am. Acad. Martimonial Lawyers (bd. govs.); mem. Decalogue Soc. (bd. govs.), Ill. Judges Assn. (dir.), Chgo. Bar Assn. (com. chmn., certificate of merit), Ill. Bar Assn. (sec. chmn.), S. Chgo. Bar Assn. (pres., bd. govs.), Am. Judicature Soc., Law Inst., Phi Beta Delta. Contbr. articles to profl. jours.; mem. editorial planning bd. Ill. Family Law, 1967. Office: 30th Floor Daley Center Chicago IL 60602 Tel (312) 793-5452

LINSHAW, JACK GOETZ, b. Phila., Feb. 19, 1937; A.B., Franklin and Marshall Coll., 1959; J.D., Villanova U., 1962. Admitted to Pa. bar, 1962, N.Y. bar, 1963; asst. trust examiner, comptroller of currency U.S. Comptroller of Currency, Phila., 1964; individual practice law, Phila., 1965; staff atty. Community Legal Services, Inc., Phila., 1966-67; asst. atty. gen. Pa. Dept. Transp., Harrisburg, 1967-69; practice law, Milford, Pa., 1969—; mem. firm Gumble, Thomson & Linshaw, Milford, 1969—; solicitor Shohola Twp. (Pa.), Dingman Twp. (Pa.) Zoning Bd. Adjustment, Milford Boro (Pa.) Zoning Bd. Adjustment. Home: Sagamore Estates Milford PA 18337 Office: 509 Broad St Milford PA 18337 Tel (717) 296-6474

LINSKY, MARTIN ALAN, b. Boston, Aug. 28, 1940; B.A., Williams Coll., 1961; LL.B., Harvard, 1964. Admitted to Mass. bar, 1965; research and legal asst. to lt. gov. Mass., 1965-66; asst. atty. gen. Commonwealth of Mass., 1967; mem. Mass. Ho. of Reps., 1967-72, asst. minority floor leader, 1971-72; fellow Inst. Politics, Harvard U., 1973; editorial writer Boston Globe, 1973-75; editor The Real Paper, Cambridge, Mass., 1975—; instr. Boston Coll. Law Sch., Newton, Mass., 1973—; election commentator WNAX TV, Boston, 1973—; cons. Ford Found. Media-Law Issues, 1974-76. Mem. Mass. Bar Assn. Contbr. articles to profl. jours. Home: 25 Thatcher St Brookline MA 02146 Office: 929 Massachusetts Ave Cambridge MA 02139 Tel (617) 492-1650

LINTON, JACK ARTHUR, b. N.Y.C., May 29, 1936; B.A., Albright Coll., 1958; J.D., N.Y. U., 1961, LL.M. in Taxation, 1966. Admitted to Pa. bar, 1962, N.Y. bar, 1963; asso. firm DeLong, Dry & Binder, Reading, Pa., 1961-63; asst. house counsel Bob Banner Assos., Inc., N.Y.C., 1963-66; partner firm DeLong, Dry, Cianci & Linton, Reading, 1967-70, Williamson, Miller, Murray & Linton, Reading, 1970-72, Gerber Linton & Pocrass, Reading, 1972—; solicitor Reading Parking Authority, 1969-76. Pres. Berks County Mental Health Assn., 1969-71; mem. Berks County Mental Health and Mental Retardation Adv. Bd., Reading Jewish Community Center. Mem. Am., N.Y. State, Pa., Berks County bar assns., The Group, Inc. Recipient Founders Day award N.Y. U., 1967. Office: 124 N 8th St Reading PA 19601 Tel (215) 374-2103

LINUS, JAMES JOSEPH, b. Phila., Feb. 18, 1930; B.B.A., U. Miami, 1954, LL.B., 1956, J.D., 1967. Admitted to Fla. bar, 1956; partner firm McCune, Hiaasen, Crum, Ferris & Gardner, Ft. Lauderdale, Fla., 1964-74; dir. Riverland Bank, Ft. Lauderdale. Mem. Am. (real estate, probate, trust coms.), Fla. bar assns. Office: McCune Hiaasen Crum Ferris Gardner 2626 E Oakland Park Blvd PO Box 14636 Fort Lauderdale FL 33306 Tel (305) 462-2000

LINZER, EDWARD, b. N.Y.C., Dec. 29, 1933; J.D., Bklyn. Coll., 1959. Admitted to N.Y. bar, 1961, Calif. bar, 1969; mng. atty. Edward Linzer & Assos., Pasadena, Calif. Mem. Pasadena Bar Assn. Office: 301 E Colorado Blvd Pasadena CA 91101 Tel (213) 795-4375

LINZY, JIM WILLIAM, b. Waco, Tex., Jan. 7, 1944; B.A., So. Meth. U., 1966, LL.D., 1969. Admitted to Tex. bar, 1969; partner firm Flood, Linzy & Thigpen, Temple, Tex., 1969—. Mem. Humanities Council, Temple. Mem. Ball County (Tex.), Tex., Am. bar assns. Home: 3204 Oakridge St Temple TX 76501 Office: PO Box 16 Temple Nat Plaza Temple TX 76501 Tel (817) 773-1663

LIPKOWITZ, IRVING DEWEY, b. N.Y.C., Sept. 23, 1899; grad. N.Y. U. Sch. Law, 1920. Admitted to N.Y. bar, 1921, U.S. Supreme Ct. bar, U.S. Tax Ct. bar; asso. firm Max D. Steuer, N.Y.C., 1918-23; partner firm Cohn & Lipkowitz, N.Y.C., 1923-26; sr. partner firm Lipkowitz & Plaut, N.Y.C., 1953—. Mem. Am., N.Y., Bklyn. bar assns., Assn. Bar City N.Y., N.Y. County Lawyers Assn. Home: 15 W 81st St New York City NY 10024 Office: 1290 Ave of Americas New York City NY 10019 Tel (212) 397-2400

LIPMAN, FREDERICK DANIEL, b. Phila., Nov. 16, 1935; A.B., Temple U., 1957; LL.B., Harvard, 1960. Admitted to Pa. bar, 1960; individual practice law, Phila., 1960-62; corporate counsel Am. Electronic Lab., Inc., Lansdale, Pa., 1962-69; asso. firm Blank, Rome, Klaus and Comisky, Phila., 1970-73, partner, 1973—. Mem. Am., Pa., Phila (officer securities law com. 1974—) bar assns., Am. Judicature Soc. Contbr. articles to legal jours. Home: 3629 Heaton Rd Huntingdon Valley PA 19006 Office: 4 Penn Center Plaza Philadelphia PA 19103 Tel (215) LO9-3700

LIPMAN, MICHEL MARTIN, b. San Francisco, June 11, 1913; A.A., San Jose State Coll.; J.D., Hastings Coll. Law, San Francisco, 1938. Admitted to Calif. bar, 1938; practiced in San Francisco, 1938-42; founder, v.p. Media Features of Am., San Francisco, 1953—; founder Point of Law, radio show, 1953—; gen. counsel Calif. Nurses Assn., San Francisco, 1967-72; dir. dept. pub. affairs State Bar Calif., 1972-75; cons. clear writing, San Francisco, 1975—. Mem. State Bar Calif. Recipient award for TV documentary Fund of the Republic, 1958, Freedom Found. award, 1954, 56, 58, Ann. award Bar Assn. San Francisco, 1958; writer of audio cassettes, tng. films, videocassettes, manuals; contbr. articles to profl. and popular publs. Office: 680 Beach St Suite 445 San Francisco CA 94109 Tel (415) 885-2807

LIPNACK, MARTIN I., b. Bklyn., Apr. 6, 1936; B.A., Bklyn Coll., 1957, J.D., 1960. Admitted to N.Y. bar, 1961, U.S. Supreme Ct. bar, 1970, Fla. bar, 1973; partner firm Applebaum and Eisenberg, Liberty, N.Y., 1968-73; asst. counsel Am. Title Ins. Co., Miami, Fla., 1973-74; partner firm Schnur and Lipnack, Ft. Lauderdale, Fla., 19—. Vice pres. Hudson Del. Council Boy Scouts Am., Middletown, N.Y., also dist. chmn.; bd. dirs. Humanitarian Found. of Ft. Lauderdale, Jewish Community Center of Ft. Lauderdale; v.p. Temple Beth Israel, Ft. Lauderdale. Mem. Am., Fla., N.Y., Broward County bar assns., Acad. Fla. Trial Lawyers, Broward Trial Lawyers Assn. Home: 7421 SW 20th St Plantation FL 33317 Office: 7880 W Oakland Park Blvd Fort Lauderdale FL 33321 Tel (305) 741-8400

LIPPE, EMIL, JR., b. Waco, Tex., Nov. 4, 1948; B.A. in Polit. Sci., Northwestern U., 1970, J.D. cum laude, 1973. Admitted to Tex. bar, 1973, U.S. Supreme Ct. bar, 1977; asso. Carrington, Coleman, Sloman, Johnson & Blumenthal, Dallas, 1973-76, Akin, Gump, Strauss, Hauer & Feld, Dallas, 1976—; lectr. communication arts Loyola U., Chgo., 1972-73. Bd. dirs. Save Open Space, Dallas, 1974-75. Mem. Am., Tex., Dallas, Dallas Jr. bar assns., Order of Coif. Author: Twenty Alternatives to the Jury System, 1971; Cases on the Jury System in the United States, 1971; bd. editors Northwestern U. Law Rev., 1972-73. Home: 7119 Vivian Ave Dallas TX 75223 Office: Republic National Bank Bldg Dallas TX 75201 Tel (214) 655-2729

LIPPE, JERRY LEONARD, b. Cleve., May 19, 1942; A.B., Miami U., Ohio, 1964; J.D., Ohio State U., 1967. Admitted to Ohio bar, 1967; asst. city atty. Columbus (Ohio), 1970, asst. city prosecutor, 1967-70; partner firm Weiner, Lippe & Cromley, Columbus, 1970—. Trustee One to One, Columbus, 1973—. Mem. Am., Ohio, Columbus bar assns., Franklin County Trial Lawyers Assn. Home: 1275 Beechlake Dr Worthington OH 43085 Office: 505 S High St Columbus OH 43215 Tel (614) 224-1238

LIPPE, MELVIN KARL, b. Chgo., Oct. 21, 1933; B.S., Northwestern U., 1955, J.D., 1958. Admitted to Ill. bar, 1958; asso. firm D'Ancona, Pflaum, Wyatt & Riskind, Chgo., 1958-61; asst. to chmn. bd. Exchange Nat. Bank of Chgo., 1961-62, asst. v.p., 1962-64, v.p., 1964-66, sr. v.p., sec. to bd. dirs., 1966-69, exec. v.p., dir., 1969-74, vice chmn. bd., 1974-76; exec. v.p., dir. Exchange Internat. Corp., 1972-74, vice chmn. bd., 1974-76; partner firm Antonow & Fink, 1977—; instr. Ill. Inst. Tech., 1960-63; dir. Am.-Israel Bank Ltd. Treas. Chgo. chpt. Am. Jewish Com., 1974—; bd. dirs., v.p. Jewish Community Centers, Chgo., 1975—. Mem. Am., Ill., Chgo. bar assns., Decalogue Soc., Phi Epsilon Pi, Tau Epsilon Rho, Beta Gamma Sigma. C.P.A., Ill.; asso. editor Northwestern U. Law Rev., 1957-58. Home: 356 Sunrise Circle Glencoe IL 60038 Office: 111 E Wacker Dr Chicago IL 60601 Tel (312) 644-3700

LIPPER, JEROME, b. N.Y.C., July 19, 1936; A.B. magna cum laude, L.I. U., 1957; L.L.B. cum laude N.Y.U., 1960, LL.M., 1963; Admitted to N.Y. State bar, 1960, U.S. Dist. Ct. bar, 1961, D.C. bar, 1970, U.S. Supreme Ct. bar, 1976; law clk. U.S. Dist. Ct., N.Y.C., 1960-61; Ford Found. Law teaching fellow Law Sch. N.Y.U., 1961-62, dir. research, asst, editor Internat. Rivers research project 1961-68; asso. firm Feldman, Kramer, Bam & Nessen, N.Y.C., 1962-65, partner, 1966-67; partner firm Fly, Shuebruk, Blume & Gaguine, N.Y.C., 1967-70, Leon, Weill & Mahony, N.Y.C., 1970—; dir. Hudson & Manhattan Corp., 1966-73, Air New Eng., 1976—. Bd. dirs. Harkness Ballet and Found., 1973-74, William Hale Harkness found., 1973-74, Talisman Found., 1976—; dir., gen. counsel Mid-Westchester YM-YWHA, Scarsdale, N.Y., 1972—; counsel to minority N.Y. State Assembly, 1966-72; pub. relations coordinator Young Men's Philanthropic League, N.Y.C., 1959-61; chmn. Emergency Com. før Hungarian Refugees, 1956; coordinator, campaign mgr. polit. campaigns, 1961—. Mem. Internat. Law Assn. (mem. com. on internat. water resources 1968—) mem. exec. com. Am. br., 1974—), Assn. Bar City N.Y. (mem. com. on fed. legislation, 1966-70, 73-75, com. on grievances, 1970-72), N.Y.U. Law Alumni Assn. (bd. dirs. 1974—), Order of Coif, Phi Alpha Theta. Contbg. author: The Law of International Drainage Basins, 1967. Mem. editorial bd. Copyright Soc., Bull., 1974—. Contbr. articles to profl. jours. Home: 15 Kensington Rd Ardsley NY 10502 Office: 261 Madison Ave New York City NY 10016 Tel (212) 687-5707

LIPPITT, HENRY FREDERICK, II, b. Providence, Jan. 8, 1915; S.B., Mass. Inst. Tech., 1936; LL.B., Harvard, 1942. Admitted to D.C. bar, 1943, N.Y. bar, 1948, Calif. bar, 1944; asso. atty. firm Gibson, Dunn & Crutcher, Los Angels, 1946-47; asst. to chief research div. U.S. AEC, N.Y.C., 1947-48; asso. firm Whitman, Ransom, Coulson & Goetz, N.Y.C., 1948-50; atty. firm Dougherty and White, N.Y.C., 1950-57; atty. So. Calif. Gas Co., Los Angeles, 1957-61; dep. gen. counsel Met. Water Dist. So. Calif., Los Angeles, 1961; individual practice law, Los Angeles, 1962—. Mem. Am., Fed. Power, Internat., Los Angeles County, Calif. bar assns., Assn. Bar City N.Y., Am. Gas Assn., Independent Natural Gas Assn., Pacific Coast Gas Assn., Calif. Conf. Pub. Utility Counsel (chmn. 19S9-61), Calif. Gas Producers Assn (exec. sec. 1961—). Contbr. articles to profl. jours. Home: 7126 Macapa Dr Los Angeles CA 90068 Office: 626 Wilshire Blvd Los Angeles CA 90017 Tel (213) 626-4821

LIPPMAN, HERBERT KELMAN, b. N.Y.C., Aug. 11, 1913; J.D., N.Y. U., 1935. Admitted to N.Y. bar, 1939, U.S. So. Dist. for N.Y. Ct. bar, 1940, U.S. Eastern Dist. for N.Y. Ct. bar, 1941; asst. dist. atty. New York County, 1942-45; individual practice law, N.Y.C., 1945—; judge Small Claims Ct. N.Y. Civil Ct., 1956—, Municipal Ct., N.Y.C., 1956-64; arbitrator Civil Ct. of New York County, 1964—; arbitrator Greater N.Y. Area Heavy Constrn. Industry, 1968—, airlines div. Internat. Brotherhood Teamsters, 1972—; mem. N.Y. State Pub. Employment Relations Bd., 1970—, N.Y. State Mediation Bd., 1970—, N.J. State Mediation Bd., 1972—. Mem. N.Y.C. Community Planning Bd., 1966-70; mem. N.Y.C. Sch. Bd., 1966-72; hearing officer N.Y.C. Parking Violations Bur., 1973—. Mem. Assn. Bar N.Y.C., N.Y. State Dist. Atty's. Assn., Am. Judges Assn. Office: 45 Rockefeller Plaza New York City NY 10020 Tel (212) 247-1595

LIPPMAN, MARSHALL ELLIOTT, b. N.Y.C., Oct. 1, 1942; B.A., Coll. City N.Y., 1963; J.D., N.Y. Law Sch., 1973. Admitted to N.Y. bar, 1974, U.S. Dist. Ct. for Eastern and So. dist. N.Y., 1974, U.S. 2d Circuit Ct. Appeals, 1975; asso. firm Graubard, Moskovitz, McGoldrick, Dannett & Horowitz, N.Y.C., 1973-74; adj. asst. prof. law, N.Y. Law Sch., 1974, asst. prof., 1974-75, asst. dean, asso. prof., 1976; asst. to gen. counsel Am. Arbitration Assn., 1972-73. Mem. Am., N.Y. State bar assns., Am. Arbitration Assn. (mem. law com.). Contbr. articles to law jours. Home: 18 Stuyvesant Oval New York City NY 10009 Office: 57 Worth St New York City NY 10013 Tel (212) 966-3500

LIPSCHULTZ, ROBERT N., b. Chgo., Sept. 6, 1922; J.D., John Marshall U., 1949. Admitted to Ill. bar, 1950; partner firm Robert N. and Charles C. Lipschultz, LaGrange, Ill., 1950-69; individual practice law, Calumet City, Ill., 1969—. Mem. Am., Ill., Chgo. bar assns., Am. Judicature Soc. Office: 2100 Sibley Blvd Calumet City IL 60409 Tel (312) 862-3050

LIPSETT, JOHN GLENN, b. Phila., Sept. 17, 1933; B.A., Swarthmore Coll., 1955; postgrad. (Fulbright scholar) U. Strasbourg (France), 1955-56; LL.B., Columbia, 1959. Admitted to N.Y. State bar, 1959, U.S. Dist. Ct. bars for Eastern and So. dists. N.Y., 1962, U.S. Supreme Ct. bar, 1970; practiced in N.Y.C., 1959—; asso. firms Chadbourne, Parke, Whiteside & Wolff, 1959-60, Steinberg & Patterson, 1960-62, Jackson, Nash, Brophy, Barringer & Brooks, 1962-70; asso. firm Boyd, Holbrook & Seward and predecessors, 1970-71, partner, 1971—; del. Jud. Dist. Conv. Democratic Party, 1973, 75. Mem. Assn. Bar City N.Y. Bd. editors Columbia Law Rev., 1957-59. Home: 535 W 110th St New York City NY 10025 Office: 420 Lexington Ave New York City NY 10017 Tel (212) 867-8280

LIPSHULTZ, STANLEY LEWIS, b. Washington, Sept. 9, 1944; B.A., Washington U., St. Louis, 1967; J.D., Am. U., 1970. Admitted to Md. bar, 1971, D.C. bar, 1971, U.S. Supreme Ct. bar, 1975; govt. loan specialist Fed. Nat. Mortgage Assn., Washington, 1970-71; asso. firm Friedman & Lipshultz, Chevy Chase, Md., 1971-72; partner firm Lipshultz & Hone, Silver Spring, Md., 1972—. Mem. bd. mgmt.

YMCA Met. Washington, Silver Spring Br., 1974, chmn. standing com., 1975—; arbitrator Health Claims Arbitration Office, Annapolis, Md., 1976—. Mem. Am., Montgomery County (Md.), Md. State, D.C. bar assns. Am. Arbitration Assn. (panel), World Peace Through Law Center, Phi Delta Phi. Home: 14937 Wellwood Rd Silver Spring MD 20904 Office: 8630 Fenton St Silver Spring MD 20910 Tel (301) 587-8500

LIPSHUTZ, ROBERT JEROME, b. Atlanta, Dec. 27, 1921; J.D., U. Ga., 1943. Admitted to Ga. bar, 1947; partner firm Lipshutz, Susmann, Sikes, Pritchard & Cohen, Atlanta, 1947-76; counsel to pres. U.S., Washington, 1977—; mem. Ga. Commn. on Compensation, 1971-75; dir. Bank of Forest Park, Asso. Credit Union. Pres. Reform Temple, Atlanta, Roxboro Valley Assn., B'nai B'rith, Atlanta; mem. Ga. Bd. Human Resources, 1972-76; chmn. Ga. 1973 Nat. Democratic Telethon; treas. Com. for Jimmy Carter and Carter/Mondale Presdl. Campaign, 1976. Mem. Am., Ga., Atlanta bar assns., Atlanta Lawyers Club. Office: White House 1600 Pennsylvania Ave Washington DC 20500 Tel (202) 456-1414

LIPSITT, WILLIAM WOODROW, b. Harrisburg, Pa., Aug. 2, 1916; A.B., Harvard, 1938, LL.B., 1941. Admitted to Pa. bar, 1946; partner firm Shelley, Reynolds & Lipsitt, Harrisburg, 1947-65; judge Ct. Common Pleas, 12th Jud. Dist. Pa., Harrisburg, 1965—; treas. Pa. Conf. State Trial Judges, 1967-72; participant Pa. Jud. Inquiry and Review Bd., 1969-74; chmn. Pa. Juvenile Ct. Judges' Commn., 1973-75, vice chmn., 1975—. Pres., Harrisburg Sch. Bd., 1957-61, Keystone Area Council Boy Scouts Am., 1969-72; bd. trustees Harrisburg Pub. Library, 1960-72; chmn. Tri-County (Pa.) Welfare Council, 1965. Mem. Dauphin County, Pa., Am. bar assns., Am. Judicature Soc., Nat. Council Juvenile Ct. Judges. Home: 2813 N 2nd St Harrisburg PA 17110 Office: Courthouse Front & Market Sts Harrisburg PA 17101 Tel (717) 255-2670

LIPSITZ, STEVEN HUGH, b. Balt., Feb. 7, 1936; A.B., Princeton U., 1958; LL.B., Columbia U., 1964. Admitted to N.Y. State bar, 1964; law clk. Hon. Edward C. McLean U.S. Dist. Ct. So. Dist. N.Y., 1964-65; with firm Bressler, Meislin & Lipsitz, N.Y.C., 1968—, partner, 1969—; dir. Experiential Systems, Inc. Mem. Am., N.Y. bar assns., Assn. Bar City N.Y. Home: 300 W End Ave New York City NY 10023 Office: 90 Broad St New York City NY 10004 Tel (212) 425-9300

LIPSON, BARRY J., b. N.Y.C., May 30, 1938; B.S. in Econs., U. Pa., 1959; J.D., Columbia, 1962; LL.M. in Trade Regulation, N.Y. U., 1968. Admitted to N.Y. State bar, 1962, Pa. bar, 1970, U.S. Supreme Ct. bar, 1967; dep. asst. atty. gen. State of N.Y., 1963-64, asst. atty. gen., 1964-67; asso. counsel, asst. sec. Block Drug Co., Inc., 1968-69; asst. sec., counsel trade regulation Koppers Co., Inc., Pitts., 1969—; dir. U.S. Chem. Corp., 1970—. Chmn. legal com. Pitts. chpt. ACLU, 1975—, bd. dirs., 1972—; bd. dirs. Pa. ACLU, 1977—. Mem. Am. (chmn. Sherman Act com. monopolization task force 1976—), Pa., Fed., N.Y. State, Allegheny County bar assns. Contbg. author: Antitrust Law Developments, 1975; contbr. articles to legal jours. Home: 117 Roup Ave Pittsburgh PA 15206 Office: 1550 Koppers Bldg Pittsburgh PA 15219 Tel (412) 391-3300 extension 496

LIPSON, JACK LOUIS, b. N.Y.C., Dec. 18, 1932; A.B., Bklyn. Coll., 1953; LL.B., Harvard U., 1956. Admitted to N.Y. State bar, D.C. bar; atty. Dept. Justice antitrust div., D.C., 1960-64; mem. firm Morrison, Murphy, Chapp & Abrams, Washington, 1964-66; partner firm Arnold & Porter, Washington, 1966—. Mem. Am. (antitrust sec.), D.C. bar assns. Home: 501S Garfield St NW Washington DC 20016 Office: 1229 19th St NW Washington DC 20036 Tel (202) 872-6908

LIPSON, MORRIS C., b. N.Y.C., July 13, 1914; grad. St. John's Coll., 1932, LL.B., 1935, LL.M., 1937. Admitted to N.Y. State bar, 1937, since practiced in N.Y.C.; individual practice law, 1937-63; mem. firm Lipson, Sadow & Marcus, 1963—; adj. instr. N.Y.C. Community Coll., Bklyn., 1974—; arbitrator Civil Ct. small claims div., N.Y.C., 1973—. Asst. dist. commr. Dept. Census, Bklyn., 1960. Mem. N.Y. County Law Assn. Home: 2023 E 70th St Brooklyn NY 11234 Office: 342 Madison Ave New York City NY 10017 Tel (212) 867-9393

LIPTON, ROBERT ISRAEL, b. N.Y.C., Dec. 11, 1920; B.C.S., U. N.C., 1942, J.D. with honors, 1946. Admitted to N.C. bar, 1946; partner firm Bryant, Lipton, Bryant & Battle, Durham, N.C., 1946-75; individual practice law, Durham, 1975—. Internat. v.p. B'nai B'rith, 1976—, mem. internat. bd. govs., 1974—, chmn. mem.s' ins. program, 1974—, pres. dist. five, 1964-65. Mem. N.C., Am., Durham County bar assns., Beta Gamma Sigma, Order of Coif. Contbr. articles to legal publs. Home: 302 Country Club Dr Durham NC 27712 Office: 1809 Chapel Hill Rd Durham NC 27707 Tel (919) 683-1302

LIPTON, ROBERT STEVEN, b. N.Y.C., May 12, 1946; B.A., N.Y. U., 1967, J.D., 1971. Admitted to N.Y. State bar, 1972, U.S. Tax Ct. bar, 1973, U.S. Customs Ct. bar, 1973, U.S. Ct. Claims bar, 1975, U.S. Supreme Ct. bar, 1975; asso. firm Curtis, Mallet-Prevost, Colt & Mosle, N.Y.C., 1971—. Mem. Am., N.Y. State, N.Y.C. bar assns., Wash. Sq. Coll. Coat of Arms Soc., Phi Beta Kappa, Pi Sigma Alpha. Editor N.Y. U. Law Rev., 1969-71. Home: 175 W 13th St New York City NY 10011 Office: 100 Wall St New York City NY 10005 Tel (212) 248-8111

LISCO, ROBERT FRED, b. Chgo., Nov. 26, 1928; J.D., DePaul U. Admitted to Ill. bar, 1951; partner firm Lisco & Field, Chgo., 1955—. Chmn. March of Dimes, Evanston, Ill. Mem. Ill., Chgo. (lectr. continuing legal edn. 1973) bar assns., Am., Ill. trial lawyers assns., Decalogue Soc. Lawyers. Office: 11 S LaSalle St Chicago IL 60603 Tel (312) ST2-5757

LISMAN, BERNARD, b. N.Y.C., July 21, 1918; Ph.B., U. Vt., 1939; LL.B., Harvard, 1942. Admitted to Vt. bar, 1942, U.S. Supreme Ct. bar, 1965; partner firm Lisman & Lisman, Burlington, Vt., 1946—; judge Chittenden (Vt.) Municipal Ct., 1949-51; trustee Vt. Law Sch., 1975—. Mem. bd. aldermen, Burlington, 1956-58; chmn. bd. Baird Children's Center, 1965-67; chmn. Vt. Indsl. Aid Bd., 1974-75. Fellow Internat. Acad. Trial Lawyers (bd. dirs. 1970-76); mem. Am., Vt. (chmn. med.-legal interprofl. com. 1975—) bar assns., Am. (bd. govs. 1970-72), Vt. (pres. 1965) trial lawyers assns. Phi Beta Kappa. Home: 205 Summit St Burlington VT 05401 Office: 191 College St Burlington VT 05401 Tel (802) 864-5756

LISS, MORRIS, b. N.Y.C., July 3, 1940; B.E.E., Coll. City N.Y., 1963; M.S., George Washington U., 1966; J.D., Catholic U. Am., 1970. Admitted to D.C. bar, 1970; partner firm Cohen & Liss, Rockville, Md., 1970-74, firm Gajarsa, Liss & Sterenbuch and predecessors, Washington, 1975—. Mem. Am. Patent Law Assn., A.B.A., Licensing Execs. Soc. Home: 11448 Beechgrove Ln Potomac MD 20854 Office: 1019 19th St NW Washington DC 20036 Tel (202) 293-2772

LISS, NORMAN, b. N.Y.C., May 7, 1932; B.S. in Econs., N.Y. U., 1952, LL.B., 1955, J.D., 1968. Admitted to N.Y. State bar, 1955. U.S. Supreme Ct. bar, 1961, U.S. Dist Ct. bar for So. Dist. N.Y., 1961, for Eastern Dist. N.Y., 1962; asso. firms Booth, Lipton & Lipton, N.Y.C., 1956-57, Seymour Detsky, N.Y.C., 1957-58; individual practice law, N.Y.C., 1958—; mem. Moot Ct. Justices N.Y. U. Law Sch.; master, arbitrator Civil Ct. of City N.Y.; mem. panel arbitrators Am. Arbitration Assn.; mem. malpractice arbitration panel Supreme Ct. of N.Y. County. Mem. exec. bd. Bronx div. Am. Cancer Soc.; chmn. Bronx Bar div. United Jewish Appeal; v.p. Bronx div. Am. Jewish Congress; mem. adv. council N.Y. U. Alumni Assn. Mem. Am., N.Y. State (speakers com. Open Classroom Project), Bronx County (N.Y.) (criminal cts. bldg. com., pub. relations com.) bar assns., N.Y. State Assn. Trial Lawyers. Recipient Distinguished Humanitarian award Insts. of Applied Human Dynamics, 1976. Home: 2727 Palisade Ave Riverdale NY 10463 Office: 200 W 57th St New York City NY 10019 Tel (212) 586-6165

LIST, ARTHUR DAVID, b. Newark, Ohio, Aug. 24, 1935; B.A. cum laude, Ohio State U., 1956, J.D. summa cum laude, 1958. Admitted to Ohio bar, 1958; since practiced in Newark, Ohio, mem. firm Jones & Jones, 1959-61; partner firm Jones, Jones & List, 1962-67, Jones, Norpell & Hervey, 1968—; solicitor City of Newark, 1962-67. Mem. Am., Ohio State, Licking County (sec. 1964-75, pres. 1975) bar assns. Home: 724 Snowdon Dr Newark OH 43055 Office: Newark Trust Bldg Newark OH 43055 Tel (614) 345-9801

LIST, ROBERT FRANK, b. Visalia, Cal., Sept. 1, 1936; B.S., Utah State U., 1959; J.D., Hastings Coll. Law, San Francisco, 1962. Admitted to Nev. bar, 1962; practice in Carson City, 1962-66; dist. atty. Carson City, 1966-70; atty gen. Nev., 1970—. Mem. Nev. Crime Commn., 1968—; mem. Commn. for Rev. Nat. Policy toward Gambling, 1972—. Chmn. Nev. Young Republicans, 1963-64; nat. vice chmn. Young Republicans, 1967-68; del. Rep. Nat. Conv., 1968, chmn. Nev. del. 1972; bd. dirs. Am. Council Young Polit. Leaders, 1972—. Mem. Nat. Assn. Atty. Gens. (exec. com. 1971—, chmn. Western region 1972-73, 75—), Am., Nev. bar assns., Utah State U., U. Cal. (pres. Sierra Nev. chpt. 1970-72) alumni assns., Sigma Alpha Epsilon, Phi Alpha Delta. Home: 2 Crest Dr Carson City NV 89701 Office: Supreme Ct Bldg Carson City NV 89701*

LITE, JOSEPH, b. N.Y.C., June 17, 1926; LL.B., Bklyn. Law Sch., 1951. Admitted to N.Y. bar, 1951, U.S. Supreme Ct. bar, 1959; individual practice law, West Islip, N.Y., 1951—; asst. county atty. Suffolk County (N.Y.), 1961-67. Mem. N.Y. State, Suffolk County (past dir.) bar assns. Home: 282 Shadybrook Ln West Islip NY 11795 Office: 239 Higbie Ln West Islip NY 11795 Tel (516) 669-3710

LITMAN, ROSLYN MARGOLIS, b. N.Y.C., Sep. 30, 1928; B.A., U. Pitts., 1949, J.D., 1952, LL.B., 1952. Admitted to Pa. bar, 1952, U.S. Supreme Ct. bar, 1953, U.S. Ct. Appeals, 1953, others; partner firm Litman, Litman, Harris & Specter, Pitts., 1952—; adj. prof. law U. Pitts., 1958—. Chmn. Pitts Pub. Parking Authority, 1970-74. Mem. Allegheny County (pres. 1974-75), Pa. (gov. 1976) Am. bar assns., Acad. Trial Lawyers of Allegheny County, Order of the Coif. Recipient Social Assistance Award Women's Am. Orgn. Rehab. Tng., 1975. Home: 1047 S Negley Ave Pittsburgh PA 15217 Office: Grant Bldg Pittsburgh PA 15219 Tel (412) 456-2000

LITMAN, SEYMOUR MARSHALL, b. N.Y.C., Apr. 7, 1918; B.A., N.Y. U., 1942; J.D., U. Va., 1941. Admitted to N.Y. bar, 1942, Fla. bar, 1969, U.S. Tax Ct. bar, 1974; individual practice law, N.Y.C., 1946-55, Mineola, N.Y., 1955-67, Miami, Fla., 1970—. Mem. Dade County Bar Assn., Fla. Bar. Home: 12605 SW 71st Ave Miami FL 33156 Office: 10 NW 14th Ave Miami FL 33125 Tel (305) 642-4811

LITNER, RICHARD JOSEPH, b. Boston, Aug. 1, 1945; B.A., Oberlin Coll., 1967; J.D., Boston U., 1970. Admitted to Mass. bar, 1970; partner firm Litner & Goldberg, Boston, 1972—. Mem. Brookline (Mass.) Council for Planning and Renewal, 1975-77; bd. dirs. Allston-Brighton YMCA. Mem. Am., Mass., Boston bar assns., Mass. Acad. Trial Attys. Home: 330 Clinton Rd Brookline MA 02146 Office: 19 Milk St Boston MA 02109 Tel (617) 482-2218

LITOWITZ, RONALD, b. Trenton, N.J., June 23, 1939; B.A., Williams Coll., 1961; LL.B., N.Y. U., 1964. Admitted to N.J. bar, 1965, N.Y. State bar, 1967; partner firm Krendler & Krendler, N.Y.C., 1975—. Home: 27 Lawrence Rd Scarsdale NY 10583 Office: 99 Park Ave 26th Floor New York City NY 10016 Tel (212) 687-8181

LITT, BARRETT STEPHEN, b. Pitts., Feb. 23, 1945; A.B., U. Calif., Berkeley, 1966; J.D., U. Calif., Los Angeles, 1969. Admitted to Calif. bar, 1970; partner firm Litt, Livezey & Taylor, Los Angeles. Mem. Los Angeles County Bar Assn., Nat. Lawyers Guild. Contbr. articles to legal publs. Office: 619 S Bonnie Brae St Los Angeles CA 90057 Tel (213) 484-8280

LITTELL, DUANE O., b. Beaver Falls, Pa., Nov. 23, 1913; B.A., Geneva Coll., 1934; LL.B., Duke U., 1938. Claim supt., regional mgr. Comml. Union/Ocean Group, 1938-44; admitted to Colo. bar, 1940; individual practice law, Denver, 1946—. Fellow Fedn. Ins. Counsel; mem. Internat. Acad. Trial Lawyers. Office: 440 Capitol Life Center Denver CO 80203 Tel (303) 222-8603

LITTENBERG, ROBERT LOUIS, b. Goshen, N.Y., July 30, 1934; student Colgate U.; B.A., U. Houston, 1954; LL.B. with honors, U. Tex., 1957. Admitted to Tex., D.C. bars, 1958, U.S. Supreme Ct. bar, 1964; atty. tax div. Dept. Justice, Washington, 1958-62; individual practice law, Los Angeles, 1962—; prof. law Southwestern U., 1965-68, U. San Fernando Valley, 1974-75, Whittier Coll., 1974—. Mem., Am., Tex., Calif., D.C., Los Angeles, Beverly Hills bar assns. Contbr. articles in field to profl. jours. Home: 3333 Red Rose Dr Encino CA 91316 Office: 1801 Century Park East Los Angeles CA 90067 Tel (213) 553-9858

LITTLE, CHARLES M., b. Pontotoc, Miss., Jan. 16, 1948; B.S. in Bus., Miss. State U., 1969, J.D., 1973. Admitted to Miss. bar, 1973; individual practice law, Tupelo, Miss., 1976—. Mem. Miss. Trial Lawyers Assn., Am. Bar Assn., Am. Trial Lawyers Assn. Home: 202 Apt 110 Milford Tupelo MS 38801 Office: 303 1/2 W Main St PO Box 1190 Tupelo MS 38801 Tel (601) 842-4726

LITTLE, DAVID WILLIAM, b. Fort Dodge, Iowa, Oct. 4, 1922; A.B., Dartmouth Coll., 1944; J.D., Northwestern U.; grad. Naval Justice Sch., Port Huaneme, Calif., 1949. Admitted to Ill. bar, 1949, Minn. bar, 1949, Wyo. bar, 1953, Ind. bar; field rep. West Pub. Co., 1949-52; individual practice law, Sheridan, Wyo., 1953-54; U.S. Commr. for Wyo., 1953-54; regional mgr. West Pub. Co., Bloomington, Ind., 1965—; state judge adv. Am. Legion, Wyo. Chmn. troop com. Boy Scouts Am., Bloomington, 1973-74; chmn. bd. deacons, bd. elders 1st Presbyterian Ch., 1966-74, chmn. bldg. fund, 1971-72; bd. dirs. Sheridan County chpt. ARC, Sheridan County Rodeo; chmn. county March of Dimes. Mem. Wyo. State, Ind. State bar assns., Northwestern U. Law Alumni Assn., Phi Delta Phi (pres. Northwestern U.). Home and Office: 3303 Browncliff Ln Bloomington IN 47401 Tel (812) 336-6686

LITTLE, DONALD CAMPBELL, b. Abilene, Kans., Jan. 29, 1901; A.B., George Washington U., 1924; postgrad. Harvard Law Sch., 1924-25; LL.B., Washburn U., 1927; grad. Nat. Coll. Trial Judges U. Nev., 1966. Admitted to Kans. bar, 1927, U.S. Supreme Ct. bar, 1942; asst. U.S. dist. atty for Dist. Kans., 1930-33; atty. Kans. Ho. of Reps. impeachments of atty. gen. and state auditor, 1933-34; chief dep. county atty. Wyandotte County, Kans., 1935-39; individual practice law, Kansas City, Kans., 1945-64, 67—; judge Kans. Dist. Ct., 29th Jud. Dist., 1965-67. Chmn. Wyandotte County Republican Party, 1956-58; mem. Kans. Civil Service Bd., 1964-65. Mem. Kans. Dist. Judges Assn. (ret.), Am. Bar Assn., SAR (Patriot medal 1964, Minute Man award 1965), Phi Kappa Psi, Delta Theta Phi. Decorated Bronze Star medal; named Hon. Citizen City of Paola, Italy, 1944, Hon. Curator Ft. Leavenworth (Kans.) Mil. Museum, 1961, Hon. Ky. Col., 1964, Distinguished Jayhawker Gov. Kans., 1964. Home: Forest Lake Bonner Springs KS 66012 Office: 7th floor Huron Bldg Kansas City KS 66101 Tel (281) 281-1903

LITTLE, EDGAR NEAL, b. Carnesville, Ga., Sept. 19, 1927; student North Ga. Coll., 1944-45, Ga. State U., 1952-53; LL.B., Atlanta Law Sch., 1950, LL.M., 1951. Admitted to Ga. bar, 1951; auditor Ga. Income Tax Dept., Atlanta, 1951-58; atty. Ga. Hwy. Dept., Atlanta, 1958-59; adminstrv. law judge Ga. Bd. Workmen's Compensation, Decatur, 1959—. Mem. Decatur-DeKalb, Ga. bar assns., State Bar Ga. Home: 1126 Allgood Rd Stone Mountain GA 30083 Office: Suite 480 One W Court Square Decatur GA 30030 Tel (404) 377-2662

LITTLE, GEORGE LESTER, JR., b. Winston-Salem, N.C., Sept. 14, 1942; B.A., Davidson Coll., 1964; J.D. with honors, U. N.C. at Chapel Hill, 1967. Admitted to N.C. bar, 1967; capt. JAGC, U.S. Army 1967-71; asso. firm Hudson, Petree, Stockton, Stockton & Robinson, Winston-Salem, 1971-75, partner, 1976—. Bd. dirs. United Way Forsyth County (N.C.), 1975—, budget chmn., 1975-76, v.p., 1977. Mem. Am., N.C., Forsyth County bar assns., N.C. State Bar, Forsyth County Jr. Bar. Home: 747 Yorkshire Rd Winston-Salem NC 27106 Office: 610 Reynolds Bldg Winston-Salem NC 27101 Tel (919) 725-2351

LITTLE, HENRY HORTON, b. Ackerville, Ala., July 30, 1906; LL.B., U. Ala., 1932, J.D., 1960. Admitted to Ala. bar, 1932; individual practice law, Luverne, Ala., 1932—; county pros. atty. Crenshaw County (Ala.), 1944-52; judge Law and Equity Ct., 1960-73; mem. Ala. State Bar Commn., 1970-73. Mem. Crenshaw County Bar Assn. (pres. 1960-76). Tel (205) 335-5703

LITTLE, JAMES DAVID, b. Troy, N.Y., Jan. 8, 1940; B.A., Siena Coll., 1962; LL.B., N.Y. Law Sch., 1965. Admitted to N.Y. State bar, 1966, U.S. Supreme Ct. bar, 1976; asso. firm Kenneally & Kenneally, 1965-68; partner firm Kenneally & Little, 1968-70; individual practice law, Glen Falls, N.Y., 1970-72; partner Little & O'Connor, Glens Falls, 1972-73, firm Little, O'Connor & Zurlo, Glens Falls, 1973—; Queensbury town justice, 1970-73; Queensbury town atty., 1973-76. Mem. Am. Judicature Soc., Am., N.Y. State, Warren County bar assns., Estate Planning Council Eastern N.Y., Am. Arbitration Assn., Warren County Magistrates Assn. (past pres.). Home: Blind Rock Rd Glens Falls NY 12801 Office: 19 W Notre Dame St Glens Falls NY 12801 Tel (518) 792-2113

LITTLE, JAMES MONROE, b. Oklahoma City, June 29, 1932; LL.B., U. Okla., 1956. Admitted to Okla. bar, 1956, U.S. Dist. Ct. western dist. Okla. bar, 1957, U.S. Supreme Ct. bar, 1963; asso. firm Conner and Little & Conner, and predecessor firms, Oklahoma City, 1957-63, partner, 1963—; lt. col. JAGC, USAR, 1974—. Dist. chmn. Last Frontier Council Boy Scouts Am., 1974—. Mem. Okla., Am., Okla. County bar assns., Okla. Trial Lawyers Assn., Comml. Law League Am. Home: 203 E Main Edmond OK 73034 Office: 105 N Hudson Oklahoma City OK 73102 Tel (405) 235-1404

LITTLEFIELD, ALEX DOWMAN, JR., b. Daytona Beach, Fla., Oct. 27, 1925; A.A., U. Fla., 1948, LL.B., 1950; postgrad U. Tex., 1953. Admitted to Fla. bar 1950; individual practice law, Daytona Beach, 1951-66; staff atty. Fla. Indsl. Commn., State of Fla. Dept. of Commerce, Tallahassee, 1966-72; asst. chief counsel Office of Legal Services and gen. counsel State of Fla. Dept. of Commerce, Tallahassee, 1972—. Mem. Fla., Fla. Govt. (pres. 1972-73) bar assns., VFW (state comdr. Fla. 1959-60), Toastmasters Internat. (area gov. 1968-69). Home: 1802 Tamiami Dr Tallahassee FL 32301 Office: 401 Collins Bldg Tallahassee FL 32304 Tel (904) 488-6556

LITTLEFIELD, NEIL OAKMAN, b. North Conway, N.H., Feb. 12, 1931; B.S., U. Maine, 1953; postgrad. (Rotary Found. fellow) U. Melbourne (Australia), 1956; LL.B., Boston U., 1957; LL.M., U. Mich., 1959, S.J.D., 1961. Admitted to Maine bar, 1957, Nebr. bar, 1959, Conn. bar, 1965; asst. prof. law Creighton U., 1959-61; asso. prof. U. Conn., 1961-65, prof., 1965-70; prof., dir. bus. planning program U. Denver, 1970—; vis. prof. Ind. U., 1966-67; cons. Neighborhood Legal Services, Hartford, Conn., 1967-68. Trustee Simsbury (Conn.) Free Library, 1964-70; mem. Simsbury Democratic Town Com., 1968; candidate for Conn. Senate, 1968. Mem. Am., Colo. bar assns., Comml. Law League, Am. Arbitration Assn. (panel arbitrators). Author: Metropolitan Area Problems and Municipal Home Rule, 1961; contbr. articles to legal jours; editor: (with others) Commercial Transactions Under the Uniform Commercial Code, Cases and Materials, 1968, 2d edit., 1974. Office: 200 W 14th Ave Denver CO 80204 Tel (303) 753-2652

LITTLEJOHN, CAMERON BRUCE, b. Pacolet, S.C., July 22, 1913; A.B., Wofford Coll., 1935, LL.D., 1968; LL.B., U. S.C., 1936, J.D., 1970. Admitted to S.C. bar, 1936; individual practice law, Spartanburg, S.C., 1936-43; mem. firm Odom, Bostick, Littlejohn & Nolen, Spartanburg, S.C., 1947-49; judge S.C. 7th dist. Circuit Ct., 1949-67; asso. justice S.C. Supreme Ct., 1967—; mem. S.C. Ho. of Reps., 1937-43, 47-49, speaker of the house, 1947-49. Trustee North Greenville Jr. Coll., 1962-67, Wofford Coll. Alumni, 1966-68; del. Democratic Nat. Conv., 1948, 64. Mem. Spartanburg County, S.C., Am. bar assns. Recipient Citizen of Year award Kiwanis Club, Spartanburg, 1975; author: Laugh With The Judge, 1974; editorial com. Trial Judges Jour., 1965-67. Home: 450 Connecticut Ave Spartanburg SC 29302 Office: Spartanburg County Courthouse Magnolia St Spartanburg SC 29304 Tel (803) 585-3363

LITTLEJOHN, JAMES MCGOWAN, b. Washington, Dec. 6, 1940; B.S. in Biol. Sci., Colo. State U., 1970; J.D., U. Denver, 1972. Admitted to Colo. bar, 1973; asso. firm Joseph P. Jenkins, Estes Park, Colo., 1973-75; partner firm Jenkins and Littlejohn, Estes Park, 1975-76; individual practice law, Estes Park, 1976—; municipal judge, Estes Park, 1976—. Coordinator Legal Aid Vols., Estes Park, 1976. Mem. Am., Colo. bar assns., Nat. Fedn. Ind. Bus. Office: 164 E Riverside Dr PO Box 1831 Estes Park CO 80517 Tel (303) 586-4653

LITTLEJOHN, WILLIAM L., b. Greenville, S.C., July 21, 1931; B.A., U. Va., 1953, LL.B., 1955. Admitted to Ill. bar, 1956; asso. firm Lord, Bissell & Brook, Chgo., 1957-61; partner firm Littlejohn, Glass & Yowell, and predecessors, Chgo., 1961—; village atty. Village of Clarendon Hills (Ill.), 1963-66. Chmn. sec., bd. dirs. Community House, Hinsdale, Ill., 1975—; bd. dirs. Godair Home, Hinsdale, 1973; bd. dirs. Graue Mill Mus., Oak Brook, Ill., 1970—. Mem. Am., Ill., Chgo. bar assns. Office: 135 S LaSalle St Suite 1211 Chicago IL 60603 Tel (312) 263-3060

LITTLETON, DONALD CAMPBELL, b. Hillsboro, Ill., Mar. 16, 1920; A.B., Antioch Coll., 1946; LL.B., St. Louis U., 1954. Admitted to Mo. bar, 1954; individual practice, St. Louis, 1954—; provisional judge St. Louis Municipal Cts., 1966. Dir. St. Louis Housing Rent Commn., 1946-47. Mem. Am. Trial Lawyers Assn., Mo., St. Louis bar assns. Home: 311 Bolton Dr Ballwin MO 63011 Office: 705 Olive St St Louis MO 63101 Tel (314) 241-6478

LITTLETON, LARRY ORMAN, b. Dallas, Dec. 24, 1941; B.A., U. Tex., Austin, 1963; J.D. with honors, 1965. Admitted to Tex. bar, 1965; asso. firm Fulbright, Crooker & Jaworski, Houston, 1965-69, Anderson, Clayton & Co., Houston, 1969-71; asso. firm Stalcup, Johnson, Meyers & Miller, Dallas, 1971-72, partner, 1972—. Mem. Am. Soc. Corp. Secs., Am., Dallas bar assns., Phi Delta Phi, Chancellors. Home: 3400 Princeton St Dallas TX 75205 Office: 2001 Bryan Tower 27th Floor Dallas TX 75201 Tel (214) 651-1700

LITTON, RALPH JOHN, b. Lock Springs, Mo., Oct. 17, 1901; LL.B., U. Idaho, 1926, B.S.Edn., 1930, J.D., 1969. Admitted to Idaho bar, 1926; individual practice law, St. Anthony, Idaho, 1932—; mem. Idaho Senate, 1954-58, chmn. judiciary and rules com., 1957-58; mem. Idaho Ho. of Reps., 1960-62, 66-72; atty. Idaho Senate, 1958-60; pros. atty. Fremont County, Idaho, 1933-39, 43-51; mem. Idaho Bar Commn., 1949-52. Mem. Am., Idaho State (pres. 1951-52) bar assns. Home: 518 E Main St Saint Anthony ID 83445 Office: Bremer Bldg Saint Anthony ID 83445 Tel (208) 624-7201

LITTY, JOHN CHARLES, JR., b. Salem, Ohio, July 28, 1935; B.S., Kent State U., 1957; J.D., Ohio State U., 1960. Admitted to Ohio bar, 1960; partner firm Harrington, Huxley & Smith, Youngstown, Ohio, 1964—; mem. nat. panel arbitrators Am. Arbitration Assn.; counsel Regional Growth Found. Mem. Ohio Def. Assn., Youngstown Claims Assn., Mahoning County (Ohio), Ohio State, Am. bar assns. Home: 8351 Chesterton Dr Poland OH 44514 Office: 1200 Mahoning Bank Bldg Youngstown OH 44503 Tel (216) 744-1111

LITWILLER, GAVIN D., b. Chgo., July 6, 1935; B.S., Bradley U., 1957; J.D., U. Denver, 1965. Admitted to Colo. bar, U.S. Dist. Ct. bar, 1966, U.S. Ct. of Appeals bar, U.S. Supreme Ct. bar, 1970; individual practice law, Rifle, Colo., 1966-72; city judge, 1969-72; asso. county judge Garfield County (Colo.), 1967-72; judge 9th Jud. Dist. Ct. Colo., Glenwood Springs, 1972—. Mem. Am., Colo., 9th Jud. Dist. bar assns., Colo. Council Juvenile Ct. Judges (pres. 1976). Home: 114 Virginia Rd Glenwood Springs CO 81601 Office: Dist Ct Garfield County Court House Glenwood Springs CO 81601 Tel (303) 945-5075

LITZ, LEONARD JOHN, b. Schenectady, N.Y., Mar. 8, 1926; B.A. in Sociology, Siena Coll., 1950; LL.B./J.D., St. John's U., Bklyn., 1952. Admitted to N.Y. bar, 1952; practiced in Schenectady, 1952-73; judge Schenectady County (N.Y.) Family Ct., 1973—; corp. counsel City of Schenectady, 1968-73. Mem. Assn. Judges of Family Ct., N.Y. State, Schenectady County bar assns. Home: 1360 Lexington Ave Schenectady NY 12309 Office: 620 State St Schenectady NY 12309 Tel (518) 382-3307

LIUZZA, BASILE ROY, b. New Orleans, Dec. 2, 1928; B.S., La. State U., 1953; J.D., 1958. Admitted to La. bar, 1958; asso. firm Hudson, Potts & Bernstein, Monroe, 1958-66, partner, 1966—. Mem. Am. Assn. R.R. Trial Lawyers, La. Bar Assn. C.P.A., La. Home: 2205 Beechwood St Monroe LA 71201 Office: PO Box 3008 Monroe LA 71201 Tel (318) 388-4400

LIVINGSTON, CHARLES HOWARD, b. Sebring, Fla., Mar. 28, 1944; B.A., Washington and Lee U., 1966; J.D., U. Fla., 1971. Admitted to Fla. bar, 1971, U.S. Ct. Appeals 5th Circuit bar, 1972, U.S. Supreme Ct. bar, 1974; asso. firm Bedell, Bedell, Dittmar, Smith & Zehmer, Jacksonville, Fla., 1971-72; asso. firm Icard, Merrill, Cullis, Timm & Furen, Sarasota, Fla., 1972-73; asst. pub. defender, spl. asst. pub. defender Sarasota County, 1973-74; partner firm Livingston & Patterson, P.A., Sarasota, 1976—. Mem. Am., Sarasota County bar assns., Fla. Bar, Assn. Trial Lawyers Am., Acad. Fla. Trial Lawyers. Office: 46 N Washington Blvd Sarasota FL 33577 Tel (813) 365-0550

LIVINGSTON, FRED, b. Batesville, Ark., Mar. 17, 1933; B.S. in Bus. Adminstrn., U. Ark., 1955; J.D., George Washington U., 1959. Admitted to Ark. bar, 1963, U.S. Supreme Ct. bar, 1967; asst. to senator, Washington, 1955-59; v.p., gen. counsel Livingston-Wiles Agy., Inc., Batesville, Ark., 1975—, Independence County Abstract Co., Batesville, 1975—. Campaign asst. to Pres. U.S., 1962, Vice Pres., 1964, 68; chmn. Batesville Housing Authority, 1963-65; bd. dirs. U. Ark. Alumni Assn., 1974—. Mem. Am., Ark., Fed., Independence County (past pres.) bar assns., Am., Ark. trial lawyers assns. Home: 1225 Dogwood Dr Batesville AR 72501 Office: Livingston Bldg 150 Broad St Batesville AR 72501 Tel (501) 793-3131

LIVINGSTON, JOHN JACOB, b. Tulsa, Apr. 23, 1936; B.B.A., U. Okla., 1959; J.D., U. Mich., 1961. Admitted to Calif. bar, 1962, Okla. bar, 1966; asso. firm McCutchen, Doyle, Brown & Enersen, San Francisco, 1963-65; partner firm Walker, Jackman & Livingston, Tulsa, 1976—. Vice pres. Tulsa chpt. Am. Heart Assn., 1975—; dist. committeeman Tulsa County Republican Party, 1967-68, mem. exec. com., 1967—; pres. Tulsa chpt. Am. Jewish Com., 1969-70. Mem. Am., Okla., Calif. bar assns., Tulsa County Title Lawyers Assn., Order of Coif, Broadway Theatre League Tulsa (v.p. 1975—). Asso. editor Mich. Law Rev., 1960-61. Home: 4870 E 68th St Apt 234 Tulsa OK 74136 Office: 1919 4th National Bank Bldg Tulsa OK 74119 Tel (918) 584-4136

LIVINGSTON, MILTON MANGOLD, JR., b. Paducah, Ky., Oct. 28, 1941; B.S. in Econs., Wharton Sch. Finance and Commerce, U. Pa., 1963; J.D., U. Ky., 1966. Admitted to Ky. bar, 1966; U.S. Supreme Ct. bar, 1971; partner firm McMurry and Livingston, Paducah, Ky., 1966—; chmn. bd., dir. M. Livingston and Co., Inc.; dir. Bank of Wingo; pros. atty. Paducah City, 1967-72; Bd. dirs. Rotary Club of Paducah, 1972—, 2d v.p., 1975, 1st v.p., 1976, pres., 1977. Mem. Am., Ky., McCracken County (sec.-treas. 1968-69) bar assns., Ky. Assn. of Trial Attys., Assn. Trial Lawyers Am., Am. Judicature Soc., Phi Delta Phi. Home: 300 Friedman Ave Paducah KY 42001 Office: Suite 713 Citizens Bank Bldg Paducah KY 42001 Tel (502) 443-6511

LIVINGSTON, ROBERT ILEY, b. Shelby County, Tenn., Feb. 21, 1928; student Memphis State U., 1949-51, Union U., 1955-57; LL.B., U. Memphis, 1954. Admitted to Tenn. bar, 1954; individual practice law, Memphis, 1954—; asst. atty. City of Memphis, 1964-65; asst. pub. defender Shelby County, 1958-59, 69-73. Mem. Tenn., Memphis-Shelby County bar assns. Office: Suite 2504 100 N Main Bldg Memphis TN 38103 Tel (901) 525-3357

LIVINGSTONE, WILLIAM EDWIN, III, b. Fort Worth, May 22, 1935; B.A., So. Meth. U., 1957, LL.B., 1960. Admitted to Tex. bar, 1960; partner firm Phinney, Hallman, Pulley & Livingstone, Dallas, 1960-72; gen. counsel Dallas Fed. Savs. and Loan Assn., 1973—. Bd. dirs. Dallas Met. YMCA, 1964-67. Mem. United States League Savs. Assns. (vice chmn. attys. com. 1977). Home: 6342 Chesley Ln Dallas TX 75214 Office: 8333 Douglas Ave Dallas TX 75225 Tel (214) 750-5140

LIZAK, CHESTER ADAM, b. Chgo., Sept. 29, 1936; B.S., DePaul U., 1961, J.D., 1963. Admitted to Ill. bar, 1963; individual practice law, Chgo., 1963-74; partner firm Schmidt, DiMonte, Baker & Lizak, Chgo., 1975—; atty. Cook County (Ill.) Forest Preserve Dist., Chgo., 1966. Mem. Am., Ill. State, Chgo. bar assns., Chgo. Council Lawyers. Contbr. articles to legal jours. Office: 7 S Dearborn St Chicago IL 60603 Tel (312) 372-7987

LLOYD, BOARDMAN, b. Concord, N.H., Jan. 8, 1942; B.A., Yale, 1964; J.D., U. Chgo., 1967. Admitted to N.Y. bar, 1968, Mass. bar, 1971; asso. firm Casey, Lane & Mittendorf, N.Y.C., 1967-69; asso. firm Choate, Hall & Stewart, Boston, 1969-75, partner, 1976—. Mem. adv. bd. Cambridge Family and Children Services, Inc.; chmn. Cambridge leadership gifts United Way. Mem. Phi Delta Phi. Home: 2 Mercer Circle Cambridge MA 02138 Office: 28 State St Boston MA 02109 Tel (617) 227-5020

LLOYD, ELLEN ANNE, b. Indpls., Jan. 13, 1925; A.B., Ind. U., 1946, LL.B. magna cum laude, 1948. Admitted to Ind. bar, 1948, U.S. Supreme Ct. bar, 1962; practiced in Brazil, Ind., 1948-50; dep. atty. gen. State of Ind., Indpls., 1957-63; dir. program sch. law codification Ind. U. Sch. Law, 1964-68; counsel firm McCrea & McCrea, Bloomington, Ind., 1968—. Mem. Order of Coif. Office: 119 S Walnut St Bloomington IN 47401 Tel (812) 336-4840

LLOYD, RJAY, b. Soda Springs, Idaho, Aug. 23, 1936; B.S. in Accounting, U. Utah, 1962; J.D., 1965; LL.M., N.Y. U., 1967. Admitted to Idaho bar, 1966; tax mgr. Ernst & Ernst, Boise, Idaho, 1966-70; mem. firm Hansen & Lloyd, Boise, 1970—; lectr. Idaho Law Found. Mem. Nat. Accounting Assn., Boise Estate Planning Council, Idaho State Tax Inst. (dir.). C.P.A., Idaho. Office: 1420 W Washington St PO Box 2780 Boise ID 83702 Tel (208) 345-5533

LLOYD, ROBERT ALLEN, b. Chgo., Aug. 3, 1941; B.S.E.E., U. Ill., 1964; J.D., Loyola U., Chgo., 1969. Admitted to Ill. bar, 1969, U.S. Patent Office, 1970; engr. Teletype Corp., Skokie, Ill., 1964-68, atty., 1969-70; patent atty. Western Electric Co., Cicero, Ill., 1971-75; mem. firm Gary, Juettner & Pyle, Chgo., 1975—. Mem. Patent Law Assn. Chgo. Office: 33 N Dearborn St Chicago IL 60602 Tel (312) 236-8123

LOBEL, MARTIN, b. Cambridge, Mass., June 19, 1941; A.B., Boston U., 1962, J.D., 1965; LL.M., Harvard, 1966. Admitted to Mass. bar, 1965, D.C. bar, 1968, U.S. Supreme Ct. bar, 1968; partner firm Lobel & Lobel, Boston, 1965-66; asst. prof. law U. Okla., Norman, 1967; Congressional fellow, Washington, 1968; legis. asst. to Senator Proxmire of Wis., Washington, 1968-72; partner firm Lobel, Novins & Lamont, Washington, 1972—; lectr. Law Sch. Am. U., Washington, 1972—; mem. FPC Nat. Gas Survey Com. Mem. Am., Mass., D.C. (chmn. consumer affairs com., mem. steering com. antitrust and consumer affairs sect.) bar assns., Order of Coif. Contbr. articles to legal revs. Home: 325 A St NE Washington DC 20002 Office: 1523 L St NW Washington DC 20005 Tel (202) 628-0066

LOBLE, LESTER HENRY, II, b. Helena, Mont., Nov. 14, 1941; A.B., Stanford, 1963; J.D. (Leaphart scholar), U. Mont., 1966. Admitted to Mont. bar, 1966; pres. firm Loble, Picotte & Pauly, P.C., Helena, 1966—. Mem. Mont. State Legislature, 1969-71; chmn. Lewis and Clark County City-County Bd. Health. Mem. Am., First Jud. Dist. bar assns., State Bar Mont. Recipient Distinguished Service award Helena Jaycees, 1970; named Outstanding Jaycee, 1970, Outstanding Young Man of Mont., 1969. Home: 716 Power St Helena MT 59601 Office: 833 N Last Chance Gulch St Helena MT 59601 Tel (406) 442-0070

LOBRANO, EDWARD POSEY, JR., b. Centreville, Miss., July 5, 1940; B.A., U. Miss., 1962, J.D., 1965. Admitted to Miss. bar, 1965; partner firm Shell, Buford, Bufkin, Callicutt & Perry, and predecessor, Jackson, Miss., 1965—; instr. Jackson Sch. Law, 1966-72, mem. Moot Ct. Bd. Mem. Am., Miss. State, Hinds County (Miss.) bar assns., Am. Trial Lawyers Assn., Miss. Def. Lawyers Assn., Phi Delta Phi. Office: PO Box 157 Jackson MS 39205 Tel (601) 948-2291

LOCHER, JOHN FRANKLIN, b. Cedar Rapids, Iowa, Feb. 2, 1946; B.A., U. Notre Dame, 1968; J.D., U. Iowa, 1972. Admitted to Iowa bar, 1972; asso. firm Wadsworth, Elderkin, Pirnie & Von Cackum, 1972-76; partner Locher & Knudten, Cedar Rapids, 1976—. Chmn. All Saints Parish Council, Major Gifts div. Regis-Lasalle High Sch. Fund Dr.; bd. dirs. Linn Area Birthright. Mem. Am., Iowa, Linn County (chmn. membership com. sec. Young Lawyers Club) bar assns. Home: 2038 4th Ave SE Cedar Rapids IA 52403 Office: 422 Brenton Financial Center Cedar Rapids IA 52406 Tel (319) 362-1164

LOCHER, RALPH SIDNEY, b. Moreni, Romania, July 24, 1915; A.B., Bluffton Coll., 1936; J.D., Western Res. U., 1939. Admitted to Ohio bar, 1939; asso. firm Davis & Young, Cleve., 1939-45, 47-48, Locher & Sarisky, Cleve., 1967-68; sec. Indsl. Commn. Ohio, 1945; sec. to Gov. Ohio, 1946, 49-53; law dir. City of Cleve., 1953-62; mayor Cleve., 1962-68; judge Ct. of Common Pleas of Cuyahoga County, 1969-72, Probate Ct. of Cuyahoga County, 1973-77; justice Ohio Supreme Ct., 1977—. Gen. chmn. safety on the streets, in bldgs. and in homes Greater Cleve. Safety Council, 1975; bd. dirs. Central YMCA, Cleve., 1954—, pres., 1974-75; bd. dirs. East End Neighborhood House, 1968-75; trustee Bluffton Coll., Parents Vol. Assn. for Retarded Children and Adults. Mem. Am., Ohio, Greater Cleve., Cuyahoga County bar assns., Am. Judicature Soc. Home: 1371 Ardoon Ave Cleveland OH 44120 Office: 30 E Broad St Columbus OH 44113

LOCHNER, H. ALLEN, b. Louisville, Aug. 14, 1912; A.B., Temple U., 1936; LL.B., U. Pa., 1939. Admitted to N.J. bar, 1941, N.Y. bar, 1943, U.S. Supreme Ct. bar, 1957; asso. atty. Arthur T. Vanderbilt, Newark, 1939-42; asso. firm Rogers & Wells, and predecessors, N.Y.C., 1942-53, partner, 1953—. Trustee Marble Men's League Found. Mem. Am., N.Y. State bar assns., Order of Coif. Home: 123 Waverly Pl New York City NY 10011 Office: Rogers & Wells 200 Park Ave 52d Floor New York City NY 10017 Tel (212) 972-7000

LOCK, JOHN RICHARD, b. Baton Rouge, Dec. 24, 1941; B.B.A. in Accounting, Tex. A. and M. U., 1964; J.D., U. Tex., 1967. Admitted to Tex. bar, 1967, U.S. Supreme Ct. bar, 1974; with Albert Caster & Co., C.P.A., Austin, Tex., 1967-68, Peat, Marwick, Mitchell & Co., Austin, 1968-72; asso. firm Small, Craig & Werkenthin, Austin, 1972-75; individual practice law, Austin, 1975—; vis. lectr. accounting and law St. Edwards U., Austin, 1975—; vis. lectr. taxation Grad. Sch. Bus., U. Tex., 1976; counsel Vaughn House, halfway home for blind. Mem. budget com. United Way, Austin; pres. Center for Profl. Accounting, Austin. Mem. Am., Travis County bar assns., Am. Judicature Soc., Am., Tex. socs. C.P.A.'s. Home: 4907 Westview Dr Austin TX 78731 Office: 1040 American Bank Tower Austin TX 78701 Tel (512) 476-6527

LOCKARD, BETTY PINE, b. Kansas City, Mo., May 12, 1933; B.S. in Edn., Central Mo. State U., 1955, M.S. in Edn., 1956; J.D., U. Mo. at Kansas City, 1961. Admitted to Mo. bar, 1961; tchr. Topeka Pub. Sch. System, 1955-56; Warrensburg (Mo.) public schl. system, 1956-58; partner firm Pine, Welling, Jones & Lockard, Warrensburg, 1961-62; probate and magistrate judge Johnson County, Mo., 1962-66; partner firm Pine & Lockard, Warrensburg, 1966-71; asso. prof. Central Mo. State U., Warrensburg, 1971—; cons. traffic mgmt. inst., 1971; condr. seminars, 1975; Show-Me Regional Planning Com., Johnson County, Mo., 1976. Active vol. Cancer Fund, Heart Fund, United Fund. Mem. Mo., Johnson County bar assns., Am. Judicature Soc., Nat. Safety Council, Mo. Police Chief's Assn., Mo. Tchrs. Assn., Community Tchrs. Assn., Kappa Delta Pi, Alpha Phi Delta, Sigma Sigma Sigma. Contbr. articles in field to profl. jours. Home: Route 5 Box 99 Warrensburg MO 64093 Office: 313 E Humphreys Central Mo State U Warrensburg MO 64093 Tel (816) 747-8549

LOCKE, JOHN HOWARD, b. Berryville, Va., Sept. 4, 1920; B.S., U. Richmond, 1941; LL.B., U. Va., 1948. Admitted to Va. bar, 1948, U.S. Supreme Ct. bar, 1970; asso. firm Gentry, Locke, Rakes & Moore, and predecessors, Roanoke, Va., 1948-51, partner, 1951—. Founder, pres. Big Bros., Roanoke, 1960. Mem. Am., Va., Roanoke City (past pres.) bar assns., Va. State Bar, Am. Jud. Soc., Internat. Assn. Ins. Counsel, Am. Coll. Trial Lawyers, Internat. Soc. Barristers (pres. 1970). Contbr. articles to legal jours. Home: 3015 Carolina Ave SW Roanoke VA 24014 Office: Suite 300 Shenandoah Bldg Roanoke VA 24004 Tel (703) 342-2921

LOCKHART, BYRON, b. Weiman, Tex., Oct. 1, 1917; B.A., Baylor U., 1940, J.D., 1941. Admitted to Tex. bar, 1941, U.S. Supreme Ct. bar, 1970; spl. agt. FBI, 1941-46; individual practice law, Austin, Tex., 1948—; spl. lectr. U. Tex., 1949-52; mem. panel arbitrators Am. Arbitration Assn. Mem. Tex. State Bar, Travis County Bar Assn. Recipient Distinguished Citizen Award, City of Austin, 1976. Office: 511 W 7th St Austin TX 78701 Tel (512) 477-3644

LOCKMAN, JOHN STEPHEN, b. Albany, N.Y., Feb. 9, 1923; student U.S. Mcht. Marine Acad., 1942-44; student Hofstra U., 1941-42, 46-47; LL.B., N.Y. U., 1950. Admitted to N.Y. bar, 1951; asso. firm Thatcher, Proffitt, Prizer, Crawley & Wood, N.Y.C., 1950-52; mem. firm Schwartz & Lockman, Massapequa, N.Y., 1952-63; judge Nassau County (N.Y.) Dist. Ct., 1964-71, Nassau County Ct., 1972—; asst. dist. atty. Nassau County, 1956-61; mem. Hempstead (N.Y.) Town Council, 1961-63; chmn. Hempstead Narcotics Guidance Council, 1970—. Chmn. dist. fin. com. Nassau County council Boy Scouts Am., 1959-60, chmn. chmn. dist. com., 1967-68; mem. parish council Sacred Heart Ch., Merrick, N.Y., 1969—. Mem. Am., Nassau County bar assns., County Judges Assn. (dir.). Office: County Courthouse 262 Old Country Rd Mineola NY 11501 Tel (516) 535-3104

LOCKWOOD, BROCTON D., b. Honolulu, Jan. 10, 1944; B.S., Oberlin Coll., 1966; J.D., Vanderbilt U., 1969. Admitted to Ill. bar, 1969; asso. firm Feirich & Lockwood, 1969-72; individual practice law, Carbondale, Ill., 1972—; asso. prof. So. Ill. U., 1972—; atty. City of Carbondale, 1972. Bd. dirs. Hill House, 1972; chmn. bd. dirs. Police and Fire depts., Carbondale, 1971. Mem. Ill., Jackson County bar assns., Am., Ill. trial lawyers assns. Home: Box 313 Carbondale IL 62901 Office: Box 543 Carbondale IL 62901 Tel (618) 549-8551

LOCKWOOD, JOHN MARSHALL, b. Woodhaven, N.Y., Jan. 25, 1913; A.B., Harvard, 1934, LL.B., 1937. Admitted to N.Y. State bar, 1938, U.S. Supreme Ct. bar, 1960; individual practice law, Huntington, N.Y., 1938-62, 75—; asst. atty. Suffolk County, N.Y., 1938; chief law asst. Dist. Ct. Suffolk County, 1964-68; asst. dist. atty., Suffolk County, 1969-74, chief appeals bur. Dist. Atty's. Office, 1973-74. Mem. N.Y., Suffolk County, Criminal bar assns., Huntington (N.Y.) Lawyers Club. Presented treatise on amendments to N.Y. State Constn., 1938. Home: 68 Greenhills Rd S Huntington NY 11746 Office: 38 New St Huntington NY 11743 Tel (516) 427-6605

LOCKWOOD, M. JUNE, b. Rochester, N.Y.; A.B., magna cum laude, Syracuse U., 1961, J.D. summa cum laude (Soroptimist fellow 1963, Bus. and Profl. Women fellow 1963), 1963. Admitted to N.Y. bar, 1963; law clk. Onondaga County (N.Y.) Ct., 1963-65, to Hon. Donald H. Mead, N.Y. State Supreme Ct., 1965—; partner firm Bucci & Lockwood, Baldwinsville, N.Y., 1965—; lectr. N.Y. State real estate broker course Onondaga Community Coll., 1972—; lectr. in field. Mem. advisory bd. Maria Regina Coll.; deacon Reformed Ch. of Syracuse. Mem. N.Y. State, Onondaga County (dir. 1971-73) bar assns., Justinian Soc. (pres. local chpt. 1962), Order of Coif, Phi Kappa Phi. Named valedictorian, recipient Moot Ct. award Syracuse U. Coll. Law, 1963. Office: 104 Syracuse St Baldwinsville NY 13027 Tel (315) 635-9944

LOCKWOOD, PETER VAN NORDEN, b. N.Y.C., Apr. 23, 1940; B.A., Harvard U., 1963, J.D., 1966. Admitted to D.C. bar, 1968, U.S. Supreme Ct. bar, 1972; law clk. to chief judge U.S. Ct. of Appeals First Circuit, 1966-67, to Justice Thurgood Marshall, U.S. Supreme Ct., 1967-68; asso. firm Caplin & Drysdale, Washington, 1968-72, partner, 1972—; trustee Mental Health Law Project, 1975—; mem. council Harvard Law Sch. Assn., 1976—. Mem. Am. Bar Assn. Home: 535 4th St SE Washington DC 20003 Office: 1101 17th St NW Washington DC 20036 Tel (202) 862-5065

LOCKWOOD, RALPH JEROME, b. Hazleton, Pa., June 23, 1905; B.A., Brown U., 1925; student Harvard Bus. Sch., 1927; LL.B., Yale, 1947. Admitted to Conn. bar, 1947; partner Lockwood & Harinstein, Bridgeport, Conn., 1958—; clk. Bridgeport City Ct., 1955-60; spl. asst. atty. gen. State of Conn., 1960-64; ct. advocate Juvenile Ct. for 1st Dist. of Conn., 1970—. Mem. Am., Conn., Bridgeport bar assns. Home: 2625 Park Ave Bridgeport CT 06605 Office: 181 Middle St Bridgeport CT 06604 Tel (203) 333-6181

LODDERS, RONALD RICHARD, b. Missoula, Mont., Apr. 29, 1948; B.S. in Philosophy, U. Mont., 1970, J.D. (Leaphart scholar), 1973. Admitted to Mont. bar, 1973; clk. judge Fed. Dist. Ct., Butte, Mont., 1973-74; asso. firm Crowley, Haughey, Hanson, Gallagher & Toole, Billings, Mont., 1974—. Mem. Am., Mont. bar assns., Am. Judicature Soc., Order of Barristers. Home: 2635 Avalon St Billings MT 59102 Office: 500 Electric Bldg Billings MT 59101 Tel (406) 252-3441

LOEB, ANDREW GOTHARD, b. N.Y.C., Dec. 18, 1944; A.B., Bowdoin Coll., 1966; J.D., Harvard, 1969; LL.M., N.Y. U., 1971. Admitted to Calif. bar, 1970, N.Y. bar, 1970; atty. VISTA, Bklyn., 1969-71; asso. firm Lowenthal & Lowenthal, San Francisco, 1971-72; counsel Calif. Dept. Ins., San Francisco, 1972-76, sr. counsel, 1976—. Mem. San Francisco Bar Assn., Assn. Calif. State Attys. Office: 100 Van Ness Ave San Francisco CA 94102 Tel (415) 557-3748

LOEB, BEN FOHL, JR., b. Nashville, May 15, 1932; B.A., Vanderbilt U., 1955, J.D., 1960. Law clk. Office Gen. Counsel Dept. Navy, Washington, 1959; admitted to Tenn. bar, 1960, U.S. Supreme Ct. bar, 1966, N.C. bar, 1975; asso. firm Crownover, Branstetter and Folk, Nashville, 1960-64; asst. prof. pub. law and govt. U. N.C., Chapel Hill, 1964-67, asso. prof., 1967-72, prof., 1972—, asst. dir. Inst. Govt., 1964—; counsel N.C. Legis. Coms. on Motor Vehicle Law, Alcoholic Beverage Control Law, Raleigh, 1970—. Mem. Am., Tenn. bar assns., Phi Beta Kappa, Phi Delta Phi. Author: Traffic Law and Highway Safety, 1970; Alcoholic Beverage Control Law, 1971; Motor Vehicle Law, 1975; Fire Protection Law, 1976. Home: 812 Emory Dr Chapel Hill NC 27514 Office: PO Box 990 Inst of Govt Chapel Hill NC 27514 Tel (919) 933-1304

LOEB, HOWARD MAX, b. N.Y.C., Jan. 13, 1946; B.A. cum laude, Syracuse U., 1968; J.D., N.Y. U., 1971. Admitted to N.Y. bar, 1972; asso. firm Bondy & Schloss, N.Y.C., 1971-75; asso. firm Kelley, Drye & Warren, N.Y.C., 1975—. Mem. Assn. Bar City N.Y. Office: 350 Park Ave New York City NY 10022 Tel (212) 752-5800

LOEBEN, ARTHUR FRANCIS, JR., b. Florence, S.C., Sept. 3, 1943; B.A., Albright Coll., 1967; J.D., Dickinson Sch. Law, 1970. Admitted to Pa. bar, 1970; asso. firm Rhodes, Sinon & Reader, Harrisburg, Pa., 1970-71; partner firm Wells, Wells & Loeben, Pottstown, Pa., 1971—; solicitor Upper Montgomery (County) Joint Auth., Pennsburg, Pa., 1975—. Chmn. cub pack Valley Forge council Boy Scouts Am., 1974—. Mem. Am., Pa., Dauphin County, Montgomery County bar assns. Contbr. articles to law jours. Office: 635 High St Pottstown PA 19464 Tel (215) 323-7465

LOEBL, JAMES DAVID, b. Chgo., July 4, 1927; A.B., Princeton, 1948; postgrad. U. Chgo., 1948-49; LL.B., Stanford, 1952. Admitted to Calif. bar, 1953, U.S. Supreme Ct. bar, 1959, Ill. bar, 1960; sec. com. on rules U.S. Ho. of Reps., 1949; dep. atty. gen. Calif. Dept. Justice, 1953-58; travel sec. to Gov. Edmund G. Brown, 1959-60; asst. to dir. Dept. Profl. and Vocational Standards, 1959-60, dep. dir., 1960, chief dep. dir., 1961, dir., 1961-63; partner firm Loebl, Bringgold, Peck & Parker and predecessors, Ventura, Calif., 1963—; dir. Employment Aptitude and Placement Assn., 1970-72; judge pro tempore Ventura County Superior Ct., 1972, 74. Asst. city atty., Ojai, Calif., 1964; mem. Ventura County Sheriffs Civil Service Exam. Bd., Ventura County Regional Sanitation Dist., 1972-75, Calif. Council on Criminal Justice, 1972—; mem. Ojai City Council, 1968—; mayor, Ojai, 1972-75; bd. dirs. Ventura County Forum of Arts, 1965, Ojai Music Festivals, 1967-68; v.p., trustee Monica Ros Sch., Ojai, 1967-74; mem. exec. com. Ventura County Assn. Govts., 1972-75. Mem. Fed., Calif., Ill., Ventura County, Los Angeles County bar assns., So. Calif. Assn. Govts. (Ojai rep. 1972-75). Home: 715 El Toro Rd Ojai CA 93023 Office: 2580 E Main St Suite 101 Ventura CA 93003 Tel (805) 648-3303

LOEFFLER, JAMES J., b. Chgo., Mar. 7, 1931; B.S., Loyola U., 1953; J.D., Northwestern U., 1956. Admitted to Ill. bar, 1956, Tex. bar, 1956; mem. firm Fulbright & Jaworski, Houston, 1956-68, partner firm, 1969—. Mem. Am., Houston bar assns., Tex. Bar Assn. (certified labor relations specialist). Home: 505 Brown Saddle Houston TX 77057 Office: 1020 Bank of SW Bldg Houston TX 77002 Tel (713) 651-5151

LOEFFLER, ROBERT HUGH, b. Chgo., May 27, 1943; A.B. magna cum laude, Harvard U., 1965; J.D. cum laude, Columbia U., 1968. Admitted to N.Y. State bar, N.Y. Ct. Appeals bar, 1969, D.C. Ct. Appeals bar, 1970, U.S. Supreme Ct. bar, 1973; asso. firm Covington & Burling, Washington, 1969-76, firm Isham, Lincoln & Beale, Washington, 1976—. Chmn. Consumer Task Force, Muskie Presdl. campaign, 1972. Mem. Am., D.C., Fec. Communications bar assns. Editor: Columbia Law Rev., 1966-68. Home: 2607 36th Pl NW Washington DC 20007 Office: 1050 17th St NW Washington DC 20036 Tel (202) 833-9730

LOESER, HANS F., b. Kassel, Germany, Sept. 28, 1920; student Coll. City N.Y., 1940-42, U. Pa., 1943-44; LL.B. magna cum laude, Harvard, 1950. Admitted to Mass. bar, 1950, U.S. Supreme Ct. bar, 1968; sect. chief U.S. Office Mil. Govt., Bavaria, Munich, Germany, 1946-47; asso. firm Foley, Hoag & Eliot, Boston, 1950-55, partner, 1956—; dir. Boston Gas Co.; mem. hearing com. Mass. Bar Overseers; Trustee Vineyard Open Land Found., Martha's Vineyard, Mass.; bd. dirs. Mass. Multiple Sclerosis Soc.; incorporator Univ. Hosp., Boston. Mem. Am., Mass. (chmn. com. on malpractice), Boston (chmn. lawyers com. for civil rights under law) bar assns. Hon. consul-gen. Republic of Senegal. Editor: Harvard Law Rev., 1948-50. Home: 78 Washington Ave Cambridge MA 02140 Office: 10 Post Office Sq Boston MA 02109 Tel (617) 482-1390

LOEVINGER, LEE, b. St. Paul, Apr. 24, 1913; B.S. summa cum laude, U. Minn., 1933, J.D., 1936. Admitted to Minn. bar, 1936, Mo. bar, 1937, U.S. Supreme Ct. bar, 1941, D.C. bar, 1966; asso. firm Watson, Ess, Groner, Barnett & Whittaker, 1936-37; trial atty., regional atty. NLRB, 1937-41; atty. antitrust div. Dept. Justice, 1941-46, asst. atty. gen. in charge antitrust div., 1961-63; partner firm Larson, Loevinger, Lindquist, Freeman & Fraser, Mpls., 1946-60; asso. justice Minn. Supreme Ct., 1960-61; commr. FCC, Washington, 1963-68; partner firm Hogan & Hartson, Washington, 1968—; gen. counsel Craig-Hallum, Inc., Mpls., 1951-60, v.p., bd. dirs. 1968-73; v.p., dir. Craig-Hallum Corp., Mpls., 1968-73; gen. counsel Gen. Securities, Inc., Mpls., 1951-60; lectr. hosp. and nursing law U. Minn., 1953-60, vis. prof. jurisprudence, 1961; professorial lectr. govt. regulation of bus. Am. U., Washington, 1968-70; U.S. del. to com. on restrictive bus. practices Orgn. for Econ. Coop. and Devel., 1961-64, vice chmn., 1963-64; U.S. del., vice chmn. Extraordinary Adminstrv. Radio Conf., Internat. Telecommunications Union, 1964, 66; mem. Adminstrv. Conf. U.S., 1972-74; spl. asst. to atty. gen. on antitrust, 1963-64; del. White House Conf. on Inflation, 1974; U.S. del. UNESCO Conf. on Mass Media, 1975. Mem. Am. (ho. of dels. 1974—), Minn. bar assns., Bar Assn. D.C., AAAS, Phi Beta Kappa, Sigma Xi, Delta Sigma Rho, Sigma Delta Chi, Phi Delta Gamma, Tau Kappa Alpha, Alpha Epsilon Rho. Author booKs and monographs including: The Law of Free Enterprise, 1949; An Introduction to Legal Logic, 1952, Spanish edit., 1954; Jurimetrics: The Methodology of Legal Inquiry, 1963; Defending Antitrust Lawsuits, 1977; contbr. articles to legal jours. Recipient Outstanding Achievement award U. Minn. Regents, 1968. Home: 5669 Bent Branch Rd Bethesda MD 20016 Office: 815 Connecticut Ave Washington DC 20006 Tel (202) 331-4530

LOEWENTHAL, CLAUDE MAURICE, b. Beziers, France, Oct. 23, 1942; B.A., U. Minn., 1965, J.D., 1968. Admitted to Minn. bar, 1969, Iowa bar, 1969; partner firm Belzer & Loewenthal, Mpls., 1971-76, firm Loewenthal & Luck, 1976—. Mem. Am., Minn. State, Hennepin County (Minn.) bar assns. Home: 5446 Richmond Curve Minneapolis MN 55410 Office: 6750 France Ave S Minneapolis MN 55435 Tel (612) 927-7771

LOFTIN, JERRY WAYNE, b. Atlanta, Oct. 17, 1949; B.A., Auburn U., 1971; J.D., U. Ga., 1974. Admitted to Ga. bar, 1974; spl. investigator Clark County (Ga.) Superior Ct., 1972-74; individual practice law, Manchester, Ga., 1974—; v.p., legal adviser F&M Bank & Trust Co., Manchester, 1975—, also dir. Chmn. Manchester Area Planning Commn., 1976—; co-chmn. March of Dimes, Meriwether County (Ga.), 1975, chmn., 1976-77; co-chmn. Boy Scouts Am. fund drive, 1974, advisor Post 94, Explorer Scouts, 1975-76; coach Midget Football, 1975-76. Mem. Am., Meriweather County (sec.-treas. 1975-76) bar assns., C. of C. Recipient Distinguished Service award Manchester Jaycees, 1976, named Outstanding Young Man of Year, 1976. Office: PO Drawer 649 Manchester GA 31816 Tel (404) 846-3441

LOFTUS, THOMAS DANIEL, b. Seattle, Nov. 8, 1930; B.A. in Polit. Sci., U. Wash., 1952, J.D., 1957. Admitted to Wash. bar, 1958, U.S. Supreme Ct. bar, 1964, U.S. Mil. Ct. Appeals bar, 1964; atty. Northwestern Mut. Ins. Co., Seattle, 1958-62, sr. atty., 1962-68; asst. gen. counsel Unigard Mut. Ins. Co., Seattle, 1969—; served to lt. col. JAGC, U.S. Army Res., 1975—, U.S. Mil. judge, 1975—; judge pro tem Seattle Municipal Ct., 1973—. Bd. dirs. Seattle Seafair, Inc., 1975—; U.S. del. Atlantic Conf. Young Polit. Leaders, Oxford, Eng., 1965. Mem. Am., Wash., Seattle-King County bar assns., Internat. Assn. Ins. Counsel, Def. Research Inst., Am. Judicature Soc., JAG Assn., Res. Officers Assn., U. Wash. Alumni Assn., Phi Delta Phi, Theta Delta Chi. Home: 3610 S King St Seattle WA 98144 Office: Financial Center 1215 4th Ave Seattle WA 98161 Tel (206) 622-4488

LOGAN, CARL MAXWELL, b. Quenemo, Kans., Mar. 20, 1942; B.A., U. Kans., 1964; J.D. cum laude, Harvard, 1967. Admitted to Kans. bar, 1967, U.S. Supreme Ct. bar, 1975; asso. firm Payne Jones, Chts., Olathe, Kans., 1967-68, partner, 1968—; mem. Johnson County Law Library Trust. Mem. Am. Kans. (certificate of appreciation 1975), Johnson County bar assns. Contbr. articles to legal jours. Home: 1086 Wyckford Rd Olathe KS 66061 Office: Tower Bldg Olathe KS 66061 Tel (913) 782-2500

LOGAN, EDWIN A., b. Winchester, Ky., Dec. 2, 1946; B.A., U. Ky., 1968, J.D., 1971. Admitted to Ky. bar, 1971, U.S. Supreme Ct. bar, 1974; atty. Dept. Econ. Security, Commonwealth of Ky., 1971; legal asst. to Gov. Ky., 1972-74; individual practice law, Frankfort, Ky., 1974—; gen. counsel Bur. Corrections Commonwealth of Ky., 1974-75. Bd. dirs. Big Bros. and Big Sisters of Frankfort, 1973—. Mem. Ky., Franklin County bar assns. Office: 308 Wilkinson St Frankfort KY 40601 Tel (502) 875-3884

LOGAN, JAMES ASHLIN, b. Wilmore, Ky., Jan. 29, 1905; A.B., Centre Coll., 1927; J.D., Case Western Res. U., 1930; postgrad. U. Cin., Oxford U. (Eng.), summer, 1972. Admitted to Ky. bar, 1930; individual practice law, Winchester, Ky., 1930-43; mem. firm Jouett & Logan, Winchester, 1937-43; spl. asst. U.S. Atty. Gen., Lexington, Ky., 1943-46; authorization officer VA, Louisville, Ky., Columbus, Ohio, 1946-49; atty. employees compensation appeals bd., D.C., 1949-51; atty., head claim dept. Inter-Ocean Ins. Co., Cin., 1951-65; individual practice law, Walton, Ky., 1965—; conciliation commr. farm debtors Nat. Bankruptcy Act, Winchester, 1935-37. Pres. Young Men's Democratic Club, Clark County, Ky., 1936; elder Presbyterian Ch., Winchester, Richwood Ch., Boone County, Ky. Mem. Ky. State, Fed. bar assns., S.A.R. (former pres. Ky. Soc., recipient Patriot's Medal 1968), Am. Legion (comdr. Daniel Boone Post, Winchester, 1947), Blue Grass Trust for Hist. Preservation, No. Ky. Heritage League. Recipient Selective Service Medal, U.S. Congress, 1946. Office: Richwood Rd Walton KY 41094 Tel (606) 485-4321

LOGAN, JAMES FRANKLIN, JR., b. Cleve., May 17, 1946; B.S., Tenn. Wesleyan Coll., 1968; J.D., U. Tenn., 1970. Admitted to Tenn. bar, 1971; asso. firm Finnell, Thompson & Scott, Cleve., 1971; partner firm Finnell, Thompson, Scott & Logan, Cleve., 1972—. Mem. Bradley County, Tenn. bar assns., Chattanooga, Tenn. trial lawyers assns., Cleve. Jaycees. Home: 3706 Woodcrest Ave Cleveland TN 37311 Office: PO Box 1476 Cleveland TN 37311 Tel (615) 472-3391

LOGAN, JAMES KENNETH, b. Quenemo, Kans., Aug. 21, 1929; A.B., Kans. U., 1952; LL.B. (now J.D.), Harvard, 1955. Admitted to Kans. bar, 1955, Calif. bar, 1956; law clerk Hon. Walter A. Huxman, U.S. Ct. Appeals 10th Circuit, 1955-56; asso. firm Gibson, Dunn & Crutcher, Los Angeles, 1956-57; asst. prof. law U. Kans., 1957-61, prof., 1961-68, dean, 1961-68; Ezra Ripley Thayer teaching fellow Harvard, 1961-62; mem. firm Payne & Jones, Chartered, Olathe, Kans., 1968—; vis. prof. law U. Tex., 1964, Stanford, 1969, U. Mich., 1976. Mem. Johnson County (Kans.) Cha rter Commn., 1975-76; trustee Ottawa U. Mem. Am., Kans., Johnson County bar assns. Author: (with Barton Leach) Future Interests and Estate Planning, 1961; Kansas Estate Administration, 3d edit., 1976. Contbr. articles in field to profl. jours. Home: 1082 Wyckford Rd Olathe KS 66061 Office: 200 E Chestnut St Olathe KS 66061 Tel (913) 782-2500

LOGAN, JOSEPH PRESCOTT, b. Topeka, Jan. 21, 1921; A.B., Dartmouth, 1942; LL.B., Harvard, 1948. Admitted to Mo. bar, 1948; asso. firm Thompson & Mitchell, St. Louis, 1948—, partner, 1957—. Pres., Ranken-Jordan Home Convalescent Crippled Children St. Louis. Mem. Am., Mo., St. Louis bar assns. Office: Thompson & Mitchell 1 Mercantile Center Saint Louis MO 63101 Tel (314) 231-7676

LOGAN, LARRY JOE, b. Humboldt, Tenn., May 17, 1946; B.S., Union U., 1970; J.D., Memphis State U., 1973. Admitted to Tenn. bar, 1974; partner firm Maddox, Lassiter, Jones & Logan, Huntingdon, Tenn., 1974—. Mem. citizens advisory com. City of McKenzie (Tenn.), 1975—. Mem. Am., Tenn. bar assns. Home: Route 1 David St McKenzie TN 38201 Office: 150 W Main St Huntingdon TN 38344 Tel (901) 986-5266

LOGAN, MORGAN N., b. Poughkeepsie, N.Y., May 2, 1933; A.B., St. Lawrence U., 1959; LL.B., Syracuse U., 1962, J.D., 1968. Admitted to N.Y. State bar, 1963, Eastern and So. dist. U.S. Dist. Ct., 1964, project atty. civil div. U.S. Corps Engrs., Hindman, Ky., 1965; individual practice law, Middle Island, N.Y., 1966—; v.p. Brookhaven Properties, Inc., Middle Island, 1971-74. Mem. Brookhaven Narcotics Guidance Counsel, 1972-73; pres. Northside Civic Assn., Middle Island, 1973-74. Mem. N.Y. State, Suffolk County bar assns., C. of C. Central Brookhaven (pres. 1973-74). Address: Half Mile Rd Middle Island NY 11953 Tel (516) 924-5030

LOHR, WALTER GEORGE, JR., b. Balt., Mar. 3, 1944; A.B., Princeton, 1966; LL.B., Yale, 1969. Admitted to Md. bar, 1969; law clk. Hon. Harrison L. Winter, U.S. Circuit judge 4th circuit, 1969-70; asso. firm Piper & Marbury, Balt., 1970-74, 1976-77, partner, 1977—; asst. Atty. Gen., Md., 1974-76. Trustee Med. Eye Bank of Md., Union Meml. Hosp., Gilman Sch. Mem. Am., Md. State bar assns., Bar Assn. of Balt. City. Home: 4307 Underwood Rd Baltimore MD 21218 Office: 25 S Charles St Baltimore MD 21201 Tel (301) 539-2530

LOISEAUX, PIERRE ROLAND, b. N.Y.C., Apr. 10, 1925; LL.B., Boston U., 1950; LL.M., N.Y. U., 1951. Admitted to Mass. bar, 1950; asst. prof. law U. Ark., 1951-53; asso. prof. law Emory U., 1953-56; prof. law U Tex., Austin, 1956-71; prof. law U. Calif. Davis, 1971—, dean, 1974—. Mem. Am., Mass. bar assns., Nat. Bankruptcy Conf., Soc. Am. Law Tchrs. Recipient Fulbright grant, 1964-65; author: Cases on Creditors' Remedies, 1966; contbr. articles in field to law jours. Office: Univ Calif Law Sch Davis CA 95616 Tel (916) 752-0243

LOISELLE, ALVA PARENT, b. Willimantic, Conn., July 4, 1910; B.S., U. Conn., 1934, LL.B., 1943. Admitted to Conn. bar, 1943; practiced in Willimantic, 1943-52; corp. counsel City of Willimantic, 1945-47, Town of Windham (Conn.), 1947-52, Town of Mansfield (Conn.), 1947-52, Town of Canterbury (Conn.), 1945-52; judge Conn. Ct. Common Pleas, 1952-57; judge Superior Ct., 1957-71, chief judge, 1970-71; justice Conn. Supreme Ct., 1971—; instr. U. Conn., 1946-52; alderman City of Willimantic, 1939-43. Mem. Windham County, Conn. State, Am. bars. Recipient Outstanding Alumni award U. Conn., 1966, U. Conn. Law Sch., 1974. Home: 110 Windham Rd Willimantic CT 06226 Office: Drawer N Sta A Hartford CT 06106 Tel (203) 566-2947

LOKEY, HAMILTON, b. Atlanta, Aug. 30, 1910; A.B., U. Ga., 1931, LL.B., 1933. Admitted to Ga. bar, 1933, U.S. Supreme Ct. bar, 1938; individual practice law, Atlanta, 1933-39, partner firm Lokey & Bowden, Atlanta, 1939—; chmn. Ga. State Bd. Bar Examiners, 1973-76; mem. Ga. Ho. of Reps., 1953-56. Mem. Am., Ga., Atlanta bar assns., Lawyers Club Atlanta, Am. Coll. Trial Lawyers, Internat. Acad. Trial Lawyers, Internat. Assn. Ins. Counsel. Home: 737 Woodward Way NW Atlanta GA 30327 Office: 2610 1st Nat Bank Tower Atlanta GA 30303 Tel (404) 658-1034

LOMBARD, RICHARD SPENCER, b. C.Z., Jan. 28, 1928; A.B., Harvard, 1949, J.D., 1952. Admitted to N.Y. State bar, 1953; asso. firm Haight, Gardner, Poor & Havens, N.Y.C., 1952-55; mem. law dept. Creole Petroleum Corp., Caracas, Venezuela, 1955-65, mgr., 1963-65; gen. counsel Esso Chem. Co., N.Y.C., 1966-69; asso. gen. counsel Humble Oil & Refining Co., Houston, 1969-71; asst. gen. counsel Exxon Corp., N.Y.C., 1971-72, asso. gen. counsel, 1972-73, gen. counsel, 1973—. Adv. com. Parker Sch. Fgn. and Comparative Law, Columbia, 1973—; adv. bd. Internat. and Comparative Law Center-Southwestern Legal Found., 1973—, vice-chmn., 1974—; adv. bd. Center of Law and Econs., Columbia, 1975—. Served with A.C., AUS, 1946-47. Fellow Am. Bar Found.; mem. Assn. Bar City N.Y., Am., N.Y. State bar assns., State Bar Tex., Am. Soc. Internat. Law, World Assn. Lawyers, Am. Judicature Soc. Author: American-Venezuelan Private International Law, 1965. Office: Exxon Corp 1251 Ave of Americas New York City NY 10020*

LOMBARDI, JEROME DANTE, b. Tarentum, Pa., Feb. 15, 1940; A.B., Columbia, 1961; LL.B., Harvard U., 1964. Admitted to Pa. bar, 1967; corp. counsel McCreary Tire & Rubber Co., Indiana, Pa., 1965-68; partner firms Ashe & Lombardi, Kittanning, Pa., 1969-75, Lombardi & Kepple, Kittanning, 1976—; chief pub. defender Armstrong County (Pa.), 1975-76; pres., chmn. D & C Assos. Co-chmn. Vandergrift (Pa.) Planning Commn., 1967-76; pres. United Cerebral Palsy of Western Pa., 1975-76; v.p., dir. Kiski Valley Med. Facility, Apollo, Pa., 1976—; bd. dirs. Kiski Area YMCA. Mem. Am., Armstrong County bar assns., Pa. Bar, Assn. Trial Lawyers Am. Home: 404 Linden St Vandergrift PA 15690 Office: Gilpin Bldg Market St Kittanning PA 16201 Tel (412) 543-2411

LOMBARDI, RICHARD CHARLES, lawyer; b. Akron, Ohio, Sept. 28, 1945; B.A., U. Akron, 1968; J.D., Ohio State U., 1970. Admitted to Ohio bar, 1971, U.S. Ct. Appeals, 6th Dist. bar, 1972; law clk. Fed. Judge, U.S. 6th Circuit Ct. Appeals, 1971-72; jr. partner law firm Loomis, Jones, Poland, Wilson & Griffith, Ravenna, Ohio, 1972—. Bd. dirs. Portage County Cancer Crusade, 1975-76; mem. Brimfield Zoning Commn., 1976—; bd. dirs. Catholic Charities, Ravenna, Ohio. Mem. Ohio State, Akron, Portage County bar assns., Omicron Delta Kappa. Home: 3809 Boydell Rd Kent OH 44240 Office: 241 S Chestnut St Ravenna OH 44266

LOMBARDO, GERALDINE, b. Hingham, Mass., Feb. 3, 1932; A.B., Suffolk U., 1968, J.D., 1970. Admitted to Mass. bar, 1971; 1st asst. clk. of ct., 1960—; individual practice law, Hingham, 1971—; corporator Hingham Instn. for Savs., 1975-76. Mem. adv. fin. com. Town of Hingham, 1973-75; mem. consumer adv. council South Shore Hosp., 1975-76. Mem. Am., Mass., Plymouth County bar assns., Mass. Dist. Ct. Clks. Assn. Home: 81 Kilby St Hingham MA 02043 Tel (617) 749-1543

LOMBARDO, JOSEPH FRANCIS, b. Phila., Sept. 11, 1933; B.S., Temple U., 1955, J.D., 1959. Admitted to Pa. bar, 1960; casualty adjuster Allstate Ins. Co., Phila., 1959-62; corp. counsel Pa. Lumbermen's Mut. Ins. Co., Phila., 1962-76; individual practice law, Phila., 1960—; dir., sec. PLM Agy., N.Y.C., 1971-76. Active Wissahickon Civic Assn., Phila., 1973—. Mem. Pa., Phila. bar assns., Justinian Soc., Temple U. Law Alumni Assn. Home: 5425 Quentin St Philadelphia PA 19128 Office: 543 Western Savs Bank Bldg Broad and Chestnut Sts Philadelphia PA 19107 Tel (215) PE5-0742

LOMENZI, JOHN PAUL, b. Rochester, N.Y., Aug. 12, 1915; student Niagara U.; LL.B., Fordham U., 1939; D.H.L. (hon.) N.Y. Inst. Tech., 1972. Admitted to N.Y. State bar, 1940, also U.S. Supreme Ct. bar; practice law, 1940-55; judge City Ct. of Rochester, 1955-61; county judge then chief judge Monroe County (N.Y.) Ct., 1961-63; Sec. state State of N.Y., 1963-73; mem. firm DeFalco, Field and Lomenzo, N.Y.C., 1973—; mem. faculty Niagara U., Rochester Inst. Tech., St. John Fisher Coll., Am. Inst. Banking. Adv. bd. Salvation Army; bd. dirs. La Guarida Meml. Settlement House, N.Y.C., Council of Social Agys.; chmn. Monroe County (N.Y.) Easter Seal Drive, Mem. Am., Rochester (past v.p.) bar assns., Am. Fedn. Bar Assns., Am. Soc. Pub. Adminstrn., Judge Advocates Assn. Office: 605 3d Ave New York City NY 10016 Tel (212) 986-2434

LONABAUGH, ELLSWORTH EUGENE, b. San Diego, Feb. 24, 1923; student U. Wyo., 1947-48; J.D., U. Colo., 1950. Admitted to Wyo. bar, 1950, Tex. bar, 1951; asso. firm Williams and Thornton, Galveston, Tex., 1951-53; partner firm Lonabaugh & Lonabaugh, Sheridan, Wyo., 1953-71, Lonabaugh & Vanderhoef, Sheridan, 1972—; atty. City Sheridan, 1957; commr. Uniform Wyo. State Laws, 1963—; mem. Wyo. Ho. of Reps., 1955-57, 67-71; commr. Wyo. State Bar, 1974-76. Mem. Am., Wyo., Tex., Sheridan County (pres. 1961-62) bar assns. Named Outstanding Man of Year, Sheridan County, 1975. Home: 441 Florence Ave Sheridan WY 82801 Office: Suite 110 50 E Loucks St Sheridan WY 82801 Tel (307) 674-4447

LONCHAR, DONALD MORRIS, JR., b. Chgo., Nov. 12, 1923; B.A., Northwestern U., 1948; J.D., DePaul U., 1955. Admitted to Ill. bar, 1955, U.S. Ct. Appeals 7th Circuit bar, 1957, U.S. Supreme Ct. bar, 1963, U.S. Ct. Mil. Appeals bar, 1963; revenue agt., spl. agt. IRS, Chgo., 1950-56; asst. states atty. Lake County (Ill.), 1957-58; asso. firm McClory, Bairstow & Anderson, Waukegan, Ill., 1958-60; partner firm McClory, Lonchar & Nordigian, Waukegan, 1960-63; sr. partner firm Lonchar & Nordigian, Waukegan, 1963—; atty. Waukegan Pub. Schs., 1967—, Zion-Benton Twp. High Sch. Dist. 126, 1970—. Pres. Waukegan Area Council Chs., 1965-66, Waukegan Exchange Club, 1966; chmn. Waukegan Grade Schs. Citizens Adv. Council, 1965-67. Mem. Am., Ill., Lake County (pres. 1973-74) bar assns., Am. Judicature Soc. Contbr. articles in field to profl. jours. Home: 1030 Flossmoor Ave Waukegan IL 60085 Office: 33 N County St Waukegan IL 60085 Tel (312) 623-0112

LONERGAN, MICHAEL MCDOWELL, b. Altadena, Calif., Aug. 18, 1944; B.A., Yale, 1966; J.D., Cornell U., 1969. Admitted to N.H. bar, 1969; partner firm Sulloway Hollis Godfrey & Soden, Concord, N.H., 1976—. Mem. N.H., Am. bar assns. Office: 9 Capitol St Concord NH 03301 Tel (603) 224-2341

LONESOME, WILLIAM LEE, b. Washington, June 24, 1907; A.B., W.Va. State Coll., 1933, H.H.D. (hon.); J.D., Howard U., 1936; LL.D., Edward Waters Coll., Wilberforce U. Admitted to W.Va. bar, 1937; individual practice law, Charleston, W.Va.; trial atty. W.Va. Rd. Commn., 1952-55; spl. aide to Gov. of W.Va., 1961-63, cons., 1955-67; commr. accounts Kanawha County (W.Va.), 1971—. Pres. Charleston Bus. and Profl. Men's Club, Charleston br. NAACP, W.Va. State Coll. Found., Inc.; trustee Wilberforce U. Mem. Am., W.Va., Kanawha County bar assns. Home: 1510 Pinewood Park St Dunbar WV 25064 Office: 507 Dickinson St Charleston WV 25301 Tel (304) 344-2569

LONG, BEVERLY MAXINE GLENN, b. Omaha, Mar. 1, 1923; A.B. in Econs., U. Chgo., 1944; J.D., Columbia, 1947. Admitted to N.Y. bar, 1948, R.I. bar, 1951, U.S. Supreme Ct. bar, 1960; asso. firm Edwards & Angell, Providence, 1950-59, partner, 1959—. Mem. adv. com. Child Welfare Services, R.I. Dept. Social Welfare, 1959-66; mem. R.I. Gov.'s Commn. on Status Women, 1965; chmn. R.I. Children's Code Commn., 1967-74; bd. dirs. R.I. Council Community Services, 1957-64, mem. task force on evaluation criminal justice programs, 1974—; mem. personnel com. Big Bros. R.I., 1964-67; bd. dirs. St. Mary's Home for Children, 1966—, chmn. service com., 1972—; chmn. budget panel United Way, 1969-70, mem. ad hoc adv. com. to exec. budget com., 1971-76, bd. dirs., 1973-74; bd. dirs. Child Welfare League Am., 1975—, mem. membership com., pub. policy com., personnel practices com., 1975—, mem. nationwide accrediation council family and children's services, 1976—; bd. dirs. R.I. Conf. Social Work, 1961-66, Children's Friend and Service, 1966-75, 76—, Providence chpt. ARC, 1967-72. Mem. Am. (adminstrn. expenses com. real property, probate and trust law sect. 1965-70, 73—, significant trust and probate decisions com. 1964-65, mem. tax aspects of decedents estates com. 1968-71, co-vice chmn. 1970-71, mem. creditors rights com. 1972-74, chmn. 1972-73), New Eng. (chmn. real property, probate and trust law sect. 1974-75), R.I. (past mem. ho. of dels., past mem. exec. com., chmn. real property, probate and trust law com. 1973-75, mem. numerous other coms.) bar assns. Recipient Pub. Service citation U. Chgo., 1958. Home: 200 Elmgrove Ave Providence RI 02906 Office: 2700 Hospital Trust Tower Providence RI 02903 Tel (401) 274-9200

LONG, DON BOYDEN, JR., b. Roanoke, Ala., Mar. 12, 1940; A.B., Columbia U., 1963; LL.B., Duke, 1966. Admitted to Ala. bar, 1966; since practiced in Birmingham, asso. firm Johnston Barton Proctor Swedlaw & Naff, 1966-71, partner, 1972—. Bd. dirs. Birmingham Pub. Library, 1974—, pres., 1975—. Mem. Am., Ala., Birmingham bar assns. Home: 2007 Warwick Ct Birmingham AL 35209 Office: 1212 Bank for Savs Bldg Birmingham AL 35203 Tel (205) 322-0616

LONG, FLETCHER, JR., b. Forrest City, Ark., Dec. 18, 1942; A.B., U. Ark., 1964, J.D., 1966. Admitted to Ark. bar, 1966; mem. staff judge adv. USMC, 1966-69; individual practice law, Forrest City, 1969—; dep. pros. atty. St. Francis County, First Jud. Dist., 1969—. Mem. St. Francis County, Ark., Am. bar assns., Am., Ark. trial lawyers assns. Home: 346 Yorktown St Forrest City AR 72335 Office: 120 S Izard PO Box 1098 Forrest City AR 72335 Tel (501) 633-2164

LONG, GEORGE ELMORE, II, b. Vicksburg, Miss., Oct. 11, 1945; B.S., Murray State U., 1968; J.D., U. Ky., 1971. Admitted to Ky. bar, 1972, Marshall County bar, 1975; asso. dir. Ky. Bar Assn., Frankfort, 1972; partner firm Cunningham & Long, Benton, Ky., 1975—. Dir. Marshall County C. of C., Lakeland Parish Center. Mem. Ky. Bar Assn. Home: Rural Route 8 Benton KY 42025 Office: 10th & Poplar Sts Benton KY 42025 Tel (502) 527-4811

LONG, HARRY SAMUEL, b. Marshall, Tex., June 22, 1928; B.B.A., U. Tex., 1960, LL.B., 1962; banking degree Rutgers U., 1969. Admitted to Tex. bar, 1962; bookkeeper, asst. to T.J. Taylor, Karnack, Tex., 1945-57; accountant Tex. Indsl. Loan Co., Austin, 1957-62; trust ops. officer Nat. Bank of Commerce, San Antonio, 1962-63; sr. v.p. 1st Security Nat. Bank, 1963-70; pres. Security 1st Mortgage Co., 1970-74; sr. v.p. 1st Security Nat. Corp., 1970-74; individual practice law, Beaumont, Tex., 1974—. Mem. Am., Tex., Jefferson County bar assns., Beaumont Estate Planners, Tex. Assn. Bank Counsel, Tex. Soc. C.P.A.'s. Author courses for Tex. Soc. C.P.A.'s. Home: 2025 Driskill Dr Beaumont TX 77706 Office: 320 San Jacinto Bldg Beaumont TX 77701 Tel (713) 835-2582

LONG, JAMES EUGENE, b. Burlington, N.C., Mar. 19, 1940; A.B., U. N.C., 1963, J.D., 1966. Admitted to N.C. bar, 1966; partner firm Long, Ridge & Long, Burlington, N.C., 1966-75; mem. N.C. House of Reps., 1970-75; chief dep. commr. of ins. N.C. Dept. of Ins., Raleigh, 1975—. Sec. N.C. Spl. Olympics, 1971-76. Mem. Am., N.C. bar assns., Alamance County Young Lawyers' Assn. (pres. 1972-75). Recipient N.C. State Employees award, 1975. Home: PO Box 335 Raleigh NC 27602 Office: Wake County Court House Raleigh NC 27611 Tel (919) 829-7343

LONG, JAMES GRANT, JR., b. Greenville, S.C., Mar. 7, 1938; A.B. in Polit. Sci., U. S.C., 1960, J.D., 1962. Admitted to S.C. bar, 1962, U.S. Supreme Ct. bar, 1967; asso. firm Perrin & Perrin, Spartanburg, S.C., 1963-66; partner firm Ward, Howell, Barnes, Long, Hudgens, and Adams, Spartanburg, 1966—; dir. Spartanburg County Legal Aid Soc., 1969-71. Mem. Am., S.C., Spartanburg County bar assns. Home: 111 Kearse Ct Spartanburg SC 29303 Office: 200 Library St Spartanburg SC 29304 Tel (803) 582-5683

LONG, JOSEPH RICHARD, b. Beardstown, Ill., Mar. 22, 1919; A.A.S., Blackburn Coll., 1939; J.D., U. Wis., 1949. Admitted to Wis. bar, 1949, U.S. Supreme Ct. bar, 1974; partner firm Blakely & Long, and predecessors, Beloit, Wis., 1948-74; individual practice law, Beloit, 1974—; vis. lectr. U. Wis. Law Sch., 1970—, co-dir. gen. practice course, 1975—; dir. trial advocacy seminars Inst. Continuing Legal Edn. for Wis., 1974—; v.p. C-Z Chem. Co., Inc., Beloit. Mem. Wis. Gov.'s Commn. on Human Rights, 1960-66; past dir. Wis. Civil Liberties Union; elder 1st Presbyn. Ch., Beloit. Mem. Am., Rock County (Wis.), Beloit bar assns., Am. Judicature Soc., Assn. Trial Lawyers Am., Law-Sci. Acad. Am., Wis. Acad. Trial Lawyers, U. Wis. Law Sch. Alumni Assn., Blackburn Coll. Alumni Assn. (past pres.), Order of Coif, Phi Kappa Phi. Bd. editors Wis. Law Rev., 1947-48. Home: 2537 Hawthorne Dr Beloit WI 53511 Office: 400 E Grand Ave Beloit WI 53511 Tel (608) 365-6681

LONG, KENNETH ROBERT, b. Camden, N.J., Oct. 21, 1940; B.A., Ohio Wesleyan U., 1962; J.D., Ohio State U., 1965; M.B.A., Miami U., 1966. Admitted to Ohio bar, 1966, Wash. bar, 1967, Pa. bar, 1972; acting adminstr. Douglas County (Ill.) Jarman Meml. Hosp., Tuscola, 1962; asso. firm Davis, Wright, Todd, Riese & Jones, Seattle, 1967-70; atty., asst. sec. Koppers Co., Inc., Pitts., 1970-75; gen. counsel, sec. Wean United, Inc., Pitts., 1975-76; gen. atty. Consol. Natural Gas Co., Pitts., 1976—. Mem. Am., Wash., Ohio, Alleghany County bar assns., Am. Soc. Corp. Secs. Home: 371 Parkway Dr Pittsburgh PA 15228 Office: 1041 4 Gateway Center Pittsburgh PA 15222 Tel (412) 471-5100

LONG, MICHAEL JOSEPH, b. Toledo, Aug. 11, 1946; A.B. in Polit. Sci., Ga. So. U., 1968; J.D., Mercer U., 1972. Admitted to Ga. bar, 1973; partner firm Wisse, Kushinka, Calhoun, Godwin and Long, Warner Robins, Ga., 1975—; city atty. Warner Robins, 1975—. Pres. Warner Robins Civitan Club, 1974-75, 75-76; bd. dirs. United Givers Fund. Mem. Am. Bar Assn., Am. Trial Lawyers Assn. Home: 209 Channing Trail Warner Robins GA 31093 Office: 1512 Watson Blvd Warner Robins GA 31093 Tel (912) 923-2617

LONG, QUENTIN VERONA, b. Okeechobee, Fla., Aug. 20, 1918; LL.B., U. Fla., 1949, J.D., 1967. Admitted to Fla. bar, 1949; atty. Fla. Rd. Dept., Tallahassee, 1949-51; practiced in Hallandale, Fla., 1951—, mem. firm Long, Crouch & Ward, firm Long and Finkel, 1975—; mem. Fla. Ho. of Reps., 1962-64; chmn. bd. Bank of Hallandale and Trust Co., 1965—, 1st Bank of Hollywood Beach, 1972—; asst. state atty. Broward County (Fla.), 1955-59, state atty., 1964-67. Mem. Am., Broward County, South Broward County bar assns., Fla. Bar, Blue Key, Delta Theta Phi. Home: 504 SW 10th Ave Fort Lauderdale FL 33312 Office: 801 E Hallandale Beach Blvd Hallandale FL 33009 Tel (305) 921-6556

LONG, RICHARD BEDELL, b. Bainbridge, N.Y., May 30, 1931; B.A., Cornell U., 1953, J.D., 1957. Admitted to N.Y. bar, 1957; partner firm Coughlin & Gerhart, and predecessor, Binghamton, N.Y., 1957—; arbitrator Am. Arbitration Assn. Trustee Syracuse U.; bd. dirs. Broome County (N.Y.) YMCA. Mem. Broome County, N.Y. State, Am. bar assns. Office: Coughlin & Gerhart One Marine Midland Plaza Binghamton NY 13901 Tel (607) 723-9511

LONG, ROBERT EDGAR, b. Roxboro, N.C., Apr. 13, 1916; A.B., Yale U., 1937; LL.B. (now J.D.), Harvard, 1940. Admitted to N.C. bar, 1940; partner firm Merritt & Long, Roxboro, 1940-42; individual practice law, Roxboro, 1946-50; partner firm Cooper, Long, Latham & Cooper, Burlington, N.C., 1953-56; partner firm Dalton & Long, Burlington, N.C., 1962-75; of counsel firm Allen, Allen, Walker & Washburn, Burlington, 1976—; adminstrv. asst. to U.S. Senator Willis Smith, 1951; spl. asst. U.S. Atty., Raleigh, N.C., 1952. Mayor City of Roxboro, 1947-51. Mem. Am., N.C., Alamance County (pres. 1967) bar assns. Home: 2907 N Fairway Dr Burlington NC 27215 Office: Suite 301 Wachovia Bldg PO Box 1087 Burlington NC 27215 Tel (919) 228-7881

LONG, THAD GLADDEN, b. Dothan, Ala., Mar. 9, 1938; A.B., Columbia, 1960; J.D., U. Va., 1963. Admitted to Ala. bar, 1963, U.S. Ct. Mil. Appeals bar, 1964, U.S. Supreme Ct. bar, 1970; asso. firm Bradley, Arant, Rose & White, Birmingham, 1963-70, partner, 1970—; lectr. law U. Ala., 1968-70. Chmn. legal com. Ala. Planning Project for Mental Retardation, Birmingham, 1967-68; legal adviser Ala. Assn. Retarded Citizens, Montgomery, 1968—; pres. Greater Birmingham Arts Alliance, bd. dirs., 1977—. Mem. Am., Ala. (chmn. antitrust sect.), Birmingham bar assns., Order of Coif, Phi Delta Phi. Recipient Ala. Assn. Retarded Children Spl. Service award, 1971; Council of Exceptional Children Appreciation award, 1972. Comments and projects editor Va. Law Rev., 1962-63; contbr. articles to legal jours. jours. Home: 3409 S Brookwood Rd Mountain Brook AL 35223 Office: 1500 Brown Marx Bldg Birmingham AL 35223 Tel (205) 252-4500

LONGACRE, JAMES ROY, b. Shelby, Ohio, June 11, 1944; B.E.E., Ohio State U., 1967; J.D., Georgetown U., 1971. Admitted to D.C. bar, 1971; agt. firm Cushman, Darby & Cushman, Washington, 1967-71, asso., 1971-72, partner, 1973—. Home: 3505 Beverly Dr Annandale VA 22042 Office: 1801 K St NW Washington DC 20006 Tel (202) 833-3000

LONGAN, FRANKLIN SISSON, b. Lincoln, Ill., June 1, 1907; student U.S. Mil. Acad., 1925-27; LL.B., U. Mont., 1936. Admitted to Mont. bar, 1936; asso. to partner firm Brown, Davis & Longan, Billings, 1936-46; sr. partner firm Longan & Holmstrom, Billings, 1946—; lectr. in field. Mem. Mont. Civil Rules Com., 1959-63, Adv. Commn. on Rules of Civil Procedure, 1963—, Mont. Jud. Nomination Commn., 1973-75; mem. Joint Med.-Legal Com. to Screen Med. Malpractice Claims, 1968—. Fellow Internat. Acad. Trial Lawyers, Am. Coll. Trial Lawyers; mem. Mont. (pres. 1959-60), Yellowstone County (pres. 1948, Order of the Roll award 1976) bar assns., Scribes. Contbr. articles to legal jours. Home: 24 Ave B Billings MT 59101 Office: Suite 319 Securities Bldg Billings MT 59101 Tel (406) 252-7127

LONGMIRE, GEORGE, b. La Follette, Tenn., Aug. 2, 1915; B.A., Lincoln Meml. U., 1939; J.D., U. N.D., 1947. Admitted to N.D. bar, 1947; agt. FBI, 1942-45; states atty. County of Grand Forks (N.D.), 1948-50; mem. N.D. State Senate, 1957-77, chmn. legis. research com., 1961-67, majority floor leader, 1969; mem. firm Longmire and Unruh, 1976—. Bd. dirs. Grand Forks City Mission and Service Center, 1950—; chmn. bd. trustees Federated Ch., Grand Forks, 1977—. Mem. Am., N.D., Grand Forks bar assns., Grand Forks C. of C. (chmn. mil. affairs com. 1977). Named Outstanding Young Man Grand Forks, N.D. Jaycees, 1950; recipient Sioux award U. N.D., 1967. Home: 3733 Belmont Rd Grand Forks ND 58201 Office: 600 DeMers Ave Grand Forks ND 58201 Tel (701) 775-0669

LONGOLUCCO, JAMES JOSEPH, b. Westerly, R.I., Oct. 19, 1936; A.B., Providence Coll., 1958; LL.B., Suffolk U., 1961. Admitted to R.I. bar, 1962; partner firm Longolucco, Parrilla & Lenihan, Westerly, R.I.; town solicitor Westerly, 1966-67, Hopkinton (R.I.), 1972-74; spl. asst. atty. gen. State of R.I., 1967-71. Mem. Am., R.I., Washington County (pres. 1974-76) bar assns., Assn. Trial Lawyers Am., Am. Judicature Soc. Home: 51 Cross St Westerly RI 02891 Office: 43 Broad St Westerly RI 02891 Tel (401) 596-0151

LONGORIA, DAVID, b. Grulla, Tex., Dec. 26, 1910; LL.B., U. Tex., 1950. Admitted to Tex. bar, 1949; since practiced in Austin, Tex., individual practice law, 1949-65; asst. atty. gen. State of Tex., 1965—. Home: 3207 Bridle Path Austin TX 78703 Office: Supreme Ct Bldg Austin TX 78701 Tel (512) 475-7501

LOOBY, JAMES GREY, b. Troy, N.Y., July 14, 1923; B.S., Siena Coll., 1949. Admitted to N.Y. bar, 1954; individual practice law, Albany, N.Y., 1954-68; counsel Monroe Abstract and Title Co., Rochester, N.Y., 1968-71, Montgomery Ward, Albany, 1971—. Mem. Albany Dem. Com., Boy Scouts Am. Mem. N.Y., Albany County bar assns., Capital Dist. Trial Lawyers Assn. Office: 28 Essex St Albany NY 12206 Tel (518) 438-4214

LOOMIE, EDWARD RAPHAEL, b. N.Y.C., Aug. 18, 1918; A.B., Columbia, 1940, J.D., 1942. Admitted to N.Y. bar, 1943; individual practice law, N.Y.C., 1946—. Home: 3904 Fulton Ave Seaford NY 11783 Office: 350 Fifth Ave New York City NY 10001 Tel (212) LW 4-3553

LOOMIS, DONALD ALVIN, b. Roseburg, Oreg., Mar. 22, 1941; B.S. in Pharmacy, Oreg. State U., 1965; J.D., Willamette U., 1968. Admitted to Oreg. bar, 1969; asso. firm Jaqua, Wheatley & Gardner, Eugene, Oreg., 1970-73, partner, 1973-74; partner firm Owens & Loomis, Eugene, 1975—. Mem. Lane County Comprehensive Health Planning Com., 1975-76. Mem. Oreg., Am., Lane County bar assns., Am., Oreg. trial lawyers assns., Oreg. Assn. Def. Counsel, Am. Soc. Pharmacy Lawyers, Nat. Health Lawyers Assn. Home: 5419 Donald St Eugene OR 97405 Office: 933 Pearl St Eugene OR 97401 Tel (503) 686-2807

LOOMIS, JOHN ELMER, b. Mauston, Wis., Apr. 25, 1924; A.B., Stanford, 1947, J.D., 1949. Admitted to Calif. bar, 1950; dep. dist. atty. Fresno County (Calif.), 1950-52, asst. county counsel, 1952-54; partner firm Staniford, Harris, Loomis & Home, Fresno, Calif., 1954—; dean, adj. prof. San Joaquin Coll. Law, Fresno, 1971-76. Mem. Am., Calif., Fresno County bar assns. Home: 3865 Wilson St Fresno CA 93704 Office: 426 T W Patterson Bldg Fresno CA 93721 Tel (209) 233-6152

LOONEY, KENNETH HEWELL, b. Birmingham, Ala., Apr. 7, 1946; B.A., Samford U., 1968; J.D., Cumberland Sch. of Law, 1971. Admitted to Ala. bar, 1971, Fla. bar, 1973; asso. firm Rives, Peterson, Pettus, Conway & Burge, Birmingham, 1971-72, firm Jack H. Harrison, Birmingham, 1972-75; individual practice law, Birmingham, 1975—. Mem. Am., Ala., Fla., Birmingham bar assns. Office: 110 Office Park Dr Suite 314 Birmingham AL 35223 Tel (205) 870-9598

LOPES, NICHOLAS FRANCIS, b. N.Y.C., Nov. 7, 1915; B.S., St. John's Coll., 1940; J.D., Fordham U., 1943. Admitted to N.Y. bar, 1943, U.S. Supreme Ct. bar, 1950; D.C. bar, 1956; asso. firm Anderson, Carew, Edelstein & Geraghty, N.Y.C., 1943-44, jr. partner, 1946-48; asso. firm Loughran & Walsh, N.Y.C., 1958-60; individual practice law, New City, N.Y., 1960—; dep. atty. gen. spl. criminal prosecutions, State of N.Y., 1944-45; counsel to Allied Commn. in Italy and chief prosecutor, Am. Mil. Govt., Rome, 1945-46; legal advisor U.S. Embassy, Rome, 1946; trial atty. criminal div. U.S. Dept. of Justice, Washington, 1950-52; spl. asst., criminal div., to atty. gen. of U.S., Washington, 1952; exec. sec., dir. Spl. Commn. Fed. Loyalty Security Program, Washington, 1953-55; asso. counsel Judiciary Com., U.S. Senate, . Washington, 1956, asst. counsel Permanet Investigating Com. and Labor Rackets Com., U.S. Senate, 1956-57; adminstr. Criminal Assigned Counsel Plan, Rockland County, N.Y., 1967—. Commr., Human Rights Commn., Rockland County, N.Y., 1963-67; sec. dir. Legal Aid Soc., Rockland County, 1966-68. Mem. N.Y. State, Am., Fed., Internat., D.C., Rockland County (pres. 1968-69) bar assns., Am. Judicature Soc., Catholic Lawyers Guild of Rockland County (pres. 1967-68). Decorated U.S. Medal of Freedom, 1947, Knight Comdr. Order of the Crown of Italy, 1946, Pontifical Order of Saint Gregory the Great, 1966. Office: Box 91 86 Maple Ave New City NY 10956 Tel (914) 634-5000

LOPEZ, FRANK A., b. Bklyn., Aug. 19, 1929; B.S., Georgetown U.; LL.B., N.Y. U. Admitted to N.Y. bar, 1963; asso. atty. criminal div. Legal Aid Soc., 1963-64; individual practice law, Bklyn., 1964—. Office: 31 Smith St Brooklyn NY 11201 Tel (212) 237-9500

LOPEZ, VINCENT CABRERA, b. Chgo., Nov. 18, 1926; A.B., U. Ill., 1949, J.D., 1958. Admitted to Ill. bar, 1958; trust dept. Continental Ill. Nat. Bank & Trust Co., Chgo., 1958-59; asst. state's atty. Cook County, Ill., 1959-61; asso. firm Hoellen & Willens, Chgo., 1961-62; individual practice law, Chgo., 1962—. Pres., Lawrence Hall Sch. for Boys, Chgo., 1971-76, Ravenswood Conservation Commn., Chgo., 1969-72, Dist. 3 Edn. Council, Chgo., 1971-72; 1st v.p. Truman Coll. Council, City Colls. of Chgo., 1975-76. Mem. Ill. Bar Assn., Am., Ill. Trial lawyers assns., Assn. U.S. Army, Airborne Assn., Civil Affairs Assn., Nat. Guard Assn. U.S., Res. Officer Assn. Office: 10 S LaSalle St Chicago IL 60640 Tel (312) 235-2222

LO PRETE, JAMES HUGH, b. Detroit, Sept. 17, 1929; A.B., U. Mich., 1951; J.D. With Distinction, 1953. Admitted to Mich. bar, 1954; practiced law, Detroit, 1953—; atty. Chrysler Corp., Detroit, 1953; asso. firm Monaghan, Campbell, LoPrete & McDonald and predecessor firms, Detroit, 1954-66, partner, 1966—; dir. Wilson-Crissman Cadillac, Inc., Thomas Hunter Corp., Drake's Batter Mix Co., Durako Paint & Color Corp.; instr. legal writing Wayne State U., 1955-56. Trustee Samuel L. Westerman Found., 1971—, sec., 1971—, treas., 1971—; trustee Presbyn. Village, Detroit, 1970—, mem. exec. com., 1974—. Mem. U. Mich. Alumni Assn. (dir. 1973-75), Am., Detroit, Oakland County bar assns., State Bar Mich. Home: 30110 Hobnail Ct Birmingham MI 48010 Office: Monaghan Campbell LoPrete & McDonald 1411 N Woodward Ave Birmingham MI 48011 Tel (313) 642-5770

LORD, GEOFFREY CRAIG, b. Boston, Apr. 12, 1946; B.A., Gettysburg Coll., 1968; J.D., U. Pa., 1971. Admitted to Pa. bar, 1972; law clerk Supreme Ct. Pa. 1971-72; asso. firm Blank, Rome, Klaus & Comisky, Phila., 1972—. Bd. mgrs. Law Alumni U. Pa. Mem. Phila., Pa. bar assns., Order of the Coif, Phi Beta Kappa. Recipient M.H. Goldstein Meml. prize, 1971, John H. Maurer Meml. prize, 1971. Home: 436 Levering Mill Rd Merion Station PA 19066 Office: 1100 Four Penn Center Plaza Philadelphia PA 19103

LORD, HERBERT MAYHEW, b. Rockland, Maine, Oct. 9, 1917, A.B., Bowdoin Coll., 1939; LL.B., Harvard, 1942. Admitted to N.Y. bar, 1942, since practiced in N.Y.C., specializing admiralty law; mem. firm Burlington, Underwood & Lord. Dir. Am. Trading Transp. Co. Guest lectr, admiralty law Practicing Law Inst., Tulane, Inst. Internat. Studies. Trustee Daycroft Sch. Greenwich, Conn. Mem. Maritime Law Assn. U.S. (sec. 1959, pres. 1974-76, exec. com. 1976—), Am. Bar Assn., Maritime Assn. Port of N.Y., India House Assn. Average Adjusters U.S., Chi Psi. Home: Lake Av Greenwich CT 06830 Office: 25 Broadway New York City NY 10004*

LORD, JOSEPH SIMON, III, b. Phila., May 21, 1912; A.B., U. Pa., 1933, LL.B., 1936; LL.D. (hon.), Suffolk U., 1975. Admitted to Pa. bar, 1936, since practiced in Phila.; law clk. Common Pleas Ct. No. 4, 1936-37; asso. firm Schnader & Lewis, 1937-46; partner firm Richter, Lord & Levy, 1946-61; U.S. atty. Eastern Dist. Pa., 1961; judge U.S. Dist. Ct., Eastern Dist. Pa., 1961—, chief judge, 1971—. Commr., Del. River Port Authority, Phila., 1961. Fellow Internat. Acad. Trial Lawyers; mem. Am., Fed., Pa., Phila. bar assns., Am. Law Inst. (adv. com., div. jurisdiction between state and fed. cts.). Home: 3011 Foxx Ln Philadelphia PA 19144 Office: US Courthouse 601 Market St Philadelphia PA 19106 Tel (215) 597-4361

LORD, RICHARD ALBERT, b. Brunswick, Maine, Dec. 23, 1935; B.A., U. Maine, 1962, LL.B., 1962. Admitted to Maine bar, 1965; practice law, Brunswick. Selectman, Town of Brunswick, 1967-69, councilman, 1970-71. Mem. Maine Bar Assn., Maine Trial Lawyers Assn., Phi Beta Kappa, Phi Kappa Phi. Office: 56 Maine St Brunswick ME 04011 Tel (207) 729-9981

LORE, IRVING ALLAN, b. Milw., Feb. 28, 1916; B.A. with honors, U. Wis., Madison, 1935, J.D. with honors (Burr W. Jones Law scholar), 1937. Admitted to Wis. bar, 1937, U.S. Supreme Ct. bar, 1942; individual practice law, Milw., 1937-43, 45—; mgmt. trustee Greater Milw. Hotel and Restaurant Industry Health and Welfare Fund, 1959—. Bd. dirs. Milw. Found., 1971-74; trustee Walter Schroeder Scholarship Fund, Marquette U., 1962—, Congregation Emanu El B'ne Jeshurun-Milw., 1970—, Mt. Sinai Med. Center, Milw., 1971—; bd. dirs. Milw. Sch. Engring., 1966—, Milw. Jewish Home for Aged, 1967—, United Way of Greater Milw., 1972—; chmn. profl. div. Greater Milw. United Fund Campaigns, 1971-72. Mem. State Bar Wis., Milw., Am. bar assns., Am. Judicature Soc., Wis. Acad. Trial Lawyers, Assn. Trial Lawyers Am., Order of Coif. Honored for distinguished service in field of human relations Wis. chpt. NCCJ, 1976; editor Wis. Law Rev., 1935-37, contbr. articles, 1935—. Home: 1610 N Prospect Ave Milwaukee WI 53202 Office: 161 W Wisconsin Ave Milwaukee WI 53203 Tel (414) 272-3619

LORE, KURT WILLIAM, b. Bklyn., July 21, 1914; B.A., Bklyn. Coll., 1936; LL.B., Columbia, 1939. Admitted to N.Y. State bar, 1939; asso. firm Smart & Farbach, N.Y.C., 1946-51; asso. firm Thacher, Proffitt & Wood, 1952-57, partner, 1957—; lectr. Columbia, 1970—, Practicing Law Inst., Am. Bar Assn.-Am. Law Inst., 1963—. Mem. Am., N.Y. State, N.Y. County, N.Y.C. bar assns. Home: 10 Plaza St Brooklyn NY 11238 Office: 40 Wall St New York City NY 10005 Tel (212) 483-5938

LORE, MARTIN MAXWELL, b. Milw., June 13, 1914; B.A., U. Wis., 1934, LL.B., 1936; LL.M., Harvard, 1937; B.C.S., Strayer Coll. Accountancy, 1939. Admitted to Wis. bar, 1936, N.Y. State bar, 1946, D.C. bar, 1947; asso. firm Rubin, Zabel & Ruppa, Milw., 1936-37; spl. atty. Office of Undersec. Treasury, Washington, 1937-38; spl. atty. office chief counsel IRS, Washington, 1938-40, trial counsel New Eng. div. tech. staff, Boston, 1940-42, N.Y. div., N.Y.C., 1942-47, tax counsel Newark, 1947-48; individual practice law, N.Y.C., 1948-72; mem. firm Zissu Lore Halper & Robson, N.Y.C., 1972-76, counsel, 1976—; lectr. in field; tax cons. Med. Econs.; pres., dir. Fed. Tax Forum, Inc. Mem. Fed., N.Y. State bar assns., Assn. Bar City N.Y., New York County Lawyers Assn., Am. Inst. C.P.A.'s, Estate Planning Council N.Y.C., Inc. (pres., dir.). Author: The Administration of the Federal Income Tax Through the U.S. Bd. of Tax Appeals, 1937; How to Win a Tax Case, 1955; Thin Capitalization, 1958; chmn. bd. editors: How to Work with the Internal Revenue Code of 1954, 1954; co-editor Jour. Taxation, 1954—. Home: 46 Broome Ave Atlantic Beach NY 11509 Office: 450 Park Ave New York City NY 10022 Tel (212) 371-3900

LORING, CHARLES ALEXIS, b. San Bernardino, Calif., June 27, 1915; student U. Redland, 1933-35, LL.D., 1962; LL.B., U. Calif. Hastings Coll. Law, San Francisco, 1938, J.D., 1938. Admitted to Calif. bar, 1938, U.S. Supreme Ct. bar, 1953; practice in Los Angeles, 1938-59; judge Calif. Superior Ct., 1959—, asst. presiding judge, 1969-70, presiding judge, 1971-72; justice pro tem Calif. Ct. Appeals, 2d Appellate Dist., 1973-75. Bd. dirs. Hastings Coll. Law Nat. Coll. Advocacy, 1971-76, Los Angeles unit Shriners Hosp. for Crippled Children, 1973-76; trustee U. Redlands, 1974-76. Mem. Hastings Coll. Law (pres. 1956), U. Redlands (pres. 1975) alumni assns., Los Angeles County Bar Assn. (trustee 1955-57). Named Man of Yr., Hastings Coll. Law, 1971, Trial Judge of Yr., Los Angeles County Trial Lawyers, 1971. Office: 111 N Hill St Los Angeles CA 90012 Tel (213) 974-5670

LORIO, KATHRYN GEORGIA VENTURATOS, b. Pitts., Feb. 15, 1949; B.A. magna cum laude, Tulane U., 1970; J.D., Loyola U. of South, 1973. Admitted to La. bar, 1973; asso. firm Deutsch, Kerrigan & Stiles, New Orleans, 1973-76; asst. prof. law Loyola U. of South, 1976—. Pres. internat. jr. aux. Am. Hellenic Ednl. Progressive Assn., 1969-70. Mem. Am., La. bar assns., Phi Beta Kappa, Phi Delta Phi. Recipient Am. Jurisprudence awards in criminal law and introduction to law, Corpus Juris Secundum award, 1971. Home: 1212 Marengo St New Orleans LA 70115 Office: Loyola U Sch Law New Orleans LA 70118 Tel (504) 865-2277

LORITZ, RICHARD FRANCIS, b. Chgo., June 13, 1941; B.A., Ill. Benedictine Coll., 1962; LL.B., DePaul U., 1965, J.D., 1968. Admitted to Ill. bar, 1966, U.S. Supreme Ct. bar, 1966; individual practice law, Chgo. and Oak Lawn, Ill., 1966—. Bd. dirs. Ill. Benedictine Coll. Assn., 1964-74. Mem. Ill. Bar Assn., SW Suburban Builders Assn., Phi Alpha Delta. Editor: DePaul Law Rev., 1965. Author: Effect of Intent on Liability under Illinois Structural Work Act, 1965; also articles in profl. jours. Office: 6305 W 95th St Oak Lawn IL 60453 Tel (312) 423-7494

LOSCH, LARRY ELSWORTH, lawyer; b. Richwood, W.Va., Apr. 14, 1945; B.S., W.Va. Inst. Tech., 1967; J.D., W.Va. U., 1970. Admitted to W.Va. bar, 1970. Partner, law firm Billheimer & Losch, Montgomery, W.Va., 1971-76; pres. Porta-Sign Advt. Inc., Quinwood, W.Va., 1969-72; pres. Armstrong Realty Co., Montgomery, W.Va., 1973—; exec. v.p. Skaggs Enterprises Inc., Montgomery, 1976; treas. Ellsworth Coal Co., Charlton Heights, W.Va., 1975—. Mem. Am., W.Va. bar assns., W.Va. Trial Lawyers Assn., W.Va. State Bar, Montgomery Area Jaycees (external v.p. 1972, internal v.p. 1976). Home and Office: Box 26 Charlton Heights WV 25040

LOSCH, ROBERT EDWARD, b. Racine, Wis., July 19, 1926; B.S., Marquette U., 1949; J.D., Georgetown U., 1953. Admitted to Wis. bar, 1953, D.C. bar, 1954; staff mem. exec. office Sec. of Navy, Washington, D.C., 1953-59; partner firm McNutt, Dudley, Easterwood & Losch, Washington, D.C., 1959—. Mem. Am., D.C., Wis., Fed. bar assns., Lawyers Literary Club (founder). Home: 2700 Calvert St Washington DC 20008 Office: 910 17th St NW Washington DC 20006 Tel (202) 296-4222

LOSER, JOE CARLTON, JR., b. Nashville, June 16, 1932; student Vanderbilt U., 1952-55; LL.B., YMCA Night Law Sch., Nashville, 1959, J.D., 1972. Admitted to Tenn. bar, 1959, U.S. Supreme Ct. bar, 1960; practiced in Nashville, 1959-65; judge Davidson County (Tenn.) Gen. Sessions Ct., 1966-69, Tenn. Circuit Ct., 10th Jud. Circuit, 1969—, presiding judge, 1972-75; mem. Tenn. Council on State-Fed. Relations, 1975—. Fellow Internat. Acad. Trial Judges; mem. Am., Tenn., Nashville bar assns., Nat. Conf. State Trial Judges, Am. Judicature Soc. Home: 5894 E Ashland Dr Nashville TN 37215 Office: 510 Met Courthouse Nashville TN 37201 Tel (615) 259-6165

LOTRIDGE, ELLOYD EROLD, b. Judsonia, Ark., Aug. 12, 1941; B.A., Trinity U., San Antonio, 1963; J.D., U. Tex., 1969; LL.M., George Washington U., 1972. Admitted to Tex. bar, 1969, Md. bar, 1970, U.S. Supreme Ct. bar, 1974; atty. ICC, Washington, 1969-70; atty. Legal Aid Bur., Inc., Cherry Hill, Md., 1970-71, chief atty., Annapolis, Md., 1971-74, dep. dir., Balt., 1974—. Mem. Tex., Md., Anne Arundal County bar assns. Home: Box 42 Grays Rd Lothian MD 20820 Office: 341 W Calvert St Baltimore MD 21202 Tel (301) 727-4580

LOTTERHOS, JULIUS LIEB, JR., b. Crystal Springs, Miss., Dec. 8, 1918; student Copiah-Lincoln Jr. Coll., 1937-38, U. Miss., 1938-39; LL.B., Jackson Sch. Law, 1949. Admitted to Miss. bar, 1949; supr. bus. enterprises div. for blind Miss. Dept. Pub. Welfare, Jackson, 1947-51; partner firm Henley, Lotterhos & Bennett, Hazlehurst, Miss., 1951—; atty. Copiah County (Miss.) Bd. Suprs., 1951—, City of Crystal Springs, 1957-69; spl. judge Miss. Circuit Ct., 14th Jud. Circuit, 1968-71; mem. Bd. Bar Commrs., 1966-67. Trustee Belhaven Coll., 1965—, pres., 1969-72; trustee Crystal Springs Schs. Mem. Am., Miss. State, Copiah County bar assns., Am. Judicature Soc., Miss. Trial Lawyers Assn., Am. Trial Lawyers Assn., Am. Soc. Hosp. Attys., Am. Soc. Law and Medicine, Comml. Law League Am. (pres. So. dist. 1970-71), Assn. Attys. for Bds. of Suprs. (pres. 1976), Nat. Assn. Civil Attys. for Counties, Sigma Delta Kappa. Recipient award for spl. service to soil and water conservation of Copiah County Soil Conservation Dist., 1974. Home: Route 2 PO Box 435 Crystal Springs MS 39059 Office: PO Box 509 Hazlehurst MS 39083 Tel (601) 894-1281

LOTTINGER, MORRIS ALBERT, JR., b. Houma, La., Aug. 12, 1937; B.A., Nicholls State U., 1962; J.D., La. State U., 1965. Admitted to La. bar, 1965; partner firm Lottinger & Lottinger, Houma, 1965-75; judge La. Ct. of Appeal, 1st Circuit, 1975—; mem. La. Ho. of Reps., 1970-75. Mem. Am., La. bar assns. Home: 109 Burkwall Dr Houma LA 70360 Office: PO Box 1268 Houma LA 70361 Tel (504) 868-4660

LOTZ, ARTHUR MERRILL, b. Bloomington, Ind., May 3, 1931; B.S., Manchester Coll., 1962; J.D., Ind. U., 1965. Admitted to Ind. bar, 1965; individual practice law, Bloomington. Bd. dirs. Salvation Army. Mem. Am., Ind. bar assns. Home: 4319 Sheffield Dr Bloomington IN 47401 Tel (812) 336-5048

LOUCKS, RICHARD RAY, b. Falls City, Nebr., Dec. 26, 1930; B.A., U. Wash., 1952, LL.B., 1956. Admitted to Wash. bar, 1956; individual practice law, Pullman, Wash., 1956—; lectr. law Wash. State U., 1956-70. Mem. Am. Trial Lawyers Assn. Contbr. articles to profl. jours. Home: NE 1510 Upper Dr Pullman WA 99163 Office: NW 715 Ritchie St Pullman WA 99163 Tel (509) 332-1176

LOUDEN, JOHN ROLLAND, b. Akron, Ohio, Nov. 10, 1940; B.S., Ohio State U., 1964; J.D., Capital U., 1969. Admitted to Ohio bar, 1969; partner firm Bainter Clay Louden & McDowell, Columbus, Ohio, 1969-70; asso. firm Hite & Hite, Utica, Ohio, 1970-72; staff Office of Atty. Gen., State of Ohio, 1972-73; asso. Harry Lewis, Columbus, 1973-74; individual practice law, Columbus, 1974—; hearing examiner Ohio Dept. Health, 1974—, Ohio Bd. Nursing Home Examiners, 1975—. Mem. Am., Ohio, Columbus bar assns. Home: 3328 Leighton Rd Columbus OH 43221 Office: 4041 N High St Columbus OH 43214 Tel (614) 268-1213

LOUDEN, WILLIAM BRUCE, b. Fairfield, Iowa, May 14, 1938; B.A. in Polit. Sci., U. Fla., 1961, J.D., 1963. Admitted to Fla. bar, 1963, Conn. bar, 1970, U.S. 2d Circuit Ct. Appeals bar, 1971, U.S. Supreme Ct. bar, 1971. Asso. firm Holland & Knight, Bartow and Lakeland, Fla., 1963-66, partner, 1967-69; asso. firm Ribicoff & Kotkin, Hartford, Conn., 1970-71, partner, 1971—; cooperating atty. ACLU, 1971—. Bd. dirs. United Fund, Lakeland, 1968, Human Relations Council, Lakeland, 1968-69, YMCA, West Hartford, 1975—; trustee Webber Coll., 1968-71. Mem. Am. (standing com. on profl. discipline 1973—), Conn., Fla. bar assns., World Assn. Lawyers, Order of Coif, Phi Beta Kappa, Sigma Chi, Phi Delta Phi. Named The Outstanding Young Man of Lakeland, Fla., 1969; editor-in-chief U. Fla. Law Rev., 1963. Home: 11 Cascade Rd West Hartford CT 06117 Office: 799 Main St Hartford CT 06103 Tel (203) 527-0781

LOUGHEAD, LEO VINCENT, b. Cleve., Aug. 16, 1916; B.B.A., Western Reserve U., 1950; LL.B., Cleve. Marshall Law Sch., 1955; J.D., Cleve. State U. 1968. Admitted to Ohio bar, 1955; real estate officer Cin. Regional Office U.S. Post Office, 1962-71; atty.-adv. U.S. Army Corps Engrs., Huntington, W.Va., 1971; mem. firm Dottore, Whitmer, Collins & Loughead, Cleve., 1972—; instr. real estate law Dyke Coll., 1974, Cuyahoga Community Coll., 1972—. Chmn. Fed. Safety Council, 1956-60; coordinator Citizens Ednl. Freedom, Cleve., 1964. Mem. Cuyahoga County Bar assn., Cleve. Area Bd. Realtors, Delta Theta Phi. Office: Park Bldg 140 Piblic Square Cleveland OH 44114 Tel (216) 351-7859

LOUGHMAN, BERNARD JOHN, SR., b. Aspen, Colo., May 17, 1899; LL.B., U. Colo., 1929, J.D., 1968. Admitted to Calif. bar, 1930; individual practice law, Ventura, Calif., 1930—; rent dir. and atty. Santa Barbara and Ventura County (Calif.), 1942-44; inheritance tax appraiser State of Calif., 1959-66. Bd. dirs. Ventura Housing Authority, 1949-55; mem. bd. appeals bldg. code, Ventura, 1954-58. Home: 358 N Catalina St Ventura CA 93003 Office: 675 E Main St Ventura CA 93001 Tel (805) 648-2781

LOUGHRIDGE, GREGORY D., b. South Bend, Ind., Apr. 7, 1948; A.B. in Polit. Sci., Ind. U., 1970; J.D., U. Notre Dame, 1973. Admitted to Ind. bar, 1973, with Assos. Corp. N.Am., South Bend, 1972-73; staff Legal Aid Soc. St. Joseph County, South Bend, 1973-76; individual practice law, South Bend, 1976—; mem. Ind. Housing Coalition, Indpls., 1973—. Mem. St. Joseph County, Ind. State bar assns. Office: 501 Lafayette Bldg 115 Lafayette Blvd South Bend IN 46601 Tel (219) 289-9228

LOUIS, FRANK ALAN, b. Bklyn., Dec. 17, 1947; A.B. cum laude, Bklyn. Coll., 1970; J.D., Rutgers U., 1973. Admitted to N.J. bar, 1973; asso. Wilbert J. Martin, Toms River, N.J., Alan J. Pogarsky, Toms River; municipal prosecutor Jackson Twp.; asst. prosecutor Ocean County (N.J.); law clk. to Hon. Henry A. Wiley. Mem. Am., N.J., Ocean County bar assns. Office: 250 Washington St Toms River NJ 08753 Tel (201) 349-0600

LOUIS, ROBERT STEVENSON, b. Santa Cruz, Calif., Dec. 23, 1935; A.B., Antelope Valley Coll., Lancaster, Calif., 1959; J.D., Hastings Coll. Law, U. Calif., 1963. Admitted to Calif. bar, 1964; dep. dist. atty. Stanislaus County (Calif.), Modesto, 1964-65; partner firm Aguilar and Louis, Modesto, 1965—. Mem. Calif. Bar Assn. (chmn. adminstrv. com. 1974-75). Home: 5848 Oakdale Rd Modesto CA 95355 Office: 1630 I St Modesto CA 95354 Tel (209) 524-4807

LOUISON, MELVIN SANFORD, b. New Bedford, Mass., July 14, 1928; LL.B. cum laude, Suffolk U., 1950. Admitted to Mass. bar, 1952, U.S. Supreme Ct. bar, 1959; partner firms Louison and Louison, Taunton, Mass., 1951-75, Louison and Cohen, Brockton, Mass., 1975—; dir. Mass. Bank & Trust Co.; mem. faculty Massoit Community Coll., 1967—, mem. adv. bd., 1974—; lectr. seminars, schs. Chmn. Better Brockton Com., 1960-61; mem. Brockton Zoning Bd. Appeals, 1962-66; chmn. Brockton Planning Bd., 1961-73. Mem. Am., Mass., Plymouth County (Mass.) bar assns., Am. Trial Lawyers Assn., Nat. Assn. Def. Lawyers in Criminal Cases, Mass. Assn. Criminal Def. Lawyers. Recipient Law Day award Order of Eagles, 1973. Home: 467 W Elm St Brockton MA 02401 Office: 495 Westgate Dr Brockton MA 02401 Tel (617) 583-8811

LOURIE, ALAN DAVID, b. Boston, Jan. 13, 1935; A.B., Harvard, 1956; M.S., U. Wis., 1958; Ph.D., U. Pa., 1965; J.D., Temple U., 1970. Admitted to Pa. bar, 1970; chemist Monsanto Co., St. Louis, 1957-59; lit. scientist, chemist, patent agt. Wyeth Labs., Radnor, Pa., 1959-64; with Smithkline Corp., Phila., 1964—, successively as patent agt., atty., asst. dir. corp. patents, dir. corp. patents, asst. gen. counsel. Mem. Am. Bar Assn., Am., Phila. Patent Law Assn., Am. Chem. Soc. Home: 1549 Willowbrook Ln Villanova PA 19085 Office: 1500 Spring Garden St Philadelphia PA 19101 Tel (215) 854-5189

LOURIE, ISADORE EDWARD, b. St. George, S.C., Aug. 4, 1932; B.A., U. S.C., 1956, LL.B., 1956. Admitted to S.C. bar, 1956; asso. firm Fulmer & Barnes, Columbia, S.C., 1956-57; partner Lourie, Drain, Airlee & Swerling, Columbia, 1957—; adminstr., legal asst. to ways and means com. S.C. Ho. of Reps., 1959-63, mem. Ho. of Reps., 1964-72; mem. S.C. Senate, 1973—. Counsel, Happy Time Center Mental Retarded Children, 1965; pres. Richland County Cancer Soc., 1959-60. Mem. S.C., Am. bar assns., Am. Trial Lawyers Assn. Named Young Man of Year City Columbia, 1959. Home: 6308 Westshore Rd Columbia SC 29206 Office: 1224 Pickens St Columbia SC 29201 Tel (803) 799-9805

LOVE, FRANCIS J., b. Harrison County, Ohio; A.B., Bethany Coll., 1924; J.D., W.Va. U., 1932. Admitted to W.Va. bar, 1932. Admitted to W.Va. bar; individual practice, Wheeling, W.Va.; mem. 80th Congress from 1st dist. W.Va. Author: Mend Your English, 1969. Home: 1153 National Rd Wheeling WV 26003

LOVE, FRANK, JR., b. Montgomery, W.Va., July 20, 1927; B.S., Washington & Lee U., 1950, LL.B., 1951. Admitted to Ga. bar, 1952, also U.S. Dist. Ct. Ga., U.S. Dist. Ct. N.C. bar, U.S. Ct. Appeals 5th Circuit bar, U.S. Ct. Appeals 4th Circuit bar; since practiced in Atlanta; asso. firm Powell, Goldstein, Frazer & Murphy, 1951-61, partner, 1961—. Fellow Am. Coll. Trial Lawyers; mem. Am., Ga., Atlanta bar assns., Lawyers Club Atlanta, Ga. Def. Lawyers Assn., Old War Horse Lawyers Club, Am. Judicature Soc. Home: 985 Foxcroft Rd Atlanta GA 30327 Office: 1100 Citizens & Southern Bank Bldg Atlanta GA 30303 Tel (404) 521-1900

LOVE, JOHN CLYDE, b. Detroit, Feb. 12, 1940; B.A., Johns Hopkins, 1962; LL.B., U. Md., 1968. Admitted to Md. bar, 1968; asso. mem. firm Cameron and Reed, Bel Air, Md., 1969-72, partner, 1972—. Mem. Am., Md., Harford County bar assns. Home: Green Oak Farm Kingsville MD 21087 Office: 30 Office St Bel Air MD 21014

LOVE, MELVIN VALESS, b. Dee, Oreg., Oct. 29, 1916; student Washington State U., 1938-41; J.D., U. Wash., 1952. Admitted to Wash. bar, 1952; asso. firm Swett & Crawford, Seattle, 1949-53, Karr, Tuttle & Campbell, Seattle, 1953-56; individual practice law, Bellevue, Wash., 1956-62; judge Municipal Ct., justice of peace, Bellevue, 1959-63; judge Bellevue Dist. Ct., 1963—. Mem. Bellevue City Council, 1953-58, mayor, 1954-56; mem. exec. com. Puget Sound Regional Planning Council, 1954-65; chmn., pres. Assn. Valley Cities, 1954-60; mem. Gov.'s Com. on Met. Problems, State Com. on Air Pollution. Mem. Wash. State, Seattle-King County, E. King County bar assns., Wash. State Magistrates Assn., Am. Judges Assn. Contbr. articles to legal jours. Home: 10431 S E 23d St Bellevue WA 98004

Office: Suite 110 Bldg 4 Benaroya Park Bellevue WA 98005 Tel (206) 454-4937

LOVE, MURRAY S., b. Pitts., Aug. 10, 1928; B.A., U. Pitts., 1948, J.D., 1954. Admitted to Pa. bar, 1955, U.S. Supreme Ct. bar, 1968; partner firm Sikov & Love, Pitts., 1957—; staff judge adv. JAGC, USAF, 1955-57; lectr. U. Pitts., Duquesne U., Hebrew U., U. Madrid, also profl. courses. Campaign worker Heart Fund, 1972-73; v.p. Tri-State div. Jewish Nat. Fund, 1973—; v.p. Congregation Beth Shalom, 1973-75; class agt. alumni giving fund U. Pitts. Law Sch.; life trustee Hebrew Free Loan Assn. Pitts. Mem. Am., Pa., Allegheny County bar assns., Allegheny County Acad. Trial Lawyers (past gov.), Assn. Trial Lawyers of Am. (pres. Western Pa. chpt. 1955-56, Pa. state committeeman 1969-74, gov. 3d circuit 1974-77), Pa. Trial Lawyers Assn. (pres. 1968-69) Am. Judicature Soc., Am. Arbitration Assn. (Pitts. accident claims adv. council), Pa. Bar Inst. (dir. 1976—), U. Pitts. Varsity Lettermen Club (pres. 1972-73), Tau Epsilon Rho, Sigma Alpha Mu, Kappa Kappa Psi. Contbr. articles to legal jours. Home: 1537 S Negley Ave Pittsburgh PA 15217 Office: 600 Plaza Bldg Pittsburgh PA 15219 Tel (412) 261-4202

LOVE, PAUL ALAN, b. Pitts., Aug. 9, 1939; B.S., U. Pitts., 1960; J.D., Dickinson Sch., Carlisle, Pa., 1963; LL.M., N.Y. U., 1964. Admitted to Pa. Supreme Ct. bar, 1964, U.S. Supreme Ct. bar, 1968; individual practice law, Pitts., 1964-75; partner firm DeCello, Manifesto, Doherty & Love, Pitts., 1976—. Bd. dirs. Hebrew Free Loan, Pitts., 1970—, Community Day Sch., Pitts., 1975—. Mem. Am., Pa., Allegheny County bar assns. Contbr. articles in field to profl. jour. Home: 2760 Mount Royal Rd Pittsburgh PA 15217 Office: Suite 200 Lawyers Bldg Pittsburgh PA 15219 Tel (412) 471-8893

LOVEJOY, ROBERT CARR, b. Janesville, Wis., Jan. 20, 1917; B.A., Yale, 1939; J.D., U. Mich., 1942. Admitted to Wis. bar, 1942; partner firm Nowlan, Mouat, Lovejoy, Wood & Cripe, and predecessors, Janesville, 1945—; instr. U. Wis. Law Sch., 1971-77. Mem. Am., 7th Jud. Circuit, Milw., Wis., Rock County bar assns., Am. Coll. Probate Counsel, Am. Judicature Soc., Legal Aid and Defenders Assn. Home: 3195 Crystal Springs Rd Janesvill WI 53545 Office: 17 N Franklin St Janesville WI 53545 Tel (608) 756-3621

LOVELACE, RICHARD MAXWELL, b. Spokane, Wash., Mar. 26, 1944; B.A., U. Tex., El Paso, 1966; J.D., U. Tex., Austin, 1970. Admitted to Tex. bar, 1969; asso. county atty. El Paso County (Tex.), 1970-71; individual practice law, El Paso, 1971—. Mem. El Paso Trial Lawyers Assn., Tex. Criminal Def. Lawyers Assn., Young Lawyers Assn. El Paso. Office: 744 Southwest Center El Paso TX 79901 Tel (915) 544-1744

LOVELAND, JOSEPH ALBERT, JR., b. Forest Hills, N.Y., Mar. 18, 1932; A.B., U. Pa., 1956; LL.B., N.Y. U., 1959. Admitted to N.Y. State bar, 1959, Calif. bar, 1966, Fla. bar, 1974; asso. firm Cravath, Swaine & Moore, N.Y.C., 1959-65; partner firm Kindel & Anderson, Los Angeles, 1965-68, Agnew, Miller & Carlson, Los Angeles, 1968-70; prin. Troy, Malin & Loveland, Los Angeles, 1970—; lectr. continuing edn. program Calif. Bar. Mem. Am., Los Angeles County bar assns., Calif. State Bar. Pomeroy scholar, 1957-59; mng. editor N.Y. U. Law Rev., 1958-59. Home: 2 Ketch St Marina del Rey CA 90291 Office: 1801 Century Park E Los Angeles CA 90017 Tel (213) 553-4441

LOVELL, ROBERT HAROLD, b. San Antonio, Dec. 5, 1944; B.S. in Marine Transp., Tex. A. and M. U., 1967; J.D., U. Tex., 1972. Admitted to Tex. bar, 1972; counsel El Paso Natural Gas Co., 1972-73, sr. counsel, Houston, 1973-74; asst. prin. counsel El Paso LNG Co., Houston, 1975—. Mem. Am., Houston bar assns., Maritime Law Assn. U.S., Phi Delta Phi. Office: El Paso LNG Co 2727 Allen Pkwy Houston TX 77019 Tel (713) 527-0421

LOVEMAN, EDWARD HERBERT, b. New Brunswick, N.J., Nov. 21, 1926; B.M.E., Bklyn. Poly. Inst., 1951; LL.B., Bklyn. Law Sch., 1961. Admitted to N.Y. bar, 1962, U.S. Patent Office bar, 1963, U.S. Ct. Custom and Patent Appeals bar, 1968; patent atty. Sperry Gyroscope Co., Great Neck, N.Y., 1959-65, Royal Typewriter Co., Hartford, Conn., 1965-66, Gen. Analine & Film Corp., N.Y.C., 1966-67; individual practice law, Huntington Station, N.Y., 1968—. Comdr., United Vets. Council of Lindenhurst (N.Y.), 1972, 76. Mem. Am., N.Y. State, Suffolk County bar assns., N.Y. Patent Law Assn. Home: PO Box 155 Great River NY 11739 Office: 789 Walt Whitman Rd Huntington Station NY 11746 Tel (516) 421-1122

LOVERDE, FRANK SANTO, b. Chgo., Mar. 5, 1905; LL.B., DePaul U., 1930. Admitted to Ill. bar, 1930; asst. corp. counsel, Chgo., 1930-31; 1st asst. referee Referee Traffic Ct., City of Chgo., 1959-64; magistrate Circuit Ct. Cook County, 1964-70, asso. judge, 1970—. Mem. Am. Bar Assn., Justinian Soc., Am. Judicature Soc. Home: 1310 Ritchie Ct Chicago IL 60610 Office: Civic Center Randolph and Clark Sts Chicago IL 60602 Tel (312) 443-8231

LOVETT, JAMES OLAN, b. Gladewater, Tex., Jan. 1, 1933; B.S., Sam Houston State U., 1959; J.D., South Tex. Coll. Law, 1970. Admitted to Tex. bar; chief criminal div. Houston Legal Found., 1971-72, chief div. civil litigation, 1972-73; partner firm Jones & Lovett, Tomball, Tex., 1973—; judge Tomball Municipal Ct., 1975—; legal profession rep. to Houston and Harris County Drug Abuse Assn., 1971-72, Pre-release program Tex. Prison System, 1972-73. Pres. Tomball chpt. Nat. Little League Baseball Inc., 1973-74; bd. dirs. Bapt. Child Care Centers, 1974, Tomball Hosp. Authority, 1972-76, Tomball C. of C., 1973-76. Mem. Am. Judges Assn., Am., Tex., Houston bar assns. Home: 219 Anna St Tomball TX 77375 Office: 200 N Cherry St Tomball TX 77375 Tel (713) 351-5636

LOVETT, LEE GILSON, b. Takoma Park, Md., Oct. 31, 1933; A.B., Principia Coll., 1955; LL.B., George Washington U., 1958. Admitted to Md. bar, 1958, D.C. bar, 1959; mem. firm Lovett and Lovett, Washington, 1960-63, firm Booth and Lovett, Washington, 1964-67, firm Pittman Lovett Ford and Hennessey, Washington, 1968—. Pres., Bullis Preparater Sch. Fathers' Club, 1970-72, Georgetown Hill and Beverly Farms PTAs, 1965, 67; chmn. Inter-community Council Citizens' Assns., Potomac, Md., 1968; gen. counsel to dist. assn. Approved Youth Clubs, Washington, 1965-68. Mem. Am., Md., FCC bar assns., Cable Pioneers Club. Contbr. articles to legal publs.; author: Interpreting FCC Broadcast Rules and Regulations, 1966, 2d edit., 1968, 3d edit., 1972. Office: 1819 H St NW Washington DC 20006 Tel (202) 293-7400

LOW, HARRY WILLIAM, b. Oakdale, Calif., Mar. 12, 1931; A.B., U. Calif., Berkeley, 1952, LL.B., 1955. Admitted to Calif. bar, 1955; teaching asso. U. Calif. at Berkeley Law Sch., 1955-56; dep. atty. gen. Calif. Dept. Justice, San Francisco, 1956-66; commr. Workmen's Compensation Commn., San Francisco, 1966; judge San Francisco Municipal Ct., 1966-74, presiding judge, 1972-73; judge Calif. Superior Ct., 1974—; mem. Calif. Council Criminal Justice, Calif. Jud. Planning Council. Chmn. bd. Edn. Center for Chinese, San Francisco, 1969—; mem. grand bd. Chinese Am. Citizens Alliance, 1970—, pres., 1975-76; commr. San Francisco Study on Schs., 1974-76; bd. dirs. Salesian Boys Club, San Francisco, NCCJ, Chinese Cultural Found., San Francisco, NE Med. Service Center of Chinatown-North Beach, San Francisco, Greater Chinatown Service Assn., San Francisco, On Lok Health Center for Aged, San Francisco, USO; trustee CORO Found., San Francisco, Grad. Theol. Union, Community Coll. Found., San Francisco. Mem. Calif. Conf. Judges (exec. bd., editor Cts. Commentary 1973-76), Am. Judges' Assn., Am. Judicature Soc., San Francisco, Calif. (research editor Law in Action and Law in the News 1958—), Am. bar assns., Queens Bench, Phi Alpha Delta. Contbr. articles to profl. publs. Tel (415) 558-3462

LOWE, DONALD VEBJORN, b. N.Platte, Nebr., June 29, 1915; student Midland Coll., 1933-35; J.D., U. Nebr., 1939. Admitted to Nebr. bar, 1939; city atty. N.Platte, 1943-45, 49-51; served to lt. JAGC, U.S. Army, 1945-47; dep. county atty. Lincoln County (Nebr.), 1947-75; individual practice law, N.Platte, 1939—; U.S. Commr., 1943-45. Mem. Nebr. State, Western Nebr., Lincoln County bar assns. Home: 918 Cedarberry Rd North Platte NE 69101 Office: 117 W 4th St North Platte NE 69101 Tel (308) 532-3911

LOWE, GEORGE ALEXANDER, b. Osawatomie, Kans., Dec. 26, 1924; A.B., U. Kans., 1948, LL.B., 1950. Admitted to Kans. bar, 1950; asst. county atty. Johnson County (Kans.), 1950-53; partner firm Lowe, Lowe & Lowe, Olathe, Kans., 1953-75, Lowe, Terry & Roberts, Olathe, 1975—; mem. Kans. Senate, 1963-65; mem. nominating commn. Kans. Supreme Ct., 1965-75; dir. 1st Nat. Bank Olathe. Pres. bd. dirs. Olathe Community Hosp., 1972-73. Fellow Am. Coll. Trial Lawyers; mem. Am. Judicature Soc., Internat. Soc. Barristers, U. Kans. Law Soc. (bd. govs., pres. 1973-74). Office: Lowe Terry & Roberts 110 W Loula St PO Box 588 Olathe KS 66061 Tel (913) 782-0422

LOWE, HERBERT BYRON, b. Decatur, Ill., June 18, 1903; B.S. in Accounting, U. Ill., 1926, LL.B., 1928. Admitted to Ill. bar, 1928, Ind. bar, 1932; individual practice law, South Bend, Ind., 1932-42, Decatur, 1942-77 partner firm Denz, Lowe & Moore, Decatur, 1977—. Mem. Ill., Macon County (pres. 1966) bar assns. Home: 3107 Lake Bluff Dr Decatur IL 62521 Office: 1055 Citizens Bldg PO Box 1527 Decatur IL 62525 Tel (217) 429-5323

LOWE, HUGH SHELLY, b. Floresville, Tex., Jan. 12, 1942; B.A., U. Tex., Austin, 1963, J.D. with high honors, 1971. Admitted to Tex. bar, 1972; law asso. Sch. Law, U. Calif., Berkeley, 1971-72; lectr. Sch. Law, U. Tex., Austin, 1972—; individual practice law, Austin, 1972—. Bd. dirs. Central Tex. ACLU, 1975—. Mem. Am., Tex., Travis County, Travis County Jr. bar assns., First Amendment Lawyers Assn., Am. Trial Lawyers Assn., Tex. Criminal Def. Lawyers Assn., Order of Coif, Chancellors. Asso. edito Tex. Law Rev., 1970-71. Home: 405 Academy St Austin TX 78704 Office: 508 W 12th St Austin TX 78701 Tel (512) 478-7463

LOWE, IRA MELVIN, b. Boston, Mar. 5, 1924; J.D., George Washington U., 1948. Admitted to D.C. bar, 1949, N.Y. bar, 1967; individual practice law, Washington, 1949—. Mem. Am. Bar Assn., Assn. Trial Attys. Home: Flat Point Farm West Tisbury MA 02575 Office: 2700 Q St NW Washington DC 20007 also One World Trade Center Suite 1535 New York City NY 10048 Tel (202) 483-6777

LOWE, JAMES ALLISON, b. Cleve., July 15, 1945; B.A., U. Pa., 1967; J.D. cum laude, Cleve. State U., 1972. Admitted to Ohio bar, 1972; since practiced in Cleve., asso. firm Berkman, Gordon & Kancelbaum, 1972-74, individual practice law, 1974-76, partner firm Sindell, Lowe & Guidubaldi, 1976—; instr. Cleve. State U. Coll. Law; legal intern Legal Aid Soc. of Cleve., 1970-72. Mem. Cleve. City Club, Jewish Community Fedn., 1974—. Mem. Am., Ohio State, Greater Cleve. bar assns., Assn. Trial Lawyers Am. Home: 3672 Lytle Rd Shaker Heights OH 44122 Office: 910 Leader Bldg Cleveland OH 44114 Tel (216) 781-8880

LOWE, JOHN WILLIAM, b. Salt Lake City, Mar. 26, 1917; A.B., U. Utah, 1937; J.D., Harvard, 1940; grad. Command and Gen. Staff Sch. U.S. Army, 1965. Admitted to Utah bar, 1940, U.S. Supreme Ct. bar, 1950; asso. firm Stephens, Brayton & Lowe, Salt Lake City, 1940-48; partner firm Brayton, Lowe & Hurley, Salt Lake City, 1948—; dir. First Fed. Savs. & Loan Assn. of Salt Lake City, 1948—, Pacific Nat. Life Ins. Co. of Salt Lake City and San Francisco, 1948-56, Arnold Machinery Co., 1971—, Pace Industries, 1976—. Mem. bd. govs. Shriners Intermountain Hosp. for Crippled Children, 1976—; pres. elect Salt Lake City Rotary Club, 1977. Mem. Utah, Am. bar assns. Home: 1624 Orchard Dr Salt Lake City UT 84106 Office: 1011 Walker Bank Bldg Salt Lake City UT 84111 Tel (801) 521-5466

LOWE, JUNG YEN, b. Honolulu, Aug. 22, 1932; B.A. in Economics, Coe Coll., 1954; J.D., Yale, 1957. Admitted to Hawaii bar, 1958, U.S. Ct. Mil. Appeals bar, 1959; U.S. Dist. Ct. Hawaii bar, 1961, U.S. Ct. Appeals 9th Circuit bar, 1973; sales adminstr. Corbin-Farnsworth, Inc., Palo Alto, Calif., 1965-67; atty. Legal Aid Soc. Hawaii, Honolulu, also dir. Economic Devel. Project, 1968-70; pres. Hawaii Economic Devel. Corp., 1970-72; partner firm Lee & Lowe, Honolulu, 1972-74; chief disciplinary counsel Supreme Ct. Hawaii, 1974—; dir. Pacific Forum, 1975—; asst. vis. prof. law U. Hawaii, 1974-75; staff officer JAG, USAF, 1958-61; mem. advisory bd. study biomass energy options for Hawaii, Stanford and U. Hawaii, 1975—; advisory com. Legal Assts. Program, U. Hawaii, 1975—; conf. on Alternative Economic Futures for Hawaii, 1973—; chmn. New Tech. for Hawaii's Future Conf., 1974; mem. Task Force for Sci. and Tech. Gov's Conf. on the Year 2000, 1970. Mem. Am., Hawaii State bar assns., Nat. Orgn. Bar Counsel. Office: Office Disciplinary Counsel Supreme Ct 1149 Bethel St Room 711 Honolulu HI 96813 Tel (808) 521-4591

LOWE, LOUIS HAMILTON, b. Taylor, Tex., June 15, 1901; LL.B., U. Tex., 1926. Admitted to Tex. bar, 1926, U.S. Supreme Ct. bar, 1967; partner Tarlton & Lowe and Kleberg Eckhart & Lowe, and predecessors, Corpus Christi, Tex., 1927-40; ret., 1974. Exec. dir. Tex. Water Code Com., 1947-48, Travis County Leagal Aid Soc., 1966-70. Mem. State Bar Tex., Travis County Bar Assn. Author: Texas Practice, vols. 6 and 6a, 1973. Address: PO Box 425 Austin TX 78767 Tel (512) 472-2995

LOWE, ROBERT CHARLES, b. Seattle, Jan. 15, 1927; B.B.A., U. Wash., 1953; LL.D., U. Denver, 1959. Admitted to Colo. bar, 1961, Alaska bar, 1961; partner firm Hughes, Thorsness, Lowe, Gantz & Clark, Anchorage, 1960-75; individual practice law, Anchorage, 1975—; chmn. bd. Peoples Bank & Trust Co., 1970—; chmn., pres., Safeco Title Agy., Inc., 1975—. Mem. Am., Alaska, Anchorage bar assns. Home: 2934 Emory St Anchorage AK 99504 Office: Suite 101 3201 C St Anchorage AK 99503 Tel (907) 276-6373

LOWE, ROBERT JOHN, b. Milw., Nov. 28, 1928; B.S., Marquette U., 1952, J.D., 1955. Admitted to Wis. bar, 1955; asso. Robert D. Jones, Milw., 1955-58; partner firm Lowe & Kozlowski, Milw., 1958-74; individual practice, Milw., 1974—. Chmn. Recreation Commn. Menomonee Falls (Wis.), 1975—. Mem. Wis. Bar Assn., Am. Arbitration Assn. (arbitrator). Office: 6430 N 76th St Milwaukee WI 53223 Tel (414) 353-4550

LOWE, SAMUEL JOSEPH, b. Upland, Pa., Sept. 30, 1936; B.S. in Music Edn., Wilkes Coll., 1958; J.D., Am. U., 1968. Admitted to D.C. bar, 1969. Supervising atty. Allstate Ins. Co., Washington, 1971-75; trial atty. firm Williams & Brown, Washington, 1975; individual practice law, Washington, 1975—. Bd. dirs. Am. Light Opera Co., Washington, 1964-66. Mem. Bar Assn. D.C., D.C. Bar Assn., Am. Arbitration Assn., Def. Research Inst., Am. Trial Lawyers Assn. Home: 4615 N Park Ave Chevy Chase MD 20015 Office: 733 15th St NW Washington DC 20005 Tel (202) 347-8411

LOWE, WILLIAM EDWARD, b. Ottumwa, Iowa, July 6, 1941; B.S., U. S.Fla., 1965; J.D., Stetson U., 1968. Admitted to Fla. bar, 1968, U.S. Supreme Ct. bar, 1975; asst. state's atty. 12th Jud. Circuit Fla., 1969; asst. county prosecutor Manatee County (Fla.), 1970-71; partner firm Lowe, Ferrell and Huie, Bradenton, Fla., 1971—; lectr. dept. police sci. St. Petersburg Jr. Coll., 1970-71; municipal judge City of Palmetto (Fla.), 1972—. Chmn., Sarasota County Selective Service Bd. Mem. Fla. Bar, Phi Alpha Delta. Office: First City Center Suite 502 1301 6th Ave W Bradenton FL 33505 Tel (813) 748-8181

LOWELL, STANLEY HERBERT, b. N.Y.C., Apr. 13, 1919; B.S.S., Coll. City N.Y., 1939; LL.B., Harvard U., 1942. Admitted to N.Y. bar, 1942, U.S. Supreme Ct. bar, 1950; asso. firm Root, Clark, Buckner & Ballantine, N.Y.C., 1942-43; asst. U.S. atty. So. Dist. N.Y., 1943-47; partner firm Lowenbraun & Lowell, N.Y.C., 1947-58, firm Corcoran, Kostelanetz, Gladstone & Lowell, N.Y.C., 1958-64, firm Gladstone & Lowell, N.Y.C., 1965-73, firm Lowell & Karassik, N.Y.C., 1973—; lectr. govt. and econs. Coll. City N.Y., 1945-47; exec. asst. to Mayor of N.Y.C., 1954-57; dep. mayor City of N.Y., 1958; chmn. N.Y.C. Commn. on Human Rights, 1960-65; adj. prof. Fordham U. Grad. Sch. of Social Service, 1972. Vice chmn. Nat. Jewish Community Relations Adv. Council; chmn. Nat. Conf. Soviet Jewry; mem. exec. bd., bd. dirs. United Jewish Appeal of Greater N.Y.; praesidium Brussels World Conf. on Soviet Jewry; pres. Citizens Com. for Children of N.Y. Mem. Assn. Bar City N.Y., N.Y. State Bar Assn., N.Y. County Lawyers Awsn. Home: 15 Paxford Ln Scarsdale NY 10583 Office: 99 Park Ave New York City NY 10016 Tel (212) 867-9595

LOWENSTEIN, EDITH, b. Cologne, Germany; came to U.S., 1934, naturalized, 1939; J.D., U. Chgo., 1939. Admitted to Ill. bar, 1939, N.Y. State bar, 1954; U.S. Supreme Ct. bar, 1947; appellate atty. Crim. div. Dept. of Justice, Washington, 1939-44, trial atty. Office of Alien Property, 1944-53; editor Interpreter Releases, N.Y.C., 1953-74; individual practice law, N.Y.C., 1958—; instr. New Sch. for Social Research, N.Y.C., 1965-66, 76, Am. Council for Nationalities Service, 1966-75. Mem. Assn. of Immigration and Nationality Lawyers (bd. govs. 1956—, chmn. N.Y. State chpt. 1966, nat. pres. 1973-74), Assn. of the Bar of the City of N.Y. (chmn. Com. on immigration and nationality 1969-72), Am. Immigration and Citizenship Conf. (dir. 1954—). Author: The Alien and the Immigration Law Ocean, 1958. Office: 25 W 43d St New York City NY 10036 Tel (212) 869-9444

LOWENSTEIN, PETER DAVID, b. N.Y.C., Dec. 31, 1935; B.A., Trinity Coll., 1958; LL.B., Georgetown U., 1961. Admitted to Conn. bar, 1962, D.C. bar, 1963, N.Y. State bar, 1963; atty. SEC, Washington, 1961-63; mem. firm Whitman & Ransom, and predecessors, N.Y.C., 1963-70, partner, 1970-73, mng. partner, 1973—. Bd. dirs. Babe Ruth League, Inc., The Children's Village Bd. dirs., sec. Grand St. Settlement, Inc., Babe Ruth Found., Inc. Mem. Assn. Bar City N.Y., N.Y. County, N.Y. State, Am., Fed., D.C., Conn. bar assns. Home: Grosset Rd Riverside CT 06878 Office: 522 Fifth Ave New York City NY 10036 Tel (212) 575-5800

LOWENTHAL, PHILIP HENRY, b. Cin., June 1, 1944; A.B., U. Calif., Berkeley, 1966, J.D., 1969. Admitted to Calif. bar, 1969, Hawaii bar, 1970; supv. atty. office of pub. defender Maui County, Hawaii, 1970—. Mem. Calif., Hawaii, Maui County (chmn. judicial liason com.) bar assns. Home: Banana Patch Haiku HI 96708 Office: 2307 Main St Wailuku HI 96793 Tel (808) 244-5371

LOWER, FREDERICK JOSEPH, JR., b. Utica, N.Y., Feb. 17, 1935; B.S., Loyola U., Los Angeles, 1956, J.D., 1964. Admitted to Calif. bar, 1965; asso. firm Chase Rotchford Downen & Drukker, Los Angeles, 1964-66, Kean & Engle, Los Angeles, 1966-68; prof. law Loyola U. Law Sch., Los Angeles, 1968-73, dean, 1973—. Mem. Am., Calif., Los Angeles County bar assns. Office: Loyola U Law Sch 1440 W 9th St Los Angeles CA 90015 Tel (213) 642-2902

LOWER, ROBERT CASSEL, b. Oak Park, Ill., Jan. 8, 1947; A.B. magna cum laude with highest honors, Harvard, 1969, J.D., 1972. Admitted to Ga. bar, 1972; asso. firm Alston, Miller & Gaines, 1972—; pres. Harvard Legal Aid Bur., 1971-72; co-founder, pres. Ga. Vol. Lawyers for the Arts, 1976—. Mem. legis. sect. Ga. Senate Dist. 40; bd. dirs. Morningside-Lenox Park Civic Assn., Atlanta, 1975-76, Atlanta Great Park Planning, Inc., 1976—; mem. Atlanta Mayor's Ad Hoc Com. for Great Park, 1975-76. Mem. Am., Ga., Atlanta bar assns. Home: 1683 N Pelham Rd NE Atlanta GA 30324 Office: 1200 Citizens & So Nat Bank Bldg Atlanta GA 30303 Tel (404) 588-0300

LOWERY, OLAN BUFORD, b. Plainview, Tex., May 11, 1930; B.S., SW Tex. State Coll.; M.A., Iowa State U.; LL.B., Baylor Coll. Admitted to Tex. bar, 1957, Pa. bar, 1968; asso. firm Dewey, Ballantine, Bushby, Palmer & Wood, N.Y.C., 1958-67; asso. Fulbright, Crocker, Freeman, Bates and Jaworski, Phila., 1967—; prof. Temple U.; cons. Land Use Task Force, Phila. Mem. Am., Pa. bar assns., AAUP. Home: 913 S 11th St Philadelphia PA 19442 Office: 1719 N Broad St Philadelphia PA 19122 Tel (215) 787-7827

LOWINGER, JOEL DAVID, b. Newark, July 8, 1939; B.A., Drew U., 1961; J.D. Fordham U., 1964; postgrad N.Y. U., 1965. Admitted to N.J. bar, 1965, U.S. Supreme Ct. bar, 1969; law clerk Middlesex County (N.J.) Ct., 1964-65; asso. firm Stevens & Mathias, Newark, 1965-68; individual practice law, Millburn, N.J., 1968—. Mem. adv. com. Millburn Twp. Rent Control, 1974. Mem. Am., N.J., Essex County bar assns. Office: 350 Millburn Ave Millburn NJ 07041 Tel (201) 376-8400

LOWMAN, GEORGE FREDERICK, lawyer; b. N.Y.C., Oct. 29, 1916; A.B., Harvard, 1938, LL.B., 1942. Admitted to Conn. bar, 1946; asso. law firm Cummings, & Lockwood, Stamford, Conn., 1946-52, partner, 1952—. Chmn. exec. com. Farrell Lines, Inc., N.Y.C., 1966—. Chmn., Darien YMCA-YWCA Fund Campaign, 1956; mem.

exec. com. Alfred W. Dater council Boy Scouts Am., 1956; chmn. Darien Cancer Fund, 1959-60; pres. bd. dirs. Silvermine Guild Artists, 1966-76. Mem. Am. (del. 1976-77), Conn. (pres. 1976-77), Stamford (pres. 1963-64) bar assns., Delta Upsilon, Kiwanis Club (pres. 1955, dir. 1952-58). Decorated Bronze Star, Legion of Merit. Home: 40 Allwood Rd Darien CT 06820 Office: Cummings & Lockwood 1 Atlantic St Stamford CT 06904

LOWNEY, MARILYN RACHEL, b. N.Y.C., Feb. 12, 1948; B.A. in Polit. Sci., and Econs., U. Md., 1969, J.D., 1972. Admitted to Md. bar, 1972, U.S. Ct. Appeals, D.C., bar, 1973; law clk. Cweiber and Edelstein, Balt., 1971; clk. Employment Security Adminstrn., State of Md., Balt., 1971; law intern Pub. Defenders office, City of Balt., 1971-72, legal advisor to urban affairs com., City Council, Balt., 1972; dir., consel Nat. Assn. Home Builders, Washington, 1973-75; legal counsel Internat. Council Shopping Centers, N.Y.C., 1975; asso. gen. counsel Md.-Nat. Capital Park and Planning Commn., 1975—. Bd. dirs. Potomac Sch. Law, Washington, 1974-75, 77—. Mem. Am., Md. State, D.C., Women's, Prince Georges County bar assns. Home: 6116 Breezewood Ct #304 Greenbelt MD 20770 Office: County Adminstrn Bldg Gov Oden Bowie Dr Upper Marlboro MD 20870

LOWREY, JOHN JUDE, b. Joliet, Ill., Oct. 28, 1939; B.S., Loyola U., Chgo., 1961; J.D., U. Denver, 1969. Admitted to Colo. bar, 1969, Ill. bar, 1970; dep. dist. atty. Colo. 1st Jud. Dist., 1969-70; asst. atty. gen. State of Ill., 1970-71, spl. asst. atty. gen., 1972, 76—; asso. firm Wildman, Harrold, Allen & Dixon, Chgo., 1971-74; individual practice law, Chgo., 1974—. Mem. Chgo., Ill., Am. bar assns., Ill., Chgo., Am. trial lawyers assns. Office: 111 W Washington St Suite 2025 Chicago IL 60602 Tel (312) 332-5433

LOWRY, GEORGE THEODORE, b. N.Y.C., Oct. 16, 1931; A.B., N.Y. U., 1953, LL.B., 1955. Admitted to N.Y. bar, 1955, U.S. Supreme Ct. bar, 1973; asso. firm Cravath, Swaine & Moore, N.Y.C., 1957-65, partner, 1965—, mng. partner, 1971-73, partner in charge European office, 1973—; dir. LeNickel Services, N.Y.C., Compagnie Generale de Radiologie, Paris. Mem. Am., N.Y. State, Internat. bar assns., Bar Assn. City N.Y., Union Nationale des Avocats. Office: 4 Place de la Concocle Paris 75008 France Tel 265-8154 also Terminal House 52 Grosvenor Gardens London SW1 England Tel 730-5203 also 1 Chase Manhattan Plaza New York City NY 10005

LOWRY, HYRUM D., b. Freedom, Utah, May 22, 1903; student U. Utah; LL.B., U. Chgo., 1930. Admitted to Utah bar, 1931; asst. atty. Salt Lake County, 1933-43, Salt Lake City, 1958-60, legal dept. Ch. Jesus Christ of Latter-Day Saints, 1960-64; asst. dist. atty., 1943-47; asst. U.S. dist. atty., 1950-52; asso. firm Kirton, McConkie, Boyer & Boyle, Salt Lake City, 1964—. Home: 2832 Commonwealth Ave Salt Lake City UT 84109 Office: 336 S 3rd E Salt Lake City UT 84111 Tel (801) 521-3680

LOWRY, ROBERT CUNNINGHAM, b. Jackson, Miss., Aug. 24, 1942; B.S. in Bus. Adminstrn., U. Ark., 1964, J.D., 1968. Admitted to Ark. bar, 1969; law clk. to chief justice Ark. Supreme Ct., 1968-69; asso. firm Chowning, Mitchell and Hamilton and predecessor, Little Rock, 1969-74; partner firm Mitchell & Lowry, Little Rock, 1974—. Bd. dirs. Youth Home, Inc., 1972-75; deacon Second Presbyterian Ch.; mem. original bd. dirs. Learning Tree Sch. Mem. Am., Ark., Pulaski County bar assns., Am., Ark. trial lawyers assns., Am. Judicature Soc. Office: 300 Spring Bldg Suite 420 Little Rock AR 72201 Tel (501) 375-7315

LOWRY, ROBERT L., b. Marlin, Tex., Nov. 11, 1918; student Delta State U., 1949; J.D., U. Houston, 1951. Admitted to Tex. bar, 1951; individual practice law, Houston, 1951-65; judge Juvenile Ct. of Harris County (Tex.), Houston, 1966—. Mem. Am. Judicature Soc., Nat Council of Juvenile Ct. Judges. Home: 1245 Ridgeley St Houston TX 77055 Office: Family Law Center Bldg Houston TX 77002 Tel (713) 228-8311

LOY, CARL LOUIS, b. Chehalis, Wash., June 10, 1916; B.A., U. Wash., 1940; LL.B., 1951. Admitted to Wash. bar, 1951; partner firm McDonald & Loy, Yakima, Wash., 1951-52; asst. atty. gen. State of Wash., Olympia, 1953-54; asst. U.S. atty., Yakima, 1954-56; partner firm Hawkins & Loy, Yakima, 1957-60, Wilson & Loy, 1960-69; judge Superior Ct. Yakima County, 1969—. Mem. exec. bd. Fort Simcoe council Boy Scouts Am., 1973-74. Mem. Am., Wash., Yakima County bar assns., Wash. Superior Ct. Judges Assn. Home: 4906 Snowmountain Rd Yakima WA 98908 Office: Yakima County Courthouse N 2d St Yakima WA 98901 Tel (509) 575-4222

LUBAROFF, MARTIN IRVING, b. Phila., May 22, 1941; A.B., Franklin and Marshall Coll., 1963; LL.B., Harvard, 1966. Admitted to Del. bar, 1967; mem. firm Richards, Layton & Finger, Wilmington, Del., 1966—. Mem. Am., Del. bar assns. Home: 211 Stone Crop Rd Northminster Wilmington DE 19810 Office: 4072 DuPont Building Wilmington DE 19899 Tel (303) 658-6541

LUBARSKY, BRUCE MARSHAL, b. San Francisco, Mar. 4, 1937; A.B., U. Calif., Berkeley, 1959, LL.B., Hastings Coll. Law, San Francisco, 1962, J.D., 1971. Admitted to Calif. Supreme Ct. bar, 1963, U.S. Supreme Ct. bar, 1971, U.S. Tax Ct., 1971, U.S. Ct. Customs and Patent Appeals bar, 1971, Fed. Ct. Appeals D.C., 1973, Calif., 1973, adminstrv. asst. San Francisco Office Dist. Atty., 1963; with JAGC, U.S. Army, Ft. Ord, Calif., 1963; partner firm Jackson, Lubarsky & Hughes, San Francisco, 1963—; instr. in bus. law San Francisco State U., 1970-71; gen. counsel Thomas A. Dooley Found., 1971—; judge pro tem San Mateo County (Calif.) Municipal Ct., 1972-73; arbitrator Am. Arbitration Assn., 1968—. Mem. Am., Calif., San Francisco, San Mateo, Fed. bar assns., Calif. Trial Lawyers Assn., Bar Assn. D.C., San Francisco Lawyers Club (gov.). Home: 301 Poett Rd Hillsborough CA 94010 Office: 1255 Post St San Francisco CA 94109 Tel (415) 776-7677

LUBART, DAVID, b. N.Y.C., Apr. 9, 1915; B.S., Bklyn. Coll., 1935; LL.B., St. John's U., 1938; Admitted to N.Y. State bar, 1938; asso. firm Paskus, Gordon & Hyman, 1938-42; mem. firm Stroock, Stroock & Lavan, N.Y.C., 1942-54, sr. partner, 1954—; sec. Browarn, Ltd., Baldwin Securities Corp.; dir. Internat. Banknote Co., Fed-Mart Corp.; sec., dir. Lambda Electronics Corp., Malt-Diastase Co., Originala Inc., Temco Service Industries Inc., Veeco Instruments Inc. Trustee, v.p. Am. Friends of Alliance Israelite Universelle; pres., trustee Tenmain Found.; sec., trustee Nerken Found.; trustee Maimonides Med. Center, Ara Found. Mem. Am., N.Y. State bar assn., Assn. Bar City of N.Y., N.Y. County Lawyers Assn., Soc. to Conquer Mental Illness, Alumni Chem. Soc. Bklyn. Coll. Home: 1020 Park Ave New York City NY 10028 Office: 61 Broadway New York City NY 10006 Tel (212) 425-5200

LUBER, LARRY BENJAMIN, b. Sikeston, Mo., July 9, 1942; B.S., SE Mo. State U., 1964; J.D., Memphis State U., 1970. Admitted to Mo. bar, 1970, Tenn. bar, 1970; law clk. to chief judge Eastern Dist. Mo., 1970; asso. firm Armstrong, Teasdale, Kramer & Vaughan, St. Louis, 1971—. Mem. Am., St. Louis bar assns. Home: 11330 Clayton St Frontenac MO 63131 Office: 611 Olive St Saint Louis MO 63101 Tel (314) 621-5070

LUBIC, ROBERT BENNETT, b. Pitts., Mar. 9, 1929; B.A., U. Pitts., 1950, J.D., 1953; M.P.L., Georgetown Law Center, 1959. Admitted to Pa. bar, 1953, U.S. Supreme Ct. bar, 1959; individual practice law, Pitts., 1955-57; atty. adviser FCC, Washington, 1957-59; individual practice law, Pitts., 1959-64; prof. law Duquesne Law Sch., 1964-65; prof. Am. U., 1965—, asso. dean, 1959-60; prof. comparative law Hebrew U., Jerusalem, 1976; arbitrator Fed. Mediation and Conciliation Service, Am. Arbitration Assn.; cons. in field. Mem. FCC Bar Assn. Home: 2813 McKinley Pl NW Washington DC 20015 Office: American U Myers Bldg Massachusetts and Nebraska Aves NW Washington DC 20016 Tel (202) 686-2613

LUBICK, DONALD CYRIL, b. Buffalo, Apr. 29, 1926; B.A. summa cum laude, U. Buffalo, 1945; J.D. magna cum laude, Harvard, 1949. Admitted to N.Y. State bar, 1950, Fla. bar, 1974; partner firm Hodgson, Russ, Andrews, Woods & Goodyear, Buffalo, 1950-61, 64—; lectr. law U. Buffalo, 1950-61; counsel U.S. Treasury Dept., 1961-64. Chmn. tax revision com. City of Buffalo, 1958-59; mem. adv. com. to select Com. on Election Law Reform, N.Y. Legislature. Mem. Am., N.Y. State, Erie County bar assns., Am. Law Inst. Recipient Exceptional Service award U.S. Treasury Dept., 1964. Home: 61 Chatham Ave Buffalo NY 14216 Office: 1800 One M & T Plaza Buffalo NY 14203 Tel (716) 856-4000

LUBIN, STANLEY, b. Bklyn., May 7, 1941; A.B., U. Mich., 1963, J.D. with honors, 1966. Admitted to D.C. bar, 1967, Mich. bar, 1968, Ariz. bar, 1972, U.S. Supreme Ct. bar, 1970, U.S. Ct. Appeals for D.C., 1967; atty. NLRB, Washington, 1966-68; asst. gen. counsel UAW, Detroit, 1968-72; asso. firm Harrison, Myers & Singer, Phoenix, 1972-74, firm McKendree & Tountas, Phoenix, 1975; partner firm McKendree & Lubin, Phoenix, 1975—; mem. Ariz. Employment Security Advisory Council, 1975-77. Mem. Ariz. State Central Com. Democratic Party, 1973—. Mem. Am., Maricopa County bar assns., State Bar Ariz., Indsl. Relations Research Assn., Ariz. Indsl. Relations Assn. (mem. exec. bd. 1973—), ACLU (dir. Ariz. chpt. 1974—). Home: 7 E Village Ct S 5219 N 44th St Phoenix AZ 85018 Office: 3443 N Central Ave Suite 1210 Phoenix AZ 85012 Tel (602) 248-9261

LUBITSKY, GERALD SAMUEL, b. Toledo, May 13, 1939; B.A., U. Toledo, 1961, J.D., 1965. Admitted to Ohio bar, 1965, U.S. Supreme Ct. bar, 1970; individual practice law, Toledo, 1965-71; partner firm Lubitsky & Lubitsky, 1972-75; partner firm Lubitsky, Neller & Post, Toledo, 1977—; instr. English, U. Toledo, 1964-65, instr. bus. law, 1966-67; mem. panel arbitrators Am. Arbitration Assn. Mem. exec. com. Toledo Bd. Jewish Edn., 1970-75. Mem. Fed., Ohio, Toledo bar assns. Home: 5266 Snowden St Toledo OH 43623 Office: 606 Madison Ave Toledo OH 43604 Tel (419) 241-3535

LUBMAN, STANLEY BERNARD, b. N.Y.C., Mar. 29, 1934; A.B. with honors, Columbia, 1955, LL.B., 1958, LL.M., 1959; student (Jervey fellow) U. de Paris, 1959-60; J.S.D. (Rockefeller Found. grantee, Fgn. Area fellow), Columbia, 1969. Admitted to N.Y. State bar, 1959, Calif. bar, 1971, D.C. bar, 1974; asso. firm Paul, Weiss, Rifkind, Wharton & Garrison, N.Y.C., 1960-61; law clk. U.S. Dist. Ct. So. Dist. N.Y., 1961-62; vis. prof. Law, U. Calif. Berkeley, 1967-68, acting asso. prof., 1968-72, lectr., 1972-74; individual practice law, Berkeley, Calif., 1972-74, Washington, 1974-76; spl. counsel firm Heller, Ehrman, White & McAuliffe, San Francisco, 1977—; vis. lectr. Law, Yale, 1976-77; mem. Nat. Com. for U.S.-China Relations, Nat. Council for U.S.-China Trade. Mem. China Council Asia Soc. (asso.), Am. Bar Assn., Phi Beta Kappa. Contbr. articles in field to profl. jours. Office: 44 Montgomery St San Francisco CA 94104 Tel (415) 981-5000

LUBOW, MARTIN, b. Pitts., May 27, 1923; B.A., U. Pitts., 1948, M.Litt., 1950; J.D., Duquesne U., 1956. Admitted to Pa. bar, 1957, since practiced in Pitts.; mem. panel Fed. Mediation and Conciliation Service. An organizer Monroeville (Pa.) Pub. Library. Mem. Am., Allegheny County bar assns., Am. Arbitration Assn. (panel arbitrators). Office: 3630 Mellon Bank Bldg 525 William Penn Pl Pittsburgh PA 15219 Tel (412) 391-5080

LUCAS, MALCOLM MILLAR, b. Berkeley, Calif., Apr. 19, 1927; B.A. in Polit. Sci., U. So. Calif., 1950, LL.B., 1953. Admitted to Calif. bar, 1954; partner firm Lucas, Deukmejian and Lucas, Long Beach, Calif., 1955-67; judge Los Angeles Superior Ct., 1967-71, U.S. Dist. Ct., Central Dist. Calif., 1971—; mem. statewide jud. process task force Calif. Council on Adminstrn. Justice, 1970-71; chmn. spl. com. on jud. reform Los Angeles Superior Ct., 1970-71; mem. select com. on trial delay Calif. Supreme Ct., 1970-71. Pres. bd. trustees Los Alamitos (Calif.) Sch. Dist., 1962. Mem. Los Angeles County, Fed., Am. bar assns. Office: 312 N Spring St Los Angeles CA 90012 Tel (213) 688-4647

LUCAS, MAXWELL DAVIS, JR., b. Memphis, Oct. 27, 1936; B.A., Vanderbilt U., 1958, LL.B., 1960. Admitted to Tenn. bar, 1960; asso. firm Clifton, Mack & Kirkpatrick, Memphis, 1960-65; partner Kirkpatrick & Lucas, Memphis, 1965—; mem. Tenn. Ho. of Reps., 1967-68. Mem. Memphis-Shelby County, Tenn., Am. bar assns., Tenn. Def. Lawyers (v.p. 1976—), Am. Judicature Soc., Trial Attys. Am. Home: 3821 S Galloway Dr Memphis TN 38111 Office: 1910 1st Nat Bank Bldg Memphis TN 38103 Tel (901) 523-7656

LUCAS, WILDER, b. St. Louis, Aug. 29, 1901; student U. Zurich, 1920, U. Lausanne (Switzerland), 1920-21; A.B., Washington U., 1924, LL.B., 1924. Admitted to Mo. bar, 1924, U.S. Supreme Ct. bar, 1931; asso. firm Bryan, William and Cave, 1924-26; individual practice law, St. Louis, 1926-41; partner firm Finley, Lucas & Arnold, and predecessors, St. Louis, 1941-59; partner firm Lucas & Murphy, St. Louis, 1963—; tchr. law Washington U., 1953; hon. Austrian consul, 1931-38. Bd. dirs., pres. internat. inst. St. Louis Soc. Crippled Children. Fellow Am. Coll. Trial Lawyers; mem. Internat. Assn. Ins. Counsel, Maritime Law Assn. U.S., Bar Assn. Met. St. Louis, Am., Mo. bar assns. Recipient Golden Hon. Austrian medal, 1957. Home: 7050 Westmoreland St University City MO 63130 Office: Suite 602 720 Olive St Saint Louis MO 63101 Tel (314) 421-0311

LUCAS, WILLIAM ERNEST, b. Walhalla, S.C., May 30, 1910; A.B., U. S.C., 1931, M.A., 1931; LL.B., Harvard, 1934. Admitted to N.Y. State bar, 1935, Ill. bar, 1936; asso. firm Thach, Dick & Burroughs, N.Y.C., 1935; practice law, Chgo., 1936-68; mem. firm McCaleb, Lucas & Brugman, Chgo., 1968—. Mem. Am., Ill. State, Chgo. bar assns., Chgo. Patent Law Assn., Phi Beta Kappa. Home: 70 Bright Oaks Circle Cary IL 60013 Office: 230 W Monroe St Chicago IL 60606 Tel (312) 236-4711

LUCCHESI, LIONEL LOUIS, b. St. Louis, Sept. 17, 1939; B.E.E., Ill. Inst. Tech., 1961; J.D., St. Louis U., 1969. Engr., Emerson Electric Co., St. Louis, 1965-69; admitted to Mo. bar, 1969; mem. firm Polster & Polster, St. Louis, 1969-74, partner, 1974—. Mem. zoning commn. City of Ballwin (Mo.), 1971—. Mem. Am. Patent Law Assn., Bar Assn. Met. St. Louis (sec. 1976—), Am., Mo. (chmn. patent and trademark com. 1976—) bar assns. Home: 644 Charbray Dr Ballwin MO 63011 Office: 1221 Locust St Saint Louis MO 63103 Tel (314) 241-6668

LUCE, DAVID LE ROY, b. Santa Rosa, Calif., July 28, 1914; A.B., U. Calif., Berkeley, 1936, LL.B., Hastings Coll. Law, San Francisco, 1940. Admitted to Calif. bar, 1940; mem. firms Cleves and Deihl, Oroville, Calif., 1947-48; individual practice law, Petaluma, Calif., 1957-58; chief spl. investment div. Calif. Franchise Tax Bd., Sacramento, 1952-53; exec. asst. criminal div. Dept. Justice, Washington, 1953-54, chief criminal sect. tax div., 1954-55, 1st asst. criminal div., 1955-56; adminstr. dir. cts. State of Alaska, Anchorage, 1959-61; dist. atty., county counsel, pub. adminstr. Lake County (Calif.), 1966—. Mem. Calif. State Bar Assn., Nat. Assn. Dist. Attys., Dist. Attys. and County Counsels' Assn. Calif., Pub. Adminstrs'. Assn., Big "C" Soc. Home: 8545 Scott Valley Rd Upper Lake CA 95485 Office: Courthouse Lakeport CA 95453 Tel (707) 263-2251

LUCE, KENNETH KLINGLE, b. Ft. Benton, Mont., Apr. 19, 1912; A.B., U. Mich., 1934, J.D., 1937. Admitted to Ohio bar, 1938, Wis. bar, 1946; asso. firm Squire, Sanders & Dempsey, Cleve., 1937-42; prof. Marquette U. Law Sch., Milw., 1945-50, 1973—; partner firm Michael, Best & Friedrich, Milw., 1950—. Mem. Am. Bar Assn., State Bar Wis. (gov. 1964—, exec. com. 1964-73), Am. Law Inst., Decorated Order of House of Orange (Netherlands), 1946. Home: 4536 N Wildwood St Milwaukee WI 53211 Office: 250 Wisconsin Ave Milwaukee WI 53202 Tel (414) 271-6560

LUCEY, CHARLES EMMET, b. Toledo, Mar. 7, 1935; B.S., Georgetown U., 1956; J.D., 1959. Admitted to D.C. bar, 1959, Fla. bar, 1959, Md. bar, 1975; counsel U.S. Treasury Dept., 1961-63; gen. counsel Support Group for Progressive Banking, 1961-66; partner firm Saxon, Maguire & Tker, 1966-71, Harrison, Lucey & Sagle, Washington, 1971—; chmn. bd., Century Nat. Bank, Bethesda, Md., 1975—. Vice-chmn. Dem. Nat. Finance Council, Dem. Nat. Com., 1974-77. Mem. Am. Bar Assn. (vice-chmn. banking com. adminstrv. law sec., 1974-75, chmn., 1975-77, vice chmn. 1977—). Home: 6134 Nevada Ave Chevy Chase MD 20015 Office: 1701 Pennsylvania Ave NW Washington DC 20006 Tel (202) 298-9030

LUCHINI, JOSEPH SANTO, b. Mologno Bergamo, Italy, Mar. 19, 1913; A.B., W.Va. U., 1936, LL.B., 1938. Admitted to W.Va. bar, U.S. Supreme Ct. bar; individual practice law, Beckley, W.Va., 1938—. Mem. Am., W.Va. State, Raleigh County bar assns. Home: 716 S Kanawha St Beckley WV 25801 Office: 224 1/2 Main St Beckley WV 25801 Tel (304) 252-4171

LUCHS, ELLIOTT STEWART, b. Bklyn., July 7, 1948; B.A., U. Calif., Irvine, 1970; J.D., Pepperdine Law Sch., 1973. Law clk. firm Garber, Sokoloff & Van Dyke, Inc., Fullerton, Calif., 1971-73, asso., 1973—; admitted to Calif. bar, 1973. Mem. Calif., Orange County trial lawyers assns., Am., Orange County (Calif.) bar assns., Calif. Workers' Compensation Applicant's Assn. Editorial bd. Pepperdine Law Sch. Law Rev., 1973. Office: 1414 W Commonwealth St Fullerton CA 92633 Tel (714) 526-2267

LUCKE, ROBERT NUMSEN, SR., b. Washington, Mar. 1, 1924; B.S., U. Md., 1950, J.D., 1959. Admitted to Md. bar, 1959; partner firm Bald, Smith & Lucke, Annapolis, Md., 1959-75, Smith & Lucke, Annapolis, 1976—; panel mem. Atty. Grievance Com. Md.; hearing officer Comptroller of Treasury of Md., 1960-62; spl. asst. county solicitor An Anne Arundel County (Md.), 1965; govt. appeals agt. SSS, 1966-72, local dir., 1972-76. Vice pres., bd. dirs. Anne Arundel County YMCA; pres. Annapolis Rotary Club. Mem. Am., Md., Anne Arundel County bar assns., Am. Trial Lawyers Assn., Severna Park (Md.) C. of C. (pres.), Am. Legion (post comdr.). Home: 5 Windward Dr Severna Park MD 21146 Office: 16 Murray Ave Annapolis MD 21401 Tel (301) 276-9712

LUCKEY, CLARENCE EDWIN, b. Eugene, Oreg., Feb. 6, 1919; B.S., U. Oreg., 1940, LL.B., 1942, J.D., 1971. Admitted to Oreg. bar, 1942, U.S. Supreme Ct. bar, 1954; dept. dist. atty. Lane County, Oreg., 1946, dist. atty., 1946-54; U.S. Atty. Dist. of Oreg., 1954-61; judge bankruptcy ct., Eugene, Oreg., 1961—; tchr. bankruptcy law Lane Community Coll., Eugene, 1974. Mem. Oreg., Lane County bar assns., Am. Judicature Soc., Nat. Conf. Bankruptcy Judges. Home: 2172 Elysium Ave Eugene OR 97401 Office: PO Box 1335 Eugene OR 97401 Tel (503) 687-6448

LUCKIE, CHARLES ADAMS, b. Montgomery, Ala., Nov. 27, 1906; LL.B., John B. Stetson U., 1931. Admitted to Fla. bar, 1931; asso. firm Rogers, Towers & Bailey, Jacksonville, Fla., 1931-41, partner, 1941-50; judge Circuit Ct., 1950—; mem. Fla. Ho. of Reps., 1941-43, 45-50. Home: 4242 Ortega Blvd Jacksonville FL 32210 Tel (904) 633-6761

LUDECKE, ALAN J., b. N.Y.C., Mar. 20, 1933; B.S., U. So. Calif., 1955; LL.B., U. Calif. at Los Angeles, 1963. Admitted to Calif. bar, 1964; mem. staff San Diego City Atty.'s Office, 1964-65; asso. firm Ludecke & Schafer, San Diego, 1965-71, firm Ludecke & Andreos, San Diego, 1972—. Mem. Am., Calif., San Diego trial lawyers assns. Named San Diego Trial Lawyers Month, 1973, 74, 76. Office: 1800 Crocker Band Bldg San Diego CA 92101 Tel (714) 232-9113

LUDGIN, ROBERT FREDERIC, b. Boston, Apr. 15, 1940; A.B., Princeton, 1962; J.D., U. Mich., 1966. Admitted to Conn. bar, 1966, U.S. 2d Circuit Ct. Appeals bar, 1967; budget examiner mil. div. Bur. Budget, Office Mgmt. and Budget, Washington, 1966-67; asso. firm Alcorn, Bakewell & Smith, Hartford, Conn., 1967-70; individual practice law, Hartford, 1971—. Mem. Am., Conn., Hartford County bar assns. Home: 286 Princeton St Hartford CT 06106 Office: 60 Washington St Hartford CT 06106 Tel (203) 549-3920

LUDLAM, WARREN VAN GILDER, JR., b. Meridian, Miss., Aug. 29, 1919; A.B. cum laude, Davidson Coll. (N.C.), 1940; LL.B., Harvard, 1943. Admitted to Tex. bar, 1944, Miss. bar, 1944, D.C. bar, 1975, U.S. Supreme Ct. bar, 1975; asso. firm Baker, Botts, Andrew & Wharton, Houston, 1943-44; asso. firm Watkins, Pyle, Ludlam, Winter & Stennis, Jackson, Miss., 1944-50, partner, 1950—, mng. partner, 1967-68; mem. nat. adv. council Practicing Law Inst., N.Y.C., 1963-75, lectr., 1965, mem. exec. com., adv. council, 1969-75; co-organizer, chmn. spl. liaison tax com. S.E. Region, IRS, 1961-62, mem. liaison com., Miss. dist. dir., 1962-63, pres., 1967-68, bd. dirs., 1964-68; past pres. Estate Planning Council Miss.; past commr. Miss. State Bar for 7th Jud. Dist., also past chmn. taxation com. Sec. ofcl. bd., past Sunday Sch. tchr. Galloway Meml. United Meth. Ch., Jackson; trustee Meth. Childrens Hosp., Jackson; past bd. dirs. St. Andrews Episcopal Day Sch., Jackson; past chmn. Hinds County chpt. Nat. Found. Infantile Paralysis, 1948; bd. mgmt. Jackson Central YMCA, 1964-66; past pres., bd. dirs. Jackson Jr. C. of C., Boys Club Jackson, Boys Club Jackson Found.; past bd. dirs. Jr. Achievement of Jackson; bd. dirs. Exchange Club Jackson, 1967-68, pres., 1969-70. Life fellow Miss. Bar Found.; mem. Am. (past com. chmn. assn. and sect. on taxation, asso. editor The Tax Lawyer 1973), D.C., Miss., Hinds County, Jackson Jr. (past pres.) bar assns., Jackson C. of C. (past com. chmn.), Phi Beta Kappa, Omicron Delta Kappa, Phi Delta Theta. Contbr. articles to profl. jours. Home: 3408 Kings Hwy Jackson MS 39216 Office: PO Box 427 20th Floor Deposit Guaranty Plaza Jackson MS 39205 Tel (601) 354-3456

LUDOLPH, ARTHUR LESLIE, b. Chgo., Nov. 25, 1888; LL.B., J.D., Chgo. Kent Coll. Law, 1915. Admitted to Ill. bar, 1915, N.Y. State bar, 1927; account exec., Mitchell, Hutchins & Co., Chgo., 1926-60, Glore, Forgan & Co., Chgo., 1960-63, Hornblower & Weeks, Hemphill, Noyes, Chgo., 1973-77. Mem. Chgo. Bar Assn. Home: 1732 Garfield Ave Aurora IL 60506 Office: Hornblower & Weeks Hemphill Noyes Inc 72 W Adams Chicago IL 60603 Tel (312) 781-6586

LUDWIG, EDMUND VINCENT, b. Phila., May 20, 1928; A.B., Harvard, 1949, LL.B., 1952. Admitted to Pa. bar, 1953; law clk. to judge Phila. Ct. Common Pleas, 1952-53; capt. JAGC, U.S. Army, 1953-56; asso. firm Duane, Morris & Heckscher, Phila., 1956-59; partner firm Barnes, Biester & Ludwig, Doylestown, Pa., 1959-68; judge Ct. of Common Pleas Bucks County (Pa.), Doylestown, 1968—; lectr. in field; chmn. juvenile ct. com. Bucks County Ct. Chmn., Youth Services Bucks County. Mem. Am., Pa., Bucks County bar assns., Juristic Soc., Am. Judicature Soc., Pa. Conf. State Trial Judges (chmn. mental health com.). Home: Office: Bucks County Court House Doylestown PA 18901 Tel (215) 348-2911

LUEBBERS, JOSEPH ALOYSIUS, b. Cin., Mar. 12, 1922; A.B., Xavier U., 1946; J.D., Chase Coll. Law, 1950. Admitted to Ohio bar, 1952, U.S. Dist. Ct. bar for So. Ohio Dist., 1961; practiced in Cin., 1963-64; adminstr. Bur. Workmen's Compensation, Indsl. Com. Ohio So. Dist., 1956-62; judge Municipal Ct., Cin., 1965-70, Ham County (Ohio) Municipal Ct., 1970—. Bd. dirs. St. Aloysius Orphange, Cin., Merci Montesorri, Cin., Men of Milford (Ohio); pres. Xavier U. Alumni Assn., Cin., 1976—. Mem. Cin., Ohio, Am. bar assns., North Am. Judges Assn., Ohio Municipal Judges Assn., Cin. Lawyers Club. Recipient award of Merit Ohio Legal Inst., 1970, Man of Year award, 1971; Outstanding Jud. Service award Ohio Supreme Ct., 1975, 76. Home: 3733 Donegal Dr Cincinnati OH 45236 Office: 1000 Main St Cincinnati OH 45202 Tel (513) 632-8310

LUIS, CARLOS WILLIAM, b. Hayfield, Minn., Mar. 19, 1919; A.B., St. Olaf Coll., 1940; B.S.L., Mpls.-Minn. Coll. Law, 1952, LL.B., 1954, J.D., 1969. Admitted to Minn. bar, 1954; tchr. and coach, Triumph, Minn., 1940-42; tchr. and prin., Shakopee, Minn., 1946-49; salesman, State Bond and Mortgage Co., New Ulm, Minn., 1949-50; with Minn. Mining and Mfg. Co., St. Paul, 1950—, graphic products group, 1950-56, corp. atty., 1956-63, asst. sec., 1963-72, acting mgr. aviation dept., 1967-68, asst. gen. counsel, 1969-72, v.p. fed. govt. affairs, 1972-74, v.p. pub. affairs and personnel relations, 1974—. Dir. St. Paul C. of C., 1975—; trustee Baptist Hosp. Fund, St. Paul, 1975—; dir. Associated Colls. of Twin Cities, 1975—, United Way of St. Paul Area, 1975—; mem. Minn. Assn. Commerce and Industry, St. Paul, 1975—. Mem. Minn. State, Ramsey County Bar Assns., Corp. Counsel Assn. Minn. Office: 3M Co 3M Center Bldg 220-14W Saint Paul MN 55101 Tel (612) 733-3461

LUKACHER, MARTIN, b. Bklyn., Dec. 29, 1931; B.E.E., Poly. Inst. N.Y., 1953; LL.B., Temple U., 1958. Admitted to D.C. bar, 1958, N.Y. State bar, 1966; patent atty. RCA Corp., 1953-63; patent counsel Gen. Dynamics Corp., 1963-71; individual practice law, Rochester, N.Y., 1971—; lectr. Am. Mgmt. Assn. Mem. Rochester Patent Law Assn. (pres. 1977), Monroe County Bar Assn. Contbr. articles to legal jours. Home: 70 Aberthaw Rd Rochester NY 14610 Office: 47 S Fitzhugh St Rochester NY 14614 Tel (716) 454-2790

LUKSCH, JOSEPH DAVID, b. Buffalo, N.Y., Jan. 17, 1930; B.A., U. Buffalo, 1957, J.D., 1958. Admitted to N.Y. State bar, 1958, Ill. bar, 1969, D.C. bar, 1972; atty. NLRB, Pitts., 1959-61, Buffalo, 1961-68; asso. firm Vedder, Price, Kaufman, Kammholz & Day, Washington, 1968-71, partner, 1972—; asst. gen. counsel labor law dept. U.S. Postal Service, Washington, 1971-72; instr. U. Buffalo, 1965-68. Mem. D.C. Bar, Fed. Bar Assn. Office: 1750 Pennsylvania Ave NW Washington DC 20006 Tel (202) 298-6445

LUM, HERMAN, b. Honolulu, Nov. 5, 1926; grad. U. Hawaii, 1946, U. Mo. Law Sch., 1950; grad. Nat. Coll. State Trial Judges, Nat. Coll. Juvenile Justice. Admitted to Hawaii bar, 1950, Fed. Dist. Ct. bar, U.S. Ct. of Appeals bar for 9th Circuit, U.S. Supreme Ct. bar, U.S. Ct. Mil. Appeals bar, U.S. Customs Ct. bar; asst. pub. prosecutor, 1950-52; chief atty. Ho. of Reps., 1955, chief clk., 1956-61; U.S. atty., 1961-67; circuit judge 1st Jud. Circuit, Honolulu, 1967—; mem. State Law Enforcement and Juvenile Delinquency Planning Agy. Chmn., Mental Health Council, Western Interstate Commn. for Higher Edn. Home: 2508 Makiki Heights Dr Honolulu HI 96822 Office: PO Box 3498 Honolulu HI 96811 Tel (808) 537-4326

LUMBARD, ELIOT HOWLAND, b. Fairhaven, Mass., May 6, 1925; B.S., U.S. Mcht. Marine Acad., 1945; B.S. in Econs., U. Pa., 1949; J.D., Columbia U., 1952. Admitted to N.Y. bar, 1953, U.S. Supreme Ct. bar, 1959; asso. firm Breed, Abbott & Morgan, N.Y.C., 1952-53, Chadbourne, Parke, Whiteside & Wolff, 1956-58; partner firm Townsend & Lewis, 1961-70, Spear & Hill, N.Y.C., 1970-75, Lumbard & Phelan, 1977—; asst. U.S. atty. So. Dist. N.Y., 1953-56; chief counsel N.Y. State Commn. Investigation, 1958-61; spl. asst. counsel for law enforcement N.Y. Gov. Rockefeller, 1961-67; criminal justice cons. N.J. Legis., 1968-69, Fla. Gov. Claude Kirk, Jr., 1967; chmn. com. on organized crime N.Y.C. Criminal Justice Coordinating Council, 1971-74; adj. prof. law City U. N.Y., 1974; chmn. bd. Palisades Life Ins. Co., 1973-75. Trustee N.Y. C. Police Found., 197, chmn. bd., 1971-74; trustee Trinity Sch. N.Y.C., 1964—; trustee Trinity Housing Co. Inc., 1969—, pres. bd., 1969-77, N.Y. State Maritime Mus., 1969—. Mem. Am., N.Y. State bar assns., Assn. Bar City N.Y., N.Y. County Lawyers Assn., Maritime Law Assn. Contbr. articles to legal jours. Home: 382 Central Park W New York City NY 10025 Office: Lumbard & Phelan One State St Plaza New York City NY 10004 Tel (212) 422-6660

LUMPKIN, CHARLES HENRY, b. Carrollton, Ga., Mar. 11, 1943; B.S., U. Ga., 1965; J.D., Emory U., 1968. Admitted to Ga. bar, 1968; mem. staff Fulton County (Ga.) Legal Services, 1967-69; asso. firm Gilbert and Head, Carrollton, Ga., 1969-73; individual practice law, Carrollton, 1973—. Mem. Carrollton City Council, 1971-73; mayor of Carrollton, 1973-75; bd. dirs. Carroll County (Ga.) March of Dimes, 1972—, chmn., 1971; bd. dirs. Oak Mountain Acad. Mem. Am., Ga., Carrollton bar assns. Office: 106 S White St Carrollton GA 30117 Tel (404) 834-0877

LUNA, MARJORIE LEE, b. South Bend, Ind., Apr. 23, 1904; LL.B., Blackstone Coll., 1938. Admitted to Mich. bar, 1938, U.S. Supreme Ct. bar, 1975; asst. pros. atty. Allegan County (Mich.), 1937, Friend of the Ct., 1939-41; circuit ct. commr., Mich., 1941-46; judge dist. ct., Kalamazoo, 1970-75, acting judge dist. and circuit cts., Kalamazoo County, 1975—. Mem. Kalamazoo County, Mich., Am. bar assns., Am. Trial Lawyers Assn. Named Woman of Year Quota Club, 1970. Home: 611 W Lovell St Kalamazoo MI 49007 Office: PO Box 9 Kalamazoo MI 49005 Tel (616) 343-3939

LUND, DANIEL PETER, b. N.Y.C., Aug. 15, 1940; A.B. cum laude, Princeton, 1962; LL.B., Columbia, 1965. Admitted to N.Y. bar, 1965, D.C. bar, 1969; asso. firm Busby Rivkin Sherman Levy and Rehm, N.Y.C., 1966-72; firm Fink, Weinberger, Fredman & Charney, N.Y.C., 1972-76; partner firm Genzer and Lund, N.Y.C., 1976—. Home: 33 Riverside Dr New York City NY 10023 Office: 444 Madison Ave New York City NY 10022 Tel (212) 759-4910

LUND, RICHARD WILLIAM, b. Salt Lake City, Mar. 1, 1913; B.A., Occidental Coll., 1935; LL.B., Harvard, 1938. Admitted to Calif. bar, 1938, U.S. Supreme Ct. bar, 1954; asso. firm Latham & Watkins, Los Angeles, 1938-45, partner, 1945—, now sr. partner. Mem. Los Angeles, Los Angeles County, Am. bar assns., Calif. State Bar, Phi Beta Kappa. Editor Harvard Law Rev., 1937-38; contbr. articles to Calif. Continuing Edn. of Bar Program. Home: 722 N Linden Dr Beverly Hills CA 90210 Office: 555 S Flower St Los Angeles CA 90071 Tel (203) 485-1234

LUND, WENDELL LUTHER, b. Prentice, Wis., Dec. 31, 1905; A.B., Augustana Coll., 1927; A.M., Columbia, 1930; LL.B., Georgetown U., 1938, J.D., 1972; Ph.D., Princeton, 1933. Admitted to D.C. bar, 1938, U.S. Supreme Ct. bar, 1944; mem. firm Lund, Levin & O'Brien, and predecessors, Washington, 1943—, Detroit, 1943-55. Sec., Mich. Adminstrv. Bd., 1941; exec. dir. Mich. Unemployment Compensation Commn., 1941-42; dir. labor prodn. div. War Prodn. Bd., 1942-43, spl. asst. to chmn., 1943; mem. War Manpower Commn., 1942-43; trustee Salem (W.Va.) Coll., 1974—; mem. bd. pensions Luth. Ch. Am., 1963-67, 70—, pres., 1967-68, 74—. Mem. Am., Fed., Inter-Am. bar assns., Bar Assn. D.C., Phi Beta Kappa. Tel (202) 331-1377

LUNDBERG, LAWRENCE BERT, b. Seattle, Jan. 18, 1947; B.A., U. Wash., 1969; J.D. cum laude, U. Minn., 1972. Admitted to Wash. bar, 1972; law clk., office of field solicitor Dept. Interior, Mpls., 1971; asso. firms Ogden, Ogden & Murphy, Seattle, 1972-75, Haugland & Sherrow, Seattle, 1975-76; partner firm Sherrow & Lundberg, Seattle, 1976—. Pres., Our Redeemer's Ch., Seattle, 1977. Mem. Seattle-King County, Snohomish County (Wash.), Wash. State, Am. bar assns., Wash. State, Am. assns. trial lawyers, Omicron Delta Epsilon. Office: 1945 Bank of Calif 900 Fourth Ave Seattle WA 98164 Tel (206) 623-3932

LUNDBORG, EDWIN ROBERT, b. Denver, Feb. 8, 1923; B.S. in Bus. Adminstrn., U. Denver, 1948, J.D., 1950. Admitted to Colo. bar, 1951; individual practice law, Denver, 1951-52, 53-57; spl. agt. atty. Office Price Stablzn., Denver, 1952-53; hearing examiner Pub. Utilities Commn. State of Colo., Denver, 1957-65; joint bd. mem. representing State of Colo. ICC, 1957—; exec. sec. Pub. Utilities Commn. State of Colo., Denver, 1965-67, commr., 1967-73, chmn., 1973—; dir. Regulatory Conf. Iowa State U. Mem. Western Conf. Pub. Service Commns. (past pres.), Nat. Assn. Regulatory Utility Commrs. (exec. com., past chmn. com. on railroads, mem. com. on communications), Transp. Law Inst. U. Denver. Home: 3302 S Oneida Way Denver CO 80224 Office: 500 State Services Bldg 1525 Sherman St Denver CO 80203 Tel (303) 892-3154

LUNDE, ASBJORN RUDOLPH, b. S.I., N.Y., July 17, 1927; A.B., Columbia, 1947, LL.B., 1949. Admitted to N.Y. bar, 1949, since practiced in N.Y.C.; with firm Kramer, Marx, Greenlee & Backus and predecessors, 1950-68, mem., 1958-68; individual practice law, 1968—; dir. numerous corps. Bd. dirs., v.p. Orchestra da Camera, Inc., N.Y.C., 1964—; bd. dirs. Sara Roby Found., N.Y.C., 1971—, The Drawing Soc., N.Y.C., 1977—. Mem. Am., N.Y. State bar assns., Assn. Bar City N.Y. Home: 1120 Park Ave New York City NY 10028 Office: 230 Park Ave New York City NY 10017

LUNDEEN, DAVID FRANKLIN, b. Fergus Falls, Minn., Oct. 28, 1932; B.A., Amherst Coll., 1954; J.D., Harvard, 1957. Admitted to Minn. bar, 1957, U.S. Ct. Mil. Appeals bar, 1957, U.S. Dist. Ct. Minn. bar, 1961, U.S. Supreme Ct. bar, 1972, U.S. 8th Circuit Ct. Appeals bar, 1973; capt. JAGC, USAR, 1957-60; asso. Field Arvesen, Donoho & Lundeen & Hoff and predecessors, 1960-61, partner, 1962—. Home: 705 Lakeside Dr Fergus Falls MN 56537 Office: 125 S Mill St Fergus Falls MN 56537 Tel (218) 736-5456

LUNDING, CHRISTOPHER HANNA, b. Evanston, Ill., June 15, 1946; B.A. magna cum laude, Harvard U., 1968; J.D., Yale U., 1971. Admitted to N.Y. bar, 1972, Fla. bar, 1972, U.S. Supreme Ct. bar, 1975; law clk. U.S. Ct. Appeals, 2d Circuit, N.Y.C., 1971-72; asso. firm Cleary, Gottlieb, Steen & Hamilton, N.Y.C., 1973—. Mem. N.Y. State Bar Assn. Contbr. article to legal jour. Office: Cleary Gottlieb et al 1 State St Plaza New York City NY 10004 Tel (212) 344-0600

LUNDQUIST, JAMES HAROLD, b. Chgo., Mar. 24, 1931; A.B., James Millikin U., 1953; J.D., John Marshall Sch. Law, 1954. Admitted to Ill. bar, 1954, N.Y. State bar, 1960, D.C. bar, 1960, U.S. Supreme Ct. bar, 1961; asso. firm Barnes, Richardson & Colburn, Chgo., 1957-60, partner, 1960—. Mem. Am. Bar Assn. (chmn. standing com. custom law 1971-76), Assn. Bar City N.Y. (com. on fed. legislation 1970-73), Assn. Customs Bar (v.p. 1976—). Office: 475 Park Ave S New York City NY 10016 also 1819 H Street Washington DC 20006 Tel (212) 725-0200 also (202) 659-8404

LUNDQUIST, ROBERT EDWARD, b. Boston, Apr. 30, 1947; A.B., Dartmouth, 1969; J.D., U. Ariz., 1973. Admitted to Ariz. bar, 1973; asso. firm Chandler, Tullar, Udall & Richmond, Tucson, 1973—. Mem. U. Ariz. Coll. Law Alumni Assn. (dir.), Am., Ariz., Pima County bar assns., Order of Coif. Exec. editor Ariz. Law Rev., 1972-73. Office: 1110 Transamerica Bldg 177 N Church St Tucson AZ 85701 Tel (602) 623-4353

LUNDY, MITCHELL MCKREE, SR., b. Philadelphia, Miss., July 10, 1922; A.B., U. Miss., 1949, LL.B., 1951, J.D., 1968. Admitted to Miss. bar, 1951; mem. firm Luncy & McConough, Grenada, Miss.; individual practice law, Grenada, 1955—; city pros. atty., Grenada; municipal ct. judge, Grenada. Mem. Grenada County, Miss. State bar assns., Phi Alpha Delta. Home: 325 Katherine Dr Grenada MS 38901 Office: 11 Evans Bldg 169 S Main St Grenada MS 38901 Tel (601) 226-1343

LUNN, STUART DOUGLAS, b. Shreveport, La., Oct. 10, 1925; B.A., La. State U., 1948, J.D., 1950. Admitted to La. bar, 1950; mem. legal dept. Shell Oil Co., New Orleans, 1950-51; partner firm Smitherman, Lunn, Hussey & Chastain, Shreveport, 1954—; dir. various bus. corps. Mem. Shreveport (pres. 1976), La., Am., Internat. bar assns. Office: 717 Comml Nat Bank Bldg Shreveport LA 71101 Tel (318) 227-1990

LUNSFORD, ALAN DWIGHT, b. Columbus, Ohio, Oct. 18, 1935; B.A., Wesleyan U., 1956; LL.B., Franklin U., 1965, J.D., 1966. Admitted to Ohio bar, 1965; accountant Ohio Nat. Bank Columbus, 1956-66; asst. pros. atty. Franklin County (Ohio), 1966-71; individual practice law, Columbus, 1971—. Mem. Columbus, Ohio, Am. bar assns. Home: 4 Sessions Dr Columbus OH 43215 Tel (614) 228-1575

LUNSFORD, LLOYD MITCHELL, b. Shelbyville, Ky., Nov. 21, 1922; B.S., U. Houston, 1950, LL.B., 1953, J.D., 1954. Admitted to Tex. bar, 1953, U.S. Supreme Ct. bar, 1963; individual practice law, S. Houston, Tex., 1953—. Mem. East End Improvement Assn., Meadowcreek Civic Club, Citizens for Good Govt. Com. Mem. Houston Bar Assn., Surburban Lawyers Assn., Nat., Tex. def. lawyers assns., Harris County Criminal Lawyers Assn. Decorated DFC, Air medal; recipient Const. Law award, West Publ. Co., St. John Garwood Law Excellence Award. Office: 411 Spencer South Houston TX 77587 Tel (713) 946-6620

LUNT, JACK, b. Hartford, Conn., Oct. 19, 1944; B.S. magna cum laude, U. Utah, 1966, J.D., 1969. Admitted to Utah bar, 1969; asso. firm Jones, Waldo, Holbrook & McDonough, Salt Lake City, 1969-73, partner, 1974—, chmn. hiring com., 1976—. Mem. Dixie Coll. Instl. Council, St. George, Utah, 1975—, Capitol Hill Commn. Utah State Bldg. Bd., Salt Lake City, 1974—; bd. dirs. Utah ACLU, 1973-75; chmn. Democratic Candidate Selection Com., Salt Lake City, 1976, Salt Lake County Dem. Conv., 1976. Mem. Am., Salt Lake County bar assns. Office: 800 Walker Bank Bldg Salt Lake City UT 84111 Tel (801) 521-3200

LUPPI, MICHAEL DENNIS, b. Medford, Mass., Aug. 12, 1946; A.B., U. Calif., Los Angeles, 1968, J.D., 1972. Admitted to Calif. bar, 1973; individual practice law, Los Angeles, 1974-75; asso. firm Myers & D'Angelo, Los Angeles, 1975—. Mem. Beverly Hills, Wilshire, Los Angeles County, Am. bar assns., State Bar Calif., Delta Theta Phi. Office: 3303 Wilshire Blvd Suite 500 Los Angeles CA 90010 Tel (213) 380-2830

LUPTON, HARVEY ARTHUR, b. Whortonsville, N.C., Sept. 1, 1909; J.D. cum laude, Wake Forest U., 1933. Admitted to N.C. bar, 1933; individual practice law, Winston-Salem, N.C., 1933-54; dist. atty. Superior Ct., Winston-Salem, 1954-65; judge Superior Ct., Winston-Salem, 1965—. Mem. Am., Fed., N.C. (v.p. 1971-72) bar assns., Conf. Superior Court Judges (pres. 1971-72). Home: 3563 Milhaven Rd Winston-Salem NC 27106 Office: Suite 510 Forsyth County Hall of Justice Winston-Salem NC 27102 Tel (919) 761-2236

LUREY, ALFRED SAUL, b. Greenville, S.C., Oct. 17, 1942; A.B., Duke U., 1964; LL.B., Harvard U., 1967. Admitted to Calif. bar, 1967, Ga. bar, 1970; law clk. 4th Circuit U.S. Ct. of Appeals, 1967-68; mem. firm Kilpatrick, Cody, Rogers, McClatchey & Regenstein, Atlanta, 1969-75, partner, 1975—; counsel, Met. Atlanta Commn. on Crime and Juvenile Delinquency, 1971-72; dir. Southeastern Bankruptcy Law Inst. Mem. Am., Atlanta bar assns., State Bars of Ga., Calif. Home: 3091 Rhodenhaven Dr NW Atlanta GA 30327 Office: 3100 Equitable Bldg Atlanta GA 30303 Tel (404) 522-3100

LURIA, SYDNEY AARON, b. N.Y.C., Feb. 2, 1908; B.A., Coll. City N.Y., 1929; LL.B., Harvard, 1934. Admitted to N.Y. bar, 1934, U.S. Supreme Ct. bar, 1942; mem. firm Larb, Luria, Glassner, Cook & Kufeld, N.Y.C., 1934—, sr. partner, 1963—. Mem. Am., N.Y. County N.Y. State bar assns., Bar Assn. City N.Y. Office: 529 Fifth Ave New York City NY 10017 Tel (212) 986-3131

LURIE, DAVID MICHAEL, b. N. Adams, Mass., Dec. 31, 1935; B.S. cum laude, Ind. U., 1958; B.S., U. Mich., 1961; LL.B., Nat. Coll. State Judiciary U. Nev., 1973. Admitted to Ind. bar, 1961, Ariz. bar, 1962; asst. atty. gen. Ariz., Phoenix, 1962-64; asst. city atty. Phoenix, 1964-67; individual practice law, Phoenix, 1967-72, 1975—; judge Ariz. Superior Ct., Maricopa County, 1972-74; asso. firm Streich, Lang, Weeks, Cardon & French, Phoenix, 1974-75; spl. counsel Ariz. Ho. of Reps., Phoenix, 1971, 77; judge pro temp City Phoenix, 1972; dir., spl. counsel Ariz. Center Law Pub. Interest, 1976—; faculty mem. Phoenix Coll., 1976—. Founder, mem. Valley (Ariz.) Big Brothers, 1965-72, officer, 1967-68, bd. dirs., 1966-72; mem. Phoenix Mountain Preservation Comm., 1972-73; bd. dirs. Temple Beth Israel, Phoenix, 1975—. Mem. Am., Maricopa County (dir.) bar assns., Maricopa County Young Lawyers Assn. (pres. 1969-70), Am. Trial Lawyers Assn. (dir. local chpt. 1972). Office: 711 Arizona Title Bldg 111 W Monroe St Phoenix AZ 85003 Tel (602) 254-5044

LURIE, HORACE LEON, b. East Palestine, Ohio, Feb. 27, 1916; student Western Res. U., 1937; LL.B., Cleve. Marshall Sch. Law, 1941, J.D., 1968. Admitted to Ohio bar, 1941, Ariz. bar, 1963; individual practice law; judge Phoenix Municipal Ct., 1973—. Mem. Ariz. State, Maricopa County bar assns. Office: 5033 N 19th Ave Room 112 Phoenix AZ 85015 Tel (602) 242-9221

LURIE, WILLIAM L., b. Latrobe, Pa., Feb. 8, 1931; B.S., Northwestern U., 1952, M.B.A., 1954, J.D., 1955. Admitted to Mich. bar, 1955, Ill. bar, 1955, N.Y. bar, 1956; with legal dept. Gen. Electric Co., N.Y.C., Syracuse, N.Y. and Charlottesville, Va., 1955-69, v.p., gen. mgr. internat. support div., 1969-72, v.p. internat. strategic planning and rev., 1972-74; v.p., gen. counsel Internat. Paper Co., N.Y.C., 1974-76, v.p. external affairs, gen. counsel, 1976, exec. v.p. diversified bus., gen. counsel, 1976—. Mem. industry adv. council Overseas Pvt. Investment Corp., 1971-73. Mem. Fgn. Policy Assn. (dir.), Brit. Am. C. of C. (dir.), Order of Coif, Beta Gamma Sigma. Office: 220 E 42d St New York City NY 10017 Tel (212) 490-6685

LUSBY, DENE LONIER, b. Balt., Aug. 6, 1933; A.B., Johns Hopkins, 1955; LL.B., U. Md., 1958. Admitted to Md. bar, 1958, U.S. Supreme Ct. bar, 1964; asso. firm Weinberg & Green, Balt., 1958-59; asst. state's atty., Balt. City, 1959-62; sr. trial atty. FTC, also anti-trust div. U.S. Dept. Justice, Washington, 1962-68; individual practice law,

Balt., 1968-72; exec. dir. Inmate Grievance Commn., State of Md., Hunt Valley, 1972—; lectr. Mem. Delta Theta Phi, Alpha Tau Omega. Home: 1813 Roland Ave Ruxton MD 21204 Office: Suite 402 Exec Plaza One Hunt Valley MD 21031 Tel (301) 667-1810

LUSTHOFF, CRAIG WILLIAM, b. Chgo., Aug. 28, 1947; B.A., Valparaiso U., 1969; J.D., DePaul U., 1974. Admitted to Ill. bar, 1974, Fla. bar, 1975; individual practice law, Westchester, Ill., 1974-76, Riverside, Ill., 1976—; bus. law instr. J. Sterling Morton High Sch. W., Berwyn, Ill., 1973—. Bd. dirs. Concordia Tchrs. Coll. Found., River Forest, Ill., 1975—; adv. com. Luth. High Sch. Assn. Greater Chgo., 1976—. Mem. Chgo., Ill. State, Am., W. Suburban, Fla. bar assns., Phi Delta Kappa, Delta Theta Phi. Office: 2914 S Harlem Ave Riverside IL 60546 Tel (312) 447-5694

LUSTIG, ROBERT M., b. Cleve., July 1, 1936; A.B., Case Western Res. U., 1957, LL.B., 1960. Admitted to Ohio bar, 1960; partner firm Lustig, Icove & Lustig, Cleve., 1961—. Mem. Am., Ohio, Cleveland, Cuyahoga County (trustee, chmn.) bar assns. Office: Leader Bldg Cleveland OH 44114 Tel (216) 241-5735

LUTHER, CHARLES WILLIAM, b. Bethany, Okla., Nov. 25, 1931; A.A., Am. River Coll., 1954; J.D., Hastings Coll. Law U. Calif., San Francisco, 1958. Admitted to Calif. bar, 1959; partner firm Luther, Luther, O'Connor & Johnson, Sacramento, 1959-70; prof. law McGeorge Sch. Law, 1965-67, asst. dean, 1967-68, asso. dean, 1968-69, prof., 1969—. Bd. dirs. Sacramento Legal Aid Soc.; bd. advisers Ct. Practice Inst., Chgo., 1971—. Mem. Am., Calif., Sacramento County bar assns., AAUP, Assn. Am. Trial Lawyers, Calif. Trial Lawyers Assn., Phi Alpha Delta. Recipient Outstanding Tchr. award McGeorge Sch. Law U. Pacific, 1973, 76; author: Survey of Torts, 1972, rev. edit., 1975; Survey of Criminal Law, 1969, rev. edit., 1975; Calif. decisions editor Community Property Jour., 1974—. Office: PO Box 2151 Fair Oaks CA 95628 Tel (916) 452-6051

LUTHER, FLORENCE JOAN, b. Bklyn., June 28, 1928; student Am. River Coll., 1959-60; J.D. magna cum laude, U. Pacific, 1962. Admitted to Calif., U.S. 9th Circuit Ct. Appeals bars, 1964; partner firm Luther, Luther, O'Connor & Johnson, Sacramento, 1964-66; research atty. Calif. 3d dist. Ct. Appeals, Sacramento, 1966-67; prof. law U. Pacific, 1967—; mem. bd. advisory Community Property Jour., 1975—. Mem. Am., Sacramento County bar assns., AAUP, Am. Judicature Soc., Iota Tau Tau, Phi Alpha Delta. Contbr. articles to profl. jours. Office: PO Box 2151 Fair Oaks CA 95628 Tel (916) 976-5400

LUTNICKI, VICTOR ANTHONY, b. Chgo., Dec. 20, 1914; B.S., Northwestern U., 1936, J.D., 1939. Admitted to Ill. bar, 1939, Mass. bar, 1946; exec. v.p. John Hancock Mut. Life Ins. Co., Boston, also dir.; chmn. bd. John Hancock Internat. Services, S.Am.; dir., mem. exec. com. Maritime Life Assurance Co., Halifax, N.S., Can.; dir., mem. exec. and finance coms. Maritime Life (Caribbean Ltd.), Trinidad, B.W.I. Chmn. bd. trustees Andover Newton Theol. Sch.; alt. rep. World Peace Through Law U.S. Mission to UN. Mem. Am. Bar Assn. (ho. of dels.), Am. Mgmt. Assn. (gen. mgmt. div. council), Phi Beta Kappa. Home: Bedford Rd Lincoln MA 01773 Office: John Hancock Pl PO Box 111 Boston MA 02117 Tel (617) 421-6100

LUTTERAL, MARGARITA NELIDA, b. Buenos Aires, Argentina, Oct. 23, 1937; LL.B., Buenos Aires U., 1963; J.D., Bklyn. Law Sch., 1972; LL.M., Harvard, 1963. Admitted to Buenos Aires bar, 1963, N.Y. State bar, 1973; asso. firm Curtis Mallet Prevost Colt & Mosle, N.Y.C., 1968-71; sr. tax editor Matthew Bender, N.Y.C., 1972—. Mem. N.Y. State, Am., Buenos Aires bar assns. Home: 301 W 45th St 12A New York City NY 10036 Office: 235 E 45th St New York City NY 10017 Tel (212) 661-5050

LUTZ, ELIZABETH MAY, b. Balt., Feb. 13, 1928; A.A., U. Balt., 1962, LL.B., 1965. Admitted to Md. bar, 1966; trust adminstrv. officer Mercantile Safe Deposit & Trust Co., Balt., 1966—. Mem. Am., Md. bar assns., Nat. Assn. Bank Women (chmn. Balt. group 1973-74). Home: 34 Acorn Circle Towson MD 21204 Office: 2 Hopkins Plaza Baltimore MD 21201 Tel (301) 237-5106

LUTZ, ROBERT EMMETT, II, b. San Diego, Apr. 8, 1946; B.A., U. So. Calif., 1968; J.D., U. Calif., Berkeley, 1971. Admitted to Calif. bar, 1971; law clk. U.S. Dist. Ct., San Diego, 1971-72; asso. firm Pillsbury, Madison & Sutro, San Francisco, 1972-73; cons., research fellow Internat. Union for Conservation of Nature and Natural Resources, Bonn, W.Ger., 1973, 74; dep. regional counsel Fed. Energy Adminstrn., San Francisco, 1974; asst. prof., dir. Inst. Coastal Law and Mgmt. U. So. Calif., Los Angeles, 1974-76; vis. prof. law U. Pacific, Sacramento, 1976—. Mem. Assn. Am. Law Schs. (chmn. sect. on environ. law 1976—), Calif., Am., Internat. bar assns., Am. Soc. Pub. Adminstrs., Phi Beta Kappa. Home: 204 Selby Ranch Rd No 5 Sacramento CA 95825 Office: 3200 5th Ave Sacramento CA 95817 Tel (916) 449-7101

LYBROOK, ROBERT BURKE, b. Gary, Ind., Jan. 11, 1914; LL.B., Ind. U., 1937. Admitted to Ind. Supreme Ct. bar, 1937, U.S. Dist. Ct. bar for So. Dist. Ind., 1937; partner firms Miller, Pogue & Lybrook, Franklin, Ind., 1946-54, Lybrook & Bradley, Nashville, Ind., 1967-72; judge 8th Jud. Circuit of Ind., 1954-66, Ind. Appellate Ct., 1970, Ind. Ct. Appeals, 1972—; pros. atty. Johnson County (Ind.), 1946-50. Mem. Ind. State Bar Assn. Home: Rural Route 8 Martinsville IN 46151 Office: 425 State House Indianapolis IN 46204 Tel (317) 633-4931

LYDERSON, DONALD JAMES, b. Everett, Wash., Apr. 5, 1938; B.A., U. Wash., 1962, J.D., 1965. Admitted to Wash. bar, 1966; partner firm Cooper & Lyderson, Everett, 1966—; city atty. City of Lake Stevens, Wash., 1974—; asst. city atty. City of Everett, 1966—. Mem. Wash., Snohomish County (v.p.) bar assns., Snohomish County Estate Planning Council (sec.). Office: PO Box 981 Everett WA 98206 Tel (206) 259-5559

LYLE, TITUS GORDON, b. Kyrock, Ky., Nov. 24, 1939; A.B., Western Ky. U., 1962; J.D., U. Ky., 1965. Admitted to Ky. bar, 1965; mem. firm Keen & Lyle, Scottsville, Ky., 1965—. Mem. Ky., Allen County, Am. bar assns., Scottsville C. of C. (sec. 1970). Home: Route 8 Scottsville KY 42164 Office: 1271 E Main St Scottsville KY 42164 Tel (502) 237-3806

LYLE, WILLIAM FRANKLIN, JR., b. Wellsburg, W.Va., Apr. 24, 1944; B.S., U.S. Air Force Acad., 1966; J.D., U. Kans., 1973. Admitted to Kans. bar, 1973; asso. firm Kenneth F. Ehling, 1973-75; partner firm Ehling & Lyle, Hutchinson, Kans., 1975—. Mem. Reno County, Kans., Am. bar assns. Home: 205 W 26th St Hutchinson KS 67501 Office: 710 Wiley Bldg Hutchinson KS 67501 Tel (316) 665-5596

LYMAN, LUKE HUDSON, b. Columbus, Ohio, Jan. 30, 1908; B.Sc., in Commerce and Adminstrn., Ohio State U., 1929, J.D., 1932. Admitted to Ohio bar, 1932; law clk. to Judge Florence E. Allen, 6th Circuit Ct. Appeals of U.S., 1934-40; clk. Am. Arbitration Assn., Cleve., 1940-42; trust legal counsel Central Nat. Bank of Cleve., 1942-63, trust officer, 1957-63, v.p., 1959-63; partner firm Burke, Haber & Berick, Cleve., 1963-66; individual practice law, Cleve., 1966—; panelist Ohio Practicing Law Inst. on Trusts, 1965, 66; instr. to C.L.U.'s., 1948-65. Trustee, soc. Lakewood (Ohio) Presbyterian Ch., 1954-60; trustee Altenheim, Cleve., 1969-75. Mem. Ohio State Bar Assn. Home: 3400 Wooster Rd Apt 220 Rocky River OH 44116 Office: 1515 East Ohio Bldg Cleveland OH 44114 Tel (216) 861-7092

LYMAN, ROBERT GEORGE, b. Albany, N.Y., Sept. 23, 1940; B.A., U. N.H., 1963; J.D., Albany Law Sch., 1969. Admitted to N.Y. bar, 1969; individual practice law, Albany, 1969—; asst. corp. counsel City of Albany, 1970-71; counsel Albany Sch. Dist., 1972-75; county atty., Albany County, 1976—. Mem. N.Y., Albany County bar assns. Home: 18 Fleetwood Ave Albany NY 12208 Office: 40 Steuben St Albany NY 12207 Tel (518) 434-0879

LYMAN, WEBSTER S., b. Columbus, Ohio, Sept. 24, 1922; B.S., Ohio State U., 1944, LL.B., 1949. Admitted to Ohio bar, 1950; mem. firm Lyman & Lyman, Columbus, 1950-74, Lyman, Lyman & Scurry, Columbus, 1974-76, Lyman, Scurry & Winkfield, Columbus, 1976—; hearing examiner Ohio Civil Rights Commn., 1974—. Mem. Nat., Columbus bar assns., Lawyers Christian Fellowship, Robert B. Elliott Law Club. Home: 1526 Demorest Rd Columbus OH 43228 Office: Suite 222 720 E Broad St Columbus OH 43215 Tel (614) 221-1158

LYNCH, ALBERT WILLIAM, b. E. Providence, R.I., June 5, 1918; A.B., Adelbert-Western Res. U., 1940; J.D., Cleveland-Marshall Law Sch., 1941. Admitted to Ohio bar, 1951; individual practice law, Cleveland, 1957—. Mem. Ohio, Greater Cleve. bar assns., Kiwanis, Masons. Home: 6400 Dellbank Dr Cleveland OH 44144 Office: 4169 Pearl Rd #311 Cleveland OH 44109 Tel (216) 741-1408

LYNCH, GEORGE PATRICK, b. Chgo., Apr. 26, 1932; B.S., U. Ill., 1957; J.D., DePaul U., 1969. Asst. atty. State of Ill., subsequently special asst. atty.; mem. firm Hardiman & Lynch, and predecessor, Chgo., 1967-75; individual practice law, Chgo., 1975—; lectr. in field. Pres. Associated Sign Contractors of Cook County (Ill.), Chgo., 1961-63. Mem. Chgo., Ill. bar assns., Ogden Hill C of C (pres. 1959-61). Contbr. articles to legal joours. Home: 2 S 703 Normandy West Oak Brook IL 60521 Office: 1 IBM Plaza Suite 2410 Chicago IL 60611 Tel (312) 822-9160

LYNCH, J. ROBERT, b. N.Y.C., Mar. 1, 1921; student Cornell U., 1940, Manhattan Coll., 1942; LL.B., Albany Law Sch., Union U., 1948. Admitted to N.Y. State bar, 1948, Fed. Dist. Ct., 1949; asso. firm Scanlon, Wright & Willmott, Watertown, N.Y., 1948; individual practice law, Lowville, N.Y., 1949-59; law asst. to N.Y. State Ct. of Claims judge, 1949-56; dist. atty. Lewis County (N.Y.), 1959; justice N.Y. Supreme Ct., Lowville, 1960—, temporary judge, appellate div., 1st dept., N.Y.C., 1974—. Chmn. Lewis County Republican Com., 1954-58. Mem. N.Y. State, Lewis County bar assns. Home: 5361 Water Terr Lowville NY 13367 Office: Lewis County Ct House Lowville NY 13367 Tel (315) 376-3413

LYNCH, JOHN FRANCIS, b. Jersey City, Feb. 6, 1909; A.B., Georgetown U., 1930; LL.B., Fordham U., 1933. Admitted to N.J. bar, 1934; asst. corp. counsel, Jersey City, 1941-49; partner firm O'Mara, Schumann, Davis & Lynch, 1949-66; judge N.J. Superior Ct., 1966—, appellate div., 1971—; v.p., chmn. legal com. N.J. Bd. Edn., 1954-66. Mem. Hudson County, N.J., Am. bar assns., Am. Judicature Soc. Asso. editor: N.J. Law Jour., 1954-66. Office: 520 Broad St Newark NJ 07102 Tel (201) 648-2616

LYNCH, PATRICK, b. Pitts., Nov. 11, 1941; B.A., Loyola U., Los Angeles, 1965, LL.B., 1966. Admitted to Calif. bar, 1967, U.S. Supreme Ct. bar, 1972; partner firm O'Melveny & Myers, Los Angeles, 1966—. Mem. Los Angeles County Bar Assn. Office: 611 W 6th St Los Angeles CA 90017 Tel (213) 621-1120

LYNCH, PATRICK WILLIAM, b. Omaha, Sept. 14, 1914; A.B., Creighton Arts Coll., 1937; J.D., Creighton Law Sch., 1938. Admitted to Nebr. bar, 1938, since practiced in Omaha, individual practice law, 1938-42, 46-49; judge Municipal Ct., 1949-54, Nebr. 4th Dist. Ct., Omaha, 1954—; mem. Nebr. Commn. Jud. Qualifications, 1967-75. Mem. Am., Nebr., Omaha bar assns., Am. Judicature Soc., Nat. Conf. State Trial Judges, Nebr. Dist. Ct. Judges' Assn. (pres. 1965), Inst. Jud. Adminstrn., Alpha Sigma Nu. Home: 2302 S 12th St Omaha NE 68108 Office: Court House Omaha NE 68102 Tel (402) 444-7007

LYNCH, ROBERT EMMET, b. Washington, Feb. 22, 1896; LL.B., Nat. U. (now George Washington U.), 1921. Admitted to U.S. Dist. Ct. bar, D.C., 1921, U.S. Ct. Appeals bar, D.C. Circuit, 1921, U.S. Supreme Ct. bar, 1924; practiced in Washington, 1921—; chief trial atty. D.C. Govt., 1928-34; adj. prof. law Columbia U. Law Sch. (now Cath. U. Law Sch.), Washington, 1928-43; gen. counsel U.S. Ho. of Reps. Com. on UnAm. Activities, 1939. Office: 821 15th St NW Washington DC 20005 Tel (202) 628-1403

LYNCH, THOMAS CAMPBELL, b. Decorah, Iowa, Jan. 5, 1923; B.S., U.S. Naval Acad., 1944; J.D., U. Iowa, 1949; served with JAGC, USNR, 1955-64; individual practice law, Decorah, 1949—; pres. Decorah Gas Co., 1963-65. Mem. Iowa, Am. bar assns., Decorah C. of C. (pres.). Home: 301 Upper Broadway Decorah IA 52101 Office: 109 1/2 W Water St Decorah IA 52101 Tel (319) 382-2218

LYNCH, VICTOR KAMERER, b. Latrobe, Pa., Sept. 9, 1929; B.S. in San. Engring., Pa. State U., 1951; LL.D., Duquesne U., 1958. Admitted to Pa. bar, 1959; design engr. and constrn. insp. Chester Engrs., Coraopolis, Pa., 1953-54, project engr., 1954-58; asso. firm Burgwin, Ruffin, Perry & Pohl, Pitts., 1959-62; partner firm Ruffin, Perry, Springer, Hazlett and Lynch, Pitts., 1962-70; asso. firm Litman Litman Harris & Specter, Pitts., 1971-74; mem. firm Lynch, Lynch, Carr & Kabala, Pitts., 1974—. Mem. Water Pollution Control Assn. Pa. (pres. 1972-73), Pa. Soc. Profl. Engrs. Recipient Sludge Shovelers award, Johnny Clearwater award. Home: 1000 Grandview Ave Pittsburgh PA 15211 Office: 3616 Mellon Bank Bldg Pittsburgh PA 15219 Tel (412) 391-1334

LYNN, ARTHUR DELLERT, JR., b. Portsmouth, Ohio, Nov. 12, 1921; student Va. Mil. Inst., 1938-39, U.S. Naval Academy, 1939-40; B.A., Ohio State U., 1941, M.A., 1943, J.D., 1948, Ph.D., 1951; postgrad. U. Mich., 1968-70. Admitted to Ohio bar, 1948, U.S. Supreme Ct. bar, 1966; instr. econs. Ohio State U., 1946-49, 50-52, asst. prof., 1952-56, asso. prof. 1956-61, prof. 1961—, prof. pub. adminstrn., 1969—, adj. prof. law, 1967—, asst. dean Coll. Commerce and Adminstrn., 1959-62, asso. dean, 1962-67, asso. dean Coll. Adminstrv. Sci., 1967-68, asso. dean faculties, 1965-70; partner firm Lynn & Lynn, Portsmouth, 1949-50; research asso. Nat. Tax Assn. Com. on Personal Property Taxation, 1952-54, research advisor com. on tax compliance costs, 1960-65, chmn. com. on model property tax assessment and equalization methods and procedures, 1961-65; cons. in field, lectr. in field; mem. Gov.'s Econ. Research Council, State of Ohio, 1966-67; bd. regents adv. com. on Title I of the Higher Edn. Act of 1965, 1965—; mem. Adv. Council on the State Tech. Services act, 1965-70, chmn. 1968-69; mem. edn. fund adv. com. Internat. Assn. Assessing Officers, 1965— budget com. United Community Council Columbus (Ohio), 1963-68. Mem. Am. Econ. Assn., Midwest Econ. Assn., Royal Econ. Soc., Ohio Council on Econ. Edn., Ohio Assn. Economists and Pol. Scis., Nat. Tax Assn. (mem. exec. com. 1965-73, pres. 1969-70), Nat. Tax Assn.-Tax Inst. Am. (sec. 1975—), Tax Inst. Am. (adv. council 1960-63), Internat. Fiscal Assn., Institut Internationale des Finances Publiques, Am., Ohio State, Fed. bar assns, Am. Soc. Pub. Adminstrn., Acad. Mgmt., Am. Pol. Sci. Assn., AAUP, AAAS, Am. Arbitration Assn., Torch Club Columbus, Rotary, Athletic Club Columbus, Nat. Lawyers Club, Nat. Economists Club., Faculty Club, Ohio Soc. N.Y., Omicron Delta Epsilon, Phi Delta Phi, Beta Gamma Sigma. Contbr. articles, reviews and reports to profl. jours. Home: 2699 Wexford Rd Columbus OH 43221 Office: Hagerty Hall Ohio State Univ 1775 S College Rd Columbus OH 43210 Tel (614) 422-0838

LYNN, BRUCE GREINER, b. Columbus, Ohio, Dec. 16, 1916; A.B., Ohio State U., 1938; J.D., Harvard, 1941. Admitted to Ohio bar, 1941; partner firm Bricker, Evatt, Barton & Eckler, Columbus. Mem. Am., Ohio State (exec. com. 1966-69), Columbus (pres. 1956-57) bar assns., Internat. Assn. Ins. Counsel, Am. Coll. Trial Lawyers. Home: 6677 Merwin Rd Worthington OH 43085 Office: 100 E Broad St Columbus OH 43215 Tel (614) 221-6651

LYNN, DONALD JUSTIN, b. Youngstown, Ohio, Jan. 9, 1891; A.B. cum laude, Harvard, 1913, LL.B., 1916. Admitted to Ohio bar, 1917, U.S. Supreme Ct. bar, 1938; sec. Cambridge (Mass.) Good Govt. League, 1913; asso. firm Harrington, Huxley & Smith, Youngstown, 1916-32, partner, 1932—; counsel RFC, Washington, 1933-34. Bd. govs. Youngstown Coll., 1934-45; trustee, v.p. Mahoning Valley Hist. Soc. Mem. Am., Mahoning County, Ohio bar assns. Home: 2356 5th Ave Youngstown OH 45504 Office: 1200 Mahoning Bank Bldg Youngstown OH 44503 Tel (216) 744-1111

LYNN, EDWARD EARL, b. Coldwater, Kans., Mar. 27, 1918; B.S., U. Ill., 1942, J.D., 1947. Admitted to Mo. bar, 1972, Ohio bar, 1961, Ill. bar, 1947; asso. firm Jenner & Block, Chgo., 1947-56, partner, 1956-57; dir., v.p., gen. counsel Gen. Dynamics Corp., St. Louis, 1971—; dir., mem. exec. com., v.p., chief legal officer Lykes-Youngstown Corp., 1969-71; dir., gen. counsel, sec. Youngstown Sheet Tube Co., 1967-71; v.p. Fairbanks, Morse & Co., Chgo., 1957-61. Bd. dirs. St. Louis Children's Hosp.; trustee Govtl. Research Council, St. Louis. Office: 7733 Forsyth Blvd Saint Louis MO 63105 Tel (314) 862-2440

LYNN, GEORGE DENNIS, JR., b. Ft. Dix, N.J., Oct. 9, 1942; B.A., U. N.C., 1964; J.D., Stetson U., 1972. Admitted to Fla. bar, 1972; mem. firm Harrison Greene Mann Rowe Stanton & Mastry, St. Petersburg, Fla., 1972—. Mem. St. Petersburg, Am., Fla. bar assns. Home: 1705 Georgia Ave NE Saint Petersburg FL 33703 Office: Florida Federal Bldg 10th floor Saint Petersburg FL 33701 Tel (813) 896-7171

LYNN, SPENCER W., b. Vanoss, Okla., Mar. 23, 1921; B.S. in Elec. Engring., U. S.C., 1941, M.S., 1942; LL.B., Oklahoma City U., 1950, J.D., 1971. Admitted to bar, 1950; individual practice law, Oklahoma City, 1950-73; trial counsel Okla. State Dept. Transp., Oklahoma City, 1973—; legal asst. Okla. Ct. Criminal Appeals, 1947-48; asso. municipal judge Oklahoma City, 1955-56. Counselor local council Boy Scouts Am., 1961-71; mem. Oklahoma County Mental Health Commn., 1968-70. Mem. Am., Okla., Oklahoma County bar assns., Am., Okla. trial lawyers assns., Mensa, Phi Delta Phi, Sigma Tau, Kappa Sigma. Office: 200 NE 21st St Oklahoma City OK 73105 Tel (405) 521-2681

LYNNE, SEYBOURN HARRIS, b. Decatur, Ala., July 25, 1907; B.S., Ala. Polytechnic Inst., 1927; LL.B., U. Ala., 1930, LL.D., 1973. Admitted to Ala. bar, 1930; individual practice law, Decatur, 1930-34; judge Morgan County (Ala.) Ct., 1934-40, Ala. Circuit Ct., 8th Circuit, 1940-42; served to lt. col. JAGC, U.S. Army, 1942-45; judge U.S. Dist. Ct., No. Dist. Ala., Birmingham, 1946-53, chief judge, 1953-73, sr. judge, 1973—. Advisory com. Meyer Found.; trustee Crippled Childrens Clinic, Birmingham, Eye Found. Hosp., Birmingham. Mem. Am., Ala., Birmingham bar assns. Home: 3323 E Briarcliff Rd Birmingham AL 35223 Office: 361 Federal Courthouse Birmingham AL 35203 Tel (205) 254-1153

LYNTON, HAROLD STEPHEN, b. N.Y.C., Nov. 2, 1909; B.A. with high orations, Yale, 1929; J.D. cum laude, Harvard, 1932. Admitted to N.Y. bar, 1933; partner firm Kaufman, Gallop, Gould, Climenko and Lynton, and predecessors, N.Y.C., 1934-51; served to capt. JAGC, U.S. Army, 1943-45; partner firm Lynton, Klein, Opton & Saslow, and predecessors, N.Y.C., 1951—; gen. counsel, dir. The Collier Cos., Naples, Fla., 1945—. Mem. Am., N.Y., N.Y.C. bar assns., N.Y. County Lawyers Assn., Phi Beta Kappa. Home: 870 United Nations Plaza New York City NY 10017 Office: 100 Park Ave New York City NY 10017 Tel (212) 683-9500

LYON, CARL FRANCIS, JR., b. Sumter, S.C., May 9, 1943; B.A., Duke U., 1965, J.D., 1968. Admitted to N.Y. State bar, 1969; asso. firm Mudge Rose Guthrie & Alexander, N.Y.C., 1968-77, partner, 1977—. Mem. Assn. Bar City N.Y., Am. Pub. Power Assn., Order of Coif. Office: 20 Broad St New York City NY 10005 Tel (212) 422-6767

LYON, DONALD WILLIAM, b. Skokie, Ill., Feb. 23, 1928; B.S., Purdue U., 1950; J.D., DePaul U., 1953; postgrad. John Marshall Law Sch., 1957-60. Admitted to Ill. bar, 1953, U.S. Supreme Ct. bar, 1959; sr. partner firm Lyon & Warman, Skokie, 1962—; village prosecutor Village of Skokie, 1961-65; coordinating prosecutor 2d Municipal Dist., 1961-65; dir. Skokie Trust & Savs. Bank, Hunter Automated Machinery Corp.; mem. adv. bd. paralegal program Mallincrodt Coll., Wilmette, Ill., 1975—; vol. legal support com. Catholic Charities, 1970—. Bus. chmn. March of Dimes, 1970; bd. dirs. St. Scholastica Fathers' Club; chmn. Mothers' March of Dimes; gen chmn. Skokie Valley United Crusade; trustee St. Lambert's troop Boy Scouts Am., Carthage Coll., Kenosha, Wis.; asso. dir. Skokie Valley Community Hosp.; mem. fin. com. Niles Township Regular Democratic Orgn.; bd. govs. Orchard Sch. for Mentally Handicapped, Orchard Center for Mental Health. Mem. Chgo., Niles Township (bd. mgrs.) bar assns. Named Man of Year, Skokie C. of C., 1963-64. Home: 7903 Lorel Ave Skokie IL 60076 Office: 4400 Oakton St Skokie IL 60076 Tel (312) 674-4410

LYON, JAMES BURROUGHS, b. N.Y.C., May 11, 1930; B.A. magna cum laude, Amherst Coll., 1952; LL.B., Yale, 1955. Admitted to Conn. bar, 1955; asso. firm Murtha, Cullina, Richter & Pinney, and predecessors, Hartford, Conn., 1956-61, partner, 1961—; adv. com. Inst. Fed. Taxation, N.Y. U., 1975—. Chmn. bd. dirs. Kingswood-Oxford Sch., W. Hartford, chmn. capital program, 1969-72; bd. dirs. Wadsworth Atheneum, Hartford, v.p., 1972—; bd. dirs. Noah Webster Found. and Hist. Soc., Inc., W. Hartford, 1965—; bd. dirs. Conn. Bar Found, v.p., 1975—; bd. dirs. Fidelco Found., Bloomfield, Conn., 1971—; corporator Mt. Sinai Hosp., Hartford, 1972—, Hartford Hosp., 1975—, St. Francis Hosp., Hartford, 1976—; trustee Old Sturbridge (Mass.) Village, 1974—; pres. N. Conn. chpt. Nat. Football Found. and Hall of Fame, 1966-69. Mem. Am., Conn., N.Y.C., Hartford County bar assns., Newcomen Soc., Phi Beta Kappa, Phi Delta Phi. Home: 25 Bishop Rd West Hartford CT 06119 Office: 101 Pearl St Hartford CT 06103

LYON, KENNETH EUGENE, JR., b. Logan, Utah, Nov. 28, 1939; B.A., San Francisco State Coll., 1963; LL.B., U. Utah, 1966. Admitted to Idaho bar, 1963, U.S. Supreme Ct. bar, 1972; individual practice law, Pocatello, Idaho, 1966—. Pres. Jefferson Sch. PTA, Pocatello, 1972-75; precinct committeeman, Pocatello, 1972-75. Mem. Am., 6th Dist. (sec. 1969) bar assns., Idaho State Bar, Am., Idaho trial lawyers assns. Home: Trail Creek Pocatello ID 83201 Office: Box 4392 Pocatello ID 83201 Tel (208) 233-1240

LYON, PHILIP KIRKLAND, b. Warren, Ark., Jan. 19, 1944; J.D. with honors, U. Ark., 1967. Admitted to Ark. bar, 1967, U.S. Supreme Ct. bar, 1970; asso. firm House, Holmes & Jewell, Little Rock, 1967-72, partner, 1972—; lectr. bus. Little Rock U., 1968-69, U. Ark. at Little Rock, 1969-72. Mem. Am., Ark., Pulaski County bar assns., Am. Soc. Personnel Adminstrn., Phi Alpha Delta. Editor Ark. Law Rev., 1966-67. Home: 10700 San Joaquin Valley Ln Little Rock AR 72212 Office: 1550 Tower Bldg Little Rock AR 72201 Tel (501) 375-9151

LYON, RICHARD KIRSHBAUM, b. Washington, Apr. 24, 1912; A.B., Dartmouth, 1933; J.D., Georgetown U., 1936. Admitted to D.C. bar, 1936, U.S. Supreme Ct. bar, 1939; asso. firm Lyon & Lyon, Washington, 1936-41; partner firm Philipson, Lyon & Chase, and predecessors, Washington, 1946-67; individual practice law, Washington, 1968—; mem. D.C. Commn. on Jud. Disabilities and Tenure, 1975—; gen. counsel Better Bus. Bur. Met. Washington, 1954—, Johnson-Humphrey Inaugural Com., 1965. Chmn., D.C. Commrs. Youth Council, 1957-60; pres. Washington Home Rule Com., 1963-66, Jewish Community Council of Greater Washington, 1962-65. Mem. Fed., FCC bar assns., D.C. Bar, Bar Assn. D.C. (dir. 1972-74). Home: 3107 Garfield St NW Washington DC 20008 Office: 1819 H St NW Washington DC 20006 Tel (202) 466-5400

LYON, ROBERT DOUGLAS, b. Los Angeles, Nov. 21, 1923; B.S., U.S. Naval Acad., 1945; LL.B., Stanford, 1949. Admitted to Calif. bar, 1950; asso. firm Lyon & Lyon, Los Angeles, 1949-55, partner, 1955—. Mem. Am., Calif., Los Angeles bar assns., Am., Los Angeles patent law assns. Home: 250 S Rimpau St Los Angeles CA 90004 Office: 800 Wilshire St Los Angeles CA 90017 Tel (213) 489-1600

LYONS, ALBERT, b. Bklyn., Feb. 17, 1907; B.A., Columbia, 1928, LL.B. Admitted to N.Y. bar, 1932; mem. firm Ruben Schwartz & Silverberg, N.Y.C.; asst. U.S. atty., Bklyn., 1936-42. Office: 450 7th Ave New York City NY 10001 Tel (212) 695-3550

LYONS, CHAMP, JR., b. Boston, Dec. 6, 1940; A.B., Harvard, 1962; LL.B., U. Ala., 1965. Admitted to Ala. bar, 1965, U.S. Supreme Ct. bar, 1973; law clk. U.S. Dist. Ct., Mobile, 1965-67; asso. firm, partner Capell, Howard, Knabe & Cobbs, Montgomery, Ala., 1967-76; partner firm Coale, Helmsing, Lyons & Sims, Mobile, 1976—; mem. adv. commn. on civil procedure Ala. Supreme Ct., 1971—. Mem. Am., Ala. bar assns., Am., Ala. law insts., Farrah Law Soc. Author: Alabama Practice, 1973; contbr. articles to law jours. Home: 229 Ridgelawn Dr E Mobile AL 36608 Office: 2750 1st Nat Bank Bldg Mobile AL 36601 Tel (205) 432-5521

LYONS, CLEM V., b. Huntington, N.Y., Sept. 4, 1931; B.S. in Pharmacy, St. John's Coll., 1954; LL.B., St. Marys U., 1962. Admitted to Tex. bar, 1962; asst. dist. atty. Bexar County (Tex.), San Antonio, 1963-66; mem. firm Southers, Goldberg & Lyons, San Antonio, 1966—. Treas., San Antonio Epilepsy Assn., 1970—. Mem. Am., Tex., San Antonio bar assns., Am., Tex., San Antonio trial lawyers assns. Home: 819 Patricia St San Antonio TX 78216 Office: 126 Villita St San Antonio TX 78205 Tel (512) 225-5251

LYONS, DENNIS GERALD, b. Passaic, N.J., Nov. 20, 1931; A.B., Holy Cross Coll., 1952; J.D., Harvard, 1955. Admitted to D.C. bar, 1955, N.Y. State bar, 1956, U.S. Supreme Ct. bar, 1960; asso. firm Shearman & Sterling, N.Y.C., 1955; atty. Office of Gen. Counsel, Dept. Air Force, Washington, 1955-58; law clk. Justice Brennan, U.S. Supreme Ct., Washington, 1958-60; asso. firm Arnold & Porter, Washington, 1960-62, partner, 1963—; mem. Pres. Johnson's Task Force on Anti-trust Laws, 1967-68. Bd. dirs. Washington Performing Arts Soc., 1975—. Mem. Am. Bar Assn., Am. Law Inst. Contbr. book revs. to mags. and jours. Home: 2500 Virginia Ave NW Washington DC 20037 Office: 1229 19th St NW Washington DC 20036 Tel (202) 872-6865

LYONS, JAMES FELTON, b. Lewiston, Idaho, Sept. 28, 1938; A.B., Stanford, 1960; J.D., U. Idaho, 1968; postgrad. Gonzaga U. Admitted to Idaho bar, 1968, U.S. Supreme Ct. bar, 1974; Justice Ct. judge Latah County, Idaho, 1966-68; partner firm Nixon, Nixon, Lyons & Bell, Bonners Ferry, Idaho, 1968—; pros. atty. Boundary County, Idaho, 1971-73; spl. atty. gen. Idaho Pub. Health Dist. No. 1, 1971—; dir. Schweitzer, Inc.; pres. Kaniksu Land & Title Co., Inc., 1969-73, Kootenai Assos., 1975—. Pres. Boundary County Hist. Soc., 1974—; mem. Idaho State Democratic Central Com., 1972—. Mem. Am. Bar Assn., Am. Acad. Forensic Sci., Am. Trial Lawyers Assn. Home: 207 Grant St Bonners Ferry ID 83805 Office: 225 Main St Bonners Ferry ID 83805 Tel (208) 267-3133

LYONS, JOHN MICHAEL, b. La Crosse, Wis., Apr. 26, 1933; student Marquette U., 1951-54; B.A., Valparaiso U., 1956, J.D., 1958. Admitted to Ind. bar, 1958, U.S. Dist. Ct. for No. and So. Dists. of Ind. bar, 1958; partner firm Pivarnik & Lyons, Valparaiso, Ind., 1958-62, Lyons, Aungst, Guastello & Allen and predecessors, Valparaiso, 1968-74; individual practice law, Valparaiso, 1974—; chief dep. pros. atty. Porter County (Ind.), 1958-62; chmn. Porter County Election Bd., 1960—; spl. lectr. Valparaiso U., 1974. Charter mem. Gary (Ind.) Diocesan Sch. Commn., 1966-70. Mem. Am. Trial Lawyers Assn., Am. Judicature Soc., Porter County (pres. 1975-76), Ind. State bar assns. Home: 201 Powderhorn Dr Valparaiso IN 46383 Office: 55 Franklin St Valparaiso IN 46383 Tel (219) 462-0597

LYONS, M. ARNOLD, b. Mpls., June 3, 1911; B.A., U. Minn., 1932, J.D., 1934. Admitted to Minn. bar, 1934, U.S. Supreme Ct. bar, 1948; partner firm Robins, Davis & Lyons, Mpls. and St. Paul, 1940—; adj. prof. Law Sch. U. Minn., Mpls., 1974-76; vis. prof. Sch. Law Hamline Univ., St. Paul, 1975-77, prof., 1977—. Mem. Am., Minn., Hennepin County bar assns., Am. Judicature Soc., Am. Arbitration Assn. (nat. panel). Editor Minn. Law Rev., 1932-34; co-author: Stein on Probate, 1976. Home: 4001 Basswood Rd Minneapolis MN 55416 Office: 33 S 5th St Minneapolis MN 55402 Tel (612) 339-4911

LYONS, PHILIP NOLAN, b. Indpls., Dec. 23, 1941; B.S., U. Calif., Berkeley, 1964; J.D., Hastings Coll., 1969. Admitted to Calif. bar, 1970, U.S. Supreme Ct. bar, 1976; v.p. Philip Lyons Co., Inc., San Francisco, 1964-69; asso. firm Chandler & Bruner, San Leandro, Calif., 1970-71, partner, 1971-72; individual practice law, San Leandro, 1972—. Mem. Calif., San Francisco, Alameda County bar assns. Office: 250 Juana Ave San Leandro CA 94577 Tel (415) 483-2255

LYONS, WILLIAM DREWRY, b. Cresco, Iowa, Oct. 10, 1927; B.S., U. Minn., 1950, J.D., 1952; C.P.C.U., Am. Inst. Property and Liability Law, 1962. Admitted to Minn. bar, 1952, Iowa bar, 1952, Nebr. bar, 1972; individual practice law, Cresco, 1952-56; asst. supt. claims Nat. Indemnity Co., Omaha, 1956-58, br. claim mgr., St. Paul, 1958-71, v.p., claim mgr., Omaha, 1971—; asso. prof. ins. N. Hennepin State Coll., 1970-71, U. Nebr. at Omaha, 1974-75. Mem. Nebr., Minn. bar assns., Central Claim Execs. Assn., Internat. Assn. Ins. Counsel, Nebr. Claimsmen Assn., Nat. Assn. Ind. Adjustors (regional adv. council). Home: 672 N 57th Ave Omaha NE 68132 Office: 4016 Farnam St Omaha NE 68131 Tel (402) 346-7400

LYSAGHT, JAMES IGNATIUS, b. N.Y.C., Oct. 2, 1924; LL.B., St. John's U., 1950. Admitted to N.Y. State bar, 1950; staff loan closing dept. Nat. City Bank, N.Y.C., 1950-52; asso. firm Alexander & Keenan, N.Y.C., 1952-57; mem. firm Hartsell, Harrington, Jacobson, & Lysaght, N.Y.C., 1957-60; trial atty., head legal dept. New Amsterdam & U.S. Casualty Ins. Cos., N.Y.C., 1960-63; individual practice law, N.Y.C., 1963—; acting police judge Village of Valley Stream, N.Y., 1963-75. Mem. Am., N.Y. State bar assns., N.Y. County Lawyers Assn., Def. Inst., N.Y. State Assn. Magistrates. Home: 70 Featherbed Ln Oakdale NY Office: 11 Park Pl New York City NY 10007 Tel (212) WO2-3050

LYSAUGHT, JOSEPH DONALD, b. Kansas City, Kans., Dec. 7, 1923; A.B., U. Kans., 1948, LL.B., 1949. Admitted to Kans. bar, 1949, U.S. Supreme Ct. bar, 1961; partner firm Weeks, Thomas, Lysaught, Bingham & Mustain, Chartered, and predecessors, Kansas City and Overland Park, Kans., 1949—; judge pro tem Dist. Ct. Wyandotte County, Kans., 1953. Mem. Am., Kans., Wyandotte County (pres. 1969), Johnson County bar assns., Am. Judicature Soc., Order of Coif. Home: 4409 W 64th St Prairie Village KS 66208 Office: 407 Capitol Federal Bldg 95th & Nall Overland Park KS 66207 Tel (913) 642-7770

LYSIAK, CONRAD CRISPIN, b. Chgo., Feb. 13, 1947; B.S. in Bus. Adminstrn., U. Tulsa, 1969, J.D., 1971. Admitted to Okla. Supreme Ct. bar, 1972, U.S. Ct. Appeals 10th Circuit bar, 1973, U.S. Supreme Ct. bar, 1975, U.S. Tax Ct., 1977; asso. firm Schuman, Milsten & Jackson, Tulsa, Okla., 1972-76; partner firm Sobel, Moran, Lysiak & Harral, Tulsa, 1976—. Mem. Am., Tulsa County bar assns., Am. Civil Liberties Union, Am. Judicature Soc. Home: 1325 A E 61st St Tulsa OK 74135 Office: Suite 505 5310 E 31st St Tulsa OK 74135 Tel (918) 664-8390

LYSLE, RICHARD SCOTT, b. Pasadena, Calif., Oct. 22, 1947; A.B., Cornell U., 1969; J.D., U. So. Calif., 1972. Admitted to Calif. bar, 1972; individual practice law, Los Angeles, 1973—. Pres., Bay Cities Democratic Club, Santa Monica, Calif., 1976; mem. 44th dist. assembly Dem. council, Santa Monica, 1974—. Mem. Lawyers Club Los Angeles County, Nat. Lawyers Guild. Home: 4182 McConnell Blvd Los Angeles CA 90066 Office: Washington Sq 400 330 Washington St Marina del Rey CA 90291 Tel (213) 822-6023

LYTAL, LAKE HENRY, JR., b. West Palm Beach, Fla., Jan. 14, 1940; B.S., Fla. State U., 1962; J.D., U. Fla., 1965. Admitted to Fla. bar, 1966; asso. firm Howell, Kirby, Montgomery, D'Aiuto & Dean, 1967-76; partner firm Montgomery, Lytal, Reiter, Denney & Searcy, West Palm Beach, 1976—; adminstv. legal asst. to Fla. Sec. of State, 1966. Mem. Am., Fla., Palm Beach County bar assns., Am. Trial Lawyers Assn., Am. Judicature Soc. Home: 517 Murfield Dr Atlantis FL 33462 Office: 2139 Palm Beach Lake Blvd West Palm Beach FL 33409 Tel (305) 686-6300

LYTCH, RUFUS ALLEN, b. Dillon, S.C., Dec. 18, 1941; B.B.A., Campbell Coll., 1966; J.D., U. N.C., 1969. Admitted to N.C. bar, 1969; asso. firm Bowen & Lytch, and predecessors, Dunn, N.C., 1969-71, partner, 1971—. Active Boy Scouts Am., 1971-72; bd. dirs. Easter Seal Soc., 1971-72; bd. deacons 1st Presbyn. Ch., Dunn, 1972-75. Mem. Am., N.C., 11th Jud. Dist. (pres. elect 1976-77), Harnett County (pres. 1976-77), N.C. State Bar assns., N.C. Acad. Trial Lawyers, Dunn Area C. of C., Chicora Country Club (pres. 1972-76, dir. 1972-76). Office: Box 151 Dunn NC 28334 Tel (919) 892-2152

LYTLE, SUSAN LEE, b. Ft. Warren, Wyo., Oct. 23, 1945; A.B. cum laude (Univ. scholar), U. Miami, Coral Gables, Fla., 1967, J.D. cum laude (Univ. scholar 1967-70, Wesley A. Sturges scholar 1969-70), 1970; LL.M. (fellow), Harvard, 1971. Admitted to Fla. bar, 1970; asso. firm Greenberg, Traurig, Hoffman, Lipoff, Quentel & Wright and predecessor, Miami, Fla., 1971-76, mem., 1976—; instr. in legal writing Boston U., fall 1970; mem. adj. faculty U. Miami Law Sch., 1974—. Active Greater Miami Jewish Fedn. Mem. Dade County (Fla.), Am. bar assns., Fla. Assn. Women Lawyers, U. Miami Law Sch. Alumni Assn. (dir. 1976—), Harvard Club of Miami, Mortar Bd., Soc. Wig and Robe, Delta Delta Delta Alumni Assn., Alpha Lambda Delta, Phi Kappa Phi. Recipient 13 Am. Jurisprudence book awards, 1967-70; editorial bd. U. Miami Law Rev., 1968-70, editor-in-chief, 1970; contbr. articles to law revs. Home: 2451 Brickell Ave Apt 21-C Miami FL 33129 Office: 1401 Brickell Ave Penthouse 1 Miami FL 33131 Tel (305) 377-3501

MAACK, ROBERT DONALD, b. Salt Lake City, July 15, 1939; student Monterey Peninsula Coll., 1963-64; B.S. cum laude, U. Utah, 1967, J.D., 1970. Admitted to Utah bar, 1970; research asst. Law Sch. Harvard U., Cambridge, Mass., 1970-71; asso. firm Pugsley, Hayes, Watkiss, Campbell & Cowley, Salt Lake City, 1971-74; partner firm Watkiss & Campbell, Salt Lake City, 1974—; pres. young lawyers sect. Utah State Bar, 1975-76, chmn. law day com., 1975; chmn. Utah Law Forum, 1970. Mem. Am. (nat. exec. council young lawyer sect. 1976—), Salt Lake County bar assns., Soc. Bar and Gavel (pres. 1972-73). Contbr. articles, mem. bd. editors Utah Law Rev., 1968-70. Home: 1615 Millcreek Way St Salt Lake City UT 84106 Office: 310 S Main St 12th Floor Salt Lake City UT 84101 Tel (801) 363-3300

MABERRY, JOHN O., b. Sayre, Okla., Jan. 23, 1905; LL.B., So. Meth. U., 1931; postgrad. U. Colo. Admitted to Okla. bar, 1931, Ark. bar, 1968; pros. atty. Beckham County (Okla.), 1931-33; county judge Beckham County Ct., 1933-37; counsel Okla. Corp. Commn., 1938-42; counsel Shell Oil Co., Los Angeles, 1942-45, Gulf Oil Corp., 1945-52, Sun Ray Oil Co., Calgary, Alta., Can., 1952-56; gen. mgr. Pacific Petroleum, 1952-58; pres. Hamilton Oil Corp., Denver, 1958-64, ret., 1964; individual practice law, Eureka Springs, Ark., 1968—. Mem. joint bd. examiners ICC, 1938-42; chmn. Alta. United Fund Com., 1952-53. Named Leading Citizen of Ark., 1974. Tel (501) 253-8788

MABIE, LEFFERTS LAMONT, b. Bronxville, N.Y., May 5, 1925; LL.B., J.D., U. Fla., 1948. Admitted to Fla. bar, 1948; individual practice law, Wauchula, Fla., 1949-65; partner firms Hopkins & Mabie, Pensacola, Fla., 1966-68, Levin, Warfield, Middlebrooks, Graff, Mabie, Rosenbloum & Magie, Pensacola, 1968—; judge Hardee County (Fla.) Ct., 1952-56. Mem. Am., 10th Jud. Circuit (pres. 1956) bar assns., Am. Judicature Soc., Acad. Fla. Trial Lawyers (pres. 1972), Soc. of Bar of 1st Jud. Circuit (pres. 1973), Assn. Trial Lawyers Am. Home: 600 Bay Cliffs Rd Gulf Breeze FL 32561 Office: 226 S Palafox St Pensacola FL 32501 Tel (904) 432-1461

MAC ARTHUR, MALCOLM DOUGLAS, b. Washington, Oct. 24, 1932; B.A., U. Wis., 1954, J.D., 1959. Admitted to Wis. bar, 1959, Calif. bar, 1961, D.C. bar, 1966, U.S. Supreme Ct. bar, 1966, U.S. Ct. Mil. Appeals bar, 1959; trial atty. antitrust div. Dept. Justice, Washington and Los Angeles, 1959-64; mem. firm Lee, To Toomey & Kent, Washington, 1964-69, partner, 1969—. Troop committee man Boy Scouts Am., Washington, 1976. Mem. Am., Fed., Wis., Calif. bar assns., Bar Assn. D.C., Order of Coif, Phi Delta Phi. Recipient award for outstanding service U.S. Atty. Gen., 1962, W.H. Page award for outstanding contbn. to Wis. Law Review, 1959; atuhor: Associations and the Antitrust Laws, 1976; contbr. articles to profl. jours. Home: 6210 Winnebago Rd Bethesda MD 20016 Office: 1200 18th St NW Washington DC 20036 Tel (202) 457-8511

MACAULAY, ANGUS HAMILTON, b. Spartanburg, S.C., Apr. 1, 1928; A.B., The Citadel, 1950; LL.B., Yale, 1955. Admitted to S.C. bar, 1955, Va. bar, 1956, U.S. Supreme Ct. bar, 1960; practiced in Richmond, Va., 1956—, partner firm Mays, Valentine, Davenport & Moore, 1961—; dir. Colonial Life & Accident Ins. Co., Columbia, S.C., 1967—. Mem. Richmond Air Pollution Control Bd., 1965—; 1st v.p. Maymont Found., Richmond, 1973—; pres. Richmond Community Action Program, Inc., 1969-70; bd. dirs. United Givers Fund, 1969-72; chmn. Richmond City Democratic Com., 1974-76; chmn. Va. 3d Dist. Dem. Com., 1975—. Mem. Richmond, Va. (chmn. sect. young lawyers 1959-60), Am. (exec. council young lawyers conf. 1960-62) bar assns., Phi Delta Phi. Recipient Gold Feather award Richmond Jaycees, 1972. Home: 502 Henri Rd Richmond VA 23226 Office: F & M Center PO Box 1122 Richmond VA 23208 Tel (804) 644-6011

MACBRIDE, THOMAS JAMISON, b. Sacramento, Mar. 25, 1914; A.B., U. Calif. at Berkeley, 1936, J.D., 1940. Admitted to Calif. bar, 1940; dep. atty. gen. Calif., 1941-42; pvt. practice, Sacramento, 1946-61; U.S. dist. judge Eastern Dist, Calif., Sacramento, 1961-67, chief judge, 1967—. Pres., Town Hall, Sacramento, 1952, N.E. area YMCA, Sacramento, 1960; mem. Nat. Commn. on Reform Fed. Criminal Laws, 1967-71. Mem. Cal. Legislature from Sacramento County, 1955-60. Bd. dirs. Sacramento YMCA. Mem. Am. Bar Assn., Am. Judicature Soc., U.S. Jud. Conf., U. Calif. Alumni Assn. (v.p. 1955, 60), Kappa Sigma, Phi Delta Phi. Home: 1800 Rockwood Dr Sacramento CA 95825 Office: 2012 US Courthouse Sacramento CA 95814*

MAC CHESNEY, BRUNSON, b. Chgo., May 21, 1909; B.A., Yale, 1931; J.D., U. Mich., 1934. Admitted to Ill. bar, 1935, U.S. Supreme Ct. bar, 1939; legal sec. SEC, 1934-35; instr. Harvard, 1935-36; asso. prof. law U. Calif. at Berkeley, 1936-38; spl. asst. atty. gen. U.S. Dept. Justice, Washington, 1938-40; faculty Northwestern U., 1940-41, prof. law, 1946-71, Edna B. Williams prof. law, 1972—; occupant chair of internat. law U.S. Naval War Coll., 1955-56; Fulbright prof. Cambridge (Eng.) U., 1951-62; pres. Library Internat. Relations, 1946; dir. Chgo. Council Fgn. Relations, 1946-49. Mem. Am., Ill., Chgo. bar assns., Am. Law Inst., Am. Soc. Internat. Law (pres. 1964-66). Decorated chevalier Legion of Honor (France), 1946. Author: International Law Situation and Documents, 1956. Acting editor in chief Am. Jour. Internat. Law, 1972. Home: 621 College Rd Lake Forest IL 60045 Office: 357 E Chicago Ave Chicago IL 60611 Tel (312) 649-8459

MAC CORMACK, DWIGHT BRADBURN, b. Great Barrington, Mass., Sept. 23, 1901; A.B., Amherst Coll., 1922; LL.B., Harvard, 1929; LL.M., Boston U., 1948; S.J.D. (hon.), New Eng. Sch. Law, 1969. Admitted to Mass. bar, 1926, Maine Fed. bar, 1953, Vt. Fed. bar, 1960; individual practice law, Boston, 1926—; counsel Mass. Spl. R.R. Commn., 1938-41, New Eng. Gov.'s R.R. Advisory Com., 1940-41; lectr. in field. Mem. Am., Boston bar assns. Contbr. articles to legal jours. Home: 16 Hillsdale Rd Arlington MA 02174 Office: 31 State St Boston MA 02109 Tel (617) 523-1300

MACDONALD, ALEXANDER BARRETT, b. Vancouver, B.C., Can., Oct. 21, 1918; B.A., U. B.C.; LL.B., Osgoode Hall Law Sch. Called to B.C. bar, created queen's counsel, 1972; former parliamentary sec. to Hon. M. J. Coldwell; former mem. Canadian Ho. of Commons; atty. gen. and minister of industry and trade devel. for B.C., 1972—. Office: Atty Gen Parliament Bldg Victoria BC V8V 4S6 Canada*

MAC DONALD, L. LLOYD, b. Marfa, Tex., July 19, 1931; B.B.A., Baylor U., 1952, LL.B., 1957. Admitted to Tex. bar, 1957; title analyst Shell Oil Co., 1957-60; individual practice law, Midland, Tex., 1960-64; partner firm Kerr, Fitz-Gerald, & Kerr, Midland, 1964-73, Turpin, Smith & Dyer, Midland, 1973—. Mem. youth com. YMCA 1962-63; bd. dirs. Salvation Army 1964—, chmn. 1969-71; bd. dirs. Midland United Way, 1973—; pres. Midland W. Rotary, 1973-74; counselor Boy Scouts Am. Mem. Midland County Bar Assn. (v.p. 1964-65), State Bar Tex., Tex. Assn. Def. Counsel. Home: 1515 Community Ln Midland TX 79701 Office: 1st Nat Bank Bldg Midland TX 79701 Tel (915) 682-2525

MAC DONALD, LEO HADLEY, SR., b. St. Louis, Mar. 15, 1934; B.S., Spring Hill Coll., 1956; J.D., St. Louis U., 1960. Admitted to Mo. bar 1960, U.S. Supreme Ct. bar, 1968; partner firm Sumner, Hanlon, Summer, MacDonald, & Nouss, P.C., St. Louis, 1970—; spl. asst. atty. gen. Mo., 1962-71; asst. circuit atty. St. Louis, 1960-69, spl. asst. circuit atty., 1969-71; instr. law St. Louis U. Law Sch., 1965-68, guest lectr. Commerce Sch., 1967-68, U.S. Narcotics Bur., 1969. Dir. B.C.

MacDonald & Co., Hadley Dean Glass Co., St. Louis. Active Boy Scouts Am. Mem. Am., Mo., St. Louis, St. Louis County bar assns., St. Louis Jr. C. of C., St. Louis County Lawyers Assn., Alpha Sigma Nu, Phi Delta Phi. Author: Termination of Parental Rights, 1962. Home: 7254 Maryland St St Louis MO 63130 Office: 7733 Forsyth Blvd Suite 700 St Louis MO 63105

MAC DONALD, RONALD BOURKE, b. Butte, Mont., Oct. 5, 1946; B.A., Gonzaga U., 1968; J.D., U. Mont., 1971. Admitted to Mont. bar, 1971; partner firm Datsopoulos & Mac Donald, Missoula, Mont., 1971—; instr. U. Mont. Sch. Law, 1975-76. Mem. Am., Mont. bar assns., Am., Mont. trial lawyers assns., Am. Judicature Soc., Young Lawyers Assn. (pres. Missoula chpt. 1974), Order of Barristers. Recipient Internat. Acad. Trial Lawyers award, 1971. Home: 217 Woodworth St Missoula MT 59801 Office: Century Plaza Bldg Suite A Missoula MT 59801 Tel (406) 728-0810

MAC DONALD, THOMAS COOK, JR., b. Atlanta, Oct. 11, 1929; B.S. in Bus. Adminstrn. with high honors, U. Fla., 1951, LL.B. with high honors, 1953. Admitted to Fla. bar, 1953; JAG, USAF, 1953-55; mem. firm Shackleford Farrior Stallings & Evans, Tampa, Fla., 1953—; legis. counsel to Gov. Fla., 1963. Fellow Am. Coll. Trial Lawyers, Am. Bar Found.; mem. U. Fla. Alumni Assn. (past pres.), Am. Law Inst., Selden Soc., Am. Bar Assn. (com. on ethics and profl. responsibility 1970-76), Fla. Bar (bd. govs. 1970-74). Recipient Distinguished Alumnus award U. Fla., 1976. Home: 1904 Holly Ln Tampa FL 33609 Office: PO Box 3324 Tampa FL 33601 Tel (813) 228-7621

MACDOUGALL, GORDON PIER, b. Bethlehem, Pa., May 31, 1930; B.A., U. Mich., 1952; grad. Columbia, 1955. Admitted to Wis. bar, 1955, N.Y. bar, 1958, D.C. bar, 1960; gen. solicitor's office N.Y. Central R.R. Co., N.Y.C., 1957-59; asso. firm LaRoe, Winn & Meerman, Washington, 1959-66; individual practice law, Washington, 1966—; spl. asst. atty. gen. Commonwealth of Pa., 1971—; spl. asst. counsel Pa. Pub. Utility Commn., Washington, 1975—. Mem. Bar Assn. D.C., Assn. ICC Practitioners, Nat. Def. Transp. Assn., Transp. Research Forum, Nat. Assn. R.R. Passengers, Maritime Adminstrv. Bar Assn. Contbr. articles to legal jours. Home: 2000 N St NW Washington DC 20036 Office: 1100 17th St NW Washington DC 20036 Tel (202) 223-9738

MAC DOUGALL, MALCOLM EDWARD, b. Denver, Jan. 26, 1938; B.S., Colo. State U., 1959; LL.D., U. Colo., 1962. Admitted to Colo. bar, 1962; clk. to judge U.S. Circuit Ct., 10th Circuit, 1962-63; atty. Denver Water Dept., 1963-65; asso. firm Saunders, Snyder & Ross, Denver, 1965-68; gen. counsel Golden Cycle Corp., Colorado Springs, 1968-71; partner firm Geddes, MacDougall & McHugh, Colorado Springs, 1971—. Mem. Colo., El Paso County (Colo.), Am. bar assns. Home: 2542 Shalimar Dr Colorado Springs CO 80915 Office: 513 Mining Exchange Bldg Colorado Springs CO 80903 Tel (303) 475-7090

MACFARLANE, GRANT, b. St. George, Utah, Apr. 1, 1899; B.A., U. Utah, 1920, LL.B., 1927, J.D., 1967. Admitted to Utah bar, 1927, U.S. Supreme Ct. bar, 1949; mem. firm Macfarlane-Cornwall, Salt Lake City, 1927-30, firm Critchlow and Critchlow, Salt Lake City, 1930-32, 36-46; individual practice law, Salt Lake City, 1946—; dep. atty. Salt Lake County, 1929-31; asst. atty. Salt Lake City, 1936-40; mem. Utah State Senate, 1939-45, pres., 1943-45; chmn. bd. Council State Govts., Chgo., 1943-45. Mem. Utah Bar Assn., Am. Judicature Soc., Pi Kappa Alpha. Recipient Distinguished Achievement award Pi Kappa Alpha, 1971; Golden award Exchange Club, 1970, Exchangite award Salt Lake Exchange Club, 1970. Office: 752 Union Pacific Bldg Salt Lake City UT 84101 Tel (801) 328-3121

MACFARLANE, HARPER, b. Chatham, Ont., Can., Jan. 26, 1901; student U. Mich., 1921; LL.B., U. Tex., 1924. Admitted to Tex. Supreme Ct. bar, 1924, U.S. Supreme Ct. bar, 1937; asso. firm Brooks, Napier, Brown & Matthews and predecessor, San Antonio, 1924-35, partner, 1935-42; partner firm Matthews, Nowlin, Macfarlane & Barrett and predecessor, San Antonio, 1942—. Mem. Am., San Antonio bar assns., State Bar Tex., Nat. Assn. R.R. Trial Counsel, Tex. Assn. Def. Counsel. Home: 1016 Wiltshire Ave San Antonio TX 78209 Office: 1500 Alamo Nat Bldg San Antonio TX 78205 Tel (512) 226-4211

MAC FARLANE, JOHN DEE, b. Pueblo, Colo., Oct. 4, 1933; A.B., Harvard, 1955; LL.B., Stanford, 1962. Admitted to Colo. bar, 1962; dep. dist. atty., Pueblo, 1962-64; partner firm McMartin & MacFarlane, 1965-68; mem. Colo. Ho. of Reps., 1965-68; mem. Colo. Senate, 1969-70; chief dep. state pub. defender, Denver, 1971-74; atty. gen. Colo., Denver, 1975—. Mem. Colo., Pueblo County (chmn. legal aid com. 1965) bar assns. Mng. editor, Stanford Law Rev., 1961-62. Home: 2080 Bellaire St Denver CO 80207 Office: 1525 Sherman St Denver CO 80203 Tel (303) 892-3611

MACFARLANE, MARGARET LAMOREAUX, b. Beaver Dam, Wis., June 24, 1916; LL.B., George Washington U., 1941. Admitted to D.C. bar, 1941, U.S. Supreme Ct. bar, 1947, Wis. bar, 1971; clk. Agr. Adjustment Adminstrn., Washington, 1934-35, jr. archivist Nat. Archives, Washington, 1935-42, adminstrv. asst., bd. econ. welfare, 1942-45, chief legal reference services GAO, 1945-71; legal researcher Wis. Hosp. Assn., Madison, 1971—. Sec., Beaver Dam Humane Soc., 1972-74. Mem. AAUW, Wis., Dodge County bar assns., Nat. Assn. Ret. Fed. Employees (sec. Beaver dam chpt.), Kappa Beta Pi. Recipient Monetary award GAO, 1956, Career Devel. award, 1967, Distinguished Service award, 1971; compiler Wis. Hosp. Law Manual, 1972, 76. Home: 328 Park Ave Beaver Dam WI 53916

MACFARLANE, ROBERT BRUCE, b. Portsmouth, Eng., Jan. 29, 1896; student Naval Architecture Admiralty Sch., Portsmouth, 1912-17; J.D., U. Richmond, 1934; came to U.S., 1924, naturalized, 1932. Admitted to Va. bar, 1932; engring. cons. Macfarlane & Sadler, Richmond, Va., 1938-60; individual practice law, Richmond, 1960—; examiner U.S. Patent Office, Richmond, 1943-45. Mem. zoning appeals City Richmond, 1950-62, planning commn., 1954-62. Mem. Va., Richmond bar assns. Home: 406 Maple Ave Richmond VA 23226 Office: Mutual Bldg Richmond VA 23219 Tel (703) 643-4145

MACGILL, HUGH CORNER, b. Balt., May 1, 1940; B.A., Yale, 1965; LL.B., U. Va., 1968; postgrad. (grad. fellow), Yale, 1970-71; (fellow in law and humanities), Harvard, 1975-76. Reginald Heber Smith community lawyer fellow, law reform unit Balt. Legal Services, 1968-69; Urban Coalition, St. Paul, 1969-70; vis. asst. prof. law, U. Conn., 1971-72, asst. prof., 1972-75, asso. prof., 1976-77, prof., 1977—; cons. U. Minn., 1969-70, Conn. Elections Commn., 1975. Bd. dirs. Conn. Humanities Council, 1976—. Mem. Am. Soc. for Legal History, Soc. for Am. Law Tchrs. Author: A Mexican Village, 1971; contbr. articles to law jours. Office: U Conn Sch Law West Hartford CT 06117 Tel (203) 523-4841

MAC GOWAN, JOHN LESLIE, b. Paris, France, Aug. 27, 1932; A.B., Middlebury Coll., 1955; J.D., U. Va., 1960. Admitted to Pa. Supreme Ct. bar, 1962, U.S. Dist. Ct. bar for Eastern Dist. Pa., 1962, U.S. Ct. Appeals bar, 3d Circuit, 1962; asso. firm Dower, McDonald & Cahn, Allentown, Pa., 1962; asso. firm Perkin, Webster & Christie, Allentown, 1963-70, partner, 1971-75; individual practice law, Allentown, 1975—. Legal counsel St. John's Luth. Ch., Allentown, 1976—. Mem. Lehigh County (Pa.), Pa., Am. bar assns. Home: 3324 Byrd Ave Allentown PA 18103 Office: Suite 403 Commonwealth Bldg PO Box 275 Allentown PA 18105 Tel (215) 437-7855

MACGREGOR, JOHN FRANKLIN, b. Ventura, Calif., Oct. 22, 1932; A.B. U. Calif. Berkeley, 1954; J.D., Golden Gate U., 1964. Admitted to Calif. bar, 1965, U.S. Dist. Ct. bar, 1965; pub. defender, Alameda County, Calif., 1965-66; lectr. law Golden Gate U., 1965-68; asso. firm Gunheim, Yturbide et al., San Francisco, 1967-75; individual practice law, San Francisco, 1975—; cons. Criminological Research Assos., Berkeley; research asso. Calif. Dept. Corrections, 1961-65; cons. Calif. State Assembly Office Research, 1968-70. Mem. Calif., Marin County bar assns., San Francisco Lawyers Club, Calif. Trial Lawyers Assn. Home: 18 Rosemont Ave San Anselmo CA 94960 Office: 1231 Market St San Francisco CA 94103 Tel (415) 861-5400

MACHEN, ARTHUR WEBSTER, JR., b. Balt., Dec. 16, 1920; A.B., Princeton U., 1942; LL.B., Harvard U., 1948. Admitted to Md. bar, 1948; asso. firm Armstrong, Machen & Eney, Balt., 1948-51; asso. firm Venable, Baetjer & Howard, Balt., 1951-57, partner, 1957—; dir. Waverly Press, Inc.; reporter Charter Bd. Balt. County, 1954; legislative draftsman Home Rule Charter, 1955; chmn. Gov.'s Commn. to Study Adminstrn. Blue Sky Laws Md., 1961, chmn. Md. Blue Sky Adv. Commn., 1962-68; mem. Commn. Revision of Corp. Laws Md., 1966; chancellor Episcopal Diocese Md., 1972—; mem. bd. mgrs. Family and Children's Soc., 1958-70, pres., 1967-69; trustee Gilman Sch., 1959-61. Mem. Balt. City, Md., Am. bar assns., Am. Judicature Soc. Contbr. articles to legal jours. Home: 1400 Malvern Ave Ruxton MD 21204 Office: 1800 Mercantile Bank & Trust Bldg Baltimore MD 21201 Tel (301) 752-6780

MACHEN, HERVEY GILBERT, b. Washington, Oct. 14, 1916; LL.B., Southeastern U., 1939, LL.M., 1941. Admitted to U.S. Dist. Ct. bar for D.C., 1939, U.S. Ct. Appeals bar for D.C., 1939, U.S. Supreme Ct. bar, 1958, Md. bar, 1940; individual practice law, Hyattsville, Md., 1941-64; partner firms Machen and Brooks and predecessor, Hyattsville, 1964-71, Machen & Aldridge, 1971—; mem. Md. Ho. of Dels., 1955-64; mem. 89th-90th Congresses from 5th Congl. Dist. Md., 1965-68; asst. state's atty. for Prince George's County, Md., 1947-50. Mem. Prince George's County (pres. 1963), Md., Am. bar assns., Sigma Delta Kappa. Home: 4107 Hamilton St Hyattsville MD 20781 Office: 4328 Farragut St Hyattsville MD 20781 Tel (301) 779-5440

MAC INTYRE, DARRELL D., b. Avoca, Wis., June 17, 1896; ed. U. Wis. Admitted to Wis. bar; asso. firm Hill, Beckwith, MacIntyre & Harrington, Madison, Wis., 1923-25; individual practice law, Madison, 1925—. Mem. Am. Trial Lawyers Assn. Home: 5122 Spring Ct Madison WI 53703 Office: 318 Trust Bldg Madison WI 53703 Tel (608) 256-0681

MACIOLEK, RICHARD D., b. Chicopee, Mass., Feb. 17, 1937; B.B.A., U. Mass., 1958; J.D., Suffolk U., 1968. Admitted to Mass. bar, 1968; asso. firms Frederick T. McCarthy, 1969-70, Langenbach, Reynolds & Aisner, 1970-73, Parker, Coulter, Daley & White, 1973—, Boston. Chmn., Zoning Bd. Appeals, Town Medway, Mass., 1971—; town moderator, Town Medway, 1974—. Mem. Am., Mass. bar assns. Office: 1 Beacon St Boston MA 02108 Tel (617) 723-4500

MACK, JAMES EDWARD, b. Atlanta, Nov. 2, 1920; B.A., George Washington U., 1943, LL.B., 1952. Admitted to D.C. bar, 1953, U.S. Supreme Ct. bar, 1977; individual practice law, D.C., 1954—. Mem. Am., D.C. bar assns., Am. Soc. Assn. Execs. Home: 9005 Congressional Ct Potomac MD 20854 Office: 5101 Wisconsin Ave Suite 504 Washington DC 20016 Tel (202) 966-7888

MACK, JOHN MELVIN, b. Chgo., July 31, 1934; B.S., Northwestern U., 1956, J.D., 1959. Admitted to Ill. bar, 1960, U.S. Supreme Ct. bar, 1974; asst. state's atty. Cook County (Ill.), 1960-64; asso. firm Orner & Wesserman, Chgo., 1964-72; partner firm Brody, Gore & Fineberg, Chgo., 1977—; arbitrator Am. Arbitration Assn. Mem. Skokie Human Relations Com., 1967-77; chmn. Skokie Task Force on Housing, 1972-74; bd. dirs. Skokie Caucus Polit. Party, 1970-77; chmn. Cub Scouts Am. Dr., Skokie, 1974-77; active B'nai B'rith, Chgo., 1961-77. Mem. Trial Lawyers Club Chgo., Soc. Trial Lawyers, Ill., Chgo. (coms. criminal law 1960-65, municipal dept. 1965-73, legal edn. 1976, ins. law 1976, circuit ct. ops. 1977) bar assns. Home: 9425 Hamlin St Evanston IL 60203 Office: 330 S Wells St Chicago IL 60606 Tel (312) 922-6828

MACK, MICHAEL RAY, b. Akron, Ohio, July 30, 1945; B.S. in Indsl. Mgmt., U. Akron, 1968, J.D., 1972. Admitted to Ohio bar, 1973; pres. Mack & Waller Co., L.P.A., Akron, 1973—. Mem. Ohio, Akron bar assns. Home: 1244 Winhurst Dr Akron OH 44313 Office: 682 W Market St Akron OH 44303 Tel (216) 434-1948

MACK, ROBERT JAMES, b. N.Y.C., Sept. 13, 1932; B.S., Georgetown U., 1954; J.D., La. State U., 1956. Admitted to La. bar, 1956; asso. firm Joseph A. Sims, Hammond, La., 1958; partner firm Sims & Mack, Hammond, 1959-73, firm Mack & O'Neal, Hammond, 1973—; lectr. La. Trial Lawyers Seminars, 1975-76. Mem. Am., La. bar assns., Am., La. trial lawyers assns. Home: 909 Holly St Hammond LA 70401 Office: PO Box 759 Hammond LA 70404 Tel (504) 345-3121

MACKALL, LAIDLER BOWIE, b. Washington, Aug. 8, 1916; A.B., Princeton U., 1938; J.D., Georgetown U., 1946. Admitted to D.C. bar, 1947; law clk. to judge D.C. Ct. Appeals, 1946-47; partner firm Steptoe & Johnson, Washington, 1948—; bd. mgrs. Nat. Conf. Bar Examiners; mem. admissions com. D.C. Ct. Appeals. Fellow Am. Coll. Trial Lawyers; mem. Am. (vice chmn. standing aviation ins. com.), D.C. bar assns., D.C. Integrated Bar, Nat. Assn. R.R. Trial Counsel, D.C. Def. Lawyers Assn., Barristers Club. Home: 4636 Hawthorne Ln NW Washington DC 20016 Office: 1250 Connecticut Ave NW Washington DC 20036 Tel (202) 223-4800

MACKAMAN, DONALD HAYES, b. Des Moines, Oct. 29, 1912; B.A., Drake U., 1933, J.D., 1935. Admitted to Iowa bar, 1935, Tex. bar, 1941, U.S. Supreme Ct. bar, 1964; atty. Campbell Taggart, Inc., Dallas, 1935—, v.p., 1959—, gen. counsel, 1966—. Chmn. bd. trustees Am. Bakers Assn. Retirement Plan. Mem. Am., Tex., Dallas bar assns., Grocery Mfrs. Assn., Tex. Mfrs. Assn., Phi Beta Kappa, Order of Coif. Home: 5337 Wateka Dr Dallas TX 75209 Office: PO Box 2640 Dallas TX 75221 Tel (214) 358-9286

MAC KAY, DONALD, b. Chgo., Nov. 29, 1897; B.S., Dartmouth, 1920, M.B.A., 1921; J.D., Chgo.-Kent Coll. Law, 1940. Admitted to Ill. bar, 1940, Wis. bar, 1956; mem. firm Petit, Olin & Overmyer, Chgo., 1941-61; individual practice law, Sister Bay, Wis., 1961—; family ct. commr., asst. dist. atty. Door County (Wis.), 1961-63. Mem. Am., Ill. State, Milw. bar assns., State Bar Wis., Door-Kewaunee Bar Assn. Home: 4209 Main St Fish Creek WI 54212 Office: 602 Bay Shore Rd Sister Bay WI 54234 Tel (414) 854-2431

MACKAY, DONALD BRUCE, b. Madison, Wis., Nov. 28, 1938; B.S., Loyola U., 1960; J.D., John Marashall Law Sch., 1963. Admitted to Ill. bar, 1963, Fed. bar, 1972; pub. defender McLean County (Ill.), 1965-70; asst. states atty. McLean County, 1963-64; partner firm Rolley & Mackay, Bloomington, Ill., 1969-71; U.S. Atty. So. Dist. Ill., Springfield, 1971—; mem. faculty Sangamon State U., Springfield; lectr. in field. Bd. govs. Ill. Defender Project, 1969-70. Mem. Ill. State Bar Assn. Home: 2178 Greenbriar St Springfield IL 62704 Office: 600 E Monroe Springfield IL 62705 Tel (217) 525-4450

MACKAY, JOHN RICHARDSON, b. Chgo., Oct. 7, 1917; J.D., John Marshall Law Sch., 1949. Admitted to Ill. bar, 1950; mem. firm John R. Mackay and Assos., Wheaton, Ill., 1974—; mem. Ill. Indsl. Pollution Control Financing Authority, 1976—; mem. Sen. Charles Percy's Com. to Study Fed. Jud. Dists. in Ill., 1975-76. Mem. Ill. State (pres. 1974-75, bd. govs. 1967—), 7th Dist. Fedn., DuPage County (pres. 1965-66) bar assns. Office: 422 W Wesley St Wheaton IL 60187 Tel (312) 690-9800

MAC KAY, ROBERT FARLEIGH, b. Phoenix, Nov. 10, 1932; B.A., Yale, 1954; LL.B., U. Calif. at Berkeley, 1961. Admitted to Calif. bar, 1962; asso. firm O'Donnell, Waiss, McComish, San Francisco, 1962-67; partner firm MacKay and MacKay, San Rafael, Calif., 1967-75; individual practice law, San Rafael, 1975—; dep. city atty., Belvedere, Calif., 1968-69, city atty., 1969-74. Mem. Calif., Marin County bar assns. Home: 210 Corte del Cerro Ignacio CA 94947 Office: 1299 Fourth St Suite 207 San Rafael CA 94901 Tel (415) 457-9262

MACKEIGAN, IAN MALCOLM, b. St. John, N.B., Can., Apr. 11, 1915; student U. Sask., 1931-32; B.A. with great distinction, Dalhousie U., 1934, M.A., 1935, LL.B., 1938; M.A., U. Toronto, 1939. Dep. adminstr. Wartime Prices and Trade Bd., Ottawa, Ont., Can., 1940-45; dept. commr. Combines Investigation Commn., Dept. Justice, Ottawa, 1945-50; partner MacKeigan, Cox & Co., Barristers, Halifax, N.S., Can., 1950-73; chief justice N.S., Halifax, 1973—; dir. Maritime Telephone. Chmn. bd. dirs. Atlantic Research Centre for Mental Retardation, 1967—; trustee Victoria Gen. Hosp., Halifax, 1968—, N.S. Research Found., 1970—, Can. Tax Found, 1963, Can. Welfare Council, 1960-62. Mem. N.S. Bar Soc. (pres. 1957), Can. Bar Assn. (v.p. 1958), Am. Coll. Trial Lawyers, Theta Kappa Pi. Home: 833 Marlborough Ave Halifax NS B3H 3G7 Canada Office: Law Courts PO Box 2314 Halifax NS Canada*

MACKEN, JAMES LEE, b. Alliance, Nebr., Feb. 17, 1929; J.D., Creighton U., 1952. Admitted to Nebr. bar, 1952, Wyo. bar, 1952; served with JAGC, U.S. Army, 1953-55; asso. firm Neighbors & Danielson, Scottsbluff, Nebr., 1955-58; county atty. Morrill County, Nebr., 1959-69; judge Scottsbluff Ct., 1969—. Pres. Bridgeport (Nebr.) Bd. Edn., 1965-68; v.p. Alliance Ednl. Service Unit 17, 1966-69; mem. Nebr. Drug Commn. Com., 1976—. Mem. Nebr. County Judges' Assn. (pres. 1975), Nat. Council Juvenile Ct. Judges, Nebr., West Nebr., 17th Dist. bars, Assn. Trial Lawyers Am., Nebr. Juvenile Justice Assn. (founder, 1st pres. 1974-75). Recipient award for traffic safety Gov. Nebr., 1975. Home: 2017 4th Ave Scottsbluff NE 69361 Office: Courthouse Gering NE 69341 Tel (308) 436-5086

MACKENZIE, WILLIAM MCALISTER, b. Chelsea, Mass., June 16, 1909; Ph.B., Brown U., 1931; LL.B., Harvard, 1934. Admitted to R.I. bar, 1934; individual practice law, Pawtucket, R.I., 1935-59; asso. justice Superior Ct. of R.I., Providence, 1959—. Home: 26 Congdon St Providence RI 02906 Office: 250 Benefit St Providence County Ct House Providence RI 02903 Tel (401) 277-3250

MACKEY, H. KENNETH, b. Wilmington, Del., Aug. 20, 1919; B.S., U. Md., 1953; J.D. cum laude, Am. U., 1955. Admitted to Md. bar, 1955; individual practice law, Elkton, Md., 1955-67; judge Circuit Ct. Cecil County (Md.), Elkton, 1967—. Home: Rural Delivery #4 Box 23 Elkton MD 21921 Office: Court House Elkton MD 21921 Tel (301) 398-0330

MACKEY, MALCOLM HAMILTON, b. Hoboken, N.J., July 20, 1929; B.A., N.Y. U., 1951; J.D., Southwestern U., 1958. Admitted to Calif. bar, 1959, since practiced in Los Angeles; asso. firm Bolton, Groff & Dunne, 1958-59; individual practice law, 1959—. Mem. Los Angeles County Democratic Com., 1966—, vice-chmn., 1970—; mem. Calif. Dem. State Central Com., 1968—; arbitrator Ins. Panel, Los Angeles County. Mem. Am., Los Angeles County bar assns., Lawyers Club Los Angeles (pres. 1976-77). Home: 5351 Vincent Ave Los Angeles CA 90041 Office: 601 W 5th St Los Angeles CA 90017 Tel (213) 624-0863

MACKEY, TERRANCE WAYNE, b. Denver, Nov. 20, 1942; A.A., Casper Coll., 1966; B.A., U. Wyo., 1968, J.D., 1970. Admitted to Wyo. bar, 1970; atty. firm King and Mackey, Jackson, Wyo., 1970-73; atty. firm Urbigkit, Mackey, Whitehead & Sullivan, Cheyenne, Wyo., 1973—; dir. juvenile delinquency study Wyo. Gov.'s Planning Com. Criminal Justice, 1969-70. Bd. dirs. Teton Mental Health Center, Jackson, 1971-73. Mem. Am. Bar Assn., Assn. Trial Lawyers Am., Wyo. Trial Lawyers Assn. (pres. 1976—), Jackson Hole C. of C. (v.p. 1972-73). Home: 706 Ridgeland St Cheyenne WY 82001 Office: 1651 Carey Ave Cheyenne WY 82001 Tel (307) 635-4271

MACKINNON, GEORGE EDWARD, b. St. Paul, Apr. 22, 1906; LL.B., U. Minn., 1929. Admitted to Minn. bar, 1929, U.S. Supreme Ct. bar, 1947, D.C. bar, 1949; asst. counsel Investors Syndicate, Mpls., 1929-42; individual practice law, Mpls., 1946, 49-53, 58-61; U.S. Atty. Dist. of Minn., 1953-58; gen. counsel, v.p. Investors Mut. Funds, Mpls., 1961-69; judge U.S. Circuit Ct. of Appeals, Washington, 1969—; mem. Minn. Ho. of Reps. from 29th Dist., 1935, 37, 39, 41; mem. 80th Congress from 3d Minn. Dist. Mem. Am., Minn. State bar assns. Author: Minn. State Reorganization Act, 1939; State Civil Service Law, 1939; Old Age Assistance Act, 1936. Home: 11333 Willowbrook Dr Potomac MD 20854 Office: 5329 US Ct House DC 20001 Tel (202) 426-7021

MACKLIN, ROBERT DOUGLAS, b. Warwick, R.I., Nov. 21, 1917; B.S., U.S. Naval Acad., 1941; LL.B., Franklin U., 1964; J.D., Capitol U., 1966. Admitted to Ohio bar, 1964, U.S. Dist Ct., So. Div. of Ohio bars, 1965, U.S. Supreme Ct. bar, 1968; asst. atty gen., State of Ohio, 1965-71, chief counsel, atty gen., 1970-71; judge Franklin County Municipal Ct., 1971—; dir. Ohio Crime Commn., 1967-69. Bd. dirs. Franklin County Crippled Children's Assn., Consumer Credit Counselling Services. Mem. Am., Ohio, Columbus bar assns., Ohio Judicial Conf., Ohio Municipal Judges Assn., Ohio Attys. Gen. Assn. (trustee). Home: 2736 Wellesley Dr Columbus OH 43221 Office: Judges Chambers City Hall Columbus OH 43215 Tel (614) 461-5655

MACKOUL, WALTER ERNEST, b. Jacksonville, Fla., Apr. 19, 1936; B.S., Jacksonville U., 1960; J.D., Stetson U., 1966. Admitted to Fla. bar, 1966; research asst. Third Dist. Ct. Appeals Fla., 1966-67; asso. firm Preddy, Haddad, Kutner & Hardy, Miami, Fla., 1967-69; adj. prof. Fla. Internat. U., Miami, 1972—. Mem. Fla. Bar, Am. Bar Assn., Am. Judicature Soc. Office: 2935 SW 3rd Ave Miami FL 33129 Tel (305) 854-3505

MAC LAREN, ROBERT IAN, II, b. West Palm Beach, Fla., Aug. 5, 1947; B.A., U. Fla., 1969, J.D., 1972. Admitted to Fla. bar, 1973; asso. firm Gunsto, Yoakley, Criser, Stewart & Hersey, Palm Beach, Fla., 1973-76; asso. firm Deschler & Reed, Boca Raton, Fla., 1976—; adminstr. asst. Fla. Ho. of Reps., 1969-70, minority leader, 1969-70. Mem. Am., Fla., Palm Beach County bar assns. Home: 755 Aurelia St Boca Raton FL 33432 Office: Boca Raton Fed Bldg 555 S Fed Hwy Boca Raton FL 33432 Tel (305) 391-3550

MAC LAUGHLIN, HARRY HUNTER, b. Breckenridge, Minn., Aug. 9, 1927; B.B.A. with distinction, U. Minn., 1949, LL.B., 1956, J.D., 1956. Admitted to Minn. Supreme Ct. bar, 1956, U.S. Supreme Ct. bar, 1971; mem. firms Larson, Loevinger, Lindquist, Freeman & Fraser, Mpls., MacLaughlin & Mondale, Mpls., Maclaughlin & Harstad, Mpls.; asso. justice Minn. Supreme Ct., 1972—; instr. law William Mitchell Coll. Law, 1958-63; lectr. U. Minn. Law Sch., 1973—. Mem. nat. advisory council SBA, 1967-69; mem. Mpls. Charter Commn., 1967-72, Minn. State Coll. Bd., 1971-72, Minn. Jud. Council, 1972. Mem. Am., Minn. State, Hennepin County (Minn.) bar assns., Beta Gamma Sigma, Phi Delta Phi. Bd. editors: Minn. Law Rev., 1954-55. Home: 2301 Oliver Ave S Minneapolis MN 55405 Office: Supreme Ct State Capitol Saint Paul MN 55155 Tel (612) 296-4033

MAC LAUGHLIN, MARLIN VANCE, JR., b. Hartford, Conn., Oct. 30, 1936; A.B. in History, Rutgers, 1958; J.D., Jones Law Sch., 1968. Admitted to Ala. bar, 1968; field mgr. St. Paul Ins. Cos., 1965-70; v.p. Roy L. Nolen Agy., Montgomery, Ala., 1970-72; regional mgr. St. Paul Title Ins. Corp., Montgomery, 1973-74, of counsel, 1974—; individual practice law, Montgomery, 1974—; spl. prosecutor City of Montgomery, 1973-75, 76—, pub. defender, 1975-76. Trustee, bd. dirs. Cradle of Confederacy R.R. Mus., New Haven R.R. Hist. and Tech. Assn.; mem. blood com. ARC, 1975—. Mem. Ala. State Bar, Am., Montgomery County bar assns., Ala. Trial Lawyers Assn., Sigma Delta Kappa. Home: 3581 Foxhall Dr Montgomery AL 36111 Office: 312 Scott St PO Box 11285 Montgomery AL 36111 Tel (205) 262-4887

MAC LEAN, JOHN H., b. Osceola, Pa., Apr. 8, 1932; B.S., Mansfield Tchrs. Coll., 1953; LL.B., Dickinson U., 1958. Admitted to Supreme Ct. Ariz. bar, 1965, U.S. Dist. Ct. bar, 1966, Supreme Ct. U.S. bar, 1971, Supreme Ct. Pa. bar, 1959; spl. agt. FBI, 1959-64; mem. firm Behrens, Mac Lean & Jacques, Phoenix, 1964—. Mem. Am., Ariz., Pa., Maricopa County bar assns., Am. Trial Lawyers Assn., Def. Research Inst. Office: Suite 2163 100 W Clarendon St Phoenix AZ 85013 Tel (602) 263-5771

MAC LEID, MATTHEW T., b. Cin., June 17, 1935; B.S., U. Cin., 1957, J.D., 1963. Admitted to Ohio bar, 1963; partner firm Thomas, Thomas & MacLeid, Cin., 1963—. Mem. men's com. Cin. Symphony Orch. Mem. Cin. Bar Assn. Recipient Freedom award Am. Legion, 1965. Office: 2350 Victory Pkwy Cincinnati OH 45206 Tel (513) 751-3600

MAC LENNAN, JOHN FINLAY, b. Washington, Nov. 11, 1948; B.A., Dickinson Coll., 1970; J.D., Cornell U., 1973. Admitted to Md. bar, 1973, Fla. bar, 1975; lt. JAGC, U.S. Naval Reserve, 1974—; legal officer Naval Drug Rehab. Center, Jacksonville, Fla., 1974, legal officer Naval Air Station, 1974-77; asso. firm Jennings, Watts, Clarke and Hamilton, 1977—. Mem., Am., Md., Fla. bar assns., Order of Coif, Phi Beta Kappa. Home: 8 Jonathan Ct Orange Park FL 32073 Office: 400 Florida Nat Bank Bldg Jacksonville FL 32201

MAC LEOD, GORDON A., b. Buffalo, Mar. 29, 1926; A.B., Hamilton Coll., 1948; J.D., Harvard, 1951. Admitted to N.Y. State bar, 1951; partner firm Hodgson, Russ, Andrews, Woods and Goodyear, Buffalo; lectr. estate planning and taxation. Mem. N.Y. State, Am., Erie City bar assns., Am. Coll. Probate Counsel. Contbr. articles to legal jours. Home: 496 Berryman Dr Snyder NY 14226 Office: 1800 One M and T Plaza Buffalo NY 14203 Tel (716) 856-4000

MAC LEOD, IAN ROBERTS, b. Erie, Pa., Aug. 6, 1931; A.B., U. Rochester, 1953; J.D., Harvard, 1959. Admitted to N.Y. State bar, 1960, Ohio bar, 1967; asso. firm Cadwalader, Wickersham & Taft, N.Y.C., 1959-65; asst. counsel Firestone Tire & Rubber Co., Akron, Ohio, 1965-69, asst. sec. and asst. counsel, 1969—. Mem. Am., Akron, Ohio State bar assns., Am. Soc. Corp. Secs. Home: 730 Ridgecrest Rd Akron OH 44303 Office: 1200 Firestone Pkwy Akron OH 44317 Tel (216) 379-6738

MAC LEOD, RODERICK MOORE, JR., b. Birmingham, Ala., Dec. 16, 1929; A.B., U. Ala., 1951; LL.B., 1953. Admitted to Ala. bar, 1953; law clk. to judge, Ala. Supreme Ct., Montgomery, 1955-56; partner firm Beddow, Embry & Beddow, Birmingham, 1956-68; atty. firm Pritchard, McCall & Jones, Birmingham, 1968-74. Mem. Am., Ala., Birmingham bar assns., Am. Trial Lawyers Assn. Home: 3033 Westmoreland Dr Birmingham AL 35223

MACMAHON, JAY ROSS, b. San Francisco, July 14, 1930; A.A., U. Calif., Berkeley, 1950, B.S., 1952; J.D., Boalt Hall, U. Calif., Berkeley, 1955. Admitted to Calif. bar, 1955; practice law, San Rafael, Calif., 1956—. Fellow Am. Coll. Probate Counsel; mem. Am., Marin County (sec. 1959-60) bar assns., State Bar Calif. (mem. taxation com. 1963-66), Am. Arbitration Assn. (nat. panel arbitrators), Lawyers Club San Francisco. Office: 960 5th Ave San Rafael CA 94901 Tel (415) 456-7500

MACMICHAEL, JAMES EDWARD, b. Bangor, Maine, Dec. 30, 1940; B.A., Bowdoin Coll., 1963; LL.B., Boston U., 1966. Admitted to Maine bar, 1966; mem. firm Wright & MacMichael, Skowhegan, Maine, 1966-76; pvt. practice law, Skowhegan, 1976—. Mem. Somerset County Commn., 1972—; bd. dirs. Kennebec Valley Mental Health Clinic, 1971-73, Sch. Adminstrv. Dist. 54, 1971. Mem. Am., Maine, Somerset County (pres. 1974-75) bar assns., Maine Central Inst. Alumni Assn. (pres. 1972-73), Maine Trial Lawyers Assn., Assn. Trial Lawyers Am. Home: 6 Coburn Ave Skowhegan ME 04976 Office: 87 Water St Skowhegan ME 04976 Tel (207) 474-9283

MAC NEIL, DONALD JOHN, b. Teaneck, N.J., Mar. 10, 1943; B.A. in English Lit., Providence Coll., 1965; J.D., U. San Diego, 1972. Admitted to Calif. bar, 1973; dep. dist. atty. San Diego, 1974—; served to maj. JAGC, USMCR, 1966—. Mem. San Diego, Calif., Am. bar assns., Order of Barristers. Office: Dist Atty's Office County Courthouse San Diego CA 92101 Tel (714) 236-2350

MACNEIL, HUGH LIVINGSTONE, b. Los Angeles, May 23, 1918; B.A., Harvard, 1939; LL.B., Loyola U., Los Angeles, 1948. Admitted to Calif. bar, 1948; with O'Melveny & Myers, Los Angeles, 1948—, partner, 1962—. Mem. Am., Calif., Los Angeles County bar assns., Am. Coll. Probate Counsel (regent), Internat. Acad. Estate and Trust Law (exec. council). Contbr. articles to legal jours. Office: 611 W 6th St Los Angeles CA 90017 Tel (213) 620-1120

MACNEIL, IAN RODERICK, b. N.Y.C., June 20, 1929; B.A. magna cum laude, U. Vt., 1950; J.D. magna cum laude, Harvard, 1955. Admitted to N.H. bar, 1956; assoc. firm Sulloway, Hollis, Godfrey & Soden, Concord, N.H., 1956-59; asst. prof. law Cornell U., 1959-62, asso. prof., 1962-63, prof. 1963-72, 74-76, Frank B. Ingersoll prof., 1976—; vis. prof. law U. East Africa, Dar es Salaam, Tanzania, 1965-67; vis. prof. law, Duke, 1971-72, prof. law, mem. Center for Advanced Studies, U. Va., Charlottesville, 1972-74; dir. Cornell U. Priorities Study, 1975. Mem. Am. Law Inst., Am., N.H. bar assns., Canadian Law Tchrs. Assn., Soc. Pub. Tchrs. Law, African Law Assn., Phi Beta Kappa. Author: Contracts, Exchange Transactions & Relationships, 1971; Bankruptcy Law in East Africa, 1966; co-author: (with Schlesinger et al) Formation of Contracts, a Study of the Common Core of Legal Systems, 1968; Morison Students and Decision Making, 1970; recipient Emil Brown Preventive Law Award, 1971. Home: 105 Devon Rd Ithaca NY 14850 Office: Cornell Law Schl Ithaca NY 14853 Tel (607) 256-3378

MAC PHAIL, JOHN ARCH, b. Johnstown, Pa., Jan. 20, 1924; B.A., Washington and Jefferson Coll., 1948; LL.B., Dickinson Sch. Law, 1951; H.L.D., Gettysburg Coll., 1971. Admitted to Pa. bar, 1952; asso. firm Brown, Swope and MacPhial, and predecessor, Gettysburg, Pa., 1952-56, partner, 1956-66; presiding judge Adams County (Pa.) Ct. Common Pleas, 1966—. Pres. Gettysburg-Adams County Torch, 1963-64, Gettysburg Community Chest, 1955-56; mem. permanent jud. commn. Synod of Trinity United Presbyn. Ch., 1971—. Mem. Am., Pa., Adams County bar assns., Pa. Conf. State Trial Judges (chmn. com. pub. relations 1974—), Nat., Pa. juvenile ct. judges assns. Recipient Distinguished Alumni award Washington and Jefferson Coll., 1971. Contbr. articles to legal jours. Home: RD 2 Gettysburg PA 17325 Office: Adams County Courthouse Gettysburg PA 17325 Tel (717) 334-6781

MACPHERSON, GILBERT PENDLETON, b. New London, Conn., May 19, 1941; B.A., U. Miami, 1964; LL.B., Stetson Coll. Law, 1967. Admitted to Fla. bar, 1967; partner firm Robinson, Macpherson, Harper & Kynes, Clearwater, Fla., 1967—; mem. anti-trust com. Fla. Bar. Pres. Belleair Civic Assn., 1977. Mem. Clearwater Bar Assn. (dir. 1975, 76). Office: PO Box 4840 Clearwater FL 33518 Tel (813) 442-9689

MACPHERSON, IAN ALEXANDER, b. Honolulu, Feb. 5, 1943; B.A. with distinction, Ariz. State Univ., 1967; J.D., 1971. Admitted to Ariz. bar, 1971; asst. atty. gen. State of Ariz., 1971—. Mem. Am., Maricopa County bar assns. Office: 1700 W Washington St Phoenix AZ 85007 Tel (602) 271-4681

MADDEN, JOHN JOSEPH, b. N.Y.C., May 27, 1946; B.A., U. Pa., 1968; J.D., Fordham U., 1975. Admitted to N.Y. bar, 1976; asso. firm Shearman & Sterling, N.Y.C., 1975—. Mem. Assn. Bar City N.Y., Am. Bar Assn. Home: 155 E 93d St New York City NY 10028 Office: 53 Wall St New York City NY 10005 Tel (212) 483-1000

MADDEN, LUCINDA NIEMAN, b. Celina, Ohio, July 4, 1899; LL.B., Franklin Law Sch., 1929, J.D., 1966. Admitted to Ohio bar, 1929, U.S. Supreme Ct. bar, 1971; individual practice law, Columbus, Ohio, 1929—. Bd. dirs. Columbus YWCA, Family and Children's Bur., Columbus; active youth activities Reorganized Ch. of Jesus Christ of Latter Day Saints. Mem. Columbus Women Lawyers (1st pres.), Columbus Bar Assn. (gov., chmn. speakers bur.). Home: 1275 Medford St Columbus OH 43209 Office: 16 E Broad St Columbus OH 43215 Tel (614) 221-4364

MADDEN, PATRICK JOHN, b. Milw., May 21, 1926; B.S., Marquette U., 1947, LL.B., 1950; LL.M., Georgetown U., 1956. Admitted to Wis. bar, 1950, U.S. Supreme Ct. bar, 1955; individual practice law, Milw., 1950-52; served with USN, office of JAG, 1953-57; city prosecutor, Milw., 1957-71; judge Milwaukee County Ct., 1972—. Mem. Wis., Milw. bar Office: 901 N 9th St Milwaukee WI 53233 Tel (414) 278-4548

MADDEN, PAUL ROBERT, b. St. Paul, Nov. 13, 1926; B.A., U. Minn., 1948; LL.B., Georgetown U., 1951. Admitted to Minn. bar, 1951, D.C. bar, 1951, Ariz. bar, 1957; asso. firm Hamilton and Hamilton, Washington, 1951-55; legal asst. to commr. Harold Patterson SEC, Washington, 1955-57; asso. firm Lewis and Roca and predecessor, Phoenix, 1957-59, partner, 1959—; sec., gen. counsel, dir. Saguaro Savings & Loan Assn., Phoenix, 1972—; asso. gen. counsel Blood Systems, Inc., BSP Ins. Co., Phoenix. Bd. dirs. Jr. Achievement of Central Ariz., Inc., 1972—, pres., 1975-76; bd. dirs. Cath. Social Services of Phoenix, 1972—. Mem. State Bar Ariz., Maricopa County (Ariz.), D.C., Am., Fed. bar assns., Fedn. Ins. Counsel, Internat. Assn. Ins. Counsel, Nat. Health Lawyers Assn., The Barristers. Home: 3732 E Pierson St Phoenix AZ 85018 Office: 100 W Washington St Phoenix AZ 85003 Tel (602) 262-5731

MADDEN, STANFORD CASIMIR, b. Kansas City, Mo., Dec. 26, 1916; J.D., U. Mo., 1939. Admitted to Mo. bar, 1939; individual practice law, Kansas City, 1939-42, 1966—; atty. Mo. Dept. Health & Welfare, 1946; Social Security Adminstrn., 1946-48; field examiner NLRB, 1948-50; atty. Office Solicitor, Dept. Labor, 1950-53; mem. firm Shughart & Thompson, 1953-56; labor relations dir. Builders' Assn., 1956-66; lectr. in field. Active Gov. Bond's Spl. Com. Pub. Employee Bargaining Mo., Fed. Mediation and Conciliation Service. Mem. Am. Arbitration Assn. (nat. panel arbitrators, 1966—), Kansas City Bar Assn. Contbr. numerous articles to law jours. Home: 6115 Oak St Kansas City MO 64113 Office: 6225 Brookside Blvd Kansas City MO 64113 Tel (816) 363-4822

MADDEN, TIMOTHY KEVIN, b. Jersey City, Nov. 6, 1939; B.S., Fairleigh Dickinson U., 1966; J.D., St. John's U., 1968. Admitted to N.J. bar, 1968; staff atty. Hudson County (N.J.) Legal Services Corp., Union City, 1968-69, staff atty., office mgr., Jersey City, 1969, exec. dir., 1969—; mem. consumer affairs com. Fed. Exec. Bd. Met. No. N.J., 1974—; mem. traffic, transp. and consumer protection com. Jersey City Citizens Adv. Council, 1975—; mem. Hudson County Ancillory Manpower Planning Bd., 1971-74. Mem. Am., N.J. State bar assns. Home: 167 Herrick Ave Teaneck NJ 07666 Office: 628 Newark Ave Jersey City NJ 07306 Tel (201) 792-6333

MADDEN, WILLIAM JOHN, b. Buffalo, Feb. 7, 1908; B.A., Holy Cross Coll., 1930; J.D., Harvard, 1934. Admitted to Mass. bar, 1934, Wash. bar, 1942; partner firm Ryan, Askren, Mathewson, Seattle, 1946-51, Bayley, Fite, Westberg, Madden, Seattle, 1951-66, Madden and Poliak, Seattle, 1966—; mem. Wash. Bar Trial Commn., 1953-54, chmn. Med.-Legal Commn., 1972-76. Mem. Wash. State, Am. bar assns., Internat. Soc. Barristers. Contbr. articles to profl. jours.; editor Wash. Bar Jour., 1948-49. Home: 3236 Hunts Point Rd Bellevue WA 98004 Office: 1411 4th Ave Bldg Seattle WA 98101 Tel (206) 682-2515

MADDEN, WILLIAM LEE, JR., b. Hastings, Nebr., Mar. 13, 1948; B.A. with distinction, Stanford, 1970; J.D., Cornell U., 1973. Admitted to Mont. bar, 1974; asso. firm Towe, Neely & Ball, Billings, Mont., 1973-75; partner firm Goetz & Madden, Bozeman, Mont., 1975—. Mem. Mont. Bar Assn., Mont. Criminal Lawyers Def. Assn. Home: PO Box 921 Bozeman MT 59715 Office: 522 W Main PO Box 1322 Bozeman MT 59715 Tel (406) 587-0618

MADDOCK, FREDERICK MCKENDRY, b. Detroit, Sept. 13, 1932; LL.B., Wayne State U., 1957. Admitted to Mich. bar, 1958; individual practice law, Detroit, 1958—; asst. city atty. City of Harper Woods (Mich.), 1963-64. Councilman City of Grosse Pointe Woods (Mich.), 1961-65; mem. Wayne County Bd. Suprs., 1964-65. Home: 656 Pear Tree Ln Grosse Pointe Woods MI 48236 Office: 28 1st St Mount Clemens MI 48043

MADDOX, DAVID J., b. Waverly, Ala., Dec. 15, 1884; B.A., U. Chgo. Admitted to Ill. bar, 1928; individual practice law, Chgo. Mem. Cook County Bar Assn. Office: 54 W Randolph St Chicago IL 60601 Tel (312) 332-3803

MADDOX, JESSIE CORNELIUS, b. Jackson, Ga., Apr. 5, 1932; student West Ga. Coll., 1954-56; B.S., U. Ga., 1959; LL.B., John Marshall Sch. Law, 1959. Admitted to Ga. bar, 1961; mem. firm Chance, Maddox & Jones, Calhoun, Ga., 1961—; atty. Gordon County (Ga.), 1965—; judge Gordon County Juvenile Ct., 1963—. Scoutmaster N.W. Ga. council Boy Scouts Am., 1959-64. Mem. Cherokee, Am., Ga. bar assns., Gordon County Bar. Recipient Gordon Watson award West Ga. Coll., 1955-56, Gold Key scholastic award Sigma Delta Kappa, 1958-59, Scholastic award in Equity, Harrison Pub. Co., 1959; named Outstanding Young Man of Year, Calhoun Jr. C. of C., 1968. Home: Route One Calhoun GA 30701 Office: 204 N Wall St Calhoun GA 30701 Tel (404) 629-4407

MADDOX, ROBERT CHARLES, b. Washington, June 23, 1943; A.A., Montgomery Coll., Rockville, Md., 1971; A.B., U. Md., 1967, J.D., 1971. Admitted to Md. bar, 1972, D.C. bar, 1972, U.S. Supreme Ct. bar, 1976; atty. Legal Aid Bur., Inc., Balt., 1971-72; asso. firm Everngam & Goldstein, Silver Spring, Md., 1972-74, Staley, Prescott & Ballman, Kensington, Md., 1974—; adj. prof. Montgomery Coll. Pres. Kiwanis Club, 1976. Mem. Am., Md. (governing council young lawyers sect., chmn. unauthorized practice law com.), D.C., Montgomery County bar assns., Phi Alpha Delta. Home: 9228 Copenhaver Dr Potomac MD 20854 Office: 5th floor Citizens Savings Bldg Kensington MD 20795 Tel (301) 933-1234

MADISON, JAMES RAYMOND, b. White Plains, N.Y., Apr. 27, 1931; B.S., Stanford, 1953, LL.B., 1959. Admitted to Calif. bar, 1960; partner firm Orrick, Herrington, Rowley & Sutclifte, San Francisco, 1968—; lectr. continuing edn. of the bar. Mem. NAACP. Mem. State Bar Calif., Calif., San Mateo County trial lawyers assns., San Francisco, San Mateo County bar assns., Lawyers Club San Francisco, ASCE, Am. Arbitration Assn., World Affairs Council No. Calif. Home: 1770 Holly Ave Menlo Park CA 94025 Office: 600 Montgomery St 12th Floor San Francisco CA 94111 Tel (415) 392-1122

MADSEN, ROY HARDING, b. Kanatuk, Alaska, Mar. 14, 1923; student Oreg. State Coll., 1941-43; LL.B., Northwestern Coll. 1953. Admitted to Oreg. bar, 1953, Alaska bar, 1962; asst. dist. atty. Clackamas County, Oreg., 1950-60; individual practice law, Oregon City, Oreg, 1960-61, Kodiak, Alaska, 1962-75; judge superior ct., Kodiak, 1975—. Regent, U. Alaska, 1970-74. Mem. Alaska, Oreg. bar assns., Am. Trial Lawyers Assn., Am. Judicature Soc. Home: 421 Upper Mill Bay Kodiak AK 99615 Office: State Court Bldg Room 52 Kodiak AK 99615 Tel (907) 486-5765

MADSON, DICK LAWRENCE, b. Keewatin, Minn., Sept. 4, 1935; B. in Mining Engring., U. Minn., 1958; J.D., William Mitchell Coll., 1962. Admitted to Minn. bar, 1962, Alaska bar, 1969; dep. pub. defender Fairbanks, Alaska, 1969-73; partner firm Cowper & Madson, Fairbanks, 1973—. Bd. dirs. Hillcrest Home for Boys, Fairbanks, 1974—, U. Fairbanks Symphony Assn., 1975—, Alaska Legal Services Corp. Mem. Alaska Bar Assn. (bd. govs. 1975—, pres. 1977—). Home: S R Box 31479 3 Mile McGrath Rd Fairbanks AK 99701 Office: Suite D Nerland Bldg Fairbanks AK 99701 Tel (907) 452-4215

MAFFEI, ALBERT, b. Eagle Creek, Oreg., Oct. 20, 1922; LL.B., Mont. State U., 1951. Admitted to Mont. bar, 1951, Oreg. bar, 1952, Alaska bar, 1953; individual practice law, Anchorage, 1954—. Mem. Alaska, Anchorage bar assns. Office: 1034 W 4th Ave Anchorage AK 99501 Tel (907) 277-2503

MAFFITT, JAMES STRAWBRIDGE, b. Raleigh, N.C., Oct. 29, 1942; A.B., Washington and Lee U., 1964, LL.B., 1966. Admitted to Va. bar, 1966, Md. bar, 1969; asso. firm Apostolou Place and Thomas, Roanoke, Va., 1966-67; partner firm Cable, McDaniel, Bowie & Bond, Balt., 1971—; trust officer Mercantile Safe Deposit & Trust Co., Balt., 1967-71. Bd. dirs. Legal Aid Bur., Inc., Balt., 1972—. Mem. Va. State, Md. State, Am. bar assns., Bar Assn. Balt. City (exec. council Young Lawyers sect. 1973—). Home: 1408 Carrollton Ave Baltimore MD 21204 Office: 1 N Charles St Baltimore MD 21201 Tel (301) 752-3650

MAG, ARTHUR, b. New Britain, Conn., Oct. 11, 1896; A.B., Yale, 1918, J.D., 1920. Admitted to Conn. bar, 1920, Mo. bar, 1920; partner firm Stinson, Mag, Thomson, McEvers & Fizzell, Kansas City, Mo., 1920—; dir. First Nat. Bank of Kansas City, First Nat. Charter Corp.

(Kansas City), Gold, Inc., Denver, Host Internat., Los Angeles, Marley Co., Kansas City, Price Candy Co., Kansas City, Rival Mfg. Co., Kansas City, Schutte Lumber Co., Z Bar Cattle Co., Hereford Redevel., Corp., L.B. Price Mercantile Co., Helzberg's Diamond Shops, Standard Milling Co., Kansas City, Rothschild & Sons, Inc., Kansas City; cons. U. Mo., 1964—; adv. trustee U. Mo. Law Found. Pres. Greater Kansas City Mental Health Found., 1952-56; mem. Nat. Adv. Council for Mental Health HEW, 1955-59; chmn. Greater Kansas City Liaison Com. Regional Med. Program for Kans. and Mo., 1952-56; mem. Gov.'s Citizens Com. on Crime and Delinquency, 1966-68; bd. curators Stephens Coll., 1967-72; trustee U. Mo., Kansas City, 1933—; mem. Citizens Study Com. on Kansas City/Jackson County Health Services, 1968; mem. Mayor's Commn. on Civil Disorder in Kansas City, 1968; co-chmn. Gov.'s Task Force on Role of Private Higher Edn. in Mo., 1970; trustee Kansas City Assn. of Trusts and Founds., Menninger Found., Menorah Med. Center Found., Midwest Research Inst. Mem. Am., Mo., Kansas City bar assns., Am. Law Inst., Lawyers Assn. of Kansas City, Assn. of Bar of N.Y.C. Home: 5049 Wornall Rd Kansas City MO 64112 Office: 2100 Ten Main Center PO Box 19251 Kansas City MO 64141 Tel (816) 842-8600

MAGARAM, PHILIP SIDNEY, b. N.Y.C., July 29, 1937; B.S. in accounting with honors, U. Calif., Los Angeles, LL.B., 1961. Admitted to Calif. bar, 1962; mem. firm Magaram, Riskin, Wayne & Minikes; chmn. bd. trustees Los Angeles County chpt. Leukemia Soc. Am., 1970—, also chmn. planned giving com. bd. govs. So. Calif. Arthritis Found., 1972—. Mem. State Bar Calif., Beverly Hills, Century City, Los Angeles County, Am. bar assns., Phi Alpha Delta, Beta Gamma Sigma, Phi Eta Sigma. Contbr. articles in field to profl. jours. Home: 8262 Skyline Dr Los Angeles CA 90046 Office: 1880 Century Park East Los Angeles CA 90067 Tel (213) 277-3135

MAGDOVITZ, LAWRENCE MAYNARD, b. Clarksdale, Miss., Aug. 21, 1937; B.A., Vanderbilt U., 1959; J.D., 1961. Admitted to Miss. bar, 1961, Tenn. bar, 1961, Ky. bar, 1962; pvt. practice law, Clarksdale, Miss., 1962—. Chmn. bd. dirs. Coahoma Legal Aid, Inc. Mem. Coahoma County, Miss., Ky. bar assns. Mem. B'nai B'rith (v.p. 1976-77). Home: 1603 Westminister Cove Clarksdale MS 38614 Office: 604 Desoto Ave Clarksdale MS 38614

MAGEE, GERALD CLAYTON, b. Mpls., May 26, 1928; B.S. in Law, U. Minn., 1952; J.D. cum laude, William Mitchell Coll. Law, 1957. Admitted to Minn. bar, 1957; claims mgr. Gen. Accident Group, Mpls., 1952-64; individual practice law, Mpls., 1964—. Mem. Am., Anoka County, Hennepin County bar assns., Trial Lawyers Assn. Home: 10446 E Mississippi Blvd Coon Rapids MN 55433 Office: 940 Midland Bank Bldg Minneapolis MN 55401 Tel (612) 339-8797

MAGEE, GERALD WAYNE, b. Waterloo, Iowa, July 20, 1943; B.A., U. Iowa, 1965, J.D., 1967. Admitted to Iowa bar, 1967; asso. firm Cudahy & Wilcox, 1967-70; partner firm Cudahy, Wilcox, Handley & Magee, 1970-74; participating shareholder firm Cudahy, Wilcox, Handley, Magee, Jefferson, Iowa, 1974-75, Cudahy, Wilcox, Handley, Magee & Polking, Jefferson, 1975—; city atty. City of Jefferson, 1976—. Mem. Am., Iowa (exec. council young lawyers sect. 1970-73), Greene County (pres. 1975) bar assns., Am. Judicature Soc., Nat., Iowa councils sch. bd. attys., Jefferson C. of C. (chmn. civic bur. 1969). Office: 206 N Wilson Ave Jefferson IA 50129 Tel (515) 386-3158

MAGEE, WARREN EGBERT, b. Washington, Apr. 27, 1908; student Strayer Coll., Washington, 1926; LL.B., American U., 1930, LL.M., 1931, LL.D., 1970. Admitted to D.C. bar, 1930, U.S. Ct. Appeals 4th Circuit bar, 1937, U.S. Ct. Claims bar, 1943, U.S. Supreme Ct. bar, 1944; partner firm Baker, Beedy & Magee, Washington, 1940-42, firm Magee, Beedy & McGovern, Washington, 1942-47, firm Magee & Bulow, Washington, 1947—. Mem. D.C. bar, Bar Assn. D.C., Am., Fed. bar assns., Am. Judicature Soc., Fedn. of Ins. Counsel. Recipient Gold medal, Pope Pius XII, 1948. Contbr. articles in med. legal jurisprudence. Home: 5009 Newport Ave Washington DC 20016 Office: Suite 304 1100 17th St NW Washington DC 20036 Tel (202) 296-7990

MAGER, TROY RICHARD, b. St. Louis, April 5, 1934; B.A., U. Mo., 1956, J.D., 1960. Admitted to Mo. bar, 1960, Ill. bar, 1971; individual practice law, Columbia, Mo., 1960-65; asst. counsel U. Mo., 1965-67, counsel, bd. curators, 1967-71; legal counsel So. Ill. U., Carbondale, 1971-75, asso. prof. law, 1975—, v.p. for devel. and services, 1972-75; asst. pros. atty. Boone County (Mo.), 1962-64. Mem. planning and zoning commn. City of Columbia, 1966-68. Mem. Am., Mo., Ill. bar assns., Am. Assn. Law Schs., Nat. Assn. Coll. and Univ. Attys. Contbr. articles in field to profl. jours. Home: 105 N Lark Ln Carbondale IL 62901 Office: 205 Law Library Southern Illinois University Carbondale IL 62901 Tel (618) 536-7711

MAGGIORE, VINCENT DOMINICK, b. Canton, Ohio, Aug. 4, 1925; student Newberry Coll., 1944-45; B.A., Ohio State U., 1949; J.D., Georgetown U., 1955. Admitted to Ariz. bar, 1955; practiced in Phoenix, 1955, 59-64; chief dep. county atty. Maricopa County (Ariz.), 1956-59; asst. atty. gen. State of Ariz., 1959-60; judge U.S. Bankruptcy Ct., Phoenix, 1964—; prof. legal asst. program Scottsdale Community Coll. Pres., St. Thomas More Soc., Phoenix, Holy Name Soc., Scottsdale, Ariz.; bd. dirs. United Fund, Phoenix. Mem. Am. Bar Assn., Am. Judicature Soc., Jud. Conf., Fed. Exec. Associated (pres. 1973-74). Recipient Lenders award of Merit Ariz. Consumer Fin. Assn., 1971; contbg. author: Willaston On Contracts, 1970. Home: 3209 Fairfield St Tempe AZ 85211 Office: Fed Bldg Phoenix AZ 85025 Tel (602) 261-4046

MAGGIPINTO, WILLIAM VITO, b. Bklyn., Nov. 19, 1915; B.A., Columbia, 1938; LL.B., 1941. Admitted to N.Y. bar, 1942; asso. firm William B. Platt, Southampton, N.Y., 1945-47; asso. firm Kenneth W. Anderson, Sag Harbor, N.Y., 1947-48; sr. partner firm Anderson, Maggipinto, Vaughn & O'Brien, and predecessor firms, Sag Harbor, 1948—; counsel Sag Harbor Savs. Bank, 1948—; counsel Town of Southampton Bd. Trustees, 1960-70; atty. Village of Sag Harbor, 1975—; commr. N.Y. State Temp. Commn. on Jud. Conduct, 1975—. Mem. village zoning bd. appeals, Southampton, 1959-63. Mem. N.Y. State, Suffolk County (dir. 1968-71; chmn. jud. com. 1971-73; 3d v.p. 1974-75, 2d v.p. 1975-76, 1st v.p. 1976-77; recipient Directors award 1975) bar assns. Office: Main St Sag Harbor NY 11963 Tel (516) 725-2222

MAGID, CECIL E., b. St. Paul, Apr. 28, 1908; B.A., U. Minn., 1934, J.D., 1937. Admitted to Minn. bar, 1937, Ill. bar, 1937; individual practice law, Chgo., 1937-40, 1962-64; partner firm Weissenbach, Hartman, Craig, Okin & Magid, Chgo., 1940-58, firm Hartman & Magid, Chgo., 1958-62, firm Grossman, Kasakoff, Magid & Silverman, Chgo., 1964-70; of counsel firm Roan & Grossman, Chgo., 1970—. Mem. Am., Chgo. bar assns. Editorial bd. U. Minn. Law Rev., 1936-37. Home: 339 N Deere Park Dr Highland Park IL 60035 Office: 120 S LaSalle St Chicago IL 60603 Tel (312) 263-3600

MAGILL, NICHOLAS HUGH, b. Clark, Colo., Sept. 4, 1920; B.S. in Law, U. Denver, 1949, LL.B., 1950. Admitted to Colo. bar, 1951, U.S. Dist. Ct. bar for Dist. of Colo., 1956; individual practice law in Steamboat Springs, Colo., 1951—; asst. dist. atty. 14th Jud. Dist. of Colo., 1954-57; town atty. Town of Steamboat Springs, 1958-74, Town of Hayden (Colo.), 1965-72. Mem. Am., Colo. (gov. 1970-72), Northwestern Colo. bar assns. Home: 885 Yahmonite St POB 100 Steamboat Springs CO 80477 Office: 119 Ninth St POB 100 Steamboat Springs CO 80477 Tel (303) 879-1515

MAGNER, JOHN CRUSE, b. Dallas, Nov. 10, 1921; LL.B., So. Meth. U., 1948. Salesman, Continental Supply Co., Ark., La., Tex., 1938-41; field office mgr. Hunt Oil Co., El Dorado, Ark., 1941-44; mem. prodn. dept., land dept. Sun Oil Co., Dallas, 1944-49; sr. v.p. Rowan Cos. Inc., drilling contractors, Houston, 1949—, also dir.; admitted to Tex. bar, 1948. Bd. dirs. Ft. Worth Jr. Achievement, 1955-69. Mem. Internat. Assn. Drilling Contractors, Am. Petroleum Inst., Am., Houston assns. petroleum landmen, Am., Tex., Houston bar assns., Tex. Mid-Continent Oil and Gas Assn. Home: 13303 Apple Tree St Houston TX 77024 Office: 1900 Post Oak Tower Houston TX 77056

MAGNOTTI, JOSPEH ERNEST, b. Bronx, N.Y., June 29, 1945; B.S., Fordham U., 1967; J.D., St. Johns U., 1971. Admitted to N.Y. State bar, 1972, Fed. Dist. Ct. bar, 1975; asso. firm Biaggi, Ehrlich & Lang, N.Y.C., 1972-74; mem. firm John S. Zachary, P.C., S.I., N.Y., 1974—; legal advisor nat. counsel Columbia Assns. in Civil Service, NAACP S.I. br. spl. asst. N.Y. State Affairs to Congressman Mario Biaggi. Mem. N.Y. State, Richmond County (dir.) bar assns. Home: 53 Uxbridge St Staten Island NY 10314 Office: 75 Little Clove Rd Staten Island NY 10301 Tel (212) 442-2828

MAGUIRE, EDWARD, b. Washington, Aug. 3, 1941; A.B., Harvard, 1963, LL.B., 1966. Admitted to Va. bar, 1967, D.C. bar, 1971; asso. firm Hunton, Williams, Gay, Powell & Gibson, Richmond, Va., 1966-69, firm Cleary, Gottlieb, Steen, & Hamilton, Washington, 1971-73; asst. chief counsel Office of Fgn. Direct Investments U.S. Dept. Commerce, Washington, 1969-71; asso. firm Cole, Corette & Bradfield, Washington, 1973—; lectr. internat. trade and investment; counsel D.C. Youth Orch., Washington, 1974—. Mem. Am., Fed. bar assns. Contbr. articles in field to profl. jours. Home: 3415 Rodman St NW Washington DC 20008 Office: 1200 17th St NW Washington DC 20036 Tel (202) 872-1414

MAGUIRE, EVERETT WILLIAM, b. San Bernardino, Calif., Jan. 2, 1928; A.A., San Bernardino Valley Coll., 1948; B.S. in Civil Engring., U. Calif., Berkeley, 1950; J.D., U. Calif., Los Angeles, 1957. Admitted to Calif. bar, 1958; civil engr. Calif. Div. Hwys., 1948, 50, 52-54, 57; atty. Calif. Dept. Pub. Works, Los Angeles, 1958-65; asso. firm Grant & Popovich, Beverly Hills, Calif., 1965-68; partner Shapiro & Maguire Law Corp., Beverly Hills, 1968—. Pres. Pacific Palisades Methodist Memorial Found., 1964-73; bd. mgrs. Palisades-Malibu YMCA, 1969—. Registered profl. engr. Mem. Calif. State Bar, Am., Los Angeles County, Santa Monica bar assns., ASCE, Soc. Am. Mil. Engrs. Office: 8500 Wilshire Blvd Suite 1026 Beverly Hills CA 90211 Tel (213) 655-5170

MAHAN, D(ANIEL) DULANY, JR., b. Hannibal, Mo., Dec. 22, 1914; A.B., U. Mo., 1936; J.D., Harvard U., 1940. Admitted to N.Y. State bar, 1941, Mo. bar, 1942; asst. atty. FTC, Washington, 1948-50; asso. firm Beneduce, MacGuire & Collins, N.Y.C., 1950-52, firm Adams & James, N.Y.C., 1952-64, firm Horst, Kurnik, Cresap & Moffitt, N.Y.C., 1964-72, firm Kurnik and Hackmann, N.Y.C., 1972—; sec. Gerling Internat. Ins., N.Y.C. and Zurich, Switzerland, 1961—. Mem. Am., N.Y. State, Internat. bar assns., Bar Assn. City N.Y., Mo. Bar Assn., World Assn. Lawyers. Home: 98 Ralph Ave White Plains NY 10606 Office: 660 Madison Ave New York City NY 10021 Tel (212) PL2-4455

MAHAN, EFFIE AYASH, b. Atlanta, May 24, 1926; LL.B., John Marshall U., 1946. Admitted to Ga. bar, 1946; individual practice law, Blairsville, Ga., 1948-66; law asst. Ga. Supreme Ct., Atlanta, 1952-76; adminstrv. law judge Ga. Bd. Workmen's Compensation, Macon, 1976—. Pres. Union County PTA, 1964-65; treas. Pres.'s Council, Atlanta, 1974-76. Mem. Ga. Assn. Women Lawyers (pres. 1972-73), Macon, Ga. bar assns., Delta Sigma Gamma. Office: 914 Georgia Power Bldg Macon GA 31201 Tel (912) 744-6060

MAHAN, ROBERT EUGENE, b. Carroll, Iowa, Oct. 23, 1946; B.S., Iowa State U., 1969; J.D., U. Iowa, 1973. Admitted to Iowa bar, 1973; since practiced in Waterloo, Iowa, asso. firm Lindeman & Yagla, 1973-75, firm Ball & Nagle, 1975-76; individual practice law, 1976—; atty. Black Hawk County Atty.'s Office, 1976—. Active, Black Hawk County Democratic Party, Waterloo, 1973-76. Mem. Am., Iowa, Black Hawk County bar assns., Am., Iowa trial lawyers assns. Home: 122 Columbia Circle Waterloo IA 50701 Office: 425 Washington St #31 Waterloo IA 50701 Tel (319) 235-6922

MAHAN, THOMAS HAROLD, b. Bozeman, Mont., Dec. 14, 1924; student Mont. State Coll., 1942-43; B.S., U.S. Mil. Acad., 1946; student in law U. Colo., summers 1954-55; B.A., U. Mont., 1956, J.D., 1956. Admitted to Mont. bar, 1956, U.S. Supreme Ct. bar, 1969; partner firm Mahan & Mahan, Helena, Mont., 1956-66; individual practice law, Helena, 1966-68; asso. firm Mahan & Strope, Helena, 1968—; spl. asst. gen. State of Mont., 1957—; dir. Mont. Legal Services Project for Health, Edn. and Welfare, 1969-72. Nat. v.p. Am. Heart Assn., 1974-75, bd. dirs., 1966-71, 74-75; pres., chmn. bd. Mont. Heart Assn., 1964-65, 70-71. Mem. State Bar Mont. (pres.), Am. Bar Assn., Am. Judicature Soc., Mont. Trial Lawyers Assn., Nat. Conf. Bar Pres.'s, Western States Bar Conf., Phi Delta Phi. Home: 1800 Silver St Helena MT 59601 Office: Northwestern Bank Bldg Room 304 Helena MT 59601 Tel (406) 442-6570

MAHER, THOMAS AUGUST, b. Bronx, N.Y., Oct. 23, 1917; B.S. in Fgn. Commerce, U. Notre Dame, 1939; J.D., Detroit Coll. Law, 1947. Admitted to Mich. bar, 1947; mgr. indsl. relations, automatic transmission div. Ford Motor Co., Cin., 1950-60, dir. personnel, 1960-65; dir. personnel Intrastate Brands Corp., Kansas City, Mo., 1965-69; individual practice law, Detroit, 1969-74; judge Juvenile div. Probate Ct., Detroit, 1975—. Bd. dirs. Soc. Retarded Children, Cin.; v.p. Greater Cin. Safety Council; mem. budget rev. commn. United Appeal, Cin.; pres. Air Control League, Cin. Mem. State Bar Mich., Am., Detroit bar assns. Home: 1247 Buckingham St Grosse Pointe Park MI 48230 Office: 1025 Forest St Detroit MI 48207 Tel (313) 833-5700

MAHERAS, THEODORE GREGORY, b. Joliet, Ill., Oct. 9, 1920; A.B., Brown U., 1941; J.D., Harvard, 1948. Admitted to Ill. bar, 1949, U.S. Supreme Ct. bar; staff judge adv. USAF, 1951-52; partner firm Economos & Reeda, Chgo., 1953-55; asst. atty. gen. Ill. Appellate Div., Chgo., 1955-61; prof., chmn. comml. law div. Roosevelt U., Chgo., 1961—; individual practice law, Chgo., 1961—; mem. staff Judge Adv. Office, USAF Res., 1950-62. Bd. dirs. Edgebrook Community Assn., 1958-62. Mem. Am., Fed., Ill. bar assns. Contbr. articles to profl. publs. Home: 6652 N Chicora Ave Chicago IL 60646 Office: 105 W Madison St Chicago IL 60602 Tel (312) 346-8565

MAHLER, STEPHEN RICHARD, b. N.Y.C., July 5, 1938; B.A., Adelphi Coll., 1960; LL.B., N.Y. U., 1964. Admitted to N.Y. bar, 1964; asst. dist. atty. Queens County, N.Y., 1966-69; partner firm Zuckerberg, Santangelo, Mahler & Harris, P.C., Kew Gardens, N.Y., 1970—; counsel N.Y. State Assembly Com. on Higher Edn., 1975-76; asso. counsel N.Y. State Assembly Med. Practice Task Force, 1977—. Chmn., Queens County chpt. N.Y. State Liberal Party, 1976—. Mem. N.Y. State, Queens County bar assns., Asst. Dist. Attys. Assn. Home: 99-25 64th Rd Rego Park NY 11374 Office: Penthouse Suite 2707 125-10 Queens Blvd Kew Gardens NY 11415 Tel (212) 268-5575

MAHONEY, DANIEL O'CONNELL, b. Mattapoisett, Mass., Nov. 30, 1928; A.B., Williams Coll., 1950; LL.B., Harvard, 1953. Admitted to Mass. bar, 1953, since practiced in Boston; asso. firm Palmer & Dodge, 1953-61, partner, 1962—; served to capt. JAGC, USAR, 1954-57. Trustee, v.p. Salem (Mass.) Hosp., 1970—. Mem. Am., Mass. (chmn. prepaid legal services com.), Boston bar assns. Home: 87 Harbor Ave Marblehead MA 01945 Office: 1 Beacon St Boston MA 02108 Tel (617) 227-4400

MAHONEY, JAMES WILLIAM, b. Walters, Okla., July 9, 1921; B.S., St. Mary's U., San Antonio, 1947; J.D., U. Fla., 1949. Admitted to Fla. bar, 1949; partner firm Mahoney Hadlow & Adams, and predecessors, Jacksonville, Fla., 1949—. Mem. Am., Fla. (chmn. real property probate trust sects. 1958-59) bar assns., Am. Judicature Soc. Office: 800 Barnett Bank Bldg Jacksonville FL 32201 Tel (904) 354-1100

MAI, HAROLD LEVERNE, b. Casper, Wyo., Apr. 5, 1928; B.A., U. Wyo., 1950, J.D., 1952. Admitted to Wyo. bar, 1952, U.S. Supreme Ct. bar, 1963; individual practice law, Cheyenne, Wyo., 1953-62, 67-71; judge Juvenile Ct., Cheyenne, 1962-67; U.S. bankruptcy judge, Cheyenne, 1971—. Mem. advisory bd. Salvation Army; bd. dirs. Am. Cancer Soc. Wyo., Inc. Mem. Am., Wyo., Laramie County bar assns., Nat. Conf. Bankruptcy Judges. Home: 5428 Walker Rd Cheyenne WY 82001 Office: US Court House 2120 Capitol Ave Cheyenne WY 82001 Tel (307) 778-2220

MAIER, HAROLD GEISTWEIT, b. Cin., Mar. 25, 1937; B.A., U. Cin., 1959, J.D., 1963; Luftbrücke Dankstipendiat Freie U., Berlin, 1959-60; LL.M., U. Mich., 1964; Ford Internat. Studies fellow U. Munich, 1964-65. Admitted to Ohio bar, 1963; asst. prof. law Vanderbilt U., Nashville, 1965-67, asso. prof., 1967-70, prof., 1970—, dir. Transnational Legal Studies, 1973—; pres. Faculty Senate, 1970-71; guest scholar Brookings Instn., Washington, 1976-77. Bd. dirs. Univ. Sch. Nashville, 1975—. Mem. Am. Soc. Internat. Law (mem. exec. council 1975—), African Law Assn., Phi Alpha Delta. Recipient Paul J. Hartman Outstanding Prof. award, 1976. Office: Vanderbilt Sch Law Nashville TN 37240 Tel (615) 322-2587

MAIER, JOSEPH FAUVER, b. Sheridan, Wyo., Nov. 6, 1920; A.A., Compton (Calif.) Jr. Coll., 1940; J.D. with honors, U. Wyo., 1947. Admitted to Wyo. bar, 1947; individual practice law, Sheridan, Wyo., 1947-49; partner firm Chaffin & Maier, Torrington, Wyo., 1949-61; individual practice law, Torrington, 1961-67; partner firm Maier & Connolly, Torrington, 1967-73; judge 1st Jud. Dist. Ct. Wyo., Cheyenne, 1973—; city atty., Torrington, 1950-72. Pres. Goshen County (Wyo.) Sch. Bd., 1969-70; pres. Wyo. Sch. Bd. Assn., 1970. Fellow Am. Coll. Probate Counsel, Internat. Acad. Trial Judges; mem. Am., Wyo., Laramie County bar assns., Wyo. Jud. Conf. (chmn. 1974-75), Torrington C. of C. (pres. 1968). Mem. bd. of editors Wyo. Law Jour., U. Wyo., 1946-47. Home: 1547 Hot Springs St Cheyenne WY 82001 Office: Box 343 Cheyenne WY 82001 Tel (307) 632-8452

MAIER, PAUL C., b. Aug. 12, 1929; B.S. in Bus. Adminstrn., U. Calif., Berkeley, 1951, J.D., 1954. Admitted to Calif. bar, 1955; asso. firm Livingston & Borregard, San Francisco, 1956-62; partner firm Herzstein & Maier, San Francisco, 1962—. Mem. City of Berkeley Planning Commn., 1975—; chmn. City of Berkeley Charter Review Com., 1972-75. Mem. Calif. State Bar, San Francisco, Am. bar assns., San Francisco Lawyers Club. Office: 500 Sansome St San Francisco CA 94111 Tel (415) 434-0610

MAIER, PETER K., b. Wurzburg, Germany, Nov. 20, 1928; B.A. cum laude, Claremont Men's Coll., 1949; J.D., U. Calif., Berkeley, 1952; LL.M. in Taxation, N.Y. U., 1953. Admitted to Calif. bar, 1953; capt. JAGC, USAF, 1953-56; trial atty., tax div. Dept. Justice, Washington, 1956-59; partner firm Bacigalupi, Elkus, Salinger & Rosenberg, San Francisco, 1959-70, firm Brookes, Maier and Wilson, San Francisco, 1970-73, firm Winokur, Schoenberg, Maier, Hammerman & Knudsen, San Francisco, 1974—; instr. Hastings Coll. Law, San Francisco, 1967, asst. prof., 1968, asso. prof., 1969-71, prof., 1971—. Mem. San Francisco Bar Assn. (chmn. tax com. 1973), San Francisco Tax Club (pres. 1973-74). Author: Recent Developments in the Income Taxation of Real Estate, 1975; The Attorney-Client Privilege in Tax Matters, 1962; Teacher's Manual, Federal Income Taxation, 1974; Deductibility of Expenses in Corporate Liquidations and Reorganizations, 1973. Home: PO Box 391 Tiburon CA 94920 Office: One California St suite 2424 San Francisco CA 94111 Tel (415) 392-8308

MAIER, RICHARD FRANKLIN, b. Massillon, Ohio, Oct. 9, 1925; B.A., Yale, 1948; J.D., U. Mich., 1951. Admitted to Ohio bar, 1951; partner firm Maier & Maier, Massillon, 1951-71; individual practice law, Massillon, 1971—; asst. city solicitor City of Massillon, 1954-55, city solicitor, 1957-63. Former dir., chpt. chmn. Massillon chpt. A.R.C.; bd. dirs., past pres. Massillon Boys Club; former chmn. Ohio Area council Boys Clubs Am., former chmn. regional com. of area council chairmen Midwest region; past pres. Massillon Rotary Club; bd. dirs. Stark Met. Housing Authority, 1971-73; rep. Ohio Legislature, 1973—; mem. legislative bd. Ohio Energy Research Devel. Agy.; legis. mem. Ohio Constnl. Revision Commn. Mem. Ohio, Stark County bar assns. Home: 1222 Providence St NE Massillon OH 44646 Office: 2200 Wales Rd NW Massillon OH 44646 Tel (216) 832-9833

MAIN, JAMES ALLEN, b. Troy, Ala., Apr. 8, 1945; B.S. in Pharmacy, Auburn U., 1968; J.D., U. Ala., 1972. Admitted to Ala. bar, 1972, U.S. Supreme Ct. bar, 1975; partner firm Burnham, Klinefelter, Halsey & Love, Anniston, Ala., 1972—. Mem. Am., Ala., Calhoun County bar assns. Home: 1029 Glenwood Terr Anniston AL 36201 Office: PO Box 1618 Anniston AL 36202 Tel (205) 237-8515

MAIN, ROBERT GORDON, b. Malone, N.Y., Sept. 29, 1917; B.A., Colgate U., 1940; J.D., Union U., 1946. Admitted to N.Y. bar, 1946; partner firm Main, Pond & Main, Malone, 1946-59; mem. N.Y. Gen.

Assembly, 1951-59; justice Supreme Ct. State N.Y., 1959—; adminstrv. judge 4th Jud. Dist., 1965-69, appellate judge 3d Jud. Dept., 1973—; asso. justice appellate div., 1974—. Mem. Franklin County (pres. 1962), N.Y. State, Am. bar assns., Fedn. Bar Assns. 4th Jud. Dist. Home: 4 Whittlesey St Malone NY 12953 Office: Franklin County Court House Malone NY 12953 Tel (518) 483-4651

MAIN, RONALD, b. Woodhaven, N.Y., Feb. 28, 1940; B.A. (Univ. scholar), U. Tulsa, 1962, J.D., 1964. Admitted to Okla. bar, 1964; asso. firms Crawford & Rizley, Tulsa, 1964-66, Houston & Klein, Inc. and predecessors, Tulsa, 1966—; adj. asst. prof. ins. U. Tulsa, 1968—; lectr. law Okla. Sch. Bus.; guest lectr. in field. Mem. Okla., Tulsa County, Am. bar assns., Phi Alpha Delta. Recipient Outstanding Service award U. Tulsa Coll. Law, 1964; author, editor: Cases and Materials On Workmen's Compensation, 1970; contbr. articles to legal jours. Home: 3926 E 58th Pl Tulsa OK 74135 Office: 1000 Sooner Fed Bldg 404 S Boston St Tulsa OK 74103 Tel (918) 583-2131

MAINE, MICHAEL ROLAND, b. Anderson, Ind., Feb. 22, 1940; A.B., DePauw U., 1961; J.D., U. Mich., 1964. Admitted to Ind. bar, 1964, U.S. Supreme Ct. bar, 1967; mem. firm Baker & Daniels, Indpls., 1964—; served with JAGC, USAF, Chanute AFB, Ill., 1965-67. Dir., Festival Music Soc., Indpls. Mem. Am., Ind., Indpls. (bd. mgrs.), 7th Circuit bar assns., Am. Judicature Soc. Home: 7001 N Central St Indianapolis IN 46220 Office: 810 Fletcher Trust Bldg Indianapolis IN 46204 Tel (317) 636-4535

MAINZ, EDWARD CHARLES, JR., b. San Antonio, June 27, 1938; B.A., St. Mary's U. of San Antonio, Tex., 1960; LL.B. magnum cum laude, 1963. Admitted to Tex. bar, 1965, U.S. Supreme Ct. bar, 1975; asst. city atty., San Antonio, 1965; asso. firm Atlas, Schwarz, Gurwitz & Bland, McAllen, Tex., 1965-69; asso. firm Palmer, Palmer & Burke, Dallas, 1969-71; asso. firm Green, Gilmore, Crutcher, Rothpletz & Burke, Dallas, 1971-72; partner firm Stalcup, Johnson, Meyers & Miller, Dallas, 1972—. Mem. Tex., Dallas, Am. (asso. editor Litigation News, 1975-76) bar assns., Am. Judicature Soc., Delta Theta Phi. Home: 10018 Windledge St Dallas TX 75238 Office: Suite 2700 2001 Bryan St Dallas TX 75201 Tel (214) 651-1700

MAIO, F. ANTHONY, b. Passaic, N.J., Mar. 30, 1937; B.S. in Mech. Engring., Stevens Inst. Tech., Hoboken, N.J., 1959; LL.B., Boston Coll., 1968. Admitted to Wis. bar, 1968, D.C. bar, 1971; partner firm Foley & Lardner, Washington. Bd. dirs. Shorewood (Wis.) ABC Program, 1970, Fairfax County (Va.) Democratic Com. Mem. Am., Fed., Wis., Milw., D.C. bar assns. Recipient commendation for lecture series Wis. Continuing Legal Edn.; contbr. articles to profl. jours. Office: 1775 Pennsylvania Ave Washington DC 20006 Tel (202) 223-4771

MAIRE, JONATHAN EDWARD, b. Detroit, Oct. 4, 1936; B.A., U. Mich., 1958; LL.B., Hastings Coll., 1964. Admitted to Calif. bar, 1964, Mich. bar, 1965; with Pros. Atty.'s Office, Ingham County, Mich., 1965-66; mem. firm Reid, Hildebrandt, King, Weed, Smith and Brown, 1966-69; municipal judge, E. Lansing, Mich., 1969-70; individual practice law, Lansing, Mich., 1969—; atty. City Leslie, Mich., 1966-76; dir. Peoples Bank of Leslie (Mich.); clk., E. Lansing Trinity Church, 1969, 75-76; bd. dirs. Camp Highfields, Onondaga, Mich., 1973; pres. Greater Lansing Youth for Christ, 1973-74. Mem. Calif., Mich., Ingham County (dir. 1974—) bar assns. Home: 1345 Sherwood Rd Williamston MI 48895 Office: 423 W Ionia St Lansing MI 48933 Tel (517) 487-3736

MAIWURM, JAMES JOHN, b. Wooster, Ohio, Dec. 5, 1948; B.A., Coll. Wooster, 1971; J.D., U. Mich., 1974. Admitted to Ohio bar, 1974; asso. firm Squire, Sanders & Dempsey, Cleve., 1974—. Mem. alumni bd. Coll. Wooster, 1975—; trustee East Side Neighborhood House, Cleve., 1976—. Mem. Am., Ohio, Greater Cleve., Cuyahoga County bar assns. Contbr. articles to legal jours. Office: 1800 Union Commerce Bldg Cleveland OH 44115 Tel (216) 696-9200

MAJESKI, EUGENE J., b. Chgo., Dec. 24, 1916; B.S., DePaul U., 1937, J.D., 1940. Admitted to Ill. bar, 1940, Calif. bar, 1946; partner firm Ropers, Majeski, Kohn, Bentley & Wagner and predecessors, Redwood City, Calif., 1950—; mem. Calif. Bar Select Com. on Malpractice Legislation. Diplomate Am. Bd. Trial Advs. Fellow Am. Coll. Trial Lawyers, Internat. Acad. Trial Lawyers; mem. San Mateo County (Calif.) Bar Assn. (pres. 1964), Calif. Assn. Def. Counsel (pres. 1966), Internat. Assn. Ins. Counsel, Nat. Assn. R.R. Trial Counsel. Office: 1125 Marshall St Redwood City CA 94063 Tel (415) 364-8200

MAJURE, GLEN ALLEN, b. Newton, Miss., May 25, 1942; B.S., Livingston (Ala.) State Coll., 1965; J.D., So. Meth. U., 1970. Admitted to Tex. bar, 1970; asso. firm Johnson, Bromberg, Leeds & Riggs, Dallas, 1970—, partner, 1975—. Mem. Barristers, Order of Coif, Phi Delta Phi. Editor-in-chief Southwestern Law Jour., 1969-70. Home: 5171 Placid Way Dallas TX 75234 Office: suite 1500 211 N Ervay Dallas TX 75201 Tel (214) 748-8811

MAKAR, JOHN, b. Smoke Run, Pa., Jan. 22, 1912; B.S., Northwestern La. State U., 1938; J.D., La. State U., 1941. Admitted to La. bar, 1941, U.S. Dist. Ct. bar, 1947, U.S. Ct. Mil. Appeals bar, 1950, U.S. Supreme Ct. bar, 1965; individual practice law, Natchitoches, La., 1946-69; partner firm Makar & Whitaker, Natchitoches, 1969—; pub. Jefferson Democrat, Jefferson Legal News, Guide Newspapers, 1950—; atty. for La. State Comptroller, 1952-56. Mem. Am., La., 10th Dist., Mil. bar assns., Asso. Ct. and Comml. Newspaper Assn. (past nat. pres.), Soc. Am. Magicians, Internat. Brotherhood Magicians (chmn. ethics and grievance com.). Home: 1407 Washington S Natchitoches LA 71457 Office: POB 775 Natchitoches LA 71457 Tel (318) 352-8204

MAKHOLM, MARK HENRY, b. Maple Valley, Wis., Jan. 10, 1915; B.A. magna cum laude, Northland Coll., 1937; LL.B., U. Wis., 1950, LL.D., 1968. Admitted to Wis. bar; asst. prof. Northland Coll., Ashland, Wis., 1937-38; high sch. tchr. Washburn, Wis., 1939-41; operational supr. E.I. DuPont de Nemours & Co., Inc., U.S. Rubber Co., Kankakee, Ill., 1941-45; high sch. tchr. West Bend, Wis., 1947-48; individual practice law, Ashland, 1950-52; atty. Sentry Ins., Stevens Point, Wis., 1952-62, v.p., gen. counsel, 1962—; dir. Sentry Ins. Mutual Co., Sentry Life Ins. Co., Sentry Indemnity Co., Sentry Life Ins. of N.Y., Dairyland Ins. Co., Sentry Corp., Middlesex Ins. Co., Patriot Gen. Ins. Co., Sentry Investment Mgmt., Inc., Dairyland Found., Inc., North Bridge Corp. Former dir. village of Park Ridge; elder Presbyterian Ch. Mem. Internat. Assn. of Ins. Counsel (mem. exec. com. 1966-69), Am. Judicature Soc., Wis. Bar Found. (dir.), Order of the Coif, Phi Delta Phi. Home: 616 Greenbriar Ave Park Ridge Stevens Point WI 54481 Office: 1421 Strongs Ave Stevens Point WI 54481 Tel (715) 344-2345

MAKI, ALLAN ABEL, b. Bklyn., May 24, 1922; A.B., Muhlenberg Coll., 1944, J.D., Columbia, 1947. Admitted to N.J. bar, 1948; partner firm Corbin & Maki, Passaic, N.J., 1948-71; individual practice law, Paterson, N.J., 1971—; dir. Greater Jersey Bancorp., N.J. Bank N.Am., Bobbink Nurseries Inc., Universal Tech., Inc., Union Bldg. and Constrn. Corp. Bd. govs. Passaic Gen. Hosp., 1968—. Mem. Am., N.J., Passaic County bar assns. Office: PO Box 4040 Paterson NJ 07509

MAKKAI, ALEXANDER JOHN, JR., b. Carteret, N.J., Apr. 30, 1943; B.A., Upsala Coll., 1965; J.D., U. Denver, 1968. Admitted to Colo. bar, 1968; partner firm Silverman and Makkai, Denver, 1968—. Mem. Colo., Denver, Adams County (Colo.) bar assns. Home: 7007 S Madison Way Littleton CO 80121 Office: 1701 W 72d Ave Denver CO 80221 Tel (303) 428-3547

MAKOWSKI, ROBERT JOHN, b. Milw., Mar. 29, 1926; Ph.B. cum laude, Marquette U., 1949, J.D., 1950. Admitted to Wis. bar, 1950; asso. firm Foley and Lardner, Milw., 1950-53; sec. Miller Brewing Co., Milw., 1953-67; asst. prof. law Marquette U., 1967-68; exec. John Conway and Assos., Milw., 1968—. Mem. Milw. Rent Control Bd., 1952-53; dir. Southeastern Wis. Coalition for Clean Air, 1971—; bd. advisors Sch. Nursing Marquette U., 1974—. Mem. Am., Wis., Milw. bar assns., Am. Soc. Law and Medicine. Contbg. author: Mandate, Maintain, Monitor, a Model for Hospital Governance. Home: 3834 S 1st St Milwaukee WI 53207 Office: 2040 W Wisconsin Ave Milwaukee WI 53233 Tel (414) 344-4084

MAKY, WALTER, b. Cleve., June 4, 1916; B.S. in Mech. Engring., Cleve. State U., 1940, J.D., 1947. Admitted to Ohio bar, 1947, U.S. Patent and Trademark Office bar, 1947, U.S. Dist. Ct. bar No. Dist. Ohio, 1950, D.C., 1967, U.S. Supreme Ct. bar, 1958, U.S. Ct. Customs and Patent Appeals bar, 1958, U.S. Ct. Appeals bar 6th Circuit, 1965; asso. firm Oberlin & Limbach, Cleve., 1945-56; partner firm Donnelly, Maky, Renner & Otto and predecessors, Cleve., 1957—. Consul of Finland for Ohio, 1952—. Mem. Am., Greater Cleve. bar assns., Am., Cleve. (pres. 1971-72) patent law assns. Home: 33320 Cromwell Dr Solon OH 44139 Office: 601 Rockwell Ave Cleveland OH 44114 Tel (216) 621-1113

MALAND, DONALD LAVERNE, b. Blue Earth, Minn., Mar. 16, 1930; B.A. cum laude, St. Olaf Coll., 1952; J.D., U. Minn., 1955. Admitted to Minn. bar, 1957; asst. to v.p. trust dept. Northwestern Nat. Bank, Mpls., 1957-59; partner firm Prindle, Maland & Stennes, Montevideo, Minn., 1959—. Vice pres. St. Olaf Coll. Alumni Bd., 1975—; pres. Our Saviors Lutheran Ch., 1966-67; city councilman, Montevideo, 1971-75. Mem. Am., Minn. State bar assns. Home: 321 N 10th St Montevideo MN 56265 Office: 102 Parkway Dr Montevideo MN 56265 Tel (612) 269-8811

MALAND, OSWALD, b. Elmore, Minn., Oct. 25, 1891; J.D., U. Minn., 1915. Admitted to Minn. bar, 1915, Iowa bar, 1916, Ill. bar, 1924; individual practice law, Mason City, Iowa, 1915-24; sr. partner firm Chapman & Cutler, Chgo., 1924-63, ret., 1963; dir. United Cities Gas Co., Nashville, 1942-76; hon. dir. Old Republic Internat. Corp. Mem. Am., Ill. bar assns. Author: Vol. 19 Fletchers Ency. of Corps. Home: 9445 Monticello Ave Evanston IL 60203

MALECKI, JAMES HENRY, b. Mpls., Mar. 23, 1936; B.B.A., U. Minn., 1957; LL.B., William Mitchell Coll., 1963. Admitted to Minn. bar, 1963; mktg. mgr. Pillsbury Co., Mpls., 1961-65; atty.-partner Gislason Law Firm, New Ulm, Minn., 1965—. Office: 1 S State St New Ulm MN 56073 Tel (507) 354-3111

MALETZ, HERBERT NAAMAN, b. Boston, Oct. 30, 1913; A.B. cum laude, Harvard, 1935, LL.B., 1939. Admitted to Mass. bar, 1939, D.C. bar, 1952, U.S. Supreme Ct. bar, U.S. Ct. of Claims bar; rev. atty. Mktg. Laws Survey, WPA, 1939-41; atty. Truman Com. of U.S. Senate, 1941-42; trial atty. antitrust div. Dept. Justice, 1946-51; asst. chief counsel, later chief counsel Office Price Stblzn., 1951-53; individual practice law, Washington, 1953-55; chief counsel Celler Antitrust Subcom., Com. on Judiciary, U.S. Ho. of Reps., 1955-61; commr. U.S. Ct. of Claims, 1961-67; judge U.S. Customs Ct., N.Y.C., 1967—. Home: 17 S Morris Ln Scarsdale NY 10583 Office: 1 Federal Pl New York City NY 10007 Tel (212) 264-2800

MALEY, CHARLES DAVID, b. Highland Park, Ill., Aug. 18, 1924; A.B., State U. Iowa, 1948; J.D., De Paul U., 1952. Admitted to Ill. bar, 1952, Fed. bar, 1952, U.S. Supreme Ct. bar, 1956; asso. firm Friedlund, Levin & Fredlund, Chgo., 1952-58; individual practice law, Chgo., 1958-68, Lake Bluff, Ill., 1966-72, Lake Forest, Ill., 1972—; receiver and trustee bankruptcy and reorganization cases, U.S. Cts., 1956-70; pub. adminstr. Lake County, 1971-73. Asst. dist. commr. North Shore Dist. council Boy Scouts Am., 1963-65; mem. Lake County Republican Central Com., 1967-72, 76—, rep. state committeeman, rep., 1971-74. Mem. Am., 7th Circuit, Ill., Chgo., Lake County bar assns., Am. Judicature Soc., Am. Arbitration Assn., Phi Gamma Delta, Phi Alpha Delta. Home: 241 W Washington St Lake Bluff IL 60044 Office: 711 McKinley Rd Lake Forest IL 60045 Tel (312) 234-5788

MALINOWSKI, ARTHUR ANTHONY, b. Chgo., Apr. 4, 1929; B.S. in Econs., DePaul U., 1956, J.D., 1960; M.S. in Indsl. Relations, Loyola U., 1958; Ph.D., Ill. Inst. Tech., 1972. Admitted to Ill. bar, 1960; instr. Inst. Indsl. Relations, Loyola U., Chgo., 1963-69, asst. prof., 1969—; lectr. dept. econs. Ill. Inst. Tech., Chgo., 1965-68; mem. Ill. Office Collective Bargaining, 1973—. Mem. Ill., Chgo. bar assns., Indsl. Relations Research Assn., Advocates Soc., Nat. Acad. Arbitrators (bd. govs. 1976—), Phi Alpha Delta, Alpha Sigma Nu, Pi Gamma Mu, Iota Sigma Epsilon. Home: 9240 Major Ave Morton Grove IL 60053 Office: 820 N Michigan Ave Chicago IL 60611 Tel (312) 670-3156

MALINOWSKI, GERALD EDWARD, b. Shamokin, Pa., Nov. 26, 1940; B.S., Bloomsburg State Coll., 1963; J.D., Dickinson Sch. Law, Carlisle, Pa., 1967. Admitted to Pa. bar, 1967; individual practice law, Mt. Carmel, Pa., 1968—; adviser to registrants SSS, Mt. Carmel, 1970—. Mem. Northumberland County (Pa.), Pa., Am. bar assns., Pa. Trial Lawyers Assn. Home: 408 N Oak St Mount Carmel PA 17851 Office: Third and Oak Sts Mount Carmel PA 17851 Tel (717) 339-4536

MALISZEWSKI, THADDEUS WALENTY, b. Hartford, Conn., Jan. 10, 1922; B.A., Wesleyan U., 1947; J.D., U. Conn., 1950. Admitted to Conn. bar, 1950, U.S. Ct. Mil. Appeals bar, 1957, U.S. Supreme Ct. bar, 1959; sales tax examiner State of Conn., Hartford, 1948; legis. asst. Hartford C. of C., 1949; sr. judge Windsor (Conn.) Municipal Ct., 1955-60; individual practice law, Hartford, 1950—; aide-de-camp Gov. Grasso's Mil. Staff, Hartford, 1976—. Chmn. Windsor chpt. ARC, 1965-66. Mem. Conn., Hartford County bar assns., Conn. Trial Lawyers Assn., Polish-Am. Congress (nat. v.p.). Contbr. articles in field to legal jours. Home: 1248 Poquonock Ave Windsor CT 06095 Office: 37 Lewis St Hartford CT 06103 Tel (203) 527-7610

MALKA, EDMOND SOLOMON, b. Sudan, Africa; LL.B., U. Chgo.; Law Licentiate, U. London, U. Jerusalem; Barrister-at-Law degree, U. Dublin; LL.D., U. Granada. Admitted to English Colonial bar, 1947, Israel bar, 1958, Irish bar, 1962, Spanish bar, 1969, N.J. bar, 1972, N.Y. bar, 1974, U.S. Supreme Ct. bar, 1976; adv. English Colonial Bar, Khartoum, Sudan, 1947-56, Israel Bar, Jerusalem, 1958-62; practiced law, Dublin, 1962-67; legal editor Am. Law Reports, Rochester, N.Y., 1968; adv. Spanish Bar, Malaga, 1969-72; asst. county prosecutor Bergen County (N.J.), 1972; dep. atty. gen. State of N.J., Trenton, 1972—. Author: English Law in a Nutshell; Comparative Talmud Jurisprudence; Sephardi Jews; Jewish Personal Law; also books in Spanish, Portuguese, Hebrew and Arabic; contbr. to Ency. Judaica, Am. Law Reports. Home: 301 W State St Trenton NJ 08618 Office: Atty Gens Office State House Annex Trenton NJ 08625 Tel (609) 292-8557

MALKIN, PETER LAURENCE, b. N.Y.C., Jan. 14, 1934; A.B. summa cum laude, Harvard, 1955, LL.B. magna cum laude, 1958. Admitted to N.Y. bar, 1958, Conn. bar, 1976; partner Wien, Lane & Malkin, N.Y.C., 1958—; mem. Empire State Bldg. Assos., 1961; east side advisory bd. Chemical Bank, 1974—; trustee Harlem Savs. Bank, 1976—; dir. Federal Compress Co., Southwide, Inc., Rapidata, Inc., WM Capital and Management Corp., Capitol Resources and Properties, Inc.; lectr. Columbia Law Sch., Practicing Law Inst. Trustee, chmn. legacy devel. com. Fedn. Jewish Philanthropies; mem. overseers Com. Univ. Resources, 1973-75, Kennedy Sch. Govt., Harvard, 1976—, Wien Internat. Scholarship Program, Brandeis U. Mem. Am., N.Y. State, Conn. bar assns., Assn. Bar City N.Y., Am. Arbitration Assn. Home: Bobolink Ln Greenwich CT 06830 Office: 60 E 42d St New York City NY 10017 Tel (212) 687-8700 also 249 Royal Palm Way Palm Beach FL 33480 Tel (305) 845-8700

MALKOFF, SOLOMON, b. Youngstown, Ohio, Apr. 24, 1918; B.A., Ohio State U., 1940, J.D., 1942. Admitted to Ohio bar, 1942; partner firm Traxler Malkoff & Boyd, and predecessor, Youngstown, 1961—; asst. dir. Youngstown Capital Improvement Program, 1955-56, Youngstown Urban Renewal Program, 1960. Mem. Mahoning County Welfare Adv. Bd., 1950-62. Mem. Am., Ohio, Trumbull County, Mahoning County bar assns., Am. Trial Lawyers Assn., Ohio Acad. Trial Lawyers. Office: 600 Mahoning Bank Bldg Youngstown OH 44503 Tel (216) 744-0291

MALLERY, THOMAS FRENCH, b. Grand Rapids, Mich., Jan. 7, 1946; B.A., U. Wis., 1964; J.D., U. Wyo., 1973. Admitted to Wis. bar, 1973; partner firm Timken, Lonsdorf & Mallery, Wausau, 1973—. Mem. Am., Wis., Marathon County bar assns. Office: 610 Jackson St PO Box 1432 Wausau WI 54401 Tel (715) 845-8234

MALLEY, JOHN WALLACE, b. Parkersburg, W.Va., Feb. 17, 1906; B.S., U.S. Naval Acad., 1927; LL.B., George Washington U., 1934; grad. Indsl. Coll. of the Armed Forces, 1941. Admitted to U.S. Ct. Appeals, 1934, U.S. Supreme Ct. bar, 1939; asso. firm Cushman, Darby & Cushman, Washington, 1934-41, partner, 1941—; lectr. patent law George Washington U., 1964-65. Mem. Am., Fed., D.C. bar assns., Am. Patent Law Assn. (bd. mgrs. 1961-64), Phi Delta Phi. Home: 24 Quincy St Chevy Chase MD 20015 Office: 1801 K St NW Washington DC 20006 Tel (202) 833-3000

MALLON, CLIFFORD PETER, b. Chgo., Oct. 5, 1935; J.D., DePaul U., 1959. Admitted to Ill. bar, 1959; served with JAGC, U.S. Army, 1960-63; asso. firm Tim J. Harrington, Chgo., 1963—. Mem. Ill. Bar Assn. Home: 10821 S Kenton St Oaklawn IL 60453 Office: 221 N LaSalle St Chicago IL 60601 Tel (312) 346-5080

MALLON, LAWRENCE GEORGE, b. Phila., Sept. 3, 1946; B.S. in Bus. Adminstrn., Georgetown U., 1967; J.D., Emory U., 1973; LL.M. in Ocean and Coastal Law, U. Miami, Coral Gables, Fla., 1974. Admitted to Ga. bar, 1973, Calif. bar, 1977; postdoctoral fellow, marine policy and ocean mgmt. scholar Woods Hole (Mass.) Oceanographic Instn., 1974-75; asst. dir. U. So. Calif. Sea Grant Program, Los Angeles, 1975-76; asso. firm Ball, Hunt, Hart, Brown, Baerwitz, Long Beach, Calif., 1976—; of counsel firm Chambers, Siefferman, Robinson, Cooper, Atlanta; lectr. in field. Mem. Am. Bar Assn. (young lawyers sect. rep. to standing com. admiralty and maritime law 1977), Marine Tech. Soc., AAAS, Am. Soc. Internat. Law, Oceanic Soc., Am. Oceanic Orgn., Law of Sea Inst., Phi Delta Phi. Author: (with Dennis M. O'Connor) Land Management Strategies, 1976; contbr. numerous articles to profl. jours. Office: 120 Linden Ave Long Beach CA 90801 Tel (213) 435-5631 also 2200 Century Pkwy NE Suite 464 Atlanta GA 30345 Tel (404) 325-9970

MALLORY, ROLAND, B.A., Calif. State U.; J.D., U. Calif. Admitted to bar; practice law, San Francisco. Mem. Am., Calif., Alameda County bar assns., Bar Assn. San Francisco, Calif., Alameda-Contra Costa trial lawyers assns. Office: Spear St Tower 1 Market Plaza Suite 560 San Francisco CA 94105 Tel (415) 777-0070

MALLOY, MICHAEL EMMETT, b. Reno, Mar. 28, 1946; B.A., U. Nev., 1968; J.D., U. San Francisco, 1971. Admitted to Nev. bar, 1971, Calif. bar, 1972; dep. atty. gen. State Nev., Carson City, 1971-72; dep. dist. atty. Washoe County (Nev.), 1972-75, asst. chief dep. dist. atty., 1975—; instr. criminal law, evidence Western Nev. Community Coll., 1975—. Bd. dir. Omega House Drug Rehab. Orgn., Reno, 1974. Mem. Am. Bar Assn., Nat. Dist. Atty's Assn., Barristers Club Nev. (former 1st v.p. young lawyers), Nev. Peace Officers Assn., Phi Alpha Delta. Office: Box 11130 Courthouse Reno NV 89510 Tel (702) 785-4240

MALMQUIST, ROBERT WARREN, b. Chgo., June 10, 1921; J.D., U. Chgo., 1948. Admitted to Ill. bar, 1948; partner firm Root & Malmquist, Morris, Ill., 1948-58; county judge, Grundy County, Ill., 1958-64; asso. circuit judge 13th Jud. Circuit Ill., Morris, 1964-71, circuit judge, 1971—; city atty., Morris, 1950-56. Mem. Grundy County Bar Assn., Ill. Judges' Assn. Recipient Silver Beaver award Boy Scouts Am., 1967. Home: 605 Vine St Morris IL 60450 Office: Court House Morris IL 60450 Tel (815) 942-0347

MALONE, BERNARD PATRICK, b. Jersey City, Oct. 24, 1935; B.S., St. Peter's Coll., 1960; LL.B., Notre Dame U., 1963. Admitted to Ind. bar, 1963, Tex. bar, 1970; with Office of Gen. Counsel FHA, Washington, 1963-66; asso. regional counsel SW region HUD, Fort Worth, 1966-68; asso. firm Locke, Purnell, Boren, Laney & Neely, Dallas, 1970—. Mem. Am., Tex. State, Dallas bar assns. Home: 6034 Meadow Rd Dallas TX 75230 Office: 3600 Republic Nat Bank Tower Dallas TX 75201 Tel (214) 744-4511

MALONE, C. WILLIAM, b. Columbus, Ohio, Mar. 8, 1927; B.Sc., Ohio State U., 1950, J.D. summa cum laude, 1952. Admitted to Ohio bar, 1952; partner firm Brownfield and Malone, Columbus, 1954-61, firm Wonnell & Malone, Columbus, 1961-73; counsel firm Power, Jones & Schneider, Columbus, 1973—. Mem. Am., Ohio State, Columbus bar assns., Order of the Coif. Mem. editorial bd. Ohio State U. Law Jour. Home: 280 Ceramic Dr Columbus OH 43214 Office: 100 E Broad St Columbus OH 43215 Tel (614) 221-7863

MALONE, JAMES LOUIS, b. Los Angeles, Dec. 22, 1931; B.A. magna cum laude, Pomona Coll., 1953; J.D., Stanford, 1959. Admitted to Calif. bar, 1961, U.S. Supreme Ct. bar, 1970, D.C. bar, 1977; asst. dean, lectr. U. Calif. Sch. Law, Los Angeles, 1961-67; dean, prof. Willamette U. Coll. Law, 1967-68; vis. prof. U. Tex. Sch. Law, 1969; sr. prin. trial atty. Fed. Maritime Commn., Washington, 1970-71; asst. gen. counsel U.S. Arms Control and Disarmament Agy., Washington, 1971-73, gen. counsel, 1973-76; U.S. rep. to Conf. of Com. on Disarmament with rank of ambassador, 1976—. Mem. Am., Calif., D.C. bar assns., Order of Coif, Phi Beta Kappa. Recipient Distinguished honor award U.S. Arms Control and Disarmament Agy., 1977; named Outstanding Young Man Am., 1967; Root-Tilden scholar N.Y. U. Sch. Law, 1953-54. Home: 7000 Elizabeth Dr McLean VA 22101 Office: 320 21st St NW Washington DC 20451 Tel (202) 632-3466

MALONE, JOHN PATRICK, JR., b. Kansas City, Mo., Aug. 3, 1944; A.B., Coll. of Holy Cross, 1966; J.D., Case Western Res. U., 1970. Admitted to Ohio bar, 1971; individual practice law, Cleve., 1971—; asst. prof. bus. law Cleve. State U., 1975—. Mem. Ohio State, Am. Cleve. bar assns., Am. Bus. Law Assn. Home: 2940 Somerton Rd Cleveland Heights OH 44118 Office: 1202 Engrs Bldg Cleveland OH 44114 Tel (216) 696-7880

MALONE, MARK JOSEPH, lawyer; b. Englewood, N.J., Apr. 24, 1945; B.A., Rutgers Coll., 1967; M.P.A., U. Okla., 1972; J.D., Rutgers U., 1973; LL.M., N.Y. U., 1977. Admitted to N.J. bar, 1973; law clk. N.J. Supreme Ct., 1973-74; dep. atty. gen. State N.J., Princeton, N.J., 1974—. Mem. Am., N.J. State bar assns. Home: 407 Washington Valley Rd Martinsville NJ 08836 Office: 13 Roszel Rd Princeton NJ 08540

MALONE, VINCENT JAMES, b. Bklyn., Feb. 28, 1904; A.B., St. John's U., N.Y.C., 1925, LL.B., 1928, S.J.D., 1929; LL.D., Siena U., 1957. Admitted to N.Y. State bar, 1930, U.S. Supreme Ct. bar, 1942; partner firm Parker, Duryee, Zunino, Malone & Carter, N.Y.C. Fellow Am. Coll. Trial Lawyers; mem. Am. Arbitration Assn., Am., N.Y. State bar assns., N.Y. County, Nassau County lawyers, Assn. Bar City N.Y., Phi Delta Phi. Home: 30 Park Ave New York City NY 10016 Office: 1 E 44th St New York City NY 10017 Tel (212) 573-9345

MALONEY, FRANK, b. Worcester, Mass., Nov. 20, 1927; B.S., U. Tex., 1953, LL.B., 1956. Admitted to Tex. bar, 1956, Mass. bar, 1969; asst. dist. atty. Travis County (Tex.), 1956-60; mem. chief law enforcement div. Atty. Gen. Tex., 1960-61; partner firm Stayton, Maloney, Hearne & Babb, Austin, Tex., 1961—; lectr. U. Tex., 1963—. Mem. Travis County, Mass., Am. bar assns., State Bar Tex., Assn. Trial Lawyers Am., Nat. Assn. Criminal Def. Lawyers, Tex. Criminal Def. Lawyers, Am. Judicature Soc., Phi Alpha Delta. Home: 311 Comet Austin TX 78746 Office: 505 W 12th St Austin TX 78701 Tel (512) 478-6641

MALONEY, GEORGE ELLIOTT, b. San Francisco, Jan. 4, 1907; A.B., U. San Francisco, 1929, J.D., 1931. Admitted to Calif. bar, 1932; atty. Aetna Casualty & Surety Co., San Francisco, 1932-36, 1938; dep. dist. atty. City San Francisco, 1943; individual practice law, San Francisco, 1943-61; judge Municipal Ct., San Francisco, 1961-76. Mem. San Francisco Bar Assn., Conf. Calif. Judges. Tel (416) 681-4533

MALONEY, JAMES PAUL, b. Chgo., Oct. 27, 1949; B.A. magna cum laude, Marquette U., 1971, J.D. cum laude, 1974. Admitted to Wis. bar, 1974, law clk. U.S. Dist. Ct. Wis., 1974-75; asso. firm Zubrensky, Padden, Graf & Bratt, Milw., 1975—. Mem. Milw. Jr. Bar Assn., Phi Beta Kappa. Home: 9419 Ridge Blvd Wauwatosa WI 53226 Office: 606 W Wisconsin Ave Milwaukee WI 53203

MALONEY, JUSTIN CLOSE, b. Spokane, Wash., Apr. 26, 1905; A.B., Gonzaga U., 1926, LL.B., 1928. Admitted to Wash. bar, 1928, U.S. Supreme Ct. bar, 1960; individual practice law, Spokane, 1928—. Mem. Wash., Spokane County bar assns., Am. Coll. Probate Counsel. Home: East 803 Nora St Spokane WA 99207 Office: Great Western Bldg Spokane WA 99201 Tel (509) 487-7960

MALONEY, MICHAEL JAMES, b. Glendale, Calif., Mar. 28, 1939; B.A., U. So. Calif.; LL.B., Loyola U. Los Angeles. Admitted to Calif. bar, 1966; partner firm Gilbert, Kelly, Crowley & Jennett, Los Angeles, 1966—. Mem. Los Angeles County Bar Assn. Office: 1541 Wilshire Blvd Los Angeles CA 90017 Tel (213) 484-2330

MALONEY, WALTER EDWARD, b. Phillipsburg, N.J., May 5, 1911; A.B., Lafayette Coll., 1933; J.D., Columbia, 1936. Admitted to N.Y. bar, 1936; asso. firm Rabenold & Scribner, N.Y.C., 1936-37, James A. Beha, 1937-39; asst. corp. counsel, N.Y.C., 1939-41; asst. gen. counsel Atlantic Gulf & W.I. Steamship Lines, Inc., 1941-42; asso. Hon. John J. Burns, gen. counsel Am. Mcht. Marine Inst., Inc., 1942-43; partner firm Burns, Currie, Maloney & Rice, and predecessors, N.Y.C., 1946-52, 55-60; partner firm Bigham, Englar, Jones & Houston, N.Y.C., 1961—; pres. Am. Mcht. Marine Inst., Inc., 1952-55. Mem. Am., N.Y. State bar assns., Maritime Law Assn. U.S., Maritime Assn. Port of N.Y. (dir., pres. 1967-69), Am. Bur. Shipping, Life Savs. Benevolent Assn. (bd. mgrs.), Transp. Assn. Am. (hon. life), India House (bd. govs., exec. com.). Home: 186 Hartshorn Dr Short Hills NJ 07078 Office: 14 Wall St New York City NY 10005 Tel (212) 732-4646

MALOUF, DONALD WINDSOR, b. San Francisco, Jan. 12, 1937; B.A., Stanford, 1958, J.D., 1961. Admitted to Calif. bar, 1962; partner firm Sedgwick, Detert, Moran & Arnold, San Francisco, 1961—. Mem. Assn. Def. Counsel, Fedn. Ins. Counsel, San Francisco, San Mateo bar assns. Home: 305 Moseley Rd Hillsborough CA 94010 Tel (415) 342-8277 Office: 111 Pine St San Francisco CA 94111 Tel (415) 982-0303

MALOY, RICHARD HARGREAVES WILLIAMS, b. N.Y.C., Aug. 5, 1926; A.B., Dartmouth Coll., 1949; J.D., Columbia U., 1953; LL.M., U. Miami, 1974. Admitted to Fla. bar, 1953; asso. firm Padgett & Teasley, Miami, Fla., 1953-58; asso. firm Scott, McCarthy, Preston, Steel & Gilleland, Miami, 1958-61, partner, 1962; partner firm Robertson, McLoed & Maloy, Coral Gables, 1965-66; prin. firm Richard H.W. Maloy & Assos., P.A., Coral Gables, 1967—; gen. counsel Wackenhut Corp., Coral Gables, 1962-64; vis. prof. law U. Miami, 1972-74. Bd. advisers Model Cities Program, Miami, 1970—. Mem. Am., Dade County (Fla.) (dir. 1971-73, v.p. 1974), Coral Gables (pres. 1969) bar assns. Author: Appellate Practice and Procedure, 1966; Bender's Florida Forms, 1968; Answers to Your Legal Problems, 1977. Contbr. articles to legal jours. Office: 370 Minorca Ave Coral Gables FL 33134 Tel (305) 443-2551

MALZ, EDWARD, b. Vienna, Austria, Aug. 31, 1924; B.A. magna cum laude, Bklyn. Coll., 1948; J.D., Bklyn. Law Sch., 1951. Admitted to N.Y. State bar, 1951, U.S. Supreme Ct. bar, 1963; individual practice law, Bklyn., 1951—; arbitrator Small Claims Ct., Kings County, Bklyn., 1965—. Mem. Bklyn. Coll. Alumni Assn. (dir. 1960—), N.Y. State, Bklyn. (editorial bd. 1964—) bar assns., Com. on Profl. Ethics, DAV, Phi Beta Kappa. Contbr. articles and book revs. to legal jours. Home: 1139 E 14th St Brooklyn NY 11230 Office: 16 Court St Brooklyn NY 11241 Tel (212) 875-1940

MANAHAN, JAMES HINCHON, b. Madelia, Minn., Aug. 27, 1936; A.B., Harvard, 1958, J.D., 1961. Admitted to Minn. bar, 1961, U.S. Supreme Ct. bar, 1972; law clk. Minn. Supreme Ct., 1961-62; practiced in Mankato, Minn., 1962—, mem. firm Farrish Zimmerman Johnson & Manahan, 1962-72, individual practice law, 1972—. Sec. Mankato Police CSC, 1971-76; chmn. Common Cause in Minn., 1974. Mem. Am. (editor Individual Rights and Responsibilities Newsletter 1975—), 6th Dist. (pres. 1974-75), Minn. State (chmn. com. victimless crimes) bar assns. Home: 218 Iota Ave Mankato MN 56001 Office: Suite 107 Madison East Mankato MN 56001 Tel (507) 387-5661

MANCHESTER, ROBERT CLEMENS, b. Paducah, Ky., Mar. 29, 1936; B.A., Centre Coll., 1958; J.D., U. Ky., 1960. Admitted to Ky. bar, 1960; mem. firms Wheeler & Marshall, 1960-63, Wheeler Marshall & Manchester, Paducah, 1963-67; individual practice law, Paducah, 1967—. Mem. McCracken County, Ky., Am. bar assns. Home: 1279 Hedge Ln Paducah KY 42001 Office: 720 Broadway Paducah KY 42001 Tel (502) 443-8268

MANDEL, FREDERICK H., b. N.Y.C., July 31, 1933; B.B.A., Coll. City N.Y., 1955; LL.B., N.Y. U., 1960, LL.M., 1965. Admitted to N.Y. bar, 1961; partner firm Mandel & Mandel, Merrick, N.Y. and N.Y.C.; asst. dir. profl. devel. Am. Inst. C.P.A.'s, 1962-67; asst. prof. C.W. Post Coll., L.I. U., 1967-70; adj. asst. prof. N.Y. U., 1961-72, Baruch Coll., 1972—. Mem. N.Y., Nassau County bar assns., Am. Inst. C.P.A.'s, N.Y. State Soc. C.P.A.'s. Editor Taxation for Accountants, 1967-76; tech. editor Jour. Taxation, 1967-76. C.P.A., N.Y. Home: 3112 Monterey Dr Merrick NY 11566 Office: 28 Merrick Ave Merrick NY 11566 also 260 Madison Ave New York City NY 10016 Tel (516) 378-2440

MANDEL, JACK KITAY, b. Erie, Pa., Sept. 26, 1936; B.A., Allegheny Coll., 1958; LL.B., U. Pa., 1961; M.A., U. Ariz., 1967. Admitted to Pa. bar, 1961, Calif. bar, 1967; asso. firm Blank, Rudanko, Klaus & Rome, Phila., 1961-62; with JAGC, USAF, 1962-66; partner firms Radensky & Mandel, Anaheim, Calif., 1967-70, Mandel & Zener, Anaheim, 1970—; asso. prof. law Western State U., Fullerton, Calif., 1970—; instr. in sociology Calif. State U., Fullerton, 1973—. Chmn. North Orange County (Calif.) Israel Bond Dr., 1972, 75, 76; mem. Calif. Democratic Central Com., 1974-76; pres. Temple Beth Tikvah, Fullerton, 1977—; trustee Allegheny Coll., 1977—. Mem. Orange County Trial Lawyers Assn. (dir. 1972-74, Orange County Trial Lawyer of Year 1974), Allegheny Coll. Alumni Soc. (chmn. So. Calif. chpt. 1968—). Office: 730 N Euclid St Suite 115 Anaheim CA 92801 Tel (714) 956-2790

MANDEL, JOSEPH DAVID, b. N.Y.C., Mar. 26, 1940; A.B., Dartmouth, 1960, M.B.A., 1961; LL.B., Yale, 1964. Admitted to Calif. bar, 1965; law clk. U.S. Ct. Appeals, 9th Circuit, Los Angeles, 1964-65; assoc. Tuttle & Taylor, Los Angeles, 1965-69, partner, 1970—. Mem. Legal Aid Found. Los Angeles, 1973—, sec., 1975—, sr. v.p., 1977—; bd. dirs. Los Angeles County Bar Found., 1975—, sec. 1976—. Mem. Los Angeles County Bar Assn. (v.p., treas. 1977—, chmn. barristers sect. 1972-73, trustee 1972-74, 76—; chmn. state bar conf. com., 1976—; chmn. membership com. 1974-76, mem. jud. com., 1975—), Calif. State Bar Assn. (mem. commn. to study bar exam. process 1973-76, mem. long range planning com. 1973—). Home: 15478 Longbow Dr Sherman Oaks CA 91403 Office: 609 S Grand Ave Los Angeles CA 90017 Tel (213) 683-0600

MANDEL, RICHARD LLOYD, b. Cleve., July 17, 1927; J.D., U. Chgo., 1950. Admitted to Ill. bar, 1950, U.S. Supreme Ct. bar, 1969; asso. firm Marcus Wexman, Chgo., 1950-57; partner firm Wexman, Mandel & Kipnis, Chgo., 1957-65, Richard L. Mandel & Assos., Chgo., 1965-70, Mandel, Lipton & Stevenson, Ltd. and predecessor, Chgo., 1970—; pub. mem. Ill. Commn. on Children, 1975—. Bd. dirs. Jewish Children's Bur. of Chgo., 1971—; bd. dirs., v.p. Citizens Com. for Children and Parents Under Stress, Inc., 1974—. Mem. Chgo. Bar Assn. (mem. com. on adoption law 1952—, chmn. 1959-62, 72-73), Child Care Assn. Ill., Chgo. Council Lawyers. Office: 10 S LaSalle St Chicago IL 60603 Tel (312) 236-7081

MANDEL, SEYMOUR, b. Mpls., Feb. 10, 1916; B.S., U. Minn., 1938, J.D., 1940. Admitted to Minn. bar, 1940; individual practice law, 1940-42; sr. partner firm Mandel & Stiegler, Mpls., 1948—. Counsel, adviser W. Broadway Devel., Inc., 1974—. Mem. Am., Minn., Hennepin County bar assns., W. Broadway Bus. Assn. Home: 2 Red Cedar Ln Minneapolis MN 55410 Office: 2006 James Ave N Minneapolis MN 55411 Tel (612) 521-3621

MANDEL, STUART K., b. Bklyn., Feb. 6, 1934; B.S., Wharton Sch. Fin., U. Pa., 1955; LL.B., U. Calif., Los Angeles, 1962. Admitted to Calif. bar, 1962; asso. firm O'Melveny & Myers, Los Angeles, 1962-68; gen. atty. ABC, Los Angeles, 1968-69, dir. labor relations and legal affairs, 1969-74, v.p. bus. affairs, 1974—. Mem. Calif., Beverly Hills bar assns., Los Angeles Copyright Soc., Order of Coif. Home: 4613 La Barca Dr Tarzana CA 91356 Office: 2040 Avenue of the Stars Century City CA 90067 Tel (213) 553-2000

MANDELKER, DANIEL ROBERT, b. Milw., July 18, 1926; B.A., U. Wis., 1947, LL.B., 1949; J.S.D., Yale, 1956. Admitted to Wis. bar; asst. prof. law Drake U., 1949-51; atty. Housing and Home Finance Agy., Washington, 1952-53; asst. prof. Ind. U., 1953-56, asso. prof., 1956-62; Ford Found. law faculty fellow, London, 1959-60; asso. prof. Washington U., 1962-63, prof., 1963—, Howard A. Stamper prof. law, 1974—; research prof. law, Columbia, 1971-72, U. Utah, summer 1975, U. Tex., summer 1976; cons. in field. Mem. Am. Bar Assn. (adv. com. housing), Am. Soc. Planning Ofcls., Order of Coif, Phi Beta Kappa, Phi Kappa Phi. Author: Green Belts and Urban Growth, English Town and Country Planning in Action, 1962; Case Studies in Land Planning and Development, 1968; Managing Our Urban Environment, 1966, 2d edit., 1971; The Zoning Dilemma, 1971; Housing Subsidies in the United States and England, 1973; New Developments in Land and Environmental Controls, 1974; co-author: (with W. R. Ewald) Street Graphics, 1971; (with R. Montgomery) Housing in America, Problems and Perspectives, 1973; (with G. Hagevik & R. K. Brail) Air Quality Management and Land Use Planning, 1974; Environmental and Land Controls Legislation, 1977; contbr. articles, monographs and texts in field to profl. jours. Home: 612 E Polo Dr Clayton MO 63105 Office: Washington Univ Sch Law St Louis MO 63130 Tel (314) 863-0100

MANDELL, HOWARD ALLYN, b. Los Angeles, Feb. 21, 1945; B.A., U. Pa., 1967; J.D., Georgetown U., 1970. Admitted to Ala. bar, 1971, D.C. bar, 1972; individual practice law, Montgomery, Ala., 1971-76; mem. firm Mandell & Boyd, Montgomery, 1976—; law clk. to chief judge U.S. Dist. Ct. Middle Dist. Ala. Mem. Am. Bar Assn., Am. Judicature Soc., Am. Trial Lawyers Assn. Office: 125 Washington Ave PO Box 2066 Montgomery AL 36103 Tel (205) 262-1666

MANDELL, LEE S., b. Newark, Apr. 22, 1941; B.A., U. Calif., San Francisco, 1963; J.D., Southwestern U., Los Angeles, 1973. Admitted to Calif. bar, 1973; asso. firm Sprague, Milligan & Beswick, San Bernardino, Calif., 1973-74; individual practice law, San Bernardino, 1974—; prof. law Citrus Belt Law Sch., Riverside, Calif., 1974-75. Mem. Am., San Bernardino County bar assns., Am., Calif. trial lawyers assns. Office: 432 N Arrowhead Ave San Bernardino CA 92401 Tel (714) 884-7181

MANDELL, SEYMOUR HERTZEL, b. Detroit, Oct. 12, 1930; B.Arch., U. Mich., 1953; J.D., Wayne State U., 1959. Admitted to Mich. bar, 1959; asst. project dir., draftsman Smith, Hinchman & Grylls, Detroit, 1951-57; office mgr. Fred Brauning & Assos., Detroit, 1958-59; pvt. practice architecture, Detroit, 1959-65, Southfield, Mich., 1966—; individual practice law, Detroit, 1959-65, Southfield, 1966—; mem. faculty Wayne State U., 1959—; spl. chmn. sub-com. on landlord-tenant legis. Detroit Bd. Commerce, 1968-69. Scoutmaster, Cub Scouts Am., 1967-70; mem. com. Detroit Mayor's Task Force, 1968-69; bd. dirs. Western Wayne County Crippled Children's Soc., 1962-64. Mem. Southfield Bar Assn., Am. Judicature Soc., Mich. Soc. Architects, AIA, Bldg. Ofcl. Conf. Am., Detroit Engring. Soc. Selected to White-Paper Bldg. Regulations Com.; co-sponsor Detroit Plumbing Code (current); guest speaker State Conv., Nat. Conf., Soc. of Plastics Industry. Home: 17445 Louise St Southfield MI 48075 Office: 17220 W 12 Mile Rd Southfield MI 48076

MANDELSTAM, CHARLES LAWRENCE, b. Brookline, Mass., July 6, 1927; B.A., Harvard, 1949; LL.B., Yale, 1952. Admitted to Conn. bar, 1952, N.Y. bar, 1953, D.C. bar, 1953; atty., office of gen. counsel Internat. Ladies' Garment Workers Union, N.Y.C., 1952-56; with firm Kaye, Scholer, Fierman, Hays & Handler, N.Y.C., 1956-60; partner firm Dornbush Mensch & Mendelstam, N.Y.C., 1968—; counsel, dir. Research Inst. for the Study of Man, 1956—; counsel Group for Ams., South Fork, Southampton, East Hampton, N.Y., 1973—, North Salem (N.Y.) Open Land Found., 1975—. Trustee Hammond Mus., North Salem, 1976—; bd. dirs. Société d'exploitation Agricole Rhodanienne, 1975—. Mem. N.Y. State, N.Y.C. bar assns. Comment editor Yale Law Jour., 1951-52. Home: 27 W 86th St New York City NY 10024 Office: 747 3d Ave New York City NY 10017 Tel (212) 935-3900

MANDICH, GEORGE D., b. Auburn, Calif., Feb. 19, 1930; A.A., Sierra Jr. Coll., 1950; B.A., U. Calif., 1957; LL.B., Hastings Coll. Law, San Francisco, 1961. Admitted to Calif. bar, 1962; individual practice law, Sacramento, 1962-72; partner firm Mandich, Clark & Barker, Sacramento, 1972—. Office: 2720 Arden Way St Sacramento CA 95825 Tel (916) 487-8613

MANDL, JOSEPH PETER, b. N.Y.C., May 20, 1900; A.B., Stanford, 1920, J.D., 1923. Admitted to Calif. bar, 1923, U.S. Supreme Ct. bar, 1933; police judge Justice's Ct., King City, Calif., 1924-33; U.S. commr. No. Dist. Calif., King City, 1930-33; counsel Fed. Emergency Adminstrn. Pub. Works, Washington, 1933-37; individual practice law, Carmel, Calif., 1924—; lt. col. JAGC, U.S. Army. Mem. Monterey County Bar Assn. Contbr. articles to legal jours. Address: 293 Hacienda Carmel Carmel CA 93921 Tel (408) 624-7155

MANDRAS, GEORGE, b. McKeesport, Pa., Jan. 17, 1930; student Johns Hopkins U., U. Pitts., Coll. City N.Y.; LL.B., U. Balt. Admitted to Md. bar, 1965; individual practice law, Balt., 1965—. Home: 918 S Ponca St Baltimore MD 21224 Office: 428 S Newkirk St Baltimore MD 21224 Tel (301) 732-3344

MANELLA, ARTHUR, b. Toronto, Ont., Can., Aug. 7, 1917; B.S., U. So. Calif., 1939, LL.B., 1941; LL.M., Harvard, 1942. Admitted to Calif. bar, 1941; partner firm Irell & Manella, Los Angeles, 1944—; spl. asst. to Atty. Gen. U.S., 1942-43; mem. planning com. U. So. Calif. Tax Inst., 1948; lectr. U. So. Calif. Sch. Law, 1951-57. Mem. Am., Los Angeles, Beverly Hills bar assns., State Bar Calif. (tax advisory commn.), Am. Law Inst., Order of Coif. Author: Current Developments in Taxation of Alimony, 1948; Non-Business versus Business Bad Debts, 1950; Capital Gains and Losses Under the Internal Revenue Code of 1954, 1955; editor-in-chief So. Calif. Law Rev., 1940-41. Office: Suite 900 1800 Ave of the Stars Los Angeles CA 90067 Tel (213) 277-1010

MANGES, GERARD HORACE, b. N.Y.C., June 19, 1934; B.A., Yale, 1956, LL.B., 1961. Admitted to N.Y. bar, 1962, D.C. bar, 1963, U.S. Supreme Ct. bar, 1967; atty. SEC, Washington, 1961-63; chief legis. asst. to Sen. Jacob K. Javits, Washington, 1963-66; asso. firm Gadsby McGuire, Hannah & Merrigan, Washington, 1966-67, White & Case, N.Y.C., 1967—. Bd. dirs., mem. exec. com. Stanley M. Isaacs Neighborhood Center, N.Y.C. Mem. Am., N.Y. State, Fed. bar assns., Bar Assn. City N.Y. Contbg. editor: Economic Development Corporations and Financing Aspects, U.S. Dept. Commerce, 1969; contbr. articles to legal jours. Home: 420 W 253d St Riverdale NY 10471 Office: White and Case 14 Wall St New York City NY 10005 Tel (212) 732-1040

MANGLER, ROBERT JAMES, b. Chgo., Aug. 15, 1930; B.S., Loyola U., Chgo., 1952; J.D., Northwestern U., 1955. Admitted to Ill. bar, 1958, U.S. Supreme Ct. bar, 1976; asst. corp. counsel City of Chgo., 1958-61, City of Evanston (Ill.), 1963-65; asso. firm McKay, Moses, McGarr & Gibbons, Chgo., 1961-63; corp. counsel Village of Wilmette (Ill.), 1965—. Mem. Chgo., Ill. State (chmn. traffic laws and cts. com. 1976-77), Am. bar assns., Phi Alpha Delta. Home: 103 Broadway Wilmette IL 60091 Office: 1200 Wilmette Ave Wilmette IL 60091 Tel (312) 251-2700

MANGUM, EUGENE KENNETH, b. Pima, Ariz., Feb. 16, 1914; J.D., U. Ariz., 1939. Admitted to Ariz. bar, 1939; legis. draftsman Ariz. Dept. Library and Archives, 1942; asso. firm Ellinwood & Ross,

Phoenix, 1942; dep. county atty. Maricopa County (Ariz.), 1946; atty. Phoenix VA., 1946-47; practiced in Casa Grande, Ariz., 1947-60; chief magistrate Phoenix City Ct., 1961-74, judge, 1975—; city atty. City of Casa Grande, 1949-60. State pres. Young Democratic Clubs Ariz., 1946-47; chmn. Pinal County (Ariz.) Dem. Party, 1948-50; active Boy Scouts Am., Alcoholism programs; bd. dirs. Ariz. Girls Ranch, Phoenix, 1961-65, Nat. Council Alcoholism, N.Y.C., 1971—. Mem. Am. Bar Assn., Phi Delta Phi. Recipient Silver Beaver award Boy Scouts Am., 1961; Paul Harris Rotary fellow, 1974; founded 1st sch. for rehab. of drunken drivers, 1966. Home: 5525 W Hazelwood St Phoenix AZ 85031 Office: 12 N 4th Ave Phoenix AZ 85003 Tel (602) 262-6681

MANGUM, HARVEY KARL, b. Pima, Ariz., Dec. 3, 1908; B.A., Gila Coll., 1928; J.D., U. Ariz., 1931. Admitted to Ariz. bar, 1931, U.S. Supreme Ct. bar, 1971; individual practice law, Flagstaff, Ariz., 1931—; mem. firms Mangum & Flick, 1947-54, Mangum & Christensen, 1956-66, Mangum, Wall & Stoops, 1968-76, Mangum, Wall, Stoops & Warden, 1977—; county atty. Coconino County (Ariz.), 1932-38; judge Ariz. Superior Ct., Flagstaff, 1939-44. Fellow Am. Coll. Trial Lawyers; mem. State Bar Ariz. (past pres.), Am. Bar Assn., Internat. Soc. Barristers, Phi Delta Phi. Home: 613 W Navajo Rd Flagstaff AZ 86002 Office: PO Box 10 222 E Birch St Flagstaff AZ 86002 Tel (602) 774-6664

MANGUM, RICHARD KARL, b. Flagstaff, Ariz., Oct. 29, 1936; B.A., U. Ariz., 1959, J.D., 1961. Admitted to Ariz. bar, 1961, U.S. Supreme Ct. bar, 1971; partner firm Mangum, Wall and Stoops, Flagstaff, 1963-76; judge Superior Ct., Coconino County, 1976—; mem. Ariz. Legis. Com. to Draft Probate Code, 1970-73. Bd. dirs. Salvation Army, Flagstaff, 1968-70. Mem. State Bar Ariz., Coconino County (Ariz.) Bar Assn. (pres. 1971-72), Am. Coll. Probate Counsel (Ariz. chmn. 1975-76). Home: 3080 N Meadowbrook St Flagstaff AZ 86002 Office: Courthouse Flagstaff AZ 86002 Tel (602) 774-5011

MANGUM, RONALD SCOTT, b. Chgo., Nov. 14, 1944; B.A., Northwestern U., 1965, J.D., 1968. Admitted to Ill. bar, 1968, U.S. Supreme Ct. bar, 1972; atty. Northwestern Univ., Evanston, Ill., 1968-74; asso. firm Lord, Bissell & Brook, Chgo., 1974-76; partner firm Liss & Mangum, Chgo., 1976—; lectr. U. Ill., Chgo. Campus extension div. Northwestern U., Evanston, Ill. Inst. Continuing Legal Edn. Vice pres. Am. Hearing Research Found., Chgo., 1972—; pres. Parkinson Research Corp., Evanston, 1970-74, 1426 Chicago Ave. Bldg. Corp., 1975-76. Mem. Ill. (assembly del. 1973—, chmn. hearings com. 1976, chmn. council state taxation sect. 1976—), Chgo. (chmn. young lawyers sect. com. jud. evaluation and reform 1976—), Am. (sect. fed. taxation exempt orgn. com.) bar assns., Nat. Assn. Coll. and Univ. Attys., Chgo. Estate Planning Council, Am. Assn. Hosp. Attys., Ill. Hosp. Assn. Author: Tax Aspects of Charitable Giving, 1976; contbr. articles Ill. Bar Jour., Newsletter of Am. Hearing Research Found.; dir. Northwestern Univ. Press, 1973. Home: 1426 Chicago Ave Evanston IL 60201 Office: Liss & Mangum 208 S LaSalle St Chicago IL 60604 Tel (312) 726-8950

MANGUS, JON LEROY, b. Flint, Mich., Oct. 27, 1941; B.A., Wheaton Coll., 1963; J.D., Northwestern U., 1966. Admitted to Ill. bar, 1967, Calif. bar, 1970; asso. Bell, Boyd, Lloyd, Haddad & Burns, Chgo., 1966-67, firm McCutchen, Doyle, Brown, Enersen, San Francisco, 1971-73; v.p., gen. counsel Krambo Corp., N.Y.C., 1973-75, San Francisco, 1976—. Mem. Ill., Calif., Am. bar assns., Order of Coif. Editorial bd. Northwestern U. Law Rev., 1964-66. Office: 2462 Filbert St San Francisc CA 94123 Tel (415) 921-8585

MANIAN, VICTOR, b. Milw., Oct. 21, 1929; student U. Wis., Milw., 1953-56; LL.B., Marquette U., 1960. Admitted to Wis. bar, 1960, U.S. Dist. Ct. bar for Eastern Dist. Wis., 1960, U.S. Supreme Ct. bar, 1967; partner firm Chittero, Griffin & Manian, Milw., 1960-65; asst. dist. atty. Milwaukee County (Wis.) Dist. Atty., 1962-69, dep. dist. atty., 1969-72; judge Milw. Children's Ct., 1972-75, Circuit Ct. 2d Judicial Circuit, Milw., 1975—; instr. Milw. Area Tech. Coll., 1966-71, U. Wis.-Milw., 1972—. Bd. dirs. Milw. Fedn. Wis. Evangelical Luth. Chs., 1970—; bd. regents Wis. Luth. Coll., 1972-77. Mem. Milw., Wis., Am. bar assns. Author: (with Thomas Gardner) Principles & Cases of the Law of Arrest, Search & Seizure, 1974; (with Thomas Gardner) Criminal Law, Principles, Cases & Readings, 1975. Office: 821 W State St Suite 601 Milwaukee WI 53233 Tel (414) 278-4480

MANIAS, GILES PETER, b. Buffalo, N.Y., Apr. 2, 1943; A.B., Canisius Coll., 1965; J.D., State U. N.Y., Buffalo, 1968; premier license den Droit Internationale Publique, Universite Libre de Bruxelles, 1969. Admitted to N.Y. State bar 1971; asso. firm Hall & McMahon, Buffalo, 1970-72; individual practice law, Buffalo, 1972-74; partner firm Gorski & Manias, 1975—; legis. counsel to mem. N.Y. Assembly. Chmn. subcom. on vol. firemen benefits N.Y. State Assembly; regional vice chmn. Catholic Charities Appeal, 1977; active Boy Scouts Am. Mem. Am., N.Y. State, Erie County (chmn. young lawyers com.) bar assns., N.Y. State Trial Lawyers. Home: 762 Crescent Ave Buffalo NY 14216 Office: 680 Elliocott Square Bldg Buffalo NY 14203 Tel (716) 856-1612

MANIFESTO, WILLIAM FRANCIS, b. Pitts., July 15, 1938; B.B.A., U. Pitts., 1960; J.D., Duquesne U., 1963. Admitted to Pa. bar, 1963; asso. firm Wirtzman, Sikov & Love, Pitts., 1963-68; partner firm DeCello, Bua & Manifesto, Pitts., 1968—; asst. dist. atty. Allegheny County, Pa., 1968-71; asso. opinion editor Allegheny County Legal Jour. Mem. Am., Western Pa. trial lawyers assns., Trial Lawyers in Criminal Ct. of Allegheny County. Home: 1700 Village Rd Glenshaw PA 15116 Office: 200 Lawyers Bldg 428 Forbes Ave Pittsburgh PA 15219 Tel (412) 471-8893

MANION, PAUL A., b. Pitts., Feb. 22, 1935; B.A., Duquesne U., 1957, LL.B., 1961. Admitted to Pa. bar, 1962, U.S. Supreme Ct. bar, 1967; law clerk to Hon. Austin L. Staley, U.S. Ct. Appeals for 3d Circuit, Pa., 1962-64; partner firm Reed Smith Shaw & McClay, Pitts., 1964—. Mem. Fed. (pres. Pitts. chpt. 1969-70), Am. (chmn. 3d circuit trial evidence com. of litigation sect. 1976—), Allegheny County (bd. govs. 1974—, past mem. exec. com. young lawyers sec., chmn. bench-bar conf. com. 1973), Pa. (chmn. com. on constl. law 1975-76) bar assns., Acad. of Trial Lawyers of Allegheny County (bd. govs., 1975-77), Jud. Conf. for U.S. Ct. Appeals for 3d Circuit. Home: 8 Glenvue Dr Pittsburgh PA 15237 Office: 747 Union Trust Bldg Pittsburgh PA 15219 Tel (412) 288-3236

MANISCALCO, PETER JOSEPH, b. St. Louis, Sept. 29, 1928; A.A., Harris Tchrs. Coll., 1952; LL.B., St. Louis U., 1956, J.D., 1969. Admitted to Mo. bar, 1956; asso. firm Stout, Kaveny, Brinkman & Sestric, St. Louis, 1957-60; asso. firm Goodwin & McGreary, St. Louis, 1960-62; magistrate 5th dist. St. Louis County, 1961-64; judge 15th circuit div., 1965-67; partner firm Pittman & Bagot, St. Louis, 1967—; asst. atty. gen. State of Mo., 1967-69. Pres. Parkway Central High Sch. PTA, St. Louis County, 1974—. Mem. Am., Mo., St. Louis County bar assns., Met. Bar Assn. St. Louis, Am. Judicature Soc. Home: 14091 Agusta Chesterfield MO 63017 Office: 7751 Carondelet Suite 406 Clayton MO 63105 Tel (314) 726-1288

MANN, CLARENCE JOHN, b. Los Angeles, July 4, 1935; B.A. summa cum laude, Wabash Coll., 1957; M.A. in Econs., LL.B., Yale U., 1963; J.D. magna cum laude, U. Bonn (Germany), 1967. Admitted to Ind. bar, 1963, Ohio bar, 1968, Ill. bar, 1974; research asst. Inst. Internat. Law U. Bonn, 1966-67; asso. firm Jones, Day, Reavis & Pogue, Cleve., 1967-72; asst. gen. counsel internat. ops. Sears, Roebuck & Co., Chgo., 1972—. Mem. advisory bd. Inst. Cultural Affairs, 1972—. Mem. Am., Inter-Am., Chgo. bar assns., Am. Soc. Internat. Law. Author: The Function of Judicial Decision in European Economic Integration, 1972; contbr. articles to legal jours., Fulbright scholar U. Bonn, 1957-59. Office: Sears Tower D/702-INT Chicago IL 60684 Tel (312) 875-9740

MANN, DAVID COTTINGHAM, b. St. Louis, Apr. 20, 1948; B.S. in Bus. Adminstrn., Murray State U., 1971; J.D., Memphis State U., 1974. Admitted to Mo. bar, 1974, U.S. Dist. Ct. bars for Western and Eastern Dists. Mo., 1975; individual practice law, Sikeston, Mo., 1974—; asst. pros. atty. Scott County, Mo., 1977—; lectr. SE Mo. State U., 1976. Mem. Scott County, Mo., Am. bar assns., Am. Trial Lawyers Assn. Office: PO Box 814 Sikeston MO 63801 Tel (314) 471-8900

MANN, FRED, b. Detroit, Aug. 29, 1945; B.A., Wayne State U., 1967; J.D., U. Mich., 1970. Admitted to Mich. bar, 1970; asso. firm Elsman, Young & O'Rourke, Detroit, 1971; individual practice law, Southfield, Mich., 1972—. Mem. Am., Oakland County (Mich.), Southfield bar assns., Govt. Contracts Assn., Comml. Law League. Office: 17350 W Ten Mile Rd Southfield MI 48075 Tel (313) 557-9220

MANN, HOWARD LAWRENCE, b. Bklyn., Dec. 10, 1941; A.B., Bklyn. Coll., 1962; LL.B. cum laude, N.Y. U., 1965. Admitted to N.Y. State bar, 1966, U.S. Dist. Ct. bar for So. and Eastern Dists. N.Y., 1968, U.S. Tax Ct. bar, 1973, U.S. Ct. Appeals for 2d Circuit bar, 1975; practiced in N.Y.C., 1966—; asso. firm Reavis & McGrath, 1967-71; asso. firm Weiss, Rosenthal, Heller, Schwartzman & Lazar, 1971-74, partner, 1974—. Mem. N.Y. Bar Assn., Order of Coif. Recipient N.Y. U. Founder's Day award, 1965; mem. N.Y. U. Law Rev., 1964. Home: 8 Romar Ave White Plains NY 10605 Office: 295 Madison Ave New York City NY 10017 Tel (212) 725-9200

MANN, JAMES LEE, b. Cleve., Feb. 3, 1943; A.B., Ohio U., 1965; J.D., Northwestern U., 1968. Admitted to Ohio bar, 1968; asso. firm Knepper, White, Richards & Miller, Columbus, Ohio, 1968-69; served with JAGC, USAF, 1969-72; asso. firm Postlewaite, Postlewaite & O'Brien, Columbus, 1969-75, partner, 1975—; asst. city solicitor City of Chillicothe (Ohio), 1973—. Mem. Admanda Twp. Zoning Commn., 1975—. Mem. Am., Ohio State, Columbus bar assns., Lions. Home: 5260 Fosnaugh Rd Stoutsville OH 43154 Office: 88 E Broad St Columbus OH 43215 Tel (614) 224-8269

MANN, JOHN MCGREGOR, b. Chgo., June 25, 1924; B.S. in Mech. Engring., U. Colo., 1949, B.S. in Bus., U. Colo., 1949; J.D., Georgetown U., 1952; M.P.L., John Marshall Law Sch., 1958. Civil engr. Hughes Constrn. Co., Washington, D.C., 1949-50; typist U.S. Patent Office, Washington, 1950, patent examiner, 1951-52; admitted to Ill. bar, 1953; patent lawyer firm McWilliams & Mann, Chgo., 1954—, partner, 1957—; sec. C.A. Young Products Corp., 1960—. Pres. Prospect Sch. PTA Clarendon Hills, Ill., 1965-66; pack chmn. Cub Scouts Pack 251, Clarendon Hills, 1967-68; vice chmn. Clarendon Hills Community Caucus, 1969-70, chmn., 1971-72; chmn. Clarendon Hills Zoning Bd. Appeals, 1973-74, mem. plan comms., 1975—. Mem. Am., Ill., Chgo. bar assns., Am., Chgo. (treas. 1973-74) patent law assns., Christian Legal Soc. (dir. 1969-72), ASME, Chgo. Engrs. Club, Patent Office Soc., Kappa Sigma, Delta Theta Phi. Author (with others): Patent, Trademark and Copyright Tax Guide, 1965, rev. edit., 1970. Contbr. articles to profl. jours. Home: 41 Golf Ave Clarendon Hills IL 60514 Office: 53 W Hackson Blvd Chicago IL 60604 Tel (312) 427-1351

MANN, KENNETH LEE, b. Long Beach, N.Y., Feb. 16, 1946; B. S., U. N.C., Chapel Hill, 1966; J.D. magna cum laude, Mercer U., 1973. Admitted to Fla. bar, 1973, U.S. Dist. Ct., 1973; asso. firm Deutsch, Deutsch, Goldberg and Young, Ft. Lauderdale, Fla., 1973-74; asso. firm Subin, Shams, Rosenbluth & Moran, Orlando, Fla., 1974—; sr. accountant Price Waterhouse & Co., Miami, Fla., 1966-70; lectr. in field. Sunday sch. tchr. Congregation Beth Israel, Macon, Ga., 1970-72, Congregation Liberal Judaism, Orlando, Fla., 1975—. Mem. Am., Orange County (com. chmn.), Fla. bar assns., Fla. Inst. Certified Public Accountants. Contbr. articles, editor-in-chief (1972-73) Mercer Law Review. Office: CNA Tower Suite 670 Box 285 Orlando FL 32802 Tel (305) 841-7470

MANN, MICHAEL BENJAMIN, b. Kissimmee, Fla., Sept. 2, 1943; B.A., Fla. State U., 1965; J.D., U. Fla., 1971. Admitted to Fla. bar, 1971; partner firm Mann & Komarek, Panama City, Fla.; city atty. Wewahitchka, Fla., 1972-75, Callaway, Fla., 1973-76, Lynn Haven, Fla., 1974—. Mem. Fla. Bar, Am., 14th Jud. Circuit, Bay County bar assns., Am. Trial Lawyers Assn. Home: 815 Iowa Ave Lynn Haven FL 32444 Office: 620 Ohio Ave Lynn Haven FL 32444 Tel (904) 265-3622

MANN, NORMAN HENRY, b. Warren, R.I., Nov. 16, 1926; B.A., Providence Coll., 1950; LL.B., Northeastern U., 1956. Admitted to R.I. bar, 1956; mem. firm Morrissey & Conley, 1956-68; asso. firm Russell C. King, 1968-73; individual practice law, Providence, 1973—. Mem. R.I. Bar Assn. Home: 46 Washington St Warren RI 02885 Office: 601 Industrial Bank Bldg Providence RI 02903

MANN, ROBERT DAVID, b. Chgo., May 27, 1941; B.A., Depauw U., 1963; J.D. Ind. U., 1966. Admitted to Ind. bar, 1966; partner firm Baker, Barnhart, Andrews, Baker & Mann, Bloomington, Ind., 1966-73, Cotner, Mann & Chapman, Bloomington, 1974—. Bd. dirs., sec. Mental Health Assn. Monroe County, 1968-74; bd. dirs. Community Mental Health Center, Bloomington, 1971—, pres., 1971-74; chmn. Bloomington Bd. Pub. Safety, 1970—. Mem. Am., Ind., Monroe County bar assns., Ind. Trial Lawyers Assn., Greater Bloomington C. of C. (sec., dir. 1970-74). Office: PO Box 176 Bloomington IN 47401 Tel (812) 332-6556

MANN, RUSSELL DUANE, b. Fairfield, Ill., Aug. 10, 1922; student So. Ill. U., 1946-48; LL.D., St. Louis U., 1951. Admitted to Ill. bar, 1951, Mo. bar, 1951, N.Mex. bar, 1952; claims rep. Fidelity & Casualty Co. N.Y., Roswell, N.Mex., 1952-53; asso. firm Atwood, Malone, Mann & Cooter, and predecessors, Roswell, 1953-56, partner, 1956—; mem. N.Mex. Bd. Bar Commrs., 1968-76; mem. bd. dirs. Prepaid Legal Services Corp. N.Mex., 1973-76; bd. dirs. Continuing Legal Edn. N.Mex., 1973-76; chmn. Bar Center Bldg. Com. State Bar N.Mex., 1974-75. Mem. Roswell (pres. 1956-57), N.Mex. (v.p. 1957-58) Jaycees, Am. Coll. Trial Lawyers, Am., N.Mex. (pres. 1973-74), Chaves County (pres.) bar assns., Nat. Conf. Bar Pres., Fedn. Ins. Counsel, N.Mex. Bar Found. (dir. 1974—), Western State Bar Conf. Home: 606 W McCune St Roswell NM 88201 Office: 502 N Main St Roswell NM 88201 Tel (505) 622-6221

MANN, WILLIAM ADEN, b. Colmesniel, Tex., June 20, 1918; B.A., U. Tex., 1939; postgrad. Harvard Grad. Sch. Bus., 1944; M.B.A., U. Kans., 1950; LL.B., George Washington U., 1956. Admitted to Tex. bar, 1956, D.C. bar, 1959, Md. bar, 1966, U.S. Supreme Ct. bar, 1965; asso. firm Bernstein, Kleinfeld & Alper, Washington, 1961-63; partner firm Swingle and Mann, Washington, 1963-71, firm Dukes, Troese, Mann & Wilson, Washington and Chevy Chase, Md., 1971-73, firm Mann & Vaughan, Chevy Chase, 1973-74, Mann, Larsen & Longest, Bethesda, Md., 1974—; dir. Lincoln Nat. Bank, Gaithersburg, Md., John Hanson Savs. & Loan Assn. Pres. PTA, Somerset, Md., 1960; trustee Somerset Sch., 1961-63. Mem. D.C., Prince George's County, Tex., Md., Montgomery County bar assns., Am. Trial Lawyers Assn. Home: 6612 Kennedy Dr Chevy Chase MD 20015 Office: Mann Bldg 7415 Arlington Rd Bethesda MD 20014 Tel (301) 656-5155

MANNING, ANNE TERESE, b. Camden, N.J., Dec. 12, 1947; B.S. in Polit. Sci., Brescia Coll., 1970; J.D., U. Tenn., 1973; postgrad. N.Y. U. Admitted to N.J. bar, 1973; asst. dep. public defender, Dept. of Public Advocate, Trenton, N.J., 1974—. Mem. Am., N.J. State, Mercer County, Camden County bar assns. Home: 1800 Klockner Rd #14 Hamilton Township NJ 08619 Office: 216-220 S Broad St Trenton NJ 08611 Tel (609) 292-4081

MANNING, JEROME ALAN, b. Bklyn., Dec. 31, 1929; B.A., N.Y. U., 1950, LL.B., 1952; LL.M., Yale U., 1953. Admitted to N.Y. bar, 1953; asso. Joseph Trachtman, N.Y.C., 1956-61; asso. firm Stroock, Stroock & Lavan, N.Y.C., 1961-64, partner, 1964—; adj. prof. law N.Y. U., 1957—; lectr. in field. Mem. N.Y. State, Am. bar assns. Home: 25 N Clover Dr Great Neck NY 10021 Office: 61 Broadway New York City NY 10006 Tel (212) 425-5200

MANNING, JOHN TAYLOR, b. Chapel Hill, N.C., Sept. 24, 1913; A.B., U. N.C., 1933, LL.B., 1936. Admitted to N.C. bar, 1936, U.S. Supreme Ct. bar, 1967; individual practice law, Durham, N.C., 1937-66, Chapel Hill, 1946-66, 74-75; partner firm Manning & Allen and predecessors, Chapel Hill, 1967-74, Graham, Manning, Cheshire & Jackson, Chael Hill, 1975—, Hillsborough, N.C., 1975—; dir. Central Carolina Bank & Trust Co., Flagler System Inc., West Palm Beach Water Co. Mem. Am., N.C. (past v.p.), 15th Dist. (past pres.), Orange County (past pres.) bar assns., 4th Jud. Circuit Ct. of Appeals Conf., N.C. State Bar Council, Chapel Hill C. of C., Phi Kappa Sigma, Am. Judicature Soc., Am. Trial Lawyers Assn., Am. Coll. Probate Councił. Home: Mint Springs Rd Chapel Hill NC 27514 Office: PO Box 578 Chapel Hill NC 27514 Tel (919) 968-4413

MANNING, MELVIN RAY, b. Smithfield, N.C., Nov. 20, 1937; J.D., U. Richmond, 1964. Admitted to Va. bar, 1964; mem. firm McCaul, Grigsvy & Pearsall, Richmond, Va., 1964—; instr. law U. Richmond, 1965-66; dir. Import Autohaus, Bon Air Realty Co., Berckman Corp.; counsel Va. Senate Commerce and Labor Com., 1968-72. Bd. dirs. St. Michael's Episcopal Sch., Richmond, 1969-72, chmn. bd., 1971-72. Mem. Va. State Bar (chmn. bar news media relations com. 1971-75; chmn. legis. com. 1975—), Am., Va. (com. labor law), Richmond, Chesterfield bar assns., McNeill Law Soc., Omicron Delta Kappa, Delta Theta Phi. Editor: U. Richmond Law Rev., 1963-64. Home: 1522 N Bon View Dr Bon Air VA 23235 Office: 320 Mutual Bldg PO Box 558 Richmond VA 23204

MANNINO, EDWARD FRANCIS, b. Abington, Pa., Dec. 5, 1941; B.A., U. Pa., 1963, LL.B., magna cum laude, 1966. Admitted to Pa. bar, 1967; asso. firm Dilworth, Paxson, Kalish & Levy, Phila., 1967-72, partner, 1972—; law clk. to judge U.S. Ct. Appeals for 3d Circuit, 1966-67. Project mgr. environ. master plan Pa. Dept. Environ. Resources, 1973; chmn. land use policy study adv. com. Pa. Land Policy Project, 1973-75; mem. Phila. Mayor's Sci. and Tech. Adv. Council, 1975—. Mem. Am. (chmn. young lawyers' environ. quality com. 1973-74, chmn. young lawyers' legal services com. 1974-75, mem. spl. com. fed. practice and procedure 1974-76), Pa., Phila. (chmn. environ. quality com. 1970-71, 73, asst. treas. 1975, gov. 1975) bar assns. Office: 2600 Fidelity Bldg Philadelphia PA 19109 Tel (215) 546-3000

MANOS, NICHOLAS, b. Youngstown, Ohio, Dec. 23, 1929; B.S. in Edn., Youngstown U., 1956; J.D., 1956. Admitted to Ohio bar, 1960; asst. dir. law, Youngstown, 1961-63; individual practice law, 1960-70; mem. Mahoning County Planning Commn., 1965-68; municipal judge, Youngstown, 1968-69; dir. law, Youngstown, 1969-71; U.S. magistrate Fed. Dist. Ct. No. Dist. Ohio Eastern Div., Youngstown, 1971—; partner firm Manos, Flask & Policy, Youngstown, 1960—; partner Beshara, Dangler, Manos, shopping center developers, St. Petersburg, Fla., 1968—. Mem. Mahoning County, Ohio, Am. bar assns., Internat. Council Shopping Centers, Nat. Council Fed. Magistrates. Home: 4030 Fairway Dr Canfield OH 44406 Office: 424 City Centre One Youngstown OH 44503 Tel (216) 746-3217

MANPEARL, GERALD, b. Milw., Dec. 27, 1937; B.S., U. Calif., Berkeley, 1960; J.D., U. Calif., Los Angeles, 1962. Admitted to Calif. bar, 1964, U.S. Dist. Ct., 1964, U.S. Supreme Ct. bar, 1972; clk. Calif. Appeals Ct. 1963-64; partner firm Baker, Ancel & Redmond, Los Angeles, 1965—; prof. law Calif. Coll. Law, 1970-72; chmn. tax com. Fgn. Trade Assn., 1975—. Mem. Am., Calif. State, Los Angeles County bar assns., Calif. Trial Lawyers Assn., World Trade Com., Los Angeles C. of C., Fgn. Trade Assn. So. Calif. Contbr. articles to profl. jours. Home: 5305 Cedros Van Nuys CA 91401 Office: 626 Wilshire Blvd Los Angeles CA 90017 Tel (213) 624-9201

MANSFIELD, ELINOR WEISS, b. Visalia, Calif., Nov. 9, 1936; A.B., Stanford, 1958, LL.B., 1962. Admitted to Calif. bar, 1963. Mem. AAUW (pres. Palo Alto chpt. 1970-72). Home: 569 Lowell Ave Palo Alto CA 94301

MANSFIELD, WILLIAM AMOS, b. Redmond, Oreg., Oct. 23, 1929; B.S., U. Oreg., 1951, J.D., 1953. Admitted to Oreg. bar, 1953; atty. JAG, USAF, Mobile, Ala., 1953-55; asst. atty. gen. State of Oreg., Salem, 1955-60; staff atty., gen. counsel U.S. Bur. Pub. Roads, Washington, 1961; city atty., Medford, Oreg., 1962-64; individual practice law, Medford, 1964—. Bd. dirs. Peter Britt Festival, 1963-65, Rogue Valley Transp. Dist., 1976; bd. trustees Children's Farm Home, 1970—. Mem. Oreg., Jackson bar assns., ACLU (bd. dirs. Oreg. 1971-77). Home: 26 Crater Lake Medford OR 97501 Office: 234 W 5th St PO Box 1721 Medford OR 97501 Tel (503) 779-2521

MANSKE, JAMES, b. Oshkosh, Wis., Aug. 26, 1948; B.S. in Govt. and Urban Affairs, U. Wis., Oshkosh, 1970, M.Urban Affairs, Milw., 1971; J.D., U. Tulsa, 1973. Admitted to Wis. bar, 1974; individual practice law, Oshkosh, 1974—. Commr., Oshkosh Area Sch. Dist. Sch. Bd., 1975—. Mem. Am. Bar Assn., Am. Trial Lawyers Assn. Home: 1212 Algoma Blvd Oshkosh WI 54901 Office: 300 Division St Oshkosh WI 54901 Tel (414) 231-6011

MANSKER, GARY F., b. Beeville, Tex., Nov. 25, 1942; B.B.A., Baylor U., 1964, LL.B., 1966. Admitted to Tex. bar, 1966; spl. agt. FBI, 1966-69; tax accountant Arthur Andersen & Co., Houston, 1969-71; partner firm Keys Russell Seaman & Mansker, Corpus Christi, Tex., 1971—. Bd. dirs. Cdrpus Christi Christian Sch., 1973—. Mem. Am., Tex., Nueces County bar assns. Contbr. articles to legal jours. Office: 1917 Bank and Trust Tower Corpus Christi TX 78477 Tel (512) 884-7484

MANSMANN, CAROL LOS, b. Pitts., Aug. 7, 1942; B.A., Duquesne U., 1964, J.D., 1967. Admitted to Pa. Supreme Ct. bar, 1967, U.S. Ct. Appeals 3rd Circuit bar, 1968, U.S. Supreme Ct. bar, 1975; law clerk to Hon. Ralph H. Smith, Jr., 1967-68; asst. dist. atty. Alleghany County (Pa.), 1968-72, also chief of appeals div.; partner firm Mansmann & Mansmann, Pitts., 1972-74, Meverry, Baxter, Cindrich, Loughren & Mansmann, Pitts., 1974—; mem. criminal procedural rules com. Pa. Supreme Ct., 1972—; asst. prof. law Duquesne U., 1974—; special asst. atty. gen. State of Pa., 1974—. Mem. profl. advisory bd. Birthright, Pitts. Mem. Alleghany County Bar Assn. Home: 323 Parkway Dr Pittsburgh PA 15228 Office: 1000 Lawyers Bldg Pittsburgh PA 15219 Tel (412) 765-2500

MANSMANN, JOHN JEROME, b. Pitts., Aug. 14, 1942; B.A., U. Dayton, 1964; postgrad. U. Fribourg (Switzerland), 1963; J.D., Duquesne U., 1967. Admitted to Pa. bar, 1967, U.S. Supreme Ct. bar, 1975; partner firm McArdle & Mansmann, Pitts., 1967-72, McVerry, Baxter, Cindrich, Loughren & Mansmann, Pitts., 1972—; spl. asst. atty. gen. Commonwealth of Pa., 1974—. Mem. Am., Pa., Allegheny County bar assn., Am. Judicature Soc. Contbr. articles to law jours. Home: 323 Parkway Dr Pittsburgh PA 15228 Office: 1000 Lawyers Bldg Pittsburgh PA 15219 Tel (412) 765-2500

MANSOUR, ANTHONY JAMES, b. Nazareth, Palestine, May 31, 1926; came to U.S., 1929, naturalized, 1947; A.A., Mott Community Coll., 1947; LL.B., Detroit Coll. Law., 1950. Admitted to Mich. bar, 1951; individual practice law, Flint, Mich., 1951-66, 72—; circuit ct. judge, Genesee County, Mich., 1966-72. Trustee Flint Osteo Hosp. Mem. Am., Mich., Genesee County bar assns. Home: 6067 Hugh St Davison MI 48423 Office: 1000 Beach St Flint MI 48502 Tel (313) 232-4184

MANTHEI, RICHARD DALE, b. Olivia, Minn., Dec. 23, 1935; B.S. in Pharmacy, S.D. State U., 1960; J.D., U. Minn., 1967; Admitted to Ind. bar, 1967, Ill. bar, 1970; atty. Eli Lilly & Co., Indpls., 1967-70; atty., Am. Hospital Supply Corp, Evanston, Ill., 1970, asst. sec., 1971—, dir. regulatory affairs, 1972—; sec., corp. counsel Annar-Stone Labs., Mt. Prospect, Ill., 19—. Pres. Grace Lutheran Ch., Libertyville, Ill., 1975. Mem. Ind., Ill., Chgo., Am. bar assns., Health Industries. Assn. (chmn. legal com. 1974-75), Health Industry Mfrs. Assn. (chmn. legal sect. 1976-77). Contbr. articles to profl. jours. Home: 884 Scott Pl Libertyville IL 60048 Office: 1740 Ridge Ave Evanston IL 60201 Tel (312) 869-2580

MANTONYA, JOHN BUTCHER, b. Columbus, Ohio, May 26, 1922; A.B., Washington and Jefferson Coll., 1944; postgrad. U. Mich., 1946-47; J.D., Ohio State U., 1949. Admitted to Ohio bar, 1949; asso. firm C.D. Lindroth, Newark, Ohio, 1949-57, partner, 1957-74; individual practice law, Newark, 1974—; mayor Village of Utica (Ohio), 1953-58. Mem. N. Fork Bd. Edn., Utica, 1962-69. Mem. Am., Ohio, Lick County bar assns. Tel (614) 349-8371

MANUCY, ORIGN ANDREW, b. Charleston, S.C., Apr. 30, 1932; B.S., N.C. State Coll., 1955; LL.B., U. Ga., 1960. Admitted to S.C. bar, 1960; individual practice law, 1963-64; asso. firm Stohey & Stoney, 1960-62; partner firm Maybank & Manucy, Charleston, 1964-76; partner firm Loundes & Manucy, Charleston, 1977—. Mem. Hibernian Soc., Charleston Trident C. of C. Home: 114 Tradd St Charleston SC 29401 Office: 27 Bendue Range Charleston SC 29401 Tel (803) 723-1688

MANUELIAN, HAIG DER, b. Watertown, Mass., May 23, 1926; B.A. summa cum laude, Tufts U., 1945; J.D., Harvard, 1948. Admitted to Mass. bar, 1948, Fla. bar, 1961; individual practice law, Boston, 1948-51, 1963—; partner firm Schlesinger & Manuelian, Boston, 1951-63. Mem. Am., Boston, Mass., Fla. bar assns., Mass. Assn. Trial Lawyers. Office: 27 State St Boston MA 02109 Tel (617) 523-1293

MANWELL, EDMUND TECUMSEH, b. Marysville, Calif., Apr. 8, 1915; A.A., Yuba Coll., Marysville, 1933; LL.B. (J.D.), Hastings Coll. Law, San Francisco, 1936. Admitted to Calif. bar, 1937, U.S. Ct. of Appeals bar 9th Circuit, U.S. Dist. Ct. bar, No. Dist. Calif., 1937; partner firm Manwell & Manwell, Marysville, 1937-67; judge Superior Ct., Yuba County, 1967-76; instr. real estate Yuba Coll., 1958-59, instr. Adult Sch., 1964; judge Justice Ct., Marysville Jud. Dist., 1953-62. Mem. exec. bd. Boy Scouts Am., 1953—, Silver Beaver award, 1958, Scouters key, 1950. Mem. Am., Yuba-Sutter (past pres.) bar assns., VFW. Home: 2122 Greely Dr Marysville CA 95901 Tel (916) 742-1116

MANZO, FRANK MICHAEL, b. Scranton, Pa., June 15, 1931; A.B. cum laude in Econs., Notre Dame U., 1952, J.D., 1956. Admitted to Pa. bar, 1956, Ind. bar, 1956, Calif. bar, 1960; individual practice law, Santa Ana, Calif., 1960—; served to capt. JAC USMC, 1956-60. Mem. Orange County Tax Assessment Appeals Bd., 1973—, chmn. 1977; trustee Orange County Law Library, 1971—, pres., 1974; commr. Orange County Harbor, Parks and Beaches Commn., 1972—. Mem. Orange County, Calif. Bar Assns., Calif. Trial Lawyers Assn. Office: 900 N Broadway St Santa Ana CA 92701 Tel (714) 547-6047

MANZO, PETER THOMAS, b. Bayonne, N.J., Feb. 16, 1947; A.B., Georgetown U., 1968; M.B.A. (Univ. scholar), Columbia, 1972; J.D. (Univ. scholar), Cornell U., 1972. Admitted to N.J. bar, 1972; asst. corp. counsel, asst. sec.-treas. N.Y. Hosp., N.Y.C., 1972-75; asst. sec. of N.Y. Hosp.-Cornell Med. Center Found., Inc., N.Y.C., 1973-75; asst. dep. pub. adv. dept. of pub. advocate Div. of Rate Counsel 1976—. Mem. N.J., Am. bar assns., Am. Soc. Law and Medicine. Columnist: The Adv., 1971-72; asso. editor Cornell Internat. Law Jour., fall 1971. Home: 95 Tracy Dr Fords NJ 08863 Office: 10 Commerce Ct Newark NJ 07102 Tel (201) 648-3684

MAR, DAVID YOU, b. Honolulu; B.A., U. Hawaii, 1937; J.D., Duke, 1947. Admitted to Hawaii bar, 1947; U.S. Dist. (Hawaii) Ct. bar, 1948; U.S. 9th Circuit Ct. Appeals, 1962, U.S. Supreme Ct. bar, 1965; dep. atty. City and County of Honolulu, 1947-55; statehood transition atty., dept. atty. gen., State of Hawaii, 1959; dep. atty. gen., 1959-62; individual practice law, Honolulu, 1956-59, 63-68; dep. corp. counsel City of Honolulu, 1969-76.

MARAGOS, TED GEORGE, b. Minot, N.D., Mar. 3, 1933; B.A., U. N.D., 1955, J.D., 1972. Admitted to N.D. bar, 1972, since practiced in Grand Forks; instr. bus. law U. N.D., 1972-74; mem. N.D. Ho. of Reps., 1960-64. Pres. bd. dirs. Greek Orthodox Ch. of Minot, 1958-64; dir. Regional Mental Health and Retardation Center of N.D., 1972-74. Mem. N.D. Bar Assn., Am. Judicature Soc., Phi Delta Theta. Hon. Indian chief Standing Rock Reservation N.D. and S.D. Office: Box 1356 Grand Forks ND 58291 Tel (701) 772-7131

MARANS, J. EUGENE, b. Butte, Mont., May 26, 1940; A.B., Harvard, 1962, LL.B., 1965. Admitted to N.Y. bar, 1966, D.C. bar, 1971; law clk. to judge U.S. Ct. Appeals, 5th Circuit, New Orleans, 1965-66; asso. firm Cleary, Gottlieb, Steen & Hamilton, N.Y.C., 1966-70, Paris, 1970-71, Washington, 1971-74, partner, Washington, 1975—; mem. N.Y. State advisory com. U.S. Commn. Civil Rights, 1969-70; mem. nat. evaluation com. on simplified method of determining eligibility in pub. assistance HEW, 1969-70; sec., counsel Bipartisan Com. on Absentee Voting, 1973—. Mem. Assn. Ams. Resident Overseas (dir. 1973—), Ripon Soc. (nat. gov. bd. 1962—, chmn. 1969-70), Am., D.C., N.Y.C. bar assns., Am. Soc. Internat. Law. Contbr. articles to legal jours. Office: 1250 Connecticut Ave NW Washington DC 20036 Tel (202) 223-2151

MARBERRY, RICHARD J., b. Watseka, Ill., July 9, 1944; B.A., Parsons Coll., 1968; J.D., John Marshall U., 1971. Admitted to Ill. bar, 1972; asst. counsel Prudential Ins. Co. Am., Chgo., 19—. Mem. Ill., Chgo. bar assns. Office: Suite 500N Prudential Plaza Chicago IL 60601 Tel (312) 861-4624

MARCELLO, DAVID ANTHONY, b. Thibodeaux, La., June 14, 1946; B.A., Williams Coll., 1968; J.D., Tulane U., 1971. Admitted to La. bar, 1971; environ. lobbyist Conservation Coalition, Baton Rouge, 1972; staff atty. New Orleans Legal Assistance Corp., 1972-73; lawyer-planner Curtis & Davis, Architects & Planners, New Orleans, 1973-74; exec. dir. La. Center for the Pub. Interest, New Orleans, 1974—; counsel Garden Dist. Assn., 1973—. Bd. dirs. Urban League, 1975-76. Fellow Inst. Politics; mem. Am., La. bar assns., ACLU (bd. dirs. 1969-76). Contbr. articles to legal jours. Office: 700 Maison Blanche Bldg New Orleans LA 70112 Tel (504) 524-8182

MARCHANT, JOHN BERTRAND, b. Oakland, Calif., June 9, 1928; B.A., U. Calif., Berkeley, 1950; J.D., U. Calif., Hastings, 1955. Admitted to Calif. bar, 1955; asso. firm Bancroft, Avery & McAllister, San Francisco, 1955-59; asst. dep. dist. atty. Alameda County, Calif., 1959-62; individual practice law, Berkeley, Calif., 1959-66; asso. firm Sedgwick, Detert, Moran & Arnold, San Francisco, 1966-73, partner, 1973—. Bd. dirs. Berkeley YMCA, 1965; St. Johns Presbyn. Ch., Berkeley, 1962-63; pres., dir. The Sea Ranch Assn., 1973-76. Mem. Am., Berkeley-Albany (pres. 1961) bar assns., North Berkeley Albany Kiwanis Club (pres. 1963), Thurston Soc., Order of Coif, Alpha Delta Phi (bd. govs. 1977—). Office: 111 Pine St San Francisco CA 94111 Tel (415) 982-0303

MARCKS, OLIVER DEWEY, b. Emmaus, Pa., May 24, 1898; B.A., Franklin and Marshall U., 1921; LL.B., Harvard U., 1924, J.D., 1969. Admitted to Mich. bar, 1925, Pa. bar, 1926; practiced law Detroit, 1925—; pres. Equitable Detroit Co., 1946—. Pres. Detroit Met. Indsl. Devel. Corp., Detroit and Wayne County Tuberculosis Found. Mem. Am., Mich., Detroit bar assns. Home: 906 Three Mile Dr Grosse Pointe MI 48230 Office: 2243 First Nat Bldg Detroit MI 48226 Tel (313) 961-2554

MARCO, ALLAN JAMES, b. Kenosha, Wis., Dec. 15, 1931; student U. Ill.; J.D., John Marshall Law Sch., 1961. Admitted to Ill. bar, 1961, U.S. Dist. Ct. bar No. Dist. Ill., 1962, U.S. Supreme Ct. bar; partner firm Marco & Mannina, Downers Grove, Ill., 1962—. Mem. Am., Ill. (mem. assembly), DuPage County (1st v.p.) bar assns., Order of John Marshall. Tel (312) 969-5556

MARCO, RICHARD JOSEPH, b. Cleve., Nov. 2, 1932; student Baldwin-Wallace Coll., 1950-53; LL.B., Cleve.-Marshall Law Sch., 1957, J.D., 1968; student real estate appraisal Case Western Res. U., 1960-61. Admitted to Ohio bar, 1957; individual practice law, Cleve., 1957-58; asst. dir. law Cleve., 1958—, chief counsel Cleve. Dept. Urban Renewal and Housing, 1968; counsel John W. Galbreath & Co., Cleve., 1968-75; partner firm Celebrezze and Marco, Cleve., 1976—. Chmn. Medina Planning and Zoning Commn., 1970-74; pres. Medina County Regional Planning Commn., 1975-76. Mem. Medina County Bar Assn., Medina County C. of C., Cleve. Cath. Lawyers Guild. Contbr. articles to legal jours., textbooks. Home: 165 Woodland Dr Medina OH 44256 Office: 4168 Rocky River Dr Cleveland OH 44135 Tel (216) 476-9030

MARCUS, BERNARD, b. Wilkes-Barre, Pa., Mar. 10, 1924; student U. Pa., 1941-43, Carnegie-Mellon U., 1943-44; LL.B., Harvard, 1948; postgrad. Loyola U. of the South, 1958. Admitted to D.C. bar, 1949, La. bar, 1958; atty., legis. reference service Library of Congress, 1949-50; acting counsel small bus. com. Ho. of Reps., 1950; atty. NLRB, Washington, Buffalo and New Orleans, 1950-57; asso. firm Deutsch, Kerrigan & Shiles, New Orleans, 1957-58, partner, 1958—; cons. State Dept., 1965-69; labor arbitrator Am. Arbitration Assn., Fed. Mediation and Conciliation Service. Pres. New Orleans Jewish Community Center, 1973-75; mem. Nat. Jewish Welfare Bd., 1974—; bd. dirs. New Orleans Jewish Welfare Bd., Jewish Family and Childrens' Service, New Orleans, Communal Hebrew Sch., New Orleans. Mem. Am., La., New Orleans (exec. com. 1971-74), D.C., Fed. bar assns. Author: Congress and the Monopoly Problem, 1950; contbr. to casebooks. Home: 630 Burdette St New Orleans LA 70118 Office: 4700 One Shell Sq New Orleans LA 70139 Tel (504) 581-5141

MARCUS, DAVID, b. Mount Kisco, N.Y., June 14, 1921; B.A., U. Ky., 1943; LL.B., Cornell U., 1945, LL.D., 1969. Admitted to N.Y. bar, 1945; law sec. to chief judge N.Y. State Ct. of Appeals, 1945-46; prin. David Marcus, N.Y.C., 1959-71; sr. partner firm Burstein & Marcus, White Plains, N.Y., 1971—; asst. atty. gen. State of N.Y., 1946-55; spl. counsel White Plains Urban Renewal Agy., 1967—. Mem. Am., N.Y. State, Westchester County bar assns., Am. Trial Lawyers Assn., Assn. Bar City N.Y. Editor-in-chief Cornell Law Rev., 1944-45. Home: 258 Soundview Ave White Plains NY 10606 Office: 2 William St White Plains NY 10601 Tel (914) 428-5700

MARCUS, JOHN RICHARD, b. St. Helena, Calif., Apr. 28, 1930; B.A., Walla Walla Coll., 1951; J.D., U. Calif., Los Angeles, 1955. Admitted to Calif. bar, 1956; individual practice law, San Bernardino, 1956-63; mem. firm Marcus & Lunsford, San Bernardino, 1963-66; partner firm Marcus & Hamilton, San Bernardino, Calif., 1974—; advocate Am. Bd. Trial Advs., 1961—; arbitrator Am. Arbitration Assn.; pres. Legal Aid Soc. San Bernardino County, 1968-69. Candidate for senator Calif. Republican Party, 1974. Mem. Calif. Trial Lawyers Assn., Law Sci. Inst. Am., Lawyers-Pilot's Bar Assn., Nat. Fedn. Ind. Bus., Navy League U.S. (pres. San Bernardino council). Office: 330 N D St suite 350 San Bernardino CA 92401 Tel (714) 884-6477

MARCUS, MARIA LENHOFF, b. Vienna, Austria, June 23, 1933; B.A., Oberlin Coll., 1954; LL.B., Yale, 1957. Admitted to N.Y. bar, 1961, U.S. Supreme Ct. bar, 1964; since practiced in N.Y.C., asso. counsel NAACP, 1961-67; asst. atty. gen. N.Y. State, 1967—; chief Litigation Bur., Atty. Gen.'s Office, 1976—; adj. prof. law N.Y. U. Law Sch. Mem. Am., N.Y. Women's bar assns., Assn. Bar City N.Y. (exec. com.). Contbr. articles to legal jours. Home: Office: 2 World Trade Center 47th Floor New York City NY 10047 Tel (212) 488-3385

MARCUS, MYRON, b. Bklyn., Feb. 4, 1933; B.A., Alfred U., 1954; J.D., Cornell U., 1960. Admitted to N.Y. bar, 1960; partner firm Fink, Weinberger, Fredman & Charney, White Plains; counsel, exec. sec. Apt. Owners Adv. Counsel Westchester; asso. counsel Builders Inst. Westchester and Putnam Counties, Inc.; counsel Sub-Contractors and Suppliers Council Westchester; guest lectr. real property sect. N.Y. State Bar Assn.; coordinator, lectr. White Plains Adult Edn., 1973-74. Pres., Soundview Area Citizens Assn., bd. counsel Family Services Westchester; city committeeman, Yonkers; county committeeman, Westchester; bd. dirs., mem. exec. com. 5th Ward Democratic Club, Yonkers; candidate N.Y. State Senate; chmn. speakers com. Yonkers Citizens for O'Connor, 1966; campaign chmn. Carmine Marasco candidate for Supreme Ct., 9th Jud. Dist., 1968; bd. dirs. men's council Jewish Community Center. Mem. Am., N.Y. State, Westchester County, White Plains bar assns., Yonkers Lawyers Assn., N.Y. Land Title Assn. Home: 14 Midchester Ave White Plains NY 10606 Office: 235 Main St White Plains NY 10601 Tel (914) 760-7550

MARCUS, RICHARD ALAN, b. N.Y.C., Aug. 25, 1933; A.B., Coll. City N.Y., 1954; LL.B., U. Va., 1959. Admitted to Va. bar, 1959, N.Y. bar, 1960, Fla. bar, 1960, Minn. bar, 1962; mem. firm Bernard C. Fuller, Miami, 1960-62, Robins, Davis & Lyons, Mpls., 1962-64; counsel Napco Industries Inc., Mpls., 1964—, also dir.; dir. Napco GmbH, Napco Export Corp., Denver Aviation Corp., Airline Support Co., Inc., Inter-Ad, Inc., Star Leasing Corp. Mem. Am. Bar Assn., Am. Mgmt. Assn. Home: 14121 Stonegate Ln Hopkins MN 55343 Office: 1600 2d St South Hopkins MN 53343 Tel (612) 935-8211

MARCUS, STEPHEN HOWARD, b. N.Y.C., June 30, 1945; B.M.E., Mass. Inst. Tech., 1967; J.D. cum laude, Harvard, 1970. Admitted to Calif. bar, 1971; asso. firm Greenberg, Bernhard, Weiss & Karma, Inc., Los Angeles, 1972-76, mem., 1976—; with JAGC, USAR, 1971-77. Mem. Los Angeles County Bar Assn., Town Hall Calif. Office: 1880 Century Park E Suite 1150 Los Angeles CA 90067 Tel (213) 553-6111

MARCUS, STEVEN EZRA, b. Bklyn., May 19, 1946; B.A., N.Y. U., 1968, J.D., 1971; LL.M., Emory U., 1975. Admitted to N.Y. State bar, 1971, Ga. bar, 1971, U.S. Dist. Ct. for No. Ga., 1971; clk. Leon, Weill & Mahoney, N.Y.C., 1970-71; asso. firm Kleiner, Herman, DeVille & Simmons, Atlanta, 1971-73; house counsel Travelers Ins. Co., Atlanta, 1973-75; individual practice law, Atlanta, 1975-76; partner firm Marcus and Gingold, Atlanta, 1976—. Mem. Atlanta Young Lawyers Assn., Am., Ga., Atlanta bar assns. Contbr. articles to legal jours. Home: 4030 Shannon Mill Rd Atlanta GA 30319 Office: 46 5th St NE Atlanta GA 30308 Tel (404) 892-0393

MARCUS, STEVEN JOEL, b. N.Y.C., Jan. 23, 1945; B.S. in Econs., U. Pa., 1966; J.D., Georgetown U., 1969. Admitted to N.Y. bar, 1970, U.S. Dist. Ct. bar for So. Dist. N.Y., 1972; asso. firm Jacob P. Lefkowitz, N.Y.C., 1971-72; partner firm Raphael and Marcus, P.C., N.Y.C., 1972—. Mem. N.Y. State, Bklyn. bar assns., Assn. Bar City N.Y., N.Y. Criminal Bar Assn., Wharton Bus. Club of N.Y. Home: 431 W 22d St New York City NY 10011 Office: 551 Fifth Ave Suite 1419 New York City NY 10017 Tel (212) 682-1480

MARDELL, FRED ROBERT, b. Chgo., Oct. 2, 1934; B.S. in Econs., DePaul U., 1955; J.D., U. Chgo., 1958. Admitted to Ill. bar, 1958; asso. firm DeVoe, Shadur & Krupp, Chgo., 1961-65; sec. Barton Brands, Inc., Chgo., v.p., 1965-72, sec. Barton Brands, Ltd., Chgo., 1972—; clk. to Ill. Appellate Ct., 1958-59; research asso. U. Chgo. Law Sch., 1958-59. Mem. Am., Ill., Chgo. bar assns., Am. Soc. Corporate Secs., Pi Gamma Mu. Asso. editor U. Chicago Law Rev. Office: 200 S Michigan Ave Chicago IL 60604 Tel (312) 431-9200

MARDEN, JOHN NEWCOMB, b. N.Y.C., Feb. 14, 1935; B.A., Yale, 1957; LL.B., Cornell U., 1960. Admitted to N.Y. bar, 1960; asso. firm Curtis, Mallet-Prevost, Colt & Mosle, N.Y.C., 1960-69, partner, 1969—. Mem. Am., N.Y. bar assns., Assn. Bar City N.Y., Yale Westchester Alumni Assn. (dir.). Home: 49 Walbrooke Rd Scarsdale NY 10583 Office: 100 Wall St New York City NY 10005 Tel (212) 248-8111

MARDER, ROBERT SHERMAN, b. Bayonne, N.J., Nov. 19, 1934; B.A., Syracuse U., 1955; LL.B., Harvard, 1958. Admitted to Iowa bar, 1960, Calif. bar, 1961; staff atty. NLRB, Washington, 1958-59, office gen. counsel Dept. Navy, Washington, 1959-60; atty. So. Pacific RR Co., San Francisco, 1960-61; asst. U.S. atty. Dept. Justice, San Francisco, 1961-66; asso. firm Benas & Kragen, Oakland, Calif. and San Francisco, 1966-68; mem. firm Garry, Dreyfus, McTernan & Brotsky, San Francisco, 1968-72; individual practice law, San Francisco, 1972—. Mem. Calif. Atty's. for Criminal Justice. Office: 2182 Greenwich St San Francisco CA 94123 Tel (415) 931-3880

MAREAN, BROWNING ENDICOTT, III, b. Beverly, Mass., Sept. 28, 1942; A.B., Stanford, 1964; J.D., U. Calif., 1969. Admitted to Calif. bar, 1970; asso. firm Gray Cary Ames & Frye, San Diego, 1969-76, partner, 1976—, resident partner, Escondido, Calif., 1976—. Mem. Am., Calif. State bar assns. Home: 3120 Bernardo Ln Escondido CA 92025 Office: 210 S Juniper suite 200 Escondido CA 92025 Tel (714) 741-2233

MARETT, ORLANDO R., b. Bklyn., Aug. 13, 1916; student Fordham U., St. John's Coll.; grad. Sch. Law St. John's U., 1947. Admitted to N.Y. State bar, 1948, U.S. Customs Ct. bar, 1971; vets. assistance officer N.Y. State Dept. Civil Service, Albany, 1946-55; asst. dir. adminstrn. of cts., 2d Dept., Bklyn., 1962-72, dep. dir.,

1972—; chmn. appeals bd. Selective Service, Fed. Eastern Dist., 1972-76. Pres. Xaverian Circle, high sch. PTA, 1967-68. Mem. Bklyn. Bar Assn., Bay Ridge, Columbian lawyers assns. Recipient meritorious service award, presdl. certificates of appreciation for work with selective service. Office: 16 Court St Brooklyn NY 11241 Tel (212) 855-7440

MARGER, BRUCE, b. N.Y.C., Oct. 3, 1932; B.S. in Accounting, U. N.C., 1954; J.D., Harvard, 1959. Admitted to Fla. bar, 1959; mem. firm Goldner, Reams, Marger, Davis, Piper & Kiernan, and predecessors, St. Petersburg, Fla., 1959—; chmn. legal advisors to Fla. Masonic Home, 1969—. Mem. Am., Fla. (chmn. various coms.) bar assns. Contbr. articles in field to legal jours. Home: 1901 80th St N St Petersburg FL 33710 Office: PO Drawer 14233 St Petersburg FL 33733 Tel (813) 896-5177

MARGER, EDWIN, b. N.Y.C., Mar. 18, 1928; B.A. in Philosophy, U. Miami (Fla.), 1951, J.D., 1953. Admitted to Fla. bar, 1953, Ga. bar, 1971; individual practice law, Miami Beach, Fla., 1953-71, Atlanta, 1971—; spl. asst. atty. gen. State of Fla., 1960-61. Pres. Biscayne Dem. Club, Miami, Fla., 1956-57, B'nai B'rith, Miami Beach Lodge, 1958-59. Fellow Am. Acad. Forensic Scis. (chmn. jurisprudence sect.); mem. Ga. Trial Lawyers Assn., Fla., Ga. (chmn. sect. environ. law 1974-75) bar assns., Ga. Assn. Criminal Def. Lawyers, World Assn. Lawyers. Office: Suite 320 6666 Powers Ferry Rd Atlanta GA 30339 Tel (404) 955-1010

MARGIN, ALAN WILLIAM, b. Bklyn., Feb. 11, 1945; B.S., N.Y. U., 1966; J.D., U. Md., 1969. Admitted to Md. bar, 1969, D.C. bar, 1970, U.S. Dist. Ct. D.C. bar, 1970, U.S. Dist. Ct. Md., 1976; asso. firm Y. Hillel Abrams, Silver Spring, Md., 1969-74; individual practice law, Chevy Chase, Md., 1974-75; partner firm Margin & Leventhal, Bethesda, Md., 1976—. Mem. Am., Md. bar assns., Bar Assn. Montgomery County, Comml. Law League Am. Office: 4350 East West Hwy Suite 204 Bethesda MD 20014 Tel (301) 986-1000

MARGOLIN, FREDERICK ALAN, b. Bklyn., June 5, 1945; B.A., Am. U., 1966; J.D., N.Y. Law Sch., 1969. Admitted to N.Y. bar, 1971; asso. firm Hesterberg & Keller, Bklyn., 1972—; asso. counsel-pub. adminstr. Kings County (N.Y.), 1972—. Mem. legacy and estates com. Jewish Nat. Fund, 1974—. Mem. Am., Bklyn. (surrogate's ct. com. 1975—), N.Y. State bar assns. Home: 1717 E 18th St Brooklyn NY 11229 Office: 32 Court St Brooklyn NY 11201 Tel (212) 875-7450

MARGOLIN, JESSE, b. N.Y.C., Nov. 19, 1928; B.A., N.Y. U., 1950; J.D., Yale, 1953. Admitted to N.Y. bar, 1954; mem. firm Becker, Ross & Stone, N.Y.C., 1953-64, partner, 1964—. Mem. Internat., Am., N.Y. State, N.Y.C. bar assns. Office: 41 E 42d St New York City NY 10017 Tel (212) 697-2310

MARGOLIN, SEYMOUR, b. N.Y.C., May 21, 1937; B.A., Hobart Coll., 1959; LL.B., Bklyn. Sch. Law, 1962. Admitted to N.Y. bar, 1962; partner Margolin & Meltzer, N.Y.C., 1969—; hearing officer Parking Violations Bur., N.Y.C. Mem. N.Y. County Lawyers Assn., N.Y. State Trial Lawyers Assn., Hosp. Fin. Mgmt. Assn. Home: 135 Willow St Brooklyn NY 11201 Office: 401 Broadway St New York City NY 10013 Tel (212) 925-6233

MARGOLIN, STEPHEN JOSEPH, b. Phila., June 9, 1945; B.A., U. Nebr., 1967, J.D., 1970. Admitted to Pa. bar, 1970; law clk. firm Nelson, Harding, Marchetti, Leonard & Tate, Lincoln, Nebr., 1969; asst. dist. atty., Phila., 1970-76; staff atty. Defenders Assn. Phila., 1976; mem. firm Fine Staud & Grossman, Phila., 1976—. Mem. Am. Bar Assn. Home: 504 Woodbrook Ln Philadelphia PA 19119 Office: 1333 Race St Philadelphia PA 19107 Tel (215) 665-0100

MARGOLIS, EMANUEL, b. Bklyn., Mar. 18, 1926; B.A., U. N.C., 1947; Ph.D., Harvard U., 1951; J.D., Yale U., 1956. Admitted to Conn. bar, 1957, Fed. bar, 1958, U.S. Supreme Ct. bar, 1969; teaching fellow Harvard U., 1949-51; instr. govt. U. Conn. at Storrs, 1951-53; asso. atty. Silberberg & Silverstein, Ansonia, Conn., 1956-60; asso. atty. Wofsey, Rosen, Kweskin & Kuriansky, Stamford, Conn., 1960-66; partner firm Wofsey, Rosen, Kweskin & Kuriansky, Stamford, 1966—. Mem. Westport (Conn.) Planning and Zoning Commn., 1971-75; mem. ACLU (nat. bd. 1975—), Am. Soc. Internat. Law, Nat. Assn. Criminal Defense Lawyers, Conn. Bar Assn. (chmn. sect. human rights and responsibilities 1971-74). Sr. editor Conn. Bar Jour., 1971—; contbr. articles to legal jours. Home: 72 Myrtle Ave Westport CT 06880 Office: 777 Summer St Stamford CT 06901 Tel (203) 327-2300

MARGOLIS, GUSTAVE SHELDON, b. Johnstown, Pa., May 6, 1921; student U. Pitts., 1938-40; J.D., 1948; A.B., U. Chgo., 1942. Admitted to Pa. bar, 1949; partner firm McWilliams, Margolis & Coppersmith, Johnstown, 1950-64, Margolis & Coppersmith, Johnstown, 1964—. Mem. Pa. Council on Arts, 1971-72; pres. Johnstown Area Arts Council, 1969-71. Mem. Pa., Cambria County (past pres.) bar assns., Somerset-Cambria Estate Planning Council, U. Pitts. Alumni Assn. (pres. Johnstown chpt. 1973-74), Order of Coif, Phi Theta Kappa, Phi Beta Kappa. Home: 1333 Menoher Blvd Johnstown PA 15905 Office: 302 Park Bldg Johnstown PA 15901 Tel (814) 536-0778

MARGOLIS, MARVIN, b. Chgo., June 21, 1927; B.S.C., Roosevelt Coll., 1949; LL.B., John Marshall Law Sch., 1962, J.D., 1970. Admitted to Ill. bar, 1962; with IRS, 1951-53, 55-67; staff Chgo. City Coll., 1967—; individual practice law, Chgo. Mem. Ill. State, Chgo. bar assns., Ill. Inst. C.P.A.'s. Home: 2722 W Jerome St Chicago IL 60645 Office: 188 W Randolph St Chicago IL 60601 Tel (312) 338-5091

MARGOLIUS, PHILIP NEAL, b. Washington, Sept. 24, 1940; B.A., Dartmouth, 1962; LL.B., Yale, 1965. Admitted to D.C. bar, 1966; partner firm Margolius, Davis & Finkelstein, Washington, 1966—; lectr. Nacrelli Bar Rev. Sch., 1975--. Vice pres. young leadership United Jewish Appeal, Washington, 1972-73; asst. treas., dir. Jewish Community Center of Greater Washington, 1973—. Mem. D.C. Bar Assn. Home: 6216 Clearwood Rd Bethesda MD 20034 Office: 1120 Connecticut Ave NW Washington DC 20036 Tel (202) 833-3939

MARIANO, WILLIAM EDWARD, b. N.Y.C., July 5, 1935; A.B., Columbia, 1956, LL.B., 1959. Admitted to N.Y. bar, 1959, U.S. Dist. Ct. So. and Eastern Dist. N.Y. bars, 1972; individual practice law, 1959—; chief counsel Select Com. on Election Law, 1969-75, N.Y. Senate Com. on Election Law, 1975—, N.Y. Senate Finance Subcom. to Study the Impact of Budget Reductions on Police and Fire Protection in N.Y.C., 1976—; chief counsel Joint Legis. Com. on Election Law, 1966-69; counsel Senate Com. on Edn., 1965; N.Y. Assembly Com. on Aviation, 1964. Home: 1 Brett Ln Bedford NY 10506 Office: 110 E 42d St New York City NY 10017 Tel (212) 697-3710

MARIASH, JULES, b. N.Y.C., July 30, 1916; LL.B., St. John's U., 1942. Admitted to N.Y. bar, 1942, U.S. Ct. Mil. Appeals, 1956, U.S. Supreme Ct. bar, 1961; mem. firm Mariash, Levy & Super, Bklyn., 1946—; mem. JAG USAFR. Bd. dirs. Sea Gate Assn. Mem. Bklyn. Bar Assn. Home: 3851 Laurel Ave Brooklyn NY 11224 Office: 166 Montague St Brooklyn NY 11201 Tel (212) 875-4380

MARIK, WAYNE JOSEPH, b. Oak Park, Ill., July 24, 1945; B.A., Marquette U., 1967, J.D., 1970. Admitted to Wis. bar, 1970; law clk. to justice Wis. Supreme Ct., Madison, 1970-71; asso. firm Thompson, Evans, Hostak & Clack, Racine, Wis., 1971-74; mem. firm Thompson & Coates, Ltd., Racine, 1975—. Trustee Racine YWCA, 1975—. Mem. Am., Racine County bar assns., State Bar Wis., Racine-Kenosha Estate Planning Council. Home: 701 Melvin Ave Racine WI 53402 Office: 840 Lake Ave PO Box 516 Racine WI 53403 Tel (414) 632-7541

MARINO, WILLIAM, b. Middle Village, N.Y., July 3, 1926; B.S., N.Y. U., 1948; J.D., St. John's Law Sch., 1952. Admitted to N.Y. bar, 1953; asso. firm McDevitt, Stricker & Needham, N.Y.C., 1953-61; partner firm Ross, Rowan & Marino, N.Y.C., 1961-71; asso. Joseph W. Conklin, Mineola, N.Y., 1971—; arbitrator Small Claims Ct., N.Y.C. Mem. N.Y. County Bar Assn. Home: 47 Foothill Ln E Northport NY 11731 Office: 88 Third Ave Mineola NY 11501 Tel (516) 248-0550

MARINOFF, MARJORIE GREENFIELD, b. Phila., Sept. 23, 1942; B.A., Barnard Coll., Columbia, 1964; LL.B. cum laude, U. Pa., 1969. Admitted to Pa. bar, 1969, U.S. Supreme Ct. bar, 1974; asso. firm Pepper Hamilton & Scheetz, Phila., 1969—. Mem. Am., Pa., Phila. (exec. com. young lawyers sect. 1971-74, sect. vice-chmn. 1972-73, Fidelity award 1976, chmn. com. on child abuse young lawyers sect. 1971—) bar assns., ACLU (dir. Phila. chpt. 1970—, dir. Pa. chpt. 1974—, sec. Phila. br. 1976—). Office: 2001 Fidelity Bldg Philadelphia PA 19109 Tel (215) 545-1234

MARINSTEIN, ELLIOTT FRED, b. N.Y.C., June 15, 1928; B.A., Bklyn. Coll., 1950; J.D., N.Y. U., 1953. Admitted to N.Y. bar, 1955, U.S. Supreme Ct. bar, 1970; individual practice law, Troy, N.Y., 1956—; asst. dist. atty. Rensselaer County (N.Y.), 1965-67; counsel Troy Charter Revision Commn., 1972-73. Vice pres. Troy Jewish Community Center, 1974-76. Mem. Am., N.Y. State, Rensselaer County (chmn. grievance com. 1972-75, 3d v.p. 1977—) bar assns., Assn. Trial Lawyers Am., Capitol Dist. Trial Lawyers Assn., N.Y. Dist. Attys. Assn., Comml. Law League Am. Home: 2354 Burdett Ave Troy NY 12180 Office: 406 Fulton St Troy NY 12181 Tel (518) 274-5034

MARIS, ARTHUR STANLEY, b. Phila., Oct. 29, 1896; B.S., U. Pa., 1921, M.E., 1924; grad. T.C. Williams Sch. Law, U. Richmond, 1964. With Chesapeake & Potomac Telephone Co., 1921-61, gen. staff supr., 1952-61; admitted to Va. bar, 1964; individual practice law, Richmond, 1964—; U.S. commr. for Eastern Dist. Va., 1966. Pres., Va. Conf. Unitarian Chs. and Fellowships, 1959-60; chmn. bd. Richmond Pub. Forum, 1965; bd. dirs. Commonwealth council Girl Scouts U.S.A., 1966-69, v.p., 1969-75. Mem. Va., Richmond bar assns., Richmond C. of C. Registered profl. engr., Va.; founder, first editor The Brown and White, student publ. Westtown; editor Punch Bowl (U. Pa.). Home: 6825 Monument Ave Richmond VA 23226 Office: 620 Mutual Bldg Richmond VA 23219 Tel (804) 648-5849

MARITOTE, ROGER FRANCIS, b. Chgo., Apr. 25, 1927; B.S. in B.A., Marquette U., Milw., 1950; LL.B., J.D., De Paul U., Chgo., 1953. Admitted to Ill. bar, 1954, U.S. Ct. Mil. Appeals bar, 1960, U.S. Supreme Ct. bar, 1960; individual practice law, Chgo., 1954-57, 67-74; asso. firm Caliendo & Connor, Chgo., 1957-60; partner firm Collins, Maritote & Roffo, Chgo., 1960-67, Roger F. Maritote, Ltd., Chgo., 1974—. Chmn. Roselle (Ill.) Zoning Bd. Appeals, 1963-73. Mem. Am., Ill., DePage County bar assns., Am. Judicature Soc., Justinian Soc. Lawyers. Contbr. to Ill. Civil Trial Evidence. Office: 188 W Randolph St Chicago IL 60601 Tel (312) 263-6397

MARK, BRIAN MICHAEL, b. Detroit, Apr. 29, 1946; B.A., U. Mich., 1967; J.D., U. Fla., 1970. Admitted to Fla. bar, 1971; asso. firm Hyzer, Knight & Lund, Miami, Fla., 1970-73; individual practice law, Miami, 1973-75; asso. gen. counsel Pan Am. Bancshares, Inc., Miami, 1975-76; mem. firm Marks, Keith, Mack & Lewis, Miami, 1976—. Mem. Am., Fla., Dade County bar assns. Office: 111 NE 1st St Miami FL 33132 Tel (305) 358-7605

MARK, JOEL, b. Los Angeles, Apr. 21, 1947; B.A., U. Calif., Berkeley, 1969; J.D., Hastings Coll. Law, U. Calif., 1972. Admitted to Calif. bar, 1972; asso. firm Macdonald, Halsted & Laybourne, Los Angeles, 1973—; disciplinary examiner State Bar of Calif., 1976-77. Mem. Am., Los Angeles bar assns., Los Angeles Assn. of Bus. Trial Lawyers, Los Angeles Jr. C. of C. (chmn. 1976). Office: 1200 Wilshire Blvd Suite 600 Los Angeles CA 90017 Tel (213) 481-1200

MARK, LEONARD JOHN, b. New Orleans, Dec. 26, 1940; B.A., Ariz. State U., 1962; LL.B., U. Ariz., 1966. Admitted to Ariz. bar, 1966; dep. pub. defender Maricopa County (Ariz.), 1966-67; asso. firm Renaud, Cook, Miller & Cordova, Phoenix, 1967-73; individual practice law, Phoenix, 1973—. Trustee, pres. Ariz. chpt. Leukemia Soc. Am., Inc., nat. trustee. Mem. Am., Ariz., Maricopa County bar assns., Ariz., Am. assns. trial lawyers. Home: 3302 E Malapai Dr Phoenix AZ 85028 Office: 1 W Madison St Phoenix AZ 85003 Tel (602) 254-6669

MARK, RICHARD MANNING, b. Omaha, Dec. 13, 1921; B.A., U. Calif., Los Angeles, 1942; J.D., U. So. Calif., 1948. Admitted to Calif. bar, 1949; individual practice law, Hollywood, Calif., 1949-50; mem. firm Kopald & Mark, Beverly Hills, Calif., 1950—. Mem. Los Angeles County, Beverly Hills bar assns. Home: 11145 Sunset Blvd Los Angeles CA 90049 Office: 8888 Olympic Blvd Beverly Hills CA 90211 Tel (213) 272-2711

MARKERT, ALLAN ROBERT, b. St. Paul, Aug. 1, 1928; B.S., U. Minn., also B.A.; B.S.L., William Mitchell Coll. Law, also LL.B., J.D. Admitted to Minn. bar, 1959; practice law, 1959-61; asst. county atty. Ramsey County (Minn.), 1961-66; dir. legal assistance of Ramsey County Legal Services for the Poor Office, OEO, 1966-68; judge Municipal Ct., 1968—. Mem. Municipal, Ramsey County ct. judges assns., Minn., Ramsey County bar assns., Am. Judges Assn., Am. Judicature Soc. Home: 2080 Roblyn St Saint Paul MN 55104 Office: Courthouse Saint Paul MN 55102 Tel (612) 298-4433

MARKEWICH, ARTHUR, b. N.Y.C., Mar. 6, 1906; B.A., Cornell U., 1926; LL.B., Columbia, 1928. Admitted to N.Y. bar, 1929; asst. dist. atty. New York County, 1930-37; magistrate N.Y.C. Ct., 1947-50; justice City Ct., N.Y.C., 1951-54, N.Y. Supreme Ct., 1955-69; judge Appellate div. N.Y. Supreme Ct. 1st Dept., 1969—. Mem. Am., N.Y. State bar assns., New York County Lawyers Assn., Assn. Bar City N.Y., Columbia Law Sch. Alumni Assn. (past dir.). Home: 175 Riverside Dr New York City NY 10024 Office: 27 Madison Ave New York City NY 10010

MARKEWICH, DANIEL, b. Bklyn., Aug. 20, 1940; B.A. magna cum laude, Harvard, 1962; LL.B. cum laude (Stone scholar), Columbia U., 1965. Admitted to N.Y. State bar, 1965, U.S. Ct. Appeals 2d Circuit bar, 1973; asst. dist. atty. N.Y. County, 1965-69; mem. firm Markewich, Rosenhaus, Markewich & Friedman, P.C. and predecessor, N.Y.C., 1969—. Mem. Assn. of Bar of City of N.Y., N.Y. Criminal Bar Assn., N.Y. County Lawyers Assn. Author: The Legal Aspects of Telephone Marketing, 1976. Home: 25 Gesner Ave S Nyack NY 10960 Office: 350 Fifth Ave New York City NY 10001 Tel (212) 563-3500

MARKEY, HOWARD THOMAS, b. Chgo., Nov. 10, 1920; J.D. cum laude, Loyola U., Chgo., 1949; M. in Patent Law, John Marshall Law Sch., 1950. Admitted to Ill. bar, 1950, practiced in Chgo., 1950-72; partner firm Parker & Carter; Parker, Markey & Plyer, 1956-72; chief judge U.S. Ct. of Customs and Patent Appeals, Washington, 1972—. Lectr. on jets, rockets, missiles and space, 1946-50, on U.S. Constitution, 1950—; instr. patent law Loyola U., 1970-71. Decorated Legion of Merit. D.F.C., Soldier's medal, Air medal, Bronze Star (U.S.); Mil. Merit Ulchi medal (Korea). Recipient George Washington Honor medal Freedoms Found., 1964. Mem. Am. Bar Assn., Am. Judicature Assn., Am. Legion (post comdr.), Air Force Assn. (pres. 1960-61, chmn. 1961-62). Home: 2350 King Pl NW Washington DC 20007 Office: 717 Madison Pl NW Washington DC 20439*

MARKHOFF, HARRIS, b. N.Y.C., Dec. 16, 1938; A.B., Columbia, 1960, LL.B., 1963. Admitted to N.Y. bar, 1963; gen. counsel Glow-Rite Corp., 1964-68; partner firm Danziger, Markhoff & Feigert, P.C., White Plains, N.Y., 1968—; lectr. in field. Mem. Am., N.Y. State, Westchester County (N.Y.) (chmn. tax sect. 1973-77) bar assns., Estate Planning Council of Westchester County (pres.). Home: Major Lockwood Ln Pound Ridge NY 10576 Office: 158 Grand St White Plains NY 10601 Tel (914) 948-1556

MARKLE, JOHN, JR., b. Allentown, Pa., July 20, 1931; B.A., Yale, 1953; LL.B., Harvard, 1958. Admitted to Pa. Supreme Ct. bar, 1959; asso. firm Drinker Biddle & Reath, Phila., 1958-64, partner, 1964—. Mem. Chester County, Pa. Republican Com., 1961-69; del. Rep. Nat. Conv., 1968; bd. dirs. Children's Aid Soc. of Pa., 1963—, pres., 1969-72; bd. dirs. Hill Sch., Pottstown, Pa., 1970—, vice chmn., 1975—. Mem. Phila., Pa., Am. bar assns., Indsl. Relations Research Assn., Indsl. Relations Assn., Am. Arbitration Assn. (nat. labor panel). Named Outstanding Young Republican in Pa., 1966-69. Home: 23 Andrews Rd Malvern PA 19355 Office: 1100 Philadelphia Nat Bank Bldg Philadelphia PA 19107 Tel (215) 491-7235

MARKLEY, GEORGE JEFFREY, b. Quito, Ecuador, Nov. 3, 1945; B.A., Colby Coll., 1967; LL.D., N.Y. U., 1970. Admitted to bar; with firm Goldstein & Peck, Bridgeport, Conn., 1970—. Mem. Conn. Bar Assn. Home: 30 Blueberry Ln Huntington CT 06484 Office: 955 Main St Bridgeport CT 06603 Tel (203) 334-9421

MARKLEY, MICHAEL MARK, b. Rogers, Ark., Dec. 8, 1946; B.A., U. Tex., Austin, 1964, J.D., 1972. Admitted to Tex. bar, 1972, U.S. Dist. Ct. bar for Western Dist. Tex., 1974; individual practice law, Austin, 1972—; pres. Rising Star Corp., 1974—; sec.-treas. Boots, Inc., 1976—. Active Austin Civic Ballet, Austin Symphony; ann. debate and duet acting judge, Austin. Mem. State Bar Tex., Travis County (Tex.), Travis County Jr., Am. bar assns.; hon. mem. Internat. Alliance of Theatrical and Stage Employees. Contbr. book revs. to legal and theatrical jours. Office: 1912 W Anderson Ln 201 Austin TX 78757 Tel (512) 458-1402

MARKOVITZ, BERNARD, b. Pitts., Apr. 17, 1939; B.A., Westminster Coll., 1961; LL.B., Duquesne U., 1965. Admitted to Pa. bar, 1965, U.S. Supreme Ct. bar; asso. firm Royston Bobb & Leonard, Pitts.; corp. treas. Ryan & Bowser Inc., Pitts.; asst. dist. atty., Allegheny County, 1966-69; trial counsel Sch. Dist. Pitts., 1969-72. Chmn. Allegheny County State Republican. Com.; mem. Govs. Justice Commn. for Pa. Mem. assn. Trial Lawyers Am., Am. Arbitration Assn. Home: 1842 Shaw Ave Pittsburgh PA 15217 Office: 1402 Grant St Pittsburgh PA 15219 Tel (412) 281-6580

MARKOVITZ, JEROME LAWRENCE, b. Phila., Nov. 29, 1909; B.S. in Econs., U. Pa., 1930, J.D., 1933. Admitted to Pa. bar, 1933, U.S. Supreme Ct. bar, 1939; partner firm Markovitz, Brooks and Cantor, Phila., 1966—; dir. Lincoln Bank. Sec. Jewish Y's and Centers, 1972—; mem. exec. com. Phila. council Boy Scouts Am.; trustee Sidney Hillman Med. Center, 1952—. Mem. Am., Fed., Pa., Phila. bar assns. Home: Apt 413B Elkins Park House Elkins Park PA 19117 Office: Suite 1032 1315 Walnut St Philadelphia PA 19107 Tel (215) KI5-4414

MARKOVITZ, MONROE, b. Elizabeth, N.J., Mar. 12, 1932; A.B., Rutgers U., 1953, J.D., 1955. Admitted to N.J. bar, 1956; individual practice law, Union, N.J., 1956—; dir., counsel The Essex Bank; counsel Builders' Assn. Met. N.J. Trustee, Jewish Ednl. Center, 1964—; trustee Congregation B'nai Israel, 1972—, Congregation Adath Jeshurn, 1966—; mem. Israel Bonds Cabinet, 1974—. Mem. N.J., Union County bar assns. Office: 1235 Morris Ave Union NJ 07083 Tel (201) 687-6600

MARKOWITZ, IRVING RICHARD, b. N.Y.C., Jan. 16, 1910; B.S., N.Y. U., 1930, J.D., 1932. Admitted to N.Y. bar, 1933; partner firm Sidney & Irving R. Markowitz, N.Y.C., 1933-51; individual practice law, Syracuse, N.Y., 1951—; mem. N.Y. State Mediation bd., 1951-61; prof. indsl. relations, Lemoyne Coll., 1966-75; cons. N.Y. State Joint Legis. Commn. on Pub. Employment, 1969; panel mem. Fed. Mediation and Conciliation Service, Am. Arbitration Assn., Center for Dispute Settlement, Pub. Employment Relations Bd., N.Y. State Mediation Bd. Mem. Soc. for Profls. in Dispute Settlements, Indsl. Relations Research Assn. Contbr. articles to profl. jours. Home and office: 1416 James Syracuse NY 13203 Tel (315) 479-5759

MARKOWITZ, LEWIS HARRISON, b. York, Pa., Aug. 28, 1933; B.A. in Govt. with distinction (Honors Coll. fellow), Conn. Wesleyan U., 1955; J.D., U. Mich., 1958. Admitted to Pa. bar, 1959, U.S. Supreme Ct. bar, 1959; partner firm Markowitz, Kagen & Griffith, York, 1959—; lectr. in field; mem. nat. panel arbitrators Am. Arbitration Assn., 1965—. Bd. dirs. Jewish Community Center, York,

1969-75, chmn. adult edn., 1968—; mem. nat. adv. com. United Synagogues Am., 1974-76; mem. Pres's. Commn. on Civil Rights, 1964. Mem. York County (dir.), Pa., Am., Fed., Internat., Inter-Am. bar assns., Am., Pa. (dir.) trial lawyers assns., Assn. ICC Practitioners, Internat. Acad. Law and Sci. (regent 1966-72), Pitts. Inst. Legal Medicine, Def. Research Inst., Trademark Soc. (asso.), Tau Epsilon Rho. Home: 108 Scarboro Dr York PA 17403 Office: 141 E Market St York PA 17405 Tel (717) 843-5526

MARKS, ALEXANDER ANDREWS, b. Montgomery, Ala., Aug. 4, 1909; A.B., Princeton, 1932; LL.B., Harvard, 1935. Admitted to Ala. bar, 1935; partner firms Murray & Marks, Montgomery, Ala., 1935-42, Yung & Marks, Montgomery, 1946-48; judge Montgomery County (Ala.) Ct. Common Pleas, 1949-61, Montgomery County Ct., 1961-75, supernumerary, 1975—; lectr. Ala. Police Acad., Montgomery, 1952-69; chmn. Montgomery Traffic Commn., 1954-62. Sr. warden St. John's Episcopal Ch., Montgomery, 1949; pres. Soc. Pioneers of Montgomery, 1966. Mem. Ala. State, Montgomery County bar assns. Home: 3313 Thomas Ave Montgomery AL 36111

MARKS, BURTON HAROLD, b. Bklyn., Sept. 17, 1932; A.B., Bklyn. Coll., 1953; LL.B., Columbia, 1956. Admitted to N.Y. bar, 1957; U.S. Dist. Cts. for so. and eastern dists. N.Y. bars, 1957; atty. Nat. Dairy Products Corp., N.Y.C., 1956-58; asso. firm Menagh, Connors & Duggan, N.Y.C., 1958-61; partner firm Manes, Lawrence, Marks & Kuperschmid, N.Y.C., 1961—. Mem. Assn. Bar City N.Y. (mem. municipal affairs com.), City Club (trustee 1971—; treas. 1971-75; pres. 1975—). Office: 250 Park Ave New York City NY 10017 Tel (212) 687-0900

MARKS, EDWARD, b. N.Y.C., Sept. 27, 1907; LL.B., N.J. Law Sch. (now Rutgers U.), 1929. Admitted to N.Y. State bar, 1931; individual practice law, Freeport, N.Y., 1931-46; asso. firm Delson, Levin & Gordon, N.Y.C., 1946-52; asso. firm Raphael Russakow, Roosevelt, N.Y., 1952-54; individual practice law, Roosevelt, 1963-68; sr. atty. realty, dept. law State of N.Y., Albany, 1968-77. Mem. Am., N.Y. State bar assns., Scribes (Am. Soc. of Writers on Legal Subjects). Author: Jensen on Mechanics Lien Law, 4th edit., 1963; (with Paperno) Criminal Law in New York, 1961; (with Maloney and Paperno) Mortgages and Mortgage Foreclosure in New York, 1963; contbr. articles to legal jours.; gen. editor Lawyers' Practical Library, 1961-63. Office: 8 River Hill Albany NY 12204 Tel (518) 436-7811

MARKS, EDWARD ARCHIBALD, JR., b. Newark, June 25, 1909; B.S., U. Va., 1931, LL.B., 1933. Admitted to Va. bar, 1932, U.S. Supreme Ct. bar, 1974; since practiced in Richmond, Va.; asso. firm Christian, Barton & Parker, 1933-36, partner firm King & Marks, 1936-45, firm Sands, Anderson & Marks and predecessors, 1945—; commr. in chancery Circuit Ct. Henrico County (Va.), 1946—, Richmond Circuit Ct., div. 1, 1948—. Tie breaker Henrico County Bd. Suprs., 1969—. Mem. Am., Va., Richmond bar assns., Am. Assn. Ins. Counsel, Def. Research Inst., Am. Coll. Trial Lawyers, Am. Judicature Soc., Order of Coif, Phi Beta Kappa. Contbr. articles to profl. jours. Home: 7200 W Franklin St Richmond VA 23226 Office: 1420 Fidelity Bldg Richmond VA 23219 Tel (804) 648-1636

MARKS, FRANK HENRY, b. Washington, Jan. 25, 1898; B.S. in Chem. Engring., George Washington U., 1922, M.S., 1924, LL.B., 1926. Admitted to D.C. bar, 1926, Ill. bar, 1928, U.S. Supreme Ct. bar, 1930; examiner U.S. Patent Office, 1928, patent counsel Kraft Co., Abbott Labs., Kimberly-Clark Corp., 1928-36; with firm Arnstein, Gluck, Weitzenfeld & Minow, Chgo., 1936-69; gen. patent counsel Sears, Roebuck and Co., Chgo., 1936-69; also artist. Recipient Order of Beaver award Boy Scouts Am., 1960; contbr. articles to legal jours.; columnist Chgo. Tribune; free-lance writer tech. and popular books; lectr. in field. Home and Office: 4940 East End Ave Chicago IL 60615 Tel (312) MU 4-3124

MARKS, HERBERT EDWARD, b. Dayton, Ohio, Nov. 3, 1935; A.B. with high distinction, U. Mich., 1957; J.D., Yale, 1960. Admitted to Ohio bar, 1960, D.C. bar, 1964, U.S. Supreme Ct. bar, 1963; served to capt. JAGC, U.S. Air Force, 1961-64; law clk. to chief judge U.S. Ct. of Claims, Washington, 1964-65; asso. firm Wilkinson, Cragun & Barker, Washington, 1965-69, partner, 1969—; asso. gen. counsel Presdl. Inaugural Com., 1969, 73; sec., gen. counsel Am. Hist. and Cultural Soc., Washington, 1970—; mem. jud. conf. com. U.S. Ct. Claims, 1969-71. Mem. Bar Assn. D.C. (chmn. Ct. of Claims com. 1974-75), Computer Law Assn. (pres. 1975-77), Am., Fed., FCC bar assns., Phi Beta Kappa. Home: 5317 Cardinal Ct Bethesda MD 20016 Office: 1735 New York Ave NW Washington DC 20006 Tel (202) 833-9800

MARKS, JACK GORDON, b. Bklyn., May 21, 1910; B.A., Washington and Lee U., 1932; J.D., Columbia, 1935. Admitted to N.Y. bar, 1936, Ariz. bar, 1954, U.S. Supreme Ct. bar, 1960; law clk. firm Hirsch, Newman, Reass & Becker, N.Y.C., 1935-37; partner firm Marks & Marks, N.Y.C., 1937-49; since practiced in Tucson; chief civil dep. sheriff, 1951-55; spl. asst. atty. gen., 1955-59, city atty., 1959-61; commr. Superior Ct., 1961-65; judge Superior Ct. Pima County, 1965—. Mem. Am., N.Y.C., Ariz., Pima County bar assns. Home: 400 Avenida de Palmas Tucson AZ 85716 Office: Division VIII Pima County Cts Bldg Tucson AZ 85701 Tel (602) 792-8381

MARKS, JEROME, lawyer; b. N.Y.C., June 24, 1931; B.S., Northwestern U., 1952, J.D., 1955. Admitted to Ill. bar, 1955; asso. law firm John B. Moser, Chgo., 1955-56; asso. law firm Koven, Koven, Salzman & Homer, Chgo., 1956-62; partner law firm Friedman & Koven, Chgo., 1962—. Co-chmn. No. Communities div. Operation Breadbasket, 1970-71. Mem. Chgo., Ill. State bar assns., Tau Delta Rho, Order of Coif. Office: 208 S LaSalle St Chicago IL 60604

MARKS, LAWRENCE JEFFREY, b. Cleve., May 9, 1942; B.A., U. Colo., 1964; J.D., U. Ariz., 1967. Admitted to Ariz. bar, 1967, also U.S. Supreme Ct. bar; bailiff, Superior Ct. Ariz., 1967-68; individual practice law, Phoenix, 1968—. Mem. Maricopa County Bar Assn., Ariz. Trial Lawyers Assn., Phi Delta Phi. Home: 3640 W Oregon St Phoenix AZ 85019 Office: 111 W Monroe Suite 141 Phoenix AZ 85003 Tel (602) 257-7750

MARKS, LEONARD H., b. Pitts., Mar. 5, 1916; B.A., U. Pitts., 1935, LL.B., 1938. Admitted to Pa. bar, 1939; individual practice law, Pitts., 1939-42; asst. to gen. counsel FCC, Washington, 1942-46; partner firm Cohn and Marks, Washington, 1946-65, 69—; dir. USIA, Washington, 1965-68; incorporator, dir. Communications Satellite Corp., 1963-65; chmn. Internat. Conf. on Communications Satellites, 1968-69; chmn. U.S. Adv. Commn. on Internat. Ednl. and Cultural Affairs, Washington, 1974—. Mem. Am., D.C. bar assns., World Assn. Lawyers, Phi Beta Kappa, Omicron Delta Kappa, Order of Coif. Contbr. articles to legal jours. Office: 1920 L St NW Washington DC 20036 Tel (202) 293-3860

MARKS, MICHAEL GEORGE, b. Davenport, Iowa, July 31, 1931; B.A., St. Ambrose Coll., 1953; J.D., U. Iowa, 1959. Admitted to Iowa bar, 1959, N.Y. bar, 1960; asso. firm Willkie Farr & Gallagher, N.Y.C., 1959-68, partner, 1969—. Mem. Am., N.Y. State bar assns. Office: 1 Chase Manhattan Plaza New York City NY 10005 Tel (212) 248-1000

MARKS, MURRY AARON, b. Carbondale, Ill., July 14, 1933; B.A., Washington U., 1954, LL.B., J.D., 1963. Admitted to Mo. bar, 1963, U.S. Dist Ct. bar, 1964, U.S. Supreme Ct. bar, 1972. Mem. exec. com. Am. Cancer Research Center, Denver. Mem. Am., St. Louis, St. Louis County bar assns., Assn. Trial Lawyers Am., Nat. Assn. Criminal Def. Lawyers, Am. Judicature Soc. Home: # 26 Williamsburg Rd St Louis MO 63141 Office: 8008 Carondelet Suite 204 Clayton MO 63105

MARKS, STANLEY JEROME, b. Milw., June 7, 1939; B.A., Cornell U., 1961; LL.B., N.Y. U., 1965. Admitted to Ariz. bar, 1966, U.S. Supreme Ct. bar, 1974; law clk. to chief justice Ariz. Supreme Ct., Phoenix, 1965-66; partner firm Langerman, Begam, Lewis, Leonard & Marks, Phoenix, 1966—. Mem. Ariz., Am. (chmn. auto. reparations com. 1971) bar assns., Assn. Trial Lawyers Am. (dir. Ariz. chpt. 1970—, state committeeman 1969-73, pres. Ariz. chpt. 1973-74), Ariz. Center Law in Pub. Interest (pres. 1976—), Maricopa County Bar Assn. Home: 5909 E Solcito Ln Scottsdale AZ 85251 Office: 1400 Arizona Title Bldg Phoenix AZ 85003 Tel (602) 254-6071

MARKS, THEODORE LEE, b. N.Y.C., Oct. 18, 1935; B.S., N.Y. U., 1956, J.D., 1958; Admitted to N.Y. bar, 1959, U.S. Supreme Ct. bar, 1964, U.S. 2d Circuit Ct. Appeals bar, 1975, U.S. Dist. Ct. for So. Dist. N.Y., 1963; since practiced in N.Y.C.; asso. firm Silver, Bernstein, Seawell, & Kaplan, 1959-65; individual practice law, 1965-71; partner firm Lee, Cash & Marks, 1971-76; partner firm Vogel, Marks & Rosenberg, 1976—. Mem. Sch. bd. selection com. Mamaroneck (N.Y.) Sch. Dist., 1975-76; co-chmn. Citizens Com. to Review Findings of Citizens Advisory Planning Com., 1976—; mem. youth bd. Larchmont (N.Y.) Temple, 1976; counsel Lower East Side Family Union, N.Y.C., 1974; chmn. young peoples group Univ. settlement N.Y.C., 1965-66; chmn. social action com. Soc. for the Advancement of Judaism, 1960. Mem. N.Y. State, Westchester County bar assns., N.Y. County Lawyers Assn., Fed. Bar Council. Office: 477 Madison Ave New York City NY 10022 Tel (212) 758-3404

MARKS, THOMAS CLARK, JR., b. Tampa, Fla., Dec. 14, 1938; B.S., Fla. State U., 1960; LL.B., Stetson U., 1963; Ph.D., U. Fla., 1971. Admitted to Fla. bar, 1963, U.S. Supreme Ct. bar, 1966; individual practice law, Tampa, 1967-69; asst. prof. polit. sci. U. So. Ala., 1971-73; asst. prof. law Stetson U., 1973-75, asso. prof., 1975—; served as capt. JAGC, U.S. Army, 1964-67, maj. Res., 1960—. Mem. Am., Fla. bar assns., Assn. Am. Law Schs. (constl. law com.) Author: (with others) Readings in Criminal Justice, 1976. Home: Office: Stetson U Coll Law Saint Petersburg FL 33707 Tel (813) 347-2124

MARKSON, ALDAN OVITER, b. N.Y.C., Nov. 23, 1929; A.B., Dartmouth, 1951; LL.B., Columbia, 1954. Admitted to N.J. bar, 1956; asso. firm Mandel, Wysoker, Desmond, Perth Amboy, N.J., 1957-60; mem. firm Pollack & Markson, Kenilworth, N.J., 1960-73; individual practice law, Kenilworth, 1974—; counsel N.J. Municipal and County Law Revision Commn., 1960-62; municipal atty., Kenilworth, 1974—, prosecutor, 1971-72; atty. Kenilworth Bd. Adjustment, 1965-70. Mem. N.J. Supreme Ct. Com. on County Dist. Cts., 1971—. Mem. N.J. Bar Assn. (chmn. com. landlord-tenant law 1971-72). Home: 42 Euclid Ave Maplewood NJ 07040 Office: 512 Boulevard Kenilworth NJ 07033 Tel (201) 272-3366

MARKSON, MARTIN, b. Bklyn., Dec. 16, 1922; B.A., Queens Coll., 1942; LL.B., Columbia, 1948. Admitted to N.Y. bar, 1948, U.S. Supreme Ct. bar, 1956; asso. firm Waldman & Waldman, N.Y.C., 1948-63, partner, 1964—; arbitrator Am. Arbitration Assn., N.Y. State Pub. Employment Relations Bd., N.J. Pub. Employment Relations Commn. Trustee Congregation Kehilath Jeshurun, N.Y.C., 1970—; v.p. Am. Zionist Fedn., 1972-76, gen. counsel, 1972—. Mem. Am., N.Y. State bar assns., Assn. Bar City N.Y., New York County Lawyers Assn. (chmn. com. on labor relations). Home: 315 E 68th St New York City NY 10021 Office: 501 Fifth Ave New York City NY 10017 Tel (212) MO1-1230

MARKSTROM, WILBUR JACK, b. South Haven, Mich., Sept. 29, 1930; B.B.A., U. Mich., 1953, J.D., 1959. Admitted to Ohio bar, 1959; asso. firm Squire, Sanders & Dempsey, Cleve., 1959-70, gen. partner, 1970—. Sec. Dunham Tavern Museum, 1968-76; v.p. Cleve. Play House Club, 1975-76. Mem. Cleve., Ohio, Am. (vice chmn. com. on pub. health care, sect. local govt. law 1976—), bar assns., Am. Soc. Hosp. Attys., Health Lawyers Assn., Nat. Health Lawyers Assn., Nat. Assn. Coll., Univ. Attys., Am. Soc. Law and Medicine. Office: 1800 Union Commerce Bldg 925 Euclid Ave Cleveland OH 44115 Tel (216) 696-9200

MARKUS, RICHARD M., b. Evanston, Ill., Apr. 16, 1930; B.S. magna cum laude, Northwestern U., 1951; J.D. cum laude, Harvard, 1954. Admitted to D.C. bar, 1954, Ohio bar, 1956, U.S. Supreme Ct. bar, 1957; atty. U.S. Dept. Justice, Washington, 1954-56; partner firm Sindell, Sindell, Bourne, Markus, Stern & Spero, Cleve., 1956-73, firm Spangenberg, Shibley, Traci, Larcione & Markus, Cleve., 1973-76; judge Ct. Common Pleas for Cuyahoga County (Ohio), Cleve., 1976—; adj. prof. Cleve. State U. Law Sch., 1960—; instr. Case Western Res. U. Law Sch., 1972—; lectr. in field; founding trustee Nat. Inst. Trial Advocacy, also faculty, 1971—. Mem. Assn. Trial Lawyers Am. (nat. pres. 1970-71), Ohio Acad. Trial Lawyers (pres. 1966-67), Ohio (council of dels. 1970—), Greater Cleve. (trustee 1967-70) bar assns., Phi Beta Kappa. Author: Trial Handbook for Ohio Lawyers, 1973; editor Harvard Law Rev., 1952-54; contbr. articles to legal jours. Home: 4769 Edenwood Rd South Euclid OH 44121 Office: Justice Center Cleveland OH 44113 Tel (216) 623-8697

MARKUS, WILLIAM HARRY, b. Pitts., Oct. 24, 1907; student Wittenberg Coll., 1924-25; B.S., U. Pitts., 1928; LL.B., Duquesne U., 1931; LL.D. (hon.), Thiel Coll., 1970. Admitted to Pa. bar, 1932, U.S. Supreme Ct. bar, 1948; solicitor West View Municipal Authority, 1942-75, McCandless Twp. Sanitary Authority, 1952—, Pine Twp. Sch. Authority, 1958-75, Western Allegheny County Municipal Authority, 1961-75, Fox Chapel Sanitary Authority, 1965—, Twp. of Pine, 1954-75, Spring Hill Savs. and Loan Assn. of Pitts., Troy Hill Fed., Concord-Liberty, Mt. Troy, Workingmens Savs. and Loan Assns., First Home Savs. Assn., Venango Fed. Savs. and Loan Assn.; counsel Pa. Savs. League, Inc., Pitts., 1958—, Pa. Municipal Authorities Assn., 1948—, Fox C Chapel Borough, 1970—. Trustee Thiel Coll., 1957-64, chmn. bd. trustees, 1963-64; trustee N. Hills Passavant Hosp., 1959—, Western Restoration Center, 1962—; pres. Lutheran Service Soc., 1955-56, Lutheran Student Found., 1955-57. Contbr. articles to monthly legal publ. Home: 756 E Madison Circle Pittsburgh PA 15229 Office: 1808 Law and Finance Bldg 425 Fourth Ave Pittsburgh PA 15219 Tel (412) 281-0235

MARLAR, DONALD FLOYD, b. Little Rock, Jan. 15, 1944; B.S., Ark. State U., 1966; J.D., U. Tulsa, 1968; LL.M., George Washington U., 1972. Admitted to Okla. bar, 1969; capt. JAGC, U.S. Army, Ft. Meade, Md., 1969-73; partner firm Pray Scott Williamson & Marlar, Tulsa, 1973—. Mem. Am., Okla., Tulsa County bar assns. Home: 3517 E 70th Pl Tulsa OK 74136 Office: 2910 4th Nat Bank Bldg Tulsa OK 74119 fTel (918) 583-1366

MARLATT, ERNEST EUGENE, b. Kenosha, Wis., Nov. 15, 1927; B.A., DePauw U., 1950; J.D., So. Meth. U., 1953. Admitted to Tex. bar, 1953; mem. legal dept. Shell Oil Co., Houston, 1953-56; individual practice law, Houston, 1957—. Mem. Tex. Bar Assn., Am. Arbitration Assn. (arbitrator 1970—), Soc. Profl. Dispute Resolution. Home: 516 S Post Oak Ln Houston TX 77056 Office: PO Box 13199 Houston TX 77019

MARLO, JOHN ALBERT, b. San Francisco, May 9, 1934; B.A. in Police Sci., San Jose State U., 1956; J.D., U. Santa Clara, 1961. Admitted to Calif. bar, 1961; practiced in Santa Cruz, Calif., 1961-73; judge Santa Cruz Municipal Ct., 1973—; mem. civil service com. Calif. Council Criminal Justice, 1965-72; instr. dept. adminstrn. of justice Cabrillo Coll., 1964—; police officer, San Jose, 1955-61; arbitrator Am. Arbitration Assn., 1968-73. Author: Police Officer and Criminal Justice, 1970. Home: 7278 Mesa Dr Aptos CA 95003 Office: 1430 Freedom Blvd Watsonville CA 95076 Tel (408) 724-1188

MARLOW, GEORGE D., b. N.Y.C., June 8, 1941; B.A., St. Lawrence U., 1963; J.D., St. John's U., 1966. Admitted to N.Y. State bar, 1967; asst. dist. atty. Queens County, N.Y., 1967-71, Dutchess County, N.Y., 1971-75; asso. firm Perry Satz, Poughkeepsie, N.Y., 1976—. Bd. dirs. Dutchess County Alcoholism Info. and Referral Center, 1976—. Mem. N.Y. State, Dutchess County bar assns. Home: RD 5 Potter Pl Hopewell Junction NY 12533 Office: 266 Mill St Poughkeepsie NY 12601 Tel (914) 454-3360 also Hopewell Plaza Hopewell Junction NY 12533 Tel (914) 226-2444

MARMELSTEIN, CHARLES MICHAEL, b. Washington, Dec. 12, 1941; B.E.E., U. Md., 1964; J.D., Am. U., 1970. Admitted to Md. bar, 1970, D.C. bar, 1971; patent examiner U.S. Patent Office, Washington, 1968-70; mem. firm Armstrong, Nikaido and Marmelstein, Washington, 1973—; asso. firm Sughrue, Rothwell, Mion, Zinn and Macpeak, Washington, 1970-73. Mem. Am., D.C. bar assns., Am. Patent Law Assn., U.S. Trademark Assn. Home: 1325 Winding Waye Ln Silver Spring MD 20902 Office: 1725 K St NW Washington DC 20006 Tel (202) 659-2930

MARMET, ROBERT ARTHUR, b. Omaha, Jan. 25, 1925; B.S., U.S. Naval Acad., 1946; LL.B., Georgetown U., 1951; LL.M., 1954. Commd. ensign USN, 1946, advanced through grades to lt., 1952; radar officer U.S.S. Portsmouth, 6th Fleet, 1946-47; communications officer, trial counsel, Naval Base, Kenitra, Morocco, 1951-53; naval aide to vice dir. Nat. Security Agy., Washington, 1953-55; ret., 1955; admitted to D.C. bar, 1951; individual practice law, Washington, 1955-61; mem. firm Marmet & Schneider, 1961-70, Marmet & Webster, 1970-73, Marmet Profl. Corp., 1973—; trustee, chmn. legal affairs com. Nat. Capital Union Presbytery, Inc. Mem. Fed. Communications Bar Assn., Am. Judicature Soc., Georgetown U. Alumni Assn. (v.p. 1965-66). Home: 5120 Cammack Dr Spring Hill MD 20016 Office: 1822 Jefferson Pl Washington DC 20036 Tel (202) 331-7300

MAROLDY, DONALD J., b. Larchmont, N.Y., Oct. 19, 1925; A.B., Fordham U., 1947, M.A., 1949, J.D., 1951. Admitted to N.Y. bar, 1952, U.S. Supreme Ct. bar, 1958; labor relations staff Mobil Oil Corp., N.Y.C. Vice-chmn., New Rochelle (N.Y.) Conservative Party, 1976—. Mem. Am., Internat. bar assns. Home: 45 Longue Vue Ave New Rochelle NY 10804 Office: 150 E 42d St New York City NY 10017 Tel (912) 883-3415

MARON, MILFORD ALVIN, b. Chgo., Jan. 21, 1926; A.B., U. So. Calif., 1949, M.A., 1953, LL.B., 1954, LL.M., 1958. Admitted to Calif. bar, 1955, U.S. Supreme Ct. bar, 1959; individual practice law, Los Angeles, 1955; dep. commr. corps. Calif. Div. Corps., Los Angeles, 1955-57; trial atty. SEC, Los Angeles, 1957-61; atty. Calif. Div. Labor Law Enforcement, Los Angeles, 1961-63; adminstrv. law judge Calif. Office Adminstrv. Hearings, Los Angeles, 1963—. Mem. State Bar Calif., Conf. Adminstrv. Law Judges (moderator panels). Contbr. articles to legal jours. Office: 314 W First St Los Angeles CA 90012 Tel (213) 620-4650

MAROVITZ, ABRAHAM LINCOLN, b. Oshkosh, Wis., Aug. 10, 1905; LL.B., Chgo.-Kent Coll. Law, 1925, J.D., 1969; L.H.D., Lincoln (Ill.) Coll., 1956, LL.D., Winston Churchill Coll., Pontiac, Ill., 1968. Admitted to Ill. bar, 1927; asst. state's atty. for Cook County (Ill.), 1927-33; practiced in Chgo., 1927-50; mem. Ill. Senate, 1938-43, 46; chmn. bd. Lincoln Nat. Bank, 1946-63; judge Cook County Superior Ct., 1950-63; chief justice Criminal Ct. of Cook County, 1958-59; judge U.S. Dist. Ct., No. Dist. Ill., 1963—, sr. judge, 1975—; mem. lawyers' adv. council U. Ill. Law Forum, 1st nat. chmn. Nat. Conf. State Ct. Trial Judges, 1958. Trustee Chgo.-Kent Coll. Law, Chgo. Med. Sch.; bd. dirs. Hebrew Theol. Coll., Anshe Sholom B'nai Israel Synagogue, Chgo.; mem. YMCA Adv. Bd. of Met. Chgo. Named Ill. Outstanding Lggislator, Ind. Voters of Ill., 1949, Man of Year Jewish Nat. Fund, 1959, Israel Bond Orgn., 1968, 73; recipient Founders' Day award Loyola U., Chgo., 1967, Ann. award of merit Decalogue Soc. Lawyers, 1968, Chgo. Press Club, 1970, Chgo. Press Photographers Assn., 1968. Office: US Courthouse Chicago IL 60604

MAROWITZ, ALBERT WARREN, b. Warren, Ohio, Sept. 21, 1912; A.B., Hiram Coll., 1934; LL.B., Youngstown U., 1942, J.D., 1969. Admitted to Ohio bar, 1942, U.S. Supreme Ct. bar, 1963; individual practice law, Warren, 1942—; tchr. real estate courses Kent State U. Pres., exec. bd. Family Service Assn., Warren, 1963-69; advisor Youngstown chpt. Parents Without Partners, 1966—. Mem. Ohio, Trumbull County (exec. com. 1974—) bar assns., Trumbull County Real Estate Bd., Tau Epsilon Rho. Office: 106 E Market St Union Savs & Trust Bldg Suite 512 Warren OH 44481 Tel (216) 399-2555

MARQUARDT, PHILIP, b. Manila, Sept. 9, 1934; B.A., U. Ariz., 1957, LL.B., 1961. Admitted to Ariz. bar, 1961; U.S. Supreme Ct. bar, 1964; judge advocate USAF, Spain, 1961-64; asst. atty. gen. Ariz., 1964-68; mem. firm Hill & Savoy, Phoenix, 1966-70; judge Superior Ct., Phoenix, 1970—. Office: Court Bldg Phoenix AZ 85003 Tel (602) 262-3851

MARQUIS, HAROLD LIONEL, b. Osceola, Iowa, Oct. 9, 1931; B.A., U. Iowa, 1954, J.D., 1960; LL.M., U. Mich., 1963. Admitted to Iowa bar, 1960, Mich. bar, 1962, Ga. bar, 1972; atty. Dow Corning Corp., Midland, Mich., 1960-62; asst. prof. law Temple U., 1963-65; prof. law Emory U., Atlanta, 1965—; vis. prof. law U. Houston,

1970-71. Mem. Ga. State Bar Assn. Contbr. articles to law jours. Home: 1858 Castleway Ln Atlanta GA 30345 Office: Law Sch Emory U Atlanta GA 30322 Tel (404) 329-6838

MARR, CARMEL CARRINGTON, b. Bklyn., June 23, 1921; B.A., Hunter Coll., 1945; J.D., Columbia, 1948. Admitted to N.Y. bar, 1948; law asst. Dyer & Stevens, N.Y.C., 1948-49; individual practice law, N.Y.C., 1949-53; adviser legal affairs U.S. Mission to UN, 1953-67; sr. legal officer UN Secretariat, 1967-68; mem. N.Y. State Human Rights Appeal Bd., 1968-71; commr. N.Y. State Pub. Service, N.Y.C., 1971—; lectr. Police Acad., 1963-67. Mem. Gov.'s Com. on Edn. and Employment of Women, 1963-64; mem. UN Devel. Corp., 1969-72, Nat. Gen. Services Pub. Adv. Council, 1969; bd. dirs. Amistad Research Center, Bklyn. Soc. for Prevention Cruelty to Children, Community Service Soc.; bd. govs. UN Assn. of U.S.A.; bd. visitors N.Y. State Sch. for Girls, Hudson, 1964-71; chmn. bd. Billie Holiday Theatre, Inc.; mem. natural gas adv. com. Fed. Energy Adminstrn. Mem. Am., Bklyn., Bklyn. Women's bar assns., Nat. Assn. Women Lawyers, Internat. Fedn. Women Lawyers, Nat. Assn. Regulatory Utility Commrs., Phi Beta Kappa, Alpha Chi Alpha. Recipient citations and medals from various civic and profl. orgns.; contbr. articles to legal jours. Office: Pub Service Commn Two World Trade Center New York City NY 10047 Tel (212) 488-4376

MARRERO, LOUIS JOHN, b. N.Y.C., May 9, 1936; A.B. in Polit. Sci., City Coll. N.Y., 1958; LL.B., St. John's Law Sch., 1963. Admitted to N.Y. State bar, 1963, U.S. Supreme Ct. bar, 1967; individual practice law, Bklyn., 1964—; asst. counsel N.Y. State Assembly, 1969, 70, 75, 76; law sec. to Justice Supreme Ct. State of N.Y., 1971-73. Mem. Republican State Com., leader, 1968-76; leader emeritus Dirksen Regular Rep. Club., 1976—; pres. Bergen Beach Civic Assn., 1967, 68, 70; v.p. and counsel Joint Council for Community Betterment; v.p. Joint Council for Better Edn.; counsel N. Canarsie Civic Assn. Mem. Bklyn. Bar Assn., Catholic Lawyers Guild, Columbian Lawyers Assn. Office: 32 Court St Brooklyn NY 11201 Tel (212) 852-1776

MARSDEN, MILO SCOVIL, JR., b. Salt Lake City, Feb. 17, 1933; B.S., U. Utah, 1959; J.D., Stanford, 1960. Admitted to Utah bar, 1960; asso. firm Parsons, Behle & Latimer, Salt Lake City, 1960-63; mem. firm Mabey Ronnow Madsen & Marsden, Salt Lake City, 1963-66, Bradford Marsden Creer & Liljenquist, Salt Lake City, 1966—. Mem. Salt Lake City CSC, 1974—, chmn., 1975—; mem. gov's. council for developmentally disabled, 1975. Mem. Am. Bar Assn. Home: 1417 Laird Circle Salt Lake City UT 84105 Office: 1700 University Club Salt Lake City UT 84111 Tel (801) 521-3800

MARSELLA, SAMUEL ANTHONY, b. White Plains, N.Y., Nov. 22, 1931; B.A., Villanova U., 1953; L.L.B., Boston U., 1956. Admitted to Mass. bar, 1956, U.S. Supreme Ct. bar, 1959, U.S. Mil. Ct. Appeals, 1959, Fed. Dist. Ct. bar, 1960; mem. firm Brooks & Wallace, Springfield, Mass., 1965-67; mem. firm Doherty, Wallace, Pillsbury & Murphy, Springfield, 1967—; city prosecutor, Springfield, Mass., 1962-64; mem. Springfield Bd. Appeals, 1965. Pres., treas., trustee Pioneer Valley Multiple Sclerosis Soc., 1960-73; trustee Bay Path Jr. Coll., 1968—. Mem. Am., Mass., Hampden County bar assns., Am. Soc. Hosp. Attys., Am. Soc. Law and Medicine, Nat. Assn. Colls. and Univ. Attys., Mass. Acad. Trial Attys. Home: 224 Chapin Terr Springfield MA 01104 Office: 1387 Main St Springfield MA 01103 Tel (413) 733-3111

MARSH, BENJAMIN FRANKLIN, b. Toledo, Apr. 30, 1927; B.A., Ohio Wesleyan U., 1950; J.D., George Washington U., 1954. Personnel officer AEC, 1950-54; admitted to Ohio bar, 1955; since practiced in Toledo, mem. firm Doyle, Lewis and Warner, 1955-71; partner firm Ritter, Boesel, Robinson & Marsh, 1971—; asst. solicitor City of Maumee (Ohio), 1959-63, solicitor, prosecutor, 1963—; asst. atty. gen. Ohio, 1969-71; adminstrv. asst. Legis. Service Commn., Columbus, Ohio, 1954-55. Mem. Lucas County Charter Commn., Toledo, 1959-60; vice-chmn. U.S. Nat. Commn. for UNESCO, mem. legal com., del. 17th Gen. Conf., Paris, 1972; pres. Toledo and Lucas County TB Soc., Citizens for Metroparks; mem. Lucas County Bd. Elections; chmn. Lucas County Rep. Exec. com., 1973-74; alt. del. Rep. Nat. Conv., 1964. Mem. Am., Ohio, Toledo bar assns., Nat. Inst. Municipal Law Officers, World Peace Through Law, Ohio Land Title Assn., Ohio Municipal League, Toledo Council World Affairs, Omicron Delta Kappa, Delta Sigma Rho, Theta Alpha Phi, Phi Delta Phi. Appointed spl. ambassador Tenth Anniversary independence of Botswana, 1976; named U.S. observor UNESCO Nat. Commn. of Africa, Addis Ababa, Ethiopia, 1974. Home: 124 W Harrison St Maumee OH 43537 Office: United Savings Bldg Toledo OH 43604 Tel (419) 241-3213

MARSH, CHARLES DICKEY, b. Chgo., Apr. 26, 1904; B.S., Kenyon Coll., 1927; LL.B., Western Reserve U., 1930. Admitted to Ohio bar, 1930, U.S. Supreme Ct. bar, 1943; asso. firm J.M. Andrus, Cleve., 1931-34; asso. firm Calhoun, McLeod & Fricke, Cleve., 1935-41; partner firm Nicola, Marsh & Gudbranson, Cleve., 1946—; foreman Cuyahoga County (Ohio) Grand Jury, 1961. Mem. Ohio, Cleve. bar assns. Home: 3251 E Monmouth Rd Cleveland Heights OH 44118 Office: 1145 Terminal Tower Cleveland OH 44113 Tel (216) 621-7227

MARSH, DANIEL ALOYSIUS, JR., b. Chgo., July 18, 1941; B.B.A., Loyola U., Chgo., 1964; J.D. with honors, John Marshall Law Sch., 1971. Admitted to Ill. bar, 1971; mgr. real estate Nat. Tea Co., Chgo., 1968-69, asst. to v.p. real estate, 1969-70; pres. D.A. Marsh & Co., Chgo., 1970-71; partner firm Forsberg, Beers & Marsh, Chgo., 1971—; adj. prof. John Marshall Law Sch., 1972—. Mem. Am., Ill., Chgo., NW Suburban bar assns. Recipient Am. Jurisprudence award. Home: Chicago IL 60614 Office: 135 S LaSalle St Chicago IL 60603 Tel (312) 782-1403

MARSH, DANIEL GABE, b. Salem, Oreg., May 14, 1937; B.A., Willamette U., 1959; J.D., U. Oreg., 1962. Admitted to Wash. bar, 1963, since practiced in Vancouver; mem. firm Landerholm, Memovich, Lansverk, Whitesides, Marsh, Morse & Wilkinson, Inc. and predecessors, 1963—; mem. Wash. Ho. of Reps., 1965-73, Wash. Senate, 1973—. Mem. Wash. Adv. Council on State Govt. Productivity, 1974-76. Mem. Am., Wash., Clark County bar assns., Am., Wash. trial lawyers assns. Home: 207 Phoenix Way Vancouver WA 98661 Office: PO Box 1086 Vancouver WA 98660 Tel (206) 696-3312

MARSH, FREDDIE DEAN, b. Pritchett, Tex., Nov. 28, 1939; A.S., Kilgore Coll., 1965; B.S., U. Houston, 1967, J.D., 1970. Admitted to Tex. bar, 1970; individual practice law, Houston, 1970-72; prosecutor City Attys. Office, Corpus Christi, Tex., 1972-73; prosecutor Hildago County (Tex.) Criminal Dist. Attys. Office, Edinburg, 1973-75; prosecutor County Attys. Office, Denton, Tex., 1975—. Mem. Am., Houston, Denton County bar assns., Tex. Dist. and County Attys. Assn., Nat. Dist. Attys. Assn. Home: 1003 Eagle 206 Denton TX 76201 Office: PO Box 718 Denton TX 76201 Tel (817) 387-4519

MARSH, JOHN SUTHERLAND, b. N.Y.C., Mar. 6, 1907; student Niagara U., 1926-27, LL.D., 1955; LL.B., Albany Law Sch., 1931. Admitted to N.Y. bar, 1932; practiced in Niagara Falls, N.Y., 1932-39; dist. atty. Niagara County (N.Y.), 1940-47; judge Niagara County Ct., 1948-53; justice N.Y. Supreme Ct., 8th Jud. Dist., 1953-65, appellate div. 4th dept., 1965-73, presiding justice, 1974—. Mem. Niagara Falls, Niagara County, N.Y. State bar assns. Home: 972 Harrison Ave Niagara Falls NY 14305 Office: Niagara County Bldg Niagara Falls NY 14302 Tel (716) 285-3503

MARSH, MALCOLM FRANCIS, b. Portland, Oreg., Sept. 24, 1928; B.S., U. Oreg., 1952, J.D., 1954. Admitted to Oreg. bar, 1954; partner firm Clark, Marsh & Lindauer, Salem, Oreg.; lawyer-del. 9th Circuit Judges Conv.; dir. Western Security Bank, Salem. Mem. Downtown Devel. Bd., Salem. Mem. Oreg., Marion County (Oreg.), Am. bar assns., Oreg. Assn. Def. Counsel. Office: 880 Liberty St NE Salem OR 97301 Tel (503) 581-1542

MARSH, RABE FERGUSON, JR., b. Greensburg, Pa., Apr. 26, 1905; A.B., Lafayette Coll., 1927; LL.B., U. Pitts., 1930. Admitted to Pa. bar, 1930; individual practice law, Greensburg, Pa., 1930-50; asst. dist. atty. Westmoreland County (Pa.), Greensburg, 1943-50; U.S. dist. judge Western Dist. Pa., Pitts., 1950—, chief judge, 1969-75, sr. judge, 1977—. Home: 905 Summit Ave Greensburg PA 15601 Office: 837 US Courthouse Pittsburgh PA 15219 Tel (412) 644-3557

MARSH, THOMAS, b. Cedar Falls, Iowa, Sept. 20, 1923; B.A., U. Iowa., 1947; J.D., U. Calif., 1952. Admitted to Calif. bar, 1953; individual practice law, Chico, Calif., 1953-55; partner firm Rich, Fuidge, Marsh & Morris, Marysville, Calif., 1955—. Mem. Yuba-Sutter (pres. 1960-61), Am. bar assns., Assn. Def. Counsel (dir. 1975-77), Am. Bd. Trial Advocates, Am. Arbitration Assn. (arbitrator 1965—). Editor Hastings Law Jour., 1951-52. Home: 585 Jones Rd Yuba City CA 95991 Office: 1129 D St Marysville CA 95901 Tel (916) 742-7371

MARSH, THOMPSON GEORGE, b. Lacon, Ill., Mar. 15, 1903; A.B., U. Denver, 1924, LL.B., 1927, M.A., 1931; LL.M., Northwestern U., 1931; S.J.D., Yale, 1935. Admitted to Colo. bar, 1927; mem. faculty law U. Denver, 1927—. Mem. Colo., Denver bar assns. Co-author, editor: American Law of Mining; contbr. articles in field to legal jours. Home: 199 Ash St Denver CO 80220 Office: Coll Law U Denver Denver CO 80204 Tel (303) 753-2654

MARSHALL, CHARLES A., JR., b. Chgo., June 15, 1934; B.A., U. Ill., 1956; J.D., Chgo.-Kent Coll. Law, 1963; Admitted to Ill. bar, 1963, U.S. Supreme Ct. bar, 1965; individual practice law, Chgo. Mem. Am., Ill., Chgo. bar assns., Am. Judicature Soc., Phi Delta Phi. Home: 5740 N Sheridan Rd Chicago IL 60660 Office: 29 S LaSalle St Chicago IL 60603 Tel (312) CE6-7953

MARSHALL, CHARLES EDWARD, b. Chgo., Feb. 19, 1939; B.S., U. Ill., 1961, J.D., Chgo.-Kent Coll. Law, 1963. Admitted to Ill. bar, 1963; mem. firm Marshall & Marshall, Somonauk, Ill., 1964—; states atty. DeKalb County (Ill.), 1970-72. Sec. Sheridan Med. Center, 1966—; bd. dirs. Open Door, Sandwich, Ill., 1974—. Mem. Am., Ill. State, DeKalb County, LaSalle County bar assns. Recipient Jaycees Outstanding Young Man award, 1973. Home: 615 N Sycamore St Somonauk IL 60552 Office: 115 E DeKalb St Somonayk IL 60552 Tel (815) 498-2521 also Sheridan IL Tel (815) 496-2521

MARSHALL, DAVID BARHYDT, b. Sheridan, Wyo., June 22, 1919; B.A., U. Va., 1941, LL.B., 1948. Admitted to Va. bar, 1947; asso. firm Paxson, Williams & Fife, Charlottesville, Va., 1947-51; partner firm Paxson Marshall & Smith, Charlottesville, 1951-73; judge Va. Dist. Ct., 16th Jud. Dist., 1973—; commonwealth's atty. Albemarle County (Va.), 1951, county atty., 1967-71. Pres. Charlottesville Ednl. Found., 1959; bd. dirs. Child & Family Service, Charlottesville. Mem. Va. State Bar (council 1970-73), Va. Bar Assn. (v.p. 1954), Am Judicature Soc., Assn. Va. Dist. Ct. Judges. Office: 606 E Market St Charlottesville VA 22901 (804) 977-1566

MARSHALL, EDMUND GOUCHER, b. Huntington, W.Va., Aug. 8, 1928; A.B., Bethany Coll., 1950; postgrad. W. Va. U., 1950-52; LL.B., U. Richmond, 1954. Admitted to W. Va. bar 1954; partner firm Marshall and St. Clair, Huntington, 1960—. Chmn. Huntington Zoning Bd. Appeals, 1965; bd. trustees Cabell Huntington Hosp., 1973. Mem. Cabell County (pres. 1968), W. Va., Am. bar assns. Office: 523 7th St Huntington WV 25701 Tel (304) 529-2421

MARSHALL, ELLIOTT DE JARNETTE, b. Front Royal, Va., Mar. 5, 1905; LL.B., George Washington U., 1930. Admitted to Va. bar, 1929; mem. firm Weaver, Armstrong & Marshall, Front Royal, 1942-46; judge 17th Jud. Circuit Ct. of Va., Front Royal, 1946-68, 26th Jud. Circuit of Va., 1969-74. Mem. Order of the Coif, Phi Delta Phi. Home: Box 856 Front Royal VA 22630 Office: Ct House Front Royal VA 22630 Tel (703) 365-3681

MARSHALL, F. JOHN, b. Oskaloosa, Iowa, Apr. 13, 1937; B.S., U. N.D. J.D., 1962. Admitted to N.D. bar; partner firm Peterson, McMenamy & Marshall, Grand Forks, N.D., 1962-65; partner firm Letnes & Marshall, Grand Forks, 1965—; 1st asst. states atty. Grand Forks County, 1959-62; spl. counsel Grand Forks County states atty's office, 1963—; atty. city Grand Forks, 1976—. Bd. dirs. Grand Forks Pub. Schs., 1962—, U. N.D. Adv. Bd., 1962—, United Fund, 1962—, United Day Nursery Sch., 1962—, United Hosp., 1962—. Adv. Bd. Mem. Grand Forks, N.D., Am. bar assns., Am. Trial Lawyers Assn. Red River Valley Horse Assn., Grand Forks Police Reserve Assn., Sigma Chi Alumni Assn., Phi Delta Phi. Office: 202 Red River Nat Bank Bldg Grand Forks ND 58201 Tel (701) 772-3408

MARSHALL, FRANK GARFIELD, b. Chgo., Oct. 28, 1894; LL.B., Northwestern U., J.D., 1970; D.H.L., Coll. Jewish Studies, Chgo., 1963. Admitted to Ill. bar, 1917; sr. partner firm Marshall & Marshall, Chgo., 1957—. Founder, Roosevelt U., 1950; chmn. bd. dirs. Spertus Coll. of Judaica. Mem. Chgo., Ill. State (privileged), Am. bar assns. Recipient Bernard G. Semel award Esco fund Am. Assn. Jewish Edn., 1960. Home: 900 N Lake Shore Dr Chicago IL 60611 Office: 10 S LaSalle St Chicago IL 60603 Tel (312) 372-3247

MARSHALL, GEORGE BADGLEY, b. Columbus, Ohio, Apr. 23, 1906; B.A., Ohio State U., 1928, LL.D., 1931; grad. Nat. Coll. State Trial Judges, Reno, Nev., 1966. Admitted to Ohio bar, 1931; practiced in Columbus, 1931-54; mem. Ohio Gen. Assembly, 1939-40, 41-42, 43-44, 47-48, 49-50; mem. Ohio Senate, 1951-52; judge Common Pleas Ct. Franklin County (Ohio), 1954—. Mem. Columbus, Ohio, Am. bar assns., Am. Judicature Soc., Phi Beta Kappa, Delta Sigma Rho, Sigma Alpha Epsilon, Phi Delta Phi. Home: 2175 W Lane Ave Columbus OH 43221 Office: Hall of Justice 369 S High St Columbus OH 43215 Tel (614) 462-3770

MARSHALL, JAMES MARKHAM, II, b. Long Beach, Calif., Aug. 30, 1940; A.B., Whitman Coll., 1962; LL.B., Stanford, 1966. Admitted to Wash. bar, 1966; field atty. NLRB, Seattle, 1966-67; asso. firm McMullen, Brooke, Knapp & Grenier, Seattle, 1967-69, Clodfelter, Lindell & Carr, Seattle, 1969-72; individual practice law, Seattle, 1973; partner firm Preston, Thorgrimson, Ellis, Holman & Fletcher, Seattle, 1973—. Pres., King County Young Democrats, 1969-70. Mem. Am., Wash., Seattle-King County, Fed., Lawyer-Pilots bar assns., Assn. Trial Lawyers Am. Office: Preston Thorgrimson et al 2000 IBM Bldg Seattle WA 98101 Tel (206) MA 3-7580

MARSHALL, JOHN TREUTLEN, b. Macon, Ga., Nov. 1, 1934; B.A., Vanderbilt U., 1956; grad. Naval Justice Sch., 1958; LL.B., Yale, 1962. Admitted to Ga. bar, 1961; partner firm Powel, Goldstein, Frazer & Murphy, Atlanta, 1967—; adj. prof. law Emory U., 1971—; prof. law Atlanta Law Sch., 1969-71; bd. dirs. Atlanta Legal Aid Soc., 1975—; mem. Atlanta Judicial Council, 1975—. Mem. Atlanta (pres. 1974-75, dir. 1971-76), Am. (del.) bar assns., Ga. Def. Lawyers Assn. Mem. editorial bd. Yale Law Jour., 1961-62; participant The Advocates, TV series Pub. Broadcasting System, 1972. Home: Office: 1100 C & S Nat Bank Bldg Atlanta GA 30303 Tel (404) 521-1900

MARSHALL, MERNA BEARMAN, b. Phila., May 27, 1933; B.S., U. Pa., 1955; LL.B., Boston U., 1958. Admitted to Pa. bar, 1959, U.S. Supreme Ct. bar, 1969; since practiced in Phila.; asso. firm Levin, Levin & Levin, 1959-60; individual practice law, 1960-61; asst. U.S. atty. eastern dist. Pa., 1961-71; judge Ct. of Common Pleas Philadelphia County, 1971—; instr. Inst. for Adminstrn. of Justice Temple U., 1975—; mem. regional ct. com. Pa. Gov.'s Justice Commn. Mem. Am., Fed., Pa., Phila. bar assns., Am. Judicature Soc., Pa. Conf. State Trial Judges. Contbr. articles in field to profl. jours. Office: 108 One E Penn Sq Bldg Philadelphia PA 19107 Tel (215) MU6-7358

MARSHALL, NELLIE MARIE, b. Balt.; LL.B., Mt. Vernon Sch. Law, 1939. Admitted to Md. bar, 1940; partner firm Marshall & Marshall, Balt., 1950-68; v.p. George J. Marshall & Sons Corp., Balt., 1964-68; judge Orphans Ct. Balt., 1954-58. Mem. Women's Bar Assn. Baltimore City (pres. 19—), Nat. Assn. Women Lawyers (chmn. Md.), UN League Lawyers, World Peace Through Law Center, Women's Civic League, Internat. Bar Assn., Internat. Bus. and Profl. Women's Conf. (del. Berne, Switzerland), Nat. Women's Party (Md. pres. 1959), Iota Tau Tau. Home: 5969 SW 1st Ct Cape Coral FL 33904 Office: 6537 Baltimore National Pike Baltimore County MD Tel (813) 542-7579

MARSHALL, SCHUYLER B., IV, b. Temple, Tex., Oct. 16, 1945; A.B., U. Tex., 1967, J.D. with honors, 1970. Admitted to Tex. bar, 1970; partner firm Thompson, Knight, Simmons & Bullion, Dallas, 1970—. Dir. Dallas County chpt. Am. Heart Assn., 1974—, Dallas Legal Services, 1974—. Mem. State Bar Tex. (trustee ins. trust, vice chmn. pub. affairs com.), Tex. Assn. Def. Counsel, Dallas, Tex., Am. bar assns., Phi Delta Phi (pres. 1970). Home: 4437 McFarlin St Dallas TX 75205 Office: 2300 Republic National Bank Bldg Dallas TX 75201 Tel (214) 655-7535

MARSHALL, SCOTT OLIVER, b. St. Louis, June 29, 1946; B.B.A. cum laude, U. Mo., Columbia, 1968, J.D., 1971. Admitted to Mo. bar, 1971, U.S. Tax Ct. bar, 1975; sr. tax cons. Peat, Marwick, Mitchell & Co., St. Louis, 1973-75; asso. firm Schramm & Morganstern, St. Louis, 1975-76, Paul H. Schramm, St. Louis, 1976; partner firm Schramm, Pines & Marshall, 1977—. Fin. and accounting officer U.S. Army Petroleum Center, Alexandria, Va. Mem. Bar Assn. Met. St. Louis, Mo. Soc. C.P.A.'s, C.P.A., Mo. Home: 609 Lockwood Ave Webster Groves MO 63119 Office: 120 S Central Ave Clayton MO 63105 Tel (314) 721-5321

MARSHALL, SHEILA HERMES, b. N.Y.C., Jan. 17, 1934; B.A., St. John's U., Bklyn., 1959; LL.B., N.Y. U., 1963. Admitted to N.Y. State bar, 1964, U.S. Supreme Ct. bar, 1967; asso. firm LeBoeuf, Lamb, Leiby & MacRae, N.Y.C., 1963-72, partner, 1973—. Mem. Am., N.Y. State bar assns. Home: 969 Park Ave New York City NY 10028 Office: 140 Broadway New York City NY 10005 Tel (212) 269-1100

MARSHALL, SYLVAN MITCHELL, b. N.Y.C., May 14, 1917; B.A., Coll. City N.Y., 1938; J.D., Harvard, 1941. Admitted to N.Y. bar, 1945, D.C. bar, 1953; asso. firm Garey & Garey, N.Y.C., 1945-51; spl. asst. to chief counsel Office of Price Stblzn., Washington, 1951-53; asso. firm Granik & Marshall, Washington, 1953-58; individual practice law, Washington, 1958-60; partner firm Marshall, Leon, Weill & Mahony, and predecessors, 1960-; spl. ambassador to inauguration Pres. of Mex., 1976; hon. consul of Finland; counsel 1st Fed. Savs. and Loan Assn. Chgo., 1st Fed. Savs. and Loan Assn. Miami (Fla.), 1st Fed. Savs. and Loan Assn. Wis., 1st Fed. Savs. and Loan Assn. Jacksonville (Fla.), Community Fed. Savs., St. Louis, Standard Fed. Savs., Cin., Franklin Soc. Fed. Savs., N.Y.C. Decorated for legal services by govts. of Panama, Finland, Brazil, Iceland, Nicaragua, Mex., Iran. Home: 2929 Ellicott St NW Washington DC 20008 Office: 1825 K St NW Washington DC 20006 Tel (202) 223-9600 also 261 Madison Ave New York City NY 10016 Tel (212) MU 7-5707

MARSHALL, TERRELL, b. Little Rock, July 14, 1908; LL.B., Ark. Law Sch., 1931. Admitted to Ark. bar, 1931, U.S. Supreme Ct. bar, 1938; asso. firm Marshall & Durbin, Little Rock, 1931-35; individual practice law, Little Rock, 1936-60; asso. with Joseph Marshall, Little Rock, 1960—; atty. Pulaski County (Ark.) Legal Aid Bur., 1938-42; trustee Ark. Law Sch., 1949-72. Bd. dirs. Ark. Property Owner's Found., 1948-65. Fellow Ark. Bar Found.; mem. Am. (reporter, contbr. Procedural Reform Survey, 1944-48, standing com. on unauthorized practice of law), Ark. (pres. 1952, exec. sec. 1939-48, standing com. on unauthorized practice of law), Pulaski County (pres. 1945) bar assns., Am. Judicature Soc. Contbg. author: Birds of Arkansas, 1951. Home: 372 Skyline Dr N Little Rock AR 72116 Office: 1012 Pyramid Bldg Little Rock AR 72201 Tel (501) 372-7069

MARSHALL, THOMAS CHARLES, b. Hartford, Conn., Dec. 12, 1941; B.A., Trinity Coll., 1963; J.D., Columbia, 1966. Admitted to Conn. bar, 1966; partner firm Weber & Marshall, New Britain, Conn., 1969—; instr. bus. law Greater Hartford Community Coll. Pres. Berlin Bd. Edn. Mem. Conn., Hartford County, New Britain bar assns. Home: 128 Cider Mill Rd Kensington CT 06037 Office: 24 Cedar St New Britain CT 06051 Tel (203) 225-9463

MARSHALL, THURGOOD, b. Balt., July 2, 1908; A.B., Lincoln U., 1930, LL.D., 1947; LL.B., Howard U., 1933, LL.D., 1954; LL.D., Va. State Coll., 1948, Morgan State Coll., 1952, Grinnell Coll., 1954,

Syracuse U., 1956, N.Y. Sch. Social Research, 1956, U. Liberia, 1960. Brandeis U., 1960, U. Mass., 1962, Jewish Theol. Sem., 1962, Wayne U., 1963, Princeton U., 1963, U. Mich., 1964, Johns Hopkins U., 1966; hon. degree Far Eastern Univ., Manila, 1968, Victoria U. of Wellington, 1968, U. Cal., 1968, U. Otago, Dunedin, New Zealand, 1968. Admitted to Md. bar, 1933; practiced in Balt., 1933-37; asst. spl. counsel N.A.A.C.P., 1936-38, spl. counsel, 1938-50, dir., counsel legal def. and ednl. fund, 1940-61; U.S. circuit judge for 2d Jud. Circuit, 1961-65; solicitor gen. U.S., 1965-67; justice U.S. Supreme Ct., 1967—. Civil rights cases argued include Tex. Primary Case, 1944, Restrictive Covenant Cases, 1948, U. Tex. and Okla. Cases, 1950, sch. segregation cases, 1952-53; visited Japan and Korea to make investigation of ct. martial cases involving Negro soldiers, 1951. Cons. Constl. Conf. on Kenya, London, 1960; rep. White House Conf. Youth and Children. Recipient Spingarn medal, 1946; Living History award Research Inst. Mem. Nat. Bar Assn., N.Y.C. County Lawyers Assn., Am. Bar Assn., Bar Assn. D.C., Alpha Phi Alpha. Home: Falls Church VA 23661 Office: Supreme Ct US Washington DC 20543*

MARSTON, WILLIAM EMMETT, b. Birmingham, Ala., Nov. 11, 1928; B.B.A., U. Miss., 1952, LL.B., 1953. Admitted to Miss. bar, 1953, Tenn. bar, 1955; law clerk to Judge Edwin R. Holmes, U.S. Ct. of Appeals, 5th Circuit, 1953-55; partner firm Martin, Tate, Morrow & Marston, P.C., Memphis, 1955—. Pres., Ole Miss Rebel Club, 1972-73. Mem. Am., Miss., Tenn. bar assns., Memphis and Shelby County (pres.) Tenn. bar assns., Law Alumni U. of Miss. (pres. 1975). Office: 705 Union Planters Nat Bank Bldg Memphis TN 38103 Tel (901) 525-5881

MARTAY, ERWIN LAWRENCE, b. N.Y.C., Oct. 16, 1908; B.S. in Law, Northwestern U., 1930, J.D., 1932. Admitted to Ill. bar, 1932; mem. Ill. Ho. of Reps.; asst. atty. gen. State of Ill., 1952-54; asst. judge Circuit Ct. Cook County, Chgo., 1965—. Active Chgo. Sch. for Retarded Children. Mem. Am., Ill., Chgo., Decalogue bar assns. Office: 1100 S Hamilton St Chicago IL 60612 Tel (312) 633-2036

MARTH, WILLIAM JAMES, b. Fond du Lac, Wis., Dec. 21, 1921; LL.B., U. Wis., 1949, J.D., 1949. Admitted to Wis. bar, 1949; mem. firm Cannon & Marth, West Bend, Wis., 1950-53, firm Marth & Marth, West Bend, 1953-73, firm Marth & Limbach, West Bend, 1973—. Office: 128 N Main St West Bend WI 53095 Tel (414) 334-3483

MARTIN, BARON HAYE, b. Boston, Sept. 14, 1926; A.B., Suffolk U., 1951, J.D., 1957; postgrad. in mgmt. U. Chgo., 1973, Nat. Coll. State Judiciary, 1975; LL.D., Saints Coll. Admitted to Mass. bar, 1958, U.S. Supreme Ct. bar, 1960; spl. asst. atty. gen. Mass., 1973; first asst. gen. counsel Mass. Bay Transit Authority, Roxbury, 1970-76; spl. justice, Roxbury, 1974—. Trustee Mass. Mental Health Found., 1970—; mem. Democratic Ward Com., 1960-70; trustee Emerson Coll., 1971—, Huntington Gen. Hosp., Boston; bd. dirs. Boston council Boy Scouts Am. Mem. Mass. Bar Assn., Mass. Trial Lawyers Assn., Mass. Spl. Justices Assn., Am. Judges Assn. Office: Roxbury Municipal Ct 84 Warren St Roxbury MA 02119

MARTIN, BEAUMONT, b. Washington, Jan. 2, 1936; B.A., George Washington U., 1956, J.D., 1959. Admitted to Tex. bar, 1965; legal officer U.S. Coast Guard, New Orleans, 1959-62; trust officer First and Mchts. Nat. Bank, Richmond, Va., 1962-63; atty. Sinclair Refining Co., Houston, 1963-67; individual practice law, Houston, 1967—. Mem. Am., Houston bar assns., State Bar Tex., Assn. Immigration and Nationality Lawyers. Home: 5719 Jason St Houston TX 77096 Office: 1123 Lehall St Houston TX 77030 Tel (713) 790-1953

MARTIN, BILLY LEE, b. Wetunka, Okla., Apr. 15, 1925; J.D., Loyola U., New Orleans, 1967. County clk. Okmulgee County, Okla., 1950-56; tax agt. Humble Oil & Refining Co. (name changed to Exxon Co. U.S.A. 1972), New Orleans, 1962-72, Houston, 1972-77; admitted to La. bar, 1967, Tex. bar, 1973; asso. firm Boatman & Laub, Okmulgee, Okla., 1977—. Mem. La. State Bar Assn., Tex. State Bar. Named outstanding student in internat. law Loyola U., 1967. Home: 1808 E 10th St Okmulgee OK 74447 Office: 800 Bell St Houston TX 77001 Tel (713) 656-2573

MARTIN, BOE WILLIS, b. Texarkana, Ark., Oct. 6, 1940; B.A. in History, Tex. A. and M. U., 1962; LL.B., U. Tex., 1964; LL.M. in Labor Law and Corp. Law, George Washington U., 1970. Admitted to U.S. Supreme Ct. bar, 1970, Tex. bar, 1964; law clk. to asso. justice Tex. Supreme Ct., 1966-67; asso. firm Law, Snakard, Brown & Gambill, and predecessor, Ft. Worth, 1967-69, 71, partner, 1972; asst. counsel U.S. Senate Labor and Pub. Welfare Com., legis. asst. to Senator Ralph W. Yarborough, 1969-70; asso. firm Stalcup, Johnson, Meyers & Miller, Dallas, 1972-74, partner, 1974—; lectr. So. Meth. U. Sch. Law, 1972, 73, 75. Mem. staff Democratic Presdl. Campaign Com., 1976. Mem. Tex., Am., Fed., Dallas bar assns., Phi Alpha Delta. Home: 9315 Seagrove St Dallas TX 75231 Office: 2001 Bryan Tower Dallas TX 75201 Tel (214) 651-1700

MARTIN, C. RABON, b. Tulsa, July 27, 1944; B.S., U. Tulsa, 1966, LL.B., 1968. Admitted to Okla. bar, 1969, U.S. Supreme Ct. bar, 1973; law clk. to judge U.S. Dist. Ct., No. Dist. Okla., Tulsa, 1967-68; dep. ct. clk. Tulsa County Dist. Ct., 1968; asso. firm Crowe & Thieman, Tulsa, 1969-73; partner firm Baker, Baker & Martin, Tulsa, 1973—; Okla. dir. Nat. Orgn. Reform Marijuana Laws, 1973—. Mem. Okla. Criminal Def. Lawyers Assn. (charter), Lawyer-Pilots Bar Assn. Tel (918) 587-1168

MARTIN, CLARENCE EUGENE, JR., b. Martinsburg, W.Va., Sept. 10, 1909; A.B., Cath. U. Am., 1931, LL.B., 1934. Admitted to W.Va. bar, 1934; mem. firm Martin & Seibert, Martinsburg, 1934-55; individual practice law, Martinsburg, 1955—; mem. W.Va. Senate, 1950-70; pros. atty. Berkeley County (W.Va.), 1940-48; chmn. bd. Mchts. & Farmers Bank, Martinsburg. Fellow Am. Bar Found., Am. Coll. Trial Lawyers; mem. W.Va., W.Va. State, Inter-Am. bar assns., Am. Judicature Soc., Nat. Assn. Ins. Counsel. Home: 107 N Rosemont Ave Martinsburg WV 25401 Office: PO Box K Martinsburg WV 25401 Tel (304) 267-8985

MARTIN, DANIEL EZEKIEL, b. Bluffton, S.C., Apr. 14, 1932; B.S., Allen U., 1954; J.D., S.C. State Coll., 1966; postgrad. Howard U., 1954-55, Wayne State U., 1968. Admitted to S.C. bar, 1966, U.S. Supreme Ct. bar, 1971; dir. Neighborhood Legal Assistance Program, Inc., Charleston, S.C., 1968-72; partner firm Moore & Martin, Charleston, 1973-74; individual practice law, Charleston, 1974—; asst. solicitor 9th Jud. Circuit, 1974—. Mem. S.C. Gov.'s Com. on Energy Council, 1973—; past fin. chmn. Palmetto dist. Coastal Carolina council Boy Scouts Am.; vice chmn. Mini-Parks, Inc., Charleston, Charleston County Bicentennial Com.; past vice chmn. Charleston County Democratic Party; past bd. dirs. Pub. Defender Corp. Charleston County; bd. dirs., legal advisor Project Pride; bd. dirs. Greater Charleston YMCA, Carolina Lowcountry chpt. ARC, S.C. Agy. Vocat. Rehab.; trustee Allen U., Emanuel A.M.E. Ch. Mem. Am., S.C., Charleston County bar assns., Charleston Trident C. of C. (dir.). Recipient Omega Psi Phi Jurisprudence Achievement award, 1974, also numerous civic awards. Home: 117 Gordon St Charleston SC 29403 Office: 61 Morris St Charleston SC 29403 Tel (803) 723-1686

MARTIN, DOUGLAS BOYD, JR., b. Bremerton, Wash., Aug. 22, 1934; B.A., U. Chgo., 1954; M.A., Johns Hopkins, 1956; LL.B., Cornell U., 1961. Admitted to D.C. bar, 1961, Calif. bar, 1964; law clk. U.S. Ct. Appeals, Washington, 1961-62; legal asst. to chmn. SEC, Washington, 1962-64; asso. firm Cotten, Seligman & Ray, San Francisco, 1964-68, partner, 1970—; asst. legal counsel Office of Fgn. Direct Investments, Dept. Commerce, Washington, 1968-69. Mem. com. on sch. dist. orgn. Marin County, Calif., 1974—; trustee Sausalito (Calif.) Sch. Dist., 1972—. Mem. San Francisco Bar Assn. Home: 77 Tomales St Sausalito CA 94965 Office: 1 Maritime Plaza Suite 1400 San Francisco CA 94111

MARTIN, EDWIN MCCAMMON, JR., b. Washington, June 22, 1942; B.A., Harvard U., 1963, LL.B., 1966. Admitted to Mass. bar, 1966; asso. firm Hale & Dorr, Boston, 1966—. Active, Robert F. Kennedy Action Corps, Boston, Hingham (Mass.) chpt. ARC. Mem. Am., Mass., Boston bar assns., Am. Soc. Internat. Law. Home: 48 Whiton St Hingham MA 02043 Office: 28 State St Boston MA 02109 Tel (617) 742-9100

MARTIN, FRANKLIN EDWIN, b. Fayetteville, N.C., Apr. 19, 1938; A.B., U. N.C., Chapel Hill, 1960, J.D., 1967. Admitted to N.C. bar, 1968; asso. firm Newsom, Graham, Strayhorn & Hedrick, Durham, N.C., 1968-72; partner firm Poisson, Barnhill, Butler & Martin, Wilmington, N.C., 1972-74; individual practice law, Wilmington, 1974—. Mem. New Hanover County (N.C.) Democratic Exec. Com., 1974-76. Mem. Am., N.C., New Hanover County bar assns., N.C. State Bar. Office: First Union Nat Bank Bldg Suite 302 PO Box 266 Wilmington NC 28401 Tel (919) 343-0196

MARTIN, GALEN A., b. E. Rainelle, W.Va., Nov. 13, 1927; B.S. in Econs., Berea Coll., 1951; postgrad. U. Tenn., Am. U.; J.D., U. Louisville, 1967. Practice law, Frankfort, Ky. Sec. Knoxville (Tenn.) Area Human Relations Council, 1957-61; exec. dir. Ky. Council on Human Relations, 1956-57; exec. dir. Ky. Commn. on Human Rights, Frankfort, 1961—. Mem. Nat. Assn. Intergroup Relations Ofcls. (pres. 1967-68, gen. council 1970-75), Am., Ky. bar assns., Louisville, Ky. beekeepers assns. Home: 5001 Hopewell Rd Louisville KY 40299 Office: 828 Capital Plaza Tower Frankfort KY 40601 Tel (502) 564-3550

MARTIN, GEORGE JOHN, JR., b. Port Chester, N.Y., June 7, 1942; A.B., Georgetown U., 1964, J.D., 1967. Admitted to N.Y. bar, 1969; asso. firm Mudge Rose Guthrie & Alexander, N.Y.C., 1967-75, partner, 1976—, resident partner Paris office, 1976—. Mem. Am. Bar Assn., Assn. Bar City N.Y., Internat. Bar Assn., Internat. Assn. Lawyers. Home: 9 Villa Sainte Foy Neuilly-Sur-Seine France 92200 Office: 12 rue de la Paix Paris France 75002 Tel 261-57-71

MARTIN, GERALD ARDEN, b. Iowa City, Mar. 3, 1943; B.A., U. Iowa, 1966, J.D., 1969. Admitted to Oreg. bar, 1969; clk. to justice Oreg. Supreme Ct., Salem, 1969-70; asso. firm McCulloch, Dezendorf, Spears & Lubersky, Portland, Oreg., 1970-71; partner firm Gray, Fancher, Holme & Hurley, Bend, Oreg., 1971—. Chmn., Deschutes County (Oreg.) chpt. March of Dimes, 1972-75. Mem. Oreg., Deshutes County bar assns. Contbr. article Iowa Law Rev. Office: 1044 Bond St Bend OR 97701 Tel (503) 382-4331

MARTIN, GRANVILLE HAROLD, b. Columbus, Ohio, Oct. 25, 1900; A.B., Ohio U., 1921; J.D., Ohio State U., 1923. Admitted to Ohio bar, 1924, Fla. bar, 1926; judge municipal ct. Ft. Lauderdale, Fla., 1932-36; individual practice law, Ft. Lauderdale, 1926—. Recipient Founder's Plaque Internat. Swimming Hall of Fame, 1965, award of merit Ohio U., Ohio State U. Alumni Assns., 1971, 73; named Broward County Sportsman of Year, 1969. Home: 2840 N Ocean Blvd Fort Lauderdale FL 33308 Office: 208 SE 6th St Fort Lauderdale FL 33301 Tel (305) 462-3724

MARTIN, HAROLD DAY, b. Rockford, Ill., May 20, 1925; student Beloit Coll., Western Ky. Coll.; LL.B., U. Louisville, 1953. Admitted to Ill. bar, 1953, Ariz. bar, 1963; formerly city atty. Loves Park, Ill.; asst. states atty. Ill., dep. atty. Maricopa County (Ariz.), 1963-68; judge Ariz. Superior Ct., Phoenix, 1968—. Mem. Am., Maricopa bar assns., Delta Theta Phi. Office: 101 W Jefferson St Phoenix AZ 85003 Tel (602) 262-3445

MARTIN, HOWARD WALLACE, b. Golden Meadow, La., Nov. 25, 1940; A.B., U. Southwestern La., 1967; J.D., La. State U., 1970. Admitted to La. bar, 1970; individual practice law, 1970-71; mem. firm Logan & Martin, La., 1971-72; pres. firm Martin & Leonard, Ltd., Lafayette, La., 1973—; congressional intern House Judiciary Com. U.S. Ho. of Reps., 1966-67. Mem. La. State, Lafayette Parish, Fifteenth Judicial Dist. Ct. bar assns., Am., La. trial lawyers assns. Home: 200 Pembroke Ln Lafayette LA 70508 Office: 201 E Main St Box 3705 Lafayette LA 70502 Tel (318) 233-4744

MARTIN, J. RAY, b. Denton, Tex., Dec. 6, 1919; B.S., North Tex. State U., 1942; J.D., Columbia, 1947. Admitted to Ill. bar, 1949, Tex. bar, 1949; practiced in Snyder, Tex., 1949-58; judge Scurry County (Tex.) Ct., 1959-62, Municipal Ct., Amarillo, Tex., 1964, Denton County (Tex.) Ct. of Law, 1971—. Mem. State Bar Assn. Tex. Office: Denton County Courthouse 2d Floor Denton TX 76201 Tel (817) 387-2514

MARTIN, JAMES ADDISON, JR., b. Danville, Va., Nov. 8, 1945; B.A., Duke Univ., 1967; M.A. in Pol. Sci., Brown U.; J.D. with honors, Emory U., 1973. Admitted to Fla. bar, 1973; law clk. Judge Paul H. Roney, 1973-74; partner firm McMullen, Everett, Logan, Marquardt & Cline, Clearwater, Fla., 1974—. Bd. dirs. Family Counseling Center, Pinellas County, Fla., Legal Aid Soc., Clearwater. Mem. Am., Fla., Clearwater bar assns. Contbr. articles in field to profl. jours. Home: 841 Bay Esplanade Clearwater Beach FL 33515 Office: PO Box 1878 400 Cleveland St Clearwater FL 33517 Tel (813) 441-8966

MARTIN, JAMES ARTHUR, b. Elmhurst, Ill., Apr. 5, 1944; B.S., U. Ill., 1965; M.S. in Math., U. Mich., 1966, J.D., 1969. Admitted to Mich. bar, 1972; asst. prof. law U. Mich., 1970-73, asso. prof. 1973-75, prof., 1975—. Mem. Com. to Revise and Consolidate Mich. Ct. Rules. Mem. Mich. Bar Assn. Home: 1105 Granger Ann Arbor MI 48104 Office: 1039 Legal Research Bldg Ann Arbor MI 48109 Tel (313) 764-2399

MARTIN, JAMES RICHARD, b. Bklyn., Nov. 14, 1937; B.A., Rutgers U., 1959; J.D., U. Houston, 1968. Admitted to Tex. bar, 1968, Calif. bar, 1970; law clk. to judge U.S. Ct. Appeals, 5th Circuit, Houston, 1968-69; partner firm Gibson, Dunn & Crutcher, Los Angeles, 1969—; lectr. in field. Contbr. articles Houston Law Rev., editor-in-chief, 1967-68. Office: 515 S Flower St Los Angeles CA 90071 Tel (213) 488-7482

MARTIN, JAMES ROBERT, JR., b. Greenville, S.C., Nov. 30, 1909; LL.B., Washington and Lee U., 1931. Admitted to S.C. bar, 1931; practice in Greenville, 1931-44; judge 13th Jud. Circuit S.C., 1944-61; U.S. judge Eastern and Western dists. S.C., 1961-67; chief judge U.S. dist. S.C., 1967—. Mem. S.C. Ho. of Reps. from Greenville County; 1943-44. Mem. Am., S.C., Greenville County bar assns. Home: 401 Crescent Ave Greenville SC 29605 Office: Federal Bldg and US Courthouse Greenville SC 29603*

MARTIN, JAMES THOMAS, b. Corinth, Miss., Mar. 5, 1936; B.E. in Chem. Engring., Vanderbilt U., 1958; LL.B., U. Va., 1964, J.D., 1970. Admitted to D.C. bar, 1965, U.S. Supreme Ct. bar, 1968; law clk. firm Pennie, Edmonds, Morton, Taylor & Adams, summer 1964; asso. firm McLean, Morton & Boustead, Washington, 1964-67, partner firm Birch, Kramer, Martin & Birch, Washington, 1967-72, Martin, Ferguson, Baker, Washington, 1972-75; individual practice law, Washington, 1975—; asso. editor Law Notes, Am. Bar Assn., 1969-71. Pres., Washington Vanderbilt Club, 1968-70, Miss. Soc. of Washington, 1972-73. Mem. Am., D.C. bar assns., Am. Patent Law Assn., Am. Chem. Soc. Contbr. articles to legal jours. Office: 1000 Connecticut Ave NW Washington DC 20036 Tel (202) 296-3650

MARTIN, JOHN CHARLES, b. Durham, N.C., Nov. 9, 1943; B.A., Wake Forest Coll., 1965, J.D., 1967. Admitted to N.C. bar, 1967; asso. firm Haywood, Denny & Miller, Durham, 1970-72, partner, 1973—; mem. Durham City Council, 1975—. Mem. Am., N.C. bar assns., Am. Judicature Soc. Home: 3808 Swarthmore Rd Durham NC 27707 Office: 201 W Main St Durham NC 27701 Tel (919) 682-5747

MARTIN, JOHN FRANCIS, b. N.Y.C., Apr. 2, 1922; B.A., N.Y. U., 1947; LL.B., Bklyn. U., 1951. Admitted to N.Y. bar, 1951, U.S. Supreme Ct. bar, 1960; since practiced in N.Y.C., partner firm Martin, Klein & Romano, 1952-54, individual practice law, 1954-69, partner firm Marshall & Martin, 1969-71, individual practice law, 1971-75, 76—; partner firm Martin & Filipowski, 1975-76. Mem. Am. Arbitration Assn., N.Y. State Trial Lawyers Assn., N.Y. State Bar Assn. Office: 342 Madison Ave New York City NY 10017 Tel (212) 279-6995

MARTIN, JOHN OVIATT, b. Cleve., Mar. 21, 1937; B.A., St. Mary's Coll., Winona, Minn., 1958; LL.B., J.D., Case-Western Res. U., Cleve., 1961. Admitted to Ohio bar, 1961, U.S. Supreme Ct. bar, 1966, U.S. Dist. Ct. bar So. Dist. Ohio, 1967; spl. agt. FBI, 1961-66; individual practice law, Fairborn, Ohio, 1966—. Pres. Miami Valley Lung Assn., Dayton, Ohio, 1973-74, Fairborn Lions Club, 1974. Mem. Ohio, Greene County (pres. 1974), Fed. bar assns., Fairborn C. of C. Home: 3851 Saint Andrews St Fairborn OH 45324 Office: 26 N Wright St Fairborn OH 45324 Tel (513) 878-8649

MARTIN, JOHN WESLEY, b. Omaha, Ga., Sept. 29, 1936; B.A. in History, Central State U., 1965; J.D., Toledo U., 1969. Admitted to Ohio bar, 1969; atty. Cleve. Legal Aid Soc., 1969-71; asst. pros. atty. Cuyahoga County (Ohio), 1971-74; individual practice law, Cleve., 1974—; arbitrator for steel industry and United Steelworkers Union. Mem. Am., Ohio, Cuyahoga County, Greater Cleve., Nat. bar assns., Assn. Trial Lawyers Am., John Harlan Law Club, Phi Alpha Delta. Reginald Heber Smith Community Lawyer fellow U. Pa., 1969. Home: 1365 East Blvd Cleveland OH 44106 Office: 1949 E 105th St Cleveland OH 44106

MARTIN, JOHN WILLIAM, b. Oakland, Calif., Apr. 27, 1913; A.B., U. Calif., 1935, LL.B., 1938. Admitted to Calif. bar, 1938, Ohio bar, 1939; asso. firm Robert L. Lamb, San Francisco, 1946-50; partner firm Dunne, Dunne & Phelps, San Francisco, 1950-63; Bledsoe, Smith, Cathart & Johnson, San Francisco, 1963-65, Price, Martin & Crabtree, Modesto, Calif., 1965—. Mem. Nat. Assn. R.R. Trial Counsel, Am., Stanislaus County (past pres.), Calif. bar assns., No. Calif. Def. Counsel Assn., Am. Bd. Trial Advocates. Home: 910 Yale Ave Modesto CA 95350 Office: PO Box 3307 Modesto CA 95353 Tel (209) 522-5231

MARTIN, JOSEPH, JR., b. San Francisco, May 21, 1915; A.B., Yale, 1936, LL.B., 1939. Admitted to N.Y. bar, 1940, Calif. bar, 1946; asso. firm Caldwalader, Wickersham & Taft, N.Y.C., 1939-41; partner firm Wallace, Garrison, Norton & Ray, San Francisco, 1946-55; partner firm Pettit, Evers & Martin, San Francisco, 1955-70, 73—; gen. counsel FTC, Washington, 1970-71; U.S. rep. Geneva Disarmament Conf., 1971-76; mem. Pres.'s Adv. Com. on Arms Control & Disarmament, 1974—. Pres., San Francisco Pub. Utilities Commn., 1956-60; treas. Calif. Republican Party; 1956-58; Rep. Nat. Committeeman for Calif., 1960-64. Mem. Am. Bar Assn., State Bar Calif. Recipient FTC Ofcl. Commendation for Outstanding Service as Gen. Counsel, 1973; Distinguished Honor award ACDA, 1973. Home: 2580 Broadway St San Francisco CA 94115 Office: 600 Montgomery St San Francisco CA 94111 Tel (415) 434-4000

MARTIN, LAWRENCE N., JR., b. White Plains, N.Y., Mar. 15, 1936; B.S., Fordham U., 1958, LL.B., 1961. Admitted to N.Y. bar, 1961, U.S. Supreme Ct. bar, 1971; enforcement atty. SEC, N.Y.C., 1961-63; asst. dist. atty. N.Y. County, N.Y.C., 1964-65; asst. dist. atty. Westchester County (N.Y.), 1968-69, judge, 1974—; sr. atty. criminal div. Westchester Legal Aid Soc., 1965-68; individual practice law, White Plains, 1969-74. Mem. Am., Westchester County bar assns., Criminal Cts. Bar Assn. Westchester. Tel (914) 682-3010

MARTIN, LEONARD ELIOT, b. Webster Grove, Mo., Aug. 22, 1917; B.A., Harvard, 1939; postgrad. Washington U., St. Louis, 1942. Admitted to Mo. bar, 1942; asso. firm Rassieur, Long & Yawitz, St. Louis, 1946-51; partner firm Stockham, Roth, Buder & Martin, St. Louis, 1952-61; partner firm Buder & Martin, St. Louis, 1962-63; individual practice law, Webster Groves, Mo., 1964-66; magistrate, 3d Dist. St. Louis County, Mo., 1967—. Mem. Am., Mo., St. Louis, St. Louis County bar assns., Am. Judicature Soc., Magistrates and Probate Judges Assn. Home: 217 Hazel Webster Groves MO 63119 Office: 7900 Carondelet Ave Clayton MO 63105 Tel (314) 889-2692

MARTIN, MALCOLM WOODS, b. St. Louis, Feb. 21, 1912; A.B., Yale, 1933; LL.B., St. Louis City Coll., 1941. Admitted to Mo. bar, 1941, U.S. Supreme Ct. bar, 1949; partner firm Peper, Martin, Jensen, Maichel & Hetlage, and predecessors, St. Louis, 1941—. Pres., St. Louis Bd. Edn., 1969-71; sec. Higher Edn. Co-ordinating Council, St. Louis, 1967—, chmn., 1973—. Mem. Am., Mo., St. Louis bar assns., Am. Judicature Soc. Home: 300 Mansion House Center apt 2210

Saint Louis MO 63102 Office: 720 Olive St Saint Louis MO 63101 Tel (314) 421-3850

MARTIN, PATRICK VINCENT, b. Bklyn., July 12, 1938; B.S., U.S. Mcht. Marine Acad., 1960; LL.B., Columbia, 1964. Admitted to N.Y. State bar, 1964, N.J., 1972, U.S. Supreme Ct. bar, 1969; asso. firm Poles, Tublin, Patestides & Stratakis, Middlesex, N.J., 1964-70, partner, 1970—. Mem. Am., N.J. bar assns., Maritime Law Assn., New York County Lawyers Assn. Address: 338 High St Middlesex NJ 08846

MARTIN, PETER WILLIAM, b. Syracuse, N.Y., Apr. 28, 1947; B.A., U. Notre Dame, 1969, J.D., 1972. Admitted to N.Y. bar, 1972, Fla. bar, 1973; staff atty. Bristol Labs. div. Bristol Myers Corp., Syracuse, 1972-73; asso. firm Nelson Stinnett Surfus Payne Hesse & Cyril, Sarasota, Fla., 1973-75; partner firm Stinnett Surfus & Martin, Sarasota, 1975—. Mem. Am., Fla., Sarasota County, N.Y. State bar assns., Am., N.Y., Fla. trial lawyers assns. Home: 1313 Hillview Dr Sarasota FL 33579 Office: 2072 Ringling Blvd Sarasota FL 33578 Tel (813) 366-3383

MARTIN, RICHARD LOUIS, b. El Reno, Okla., Sept. 14, 1914; LL.B., LaSalle Extension U. Admitted to Ark. bar, 1947; dep. pros. atty., 1948-50; partner firm Martin, Vater & Snyder, and predecessors, Ft. Smith, Ark., 1950—; clk. Municipal Ct., 1939-42, Circuit Ct., 1947-48. Mem. exec. bd. Westark Area council Boy Scouts Am., 1958-68; chmn. bd. First Christian Ch., Ft. Smith, 1958-60, 72-73; pres. Twin City Council Chs., 1960-62; bd. dirs., exec. com. Christian Chs. (Disciples of Christ) in Ark., 1970—, mem. gen. bd. and adminstrv. com., 1970—; mem. regional bd. NCCJ, 1972—; mem. bd. govs. Nat. Council Chs., 1976—; chmn. Sebastian County (Ark.) campaign Am. Cancer Soc., 1976; bd. dirs. Christian Ch. Found. Fellow Am. Coll. Probate Counsel; mem. Am., Ark., Sebastian County bar assns., Am. Judicature Soc., Western Ark. Estate Planning Council (pres. 1965-66). Recipient Silver Beaver award Boy Scouts Am. Home: 7718 Westminister Pl Fort Smith AR 72903 Office: 505 First Nat Bank Bldg Fort Smith AR 72901 Tel (501) 782-4028

MARTIN, ROGER LESLIE, b. Webster, N.Y., Jan. 12, 1924; B.S. in Engring., U. Mich., 1948; LL.B., Fordham U., 1951. Admitted to Fla., D.C., Va. bars; corporate patent atty. Kaiser Aluminum and Chem. Corp., Baton Rouge, 1951-52, Washington, 1953-55, Harshaw Chem. Co., Cleve., 1955-56; partner firm Baldwin & Martin, Jacksonville, Fla., 1957-63; individual practice law, Orlando, Fla., 1963—. Mem. govt. study commn., Seminole County, Fla., 1973. Mem. Am. Patent Law Assn. Home: 322 Broadview Ave Altamonte Springs FL 32701 Office: PO Box 604 697 E Altamonte Dr Altamonte Springs FL 32701 Tel (305) 830-0733

MARTIN, SAMUEL THOMAS, b. Lynchburg, Va., Sept. 27, 1913; J.D., Washington and Lee U., 1938. Admitted to Va. bar, 1937; individual practice law, Lynchburg, 1938-54, partner firm Martin, Taylor, Fralin & Freeman and predecessor, Lynchburg, 1954—; commr. accounts Circuit Ct. Lynchburg; mem. Va. Ho. of Dels., 1944-48. Mem. Am., Va., Lynchburg (pres. 1960) bar assns., Lynchburg Kiwanis Club (pres. 1947). Home: 1644 Spottswood Pl Lynchburg VA 24503 Office: 1003 Church St Lynchburg VA 24504 Tel (804) 845-3461

MARTIN, SCOTT ALFRED, b. Grand Rapids, Mich., Apr. 21, 1946; B.A., U. Calif., Riverside, 1968; J.D., U. Calif. Hastings Coll. Law, San Francisco, 1973. Admitted to Calif. bar, 1973; asso. firm Reid, Babbage & Coil, Riverside, 1974; mem. firm Hillsinger & Costanzo, Los Angeles, 1974—. Mem. Am., Orange County bar assns., Orange County Trial Lawyers assn., So. Calif. Def. Counsel Assn., Barristers Orange County. Office: 2232 SE Bristol St Suite 204 Santa Ana CA 92707 Tel (714) 754-0855

MARTIN, THOMAS FRANCIS, b. Huron, S.D., Dec. 4, 1940; B.A., Huron Coll., 1962; J.D. cum laude, U. S.D., 1965. Admitted to S.D. bar, 1965; since practiced in Brookings, S.D., partner firm McCann & Martin, 1965-68; v.p. firm McCann, Martin & Mickelson, 1968—; city atty. Brookings, 1965-66; states atty. S.D., 1967-70. Mem. S.D. State Bar, S.D., Am. trial lawyers assns., Am. Bar Assn., Brookings C. of C. (pres. 1972). Home: 1913 Derdall Dr Brookings SD 57006 Office: 317 6th Ave Brookings SD 57006 Tel (605) 692-6163

MARTIN, WILLARD GORDON, JR., b. Boston, Dec. 12, 1937; A.B., Bates Coll., 1959; LL.B., Harvard U., 1962. Admitted to N.H. bar, 1962; asso. firm Nighswander, Lord, Martin & Killkelley, Laconia, N.H., 1962—; bar examiner, N.H. Bar, 1972—; asso. justice Laconia Dist. Ct., 1973—; city solicitor Laconia, 1963-66; atty. Belknap County (N.H.), 1967-68; rep. to N.H. Gen. Ct., 1969-70; mem. N.H. Judicial Council, 1971-75. Mem. Belknap County, N.H., Am. bar assns. Home: RFD 4 Glidden Rd Laconia NH 03246 Office 1 Mill Plaza Laconia NH 03246 Tel (603) 524-4121

MARTIN, WILLIAM CABINESS, b. Roba, Ala., June 17, 1911; A.B., George Washington U., 1936, J.D., 1938; J.D.S., Nat. U., 1939. Admitted to Fla. bar, 1939, D.C. bar, 1939, U.S. Supreme Ct. bar, 1946; asst. adminstr. patronage com. U.S. Ho. of Reps., 1937-38, appropriations com., 1938-40; asst. corp. counsel D.C., 1940-42; dep. commr. Fla. Indsl. Commn., Miami, 1946-48. Active Big Bros., Dade County, Fla., 1959—; chmn. troop 7 Boy Scouts Am., Coral Gables, Fla., 1972—; chmn. Dade County Dem. Exec. Com., 1960-64. Mem. Fed. (v.p. S. Fla. chpt. 1960), Dade County (pres. 1959-60) bar assns. Home: 1261 Coral Wy Coral Gables FL 33134 Office: Suite 808 Douglas Centre 2600 Douglas Rd Coral Gables FL 33134 Tel (305) 442-2355

MARTIN, WILLIAM DISKIN, b. Pitts., Mar. 1, 1920; B.A., St. Francis Coll., 1942; J.D., Duquesne U. Admitted to Pa. bar, 1957; partner firm Nairn & Martin, Pitts., 1957—; asst. dist. atty. Allegheny County, 1957—; dir. Allegheny Regional Narcotic Task Force, 1972-75; solicitor Allegheny County Ancient Order of Hibernians, 1976—. Home: 2483 Summit St Bethel Park PA 15102 Office: 500 Law and Finance Bldg Pittsburgh PA 15219 Tel (412) 281-0750

MARTIN, WILLIAM OSCAR, JR., b. Glendale, Calif., Jan. 25, 1948; B.A., Monmouth (Ill.) Coll., 1970; J.D., U. Ill., Champaign, 1973. Admitted to Ill. bar, 1973; asso. firm Samuels, Miller, Schroeder, Jackson & Sly, Decatur, Ill., 1973—; asso. prof. bus. law Richland Community Coll., Decatur, 1974—. Atty., bd. dirs. Boys' Club Decatur. Mem. Am., Ill. (civil practice and procedure sect. com.), Macon County bar assns. Contbr. to Chgo. Daily Law Bull. Home: 219 Austin Ave Decatur IL 62522 Office: PO Box 1359 Decatur IL 62525 Tel (217) 429-4325

MARTINDALE, EVERETT OTTO, b. Little Rock, Mar. 27, 1947; B.A., Ouachita Bapt. U., 1970; J.D., U. Ark., 1974. Admitted to Ark. bar, 1974; asso. firm Matthews, Portle, Osterloh & Weber, Little Rock, 1974—. Active Big Bros. Pulaski County, 1970—, 1st Bapt. Ch., Little Rock; coach Little Rock YMCA, 1971. Mem. Am., Ark., Pulaski County bar assns. Home: 306 Midland St Little Rock AR 72205 Office: 10121 Rodney Parham Rd Little Rock AR 72209 Tel (501) 224-4000

MARTINDALE, JAMES VAUGHAN, b. Chgo., Oct. 16, 1894; student Bklyn. Poly. Prep. Sch., 1911. Vice pres., sec. Martindale-Hubbell, Inc., Summit, N.J., 1930-46, pres., treas., 1947-57, dir., 1930—, chmn. bd. dirs., 1943-46, 57—; pres. Bar Register Co., Inc., Summit, 1947-57, dir., 1935—; cons. to Survey Legal Profession, 1949-52. Home: 189 Rugby Rd Brooklyn NY 11226 Office: 1 Prospect St Summit NJ 07901*

MARTINEZ, ANTONIO CLAUDIO, b. Santiago, Dominican Republic, Sept. 7, 1926, came to U.S., 1933, naturalized, 1938; A.B., Hunter Coll., 1950; LL.B., Bklyn. Law Sch., 1956, J.D., 1956; Admitted to N.Y. bar, 1956, U.S. Supreme Ct. bar, 1966; law clk. firm William L. Standard, N.Y.C., 1950-55; treasury enforcement agt. Treasury Dept., N.Y.C., 1956; partner firm Kahn and Martinez, N.Y.C., 1957-59; individual practice law, N.Y.C., 1960—. Mem. Am., N.Y. State, Inter Am., Western Hemisphere (pres. 1975-77) bar assns., N.Y. County Lawyers Assn., Puerto Rican Bar Assn. N.Y. (dir. 1967-68), Fed. Bar Council, Assn. Immigration and Nationality Lawyers (dir. 1977-80), Am. Soc. Internat. Law. Home: 62-33 Dieterle Crescent Rego Park NY 11374 Office: 324 W 14th St New York City NY 10014 Tel (212) 989-0404

MARTINEZ, MARIO J., b. El Paso, Tex., Sept. 5, 1935; A.B., U. Tex., El Paso, 1957; LL.B., U. Tex., 1963. Admitted to Tex. bar, 1963; asst. U.S. atty. Western Dist. Tex., 1965-67, U.S. commr., 1967-71, U.S. magistrate, 1971-73; pres. Mario J. Martinez, Inc., El Paso, 1974—. Pres. Catholic Counseling Service, 1973; bd. dirs. Campfire Girls, 1971—. Mem. Am., El Paso County (dir. 1973-75) bar assns., State Bar Tex. (mem. grievance com. 1974—), Am., Tex. trial lawyers assns. Office: 600 Myrtle St El Paso TX 79901 Tel (915) 532-2638

MARTINEZ, MEL R., b. Cuba, Oct. 23, 1946; B.A., Fla. State U., 1969, J.D., 1973. Admitted to Fla. bar, 1973; partner firm Billings, Frederick, Wooten & Honeywell, Orlando, Fla., 1973—; adminstrv. asst. to sec. of state State of Fla., 1969-70; trustee Orange County Legal Aid Soc., 1975—. Mem. Am., Fla., Orange County bar assns., Assn. Trial Lawyers Am., Fla. Acad. Trial Lawyers, Fla. State U. Boosters, Inc (dir.), Fla. State U. Coll. Law Alumni Assn. (dir.), Phi Delta Phi. Home: 1005 Lancaster Dr Orlando FL 32806 Office: 236 S Lucerne Circle Orlando FL 32801 Tel (305) 843-7060

MARTINEZ, ROBERT PAUL, b. Bklyn., Sept. 8, 1946; A.B., Boston Coll., 1967; J.D., N.Y. U., 1970. Admitted to N.J. bar, 1970; individual practice law, Trenton, 1970-74; dep. atty. gen., spl. asst. to atty. gen. State of N.J., Trenton, 1974—; gen. counsel N.J. Sch. Bds. Assn., 1970-74. Mem. N.J. Pub. Broadcast Authority, 1974-77; chmn. Gov.'s Task Force on Casino Gambling, 1976-77. Mem. Am., N.J. bar assns. Co-author: Basic School Law, 1970. Home: 105 Renfrew Ave Trenton NJ 08618 Office: State House Annex Trenton NJ 08625 Tel (609) 292-1570

MARTINEZ-CID, RICARDO, b. Havana, Cuba, May 9, 1950; B.A., U. Fla., 1970, J.D., with honors, 1972. Admitted to Fla. bar, 1973; asso. firm Steel, Hector & Davis, Miami, Fla., 1972-76, Martinez-Cid & Suarez, 1977—. Mem. Internat., Am., Fla. bar assns., Order of Coif, Phi Beta Kappa. Office: SE First National Bank of Coral Way Bldg 1699 Coral Way Suite 315 Miami FL 33145 Tel (305) 856-7976

MARTINI, EILEEN TULIPAN, b. Jersey City, Sept. 29, 1944; B.A., Jersey City State Coll., 1965; J.D., Rutgers U., 1972. Admitted to N.J. bar, 1972; law clk. Hudson County Legal Services, 1970-72; individual practice law, Jersey City, 1972—; asst. county counsel Hudson County, N.J., 1976—; legislative counsel to mayor city Jersey City, 1972-76; mem. legislative action com. N.J. Conf. Mayors, 1972—, staff rep. of mayor Jersey City to U.S. Conf. Mayors, 1974-76. Trustee Jersey City State Coll., 1976—; legal counsel NOW, Jersey City chpt. 1974—; mem. state bd. trustees N.J. Civil Liberties Union, 1975—; bd. dirs. Hudson County Legal Services Inc., 1974—; mem. Hudson County Women's Polit. Caucus, 1974—. Mem. N.J., Hudson County bar assns. Office: 26 Journal Square Jersey City NJ 07306 Tel (201) 963-0444

MARTINIS, JOSEPH A., b. N.Y.C., Mar. 6, 1906; LL.B., Fordham U., 1928. Admitted to N.Y. State bar, 1930; partner firm Martinis & Kraf, N.Y.C., 1930-50; mem. N.Y. State Legislature from Bronx, 1947-50; magistrate, N.Y.C., 1950-59; justice Ct. of Spl. Sessions, 1959-60; acting judge County Ct. of Bronx County, N.Y., 1960-63; criminat ct. judge, N.Y.C., acting justice Supreme Ct., N.Y.C., 1963—. Mem. Bronx County Bar Assn. Contbr. articles to profl. jours. Home: 3616 Henry Hudson Pkwy Riverdale NY 10463 Office: 100 Centre St New York City NY 10013

MARTINSON, LLOYD GAINES, b. St. Louis, Nov. 22, 1919; B.S. in Bus., U. Idaho, 1949, J.D., 1950; Admitted to Idaho bar, 1950; individual practice law, Moscow, Idaho, 1950—; probate judge Latah County Ct., Idaho, 1952-53, pros. atty., 1954-57. Mem. Phi Alpha Delta. Home: 1122 E B St Moscow ID 83843 Office: 124 E 3d St Moscow ID 83843

MARTLAND, RONALD, b. Liverpool, Eng., Feb. 10, 1907; B.A., U. Alta. (Can.), Edmonton, 1926, LL.B., 1928, LL.D., 1964; B.A. Oxford (Eng.) U., 1930, B.C.L., 1931, M.A., 1935. Called to Alta. bar, 1932, created King's counsel, 1943; practiced law in Edmonton, 1932-48; justice Supreme Ct. of Can., 1958—; hon. prof. faculty of law U. Alta. Mem. Canadian Bar Assn. Home: 55 Placel Rd Rockcliffe Park ON Canada Office: Supreme Ct of Canada Wellington St Ottawa ON K1A OJ1 Canada*

MARTONE, MICHAEL ROBERT, b. Glen Cove, N.Y., Sept. 27, 1934; B.S., Lehigh U., 1956; LL.B., N.Y. Law Sch., 1959, J.D., 1959. Admitted to N.Y. bar, 1959; asso. firm Suozzi & Sordi, Glen Cove, N.Y., 1959-60; partner firm Nicholas A. Sordi, Glen Cove, 1960-61; dep. county atty. Nassau County (N.Y.), Mineola, 1961-68, sr. dep. county atty., 1968-70; individual practice law, Mineola, 1970-72; v.p. firm Koeppel Sommer Lesnick & Martone, Mineola, 1973—; spl. atty. City of Glen Cove, 1974; condemnation atty. Glen Cove Urban Renewal Agy., 1973—; lectr. Adelphi U., Hofstra U.; sec. Nassau County Legal Aid Soc., 1968—. Chmn. Glen Cove Bd. Fire Commrs., 1959-71; commr. pub. safety City of Glen Cove, 1971-73. Mem. Nassau, North Shore lawyers, Nassau, N.Y., Am. bar assns., Columbia Soc. Real Estate Appraisers. Home: 37 Oak Ln Glen Cove NY 11542 Office: 220 Old Country Rd Mineola NY 11501 Tel (516) 747-6300

MARTY, LAWRENCE A., b. Leigh, Nebr., June 17, 1926; student Wayne State U., 1944-46, Creighton Sch. Law, 1946-48; J.D., U. Wyo., 1954. Admitted to Wyo. bar, 1954; individual practice, Green River, Wyo., 1954-67; partner firm Marty & Clark, Green River, 1967-74; partner firm Marty & Ragsdale, Green River, Wyo., 1975—; judge Green River Municipal Ct., 1956-58; U.S. Magistrate Dist. Wyo., 1958—. Active Republican State Com. Sweetwater County (Wyo.), alt. del. Rep. Nat. Conv., 1964. Mem. Am., Wyo., Sweetwater County bar assns., Wyo. State Bar Commnrs. Office: Box 231 Green River WY 82935 Tel (307) 875-3235

MARVEL, JAMES K., b. Webster City, Iowa, Oct. 4, 1947; B.A., U. Iowa, 1970, J.D., 1973. Admitted to Iowa bar, 1973; asso. firm Karr, Karr & Karr, Webster City, 1973-75; individual practice law, Pella, Iowa, 1975—; instr. in bus. law Central Coll., Pella, 1975—. Pres. Webster City United Fund, 1973-75. Mem. Marion County (Iowa), Iowa State, Am. bar assns. Home: 1302 Main St Pella IA 50219 Office: 716 Main St Pella IA 50219 Tel (515) 628-4513

MARVIN, LAWRENCE WARREN, JR., b. Sacramento, Dec. 25, 1927; B.A., U. Calif., Berkeley, 1949; J.D., U. San Francisco, 1953. Admitted to Calif. bar, 1954; research atty. Calif. 3d Dist. Ct. Appeal, 1955-58; dep. dist. atty. Sacramento County, 1958; asso. firm Fitzwilliam, Memering, Stumbos & DeMers, Sacramento, 1958-62; sr. partner firm Barrett, Marvin, Good & Newlan, Sacramento, 1962-69, Redding, Calif., 1965-69; judge Municipal Ct., Sacramento, 1969—, presiding judge, 1974-75; founding pres. Barristers Club of Sacramento, 1956, sec., 1958; panelist Inst. Calif. Center Judicial Edn. and Research, 1975, chmn. planning com., 1976. Active Boy Scouts Am., 1966-68; v.p. Land Park Little League, Sacramento, 1968. Mem. Conf. Calif. Judges. Office: Sacramento County Courthouse 720-9th St Sacramento CA 95814 Tel (916) 440-5511

MARWEDEL, WARREN JOHN, b. Chgo., July 3, 1944; B.S., U.S. Merchant Marine Acad., 1966; J.D., Loyola U., 1972. Admitted to Ill. bar, 1972, Fed. bar, 1972, U.S. Supreme Ct., 1976; mem. firm Bradley, Eaton, Jackman & McGovern, Chgo., 1972-77, Haskell and Perrin, Chgo., 1977—. Mem. Chgo., Ill., Am. bar assns., Maritime Law Assn. Contbr. article to profl. jour. Home: 6625 N Kilpatrick Ave Lincolnwood IL 60646 Office: 218 S La Salle St Chicago IL 60604

MARX, RICHARD BENJAMIN, b. N.Y.C., June 17, 1932; B.A., Hobart Coll., 1954; LL.B., N.Y. U., 1957. Admitted to N.Y. bar, 1958, U.S. Supreme Ct. bar, 1964, Fla. bar, 1965, U.S. Ct. Appeals bar for 5th Circuit, 1965, 2d Circuit, 1975, U.S. Dist. Ct. bar for So. Dist. Fla., 1965, So. Dist. N.Y.; individual practice law, Miami, Fla., 1965-72, 75—; partner firm Frank, Strelkow and Marx, Miami Beach, Fla., 1965-72, Marx and Squitero, 1972-75; municipal judge City of Sweetwater, Fla., 1966; arbitrator N.Y. Stock Exchange, 1972—. Mem. Am., Dade County, Fla. bar assns., Am. Judicature Soc., Am. Trial Lawyers Assn., Acad. Fla. Trial Lawyers. Contbr. articles to profl. jours. Home: 6280 SW 116th St Miami FL 33156 Office: 2951 S Bayshore Dr Suite 7A Miami FL 33133 Tel (305) 443-4832

MARYE, EDWARD AVONMORE, JR., b. Madisonville, Ky., Apr. 1, 1927; LL.B., U. Ky., 1951. Admitted to Ky. bar, 1951, U.S. Tax Ct. bar, 1975; individual practice law, Versailles, Ky., 1951-68; Mt. Sterling, Ky., 1968—; spl. counsel Ky. Dept. Revenue, 1956-57; asst. atty. gen. Ky. Dept. Hwys., 1957-60; city atty. City of Versailles, 1961-65; judge Versailles City Ct., 1966-67, Mt. Sterling City Ct., 1973-74; county atty. Woodford County (Ky.), 1967-68; judge pro-tem Montgomery County (Ky.) Ct., 1975—; mem. Gov. Ky. Spl. Com. on Water Resources, 1969. Del. Lexington (Ky.) Diocese Episcopal Conv., 1967, 69, 71, 73, 75; alt. del. Gen. Conv. Episc. Ch., Mpls.-St. Paul, 1976. Mem. Am., Ky. (ho. of dels. 1968), Woodford County (pres. 1961-62), Montgomery County bar assns., 21st Jud. Dist. Pub. Defenders (chmn. 1973—), Phi Delta Phi, Phi Kappa Tau (nat. pres. 1975—). Office: 50 Broadway Mount Sterling KY 40353 Tel (606) 498-2430

MARZETTI, LAWRENCE ANTHONY, b. Jamaica, N.Y., Feb. 17, 1944; B.A. in Econs., Boston Coll., 1966; J.D., Georgetown U., 1970. Admitted to Md. bar, 1970, Washington bar, 1971; partner firm Allen & Marzetti, Oxon Hill, Md., 1972—. Mem. Am., Md. State, Prince George's County bar assns. Home: 13007 Venango Rd Oxon Hill MD 20022 Office: 6188 Oxon Hill Rd Oxon Hill MD 20021 Tel (301) 839-3600

MARZULLA, ROGER JOSEPH, b. Glendale, Calif., Aug. 12, 1947; B.A., U. Santa Clara, 1968; J.D., Santa Clara Law Sch., 1971. Admitted to Calif. bar, 1972, U.S. Supreme Ct. bar, 1975; partner firm Mager & Matthews, San Jose, Calif., 1971—; prof. internat. law San Jose State U., 1975. Mem. Italian-Am. Bicentennial Comm. Mem. Am., Calif., Santa Clara bar assns., Am., Calif., Santa Clara trial lawyers assns. Editorial bd. Santa Clara Law Rev. Office: Suite 600 Bank of America Bldg 12 S 1st St San Jose CA 95113 Tel (408) 298-0456

MARZULLI, JOHN A., b. Newark, June 12, 1923; B.S., Seton Hall U., 1950; LL.B., Rutgers U., 1948, J.D., 1968. Admitted to N.J. bar, 1948; individual practice law, Newark, 1948-66; judge Essex County (N.J.) Dist. Ct., 1966-68, presiding judge, 1968-71; judge Essex County Ct., 1971-74, Superior Ct., 1974—. Mem. Am., N.J. State, Essex County bar assns. Home: 102 Summit Ave Upper Montclair NJ 07043 Office: New Courts Bldg Newark NJ 07102

MASCHER, GILBERT ERNSTINE, b. Indpls., Dec. 17, 1945; B.S. in Mgmt. and Adminstrn., Ind. U., 1967; J.D., 1973. Admitted to Ind. bar, 1973; chief hearing officer legal div. Ind. Dept. Revenue, Indpls., 1973-74; asst. corp. counsel City of Indpls., 1976—; partner firm Elrod & Elrod, Indpls., 1975—. Pres. Beta of Sigma Pi Found., Inc., 1972—. Mem. Am., Ind., Indpls. bar assns. Office: 803 1st Federal Bldg Indianapolis IN 46204 Tel (317) 637-2527

MASCOLO, FREDERIC E., b. Waterbury, Conn., July 24, 1929; B.S., Seton Hall U., 1951; LL.B., Georgetown U., 1953. Admitted to Conn. bar, 1954; partner firm Mascolo, Mascolo, Rinaldi & Carolan, P.C., Waterbury, Conn., 1953—; judge Conn. Probate Ct., Dist. of Waterbury, 1971—; pres., chief judge Probate Assembly and Judges of the State of Conn., 1975—. Comptroller City of Waterbury, 1964-66; pres. Waterbury Baseball, 1973—. Mem. Am., Conn., Waterbury bar assns. Home: 47 Shiring Ln Waterbury CT 06708 Office: 835-12 Wolcott St Waterbury CT 06705 Tel (203) 574-5300

MASERITZ, GUY B., b. Balt., June 5, 1937; B.A., Johns Hopkins, 1959, M.A. in Econs., 1961; LL.B., U. Md., 1966. Admitted to Md. bar, 1966, D.C. bar, 1968, U.S. Supreme Ct. bar, 1975; atty. SEC, 1966-70; counsel SEC Instnl. Investor Study, 1971; asst. gen. counsel Am. Life Ins. Assn., 1971-73; atty. evaluation sect. antitrust div. Dept. Justice, Washington, 1974-76, chief legislative unit, 1976—; lectr. econs. U. Md., 1967-71. Atty. Legal Aid Soc., 1968. Chmn. election monitoring com. Village of Wilde Lake, Columbia, Md., 1971. Mem. Am., D.C. bar assns. Recipient Outstanding Performance award Dept. Justice, 1975, 77; editorial staff Md. Law Rev.; author: Dept. of Justice Report on the Pricing and Marketing of Insurance, 1977. Home: 10510 Green Mountain Circle Columbia MD 21044 Office: 10th and Pennsylvania Ave Washington DC 20532 Tel (202) 739-2497

MASETTO, SANDRA LYNNE, b. Phoenix, Sept. 4, 1945; B.A., U. Ariz., 1963; M.A., 1968; J.D., Ariz. State U., 1971. Admitted to Ariz. bar, 1971; mem. firm Fredrick E. Kallof, Phoenix, 1971-76; spl. asst. to Gov., Ariz., 1976—; mem. Maricopa County Fair Commn., 1976—, Commn. on Status of Women, Phoenix, 1975—. Mem. Maricopa County Assn. Govt's. (criminal planning com., 1974—), Bus. & Profl. Women, Ariz., Maricopa County, Ariz. bar assns. Home: 5721 N 19th Dr Phoenix AZ 85015 Office: Ariz State Capitol Phoenix AZ 85007

MASIN, JEFF STUART, b. Bronx, N.Y., Feb. 14, 1947; B.A., Rutgers U., 1968, J.D., 1971. Admitted to N.J. bar, 1971, U.S. Supreme Ct. bar, 1976; law sec. to judge appellate div. N.J. Superior Ct., 1971-72; asst. prosecutor Atlantic County (N.J.), 1972-76; asso. firm Archer, Greiner & Read, Haddonfield, N.J., 1976—. Mem. Am., N.J., Atlantic, Camden County bar assns., Asst. Prosecutors Assn. N.J. Contbr. article to legal jour. Home: 128 Henfield Ave Cherry Hill NJ 08003 Office: 1 Centennial Sq Haddonfield NJ 08033 Tel (609) 795-2121

MASINTER, ALLAN HOWARD, b. Huntington, W.Va., Dec. 9, 1927; A.B., W.Va. U., 1950, J.D., 1966. Admitted to W.Va., bar, 1966; partner firm Lewis Ciccarello Masinter & Friedberg, and predecessors, Charleston, 1968—. Mem. Am., W.Va., Kanawha County bar assns., Am., W.Va. (pres. 1977—) trial lawyers assns., Lawyer-Pilots Bar Assn. Office: 6th floor L & S Bldg 812 Quarrier St Charleston WV 25301 Tel (304) 343-8891

MASINTER, EDGAR MARTIN, b. Huntington, W.Va., Jan. 2, 1931; A.B., Princeton U., 1952; LL.B., Harvard U., 1955. Admitted to D.C. bar, 1955, N.Y. bar, 1958; asso. firm Simpson Thacher & Bartlett, N.Y.C., 1957-66, partner, 1966—. Mem. Am. Bar Assn., Assn. Bar City N.Y.

MASINTER, EDWIN MICHAEL, b. Roanoke, Va., Aug. 11, 1937; B.S., Washington and Lee U., 1958, LL.B. magna cume laude, 1961; LL.M., N.Y. U., 1962. Admitted to Va. bar, 1961, Ga. bar, 1962; since practiced in Atlanta, asso. firm Hansell, Post, Brandon & Dorsey, 1962-64, partner, 1965—. Mem. Am., Ga., Atlanta bar assns., Lawyers Club Atlanta. Home: 560 Twin Springs Rd NW Atlanta GA 30327 Office: 3300 1st Nat Bank Tower Atlanta GA 30303 Tel (404) 581-8148

MASLIN, HARVEY LAWRENCE, b. Chgo., Oct. 22, 1939; B.S. in Pub. Adminstrn., U. Ariz., 1961, J.D., 1964. Admitted to Ariz. bar, 1964, Calif. bar, 1966; jr. partner firm Maslin, Rotundo & Maslin, Sherman Oaks, Calif., 1966-67; v.p., gen. counsel, asst. sec., mgr. internat. dept. Western Temporary Services, Inc., San Francisco, 1967—; dir. Western Staff Services (U.K.) Ltd., London, Western Girl (N.Z.) Ltd., Aukland. Mem. Am., Ariz., Calif. bar assns., Phi Alpha Delta. Contbr. articles to personnel mgmt. mags. Home: 611 Creekmore Ct Walnut Creek CA 94598 Office: 101 Howard St Western Temporary Services San Francisco CA 94105 Tel (415) 981-8480

MASON, ARTHUR DAVID, b. Cambridge, Mass., Mar. 13, 1941; B.S. in Indsl. and Labor Relations, Cornell U., 1963; J.D., Boston Coll., 1966. Admitted to Mass. bar, 1966, D.C. bar, 1973; asso. firm Stadfeld, Prague & Henkoff, 1968-69; atty. SEC, 1969-71; asso. firm Gadsby & Hannah, 1971-72; partner firm Dickstein, Shapriro & Morin, Washington, 1972—; cons. Pres.'s Commn. on Review of Nat. Policy Towards Gambling. U.S. del. to WHO. 1976; candidate for Congress 4th Dist. Mass., 1976; New Eng. bd. dirs. B'nai B'rith Anti-Defamation League; profl. chmn. Mass. United Way; Mass. benefit dir. Heart Fund. Mem. Am., Fed., D.C., Boston bar assns. Recipient Meritorious Service award Italian-Am. Civil League Am., 1976; Distinguished Service award Internat. Brotherhood Police Officers, 1975. Home: 177 Buckminster Rd Brookline MA 02146 Office: 2101 L St NW Washington DC 20037 Tel (202) 785-9700

MASON, ERNEST EDWARD, b. Gainestown, Ala., Mar. 19, 1904; B.A., U. Fla., 1925, J.D., 1928. Admitted to Fla. bar, 1928; since practiced in Pensacola, Fla., individual practice law, 1928-41; judge Ct. of Record of Escambia County, 1941-60, 1st Jud. Circuit Ct. Fla., 1960—; mem. Fla. Legislature, 1930-32; city atty., 1933-41. Pres., Am. Lung Assn., 1969-70; chmn. Pensacola chpt. ARC, 1944-45. Recipient Will Ross medal 1973. Mem. Am. Bar Assn. Recipient Good Govt. award Fla. Jaycees, 1959. Home: 1525 E Lakeview Ave Pensacola FL 32503 Office: County Ct House PO Box 12007-32589 Pensacola FL 32501 Tel (904) 433-2421

MASON, GEORGE JEFFERSON, III, b. Dallas, Aug. 11, 1947; B.B.A., Baylor U., 1969, J.D., 1972; student Hebrew U., Jerusalem, Israel, 1970. Admitted to Tex. bar, 1972; asso. firm Lane, Savage, Counts and Winn, Dallas, 1973—; election inspector Tex. Sec. State, Dallas County, 1975-76. Mem. Tex., Dallas bar assns., Delta Theta Phi. Home: 10406 Estate Ln Dallas TX 75238 Office: 3330 Republic National Bank Bldg Dallas TX 75201 Tel (214) 741-3633

MASON, HARRY GEORGE, b. Bklyn., Apr. 28, 1921; student Bowling Green State U., 1938-39, 48-49; LL.B. cum laude, St. Johns U., Bklyn., 1951; LL.M. in Taxation, N.Y. U., 1952; postgrad. in accounting and mgmt. Rutgers U., 1953-55. Admitted to N.Y. bar, 1951, U.S. Supreme Ct. bar, 1960, U.S. Tax Ct. bar, 1966, Fla. bar, 1972; counsel, asst. sec. Tung-Sol Electric, Inc., (now Studebaker-Worthington Inc.), Newark, 1956-63; sr. tax atty. Am. Can Co., Greenwich, Conn., 1963-70; tax counsel GAC Corp., Miami, Fla., 1970-71; dir. taxes Gen. Devel. Corp., Miami, 1972—; adv. bd. Tax Mgmt., Inc.; dir., treas. Fed. Excise Tax Council. Mem. Tax Execs. Inst. (pres. South Fla. chpt. 1971-72, chmn. subcom. on depletion and depreciation), Am., N.Y. bar assns., N.J., Conn. mfrs. assns., Asso. Industries N.Y., N.Y. Tax Soc. Home: 1461 Mendavia Ave Coral Gables FL 33146 Office: 1111 S Bayshore Dr Miami FL 33131 Tel (305) 350-1288

MASON, JOHN L., b. Cin., Dec. 9, 1921; B.B.A., U. Cin., 1947, J.D. Admitted to Ohio bar, 1948; pres. Ct. Index Press, Inc., Cin., 1973—, Anderson Pub. Co., 1974—. Mem. Ohio, Cin. bar assns. Office: 646 Main St Cincinnati OH 45201 Tel (513) 421-4393

MASON, JOSEPH CROWDER, JR., b. Norfolk, Va., Sept. 4, 1928; B.Ch.E., N.C. State U., 1952; M.Ch.E., Villanova U., 1960; J.D., Temple U., 1962. Admitted to Pa. bar, 1963, Ill. bar, 1966, U.S. Supreme Ct. bar, 1973; patent atty. Sun Oil Co., Phila., 1963; mgr. contracts, 1964; sr. patent atty. Celanese Corp., Charlotte, N.C., 1965; gen. patent atty. UOP, Inc., Des Plaines, Ill., 1966-69, counsel office of the pres. UOP Process div., 1969-74, gen. counsel litigation, 1974—. Mem. citizens fin. com. Dist. 103 Sch. Bd., Lincolnshire, Ill. Mem. Am. Inst. Chem. Engrs., Am., Ill. bar assns., Am. Patent Law Assn., Licensing Execs. Soc. Recipient Albert M. Cohen award for outstanding service to Temple Law Sch., 1962. Home: 8 Anglican Ln Lincolnshire Deerfield IL 60015 Office: 20 UOP Plaza Des Plaines IL 60016 Tel (312) 391-2521

MASON, LESLIE LONGSTREET, JR., b. Charleston, W.Va., Dec. 8, 1926; student Purdue U., Lafayette, Ind., 1944-45, 47-48; LL.B., Washington and Lee U., 1951. Admitted to Va. bar, 1954; practiced law in Powhatan, Va., 1955-74; judge Powhatan County (Va.) Ct., 1956-74, Va. Dist. Ct., 11th Jud. Dist., 1974—. Home: The Glebe PO Box 1 Powhatan VA 23139 Tel (804) 598-3221

MASON, MEARLE DELBERT, b. Nowata, Okla., Mar. 1, 1921; B.A., Pittsburg (Kans.) State Coll., 1943; J.D., U. Mich., 1949. Admitted to Kans. bar, 1949; partner firm Hill & Mason, Wichita, Kans., 1950—; atty. City of Mulvane, Kans., 1971—; municipal judge City of Wichita, 1973—; pres. Prepaid Legal Services Kans., 1973-74. Mem. Westside Kiwanis, Wichita (pres.), Pleasant Valley Lions Club, Wichita (pres.), Kans. Trial Lawyers Assn., Kans., Wichita (pres. 1975-76) bar assns. Home: 3109 N St Clair Wichita KS 67204 Office: 810 W Douglas Suite C Wichita KS 67203 Tel (316) 265-3247

MASON, MICHAEL GENE, b. Cin., Mar. 21, 1943; B.B.A. cum laude, U. Cin., 1965, J.D., 1968. Admitted to Ohio bar, 1968; sr. tax accountant Haskins & Sells, Cin., 1969-72; asst. prof. accounting and bus. law U. Cin., 1972—; staff cons. Minn. Systems Research, Inc. (Mpls.). Mem. Am. Bar Assn., Am. Inst. C.P.A.'s, Ohio Soc. C.P.A.'s. Home: 8004 Higgins Ct Cincinnati OH 45242 Office: 568 French Hall University of Cincinnati Cincinnati OH 45221 Tel (513) 475-5906

MASON, MILTON DONALD, b. Twin Valley, Minn., Oct. 5, 1904; B.A., Macalester Coll., 1926; J.D., William Mitchell Coll. Law, 1932. Admitted to Minn. bar, 1933; partner firm Dailey, Mason & Mason, (later Mason & Mason), Mankato, Minn., 1933-49; atty. Blue Earth County, Minn., 1939-49; judge Minn. Dist. Ct., Mankato, 1949-74; served Minn. Supreme Ct., St. Paul, 1972. Bd. dirs. YMCA, Mankato, 1938-52, Salvation Army, 1968—. Mem. Am., Minn. bar assns., Am. Judicature Soc., Inst. Jud. Adminstrn., Nat. Conf. State Trial Judges (former regional rep., del.), Minn. County Atty's. Assn. (former pres.), Minn. Dist. Judges' Assn. (former pres.). Home: 2021 Roe Crest Dr Mankato MN 56001 Office: Courthouse Mankato MN 56001 Tel (507) 625-3031

MASON, RICHARD DEAN, b. Sickles, Okla., Aug. 2, 1906; B.S., U. Okla., 1929, A.B., 1931, E.E., 1931; M.S., Mass. Inst. Tech., 1931; LL.B., George Washington U., 1935. Admitted to D.C. bar, 1935, Ill. bar, 1938; engr. Gen. Electric Co., 1929-31, mem. patent dept., 1931-35, atty. 1935; atty. Hazeltine Corp., N.Y.C., 1936; mem. firm Davis, Lindsey, Smith & Shonts, Chgo., 1937-43, firm Miller, Dodds & Mason, Chgo., 1944-48; partner firm Mason, Kolehmainen, Rathburn & Wyss, Chgo., 1948—; lectr. patent law U. Okla., 1949-50; advisor to research depts. U. Ariz., Ariz. State U., U. N.Mex., 1974—. Mem. Am., Ill., Chgo. bar assns., Chgo. Patent Law Assn., Ill. C. of C., Phi Kappa Psi, Sigma Tau, Phi Delta Phi. Home: 970 Green Bay Rd Winnetka IL 60093 Office: 20 N Wacker Dr Chicago IL 60606 Tel (312) 346-1677

MASON, ROBERT LEE, b. Dallas, Jan. 22, 1936; B.A., U. Tulsa, 1960, LL.B., 1963. Admitted to Okla. bar, 1963; asso. firm Wheeler, Wheeler & Wheeler, Tulsa, 1963-64; partner firm Mason & Mason, Tulsa, 1965-75; individual practice law, Tulsa, 1975—; dept. ct. clk, Tulsa County, Tulsa, 1960-63. Mem. Am., Okla. bar assns., Nat., Okla. assns. trial lawyers. Home: 8410 E 25th Pl Tulsa OK 74129 Office: 704 Beacon Bldg Tulsa OK 74103 Tel (918) 583-1104

MASON, SHANNON TAYLOR, JR., b. Norfolk, Va., Dec. 13, 1933; B.A., Old Dominion U., 1959; B.C.L., Marshall-Wythe Sch. Law, 1962. Admitted to Va. Supreme Ct. of Appeals bar, 1962, U.S. Dist. Ct. bar for Eastern Dist. Va., 1962; law clk. to Hon. Walter H. Hoffman, U.S. Dist. Ct. for Eastern Dist. Va., 1962-63; partner firms Preston, Preston, Wilson & Mason, Norfolk and Newport News, Va., 1963-72, Ferguson & Mason, Newport News, 1972—; substitute judge Newport News Gen. Dist. Cts., 1972—. Bd. visitors Old Dominion U. Mem. Norfolk-Portsmouth, Newport News, Va. State, Am. bar assns., Va. State Bar, Va. Trial Lawyers Assn. Home: 13 Moyer Rd Newport News VA 23602 Office: 225 28th St Newport News VA 23607 Tel (804) 245-3843

MASON, WILLIAM CLARENCE, b. Fayetteville, Tenn., Feb. 17, 1936; B.A., David Lipscomb Coll., 1958; J.D., Vanderbilt U., 1961. Admitted to Tenn. bar, 1961; partner firm Womack & Mason, Fayetteville, 1964—. Mem. Tenn. Bd. Pardons, Paroles and Probation, 1964-67; mayor City of Fayetteville, 1976—. Mem. Am., Tenn., Fayetteville bar assns., Am. Trial Lawyers Assn. Home: 1226 Huntsville Hwy Fayetteville TN 37334 Office: 311 E Market St Fayetteville TN 37334

MASON, WILLIAM ERNEST, b. Oak Park, Ill., July 16, 1919; student Ill. Inst. Tech., 1937-38, U. Ill., 1946-47; LL.B., George Washington U., 1949. Admitted to Ill. bar, 1949, U.S. Supreme Ct. bar, 1963; atty. Pioneer Publishing Co., Oak Park, 1950-58; asst. States' Atty. Cook County, Ill., 1958-60; atty. Park Dist. Oak Park, 1960-72; individual practice law, Oak Park, Ill., 1960—. Mem. Am., Ill. State, Chgo., West Suburban (pres. 1973) bar assns., Am. Judicature Soc. Home: 546 Fern Ave Elmhurst IL 60126 Office: 840 S Oak Park Ave Oak Park IL 60304 Tel (312) 383-6626

MASSA, JOSEPH ANTHONY, JR., b. Warren, Pa., July 12, 1941; B.A. in Economics, U. Notre Dame, 1963; J.D., Cleve. State U., 1968. Admitted to Pa. bar, 1969; individual practice law, Warren, Pa., 1969—; solicitor Warren County Sch. Dist., 1973—, Youngsville (Pa.) Borough, 1971—; pub. defender 37th Judicial Dist. Pa., 1969—; instr. criminology Indiana U. Pa., 1972—. Mem. Warren County Jail Adv. Com., 1971; bd. dirs. Warren Sheltered Workshop, 1970. Mem. Warren County, Pa., Am. bar assns., Pa. Trial Lawyers Assn., Nat. Coll. Criminal Defense Atty.'s, Nat. Pub. Defenders Assn., Pa. Borough Solicitor's Assn., Pa. Sch. Bd. Solicitors Assn. Home: 108 Monroe St Warren PA 16365 Office: Penn Bank Bldg Warren PA 16365 Tel (814) 723-4522

MASSEL, ELIHU SAUL, b. Bklyn., May 3, 1940; B.A., Alfred U., 1962; J.D., N.Y. U., 1965; Admitted to N.Y. State bar, 1966, U.S. Supreme Ct. bar, 1970; individual practice law, N.Y.C., 1972—; law guardian Legal Aid Soc. Family Ct. Br., N.Y.C., 1966-67; asso. firm Henry Abrams, N.Y.C., 1967-69; asst. atty. gen. N.Y. State Dept. Law, 1969-72. Mem. Assn. Immigration and Nationality Lawyers (chmn. N.Y. chpt. 1976-77), Am., N.Y. State, Queens County bar assns., Assn. Bar City N.Y. Bd. dirs. Am. Youth Hostels Inc., 1970—; bd. dirs. N.Y. ch Met. N.Y. Council Am. Youth Hostels Inc., 1969—, pres. 1971-74; bd. dirs. N.Y. Chpt. Leukemia Soc., 1976—. Home: 46 Carman Rd Scarsdale NY 10583 Office: 122 E 42nd St New York City NY 10017 Tel (212) OX 7 0133

MASSEY, ALBERT PAUL, JR., b. Phila., Jan. 27, 1940; B.S. in Econs., Villanova U., 1961, J.D., 1964. Admitted to Pa. bar, 1965, U.S. Supreme Ct. bar, 1970; individual practice law, West Chester, Pa., 1964-66; partner firm Riley & Massey, Paoli, Pa., 1966-69, firm Lentz, Riley, Cantor, Kilgore & Massey, Paoli, 1969—. Bd. dirs. Bryn Mawr (Pa.) Hosp., 1970—, Daemion House, Berwyn, Pa., 1972—, Paoli Fire Co., 1975—, Main Line C. of C., 1975—; fin. chmn. Republican Party of Chester County (Pa.), 1976—. Mem. Chester County, Pa. (chmn. sect. young lawyers 1974-75, ho. of dels. 1976—), Am. bar assns., Villanova U. Law Alumni Assn. (pres. 1970), Upper Main Line Condrs. Assn. (dir. 1974—). Bd. editors Villanova Law Rev., 1962-64. Office: 30 Darby Rd Paoli PA 19301 Tel (215) 647-3310

MASSEY, BERT V., II, b. Brownwood, Tex., Oct. 3, 1943; B.A., U. Tex., 1967, J.D., 1969. Admitted to Tex. bar, 1969; atty. Vet.'s Land Bd. Tex., Austin, 1969-70; asso. firm Baker, Foreman & Boudreaux, Dallas, 1970-72; partner Brown County Abstract Co., Brownwood, 1972—; individual practice law, Brownwood, 1972—; mayor pro tem City of Brownwood, 1976—. Bd. dirs. Heart of Tex. council Girl Scouts U.S.A., 1975—, Brown County Cancer Soc., 1976—. Mem. Am., Brown County (sec.-treas. 1975—), Brownwood bar assns., Tex. Land Title Assn. (chmn. legis. com. 1976—), Brownwood C. of C. (dir. 1974—). Office: PO Box 819 303 N Center Ave Brownwood TX 76801 Tel (915) 646-6591

MASSEY, FRANK AUBREY, b. Ellis County, Tex., Nov. 28, 1911; student pub. schs., Fort Worth. Admitted to Tex. bar, 1937; partner firm Massey, Mobley Turner & Hudspeth, Abilene, Tex., 1937-43; individual practice law, Ft. Worth, 1945-53; chief justice Ct. Civil Appeals, 2d Dist., Ft. Worth, 1953—. Mem. Ft. Worth City Planning Bd., 1957-58. Mem. State Bar Tex., Tex. Jud. Conf. Home: 5101 Curzon St Fort Worth TX 76107 Office: Civil Courts Bldg Fort Worth TX 76102 Tel (807) 334-1166

MASSEY, GARY EARL, b. Lakeland, Fla., Nov. 3, 1946; B.S., U. Fla., 1968, J.D., 1971. Admitted to Fla. bar, 1971; asso. firm Henderson, Franklin, Starnes & Holt, Ft. Myers, Fla., 1971-73; asso. firm James C. Fisher, Altamonte Springs, Fla., 1973-74; partner firm Brock, Massey, Weldon & Baum, Altamonte Springs, 1974—; city atty. Lake Mary, Fla., 1975—, Winter Springs, Fla., 1975—. Chmn. human rights advocacy com. East Central Fla. region Sertoma Internat., 1974-75; bd. dirs. Seminole County Legal Aid Soc., 1976—. Mem. Am. Arbitration Assn., Am., Fla., Seminole County bar assns. Home: 1720 Lake Waumpi Dr Maitland FL 32751 Office: 355 E Semoran Blvd Altamonte Springs FL 32701 Tel (305) 834-8111

MASSEY, THOMAS CADE, b. San Angelo, Tex., Mar. 5, 1931; B.A., U. Tex., 1959, J.D., 1960. Admitted to Tex. bar, 1960; city atty. City of Graham (Tex.), 1960-63, 64-65; partner firm Logan Lear Massey & Gossett, San Angelo, 1966-74; individual practice law, San Angelo, 1974—. Mem. Tex. Ho. of Reps., 1972—, San Angelo Commn. on Status of Women, 1970-72; active Am. Cancer Soc., 1965-67. Mem. Tex., Tom Green County bar assns. Home: 1909 Douglas Dr San Angelo TX 76901 Office: 107 S Irving St San Angelo TX 76901 Tel (915) 653-2448

MASSMAN, JOSEPH ROY, b. Corpus Christi, Tex., Oct. 12, 1943; A.B., Carroll Coll., 1966; J.D., U. Miss., 1972. Admitted to Miss. bar, 1972, Mont. bar, 1973; clk. to Justice Daly, Mont. Supreme Ct., 1972-73; counsel Mont. local govt. study commn., 1973; tax counsel Mont. Dept. Revenue, Helena, 1974-76; individual practice law, Helena, 1976—. Mem. Mont., Helena bar assns., Phi Alpha Delta. Home: 1426 Boulder Ave Helena MT 59601 Office: Box 804 Helena MT 59601 Tel (406) 442-2111

MASTERS, ALBERT EDWARD, b. Dallas, June 3, 1945; B.A., North Tex. State U., 1966; J.D., So. Meth. U., 1969. Admitted to Tex. bar, 1969; asso. firm Fannin and Harper, Dallas, 1969; with JAGC, USN, 1970-74; asso. firm W. Doyle Elliott, Friona, Tex., 1976—; city atty. City of Friona, 1976—. Mem. Dallas County, Am., Parmer County (Tex.) bar assns. Recipient Russell Baker Moot Ct. award, 1967. Home: 37 1300 N Walnut St Friona TX 79035 Office: 901 Main St Friona TX 79035 Tel (806) 247-2778

MASTERSON, BERNARD JOSEPH, b. Chgo., Mar. 10, 1919; B.B.A., U. Fla., 1941, LL.B., 1952. Admitted to Fla. bar, 1952; mem. firm Masterson, Meros & Lloyd, and predecessors, 1952-60, firm Masterson, Rogers & Patterson, and predecessors, St. Petersburg, Fla., 1960—. Mem. Fla. Med. Malpractice Commn., 1975—. Fellow Am. Coll. Trial Lawyers; mem. Am. Judicature Soc., Am., Fla., St. Petersburg bar assns., Acad. Fla. Trial Lawyers (pres. 1975-76). Home: 416 Villa Grande St Petersburg FL 33707 Office: 447 Third Ave North St Petersburg FL 33701 Tel (813) 896-3641

MASTERSON, WILLIAM ANTHONY, b. N.Y.C., June 25, 1931; B.A., U. Calif., Los Angeles, 1953, J.D., 1958. Admitted to Calif. bar, 1959, U.S. Supreme Ct. bar, 1965; asso. firm Sheppard, Mullin, Richter & Hampton, Los Angeles, 1958-63, partner, 1963—; supr. corporate litigation Litton Industries, Inc., Beverly Hills, Calif., 1966-68. Fellow Am. Coll. Trial Lawyers; mem. Assn. Bus. Trial Lawyers (pres. 1975-76), Order of Coif. Office: 333 S Hope St Los Angeles CA 90071 Tel (213) 620-1780

MASTOR, GEORGE CONSTANDINE, b. Bemidji, Minn., Dec. 2, 1925; B.S. in Law, U. Minn., 1949, LL.B., 1952. Admitted to Minn. bar, 1952, since practiced in Mpls.; partner firm Mastor and Mattson, 1953—. Mem. Minn. (sec. 1970-74, pres. 1975-76), Hennepin County (pres. 1968-69) bar assns., Am. Right of Way Assn. (pres. Tri-State chpt. 1962). Home: 7421 Kellogg Ave Edina MN 55435 Office: Peavey Bldg Minneapolis MN 55402*

MASTRANGELO, JOSEPH NICHOLAS, b. N.Y.C., July 12, 1914; student N.Y. U., 1931-35; J.D., Fordham U., 1940. Admitted to N.Y. bar, 1942; asso. atty. Workmen's Compensation Bd., N.Y.C., 1954—, referee, 1954-71. Home: 72 Barrow St New York City NY 10014 Office: 2 World Trade Center New York City NY 10047 Tel (212) 488-3095

MATAN, EUGENE LOUIS, b. Chgo., May 29, 1931; B.A., Ohio State U., 1953, J.D. summa cum laude, 1958. Admitted to Ohio bar, 1958; mem. firm Matan, Rinehart & Smith, Columbus, 1975—. Mem. Am., Ohio, Columbus bar assns., Ohio Acad. Trial Lawyers, Am.,

Franklin County (trustee) trial lawyers assns., Phi Alpha Delta. Office: 16 E Broad St Columbus OH 43215 Tel (614) 228-2678

MATEER, DON METZ, b. Evanston, Ill., July 29, 1945; B.A., U. Mich., 1967; J.D., U. Ill., 1971. Admitted to Ill. bar, 1971, U.S. Dist. Ct. No. Dist. Ill. bar, 1972, U.S. Ct. Appeals 7th Circuit bar, 1974; asso. firm Gilbert, Powers, Mateer & Erickson, and predecessor, Rockford, Ill., 1971-75, partner, 1975—; dir. Gases & Arc Supply, 1973—; arbitrator Am. Arbitration Assn., 1976—. Mem. Am., Ill., Winnebago County bar assns. Home: 5823 Hoylake Dr Rockford IL 61107 Office: 3106 N Rocton Ave Rockford IL 61103 Tel (815) 968-7536

MATHENY, TOM HARRELL, b. Houston; B.A., Southeastern La. U., 1954; J.D., Tulane U., 1957. Admitted to La. bar, 1957; partner firm Pittman & Matheny, Hammond, La., 1957—; trust counsel First Guaranty Bank; v.p. So. Brick Supply, Inc.; past mem. faculty Holy Cross Coll., New Orleans, Southeastern La. U. Dist. lay leader Methodist Ch., Baton Rouge Dist., 1960-64; bd. dirs., chmn. fin. com. La. Interch. Conf.; mem. Council on Ministries, La. Ann. Conf.; mem. Commn. on Higher Edn. La. Area Council; chmn. Conf. Bd. of Laity, 1965—; mem. Dist. council Boy Scouts Am., 1957-66, chmn. advancement com., 1960-64, mem. exec. bd. Istrouma council, 1966—; chmn. crime control com. Goals for La.; pres. Masonic Youth Found. La., 1970-71, La. Alumni Council, Tangipahoa Parish Mental Health Assn.; pres., bd. dirs. La. Mental Health Assn., 1973—; sec. Chep Morrison Scholarship Found.; bd. dirs. Tangipahoa Parish chpt. ARC, 1957-67, Southeastern Devel. Found., La. Moral and Civic Found.; hon. trustee John F. Kennedy Coll.; dist. gov. Supreme council Order DeMolay, 1964—. Mem. Am., La. (gen. chmn. com. on legal aid, chmn. com. on prison reform), 21st Jud. Dist. (v.p. 1967-68, 71-72) bar assns., Am., La. trial lawyers assns., Acad. Polit. Sci., Am. Judicature Soc., Comml. Law League Am., Law-Sci. Inst., World Peace through Law Acad., Am. Acad. Polit. and Social Sci., Internat. Acad. Law and Sci., Nat. Lawyers Club, Assn. Nat. Colls. and Univs. Attys., Am. Coll. Mortgage Attys., Inc., Southeastern Alumni Assn. (pres. 1961-62, dir. Tangipahoa Parish chpt.), Tulane Sch. Law Alumni Assn., Hammond Assn. Commerce (dir. 1960-65), La. Hist. Assn., UN Assn., Friends of Cabildo, Internat. Platform Assn., Nat. Hist. Soc. La. Ann. Conf., Phi Alpha Delta. Home: PO Box 221 Hammond LA 70404 Office: PO Box 1598 Hammond LA 70404 Tel (504) 345-3367

MATHERS, WILLIAM HARRIS, b. Newport, R.I., Aug. 27, 1914; A.B., Dartmouth Coll., 1935; J.D., Yale, 1938. Admitted to N.Y. bar, 1940; with Milbank, Tweed & Hope, 1938-48; mem. Milbank, Tweed, Hope & Hadley, 1948-57; v.p., sec., dir. Yale & Towne Mfg. Co., Stamford, Conn., 1957-60; partner firm Chadbourne, Parke, Whiteside & Wolff, 1960—. Mayor Village of Cove Neck, N.Y. Trustee Barnard Coll., 1958-69. Mem. Am., N.Y. State, Nassau County bar assns., Assn. Bar City of N.Y., New Eng. Soc. in City of N.Y., Phi Beta Kappa. Home: Cove Neck Rd Cove Neck Oyster Bay NY 11771 Office: 30 Rockefeller Plaza New York City NY 10020*

MATHES, PATRICIA ANN, b. New Orleans, Aug. 15; B.A., Barat Coll. Sacred Heart, 1969, J.D., Tulane U., 1972. Admitted to La. bar, 1972; asso. firm deVerges and deVerges, New Orleans, 1972-76; land rep. Chevron Oil Co., New Orleans, 1976—; prof. bus. law Loyola Univ., New Orleans, 1975. Mem. La. Bar Assn. Office: 1111 Tulane Ave New Orleans LA 70112 Tel (504) 521-6367

MATHES, STEPHEN JON, b. N.Y.C., Mar. 18, 1945; B.A., U. Pa., 1967, J.D., 1970. Admitted to N.Y. bar, 1971, Pa. bar, 1972; clk. to judge U.S. Ct. Appeals 3d Circuit, Phila., 1970-71; asso. firm Dilworth, Paxson, Kalish & Levy, Phila., 1972-77, partner, 1977—. Mem. Am., Pa., Phila. bar assns. Home: 607 E Durham St Philadelphia PA 19119 Office: 2600 Fidelity Bldg Philadelphia PA 19109 Tel (215) KI6-3000

MATHEWS, CLIFFORD LAURENCE, JR. (LARRY), b. Nashville, Mar. 26, 1943; B.A., So. Methodist U., 1965, J.D., 1968. Admitted to Tex. bar, 1968; law clk. to U.S. dist. judge, El Paso, Tex.; asst. dist. atty., El Paso, 1970-71; asso. firm T. Udell Moore, El Paso, 1971-72; individual practice law, El Paso, 1972-74; partner firm Johnson, Allen & Aycock, El Paso, 1974-75; 1st asst. to fed. pub. defender Western Dist. Tex., 1975—; lectr. constl. law El Paso Community Coll., 1973; spl. prosecutor on pornography City of El Paso, 1974. Mem. Fed., Tex. bar assns., Tex. Criminal Def. Lawyers Assn. Contbr. articles in field to profl. jours. Home: 10035 Montwood Apt 12 El Paso TX 79925 Office: Suite 800 Mills Building El Paso TX 79901 Tel (915) 543-7295

MATHEWS, ROBERT ELDEN, b. Waterville, Maine, Apr. 17, 1894; s. Shailer and Mary Philbrick (Elden) M.; A.B., Yale U., 1915; J.D. cum laude, U. Chgo., 1920; Admitted to Ill. bar, 1921; gen. practice with Frederick A. Brown, Chgo., 1920-22; instr. U. Chgo. Law Sch., 1922; asso. prof. U. Mont., 1922-24; prof. law Ohio State U., Columbus, 1924-64, prof. emeritus, 1964; prof. law U. Tex., Austin, 1966-72; vis. prof. law Columbia, 1928-29; vis. prof. Indian Law Inst., cons. on legal studies, New Delhi, 1961-62; vis. prof. Harvard Law Sch., 1963-64; mem. faculty orientation program Am. law Princeton, 1965. Mem. Office of Gen. Counsel Bd. Econ. Warfare and Fgn. Econ. Adminstrn., Washington, 1942-44 (on leave from Ohio State U.); mem. U.S. Labor Mission to Bolivia, 1943; asso. gen. counsel Nat. War Labor Bd., 1944-45, pub. mem. and co-chmn. appeals com., 1945. Chmn. Boulder Conf. Edn. for Pub. Responsibility, 1956; chmn. local bd. No. 18, Selective Service Adminstrn., Columbus, 1940-42; pres. League Ohio Law Schs., 1947; chmn. Nat. Conf. Tng. Law Students in Labor Relations, 1947; pres. Assn. Am. Law Schs., 1952; mem. U.S. Nat. Commn. for UNESCO, 1951-55. Mem. Internat. Soc. Labor Law and Social Legislation (chmn. U.S. nat. com., 1958-61; mem. internat. exec. com. 1958-61, nat. exec. com. 1958—), Nat. Acad. Arbitrators (mem. labor law group 1947—, chmn. 1947-58), Am. Bar Assn. (council sect. legal edn. 1953-61), ACLU (nat. com. 1955-70), AAUP (nat. council 1936-39), World Peace through Law Center (exec. com. sect. legal edn. 1972—), Soc. Am. Law Tchrs., Order of Coif (hon.), Elihu (Yale), Phi Beta Kappa (hon.), Beta Theta Pi, Phi Delta Phi. Compiler: Mathews' Revision of Mechem's Cases on Partnership, 1935; Mathews' Cases on Agency and Partnership, 1958. Editor in chief: Labor Relations and the Law, 1953; The Employment Relation and the Law, 1955; editor Legal Edn. and Public Responsibility, 1960; participating editor Labor Relations and Social Problems, 1971-77. Author: Problems Illustrative of the Responsibilities of Members of the Legal Profession, 1955, 6th edit., 1974. Contbr. Ohio Jurisprudence, also legal publs. Home: 4614 Lakeview Dr Austin TX 78731 Office: Coll Law U Tex 2500 Red River St Austin TX 78705 Tel (512) 471-5151

MATHEWS, RODERICK B., b. Lawton, Okla., Mar. 12, 1941; B.A., Hampden-Sydney Coll., 1963; LL.B., U. Richmond, 1966. Admitted to Va. bar, 1966; since practiced Richmond, Va., asso. firm Christian, Barton, Parker, Epps & Brent, 1966-72; partner firm Christian, Barton, Epps, Brent & Chappell, 1972—. Mem. Va., Am. bar assns., Va. State Bar. Home: 8108 University Dr Richmond VA 23229 Office: 1200 Mutual Bldg 909 E Main St Richmond VA 23219 Tel (804) 644-7851

MATHEWS, WESLEY HERBERT, b. Duluth, Minn., Sept. 25, 1930; A.B., San Diego State U., 1952; J.D., U. Calif., Los Angeles, 1955. Admitted to Calif. bar, 1956, U.S. Supreme Ct. bar, 1960; dep. city atty. City of San Diego, 1956-57; partner firm Hauslein & Mathews, San Diego, 1957-63; sr. partner firm Mathews Bergen Vodicka & Potash, and predecessor, San Diego, 1965—. Certified specialist criminal law Calif. State Bar. Mem. Am., Calif., San Diego County bar assns., Am., Calif. trial lawyers assns., Nat. Coll. Criminal Def. Lawyers. Office: Suite 652 121 Broadway San Diego CA 92101 Tel (714) 234-8331

MATHEWSON, GEORGE ATTERBURY, b. Paterson, N.J., Mar. 31, 1935; A.B., Amherst Coll., 1957; LL.B., Cornell U., 1960; LL.M., U. Mich., 1961. Admitted to N.Y. bar, 1963; atty. office spl. legal assts., trial atty. FTC, Washington, 1963-65; individual practice law, Syracuse, N.Y., 1967-72, 73—; regional atty. N.Y. State Dept. Environ. Conservation, Liverpool, N.Y., 1972-73. Deacon, Presbyn. Ch. Liverpool (N.Y.), 1973-74. Mem. Fed., N.Y. State, Onondaga County bar assns., Am. Judicature Soc., Southside Businessmen Syracuse (dir. 1971-72), Phi Delta Phi. Home: 4786 Makyes Rd Syracuse NY 13215 Office: 4304 S Salina St Syracuse NY 13205 Tel (315) 492-3363

MATHIAS, JOSEPH MARSHALL, b. Frankfort, Ky., Jan. 23, 1914; A.B., U. Md., 1935; LL.B., Southeastern U., 1942. Admitted to Md. bar, 1942; partner firms Moorman and Mathias, Bethesda, Md., 1946-50, Jones, Mathias & O'Brien, Bethesda and Silver Spring, Md., 1950-65; judge Md. Tax Ct., 1959-65, 6th Jud. Circuit Ct. of Md. in Montgomery County, 1965—; adminstrv. judge Montgomery County Circuit Ct., 1969-75, 6th Jud. Circuit Md., 1975—. Mem. Md. Jud. Conf., Am., Md. bar assns., Am. Judicature Soc. Home: 10011 Summit Ave Kensington MD 20795 Office: Courthouse Rockville MD 20850 Tel (301) 279-8281

MATHIAS, ROBERT B., b. Shepherdstown, W.Va., June 28, 1916; LL.B., Nat. U., 1947. Admitted to Md. bar, 1947; sr. mem. firm Mathias, Mathias & Dotson, 1947-65; judge 7th Jud. Circuit Ct., Prince George's County, Upper Marlboro, Md., 1965—; county atty. Prince George's County, 1955-65. Mem. Nat. Coll. State Trial Judges (faculty advisor 1974), Nat. (pres. 1964-65), Md. (pres. 1963-64) county civil attys. assns. Office: Court House Upper Marlboro MD 20870 Tel (301) 627-3000

MATHIS, LEWIS HENDERSON, b. Blytheville, Ark., Apr. 21, 1942; B.S. in Bus. Adminstrn., U. Ark., 1965, LL.B., 1968; LL.M., George Washington U., 1972. Admitted to Ark. bar, 1968; asso. firm Friday, Eldredge & Clark, Little Rock, 1976—; lectr. law U. Ark., Mem. Am., Ark. bar assns. Office: 2000 First National Bldg Little Rock AR 72315 Tel (501) 376-2011

MATHIS, WILLIAM LOWREY, b. Jackson, Tenn., Dec. 19, 1926; B.S., Duke, 1947; J.D., George Washington U., 1951. Admitted to D.C. bar, 1951, Fla. bar, 1972; asso. firm Swecker & Mathis, Washington, 1952-60, Burns, Doane, Swecker & Mathis, Washington, 1961—; adj. prof. Georgetown U. Law Center, 1974—. Mem. Am., D.C. bar assns., Am. Patent Law Assn. (sec. 1969-72). Home: 3709 Chanel Rd Annandale VA 22003 Office: 815 Connecticut Ave NW Washington DC 20006 Tel (202) 298-9185

MATIA, DAVID THOMAS, b. Cleve., Nov. 20, 1928; B.S., John Carroll U., 1950; LL.B., Case Western Res. U., 1957. Admitted to Ohio bar, 1957; judge Cuyahoga County (Ohio) Ct. Common Pleas, 1971—; mem. Ohio Ho. of Reps., 1959-64, Ohio Senate, 1965-66; law dir. City of Independence (Ohio), 1968-69. Mem. Ohio, Cuyahoga, Cleve. bar assns. Recipient Outstanding Jud. Service awards Ohio Supreme Ct., 1972, 73, 74, 75, 76. Office: 1 Lakeside Ave Cleveland OH 44113 Tel (216) 623-8752

MATIAS, ROBERT WILLIAM, b. Cedar Rapids, Iowa, Apr. 12, 1937; B.A., Coe Coll., 1959; LL.B., U. Iowa, 1961. Admitted to Iowa bar, 1961; asst. atty. Linn County, Iowa, 1963-64; individual practice law, Cedar Rapids, 1961—. Mem. Am., Linn County bar assns., Am. Trial Lawyers Assn. Home: 365 Park Terr SE Cedar Rapids IA 52403 Office: 810 Dows Bldg Cedar Rapids IA 52401 Tel (319) 364-1538

MATIAS, THOMAS REDMOND, b. Binghamton, N.Y., May 26, 1931; B.A., State U. N.Y., 1953, M.B.A., Cornell U., 1958, LL.D., 1959. Admitted to N.Y. State bar, 1960; student intern IRS, Washington, 1958, Exec. Office of Pres., 1957; atty. GAO, Washington, 1960-62, trial atty. FMC, 1962-65; regulatory atty. Western Union Telegraph Co., N.Y.C., 1965-69, ITT, 1969-72; adminstrv. law judge N.Y. Pub. Service Commn., Albany, 1972—. Mem. N.Y. State Bar Assn., Cornell Law Assn., Phi Delta Phi. Home: 37 Douglas Rd Delmar NY 12054 Office: Empire State Plaza Albany NY 12223

MATKIN, RAYMOND CLYDE, b. Waco, Tex., Nov. 21, 1946; B.B.A., Baylor U., 1968, J.D., 1971. Admitted to Tex. bar, 1971; chief felony prosecutor McLennan County Dist. Atty's. Office, Waco, 1971—. Mem. State Bar Tex. Home: 909 Baylor #309 Waco TX 76706 Office: 302 Court House Annex Waco TX 76706 Tel (817) 756-7171

MATNEY, HAROLD VERNON, b. Kansas City, Mo., July 16, 1942; B.A., Ottawa U., 1969; J.D., U. Kans., 1973. Admitted to Kans. bar, 1974; partner firm Matney & Roth, Ottawa, 1974—. Trustee Franklin County Hist. Soc.; chmn. bd. trustees Curry Ministerial Scholarship Fund. Mem. Am., Kans. bar assns., Am., Kans. trial lawyers assns. Office: 101 W 2d St Ottawa KS 66067 Tel (913) 242-7944

MATONIS, JOHN JOSEPH, b. Phila., June 7, 1936; B.S., St Joseph's Coll.; J.D., Temple U., 1965. Admitted to Pa. bar, D.C. bar, Calif. bar, U.S. Supreme Ct. bar, 1970; asso. firm Richter, Lord, Cavanaugh, McCartney & Raynes, Phila., 1967-68; individual practice law, Washington, 1968—; asso. firm Walter Maund, San Diego, 1976—; mem. lawyer's adv. com. mental health rules Superior Ct. D.C., 1972-73; founder; lectr. Citizens Courtroom Workshop, 1975—. Mem. Bar Assn. D.C. (chmn. mental health commitment affairs subcom. 1971-72), Am. Trial Lawyer's Assn. (chmn. mental health statutes com. 1969-71), Citizens for Truth in Nutrition (counsel 1974-76), Internat. Assn. Cancer Victims and Friends (treas. 1976-77). Recipient Atty. of Year award Nat. Justice Found., 1973. Tel (202) 338-4200

MATTESON, J. HAROLD, b. Swissvale, Pa., July 31, 1909; B.S. in Edn., U. Miami, 1932, LL.B., 1933, J.D., 1966; student Columbia, 1931, U. Va., 1930. Admitted to Fla. bar, 1933; asst. circulation mgr. Miami (Fla.) Daily News, 1932; religious news editor Sta. WIOD, Miami, 1943; so. regional dir. NCCJ, Miami, 1943-45; tchr. Dade County (Fla.) Pub. Schs., 1932-42, vis. tchr., 1945-52; asst. dir. site planning Dade County Schs., 1953-73; ret., 1973. Mem. Dade County Bar Assn. (life). Home: 11801 Northtrail Ave Tampa FL 33617 Tel (813) 988-5582

MATTHEWS, ARCHIBALD MORGAN, b. Johnstown, Pa., Mar. 27, 1902; A.B., Washington and Jefferson Coll., 1923; LL.B., U. Pitts., 1927, J.D., 1968. Admitted to Pa. bar, 1927, U.S. Supreme Ct. bar, 1937; individual practice law, Somerset, Pa., 1927—; asso. William R. Hughes, Somerset, 1970—; dist. atty. Somerset County (Pa.), 1936-44; dep. atty. gen. State of Pa., Harrisburg, 1950-58; dir. civil def. County of Somerset, 1950—. Mem. Am., Pa., Somerset County bar assns. Home: N Rosina Ave and Felgar Rd Somerset PA 15501 Office: 110 E Union St Somerset PA 15501 Tel (814) 445-5483

MATTHEWS, ARTHUR LAMAR, JR., b. Sarasota, Fla., Nov. 6, 1939; A.B., Stetson U., 1961; LL.B., U. Fla., 1964, J.D., 1967. Admitted to Fla. bar, 1964; asso. firm Dye & Dye, Bradenton, Fla., 1964-68, partner, 1968; asso. firm Williams, Parker, Harrison, Dietz & Getzen, Sarasota, 1969-71, partner, 1972—; asst. state's atty. 12th Jud. Circuit Fla., 1968-69; instr. paralegal edn. Manatee Jr. Coll., 1975—. Bd. dirs. Fla. West Coast Symphony, 1974—, Sarasota United Appeal, 1976. Mem. Fla. Bar (pres. young lawyers sect. 1975-76, ex officio mem. bar bd. govs. 1975-76), Sarasota County, Am. bar assns., Fla. Acad. Trial Lawyers, Am. Trial Lawyers Assn., Phi Delta Phi. Office: 1550 Ringling Blvd Sarasota FL 33578 Tel (813) 366-4800

MATTHEWS, BYRON STEWART, b. Evanston, Ill., June 2, 1928; B.A., Northwestern U., 1949, J.D., 1952. Admitted to Ill. bar, 1952, Okla. bar, 1967; individual practice law, Ill., 1952-66; individual practice law, Tulsa, 1967-70; atty. Legal Aid Soc., Tulsa, 1970—; faculty John Marshall Law Sch., 1958-66, Lawyers Inst., 1958-66. Mem. Am., Okla. bar assns. Contbr. articles to profl. jours.

MATTHEWS, CHARLES EDWARD, b. White Plains, N.Y., Nov. 15, 1946; B.A., Fordham Coll., 1968; J.D., Columbia, 1971. Admitted to N.Y. bar, 1972; asso. firm Spengler, Carlson, Gubar, Churchill & Brodsky, N.Y.C., 1971—. Asso., Columbia Law Rev., 1970-71. Home: 358 Church St White Plains NY 10603 Office: 280 Park Ave New York City NY 10017 Tel (212) 682-4444

MATTHEWS, CHARLES WILBURN, b. Houston, Feb. 27, 1945; B.A., U. Tex., 1967; J.D., U. Houston, 1970. Admitted to Tex. bar, 1970, U.S. Supreme Ct. bar, 1975; individual practice law, Houston, 1970-71; atty. Humble Oil & Refining Co. (now Exxon Co.), Houston, 1971—. Mem. Am., Tex., Houston, Houston Jr. bar assns., Def. Research Inst. Home: 10206 Briar Rose Houston TX 77042 Office: 800 Bell St Houston TX 77001 Tel (713) 656-3453

MATTHEWS, CLARK J., II, ed. So. Meth. U., 1959, J.D., 1961. With SEC, 1961-63; law clk. U.S. Dist. Ct., 1963-65; atty. Southland Corp., Dallas 1965-73, v.p., gen. counsel, 1973—. Office: 2828 N Haskell Ave Dallas TX 75221*

MATTHEWS, F. BYRON, b. Ft. Worth, Apr. 13, 1912; LL.B., Baylor U., 1934. Admitted to Tex. bar, 1934; asst. dist. atty. Tarrant County, Tex., 1934-38; individual practice law, Ft. Worth, 1938-63; judge Tex. Dist. Ct., Ft. Worth, 1963—. Home: 412 Matthews Dr Arlington TX 76012 Office: Criminal Cts Bldg Fort Worth TX 76012 Tel (817) 334-1350

MATTHEWS, JOLLY WALTER, b. Houston, June 12, 1940; B.S., Miss. Coll., 1968; J.D., U. Miss., 1971. Admitted to Miss. bar, 1971; asso. firm Estes & Blackwell, Gulfport, Miss., 1971-72, firm Zachary, Weldy & Ingram, Hattiesburg, Miss., 1972-75; partner firm Ingram & Matthews, Hattiesburg, 1975—. Mem. Am., Miss., S. Central Miss. bar assns., Miss. Trial Lawyers Assn. Home: 910 S 34th Ave Hattiesburg MS 39401 Office: 307 W Pine St Hattiesburg MS 39401 Tel (601) 545-2211

MATTHEWS, RODERICK JON, b. Madison, Wis., Mar. 4, 1946; B.A., U. Wis., 1968; J.D., Harvard, 1973. Admitted to Wis. bar, 1973; partner firm Sieker & Matthews, Madison, 1973—; lectr. grad. sch. bus. U. Wis., 1974—. Mem. Dane County Bd. Suprs., Madison, 1974—; mem. Dane County Judiciary and Legis. Com., 1974—, chmn. 1976—. Mem. Am., Wis., Dane County bar assns. Home: 1320 Chandler St Madison WI 53715 Office: 119 Monona Ave Madison WI 53703 Tel (608) 257-4303

MATTHEWS, THOMAS CLARK, JR., b. Lewistown, Pa., Oct. 7, 1931; A.B. cum laude, Princeton U., 1953; LL.B., U. Va., 1958. Admitted to Va. bar, 1958, D.C., 1959, U.S. Supreme Ct. bar, 1961; law clk. to Judge Warren E. Burger, U.S. Ct. Appeals D.C., 1958-59; with firm Weaver & Glassie, Washington, 1959-67, firm Wald, Harkrader & Ross, Washington, 1967—; spl. counsel Commn. Polit. Activity Govt. Personnel, Washington, 1967. Bd. dirs. D.C. chpt. ARC, 1967-76. Mem. Am., Fed., D.C. bar assns. Home: 3111 Garfield St NW Washington DC 20007 Office: 1320 19th St NW Washington DC 20036 Tel (202) 296-2121

MATTHEWS, WILLIAM LEWIS, JR., b. Livermore, Ky., Jan. 13, 1918; A.B., Western Ky. U., 1941; J.D., U. Ky., 1941; LL.M., U. Mich., 1946; S.J.D., 1950. Admitted to Ky. bar, 1941; research fellow, U. Mich., 1941-42; individual practice law, Bowling Green, Ky., 1946-47; asso. prof. law U. Ky., 1947-49; prof., 1947-74; acting dean, coll. of law, 1951-52, 56, 57, dean, 1957-71, alumni distinguished prof. law, 1974—; vis. prof. law, U. N.C., summer 1959, U. Mich., summer 1962, N.Y. U., 1966-67; mem. Nat. Conf. Uniform State Laws, 1968-73; mem. pub. service commn., State of Ky., 1975-76. Mem. Am., Ky. State, Fayette County bar assns., Order of the Coif, Omicron Delta Kappa. Contbr. articles to law jours. Home: 1752 Mooreland Lexington KY 40502 Office: Room 120 Coll Law U Ky Lexington KY 40506 Tel (606) 257-3998

MATTHEWS, WILLIAM PHILIP, b. Newton, Mass., Apr. 24, 1934; B.S., Boston Coll., 1957; J.D., New Eng. Sch. Law, 1962. Admitted to Mass. bar, 1962; staff atty. Mass. Defenders Com., Boston, 1963; partner firm Matthews Nicolazzo & Harrington, Newton, 1963-70, firm Freeto Winslow Uehlein & Matthews, Auburndale, Mass., 1975—; dir. marginally indigent program Newton Dist. Ct., 1973-76. Mem. Newton Bd. Aldermen, 1966-70. Mem. Am., Mass. bar assns. Office: 335 Auburn St Auburndale MA 02166 Tel (617) 969-1500

MATTHIAS, RUSSELL HOWARD, lawyer; b. Milw., Aug. 7, 1906; A.B., Northwestern U., 1929, J.D., 1932. Admitted to Ill. bar, 1933; partner law firm Meyers and Matthias (and predecessor firm), Chgo., 1949-59, sr. partner, 1959—; spl. asst. to Atty. Gen. U.S., 1934-35. Trustee, Village of Kenilworth, Ill., 1959-66, pres., 1966-70. Mem. Am., Ill., Chgo. bar assns., Internat. Assn. Life Ins. Counsel. Home: 1500 Sheridan Rd Wilmette IL 60091 Office: 230 W Monroe St Chicago IL 60061

MATTHIES, MARY TILLMAN, b. Baton Rouge, Mar. 22, 1948; B.S., Okla. State U., 1969; J.D., U. Tulsa, 1972. Admitted to Okla. bar, 1973, U.S. Supreme Ct. bar, 1976; asso. firm Kothe, Nichols & Wolfe, Inc., Tulsa, 1972-76, partner, 1976—; mem. Women's Task Force Tulsa Community Relations Commn., 1972-73. Mem. Am., Okla., Tulsa County bar assns., Phi Delta Phi. Contbr. articles to legal jours. Home: 1722 S Carson St Tulsa OK 74119 Office: 124 E 4th St Tulsa OK 74103 Tel (918) 584-5182

MATTICKS, KENNETH RUDOLPH, b. Pitts., July 14, 1946; B.A., U. Cin., 1968, J.D., 1971. Admitted to Ohio bar, 1971; asso. firm Graydon, Head & Ritchey, Cin., 1971-74; partner firm Matticks & Giannestras, Wilmington, Ohio, 1974-75; individual practice law, Wilmington, 1975—. Mem. Wilmington Vol. Firefighters, 1974—; pres. Clinton County (Ohio), Mental Health Center, 1975-77; elder Presbyn. Ch. of Wilmington, 1976. Mem. Clinton County, Ohio State bar assns., Buckeye Firefighters, Ohio State Fireman's Assn. Home: 74 Fulton St Wilmington OH 45177 Office: 19 S South St Wilmington OH 45177 Tel (513) 382-1366

MATTIONI, JOHN, b. Phila., Dec. 18, 1935; B.S., U.S. Mcht. Marine Acad., 1957; J.D. (Barenkopf scholar), Temple U., 1964. Admitted to Pa. bar, 1965, D.C. bar, 1965, U.S. Supreme Ct. bar, 1971; law clk. to judge Common Pleas Ct., 1964-67; asst. city solicitor City of Phila., 1967-71, dep. solicitor, 1971-72, dep. solicitor litigation div., 1972-74; mem. firm Mattioni, Mattioni & Mattioni, Phila., 1965—; instr. law Del. Law Sch., 1974, Temple U., 1974-76. Mem. Phila. Bar Assn., Maritime Law Assn., Marine Tech. Soc. Recipient J. Howard Reber award, 1964, Sarah A. Shull award, A. J. Davis award, 1964, Phi Alpha Delta award, 1962, Thomas Skelton Harrison Found. grantee, 1963. Editor in chief Temple Law Quar., 1964. Office: 400 1 E Penn Square Bldg Philadelphia PA 19107 Tel (215) 563-7924

MATTIS, JAMES MELVIN, b. McConnellsville, Ohio, July 12, 1942; B.A. in Polit. Sci., Central Washington State Coll., 1964; J.D., U. Wash., 1967. Admitted to Wash. bar, 1967, Oreg. bar, 1968; legal cons. Bur. of Govt. Research & Service U. Oreg., 1967—, asst. prof. community service and pub. affairs, 1970—, mem. legis. interim judiciary advisory com. on traffic code, 1973-75; cons. League Oreg. Cities, Assn. Oreg. Counties, others; legal counsel Columbia Regional Assn. Govts., 1973-74. Elder Westminister Presbyterian Ch., Eugene, Oreg., 1976—. Mem. Am., Lane County bar assns., Oreg. State Bar, Wash. State Bar. Contbr. articles in field to profl. jours. Home: 2015 Ridgeway Dr Eugene OR 97401 Office: PO Box 3177 Eugene OR 97403 Tel (503) 686-5232

MATTOCH, IAN LESLIE, b. Honolulu, July 13, 1943; B.A., Occidental Coll., 1965; J.D., Northwestern U., 1968. Admitted to Nebr. bar, 1968, Hawaii bar, 1969; asso. firm Cades, Schutte, Flemming & Wright, Honolulu, 1968-70; partner firm Mattoch, Kemper & Brown, Honolulu, 1970-75; individual practice law, Honolulu, 1975—; tchr. Punahou Sch., Honolulu, 1968-76. Mem. Am., Hawaii (dir. young lawyers sect.) bar assns. Contbr., editor Hawaii Bar Jour., 1969-71. Office: 841 Bishop St Honolulu HI 96813 Tel (808) 523-2451

MATTOX, JOHN DWIGHT, b. Jesup, Ga., Oct. 29, 1917; A.B., Mercer U., 1939, LL.B., 1948. Admitted to Ga. bar, 1948; mem. firm Turpin & Lane, Macon, Ga., 1948-51, partner, 1951-56; regional counsel Fed. Nat. Mortgage Assn., Atlanta, 1957-59; partner firm Adams & Mattox, Jesup, 1959-61; individual practice law, Jesup, 1961—; pres. Macon Legal Aid Soc., 1953-54. Pres., Macon Community Planning Council, 1951-52; charter mem. Wayne County Indsl. Devel. Authority, 1963—; mem. City of Jesup Planning and Zoning Commn., 1965—. Mem. Am., Macon (past pres.), Jesup (past pres.) bar assns., Brunswick Jud. Circuit Bar Assn. (past pres.), State Bar Ga. (legal aid com., past mem. bd. govs.), Am. Judicature Soc. Named Man of Year in Macon, Young Peoples League for Better Govt. in Bibb County, 1953. Home: 417 N Mahogany St Jesup GA 31545 Office: 356 E Cherry St Jesup GA 31545 Tel (912) 427-7783

MATTSON, GEORGE TAUNO, b. Seattle, Dec. 7, 1942; B.A., U. Wash., 1964, LL.B., 1966. Admitted to Wash. bar, 1966; since practiced in Seattle and Renton, Wash.; staff atty. Legal Services Center, Seattle, 1966-67; dep. pros. atty. King County, (Wash.), 1968-70; individual practice law, Seattle, 1970-71; judge Renton dist. King County Dist. Ct., 1971—. Bd. dirs. Renton Area Youth Services, 1971—, chmn., 1973; citizens adv. bd. Alcohol and Drug Abuse Inst., U. Wash., 1974—; adv. bd. King County Dept. Rehab., 1975—. Mem. Am. Judges Assn., Am. Judicature Soc., Wash. State (pres.), King County magistrates assns. Office: 200 Mill St Renton WA 98055 Tel (206) 226-3511

MATTSON, MARCUS, b. Ogden, Utah, July 3, 1904; B.A., U. Calif., Berkeley, 1927, J.D., 1930. Admitted to Calif. bar, 1930; asso. firm Lawler, Felix & Hall, Los Angeles, 1930-41, sr. partner, 1941—; mem. advisory council on rules of practice and procedure FTC, 1970-74; bd. dirs. Pacific Legal Found., 1974—. Bd. dirs. R. M. Pyles Boys Camp, Hunting Beach, Calif., 1967—. Fellow Am. Coll. Trial Lawyers (regent 1973—, chmn. com. on minimum qualifications of trial lawyers 1973—); mem. Am. Bar Assn. (chmn. sect. antitrust law 1965-66), State Bar Calif. (v.p. bd. govs. 1959-60), Los Angeles County Bar, Am., Los Angeles County (dir.) bar founds. Home: 515 N Cherokee Ave Los Angeles CA 90004 Office: 605 W Olympic Blvd Los Angeles CA 90015 Tel (213) 620-0060

MATUSICK, MITCHELL M., b. Dery, Pa., May 16, 1928; LL.B., U. Buffalo, 1953. Admitted to bar; partner firm Lovalo, Matusick & Spadafora, Buffalo, 1953—; counsel Buffalo Gear, Inc. Mem. Erie County Bar Assn. Home: 6845 Picture Lake Dr Hamburg NY 14075 Office: 958 Ellicott Sq Bldg Buffalo NY 14203 Tel (716) 854-1111

MATUSOW, DONALD EDWARD, b. Phila., Dec. 29, 1942; B.S., Ursinus Coll., 1964; J.D., Temple U., 1967. Admitted to Pa. bar, 1968; since practiced in Phila.; law clk. U.S. Dist. Ct. for Eastern Dist. Pa. 1967-68; asso. firm Wolf, Block, Schorr & Solis-Cohen, 1968-71; partner firm Litvin, Blumberg, Matusow & Young, 1971—; mem. Pa. Civil Jud. Com., 1972—; staff lawyer Community Legal Services Phila., 1969-71. Mem. Phila. bar assn., Pa., Phila. trial lawyers assns. Contbr. article to profl. jours. Home: 1611 Winston Rd Gladwyne PA 19035 Office: 210 W Washington Sq 5th Floor Philadelphia PA 19106 Tel (215) 925-4500

MAU, CHUCK, b. Honolulu, Hawaii, Jan. 10, 1907; B.A., U. Colo., 1933, LL.B., 1933. Admitted to Hawaii bar, 1935; dep. atty. gen. Hawaii, 1936-40; individual practice Honolulu, 1940-50, 1951—; judge Hawaii Tax Appeal Ct., 1948, 1st Circuit Ct. Hawaii, 1950-51; sr. partner firm Mau, Mau & White, 1975—; mem. bd. suprs. city and county Honolulu, 1940-46, 48-50; mem. bd. examiners Hawaii Bar, 1949. Del. Democratic nat. conv., 1948, Hawaii Const. Conv., 1950, chmn. central com. Dem. party Hawaii 1950; pres. Oahu chpt. Assn. Crippled Children and Adults, 1957-60; pres. Hawaii chpt. 1961-62, nat. trustee 1961-62, hon. life dir., 1973; v. chmn. governing bd. Hawaii chpt. Arthritis Found., 1965-71; bd. dirs. Kokokahi Trust, Kapiolani Maternity and Bynecol. Hosp., Leahi Hosp., Honolulu Community Theatre, Hawaii Child and Family Services; chmn. Honolulum Symphony Fund Dr., 1962; mem. adv. com. to Standing com. on edn. about communism and contrast with liberty under law, 1968—, mem. adv. com. Hawaii chpt. Am. Freedom. Found., 1971—. Mem. Am. (adv. com. unauthorized practice law 1967—), Hawaii bar assns. Recipient alumni award U. Colo., 1954, named to Hall Fame "C" Club, 1969, named law father year, Honolulu C. of C., 1957. Home: 3077 La Pietra Circle Honolulu HI 96815 Office: Suite 408 Hawaii Nat Bank Bldg 116 S King St Honolulu HI 96813 Tel (808) 536-3451

MAUD, OLIVER HUDSON, b. Florence, Ariz., Aug. 29, 1936; B.A. in Bus. Adminstrn., U. Ariz., 1958, J.D., 1965. Admitted to Ariz. bar, 1965; asso. firm Robertson, Childers, Everett, Burke & Drackman, Tucson, 1966-68; partner firm Estes, Browning, Maud & Zlaket, Tucson, 1968-70; partner firm Maupin, Wilson & Maud, Phoenix, 1970-73; individual practice law, Case Grande, Ariz., 1973—. Mem. Am. Bar Assn., State Bar Ariz. Home: Route 1 Box 17E Coolidge AZ 85228 Office: 121 W Florence Blvd Suite G Casa Grande AZ 85222 Tel (602) 836-2202

MAUHS, PETER MYERS, b. Albany, N.Y., Sept. 12, 1931; B.A., Colgate U., 1954; LL.B., Albany Law Sch., 1957. Admitted to N.Y. bar, 1959; county atty. Schoharie County, N.Y., 1965-68, 76—; atty. Fed. Land Bank of Springfield, 1974—, Mohawk-Schoharie Production Credit Assn., 1974—, N.Y. State Guernsey Breeders Coop., Inc., 1960-75, Schoharie County Coop. Dairies, Inc., 1960-74, Farmers Home Adminstrn., 1960-68. Mem. N.Y. State, Schoharie County (pres. 1970), bar assns., N.Y. State Trial Lawyers Assn. Home: R D Cobleskill NY 12043 Office: Box 129 Cobleskill NY 12043 Tel (518) 234-3525

MAULSBY, ALLEN FARISH, b. Balt., May 21, 1922; A.B., Williams Coll., Williamstown, Mass., 1944; LL.B., U. Va., 1946. Admitted to Md. bar, 1947, N.Y. bar, 1950; law clk. Hon. Morris A. Soper, judge U.S. Circuit Ct. Appeals 4th Circuit, 1946-47; mem. firm Cravath, Swaine & Moore, N.Y.C., 1947-57, partner, 1958—. Mem. rector council, vestry St. James Episcopal Ch., N.Y.C., 1962-68; dir. St. James chpt. Brotherhood of St. Andrew, N.Y.C.; trustee The Spence Sch., N.Y.C., The Five Points House, N.Y.C., Woodycrest Five Points Child Care, N.Y.C.; dir. Episcopal Ch. Found., N.Y.C., 1973. Mem. Am. Coll. Trial Lawyers, Am., N.Y. State, Fed. bar assns., Assn. Bar of N.Y., N.Y. County Lawyers Assn. Office: 1 Chase Manhattan Plaza New York City NY 10005 Tel (212) 422-3000

MAUPIN, ROBERT WADE, b. Carrollton, Mo., Apr. 24, 1932; A.B., U. Mo., 1954, J.D., 1959. Admitted to Mo. bar, 1959; law dept. Mo. Farmers Assn., 1959—, asst. gen. counsel, 1966—, sec., 1973—. Mem. Am. Judicature Soc., Am., Mo. bar assns. Office: 201 S 7th St Columbia MO 65201 Tel (314) 874-5111

MAURER, ALVIN EARL, JR., b. Minersville, Pa., Sept. 10, 1920; B.J., Pa. State U., 1942; J.D., U. Pa., 1945. Admitted to Pa. bar, 1946; individual practice law, Pottsville, Pa., 1946—; workman's compensation referee State of Pa., Frackville, 1967-71. Mem. Schuylkill County (Pa.), Pa., Am. bar assns. Home: 465 Sunbury St Minersville PA 17954 Office: 212 Thompson Bldg Pottsville PA 17901 Tel (717) 622-4260

MAURER, JAMES RICHARDSON, b. Tulsa, June 9, 1930; B.A., Stanford, 1951, LL.B. (Newhouse scholar), 1953. Admitted to Wash. bar, 1954, Calif. bar, 1955; contract coordinator Boeing Co., Seattle, 1953-54; staff asst. atty. Ryan Aero. Co., San Diego, 1955-57, tax counsel, 1958-59, legal counsel, 1960-68; partner firm Madruga & Maurer, Indio, Calif., 1968-69; asst. gen. counsel Electro Optical Systems, Pasadena, Calif., 1969-70; asst. gen. counsel Brown Co., Pasadena, 1970-71, gen. counsel, 1971—, v.p. and sec., 1971—, also dir. Mem. Am., Los Angeles bar assns., Am. Soc. Corporate Secs. Editorial bd. Stanford Law Rev., 1952-53. Home: 286 E Alegria Ave Sierra Madre CA 91024 Office: 251 S Lake Ave Pasadena CA 91101 Tel (213) 684-1800

MAURER, RICHARD SCOTT, b. Cleve., July 16, 1917; A.B., Ohio Wesleyan U., 1938; J.D., Yale, 1941. Admitted to Ohio bar, 1941, Tenn. bar, 1944, Ga. bar, 1954; mem. legal staff CAB, Washington, 1941-43; staff atty. Chicago & So. Air Lines, Memphis, 1943-53, v.p., gen. counsel, 1953; with Delta Air Lines, Atlanta, 1953—, sec., 1960—, gen. counsel, 1965—, sr. v.p., 1967—, also dir. Pres. Memphis Better Bus. Bur.; mem. Atlanta Salvation Army Adv. Bd., chmn., 1971-72. Mem. Am. (chmn. sect. ins., negligence and compensation law 1973-74), Ga., Atlanta bar assns., Am. Soc. Corporate Secs. (chmn. bd. 1976-77), Phi Beta Kappa, Omicron Delta Kappa, Phi Gamma Delta. Tel (404) 762-2441

MAURER, ROBERT HENRY, b. Minersville, Pa., June 7, 1923; B.A., Pa. State U., 1947; LL.B., Dickinson Sch. Law, 1950. Admitted to Pa. bar, 1951; dep. atty. gen. Commonwealth Pa., Harrisburg, 1952-55; asso. firm McNees, Wallace and Nurick, Harrisburg, 1956-61; individual practice law, assn. mgmt., Harrisburg, 1961—; counsel, exec. dir. Pa. Assn. Broadcasters, Harrisburg, 1961—; counsel, exec. v.p. Pa. Bakers Assn., Harrisburg, 1963—; counsel, exec. dir. Pa. Car and Truck Renting and Leasing Assn., Harrisburg, 1961—; counsel Pa. Soc. Profl. Engrs., 1962—, Pa. Restaurant Assn., 1969—; Pa. counsel Am. Mut. Ins. Alliance, Chgo. Mem. Pa., Dauphin County bar assns. Home: 309 S 31st St Green Acres Harrisburg PA 17109 Office: 407 N Front St Harrisburg PA 17101 Tel (717) 236-9522

MAURIN, J. PAUL, III, b. Kansas City, Mo., Sept. 13, 1946; B.A., Creighton U., 1968, J.D., 1971. Admitted to Kans. bar, 1972, Nebr. bar, 1972; individual practice law, Kansas City, Kans., 1972-74; partner firm Maurin, McCamish & Vader, Kansas City, Kans., 1974—; judge pro tem Magistrate Ct. Wyandotte County (Kans.), 1976, Kansas City (Kans.) Municipal Ct., 1976, Wyandotte County Juvenile Ct., 1974—; asst. dist. judge pro tem Dist. Ct. Wyandotte County Juvenile Dept., 1977—. Pres., Westheight Manor S. Community Devel. Group; legal council Children and Youth Commn.; mem. Kans. Council Crime and Delinquency. Mem. Am., Kans., Nebr. bar assns., Am., Kans. trial lawyers assns. Home: 1200 Hoel Pkwy Kansas City KS 66102 Office: 845 Armstrong St PO Box F Kansas City KS 66101 Tel (913) 371-8383

MAUTONE, ANTHONY RAY, b. Newark, May 3, 1943; B.S. in Psychology, Villanova U., 1964; LL.B., Seton Hall U., 1967. Admitted to N.J. bar, 1969; first asst. prosecutor Essex County Prosecutors Office, Newark, 1969—. Mem. Nat. Dist. Attys. Assn., County Prosecutors Assn. N.J., N.J., Essex County bar assns. Office: Essex County Courts Bldg Newark NJ 07102 Tel (201) 961-7429

MAUZY, OSCAR HOLCOMBE, b. Houston, Nov. 9, 1926; B.B.A., U. Tex., 1950, S.J.D., 1952. Admitted to Tex. bar, 1951, U.S. Supreme Ct. bar, 1957; partner, firm Mullinax, Wells, Mauzy & Baab, Inc., Dallas, 1952—. Mem. Dallas, Tex., Am. Trial Lawyers Assns., Dallas Bar Assn., State Bar Tex. Home: 904 Evergreen Hill Rd Dallas TX 75208 Office: 8204 Elmbrook Dr Suite 200 Dallas TX 75247 Tel (214) 630-3672

MAW, CARLYLE ELWOOD, b. Provo, Utah, Oct. 13, 1903; B.S., Brigham Young U., 1925; LL.B., Harvard, 1928. Admitted to N.Y. State bar, 1929, D.C. bar, 1976; asso. firm Cravath, Swaine & Moore, N.Y.C., 1928-33, 1934-38, mem. firm 1939-73, counsel, 1976—; legal advisor Dept. State, 1973-74; chief delegation, spl. rep. of Pres. to Law of Sea Conf., 1975; spl. rep. to Govt. of Peru in Marcona Negotiations, 1976; undersec. state for security assistance Dept. State, D.C., 1974-76; cons. security assistance and law of sea matters Dept. State, 1976—. Fellow Am., N.Y. bar founds.; mem. Am., N. Y. State, Internat., Inter-Am. bar assns., Assn. Bar City N.Y., Internat. Law Assn., Union Internationale des Avocats, Am. Soc. Internat. Law. Contbr. articles to legal jours. Home: 870 UN Plaza New York City NY 10017 Office: 1 Chase Manhattan Plaza New York City NY 10005 Tel (212) 422-3000

MAW, GRANT S., b. Ogden, Utah, Aug. 18, 1926; A.A., Weber Jr. Coll., 1948; B.S. in History, U. Utah, 1951, LL.B., 1954, J.D., 1967. Admitted to Utah bar, 1955; individual practice law, Ogden, 1955-66; atty.-advisor Odgen Air Logistics Command, Hill AFB, 1967—; U.S. commr. No. Div. Dist. Utah, 1957-60; instr. Weber State Coll., Ogden. Home: 1346 36th St Ogden UT 84403 Tel (801) 777-6753

MAW, HERBERT BROWN, b. Ogden, Utah, Mar. 11, 1893; LL.B., U. Utah, 1916, B.S., 1923; M.A., Northwestern U., 1926, J.D., 1927. Admitted to Utah bar, 1916, Fed. bar, 1920; mem. Utah State Senate, 1929-39, pres. Sen., 1935-39; gov. Utah, 1941-49; prof. U. Utah, Salt Lake City, 1923-32, dean men, 1932-40; individual practice, Salt Lake City; referee in bankruptcy U.S. Dist. Ct. of Utah, 1967-70. Home: 1212 Yale Ave Salt Lake City UT 84105 Office: 309 Boston Bldg Salt Lake City UT 84111 Tel (801) 359-3871

MAX, HERBERT B., b. Newark, May 24, 1931; B.A., Columbia Coll., 1952, LL.B., 1954. Admitted to N.Y. bar, 1958; asso. firm Delson & Gordon, N.Y.C., 1960-65; individual practice law, N.Y.C., 1965—; chmn. bd. Denver Instrument Corp. 1975—. Mem. Am. N.Y. State Bar Assns., Assn. Bar City N.Y. Asso. editor: N.Y. State Legislative Annual, 1958, 1959. Office: 77 Water St New York City NY 10005 Tel (212) 437-7132

MAXEINER, PHILIP ARTHUR, b. Sioux City, Iowa, Apr. 24, 1913; B.S. in Bus. Adminstrn., Washington U., St. Louis, 1933, J.D., 1936. Admitted to Mo. bar, 1936, U.S. Supreme Ct. bar, 1943; mem. firm Lewis, Rice, Tucker, Allen & Chubb, St. Louis, 1936—; dir. Gen. Metal Products Co., Midland Container Corp.; municipal judge City of Ladue (Mo.), 1969-73. Bd. dirs. Campus YMCA, 1948—. Mem. Am., Fed., Mo. bar assns., Am. Judicature Soc. Recipient Legion of Merit. Home: 22 Woodcrest Dr Ladue MO 63124 Office: 611 Olive St St Louis MO 63101 Tel (314) 231-5833

MAXFIELD, GUY BUDD, b. Galesburg, Ill., May 4, 1933; A.B., Augustana Coll., 1955; J.D., U. Mich., 1958. Admitted to N.Y. bar, 1959; asso. firm White & Case, N.Y.C., 1958-63; prof. law N.Y. U., N.Y.C., 1963—; partner firm Gifford, Woody, Carter & Hays, N.Y.C., 1972—; cons. Commonwealth P.R., 1968-69. Mem. Am., N.Y. (com. vice chmn. 1969-70) bar assns. Author: The Federal Estate and Gift Taxes, 2d edit., 1967; Federal Estate and Gift Taxation, 3d edit., 1974; contbr. articles to legal jours. Home: 37 Washington Sq W New York City NY 10011 Office: 14 Wall St New York City NY 10005 Tel (212) 349-7400

MAXFIELD, PETER CHARLES, b. Scottsbluff, Nebr., May 10, 1941; A.B., Regis Coll., 1963; J.D., U. Denver, 1966; LL.M., Harvard, 1968. Admitted to Colo. bar, 1966, Wyo. bar, 1969; atty. U.S. Dept. Justice, Washington, 1966-67; asso. firm Hindry, Erickson & Meyer, Denver, 1968-69; asst. prof. law U. Wyo., 1969-72, asso. prof., 1972-75, prof., 1975—; vis. prof. law U. N.M., 1972-73. Author: Income Taxation of Mining Ops., 1st edit., 1973; 2nd edit., 1975; Natural Resources on Indian Lands, 1977. Home: 1727 Rainbow Laramie WY 82070 Office: U Wyo Coll Law Laramie WY 82070 Tel (307) 766-5262

MAXWELL, DONALD, b. Johnstown, Pa., Aug. 22, 1933; A.B., Duke, 1955; J.D., U. Mich., 1960. Admitted to Ariz. bar, 1961, U.S. Supreme Ct. bar, 1965; legal asst. to Chief Justice Supreme Ct. Ariz., 1960-62; asso. firm Botsford, Shumway & Wilson, 1962-64; sr. partner firm Maxwell, Johnson & Smith, 1964-75; individual practice law, Scottsdale, Ariz., 1975—; pres. Ironwood Land Co., Tonto Hills Water Co.; tchr. govtl. law Scottsdale High Sch. Mem. adv. council Salvation Army; dir. Scottsdale C. of C., Jackson Charitable Fund; dir. YMCA, 1970; pres. Scottsdale Paradise Valley Young Republicans; mem. Nat. Presdl. Surrogate Advance Team, 1972; pres. Little League, PTA. Mem. Am., Ariz., Maricopa County, Scottsdale bar assns., Am. Arbitration Assn. (nat. bd.). Contbr. guest editorials to Ariz. Weekly Gazette. Home: 4626 E Arcadia Ln Phoenix AZ 85018 Office: 7060 Main St Scottsdale AZ 85251 Tel (602) 947-7201

MAXWELL, GEORGE SMALL, b. Rawal Pindi, Punjab, Pakistan, Feb. 8, 1906 (parents Am. citizens); A.B., Westminster (Pa.), Coll., S.T.B., 1926; Princeton, 1929; LL.B., Cleve.-Marshall Law Sch., 1954; J.D., Cleve. State U., 1969. Admitted to Ohio bar, 1955; asst. pastor Vance Meml. Ch., Wheeling, W.Va., 1929-31; pastor 1st Presbyterian Ch., Waynesburg, Pa., 1931-41, 1st Presbyterian Ch., Mt. Lebanon, Pa., 1941-45; vice-chmn. nat. appeals com. War Labor Bd., Washington, 1945; dir. Wage Stblzn. Bd., 5th Dist., Cleve., 1946-47; sec-treas. Steel Truckers Employers Assn., Cleve., 1947-70; exec. sec. Central States Employers Assn., Chgo., 1957-58. Office: 1104 One Public Sq Cleveland OH 44113 Tel (216) 566-9028

MAXWELL, HOWARD JAMES, b. East Hampton, Conn., Feb. 24, 1922; A.B., Dickinson Coll., 1948; LL.B., U. Conn., 1952. Admitted to Conn. bar, 1952, U.S. Ct. Appeals bar, 2d Circuit, 1957; staff Aetna Ins. Co., 1948-52; partner firms Steele, Collins & Maxwell, 1954-60, Steele & Maxwell, 1960-67, Tracy & Maxwell, Hartford, Conn.,

1967—; legal adviser CAC; asso. dir. Bank & Trust Co. Chmn. Republican Town Com. Mem. Hartford, Conn., Middletown, Middlesex bar assns., Beta Theta Pi (asst. sec.). Home: 67 Wardsell Rd West Hartford CT 06107 Office: 99 Pratt St Hartford CT 06103 Tel (203) 278-6010

MAXWELL, LILLIENSTEIN JULIUS, b. N.Y.C., Dec. 18, 1927; A.B., Coll. City N.Y., 1949; LL.B., Columbia, 1952. Admitted to N.Y. bar, 1952, U.S. Supreme Ct. bar, 1973; partner firm Rich, Krinsly, Poses, Katz, & Lillienstein, N.Y.C., 1952—; village atty. Village of Ardsley (N.Y.), 1971—. Trustee Village of Ardsley, 1968-71; chmn. Ardsley Library Study Com., 1967-68; atty.-mem. Ardsley Narcotics Guidance Council, 1972—. Mem. N.Y. County Lawyers Assn. Office: 99 Park Ave New York City NY 10016 Tel (212) 867-7200

MAXWELL, RALPH BERNARD BORDEN, b. Devils Lake, N.D., Nov. 26, 1919; B.C.S., U. N.D., 1941, L.L.B., 1947. Admitted to N.D. bar, 1947; state's atty. Rolette County (N.D.), 1949-53; U.S. dist. atty. for N.D., 1954, asst. U.S. dist. atty., 1955-58; practiced in West Fargo, N.D., 1958-67; judge N.D. 1st Jud. Dist. Ct., 1967—; del. N.D. Constl. Conv., 1972. Mem. Am., Cass County (pres. 1961-62), N.D. bar assns., Am. Judicature Soc., State Jud. Council, Order of Coif. Home: 501 9th Ave W West Fargo ND 58078 Office: Cass County Courthouse Fargo ND 58102 Tel (701) 237-3131

MAXWELL, ROBERT EARL, b. Elkins, W.Va., Mar. 15, 1924; student Davis and Elkins Coll.; LL.B., W.Va. U., 1949. Admitted to W.Va. bar, 1949; practiced in Randolph County, 1949; pros. atty. Randolph County, 1952-61; U.S. atty. for No. Dist. W.Va., 1961-64; judge U.S. Dist. Ct. for No. Dist. W.Va., Elkins, 1965—, now chief judge. Del., Democratic Nat. Conv., 1956, 64. Mem. Am., W.Va., Randolph County bar assns., W.Va. State Bar, Am. Legion. Home: Elkins WV 26241 Office: US Courthouse Elkins WV 26241*

MAXWELL, ROLAND, b. Marion, Iowa, Jan. 27, 1901; A.B., U. So. Calif., 1922, J.D., 1923. Admitted to Calif. bar, 1922, U.S. Supreme Ct. bar, 1938; practiced in Los Angeles, 1922-25, Pasadena, 1925—. Bd. dirs. Nat. Interfrat. Found., N.Y.C.; bd. dirs. gen. counsel Methodist Hosp. So. Calif., Arcadia, also former pres.; pres. Hosp. Found. So. Calif., Ariz. Conf. United Meth. Ch.; trustee, sec. Pasadena Meth. Found.; bd. dirs. Phi Kappa Tau Found. Mem. Am., Los Angeles County, Pasadena bar assns., Pasadena C. of C., Pasadena Tournament Roses Assn., Coleman Chamber Music Assn. (treas.). Named Pasadena's Outstanding Young Man, U.S. Jr. C. of C., 1933. Home: 200 Los Altos Dr Pasadena CA 91105 Office: 301 E Colorado Blvd Suite 628 Pasadena CA 91101 Tel (213) 796-2664

MAXWELL, STEPHEN LLOYD, b. St. Paul, Jan. 12, 1921; B.A., Morehouse Coll., 1942; B.S.L., St. Paul Coll. Law, 1951, J.D., 1953. Admitted to Minn. bar, 1953, Ill. bar, 1955; individual practice law, St. Paul, 1953-59; asst. county atty. Ramsey County (Minn.), 1959-64, 67; corp. counsel City of St. Paul, 1964-66; judge Municipal Ct., St. Paul, 1967-68; judge Dist. Ct. of Minn., St. Paul, 1968—. Bd. regents St. John's U., Collegeville, Minn., 1972—; v.p. Many Waters area council Boy Scouts Am., 1975—; corporate mem. United Hosps., Inc., St. Paul, 1975—. Mem. Minn., Ramsey County, Nat. bar assns., St. Paul-Mpls. Com. Fgn. Relations. Home: 882 Carroll Ave St Paul MN 55104 Office: 1309 Ct House Saint Paul MN 55102 Tel (612) 298-4808

MAY, GEORGE WILLIS, b. Fairmont, W.Va., Sept. 18, 1922; A.B., W.Va. U., 1943, J.D., 1946. Admitted to W.Va. bar, 1946; individual practice law, Fairmont, 1946—; pres. First Exchange Bank, Mannington, W.Va., 1968—. Pres. Union Mission of Fairmont, 1970-71. Mem. Am. Trial Lawyers Assn., Am., Marion County, (pres. 1959), W.Va. (dir. 1970-73) bar assns. Home: 1148 Avalon Rd Fairmont WV 26554 Office: 502 First Nat Bank PO Box 1108 Fairmont WV 26554 Tel (304) 363-5840

MAY, NELL CLEVELAND, b. Fulton, Miss., Sept. 11, 1923; B.A., Blue Mountain (Miss.) Coll., 1944; grad. Delta State Coll., Cleveland, Miss., 1948. Admitted to Miss. bar, 1964; Owner firm Arthur T. Cleveland, Fulton, Miss.; dir., atty., sec. Tombigbee Bank and Trust Co., Fulton, 1975—. Dir. Regional Rehab. Center, Inc., Tupelo, Miss., 1961—, also chmn. Mem. Miss., Itawamba County bar assns. Home: 513 S Cummings St Fulton MS 38843 Office: PO Box 538 111 S Gaither St Fulton MS 38843 Tel (601) 862-2766

MAY, RICHARD HERBERT, b. Wilmington, Del., Feb. 19, 1935; A.B., Hamilton Coll., 1957; LL.B., Cornell U., 1960. Admitted to Del. bar, 1960, U.S. Supreme Ct. bar, 1965; asso. firm Young Conaway Stargatt & Taylor, Wilmington, Del., 1960-64, partner, 1964—; instr. law Brandywine Coll., Wilmington, 1960—. Mem. session Westminster Presbyterian Ch., Wilmington, 1974—; dir. Delaware Cancer Soc., 1968-70. Mem. Del. State, Am., New Castle County bar assns. Home: 107 Willow Spring Rd Wilmington DE 19807 Office: 1401 Market Tower Wilmington DE 19899 Tel (302) 571-6630

MAY, ROBERT A., b. Grand Rapids, Mich., May 8, 1911; A.B., U. Mich., 1933, J.D., 1936. Admitted to Mich. bar, 1936, Ariz. bar, 1941, U.S. Supreme Ct. bar, 1960; asso. firm Clifford Mitts, Grand Rapids, 1936-41; mem. firm Darnell & Robertson, Tucson, 1943-44; individual practice law, Tucson, 1944-55; mem. firm May, Lesher & Dees, Tucson, 1955-60, May & Dees, Tucson, 1960-75, May, Dees & Barassi, Tucson, 1975—; dir., gen. counsel St. Luke's in the Desert, 1944—, chief exec. officer, 1964-76, pres. emeritus, 1976; treas. Desert Sanitorium, Inc., 1943-45; adv. bd. Tucson Med. Center, 1946-49; Ariz. state chmn. Joint Editorial Bd. for Uniform Probate Code, Ariz., 1972—, mem. legis. council com. on revision of probate code, 1970-72; bd. dirs. Pima County Legal Aid Soc., Inc., 1952-77, emeritus, 1977—, pres., 1958-60. Co-founder Tucson Conv. Bur., 1945-74, exec. bd., 1957-67; founding mem., exec. bd. Tucson Council Chs., chmn. fin. com., 1948-64, pres., 1956-58; v.p. Ariz. Council Chs., 1956-58; chancellor Episcopal Parish, 1943—, vestryman, 1943-73, 74-77, rector's warden, 1977—; vice chancellor Diocese of Ariz., 1959—; vice chmn. field and hosp. com. ARC, 1942-45; regional chmn. U. Mich. Law Sch. Fund, 1963-66, mem. nat. com. on fund, 1967-72; co-founder U. Ariz. Law Sch. Fund; visitors com. U. Mich. Law Sch., 1964-67; mem. Citizen's Adv. Com for Pub. Schs., 1944-46; co-founder Def. Info. Office. Fellow Am. Coll. Probate Counsel (regent 1966-69, 73-77), Am. Bar Found.; mem. Am. Bar Assn. (standing com. on client security fund 1968-73, vice chmn. ins. sec., health law ins. com. 1958-70, chmn. 1970-72), State Bar Ariz. (vice chmn. group ins. com. 1952-55, chmn. 1955-72, chmn. bd. trustees client security fund 1960—, com. for revision probate code 1942-44), Pima County Bar Assn. (pres. 1955-56), Fed., Internat. bar assns., So. Ariz. Estate Planning Council (co-founder, charter pres. 1956), Internat. Assn. Ins. Counsel, Internat. Acad. Law and Sci., Am. Judicature Soc. (dir. 1963-67), Nat. Coll. Probate Judges, Assn. Ins. Attys. (past dir.), Ariz. Pioneer Soc., Def. Research Inst. (charter mem.), Tucson C. of C., U. Mich. Alumni Assn. (pres. Grand Rapids 1938-40, Tucson, 1945-50, 76-77, dir. 8th dist. 1943-46), Phi Sigma Kappa (founder, charter pres. Tucson Alumni Club 1960-74). Home: 1915 E Third St Tucson AZ 85719 Office: 3d Floor United Bank Bldg 120 W Broadway Tucson AZ 85701 Tel (602) 624-2301

MAY, RONALD ALAN, b. Waterloo, Iowa, Sept. 8, 1928; B.A., U. Iowa, 1950; LL.B., Vanderbilt U., 1953. Admitted to Ark. bar, 1953; mem. firm Daggett & Daggett, Marianna, Ark., 1953-58; asso. and partner firm Wright, Lindsey & Jennings, Little Rock, 1958—. Mem. Am. Bar Assn. (chmn. sci. and tech. sect. 1975-76). Editor: Automated Law Research, 1973; Sense and Systems in Automated Law Research, 1975; contbr. articles to legal jours. Home: 420 Midland Little Rock AR 72205 Office: 2200 Worthen Bank Bldg Little Rock AR 72201 Tel (501) 371-0808

MAY, TIMOTHY JAMES, b. Denver, Aug. 3, 1932; B.A., Catholic U. Am., 1954; LL.B., Georgetown U., 1957, LL.M., 1960. Admitted to D.C. bar, 1957, U.S. Supreme Ct. bar, 1961; law clk. to judge U.S. Ct. Appeals, D.C. Circuit, 1957-58; asso. firm Covington & Burling, Washington, D.C., 1958-61; cons. to pres. U.S., 1961-62; acting chief counsel Senate Armed Services subcom., 1962-63; mng. dir. Fed. Maritime Commn., 1963-66; U.S. rep. to Internat. Maritime Confs., Paris, London, 1964-66; gen. counsel U.S. Post Office Dept., 1966-69; sr. partner firm Patton, Boggs & Blow, Washington, 1969—. Nat. dir. Citizens for Presdl. vote, 1961. Mem. Am., Fed., Postal Rate, Maritime bar assns. Contbr. articles to profl. jours. Recipient presdl. award, 1964; Arthur Flemming award Jaycees, 1966; Jump Meml. Found. award achievement in pub. adminstrn., 1965, 66, 67; Benjamin Franklin award U.S. Postal Service, 1969; named young lawyer year Fed. Bar Assn., 1967. Home: 3828 52d St NW Washington DC 20016 Office: 1200 17th St NW Washington DC 20036 Tel (202) 223-4040

MAYBANK, BURNET RHETT, b. Charleston, S.C., May 2, 1924; student The Citadel; B.S., U. S.C., 1950, LL.B., 1950. Admitted to S.C. bar, 1950; sr. partner firm Maybank & Manucy, Charleston; mem. S.C. Ho. of Reps., 1952-58; lt. gov. S.C., 1958-62. Mem. Am., S.C., Charleston County bar assns. Home: 1886 Houghton Dr Charleston SC 29412 Office: Maybank & Manucy PO Box 126 Charleston SC 29402 Tel (803) 722-1674 also 722-4735

MAYBERRY, HERBERT SYLVESTER, b. Enid, Okla., Jan. 20, 1927; B.S. in Geology, U. Okla., 1949; J.D., U. Denver, 1959. Admitted to Colo. bar, 1959, Okla. bar, 1967; geologist Shell Oil Co., Denver, 1949-58; sec., mgr., counsel Ball Assos., Ltd., Denver, 1958-65; exec. asst. Western Geophys. Co. Am., Shreveport, La., 1965-66; v.p., sec., gen. counsel McAlester Fuel Co. (Okla.), 1966—. Mem. Am., Okla., Colo. bar assns., Southwest Legal Found., Am. Assn. Petroleum Geologists, Assn. Profl. Geol. Scientists. Home: 1807 Cardinal Ln McAlester OK 74501 Office: PO Box 907 McAlester OK 74501 Tel (918) 423-5050

MAYDEW, MARVIN WAYNE, b. Lebanon, Kans., June 12, 1926; B.B.A., Washburn U., 1966, J.D., 1969. Admitted to Kans. bar, 1969; prin. Marvin W. Maydew, C.P.A., Topeka; mem. Kans. Bd. Accountancy, 1971-74, chmn., 1974; chmn. 20th Ann. Kans. Tax Conf., 1970. Mem. Am., Kans., Topeka bar assns., Am. Judicature Soc., Kans. Soc. of C.P.A.'s (bd. dirs. 1968-71, 1974-77), Am. Inst. C.P.A.'s, Am. Accounting Assn. Home: 1429 Ward Pkwy Topeka KS 66606 Office: Suite 600 820 Quincy St Topeka KS 66612 Tel (913) 234-6673

MAYER, EUGENE DONALD, b. Bridgewater, S.D., Sept. 15, 1926; LL.B., U. S.D., 1951. Admitted to S.D. bar, 1951; partner firm Riter, Mayer, Hofer & Riter, Pierre, S.D., 1951—; states atty. Hughs County, 1955-58; asst. atty. City Pierre, 1951—. Mem. Am. Bar Assn., State Bar of S.D., Pierre C. of C. (pres., 1975-76). Home: 220 N Van Buren St Pierre SD 57501 Office: 319 S Coteau St Pierre SD 57501 Tel (605) 224-5826

MAYER, JAMES JOSEPH, b. Shelby, Ohio, Oct. 13, 1920; student DeSales Coll., 1938-40; J.D., Ohio No. U., 1946. Admitted to Ohio bar, 1947, U.S. Supreme Ct. bar, 1959; practiced in Shelby, 1947-49, Mansfield, Ohio, 1949-59; judge Richland County (Ohio) Ct. Common Pleas, 1959—, Muskingum Watershed Conservancy Dist., 1959—; asst. pros. atty. Richland County, 1949-52. Mem. Ohio Bar, Richland County Bar Assn., Common Pleas Judges Assn. Recipient certificate of appreciation SSS, 1972; Carl V. Weygandt award Ohio Supreme Ct., 1972, 73, Outstanding Judicial Service awards, 1974, 75, Superior Judicial Service award, 1976; testimonial Richland Bar Assn., Richland County Med. Soc. and Citizens of Richland County, 1974, Chalk and Slate award Mansfield Edn. Assn., 1975, testimonial Richland County Council AFL-CIO, 1975, Ohio 110th Gen. Assembly award, 1972. Home: Rural Delivery 11 Fleming Falls Rd Mansfield OH 44903 Office: 50 Park Ave E Mansfield OH 44902 Tel (419) 524-4004

MAYER, MICHAEL FORD, b. White Plains, N.Y., Sept. 8, 1917; B.S. cum laude, Harvard, 1939; LL.B., Yale, 1942. Admitted to N.Y. bar, 1943; asso. firm Greenbaum, Wolff & Ernst, N.Y.C., 1946-47, Spring & Eastman, N.Y.C., 1947-56, partner, 1956-67; mem. firm Sargoy & Stein, N.Y.C., 1967-68; partner firm Mayer & Bucher, N.Y.C., 1968—; exec. dir., gen. counsel Internat. Film Importers & Distbrs. of Am., Inc., N.Y.C., 1959-68; tchr. New Sch. Social Research, N.Y.C., 1971—. Mem. Am., N.Y.C., Westchester County bar assns., Fed. Bar Council. Author: Divorce and Annulment in the Fifty States, 1967; What You Should Know About Libel and Slander, 1968; Rights of Privacy, 1972; The Film Industries, 1973; contbr. articles to legal jours. Home: 9 Inverness Rd Scarsdale NY 10583 Office: 111 W 57th St New York City NY 10019 Tel (212) 581-4577

MAYER, VELIA ANN, b. Titus County, Tex., Feb. 13, 1943; student Millsaps Coll.; B.A., U. Miss., 1965, J.D., 1968. Admitted to Miss. bar, 1968, U.S. Dist. Ct. bar No. Dist. Miss., So. Dist. Miss., U.S. Ct. Appeals bar, 5th Circuit; legal research asst. to Justice Tom P. Brady, Miss. Supreme Ct., 1968-69; spl. asst. atty. gen. Miss. Atty. Gen's Office, Jackson, 1969-71; asso. firm Watkins & Eager, Jackson, 1971-75, partner, 1976—. Mem. Am., Miss., Hinds County (Miss.) bar assns., Jackson Young Lawyers' Assn., Am. Judicature Soc. Home: 787 Arlington St Jackson MS 39202 Office: PO Box 650 800 Plaza Bldg Jackson MS 39205 Tel (601) 948-6470

MAYES, BOB IVAN, b. Farmington, Ark., Jan. 18, 1938; B.A., U. Ark., 1965, LL.B., 1967. Admitted to Ark. bar, 1967; individual practice law, Fayetteville, Ark., 1967-68; judge Juvenile Ct. Washington County (Ark.), Fayetteville, 1968—. Mem. advisory council Youth Services Planning Bd. Mem. Am., Ark., Washington County bar assns., Nat. Juvenile Judges' Assn., Ark. Juvenile Justice Assn. Home: Forest Hills Rd Fayetteville AR 72701 Office: PO Box 388 Fayetteville AR 72701 Tel (501) 443-5731

MAYES, FREDERICK WILLIAM, b. Denton County, Tex., Mar. 29, 1917; LL.B., So. Meth. U., 1942. Admitted to Tex. bar, 1942; individual practice law, Dallas, 1942—; ind. ins. broker, Dallas, 1952—. Home and Office: 3930 Northaven St Dallas TX 75229 Tel (214) 352-6469

MAYES, S. HUBERT, JR., b. Little Rock, Sept. 6, 1931; J.D., U. Ark., 1954. Admitted to Ark. bar, 1954; asst. sec. Ark. State Senate, 1953; atty. Ark. State Revenue Dept., 1954-55; dep. pros. atty. 6th Judicial Dist., Ark., 1957-58; spl. asst. atty. gen. State of Ark., 1963; partner firm Mayes & Murray, Little Rock. Mem. Am., Ark., Pulaski County bar assns., Defense Research Inst., Ark., Am. trial lawyers assns. Home: 2021 Beechwood St Little Rock AR 72207 Office: 2248 First National Bldg Little Rock AR 72201 Tel (501) 375-9952

MAYES, WILLIAM ROBERT, b. Kirkland, Wash., May 30, 1925; student Pasadena City Coll.; grad. Southwestern U., 1955. Admitted to Calif. bar, 1955; practice law, 1955-71; judge Municipal Ct., West Covina, Calif., 1971—; arbitrator Am. Arbitration Assn., 1960-61. Mem. Los Angeles County, Am., Pomona Valley, Citrus (charter, pres. 1960-61) bar assns., Azusa (Calif.) C. of C. (pres. 1960-61, life).

MAYEUX, DONALD LYNN, b. Mamou, La., Sept. 8, 1941; B.S., La. State U., 1962, J.D., 1968. Admitted to La. bar, 1968; asso. firm Devillier and Ardoin, Eunice, La., 1968-69; partner firm Guillory, McGee and Mayeux, Eunice, 1969—; mem. St. Landry Parish (La.) Indigent Defendant's Bd., 1974—; instr. Dale Carnegie courses, Eunice, 1972—. Chmn. St. Landry Parish March of Dimes Assn., 1973—; chmn. Eunice Democratic exec. com., 1973—; v.p. ch. parish council, lay minister St. Thomas Moore Parish, Eunice. Mem. Am., La., St. Landry Parish bar assns., La. Trial Lawyers Assn., Eunice Jaycees (pres. 1969; named Outstanding Young Man in Eunice 1971; Outstanding Eunice Jaycee 1969). Home: 200 Pinecrest Eunice LA 70535 Office: 140 N 2d St Eunice LA 70535 Tel (318) 457-5213

MAYFIELD, CHARLES RUSSELL, JR., b. Bay Springs, Miss., Nov. 20, 1927; B.S., U. Miss., 1947, LL.B., 1950. Admitted to Miss. bar, 1950; individual practice law, Jackson, Miss., 1950—. Home: 5420 Marblehead Dr Jackson MS 39211 Office: Suite 205 518 E Capitol St Jackson MS 39205 Tel (601) 948-3590

MAYFIELD, REID KERRIN, b. Durant, Okla., Feb. 8, 1937; B.A., Southeastern State Coll., Durant, 1959; J.D., Oklahoma City U., 1966. Patrolman, Oklahoma City Police Dept., 1960-65; agt. Okla. Alcoholic Beverage Control Bd., Oklahoma City, 1965-66; admitted to Okla. bar, 1966; judge McCurtain County (Okla.) Ct., 1967-68; asso. dist. judge McCurtain County Dist. Ct., 1969-70; individual practice law, Atoka, Okla., 1971—; asst. dist. atty. Atoka County, 1971-72, 76—; town atty. Town of Tushka (Okla.) and Town of Stringtown (Okla.), 1972-76; city atty. City of Atoka, 1976—. Mem. Chickasaw Multi-county Library Bd., 1973—, vice chmn., 1974-75, chmn., 1975-76. Mem. Okla. Bar Assn. Home: 304 S Mississippi Ave Atoka OK 74525 Office: 229 E Court St Atoka OK 74525 Tel (405) 889-5213

MAYFIELD, ROBERT USHER, b. Temple, Tex., Mar. 3, 1947; student InterAm. U., Saltilio, Mexico, summer 1963, Harvard, 1967, U. Edinburgh (Scotland), summer 1970; B.A., U. Tex., 1971, J.D., 1972. Page, U.S. Congress, summer 1960; mem. staff Senator J. P. Word, Austin, Tex., legis. sessions 1967, 69, 71; law clk. firm Byron Lockhart, Austin, 1971-72; admitted to Tex. bar, 1972; asso. firms Wheat, Wheat & Stafford, Woodville, Tex., 1972-73, Thomas & Burdett, Hereford, Tex., 1973-77; co-owner, gen. counsel Tolmay Enterprises, Inc., 1977—. Chmn. bd. dirs. Hereford Day Care Center, 1974—; v.p., founding dir. Hereford YMCA, 1976—; chmn. environ. com. Hereford C. of C., 1976. Home: 10144 Aspen St Austin TX 78758 Office: 13207 Research St Austin TX 78759

MAYFIELD, WILLIAM STEPHEN, b. Gary, Ind., Mar. 2, 1919; A.B., Detroit Inst. Tech., 1946; J.D., Detroit Coll. Law, 1949. Admitted to Mich. bar, 1949; asso. firm Lewis, Rowlette, Brown, Wanzo and Bell, Detroit, 1949-51; atty. U.S. Office Price Stablzn., Washington, 1951-53; referee, friend of the court, Detroit, 1953-72; prof. law So. U., Baton Rouge, 1972—. Mem. regional bd. Boy Scouts Am., 1962-63. Mem. Am., Mich., Nat., Wolverine bar assns., Louis A. Martinet Legal Soc., Detroit Coll. Law Alumni Assn., World Assn. Law Profs., Comml. Law League of Am., Am. Fedn. Tchrs., Ret. Officers Assn., Delta Theta Phi. Home: PO Box 73823 Baton Rouge LA 70807 Office: Southern U Sch Law Baton Rouge LA 70813 Tel (504) 771-3776

MAYNARD, GEORGE FLEMING, b. Montgomery, Ala., Mar. 10, 1931; B.A., Washington and Lee U., 1953; LL.B., U. Va., 1956. Admitted to Va. bar, 1956, Miss. bar, 1956, Ala. bar, 1957; asso. firm Cabaniss, Johnson, Gardner, Dumas & O'Neal, Birmingham, Ala., 1957-63, partner, 1963—. Mem. Am., Ala., Miss., Va. bar assns., Am. Law Inst. Office: 1900 1st National-Southern Natural Bldg Birmingham AL 35203 Tel (205) 252-8800

MAYNARD, WILLIAM, b. Plymouth, N.H., Apr. 25, 1917; student U. N.H.; LL.B., Boston U., 1942. Admitted to N.H. bar, 1944, U.S. Supreme Ct. bar, 1963; asst. U.S. Atty., N.H., 1954-59; legal counsel Gov., N.H., 1959; atty. gen. State of N.H., 1961-66; chmn. N.H. State Tax Commn., 1969-73; individual practice law, Concord, N.H., 1966-69; mem. firm Maynard, Perkins & Phillips, Concord, 1977—. Mem. N.H., Grafton County, Merrimack County bar assns. Office: 87 N State St Concord NH 03301 Tel (603) 225-6603

MAYNE, ARLOW WESLEY, b. nr. Ky., Sept. 17, 1921; student Cumberland Coll., 1946-48; LL.B., U. Ky., 1951. Admitted to Ky. bar, 1951-since practiced in Ashland, with law dept. Ashland Oil, Inc., 1951-62, asst. sec., 1962-65, gen. counsel, 1965—, adminstrv. v.p., 1966—. Mem. Ashland Jr. C. of C., Am., Ky., Boyd County (pres. 1964-65) bar assns., Phi Alpha Delta. Home: 117 Mt Savage Dr Ashland KY 41101 Office: 1409 Winchester Ave Ashland KY 41101*

MAYO, JOHN TYLER, b. Goshen, N.Y., Sept. 10, 1933; A.B., Colgate U., 1954; J.D., Columbia U., 1960. Admitted to N.Y. State bar, 1960, U.S. Supreme Ct. bar, 1964; asso. firm Mayer, Kissel, Matz & Seward, N.Y.C., 1960-62; partner firm Mayo & Mayo, Goshen, 1962—; dir. Goshen Savs. & Loan. Mem. Goshen (pres. 1977), Orange County (dir. 1974—, v.p. 1976—), N.Y. State, Am. bar assns. Home: Owens Rd Goshen NY 10924 Office: 154 Main St Goshen NY 10924

MAYO, LOUIS HARKEY, b. Prestonburg, Ky., May 18, 1918; B.S., U.S. Naval Acad., 1940; LL.B., U. Va., 1949; J.S.D., Yale, 1953. Admitted to Va. bar, 1949; faculty George Washington U., 1950—; mem. Nat. Law Center, 1950-58, acting dean, 1958-59; dean Grad. Sch. Pub. Law, 1960-66; v.p. for policy studies and spl. projects, 1966—, dir. program policy studies in sci. and tech., 1966—; mem.

Nat. Acad. Scis. Panel on Tech. Assessment, 1968-69, Nat. Acad. Public Adminstrn. Panel on Tech. Assessment, 1970—; adv. group Internat. Soc. for Tech. Assessment, 1973—; Am. Bar Found. Com. on the Law of Outer Space, 1964-65; counsellor Center for Policy Scis. Mem. Am., Va., Fed., D.C. bar assns. Co-author: Network Broadcasting, 1957; contbr. articles, monographs in field to legal jours. Home: 3018 Wallace Dr Falls Church VA 22042 Office: Room 714 Academic Library George Washington U Washington DC 20052 Tel (202) 676-7382

MAYS, RICHARD DUDLEY, b. Dallas, Dec. 28, 1939; B.B.A., U. Tex., 1962, J.D., 1965. Admitted to Tex. bar, 1965; partner firm Mays & Mays, Dallas, 1965-67; asst. dist. atty. Dallas County, 1967-73; judge 204th Jud. Dist. Ct., Dallas, 1973—. Democratic Precinct chmn., Dallas, 1966. Mem. Dallas, Tex. bar assns. Home: 3601 Caruth St Dallas TX 75225 Office: Dallas County Ct House Dallas TX 75202 Tel (214) 749-8452

MAZANDER, EARL JOSEPH, b. Coulterville, Ill., Nov. 5, 1932; LL.B., U. Ark. Admitted to Ark. bar, 1960; municipal judge, Hot Springs, Ark., 1967—. Mem. Ark., Garland County bar assns., Am. Legion, VFW. Home: 400 Bayles St Hot Springs AR 71901 Office: City Hall Hot Springs AR 71901 Tel (501) 624-3281

MAZEL, WILLIAM, b. Norfolk, Va., Apr. 24, 1930; A.A., Norfolk Coll. of William & Mary U., 1949; J.D., U. Richmond, 1951. Admitted to Va. bar, 1952; individual practice law, Norfolk, 1955—; asso. prof. bus. law Old Dominion U., Norfolk, 1966—; mem. various univ. coms. Pres., Hebrew Acad. Tidewater; dir. Tidewater Community Sch. Mem. Am., Va. bar assns., Am. Judicature Soc. Contbr. articles in field to legal jours. Home: 437 Hariton Ct Norfolk VA 23505 Office: 705 One Main Plaza E Norfolk VA 23510 Tel (804) 622-1909

MAZOR, LESTER JAY, b. Chgo., Dec. 12, 1936; A.B., Stanford, 1957, J.D., 1960. Admitted to Utah bar, 1962; law clk. judge Warren E. Burger, U.S. Ct. Appeals, D.C. Circuit, 1960-61; instr. U. Va. Law Sch., Charlottesville, 1961-62; asst. prof. U. Utah Sch. Law, Salt Lake City, 1962-66, asso. prof., 1966-69, prof., 1969-70; Henry R. Luce prof. law Hampshire Coll., Amherst, Mass., 1970-75, prof., 1975—; vis. prof. law Stanford, 1967-68, State U. N.Y. at Buffalo, 1973-74, U. Conn., 1972, 76-77. Mem. Am. (com. reporter 1965-69), Utah bar assns., Law and Soc. Assn., Am. Soc. Legal History. Co-editor: Introduction to the Study of Law, 1970. Home: 125 Potwine Ln Amherst MA 01002 Office: Hampshire Coll Amherst MA 01002 Tel (413) 549-4600

MAZUR, JAMES ANDREW, b. Port Clinton, Ohio, Apr. 24, 1941; B.B.A., U. Toledo, 1963; J.D., Cleveland Marshall Law Sch., 1968. Admitted to Ohio bar, 1968, U.S. Dist. Ct. bar, 1970; mem. mgmt. and labor relations staff Chevrolet Cleve., Cleve., 1963-68; partner firm Osterland & Mazur, N. Royalton, Ohio, 1969—. Chmn. Democratic Party, Ottawa County, central committeeman, Danbury Twp. Mem. Am., Ohio, Greater Cleve. bar assns., Delta Theta Phi. Home: 340 N Sackett St Lakeside OH 43440 Office: 7029 Royalton Rd N Royalton OH 44133 Tel (216) 237-8284

MAZURSKY, CHARLES JAY, b. Madison, Wis., Aug. 12, 1941; B.A., U. Wis., 1963; J.D., Hastings Coll. Law U. Calif., 1969. Admitted to Calif. bar, 1970; asso. firm Dryden, Harrington & Swartz, Los Angeles, 1969-75, partner, 1975—. Mem. Calif., Los Angeles County bar assns. Home: 157 S Vista St Los Angeles CA 90036 Office: One Wilshire Bldg Los Angeles CA 90017 Tel (213) 628-2184

MAZZA, ANTHONY JOSEPH, b. N.Y.C., Oct. 23, 1945; LL.B., Fordham Coll., 1967, J.D., 1970. Admitted to N.Y. bar, 1971, Colo bar, 1971, U.S. Dist. Ct. bar for Dist. Colo., 1971; law clk. firm Mudge, Rose, Gutham & Alexander, N.Y.C., 1968; partner firm Slemon, Mazza & La Salle, P.C., Aspen, Colo., 1970-75, 77—. Mem. Fordham Law Rev., 1968-69. Office: Mountain Plaza Bldg Aspen CO 81611 Tel (303) 925-2043

MAZZIA, ALEXANDER LLORET, b. N.Y.C., May 12, 1924; B.S. with high distinction in Mech. Engring., U. Rochester, 1945; J.D., U. So. Calif., 1957. Admitted to Calif. bar, 1958; individual practice law, Torrance, Calif., 1958—; prof. law Western State U. Coll. law, Orange County, Calif., 1972—. Pres. Torrance Democrats Inc., 1972,73,74. Mem. Phi Beta Kappa, Phi Delta Phi. Home: 348 Via Almar Palos Verdes Estates CA 90274 Office: 1405 Sartori Ave Torrance CA 90501 Tel (213) 328-0792

MCADAM, PATRICK MICHAEL, b. Los Angeles, Jan. 24, 1946; B.B.A., Loyola U., Los Angeles, 1967, J.D., 1970. Admitted Calif. bar, 1971, U.S. Fed. Dist. 9th Ct., 1972, also Central and So. Dist.; asso. firm Iverson, Yoakum, Papiano & Hatch, Los Angeles, 1971—. Mem. Los Angeles, Am. bar assns., Assn. So. Calif. Ins. Def. Council, State Bar Calif., Assn. Bus. Trial Lawyers. Office: 611 W 6th St Suite 1900 Los Angeles CA 90017

MC ADAMS, HERBERT HALL, b. Jonesboro, Ark., June 6, 1915; B.S., Northwestern U., 1937; postgrad. Harvard, 1937-38, Loyola U., Chgo., 1938-39; J.D., U. Ark., 1940. Admitted to Ark. bar, 1940, U.S. Supreme Ct. bar, 1944; pres. Home Fed. Savs. & Loan Assn., Jonesboro, 1954-67, chmn. bd., 1954-76; chmn. bd., chief exec. officer Citizens Bank of Jonesboro, 1959—, Union Nat. Bank of Little Rock, 1970—; dir. Ark. La. Gas Co., Shreveport; mem. Ark. Bd. Bar Examiners, 1950-55, Ark. Uniform Code Commn., 1964-66; commr. Nat. Assn. Commns. Uniform State Laws, 1961-66; patron Ark. Bar Found., 1972. Chmn., Metrocentre Improvement Dist. Little Rock, 1973-75, Ark. Indsl. Devel. Commn., 1967-72, Ark. State U. Found., 1977—; mem. Ark. Council on Econ. Edn., 1972; trustee Ark. Children's Hosp., 1973—. Mem. Am., Ark. (mem. coms.), Pulaski County, Craighead County (pres. 1953-54) bar assns., Ark., Am. bankers assns. Home: 47 Edgehill Rd Little Rock AR 72207 Office: Union National Bank Bldg Little Rock AR 72203 Tel (501) 378-4000

MC ALEAR, ALLEN LEE, b. Havre, Mont., Mar. 25, 1928; student U. Nev., 1948, U. Oreg., 1948-50; J.D., U. Mont., 1953. Admitted to Mont. bar, 1953; individual practice law, Bridger, Mont., 1953-57, Bozeman, Mont., 1957—. Chmn. Democratic Central Com., 1966-70; pres. chpt. 18 Am. Contract Bridge League, 1968-72. Mem. Phi Delta Phi. Home: Meadowlark Addition Bozeman MT 59715 Office: Story Block 3 - 5 Bozeman MT 59715 Tel (406) 587-3462

MC ALLEN, HENRY RAYMOND HAMILTON, b. Chgo., Apr. 23, 1938; A.B., Ohio U., 1961; J.D., U. Mich., 1964. Admitted to Ohio bar, 1965; asso. firm F. T. Eagleson Jr., Columbus, Ohio, 1965; atty. examiner Pub. Utilities Commn. of Ohio, Columbus, 1966-68; individual practice law, Columbus, 1968-77; asst. pub. defender Ohio Pub. Defender Commn., Columbus, 1977—. Mem. Am., Ohio, Columbus bar assns., Am. Judicature Soc. Office: 20 E Broad St Columbus OH 43215 Tel (614) 466-5393

MC ALLISTER, JOHN DUNHAM, b. Houston County, Ga., Aug. 18, 1945; B.A., Ga. State Coll., 1967; J.D., U. Ga., 1970. Admitted to Ga. bar, 1970; legal counsel Ga. Municipal Assn., Atlanta, 1970-71; mem. firm Charles J. Driebe, Jonesboro, Ga., 1971-74; individual practice law, 1975-76; mem. firm Margot S. Roberts, 1976—. Mem., chmn. State of Ga. Bldg. Adminstrv. Bd., 1970-73. Mem. Am. (state bd. govs. 1977—), Clayton County (pres. 1974-75) bar assns., Ga. Assn. Criminal Def. Lawyers (v.p. 1977—), Lawyers Club of Atlanta. Home: 202 S Main St Jonesboro GA 30236 Office: 148 S Main St Jonesboro GA 30236 Tel (404) 477-5050

MC ALLISTER, NEWMAN ELWOOD, b. Shreveport, La., Oct. 29, 1942; B.A., U. Mo., Kansas City, 1964; J.D., 1967. Admitted to Mo. bar, 1967, Colo. bar, 1971; asso. firm Achtenberg, Sandler & Balkin, Kansas City, Mo., 1967-68, 1969-71; jr. partner firm Gibson, Gerdes & Campbell, Colorado Springs, 1971-77, gen. partner, 1977—. Mem. Colo., El Paso County bar assns. Recipient Man of the Year award Soc. Preservation and Encouragement Barber Shop Quartet Singing in Am., 1975. Home: 8740 Chipita Park Rd Cascade CO 80809 Office: 310 Mining Exchange Building Colorado Springs CO 80903 Tel (303) 636-3866

MC ALLISTER, WILLIAM MENZIES, b. Portland, Oreg., Nov. 2, 1905; LL.B., Willamette U., 1928, LL.D., 1963. Admitted to Oreg. bar, 1928, Wash. bar, 1929; individual practice law, Medford, Oreg., 1931-56; judge Oreg. Supreme Ct., Salem, 1956-76, chief justice, 1959-66. Representative, Oreg. State Legislature, 1937-44, Speaker of House, 1943-44, Senator, 1949. Mem. Am. Bar Assn., Inst. Jud. Adminstrn., Nat. Legal Aid and Defense Assn., Nat. Council on Crime and Delinquency, Delta Theta Phi. Named Distinguished Law Alumni Willamette U., 1976. Home: 3403 Country Club Dr S Salem OR 97302 Tel (503) 364-5166

MCAMIS, EDWIN EARL, b. Cape Girardeau, Mo., Aug. 8, 1934; A.B., Harvard, 1956, LL.B., 1959. Admitted to N.Y. bar, 1960, U.S. Supreme Ct. bar, 1965; asso. firms Webster, Sheffield & Chrystie, N.Y.C., 1959-61, Regan Goldfarb Powell & Quinn, N.Y.C., 1962-65; asso. firm Lovejoy, Wasson, Lundgren & Ashton, N.Y.C., 1965-69, partner, 1969—. Mem. Assn. Bar City N.Y. (fed. cts. com. 1975—), Am. Bar Assn. (charter mem. sect. on litigation 1972—, Selden Soc. Home: 310 W 72d St New York City NY 10023 Office: 250 Park Ave New York City NY 10017 Tel (212) 697-4100

MC ANANY, PATRICK DALY, b. Sweetwater, Tex., Nov. 18, 1943; B.A., Rockhurst Coll., Kansas City, Mo., 1965; J.D., U. Mo., 1968, LL.M., 1971. Admitted to Kans. bar, 1973, Mo. bar, 1968, N.Y. bar, 1973; asso. firm Miller & O'Laughlin, Kansas City, Mo., 1968-70; asst. div. atty. Mobil Oil Corp., N.Y.C., 1970-73; mem. firm McAnany, Van Cleave & Phillips, Kansas City, Kans., 1973—. Mem. Kansas City, Johnson County, Wyansott County bar assns. Office: 4140 W 71st St Prairie Village KS 66208 Tel (913) 831-4040

MCANANY, PATRICK DAMIEN, b. Kansas City, Kans., Feb. 28, 1930; A.B., Rockhurst Coll., 1951; M.A., St. Louis U., 1958, St.L., 1964; J.D., Harvard, 1960. Admitted to Mo. bar, 1960, Ill. bar, 1972; asso. firm Moser, Marsalek, St. Louis, 1960, Morris A. Shenker, St. Louis, 1961; asst. to asso. prof. law U. St. Louis, 1965-69; research asso. U. Chgo. Law Sch., 1969-70; dir. Council on Diagnosis and Evaluation of Criminal Defendants, Chgo., 1969-71; asso. prof. criminal justice U. Ill., Chgo. Circle, 1971—; reporter Ill. Unified Code of Corrections, 1969-71. Chmn., Narcotics Service Council, St. Louis, 1967-69; pres. Fondo Rehabilitacion Empleyo y Economato, Inc., Chgo., 1975—. Mem. Am., Chgo bar assns., Chgo. Council Lawyers, Acad. Criminal Justice Scis. Recipient Meritorious Achievement award Ill. Acad. Criminology, 1973; author: Contemporary Punishment, 1972; contbr. articles in field to profl. jours. Home: 732 S East Ave Oak Park IL 60304 Office: Dept Criminal Justice U Ill Chicago Circle PO Box 4348 Chicago IL 60680

MC ANDREW, THOMAS JOSEPH, b. Providence, Oct. 19, 1945; B.A., Providence Coll., 1968; J.D., Am. U., 1971; LL.M., Georgetown U., 1973. Admitted to R.I. bar, 1971, D.C. bar, 1972; trial atty. CAB, Washington, 1971-72; legal asst. to mem. NLRB, Washington, 1972-73; labor relations officer R.I. Dept. Edn., Providence, 1973-74, dep. asst. commr. edn., 1974—; adj. prof. law U. R.I. Trustee John E. Fogarty Found. for Retarded. Mem. Am., Fed. bar assns., Practicing Labor Lawyers Club Washington. U.S. Office Edn. grantee, 1976-77. Home: 96 Meredith Dr Cranston RI 02920 Office: 199 Promenade St Providence RI 02908 Tel (401) 277-2042

MC ANDREWS, JAMES PATRICK, b. Cardondale, Pa., May 11, 1929; B.S. in Accounting, U. Scranton, 1949; LL.B., Fordham U., 1952; real estate inst. certificate N.Y. U., 1972. Admitted to N.Y. state bar, 1953, U.S. Supreme Ct. bar, 1960, Ohio bar, 1974; asso. with James F. McManus, Levittown, N.Y., 1955; atty. Emigrant Savs. Bank, N.Y.C., 1955-68; counsel Tchrs. Ins. and Annuity Assn., N.Y.C., 1968-73; asso. firm Thompson, Hine & Flory, Cleve., 1973-74, partner, 1974—. Mem. Am., Ohio bar assns., Bar Assn. Greater Cleve., Am. Land Title Assn., Urban Land Inst. Contbr. articles to legal jours. Home: 2971 Litchfield Rd Shaker Heights OH 44120 Office: 1100 Nat City Bank Bldg Cleveland OH 44114 Tel (216) 241-1880

MC ARA, HARRY BERNARD, b. Flint, Mich., Aug. 9, 1919; ed. Sch. Law U. Detroit. Admitted to Mich. bar, 1952; partner firms Devine & McAra, 1952-60, McAra & Palmer, 1960-73; judge Genesee County (Mich.) Circuit Ct., 1973—; twp. atty. Fenton Twp. (Mich.), 1960-72. Bd. dirs. YMCA Boys Farm; mem. Lake Fenton Citizens Advisory Com. Mem. Am. Judicature Soc., Mich. State Judges Assns. Home: 13363 Lakeshore Dr Fenton MI 48430 Office: 501 Courthouse 900 S Saginaw St Flint MI 48502 Tel (313) 766-8623

MC ARDLE, PATRICK FRANCIS, b. Pitts., Mar. 17, 1945; B.A., U. Pa., 1967; J.D., U. Pitts., 1970. Admitted to Pa. bar, 1970; partner firm McArdle, Henderson, Caroselli, Spagnolli & Beachler, Pitts., 1970—. Mem. Am., Allegheny County bar assns., Assn. Trial Lawyers Am. Home: 360 Morrison Dr Pittsburgh PA 15216 Office: 1100 Law & Finance Bldg Pittsburgh PA 15219 Tel (412) 391-9860

MC ARTHUR, SCOTT, b. Olympia, Wash., Nov. 9, 1932; A.B., U. Puget Sound, 1955; M.S., U. Oreg., 1958; J.D., Lewis and Clark Coll., 1966. Admitted to Oreg. bar, 1966, U.S. Supreme Ct. bar, 1973; partner firm McArthur & Horner, Monmouth, Oreg., 1967—; judge Falls City (Oreg.) Municipal Ct., 1968—. Mem. Oreg. State Bar (chmn. com. on econs. of practice 1975-76), Am., 12th Jud. Dist. (pres. 1973-74) bar assns., Oreg. Municipal Judges Assn. Contbr. articles to legal jours. Home: 520 S College St Monmouth OR 97361 Office: 110 N Atwater St Monmouth OR 97361 Tel (503) 838-0251

MC ATEE, JOHN J., JR., b. St. Louis, Mo., Nov. 23, 1936; A.B., Princeton U., 1958; LL.B., Yale, 1963. Admitted to N.Y. bar, 1964; asso. firm Davis Polk & Wardwell, N.Y.C., 1963-69, mem., 1969—. Pres., chief exec. officer Long Island Coll. Hosp., 1974-75, now vice-chmn. bd. regents; exec. com. Bklyn. Inst. of Arts & Scis., The Ethel Walker Sch., Simsbury, Conn. Mem. Internat., Am., N.Y. State bar assns., Bar Assn. City of N.Y. (com. on securities regulation). Contbr. articles to legal jours. Home: 237 Roundhill Rd Greenwich CT 06830 Office: One Chase Manhattan Plaza New York City NY 10005 Tel (212) 826-6938

MCAULAY, JOHN JAMES, b. Muskogee, Okla., July 11, 1912; A.B., Loyola U., New Orleans, 1936, LL.B., 1940, J.D., 1968; LL.M., Harvard, 1942. Admitted to La. bar, 1940; mem. faculty Loyola U., New Orleans, 1940-41, 1946-62, asst. dean, 1962-66, asso. dean, 1971—; vis. prof. law La. State U., spring 1965; reporter Statutory Revision Project, La. State Law Inst., 1947-49. Mem. Am., La., New Orleans bar assns., Am. Judicature Soc., La. State Law Inst., Phi Alpha Delta. Home: 1509 Audubon St New Orleans LA 70118 Office: Loyola U Sch Law New Orleans LA 70118 Tel (504) 865-2261

MC AULIFFE, GERARD STEPHEN, b. Boston, Sept. 2, 1946; A.B., Stonehill Coll., 1968; J.D., U. Maine, 1971. Admitted to Mass. bar, 1971, Maine bar, 1971; law clk. to Chief Justice Armand A. Dufiesne, Supreme Jud. Ct. of Maine, 1971-72; asso. firm Frank J. McGee, Marshfield, Mass., 1972-75; partner firm McParland and McAuliffe, Quincy, Mass., 1975—; instr. in legal research U. Maine, 1971; lectr. in law enforcement Northeastern U., 1975—. Mem. Am., Mass., Quincy bar assns. Office: 190 School St Quincy MA 02169 Tel (617) 471-0700

MC AVOY, JOHN JOSEPH, b. Worley, Idaho, June 28, 1933; B.A., U. Idaho, 1954, LL.B., 1958; LL.M., Yale, 1959. Admitted to Idaho bar, 1958, U.S. Supreme Ct. bar, 1962, N.Y. State bar, 1963, U.S. Tax Ct. bar, 1969, D.C. bar, 1976; asst. prof. law George Washington U., Washington, 1959-62; staff atty. Senate Subcom. on Armed Forces, 1962; asso. firm White & Case, N.Y.C., 1963, partner, 1972—; cons. Samuel Rubin Found., 1969-70; dir. Agfa Gevaert, Inc., mem. panel comml. arbitrators Am. Arbitration Assn. Bd. dirs. N.Y. Civil Liberties Union. Mem. Assn. of Bar N.Y.C., Phi Beta Kappa, Phi Alpha Delta. Author, speaker in civil liberties field. Home: 1 Gracie Terr New York City NY 10028 Office: 14 Wall St New York City NY 10005 Tel (212) 732-1040

MCBREARTY, WILLIAM JAMES, b. Detroit, Oct. 21, 1901; A.B., U. Detroit, 1923, LL.B., 1926. Admitted to Mich. bar, 1926, Ohio bar, 1960; sr. trial atty., City of Detroit, 1927-44; chmn. Mich. Pub. Service Commn., 1944-47; state bar commnrs., 1953-70; individual practice law, Detroit; chmn. Mich. Employment Security Appeal Bd., 1974—. Mem. City of Detroit Bd. Zoning Appeals, 1950-61. Mem. Detroit, Mich. State, Am. bar assns. Home: 349 Merriweather Rd Grosse Pointe Farms MI 48236 Office: 7310 Woodward Ave Detroit MI 48202 Tel (313) 876-5230

MC BRIDE, LLOYD MERRILL, b. Corydon, Iowa, July 20, 1908; B.A., Carleton Coll., 1930; J.D., Northwestern U., 1934. Admitted to Ill. bar, 1934, U.S. Supreme Ct. bar, 1947; partner firm McBride, Baker, Wienke & Schlosser, and predecessors, Chgo., 1940—; dir., mem. exec. com. Morton-Norwich Products, Inc.; dir. Wallace Bus. Forms, Inc., Stenographic Machines, Inc., Vermilion Corp., Bayou Corp., Bornquist, Inc., Frederic Ryder Co., Stenning Industries, Inc., Morton Industries of Can., Ltd., Essex Terminal Rwy. Co., Canadian Salt Co. Ltd., Morton Terminal Ltd. Trustee Carleton Coll., Morton Arboretum. Mem. Am., Ill., Chgo. bar assns. Home: 1550 N State Pkwy Chicago IL 60610 Office: 110 N Wacker Dr Chicago IL 60606 Tel (312) 346-6191

MC BRIDE, ROBERT L., b. Hillsboro, Ohio, Dec. 26, 1909; A.B., Washington and Lee U., 1932; LL.B., U. Cin., 1935. Admitted to Ohio bar, 1935; partner firm McBride & McBride, Hillsboro, 1936—; dir. Hillsboro Bank & Savs. Co. Mem. Highland County Bar Assn. Home: 232 E Walnut St Hillsboro OH 45133 Office: Hillsboro Bank Bldg Hillsboro OH 45133 Tel (513) 393-1515

MC BRIDE, STEPHEN ALAN, b. Hartford, Conn., Jan. 17, 1944; A.B. in Polit. Sci., Providence Coll., 1966; J.D., Villanova U., 1969. Admitted to Pa. bar, 1969; asso. firm Goodis, Greenfield, Narin & Mann, Phila., 1969-70; asso. firm Kassab, Cherry, Curran & Archbold, Media, Pa., 1970—. Mem. Del. County, Pa. bar assns. Home: 500 Hidden Valley Rd Chester PA 19014 Office: 214 N Jackson St Media PA 19063 Tel (215) 565-3800

MC BRIDE, THOMAS MATTHEW, III, b. New Orleans, July 19, 1923; LL.B., Tulane U., 1950. Admitted to La. bar, 1950, U.S. Dist. Ct. for Eastern Dist. La. bar, 1950, U.S. Dist. Ct. for so. dist. Miss. bar, 1956, U.S. 5th Circuit Ct. Appeals bar, U.S. Supreme Ct. bar, 1972; asso. firm Prowell & Viosca, New Orleans, 1950-55; partner firm Tillery & McBride, Arabi, La., 1955-62; partner firm McBride, Bopp & Perez, Arabi, 1963-68; partner firm McBride & Tonry, Chalmette, La., 1969-73; individual practice law, Chalmette, 1973—; spl. counsel SBA, 1956; atty.-sheriff St. Bernard Parish, La., 1973—. Chmn., St. Bernard Social Welfare Com., 1963; bd. dirs. Children's Bur. New Orleans, 1966-68. Mem. Fed., La. State, St. Bernard Parish, Plaquemines Parish bar assns., Am. Trial Lawyers Assn., VFW (comdr. Orleans parish council 1953-54), Rotary (pres. St. Bernard Parish, 1965), Greater New Orleans C. of C. (dir. St. Bernard council 1966-68). Home: 50 Carolyn Ct Arabi LA 70032 Office: 8901 W Judge Perez Chalmette LA 70043 Tel (504) 271-3484

MC BRYDE, THOMAS HENRY, b. New Albany, Miss., Oct. 26, 1925; B.S., U.S. Mil. Acad., 1946; LL.B., U. Va., 1952. Admitted to Va. bar, 1952, N.Y. bar, 1959; with Judge Adv. Gen's Corps U.S. Army, 1952-57, instr. in law U.S. Mil. Acad., 1956-57; asso. firm Rogers & Wells and predecessors, N.Y.C., 1957-60, 61-65, partner, 1965—; asst. counsel N.Y. State Banking Dept., N.Y.C., 1960-61; chief counsel N.Y. State Joint Legislature Com. to Revise Banking Law, 1962-65, minority counsel, 1965-66; mem. N.Y. Banking Supt's. Adv. Com. on Supervision of Mut. Instns., 1966-67. Mem. Am., N.Y. State bar assns., Va. State Bar (asso.), Am. Arbitration Assn. (comml. panel 1976—), Order of Coif. Office: 200 Park Ave New York City NY 10017 Tel (212) 972-7000

MC BURNETT, KENNETH STEWARD, b. Cedartown, Ga., Nov. 6, 1931; B.S., U.S. Naval Postgrad. Sch., Monterey, Calif., 1968; J.D., U. Ga., 1974. Admitted to Ga. bar, 1974; city atty., Richmond Hill, Ga.; county atty., Bryan County, Ga. Mem. Pembroke Hosp. Authority. Mem. Am., Ga., Atlantic Jud. Circuit bar assns. Home and office: PO Box 1041 Pembroke GA 31321 Tel (912) 653-4383

MC CABE, DAVID ALLEN, b. N.Y.C., Aug. 2, 1940; B.A., Princeton U., 1962; LL.B., Columbia U., 1966. Admitted to N.Y. bar, 1967; asso. firm Shearman & Sterling, N.Y.C., 1966-74, partner, 1974—; dir. Dequssa, Inc., 1972—. Office: 52 Wall St New York City NY 10005 Tel (212) 483-1000

MC CABE, EDWARD L., b. Williamsport, Ind., Jan. 18, 1901. B.A., Wabash Coll., 1922; Admitted to Ind. bar, 1922; pros. atty. 21st Jud. Circuit, 1941-44, 58-70, chief dep. pros. atty., 1970—. Mem. Warren County (Ind.), Ind. State, Am. bar assns. Office: 113 N Monroe St Williamsport IN 47993 Tel (317) 764-2476

MC CABE, MICHAEL KENNETT, b. St. Louis, Oct. 10, 1945; B.A., U. Mo., 1968, J.D., 1970. Admitted to Iowa bar, 1976; asst. counsel Mo. State Hwy. Commn., Jefferson City, 1970-73; sr. counsel Mo. Pub. Service Commn., Jefferson City, 1973-76; atty. Iowa Power & Light Co., Des Moines, 1976—; chmn. adminstrv. appeals subcom. Mo. Bar, 1974-76. Bd. dirs. Iowa Soc. Prevention Blindness, 1977—. Mem. Am., Iowa, Mo. bar assns., Fed. Power Bar, Phi Delta Phi. Home: 3921 Mary Lynn St Urbandale IA 50322 Office: 666 Grand Ave Des Moines IA 50309 Tel (515) 281-2351

MC CABE, ROBERT FOURCE, JR., b. Pitcairn, Pa., Oct. 12, 1936; A.B., U. Pitts., 1957, J.D., 1960; student Oxford (Eng.) U., 1956. Admitted to Pa. bar, 1961; partner firm Lindsay McGinnis McCandless & McCabe, Pitts., 1966—; solicitor Borough of Pitcairn, 1967-76. Mem. Am., Allegheny County bar assns. Home: 106 Himalaya Rd Monroeville PA 15146 Office: Lindsay McGinnis McCandless & McCabe 930 Grant Bldg Pittsburgh PA 15219 Tel (412) 471-2420

MC CABE, STEPHEN MICHAEL, b. N.Y.C., Feb. 26, 1941; B.A., Seton Hall U., 1962, J.D., 1965. Admitted to N.Y. bar, 1966, U.S. Supreme Ct. bar, 1972; asso. firm William H. Morris, N.Y.C., 1966-69, firm George B. McPhillips, Mineola, N.Y., 1969-72; partner firm McCabe & Nicolini, Mineola, 1972—. Mem. Am., N.Y., Nassau County bar assns., Def. Research Inst., Lawyer Pilots Bar Assn. Home: 253 Hempstead Ave Rockville Centre NY 11570 Office: 290 Old Country Rd Mineola NY 11501 Tel (516) 741-6299

MC CAFFERY, JOSEPH JAMES, JR., b. Butte, Mont., July 15, 1908; B.A., Stanford U., 1930; J.D., U. Mont., 1934. Admitted to Mont. bar, 1934; mem. firm McCaffery & Peterson, P.C. and predecessors, Butte, 1934-67, pres., 1967—; atty. Reconstrn. Finance Corp., Washington, 1935-36; spl. asst. atty. gen., 1949-57; mem. adv. bd. Gonzaga Law Council, 1967-71. Vice-chmn. Mont. Fish and Game Commn., 1969-71; chmn. Mont. Com. Lawyers for Johnson and Humphrey; trustee, U. Mont., 1949-51; mem. Selective Service Appeal Bd., 1949-69; chmn. Red Cross, 1959, Community Chest, 1959; trustee-at-large U. Mont. Law Sch., 1969-71. Fellow Internat. Acad. Trial Lawyers, Law Sci. Acad.; mem. Am., Mont. (pres. 1969-70), Silver Bow County bar assns., Am., Mont. (dir. 1969-70) trial lawyers assns. Home: 106 Rampart Dr Butte MT 59701 Office: 27 W Broadway St Butte MT 59701 Tel (406) 792-1221

MCCAFFREY, CARLYN SUNDBERG, b. N.Y.C., Jan. 7, 1942; A.B., George Washington U., 1963; LL.B., N.Y. U., 1967, LL.M., 1974. Admitted to N.Y. State bar, 1974; law clk. to chief judge Calif. Supreme Ct., San Francisco, 1967-68; instr. law N.Y. U., 1968-70, asst. prof., 1970-74, adj. asst. prof., 1975--; asso. firm Weil, Gotshal & Manges, N.Y.C., 1974—. Mem. adv. bd. N.Y. State Tax Commn., 1976—. Mem. N.Y. State Bar Assn. Home: 35 Fifth Ave New York City NY 10003 Office: 767 Fifth Ave New York City NY 10022 Tel (212) 758-7800

MC CAFFREY, JOHN WARREN, b. Chgo., May 12, 1900; B.S., Armour Inst. Tech., 1922, Chem.E., 1925; LL.B., Chgo. Kent Coll., 1930. Admitted to Ill. bar, 1933; engr. and lawyer for Universal Oil Products Corp., Chgo., 1930-43; contracting officer rep. Ordnance Dept. U.S. Army, 1943-45; atty. Chgo. Bd. Selective Service, 1941-46; counsel Nat. Metal Trade Assn., Chgo., 1945-49; owner, mgr. Patent and Engring Service Co., Chgo., 1950-65; judge Circuit Ct. Cook County, Ill., 1965-71. Trustee Ill. Inst. Tech., 1940-43. Mem. Ill. Bar Assn., Patent Law Assn. Chgo. Named Man of Yr., Ill. Inst. Tech., 1972. Home: 1200 Greenwood Ave Wilmette IL 60091 Tel (312) 251-0426

MC CAFFREY, STEPHEN CONOLLEY, b. San Mateo, Calif., Jan. 21, 1945; B.A., U. Colo., 1967; J.D., U. Calif. Boalt Hall, Berkeley, 1971; Dr.Jur. magna cum laude, U. Cologne (W.Ger.), 1974. Admitted to Calif. bar, 1973; research fellow Max Planck Inst. for Fgn. Pvt. Law and Pvt. Internat. Law, Hamburg, Germany, 1972; asso. prof. law Southwestern U. Sch. Law, Los Angeles, 1974—; research fellow Max Planck Assn., Hamburg, 1972, Alexander von Humboldt Found., Bad Godesberg, Germany, 1973-74; cons. com. on environ. law Internat. Union for Conservation of Nature. Mem. Calif. State Bar, Am., Internat. bar assns., Am. Soc. Internat. Law, Internat. Council Environ. Law, Sierra Club. Contbr. articles to profl. publs. Office: 675 S Westmoreland Ave Los Angeles CA 90005 Tel (213) 380-4800

MCCAIN, WILBUR TEAL, b. Colfax, La., Oct. 19, 1913; B.A., Northwestern State U., Natchitoches, La., 1938; LL.B., 1943; J.D., La. State U., Baton Rouge, 1968. Admitted to La. bar, 1943, U.S. Supreme Ct. bar, 1971; individual practice law, Colfax, 1943—; spl. asst. atty. gen. State of La., also atty. Bank of Montgomery (La.), 1959—, Colfax Banking Co., 1968—; city atty. Montgomery, 1959—; judge La. 35th Jud. Dist., 1977—. Bd. dirs. Attakapas council Boy Scouts Am.; mem. La. Ho. of Reps., 1940-48; chmn. Grant Parish Democratic Com.; mem. La. State Dem. Central Com., 1972—. Mem. La. (charter), Alexandria, Grant, Winn bar assns., La. Trial Lawyers Assn. (charter), Am. Trial Lawyers, Am. Judicature Soc., Municipal Attys. Assn. Recipient Outstanding Civic Leader Am. (plaque) Lions, 1967; Outstanding Hwy. Bd. Mem., Central La. Mayors Assn., 1967. Home: 401 2d St Colfax LA 71417 Office: Courthouse POB 223 Colfax LA 71414 Tel (381) 627-3244

MC CALEB, JOE WALLACE, b. Nashville, Tenn., Dec. 9, 1941; A.B. in History, Union U., 1964; postgrad. George Peabody Coll., 1965-66; J.D., Memphis State U., 1970. Admitted to Tenn. bar, 1971; law clk. to justice Tenn. Supreme Ct., 1970-71; atty. div. water quality control Tenn. Dept. Pub. Health, Nashville, 1971-73, div. solid waste mgmt., 1973-74, Bur. Environ. Health Services, 1974-77; pvt. practice law, Hendersonville, Tenn., 1977—. Am., Sumner County, Tenn. bar assns., Nashville Barrister's Club, Phi Delta Phi. Office: 394 W Main St Hendersonville TN 37075 Tel (615) 822-1610

MCCALL, HOBBY HALBERT, b. Dallas, May 16, 1919; student Southwestern U., 1936-38; U. Tex., 1938-39; LL.B., So. Methodist U., 1942. Admitted to Tex. bar, 1943; atty. appeals div. IRS, Pitts., 1946-49; mem. firm McCall, Parkhurst & Horton, Dallas, 1949—. Bd. dirs. Camp Brady Spruce, YMCA, 1952—, chmn., 1963-64; bd. dirs. Douglas MacArthur Acad. Freedom, 1963—, vice chmn., 1963-70; trustee Dallas Community Coll. Found., 1974—. Mem. Am. Bar Assn. (chmn. local govt. law sect. 1974-75). Home: 4220 Versailles St Dallas TX 75205 Office: 1400 Mercantile Bank Bldg Dallas TX 75201 Tel (214) 748-9501

MC CALL, MICHAEL WILLIAM, b. Gordon, Nebr., Sept. 12, 1943; B.A., U. Wyo., 1971, J.D., 1971. Admitted to Wyo. bar, 1971, U.S. Supreme Ct. bar, 1976; spl asst. atty. gen. State of Wyo. (Office of State Engr.), Cheyenne, 1971-73; partner firm Borthwick and McCall, Cheyenne, 1973—; pub. defender Laramie County, sec., bd. dirs., 1974—. Active Laramie County Cancer Soc., 1972-73, v.p., 1973-74, pres., 1974-75; bd. dirs. SE Mental Health Center, 1974. Mem. Am. Bar Assn. (mem. natural resources sect. law student div. 1967-71), Wyo., Laramie County bar assns. Recipient Layman Advocacy award U. Wyo. Law Sch., 1971. Home: 6219 Buffalo Ave Cheyenne WY 82001 Office: PO Box 1124 Suite 201 Teton Bldg Cheyenne WY 82001 Tel (307) 635-2433

MCCALLUM, DONALD ROY, b. Appleton, Wis., July 21, 1930; B.S., U. Wis., 1957; J.D., 1960. Admitted to Wis. bar, 1960, U.S. Dist. Ct. bar, 1960, U.S. Ct. Appeals, 1968, U.S. Supreme Ct. bar, 1976; dep. dist. atty. Dane County, Wis., 1961-66; asso. firm Jasper, Winner, Perina & Rouse, Madison, 1966-70; partner firm Winner, McCallum & Hendee, Madison, 1970—; lectr. law U. Wis., Madison, 1965; bd. dirs. Dane County Legal Services Center, 1968—. Chmn. Dane County chpt. National Brotherhood Assn., 1965—. Mem. Am., Dane County (chmn. criminal law com. 1969-74) bar assns., State Bar of Wis., Assn. Trial Lawyers Am., Phi Delta Phi. Home: Route 3 Stoughton WI 53589 Office: 111 S Fairchild St Madison WI 53703 Tel (608) 257-0257

MC CALLUM, DONALD VERNE, b. Council, Idaho, Nov. 26, 1913; student Reed Coll., 1939-40, Willamette U., 1940-42; LL.B., N.Y. U., 1951. Admitted to Oreg. bar, 1942, U.S. Supreme Ct. bar, 1953; individual practice law, Baker, Oreg., 1942-50, Portland, Oreg., 1957-70, Bend, Oreg., 1970—; exec. v.p. Safeco Title Ins. Co., Los Angeles, 1954-57; pres. Title & Trust Co. Oreg., Portland, 1957-66, Sunriver Properties, Inc. (Oreg.), 1965-71. Bd. dirs. Central Oreg. Symphony Soc., 1973—; adv. bd. St. Charles Med. Center, 1973—; chmn. Oreg. State Bar World Peace Through Law Com., 1970. Mem. Am., Oreg. bar assns. Home: Central Ln Sunriver OR 97701 Office: 265 Red Oaks Sq Bend OR 97701 Tel (503) 382-4990

MC CALLY, CHARLES THOMAS, b. Washington, Jan. 24, 1929; A.A., Am. U., 1952; LL.B., George Washington U., 1953. Admitted to D.C. bar, 1954; asst. U.S. atty. for D.C., 1959-61; partner firm Craighill, Mayfield & McCally, Washington, 1961—. Mem. Delta Theta Phi. Home: 690 Old Stage Rd Rockville MD 20852 Office: Suite 901 725 15th St NW Washington DC 20005 also 7401 Wisconsin Ave Bethesda MD 20014 Tel (202) 347-4444 also Tel (301) 881-0017

MC CANDLESS, GEORGE CURRYER, b. Indpls., Feb. 16, 1903; B.S., Butler U., 1925; LL.B., Ind. Law Sch., 1927. Admitted to Ind. bar, 1927, Ohio bar, 1930; individual practice law, Hamilton, Ohio, 1930—; mem. Ohio Ho. of Reps., 1939-40, 42-46, Ohio State Senate, 1947-50. Mem. Butler County Bar Assn. Home: 728 Elmwood St Hamilton OH 45013 Office: 513 Rentschler Bldg Hamilton OH 45011 Tel (513) 892-1147

MC CANDLESS, RICHARD LEE, b. Butler, Pa., May 30, 1934; A.B., Haverford Coll., 1955; M.Ed., Temple U., 1957; LL.B., Dickinson Sch. Law, 1960. Admitted to Pa. bar, 1960; asso. with Lee C. McCandless, Butler, Pa., 1960-67; individual practice law, Butler, 1967-69; mem. firm Coulter, Gilchrist, Dillon & McCandless, Butler, 1970-76, firm Dillon McCandless, King & Kemper, 1977—; dir. Butler Cons. Discount Co., 1970—. Chmn. fund raising Cerebral Palsy of Butler and Lawrence Counties, 1970; bd. dirs. Butler County br. Pa. Assn. for Blind, 1970, v.p., 1971—; mem. Butler County Br. for Crippled Children and Adults, Butler County United Fund, 1964-65; bd. dirs. Pa. Harness Horsemen's Assn., 1975—. Mem. Butler County, Pa., Am. bar assns., Fraternal Order Police. Named Elk of Year, Butler Lodge, 1968. Home: 206 Bluegrass Dr Butler PA 16001 Office: 128 W Diamond St Butler PA 16001 Tel (412) 283-2200

MC CANN, JOHN FRANCIS, JR., b. Indpls., Mar. 21, 1929; B.S. with distinction, St. Joseph's Coll., Rensselaer, Ind., 1951; J.D., Ind. U., 1954. Admitted to Ind. bar, 1954; dep. reporter Ind. Supreme Ct., 1950-53; atty. U.S. Chief Attys. Office, Indpls., 1957-60; dep. prosecutor Marion County (Ind.), 1960-62; prosecutor City of Indpls., 1962-64, atty., 1964-67; partner firm McCann & Lonbarger, Indpls., 1962—. Chmn. bd. dirs. Village of Woodland Lake, Ind.; bd. dirs. St. Joseph Coll., 1957-66. Mem. Indpls. Bar Assn. Home: 1202 N Audubon Rd Indianapolis IN 46219 Office: 4219 E Michigan St Indianapolis IN 46201 Tel (317) 357-6416

MC CANN, JOHN JOSEPH, b. Rochester, N.Y., Jan. 1, 1942; A.A., Adirondack Community Coll., 1966; A.B., Georgetown U., 1969; J.D., Syracuse Law Sch., 1972. Admitted to N.Y. bar, 1973; asso. firm McPhillips, Fitzgerald & Meyer, Glens Falls, N.Y., 1972-74; partner firm Leggett, Smith & McCann, P.C., Chestertown, N.Y., 1974-76; asst. U.S. atty. no. Dist. N.Y. Dept. Justice, 1976—; town atty. Town of Horricon (N.Y.), 1975-76. Bd. dirs. Adirondack Tri-County Nursing Home, North Creek, N.Y., 1976—. Mem. N.Y. State, Am., Warren County (N.Y.) bar assns. Home: 104 Wilkinson Pl Baldwinsville NY 13027 Tel (315) 473-6660

MCCANN, MICHAEL EARL, b. Brookings, S.D., Oct. 26, 1943; B.A., Marietta Coll., 1966; J.D., U. S.D., 1972. Admitted to S.D. bar, 1972; mem. firm McCann, Martin & Mickelson, Brookings, 1972—. Mem. Am., S.D. bar assns. Home: 1912 State St Brookings SD 57006 Office: 317 6th Ave Brookings SD 57006 Tel (606) 692-6163

MC CANN, RICHARD EUGENE, b. Billings, Mont., Aug. 13, 1939; B.A. magna cum laude, Rocky Mountain Coll., 1965; J.D. with high honors, U. Mont., 1972. Personnel mgmt. specialist U.S. Bur. Reclamation Dept. Interior, Ephrata, Wash., 1965-69; admitted to Mont. bar, 1972; law clk. to Hon. William J. Jameson, judge U.S. Dist. Ct. for Dist. Mont, 1972-73; asso. firm Crowley, Haughey, Hanson, Gallagher & Toole, Billings, 1973—. Trustee Rocky Mountain Coll., 1973—. Mem. Am., Mont., Yellowstone County (Mont.) bar assns., Am. Judicature Soc. Editor-in-chief Mont. Law Rev., 1971-72; contbr. articles to legal jours. Office: 500 Electric Bldg Billings MT 59101 Tel (406) 252-3441

MC CANN, WILLIAM VERN, b. Lewiston, Idaho, June 10, 1943; B.S., U. Idaho, 1966, J.D., 1969. Admitted to Idaho bar, 1969, U.S. Supreme Ct. bar, 1974; individual practice law, Lewiston, 1969—; legal counsel U.S. Jaycees, 1975-76, Idaho Jaycees, 1971-72. Pres., Lewis-Clark Council on Youth, 1971; bd. dirs. United Fund, 1972-76, Lewiston Roundup Assn., 1973-76; service club chmn. Lewiston Community Center, 1973. Mem. Am., Idaho, Clearwater bar assns., Lewis-Clark Pilots Assn. (pres. 1976). Recipient Lewiston-Clarkston Legal Secs. Assn. Boss of Year, 1970, Lewiston Jaycees Key Man award. Home: 100 Thiessen Rd Lewiston ID 83501 Office: 931 Bryden Ave Lewiston ID 83501 Tel (208) 743-5517

MCCARTAN, PATRICK F., b. Cleve., Aug. 3, 1934; A.B., U. Notre Dame, 1956, LL.B., 1959. Admitted to Ohio bar, 1960; law clk. to Justice Whittaker, U.S. Supreme Ct., 1959; now with firm Jones, Day, Reavis & Pogue, Cleve. Fellow Am. Coll. Trial Lawyers; mem. Bar Assn. Greater Cleve. (pres. 1977—). Office: 1700 Union Commerce Bldg Cleveland OH 44115 Tel (216) 696-3939*

MC CARTER, CHARLES CHASE, b. Pleasanton, Kans., Mar. 17, 1926; B.A., Principia Coll., 1950; J.D., Washburn U., 1953; LL.M., Yale, 1954. Admitted to Kans. bar, 1953, U.S. Supreme Ct. bar, 1962, Mo. bar, 1968; asst. atty. gen. State of Kans., Topeka, 1954-57; counsel FCC, D.C., 1957-58; asso. firm Weigard, Curfman, Brainerd, Harris and Kaufman, Wichita, Kans., 1958-61; gen. counsel Kans. Corp. Commn., Topeka, 1961-63; partner firm McCarter, Frizzell & Wettig, Wichita, 1963-68, McCarter & Badger, Wichita, 1968-73; individual practice law, St. Louis, 1968-76; partner firm McCarter & Greenley, St. Louis, 1976—; law lectr. Washburn Law Sch., Topeka, 1956-57; Tex. mem. legal com. Interstate Oil Compact Commn., 1961; mem. govtl. adv. council Gulf Oil Corp., 1977—. Chmn. Human Relations Devel. Adv. Bd., Wichita, 1967-68; bd. dirs. Peace Haven Assn., Inc., 1972-73. Mem. Am., Kans., Mo. bar assns. Contbr. articles to profl. jours.; asso. editor Washburn U. Law Rev., 1952-53. Home: 23 Chapel Hill Estates St Louis MO 63131 Office: Suite 700 230 S Bemiston St St Louis MO 63105 Tel (314) 725-7556

MC CARTER, LOWELL HAROLD, b. Alma, Mich., Aug. 4, 1934; B.S. in Chem. Engring., Purdue U., 1957; J.D., John Marshall Sch. Law, 1962. Admitted to Ind., Ill. bars, 1962, Mich. bar, 1965, Mass. bar, 1968; law clk. Pretzel, Stouffer, Nolan & Rooney, Chgo., 1961-63; examiner U.S. Patent and Trademark Office, Washington, 1963-64; asso. patent atty. BASF Wyandotte (Mich.) Chem. Co., 1964-67; patent counsel Ledgemont Lab., Kennecott Copper Corp., Lexington, Mass., 1967—; instr. bus. law Middlesex Community Coll., Bedford, Mass. Chmn., Carlisle (Mass.) Town Bldg. Com., 1973-74; mgr. Carlise Pee Wee Baseball League, 1976. Mem. Am., Mass. (intellectual property com.) bar assns., Am. Patent Law Assn. (edn., pub. info. coms.). Home: 150 Peter Hans Rd Carlisle MA 01741 Office: 128 Spring St Lexington MA 02173 Tel (617) 862-8268

MC CARTHA, C. EUGENE, b. Leeseville, S.C., Mar. 13, 1934; A.B., Mich. State U., 1955; LL.B., Duke U., 1958. Admitted to N.C. bar, 1958; partner firm Mc Cartha & Goines, Charlotte, N.C. Mem. 26th Judicial Dist., N.C., Am. bar assns., N.C. Acad. Trial Lawyers. Home: 2440 Sedley Rd Charlotte NC 28211 Office: 1805 Southern Nat Center Charlotte NC 28211 Tel (704) 377-1666

MC CARTHY, CHARLES JOSEPH, b. Providence, June 19, 1907; A.B., Providence Coll., 1927; LL.B., Yale U., 1930. Admitted to N.Y. state bar, 1932, R.I. bar, 1933, Tenn. bar, 1934, D.C. bar, 1967, U.S. Supreme Ct. bar, 1935; law clk., firm Rushmore, Bisbee & Stern, N.Y.C., 1930-31, asso., 1931-32; instr. Providence Coll., 1932-34; individual practice law, Providence, 1932-34; atty. RFC, N.Y.C., 1934; atty. TVA, Knoxville, Tenn., 1934-38, asst. gen. counsel, solicitor, 1939-58, gen. counsel, 1958-67; spl. asst. to U.S. Atty. Gen., Washington, 1938-39; partner firm Belnap, McCarthy, Spencer, Sweeney & Harkaway and predecessor firms, Washington, 1967—. Mem. Am., Fed., Fed. Power bar assns., Assn. ICC Practitioners. Contbr. articles to profl. jours. Home: 6401 Lakeview Dr Falls Church VA 22041 Office: 1750 Pennsylvania Ave NW Washington DC 20006 Tel (202) 393-5710

MC CARTHY, DENNIS, b. N.Y.C., Oct. 4, 1912; student Stanford, 1932-35; J.D., Georgetown U., 1939. Admitted to D.C. bar, 1939, Colo. bar, 1943, Utah bar, 1946; asst. U.S. atty., Washington, 1940-43; sr. mem. firm Van Cott, Bagley, Cornwall & McCarthy, Salt Lake City, 1946—. Fellow Am. Bar Found. (state chmn. 1977—); mem. Salt Lake County (pres. 1957-58), Utah State, Am. bar assns. Home: 2408 Haven Ln Salt Lake City UT 84117 Office: 141 E First South St Salt Lake City UT 84111 Tel (801) 532-3333

MC CARTHY, DENNIS KEVIN, b. Ironton, Ohio, Nov. 25, 1941; B.A. in History, U. Cin., 1965; J.D., Chase Coll., Park Hills, Ky., 1973. Admitted to Ohio, Ky. bars, 1973; credit supr. Procter & Gamble Co., Cin., 1967-73, transp. analyst, 1973—. Mem. Am., Ky., Ohio, Cin. bar assns. Office: 599 E 6th St Cincinnati OH 45202 Tel (513) 562-2881

MCCARTHY, J. THOMAS, b. Detroit, July 2, 1937; B.S., U. Detroit, 1960; J.D., U. Mich., 1963. Asso. firm Julian Caplan, San Francisco, 1963-66; admitted to Calif. bar, 1964, U.S. Patent and Trademark bar, 1964; prof. law U. San Francisco, 1966—; vis. prof. Univ. Coll., Dublin, Ireland, summer 1975; legal cons. Townsend & Townsend, San Francisco, 1974—; mem. Calif. Atty. Gen.'s Consumer Protection Task Force; vis. prof. U. Calif. at Berkeley, 1976-77. Mem. San Francisco Patent Law Assn., IEEE, Nat. Panel Consumer Arbitrators. Recipient Watson award Am. Patent Law Assn., 1965. Author: McCarthy on Trademarks and Unfair Competition, 2 vols., 1973; contbr. articles to legal jours. Office: 2130 Fulton St San Francisco CA 94117 Tel (415) 666-6517

MC CARTHY, JOHN ALOYSIUS MARTIN, b. Phila., July 6, 1901; B.S. in Economics, Univ. Pa., 1924; J.D., Temple U., 1928. Admitted to Pa. bar, 1928; individual practice law, Phila.; spl. dep. atty. gen. State of Pa., 1938-39; mem. Pa. Civil Service Commn., Harrisburg, 1942—, chmn., 1976—; mem. Philadelphia County Bd. Law Examiners, chmn., 1964-68, sec., 1968-72. Mem. Phila. Bar Assn. Home: 6344 Woodbine Ave Philadelphia PA 19151 Office: 527-29 Western Savings Bank Building Philadelphia PA 19107 Tel (215) 545-2252

MC CARTHY, JOHN BURKE, b. Springfield, Ill., Aug. 28, 1926; Ph.B., Marquette U., 1950, J.D., 1956. Admitted to Wis. bar, 1956, U.S. Supreme Ct. bar, 1972; asso. firm Schloemer Stoltz & Merriam, West Bend, Wis., 1956-58; staff counsel State Bar of Wis., Madison, 1958-74, grievance adminstr., 1974—; col. JAGC, U.S. Army Res., 1972. Bd. dirs. Cath. Social Service Agy., Madison, 1973—, pres., 1976. Mem. Am., Wis., Dane County bar assns., Nat. Orgn. Bar Counsel. Office: State Bar of Wis 402 W Wilson St Madison WI 53703 Tel (608) 257-3838

MC CARTHY, JOHN JUSTIN, b. Phila., Sept. 14, 1896; student Wharton Sch. U. Pa., 1917, Temple U., 1941. Admitted to Pa. bar, 1944, Hawaii bar, 1953, Calif. bar, 1955. Pres. McCarthy Bros., Inc., Phila., 1919-42; individual practice law, Guam and Honolulu,

1950-54; individual practice, La Jolla, Calif, 1954—. Mem. Phila., Pa., Guam, Honolulu, San Diego, Fed. bar assns., Phi Alpha Delta. Office: PO Box 6 La Jolla Shores Dr La Jolla CA 92037

MC CARTHY, MAURICE JOSEPH, b. Chgo., June 27, 1938; A.B., Loyola U., Chgo., 1960, J.D., 1963. Admitted to Ill. bar, 1963, U.S. Supreme Ct. bar, 1968; partner firm McCarthy & Clements, Chgo., 1963—; adj. prof. John Marshall Law Sch. Mem. Am., Chgo., Ill. bar assns., Am., Ill. trial lawyers assns., Appellate Lawyers Assn., Bar Assn. 7th Fed. Circuit. Office: 55 E Monroe St Chicago IL 60603 Tel (312) 372-8893

MC CARTHY, MICHAEL CHARLES, b. Farmington, Mo., Sept. 12, 1914; A.A., U. Mo., 1935, J.D., 1939. Admitted to Mo. bar, 1939, Nebr. bar, 1946; partner firms Damron & McCarthy, Farmington, 1939-41, McCarthy, McCarthy & Vyhnalek and predecessors, North Platte, Neb., 1946—; spl. agt. FBI, Phila., Providence and Washington, 1942-44; agt. OSS, China, 1944-46; dir. Mut. Bldg. & Loan Assn. of North Platte, 1949—. Bd. dirs. North Platte Meml. Hosp., 1953-75; mem. North Platte Bd. Edn., 1957-60, pres., 1959-60; chmn. North Platte Bd. Pub. Works, 1960-72. Fellow Am. Coll. Probate Counsel; mem. Lincoln County (Nebr.), Western Nebr., Nebr., Am. bar assns. Home: 225 McDonald Ave North Platte NE 69101 Office: 121 W 2d St North Platte NE 69101 Tel (308) 532-0551

MC CARTHY, PATRICK JOSEPH, b. Hanford, Calif., June 1, 1919; B.S., U. Calif., Berkeley, 1940; postgrad. Sch. Bus. Adminstrn. Harvard, 1941, 44; J.D., U. San Francisco, 1946. Admitted to Calif. bar, 1946; partner firm Wells & McCarthy, Sacramento, McCarthy & Crow, Sacramento; individual practice law, Graeagle, Calif., 1971—. Mem. Calif. State, Sacramento City, Plumas County (Calif.) bar assns., Calif. State Bd. Accountancy, Assn. Trial Lawyers Am. (asso. editor in tort and R.R. law 1956—). Licensed pub. accountant, Calif. Office: Hwy 89 PO Box 13 Graeagle CA 96103 Tel (916) 836-2784

MCCARTHY, RANDOLPH, JR., b. Bklyn., July 17, 1934; B.B.A., St. Johns U., 1961; J.D., Ohio State U., 1966. Admitted to Mich. bar, 1966; salesman Doubleday Co., Inc., Garden City, N.Y., 1961-63; asso. law firm Troff, Lilly, Piatt, File & Doyle, 1966-68; partner law firm Sloan & McCarthy, Kalamazoo, Mich., 1968-74; individual practice law, Kalamazoo, Mich., 1974—. Mem. Am., Mich., Kalamazoo County bar assns., Am. Trial Lawyers Assn. Home: 10592 W M Ave Kalamazoo MI 49009 Office: 291 Park Bldg 132 W South St Kalamazoo MI 49006 Tel (616) 343-8410

MC CARTNEY, FRANK HOWARD, b. Maysville, Ky., Sept. 30, 1949; B.A. with honors, U. Ky., 1971, J.D. with honors, 1974. Admitted to Ky. bar, 1974, U.S. Dist. Ct. bar for Eastern Dist. Ky., 1974; partner firm Suit, McCartney & Price, Flemingsburg, Ky., 1974—; asst. county atty. Fleming County, Ky., 1976. Mem. Northeastern Ky. Crime Council, 1974-76; mem. Buffalo Trace Advisory Bd., Maysville, 1975—; elder Flemingsburg Christian Ch., 1976. Mem. Ky., Am. bar assns., Order of Coif. Recipient 13th Region Wilkerson award Phi Gamma Delta, 1971, Cite and Substance award Ky. Law Jour., 1974, Ky. Jaycees Speak-Up award, 1975; mem. staff Ky. Law Jour., 1972-74. Home: Rural Route 3 Box 231 Flemingsburg KY 41041 Office: 108 E Water St Flemingsburg KY 41041 Tel (606) 845-7131

MC CARTNEY, ROBERT CHARLES, b. Pitts., May 3, 1934; A.B., Princeton, 1956; J.D., Harvard, 1959. Admitted to D.C. bar, 1959, Pa. bar, 1960; asso. firm Eckert, Seamans, Cherin and Mellott, Pittsburgh, 1959-64, partner firm, 1965—; sec. Ryan Homes, Inc., 1973—; solicitor N. Pittsburgh Community Devel. Corp., 1968-76, alt. dir.; solicitor, mem. McCandless Indsl. Devel. Authority, 1972—; mem. McCandless Twp. Study Commn., 1973-74; dir., sec. Washington Trotting Assn., 1973—. Mem. Allegheny County, Pa., Am. bar assns. Home: 9843 Woodland Rd-N Pittsburgh PA 15237 Office: 42d Floor 600 Grant St Pittsburgh PA 15219 Tel (412) 566-6000

MCCARTY, JOHN JAMES, b. Carbondale, Pa., June 12, 1931; A.B., U. Scranton, 1952; LL.B., U. Pa., 1955. Admitted to Pa. bar, 1955; served as legal officer USMCR, 1955-58; asso. firm Richter, Lord, Toll, Cavanaugh, McCarty & Raynes and predecessors, Phila., 1959-67, partner, 1967-69; partner firm Raynes, McCarty & Binder, Phila., 1969—. Mem. Phila., Pa., Am. bar assns., Phila., Pa., Am. trial lawyers assns. Office: 1845 Walnut St Philadelphia PA 19103 Tel (215) LO8-6190

MC CARTY, JOSEPH COFFEE, III, b. Corpus Christi, Tex., Oct. 7, 1944; B.A., U. Miss., 1966; J.D., Vanderbuilt U., 1971. Admitted to Tenn. bar, 1971; asso. firm Thomason, Crawford & Hendrix, Memphis, 1972-75, partner, 1975-77; mem. firm Waring, Cox, James, Sklar & Allen, 1977—. Bd. govs. Inst. Medicine and Religion, 1976—. Mem. Memphis-Shelby County, Tenn., Am. (vice chmn. econs. of law office mgmt. com. 1975—) bar assns., Phi Delta Phi. Home: 2096 Firefly Cove Memphis TN 38138 Office: 2000 Sterick Bldg Memphis TN 38103 Tel (901) 525-8721

MCCARTY, VIRGINIA DILL (MRS. MENDEL O. MCCARTY), b. Plainfield, Ind., Dec. 15, 1924; A.B., Ind. U., 1946, LL.B., 1950. Admitted to Ind. bar, 1950; with Wasson's Dept. Store, Indpls., 1950; legal staff OPS, Indpls., 1950-52, final title examiner Union Title Co., Indpls., 1952-53; dep. atty. gen. Ind., 1965-66, asst. atty. gen., 1966-69; partner law firm Dillon, Kelley, McCarty, Hardamon, & Cohen, Indpls., 1969-77; chief counsel Marion County Prosecutor's Office, 1975-76; pres. Dill-Fields Implement Co., Inc., Greenfield, Ind., 1967-77; U.S. atty. for So. Ind., 1977—; mem. and sec.-treas. Ind. Bd. Law Examiners, 1971-75, v.p., 1975—. Mem. Indpls. Mayor's Task Force Women, 1972-74, chairperson legal status com., 1974—. Pres. Greater Indpls. Women's Polit. Caucas, 1971-74, Ind. Women's Polit. Caucus, 1972-73; precinct vice committeeman, 1966-69, 74-76; chairperson orgn. com. Nat. Women's Polit. Caucus, 1973-75; v.p. Hoosiers for Equal Rights Amendment, 1973-74; mem. Gov.'s Commn. on Privacy, 1975-77; Democratic nominee for atty. gen. Ind., 1976. Bd. dirs. Ind. Lawyer's Com., 1974-77, Concord Center, 1968-72, INFO, Inc., 1972-77. Mem. Ind., Indpls. (legis. chmn. 1972) bar assns., Order of Coif, Phi Beta Kappa. Home: 5809 Washington Blvd Indianapolis IN 46220 Office: Old Federal Bldg Room 246 Indianapolis IN 46204

MC CASLIN, HUEY LEON, b. Royal, Ark., Oct. 3, 1931; B.S., U. Oreg., 1956, U. Kans., 1960; LL.B., LaSalle Extension U., 1968. Admitted to Calif. bar, 1968; with Cal Farm Ins. Co., Yuba City, 1959-68; dep. dist. atty. County df Yuba (Calif.), 1970-74; individual practice law, Yuba City, 1968—; mem. panel of arbitrators Am. Arbitration Assn., 1969—. Sec.-treas. Yuba-Sutter Democratic Central Com., 1960-64; treas. Buttes area chpt. Boy Scouts Am., 1967; sec. superior Claims Assn., 1962. Mem. Am. Judicature Soc., Am., Calif., Yuba-Sutter bar assns. Home: 1096 Briar Ln Yuba City CA 95991 Office: 1343 Gray Ave Yuba City CA 95991 Tel (916) 674-3099

MC CAULEY, RICHARD GRAY, b. Balt., June 17, 1940; B.A. cum laude, Williams Coll., 1962; LL.B., U. Va., 1965. Admitted to Md. bar, 1965, U.S. Supreme Ct. bar, 1969; asso. firm Piper & Marbury, Balt., 1965-69; asst. atty. gen. Md., 1969-71; sr. v.p., gen. counsel, sec. Rouse Co. and subsidiaries, Columbia, Md., 1971—; gen. counsel Howard Research and Devel. Corp., Columbia, Md., 1972—. lectr. Am. Law Inst. Bd. dirs. Columbia Park and Recreation Assn., 1972—, chmn. exec. com., 1972—. Mem. Md. State, Am. bar assns., Bar Assn. Balt. City, Am. Judicature Soc., Urban Land Inst., Jr. Bar Assn. Balt. City (pres. 1972-73). Office: Rouse Co Little Patuxent Parkway Columbia MD 21044 Tel (301) 992-6400

MCCAW, ROBERT BRUCE, b. Durham, N.C., Dec. 24, 1943; B.S. in Math, Georgetown U., 1965; J.D., U. Va., 1970. Admitted to Va. bar, 1970, D.C. bar, 1971, U.S. Supreme Ct. bar, 1974; law clk. to justice Hugo L. Black, U.S. Supreme Ct., 1970-71; atty. firm Wilmer, Cutler & Pickering, Washington, 1971—. Bd. dirs. Lake Anne Nursery Kindergarten, 1977—. Mem. Va. (environ. law com. 1975—), D.C. bar assns. Office: 1666 K St NW Washington DC 20006 Tel (202) 872-6349

MC CLAIN, WILLIAM ASBURY, b. Sweetwater, Tenn., Apr. 1, 1901; B.S., Davidson Coll. 1924; LL.B., U. Va. 1927. Admitted to Tenn. bar, 1927, Ga. bar, 1928; asso. firm Watkins Asbill & Watkins, 1928-31, Hooper & Hooper, Atlanta, 1931-35; atty., gen. counsel's office SEC, Washington, 1935-38, southeastern regional counsel, Atlanta, 1938-46; partner firm Candler, Cox, McClain & Andrews, Atlanta, 1946-70, McClain, Mellen, Bowling & Hickman, Atlanta, 1970—; asst. atty. gen. State of Ga., 1932; spl. asst. atty. gen. Atty. Gen. U.S., 1943; officer numerous cos. Spl. v.p. Ga. Hort. Soc.; trustee Episcopal Radio-TV Found., Inc., Atlanta, Diocesan Found., Inc., Atlanta, Lovett Sch., Atlanta. Mem. Atlanta Lawyers Club, Am., Atlanta bar assns., Am. Judicature Soc., Beta Theta Pi. Recipient citation Ga. Hort. Soc., 1975, Spl. Trustee's award Bd. Trustees Lovett Sch., 1975. Home: 1776 W Wesley Rd NW Atlanta GA 30327 Office: 225 Peachtree St NW Atlanta GA 30303 Tel (414) 577-9411

MC CLAIN, WILLIAM LEO, b. Marshall, Minn., May 23, 1925; B.S.L., U. Mpls.; LL.B., St. Paul Coll. Law, 1951. Admitted to Minn. bar, 1951, Ariz. bar, 1956; title examiner Phoenix Title & Trust Co., 1954-56; individual practice law, Phoenix, 1956—. Mem. Ariz., Minn., Maricopa County bar assns., Am., Ariz., Phoenix trial lawyers assns., Delta Theta Phi. Home: 4319 N 78th St Scottsdale AZ 85251 Office: 111 W Monroe St Phoenix AZ 85003 Tel (602) 252-7685

MC CLATCHEY, DEVEREAUX FORE, b. Marietta, Ga., June 1, 1906; B.Ph., Emory U., 1926, LL.B., 1929. Admitted to Ga. bar, 1927; asso. Harold Hirsch, Atlanta, 1930-31, firm Hirsch & Smith, Atlanta, 1931-36; partner firm Kilpatrick, Cody, Rogers, McClatchey & Regenstein, Atlanta, 1936—; mem. Ga. Ho. of Reps., 1965-70; gen. counsel Nat. Assn. Life Cos., Atlanta; v.p., dir., mem. exec. com. Coastal States Life Ins. Co.; dir. Fulton Nat. Bank, Randall Bros., Inc. Mem. Atlanta Bd. Edn., 1937-57, pres., 1953-57; pres. Atlanta Symphony Guild, 1947-49. Fellow Am. Coll. Probate Counsel; mem. Am., Ga., Atlanta (pres. 1950-51) bar assns., Atlanta Lawyers Club, Am. Law Inst., Am. Judicature Soc. Home: 66 Avery Dr NE Atlanta GA 30309 Office: 3100 Equitable Bldg Atlanta GA 30303 Tel (404) 522-3100

MCCLEARN, WILLIAM, Pres. Denver Bar Assn., 1977—. Office: 730-17th St Suite 520 Denver CO 80204 Tel (303) 292-9200*

MC CLELLAN, CHARLES E., b. Moline, Ill., Nov. 2, 1936; B.S. with honors U. Ill., 1958; J.D., DePaul U., 1965. Admitted to Ill. bar, 1966, also U.S. Supreme Ct. bar; asso. firm Riordan, Malone, & Schlax, Chgo., 1967-70; tax atty. Jewel Cos., Chgo., 1970—; lectr. John Marshall Law Sch., 1967-68. Chmn. Com. on Edn., Oak Park, Ill., 1975-76. Mem. Am., Chgo., Ill. bar assns., Chgo. Tax Club (chmn. ann. tax sem. 1975), Chgo. Tax Execs. Inst. (2d v.p. 1976). Editor: Law of Federal Income Tax, 1967-70. Office: 5725 E River Rd Chicago IL 60304 Tel (312) 693-6000

MC CLELLAN, JOSEPH LEE, b. Billings, Okla., June 8, 1920; B.S.C.E., Iowa State U., 1942; LL.B., Okla. U., 1948. Admitted to Okla. bar, 1948, Tex. bar, 1968; practiced in Perry, Okla., 1948-50; asst. county atty. Noble County, Okla., 1948-50; atty. Continental Oil Co., Ponca City, Okla., 1950 and Following, then sr. atty., then gen. atty., sr. counsel, Houston, 1967—. Mem. Okla., Tex., Am. bar assns. Office: PO Box 2197 Houston TX 77001 Tel (713) 965-2385

MC CLELLAN, OLIVER BARR, b. Cuero, Tex., Dec. 12, 1939; B.A. with honors, U. Tex., 1961, LL.B., 1964, J.D., 1964. Admitted to Tex. bar, 1964; legal asst. to mem. NLRB, Washington, 1964; legal-tech. adv. to commr. FPC, Washington, 1964-66; asso. firm Clark, Thomas, Winters & Shapiro, Austin, Tex., 1966-70, partner, 1970—; legis. asst. Tex. Ho. of Reps., 1963; auditor Tex. Indsl. Accident Bd., 1961-63. Mem. Citizens Charter Study Commn., 1969, 75; mem. Austin Goals Commn., 1972; chmn. bd. ARC, Central Tex., 1972-76; pres. Kappa Alpha Scholarship Found., 1969-76; pres. Little League, W. Austin, 1969-75. Mem. Am. (chmn. spl. com AEC licensing 1968-70), Tex., Fed., Fed. Power, Travis County bar assns. Contbr. articles to legal jours. Home: 2904 Bowman Ave Austin TX 78703 Office: 12th Floor Capital Nat Bank Bldg POB 1148 Austin TX 78767 Tel (512) 472-8442

MC CLELLAND, JAMES RALPH, JR., b. Stone Mountain, Ga., Oct. 16, 1916; A.B., Davidson Coll., 1937; LL.B., Atlanta Law Sch., 1941; postgrad. Emory U. Law Sch., 1946-47. Admitted to Ga. bar, 1940; practiced in Atlanta, 1946—, asso. firm George & John L. Westmoreland, 1946-54, partner firm Matthews & McClelland, 1955-67, individual practice law, 1967—; mem. Ga. Ho. of Reps., 1957-65. Mem. Atlanta Bar Assn. (pres. 1957-58), State Bar Ga., Lawyers Club of Atlanta, Am. Judicature Soc., Ga., Am. trial lawyers assns., World Assn. Lawyers (founding), Delta Theta Phi. Office: Suite 320-6666 Powers Ferry Rd NW Atlanta GA 30339 Tel (404) 955-1010

MC CLELLAND, LINDLEY ROSSITER, b. Girard, Pa., Apr. 7, 1916; B.A., U. Pitts., 1938; LL.B., U. Pa., 1941. Admitted to Pa. bar, 1943; mem. firms Rossiter, Benacci & McClelland, 1946-57, Good, McClelland & Brabender, 1957-67; judge, Erie, Pa., 1967—; asst. dist. atty. Erie County (Pa.), 1947-56, solicitor for clk. for courts, 1956-60, county solicitor, 1960-64, dist. atty., 1966-67. Incorporator St. Vincent Med. Center. Mem. Erie County, Pa. bar assns. Contbr. articles to legal jours. Home: 5898 Overlook Dr Erie PA 16505 Office: 106 W 6th St Erie PA 16501 Tel (814) 455-6346

MC CLELLAND, LLOYD SHAW, b. Bellevue, Pa., Feb. 1, 1922; student Carnegie Inst. Tech., 1940-42; LL.B., Northwestern U., 1944. Admitted to Ill. bar, 1945; asso. firm Sidley, Austin, Burgess & Harper, Chgo., 1945-50; atty. law dept. Sears, Roebuck and Co., Chgo., 1950-61, asst. sec., 1961-71, sec., gen. counsel, 1971—, v.p., 1973—; dir. Western Forge Corp., Colorado Springs, Colo. Mem. Chgo., Am. bar assns., Am. Soc. Corp. Secs. Inc., Assn. Gen. Counsel, Legal Club of Chgo., Law Club of Chgo. Home: 72 Canterbury E Northfield IL 60093 Office: Sears Tower D/766 Chicago IL 60684 Tel (312) 875-5766

MC CLINTON, MICHAEL CRAIG, b. Auburn, Wash., Jan. 10, 1947; B.A., U. South Calif., Los Angeles, 1969; J.D., Willamette U., 1972. Admitted to Oreg. bar, 1972; asso. firm Clark, Marsh & Lindauer, Salem, Oreg., 1972-76, partner, 1976—; pres. bd. dirs. Marion-Polk Legal Aid. Mem. Marion County (Oreg.), Oreg. State, Am. bar assns., Oreg. Assn. Def. Counsel. Office: 880 Liberty St NE Salem OR 97301 Tel (503) 1542

MC CLOSKEY, JAMES BOSWELL, b. Pitts., June 11, 1945; A.B., Drury Coll., Springfield, Mo., 1967; J.D., U. Mo., Columbia, 1970. Admitted to Mo. bar, 1970; solicitor Western Region law dept. Norfolk and Western Railway Co., St. Louis, 1970-73, asst. gen. atty., 1973-75, asst. gen. solicitor, 1975—. Mem. Am. Bar Assn., Conf. of Freight Loss and Damage Counsel, Ind., Ill., Iowa railroad assns., Mo. R.R. Com. (vice chmn.). Home: 303 Quail Village Ct Ballwin MO 63011 Office: 1667 Railway Exchange Bldg 611 Olive St Saint Louis MO 63011 Tel (314) 425-8845

MC CLOW, THOMAS ALAN, b. Detroit, Apr. 25, 1944; B.S., Mich. State U., 1966; J.D., Loyola U., Chgo., 1969. Admitted to Ill. bar, 1969, U.S. Supreme Ct. bar, 1973; asso. firm Douglas F. Comstock, Geneva, Ill., 1970-73, firm John L. Nickels, Elburn, Ill., 1973—; pub. adminstr., conservator and guardian Kane County (Ill.), 1975—. Bd. dirs. Kane County Council Econ. Opportunity, 1971-73, Tri-City Youth Project, 1972-73; faculty dean Fox Valley Parent Edn. Center, 1974-76. Mem. Ill., Kane County, Chgo. bar assns. Home: 36 W 957 Tree Top Ln Saint Charles IL 60174 Office: 130 N Main St PO Box AC Elburn IL 60119 Tel (312) 365-6441

MC CLOY, JOHN JAY, b. Phila., Mar. 31, 1895; B.A., Amherst Coll., 1916, LL.D. (hon.); LL.B., Harvard, 1921, LL.D., (hon.); LL.D. (hon.), Boston Coll., Brown U., Colby Coll., Columbia, Dartmouth, Franklin and Marshall U., Haverford Coll., Lehigh U., N.Y. U., Middlebury Coll., Princeton, Syracuse U., Trinity U., U. Md., U. Notre Dame, U. Pa., Swarthmore Coll., Yale, Williams Coll., Wilmington Coll. Admitted to N.Y. bar, 1922; partner firm Milbank, Tweed, Hadley & McCloy, N.Y.C., 1963—; chmn. exec. com. Squibb Corp.; dir. Dreyfus Corp., Mercedes-Benz of N.Am., Olinkraft, Inc.; past dir. Allied Chem. Corp., AT&T, Chase Manhattan Bank, Met. Life Ins. Co., Westinghouse Electric Corp.; pres. World Bank, 1947-49; chmn. Com. for Modern Cts., Inc., Am. Council on Germany, Inc. Asst. sec. war, 1941-45; U.S. mil. gov. U.S. high commr. for Germany, 1949-52; adviser on disarmament matter to Pres. Kennedy, until 1961; mem. Pres.'s Commn. to Investigate Assassination Pres. Kennedy, 1963; chmn. Gen. Adv. Com. on Disarmament, until 1974; past chmn. bd. UN Devel. Corp.; hon. chmn. bd. Council Fgn. Relations, Inc., Internat. House, Atlantic Inst.; hon. bd. dirs. Acad. Polit. Sci., Columbia; fellow of bd. Johns Hopkins; trustee, mem. adv. bd. George C. Marshall Research Found.; mem. hon. com. German Marshall Fund of U.S.; hon. chmn. bd. trustees, trustee emeritus Amherst Coll.; hon. trustee Deerfield Acad., Lenox Hill Hosp.; treas., trustee Am. Sch. Classical Studies, Athens, Greece; mem. exec. com. Salk Inst., La Jolla, Calif. trustee John M. Olin Found. Mem. Am., Fed., N.Y. State, N.J., D.C. bar assns., Assn. Bar City N.Y., N.Y. County Lawyers Assn., Am. Soc. Internat. Law. Decorated D.S.M., Medal of Freedom, grand cross Order of Merit (Fed. Republic Germany), grand officer Legion of Honor (France), grand officer Order of Merit (Italy); hon. mem. senate Johann Wolfgang Goethe U., Frankfurt, Gy and Friedrich Wilhelm U., Bonn; hon. citizen Free U. Berlin; author: The Challenge to American Foreign Policy, 1953. Office: 1 Chase Manhattan Plaza New York City NY 10005 Tel (212) 422-2660

MC CLUGGAGE, MICHAEL LEE, b. Coshocton, Ohio, Mar. 9, 1947; B.A., Ohio Wesleyan U., 1969; J.D., U. Chgo., 1972. Admitted to Ill. bar, 1972, U.S. Dist. Ct. bar, 1972; asso. firm Wildman, Harrold, Allen and Dixon, 1972—. Mem. Am., Ill., Chgo. bar assns., Chgo. Council Lawyers, Phi Beta Kappa. Home: 451 W Wrightwood St Chicago IL 60614 Office: One IBM Plaza Chicago IL 60611 Tel (312) 222-0400

MC CLUNG, DANIEL COLEMAN, b. Butler, Okla., Mar. 9, 1924; B.S. in Geology, U. Okla., 1950, J.D., 1966. Admitted to Okla. bar, 1966; individual practice law, Blackwell, Okla., 1966—; asst. county atty. Kay County (Okla.), 1967; municipal judge, Blackwell, 1968-72. Mem. Okla. Bar Assn., Okla. Trial Lawyers Assn. (probate editor The Advocate, 1971—). Home: 417 Bel Aire St Blackwell OK 74631 Office: 118 S 1st St PO Box 404 Blackwell OK 74631 Tel (405) 363-0800

MC CLUNG, RICHARD GOEHRING, b. Butler, Pa., June 26, 1913; A.B., Princeton, 1935; certificate Harvard Bus. Sch., 1937; J.D., Yale, 1939. Admitted to N.Y. bar, 1940, Pa. bar, 1940, U.S. Supreme Ct. bar, 1944, U.S. Dist. Ct. bar, 1946; asso. firm Davis Polk & Wardwell, N.Y.C., 1939-42, Carter, Ledyard & Milburn, N.Y.C., 1946-48, partner, 1948—. Trustee, Youth Consultation Service Diocese of N.Y., Inc., 1948-56, pres., 1954-56; mem. Met. Opera Guild, Inc., 1957-66, head publs. com., 1961-65; trustee Greenwich (Conn.) Center for Child and Family Welfare, 1958-64, Greenwich Country Day Sch., 1964-72, pres. bd. trustees, 1968-71; trustee Greenwich Hosp. Assn., 1966—, v.p., 1975—; mem. vestry St. Barnabas Ch., 1976—; mem. Greenwich Historic Dist. Commn., 1975—; mem. Democratic Town Com. Greenwich, 1972-74. Mem. Am., N.Y. State, N.Y.C. bar assns. Home: 30 Winding Ln Greenwich CT 06830 Office: 2 Wall St New York City NY 10005 Tel (212) RE2-3200

MC CLURE, ALFRED EDWARD, b. Jersey City, May 29, 1944; A.B., Rutgers U., 1965; J.D., Seton Hall U., 1969. Admitted to Ind. bar, 1969; dir. research City Fed. Savs. and Loan Assn., Elizabeth, N.J., 1965-69; v.p., chief counsel Nat. Homes Acceptance Corp., Lafayette, Ind., 1969-74; partner firm McClure & Rosenthal, Lafayette, 1974—. Vice-pres. Family Service Agy. of Tippecanoe County, 1974-76. Mem. Am. (com. housing and urban renewal, local govt. sect.), Ind. (chmn. real estate div. 1969-76) bar assns., Mortgage Bankers Assn. Am. Office: 1709 Teal Rd Lafayette IN 47905 Tel (317) 474-4402

MCCLURE, CHARLES DAVIS, b. Birmingham, Ala., May 22, 1935; B.S.J., U. Fla., 1957; LL.B., Stetson U., 1963. Admitted to Fla. bar, 1963; atty. Fla. Rd. Dept., Tallahassee; gen. counsel to Comptroller Fla., Tallahassee, 1963-67; individual practice law, Tallahassee, 1967-73; U.S. commr. U.S. Dist. Ct. No. Fla., 1968-72; judge Leon County (Fla.) Ct., 1973—. Mem. Tallahassee, Fla. bar assns., Sigma Alpha Epsilon, Sigma Delta Chi (pres. chpt. 1971).

Author: (with Klein Wigginton) Organizing and Advising Small Businesses, 1969. Home: 3119 Middlebrook Circle Tallahassee FL 32303 Office: Leon County Courthouse Tallahassee FL 32301 Tel (904) 488-7387

MCCLURE, GEORGE WALKER, b. Shaowu, China, Nov. 15, 1919; A.B., U. Calif., Berkeley, 1940, J.D., 1949. Admitted to Calif. bar, 1950, U.S. Supreme Ct. bar, 1958; since practiced in Contra Costra County, Calif., dep. dist. atty., 1950-69, chief dep. county counsel, 1969—. Mem. Calif. Bar (com. adminstrn. justice 1968—), Contra Costa County Bar Assn. (dir. 1960-75); Phi Beta Kappa. Home: 3761 Canyon Way Martinez CA 94553 Office: PO Box 69 Martinez CA 94553 Tel (415) 372-2053

MC CLURE, JOHN CHARLES, b. Union City, Ind., July 22, 1945; A.B., Miami U., Oxford, Ohio, 1967; J.D., Ohio State U., 1970. Admitted to Colo., Ohio bars, 1971; dep. pub. defender, Alamosa, Colo., 1971-73; partner firm Smith & McClure, Alamosa, 1973-74, firm McClure & Jacobs, Alamosa, 1974—. Mem. San Luis Valley (pres. 1976-77), Colo., Am. bar assns., Colo. Trial Lawyers Assn. Home: 2200 Thomas Ave Alamosa CO 81101 Office: 915 4th St Alamosa CO 81101 Tel (303) 589-6603

MC CLURE, WILLIAM PENDLETON, b. D.C., May 25, 1925; B.S. in Econs., U. Pa., 1949; J.D. with honors, George Washington U., 1951, LL.M., 1954; postgrad. Hague Acad. Internat. Law (Holland), 1952. Admitted to D.C. bar, 1951, U.S. Supreme Ct. bar, 1954, M.D. bar, 1957; sr. partner firm McClure & Trotter, D.C., 1952—. Chmn. D.C. div. Crusade Against Cancer, Am. Cancer Soc., 1966-67. Mem. Am. Bar Assn., Bar Assn. D.C., Am. Judicature Soc., Order of Coif, Phi Delta Phi, Phi Delta Theta. Home: 9505 Brook Dr Bethesda MD 20034 Office: 1100 Conn Ave NW Washington DC 20036 Tel (202) 659-3400

MCCLUSKEY, JOSEPH J., b. Middleport, Pa., Dec. 9, 1928; A.B., Franklin and Marshall Coll., 1948-52; LL.B., Temple U., 1960. Admitted to Pa. bar, 1962; individual practice law, Hazleton, Pa., 1962—; solicitor Hazle Twp. Sch. Dist., 1963-66, City of Hazleton, 1966-68, Hazle Twp., 1966-70. Mem. Am., Pa. trial lawyers assns., Luzerne Law and Library Assn. Home: 996 E Chestnut St Hazleton PA 18201 Office: 312-313 Northeastern Bldg Hazleton PA 18201 Tel (717) 455-3754

MC COLLOUGH, WILLIAM BRYANT, JR., b. Birmingham, Ala., Feb. 23, 1929; B.S. U. Ala., 1953, LL.B., 1956. Admitted to Ala. bar, 1956; partner firm McCollough & McCollough, Birmingham, 1956—. Mem. Birmingham, Ala. bar assns. Home: RFD 13 Box 776 Birmingham AL 35243 Office: 908-14 Frank Nelson Building Birmingham AL 35203 Tel (205) 322-2653

MC COLLUM, IRA WILLIAM, JR., b. Brooksville, Fla., July 12, 1944; B.A., U. Fla., 1965, J.D., 1968. Admitted to Fla. bar, 1968; asso. firm Pitts, Eubanks, Ross & Rumberger, Orlando, Fla., 1973-75, partner firm, 1975—; served to lt. USNR Judge Adv. Gen., 1969-72, mil. judge, 1970. Chmn. Republican. exec. com. Seminole County, Fla., 1976—. Mem. Fla. Bar, Am., Orange County (exec. council 1975—) bar assns., Phi Delta Phi, Omicron Delta Kappa, Fla. Blue Key (pres. 1968). Mem. U. Fla. Hall of Fame. Home: 1010 Cathy Dr Altamonte Springs FL 32701 Office: 605 E Robinson St Orlando FL 32801 Tel (305) 425-4251

MC COLLUM, JAMES TERRY, b. Urbana, Ill., Dec. 24, 1934; B.S. in Geology, U. Ill., 1956, J.D., 1962. Admitted to N.Y. state Bar, 1962, U.S. Supreme Ct. bar, 1966, U.S. Ct. Mil. Appeals, 1966; asso. firm Kaman, Berlove & Kaman, Rochester, N.Y., 1962-66; partner firm DiGennaro & McCollum, Rochester, 1967; asso. firm Dutcher, Witt, Sidoti & Considine, Rochester, 1967-72; individual practice law, Rochester, 1972—. Mem. Monroe County, N.Y. State bar assns., Council Scottish Clan Assns. (sec. 1975—), Rochester Regional Chpt. Equal Rights for Fathers New York State (bd. dirs. 1976—), Am. Humanist Assn. (pres. Rochester chpt. 1964; counselor), Rochester Fedn. Western Round and Square Dance Clubs, Inc., (pres. 1973-74), Am. United for Separation Church and State (dir. chpt. 1967—). Home: 522 Goodman St S Rochester NY 14607 Office: 200 Times Square Bldg Rochester NY 14614 Tel (716) 232-7272

MC COMB, JOHN ARCHIE, b. Green Bay, Wis., May 29, 1919; B.A., U. Wis., Madison, 1942, LL.B., 1948. Admitted to Wis. bar, 1948; with Hardware Mut. Co., 1948-67, dist. mgr., Stevens Point, Wis., Minn., N.D. and S.D., 1960-63, resident v.p., 1963-67; v.p. claims Sentry Ins. Mut. Co., Sentry Life Ins. Co. and Sentry Indeminity Co., Stevens Point, 1967-77; mng. dir. ins. ops. U.K., London, 1977—; gov. Ins. Crime Prevention Inst., 1974-75. Chmn. bd. dirs. St. Michaels Hosp., Stevens Point, 1967—; bd. dirs. Stevens Point Humane Soc., 1973-74; pres. Stevens Point YMCA, 1974-75. Mem. Internat. Assn. Ins. Counsel (v.p. 1972-75), Am. Mut. Ins. Alliance (claims exec. com. 1975-76), Ins. Crime Prevention Inst. Home: 55 Maplewood Dr Stevens Point WI 54481 Office: Sentry Offices UK 56 Leadenhall St London EC3 England Tel 01-481-3464

MC COMB, MARSHALL FRANCIS, b. Denver, May 6, 1894; A.B., Stanford; J.D., Yale; LL.D., Loyola U., Los Angeles, U. San Fernando Valley, Western State U., Anaheim, Calif. Admitted to Calif. bar, 1920, practice law, 1920-27; judge Los Angeles Superior Ct., 1927-35; justice Calif. Ct. Appeal, 2d Appellate Dist., 1935-36; asso. justice Calif. Supreme Ct., 1956—; instr. in constitutional and bus. law U. Calif., Los Angeles; prof. law U. So. Calif., Loyola U. Mem. Am., Hollywood (Calif.), Los Angeles bar assns., Delta Theta Phi, Sigma Delta Kappa. Home: 2550 Filbert St San Francisco CA 94123 Office: State Bldg 350 McAllister St Room 4042 San Francisco CA 94102 Tel (415) 557-3436

MCCONN, JOHN L., JR., b. Tulsa, 1923; student Rice U.; LL.B., U. Tex., 1949. Admitted to Tex. bar, 1949; now mem. firm Butler, Binion, Rice, Cook & Knapp, Houston. Fellow Am. Coll. Trial Lawyers; mem. Am., Houston (pres. 1976-77) bar assns., State Bar Tex., Internat. Assn. Ins. Counsel, Tex. (v.p. 1968-69, 69-70), Houston (pres. 1971-72) assns. def. counsel, Phi Alpha Delta. Office: 1100 Esperson Bldg Houston TX 77002 Tel (713) 237-3181*

MC CONNAUGHEY, GEORGE CARLTON, JR., b. Hillsboro, Ohio, Aug. 9, 1925; B.A., Denison U., 1949; LL.B., Ohio State U., 1951, J.D., 1967. Admitted to Ohio bar, 1951; asst. atty. gen. Ohio, 1951-54; partner firm McConnaughey & McConnaughey, Columbus, Ohio, 1954-57, McConnaughey, McConnaughey & Stradley, Columbus, 1957-62, Laylin, McConnaughey & Stradley, Columbus, 1962-67, George, Greek, King, McMahon & McConnaughey, Columbus, 1967—; dir., sec. Mid-Continent Telephone Corp., Hudson, Ohio, N.Am. Broadcasting Co. (WMNI Radio, Columbus); dir. Newark Telephone Co. (Ohio). Trustee Columbus Town Meeting Assn., pres., 1974-76; trustee Buckeye Boys Ranch; pres. Upper Arlington Bd. Edn., 1967-69, mem., 1962-70; chmn. Ohio Young Republicans, 1956; U.S. Presdl. elector, 1956. Mem. Am., Ohio, Columbus bar assns., Am. Judicature Soc. Home: 1969 Andover Rd Columbus OH 43212 Office: 100 E Broad St Columbus OH 43215 Tel (614) 228-1541

MCCONNELL, BEVERLY J., b. Chgo., Mar. 10, 1931; B.A., U. Ariz., 1953; J.D., 1955. Admitted to Ariz. bar, 1955; atty. Pinal County (Ariz.) Attys. Office, Florence, 1955-58; partner firm Wilson, McConnell & Moroney and predecessor, Phoenix, 1958—. Mem. Comml. Law League Am., Ariz. State, Maricopa (county Ariz.) bar assns. Office: 114 W Adams St Phoenix AZ 85003 Tel (602) 258-8455

MC CONNELL, E(ARL) JOHN, b. Tulsa, Feb. 25, 1940; B.A., Pa. State U., 1963; J.D., Dickinson Sch. Law, 1966. Admitted to Hawaii bar, 1969, U.S. Dist. Ct. bar for Dist. Hawaii, 1969, U.S. Ct. Appeals bar, 9th Circuit, 1973; asso. firm Pudgett, Greeley, Marumoto & Akinaka, Honolulu, 1969-70; dep. atty. gen. State of Hawaii, Honolulu, 1970-75; dep. dir. Hawaii Dept. Regulatory Agys., Honolulu, 1975—; dir. Inst. Continuing Legal Edn., 1976-77. Central committeeman Hawaii Democratic Party, 1976—; platform chmn. state conv., 1976. Mem. Hawaii State Bar Assn. (chmn. com. atty.-client relations 1977). Home: 4068 Round Top Dr Honolulu HI 96822 Office: 1010 Richards St Honolulu HI 96813 Tel (808) 548-7589

MC CONNELL, JAMES GUY, b. Hinsdale, Ill., Sept. 24, 1947; B.S. in Journalism, Iowa State U., 1969; J.D., Northwestern U., 1973. Admitted to Ill. bar, 1973; asst. dir. research Am. Judicature Soc., Chgo., 1972-73; asso. firm Rooks, Pitts, Fullagar & Poust, Chgo., 1973—. Mem. Sch. Dist. 102 Bd. Edn., LaGrange Park, Ill., 1975-76. Mem. Am., Ill. State, Chgo. bar assns., Am. Judicature Soc., Trial Lawyers Club of Chgo. Contbr. articles to profl. jours. Office: 208 S LaSalle St Chicago IL 60604 Tel (312) 372-5600

MC CONNELL, JUDITH DOBSON, b. Lincoln, Nebr., Feb. 10, 1944; B.A., U. Calif., Berkeley, 1966, J.D., 1969. Admitted to Calif. bar, 1970; atty. Calif. Dept. Transp., San Diego, 1969-76; partner firm Reed, McConnell & Sullivan, San Diego, 1976—; referee State Bar Disciplinary Bd., 1976—; dir. San Diego County Water Authority, 1972-75. Mem. San Diego County Bar Assn., Lawyers Club San Diego, Calif. Women Lawyers Assn., Phi Beta Kappa. Office: 1007 Fifth Ave Suite 412 San Diego CA 92101 Tel (714) 239-9601

MCCORD, GRACE DOERING, b. Cleve., June 16, 1890; A.B., Case Western Res. U., 1911; J.D. magna cum laude, Baldwin Wallace Coll., 1925; LL.M., Cleve.-Marshall Law Sch. Cleve. State U., 1927. Tchr. pub. high schs., Ohio, 1911-20; mem. staff Albuquerque Morning Jour., 1920; admitted to N.Mex. bar, 1925, Ohio bar, 1931, U.S. Supreme Ct. bar, 1960; asso. firm John F. Simms, Albuquerque, 1925-26; law asst. Ohio Ct. Appeals, 8th Dist., 1926-33; asso. firm Doering, Doering & Doering, Cleve., 1933—; prof. appellate practice and procedure Cleve.-Marshall Law Sch., Cleve. State U., 1933-38; asst. dir. law City of Cleve., 1935-42; lectr. in field. Trustee Legal Aid Soc., Cleve. Fellow Ohio State Bar Found.; mem. Am. (ho. of dels. 1957, 58-59), Ohio (life mem., Recognition award 1976), Cuyahoga County (trustee 1938-49, life mem., Recognition award 1969), Greater Cleve. (hon., Recognition award 1975) bar assns., Am. Judicature Soc., Internat. Fedn. Women Lawyers, Nat. Assn. Women Lawyers (pres. 1957-58), Czechoslovac Soc. Am. (hon.), Phi Beta Kappa, Phi Alpha Delta. Recipient citation Case Western Res. U. Bd. Govs., 1963; Recognition award Women Lawyers Club Cleve., 1956; author: (with John Sherman Long) McCord of Alaska: Statesman for the Last Frontier, 1975; contbr. articles to legal jours. Home: 14269 Cedar Rd Cleveland OH 44121 Office: Doering Bldg 5484 Broadway Cleveland OH 44127 Tel (216) 341-0122

MCCORD, GUYTE PIERCE, JR., b. Tallahassee, Sept. 23, 1914; student Davidson Coll., 1933-34; B.A., U. Fla., 1940, J.D., 1940. Admitted to Fla. bar, 1940, U.S. Supreme Ct. bar, 1945, U.S. 5th Circuit Ct. Appeals bar, 1956; practiced in Tallahassee, 1940-60; judge Fla. 2d Jud. Circuit Ct., 1960-74, Fla. Dist. Ct. Appeal, 1st Dist., 1974—; dep. commr. Fla. Indsl. Commn., 1946-47; pros. atty. Leon County (Fla.), 1947-48; asst. gen. counsel Fla. Pub. Service Commn., 1949-60; chmn. Fla. Conf. Circuit Judges, 1972. Pres. Murat House Assn., Tallahassee, 1967-69; bd. dirs. Fla. Heritage Found., 1969-70, mem. exec. com., 1965-69; edlder 1st Presbyn. Ch., Tallahassee. Mem. Fla. Bar, Am., Tallahassee bar assns., Phi Delta Phi, Sigma Alpha Epsilon. Home: 502 S Ride St Tallahassee FL 32303 Office: PO Box 1028 Tallahassee FL 32302 Tel (904) 488-1675

MCCORD, ROBERT BRYAN, b. Atlanta, Apr. 28, 1917; B.S., Ga. State-Woodrow Wilson Coll. Law, 1945, LL.B., 1947. Admitted to Ga. bar, 1947; partner firm McCord, Cooper & Voyles and predecessor firms, Hapeville, Ga., 1950-67, sr. partner, 1967—. City atty., Hapeville, 1954-64. Mem. Am., Ga., Atlanta bar assns., Lawyers Club Atlanta, Hapeville C. of C. (pres. 1953-54), Travellers Protective Assn. (sec. treas. 1970-77). Club: Exchange of Hapeville, Ga. Dist. Exchange. Home: 347 Northwoods Pl Hapeville GA 30354 Office: 201 Jackson Bldg 535 Central Ave Hapeville GA 30354

MC CORD, ROBERT LEE, JR., b. Needles, Calif., Dec. 27, 1941; A.B. in Polit. Sci., U. Calif., Santa Barbara, 1963; postgrad. U. Calif., Hastings Coll. Law, 1963-65, LL.D., 1970. Admitted to Calif. bar, 1970; dep. dist. atty. Ventura County (Calif.), 1970-72; partner firm Holt, Taylor and McCord, Ventura, Calif., 1972—; prof. Ventura Sch. Law, 1972-74. Mem. Calif. Trial Lawyers Assn., Calif., Ventura (chmn. continuing edn. of the bar 1972-76) bar assns. Office: 78 N Ash St Ventura CA 93001 Tel (805) 643-8655

MC CORD, WILLIAM KEITH, b. Alamo, Tenn., Jan. 29, 1933; B.A., U. Tenn., 1955; J.D., 1960; B.D., Duke, 1958. Admitted to Tenn. bar, 1960; mem. firm Egerton, McAfee, Armistead, Davis & McCord, Knoxville, 1960-75; partner firm McCord & Cockrill, Knoxville, 1976—. Mem. Am., Tenn. bar assns. Office: 601 Concord St Knoxville TN 37919 Tel (615) 637-5252

MC CORKINDALE, DOUGLAS HAMILTON, b. N.Y.C., June 14, 1939; B.A., Columbia, 1961, LL.B. cum laude, 1964. Admitted to N.Y. bar, 1964; asso. firm Thacher, Proffitt & Wood, N.Y.C., 1964-70, partner, 1970-71; v.p., gen. counsel, sec. Gannett Co., Inc., Rochester, N.Y., 1971-76, sr. v.p. finance and law, 1977—. Mem. Am., N.Y. bar assns. Home: 1194 East Ave Rochester NY 14607 Office: Lincoln Tower Rochester NY 14604 Tel (716) 546-8600

MC CORKINDALE, ROBERT WILLIAM, II, b. Joplin, Mo., Mar. 12, 1943; J.D., U. Ark., 1968. Admitted to Ark. bar, 1968; partner firm Shouse & McCorkindale, Harrison, Ark., 1968-69, Walker, Campbell & McCorkindale, Harrison, 1970—; atty. City of Harrison, 1971. Mem. Am., Ark., Boone County bar assns. Home: 1609 Brentwood St Harrison AR 72601 Office: 218 E Ridge St Harrison AR 72601 Tel (501) 741-3448

MC CORMAC, JOHN WAVERLY, b. Zanesville, Ohio, Feb. 8, 1926; B.S., Muskingum Coll., 1951; J.D., Capital U., 1961. Admitted to Ohio bar, 1961; asso. firm Schwenker, Teaford, Brothers & Bernard, Columbus, Ohio, 1961-65; dean Capital U. Law Sch., Columbus, 1966-71, prof. law, 1965-74; judge Tenth Dist. Ct. of Appeals, Columbus, 1974—. Mem. Am., Ohio (council of dels. 1973-77), Columbus (pres. 1975-76) bar assns., Am. Judicature Soc., League of Ohio Law Schs. (pres. 1970). Author: Ohio Civil Rules Practice, 1970; Ohio Civil Practice, vol. I, 1971, vol. II, 1976. Home: 395 Longfellow Ave Worthington OH 43085 Office: 369 S High St Columbus OH 43215 Tel (614) 462-3610

MC CORMACK, EDWARD JOSEPH, JR., b. Boston, Aug. 29, 1923; student Colby Coll.; B.S., U.S. Naval Acad.; J.D. cum laude, Boston U. Admitted to Mass. bar, 1952, U.S. Supreme Ct. bar, 1955, D.C. bar, 1965; mem. firm McCormack & Doyle, Boston, 1952-58; atty. gen. State of Mass., 1958-63; mem. firm McCormack & Zimble, Boston, 1963—; master Boston sch. desegregation, 1975. Mem. Boston City Council, 1954-58, Mayor's Com. on Violence, 1976; chmn. Com. for Boston, 1976. Mem. Mass. Bar, Am. Bar Assn., Am. Trial Lawyers Assn., Mass. Acad. Trial Attys. Home: Jamaicaway Tower Jamaica Plain MA 02130 Office: 19 Congress St Boston MA 02109 Tel (617) 227-4500

MC CORMACK, FRANCIS XAVIER, b. N.Y.C., July 9, 1929; A.B. cum laude, St. Francis Coll., Bklyn., 1951; LL.B., Columbia, 1954. Admitted to N.Y. bar, 1955, Mich. bar, 1963, Calif. bar, 1974, Pa. bar, 1975; asso. firm Cravath, Swaine & Moore, N.Y.C., 1956-62; atty. Ford Motor Co., 1962-64, asst. gen. counsel, 1970-72; v.p., gen. counsel, sec. Philco-Ford, Phila., 1964-72; v.p. Atlantic Richfield Co., Los Angeles, 1972-73, gen. counsel, 1972—, sr. v.p., 1973—. Mem. Am. Petroleum Inst. Home: 975 Singing Wood Dr Arcadia CA 91006 Office: 515 S Flower St Los Angeles CA 90071 Tel (213) 486-1774

MCCORMACK, WILLIAM JOSEPH, b. W.Orange, N.J., July 12, 1902; LL.B., Rutgers, 1925. Admitted to N.J. bar, 1925; individual practice law, Orange, 1925-52, East Orange, 1954—; asso. firm Milton, McNulty and Augelli, Jersey City, 1952-54; asst. atty. gen., N.J., 1934-44; deputy atty. gen., N.J., 1954-73. Mem. N.J., Essex County bar assns., NRC. Author: A Taking Without an Invasion of Land, 1966; The Gallant Case: A New Look at Just Compensation, 1967; Justice for All?, 1975; Compensable and Non Compensable Items in Eminent Domain, 1969; Procedures Under the Eminent Domain Act of 1971, 1973. Home: 19 Dartmouth Rd West Orange NJ 07052 Office: 555 William St East Orange NJ 07017 Tel (201) 673-0008

MC CORMICK, EDWARD JAMES, JR., b. Toledo, May 11, 1921; B.S., John Carroll U., 1942; J.D., Case Western Res. U., 1948. Admitted to Ohio bar, 1948; mem. firm Mulholland, Hickey, Lyman, McCormick, Fisher & Hickey, and predecessors, Toledo, 1948—, jr. partner, 1954-60, sr. partner and office mgr., 1960—. Active Toledo C. of C., Toledo Municipal League; past pres. Toledo Small Bus. Assn., Lucas County Cancer Soc.; mem. Toledo Port Authority Advisory Bd. Mem. Am., Ohio, Lucas County, Toledo bar assns., Immigration and Nationalization Lawyers Assn., Am. Trial Lawyers Assn., Am. Judicature Soc., Toledo Power Squadron, Toledo Zool. Soc., Toledo Art Museum. Named Outstanding Young Man, Toledo Jaycees, 1952, Woodman of the World, 1953. Home: 3161 Haughton Ave Toledo OH 43606 Office: 741 Nat Bank Bldg Toledo OH 43604 Tel (419) 243-6251

MC CORMICK, HARVEY LEE, b. Tyler, Tex., Aug. 14, 1919; J.D., Marquette U., 1948. Admitted to Wis. bar, 1948, Mo. bar, 1971; mng. atty., law reform appeals sect. Legal Aid Defender Soc. Greater Kansas City (Mo.), 1970-72; asso. prof. law N.C. Coll. Law Sch., Durham, 1948-52; adminstrv. law judge Bur. Hearings Appeals, Social Security Adminstrn., Kansas City, Mo., 1972—. Author: Social Security Claims and Procedures, 1973; Medicare-Medicaid Claims and Procedures, 1977. Address: 5613 N Tullis St Kansas City MO 64119 Tel (816) 374-2106

MC CORMICK, ROSEBUD HORNE, b. Yonkers, Ga., Sept. 20, 1900; student law under practicing lawyer; admitted to Ga. bar; asso. firm Borris & McCormick; mem. firm Strozier, Gower & McCormick; individual practice law, 1957-72; ret., 1972; former ct. reporter, Cordele (Ga.) Judicial Circuit. Mem. adminstrv. bd. Cordele United Meth. Ch. Recipient Bicentennial award Cordele Judicial Circuit. Address: Local Realty Bldg Cordele GA 31015

MC CORQUODALE, JOSEPH C., b. Jackson, Ala., Aug. 8, 1945; B.S. in Math., U. Ala., 1967, J.D., 1971. Admitted to Ala. bar, 1971; partner firm McCorquodale & McCorquodale, Jackson, 1971—. Chmn. Clarke County (Ala.) March of Dimes; mem. bd. adminstrs. 1st Meth. Ch., Jackson. Mem. Am., Ala. bar assns., Ala., Am. trial lawyers assns. Home: 415 Rose Street Jackson AL 36545 Office: 240 Commerce St Jackson AL 36545 Tel (205) 246-9015

MC COWN, SUE VICK, b. Cornelius, N.C., May 25, 1926; A.B., Greensboro Coll., 1946; J.D., Duke Law Sch., 1950. Admitted to N.C. State Bar, 1950; partner firm McCown and McCown, Manteo, N.C., 1950—. Mem. Dare County Bd. Elections. Mem. N.C. Bar Assn. Home: 11 Mother Vineyard Rd Manteo NC 27954 Office: Sir Walter Raleigh Ave Manteo NC 27954 Tel (919) 473-2192

MC COY, DONALD B., b. Phila., Nov. 25, 1938; B.A. in English, Villanova U., 1960; J.D., Temple U., 1968. Admitted to Pa bar, 1969; served to lt. comdr. USN, 1960-68; mng. partner firm Dean & McCoy, Langhorne, Pa., 1970—; mem. courthouse com. Bucks County Bar Assn.; chmn. ethics com. Middletown Businessmen's Assn., Pres. Levittown Exchange Club; chmn. legislative sub-com. Bucks County C. of C., also bd. dirs.; Solicitor Council Rock Sch. Dist. Mem. Am., Pa., Bucks County bar assns., Phi Alpha Delta. Office: 407 E Lincoln Hwy Langhorne PA 19047 Tel (215) 757-7673

MC COY, WILLIAM CHARLES, JR., b. Akron, Ohio, Dec. 10, 1923; B.S. in Engring., Princeton U.; LL.B., Western Res. U., 1949. Admitted to Ohio bar, 1951, U.S. Supreme Ct. bar, 1963; partner firm McCoy, Greene & TeGrotenhuis, Cleve., 1956-69; partner firm McCoy, Greene & Howell, Cleve., 1969-73; partner firm Bosworth, Sessions & McCoy Cleve., 1973—. Trustee, sec. Hawken Sch., 1970—; trustee, treas. Ohio Conservation Found., 1976—; trustee Bolton Found., 1973—. Mem. Greater Cleve., Am. bar assns. Home: Shaker Blvd Chagrin Falls OH 44022 Office: 625 Nat City Bank Bldg Cleveland OH 44114 Tel (216) 781-9050

MC CRAY, WENDELL PATRICK, b. Cissna Park, Ill., July 19, 1921; B.A. in Edn., Ill. State Normal U., 1946; J.D., Chgo. Kent Coll. Law, 1951. Admitted to Ill. bar, 1951, Calif. bar, 1963, U.S. Supreme Ct. bar, 1973; law clk. to U.S. Dist. Judge Wham, Eastern Dist. Ill., 1953-56; referee in bankruptcy U.S. Dist. Ct., Eastern Dist. Ill.; practiced in Santa Ana, Calif., 1963-72; judge Westminster (Calif.) Municipal Ct., 1972—. Mem. Ill. Ill. State, Am. bar assns., Calif. Conf. Judges Assn., Am. Bd. Trial Advs., Phi Delta Phi. Office: 8144 Westminster Blvd Westminster CA 92683

MC CREADY, WILLIAM SAMUEL, b. Toledo, Apr. 5, 1944; B.A., Ohio State U., 1966; J.D., U. Toledo, 1969. Admitted to Ohio bar, 1970; asso. firm Ritter, Boesel, Robinson & Marsh, Toledo, 1970; city prosecutor City of Maumee (Ohio), 1971-75, asst. solicitor, 1971—. Mem. Toledo, Ohio, Am. bar assns., Home: 214 W Dudley St Maumee OH 43537 Office: 610 United Savs Bldg Toledo OH 43604 Tel (419) 241-3213

MC CREARY, ROBERT GROSVENOR, JR., b. Cleve., Apr. 30, 1918; A.B., Amherst Coll., 1940; LL.B., Case Western U., 1947. Admitted to Ohio bar, 1947, Fed. bar, 1948; partner firm Arter & Hadden, Cleve., 1958—; instr. admiralty law Case Western Reserve Sch. Law, 1965, 66, 76. Mem. Am., Ohio State bar assns., Bar Assn. Greater Cleve. (pres. 1974-75), Maritime Law Assn. Recipient award best paper Nat. Safety Council Marine Sect., 1976. Home: 23300 Stanford Rd Shaker Heights OH 44122 Office: 1144 Union Commerce Blvd Cleveland OH 44115 Tel (216) 696-1144

MCCREE, WADE HAMPTON, JR., b. Des Moines, July 3, 1920; A.B. summa cum laude, Fisk U., 1941; LL.B., Harvard, 1944, LL.D., 1969; LL.D., Tuskegee Inst., 1963, Wayne State U., 1964, Detroit Coll. Law, 1965, U. Detroit, 1968, Mich. State U., 1971, U. Mich., 1971, Oakland U., 1974, Lewis and Clark U., 1976, Northwestern U., 1976; Litt.D., Centre Coll., Danville, Ky., 1976. Admitted to Mich. bar, 1948; since practiced in Detroit, individual practice law, 1948-52; commr. Workmen's Compensation Commn., 1954-61; judge U.S. Dist. Ct., 1961-66, U.S. Circuit Ct., 1966—; adj. prof. law Wayne State U., 1963-65, Ind. U., summer 1970, U. Detroit, 1976. Vice pres. United Found.; bd. dirs. Detroit Symphony, Greater Mich. Found., Henry Ford Hosp., Met. Hosp., Harvard Overseer, Fisk U.; chmn. bd. dirs. Higher Edn. Opportunities Com. Mem. Am. Bar Assn., Am. Law Inst., Am. Judicature Soc., Inst. Jud. Adminstrn. Home: 1324 Nicolet Pl Detroit MI 48207 Office: 700 US Court House Detroit MI 48226 Tel (313) 226-6014

MC CRIGHT, LEWIS REGINALD, b. Benton, Ark., Aug. 26, 1915; B.S. in Bus. Adminstrn. (Am. Banking Assn. scholar), U. Ark., 1938; postgrad. U. Tex., 1946-47; LL.B. (Pat C. Herrington award), Ark. Law Sch. (now U. Ark. Law Sch.), 1951. Admitted to Ark. bar, 1951, U.S. Tax Ct. bar, 1951, U.S. Supreme Ct. bar, 1957; partner firm McCright, Eldridge, Massey & Co., C.P.A.'s, Little Rock, 1965-68; individual practice law, Little Rock, 1951—. C.P.A., Ark. Mem. Ark. Bar Assn., Ark. Soc. C.P.A.'s (pres. 1958-59), Am. Inst. C.P.A.'s. Home: 7123 W Markham St Little Rock AR 72205 Office: 4942 W Markham St Little Rock AR 72205 Tel (501) 663-2066

MC CROOM, EDDIE WINTHER, b. Memphis, Sept. 11, 1932; B.S., Ark. Agrl., Mech. and Normal Coll., 1955; LL.B., Western Res. U., 1962. Admitted to Ohio bar, 1962; asso. firm Barry & Johnson, Cin., 1963-64; individual practice law, Cin., 1971-73; mem. firm Breckeridge & Haynes, Youngstown, Ohio, 1976—; 1st asst. dist. atty. Office Dept. Justice, Cin., 1965-70; mem. Ohio Civil Rights Commn., 1962; coordinator Ohio Equal Employment Opportunity, 1972. Mem. Cin., Ohio State, Fed. bar assns. Author: A First Look At The Ohio Civil Rights Commn., 1961. Office: Suite 419 Legal Arts Centre Youngstown OH 44503 Tel (216) 744-5139

MC CRORY, J. WALTER, b. Johnston, Pa., Dec. 11, 1941; B.A., Fla. State U., 1963; postgrad. in accounting George Washington U., 1965-66; J.D. U. Fla., 1969. Admitted to Fla. bar, 1970; accountant Moore, Cloud & Richardson, Gainesville, Fla., 1967-69; mem. firm Rimes, Greaton & Murphy, Ft. Lauderdale, Fla., 1970-72; asst. pub. defender Broward County (Fla.), 1972-74; individual practice law, Ft. Lauderdale, 1972-76; mem. firm McCrory, Chappell, Brandt & Gore, Ft. Lauderdale, 1976—. Area capt. United Fund; mem. pres. club Broward Community Coll., hon. trustee. Mem. Estate Planning Council Broward County, Fla. Inst. C.P.A.'s, Phi Delta Phi (asst. province pres.). Home: 2857 NE 25th St Fort Lauderdale FL 33305 Office: 1040 Bayview Dr Fort Lauderdale FL 33304 Tel (305) 565-2767

MC CRORY, THOMAS MILTON, III, b. Dallas, Sept. 2, 1945; B.B.A., Baylor U., 1968, J.D., 1970. Admitted to Tex. bar, 1970; partner firm Freeman & McCrory, Dallas, 1970—; gen. counsel Preston State Bank, Dallas. Mem. State Bar Tex., Am., Dallas (vice-chmn. unauthorized practice com. 1976, mem. ethics com.) bar assns., Tex. Assn. Bank Counsel. Office: 400 Preston State Bank Bldg Dallas TX 75225 Tel (214) 691-5660

MC CRURY, PHILLIP WAYNE, b. St. Peter, Minn., Aug. 29, 1944; B.A., U. Tex., 1966, J.D., 1968; grad. Nat. Coll. Dist. Attys., 1970. Admitted to Tex. bar, 1968, U.S. Supreme Ct. bar, 1976; asso. firm Shafer, Gilliland, Davis, Bunton & McCollum, Odessa, Tex., 1968-70; asst. dist. atty., Nueces County, Tex., 1970-73; partner firm Auforth, Keas, McCrury, Karchmer & Haas, Corpus Christi, Tex., 1973—; mem. Nueces County Juvenile Ct. Advisory Bd. Pres. bd. S. Tex. Lighthouse Blind. Faculty advisor Nat. Coll. Dist. Attys., 1971. Office: 3318 S Alameda St Corpus Christi TX 78411 Tel (512) 854-1071

MC CUBBIN, NICHOLAS DAVID, b. Oneida, Ky., July 10, 1941; B.S., U. Ky., 1963; M.Div., So. Bapt. Theol. Sem., 1968; J.D., U. Louisville, 1971. Admitted to Ky. bar, 1971, U.S. Supreme Ct. bar, 1974; dist. atty. Bur. Hwys. Commonwealth Ky., Frankfort, Manchester and Somerset, 1971-74; asst. resident counsel E. Ky. Power Coop., Inc., Winchester, 1974—. Dir., Somerset Community Coll. Sports Assn., 1973-74; active Ky. Hist. Soc., Frankfort, 1974—, Ky. Assn. Mental Health, Louisville, 1974—; tchr., mem. fin., budget and constn. coms. Trinity Bapt. Ch., Lexington, Ky., 1974—. Mem. Internat., Am., Ky., Pulaski County bar assns., Assn. Trial Lawyers Am., World Peace Through Law Center, Ky. Assn. Trial Attys., Nat. Assn. Criminal Def. Lawyers, Am. Judicature Soc., Somerset-Pulaski County and Jr. chambers commerce. Home: 1831 Cantrill Dr Lexington KY 40505 Office: Box 707 Winchester KY 40391 Tel (606) 744-4812

MC CUBBREY, JAMES BRUCE, b. Grosse Pointe, Mich., Feb. 25, 1936; B.S.E., U. Mich., 1958, J.D., 1961. Admitted to Ill. bar, 1961, Calif. bar, 1966; asso. firm Mueller, Aichele & Rauner, Chgo., 1961-65, Fitch, Even, Tabin & Luedeka, Chgo. and San Francisco, 1965—. Mem. Am. Bar Assn., State Bar Calif., Bar Assn. San Francisco, Patent Law Assn. Chgo., San Francisco Patent Law Assn. Home: 929 Greenhill Rd Mill Valley CA 94941 Office: 235 Montgomery St San Francisco CA 94104 Tel (415) 981-8008

MC CUE, JOHN BERCHMANS, b. Pitts., June 22, 1921; B.A., Pa. State U., 1942; J.D., U. Pitts., 1948. Admitted to Pa. bar, 1949, U.S. Supreme Ct. bar, 1966; individual practice law, Kittanning, Pa., 1949-63; partner firm McCue and Bertocchi, Kittanning, 1963—; mem. Pa. Gen. Assembly, 1963-64, 71-76. Mem. Am., Pa., Armstrong County bar assns., Judge. Advs. Assn. Home: R D 7 Kittanning PA 16201 Office: 217 Market St Kittanning PA 16201 Tel (412) 543-7351

MC CULLOH, CLYDE COSTON, b. Haskell, Tex., July 7, 1902; A.B., U. N.Mex., 1925; postgrad. U. So. Calif., 1929-30. Admitted to Calif. bar, 1930, N.Mex. bar, 1932; atty. N.Mex. State Tax Commn., Santa Fe, 1937-41, 49-51; asst. atty. gen. State N.Mex., 1941-44, 53-54, atty. gen., 1944-49; judge N.Mex. Dist. Ct. 11th Jud. Dist., Aztec, 1955-68; ret., 1968; pres. N.Mex. State Bar, 1947-48. Mem. Am. Bar Assn. Home: 1133 Chaco Ave Farmington NM 87401

MCCULLOUGH, DALE PATRICK, b. Marshall County, Minn., Mar. 20, 1944; B.A., Bemidji State Coll.; J.D., William Mitchell Coll., 1971. Admitted to Minn. bar, 1971; individual practice law; atty. Phalen Area Community Council, 1972. Mem. Ramsey County (vice chmn. family law com., mem. med.-legal com., criminal law com.), Washington, Minn., Am. bar assns., Am., Minn. trial lawyers assns. Home: 16363 Norell Ave N Marine-on-Saint Croix MN 55047 Office: 1073 Payne Ave Saint Paul MN 55101 Tel (612) 772-3446

MC CULLOUGH, FRANK WITCHER, JR., b. Huntington, W.Va., Dec. 4, 1920; B.A., Tulane U., 1943; LL.B., W.Va. U., 1949. Admitted to W.Va. bar, 1949; partner firm McCabe and McCullough, Charleston, W.Va., 1956—. Officer, dir. local corps Charleston CSC, 1952-77; pres. Legal Aid Soc. Kanawha County (W.Va.), 1957. Mem. Am. (former program dir., recipient service citation 1951), W.Va. (exec. sec.-treas. 1959—), Kanawha County bar assns., Am. Judicature Soc., SAR (past pres. local chpt.), Phi Delta Phi. Home: 1405 Ravinia Rd Charleston WV 25314 Office: Security Bldg Charleston WV 25301

MC CULLOUGH, JOHN ARTHUR, b. Washington, Oct. 27, 1945; A.B., Princeton U., 1967; J.D., Yale U., 1970. Admitted to D.C. bar, 1971; asst. counsel Office of Gen. Counsel, Dept. Navy, Washington, 1970-72; asso. firm Jones, Day, Reavis & Pogue, Washington, 1972—. Mem. Am., D.C. bar assns., Am. Soc. Internat. Law, Nat. Contract Mgmt. Assn. Home: 1600 S Eads 635-S Arlington VA 22202 Office: 1100 Connecticut Ave NW Washington DC 20036 Tel (202) 452-5847

MC CUNE, JOHN JENNINGS, b. East Lansing, Mich., Mar. 20, 1919; student Lawrence Coll., 1937-38; A.B., U. Mich., 1941; LL.B., U.Mich., 1949. Admitted to Mich. bar, 1949, Nev. bar, 1960, U.S. Supreme Ct. bar, 1964; individual practice law, Lansing, Mich., 1949-59, Reno, 1960—; mem. Mich. Ho. of Reps., 1952-56; law lectr. Mich. State U., 1949-50; asst. pros. atty. Ingham County (Mich.), 1950-51. Mem. Am., Washoe County (Nev.) bar assns., state bars Mich., Nev., Phi Alpha Delta. Named Hon. Alumnus Mich. State U., 1955; editor Inter Alia, Nev. State Bar Jour., 1963—. Home: 1311 Humboldt St Reno NV 89509 Office: 241 Ridge St Reno NV 89501 Tel (702) 786-0697

MC CURDY, JOSEPH PATRICK, b. Balt., Nov. 1, 1940; A.B., Loyola Coll., 1962, LL.B., Villanova U., 1965. Admitted to Md. bar, 1966; trust adminstr. Union Trust Co. Md., 1965-66; staff atty. Legal Aid Bureau, Inc., 1966-68; asso. firm Goodman, Meagher and Enoch, Md., 1968-72; asso. firm Gallagher, Evelius and Jones, Balt., 1972—. Mem. Md., Balt. bar assns. Home: 227 Chancery Rd Baltimore MD 21218 Office: 1100 One Charles Center Baltimore MD 21201 Tel (301) 727-7702

MC CUTCHAN, GORDON EUGENE, b. Buffalo, Sept. 30, 1935; B.A., Cornell U., 1956, M.B.A., 1958, LL.B., 1959. Admitted to N.Y. bar, 1959, Ohio bar, 1964; individual practice law, Rome, N.Y., 1959-61; atty., advisor SEC, Washington, 1961-64; mem. Office of Gen. Counsel, Nationwide Ins. Cos., Columbus, Ohio, 1964—, v.p., asso. gen. counsel, 1973—; partner firm Wagner, Schmidt, McCutchan, Hank & Birkhimer, Columbus, 1964—. Mem. Fed., Columbus, Ohio, Am. bar assns., Assn. Life Ins. Counsel. Home: 2376 Oxford Rd Columbus OH 43221 Office: One Nationwide Plaza Columbus OH 43215 Tel (614) 227-7612

MC DADE, JOHN MICHAEL, b. Amarillo, Tex., Jan. 31, 1940; B.S. in Internat. Affairs, Georgetown U., 1963; J.D., U. San Diego, 1968. Admitted to Calif. bar, 1970, Fed. bar, 1970; prin., tchr. St. Augustine Sch. San Diego, 1964-70; individual practice law, San Diego, Calif., 1970-72; partner firm Bourne, McDade, Moon & Cline, San Diego, 1972-75; partner firm McDade & Treitler, San Diego, 1975—. Pres. Republican Assos. San Diego, 1974—, mem. Republican County Central Com., San Diego, 1966-74. Mem. Calif., San Diego County bar assns. Asso. editor San Diego Law Rev., 1966-68. Home: 1218 Bernita Rd El Cajon CA 92020 Office: 8334 Clairemont Mesa Blvd Suite 207 San Diego CA 92111 Tel(714) 292-0671

MC DAID, EDWARD B., b. Phila., Sept. 19, 1945; B.A., Stetson U., 1966; J.D., Dickinson Sch. Law, 1969. Admitted to Pa. bar, 1969; mem. firm Farage & Shrager, Phila., 1969—. Mem. Am., Pa. trial lawyers assns. Office: 836 Suburban Station Philadelphia PA 19103 Tel (215) 563-3973

MC DANIEL, DOUTHIT YOUNG, b. Granger, Tex., Sept. 23, 1898; B.A., Baylor U., 1919; LL.B., U. Tex., 1922. Admitted to Tex. bar, 1922; municipal judge City Waco, Tex., 1930-36; judge McLennan County, Tex., 1937-48; dist. judge 74th Jud. Dist. Tex., 1949-67; individual practice law, Waco, 1967—; instr. Baylor U., Waco, 1944-49. Mem. Waco-McLennan Bar Assn. Recipient Good Govt. award Waco Jr. C. of C., Dedicated Service award County Judges and Commr. Assn. Tex., plaque Waco-McLennan Bar Assn. Home and Office: 532 N 32d St Waco TX 67607 Tel (817) 652-8164

MC DANIEL, EDWARD EUGENE, b. Memphis, July 21, 1936; A.B., Howard U., Washington, 1958; J.D., Golden Gate Coll., San Francisco, 1967. Admitted to Calif. bar, 1968; examiner Bur. Employees' Compensation, U.S. Dept. Labor, Boston, 1961-64, NLRB, San Francisco, 1964-68; mem. bd. arbitration U.S. Steel Corp./United Steelworkers Am., Pitts., 1969-75; impartial umpire Alan Wood Steel Co./United Steelworkers Am., Conshohocken, Pa., 1971-74; arbitrator Am. Arbitration Assn., Fed. Mediation and Conciliation Service, Pa. Bur. Mediation Panels, 1971—; panel arbitrator ERDA and various U.S. contractors/unions, 1973—; panel arbitrator baseball players' salary disputes Major League Baseball Club Assn./Major League Baseball Players Assn., N.Y.C., 1973-74; permanent arbitrator Am. Can Co./United Steelworkers Am., Greenwich, Conn., 1975—; spl. arbitrator U.S. Steel Corp./United Steelworkers Am., Pitts., 1975—; panel arbitrator Bituminous Contractors' Assn./United Mine Workers Am., Washington, 1975—; impartial umpire Noranda Aluminum Co. Can./United Steelworkers Am., Sikeston, Mo., 1976—. Mem. State Bar Calif., Am. Bar Assn., Nat. Acad. Arbitrators. Home: 116 S Homewood Ave Pittsburgh PA 15208 Office: The Bigelow Suite 1624 Pittsburgh PA 15219

MC DANIEL, JAMES EDWIN, b. Dexter, Mo., Nov. 22, 1931; A.B., Washington U., 1957, LL.B., 1959. Admitted to Mo. bar, 1959, U.S. Supreme Ct. bar, 1966; partner firm Barnard & Baer, St. Louis, 1961—. Trustee First Congregational Ch., St. Louis. Mem. Am. Bar Assn. (mem. ho. of dels. 1976—, Mo. Bar Assn. (gov. 1974—), Bar Assn. Met. St. Louis (pres. 1972), Assn. Def. Counsel (past pres.), Phi Delta Phi. Home: 767 Elmwood St St Louis MO 63122 Office: Suite 1400 818 Olive St St Louis MO 63101 Tel (314) 241-5500

MC DANIEL, LESLIE BRUCE, b. Dillon, S.C., May 26, 1933; B.S., Wake Forest Coll., 1955, J.D., 1958. Admitted to N.C. bar, 1958, Ga. bar, 1963, U.S. Supreme Ct. bar, 1971; staff atty. Securities & Exchange Commission, Atlanta, 1962-66; since practiced in Raleigh, N.C., mem. firm Cris, Twiggs & Wells, 1967-68, individual practice law, 1969, mem. firm McDaniel & Fogel, 1970—; judge adv. gen. USAF 1959-61. Mem. Raleigh Jaycees 1967-69. Mem. N.C. State, N.C., Fed., Am. Bar Assns. Contbr. articles to legal jours. Home: 1201 Granada Dr Raleigh NC 27612 Office: Box 1182 612 Branch Bank 333 Fayetteville St Raleigh NC 27601 Tel (919) 828-4486

MC DANIEL, MILDRED LEE, b. Paris, Ky., Aug. 3, 1915; A.B., U. Ky., 1938, M.A., 1950; J.D., U. Miami, 1955. Admitted to Fla. bar 1955; individual practice law, Hollywood, Fla., 1955-75, Ft. Lauderdale, 1955-75, Miami, 1961—; asso. prof. govt. Miami Dade Community Coll., 1961—. Mem. Am., Fla. bar assns., Am., So. polit. sci. assns. Home: 540 Reinante Ave Miami FL 33156 Tel (305) 666-3242

MC DANIEL, NICHOLAS CALVIN, b. Warrenton, N.C., Oct. 29, 1937; B.S. in Engring., U. Tenn., 1961; M.B.A., Ga. State U., 1974; J.D., Emory U., 1965. Admitted to Ga. bar, 1965, Tenn. bar 1966; v.p., Dean Witter & Co., Inc., San Francisco, 1976—; sr. v.p. Asset Mgmt. Atlanta, 1975-76; mem. firm Withers & McDaniel, Atlanta, 1965-70, partner, 1970-73; lectr. Ga. State U., 1970-74. Mem. Inst. Certified Fin. Planners (nat. pres.), Internat. Assn. Fin. Planners (dir. 1975-77, pres. Ga. chpt. 1975-76). Home: 9220 Huntcliff Trace NE Atlanta GA 30338 also 101 Bella Vista Ave Belvedere CA 94920 Office: 45 Montgomery St San Francisco CA 94120 Tel (415) 392-7200

MC DANIEL, PAUL REESE, b. Sabetha, Kans., Jan. 28, 1936; B.A., U. Okla., 1958; LL.B., Harvard, 1961. Admitted to Okla. bar, 1961; asso. firm Crowe, Dunlevy, Thweatt, Swinford, Johnson & Burdick, Oklahoma City, 1961-67; atty-adviser, acting asso. tax legis. counsel Office of Tax Legis. Counsel, Dept. Treasury, Washington, 1967-69; spl. asst. to Senator Albert Gore, Washington, 1967-70; prof. law Boston Coll., 1970—; spl. tax cons. Hill & Barlow, Boston, 1973—; cons. U.S. Senate Judiciary Com. sub-com. on adminstrv. practices, 1976—. Bd. dirs. Newton (Mass.) Community Devel. Found., 1975—. Mem. Am. Bar Assn., Nat. Tax Assn.-Tax Inst. Am., Internat. Fiscal Assn. Recipient Meritorious Service award Dept. Treasury, 1969; Sr. Fulbright-Hays scholar, 1976; author: (with others) Federal Income Taxation, vol. 1, 1972, vol. 2, 1973; Federal Wealth Transfer Taxation, 1977; contbr. articles to legal publs. Home: 27 Orient Ave Newton MA 02159 Office: 885 Centre St Newton Centre MA 02159 Tel (617) 969-0100

MC DANIEL, ROBERT J., b. Lexington, Ky., Feb. 27, 1943; B.S. in Psychology, U. Ky., 1964, J.D., 1967. Admitted to Ky. bar, 1967, U.S. Supreme Ct. bar, 1971; legal clk. U.S. Army, 1968-70; individual practice law, Paris, Ky., 1971—. Chmn. local Easter Seal Soc., 1973-76. Mem. Ky. Bar Assn., Ky. Defenders Assn. (chmn.), Bourbon County Legal Aid Soc. Home: 305 Robin Rd Paris KY 40361 Office: 226 Main St Paris KY 40361 Tel (606) 987-1423

MCDANIELS, WILLIAM E., b. Needham, Mass., July 1, 1941; B.A., Williams Coll., 1963; J.D., Georgetown U., 1966; grad. fellow U. Pa., 1966-68. Admitted to D.C. bar, 1967; staff atty. Pub. Defender Office, Phila., 1966-68; atty. firm Williams & Connolly, Washington, 1968-75, partner, 1976—; adj. prof. evidence and criminal law Georgetown U. Law Center, 1970—. Mem. Am. Bar Assn. Home: 2952 Newark St NW Washington DC 20008 Office: 1000 Hill Bldg Washington DC 20006

MC DARRIS, JOSEPH CHARLES, b. Beech, N.C., Sept. 2, 1917; B.S., Berea Coll., 1938; LL.B., Wake Forest U., 1960, S.J.D., 1960. Admitted to N.C. bar, U.S. Dist. Ct. bar, 1960; partner firm Ferguson & McDarris, Waynesville, N.C., 1960-65; individual practice law, Waynesville, 1965-73; judge 30th Jud. Dist., Waynesville, 1973—; atty. Haywood County (N.C.) Dept. Social Services, 1963-73; atty. Town of Waynesville, 1966-73; atty. Asheville Production Credit Assn., 1966-73. Mem. Am., N.C. bar assns., Am. Legion, VFW. Home: 103 Walnut St Waynesville NC 28786 Office: County Court House Main St Waynesville NC 28786 Tel (704) 456-3540

MC DERMOTT, EDWARD ALOYSIUS, b. Dubuque, Iowa, June 28, 1920; A.B., Loras Coll., 1939, J.D. (hon.), 1973; J.D., U. Iowa, 1942; J.D. (hon.), Xavier U., 1962. Admitted to Iowa bar, 1942, Nebr. bar, 1942, D.C. bar, 1965, U.S. Supreme Ct. bar, 1960; atty. law dept. Montgomery Ward and Co., Chgo., 1943-46; asso. firm O'Connor, Thomas and O'Connor, Dubuque, 1946-50; partner firm O'Conner, Thomas, McDermott and Wright, Dubuque, 1951-61, firm Hogan and Hartson, Washington, 1965—; chief counsel U.S. Senate subcom. on privileges and elections, 1950-51; mem. uniform laws commn., 1958-62; dep. dir. U.S. Office Civil and Def. Mobilization, 1961-62; dir. White House Office of Emergency Planning, 1962-65; mem. NSC, 1962-65; U.S. del. to non-mil. coms. NATO, 1962-65. Trustee Colgate U., 1970-75; regent U. Santa Clara, 1969-74, Coll. Notre Dame, 1972—, Loras Coll., 1976—; bd. dirs. Indsl. Coll. of Armed Forces, 1964-69, Iowa Law Sch. Found., 1973—; bd. dirs., officer Am. Irish Found., 1969—; bd. advisors Lynchburg Coll., 1970—. Mem. Am., Iowa, D.C. bar assns., Nat. Lawyers Club, Am. Judicature Soc. Named to Knights of Malta, Knights of the Equestrian Order of the Holy Sepulchre; recipient AMVETS Nat. award, 1965. Home: 5400 Albemarle St NW Westmoreland Hills Washington DC 20016 Office: 815 Connecticut Ave NW Washington DC 20006 Tel (202) 331-4637

MC DERMOTT, FRANCIS O., b. Denver, Feb. 25, 1933; student Creighton U., 1951-53, George Washington U., 1953-56; LL.B., Am. U., 1960. Admitted to D.C. bar 1960; trial atty. Office of Regional Council, Phila. region, Washington Br., 1961-65; profl. staff mem. Com. on Finance U.S. Senate, Washington, 1965-68; tax counsel Assn. of Am. R.R.s, 1968-73; mem. firm Hopkins, Sutter, Mulroy, Davis & Cromartie, Washington, 1973—. Mem. Am., Fed., D.C. Bar assns. Office: 1750 K St S 110 Washington DC 20006 Tel (202) 785-8787

MC DERMOTT, JOHN EMORY, b. Ravenna, Ohio, Oct. 25, 1946; B.A., Ohio Wesleyan U., 1968; J.D., Harvard, 1971. Admitted to Calif. bar, 1972; asso. firm Latham & Watkins, Los Angeles, 1971-72; staff atty. Western Center on Law and Poverty, Los Angeles, 1972-74, dir. litigation, 1975—; dep. city atty. City of Los Angeles, 1974-75; adj. lectr. on law U. So. Calif., Los Angeles, 1973-74, 74-75, 76-77; Distinguished lectr., U. So. Calif. Sch. Pub. Adminstrn., 1976; mem. legal advocacy study group Los Angeles Area Developmental Disabilities Bd., 1976. Mem. Am., Calif. bar assns. Editor: Indeterminancy in Education, 1976. Office: 1709 W 8th St Los Angeles CA 90017 Tel (213) 483-1491

MC DERMOTT, JOHN HENRY, b. Evanston, Ill., June 23, 1931; B.A., Williams Coll., 1953; J.D., U. Mich., 1956. Admitted to Mich. bar, 1955, Ill. bar, 1956; with JAGC, U.S. Air Force, Reno, 1956-58; asso. firm McDermott, Will & Emery, Chgo., 1956-64, partner, 1964—. Mem. Ill., Chgo., Am. bar assns., State Bar Mich. Home: 714 Park Ln Winnetka IL 60093 Office: 111 W Monroe St Chicago IL 60603 Tel (312) 372-2000

MCDERMOTT, PETER D., b. Pocatello, Idaho, Sept. 23, 1939; B.A., Idaho State U., 1964; LL.B., U. Idaho, 1968. Admitted to Idaho bar, 1968; partner firm McDermott & McDermott, Pocatello; pub. defender 6th Jud. Dist. Idaho; instr. criminal law Idaho State U. Mem. Am., Idaho trial lawyers assns., Nat. Assn. Pub. Defenders. Home: Crystal Springs Dr Pocatello ID 83201 Office: PO Box 3 Pocatello ID 83201 Tel (208) 232-3162

MC DERMOTT, ROBERT FRANCIS, JR., b. Cambridge, Mass., Nov. 3, 1945; A.B., Harvard, 1967; LL.B., Yale, 1970. Admitted to Conn. bar, 1970, Ga. bar, 1973, Va. bar, 1976; staff asst. to Pres. of U.S., Washington, 1971-72; asso. firm Alston, Miller & Gaines, Atlanta, 1973-74; staff asst. to dep. atty. gen. Dept. of Justice, Washington, 1974-75, asso. dep. atty. gen., 1975; asst. U.S. atty. E. Dist. of Va., Alexandria, 1976—. Office: 117 S Washington St Alexandria VA 22314 Tel (703) 557-9100

MC DERMOTT, ROBERT JOSEPH, b. Bklyn., Sept. 5, 1944; A.B., Georgetown U., 1966; J.D., N.Y. U., 1970, LL.M. in Taxation, 1974. Admitted to N.Y. bar, 1971; asso. firm Dewey, Ballantine, Bushby, Palmer & Wood, N.Y.C., 1970—. Mem. Am. Bar Assn. Home: 875 West End Ave New York City NY 10025 Office: 140 Broadway New York City NY 10005 Tel (212) DI 4-8000

MCDERMOTT, THOMAS JOHN, JR., b. Santa Monica, Calif., Mar. 23, 1931; B.A., U. Calif., Los Angeles, 1953, J.D., 1958. Admitted to Calif. bar, 1958; asso. firm Gray, Binkley & Pfaelzer, Los Angeles, 1958-64; partner firm Gray, Pfaelzer & Robertson, Los Angeles, 1964-67, Kadison, Pfaelzer, Woodard, Quinn & Rossi, Los Angeles, 1967—. Sec. bd. govs. Performing Arts Council of Music Center, Los Angeles. Mem. Am., Los Angeles County bar assns., State Bar Calif., Order of Coif. Home: 505 N Foothill Rd Beverly Hills CA 90210 Office: 611 W 6th St Los Angeles CA 90017 Tel (213) 626-1251

MC DONALD, ANGUS WILLIAM, b. Louisville, May 29, 1912; LL.B., U. Va., 1935. Admitted to Ken. bar, 1935; since practiced in Lexington, Ken., partner firm McDonald, Alford & Roszell (and predecessors), 1936—; spl. agt. FBI, 1942-45. Mem. Am., Ken., Fayette County Bar Assns. Home: 7 Deepwood Dr Lexington KY 40505 Office: PO Box 1808 Lexington KY 40501 Tel (606) 252-8981

MC DONALD, BEN F., b. Austin, Tex., Oct. 28, 1925; B.A. in Bus. and Econs., U. Tex., 1944, LL.B., 1949. Admitted to Tex. bar, 1949, U.S. Ct. Appeal bar, 1954, U.S. Supreme Ct. bar, 1968; trial atty. U.S. Atty. Gen.'s Office, 1949, 50; asso. firm Warren & Gross, Corpus Christi, Tex., 1950-51; partner firm Warren & McDonald, 1951-56; with firm McDonald, Spann & Smith, 1956-74; exec. dir. Govs. Office Tex. Dept. Community Affairs, 1974—; mayor City of Corpus Christi, 1961-63. Mem. Corpus Christi Human Relations Council (chmn.), Corpus Christi, Tex. bar assns. Office: 900 Wilson Bldg Corpus Christi TX 78401 Tel (512) 884-8221

MC DONALD, CHARLES EUGENE, b. Canyon, Tex., Feb. 21, 1927; B.S., W. Tex. State Normal Coll., 1948; J.D., U. Tex., 1953. Admitted to Tex. bar, 1953; individual practice law, Bangs, Tex., 1953—. Office: 106 S 1st St Bangs TX 76823

MC DONALD, DANIEL PATRICK, b. Darlington, Wis., June 21, 1942; B.S., Marquette U., 1964, J.D., 1966. Admitted to Wis. bar, 1966; practiced in Darlington, 1968-69; dist. atty., commr. family ct. Lafayette County (Wis.), 1969-71; judge Lafayette County Ct., 1971—; mem. S.W. Wis. Regional Criminal Justice Council, 1969—, chmn., 1971-72. Mem. Wis. State, Lafayette County bar assns. Home: Willow Springs Ln Darlington WI 53530 Office: Lafayette County Courthouse Darlington WI 53530 Tel (608) 776-2311

MCDONALD, EARL EARNEST, b. Albion, Ind., Feb. 11, 1906; A.B., DePauw U., 1927; M.A., U. Mich., 1931. Admitted to Mich. bar, 1938, U.S. Supreme Ct. bar, 1964; tchr. pub. schs., Mt. Morris, Marine City and Lansing, Mich., 1927-43; individual practice law, Lansing, 1938-43; asst. pros. atty. Ingham County, Mich., 1943-45, chief asst. prosecutor, 1945-50; municipal judge Lansing, Mich., 1960-70, sr. judge dist. ct., Lansing, 1971-72; vis. dist. judge, 1974—; instr. bus. law Am. Inst. Banking, Lansing, 1943-62, Mich. State U., Lansing, 1958-66; active ct. legis. reforms, 1950-70; lectr. in field. Mem. Mich., Ingham County bar assns., Am. Judges Assn. Contbr. articles to legal jours. Home: 1018 W Lapeer St Lansing MI 48915

MCDONALD, FRANK GOODALL, b. Meridian, Tex., Apr. 9, 1916; student Hill Jr. Coll., 1934; A.B., Baylor U., 1936; LL.B., J.D., U. Tex., 1938; grad. U.S. Army Command and Gen. Staff Coll., 1961. Admitted to Tex. bar, 1938, U.S. Supreme Ct. bar, 1942; individual practice law, Hillsboro, Tex., 1938-40; judge Dist. Ct., 66th Dist., Hillsboro, 1947-53; chief justice Tex. Civil Appeals Ct., 10th Dist., Waco, 1953—. Mem. Tex., Waco-McLennan County bar assns. Home: 2407 Starr St Waco TX 76710 Office: Courthouse 4th Floor Waco TX 76701 Tel (817) 753-7341

MCDONALD, FRED JAMES, b. Paris, Tex., Aug. 6, 1917; student Oklahoma City U., 1948; J.D., U. Okla., 1955; LL.M., U. Mich., 1965. Admitted to Okla. bar, U.S. Dist. Ct. bar, 1955; prof. bus. law and ins. Okla. State U., Stillwater, 1955-68; prof. law, dir. legal clin. edn. Oklahoma City U., 1968—; cons. in field. Mem. Okla. Bar Assn., Nat. Rifle Assn., Res. Officers Assn., Phi Delta Phi. Contbr. articles in field to profl. jours. Home: 4637 NW 70th St Oklahoma City OK 73132 Office: 2301 N Blackwelder St Oklahoma City OK 73106 Tel (405) 525-5411

MCDONALD, GARY RONALD, b. Saginaw, Mich., Feb. 3, 1940; B.B.A., U. Mich., 1962; J.D., Wayne State U., 1965. Admitted to Mich. bar, 1965, U.S. Supreme Ct. bar, 1967; individual practice law, Saginaw, 1965-72; mem. firm Moskal, McDonald, McDonald, Callison, Callison & Weinstein, 1965-72; judge Mich. 70th Dist. Ct., 1972-76; circuit judge 10th Jud. Circuit Mich., 1976—; sec. exec. com. Region Law Enforcement Council, Essexville, Mich.; chmn. criminal justice co-ordinating com. Saginaw County (Mich.) Office Criminal Justice. Mem. adv. council Insight Internat. Inc., Saginaw. Mem. Am. Judicature Soc., Am., Mich. trial lawyers assns., State Bar Mich., Saginaw County Bar Assn. Office: 115 S Michigan Ave Saginaw MI 48602 Tel (517) 793-9100

MC DONALD, GEORGE EDWARD, b. Alameda, Calif., July 25, 1920; B.A. in Philosophy, U. San Francisco, 1945, LL.D., 1949. Admitted to Calif. bar, 1950; practiced in Alameda, 1950-64; judge Municipal Ct., Alameda, 1964—; inheritance tax appraiser Calif. State, 1959-64, Treas. Alameda County Democratic Central Com., 1950-64; chmn. Alameda chpt. Cerebral Palsy Assn., 1952-63; chmn. Salvation Army, Alameda, 1964—. Mem. Alameda County Bar Assn., St. Thomas More Soc., Alameda County Municipal Ct. Judges Assn. Office: Alameda Municipal Ct 1516 Oak St Alameda CA 94501 Tel (415) 522-5050

MC DONALD, HARRY WILLIAM, b. Cohoes, N.Y., June 13, 1917; student Rensselaer Poly. Inst., 1937; LL.B., Albany, 1940. Admitted to N.Y. bar, 1941; rep. Hartford Accident & Indemnity Co., Albany, 1941-45; regional atty. N.Y. State Labor Relations Bd., Albany, 1945—. Trustee Cohoes Mem. Hosp. Assn. Mem. Am., N.Y. bar assns. Home: 25 James St Cohoes NY 12047 Office: 88 Remsen St Cohoes NY 12047 Tel (518) 237-2040

MC DONALD, JAMES OWEN, b. Schenectady, Aug. 5, 1927; A.B., Syracuse U., 1949; J.D., DePaul U., 1955; certificate Environ. Mgmt. Inst., U. So. Calif., 1976. Admitted to Ill. bar, 1956; individual practice law, Chgo., 1956-57; dir. constrn. grants region V, EPA, Chgo., 1967-71, dir. enforcement, 1971—. Mem. Ill. State Bar Assn., Nat., Chgo. Audubon socs., Nat. Geog. Soc., Sierra Club, Am. Birding Assn. Recipient Gold medal for Exceptional Service, EPA, 1971. Home: 1760 W Jarvis Ave Chicago IL 60626 Office: 230 S Dearborn St Chicago IL 60604 Tel (312) 353-2076

MC DONALD, JAMES ROBERT, b. Greensburg, Pa., Dec. 9, 1940; B.A., St. Vincent Coll., 1966; J.D., Duquesne U., 1969. Admitted to Pa. Supreme Ct. bar, 1970; individual practice law, Greensburg, 1969—; owner J. M. Abstract Co. Mem. Pa. Bar Assn., Westmoreland County (Pa.) Bar. Home: 409 Sheffield Dr Greensburg PA 15601 Office: 13 N Maple Ave Greensburg PA 15601 Tel (412) 836-0061

MC DONALD, JOHN RICHARD, b. Connersville, Ind., Aug. 8, 1933; B.A., U. Ariz., 1957, LL.B., 1960. Admitted to Ariz. bar, 1960, U.S. Supreme Ct. bar, 1971; asso. firm Richard N. Roylston, 1960-62; individual practice law, 1962-65; partner firm McDonald & Rykken, Tucson, 1965-68, DeConcini, McDonald, Brammer & Yetwin, and predecessors, Tucson, 1968—. Bd. dirs. Tucson Assn. for Blind, 1966—, v.p., 1967-73; bd. dirs. Comstock Children's Hosp., 1964—, pres., 1970-71; bd. dirs. Skyline Bel Aire Community Assn., 1972-74, pres., 1972-73; clk. bd. trustees Catalina Foothills Sch. Dist., 1976—; precinct committeeman Republican Party, 1964-66. Mem. Am., Ariz., Pima County bar assns. Office: 240 N Stone St Tucson AZ 85701 Tel (602) 623-3411

MC DONALD, JOHN WILLIAM, b. Hollister, Calif., Feb. 17, 1925; B.A., U. Calif., 1947; LL.B., Hastings Coll. Law, San Francisco, 1950. Admitted to Calif. bar, 1951; law clk. Calif. Dist. Ct. Appeals, San Francisco, 1951-52; partner firm Clewe, Blade & McDonald, Oroville, Calif., 1952-60; mem. firm Boccardo, Blum, Lull, Niland & Bell, San Jose, Calif., 1960—. Mem. Am. Bar Assn., Am., Calif. trial lawyers assns. Office: 111 W Saint John St San Jose CA 95113 Tel (408) 298-5678

MC DONALD, JOHN WILLIAM, JR., b. Cody, Wyo., Dec. 30, 1935; B.S., U. Mont., 1958, J.D., 1961. Admitted to Mont. bar, 1961; partner firm McDonald & Josephson, Livingston, Mont. and Big Timber, Mont., 1962-70; individual practice law, 1970-72; partner firm McDonald & Blackwood, Livingston, 1972—; dep. atty. Park County (Mont.), 1965-75; instr. U. Mont., Missoula, 1961-62. Trustee Livingston Meml. Hosp. Assn., 1975—, v.p., 1976. Mem. Am., Mont., Park-Sweetgrass (pres. 1976) bar assns. Home: 617 S 12th St Livingston MT 59047 Office: 116 W Callender St Livingston MT 59047 Tel (406) 222-2941

MC DONALD, LAURIER BERNARD, b. Memphis, Oct. 3, 1931; B.A., Tex. A. and I. U., 1957; J.D., U. Tex., 1961. Admitted to Tex. bar, 1961, U.S. Supreme Ct. bar, 1964; partner firm Pena, McDonald, Prestia & Zipp, Edinburg, Tex., 1966—; agt. FBI, Quantico, Va., 1961, Tampa, Fla., 1962, Washington, 1963, San Juan, P.R., 1964, N.Y.C., 1965; vis. lectr., prof. Pan. Am. U.; guest lectr. Immigration and Nationality Symposiums, Seminars; del. to joint confs. Soviet-U.S., Moscow, 1974, 76. Mem. Am. Bar Assn., Assn. Immigration and Nationality Lawyers (past pres. Tex. chpt.). Home: 1027 S 12th St Edinburg TX 78539 Office: 600 S Hwy 281 Edinburg TX 78539 Tel (512) 383-6251

MCDONALD, MARK T., b. 1935; B.A., Prairie View A. and M. U.; LL.B., Tex. So. U. Admitted to Tex. bar, 1962; now partner firm McDonald & McDonald, Houston. Mem. Nat. Bar Assn. (pres. 1977—). Office: 1834 Southmore Blvd Suite 203 Houston TX 77004*

MCDONALD, RICHARD EDWARD, b. Pontiac, Mich., June 10, 1929; student Santa Ana (Calif.) Coll., 1954. Flint (Mich.) Jr. Coll., 1954-55; B.S. (Alumni scholar), Wayne State U., 1957, M.E., 1959; postgrad. U. Mich., 1957, Pepperdine Coll., Los Angeles, 1961-62, 65, U. So. Calif., 1964-65, U. Calif., Los Angeles, 1964, Detroit Coll. Law, 1965-66; J.D., U. Calif., Los Angeles, 1967. Warehouse clk. Mich. CSC, Pontiac State Hosp., 1948, Mich. Liquor Control Commn., 1950-52; ct. recorder, clk. USMC Air Sta., El Toro, Calif., 1952-54; tchr. Detroit City Schs., 1956-59; tchr. Compton (Calif.) Union High Sch. Dist., 1959-65, curriculum chmn. bus. edn., 1965-66; faculty Compton Coll., 1961-65; admitted to Mich. bar; individual practice law, Flint, 1968—; atty. Model Cities Program, 1970-71; hearing referee Mich. Civil Rights Commn., 1970—. Active, NAACP, Urban League of Flint; bd. dirs. Greater Flint Opportunities Industrialization Center, Legal Aid Soc. Eastern Mich., Ridgecrest Apts. Mem. Am., Nat., Genesee County bar assns., Am. Trial Lawyers Assn. (treas. 1970-71), C. of C. Greater Flint. Recipient Smead Mfg. Co. award, 1957; named Most Outstanding Student, Detroit Bus. Tchrs. Assn., 1957; contbr. articles to profl. publs. Office: 2217 Detroit St Flint MI 48503 Tel (313) 239-3666

MC DONALD, TERRENCE WHITTY, b. Detroit, May 3, 1943; B.A., U. Notre Dame, 1971; J.D., St. Mary's Sch. Law, 1973. Admitted to Tex. bar, 1973, U.S. Ct. Appeals bar, 5th Circuit, 1974; U.S. Dist. Ct. bar, Western Dist. Tex., 1975; asso. firm Nicholas & Barrera, Inc., San Antonio, 1973—; instr. legal research and writing St. Mary's Law Sch., 1972-73, adj. prof. criminal law and criminal procedure, 1975—. Bd. dirs. San Antonio Literacy Council, 1976—. Mem. State Bar Tex., Am. Bar Assn., Tex. Criminal Def. Lawyers Assn., Phi Delta Phi. Notes editor St. Mary's Law Jour., 1972-73. Home: 209 Madison St San Antonio TX 78204 Office: 424 E Nueva St San Antonio TX 78205 Tel (512) 224-5811

MC DONALD, THOMAS ALEXANDER, b. Chgo., Aug. 20, 1942; A.B., Georgetown U., 1965; J.D., Loyola U., Chgo., 1968. Admitted to Ill. bar, 1969; asso. firm Clausen, Miller, Gorman, Caffrey & Witous, Chgo., 1969-76, partner, 1976—. Mem. Am., Ill., Chgo. bar assns., Trial Lawyers Club Chgo. Home: 107 N Carriage Rd Barrington IL 60010 Office: 135 S LaSalle St Chicago IL 60603 Tel (312) 346-6200

MCDONALD, THOMAS DONALD, b. Lakewood, Ohio, Jan. 8, 1928; A.B., DePauw U., 1950; LL.B., Ohio State U., 1952. Admitted to Ohio bar, 1953, U.S. Supreme Ct. bar, 1963; mem. firm McDonald, Hopkins & Hardy, and predecessors, Cleve., 1953—. Mem. Am., Ohio State, Cuyahoga County (pres. 1976-77) bar assns., Bar Assn. Greater Cleve., Assn. Trial Lawyers Am., Ohio Acad. Trial Lawyers, Cleve. Acad. Trial Attys. (pres. 1967-68). Home: 21800 Lake Rd Rocky River OH 44116 Office: 1105 E Ohio Bldg Cleveland OH 44114 Tel (216) 621-3480

MCDONALD, WILLIAM JAMES, b. N.Y.C., Apr. 17, 1927; B.S., Holy Cross Coll., 1949; J.D., Georgetown U., 1952. Admitted to N.Y. bar, 1952, also U.S. Supreme Ct. bar; asso. firm Clark, Carr & Ellis, N.Y.C., 1952-69, partner, 1963-69; v.p., gen. counsel Union Pacific RR Co. and subsidiaries, 1968, v.p. law dept., 1969; v.p., gen. counsel Union Pacific Corp., 1969-73, sr. v.p. law, 1973—; dir. Los Angeles and Salt Lake RR, Oreg. Wash. RR & Nav., Spokane Internat., St. Joseph & Grand Island RR, Oregon Short Line RR, Union Pacific Land Resources & Upland Industries. Mem. bd. edn. Archdiocese of N.Y.; mem. Cardinal's Com. for Edn. in Archdiocese, 1970, Cardinal's Com. of Laity, 1969. Mem. Assn. Bar City N.Y. (com. securities regulation 1962-67), Assn. Am. Railroad. (legal affairs com., chmn. various subcoms.), Am. Bar Assn. (mem. council; chmn. railroad com. pub. utilities sect.). Contbr. articles to profl. jours. Home: 11 Axtell Dr Scarsdale NY 10583 Office: 345 Park Ave New York City NY 10022 Tel (212) 826-8220

MC DONOUGH, DAYLE CROCKETT, b. Cameron, Mo., Dec. 14, 1891; LL.B. cum laude, U. Mo., Columbia, 1912, J.D. cum laude, 1969. Admitted to Mo. bar, 1912; practiced in Kansas City, Mo., 1913-17; supr. Bur. of War Risk Ins., Washington, 1918-19; Am. consul State Dept., Washington, 1919-24, commd. fgn. service officer, 1924; consul Concepcion, Chile, 1919-22, La Paz, Bolivia, 1922-25, Caracas, Venezuela, 1925-26, Guadalajara, Mexico, 1926, Sydney, Australia, 1926-29; consul gen. Bombay, India, 1931-34, Guayaquil, Ecuador, 1934-37, Monterrey, Mexico, 1938-41; consul gen., 1st sec. Santiago, Chile, 1941-43; consul gen. Glasgow, Scotland, 1945-51, London, Eng., 1949; probate judge, ex officio magistrate DeKalb County (Mo.) Ct., 1957—. Mem. Mo. Bar Assn., Am. Fgn. Service Assn., Order of Coif, Delta Sigma Rho, Phi Delta Phi. Home: 608 S Water St Maysville MO 64469 Office: Courthouse Maysville MO 64469 Tel (816) 449-5400

MC DONOUGH, DONALD JOSEPH, b. Bklyn., Mar. 19, 1918; B.A., Georgetown U., 1939; LL.B., Fordham U., 1942. Admitted to N.Y. bar, 1942; individual practice law, Bklyn. Mem. N.Y. State, Nassau bar assns. Home: 25 Nassau Blvd Garden City NY 11530 Office: 16 Court St Brooklyn NY 11241 Tel (212) 852-1051

MC DONOUGH, EDWARD JOSEPH, b. Salt Lake City, Nov. 24, 1938; student U. Notre Dame, 1957-58; A.B., U. Utah, 1962, M.A., 1966, J.D., 1970. Admitted to Utah bar, 1970; partner firm Jones, Waldo, Holbook & McDonough, Salt Lake City, 1970—. Home: 1514 Preston St Salt Lake City UT 84108 Office: 800 Walker Bank Bldg Salt Lake City UT 84111 Tel (801) 521-3200

MC DONOUGH, JAMES GREGORY, b. Carbondale, Pa., Oct. 19, 1939; B.S., U. Scranton, 1962; J.D., U. Pa., 1969. Admitted to Pa. bar, 1965; law clk. to judge U.S. Dist. Ct., 1965-67; partner firm Judd, Schuessel & McDonough, Carbondale, 1969—; solicitor County of Lackawanna (Pa.), 1972-73, City of Carbondale, 1974—, Greenfield Twp. (Pa.), 1972-74, Lackawanna County Transit Authority, 1973—. Mem. Am. Bar Assn., Am., Pa. trial lawyers assns. Home: RD #1 Carbondale PA 18407 Office: 11-13 Park Pl Carbondale PA 18407 Tel (717) 282-1515

MCDONOUGH, JAMES NORMAN, b. Toledo, Mar. 2, 1911; A.B., St. John's U., 1931; J.D., Case Western Res. U., 1936, LL.M., 1937. Admitted to Ohio bar, 1936; teaching fellow N.Y. U. Law Sch., N.Y.C., 1937-39; instr. Law Sch. Loyola U., Los Angeles, 1939-40; mem. editorial staff Catholic Press Union, Inc., Cleve., 1940-43, 1946-47; lectr. Case Western Res. U., Cleve., 1947, asst. prof., 1947-48, asso. prof., faculty adviser law rev., 1948-51, prof., 1951-53; prof. St. Louis U. Law Sch., 1953—, dean, 1953-62; mem. adv. bd. St. Louis County Pub. Defender, 1963—. Mem. Mo. adv. com. U.S. Com. Civil Rights, 1959-61, chmn., 1960-61; bd. dirs. Legal Aid Soc. City and County St. Louis, 1957-64; mem. University City (Mo.) Human Relations Commn., 1962-65, vice chmn., 1963-65. Mem. Am. Law Inst., Am., Ohio, Met. St. Louis bar assns., Inst. Internat. D'Etude et de Documentation en Matière de Concurrence Commerciale, Order of Coif, Delta Theta Phi, John Henry Newman Honor Soc. Author: (with others) Juvenile Court Handbook, 1970; contbr. articles to legal jours. Home: 515 Purdue Ave University City MO 63130 Office: 3642 Lindell Blvd Saint Louis MO 63108 Tel (314) 535-3300

MC DONOUGH, JOSEPH PATRICK, b. Portland, Maine, Aug. 13, 1914; J.D. with honors, Suffolk U., 1940. Admitted to Mass. bar, 1946; individual practice law, Quincy, Mass. Chmn. Quincy Rent Control Bd., 1953. Mem. Am., Mass., Boston, Quincy bar assns., Am. Trial Lawyers Assn. Office: 1372 Hancock St Quincy MA 02169 Tel (617) 479-4100

MC DONOUGH, PATRICK JOHN, b. Pittsfield, Mass., July 6, 1948; B.A., U. Notre Dame, 1970, M.A. in Govt., 1973, J.D., 1973. Admitted to Mass. bar, 1973; counsel Nat. Center for Law and the Handicapped, South Bend, Ind., 1974; legal counsel Mass. Bur. Developmental Disabilities, Boston, 1974-75; gen. counsel Mass. Office of Fed. and State Resources, Boston, 1975—; cons. Urban

Coalition, South Bend, 1973. Mem. com. human rights Mass. Developmental Disabilities, 1975—. Mem. Mass. (mem. sec. family law), Am. bar assns. Contbr. articles to profl. jours. Home: Butler Ave Manchester MA 01944 Office: Room 540 State House Boston MA 02133 Tel (617) 727-4178

MC DONOUGH, ROGER JAMES, b. Salt Lake City, Utah, Apr. 17, 1934; LL.B., U. Utah, 1959. Admitted to Utah bar, 1959; mem. firm Jones, Wald, Holbrook & McDonough, Salt Lake City, 1959-76. Mem. Am. Judicature Soc., Am. Bar Assn. Contbr. articles to legal jours. Home: 2133 Broadmore St Salt Lake City UT 84111 Office: 800 Walker Bank Bldg Salt Lake City UT 84111 Tel (801) 521-3200

MC DONOUGH, THOMAS JOSEPH, b. N.Y.C., Jan. 20, 1934; B.A., Manhattan Coll., 1952; B.A., Queens Coll., 1956; LL.B., N.Y. U., 1962. Admitted to N.Y. bar, 1962, U.S. Ct. Appeals bar, 1964; asso. firm George Conway, N.Y.C., 1962-63, firm J. Robert Morris, N.Y.C., 1962-65; mem. firm Bigham, Englar, Jones & Houston, N.Y.C., 1965-70, firm Miller & Mannix, Lake George, N.Y., 1970-76; individual practice law, Glens Falls, N.Y., 1976—. Mem. Maritime Law Assn. U.S., N.Y. State, Warren County, Am. bar assns. Home: 28 Twicwood Ln Glens Falls NY 12801 Office: Lake George Rd Glens Falls NY 12801 Tel (518) 792-0915

MCDONOUGH, WILLIAM GRADY, b. McMinnville, Tenn., Oct. 23, 1898; student Middle Tenn. State Normal, 1919-21; LL.B., Cumberland U., 1924. Admitted to Tenn. bar, 1925; mem. Tenn. Ho. of Reps., 1926-28; mem. Tenn. Bd. Pardons, 1933-34; postmaster McMinnville, 1934-38; judge Warreb County (Tenn.) Ct. Gen. Sessions, 1941-42, 1966-74; practice law, McMinnville. Mem. Tenn., McMinnville (past pres.) bar assns. Recipient Community Leader Am. award Community Leaders Am. Bd., 1969. Home: 104 Oakhill Dr McMinnville TN 37110 Office: 102 N Chancery St McMinnville TN 37110 Tel (615) 473-5925

MCDOUGAL, MYRES SMITH, b. 1906; B.C.L., Oxford (Eng.) U., 1930; J.S.D., Yale U., 1931; LL.B., U. Miss., 1935, Northwestern U., 1966, York U., 1970. Admitted to Miss. bar, 1935; teaching fellow U. Miss., 1925-27; asst. prof. U. Ill., 1931-34; vis. asso. prof. Yale U., 1934-35, asso. prof. law, 1935-39, prof., 1939—, William K. Townsend prof., 1944-58, Sterling prof. law, 1959-76; vis. prof. Cairo U., 1959-60, N.Y. Law Sch., 1976—; vis. Distinguished prof. Temple U., 1976; asst. gen. counsel Lend Lease Adminstrn., 1942; gen. counsel Office Relief and Rehab. Ops. Dept. State, 1943; mem. U.S. panel Permanent Ct. Arbitration, 1963-69. Mem. Am. Law Inst., Institut de Droit International, Am. Soc. Internat. Law (pres. 1958, hon. pres. 1973-76, Manley O. Hudson award 1976), Internat. Law Assn., Am. Assn. Law Schs. (pres. 1966). Author: Law and Minimum World Public Order: The Regulation of International Coercion, 1961; The Public Order of the Oceans: A Contemporary International Law of the Sea, 1962; Law and Public Order in Space, 1963. Office: Yale U Sch Law New Haven CT 06520*

MC DOWELL, DANIEL GRAY, b. Knoxville, Tenn., May 23, 1942; B.S., Auburn U., 1964; LL.B., U. Ala., 1967. Admitted to Ala. bar, 1967, U.S. Supreme Ct. bar; asso. firm Bedford & Bedford, 1967-73; partner firm Fine, McDowell & Mansell, Russellville, 1973—. Chmn. Facilities Com. Muscle Shoals Comprehensive Health Planning Council, 1974-76; dir. Franklin County Am. Red Cross, 1976; dir. Franklin County United Fund, 1976. Mem. Ala. Trial Lawyers, Assn. Trial Lawyers Am., Am. Judicature Soc., Am., Franklin County (pres. 1976-77) bar assns. Home: Route 1 Spruce Pine AL 35585 Office: 507 N Jackson Ave Russellville AL 35653 Tel (205) 332-1660

MC DOWELL, JOSEPH FRANCIS, III, b. Manchester, N.H., Oct. 22, 1946; B.S., Providence Coll., 1968; J.D., Suffolk U., 1971. Admitted to N.H. bar, 1971, U.S. Dist. Ct., 1971, U.S. Ct. Appeals 1st Circuit bar, 1973, U.S. Supreme Ct. bar, 1976; asso. firm Alexander J. Kalinski, Manchester, 1971-73; partner firm Craig, Wenners, Craig & Mc Dowell, Manchester, 1973—. Mem. N.H., Manchester bar assns. Editor: Suffolk U. Law Review, 1970-71. Contbr. articles in field to profl. jours. Office: 84 Bay St Manchester NH 03104 Tel (603) 669-3970

MC DOWELL COOPER, PATSY JO, b. San Marcos, Tex., July 3, 1930; B.A., Tulane U., 1951; J.D., La. State U., 1958. Admitted to La. bar, 1958, Tex. bar, 1965; partner La. State Abstract Co., Napoleonville, 1943-56; gen. counsel Legal Aid Soc., Baton Rouge, 1958-61; asso. firm Kelton & Taylor, Baton Rouge, 1962-67; individual practice law, Baton Rouge, 1967—. Mem. Am. (recipient Harrison Tweed award 1958), La., Tex., Baton Rouge bar assns., Baton Rouge Bus. and Profl. Women's Club, Am. Judicature Soc., Phi Alpha Delta. Home: 9116 Redbud St Baton Rouge LA 70815 Office: Suite 1 9255 Florida Blvd Baton Rouge LA 70815 Tel (504) 924-4266

MC EACHEN, RICHARD EDWARD, b. Omaha, Sept. 24, 1933; B.S., U. Kan., 1955; J.D., U. Mich., 1961. Admitted to Mo. bar, 1961; asso. firm Hillix, Hall, Hasburgh, Brown & Hoffhaus, Kansas City, Mo., 1961-62; trust officer, v.p. 1st Nat. Bank of Kansas City, 1962-74, sr. v.p., 1974-75; sr. v.p. Commerce Bank of Kansas City, N.A., 1975—. Mem. advisory council Future Farmers Am., Kansas City, 1970—; gov. Am. Royal Livestock and Horse Show Assn., 1970—; bd. dirs. Harry S. Truman Med. Center, Kansas City, 1974—. Mem. Mo., Kansas City bar assns., Lawyers Assn. of Kansas City, Am. Inst. Banking, Mo. Bankers Assn. Office: Commerce Bank of Kansas City NA PO Box 248 Kansas City MO 64141 Tel (816) 234-2562

MC EACHERN, CLEMENT LEE, b. Union, S.C., Jan. 18, 1910; B.S., Furman U., 1930; LL.B., Georgetown U., 1939; postgrad. U. Mich., 1946. Admitted to Miss. bar, 1939, S.C. bar, 1947; atty. antitrust div. Dept. Justice, Washington, 1940, N.Y.C., 1943, civil div., Washington, 1948-49; atty. Am. Cyanamid Corp., Stamford, Conn., 1947-48; gen. practice law, Greenville, S.C., 1949—. Mem. S.C. Bar Assn. Home: 535 Wembley Rd Greenville SC 29607 Office: Suite 602 SC Nat Bank Bldg Greenville SC 29601 Tel (803) 235-8217

MC EACHERN, JOHN HUGH, b. Portsmouth, N.H., Jan. 3, 1940; B.S., U. N.H., 1962; LL.B., Boston U., 1965. Admitted to N.H. bar, 1965, Mass. bar, 1965, U.S. Ct. Military Appeals bar, 1965, Maine bar, 1972, Fed. bar, 1972, U.S. Supreme Ct. bar, 1976; served to capt. JAGC, 1965-68; asso. firm Sheean, Phinney, Bass & Green, Manchester, N.H., 1968-70; incorporator firm Shaines, Madrigan and McEachern, Portsmouth, N.H., 1970—. Del. Democratic State Conv., Portsmouth, 1962; chmn. Hampton Democratice Com., Hampton, N.H., 1973—. Mem. Am. Judicature Soc., Fed., Am., N.H. bar assns., Am. Trial Lawyers Assn. Home: N Shore Rd Hampton NH 03842 Office: 25 Maplewood Ave Portsmouth NH 03801 Tel (603) 436-3110

MC EACHIN, ARCHIBALD BRUCE, b. Tuscaloosa, Ala., Jan. 19, 1910; A.B., U. Ala., 1931, LL.B., 1933. Admitted to Ala. bar, 1933; asso. firm H.A. and D.K. Jones, Tuscaloosa, 1933-40; sr. partner firm Jones, McEachin, Ormond & Fulton, Tuscaloosa, 1964—. Sec. bd. deacons First Baptist Ch., Tuscaloosa, 1951-53; bd. dirs. Tuscaloosa chpt. ARC, 1949-50. Mem. Internat. Assn. Ins. Counsel, Nat. Assn. R.R. Trial Counsel, Tuscaloosa County Bar Assn. (past pres.). Home: 1718 8th St Tuscaloosa AL 35401 Office: 403 First Nat Bank Bldg Tuscaloosa AL 35401 Tel (205) 349-2500

MCEACHIN, DANIEL MALLOY, b. Florence, S.C., Aug. 2, 1925; student Davidson Coll., 1942-43; LL.B., U. S.C., 1949. Admitted to S.C. bar, 1949, U.S. Dist. Ct. bar for Dist. S.C., 1949, U.S. 5th Circuit Ct. Appeals bar, 1955; mem. firm McEachin, & McEachin, Florence, 1949-74; judge Civil and Criminal Cts., Florence, 1974-75; spl. judge Circuit Ct. S.C., 1975—; mem. S.C. Com. on Grievances and Discipline, 1970-73. Mem. S.C., Florence County bars. Home: 1007 Wentworth St Florence SC 29501 Office: Complex Bldg Florence SC 29501 Tel (803) 665-3052

MC ELDREW, JAMES JOSEPH, b. Phila., May 14, 1924; B.S., St. Joseph's U., 1950; LL.D., Rutgers U., 1953. Admitted to Pa. bar, 1954; sr. partner firm McEldrew, Hanamirian, Quinn & D'Amico, Phila., 1966—. Mem. Am., Phila. bar assns., Def. Counsel Assn., Defense Research Inst. Home: 915 Wilde Ave Drexel Hill PA 19026 Office: 800 Architects Building 117 South 17th St Philadelphia PA 19103

MC ELHANEY, JOHN CORAL, b. Plainview, Nebr., May 3, 1932; B.A., U. Nebr., 1953, J.D., 1958. Admitted to Nebr. bar, 1958, Wis. bar, 1964; teaching research asso. U. Nebr. Coll. Law, 1958-59; spl. asst. atty. gen. Nebr., 1959; asso. firm Chambers, Holland, Dudgeon & Hastings, Lincoln, Nebr., 1959-63; trust officer Comml. and Savs. Bank, Monroe, Wis., 1963—, v.p., 1973—. Chmn., Mayor's Citizens Adv. Com., Monroe, 1968. Mem. Nebr. State, Wis. State, Green County (pres. 1967) bar assns., Wis. Trustees Assn., Monroe Jaycees (dir. 1966). Home: 1726 Country Ln Monroe WI 53566 Office: 1717 10th St Monroe WI 53566 Tel (608) 328-4000

MC ELHANEY, LELAND PAUL, b. Oakland, Calif., Sept. 3, 1941; B.P. Sci., U. Calif., Berkeley, 1963, J.D., 1966. Admitted to Calif. bar, 1966, U.S. Supreme Ct. bar, 1976; asso. firm Cosgrove, Cramer, Rindge, & Barnum, Los Angeles, 1969—. Mem. Calif. State, Los Angeles County bar assns. Office: 611 W 6th St Los Angeles CA 90017 Tel (213) 629-1450

MC ELROY, BERT, b. Altus, Okla., Sept. 24, 1917; LL.B., U. Okla., 1941; postgrad. N.Y. U., 1943. Admitted to Okla. bar, 1941; legal and claims officer transp. corps, defense counsel gen. cts. marshal, U.S. Army, 1942-46, mem. staff Judge Adv. Gen.'s Corps, 1950-51; partner firm Sanders, McElroy & Carpenter, Tulsa, 1951—; v.p. Denver Corp.; chmn. bd. Lakeside State Bank, Oologah, Okla. Pres., Tulsa County Young Republicans, 1947-48; pres. Tulsa County Rep. Minutemen, 1951-52; Tulsa County Rep. chmn., 1952-54, 65-67; Rep. state committeeman, 1954-62, 67-69; law mem. Okla. Mental Health Bd., 1964—, chmn., 1968-70; dir. Tulsa Boys' Home; chmn. bd. of deacons 1st Baptist Ch. Tulsa; pres. Baptist Laymen's Orgn.; mem. advisory com. Tulsa Jr. Coll.; bd. dirs. Okla. U. Law Center. Fellow Am. Coll. Probate Counsel, Am. Judicature Soc., Am. Bar Assn., Am. Bar Found., Am. Coll. Trial Lawyers; mem. Okla., Tulsa County (pres. 1972) bar assns., Jud. Council Okla., Nat. Conf. Commrs. on Uniform State Laws (Okla. commr. 1967—). Home: 1382 E 27th St Tulsa OK 74114 Office: Suite 205 Denver Bldg 624 S Denver Ave Tulsa OK 74119

MCELROY, BERT COLYAR, b. Pearl River, N.Y., Nov. 22, 1943; student U. Okla., 1961-64; LL.B., U. Tulsa, 1967. Admitted to Okla. bar, 1967, U.S. Supreme Ct. bar, 1974. asso. firm Sanders, McElroy & Carpenter, Tulsa, 1967-73; partner firm McElroy, Naylor & Williams, Tulsa, 1973-76; individual practice law, Tulsa, 1976—; legal mem. Tulsa Emergency Med. Services Council, 1974--. Mem. Tulsa Charter Revision Commn., 1974; bd. dirs., v.p. Green County chpt. Nat. Multiple Sclerosis Soc., 1974—. Mem. Am., Okla. (pres. young lawyers conf. 1972, chmn. gen. practice sect. 1974, mem. law schs. com. 1975—), Tulsa County (exec. com. 1974-75, named outstanding jr. mem. 1974) bar assns., Am. Judicature Soc., Okla. Trial Lawyers Assn., Order Curule Chair, Phi Alpha Delta. Notes and comments editor Tulsa Law Jour., 1966-67; recipient Am. Jurisprudence award, 1967; Corpus Juris Secundum award, 1967. Office: 1850 S Boulder Ave Tulsa OK 74119 Tel (918) 583-7046

MC ELROY, JIMMY E., b. Horn Lake, Miss., Nov. 13, 1944; B.S., Delta State Coll., 1966, M.S., 1966; J.D., Memphis State U., 1973. Admitted to Tenn. bar, 1973, Miss. bar, 1973; individual practice, Fulton, Miss., 1973—; pros. atty. Itawamba County, Miss., 1976—. Mem. Am., Miss., Tenn., Itawamba County bar assns. Home: PO Box 521 Fulton MS 38843 Office: Crane Bldg 304 W Wiygul St Fulton MS 38843 Tel (601) 862-2240

MC ELVAIN, MICHAEL BLAINE, b. Macomb, Ill., Aug. 14, 1947; B.S., U. Ill., 1969, J.D., 1972. Admitted to Ill. bar, 1972, U.S. Supreme Ct. bar, 1972; partner firm Thomson, Thomson, Zanoni & Flynn, Bloomington, Ill. Mem. Am., Ill. McLean County bar assns., Am., Ill. trial lawyers assns. Home: 222 Ivanhoe St Bloomington IL 61701 Office: 105 N Center St Bloomington IL 61701 Tel (309) 829-7069

MCELWEE, CLAUDE WEBSTER, JR., b. St. Louis, Nov. 19, 1940; A.B., U. Mo. at Columbia, 1962, J.D., 1964; student U.S. Army Command and Gen. Staff Coll., 1975. Admitted to Mo. bar, 1964, U.S. Ct. Mil. Appeals bar, 1969, U.S. Supreme Ct. bar, 1969; partner firm McElwee and McElwee, St. Louis, 1964—; maj. JAGC, USAR, 1962—; pros. atty. City of Brentwood (Mo.), 1973—; spl. asst. atty. gen. State of Mo., 1965-70. Gen. counsel St. Louis Opportunities Industrialization Centers, 1973—; pres. U. Mo. Law Alumni Assn., 1977-78. Mem. Am. Bar Assn., Mo. Bar, Bar Assn. St. Louis (sec. 1974). Home: 11 York Hills Brentwood MO 63144 Office: 706 Chestnut St Saint Louis MO 63101 Tel (314) 421-5442

MC EVILLEY, ROBERT MICHAEL, b. Cin., Feb. 26, 1946; A.B., Marquette U., 1968; J.D., No. Ky. State Coll., 1974. Admitted to Ohio bar, 1974; asso. firm Doggett & Wais, Cin., 1974—; asst. pros. atty. Hamilton County, Ohio, 1974—. Mem. Am., Ohio, Cin. bar assns. Home: 3316 Ashwood Dr Cincinnati OH 45213 Office: 1014 Vine St Cincinnati OH 45202 Tel (513) 241-6116

MC FADDEN, FRANK HAMPTON, b. Oxford, Miss., Nov. 20, 1925; B.A., U. Miss., 1950; LL.B., Yale, 1955. Admitted to N.Y. bar, 1956, Ala. bar, 1959; asso. firm Lord, Day & Lord, N.Y.C., 1955-58; asso. firm Bradley, Arant, Rose & White, Birmingham, Ala., 1958-63, partner, 1963-69; judge U.S. Dist. Ct., No. Dist. Ala., 1969—, chief judge, 1973. Home: 3015 Briarcliff Rd Birmingham AL 35223 Office: Fed Courthouse Birmingham AL 35203 Tel (205) 254-1706

MCFADDEN, JACK DAVID, b. Charleston, W.Va., Dec. 11, 1936; B.A., Morris Harvey Coll., 1967; J.D., W.Va. U., 1970. Admitted to W.Va. bar, 1970, Fed. bar, 1970, Fla. bar, 1970; asso. law firm Wagner & Bertone, Holly Hill, Fla., 1970-72; partner law firm Hoffman, Hendry, Parker and Smith, Daytona Beach, Fla., 1972-75; pvt. practice law, Daytona Beach, Fla., 1975—. Mem. W.Va. State, Fla. State, Am. bar assns., Acad. Fla. Trial Lawyers, Am. Judicature Soc. Home: 991 Parkwood Dr Ormond Beach FL 32074 Office: 100 Seabreeze Blvd Daytona Beach FL 32018

MC FADDEN, JOSEPH JAMES, b. Boise, Idaho, May 3, 1916; student U. Idaho, Pocatello, 1934-35; B.S. in Bus., U. Idaho, Moscow, 1937, postgrad. Coll. Law, 1938. Admitted to Idaho bar, 1940, U.S. Dist. Ct. bar for Dist. Idaho, 1953; ct. reporter Dist. Ct., 1938-42; practiced in Hailey, Idaho, 1946-60; justice Idaho Supreme Ct., 1960—, chief justice, 1966, 69-70, 76-77; pros. atty. City of Hailey, 1948-52, 54-60. Pres. Idaho Boys State, 1961-62. Mem. Am. Bar Assn., Am. Judicature Soc. (dir. 1969-70). Recipient award of Merit U. Idaho Coll. Law, 1976. Home: 2110 N Curtis St Boise ID 83704 Office: Supreme Ct Bldg Boise ID 83720 Tel (209) 375-3464

MC FADDEN, THOMAS JOSEPH, b. S.I., N.Y., May 1, 1900; A.B., Cornell U., 1922, J.D., 1925; postgrad. Yale Law Sch., 1927-28. Admitted to N.Y. bar, 1928, D.C. bar, 1934, U.S. Supreme Ct. bar, 1935; spl. asst. to atty. gen. Dept. Justice, 1928-29; counsel mgr. Nat. Paint, Varnish and Lacquer Assn., Washington, 1929-34; partner firm Donovan, Leisure, Newton & Irvine, N.Y.C., 1934—. Mem. Am., Fed., N.Y. State bar assns., Cath. Lawyers Guild N.Y.C. Home: Pinehurst Ave and 183d St New York City NY 10033 Office: 30 Rockefeller Plaza New York City NY 10020 Tel (212) 489-4100

MCFARLAND, CARL, b. Seattle, Oct. 6, 1904; B.A., U. Mont., 1928; M.A., 1929, LL.B., 1930, LL.D. (hon.), 1949; S.J.D., Harvard, 1932; LL.D., (hon.), Carroll Coll., 1973. Admitted to Mont. bar, 1930, D.C. bar, 1937, Va. bar, 1967, U.S. Supreme Ct. bar, 1933; partner firm Toomey and McFarland, Helena, Mont., 1932-33; spl. asst. to atty. gen. U.S. Dept. Justice, Washington, 1933-37, asst. atty. gen., 1937-39; mem. firm Cummings & Stanley, Washington, 1939-44; partner firm McFarland & Sellers, Washington, 1946-51; pres. U. Mont., Missoula, 1951-58; prof. law U. Va., Charlottesville, 1958-75; prof. emeritus, 1975—; mem. Atty. Gen's Com. Adminstrv. Procedure, Washington, 1939-41; second Hoover Commn. Task Force Adminstrv. Law, Washington, 1954-55, bd. Helena, Mont. br. Fed. Res. Bank, Mpls., 1951-58. Mem. Am. Law Inst., Am. Bar Assn. (Ross award 1934, Ho. of Dels. 1949, medal 1946), Am. Soc. Internat. Law. Author: Judicial Control of Federal Trade Commission and Interstate Commerce Commission, 1933; (with Arthur Vanderbilt) Administrative Law, 1947, 52; (with Homer Cummings) Federal Justice, 1937; Administrative Procedures and Public Lands, 1969. Home: Turner Mountain Ivy VA 22945 Office: Law School University Virginia Charlottesville VA 22901 Tel (804) 924-3458

MC FARLAND, NATHANIEL MARTIN, b. Dalton, Ga., Nov. 7, 1915; student Monroe A. and M. Coll., 1934; LL.B., Atlanta Law Sch., 1937; LL.M. Woodrow Coll. Law, 1938; postgrad. U. Ga., 1943-44. Admitted to Ga. bar, 1938, U.S. Ct. Appeals bar, 1938, U.S. Supreme Ct. bar, 1950; judge city ct., Decatur, Ga., 1946-53; asst. city atty., Atlanta, 1955-73; partner firm Murphy, McFarland & Turoff, Decatur, Ga., 1960-73; individual practice law, Decatur, 1973—. Mem. State bar of Ga., Atlanta Bar Assn., Old Warhorse Lawyers Club, Rotary, Masons, Shriners. Home: 3669 Calumet Rd Decatur GA 30034 Office: S DeKalb Office Park Suite 105 3011 Rainbow Dr Decatur GA 30034 Tel (404) 241-2671

MC FERRIN, PHILIP NORTH, b. Gainesville, Fla., Oct. 11, 1942; A.B., Dartmouth, 1964; LL.B., U. Va., 1967. Admitted to Va. bar, 1967, Tenn. bar, 1974; capt. U.S. Army JAGC, 1967-71; atty., advisor U.S. Tax Ct., Washington, 1971-74; asso. firm Canada, Russell & Turner, Memphis, 1974—. Mem. Am., Tenn., Memphis and Shelby County bar assns. Decorated Bronze Star. Home: 48 N Alicia Dr Memphis TN 38112 Office: 12th Floor Union Planters Bank Bldg Memphis TN 38103 Tel (901) 521-1111

MC GAHEE, JACK EZELLE, b. Augusta, Ga., May 16, 1920; A.B., U. Ga., 1941, LL.B., 1948. Admitted to Ga. bar, 1948; since practiced in Augusta, 1948—, partner firm McGahee Plunkett Benning & Fletcher, 1952—; asso. judge Ga. State Ct., Richmond County, 1968-73. Pres., Ga.-Carolina council Boy Scouts Am., 1969; bd. dirs. Richmond County unit Am. Cancer Soc., 1974—. Mem. Am., Augusta (past pres.) bar assns., State Bar Ga. (past mem. bd. govs.), Ga., Am. trial lawyers assns., Am. Judicature Soc., Phi Delta Phi. Home: 604 Wellesley Dr Augusta GA 30904 Office: 507 Telfair St Augusta GA 30902 Tel (404) 724-7021

MC GANN, W(ILLIAM) THOMAS, b. Moorestown, N.J., Oct. 20, 1911; student Coll. S. Jersey, 1932; J.D., Rutgers U., 1936. Admitted to N.J. bar, 1939; individual practice, Moorestown, 1939—; asst. U.S. atty. Dist. N.J., 1951-53; judge Burlington County (N.J.) Ct., Mt. Holly, 1955-66, N.J. Superior Ct., Mt. Holly, 1966-76; of counsel firm Hartman, Schlesinger, Schlosser and Faxon, Mt. Holly, 1976—. Mem. Moorestown Human Relations Council, 1948-49, Moorestown Planning Bd., 1949-51. Mem. Am., N.J., Burlington County bar assns. Home: 740 Signal Light Rd Moorestown NJ 08057 Office: 129 High St Mount Holly NJ 08060 Tel (609) 267-3050

MCGARITY, EDMUND CODY, JR., b. Birmingham, Ala., Nov. 8, 1928; B.S., Auburn U., 1951; LL.B., Jones Law Sch., 1964. Admitted to Ala. bar, 1964; controller, treas., v.p., adminstrv. v.p. U.S. Pipe and Foundry Co., Birmingham, 1953-75; adminstrv. v.p. U.S. Home Corp., Clearwater, Fla., 1975-76; v.p. Harrison Industries, Inc., Birmingham, 1976—, Structural Wood Systems, Inc., Birmingham, 1976—. Pres., Shades Mountain Community Park, Inc., Birmingham, 1966; sr. warden All Saints Episcopal Ch., Birmingham, 1968. Mem. Fin. Execs. Inst., Lamda Chi Alpha, Delta Sigma Pi, Phi Kappa Phi. Home: 1732 Cedarwood Rd Birmingham AL 35216 Office: Suite 105 2 Metroplex Dr Birmingham AL 35209 Tel (205) 871-4098

MC GARY, THOMAS HUGH, b. Milburn, Ky., Mar. 6, 1938; A.B., Elmhurst Coll., 1961; J.D., U. Chgo., 1964. Admitted to Ill. bar, 1964; asst. atty. gen. State Ill., Springfield, 1965-67, supr. consumer credit div., 1967-70; individual practice law, Springfield, 1970—; village atty., Riverton, Ill., 1973—, Spaulding, Ill., 1974—; dir. Citizens Bank Edinburg, Ill., Schuyler State Bank, Rushville, Ill., Lincoln Savs. & Loan, Pawnee, Ill., Bank of Kenney (Ill.). Mem. vestry, lay reader St. Paul's Episcopal Cathedral, Springfield, 1967—. Mem. Am. Judicature Soc., Am., Ill. State, Sangamon County bar assns., Springfield Art Assn., Springfield Symphony Assn., Phi Delta Phi. Home: 1520 Bates Ave Springfield IL 62704 Office: 911 Ridgeley Bldg 502 E Monroe Springfield IL 62701 Tel (217) 753-1767

MC GEADY, MANUS EAMONN, b. Balt., Oct. 20, 1932; B.A., Johns Hopkins, 1961; J.D., U. Balt., 1964. Admitted to Md. bar, 1964; asst. to v.p., asst. mgr. indsl. relations Md. Shipbldg. and Drydock Co., Balt., 1958-63; pres. Martin G. Imbach, Inc., Balt., 1964—. Advisor Jr. Achievement, 1959-63; pres. Santa Claus Anonymous, 1967; loaned exec. Central Md. United Fund, 1957; coach, dir. Roland Park Little League, 1969-75. Mem. Engring. Soc. Balt. (chmn. civic affairs com. 1972-77), Md. Bar Assn. (mem. environ. law com. 1975—, spl. com. on offshore drilling 1974-76), Balt. City Assn., Am. Judicature Soc., Soc. Am. Mil. Engrs., Soc. Indsl. Archeologists, Hibernian Soc. of Balt. Contbr. articles to profl. jours. Home: 206 Enfield Rd Baltimore MD 21212 Office: 1403 Fidelity Bldg Baltimore MD 21201 Tel (301) 539-3327

MC GEE, CHARLES MICHAEL, b. Salt Lake City, June 11, 1945; B.A., U. Pacific, 1966; J.D., U. Denver, 1969. Admitted to Nev. bar, 1969, U.S. Ct. Mil. Appeals bar, 1970, Calif. bar, 1973; served to capt. JAGC, U.S. Army, 1970-73; asso. firm Sanford, Sanford, Fahrenkopf & Mousel, Reno, 1973-75; partner firm Sanford, Sanford & McGee, Reno, 1976—; mem. med. legal screening panel, unauthorized practice law com. State Bar Nev.; guest instr. Sparks High Sch., U. Nev. Mem. Am., Washoe County, San Francisco bar assns., Am. Judicature Soc. Office: PO Box 1249 Reno NV 89504 Tel (702) 322-9166

MCGEE, GLEN MERL, lawyer; b. Henderson, Iowa, Dec. 12, 1927; B.A., U. No. Iowa, 1949; J.D., U. Iowa, 1955. Admitted to Iowa, U.S. Dist. Ct. bars, 1955; spl. agt. FBI, Seattle, 1956-57; pvt. practice law, Glenwood, Iowa, 1957-59; partner firm Thomas, McGee & Thomas, Glenwood, 1959—; dir., atty. Mills County Savs. & Loan Assn., Glenwood, 1962—. Atty., Mills County, Iowa, 1959-67. Mem. Iowa, Southwest Iowa bar assns. Home: 607 2d St Glenwood IA 51534 Office: 10 N Walnut St Glenwood IA 51534

MC GEE, JOSEPH HALSTEAD, b. Charleston, S.C., Apr. 6, 1929; B.A., Washington and Lee U., 1950, LL.B., 1952. Admitted to S.C. bar, 1956; individual practice law, Charleston, 1956-62; partner firm Buist, Moore, Smythe & McGee, and predecessor, Charleston, 1962—; mem. S.C. Ho. of Reps., 1962-68, Charleston City Council, 1971-75. Vice pres. S.C. Tricentennial Commn.; pres. Hist. Charleston Found., S.C. Hist. Soc.; trustee Nat. Trust Hist. Preservation. Mem. Charleston, S.C. (exec. com. 1970), Am. bar assns., Def. Research Inst. Home: 131 Church St Charleston SC 29401 Office: 5 Exchange St PO Box 999 Charleston SC 29402 Tel (803) 722-8375

MCGEE, MICHAEL HENRY, b. Rock Hill, S.C., Dec. 6, 1943; B.A., U. N.C., Chapel Hill, 1968, J.D., 1971. Admitted to N.C. bar, 1971; staff atty. High Point (N.C.) Legal Services Assn., 1972-74; dist. counsel Equal Employment Opportunity Commn., Charlotte, N.C., 1974-76; individual practice law, Charlotte, 1976—. Chmn. bd. dirs. High Point Youth Services Bur., 1972-74; mem. Mecklenburg County Commn. Status of Women, 1976-77, N.C. Human Relations Council, 1977—. Mem. Fed., N.C. State bar assns., Sierra Club. Contbr. articles to legal publs. Home: 412 E Kingston Ave Charlotte NC 28203 Office: 1021 Kenilworth Ave Charlotte NC 28204 Tel (704) 377-2148

MC GEE, WILLIAM SEARS, b. Houston, Sept. 29, 1917; student Rice Inst.; LL.B., U. Tex., 1940. Admitted to Tex. bar; asso. firm Sears, Blades, Moore & Kennerly, Houston, 1940-43, 46-48, 55-58; judge County Ct., Houston, 1948-54, 151st Dist. Ct., 1955, 55th Dist. Ct., 1958-69; asso. justice Supreme Ct. Tex., Austin, 1969—. Bd. dirs. YMCA, Houston; mem. Houston Community Council, 1948-54; past pres. Houston Council for Deaf Children. Mem. Am., Houston, Houston Jr. (v.p. Houston jr. sect.) bar assns., Am. Judicature Soc., Tex. Bar Found., Phi Delta Theta. Home: 2300 Quarry Rd Austin TX 78703 Office: PO Box 12248 Capital Station Austin TX 78711 Tel (512) 475-3623

MC GEENEY, JOHN STEPHEN, b. Woodhaven, N.Y., Dec. 22, 1934; B.A., Amherst Coll., 1956; LL.B., Harvard U., 1959. Admitted to N.Y. bar, 1960, Conn. bar, 1960; partner firm Cummings and Lockwood, Stamford, Conn., 1959—; dir. various corps. and founds. Founding mem. Stamford Equal Economic Council. Mem. Am., Conn., Stamford bar assns. Home: 550 White Oak Shade Rd New Canaan CT 06840 Office: Cummings and Lockwood 1 Atlantic St Stamford CT 06904 Tel (203) 327-1700

MC GEOUGH, ROBERT SAUNDERS, b. Chgo., Aug. 30, 1930; A.B., Duke, 1952; LL.B., U. Mich., 1959. Admitted to Ohio bar, 1959; partner firm Dennison & McGeough, Warren, Ohio, 1959-64; asso. firm Hoppe, Day & Ford, Warren, 1964-69; partner firm Hoppe, Frey, Hewitt & Milligan, Warren, 1969—. Pres., Warren Exchange Club, 1964; trustee Children's Rehab. Center, Warren, 1972—, sec., 1976; co-chmn. profl. div. United Way, Trumbull County, Ohio, 1976. Mem. Ohio, Am. bar assns. Home: 3264 Crescent Dr NE Warren OH 44483 Office: 500 Second National Tower Warren OH 44481 Tel (216) 392-1541

MC GHEE, JOHN ROBERT, b. Huntington, W.Va., Jan. 1, 1930; B.S., U. Ky., 1952; J.D., W.Va. U., 1957. Admitted to W.Va. bar, 1957; individual practice law, Marlington, W.Va., 1957-58, Bluefield, W.Va., 1958-69; mem. firm Kwass, Stone, McGhee & Feuehtenberger, Bluefield, 1969—; part time municipal judge, 1964—; U.S. Commr. for So. Dist. W.Va., 1960-68. Mem. W.Va. State Bar, W.Va., Mercer County bar assns., Phi Delta Phi. Home: 1023 Dogwood Ln Bluefield WV 24701 Office: 325 Federal St Bluefield WV 24701 Tel (304) 327-8193

MCGIFFERT, DAVID ELIOT, b. Boston, June 26, 1927; A.B., Harvard U., 1949, LL.B., 1953. Admitted to D.C. bar, 1954, U.S. Supreme Ct. bar, 1958; asso. mem. firm Covington & Burling, Washington, 1953-61, partner, 1969-77; asst. sec. def. for internat. security affairs, 1977—; lectr. in field; asst. to sec. def. legis. affairs, 1962-65; under sec. Army, 1966-69. Mem. Am., D.C. bar assns., Am. Soc. Internat. Law. Home: 3461 Macomb St NW Washington DC 20016 Office: Pentagon Washington DC 20301

MC GILL, DENNIS WALTER, b. Dallas, Oct. 2, 1941; B.S. in Psychology, Tex. A. and M. U., 1965; LL.B., U. Tex., 1968. Admitted to Tex. bar, 1968, U.S. Supreme Ct. bar, 1975; asso. with Travis D. Shelton, Lubbock, Tex., 1970—; legal counsel Tex. Jaycees, 1976, 77-78. Bd. dirs. Lubbock Meals on Wheels, 1972—, Lubbock ARC, 1972-75, Lubbock council Camp Fire Girls, 1972-75, Lubbock Juvenile Detention Center, 1972—, Lubbock March of Dimes, 1977—, Lubbock Family Service Assn., 1977—; active United Way. Mem. Tex. Criminal Def. Lawyers, Tex. Trial Lawyers, Am., Tex., Lubbock County bar assns., Lubock County Jr. Bar, South Plains Trial Lawyers, Delta Theta Phi. Named Outstanding Young Man of Lubbock, 1972, One of Five Outstanding Young Texans, 1973. Home: 5763 38th St Lubbock TX 79415 Office: 1507 13th St Lubbock TX 79401 Tel (806) 763-5201

MC GILL, ROBERT JACKSON, b. Albany, Ga., Oct. 22, 1944; B.S., U. Ala., 1969; J.D., U. Fla., 1971. Admitted to Fla. bar, U.S. Dist. Ct. bar for Middle Dist. Fla.; asst. pub. defender 12th Jud. Circuit Fla., Sarasota, 1975; partner firms Lee & McGill, Sarasota, 1974, Berg & McGill, Venice, Fla., 1975, Korp, Wheeler, & McGill, Venice, 1976—. Mem. Am. Trial Lawyers Assn., Acad. Fla. Trial Lawyers. Home: 519 Peach St Venice FL 33593 Office: 609 S Tamiami Trail Venice FL 33595 Tel (813) 485-5486

MC GILLICUDDY, DENNIS JOSEPH, b. Phila., Dec. 10, 1941; B.A., U. Fla., 1963, J.D., 1966. Admitted to Fla. bar, 1966; law clk. U.S. Dist. Ct. Judge, Middle Dist. Fla., Jacksonville, Fla., 1966-67; asso. firm Holland and Knight, Lakeland, Fla., 1967-68; v.p., gen. counsel Micanopy Cable TV, Inc., Alachua, Fla., 1968-71; pres. Coaxial Communications, Inc., Sarasota, Fla., 1971-76; pres. Cablenet Internat. Corp., 1974—; Telecoinema of Columbus, Inc., 1974—. Home: 3827 Flamingo Ave Sarasota FL 33581 Office: 5111 Ocean Blvd Sarasota FL 33581 Tel (813) 349-2770

MCGILLIVRAY, WILLIAM A., Now chief justice appellate div. Supreme Ct. of Alta. (Can.), Edmonton. Office: Supreme Ct Edmonton AB Canada*

MC GINITY, LEO FRANCIS, b. Garden City, N.Y., Aug. 9, 1927; A.B., Georgetown U., 1950; LL.B., N.Y. U., 1954. Admitted to N.Y. State bar, 1954; U.S. Supreme Ct. bar, 1960; individual practice law, Mineola, N.Y., 1954-73; partner firm McGinity, Bernstein, D'Amato & Hurley, Mineola, 1973-76; county ct. judge Nassau County (N.Y.), 1976—; town councilman Hempstead (N.Y.), 1969-76. Trustee Mercy Hosp., Rockville Centre, 1966—. Mem. Nassau County Bar Assn., Nassau Lawyers Assn., Nassau County Criminal Cts. Bar Assn. (pres. 1964), Nassau County Criminal Coordinating Com. Home: 1427 Dartmouth St Baldwin NY 11510 Office: Nassau County Courthourse 262 Old Country Rd Mineola NY 11501 Tel (516) 535-5640

MC GINN, GARRY P., b. Mangum, Okla., Oct. 19, 1938; B.B.A., U. Okla.; J.D., Oklahoma City U. Admitted to Okla. bar, 1966; asso. judge Okla. Dist. Ct., 1968—. Home: 1607 W Ave D Elk City OK 73644 Office: Courthouse Sayre OK 73644 Tel (405) 928-3528

MCGINNES, JAMES MARC, b. Murray, Utah, Sept. 27, 1941; B.A., Stanford, 1963; J.D., U. Calif., Berkeley, 1966; postgrad. U. Nancy (France), 1967. Admitted to Calif. bar, 1967; asso. firm Thelen, Marrin, Johnson, & Bridges, San Francisco, 1967-69; asso. firm Westwick, Collison & Talaga, Santa Barbara, Calif., 1969-71; individual pratice law, Santa Barbara, 1971—; lectr. in environ. law U. Calif., Santa Barbara, 197, Calif. Law Inst., Santa Barbara, 1976. Pres. Community Environ. Council, Inc., Santa Barbara, 1972-75; mem. gen. plan goals com. Council on Population and Environment, Chgo. Mem. Calif., Santa Barbara County bar assns. Author: Principles of Environmental Law, 1973. Home: 1088 E Mountain Dr Santa Barbara CA 93109 Office: 100S Santa Barbara St Santa Barbara CA 93101 Tel (805) 963-7739

MC GINNIS, JOHN ROBERT, b. Greenup, Ky., Jan. 15, 1943; B.S., Morehead State U., 1965; J.D., U. Ky., 1968. Admitted to Ky. bar, 1969; instr. Easter Ky. U. Sch. Law Enforcement, Richmond, 1968; mem. firm McGinnis & Leslie, and predecessors, Greenup, 1969—. Mem. Lansdowne Mental Health Bd. Mem. Greenup County, Boyd County bar assns., Jaycees. Home: Front St Greenup KY 41144 Office: Braden Bldg Greenup KY 41144 Tel (606) 473-9817

MC GINNIS, ROBERT CAMPBELL, b. Dallas, Jan. 1, 1918; A.B., U. Tex., Austin, 1938; LL.B., Yale, 1941. Admitted to Tex. bar, 1941, Ohio bar, 1942; asso. firm Squire, Sanders & Dempsey, Cleve., 1941-42; instr. So. Meth. U. Law Sch., 1946; asso. firm Carrington Gowan Johnson & Walker, Dallas, 1946-49; asso. firm Powell, Wirtz and Rauhut, Austin, 1949-50; partner firm McGinnis, Lochridge & Kilgore, Austin, 1950—; vis. prof. law U. Tex., 1963-64; dir. Tex. State Bank—Austin; mem. Tex. Jud. Qualifications Commn., 1971—, chmn., 1976—. Bd. dirs. YMCA, Austin, 1949-53, Austin Cancer Soc., 1955-59. Mem. Am., Travis County (Tex.) (pres. 1962-63) bar assns., State Bar Tex. (chmn. adminstrv. law com. 1968-69, chmn. probate sect. 1973-74). Home: 2708 Scenic Dr Austin TX 78703 Office: 900 Congress Ave Austin TX 78703 Tel (512) 476-6982

MC GLINN, FRANK CRESSON POTTS, b. Phila., Nov. 19, 1914; A.B., U. N.C., 1937; J.D., U. Pa., 1940; LL.D. (hon.), Villanova U., 1970. Admitted to Pa. bar, 1941; marine counsel, Reliance Ins. Co., Phila., 1941-42; asso. firm Pepper, Bodine, Hamilton Stokes, Phila., 1946-53; with Fidelity Bank, Phila., 1957—. Mem. bd. dirs. Fgn. Policy Assn., 1976—; mem. bd. dirs. and mem. exec. com. William Penn Found.; trustee Citizens Research Found., 1974; mem. U.S. Nat. Com. for UNESCO, 1969—; mem. advisory com. World Affairs Council, mem. Independence Nat. Hist. Park advisory com., 1969; hon. trustee Temple U.; mem. exec. com. Catholic Charities Appeal, 1960—; mem. exec. com. United Way. Mem. Phila. (chmn. pub. relations com. 1962-63, mem. nat. indsl. conf. bd., sr. mktg. execs. panel), Pa., Am. bar assns., Sharswood Law Club, Pub. Relations Soc. Am. Decorated Purple Heart, knight comdr. Equestrian Order of St. Gregory the Great, 1976, Knight of Malta, Stella Della Solidarieta (Italy), 1948; recipient Richard Allen award, 1975, Nat. Cystic Fibrosis Found. Man of Year award, 1969, NCCJ Nat. Human Relations award, 1967; named hon. mem. Mother Bethel A.M.E. Church, 1976. Home: 729 Millbrook Ln Haverford PA 19026 Office: 135 S Broad St Philadelphia PA 19109 Tel (215) 985-8113

MC GOFFIN, KEITH DONALD, b. Tacoma, Sept. 12, 1930; LL.B., Gonzaga U., 1954. Admitted to Wash. bar, 1954; chief civil dep. pros. atty. Pierce County (Wash.), 1955-64; partner firm Steele & McGoffin, Tacoma, 1964-67, firm Rovai, McGoffin, Turner & Mason, and predecessor, Tacoma, 1966—. Bd. dirs. Mountainview Gen. Hosp., Tacoma, 1965-70, Beckonridge Homeowners Assn., Tacoma, 1966-74. Mem. Wash. State Bar. Home: 4602 Merry Ln W Tacoma WA 98466 Office: 818 S Yakima St Tacoma WA 98405 Tel (206) 272-9303

MCGOLDRICK, MICHAEL JOHN, b. Phila., Nov. 16, 1948; student Javeriana U., Bogota, Columbia, 1968; B.A. magna cum laude, LaSalle Coll., 1970; J.D., U. Notre Dame, 1973; A.D., U. Va., 1974; LL.M. in Taxation, N.Y. U., 1975, LL.M. in Corporate and Comml. Law, 1976. Admitted to Pa. bar, 1973, N.J. bar, 1974, Mil. Ct. Appeals bar, 1974; asso. firm Harvey, Pennington, Herting & Renneisen, Phila., 1974—; capt. JAGC, U.S. Army, Ft. Dix, N.J., 1974—. Mem. K.C. Mem. Pa., N.J., Am. bar assns. Contbr. article to legal jour. Home: 1241 B Cedar St Fort Dix NJ 08640 Office: 7 Penn Center 17th and Market Sts Philadelphia PA 19103 Tel (215) LO3-4470

MC GONIGAL, RICHARD M., b. Cleve., May 4, 1940; A.B., Harvard, 1962; J.D., Columbia, 1965. Admitted to Ohio bar, 1965; asso. firm Squire, Sanders & Dempsey, Cleve., 1965-75, partner, 1975—. Mem. Am., Fed., Ohio, Cleve. bar assns., Computer Law Assn. Editor in chief of Jurimetrics Jour., 1975—. Office: 1800 Union Commerce Bldg Cleveland OH 44115 Tel (216) 696-9200

MC GOVERN, CHARLES JOSEPH, b. Providence, Mar. 16, 1920; A.B., Providence Coll., 1941; LL.B., Harvard, 1944. Admitted to R.I. bar, 1948, U.S. Dist. Ct. for Dist. R.I. bar, 1949, U.S. 1st Circuit Ct. Appeals bar, 1969; partner firm Coffey, McGovern & Novogroski, Providence, 1948—; mem. R.I. Jud. Council, 1975—. Mem. Warwick (R.I.) Bd. Pub. Safety, 1965-74, chmn., 1967-74. Mem. Am., R.I., Kent County (R.I.) bar assns. Home: 395 Spring Green Rd Warwick RI 02888 Office: 1015 Hosp Trust Bldg 15 Westminster St Providence RI 02903 Tel (401) 274-1144

MCGOVERN, CLEMONT, JR., b. Chester, Pa., Oct. 9, 1934; B.A., St. Joseph's Coll., 1956; LL.B., U. Pa., 1959. Admitted to Pa. bar, U.S. Supreme Ct. bar; indivdual practice law, Chester, 1963; asso. firm Albert E. Smith, 1963-65; asso. with Edward D. McLaughlin and Charles C. Keeler, Chester, 1965-68; partner firm deFuria and Larkin, Chester, 1968-70, firm Fronefield, deFuria & Petrikin, Media and Chester, 1970-74. Mem. Delaware Valley Regional Planning Commn.; mem. exec. com. Phila. Archdiocesan Sch. Bd.; chmn. Southeastern Dist. Pa. League Cities, Cancer Fund. Dr., Chester; mem. Chester Bicentennial Com.; committeeman 1st ward 2d precinct Republican Party. Home: 903 E 20th Chester PA 19013 Office: Courthouse Media PA 19063 Tel (215) 891-2168

MC GOVERN, MARGARET FRANCES, b. Boston, Aug. 15, 1924; student Emanuel Coll., 1944; LL.B., Boston U., 1946. Admitted to Mass. bar, 1946, U.S. Supreme Ct. bar, 1949; partner firm McGovern & McGovern, Boston, 1946-72, Miller & McGovern, Boston, 1972—; corp. counsel City of Boston, 1956-60. Bd. dirs. Friends Boston Assn. Retarded Children, 1955-60; active Nat. Found. Infantile Paralysis, 1956-60; dir., Mass. chmn. Mothers March. Mem. Am., Mass. bar assns., Am. Acad. Matrimonial Lawyers, Justinian Law Soc. Named hon. col. USAF, 1954. Home: 310 Commonwealth Ave Newton MA 02167 Office: 44 School St Boston MA 02108 Tel (617) 332-1682

MC GOVERN, SHEILA ELIZABETH, b. Cambridge, Mass., Dec. 12, 1936; grad. Boston Coll. Sch. Edn., 1957; J.D., Boston Coll., 1960. Admitted to Mass. bar, 1960; equity clk. and asst. register Middlesex (Mass.) Probate Ct., 1962-74, judge, 1974—. Vice-chmn. bd. trustees Cambridge Hosp., 1975—; mem. Task Force for Creation of New Health Policy Bd. for City of Cambridge, 1975—. Mem. Mass. Assn. Women Lawyers (past pres.), Boston Coll. Law Sch. Alumni Assn. (pres.). Author: Massachusetts Probate Practise System, 1966; Massachusetts Divorce Practise System, 1970. Office: Middlesex Probate Court East Cambridge MA 02141 Tel (617) 494-4530

MCGOVERN, THOMAS HIGGINS, b. Lowell, Mass., Sept. 19, 1902; A.B., Loyola U., Los Angeles, 1924, LL.B., 1926, J.D., 1928. Admitted to Calif. bar, 1926; partner frim Macdonald, Halsted & Laybourne and predecessor firms, Los Angeles, 1948--. Mem. Am., Los Angeles County bar assns., State Bar Calif. Home: 215 25th St Santa Monica CA 90402 Office: 1200 Wilshire Blvd Los Angeles CA 90017 Tel (213) 481-1200

MC GOVERN, WALTER THOMAS, b. Seattle, May 24, 1922; student U. Santa Clara (Calif.), 1940-43; B.A., U. Wash., Seattle, 1948, LL.B., 1950. Admitted to Wash. bar, 1950; asso. firm Kerr, McCord & Moen, Seattle, 1950-58; judge Seattle Municipal Ct., 1958-64, King County Superior Ct., 1965-67; asso. justice Wash. Supreme Ct., 1968-70; judge U.S. Dist. Ct., Seattle, 1971—, chief judge, 1976—. Mem. council Gonzaga U. Sch. Law; mem. vis. com. U. Wash. Sch. Law. Mem. Am., Wash., Seattle-King County bar assns., Am. Judicature Soc. Home: 4600 NE 40th St Seattle WA 98105 Office: US Courthouse 1010 5th Ave Seattle WA 98104 Tel (206) 442-5410

MCGOWAN, HAROLD XAVIER, b. N.Y.C., Aug. 26, 1913; A.B., Fordham U., 1935; LL.B., Bklyn. Law Sch., 1937; LL.M., N.Y. U., 1952. Admitted to N.Y. bar, 1938, U.S. Supreme Ct. bar, 1959; asst. dist. atty. N.Y. County, 1938-54; dir. law div. Waterfront Commn. N.Y. Harbor, 1954-68; individual practice law, N.Y.C., 1955—; adj. prof. law N.Y. U., 1957—. Councilman, City of Long Beach (N.Y.), 1958-62, asso. tax assessor, 1962-69. Mem. Nassau County, N.Y.C. bar assns., Long Beach Lawyers Assn. Home: 811 E Walnut St Long Beach NY 11561 Office: 299 Broadway New York City NY 10007 Tel (212) 227-4855

MC GRATH, DONALD, II, b. Los Angeles, May 5, 1941; B.S., U. Ariz., 1963, J.D., 1968. Admitted to Ariz. bar, 1968, Calif. bar, 1969; intern Senator Paul Fannin, Washington, summer 1967; mem. senatorial campaign staff Senator Barry M. Goldwater, Phoenix, 1968; asso. firm Orfield, Thompson, Bunker & Sullivan, San Diego, 1969-72; partner firm Thompson, Bunker, Sullivan & McGrath, San Diego, 1972-76, Thompson, Sullivan, McGrath & McDonald, San Diego, 1976—. Mem. State Bar Ariz., State Bar Calif., San Diego County Bar Assn., Calif. Trial Lawyers Assn., Greater San Diego County Barristers (v.p., dir. 1973-74). Office: 1200 Third Ave Suite 1405 San Diego CA 92101 Tel (714) 234-6781

MC GRATH, GEORGE WILLIAM, JR., b. Newark, Oct. 23, 1922; A.B., Princeton, 1943; LL.B., Harvard, 1950. Admitted to N.Y. bar, 1951; asso. firm Sage, Gray, Todd & Sims, N.Y.C., 1950-57, partner, 1958—. Mem. Am., N.Y. State bar assns., Assn. Bar City N.Y. Home: 172 Flowerhill Rd Huntington NY 11743 Office: 140 Broadway New York City NY 10005 Tel (212) 248-1100

MCGRATH, JOHN FRANCIS, b. Chgo., Apr. 13, 1926; B.A., Loyola U., Chgo., 1947; J.D., U. Colo., 1950. Admitted to Colo. bar, 1950, Ill. bar, 1950; partner firm Kettelkamp, McGrath, Vento, Pueblo, Colo., 1950-67; judge U.S. Bankruptcy Ct., Denver, 1967—; dep. dist. atty. Pueblo County (Colo.), 1953-57. Pres. Pueblo Symphony, Pueblo Broadway Theatre League. Mem. Colo., Pueblo County (sec.) bar assns., Phi Alpha Delta, Alpha Delta Gamma. Home: 1490 Findlay Way Boulder CO 80303 Office: 108 US Courthouse Denver CO 80202 Tel (303) 837-4045

MC GRATH, JOHN JOSEPH, b. Bronxville, N.Y., Jan. 8, 1926; B.A., Yale, 1950; J.D., U. Conn., 1956. Admitted to Conn. bar, 1957, U.S. Dist. Ct., 1960, U.S. Tax Ct. bar, 1964; asst. traffic mgr. Port of Boston Authority, 1950-53; supr. Conn. Gen. Life Ins. Co., Hartford, 1953-56; asso. trust officer New Britain Nat. Bank (Conn.), 1956-58; with firm Murtha, Cullina, Richter & Pinney, Hartford, 1958—, partner, 1961—. Capt. Simsbury (Conn.) Community Fund, 1969; trustee Alleluia House, Inc., Avon, Conn., 1970—; chmn. Yale Alumni Schs. Com., Hartford, 1974—, v.p., 1975—. Mem. Am.,

Conn., Hartford County bar assns., Hartford Estate and Bus. Planning Council. Contbr. articles to legal jours. Home: 7 Country Club Dr West Simsbury CT 06092 Office: 101 Pearl St Hartford CT 06103 Tel (203) 549-4500

MC GRATH, J(OHN) NICHOLAS, JR., b. Los Angeles, Feb. 12, 1940; B.A. with honors, Lehigh U., 1962; LL.B. magna cum laude, Columbia U., 1965. Admitted to D.C. bar, 1966, Calif. bar, 1969, U.S. Supreme Ct. bar, 1970, Colo. bar, 1971; law clk. to U.S. Ct. Appeals, D.C. Circuit, 1965-66, to Justice Thurgood Marshall, U.S. Supreme Ct., 1967-68; asst. to solicitor gen. Dept. Justice, Washington, 1966-67; asso. firm Pillsbury, Madison & Sutro, San Francisco, 1968-70; asso. firm Clark, Oates & Austin, Aspen, Colo., 1970-72; partner firm Oates, Austin, McGrath & Jordan, 1972—. Mem. Pitkin County (pres. 1977), Colo., Calif., D.C. bar assns., Am. Trial Lawyers Assn. Office: 600 E Hopkins St Suite 204 Aspen CO 81611 Tel (303) 925-2600

MCGRATH, ROBERT GEORGE, b. Oakland, Calif., Oct. 18, 1943; A.B., U. Calif., Berkeley, 1965; J.D., Hastings Coll. Law, U. Calif., 1968. Admitted to Calif. bar, 1969; dep. pub. defender Contra Costa County (Calif.), 1969-73; asso. firm Rockwell & Rogers, Antioch, Calif., 1973-75; partner firm Rockwell, Rogers & McGrath, Antioch, 1975—. Mem. Contra Costa County Democratic Central Com., 1971—, treas., 1973—; bd. dirs. Contra Costa County Atty.'s Reference Panel, 1976. Mem. Am., Contra Costa County (dir. 1976) bar assns. Office: 113 G St Antioch CA 94509 Tel (415) 757-4545

MC GRATH, WILLIAM JOSEPH, b. Oceanside, N.Y., May 20, 1929; B.B.A., U. Cin., 1951, J.D., 1961; M.B.A., Xavier U., Cin., 1956. Admitted to Ohio bar, 1961, U.S. Supreme Ct. bar, 1964; project adminstr. Honeywell Inc., Mpls., 1962-64; individual practice law, Dayton, Ohio, 1964—; instr. Air Force Inst., Dayton, 1964-71; asso. prof. bus. law Wright State U., 1971—. Mem. Am. Bus. Law Assn., Dayton, Ohio, Fed. bar assns. Author: (with R. Shearer) Terminating the Breaching Contractor, the Problem and a Possible Solution, 1973 (Nat. Contract Mgmt. Assn. 1st Place award). Office: 2412 Far Hills Ave Dayton OH 45419 Tel (513) 298-4105

MC GRAW, ARTICE LEE, b. Pensacola, Fla., Sept. 16, 1943; B.S., U. So. Miss., 1965; J.D., Cumberland Sch. Law, Samford U., 1968. Admitted to Ala. bar, 1968, Fla. bar, 1969; partner firm Cetti & McGraw, Pensacola, Fla. Mem. Ala., Fla. bar assns. Home: 205 Palmett Rd Gulf Breeze FL 32561 Office: 26 E Garden St Pensacola FL 32501 Tel (904) 438-4036

MCGREGOR, CALVIN CAMP, b. Honolulu, Aug. 25, 1915; A.B., U. Hawaii, 1937, J.D., Harvard, 1940. Admitted to Hawaii bar, 1940; dist. judge, Hawaii, 1946-53, circuit judge, 1953-58; partner firm King & McGregor, Honolulu, 1958—; head U.S. del. UNESCO meeting, Singapore, 1971. Vice pres. Hawaiian Civic Club; treas., dir. Met. Honolulu YMCA; mem. Hawaii Senate, 1959-62. Mem. Am., Hawaii bar assns. Home: 1594 Alewa Dr Honolulu HI 96817 Office: 394 Alexander Young Bldg Honolulu HI 96813 Tel (808) 536-4659

MC GREGOR, DOUGLAS WEAR, b. Springfield, Mo., Oct. 7, 1902; LL.B., U. Tex., 1926. Admitted to Tex. bar, 1926, Ind. bar, 1949; individual practice law, Houston; U.S. atty. So. Dist. Tex., 1934-44; partner firm Simmons, McGregor & Arnold, Houston, 1937-38, McGregor, Sewell & Junell, Houston, 1950-64; asst. atty. gen. U.S., 1946, dep. atty. gen., 1947. Mem. Am., Tex. bar assns. Home: 5938 Stones Throw St Houston TX 77057 Tel (713) 782-7479

MC GREW, THOMAS JAMES, b. Wilkes-Barre, Pa., Jan. 21, 1942; A.B. in English Lit. and Philosophy, U. Scranton, 1963; J.D., U. Pa., 1970. Admitted to D.C. bar, 1970, U.S. Supreme Ct. bar, 1973; atty. Arnold & Porter, Washington, 1970—. Mem. Am. Bar Assn., D.C. Bar. Editor U. Pa. Law Rev., 1970. Home: 3909 Virgilia St Chevy Chase MD 20015 Office: 1229 19th St NW Washington DC 20036 Tel (202) 872-6925

MC GRUDER, JAMES PATRICK, b. Los Angeles, Mar. 11, 1926; J.D., U. Denver, 1953. Admitted to Colo. bar, 1954, Calif. bar, 1972; asst. city atty., Denver, 1954-61; asst. U.S. atty., Denver, 1961-64; asst. resident atty. Prudential Ins. Co., Los Angeles, 1964-70, resident atty., 1970—. Mem. Colo., Calif. bar assns. Home: 10036 Shoshone Ave Northridge CA 91325 Office: Prudential Ins Co 2049 Century Park E Los Angeles CA 90067 Tel (213) 277-1400

MC GUINN, JOHN ALBERT, b. Hartford, Conn., June 17, 1934; A.B., Holy Cross Coll., 1956; LL.B., Georgetown U., 1959, LL.M., 1961. Admitted to Conn. bar, 1959, U.S. Ct. Appeals bar for D.C., 1960, U.S. Supreme Ct. bar, 1964; law clk. U.S. Ct. of Appeals for D.C. Circuit, 1959-60; asso. firm Patterson, Belknap & Farmer, Washington, 1960-68; partner firm Farmer, Shibley, McGuinn & Flood, Washington, 1968—; adj. prof. labor law Georgetown U., 1964-72. Mem. Am., Fed., D.C. bar assns. Home: 3749 Upton St NW Washington DC 20016 Office: 1120 Connecticut Ave NW Washington DC 20036 Tel (202) 331-7311

MC GUINN, MARTIN GREGORY, JR., b. Phila., Sept. 9, 1942; A.B., Villanova U., 1964, J.D., 1967. Admitted to Pa. bar, 1967, N.Y. State bar, 1970; served as capt. USMC, 1967-70; asso. firm Sullivan & Cromwell, N.Y.C., 1970—. Mem. bd. consultors Villanova Law Sch., 1971—. Mem. Assn. Bar City N.Y., N.Y. State Bar Assn., Council N.Y. Law Assos. Editor in chief Villanova Law Rev., 1966-67. Home: 80 E End Ave Apt 9-H New York City NY 10028 Office: 48 Wall Street New York City NY 10005 Tel (212) 952-8133

MC GUIRE, DAVID FRANCIS, b. Dubuque, Iowa, Aug. 22, 1929; B.S., Loras Coll., 1949; J.D., U. Iowa, 1952. Admitted to Iowa bar, 1952; partner firm Martin & McGuire, Cedar Rapids, Iowa, 1954-59, McGuire Bernau & Culver, Cedar Rapids, 1959-66; individual practice law, Cedar Rapids, 1966—; city atty. Cedar Rapids, 1958—. Mem. Am., Iowa, Linn County bar assns., Iowa Municipal Attys. Assn., Nat. Inst. Municipal Law Officers (state chmn.). Home: 4350 Eaglemere Ct SE Cedar Rapids IA 52403 Office: 214 First Ave Bldg Cedar Rapids IA 52401 Tel (319) 363-2601

MC GUIRE, ELMER JAMES, b. Kansas City, Mo., Feb. 10, 1914; A.B., U. Calif., 1936; J.D., 1948. Admitted to Calif. bar, 1948; partner firm O'Gara and McGuire, San Francisco, 1949—; lectr. Calif. Continuing Edn. of Bar, 1964. Mem. Am., San Francisco, Alameda County bar assns., Calif. Trial Lawyers Assn., Am. Judicature Soc., Phi Delta Phi. Home: 889 Longridge Rd Oakland CA 94610 Office: Suite 950 Alcoa Bldg 1 Maritime Plaza San Francisco CA 94111 Tel (415) 433-2250

MCGUIRE, JOSEPH THOMAS, b. Oak Park, Ill., Nov. 14, 1925; A.B., Loyola U., Chgo., 1948, J.D. cum laude, 1953. Admitted to Ill. bar, 1953; asso. firm Morgan, Halligan and Lanoff, Chgo., 1954-60; partner firm Perz and McGuire, Chgo., 1960—. Mem. fund raising cons. Skokie Valley Community Hosp., St. Joan of Arc Church. Mem. Ill., Am. Trial Lawyers Assns., Chgo., Am., Ill. State bar assns., Cath. Lawyers Guild. Contbr. articles to legal publ. Home: 3930 Enfield St Skokie IL 60076 Office: 228 N LaSalle St Chicago IL 60601 Tel (312) 372-8282

MC GUIRE, WALTER R., b. Asheville, N.C., Dec. 8, 1913; A.B., U. N.C., 1936, LL.B., 1937. Admitted to N.C. bar, 1937; since practiced law in Asheville; mem. firm Bernard & Parker, 1952-53, Bernard, Parker & McGuire, 1953-56, Parker & McGuire, 1956-60, Parker, McGuire & Baley, 1960-68, McGuire & Wood, 1973, McGuire, Wood, Erwin & Crow, 1973—; mem. N.C. Bd. Law Examiners, 1972—. Trustee Pack Meml. Library, Asheville, 1959—. Mem. Am., N.C. State, Brevoort County bar assns. Home: 61 Kimberly Knoll Asheville NC 28804 Office: PO Box 1411 705 First Union Nat Bank Bldg Asheville NC 28802 Tel (704) 254-8806

MC HANEY, FLAKE L., b. White Oak, Mo., Sept. 25, 1920; A.B. in Econs. with distinction, U. Mo., 1942; LL.B., Harvard U., 1948. Admitted to Mo. bar, 1948, U.S. Dist. Ct. bar for Eastern Dist. Mo., 1950; sr. partner firm McHaney, Billings & Welman, Kennett, Mo., to 1972; judge Mo. Circuit Ct., 35th Jud. Circuit, 1973—; mem. faculty Nat. Inst. Trial Advocacy, Boulder, Colo., 1973—; spl. lectr. Washington U. Sch. Law, St. Louis, U. Mo. Sch. Law. Fellow Am. Bar Found., Am. Coll. Trial Lawyers, Am. Coll. Probate Counsel; mem. Am. Law Inst., Mo. Bar Assn. (gov.), Mo. Bar Found. (trustee). Home: 1111 White Oaks Pl Kennett MO 63857 Office: PO Box 507 Kennett MO 63857 Tel (314) 888-9133

MCHARDY, LOUIS WILLIAM, b. Baton Rouge, Oct. 31, 1930; B.A., La. State U., 1951, M.S.W., 1956. Probation officer, then chief probation officer Family Ct., Baton Rouge, 1955-64; dir. ct. services Juvenile Ct., St. Louis, 1965-72; exec. dir. Nat. Council Juvenile Ct. Judges, Reno, 1972—, also dean Nat. Coll. Juvenile Justice; adj. prof. jud. adminstrn. U. Nev., 1972—. Mem. Mo. Law Enforcement Assistance Council, 1969-72; exec. dir. Nat. Juvenile Ct. Found., 1972—. Mem. exec. bd. Nev. area council Boy Scouts Am.; bd. dirs. Nev. Catholic Welfare Bur. Mem. Am. Soc. Assn. Execs., Internat. Assn. Youth Ct. Magistrates (hon. v.p. 1974—). Editor, pub. jours. in field. Home: 4265 Ross Dr Reno NV 89502 Office: 118 Judicial Coll Bldg Univ Nev Reno NV 89507*

MCHARG, M. JANE, b. Fond-du-Lac, Wis., July 13, 1946; B.B.A., U. Iowa, 1968, J.D., M.A. in Accounting, 1971. Admitted to Iowa bar, 1971; accountant firm H.G. Petershagen, C.P.A., Iowa City, 1971-72; Friend of Ct. atty. Linn County (Iowa), Cedar Rapids, 1972—; jud. magistrate Iowa County, Marengo, 1973—. Mem. Am., Iowa State, Iowa County, Linn County bar assns., Nat. Reciprocal Family Support Enforcement Assn., U. Iowa Alumni Assn., Phi Gamma Nu, Kappa Beta Pi. Home: 304 Washington St Victor IA 52347 Office: Linn County Courthouse Cedar Rapids IA 52401 Tel (319) 398-3595

MCHOSE, JOHN CRESCO, b. Springfield, Mass., Sept. 19, 1902; A.B., Stanford, 1924, J.D., 1927. Admitted to Calif. bar, 1927, D.C. bar, 1970, U.S. Supreme Ct. bar, 1962; mem. firm Lillick McHose & Charles, and predecessors, Los Angeles, 1927—; mem. U.S. Supreme Ct. Com. on Admiralty Rules, 1966-72. Mem. Am., Calif. State, Internat. bar assns., Am. Bar Found., Maritime Law Assn. U.S. (pres. 1970-72), Los Angeles C. of C. (dir., v.p. 1958-64). Contbr. articles to legal jours. Home: 32859 Seagate Dr Rancho Palos Verdes CA 90274 Office: 611 W 6th St Los Angeles CA 90017 Tel (213) 620-9000

MCHUGH, JAMES LENAHAN, JR., b. Pitts., June 28, 1937; B.A., Duquesne U., 1959; J.D., Villanova U., 1962. Admitted to D.C. bar, 1962; law clk. to chief judge U.S. Dist. Ct., Eastern Dist. Pa., 1962-63, to asso. justice U.S. Supreme Ct., Washington, 1963-64; Served with JAG AUS, 1964-67; asso. firm Steptoe & Johnson, Washington, 1967-70, partner, 1970—; bd. cons. Villanova Law Sch., 1973—, chmn. bd., 1977—; Dir. Robert F. Kennedy Meml. Washington Lawyers Project, 1972-74. Mem. Am., D.C., Fed. Power Bar assns., Coif, Barristers. Editor-in-chief Villanova Law Review, 1961-62. Home: 5603 Albia Rd Bethesda MD 20016 Office: 1250 Connecticut Ave N W Washington DC 20036 Tel (202) 862-2250

MCHUGH, KENNTH ROBERT, b. Manchester, N.H., July 18, 1944; B.A., St. Anselm's Coll., 1966; J.D., Suffolk U., 1969. Admitted to N.H. bar, 1969; asso. firm Emile R. Bussiere, Manchester, 1969—; justice Hooksett (N.H.) Dist. Ct., 1976—. Mem. Am., N.H., Manchester bar assns. Office: 15 North St Manchester NH 03104

MC INERNEY, DENIS, b. N.Y.C., May 31, 1925; B.S., Fordham U., 1948, J.D. cum laude, 1951. Admitted to N.Y. State bar, 1951, U.S. Supreme Ct. bar, 1960, D.C. bar, 1961; asso. firm Cahill Gordon & Reindel, N.Y.C., 1951-61, partner, 1962—. Fellow Am. Coll. Trial Lawyers, Am. Bar Found.; mem. N.Y. State 1st Dept. Com. on Character and Fitness for Admission to Bar, Am., N.Y. State (chmn. com. cts. appellate jurisdiction, mem. ho. dels.), N.Y. County bar assns., Assn. Bar City N.Y., Practising Law Inst. (lectr.). Home: 119 N Chatsworth Ave Larchmont NY 10538 Office: Cahill Gordon & Reindel 80 Pine St New York City NY 10005 Tel (212) 825-0100

MC INERNEY, DONALD BURTON, b. Chgo., Feb. 23, 1934; B.S., U. Wis., 1959; J.D., Ill. Inst. Tech. Chgo.-Kent Coll. Law, 1968; M.B.A., U. Chgo., 1975. Dir. of program practices CBS-TV, Chgo., 1961-66; admitted to Ill. bar, 1968; atty. Continental Ill. Nat. Bank and Trust Co., Chgo., 1968-71, trust officer, 1971-73, 2d v.p., 1973-76, mgr. trust personal agy. div., 1975—, v.p., 1976—. Mem. Chgo., Ill. State, Am. bar assns., Law Club, Chgo. Estate Planning Council, Am. Inst. Banking, Ill. Inst. Tech. Chgo. Kent (pres. 1977—), U. Chgo. alumni assns. Home: 1318 Kenton Rd Deerfield IL 60015 Office: 231 S LaSalle St Chicago IL 60693 Tel (312) 828-3580

MC INERNEY, GEORGE FRANCIS XAVIER, b. Bklyn., Feb. 2, 1917; B.A., Washington and Lee U., 1939, LL.B., 1941. Admitted to N.Y. bar, 1944; partner firm Mc Inerney & Mc Inerney, Bay Shore, N.Y., 1944-53; town atty. Town of Islip (N.Y.), 1953-63; judge Suffolk County (N.Y.), 1963-69; justice N.Y. State Supreme Ct., Suffolk County, 1969—. Playwright: Nor All Your Tears, 1965. Home: 164 McConnell Ave Bayport NY 11705 Office: 559 Middle Rd Bayport NY 11705 Tel (516) HR2-1033

MCINERNEY, KEVIN JOSEPH, b. Washington, Nov. 29, 1942; B.S.S., Fordham U., 1964; LL.B., Yale, 1967. Admitted to D.C. bar, 1968, N.Y. bar, 1968, Fla. bar, 1968, Calif. bar, 1970, U.S. Supreme Ct. bar, 1975; asst. U.S. atty. So. Dist. N.Y., 1968-69; asst. U.S. atty. So. Dist. Calif., 1969-70; individual practice law, San Diego, 1970-72; partner firm McInerney, Milchen & Frank, San Diego, 1972—; chmn. San Diego Fed. Ct. Com. Mem. Assn. Immigration and Nationality Lawyers, Am., Fed., Calif., N.Y., San Diego bar assns. Office: 110 W A St 1690 San Diego CA 92101 Tel (714) 238-1888

MCINERNY, JOHN SMITH, b. Merced, Calif., Aug. 22, 1928; B.S. in Econs., U. Santa Clara, 1949, J.D., 1954. Admitted to Calif. bar, 1955; dep. atty. gen. State of Calif., San Francisco, 1954-63; legal adviser, clemency sec. to Gov., Sacramento, 1963-66; judge Calif. Superior Ct. for Santa Clara County, 1966—; mil. judge JAGC, USAR, 1970—. Mem. Conf. Calif. Judges, Santa Clara County Bar Assn., Judge Adv. Assn., Calif. State Bar (past chmn. commn. criminal law). Office: 191 N 1st St San Jose CA 95113 Tel (408) 299-3415

MCINNIS, EMMETT EMORY, JR., b. McAlester, Okla., Sept. 12, 1920; B.S., Northwestern U., 1945; LL.B., Yale, 1948. Admitted to Wash. bar, 1951, U.S. Supreme Ct. bar, 1958; individual practice law, Seattle, 1951—; lectr. in field. Elder, Presbyterian Ch. Mem. Am., Wash., Seattle-King County bar assns., Estate Planning Council Seattle (pres. 1973). Office: 1111 Seattle Tower Seattle WA 98101 Tel (206) 623-6624

MC INNIS, JOHN ROBERT, b. Gt. Falls, Mont., Aug. 26, 1935; B.A., Carroll Coll., 1959; M.B.A. in Accounting, U. Calif. at Los Angeles, 1961; J.D., Georgetown U., 1965, LL.M. in Taxation, 1967. Accountant, FTC, Washington, 1962-64; admitted to Mont. bar, 1964, U.S. Tax Ct. bar, 1966; trial atty. FTC, 1964-66; individual practice law, Missoula, Mont., 1966—. Trustee Carroll Coll., Helena, Mont., 1972—. Mem. Am., Mont., Western Mont. bar assns., Nat. Assn. Attys.-C.P.A.'s. Home: 3024 Queen St Missoula MT 59801 Office: 199 West Pine St Missoula MT 59801 Tel (406) 728-1200

MC INTEE, MICHAEL RAY, b. Northgate, N.D., Aug. 5, 1921; B.S., U. N.D., 1943, J.D., 1953. Admitted to N.D. bar, 1953; partner firm McIntee & Whisenand, Williston, N.D., 1953-68, sr. partner, 1968—; states atty. Williams County (N.D.), 1956-60. Mem. Am., N.D. (pres. 1972-73), Williams County bar assns., Am. Soc. Hosp. Attys., Am. Trial Lawyers Assn. Home: 1208 4th Ave E Williston ND 58801 Office: PO Box 1307 Williston ND 58801 Tel (701) 572-6781

MC INTIRE, ROBERT EDWARD, b. Champaign, Ill., Jan. 18, 1947; B.A. in English, U. Ill., 1968, J.D., 1972. Admitted to Ill. bar, 1972; asso. firm Edward A. McIntire, 1972; asst. states atty. Kankakee County, Ill., 1972-74; asso. firm Arnold, Gesell, & Schwulst, Bloomington, Ill., 1974-76; individual practice law, Bloomington, 1976—; asst. pub. defender McLean County, Ill., 1974-76; pub. defender Woodford County, Ill., 1976—. Mem. Ill., McLean County bar assns., Ill. Pub. Defenders Assn. Asst. editor: U. Ill. Law Forum, 1970-71. Home: 701 S Mercer St Bloomington IL 61701 Office: 2205 E Washington St PO Box 35 Bloomington IL 61701 Tel (309) 663-6444

MCINTOSH, DAVID FOREMEN, b. Chgo., Dec. 29, 1929; B.S., U.S. Coast Guard Acad., 1952; J.D., George Washington U., 1960; LL.M., U. Miami, 1972. Admitted to D.C. bar, 1960, Alaska bar, 1965, Fla. bar, 1972; commd. ensign U.S. Coast Guard, 1952, advanced through grades to commdr., 1969; retired, 1973; asst. U.S. Atty., So. Dist., Fla., 1973-77; mem. firm Corlett, Merritt, Killian & Sikes, Miami, Fla., 1977—; mil. judge, 1963-73. Dir., USCG Fed. Credit Union, 1969-76, v.p., 1972. Mem. Am. Arbitration Assn., Dade County Bar Assn., Order Coif. Office: 116 W Flagler St Miami FL 33130 Tel (305) 337-8931

MC INTOSH, EDWARD DALTON, b. Marlin, Tex., Dec. 19, 1932; B.B.A., U. Tex., 1956, LL.B., 1960. Admitted to Tex. bar, 1960; partner firm Banner, McIntosh & Dobbs, Wichita Falls, Tex., 1960—. Mem. Wichita County (Tex.) (pres. 1972-73, dir.), Am. bar assns., State Bar Tex. (dir. 1975—), Am. Trial Lawyers Assn., Tex. Trial Lawyers, Am. Judicature Soc. Office: 1200 Hamilton Bldg Wichita Falls TX 76301 Tel (817) 723-6644

MCINTOSH, RUSSELL HUGH, b. Danville, Ga., Feb. 22, 1915; B.A., U. Fla., 1937, M.A., 1941, J.D., 1949. Admitted to Fla. bar, 1949; individual practice law, W. Palm Beach, Fla., 1949-57; partner firm Ives, McIntosh & Davis, W. Palm Beach, 1957-60; judge Palm Beach County (Fla.) Criminal Ct. of Record, 1960-73, Palm Beach County Circuit Ct., 1973—. Mem. Palm Beach County Bar Assn. Editor U. Fla. Law Rev., 1948. Home: 3218 Alton Rd West Palm Beach FL 33405 Office: Palm Beach County Courthouse Rm 412 West Palm Beach FL 33401 Tel (305) 837-2439

MC INTYRE, DAVID L., b. Ithaca, N.Y., Oct. 14, 1941; B.A., Valparaiso U., 1963; LL.B., State U. N.Y., Buffalo, 1966. Admitted to N.Y. bar, 1966, U.S. Supreme Ct. bar, 1970; asso. firm Chester S. Grove, 1966-70; individual practice law, 1971-73; partner firm McIntyre, Smith, Foltz & May, 1973-76; partner firm McIntyre & Smith, P.C., Lockport, N.Y., 1976—; atty. Town of Hartland, 1968—. Bd. dirs. Niagara County Council Girl Scouts U.S.A., 1971-75. Mem. N.Y., Niagara County, Lockport bar assns., Am. Judicature Soc. Office: 415 S Transit St Lockport NY 14094 Tel (716) 434-6214

MC KAY, BARRIE GUNN, b. Huntsville, Utah, Aug. 17, 1930; B.A. in Accounting and Econs., Brigham Young U., 1958; J.D., U. Chgo., 1961. Admitted to Utah bar, 1961; since practiced in Salt Lake City; asso. firm McKay & Burton, 1961-69, partner, 1969-71; partner firm McKay, Burton, McMurray & Thurman, 1971—; legal sec. Utah Restaurant Assn., 1967—; dir. Utaho Corp., 1964—. Guide on Mormon Temple Sq., 1967-76; scoutmaster, instl. rep. Boy Scouts Am., 1964—. Mem. Am. (mem. tax sect.), Utah State (mem. tax sect.) bar assns., Salt Lake City C. of C., Brigham Young U. Alumni Assn. (bd. dirs. 1973—), Utah Restaurant Assn. (exec. sec. 1964-67). Recipient Spl. award Brigham Young U. Devel. Office, 1974. Home: 564 E 1700 S Bountiful UT 84010 Office: 500 Kennecott Bldg Salt Lake City UT 84133

MC KAY, CONNALLY, b. Eddy, Tex., Sept. 22, 1914; LL.B., Baylor U., 1937. Admitted to Tex. bar, 1937; county atty. Wood County (Tex.), 1941-43, 46; dist. atty. Smith, Wood and Upshur counties (Tex.), 1946-49; referee in bankruptcy Eastern Dist. Tex., 1949-52; judge 114th Jud. Dist., 1953-69; asso. justice Tex. 12th Ct. of Civil Appeals, 1969—; mem. Tex. Jud. Qualifications Commn., 1966-69; dir. Citizens 1st Nat. Bank of Tyler, E. Tex. Savs. & Loan Assn. Pres., East Tex. Fair Assn., 1960, Baylor U. Ex-Students' Assn., 1963, Tyler (Tex.) Indsl. Found., 1966-67, East Tex. Hosp. Found., 1970-72, Tex. Rose Festival Assn., 1974; trustee Baylor U. Coll. Dentistry. Recipient T. B. Butler award as Outstanding Citizen of Tyler T.B. Butler Pub. Co., 1965. Home: 3110 Belmead Ln Tyler TX 75701 Office: 306 Smith County Courthouse Tyler TX 75702 Tel (214) 593-8471

MC KAY, DOUGLAS, JR., b. Columbia, S.C., Aug. 12, 1917; B.A., U. S.C., 1939; LL.B., S.C. Law Sch., 1941. Admitted to S.C. bar, 1941, U.S. Ct. Appeals bar, 1948, U.S. Supreme Ct. bar, 1971; asso. firm Douglas McKay, 1941-46; partner firm McKay and McKay, 1946-54; partner firm McKay, Sherrill, Walker & Townsend, and predecessors, 1954—; chmn. Advisory Com. Improvement of Workmen's Compensation Laws S.C. Mem. Am. Law Inst., Assn. Railroad Trial Counsel, Internat. Assn. Ins. Counsel, Am., S.C., Richland County (sec. 1945-46) bar assns. Office: 1340 Bull St PO Drawer 447 Columbia SC 29202 Tel (803) 771-8880

MCKAY, RALPH EDWARD, b. Bayonne, N.J., Aug. 18, 1945; B.S., St. Peter's Coll., 1967; J.D. cum laude, Seton Hall U., 1972. Admitted to N.J. bar, 1972; asst. prosecutor Ocean County (N.J.), 1972-76; spl. dep. atty. gen. State N.J., 1973—; individual practice law, Toms River, N.J., 1973—. Mem. Am., N.J., Ocean County bar assns., Law Assn. U.S. Home: 14 Harpoon St Beachwood NJ 08722 Office: 125 Washington St Toms River NJ 08753 Tel (201) 349-0696

MCKAY, ROBERT BUDGE, b. Wichita, Kans., Aug. 11, 1919; B.S., U. Kans., 1940; J.D., Yale, 1947; LL.D. hon., Mt. St. Mary's Coll., Seton Hall Coll., Emory U., 1973. Admitted to D.C., Kans. bars, 1948, N.Y. bar, 1973; atty. Dept. Justice, Washington, 1947-50; asso. prof. law Emory U., Atlanta, 1950-53; prof. law N.Y. U., 1953-75, dean, 1967-75; dir. Justice Program Aspen Inst., N.Y.C., 1975—. Pres., Legal Aid Soc. N.Y.C., 1975—; chmn. N.Y. State Spl. Commn. Attica, N.Y.C., 1971-72, Citizens Union, N.Y.C., 1971—; vice chmn. Nat. News Council, N.Y.C., 1973—. Mem. Am. (comm. chmn.), N.Y., N.Y.C. (chmn. exec. com.) bar assns., Am. Law Inst., Am. Judicature Soc. Author: Apportionment, 1965; recipient William Nelson Gromwell medal, Am. Friends Hebrew U., 1973, Arthur T. Vanderbilt medal, 1975, Albert Gallatin medal, 1973. Home: 29 Washington Sq W New York City NY 10011 Office: 36 W 44th St New York City NY 10036 Tel (212) 730-0168

MC KEAG, GEORGE WILSON, b. Washington, Pa., July 31, 1905; B.A., Swarthmore Coll., 1927; LL.B., U. Pa., 1930. Admitted to Pa. bar, 1930, U.S. Supreme Ct. bar, 1938; individual practice law, Phila., 1930-42, 64-66; partner firm Philips, Farran & McKeag, Phila., 1946-56; of counsel firm Morgan, Lewis & Bockius, Phila., 1966—; pres. Prospect Park (Pa.) State Bank, 1953-56; v.p. Broad St. Trust Co., Phila., 1956-64; counsel Office of Gen. Assembly of United Presbyterian Ch. U.S.A.; solicitor United Presbyn. Found., Phila. and N.Y.C., 1942—, v.p., 1972—. Mem. Phila., Pa., Am. bar assns. Contbr. articles to legal jours. Home: 645 Parrish Rd Swarthmore PA 19081 Office: 123 S Broad St Philadelphia PA 19109 Tel (215) 491-9200

MCKEE, JAMES CLAY, b. Salt Lake City, Sept. 1, 1942; B.S., U. Utah, 1965, J.D., 1968. Admitted to Utah bar, 1968; individual practice law, Salt Lake City, 1971; dep. county atty. Salt Lake County, 1971; atty. Office Dist. Counsel, U.S. VA, Salt Lake City, 1971—. Chmn., Jim Bridger Explorer dist. Gt. Salt Lake council Boy Scouts Am., 1974-76; bd. dirs. Ft. Douglas Mil. Mus. Assn., 1974—. Mem. Am., Utah, Fed. (v.p. Utah chpt. 1977), Salt Lake County bar assns., Am. Judicature Soc., Assn. U.S. Army, Res. Officers Assn. Home: 374 Williams Ave Salt Lake City UT 84111 Office: 125 S State St Salt Lake City UT 84111 Tel (801) 524-5950

MC KEE, ROBERT SMITH, b. Martins Ferry, Ohio, Dec. 1, 1921; B.S. in Commerce, U. Va., 1948; LL.B., U. Houston, 1959. Admitted to Tex. bar, 1959; accountant H.S. Hutzell, Wheeling, W.Va., 1948-50; treas. Compania Industrial Comercial del Sur S.A., Montevideo, Uruguay, 1950-53; v.p., treas. Transco Cos., Inc., Houston, 1953—. Mem. Am. Gas Assn., Am. Bar Assn., Interstate Natural Gas Assn. Am. (treas.). Home: 5214 Darnell St Houston TX 77096 Office: 2700 S Post Oak St Houston TX 77098 Tel (713) 626-8100

MC KEE, WILLIAM DAVID, b. N.Y.C., Aug. 11, 1926; B.M.E., Duke, 1946; LL.B., Columbia, 1949. Admitted to Calif. bar, 1949; asst. to dir. Am. Law Inst., Berkeley, Calif., 1949-50; asso. firm Orrick, Herrington, Rowley & Sutcliffe, San Francisco, 1950-57, partner, 1958—; lectr. law U. Calif., Berkeley, 1952-60; dir. Golden West Fin. Corp., 1970—. Mem. Am., Calif. (chmn. tax sect. 1956—), San Francisco bar assns. Mem. adv. com. Hastings Law Jour., 1960—; contbr. articles to legal jours. Home: 1271 Redwood Ln Lafayette CA 94549 Office: 600 Montgomery St San Francisco CA 94111 Tel (415) 392-1122

MC KEEVER, JOHN HENRY, b. Allentown, Pa., Aug. 31, 1925; A.B. cum laude, Princeton, 1948; J.D., U. Pa., 1951. Admitted to Pa. bar, 1952; asso. firm Butz Hudders Tallman & Rupp, Allentown, 1952-57; individual practice law, Allentown, 1957—; counsel, dir. banks and bus. corps. Mem. Am., Pa., Lehigh County (Pa.) bar assns. Home: RD 1 Danielsville PA 18038 Office: 1444 Hamilton St PO Box 1886 Allentown PA 18105 Tel (215) 432-1671

MCKEGNEY, BRIAN P., b. N.Y.C., May 6, 1940; A.B., Belmont Abbey Coll., 1963; J.D., Western Reserve U., 1966. Admitted to N.Y. bar, 1968, U.S. Customs Ct., 1971, U.S. Dist. Ct., So. Dist., Eastern Dist., 1977; asso. law firm Otis & Edelman, N.Y.C., 1966-68, partner, 1968-71; partner firm Shanley, McKegney, Dolan & Wallman, N.Y.C., 1971—; instr. civil practice N.Y. U., 1973. Mem. N.Y. State, Westchester County bar assns., N.Y. State Assn. Trial Lawyers, Guild Catholic Lawyers. Home: Lois Pl RFD 2 Katonah NY 10536 Office: 233 Broadway New York City NY 10007 Tel (212) 267-0700

MC KELVEY, JUDITH GRANT, b. Milw., July 19, 1935; B.S., U. Wis., 1957, J.D., 1959. Admitted to Wis. bar, 1959, Calif. bar, 1968; lectr. U. Md. European div., 1967-68; asst. prof. law Golden Gate U., 1968-71, asso. prof., 1971-74, prof., 1974, dean, 1974—. Mem. San Francisco Lawyers Com. for Urban Affairs (dir. 1977—), Bar Assn. San Francisco (dir. 1975-77), Calif. Women Lawyers (pres. 1975-76, dir. 1976-77). Office: 536 Mission St San Francisco CA 94105 Tel (415) 391-7800

MC KENNA, ALVIN JAMES, b. New Orleans, Aug. 17, 1943; A.B., Canisius Coll., 1963; J.D., U. Notre Dame, 1966. Admitted to N.Y. bar, 1966, Ohio bar, 1967; clerk U.S. Dist. judge So. Dist. Ohio, Columbus, 1966-68; asst. U.S. Atty. So. Dist. Ohio, 1968-70; partner firm Alexander, Ebinger, Holschuh, Fisher & McAlister, Columbus, 1970—. Mem. City Council Gahanna, Ohio (pres. 1973), mem. bd. Gahanna Community Improvement Corp. Mem. Am., Fed., Ohio State, Columbus bar assns. Selected one of Ten Outstanding Young Men in Columbus 1974. Home: 202 Academy Ct Gahanna OH 43230 Office: 17 S High St Columbus OH 43215 Tel (614) 221-6345

MC KENNA, DAVID WILLIAM, b. Rushville, Nebr., Sept. 7, 1945; B.A., Macalester Coll., St. Paul, 1967; J.D., U. Minn., 1970. Admitted to Minn. bar, 1970; mem. firm Erickson, Zierke, Kuderer, Utermarck & McKenna, Fairmont, Minn., 1971-76; dir. Econ. Crimes Control Project, Office Atty. Gen. State of Minn., St. Paul, 1976—; asst. atty. Martin County (Minn.), Fairmont, 1971-76. Mem. Am., Minn., Martin County, 17th Jud. Dist. bar assns., Assn. Trial Lawyers Am., Nat. Dist. Attys. Assn., Minn. County Attys. Assn. Office: 122 Veterans Service Bldg Saint Paul MN 55155 Tel (612) 296-8430

MC KENNA, JAMES ALOYSIUS, JR., b. Poughkeepsie, N.Y., July 1, 1918; student Manhattan Coll., 1934-35; B.S., Catholic U. Am., 1938; LL.B., Georgetown U., 1942. Admitted to D.C. bar, 1941, U.S. Supreme Ct. bar, 1947; counsel CAB, Washington, 1941-42; asst. to gen. counsel Office Alien Property Custodian, Washington, 1942-44; partner firm Haley, McKenna & Wilkinson, Washington, 1948-52, McKenna, Wilkinson and Kittner, Washington, 1952—; owner, pres. radio sta. WCMB, WSFM, Harrisburg, Pa., sta. KQRS, KQRS-FM, Mpls., WWQM, WMAD-FM, Madison, Wis., also dir.; co-owner, v.p. sta. WAWA, WAWA-FM, Milw. Mem. Am., D.C., Fed. Communications bar assns., IEEE, Georgetown U. Alumni Assn., Delta Theta Phi. Home: 5219 Oakland Rd Chevy Chase MD 20015 Office: 1150 17th St NW Washington DC 20036 Tel (202) 296-1600

MC KENRY, JAMES REINHARDT, b. Richmond, Va., Apr. 27, 1935; B.S., U. Va., 1958, LL.B., 1962, J.D., 1970. Admitted to Va. bar, 1962, U.S. Supreme Ct. bar, 1971; partner firm Brydges, Broyles & McKenry, Virginia Beach, 1962-73, firm Broyles, McKenry & Gorry, Virginia Beach, 1973-76; individual practice law, Virginia Beach, 1976—; mem. Va. Commonwealth Task Force on Criminal Justice Goals and Objectives, 1975-77. Chmn. ann. fund dr. Tidewater Heart Assn., Virginia Beach; legal advisor Virginia Beach Rescue Squad; bd. dirs. United Community Fund, Virginia Beach. Mem. Va. State Bar (chmn. criminal law sect. 1976), Am. (vice chmn. membership com. criminal justice sect.), Va., Virginia Beach (pres. 1973) bar assns. Office: 402 Beach Tower 3330 Pacific Ave Virginia Beach VA 23451 Tel (803) 425-5484

MC KENZIE, ANN LLEWELLYN, b. Oxford, N.C., Dec. 18, 1925; student U. N.C., 1942-44, Cert. of Laws, 1955. Admitted to N.C. bar, 1955, Md. bar, 1958; mem. firm Llewellyn & Green, Concord, N.C., 1955-57, Llewellyn & McKenzie, Concord, 1958-60, Llewellyn, McKenzie & Llewellyn, 1960-66; individual practice law, Balt. and Concord, 1966—. Mem. N.C. State, Md., Balt. bar assns., Women's Bar Assn. Md. Home: 500 Druid Hill Ave Baltimore MD 21201 Office: suite 47 3 E Lexington St Baltimore MD 21202 Tel (301) 752-3696

MCKENZIE, CLAUDE FLEATUS, b. Athens, Tenn., Jan. 16, 1930; B.A., Duke U., 1948-52; LL.B., Mt. Vernon Sch. Law, 1958; J.D., U. Balt., 1970. Admitted to Md. bar 1960, Md. Ct. Appeals bar, 1960, Balt. City Supreme Bench, 1960, U.S. Dist. Ct. of Md., 1962; individual practice law, Balt., 1960—. Pres. Seton Hill Assn., Balt., 1973-74; mem. Mayor's Com. Downtown Balt., 1976-77. Mem. Md. Trial Lawyers Assn., Md., Balt. bar assns., Md. Crime Investigating Commn. Home: 500 Druid Hill Ave Baltimore MD 21201 Office: One Charles Center Suite 516 Baltimore MD 21201 Tel (301) 539-7550

MCKENZIE, HORACE HOUSTON, b. Prescott, Ark., Mar. 6, 1905; student Henderson Brown Coll., 1921-22. Admitted to Ark. bar, 1933, U.S. Dist. Ct., 1933 U.S. Dist. Ct. Western Dist. Ark. bar, 1948, U.S. Supreme Ct. bar, 1960; individual practice law, Prescott, Ark., 1933-47, partner firm Tompkins, McKenzie & McRae, Prescott, Ark., mem. Ark. Statutes Revision Co., 1961-64; mem. Ark. State Bar Exam. Bd., 1965-70. Pres. Prescott Sch. Bd., 1960-65; chmn. bd. stewards, First Methodist Ch., Prescott, 1947-51, 60-64. Fellow Am. Coll. Trial Lawyers; mem. SW, Ark., Am. bar assns., Internat. Soc. Barristers. Home: 604 E Main St Prescott AR 71857 Office: McKenzie Bldg E 2nd St Prescott AZ 71857 Tel (501) 887-2601

MC KENZIE, SAM PHILLIPS, b. Blytheville, Ark., Oct. 30, 1920; LL.B. with 1st honors, U. Ga., 1944. Admitted to Ga. bar, 1944; mem. firm Carter, Carter & McKenzie, Atlanta, 1944-49, McKenzie, Kaler & Shulman, Atlanta, 1949-56; individual practice law, Atlanta, 1956-62; judge Ga. Superior Ct., Atlanta Jud. Circuit, 1962—; lectr. Atlanta Law Sch., 1944-64. Pres. Atlanta Tb Assn., 1956-58, dir., 1963-64; pres. Cath. Social Services, 1956-59; Ga. mem. Council for Christian Unity, 1963; pres. bd. dirs. Holy Family Hosp., 1964-66. Mem. Am., Ga., Atlanta bar assns., Nat. Conf. State Trial Judges (exec. com., vice chmn. 1969-70), Am. Law Inst., Phi Delta Theta (internat. pres. 1962-64). Named Atlanta Young Man of Year Jr. C. of C. of Atlanta, 1948; co-author: State Trial Judge's Book, 2d edit., 1969. Home: 3370 E Wood Valley Rd NW Atlanta GA 30327 Office: 816 Fulton County Courthouse Atlanta GA 30303 Tel (404) 572-2404

MC KENZIE, WILLIAM HERBERT, b. Vienna, Ill., Dec. 2, 1938; B.A., Blackburn Coll., 1960; J.D., Calif. Western Sch. Law, San Diego, 1967. Admitted to Calif. bar, 1967; asst. counsel Regents U. Calif., Berkeley, 1968-71; asst. county counsel El Dorado County, Placerville, Calif., 1971-73; partner firm Donley & McKenzie, San Luis Obispo, 1973—. Treas. San Luis Obispo County Legal Aid, 1975—. Mem. Calif., San Luis Obispo County bar assns. Contbr. articles to profl. jours. Office: 1270 Peach St San Luis Obispo CA 93401 Tel (805) 544-7540

MC KEOWN, CHARLES JOSEPH, b. Joliet, Ill., Oct. 9, 1908; J.D., U. Ill., 1931. Admitted to Ill. bar, 1931, U.S. Supreme Ct. bar, 1941; partner firm McKeown Fitzgerald Zollner Buck & Sangmeister & Hutchison, and predecessors, Joliet, Ill., 1936—; asst. state's atty. Will County, Ill., 1933-36; asst. city atty. Joliet, Ill., 1937-39, city atty., 1939-43; legal counsel Joliet Park Dist., 1952-73. Pres., Rainbow council Boy Scouts Am., 1952-53, Joliet YMCA, 1959; sec. Silver Cross Hosp., 1954—. Mem. Am., Ill., Will County (past pres.) bar assns. Home: 1314 Sherwood Pl Joliet IL 60435 Office: 2455 Glenwood Ave Joliet IL 60435 Tel (815) 729-4800

MC KERALL, SAMUEL GRAHAM, b. Birmingham, Ala., Aug. 3, 1939; B.A., U. Ala., 1961, J.D., 1971. Admitted to Ala. bar, 1971, U.S. Supreme Ct. bar, 1975; asso. firm Johnston & Shores, Birmingham, 1971-75; partner firm Shores & McKerall, Foley, Ala., 1975—; mem. com. on Ala. code revision Ala. State Bar, 1975. Mem. Am. Bar Assn. Home: 310 W Shriver Ave Summerdale AL 36535 Office: PO Box 788 Ala Hwy 59 S Foley AL 36535 Tel (205) 943-1571

MC KIE, EDWARD FOSS, b. Albany, N.Y., Oct. 29, 1924; B.E.E., Rensselaer Poly. Inst., 1948; LL.B., Georgetown U., 1952. Admitted to D.C. bar, 1952, U.S. Supreme Ct. bar, 1958; asso. firm Pennie Edwards Morton Barrows & Taylor, Washington, 1949-52, Stone Boyden and Mack, Washington, 1952-56, Burns Doane Benedict & Irons, Washington, 1956-60; mem. firm Schuyler Birch Swindler McKie and Beckett, Washington, 1960—; adj. prof. Georgetown Law Sch., 1963-67; adv. com. U.S. Patent and Trademark Office, 1976—, U.S. State Dept., 1968-76. Mem. Am. Patent Law Assn. (pres. 1975-76), Am. Bar Assn. (chmn. sect. patent, trademark and copyright law 1967-68). Contbr. articles to legal jours. Office: 1000 Connecticut Ave Washington DC 20036 Tel (202) 296-5500

MC KIERNAN, JOHN SAMMON, b. Providence, Oct. 15, 1911; A.B. cum laude, Notre Dame U., 1934; LL.B., Boston U., 1937. Admitted to R.I. bar, 1937; asso. firm McKiernan, McElroy & Going, 1941; legal advisor Providence Civil Service Comm., also roving clk. Gen. Assembly, 1941-42; chmn. Providence Fair Rents Com., 1941; 1st asst. city solicitor City of Providence, 1942-43, 46-47; gov. State of R.I., 1950-51, lt. gov., 1947-56; asso. justice Superior Ct., Providence, 1956—. Mem. R.I. Bar Assn. Home: 75 Hilltop Dr PO of Warwick East Greenwich RI 02818 Office: Providence County Court House 250 Benefit St Providence RI 02903 Tel (401) 277-3250

MC KIM, WILLIAM JAMES, b. Ellwood City, Pa., Sept. 12, 1946; B.S., Duquesne U., 1968, J.D., 1971. Admitted to Pa. bar, 1971; clk. U.S. Ct. Appeals, 3d Circuit, Phila., 1972-74; atty., law dept. U.S. Steel Corp., Pitts., 1974—. Mem. Am., Pa., Fed. (treas. local chpt.), Allegheny County bar assns. Editor: Duquesne Law Rev. Home: 144 Oakville Dr Apt 1A Pittsburgh PA 15220 Office: 600 Grant St Pittsburgh PA 15230 Tel (412) 433-2939

MC KINLEY, WILLIAM, b. Freeport, N.Y., Oct. 8, 1903; B.A., Cornell U., 1925; J.D., Fordham U., 1927. Admitted to N.Y. bar, 1928, U.S. Supreme Ct. bar, 1956; individual practice law, White Plains, 1928—; mem. White Plains CSC, until 1942; acting city judge, White Plains, 1942-46, city judge, 1946-48, dep. corp. counsel, 1949-52, corp. counsel, 1953-68. Mem. Planning Bd., White Plains, 1950-68, Traffic Commn., 1953-68, Real Estate Com. and Charter Revision Com., City of White Plains, 1960-68; vol. fireman, White Plains, 1942—; v.p. Mamoroneck Ave. Sch. PTA, 1943; chmn. White Plains Heart Fund campaigns, 1957-67; capt. drives Community Chest, 1943-49; candidate for mayor, White Plains, 1957; pres. White Plains Young Mens Republican Club, 1937-38; pres. Gedney Farm Assn., 1972-73. Mem. Am., N.Y. State (chmn., mem. exec. com. mcpl. law sect.), Westchester County, White Plains bar assns., N.Y. State Assn. Corp. Counsels (past pres.), Nat. Inst. Mcpl. Law Officers (chmn. N.Y. State 1965), White Plains, St. Agnes hosp. assns., Westchester County Hist. Soc., Alpha Tau Omega, Delta Theta Phi. Home: 24 Ridgeway Circle White Plains NY 10605 Office: 1 N Broadway White Plains NY 10601 Tel (914) 949-7100

MC KINLEY, WILLIAM WEBSTER, b. Des Moines, Jan. 3, 1926; B.A., U. Iowa, 1949, J.D., 1950. Admitted to Iowa bar, 1950; atty. Employers Mutual Casualty Co. Des Moines, 1950-53; partner firm Redfern, McKinley, Olson & Mason, Cedar Falls, Iowa, 1953—; atty. City Cedar Falls, 1959-63, mayor, 1963-71. Trustee Cedar Falls Municipal Utilities, 1971-75. Mem. Am., Iowa, Black Hawk bar assns., Am., Iowa trial lawyers assns., League Iowa Municipalities (dir., 1965-68). Named Representative Citizen, Cedar Falls C. of C., 1976. Home: 1917 Tremont St Cedar Falls IA 50613 Office: 315 Clay St Cedar Falls IA 50613 Tel (319) 277-6830

MC KINNEY, E. MELVILLE, b. Oakland, Calif., Apr. 6, 1939; B.A., U. Pacific, 1960; LL.B., U. Calif., 1963. Admitted to Calif. State bar, 1964; asso. firm Cresswell, Davis & Lamborn, Oakland, 1964-68; asso. firm. Crosby, Heafey, Roach & May 1968-70, mem. firm, 1970—. Active Sierra Club; active Big Bros. of Am. Mem. Calif. Bar Assn., Nat. Assn. of R.R. Trial Lawyers. Home: 3139 Via Larga Alamo CA 95407 Office: 1939 Harrison St Oakland CA 94612 Tel (415) 834-4820

MCKINNEY, RUSSELL R., b. Visalia, Calif., Sept. 26, 1942; B.A., Stanford, 1964; J.D., U. Calif., San Francisco, 1967. Admitted to Calif. bar, 1968, U.S. Supreme Ct. bar, 1971; partner firm McKinney & Hendrix, Visalia, 1968—; mem. Calif. Atty. Gen.'s Vol. Adv. Council, 1972—. Mem. Calif., Tulare County bar assns., Am. Judicature Soc., Calif. (gov. 1971-75, 76—), Tulare County (chpt. pres. 1971-73) trial lawyers assns., Visalia C. of C. Asso. editor Calif. Trial Lawyers Assn. Jour., 1973. Office: 220 S Mooney Blvd Visalia CA 93277 Tel (209) 732-3471

MCKINNEY, SAMUEL ROBERT, b. Tiffin, Ohio, Oct. 24, 1912; A.B., Case-Western Res. U., 1934, LL.B., 1937. Admitted to Ohio bar, 1937; individual practice law, Tiffin, 1937—. Pres. Tiffin YM-YWCA. Mem. Seneca County (Ohio) (pres.), Ohio State bar assns. Home: 125 Winfield Dr Tiffin OH 44883 Office: 108 E Market St Tiffin OH 44883 Tel (419) 447-0812

MC KINNON, DAN A., III, b. Rochester, Minn., June 27, 1939; B.S., U. N.Mex., 1962; LL.B., U. Colo., 1965. Admitted to N.Mex. bar, 1966, U.S. Dist. Ct. bar for Dist. N.Mex., 1966, U.S. Ct. Appeals bar, 10th Circuit, 1966; asso. firm Marron & McKinnon and predecessors, Albuquerque, 1966-68, partner, 1968—; mem. Com. to Implement Standards of Criminal Justice in N.Mex., 1970-73; cooperating atty. N.Mex. Civil Liberties Union. Mem. Albuquerque Bd. Edn., 1971-77; mem. governing bd. Albuquerque Tech.-Vocat. Inst., 1971-77; mem. N.Mex. Gov's. Commn. on Pub. Broadcasting, 1975—. Mem. N.Mex. State, Albuquerque bar assns., Am. Judicature Soc. Home: 4401 Dietz Loop NW Albuquerque NM 87107 Office: 406 Sandia Savings Bldg 400 Gold Ave SW Albuquerque NM 87102 Tel (505) 247-4051

MCKINNON, KENNETH PERRY, b. Washington, Nov. 19, 1943; B.S., U. Md., 1965; J.D., Georgetown U., 1968. Admitted to D.C. bar, 1968, U.S. Supreme Ct. bar, 1972; atty. Office of Gen. Counsel, GAO, Washington, 1968-71; asso. firm Stroock & Stroock & Lavan, Washington, 1972—; mem. legal adv. council Complaince Rev. Commn., Democratic Nat. Com., 1975-76. Mem. Am., Fed. bar assns., Bar Assn. D.C. Home: 2445 California St NW Washington DC 20008 Office: 1150 17th St NW Washington DC 20036

MCKINSTRY, TAFT AVENT, b. Versailles, Ky., July 17, 1946; B.A., U. Ky., 1969, J.D., 1972. Admitted to Ky. bar, 1972; asso. firm Fowler, Rouse, Measle & Bell, Lexington, Ky., 1972—. Bd. dirs. Lexington-Fayette County Historic Commn., 1974—, Lexington Living Arts and Scis. Center, 1976—; mem. Lexington Jr. League, 1969—. Mem. Am., Ky., Fayette County (sec. 1973-74) bar assns. Editorial staff U. Ky. Coll. Law Jour., 1970-72. Office: 4-A Citizens Bank Sq Lexington KY 40507 Tel (606) 252-6731

MC KINZIE, JOHN FRANCIS, b. Pontiac, Ill., Nov. 30, 1925; B.S., U. Ill., 1950, J.D., 1951. Admitted to Ill. bar, 1951; asso. firm Thomas & Mulliken, Champaign, Ill., 1951-53; v.p. Union Ins. Group, Bloomington, Ill., 1953-76; exec. v.p. Meridian Mut. Ins. Co., Indpls., 1976—; sec., dir. Am. Union Life Ins. Co., 1959—; gen. counsel Mid-Am. Fin. Corp. and United Services Agy., Inc., 1968—; mem. law adv. bd. U. Ill., 1956-58. Mem. adv. bd. St. Joseph's Hosp., Bloomington, 1968-75, pres., 1970-71; mem. bd. edn. Diocese Peoria, Ill., 1970-76, pres., 1973-75. Mem. Ill., McLean County bar assns.,

Soc. CPCU. Home: 6425 N Kingswood Dr Indianapolis IN 46256 Office: 2955 N Meridian St Indianapolis IN 46208 Tel (317) 923-6371

MC KITRICK, MICHAEL JOSEPH, b. Marion, Ind., May 12, 1948; student So. Ill. U., 1968-69; B.A., No. Ill. U., 1970; J.D., U. Iowa, 1973. Admitted to Iowa, Mo. bars, 1973, Ill. bar, 1975; asso. firm Schramm & Morganstern, St. Louis, 1973-76; asso. firm Gallop Johnson Godiner Morganstern & Crebs, St. Louis, 1976—. Mem. Ill., Mo., St. Louis County, St. Louis (pub. edn. com.) bar assns. Editorial bd. Iowa Law Rev., 1972-73. Contbr. articles to legal jours. Home: 8907 Ulysses Ct Saint Louis MO 63123 Office: 7733 Forsyth Blvd Suite 1800 Saint Louis MO 63105 Tel (314) 862-1200

MC KONE, THOMAS CHRISTOPHER, b. Hartford, Conn., Oct. 31, 1917; A.B. cum laude, Coll. Holy Cross, 1940; LL.B., U. Conn., 1949. Admitted to Conn. bar, 1949; clk. Hartford Probate Ct., 1949-58; stockholder firm Reid & Riege, R.C., Hartford, 1958—. Fellow Internat. Soc. Barristers, Am. Coll. Probate Counsel; mem. Am., Conn. (exec. com. probate sect. 1966—), Hartford County (chmn. probate com. 1966—) bar assns. Author: (with others) Connecticut General Statues, annotated rev., 1958; Probate Courts and Procedure. Home: 5 Drury Ln W Hartford CT 06107 Office: 1 Constitution Plaza Hartford CT 06103 Tel (203) 278-1150

MC KOOL, MIKE, b. Mexico City, Dec. 30, 1918; B.A., George Washington U., 1942; LL.B., So. Methodist U., 1946. Admitted to Tex. bar, 1946, also U.S. Ct. Appeals bar, U.S. Supreme Ct. bar; partner firm McKool, McKool, McKool, Shoemaker & Vassallo and predecessors, Dallas, 1946—; mem. Tex. Senate, 1969-73. Mem. Am., Tex., Dallas bar assns., Am., Tex., Dallas trial lawyers assns. Home: 6900 Royal Ln Dallas TX 75230 Office: 5025 N Central Expressway Dallas TX 75205 Tel (214) 521-7500

MCKRAY, GEORGE ALEXANDER, b. San Francisco, Feb. 28, 1926; A.B., U. Calif., 1948, M.S., 1954, M.P.H., 1957; J.D., U. San Francisco, 1958; LL.M., N.Y. U., 1962. Admitted to Calif. bar, 1960, D.C. bar, 1961; adminstrv. asst. to chief, div. preventive med. services Calif. Dept. Pub. Health, 1957-58; adminstrv. asst., asst. to chief Bur. Food and Drug Inspections, 1958-59; research program analyst, research grant br. div. gen. med. sci. NIH, Bethesda, Md., 1960-61; individual practice law, San Francisco, 1963—. Mem. Am., San Francisco bar assns., Am., Calif. trial lawyers assns., San Francisco Lawyers Club, AAAS, Sigma Xi, Delta Omega. Office: Suite 850 235 Montgomery St San Francisco CA 94104 Tel (415) 781-4368

MC LAFFERTY, BERNARD JOSEPH, b. Phila., July 13, 1936; B.S., St. Joseph's Coll., 1958; LL.B., Villanova U., 1961. Admitted to Pa. bar, 1962, U.S. Supreme Ct. bar, 1976; asst. dist. atty. Montgomery County, Pa., 1964-65; asst. county solicitor Montgomery County, 1968—; mem. firm McLafferty & Edelmayer, P.C., Norristown, Pa., 1969—. Mem. Am., Pa., Montgomery bar assns., Montgomery County Estate Planning Council, Am. Assn. of Trial Lawyers, Pa., Montgomery trial lawyers assns. Home: 814 E Gravers Ln Wyndmoor PA 19118 Office: 325 Swede St Norristown PA 19401 Tel (215) 279-2440

MCLAIN, EUGENE MILTON, JR., b. Clay County, Ala., Feb. 14, 1931; B.S., Auburn U., 1953; postgrad. Cambridge U. (Eng.) 1953-54, economics U. Ala. 1959. Admitted to Ala. bar 1959; mem. firm Bell, Richardson, Cleary, McLain & Tucker, Huntsville, Ala., 1959-73; mem. Ho. of Reps. State of Ala. 1966-70, mem. State Senate, State of Ala., 1970-74; owner, mgr. Gene McLain Real Estate, Huntsville, 1976—. Mem. Huntsville, Madison County bar assns., Young Lawyers of Ala. (pres. 1962), Elks, Masons, Rotarians. Recipient 4 Outstanding Young Men of Ala. award, 1960. George Washington Honor medal, Freedoms Found., Valley Forge, 1955, Good Govt. award Huntsville, 1970. Home: 4101 Piedmont Dr SE Huntsville AL 35802 Office: 1402-B N Memorial Pkwy Huntsville AL 35801 Tel (205) 533-3413

MCLAIN, MAURICE CLAYTON, b. Hillsboro, Tex., Sept. 22, 1929; B.A. in Math., N. Tex. State U., 1950; J.D., So. Methodist U., 1962. Admitted to Tex. bar, 1962, U.S. Supreme Ct. bar, 1976; engring. contracts coordinator Vought Aerospace div. LTV Corp., Dallas, 1961-64; asso. firm Abney & Burleson, Dallas, 1964-66; counsel Fed. Nat. Mortgage Assn., Dallas, 1966-69; v.p., counsel USLIFE Real Estate Services Corp., Dallas, 1970—; mem. real property adv. commn. Tex. Bd. Legal Specialization, State Bar Tex. Mem. Am., Tex., Dallas, Fed. bar assns., Am. Judicature Soc., Real Estate Fin. Execs. Assn. (officer, dir.), Phi Delta Phi. Home: 3908 Royal Ln Dallas TX 75229 Office: 6500 Harry Hines Blvd Dallas TX 75235 Tel (214) 357-1861

MC LANE, DAVID GLENN, b. Dallas, Jan. 17, 1943; B.A., So. Methodist U., 1963, LL.B., 1966. Admitted to Tex. bar, 1966, U.S. Supreme Ct. bar, 1971; briefing atty. Supreme Ct. Tex., Austin, 1966-67; asso. firm Wynne & Jaffe, Dallas, 1967-73, partner, 1973—; bd. dirs. Southwest Pension Conf., 1975—, v.p., pres. elect, 1977-78. Mem. State Bar of Tex., Am. Bar Assn., So. Methodist U. Alumni Assn. (exec. com. 1972—). Editor: Southwestern Law Jour., 1965-66, Incorporation Planning in Texas, 1977. Home: 3712 Miramar Ave Dallas TX 75205 Office: 1000 LTV Tower Dallas TX 75201 Tel (214) 748-7211

MC LANE, FREDERICK BERG, b. Long Beach, Calif., July 24, 1941; B.A., Stanford U., 1963; LL.B., Yale U., 1966. Admitted to Calif. bar, 1967; asso. prof. law U. Miss., Oxford, 1966-68; asso. firm O'Melveny & Myers, Los Angeles, 1968-74, partner, 1975—. Bd. dirs. N. Miss. Rural Legal Services, 1966-68, chmn., 1966-68; bd. dirs. Legal Aid Found. Los Angeles, 1974—. Mem. Am., Los Angeles County bar assns. Bd. editors Yale Law Jour., 1964-66. Home: 3553 Willow Crest Ave Studio City CA 91604 Office: 611 W 6th St Los Angeles CA 90017 Tel (213) 620-1120

MCLANE, H. ARTHUR, b. Valdosta, Ga., Apr. 2, 1939; B.A., Emory U., 1961; J.D., U. Ga., 1964. Admitted to Ga. bar, 1963, U.S. Supreme Ct. bar, 1972; practiced in Valdosta, 1963—; sr. partner firm McLane, Dover & Sherwood, Valdosta; judge Ga. State Ct. of Lowndes County, 1974—; atty. Lowndes County, 1965-72, Lowndes County Bd. Health, 1966-72, Echols County (Ga.) Bd. Edn., 1967—. Mem. Valdosta Area Vo-Tech Advisory Bd., 1968—; pres. bd. dirs. Valdosta Boy's Club, 1971-72; trustee Park Ave. United Methodist Ch., Valdosta, 1972—. Mem. State Bar Ga., So. Circuit, Valdosta (pres. 1974) bar assns., Am. Judicature Soc., Gridiron, Blue Key, Phi Delta Phi, Phi Kappa Phi. Contbr. articles to Ga. Bar Jour. Home: 2306 Pinecliff Dr Valdosta GA 31601 Office: 504 N Patterson St PO Box 505 Valdosta GA 31601 Tel (912) 244-6721

MC LANE, JOHN PATRICK, b. Auburn, N.Y., Aug. 7, 1943; A.B. magna cum laude, Niagara U., 1965; J.D., cum laude, Columbia, 1968. Admitted to N.Y. bar, 1968, U.S. Supreme Ct. bar, 1973; confidential law clk. to Hon. Edmund Port, U.S. Dist. Judge for No. Dist. N.Y., 1968-70; partner firm Boyle, Lipski & McLane, Auburn, 1970—; magistrate U.S. Dist. for No. Dist. N.Y., 1971—. Bd. dirs., treas. Auburn YMCA, 1973—. Mem. Cayuga County (N.Y.), N.Y. State, Am. bar assns. Home: 8 Emma St Auburn NY 13021 Office: 302 Nat Bank Bldg Auburn NY 13021 Tel (315) 253-0326

MC LANE, JOHN ROY, JR., b. Manchester, N.H., Feb. 19, 1916; LL.B., Dartmouth Coll., 1938; Harvard U., 1941. Admitted to N.H. bar, 1941; partner firm McLane, Graf, Greene, Raulerson & Middleton, Manchester, 1945—; dir. First Fin. Group N.H., Inc., Manchester Gas Co. Trustee, clk. St. Paul's Sch., Concord, N.H., 1952—; trustee N.H. State Hosp., 1949-62; bd. dirs. Child and Family Services N.H., 1946-71, pres., 1963-71; trustee, sec. Norwin S. and Elizabeth N. Bean Found., 1967—; bd. dirs. Council Founds., 1968-74, chmn., 1970-72; pres. N.H. Performing Arts Center, 1974—. Mem. Am., N.H., Manchester bar assns. Office: 40 Stark St Box 326 Manchester NH 03105 Tel (603) 625-6464

MC LANE, MALCOLM, b. Manchester, N.H., Oct. 3, 1924; A.B., Dartmouth, 1948; B.A. in Jurisprudence, Oxford (Eng.) U., 1950; J.D., Harvard, 1952. Admitted to N.H. bar, 1952; asso. firm Orr & Reno, Concord, N.H., 1952-55, partner, 1955—; mem. Concord City Council, 1957-76, N.H. Exec. Council, 1977—; mayor City of Concord, 1970-76. Mem. N.H., Am. bar assns. Home: 5 Auburn St Concord NH 03301 Office: 95 N Main St Concord NH 03301 Tel (603) 224-2381

MC LAREN, JOHN WALLACE, b. N.Y.C., Sept. 5, 1915; B.E.E., Manhattan Coll., 1949; LL.B., Fordham U., 1953, LL.D., 1968; LL.M., N.Y. U., 1955. With trust dept. Guaranty Trust Co., N.Y.C., 1934-41; admitted to N.Y. bar, 1953, Conn. bar, 1955, Calif. bar, 1966; mem. legal staff firm Pennie, Edmonds, Morton, Barrows, & Taylor, N.Y.C., 1949-51; atty. Sperry Gyroscope Co., L.I., N.Y., 1951-54; corp. counsel Perkin-Elmer Corp., Norwalk, Conn., 1954-58; sec., gen. counsel Daystrom, Inc., Murray Hill, N.J., 1959-61, asst. v.p., 1961-62, v.p., gen. counsel, 1962-64; individual practice law, Hartford, Conn., 1964-66, San Diego, 1966—, LaJolla, Calif., 1967—; asst. v.p. Schlumberge SW Corp, 1961-62; v.p., sec., dir. Advance Adv. Service, Inc., Benton Harbor, Mich., 1959-64; sec. dir. Daystrom Ltd., Toronto, Ont., Can., 1959-64; sec. Daystrom Overseas, Ltd. Geneva, Switzerland, 1959-64; v.p. asst. treas. Daystrom Realty Corp., Murray Hill, N.J., 1959-64; sec. dir. Ford Engrng. Co., Inc. Los Angeles, 1959-64, Heath Co., Benton Harbor, 1959-64; asst. sec. dir. Daystrom Weston, Inc., Ponce, P.R., 1959-64; v.p., gen. counsel Weston Electronics, Inc., Newark, 1965, also dir. Mem. IEEE, Instrument Soc. Am., Am. Soc. Corp. Secs., Am. Bar Assn. Home: Fairway Rd La Jolla CA 92037 Office: 6969 Fairway Rd La Jolla CA 92037 also San Diego CA Tel (714) 454-2239

MCLARIO, JOHN J., b. Pontiac, Mich., Mar. 2, 1925; B.A., Bob Jones U., 1950; J.D., Marquette U., 1953; H.H.D., Maranatha Baptist Bible Coll., 1973. Admitted to Wis. bar, 1953, Fla. bar, 1971; practiced law, Menomonee Falls, Wis., 1953—; head legal dept. Continental Casualty Co., 1953-54; mem. firm McLario, Bernoski & Reid, 1957—; lectr. Bob Jones U., 1976. Chmn. campaigns ARC, March of Dimes, YMCA; chmn. Menomonee Falls Zoning Bd. Appeals; pres. Menomonee Falls Sch. Bd.; mem. Wis. State Coop. Ednl. Assn.; chmn. Menomonee Falls Ednl. Com., 1976-77; pres. Christian Vision; trustee Bob Jones U., recipient alumni citation, 1971, named alumni of year, 1973; trustee, mem. Christian Legal Def. and Ednl. Fund Maranatha Bapt. Bible Coll. Mem. Wis., Fla. bar assns., Am. Trial Lawyers Assn., Wis. Acad. Trial Lawyers, Christian Legal Soc., Am. Arbitration Assn. (arbitrator). Home: W142 N7919 Thorndell Dr Menomonee Falls WI 53051 Office: N88 W16783 Main St Menomonee Falls WI 53051 Tel (414) 251-4210

MC LARRY, GEORGE CHURCH, b. Memphis, Nov. 17, 1938; B.A., Stetson U., 1960, LL.B., 1963. Admitted to Fla. bar, 1963; since practiced in Orlando, Fla., asso. firm Giles, Hedrick and Robinson, 1963-65, partner firm Hoequist and McLarry, 1965—. Mem. Fla. Council of Internat. Devel. (div. Fla. Dept. Commerce); chmn. local sch. advisory com. Mem. Fla. Bar Assn. (internat. law com.), Am. Bar Assn. (internat. law sec.), Phi Delta Phi. Home: 4918 Gramont Ave Orlando FL 32809 Office: Suite 135 3319 Maguire Blvd Orlando FL 32803 Tel (305) 894-7911

MCLAUGHLIN, EDWARD FRANCIS, b. Skaneateles, N.Y., Mar. 12, 1909; A.B., Niagara U., 1933; LL.B., N.Y. Law Sch., 1939, J.D., 1968. Admitted to N.Y. bar, 1939, Ill. bar, 1945, U.S. Supreme Ct. bar, 1970; atty. legal dept. Royal-Liverpool Ins. Group, N.Y.C., 1939-42; atty. Chgo. VA, 1945-46, solicitor's office, Washington, 1946-47; supervising atty. AEC, Schenectady, 1947-48; mem. firms Hiscock, Cowie, Bruce, Lee & Mawhinney, Syracuse, N.Y., 1948-59, O'Shea, Griffin, Jones, & McLaughlin, Rome, N.Y., 1959-73; justice N.Y. Supreme Ct., 5th Jud. Dist., 1973—. Chmn. profl. com. United Fund, Rome, N.Y., 1968-70; mem. exec. bd. Iroquois council Boy Scouts Am., Rome. Mem. Am., N.Y. State (ho. of dels. 1972-74, chmn. sect. trial lawyers 1971-72), Oneida County (pres. 1971-72) bar assns. Home: 1756 N George St Rome NY 13440 Office: Supreme Ct Chambers Oneida County Courthouse Rome NY 13440 Tel (315) 336-0772

MCLAUGHLIN, HAROLD J., b. N.Y.C., June 22, 1905; B.S., N.Y. U., 1926, Indsl. Engr., 1927, J.D., 1928, S.J.D., 1930. Admitted to N.Y. State bar, 1930, U.S. Supreme Ct bar, 1939; mem. firm McLaughlin & Hannon, N.Y.C., 1930-39; justice Municipal Ct. City N.Y., 1939-62. pres. justice, 1959-62; judge Civil Ct. N.Y., 1962-66; justice Supreme Ct. State N.Y., 1966-76, ret., 1976; mem. firm McLaughlin, McLaughlin & Neimark, Bklyn., 1976—. Mem. Bklyn. Bar Assn. Home: 3623 Ave T Brooklyn NY 11234 Office: 32 Court St Brooklyn NY 11201 Tel (212) 858-8080

MC LAUGHLIN, JOSEPH MAILEY, b. Los Angeles, July 10, 1928; J.D., Loyola U., Los Angeles, 1955. Admitted to Calif. bar, 1955, U.S. Supreme Ct. bar, 1959; mem. firm McLaughlin and Irvin, Los Angeles, 1955—, San Francisco, 1969—; lectr. in labor relations Loyola U., Los Angeles, 1958-60. Mem. San Francisco, Long Beach (Calif.), Los Angeles County, Fed., Am., Inter-Am. bar assns., State Bar Calif., Am. Judicature Soc., Am. Soc. Internat. Law. Office: 800 W Sixth St Suite 300 Los Angeles CA 90017 Tel (213) 485-1351 also One California St Suite 1935 San Francisco CA 94111

MCLAUGHLIN, ROBERT FRANCIS, b. Mountain Home, Idaho, July 11, 1920; B.A., U. Idaho, 1948, LL.B., 1950, J.D., 1960. Admitted to Idaho bar, 1950, U.S. Dist. Ct. for Idaho bar, 1950, U.S. Supreme Ct. bar, 1957, U.S. 9th Circuit Ct. Appeals bar, 1970; individual practice law, Mountain Home, 1950—; pros. atty. Elmore County, 1950-60; city atty., Mountain Home, 1962-66; city atty., Glenns Ferry, Idaho, 1952-54, 59-67. Chmn. fund drive Boy Scouts Am., 1953; Democratic nominee U.S. Senate, 1960; mem. Kennedy-Johnson Natural Resources Com., 1960; chmn. Idaho Vets for Johnson-Humphrey, 1964. Mem. Idaho State Bar Assn., Assn. Trial Lawyers Am. (pres. Idaho chpt. 1968-70), U. Idaho Law Sch. Alumni Assn. (pres. 1961-66), Idaho Pros. Attys. Assn. (pres. 1959-60). Home: 1120 N 8th East St Mountain Home ID 83647 Office: 700 N 3rd East St Mountain Home ID 83647 Tel (208) 578-4438

MCLAUGHLIN, STEPHEN FRANK, b. St. Louis, Apr. 10, 1945; B.A. in Econs. with honors, U. Oreg., 1967, B.S. in Bus. Adminstrn., 1967; J.D., Duke, 1972; LL.M. in Fed. Taxation, Emory U., 1977. Admitted to Ga. bar, 1972; asso. firm Troutman, Sanders, Lockerman & Ashmore, Atlanta, 1972—. Mem. Am., Atlanta bar assns., State Bar Ga. (chmn. air rights legislation com. real property sect. 1974-75, chmn. supplying legal services com. young lawyers sect. 1975—), Order of Coif, Phi Beta Kappa, Phi Eta Sigma. Mem. editorial bd. Duke Law Jour., 1971-72. Office: 1400 Candler Bldg Atlanta GA 30303 Tel (404) 658-8000

MC LAUGHLIN, THOMAS E., b. Albany, N.Y., May 2, 1935; B.A., U. Detroit, 1962; J.D., U. Md., 1969. Admitted to Md. bar, 1969, Wash. bar, 1974, U.S. Supreme Ct. bar, 1974; dep. regional dir. HEW, Washington, 1961, Seattle, 1969-76; individual practice law, 1976—. Chmn. parent adv. com. Issaquah Sch. Bd. Mem. Md., Am., Wash. State bar assns., Am. Jurisprudence Assn. Home: 16138 S E 145th Pl Renton WA 98055 Office: 2010 Pacific Bldg 3rd & Columbia Seattle WA 98104 Tel (206) 682-5322

MCLAUGHLIN, THOMAS JOHN, b. N.Y.C., July 9, 1930; B.B.A., Manhattan Coll., 1954; M.B.A., U. Ariz., 1955; J.D., U. Chgo., 1960. Admitted to Ariz. bar, 1961; asst. atty. City of Phoenix, 1962-64; individual practice law, Phoenix, 1964—; instr. Phoenix Coll., 1965-68. Mem. Am. Trial Lawyers Assn., Maricopa County Bar Assn., Am. Arbitration Assn. Office: 810 Luhrs Tower 45 W Jefferson St Phoenix AZ 85003 Tel (602) 258-5726

MC LEAN, BRUCE CHARLES, b. Waterville, N.Y., May 11, 1924; A.B., Hamilton Coll., 1946; LL.B., Cornell U., 1951. Admitted to N.Y. State bar, 1951; mem. firm Kernan & Kernan, Utica, N.Y., 1951-55; dir. legal affairs, asst. sec. Mohawk Airlines, Inc., Utica, 1955-57, sec., dir. legal affairs, 1957-63, v.p. corporate affairs, sec., 1963-67, v.p., gen. counsel, sec., 1967-68, dir., sr. v.p., gen. counsel, dir. wholly-owned subs., 1968-72; counsel N.Y. State Power Authority, 1972—. Past pres. Family Service Assn. of Greater Utica, Inc.; pres. Home of the Good Shepherd; dir. Oneida County Indsl. Devel. Corp.; past chmn. bd. trustees Mohawk Valley Community Coll., now trustee emeritus; past pres., trustee, elder New Hartford Presbyterian Ch.; dir. Utica YMCA, Cosmopolitan Center, Nat. council Boy Scouts Am. for Greater Utica. Mem. Am., N.Y. State, Oneida County bar assns. Home: 66 Paris Rd New Hartford NY 13413 Office: 66 Paris Rd New Hartford NY 13413 Tel (315) 797-0238

MCLEAN, EDWARD PAUL, b. Anaconda, Mont., Apr. 12, 1946; B.S. in Bus. Adminstrn., U. Mont., 1969, J.D., 1973. Admitted to Mont. bar, 1973; dep. county atty. Missoula County (Mont.), Missoula, 1973-76, chief criminal dep., 1976—. Active United Givers, Missoula, Missoula County United Way, Boy Scouts Am.; day camp dir. Cub Scouts Am., 1977. Mem. Am., Mont., Western Mont. bar assns., Young Lawyers Assn. Home: 223 E Sussex St Missoula MT 59801 Office: 200 W Broadway Missoula MT 59801 Tel (406) 543-3111

MCLEAN, JOHN JOSEPH, JR., b. Pitts., Aug. 28, 1927; B.S., Mt. St. Mary's Coll., 1950; LL.B., Harvard, 1953. Admitted to Pa. bar, 1954; partner firm Spinelli and McLean, Pitts., 1954-66; judge Common Pleas Ct. Allegheny County, Pitts., 1966-76; partner firm Buchanan, Ingersoll, Rodewald, Kyle & Buerger, Pitts., 1976—; adj. prof. law Pitts., 1971-76; mem. Pa. Civil Procedural Rules Com., 1973—. Bd. prison insps. Allegheny County, 1966-76. Mem. Am., Pa., Allegheny County bar assns., Assn. Trial Lawyers Am. Home: 3883 Chester St Munhall PA 15120 Office: 600 Grant St Pittsburgh PA 15219 Tel (412) 562-8961

MCLELLAN, GERALD DAVID, b. Holyoke, Mass., Aug. 2, 1935; B.A., U. Mass., 1957; J.D., St. John's U., Queens, N.Y., 1960. Admitted to Mass. bar, 1960, N.Y. bar, 1960; asso. firm Bailey & Muller, N.Y.C., 1960-61, firm Resnic, Beauregard, Resnic, Holyoke, Mass., 1961-63, Davenport, Millane & McLellan, Holyoke, 1965-72; individual practice law, Holyoke, 1963-65; spl. judge Probate Ct., 1972-73, Worcester County (Mass.) Probate Ct., 1973—; lectr. Boston Coll. Law Sch., 1975-76; instr. New Eng. Law Sch. Bd. dirs. Holyoke Hosp., 1970-71; pres. Pioneer Valley Estate Planning Council, Hampshire and Franklin Counties. Mem. Mass., N.Y. State, Fed. bar assns. Recipient Bancroft Whitney award Bancrof Whitney Pub. Co., 1960; bd. editors Family Law Quar.; contbr. articles to legal publs. Home: 333 Shays St Amherst MA 01002 Office: 2 Main St Worcester MA 01608 Tel (617) 753-7349

MCLELLAND, D(AVID) MARSH, b. Iredell County, N.C., Feb. 16, 1921; A.B., U. N.C., Chapel Hill, 1942, J.D., 1948. Admitted to N.C. bar, 1948; practiced in Burlington, N.C., 1948-53; clk. Alamance County Superior Ct., 1953-68; ex-officio judge, Alamance County Probate Ct., 1953-68; judge Alamance County Juvenile Ct., 1953-68, N.C. Gen. Ct. of Justice, Dist. Ct. Div., 1968-72; resident judge Superior Ct. Div., 15th Jud. Dist., 1972—. Mem. Am., N.C. bar assns. Home: 2018 Nottingham Ln Burlington NC 27215 Office: PO Box 575 Graham NC 27253 Tel (919) 228-6491

MC LENDON, MELBURNE DEKALB, b. Atlanta, Apr. 21, 1921; LL.B., U. Ga., 1948. Admitted to Ga. bar, 1949; practice law, Atlanta. Troop leader Boy Scouts Am., Atlanta, 1962-72. Mem. Am., Ga., Atlanta bar assns., Am. Judicature Soc., World Peace Through Law, Ga. Defense Lawyers Assn. (mem. exec. com.), Internat. Assn. Ins. Counsel (mem. various coms. 1969—). Home: 785 Starlight Ln Atlanta GA 30342 Office: 1810 1st Nat Bank Tower Atlanta GA 30303 Tel (404) 658-9220

MC LEOD, CLARENCE E., b. Cleve., Feb. 14, 1920; A.B., Howard U., 1941; LL.D., Cleve. State Law Sch., 1949. Admitted to Ohio bar, 1950, U.S. Supreme Ct. bar, 1958; asst. atty. gen. Ohio, 1952-57; atty.-in-charge Cleve. Legal Aid Soc., 1967-72; chmn. Ohio Pardon and Parole Commn., 1957-59. Office: 1516 E 107th St Cleveland OH 44106 Tel (216) 229-6040

MCLEOD, DANIEL ROGERS, b. Sumter, S.C., Oct. 6, 1913; student Wofford Coll., 1931-32; LL.B., U. S.C., 1948. Admitted to S.C. bar, 1948; asst. atty. gen. S.C., 1950-58; atty. gen., 1958—. Mem. Am., S.C. bar assns. Home: 4511 Landgrave Rd Columbia SC 29206 Office: Wade Hampton Office Bldg Columbia SC 29201*

MCLEOD, LARRY VARNADOE, b. Ellaville, Ga., Nov. 11, 1932; A.B., U. Ga., 1959, J.D., 1954. Admitted to Ga. bar, 1955, U.S. Supreme Ct. bar, 1965; with Crawford & Co., Athens, Ga., 1954-56; individual practice law, Athens, 1956-63; mem. firm McLeod & Galis, Athens, 1963-65, Erwin, Epting, Gibson & McLeod, Athens, 1965—; judge Magistrates Ct. of Clarke County (Ga.), 1962-68; instr. Sch Bus., U. Ga., 1958-68, Sch. Law, 1959—; mem. faculty Ga. Banking Sch., 1965—; lectr. profl. courses. Vestryman, Emanuel Episcopal Ch., Athens. Fellow Am. Coll Probate Counsel; mem. Am., Western Circuit (past pres.), Athens bar assns., State Bar Ga. (chmn. fiduciary law sect. 1973-74, past chmn. uniform comml. laws com., banking law com., vice chmn. continuing legal edn. com., mem. adv. com. on revision state banking laws, mem. fiduciary law study com., uniform comml. code study com.), Am. (adv. com. Joint Commn. on Accreditation Hosps.), Ga. (charter mem., past pres.) socs. hosp. attys. Author monographs and articles in field. Home: 382 Woodward Way Athens GA 30601 Office: PO Box 1587 Athens GA 30603 Tel (404) 549-9400

MCLEOD, MURRAY ALLAN, b. Detroit, June 9, 1932; student Capital U., 1951-54, Seattle U., 1957-58; J.D., U. Wash., 1961. Admitted to Wash. bar, 1961; law clk. King County (Wash.) Superior Ct., Seattle, 1961-62; dep. pros. atty. King County, 1962-63; individual practice law, Kent, Wash., 1963-67; judge Aukeen Dist. Ct., King County, 1967—; lectr. Nat. Coll. State Judiciary, Reno, Am. Acad. Jud. Edn., Washington, Green River Coll., Auburn, Wash.; founder, project dir. Project Escape Alcoholism Ct. S. King County, 1971-75. Bd. dirs. Am. Cancer Soc., King County, 1968-74, Valley Cities (Wash.) Bd. Mental Health, 1968-70, Catherine Blake Home for the Retarded, Kent, 1974-75, Children's Home Soc. Wash., Seattle, 1974-76, Kent Valley Youth Services, 1968-71. Mem. Am., Wash., Seattle-King County, S. King County bar assns., Am. Judges Assn., Nat. Conf. Spl. Judges, Wash., King County magistrates assns. Editor criminal law sect. Wash. State Manual for Cts. of Ltd. Jurisdiction, 1972-74; guest columnist Valley Papers, King County. Office: 810 28th St NE Auburn WA 98002 Tel (206) UL2-5233

MC LEOD, WALTON JAMES, III, b. Walterboro, S.C., June 30, 1937; B.A., Yale, 1959; LL.B., U. S.C., 1964; postgrad. U. Minn. Sch. Pub. Health, summer 1972, Nat. Coll. State Judiciary, U. Nev., summer 1973. Admitted to S.C. bar, 1964, U.S. Supreme Ct. bar, 1974; law clk. to chief U.S. Circuit Judge Clement F. Haynsworth, Richmond, Va., 1964-65; asso. firm Pope & Schumpert, Newberry, S.C., 1965-67; asst. U.S. atty., Columbia, 1967-68; gen. counsel S.C. Pollution Control Authority, Columbia, 1968-70, S.C. Dept. Health and Environ. Control, Columbia, 1968—; judge Newberry County Magistrates Ct., Little Mountain, 1973—; adj. faculty mem. Golden Gate U., Shaw AFB, S.C., summer 1976; acting coroner Newberry County, 1975; lt. comdr. JAGC, USNR, 1970—. Chmn. Newberry County Prisoner Aid Project, 1965-66, March of Dimes, Newberry, 1966, Boy Scouts Camping and Activities Com., 1965-67, Columbia area Yale Alumni Com., 1972—, Central Midlands Com. on Historic Preservation, 1976—; exec. dir. Newberry Young Democrats, 1965-67; treas. S.C. Young Dems., 1967-68; campaign chmn. Newberry County Dem. Party, 1966, mem. exec. com., 1972-76, alt. state committeeman, 1974-76; pres. Newberry Jaycees, 1967; bd. dirs. S.C. Bd. Certification Environ. Systems Operators, Newberry County Planning Commn., S.C. Nuclear Adv. Council, Central Midlands Regional Planning Council, Newberry County Devel. Bd. Mem. Am., S.C., Richland County bar assns., S.C. Magistrates Assn. (pres. 1976—, Distinguished Jud. Achievement award 1975), Nat. Conf. Spl. Ct. Judges (chmn. rural cts. com. 1975-76), Judge Advs. Assn., Phi Delta Phi. Named Outstanding Jaycee of Newberry, 1967; author: Legal Perspectives of Environmental Health, 1973; Environmental Quality Law, 1975; contbr. articles to legal jours. Home: Reunion Dr Little Mountain SC 29075 Office: 2600 Bull St Columbia SC 29201 Tel (803) 758-5658

MCLOONE, JOHN HENRY, IV, b. Waseca, Minn., May 28, 1939; student St. John U., 1959-61, U. Minn., 1961-62; A.B., St. Thomas U., 1963; J.D., William Mitchell U., 1970. Admitted to Minn. bar, 1970; individual practice law, Waseca, 1970—. Mem. Minn. State, Am. bar assns., Minn., Am. trial lawyers assns. Home: Rural Route 4 Waseca MN 56093 Office: 111 N State St Waseca MN 56093 Tel (507) 835-3378

MC LURE, JOSEPH HAMIL, JR., b. Atlanta, June 22, 1932; B.A., U. Ala., 1953; LL.B., Emory U., 1955. Admitted to Ga. bar, 1955; judge adv. USAF, 1955-57; individual practice law, Atlanta, 1957-58; atty. NLRB, Atlanta, 1958-65; labor relations counsel The Coca-Cola Co., Atlanta. Mem. Am., Ga., Atlanta bar assns. Office: 310 North Ave NW Atlanta GA 30313 Tel (404) 897-3676

MC MAHAN, PARKER FRANK, JR., b. Chgo., June 20, 1938; B.A., Beloit Coll., 1960; J.D., Chgo. Kent Coll. Law, 1967. Admitted to Ill. bar, 1968; asso. firm Brown, Stine, Cook & Hanson, Chgo., 1968-70, partner, 1971-72; individual practice law, Chgo., 1972—. Trustee Gail Borden Pub. Library Dist., 1974—; advisor Parents Without Partners, 1971—, Family Service Assn., Elgin, 1972-74. Mem. Ill., Am. bar assns., Comml. Law Am. Fellow Comml. Law Found. Home: 1010 Douglas Rd Route 1 Elgin IL 60120 Office: 208 S LaSalle St Chicago IL 60603 Tel (312) 641-0626

MC MAHON, JOHN JOSEPH, b. Cleve., Mar. 26, 1909; B.A., John Carroll U., 1934; LL.B., Western Res. U., 1937. Admitted to Ohio bar, 1937; asst. prosecutor City of Cleve., 1941-43; trial counsel Cleve. Transit System, 1943-44; partner firm McMahon & McMahon, Cleve., 1944-50; sr. partner McMahon & Friel, 1950-62; judge Common Pleas Ct., Cleve., 1962—. Active Cleve. Welfare Fedn., Citizens Council for Health and Welfare, Citizens League, Cleveland Heights Democratic Club. Fellow Cleve. Acad. Trial Attys.; mem. Am. Judicature Soc., Ohio (del.), Cuyahoga County (life mem. bd. trustees, pres. 1960), Greater Cleve. bar assns. Home: 34855 Dogwood Ln Solon OH 44139 Office: 1200 Ontario Justice Center Tower Cleveland OH 44113 Tel (216) 623-8758

MC MAHON, PAUL JOSEPH, b. Phila., Aug. 19, 1947; B.A., Swarthmore Coll., 1969; J.D., U. Pa., 1972. Admitted to Pa. bar, 1972; asso. firm David Berger, Phila., 1972-76; partner firm Barrack, Rodos & McMahon, Phila., 1976—; instr. Swarthmore Coll. Mem. Am., Phila., Pa. bar assns. Office: 2000 Market St Philadelphia PA 19103 Tel (215) 963-0600

MCMAHON, RAYMOND JOHN, b. Pawtucket, R.I., Dec. 23, 1921; A.B., Dartmouth, 1943; LL.B., Harvard, 1945. Admitted to Mass. bar, 1945, R.I. bar, 1946; trial counsel, atty. Nuremberg (Germany) War Crimes Trials, 1946-47; partner firm McMahon & McMahon, Providence, 1948—. Mem. Am. Coll. Probate Counsel, Am., R.I. bar assns. Office: 111 Westminster St Providence RI 02903 Tel (401) 331-2341

MC MAHON, RICHARD LEE, b. Wilmington, Del., Apr. 15, 1932; B.A., Wesleyan U., 1953; LL.B. cum laude, U. Pa., 1956. Admitted to Del. bar, 1957, D.C. bar, 1956; asso. firm Potter Anderson & Corroon, Wilmington, 1957-65, partner, 1965—. Mem. Am., Del. bar assns. Editor: U. Pa. Law Review, 1954-56. Office: 350 Delaware Trust Bldg Wilmington DE 19801 Tel (302) 658-6771

MCMAHON, ROY FRANKLIN, b. Cleve., July 27, 1909; B.S., Case Western Res. U., 1928-31; LL.B., Ohio No. U., 1934, J.D., 1967. Admitted to Ohio bar, 1935, U.S. Supreme Ct. bar, 1938; practiced in Cleve., 1935-57; judge Cuyahoga County (Ohio) Ct. Common Pleas, 1957—; mem. Ohio Ho. of Reps., 1947-48, 51-52, 53-54. Mem. Am., Ohio, Cuyahoga County bar assns., Bar Assn. Greater Cleve., Am. Judicature Soc., Nat. Trial Judges Assn., Ohio State Common Pleas Judges Assn. Recipient Outstanding Jud. Service award Ohio Supreme Ct., 1973, 74, 75, Distinguished Service award Delta Theta Phi, 1975. Home: 31739 Shaker Blvd Pepper Pike OH 44124 Office: Courtroom D (NE) 22d Floor Courts Tower Justice Center 1200 Ontario St Cleveland OH 44113 Tel (216) 623-8748

MC MAHON, THOMAS JOHN, b. Syracuse, N.Y., June 17, 1929; A.B. magna cum laude, Holy Cross Coll., 1951; J.D., Georgetown U., 1957. Admitted to D.C. bar, 1957, N.Y. bar, 1957, Conn. bar, 1960, Pa. bar, 1964, Mass. bar, 1971; with U.S. Naval Res., 1951—, capt. JAGC, 1976—; individual practice law, N.Y.C., 1957-59, Norwalk, Conn., 1960; atty. Am. Cyanamid Co., Stamford, Conn., 1961-63, Gulf Oil Corp., Pitts., 1964-69, Gillette Co., Boston, 1969-74; asso. prof. law Suffolk U., Boston, 1974—. Pres., Westport (Conn.) Young Republican Club, 1963. Mem. Mass. Bar Assn., Boston Patent Law Assn., Naval Res. Assn., Naval Res. Lawyers Assn., Res. Officers Assn. Home: PO Box 28 Walpole MA 02081 Office: Suffolk U Law Sch 41 Temple St Boston MA 02114 Tel (617) 723-4700 x 169

MCMAHON, WILLIAM ROBERT, b. Rochester, N.Y., Jan. 12, 1944; B.S., Tri-State U., 1967; J.D., U. Toledo, 1970. Admitted to Ohio bar, 1971, U.S. Supreme Ct. bar, 1975; individual practice law, Tiffin, Ohio, 1971—; asst. pros. atty. Seneca County (Ohio), 1971-72, spl. asst. pros. atty., 1973; legal counsel Tiffin Area Jaycees, 1971-72. Trustee Project Aide; bd. dirs. United Way Tiffin, Inc. 1973-76; budget chmn. Betty Jane Rehab. Center, 1972-74, trustee, 1974—; trustee Tiffin U.; adv. K.C., 1973—; trustee Tiffin Area Physicians Placement Fund, 1976—. Mem. Am., Ohio State, Seneca County, Toledo bar assns., Am., Ohio acads. trial lawyers, Am. Judicature Soc., Tiffin Area C. of C. (dir. 1972-76). Named Jaycee of Month, Tiffin Area Jaycees, 1972. Home: 162 Hampden Park Tiffin OH 44883 Office: 174 Jefferson St Tiffin OH 44883 Tel (419) 447-9073

MC MANUS, EDWARD JOSEPH, b. Keokuk, Iowa, Feb. 9, 1920; student St. Ambrose Coll., 1936-38; B.A., U. Iowa, 1940, J.D., 1942. Admitted to Iowa bar, 1942; practiced in Keokuk, 1946-62; chief judge U.S. Dist. Ct., No. Dist. Iowa, 1962—; city atty. City of Keokuk, 1946-55; mem. Iowa Senate, 1955-59; lt gov. State of Iowa, 1959-62. Mem. Iowa Devel. Commn., 1957-59; del. Democratic Nat. Conv., 1956-60. Mem. Order Coif. Office: POB 5005 Cedar Rapids IA 52407

MC MANUS, GERALD LYNDON, b. Mpls., July 13, 1933; B.A., Coll. St. Thomas, 1957; J.D., William Mitchell Coll., 1969. Admitted to Minn. bar, 1970, U.S. Supreme Ct. bar, 1973; legal editor West Pub. Co., St. Paul, 1970-71; individual practice law, Wabasha, Minn., 1971—. Cubmaster, Gamehaven council Boy Scouts Am., 1975-76; chmn. wagon train scroll Wabasha Bicentennial com., 1976. Mem. Wabasha C of C (sec.-treas. 1971-74), Am., Minn. State, Third Dist. (dir. 1976—) bar assns. Recipient Am. Jurisprudence certificate of award William Mitchell Coll. Law, 1966. Home: 423 W Lawrence Blvd Wabasha MN 55981 Office: PO Box 149 Wabasha MN 55981 Tel (612) 565-3838

MC MANUS, JOHN EDWARD, b. Washington, Aug. 6, 1944; B.S., U. So. Miss., 1966; LL.B., Memphis State U., 1972. Admitted to Tenn. bar, 1972; asso. firm Farris, Hancock, Gilman, Branan & Lanier, Memphis; partner firm McManus & Holloman, Memphis; asso. prof. Memphis State U. Lectr., advisor Parents Without Partners; advisor to civic drug control groups. Mem. Tenn., Memphis, Shelby County bar assns. Contbr. articles in field to legal jours. Home: 8370 Armscote St Memphis TN Office: 100 N Main St Suite 3021 Memphis TN 38103 Tel (901) 523-8865

MC MANUS, OWEN BERNARD, b. Pitts., Mar. 25, 1924; B.S., U. Pitts., 1946, LL.B., 1948, J.D., 1968. Admitted to Pa. bar, 1949, U.S. Supreme Ct. bar, 1970; asst. dist. atty. Allegheny County (Pa.), 1949-51; partner firm Brandt, McManus, Brandt & Malone, Pitts., 1951-76; gen. partner firm Baskin, Boreman, Wilner, Sachs, Gondelman & Craig, Pitts., 1976—; dep. atty. gen. Pa. Pub. Utilities Commn., 1955-56; solicitor Borough of Bethel Park (Pa.), 1953—, South Park Twp. (Pa.), 1953-65, Peters Twp. (Pa.), 1967-69. Vice pres. bd. dirs. Pace Sch., Pitts. Mem. Pa., Allegheny County bar assns., Am. Judicature Soc. Home: 940 Dorseyville Rd Pittsburgh PA 15238 Office: 10th floor Frick Bldg Pittsburgh PA 15219 Tel (412) 562-8688

MC MANUS, RICHARD GRISWOLD, JR., b. Rockville Centre, N.Y., May 12, 1943; B.B.A., U. Notre Dame, 1965; J.D., U. Denver, 1970. Admitted to Colo. bar, 1970, U.S. Supreme Ct. bar, 1974; asst. atty. gen. State of Colo., Denver, 1970—. Republican precinct committeeman, 1974—. Mem. Am., Colo., Denver bar assns., Colo. Correctional Assn. (dir. 1975-76). Home: 1640 Ivy St Denver CO 80220 Office: State Services Bldg 1525 Sherman St Denver CO 80203 Tel (303) 892-3611

MC MANUS, RICHARD PHILIP, b. Keokuk, Iowa, Oct. 20, 1929; B.A., St. Ambrose Coll., 1949; J.D., U. Mich., 1952; M.B.A. (with honors), Roosevelt U., 1965. Admitted to Iowa bar, 1952, Ill. bar, 1958; partner firm McManus & McManus, Keokuk, 1953-63; regional counsel Naval Facilities Engring. Command, Great Lakes, Ill., 1963-66; atty. Household Fin. Corp., Chgo., 1966-69, 71-75, asst. dir. planning and devel. dept., 1969-70, v.p., dir.-law, 1975—. Trustee Village of Lake Bluff (Ill.), 1973—; chmn. Democratic Com., Lee County, Iowa, 1961-63. Mem. Am., Fed., Ill., Chgo. bar assns., Nat. Consumer Fin. Assn. (chmn. law subcom. on consumer credit ins. 1975—), Conf. Personal Fin. Law, Consumer Credit Ins. Assn. Contbr. articles to legal jours. Home: 253 W Sheridan Pl Lake Bluff IL 60044 Office: 3200 Prudential Plaza Chicago IL 60601 Tel (312) 944-7174

MCMANUS, VERNON C., b. Eunice, La., Feb. 19, 1938; B.S., La. State U., 1964, J.D., 1967. Admitted to La. bar, 1968; individual practice law, Eunice, 1968-73; partner firm Tate & McManus, Eunice, 1973—. Mem. St. Landry Parish Sch. Bd. Mem. La. (ho. dels.), St. Landry Parish (v.p.) bar assns., Am., La. trial lawyers assns. Office: PO Box 666 Eunice LA 70535 Tel (318) 457-2256

MC MATH, SIDNEY SANDERS, b. Columbia County, Ark., June 14, 1912; B.A., LL.B., U. Ark., 1936. Admitted to bar; pros. atty. Ark. 18th Judicial Dist., after 1946; past gov. State of Ark.; sr. mem. firm McMath, Leatherman & Woods, Little Rock. Fellow Internat. Acad. Trial Lawyers (pres. elect), Internat. Soc. Barristers; mem. Am., Ark. bar assns. Home: 22 E Palisades Dr Little Rock AR 72207 Office: 711 W 3d St Little Rock AR 72201

MC MEANS, WALTER SHEPPARD, b. Birmingham, Ala., May 26, 1929; B.B.A., U. Houston, 1953, J.D., 1960. Admitted to Tex. bar, 1960, U.S. Supreme Ct. bar, 1975; individual practice law, Houston, 1960—; mem. Sugar Land (Tex.) City Council, 1974—. Mem. Phi Delta Phi. Office: 1400 Fannin Bank Bldg Houston TX 77030 Tel (713) 790-1350

MC MENAMIN, HUGH J., b. Scranton, Pa., Sept. 24, 1916; B.S., Yale, 1938, LL.D., 1941. Admitted to Pa. bar, 1947; U.S. Dist. Ct. Middle Dist. Pa. bar, 1947, U.S. Ct. Appeals for 3d Circuit bar, 1947; asso. firm Henkelman, McMenamin, Kreder & O'Connell, Scranton, Pa., 1942-52, partner, 1952—. Mem. Pa. State Senate, 1950-62. Mem. Am., Pa., County bar assns., Coll. Trial Lawyers, Def. Research Inst. Home: Bellefonte Apts Capri Bldg Lake Scranton Rd Scranton PA 18505 Office: 200 Northeastern Bank Bldg Scranton PA 18503 Tel (717) 346-7922

MC MICHAEL, ROBERT LEE, b. Neosho, Mo., Apr. 8, 1920; LL.B., U. Colo., 1949. Admitted to Colo. bar, 1950; individual practice law, Pueblo, Colo., 1950—; legal adviser Pueblo Army Depot U.S. Army, 1953-64. Mem. Colo. Bar Assn. Named Colo. Eagle of Year Fraternal Order of Eagles, 1972; recipient Spl. plaque Pueblo Optimist Club, 1974. Home: 1229 Suncrest Ln Pueblo CO 81005 Office: 616 W Abriendo St Pueblo CO 81004 Tel (303) 543-3792

MCMILLAN, HENRY WILLIAM, b. Hope, Ark., Aug. 31, 1909; student Ouachita Bapt. Coll., 1930, Tex. U. Law Sch., 1931-34. Admitted to Ark. bar, 1934; mem. firm McMillan, Turner & McCorkle and predecessor, Arkadelphia, Ark., 1934—. Pres. Ouachita River Valley Assn., 1950-61; trustee Ark. Coll., 1941—, Ross Found., 1967—. Mem. Clark County, Ark., Am. bar assns. Recipient Outstanding Lawyer award Ark. Bar Found., 1970-71. Home: 210 5th St Arkadelphia AR 71923 Office: 929 Main St Arkadelphia AR 71923 Tel (501) 246-2468

MC MILLAN, JAMES BRYAN, b. Goldsboro, N.C., Dec. 19, 1916; A.A., Presbyn. Jr. Coll., Maxton, N.C., 1934; A.B., U. N.C., 1937; LL.B., Harvard, 1940, postgrad. in trial advocacy, 1975. Admitted to N.C. bar, 1941; mem. staff N.C. Atty. Gen., 1940-42; partner firm Helms, Mulliss, McMillan & Johnston, Charlotte, N.C., 1946-68; judge U.S. Dist. Ct., Western Dist. N.C., 1968—; judge pro tem Charlotte City Ct., 1947-51; mem. N.C. Cts. Commn., 1963-71; mem. faculty Nat. Inst. Trial Advocacy, Boulder, Colo., 1973—. Mem. permanent judicial commn. Presbyn. Ch. U.S., 1975—. Fellow Internat. Acad. Trial Lawyers; mem. Am., 26th Dist. (pres. 1957-58), N.C. (pres. 1960-61) bar assns., United World Federalists, St. Andrews Coll. Alumni Assn. (pres. 1965-66), Golden Fleece, Order of Coif, Omicron Delta Kappa. Recipient Algernon Sydney Sullivan award St. Andrews Presbyn. Coll., 1971. Home: 1930 Mecklenburg Ave Charlotte NC 28205 Office: US Dist Ct Charlotte NC 28201 Tel (704) 372-7365

MCMILLIAN, THEODORE, b. St. Louis, Jan. 28, 1919; B.S., Lincoln U., 1941; J.D., St. Louis U., 1949. Admitted to Mo. bar, 1949; partner firm Lynch & McMillian, St. Louis, 1949-52; asst. circuit atty., St. Louis, 1952-56; judge 2d Jud. Circuit, St. Louis, 1956-72; judge Mo. Ct. Appeals, St. Louis, 1972—; faculty Nat. Coll. Judiciary U. Nev., 1970—, Nat. Coll. Juvenile Justice U. Nev., 1970—; asso. prof. U. Mo.-St. Louis; lectr. law St. Louis U. Chmn. Human Devel. Corp., 1964—; Minority Economic Devel. Agency, 1972—; bd. mgrs. Herbert Hoover Boys Club, 1970; mem. exec. com Urban League; bd. dirs. Tower Village; trustee Blue Cross Hosp. Services, 1970—. Mem. Phi Beta Kappa, Alpha Sigma Nu. Recipient Alumni Merit award St. Louis U. Home: Office: Civil Cts Bldg 12th and Market Sts St Louis MO 63101 Tel (314) 453-4606

MC MINN, BENJAMIN CLARK, b. El Dorado, Ark., Dec. 30, 1938; B.A., Tulane U., 1960; student U. Madrid, 1960-61, Kansai U. Fgn. Studies, Osaka, Japan, 1968, So. Meth. U., 1962-64; J.D., U. Ark., 1968. Admitted to Ark. bar, 1968, U.S. Supreme Ct. bar, 1972; gen. counsel Ark. Pub. Service Commn., Little Rock, 1968-72; individual practice law, Little Rock, 1973—. Pres., Ark. Easter Seal Soc., 1970-72. Mem. Am., Ark., Pulaski County bar assns., Am. Judicature Soc., Fed. Power Bar Assn. Office: 1275 Tower Bldg Little Rock AR 72201 Tel (501) 372-5007

MC MONIES, WALTER WITTENBERG, JR., b. Portland, Oreg., May 11, 1947; B.A., Yale, 1969, J.D., 1972. Admitted to Calif. bar, 1973, Oreg. bar, 1974; asso. firm Pillsbury, Madison & Sutro, San Francisco, 1972-74; dep. regional counsel Region IX Fed. Energy Adminstrn., San Francisco, 1974-76; individual practice law, Portland, 1976—. Mem. Calif., Oreg. bar assns. Home and Office: 815 SW Vista Ave Portland OR 97205

MC MULLEN, NEIL CAMPBELL, b. Tampa, Fla., Aug. 30, 1913; student Emory U., 1933; A.B. and J.D., U. Fla., 1937. Admitted to Fla. bar, 1937; practiced in Tampa, 1937-60; judge Fla. 13th Jud. Circuit Ct., Tampa, 1960—, chief judge, 1971-73; mem. Fla. Ho. of Reps., 1942-50; asst. county prosecutor Hillsborough County (Fla.), 1944; asst. city atty. City of Tampa, 1956-60. Chmn. Twin Bays Dist council Boy Scouts Am. Mem. Am., Tampa, Hillsborough County (pres. 1951), Fla. (pres. sect. jr. bar 1942) bar assns., Nat. Conf. State Trial Judges, Am. Judicature Soc., Kappa Alpha. Recipient Silver Beaver award Boy Scouts Am. Office: Hillsborough County Courthouse Tampa FL 33602 Tel (813) 229-2365

MC MULLEN, WAYLON ELWOOD, b. Oklahoma City, June 26, 1946; B.A., Baylor U., 1970, J.D., 1971. Admitted to Tex. bar, 1971; partner firm McMullen & Assos., Dallas, 1971-73; partner firm McMullen & Porter, Dallas, 1973—. Mem. Am., Tex., Dallas bar assns., Am., Tex., Dallas trial lawyers assns. Office: 12700 Park Central Pl Suite 1603 Dallas TX 75251 Tel (214) 387-4844

MC MULLIN, JOSEPH BRYANT, b. Oskaloosa, Iowa, Aug. 8, 1923; B.A., U. Okla., 1950, LL.B., 1951, J.D., 1968. Admitted to Okla. bar, 1950, U.S. Supreme Ct. bar, 1959, Calif. bar, 1968; served to lt. col. JAGC, USAF, 1950-67, ret., 1967; individual practice law, Altadena, Calif., 1967—. Chmn., Altadena Town Council, 1975—; pres. Altadena Rotary, 1974-75. Mem. Okla., Am., Calif., Los Angeles County, Pasadena bar assns., Judge Advs. Assn., Lawyers Club Los Angeles, Ret. Officers Assn. (pres. local chpt. 1973), Mil. Order of World Wars (comdr. local chpt. 1971-72), Am. Legion (post comdr. 1970-71), Altadena C. of C. (named Altadena's Outstanding

Citizen 1974, dir. 1977—). Home: 2195 Crescent Dr Altadena CA 91001 Office: 2257 N Lake Ave Altadena CA 91001 Tel (213) 681-4408

MC MURCHIE, BOYD LEIPER, b. Ontario, Oreg., Sept. 7, 1937; B.A., U. S.D., 1961, LL.B., 1963; grad. Nat. Coll. State Judiciary U. Nev. Admitted to S.D. bar, 1963; mem. firm Brown & Lindley and predecessor, Chamberlain, S.D., 1963-70; U.S. commr. and magistrate, 1966-75; judge S.C. Circuit Ct., 4th Jud. Circuit, 1975—; state's atty. Brule County (S.D.), Lyman County (S.D.); city atty. City of Chamberlain. Mem. S.D. Bar, S.D. Judges Assn., S.D., Am. trial lawyers assns., Delta Theta Phi. Home: 208 Alcott St Chamberlain SD 57325 Office: Brule County Courthouse Chamberlain SD 57325 Tel (605) 734-6574

MCMURRAY, ROBERT L., b. Waynesboro, Pa., June 26, 1929; B.S. in Bus. Adminstrn., U. Mo., 1951; also postgrad. in Law; LL.B., Vanderbilt U., 1954; postgrad. in Taxation, N.Y.U., 1959-60. Admitted to Tenn. bar, 1954, U.S. Supreme Ct. bar, 1971; partner firm Bell, Painter, McMurray, Callaway, Brown & Mashburn, Cleveland, Tenn. Fellow Am. Coll. Probate Counsel; mem. Am., Tenn. (pres. 1977-78), Bradley County bar assns., Internat. Assn. Ins. Counsel, Assn. Ins. Attys., Order of Coif, Phi Delta Phi. Editorial bd. Vanderbilt Law Rev., 1954. Office: PO Box 1169 Merchants Bank Bldg Cleveland TN 37311 Tel (615) 476-8541*

MCMURTRY, ROY, Now atty. gen. Province of Ont. (Can.), Toronto. Office: 18 King St E Toronto ON M5C 1C5 Canada*

MC NAIR, ROBERT EVANDER, b. Cades, S.C., Dec. 14, 1923; A.B., U. S.C., 1947, LL.B., 1948. Admitted to S.C. bar, 1948; mem. S.C. House of Reps., 1951-62; lt. gov. State of S.C., 1962-65; gov., 1965-71; sr. partner firm McNair, Konduros, Corley, Singletary & Dibble, Columbia, S.C., 1971—; chmn. Nat. Conf. of Lt. Govs., 1965-66, Edn. Commn. of the States, 1968-69, So. Govs. Conf., 1968-69, Nat. Democratic Govs. Conf., 1968-69. Mem. arrangements com. Dem. Nat. Conv., 1976. Mem. S.C. Bar, Am., Richland County bar assns. Office: PO Box 11895 Columbia SC 29211 Tel (803) 799-9800

MC NALLEY, LEO ARTHUR, b. Michigan Valley, Kans., Nov. 12, 1899; A.B., U. Kans., 1923, LL.B., 1925. Admitted to Kans. bar, 1925, Fla. bar, 1926; individual practice law, Miami Beach, Fla., 1926-27, Minneapolis, Kans., 1927-61; judge 28th and 30th Jud. Dist., Salina, Kans., 1961-71; of counsel firm Clark, Mize & Linville, Salina, 1971—; atty. Ottawa County (Kans.), 1929-35; chmn. Kans. Jud. Commn., 1974. Mem. Kans. Dist. Judges Assn. (pres. 1967), Am. (ho. of dels. 1966-68), Fla., Kans. (pres. 1968-69), Northwest Kans., Salina bar assns. Home: 675 Jaran St Salina KS 67401 Office: 129 S 8th St PO Box 624 Salina KS 67401 Tel (913) 823-6325

MC NALLY, HARRY DONALD, b. Akron, Ohio, Jan. 6, 1944; B.S., Ohio State U., 1965; J.D., U. Akron, 1970. Admitted to Mich. bar, 1971, Ohio bar, 1972; accountant Terex div. Gen. Motors, Hudson, Ohio, 1965-70; with tax. dept. Gen. Motors. Corp., Detroit, 1970-72; tax. atty., Roadway Express, Inc., Akron, 1972-74, dir. tax dept., 1974—. Mem. Akron, Ohio State, Mich., Am. bar assns. Office: 1077 Gorge Blvd Akron OH 44309 Tel (216) 434-1641

MCNALLY, JAMES BENNETT MICHAEL, b. Jersey City, Apr. 5, 1896; A.B., St. John's U., Bklyn., 1917, LL.D., 1945; LL.B., Fordham U., 1920, LL.D., 1955; LL.D., Manhattan Coll., 1954, Assumption Coll., 1956. Admitted to N.Y. bar, 1920; practiced in N.Y.C.; U.S. atty. for So. Dist. N.Y., 1943-44; justice N.Y. Supreme Ct., 1945-56, chmn. bd. justices, 1953-59; asso. justice appellate div., 1956-73; counsel firm Seward & Kinsel, N.Y.C., 1973—; prof. law St. John's U., 1925-32. Home: 240 Central Park S New York City NY 10019 Office: 63 Wall St New York City NY 10005 Tel (212) 248-2800

MC NALLY, JAMES MICHAEL, b. Sioux City, Iowa, Oct. 23, 1934; J.D., U. S.D., 1961. Admitted to Iowa bar, 1961, Calif. bar, 1970; asst. U.S. atty., Iowa, Sioux City, 1962-64; mem. Iowa Senate, 1965-67; individual practice law, Ventura, Calif., 1967—. Mem. Calif. Attys. for Criminal Justice. Contbr. articles to S.D. Law Rev. Office: 5755 Valentine Rd Ventura CA 93003 Tel (805) 644-7136

MC NALLY, JOHN JOSEPH, b. N.Y.C., July 1, 1927; A.B., Coll. Holy Cross, Worcester, Mass., 1950; LL.B., Harvard, 1953. Admitted to N.Y. bar, 1953; asso. firm White & Case, N.Y.C., 1953-63, partner, 1964—; dir. Holly Sugar Corp., 1973—; panelist in field. Trustee, Caedmon Sch., N.Y.C., 1968—. Mem. Am., N.Y. State bar assns., Bar Assn. City N.Y., New York County Lawyers Assn. Home: 58 Avon Rd Bronxville NY 10708 Office: 14 Wall St New York City NY 10005 Tel (212) 732-1040

MCNALLY, RAYMOND FORREST, JR., b. Chillicothe, Mo., May 23, 1911; A.B., Georgetown U., 1932; J.D., Loyola U., Chgo., 1936. Admitted to Ill. bar, 1936, Mo. bar, 1946; asso. in practice with Joseph F. Elward, Chgo., 1937-41; individual practice law, St. Louis, 1946—; spl. asst. city counselor assigned Citizens Milk Investigation Com., St. Louis, 1947-48; atty. Met. St. Louis Sewer Dist. Investigation, 1963; spl. counsel St. Louis County Council, 1966. Mem. St. Louis Area Rent Adv. Bd., 1950-52, chmn., 1952-53; chmn. St. Louis County Air Pollution Appeal Bd., 1967-72; mem. St. Louis County Bd. Police Commrs., 1972-75. Mem. Am., Mo. (gov. 1956-58), St. Louis (v.p. 1955-56) bar assns. Home: 7330 Pershing Ave St Louis MO 63130 Office: 611 Olive St St Louis MO 63101 Tel (314) 621-1614

MCNAMAR, DAVID FRED, b. Terre Haute, Ind., Mar. 26, 1940; B.S., Purdue U., 1962; J.D., Ind. U., 1968. Admitted to Ind. bar, 1968, U.S. Supreme Ct. bar, 1974; asso. firm Steers, Sullivan, McNamar & Rogers, and predecessors, Indpls., 1968-70, partner, 1970—. Bd. dirs. Chapel Glen Club, Inc. (pres. 1973, chmn. bd. dirs. 1973); deacon, elder John Knox United Presbyterian Ch., Indpls., 1973-76. Mem. Am., Ind., Indpls. (bd. mgrs.) bar assns., Nat. Health Lawyers Assn. Home: 710 Fenster Ct Indianapolis IN 46234 Office: Steers Sullivan et al 45 N Pennsylvania St Suite 312 Indianapolis IN 46204 Tel (317) 636-3471

MC NAMARA, A.J., b. New Orleans, June 9, 1936; B.S. in Petroleum Engring., La. State U., 1959; J.D., Loyola U., New Orleans, 1968. With Eggelhof Engrs., Inc., New Orleans, 1962-63; claim rep. Aetna Life & Casualty Co., New Orleans, 1963-66; admitted to La. bar, 1968, U.S. Supreme Ct. bar, 1971; law clk. U.S. Dist. Ct. for Eastern La., 1966-68; mem. firm Mouton Roy Carmouche Hailey Bivens & McNamara, Metairie, La., 1972—; individual practice law, New Orleans, 1968-72; mem. La. Ho. of Reps., 1975—. Mem. New Orleans, La., Am. bar assns., Maritime Law Assn. U.S., Am. Trial Lawyers Assn., La. Def. Lawyers Assn. Recipient Law Sch. award Bancroft-Whitney Pub. Co., 1968. Home: 1224 Beverly Gardens Dr Metairie LA 70002 Office: 3301 N Causeway Blvd Suite 643 Metairie LA 70002 Tel (504) 834-9252

MC NAMARA, JOHN JOSEPH, JR., b. Bklyn., July 15, 1915; A.B., Fordham U., 1937, J.D., 1941. Admitted to N.Y. bar, 1941; confidential clk. Judge Bernard Ryan, N.Y. State Ct. Claims, Albany, 1946-57, chief law asst., 1957—; cons. N.Y. State Comm. Eminent Domain, Albany, 1973. Mem. Bklyn, N.Y. (exec. com., chmn. com. legis.) bar assns. Contbr. articles to St. John's Law Rev., N.Y. State Bar Assn. Real Property Sect. Newsletter. Home: 379 Quail St Albany NY 12208 Office: NY State Court of Claims Justice Bldg Empire State Plaza Albany NY 12223 Tel (518) 465-8881

MCNAMARA, PAUL, b. Boston, Feb. 14, 1941; B.A., Boston Coll., 1962, LL.B., 1965. Admitted to Mass. Bar Assn., 1965, Fed. bar, 1966; partner firm Csaplar & Bok, Boston, 1972—. Mem. Mass., Boston bar assns., Am. Land Title Assn. Office: One Winthrop Square Boston MA 02110 Tel (617) 357-4400

MC NAMARA, WILLIAM ALBINUS, b. Superior, Wis., Mar. 1, 1909; B.A., U. Wis., 1930, M.A., 1931, LL.B., 1934. Admitted to Wis. bar, 1934; accountant Frzer & Torbett, C.P.A.'s., Chgo., 1934-35; sec. bondholders; com. Chgo. Title & Trust Co., 1935-36; sec. Curt G. Joa, Inc., Sheboygan Falls, Wis., 1936-37, now dir.; partner firm Cavanaugh & McNamara, Madison, Wis., 1937-42, Rieser, Mathys, McNamara & Stafford, Madison, 1942-58; with Madison Gas & Electric Co., 1958—, fin. v.p., 1958-74, sr. v.p. fin. 1974—, also dir.; dir. 1st Fed. Savs. & Loan Assn. Mem. Dane County (Wis.), Am. bar assns., State Bar Wis. (c(chmn. taxation 1950-51), Am. Gas Assn., Wis. Utility Assn. (dir.), Greater Madison C. of C. (pres. 1962, dir. 1960-63). Home: 112 Roby Rd Madison WI 53705 Office: 100 N Fairchild St Madison WI 53703 Tel (608) 252-7013

MC NATT, ISAAC CLENN, b. Bladen County, N.C., Nov. 19, 1916; B.S. with high honors, Hampton Inst., 1937; J.D. magna cum laude, St. John's U., 1945. Admitted to N.Y. bar, 1946, N.J. bar, 1968; individual practice law, N.Y.C., 1946—, Teaneck, N.J., 1968—. Dep. mayor Twp. of Teaneck, 1970-74; chmn. Teaneck Bicentennial Com., 1974-76. Mem. Am., Bergen County, N.J., Garden State (past pres.) bar assns., Am. Arbitration Assn. Home: 125 Voorhees St Teaneck NJ 07666 Office: 1420 The Plaza Teaneck NJ 07666 also 848 Saint Nicholas Ave New York City NY 10031 Tel (201) 837-1818 or (212) 283-2400

MC NEEL, JASON NILES, b. Louisville, Miss., Mar. 12, 1947; A.B., Miss. State U., 1969; J.D., U. Miss., 1972. Admitted to Miss. bar, 1972; dist. atty. Fifth Circuit Ct. Dist. Miss., Louisville, 1976—. Mem. Am., Miss. bar assns., Miss. Prosecutors Assn. Home: 509 E College St Louisville MS 39339 Office: 405 Main St Louisville MS 39339 Tel (601) 773-2041

MC NEILL, WALTER GILES, b. Mt. Vernon, N.Y., Oct. 13, 1935; B.S., Tufts U., 1957; LL.B., N.Y. U., 1960. Admitted to N.Y. State bar 1960, U.S. Supreme Ct. bar 1968; Mem. firm Brown, Wood, Ivey, Mitchell & Petty, and predecessors, N.Y.C., 1964—. Mem. Am. Bar Assn., Assn. of the Bar of the City of N.Y. Office: One Liberty Plaza New York City NY 10006 Tel (212) 349-7500

MCNELIS, CHARLES ANTHONY, b. Jim Thorpe, Pa., Sept. 10, 1919; LL.B., Fordham U., 1950. Admitted to N.Y. bar, 1950, D.C. bar, 1966, U.S. Supreme Ct. bar, 1954; sr. trial atty., criminal sect., tax div. U.S. Dept. Justice, Washington, 1950-69; trial counsel firm Welch & Morgan, Washington, 1970—. Mem. Am., D.C. bar assns. Home: 10212 Farnham Dr Bethesda MD 20014 Office: 900 17th St Washington DC 20006 Tel (202) 296-5151

MC NETT, JOHN CAMERON, b. Ft. Wayne, Ind., July 17, 1944; B.S., Purdue U., 1967; J.D., George Washington U., 1970. Admitted to Ind. bar, 1970; asso. firm Woodard, Weikart, Emhardt & Naughton, Indpls., 1970-73, partner, 1974—. Mem. Indpls., 7th Fed. Circuit, Ind. State (vice chmn. patent, trademark and copyright sect.) bar assns., IEEE (chmn. profl. activities com. central Ind. sect. 1975—), Am. Chem. Soc., Indpls. Sci. and Engring. Found. Home: 6160 N Sherman Dr Indianapolis IN 46220 Office: One Indiana Sq Suite 2670 Indianapolis IN 46204 Tel (317) 634-3456

MC NEVIN, MICHAEL TUCKER, b. Chgo., Aug. 21, 1934; B.A., U. N.Mex., 1956; Litt. B., Oxford U., 1964; LL.B., Harvard, 1966. Admitted to N.Y. State bar, 1967; since practiced in N.Y.C., mem. staff New Yorker mag., 1966-70; mem. firm Thacher, Proffitt & Wood, 1972—. Contbr. articles to New Yorker Mag. Home: 444 E 82d New York City NY 10028 Office: 40 Wall St New York City NY 10005 Tel (212) 483-5804

MC NEW, ROBERT ALTON, b. Mt. Vernon, Ohio, July 31, 1938; B.S., La. State U., 1961; J.D., George Washington U., 1968. Admitted to Ohio bar, 1968; trial atty., antitrust div. Dept. Justice, Cleve., 1968-75, asst. chief antitrust div., N.Y.C., 1975—. Mem. Plainview (N.Y.)-Old Bethpage Central Sch. Dist. Bd. Edn., 1976—. Mem. Am. Bar Assn. Home: 19 Richard Ct Plainview NY 11803 Office: 26 Federal Plaza Suite 3630 New York City NY 10007 Tel (212) 264-0394

MC NICHOLAS, JAMES DONALD, b. Marenisco, Mich., Apr. 23, 1918; A.B., U. Mich., 1940, J.D., 1948. Admitted to Mich. bar, 1948, Tex. bar, 1949; asso. firm Keith, Mehaffy & Weber, 1960-68, McNicholas & Crawford, 1964-69, Benckenstein, McNicholas, Oxford, Radford & Johnson, Beaumont, Tex., 1969—; pres. Beaumont Savs. & Loan Assn., 1960-68, hon. chmn. bd., 1968—. Mayor City of Beaumont, 1968-70; former chmn. Beaumont Planning and Zoning Commn.; former dir. Family Services, YMCA, Trinity-Neches council Boy Scouts Am., Golden Triangle Criminal Justice Council, Schlesinger's Geriatric Center; chmn. Greater E. Tex. Health Systems Agy., Inc.; mem. bd. Jefferson County Coalition for Crime Prevention. Fellow Tex. Bar Found.; mem. Am., Mich., Tex., Jefferson County (pres. 1967-68) bar assns., Tex. Assn. Def. Counsel, Phi Delta Phi. Home: 108 W Caldwood Dr Beaumont TX 77707 Office: PO Drawer 150 Beaumont TX 77704 Tel (713) 833-9182

MC NICHOLAS, JOHN PATRICK, III, b. Los Angeles, Aug. 18, 1936; B.A., U. Calif., Los Angeles, 1958; ed. Loyola Law Sch., Los Angeles, 1958-62. Admitted to Calif. bar, 1962, U.S. Dist. Ct. Central Dist. Calif. bar, 1962, U.S. Supreme Ct. bar, 1976; partner firm Morgan, Wenzel & McNicholas, Los Angeles, 1969—. Diplomate Am. Bd. Trial Advocates. Mem. Assn. So. Calif. Defense Counsel, Am., Los Angeles County bar assns., Am. Jud. Soc., Phi Delta Phi. Office: 1545 Wilshire St Suite 800 Los Angeles CA 90017 Tel (213) 483-1961

MC NICHOLAS, MICHAEL JOSEPH, b. Bayonne, N.J., Dec. 12, 1923; B.S. in Biology, So. Meth. U., Dallas, 1949, LL.B., 1953. Admitted to Tex. bar, 1953; individual practice law, Dallas, 1964—. Mem. Tex., Dallas bar assns. Office: 812 Main Bank Bldg Dallas TX 75202 Tel (214) 741-3795

MC NICHOLS, JOHN FRANCIS, b. Chgo., Aug. 6, 1935; LL.B., DePaul U., 1961, J.D., 1973. Admitted to Ill. bar, 1961, Fla. bar; 1st asst. state's atty. McLean County (Ill.), Bloomington, 1965-68; dist. defender Ill. Defender Project, Springfield, 1970-74; project coordinator ct. aid victim/witness program Dade County (Fla.) Criminal Cts., Miami, 1976-77. Mem. Ill., McLean County (chmn. legal aid 1968-69) bar assns. Author: (with others) Handbook for Florida Marine Law Enforcement Officers, 1976; Legal Problems on the Continental Shelf of Florida, 1976; Florida Sea Grant, 1976. Home: 3301 N State Rd #7 Hollywood FL 33021 Office: 1351 NW 12th St Miami FL 33125 Tel (305) 547-7820

MC NICHOLS, JOHN JOSEPH, b. Chgo., Jan. 8, 1927; Ph.B. (Chgo. Tribune scholar), Loyola U., Chgo., 1949, J.D., 1953. Supr. workmen's compensation claims Zurich-Am. Ins. Co., Chgo., 1950-54; admitted to Ill. bar, 1953, U.S. Supreme Ct. bar, 1963; mem. firm Asher, Greenfield, Goodstein, Pavalon & Segall, Chgo., 1954—; mem. Ill. Ho. of Reps., 1965-66. Mem. Dem. Central Com. of Cook County, 1965-66; Dem. committeeman Proviso Twp. (Ill.), 1965-66. Mem. Am., Ill. State, Chgo. bar assns., Workmen's Compensation Lawyers Assn. (past pres.). Recipient Outstanding Freshman Legislator award Ind. Voters of Ill., 1965. Home: 722 Benton Ct Elmhurst IL 60126 Office: 228 N LaSalle St Chicago IL 60601 Tel (312) 263-1500

MCNICHOLS, RAY, b. Bonners Ferry, Idaho, June 16, 1914; LL.B., U. Idaho, 1950. Admitted to Idaho bar, 1950, U.S. Supreme Ct. bar; practice, Orofino, Idaho, 1950-64; U.S. dist judge Dist. Idaho, Boise, 1964—. Mem. Phi Delta Theta, Phi Alpha Delta. Home: 1923 S Roosevelt Boise ID 83701 Office: US Ct Bldg 550 W Fort St Boise ID 83724*

MC NICHOLS, STEPHEN LUCID ROBERT, JR., b. Denver, June 5, 1943; B.A., Pomona Coll., 1965; J.D., U. Calif., 1968. Admitted to Colo. bar, 1968, Calif. bar, 1969; dep. dist. atty. San Luis Obispo County (Calif.), 1969-72; asso. firm Varni, Fraser, Hartwell & Van Blois, Hayward, Calif., 1972-75, partner, 1976—; mem. com. adminstrn. justice Calif. State Bar, 1975—. Mem. Morro Bay (Calif.) Planning Commn., 1970—, chmn., 1972. Mem. Am., Calif. trial lawyers assns., Barristers' Club Alameda County (dir. 1974-75), Alameda County, So. Alameda County (dir., 1975—) bar assns. Recipient George Burgess prize Pomona Coll., 1965. Office: Suite 606 22300 Foothill Blvd Hayward CA 94543 Tel (415) 886-5000

MCNULTY, JOHN KENT, b. Buffalo, Oct. 13, 1934; A.B. with high honors, Swarthmore Coll., 1956; LL.B., Yale, 1959. Admitted to Ohio bar, 1961, U.S. Supreme Ct. bar, 1964; law clerk Mr. Justice Hugo L. Black, Asso. Justice U.S. Supreme Ct., Washington, 1959-60; vis. prof. U. Tex. Sch. Law, summer 1960; asso. firm Jones, Day, Cockley and Reavis, Cleve., 1960-64; acting asso. prof. law, prof. law U. Calif. Sch. Law, Berkeley, 1964—; counsel Baker & McKenzie, San Francisco, 1974-75. Mem. Am. Bar Assn. (taxation sec.), Am. Law Inst., Internat. Fiscal Assn., Order of the Coif, Phi Beta Kappa. Guggenheim fellow, 1977. Author: (with Kragen) Federal Income Taxation, 1974; Federal Income Taxation of Individuals, 1972; Federal Estate and Gift Taxation, 1973. Home: 439 Spruce St Berkeley CA 94708 Office: 389 Boalt Hall (Sch Law) U Calif Berkeley CA 94720 Tel (415) 642-1828

MCNULTY, PATRICK JAMES, b. L'Anse, Mich., May 18, 1922; B.S.Law, U. Minn., 1948, J.D., 1949. Admitted to Minn. bar, 1949; partner firm Bouschor & McNulty, Duluth, Minn., 1950-68; individual practice law, Duluth, 1968—; judge U.S. Bankruptcy Ct., Duluth, 1968—; magistrate U.S. Dist. Ct., Duluth, 1969—; lectr. Minn. Continuing Legal Edn. Program, 1973-76. Mem. Duluth Charter Commn., 1960-65, Duluth Bd. Housing Appeals, 1968-70. Mem. Minn. State Bar, Am., 6th Jud. (pres.) bar assns., Am., Minn. trial lawyers assns., U.S. Conf. Bankruptcy Judges, U.S. Conf. U.S. Magistrates. Home: 410 Aspen Ln Duluth MN 55804 Office: 412 US Courthouse Duluth MN 55802 also 400 Alworth Bldg Duluth MN 55802 Tel (218) 722-6692

MC NUTT, ROBERT DONALD, b. Colby, Kans., July 6, 1921; B.S. Commerce, U. Nebr., 1947, LL.B., 1949, J.D., 1949. Admitted to Nebr. bar, 1949; asso. firm Van Pelt, Marti and O'Gara, Lincoln, Nebr., 1949-54; trust officer 1st Trust Co., Lincoln, 1954-61; v.p., trust officer Santa Barbara Nat. Bank (Calif.), 1961-63; v.p. Met. Bank, Hollywood, Calif., 1963-65; asst. prof. law Calif. State U., Northridge, 1965-69, asso. prof., 1969-73, prof., 1973—; mem. Nebr. Senate, 1951-55. Mem. Los Angeles Bd. Pub. Utilities, 1965-74, pres., 1970-73. Mem. Nebr. State Bar Assn., Am. Bus. Law Assn. Recipient Distinguished Prof. award Calif. State U., Northridge, 1975. Home: 8934 Rathburn St Northridge CA 91325 Office: 18111 Nordhoff St Northridge CA 91330 Tel (213) 885-2460

MC PARTLIN, GEORGE G., b. International Falls, Minn., Oct. 20, 1909; LL.B., St. Paul Coll., 1936. Admitted to Minn. bar, 1940, U.S. Dist. Ct. bar, 1940; individual practice law, St. Paul, 1940-73; U.S. magistrate, St. Paul, part-time 1971-73, 73—. Mem. St. Paul Planning Bd., 1952-73, Zoning Bd., 1954-73; mem. Minn. Boxing Commn., 1970-75. Mem. Am., Minn., Ramsey County bar assns., Nat. Assn. Criminal Def. Attys. Home: 905 Lakeview Ave St Paul MN 55117 Office: 778 US Courthouse 316 N Robert St St Paul MN 55101 Tel (612) 725-7181

MCPHERON, ALAN BEAUMONT, b. McAlester, Okla., July 6, 1914; LL.B., Okla. U., 1937. Admitted to Okla. bar, 1937; practiced in Durant, Okla., 1937—; asst. county atty. Bryan County, Okla., 1939-42, county atty., 1942-43; judge Okla. Dist. Ct., 19th Dist., 1965-75; chmn. War Vets. Commn. of Okla., 1949-51; mem. bd. rev. Okla. Employment Security Commn., 1951-59. Mem. Okla., Am. bar assns. Home: 2010 W Live Oak St Durant OK 74701 Office: 116 N 3d St Durant OK 74701 Tel (405) 924-7300

MC PHERSON, BILLY JACK, b. Oneonta, Ala., Aug. 18, 1935; A.B., Lincoln Meml. U., Harrogate, Tenn., 1956; J.D., Cumberland Sch. Law, Birmingham, Ala., 1968. Claims rep. Security of New Haven, 1960-61, Statemans Group, Birmingham, 1961-65, St. Paul Ins. Co., Birmingham, 1965-69; admitted to Ala. bar, 1969; individual practice law, Oneonta, 1969—. Mem. Am. Bar Assn., Am. Judicature Soc., Ala. Criminal Def. Lawyers, Ala. Trial Lawyers Assn. Home: Route 2 Red Oak Rd Oneonta AL 35121 Office: 229 2d Ave E Oneonta AL 35121 Tel (205) 625-3462

MC PHERSON, DONALD PAXTON, JR., b. Chambersburg, Pa., Oct. 6, 1906; A.B., Princeton, 1928, LL.B., Harvard, 1931. Admitted to Pa. bar, 1934; practiced in Phila., 1934-35; partner firm McPherson and McPherson, Gettysburg, Pa., 1936-37; individual practice law, Gettysburg, 1937-44, 46—; mem. Pa. Senate, 1948-56, chmn. com. on constl. changes and fed. relations, 1951-53, chmn. judiciary gen. com., 1955; mem. ICC, 1956-63, chmn. div. 1, 1962, vice chmn. ICC, 1963. Trustee Gettysburg Presbyn. Ch., 1938-44, Landon Sch., Bethesda, Md., 1958-60, Wilson Coll., Chambersburg, 1953-63; sec. Adams County Mut. Fire Ins. Co., Gettysburg, 1937-50; pres. Evergreen Cemetery Assn., 1946-56, Gilliland Presbyn. Home, Gettysburg, 1951-66. Mem. Adams County (Pa.), Pa., Am. bar assns., Am. Judicature Soc. Office: 126 Baltimore St Gettysburg PA 17325 Tel (717) 334-3105

MC PHERSON, DONALD PAXTON, III, b. Balt., Aug. 9, 1941; A.B., Princeton, 1963; LL.B., Columbia, 1966. Admitted to Md. bar, 1966; with firm Piper & Marbury, Balt., 1966—. Mem. Am., Md. bar assns. Office: 2000 First Md Bldg 25 S Charles St Baltimore MD 21201 Tel (301) 539-2530

MCPHERSON, HARRY CUMMINGS, JR., b. Tyler, Tex., Aug. 22, 1929; B.A., U. of South, 1949; LL.B., U. Tex., 1956. Admitted to Tex. bar, 1956, D.C. bar, 1969; gen. counsel Senate Democratic Policy Com., Washington, 1963, dep. under-sec. Dept. Army, 1963-64; asst. sec. State, 1964-65; spl. counsel to Pres. U.S., 1965-69; partner firm Verner, Liipfort, Bernhard & McPherson, Washington, 1969—. Vice-chmn. J.F. Kennedy Center for Performing Arts, Washington, 1969-76, gen. counsel, 1977—; bd. dirs. Council on Fgn. Relations, 1973—. Author: A Political Education, 1972. Home: 30 West Irving St Chase Chase MD 20015 Office: 1660 L St NW Washington DC 20036 Tel (202) 452-7426

MC QUADE, HENRY FORD, b. Pocatello, Idaho, Oct. 11, 1915; B.A., U. Idaho, 1940, LL.B., 1943. Admitted to Idaho bar, 1946; pros. atty. Bannock County, Idaho, 1947-51, dist. judge, Boise, Idaho, 1951-56; chief justice Idaho Supreme Ct., Boise, 1964-65, 71-73, 75-76; dep. adminstr. policy devel. Law Enforcement Assistance Adminstrn., Dept. Justice, Washington, 1976; adminstrv. law judge U.S. Occupational Safety and Health Rev. Commn., 1976—; mem. Nat. Advisory Commn. on Criminal Justice Standards and Goals, Washington, 1971-73. Active ARC, Boise, 1969-75. Mem. Am., Idaho bar assns., Am. Judicial Soc., Phi Alpha Delta.

MCQUARY, RAY JACKSON, b. Austin, Tex., Jan. 23, 1940; B.S., U.S. Mil. Acad., 1963; J.D., U. Tex., Austin, 1972. Admitted to Tex. bar, 1972; staff counsel for inmates Tex. Dept. Corrections, Rosharon, 1972—. Home: Route 2 Box 376 Rosharon TX 77583 Office: Route 2 Box 59 Rosharon TX 77583 Tel (713) 595-3434

MC QUEEN, C. RICHARD, b. Columbus, Ind., Aug. 25, 1936; B.A., DePauw U., 1958; J.D., Duke U., 1961. Admitted to Ind. bar, 1961, Ga. bar, 1964; asso. firm Greene, Buckley, Derieux & Jones, Atlanta, 1963-68, partner, 1968—. Mem. Ind., Ga., Atlanta bar assns., Lawyers Club of Atlanta, Southeastern Bankruptcy Law Inst., Inc. (dir.). Home: 445 Pineland Rd NW Atlanta GA 30342 Office: Suite 1515 225 Peachtree St NE Atlanta GA 30303 Tel (404) 522-3541

MCQUILLAN, JAMES MICHAEL, b. Greeley, Nebr., Apr. 14, 1942; J.D., Creighton U., 1966. Admitted to Nebr. bar, 1966, U.S. Tax Ct. bar, 1973; partner firm McGinley, Lane, Mueller, Shanahan, McQuillan & Gale, Ogallala, Nebr., 1968—. Mem. Ogallala Airport Authority, 1968-70. Mem. Am., Nebr. State, Western Nebr., Keith County (pres. 1974-75) bar assns., Am. Judicature Soc. Home: 1231 E A St Ogallala NE 69153 Office: 401 N Spruce St Ogallala NE 69153

MC QUOID, RONALD RICHARD, b. Los Angeles, Mar. 5, 1933; LL.B., Loyola U., Los Angeles, 1965. Admitted to Calif. bar, 1966; asso. firm Murchison & Cumming, Los Angeles, 1966-71, partner, 1971—. Mem. underwater safety com. County of Los Angeles, 1973—. Mem. So. Calif. Def. Counsel, Wilshire Bar Assn. (dir.). Office: 680 Wilshire Pl Los Angeles CA 90075 Tel (213) 382-7321

MC RAE, DONALD JAMES, b. Kewanee, Ill., May 5, 1926; B.S., Northwestern U., 1948, J.D., 1951. Admitted to Ill. Supreme Ct. bar, 1951, U.S. Dist. Ct. bar, 1954; individual practice law, Kewanee, Ill., 1951—. Mem. Ill., Henry County bar assns. (past pres. county assn.), Am., Ill. trial lawyers assns. Office: 217 W 2d St Kewanee IL 61443 Tel (309) 853-4357

MCRAE, GORDON LARUE, b. Swanville, Minn., Oct. 18, 1914; B.S. in Law, U. Minn., 1947, LL.B., 1948. Admitted to Minn. bar, 1948, U.S. Ct. of Appeals bar, 1949; law clk. to U.S. Dist. Ct. Judge, Mpls., 1948-50; individual practice law, Bemidji, Minn., 1951-52, 54-62; asst. counsel Northwestern Mut. Life Ins. Co., Milw., 1952-54; judge Minn. Dist. Ct., Internat. Falls, 1964—; mem. Minn. Bd. Jud. Standards, 1974—; mem. com. on Minn. jury instructions guides. Mem. Am., Minn. bar assns., Am. Judicature Soc., Bemidji C. of C. (dir. 1958-62), Phi Delta Phi. Home: 119 Riverview Blvd International Falls MN 56649 Office: Dist Ct Chambers International Falls MN 56649 Tel (218) 283-2963

MCRAE, HAMILTON EUGENE, JR., b. Arkadelphia, Ark., Feb. 9, 1905; student U. Ark., 1922-24; LL.B., U. Tex., 1928. Admitted to Tex. bar, 1928; mem. firm Conner & McRae, Eastland, Tex., 1928-32; mem. firm McRae & McRae, Eastland, 1932-36; mem. firm Stubbeman, McRae & Sealy, Midland, Tex., 1936-57; mem. firm Stubbeman, McRae, Sealy, Laughlin & Browder and predecessor, Midland, 1957—. Trustee Austin Presbyn. Theol. Sem., Austin, 1958-65, Tex. Presbyn. Found., Dallas, 1958-65; bd. dirs. Mus. S.W., Midland Coll. Found., Permian Basin Petroleum Mus. Library and Hall Fame, Midland; mem. adv. com. United Way Midland. Mem. Am., Tex., Midland, Fed. Power bar assns. Home: 406 South L St Midland TX 79701 Office: PO Box 1540 Midland TX 79702 Tel (915) 682-1616

MCRAE, HAMILTON EUGENE, III, b. Midland, Tex., Oct. 29, 1937; B.E.E., U. Ariz., 1961, J.D., 1967. Admitted to Ariz. bar, 1967; asso. firm Jennings, Strouss & Salmon, Phoenix, 1967-71, partner, 1971—; instr. in field, 1974—. Mem. Am. Inst. Mining Engrs., U. Ariz. Alumni Assn., Am., Ariz., Maricopa County bar assns., Phi Gamma Delta (trustees ednl. found. 1974—). Contbr. articles in field to legal jours. Home: 8101 N 47th St Paradise Valley AZ 85253 Office: 111 W Monroe St Phoenix AZ 85003 Tel (602) 262-5873

MCRAE, ROBERT MALCOLM, b. Memphis, Dec. 31, 1921; B.A., Vanderbilt U., 1943; LL.B., U. Va., 1948. Admitted to Tenn. bar, 1948; Asso. firm Apperson, Crump, Duzane & McRae and predecessor, Memphis, 1948-54, partner, 1954-59; partner firm Larkey, Dudley, Blanchard, & McRae, Memphis, 1959-64; judge Shelby County Circuit Ct., div. 8, 1964-66, U.S. Dist. Ct., Western Dist. Tenn., 1966—; asst. city atty. City of Memphis, 1961-64. Pres. Memphis Little Theatre, 1959-60, Episcopal Churchmen of Tenn., 1965; sr. warden Ch. of Holy Communion, Memphis, 1958-59, 64-65. Mem. Am., Tenn. (chmn. com. discipline and ethics 1963-64), Memphis and Shelby County (hon., dir. 1958-61) bar assns., Dist. Judges Assn. of 6th Circuit (pres. 1975-76). Editorial bd. U. Va. Law Rev., 1947-48. Office: 167 N Main St Memphis TN 38103 Tel (901) 521-3200

MC REYNOLDS, LARRY STEVEN, b. Kirksville, Mo., Apr. 3, 1940; B.S., Kans. State U., 1963; J.D., U. Denver, 1970. Admitted to Colo. bar, 1971, Ga. bar, 1971; partner firm Stokes & Shapiro, Atlanta, 1974—; engr. McDonnell Douglas Corp., Huntington Beach, Calif., 1965-68, Brown Engring. Co., Inc., Huntsville, Ala., 1963-65. Mem. Am., Colo., Atlanta bar assns., State Bar Ga. Contbr. articles to engring. and legal jours. Home: 1563 Hidden Hills Pkwy Stone Mountain GA 30083 Office: Stokes & Shapiro 2300 First Nat Bank Tower Atlanta GA 30303 Tel (404) 658-9050

MC SWAIN, ANGUS STEWART, JR., b. Bryan, Tex., Nov. 26, 1923; B.S., Tex. A & M U., 1947; J.D., Baylor U., 1949; LL.M., U. Mich., 1951. Admitted to Tex. bar, 1949; asst. prof. law Baylor U., Waco, Tex., 1949-50, asso. prof., 1951-56, prof., 1956—, dean, 1965—. Fellow Am. Bar Found.; mem. Am., Tex. bar assns., Am. Arbitration Assn., Phi Alpha Delta, Tau Beta Pi. Author: (with Norvell) Cases and Material on Tex. Land Practice, 1951; (with Norvell and Simpkins) Cases and Materials on Texas Land Practice, 1968; Supplemental Cases and Materials on Property, 1965; (with Wendorf) Cases and Materials on Texas Trust and Probate Administration, 1965; contbr. articles to legal jours. Home: 4600 Kenny Ln Waco TX 76710 Office: Law Sch Baylor U Waco TX 76703 Tel (817) 755-1911

MCSWEEN, JAMES CARTY, JR., b. Newport, Tenn., Sept. 14, 1930; A.B., U. Chattanooga, 1952; LL.B., U. Tenn., 1953. Admitted to Tenn. bar, 1954; individual practice law, Newport, 1954—; served with JAGC, U.S. Army, 1954-57; U.S. magistrate, 1962—; spl. chancellor 13th Chancery Div., 1976—. Mem. Newport Bd. Edn., 1974—; mem. regional planning commn., 1969—; dir. Cocke County Meml. Hosp. Assn., 1974—. Mem. Am., Tenn. bar assns., Am. Judicature Soc. Home: 503 Cherokee Newport TN 37821 Office: PO Box 326 Newport TN 37821 Tel (615) 623-7271

MC SWINEY, FRANCIS GRAHAM, b. Concord, N.H., Oct. 7, 1942; A.B. in History, Stanford, 1966; J.D. cum laude, Boston U., 1969. Admitted to N.H. bar, 1969; law clk. U.S. Dist. Ct., Dist. N.H., 1969-70; asso. firm Hall Morse, Gallagher & Anderson, Concord, N.H., 1970-73; partner firm McSwiney, Jones & Semple, New London, N.H., 1973—; vis. asst. prof. bus. law Colby-Sawyer Coll., 1973—; spl. justice New London Dist. Ct., 1976—. Vol. fireman New London Fire Dept., 1971—; bd. dirs. New London Hosp. Assn., 1973—, v.p., 1974-77, pres., 1977—; chmn. exec. com. 1st Bapt. Ch. of New London, 1974. Mem. N.H. (chmn. com. new lawyers 1973), Am., Merrimack County (exec. com. 1976—) bar assns. Recipient book awards in medicolegal problems in trial practice and fed. taxation Bancroft-Whitney Co.; jr. editor Boston U. Law Rev., 1967-68, sr. editor, 1968-69. Office: PO Box 167 Main St New London NH 03257 Tel (603) 526-6955

MC TAVISH, GLENN ALEXANDER, b. Elgin, Ill., Aug. 1, 1917; B.S., U. Ill., 1939, LL.B., 1941. Admitted to Ill. bar, 1941; partner firm Walker & Atwood, Chgo., 1946-56; individual practice law, Chgo., 1956-61; partner firm Bernstein & Ganellen, Chgo., 1961-69; sr. atty. Trans Union Corp., Chgo., 1969-73, asst. gen. counsel, 1973—. Home: 115 N McLean Blvd Elgin IL 60120 Office: 90 Half Day Rd Lincolnshire IL 60015 Tel (312) 295-4313

MC TEER, CHARLES VICTOR, b. Balt., Sept. 25, 1948; B.A., Western Md. Coll., 1969; J.D., Rutgers U., 1972. Admitted to Md. bar, 1972, Miss. bar, 1973; staff atty. N. Miss. Rural Legal Services, Greenwood, 1972-73; partner firm McTeer, Walls Bailey and Buck, Greenville, Miss., 1974—; mem. bd. attys. Center for Constl. Rights, N.Y.C. Trustee Rust Coll., 1975—, New Hope 1st Baptist Ch., Greenville. Mem. Am., Fed., Miss. (sec. Washington County 1976) bar assns., Am. Judicature Soc., Nat. Conf. Black Lawyers, Am. Trial Lawyers Assn. Home: 817 S Washington Ave Greenville MS 38701 Office: 819 Main St Greenville MS 38701 Tel (601) 335-6001

MC TIGHE, PAUL FRANCIS, JR., b. Pitts., Aug. 19, 1948; B.A., U. Pitts., 1970, J.D., U. Tulsa, 1972. Admitted to Okla. bar, 1973; legal intern firm Gable, Gotwals, Rubin, Fox, Johnson & Baker, Tulsa, 1972-73; individual practice law, Tulsa, 1973—. Mem. Am., Tulsa County bar assns. Mem. staff Tulsa U. Law Jour., 1971-72. Home: 1050 E 61st St # 55 Tulsa OK 74136 Office: 424 Beacon Bldg Tulsa OK 74103 Tel (918) 582-8850

MC VAY, WILLIAM WALTER, b. Pitts., Jan. 25, 1933; A.B., Allegheny Coll., 1954; LL.B., U. Pitts., 1958. Admitted to Pa. bar, 1958, Fed. bar, 1958, U.S. Supreme Ct. bar, 1965; partner firm McArdle, Mc Laughlin and Mc Vay, Pitts. Mem. Am., Allegheny County (chmn. young lawyers sect. 1965), Pa. bar assns., Assn. Trial Lawyers Am., Pa. Trial Lawyers Assn., Acad. Trial Lawyers Allegheny County. Home: 230 Warwick Dr Pittsburgh PA 15219 Office: 618 Frick Bldg Pittsburgh PA 15219 Tel (412) 471-3250

MC VEY, HENRY HANNA, III, b. Richmond, Va., Aug. 12, 1935; B.S., B.A. magna cum laude, Hampden-Sydney Coll., 1957; LL.B., U. Va., 1960. Admitted to Va. bar, 1960, U.S. Supreme Ct. bar, 1970; mem. firm Battle, Neal, Harris, Minor & Williams, Richmond, 1960-66, (named changed to McGuire, Woods & Battle), Richmond, 1966—. Mem. Richmond, Va., Am. bar assns., Fedn. of Ins. Counsel, Phi Beta Kappa, Omicron Delta Kappa. Home: 1808 Hanover Ave Richmond VA 23220 Office: 1400 Ross Bldg 801 E Main St Richmond VA 23219 Tel (804) 644-4131

MC VEY, WALTER LEWIS, JR., b. Independence, Kan., Feb. 19, 1922; B.A., U. Kan., 1947, J.D., 1948; M.A., Ga. State U., 1976. Admitted to Kan. bar, 1948, U.S. Supreme Ct. bar, 1961, Ga. bar, 1965; partner firm McVey, McVey & McVey, Independence, Kan., 1948-55; individual practice law, Independence, 1955-60, Atlanta, 1965—; mem. Kan. Ho. of Reps., 1949-52; judge Independence City Ct., 1952-56; mem. Kan. Senate, 1957-60; mem. 87th Congress from 3d Dist. Kans. Mgmt. cons., Atlanta, 1964—; adj. prof. polit. sci. Ga. State U., 1968—, DeKalb Coll., 1968—. Mem. State Bar Ga., Former Mems. Congress, Inc., Ga. Polit. Sci. Assn. Author fed. aids manual for Ga. municipalities, 1966. Home: 712 E Paces Ferry Rd NE Atlanta GA 30305 Office: PO Box 18505 Atlanta GA 30326 Tel (404) 261-5816

MC WHINNIE, WILLIAM JAMES, b. San Pedro, Calif., July 17, 1920; B.A., U. So. Calif., 1943, LL.B., 1944, LL.M., 1944. Admitted to Calif. bar, 1944; individual practice law, San Pedro, 1944—. Bd. dirs. San Pedro Hosp., Boys' Club, YMCA. Mem. Am., Harbor bar assns. Office: 757 W 9A St San Pedro CA 90731 Tel (213) 833-1313

MC WHORTER, JOHN LEE, b. Dallas, Sept. 19, 1937; B.S., Okla. State U., 1959; J.D., Memphis State U., 1965. Admitted to Tenn. bar, 1965; partner firm Hoffman, Hughes, McWhorter & Wener, Memphis, 1965—. Mem. Am., Memphis, Shelby County bar assns., Am., Tenn. trial lawyers assns. Home: 5911 Brierhaven Ave Memphis TN 38138 Office: 100 N Main St Memphis TN 38103 Tel (901) 525-2496

MC WHORTER, ROBERT TWEEDY, JR., b. Sheffield, Ala., Sept. 28, 1943; B.S. in Banking, U. Ala., 1965; J.D., Cumberland Sch. Law, 1969. Admitted to Ala. bar, 1969; trust dept. First Nat. Bank of Decatur (Ala.), 1969-71; individual practice law, Decatur, 1971—; judge City of Decatur, 1971-73, Morgan County (Ala.) Ct., 1973—. Home: 2010 Stratford Rd Decatur AL 35601 Office: 1301 6th Ave SE Decatur AL 35601 Tel (205) 350-1466

MC WHORTER, WILLIAM HARRISON, JR., b. Athens, Ga., Jan. 3, 1945; B.S. in Bus. Adminstrn., U. Ga., 1967, J.D., 1970. Admitted to Ga. bar, 1970, La. bar, 1971; served with JAG, USAF, 1970-74; mem. firm Smith, Shepherd & Gary, Swainsboro, Ga., 1974-75; partner firm Shepherd, Gary & McWhorter, Swainsboro, 1976—. Chmn. Emanuel County Heart Fund, 1975; bd. United Fund, 1975-76. Mem. La., Ga., Emanuel County bar assns. Home: 105 Lakewood Dr Swainsboro GA 30401 Office: PO Box 99 Swainsboro GA 30401 Tel (912) 237-7551

MC WILLIAMS, HOWARD CLIFTON, b. Ebensburg, Pa., May 26, 1918; B.A., Pa. State U., 1940; LL.B., U. Pa., 1943; postgrad. Harvard, 1946. Admitted to Pa. bar, 1943; partner firm McWilliams, Margolis & Coppersmith, Johnstown, 1946-55; pres. judge Ct. Common Pleas, Ebensburg, 1955—; dir., sec. Johnstown (Pa.) Traction Co. Past pres. Johnstown Symphony Orch.; bd. dirs. Community Chest. Mem. Pa., Cambria County bar assns., Pa. Trial Judges Assn. (exec. com. 1970), Pa. Juvenile Ct. Judges Assn. Named Outstanding Sr., Pa. State U., 1940. Home: 510 Pennsylvania Ave Johnstown PA 15905 Office: Courthouse Ebensburg PA 15931 Tel (814) 472-7590

MC WILLIAMS, JOHN GLENN, b. Columbus, Ohio, Oct. 20, 1947; B.S., Ohio State U., 1969; J.D., Duke, 1972. Admitted to Calif. bar, 1972; tax mgr. Price Waterhouse and Co., San Francisco, 1972-76; asst. prof. law and accounting San Francisco State U., 1976—; speaker Am. Mgmt. Assn. Mem. Am., San Francisco bar assns., Am. Inst. C.P.A.'s, Calif. Soc. C.P.A.'s, Calif. Tax Reform Assn. Office: San Francisco State U 1600 Holloway St San Francisco CA 94132 Tel (415) 469-1270

MC WILLIAMS, STANLEY REED, b. Sulphur Springs, Tex., June 7, 1947; B.A., U. Tex., Arlington, 1969; J.D., Tex. Tech. U., 1972. Admitted to Tex. bar, 1972; clk. firm Nelson McClesky, Harriger & Brazill, Lubbock, Tex., 1970-72; asso. firm Abernathy & Orr, McKinney, Tex., 1972—. Officer, dir. McKinney Jaycees; bd. dirs. McKinney Boys Club; mem. planning and zoning com. City of McKinney; sec. adminstrv. bd. 1st United Methodist Ch. Mem. Am., Tex., North Tex. (pres.), Tex. Jr., Collin County bar assns. Named Key Man of Year McKinney Jaycees, 1975. Home: 313 Westpark St McKinney TX 75069 Office: 112 W Virginia St McKinney TX 75069 Tel (214) 542-2661

MEACHAM, MARGIE MILLHONE, b. Omaha, Feb. 4, 1930; LL.B., U. Wyo., 1952, J.D., 1954; postgrad. Northwestern U. Sch. Law, 1971, Am. Acad. Jud. Edn., 1972. Admitted to Wyo. bar, 1954; instr. U. Wyo. Coll. Law, 1953-55; asso. firm Jerry W. Housel, Cody, Wyo., 1955-56, 62-68; individual practice law, Cody, 1968-73, Rawlins, Wyo., 1973—; justice of the peace Park County, Wyo., 1955-56, 64-65, Carbon County, Wyo., 1975—; judge Cody Municipal Ct., 1963-73; Wyo. jud. rep. Law Enforcement Acad. Adv. Bd. Mem. Park County Mental Health Bd., 1970-73, Carbon County Mental Health Bd., 1973-74. Mem. Carbon County, Park County (pres. 1965-66) bar assns., Wyo. Bar, Am. Judicature Soc., N.Am. Judges Assn., Wyo. Minor Ct. Judges Assn. Home: 309 W Walnut St Rawlins WY 82301 Office: Courthouse Rawlins WY 82301 Tel (307) 324-2746

MEAD, JOHN TENNEY, b. Evanston, Ill., July 6, 1928; B.A., Princeton, 1951; J.D., U. Chgo., 1955. Admitted to Ill. bar, 1956; spl. asst. atty. gen. State of Ill., Chgo., 1966—; partner firm Notz, Craven, Mead, Maloney & Price, Chgo., 1967—. Pres., Lincoln Park Conservation Assn., Chgo., 1969-70, Barrington (Ill.) Countryside Assn., 1975—. Mem. Chgo., McHenry County, Ill. bar assns. Office: 1911 100 W Monroe St Chicago IL 60603 Tel (312) CE6-1100

MEAD, PENFIELD COMSTOCK, b. New Canaan, Conn., Mar. 26, 1920; grad. Yale Law Sch., 1948. Admitted to Conn. bar, 1948; partner firm Mead & Bromley, and predecessors, Stamford, Conn., 1948—; prosecutor New Canaan Town Ct., 1953-60; judge of probate Dist. of New Canaan, 1974—; trustee New Canaan Savs. Bank. Bd. dirs. New Canaan Nature Center, Family and Children Services of Stamford, Salvation Army, Stamford, Camp Mohawk, Cornwall, Conn. Mem. Am., Conn., New Canaan, Stamford bar assns., Am. Trial Lawyers Assn. Home: 284 Park St New Canaan CT 06840 Office: 41 Bank St Stamford CT 06901 Tel (203) 325-4477

MEAD, WAYLAND MCCON, b. Roxbury, N.Y., Nov. 25, 1931; B.S., Cornell U., 1953, LL.B., 1958, J.D., 1970. Admitted to N.Y. bar, 1958; asso. firm Sage, Gray, Todd & Sims, N.Y.C., 1958-59, Lee, McCarthy & DeRosa, N.Y.C., 1970-75; atty. Mut. Ins. Rating Bur., N.Y.C., 1959-62, Mut. Advisory Assn., N.Y.C., 1959-62, The Continental Ins. Cos., N.Y.C., 1962-65, Am. Home Assurance Co., N.Y.C., 1965-69; v.p., gen. counsel Am. Internat. Group, Inc., N.Y.C., 1975—. Mem. Am. Bar Assn. Home: 22 Lucille Ct Massapequa NY 11758 Office: 102 Maiden Ln New York City NY 10005 Tel (212) 791-7453

MEADE, RICHARD CRAIG, b. Phila., Apr. 20, 1939; B.A., Cornell U., 1960; J.D., Columbia U., 1964; student Faculte de Droit, U. Paris, 1962-63, Institut d'Etudes, Poliques de Paris, 1968. Admitted to N.Y. State bar, 1965, D.C. bar, 1968; asso. firm Barnes, Richardson & Colburn, N.Y.C., 1964-66; partner firm Freeman, Meade, Wasserman & Schneider and Predecessors, N.Y.C., 1966—, partner firm Meade, Wasseman & Freeman, and Predecessors, Paris, France, 1971—. Dir. Parents Assn. Ecole Active Bilanque, Paris, 1977; pres. Internat. Wine and Food Soc. (Paris), 1976—. Mem. N.Y. County Lawyers Assn., Am. Bar Assn., Am. Fgn. Law Assn., Internat. Bar Assn., Am. Soc. Internat. Law. Home: 20 rue Alphonse de Neuville Paris France 75017 Office: 53 Boulevard de Courcelles Paris 75008 France Tel 267 53 97 766 29 31

MEADOR, DANIEL JOHN, b. Selma, Ala., Dec. 7, 1926; B.S., Auburn U., 1949; J.D., U. Ala., 1951; LL.M., Harvard, 1954. Admitted to Ala. bar, 1951, Va. bar, 1961, U.S. Supreme Ct. bar, 1955; law clk. Justice Hugo L. Black, U.S. Supreme Ct., 1954-55; practiced in Birmingham, Ala., 1955-57; asso. prof. law U. Va., 1957-61, prof., 1961-66; Fulbright lectr., Eng., 1965-66; prof., dean Sch. Law U. Ala., 1966-70; James Monroe prof. law U. Va., 1970-77; asst. atty. gen. Office Improvement Adminstrn. Justice, Dept. Justice, Washington, 1977—; served with JAGC, U.S. Army, 1951-53; mem. Adv. Council Appellate Justice, 1971-75; chmn. cts. task force Nat. Adv. Commn. on Criminal Justice, Standards, and Goals, 1971-73; dir. appellate justice project Nat. Center for State Cts., 1972-74. Mem. Am. Law Inst., Am., Va., Ala. bar assns., Am. Judicature Soc. (dir.), Am. Soc. Legal History (past dir.), Phi Delta Phi, Order of Coif, Raven Soc. Author: Preludes to Gideon, 1966; Appellate Courts: Staff and Process in the Crisis of Volume, 1974; Criminal Appeals: English Practices and American Reforms, 1972; Mr. Justice Black and His Books, 1974; (with P. Carrington and M. Rosenberg) Justice on Appeal, 1976. Contbr. articles to legal jours. Home: Flordon Dr Charlottesville VA 22901 Office: Office Improvements Adminstrn Justice Dept Justice Washington DC 20530

MEAGHER, JOHN HENRY, b. Worcester, Mass., Dec. 7, 1908; B.A., Harvard, 1931, LL.B., 1934. Admitted to Mass. bar, 1934, U.S. Supreme Ct. bar, 1939; since practiced law in Worcester, mem. firm Zaeder & Bianchi, 1934-40, Ceaty, Meagher & MacCarthy, 1945-51; judge Mass. Superior Ct., Worcester, 1951—, sec. of justices, 1972—, sr. justice, 1973—; pres. Worcester County Law Library, 1975—. Treas., Democratic Campaign, Mass., 1948, 50. Mem. Am. Law Inst., Mass., Am., Worcester (pres 1948) bar assns., Am. Antiquarian Soc. Home: 95 Commodore Rd Worcester MA 01602 Office: Superior Ct Boston MA 02108 Tel (617) 756-2241

MEAGHER, THOMAS FRANCIS, b. N.Y.C., Aug. 26, 1926; B.A., Fordham U., 1950; LL.B., St. John's U., 1955; LL.M., N.Y. U., 1959. Admitted to N.Y. State bar, 1955, U.S. Dist. Ct. bar, 1956; atty. of record Liberty Mut. Ins. Co., Queens, N.Y., 1961-66; partner firm DeBlasio & Meagher, and predecessor, N.Y.C., 1966—. Mem. N.Y. State, Queens County, Bronx County, Westchester County bar assns., Yonkers Lawyers Assn., Am. Trial Lawyers Assn., Catholic Lawyers Guild, Practicing Law Inst. (lectr.). Home: Office: 233 Broadway New York City NY 10007 Tel (212) 227-6750

MEALEY, CATHERINE ELIZABETH, b. Ames, Iowa, Apr. 4, 1928; B.A., U. Iowa, 1950, M.A., 1951, J.D., 1957; M. Law Librarianship, U. Wash., 1962. Admitted to Iowa bar, 1957, Wyo. bar, 1965; individual practice law, Flagstaff, Ariz., 1958-60; asst. prof., librarian U. Wyo., 1962-67, asso. prof., 1967-76, prof., 1976—. Mem. Wyo. Bar Assn. Home: 121 Ivinson St Laramie WY 82070 Office: Coll Law U Wyo Laramie WY 82071 Tel (307) 766-5175

MEANS, CYRIL CHESNUT, JR., b. Phila., Dec. 21, 1918; A.B., Harvard, 1938, LL.M., 1948; J.D., Wayne State U., 1941. Admitted to Mich. bar, 1941, U.S. Supreme Ct. bar, 1946; law sec. to Justice Henry M. Butzel of Mich. Supreme Ct., 1941-42; asso. prof. law Detroit Coll. Law, 1946-47; asst. prof. law Stanford (Calif.), 1948-50; legal advisor Office of U.S. High Commr. Germany, 1950-54; arbitration dir. N.Y. Stock Exchange, 1955-56; exec. v.p., dir. Tech. Studies, Inc., N.Y.C., 1957—; chmn. bd. trustees Trent Sch., N.Y.C., 1963-64, dean, 1964-65; projects coordinator Western Australia Devel. Corp., N.Y.C., 1965-66; asst. prof. N.Y. Law Sch., 1969-70, asso. prof., 1970-73, prof., 1973—; mem. N.Y. State Gov.'s Commn. to Rev. N.Y. State's Abortion Law, 1968; chmn. legal com. Nat. Abortion Rights Action League, 1970—; mem. advisory com. on population affairs to sec. HEW, 1975—. Mem. Am. Soc. Internat. Law, Am., N.Y.C. bar assns., Selden Soc., Am. Soc. Legal History. Author: The Law of N.Y. Concerning Abortion and the Status of the Fetus, 1964-1968: A Case of Cessation of Constitutionality, 1968; The Phoenix of Abortional Freedom, 1971. Home: 1199 Park Ave Apt 7-H New York City NY 10028 Tel (212) 289-5163 Office: New York Law Sch 57 Worth St New York City NY 10013 Tel (212) 966-3500 also Salt Island Rd (Brier Neck) Gloucester MA 01930 Tel (617) 281-2446

MEANS, ERNEST ELMER, b. Akron, Ohio, July 6, 1918; A.B., Wittenberg U., 1948; Ph.D., U. Wis., 1958; LL.B., U. Fla., 1964. Admitted to Fla. bar, 1964; asst. prof. polit. sci. The Citadel, 1952-54; asso. prof. Fla. State U., 1954-62; research aide Fla. Supreme Ct., 1964-67; dir. statutory revision Fla. Legislature, Tallahassee, 1967—; asso. mem., sec. Fla. Commn. for Uniform State Laws, 1967—. Mem. Am. Polit. Sci. Assn. Office: Holland Bldg Tallahassee FL 32304 Tel (904) 488-8403

MEANS, WILLIAM WALTER, b. Sand Springs, Okla., Mar. 29, 1933; J.D., U. Tulsa, 1961. Admitted to Okla. bar, 1961; practiced in Tulsa, 1961-62; asst. pub. defender Tulsa County (Okla.), 1961, asst. county atty., 1962-66, chief civil asst.-county atty., 1966-67; judge Tulsa County Ct. Common Pleas, 1967-69; asso. judge Okla. Dist. Ct., Tulsa-Pawnee Counties Jud. Administrv. Dist., 1969-71, dist. judge, 1971—, presiding judge, 1975—; judge trial div. Ct. on the Judiciary, State of Okla., 1975, 76; mem. Ct. Bank Rev., 1976—; adj. asso. prof. U. Tulsa Coll. Law, 1974—. Mem. Tulsa County, Okla., Am. bar assns., Am. Judicature Soc., Okla. Jud. Conf. (pres. 1973). Office: Tulsa County Courthouse 5th and Denver Sts Tulsa OK 74103 Tel (918) 584-0471

MEARA, J. WILLIAM, b. Mendota, Ill., Jan. 23, 1916; B.S. in Commerce and Law, U. Ill., 1938; J.D., U. S.D., 1940. Admitted to Ill. bar, 1940; individual practice law, Bloomington, Ill., 1940-76; gen. counsel The How Inc., 1958-76, Kickapoo Water Co., 1964-76, T & P Heating & Cooling Co., 1964-76, Advanced Electronics Industries, Inc., 1975-76. Alderman, City of Bloomington, 1947-50; pres. Tb Assn., 1949, 50, 51; pres. PTA, 1952, 59; treas. county chpt. Assn. for Crippled, 1953-56; v.p. Lake Bloomington Assn., 1960-61; dist. bd. chmn. Boy Scouts Am., 1965; mem. McLean County Bd. Suprs., 1967-72; pres. Bloomington Kiwanis, 1957, lt. govt. Ill.-Iowa, 1963. Mem. Am., Ill. State, McLean County (pres. 1964) bar assns., Phi Delta Phi. Home: 1014 E Jefferson St Bloomington IL 61701 Office: 500 Meara Bldg Bloomington IL 61701 Tel (309) 828-3371

MEBANE, DAVID CUMMINS, b. Toledo, Dec. 18, 1933; B.S. in Bus. Adminstrn., Ariz. State U., 1957; LL.B., U. Wis., 1960. Admitted to Wis. bar, 1960; with Judge Adv. Gen. Corps, USAF, 1960-63; atty., trust officer 1st Wis. Nat. Bank, Oshkosh, 1963-66; individual practice law, Ripon, Wis., 1966; dep. dist. atty. Dane County, Wis., 1966-69; asst. atty. gen., adminstr. div. criminal investigation Wis. Dept. Justice, 1970-71; dep. atty. gen. Wis., 1972-73; U.S. atty. Western Dist. Wis., Madison, 1974—; chmn. State Fed. Law Enforcement Commn. Wis. Mem. State Bar Wis., Am, Dane County (Wis.) bar assns. Home: 6602 Montclair Ln Madison WI 53711 Office: PO Box 112 Madison WI 53701 Tel (608) 252-5158

MEBANE, FRANK CARTER, JR., b. Durham, N.C., May 30, 1906; A.B., Princeton, 1927; LL.B., N.Y. Law Sch., 1930; postgrad. in Patent Law, Columbia U. Extension, 1940-41. Admitted to N.Y. bar, 1931, U.S. Supreme Ct. bar, 1939; asso. firm Strange Myers Hinds & Wight, N.Y.C., 1932-42; individual practice law, S.I., N.Y., 1949—; labor relations staff Western Electric Co., South Kearny, N.J., 1942-49. Trustee S.I. Zool. Soc. Mem. Richmond County Bar Assn. Tel (212) 273-4663

MEBEL, ROBERT E., b. Bklyn., July 7, 1903; B.A., Columbia, 1923, LL.B./J.D., 1925. Admitted to N.Y. bar, 1925; individual practice law, N.Y.C., 1926-76; mem. firm Mebel & Sessa, Bklyn., 1976—. Mem. Bklyn. Bar Assn., Bklyn. Municipal Club. Home: 240 Central Park S New York City NY 10019 Office: 188 Montague St Brooklyn NY 11201 Tel (212) MA 5-0030

MEDALIE, RICHARD JAMES, b. Duluth, Minn., July 21, 1929; B.A. summa cum laude, U. Minn., 1952; certificate U. London, 1953; A.M., Harvard, 1955, J.D. cum laude, 1958. Admitted to D.C. bar, 1958, N.Y. bar, 1962, Supreme Ct. U.S. bar, 1961; law clk. U.S. Ct. Appeals for D.C. Circuit, 1958-59; asst. to Solicitor Gen. of U.S., 1960-62; asso. firm Kaye, Scholer, Fierman, Hays & Handler, N.Y.C., 1962-65; dep. dir. Ford Found. Inst. Criminal Law and Procedure, Georgetown U. Law Center, 1965-68; partner firm Friedman, Medalie & Ochs and predecessors, Washington, 1968—; adj. prof. adminstrv. and criminal law Georgetown U., 1967-70; mem. panel arbitrators Am. Arbitration Assn., 1964—; chmn. criminal law task force and personnel com. D.C. Law Revision Commn., 1975—. Mem. Am. Law Inst., D.C. Unified Bar, Am., N.Y. State bar assns., Assn. Bar City N.Y., Harvard Law Sch. Assn. D.C. (pres.), Phi Beta Kappa, Phi Alpha Theta. Fulbright scholar U. London, 1952-53; Ford fellow, 1954-55; author: From Escobedo to Miranda, the Anatomy of a Supreme Court Decision, 1966; (with others) Federal Consumer Safety Legislation, 1970; editor: (with others) Crime: a Community Responds, 1967; contbr. articles profl. jours. Home: 3113 Macomb St NW Washington DC 20008 Office: 1700 Pennsylvania Ave NW Washington DC 20006 Tel (202) 393-7110

MEDLAND, MICHAEL FRANCIS, b. N.Y.C., Sept. 28, 1941; B.S. in Commerce, St. Louis U., 1963, J.D., 1971. Admitted to Mo. bar, 1972, Wis. bar, 1972; mgr. group ins. renewal underwriting Gen. Am. Life Ins. Co., St. Louis, 1966-72; asst. dir. govt. and industry relations CUNA Mut. Ins. Soc., Madison, Wis., 1972—. Pres. Aldo Leopold Sch. Parent-Faculty Orgn., Madison, Wis., 1975-76; pres. bd. dirs. St. James Sch., Madison, 1976—. Mem. Mo. Bar Assn., State Bar Wis., Am. Soc. C.L.U.'s. Office: CUNA Mut Ins Soc PO Box 391 Madison WI 53701 Tel (608) 238-5851

MEDLIN, ELMER JAMES, b. Gorham, Ill., Jan. 6, 1914; LL.B., Chgo. Kent Coll., 1937, J.D., 1969. Admitted to Ill. bar, 1937; Judge City of Carbondale (Ill.), 1938-46; pub. defender Jackson County (Ill.), 1951-68; mem. firm Medlin, Zimmer & Medlin, Carbondale, 1951—; pres. Univ. Bank of Carbondale, 1972—. Mem. Am., Ill., Jackson County bar assns. Office: 818 W Main St Carbondale IL 62901 Tel (618) 457-4164

MEDOFF, M. CRAIG, b. Phila., Mar. 11, 1919; B.S., U. Pa., 1948; J.D., Harvard U., 1951. Admitted to Calif. bar, 1952; trust officer Citizen's Nat. Bank, Los Angeles, 1952-54; individual practice law, Santa Monica, Calif., 1954—; dir. pvt. corps., Los Angeles. Chmn. bd. Pacific Palisades Youth Center, 1956-57, pres., 1957-58; bd. dirs. Brentwood (Calif.) Property Owners Assn., 1976-77. Mem. Am., Los Angeles, Santa Monica bar assns., Los Angeles Trial Lawyers Assn., Lawyers Club Los Angeles. Office: Suite 302 100 Wilshire Blvd Santa Monica Blvd Santa Monica CA 90401 Tel (213) 459-0769

MEDVECKY, THOMAS EDWARD, b. Bridgeport, Conn., Apr. 22, 1937; A.B., Bowdoin Coll., 1959; LL.B., St. John's U., 1962. Admitted to Conn. bar, 1962; asso. firm Louis Katz, Danbury, Conn., 1963-68; individual practice law, Bethel, Conn., 1968—; asst. town counsel Bethel, 1963-67; asso. dir. State Nat. Bank Conn. Mem. budget cm. Danbury Community Chest, 1966-68. Mem. Am., Conn., Danbury bar assns. Recipient Am. Jurisprudence award, 1962. Office: 99 Greenwood Ave Bethel CT 06801 Tel (203) 744-6200

MEE, WILLIAM HENRY, b. N.Y.C., Jan. 5, 1920; B.A., L.I. U., 1948; J.D., N.Y. U., 1950. Admitted to N.J. bar, 1951, N.Mex. bar, 1966; partner firm Citta & Mee, Toms River, N.J., 1951-52, Huber & Mee, Toms River, 1953-66; sr. atty. N.Mex. Legis. Council, Santa Fe, 1966—; magistrate Borough Beachwood (N.J.) Municipal Ct., 1951-52; atty. Borough Beachwood, 1952-65, Twp. Berkeley (N.J.), 1959-65. Mem. Am., N.J., Ocean County bar assns. Home: Route 2 Box 310 US Hwy 14 Santa Fe NM 87501 Office: Room 334 State Capitol Santa Fe NM 87503 Tel (505) 827-3141

MEEHAN, JOHN FRANCIS, b. Goshen, N.Y., Oct. 8, 1920; student, Coll. of Holy Cross; LL.B., N.Y. U., 1949. Admitted to N.Y. State bar, 1950; individual practice law, Goshen, 1950-74; partner firm Meehan & Fink, Goshen, 1975—; town atty. Town of Chester (N.Y.), 1974—; atty. Goshen Savs. & Loan Assn., 1960—, pres., 1975—, dir., 1975—; police judge Village of Goshen, 1951-62. Mem. Goshen (pres. 1974), Or County (dir. 1970-72, 75—) bar assns. Home: 51 S South St Goshen NY 10924 Office: Rt 17M Goshen NY 10924 Tel (914) 294-5421

MEEHAN, ROBERT PATRICK, b. Pittston, Pa., Feb. 11, 1947; B.A., U. Scranton, 1969; J.D., Dickinson Sch. Law, 1972. Admitted to Pa. bar, 1972; dep. counsel, dept. auditor gen. Commonwealth of Pa., Harrisburg, 1972—; solicitor Twin Lakes Park South (Pa.) Civic Assn., 1973—; adv. Harrisburg council K.C., 1976—. Pres., St. Catherine Laboure Athletic Assn., 1976—; pres. Dauphin Deanery, Harrisburg Cath. Youth Orgn., Boys Grade Sch. Basketball League, 1976—. Mem. Pa. Bar Assn. Home: 983 Galion St Harrisburg PA 17111 Office: 224 Finance Bldg Harrisburg PA 17102 Tel (717) 787-4546

MEEKER, DAVID NELSON, b. Ann Arbor, Mich., Mar. 10, 1949; A.B., Dartmouth Coll.; J.D., Case Western Res. U. Admitted to Ohio bar, 1974; atty. Hobart Corp., Troy, Ohio, 1974—. Trustee Children's Med. Center, Dayton, Ohio, 1975—. Mem. Am., Ohio, Miami County bar assns. Home: 1700 Swailes Rd Troy OH 45373 Office: Hobart Corp Troy OH 45373 Tel (513) 335-7171

MEEKER, MICHAEL DAVID, b. Asheville, N.C., June 13, 1947; B.S. in Bus. Adminstrn., U. N.C., 1969, J.D. with honors, 1972. Admitted to N.C. bar, 1972; asso. firm Brooks, Pierce, McLendon, Humphrey & Leonard, Greensboro, N.C., 1972—. Mem. Am., N.C., Greensboro bar assns., Order of Coif, Beta Gamma Sigma. Home: 804 Meade Dr Greensboro NC 27410 Office: PO Drawer U 201 N Elm St Greensboro NC 27402 Tel (919) 373-8850

MEEKS, CORDELL DAVID, JR., b. Kansas City, Kans., Dec. 17, 1942; A.B., U. Kans., 1964, J.D., 1967; Reginald Heber Smith Community Lawyer fellow in poverty law U. Pa., 1967-68; admitted to Kans. bar, 1968, Fed. Ct. bar, 1968, U.S. Supreme Ct. bar, 1971; sr. partner firm Meeks & Sutherland, Kansas City, Kans., 1972—; judge Municipal Ct. Kansas City, 1976—; dir. Douglass State Bank, Kansas City. Chmn. Wyandotte County chpt. ARC, 1973-74; chmn. Wyandotte County Legal Aid Soc., Inc., 1973-75; active Am. Cancer Soc., N.E. Adv. Bd. Wyandotte County Mental Health Assn.; bd. dirs. Jr. Achievement Greater Kansas City. Mem. Wyandotte County Bar Assn., Am. Trial Lawyers Assn. Home: 7915 Walker St Kansas City KS 66112 Office: One Gateway Center Bldg Suite 115 Kansas City KS 66101 Tel (913) 281-5674

MEER, JESSE ROSS, b. N.Y.C., Nov. 18, 1931; A.B., Bklyn. Coll., 1953; LL.B., Harvard, 1958. Admitted to N.Y. State bar, 1958; asso. firm Berlack, Israel & Liberman, N.Y.C., 1958-63, partner firm, 1964—; lectr. Practising Law Inst., 1963-64, AMR Internat., Inc., 1975-76. Trustee, Community Temple Beth Ohr, Bklyn., 1966—. Mem. Bar Assn. City N.Y., N.Y. Law Inst. Home: 789 E 18th St Brooklyn NY 11230 Office: 26 Broadway New York City NY 10004 Tel (212) 248-6900

MEGLIO, JOHN JOSEPH, b. Bklyn., Aug. 15, 1936; B.A., St. John's U., 1957, LL.B., 1960; LL.M., N.Y. U., 1968. Admitted to N.Y. State bar, 1961, Calif. bar, 1971; spl. research asst. Am. Bar Found., Chgo., 1968-70; individual practice of law, N.Y.C., 1970—; asst. dist. atty. State of N.Y. State, Kings County, 1965-68. Mem. Am., N.Y. State, Bklyn. bar assns., Nat. Dist. Atty. Assn. Office: 555 Madison Ave New York City NY 10022 Tel (212) 355-1660

MEHLER, IRVING MARTIN, b. N.Y.C., Feb. 7, 1914; LL.B., St. John's U., N.Y.C., 1941; LL.M., Bklyn. Law Sch., 1951; J.D., , U. Chgo., 1953. Admitted to N.Y. bar, 1943, U.S. Supreme Ct. bar, 1948, Colo. bar, 1954; individual practice law, N.Y.C., 1946-52, Colo., 1960-64; editor of opinions Colo. Supreme Ct., Denver, 1964—; prof. law Westminster Law Sch., 1955-57, also asst. dean; asst. prof. law U. Denver, 1957-60. Chmn. bd. edn. Hillel Acad., Denver, 1960-67. Mem. Colo., Denver bar assns. Recipient Peppercorns award, 1960; Masonic Certificate of Merit, 1976. Author: Effective Legal Communication, 1975; contbr. articles to legal jours. Home: 1555 Winona Ct Denver CO 80204 Office: 205 State Capitol Bldg Denver CO 80203 Tel (303) 892-2421

MEHRTENS, WILLIAM OSBORNE, JR., b. Miami Beach, Fla., Nov. 20, 1945; B.S., U. Fla., 1968; J.D. magna cum laude, Fla. State U., 1971. Admitted to Fla. bar, 1971, U.S. Supreme Ct. bar, 1974; asso. firm Smathers & Thompson, Miami, Fla., 1971—. Mem. Am., Fla., Dade County (dir. 1973-76) bar assns., Dade County Def. Bar Assn., Am. Judicature Soc., Phi Delta Phi. Recipient Am. Jurisprudence award Bancroft-Whitney Co., 1969. Home: 1441 SW 11th St Miami FL 33135 Office: 1301 Alfred I DuPont Bldg Miami FL 33131 Tel (305) 379-6523

MEIER, STEVEN KENNETH, b. N.Y.C., June 23, 1945; B.A., State U. N.Y., Buffalo, 1967; J.D., St. John's U., 1971. Admitted to N.Y. State bar, 1972, U.S. Dist. So. N.Y. bar, 1974, Eastern N.Y. bar, 1974, U.S. Supreme Ct. bar, 1976; mem. firm Robinowitz & Bianchi, White Plains, N.Y., 1971-73; mem. firm Corwin & Frey, N.Y.C., 1973—; arbitrator City Ct., White Plains, 1973. Dir. Ukiyo-e Soc. Am., Inc., N.Y.C., 1975—. Mem. Am., N.Y. State, Westchester County bar assns. Office: 50 E 42d St New York City NY 10017 Tel (212) 986-3070

MEIER, WILLIAM CHARLES, b. St. Paul, Apr. 13, 1920; B.S., U. Minn., 1942, J.D., 1947. Admitted to Minn. bar, 1947; asso. firm Hoffmann, Donahue, Graff & Meier, St. Pual, 1947-52; partner firm Meier, Kennedy & Quinn, St. Paul, 1952—. Mem. Am., Minn. (gov. 1975—), Ramsey County (past pres., sec., chmn. ethics com. 1967-72) bar assns. Home: 214 W Marie Ave West St Paul MN 55118 Office: 430 Minnesota Bldg St Paul MN 55101 Tel (612) 226-8844

MEIER, WILLIAM HENRY, b. Lincoln, Nebr., Dec. 23, 1904; A.B., U. Nebr., 1926, D.D., 1930. Admitted to Nebr. bar, 1930, U.S. Supreme Ct. bar, 1971; spl. agt. FBI, 1930-31; individual practice law, Lincoln, 1931-32; atty. Fed. Land Bank, Omaha, 1933-36; individual practice law, Minden, Nebr., 1936-67; sr. partner firm Meier & Adkins, Minden, 1967—; asst. U.S. atty. Nebr., 1941-43; county atty. Kearney County (Nebr.), 1958-67; city atty. Minden, 1971—; mem. Nebr. Ho. of Reps., 1932-33. Mem. Minden Sch. Bd., 1945-48; mem. Kearney County Sch. Reorgn. Com., 1949-54. Mem. Nebr. State (pres. gen. practice sect. 1975), Nebr. Tenth Jud. Dist. bar assns., Delta Theta Phi. Recipient Man of Year award Minden C. of C., 1950. Home: 305 N Tower Ave Minden NE 68959 Office: 401 E 4th St Suite 102-104 Minden NE 68959 Tel (308) 832-2150

MEIERING, MARK CARL, b. Roswell, N.Mex., Sept. 28, 1944; B.B.A., U. Notre Dame, 1966; J.D., N.Y. U., 1969. Admitted to N.Mex. bar, 1970, U.S. Ct. Appeals 10th Circuit bar, 1971; law clerk Honorable D.C. Hill U.S. Ct. Appeals 10th Circuit, 1969-71; asst. U.S. atty. Dist. N.Mex., Albuquerque, 1971-76; asso. firm Rodey, Dickason, Sloan, Akin & Robb, Albuquerque, 1976—. Mem. Am., Fed. bar assns., Fed. Bar Assn. N.Mex. (treas. 1972). Recipient Herman Crown award U. Notre Dame, 1966; Wickersham award N.Y. U., 1969. Office: 20 First Plaza Suite 700 Albuquerque NM 87103 Tel (505) 765-5900

MEIKLEJOHN, ALVIN JERRY, JR., b. Omaha, Nebr., June 18, 1923; B.S., U. Denver, 1951, B.A., 1951, J.D., 1951. Admitted to Colo. bar, 1951; asso. firm Jones, Meiklejohn, Kehl & Lyons, and predecessors, Denver, 1954—, partner firm, 1957—; chmn. Transp. Law Inst., 1967-74. Mem. bd. edn. Jefferson County Sch. Dist. R-1, 1971—, pres., 1973-76. Mem. Arvada C. of C. (bd. dirs. 1973—), Colo. Assn. Sch. Bds. (pres. 1976—), Nat. Sch. Bds. Assn. (bd. dirs. 1976—), Colo. Soc. C.P.A.'s, Am. Inst. C.P.A.'s, Denver, Colo., Am. bar assns., Motor Carrier Lawyers Assn. (past pres., mem. exec. com. 1968—). Home: 7540 Kline Dr Arvada CO 80005 Office: 1600 Lincoln Center Bldg 1660 Lincoln St Denver CO 80264 Tel (303) 534-3245

MEILINGER, REX FREDERICK, b. Sandwich, Ill., Apr. 23, 1921; B.S., U. Ill., 1943; J.D., Northwestern U., 1950. Admitted to Ill. bar, 1950; partner firm Givler, Meilinger, Casey & Flanders, and predecessors, Aurora, Ill., 1950-67; individual practice law, Aurora, 1967-71; judge 16th Jud. Circuit Ct., DeKalb, Kane, and Kendall Counties, Sycamore, Ill., 1971—. Mem. Am., Ill., DeKalb and Kane Counties bar assns. Home: 201 E 4th St Sandwich IL 60548 Office: Court House Sycamore IL 60178 Tel (815) 895-9161

MEILMAN, SIDNEY, b. N.Y.C., Nov. 25, 1913; student City U. N.Y., 1930-34; LL.B., Bklyn. Law Sch., St. Lawrence U., 1937. Admitted to N.Y. State bar, 1939; acting village justice Tuckahoe, N.Y., 1962-66; with U.S. Dept. Labor, 1941-51; individual practice law, 1951—. Active Bronxille-Eastchester-Tuckahoe United Way., 1956-76, dir., 1971-74, sec.-treas., 1974-75; mem. law com. Family Consultation Service, Eastchester, N.Y., 1975-77. Mem. Eastchester (pres. 1975-76), Westchester County (vice chmn. labor law com. 1975-77) Bar assns., N.Y. State, Westchester County Magistrates assns., Am. Arbitration Assn. (Fed. Labor panel). Home: 165 Park Dr Eastchester NY 10707 Office: 705 Bronx River Rd Yonkers NY 10704 Tel (914) 776-6600

MEINDL, GERALD JAMES, b. Oregon City, Oreg., Sept. 24, 1907; B.S., U. Oreg., 1929; J.D., George Washington U., 1933. Admitted to D.C. bar, 1932, Oreg. bar, 1933, U.S. Supreme Ct. bar, 1941; atty. war risk ins. Oreg. Dept. Justice, Portland, 1934-40; individual practice law, Portland, 1940—. Mem. Order of the Coif, Delta Theta Phi. Home: 1948 SW Edgewood Rd Portland OR 97201 Office: 2545 SW Terwilliger Blvd Portland OR 97201 Tel (503) 222-9396

MEINSTER, J. BARRY, b. Balt., Feb. 23, 1947; B.S., U. Md., 1969, J.D., 1973. Admitted to Md. bar, 1973; law clk. Supreme Bench Balt., 1970-73; individual practice law, Balt., 1974—. Mem. Md. State Bar Assn., Assn. Trial Lawyers Am. Home: 4619 Devilen Circle Pikesville MD 21208 Office: Suite 302 222 Saint Paul Pl Baltimore MD 21202 Tel (301) 331-0111

MEIR, DENNIS SCOTT, b. N.Y.C., May 23, 1945; A.B., Amherst Coll.; J.D., Harvard U. Admitted to Ga. bar, 1972; mem. firm Kilpatrick, Cody, Rogers, McClutchy & Regenstein, Atlanta, 1972—. Mem. Am. Bar Assn., State Bar Ga. Home: 732 Starlight Ct NE Atlanta GA 30342 Office: 3100 Equitable Bldg Atlanta GA 30303

MEISEL, GEORGE IRA, b. Cleve., May 5, 1920; A.B., Case Western Res. U., 1942; LL.B., Harvard U., 1948. Admitted to Ohio bar, 1948; asso. firm Williams, Eversman & Morgan, Toledo, 1948-51; asso. firm Squire, Sanders & Dempsey, Cleve., 1951-58, partner, 1958—. Mem. Am. (founding chmn. sect. litigation 1973-74), Ohio bar assns., Bar Assn. Greater Cleve. (pres. 1975—), Am. Coll. Trial Lawyers, Internat. Assn. Ins. Counsel (chmn. def. research com. 1976—, mem. exec. com. 1977—). Contbr. articles to Otolaryngology and legal jours. Home: 2691 Wadsworth St Shaker Heights OH 44122 Office: Union Commerce Bldg Cleveland OH 44115 Tel (216) 696-9200

MEISELMAN, LEONARD JOHN, b. Bklyn., June 19, 1919; LL.B., St. Johns U., 1940. Admitted to N.Y. bar, 1940, U.S. Ct. of Claims bar, 1949, U.S. Tax Ct. bar, 1947, U.S. Supreme Ct. bar; asso. firm Black, Varian & Simon, N.Y.C., 1940, firm Spellman, Rosenblatt & Enselman, N.Y.C., 1940-41; asst. corp. counsel N.Y.C., 1944-47; individual practice law, N.Y.C., 1948-59; partner firm Meiselman, Boland, Reilly & Pittoni, and predecessors, Mineola, N.Y., 1959—; lectr. real property Coll. City N.Y., 1945-48, Bklyn. Coll., 1949-66; adj. prof. real property N.Y. Inst. Tech., Old Westbury, 1976; pros. atty. Village of East Hills, N.Y., 1955-59, acting police justice, 1959-65; arbitrator Nat. Panel of Arbitrators, Am. Arbitration Assn., 1965—. Mem. N.Y. County Lawyers Assn., Fed. Bar Assn., Bar Assn. Nassau County (dir.), N.Y. Trial Lawyers Assn., Nassau and Suffolk bar assns. Contbr. articles to legal jours. Home: Woodhollow Rd East Hills Roslyn Heights NY 11577 Office: 54 Willis Ave Mineola NY 11501 Tel (516) 248-2400

MEISENHOLDER, ROBERT, b. Mitchell, S.D., Mar. 15, 1915; B.A., U. S.D., 1936; J.D., U. Mich., 1939, S.J.D. (Cook Meml. fellow), 1942. Admitted to S.D. bar, 1939, N.Y. bar, 1941, Ohio bar, 1952; asso. firm Chadbourne, Wallace, Parke and Whiteside, N.Y.C., 1941-43, 46-47; prof. law. U. Miami (Fla.), 1947-51; asso. atty. Office Gen. Counsel, Navy Dept., Dayton, Ohio, 1951-52; prof. law U. Cin., 1952-54, U. Wash., Seattle, 1954—; vis. prof. Emory U., 1948, U. Ariz., 1950, U. Mich., 1958-59. Mem. evidence task force Wash. Jud. Council, 1976; chmn. com. fed. rules Wash. State Bar Assn., 1970-73; chmn. sect. jud. adminstrn. Seattle-King County Bar Assn., 1970-73. Chmn. Citizens Adv. Land Use Com., Bellevue, Wash., 1973-74. Mem. N.Y. State Bar Assn., AAUP, Antique Wireless Assn., Order of Coif, Phi Beta Kappa, Phi Delta Phi, Tau Kappa Alpha. Author: Commentaries on New Washington Rules of Pleading, Practice and Procedure, 1959; Washington Evidence Law and Practice, 1965; West's Federal Forms, vols. 2-4, 1967-70; (with others) Cases and Materials on Procedure Before Trial, 1968; contbg. author: McCormick Evidence, 2d edit., 1972; (with Broun) Problems in Evidence, 1973; (with others) Cases and Materials on Civil Procedure, 1975. Office: U of Wash Sch of Law Seattle WA 98150 Tel (206) 543-4907

MEISLIN, BERNARD JOSHUA, b. N.Y.C., Nov. 10, 1927; B.A., U. Mich., 1948; LL.B., Harvard, 1951; LL.M., N.Y. U., 1954. Admitted to N.Y. bar, 1951, N.J. bar, 1976; asso. firm Orr & Brennan, Bklyn., 1951-61; partner firm Bressler Meislin & Lipsitz, N.Y.C., 1961—. Mem. N.Y. State Bar Assn. Author: Jewish Law in American Tribunals, 1976; contbg. author: Stock Market Handbook, 1970; co-author tax notes Nichols Cyclopedia of Legal Forms, Vols. 1, 3, 7, 7A, 8, 9, 9A, 1958-63. Editor: (with B. Bressler) New York Lawyer's Manual, 1961-70. Contbr. articles to legal jours. Home: 73 Athens Rd Short Hills NJ 07078 Office: 90 Broad St New York City NY 10004 Tel (212) HA 5-9300

MEISSNER, WENDELL EUGENE, b. Omaha, July 1, 1940; B.A., U. Nebr. Omaha, 1963, J.D., Creighton U., 1966. Admitted to Nebr. bar, 1966; partner firm Meissner & Meissner, Omaha, 1966—. Home: 7623 State St Ralston NE 67127 Office: 4819 S 24th St Omaha NE 68107 Tel (402) 731-0973

MEISTRELL, GERARD MOODY, b. Bklyn., May 21, 1941; A.B., Princeton, 1963; J.D., Harvard, 1966. Admitted to N.Y. bar, 1966; partner firm Cahill Gordon & Reindel, N.Y.C., 1974—. Mem. Assn. Bar City N.Y., N.Y. State Bar Assn. Office: 80 Pine St New York City NY 10005 Tel (212) 825-0100

MEJDA, JAMES JOHN, b. Chgo., Sept. 6, 1912; certificate arts Morton Coll., 1932; J.D., DePaul U., 1935; postgrad. Nat. Coll. State Judiciary U. Colo., 1966, U. Nev., 1971. Admitted to Ill. bar, 1935, U.S. Dist. Ct. bar, No. Dist. Ill., 1941; practiced in Chgo. and suburbs, 1935-64; judge Circuit Ct. Cook County (Ill.), 1964-76; judge Ill. Appellate Ct., 1st dist., 1973—, presiding judge 3d div., 1976, mem. 1st dist. exec. com., 1976; asst. atty. gen. State of Ill., 1961-64; chief legal dep. Ill. State Toll Hwy. Commn., 1961-64; pres. Village of Stickney (Ill.), 1949-64; justice of peace Stickney Twp., 1937-41; committeeman Stickney Twp. Democratic Party, 1942-54, 58-64; police magistrate Village of Stickney, 1947-49; arbitrator Ill. Indsl. Commn., 1949-53. Mem. Am., Ill. State, Chgo., West Suburban bar assns., Bohemian Lawyers Assn. Chgo., Ill. Judges Assn., Delta Theta Phi, Pi Gamma Mu. Office: Richard J Daley Center Chicago IL 60602 Tel (312) 793-5408

MELAMED, ARTHUR DOUGLAS, b. Mpls., Dec. 3, 1945; B.A., Yale, 1967; J.D., Harvard, 1970. Admitted to D.C. bar, 1970; law clk. to judge U.S. Ct. Appeals 9th Circuit, San Francisco, 1970-71; asso. firm Wilmer, Cutler & Pickering, Washington, 1971—. Office: 1666 K St NW Washington DC 20006 Tel (202) 872-6000

MELAT, JUSTIN RICHARD, b. Hobert, Ind., July 24, 1940; B.S. in English and History, Tenn. State U., 1965; J.D., U. Tenn., 1968. Admitted to Colo. bar, 1969; since practiced in Colorado Springs, Colo., asso. firm Rector, Kane, Donley & Wills, 1970-71, partner firm Rector, Melat & Wheeler, 1971-76, firm Melat & Wheeler, 1976—; v.p. Tenn. State U., 1963-64; instr. El Paso County Trial Advocacy Sch. Mem. Def. Research Inst., Am., Colorado Springs (v.p.) trial lawyers assns., Am. Arbitration Assn. (panel), El Pas County, Colo. bar assns., Def. Lawyers Assn. Home: 4304 Meadowview Ct Colorado Springs CO 80917 Office: 120 E Moreno Ave Colorado Springs CO 80903 Tel (303) 475-0304

MELBARDIS, WOLFGANG ALEXANDER, b. Bayreuth, Germany, June 21, 1946; B.A., Hartwick Coll., Oneonta, N.Y., 1968; J.D., St. John's U., N.Y.C., 1971; M.B.A., L.I.U., 1977. Admitted to N.Y. State bar, 1972, U.S. Ct. Military Appeals bar, 1972; prosecutor, def. counsel Hdqrs. 1st Cavalry Div., Fort Hood, Tex., 1972-74, legal assistance officer, 1974; asst. prof. law U.S. Military Acad., 1974-77, also claims officer, Mem. Am., N.Y. State bar assns., Res. Officers Assn. Home: 70 Knightsbridge Rd Great Neck NY 11021 Office: 3-31 Thayer Rd West Point NY 10996 Tel (914) 446-9512

MELBYE, RICHARD BRENTON, b. Berkeley, Calif., Dec. 8, 1933; A.B., U. Calif., 1955, LL.B., J.D., 1958. Admitted to Calif. bar, 1959; asso. firm James P. Shovlin, Jr., San Francisco, 1958-63; partner firm Kane, Owen & Melbye (now Owen, Melbye & Rohlff), Redwood City, Calif., 1963—. Bd. dirs. Atherton (Calif.) Little League, 1969-75. Mem. Calif., Santa Clara trial lawyers assns., Am., Calif. State, San Francisco, San Mateo (bench and bar com. 1970-71), Santa Clara County bar assns., Assn. Def. Counsel No. Calif. (bd. govs. 1974-75). Home: 36 Middlefield Rd Atherton CA 94025 Office: 700 Jefferson Ave Redwood City CA 94063 Tel (415) 364-6500

MELCHER, WILLIAM CHARLES, b. Allentown, Pa., Oct. 14, 1942; A.B. in Econs., San Francisco State U., 1965; J.D., Golden Gate U., 1969. Admitted to Calif. bar, 1970, Fed. bar, 1970; instr. Mid Valley Coll. Law, Encino, Calif., 1971-74; dean Golden West U. Sch. Law, Santa Monica, Calif., 1974; dep. dist. atty. Los Angeles County, Calif., 1970-76; pres. WCM Prodns., Hollywood, Calif., 1976—; feature columnist Acad. Country Music Chronicle. Mem. State Bar Calif., Acad. Country Music, Country Music Assn. Nashville, U.S. Power Squadron. Office: 4520 Larkwood Ave Woodland Hills CA 91364 Tel (213) 888-9750

MELCHERT, PAUL AUGUST, b. Murdo, S.D., Oct. 22, 1935; B.A., Valparaiso U., 1956, LL.B., 1958. Admitted to Minn. bar, U.S. Dist. Ct. bar, 1958; with firm Glaeser & Melchert, Waconia, Minn., asso., 1958-62, partner, 1962-66; individual practice law, Waconia, Minn., 1966-69; partner firm Melchert, Hubert, Howe & Young, Waconia, 1969—. Mem. Am., Minn. bar assns. Office: 1st Nat Bank Bldg Waconia MN 55387 Tel (612) 442-2154

MELCHIOR, KURT WERNER, b. Essen, Germany, Oct. 30, 1924; Ph.B., U. Chgo., 1943, M.A., 1949; LL.B., Yale, 1951. Admitted to Ill. bar, 1951, D.C. bar, 1951, Calif. bar, 1957; atty. preparedness com. U.S. Senate, 1951-52, Office Price Stabilization, 1952-53, Dept. Justice, 1953-56; asso. firm Landels, Weigel & Ripley, San Francisco, 1956-57, firm Freed & Freed, San Francisco, 1957-60; asso. firm Severson, Werson, Berke & Melchior, and predecessors, San Francisco, 1960-63, partner, 1963—; lectr. Golden Gate U. Sch. Law, 1961-67. Mem. Calif. Gov's. Commn. on Family, 1966; mem. bd. dirs. Nat. Assn. Mental Health, 1966-72, chmn. litigation panel, 1973-75; pres. French Am. Bilingual Sch., 1974-75; law mem. Human Research Com., Pacific Med. Center, 1973-75; pres. San Francisco Assn. Mental Health, 1960-61; pres. San Francisco Suicide Prevention, 1963-65. Mem. State Bar Calif. (bd. govs., 1975—, v.p. 1977—, corp. law com. 1974-75, lectr. continuing legal edn., past del. conf. of dels.), Bar Assn. San Francisco (dir., 1973-75), Am., Fed. bar assns., Lawyers' Club San Francisco, Order Coif. Home: 159 Miraloma Dr San Francisco CA 94127 Office: 1 Embarcadero Center San Francisco CA 94111 Tel (415) 398-3344

MELENDRES, ARTHUR DAVID, b. Albuquerque, Dec. 19, 1943; B.A., U. N. Mex., 1965, J.D., 1971. Admitted to N. Mex. bar, 1971; law clk. to judge U.S. Dist. Ct., 1971; partner firm Modrall, Sperling, Roehl, Harris & Sisk, Albuquerque, 1971—; mem. municipal rules com. N. Mex. Supreme Ct., 1976—. Mem. Albuquerque Employee Relations bd., 1974-75; mem. state central com. Democratic Party N. Mex., 1974-76; bd. dirs. Albuquerque Legal Aid Soc., 1976—, Bernalillo County ARC, 1973—. Mem. Am., Albuquerque (bd. dirs. 1975—) bar assns., State Bar N. Mex. (chmn. legis. com. 1976—, chmn. long-range planning 1976—), N. Mex. Bar Assn. (pres. young lawyers sect. 1974-75, service award 1975). Home: 929 Quincy St NE Albuquerque NM 87110 Office: 800 Public Service Bldg PO Box 2168 Albuquerque NM 87103 Tel (505) 243-4511

MELIA, ALOYSIUS JAMES, b. N.Y.C., Feb. 8, 1915; A.B., Fordham U., 1935, J.D., 1938. Admitted to N.Y. bar, 1939, U.S. Dist. Ct. bar, 1946, U.S. Ct. of Appeals bar, 1947; asso. firm O'Malley and Wilson, N.Y.C., 1939-41; asst. dist. atty. N.Y. County, 1942-56; dep. police commn., 1956-60, 63-68; gen. counsel N.Y.C. Housing and Redevel. Bd., 1960-63; judge N.Y.C. Criminal Ct., 1968-71; acting justice N.Y. State Supreme Ct., N.Y.C., 1971—; lectr. Coll. City N.Y., 1958-60, N.Y. Law Sch., 1961-63, N.Y. U., 1965-68, N.Y.C. Practicing Law Inst., 1950-65. Mem. N.Y.C. Bar Assn. Office: 100 Centre St New York City NY 10013 Tel (212) 374-5870

MELICH, MITCHELL, b. Bingham Canyon, Utah, Feb. 1, 1912; LL.B., U. Utah, 1934. Admitted to Utah bar, 1934; practice law, Moab, Utah, 1934-63; city atty., Moab, 1934-55; county atty., Grand County (Utah), 1940-42; mem. Utah Senate, 1942-50, minority leader, 1949-50; pres., dir. Uranium Reduction Co., Moab, 1954-62; sec., dir. Utex Exploration Co., Moab, 1953-62; treas., dir. New Park Mining Co., Moab, 1962-65; cons. to pres. Atlas Minerals div. Atlas Corp., 1962-67; cons. on staff Congressman Sherman P. Lloyd of Utah, 1967-68; solicitor U.S. Dept. Interior, Washington, 1969-73; partner firm Ray, Quinney & Nebeker, Salt Lake City, 1973—; dir. First Security Bank Utah. Mem. Colo. River Com. Utah, 1945-47, Utah Water and Power Bd., 1947, Utah Legis. Council, 1949-54; chmn. Citizens Adv. Com. Higher Edn., 1968; bd. regents U. Utah, 1961-65, mem. devel. fund com., nat. adv. council, 1968-73; bd. dirs. St. Marks Hosp., 1973—. Mem. Am. Bar Assn., Utah State Bar. Recipient Distinguished Alumni award U. Utah, 1969. Home: 900 Donner Way Salt Lake City UT 84108 Office: Deseret Bldg Salt Lake City UT 84111 Tel (801) 532-1500

MELIN, ROBERT ARTHUR, b. Milw., Sept. 13, 1940; B.A. summa cum laude, Marquette U., 1962, J.D., 1966; certificate U. Va. Law Sch., 1967. Admitted to Wis. bar, 1966, U.S. Supreme Ct. bar, 1975; law clerk Fed. Judge John W. Reynolds, U.S. Dist. Ct. Eastern Dist. Wis., 1966; capt. Judge Adv. Gen., 1967-70; lectr. in law Haile Sellassie I U. Law Faculty, Addis Ababa, Ethiopia, 1971-72; mem. firm Walther & Halling, Milw., 1973-74, Schroeder, Gedlen, Riester & Moerke, Milw., 1974—. Chmn. Milw. County Young Democrats, 1963-64. Mem. Am., Wis., Milw., Milw. Jr. bar assns., Nat. Legal Aid and Defender Assn., Delta Theta Phi, Phi Alpha Theta, Pi Gamma Mu. Author: Evidence in Ethiopia, 1972; also chpt. on Ethiopia in Ann. Survey African Law 1970, 1974; contbr. articles to legal jours.; asso. editor Marquette Law Rev., 1964-65. Home: 8108 N Whitney Rd Milwaukee WI 53217 Office: 212 W Wisconsin Ave Milwaukee WI 53203 Tel (414) 272-4060

MELLING, BRIAN JAMES, b. Cleve., Oct. 21, 1949; B.A., Mount Union Coll., 1971; J.D., Ohio No. U., 1974. Admitted to Ohio bar, 1974; individual practice law, Bedford, Ohio, 1974—; prosecutor City of Bedford, 1975—, law dir., 1976—. Mem. Am., Ohio, Cleve., S.E. bar Assns. Home: Ennis Ave Bedford OH 44146 Office: 680 Broadway Bedford OH 44146 Tel (216) 232-0994

MELOY, LORETTA, b. Shelbyville, Ind., Apr. 26, 1924; B.S., Ind. U., 1942, J.D., 1968. Admitted to Ind. bar, 1969; individual practice law, Shelbyville, 1969—; judge, Shelbyville, 1972-75. Mem. Ind. State, Shelby County bar assns. Office: PO Box 454 Shelbyville IN 46176 Tel (317) 398-9211

MELOY, PETER GEORGE, b. Townsend, Mont., Feb. 22, 1908; J.D., U. Mont., 1936. Admitted to Mont. bar, 1936; past sr. partner firm Meloy, Kline & Niklas, Helena, Mont.; judge Mont. 1st Jud. Dist. Ct., Helena, 1972—. Home: 1317 9th Ave Helena MT 59601 Office: Court House Helena MT 59601 Tel (406) 442-6070

MELOY, THOMAS CLIFFORD, b. Akron, Ohio, July 19, 1940; B.A., Kent State U., 1962; J.D., Western Res. U., 1965. Admitted to Ohio bar, 1970; claims atty. Nationwide Ins. Co., 1965-76; partner firm Shoemaker, Comanor and Meloy, Cuyahoga Falls, Ohio, 1976—; regional coordinator Rehab. Nationwide Ins. Co. No. Ohio, 1972-75. Mem. Am., Akron, Ohio bar assns., Ohio Def. Assn. Home: 118 Mayfield Ave Akron OH 44313 Office: 116 Portage Trail Cuyahoga Falls OH 44221 Tel (216) 929-3168

MELTON, EMORY LEON, b. McDowell, Mo., June 20, 1923; LL.B., U. Mo., 1945. Admitted to Mo. bar, 1944; individual practice law, Cassville, Mo., 1947—; pros. atty. Barry County, Mo., 1947-51; mem. Mo. Senate, 1973—. Mem. Mo. Bar Assn. Home: Route 1 Cassville MO 65625 Office: 201 W 9th St Cassville MO 65625 Tel (417) 847-4144

MELTON, HOWELL WEBSTER, b. Atlanta, Dec. 15, 1923; LL.B., U. Fla., 1948, J.D., 1967. Admitted to Fla. bar, 1948, U.S. Supreme Ct. bar, 1960; asso. firm Upchurch, Melton & Upchurch, St. Augustine, 1948-60; judge Circuit Ct., 7th Jud. Circuit Fla., 1961—. Chmn. bd. stewards, trustee Grace Methodist Ch., St. Augustine; chmn. ofcl. bd. 1st Meth. Ch., St. Augustine; mem. Bd. Social Welfare, Dist. 5 and St. Johns County, 1955-56, Health Planning Council, Jacksonville Area, Inc.; v.p., gen. chmn. fund raising campaign Community Chest-United Fund of St. Augustine and St. Johns County, 1957, also bd. dirs.; pres. St. Johns County Welfare Fedn.; sec. St. Johns County Blood Bank; v.p., bd. dirs. St. Augustine YMCA; pres., bd. dirs., chmn. bd. trustees Flagler Hosp., St. Augustine; v.p. St. Johns County Mental Health Assn.; mem. adv. bd. N.Fla. council Boy Scouts Am. Mem. Am., Fla. (past chmn. Council of Bar Pres.'s, past dir. Jr. Bar sect.), St. Johns County (past pres.) bar assns., Am. Judicature Soc., Nat. Conf. State Trial Judges, Fla. Conf. Circuit Judges (sec.-treas. 1972, chmn. 1974, exec. com. 1975—), Am. Legion, U. Fla. Alumni Assn. (past dist. v.p.), St. Augustine and St. Johns County C. of C. (dir. 1957-58, v.p. 1958), Phi Delta Phi, Phi Delta Theta. Recipient Distinguished Service award St. Augustine Jr. C. of C., 1953. Home: 41 Carrera St Saint Augustine FL 32084 Office: St Johns County Courthouse Saint Augustine FL 32084 Tel (904) 824-8131

MELTON, MICHAEL WARD, b. Chgo., Mar. 13, 1946; B.A., Princeton, 1968; J.D., U. So. Calif., 1973. Admitted to Calif. bar, 1973; asso. firm Kindel & Anderson, Los Angeles, 1973—. Mem. Am., Calif., Los Angeles County bar assns., Order of Coif. Editor So. Calif. Law Rev., 1973. Office: 555 S Flower St Los Angeles CA 90071 Tel (213) 680-222

MELTON, WILLIAM DUDLEY, b. Pineapple, Ala., June 30, 1943; B.S., Auburn U., 1963; J.D., U. Ala., 1966. Admitted to Ala. bar, 1966, U.S. Supreme Ct. bar, 1971, U.S. Ct. Appeals 5th Circuit bar, 1972; individual practice law, Evergreen, Ala.; spl. asst. atty. gen. State of Ala., 1972—. Mem. Ala. Ho. of Reps., 1967-71, Ala. Senate, 1973-74. Mem. Am., Ala. (bd. govs. 1975-76) trial lawyers assns., Fed., Ala., Conecuh County bar assns., Am. Judicature Soc. Mem. editorial bd. Ala. Lawyer, 1973-77. Office: Rutland-Price Bldg Evergreen AL 36401 Tel (205) 578-2423

MELTZER, BERNARD DAVID, b. Phila., Nov. 21, 1914; A.B., U. Chgo., 1935, J.D., 1937; LL.M., Harvard, 1938. Admitted to Ill. bar, 1938; atty., spl. asst. to chmn. SEC, 1938-40; asso. firm Mayer, Meyer, Austrian & Platt, Chgo., 1940; spl. asst. to asst. sec. state, also acting chief fgn. funds control div. div. State 1941-43; trial counsel U.S. staff Internat. Nuremberg War Trials, 1945-46; from professorial lectr. to prof. law U. Chgo. Law Sch., 1946—. Hearing commr. NPA, 1952-53; labor arbitrator; spl. master U.S. Ct. Appeals for D.C., 1963-64; bd. publs. U. Chgo., 1965-67, chmn., 1967-68; mem. Gov. Ill. Adv. Commn. Labor-Mgmt. Policy for Pub. Employees in Ill., 1966-67; cons. U.S. Dept. Labor, 1969-70. Bd. dirs. High Park Community Conf., 1954-56, S.E. Chgo. Commn., 1956-57. Mem. Am. (co-chmn. com. devel. law under NLRA 1959-60; mem. spl. com. transp. strikes), Ill., Chgo. (bd. mgrs. 1972-73) bar assns., Nat. Acad. Arbitrators, Am. Law Inst., Am. Acad. Arts and Scis., Phi Beta Kappa, Order of Coif. Author: (with W.G. Katz) Cases and Materials on Business Corporations, 1949; Labor Law Cases, Materials and Problems, 1970, supplement, 1972, 75; also articles. Home: 1219 E 50th St Chicago IL 60615*

MELTZER, BRIAN, b. Chgo., Apr. 15, 1944; A.B. in Math., Cornell U., 1966; J.D., Harvard U., 1969. Admitted to Ill. bar, 1969; asso. firm D'ancona, Pflaum, Wyatt & Riskind, Chgo., 1969-71; asso. firm Schwartz & Freeman, Chgo., 1971-76, partner, 1976—; instr. Central YMCA Community Coll.; speaker Ill. Inst. Continuing Legal Edn., Ill. Condominium Law Program, 1977; instr. Northwestern U. Mem.

Chgo. Bar Assn., Chgo. Council Lawyers. Contbr. articles to legal jours. Home: 3400 Lake Shore Dr apt 4C Chicago IL 60657 Office: Suite 4530 One IBM Plaza Chicago IL 60611 Tel (312) 222-0800

MELVILLE, CHARLES HARTLEY, b. Cin., Jan. 18, 1937; A.B., Princeton, 19S9; LL.B., U. Cin., 1962. Admitted to Ohio bar, 1962; asso. firm Yungblut, Melville, Strasser & Foster, Cin., 1962-67; partner firm Melville, Strasser, Foster & Hoffman, 1967-72; gen. counsel Senco Products Inc., Cin., 1973-74, v.p., 1974—; lectr. U. Cin., 1963-73. Mem. Cin. Bar Assn. Home: 434 Oliver Rd Cincinnati OH 45215 Office: 8485 Broadwell Rd Cincinnati OH 45244 Tel (513) 474-3000

MELVIN, JAMES RADCLIFFE, b. Whiteville, N.C., Dec. 6, 1942; A.A., Wingate Coll., 1962; B.A., Wake Forest U., 1964, J.D., 1966. Admitted to N.C. bar, 1966; individual practice law, Elizabethtown, N.C., 1969-70; partner firm Moore and Melvin, Elizabethtown, 1971—. Commr., Town of White Lake (N.C.), 1969-73; bd. dirs. N.C. Blueberry Festival, 1970-73, Four County Community Services, 1973—. Mem. Am., N.C. 13th Dist. (pres. 1974-75) bar assns., Am. Judicature Soc., Phi Alpha Delta. Home: Dublin Rd Elizabethtown NC 28337 Office: PO Box 875 Courthouse Dr Elizabethtown NC 28337 Tel (919) 862-2544

MENAPACE, RALPH C., JR., b. Mt. Carmel, Pa., Nov. 24, 1931; B.A., Yale, 1953, LL.B., 1956. Admitted to N.Y. bar, 1957; asso. firm Cahill, Gordon & Reindel, N.Y.C., 1956-65, partner, 1966—; counsel, bd. dirs. Municipal Art Soc., N.Y.C., 1970—, Central Park Community Fund, 1975—. Mem. Internat., N.Y. State bar assns., Assn. Bar City N.Y. Home: 1115 Fifth Ave New York City NY 10028 Office: 80 Pine St New York City NY 10005 Tel (212) 825-0100

MENDELSOHN, ALLAN IRVING, b. Chgo., May 15, 1932; S.B., U. Ill., 1954, LL.B., 1955; LL.M., Harvard U., 1956; Diplome, The Sorbonne, Paris, 1962. Admitted to Ill. bar, 1955, D.C. bar, 1966, U.S. Supreme Ct. bar, 1961; served with JAGC, 1956-59; atty. Office Gen. Counsel Appellate Litigation, NLRB, Washington, 1959-62; mem. staff office legal adviser Dept. State, Washington, 1963-68; asso. firm Glassie, Pewett, Beebe & Shanks, 1968-70, partner 1970—; cons. UN Commn. Internat. Trade Law, 1971-72, U.S. Senate Com. Pub. Works, 1971—, U.S. Dept. Interior, 1972-75; U.S. del to U.S. Diplomatic Internat. Confs. Pvt. Internat. Air and Maritime Law, 1963-68; fgn. claims commr. U.S. Army, Beirut, Lebanon, 1958. Mem. Am., D.C. bar assns., Walter Reed Soc. Contbr. articles to legal jours. Home: 3310 Cathedral Ave Washington DC 20008 Office: 1737 H St NW Washington DC 20006 Tel (202) 466-4310

MENDELSON, LEONARD MELVIN, b. Pitts., May 20, 1923; A.B., U. Mich., 1947; J.D., Yale, 1950. Admitted to Pa. bar, 1951, U.S. Supreme Ct. bar, 1955; mem. firm Hollinshead and Mendelson, Pitts., chmn. bd., 1974—. Mem. Pitts. Bd. Pub. Edn., 1975-76. Mem. Allegheny County (chmn. lawyer realty joint com. Pitts. chpt. 1971-72), Pa., Am. bar assns. Home: 138 Hartwood Dr Pittsburgh PA 15208 Office: 3010 Mellon Bank Bldg Pittsburgh PA 15219 Tel (412) 281-2222

MENDELSON, WILLIAM, b. Cleve., Oct. 27, 1904; B.A., Ohio State U., 1926; LL.B., Case Western Reserve U., 1928, J.D., 1968. Admitted to Ohio bar, 1928; since practiced in Cleve.; mem. firm Mendelson & Mendelson, 1928-47, mem. firm Benesch, Friedlander, Coplan & Aronoff, and predecessors, 1947-75, of counsel, 1975—. Mem. Greater Cleve., Ohio bar assns. Home: 1 Bratenahi Pl Bratenahl OH 44108 Office: 1100 Citizens Bldg Cleveland OH 44114 Tel (216) 696-1600

MENDICINO, V. FRANK, b. Denver, June 26, 1939; B.S., U. Wyo., 1962, J.D. with honors, 1970. Admitted to Wyo. bar, 1970, Fed. bar, 1970, U.S. Supreme Ct. bar, 1976; mem. firm Smith, Stanfield, & Mendicino, Laramie, Wyo., 1970-75; asst. city atty., Laramie, 1970-75; justice of the peace, Albany County, Wyo., 1970-72; mem. Wyo. Legislature, 1973-74; atty. gen. State of Wyo., Cheyenne, 1975—. Pres., Albany County United Fund, 1973; trustee Cathedral Home Children, 1970-74. Mem. Albany County, Wyo., Am. bar assns. Recipient state and local distinguished service awards Wyo. and Laramie Jaycees, 1973. Home: 3711 Dover Rd Cheyenne WY 82001 Office: 123 Capitol Bldg Cheyenne WY 82002 Tel (307) 777-7841

MENEFEE, CHARLES CULL, b. Ann Arbor, Mich., Aug. 13; A.B., U. Mich., 1934, LL.B., 1937. Admitted to Mich. bar, 1937; asso. firm Roscoe O. Bonisteel, Ann Arbor, 1939-53; individual practice law, Ann Arbor, 1954-58, Rogers City, Mich., 1958—; ct. commr., 1942-52; judge Presque Isle County (Mich.) Probate Ct., 1971—; city atty. City of Rogers City, 1958-76; mem. Ann Arbor City Council, 1953-57. Mem. Mich. State, 26th Jud. Circuit bar assns. Home: 481 W Erie St Rogers City MI 49779 Office: 124 S Third St Rogers City MI 49779 Tel (517) 734-2090

MENGSHOL, JOHN GILBERT, b. Berkeley, Calif., Feb. 3, 1937; B.S. in Chem. Engring., U. Calif., Berkeley, 1959, J.D., 1966. Admitted to Calif. bar, 1966, U.S. Supreme Ct. bar, 1971, U.S. Tax Ct. bar, 1973; asso. firm Thomas, Snell, Jamison, Russell, Williamson & Asperger, Fresno, Calif., 1966-69, partner, 1970—. Bd. dirs. Fresno Arts Center, 1971—, pres., 1972-74. Mem. State Bar Calif., Am., Fresno County bar assns. Office: Fresno's Townehouse Fresno CA 93710 Tel (209) 442-0600

MENKE, DAVID JOHN, b. Milw., Oct. 17, 1941; B.S. in Econs., U. Wis., 1964; J.D., Syracuse U., 1969. Admitted to N.Y. bar, 1970; mem. legal dept. Mut. of N.Y. Life Ins. Co., N.Y.C., 1969-70; asst. dist. atty. Broome County (N.Y.), Binghamton, 1970-71; asso. firm Gent & Egan, Binghamton, 1971-75; individual practice law, Binghamton, 1976—. Trustee Susquehanna Sch., Binghamton. Mem. Broome County, N.Y. State, Am. bar assns., Comml. Law League Am., Phi Alpha Delta. Home: 1004 So Pines Dr Endwell NY 13760 Office: 19 Chenango St Binghamton NY 13901 Tel (607) 724-3300

MENNELL, ROBERT LEE, b. Boston, Mar. 5, 1934; B.A., U. Calif. at Los Angeles, 1955; J.D., Harvard, 1962. Admitted to Calif. bar, 1963; asso. firm Voegelin, Barton, Harris & Callister (now Voegelin & Barton), Los Angeles, 1962-68; individual practice law, Encino, Calif., 1968-70; prof. law Southwestern U., Los Angeles, 1968—; vis. prof. Law Sch. Notre Dame U., 1975-76. Mem. State Bar Calif., Am., Los Angeles County bar assns. Author: California Decedents' Estates, 1973; Editorial bd. Community Property Jour., 1975—. contbr. articles to legal jours. Home: 3707 Sapphire Dr Encino CA 91436 Office: 675 S Westmoreland Ave Los Angeles CA 90005 Tel (213) 380-4800

MENOR, BENJAMIN, b. San Nicholas, Philippines, Sept. 27, 1922; B.S., U. Hawaii, 1950; LL.B., Boston U., 1952. Admitted to Hawaii bar, 1953; individual practice law, Hilo, Hawaii, 1959-69; county atty., Hilo, 1953-59; mem. Hawaii State Senate, 1962-66; state dist. ct. magistrate, Hilo, 1967-69; judge Circuit Ct., Hilo, 1969-74; asso. justice Hawaii Supreme Ct., Honolulu, 1974—. Mem. Hawaii Bar Assn. Recipient Pub. Office award Philippines Govt., 1974. Home: 95301 Mahapili Ct Mililani Town HI 96789 Office: Supreme Ct Hawaii PO Box 2560 Honolulu HI 96804 Tel (808) 548-3250

MENSH, MYRON JOSEPH, b. Vero Beach, Fla., May 24, 1939; B.A., Emory U., 1961; postgrad U. Fla., 1961-62; J.D., Stetson U., 1964. Admitted to Fla. bar, 1964; partner firm Mensh, Mensh, Zacur & Graham, St. Petersburg, Fla., 1965-75; asso. judge, Maderia Beach, Fla., 1965-66; asst. state atty. 6th Jud. Circuit, St. Petersburg, 1967—. Founder, pres. Temple Hillel, Inc., St. Petersburg, 1972—. Mem. Am., Fla., St. Petersburg bar assns., Lawyers Title Guaranty Fund, Fla. Presecuting Attys. Assn. Office: 5200 Central Ave Saint Petersburg FL 33707 Tel (813) 381-0051

MENSH, SAMUEL LIONEL, b. Cisna, Poland, Feb. 8, 1912; LL.B., Nat. U., 1938, LL.M., 1939, M.P.L., 1939. Admitted to D.C. bar, 1938, D.C. Fed. Ct. Appeals bar, 1938; individual practice law, Washington, 1938—. Mem. Am. Trial Lawyers Assn. Home: 1131 University Ave Silver Spring MD 20902 Office: 815 15th St NW Washington DC 20005 Tel (202) 347-9411

MENSORE, JOHN JOSEPH, b. New Martinsville, W.Va., Aug. 4, 1938; B.A., Wheeling Coll., 1960; J.D., W.Va. U., 1963. Admitted to W.Va. bar, 1963; partner Mensore & Mensore, New Martinsville, 1965—; v.p., gen. mgr. J.C. Mensore Distbr., Inc., New Martinsville, 1969—. Bd. dirs. No. W.Va. Blue Cross-Blue Shield, 1965—, exec. bd., 1976—; bd. dirs. Wetzel County Hosp., New Martinsville, 1965—; bd. dirs., treas. Jr. Achievement Greater New Martinsville Area, 1965—. Mem. Am., W.Va., Wetzel County bar assns., Phi Delta Phi. Home: 343 Clark Dr New Martinsville WV 26155 Office: 267 Main St New Martinsville WV 26155 Tel (304) 455-1700

MENSORE, TULANE BOUCH, b. Weston, W.Va., Feb. 2, 1940; A.B., W.Va. U., 1961, J.D., 1964. Admitted to W.Va. bar, 1964; partner Mensore & Mensore, New Martinsville, W.Va., 1965—; sec.-treas. J.C. Mensore Distbr., Inc., New Martinsville, 1969—. Mem. New Martinsville Civic League, Wetzel County Hosp. Aux., New Martinsville, 1966—; bd. dirs. Citizens Scholarship Found. of New Martinsville, 1974-77, Friends of WWVU-TV, Morgantown, W.Va., 1974—. Mem. Am., W.Va., Wetzel County bar assns. Home: 343 Clark Dr New Martinsville WV 26155 Office: 267 Main St New Martinsville WV 26155 Tel (304) 455-1700

MENTSCHIKOFF, SOIA, b. Moscow, Apr. 2, 1915 (parents Am. citizens); A.B., Hunter Coll., 1934; LL.B., Columbia, 1937; LL.D. (hon.), Smith Coll., 1967, Syracuse U., 1974, Boston Coll., 1974, Boston U., 1974, Layfette Coll., 1974, U. Puget Sound Sch. Law, 1976. Admitted to N.Y. bar, 1938, Ill. bar, 1956; asso. firm Scandrett, Tuttle & Chalaire, N.Y.C., 1937-41; asso. firm Spence, Windels, Walser, Hotchkiss & Angell, N.Y.C., 1941-44, partner, 1944-45; partner firm Spencer Hotchkiss Parker & Duryee, N.Y.C., 1945-49; vis. prof. Harvard Law Sch., Cambridge, Mass., 1947-49; prof. U. Chgo. Law Sch., 1951-74; vis. prof. U. Miami (Fla.) Law Sch., 1968, distinguished cons. and asso. of faculty, 1968-71, distinguished vis. prof., 1971-74, dean Sch. Law, 1974—; mem. council Nat. Endowment for the Humanities, 1965-71; cons. AID, 1966-69; cons. permanent editorial bd. Uniform Comml. Code, 1962—. Mem. Am. Law Inst. (life), Am. Bar Assn., Bar Assn. City N.Y., Am. Acad. Arts and Scis. Home: 1012 San Pedro Ave Coral Gables FL 33156 Office: U Miami Sch Law PO Box 248087 Coral Gables FL 33124 Tel (305) 284-2392

MENZIES, WALTER ROBERT, b. Cheyenne, Wyo., Jan. 22, 1902; J.D., Marquette U., 1927. Admitted to Wis. bar, 1927; individual practice law, Menomonee Falls, Wis., 1927—; municipal judge, Butler, Wis., 1960-74. Mem. Butler Planning Commn., 1955-75. Mem. Am. Power Boat Assn. Home: 12902 W Lancaster Ave Butler WI 53006 Office: N 48 W 14170 Hampton Rd Menomonee Falls WI 53051 Tel (414) 781-6620

MERCER, GRADY, b. Beulaville, N.C., Jan. 18, 1906; A.B. in Edn., LL.B., U. N.C. Admitted to N.C. bar, 1939; asso. firm Mercer, Thigpen & Mercer, Kenansville, N.C.; senator N.C. Gen. Assembly, 1959. Address: Kenansville NC 28349 Tel (919) 296-6151

MERCER, HELEN ROUNTREE, b. San Francisco, Apr. 29, 1913; B.A., U. Calif., Los Angeles, 1934; LL.B., Southwestern U of Law, 1937. Admitted to Calif. bar, 1938; atty. Title Ins. & Trust Co., Ventura, Calif., 1959-69; individual practice law, Ventura, 1969—. Sec. bd. dirs. Girl Scouts U.S.A., Ventura, 1952-54. Mem. Phi Delta Delta (pres. Santa Barbara Alumni chpt. 1967-68). Home: 4475 Whittier St Ventura CA 93003 Office: 21 S California St Suite 305 Ventura CA 93001 Tel (805) 683-7701

MERCURIO, DANTE JERALDO, b. Bloomfield, N.J., Sept. 9, 1921; A.B., Montclair State Coll., 1949; LL.B., Rutgers U., 1957. Admitted to N.J. bar, 1958; clk. municipal ct., Bloomfield, 1951-74; individual practice law, Bloomfield, 1974—; judge adv. Am. Legion, Post 201, Livingston, N.J. Mem. Lawyers Club Bloomfield (pres. 1970). Home: 37 N Westgate Rd Livingston NJ 07039 Office: 316 Broad St Bloomfield NJ 07003 Tel (201) 743-1110

MERDES, EDWARD ANTHONY, b. Leetsdale, Pa., Jan. 12, 1926; B.S. in Indsl. Labor Relations, Cornell U., 1949, LL.B., 1951; Admitted to N.Y. bar, 1951, Alaska bar, 1952; asst. U.S. atty., Juneau, Alaska, 1952-53; asst. atty. gen. Ter. Alaska, 1953-57; partner firm McNealy & Merdes, Fairbanks, Alaska, 1957-66; sr. partner firm Merdes, Schaible et al, Fairbanks, 1966—; mem. Alaska Senate, 1968-72. Mem. Am., Alaska bar assns., Jaycees (world pres. 1966). Office: Merdes Schaible Box 810 Fairbanks AK 99701 Tel (907) 452-1855

MEREDITH, ARTHUR SUTPHEN, b. Somerville, N.J., Apr. 19, 1923; A.B., Rutgers U., 1947, LL.B., 1950. Admitted to N.J. bar, 1951; partner firm Meredith & Norris, Somerville, 1951-68; judge Somerset County (N.J.) Ct., 1968-73, N.J. Superior Ct., 1973—; prosecutor Somerset County, 1959-65; atty. Borough Somerville, 1966-67. Mem. Somerville Borough Council, 1950-52; vice chmn. Somerset County Democratic Com., 1953-54, chmn., 1954-58; v.p. Somerset Valley Community Chest, 1951; pres. Somerset County Council Social Agys., 1950; del. N.J. Constl. Conv., 1966. Mem. Somerset County, N.J., Am. bar assns., N.J. Prosecutors Assn. (v.p.). Home: 198 W High St Somerville NJ 08876 Office: Courthouse W Main St Somerville NJ 08876 Tel (201) 725-4700

MEREDITH, JAMES HARGROVE, b. Wedderburn, Oreg., Aug. 25, 1914; A.B., U. Mo., 1936, LL.B., 1937. Admitted to Mo. bar, 1937, D.C. bar, 1961; practiced in Portageville and New Madrid, Mo., 1937-41; asst. pros. atty. New Madrid County (Mo.), 1937-41; spl. agt. FBI, 1942-44; practice in Portageville, 1946-49; legal counsel Gov. of Mo., 1949-50; chief counsel Mo. Div. Ins., 1950-52; mem. firm Lowenhaupt, Chasnoff, Waite & Stolar, St. Louis, 1952-56; partner firm Stolar, Kuhlman & Meredith, St. Louis, 1956-61, Cook, Meredith, Murphy & English, St. Louis, 1961-62, Stuart & Meredith, Washington, 1961-62; judge U.S. Dist. Ct., Eastern Dist. Mo., 1962—, chief judge, 1971—. Trustee Mo. U. Law Sch. Found., 1963-69, Eastern Mo. chpt. Arthritis and Rheumatism Found., 1964-74, Friends of Mo. Library Assn., 1965. Mem. Mo. Acad. Squires, U.S. Jud. Conf., Am., Mo., St. Louis, Fed. bar assns., Lawyers Assn., Bar Assn. D.C., Order of Coif, Sigma Chi, Phi Delta Phi. Home: 625 S Skinker St Saint Louis MO 63105 Office: 324 US Courthouse and Custom House 1114 Market St Saint Louis MO 63101 Tel (314) 425-4217

MEREDITH, SAMUEL EDWARD, b. Milford, Del., May 17, 1938; A.B., Dickinson Coll., 1960; J.D., Golden Gate Sch. Law, 1967. Admitted to Calif. bar, 1968; atty. Safeco Ins. Co., Burlingame, Calif., 1968-72; partner firm Goshkin, Pollatsek, Meredith & Lee, San Francisco, 1972—. Mem. Am., Calif., San Francisco bar assns., Assn. Def. Attys., No. Calif. Assn. Compensation Def. Attys. Home: 2753 Ramona St Palo Alto CA 94306 Office: 111 Pine St San Francisco CA 94111 Tel (415) 981-1400

MERIAM, HAROLD AUSTIN, JR., b. N.Y.C., May 5, 1920; student Fordham U., 1939-42; LL.B. summa cum laude, Bklyn. Law Sch., 1948. Admitted to N.Y. bar, 1949; asso. firm Wagner, Quillinan, Wagner & Tennant, N.Y.C., 1948-49; law asst. to asso. judge N.Y. Ct. Appeals, 1950-53; asso. firm Cullen and Dykman, Bklyn., 1953-64, partner 1965—; cons. Joint Legis. Com. Ct. Reorgn. N.Y., 1966-67. N.Y. Temporary Commn. Estates, 1963-67; cons. judiciary N.Y. Constl. Conv., 1967; mem. com. advise and consult Jud. Conf. Civil Practice Law and Rules N.Y., 1969—. Bd. dirs. SE Nassau Guidance Center, 1965, Brookwood Child Care, 1965; v.p. Bklyn. Bur. Community Service, 1972—. Mem. Bklyn., Queens, N.Y. State (chairman elect trusts and estate law sect. 1976—) bar assns., Am. Coll. Probate Counsel. Home: 1404 Delile Pl Wantagh NY 11793 Office: 177 Montague St Brooklyn NY 11201 Tel (212) 855-9000

MERIDETH, H.L., b. Greenville, Miss., Dec. 7, 1930; B.S., Miss. State U., 1953; LL.B., U. Miss., 1958. Admitted to Miss. bar, 1958; individual practice law, Greenville, 1958-64; sr. partner firm Robertshaw & Merideth, Greenville, 1964—; mem. Miss. Legislature, 1960—. Mem. Am., Miss., Washington County bar assns. Named Greenville's Outstanding Young Man, 1960. Home: 7 N Plantation Dr Greenville MS 38701 Office: PO Box 1498 Greenville MS 38701 Tel (601) 378-2171

MERKEL, CHARLES MICHAEL, b. Nashville, Nov. 2, 1941; B.A., U. Miss., 1963, J.D., 1966; LL.M., Georgetown U., 1969. Admitted to Miss. bar, 1966, U.S. Supreme Ct. bar, 1969; trial atty., tax div. Dept. Justice, Washington, 1966-70; partner firm Dunbar & Merkel, Clarksdale, Miss., 1971-73, Holcomb Dunbar Connell Merkel & Tollison, Clarksdale, 1973—; city judge, Clarksdale, 1974—. Fin. chmn. Boy Scouts Am. Mem. Miss., Am. bar assns., Am. trial lawyers assns., Clarksdale C. of C., Phi Delta Phi. Home: 101 Cypress St Clarksdale MS 38614 Office: 152 Delta St Clarksdale MS 38614 Tel (601) 627-2241

MERKEL, EDWARD W., b. Cin., May 4, 1908; A.B., Dartmouth, 1929; J.D., Harvard, 1932. Admitted to Ohio bar, 1932, U.S. Supreme Ct. bar, 1935; asso. firm Gilbert Bettmen, Cin., 1932-35; asso. firm Dinsmore, Shehl, Sawyer, Cin., 1935-43, partner, 1945-55; legal dir. Procter & Gamble, Cin., 1955-67, sec., 1962-67. Mem. Cin., Ohio, Am. bar assns. Home: 1617 E McMillan St Apt 203 Cincinnati OH 45206

MERKER, HOWARD BURTON, b. Balt., Oct. 15, 1930; Ph.B., Loyola Coll., Balt., 1952; J.D., U. Balt., 1958. Admitted to Md. bar, 1959; asso. trial magistrate, Balt., 1966-70; dep. state's atty. Balt. County, Md., 1975—. Chmn. N.W. Area Ednl. Adv. Council. Mem. Nat. Dist. Attys. Assn., Am., Md. bar assns., Nat. Council Juvenile Cts., Trial Judges Assn. Md. Home: 6711 Chokeberry Rd Baltimore MD 21209 Office: States Attorneys Office Court House Towson MD 21204 Tel (301) 494-3500

MERKIN, WILLIAM LESLIE, b. N.Y.C., Apr. 30, 1929; B.A., U. Tex., 1950; J.D., St. Mary's U., 1953. Admitted to Tex. bar, 1953, U.S. Supreme Ct. bar, 1970, since practiced in El Paso, Tex., partner firm Pearson & Merkin, 1957-58, individual practice law, 1959-70, sr. partner firm Merkin & Gibson, 1971—; lectr. Tex. Western Coll., 1957-59, JAG, U.S. Army, 1954-56. Pres., B'Nai Brith El Paso, 1961; mem. SW Regional commn. Anti-Defamation League. Mem. Tex., El Paso bar assns., Tex., El Paso (dir.) trial lawyers assns., Assn. Trial Lawyers Am. Home: 829 Cherry Hill Ln El Paso TX 79912 Office: Suite 510 Bassett Tower El Paso TX 79901 Tel (915) 533-4433

MEROW, JOHN EDWARD, b. Little Valley, N.Y., Dec. 20, 1929; student U. Calif., Los Angeles, 1947-48; B.S.E., U. Mich., 1952; J.D., Harvard, 1958. Admitted to N.Y. bar, 1958, U.S. Supreme Ct. bar, 1971; asso. firm Sullivan & Cromwell, N.Y.C., 1958-64, partner, 1965—; dir. Kaiser Aluminum & Chem. Corp., Kaiser Aluminum & Chem. Sales, Inc., Kaiser Bauxite Co., Broad St. Investing Corp., Nat. Investors Corp., Union Cash Mgmt. Fund, Inc., Union Capital Fund, Inc., Union Income Fund, Inc. Mem. adv. council Center Study of Fin. Instns of U. Pa.; trustee Prot. Episcopal Soc. Promoting Religion and Learning in State of N.Y. Mem. Assn. Bar City N.Y., Am., N.Y. State bar assns., N.Y. Law Inst., Union Internationale des Avocats. Home: 350 E 69th St New York City NY 10021 Office: 48 Wall St New York City NY 10005 Tel (212) 952-8138

MERRELL, BROWNELL, JR., b. Pasadena, Calif., Oct. 12, 1939; student Stanford, 1957-59; A.B., Northwestern U., 1961; LL.B., Stanford, 1964. Admitted to Calif. bar, U.S. Supreme Ct. bar, 1972; asso. firm Walker, Wright, Tyler & Ward, Los Angeles, 1965-66; partner firm Dietsch, Gates, Morris & Merrell and predecessor firms, Los Angeles, 1967—; mem. hearing sub-com. Calif. State Bar Examiners, 1975—. Mem. Am. (litigation sect.), Calif. bar assns., World Affairs Council, Calif. Assn. Pub. Utilities Counsel, Phi Beta Kappa. Office: 800 Wilshire Blvd Los Angeles CA 90017 Tel (213) 680-0140

MERRELL, EDGAR SANFORD KEEN, b. Lowville, N.Y., Aug. 7, 1926; B.A., St. Lawrence U., 1949; LL.B., Syracuse U., 1952. Admitted to N.Y. bar, 1953; partner firm Merrell & Merrell, Lowville, 1953—; atty. N.Y. State Tax Commn., 1954-58, 75-77; dir. Nat. Bank No. N.Y. Mem. Lowville Sch. Bd., 1954-67; area dir. N.Y. State Sch. Bd. Assn.; mem. vestry Trinity Ch.; bd. dirs. Lewis County Heart Assn.; treas. Lowville Cemetery Assn., chmn. Lewis County March of Dimes, 1955. Mem. Am., N.Y. State, Lewis County bar assns., Phi

Delta Phi. Home: 48 Collins Lowville NY 13367 Office: 37 Shady Ave Lowville NY 13367 Tel (315) 376-6565

MERRELL, LOUIS JACOB, b. Obobesti, Romania, Dec. 26, 1892; B.A., Coll. City N.Y., 1913; J.D., N.Y. U., 1920. Sec. to editor-in-chief, sec. editorial dept. N.Y. Times, N.Y.C., 1912-17; admitted to N.Y. bar, 1920, U.S. Supreme Ct. bar, 1943; asso. firm Feiner & Maass, N.Y.C., 1920-22; partner firm Moss & Merrell, and predecessors, N.Y.C., 1922-46; individual practice law, Bklyn., 1946—; instr. law Coll. City N.Y. Sch. Bus. and Civic Adminstrn., 1923-24; mem. N.Y.C. Mayor's Com. on Judiciary, 1962-73; pres. emeritus N.Y. Legis. Service Inc. Chmn., Kings County (N.Y.) Liberal Party, 1958-60. Fellow N.Y. Bar Found.; mem. N.Y. State (chmn. com. to cooperate with law revision commn. 1956-57), Bklyn. (pres. 1957-58) bar assns., Assn. Bar City N.Y., Phi Beta Kappa. Contbr. articles to legal jours. Home: 180 West End Ave New York City NY 10023 Office: 16 Court St Brooklyn NY 11241 Tel (212) UL 8-1502

MERRIAM, RONALD C., b. 1916; B.A., Albertus Magnus Coll.; law degree, Am. U. Called to Ont. bar, 1948; now exec. dir. Canadian Bar Assn., Ottawa. Office: 90 Sparks St Ottawa ON K1P 5B4 Canada*

MERRICK, IVAN EDWARD, b. St. Regis, Mont., Sept. 20, 1915; J.D., U. Wash., 1938; S.T.B., Gen. Theol. Sem., 1952. Admitted to Wash. bar, 1938, U.S. Supreme Ct. bar, 1954; since practiced in Seattle, asso. firm Padden & Moriarty, 1938-39; partner firm Merrick & Merrick, 1939-41; asso. firm Padden & Moriarty, 1945-49, partner, 1949—; mem. firm Robbins, Merrick & Kraft, 1970—; priest, Episcopal Ch., 1951-69; chmn. Mental Health and Mental Retardation Advisory Council, State of Wash., 1970-73; mem. Comprensive Health Planning Com., Region IX, USPHS, 1965-72. Chmn. standing com. Diocese of Olympia, 1975-76; pres. Found. for the Handicapped, 1975—; chmn. Children's Home Soc. Wash., 1973-75. Mem. Am., Wash State (chmn. family law com. 1969-72), Seattle-King County bar assns. Home: 6235 NE Princeton Way Seattle WA 98115 Office: 1012 Seattle Tower Seattle WA 98101 Tel (206) 624-8822

MERRIFIELD, LEROY SORENSON, b. Mpls. Nov. 18, 1917; B.A., U. Minn., 1938, LL.B., 1941; M. Pub. Adminstrn., Harvard, 1942, S.J.D., 1956. Admitted to Minn. bar, 1941, U.S. Supreme Ct. bar, 1957; lawyer Office Price Adminstrn., Boston, 1942; lawyer anti-trust div. U.S. Dept. Justice, Washington, 1946-47; asst. prof. Nat. Law Center George Washington U., Washington, 1947, asso. prof., 1948, prof., 1956—, acting dean, 1948-49; labor arbitrator Am. Arbitration Assn., Fed. Mediation and Conciliation Service, 1966—; cons. Commn. on Govt. Security, 1956-57; referee Nat. Railroad Adjustment Bd., 1958; mem. HEW reviewing authority on civil rights, 1968; advisor U.S. Civil Service Commn. Bd. of Appeals and Rev., 1970. Mem. Am., Fed. bar assns., Internat. Soc. Labor Law and Social Legislation, Phi Beta Kappa. Fulbright scholar, 1951; Ford Found. fellow, 1963-64; author: (with Smith and Rothschild) Materials and Cases on Collective Bargaining and Labor Arbitration, 1970; (with Smith and St. Antoine) Cases and Materials on Labor Relations Law, 1974; note editor Minn. Law Rev., 1940-41. Home: 1907 Martha's Rd Alexandria VA 22307 Office: Nat Law Center George Washington U Washington DC 20052 Tel (202) 676-6745

MERRILL, ABEL JAY, b. Balt., Mar. 25, 1938; B.A., Colgate U., 1959; LL.B., U. Md., 1964. Admitted to Md. bar, 1964; law clk. to chief judge U.S. Ct. Appeals, Balt., 1964-65; asso. firm Gordon, Feinblatt & Rothman, Balt., 1965-70; individual practice law, Annapolis, Md., 1970-72; prin. firm Merrill & Lilly, Profl. Assn., Annapolis, 1972—; mem. inquiry com. Atty. Grievance Commn. Md., 1975—. Mem. Am., Md., Anne Arundel County (chmn. com. unauthorized practice law 1975—) bar assns. Asst. editor Md. Law Rev., 1962-63. Office: Maryland Nat Bldg 160 South St Annapolis MD 21404 Tel (301) 263-9360

MERRILL, ALLEN HUNTER, b. Eufaula, Ala., Aug. 24, 1917; A.B., U. N.C., 1939; J.D., Yale, 1942. Admitted to N.Y. bar, 1947; asso. firm Cravath, Swaine & More, N.Y.C., 1946-56, partner, 1957—. Pres. Recording for the Blind, Inc., N.Y.C., 1963-69, chmn., 1968-69, dir., 1959—. Mem. Am., Internat., N.Y. State bar assns., Union Internat. des Avocats, Phi Beta Kappa. Office: 1 Chase Manhattan Plaza New York City NY 10005 Tel (212) HA2-3000

MERRILL, BURTON, b. Chgo., Oct. 7, 1933; J.D., U. So. Calif., 1966. Admitted to Calif. bar, 1966; sr. research atty. Calif. Ct. Appeals, Los Angeles; prof. law Southwestern U., Los Angeles, 1971—. Mem. Am., Los Angeles County bar assns. Office: 675 S Westmoreland Ave Los Angeles CA 90005 Tel (213) 388-0848

MERRILL, LARUE HENDRICKS, b. Richmond, Utah, Aug. 3, 1895; student Brigham Young Coll., 1916; B.S., Utah State U., 1927; LL.B., Nat. U., 1934, J.S.D., 1935. Admitted to Idaho bar, 1936; individual practice law, Idaho Falls, Idaho, 1936-77, ret., 1976; tchr. pub. schs. Murtaugh, Idaho, 1922-26; supt. schs. Victor, Idaho, 1927-29, McCammon, Idaho, 1929-32; pres. Larch & Merrill Corp., Idaho Falls, 1942-47; speaker in field. Pres., McCammon PTA, 1929-30; bd. dirs. Community Chest, Idaho Falls; bd. dirs. Teton Peaks Council Boy Scouts Am., pres. Silver Beavers Colony #2, 1970. Author: Alma Merrill Family Books. Home: 104 E 21st St Idaho Falls ID 83401 Tel (208) 522-0965

MERRILL, LAWRENCE EVERETT, b. Springfield, Mass., July 27, 1944; B.A. cum laude, Amherst Coll., 1966; J.D., N.Y. U., 1969. Admitted to Maine bar, 1969; asso. firm Rudman, Rudman & Carter, Bangor, Maine, 1969-73, partner, 1974—; instr. evening program Beal Coll., Bangor, 1974—; asst. sec. Maine Bar Assn. Mut. Title Ins. Co., 1973—. Mem. Am., Maine, Penobscot County (sec.-treas. 1973—) bar assns. Home: 120 Hudson Rd Bangor ME 04401 Office: 84 Harlow St Bangor ME 04401 Tel (207) 947-4501

MERRILL, RAYMOND KAY, b. Wheaton, Ill., Aug. 8, 1916; student Central YMCA Coll., 1938; LL.B., J.D., Chgo.-Kent Coll. Law, 1942. Admitted to Ill. bar, 1942; atty. Chgo, Milw., St. Paul and Pacific R.R. Co., Chgo., 1946-48, asst. gen. solicitor, 1948-55, gen. atty., commerce counsel, 1956-61, gen. solicitor, 1961-70, v.p. law, 1970—. Mem. Kane County, Ill. State, Am. bar assns. Home: 254 S Clifton Ave Elgin IL 60120 Office: 516 W Jackson Blvd Chicago IL 60606 Tel (312) 648-3836

MERRILL, WALTER JAMES, b. Anniston, Ala., Sept. 30, 1912; B.A., U. Ala., 1931, LL.B., 1934. Admitted to Ala. bar, 1934, U.S. Ct. Appeals 5th Circuit bar, 1952; partner firm Merrill, Jones & Merrill, Anniston, 1934-41; partner firm Knox, Jones, Woolf & Merrill, Anniston, 1947-75; pres. firm Merrill, Porch, Doster & Dillon, Anniston, 1975—; mem. Ala. Appellate Rules com., 1974—. Fellow Am. Coll. Trial Lawyers; mem. Ala., Am. bar assns., Ala. Law Inst., Defense Research Inst. Home: 226 Crestview Rd Anniston AL 36201 Office: 500 First Nat Bank Bldg Anniston AL 36201 Tel (205) 237-2871

MERRILL, WILLIAM HENRY, JR., b. Indpls., Apr. 11, 1942; B.S., Butler U., 1965; J.D., Ind. U., 1967. Admitted to Ind. bar, 1967, U.S. Dist. Ct. bar for So. Dist. Ind. 1967; trust officer Mchts. Nat. Bank & Trust Co., Indpls., 1967-69; gen. counsel Everett I. Brown Co., Indpls., 1969—; v.p., gen. counsel Landeco Inc., Indpls. Mem. Carmel (Ind.) Planning Commn., 1974-75, 77—. Mem. Am., Ind. State, Indpls. bar assns., Bar Assn. 7th Fed. Circuit, Am. Judicature Soc. Office: 5406 W Bradbury Ave Indianapolis IN 46241 Tel (317) 244-2881

MERRIMAN, JOHN ALLEN, b. Knoxville, Iowa, Aug. 13, 1942; A.B., Northwestern U., 1964; LL.B., Columbia, 1967. Admitted to Iowa bar, 1967, U.S. Tax Ct. bar, 1968; asso. firm Gamble, Riepe, Martin & Webster, Des Moines, 1967-69; asso. counsel Equitable Life Ins. Co., Des Moines, 1969-75; partner firm Mumford, Schrage, Merriman, Des Moines, 1976—. Chmn. Polk County (Iowa) Republican Party, 1974—; del. Rep. Nat. Conv., 1976. Mem. Am., Iowa, Polk County bar assns. Home: 4290 NW 46St Pl Des Moines IA 50323 Office: 1001 Equitable Bldg Des Moines IA 50309 Tel (515) 245-6710

MERRITT, BRUCE GORDON, b. Iowa City, Iowa, Oct. 4, 1946; A.B. magna cum laude Occidental Coll., 1968; J.D., magna cum laude, Harvard, 1972. Admitted to Calif. bar, 1973; asso. firm Markbys, London, 1972-73; asso. firm Nossaman, Krueger & Marsh, Los Angeles, 1973—. Mem. Am. (mem. ad hoc com on internat. aspects of natural resources, internat. law sect.), Los Angeles County (mem. internat. law and human rights sects.) bar assns. Contbg. author: An Evaluation of the U.S. Govt. in its Relationships to U.S. firms in International Petroleum Affairs, 1975; contbr. articles to profl. jours. Office: 445 S Figueroa St 30th Floor Los Angeles CA 90071 Tel (213) 628-5221

MERRITT, HARLEY ALFRED, b. Los Angeles, June 21, 1943; LL.B., Lincoln U., 1972. Admitted to Calif. bar, 1972; asso. law offices of Darrell W. Stevens, Oroville, Calif., 1972—. Mem. Am., Calif. Bar Assns., Oroville C. of C., (V.O.T.E. Com. 1974). Home: 78 Brookdale Ct Oroville CA 95965 Office: 1650 Lincoln St Oroville CA 95965 Tel (916) 533-0661

MERRITT, JAMES SCOTT, JR., b. Knoxville, Tenn., Nov. 7, 1939; B.A., Yale, 1961; LL.B., U. Va., 1964. Admitted to Mo. bar, 1964; asso. firm Stinson Mag Thomson McEvers & Fizzell, Kansas City, Mo., 1964-68, partner, 1968—. Mem. exec. com. Kansas City Conservatory of Music. Mem. Am. Bar Assn., Kansas City Lawyers Assn. Office: 2100 Ten Main Center Kansas City MO 64105 Tel (816) 842-8600

MERRITT, ROBERT LLOYD, b. N.Y.C., Sept. 24, 1919; B.S. cum laude, City Coll N.Y., 1939; LL.B. (James Kent scholar), Columbia U., 1942. Admitted to N.Y. State bar, 1942, Ohio bar, 1951, U.S. Supreme Ct. bar, 1952; partner firm Guren, Merritt, Sogg & Cohen, and predecessors, Cleve., 1958—. Trustee Cleve. Pub. Library, 1968-74, pres., 1970-72, v.p., 1972-74. Mem. Am., Greater Cleve. (trustee 1968-71) bar assns. Contbr. articles to legal jours. Home: 2481 Edgehill Rd Cleveland Heights OH 44106 Office: 650 Terminal Tower Cleveland OH 44113 Tel (216) 696-8550

MERRYMAN, JOHN HENRY, b. Portland, Oreg., Feb. 24, 1920; B.S., U. Portland, 1943; M.S., U. Notre Dame, 1944, J.D., 1947; LL.M., N.Y. U., 1950, J.S.D., 1955. Mem. faculty U. Santa Clara (Calif.), 1948-53; mem. faculty Stanford Sch. Law, 1953—, prof., 1960-71, Nelson B. and Marie B. Sweitzer prof., 1971—; vis. prof. Law Sch. N.Y. U., 1950, U. Rome, 1963-64; vis. research prof. Center Planning and Econ. Research, Athens, Greece, 1962, 64; mem. Internat. Faculty Comparative Law, Strasbourg, France, 1964, 69, Mexico, 1965; Fulbright research scholar and vis. research prof. Max Planck Institut fur auslandisches und internationales Privatrecht, Hamburg, W.Ger., 1968-69; mem. Atty. Gen. Calif. Adv. Com. on Civil Rights, 1960-63. Mem. No. Calif. ACLU (dir. 1955-68, chmn. 1957-61). Recipient Silver medal U. Rome, 1964; decorated officer Order Merit Italian Republic; author: The Civil Law Tradition, 1969, Spanish edit., 1971, Italian, 1973; (with M. Cappelletti and J. Perillo) The Italian Legal System: An Introduction, 1967; Some Problems of Greek Shoreland Development, in Greek, 1966, in English, 1965; (with others) American Law of Property, 1952; contbr. articles to legal jours. Home: 835 Pine Hill Rd Stanford CA 94305 Office: Sch Law Stanford U Stanford CA 94305 Tel (415) 497-2473

MERSHON, JERRY L., b. Oakley, Kans., Sept. 25, 1933; B.S., Kans. State U., 1955; LL.B., J.D., Washburn Sch. Law, 1961. Admitted to Kans. bar, 1961; individual practice law, Manhattan, Kans., 1961-65; judge Probate & Juvenile Ct. Riley County (Kans.), Manhattan, 1965—; lectr., faculty mem. Nat. Coll. Dist. Attys., Houston, 1974. Active Riley County Mental Health Assn.; mem. Gov.'s Com. on Criminal Adminstrn., 1975-79. Mem. Am., Riley County, Kans. bar assns., Kans. Spl Ct. Judges Assn. (Kans. del. 1973-75), Am. Judicature Soc. Home: 1905 Indiana Ln Manhattan KS 66502 Office: Ct Annex Bldg 5th & Poyntz Sts Manhattan KS 66502 Tel (913) 776-9235

MERSKY, ROY MARTIN, b. N.Y.C., Sept. 1, 1925. B.S., U. Wis., 1948, J.D., 1952, M.A.inL.S., 1953. Admitted to Wis. bar, 1952, Tex. bar, 1972, U.S. Supreme Ct. bar, 1970; individual practice law, Madison, Wis., 1952-54; chief readers' and reference service Yale Law Library, 1954-59; dir. Wash. State Law Library, 1959-63; exec. sec. jud. council, commr. Wash. Ct. Report, 1959-63; prof. law, law librarian U. Colo., 1963-65, U. Tex., 1965—; interim-dir. Jewish nat. and univ. library Hebrew U., Jerusalem, 1972-73. Mem. Am. Bar Assn., ALA, Assn. Am. Law Schs., Am. Assn. Law Libraries, Scribes, ACLU, AAUP. Author: (with Jacobstein) Fundamentals of Legal Research, 4th edit., 1973; Water Law Bibliography and Supplements, 1966, 69, 74; Index to Periodical Articles Related to Law, 1976; An Introduction and Compilation of Senate Judicial Hearings and Reports to Accompany Successful Nominations to the Supreme Court of the United States, 1916-1972, 1975. Home: 1419 Gaston Ave Austin TX 78703 Office: 2500 Red River St Austin TX 78705 Tel (512) 471-1336

MERTENS, WILLIAM, b. N.Y.C., May 20, 1910; A.B., Wesleyan U., Middletown, Conn., 1931; J.D., Harvard, 1934. Admitted to N.Y. bar, 1934; practiced in N.Y.C.; dep. asst. dist. atty. New York County, 1938-41; dep. supt. banks, gen. counsel N.Y. State Dept. Banking, 1945; counsel Com. Installment Financing, N.Y. State Legislature, 1947-49; spl. counsel N.Y. State Dept. Ins., 1951-53; asso. counsel N.Y. Joint Legis. Com. on Ct. Reorgn., 1961-63; justice N.Y.C. City Ct., 1950; judge N.Y.C. Civil Ct., 1967—; acting justice N.Y. Supreme Ct., 1974—; chmn. Nat. Conf. Spl. Ct. Judges, 1972-73. Mem. Am., N.Y. State bar assns., Assn. Bar City N.Y., New York County Lawyers Assn., Am. Judicature Soc., Am. Judges Assn. (award for dedication to justice 1975), Phi Beta Kappa. Home: 630 Park Ave New York City NY 10021 Office: 111 Centre St New York City NY 10013 Tel (212) 374-8073

MERTZ, FRANCIS JAMES, b. Newark, Sept. 24, 1937; B.A., St. Peter's Coll., 1958; J.D., N.Y.U., 1961. Admitted to N.J. bar, 1966; exec. v.p. St. Peter's Coll., Jersey City, 1962—; dir. Comml. Trust Co., N.J. Edn. Computer Network. Trustee Felician Coll., 1973—, Jersey City Edn. Center, 1975—; chmn. Hudson County Cath. Community Services, 1977—. Mem. Am., N.J. bar assns., Nat. Assn. Coll. and Univ. Attys., Assn. Ind. Colls. and Univs. in N.J. (dir.), N.J. Assn. Colls. and Univs. (treas., dir. 1977—). Home: 60 Bayberry Ln Watchung NJ 07060 Office: St Peter's Coll 2641 Kennedy Blvd Jersey City NJ 07306 Tel (201) 333-4400

MERVIS, STANLEY HOWARD, b. Portsmouth, Va., July 12, 1927; B.S., Coll. William and Mary, 1947, J.D., 1950. Admitted to Va. bar, 1949, N.Y. bar, 1950, Mass. bar, 1957, U.S. Supreme Ct. bar, 1958; asst. legal editor Prentice-Hall, Inc., N.Y.C., 1950-51; patent examiner U.S. Patent Office, Washington, 1951-54; patent atty. Polaroid Corp., Cambridge, Mass., 1954—, asso. patent counsel, 1969—. Mem. Am. Bar Assn., Am. (chmn. chem. practice com. 1974-76), Boston patent law assns. Home: 11 Nod Hill Rd Newton Highlands MA 02161 Office: Polaroid Corp 549 Technology Sq Cambridge MA 02139 Tel (617) 864-6000

MESERVEY, FREDERICK WILLIAM, b. Norwalk, Conn., Mar. 7, 1930; A.B., Hamilton Coll., 1951; LL.B., Cornell U., 1954. Admitted to N.Y. State bar, 1955; asso. firm White & Case, N.Y.C., 1956-59; mem. firm Toaz, Buck, Myers & Brower, Huntington, N.Y., 1959-63, partner, 1963-75; partner firm Curto, Meservey & Armstrong, Huntington, 1975—. Chmn., Suffolk County (N.Y.) chpt. ARC, 1970-75; bd. dirs. Huntington YMCA, 1970-75. Mem. New York State (exec. com. trusts and estates sect. 1974—), Suffolk County bar assns., Vis. Homemakers Assn. Suffolk County (dir. 1975—). Home: 3 Woodlot Ln Huntington NY 11743 Office: 7 High St Huntington NY 11743 Tel (516) 271-7500

MESERVY, JAY ALONZO, b. Logan, Utah, Oct. 30, 1933; B.A. in Speech and Theatre, U. Conn., 1957; LL.B., U. Utah, 1963, J.D., 1967. Admitted to Utah bar, 1963; law clk. to justice Utah Supreme Ct., 1962-63; partner firm Greenwood & Meservy, Salt Lake City, 1963-71; individual practice law, Salt Lake City, 1971-72; partner firm Verhaaren & Meservy, Salt Lake City, 1972—. Mem. Am., Utah, Salt Lake County, Davis County bar assns., Utah Pub. Health Assn., Am. Trial Lawyers. Office: 466 E 500 S Salt Lake City UT 84111 Tel (801) 322-5555

MESHBESHER, RONALD I., b. Mpls., May 18, 1933; B.S.L., U. Minn., 1955, J.D., 1957. Admitted to Minn. bar, 1957, U.S. Supreme Ct., 1966; asst. prosecuting atty. Hennepin County, Mpls., 1958-61; partner firm Meshbesher, Singer & Spence, Mpls., 1961—. Prof., permanent faculty lectr. Nat. Coll. Criminal Defense Lawyers and Pub. Defenders. Mem. Gov.'s Commn. Law Enforcement, Adminstrn. Justice and Corrections, Minn., 1967. Mem. Internat. Acad. Trial Lawyers, Am. Bd. Trial Advocates, Am. Acad. Forensic Scis., Assn. Trial Lawyers Am., Nat. Assn. Criminal Defense Lawyers, Am., Minn. State bar assns., Minn. Trial Lawyers Assn. (pres. 1973-74). Contbr. articles in field to legal jours. Office: 1616 Park Ave Minneapolis MN 55404 Tel (612) 339-9121

MESHON, MAX, b. Phila., Aug. 8, 1917; J.D., Temple U., 1952. Admitted to Pa. bar, 1953, U.S. Supreme Ct. bar, 1959; asso. firm Freedman Landy & Lorry, Phila., 1953-54; sr. partner firm Eilberg Meshon & Brener, Phila., 1954-68, firm Meshon & Brener, Phila., 1968—; clk. Ct. Common Pleas of Philadelphia County, 1952-53. Nat. commr. adult edn. B'nai B'rith, 1965—. Mem. Am., Pa., Phila. bar assns., Am. Trial Lawyers Assn., Pitts. Med.-Legal Soc. Editor-in-chief Temple Law Quarterly, 1950-52. Home: 104 Overbrook Pkwy Philadelphia PA 19151 Office: One E Penn Sq Philadelphia PA 19107 Tel (215) LO4-0600

MESIROV, CLARENCE, b. Phila., Nov. 3, 1905; B.S. in Econs., U. Pa., 1927, J.D., 1930. Admitted to Pa. bar, 1930; individual practice law, Phila., 1930—. Chmn., U. Pa. 50th reunion gift com., 1977. Mem. Law Acad. Phila. (pres. 1935). Home: 1208 N Woodbine Ave Narberth PA 19072 Office: Fidelity Bldg 15th floor Philadelphia PA 19109 Tel (215) 893-5089

MESIROV, LEON I., b. Phila., Jan. 19, 1912; A.B., U. Pa., 1931, J.D., 1934. Admitted to Pa. bar, 1934; asso. firm Mesirov & Leonards, Phila., 1934-48, partner, 1948-59; partner firm Mesirov, Gelman, Jaffe & Cramer, and predecessors, Phila., 1959—; counsel Registration Commn., Phila., 1937-39; dep. to city solicitor City of Phila., 1952; mem. CSC, 1952-70. Mem. Am., Pa., Phila. bar assns., Phila. Lawyers Club, Order of Coif. Home: 2131 Saint James Pl Philadelphia PA 19103 Office: 15th floor The Fidelity Bldg Philadelphia PA 19109 Tel (215) 893-5010

MESIROW, CHARLES MICHAEL, b. Los Angeles, May 8, 1946; A.B., U. Calif., 1968; J.D., Calif. Western Sch. Law, 1971. Admitted to Calif. bar, 1972; dep. dist. atty. Santa Clara County Dist., San Jose, Calif., 1972-76; partner firm Mesirow and Fink, 1977—; prof. Foothill Coll. 1972—. Mem. Am., Santa Clara County bar assns., Calif. Dist. Atty. Assn. Home: 2325 Eastridge Ave Apt 612 Menlo Park CA 94025 Office: 4000 Moorpark Ave Suite 204 San Jose CA 95117 Tel (408) 249-5152

MESIROW, HAROLD ESIAH, b. Washington, Oct. 25, 1932; B.A., George Washington U., 1954, LL.B., 1957. Admitted to D.C. bar, 1957; law clk. U.S. Dist. Ct. for D.C., 1957-58; asso. firm Macleay, Lynch, Bernhard & Gregg, Washington, 1958-61, partner, 1961-67; partner firm Hydeman, Mason & Goodell, Washington, 1967—; ocean carrier editor ICC Practitioners Assn. Mem. Am., D.C. bar assns., Maritime Adminstrv. Bar Assn., ICC Practitioners Assn. Home: 7908 Cindy Ln Bethesda MD 20034 Office: 1220 19th St NW Washington DC 20036 Tel (202) 833-9040

MESROBIAN, RICHARD CHARLES, b. Highland Park, Mich., Aug. 22, 1926; A.B., Western Res. U., 1949, J.D., 1952. Admitted to Ohio bar, 1952; individual practice law, Cleve., 1952—; prosecutor Newburgh Heights (Ohio), 1960-66, councilman, 1970—. Mem. Ohio, Cuyahoga bar assns., Nat. Assn. Criminal Def. Lawyers. Home: 3712 Washington Park Blvd Newburgh Hts OH 44105 Office: 410 Leader Bldg Cleveland OH 44114 Tel (216) 696-8292

MESSENGER, DONALD BURDETT WHITE, b. Federalsburg, Md., Sept. 11, 1935; B.A., Washington Coll., 1957; LL.D. cum laude, Washington and Lee U., 1960. Admitted to Md. bar, 1960, D.C. bar, 1963; asso. firm Marvin Smith, Denton, Md., 1960, firm Duckett,

Orem Christie & Beckett, Hyattsville, Md., 1961-64; founding partner firm Messenger, Lynch, Hills & Miller, Beltsville, Md., 1964—; atty. Town of Berwyn Heights (Md.), 1967, Prince George County (Md.) Election Bd., Upper Marlboro, 1966-68. Bd. mgmt. Prince George's County (Md.) YMCA, Beltsville, 1971-74; chmn. Prince George's Consumer Protection Commn., Upper Marlboro, 1971-73; mem. Howard County (Md.) Bi Partisan Redistricting Commn., Ellicott City, 1974-75. Mem. Am., Md., D.C., Prince George's County bar assns. Home: 10497 Graeloch Rd Laurel MD 20810 Office: 5010 Sunnyside Ave Beltsville MD 20705 Tel (301) 474-2300

MESSER, DORIS EILEEN, b. New Boston, Ohio, June 9, 1914; LL.B., Ohio State U., 1938, J.D., 1970. Admitted to Ohio bar, 1938; atty. Ohio Bur. Unemployment Compensation, Columbus, 1939-42; research dir. F&R Lazarus & Co. div. Federated Dept. Stores, Inc., Columbus, Ohio, 1942-49, asst. to controller, 1949-52, legal counsel, 1952—. Mem. Minerva Park (Ohio) City Council, 1965-68. Mem. Columbus Bar Assn., Columbus Assn. Retail and Service Credit, Women Lawyers Columbus. Home: 2111 Ferris Rd Columbus OH 43224 Office: F&R Lazarus & Co 236 E Town St Columbus OH 43215 Tel (614) 463-2446

MESSERMAN, ROBERT HERMAN, b. Atlantic City, N.J., Dec. 1, 1938; B.S., N.Y. U., 1960; J.D., Temple U., 1963; Ed.D., U. Sarasota, 1976. Admitted to N.J. bar, 1964, Pa. bar, 1964; asst. gen. claims atty. Southeastern Pa. Transp. Authority, Phila., 1972—; adj. asst. prof. bus. law Rutgers U., Camden, N.J., 1971—; lectr. bus. law Wharton Sch. U. Pa., 1976—; mem. nat. panel arbitrators Am. Arbitration Assn., 1966—. Democratic committeeman, Phila., 1965-67; Dem. dist. leader, Cherry Hill, N.J., 1976—; mem. Springbrook Civic Assn. Mem. Am., N.J., Pa., Phila., Camden County bar assns., Am. Bus. Law Assn., Northeastern Regional Bus. Law Assn. Home: 502 Arthur Dr Cherry Hill NJ 08003 Office: 211 S Broad St Philadelphia PA 19107 Tel (215) KI6-4402 also 1500 N Kings Hwy Cherry Hill NJ 08034 Tel (609) 428-5566

MESSINGER, BARRY WILLIAM, b. N.Y.C., Oct. 31, 1944; B.A., U. Vt., 1965; J.D., Am. U., 1968. Admitted to N.Y. bar, 1970, U.S. Supreme Ct. bar, 1973; asso. dir. bus. affairs CBS News, N.Y.C., 1973—; asst. counsel Motion Picture Assn. Am., N.Y.C., 1969-73; served as legal assistance officer, 1st lt. USAR, Ft. Sill, Okla., 1968-69, mem. nat. panel arbitrators Am. Arbitration Assn., 1970—. Mem. Assn. Bar City N.Y., Am., N.Y. State bar assns. Home: 36 Maxwell Ln Englishtown NJ 07726 Office: care CBS Inc 524 W 57th St New York City NY 10019 Tel (212) 975-6157

MESSINGER, STANLEY, b. N.Y.C., May 21, 1938; B.A., U. Vt., 1960; LL.B., Syracuse U., 1963, J.D., 1968. Admitted to N.Y. bar, 1964, U.S. Supreme Ct. bar, 1970; trial asst. firm Fuchsberg & Fuchsberg, N.Y.C., 1963-65; asso. firm Butler, Jablow & Geller, N.Y.C., 1965-66, Arthur A. Herman, Mt. Vernon, N.Y., 1967-69; individual practice law, Mt. Vernon, 1969-73; partner firm Messinger, Alperin & Hufjay, Mt. Vernon, 1973—; arbitrator Small Claims Ct. Panel, Mt. Vernon. Pres. Birchwood Ln. Civic Assn., Hartsdale, N.Y.; bd. govs. Greenburgh (N.Y.) Council Civic Assn. Mem. Am., N.Y., Westchester County (sec. family and matrimonial law sect.), Mt. Vernon (past v.p., treas.) bar assns., Am., N.Y. State trial lawyers assns. Home: 25 Birchwood Ln Hartsdale NY 10530 Office: 22 W 1st St Mount Vernon NY 10550 Tel (914) 664-4480

MESSNER, ROBERT THOMAS, b. McKeesport, Pa., Mar. 27, 1938; B.A., Dartmouth Coll., 1960; LL.B., U. Pa., 1963. Admitted to Pa. bar, 1965; asso. firm Rose, Schmidt & Dixon, Pitts., 1965-68; asst. dir. employee relations G.C. Murphy Co., McKeesport, 1968-70, asst. sec., 1970-74, corporate sec., 1974—, gen. counsel, 1975—, v.p., 1976—; dir. G.C. Murphy Found. Dir. McKeesport YMCA; chmn. Republican registration Allegheny County (Pa.), Pitts., 1967; mem. advisory bd. Pa. Human Relations Commn., McKeesport, 1968, 69. Mem. McKeesport C. of C. (dir.), Am. Soc. Corporate Secs., Am., Pa., Allegheny County bar assns. Home: 1061 Blackridge Rd Pittsburgh PA 15235 Office: 531 Fifth Ave McKeesport PA 15132 Tel (412) 664-4441

METCALF, BERTRAM BRAUNNE, b. Milw., Oct. 24, 1911; B.A., U. Iowa, 1934, J.D., 1936. Admitted to Iowa bar, 1936; mem. firm Metcalf & Metcalf, Davenport, Iowa, 1936-42, 1945-51; individual practice law, Davenport, 1951-63; judge municipal ct., Davenport, 1963-72; asst. city atty., Davenport, 1972-73; individual practice law, Davenport, 1973—; justice of peace, 1956-62, juvenile judge, 1965-71. Pres. Scott County Mental Health Assn. Mem. Am., Iowa State, Scott County bar assns. Home: 3231 Kenwood Ave Davenport IA 52807 Office: 712 Kahl Bldg Davenport IA 52801 Tel (319) 324-4312

METCALF, FRED HUGHES, b. New Brunswick, N.J., Feb. 22, 1922; B.S. in B.A., U. Mo., 1943, LL.B., 1948. Admitted to Mo. bar, 1948; asst. city counselor, Kansas City, Mo., 1948-52; atty. Comml. Union, Kansas City, 1953—. Mem. Republican County Com., Kansas City, 1954-60. Mem. Mo. Bar Assn. Home: 8900 Horton St Overland Park KS 66207 Office: 211 W Armour Blvd Kansas City MO 64111 Tel (816) 753-6700

METCALF, RICHARD IRVING, b. Newark, N.Y., June 12, 1942; B.S., Bowling Green State U., 1964; J.D., Syracuse U., 1967. Admitted to Wis. bar, 1967, Tex. bar, 1972; atty. pres.'s dept. and law dept. Northwestern Mut. Life Ins. Co., Milw., 1967-69; mem. firm Davis, Kuelthau, Vergeront, Stover & Leichtfuss, Milw., 1969-72, Locke, Purnell, Boren, Laney & Neely, Dallas, 1972—. Mem. Am., Wis., Tex. bar assns., Phi Delta Phi. Case notes editor Syracuse Law Rev., 1966-67. Home: 7132 Leameadow Dallas TX 75248 Office: 3600 Republic Bank Tower Dallas TX 75201 Tel (214) 744-4511

METCALF, WALKER N., b. San Antonio, Mar. 24, 1929; B.B.A., U. Tex., 1955, J.D., 1957. Admitted to Tex. bar, 1957, U.S. Supreme Ct. bar, 1961; individual practice law, Lubbock, Tex., 1957—; served to lt. col. JAGC, USAR. Mem. Lubbock Econs. Council. Mem. Tex. State Bar, Am. Bar Assn. Office: 1005 15th St Lubbock TX 79401 Tel (806) 763-7306

METHENY, FRED RAY, JR., b. Jan. 23, 1922; B.S., U. Nebr., 1947, LL.B., 1949. Admitted to Nebr. bar, 1949, Calif. bar, 1955; spl. agt. FBI, Washington, 1949-53; dep. counsel Los Angeles County, 1955-58; practice law, Los Angeles, 1958-61; asst. city atty. City of Pasadena (Calif.), 1961-66, Palm Springs (Calif.), Indian Wells (Calif.), 1966-71; judge Riverside County (Calif.) Superior Ct., 1971—. Bd. dirs. Desert Hosp. Child Care Study Div., Palm Springs, Palm Springs Boys' Club; bd. cons. Children's Village, Internat. Orphans, Inc., Los Angeles. Mem. Am., Desert bar assns., Conf. Calif. Judges. Contbr. articles to legal publs. Office: 46-209 Oasis St Indio CA 92201 Tel (714) 347-8511

METTELHORST, LOUIS C., b. Chgo., Nov. 9, 1913; B.A., Northwestern U., 1934, J.D., 1937; M.Patent Law, John Marshall Sch. Law, 1947. Admitted to Ill. bar, 1937, U.S. Supreme Ct. bar, 1975; with claim dept. Kemper Ins. Co., Chgo., 1940-43; individual practice law, Chgo., 1940—; arbitrator Am. Arbitration Assn., 1967—. Dist. chmn., council v.p., exec. bd. mem. N.W. Suburban council Boy Scouts Am. (Silver Beaver award); mem. Camp Fire Girls, Chgo. Met. Council, Park Ridge (Ill.) Police Recognition Bd., 1972-75. Mem. Am., Ill. Chgo. bar assns. Home: 42F Root St Park Ridge IL 60068 Office: 10 S LaSalle St Chicago IL 60603 Tel (312) FR 2-3219

METTLER, GEORGE, b. Jersey City, Sept. 6, 1938; B.S.E.E., Newark Coll. Engring., 1961; J.D., Seton Hall Law Sch., 1971. Admitted to N.J. Bar, 1971; design engr. Bendix, Simmonds Precision, and RCA, 1961-71; individual practice law, Ramsey and East Orange, N.J., 1971—; U.S. atty. U.S. Court Appeals Third Circuit, 1973. Mem. Am., Bergen County Bar. Assns., IEEE. Home: 263 N Central Ave Ramsey NJ 07446 Office: 62 Halsted St East Orange NJ 07019 Tel (201) 676-9300 also 70 Franklin Turnpike Ramsey NJ 07446

METZ, ALAN L., b. Forrest, Ill., Apr. 4, 1941; B.A., U. Ill., 1963, J.D. with honors, 1970. Admitted to Ill. bar, 1970; asso. firm Jenner & Block, Chgo., 1970-76, partner, 1976—. Mem. Am., Chgo. (def. of prisoners com.), Ill. bar assns., Am. Arbitration Assn. (comml. panel), Order of Coif. Contbr. articles to legal jours. Office: Jenner & Block One IBM Plaza Chicago IL 60611 Tel (312) 222-9350

METZGAR, BERNARD PAUL, b. Albuquerque, Nov. 29, 1936; B.A. in Econs. and Govt., U. N.Mex., 1962; LL.B., Georgetown U., 1966. Admitted to N. Mex. bar, 1966; staff atty. Legal Aid Soc. of Albuquerque, 1966-68, dir., 1969—, pres. bd., 1969-73; sr. partner firm Lamb, Metzgar, Franklin & Lines, Profl. Assn., Albuquerque, 1968—; mem. N.Mex. advisory council Legal Services Corp., 1976—. Founder Epilepsy Found. of N.Mex Inc., Albuquerque, 1970; mem. N.Mex. Metropolitan Boundaries Commn., 1973-75. Mem. Am., N.Mex., Albuquerque bar assns., Nat. Legal Aid, Defender Assn., Delta Theta Phi. Home: 9508 Parsifal Pl NE Albuquerque NM 87111 Office: Suite 1010 Bank of N Mex Bldg PO Box 987 Albuquerque NM 87103 Tel (505) 247-0107

METZGER, DAVID PHILLIP, b. Milw., Apr. 25, 1948; B.A., U. Wis., 1970, J.D., 1974. Admitted to Wis. bar 1974; adminstrv. asst., mem. congl. staff U.S. Ho. of Reps., Washington, 1975—, subcom. counsel Small Bus. Com., 1977—. Home: 619 7th St NE Washington DC 20002 Office: 2361 Rayburn Bldg Washington DC 20515 Tel (202) 225-5821

METZGER, MELVIN, b. N.Y.C., Oct. 6, 1928; B.B.A., Coll. City N.Y., 1949; J.D., Bklyn. Coll., 1951, LL.M., 1975. Admitted to N.Y. bar, 1951, U.S. Supreme Ct. bar, 1968, U.S. Ct. Mil. Appeals bar, 1954, U.S. Tax Ct. bar, 1955; individual practice law, Flushing, N.Y., 1955—. Chmn. bd. Yeshiva High Sch. of Queens (N.Y.), 1973-76, pres., 1976—. Mem. Am., Queens, Fed., N.Y. County bar assns., Am., N.Y. assns. c.p.a.-attys. Office: 176-60 Union Turnpike Flushing NY 11366 Tel (212) 380-5200

METZNER, ARCH LOUIS, JR., b. Wheeling, W.Va., Oct. 16, 1913; A.B., Princeton, 1932; J.D., U. Denver, 1949. With Wheeling (W.Va.) Dollar Savings & Trust Co., 1936-42; admitted to Colo. bar, 1949; atty. United Bank Denver, 1946-69, sr. v.p., 1964-69; adj. prof. U. Denver, 1970—. Mem. Denver Art Museum, pres., 1950-62; treas. Denver Zool. Found., 1965-70; vice-chmn. Urban League Colo. Mem. Colo., Denver bar assns. Recipient Award of Merit Colo. Bar Assn., 1968. Home and Office: 1776 Forest Pkwy Denver CO 80220 Tel (303) 377-1832

METZNER, CARROLL EDWIN, b. Milw., Apr. 24, 1919; B.S., Northwestern U., 1941; LL.B., U. Wis., 1943. Admitted to Wis. bar, 1944; asso. firm Bell, Metzner & Seibold, and predecessors, Madison, Wis., 1943-51, partner, 1951—. Mem. Madison City Council, 1951-56; Wis. State Assembly, 1955-59. Mem. Am., Dane County bar assns., Fedn. Ins. Counsel, Ins. Trial Council Wis., Def. Research Inst. Contbr. articles in field to profl. jours. Home: 733 Huron Hill Madison WI 53711 Office: 222 W Washington Ave PO Box 1807 Madison WI 53701 Tel (608) 257-3764

MEWHORT, DONALD MILTON, JR., b. Toledo, Oct. 30, 1940; A.B. in Accounting, Duke, 1962, LL.B., 1965. Admitted to Ohio bar, 1965; asso. firm Shumaker, Loop & Kendrick, Toledo, 1965-70, partner, 1971—, mng. partner, 1977—. Trustee, Epworth United Meth. Ch., 1973-76; v.p. United Central Services, Inc., 1974—; trustee Boys Club of Toledo, 1975—. Mem. Toledo (exec. com.), Ohio State (bd. govs. labor law sect.), Am., Toledo Jr. (pres. 1974-75) bar assns., Am. Judicature Soc. Home: 4449 Lancelot Rd Toledo OH 43623 Office: 811 Madison Ave Suite 500 Toledo OH 43624 Tel (419) 241-4201

MEYER, ALFRED WILLIAM, b. Valparaiso, Ind., Nov. 19, 1927; A.B., Valparaiso U., 1948, J.D., 1950; LL.M., Harvard, 1951. Admitted to Ill. bar, 1950; judge advocate U.S. Army, 1951-54; mem. law faculty Ind. U., Bloomington, 1954-61; prof. law Valparaiso U., 1962—, dean, 1969—. Mem. Ind. Bar Assn. Cardozo fellow, 1962-63; contbr. articles in field to profl. jours. Office: Valparaiso U Sch Law Valparaiso IN 46383 Tel (219) 464-5434

MEYER, BERNARD STERN, b. Balt., June 7, 1916; B.S., Johns Hopkins, 1936; LL.B., U. Md., 1938. Admitted to Md. bar, 1938, D.C. bar, 1947, N.Y. bar, 1947; asso. firm Fisher & Fisher, Balt., 1938-41; atty. U.S. Treasury, Gen. Counsels Office, Washington, 1941-43; individual practice law, N.Y.C., 1947-54; mem. firm Meyer, Fink, Weinberger & Juliano, N.Y.C., 1954-58; justice N.Y. State Supreme Ct., 1958-72; mem. firm Fink, Weinberger, Meyer, & Charney, N.Y.C., 1973-74; mem. firm Meyer, English & Cianciulli, Mineola, counsel Fink, Weinberger, Fredman & Charney, N.Y.C., 1975—; spl. dep. atty. gen. N.Y. charge spl. Attica investigation, 1975. Founder United Fund L.I., 1967; pres. Health and Welfare Council Nassau County, 1963-64; chmn. adv. com. N.Y. Code Evidence; mem. bd. dirs. Nat. Coll. State Judiciary, 1968—. Mem. Am. (sec. lawyers conf. 1976—), N.Y. State (chmn. jud. sect. 1971-72), N.Y. County, Nassau County bar assns., Assn. Bar City N.Y. (chmn. com. matrimonial law), New York, Nassau county lawyers assns., Nat. Conf. State Trial Judges (chmn.), Assn. Supreme Ct. Justices (pres. 1971-72), Order of Coif. Recipient Distinguished Service award L.I. Press, 1968; contbr. articles to legal periodicals. Home: 161 Ocean Ave Woodmere NY 11598 Office: 160 Mineola Blvd Mineola NY 11501 Tel (516) 741-6565

MEYER, DAVID NATHAN, b. N.Y.C., Aug. 14, 1946; B.A. cum laude, Yeshiva U., 1968, B.H.L., 1968; J.D. cum laude N.Y. U., 1972. Admitted to N.Y. bar, 1972, U.S. 2d Circuit Ct. Appeals, 1976, U.S. So. and Eastern Dist. Cts. N.Y., 1976; asso. firm Aranow, Brodsky, Bohlinger, Benetar & Einhorn, N.Y.C., 1972-74, Fried, Frank, Harris, Shriver & Jacobson, N.Y.C., 1974-77; mem. legal dept. Viacom Internat., Inc., 1977—. Mem. Am. Bar Assn., N.Y. County Lawyers Assn. Contbr. articles to legal jours. Home: 170 W End Ave Apt 16C New York City NY 10023 Office: 1211 Ave of the Americas New York City NY 10036 Tel (212) 575-5175

MEYER, DWAINE FREDRIC, b. Dallas Center, Iowa, Nov. 16, 1929; B.S., Iowa State U., Ames, 1952; J.D., Drake U., 1957. Admitted to Iowa bar, 1957; individual practice law, Oskaloosa, Iowa, 1957-63, Pella, Iowa, 1963—; jud. magistrate Marion County (Iowa), 1973—; FM broadcaster. Chmn. Marion County Bd. Health, 1969—. Mem. Iowa Assn. Jud. Magistrates (pres.), Iowa, Marion County, Pella bar assns. Office: 810 Main St Pella IA 50219 Tel (515) 628-2323

MEYER, FERD. CHARLES, JR., b. San Antonio, Tex., Sept. 30, 1939; student Tulane U., 1957-58; B.B.A., U. Tex., 1961, LL.B., 1964. Admitted to U.S. Supreme Ct. bar, 1965, Tex. bar, 1966; partner firm Matthews, Nowlin, MacFarlane & Barrett, San Antonio, 1966—; div. atty. So. Pacific Co., San Antonio, 1966—. Trustee Tex. Mil. Inst., 1974—. Mem. Am., Tex., San Antonio bar assns., Tex. Assn. Def. Counsel, Nat. Assn. R.R. Trial Counsel. Home: 601 Morningside Dr San Antonio TX 78209 Office: 1500 Alamo Nat Bldg San Antonio TX 78205 Tel (512) 226-4211

MEYER, GEORGE HERBERT, b. Detroit, Feb. 28, 1928; A.B., U. Mich., 1949; J.D., Harvard, 1952; certificate Oxford U., Eng., 1955; LL.M., Wayne State U., 1962. Admitted to D.C. bar, 1952, Mich. bar, 1953; served as 1st lt. JAGD, U.S. Air Force, 1952-55; asso. firm Fischer, Franklin & Ford, Detroit, 1956-63, mem., 1963-74; individual practice law, Bloomfield Hills, Mich., 1974—. Chmn. Birmingham (Mich.) Bd. Housing Appeals, 1964-68; vice chmn. Birmingham Bd. Zoning Appeals, 1966-69; mem. Birmingham Planning Bd., 1968-70; chmn. Detroit Sci. Mus. Soc., 1974—; exec. bd. Detroit Area council Boy Scouts Am., 1976—; trustee Bloomfield Village, 1976—. Mem. State Bar Mich., Am., Fed., Oakland County, Detroit bar assns., Harvard Law Sch. Assn. Mich. (pres. 1970—), Phi Beta Kappa. Home: 1228 Sandringham Way Birmingham MI 48010 Office: 100 W Long Lake Rd Bloomfield Hills MI 48013 Tel (313) 647-5111

MEYER, GEORGE SPINA, b. N.Y.C., Aug. 31, 1939; B.S., Tulane U., 1965; J.D., Loyola U., New Orleans, 1967. Admitted to D.C. bar, 1968, La. bar, 1970, Colo. bar, 1970; asst. judge adv. U.S. Air Force, 1968-71; partner firm Kierr Gainsburgh Benjamin Fallon & Lewis, New Orleans, 1971—. Mem. Am. Trial Lawyers Assn., Am., Fed., La., New Orleans bar assns. Home: 379 Fairfield Ave Gretna LA 70053 Office: Kierr Gainsburgh Benjamin Fallon & Lewis 1718 First Nat Bank of Commerce Bldg New Orleans LA 70112 Tel (504) 522-2304

MEYER, HOWARD NICHOLAS, b. Bklyn., Oct. 15, 1914; B.A., Columbia U., 1934, LL.B., 1936. Admitted to N.Y. bar, 1937, U.S. Supreme Ct. bar, 1951; corporate atty. Schlenley Distillers Corp., 1936-39; spl. asst. U.S. atty. gen., claims div., N.Y.C., 1942-48; practice law N.Y.C., 1948—; with Wolf, Popper, Ross & Wolf, 1949-51; parnter firm Abzug & Meyer, 1952-54; with O'Dwyer & Bernstein, 1954-73; panel arbitrator N.Y. State Mediation Bd., 1971, Am. Arbitration Assn., 1974; N.J. Mediation Bd., 1974; Active Boy Scouts Am.; mem. better edn. com. Rockville Center Bd. Edn. Adv. Com., 1954-56. Mem. NAACP, Assn. Study Negro Life and History, NOW, ACLU, Authors Guild Am., N.Y. State, N.Y.C. bar assns., N.Y. County Lawyers Assn. Author: Let Us Have Peace, 1966; Colonel of the Black Regiment, 1967; The Amendent That Refused to Die, 1973. Editor: Army Life in a Black Regiment, 1962; Integrating America's Heritage, 1969; Herndon's Let Me Live, 1970. Home: 76 Tarence St Rockville Centre NY 11570 Office: 270 Madison Ave New York City NY 10016 Tel (212) 685-9800

MEYER, IVAN ISAK, b. Nonnenweier, Baden, Germany, Nov. 21, 1901; Dr. Juris Utriusque, U. Freiburg (Germany), 1924; LL.B., Fordham U., 1939, Ph.D., 1943, J.D., 1968. Admitted to German bar, 1928, N.Y. State bar, 1944, U.S. Supreme Ct. bar, 1960; individual practice law, N.Y.C. Mem. N.Y. County Bar Assn. Author Jubilaeumsschrift der Juedischen, Gemeinde Nennenweier, Baden, 1927. Office: 40 Exchange Pl New York City NY 10005 Tel (212) 425-4224

MEYER, M. HOLT, b. Hong Kong, Sept. 28, 1930; A.B., Harvard, 1952; LL.B., Columbia, 1958. Admitted to N.Y. bar, 1958; asso. firm H.A. and C.E. Heydt, N.Y.C., 1958-59, Fleischmann Jaeckle Stokes & Hitchcock (now Webster & Sheffield), N.Y.C., 1959-66; judge N.Y. State Family Ct., 1973—; asst. to Mayor John Lindsay, N.Y.C., 1966-73; chmn. Mayor's Urban Action Task Force for Richmond County, 1967-73. Mem. Family Ct. Judges Assn. N.Y.C. (dir.), Am., N.Y. State, N.Y.C., Richmond County bar assns. Home: 966 Bard Ave Staten Island NY 10301 Office: 100 Richmond Terr Staten Island NY 10301 Tel (212) 442-4412

MEYER, MICHAEL EDWIN, b. Chgo., Oct. 23, 1942; B.S., U. Wis., 1964; J.D., U. Chgo., 1967. Admitted to Calif. bar, 1968, U.S. Supreme Ct. bar, 1971; asso. firm Lillick McHose & Charles, Los Angeles, 1967-74, partner, 1974—; judge pro tempore Beverly Hills (Calif.) Municipal Ct., 1974-76. Mem. cabinet U. Chgo., 1972-75. Mem. Am., Calif., Los Angeles, Beverly Hills bar assns., Copyright Soc., Japan Am. Soc., Fgn. Trade Assn., Brazil-Calif. Trade Assn., Calif. Trial Lawyers Assn. Home: 4105 Pacific Ave Marina Del Rey CA 90291 Office: 707 W Wilshire Blvd Los Angeles CA 90017 Tel (213) 620-9000

MEYER, PAUL EDWARD, b. Erie, Pa., Oct. 23, 1947; B.A., Kent State U., 1969; J.D., Cleve. State U., 1974. Admitted to Ohio bar, 1974; investigator Ohio Civil Rights Commn., Akron and Cleve., 1972-73; law clk. Ashtabula County (Ohio) Ct. Common Pleas, 1974; judge adv. U.S. Marine Corps, Akron, 1974—. Mem. Ohio State Bar Assn. Home and Office: 1375 N Revere Rd Akron OH 44313 Tel (216) 836-8740

MEYER, PAUL RICHARD, b. St. Louis, Apr. 12, 1925; A.B. with honors, Columbia, 1949; J.D., Yale, 1952. Admitted to Oreg. bar, 1953, Calif. bar, 1953, N.Y. bar, 1953; teaching asst. Law Sch. Yale, 1951-52; teaching asso. U. Calif. Sch. Law, Berkeley, 1952-53; asso. firm King, Miller, Anderson, Nash & Yerke, Portland, Oreg., 1953-59; partner firm Kobin & Meyer, Portland, Oreg., 1960—; mem. panel arbitrators Am. Arbitration Assn. Bd. dirs. Oreg. affiliate ACLU, 1955-71, nat. bd. dirs., 1971—, mem. exec. com. nat. bd., 1976—; trustee Congregation Beth Israel, 1969-74, sec. bd. trustees, 1971-74; bd. dirs. Friends of Chamber Music, Portland, 1970—, pres., 1974-75.

Mem. Oreg. State Bar (lectr.), Multnomah County (Oreg.), Am. bar assns., Phi Beta Kappa. Contbr. articles to profl. publs. Home: 602 NW Skyline Crest Portland OR 97229 Office: Suite 800 610 SW Alder St Portland OR 97205 Tel (503) 223-1107

MEYER, RAUER LEWIS, b. Washington, Jan. 19, 1948; A.B., Brown U., 1969; J.D., Harvard U., 1973. Admitted to Calif. bar, 1973; asso. firm Wyman, Bautzer, Rothman & Kuchel, Los Angeles, 1973—. Mem. Am. Bar Assn. Home: 5094 Point Dume Canyon Rd Malibu CA 90265 Office: 2049 Century Park E Los Angeles CA 90067 Tel (213) 556-8000

MEYER, RICHARD EDWARD, b. Bklyn., Mar. 18, 1930; B.S., Wagner Coll., 1951; LL.B., N.Y. Law Sch., 1960. Admitted to N.Y. State bar, 1961, U.S. Dist. Ct. bar for So. and Eastern Dists. N.Y., 1963, U.S. Ct. Appeals bar 2d Circuit, 1966; asso. firm Foley & Martin, N.Y.C., 1962-70; asso. firm McHugh, Heckman, Smith & Leonard (merger Foley & Martin and McHugh, Heckman, Smith & Leonard), N.Y.C., 1970-75, partner, 1976—. Home: 112 Alpine St Yonkers NY 10710 Office: 80 Pine St New York City NY 10005 Tel (212) 422-0222

MEYER, RICHARD MARTIN, b. N.Y.C., Jan. 11, 1934; B.A., Yale, 1955, LL.B., 1958. Admitted to N.Y. bar, 1959, U.S. Supreme Ct. bar, 1969; atty. U.S. Dept. Justice, Washington, 1958-60; asso. firm Hays, Sklar & Herzberg, N.Y.C., 1960-61; spl. counsel U.S. SEC, Washington, 1961-65; asso. firm Pomerantz, Levy, Haudek & Block, N.Y.C., 1965-70, partner, 1970—. Mem. Fed. Bar Council, Bar Assn. City N.Y., N.Y. County Lawyers Assn. Editor: Yale Law Jour., 1957-58; contbr. articles in field to profl. jours. Home: 75 Maywood Rd New Rochelle NY 10804 Office: 295 Madison Ave New York City NY 10017 Tel (212) 532-4800

MEYER, RICHARD STEVEN, b. N.Y.C., Dec. 3, 1944; B.S. in Econs., U. Pa., 1965; LL.B., Yale, 1968. Admitted to Pa. bar, 1968; dep. atty. gen. Commonwealth of Pa., Harrisburg, 1968-69; asso. firm Wolf, Bloch, Schorr & Solis-Cohen, Phila., 1969-73, Dilworth, Paxson, Kalish & Levy, Phila., 1973-75, partner, 1975—; participant Employment Discrimination Referral Project, Phila., 1972—. Mem. Am., Pa., Phila. bar assns. Home: 1919 Panama St Philadelphia PA 19103 Office: 123 S Broad St Philadelphia PA 19109 Tel (215) 546-3000

MEYER, RUDOLF SELIGMANN, b. Hamburg, Germany, Jan. 6, 1926; came to U.S., 1938, naturalized, 1943; LL.B., Bklyn. Law Sch., 1951. Admitted to N.Y. State bar, 1951; individual practice law, N.Y.C., 1951-76; sec. to judge Supreme Ct., Kings County, N.Y., 1975—. Mem. N.Y. State Bar Assn. Home: 1566 52nd St Brooklyn NY 11219 Office: 16 Court St Brooklyn NY 11241

MEYER, SIGMUND O., b. Butte, Mont., Apr. 22, 1912; B.A., U. So. Calif., 1934, J.D., 1936. Admitted to Mont. bar, 1937, U.S. Supreme Ct. bar, 1947; individual practice law, Butte. Mem. Am., Mont., Silver Bow County bar assns. Home: 3400 St Ann St Butte MT 59701 Office: 519 Metals Bldg PO Box 508 Butte MT 59701 Tel (406) 792-6755

MEYER, STEPHEN H., b. Warrensburg, Mo., Mar. 22, 1948; B.A. cum laude, Concordia Sr. Coll., Ft. Wayne, Ind., 1968-70; J.D., Valparaiso U., 1973. Admitted to Ind. bar, 1973, Iowa bar, 1973, U.S. Supreme Ct. bar, 1976; partner firm Chudom & Meyer, Schererville, Ind., 1974—; atty. Town of Hebron Plan Commn., 1975—. Election commr., Lake County, Ind., 1972. Mem. Am., Ind. bar assns., Am., Ind. trial lawyers assns., Am. Judicature Soc. Note Editor: Valparaiso U. Law Rev., 1972-73. Office: 833 W Lincoln Hwy Schererville IN 46375 Tel (219) 838-9444

MEYER, WALTER GEORGE, JR., b. Akron, Ohio, Mar. 21, 1939; B.S., Oreg. State U., 1961; J.D., Ind. U., 1964. Admitted to Ind. bar, 1964, Wash. bar, 1965; lawyer Office of Regional Solicitor, U.S. Dept. Interior, Portland, Oreg., 1964-65; law clk. to judge U.S. Dist. Ct. Western Dist. Wash., Seattle, 1965-66; asso. firm Elvidge, Watt, Veblen, Tewell & Venables, Seattle, 1966-67; asso. firm Palmer, Willis, McArdle & Meyer, Yakima, Wash., 1967-69, partner, 1969-72; asso. firm Halverson, Applegate & McDonald, Yakima, 1973-75, partner, 1975—. Mem. Am., Wash. State, Yakima County bar assns. Home: 4902 Scenic Terr Yakima WA 98908 Office: 415 N 3d St Yakima WA 98907 Tel (509) 575-6611

MEYEROFF, ROBERT NEIL, b. Milw., Aug. 28, 1946; A.B., U. Wis., Madison, 1968, J.D., 1971. Admitted to Wis. bar; with IRS, Milw., 1971-72; asso. Herbert L. Usow, Milw., 1972—. Address: 606 W Wisconsin St Suite 1100 Milwaukee WI 53203 Tel (414) 272-7800

MEYERS, BRUCE FRANCE, b. Seattle, Aug. 10, 1925; B.S. in Geology, U. Wash., 1948; B.A. in Law, U. Wash., 1950; J.D. with honors, George Washington U., 1963; postgrad. Brown U., 1966-67; Commd. 2d lt. USMC, 1945, advanced through grades to col.; comdr. rifle co. in Korea, 1951, bn. comdr. in 6th Fleet landing force, 1966, regt. comdr. 26th Marine Regiment and Khe Sanh combat base, Vietnam, 1968; ret., 1970; admitted to Va. bar, 1970, Wash. bar, 1971, U.S. Supreme Ct. bar, 1974; mgr. firm Lane, Powell, Moss & Miller, Seattle, 1970-71; mem. firm Reed, McClure, Moceri & Thonn, Seattle, 1971-74; asst. prof. law U. Puget Sound, 1974—, asst. dean Sch. Law, 1974-75, asso. dean, 1975—; White House Aide, 1960; dep. asst. for legis. affairs to Sec. Def., 1960-63. Vice chmn. Seattle Downtown YMCA, 1972-74. Mem. Am., Va., Wash. bar assns., Am. Assn. Law Schs., Order of Coif, Phi Delta Phi. Contbr. articles to mil. publs.; editorial bd. George Washington U. Law Rev., 1963-64. Home: 6914 W Mercer Way Mercer Island WA 98040 Office: Sch of Law U Puget Sound 8811 S Tacoma Way Tacoma WA 98499 Tel (206) 756-3393

MEYERS, CHARLES JARVIS, b. Dallas, Aug. 7, 1925; B.A., Rice U., 1949; LL.B., U. Tex., 1949; LL.M., Columbia, 1953, J.S.D., 1964. Admitted to Tex. bar, 1949; asst. prof. law U. Tex. at Austin, 1949-52; asso. prof., 1952-54; asso. prof. law Columbia, 1954-57, prof., 1957-62; prof. law Stanford U. (Calif.), 1962—, Charles A. Beardsley prof., 1971-76, Richard E. Lang prof., dean sch. law, 1976—; vis. prof. U. Minn., Mpls., 1953-54, Cornell U., 1961, U. Mich., 1963, U. Utah, 1965, U. Chile, Santiago, 1968-69; dir. Pub. Advocates Inc., San Francisco, 1971—; asst. gen. counsel Nat. Water Commn., 1970-73. Mem. Am. Law Inst., Am. Bar Assn., Assn. Am. Law Schs. (pres. 1975), Order Coif, Phi Beta Kappa, Phi Delta Phi. Author: (with H.R. Williams) Oil and Gas Law, 1959; (with A.D. Tarlock) Water Resource Management, 1971; Cases on Oil and Gas Law, 3d edit., 1974; Legal-Economic Aspects of Environmental Protection, 1971. Home: 730 Frenchman's Rd Stanford CA 94305 Office: Stanford Law Sch Stanford CA 94305 Tel (415) 497-4455

MEYERS, DAVID S., b. Cleve., Mar. 6, 1928; A.B., Allegheny Coll., 1949; LL.B., U. Mich., 1952. Admitted to Ohio bar, 1952, Mich. bar, 1952; served to capt. JAGC, USAF, 1952-54; mgr. tax dept. Arthur Andersen & Co., Cleve., 1954-60; partner firm Meyers, Stevens & Rea, Cleve., 1960—. Bd. dirs., United Torch, Cleve., 1957; treas., bd. dirs. Suicide Prevention Bur., Cleve., 1974-77. Mem. Ohio, Cleve. bar assns., Ohio Soc. C.P.A.'s.

MEYERS, DONALD DEAN, b. McClusky, N.D., Nov. 22, 1930; B.S., N.D. State U., 1952; J.D., U. Mich., 1957; postgrad. U. Cambridge (Eng.), 1957-58. Admitted to Ariz. bar, 1958; partner firm Shimmel, Hill, Kleindienst & Bishop, 1960-68; individual practice law, Phoenix, 1968—; asst. county atty. Maricopa County (Ariz.), 1958-60. Pres. Fiesta Bowl, 1972; founder, bd. dirs. Phoenix Men's Arts Council, Phoenix Men's Symphony Assn., Bus. Men's Polit. Com. Ariz. Mem. Am., Ariz., Maricopa County bar assns., Am. Assn. Hops. Attys. Office: 3003 N Central St Suite 1901 Phoenix AZ 85012 Tel (602) 264-2571

MEYERS, ERIC BARTON, b. Washington, Oct. 7, 1942; A.B., Trinity Coll., 1965; J.D. with honors, George Washington U., 1968. Admitted to N.Y. bar, 1968, Fla. bar, 1971, U.S. Supreme Ct. bar, 1972; summer asso. firm Arnold and Porter, Washington, 1967; asso. firm Hughes Hubbard & Reed, N.Y.C., 1968-71; asso. firm Shutts & Bowen, Miami, Fla., 1971-73, partner, 1974—. Bd. dirs. S. Fla. Cystic Fibrosis Found., 1975-76. Mem. Am., Fla., Dade County bar assns., Am. Judicature Soc. Home: 5740 SW 113th St Miami FL 33157 Office: 1000 First Nat Bank Bldg Miami FL 33131 Tel (305) 358-6300

MEYERS, GERSON ELLIS, b. Chgo., Oct. 13, 1935; S.B., Mass. Inst. Tech., 1957; LL.B., Georgetown U., 1963. Admitted to Va. bar, 1963, Ill. bar, 1963, U.S. Patent Office bar, 1963, U.S. Supreme Ct. bar, 1968, U.S. Ct. Mil. Appeals bar, 1968, U.S. Ct. Claims bar, 1976; examiner U.S. Patent Office, Washington, 1960-63; asso. firm Anderson, Luedeka, Fitch, Even & Tabin, Chgo., 1963-64; asso. firm Dressler, Goldsmith, Clement, Gordon & Shore, Chgo., 1964-71, mem., 1972—; served to comdr. JAGC, USNR. Mem. Northbrook (Ill.) Bd. Edn., 1960-63. Mem. Am., Ill. State, Chgo. bar assns., Chgo. Patent Law Assn., Phi Alpha Delta. Home: 4020 Brittany Ct Northbrook IL 60062 Office: 1800 Prudential Plaza Chicago IL 60601 Tel (312) 527-4025

MEYERS, JAMES WILLIAM, b. Natick, Mass., Sept. 16, 1942; B.S.A. with high honors, Bentley Coll., 1964; J.D., Harvard, 1970. Sr. accountant Ernst & Ernst, Boston, 1964-67; trial atty., criminal div. Dept. Justice, Washington, 1970-72; chief appellate sect., Office U.S. Atty., So. Dist. Calif., 1972-76; U.S. Bankruptcy judge So. Dist. Calif., San Diego, 1976—. Mem. Am. Bar Assn. Office: US Courthouse 940 Front St San Diego CA 92189 Tel (714) 293-5622

MEYERS, ORIN CHRISTOPHER, II, b. Shawnee, Okla., May 6, 1944; B.B.A., U. Okla., 1966, J.D., 1969; LL.M., Georgetown U., 1972. Admitted to Okla. bar, 1969, U.S. Supreme Ct. bar, 1973; with Arthur Andersen & Co., Oklahoma City, 1969-70; partner firm Godlove Joynes Garrett & Meyers, Lawton, Okla., 1972—. Bd. dirs. Okla. Inst. Taxation. Mem. Am., Okla. bar assns. Office: 802 C Ave Lawton OK 73501 Tel (405) 353-6700

MEYERSON, EDWARD PAUL, b. N.Y.C., May 26, 1941; B.S., U. Tampa, 1964; J.D., Cumberland Sch. Law, Samford U., 1969. Admitted to Ala. bar, 1969, Fla. bar, 1969; partner firm Denaburg, Schoel, Meyerson & Ogle, Birmingham, Ala., 1969—; gen. counsel Ala. chpt. Am. Subcontractors Assn. Mem. Ala., Fla., Birmingham bar assns., Comml. Law League Am. Named Outstanding Young Leader of Tampa Tampa C. of C., 1964. Office: 1000 Brown Marx Bldg Birmingham AL 35203 Tel (205) 328-5760

MEYERSON, STANLEY PHILLIP, b. Spartanburg, S.C., Apr. 13, 1916; student Ga. Inst. Tech., 1933-34; A.B., Duke, 1937, J.D., 1939. Admitted to S.C. bar, 1939, N.Y. bar, 1940, Ga. bar, 1945; individual practice law, N.Y.C., 1939-41; lumber atty., southeastern region Office Price Adminstrn., Atlanta, 1942-43; partner firm Hatcher, Meyerson, Oxford & Irvin, Atlanta, 1950—; adj. prof. law Ga. State U., 1945-47. Sec., trustee Phoenix Soc. of Atlanta, 1975-76; trustee Annandale at Suwanee (Ga.), 1970-76. Mem. Am., Fed., Atlanta (sec.-treas. 1961-62) bar assns., Lawyers Club of Atlanta (chmn. practice com. 1960), State Bar Ga. (chmn. tax com. 1966), Am. Judicature Soc., Am. Coll. Mortgage Attys., Newcomen Soc. Contbr. articles to legal jours. Home: 975 Nawench Dr NW Atlanta GA 30327 Office: 40 Marietta St NW Atlanta GA 30303 Tel (404) 525-3404

MICALI, THOMAS AGATINO, b. Chgo., Dec. 2, 1914; A.B., U. Ill., 1936, J.D., 1939. Admitted to Ill. bar, 1939; individual practice law, Chgo., 1939-41; mem. staff law dept. Pullman-Standard Car Mfg. Co., Chgo., 1947-53, gen. counsel, 1953-57, gen. counsel Pullman Inc., 1957. v.p., 1959-69, dir., 1974—, pres. Pullman Trailmobile, 1971—. Mem. Am., Ill., Chgo. Bar assns. Home: 1301 Plum Tree Ln Winnetka IL 60093 Office: 200 E Randolph Dr Chicago IL 60601 Tel (312) 322-7680

MICCI, EUGENE DAVID, b. Derby, Conn., Aug. 17, 1945; B.A. in Govt., Fairfield U., 1967; J.D., Boston U., 1970. Admitted to Conn. bar, 1970, U.S. Supreme Ct. bar, 1975; asso. firm Cohen, Sylvester & Micci, and predecessors, Shelton, Conn., 1971-76, partner, 1976—; legis. commr. State of Conn., 1976—; mayor City of Derby, 1973-76. Mem. Conn., Valley bar assns. Recipient Outstanding Alumni award Fairfield U., 1974. Home: 30 Lewis St Derby CT 06418 Office: 433 Howe Ave Shelton CT 06484 Tel (203) 735-3364

MICHAEL, JAMES HARRY, JR., b. Charlottesville, Va., Oct. 17, 1918; B.S., U. Va., 1940, LL.B., 1942. Admitted to Va. bar, 1942, practiced in Charlottesville, 1946—; mem. firm Michael & Dent, Ltd., 1946—; asso. judge Charlottesville Juvenile and Domestic Relations Ct., 1954-67; spl. master patent cases U.S. Dist. Ct. for Western Va., 1960-70; mem. Va. Senate, 1967—; spl. counsel various sch. bds. Chmn. exec. com., governing bd. Council State Govts., 1975-76; mem. Va. Crime Commn., Va. Code Commn.; mem. Commn. on Interstate Cooperation; mem. Charlottesville-Albemarle Rescue Squad, Charlottesville Com. Fgn. Relations; mem. Charlottesville Pub. Sch. Bd., 1951-62, vice chmn., 1961; bd. govs. St. Anne's-Belfield Sch., 1952-76, St. Anne's-Belfield, Inc., 1967—; chmn. Va. State Coal and Energy Commn. Mem. Am., Va., Charlottesville-Albemarle bar assns., Am. Trial Lawyers Assn., Am. Judicature Soc. Home: 900 Rugby Rd Charlottesville VA 22903 Office: PO Box 1070 Charlottesville VA 22902 Tel (804) 977-8880

MICHAEL, KAISER, JR., b. Albuquerque, Sept. 28, 1932; B.B.A., U. N.Mex., 1955; J.D., U. Denver, 1957. Admitted to N.Mex. bar, 1957, U.S. Supreme Ct. bar, 1973; asst. staff judge adv. USAF, Webb AFB, Tex., 1957-59; asst. dist. atty. First Jud. Dist. N.Mex., 1959-60, Second Jud. Dist. N.Mex., 1961-62; partner firm Knight, Sullivan, Villella, Skarsgard & Michael, and predecessors, Albuquerque, 1962—; commr. State Bar N.Mex., 1973—; chmn. ct. com. Met. Criminal Justice Coordinating Council, 1973—. Pres. Kidney Found. N.Mex., 1976—. Mem. Am., N.Mex., Albuquerque (pres. 1971-72) bar assns., Am., N.Mex. trial lawyers assns., Am. Judicature Soc. Named Outstanding External Chmn., N.Mex. C. of C., 1961-62. Home: 4317 Royene St NE Albuquerque NM 87110 Office: 6022 Constitution Ave NE Albuquerque NM 87110 Tel (505) 265-8446

MICHAEL, NELSON MARSHALL, b. Keyser, W.Va., Mar. 4, 1948; B.S. in History, Frostburg State Coll., 1970; J.D., W.Va. U., 1973. Admitted to W.Va. bar, 1973; asso. firm James H. Swadley, Jr., Keyser, 1973-75; partner firm Swadley, Michael & Barr, Keyser, 1975—; pros. atty. Mineral County (W.Va.), 1977—. Mem. Am., W.Va State, Mineral County bar assns., Keyser-Mineral County C. of C., Phi Alpha Delta. Home: Limestone Rd Keyser WV 26726 Office: 119 West St Keyser WV 26726 Tel (304) 788-0300

MICHAEL, RICHARD ALEXANDER, b. Chgo., May 7, 1933; B.S., Loyola, Chgo., 1955, J.D. magna cum laude, 1958; LL.M., U. Ill., 1960. Admitted to Ill. bar, 1958; asst. prof. Loyola U. of New Orleans, 1959-63; staff La. Legis. Counsel, Baton Rouge, 1959-62; chief appellate div. Office Atty. Gen. State Ill., Chgo., 1964-67; prof. law Loyola U. of Chgo., 1967—, gen. counsel, 1968-73; clk. judge Daniel Ward Ill. Supreme Ct., 1972; cons. Assessor Cook County (Ill.), 1972-73; cons. corp. counsel City Chgo., 1974-75; prof. Ill. Jud. Conf., 1967—; lectr. in field. Mem. Am., Ill. (publs. com.), Chgo. bar assns., Am. Judicature Soc. Contbr. articles to Loyola Law Review, Loyola Law Jour., Chgo. Bar Record, Ill. Bar Jour. Home: 6101 N Sheridan Rd E Chicago IL 60660 Office: 41 E Pearson St Chicago IL 60611 Tel (312) 670-2940

MICHAELREE, JACK MORRELL, b. Effingham, Ill., Sept. 6, 1925; B.S., U. Notre Dame, 1950, J.D., 1951. Admitted to Ill. bar, 1951; mem. firm Michaelree and Michaelree, Effingham, 1951-58; judge Effingham County Ct., 1958-64; asso. judge 4th Circuit Ill., 1964-71, judge, 1971—. Mem. Effingham County, Ill. bar assns., Ill. Judge's Assn. Home and Office: POB 632 Effingham IL 62401 Tel (217) 342-6166

MICHAELS, DAVID SETH, b. Newark, Oct. 9, 1946; B.A., Amherst Coll., 1968; J.D., U. Mich., 1972. Admitted to Tenn. bar, 1972, Miss. bar, 1972; Reginald Heber Smith Community Lawyer fellow, Jackson, Miss., 1973-75, Memphis, 1972-73; gen. counsel Miss. Mental Health Project, Jackson, 1973-77. Mem. Miss., Hinds County, Am. bar assns.

MICHAELSEN, HOWARD KENNETH, b. Odessa, Wash., May 1, 1927; B.A. in Social Studies Edn., Wash. State U., 1953; J.D., Gonzaga U., 1958. Admitted to Wash. bar, 1959; mem. firm Michaelsen & Lee, Spokane, Wash., 1959—. Mem. Lilac Festival, Spokane, 1974—. Mem. Wash., Spokane County bar assns., Am. Trial Lawyers Assn. Home: 5611 N Ash St Spokane WA 99208 Office: 4407 N Division St Spokane WA 99207 Tel (509) 489-9430

MICHAELSON, BENJAMIN, JR., b. Annapolis, Md., May 30, 1936; B.A. in English, U. Va., 1957; J.D., U. Md., 1962. Admitted to Md. bar, 1962; asso. firm Goodman, Bloom & Michaelson, Annapolis, 1962-63; individual practice law, Annapolis, 1963-73; sr. partner firm Michaelson & Christhilf, P.A., Annapolis, 1973—; counsel Anne Arundel County (Md.) Bd. Edn., 1966-76; gen. counsel, dir. Annapolis Fed. Savs. & Loan Assn., 1965—. Pres. Severna Park (Md.) Jaycees, 1963-64; state legal counsel Md. Jaycees, 1965-65; nat. dir. U.S. Jaycees, 1965-66. Mem. Am., Md., Anne Arundel County (exec. com.) bar assns., Delta Theta Phi. Recipient Outstanding Young Man award, Severna Park, 1965. Home: Rt 2 Holly Beach Farm Annapolis MD 21401 Office: 215 Main St PO Box 11 Annapolis MD 21401 Tel (301) 267-8178

MICHAELSON, JULIUS COOLEY, b. Salem, Mass., Jan. 26, 1922; LL.B., Boston U., 1947; M.A., Brown U., 1967. Admitted to Mass. bar, 1947, R.I. bar, 1948; asso. firm Abedon, Michaelson, Stanzler & Biener, Providence, 1955-74; atty. gen. R.I., Providence, 1975—. Mem. R.I. Senate, 1963-74. Mem. Am., R.I. (pres. 1973) bar assns., Am. Trial Lawyers Assn. Office: Providence County Court House 250 Benefit St Providence RI 02903 Tel (401) 831-6850

MICHAELSON, KENT W., b. Wauwatosa, Wis., June 21, 1921; B.S.L., Northwestern U., 1948, LL.B., 1950. Admitted to Wis. bar, 1950, Nev. bar, 1968; asso. firm Kivett & Kasdorf, Milw., 1950-53; field adjuster Ohio Casualty Ins. Co., 1953-55; claims mgr. Nat. Union Ins. Co., Los Angeles, 1955-66, home office examiner, Pitts., 1966-67; asso. firm Morse & Graves, Las Vegas, Nev., 1968-69; asso. firm Cromer, Barker, Michaelson, and predecessor, Las Vegas, 1969-71, partner, 1971—. Mem. Wis., Nev., Clark County, Am. bar assns. Office: 514 S 3d St Las Vegas NV 89101 Tel (702) 384-4012

MICHAUD, FREDERICK CHARLES, b. Winterset, Iowa, Nov. 22, 1940; A.B., Stanford, 1962; J.D., U. Calif., Berkeley, 1965. Admitted to Calif. bar, 1966, U.S. Supreme Ct. bar, 1971; dep. dist. atty. Santa Clara County (Calif.), 1966-67; partner firm Griswold, Michaud & Halliday, San Jose, Calif., 1968—. Mem. Calif. (chmn. council chpt. pres.'s 1976), Santa Clara (pres. 1975-76) trial lawyers assns., Am., Santa Clara (chmn. torts sect. 1976, med.-legal com. 1976) bar assns., Am. Trial Lawyers Assn. Home: 27709 Via Cerro Gordo Los Altos Hills CA 94022 Office: 12 S 1st St San Jose CA 95113 Tel (408) 295-7574

MICHEEL, RICHARD ARTHUR, b. Davenport, Iowa, Dec. 19, 1920; B.S., St. Ambrose Coll., 1943; LL.B., Georgetown U., 1948. Admitted to Iowa bar, 1951, D.C. bar, 1952; asso. firm Robert Sheriff and Moss, Washington, 1972-76; asso. with Daniel Honig, Washington, 1976—. Mem. D.C. Bar Assn., Counsellors. Home: 5507 Jordan Rd Bethesda MD 20016 Office: 1819 H St NW Washington DC 20006 Tel (202) 872-0702

MICHEL, CLIFFORD LLOYD, b. N.Y.C., Aug. 9, 1939; A.B. cum laude, Princeton, 1961; J.D., Yale, 1964. Admitted to N.Y. bar, 1964, French bar, 1972, U.S. Supreme Ct. bar, 1972; asso. firm Cahill, Gordon & Reindel, N.Y.C., 1964-71, partner, 1972—, assigned to Europe, 1967-69; dir. Cities Service Co., Dome Mines Ltd., Sigma Mines (Que.) Ltd. Mem. exec. com. gift of health campaign Am. Hosp. of Paris. Mem. Am., N.Y. State, N.Y. County bar assns., Am. Soc. Internat. Law, Am. Judicature Soc., Assn. Nationale des Conseils Juridique. Home: St Bernards Rd Gladstone NJ 07934 Office: 80 Pine St New York City NY 10005 Tel (212) 825-0100 also (212) 344-1090

MICHELMAN, LEONARD STANLEY, b. Bklyn., Mar. 12, 1923; Sc. B. in Physics, Brown U., postgrad. U. Tenn., 1944; LL.B., Boston U., 1948; M. Patent Law, George Washington U., 1950. Admitted to Mass. bar, 1949, U.S. Patent Ct. bar, 1951; examiner U.S. Patent Office, Washington, 1948-51; asso. firm Bacon, Weltman & Cohen, Springfield, Mass., 1951-52; individual practice law, Springfield,

1953—. Past pres. Rental Housing Assn. Mem. Mass., Hampden County bar assns., Am. Patent Law Assn. (mem. unfair competition com.), Patent Office Soc., Am. Arbitration Assn. (arbitrator), Tau Epsilon Rho. Contbr. articles in field to Patent Office Jour. Home: 172 Lynnwood Longmeadow MA 01106 Office: 1333 E Columbus Ave Springfield MA 01105 Tel (413) 737-1166

MICHELS, FREDRIC EARL, b. Chgo., Apr. 3, 1947; B.A., Ind. U., 1970; J.D., U. Louisville, 1973. Admitted to Ky. bar, 1973; asst. city law dir. City of Louisville, 1974; partner firm Gittleman, Charney & Michels, Louisville, 1974-75; individual practice law, Louisville, 1975—. Mem. Am., Ky., Louisville bar assns., Am. Trial Lawyers Assn. Home: 3117 Dell Brooke Ave Louisville KY 40220 Office: Suite 500 310 W Liberty St Louisville KY 40202 Tel (502) 585-4552

MICHELSEN, ROLF THOMPSON, b. Bklyn., May 15, 1899; B.A., Amherst Coll., 1921; J.D., Harvard, 1924. Admitted to N.Y. bar, 1929, U.S. Supreme Ct. bar, 1946; partner firm Hatch & Wolfe, N.Y.C., 1936-40, Michelsen & Chamberlain, N.Y.C., 1940-45, Michelsen & Elliott, N.Y.C., 1945-55, Pyne, Brush, Smith & Michelsen, N.Y.C., 1955-60, Brush & Michelsen, N.Y.C., 1960-62; individual practice law, N.Y.C., 1962-68, Bellport, N.Y., 1968—. Commr. of appraisal Del. Watershed for N.Y.C., 1938-40, 44-46. Mem. Am., Suffolk County bar assns., Assn. Bar City N.Y., Maritime Law Assn. U.S.A., Am. Arbitration Assn. (mem. panel N.Y.C.). Decorated knight 1st class Royal Order of Saint Olav (Norway). Home: 71 S Howells Point Rd Bellport NY 11713 Tel (516) 286-8286

MICHELSEN, WAYNE ROWLAND, b. Chgo., Mar. 22, 1924; B.B.A., Northwestern U., 1949, J.D., 1953. Admitted to Ill. bar, 1953; owner real estate bus., Chgo., 1947-67; individual practice law, Chgo., 1953-67; mgr. escrow dept. Pioneer Nat. Title Ins. Co., Chgo., 1967-69, nat. title officer, 1969-70; mgr. real estate loan dept. Ill. State Bank, 1970-72; mgr. ops. Employee Transfer Corp. subs. Chgo. Title & Trust Co., 1972-75, ops. counsel, 1975—; instr. real estate, 1973—. Office: 20 N Wacker Dr Chicago IL 60606 Tel (312) 630-2978

MICHELSON, HORACE, b. Somerville, N.J., Mar. 28, 1919; A.B., Rutgers U., 1940, A.M., 1941; LL.B., Columbia, U., 1947. Admitted to N.Y. bar, 1948; asso. firm Moses & Singer, N.Y.C., 1948-56, mem. firm, 1957—. Mem. Am., N.Y. State, N.Y. County bar assns., Phi Beta Kappa. Editor Columbia Law Rev., 1946-47. Home: 70 E 10th St New York City NY 10003 Office: 51 W 51st St New York City NY 10019 Tel (212) 581-9000

MICHELSON, MARK AVRAM, b. Cambridge, Mass., Apr. 28, 1935; A.B. magna cum laude, Harvard, 1957, LL.B. cum laude, 1962. Admitted to Mass. bar, 1962, U.S. Supreme Ct. bar, 1972; law clk. Supreme Judicial Ct. Mass., 1962-63; asso. firm Choate, Hall & Stewart, Boston, 1963-69, partner 1970—. Chmn. Commn. on Law and Social Action, Am. Jewish Cong., 1969-72; v.p., Citizens Housing and Planning Assn., 1974-76, pres., 1976—; chmn. Brookline Rent Control Bd., 1971-72; mem. Town Meeting, Brookline, 1972—. Mem. Am. Law Inst. Office: 28 State St Boston MA 02109 Tel (617) 227-5020

MICHELSON, ROBERT, b. St. Louis, Dec. 23, 1944; B.A., Beloit (Wis.) Coll., 1967; student U. Wales, Bangor, 1965-66; J.D., Duke, 1972. Admitted to Wis. bar, 1972; asso. firm Foley and Capwell, Racine, Wis., 1972-73; partner firm Goodman and Michelson, Racine, 1973—; municipal judge City of Racine, 1974, 76; mem. SE Wis. Council on Criminal Justice, 1975-76. Mem. exec. bd. Racine County (Wis.) Democratic Party, 1972—; chmn. adv. com. Racine County Bd. Welfare, 1973-74. Mem. Wis., Racine County bar assns., Am. Trial Lawyers Assn. Recipient Advocacy award Internat. Acad. Trial Lawyers, 1972. Office: 440 Main St Racine WI 53403 Tel (414) 637-7488

MICHELSTETTER, STANLEY HUBERT, b. Milw., July 8, 1946; B.A. in Math., U. Wis., 1968, J.D., 1972. Admitted to Wis. bar, 1972; atty.-mediator Wis. Employment Relations Comm., Milw., 1972—. Mem. Am., Wis., Milw. bar assns., Indsl. Relations Research Assn., Soc. Profls. Dispute Resolution, Am. Arbitration Assn. (labor arbitration panel). Home: 1500 W Green Brook Rd Milwaukee WI 53217 Office: Room 560 819 N 6th St Milwaukee WI 53203 Tel (414) 224-4597

MICHENER, JOHN HAROLD, b. Wichita, Kans., Oct. 6, 1925; B.A. (Summerfield scholar), U. Kans., 1948, M.A., 1949; Ph.D. (Univ. fellow), U. Calif., Berkeley, 1956; J.D., U. Md., 1962. Admitted to Md. bar, 1962; with Social Security Adminstrn., Balt., 1966—, chief ins. compliance staff, 1966, dir. health ins. appraisal staff, 1967-75, mem. mgmt. coordination and spl. projects staff, 1975-77, dir. mgmt. staff Office of Mgmt. and Adminstrn., 1977—; co-dir. Balt. City Housing Ct. Clinic, 1973—. Mem. Balt. City Bd. Municipal and Zoning Appeals, 1976—; pres. Nat. Neighbors, Phila., 1973-74, Balt. Neighborhoods, Inc., 1973-75, Sponsors of Open Housing Investment, Washington, 1975-76, Citizens Planning and Housing Assn., Balt., 1975-76; bd. dirs. Fund for an Open Soc., Phila., 1975—; bd. dirs., chmn. Middle Atlantic region exec. com. Am. Friends Service Com., 1976—. Mem. Am. Bar Assn., Am. Polit. Sci. Assn., Am. Soc. Pub. Adminstrn., Order of Coif, Phi Beta Kappa. Home: 2616 Talbot Rd Windsor Hills Baltimore MD 21216 Office: 800 Altmeyer Bldg Social Security Administration Woodlawn MD 21235 Tel (301) 594-3164

MICHIE, DANIEL BOORSE, JR., b. Phila., July 28, 1922; S.B., Harvard, 1943; LL.B., U. Va., 1948. Admitted to Pa. bar, 1949; since practiced in Phila., asso. firm Harry J. Alker, 1949, Kephart & Kephart, 1950-51, Fell & Spalding, 1952-53, partner firm, 1954-68, Fell, Spalding, Goff & Rubin, 1969—; spl. master U.S. Ct. Appeals for 3d Circuit, 1970—; solicitor Twp. of Abington (Pa.), 1958—; chmn. adv. com. on probation of Pa., 1966—; chmn. bd. trustees Phila. Prisons, 1968-71; pres. Phila. Crime Commn., 1960-63. Pres. Phila. Fellowship Comm., 1970-71; pres. area com. for econ. edn., Phila., 1971-77, Nat. Assn. Citizens Crime Commns., 1961-62; Unitarian Universalist Service Com., Boston, 1969-72, Phila. Council for Internat. Visitors, 1957-60. Mem. Phila., Pa. (chmn. sect. real property, probate and trust law 1977—, ho. of dels. 1971—, chmn. rules and calendar com. 1975—), Am., Fed. bar assns., Am. Judicature Soc., NCCJ (co-chmn. S.Jersey region 1967-71, nat. bd. govs. 1971—), Navy League of U.S. (pres. Phila. council 1976—). Recipient Silver Beaver award Boy Scouts Am., 1961. Home: PO Box 8 1129 Wrack Rd Meadowbrook PA 19046 Office: 510 Walnut St Suite 1800 Philadelphia PA 19106 Tel (215) 925-8300

MICK, HOWARD HAROLD, b. Newton, Kans., Oct. 21, 1934; B.S. in Bus., U. Colo., 1958, LL.B., 1958. Admitted to Colo. bar, 1958, Mo. bar, 1959; asso. firm Stinson, Mag, Thomson, McEvers & Fizzell, Kansas City, Mo., 1959-62, mem., 1962—; dir. Electro-Dynamics Corp. Mem. Assn. Bank Holding Cos. (mem. lawyers' com.), Am., Kansas City bar assns., Lawyers Assn. Kansas City. Office: 2100 Ten Main Center Kansas City MO 64106 Tel (816) 842-8600

MICK, ROBERT WYATT, JR., b. Sturgis, Mich., Jan. 14, 1929; B.B.A., U. Mich., 1950; J.D., 1953. Admitted to Mich. bar, 1954, Ind. bar, 1959; partner firm Bingham, Loughlin, Means & Mick, Mishawaka, Ind., 1959—; dep. pros. atty., St. Joseph County, Ind., 1963; city atty. City of Mishawaka, 1964—. Mem. Ind. Commn. Aging and Aged, 1973—; bd. dirs. Real Services of St. Joseph County, 1966—, pres., 1974-75. Mem. Am., Fed., Ind., St. Joseph County bar assns., State Bar Mich. Home: 507 Edgewater Dr Mishawaka IN 46544 Office: 400 Lincoln Way E Mishawaka IN 46544 Tel (219) 255-9616

MICKEL, CHARLES J., b. Winner, S.D., Dec. 28, 1938; B.A., U. S.D., 1960, M.A., 1962, J.D. with honors, 1968. Admitted to S.D. bar, 1968; dep. state atty. Pennington County (S.D.), 1969-71, asst. pub. defender, 1973-74; partner firm Mickel, Moore & Pokela, Rapid City, S.D., 1971—; law clk. Fed. Dist. Ct., Aberdeen, S.D., 1968-69, S.D. Supreme Ct., Pierre, 1969; chmn. S.D. Juvenile Justice Com., 1976—; mem. S.D. Ho. of Reps., 1975-77. Bd. dirs. Black Hills Legal Services, 1974—, Western S.D. Community Action, 1970-72; mem. S.D. Bd. Environ. Protection, 1977—. Mem. S.D., Pennington County bar assns. Home: Box 456 Suburban Route Rapid City SD 57701 Office: 625 9th St Rapid City SD 57709 Tel (605) 348-2471

MICKELWAIT, LOWELL PITZER, b. Glenwood, Iowa, Nov. 15, 1905; A.B., U. Wash., 1928, LL.B. cum laude, 1930. Admitted to Wash. bar, 1930, U.S. Supreme Ct. bar, 1936; since practiced in Seattle, partner firm Holman, Mckelwait, Marian, Blacks & Perkins, 1930-62; dir., v.p., indsl. and pub. relations The Boeing Co., 1962-72; of counsel Perkins, Coie Stone, Olsen & Williams; dir. Puget Sound Power & Light Co., 1960—; dir. Pacific Northwest Bell Telephone Co., 1966-76. Chmn. Norman Archibald Charitable Found., 1976—; campaign chmn. Seattle-King County Community Chest, 1950, pres. 1963; pres. United Good Neighbor Fund, 1956, 61; chmn. Seattle-King County Bicentenial Commn., 1976; chmn. King County Design Commn., 1968—; pres. Pacific Sci. Center Found., 1972-73, chmn. bd., 1974-75. Mem. Am., Wash., King County bar assns., Order of Coif, Seattle C. of C. (pres. 1972-73), Phi Delta Phi, Phi Gamma Delta. Home: 1551 NW 195th Seattle WA 98177 Office: 1900 Washington Bldg Seattle WA 98101 Tel (206) 682-8770

MICKUM, GEORGE BRENT, III, b. Washington, Jan. 13, 1928; B.S., Georgetown U., 1949, LL.B., 1952; law clk. judge U.S. Ct. Appeals D.C. Circuit, Washington, 1952-53; law clk. to asso. justice Supreme Ct. U.S., 1953-54; partner firm Steptoe & Johnson, Washington, 1954—. Mem. Bar Assn. D.C., D.C., Fed. Power, Am. bar assns., Am. Judicature Soc. Home: 44 Grafton St Chevy Chase MD 20015 Office: 1250 Connecticut Ave NW Washington DC 20036 Tel (202) 862-2105

MIDDLEKAUFF, ROGER DAVID, b. Cleve., May 6, 1935; B.Chem. Engring., Cornell U., 1958; J.D. cum laude, Northwestern U., 1964. Admitted to Ohio bar, 1964, D.C. bar, 1966, U.S. Supreme Ct. bar, 1974; asso. firm Roetzel & Andress, Akron, Ohio, 1964-66, Kirkland, Ellis & Rowe, Washington, 1966-69; asso. firm Bonner, Thompson, Kaplan & O'Connell, Washington, 1969-72, partner, 1973—; mem. adv. com. extension service project Dept. Agr., 1976—; mem. adv. com. solar energy project ERDA, 1975; indsl. observer Codex Alimentarius Commn., 11th session, 1976. Chmn. air quality task force Met. Washington Bd. Trade, 1972-74, chmn. energy task force, 1974-75, vice chmn. community devel. bur, 1977; chmn. Arthur S. Flemming Awards Commn., 1969-70; vol. gen. counsel Episcopal Found. for Drama, 1976-77, Scotland Community Devel. Assn., 1971-73, Congregations United for Shelter, 1971-73, Iona House, 1974-77; sr. warden St. Columba's Episc. Ch., Washington, 1975—; mem. lawyer's panel Pres. Ford Com., 1976. Mem. D.C. Unified, D.C. Vol., Am. bar assns., Order of Coif. Contbr. articles to legal jours.; editor Practising Law Inst. Office: 900 17th St NW Washington DC 20006 Tel (202) 659-4660

MIDDLETON, BISSELL JENKINS, b. Charleston, S.C., Sept. 6, 1926; A.B., Princeton U., 1949; J.D., Harvard U., 1952. Admitted to N.Y. State bar, 1952, D.C. bar, 1969, U.S. Supreme Ct. bar, 1955; asso. firm Root, Ballentine, Bushby, Palmer & Wood, N.Y.C., 1952; trial atty. appellate sect. civil. div. Dept. Justice, 1955-58; counsel Export-Import Bank U.S., Washington, 1958-65, v.p. program planning and info., 1966-69, v.p. fin., 1969; of counsel Patton, Boggs & Blow, Washington, 1971—; partner firm Nixon, Hargrave, Devans & Doyle, Washington, 1972—. Bd. dirs. Country Day Sch., McLean, Va. 1974—; trustee New Eng. Coll., Henniker, N.H., 1976—. Mem. Washington Fgn. Law Soc. (v.p.), Bar Assn. D.C., Am., Fed. (past chmn. fgn. fin. com.) bar assns., Am. Soc. Internat. Law, Phi Beta Kappa. Author chpt. in A Lawyer's Guide to International Business Transactions, 1963; (with Nathaniel McKitterick) The Bankers of the Rich and the Bankers of the Poor: The Role of Export Credit in Development Finance, 1972. Home: 1203 Towlston Rd Great Falls VA 22066 Office: 1666 K St NW Suite 701 Washington DC 20006 Tel (202) 872-0044

MIDDLETON, JACK BAER, b. Phila., Jan. 13, 1929; B.A., Lafayette Coll., 1950; J.D., Boston U., 1956. Admitted to N.H. bar, 1956, U.S. 1st Circuit Ct. Appeals bar, 1957, U.S. Supreme Ct. bar, 1972; asso. firm McLane, Graf, Greene, Rauberson & Middleton and predecessor, Manchester, N.H., 1956-62, partner, 1962—; spl. judge Merrimack Dist. Ct., 1962—; mem. N.H. Commn. Uniform State Laws, 1971-75. Mem. Bedford (N.H.) Sch. Bd., 1960-66. Mem. Am., N.H., Manchester bar assns. Author: (with G. Marshall Abbey) Summary of New Hampshire Law, 1964; (with Guenther and De Grandpre) Compendium of New Hampshire Law, 1969; (with Robert Chiesa) Trial of a Wrongful Death Action in N.H., 1977. Home: N Amherst Rd Bedford NH 03102 Office: 40 Stark St Manchester NH 03101 Tel (603) 625-6464

MIDDLETON, JAMES BOLAND, b. Columbus, Ga., Aug. 19, 1934; B.A., Georgia State U., 1964; J.D., Woodrow Wilson Coll. of Law, 1972. Admitted to Ga. bar, 1972, U.S. Patent Office bar, 1973; asso. firm Jones, Thomas & Ashew, Atlanta, 1972-76; individual practice law, Decatur, Ga., 1976—. Mem. Am., Ga. (treas. individual rights sect. 1976-77), Atlanta Decatur-DeKalb bar assns., Am. Patent Law Assn., Editorial bd. The Atlanta Lawyer, 1975—; contbr. articles to profl. jours. Home: 1155 McConnell Dr Decatur GA 30033 Office: 212 Trust Bldg PO Box P Decatur GA 30031 Tel (404) 377-5327

MIDLER, JOSEPH M., b. N.Y.C., Sept. 25, 1921; B.A., Bklyn. Coll., 1945; LL.B., Columbia, 1947. Admitted to N.Y. bar, 1947; asso. firm Engel, Judge & Miller, N.Y.C., 1949-59; partner firm Safir, Kahn, Midler & Simon, N.Y.C., 1972-77, firm Bobrow Greenapple Burton Distler & Midler, 1977—. Active Boy Scouts Am. Mem. Am. Arbitration Assn. (panel), Assn. Bar City N.Y. Recipient Silver Beaver award Boy Scouts Am. Home: 877 Port Dr Mamaroneck NY 10543 Office: 919 Third Ave New York City NY 10022 Tel (212) 752-2604

MIDONICK, MILLARD LESSER, b. N.Y.C., May 24, 1914; A.B., Columbia U., 1934, J.D., 1936. Admitted to N.Y. bar, 1937, U.S. Supreme Ct. bar, 1954; trial examiner, trial atty. NLRB, N.Y.C. and Washington, 1937-46; mem. firm Polier, Midonick and Zinsser, N.Y.C., 1946-62; justice N.Y.C. Municipal Ct., 1956; judge N.Y. State Family Ct., 1962-71, Surrogate Ct., N.Y. County, 1972—; lectr. in field. Bd. dirs., bd. visitors Columbia U. Sch. Law; bd. dirs. Beth Israel Hosp., other civic orgns. Mem. Assn. Bar City N.Y. (lectr. continuing edn.), New York County Lawyers Assn., Assn. Judges of Family Ct. of State N.Y. (chmn. constitutional conv. 1966-67), Am., N.Y. State bar assns., Surrogates' Assn. State N.Y., Nat. Council Probate Judges (lectr. 1976). Recipient award for best legis. program Nat. Council Juvenile Ct. Judges, 1967; author: Children, Parents and the Courts: Juvenile Delinquency, Ungovernability and Neglect, 1972; editor Columbia Law Rev. Office: 31 Chambers St New York City NY 10007 Tel (212) 374-8280

MIERS, HARRIET ELLAN, b. Dallas, Aug. 10, 1945; B.S. in Math., So. Meth. U., 1967, J.D., 1970. Admitted to Tex. bar, 1970; summer intern firm Belli, Ashe, Ellison, Choulos & Lieff, San Francisco, 1969; law clk. to chief judge U.S. Dist. Ct. for No. Dist. Tex., 1970-72; asso. firm Locke, Purnell, Boren, Laney & Neely, Dallas, 1972—. Third v.p., program chmn., bd. dirs. YWCA Met. Dallas; bd. dirs. Dallas Legal Services Found. Mem. Dallas (sec.-treas.), Am. bar assns., State Bar Tex. (vice chmn. sect. antitrust). Home: 5414 Walnut Hill Ln Dallas TX 75219 Office: 3600 Republic Bank Tower Dallas TX 75201 Tel (204) 744-4511

MIES, JAMES EDWARD, b. Garrett, Ind., July 21, 1928; J.D., U. Detroit, 1951. Admitted to Mich. bar, 1952; partner firm Brashear, Brashear, Mies and Duggan, Detroit, Livonia, Mich., 1953-68; judge 16th Dist. Ct., Livonia, Mich., 1969—; mem. Mich. Jud. Tenure Commn., 1975—; faculty Am. Acad. Jud. Edn., Washington, Center for Adminstrn. of Justice, Detroit. Trustee Mich. Cancer Found., Detroit, 1963—; mem. Wayne Center Retarded and Developmentally Disabled, Detroit, 1975—; bd. dirs. Community Opportunity Center, Livonia, 1965—; chmn. Livonia Charter Commn., Livonia, 1966-68. Mem. Am., Mich., Livonia bar assns., Am. Judges Assn., Mich. Dist. Judges Assn. Home: 9612 Berwick St Livonia MI 48150 Office: 15140 Farmington Rd Livonia MI 48154 Tel (313) 522-5900

MIGDAL, SHELDON PAUL, b. Chgo., July 3, 1936; B.S., U. Ill., 1958, J.D., Northwestern U., 1961. Admitted to Ill. bar, 1961; atty. Tax div. U.S. Dept. Justice, Washington, 1961-67; asso. firm Dixon, Todhunter, Knouff & Holmes, Chgo., 1968-68; partner firm Wildman, Harrold, Allen & Dixon, Chgo., 1968—. Exec. v.p., bd. dirs. Better Boys Found., Chgo., 1969—. Mem. Am., Chgo., Ill. bar assns., Am. Inst. C.P.A.'s, Ill. Soc. C.P.A.'s. C.P.A., Ill. Office: Suite 3000 1 IBM Plaza Chicago IL 60611 Tel (312) 222-0400

MIHALICH, GILFERT MATTHEW, b. Monessen, Pa., July 12, 1926; B.A., Duquesne U., 1948; J.D., U. Pitts., 1957. Admitted to Pa. bar, 1957, U.S. Supreme Ct. bar; law clk. Ct. Common Pleas Westmoreland County (Pa.) and Supreme Ct. Pa.; individual practice law, Monessen, to 1971; city solicitor, Monessen; asst. dist. atty.; solicitor Westmoreland County Law Enforcement Officers Assn.; judge Ct. Common Pleas Westmoreland County, Greensburg, Pa., 1971—; instr. criminal law Indiana U. Pa.; Past chmn. Westmoreland County Prison Bd.; mem. Pa. Gov.'s Justice Commn.; past chmn. Monessen Mayor's Adv. Com., Mayor's Adv. Com. on Minority Housing; past area chmn. blood program ARC; past chmn. Monessen Cancer Crusade; adv. bd. Salvation Army; bd. dirs. Westmoreland County Cancer Crusade. Mem. Pa. Conf. State Trial Judges. Home: 1011 Dennis Ave Monessen PA 15062 Tel (412) 834-2191

MIKELL, BERNARD JOSEPH, JR., b. N.Y.C.; B.A., Hamilton Coll., 1960; LL.B., U. Va., 1969. Admitted to Calif. bar, 1970; asso. Cushing, Cullivan, Hancock & Rothert, San Francisco, 1970-71; counsel Great Western Savings & Loan Assn., San Francisco, 1971-73; legis. advocate Calif. Savings & Loan League, Los Angeles, Sacramento, 1973-76; v.p., gen. counsel Calif. Housing Finance Agy., Sacramento, 1976—. Office: 301 Capitol Mall Suite 403 Sacramento CA 95814 Tel (916) 322-3991

MIKLICH, THOMAS ROBERT, b. Cleve., Apr. 17, 1947; B.B.A., Cleve. State U., 1969, J.D., 1973. Admitted to Ohio bar, 1974; asst. sec., corporate dir. taxes, Sherwin-Williams Co., Cleve., 1969—. Mem. Ohio Bar Assn., Ohio Soc. C.P.A.'s, Am. Inst. C.P.A.'s, Tax Exec. Inst. Office: 101 Prospect Ave NW Cleveland OH 44115 Tel (216) 566-2573

MILAM, JESSE RUSH, III, b. Waco, Tex., Sept. 13, 1948; student Ga. Inst. Tech., 1966-69; J.D., Baylor U., 1972. Admitted to Tex. bar, 1972; individual practice law, Waco; city atty. City of Killeen, Tex., 1973—. Mem. Am., Bell-Lampasas-Mills Counties, Tex. bar assns., Tex. Trial Lawyer's Assn., Tex. City Atty.'s Assn. Home: 607 Goodnight St Killeen TX 76541 Office: 400 N 2d St Killeen TX 76541 Tel (817) 634-2191

MILAM, KENNETH EWING, b. Tupelo, Miss., July 11, 1944; B.A., U. Miss., 1966, J.D., 1969. Admitted to Miss. bar, 1969; asso. firm Lumpkin, Holland & Ray, Tupelo, 1971-74; partner firm Jolly, Holloman & Miller, Tupelo, 1974-75, firm Jolly & Miller, Jackson, Miss., 1976—. Mem. Am., Fed., Hinds County (sec. 1972) bar assns., Am. Soc. Hosp. Attys., Phi Delta Phi. Office: PO Box 2366 Jackson MS 39205 Tel (601) 948-3131

MILANO, SALVATORE MICHAEL, b. N.Y.C., Aug. 19, 1921; B.S., Fordham U., 1942, LL.B., 1949, J.D., 1968. Admitted to N.Y. bar, 1949; individual practice law, Lynbrook, N.Y., 1949—. Mem. Planning Bd. Village Rockville Centre, N.Y., 1968— (vice-chmn.). Mem. N.Y. State and Nassau County bar assns. Home: 59 Berkshire Rd Rockville Centre NY 11570 Office: 2 Broadway Lynbrook NY 11563 Tel (516) 599-2750

MILBERG, LAWRENCE, b. Bklyn., Oct. 3, 1913; B.A., N.Y. U., 1933; J.D., Harvard, 1936. Admitted to N.Y. bar, 1937, U.S. Supreme Ct. bar, 1961; partner firm Blumberg, Singer, Ross & Gordon, N.Y.C., 1959-60, firm Milberg & Levy, N.Y.C., 1961-68, firm Leibowitt, Milberg, Weiss & Fox, N.Y.C., 1968-72, firm Milberg, Weiss, Bershad & Specthrie, N.Y.C., 1972—. Mem. Am., N.Y. bar assns., Fed. Bar Council, Assn. Bar City N.Y., Phi Beta Kappa. Office: 1 Pennsylvania Plaza New York City NY 10001 Tel (212) 594-5300

MILBURN, HERBERT THEODORE (TED), b. Cleve., May 26, 1931; B.S., East Tenn. State U., 1953; J.D., U. Tenn., 1959; grad. Nat. Coll. State Judiciary, U. Nev., 1975. Admitted to Tenn. bar, 1959; mem. firm Bishop, Thomas, Leitner, Mann & Milburn, and predecessor, 1959-73; judge, 1973—; spl. judge Tenn. Ct. Appeals, Eastern Sect., 1976. Mem. Chattanooga (sec.-treas. 1967), Tenn., Am. bar assns. Home: 910 Crownpoint Rd W Signal Mountain TN 37377 Office: Hamilton County Courthouse Chattanooga TN 37402 Tel (615) 757-2538

MILBURN, LAIRD THOMAS, b. Santa Maria, Calif., Mar. 9, 1942; B.A., U. Colo., Boulder, 1965; J.D., U. Denver, 1971. Admitted to Colo. bar, 1972, U.S. Dist. Ct. Colo. bar, 1972; partner firm Graham & Dufford, Grand Junction, Colo., 1974—; mem. bd. dirs. Colo. Rural Legal Services, 1972—, chmn., 1974-75. Chmn. Mesa County Democratic Central Com., 1975—. Mem. Am., Colo. bar assns., Colo. Trial Lawyers Assn. Home: 2000 N 6th St Grand Junction CO 81501 Office: Suite 900 Valley Federal Plaza Grand Junction CO 81501 Tel (303) 242-4614

MILDE, WALTER LYALL, b. Cleve., July 26, 1934; A.B., Harvard, 1955, LL.B., 1958. Admitted to Ohio bar, 1958, U.S. Supreme Ct. bar, 1962; asso. firm Squire, Sanders & Dempsey, Cleve., 1958-59, 62-69, partner, 1969—; mem. office of gen. counsel dept. of Air Force, U.S. Dept. Defense, Washington, 1959-62. Mem. Ohio, Fed., Cleve. bar assns. Office: 1800 Union Commerce Bldg Cleveland OH 44115 Tel (216) 696-9200

MILES, BRADLEY CARSON, b. San Angelo, Tex., Apr. 28, 1934; B.B.A., U. Tex., Austin, 1957, J.D., 1958. Admitted to Tex. bar, 1958, U.S. Supreme Ct. bar, 1967; atty. Taylor County (Tex.), 1961-63, 42d Jud. Dist., Abilene, Tex., 1963-67; judge Taylor County Ct., 1967-69; individual practice law, San Angelo, 1969—. Pres. advisory devel. bd. So. Bapt. Radio-TV Commn., Ft. Worth, Tex., 1970-72; dir. Tom Green County (Tex.) Child Welfare Dept., 1975—, San Angelo Symphony Orch., 1976-78. Mem. Tex., Tom Green County bar assns., Tex. Criminal Defense Lawyers Assn., San Angelo Estate Planning Council. Home: 2138 Sul Ross St San Angelo TX 76901 Office: Box 5067 San Angelo TX 76902 Tel (915) 653-3688

MILES, CATHERINE E., b. Reform, Ala., Dec. 24; B.S., U. Ala., 1949, M.S., 1950, Ph.D., 1953; J.D., Emory U., 1963. Indsl. accountant Batson-Cook Co., West Point, Ga., 1937-42; asst. prof. accounting Ga. State U., 1952-55, asso. prof., 1956-58, prof., 1958—, chmn. accounting dept., 1955—; admitted to Ga. bar. Mem. Am. Accounting Assn. (nat. sec. 1969-70), Am. Bar Assn., Am. Soc. Women Accountants, State Bar Ga., Ga. Assn. Accounting Instrs., Ga. Soc. C.P.A.'s, Nat. Assn. Accountants, Beta Alpha Psi, Beta Gamma Sigma, Phi Chi Theta., Omicron Delta Kappa. Named Woman of Year in Edn., author: (with Joseph E. Lane, Jr.) Business and Personal Taxes, 1973, 74, 75; contbr. articles to legal jours. Office: Accounting Dept Ga State U Atlanta GA 30303 Tel (404) 658-2611

MILES, JAMES RICHARD, b. Dayton, Ohio, June 25, 1937; B.A., Ohio State U., 1959, J.D., 1961; LL.M., U. Mich., 1973; postgrad. Hague Acad. Pub. Internat. Law, 1975. Admitted to Ohio bar, 1961; with JAGC, USAF, 1962-66, commd. capt., 1968, advanced through grades to lt. col., 1975; staff Hdqrs., Washington, 1973—; asso. firm Smith & Schnacke, Dayton, 1966-68. Trustee Divine Sci. Ch., Washington, 1975—. Mem. Am. (vice chmn. com. internat. comparative criminal law), Fed., Ohio State bar assns., Am. Soc. Internat. Law, Order of Coif. Contbr. articles to legal publs.; casenote editor Ohio State Law Jour., 1960-61. Home: 145 W Norman Ave Dayton OH 45405 Office: Hdqrs USAF Judge Adv Dept I Washington DC 20316 Tel (202) OX 3 5850

MILES, MANDERSON LEHR, b. Beloit, Wis., Jan. 17, 1947; B.B.A., U. Okla., 1969; J.D., U. Idaho, 1972. Admitted to Idaho bar, 1973; partner firm Knowlton & Miles, Lewiston, Idaho, 1972—; pub. defender Nez Perce County (Idaho), 1972—. Bd. dirs. North Idaho Children's Home, Lewiston, 1975-76. Mem. Am. Trial Lawyers Assn., Am., Idaho bar assns., North Idaho Trial Lawyers (pres. 1975), Ducks Unltd. (dir. Lewis-Clark chpt. 1975-76). Home: 940 Stewart St Lewiston ID 83501 Office: 312 17th St Lewiston ID 83501 Tel (208) 746-0103

MILES, ROBERT LAFOLLETTE, b. Big Rapids, Mich., Sept. 8, 1911; J.D., Detroit Coll. Law, 1936. Admitted to Mich. bar, 1936, U.S. Dist. Ct. bar, 1938, U.S. Supreme Ct. bar, 1962, U.S. Circuit Ct. of Appeals bar, 1972; pros. atty., Mecosta County, Mich., 1939-42; individual practice law, 1946-75; probate judge Mecosta County, 1972-75; judge Dist. Ct., Mecosta and Osceola Counties (Mich.), Big Rapids, 1975—. Mem. 27th Jud. Dist., Mecosta-Osceola bar assns., Am., Mich. trial lawyers' assns., Nat. Council Juvenile Ct. Judges. Home: 120 Cedar St Big Rapids MI 49307 Office: Dist Ct Mecosta County Bldg 400 Elm St Big Rapids MI 49307 Tel (616) 796-8631

MILES, ROY ADAIR, b. Rutherford County, Tenn., Sept. 22, 1898; LL.B. Vanderbilt U., 1921. Admitted to Tenn. bar, 1921; partner firm Miles, Butler, Corbitt & McCall, Nashville, 1941-58; judge Tenn. Circuit Ct., 10th Jud. Circuit, 1958-74; of counsel firm Dale, Thompson & Miles, Nashville, 1974—; pres. Tenn. Jud. Conf., 1961-62; mem. exec. com. Nat. Conf. State Trial Judges, 1969-71; mem. Tenn. Jud. Council, 1969-75. Home: 3601 Saratoga Dr Nashville TN 37205 Office: Dale Thompson & Miles Suite 1406 Nashville Trust Bldg Nashville TN 37201 Tel (615) 255-7443

MILEY, RICHARD EDWIN, b. Charleston, S.C., Jan. 28, 1945; B.A., Clemson U., 1967; J.D., Emory U., 1973. Admitted to S.C. bar, 1974, Ga. bar, 1974; law clk. to judge U.S. Dist. Ct., 1974-75; asso. firm Nixon, Yow, Waller & Capers, Augusta, Ga., 1975—; asso. prof. Augusta Law Sch. Mem. Am., S.C. bar assns., N. Augusta C. of C. Home: 2024 Pisgah Rd North Augusta SC 29841 Tel (404) 722-7541

MILFORD, CHARLES PICKENS, b. Jacksonville, Fla., Aug. 16, 1939; B.A., U. Fla., 1961, J.D., 1964. Admitted to Fla. bar, 1964; since practiced in Jacksonville; asso. firm Mathews, Osborne & Ehrilich, 1967-68; asso. counsel Fla. State Bd. Health, 1968-69; asso. firm MacLean & Brooke, 1969-72; house counsel Winn-Dixie Stores, Inc., 1972—. Campaign dir., bd. dirs. N.E. chpt. March of Dimes, 1975-76; v.p., bd. dirs. Jacksonville Mental Health Assn. Mem. Jacksonville (dir.), Fla., Am. bar assns. Home: 3818 Barkdale Ct Jacksonville FL 32211 Office: PO Box B Jacksonville FL 32203 Tel (904) 783-1800

MILGRIM, ROGER MICHAEL, b. N.Y.C., Mar. 22, 1937; A.B., U. Pa., 1958; LL.B., N.Y. U., 1961, LL.M., 1962. Admitted to N.Y. bar, 1961, U.S. Supreme Ct. bar, 1974; asso. firm Baker & McKenzie, Paris, 1963-65, Nixon Mudge Rose Guthrie & Alexander, N.Y.C., 1965-68; mem. firm Milgrim Thomajan & Jacobs, N.Y.C., 1968—; adj. prof. N.Y. U. Sch. Law, 1975—, N.Y. U. Inst. Comparative Law, 1976—. Trustee Bklyn. Hosp. Mem. Assn. Bar City N.Y., N.Y. State, Am. bar assns., N.Y. U. Law Alumni Assn. (dir. 1972-76). Author: Trade Secrets, 1967. Home: 2 Montague Terr Brooklyn NY 11201 Office: Suite 750 25 Broadway New York City NY 10004

MILKMAN, MURRAY, b. Scranton, Pa., Dec. 6, 1929; A.B. in Polit. Sci., Temple U., 1951; LL.B., U. Pa., 1954. Admitted to D.C. bar, 1954, Pa. bar, 1955, N.J. bar, 1965; asso. firm Berger & Gelman, Phila., 1957-59, Ochman & Greenberg, Phila., 1959-60, Berger & Stein, Phila., 1960-64; asst. counsel Ronson Corp., Woodbridge, N.J., 1964-66; asst. counsel Pa. Power & Light Co., Allentown, 1966—. Mem. Allentown Human Relations Commn., 1973—. Mem. Pa., Lehigh County bar assns. Home: 3044 Greenleaf St Allentown PA 18104 Office: 2 N 9th St Allentown PA 18101 Tel (215) 821-5725

MILLARD, A. MARTIN, b. Nashville, Kans., Oct. 3, 1917; A.B., Washburn U., 1951, J.D., 1970. Admitted to Kans. bar, 1941, U.S. Supreme Ct. bar, 1972; individual practice law, Wichita, Kans., 1941—; state prosecutor, Wichita. Mem. Kans. Bar Assn. Home: Route 1 Towanda KS 67144 Office: 7701 E Kellogg St Wichita KS 67207 Tel (316) 682-7307

MILLARD, MARK STANTON, b. Los Angeles, Apr. 9, 1938; B.S. in Finance, U. So. Calif., 1960, LL.B., 1963. Admitted to Calif. bar, 1964; asso. firm Hurwit & Hurwit, Orange, Calif., 1964-68; partner firm Oster, Millard & Suchman, Santa Ana, Calif., 1968—. Mem. Am., Orange County bar assns., Calif., Orange County trial lawyers assns. Office: 444 W 10th St Santa Ana CA 92701 Tel (714) 543-8447

MILLEDGE, ALLAN FRANCIS, b. Miami, Fla., Oct. 21, 1930; A.B., U. N.C., 1951; LL.B. cum laude, Harvard, 1955, J.D., 1969. Admitted to Fla. bar, 1955; U.S. 5th Circuit Ct. Appeals bar, 1958; U.S. Supreme Ct. bar, 1959; asst. atty. gen. State Fla., Tallahassee, 1957-59; asso. firm Nichols, Gaither, Green, Frates & Beckham, Miami, 1959-62; partner firm Milledge & Hermellee and predecessors, 1962—. Chmn. met. youth adv. bd. Dade County, Fla., 1965-67; chmn. environ. head mgmt. study com., 1972-74. Mem. Am., Fla. Dade County bar assns., Harvard Law Sch. Assn. Fla. (pres. 1969-70), Phi Beta Kappa. Home: 2935 Day Ave Miami FL 33133 Office: 2699 S Bayshore Dr Miami FL 33133 Tel (305) 858-5660

MILLER, ANDREW PICKENS, b. Fairfax, Va., Dec. 21, 1932; A.B. magna cum laude, Princeton, 1954; LL.B., U. Va., 1960. Admitted to Va. bar, 1960; partner firm Penn, Stuart & Miller, Abingdon, Va., 1963-69; atty. gen. Commonwealth of Va., Richmond, 1970-77. Sec.-treas., bd. dirs. The Barter Found. Inc., 1962-69; pres. Washington County United Fund, Inc., Abingdon, 1963-64, Va. Highlands Festival, Inc., Abingdon, 1963-65; trustee King Coll., Bristol, Tenn., 1966-74; chmn. Law Day Observance, Commonwealth Va., 1966; mem. adv. com. Old Dominion Found. dirs. SWTb and Respiratory Diseases Assn., 1967-69; mem. adv. bd. Ams. for Effective Law Enforcement, Inc., 1973—, Center for Oceans Law and Policy, 1975—. Fellow Am. Bar Found.; mem. Am. (ho. of dels. 1971-76), Va. (chmn. young lawyers sect. 1967-68, mem. com. constl. revision 1968-69) bar assns., So. Conf. Attys. Gen. (chmn. 1973-74), Nat. Assn. Attys. Gen. (chmn. anti-trust com. 1971-76, mem. exec. com. 1973-74, Wyman Meml. award 1976), Am. Judicature Soc. (dir. 1973-76, exec. com. 1974-76), Raven Soc., Order of Coif, Phi Beta Kappa. Recipient Distinguished Service award Jaycees, 1963. Home: 13 Glenbrooke Circle W Richmond VA 23229

MILLER, BRUCE LYMAN, b. Siloam Springs, Ark., June 19, 1913; B.A., LL.B., U. Ark., 1937; postgrad. Harvard Law Sch., 1946. Admitted to Tex. bar, 1937, Ark. bar, 1937, U.S. Supreme Ct. bar, 1963; asso. firm Cutrer & Murfee, Houston, 1937-40, Clark, Carr & Ellis, N.Y.C., 1946-48; individual practice law, Hereford, Tex., 1949—. Troop leader Boy Scouts Am., 1956-58, regional bd. dirs., 1965-69; bd. dirs. Regional Alcoholism Authority; chmn. Deaf Smith Council on Alcoholism, 1970-71. Mem. Am., Tex. (chmn. grievance com. 1952-61), 69th Jud. Dist. (pres. 1957) bar assns. Home: Harrison Hwy Box 1111 Hereford TX 79045 Office: 315 Sampson Box 1111 Hereford TX 79045 Tel (806) 364-1011

MILLER, BRUCE SHERWOOD, b. Balt., July 20, 1943; B.A., Pa. State U., 1965; J.D., Dickinson Sch. Law, 1968. Admitted to Pa. bar, 1968; asso. firm Laputka, Bayless, Ecker & Cohn, Hazleton, Pa., 1968-73, partner, 1973—; asst. pub. defender, Luzerne County, Pa., 1970—; cooperating counsel ACLU, 1972—, NOW, 1974—. Mem. nat. discriminations com. B'nai B'rith, 1972—, pres. eastern Pa. council, 1973-74. Mem. Am., Pa., Luzerne County bar assns. Office: 605 Citizens Bank Bldg Hazleton PA 18201 Tel (717) 455-4731

MILLER, C.A. SEARCY, b. Bryan, Tex., Oct. 25, 1936; B.A., U. Tex., 1958; J.D., Baylor U., 1962. Admitted to Tex. bar, 1962, U.S. 5th Circuit Ct. Appeals bar, 1970, U.S. Supreme Ct. bar, 1971; asst. city atty., Waco, Tex., 1962-63, city atty., Cedar Hill, Tex., 1963-73; partner firm Anderson, Henley, Shields & Miller, Dallas, 1973—; Law Day speaker, Dallas, 1970. Dir. Visiting Nurses Assn., Dallas, 1968-74; mem. planning commn. City of Univ. Park, Tex., 1970-71; mem. sustaining campaign Park Cities YMCA, Dallas, 1976—; mem. Highland Park Sports Club, 1976—. Mem. Am. (mem. forum com. on health law), Tex., Dallas (mem. legal ethics com. 1970) bar assns., Tex. Assn. Hospital Attys., Tex., Dallas Assn. defense counsel, Am. Soc. Hospital Attys., Phi Alpha Delta. Contbr. articles to legal jours. Home: 3202 Princeton Ave Dallas TX 75205 Office: 3100 Fidelity Union Tower Dallas TX 75201 Tel (214) 742-1161

MILLER, CREIGHTON EUGENE, b. Cleve., Sept. 26, 1922; A.B., U. Notre Dame, 1944; LL.B., Yale, 1947. Admitted to Ohio bar, 1947; individual practice law, Cleve., 1947—; asst. atty. gen. State of Ohio, 1949-50; regional enforcement dir. Office of Price Stablzn., Mich., Ohio and Ky., 1951-52; pres. Telerama Cable TV Co., Cleve., 1964-72; founder, legal counsel Nat. Football League Players Assn. Pres., Cleve. Dist. Golf Assn., 1970—; trustee Huron Rd. Hosp., 1972-76. Mem. Am., Ohio, Greater Cleve. bar assns., Maritime Law Assn. Named to Nat. Football Found. and Hall of Fame, 1976, All Am. Football Team, 1943, Del. Sports Hall of Fame, 1976. Home: 19901 Van Aken Blvd Shaker Heights OH 44122 Office: 1610 Euclid Ave Cleveland OH 44115 Tel (216) 861-6007

MILLER, DALE KEITH, b. St. Joseph, Mo., Nov. 2, 1946; B.S.B.A. in Econs., U. Mo., Columbia, 1968, J.D., 1973. Admitted to Mo. bar, 1973, U.S. Dist. Ct. bar for Western Dist. Mo., 1973; partner firm Sears and Miller, Savannah, Mo., 1973—; city atty. City of Savannah, 1973-76; dep. juvenile officer Andrew County, Mo., 1975-76, pros. atty., 1977—. Tel (816) 324-3712

MILLER, DAVID GLEN, b. Los Angeles, Mar. 8, 1940; B.A., Antioch Coll., 1964; J.D., Calif. Western U., 1967. Atty., NLRB, Los Angeles, 1967-68; admitted to Calif. bar, 1968, Ohio bar, 1968; mem. firms Smith & Schnacke, Dayton, Ohio, 1968-69, Loeb & Loeb, Los Angeles, 1969-74, Paterson & Taggart, Palos Verdes Estates, Calif., 1974—. Mem. Los Angeles County Bar, Beverly Hills (Calif.), Am. bar assns. Office: 2550 Via Fejon-3N Palos Verdes Estates CA 90274 Tel (213) 378-9437

MILLER, DAVID LYLE, b. Vincennes, Ind., Nov. 18, 1939; student Vincennes U., 1957-59; A.B., Ind. U., 1962, J.D., 1968. Admitted to Ind. bar; partner firm Miller & Miller, Vincennes, Ind., 1968—; dep. pros. atty. Knox County (Ind.), 1969-71, 72-73, police legal advisor, 1971-72. Chmn. Knox County ARC, 1972, blood chmn., 1973—. Mem. Ind., Knox County bar assns. Home: 414 McKenney Rd Vincennes IN 47591 Office: 402 American Bank Bldg Vincennes IN 47591 Tel (812) 882-8957

MILLER, EDWIN HENRY, b. Balt., Dec. 28, 1918; A.B., Washington and Lee U., 1940; LL.B., U. Md., 1947, J.D., 1969. Admitted to Md. bar, 1947; U.S. magistrate, Hagerstown, Md., 1954—; magistrate State of Md., 1957-58; mem. st. bd. License Commrs. Washington County (Md.), 1967-76; mem. adv. bd. Md. State Bank, 1975—. Pres. Washington County Mental Health Assn., 1962; bd. dirs. Md. Mental Health Assn., 1962-63; div. chmn. United Fund campaign, 1962; dir. ch. council Trinity Luth. Ch., 1962-66. Mem. Am., Md. State (v.p. 1966), Washington County (pres. 1963-64) bar assns., Gamma Eta Gamma. Home: 14519 Manor Park Dr Rockville MD 20853 Office: 82 W Washington St Hagerstown MD 21740 Tel (301) 731-1234

MILLER, EUGENE CARLISLE, JR., b. Indpls., Jan. 16, 1929; A.B., Wesleyan U., 1950; LL.B., Harvard, 1953. Admitted to Ind. bar, 1953; asso. firm Barnes, Hickam, Pantzer and Boyd, Indpls., 1953, 57-60, partner, 1960—; served to capt. JAGC, U.S. Army, 1954-57. Bd. dirs. Indpls Settlements, Inc., 1965-70; bd. dirs. Christamore House, 1958-64, sec., 1958-64, pres., 1967-69; bd. dirs. Happy Hollow Children's Camp, Inc., 1964—, pres., 1971-72; vestryman St. Paul's Episcopal Ch. Mem. Indpls. (chmn. United Way com.), Ind. State, Am. bar assns., Bar Assn. 7th Fed. Circuit (chmn. membership com.), Am. Judicature Soc., Lawyers Club Indpls. (pres. 1974-75). Office: 1313 Merchants Bank Bldg Indianapolis IN 46204 Tel (317) 638-1313

MILLER, FRANCES HALL, b. Boston, Dec. 25, 1938; A.B., Mt. Holyoke Coll., 1960; J.D., Boston U., 1965; postgrad London Sch. Econs., 1965-66. Admitted to Mass. bar, 1966; instr. Boston U. Sch. Law, 1968-71, lectr., 1971-73, adj. asso. prof., 1973-75, asso. prof., 1975—; asso. firm Powers & Hall, Boston, 1972-76; of counsel firm Bowker, Elmes, Perkins, Mecsas & Gerrard, Boston, 1976—; commr. Mass. Rate Setting Commn., 1974. Mem. Hill-Burton State Adv. Com., Boston, 1972-74; mem. Champ State Com., Boston, 1974—; mem. Mass. Health Facilities Appeals Bd., Boston, 1974—; trustee Mt. Holyoke Coll., 1976—. Mem. Am. Soc. Law and Medicine (asso. editor of newsletter, exec. council), Mass. Bar Assn., Mass. Assn. Women Lawyers, Phi Beta Kappa (hon.). Contbr. articles in field to profl. jours. Home: 42 Cliff Rd Wellesley MA 02181 Office: 765 Commonwealth Ave Boston MA 02215 Tel (617) 353-4421

MILLER, FRANK WILLIAM, b. Appleton, Wis., May 15, 1921; B.A., U. Wis., 1946, LL.B., 1948, S.J.D., 1954. Admitted to Wis. bar, 1948; faculty Washington U., St. Louis, 1948—, Coles prof. law, 1961-65, James Carr prof. criminal jurisprudence, 1965—. Mem. Am. Bar Assn. Author: (with A. C. Becht) The Test of Factual Causation in Negligence and Strict Liability Cases, 1961; Prosecution: The Decision to Charge a Suspect with a Crime, 1969. Editor: (with R. Dawson, G. Dix and R. Parnas) Criminal Justice Administration, 2d edit., 1976; Sentencing and the Correctional Process, 2d edit., 1976; The Mental Health Process, 2d edit., 1976; The Juvenile Justice Process, 1976. Home: 9 Fairwainds Ct Olivette MO 63132 Office: Sch Law Washington U Saint Louis MO 63130 Tel (314) 863-0100

MILLER, FREDERICK HUGUENIN, b. Kansas City, Mo., Aug. 20, 1939; B.S., U. Wis., 1963, J.D., 1967. Admitted to Wis. bar, 1967; asst. legal counsel Gov. State of Wis., 1967-68, legal counsel, 1968-69; dep. dist. atty. Dane County (Wis.), 1969-70; partner firm Miller and Rothstein, Madison, Wis., 1971-77; asst. legal counsel Wis. Dept. Health and Social Services, 1977—. Deacon Christ Presbyn. Ch., Madison, 1967; bd. dirs. Madison Legal Aid, Dane County Legal Aid. Mem. Nat. Assn. Extradition Ofcls. (v.p. 1968-69, life asso.), Wis., Dane County bar assns., Wis. Jud. Council (reporter criminal procedure revision). Home and Office: 1415 Main St Cross Plains WI 53528

MILLER, GARNET EDWARD, b. Erwin, Tenn., Jan. 28, 1913; A.B., Carson-Newman Coll., 1933; J.D., Duke, 1936. Admitted to N.C. bar, 1936, Tenn. bar, 1939, also U.S. Tax Ct. bar; practiced in Asheboro, N.C., 1936—; partner firm Miller, Beck, O'Briant & Glass, 1953—; individual practice law, 1936-53; served with JAGC, U.S. Army, 1943-45. Fellow Am. Coll. Trial Lawyers, Internat. Soc. Barristers, Am. Coll. Probate Counsel; mem. N.C. (bd. govs. 1961-64, 72-73, v.p. 1972-73), Am. bar assns. Home: 818 Worth St Asheboro NC 27203 Office: 115 S Fayetteville St Asheboro NC 27203 Tel (919) 625-5123

MILLER, GEORGE J., b. Charlotte, N.C., Dec. 1, 1926; B.S., U. N.C., 1950, LL.B., 1953. Admitted to N.C. bar, 1953, U.S. Dist. Ct. bar for Western Dist. N.C., 1953, U.S. Ct. Appeals bar, 4th Circuit, 1965; pros. atty. City of Charlotte Criminal (Recorder's) Ct., 1957-61; now partner firm Welling and Miller, Charlotte. Mem. 26th Jud. Dist., N.C., Am. bar assns., N.C. State Bar (councilor 1968-74, pres. 1976—), Am. Judicature Soc., Phi Alpha Delta. Office: Equity Bldg Suite 1 701 E Trade St Charlotte NC 28202 Tel (704) 372-6644*

MILLER, GEORGE MILTON, b. Cleve., May 30, 1943; B.A., Ursinus Coll., 1965; J.D., Case Western Res. U., 1968. Admitted to Ohio bar, 1968; law clk. Cuyahoga County Common Pleas Ct., 1970-73; staff atty. Summit County (Ohio) Legal Aid, 1973-76; referee Domestic Relations Ct. Summit County, Akron, 1976—. Mem. Akron Bar Assn. Home: 4079 Darrow Rd Stow OH 44224 Office: Summit County Courthouse Akron OH 44308 Tel (216) 379-5327

MILLER, GERALDENE YOUNT, b. Galena, Kans., Oct. 27, 1928; A.B., U. Kans., 1951; J.D., U. Mo., 1958. Admitted to Kans. bar, 1958, Iowa bar, 1959, Okla. bar, 1960; individual practice law, Ponca City, Okla., 58—. Mem. Okla., Kay County bar assns., Phi Alpha Delta. Home: 727 Monument Rd Ponca City OK 74601 Office: PO Box 547 Ponca City OK 74601 Tel (405) 765-6697

MILLER, HARBAUGH, b. Wilkinsburg, Pa., July 23, 1902; B.S., U. Pitts., 1922, J.D., 1925. Admitted to Pa. bar, 1925; partner firm Miller Entwisle & Duff, Pitts., 1955—. Trustee emeritus U. Pitts.; pres. Goodwill Industries, 1958-61, Pitts. YMCA, 1956-58. Fellow Am. Bar Found., Am. Coll. Probate Counsel; mem. Am. Law Inst., Am. Judicature Soc., Am. (ho. of dels.), Pa., Allegheny County (pres. 1955) bar assns., SAR (chpt. pres. 1940), Phi Delta Theta, Omicron Delta Kappa, Beta Gamma Sigma, Phi Delta Phi. Home: 154 N Bellefield Ave Pittsburgh PA 15213 Office: Frick Bldg Pittsburgh PA 15219

MILLER, HARRY J., b. Chgo., Sept. 3, 1904; student U. Calif., Los Angeles; B.A., U. So. Calif., LL.B. Admitted to Calif. bar, 1929; individual practice law, Los Angeles; of counsel firm Pacht Ross Warne Bernhard & Sears, Los Angeles. Mem. Los Angeles, Beverly Hills (Calif.) bar assns. Office: Suite 500 1800 Avenue of the Stars Los Angeles CA 90067 Tel (213) 277-1000

MILLER, HARVEY ALVIN, JR., b. Pitts., Sept. 1, 1918; A.B., Grove City Coll., 1940; J.D., U. Pitts., 1947. Admitted to Pa. bar, 1948, U.S. Supreme Ct. bar, 1955; partner firm Miller & Miller, Pitts., 1948—. Trustee, mem. exec. com. Grove City Coll., 1954—; trustee, mem. legal com. N. Hills Passavant Hosp., Pitts., 1970—. Mem. Am., Allegheny County bar assns. Office: 1105 Porter Bldg Pittsburgh PA 15219 Tel (412) 471-7796

MILLER, HENRY GEORGE, b. Bklyn., Feb. 18, 1931; B.A., St. John's U., 1952, J.D., 1959; postgrad. Columbia, N.Y. U. Admitted to N.Y. bar, 1959; asso. firm Lawless & Lynch, N.Y.C., 1959-62, Bachkoff, Miller & Steger, N.Y.C., 1962-67; partner firm Clark, Gagliardi & Miller, White Plains, N.Y., 1967—; lectr. Practising Law Inst., Fordham Law Sch., St. John's Law Sch., various profl. assns. Fellow Am. Coll. Trial Lawyers, Internat. Acad. Trial Lawyers, N.Y. Bar Found.; mem. Internat. Assn. Ins. Counsel, Fedn. Ins. Counsel, Assn. Trial Lawyers Am., N.Y. State Trial Lawyers Assn. (dir.), Def. Assn. N.Y. (dir.). Moderator radio shows on the law; has appeared on radio and TV shows; contbr. articles to legal jours. Office: 175 Main St White Plains NY 10601 Tel (914) 946-8900

MILLER, HOWARD BENJAMIN, b. Newark, July 11, 1937; A.B., Pepperdine U., 1957; J.D., U. Chgo., 1960. Admitted to Calif. bar, 1961; law clk. to Justice Roger J. Traynor of Calif. Supreme Ct., 1960-61; practiced in Los Angeles, 1961-65; asso. prof. law U. So. Calif., 1965-69, prof., 1969—, asso. dean Law Center, 1967-68. Bd. dirs. Calif. Rural Legal Assistance, 1967-69; chmn. bd. Western Center on Law and Poverty, Los Angeles, 1968-69; mem. Los Angeles City Bd. Edn., 1976—. Mem. State Bar Calif. Recipient Alumni award for Pub. Service U. Chgo., 1973; editor-in-chief U. Chgo. Law Rev., 1959-60; advocate The Advocates, nat. pub. TV program, 1969-73; host At One With program Sta. KNBC-TV, Los Angeles, 1975—. Office: U So Calif Law Center University Park Los Angeles CA 90007 Tel (213) 741-7984

MILLER, HOWARD J., b. Denver, Feb. 14, 1929; B.S. in Law, U. Denver, 1951, LL.B., 1953. Admitted to Colo. Supreme Ct. bar, 1954, U.S. Dist. Ct. Colo. bar, 1959; individual practice law, Denver, 1957-62; partner firm Cain, Holland, Miller & Tobey, Jefferson County, Colo., 1963; individual practice law, Wheat Ridge, Colo., 1964—. Mem. Colo. First Judicial Dist. Bar Assn., Phi Alpha Delta. Home: 4480 Yarrow St Wheat Ridge CO 80033 Office: 3798 Marshall St Wheat Ridge CO 80033 Tel (303) 424-7831

MILLER, IRVING NOEL, b. Highland Park, Mich., June 29, 1935; B. Commerce, U. Detroit, 1959; J.D., Woodrow Wilson Coll., 1971. Admitted to Ga. bar, 1973; law clk. firm Lord, Bissell & Kadyk, Chgo., 1961-62; individual practice law, Atlanta, 1973—. Mem. Am., Ga., Atlanta bar assns. Office: 3390 Peachtree Rd NE Atlanta GA 30357 Tel (404) 577-3665

MILLER, IVAN LAWRENCE, b. Cleve., Feb. 2, 1914; A.B., Case Western Res. U., 1936, J.D., 1938; postgrad. Harvard Grad. Sch. Bus. Adminstrn., 1943, Inns of Ct., Middle Temple, London, 1945. Admitted to Ohio bar, 1938, U.S. Supreme Ct. bar, 1960; practice law, Cleve., 1938-41, 46-68; served to maj. JAGC, AUS, 1941-46; partner firm Ziegler, Metzger, Miller & Hoppe, Cleve., 1968—; consul Belgium (Ohio), 1962—; legal adviser to Brit. Consulate Gen., 1958—, to Canadian Consulate and Trade Commn., 1964—. Mem. bd. overseers Case Western Res. U., 1972-76. Fellow Royal Soc. Arts (Gt. Britain); mem. Fed. (pres. Cleve. chpt. 1974-75), Am., Ohio State bar assns., Bar Assn. Greater Cleve. (trustee 1953-55), Consular Corps Coll. (Consul of Year 1974), Soc. Benchers of Case Western Res. U. Decorated Bronze Star, Officer Brit. Empire, Knight in Order of Crown and Mil. Cross (Belgium), Ohio Commodore. Home: 2482 Derbyshire Rd Cleveland Heights OH 44106 Office: 1670 Union Commerce Bldg Cleveland OH 44115 Tel (216) 781-5470

MILLER, JACK BURLESON, b. San Saba, Tex., Oct. 21, 1921; B.S., Tex. Agrl. & Mech. U., 1943; LL.B., U. Tex., 1948. Admitted to Tex. bar, 1948; county judge San Saba County (Tex.), 1948-51; dist. atty. 33d Jud. Dist., San Saba, 1954-60; judge 33d Jud. Dist. Ct., San Saba, 1960-76; mem. Tex. Advisory Com. Legal Services Corp. Mem. Am., Tex., Hill Country bar assns. (pres. local assn. 1968-69). Home: 502 W Commerce St San Saba TX 76877

MILLER, JACK EVERETT, b. Monroe, La., Dec. 10, 1921; student Ga. Tech., 1942-43; grad. Gilbert Johnson Law Sch., 1948. Admitted to Ga. bar, 1948, U.S. Ct. Mil. Appeals bar, U.S. Supreme Ct. bar; individual practice law, Savannah. Lt. col. JAG, U.S. Army, ret. Mem. Ga., Savannah bar assns.

MILLER, JACK HOLLY, b. Navasota, Tex., Dec. 12, 1921; B.S., U. Houston, 1950, LL.B., Bates Coll. Law, 1951. Admitted to Tex. bar, 1951, La. bar, 1969; practiced in Houston, 1951; title clk. abstract title and div. order Standard Oil Co., Houston, 1951-56; supr. land titles, units and agreements Gulf Oil Corp., Houston, 1956-57, Shreveport, La., 1958, New Orleans, 1959—; asst. to dir. Houston Legal Aid, 1951. Mem. New Orleans Bar Assn., Petroleum Landmen's Assn. Home: 156 Elaine Ave Harahan LA 70123 Office: Gulf Oil Corp PO Box 61590 New Orleans LA 70161 Tel (504) 566-2216

MILLER, JACOB WILLIS, b. Louisville, Sept. 5, 1927; B.S. in Pharmacy, U. Ky., 1951; J.D., Washburn U. Topeka, 1964. Admitted to Kans. bar, 1964; pres. Miller's U. Village Drug, Inc., Topeka, 1961—. Democratic candidate in primaries for U.S. Ho. of Reps., 1974, in gen. election for Kans. State Senate, 1976. Mem. Kans. (pres. 1970, recipient Bowl of Hygeia for Outstanding Community Service 1976), Am. (speaker ho. of dels. 1973-74) pharm. assns. Named Distinguished Alumnus in Pharmacy, U. Ky., 1975. Office: 2605 W 21st St Topeka KS 66604 Tel (913) 232-0568

MILLER, JAMES BRYAN, b. Roanoke, Va., Aug. 12, 1932; B.A. in Econs., U. Va., 1954; J.D., Am. U., 1960. Admitted to Va. bar, 1961, D.C. bar, 1961; individual practice law, Arlington, Va. and Washington, 1961-62, 67-69; partner firm Johnson, Miller & Labriskie, and predecessor, Arlington and Washington, 1962-67, firm Miller, Miller, Patterson & Reese, Arlington and Washington, 1969—; arbitrator Am. Arbitration Assn., 1967—; instr. No. Va. Police Acad., 1969—. Mem. Va. State, D.C., Am. bar assns., Am. Judicature Soc., Am. Trial Lawyers Assn., Confrérie de la Chaine des Rotisseurs. Office: 2701 N Pershing Dr Arlington VA 22201 Tel (703) 522-2422

MILLER, JAMES M., b. Springhill, La., Oct. 30, 1942; J.D., La. State U., 1969. Admitted to La. bar, 1969; asso. firm Hayes Harkey Smith & Cascio, Monroe, La., 1969-73; partner firm Hamilton Carroll & Miller, Oak Grove, La., 1973—. Mem. Am., La., Fifth Jud. Dist. (past pres.) bar assns. Named Jaycee of Year, 1974. Address: Drawer 340 Oak Grove LA 71263 Tel (501) 428-2383

MILLER, JAMES PAUL, b. Circleville, Ohio, June 21, 1938; B.S.C., Ohio U., 1960; J.D., Ohio State U., 1963. Admitted to Ohio bar, 1963, U.S. Dist. Ct. So. Dist. Ohio bar, 1965, U.S. Supreme Ct. bar, 1971; asso. firm Buckley & Miller and predecessors, 1963-65, partner, 1965—; prosecutor City of Wilmington, Ohio, 1964-68, solicitor, 1969-75. Pres. ARC, Wilmington, 1966. Mem. Am., Ohio State Clinton County (pres. 1975-76) bar assns., Am. Judicature Soc., Wilmington C. of C. (dir. 1968-70). Recipient Distinguished Service award Wilmington Jaycees, 1970; contbr. articles to law reviews. Home: 1073 Warren Dr Wilmington OH 45177 Office: 145 N South Wilmington OH 45177 Tel (513) 382-0946

MILLER, JEFFORDS DONALSON, b. Kissimmee, Fla., Jan. 13, 1936; A.B., Rollins Coll., 1959, M.A., 1964; J.D., Cumberland Law Sch., 1967. Admitted to Ala. bar, 1967, Fla. bar, 1967; individual practice law, Birmingham, Ala., 1967, Kissimmee, Fla., 1968; asst. state atty., Kissimmee, 1969; div. chief, office of state atty. Osceola County, Kissimmee, 1973—; law clk. for U.S. Dist. Ct. Judge H. H. Grooms, Birmingham, 1968; instr. criminal justice program Valencia Jr. Coll., 1971, Rollins Coll., 1972-74. Mem. Fla., Ala. bars, Nat. Dist. Attys. Assn., Fla. Pros. Attys. Assn., Orange and Osceola County bar assns., Phi Delta Phi. Home: 903 S Thacker Ave Kissimmee FL 32741 Office: Office of State Atty Osceola County Courthouse Kissimmee FL 32741 Tel (305) 847-7691

MILLER, JERRE AUSTIN, b. Hopkins, Minn., Jan. 25, 1932; B.A., St. John's U., 1954; LL.B., William Mitchell Coll. Law, 1962. Admitted to Minn. bar, 1962; partner firm Besely Otto Miller & Keefe, Hopkins, 1962—. Mem. Hopkins Planning Commn., 1966-69, councilman, 1969-75, mayor, 1975—. Mem. Hennepin County (Minn.), Minn. State bars. Home: 125 15th Ave N Hopkins MN 55343 Office: 203 NW Nat Bank Bldg Hopkins MN 55343 Tel (612) 938-7635

MILLER, JOEL, b. N.Y.C., Mar. 3, 1921; B.M.E., Bklyn. Poly. Inst., 1949; J.D. cum laude, U. Miami, Coral Gables, Fla., 1952. Admitted to Fla. bar, 1952, U.S. Supreme Ct. bar, 1958; partner firm Miller & Capp, Ft. Lauderdale, Fla., 1965-69, Miller & Squire, Ft. Lauderdale, 1969—; judge Wilton Manors (Fla.) Municipal Ct., 1973—, Sunrise (Fla.) Municipal Ct., 1975—. Bd. dirs. Broward County (Fla.) Legal Aid. Mem. Broward County Criminal Def. Lawyers Assn., Am. Trial Lawyers Assn. Office: 500 NE 3d Ave Fort Lauderdale FL 33301 Tel (305) 764-3211

MILLER, JOEL ENOCH, b. N.Y.C., June 28, 1932; A.B., Columbia, 1954, J.D., 1956; LL.M., N.Y. U., 1964. Admitted to N.Y. bar, 1957; law sec. U.S. 2d Circuit Ct. Appeals, N.Y.C., 1956-57; asso. firm Paul, Weiss, Rifkind, Wharton & Garrison, N.Y.C., 1957-60; asso., partner, sr. partner, of counsel firm Demov, Morris, Levin & Shein, N.Y.C., 1961-70; partner firm Paley & Miller, N.Y.C., 1974-76; individual practice law, Flushing, N.Y., 1971—; adj. faculty law St. John's U., 1976—; served to capt. JAGC, U.S. Army Res., 1958-64. Mem. Am., N.Y. State bar assns. Author: Federal Taxation of Trusts, 1968; contbr. articles to legal jours. Home and Office: 73-11 184th St Flushing NY 11366 Tel (212) 454-2632

MILLER, JOEL LAWRENCE, b. Chgo., Sept. 17, 1935; B.S., U. Ill., 1957; J.D., Northwestern U., 1961. Admitted to Ill. bar, 1961; hearing referee State of Ill. Dept. Revenue, Chgo., 1961-64; asso. firm Burton, Isaacs, Dixon & Wynne, Chgo., 1964-67; partner firm Burton, Isaacs, Bockelman & Miller, Chgo., 1968-70, firm Levy & Erens, Chgo., 1970—; lectr. John Marshall Sch. Law, Chgo., 1962-65. Treas., v.p. asso. bd. trustees Mount Sinai Hosp. Med. Center, Chgo., 1967-71. Mem. Am., Ill. State bar assns. Asso. editor Northwestern U. Law Rev. Home: 1590 Hawthorne Ln Highland Park IL 60035 Office: 208 S La Salle St Chicago IL 60604 Tel (312) 368-9500

MILLER, JOHN ALLEN, b. Goshen, Ind., Apr. 9, 1937; LL.B., Stetson U., 1960. Admitted to Fla. bar, 1960, U.S. Tax Ct. bar, 1971, U.S. Ct. Customs bar, 1971; since practiced in Ft. Lauderdale, Fla., mem. trust dept. 1st Nat. Bank, 1960-61; individual practice law, 1961-68; judge Juvenile Ct. Broward County, 1968-72, 17th Jud. Circuit Ct. State of Fla., 1972—; lectr. Fla. Police Standards Council. Mem. Mayor's Com. on Coll. Spring Vacation, City of Ft. Lauderdale, 1961, Mayor's Com. on Drug Abuse, 1971; pres. Broward County 4-H Found., 1973—; mem. New River Dist. Scoutmasters' Tng. Council. Mem. Nat. Council Juvenile Ct. Judges, Fla. Circuit Judges Assn. (lectr. continuing edn. seminars), Blue Ridge Inst. (treas. 1970—), Internat. Assn. Chiefs of Police (guest lectr.), Am., Fla. (continuing edn. lectr.) bar assns. Home Office: Broward County Courthouse 201 SE 6th St Fort Lauderdale FL 33301 Tel (305) 765-5929

MILLER, JOHN GARY, b. Idaho Falls, Idaho, June 16, 1938; B.A., U. Colo., 1961, J.D., 1965. Admitted to Colo. bar, 1965; judge Longmont (Colo.) Municipal Ct., 1965-76, Westminister (Colo.) Municipal Ct., 1972—. Mem. Colo., Am. (award for jud. excellence 1971) bar assns., Colo. Municipal Judges Assn. (pres. 1970-71), Am. Judges Assn. (gov. 1972—). Office: PO Box 215 Longmont CO 80501 Tel (303) 776-8880

MILLER, JOHN PHILIP, b. Balt., June 14, 1948; B.A., Gettysburg Coll., 1970; J.D., Washington and Lee U., 1973. Admitted to Md. bar, 1973, Ga. bar, 1976; asst. state's atty. Balt., 1973-74; asso. firm Israelson, Pines and Jackson, Balt., 1974-75; atty. So. Bell Tel. & Tel. Co., Atlanta, 1976-77; asso. firm Kaplan, Heyman, Greenberg, Engelman & Belgrad, Balt., 1977—. Mem. Am., Md., Ga. bar assns., Am. Trial Lawyers Assn., Delta Theta Phi, Pi Lambda Sigma. Office: 10th Floor Sun Life Bldg Charles and Redwood Sts Baltimore MD 21201 Tel (301) 539-6967

MILLER, JOHN SAMUEL, JR., b. Eutaw, Ala., July 1, 1936; B.S., Fla. State U., 1961, J.D., 1968. Admitted to Fla. bar, 1969; partner firm La Capra, Miller & Wiser, Tallahassee, Fla., 1969—; dir. Judicial Council Fla., 1965-69; spl. master U.S. Bankruptcy Ct. No. Dist. Fla. Mem. Soc. Cincinnati, State S.C., Tallahassee Quarterback Club, Fla. State U. Alumni Assn. Mem. Tallahassee, Fla., Am. Bar Assns. Office: 225 S Gadsden St Tallahassee FL 32302 Tel (904) 222-8021

MILLER, KENNETH K., b. Brice, Ohio, Mar. 11, 1912; A.B., George Washington U., 1934, LL.B., 1937. Admitted to D.C. bar, 1936, Ill. bar, 1938, Ariz. bar, 1971; with Chgo. Motor Club, 1937-41; mem. staff Labor Relations Assos., Chgo., 1941-45; pres. Commonwealth Products, Kalamazoo, 1945-58; Active, 7th Ave Boys Club, Phoenix. Mem. Ariz., Maricopa County bar assns., Am. Legion. Home: 25418 Wyoming Ave Sun Lakes AZ 85224 Office: 80 E Columbus Ave Phoenix AZ 85012 Tel (602) 264-3250

MILLER, KENNETH RAY, b. Fairmont, W.Va., Feb. 15, 1943; B.S., Fairmont State Coll., 1965; M.S., W.Va. U., 1967, J.D., 1972. Admitted to W.Va. bar, 1972; asso. law firm Furbee, Amos, Webb & Critchfield, Fairmont, W.Va., 1972-76, partner, 1976—. Mem. Marion County Planning Commn., 1972—; mem. Marion County Landfill Bd., 1974—; vestryman, trustee Christ Episcopal Ch.; mem. Fairmont State Coll. Adv. Com. Mem. W.Va., Marion County, Am. bar assns., W.Va. Trial Lawyers Assn., Fairmont Jaycees. Home: 1320 Peacock Ln Fairmont WV 26554 Office: PO Box 1189 Fairmont WV 26554 Tel (304) 363-8800

MILLER, LAMBERT HENRY, b. Groton, S.D., Aug. 31, 1907; A.B., George Washington U., 1932, J.D., 1936, LL.M., 1937. Admitted to D.C. bar, 1937, U.S. Supreme Ct. bar, 1941; gen. counsel Nat. Assn. Mfrs., Washington, 1949-72, sr. v.p., gen. counsel, 1969-72; counsel Hamel, Park, McCabe & Saunders, 1972—; adj. prof. trade assn. law Georgetown U. Grad. Sch. Law, 1957-59; legal advisor industry mems. Nat. War Labor Bd., 1942-43. Mem. Am., D.C. bar assns., Editor, pub. Nat. Assn. Mfrs. Law Digest, 1949-59. Home: 610 N 11th St Falls Church VA 22046 Office: 1776 F St NW Washington DC 20006 Tel (202) 785-1234

MILLER, LEE FORSTER, JR., b. Bristol, Va., Aug. 8, 1928; B.A., U. Tenn., 1950; J.D., Georgetown U., 1958. Admitted to D.C. bar, 1959, Tenn. bar, 1959; asso. firm Miller & Miller, Johnson City, Tenn., 1959-67, firm Wrape & Hernly, Memphis, 1967-70; dep. dir. Memphis and Shelby County Legal Services, 1970—. Mem. Memphis and Shelby County Bar Assn. Home: 4304 Nellwood Ln Memphis TN 38117 Office: 325 Dermon Bldg Memphis TN 38103 Tel (901) 526-5132

MILLER, LORRAINE DAWN, b. N.Y.C.; A.B., N.Y. U., 1948, LL.M., 1958, J.D., 1968, S.J.D., 1968. Admitted to N.Y. bar, 1952, U.S. Dist. Ct. bar, 1954, U.S. Supreme Ct. bar, 1960; asst. corp. counsel City N.Y., 1954; counsel to City Council Pres., N.Y.C., 1969; spl. counsel N.Y. State Assembly Minority Leader, 1971-73; counsel N.Y. State Senate Dep. Minority Leader, 1976; judge Civil Ct. City N.Y., 1976—; chmn. N.Y.C. Housing Ct. Council, 1975-76; lectr. New Sch. Social Research. Trustee Boys Brotherhood Republic and Camp Wabenaki, N.Y.C., 1963-77; chmn. March of Dimes, N.Y.C., 1961-70. Mem. N.Y. County Lawyers Assn., N.Y. Womens Bar Assn., N.Y. State Trial Lawyers Assn., Nat. Assn. Housing and Redevel. Ofcls., Inst. Jud. Adminstrn., N.Y. U. Law Sch. Alumni Assn. (dir.), Citizens Housing and Planning Council (dir.). Author: Revolutionary Milestones in Law of Landlord and Tenant, 1967; recipient Humanitarian of Community award Cancer Care, 1966. Office: Civil Ct City NY 111 Centre St New York City NY 10013 Tel (212) 227-5070

MILLER, LOUIS RICE, b. Frankfort, Ind., Feb. 28, 1914; A.B., U. Chgo., 1935, J.D., 1937. Admitted to Ill. bar, 1938; asso. firm Gardner, Carton & Douglas, Chgo., 1937-40; with Armour & Co., Chgo., 1940—, asst. gen. counsel, 1957-67, v.p., gen. counsel, sec., 1967—, v.p. law, 1977; v.p., gen. counsel Greyhound Corp., Phoenix, 1972—, v.p. law, 1977. Mem. Am., Chgo. bar assns., Assn. Gen. Counsel. Office: Greyhound Corp Phoenix AZ 85077 Tel (602) 248-5730

MILLER, MARTEEN JAMES, b. Modesto, Calif., Feb. 4, 1930; B.A., San Francisco State U., 1958; LL.D., U. San Francisco, 1961; postgrad. in Psychiatry and Law, U. So. Calif., 1975. Admitted to Calif. bar, 1962; law clk. Sonoma County (Calif.) Pub. Defender, 1961; asst. pub. defender Sonoma County, 1962-66, pub. defender, 1966—; faculty law Empire Law Sch., 1974—. Mem. Am., Calif., Sonoma County bar assns., Calif. Pub. Defenders Assn. Recipient Bur. Nat. Affairs award. Office: 2555 Mendocino Ave Santa Rosa CA 95401 Tel (707) 527-2791

MILLER, MARVIN DAVID, b. Los Angeles, Oct. 3, 1934; B.A., U. Calif., Los Angeles, 1956; LL.B., Harvard U., 1959. Admitted to Calif. bar, 1960; pres. Regis Corp., Beverly Hills, Calif., 1963—. Commr., Citizens Advisory Commn., on Community Devel., Los Angeles County. Mem. Am., Calif. bar assns. Office: 8383 Wilshire Blvd Beverly Hills CA 90211 Tel (213) 653-5503

MILLER, OVVIE, b. Bklyn., July 14, 1935; B.A., U. Calif., Los Angeles, 1961; J.D., Harvard, 1961. Admitted to Calif. bar, 1962; law clerk Judge William M. Byrne, U.S. Dist. Ct. So. Dist. Calif., 1961-62; asso. firm Weber, Schwartz & Alschuler, Beverly Hills, Calif., 1962-66; partner firm Gold & Miller, Beverly Hills, 1966-69; asso. firm Hertzberg & Childs, Beverly Hills, 1969, partner, 1969—. Pres. Westside Jewish Community Center, Los Angeles, 1974-76; pres. Jewish Centers Assn., Los Angeles, 1976—. Fellow Am. Acad. Matrimonial Lawyers; mem. State Bar of Calif., Am., Los Angeles County, Beverly Hills (bd. gov. 1970-73) bar assns. Contbr. articles in field to profl. jours. Office: 9454 Wilshire Blvd Beverly Hills CA 90212 Tel (213) 278-8460

MILLER, PAUL A., b. Detroit, Jan. 1, 1941; B.S., U. Fla., 1963, J.D., 1971. Admitted to Fla. bar, 1972; individual practice law, Orlando, Fla.; advisor Valencia Community Coll., 1974—. Mem. Am., Fla., Orange County bar assns. Home: 2863 Sanbina Winter Park FL 32789 Office: 3438 Lawton Rd Suite 200 Orlando FL 32803 Tel (305) 894-2345

MILLER, PAUL DANIEL, b. Butte, Mont., Mar. 1, 1941; B.A., U. Mont., 1963, J.D., 1966. Admitted to Mont. bar, 1966; law clk. Mont. Supreme Ct., Missoula, 1966; asso. firm Alexander, Kuenning & Hall, Great Falls, Mont., 1966-69; partner firm Alexander, Kuenning, Miller & Ugrin, Great Falls, Mont., 1969—; asst. prof. U. Mont., 1966-67. Bd. dirs. Great Falls YMCA; trustee Mont. Deaconess Med. Center, Great Falls; bd. dirs. Great Falls Children's Receiving Home. Mem. Mont., Am. bar assns., Am. Inst. C.P.A.'s, Mont Soc. C.P.A.'s. Home: 3220 4th Ave S Great Falls MT 59403 Office: Box 1744 Great Falls MT 59401 Tel (406) 727-5666

MILLER, R. TERRY, b. San Jose, Calif., Feb. 28, 1947; B.A., U. Calif., 1968; J.D., So. Methodist U., 1971. Admitted to Tex. bar, 1971; asso. firm Hewett, Johnson, Swanson & Barbee, 1971-72; house counsel Am. Housing Resources, Inc., 1972; asso. firm Nichols and Co., 1973-74; partner firm Baker, Glast, Riddle & Tuttle, Dallas, 1975—. Fund raiser United Fund, 1975. Mem. Tex., Dallas bar assns. Editor: Southwestern Law Jour., 1971. Home: 6933 Vista Willow St Dallas TX 75240 Office: 2001 Bryan Tower Dallas TX 75201 Tel (214) 651-0500

MILLER, RAYMOND CHARLES, b. Meadville, Pa., July 25, 1906; student Allegheny Coll., 1926-29; B.S., U. Pitts., 1931, LL.B., 1934. Admitted to Pa. bar, 1934; U.S. conciliation commr. Dept. Justice, Crawford County, Pa., 1937-39; referee Bankruptcy Ct. Crawford County, 1940-42; dep. atty. gen. State of Pa., Harrisburg, 1943-74; individual practice law, Meadville, 1974—. Mem. Pa., Crawford County bar assns., Delta Theta Phi. Home and Office: Box 12 322 N Main St Meadville PA 16335 Tel (814) 336-1551

MILLER, REED, b. Fairmont, W.Va., Dec. 1, 1918; A.B., W.Va. U., 1939, LL.B., 1941. Admitted to W.Va. bar, 1941, N.Y. bar, 1945, D.C. bar, 1946; now with firm Arnold & Porter, Washington. Mem. Fed. Communications Bar Assn. (pres. 1975-76), Phi Beta Kappa. Asso. student editor W.Va. Law Quar., 1940-41. Office: 1229 19th St NW Washington DC 20036 Tel (202) 872-6700*

MILLER, RICHARD ISAAC, b. N.Y.C., May 28, 1929; A.A., U. Calif. at Berkeley, 1948; B.A., 1950; J.D., Yale, 1953; postgrad. Harvard, 1956. Admitted to N.Y. State bar, 1955, Mass. bar, 1956; judge adv. U.S. Air Force, 1953-55; resident counsel Baird Atomic, Inc., Cambridge, Mass., 1955-57; sr. asso. Morrison, Mahoney & Miller, Boston, 1957-66; v.p. Harbridge House, Inc., Boston, 1966—; asst. adminstr. Mass. Inst. Tech. Lincoln Lab., 1958-59; v.p., treas., gen. counsel Diffraction Ltd., Inc., 1960-66. Mem. Lexington Town Meeting, 1960-71; chmn. bd. trustees Cambridge Opera Workshop, 1965-68; dir. Lyric Opera Co., Boston, 1972—. Mem. Am., N.Y. State, Boston bar assns. Nat. Endowment for Humanities fellow, 1976. Author: Legal Aspects of Technology Utilization, 1974; The Law of War, 1975. Tel (617) 267-6410

MILLER, RICHARD SHERWIN, b. Boston, Dec. 11, 1930; B.S., Boston U., 1951, J.D. magna cum laude, 1956; LL.M., Yale, 1959. Admitted to Mass. bar, 1956, Mich. bar, 1961; individual practice law, Boston, 1956-58; asso. prof. and prof. law Wayne State U., Detroit, 1959-65, Ohio State U., Columbus, 1965-73, dir. clin. and interdisciplinary programs, 1971-73; prof. law U. Hawaii, Honolulu, 1973—; legal dir. Ohio OSHA Project, Columbus, 1973. Mem. TV for Youth Adv. Group, Honolulu, 1975—, Hawaii Com. Legal Edn. for Youth, Honolulu, 1974—. Mem. Am. Bar Assn., Soc. Am. Law Tchrs. Editor-in-chief Boston U. Law Rev., 1955-56; editor: (with R. Stanger) Essays on Expropriations, 1967. Author: Courts and the Law: An Introduction to our Legal System, 1971. Producer, moderator Law Forum, Ednl. TV, Columbus, 1968. Home: 315 Iliaina St Kailua HI 96734 Office: U Hawaii Sch Law Honolulu HI 96822 Tel (808) 948-8636

MILLER, ROBERT, b. N.Y.C., Dec. 5, 1930; B.A., Princeton, 1952; LL.B., Columbia, 1957. Admitted to N.Y. bar, 1958; asso. firm Miller & McCarthy (formerly Scribner & Miller), 1957-65, partner, 1965—. Mem. Assn. Bar City N.Y., Am., N.Y. State bar assns., N.Y. County Lawyers Assn. Office: One Battery Park Plaza New York City NY 10708 Tel (212) 269-8060

MILLER, ROBERT ARTHUR, b. Aberdeen, S.D., Aug. 28, 1939; B.B.A., U. S.D., 1961, J.D., 1963. Admitted to S.D. bar, 1963; asst. atty. gen. State of S.D., 1963-65; individual practice law, Philip, S.D., 1965-71; state's atty. Haakon County (S.D.) and city atty. Philip, 1965-71; judge Circuit Ct. S.D., 1971—, presiding judge 6th Circuit, 1975—. Mem. S.D. Judges Assn. (pres. 1976), State Bar S.D. (jud. council), Philip C. of C. (v.p. 1970). Home: 316 N Van Buren St Pierre SD 57501 Office: PO Box 1112 Pierre SD 57501 Tel (605) 224-3711

MILLER, ROBERT CARL, b. Schenectady, June 14, 1943; B.B.A., St. Bernardine of Siena Coll., 1965; J.D., Albany Law Sch. Union U., 1968; LL.M. in Taxation, N.Y. U., 1974. Admitted to N.Y. bar, 1969, U.S. Tax Ct. bar, 1971; asso. firm Tate and Tate, Albany, N.Y. Mem. Albany County, N.Y. State bar assns., N.Y. State Soc. C.P.A.'s, Am. Assn. Atty.-C.P.A.'s. Office: 1698 Central Ave Albany NY 12205 Tel (518) 869-3531

MILLER, ROBERT FRIEND, b. Cleve., Nov. 3, 1922; A.B., Dartmouth, 1944; LL.B., U. Ariz., 1950. Admitted to Ariz. bar, 1950; dep. county atty. Pima County (Ariz.), 1951-52; individual practice law, Tucson, 1952-57; partner firm Merchant, Parkman, Miller & Pitt, Tucson, 1957-64, firm Miller & Pitt, Tucson, 1964-68, firm Miller, Pitt & Feldman, Tucson, 1968—. Fellow Am. Coll. Trial Lawyers, Internat. Acad. Trial Lawyers; mem. Assn. Trial Lawyers Am., Pima County Bar Assn. (exec. com. 1970-74, pres. 1973-74). Office: 111 S Church Ave Tucson AZ 85701 Tel (602) 792-3836

MILLER, ROBERT JOSEPH, b. Evanston, Ill., Mar. 30, 1945; B.A. in Polit. Sci., Santa Clara U., 1967; J.D., Loyola U., Los Angeles, 1971. Admitted to Nev. bar, 1971; dep. dist. atty. Clark County Dist. Atty., Las Vegas, Nev., 1971-73, 75; legal adviser Las Vegas Met. Police Dept., 1973-75; justice of the peace Las Vegas Twp., 1975—. Bd. dirs., v.p. YMCA, Las Vegas; bd. dirs. Big Bros. So. Nev., Goodwill Industries of So. Nev.; chpt. founder Lawyers vs. Doctors basketball game Am. Cancer Soc., Las Vegas, 1974, dir. Clark County, Nev. chpts.; mem. advisory bd. Raleigh Hills Hosp., Las Vegas; bd. dirs. chpt. Nat. Multiple Sclerosis Soc., Fitzimmons Hosp., Las Vegas. Mem. Nev. State, Clark County bar assns. Recipient Good Fellow award City of Hope, 1975. Office: 200 E Carson St Las Vegas NV 89101 Tel (702) 386-4011

MILLER, ROBERT NOLEN, b. Monmouth, Ill., May 30, 1940; B.A., Cornell U., 1962; LL.B., J.D., U. Colo., 1965. Admitted to Colo. bar, 1965; asso. firm Marshall Quiat, Denver, 1965-66; asso. firm Fischer & Beatty, Ft. Collins, Colo., 1969-70; dist. atty. 19th Jud. Dist., Greeley, Colo., 1971—. Bd. dirs. Legal Aid Clinic U. Colo., 1965, Boys' Club of Greeley, 1971—; capt. United Way, Greeley, 1974; chmn. Christian enlistment First Congregational Ch., Greeley, 1976; mem. exec. com. Nat. Asthma Center, Greeley, 1976. Mem. Colo., Weld County bar assns., Nat., Colo. (pres.) dist. attys. assns. Office: PO Box 1167 Greeley CO 80631 Tel (303) 356-4000

MILLER, ROBERT STEVEN, b. New Brunswick, N.J., June 23, 1942; A.B., Duke, 1964; J.D., U. Fla., 1966. Admitted to Fla. bar, 1967, N.J. bar, 1968, U.S. Supreme Ct. bar, 1974; atty. Corp. Trust Co., N.Y.C., 1968-70, Lums Restaurant Corp., Miami, Fla., 1970-71; individual practice law, Ft. Lauderdale, Fla., 1971—; atty. City of Hallandale (Fla.), 1973—. Mem. Broward County Lawyers Assn., Am., Broward County bar assns. Office: 201 SE 2nd St Fort Lauderdale FL 33301 Tel (305) 463-2992 also 2500 E Hallandale Beach Blvd Suite 711 Hallandale FL 33009 Tel (305) 456-7111

MILLER, ROGER JAMES, b. Yankton, S.D., Oct. 6, 1947; B.B.A., U. Nebr., 1970, J.D., 1973. Admitted to Nebr., Colo. bars, 1973; partner firm Nelson, Harding, Marchetti, Leonard & Tate, Lincoln, Nebr., 1973-76, Omaha, 1976—. Program chmn., exec. com. Lancaster County (Nebr.) Young Republicans, 1975; platform com. Douglas County (Nebr.) Rep. Party, 1976—. Mem. Omaha, Nebr., Colo., Am. (co-chmn. Nebr. constrn. com. litigation sect. 1976—) bar assns., Phi Delta Phi (magister local chpt.). Home: 14112 Pine St Omaha NE 68144 Office: 820 Nebraska Savings Bldg 1623 Farnam St Omaha NE 68102 Tel (402) 348-0832

MILLER, SCOTT TOWER, b. Princeton, Ind., Mar. 13, 1941; Sci. degree, Ky. Mil. Inst., 1959; B.A., U. Louisville, 1965, J.D., 1968. Admitted to Ind. bar, 1968, Fla. bar, 1969; asso. firm Prentice & Prentice, Jeffersonville, Ind., 1968-69; deputy atty. gen. Ind. Atty. Gen.'s Office, Indpls., 1969-70, asst. atty. gen., 1970-71; asst. U.S. Atty. So. Dist. Ind., 1971-72; spl. atty. U.S. Dept. Justice, Indpls., 1972-73; circuit judge 3d Judicial Circuit, Harrison-Crawford Circuit Cts., Corydon, Ind., 1973—. Mem. adv. bds. Harrison County Mental Health Satellite Program, 1973—, regional youth services program, 1973—; bd. dirs. Ind. Criminal Justice Regional Planning Bd., 1974—; Ind. Judicial Center Bd. advisors. Mem. Am. Judicature Soc., Ind., Fla. bar assns., Ind. Judges Assn., Juvenile Judges Assn., Juvenile Judges Council. Home: Rt 2 Box 128-C Corydon IN 47112 Office: Court House Corydon IN 47112 Tel (812) 738-2191

MILLER, SIGMUND LAWRENCE, b. N.Y.C., Feb. 13, 1912; A.B., U. Pa., 1932; LL.B., Harvard, 1935. Admitted to Conn. bar, 1935, Mass. bar, 1935; individual practice law, Bridgeport, Conn., 1935-45; sr. partner firms Miller & Burstein, Bridgeport, 1946-59, Miller & Baroff, Bridgeport, 1960-69; individual practice law, Bridgeport, 1969-72; pres. Sigmund L. Miller, P.C., Bridgeport, 1972—. Pres., chmn. bd., trustee Park City Hosp., Bridgeport, 1952—; trustee Conn. Hosp. Assn., 1959-61. Mem. Bridgeport, Conn., Am. bar assns. Home: 66 Teller Rd Trumbull CT 06611 Office: 855 Main St Bridgeport CT 06604 Tel (203) 334-0191

MILLER, SIMON GERALD (JERRY), b. East St. Louis, Ill., May 5, 1942; B.B.A., Washington U., St. Louis, 1965; J.D., U. Mo., 1969. Admitted to Mo. bar, 1969; pub. defender St. Louis County (Mo.), 1969-72; individual practice law, Clayton, Mo., 1972—; lectr. in field. Mem. Am., Mo., St. Louis County, Met. St. Louis bar assns. Office: Suite 532T 225 S Meramec Ave Clayton MO 63105 Tel (314) 726-5100

MILLER, THOMAS ALLISON, SR., b. Tanner, Ala., Sept. 4, 1918; LL.B., U. Miami (Fla.), 1953; B.S. in Bus. Adminstrn., U. Tampa, 1959. Owner, mgr. White Hut restaurant, Tampa, Fla., 1946-52; admitted to Fla. bar, 1953; practiced in Tampa, 1953-61; judge Indsl. Claims Ct., 1961-69, Hillsborough County (Fla.) Ct., 1972—. Chaplain, judge adv. Am. Legion of Fla., 1971-72; chaplain Fla. 40 and 8 soc., 1976. Mem. Fla. Bar., Am., Hillsborough County bar assns., Conf. County Ct. Judges of Fla. (sec. 1973, v.p. 1974, treas. 1975). Home: 1005 W Idlewild Ave Tampa FL 33604 Office: Courthouse Annex Room 202 Tampa FL 33602 Tel (813) 229-0507

MILLER, THOMAS MARSHALL, b. Mineral Wells, Tex., Oct. 19, 1910; LL.B., Houston Law Sch., 1935. Admitted to Tex. bar, 1935, Ga. bar, 1955; reporter, office mgr. Dun & Bradstreet, Ft. Worth and Houston, 1925-42; v.p.-traffic and sales Chgo. & So. Air Lines, Memphis, 1942-53; with Delta Air Lines, Atlanta, 1953—, sr. v.p., 1953-73, dir., mktg. cons., 1973—. Pres., chmn. Atlanta Conv. Bur., 1966-69. Mem. Am. Soc. Traffic and Transp., Inst. Certified Travel Agts. (vice chmn. emeritus). Home: 19 Marsh Dr Hilton Head Island SC 29928 Office: 145 15th St NE #847 Atlanta GA 30309 Tel (404) 892-0281

MILLER, THOMAS OLLIE, b. Lusk, Wyo., July 24, 1898; LL.B., Am. Extension U., Los Angeles, 1927. Admitted to Wyo. bar, 1927; individual practice law, Casper, Wyo., 1927-30, Lusk, 1930-57, Cheyenne, Wyo., 1970—; partner firm Miller, Suyematsu, Crowley & Duncan, Cheyenne, 1960-70; mem. Wyo. Senate, 1953-57; atty. gen. State of Wyo., 1957-60. Fellow Am. Bar Found.; mem. Am., Laramie County (Wyo.) bar assns., Wyo. State Bar (pres. 1957-58), Am. Judicature Soc. Home and Office: PO Box 287 Cheyenne WY 92001 Tel (307) 634-9669

MILLER, THORMUND AUBREY, b. Pocatello, Idaho, July 14, 1919; B.A., Reed Coll., Portland, Oreg., 1941; LL.B., Columbia, 1948; postgrad. Harvard Grad. Sch. Bus., 1961. Admitted to Calif. bar, 1949, D.C. bar, 1951, U.S. Supreme Ct. bar, 1960; asso. firm McCutchen, Thomas, Matthews, Griffiths & Greene, San Francisco, 1948-50; atty. So. Pacific Transp. Co., Washington, 1950-56, asst. gen. atty., 1956-59, gen. atty., 1959-66, sr. gen. atty., San Francisco, 1966-75, gen. solicitor, 1975—; gen. counsel So. Pacific Communications Co., San Francisco, 1973—, also dir.; dir. Tops On Line Services, Inc. Mem. State Bar Calif., Am. Bar Assn., ICC Practitioners Assn., Transp. Research Forum, FCC Bar Assn., Phi Delta Phi. Home: 228 Polhemus Ave Atherton CA 94025 Office: 1 Market Plaza San Francisco CA 94105 Tel (415) 362-1212

MILLER, TIMOTHY JAY, b. Inglewood, Calif., Jan. 4, 1939; B.S. in Accounting, U. So. Calif., 1961, LL.B., 1964. Admitted to Calif. bar, 1965, U.S. Tax Ct., 1965; since practiced in Los Angeles, asso. firm Cosgrove, Cramer, Rindge & Barnum, 1965-68, individual practice law, 1968-70, partner Ebben Ebben and Brown, 1970—. Bd. dirs. Inter-community Child Guidence Guild, 1976—. Mem. Newport Harbor (Calif.) C. of C., Am., Los Angeles County bar assns. Home: 9045 Lindante Dr Whittier CA 90603 Office: 615 S Flower St Los Angeles CA 90017 Tel (213) 624-1001 also 610 Newport Center Dr Newport Beach CA 92660 (714) 644-4181

MILLER, WILLIAM EDWARD, b. Lockport, N.Y., Mar. 22, 1914; B.A., Notre Dame U., 1935; LL.B., Albany U., 1938. Admitted to N.Y. bar, 1938; partner firm Holly and Miller, Lockport, 1939-51; mem. U.S. Ho. of Reps., 1951-65; partner firm Miller, Farmelo, Cane & Greene, Buffalo, 1961—; U.S. commr. Western Dist. N.Y., 1939-42; asst. dist. atty. Niagara County (N.Y.), 1946-48, dist. atty., 1948-51; Republican candidate for Vice Pres. of U.S., 1964. Mem. N.Y., Erie County, Niagara County bar assns. Home: 418 Willow St Lockport NY 14094 Office: 1601 Liberty Bank Bldg Buffalo NY 14202 Tel (716) 853-3040

MILLER, WILLIAM JAMES, b. Lawrence, Kans., Oct. 15, 1924; B.S. in Engring., U. Kans., 1950; J.D., U. Mo., 1958. Admitted to Kans. bar, 1958, Iowa bar, 1958, Okla. bar, 1960, Patent bar, 1958; mgr. engring. quality control Communications Accessories Co., Kansas City, Mo., 1955-58; asst. Collins Radio Co., Cedar Rapids, Iowa, 1958-59, atty. Continental Oil Co., Ponca City, Okla., 1959—. Pres. First United Methodist Ch., Ponca City, also adult Sunday sch. tchr.; treas. Woodland's PTA, Ponca City. Mem. Okla. Patent Bar Assn., Am., Okla. bar assns., Internat. Patent Bar, C. of C., Phi Alpha Delta. Home: 727 Monument Rd Ponca City OK 74601 Office: PO Box 547 Ponca City OK 74601 Tel (405) 765-6697

MILLER, WILLIAM JESSE, JR., b. Columbus, Kans., Nov. 5, 1925; B.S. in Bus. Adminstrn., U. Kans., 1948; J.D., Washburn U., Topeka, Kans., 1952. Admitted to Kans. bar, U.S. Dist. Ct. bar, 1952; individual practice law, Sabetha, Kans., 1952-54; v.p., gen. counsel Security Benefit Life Ins. Co., Topeka, 1954-75, pres., 1975—. Mem. Kans., Am., Topeka bar assns., Kans. Assn. Commerce and Industry (dir., v.p.), Topeka C. of C. (dir.), Assn. Life Ins. Counsel. Author: Life Insurance Law of Kansas, 1974. Home: 2824 Plass St Topeka KS 66611 Office: 700 Harrison St Topeka KS 66636 Tel (913) 259-3000

MILLER, WILLIAM SCOTT, JR., b. Williford, Ark., Apr. 15, 1921; B.S. summa cum laude, Miss. State U., 1943; LL.B., Ark. Law Sch., 1949. Admitted to Ark. bar, 1948; asso. firm E. Charles Eichenbaum, Little Rock, 1949-57; partner firm Eichenbaum, Scott, Miller, Crockett & Darr, Little Rock, 1957—; mem. nat. adv. group Commr. Internal Revenue, 1973-74; lectr. Ark. Soc. C.P.A.'s, Ark. Law Sch., 1965. Pres., trustee Baptist Med. Center System, 1974-75; v.p. Little Rock Boys' Club, 1976—; pres. Ark. Assn. AAU, 1972. Mem. Ark., Am., Pulaski County (pres. 1964-65) bar assns., Am. Judicature Soc. Home: 3205 Shenandoah Valley Little Rock AR 72212 Office: 600 Tower Bldg Little Rock AR 72201 Tel (501) 376-4531

MILLER, WILLIAM STEWART, b. Pasadena, Calif. July 24, 1934; J.D., Hastings Coll., San Francisco, 1960. Admitted to Calif. bar, 1961; partner firm Cress and Miller, Blythe, Calif., 1961-63; individual practice law, Blythe, 1963-75; judge Palo Verde Jud. Dist., Blythe, 1966-76; municipal ct. Desert Municipal Ct., Blythe, 1976—. Office: 260 N Spring St Blythe CA 92225 Tel (714) 922-8128

MILLER, WILLIS LINTON, III, b. Valdosta, Ga., Oct. 19, 1947; B.A., Emory U., 1969, J.D., 1972. Admitted to Ga. bar; individual practice law, Valdosta, 1973-75; with firm Banham & Bennett, Valdosta, 1976—. Mem. Am., Valdosta bar assns., State Bar Ga., Trial Lawyers Assn. Ga. Home: 2367 Young Dr Valdosta GA 31601 Office: Suite 201 509 N Patterson St Valdosta GA 31601 Tel (912) 242-0314

MILLIGAN, DAVID TIMOTHY, b. Columbus, Ohio, Dec. 13, 1943; B.A., Ohio State U., 1965, J.D. cum laude, 1968. Admitted to Ohio bar, 1968; law clk. Ohio Supreme Ct., 1968-69; asst. clk. Ohio Ho. of Reps., Columbus, 1971-72; partner firm Milligan, Milligan & Milligan, Westerville, Ohio, 1969—; exec. sec., legal counsel Ohio Info. Com.; chmn. Columbus Bd. of License Appeals, 1975—. Mem. Am., Ohio, Columbus bar assns., Franklin County Trial Lawyers Assn. Home: 3825 Dempsey Rd Westerville OH 43081 Office: 3791 Dempsey Rd Westerville OH 43081 Tel (614) 891-6363

MILLIGAN, FRED, SR., b. Upper Sandusky, Ohio, Nov. 14, 1906; B.A., Ohio State U., 1928; LL.B., Franklin U., 1934; J.D., Capital U., 1966. Admitted to Ohio bar, 1933, U.S. Supreme Ct. bar, 1954; sr. partner firm Milligan, Milligan & Milligan, Westerville, Ohio, 1974—; asst. atty. gen. Ohio, 1933-37; exec. sec. Ohio Adminstrv. Law Commn., 1942; dir. Ohio Dept. Commerce, 1947-49; asst. dir. Fed. Commn. Intergovtl. Relations, 1953-54. Pres. Ohio Info. Com., 1966—; pres. Central Ohio council Boy Scouts Am., 1949-51, Franklin County Hist. Soc., 1954-56; trustee Columbus Town Meeting, 1957-64, Blendon Twp., Franklin County, 1971—, Westerville Area C. of C., 1977 Westerville Pub. Library, 1977; v.p. bd. trustees Concord Counselling Service, 1977. Mem. Am., Ohio, Columbus bar assns., Columbus C. of C., Phi Delta Phi. Home: 3785 Dempsey Rd Westerville OH 43081 Office: 3791 Dempsey Rd Westerville OH 43081 Tel (614) 891-6363

MILLIGAN, FRED J., JR., b. Columbus, Ohio, Aug. 23, 1942; B.A., Ohio State U., 1964, J.D., 1967. Admitted to Ohio bar, 1967; partner firm Milligan, Milligan & Milligan, Westerville, Ohio, 1968—. Pres. bd. trustees Central Coll. United Presbyn. Ch., 1975; exec. bd. Central Ohio council Boy Scouts Am., 1973-76. Mem. Columbus, Ohio bar assns. Home: 3839 Dempsey Rd Westerville OH 43081 Office: 3791 Dempsey Rd Westerville OH 43081 Tel (614) 891-6363

MILLIGAN, JOHN THOMAS, b. Detroit, Oct. 18, 1929; B.A., Miami U., Oxford, Ohio, 1951; J.D., U. Mich., 1956. Admitted to Mich. bar, 1956, Ohio bar, 1957; partner firm Hoppe, Frey, Hewitt & Milligan, Warren, Ohio, 1956—; dir. Trumbull Savs. & Loan Co., Warren, 1972—, Reese Tool & Supply Co., Warren, 1974—, I.J. Investment Co., Inc., Warren, 1976; sec. Taylor-Winfield Corp., Warren, 1968. Trustee, Trumbull Meml. Hosp., Warren, 1968—, First Presbyn. Ch. Warren, 1975—. Mem. Am., Ohio, Trumbull County bar assns., Warren Area C. of C. (dir. 1970-74). Recipient Distinguished Service award Family Service Assn., 1974. Home: 266 Country Club Dr Warren OH 44484 Office: 500 Second National Tower Warren OH 44481 Tel (216) 392-1541

MILLIGAN, WILLIAM WEST, b. Bellefontaine, Ohio, Dec. 24, 1923; LL.B., Hiram Coll., 1948; J.D., U. Mich., 1951. Admitted to Ohio bar, 1951; practiced in Sidney, Ohio, 1953-54, 56; asst. counsel judiciary com. U.S. Ho. of Reps., 1955; mem. Ohio Ho. of Reps., 1957-64; individual practice law, Sidney, 1956-69; U.S. atty for So. Dist. Ohio, 1969—; pres. Milligan Hill Co., Sidney. Mem. Fed., Columbus, Ohio, Am. bar assns., Am. Judicature Soc. (trustee). Author: (with others) Ohio Forms of Pleading and Practice, 1969. Home: 150 W Beechwold Blvd Columbus OH 43214 Office: 85 Marconi Blvd Columbus OH 43215 Tel (614) 469-5715

MILLIKEN, CHARLES BUCKLAND, b. New Haven, June 2, 1931; B.A., Yale, 1952; J.D., Harvard, 1957. Admitted to Conn. bar, 1957; asso. firm Shipman & Goodwin, Hartford, Conn., 1957-60, partner firm, 1961—; dir. Acromold Products Corp. Trustee Westminster Sch., Simsbury, Conn., 1969—, sec., 1970-74, chmn., 1974—; bd. dirs. Greater Hartford Arts Council, 1971—; bd. dirs. Symphony Soc. of Greater Hartford, 1959-75, sec., 1960-62, pres., 1962-64. Fellow Am. Coll. Probate Counsel; mem. Am., Conn. (lectr.), Hartford County bar assns. Author: (with Alex Lloyd) The Service Business: Partnership or Corporation, 1969. Home: 104 Whetten Rd West Hartford CT 06117 Office: 799 Main St Hartford CT 06103 Tel (203) 549-4770

MILLIKEN, PAUL EDWIN, b. Akron, Ohio, Dec. 31, 1928; B.S. in Edn., Ohio State U., 1953; J.D., U. Akron, 1963. Trainee, Goodyear Aircraft Corp., Akron, 1955-57; patent adminstr. Goodyear Aerospace Corp., Akron, 1957-64; admitted to Ohio bar, 1963, U.S. Patent Office bar, 1964; patent atty. Goodyear Tire & Rubber Co., 1964-77, Goodyear Aerospace Corp., Akron, 1977—. Mem. Akron Bar Assn., Cleve. Patent Law Assn. Holder 8 U.S. patents and numerous foreign patents. Home: 9061 Wall St NW Massillon OH 44646 Office: Goodyear Aerospace Corp Akron OH 44315 Tel (216) 794-3894

MILLIN, PAUL H., b. Warren, Pa., Feb. 7, 1944; B.A., Maryville (Tenn.) Coll., 1966; J.D., U. Tenn., Knoxville, 1969. Admitted to Pa. bar, 1970; partner firm Swanson, Beverino & Millin, P.C., Warren,

1971—; dist. atty., Forest County, Pa., 1972—. Mem. Am., Pa., Forest County (pres.) bar assns., Am., Trial Lawyers Assn., Nat. Dist. Attys. Assn., Pa. Dist. Attys. Assn., Am. Arbitration Assn. Office: Elm St Tionesta PA 16353 Tel (814) 755-3581

MILLION, ELMER MAYSE, b. Pond Creek, Okla., Dec. 10, 1912; A.B., Southwestern Okla. State U., 1936; LL.B., U. Okla., 1935; S.J.D. (Sterling fellow), Yale, 1938. Admitted to Okla. bar, 1935, U.S. Supreme Ct. bar, 1944; individual practice law, Weatherford and Norman, Okla., 1935-36; sr. atty. U.S. Dept. Justice, Washington, 1943-46, Office of Alien Property Custodian, Washington, 1946; prof. law N.Y. U., N.Y.C., 1947-70, U. Okla., Norman, 1970—; hearing officer U.S. Dept. Justice, 1943-45; faculty mem. Inter-Am. Law Inst., 1948-68. Pres., Fairlington (Va.) Civic Assn., 1944-45; dir. Maternity Consultation Service, N.Y.C., 1949-55; dir. Greenwich Village Montessori Sch., 1966-69. Mem. Am., Okla. bar assns., Am. Trial Lawyers' Assn., Phi Alpha Delta. Author: (with Walsh and Niles) Cases on Property, 3 vols., 1951-57; contbr. articles in field to legal jours.; dir. N.Y. U. Intramural Law Rev., 1954-64; gen. editor Okla. Practice Methods, 1970—. Home: 2530 Beaurue Dr Norman OK 73069 Office: 300 Timberdell Rd Norman OK 73019 Tel (405) 325-4011

MILLIOUS, JOSEPH MARCELLUS, b. Fremont, Ohio, May 16, 1914; A.B., Ohio State U., 1935; J.D., Capital U., 1951. Admitted to Ohio bar, 1952, U.S. Supreme Ct. bar, 1970; credit mgr. Capital City Products Co., Columbus, Ohio, 1935-42; asst. to pres. and dir. indsl. relations Universal Concrete Pipe Co., Columbus, 1945-53; counsel, dir. indsl. relations Columbus (Ohio) Bolt & Forging, 1953-63; mem. firm Speer, Mackey & Millious, Columbus, 1963-70; mem. firm Tingley, Hurd & Emens, Columbus, 1970—; lectr. Franklin U., 1962—; dir. labor relations State of Ohio, 1975-76. Pres. Franklin County Mental Health Assn., 1968; pres., chmn. of bd. English Speaking Union, 1971—; mem. bd. dirs. Navy League, 1973. Mem. Columbus, Ohio, Am. (mem. labor com.) bar assns., Am. Arbitration Assn. (arbitration panel), Fed. Mediation and Conciliation Service. Contbr. articles to publs. Home: 2014 Beverly St Columbus OH 43221 Office: 250 E Broad St Columbus OH 43215 Tel (614) 221-6527

MILLMAN, MAX R., b. N.Y.C., April 17, 1915; B.S., Coll. City N.Y., 1937; J.D. (hon.), George Washington U., 1950. Admitted to D.C. bar, 1950, Pa. bar, 1960; patent examiner Caesar & Rivise, Phila., 1945-48, patent atty., 1951-58; partner firm Millman & Jacobs, Phila., 1958—. Mem. Phila., D.C. bar assns., Am., Phila. patent law assns. Home: Chestnut St Philadelphia PA 19103 Office: 828 Suburban Station Bldg Philadelphia PA 19103 Tel (215) LO4-2234

MILLMAN, RICHARD MARTIN, b. Newark, July 7, 1937; B.A., Brandeis U., 1957; LL.B., Georgetown U., 1960. Admitted to D.C. bar, 1961, Md. bar, 1968, U.S. Supreme Ct. bar, 1965; law clk. to chief judge U.S. Ct. Appeals 4th Circuit, 1960; individual practice law, Washington, 1961-76; mem. firm Millman & Broder, Washington, 1976—. Mem. Montgomery County Council Fin. Adv. Com., 1967-69, Montgomery County Council Task Force on Taxation, 1967; mem. Com. on Adminstrn. Justice in D.C., 1967; mem. Md. Gov's Com. on Employment of Handicapped, 1967; mem. housing task force com. Nat. Council Sr. Citizens, 1972; co-chmn. Brandeis U. Ann. Givers Fund, Greater Washington Area, 1971; mem. Md. Commn. on Jud. Reform, 1974-75; bd. dirs. Md. div. Am. Trauma Soc., 1974, treas., 1975. Mem. Am., Fed., Internat., Md., D.C. bar assns., Am. Trial Lawyers Assn., Nat. Assn. Def. Lawyers in Criminal Cases, Phi Delta Phi. Office: 1730 M St NW Washington DC 20036 Tel (202) 296-4490

MILLS, CAROLYN BUTTLES, b. Huntsville, Ala., Aug. 13, 1947; B.S., U. So. Miss., 1969, M.S., 1970; J.D., U. Miss., 1973. Admitted to Miss. bar, 1973; staff atty., adminstrv. asst. Miss. Bar Legal Services, Inc., Jackson, 1973-76; spl. asst. atty. gen. State of Miss., Jackson, 1976—; instr. polit. sci. Miss. Coll., Clinton, 1975. Mem. Miss., Hinds County, Am. bar assns., Jackson Young Lawyers, Miss. Women Lawyers. Home: 208 Simmons Pl Clinton MS 39056 Office: PO Box 220 Jackson MS 39205 Tel (601) 354-7130

MILLS, CLARENCE R., JR., b. N.Y.C., Nov. 9, 1918; B.S., Wayne State U.; LL.B., Ind. U. Admitted to Ind. bar, 1956, U.S. Ct. Mil. Appeals bar, 1957, U.S. Supreme Ct. bar, 1970; since practiced in Indpls., individual practice law; dep. atty. gen., dep. prosecutor; judge Marion County Municipal Ct. Active Indpls. Hist. Preservation Com., Arthritis Found. Mem. Am., Ind., Indpls. bar assns., Am. Judicature Soc., Ind. Judge Assn. Contbr. articles to legal jours. Home: 8751 Guilford Ave Indianapolis IN 46240 Office: Marion County Municipal Ct Rm 2 W306 City-County Bldg Indianapolis IN 46203 Tel (317) 633-3933

MILLS, DON BURTON, b. Barbourville, Ky., Jan. 29, 1930; B.A., U. Ky., 1956, J.D., 1959. Admitted to Ky. bar, 1960; individual practice law, Barbourville, 1960—; city atty. City of Barbourville, 1960-71, mem. planning commn., 1962-77; commonwealth atty., 27th jud. dist., Knox and Laurel Counties, Ky., 1977—. Mem. Am., State of Ky., Knox County bar assns., Knox County C. of C. (pres. 1967-68). Home: 100 Mills St Barbourville KY 40906 Office: 103 Liberty St Barbourville KY 40906 Tel (606) 546-3239

MILLS, DON HARPER, b. Peking, China, July 29, 1927; B.S., U. Cin., 1950, M.D., 1953; J.D., U. So. Calif., 1958. Intern, Los Angeles County Gen. Hosp., 1953-54; fellow in pathology, Med. Sch. U. So. Calif., 1954-55; admitted to Calif. bar, 1958; admitting physician Los Angeles Gen. Hosp., 1954-57, attending staff dept. pathology, 1959—; asst. in pathology Hosp. of the Good Samaritan, Los Angeles, 1956-65, consulting staff dept. pathology, 1967-72, affiliating staff, 1972—; dep. med. examiner Office of Los Angeles County Med. Examiner-Coroner, 1957-61; cons. in forensic medicine, Los Angeles, 1958—; instr. pathology Sch. Medicine, U. So. Calif., 1958-62, asst. clin. prof., 1962-65, asso. clin. prof., 1965-69, clin. prof., 1969—; instr. legal medicine Sch. of Medicine, Loma Linda U., 1960-66, asso. clin. prof. humanities, 1966—; research cons. HEW Sec.'s Commn. on Med. Malpractice, 1972-73; cons. Armed Forces Inst. Pathology, Dept. Army, Washington, 1975—, Nat. Center for Health Services Research, HEW, 1975—; expert cons. Office of the Sec. HEW, 1975—. Mem. adv. council Assembly Select Com. on Med. Malpractice, State of Calif., 1973-75. Fellow Am. Coll. Legal Medicine (bd. govs. 1970—, pres. 1974-76, editorial bd. jour. 1972—), Am. Acad. Forensic Scis. (editorial bd. jour. 1965—, Merit award 1974); mem. Am. (editorial bd. jour. 1973—), Calif., Los Angeles County med. assns., Assn. Am. Med. Colls., AAAS, Am., Los Angeles County bar assns., Am. Judicature Soc., Drug Info. Assn., Kansas City Surg. Soc. (hon.), N.Y. Acad. Scis., Am. Soc. Hosp. Attys., Alpha Omega Alpha, Order of Coif. Recipient Peter T. Kilgour prize U. Cin., 1953; mem. editorial bd. So. Calif. Law Rev., 1956-58, Medical Alert Communications, 1973-75; column editor Newsletter of Long Beach Med. Assn., 1960-75, Jour. Am. Osteopathic Assn., 1965—, Ortho Panel, 1970—; exec. editor Trauma, 1964—; editorial cons. Physician's Legal Brief, 1965-75, Surgical Advances, 1970-74, Hazards of Medication, 1971. Home: 1141 Los Altos Ave Long Beach CA 90815 Office: 600 S Commonwealth Ave Suite 1702 Los Angeles CA 90005 Tel (213) 480-1900

MILLS, JERRY WOODROW, b. Springfield, Mo., July 17, 1940; B.E.E., Tex. A. and M. U., 1963; J.D., Georgetown U., 1967. Admitted to Tex. bar, 1967; asso. firm Burns, Doane, Swecker & Mathis, Washington, 1965-67; partner firm Richards, Harris & Medlock, Dallas, 1967—. Mem. Am., Tex. Jr. (treas. 1974-75), Dallas (Outstanding Young Lawyer 1975), Dallas Jr. (pres. 1971) bar assns., State Bar Tex. Home: 9417 Trailhill Dr Dallas TX 75238 Office: 2900 1 Main Pl Dallas TX 75250 Tel (214) 742-8013

MILLS, JOHN MCLAURIN, b. Wilmington, N.C., Apr. 22, 1915; student U. N.C., 1933-35; LL.B., U. S.C., 1939, J.D., 1970. Admitted to S.C. bar, 1939; practiced in Bennettsville, S.C., 1945-67; judge Marlboro County (S.C.) Ct., 1967—; county atty. Marlboro County, 1960-67. Mem. S.C., Am. bar assns., Marlboro County Bar Assn. (pres. 1964-67), Order Wig and Robe, Phi Delta Phi. Home: 2009 W Main Extension Bennettsville SC 29512 Office: 114 N Liberty St Bennettsville SC 29512 Tel (803) 479-3601

MILLS, RICHARD HENRY, b. Beardstown, Ill., July 19, 1929; B.A., Ill. Coll., 1951; J.D., Mercer U., 1957. Admitted to Ill. bar, 1957; practiced in Virginia, Ill., 1957-66; judge 8th Jud. Circuit Ct. of Ill., 1966-76; justice Appellate Ct. Ill., 1976—; legal adviser Ill. Youth Commn., 1958-60; state's atty. Cass County (Ill.), 1960-64; mem. Ill. Supreme Ct. Rules Com., 1963—; chmn. Ill. Supreme Ct. Com. on Criminal Law Seminars for Judges, 1971-76; lt. col. JAGC, USAR, Korea, 1953-54. Mem. exec. bd. Abraham Lincoln council Boy Scouts Am.; mem. adminstrv. bd. Presbyn. Ch., Virginia. Mem. Am. (Finch award 1974), Ill. State (chmn. sect. criminal law 1967-68, sect. jud. adminstrn. 1972-73), Chgo., Cass County (pres. 1962-64, 75-76) bar assns., Am. Judicature Soc., Nat. Conf. State Trial Judges, Ill. Judges Assn. Recipient George Washington Honor medal Freedoms Found., 1969, 73, 75; Eagle Scout award Boy Scouts Am., 1943, Silver Beaver award, 1975. Contbr. articles to legal jours.; editorial bd. Mercer Law Rev., 1956-57. Home: 342 S Cass St Virginia IL 62691 Office: Courthouse Virginia IL 62691 Tel (217) 452-3220

MILLS, STUART BRUCE, b. Buffalo, May 22, 1949; B.S., Nebr. Wesleyan U., 1971; J.D., U. Nebr., 1972. Admitted to Nebr. bar, 1973; asso. firm Samuelson & Mills, 1973-74, partner, 1974—; dep. county atty. Thurston, 1973, 74. Mem. Nebr. Bar Assn. Home: Box 381 Pender NE 68047 Office: 309 Main St Pender NE 68047 Tel (402) 385-3404

MILLS, WILLIAM HAYES, b. Gordo, Ala., Mar. 30, 1931; LL.B., U. Ala., 1956. Admitted to Ala. bar, 1956, U.S. Dist. Ct. No. Dist. Ala. bar, 1956, U.S. Ct. Appeals 5th Circuit bar, 1959, 4th Circuit bar, 1970, U.S. Supreme Ct. bar, 1971; asso. firm Rogers, Howard & Redden, Birmingham, Ala., 1956-60; partner firm Rogers, Howard, Redden & Mills, Birmingham, 1961—. Mem. Birmingham, Ala., Am. bar assns., Ala. Trial Lawyers Assn., Assn. Trial Lawyers Am. Editor-in-chief Ala. Law Rev., 1955. Home: 1418 Sharpsburg Circle Birmingham AL 35213 Office: 1033 Frank Nelson Bldg Birmingham AL 35203 Tel (205) 251-5138

MILLSAP, RICHARD, b. Alton, Mo., June 18, 1925; B.A., U. Mo. at Kansas City, 1949, J.D., 1950. Admitted to Kans. bar, 1950, Mo. bar, 1967; asso. firm Stanley, Schroeder, Weeks, Thomas & Lysaught, Kansas City, Kans., 1951-67, sr. partner, 1960-67; partner firm Kirby, Millsap & Lewis, Springfield, Mo., 1967-69; dir. edn. Mo. Bar, Jefferson City, 1969-75; asso. firm Weeks, Thomas, Lysaught, Bingham & Mustain, Overland Park, Kans., 1975—; atty. Wyandotte Twp. Bd., 1966. Bd. govs. Veteran's Quindaro Homes, Inc., 1955-57, pres., 1956-57; bd. govs. Camp Fire Girls, 1963-65; pres. Republicans for Action, 1964-66. Mem. Am., Kans., Johnson County bar assns., U. Mo. at Kansas City Law Found. Co-author: Missouri Civil Trial Practice, 1976. Home: 10114 W 65th Dr Shawnee Mission KS 66203 Office: 407 Capitol Federal Bldg 95th and Nall Overland Park KS 66207 Tel (913) 642-7770

MILLSTONE, PHILLIP ARTHUR, b. Youngstown, Ohio, Dec. 20, 1909; A.B., Ohio State U., 1930, LL.B., 1932, J.D., 1932. Admitted to Ohio bar, 1932; individual practice law, Youngstown, 1932-43, 46-65; sr. partner firm Millstone and Kannensohn, Youngstown, 1965—; sec. Mahoning County (Ohio) Bldg. Commn. for Courthouse Annex, 1954-55. Mem. Youngstown Zoning Commn., 1965-70. Mem. Mahoning County, Ohio State, Am. bar assns. Home: 2318 Selma Ave Youngstown OH 44504 Office: 810 Mahoning Bank Bldg Youngstown OH 44503 Tel (216) 743-5181

MILLWARD, GUY EARL, JR., b. New Brunswick, N.J., May 17, 1947; B.A., Union Coll., 1969; J.D., U. Louisville, 1973. Admitted to Ky. bar, 1973; asso. firm Rose & Martin, Williamsburg, Ky., 1973-74; individual practice law, Barbourville, Ky., 1974—. Adv. com. Knox County Gen. Hosp., 1975-76. Mem. Am., Ky., Knox County (pres. 1977—) bar assns., Assn. Trial Lawyers Am. Home: Edgewood Dr Barbourville KY 40906 Office: 119 Cole Ct Barbourville KY 40906 Tel (606) 546-5114

MILLWARD, WAYNE FOSTER, b. Camden, N.J., June 3, 1935; B.S., Ursinus Coll., Pa., 1957; J.D., Am. U., 1968. Admitted to Md. bar, 1969, U.S. Supreme Ct. bar, 1973; hearings rep. Reed, Roberts Assos., Inc., Arlington, Va., 1968-71, v.p., 1971-76, sr. v.p., Garden City, N.Y., 1976—. Mem. bd. appeals City of Rockville (Md.), 1971-72, mem. park recreation adv. bd., 1969-71; pres. Twinbrook Citizens Assn., Rockville, 1970-71. Contbr. articles to legal jours. Office: Reed Roberts Assos Inc 118 7th St Garden City NY 11530 Tel (516) 248-6900

MILNES, GREGORY EARL, b. Medford, Oreg., Mar. 5, 1939; B.A., Willamette U., 1961, J.D., 1964. Legis. corr. Stas. KMED Radio, KMED-TV, Medford, Oreg., 1961, 63; admitted to Oreg. bar, 1964; law clk. Oreg. Pub. Utility Commr., Salem, 1963-64; gen. atty. FCC, Washington, 1964-66; dep. dist. atty. Washington County (Oreg.), 1967-69, chief dep. dist. atty., 1968-69; judge Washington County (Oreg.) Dist. Ct., 1969-75, Washington County Circuit Ct., 1975—. Chmn. Washington County Drug Abuse Council, 1972-76; chmn. criminal justice com. Columbia Region Assn. Govts., Portland, Oreg., 1972—; mem. Washington County Welfare Advisory Com. Mem. Oreg. State, Washington County bars, Am. Bar Assn., Am. Judicature Soc., Oreg. Jud. Conf. Recipient Beaverton Area Distinguished Service award Beaverton Jaycees, 1974; named 1 of Oreg.'s 5 Outstanding Young Men Oreg. Jaycees, 1974. Home: 740 SE 24th Ave Hillsboro OR 97123 Office: 302 Courthouse Hillsboro OR 97123

MILOSTAN, HARRY, b. Alpena, Mich., Sept. 25, 1920; B.A. in Bus. Adminstrn., Mich. State U.; J.D., U. Detroit. Admitted to Mich. bar; individual practice law, Mt. Clemens, Mich. Contbr. articles on Slavic Peoples to newspapers; editor-in-chief U. Detroit Law Jour. Home: 48855 N Gratiot Ave Mount Clemens MI 48043 Office: 48855 N Gratiot Ave Mount Clemens MI 48043 Tel (313) 949-9222

MILSTEIN, RICHARD SHERMAN, b. Westfield, Mass., May 9, 1926; A.B., Harvard, 1948; J.D., Boston U., 1952. Admitted to Mass. bar, 1952, U.S. Supreme Ct. bar, 1960; asso. firm Ely King Corcoran Milstein & Beaudry, Springfield, Mass., 1954-59, partner, 1959—; adminstr. com. on continuing legal edn. Mass. Bar Assn., 1960-69; dir. Mass. Continuing Legal Edn., Inc., 1969-76; exec. dir. New Eng. Law Inst., 1975-76; instr. Western New Eng. Law Sch., Springfield, 1962-65, 75-77; dir. Mass. continuing legal edn. New Eng. Law Inst., 1976—. Mem. Mass. Gov.'s Spl. Commn. to Revise Securities Laws, 1970-73; mem. Gov.'s Jud. Nominating Commn., 1975—. Chmn. personnel policy bd. City of Westfield (Mass.), 1962-67; trustee Horace Smith Fund; Westfield Acad.; v.p. Sta. WGBY, Pub. TV, 1972; corporator Springfield Symphony Orch., 1977. Mem. Am. Law Inst., Am. Bar Found., Mass. (future planning com. 1976—, edn. com. 1976—), Hampden (exec. com. 1972—), Am., Boston (corp. law com.) bar assns., Scribes. Editorial bd. Mass. Law Quar., 1960-76. Home: 140 Chestnut St Springfield MA 01103 Office: 1387 Main St Springfield MA 01103 Tel (413) 781-1920

MILSTEN, DAVID RANDOLPH, b. Coalgate, Okla., Sept. 29, 1903; B.A., U. Okla., 1925, LL.B., 1928; postgrad. Yale, 1926. Admitted to Okla. bar, 1928; individual practice law, Tulsa; asst. dist. atty. Tulsa County, 1928-30; legal counsel Tulsa Opera Inc. Hon. trustee and past pres. Temple Israel. Mem. Thomas Gilcrease Inst. Am. History and Art (dir. emeritus, past pres., past chmn. bd.), Sigma Alpha Mu. Author: Biography, Appreciation of Will Rogers, 1935; Howdy Folks (poem), 1938; Before My Night (poems), 1962; Thomas Gilcrease, 1969. Home: 3905 S Florence Pl Tulsa OK 74105 Office: Tower Suite Philtower Bldg Tulsa OK 74103 Tel (918) 583-7575

MILTENBERGER, ROBERT HENRY, II, b. Dayton, Ohio, Oct. 10, 1934; A.B. cum laude, Harvard, 1956; J.D., U. Mich., 1959. Admitted to N.Y. bar, 1960; asso. firm Hodgson, Russ, Andrews, Woods and Goodyear, Buffalo, 1960—, gen. partner, 1968—; lectr. continuing edn. program N.Y. State Bar Assn. Mem. Am., N.Y. State, Erie County bar assns. Office: 18th Floor One M & T Plaza Buffalo NY 14203 Tel (716) 856-4000

MILTNER, FRANK HENRY, b. Lake City, Mich., Nov. 9, 1918; A.B., U. Notre Dame, 1940; LL.B., U. Mich., 1943. Admitted to Mich. bar, 1943; partner firm Miltner & Miltner, Cadillac, Mich., 1946-69; pros. atty. Wexford County (Mich.), Cadillac, 1947-50; recorders judge City of Cadillac, 1958-66; judge Probate Ct. Wexford County, Cadillac, 1966-68, 84th Jud. Dist. Ct., Cadillac, 1969—; state judge adv. Mich. N.G., 1970-74. Pres., bd. dirs. Cadillac Indsl. Fund Inc. Mem. Am., Mich. bar assns., Mich. Dist. Judges Assn., Cadillac Area C. of C. (former dir.). Home: 443 E Division St Cadillac MI 49601 Office: Court House Cadillac MI 49601 Tel (616) 775-8582

MINAS, SETRAK BENJAMIN, b. Worcester, Mass., Mar. 20, 1908; B.S., Boston U., 1930, J.D., 1933, LL.M., 1937. Admitted to Mass. bar, 1933, Fed. bar, 1937; partner law firm Minas, Preble and Lawrence, Boston, 1937-42; pvt. practice law, Rockport, Mass., 1946—; part time sr. lectr. bus. law Northeastern U., 1945—. Mem. Commn. Indsl. Devel., Rockport, Mass., 1973-76. Mem. Mass. Bar Assn., Am. Judicature Soc., Knights of Malta, Am. Catholic Fedn. Austrian, German, Swiss Univ. Profs. Home: Box 1 Rockport MA 01966

MINCER, GLENN CLAUDE, b. Cozad, Nebr., Feb. 16, 1899; A.B., Nebr. State Coll., 1921; postgrad. Columbia U., 1920; J.D., U. Nebr., 1925. Admitted to Nebr. bar, 1925, Fla. bar, 1925; tchr., Nebr., Colo., 1921-23; judge municipal ct., Miami Beach, Fla., 1930; mem. Fla. legis., 1935; asst. solicitor, Dade County, Fla., 1936-45, states atty., 1945-53, asst. states atty., 1953-64. Mem. Elks., Am. Legion. Home and office: 45 Salmanca Ave Coral Gables FL 33134 Tel (305) 443-6134

MINER, RUTH MIRIAM, b. Dec. 13, 1893; B.A., Wellesley Coll., 1916; LL.B., Union U., 1920, J.D., 1970. Admitted to N.Y. bar, 1921; atty. Albany (N.Y.) Legal Aid Soc., 1922-25; law clk. N.Y. Supreme Ct., 1924-30; atty. Town of Bethlehem (N.Y.), 1926-34; asst. counsel N.Y. Legis. Bill Drafting Commn., 1940-42; sr. partner firm Miner, Feeney & Ford, Albany, 1963—; pres. Main Bros. Oil Co., Delmar, N.Y., 1972—, Main Bros. Industries, Inc., 1973—. Past pres., dir. Albany Legal Aid Soc. Mem. Mohawk and Hudson River Humane Soc., past dir.; past dir. Family and Children's Service of Albany, Inc.; past dir. Sr. Citizens Center, Inc.; active Girl Scouts U.S.A., past council mem. Albany County council; dir. Albany Girls Club; mem. N.Y. State Rep. Com., N.Y. State Fedn. Rep. Women's Clubs, Inc., Albany County Rep. Com., also vice-chmn., 1940-50, mem. exec. com., 1940-54; hon. mem. N.Y. State Election Commn., 1958—; past mem. gen. bd. Nat. Council Chs. Christ in Am., Albany County Council Religious Edn.; mem., dir., past pres. City Club Albany; mem. Bethleham Hist. Soc.; past trustee Albany Acad. for Girls, mem. alumnae council, past pres. alumni assn. trustee Albany Law Sch., Union U., Charlton Sch. for Girls. Mem. Nat. Assn. Legal Aid Orgns. (past mem. exec. com.), Nat. Council on Crime and Delinquency, Am., N.Y. State, Albany County bar assns., N.Y. State, Nat. assns. women lawyers, Albany County Council Social Agys., Nat. Women's Party, DAR, AAUW, N.Y. State Bus. and Profl. Women's Club, YWCA, Delmar Progress Club, UN. Assn. (Albany chpt.), Am. Judicature Soc., Rep. Women of the Legislature. Office: 100 State St Albany NY 12207 Tel (518) 465-5294

MINER, ZELLIE, b. New Haven, Mar. 2, 1907; A.B., Western Res. U., 1927, LL.B., 1929. Admitted to Ohio bar, 1929, U.S. Dist. Ct. bar No. Dist. Ohio, 1935; regional rent atty. O.P.A., 1942-47; partner firm Weiner & Miner, Cleve., 1929-69; individual practice law, Cleve., 1970—; conducted bar review course for Ohio bar, 1929-69, Miner Bar Review Course, 1970—, seminar on uniform comml. code Cuyahoga Bar Assn. Mem. Am., Ohio, Greater Cleve., Cuyahoga County bar assns. Author: (with others) Ohio Methods of Practice, Vols. 1 and 2, 1957. Home: 3446 Old Green Rd Beachwood OH 44122 Office: 230 Leader Bldg Cleveland OH 44114 Tel (216) 781-5025

MINGE, DAVID, b. Clarkfield, Minn., Mar. 19, 1942; B.A., St. Olaf Coll., 1964; J.D., U. Chgo., 1967. Admitted to Minn. bar, 1967; asso. firm Faegre & Benson, Mpls., 1967-70; asst. prof. law U. Wyo., 1970-74, asso. prof., 1974—; cons. U.S. Ho. of Reps. Judiciary Com., 1975; Fulbright lectr. law U. Helsinki (Finland), 1976. Vice chmn. Mpls. Model Cities Citizen Com., 1968-69. Author: Effect of Law on County and Municipal Expenditures, 1975. Home: 1406 Custer St Laramie WY 82070 Office: Coll of Law U of Wyo Laramie WY 82071 Tel (307) 766-6107

MINKOWITZ, MARTIN, b. Bklyn., Feb. 7, 1939; A.A., Bklyn. Coll., 1959, B.A., 1961; LL.B., Bklyn. Law Sch., 1963, LL.M., 1965, J.D., 1967. Admitted to N.Y. State bar, 1963, U.S. Supreme Ct. bar, 1967; partner firm Minkowitz & Rosenbluth, N.Y.C., 1964-76; hearing officer N.Y.C. Parking Violations Bur., 1970-76; instr. bus. law City U. N.Y., 1975—; gen. counsel N.Y. State Workmen's Compensation Bd., 1976—. Mem. Am., N.Y. State bar assns., Assn. Bar City N.Y., N.Y. County Lawyers Assn., Am. Arbitration Assn. (arbitrator 1976), Bklyn. Law Sch. Alumni Assn. Author: Rent Stabilization and Control Laws of New York, 1972. Office: Two World Trade Center New York City NY 10017 Tel (212) 488-3095

MINKS, MERLE EDWARD, b. Fisher, Ill., May 10, 1917; B.A., Knox Coll., 1939; LL.B., U. Tex., 1948. Admitted to Tex. bar, 1948, Pa. bar, 1970; atty. Gulf Oil Corp., Houston, 1948—; chief counsel Wilshire Oil Co. of Calif., Los Angeles, 1960-63, regional atty. Gulf Oil Corp., Los Angeles, 1963-67, asso. gen. counsel Gulf Oil Co.-Eastern Hemisphere, London, 1967-69, corporate gen. counsel, Pitts., 1969—. Bd. dirs. YMCA of Pitts., Pitts.-Allegheny County chpt. ARC, Allegheny Trails council Boy Scouts Am.; trustee Knox Coll.; advisory com. Parker Sch., Internat. and Comparative Law Center, Internat. Oil and Gas Ednl. Center. Mem. Tex., Pa., Am. bar assns., Assn. of Gen. Counsel (v.p., mem. exec. com.). Home: 106 Hickory Hill Rd Pittsburgh PA 15238 Office: PO Box 1166 Pittsburgh PA 15230 Tel (412) 263-5136

MINNARD, LAWRENCE ROBERT, b. Niagara Falls, N.Y., Oct. 6, 1943; B.S. in Edn., Ohio No. U., 1961, J.D., 1968. Admitted to Ohio bar, 1968; asso. firm Navarre, Rizor & DaPore, Lima, Ohio, 1971—. Mem. Am., Ohio bar assns., Am., Ohio trial lawyers assns. Home: 2116 W High St Lima OH 45805 Office: 130 W North St Lima OH 45801 Tel (119) 227-8737

MINNICK, MALCOLM DAVID, b. Indpls., July 5, 1946; B.A., U. Mich., 1968, J.D., 1972. Admitted to Calif. bar, 1972; asso. firm Lillick, McHose & Charles, Los Angeles, 1972—. Mem. Am., Los Angeles bar assns., Fin. Lawyers Conf., Beta Theta Pi. Office: 707 Wilshire Blvd Los Angeles CA 90017 Tel (213) 620-9000

MINNITI, JOSEPH A., b. Port Chester, N.Y., Oct. 25, 1928; A.B., St. Lawrence U., 1954; J.D., Syracuse U., 1957. Admitted to N.Y. State bar, 1958; trial atty. Thomas J. Flood, N.Y.C., 1957-62; individual practice law, Mamaroneck, N.Y., 1962-75; partner firm Minniti & Pirro, Mamaroneck, 1975-76, Minniti, Pirro & Monsell, Mamaroneck, 1976—; atty. Police Benevolent Assn., Mamaroneck, 1963-69, Westchester County Police Conf., 1967-68. Mem. Village of Mamaroneck Bicentennial Com., 1976; mem. Zoning Law Study Commn., Mamaroneck, 1976. Mem. Am., N.Y. State, Westchester County, Mamaroneck, Harrison Larchmont bar assns., Am. Trial Lawyers Assn., Phi Delta Phi. Home: 280 Murray Ave Larchmont NY 10538 Office: 100 Mamaroneck Ave Mamaroneck NY 10543 Tel (914) 698-9300

MINNO, FRANCES PATRICIA FRAHER, b. Lynn, Mass., July 25, 1930; B.A., Manhattanville Coll., 1951; LL.B., Harvard, 1954. Admitted to Mass. bar, 1954, Pa. bar, 1960, U.S. Supreme Ct. bar, 1961; adj. prof. law U. Pitts., 1967—. Trustee Shady Side Acad., Pitts., 1973-76. Mem. Soc. Hosp Attys. (charter), Allegheny County Bar Assn. Co-author: Problems in Hospital Law, 1973; History and Law of Nursing, 1976. Home: 650 Morewood Ave Pittsburgh PA 15213 Office: 1400 Lawyers Bldg Pittsburgh PA 15219 Tel (412) 281-6225

MINOR, JAMES BERYLL, b. Fairmont, W.Va., June 1, 1919; B.A., George Washington U., 1943, LL.B., 1945. Admitted to D.C. bar, 1945, Md. bar, 1974; legis. counsel War Assets Adminstrn., Washington, 1947-49; dep. chief legis. div. USAF, Washington, 1949-61; dir. rules codification, asso. gen. counsel FAA, Washington, 1961-67; asst. gen. counsel Dept. Transp., Washington, 1967-70, dep. asst. sec., 1970-71; gen. counsel U.S. Price Commn., Washington, 1972-73; individual practice law, Chevy Chase, Md., 1973—; adj. prof. Antioch Sch. Law, 1974-77. Mem. Am. (chmn. standing com. on legal drafting), D.C., Md., Montgomery County (Md.) bar assns. Home: 3104 Kent St Kensington MD 20795 Office: Suite 201 8520 Connecticut Ave Chevy Chase MD 20015 Tel (301) 652-0546

MINOR, JOHN CHRISTOPHER, b. Hobbs, N.Mex., Oct. 20, 1942; student U. Santa Clara, 1960-64; B.S., Willamette U., 1964, J.D., 1967. Admitted to Oreg. bar, 1967, U.S. Supreme Ct. bar, 1972; dep. dist. atty. Lincoln County (Oreg.), 1968-69; asso. firm Minor & Yeck, and predecessors, Newport, Oreg., 1969-70, partner, 1970—; atty. City of Newport, 1975—, Port of Newport, 1975—; counsel Lincoln County, 1975—; atty. Pac Community Hosp., Newport, 1971—; judge Newport Municipal Ct., 1970-72. Pres. Lincoln County ARC, 1972-73. Mem. Am., Oreg., Lincoln County (pres. 1970-71), Oreg. State Bar (chmn. com. on uniform state laws 1972-73). Home: Big Creek Rd Newport OR 97365 Office: 236 W Olive St Newport OR 97365 Tel (503) 265-8888

MINOW, NEWTON NORMAN, b. Milw., Jan. 17, 1926; B.S., Northwestern U., 1948, J.D., 1950, LL.D. (hon.), 1965; LL.D. (hon.), Brandeis U., 1963, U. Wis., 1963, Columbia, 1972. Admitted to Ill. bar, 1950, U.S. Dist. Ct. bar for Calif., 1972; asso. firm Mayer, Brown & Platt, Chgo., 1950-51, 53-55; law clk. to Chief Justice Fred M. Vinson, U.S. Supreme Ct., 1951-52; adminstrv. asst. to Gov. Adlai E. Stevenson, Ill., 1952-53; partner firm Stevenson, Rifkind & Wirtz, Chgo., 1955-61; chmn. FCC, Washington, 1961-63; exec. v.p., gen. counsel, dir. Ency. Brit., Inc., 1963-65; asso. firm Sidley & Austin and predecessor, Chgo., 1965—; dir. Aetna Casualty & Surety Co. Ill., Aetna Life Ins. Co. Ill.; trustee Rand Corp., 1965—, chmn., 1970-72; chmn. Arthur Anderson & Co. Pub. Review Bd., 1975—; mem. adv. bd. Pan Am. Internat., 1977—; professorial lectr. Northwestern U., Medill Sch. Journalism. Co-chmn. steering com. League Women Voters Debate Project; bd. dirs., past chmn. Chgo. Ednl. Television Assn.; bd. dirs. Acad. for Ednl. Devel., Adler Planetarium, Chgo. Orchestral Assn.; trustee Mayo Found., Northwestern U., U. Notre Dame; chmn. Bi-Partisan Study of Campaign Costs in Electronic Era, Twentieth Century Fund; chmn. bd. overseers Jewish Theol. Sem. Am.; bd. govs. Pub. Broadcasting Service; mem. Chgo. Com., Council Fgn. Relations, Internat. Broadcast Inst., Nat. Acad. Television Arts and Scis. Fellow Am. Bar Found.; mem. Am., Ill., Wis., Chgo. bar assns., Am. Judicature Soc., Am. Soc. Internat. Law, Law Club, Legal Club, Econ. Club Chgo. (dir.). Recipient John Henry Wigmore award Northwestern U. Sch. Law, 1950, George Foster Peabody Broadcasting award, 1961, Dr. Lee DeForest award Nat. Assn. for Better Radio and Television, 1962, Distinguished Service award Phi Beta Kappa, 1965; named One of Ten Outstanding Young Men in Chgo., Jr. C. of C. and Industry, 1960, One of America's Ten Outstanding Young Men, 1961; author: Equal Time: The Private Broadcaster and The Public Interest, 1964; (with John B. Martin, Lee M. Mitchell) Presidential Television, 1973; contbr. to As We Knew Adlai, 1966. Home: 375 Palos Rd Glencoe IL 60022 Office: One First Nat Plaza Suite 4800 Chicago IL 60603 Tel (312) 329-5555

MINTER, ALAN HUNTRESS, b. San Antonio, Feb. 21, 1939; student Brown U., 1957-59; B.A., U. Tex., 1962, J.D., 1965. Admitted to Tex. bar, 1965, U.S. Supreme Ct. bar, 1971; asst. atty. gen. State Tex., Austin, 1965-71; individual practice law, Austin, 1971—; govt. appeal agt. Local Draft Bd. 119, Austin, 1971-72; adv. com. Tex. Constl. Revision Com., 1973. Adv. bd. history aviation collection Univ. Tex., Austin, recipient Burnelli Aviation medal; trustee St. Andrew's Episcopal Sch., Austin, 1973-76, chmn. property com., 1975-76; bd. dirs. Austin Heritage Soc., 1974—; mem. ad hoc hist. zoning com. City Austin, 1973. Mem. Am., Travis County, Austin Jr. (co-chmn. publicity com., 1967, chmn. law enforcement, traffic safety com., 1968) bar assns., Sheriffs Assn. Tex., Comml. Law League Am., Am. Trial Lawyers Assn., Tex. Old Forts and Missions Restoration Assn., Assn. Tex. Pioneers, Old Trail Drivers Assn. Tex., Phi Alpha Delta. Contbr. article Tex. Hist. Assn. Quart. Home: 1602 W Lynn St Austin TX 78703 Office: 500 W 16th St Austin TX 78701 Tel (512) 478-1075

MINTER, LLOYD GEORGE, b. Pocasset, Okla., Nov. 2, 1918; B.A., Okla. Baptist U., 1940; J.D., U. Okla., 1943. Admitted to Okla. bar, 1943; asso. firm Rainey, Flynn, Green & Anderson, Oklahoma City, 1943; mem. legal staff Phillips Petroleum Co., Oklahoma City, 1943-49, Bartlesville, 1949—, v.p., gen. counsel, dir., mem. exec. com., 1971-74, sr. v.p., gen. counsel, dir., mem. exec. com., 1974—. Mem. adv. bd. Internat. Oil and Gas Ednl. Center, Okla. U. Law Center. Mem. Am., Okla., Washington County bar assns., Mid-Continent Oil and Gas Assn., Am. Petroleum Inst., Ind. Petroleum Assn., Am. Judicature Soc., Bartlesville C. of C., Phi Kappa Delta, Phi Delta Phi. Recipient Outstanding Alumni award Okla. Bapt. U., 1961. Home: 2112 Skyline Dr Bartlesville OK 74003 Office: 18 Phillips Bldg Bartlesville OK 74004 Tel (918) 661-3834

MINTO, ROBERT WARREN, JR., b. Kirkland, Wash., Apr. 13, 1947; B.B.A., U. Wash., 1969; J.D., U. Mont., 1973. Admitted to Mont. bar, 1973, U.S. Tax Ct. bar, 1976; asso. firm Worden, Thane & Haines, Missoula, Mont., 1973—; gen. counsel Larry Larson & Assos., Missoula, 1973—, Missoula Planned Parenthood, 1974-75. Mem. Mont., Western Mont., Am. bar assns. Recipient Scholastic Achievement award Bur. Nat. Affairs, 1973. Home: 912 Parkview Way Missoula MT 59801 Office: 220 Savings Center Missoula MT 59801 Tel (406) 543-8251

MINTON, JERRY DAVIS, b. Ft. Worth, Aug. 13, 1928; B.B.A., U. Tex., Austin, 1949, J.D., 1960; grad. Nat. Trust Sch., Northwestern U., 1960. Sr. v.p., exec. trust officer 1st Nat. Bank, Ft. Worth, 1965—; dir. State Nat. Bank, Odessa, Tex., 1973—; lectr. Southwestern Grad. Sch. Banking; mem. adv. council program exec. profs. U. Tex. Coll. Bus., Arlington. Trustee, 1st v.p. All Saints Episcopal Hosp.; exec. bd. Longhorn council Boy Scouts Am.; bd. dirs. Ft. Worth Art Assn.; trustee, treas. Hist. Ft. Worth, Inc.; mem. aviation bd. Ft. Worth City Council. Mem. Am. Bar Assn., State Bar Tex., Ft. Worth-Tarrant County Bar Assn., Am., Tex. (chmn. trust div. 1975-76) bankers assns., Ft. Worth Bus., Estate Council (chmn. 1972-73), Air Force Assn., Tex. Christian U. Mgmt. Alumni Assn. (pres. 1975). Decorated D.F.C., Air medal with 3 oak leaf clusters; named Outstanding Young Lawyer of Ft. Worth, 1967. Tel (817) 390-6900

MINTON, LARRY CHARLES, lawyer; b. International Falls, Minn., July 18, 1945; B.A., U. N.D., 1967; J.D., U. Minn., 1970. Admitted to Minn. bar, 1970, Fed. Dist. Ct. Minn., 1971; investment atty. Law Dept., Northwestern Nat. Life Ins. Co., Mpls., 1970-71; partner law firm Naughtin, Mulvahill & Minton, Hibbing, Minn., 1972—; instr. bus. law Hibbing Community Coll., 1974-76; dir. CWDC Industries, Hibbing, Minn., 1976—. Bd. dirs. Life Enrichment for Elderly, Inc., 1976—. Mem. Minn. State, Am., Range bar assns., Hibbing Lions Club (dir. 1973-74). Office: 201 1st Nat Bank Bldg Hibbing MN 55746

MINTZ, M. J., b. Phila., Oct. 29, 1940; B.S., Temple U., 1961, J.D., 1968. Admitted to D.C. bar, 1969; atty., adviser to judge U.S. Tax Ct., Washington, 1968-70; asst. gen. counsel Cost of Living Council, Washington, 1971-73; partner firm Dickstein, Shapiro & Morin, Washington, 1973—; adj. prof. law Internat. Sch. Law, Washington, 1974—. Mem. D.C. Bar, Bar Assn. D.C., Am. Bar Assn., Am. Inst. C.P.A.'s. Office: 2101 L St NW Washington DC 20037 Tel (202) 785-9700

MINTZ, SEYMOUR STANLEY, b. Newark, Mar. 7, 1912; A.B., George Washington U., 1933, J.D., 1936. Admitted to D.C. bar, 1936; atty. Office Undersec. Treasury, 1937-38, Office Chief Counsel, IRS, 1938-42; asso. firm Hogan & Hartson, Washington, 1946-49, partner, 1949—; dir. Republic Steel Corp., Cleve., Dynalectron Corp., Washington; adj. prof. Georgetown U. Law Sch., 1952-55; mem. adv. group to commr. Internal Revenue, 1961. Mem. Am., Fed., D.C. bar assns., Am. Law Inst., Order of Coif. Contbr. articles to profl. jours. Office: 815 Connecticut Ave NW Washington DC 20006 Tel (202) 331-4608

MIRABEL, JOSEPH THOMAS, b. Bklyn., May 22, 1916; LL.B., St. John's U., 1947. Admitted to N.Y. bar, 1947; practice law, Huntington, N.Y. Fellow Am. Coll. Trial Lawyers; mem. N.Y. State (sec.), Nassau and Suffolk County (N.Y.) (exec. com.), Nassau County, Suffolk County bar assns. Columbian Lawyers Assn., Assn. Trial Lawyers Am. Author: (with others) Law of Negligence. Office: 56 E Carver St Huntington NY 11743 Tel (516) 271-3800

MIRABILE, THOMAS JOSEPH, b. Bklyn., Mar. 22, 1908; B.C.S., Sch. Commerce N.Y. U., 1927; LL.B., Bklyn. Law Sch., 1930; grad. Nat. Coll. State Trial Judges U. Nev., 1967. Admitted to N.Y. bar, 1932; practice law in N.Y.C.; mem. N.Y.C. Council, 1947-60; judge Municipal Ct., N.Y.C., 1960-61, N.Y.C. Civil Ct., 1962-72; justice N.Y. State Supreme Ct., Bklyn., 1973—. Mem. Am. Bar Assn., Bklyn. Bar, Kings County (N.Y.) Criminal Bar, Columbian Lawyers Assn., Am. Justinian Soc. of Jurists, Bklyn. Soc. Architects (hon. life). Home: 85-26 Edgerton Blvd Jamaica NY 11432 Office: 360 Adams St Brooklyn NY 11201 Tel (212) 643-3195

MIRARCHI, CHARLES P., JR., b. Phila., Aug. 27, 1924; B.S., Temple U., 1944, J.D., 1948. Admitted to Pa. bar, 1948, U.S. Supreme Ct. bar; since practiced in Phila., partner firm Mirarchi, De Fino & Coppolino, 1948-71; judge Ct. of Common Pleas, 1971—; trustee Phila. Prisons, 1968-71; adj. prof. law Del. Law Sch., 1975—. Dist. chmn. Boy Scouts Am.; active charity fund-raising drives. Mem. Pa. Conf. State Trial Judges (exec. mem.), Am., Pa., Phila. bar assns., The Justinian Soc., Am. Judicature Soc., St. Thomas More Soc. Recipient Service awards various orgns. Home: 1329 Morris St Philadelphia PA 19148 Office: 336 City Hall Philadelphia PA 19107 Tel (215) MU6-7342

MIRASSOU, JEAN BERNARD, b. Los Angeles, Apr. 1, 1929; B.S., Loyola U., 1951; LL.B., U. So. Calif., 1958. Admitted to Calif. bar, 1958; asso. firm MacFaden & Hall, Calif., 1958-60; mem. firm Hall & Mirassou, 1960-68, Wegener & Mirassou, 1968-76, Wegener, Mirassou & Clark, Redondo Beach, Calif., 1976—; city atty. City of Hermosa Beach, 1968—. City councilman, Redondo Beach, 1961-65. Mem. State Bar Calif., South Bay, Los Angeles County, Am. bar assns., Comml. Law League Am. Home: 200 Vista del Parque Redondo Beach CA 90277 Office: 1611 S Pacific Coast Hwy Redondo Beach CA 90277 Tel (213) 540-5201

MIRICK, JOHN ODLIN, b. Worcester, Mass., Nov. 27, 1946; B.A. magna cum laude, Amherst Coll., 1968; M.A., U. London, 1969; J.D. cum laude, Harvard, 1972. Admitted to Mass. bar, 1972; asso. firm Hale & Dorr, Boston, 1972-76, Mirick, O'Connell, DeMallie & Lougee, Worcester, 1976—. Mem. Am., Mass. bar assns. Office: 1700 Mechanics National Tower Worcester MA 01608 Tel (617) 799-0541

MIRIKITANI, CARL KUNIO, b. Honolulu, Jan. 16, 1948; B.A. magna cum laude, Oberlin Coll., 1969; J.D., U. Chgo., 1972. Admitted to Hawaii bar, 1972; law clerk to Justice Bernard H. Levinson Hawaii Supreme Ct., Honolulu, 1972; partner firm Goodsill, Anderson & Quinn, Honolulu, 1977—. Active Republican Party of Hawaii, Honolulu, 1973—; del. Republican Nat. Conv., 1976. Mem. Hawaii State Bar Assn., Order Coif, Phi Beta Kappa. Mem. Chgo. Law Rev. Tel (808) 531-5066

MIRMAN, JOEL HARVEY, b. Toledo, Dec. 3, 1941; B.B.A., Ohio U., 1963; J.D., Ohio State U., 1966. Admitted to Ohio bar, 1966, U.S. Supreme Ct. bar, 1972; asso. firm Topper, Alloway, Goodman, DeLeone & Duffey, Columbus, Ohio, 1966-71, partner, 1971—; lectr. Ohio Legal Inst., 1973-75, Ohio Jud. Conf., 1976. Mem. Ohio Elections Commn., 1976—. Mem. Am., Ohio, Columbus bar assns. Home: 872 Harvest Ln Ct Columbus OH 43213 Office: 17 S High St Columbus OH 43215 Tel (614) 221-2341

MISHEFF, ALEXANDER PETER, b. Red Wing, Minn., Feb. 15, 1934; A.B. cum laude, Harvard, 1956, LL.B., 1959. Admitted to Ill. bar, 1960; with Continental Ill. Nat. Bank & Trust Co., Chgo., 1960—, asst. sec., 1964-68, trust officer, 1968-71, trust counsel, 1971-76, sr. atty., 1976—; lectr. trust and estate law. Mem. Chgo. Bar Assn. Contbr. to Trust Administration in Illinois, 1976. Home: 910 N Lake Shore Dr apt 2316 Chicago IL 60611 Office: 231 S LaSalle St Room 1787 Chicago IL 60693 Tel (312) 828-6922

MISHKIN, ESAU JACOB, b. Morristown, N.J., July 1, 1918; B.A., Drew U., 1939; LL.B., Bklyn. Law Sch., 1946, J.D., 1967. Admitted to N.Y. State bar, 1946, Fla. bar, 1958, U.S. Supreme Ct. bar, 1956; individual practice law, Mineola, N.Y., 1952-64, 68—, Sarasota, Fla., 1958—; sr. partner firm Mishkin, Miner, Harwood & Semel, Garden City, N.Y., 1964-68. Atty., dir. Roslyn Vis. Nurses Assn., North Shore Vis. Nurses Assn., 1969-75. Mem. Nassau County Bar Assn., N.Y. County Lawyers Assn., The Fla. Bar (exec. mem. trial tactics commn. 1962-66), N.Y. State Assn. Trial Lawyers (dir. 1952-65, gov. 19th dist. 1965—), Am. Trial Lawyers Assn. (asso. editor in tort law 1952—), Met. Trial Lawyers Assn., Nassau-Suffolk Trial Lawyers Assn., Nassau Lawyers Assn. L.I. Office: 370 E Old Country Rd Garden City NY 11530 Tel (516) 741-4114

MISHKIN, PAUL J., b. Trenton, N.J., Jan. 1, 1927; A.B., Columbia, 1947, LL.B., 1950; M.A. (hon.), U. Pa., 1971. Admitted to N.Y. bar, 1950, U.S. Supreme Ct. bar, 1958; law faculty U. Pa., 1950-73; prof. Law U. Calif. at Berkeley, 1973-75, Emanuel S. Heller prof., 1975—; faculty Salzburg Seminar in Am. Studies, 1974; Charles Inglis Thompson guest prof. U. Colo., 1975; cons. City of Phila., 1953; reporter Am. Law Inst. study div. jurisdiction between state and fed. cts., 1960-65. Trustee Jewish Publ. Soc. Am., 1966-75. Fellow Am. Acad. Arts and Scis., Am. Bar Found.; mem. Am. Law Inst., Phi Beta Kappa. Author: (with Morris) On Law in Courts, 1965; (with Bator, Shapiro and Wechsler) Federal Courts and the Federal System, 1973, Supplement, 1977. Contbr. articles in field to legal jours. Center for Advanced Study in the Behavioral Sciences fellow, 1964-65; Rockefeller Found. research grantee, 1956. Home: 91 Stonewall Rd Berkeley CA 94705 Office: Boalt Hall U Calif Berkeley CA 94720 Tel (415) 642-1860

MISHLER, JACOB, b. N.Y.C., Apr. 20, 1911; B.S., N.Y.C., 1931, J.D., 1933. Admitted to N.Y. State bar, 1934; practiced in Long Island City, N.Y., 1934-59; justice N.Y. Supreme Ct., 10th Jud. Dist., 1959-60; U.S. dist. judge Eastern Dist. N.Y., 1960-69, chief judge, 1969—. Mem. Electoral Coll., 1952. Bd. dirs. Boys Club Queens. Mem. Queens County bar Assn. Home: Birchwood Towers Forest Hills Queens NY 11827 Office: Courthouse 225 Cadman Plaza E Brooklyn NY 11201*

MISROCK, S. LESLIE, b. Jersey City, Feb. 26, 1928; B.S., Mass. Inst. Tech., 1955; A.M., Columbia, 1956; LL.B., Fordham U., 1959. Admitted to N.Y. bar, 1960, U.S. Supreme Ct. bar, 1976; asso. firm Pennie & Edmonds, and predecessors, N.Y.C., 1955-63, partner, 1964—, sr. partner, 1972—. Fellow Am. Inst. Chemists, Chem. Soc. (London), Am. Chem. Soc.; mem. Am. Bar Assn., Am., N.Y. patent law assns., Assn. Bar City N.Y. Home: 74 Hilltop Dr Chappaqua NY 10514 Office: 330 Madison Ave New York City NY 10017 Tel (212) 986-8686

MISSAN, RICHARD SHERMAN, b. New Haven, Conn., Oct. 5, 1933; B.A., Yale, 1955, J.D., 1958. Admitted to N.Y. bar, 1959; asso. law firm Marshall, Bratter, Greene, Allison, & Tucker, N.Y.C., 1959-62; asso. law firm Kaye, Scholer, Fierman, Hays & Handler, N.Y.C., 1962-67; partner law firm Schoenfeld & Jacobs, N.Y.C., 1968—. Mem. Assn. of Bar of City N.Y., Fed. Bar Council, Am., N.Y. State bar assns. Home: 301 E 78th St New York City NY 10021 Office: 225 W 44th St New York City NY 10036

MITCHELL, ALDUS SAMUEL, b. Birmingham, Ala., June 24, 1930; B.A., Lincoln U., 1955; J.D., U. Chgo., 1958. Admitted to Ill. bar, 1958, U.S. Supreme Ct. bar, 1971; asso. firm Amiel G. Hall, Chgo., 1958-59; partner firm Posey & Mitchell, Chgo., 1959-66; asso. firm McCoy Ming & Black, Chgo., 1966-76; prin. firm Mitchell Hall & Jones, Chgo., 1976—. Chmn. com. legal redress Chgo. chpt. NAACP, 1975-76, pres. South Shore chpt., 1976-78. Mem. Ill. State, Chgo., Cook County (Ill.) bar assns. Office: 110 S Dearborn St Chicago IL 60603 Tel (312) 346-6789

MITCHELL, BRADFORD WILLIAM, b. Lewiston, Maine, Aug. 14, 1927; student U. Maine, 1947-49; LL.B., Boston U., 1952. Admitted to Maine bar, 1952, Mass. bar, 1952, N.H. bar, 1967, Pa. bar, 1976, U.S. Supreme Ct. bar, 1971, U.S. Ct. Mil. Appeals bar, 1974; served to capt. JAGC, U.S. Army, 1952-59; asst. gen. counsel Am. Mut. Liability Ins. Co., Wakefield, Mass., 1959-67, asst. v.p., 1963-67; gen. counsel Nat. Grange Mut. Ins. Co., Keene, N.H., 1967-73, also dir., corporate sec., 1971-75, exec. v.p., 1973-75; pres. Harleysville (Pa.) Mut. Ins. Co., 1976—, also dir. Chmn. campaign Monadnock United Fund, Keene, 1974, Am. Cancer Soc., Keene,

1973, chmn. City of Keene Sunday Sales Com., 1971; pres. Keene PTA, 1970. Mem. Am., N.H. bar assns., Keene C. of C. (pres. 1973). Contbr. articles to jours. and newspapers. Home: 54 Water Crest Dr Doylestown PA 18901 Office: 355 Maple Ave Harleysville PA 19438

MITCHELL, DALE BRYANT, b. Centralia, Ill., Sept. 26, 1940; B.S., Murray State Coll., 1963; J.D., U. Ky., 1966. Admitted to Ky. bar, 1967; dist. atty. Commonwealth of Ky. Dept. Hwys., 1967; legal staff to commr. Ky. Dept. Pub. Safety, Frankfort, 1968-69; partner firm Martin, Scalf & Mitchell, Corbin, Ky., 1969-70, Burns, Maricle & Mitchell, Manchester and Somerset, Ky., 1970-72, Mitchell & Gillum, Somerset, 1975—; individual practice law, Somerset, 1972-75. Bd. dirs. Somerset YMCA. Mem. Am. Judicature Soc., Ky., Pulaski bar assns. Home: 509 Cardinal Dr Somerset KY 42501 Office: 102 W Columbia St PO Box 111 Somerset KY 42501 Tel (606) 679-6347

MITCHELL, DAVID WALKER, b. Oakland, Calif., Nov. 11, 1935; A.B., Stanford, 1957; J.D., Harvard, 1960. Admitted to Calif. bar, 1961, U.S. Supreme Ct. bar, 1975; asso. firm Kindel & Anderson, Los Angeles, 1961-65, Weir, Hopkins, Donovan & Zavlaris, San Jose, Calif., 1965-67; mem. firm Hopkins & Carley, and predecessors, San Jose, 1967—; mem. bd. dirs. Com. Trust, Santa Clara Co., 1975—. Bd. dirs. Miramonte Mental Health Services, 1970-76, Friends Outside, 1965-74. Mem. Am., Calif., Santa Clara County bar assns., San Jose C. of C. (dir. 1974—). Office: 101 Park Center Plaza San Jose CA 95113 Tel (408) 286-9800

MITCHELL, DEAN WADE, b. Woodward, Iowa, May 22, 1917; J.D., Drake U., 1940. Admitted to Iowa bar, 1940; practiced in Des Moines, 1940-41; claims adjuster Farmers Ins. Group, Los Angeles, 1941-42, br. claims mgr., Des Moines, 1942-45, Kansas City, Mo., 1945-48; asst. mgr. Iowa Farm Mut. Ins. Co., Des Moines, 1948-51, Iowa Mut. Hail Co., Des Moines, 1951-53, Iowa Life Co., Des Moines, 1953-57; gen. mgr. Farm Bur. Mut. and Farm Bur. Life cos., West Des Moines, 1957—, exec. v.p., 1963—; pres. PFS Mgmt. Services, Inc. Bd. dirs. Health Planning Assembly of Polk County (Iowa), Des Moines YMCA; mem. ways and means com. Nat. Assn. Retarded Citizens. Mem. Nat. Assn. Ind. Insurers (chmn. 1976), Iowa, Am., Polk County bar assns., Iowa Ins. Inst., Delta Theta Phi. Home: Route 1 Bouton IA 50039 Office: 5400 University St West Des Moines IA 50265 Tel (515) 225-5661

MITCHELL, GEORGE ALBERT, b. Warrior, Ala., Oct. 4, 1901; B.A., Samford U., 1932, B.S., 1933, M.A., 1935, LL.B., 1942, J.D., 1968. Admitted to Ala. bar, 1943; tchr. Jefferson (Ala.) County schs., 1922-30; dep. sheriff Jefferson County., 1935-47; tchr. math Tarrant (Ala.) High Sch., 1947-51; supt. Tarrant (Ala.) Pub. Sch. system, 1951-62; asso. firm Emond and Vines, Birmingham, Ala., 1962-68; dep. dist. atty. Jefferson County, 1968-71; individual practice law, Birmingham, 1971—. Pres. Tarrant Tchrs. Assn., 1935-37. Mem. Am., Ala., Birmingham bar assns. Home: 3527 W Lakeside Dr Birmingham AL 35243 Office: 710 Massey Bldg Birmingham AL 35203 Tel (205) 324-6611

MITCHELL, HENRY VINCENT EDWARDS, b. Wilkes-Barre, Pa., Dec. 10, 1915; B.A., Williams Coll., 1938; LL.B., Yale U., 1941. Admitted to D.C. bar, 1941, Oreg. bar, 1942, Ohio bar, 1942; asso. firm Bowman & Bailey, Springfield, Ohio, 1941-42; atty. Bonneville Power Adminstrn., Oreg., 1942-43; asso. firm McAfee, Hanning, Newcomer, Hazlett & Wheeler, Cleve., 1943-67, Squire, Sanders & Dempsey, Cleve., 1967—. Mem. Am., Fed., Ohio, D.C., Cuyahoga County, Greater Cleve. bar assns., Am. Coll. Trial Lawyers. Office: 1800 Union Commerce Bldg Euclid Ave Cleveland OH 44115 Tel (216) 696-9200

MITCHELL, JACK HARRIS, III, b. Birmingham, Ala., Sept. 9, 1947; B.S. in Chem. Engring., Clemson U., 1969; J.D., Vanderbilt U., 1972. Admitted to Tenn. bar, 1972, S.C. bar, 1973; served with JAGC, USAF, 1972-73; asso. Horton, Greenville, S.C., 1973; prin. Dillard & Mitchell, P.A., Greenville, 1973—. Mem. Greenville County (S.C.), Am. bar assns., S.C. Bar. Office: 119 Manly St Greenville SC 29601 Tel (803) 271-8610

MITCHELL, JOHN ANDREW, b. Schenectady, Apr. 23, 1934; B.S., St. Lawrence U., 19—; LL.B., Mich. U., 1961. Admitted to Calif. bar, 1961; law clk. to judge, San Diego, 1961-62; asst. U.S. atty., Los Angeles, 1962-65, San Diego, 1966-68; asso., trial lawyer firm Dryden, Harrington & Schwartz, Los Angeles, 1965-66; partner, trial lawyer firm Sullivan, Jones & Mitchell, San Diego, 1968-70; partner, trial lawyer firm Mitchell, Schmidt, D'Amico, McCabe & Stutz, San Diego, 1970—; staff atty. Calif. Gov's. Commn. on Los Angeles Riots, 1965. Mem. Calif., San Diego, Am. bar assns., Calif., San Diego trial lawyers assns., Am. Bd. Trial Advocates. Home: 10831 Melva Rd La Mesa CA 92041 Office: 2170 4th Ave San Diego CA 92101 Tel (714) 236-1133

MITCHELL, JOHN J., JR., b. Washington, Jan. 30, 1933; B.A., Pomona Coll., 1958; J.D., Hastings Coll. Law, 1963. Admitted to Calif. bar, 1964, U.S. Supreme Ct. bar, 1969, U.S. Ct. Appeals bar 9th Circuit, 1964, U.S. Dist. Ct. bars No. and So. Dists. Calif., 1964; asso. firm Ross & Harris, Santa Barbara, Calif., 1964-65; dep. county counsel, Santa Barbara, 1965-73; individual practice law, Santa Barbara, 1973—. Mem. adv. bd. Salvation Army, 1966—, chmn., 1975-77; mem. profl. com. Santa Barbara Mus. Art, 1976; trustee Hastings Law Center Found. Mem. Santa Barbara County Bar Assn. Office: PO Box 4601 Santa Barbara CA 93103 Tel (805) 969-0100

MITCHELL, JOHN JOSEPH, b. Malden, Mass., Dec. 26, 1926; student Georgetown U., 1946-49; LL.B., Am. U., 1956. Admitted to Md. bar, 1957, D.C. bar, 1958, U.S. Supreme Ct. bar, 1963; asso. firm Vance V. Vaughan, Brentwood, Md., 1957-58, firm Miazga & Miazga, Riverdale, Md., 1958-62; partner firm Domahue, Ehrmantraut and Mitchell, Rockville, Md., 1962-68; pub. defender Montgomery County (Md.), 1968-72, Md. 6th Dist., 1972-73; judge Montgomery County Dist. Ct., 6th Dist., 1973, Montgomery County Circuit Ct., 6th Dist., 1973—; mem. Montgomery County Criminal Justice Commn., 1968-72; mem. Md. Gov.'s Commn. on Law Enforcement, 1969-72; chmn. Dist. 6 Adv. Bd. for Pub. Defender System Md., 1975—. Mem. Montgomery County Drug Abuse Commn., 1970-72; co-founder Prince George's County (Md.) Legal Aid Bur., 1960. Mem. Am., Md. State, Montgomery County bar assns., Md. Jud. Conf., Md. State's Atty. Assn. Home: 4925 Flanders Ave Kensington MD 20795 Office: 27 Courthouse Sq Rockville MD 20850 Tel (301) 279-8352

MITCHELL, LEE MARK, b. Albany, N.Y., Apr. 16, 1943; A.B., Wesleyan U., Middletown, Conn., 1965; J.D., U. Chgo., 1968. Admitted to Ill. bar, 1968, D.C. bar, 1969, U.S. Supreme Ct. bar, 1972; asso. firm Leibman, Williams, Bennett, Baird and Minow, Chgo., 1968-69, Washington, 1969-72; mem. firm Sidley and Austin, Washington, 1972—, partner, 1974—; co-dir. Twentieth Century Fund, Polit. Access to TV Project, 1971-72, rapporteur Task Force on Pub. Affairs TV, 1974; del. Brit. Legislators' Conf. on Govt. and Media, Eng., 1974; adv. com. on clin. edn. Law. Sch., U. Chgo., 1975—. Mem. Fed. Communications, Fed., Chgo. bar assns., Am. Arbitration Assn., Nat. Lawyers Club, Nat. Press Club. Author: Presidential Television, 1973; Broadcasting the Legislature, 1974; contbr. articles to books, publs. Home: 1323 Kirby Rd McLean VA 22101 Office: 1730 Pennsylvania Ave NW Washington DC 20006 Tel (202) 624-9000

MITCHELL, LEROY WILLIAM, b. Murphysboro, Ill., July 26, 1927; B.E.E., Rose Poly. Inst., 1949; J.D., DePaul U., 1954. Mem. firm Leydig, Voit, Osann, Mayer & Holt, Ltd., Chgo. and Rockford, Ill., 1953—; admitted to Ill. bar, 1955, U.S. Patent Office bar, 1955. Pres. Lake Summerset Assn., Durand, Ill., 1972-73. Mem. Am., Chgo., Winnebago County (Ill.) bar assns., Am., Chgo. patent law assns., IEEE, Am. Legion, Lambda Chi Alpha, Tau Beta Pi, Delta Theta Phi. Office: 815 N Church St Rockford IL 61103 Tel (815) 963-7661

MITCHELL, MILTON, b. Rochester, N.Y., Apr. 6, 1916; J.D., George Washington U., 1942. Admitted to D.C. bar, 1941, U.S. Supreme Ct., 1966; atty. Bur. Customs, Washington, 1945-50; asst. chief protocol Dept. State, Washington, 1950-64, sr. atty., 1964-69; lectr. internat. law Nat. Law Center, George Washington U., Washington, 1964—; gen. counsel Accuracy In Media, Inc., Washington, 1973—. Mem. Fed. Bar Assn. Home and Office: 9510 Hale St Silver Spring MD 20910 Tel (301) 585-4663

MITCHELL, PATRICK HOWARD, b. Enumclaw, Wash., July 12, 1941; B.A., Willamette U., 1963; J.D., Stanford U., 1969. Admitted to Calif. bar, 1970, D.C. bar, 1970, U.S. Supreme Ct. bar, 1973; spl. counsel U.S. Senate Com. on Internal and Insular Affairs, 1969; asso. firm Ely Duncan, Washington, 1970; partner firm Duncan, Allen & Mitchell, Washington, 1970—; v.p. Am. Bus. Assn. Zaire, 1975-76, pres., 1976-77. Mem. Am., Fed. Power bar assns., Internat. Law Assn. Contbr. articles to legal jours. Home: BP 12368 Kinshasa 1 Zaire Office: 1775 K St NW Washington DC 20006 Tel (202) 833-2300

MITCHELL, RANDALL LARRABEE, b. Chgo., June 15, 1942; B.A., U. Mich., 1964; J.D., U. Ill., 1967. Admitted to Ill. bar, 1967, U.S. Dist. Ct. bar, 1971, Circuit Ct. Appeals, 1971; asso. firm Chapman & Cutler, Chgo., 1971—. Mem. Am., Ill. bar assns. Home: 207 Maple Rd Barrington IL 60010 Office: 111 W Monroe St Chicago IL 60603 Tel (312) 726-6130

MITCHELL, ROBERT CHARLES, b. N.Y.C., Aug. 4, 1940; A.B., Dartmouth, 1962; M.B.A., U. Pitts., 1964, LL.B., 1967, J.D., 1970. Admitted to Pa. bar, 1968, U.S. Supreme Ct. bar, 1971; since practiced in Pitts.; individual practice, 1967-68; law clk. U.S. Dist. Ct., 1968-72, magistrate, U.S. Dist. Ct. Western Pa., 1972—. Mem. Am., Pa., Allegheny County bar assns., Am. Judicature Soc. Office: 501 US Post Office and Courthouse Pittsburgh PA 15219 Tel (412) 644-3548

MITCHELL, ROBERT LAURIE, b. Washington, Jan. 30, 1923; B.A., U. Md., 1949; LL.B. (now J.D.), Emory U., 1954. Admitted to Md. bar, 1959, U.S. Ct. Mil. Appeals, 1960, U.S. Supreme Ct. bar, 1963; served with U.S. Air Force, 1942-46, 50-68; individual practice law, La Plata, Md., 1968-74; partner firm Mitchell & Ellinger, La Plata, 1975—. Bd. govs. Charles County (Md.) Bicentennial Com., Inc., La Plata, 1975, Charles County Children's Aid Soc., La Plata, 1976—. Mem. Md., Charles County (pres. 1970) bar assns., Trial Judges Assn. Md., Air Force Assn., Ret. Officers Assn. Home: Oak Grove Box 966 La Plata MD 20646 Office: Box 966 114 La Grange Ave La Plata MD 20646 Tel (301) 934-4292

MITCHELL, STEPHENS, b. Atlanta, Jan. 14, 1896; A.B., U. Ga., 1915; LL.B., 1919. Admitted to Ga. bar, 1920; 1935; partner firm Mitchell & Mitchell, Atlanta, 1919-56, firm Mitchell, Clarke, Pate & Anderson, Atlanta, 1956—. Pres., Atlanta Hist. Soc., 1956-58, chmn., 1958-67; mem. Conf. Soc. St. Vincent DePaul. Mem. Am., Internat., Ga., Atlanta (pres. 1937) bar assns., Lawyers Club Atlanta (pres. 1933). Author: (with Powell) Actions for Land, 1946; Real Property in Georgia, 1945. Home: 3358 Habersham Rd NW Atlanta GA 30305 Office: 600 Atlanta Fed Savings Bldg Atlanta GA 30303 Tel (404) 577-6010

MITCHELL, STUART MALCOLM, b. Bklyn., Aug. 8, 1932; B.A., Bklyn. Coll., 1954; LL.B., St. John's U., 1956. Admitted to N.Y. bar, 1957; asso. firm Roosevelt & Frieden, N.Y.C., 1956-58, firm Crisona Bros., N.Y.C., 1958-60; individual practice law, Nyack, N.Y., 1960—; lectr. bus. law Rockland Community Coll., Suffern, N.Y., 1968, Dominican Coll., Blauvelt, N.Y., 1974. Mem. N.Y., Rockland County bar assns., Nyack C. of C. Office: 81 1st Ave Nyack NY 10960 Tel (914) 358-4300

MITCHELL, WALTER LOUIS, III, b. Orange, N.J., Feb. 20, 1945; B.A., Yale U., 1967; J.D., Boston U., 1970. Admitted to N.H. bar, 1970; partner firm Nighswander Lord Martin & Killikelley, Laconia, N.H. Mem. Meredith (N.H.) Planning Bd., 1975—; chmn., 1976-77. Mem. Am., N.H., Belknap County bar assns. Home: RFD 3 Keyser Rd Meredith NH 03253 Office: PO Box 189 1 Mill Plaza Laconia NH 03246 Tel (603) 524-4121

MITCHELL, WILLIAM BUFORD, b. Musella, Ga., Apr. 7, 1911; student Mercer U., 1927-28. Admitted to Ga. bar, 1935; individual practice law, Roberta, Ga., 1935-36, Forsyth, Ga., 1936—. State rep., Gen. Assembly Ga., 1943-49; dist. sec. Lions Internat., 1942. Mem. State Bar Ga., Flint Circuit Bar Assn. (pres., 1967-68), Ga. Trial Lawyers' Assn. Home: 100 W Johnston St Forsyth GA 31029 Office: 90 W Johnston St Forsyth GA 31029 Tel (912) 994-5238

MITHERZ, HAROLD, b. N.Y.C., July 15, 1917; B.S., N.Y. U., 1938, LL.B., 1940, J.D., 1968. Admitted to N.Y. State bar, 1941, U.S. Supreme Ct. bar; since practiced in N.Y.C., individual practice law, 1946-50; asso., partner firm Tanzer, Mullaney, Mitherz & Pratt, to 1975; of counsel Kurzman & Frank, 1975—; dir. Whatman, Reeve Angel Inc., Maidstone, Kent, Eng., 1959-76; asso. justice Village of Thomaston (N.Y.), 1975-76, justice, 1977—, trustee, 1966-68. Mem. Am., N.Y. State bar assns., N.Y. County Lawyers Assn. Home: 7 Grace Ct N Great Neck NY 11021 Office: 230 Park Ave New York City NY 10017 Tel (212) 867-9500

MITTEL, ROBERT EDMOND, b. San Francisco, Mar. 14, 1941; A.B., U. Calif., 1963; LL.B., Hastings Coll. Law, 1966. Admitted to Calif. bar, 1963, Maine bar, 1969, Fed. bar, 1969, U.S. Ct. Appeals, bar, 1970; mem. Pine Tree Legal Assistance, Portland, Maine, 1968-76, dir. litigation unit, 1968-76; atty. Eastern Indian Research Project, Portland, 1972-73; asso. firm Sewall & White, Portland, 1976—. Mem. Maine Bar Assn., ACLU. Office: 80 Exchange St Portland ME 04111 Tel (207) 775-3101

MITTLEBEELER, EMMET VAUGHN, b. Louisville, Aug. 8, 1915; B.A., U. Louisville, 1936, LL.B., 1939, J.D., 1970; M.A., U. Chgo., 1950, Ph.D., 1951. Admitted to Ky. bar, 1939, U.S. Supreme Ct. bar, 1953; mem. staff Legal Aid Soc. Louisville, 1939-40; clk. Ky. Statute Revision Commn., Frankfort, 1940-42; asst. atty. gen. Office Atty. Gen. Ky., Frankfort, 1945-48; individual practice law, Louisville, and lectr. U. Louisville, 1948, 51-53; asst. prof. govt. and pub. adminstrn. Am. U., 1954-57, asso. prof., 1957-61, prof., 1961—; asst. to Congressman John M. Robsion, Jr., 1953-54; Fulbright-Hays prof. U. Coll. Rhodesia and Nyasaland, Salisbury, So. Rhodesia, 1962-63; vis. prof. Faculty Law, Inst. Adminstrn. U. Ife, Ile-Ife and Ibadan, Nigeria, 1969-70; Fulbright Hays prof. Inst. Adminstrn. Ahmadu Bello U., Zaria, Nigeria, 1976-77; cons. in field. Mem. Ky. Bar Assn., Am. Polit. Sci. Assn., AAUP, African Law Assn., Ky. Hist. Soc., Filson Club, Phi Alpha Delta, Pi Sigma Alpha. Author: African Custom and Western Law, 1976; contbr. publs.; contbg. editor: Dictionary of Political Science, 1964. Home: 2007 Grasmere Dr Louisville KY 40205 Office: Am U Washington DC 20016 Tel (212) 686-2377

MITTLER, AUSTIN STUART, b. Far Rockaway, N.Y., Apr. 2, 1939; B.A., Dartmouth Coll., 1960; LL.B., N.Y. U., 1963. Admitted to N.Y. State bar, 1963, D.C. bar, 1968; legal research asst. Dist. Atty.'s Office Queens County (N.Y.), 1961; summer asst. U.S. Atty.'s Office, Eastern Dist. N.Y., 1962; trial atty. criminal div. U.S. Dept. Justice, 1963-66, spl. asst. U.S. atty., 1966; law sec. to justice Supreme Ct. Queens County, 1966; spl. atty. criminal div. U.S. Dept. Justice, 1967, staff asst. to asst. atty. gen., 1967-68; mem. firm Hogan and Hartson, Washington, 1968—. Mem. Am., D.C. bar assns., N.Y. U. Law Alumni Assn., Am. Judicature Soc. Home: 9002 Shad Ln Potomac MD 20854 Office: 815 Connecticut Ave NW Washington DC 20006 Tel (202) 331-4582

MITZNER, IRA ROBERT, b. Bklyn., July 24, 1947; B.A. in Polit. Sci. cum laude, Brown U., 1969; J.D., Georgetown U., 1973. Admitted to D.C. bar, 1973; asso. firm Dickstein, Shapiro & Morin, Washington, 1973—, law clk., 1971-73. Mem. Am., D.C. bar assns. Office: 2101 L St NW Washington DC 20037

MIUCCIO, ALEXANDER A., b. N.Y.C., Aug. 1, 1934; B.S., Fordham U., 1955; LL.B., St. John's U., 1958. Admitted to N.Y. bar, 1959; partner firm Altieri, Kushner & Miuccio, N.Y.C., 1969—. Office: 41 E 42d St New York City NY 10017 Tel (212) 687-2055

MIXTER, FRANK GLEN, b. Fairgrove, Mich., Apr. 24, 1899; LL.M., Detroit Coll. Law, 1924. Admitted to Mich. bar, 1925; individual practice law, Detroit, 1925-65; sch. atty. City of Lincoln Park, Mich., 1925-33, 51-65, city atty., 1929-35. Mem. Lincoln Park Library Commn., 1931-36, Lincoln Park Bd. Edn., 1933-51. Mem. Mich. Bar Assn. (award 1975). Office: 1100 Southfield Rd Lincoln Park MI 48146 Tel (313) 382-4411

MIYASAKI, SHUICHI, b. Paauilo, Hawaii, Aug. 6, 1928; B.S. in Civil engring., U. Hawaii, 1951; J.D., U. Minn., 1957; LL.M. in Taxation with honors, Georgetown U., 1959. Civil engr. Japan Constrn. Agy., Tokyo, 1953-54; admitted to Minn. bar, 1957, Hawaii bar, 1959; examiner U.S. Patent Office, Washington, 1957-59; dep. atty. gen. State of Hawaii, 1960-61; mem. firm Okumura Takushi Funaki & Wee, Honolulu, 1961—; atty. Hawaii Senate, 1961; chief counsel Hawaii Senate Ways and Means Com., 1962, Senate Judiciary Com., 1967-70; mem. staff Judge Adv. Gen. Corps USAR, 1963—. Instnl. rep. Aloha council Boy Scouts Am., 1963—; exec. com., sec., dir. Legal Aid Soc. Hawaii, 1970-72. Mem. Am., Hawaii (chmn. legis. com. 1975-76) bar assns., U.S. Patent Office Soc., Hawaii Estate Planning Council, Phi Delta Phi. Home: 1552 Bertram St Honolulu HI 96816 Office: suite 500 Alexander Young Bldg 1015 Bishop St Honolulu HI 96813 Tel (808) 536-1791

MIZE, ARNOLD MAX, b. Soldier, Kans., Jan. 28, 1940; B.B.A., Washburn U., Topeka, 1961, J.D., 1964. Admitted to Kans. bar, 1964; individual practice law, Derby, Kans., 1964—. Former pres. Derby C. of C.. Mem. Am., Kans., Wichita bar assns. Recipient Am. Jurisprudence prize; Nat. Americanism certificate Am. Legion. Office: 212 E Madison St Derby KS 67037 Tel (316) 788-2859

MIZE, WEBB MORSE, b. Forest, Miss., Mar. 19, 1910; student Millsaps Coll., 1926-27; B.A., U. Miss., 1930, LL.B., 1932, J.D., 1968. Admitted to Miss. bar, 1932; partner firm Mize, Thompson & Mize, Gulfport, Miss., 1932-71, Mize, Thompson & Blass, 1971—; asst. atty. gen. State of Miss., Jackson, 1936-37. Fellow Am. Coll. Probate Counsel, Miss. Bar Found.; mem. Am. Bar Assn. Home: 9 Mockingbird Ln Gulfport MS 39501 Office: 310 Gulf Nat Bank Bldg Gulfport MS 39501 Tel (601) 863-2612

MLSNA, TIMOTHY MARTIN, b. Berwyn, Ill., Feb. 13, 1947; B.A., MacMurray Coll., 1969; J.D. cum laude, Northwestern U., 1974. Admitted to Ill. bar. 1974, U.S. Dist. Ct. bar, 1974; asso. firm McDermott, Will & Emery, Chicago, Ill., 1974—. Mem. Am., Ill., Chgo. bar assns. Office: 111 W Monroe St Chicago IL 60603 Tel (312) 372-2000

MMAHAT, JOHN ANTHONY, b. New Orleans, Sept. 5, 1931; B.A., Tulane U., 1956, J.D., 1958. Admitted to La. bar, 1958; sr. partner firm Mmahat, Gagliano, Duffy & Giordano, Metairie, La. Mem. Delgado Art Mus.; Democratic presdl. elector, 1976. Mem. Fed., Am., New Orleans, Jefferson bar assns., Am. Coll. Mortgage Attys., La. Landmark Soc., Friends Cabildo. Home: 1239 1st St New Orleans LA 70130 Office: 5500 Veterans Meml Blvd Metairie LA 70003 Tel (504) 887-6962

MNOOKIN, ROBERT HARRIS, b. Kansas City, Mo., Feb. 4, 1942; A.B., Harvard, 1964, LL.B., 1968. Admitted to D.C. bar, 1969, Calif. bar, 1970; asso. firm Howard, Prim, Smith, Rice & Downs, San Francisco, 1970-72, counsel, 1972—; lectr. U. Calif., Berkeley, 1972, dir. childhood and govt. project, 1972-74, acting prof. law, 1973-75, prof., 1975—. Mem. overseer's com. to visit law sch. Harvard, 1972—; chmn., bd. trustees Berkeley Pub. Library, 1973—. Mem. Am., Calif., San Francisco bar assns. Contbr. articles in field to profl. jours. Home: 9 The Uplands Berkeley CA 94705 Office: 342 Boalt Hall U Calif Berkeley CA 94720 Tel (415) 642-5980

MOBERLY, ROBERT JAMES, b. Dayton, Ohio, Dec. 22, 1933; B.S. in Indsl. Engring., Gen. Motors Inst., 1956; J.D., U. San Diego, 1969. Admitted to Calif. bar, 1971; COMSAT Missions program mgr. Convair div. Gen. Dynamics Corp., San Diego, after 1956; asso. firm Lefebvre and Sims, San Diego, 1971—. Pres. Kearny Mesa Pop Warner Football League, San Diego, 1968-69; pres. Serra Mesa Little League, San Diego, 1968. Mem. Calif., San Diego County bar assns., Am. Mgmt. Assn. Home: 11082 Promesa Dr San Diego CA 92124 Office: 110 W C St Suite 1700 San Diego CA 92101 Tel (714) 239-0202

MOBILLE, GEORGE THOMAS, b. South Bend, Ind., July 27, 1925; B.S. in Chem. Engring., Notre Dame U., 1948; LL.B., Cornell U., 1951. Admitted to N.Y. State bar, 1951, D.C. bar, 1952; sr. partner firm Cushman, Darby and Cushman, Washington, 1951—; vis. lectr. Cath. U. Law Sch. Mem. Am., D.C., N.Y. State bar assns., Am. Patent Law Assn., U.S. Trademark Assn. Contbr. articles to legal jours. Home: 5210 Portsmouth Rd Washington DC 20016 Office: Cushman Darby & Cushman 1801 K St NW Washington DC 20006 Tel (202) 833-3000

MOBLEY, JOHN HOMER, II, b. Shreveport, La., Apr. 21, 1930; A.B., U. Ga., 1951, J.D., 1953. Admitted to Ga. bar, 1952; served with JAGC, USAF, 1953-55; practiced in Atlanta, 1955—, individual practice law, 1955; partner firms Kelley & Mobley, 1956-63, Gambrell & Mobley, 1963—. Mem. State Bar Ga., Am., Atlanta bar assns., Am. Judicature Soc., Lawyers Club, Gridiron, Phi Delta Phi, Kappa Alpha. Office: 3900 1st Nat Bank Tower Atlanta GA 30303 Tel (404) 658-9150

MOBLEY, JOHN WESLEY, b. Mobile, Ala., Feb. 28, 1925; student Ala. Poly. Inst., 1942-43, Springhill Coll., 1947-49; LL.B., U. Ala., 1952, J.D., 1969. Admitted to Ala. bar, 1952, U.S. Dist. Ct. bar, 1954, U.S. Tax Ct. bar, 1957, ICC bar, 1957; individual practice law, Mobile, Ala., 1952-54; asso. firm Howell & Johnston, Mobile, 1954-55; asso. to partner firm Holberg, Tully & Aldridge, Mobile, 1955-61; asst. U.S. atty. So. Dist. Ala., Mobile, 1961-63; partner firm Hamilton, Denniston, Butler & Riddick, Mobile, 1963-66; U.S. commr. So. Dist. Ala., Mobile, 1965-66; corp. counsel Internat. Paper Co., Mobile, 1966—; instr. Springhill Coll., 1952-54, Am. Coll. Life Underwriters, 1963-65; mem. Greater Mobile Mental Health-Mental Retardation Bd. Pres., Children's Dental Clinic, Mobile County Assn. Mental Health, Mobile Mental Health Center, Family Counsel Center, PTA Augusta Evans Sch., Mobile; bd. dirs. Community Chest Mobile, United Cerebral Palsy Assn. Mobile, Sr. Citizens Services Inc., Gordon Smith Center; mem. adv. com. SW Ala. Health Planning Council. Mem. Am., Fed. bar assns., Mobile, Ala. chambers commerce, Nat. Forest Products Assn., U. Ala. Alumni Assn. (past pres., dir.), Phi Delta Phi. Home: 211 Woodlands Ave Mobile AL 36607 Office: PO Box 2328 Mobile AL 36601 Tel (205) 457-8911

MOCH, ROBERT GASTON, b. Montesano, Wash., June 20, 1914; B.A., U. Wash., 1936; J.D., Harvard, 1941. Admitted to Mass. bar, 1941, Wash. bar, 1945; asso. firm Herrick, Smith, Donald, Farley & Ketchum, Boston, 1941-45; asso. firm Eggerman, Rosling & Williams, Seattle, 1945-50, Weter, Robert & Shefelman, Seattle, 1950-53; partner firm Roberts, Shefelman, Lawrence, Gay & Moch, Seattle, 1953—; del. Nat. Conf. Law and Poverty, Washington, 1965, Nat. Defender Conf., 1969; chmn. King County (Wash.) Pub. Defender Advisory Com., 1970. Trustee Seattle-King County Legal Aid Bur., 1966-72. Mem. Am., Wash., Seattle-King County (trustee 1966-69) bar assns., Phi Beta Kappa, Phi Delta Phi, Alpha Kappa Psi, Beta Gamma Sigma. Home: 3414 Hunts Point Rd Bellevue WA 98004 Office: 1818 IBM Bldg Seattle WA 98101 Office: Tel (206) 622-1818

MOCK, DONALD JOSEPH, b. Chgo., July 24, 1928; B.S., Loyola U., Chgo., 1951; LL.D., 1953. Admitted to Ill. bar, 1954; individual practice law, Itasca, Ill., 1954—; magistrate, Wood Dale, Ill., 1956-64. Pres. Driscoll Parents Assn., Driscoll High Schl., Addison, Ill., 1975—. Mem. Am., Ill., DuPage County bar assns., Am. Judicature Soc., Assn. Trial Lawyers Am., Loyola Law Alumni Assn., Phi Alpha Delta. Contbr. articles to law jours. Home: 178 Forest Glen Wood Dale IL 60191 Office: 308 W Irving Park Rd Itasca IL 60143 Tel (312) 773-9690

MODECKI, CARL ALBERT, b. Newark, June 16, 1941; A.B., U. Ky., 1964; LL.B., George Washington U., 1967. Admitted to Va. bar, 1967, Wis. bar, 1969, Mass. bar, 1976; asst. dir. legal dept. Am. Automobile Assn., Washington, D.C., 1967-69, gen. counsel Wis. div. Madison, 1969-70; exec. dir. Mass. Bar Assn., Boston, 1971—. Vice chmn. Swampscott Sch. Building Com., 1974—; bd. dirs. George Washington U. Law Sch. Alumni Assn. Mem. Am., Wis., Va., Mass., New Eng. (sec.-treas.) bar assns., Am. Soc. Assn. Execs. Home: 93 Magnolia Rd Swampscott MA 01907 Office: 1 Center Plaza Boston MA 02108 Tel (617) 523-4529

MOELLERING, ALFRED WILLIAM, b. Ft. Wayne, Ind., Dec. 13, 1926; B.S. in Bus., Ind. U., 1951, LL.B., 1953. Admitted to Ind. bar, 1953, U.S. Dist. Ct. bar, U.S. Supreme Ct. bar, 1962; individual practice law, Ft. Wayne, 1954-62; U.S. atty. No. Dist. Ind., Ft. Wayne, 1962-70; judge Allen County (Ind.) Superior Ct., Ft. Wayne, 1971—. Pres., Festival Music Theatre, 1956-57; bd. dirs. Ft. Wayne Ballet, 1957-59; bd. dirs. Ft. Wayne Philharmonic Orch., 1968-71; sec.-treas. Future Security, Inc. Mem. Am., Ind., Allen County bar assns., Am. Judicature Soc., Phi Delta Phi. Contbr. articles in field to legal jours. Home: 5120 DeRome Dr Fort Wayne IN 46815 Office: Allen County Court House Fort Wayne IN 46802 Tel (219) 423-7251

MOENING, RONALD SYLVESTER, b. Lima, Ohio, June 13, 1948; A.B. cum laude, Xavier U., 1970; J.D. cum laude, U. Toledo, 1973. Admitted to Ohio bar, 1973; asso. firm Robison Curphey & O'Connell, Toledo, 1973—. Mem. Delta Theta Phi. Home: 3134 Muirfield St Toledo OH 43614 Office: 425 Libbey Owens Ford Bldg Toledo OH 43624 Tel (419) 255-3100

MOENSSENS, ANDRE ACHILLES, b. Hoboken, Belgium, Jan. 13, 1930; J.D., Chgo.-Kent Coll. Law, 1966; LL.M., Northwestern U., 1967. Admitted to Ill. bar, 1966, U.S. Supreme Ct. bar, 1972, Va. bar, 1974; prof. law Chgo.-Kent Coll. Law, 1967-73; prof. law, dir. Inst. Criminal Justice U. Richmond (Va.), 1973—; individual practice law, Chgo. and Richmond, 1966—; cons. in field. Fellow Am. Acad. Forensic Scis. (sec.-treas. 1974—, chmn. jurisprudence sect. 1972); mem. Internat. Assn. for Identification (asso.), Ill., Va., Richmond bar assns. Author: Fingerprints and the Law, 1969; Fingerprint Techniques, 1972; co-author: Cases and Comments on Criminal Law, 1973; sr. co-author: Scientific Evidence in Criminal Cases, 1973; Direct and Cross Examination of Experts, 1977; contbr. articles in field to profl. jours. Office: T C Williams Sch Law Univ Richmond Richmond VA 23173 Tel (804) 285-6410

MOFFAT, RICHARD HOWE, b. Salt Lake City, Dec. 17, 1931; B.S., U. Utah, 1953; J.D., Stanford, 1956. Admitted to Utah bar, 1956, since practiced in Salt Lake City; pres. firm Moffat, Welling & Paulsen, 1957—; commr. Utah State Bar, 1972—. Mem. Utah Bd. Alcoholism and Other Addictive Drugs, 1964-72; mem. governing bd. Utah Legal Services Corp., 1970—, chmn. personnel com., 1972—; mem. Utah Commn. Jud. Qualification and Removal, 1974-77, chmn., 1976-77; mem. Supreme Ct. Jud. Nominating Commn., 1975—; founder, pres. South Cottonwood, Inc. Mem. Am., Utah, Salt Lake County (pres. 1969-70) bar assns. Home: 1122 Vine St Salt Lake City UT 84121 Office: 9th Floor Tribune Bldg Salt Lake City UT 84111 Tel (801) 521-7500

MOFFETT, JOHN JAMES, b. Canton, Ohio, May 2, 1946; B.A., Ohio State U., 1969, B.S. in Edn., 1971, J.D., 1971. Admitted to Ohio bar, 1972; asso. firm Cope & Moffett, Carrollton, Ohio, 1972-74; individual practice law, Carrollton, 1974—; solicitor Village of E. Sparta (Ohio). Mem. sch. bd. Carrollton Exempted Village; pres. Carroll County (Ohio) Heart Assn.; trustee St. Luke's Home for Aging, N. Canton. Mem. Carroll County, Ohio (ethics com.), Am. bar assns. Home: 420 Abrahims Ave Carrollton OH 44615 Office: 71 Public Sq Carrollton OH 44615 Tel (216) 627-7116

MOFFITT, ROY BRATTON, b. Greensboro, N.C., Sept. 11, 1927; B. Geol. Engring., N.C. State U., 1952, profl. degree Ceramic Engr., 1957, B.S., 1961; J.D., George Washington U., 1966. Admitted to D.C. bar, 1967, N.C. bar, 1968; indsl. engr. U.S. Steel, Birmingham, Ala., 1952-54; instr. N.C. State U., 1954-57, asso. prof., 1957-63; examiner U.S. Patent Office, 1963-68; coordinator patent activities Superior Continental Corp., Hickory, N.C., 1968-69, patent counsel, 1969-73, sec., legal counsel 1973-77; individual practice law, 1977—. Mem. N.C., Catawba, Am. bar assns. Patentee in field; contbr. articles to profl. jours. Home: Box 675 Route 10 Hickory NC 28601 Office: 1928 Main Ave Hickory NC 28601 Tel (704) 328-2171

MOFFITT, WILLIAM ALBERT, JR., b. St. Louis, June 19, 1919; B.A. magna cum laude, St. Louis U., 1941, LL.B., 1948, J.D., 1969. Admitted to Mo. bar, 1948, U.S. Supreme Ct. bar, 1956, Tax Ct. U.S. bar, 1968; asso. firm Cox, Cox & Cox, St. Louis, 1949-61; partner firm Cox, Moffitt & Cox and predecessors, St. Louis, 1961—; asst. to dir. pub. relations St. Louis U., 1946-48, lectr., 1948-53, 60-61; lectr. St. Louis Bar Assn. and Washington U., 1962-63; spl. asst. atty. gen. Mo., 1968; mcpl. judge, Village of Bel-Ridge, 1970-71. Mem., sec. Planning and Zoning Commn., Bellefontaine Neighbors, Mo., 1959-65; bd. dirs. St. Louis Chronic Hosp. Welfare Assn., Inc. Mem. Am., Mo. (chmn. civil practice and procedure com. 1963-64), St. Louis bar assns., Lawyers Assn. St. Louis, Cath. Lawyers Guild St. Louis. Home: 622 Chamblee Ln Saint Louis MO 63141 Office: 612 The Plaza Tower 111 W Port Plaza Saint Louis MO 63141 Tel (314) 434-3883

MOGAVERO, JOSEPH ANTHONY, b. Cooperstown, N.Y., Nov. 10, 1927; B.M.E., Clarkson Coll., 1950; LL.B., Albany Coll., 1953, J.D., 1968. Admitted to N.Y. bar, 1953; clk. N.Y. State Attys. Gen.'s Office, Albany, 1950-53; dist. atty. Otsego County (N.Y.), Cooperstown, 1960-69; partner firm Latham and Mogavero, Unadilla, N.Y., 1957-71; judge Otsego County, 1971—. Mem. N.Y. State, Otsego County (past pres.) bar assns., N.Y. State County Judges Assn. Home: 132 Old Main St Unadilla NY 13849 Office: County Office Bldg Cooperstown NY 13326 Tel (607) 547-4264

MOHLER, MARTIN EDWARD, b. Toledo, Apr. 4, 1948; B.A. cum laude, John Carroll U., 1970; J.D., Toledo U., 1973. Admitted to Ohio bar, 1973; asso. firm MacDaniels & Mohler, Toledo, 1974; mem. firm Mohler Christiansen & Covrett, Toledo, 1975—; chmn. law dept. Davis Jr. Coll., 1974-76. Mem. Am., Ohio, Toledo, Lucas County bar assns. Home: 3805 Grantley Rd Toledo OH 43613 Office: 464 Spitzer Bldg Toledo OH 43604 Tel (419) 243-8550

MOHR, ANTHONY JAMES, b. Los Angeles, May 11, 1947; B.A. cum laude, Wesleyan U., 1969; J.D., Columbia, 1972; diploma in comparative law with honors, Faculté Internationale pour l'Enseignement du Droit Comparé, 1975. Admitted to Calif. bar, 1972, D.C. bar, 1976; law clk. Hon. A. Andrew Hauk, U.S. Dist. Ct. Central Dist. Calif., 1972-73; asso. firm Schwartz, Alschuler & Grossman, Los Angeles, 1973-75; of counsel firm Radomile & Roach, Los Angeles, 1976—; co-host Theta Cable Pub. Access TV series on law and soc., Los Angeles, 1973-74. Mem. nat. adv. council Center for Study of the Presidency, 1974—; del. White House Conf. on Youth, Estes Park, Colo., 1971; mem. Los Angeles Dist. Atty.'s Adv. Council, 1976—. Mem. Beverly Hills Bar Assn. (bd. govs.), Barristers of Beverly Hills Bar Assn. (treas.), Am., Los Angeles County bar assns., Phi Delta Phi, Phi Beta Kappa. Contbr. articles to legal jours. Home: 233 S Barrington Ave Los Angeles CA 90049 Office: 1880 Century Park E Los Angeles CA 90067 Tel (213) 553-5918 or 277-3007

MOISE, IRWIN STERN, b. Santa Rosa, N.Mex., Dec. 1, 1906; J.D., U. Mich., 1928; LL.D., Highlands U., 1963. Admitted to N.Mex. bar, 1928, Ill. bar, 1960; individual practice law, Tucumcari, N.Mex., 1928-33; dep. adminstr. NRA, Washington, 1934-36; state dir. FHA, Santa Fe, 1936; dist. judge, Las Vegas, N.Mex., 1937-43; individual practice, Albuquerque, 1946-59; justice N.Mex. Supreme Ct., 1959-69, chief justice, 1969-70; mem. firm Sutin, Thayer & Browne, Albuquerque, 1970—. Mem. Am., N.Mex., Albuquerque bar assns. Home: 4715 Marquette St NE Albuquerque NM 87108 Office: 600 First Plaza Bldg Albuquerque NM 81102 Tel (505) 842-8200

MOKOTOFF, HAROLD S., b. N.Y.C., Aug. 24, 1910; LL.B., St. Johns U., 1932. Admitted to N.Y. bar, 1933; arbitrator N.Y.C. Municipal Ct., Am. Arbitration Assn. Pres. Great Neck Estates (N.Y.) Civic Assn. Mem. Bklyn. (ethics com.), Nassau County (N.Y.), Fed. bar assns. Home: 2 Amherst Rd E Great Neck NY 11021 Office: 2 Pennsylvania Plaza New York City NY 10001 Tel (212) 594-0660

MOLAISON, JOHN JACKSON, SR., b. Gretna, La., Aug. 22, 1929; J.D., Loyola U., New Orleans, 1960. Admitted to La. bar, 1960; partner firm Molaison & Molaison, Gretna, 1960-67; judge Jefferson Parish (La.) Ct., 2d Parish Ct., 1967—. Mem. Jefferson Parish Criminal Bar Assn., Jefferson Parish Bar Assn. Home: 2517 Vulcan Dr Harvey LA 70058 Office: Second Parish Ct Gretna Courthouse Gretna LA 70053 Tel (504) 367-6611

MOLDAUER, IRVING, b. Bklyn., Sept. 23, 1906; LL.B., St. Lawrence U., 1927. Admitted to N.Y. State bar, 1928, U.S. Supreme Ct. bar, 1959; law clk., asso. firm Hirsh, Newman & Reass, N.Y.C., 1922-29; asso. firm Hirsh, Newman, Reass & Becker, N.Y.C., 1929-33, partner, 1933-42; partner firm Moldauer & Tepper, N.Y.C., 1955-56, Moldauer & Katz, 1962-69; individual practice law, N.Y.C., 1969—. Mem. Bklyn., Nassau County, N.Y. State, Am. bar assns., Assn. Bar City N.Y. Home: 18 Pine St Woodmere NY 11598 Office: 1501 Broadway New York City NY 10036 Tel (212) 398-9760

MOLDAVAN, MICHAEL STEPHEN, b. Atlanta, Sept. 22, 1948; B.B.A. with honors, Ga. State U., 1970; J.D. (scholar), U. Ga., 1973. Admitted to Ga. bar, 1974; asso. firm Sam Calhoun, Jr., Chatsworth, Ga., 1973-75; individual practice law, Chatsworth, 1975—; instr. continuing edn. program Dalton (Ga.) Jr. Coll., 1976—; instr. bus. law Reinhardt Coll., Waleska, Ga., 1976—. Vol. probation officer Murray County (Ga.), 1975—; dir. N. Ga. Area Community Action Assn., Chatsworth; active adv. council Murray County Drug Council. Mem. Am., Ga., Conasauga bar assns., Murray County Home Builders Assn. (past officer). Home: Route 1 Box 219 Chatsworth GA 30705 Office: 114 1/2 3rd Ave Chatsworth GA 30705 Tel (404) 695-6414

MOLINE, HARRY O., JR., b. St. Louis, Sept. 7, 1934; A.B. in Econs., Drury Coll., 1956; J.D., Washington U., St. Louis, 1962. Admitted to Mo. bar, 1962; atty.-in-charge St. Louis br. office SEC, 1962-69; asso. firm Thomas, Busse, Weis, Cullen & Godfrey, St. Louis, 1969-73; partner firm Moline, Tegethoff & Ottsen, St. Louis, 1973—. Mem. Met. Bar Assn. St. Louis. Home: 10631 Mentz Hill Acres Saint Louis MO 63128 Office: Suite 550 7701 Forsyth Blvd Saint Louis MO 63105 Tel (314) 725-3200

MOLINS, MARCEL, b. Granollers, Spain, Nov. 1, 1936; came to U.S., 1963; J.D., Barcelona U., 1958; diplomas comparative law seminars Strasburg Comparative Law Sch., 1961-62; LL.M., Northwestern U., 1964; J.D., Loyola U., 1966. Admitted to Barcelona bar, 1958, Madrid bar, 1966, Ill. bar, 1967; individual practice law, Barcelona, 1959-61; asso. firm Baker & McKenzie, Chgo., 1964-70, partner, 1970—; tchr. Lawyers Inst., John Marshall U., 1968-69. Mem. Barcelona, Madrid, Chgo., Ill. bar assns. Home: 6033 N Sheridan Rd Chicago IL 60660 Office: Prudential Plaza Chicago IL 60601 Tel (312) 565-0025

MOLL, JON HOYT, b. Wauseon, Ohio, Sept. 5, 1942; A.B. in Polit. Sci., Ind. U., 1964, J.D., 1967. Admitted to Ind. bar, 1967; served as lt. JAGC, USN, 1967-71; asso. firm Defur, Voran, Hanley, Radcliff & Reed, Muncie, Ind., 1971-74, partner, 1974—. Bd. dirs. Delaware County Mental Health Clinic, 1973-75, pres., 1975; bd. dirs. Comprehensive Mental Health Services E.Central Ind., 1975-76; adv. bd. child mental health div. Ind. Dept. Mental Health, 1976; bd. dirs. Central Ind. Health Services Agy., 1976. Mem. Am., Ind., Muncie bar assns., Order of Coif. Home: 2610 W Berwyn Rd Muncie IN 47304 Office: 320 S High St Muncie IN 47305 Tel (317) 288-3651

MOLLENKAMP, ALAN LEE, b. Toledo, Oct. 13, 1946; B.A., U. Toledo, 1969; J.D., Loyola U., Los Angeles, 1973. Admitted to Ohio bar, 1974; individual practice law, Toledo, 1974; asso. firm Winchester, Douglas, Lydy & Mollenkamp, Toledo, 1974—. Home: 3301 E Lincolnshire St Toledo OH 43606 Office: 1045 Spitzer Bldg Toledo OH 43604 Tel (419) 248-4677

MOLLIGAN, PETER NICHOLAS, b. New Orleans, Mar. 8, 1938; B.A., La. State U., 1960; J.D., San Francisco U., 1970. Admitted to Calif. bar, 1970; served as lt. JAGC, USN, 1960-63; regional claims mgr. Govt. Employees Ins. Cos., San Francisco, 1963-70; partner, treas. firm Hoberg, Finger & Brown, San Francisco, 1970—. Mem. Calif., San Francisco trial lawyers assns., Am., Calif., San Francisco bar assns., Lawyers Club San Francisco, Inner Circle Advocates. Office: 703 Market St San Francisco CA 94103 Tel (415) 543-9464

MOLLOY, JOHN JOSEPH, III, b. San Antonio, Aug. 8, 1946; B.S., U. So. Calif., 1968, J.D., 1972. Admitted to Calif. bar, 1972; asso. firm Sheppard, Mullin, Richter & Hampton, Los Angeles, 1972—. Active Los Angeles Jr. C. of C. Mem. Am., Los Angeles County bar assns., State Bar Calif. Office: 333 S Hope St Los Angeles CA 90071 Tel (213) 620-1780

MOLLOY, ROBERT THOMAS, b. Tyron, N.C., May 20, 1917; B.S.S., City Coll. N.Y., 1938; Naumberg scholar Downing Coll., U. Cambridge, Eng., 1936; LL.B., Yale 1941, J.D., 1970. Admitted to N.Y. bar, 1941, D.C. bar, 1955, Va. bar, 1970; asso. firm Milbank, Tweed, Hadley & McCloy, and predecessor firms, N.Y.C., 1941, 46-55; asso. firm Dudley, Jones & Ostman, and successor firms, Washington, 1955-56, partner, 1956; partner firm Molloy, Simpson & Johnson and predecessor firms, Washington, 1965—; pres. Molloy, Simpson & Johnson, P.C., Vienna, Va., 1971—; spl. counsel Hale Russell Gray Seaman & Burkett, N.Y.C., 1958—; spl. counsel Bose, McKinney & Evans, Indpls., 1969—. Mem. D.C., Va., N.Y. State, Fed., Am. bar assns., Assn. Bar City N.Y., University Club, Metropolitan Club. Author: Federal Income Taxation of Corporation, 1972; contbr. articles to profl. jours. Home: 1026 16th St NW Washington DC 20036 Office: 1900 L St NW Washington DC 20036 Tel (202) 659-8877

MOLTZ, MARTIN PAUL, b. Chgo., Nov. 22, 1944; B.A., U. Ill., 1966; J.D., U. Okla., 1969. Admitted to Ill. bar, 1971, Fla. bar, 1976; asst. state's atty. Cook County (Ill.), 1971-72; staff atty. Ill. State's Attys. Assn., Elgin, 1972—. Mem. Am., Ill. State, Chgo. bar assns., Fla. Bar, Phi Alpha Delta. Home: 7306 N Winchester Ave Chicago IL 60626 Office: 35 Fountain Sq Plaza Elgin IL 60120 Tel (312) 697-0020

MOLTZEN, EDWARD WILLIS, b. Chgo., Apr. 20, 1944; B.A., North Park Coll., 1965; J.D., John Marshall Law Sch., 1968. Admitted to Ill. bar, 1968; asso. firm Orner & Wasserman, Chgo., 1968-69; asso. firm Van Duzer, Geshon, Jordan & Petersen, Chgo., 1969-76, partner firm, 1976—. Bd. dirs. Orland Park (Ill.) Community Chest, 1971-74. Mem. Ill. State Bar Assn., Delta Theta Phi. Home: 13 Kohlwood Dr Mokena IL 60448 Office: 222 W Adams St Chicago IL 60606 Tel (312) 977-8095

MONACO, RAYMOND WILLIAM, b. Providence, Feb. 10, 1918; B.S., Holy Cross Coll., 1941; LL.B., Georgetown U., 1948. Admitted to R.I. bar, 1949; individual practice law, Providence, 1949—; assoc. counsel Nat. Football League Alumni Assn., Indpls., 1968—. Mem. Aurora Civic Assn.; bd. dirs. Holy Cross Coll. Home: 1 Grove Ave N Providence RI 02911 Office: 1111 Industrial Bank Bldg Providence RI 02903 Tel (401) 421-1170

MONAGHAN, BERNARD ANDREW, b. Birmingham, Ala., Jan. 28, 1916; B.A., Birmingham-So. Coll., 1934, L.H.D., 1967; LL.B., Harvard, 1937; B.A. (Rhodes scholar), Oxford (Eng.) U., 1939. Admitted to Ala. bar, 1937, U.S. Supreme Ct. bar, 1944; asso. firm Bradley, Arant, Rose & White, and predecessors, 1939-48, partner, 1948-58; counselor Dept. Army, 1952-53; exec. v.p. Vulcan Materials Co., Birmingham, 1958-59, pres., chief exec. officer, 1959—. Bd. dirs. Bapt. Hosp. Found., Ala. regional chpt. NCCJ; trustee Birmingham-So. Coll., So. Research Inst., Ireland Found., Rushton Lectures; bd. govs. Indian Springs Sch.; mem. nat. execs. com. Nat. Council Crime and Delinquency. Mem. Ala., Birmingham bar assns., Phi Beta Kappa, Alpha Tau Omega. Named Gold Knight of Mgmt., Nat. Mgmt. Assn., 1967. Home: Dell Rd Birmingham AL 35223 Office: 1 Metroplex Dr Birmingham AL 35209 Tel (205) 877-3179

MONAGHAN, KEVIN PAUL, b. N.Y.C., Apr. 8, 1939; B.A., Fordham U., 1962; LL.B., Cornell U., 1965. Admitted to N.Y. State bar, 1965, Calif. bar, 1968; asso. firm McCanliss & Early, N.Y.C., 1965-67; counsel Jenkins & Perry, San Diego, 1968-76; partner firm Hahn, Cazier, Hoegh & Leff, San Diego, 1976—; dir. IMED Corp. Mem. Calif. Broker Dealers Compliance Assn. (pres. 1974-75, advisory bd. 1976—), Am. Bar Assn. (mem. sec. corporate, banking-bus. law, subcom. on broker-dealers of fed. regulation of securities com.), San Diego Corporate Fin. Counsel, Cuyamaca Club (bd. govs.). Contbr. articles to profl. jours.; editor Privately Held

Growth Cos., 1974. Home: 13086 Old Barona Rd Lakeside CA 92040 Office: 1010 2d Ave Suite 2222 San Diego CA 92101 Tel (714) 231-8911

MONASCH, BURTON ISADORE, b. Bklyn., Mar. 9, 1927; A.B., N.Y. Univ., 1949; LL.B., Yale, 1952. Admitted to N.Y. bar, 1952; asso. firm Hess Mela Segall Popkin & Guterman, N.Y.C., 1952-59; partner firm Berger Monasch & Berger, N.Y.C., 1959-69, firm Monasch Chazen Stream & Feinberg, N.Y.C., 1969—. Mem. Am., N.Y. bar assns., Assn. Bar City N.Y., Am. Acad. Matrimonial Lawyers (pres. 1974—). Home: 102 Flamingo Rd Roslyn NY 11576 Office: 777 3d Ave New York City NY 10017 Tel (212) 759-7220

MONCREIFF, ROBERT PHILIP, b. Evanston, Ill., Mar. 26, 1930; B.A., Yale, 1952, Oxford U., 1954; LL.B., Harvard, 1957. Admitted to Mass. bar, 1957; mem. firm Palmer & Dodge, Boston, 1957—. Councillor, City of Cambridge (Mass.), 1970-73; chmn. Cambridge Bicentennial Corp., 1974—. Mem. Am., Boston bar assns. Home: 11 Gray Gardens Cambridge MA 02138 Office: One Beacon St Boston MA 02108 Tel (617) 227-4400

MONE, PETER JOHN, b. Brockton, Mass., Apr. 8, 1940; A.B. cum laude, Bowdoin Coll., Brunswick, Maine, 1962; J.D., U. Chgo., 1965. Admitted to Ill. bar, 1965; partner firm Baker & McKenzie, Chgo., 1968—. Mem. Am., Ill., Chgo. bar assns., Chgo. Trial Lawyers Assn., Soc. Trial Lawyers, Def. Research Inst. Office: Suite 2700 Prudential Plaza Chicago IL 60601 Tel (312) 565-0025

MONEYMAKER, RICHARD MICHAEL, b. Los Angeles, May 17, 1936; B.A., Yale, 1957; J.D., U. Calif., Berkeley, 1960. Admitted to Calif. bar, 1961, U.S. Supreme Ct. bar, 1967; asso. counsel Bank of Am., Los Angeles, 1961-62; partner firm Tiernan & Moneymaker, Los Angeles, 1962-71; partner, pres. firm Moneymaker & Wolfson, Los Angeles, 1971-77, owner, 1977—. Pres. Pacific Coast Rugby Football Union, 1965—; v.p. U.S. Rugby Football Union, 1975—; sec. Los Angeles-Auckland Sister City Com., 1971—; mem. Los Feliz Improvement Assn., 1965—, pres., 1977—; asso. bd. mem. Calif. Mus. Sci. and Industry, 1965—; bd. dirs. So. Calif. Yale Scholarship Fund Found., 1975—. Mem. Lawyers Club Los Angeles, Los Angeles County Bar Assn., Yale Club So. Calif. (dir.). Home: 4768 Bryn Mawr Rd Los Angeles CA 90027 Office: 700 S Flower St Suite 1702 Los Angeles CA 90017 Tel (213) 622-1088

MONGE, JAY PARRY, b. N.Y.C., Mar. 15, 1943; A.B., Harvard, 1966; LL.B., U. Va., 1969. Admitted to Ill. bar, 1969; asso. firm Mayer, Brown & Platt, Chgo., 1969-75, partner, 1976—. Asso. Rush-Presbyterian St. Luke's Med. Center. Mem. Am. Bar Assn. Home: 983 Morningside Dr Lake Forest IL 60045 Office: Room 1955 231 S LaSalle St Chicago IL 60604 Tel (312) 782-0600

MONGIARDO, DANTE PETER, b. Paterson, N.J., Aug. 10, 1945; B.A., Seton Hall U., 1967; J.D., N.Y. Law Sch., 1970. Admitted to N.J. bar, 1970, U.S. Supreme Ct. bar, 1974; law clk. to judge Morris County Ct., Morristown, N.J., 1970-72; asso. firm Frank A. Paglianite, West Caldwell, N.J., 1971-72; asst. county prosecutor Passaic County, Paterson, N.J., 1972—; police legal advisor Passaic County, 1975—. Mem. Am., N.J. bar assns., Nat. Dist. Attys. Assn., N.J. Prosecutors Assn., N.J. Asst. Prosecutors Assn. Contbr. to Search and Seizure Law Report, 1976. Office: New Court House Hamilton St Paterson NJ 07505 Tel (201) 525-5000

MONK, ROBERT L., b. Santa Barbara, Calif., Oct. 11, 1940; A.B., U. Calif., Santa Barbara, 1962; J.D., U. Calif., Berkeley, 1965. Admitted to Calif. bar, 1966; aide to criminal procedure com. Calif. State Legislature, Sacramento, 1965-66; staff atty. State of Calif., Sacramento, 1966-67; dep. dist. atty. County of Santa Barbara, 1967-70; individual practice law, Santa Barbara, 1970—; juvenile ct. referee, 1972—. Mem. Santa Barbara Bd. Harbor Commrs., 1970-73, chmn., 1972-73. Mem. Calif., Santa Barbara County bar assns., Am. Judicature Soc., Calif. Trial Lawyers Assn., Barristers Club Santa Barbara County (pres. 1972). Office: 211 E Victoria St Suite D Santa Barbara CA 93101 Tel (805) 963-1994

MONNING, WRIGHT BRUCE, b. Dallas, Apr. 28, 1948; B.B.A., So. Meth. U., 1970, J.D., 1972. Admitted to Tex. bar, 1973, U.S. Supreme Ct. bar, 1967; mem. firm McKenzie & Baer, Dallas, 1973-75, Wynne & Wynne, Wills Point, Tex., 1975—. Bd. dirs. Van Zandt County Child Welfare Unit. Mem. Van Zandt County, Dallas, Am. bar assns., Dallas Jr. Bar Assn. (past dir.), State Bar Tex. Home: 439 W James Wills Point TX 75169 Office: 137 W James PO Box 487 Wills Point TX 75169 Tel (214) 873-2531

MONSON, DANIEL LEROY, b. Milw., Apr. 12, 1920; B.S., U. Wis., 1948, J.D., 1950. Admitted to Wis. bar, 1950, U.S. Supreme Ct. bar, 1962; atty., office of gen. counsel U.S. Dept. Agr., Washington, 1951-61; asst. gen. counsel FCA, Washington, 1961-73, gen. counsel, dep. gov., 1973—; steering com. Symposium on Coops. and the Law, U. Wis. Pres., Springfield (Va.) Community Theatre; bd. dirs. FCA Credit Union. Home: 6703 Emporia Ct Springfield VA 22152 Office: FCA 490 L'Enfant Plaza Washington DC 20578 Tel (202) 755-2136

MONSON, TERRY LEWIS, b. Fargo, N.D., Jan. 5, 1947; B.A., N.D. State U., 1969; J.D., Northwestern U., 1972. Admitted to Iowa bar, 1972; asso. firm Ahlers, Cooney, Dorweiler, Haynie & Smith, Des Moines, 1972—. Bd. dirs., v.p. Child Devel. Care Center, 1975—. Mem. Polk County, Iowa State, Am. bar assns. Office: 920 Liberty Bldg Des Moines IA 50309 Tel (515) 243-7611

MONTAGUE, HARRY LADDIE, JR., b. Phila., July 28, 1938; B.A., U. Pa., 1960; LL.B., Dickinson Sch. Law, 1963. Admitted to Pa. bar, 1964, D.C. bar, 1964; asso. firm Cohen, Shapiro, Berger, Polisher & Cohen, Phila., 1964-70, David Berger, P.A., Phila., 1970-76, film Berger & Montague, 1977—. Trustee St. Peter's Sch., Phila., 1973—. Mem. Am., Phila. (mem. exec. com. young lawyers' sect. 1968-70) bar assns., Antitrust Inst. Mem. bd. editors Dickinson Law Rev., 1962-63. Office: 1622 Locust St Philadelphia PA 19103 Tel (215) 732-8000

MONTAGUE, MALCOLM JOHN, b. Portland, Oreg., June 1, 1929; B.S. in Social Sci., U. Oreg., 1951, J.D., 1954. Admitted to Oreg. bar, 1954; served with Office Staff Judge Adv., Lackland AFB, Tex., 1954-56; asso. firm Robert R. Rankin, Portland, 1956-58; atty. Office of City Atty., Portland, 1958-60; partner firm Williams, Montague, Stark, Hiefield & Norville, Portland, 1960-75, White, Sutherland, Parks & Allen, Portland, 1976—; instr. NW Coll. Law, Portland, 1958-69, also profl. courses; judge pro tem Oreg. Dist. and Circuit Cts., 1976—. Mem. Am. (attributions sub com. com. on taxation), Oreg. (sec. com. corp. and partnership law) bar assns., Oreg. Securities Law Assn. Contbr. articles to profl. publs. Home: 3960 SW Wapato St Portland OR 97201 Office: 1200 Jackson Tower 806 SW Broadway Portland OR 97205 Tel (503) 224-4840

MONTAGUE, ODEN WALTER, b. Aurora, N.C., Nov. 17, 1919; B.A., Coll. of William and Mary, 1949, LL.B., 1951. Admitted to Va. bar, 1950; individual practice law, Hampton, Va., 1951-52; staff officer CIA, Washington, 1952-72, South Vietnam, 1972; prosecutor Commonwealth of Va. Atty.'s Office, Norfolk, 1972-76; asst. commonwealth atty. Circuit Cts., Norfolk, 1976—. Mem. Nat. Dist. Attys. Assn., Va. State Bar, Baylake Pines Civic Assn. Home: 4324 John Silver Rd Virginia Beach VA 23455 Office: 800 E City Hall Ave Norfolk VA 23501 Tel (804) 441-2945

MONTAGUE, ROBERT LATANE, b. Washington, Sept. 18, 1935; B.A., U. Va., 1956, LL.B., 1961. Admitted to Va. bar, 1961, Ky. bar, 1961, U.S. Supreme Ct. bar, 1965, D.C. bar, 1966; asst. atty. gen. State of Ky., Frankfort, 1961-64; asso. firm Howard W. Smith, Jr., Alexandria, Va., 1964-66, Lambert, Brown & Furlow, Washington, 1965-69; individual practice law, Alexandria, Va., 1969—; mem. planning com. World Peace Through Law Center, 1967-69. Pres., Historic Alexandria Found., 1968-70, Old Town Civic Assn., 1971-73, No. Va. Conservation Council, 1973-74; chmn. Alexandria Bea Beautification Com., 1968-70, Alexandria Environ. Policy Commn., 1970-73, Nat. Capital Area chpt. March of Dimes, 1972-74; bd. dirs. Assn. Preservation Va. Antiquities. Mem. Am. Judicature Soc., Am. Soc. Internat. Law, Am., Ky., Va. (chmn. environ. law com. 1972-75), Alexandria bar assns., Nat. Health Agencies Council (v.p. 1976-77). Contbr. articles in field to legal jours. Home: 207 Prince St Alexandria VA 22314 Office: 1007 King St Alexandria VA 22314 also Urbanna VA 23175

MONTALBANO, ANTHONY, b. Bklyn., Nov. 2, 1939; A.B., Georgetown U., 1961; LL.B., Fordham U., 1964. Admitted to N.Y. bar, 1965; partner firm Hirshfeld, Birbrower, Montalbano & Condon, and prgdecessors, New City, N.Y., 1965—; gen. counsel Registrar & Transfer Co.; closing atty. Union Savs. Ban, New City. Pres., Clarkstown Democratic Club, 1975. Mem. Rockland County, N.Y. State, Am. bar assns., New York C. of C. (dir. 1975—), First Unitarian Soc. Rockland County (chmn. bd. trustees 1976). Home: 20 Prides Crossing New City NY 10956 Office: 20 Squadron Blvd New City NY 10956

MONTALBANO, BERNARD BART, b. Passaic, N.J., Nov. 23, 1944; B.S. in Accounting, Fairleigh Dickinson U., 1966; J.D., N.Y. U., 1969. Admitted to N.J. bar, 1969; law clk; 1969-70; asst. county prosecutor, Passaic, 1969-71; individual practice law, Clifton, N.J., 1971—. Mem. Am., N.J., Passaic County bar assns. Office: 805 Clifton Ave Clifton NJ 07013 Tel (201) 779-7904

MONTANTE, JAMES, b. Pittston, Pa., Nov. 15, 1907; B.A., U. Mich., 1928, LL.B., 1930. Admitted to Mich. bar, 1930; individual practice law, Detroit, 1930-61; judge Circuit Ct. Wayne County (Mich.), Detroit, 1961—. Mem. Italian-Am. Lawyers Club Mich. (pres. 1938), Nat. Lawyers Guild (pres. Detroit chpt. 1948), Detroit Bar Assn. (pres. 1961), State Bar Mich., Mich. State Judges Assn. (pres. 1973-74). Office: 1507 City-County Bldg Detroit MI 48226 Tel (313) 224-5213

MONTANTE, PHILIP JOSEPH, JR., b. Buffalo, Jan. 30, 1945; B.B.A., Drake Coll., 1966; M.Ed., Fla. Atlantic U., 1967; J.D., Samford U., 1971. Admitted to Fla. bar, 1971, U.S. Supreme Ct. bar, 1976; asst. state atty. Fla., 1971-75; spl. asst. atty. gen. State of Fla., 1975-76; partner firm Tyson and Montante, Ft. Lauderdale, Fla., 1975-76; mem. firm Sturrup and Della Donna, Ft. Lauderdale, 1976—; chief judge municipal ct., Margate, Fla., 1975-77; spl. cons. Fla. Organized Crime Control Council, Gov's. Commn. on Criminal Justice; commd. by gov. to jud. nominating commn., 1975-79; chmn. profl. ethics com. Broward County Bar; mem. profl. ethics com. Fla. Bar. Bd. dirs. Community Service Council; trustee Ft. Lauderdale Coll. Mem. Am. Bar Assn., Am. Trial Lawyers Assn., Am. Judicature Soc., AAUP, Nat. Council on Crime and Delinquency, Nat. Dist. Attys. Assn. Named Outstanding Young Man Am., 1976; author: Florida's Consumer Fraud Laws - A Compilation, 1973; contbg. author: Organized Crime Deskbook for Florida Prosecutors. Office: 2601 E Oakland Park Blvd Fort Lauderdale FL 33306 Tel (305) 563-2600

MONTECALVO, VINCENT JOSEPH, b. Providence, Aug. 30, 1941; B.S. in Bus. Adminstrn., Bryant Coll., 1966; J.D., Suffolk U., 1969. Admitted to R.I. bar, 1969, U.S. Dist. Ct. for Dist. R.I. bar, 1971; staff atty. R.I. Legal Services Inc., Pawtucket, 1970-73; asso. firm Hawkins & Hoopis, Providence, 1973—; asst. legal counsel for child welfare services R.I. Dept. Social, Rehab. Services, 1974—. Mem. R.I., Am. bar assns. Home: 52 Alexander St North Providence RI 02904 Office: 134 Francis St Providence RI 02903 Tel (401) 421-7000

MONTENEGRO, NICHOLAS CHARLES, b. Weehawkin, N.J., Nov. 3, 1942; B.A., Seton Hall U., 1963, J.D., 1969. Law clk. Hudson County (N.J.) Legal Services, 1967-69; staff atty., 1969-71; admitted to N.J. bar, 1969, Fla. bar, 1970; chief counsel N.J. Regional Drug Abuse Agy., Jersey City, 1971-72; partner firm Cornblatt & Montenegro, Brick Town, N.J., 1972-74; individual practice law, Brick Town, 1974—; acting magistrate City of Brick Town; pub. defender, Brick Town. Mem. local draft bd. Mem. Am., N.J., Fla., Ocean County bar assns. Named Jaycee of Month Brick Town Jaycees, 1974, 75, 76. Home: 485 Amherst Dr Brick Town NJ 08723 Office: 254 Brick Blvd Brick Town NJ 08723 Tel (201) 477-9600

MONTEVERDE, TOM P., b. Pitts., May 13, 1927; A.B. summa cum laude, U. Pitts., 1948; LL.B., Dickinson Sch. Law, 1951. Admitted to Pa. Supreme Ct. bar, 1952, also U.S. Supreme Ct. bar and others; asso. firm James J. Burns, Jr., Pitts., 1951-55; asso. firm Schnader, Harrison, Segal & Lewis, Phila., 1955-60, partner, 1960-70; partner firm Pelino, Wasserstrom, Chucas & Monteverde, Phila., 1971—; lectr. in field; vol. lawyer Miss. Project Lawyers Com. for Civil Rights, 1967; co-chmn. Dickinson Law Sch. Forum for Continuing Edn., 1973-76. Mem. Am., Pa., Phila., Allegheny County (Pa.) bar assns., Am. Trial Lawyers Assn., Phila. Trial Lawyers Assn., Am. Arbitration Assn., Lawyers Com. for Civil Rights Under Law, ACLU. Home: 411 E Willow Grove Ave Philadelphia PA 19118 Office: 2300 Packard Bldg 15th and Chestnut Sts Philadelphia PA 19102 Tel (215) 665-1440

MONTGOMERY, C.P., JR., b. Newport News, Va., Dec. 4, 1936; A.B., Dartmouth, 1959; LL.B., U. Va., 1965. Admitted to Va. bar, 1965; asst. commonwealth atty. Arlington County (Va.), 1965-66; asst. U.S. atty. for Eastern Va., Alexandria, 1967-71; asso. firm Herrell Campbell & Lawson, Arlington, Va., 1971-76; individual practice law, Vienna, Va., 1976—; spl. hearing officer U.S. Dept. Justice, 1967-68. Mem. Am., Arlington County, Fairfax County bar assns. Recipient Spl. Achievement award U.S. Dept. Justice, 1970. Home: 7303 Idylbrook Ct Falls Church VA 22043 Office: 8320 Old Courthouse Rd Suite 305 Vienna VA 22180 Tel (703) 821-1172

MONTGOMERY, CHARLES BARRY, b. Latrobe, Pa., Apr. 17, 1937; B.A., Muskingum Coll., New Concord, Ohio, 1959; J.D., U. Mich., 1962. Admitted to Ill. Supreme Ct. bar, 1962, U.S. Supreme Ct. bar, 1971; asso. firm Jacobs & McKenna, Chgo., 1962-67; partner firm Jacobs, Williams & Montgomery, Chgo., 1967—. Bd. dirs. Presbyterian Home, Evanston, Ill.; trustee Muskingum Coll. Mem. Am., Ill., Chgo. bar assns., Am. Arbitration Assn., Soc. Trial Lawyers, Internat. Assn. Ins. Council, Ill. Defense Counsel. Home: 313 Wisconsin Row Chicago IL 60614 Office: 20 N Wacker Dr Chicago IL 60606 Tel (312) 443-3242

MONTGOMERY, DAVID ROGERS, b. Roanoke, Va., Sept. 3, 1947; B.A., U. Va., 1969; J.D., U. Ga., 1972. Admitted to Ga. bar, 1972, U.S. Supreme Ct. bar, 1976; partner firm Hudson and Montgomery, Athens, Ga., 1972—. Mem. Am. Bar Assn., Am., Ga. trial lawyers assns. Home: Lexington GA 30648 Office: 316 So Mutual Bldg Athens GA 30601 Tel (404) 549-9823

MONTGOMERY, EDMUND WARREN, II, b. Yazoo City, Miss., Feb. 10, 1920; B.A., U. Miss., 1941, LL.B., 1947, J.D., 1968. Admitted to Miss. bar, 1947; sr. partner firm Howie, Montgomery & Montjoy, and predecessors, Jackson, Miss., 1947—; dep. comdt. Judge Adv. Gen's. Sch., U.S. Army, U. Va., 1970-71, chief judge U.S. Army Judiciary, Washington, 1971-75. Recipient Legion Merit, Legal Services, USAR, 1975, Meritorious Service medal, 1971; Legis. commendation State of Miss., 1974. Office: Suite 1224 Deposit Guaranty Plaza Jackson MI 39205 Tel (601) 948-6321

MONTGOMERY, EDWARD RUTHERFORD PAUL, b. Long Beach, Calif., June 16, 1922; A.B., U. Calif., Berkeley, 1947, LL.B., 1950. Admitted to Calif. bar, 1951; atty., jud. council Calif. Supreme Ct., San Francisco, 1951-52; atty. Fed. Land Bank, Berkeley, 1952-55; since practiced in Pasadena, Calif., partner firm Millikan, Montgomery, Olafson & Hardy, 1955-76, Montgomery & Lightfoot, 1976—. Mem. Am., Los Angeles, Pasadena bar assns. Office: 151 S El Molino Ave #303 Pasadena CA 91101 Tel (213) 577-1382

MONTGOMERY, H. GORDON, b. Ft. Worth, Feb. 11, 1922; B.A., Hardin-Simms U., 1945; M.A., Universidad de les Americas, 1967; J.D., U. Tex., 1949. Admitted to Tex. bar, 1949; partner firm Cox, Bradbury & Montgomery, Abilene, Tex., 1949-53; asst. dist. atty. Dallas, 1953-63; individual practice law, Mexico City, 1963-65; U.S. Area counsel HUD, P.R., San Antonio, 1965—. Home: 123 Brackenridge Apt 344 San Antonio TX 78209 Office: PO Box 9163 San Antonio TX 78285 Tel (512) 229-6770

MONTGOMERY, JEFF, b. Winfield, Tex., Jan. 11, 1920; B.S. in Petroleum Engring., Tex. A. and M. Coll., 1941; postgrad. Harvard Sch. Bus. Adminstrn., 1941-42; J.D., George Washington U., 1948. Admitted to Tex. bar, 1948; partner firm Klapproth, Hamilton & Montgomery, Midland, Tex., 1948-50; mgr. Tex. Crude Oil Co., Ft. Worth, 1950-53; cons. petroleum engring., Ft. Worth, 1953-54; v.p., dir. Murmanill Corp., Dallas, 1954-56; pres., dir. Kirby Industries, Inc., Houston, 1956-73, chmn. bd., 1973—; chmn. bd. Kirby Exploration Co., 1976—, Caribbean Finance Co., 1976—; dir. Cullen Center Bank & Trust Co., Houston, 1969—. Chmn. welfare com. Salvation Army Advisory Bd., Houston, 1965-69; bd. dirs. United Fund, Houston, 1971-73, Alley Theatre, Houston, 1973-76; trustee U. St. Thomas. Mem. Am. Inst. Mining, Metall, Petroleum Engrs., Am. Assn. Petroleum Geologists (asso.), Tex. Mid-Continent Oil, Gas Assn. (dir., exec. com.), Ind. Petroleum Assn. Am. (exec. com. 1973-75), Am. Petroleum Inst., Am. Inst. Mgmt., Am. Bar Assn., State Bar Tex., Nat. Petroleum Council, Order of Coif, Tau Beta Pi, Phi Delta Phi. Home: 2212 Del Monte Dr Houston TX 77019 Office: PO Box 1745 Houston TX 77001 Tel (713) 629-9370

MONTGOMERY, JOHN MICHAEL, b. Starkville, Miss., Dec. 4, 1947; B.S., Miss. State U., 1971; J.D., U. Miss., 1973. Admitted to Miss. bar, 1973; individual practice law, Starkville, 1973—; asst. dist. atty., Starkville; capt. Judge Adv. Gen. Corps Miss. Army Nat. Guard. Mem. Miss. Trial Lawyers Assn., Miss. Prosecutors Assn., Nat. Dist. Atty. Assn. Home: 409 Myrtle St Starkville MS 39759 Office: Box 891 Starkville MS 39759 Tel (601) 323-6916

MONTGOMERY, KENNETH FLOYD, b. Apalachicola, Fla., Apr. 15, 1903; A.B., Dartmouth, 1925; J.D. (scholar), Harvard, 1928; L.H.D., Columbia; L.H.D., Miles Coll. Admitted to Ill. bar, 1928; asso. firm Wilson & McIlvaine, Chgo., 1928-40, partner, 1940—; vis. com. mem. U. Chgo. Law Sch., Stanford Law Sch., Notre Dame Law Sch. Trustee Rush-Presbyterian-St. Luke's Hosp., Chgo.; charter trustee Lake Forest (Ill.) Coll. Mem. Am., Ill., Chgo. bar assns. Home: 24 Bridlewood Rd Northbrook IL 60062 Office: 135 S LaSalle St Rm 2300 Chicago IL 60603 Tel (312) 263-1212

MONTGOMERY, LUTHER SIDNEY, b. Tickfaw, La., Nov. 11, 1911; student E. Tex. Bapt. Coll., 1931-32; LL.B., La. State U., 1938. Admitted to La. bar, 1940; spl. agent FBI, 1941-45; commr. wildlife and fisheries State of La., 1945-48; practice law, Shreveport, La. Mem. La. Bar Assn. Home: 536 Jordan St Shreveport LA 71101 Office: 622 Lane Bldg Shreveport LA 71101 Tel (318) 221-7589

MONTGOMERY, PAUL, JR., b. Laurel, Miss., Nov. 26, 1935; B.S., La. State U., 1956; LL.B., U. Miss., 1963, J.D., 1968; M.R.E., New Orleans Baptist Theol. Sem., 1969. Admitted to Miss. bar, 1963, Ga. bar, 1974; atty. Callon Petroleum Co., Natchez, Miss., 1964-68; ednl. ministry Ga. Baptist Chs., various cities, 1970-72; dir. devel. Ga. Baptist Found., Atlanta, 1973—. Mem. Am. Bar Assn. Home: 1306 N Shady Grove Ct Stone Mountain GA 30083 Office: 2930 Flowers Rd S Atlanta GA 30341 Tel (404) 455-0404

MONTGOMERY, SETH DAVID, b. Santa Fe, N.Mex., Feb. 16, 1937; A.B., Princeton U., 1959; LL.B., Stanford U., 1965. Admitted to N.Mex. bar, 1965, U.S. Tax Ct. bar, 1976; asso. atty. firm Montgomery, Andrews & Hannahs, Santa Fe, 1965-67, partner 1968—; chmn. N.Mex. State Adv. Council to Legal Services Corp., 1976—; vis. instr. U. N.Mex. Sch. Law, 1970-71; mem. N.Mex. Supreme Ct. Adv. Com. on Statutes. Trustee Santa Fe Prep. Sch., 1968-74, Legal Aid Soc. Santa Fe, 1968-76. Mem. Am. Bar Assn., Am. Judicature Soc., Bar Assn. 1st Judicial Dist. Office: 325 Paseo de Peralta Santa Fe NM 87501 Tel (505) 982-3873

MONTGOMERY, WILLIAM ADAM, b. Evanston, Ill., May 22, 1933; B.A., Williams Coll., 1955; LL.B., Harvard U., 1958. Admitted to D.C. bar, 1958, Ill. bar, 1958; atty. appellate sect. civil div. Dept. Justice, Washington, 1958-60; asso. firm Schiff, Harding & Waite, Chgo., 1960-68, partner, 1968—. Bd. trustees Inst. Psychoanalysis, Chgo., 1976; mem. caucus com. Village of Winnetka, 1974-75; alumni adminstr. Tyng Bequest, Williams Coll., 1976. Mem. Am., Chgo., Ill. bar assns., Bar Assn. Seventh Fed. Circuit, Williams Alumni Assn. Chgo. (pres. 1970-72). Office: 7200 Sears Tower 233 S Wacker St Chicago IL 60606 Tel (312) 876-1000

MONTIE, GARY ARTHUR, b. Milw., Feb. 12, 1948; B.S., U. Wis., 1970, J.D., 1973. Admitted to Wis. bar, U.S. Dist. Ct. bar, 1973; asso. firm Donald S. Eisenberg & Assos., Madison, Wis., 1973-74; hearing examiner State of Wis. Dept. Health and Social Services, 1974-75; partner firm Montie, Wadsack & Youngerman, Madison, 1975—; supervising atty. Community Law Offices, Madison, 1975—; legal advisor Madison Tenant Union, 1974-75. Mem. Am. Bar Assn., Am. Trial Lawyers Assn. Home: 136 Lathrop St Madison WI 53705 Office: 222 S Hamilton St Madison WI 53703 Tel (608) 257-4580

MONTOYA, SAMUEL ZACHARY, b. Pena Blanca, N.Mex., Dec. 2, 1916; A.B., U. N.Mex., 1936; LL.B., Georgetown U., 1941. Admitted to N.Mex. bar, 1941; practiced in Santa Fe, 1946-58, mem. firm Andrews and Montoya, 1957-58; city atty. City of Santa Fe, 1955-58; judge N.Mex. Dist. Ct., 1st Jud. Dist., 1959-71; justice N.Mex. Supreme Ct., 1971-76; mem. Santa Fe City Council, 1949-54; U.S. del. Inter-Am. Conf. Attys. Gen., Mexico City, 1963; chmn. N.Mex. adv. com. Nat. Commn. on Civil Rights, 1959-63. Treas., N.Mex. Democratic Party, 1957-58; chmn. bd. dirs. N.Mex. State Hosp., Las Vegas, 1959-61. Mem. Nat. Council Juvenile Ct. Judges (v.p. 1969-71), Nat. Council Crime and Delinquency (adv. council on judges 1967-70), N.Mex. Jud. Conf. (pres. 1970-71), Santa Fe County Bar Assn. (pres. 1951-52), Pi Sigma Alpha. Decorated Bronze Star. Home and Office: 216 Sombrio Dr Santa Fe NM 87501 Tel (505) 983-8545

MOODY, BLAIR, JR., b. Detroit, Feb. 27, 1928; B.A. in Econs., U. Mich., 1949, LL.B., 1952; grad. Nat. Coll. State Trial Judges, 1966. News reporter Detroit News, 1948-49, Washington Post, 1952; admitted to Mich. bar, 1952; served with JAGC, USAF, 1952-53; partner firm Sullivan, Eames, Moody & Petrillo, Detroit, 1953-65; judge 3d Mich. Circuit Ct., 1965-76; justice Mich. Supreme Ct., 1977—. Elder Meml. Presbyn. Ch.; mem. adv. bd. We Care, Inc.; active PTA, Little League, Vol. Probation Program. Mem. Detroit, Mich., Am. bar assns., Mich. Judges Assn. (v.p., exec. bd.), Phi Delta Phi, Phi Delta Theta. Home: 69 Willow Tree Pl Grosse Pointe Shores MI 48236 Office: 1425 Lafayette Bldg Detroit MI 48226 Tel (313) 256-9628

MOODY, CHESLEY GARY, b. New London, Conn., July 14, 1944; B.S. in Advt., U. Fla., 1968, J.D., 1971. Admitted to Fla. bar, 1971; partner firm Koch & Moody, Gainesville, Fla., 1971-72, Miller & Moody, Gainesville, 1972-75, Moody & Reed, Gainesville, 1975—; agt. St. Paul Title Ins. Co.; mem. Lawyers Title Guaranty Fund. Mem. Am., Fla. trial lawyers assns., 8th Jud. Bar Assn. Home: 4233 NW 32d St Gainesville FL 32605 Office: 605 NE 1st St Gainesville FL 32601 Tel (904) 373-6791

MOODY, EARLE FARLEY, II, b. Dothan, Ala., Nov. 23, 1944; B.S., U. Ala., 1968; J.D., Cumberland Sch. Law, 1973. Admitted to Ala. bar, 1973, Fla. bar, 1974; clk., presiding judge Ala. Ct. Civil Appeals, Montgomery, 1973-74; individual practice law, Birmingham, Ala., 1974—; spl. asst. atty. gen. State of Ala., 1975—. Mem. Am., Birmingham, Ala., Fla. bar assns. Home: 2301 Lullwater Rd Birmingham AL 35243 Office: 500 Southland Dr Birmingham AL 55226 Tel (205) 823-5968

MOODY, JAMES SHELTON, b. Plant City, Fla., Dec. 29, 1914; student Washington and Lee U., 1933-34; B.S. in Bus. Adminstrn. with honors, U. Fla., 1959, J.D. with honors, 1939. Admitted to Fla. bar, 1939; partner firm Trinkle & Moody, Plant City, 1939-57; judge Fla. Circuit Ct., 13th Jud. Circuit, 1957—, presiding judge, 1963-65; mem. Fla. Ho. of Reps., 1948-57; mem. Fla. Jud. Qualifications Commn., 1969-75, vice chmn., 1974-75; chmn. Fla. Conf. Circuit Judges, 1970; dir. Hillsboro Bank, Plant City, Sunshine State Fed. Savings & Loan Assn., Plant City. Bd. dirs. Strawberry Festival Assn., Plant City; mem. exec. bd. Gulf Ridge council Boy Scouts Am.; elder 1st Presbyn. Ch., Plant City. Mem. Hillsborough County, Fla. bar assns. Named Most Valuable Rep. Fla. Press, 1957, Most Valuable Mem. Legislature Fla. Legislature, 1957. Home: 803 N Collins St Plant City FL 33566 Office: Hillsborough County Courthouse Tampa FL 33602 Tel (813) 229-1682

MOODY, LIZABETH ANN, b. Johnson City, Tenn., July 11, 1934; A.B., Columbia, 1956; LL.B., Yale, 1959. Admitted to Conn. bar, 1959, Ohio bar, 1960; asso. firm Goldstein & Peck, Bridgeport, Conn., 1959-60; asso. firm Slough & Slough, Cleve., 1960-61, 63-66; asso. firm Gottfried, Ginsberg, Guren & Merrit, Cleve., 1962; partner firm Metzenbaum, Gaines, Finley & Stern, Cleve., 1967-71; asso. prof. law Cleve. State U., 1970-73, prof. law, 1973—; mem. civil rights reviewing authority HEW, 1974—; sec., gen. counsel United Mfg. Co., 1969-71; dir. Allied Steel & Tractor Co.; dir., sec. Penril Corp., 1968-71; sec. Com Corp., Inc., 1969-71. Mem. Ohio Pub. Defender Commn., 1976—; mem. advisory council Ohio Bur. Employment Services, 1970-74; pres., trustee Women's Law Fund, 1972—. Mem. Bar Assn. Greater Cleveland (trustee 1973-76), Am. Bar Assn., Am. Assn. Law Schs. (exec. com. 1976—), Soc. Am. Law Tchrs., Nat. Assn. Women Lawyers. Author: Smith's Review of Estates, Trusts and Administration, 1973; Smith's Review of Corporations, 1976; contbr. articles to profl. jours.; recipient Meritorious service award Bar Assn. Greater Cleve., 1973, award Ams. for Democratic Action, 1976. Home: 17210 Parkland Dr Shaker Heights OH 44120 Office: Coll Law Cleve State Univ Cleveland OH 44115 Tel (216) 687-2348

MOODY, NANCY PAXTON, b. Austin, Tex., Sept. 20, 1932; student Sweet Briar (Va.) Coll., 1950-51; B.A., U. Tex., 1956, LL.B., 1958. Admitted to Tex. bar, 1958; asso. firm Moody, Robertson and Moody, Austin, 1958-59; individual practice law, Austin, 1960—; parliamentarian 56th Legis. Tex. Senate, 1959. Trustee United Fund, Brownsville, Tex., 1960-63; bd. dirs. Austin Child Guidance Center, 1964-69. Mem. State Bar Tex., Am. Bar Assn. Office: PO Box 5128 Austin TX 78763 Tel (512) 478-4012

MOODY, ROBERT CARROLL, b. Richmond, Ky., Aug. 13, 1937; B.A., U. Ky., 1959, J.D., 1968. Admitted to Ky. bar, 1968; partner firm Moody, Fagan & Moody, Richmond, 1968-76; individual practice law, Richmond, 1976—; asst. prof. law enforcement Eastern Ky. U., 1969-74; city atty. City of Richmond, 1974—. Chmn. Cancer Soc. Crusade, Richmond, 1976; bd. dirs. Madison County (Ky.) Ambulance Service, Madison County Red Cross. Mem. Madison County, Ky. bar assns., Municipal Attys. Assn. Ky. Home: Route 1 PO Box 118 Berea KY 40403 Office: PO Box 675 101 E Irvine St Richmond KY 40475 Tel (606) 623-7333

MOODY, RONALD HUDSON, b. Waco, Tex., Apr. 16, 1943; LL.B., Baylor U., 1967. Admitted to Tex. bar, 1967; pros. atty. McLennan County (Tex.) Dist. Attys. Office, Waco, 1967-68; judge Kaufman County (Tex.), 1969-72; partner firm Moody & Crow, Waco, 1972—. Mem. Tex., McLennan County bar assns. Office: 3801 W Waco Dr Waco TX 76710 Tel (817) 753-6455

MOODY, STEVE EARL, b. Washington, Apr. 21, 1945; A.B., Mercer U., Macon, Ga., 1967, J.D., 1970. Admitted to Fla. bar, 1971; asso. firm Watson, Hubert & Davis, Ft. Lauderdale, Fla., 1971-73; partner firm Moody & Jones, and predecessors, Ft. Lauderdale, 1973—. Mem. Am., Fla., Broward County bar assns., Fla., Broward County trial lawyers assns. Office: 3661 W Oakland Park Blvd Fort Lauderdale FL 33311 Tel (305) 733-8505

MOOERS, EDWIN ABNER, JR., b. Washington, Nov. 10, 1916; student Mt. St. Mary's Coll.; B.A., George Washington U., 1938; J.D., Am. U., 1941. Admitted to D.C. bar, 1942, U.S. Supreme Ct. bar, 1947; asso. firm Hamilton and Hamilton, Washington, 1944-52; partner firm Mooers and Marmorstone, Washington, 1952—; adj. prof. Law Sch., Am. U., 1957—; lectr. Practising Law Inst., 1970-73; dist. counsel Gen. Electric Co. and Hotpoint Co., 1952-65. Mem. D.C. Bar Assn., Am. Trial Lawyers Assn. (spl. award 1972), Phi Alpha Delta (spl. award 1968). Author: Digest of the Law of Wills and Probate Procedure for D.C. for Practising Law Inst., 1970. Home: 5005 Belt Rd NW Washington DC 20016 Office: 1400 20th St NW Washington DC 20036 Tel (202) 296-3744

MOON, ALBERT IVAN, JR., b. Tucson, Jan. 25, 1931; B.S., Carnegie-Mellon U., 1952; J.D., U. Calif., Los Angeles, 1961. Admitted to Calif. bar, 1962, U.S. Supreme Ct. bar, 1968, Hawaii bar, 1971, Trust Terr. Pacific bar, 1973; test engr. Convair Co., Pomona, Calif., 1952-55; project engr. Aerophysics Devel. Corp., Santa Barbara, Calif., 1955-58; individual practice law, Oxnard, Calif., 1961-62; asst. counsel The Aerospace Corp., El Segundo, Calif., 1962-65; corp. counsel Holmes & Narver, Inc., Los Angeles, 1965-70; v.p., gen. counsel ONC Motor Freight System, Palo Alto, Calif., 1970-71; partner firm Ashford & Wriston, Honolulu, 1971—; arbitrator Am. Arbitration Assn. Mem. Am., Hawaii, Calif. bar assns. Contbr. article to Jour. Air Law and Commerce. Home: 46-305 Ikiiki St Kaneohe HI 96744 Office: 235 Queen St Honolulu HI 96810 Tel (808) 524-4787

MOON, DAVID CARROLL, b. Topeka, Aug. 13, 1941; A.B. cum laude, Occidental Coll., Los Angeles, 1963; postgrad. London Sch. Econs., 1964-65; M.A. Fletcher Sch. Law and Diplomacy, 1964; J.D., U. Calif., Berkeley, 1968. Admitted to Calif. bar, 1969, U.S. Supreme Ct. bar, 1973; asso. firm Milbank, Tweed, Hadley & McCloy, N.Y.C., 1968-70; dir. Solano County Legal Assistance, Vallejo, Calif., 1971; directing atty. San Francisco Neighborhood Legal Assistance, 1971-76; asst. dist. atty., San Francisco, 1976—; lectr. Golden Gate Coll. Law., San Francisco. Chmn. non-victim crime com. San Francisco Barristers' Club, 1976; del. Calif. State Bar Conv., 1976. Mem. San Francisco Bar Assn. (mem. spl. com. revision fed. ct. appellate system), Calif. State Bar (com. on pub. interest law practice 1976—), Phi Beta Kappa. Contbr. articles to legal jours. Office: 880 Bryant St San Francisco CA 94103 Tel (415) 553-1821

MOON, FRED ARNOLD, b. Miller, Dakota Ter., Jan. 4, 1887; grad. U. Mo., 1908. Admitted to Mo. bar, 1908; city atty., Springfield, Mo., 1914-1920; gen. counsel Indsl. Loan & Investment Co., Springfield, 1929-68, Springfield Garment Mfg. Co., 1944-67, Union Stock Yards, Springfield, 1934-77, Commerce Bank, Springfield, 1930-76. Del. Democratic Nat. Conv., 1940; mem. Greene County Library Bd., 1952. Mem. Mo., Greene County bar assns. Recipient Certificate of Appreciation, Pres. of the U.S., 1942, Commerce Bank, 1974, Certificate of Appreciation Library Award, Springfield-Greene County, 1975. Home: 2049 Brentwood Springfield MO 65804 Office: 1705 N Jefferson Springfield MO 65803 Tel (417) 862-3704

MOONEY, GERALD KENNETH, b. Spokane, Wash., July 20, 1943; B.A., St. Vincent Coll., 1965; J.D., Gonzaga Sch., 1969. Admitted to Wash. bar, 1970; clk. Supreme Ct. Wash., Olympia, 1969-72, sr. counsel House Judiciary Com. Wash. Legislature, 1973-75, partner firm Mooney & Cullen, 1972-73, Mooney, Cullen & Holm, 1973—; mem. Legis. Com. Wash. State Bar Assn. 1975—, exec. bd. Real Property Probate and Trust sect. Wash. State Bar Assn. 1976—. Division chmn. United Way Thurston County, 1976, mem. bd. Olympia C. of C. (chmn. congl. and legis. affairs com. 1975-76); county chmn. Rosellini for Governor campaign 1972, state coordinator Brown for President 1976. Mem. Am. (mem. service contracts com., pub. contract law sect.), Wash. State, Thurston-Mason County bar assns., Wash. State Trial Lawyers Assn. Author: (with Golob) Practitioners Guide: Washington Criminal Code, 1976, supplement, 1977; exec. editor, co-author: Construction Liens and Claims, 1968-69, contbr. articles to legal jours. Home: Rt 9 Box 378 Olympia WA 98506 Office: Suite 301 201 W 5th Ave Olympia WA 98501 Tel (206) 943-6747

MOONEY, ROBERT PHILLIP, b. Cleve., Sept. 16, 1926; student Miami U., 1944, 46-48; J.D., U. Cin., 1950; postgrad. Harvard Law Sch., 1950-51. Admitted to Ohio bar, 1950, U.S. Supreme Ct. bar, 1973; since practiced in Cleve., atty. Harris Intertype Corp., 1951-58; asso. counsel, asst. sec. Hupp Corp., 1958-67; gen. counsel, asst. sec. Harshaw Chem. Co., 1967—. Mem. Ohio, Cleve. bar assns., Am. Soc. Corporate Secs., Delta Upsilon, Phi Alpha Delta. Home: 84 E 194th St Euclid OH 44119 Office: 1945 E 97th St Cleveland OH 44106 Tel (216) 721-8300

MOORADIAN, CARL EDWARD, b. Niagara Falls, N.Y., Feb. 2, 1942; A.B., Brown U., 1964; LL.B., State U. N.Y., Buffalo, 1967, J.D., 1968. Admitted to N.Y. bar, 1967; asso. firm A. Russell Leone, Niagara Falls, 1969-74, also asst. to N.Y. State Estate Tax Atty. for Niagara County, 1969-74; asst. corp. counsel City of Niagara Falls, 1974-75, corp. counsel, 1975—; individual practice law, Niagara Falls, 1974—. Mem. Niagara Falls Human Relations Commn., 1973-75. Mem. Am., N.Y. State, Niagara County, Niagara Falls bar assns., Nat. Inst. Municipal Legal Officers. Office: 324 Pine Ave Niagara Falls NY 14301 Tel (716) 284-9660

MOORE, ALFRED, b. Hattiesburg, Miss., May 28, 1912; B.A., U. So. Miss., 1934, LL.B., 1936. Admitted to Miss. bar, 1936; partner firm Moore, Jones & Moore, Hattiesburg, 1961—; pres. First Magnolia Fed. Savs. and Loan Assn., Hattiesburg, 1968—; adv. com. Miss. Employment Security Commn., 1962—. Active U. So. Miss. Found., Hattiesburg; former pres. Hattiesburg Civic Assn. Mem. Am., S. Central (past pres.) bar assns., Miss. State Bar, Miss. Bar Found., U.S. Savs. and Loan League (dir.), Am. Judicature Soc., Fed. Home Loan Bank Bd. (past dir.), Hattiesburg C. of C. (dir., past pres.), U. So. Miss., U. Miss. alumni assns. Home: 2312 Carriage Rd Hattiesburg MS 39401 Office: 130 W Front St Hattiesburg MS 39401 Tel (601) 544-1700

MOORE, ANDREW GIVEN TOBIAS, II, b. New Orleans, Nov. 25, 1935; B.B.A., Tulane U., 1958, J.D., 1960. Admitted to La. bar, 1960, Del. bar, 1963; partner firm Killoran & Van Brunt, Wilmington, Del., 1964-76, Connolly, Bove & Lodge, Wilmington, 1976—; with JAGC, USAF, 1960-63; law clk. to chief justice Del. Supreme Ct., 1963; mem. Del. Bd. Accountancy, 1965-72; mem. Del. Bd. Bar Examiners, 1975—. Mem. Am., La., Del. (v.p.) bar assns. Contbr. article to legal jour. Home: 11 Red Oak Rd Wilmington DE 19806 Office: 1800 Farmers Bank Bldg Wilmington DE 19899 Tel (302) 658-9141

MOORE, ARNOLD CARMICHAEL, b. McDonough, Ga., June 9, 1935; B.A., Emory U., 1957, LL.B., U. Ga., 1960; LL.M., N.Y. U., 1961. Admitted to Ga. bar, 1959; partner firm Troutman, Sanders, Lockerman & Ashmore, Atlanta, 1970—. Mem. Am., Ga., Atlanta bar assns., Lawyers Club Atlanta. Home: 3835 Vermont Rd Atlanta GA 30319 Office: 1400 Candler Bldg Atlanta GA 30303 Tel (404) 658-8076

MOORE, ARTHUR WILLIAM, b. Erie, Pa., Feb. 10, 1920; B.S. in Econs., U. Pa., 1941; LL.B., Georgetown U., 1948. Admitted to Ohio bar, 1949, D.C. bar, 1949; partner firm Taggart Cox Moore & Hays, Wooster, Ohio, 1949-71; individual practice law, Wooster, 1972—. Bd. dirs. Red Cross Wayne County, 1971—, Wooster YMCA, 1972, Wooster C. of C., 1960. Mem. Wayne County, Ohio, Am. bar assns. Home: 201 Holmes Blvd Wooster OH 44691 Office: 146 E Liberty St Wooster OH 44691 Tel (216) 262-6333

MOORE, BEVERLY COOPER, b. Greensboro, N.C., Dec. 8, 1909; A.B., U. N.C., 1931; LL.B., J.D., Yale, 1934. Admitted to N.C. bar, 1934; individual practice law, Greensboro, 1934-42; partner firm Smith, Moore, Smith, Schell & Hunter and predecessors, Greensboro, 1945—; mem. N.C. Gen. Assembly, 1941-43. Fellow Am. Coll. Trial Lawyers, Am. Bar Found.; mem. Greensboro (pres. 1949-50), N.C. (pres. 1958-59) bar assns., Am. Law Inst., Am. Bar Assn. (mem. ho. of dels. 1962—, bd. govs. 1970-73). Home: 906 Country Club Dr Greensboro NC 27408 Office: PO Drawer G Greensboro NC 27420 Tel (919) 378-1450

MOORE, CHARLES EDWIN, b. Des Moines, Aug. 2, 1903; LL.B., Drake U., 1927. Admitted to Ia. bar, 1927; gen. practice, Des Moines, 1927-34; asst. county atty. Polk County, 1934-36; judge Des Moines Municipal Ct., 1936-43, 9th Jud. dist. Ia. Dist. Ct., 1942-62; justice Ia. Supreme Ct., 1962—, now chief justice; part-time instr. Drake U. Law Sch., 1941-62. Mem. Am., Ia., Polk County bar assns. Republican. Methodist. Mason (33 deg., Shriner). Home: 1540 Guthrie Ave Des Moines IA 50316 Office: State House Des Moines IA 50316*

MOORE, CHARLES RAPHAEL, JR., b. St. John's, Nfld., Can., Jan. 11, 1934; B.S., U. R.I., 1958; LL.D., Boston Coll., 1962; LL.M. In Taxation, Boston U., 1964. Admitted to Conn. bar, 1963, Mass. bar, 1964; individual practice law, Hartford, Conn., 1964-68; asso. firm Gross Hyde & Williams, Hartford, 1968-71, partner, 1971—; dir. Charles Parker Corp., Union Mfg. Corp. Mem. Am., Conn. (chmn. com. liaison with accountants), Hartford County (Conn.) (chmn. com. continuing legal edn.) bar assns. Home: Harbor View North Essex CT 06426 Office: 799 Main St Hartford CT 06103 Tel (203) 278-1420

MOORE, CHARLES ROY, b. Maynardville, Tenn., Jan. 31, 1910. Admitted to Tenn. bar, 1933, U.S. Supreme Ct. bar, 1939; individual practice law, Maynardville, 1932-36; with FTC, Washington, atty., 1936—; atty. in charge food and drug sect., legal adviser to bur. field ops., atty. in charge field ops.; individual practice law, Maynardville, 1971—; city atty. City of Maynardville, 1971-76; county atty. County of Union, 19—. Recipient Distinguished Service award FTC, 1958; award of Merit Nat. Civil Service League, 1975; contbr. articles to law revs. Office: Spring St Maynardville TN 37807 Tel (615) 992-8101

MOORE, DAVID BROWNING, b. Carroll, Iowa, May 25, 1943; B.S., N.W. Mo. U., 1965; J.D., U. Iowa, 1968. Admitted to Iowa bar, 1968; county atty., Shelby County, Iowa, 1969-72; partner firm Louis, Moore & Kohorst, Harlan, Iowa, 1970—; chmn. Shelby County Crime Commn., 1969—; mem. S.W. Iowa Crime Commn., 1971—; mem. Iowa Crime Commn., 1974-75. Chmn., Shelby County Republican party, 1974-76. Mem. Iowa, S.W. Iowa, Shelby County (pres. 1975-76) bar assns. Home: 1808 18th St Harlan IA 51537 Office: 602 B Market St Harlan IA 51537 Tel (712) 755-3156

MOORE, DWIGHT BROWN, b. Keokuk, Iowa, Dec. 20, 1931; B.A., U. Md., 1953; LL.B., U. Va., 1956. Admitted to Va. bar, 1956, Ohio bar, 1962, Ill. bar, 1973; trial atty., antitrust div. U.S. Justice Dept., Cleve., 1956-72, asst. chief, Cleve., 1968-72, chief, Los Angeles, 1975—; individual practice law, Chgo., 1973-74. Office: 1444 US Court House Los Angeles CA 90012 Tel (213) 688-2500

MOORE, E. DON, b. Sardis, Miss., Sept. 6, 1923; LL.B., Jackson Sch. Law, 1948. Admitted to Miss. bar, 1948; br. mgr. Zurich Ins. Co., 1951-72, sr. v.p., Jackson, Miss., 1972—. Mem. Miss. Ins. Council (past pres.), Miss. Soc. CPCU (past pres.). Club: Servian. Home: 4830 Northampton St Jackson MS 39211 Office: PO Box 5137 Jackson MS 39216 Tel (601) 939-0440

MOORE, E. JAMES, b. Forsyth County, N.C., July 17, 1926; B.S., Wake Forest U., 1949, LL.B., 1951, J.D., 1970. Admitted to N.C. bar, 1951; asso. firm Lassiter Moore & Van Allen, Charlotte, N.C., 1952-53; since practiced in Wilkesboro, N.C., individual practice, 1953-55, 60-68, 69—, partner firm Porter & Moore, 1955-60, Moore & Moore, 1969; mayor and judge mayor's ct. N.Wilkesboro, N.C., 1961-63; judge Wilkes County Spl. Ct., 1964-65. Mem. Am., N.C. bar assns., N.C. Assn. Municipal Attys., Wilkes C. of C. (dir.). Active rev. of municipal laws. Home: 2 Eastover Dr North Wilkesboro NC 28659 Office: 924 B St North Wilkesboro NC 28659 Tel (919) 667-1129

MOORE, EMERSON LOGAN, b. Indpls., Sept. 26, 1943; A.B., Brown U., 1965; J.D., U. Ill., 1968. Admitted to Ill. bar, 1968, U.S. Dist. Ct. bar, 1976, asst. state's atty. Champaign County, Ill., 1968-72; asso. firm Lemna & Lee, Tuscola, Ill., 1972-74, partner, 1975-76; partner firm Lemna & Moore, 1977—; city atty., Arcola, Ill., 1974—. Advisor Law Explorer Post Boy Scouts Am., Tuscola, 1975—; chmn. Arcola Citizens Advisory Com., 1976—. Mem. Ill., Douglas County bar assns. Home: 363 W Main St Arcola IL 61910 Office: 401 S Main Tuscola IL 61953 Tel (217) 253-2383

MOORE, ESCUM LIONEL, JR., b. Lexington, Ky., Sept. 8, 1942; A.B., U. Ky., 1964, J.D., 1966. Admitted to Ky. bar, 1966; law clk. U.S. Dist. Judge Eastern Dist. Ky., 1966-67; partner firm Turley, Savage & Moore, Lexington, 1967—; adj. prof. law U. Ky., 1973—. Mem. Am., Ky., Fayette County bar assns., Am. Judicature Soc., U. Ky. Alumni Assn. (dir.). Home: 340 Hart Rd Lexington KY 40502 Office: 134 N Limestone St Lexington KY 40507 Tel (606) 252-1705

MOORE, GEORGE CRAWFORD JACKSON, b. Chattanooga, Dec. 9, 1942; B.A., U. Fla., 1963; B. Ph., St. Andrews (Scotland) U., 1966; B.A. in English Law, Cambridge (Eng.) U., 1968, M.A., 1973, LL.B. in Internat. Law, 1969. Admitted to English bar, 1970, Jamaican bar, 1971, Fla. bar, 1972, Turks and Caicos Islands (W.I.)

bar, 1974, U.S. Supreme Ct. bar, 1976; legis. asst. to Senator Charles McC. Mathias, Jr., Washington, 1970-72; asst. pub. defender Fla. 15th Jud. Circuit, West Palm Beach, 1973; individual practice law, West Palm Beach, Fla., 1973—, Turks and Caicos Islands, 1974—; founder, dir. law careers program pub. and pvt. schs., Boca Raton, Fla.; of counsel firm Bratten & Harris, West Palm Beach; barrister-at-law Inner Temple, London. Mem. Am. Soc. Internat. Law, Brit. Inst. Internat. and Comparative Law, Am., Inter-Am., Palm Beach County (chmn. com. internat. law) bar assns., Fla. Bar, Southeastern Admiralty Law Inst., U.S. Maritime Law Assn., Cambridge U. Grads. Students Union (pres. 1969). Co-author: Turks and Caicos Island, 1975. Home: 500 N Congress St Apt 207 West Palm Beach FL 33401 Office: 500 Comeau Bldg 319 Clematis St West Palm Beach FL 33401 Tel (305) 659-2400

MOORE, GEORGE ELLIS, b. Long Beach, Calif., Mar. 31, 1936; B.S. in Indsl. Mgmt., U. So. Calif., 1957; J.D., Loyola U., Los Angeles, 1964. Admitted to Calif. bar, 1965; partner firm Belcher, Henzie & Biegenzahn, Los Angeles, 1965-73, firm Harney & Moore, Los Angeles, 1973—; lectr. Calif. Continuing Edn. of the Bar, Bridging the Gap, Bd. dirs. Escape Homeowners Assn., 1975—. Mem. Am., Calif., Los Angeles County bar assns., Am. Bd. Trial Advs., Los Angeles Trial Lawyers Assn. (dir.). Home: 2427 Chislehurst Dr Los Angeles CA 90027 Office: 650 S Grand Ave Suite 1200 Los Angeles CA 90017 Tel (213) 626-8761

MOORE, GEORGE ROBERT, b. Washington, Pa., Jan. 10, 1943; B.A., Washington and Jefferson Coll., 1964; J.D., Vanderbilt U., 1967. Admitted to Pa. bar, 1968; with JAGC, USMC, 1968-71; law clk. to judge U.S. Dist. Ct. for Western Dist. Pa., 1971-72; asso. firm Eckert Seamans Cherin & Mellott, Pitts., 1972—. Office: 42d floor 600 Grant St Pittsburgh PA 15219 Tel (412) 566-6000

MOORE, JAMES WALTERS, b. Johnstown, Pa., Jan. 20, 1928; A.B. in Govt. and Pub. Adminstrn., Dartmouth, 1950; LL.B., U. Pa., 1956. Admitted to Pa. bar, 1957, Mass. bar, 1962; asso. firm Duane, Morris & Heckscher, Phila., 1956-61; sec., gen. counsel Itek Corp., Lexington, Mass., 1961—. Mem. Am., Boston bar assns., Am. Soc. Corporates Secs., Internat. Fiscal Assn. Home: 116 Meadowbrook Rd Weston MA 02193 Office: 10 Maguire Rd Lexington MA 02173 Tel (617) 276-3015

MOORE, JOHN ADAMS, JR., b. Oshkosh, Wis., Dec. 5, 1943; B.S., U. Wis. at Madison, 1966, J.D., 1969. Admitted to Wis. bar, 1969, Wash. State bar, 1971; dep. pros. atty. Yakima County (Wash.), Yakima, 1971-73; individual practice law, Yakima, 1973—; instr. Yakima Valley Community Coll., 1974. Bd. dirs. Cath. Family and Child Services, 1976. Mem. Wis., Yakima County, Wash. State bar assns. Home: Rural Route 6 Box 319 A Yakima WA 98908 Office: 516 Miller Bldg Yakima WA 98901 Tel (509) 457-4126

MOORE, JOHN CHAMBERLAIN, b. Auburn, N.Y., May 7, 1915; B.A., Yale U., 1938, LL.B., 1941. Admitted to N.Y. State bar, 1942, U.S. Supreme Ct. bar, 1972; asso. firm Haight, Gardner, Poor & Havens, and predecessors, N.Y.C., 1941-48, partner, 1949—. Vestryman and warden St. John's Ch.,, Pleasantville, N.Y., 1949-51, 66-68; active Boy Scouts Am., 1954—, scout commr. Washington Irving council, White Plains, N.Y., 1959-63, Greenwich (Conn.) council, 1973—. Mem. Maritime Law Assn. U.S. (exec. com. 1952-55, sec. 1956-59, v.p. 1966-68, chmn. com. on bills of lading 1952—), Comité Maritime Internationale. Home: 232 Riverside Ave Riverside CT 06878 Office: One State St Plaza New York City NY 10004 Tel (212) 344-6800

MOORE, JOHN CHARLES, b. El Paso, Tex., Dec. 17, 1943; B.A., Washington and Lee U., 1966, J.D., 1973; M.A., Northwestern U., 1967; postgrad. Universitaet Tuebingen, W.Ger., 1968. Admitted to Va. bar, 1973; asso. firm Mays, Valentine, Davenport & Moore, Richmond, Va., 1973-76; partner firm Coates & Comess, Richmond, 1976; partner firm Coates, Comess, Settle, Moore & Taylor, Richmond, 1977—; adj. prof. bus. law Va. Commonwealth U., 1976. Mem. service bd. First Baptist Ch., Richmond; bd. dirs. Sr. Center, Inc., Richmond. Mem. Am., Va., Richmond bar assns., Va. State Bar, Phi Beta Kappa, Omicron Delta Kappa. Home: 4406 S Ashlawn Dr Richmond VA 23221 Office: 113 N Foushee St Richmond VA 23220

MOORE, JOHN LEE, b. Ortonville, Minn., Sept. 27, 1931; B.A., Beloit Coll., 1953; J.D., Northwestern U., 1956. Admitted to Ill. bar, 1957; with Country Mut. Ins. Co., Chgo., 1956-58; mem. firm Garard & Moore, Oregon, Ill., 1958-64; state's atty. Ogle County, 1964-68; magistrate 15th Circuit Ct. of Ill., Oregon, 1968-70; judge 15th Jud. Circuit Ct. of Ill., Oregon, 1970—; mem. NW Ill. Criminal Justice Commn., 1973—, vice chmn., 1975-76. Mem. Am., Ill. bar assns., Am. Judicature Soc., Juveniles Judges Assn. Home: 500 North 4th St Oregon IL 61061 Office: Ct House Oregon IL 61061 Tel (815) 732-2004

MOORE, JOSEPH WILLIAM, b. Braddock, Pa., Dec. 17, 1925; B.A. magna cum laude, U. Pitts., 1946-50, J.D., 1953. Admitted to Pa. bar, 1954; law clk. firm Reed, Smith, Shaw & McClay, Pitts., 1953-54; asso. firm Baker, Watts & Woods, Pitts., 1954-55; atty. advisor, asst. security officer Bur. Ordnance, U.S. Dept. Navy, Washington, 1955-59; asst. dir. contracts Cleve. Pneumatic Industries, 1959-60; individual practice law, Pitts., 1960-61; asst. adminstr. contracts Nuclear Sci. & Engring. Corp., Pitts., 1961; registered rep., account exec. W.H. Babbitt & Co., Inc., Pitts., 1962-63; atty. advisor real estate div. C.E., U.S. Dept. Army, Pitts., 1963-67; title officer Union Title div. Commonwealth Land Title Ins. Co., Pitts., 1967—. Legal counsel, treas. Pitts. Opera Guild, 1962-63; active Pitts., Washington County history and landmarks founds., Western Pa., Washington County hist. socs., Nat. Trust for Historic Preservation, others. Mem. Allegheny County Bar Assn., John Marshall Club, Phi Alpha Theta. Recipient award for civilian service Dept. Army, 1967. Home: Moore-McKennan Farm RD 6 Box 1 Washington PA 15301 Office: 210 Grant St Pittsburgh PA 15219 Tel (412) 471-1492

MOORE, LARRY, b. Fremont, Ohio, Dec. 24, 1939; B.S. in Pharmacy, Ohio State U., 1965; J.D., Howard U., 1973. Admitted to Mich. bar; registered pharmacist, 1965-71; law clk. firm Covington & Burling, Washington, 1972; asso. firm Miller, Canfield, Paddock & Stone, Detroit, 1973-75; trial atty. Dept. Justice, Washington, 1976—; cons. minority career devel. Am. Pharm. Assn., 1971, D.C. Dept. Housing and Community Devel., 1975. Mem. Am., Mich. bar assns., D.C. Pharmacy Assn. Recipient Am. Jurisprudence award for excellence. Home: 11501 Regnid Dr Wheaton MD 20902 Office: Dept of Justice 10th and Constitution Ave Washington DC 20530 Tel (202) 739-3785

MOORE, LEWIS LESTER, b. Madison, Wis., Dec. 31, 1928; B.A., San Francisco State U., 1956; LL.D., Lincoln U., 1964. Admitted to Calif. Supreme Ct. bar, 1965, U.S. Ct. Appeals bar, 1965; tchr. Westmoor High Sch., Daly City, Calif., 1957-66; individual practice law, Redwood City, Calif., 1966—. Mem. San Mateo County, Calif. State bar assns., San Mateo County, Calif., Am. trial lawyers assns. Recipient Am. Jurisprudence award Lincoln U. Sch. of Law, 1964. Home: 1819 Eaton St San Carlos CA 94070 Office: 755 Brewster St Redwood City CA 94063 Tel (415) 365-4950

MOORE, LOGAN, b. San Bernadino, Calif., Aug. 24, 1925; J.D., Santa Clara U., 1951. Admitted to Calif. bar, 1952; individual practice law, Garden Grove, Calif., 1952-65; judge Municipal Ct., Anaheim, Calif., 1965—; faculty Trial Judges Coll., 1968-75. Active United Fund, Garden Grove; active Orange County Child Guidance, Garden Grove. Mem. Orange County Bar Assn., Calif. Conf. Judges (chmn. municipal cts. com. 1972). Home: 1564 Tonia Ln Anaheim CA 92802 Office: 1275 N Berkeley St Fullerton CA 92632 Tel (714) 870-4100

MOORE, MICHAEL CARL, b. Spokane, Wash., Aug. 26, 1942; B.A., Dartmouth, 1964; J.D., U. Idaho, 1968. Admitted to Idaho bar, 1968; asso. firm Rapaich & Knutson, Lewiston, Idaho, 1968-69; dir. atty. Lewis-Clark Legal Services, Lewiston, 1970; individual practice law, Lewiston, 1971—; city atty. City of Lewiston, 1971—; vis. lectr. in law U. Idaho, 1974—. Bd. dirs. Luna House Hist. Soc., Lewiston, 1974—. Mem. Am., Clearwater (county, Idaho) bar assns., Idaho State Bar. Home: 1217 3d St Lewiston ID 83501 Office: Kettenbach Bldg 128 Main St Lewiston ID 83501 Tel (208) 746-3321

MOORE, MICHAEL CLEVELAND, b. Gadsden, Ala., Apr. 8, 1946; A.B., Samford U., 1967, J.D., Cumberland Sch. Law, 1971. Admitted to Ala. bar, U.S. Dist. Ct. for No. Dist. Ala. bar, 1971; law clk. firm Rogers, Howard, Redden & Mills, Birmingham, Ala., 1968, to Judge L. Charles Wright, Ala. Ct. Civil Appeals, 1971; asso. firm Watson & Fay, Huntsville, Ala., 1971-74; mem. firm Watson, Moore & Mason, Huntsville, 1974—; instr. Ala. Ct. referral Driving While Intoxicated Program for City of Huntsville; agt. Commerce Guaranty Title Ins. Corp., Mid-South Title Ins. Corp. Mem. Huntsville-Madison County Indsl. Devel. Com. Mem. Am. (law sch. liaison com.), Huntsville Madison County (sec., chmn. com. on self-indexing system) bar assns., Ala., Am. trial lawyers assns., Am. Judicature Soc., Cumberland Law Sch. Alumni Assn., Huntsville C. of C., Huntsville Homebuilders Assn. Home: 1016 Toney Dr SE Huntsville AL 35802 Office: 920 Franklin St SE Huntsville AL 35801 Tel (205) 536-7423

MOORE, MICHAEL SCOTT, b. Portland, Oreg., July 31, 1943; A.B., Honors Coll. U. Oreg., 1964; LL.B., Harvard, 1967. Admitted to Calif. bar, 1969; researcher U. Conn., 1967; instr. Sch. Law U. Calif., Berkeley, 1969-70; mem. firm Howard, Prim, Rice, Nemerovski, Canady & Pollak, San Francisco, 1968-72; asso. prof. law U. Kans., 1972-77; fellow in law and humanities Harvard, 1973-74, sr. fellow, 1976-77; asso. prof. law U. So. Calif. Law Center, 1977—. Mem. Internat. Assn. Philosophy Law, Social Philosophy, Am. Soc. Polit. and Legal Philosophy, Mind Assn., Phi Beta Kappa. Contbr. articles to legal jours., articles on mental illness to philos. and psychiat. jours. Office: U So Calif Law Center University Park Los Angeles CA 90007 Tel (213) 741-5063

MOORE, RALPH JOSEPH, JR., b. St. Paul, Sept. 29, 1932; B.A. summa cum laude, Yale, 1954; LL.B., U. Calif., Berkeley, 1959; postgrad. Cambridge (Eng.) U., 1961. Admitted to Calif. bar, 1961, D.C. bar, 1965, Md. bar, 1972, U.S. Supreme Ct. bar, 1964; law clk. to chief justice U.S. Supreme Ct., 1959-60; asso. firm Stark & Champlin, Oakland, Calif., 1960-63; atty. policy planning sect. antitrust div. Dept. Justice, Washington, 1963; asso. firm Shea & Gardner, Washington, 1964-66, partner, 1966—. Mem. citizens advisory bd. Rosewood (Md.) State Hosp., 1972-77, chmn., 1972-73; mem. Md. Gov.'s Commn. on Edn. of Handicapped, 1975—; mem. advisory com. on edn. of severely and profoundly handicapped Md. Bd. Edn., 1975—; bd. dirs. Md. Assn. Retarded Citizens, 1972-76, Cerebral Palsy Assn. Montgomery County, 1972—, Montgomery County Assn. Retarded Citizens, 1972—, Coop. Sch. for Handicapped Children, 1970-73. Mem. Am., Md. bar assns., Bar Assn. D.C., State Bar Calif., Phi Alpha Delta, Order of Coif, Phi Beta Kappa. Home: 6805 Laverock Ct Bethesda MD 20034 Office: 734 15th St NW Washington DC 20005 Tel (202) 737-1255

MOORE, RICHARD INGRAM, b. Flushing, N.Y., Feb. 16, 1939; A.B., Duke, 1960; LL.B., Boston U., 1963. Admitted to D.C. bar, 1964, Pa. bar, 1966; asso. firm John W. Dean, III, Penndel, Pa., 1966-67, firm Power, Bowen & Valimont, Doylestown, Pa., 1967-71; partner firm Durben & Moore, Morrisville, Pa., 1971-73; individual practice law, Southampton, Pa., 1973—; law clk. Hon. William Hart Rufe, III, 1974—. Mem. Council Rock Sch. Bd., Bucks County, Pa., 1969-71; v.p., gen. counsel Bucks County Council on Alcoholism, Doylestown, 1975—; bd. dirs. TODAY, INC., Newtown and Southampton, Pa.; bd. dirs., mem. adv. bd. R.A.P., Newtown. Approved atty. Comml. Law League. Mem. Am., Pa., Bucks County bar assns., Pa. Trial Lawyers Assn. Office: 736 2d St Pike Southampton PA 18966 Tel (215) 322-1908

MOORE, RICHMOND, JR., b. Richmond, Va., July 4, 1911: A.B., U. Va., 1933, LL.B., 1936. Admitted to Va. bar, 1936; partner firm Mays, Valentine, Davenport & Moore, and predecessor. Richmond, 1967—; dir. So. Bank and Trust Co., 1964-67, Home Beneficial Life Ins. Co., 1966—. Pres. Westhampton Citizens Assn., 1959; bd. dirs. The Retreat Hosp., 1949—; elder, trustee Presbyn. Ch. Mem. Am., Va., Richmond (pres. 1971) bar assns., Estate Planning Council Richmond (pres. 1958), Assn. Life Ins. Counsel, Phi Beta Kappa, Delta Psi, Phi Delta Phi, Raven Soc. Home: 10 Huntly Rd Richmond VA 23226 Office: F & M Center 1111 E Main St Richmond VA 23219 Tel (804) 644-6011

MOORE, ROBERT MADISON, b. New Orleans, June 21, 1925; B.B.A., Tulane U., 1948; J.D., U. Va., 1952; LL.M., N.Y. U., 1953. Admitted to La. bar, 1955, Calif. bar, 1972, U.S. Supreme Ct. bar, 1962; asst. to pres. and gen. counsel Underwear Inst., N.Y.C., 1953-55; mem. firm Curtis, Foster & Dillon, New Orleans, 1955-56; asst. gen. atty. Standard Fruit & S.S. Co., New Orleans, 1957-60, gen. atty., 1960-72, sec., 1964-72; gen. counsel Castle & Cooke, Inc., Honolulu, 1972—, v.p., 1974—; asst. atty. gen. La., 1956-58. Mem. Met. Crime Commn. New Orleans, 1968-72; bd. dirs. Le Petit Theatre du Vieux Carre, 1969-72. Mem. Am., Calif., Hawaii, La., N.Y., Inter-Am. bar assns., Maritime Law Assn. Food Law Inst. fellow, 1952-53. Home: 7 Presidio Ave San Francisco CA 94115 Office: 50 California St San Francisco CA 94111 Tel (415) 986-3000

MOORE, ROY DEAN, b. Chickasha, Okla., Jan. 15, 1940; B.A. in Speech Edn., Central State U., Edmond, Okla., 1962, M.Ed. in Secondary Adminstrn., 1966; J.D., Oklahoma City U., 1970. Admitted to Okla. bar, 1970; pros. atty. City of Lawton (Okla.), 1970-71; spl. judge Okla. Dist. Ct., 5th Jud. Dist., 1971-72; individual practice law, Lawton, 1973—. Pres. Comanche County (Okla.) Mental Health Assn., 1972-73, dir., 1972—; bd. dirs. Okla. Assn. Mental Health, 1973—; del. from Okla. to Republican Nat. Conv., 1976. Recipient Service award Nat. Assn. Mental Health, 1974. Home: 2114 Atlanta St Lawton OK 73501 Office: 906 C Ave Lawton OK 73501 Tel (405) 355-8800

MOORE, STANLEY DONALD, b. Visalia, Calif., Mar. 22, 1940; B.A., Whitman 1962; J.D., Gonzaga U., 1969. Admitted to Wash. bar, 1969; asst. Wash. State Atty. Gen.. Spokane, 1969-70; asso. firm Winston, Repsold & McNichols, Spokane, 1970-74; partner firm Winston, Cashatt, Repsold, McNichols, Connelly & Driscoll, Spokane, 1974—. Mem. Wash. State Citizens Adv. Com. on Dept. Social and Health Services, 1972—, chmn., 1972-76. Mem. Wash. Trial Lawyers Assn. Home: W 833 Shoshone Pl Spokane WA 99203 Office: 5th Floor Spokane and Eastern Bldg Spokane WA 99201 Tel (509) 838-6131

MOORE, TERENCE LEE, b. Louisville, Nov. 2, 1941; B.S., U. Louisville, 1967, J.D., 1969. Admitted to Ky. bar, 1969; asso. firm Alan N. Leibson, P.S.C., Louisville, 1969-70; individual practice law, Covington, Ky., 1970-74; mem. firm Blakely, Moore & Gettys, Covington, 1974—; law clk. Jefferson Circuit Ct., Louisville, 1966-68. Mem. Am., Ky. trial lawyers assns., Soc. of Law and Medicine. Home: 107-J Winding Way Covington KY 41011 Office: 106 E 3rd St Covington KY 41011 Tel (606) 431-2130

MOORE, THOMAS JEFFERSON, b. Loganville, Ga., June 2, 1919; B.S., Furman U., 1940; LL.B., Emory U., 1949, LL.D. Engr., So. Bell Tel. & Tel. Co., Atlanta, 1940-49, atty., 1950-67; admitted to Ga. bar, 1950; atty. So. Central Bell Tel. & Tel. Co., Birmingham, Ala., 1967-73; individual practice law, Grayson, Ga.; justice of the peace Bay Creek Dist., 1976—. Mem. Guinnett County (Ga.) Sch. Bd., 1948-58. Mem. Guinnett County, Ga. bar assns. Address: 1785 Hwy 20 Grayson GA 30221 Tel (404) 963-9001

MOORE, THOMAS MICHAEL, JR., b. San Francisco. Sept. 10, 1931; B.A., U. Calif., Berkeley, 1953; J.D., Hastings Coll. Law, U. Calif., 1958. Admitted to Calif. bar, 1959; U.S. Supreme Ct. bar, 1967; asst. dist. atty., chief prosecutor Monterey County, Calif., 1959-64; partner firm Hudson & Martin, Ferrante & Street, Monterey, Calif., 1964-67; dir. Peace Corps- Senegal Africa, 1967-70; individual practice law, Monterey, 1970-72; judge pro tem, referee Juvenile Ct. and Superior Ct., Salinas, Calif., 1972—; prof. Golden Gate U. Grad. Div., 1974—. Mem. Calif., Monterey bar assns., Phi Alpha Delta. Home: Toyon Way Carmel Valley CA 93924 Office: Juvenile Ct 1422 Natividad St Salinas CA 93901 Tel (408) 758-1081

MOORE, THOMAS RONALD, b. Duluth, Minn., Mar. 27, 1932; B.A. magna cum laude, Yale, 1954; J.D., Harvard, 1957; LL.M. in Taxation, N.Y. U., 1961. Admitted to N.Y. bar, 1958, U.S. Supreme Ct. bar, 1965; tutor Harvard Law Sch. Internat. Program in Taxation, 1956-57; asso. firm Dewey, Ballantine, Bushby, Palmer & Wood, N.Y.C., 1957-65; asso. firm Breed, Abbott & Morgan, N.Y.C., 1965-66, partner, 1967—; sec., dir. Broad Hollow Estates, Inc., H. Malcolm Teare Agy., Inc.; lectr. Practising Law Inst. N.Y.C., Las Vegas, New Orleans, Cornell Law Sch., N.Y. U., Inst. Fed. Taxation, So. Fed. Tax Inst., Condyne, U. Hartford Tax Inst. Pres., bd. dirs. Nat. Soc. Prevention Blindness; sec., treas., trustee A.D. Henderson Found. Del.; trustee A.D. Henderson Found. Fla.; bd. dirs. Theatre, Inc. (Phoenix Theatre), N.Y.C. Mem. Am., N.Y. State bar assns., Assn. Bar City N.Y. Co-author: Estate Planning and the Close Corporation, 1970. Mem. editorial bd. The Tax Lawyer, 1969-72. Contbr. articles to profl. jours. Office: 1 Chase Manhattan Plaza New York City NY 10005

MOORE, WILLIAM BOWDITCH, b. Hillsdale, Mich., Feb. 25, 1934; B.A., U. N.C., 1956; LL.B., U. Va., 1962. Admitted to Va. bar, 1962, U.S. Supreme Ct. bar, 1963; partner firm Phillips, Kendrick, Gearheart & Aylor, Arlington, Va., 1968—. Pres., chmn. bd. trustees Nat. Orthopedic Hosp., Arlington. Mem. Arlington County (pres. 1976-77), Am., Va. State bar assns. Recipient Distinguished Service award Arlington Jaycees, 1969. Home: 4717 24th Rd N Arlington VA 22207 Office: 2009 14th St N Arlington VA 22201 Tel (703) 527-8100

MOORE, WILLIAM CLARENCE, b. Richland, Ga., Feb. 17, 1942; A.B., Mercer U., 1964, J.D., 1966. Admitted to Ga. bar, 1965; served to capt. JAGC, U.S. Army, Ft. Benning, Ga., 1966-70; partner firm Moore & Worthington, Columbus, Ga., 1970—. Mem. Am. Bar Assn., Ga. Trial Lawyers Assn., Columbus Lawyers Club. Office: 908 2d Ave Columbus GA 31901 Tel (404) 324-5606

MOORE, WILLIAM THEODORE, JR., b. Bainbridge, Ga., May 7, 1940; A.A., Ga. Mil. Coll., 1960; student U. Ga., 1960-61, J.D., 1964. Admitted to Ga. bar, 1964; asso. firms Pierce, Ranitz & Lee, Savannah, Ga., 1964-65, Richardson, Doremus & Karsman, Savannah, 1965-68; partner firm Corish, Smith, Remler & Moore, Savannah, 1968—; atty. Savannah-Chatham Bd. Edn., 1975—. Mem. Chatham County (Ga.) Zoning Bd. Appeals, 1972-75; sec. Coastal Plains chpt. Ga. Conservancy, 1972-73. Mem. Am. Judicature Soc., Nat. Orgn. and Legal Problems of Edn., Savannah Estate Planning Council (pres. 1976—), State Bar Ga. (exec. council sect. younger lawyers 1968-75, mem. grievance tribunal for Eastern Circuit), Savannah Bar Assn. (pres. younger lawyers 1968), U. Ga. Law Sch. Assn. Council (council 1976—), Phi Delta Phi. Recipient certificate of performance State Bar Ga. Younger Lawyers Sect., 1975; contbr. articles to legal jours. Home: 712 Bradley Point Rd Savannah GA 31410 Office: 123 Abercorn St Savannah GA 31401 Tel (912) 236-7167

MOORE, WILLIAM TYLER, b. Robertson County, Tex., Apr. 9, 1918; B.S. in Econs., Tex. A. and M. U., 1940; LL.B., U. Tex., 1949. Admitted to Tex. bar, 1948, since practiced in Bryan; mem. firm Moore, Culpepper & Moore, 1975—; mem. Tex. Ho. of Reps., 1946-48, Tex. Senate, 1948—. Home: 1204 Sul Ross St Bryan TX 77801 Office: 302 Post Office St Bryan TX 77801 Tel (713) 823-8178

MOORE, WINSOR CARL, b. Mt. Pleasant, Iowa, Jan. 13, 1911; B.A., Central YMCA Coll., 1935; J.D., George Washington U., 1937; LL.M., Cath. U. Am., 1939; B.S. in B.A., U. Omaha, 1949. Admitted to D.C. bar, 1938, Nebr. bar, 1954, Colo. bar, 1969; prof. law Creighton U., Omaha, 1946-69; individual practice law, Ft. Collins, Colo., 1969—; mem. firm Wolfe & Moore, Fort Collins. Mem. Am. Soc. Questioned Document Examiners (hon.), Am., Nebr., Colo. bar assns., Phi Alpha Delta. Author: Nebraska Practice—Practice Methods and Forms, 9 vols., 1968; (with Shkolnick) Uniform Commercial Code with Forms—Nebraska Practice, 2 vols., 1965; contbr. articles to legal jours. Home: 1912 Kedron Dr Fort Collins CO 80521 Office: 40 1 1st National Tower PO Box 1943 Fort Collins CO 80522 Tel (303) 493-8787

MOORHEAD, DIXON DOUGHTY, b. Belvidere, Ill., Sept. 20, 1913; B.S., U. Ill., 1936; J.D., Chgo. Kent Coll., 1941; grad. U. Calif. Grad. Sch. Bus. Adminstrn. Exec. Tng. Program, 1964. Admitted to Ill. bar, 1941, Mich., 1946, Calif bar, 1957; individual practice law,

Sault Ste. Marie, Mich., 1946-56; atty., v.p. law dept. United Calif. Bank, Los Angeles, 1956-62; pres. Wilshire Nat. Bank, Los Angeles, 1962-65; pres. Comml. and Farmers Nat. Bank, Oxnard, Calif., 1965-68; individual practice law, Ventura, Calif., 1968—. Mem. harbor commn. Ventura County (Calif.), 1975—. Mem. Ill., Mich., Calif., Ventura County bar assns. Office: 168 N Brent St Ventura CA 93003 Tel (805) 648-2400

MOORHEAD, JOHN THOMAS, b. Albany, N.Y., May 22, 1899; LL.B., La Salle U., 1937, So. Law U., 1950, Memphis State U., 1967. Admitted to Tenn. bar, 1950, U.S. Supreme Ct. bar, 1971; individual practice law, Memphis, 1950—. Office: Suite 436 Commerce Title Bldg 12 S Mid America Mall Memphis TN 38103 Tel (901) 525-6378

MOORMAN, JAMES W., b. Pitts., Nov. 22, 1937; A.B., LL.B., Duke U. With firm Davis, Polk & Wardell, N.Y.C., 1963-66; trial atty. Land and Natural Resources div. Dept. Justice, 1966-69, asst. atty. gen., Washington, 1977—; staff atty. Center for Law and Social Policy, 1969-71; exec. dir. Sierra Club Legal Def. Fund, Inc., 1971-74, staff atty., 1977—. Office: US Dept Justice Land and Natural Resources Div Constitution Ave and 10th St NW Washington DC 20530*

MOORMAN, JOHN KENNETH, b. Roanoke, Va., Feb. 1, 1941; B.A., U. Va., 1963, LL.B., 1966. Admitted to Va. bar, 1966, Ga. bar, 1969; asso. firm Long, Weinberg, Ansley, & Wheeler, Atlanta, 1968-72, partner, 1973—. Mem. Am., Va. Ga., Atlanta bar assns., Am. Judicature Soc., Ga. Def. Lawyers Assn. Home: 45 Brighton Rd Atlanta GA 30309 Office: 3000 Equitable Bldg 100 Peachtree St Atlanta GA 30303 Tel (404) 525-5903

MOOSBRUGGER, GORDON CHARLES, b. St. Paul, Oct. 31, 1926; LL.B., St. Paul Coll. Law (now William Mitchell Coll. Law), 1954. Admitted to Minn. bar, 1954; asso. firm Robert P. Liesch, St. Paul, 1954, 56; spl. asst. atty. gen. State of Minn., 1957-67; asst. corp. counsel City of St. Paul, 1967-68; individual practice law, St. Paul, 1968—. Mem. Minn. Bar Assn. Home: 13956 N 10th St Stillwater MN 55082 Office: 807 Degree of Honor Bldg Saint Paul MN 55101 Tel (612) 224-3879

MOOSSA, WALTER JOSEPH, b. Worcester, Mass., Mar. 13, 1908; LL.B., Suffolk U., 1930, LL.D., 1930. Admitted to Mass. bar, 1930, U.S. Supreme Ct. bar, 1933; mem. firm Moossa and Dumas, Worcester, Mass., 1930-62; first judge of First Dist. Ct. Eastern Worcester, Westborough, Mass., 1962—; mem. adminstrv. com. of dist. cts. on mental health. Chmn. Lake Quinsigamond Commn., Worcester, Mass., 1949-64. Mem. Worcester County, Mass. bar assns., Am. Judges Assn., Nat. Council Juvenile Ct. Judges, Am. Judicature Soc., Dist. Ct. Judges of Mass. Home: 295 Turnpike Rd Apt 216N Westborough MA 01581 Office: 175 Milk St Westborough MA 01581 Tel (617) 366-8266

MOOTS, PHILIP ROY, b. Bellefountaine, Ohio, June 10, 1940; B.A. cum laude, Ohio State U., 1962; J.D., Harvard, 1965. Admitted to Ohio bar, 1965; partner firm Dunbar, Kienzle & Murphey, Columbus, Ohio, 1965-71; legal advisor Dept. Indsl. Relations State of Ohio, Columbus, 1971-72, dep. dir. Dept. Commerce, 1972; exec. asst. to gov. State of Ohio, Columbus, 1972-75; partner firm Moots, Hultin, Weinberger & Cope, Columbus, 1976—; adj. prof. law Ohio State U., 1972—. Chmn., Commn. Higher Edn. United Methodist Ch. Ohio; trustee United Theol. Sch.; bd. dirs., adminstrv. v.p. South Side Settlement House. Mem. Am., Ohio, Columbus bar assns., Phi Beta Kappa, Phi Alpha Theta. Home: 149 W Kenworth Rd Columbus OH 43214 Office: 21 E State St Columbus OH 43215 Tel (614) 221-3121

MORAIN, JAMES HUBERT, b. Hays, Kans., Nov. 22, 1934; B.B.A., Kans. State U., 1959; J.D., Washburn U., 1970. Mgr., Kans. Claims Service, Liberal, 1960-65; adjuster Gen. Adjustment Bur., 1965-68; clk. reader Kans. Senate, 1969-70; admitted to Kans. bar, 1970; partner firm Vance Hobble Neubauer Nordling Sharp & McQueen, Liberal, 1970—. Chmn., Seward County (Kans.) Cancer Crusade, 1971; team leader United Fund Seward County, 1971-72. Mem. Kans., S.W. Kans., Seward County (pres. 1977), Am. bar assns., Lawyer-Pilots Bar. Home: 808 Maple St Liberal KS 67901 Office: 419 N Kansas St Liberal KS 67901 Tel (306) 624-2548

MORALES, JOSEPH ANTHONY, b. Managua, Nicaragua, Nov. 12, 1937; B.S., San Francisco State U., 1959; J.D., Hastings Coll. Law, 1964. Admitted to Calif. bar, 1965; individual practice law, San Francisco, 1965—. Mem. Bd. Assessment Appeals City and County of San Francisco, 1976—; bd. dirs. Golden Gate chpt. ARC. Mem. Calif., San Francisco, San Mateo bar assns., San Francisco State U. Alumni Assn. (dir.). Office: 1255 Post St San Francisco CA 94109 Tel (415) 885-5758

MORALES, JULIO KAREL, b. Havana, Cuba, Jan. 17, 1948; B.A., Carroll Coll., 1969; J.D., U. Mont., 1972. Admitted to Mont. bar, 1972, U.S. Ct. Mil. Appeals bar, 1972; clk. to asso. justice Mont. Supreme Ct., 1972; individual practice law, Missoula, Mont., 1973—. Bd. dirs. Missoula Exchange Club, 1974. Mem. Am. (Law Day award 1974, 76), Mont. (chmn. law day com. 1974—, dir. young lawyers sect. 1976—) bar assns., Am. Judicature Soc., Phi Delta Phi. Home: 213 Pattee Creek Dr Missoula MT 59801 Office: Western Bank Bldg Missoula MT 59801 Tel (406) 543-6557

MORALES, NESTOR, b. Tampa, Fla., Mar. 25, 1909; LL.B., U. Fla., 1935. Admitted to Fla. bar, 1935; individual practice law, Miami, Fla., 1935—; hon. vice consul of Nicaragua, 1948—. Mem. Am. Judicature Soc., Dade County Bar Assn. (chmn. speakers com.). Author legal booklets. Home: 645 Solano Prado Coral Gables FL 33156 Office: 2279 Coral Way Miami FL 33145 Tel (305) 854-8550

MORAN, FRANCES MARY, b. Brockton, Mass., June 14, 1912; A.B., Boston U., 1933; J.D., Northeastern U., 1943. Admitted to Mass. bar, 1943; asso. firm Warner & Stackpole, Boston, 1943-51; with Century Shares Trust, Boston, 1951-53, Mass. Natural Resources Dept., Boston, 1953-55; legal cons. Mass. Water Resources Commn., 1955-58; v.p. Keystone Co. of Boston, 1958—; mem. adv. bd. Essex County Bank & Trust, 1976—; trustee Beverly Hosp., 1973—. Mem. Beverly (Mass.) Conservation Commn., 1958-65; trustee Beverly Pub. Library, 1974—. Mem. Mass. Bar Assn. Author: Highlights of Pension Reform Act, 1974. Home: 25 Albany Circle Beverly MA 01915 Office: 99 High St Boston MA 02104 Tel (617) 338-3333

MORAN, HUGH ANDERSON, III, b. Shanghai, China, May 30, 1912 (parents Am. citizens); student Stanford, 1931-33, J.D., 1939; B.S., Cornell U., 1936. Admitted to Calif. bar, 1941; law clk. firm Robert Beale, San Francisco, 1939-40; atty. land dept. Shell Oil Co., Los Angeles, 1941-42; asso. firm Salisbury, Robinson & Knudsen, Los Angeles, 1942-46; individual practice law, Los Angeles, 1945-52; partner firm Stone, Moran & Anderson and predecessor, Pasadena, Calif., 1952-66; individual practice law, Pasadena, 1966—; officer, dir., gen. counsel Strait Door & Plywood Corp., Whitings Automotive Inc.. Pacific Universal Products Corp., Calvex Corp., Brown & Welin Pharmacy, Milton S. Weber Inc.; gen. counsel, officer Premier Plating Works, Caine, Farber & Gordon Inc., R. Bob Roberts, Inc. Mem. Am., Internat., Calif., Los Angeles, Pasadena bar assns., Am. Arbitration Assn. (nat. panel arbitrators), Phi Alpha Delta. Office: Suite 301 61 S Lake Ave Pasadena CA 91101 Tel (213) 449-4716 also (213) 684-0776

MORAN, ROBERT RUSSELL, b. David City, Nebr., Nov. 29, 1926; S.Sc.L., U. Neb., 1949, LL.B., 1951. Admitted to Neb. bar, 1951, U.S. Dist. Ct. bar for Dist. Nebr., 1951; individual practice law, Hemingford, Nebr., 1951-52; county atty. Box Butte County (Nebr.), 1952-57; partner firm Gantz, Hein and Moran, Alliance, Nebr., 1957-66; judge Nebr. Dist. Ct., 16th Jud. Dist. Nebr., 1966—. Mem. Nebr. (award of spl. merit 1974), Am. bar assns., Nebr. Dist. Judges Assn. (pres. 1974). Home: 806 Laramie Ave Alliance NE 69301 Office: Courthouse Alliance NE 69301 Tel (308) 762-3376

MORAN, THOMAS JOSEPH, b. Waukegan, Ill., July 17, 1920; B.A., Lake Forest Coll., 1947; J.D., Chgo.-Kent Coll. Law, 1950. Admitted to Ill. bar; individual practice law, 1950-56; state's atty. Lake County (Ill.), 1956-58; judge Probate Ct. Lake County, 1958-61; judge 19th Jud. Circuit Ct. Ill., 1961-64; justice Appelate Ct. Ill., 2d Dist., Waukegan, after 1964; justice Ill. Supreme Ct., 1976—; adj. prof. N.Y. U., La. State U. Mem. Inst. Jud. Adminstrn., Am. Judicature Soc., Am., Ill., Lake County bar assns. Office: 215 N Utica St Waukegan IL 60085 Tel (312) 623-1333

MORATZKA, TIMOTHY DEAN, b. Sioux Falls, S.D., Nov. 4, 1944; B.S., Augustana Coll., Sioux Falls, S.D., 1966; J.D., U. Tenn., 1969. Admitted to Minn. bar, 1971; mem. firm Lawrence Costello & Moratzka, Hastings, Red Wing and Cannon Falls (all Minn.), 1971—; trustee in bankruptcy U.S. 3d Div. Dist. Ct. Minn., St. Paul, 1972—. Mem. Am., Fed., Minn. bar assns., Am. Judicature Soc., Delta Theta Phi. Contbr. articles to legal jours. Home: 2020 Nininger Rd Hastings MN 55033 Tel (612) 437-7740

MORE, TIMOTHY TRENCHARD, b. Cin., Aug. 4, 1945; B.A., Yale, 1967; LL.B., U. Va., 1970. Admitted to R.I. bar, 1970; asso. firm Edwards & Angell, Providence, 1970-76, partner, 1976—. Trustee exec. bd. Providence Found., 1974; mem. exec. com. Yale Assn. R.I., 1976; vestryman Grace Ch., Providence, 1976. Mem. R.I. Bar Assn.

MOREHEAD, DWIGHT HOYT, b. Columbus, Ohio, June 19, 1912; B.A. cum laude, Ohio State U., 1934, M.A., 1936, J.D., 1938. Admitted to Ohio bar, 1938; asso. firm Watson Davis & Joseph, Columbus, 1938-42; asso. firm Fuller Henry Hodge & Snyder, Toledo, 1942-50, partner, 1950-56; mem. legal dept. Owens-Ill., Inc., Toledo, 1956-77, sec., 1969-77, asst. gen. counsel, 1976-77; partner firm Fuller, Henry, Hodge & Snyder, Toledo, 1977—. Mem. Am., Ohio, Toledo, Fed. bar assns., Am. Soc. Corporate Secs., Assn. ICC Practitioners, Phi Beta Kappa, Delta Theta Phi. Home: 4411 Bonniebrook Rd Toledo OH 43615 Office: 1200 Edison Plaza 300 Madison Ave Toledo OH 43604 Tel (419) 255-8220

MORELAND, JAMES ALFRED, b. Newark, Apr. 5, 1940; A.B., Brown U., 1961; J.D., U. Chgo., 1964; LL.M., Boston U., 1967. Admitted to Mass. bar, Fla. bar, U.S. Tax Ct. bar; asso. firm Hill & Barlow, Boston and Martha's Vineyard, Mass., 1964-67, Maguire, Voorhis & Wells, Orlando, Fla., 1967-72, Turnbull, Abner & Daniels, Winter Park, Fla., 1972-74, partner, 1974-75; prin. firm Moreland & Cunningham, Winter Park, 1975—; municipal judge City of Winter Park, 1975-77. Chmn. Winter Park Planning and Zoning Commn., 1972-75; mem. Winter Park Civil Service Bd., 1977—. Mem. Am. Bar Assn. Contbr. to Manual on Fla. Will Drafting and Estate Planning, 1968 rev. edit., 1973. Home: 1618 Neola Trail Winter Park FL 32788 Office: PO Box 1298 Winter Park FL 32790 Tel (305) 628-0884

MORELAND, JOHN NORBERT, b. Mason City, Iowa, May 4, 1936; B.A. cum laude, Notre Dame U., 1958, J.D., 1961. Admitted to Iowa bar, 1961; individual practice law, Ottumwa, Iowa, 1961-64, 74-; partner firm Bookin & Moreland, 1964-65, Moreland & Vinyard, 1969-74; asst. county atty. Wapello County (Iowa), 1961-64; alt. judge Ottumwa Municipal Ct., 1966-70. Pres., bd. dirs. Ottumwa Cath. Sch. System, 1967-68, 69-72; pres. Am. Home Finding Assn., 1967-69; mem. Ottumwa Adv. Council, 1965-67, Ottumwa Airport Commn., 1963-65. Mem. Am., Iowa, 8th Jud. Dist., Wapello County (pres. 1968-69) bar assns. Home: 139 E Maple St Ottumwa IA 52501 Office: 211 1/2 E Main St PO Box 247 Ottumwa IA 52501 Tel (515) 682-8326

MORELLI, ARNOLD, b. Cin., June 28, 1928; B.A., Univ. Cin., 1951; LL.B., Harvard, 1955. Admitted to Ohio bar, 1955; asso. firm Squire, Sanders & Dempsey, Cleve., 1955-57; asso. firm Paxton & Seasongood, Cin., 1957-61; asst. U.S. atty., Cin., 1961-66; partner firm Bauer, Morelli & Heyd Co., Cin., 1966—; lectr. law Univ. Cin., Chase Law Sch., Cin. Mariemont Bd. Edn., Ohio, 1974. Mem. Am., Ohio, Cin. bar assns. Home: 6507 Mariemont Ave Mariemont OH 45227 Office: 503 Executive Bldg 35 E 7th St Cincinnati OH 45202 Tel (513) 241-3676

MORELLI, FRED MICHAEL, JR., b. Chgo., Sept. 23, 1941; B.A., U. Notre Dame, 1963, LL.B., 1966. Admitted to Ill. bar, 1966; individual practice law, Aurora; pub. defender, Kane County, Ill., 1967—. Mem. Ill., Chgo., Kane County bar assns. Office: 403 W Galena Blvd Aurora IL 60506 Tel (312) 897-1172

MORENO, WILLIAM FRANK, b. Oak Park, Ill., Mar. 12, 1930; J.D., DePaul U., 1956. Admitted to Calif. bar, 1957; since practiced in Salinas, Calif., partner firm Stewart & Moreno, 1957-64, Moreno & Parmelee, 1964-66; partner firm Moreno, Branner & Carnazzo, and predecessor, 1966-72, pres., 1963-72; judge Municipal Ct. Salinas Jud. Dist., 1972—. Pres. Italian Catholic Fedn., 1970; founder Hartneu Newman Found., Monterey County Legal Aid Soc., Salinas Valley Council Alcoholism, Sun St. Center. Mem. Conf. Calif. Judges, Calif. Bar Assn., Am. Trial Lawyers' Assn., Salinas C. of C. (v.p. 1971-72). Office: PO Box 1409 Ct House Salinas CA 93901 Tel (408) 424-8611

MOREY, RANDALL EDWARD, b. Spooner, Wis., Sept. 15, 1923; Ph.D., U. Wis., 1948, LL.D., 1949. Admitted to Wis. bar, 1949; individual practice law, Mondovi, Wis., 1949-54; partner firm Whelan & Morey, Mondovi, 1954-71; mem. firm Whelan, Morey & Ricci, Mondovi, 1971—. Pres. Mondovi Community Chest, 1960-65. Mondovi Sch. Bd., 1968—; pres. Wis. layman's fellowship United Ch. of Christ, 1962. Mem. State Bar Assn. Wis., Am., Tri-County (sec. 1958, pres. 1974) bar assns., Wis. Acad. Trial Lawyers, Am. Trial Lawyers Assn., Def. Research Inst. Home: 409 Parker Ave Mondovi WI 54755 Office: 224 W Main St Mondovi WI 54755 Tel (715) 926-4225

MOREY, THOMAS MCKINLEY, b. Chgo., Aug. 22, 1933; B.S., Western Ill. U., 1959; LL.B., Chgo.-Kent Coll. Law, 1962. Admitted to Ill. bar, 1963; partner firm Moore, Morey & Coleman, Midlothian, Ill., 1963-66; asst. atty. gen. State of Ill., 1965-66; counsel Hartford Ins. Co., Chgo., 1966-68; mem. firm Querrey, Harrow, Gulanick & Kennedy, Chgo., 1968—. Mem. Am., Ill., Chgo., S. Suburban bar assns., Trial Lawyers Club Chgo. Home: 2813 Greenwood Hazel Crest IL 60429 Office: 135 S LaSalle St Chicago IL 60603 Tel (312) 236-9850

MORFORD, DOUGLAS HARRY, b. Redbank, N.J., Mar. 30, 1944; B.S., Fla. State U., 1966, J.D. with high honors, 1969. Admitted to Fla. bar, 1969, U.S. Ct. Mil. Appeals bar, 1970, U.S. Supreme Ct. bar, 1973; with JAGC, U.S. Air Force, 1969-72; mem. firm Ulmer Murchison Ashby & Ball, Jacksonville, Fla., 1972—; editor State Pub. Defender Trial Handbook, 1967-69. Mem. Am., Jacksonville bar assns., Fla. Bar. Home: 1935 Largo Rd Jacksonville FL 32207 Office: 1600 Atlantic Bank Bldg PO Box 479 Jacksonville FL 32201 Tel (904) 354-5652

MORGAN, BUCKLYN MONTE, b. Phoenix, Oct. 16, 1942; B.S., Ariz. State U., 1965; J.D., U. Ariz., 1971. Admitted to Ariz. bar, 1971; partner firm Morgan Cord & Keppel, Scottsdale, Ariz. Mem. Am., Scottsdale (dir.) bar assns., Am. Trial Lawyers Assn., Scottsdale C. of C. (chmn. polit. action task force). Address: 7505 E Main St Scottsdale AZ 85251 Tel (602) 994-0345

MORGAN, DENNIS WILLIAM, b. Buffalo, Nov. 3, 1948; B.A., Syracuse U., 1970; J.D., Gonzaga U., 1973. Admitted to Wash. bar, 1973; asso. firm Cross and Morgan, and predecessor, Ritzville, Wash., 1973-74, partner, 1975—; mem. Ritzville City Council, 1974-75. Mem. Ritzville Vol. Fire Dept., 1974—. Mem. Am., Wash. State, Adams County (Wash.) bar assns., Wash. State Trial Lawyers Assn. Office: 120 W Main St Ritzville WA 99169 Tel (509) 659-0600

MORGAN, DONALD LEE, b. Houston, Jan. 21, 1934; A.B., Harvard U., 1956, LL.B., 1962. Admitted to D.C. bar, 1962, U.S. Supreme Ct. bar, 1969; asso. firm Cleary, Gottlieb, Steen & Hamilton, Washington, 1962-69, partner, 1970—. Mem. D.C. Bar (hearing com. #4 1975), Am. Bar Assn. Office: 1250 Connecticut Ave NW Washington DC 20036 Tel (202) 223-2151

MORGAN, EARL ADAMS, b. Roseland, La., June 24, 1915; B.A., La. State U., 1937, B.S. in Library Sci., 1938, J.D., 1947- Admitted to La. bar, 1947, U.S. Supreme Ct. bar, 1968; commd. 2d lt. USAF, 1942; advanced through grades to col., 1969; mem., chmn. USAF Bd. Review, 1951-55, 1962-65; staff judge adv. Chanute Air Force Base, Ill., 1955-58; dir. internat. law USAF, Europe, 1959-62; chief internat. law div. Office of JAG, 1965-66; dep. staff judge adv. Mil. Airlift Command, 1966-69; ret., 1969; dir. law library La. State U. Law Sch., Baton Rouge, 1970, dir. law library, asso. prof. law, 1971-74; individual practice law, Baton Rouge, 1974—. Mem. La. State, Am., Fed., Inter-Am. bar assns., Order of Coif. Recipient Legion of Merit, 1963, 66; bd. editors La. Law Rev., 1940-41. Home: 12335 Buckingham Ave Baton Rouge LA 70815 Office: 4531 North Boulevard Baton Rouge LA 70806 Tel (504) 925-0985

MORGAN, EARL EDWARD, b. O'Fallons, Nebr., Aug. 9, 1918; LL.B., U. Nebr., 1947. Admitted to Nebr. bar, 1947; individual practice law, N. Platte, Nebr., 1947—. Mem. Am., Nebr. bar assns. Home: Tryon Route N Platte NE 69101 Office: 212 N Dewey St N Platte NE 69101 Tel (308) 532-5090

MORGAN, EVERETTE LEE, b. Statesville, N.C., May 21, 1927; A.B., Duke, 1951; LL.B., U. S.C., 1953. Admitted to S.C. bar, 1953, U.S. Supreme Ct. bar, 1961; partner firm Hyman, Morgan, Brown, Saleeby, Giffords & Rushton, Florence, S.C., 1955—; U.S. commr. S.C. dist., Florence, 1966-70; U.S. magistrate S.C. dist., Florence, 1970-74. Mem. Am., S.C., Florence County (past pres.) Florence bar assns., S.C. Def. Attys. Assn., Am. Trial Lawyers Assn. Home: 1600 W Hillside Ave Florence SC 29501 Office: 170 Court House Sq Florence SC 29501 Tel (803) 662-6321

MORGAN, FRANK WILLIAM, b. Queens, N.Y., Jan. 31, 1938; B.A. in Econs., Queens Coll., 1959; LL.B., Fordham U., 1963, J.D., 1967. Admitted to N.Y. bar, 1963, U.S. Supreme Ct. bar, 1972, Pa. bar, 1976; asso. firm Jackson, Nash, Brophy, Barringer & Brooks, N.Y.C., 1963-67; asst. v.p. Walston & Co., Inc., N.Y.C., 1970-71; sr. counsel Gulf Oil Corp., Pitts., 1971—. Mem. Am., N.Y.C. bar assns. Recipient Man of Year award Albertson Roslyn Hts. Rep. Com., 1971; Am. Jurisprudence prize Am. Judicature Soc., 1963. Office: PO Box 1166 Pittsburgh PA 15230 Tel (412) 391-2400

MORGAN, GEORGE TAD, b. Elgin, Ill., Sept. 25, 1933; B.S., Northwestern U., 1955, J.D., 1958. Admitted to Ill. bar, 1958; individual practice law, Elgin, 1958-64; with Montgomery Ward Co., Chgo., 1964—, asst. gen. counsel, 1971—. Mem. Chgo., Am. bar assns. C.P.A., Ill. Office: One Montgomery Ward Plaza Chicago IL 60671 Tel (312) 467-2230

MORGAN, GERALD D., JR., b. Washington, D.C., Mar. 1, 1937; B.A., Amherst Coll., 1959; M.A., Oxford U., Oxford, Eng., 1962; LL.N., Columbia U., 1965. Admitted to N.Y. state bar, 1966; atty. firm Hale, Russell & Stentzel, N.Y.C., 1965-70; atty. adv. U.S. Dept. State AID, 1970-71; atty. advisor Overseas Pvt. Investment Corp., 1971-72, sr. counsel for ins., 1972-75, v.p., gen. counsel, 1975-76; gen. counsel U.S. Dept. State AID, Washington, D.C., 1976—. Mem. N.Y. State, Am., Fed. bar assns., Assn. Bar City N.Y., Am. Economic Assn., Phi Beta Kappa. Home: 1661 Crescent Place N W Apt 308 Washington DC 20009 Office: 21st and Virginia Ave N W Room 6895 US Dept State Washington DC 20523 Tel (202) 632-8548

MORGAN, GLEN B., b. Cleve., June 25, 1928; B.B.A., Case Res. U., 1951, LL.B., 1954. Admitted to Ohio bar, 1954; atty. Cleve. Electric Illuminating Co., 1957-65, McNeal and Schick, Cleve., 1955-57; partner firm Zidar, Morgan and Burns, Cleve., 1965—; dir. law city of Macedonia (Ohio), 1965—; atty. N. Hills Water Dist., 1968-77, Northfield Center Twp., 1968—, Sagamore Hills Twp., 1968—. Mem. Ohio, Cleve. bar assns. Office: 75 Public Square Suite 810 Cleveland OH 44113 Tel (216) 621-4636

MORGAN, JACK MCGEE, b. Portales, N.Mex., Jan. 15, 1924; B.B.A., LL.B., U. Tex. Admitted to N.Mex. bar, 1970; practice law, Farmington; mem. N.Mex. Senate, 1973—, mem. finance conservation com.; vice chmn. subcom. on coal, lignite & mining; mem. S.W. Regional Energy Council. Mem. Am., N.Mex., San Juan County bar assns., C. of C. Home: 4113 Skyline Dr Farmington NM 87401 Office: PO Box 2151 Farmington NM 87401 Tel (505) 325-4433

MORGAN, JACK WALLACE, b. Inglewood, Calif., May 4, 1937; B.A. in Polit. Sci., U. So. Calif., 1959, J.D., 1962, LL.M., 1964. Admitted to Calif. bar, 1963, U.S. Supreme Ct. bar, 1972; law clk. firm Cadoo & Tretheway, Inglewood, 1962; asso., firm Cadoo, Tretheway & McGinn, Inglewood, 1963-64; partner firm Cadoo, Tretheway, McGinn & Morgan, Inglewood and Marina del Rey, Calif., 1965—; state inheritance tax referee Torrance, Long Beach and Norwalk superior cts., 1968—. Mem. Los Angeles, So. Bay, Marina del Rey, Inglewood bar assns., Calif. Assn. Realtors (legal affairs com.), Marina del Rey C. of C. (dir. 1971-75, pres. 1975-76. chmn. bd. 1976-77). Recipient commendations for outstanding community service Calif. State Assembly, County of Los Angeles. Office: 4560 S Admiralty Way Suite 110 Marina del Rey CA 90291 Tel (213) 822-2066

MORGAN, JAMES HARVEY, b. Cedarburg, Wis., May 14, 1947; B.A., U. Wis. at Madison, 1965-70, J.D., 1972. Admitted to Wis. bar, 1972, Fed. bar, 1972; asst. dist. atty. Outagamie County, Wis., 1972-73; partner firm Elliott & Morgan, Chilton, Wis., 1973-74; asso. firm Block and Seymour, Appleton, Wis., 1974-75; partner firm Hurth, Husting & Morgan, Cedarburg, Wis., 1975—. Mem. Ozaukee County Emergency Med. Services Bd., 1975—. Mem. Wis., Ozaukee County, Am. bar assns., Assn. Trial Lawyers Am. Office: W62 N573 Washington Ave Cedarburg WI 53012 Tel (414) 0990

MORGAN, JAMES ROBERT, b. Oshkosh, Wis., June 13, 1926; student Oshkosh State U., 1946-48; B.S., U. Wis., 1960, LL.B., 1952, postgrad., 1954-57. Admitted to Wis. bar, 1952; research atty. Wis. Taxpayers Alliance, Madison, 1953-64, exec. v.p., 1971-75, pres., 1975—; sec. Wis. Dept. Revenue. 1965-71; cons. Wis. Blue Ribbon Tax Study Com., 1959, Wis. Gold Ribbon Com., 1963; mem. Gov.'s Medicare Task Force, 1966, Commn- on Interstate Cooperation, 1966-70; vice chmn. Gov.'s Task Force on Local Govt. Fin. and Orgn., 1969; chmn. Legis. Council Spl. Com. on County Home Rule, 1971-73; mem. Spl. Legis. Com. on Taxation of Agr. Land, 1974; mem. Gov.'s Com. on State-Local Relations and Finance, 1976; mem. Spl. Legis. Com. on Occupational Licensing, 1976; mem. Wis. State Personnel Bd. Pres. Diocesan Council of Madison, 1970-72. Mem. Midwest (past pres.), Nat. (past pres.) assns. tax adminstrs. Home: 216 Virginia Terr Madison WI 53705 Office: 335 W Wilson St Madison WI 53703 Tel (608) 255-4581

MORGAN, JO VALENTINE, JR., b. Washington, June 26, 1920; A.B. magna cum laude, Princeton, 1972; LL.B., Yale, 1947. Admitted to D.C. bar, 1948, Md. bar, 1948; asso. firm Whiteford, Hart, Carmody & Wilson, Washington, 1948-53, partner, 1953-76, sr. partner, 1976—; gen. counsel, mem. adv. bd. Nat. Bank Washington, 1965—; gen. counsel, dir. Chesapeake Instrument Corp., 1962-74. Pres. Sumner Citizens Assn., 1958-60, Westmoreland Citizens Assn., 1953-54. Montgomery County Humane Soc., 1973-75. Fellow Am. Coll. Trial Lawyers; mem. D.C. (dir. 1957-58, 73-75), Am. bar assns., Lawyers Club, Order of Coif, Barristers Club. Home: 5120 Westpath Way Sumner MD 20016 Office: 1050 17th St Washington DC 20036 Tel (202) 466-3930

MORGAN, JOHN JOSEPH, b. Phila., Dec. 15, 1945; B.A., St. Vincent Coll., 1967; J.D., Rutgers U., 1973. Staff atty. Neighborhood Legal Services Assn., Butler, Pa., 1973-76, also dir.; individual practice law, Butler, 1976—; mem. staff Pub. Defenders Office, 1976—; mem. Pa. Bar Assn. Home: 976 Whitestown Rd Butler PA 16001 Office: 249 S Main St Butler PA 16001 Tel (412) 283-2992

MORGAN, JOHN RULON, b. Spanish Fork, Utah, Jan. 2, 1902; B.A., Brigham Young U., 1923; J.D., U. Utah, 1926. Admitted to Utah bar, 1926; mem. firm Morgan & Morgan, Provo, Utah, 1926-35, Morgan & Payne, Provo, 1935—. Del. Republican Nat. Conv., 1940, 52, 60, 64; mem. Nat. council Boy Scouts Am., 1950—, recipient Silver Beaver award, 1965; pres. Nat. Soc. Sons Utah Pioneers and Sons and Daus. of Utah Pioneers, Provo, 1960—; mem. Utah Bd. Civil Def., 1960. Mem. Utah State, Utah County (pres. 1960), Am. bar assns., Brigham Young U., U. Utah alumni assns., Delta Theta Phi. Recipient (with Fern Morgan) Civic award as outstanding couple of Provo Sons and Daus. Utah Pioneers, 1975. Office: 128 E Center St Provo UT 84601 Tel (801) 373-3733

MORGAN, PATRICK JOSEPH, b. Bklyn., July 15, 1935; A.B., Fordham U., 1957, LL.B., 1960. Admitted to N.Y. State bar, 1961; counsel Union Carbide Corp., 1961—, also asso. internat. counsel, area counsel for Far East. Mem. Am. (antitrust, internat. law, corp. and bus. law coms.), N.Y. State bar assns., Internat. Law Assn. Contbr. articles to legal jours. Home: 760 Valley Rd New Canaan CT 06840 Office: 270 Park Ave New York City NY 10017 Tel (212) 551-2281

MORGAN, RICHARD MOORE, b. Hamlet, N.C., July 18, 1940; A.B., Davidson Coll., 1962; J.D., Duke, 1965. Admitted to N.C. bar, 1965; mem. firm Stevens, McGhee, Morgan & Lennon, Wilmington, N.C., 1968—. Trustee, New Hanover County Retirement System, 1975—; bd. dirs. Lower Cape Fear Council for the Arts, 1975. Mem. N.C., New Hanover County bar assns. Decorated Bronze Star. Home: 1123 Princeton Dr Wilmington NC 28401 Office: suite 409 Wachovia Bank Bldg Wilmington NC 28401 Tel (919) 763-3666

MORGAN, ROBERT DALE, b. Peoria, Ill., May 27, 1912; A.B., Bradley Poly. Inst., 1934; J.D., U. Chgo., 1937. Admitted to Ill. bar, 1937, U.S. Supreme Ct. bar, 1947; asso. firm Morgan, Pendarvis & Morgan, and predecessors, Peoria, 1937-38, partner, 1938-42, 46-57, Davis, Morgan & Witherell, Peoria, 1957-67; judge U.S. Dist. Ct. for So. Ill., 1967—, chief judge, 1972—. U.S. Commr., Peoria, 1938-46; pres. Peoria YMCA, 1947-52; mayor Peoria, 1953-57; trustee Bradley U., 1957—; bd. dirs. Peoria Bd. Med. Edn., 1968—. Mem. Am., Ill., Peoria County bar assns., Am. Judicature Soc. Home: 4943 N Grand View Dr Peoria IL 61614 Office: 216 Federal Bldg Peoria IL 61601 Tel (309) 671-7115

MORGAN, SARA POSEY, b. Andrews, N.C., May 11, 1915; B.S., Asheville Coll., 1942; M.S., U. Tenn., 1944; postgrad. U. N.C., 1945, Case Inst. Tech. (Republic Steel fellow), 1956; J.D., Samford U., 1969. Admitted to Ala. bar, 1969; prof. bus. law Coll. Bus., U. Montevallo (Ala.), 1969—; individual practice law, Montevallo, 1969—; asso. prof. Ala. Coll., Montevallo, 1954-71; program specialist distbn. and mktg. U.S. Office Edn., Washington, 1966. Pres., Shelby County unit. Am. Cancer Soc., 1975-76. Mem. Am., Ala. bar assns., AAUW, Southeastern Regional Bus. Law Assn. (pres. 1974-75), DAR, Phi Alpha Delta. Hayes-Fulbright grantee, Poland, 1974. Contbr. articles to legal jours. Home: 346 Moody St N Montevallo AL 35115 Office: U Montevallo Montevallo AL 35115 Tel (205) 665-2521

MORGAN, WILLIAM MARSHALL, b. N.Y.C., Feb. 8, 1922; B.A., U. Pitts., 1947; J.D., U. So. Calif., 1950. Admitted to Calif. bar, 1950; since practiced in Los Angeles; atty. City of Los Angeles, 1950-52; partner firm Jarrett & Morgan, 1953-61, firm Morgan, Wenzel & McNicholas, 1961—. Mem. Am., Calif. State bar assns., Am. Bd. Trial Advocates, Internat. Acad. Trial Lawyers, Internat. Assn. Ins. Counsel. Office: 1545 Wilshire Blvd Los Angeles CA 90017 Tel (213) 483-1961

MORGANSTERN, GERALD H., b. N.Y.C., Dec. 19, 1942; B.S., U. Pa., 1963; LL.B., Columbia, 1966. Admitted to N.Y. bar, 1967; asso. firm Hofheimer, Gartlir, Gottlieb & Gross, N.Y.C., 1967-73, partner, 1973—. Bd. dirs., counsel The Bridge, Inc., N.Y.C., 1975—; mem. adult edn. adv. com., long range planning com. Union Free Sch. Dist. 14, Hewlett, N.Y., 1975—. Mem. Am., N.Y. State bar assns., Assn. Bar City N.Y. Office: 100 Park Ave New York City NY 10017 Tel (212) 725-0400

MORGANSTERN, RAMON JEROME, b. St. Louis, Dec. 14, 1932; A.B., Washington U., 1955, J.D., 1957. Admitted to Mo. bar, 1957; asso. atty. firm Husch, Eppenberger, Donahue, Elson & Cornfeld, St. Louis, 1959-65; individual practice law, St. Louis, 1965-69; partner firm Schramm & Morganstern, St. Louis, 1970-76; partner firm Gallop, Johnson, Godiner, Morganstern & Crebs, St. Louis, 1976—. Pres., St. Louis Met. Council on Devel. Disabilities, 1971-77; bd. dirs. St. Louis Assn. Retarded Children, 1976—, St. Louis County Assn. Spl. Children, 1975—; Mo. Assn. Children with Learning Disabilities, 1974—, Spl. Offender Council, 1976—. Mem. Mo., St. Louis Met., St. Louis County, Am. bar assns., Phi Beta Kappa, Pi Sigma Alpha, Phi Delta Phi, Phi Eta Sigma. Home: 1328 Benbush Dr St Louis MO 63141 Office: 7733 Forsyth Blvd Suite 1800 St Louis MO 63105 Tel (314) 862-1200

MORGENS, WARREN KENDALL, b. Oklahoma City, May 25, 1940; B.S. in Bus. Adminstrn., Washington U., St. Louis, 1961, J.D., 1964. Admitted to Mo. bar, 1964, U.S. Supreme Ct. bar, 1968; with JAG, U.S. Navy, 1964-68, lt. comdr. Res., 1971—; atty. Office Gen. Counsel, SEC, Washington, 1968-69; asst. atty. gen., chief counsel St. Louis Atty. Gen.'s Office, State of Mo., 1969-72; partner firm Park Craft & Morgens, Kansas City, Mo., 1973-76; DeWitt Zeldin & Morgens, Kansas City, 1976—. State mgr. fed. polit. campaigns. Mem. St. Louis, Kansas City bar assns. Home: 121 Ward Pkwy Kansas City MO 64112 Office: Ten Main Center Upper Plaza Kansas City MO 64105 Tel (816) 474-3000

MORHOUS, LAWRENCE EUGENE, b. Okinawa, Mar. 16, 1947; B.S. in Bus. Mgmt., U. Va., 1969; J.D., Washington and Lee U., 1972. Admitted to W.Va. bar, 1972; partner firm Hudgins, Coulling, Brewster & Morhous, Bluefield, W.Va., 1972—. Mem. W.Va. State, Mercer County (W.Va.) bar assns. Office: PO Box 529 Bluefield WV 24701 Tel (304) 325-9179

MORI, JUN, b. San Francisco, Dec. 13, 1929; B.A., U. Calif., Los Angeles, 1955; J.D., U. So. Calif., 1958; LL.B. Waseda Univ., Tokyo, 1951. Admitted to Calif. bar, 1959, U.S. Supreme Ct. bar, 1971; dep. commr. corps., State of Calif., 1959-60; sr. partner firm Mori & Katayama, Los Angeles, 1960—. Chmn. Los Angeles-Nagoya Sister City Affiliation, 1965-66. Mem. Am., Los Angeles County bar assns., Am. Jud. Soc. Home: 2219 Cheswic Ln Los Angeles CA 90027 Office: 700 S Flower St Suite 410 Los Angeles CA 90017 Tel (213) 624-7621

MORIARTY, JOHN VAL, b. Indpls., July 11, 1940; B.S. in Aero. Engring., Notre Dame U., 1963; M.B.A., Ind. U., 1967, J.D., 1969. Admitted to Ind. bar, 1969; partner firm Woodard, Weikart, Emhardt & Naughton, Indpls., 1969—; trial dep. Marion County (Ind.) Prosecutor's Office, 1975-76. Mem. Indpls., Ind. State, Am. bar assns., Ind. Soc. Profl. Engrs. Home: 7620 Camelback Dr Indianapolis IN 46250 Office: 111 Monument Circle Indianapolis IN 46204 Tel (317) 634-3455

MORIARTY, MAURICE JAMES, b. Chgo., Nov. 15, 1924; A.B., U. Ill., 1948; LL.B., U. Notre Dame, 1951, J.D., 1969. Admitted to Ill. bar, 1952, U.S. Supreme Ct., 1956, U.S. Ct. Appeals, 1954; pres. Moriarty, Rose & Hultquist, Ltd., Chgo., 1952—; dir. numerous domestic, fgn. corps. Mem. Am., Ill., Chgo. Fed. bar assns., Am., Ill., Chgo. Trial Lawyers Assns., Am. Judicature Soc. Contbr. articles to profl. jours. Home: 505 N Lake Shore Dr Apt 5706 Chicago IL 60611 Office: 150 N Wacker Dr Chicago IL 60606

MORIEARTY, SCOTT CARSON, b. Bloomington, Ill., Dec. 18, 1946; A.B., Harvard, 1969, J.D., 1972. Admitted to Mass. bar, 1972; asso. firm Foley, Hoag & Eliot, Boston, 1972-74, 76-77; asst. prof. Coll. Law, U. Ill., Champaign, 1974-76. Mem. Mass. Bar Assn. Editor Harvard Law Rev., 1970-72. Office: 10 Post Office Sq Boston MA 02109 Tel (617) 482-1390

MORING, JOHN FREDERICK, b. Farmville, Va., Oct. 30, 1935; B.S., Va. Polytech. Inst., 1957; J.D., George Washington U., 1961. Admitted to Va. bar, 1961, D.C. bar, 1962, U.S. Supreme Ct. bar, 1968; asso. firm Morgan, Lewis & Bockius, D.C., 1961-68, partner firm, 1969—. Republican candidate for Va. Ho. of Dels., 21st Dist., Alexandria, 1973; mem. Alexandria City Rep. Com., 1973—, chmn. candidate recruitment com., 1975; pres. Sterling Citizens Assn., 1971—. Mem. Fed. Power (sec. 1965-68, chmn. program com. 1969), Am. (v. chmn. natural gas com., natural resources law sec. 1975—) bar assns. Contbr. articles to profl. jours. Home: 3513 Sterling Ave Alexandria VA 22304 Office: 1800 M St NW Washington DC 20036 Tel (202) 872-5013

MORINGIELLO, THOMAS G., b. Bklyn., N.Y., Dec. 8, 1933; B.A., St. John's U., 1955, LL.B., 1958. Admitted to N.Y. bar, U.S. Supreme Ct. bar; individual practice law, N.Y.C., 1963—; dir Hadrian Constrn. Ltd., London, Eng., Interblock Ltd., London, Eng. Mem. NY. State Trial Lawyers Assn., Assn. Bar City N.Y., Queens Bar Assn., St. John's U. Coll. Alumni Assn. (pres. 1960-70). Office: 126 E 35th St New York City NY 10016 Tel (212) 788-6364

MORITZ, ARTHUR MARS, b. Guatemala, June 22, 1897; B.A., Coll. City N.Y., 1919; LL.B., Columbia, 1922. Librarian asst. N.Y. Pub. Library, N.Y.C., 1910-21; admitted to N.Y. bar, 1923, Mass. bar, 1931, U.S. Supreme Ct. bar, 1934; asso. firm Morris Hillquit, N.Y.C., 1923-27; individual practice law, N.Y.C., 1927—. Mem. Assn. Bar City N.Y., New York County Lawyers Assn., N.Y. State, Am. bar assns. Home: 1 Richelieu Rd Scarsdale NY 10583 Office: 551 Fifth Ave New York City NY 10017 Tel (212) MU 2-8544

MORITZ, CLINTON R., b. Buffalo Lake, Minn.. Nov. 12, 1923; student Gustavus Adolphus Coll., St. Peter, Minn., 1941-43, 46, St. Olaf Coll., 1943-44; B.S. in Law, LL.B., St. Paul Coll. Law, 1951; J.D., William Mitchell Coll. Law, 1969. Admitted to Minn. bar, 1951; practice law, Wells, Minn., 1951-56; escrow officer Minn. Title Co., Mpls., 1956-65; corp. counsel White Investment Co., Mpls., 1965-67; title examiner North Star Title Co., Mpls., 1967-71; asso. counsel Miles Cos., Mpls., 1971—. Mem. Wells City Council, 1955-56. Mem. Minn. (pub. relations com. 1953-63), Hennepin County bar assns., Delta Theta Phi. Author: Examining Titles for Title Insurance, 1964. Home: 6710 Stevens Ave S Richfield MN 55423 Office: 4500 Lyndale Ave N Minneapolis MN 55412 Tel (612) 588-9796

MORITZ, MICHAEL EVERETT, b. Marion, Ohio, Mar. 30, 1933; B.S., Ohio State U., 1958, J.D. summa cum laude, 1961. Admitted to Ohio bar, 1961; asso. firm Dunbar Kienzle & Murphey, Columbus, Ohio, 1961-65, partner, 1966-72; partner firm Moritz McClure Hughes & Hadley, Columbus, 1972—; dir. Cardinal Foods, Inc., Pharmacy Systems, Inc., others; adj. prof. Capital U. Law Sch., 1969-70; lectr. Ohio Legal Center Inst., 1967. Chmn. legal div. United Appeal of Franklin County, 1964; pres. Capital City Young Republican Club, 1966, mem. Franklin County Rep. Exec. Com., 1966—; trustee Omicron Deuteron Assn., 1964-71, pres., 1970. Mem. Am., Ohio, Columbus bar assns., Am. Judicature Soc., Order of Coif, Phi Gamma Delta, Beta Gamma Sigma. Recipient Distinguished Service award Columbus Jr. C. of C., 1966. Home: 1110 Kingsdale Terr Columbus OH 43220 Office: 150 E Broad St Columbus OH 43215 Tel (614) 224-0888

MORITZ, PRESTON WILLIAM, b. North Catasauqua, Pa., June 16, 1939; student U.S. Coast Guard Acad., 1958-60; B.A., Moravian Coll., 1963; J.D., Dickinson Sch. Law, 1966. Admitted to Pa. bar, 1966; asso. law firm Brose, Poswistilo & LaBarr, Easton, Pa., 1966-70; v.p. Lehigh Valley Title Co., Easton, Pa., 1968-70; partner law firm Peters, Moritz & Peischl, Nazareth, Pa., 1970—. Vice-chmn. service Minsi Trail Council Boy Scouts Am., 1975-76. Mem. exec. bd. Northampton County Am. Cancer Soc.; bd. dirs. Lehigh Valley Football All-Star Game. Mem. Northampton County, Pa. bar assns., Nazareth Area C. of C. (pres. 1977—). Home: 305 E Center St Nazareth PA 18064 Office: Center Square Nazareth PA 18064

MORNINGSTAR, MARSHALL ALBERT, II, b. Staunton, Va., Nov. 15, 1946; B.S., U. Md., 1968; J.D., U. Balt., 1973. Admitted to Md. bar, 1973; staff Legal Aid Bur., Westminster, Md., 1973; partner firm Zimmerman, Aldridge & Dwyer, Frederick, Md., 1973—. Crusade chmn. Frederick County chpt. Am. Cancer Soc., 1974-75, pres., 1975—; v.p., dir. Frederick Sertoma Club, 1975—. Mem. Am., Md., Frederick County bar assns., Frederick C. of C. (dir. 1976—). Home: Route 3 Ruhland Dr Frederick MD 21701 Office: 120 W Church St Frederick MD 21701 Tel (301) 663-5191

MORONEY, DENNIS PATRICK, b. Milw., Apr. 16, 1947; B.A. in History, Regis Coll., 1969; J.D., Marquette U., 1973. Admitted to Wis. bar, 1973, U.S. Dist. Ct. Eastern and Western Dist. Wis., 1973; lendor First Wis. Nat. Bank Milw., 1969-73; partner firm McMahon & Moroney, Milw., 1973—. Active United Fund, 1969-70, 76. Mem. Wis., Milw., Milw. Jr. bar assns., Delta Theta Phi. Named to Wis. Men of Distinction, 1976; Author: Buy Now-Pay Later, 1969. Home: 2424 N 62d St Wauwatosa WI 53213 Office: 710 N Plankinton Ave Milwaukee WI 53203 Tel (414) 276-8985

MORONY, JEAN, b. Topeka, Mar. 21, 1912; A.B., Stanford, 1932, M.A., 1933; J.D., Hastings Coll. Law U. Calif., 1936. Admitted to Calif. bar, 1936, U.S. Supreme Ct. bar, 1955; dep. atty. gen. Calif., 1937-39; police judge, City of Chico, 1939-42; U.S. conciliation commr. for Butte County, 1940-42; served to capt. JAGC, AUS, 1942-46; asst. city atty., Chico, 1946-61; judge Butte County Superior Ct., Oroville, Calif., 1961—; faculty Calif. Coll. Trial Judges, U. Calif., 1971-72; mem. exec. com., chmn. Superior Ct. com. Jud. Council Calif., 1969-73; justice pro tem Ct. of Appeals 3d Dist., 1972; mem. adv. com. for Center Jour., Calif. Center for Jud. Edn. and Research, 1973-77, adv. com. Juvenile Ct. Inst., 1974, chmn. new trial ct. judges orientation planning com., 1976—; mem. video tape adv. com. McGeorge Sch. Law, U. of Pacific, 1974-75; bd. dirs. No. Calif. Criminal Justice Trng. and Edn. System, 1974-76; chmn. uniform rules com. Superior Cts. 3d Appellate Dist., 1970—; chmn. by-laws com. Conf. Calif. Judges, 1976—. Chmn., Chico Airport Commn., 1946-48; bd. dirs. 3d Agrl. Dist. Fair Assn., 1940-61, pres., 1960-61. Mem. Am., Butte County (pres. 1953) bar assns., Am. Judicature Soc., Nat. Council Juvenile Ct. Judges, Calif. Conf. Judges, Conf. State Bar Dels. (v.p. 1959-61, mem. exec. com.), Pi Sigma Alpha. Phi Alpha Delta. Author, Manual on California Government, 1938, rev. edit., 1973. Office: Butte County Court House 1 Court St Oroville CA 95965 Tel (916) 534-4611

MORRELL, MALCOLM ELMER, JR., b. Portland, Maine, Aug. 25, 1927; A.B., Bowdoin Coll., 1949, LL.B., 1952. Admitted to Maine bar, 1952; asso. firm Eaton, Peabody, Bradford & Veague, Bangor, Maine, 1954-58, partner, 1958—; trustee Maine Central Inst., 1968—, v.p., 1971-73; mem. bd. overseers Bowdoin Coll., 1974—; mem. alumni council Bowdoin Coll., 1969-72, pres., 1972. Fin. chmn. Katahdin Area Council Boy Scouts Am., 1964; dir. Bangor Children's Home, 1958—, pres., 1961-68; dir. Bangor YMCA, 1965-71, pres., 1969-71; trustee All Souls Congregational Ch., 1970-74, moderator, 1974; dir. United Way of Penobscot Valley, 1976—. Mem. Penobscot County (pres., 1975), Maine State, Am. (mem. labor relations, corp. banking, bus. law sects.) Bar Assns. Home: 120 Royal Rd Bangor ME 04401 Office: 6 State St Bangor ME 04401 Tel (207) 947-0111

MORRILL, DAVID EARL, b. Sturgis, S.D., Aug. 11, 1932; B.S. in Bus. Adminstrn., U. S.D., 1954, J.D., 1956. Admitted to S.D. bar, 1956; atty. City of Sturgis (S.D.), 1956-66; gen. counsel Black Hills Power & Light Co., Rapid City, S.D., 1968—. Mem. S.D. Bd. Regents for Higher Edn., 1975—; pres. S.D. League Municipalities, 1960-61. Mem. Am. Bar Assn., Am. Judicature Soc., S.D. Trial Lawyers Assn. Home: 1440 Sherman St Sturgis SD 57785 Office: PO Box 580 Sturgis SD 57785 Tel (605) 347-2551

MORRIS, BENJAMIN GORDON, b. Quinter, Kans., Jan. 5, 1940; A.B., U. Kans., 1962, J.D., 1966; postgrad. Instituto Interamericano de Educacion Politica, San José, Costa Rica, 1962. Admitted to Kans, bar, 1966, Mo. bar, 1967, Fla. bar, 1972; dir. activities Mo. Bar, Jefferson City, 1966; asst. dean Sch. Law U. Kans., 1967-69; trust officer Exchanger Nat. Bank, Tampa, Fla., 1969-72, v.p., 1972-74; v.p., sec. Exchange Bankcorp., Inc., Tampa, 1974—; mem. Kans. Ho. of Reps., 1964-66. Pres. Hillsborough County chpt. Am. Heart Assn., 1977; vice-chmn. Hillsborough County Emergency Med. Services Council, 1977; chmn. edn. council Greater Tampa C. of C. 1975. Mem. Am., Fla., Hillsborough County bar assns. Contbr. articles to law jour. Home: 501 W Davis Blvd Tampa FL 33606 Office: Suite 2112 Exchange Nat Bank Bldg Tampa FL 33602 Tel (813) 224-5326

MORRIS, BETTY BRYANT, b. Mountain Grove, Mo., Oct. 9, 1940; J.D., Whittier Coll. Sch. Law, 1968; certificate U. So. Calif., 1970; postgrad Inst. Electronic Tech. Writing. Admitted to Calif. bar, 1969; asso. trust counsel Security Pacific Nat. Bank, Los Angeles, 1969-73; asst. counsel Union Bank, Los Angeles, 1973-74, asso. counsel, 1974—; corp. sec. Union Internat. Bank, Los Angeles, 1974—; advisory council Los Angeles County Dist. Atty. Past pres. advisory council Central Advisory Bd. Los Angeles City Sch. Dist.; mem. Calif. Job Creation Bd.; exec. advisory bd. Career Planning Center. Mem. Calif. Elected Womens Assns., League Women Voters NOW, Calif.

Women Lawyers (founder), Am. Arbitration Assn., Nat. Bus. and Profl. Women Los Angeles (former pres.), Am. Inst. Banking, Fin. Lawyers Conf., Internat., Nat. (regional dir.) assns. women lawyers, Center Law in the Pub. Interest, Women Lawyers Assn. Los Angeles (former pres.), Women's Coalition (past sec., treas.), Los Angeles County Bar Assn. (trustee), Whittier Coll. Sch. Law Alumni Assn. (past pres.), Phi Alpha Delta. Recipient Outstanding Career Woman certificate, Calif. Fedn. Bus. and Profl. Women, 1973, Outstanding Vol. Service certificate, Union Bank, 1976, Outstanding Vol. Service resolution City of Los Angeles, 1976, resolution of appreciation Calif. Legislature, 1976. Office: 445 S Figueroa St Los Angeles CA 90071 Tel (213) 687-6286

MORRIS, CARLOSS, b. Galveston, Tex., June 7, 1915; B.A., Rice Inst., 1936; J.D., U. Tex., 1939. Admitted to Tex. bar, 1938; sr. partner Morris, Harris, McCanne, Tinsley & Snowden, Houston, 1942—; chmn. bd., co-chief exec. officer Stewart Info. Services Corp., 1975—; chmn. bd. Stewart Title Guaranty Co., 1975—. Pres., Star of Hope Mission, 1951—, Tex. Safety Assn., 1950-51; chmn. Interdisciplinary Commn. on Housing and Urban Growth, 1974—; trustee Baylor U., 1952-72, past vice chmn. bd., trustee Baylor Coll. Medicine, chmn., 1968; bd. dirs. Goodwill Industries; bd. dirs., exec. com. Billy Graham Evangelistic Assn.; trustee Oldham Little Ch. Found., B.M. Woltman Found. Fellow Am., Tex. bar founds.; mem. Am. (past chmn. younger lawyers sect., past del., mem. council real property, probate and trust sect.), Tex. bar assns., Chancellors, Order of Coif, Phi Delta Phi, Alpha Tau Omega. Home: 3996 Inverness Ln Houston TX 77019 Office: 2200 W Loop S Suite 225 Houston TX 77027 Tel (713) 627-1520

MORRIS, DAVID JOHN, b. Helena, Mont., Feb. 6, 1941; B.A. with honors, U. Mont., 1963; J.D., U. Calif. at Berkeley, 1966. Admitted to Calif. bar, 1967; asso. firm Baker, Ancel & Redmond, Los Angeles, beginning in 1966, subsequently partner. Mem. Am., Los Angeles County bar assns. Home: 15416 Brownwood Pl Los Angeles CA 90024 Office: 626 Wilshire Blvd Suite 700 Los Angeles CA 90017 Tel (213) 624-9201

MORRIS, DEWAYNE NEAL, b. Cullman, Ala., June 30, 1931; B.A., U. Ala., 1957, LL.B., 1958. Admitted to Ala. bar, 1958; individual practice law, Birmingham, Ala., 1958-59; chmn. Jefferson County (Ala.) Bd. of Equalization, Birmingham, 1959-63; real estate mgr. Ala. Farm Bur. Ins. Cos., Montgomery, 1963-64; partner firm Markstein & Morris, Birmingham, 1964—. Mem. Club of All Nations (pres. 1962-63). Mem. Am., Ala., Birmingham bar assns. Home: 900 Conroy Rd Birmingham AL 35222 Office: 512 Massey Bldg Birmingham AL 35203 Tel (205) 254-3880

MORRIS, EARL FRANKLIN, b. Byesville, Ohio, Apr. 5, 1909; A.B., Wittenberg U., 1930, LL.D. (hon.), 1955; J.D., Harvard, 1933; LL.D. (hon.) Willamette U., 1967, Valparaiso U., 1968, Findlay Coll., 1971, Dickinson Sch. Law, 1974. Admitted to Ohio bar, 1933, U.S. Supreme Ct. bar, 1946; asso. firm Wright, Harlor, Morris & Arnold, Columbus, Ohio, 1933-34, partner, 1935—; spl. counsel Midland Mut. Life Ins. Co., 1938—. Bd. dirs. Wittenberg U., 1948—, chmn., 1973—; bd. dirs. Ohio Found. Ind. Colls., 1953—, Assn. Ind. Colls. and Univs. of Ohio, 1970—; moderator Columbus Town Meeting, 1938-74. Mem. Am. (pres. 1967-68), Ohio State (pres. 1956-57), Columbus (pres. 1949-50) bar assns., Am. Bar Found., Am. Law Inst., Am. Judicature Soc. (chmn. bd. dirs. 1970-72), Inst. Jud. Adminstrn., Inst. for Ct. Mgmt. (chmn. bd. trustees 1973—), Am. Coll. Trial Lawyers, Internat. Bar Assn., Nat. Conf. Bar Pres's, (chmn. 1961-62), Assn. Life Ins. Counsel, Phi Delta Phi (hon.). Contbr. articles to legal jours. Home: 2531 Fair Ave Columbus OH 43209 Office: 37 W Broad St Columbus OH 43215 Tel (614) 224-4125

MORRIS, EUGENE JEROME, b. N.Y.C., Oct. 14, 1910; B.S.S., Coll. City N.Y., 1931; LL.B., St. Johns U., 1934. Admitted to N.Y. bar, 1935, U.S. Supreme Ct. bar, 1940; atty. N.Y. Mortgage Commn., N.Y.C., 1935-37; asso. firm Natanson, Pack & Scholer, N.Y.C., 1937-45; mem. firm Demov, Morris, Levin & Shein, N.Y.C., 1946—; instr. law real property N.Y. Law Sch., 1946-47; lectr., seminar chmn. New Sch. Social Research, N.Y. U., Practicing Law Inst. Mem. Am. Bar Assn., Assn. Bar City N.Y., N.Y. County Lawyers Assn. Contbr. articles to law revs.; editor weekly column N.Y. Law Jour., 1965—. Home: 200 Central Park S New York City NY 10019 Office: Demov Morris Levin Shein 40 W 57th St New York City NY 10019 Tel (212) 757-5050

MORRIS, FRANK ROCKWELL, JR., b. Jackson, Mich., July 1, 1929; B.A., Yale U., 1952; J.D., U. Mich., 1957. Admitted to Ohio bar, 1958; partner firm Porter, Wright, Morris and Arthur, Columbus, Ohio, 1957—; dir. Ironsides Co., Columbus, 1960—, Rimrock Corp., Columbus, 1965—, Dollar Fin. Inc., Columbus, 1977—. Pres. bd. trustees The Columbus Acad., 1972-74. Fellow Ohio State Bar Found.; mem. Am. (council corp., banking and bus. law sect. 1974—), Ohio State (chmn. corporation law com. 1974-76), Columbus bar assns., Phi Delta Phi. Home: 216 S Columbia Ave Columbus OH 43209 Office: 37 W Broad St Columbus OH 43215 Tel (614) 224-4125

MORRIS, GARY J., b. St. Louis, Sept. 7, 1936; A.B., Washington U., St. Louis, 1958, J.D., 1960. Admitted to Mo. bar, 1960, U.S. Supreme Ct. bar, 1971; individual practice law, Clayton, Mo., 1961-67; co-founder, partner firm Carp & Morris, Clayton, 1968—; gen. counsel, exec. dir. Coin Machine Operators Assn., Inc., St. Louis, 1968—. Active United Way, Jewish Fedn. St. Louis. Mem. Am., Mo., St. Louis County (chmn. com. econs. and law office mgmt. 1973-75), Met. St. Louis bar assns., Assn. Trial Lawyers Am. Home: 200 Brooktrail Ct Creve Coeur MO 63141 Office: 225 S Meramec Ave Clayton MO 63105 Tel (314) 727-7200

MORRIS, HARVEY BLAND, b. Athens, Ala., July 20, 1942; B.S., U. Ala., 1965, J.D., 1966. Admitted to Ala. bar, 1966; mem. firm Walker, Morris & Smith, Huntsville, Ala., 1966-69, partner, 1969—. Mem. Ala. Trial Lawyers Assn., Ala. Def. Lawyers Assn., Ala. Criminal Lawyers Assn., Assn. Trial Lawyers Am., Huntsville-Madison County C. of C. Home: 2024 Memorial Pkwy Huntsville AL 35810 Office: 604 Madison St Huntsville AL 35801 Tel (205) 533-5941

MORRIS, JACK IRVING, b. Dec. 15, 1928; B.S., U. Buffalo, 1952, LL.B., 1953, J.D., 1968. Admitted to N.Y. State bar, 1953; asso. Elton M. Dale, Kenmore, N.Y., 1952-62; individual practice law, West Seneca, N.Y., 1953-71; partner firm Schroeder & Morris, Accountants, West Seneca, 1951-53; partner firm Morris & Bray, Buffalo, 1971—; atty. Town of West Seneca, 1956-65; atty. Erie County Sewer Dists. 1 and 3, 1959-64; mem. commn. N.Y. State Office for Local Govt., 1960-64; mem. N.Y. State Commn. on Suburban Town Law, 1963-64; chmn. resolutions com. N.Y. State Assn. Towns, 1964-65; dir. Morlawn Realty, Inc., 1299 Union Rd., Inc., Regent Resort Motel, Inc., Morhead Properties Ltd., 626 N Birch Rd, Inc., Sherman Purebred Farms. Chmn. indsl. com. Community Chest; chmn. bus. sect. Buffalo Philharmonic Orch. Mem. Nat. Arbitration Assn., N.Y. State, Am., Erie County bar assns. Home: 948 Main St West Seneca NY 14224 Office: 1299 Union Rd Buffalo NY 14224 Tel (716) 674-9100

MORRIS, JAMES WALLIS, b. Marion, Ky., Nov. 6, 1944; B.A., Murray State U., 1967; M.A., U. Ky., 1969; J.D., Vanderbilt U., 1971. Admitted to S.C. bar; asso. firm Nelson, Mullins, Grier & Scarborough, Columbia, S.C., 1971-74; individual practice law, 1974-75; partner firm Morris, Medlin & Perry, Columbia, 1975—. Founder Nashville chpt. Big Bros. Am., 1970-71; chmn. profl. com. Am. Cancer Soc. Mem. S.C., Am. bar assns., Comml. Bar Assn., Am. Trial Lawyers Assn. Author: Retirement and Vacation Lot Sales: The Full Disclosure Act, 1976. Home: 5420 Slyvan Dr Columbia SC 29206 Office: PO Box 11865 Columbia SC 29201 Tel (803) 779-6767

MORRIS, JOE CRAVEN, b. Jackson, Tenn., Oct. 11, 1935; B.A., Lambuth Coll., 1959; LL.B., U. Tenn., 1960. Admitted to Tenn. bar, 1961; law clk. U.S. Dist. Ct. Western Dist. Tenn., 1962-63; with firm Wrape and Hernly, Memphis and Washington, 1963-64; field rep. Congressman Ray Blanton of Tenn., 1966-69; municipal judge, Jackson, 1972-76; chanellor State of Tenn., Jackson, 1976—. Bd. dirs. Jackson Mental Health Center, 1968-71. Mem. Am., Tenn., Jackson, Madison County bar assns. Home: 43 Shadowlawn St Jackson TN 38301 Office: Madison County Courthouse Jackson TN 38301 Tel (901) 427-1286

MORRIS, JOHN EDWARD, b. N.Y.C., Sept. 30, 1916; A.B., Coll. City N.Y., 1937; A.M., Columbia, 1938; J.D., Harvard, 1942. Admitted to N.Y. bar, 1942; asso. firm Clarke & Reilly, N.Y.C., 1946-50; sr. partner firm Morris, Duffy, Ivone & Jensen, N.Y.C., 1950—. Mem. Am., N.Y., Bronx County bar assns., Am. Arbitration Assn. (arbitrator 1955—), N.Y. County Lawyers Assn., Internat. Assn. Ins. Counsel, Def. Research Inst., Harvard Law Sch. Assn. N.Y.C. Home: 9 Meadowlark Dr W Nyack NY 10994 Office: 233 Broadway New York City NY 10007 Tel (212) 766-1888

MORRIS, JOHN WHELCHEL, b. Gainesville, Ga., Jan. 7, 1945; B.A., Yale, 1967; J.D., U. Pa., 1970. Admitted to Pa. bar, 1970; asso. firm Clark, Ladner, Fortenbaugh & Young, Phila., 1970-73, Pierson, Jones & Nelson, 1973-74; 1st asst. dist. atty. Phila., 1975—; lectr. Temple U., 1971—. Mem. Pa., Phila. bar assns., Nat. Dist. Attys. Assn. Home: 1210 Pine St Philadelphia PA 19107 Office: 1600 PNB Bldg Philadelphia PA 19107 Tel (215) 665-0800

MORRIS, JOHN WILBERT, JR., b. Fortuna, Calif., Feb. 5, 1939; B.S., Fresno State Coll., 1964; J.D., San Francisco Law Sch., 1972. Admitted to Calif. bar, 1972; asso. partner firm Boccardo, Blum, Lull, Niland & Bell, San Francisco, 1972—, Boccardo Offices, Los Angeles, 1972—; lectr. in field. Pres. Fresno (Calif.) Young Republicans, 1966-67. Mem. San Francisco County Bar Assn. Office: 1 California St Suite 1700 San Francisco CA 94111 Tel (415) 391-3700

MORRIS, JOSEPH WILSON, b. Rice County, Kans., Apr. 28, 1922; A.B., Washburn U., 1943, J.D., 1947; LL.M., U. Mich., 1948, S.J.D., 1955. Admitted to Kans. bar, 1947, Okla. bar, 1949; with Shell Oil Co., Tulsa, N.Y.C., 1948-60; asso. gen. counsel Amerada Petroleum Corp., Tulsa, 1960-67, gen. counsel, 1967-69, v.p., gen. counsel, 1969-72; dean Coll. Law U. Tulsa, 1972-74; now chief judge U.S. Dist. Ct. Mem. Okla. State Regents Higher Edn., 1970-73. Mem. Tulsa County (pres. 1971), Muskogee County, Okla., Am. bar assns., Am. Judicature Soc., Am. Law Inst. Contbr. articles to legal jours. Home: Rt 3 Box 132 Muskogee OK 74401 Office: PO Box 828 Muskogee OK 74401 Tel (918) 683-4321

MORRIS, NORVAL, b. Auckland, New Zealand, Oct. 1, 1923; LL.B., U. Melbourne (Australia), 1946, LL.M., 1947; Ph.D. in Criminology (Hutchinson Silver medal 1950), London (Eng.) Sch. Econs., 1949. Asst. lectr. London Sch. Econs., 1949-50; sr. lectr. law U. Melbourne, 1950-58, prof. criminology, 1955-58; called to Australian bar, 1953; Ezra Ripley Thayer teaching fellow Harvard Law Sch., 1955-56, vis. prof., 1961-62; Boynthon prof., dean faculty law U. Adelaide (Australia), 1958-62; dir. UN Inst. Prevention Crime and Treatment of Offenders, Tokyo, Japan, 1962-64; Julius Kreeger prof. law and criminology, dir. Center Studies Criminal Justice, U. Chgo., 1964—; now dean Law Sch.; chmn. Commn. Inquiry Capital Punishment in Ceylon, 1958-59; mem. Social Sci. Research Council Australia, 1958-59; Australian del. confs. div. human rights and sect. social def. UN, 1955-66, mem. standing adv. com. experts prevention crime and treatment offenders; pres. Ill. Gov.'s Adv. Com. on Adult Offenders. Served with Australian Army, World War II; PTO. Decorated Japanese Order Sacred Treasure 3d Class. Author: The Habitual Criminal, 1951; Report of the Commission of Inquiry on Capital Punishment, 1959; (with W. Morison and R. Sharwood) Cases in Torts, 1962; (with Colin Howard) Studies in Criminal Law, 1964; (with G. Hawkins) The Honest Politicians Guide to Crime Control, 1970. Internat. editorial bd. Excerpta Criminologica 1960. Home: 1207 E 50th St Chicago IL 60637*

MORRIS, REGINALD PHILIP, b. Madisonville, Va., Jan. 13, 1935; B.A., U. Richmond, 1960, J.D., 1964. Admitted to Va. bar, 1965, U.S. Supreme Ct. bar, 1975; v.p. Allen, Allen, Allen & Allen, P.A., Richmond, Va., 1958—; substitute judge Chesterfield Gen. Dist. Ct., 1974—, Chesterfield Juvenile and Domestic Relations Ct., 1975—, Colonial Heights Gen. Dist. Ct., 1975—, Colonial Heights Juvenile and Domestic Relations Ct., 1975—. Bd. dirs. Chester Civitan Club 1970-75, Chester Sports Boosters, Inc., Chester Little League; mem. Chester Jaycees, Izaak Walton League of Am.; deacon Chester Presbyterian Ch., 1970-73. Mem. Am., Va., Chesterfield Colonial Heights, Richmond, bar assns., Am., Va., Richmond assns. trial lawyers, Am. Judicature Soc., Law Sci. Acad. Am., Richmond Jr. Bar. Home: 11612 Boyd Rd Chester VA 23831 Office: 1809 Staples Mill Rd Richmond VA 23230 Tel (804) 359-9151

MORRIS, RICHARD SCOTT, b. Oklahoma City, Okla., July 28, 1932; J.D., U. N.Mex., 1960. Admitted to N.Mex. bar, 1961; atty. N.Mex. Oil Conservation Commn., Sante Fe, 1960-62; partner firm Montgomery, Federiei, Andrews, Hannahs & Morris, Sante Fe, 1962-73; v.p., asso. gen. counsel El Paso Nat. Gas Co. (Tex.), 1973—. Mem. Am., N.Mex. bar assns. Office: PO Box 1492 El Paso TX 79978 Tel (915) 543-3345

MORRIS, THOMAS JEFFERSON, b. Pearson, Ga., Apr. 17, 1910; B.A., Rollins Coll., 1933; LL.B., Yale, 1936; grad. Trial State Judges Coll., Reno, Nev., 1970. Admitted to N.H. bar, 1937; asst. to pres. Stoneleigh Coll., 1936-43, now prof.; partner firm Morris, Griffin & Harrington, Portsmouth, N.H., 1948-57; judge Rye (N.H.) Municipal Ct., 1955-57; asso. justice N.H. Superior Ct., 1957-75. Trustee Rye Pub. Library. Mem. Am., N.H. bar assns., Am. Judicature Soc. Home: 11 Washington Rd Rye NH 03870 Tel (603) 436-5357

MORRIS, WALTER A., JR., b. 1921; A.B., Holy Cross Coll., 1942; LL.B., Columbia 1947. Admitted to N.Y. bar; with firm Shearman & Sterling & Wright, 1947-57; asst. gen. counsel. asst. sec. W.R. Grace & Co., 1957-69; asst. gen. counsel Consol. Edison Co. N.Y. Inc., N.Y.C., 1969-70, sec. asst. gen. counsel, 1970-73, gen. counsel, 1973—. Mem. Am. Soc. Corp. Secs. (pres. N.Y. group, dir.). Office: 4 Irving Pl New York City NY 10003*

MORRIS, WALTER EDMUND, b. Punxsutawney, Pa., June 10, 1891; B.S., Oreg. State Coll., 1912; LL.B., J.D., U. Mich., 1916. Admitted to Pa. bar, 1917; individual practice law, Punxsutawney, 1917—; atty. Savs. & Trust Co., Punxsutawney br.; dist. atty., 1922-33; mem. Pa. Senate, 1962-64. Mem. Am., Pa., Jefferson County bar assns. Home: 209 Dinsmore Ave Punxsutawney PA 15767 Office: 5-6 Swartz Bldg Mahoning St Punxsutawney PA 15767 Tel (814) 938-4300

MORRIS, WILLIAM ROBERTS, b. Shelby, Ohio, June 15, 1907; B.A., Bethany Coll., 1929; LL.B., U. Mich., 1932. Admitted to Ohio bar, 1932; individual practice law, Shelby, 1932—; judge Shelby Municipal Ct., 1959-69; mayor City of Shelby, 1940-43, 52-56; pres. Richland County (Ohio) Bar, 1964-65. Mem. Am., Ohio, Richland County bar assns. Home: 47 Grand Blvd Shelby OH 44875 Office: 23 W Main St Shelby OH 44875 Tel (419) 342-4337

MORRISON, DOUGLAS WILLIAM, b. Lovell, Wyo., Apr. 7, 1940; B.S. magna cum laude, Brigham Young U., 1964; postgrad. N.Y. U. Sch. Law, 1964-65; J.D., U. Utah, 1968. Admitted to Utah bar, 1968, D.C. bar, 1969, U.S. Supreme Ct. bar, 1974; asso. firm Jones Waldo Holbrook & McDonough, Salt Lake City, 1968-69, Wilkinson Cragun & Barker, Washington, 1969-70, Fabian & Clendenin, Salt Lake City, 1970-71; individual practice law, Provo, Utah, 1971—; asst. to dean Coll. Bus., Brigham Young U., Provo, 1963-64, lectr., 1971—. Coach Little League, 1975-76; cubmaster Boy Scouts Am., 1976—; missionary Gulf States, Ch. of Jesus Christ of Latter-day Saints, 1960-62, mem. high council, 1974-76. Mem. Am. Inst. C.P.A.'s, Nat. Soc. Pub. Accountants, Am. Assn. Atty.-C.P.A.'s, Am. Bar Assn., Order of Coif. Mem. Mormon Tabernacle Choir, 1967-69. Home: 3326 Navajo Ln Provo UT 84601 Office: 1675 N 200 W Provo UT 84601 Tel (801) 375-2221

MORRISON, DWIGHT EDWARD, b. Boone, Iowa, Nov. 19, 1919; B.S., Iowa State U., 1942; A.M., Columbia, 1944, Ph.D., 1946; J.D., Ind. U., 1968. Admitted to Ind. bar, 1968; sr. organic chemist Eli Lilly & Co., Indpls., 1945-62, patent technician, 1962-67, patent agt., 1967-68, patent atty., 1968—. Mem. Ind. (sec.-treas. patent copyright and trademark sect. 1973-74), Am. bar assns. Home: 250 Williams Dr Indianapolis IN 46260 Office: 307 E McCarty St Indianapolis IN 46206 Tel (317) 462-4441

MORRISON, HENDERSON WILLIAM, b. N.Y.C., July 4, 1915; certificate St. John's Coll., 1937; LL.B., Fordham U., 1941. Admitted to N.Y. State bar, 1941; asso. firm George M. Levy, Mineola N.Y., 1945-49; partner firm Edwards, Froehlich & McDonough, Mineola, 1949-59; partner firm Morrison & Dougherty, Garden City, N.Y., 1959-64; judge Nassau County Dist. Ct., 1964-73; judge County Ct., Nassau County, 1973, adminstrv. judge, 1973—. Mem. advisory bd. St. Anthony's Guidance Clinic, 1958—; vol. of year Mental Health and Geriatrics div. Catholic Charities, Diocese of Rockville Centre; former pres. Garden City Republican Club. Mem. Catholic Lawyers Guild (former pres.), Nassau Lawyers Assn. Nat. Assn. of CIC Agts., Fordham Law Rev. Assn., Fordham Law Alumni Assn. Mem. editorial staff Fordham Law Review. Home: 14 Cedar Pl Garden City NY 11530 Office: 262 Old Country Rd Mineola NY 11501 Tel (516) 535-2065

MORRISON, JAMES LAWRENCE, b. Decatur, Ill., Aug. 14, 1927; A.B., Millikin U., Decatur, 1950; J.D., U. Ill., 1951; A.M.P., Harvard, 1974. Admitted to Ill. bar, 1951; atty. Swift & Co., 1951-57, tax counsel, 1957-68, mgr. tax div., 1968-73; dir. taxes Esmark, Inc., Chgo., 1973-74, asst. controller taxes, 1974-77, asst. gen. counsel, dir. govt. affairs, 1977—; mem. Esmark Pension Bd., 1975—, Esmark Found. Bd., 1976-77. Vice pres., dir. Chgo. Jr. Assn. Commerce and Industry, 1957-62; bd. dirs. Joint Civic Com. on Elections, 1954-62; pres., chmn. bd. Citizens Greater Chgo., 1965-67; active Boy Scouts Am. Mem. Am., Ill., Chgo. bar assns., Tax Exec. Inst., Chgo. Assn. Commerce and Industry. Recipient Distinguished Service award Chgo. Jaycees, 1967, Trail Blazer award, Silver Beaver award, Boy Scouts Am., 1974. Office: 1725 K St NW Washington DC 20006 Tel (202) 223-4894

MORRISON, JAMES LOWRY, b. Kansas City, Mo., Dec. 28, 1925; student Cornell Coll., 1946, Grinnell Coll., 1946-47; LL.B., Drake U., 1950. Admitted to Iowa bar, 1950, Nebr. bar, 1952; spl. agt. FBI, 1951; sec., treas. Nebr. Telephone Assn., Lincoln, 1952-56; dir. of gen. info. and gen. comml. supt. W. Coast Telephone Co., Everett, Wash., 1956-62; asst. sec. Continental Telephone Co., Clayton, Mo., 1962-63; gen. counsel Iowa-Ill. Telephone Co., New London, Ia., 1963-65; individual practice law, Mt. Pleasant, Iowa, 1965-76; asst. v.p. and trust officer Citizens Bank & Trust Co., Park Ridge, Ill., 1976—; county atty. Henry County, Iowa, 1967-71. Mem. Iowa, Nebr. bar assns. Office: 1 S Northwest Highway Park Ridge IL 60068 Tel (312) 825-7000

MORRISON, JOHN HORTON, b. St. Paul, Sept. 15, 1933; B.B.A., U. N.Mex., 1955; B.A., U. Oxford, 1957, M.A., 1961; J.D., Harvard, 1962. Admitted to Ill. bar, 1962, U.S. Supreme Ct. bar, 1965; asso. firm Kirkland & Ellis, Chgo., 1962-67, partner, 1968—. Mem. Am., Ill. bar assns. Home: 2717 Lincoln St Evanston IL 60201 Office: Suite 5800 200 E Randolph Dr Chicago IL 60601 Tel (312) 861-2252

MORRISON, KEITH EVERETT, b. Hoisington, Kans., Feb. 9, 1910; A.B., U. Kans., 1931; M.S., U. Wyoming, 1939; LL.B., Yale, 1948. Admitted to Kans. bar, 1949; U.S. Dist. Ct. for Kans., 1949; Tex. bar, 1956; faculty law U. Tex., Austin, 1948—, William Stamps Farish prof. law, 1969—; agr. economist, U. Wyo., 1939-41. Mem. Am., Tex. bar assns. Author: (with others) The Study of Federal Tax Law, 19—. Home: 4600 Ridge Oak Dr Austin TX 78731 Office: Law Sch Univ Tex 2500 Red River Rd Austin TX 78705 Tel (512) 471-5151

MORRISON, MICHAEL PATRICK, b. Hinsdale, Ill., Feb. 21, 1944; B.A., Mich. State U., 1967; J.D., U. Tex., 1972. Admitted to Ill. bar, 1972; asso. firm McDermott, Will & Emery, Chgo., 1972—; lectr. in mil. law USAF Officer Tng. Sch., 1970-72. Mem. Am., Ill., Chgo., bar assns. Office: 111 W Monroe St Chicago IL 60603 Tel (312) 372-2000

MORRISON, STEPHEN GERALD, b. Cambridge, Mass., Sept. 22, 1913; LL.B., Boston Coll., 1949. Admitted to Mass. bar, 1949; asso. prof. law, law librarian Boston Coll., 1949—. Mem. Mass. Bar Assn. Home: 373 Medford St Somerville MA 02145 Tel (617) 625-5289

MORRISS, WILL A., JR., b. Kerrville, Tex., Aug. 26, 1903; B.A., U. Tex., 1924, LL.B., 1926. Admitted to Tex. bar, 1926; partner firm Morriss & Morriss, 1926-46, Morriss, Morriss & Boatwright, 1947-49, Morriss, Morriss, Boatwright & Lewis, San Antonio, 1950-64, Morriss, Boatwright, Lewis & Davis, San Antonio, 1965—. Pres. San Antonio YMCA, 1943-44; chmn. Bexar County (Tex.) Democratic Exec. Com., 1934-44. Mem. Am., Tex., San Antonio bar assns., Am. Judicature Soc., Am., San Antonio trial lawyers assns., Phi Delta Phi. Home: 114 Brittany Dr San Antonio TX 78212 Office: 1215 Nat Bank Commerce Bldg San Antonio TX 78205 Tel (512) 227-8304

MORRISSETTE, PETER JOSEPH, b. Providence, May 9, 1943; B.A., Dartmouth, 1965; LL.B., J.D., Boston U., 1968. Admitted to Vt. bar, 1960; asso. firm John A. Swainbank, St. Johnsbury, Vt., 1968-70; partner firm Swainbank, Gensburg & Morrissette, St. Johnsbury, 1970-75, Swainbank, Morrissette & Neylon, St. Johnsbury, 1976—; town and village atty. Lyndon (Vt.), 1970—. Mem. exec. com. Lyndon Inst., 1975—. Mem. Am., Vt., Caledonia County bar assns. Home: 31 Williams St Lyndonville VT 05651 Office: 83 Eastern Ave Saint Johnsbury VT 05819 Tel (802) 748-5157

MORRISSEY, JOHN C., b. 1914; M.B.A., LL.B., Yale U., J.S.D., N.Y.U., 1951. Asso. firm Dorsey & Adams, 1940-41, 46-50; counsel Office of Sec. of Def., Dept. Def., Washington, 1950-52; acting gen. counsel Def. Electric Power Adminstrn., 1952-53; atty. Pacific Gas & Electric Co., San Francisco, 1953-70, asso. gen. counsel, 1970-75, v.p., gen. counsel, 1975—. Office: 77 Beale St San Francisco CA 94106*

MORRISSON, ALAN STUART, b. St. Louis, Dec. 24, 1937; B.A., Valparaiso U., 1959, J.D., 1962; Admitted to Ind. bar, 1962, U.S. Supreme Ct. bar, 1976; asst. counsel Midwestern United Life Ins. Co., Ft. Wayne, Ind., 1962-66; asst. prof. Valparaiso U., 1966-69; adj. prof. law, 1969—; partner firm Hoeppner, Wagner & Evans, Valparaiso, Ind., 1969—. Vice-chmn. Valparaiso U. Community Campaign, 1971, 72, 76. Mem. Am., Ind. Porter County Bar Assns., Nat. Assn. Coll. and Univ. Attys., Valparaiso U. Alumni Assn. (v.p. 1970-73). Office: 101 Lincolnway Valparaiso IN 46383 Tel (219) 464-4961

MORROW, FRANK AARON, b. Ft. Benjamin Harrison, Ind., Dec. 15, 1932; A.B., DePauw U., 1955; A.M., U. Mich., 1959, Ph.D., 1964; J.D., U. Wash., 1971. Admitted to Wash. bar, 1972; prof. philosophy U. Ky., Lexington, 1962-64, No. Ill. U., DeKalb, 1964-66, Western Wash. State Coll., Bellingham, 1966-75; individual practice law, Bellingham, 1972—; commr. Superior Ct. Whatcom County, Wash., 1975—. Mem. Am., Wash. bar assns. Contbr. article to Ethics. Home: 2706 Northwest Ave Bellingham WA 98225 Office: 423 Bellingham National Bank Bldg Bellingham WA 98225 Tel (206) 676-1262

MORROW, JOHN PAUL, b. Mpls., July 16, 1932; B.B.A., U. Wis., 1955, J.D., 1956. Admitted to Wis. bar, 1957; partner Morrow, Pope & Angel, Dodgeville, Wis., 1957—; dist. atty. Iowa County (Wis.) 1960-62, 65-66; chmn. postgrad. legal edn. com. State Bar Wis., 1976-77. Pres. Dodgeville Gen. Hosp., 1960-62, bd. dirs., 1958-69. Mem. Am., Wis., Iowa County bar assns., Am. Judicature Soc., Am., Wis. trial lawyers assns., Dodgeville C. of C. (past pres.). Home: 110 N Main St Dodgeville WI 53533 Office: 103 W Merrimac St Dodgeville WI 53533 Tel (608) 935-3346

MORSE, DAVID ABNER, b. N.Y.C., May 31, 1907; B.A., Rutgers U., 1929, LL.D., 1957; LL.B., Harvard, 1932; LL.D., U. Geneva, 1962, U. Strasbourg, 1968; D. Social Scis. (hon.), Laval U., Que., 1969; L.H.D., Brandeis U., 1971. Admitted to N.J. bar, 1932, N.Y. bar, 1972, D.C. bar, 1972; since practiced in Washington, chief counsel Petroleum Labor Policy Bd., Dept. Interior, spl. asst. to U.S. Atty. Gen., 1934-35; regional atty. NLRB, 1935-38, gen. counsel, 1945-46; Under Sec. of Labor, 1946-48; dir. gen. ILO, 1948-70; advisor, adminstr. UN Devel. Program, 1970. Chmn. bd. French Internat. Sch., 1976. Mem. Am. Arbitration Assn. (nat. panel). Recipient Meritorious Pub. Service award Sidney Hillman Found., 1969. Home: 3421 Prospect St NW Washington DC 20007 Office: 1156 15th St NW Washington DC 20005 Tel (202) 331-4066

MORSE, FRANK PATRICK, b. Springfield, Mass., Aug. 7, 1944; B.A. magna cum laude, Stanford, 1966; J.D., Harvard, 1969. Admitted to Calif. bar, 1970, U.S. Supreme Ct. bar, 1974, D.C. bar, 1976; asso. firm Sheppard, Mullin, Richter & Hampton, Los Angeles, 1969-73; dep. dist. atty. Los Angeles Dist. Atty's. Office, 1973-75; spl. counsel Summa Corp., Las Vegas, Nev., 1975—; lectr. U. So. Calif. Grad. Sch., U. Calif., Irvine; examiner Calif. State Bar. Mem. Calif. State Bar (del. conv. 1972, 73), Phi Beta Kappa Alumni Assn. (treas.). Office: 4045 Spencer St Las Vegas NV 89101 Tel (702) 733-0123

MORSE, GEORGE PATRICK, b. Milw., Mar. 17, 1917; LL.B., George Washington U., 1951, J.D., 1951. Admitted to D.C. bar, 1951, Md. bar, 1958; aide to dir. for war crimes OSS, Washington, 1945, Nurnberg, Ger., 1945-46; security officer CIA, Washington, 1946-51; dir. security USPHS, Washington, 1951-53; chief personnel security div. Dept. HEW, 1953-55, dir. safety and protection mgmt. NIH, 1955-70; individual practice law Washington, 1970—, Silver Spring, Md., 1970—; dir. George P. Morse & Assos., Cons., 1970—. Exec. dir. community devel. com. Religious of Jesus and Mary, Md., 1961—. Mem. Am. (chmn. civil service law com. 1968-70), D.C., Montgomery County bar assns., Am. Soc. Indsl. Security. Recipient citation K.C., 1965, citation for fed. service Pres. of U.S., 1970; author: Protecting the Health Care Facility, 1974; contbr. articles to legal jours. Office: 9402 Stateside Ct Silver Spring MD 20903 Tel (301) 434-3245

MORSE, JACK OSBORN, b. Atlanta, May 17, 1947; B.A., Duke U., 1969; J.D., U. Ga., 1972. Admitted to Ga. bar, 1972; partner firm Gambrell, Russell, Killorin & Forbes, Atlanta, 1973—. Mem. Am., Ga., Atlanta bar assns., Phi Delta Phi. Home: 2567 Hyde Manor Dr Atlanta GA 30327 Office: 4000 First Nat Bank Tower Atlanta GA 30303 Tel (404) 658-1620

MORSE, JOHN HARLEIGH, b. Estherville, Iowa, Sept. 22, 1910; B.A., U. Iowa, 1930; M.B.A., Harvard, 1932; J.D., Yale, 1935. Admitted to N.Y. bar, 1936, U.S. Supreme Ct. bar, 1946; mem. legal staff firm Carter, Ledyard & Milburn, N.Y.C., 1935-36; asso. firm Cravath, Swaine & Moore, N.Y.C., 1936-46, partner, 1946-76. Mem. Am. Bar Assn. (chmn. sect. labor law 1961-62). Office: 3700 Time-Life Bldg 110 W 51st St New York City NY 10020 Tel (212) 582-8837

MORSE, M. MITCHELL, b. Plainfield, N.J., Nov. 23, 1942; A.B. cum laude, Brown U., 1964; J.D., Stanford, 1967. Admitted to Calif. bar, 1968, Conn. bar, 1969, U.S. Supreme Ct. bar, 1973; since practiced in New Haven, asso. firm Jacobs, Jacobs & Grudberg, 1968-74, partner, 1974—; vis. instr. Yale, 1970-75. Mem. Conn. (dir. 1974—), New Haven (chmn. 1973-75) civil liberties unions, Conn. Bar Assn., Conn. Trial Lawyers Assn. (pres. 1977—), Order of Coif, Phi Beta Kappa. Contbr. articles to legal jours. Home: 95 Olive St New Haven CT 06511 Office: 350 Orange St New Haven CT 06503 Tel (203) 772-3100

MORSE, TERRENCE JAMES, b. Van Wert, Ohio, Jan. 13, 1948; B.A. with distinction in History, Ohio State U., 1970, J.D. cum laude, 1972. Admitted to Ohio bar, 1973; partner firm Carlile, Patchen, Murphy & Allison, Columbus, Ohio, 1976—. Ward com. person Democratic Party; mem. exec. com. Franklin County Dem. Party, 1973-75; trustee Alvis House, Half-Way House for Prisoners, 1977—. Mem. Columbus Bar Assn. (municipal ct., civil disorder, speakers' bur. coms.), Ohio, Am. bar assns., Ohio, Am. trial lawyers assns., Phi Beta Kappa. Home: 9748 Grandview Ave Pickerington OH 43147 Office: 100 E Broad St Columbus OH 43215 Tel (614) 228-6135

MORTENSEN, GENE LEROY, b. Fargo, N.D., Jan. 1, 1942; B.S., Bemidji State Coll., 1965; J.D., U. Tulsa, 1967. Admitted to Okla. bar, 1968, U.S. Supreme Ct. bar, 1972; asso. firm Rosenstein, Fist & Ringold, Tulsa, 1968-72, mem. firm, 1972—. Mem. Am., Okla., Tulsa County bar assns., Am. Judicature Soc. Editor-in-chief Tulsa Law Jour., 1967. Home: 1956 E 34th St Tulsa OK 74105 Office: 525 S Main St Tulsa OK 74103 Tel (918) 585-9211

MORTENSEN, IRVAL LAFAUN, b. Pima, Ariz., Mar. 20, 1935; B.S., Ariz. State U., 1959; LL.B., U. Ariz., 1962. Admitted to Ariz. bar, 1962; county atty. Graham County, Ariz., 1963-68; partner firm Richardson & Mortensen, Safford, Ariz., 1969—. Bd. dirs. Mt. Graham Hosp., 1972—. Mem. Ariz. (mem. bd. govs. 1976—), Graham County bar assns. Home: 1311 Chaparral Dr Safford AZ 85546 Office: 516 Main St Safford AZ 85546 Tel (602) 428-2700

MORTIMER, HARVEY WARD, b. Washington, Sept. 4, 1911; A.B., Princeton, 1932; student chem. engring. Columbia, 1933; LL.B., St. Lawrence U., 1936; J.D., Bklyn. Law Sch., 1950. Admitted to N.Y. bar, 1937; patent atty. U.S. Rubber Co., N.Y.C., 1937-46; contracting and legal officer Signal Corps, AUS, 1942-46; partner firm Darby & Darby, N.Y.C., 1947—. Trustee Montclair (N.J.) Hist. Soc. Mem. Am., Fed. bar assns., N.Y., N.J. (pres. 1954-55) patent law assns. Home: 109 Alexander Ave Upper Montclair NJ 07043 Office: 405 Lexington Ave New York City NY 10017 Tel (212) OX 7-7660

MORTIMER, WENDELL REED, JR., b. Alhambra, Calif., Apr. 7, 1937; A.B., Occidental Coll., Los Angeles, 1958; LL.B., U. So. Calif., 1965, J.D., 1965. Admitted to Calif. bar, 1966; trial atty. Calif. Legal Div., Los Angeles, 1966-73; partner firm Thelen, Marrin, Johnson & Bridges, Los Angeles, 1973—; arbitrator nat. panel Am. Arbitration Assn., 1970—; arbitrator Calif. Superior Ct., 1972—. Mem. Los Angeles County, San Francisco, Pasadena (Calif.), Am. bar assns., State Bar Calif. (del. 1973-76), Phi Delta Phi. Office: Suite 4400 555 S Flower St Los Angeles CA 90071 Tel (213) 627-8265

MORTON, DAVID HUGHES, b. St. Joseph, Mo., Apr. 17, 1922; A.B., U. Mich., 1943, LL.B., 1949. Admitted to Mo. bar, 1949; asso. firm W.M.Morton, St. Joseph, 1949-53; partner firm Morton & Morton, St. Joseph, 1953-70, firm Morton, Reed and Counts, St. Joseph, 1970—. Chmn. Mo. Arts Council, 1973-75; bd. dirs., pres. Albrecht Art Mus., 1966-68; bd. dirs. Kansas City Art Inst.; pres. St. Joseph Symphony Soc., 1959-64; trustee Noyes Home for Children. Mem. Am., Mo. (chmn. pub. relations com. 1958-60), St. Joseph (pres. 1962, treas. 1954-61) bar assns., Am. Judicature Soc., Phi Delta Phi. Home: 809 N Noyes Blvd Saint Joseph MO 64506 Office: Suite 702 Corby Bldg Saint Joseph MO 64501 Tel (816) 232-8411

MORTON, JOSEPH NEIL, b. Mpls., Sept. 8, 1902; B.A., U. Minn., 1923; J.D., Harvard, 1926. Admitted to Minn. Supreme Ct. bar. 1926, U.S. Ct. Appeals 8th Circuit bar, 1929, U.S. Supreme Ct. bar, 1949, U.S. Ct. Claims bar, 1953; partner firm Sanborn, Graves, Appel, Andre & Morton, and predecessors, St. Paul, 1926-39; partner firm Appel & Morton, St. Paul, 1939-41; mem. firm Briggs and Morgan, and predecessors, St. Paul, 1941—. Pres. St. Paul Bd. Edn., 1951-55. Mem. Am., Minn. (treas. 1939-43), Ramsey County (pres. 1950-51) bar assns. Office: 2200 First National Bank Bldg Saint Paul MN 55101 Tel (612) 291-1215

MORTON, RICHARD PAGE, b. Keysville, Va., Sept. 12, 1901; B.A., Hampden Sydney Coll., 1923; J.D., U. Va., 1927. Admitted to Va. bar, 1926; trial justice Charlotte County (Va.), 1934-35; commonwealth's atty. Charlotte County, 1936-55; judge Charlotte County Gen. Dist. Ct., 1956—. Pres., Charlotte County United Fund; bd. trustees Patrick Henry Meml. Found. Mem. Va. Bar Assn., County & Municipal Judges Assn. Va. (pres. 1963-64). Home: PO Box 177 Charlotte Court House VA 23923 Office: same Tel (804) 542-5600

MORTON, WADE HAMPTON, JR., b. Birmingham, Ala., Jan. 13, 1940; B.S. in Commerce and Bus. Adminstrn., U. Ala., 1962, LL.B., 1964. Admitted to Ala. bar, 1964; with JAGC, U.S. Army, 1964-67; asso. firm Hubbard & Waldrop, Tuscaloosa, Ala., 1967-69, Wallace & Ellis, Columbiana. Ala., 1969-71; individual practice law, Columbiana, 1971—. Mem. Am., Ala., Shelby County (Ala.) bar assns., Ala. Trial Lawyers Assn., U. Ala. Alumni Assn. (pres. Shelby County chpt. 1974). Editorial bd. Ala. Law Rev., 1963-64. Office: S Main St PO Box 1227 Columbiana AL 35051 Tel (205) 669-6667

MORTON, WOOLRIDGE BROWN, JR., b. N.Y.C., Nov. 11, 1914; B.S., U. Va., 1936, LL.B., 1938. Admitted to Va. bar, 1938, N.Y. bar, 1940, D.C. bar, 1951; asso., partner Pennie, Davis, Marvin & Edmonds and successors, N.Y.C., 1938-64; partner firm Morton, Bernard, Brown, Roberts & Sutherland, and predecessors, Washington, 1964—; lectr. law U. Va., 1959—; mem. advisory com. on civil rules to com. on practice and procedure Jud. Conf. of the U.S., 1961-71. Mem. Am. Bar Assn. (co-chmn. nat. conf. of lawyers and scientists 1975—), Am. Patent Law Assn. (pres. 1964-65, del. to Am. Bar Assn. 1965—), Va. State Bar (vice chmn. patent sect. 1976-77). Home: Morland off Route 641 King George VA 22485 Tel (202) 457-4600

MOSCATO, JAMES RICHARD, b. Cianciana, Sicily, Italy, May 3, 1908; A.B., Ohio State U., 1931, B.S. in Edn., 1932. Admitted to Ohio bar, 1942; solicitor Village of Rayland, 1950-68; asst. atty. gen. State of Ohio, 1955-59; asst. dist. atty., Jefferson County, Ohio; justice of peace, 1949-59. City councilman, 1934-35. Mem. Am., Ohio State, Jefferson County, Belmont bar assns., Am. Trial Lawyers Assn., Ohio Trial Lawyers. Home: 126 Sinclair Ave Yorkville OH 43971 Office: 104 1/2 S 4th St Martins Ferry OH 43935 (614) 633-2601

MOSCATO, LOUIS V., b. Bklyn., Jan. 3, 1909; grad., Columbia Coll., 1932; L.L.B., Bklyn. Law Sch., 1933. Admitted to N.Y. bar, 1934, U.S. Eastern Dist. Ct. bar, 1940; mem. firm Curtis, Studwell & Moscato, Bklyn., 1950—; law tchr. Am. Academy McAllister Inst. 1960-76. Mem. Phi Delta Phi. Home: E 1802 Amsterdam Ave Marietta GA 30067 Office: 164 Montague St Brooklyn NY 11201

MOSEBACH, BARRY NATHAN, b. York, Pa., Nov. 25, 1942; A.B., Pa. State U., 1964; J.D., Dickinson Coll., 1967; LL.M., N.Y. U., 1974. Admitted to Pa. bar, 1967, N.J. bar, 1970, U.S. Supreme Ct. bar, 1971; with office of regional counsel IRS, Phila. and Newark, 1967-72; partner firm Dower, Mosebach & Co., Allentown, Pa., 1972—; prof. Cedar Crest Coll., Allentown, 1976—. Mem. Am., Pa., N.J. bar assns. Home: 2538 Nevada St Allentown PA 18103 Office: 12 N 7th St Allentown PA 18101 Tel (215) 821-1116

MOSELEY, CAROL ELIZABETH, b. Chgo., Aug. 16, 1947; B.A., U. Ill., 1969; J.D., U. Chgo., 1972. Admitted to Ill. bar, 1973; asso. firm Mayer, Brown & Platt, 1970, firm Ross, Hardies, O'Keefe, Babcock & Parsons, 1971; asso. firm Davis, Miner & Barnhill, 1972-73; asst. U.S. atty. No. Dist. Ill., Chgo., 1973—. Mem. Ill., Fed., Cook County bar assns. Office: 219 S Dearborn St Chicago IL 60602 Tel (312) 353-5437

MOSELEY, GEORGE BOSWELL, III, b. Cleve., Nov. 21, 1944; B.S. in Econs., Ohio State U.. 1963; M.B.A., Harvard, 1965; J.D., U. Mich., 1970. Admitted to Mass. bar, 1971, Calif. bar, 1972, Conn. bar, 1973; research asso. Harvard Sch. Pub. Health, Boston, 1971-74; vis. lectr. Harvard Med. Sch., Boston, 1976—; asst. gen. counsel, spl. asst. atty. gen. Commonwealth of Mass., Boston, 1974—; asst. sec. Govt. of Mauritius, Port Louis, 1965-66. Bd. dirs. Boston Food Coop., 1974—. Mem. Am., Calif. bar assns., Nat. Health Lawyers Assn. Contbr. articles to legal jours. Home: Old South Rd Litchfield CT 06759 Office: State House Room 109 Boston MA 02133 Tel (617) 727-8038

MOSELEY, JAMES ALVIS, b. Galveston, Tex., Nov. 22, 1934; B.A., Tex. A. and M. U., 1957; J.D., S. Tex. Coll. Law, 1965. Admitted to Tex. bar, 1965; asst. dist. atty. for Harris County (Tex.), 1965—. Mem. State Bar Tex., Nat. Dist. Attys. Assn., Tex. Dist. and County Attys. Assn. Home: 9738 Tappenbeck St Houston TX 77055 Office: 301 San Jacinto St Houston TX 77002 Tel (713) 221-6154

MOSELEY, JOHN RUTHERFORD, b. Glastonbury, Conn., June 24, 1911; student R.I. State Coll., 1927-29; LL.B., Northeastern U., Springfield, Mass., 1940. Admitted to Mass. bar, 1941; individual practice law, Greenfield, Mass.; asst. clk. of cts. Franklin County (Mass.), 1958-60, clk. of cts., 1961—. Mem. Franklin County (pres.), Mass. bar assns. Home: Central St Montague MA 01351 Tel (413) 774-4388

MOSES, HAMILTON, JR., b. Chgo., Nov. 16, 1909; A.B., Amherst Coll., 1931; J.D., Harvard, 1934. Admitted to Ill. bar, 1934, U.S. Supreme Ct. bar, 1935; asso. firm Moses, Bachrach & Kennedy, Chgo., 1934-36, partner, 1936-41; exec. v.p. Dunwoody & O'Bryan & Co., Factors, Chgo., 1946-47; founder, pres. Rawleigh, Moses & Co., Inc., Factors, Chgo., 1948-76; cons., dir. internat. factoring Assos. Comml. Corp., Chgo., 1976—; mem. legal com. Factors Chain Internat., Amsterdam, Holland, 1974-76; contbr. Internat. Inst. Unification of Pvt. Law, Rome; dir. Nat. Comml. Fin. Conf., N.Y.C. Pres. Chase House, 1960-64, Assn. House, 1965-68; trustee Episcopal Charities, 1972—; warden Christ Ch., Winnetka, Ill., 1971-73. Mem. Chgo. Bar Assn. Contbr. Internat. Bus. Mag. Home: 633 Sheridan Rd Winnetka IL 60093 Office: 55 E Monroe St Chicago IL 60603 Tel (312) 781-5800

MOSES, PAUL E., b. Latrobe, Pa., Nov. 12, 1927; A.B., U. Chgo., 1949, J.D., 1952. Admitted to Pa. bar, 1953, U.S. Supreme Ct. bar, 1962; asso. firm Evans Ivory & Evans, Pitts., 1953-66, partner, 1966—; instr. Duquesne U. Law Sch., 1956-58. Mem. citizens adv. bd. Forbes Hosp. System, 1973—. Mem. Allegheny County, Pa., Am. bar assns., Allegheny County Acad. Trial Lawyers. Office: 711 Frich Bldg Pittsburgh PA 15219

MOSES, RAY EDWARD, b. Houston, Jan. 9, 1941; B.A., U. Tex., 1962, J.D., 1965; LL.M., Northwestern U., 1970. Admitted to Tex. bar, 1965. Briefing atty. Ct. Criminal Appeals, Austin, Tex., 1965-66; asst. dist. atty. Harris County, Tex., 1966-68; spl. asst. U.S. atty., Houston, 1969-70; prof. law S. Tex. Coll., 1970—; vis. prof. So. Meth. U., 1973-74; mem. Tex. Bd. Legal Specialization, 1974-75; mem. Tex. Criminal Def. Lawyers Skills Training Project, 1973; Ford fellow Northwestern U. Prosecution and Defense Program, 1972; vis. scholar Harvard Coll., 1976. Author: Scientific Evidence in Criminal Cases, 1973; Criminal Defense Sourcebook, 1974. Home: 5318 Green Springs Houston TX 77066 Office: 1303 San Jacinto Houston TX 77002 Tel (713) 659-8040

MOSESIAN, PAUL SUREN, b. Fresno, Calif., Apr. 17, 1938; B.S., U. Calif., Berkeley, 1960, J.D., 1963. Admitted to Calif. bar, 1964; individual practice law, Fresno, 1964—. Chmn. David of Sassoon Assn., 1970-73; active Fresno YMCA, 1964—, Boy Scouts Am., 1965-66. Mem. Calif., Fresno County bar assns., Calif. Trial Lawyers Assn., Phi Alpha Delta. Office: Suite 515 Fresno TowneHouse Fresno CA 93721 Tel (209) 485-2162

MOSIER, DAVID CLAUDE, b. Martinsville, Ind., Sept. 15, 1938; B.S., Ind. U., 1961, LL.B., 1965. Admitted to Ind. bar, 1965, U.S. Supreme Ct. bar, 1971; judge Portland (Ind.) City Ct., 1965-68, Columbus (Ind.) City Ct., 1971-75; mem. firm Hinkle, Mosier, Racster, Portland, 1965-71, Marshall & Mosier, 1972-74, Mosier & Silva, Columbus, 1975—. Chmn. Ind. Nature Conservancy, 1972-75; bd. dirs. Ind. Outdoor Edn., Inc. Mem. Am. Trial Lawyers Assn., Ind., Barth County bar assns., Legal Services, Inc. Home: Rural Route 2 POB 169A Nashville IN 47448 Office: 205 Washington St Columbus IN 47201 Tel (812) 376-9285

MOSK, RICHARD MITCHELL, b. Los Angeles, May 18, 1939; A.B., Stanford U., 1960; J.D., Harvard, 1963. Admitted to Calif. bar, 1964, U.S. Supreme Ct. bar, 1969; mem. staff Pres's. Commn. Assassination Pres. Kennedy, Washington, 1964; law clk. justice Mathew Tobriner, Calif. Supreme Ct., San Francisco, 1964-65; mem. firm Mitchell, Silberberg & Knupp, Los Angeles, 1965—; dep. fed. pub. atty., Los Angeles, 1975-76; mem. Los Angeles County Jud. Procedures Commn., 1973—. Mem., fire bd. inquiry Los Angeles County and City, 1971. Mem. Am., Los Angeles, Beverly Hills, Fed. (pres. local chpt., 1971-72) bar assns., Am. Judicature Soc. Contbr. articles Los Angeles Bar Bull., Case and Comment, Ark. Bar Jour., Los Angeles Times and others. Home: 1531 San Ysidro Dr Beverly Hills CA 90210 Office: 1800 Century Park E St Los Angeles CA 90067

MOSK, STANLEY, b. San Antonio, Sept. 4, 1912; Ph.B., U. Chgo., 1933; student Hague Acad. Internat. Law, 1970; LL.D., U. Pacific, 1970, U. San Diego, 1971, U. Santa Clara, 1976. Admitted to Calif. bar, 1935, U.S. Supreme Ct. bar, 1956; sec., legal advisor Gov. Calif., 1939-42; judge Superior Ct., Los Angeles, 1943-58; atty. gen. State Calif., 1959-64; justice Calif. Supreme Ct., San Francisco, 1964—; mem. Anglo-Am. Mission Appellate Cts., 1961-62; lectr. Distinguished Am's. program Dept. State, 1965. Bd. regents Univ. Calif., 1940; pres. Vista del Mar Child-Care Service, Los Angeles, 1954-58; chmn. San Francisco Film Festival, 1967, Thanks to Scandinavia Fund, 1967-68; mem. Town Hall, Los Angeles. Mem. Am., San Francisco, Los Angeles, Santa Monica bar assns., Am. Judicature Soc., Lawyers Club San Francisco, Los Angeles. Recipient Distinguished Alumnus award, Univ. Chgo., 1958; contbr. numerous articles to law reviews and profl. jours. Office: State Bldg San Francisco CA 94102 Tel (415) 557-3565

MOSKOVITZ, MYRON, b. San Francisco, Nov. 23, 1938; B.S., U. Calif., 1960, LL.B., 1964. Admitted to Calif. bar, 1965, U.S. Supreme Ct. bar, 1971; law clk. to judge Calif. Supreme Ct., 1964-65; directing atty. Calif. Rural Legal Assistance, Marysville, 1967-68; chief atty. Nat. Housing Law Project, Berkeley, Calif., 1968-72; prof. law Golden Gate U., San Francisco, 1972—. Chmn. Calif. Commn. Housing and Community Devel., 1976—. Mem. Nat. Lawyers Guild. Author: California Eviction Defense Manual, 1971; California Tenants Handbook, 1972; contbr. articles to legal jours. Home: 2371 Eunice St Berkeley CA 94708 Office: 536 Mission St San Francisco CA 94105 Tel (415) 391-7800

MOSLANDER, CARL EDMOND, b. Bartlesville, Okla., Dec. 30, 1925; LL.B., U. Okla., 1951, J.D., 1970. Admitted to Okla. bar, 1951; practiced in Oklahoma City, 1951—; asso. firm Hammer & Clift, 1955-63, Farmer & Kerr, 1963-68; individual practice law, 1968—. Mem. Am., Okla. bar assns., Am. Trial Lawyers Assn., Delta Theta Phi. Home: 5100 NW 27th St Oklahoma City OK 73127 Office: 4308 NW 23d St Oklahoma City OK 73107 Tel (405) 946-5533

MOSMAN, ROY EARL, b. Boise, Idaho, June 28, 1932; B.S., U. Idaho, 1953; R.P.T., Med. Coll. Va., 1954; LL.B., U. Oreg., 1959. Admitted to Idaho bar, 1960; individual practice law, Lewiston, 1960-69; partner firm Blake, Feeney, and Mosman, Lewiston, Idaho, 1969-74; pros. atty. Nez Perce County (Idaho), 1962-74; judge Dist. Ct. 2d Jud. Dist., 1971—. Bd. dirs. North Idaho Children's Home, Lewiston, Lewiston Boy's Club. Mem. Idaho Trial Lawyers Assn. Home: 615 Moore St Moscow ID 83843 Office: PO Box 9226 Moscow ID 83843 Tel (208) 882-3022

MOSS, CHARLES MALCOLM, b. Sullivan, Ind., Apr. 18, 1905; B.A., Vanderbilt U., 1927; J.D., U. Chgo., 1930. Admitted to Ill. bar, 1933, Calif. bar, 1947; asso. firm Wolf, Shaugnessy & Davis, Chgo., 1931-34; with Prudential Ins. Co. Am., 1934-64, counsel Mid-Am. home office, Chgo., 1954-64, asso. gen. solicitor, 1961-64; gen. counsel Am. Life Conv., 1964-73; v.p., gen. counsel Am. Life Ins. Assn., 1973; of counsel firm Schiff, Hardin & Waite, Chgo., 1973—. Mem. Assn. Life Ins. Counsel, Am. (chmn. Am. Bar Center facilities spl. com. 1963-67, chmn. life ins. law com., ins., negligence and compensation sect., 1966-67, chmn. lawyer placement info. spl. com. 1967-72, editor newsletter 1962-65), Ill. (bd. govs. 1962-67, chmn. ins. program com. 1964-65, past vice chmn. sec. ins. law, past chmn. corporate law depts. sect., past mem. council sect. real estate law), Chgo. (chmn. corporate law depts. com.) bar assns., Bar Assn. 7th Jud. Circuit, State Bar Calif., Ill. C. of C., Phi Beta Kappa, Sigma Alpha Epsilon, Phi Delta Phi, Omicron Delta Gamma. Home: 106 Westmoreland Dr Wilmette IL 60091 Office: 7200 Sears Tower 233 S Wacker Dr Chicago IL 60606 Tel (312) 876-1000

MOSS, GLEN LEE, b. Los Angeles, Mar. 18, 1943; B.Sc., U. Calif., Los Angeles, 1965; J.D., U. Calif., Berkeley, 1968. Admitted to Calif., U.S. Dist. Ct. No. Calif. U.S. Ct. Appeals 9th Circuit bars, 1969, U.S. Tax Ct. bar, 1972; since practiced in Hayward, Calif.; individual practice law, 1969-72, 73—; partner firm Baker & Moss, 1972-73; lectr. Law Golden Gate U., 1974—; instr. Law Chabot Coll., 1975—; mem. nat. bd. arbitrators, Am. Arbitration Assn. Mem. ACLU (dir. Berkeley, Albany, Kensington branch), mem. Beta Gamma Sigma, Pi Sigma Alpha. Home: 512 Neilson Berkeley CA 94707 Office: Hayward Air Plaza Bldg 22693 Hesperian Blvd Suite 175 Hayward CA 94541 Tel (415) 785-5266

MOSS, GORDON WALTER, b. Mt. Vernon, Wash., Dec. 17, 1920; B.A., U. Wash., 1942; LL.B., Stanford, 1948. Admitted to State of Wash. bar, 1948; mem. firm Lane, Powell, Moss & Miller, Seattle, 1948—. Mem. King County, Am., Wash. State Bar assns., Maritime Law Assn. Home: 6205 S E 27th St Mercer Island WA 98040 Office: 1700 Washington Bldg Seattle WA 98101 Tel (206) 223-7020

MOSS, HERBERT ALLEN, b. N.Y.C., Jan. 18, 1934; B.A., Coll. City N.Y., 1955; LL.B., N.Y. U., 1962, LL.M. in Labor Law, 1964. Admitted to N.Y. State bar, 1962, Calif. bar, 1965; atty. NLRB, Newark and Los Angeles, 1962-67; individual practice law, Santa Ana, Calif., 1968—; lectr. labor law U. Calif., Los Angeles and Irvine, 1969—. Mem. Orange County Republican Central Com., 1975—. Mem. Am. Bar Assn. Contbr. articles to legal jours. Office: 888 N Main St Santa Ana CA 92701 Tel (714) 547-7712

MOSS, HERBERT KENTON, b. St. Louis, Dec. 5, 1910; A.B., Washington U., St. Louis, 1933, LL.B., 1933. Admitted to Mo. bar, 1933; with FBI, 1934-61, spl. agt. in charge, Louisville, 1940-44, Savannah, Ga., 1944-45; asst. spl. agt. in charge, St. Louis, 1945-61; presiding judge Jefferson County (Mo.) Ct., 1963-64; judge Mo. Circuit Ct., 23d Jud. Circuit, 1965-77. Chmn. Jefferson County Planning and Zoning Commn., 1963-64. Mem. Am. Bar Assn., Am. Judicature Soc. Home: Route 2 PO Box 84 Hillsboro MO 63050 Office: Courthouse Hillsboro MO 63050 Tel (314) 789-2442

MOSSAWIR, HARVE H., JR., b. Morton, Miss., Aug. 9, 1942; B.A. with honors, U. Ala., 1964; M.A. (Fulbright scholar), U. Manchester (Eng.), 1965; J.D. with honors, U. Chgo., 1968. Admitted to Calif. bar, 1970; partner firm Irell & Manella, Los Angeles, 1969—; asst. prof. law U. Ala., 1968-69. Bd. dirs., v.p. Santa Monica (Calif.) Parents Nursery Sch., 1973-75. Mem. Am., Calif. bar assns., Order Coif, Phi Beta Kappa, Phi Alpha Theta, Pi Sigma Alpha, Delta Sigma Rho, Tau Kappa Alpha. Contbr. articles in field to profl. jours. Home: 2950 Mandeville Canyon Los Angeles CA 90049 Office: 1800 Ave of the Stars Los Angeles CA 90067 Tel (213) 277-1010

MOSSMAN, KEITH, b. Vinton, Iowa, Jan. 29, 1921; B.A., Ill. Coll., 1942; J.D., U. Ill., 1948. Admitted to Ill. bar, 1947, Iowa bar, 1948, U.S. Supreme Ct. bar, 1966; partner firm Mossman & Grote, Vinton, 1948—; pros. atty. Benton County, Iowa, 1951-69. Mem. Nat. Dist. Atty's. Assn. (pres. 1963-64), Am. (chmn., criminal justice sect., 1973-74, del. 1976-77), Iowa bar assns., Internat. Soc. Barristers, Iowa Acad. Trial Lawyers, Am. Judicature Soc. Contbr. articles to Psychology Today, Am. Criminal Law Review, Judges Jour., Am. Trial Lawyers Jours., Am. Bar Assn. Jour. Home: 1503 Washington Dr Vinton IA 52349 Office: 122 E 4th St Vinton IA 52349 Tel (319) 472-2396

MOTSINGER, JOHN FAIRBANKS, JR., b. Winston-Salem, N.C., Jan. 6, 1930; B.S., U. N.C., 1953; LL.B., U. Miami (Fla.), 1956. Admitted to N.C. bar, 1956, Fla. bar, 1956; mem. firm Johnson Motsinger Trismen & Sharp, Orlando, Fla. Chmn. Central Fla. Heart Assn., 1963; mem. Orange County Civic Facilities Bd., 1975, 76. Mem. Phi Beta Kappa, Beta Gamma Sigma. Home: 5565 Jessamine Ln Orlando FL 32809 Office: 100 E Robinson St Orlando FL 32801 Tel (305) 841-7350

MOTTL, RONALD MILTON, b. Cleve., Feb. 6, 1934; B.S., U. Notre Dame, 1956, LL.B., 1957. Admitted to Ohio bar, 1957; asst. law dir. City of Cleve., 1958-60; pres. Parma (Ohio) City Council, 1962-66; mem. Ohio Ho. of Reps., 1967-69, Ohio Senate, 1969-74; mem. U.S. Ho. of Reps. for 23d Dist. Ohio, 1974—. Mem. Am., Ohio, Cuyahoga County, Cleve. bar assns., Am. Trial Lawyers Assn. Home: 7713 Wake Robin Dr Parma OH 44129 Office: 1233 Longworth Bldg Washington DC 20515 Tel (202) 225-5731

MOTZ, JOHN FREDERICK, b. Balt., Dec. 30, 1942; A.B., Wesleyan U., 1964; LL.B., U. Va., 1967. Admitted to Md. bar, 1967, Fed. bar, 1967; law clk. to judge U.S. Ct. Appeals 4th Circuit, 1967-68; asst. U.S. Atty. Dist. Md., 1969-71; partner firm Venable, Baetjer, & Howard, Balt., 1976—; asst. to constitutional conv. commn. Md., 1967. Trustee Friends Sch. Balt., 1972—, chmn., 1976—; mem. Balt. City Social Services Adv. Com., 1974—. Mem. Am., Md., Balt. City bar assns. Contbr. articles to profl. jours. Office: 1800 Mercantile Bank and Trust Bldg Baltimore MD 21218 Tel (301) 752-6780

MOUAT, WILLIAM GAVIN, b. Myers, Mont., Apr. 5, 1919; B.A., U. Idaho, 1944; LL.B., U. Mont., 1947, J.D., 1947. Admitted to Mont. bar, 1947; individual practice law, Billings, Mont., 1950-75; sr. partner firm Mouat & Martinson, Billings, 1976—. Mem. Am., Mont., Yellowstone County (Mont.) bar assns., Am. Judicature Soc. Home: 825 Parkhill Dr Billings MT 59102 Office: 805 Midland Nat Bank Bldg Billings MT 59101 Tel (406) 248-7831

MOUKAD, JOSEPH ELIAS, b. N.Y.C., Dec. 30, 1910; B.A., Columbia Coll., 1931; LL.B., St. John's U., 1934. Admitted to N.Y. bar, 1935, U.S. Supreme Ct. bar, 1955. With N.Y. Life Ins. Co., N.Y.C., 1933-42; individual practice law, N.Y.C., 1946-58; partner firm Mullane & Moukad, N.Y.C., 1958-68, firm Cusack & Stiles, 1969—. Mem. Am., N.Y. State bar assns., N.Y. County Lawyers Assn. (chmn. com. on lawyer placement 1963-71), Guild Cath. Lawyers (gov. 1958-61, 62-65), Columbia Coll. and Law Sch. alumni assns., Am. Judicature Soc., Am. Legion. Home: 505 E 14th St New York City NY 10009 Office: 61 Broadway New York City NY 10006 Tel (212) 480-0400

MOUL, WILLIAM CHARLES, b. Columbus, Jan. 12, 1940; B.A., Miami U., Oxford, Ohio, 1961; J.D., Ohio State U., 1964. Admitted to Ohio bar, 1964; partner firm George, Greek, King, McMahon & McConnaughey, Columbus, 1970—. Mem. Ohio State, Columbus bar assns., Lawyers Club Columbus (pres. 1976—). Home: 2512 Danvers Ct Columbus OH 43220 Office: 100 E Broad St Columbus OH 43215 Tel (614) 228-1541

MOULE, REID S., b. Buffalo, Apr. 14, 1908; LL.B., U. Buffalo, 1931; L.H.D., Medaille Coll., 1972. Admitted to N.Y. State bar, 1932; individual practice law, Buffalo, 1932-58; justice Supreme Ct. of N.Y. State, Buffalo, 1959-68; justice Appellate Div. Supreme Ct. of N.Y. State, Buffalo, 1969—. Trustee Hobart and William Smith Colls., 1970-75, hon. trustee, 1975; bd. mgrs. Buffalo, Erie County Hist. Soc.; chmn., mem. Council of State U. Coll. at Buffalo, 1954-58; mem. N.Y. State Commn. Revision and Simplification of Constitution, 1956, 57. Mem. Am., N.Y. State, Erie County bar assns. Recipient Award Hobart and William Smith Colls., 1972; Distinguished Alumnus Award U. Buffalo Law Sch. Alumni Assn., 1970. Home: 281 Nottingham Terr Buffalo NY 14216 Office: Erie County Hall Buffalo NY 14202 Tel (716) 852-1291

MOULTON, ROBERT ELLIS, b. Wilder, Idaho, Aug. 24, 1927; B.A., U. Idaho, 1950; J.D., U. Oreg., 1958. Admitted to Oreg. bar, 1958; research asso. bur. municipal research and service U. Oreg., 1950-55; cons. League Oreg. Cities, Eugene, 1959; partner firm Moulton & Morris, Eugene, 1958-60; individual practice law, Eugene, 1960-65; partner firm Vonderheit, Hershner, Hunter, Miller, Moulton & Andrews, and predecessors, Eugene, 1965—; research asso. Lane County (Oreg.) Charter Com., 1960-62; chmn. Central Lane Met. Study Commn., 1970-72. Mem. Eugene Human Rights Commn., 1964-66; bd. govs. Met. Civic Club for Eugene and Springfield, Oreg., 1966-68. Mem. Am. Bar Assn., State Bar Oreg. (chmn. local govt. com. 1964-65; mem. mineral pub. lands and water law commn. 1967-68; local govt. com. 1971-74), Phi Beta Kappa. Home: 294 Sterling Dr Eugene OR 97404 Office: 260 E 11th Ave Eugene OR 97401 Tel (506) 686-8511

MOUNTAIN, CLINTON DELAINE, b. Pisgah, Ala., Aug. 17, 1941; B.A., U. Ala., 1965, J.D., 1968. Admitted to Ala. bar, 1968; asso. firm Skidmore, Skidmore & Crownover, Tuscaloosa, 1968-70; partner firm Skidmore, Skidmore, Crownover & Mountain, Tuscaloosa, 1970-72; individual practice law, Tuscaloosa, 1972—; instr. legal studies U. Ala., 1969—. Mem. Com. Pub. Safety, City of Tuscaloosa, 1973—. Mem. Ala. Trial Lawyers Assn. Home: 50 Sherwood Dr Tuscaloosa AL 35401 Office: 2600 Seventh St Tuscaloosa AL 35401 Tel (205) 349-1740

MOUNTS, MELVIN ELMER, JR., b. Washington, Pa., June 28, 1940; B.A., Washington and Jefferson Coll., 1962; M.L.S., Rutgers U., 1964; J.D., Seton Hall U., 1969. Admitted to N.J. bar, 1969, U.S. Supreme Ct. bar, 1976; trainee Newark (N.J.) Pub. Library, 1962-64, reference librarian, 1964-69; rules analyst N.J. div. Adminstrv. Procedure, 1969-70; dep. atty. gen. N.J. Dept. Law and Pub. Safety, Trenton, 1970—. Mem. N.J., Essex County bar assns. Home: 61 Rock Spring Ave West Orange NJ 07052 Office: State House Annex Trenton NJ 08625 Tel (609) 292-8566

MOUSHEGIAN, JAMES, b. Washington, Aug. 28, 1944; B.S. in Bus. Adminstrn., E. Carolina U., 1966; J.D., U. Ga., 1969. Admitted to Va. bar, 1969, Calif. bar, 1971; mem. firm Bruce D. Starkey, San Francisco, 1971-74; mem. firm Gordon & Rees, San Francisco, 1974-76, partner, 1976—. Mem. Calif., Va., San Francisco bar assns., Assn. Defense Counsel. Home: 52 Filbert Ave Sausalito CA 94965 Office: 235 Montgomery St Suite 1530 San Francisco CA 94104 Tel (415) 986-8041

MOUSHEY, CHARLES L., b. Alliance, Ohio, 1917; student Ohio State U., So. Meth. U.; LL.B., William McKinley Sch. Law, 1947. Admitted to Ohio bar, 1948, U.S. Supreme Ct. bar, 1961; mem. firm Gwin, Moushey & Tangi, Alliance. Pres. CSC Alliance, 1956—. Mem. Ohio, Stark County bar assns., Ohio Acad. Lawyers. Home: 2460 Ridgewood Ave Alliance OH 44601 Office: 119 E State St Alliance OH 44601 Tel (216) 821-5330

MOUTINHO, MANUEL, JR., b. Ludlow, Mass., Feb. 20, 1931; B.A., U. Va., 1953; J.D., Boston Coll., 1958. Admitted to Mass. bar, 1958, U.S. Supreme Ct. bar, 1963; town counsel Ludlow (Mass.), 1960-72, probation officer, 1960—; chief probation officer Dist. Ct., Springfield, Mass., 1973—. Chmn. Pioneer Valley Multiple Sclerosis Soc., 1974; pres. Lusitania Inst., 1965. Mem. Hampden County Bar Assn. Home: 24 Lehigh St Ludlow MA 01056

MOWBRAY, JOHN CODE, b. Bradford, Ill., Sept. 20, 1918; B.A., Western Ill. U., 1940, L.H.D. (hon.), 1976; postgrad. U. Va., 1944, Northwestern U., 1945; J.D. cum laude, U. Notre Dame, 1949. Admitted to Nev. bar, 1949, Ill. bar, 1950; chief dep. dist. atty. Clark County, Las Vegas, Nev., 1949-53; individual practice law, Las Vegas, 1949-57; U.S. referee in bankruptcy for Dist. of Nev., 1957-59; mem. U.S. Jud. Conf. for 9th Circuit, 1957-59; dist. judge 8th Jud. Dist. Nev., Las Vegas, 1959-67; justice Supreme Ct. Nev., Carson City, 1967—; faculty adviser Nat. Coll. State Trial Judges, U. Pa., summer 1967; founder pub. defender program in Nev. under Ford Found. grant, 1965. Vice pres. Boulder Dam Area council Boy Scouts Am., 1960-70, bd. dirs. Nev. Area council, 1967—; pres. City of Hope, 1963-64, Nat. Council Christians and Jews, 1965-66; v.p. YMCA, 1964—. Mem. Am., Nev., Ill. bar assns., Am. Judicature Soc. Recipient George Washington Honor medals Freedoms Found. at Valley Forge, 1964, 69; Silver Beaver award Boy Scouts Am., 1966; Equal Justice award for Western States, NAACP, 1970; Gen. MacArthur Medal award Nat. SAR, 1971; Outstanding Alumni award Western Ill. U., 1971; Mowbray Hall named in his honor Western Ill. U., 1974. Home: 1815 S 15th St Las Vegas NV 89104 Office: Supreme Ct Nev Capitol Complex Carson City NV 89710 Tel (702) 885-5176

MOWRER, FREDERICK MARTIN, b. Huntington, Ind., Nov. 14, 1919; B.S., Ind. U., 1949, LL.B., 1949. Admitted to Ind. bar, 1949, N.Mex. bar, 1963; mem. firm Lesh & Lesh, Huntington, 1949-58; pros. atty. Huntington County, 1952-54; judge Huntington, 1958-63; asst. city atty., Huntington, 1963-68; judge Albuquerque Municipal Ct., 1968—; instr. bus. law Huntington Coll., 1955. Active Polio Found., United Fund, ARC. Home: 10016 Inca Ct NE Albuquerque NM 87111 Office: 401 Marquette NW Albuquerque NM 87103 Tel (505) 766-7846

MOWRY, JAMES BEDELL, b. Atlanta, June 12, 1935; A.B.J., U. Ga., 1958, LL.B., 1964. Admitted to Ga. bar, 1970; asso. firm Smith, Cohen, Ringel, Kohler, Martin & Lowe, Atlanta, 1970-72; asso. firm Arnall, Golden & Gregory, Atlanta, 1972—. Sec., treas. Exchange Club of Atlanta, 1975—, chmn. youth com., 1974-75. Mem. State Bar Ga., Atlanta Bar Assn., Lawyers Club Atlanta. Named boss of the year, Gate City Charter chpt. Am. Bus. Women's Assn., 1974. Home: 2573 Bentbrook Ct Atlanta GA 30360 Office: 1000 Fulton Federal Bldg Atlanta GA 30303 Tel (404) 577-5100

MOXLEY, CHARLES JOSEPH, JR., b. Balt., Feb. 22, 1944; B.A. in Polit. Sci., Fordham U., 1965. M.A. in Russian Area Studies, 1966; J.D., Columbia, 1969. Admitted to N.Y. bar, 1969; law clk. to judge U.S. Dist. Ct., So. Dist. N.Y., 1969-70; asso. firm Davis Polk & Wardwell, N.Y.C., 1970—. Mem. Bar Assn. City N.Y., Am., N.Y. State bar assns., New York County Lawyers Assn., Am. Soc. Internat-Law. Home: 2 Fifth Ave New York City NY 10011 Office: 1 Chase Manhattan Plaza New York City NY 10005 Tel (212) HA 2-3400

MOYA, CLARENCE BENJAMIN, b. Belen, N.Mex., Oct. 7, 1940; A.B., Princeton, 1962; J.D., U. N.Mex., 1970. Admitted to N.Mex. bar, 1970; fellow Harvard, 1970-71; advisor Law Enforcement Assistance Adminstrn., Albuquerque, 1972; dep. gen. counsel Mexican Am. Legal Defense Fund, San Francisco, 1972-73; asso. prof. law U. Utah, 1973-76; asso. firm Pillsbury, Madison & Sutro, San Francisco, 1976—; advisor Utah State Bd. Higher Edn., 1973-76; Equal Opportunity Commn. U. Utah, 1973-76. Mem. Mexican Am. Lawyers Orgn. Contbr. articles in field to law jours. Home: 1630 Jones St San Francisco CA 94109 Office: 225 Bush St San Francisco CA 94104 Tel (415) 983-1732

MOYA, PATRICK ROBERT, b. Belen, N.Mex., Nov. 7, 1944; A.B., Princeton, 1966; J.D., Stanford, 1969. Admitted to Calif. bar, 1970, Ariz. bar, 1970, D.C. bar, 1970, U.S. Supreme Ct. bar, 1973; asso. firm Lewis and Roca, Phoenix, 1969-73, partner, 1973—; instr. Ariz. State U. Law Sch., 1972; mem. securities com. State Bar Ariz., 1974—. Mem. bd. adjustment Paradise Valley, Ariz., 1976—; dir. Phoenix Little Theatre, 1973-74, U. Club of Phoenix, 1973—, v.p., 1976-77, pres., 1977—; dir. Phoenix Mens Arts Council, 1973—, sec., 1973-74; dir. Interfaith Counseling Service, Scottsdale, Ariz., 1973-74; Republican precinct committeeman, Maricopa County, Ariz., 1976—. Mem. Am., Ariz., Calif., D.C., Maricopa County bar assns. Home: 5119 E Desert Park Ln Paradise Valley AZ 85253 Office: 100 W Washington St Phoenix AZ 85003 Tel (602) 262-5733

MOYE, H. ALLEN, b. Newnan, Ga., Mar. 29, 1948; B.A., Emory U., 1970; J.D., U. Ga., 1973. Admitted to Ga. bar, 1973; atty. Ga. Indigent Legal Services, Gainesville, 1972; research asst. Dist. Atty's Assn. of Ga., Atlanta, 1973-74; asst. dist. atty. Atlanta Jud. Circuit, 1974—. Mem. exec. com. DeKalb County (Ga.) and 4th Congl. Dist. Republican parties, 1975—; gen counsel Ga. Fedn. Young Republican Clubs, 1976—. Mem. State Bar Ga., Atlanta, Am. bar assns., Pros. Attys. Counsel Ga. Office: 301 Fulton County Courthouse 136 Pryor St SW Atlanta GA 30303 Tel (404) 572-2328

MOYE, JOHN EDWARD, b. Deadwood, S.D., Aug. 15, 1944; B.B.A., U. Notre Dame, 1965; J.D. with distinction, Cornell U., 1968. Admitted to N.Y. bar, 1968, Colo. bar, 1971; prof. law U. Denver, 1969-76; partner firm Head, Moye, Carver & Ray, Denver, 1976—; chmn. Colo. Uniform Comml. Code Revision Commn. cons. in field. Bd. dirs. Denver Council of Arts and Humanities, Colo. Rural Legal Services, Continuing Legal Edn. in Colo. Inc. Mem. Am., N.Y., Colo., Denver bar assns., Comml. Law League. Author: Business Organizations, 1974; Student Guide to Corporations, 1975; (with R. Forrester) Federal Jurisdiction, 1977; Commercial Transactions Under the UCC, 1976. Office: 200 W 14th Ave Denver CO 80204 also 828 17th St Suite 810 Denver CO 80202 Tel (303) 623-1770

MOYER, JOHN THOMAS, b. Barberton, Ohio, July 23, 1939; A.B., Ohio U., 1961; J.D., Ohio No. U., 1964. Admitted to Ohio bar, 1964; partner firm Moyer & Moyer, Barberton, 1964—. Home: 970 Andrews Rd Medina OH 44216 Office: 312 Marshall Bldg Barberton OH 44203 Tel (216) 745-3147

MOYERMAN, H. BARRY, b. Phila., Apr. 16, 1925; B.S., Drexel U., 1948; LL.B., Temple U., 1953. Admitted to Pa. bar, 1955, Washington D.C. bar, 1956; atty. Atlas Powder Co., Wilmington, Del., 1956-59; partner firm Bilker, Kimmelman & Moyerman, Phila., 1960-66; chief patent counsel Air Products & Chemicals, Inc., Allentown, Pa., 1967—. Mem. Phila. Patent Law Assn., Assn. Corp. Patent Counsel. Home: 235 Bridge St Catasauqua PA 18032 Office: PO Box 538 Allentown PA 18105 Tel (215) 398-8519

MOYES, VIOLET DAVISON, b. Quincy, Mass., Oct. 27, 1919; J.D., Northeastern U., 1942. Admitted to Mass. bar, 1943; with John Hancock Mut. Life Ins. Co., Boston, 1937—, dir. tech. services, 1967—. Mem. Mass. Bar Assn., Women Marine Assn., Kappa Beta Pi. Home: 13 Willow Ave Wollaston MA 02170 Office: John Hancock Pl Boston MA 02117 Tel (617) 421-6554

MOYLAN, CHARLES ELLSWORTH, JR., b. Balt., Dec. 14, 1930; B.A., Johns Hopkins, 1952; J.D., U. Md., 1955. Admitted to Md. bar, 1957, since practiced in Balt., asst. city solicitor, Balt., 1958; asst. state's atty., 1959-62, dep. state's atty., 1963, state's atty., 1964-70; asso. judge Md. Ct. Spl. Appeals, 1970—; prof. criminal law U. Balt., 1963-68; mem. faculty Nat. Coll. Dist. Attys., Am. Acad. Jud. Edn.; lectr. in field. Trustee Hood Coll., Frederick, Md. Mem. Am., Md., Balt. bar assns., Md. State's Attys.' Assn. (pres. 1966-68), Nat. Dist. Attys.' Assn. (v.p. 1968-70, named Outstanding Prosecutor 1968), The Selden Soc. Contbr. articles in field to profl. jours. Home: 3 Millbrook Rd Baltimore MD 21218 Office: 1214 One S Calvert Bldg Baltimore and Calvert Sts Baltimore MD 21202 Tel (301) 727-2470

MOYNAHAN, BERNARD THOMAS, JR., b. Akron, Ohio, Dec. 29, 1918; A.B. with distinction, U. Ky., 1935, LL.B., 1938. Admitted to Ky. bar, 1940; individual practice law, Nicholasville, Ky., 1940-42; county atty. Jessamine County, (Ky.), Nicholasville, 1946-54; mem. firm Watts & Moynahan, Nicholasville, 1949-61; U.S. Atty. Eastern Dist. Ky., Lexington, 1961-63; judge U.S. Dist. Ct., Lexington, 1963-69, chief judge, 1969—. Mem. Ky. (merit award 1974), Jessamine County bar assns. Mem. editorial staff Ky. law Jour., 1936-38. Home: Route 2 Nicholasville KY 40356 Office: Fed Bldg Room 321 Lexington KY 40501 Tel (606) 252-2312

MOYNIHAN, MICHAEL CLIFFORD, b. Manchester, Conn., Oct. 6, 1897; LL.B., Willamette U., 1927; postgrad. U. Wash., 1945. Admitted to Oreg. bar, 1927; individual practice law, Lebanon, Oreg., 1927—. Mem. Oreg. Bar Assn. Home and office: 3295 S Tucker Ln Lebanon OR 97355 Tel (502) 258-8654

MOZOLA, (FRANK) JOHN, b. Houston, June 24, 1948; B.B.A. with honors, U. Tex., Austin, 1970, J.D. cum laude, 1973. Admitted to Tex. bar, 1973; asso. firm Underwood, Wilson, Sutton, Berry, Stein & Johnson, Attys., Amarillo, Tex., 1973—. Trustee, Amarillo Opportunity House. Mem. Amarillo Bar Assn. Office: PO Box 9158 Amarillo TX 79105 Tel (806) 376-5613

MROTEK, RYSZARD STANISLAW, b. Lwow, Poland, July 13, 1932; B.A. in Govt. and Internat. Relations, U. Conn., 1956, J.D., 1964. Admitted to Conn. bar, 1967, U.S. Dist. Ct. bar, 1967, U.S. Ct. Appeals bar, 1967, U.S. Supreme Ct. bar, 1970; atty. group div. Aetna Life & Casualty Co., Hartford, Conn., 1965-66; partner firm Saxe, Friedle & Mrotek, New Britain, Conn., 1968-69; partner, v.p. firm Kozloski & Mrotek, New Britain and Hartford, 1974—; atty. U.S. VA. Mem. Conn. Bar Assn., Am. Trial Lawyers Assn., Assn. Immigration and Nationality Lawyers, Am. Soc. Internat. Law, Polish-Am. Congress (nat. dir., state pres.), Polish-Hungarian World Fedn. (past nat. dir.), Polish Nat. Alliance, Polish-Am. Falcons, Captive Nations Assembly, Kosciuszko Found., Polish Immigration Com., Polish Home Army Veterans Assn., Berlin Human Relations Council, NAACP (legal counsel New Britain chpt.). Contbr. articles and satirical poetry to various publs. Home: 285 Southington Rd Kensington CT 06037 Office: Suite 4 360 Main St Hartford CT 06106 Tel (203) 525-5770

MUCKLESTONE, ROBERT STANLEY, b. Seattle, May 15, 1929; B.S., U. Wash., 1953, J.D., 1954. Admitted to Wash. bar, 1954; asso. firm Perkins, Coie, Stone & Williams, Seattle, 1954-63, partner, 1963—. Chmn. bd. trustees Pacific N.W. Aviation Hist. Found., Seattle, 1975—. Mem. Am. Coll. Probate Counsel, Am. Bar Found., Seattle Estate Planning Council (pres.), Am. Bar Assn. (chmn. sect. young lawyers 1964-65, mem. ho. of dels. 1965-67, 76—). Author: (with John Huston) General Considerations—Tax Management Estates, Gifts and Trusts Portfolios, 1971; Washington Probate Practice, Procedure and Tax Manual, vol. 1, 1973, vol. 2, 1975. Home: 5201 NE 43d St Seattle WA 98105 Office: 1900 Washington Bldg Seattle WA 98101 Tel (206) 682-8770

MUDD, JOHN OTIS, b. Missoula, Mont., July 15, 1943; B.A., Cath. U. Am., 1965, M.A., 1966; J.D., U. Mont., 1973. Admitted to Mont. bar, 1973; partner firm Mulroney, Delaney, Dalby & Mudd, Missoula, 1973—; lectr. U. Mont. Sch. Law, 1973-74, 75-76. Exec. dir. Mont. Boys' State ann. seminar in govt. Mem. Am., Western Mont. bar assns., Am. Arbitration Assn., Am. Judicature Soc., Am. Soc. Writers on Legal Subjects. Editor and chief Mont. Law Rev., 1972-73. Office: PO Box 8228 Missoula MT 59801 Tel (406) 721-2550

MUDGE, RICHARD TREEN, b. Hollywood, Calif., Mar. 2, 1931; A.B., Fresno State U., 1952; J.D., U. Calif. at Los Angeles, 1957. Admitted to Calif. bar, 1959; individual practice law, Laguna Hills, Calif., 1959—; instr. adult edn. Saddleback Unified Sch. Dist. Mem. Orange County Bar Assn. Office: 23521 Paseo De Valencia suite 213 Laguna Hills CA 92653 Tel (714) 837-6030

MUELLER, ALVIN REUBEN, b. Arlington, Minn., Nov. 13, 1921; B.A., Gustavus Adolphus Coll., 1943; LL.B., St. Paul Coll. Law, 1952. Admitted to Minn. bar, 1953; spl. asst. atty. gen. Minn. Atty. Gen., St. Paul, 1953-55; partner firm Kunz, Mueller & Kroening, New Ulm, Minn., 1963—; asst. city atty. City of New Ulm, 1960-67, city atty., 1967-68; mem. dist. advisory council SBA. Pres. New Ulm Lions Club. Mem. Minn. State, Am. bar assns., Am. Judicature Soc., Assn. Trial Lawyers Am. Home: 306 Monument St New Ulm MN 56073 Office: 512 2d St N New Ulm MN 56073 Tel (507) 354-3158

MUELLER, GEORGE PAUL, b. St. Louis, Aug. 29, 1916; J.D., Washington U., St. Louis, 1938. Admitted to Mo. bar, 1938; with Terminal R.R. Assn. of St. Louis, 1946—, gen. counsel, 1957—, v.p., 1960—, sec., 1964—. Chmn. Police and Fireman's Retirement Bd., Richmond Heights, Mo., 1966—; mem. Richmond Heights Bd. Adjustment, 1973—. Mem. Am. Bar Assn., Mo. Bar, Bar Assn. St. Louis. Home: 7733 Brookline Terr Richmond Heights MO 63117 Office: 906 Olive St Saint Louis MO 63101 Tel (314) 342-4318

MUELLER, RICHARD EDWARD, b. Chgo., Mar. 22, 1927; B.S., Northwestern U., 1949, LL.B., 1951. Admitted to Ill. bar, 1951; partner firm Lord, Bissell & Brook, Chgo., 1961—. Mem. Am., Ill., Chgo. bar assns., Ill. Def. Counsel. Home: 5057 N Mango Chicago IL 60630 Office: 115 S LaSalle St Chicago IL 60603 Tel (312) 443-0234

MUFFOLETT, JOSEPH ROBERT, b. Balt., May 15, 1934; B.S., Loyola Coll., Balt., 1956; LL.B., U. Md., 1959, J.D., 1960. Admitted to Md. bar, 1959; individual practice law, Monkton, Md., 1959—; v.p., chief counsel AFL-CIO Am. Fedn. Govt. Employer 1923, 1963-68. Vice pres. Luthernville (Md.) Improvement Assn., 1964-69. Mem. Md., Fed. bar assns., U. Md., Loyola Coll. alumni assns., Gamma Eta Gamma. Office: 2154 Monkton Rd Monkton MD 21111 Tel (301) 472-4362

MUIR, J. DAPRAY, b. Washington, Nov. 9, 1936; J.D., U. Va., 1964; A.B., Williams Coll., 1958. Admitted to Va., Md. and D.C. bars, 1964, U.S. Supreme Ct. bar, 1967; law clk. U.S. Dist. Ct. for D.C., 1964-65; asso. firm Hanson, Cobb & O'Brien, Washington, 1965-69, Steptoe & Johnson, Washington, 1969-71; staff asst. to Pres. U.S., Washington, 1971; asst. legal adviser for econ and bus. affairs Dept. State, Washington, 1972-74; partner firm Muir & Stolper, Washington, 1976—. Mem. Am. (co-chmn. com. internat. econ. orgns., internat. law sect.), D.C. bar assns., Am. Soc. Internat. Law, The Barristers. Contbr. articles to legal jours; adv. bd. Jour. Internat. Law and Econs., 1974—. Home: 2905 Woodland Dr Washington DC 20008 Office: 1819 H St NW Washington DC 20006 Tel (202) 223-2500

MUIRHEAD, JAMES RUSSELL, b. Phillipsburg, Pa., Apr. 11, 1941; A.B., Cornell U., 1963, LL.B., 1966. Admitted to N.H. bar, 1966; mem. firm McLane Graf Greene Raulerson & Middleton, Manchester, N.H., 1966—; pres. N.H. Legal Services, 1975. Mem. Am., N.H. (bd. govs. 1970-73, 75-77), Manchester bar assns. Office: McLane Graf Greene Raulerson & Middleton 40 Stark St Manchester NH 03101 Tel (603) 625-6464

MULCHINOCK, DAVID STEWARD, b. Allentown, Pa., Feb. 10, 1945; A.B., Georgetown U., 1967; J.D., Cornell U., 1970. Admitted to N.Y. State bar, 1971, N.J. bar, 1974; asso. firm Hale, Grant, Meyerson, O'Brien & McCormick, N.Y.C., 1970-72, partner, 1972—; individual practice law, Princeton, N.J., 1974—. Mem. Am., N.Y. State, Princeton, N.J. bar assns., Assn. Bar City N.Y. Home: 19 Moran Ave Princeton NJ 08540 Office: 100 E 42d St New York City NY 10017 also One Palmer Sq Princeton NJ 08540 Tel (212) 867-2310

MULDER, JOHN, b. Holland, Mich., Feb. 5, 1906; A.B., Hope Coll., Holland, 1928; J.D., Harvard, 1931. Admitted to Ill. bar, 1932; individual practice law, Chgo., 1932—; master in chancery Circuit Ct. Cook County (Ill.), 1942-48. Mem. Am., Ill. State, Chgo. bar assns. Home: 5858 N Kenneth Ave Chicago IL 60646 Office: 135 S LaSalle St Chicago IL 60603 Tel (312) 263-0420

MULFORD, JON K., b. Camden, N.J., Mar. 12, 1938; B.A., Hamilton Coll., 1960; M.A., Vanderbilt U., 1963; J.D., U. Colo., 1966. Admitted to Colo. bar, 1966; asso. firm Dawson, Nagel, Sherman & Howard, Denver, 1966-67; mem. firm Mulford & Love, Granby, Colo., 1967-74; individual practice law, Aspen, Colo., 1974—; atty. Grand County (Colo.), 1968-72. Mem. Am., Colo. (chmn. legal assts. com. 1972-73), NW Colo. (pres. 1971) bar assns. Office: 600 E Hopkins Ave Aspen CO 81611 Tel (303) 925-8780

MULKEY, ANTHA, b. Cartecay, Ga., Oct. 31, 1909; B.S. in Commerce, U. Ga., 1935; LL.B., Woodrow Wilson Coll., 1942; J.D., Emory U., 1949. Admitted to Ga. bar, 1942, U.S. Supreme Ct. bar, 1949; mem. firm King & Spalding, Atlanta, 1942—. Mem. Am., Atlanta bar assns., State Bar Ga. Home: 630 Bellemeade Ave NW Atlanta GA 30318 Office: 2500 Trust Co Tower Atlanta GA 30303

MULLALLY, LAWRENCE ELWYN, b. Oakland, Calif., Mar. 14, 1913; A.B., U. Calif., Berkeley, 1935, J.D., 1938. Admitted to Calif. bar, 1938, U.S. Dist. Ct. bar, for Dist. San Francisco and Sacramento, 1938, U.S. Ct. Appeals bar, 9th Circuit, 1938; atty. FCA, Washington, 1939-41; with JAGC, U.S. Army, 1941-46; asso. firms Cooley, Crowley & Gither, San Francisco, 1946-47, Keith, Creede & Sedgwick, San Francisco, 1947-51; partner firm Mullally & Bennett, Oakland, Calif., 1951-53, Mullally & Wines, Oakland, 1953-57, Mullally & McCorkindale, Oakland, 1957-65; individual practice law, Oakland, 1965—; lectr. Continuing Edn. of Bar, 1955-63. Mem. Calif. State Bar, Am. (contbr. articles to jour.), Alameda County (Calif.) (chmn. com. judges liaison 1974) bar assns., Def. Counsel Assn., Am. Bd. Trial Advs. Bd. editors Housing Legal Digest. Office: 1005 Central Bldg 436-14th St Oakland CA 94612 Tel (415) 444-0992

MULLAN, JAMES BOYD, b. Rochester, N.Y., May 7, 1903; B.S., Colgate U., 1925; LL.B., Syracuse U., 1930. Admitted to N.Y. State bar, 1931; mem. firm Moser and Reif, Rochester, 1930-40, Moser, Johnson and Reif, Rochester, 1940-66, Johnson, Reif and Mullan, Rochester, 1966—. Sch. dir., Brighton, N.Y., 1953; pres. Travelers Aid, 1950, Nat. Travelers Aid. Soc., 1952; life mem. bd. visitors Syracuse U. Coll. Law. Fellow Am., N.Y. State bar founds.; mem. Am. Judicature Soc., Monroe County (trustee 1969), N.Y. State (pres. 1961, life mem. ho. of dels.) bar assns., Fedn. Bar Assn. Western N.Y. (pres.), Am. Coll. Trial Lawyers. Home: 44 Avalon Dr Rochester NY 14618 Office: 47 S Fitzhugh St Rochester NY 14614 Tel (716) 262-5725

MULLANE, KENNETH JAMES, b. N.Y.C., Mar. 17, 1909; A.B., Mt. St. Mary's Coll., 1929; postgrad. Columbia, 1929-30; J.D., Harvard, 1933. Admitted to N.Y. bar, 1934, U.S. Supreme Ct. bar, 1949; asso. firm Philip J. Dunn, N.Y.C., 1934-39; individual practice law, N.Y.C., 1939-45, 1951-57; partner firm Cary & Mullane, N.Y.C., 1945-51, Mullane and Moukad, N.Y.C., 1957-69; individual practice law, N.Y.C., 1969—; lectr. Practising Law Inst., N.Y.C.; gen. counsel, sec., dir. Dioptric Instrument Corp., N.Y.C., 1942-44. Bd. dirs. Trafalger Hosp., N.Y.C., 1966-67. Fellow Am. Coll. Probate Counsel; mem. Am., N.Y. bar assns., N.Y. County Lawyers Assn., Guild Catholic Lawyers. Home: 468 Riverside Dr New York City NY 10027 Office: 70 Pine St New York City NY 10005 Tel (212) 344-1280

MULLANY, WILLIAM CHRISTOPHER, b. N.Y.C., Dec. 24, 1926; B.A., St. John's U., 1951, J.D., 1953. Admitted to N.Y. bar, 1958; asso. firm Ryder & Costello, Carmel, N.Y., 1958-59; with Hartford Ins. Co. (Conn.), 1960-66; partner firm Saccoman & Mullany, Kingston, N.Y., 1966-70; individual practice law, Kingston, 1970—; mem. appeals bd. N.Y. State Dept. Motor Vehicles, 1975—; atty. Town of New Paltz Planning Bd., 1976—; mem. panel arbitrators Am. Arbitration Assn., 1969—; town atty. Town of Rochester, 1975; estate tax atty. for Putnam County, State of N.Y., 1968-69. Bd. dirs. Am. Cancer Soc., 1975—; pres. bd. trustees Kingston Area Library, 1974-76; asso. appeal agt. U.S. Selective Service, Kingston, 1968-71; former bd. dirs. ARC, Ulster County Boy Scouts Am. Mem. Am., N.Y. State, Ulster County (dir.) bar assns. Home: RD 7 Elmendorf Dr Kingston NY 12401 Office: 101 Green St Kingston NY 12401 Tel (914) 338-2935

MULLENDORE, BERTRUM NOEL, b. Howard, Kans., Sept. 5, 1901; LL.B., Washburn U., 1924, J.D., 1970. Admitted to Kans. bar, 1924; individual practice law, Howard, 1928—; spl. asst. atty. gen. State of Kans., 1931-72; city atty. City of Howard, Chmn. bd. edn. Howard Pub. Schs. Mem. Kans. Bar Assn. Home: 408 Pennsylvania Ave Howard KS 67349 Office: 120 W Randolph St Howard KS 67349 Tel (316) 374-2236

MULLENS, RICHARD ARNOLD, b. Cheyenne, Wyo., Apr. 15, 1918; B.A., U. Wyo., 1940, J.D., 1942. Admitted to Wyo. bar, 1942, D.C. bar, 1954; atty. chief counsel's office IRS, Washington, 1946-52; legal adv. staff U.S. Treasury, Washington, 1952-54; asso. firm Hogan & Hartson, Washington, 1954-60; partner firm Silverstein & Mullens, Washington, 1960—. Mem. governing bd. Nat. Cathedral Sch. Girls, 1966-72. Mem. Am., D.C., Wyo. State bar assns., Def. Orientation Conf. Assn. Contbr. articles to profl. jours.; editor Tax Exec. Mag., 1964-70. Office: 1776 K St NW Washington DC 20006 Tel (202) 452-7930

MULLER, FREDERICK ARTHUR, b. Center Moriches, N.Y., Dec. 18, 1937; B.A., U. Rochester, 1960; J.D., U. Chgo., 1963. Admitted to Ill. bar, 1963, N.Y. bar, 1964, Ct. Mil. Appeals Bar, 1965; served to capt., JAGC, U.S. Air Force, 1964-67; sr. law clk. to judge N.Y. Ct. Appeals, Albany, 1968-69, 72; asso. firm Hodgson, Russ, Andrews, Woods & Goodyear, Buffalo, 1969-72; sr. staff atty. N.Y. Ct. Appeals, Albany, 1973—; cons. staff atty. N.Y. State Ct. Judiciary, Albany, 1973. Bd. dirs. N.Y. State Credit Union League, Hudson Valley (N.Y.) div., 1965; mem. budget com. United Fund Albany, 1975—; exec. com. Baptist Assn. Western N.Y., Buffalo, 1969. Mem. N.Y. Bar Assn., Phi Delta Phi, Phi Beta Kappa. Editor: Ct. Appeals Decisions Without Opinion, 1973—. Home: 47 Hiawatha Dr Guilderland NY 12084 Office: Court of Appeals Hall Eagle St Albany NY 12207 Tel (518) 474-2281

MULLER, JOHN, b. N.Y.C., Nov. 20, 1947 jB.A., U. Notre Dame, 1969; J.D., George Washington U., 1973. Admitted to Ind. bar, 1973; asso. mem. firm Steers, Klee, Sullivan, McNamar & Rogers, Indpls., 1973-75, Compton, Coons, Fetta & Thompson, Indpls., 1975—; atty. Marion County (Ind.) Prosecutor's Office, 1975-76; pub. defender Marion County Criminal Ct. 111, 1976—; asso. prof. bus. law Marion Coll., Indpls., 1975; investigator pub. defender service, Washington, 1969-72. Mem. Am., Ind., Indpls. bar assns. Home: 3964 Braddock Dr Indianapolis IN 46268 Office: Suite 700 107 N Pennsylvania St Indianapolis IN 46204

MULLER, RICHARD L., b. New Orleans, Apr. 13, 1942; B.E.E., La. State U., 1965; J.D., Loyola U. of South, New Orleans, 1971. Engr., South Central Bell Co., 1965-67, comml. mgr., 1967-68; sales engr. control systems Westinghouse Electric Corp., New Orleans, 1968-71; asso. firm Foley Judell Beck Bewley & Landwear, New Orleans, 1971-72, firm Robert Anderson, Covington, La., 1972-73; partner firm Massony & Muller, Mandeville, La., 1973—. Bd. dirs. Miss La. Pageant, Monroe, 1968. Mem. La., Am. Covington (pres. 1975-76), St. Tammany Parish (La.) bar assns., Am., La. trial lawyers assns., Eta Kappa Nu. Recipient Am. Jurisprudence awards. Home: 3514 Joyce Dr Mandeville LA 70448 Office: 298 Oakwood Dr Mandeville LA 70448

MULLIGAN, JAMES M., b. Wilmington, Del., Sept. 5, 1932; B.S., St. Joseph's Coll., 1954; J.D. (Owen J. Roberts Scholar), U. Pa., 1957. Admitted to Pa. bar, 1958, Del. bar, 1958, U.S. Supreme Ct. bar, 1965; asso. firm Pepper, Bodine, Frick, Sheetz & Hamilton, Phila., 1957-58; asso. firm Connolly, Bove & Lodge, Wilmington, 1958-64, partner, 1964—; instr. Wharton Sch. Fin. and Commerce, U. Pa., Phila., 1955-57; asst. city solicitor City of Wilmington, 1958-64. Mem. Am., Pa., Del. bar assns., Am. Judicature Soc. Home: 510 Kerfoot Farm Rd Wilmington DE 19803 Office: 1800 Farmers Bank Bldg 919 Market St Wilmington DE 19899 Tel (302) 658-9141

MULLIGAN, WILLIAM HUGHES, b. N.Y.C., Mar. 5, 1918; A.B. cum laude, Fordham U., 1939, J.D. cum laude, 1942, LL.D., 1975; LL.D., St. Peter's Coll., Jersey City, 1966, Iona Coll., 1972, Bklyn. Law Sch., 1972, Villanova U., 1974; L.H.D., Siena Coll., 1967. Admitted to N.Y. State bar, 1942; law faculty U., 1946—, Wilkinson prof. law, 1962-71, dean Sch. Law, 1956-71, adj. prof., 1971—; judge U.S. Ct. Appeals, 2d Circuit, N.Y.C., 1971—; chmn. Citizens Com. on Reapportionment, 1964, Examining Bd. Manhattan and Bronx (N.Y.) Surface Transit Operating Authority, 1964-71; mem. N.Y. State Constl. Conv., 1965, gen. counsel Republican dels., 1967; mem. adv. council N.Y. State Labor and Mgmt. Improper Practices Act, 1968-71; mem. N.Y. State Com. to Revise Legis. and Judiciary Salaries, 1970-71, N.Y. State Com. on Adminstrn. Cts., 1970-71. Mem. Am., N.Y. State bar assns. Recipient St. John de La Salle medal Manhattan Coll., 1967, Encaenia medal Fordham Coll., 1966, Alumni medal Fordham U. Law Sch., 1971. Office: One Federal Plaza New York City NY 10007 Tel (212) 791-0930

MULLIGAN, WILLIAM JOSEPH, b. Milw., May 20, 1936; B.S., Marquette U., 1958, LL.B., 1960; M.S., U. Wis., 1965. Admitted to Wis. bar, 1960, Fed. bar, 1960, U.S. Supreme Ct. bar, 1963, U.S. Tax Ct. bar, 1972; asst. U.S. atty. Eastern Wis., Milw., 1960-65. U.S. Atty., 1974—; atty. Wis. Telephone Co., Milw., 1966-70; asso. firm Hayes, Peck, Perry & Gerlach, Milw., 1970-72, asso. firm Schroeder, Gedlen, Riester & Moerke, Milw., 1972-74; spl. asst. No. Dist. Ill., Chgo., 1976—; chmn. Fed. State Law Enforcement Commn. of Wis., 1974—. Bd. mem., v.p. Legal Aid Soc. Milw., 1967-74; mem. United Community Services of Greater Milw., Inc., 1972-74; scout leader, treas. Boy Scouts Am. Troop # 15 Milw., 1975—. Mem. Milw. Jr. Bar Assn. (pres. 1972-73), State Bar Wis. (bd. govs. 1973-74, chmn. criminal law sect. 1965-67), Fed. (pres. Milw. chpt. 1972-73), Milw. (law day chmn. 1976—) bar assns., Bar Assn. 7th Circuit (Wis. co-chmn. criminal law sect. 1973—), Wis. Acad. Trial Lawyers (treas. Milw. chpt. 1971-73), Wis. Dist. Attys. Assn. Contbr. articles to legal jours. Office: 330 Fed Bldg 517 E Wisconsin Ave Milwaukee WI 53202 Tel (414) 224-1441

MULLIKIN, BERNIE, JR., b. Memphis, June 29, 1927; student Memphis State U.; LL.B., So. Law U., 1951. Admitted to Tenn. bar, 1951; individual practice law, Memphis, 1965—. Pres. Avon Summerview Civic Club; pres. bd. mgmt. T. Walder Lewis YMCA. Mem. Am., Tenn., Memphis, Shelby County bar assns. Home: 935 N Mendenhall St Memphis TN 38122 Office: 3015 One Hundred N Main Bldg Memphis TN 38103 Tel (901) 523-1508

MULLIN, JOHN STANLEY, b. Los Angeles, July 14, 1907; A.B., Stanford, 1930; LL.B., Harvard, 1933. Admitted to Calif. bar, 1933, U.S. Supreme Ct. bar, 1950; partner firm Sheppard, Mullin, Richter & Hampton, Los Angeles, 1936—. Commr., Los Angeles Dept. Water and Power, 1959-62. Mem. State Bar Calif., Los Angeles County, N.Y., Am. (chmn. sect. real property, probate and trust law 1958-59, chmn. standing com. clients' security funds 1970-73, co-chmn. nat. conf. lawyers and titles ins. cos. and abstractors 1976—, mem. spl. com. residential real estate transactions 1972-73, mem. ho. dels. 1968-76) bar assns. Office: 333 S Hope St Los Angeles CA 90071 Tel (213) 620-1780

MULLIN, WILLIAM SCHOFIELD, b. Milw., Mar. 17, 1938; A.B., Dartmouth, 1960; J.D., Harvard, 1966. Admitted to Ill. bar, 1966, Calif. bar, 1972; asso. Kirkland & Ellis, Chgo., 1966-71, partner, 1972, Schofield & Millin, La Jolla, Calif., 1972-74; prin. firm Woolley & Mullin, La Jolla, 1974—; referee Calif. State Inheritance tax, San Diego County, 1975—. Trustee La Jolla United Methodist Ch., 1974—. Home: 5520 Via Callado La Jolla CA 92037 Office: 1129 Wall St PO Box 2364 La Jolla CA 92038 Tel (714) 454-8851

MULLINIX, THOMAS MAURICE, b. Kansas City, Kans., Mar. 18, 1945; A.B., U. Kans., Lawrence, 1967, J.D., 1970. Admitted to Kans. bar, 1971; asso. firm Steinegen & Reid, Kansas City, Kans., 1971-73; mem. firm Evans and Mullinix, Kansas City, 1973—. Mem. Kans., Mo., Am., Wyandotte County (sec. 1976), Kansas City bar assns., Kans. Trial Lawyers Assn. Home: 2110 N 86th St Terr Kansas City KS 66109 Office: 288 New Brotherhood Bldg Kansas City KS 66101 Tel (913) 621-1200

MULLINS, LESLIE MORRIS, b. Coeburn, Va., Apr. 19, 1917; B.A., Emory and Henry Coll., 1940; LL.B., U. Va., 1942, J.D., 1970. Admitted to Va. bar, 1942; mem. firm Greear, Bowen, Mullins & Winston, Norton, Va., 1946-74, Mullins, Winston & Robinson, 1975—. Chmn. Eastern Wise County unit ARC, 1946-53; mem. town council, Coeburn, 1946-53. Fellow Am. Coll. Trial Lawyers; mem. Am. Assn. R.R. Trial Lawyers, Va. Defense Attys., Defense Research Inst., Va. Trial Lawyers Assn., Wise County Bar Assn. (pres. 1960), Va. State Bar Assn. (v.p. 1956, 72). Mem. editorial bd. U. Va. Law Rev., 1942. Home: 315 Henry St Norton VA 24273 Office: 32 7th St Norton VA 24273 Tel (703) 679-3110

MULLINS, RAYMOND GLENN, b. Detroit, Mar. 28, 1943; B.A. in Econs., Howard U., 1965; J.D., U. Mich., 1973. Admitted to Mich. bar, 1973, U.S. Dist. Ct. bar for Eastern Dist. Mich., 1973, U.S. Ct. Appeals bar, 6th Circuit, 1976; clk. to Hon. Damon J. Keith U.S. Dist. Ct. for Eastern Dist. Mich., 1973-74; individual practice law, Ypsilanti, Mich., 1974—; dir. Park View Apts. Mem. Ypsilanti Tax Rev. Bd., 1975; bd. dirs. Washtenaw County (Mich.) Legal Aid. Mem. NAACP., Omega Psi Phi. Office: 117 Pearl St Ypsilanti MI 48197 Tel (313) 485-7517

MULLINS, ROGER WAYNE, b. Bluefield, Va., Feb. 6, 1944; B.S., U. Ala., 1968, J.D., 1971. Admitted to Va. bar, 1971; pvt. practice, Tazewell, Va., 1971-77; asst. pros. atty. Tazewell County, 1977—. Mem. Am., Tazewell (v.p. 1976—) bar assns., Va. State Bar, Va. Trial Lawyers Assn. (dist. v.p., bd. govs. 1976—), Alpha Kappa Psi. Office: Main St Tazewell VA 24651 Tel (703) 988-4390

MULLIS, GERALD SPENCER, b. Dublin, Ga., Sept. 14, 1926; LL.B., Mercer U., 1951, J.D., 1955. Admitted to Ga. bar, 1951; partner firms Phillips & Mullis, Macon, Ga., 1955-61, Mullis, Reynolds, Marshall & Horne, Macon, 1969—; sec.-treas. Macon Legal Aid Soc., 1960, v.p., 1961, pres., 1962. Bd. dirs. Macon Community Planning Council, 1961-63, Family Counselling, Macon, 1975—. Mem. Am., Ga. (v.p. 1972-74) trial lawyers assns., Macon Bar Assn. Author: (with George E. Saliba) Georgia Annotations Under Restatement of Law of Torts, 1955. Home: 247 Idle Wild Rd Macon GA 31204 Office: 612 Georgia Power Bldg Macon GA 31201 Tel (912) 746-9623

MULLOY, WARREN DAVIS, b. Upper Darby, Pa., Jan. 29, 1930; A.B., Dartmouth, 1951; J.D., U. Pa., 1954. Admitted to Pa. bar, 1955, ICC bar, 1955, U.S. Supreme Ct. bar, 1962; law clk. firm White Williams & Scott, Phila., 1954-55, asso., 1955-57; asst. U.S. atty. eastern dist. Pa., Phila., 1955-57, chief civil div., 1969-72, first asst. U.S. atty., 1972; mem. firm David Berger, Phila., 1972—; house counsel Pa. R.R. Co., Phila., 1957-69; instr. Acad. Advanced Traffic, Phila., 1965-70. Dir. Rise Tree Media Sch. Bd., 1967-72, v.p., 1971, pres., 1972; mem. exec. bd. Del. County Chpt. March of Dimes, 1968-72; dir. Upper Providence Twp. Citizens Assn., 1968—. Mem. Phila., Fed. bar assns., Am. Arbitration Assn. Office: 1622 Locust St Philadelphia PA 19103 Tel (215) 732-8000

MULOCK, EDWIN THOMAS, b. Tuscaloosa, Ala., Nov. 7, 1943; B.S. in Bus. Adminstrn., Stetson U., 1965; J.D., Stetson U., St. Petersburg, 1968. Admitted to Fla. bar, 1968; asso. with William Kimball, Bradenton, Fla., 1968-69; partner firm Talley, Matthews & Mulock, Bradenton, 1969-72, Matthews & Mulock, Bradenton, 1972-74, Kearney, Matthews & Mulock, Bradenton, 1974-75, Kearney & Mulock, Bradenton, 1976—; asst. pub. defender, Manatee County, Fla., 1969-72, asst. state atty., Manatee County, 1974-75; instr. Manatee County Jr. Coll., 1972-74. Active Bradenton ARC, United Fund, DeSoto Boys Club, Hernando DeSoto Soc., Jaycees, Sertoma Club, Manatee County YMCA, Mental Health Bd., C. of C., High Sch advisory com., Blood Bank. Mem. Am. Trial Lawyers Assn., Nat. Dist. Attys. Assn., Legal Forum Com., Acad. Fla. Trial Lawyers, Am., Manatee County bar assns. Home: 1604 80th St NW Bradenton FL 33505 Office: 519 13th St W Bradenton FL 33505 Tel (813) 748-2104

MULREANY, ROBERT HENRY, b. Bklyn., Aug. 5, 1915; LL.B., N.Y. U., 1940. Admitted to N.Y. bar, 1940; sr. partner firm De Forest & Duer, N.Y.C., 1949—; pres. Provident Loan Soc. of N.Y., N.Y.C., 1955—; sec., gen. counsel, dir. Hackensack Water Co., Weehawken, N.J., 1954—; mayor City of Westfield (N.J.), 1965-68; dir. Nat. State Bank of Elizabeth (N.J.). Trustee John A. Hartford Found. Inc., Smith Richardson Found., Inc., Tuskegee Inst.. Council on Social Work Edn., N.Y.C., Overlook Hosp., Summit, N.J.; pres. Westfield Bd. Edn., 1959-62; chmn. N.Y.C. Advisory Com. on Pub. Welfare, 1963-67. Mem. Am. Bar Assn., Assn. Bar City N.Y. Contbr. articles to profl. publs. Home: 736 Norgate St Westfield NJ 07090 Office: 20 Exchange Pl New York City NY 10005 Tel (212) 269-0230

MULROY, THOMAS MICHAEL, b. Pitts., Oct. 16, 1948; A.B., John Carroll U., 1970; postgrad. London Sch. Econs., 1972; J.D., U. Notre Dame, 1973. Admitted to Pa. bar, 1973; asso. firm Wick, Vupno, & Lavelle, Pitts., 1973-75; individual practice law, Pitts., 1975—. Mem. Am., Pa., Allegheny County bar assns., ICC Practitioners Assn. Home: 1158 Pennsbury Blvd N Pittsburgh PA 15205 Office: 800 Lawyers Bldg Pittsburgh PA 15219 Tel (412) 261-4970

MULTER, ABRAHAM JACOB, b. N.Y.C., Dec. 24, 1900; LL.B., St. Lawrence U., 1921; LL.M., Bkyn. Law Sch., 1922; LL.D., Yeshiva U., 1963. Admitted to N.Y. bar, 1923, U.S. Dist. Ct. bar for Eastern and So. Dists. N.Y., 1925, U.S. Supreme Ct. bar, 1947; partner firm Multer & Multer, N.Y.C., 1923-30, Rafiel & Multer, N.Y.C., 1943-47, Multer, Nova & Seymour, N.Y.C., 1948-67; individual practice law, N.Y.C., 1930-43; justice N.Y. Supreme Ct., Bklyn., 1968-77; mem. 80th-89th Congresses from 13th N.Y. Dist.; spl. asst. atty. gen. in charge of election matters N.Y. State, 1930-40; counsel N.Y. State Assembly, 1934-37, N.Y.C. Councilman's Investigating Com., 1943; counsel N.Y.C. Mayor, 1946-47; chmn. N.Y. State Law Com., 1965-67, Kings County (N.Y.) Law Com., 1950-67; adj. prof. Bklyn. Law Sch., 1976—. Mem. Am., Bklyn., Inter-Am. bar assns., Am. Soc. Internat. Law, Am. Judicature Soc., Internat. Assn. Jewish Jurists and Lawyers, Assn. Supreme Ct. Justices, Bklyn. Law Sch. Alumni Assn. (pres.). Recipient awards Am. Legion, VFW, Jewish War Vets., Boy Scouts Am., Bklyn. Jewish Community Council, numerous others. Home: 1397 E 21st St Brooklyn NY 11210 Office: Supreme Ct Civic Center Brooklyn NY 11201 Tel (212) 643-5254

MULTZ, CARROLL EDWARD, b. Helena, Mont., Aug. 16, 1936; B.S., U. Mont., 1958, J.D., 1961. Admitted to Mont. bar, 1961, Colo. bar, 1964; marshall, law clk. Mont. Supreme Ct., Helena, 1961-62; asst. atty. gen. State of Mont., Helena, 1962-63; individual practice law, Denver and Steamboat Springs, Colo., 1964-68; chief trial dep. Dist. Attys. Office 4th Jud. Dist., Colorado Springs, 1968-72; partner firm Multz, Riggs & Sandler, Colorado Springs, 1972-74; dist. atty. 14th Jud. Dist., Craig, Colo., 1974—; pres. Continuing Legal Edn. in Colo., Inc. Chmn. Moffat County (Colo.) March of Dimes, Craig, 1974—; bd. dirs. Western Colo. council Boy Scouts Am., 1974—; dir. Moffat County Alcohol and Drug Abuse Adv. Council, 1975—. Mem. Am. Trial Lawyers Assn., Nat., Colo. dist. attys. assns., Am., Colo. (chmn. criminal law sect. 1974-75), Northwestern Colo. bar assns. Recipient award of Excellence Cablevision TV Channel 3, 1972; Mark L. Shepherd award Craig Jaycees, 1975; Man of Year award The Daily Press, 1975. Contbr. legal handbooks. Chmn. editorial bd. The Colo. Lawyer, 1976—. Home: 780 Bridger Circle Craig CO 81625 Office: Moffat County Courthouse Craig CO 81625 Tel (303) 824-3904

MULVEHILL, JOHN HENRY, b. Louisville, Jan. 20, 1934; B.A., St. Johns Coll., 1955; J.D., Georgetown U., 1958; LL.M., N.Y. U., 1964. Admitted to N.Y. bar, 1959; mem. firm Casper Ughetta, N.Y.C., 1959-61; mem. legal dept. Liberty Mutual Ins. Co., 1961—; partner firm Fuhrman & Mulvehill, Smithtown, N.Y., 1970-76. State committeeman N.Y. Conservative Party. Mem. Am., N.Y., Suffolk County bar assns., Huntington Lawyers Club, Nassau-Suffolk Trial Lawyers. Home: 6 Kaylor Ct Cold Spring Harbor NY 11724 Office: 11 Route 111 Smithtown NY 11787 Tel (516) 724-9510

MULVIHILL, JAMES FRANCIS, b. Paterson, N.J., Oct. 23, 1938; B.A., Montclair State Coll., 1960; M.A., U. Notre Dame, 1961; J.D., Seton Hall U., 1971. Admitted to N.J. bar, 1971; dep. atty. gen., div. criminal justice State of N.J., 1972—. Mem. West Orange (N.J.) Environ. Commn., 1972-74. Home: 5 2d Ave SeaGirt NJ 08750 Office: 13 Roszel Rd Princeton NJ 08540 Tel (609) 452-9500

MULY, CARL ARNETT, b. Balt., June 30, 1933; B.A., Johns Hopkins, 1957; J.D., U. Balt., 1962. Admitted to Md. bar, 1963; partner firm Mezger & Mezger, Balt.; served to lt. comdr. JAGC. Mem. Savs. and Loan Lawyers Md., Inc. (sec.-treas.), Balt. City Bar Assn., Phi Gamma Delta, Sigma Delta Kappa. Home: 3545 Rogers Ave Ellicott City MD 21043 Office: 655 Crain Hwy SE Glen Burnie MD 21061

MUNDAY, MELVIN WAYNE, b. Granite Falls, N.C., Jan. 11, 1931; A.B., Lenoir Rhyne Coll., 1952; J.D., Georgetown U., 1961. Admitted to Md. bar, 1962; with firm Mudd & Mudd (now Mudd, Mudd, Munday & Heinze, P.A.), La Plata, Md., 1962—, pres., 1976—; spl. asst. atty. gen. State of Md., 1975—. Mem. Assn. Md. Hosp. Attys., Md. State Bar Assn. Home: Route 6 E La Plata MD 20646 Office: 111 La Grange Ave La Plata MD 20646 Tel (301) 934-9541

MUNDHEIM, ROBERT HARRY, b. Hamburg, Germany, Feb. 24, 1933; B.A., Harvard, 1954, LL.B., 1957. Admitted to N.Y. State bar, 1958; asso. firm Shearman & Stirling, N.Y.C., 1957-61; counsel SEC, Washington, 1962-63; asso. prof. law Duke, 1965; Fred Carr Prof. law U. Pa., 1965—; dir. U. Pa. Law Sch. Center for Study Fin. Instns., 1969—. Mem. Am. Law Inst., Am. Bar Assn. Author: The Outside Director of the Public Corporation, 1976. Home: 4628 Pine St Philadelphia PA 19143 Office: 3400 Chestnut St Philadelphia PA 19174 Tel (215) 243-7463

MUNDY, JOHN ELLIS, b. Jonesboro, Ga., Nov. 29, 1894; A.B., U. Ga., 1917, LL.B., 1918. Admitted to Ga. bar, 1918; asst. U.S. atty., No. Dist. Ga., 1934-46, U.S. dist. atty., 1946-53, referee in Bankruptcy Ct., 1954-68; judge Juvenile Ct., Clayton County, Ga., 1971-72; mem. Ga. Ho. of Reps., 1929-32. Author: Around A Town Named for Jones, 1973. Home and Office: 9116 Fayetteville Rd Jonesboro GA 30237 Tel (404) 478-7438

MUNK, MILTON VINCENT, JR., b. Connellsville, Pa., Dec. 19, 1935; B.A., U. Notre Dame, 1957, LL.B., 1959. Admitted to Pa. bar, 1960; individual practice law, Mt. Pleasant, Pa., 1960-76; partner firm Munk & Flaherty, Mt. Pleasant, 1977—; solicitor Borough of Mt. Pleasant, 1965—. Mem. Pa., Am. bar assns., Am. Judicature Soc. Home: RD 2 Mount Pleasant PA 15666 Office: 450 Main St Mount Pleasant PA 15666 Tel (412) 547-3542

MUNLEY, ROBERT WILLIAM, b. Archbald, Pa., Nov. 22, 1930; B.S., U. Scranton, 1952. Admitted to Pa. bar, 1959; atty. Munley & Munley, 1959—; asst. dist. atty. Lackawanna County (Pa.), 1960-69. Bd. dirs. Lourdsmont Sch., Clarks Summit, Pa.; solicitor Valley View Sch. Dist., Archbald, 1972—. Mem. Am., Pa. bar assns., Pa. Trial Lawyers Assn. Home: 352 Main St Archbald PA 18403 Office: 5th floor 400 Spruce St Dime Bank Bldg Scranton PA 18503 Tel (717) 346-7401

MUNRO, DONALD LIONEL, b. Superior, Wis., Nov. 10, 1917; LL.B., Detroit Coll. Law, 1944. Admitted to Mich. bar, 1944; practiced in Detroit, 1945-46, Ontonagon, Mich., 1946-67; prosecuting atty. Ontonagon County (Mich.), 1949-56, 63-64; judge Mich. Circuit Ct., 32d Jud. Circuit, 1967—. Mem. Mich. State Bar Assn., Mich. Judges Assn. Home: Star Route PO Box 132 Ontonagon MI 49953 Office: 601 Trap St Ontonagon MI 49953 Tel (906) 884-4699

MUNRO, ROBERT FOWLIS, b. Lafayette, Ind., May 26, 1919; B.S., Purdue U., 1940; J.D., Ind. U., 1949. Admitted to Ind. bar, 1949, U.S. Dist. Ct. bar for No. Dist. Ind., 1955; asso. firm Vaughan & Vaughan, Lafayette, 1949-50; partner firm Ball & Munro, Lafayette, 1950-54; dep. pros. atty. Tippecanoe County (Ind.), 1950-51, pros. atty., 1952-58; judge Tippecanoe County Superior Ct., 1959—. Mem. Tippecanoe County, Ind. State bar assns., Order of Coif. Contbr. to Ind. Law Jour., Columbia Law Rev. Home: 455 S 8th St Lafayette IN 47901 Office: Tippecanoe County Courthouse Lafayette IN 47901 Tel (317) 742-7060

MUNROE, WILLIAM CALVIN, JR., b. Providence, Feb. 21, 1929; A.B., Brown, U., 1950; LL.B., Harvard, 1953. Admitted to Mass. bar, 1957; asso. firm Russell, Plummer & Rutherford, Boston, 1957-59; asst. fgn. counsel USM Corp., Boston, 1959-69, internat. counsel, 1970—. Mem. Lincoln (Mass.) Fin. Com., 1973—, chmn., 1975—. Mem. Am., Boston bar assns. Office: 140 Federal St Boston MA 02107 Tel (617) 542-9100

MUNS, EDWARD CARROL, b. Brownwood, Tex., Dec. 5, 1937; B.C.E., U. Ariz., 1961; J.D., U. Calif., Berkeley, 1971. Admitted to Calif. bar, 1972; engr. Morrison-Knudsen Co., Boise, Idaho, 1963-68; asso. firm Davis, Craig & Bartalini, Alameda, Calif., 1972; asso. firm White, Price, Peterson & Robinson, San Diego, 1972-76, partner, 1976-77; partner firm Peterson, Gamer, Muns, Branton & Price, San Diego, 1977—; lectr. Calif. Western Sch. Law, 1974—. Bd. dirs. Center City Assn., San Diego, 1974-75. Mem. San Diego County, Am. bar assns., State Bar Calif. Office: 530 B St Suite 2300 San Diego CA 92101 Tel (714) 234-0361

MUNSON, EARL HENRY, JR., b. Edgerton, Wis., Jan. 15, 1935; B.S., U. Wis., 1957, LL.B., 1959. Admitted to Wis. bar, 1959; Wis. Supreme Ct. bar, 1959, U.S. Ct. of Mil. Appeals bar, 1962; lt. comdr. JAGC, USN, 1959-62; asst. dist. atty. Dane County (Wis.), 1963-65; mem. firm LaFollette, Sinykin, Anderson & Munson, Madison, Wis., 1965—. Bd. dirs. Legal Services Center of Dane County, 1962-77, pres., 1974-77. Mem. Am., Dane County bar assns., State Bar Wis. (bd. govs. 1976), Bar Assn. 7th Fed. Center, Am. Trial Lawyers Assn., Phi Beta Kappa, Order of Coif. Home: 126 Marinette Trail Madison WI 53705 Office: 222 W Washington Ave Madison WI 53703 Tel (608) 257-3911

MUNSON, EDWIN PALMER, b. Richmond, Va., Aug. 21, 1935; B.S. in Commerce, U. Va., 1957, LL.B., 1963. Admitted to Va. bar, 1963; asso. firm Williams, Mullen & Christian, Richmond, 1963-72; sec., resident counsel, contract officer Va. Blue Cross and Blue Shield, Richmond, 1972—. Commr. Richmond Redevel. and Housing Authority. Mem. Va. Richmond, Am. bar assns. Home: 4410 Patterson Ave Richmond VA 23221 Office: 2015 Staples Mill Rd Richmond VA 23230 Tel (804) 359-7283

MUNSON, GEORGE KIBBY, b. Rochester, N.Y., May 15, 1893; A.B., U. Rochester, 1914; LL.B., George Washington U., 1924. Admitted to D.C. bar, 1924, Md. bar, 1933, U.S. Supreme Ct. bar, 1955; mem. firm Hitt and Munson, Washington, 1927-40; mem. firm Roberts & McInnis, and successors, Washington, 1942-72; partner firm Bird & Tansill, Washington, 1972—; spl. examiner Mixed Claims Commn., U.S. and Germany, 1929-30; dep. asst. atty. gen. Ga. to represent Ga. Pub. Service Commn., 1953-54. Mem. Am., D.C. bar assns., Am. Judicature Soc., Order of Coif, Phi Delta Phi. Home: 7500 Meadow Ln Chevy Chase MD 20015 Office: 1140 Connecticut Ave NW Washington DC 20036 Tel (202) 833-2266

MUNSON, PETER J., b. N.Y.C., Dec. 7, 1947; B.A. in Econs., City Coll. N.Y., 1969; J.D., Stetson Coll. Law, 1972. Admitted to Fla. bar, 1972; partner firm Yancey & Munson, Lakeland, Fla., 1972-76, Munson & Anderson, 1976—; program atty. Fla. Dept. Health and Rehab. Services, 1975—; pros. atty. City of Lakeland, 1975-76, municipal ct. judge, 1976-77; lectr. Fla. So. Coll., 1977—. Bd. dirs. Walola Chapel and Retreat, Winter Haven, Fla., Kiwanis Club of Lakeland, Concerned People, Central Fla. Health Council. Mem. Am., Fla., Lakeland, 10th Jud. Circuit bar assns. Home: 1117 Hunt Ave Lakeland FL 33801 Office: 414 Marble Arcade Lakeland FL 33801 Tel (813) 688-5501

MUNSTER, JOE HENRY, JR., b. Austin, Tex., July 28, 1912; B.A. summa cum laude, U. Tex., 1933, M.A., 1933, J.D. summa cum laude, 1936; S.J.D., Northwestern U., 1952. Admitted to Tex. bar, 1936, Ct. of Mil. Appeals bar, 1953; individual practice law, Austin, 1936-41; commd. lt. (j.g.) USN, 1941; advanced through grades to capt., 1954; dist. legal officer 15th Naval Dist., 1947-49, 13th Naval Dist., 1955-57; gen. insp. Office JAG, 1952-55; comdg. officer U.S. Naval Justice Sch., 1957-60; asst. JAG, 1960-61; spl. council of sec. navy, 1961, ret., 1961; prof. law Western Res. U., 1961-66; prof. law Hasting Law Sch. U. Calif., 1966—, asst. dean, 1966-67, asso. dean, 1967-71. Mem. Am., Fed. Tex., San Francisco, bar assns., AAUP, Am. Econ. Assn., Chancellors, Assn. Am. Law Schs. (chmn. com. on pre-legal edn. and admission to law sch. 1972, chmn. sect. 1973, sec. 1975, Hastings Coll. Law rep. 1972—), Order of Coif, Phi Beta Kappa. Contbr. articles to profl. jours. Home: 999 Green St 902 San Francisco CA 94133 Office: 198 Mc Allister St San Francisco CA 94102 Tel (415) 557-1305

MUNTZ, JOHN CONYNE, b. Ada, Okla., Feb. 5, 1940; B.S., U. Okla., 1965, J.D., 1968. Admitted to Okla. bar, 1968, U.S. Dist. Ct., 1968; asst. dist. atty., Duncan, Okla., 1968-70; partner firm Bounds & Muntz, Hugo, Okla., 1970-73, individual practice law, Hugo., 1973—; U.D. magistrate, 1971—. Chmn. Choctaw County chpt. ARC, 1973—. Mem. Am., Okla. bar assns. Office: 111 N 3d St Hugo OK 74743 Tel (405) 826-3373

MUNZER, STEPHEN IRA, b. N.Y.C., Mar. 15, 1939; A.B., Brown U., 1960; LL.B., Cornell U., 1963. Admitted to N.Y. State bar, 1964, U.S. Supreme Ct. bar, 1974; asso. firm Amen Weisman & Butler, N.Y.C., 1965-69; partner firm Sobol Munzer & Linck, N.Y.C., 1970—. Mem. N.Y. State Bar Assn., Assn. Bar City N.Y. (real property law com.). Home: 850 Park Ave New York City NY 10021 Office: 295 Madison Ave New York City NY 10017 Tel (212) 685-6945

MURA, PAUL EUGENE, b. Rochester, N.Y., June 17, 1938; B.A., St. John Fisher Coll., 1960; LL.B., Union U., 1963, J.D., 1968. Admitted to N.Y. State bar, 1964, U.S. Supreme Ct. bar, 1973; asso. firm Wilson, Trinker & Gilbert, Rochester, 1963-64; asst. dist. atty. Monroe County (N.Y.), 1964-67; mem. firm Johnson, Reif & Mullan, Rochester, 1967; individual practice law, Rochester, 1967—; staff atty., asst. sec. Eastman Savs. and Loan Assn. Mem. Am., N.Y. State, Monroe County bar assns., N.Y. State Dist. Attys. Assn. Home: 3236 Culver Rd Rochester NY 14622 Office: 377 State St Rochester NY 14650 also 25 E Main St Rochester NY 14614 Tel (716) 454-1350 and 724-4217

MURAOKA, MAMORU, b. Hilo, Hawaii, May 14, 1927; B.S., Ind. U., 1963, J.D., 1966. Admitted to Minn. bar, 1967; legal editor West Pub. Co., St. Paul, 1966—. Mem. Am., Minn., Hennepin County (Minn.) bar assns. Home: 6329 Barrie Rd Edina MN 55435 Office: 50 Kellogg Blvd Saint Paul MN 55102 Tel (612) 228-2588

MURCHISON, DAVID CLAUDIUS, b. N.Y.C., Aug. 19, 1923; A.A., George Washington U., 1946, J.D. with honors, 1949. Admitted to D.C. bar, 1949, U.S. Supreme Ct. bar, 1953; legal asst. to Under Sec. Army, Washington, 1949-51, asso. gen. counsel Small Def. Plants Adminstrn., 1952-53; legal advisor, asst. to chmn. FTC, Washington, 1953-55; partner firm Howrey & Simon, Washington, 1955—; legal advisor to U.S. del. UN Econ. and Social Council, 1955. Mem. N.Y. State, Am., Fed. bar assns., Bar Assn. D.C., Am. Soc. Internat. Law, Order of Coif. Home: 5417 Blackstone Rd Westmoreland Hills MD 20016 Office: 1730 Pennsylvania Ave NW Washington DC 20006 Tel (202) 783-0880

MURCHISON, NEIL BRYANT, b. Tyrone, Pa., July 29, 1940; A.B., Franklin and Marshall Coll., 1962; J.D., Dickinson Law Sch., 1965. Admitted to Pa. Supreme Ct. bar, 1965, U.S. Ct. Mil. Appeals bar, 1966, Blair County Ct. of Common Pleas bar, 1970, U.S. Dist. Ct. Western Dist. Pa. bar, 1971; served with JAGC, U.S. Navy, 1965-69; asso. firm John F. Sullivan, 1970-73; partner firm Sullivan and

Murchison, Altoona, Pa., 1973—. Mem. Pa., Blair County bar assns., Altoona Area C. of C. Home: 1800 Bell Ave Altoona PA 16602 Office: 2229 Broad Ave Altoona PA 16601 Tel (814) 946-0252

MURDEN, WILLIAM JESSE, b. Peekskill, N.Y., Apr. 20, 1923; A.B., N.Y. U., 1950; LL.B., Bklyn. Law Sch., 1953. Admitted to N.Y. bar, 1954; individual practice law, Peekskill, 1954—; judge City Ct., Peekskill, 1976, mayor, 1966-69. Mem. Am., N.Y., Westchester, Peekskill bar assns. Office: 44 N Division St Peekskill NY 10566 Tel (914) 737-5511

MURDOCH, CONVERSE, b. Washington, Pa., Aug. 27, 1919; A.B., Bowdoin Coll., 1941; J.D., Columbia, 1947; LL.M., Georgetown U., 1951. Admitted to N.Y. bar, 1947, Pa. bar, 1954, Del. bar, 1961; asso. firm Dechert Price & Rhoads, Phila., 1954-61, firm Potter, Anderson & Corroon, Wilmington, Del., 1961-69; pres. firm Murdoch & Walsh, Wilmington, 1970—; spl. atty., office of chief counsel IRS, Washington, 1948-52, spl. asst. to chief counsel, 1952-54. Pres. Wynnewood (Pa.) Civic Assn., 1959-60; chmn. "The Group", 1974—. Mem. Am., Del. (chmn. tax com. 1975—), Fed. (pres. Del. chpt.) bar assns., Am. Acad. Tax Practice (dean 1962—). Lectr. tax. insts.; lectr., mem. planning com. Del. Tax Inst., 1970-76; contbr. articles to legal jours. Office: Box 949 Wilmington DE 19899 Tel (302) 658-8662

MURNAGHAN, FRANCIS DOMINIC, JR., b. Balt., June 20, 1920; B.A., Johns Hopkins, 1941; LL.B., Harvard; 1948. Admitted to Md. bar, 1949; asso. firm Barnes, Dechert, Price, Smith & Clark, Phila., 1948-50; staff atty. Office of Gen. Counsel, U.S. High Commr. for Germany, 1950-52; asst. atty. gen. State of Md., 1952-54; asso. firm Venable, Baetjer & Howard, Balt., 1952-57, partner, 1957—. Chmn. Charter Revision Commn. of Balt., 1963-64; trustee Walters Art Gallery, 1961, pres., 1963—; pres. Sch. Bd. of Balt., 1967-70. Mem. Am., Md., Balt. bar assns., Am. Coll. Trial Lawyers. Home: 15 W Mount Vernon Pl Baltimore MD 21201 Office: 1800 Mercantile Bank and Trust Bldg 2 Hopkins Plaza Baltimore MD 21201 Tel (301) 752-6780

MUROV, OSCAR, b. Bklyn., Feb. 11, 1911; student St. John's Coll., 1929, LL.B., 1932. Admitted to N.Y. bar, 1934, U.S. Supreme Ct. bar, 1949; individual practice law, Lindenhurst, N.Y., 1934-67; judge Dist. Ct. Suffolk County, Lindenhurst, 1967-74; county judge Suffolk County, Lindenhurst, 1974—; village atty. Lindenhurst, police justice; counsel Lindenhurst, Wyandanch and Copiague sch. dists.; counsel Town of Babylon (N.Y.). Founder, Lindenhurst Meml. Library; past pres., bd. dirs. Lindenhurst Hebrew Congregation, now hon. trustee; bd. dirs. Babylon Town Symphony. Mem. Am., N.Y. State, Suffolk County bar assns., Lindenhurst C. of C. (past pres.). Home: 480 S 2d St Lindenhurst NY 11757 Office: 152 W Hoffman Ave Lindenhurst NY 11757 Tel (516) 226-2955

MURPHEY, ELWOOD, b. Berkeley, Calif., Oct. 9, 1909; A.B., U. Calif., Berkeley, 1930, J.D., 1933. Admitted to Calif. bar, 1933; dep. dist. atty. El Dorado (Calif.), 1933-35; asso. firm McClymonds, Wells and Wilson, Oakland, Calif., 1935-41, partner firm Wells, Murphey and Coffey, and predecessors, Oakland, 1941-60; gen. counsel, sec., v.p., sr. v.p., pres., vice chmn. bd. ISI Corp., San Francisco, 1960—, chmn. bd. ISI Trust Fund; pres. ISI Growth and Income Funds. Mem. State Bar Calif., Alameda County Bar Assn. (exec. com. 1952-56, v.p. 1954, pres. 1955). Home: 28 Kerr Ave Kensington CA 94707 Office: 100 California St San Francisco CA 94111 Tel (415) 392-6869

MURPHY, BURKETTE DEAN, III, lawyer; b. Atlanta, Nov. 6, 1947; B.A., Mercer U., 1969, J.D., 1972. Admitted to Ga. bar, 1973; mem. firm Watson, Brown, Foster and Murphy, Jonesboro, Ga., 1975—. Mem. State Bar of Ga., Am., Clayton County, Fayette County bar assns. Home: 175 DeVilla Trace Route 5 Fayetteville GA 30214 Office: 101 N Main St Jonesboro GA 30236

MURPHY, CHARLES SPRINGS, b. Wallace, N.C., Aug. 20, 1909; A.B., Duke, 1931, LL.B., 1934, LL.D. (hon.), 1967. Admitted to N.C. bar, 1933, D.C. bar, 1947, U.S. Supreme Ct. bar, 1944; asst. legis. counsel U.S. Senate, 1934-47; adminstrv. asst. to Pres. of U.S., 1947-50, spl. counsel, 1950-53; partner firm Morison, Murphy, Clapp & Abrams, and predecessors, Washington, 1953-61, partner, 1969—; U.S. Under-Sec. Agr., 1961-65; chmn. CAB, 1965-68; counselor Pres. of U.S., 1968-69; pres. Commodity Credit Corp., Washington, 1961-65; gen. counsel Frontier Airlines, Inc., Denver, 1971—. Pres. Harry S. Truman Library Inst., Independence, Mo., 1977—; gen. counsel Harry S. Truman Scholarship Found., Washington, 1976—; trustee Duke U., Durham, N.C., 1969—, bd. visitors, 1973—. Mem. Am., Fed., D.C., N.C. bar assns., D.C. Bar, N.C. Bar. Office: Morison Murphy et al 1776 K St NW Washington DC 20006 Tel (202) 293-6260

MURPHY, CHRISTOPHER JOSEPH, III, b. Washington, Apr. 24, 1946; B.A., U. Notre Dame, 1968; J.D., U. Va., 1971; M.B.A. with distinction, Harvard, 1973. Admitted to Va. bar, 1971; dir. FBT Bancorp., Inc., South Bend, Ind., 1972; prin. The Research Group, Inc., Charlottesville, Va., 1969-72; exec. trainee Citicorp. subs. Group, group mgmt. office, N.Y.C., 1973-74, area dir. Citicorp. Mgmt. Services Corp., St. Louis, 1974-75; asst. to chief operating officer Nationwide Fin. Services Corp., citicorp., St. Louis, 1975; v.p. Citicorp., ins. and liability products, 1975-76; sr. v.p. FBT Bancorp., Inc.; v.p. planning and services div. First Bank & Trust Co., South Bend, 1976—, pres., chief exec. officer, 1977—. Mem. Am. Bar Assn. Home: 1237 E Jefferson Blvd South Bend IN 46617 Office: 414 First Bank & Trust Bldg South Bend IN 46601 Tel (219) 284-3218

MURPHY, DAVID, b. Joliet, Ill., Jan. 1, 1917; J.D., DePaul U., 1940. Admitted to Ill. bar, 1941; individual practice law, Joliet, 1941—; atty. Joliet Twp., 1961-69; pub. adminstr. Will County (Ill.), 1966-72. Tel (815) 726-5040

MURPHY, DENIS JAMES, b. Hempstead, N.Y., Sept. 21, 1938; B.A., Lehigh U., 1960; J.D., Georgetown U., 1964. Admitted to Ohio bar, 1964, Conn. bar, 1964; asso. firm Baldwin Nichol and Menapace, Columbus, Ohio, 1965-67; partner firm Carlile Patchen Murphy & Allison, Columbus, 1967—; adj. prof. Ohio State U. Coll. Law, 1974—. Mem. Am., Ohio, Columbus bar assns., Am., Ohio, Franklin City trial lawyers assns., Am. Arbitration Assn. Home: 987 Grandview Ave Columbus OH 43212 Office: 100 E Broad St Columbus OH 43215 Tel (614) 228-6135

MURPHY, EARL FINBAR, b. Indpls., Nov. 1, 1928; A.B., Butler U., 1949, M.A., 1954; J.D., Ind. U., 1952; LL.M., Yale, 1955, J.S.D., 1959. Admitted to Ind. bar, 1952; individual practice law, Indpls., 1952-54; asst. prof. Harpur Coll., State U. N.Y. at Binghamton, 1955-57; Rockefeller fellow U. Wis. Law Sch., Madison, 1957-58; asst. prof. Temple U. Sch. Law, Phila., 1958-60, asso. prof., 1960-65, prof. law, 1965-69; prof. law Ohio State U. Coll. Law, Columbus, 1969—. Chmn. Ohio Environ. Bd. Rev., 1972-74. Mem. Am. (spl. com. on energy law 1976—), Inter-Am., Ind., Fed. bar assns., Am. Soc. Legal History, World Soc. Ekistics. Author: Water Purity, 1961; Governing Nature, 1967; Man and His Environment: Law, 1971. Home: 57 E Mithoff St Columbus OH 43206 Office: 1659 N High St Columbus OH 43210 Tel (614) 422-4796

MURPHY, EDWARD ELIAS, JR., b. St. Louis, Dec. 21, 1925; A.B., Washington U., St. Louis, 1947; J.D., Harvard, 1950. Admitted to Mo. bar, 1950, U.S. Supreme Ct. bar, 1972; asso. firm Coburn, Storckman & Croft, St. Louis, 1950-55; individual practice law, St. Louis, 1955-60; partner firm Murphy, Kortenhof & Ely, St. Louis, 1960-73; pres. firm Murphy-McCarthy Assos., Clayton, Mo., 1973—. Councilman St. Louis County, Mo., 1960-64; mem. charter commn., 1967, planning commn., 1971-76. Mem. Am. Bar Assn., Mo. Bar, Bar Assn. Met. St. Louis. Home: 9967 Holliston Ct Saint Louis MO 63124 Office: 120 S Central Ave Clayton MO 63105 Tel (314) 725-5440

MURPHY, GALVIN PALMER, b. Albany, N.Y., May 26, 1926; student Bates Coll.; A.B., Tufts Coll., 1949; J.D., Harvard Law Sch., 1954. Admitted to N.Y. bar, 1955, Fed. bar, 1955; asso. firm Dewey, Ballantine, Bushby, Palmer & Wood, N.Y.C., 1954-61; internat. counsel Standard Brands Inc., N.Y.C., 1961-64, dir. internat. planning and devel., 1964-72; asst. gen. counsel J.P. Stevens & Co., Inc., N.Y.C., 1972—; lectr. Northeastern U., Boston, 1952-53, N.Y. U., 1972—; pres. Friendly Homes, Inc., NY.C., 1959—; dir. Fiduciary Councel, Inc., N.Y.C., 1970-72. Trustee Mercy Coll., Dobbs Ferry, N.Y., 1972—; mem. U.S. Olympic Team, Mexico City, 1968. Mem. Am. Arbitration Assn. (arbitrator 1972—), Lawyers Assn. Textile Industry Inc. (gov. 1975—), Am. Irish Hist. Soc. (sec. 1972—), Assn. Bar City N.Y., Internat. Bar Assn. Contbr. articles to profl. jours. Home: 315 E 72d St New York City NY 10021 Office: 1185 Ave Americas New York City NY 10036 Tel (212) 575-3502

MURPHY, HARRIET LOUISE M., b. Atlanta, June 6, 1927; A.B., Spelman Coll., 1949; M.A., Atlanta U., 1952; J.D., U. Tex., 1969. Admitted to Tex. bar, 1969. Instr. social scis. So. U., 1954-56; asst. prof. polit. sci. Prairie View A. and M. U., 1956-60; instr. Longview (Tex.) Ind. Sch. Dist., 1960-66; prof. govt. Huston-Tillotson Coll., 1966—; individual practice law, Austin, Tex., 1971—; relief judge Austin Ct., 1973—. Mem. advisory com. on African affairs Dept. State, 1970-72; mem. diplomatic mission to South Africa, 1972; chmn. legal redress NAACP., Austin, 1971-73; mem. advisory com. on spl. edn. Austin Ind. Sch. Dist., 1975—; mem. heritage com. Austin Bicentennial Commn., 1975—; v.p. Austin Urban League, 1976—; del. Democratic nat. conv., 1976; presdl. elector, 1976. Mem. Am., Tex., Travis County (Tex.), Nat. bar assns., Tex. Municipal Judges Assn., Zeta Sorority (Woman in Law 1974), Delta Sorority (Woman Breaking New Ground award 1974). Named Woman of Month Am. Nat. Bank, Austin, 1973. Home: 6635 Greensboro Dr Austin TX 78723 Office: 1701A Rosewood Ave Austin TX 78702 also Huston-Tillotson Coll Austin TX 78723 Tel (512) 476-7421

MURPHY, HENRY L., JR., b. Hyannis, Mass., Nov. 27, 1941; A.B., Georgetown U., 1964; J.D., Suffolk U., 1968; postgrad. Boston U. Law Sch., 1970. Admitted to Mass. bar, 1968; clk. 1st Dist. Ct., Barnstable, Mass., 1968-70; partner firm Smith, Murphy, Hyannis, 1970—; town counsel Town of Barnstable, 1973—; instr. Northeastern U., 1968-70. Dir., adminstrv. mgr. Edward Bangs Kelley and Eliza Kelley Found., 1970—; gov. Cape Cod Conservatory of Music and Art, 1973—. Mem. Am. Judicature Soc., Am., Mass., Barnstable County bar assns., Phi Alpha Delta. Home: 176 Bay Ln Centerville MA 02632 Office: 239 Main St Hyannis MA 02601 Tel (617) 775-3116

MURPHY, JAMES MICHAEL, b. Spokane, Jan. 21, 1943; B.A., Eastern Wash. State Coll., 1965; J.D., Gonzaga U., 1973. Admitted to Wash. Supreme Ct. bar, 1973; law clk. firm Morrison, Huppin, Ewing & Anderson, Spokane, 1971-72; law clk. Hon. Marshall A. Neill Chief Judge U.S. Dist. Ct. Eastern Dist. Wash., 1972-74; asst. atty. gen. dept. social and health services State of Wash., Spokane, 1975-76; asst. atty. gen. Edn. and Consumer Protection, Spokane, 1976—. Mem. advisory bd. Suspected Child Abuse & Neglect Assn., Spokane, 1974—; pres. bd. dirs. Native Am. Legal Services Program, Spokane, 1975—. Mem. Am., Wash., Spokane County (trustee 1975—) bar assns. Home: N 6415 Catherine St Spokane WA 99208 Office: 1305 Old National Bank Bldg Spokane WA 99201 Tel (509) 456-3123

MURPHY, JAMES PATRICK, b. Missoula, Mont., Feb. 9, 1944; B.A., Amherst Coll., 1966; J.D., U. Mont., 1969. Admitted to Mont. bar, 1969; law clk. to dist. judge, Billings, Mont., 1969-71; partner firm Berger, Anderson, Sinclair & Murphy, Billings, 1971—; lectr. high schs. Mem. Am., Mont., Yellowstone County bar assns., Am., Mont. trial lawyers assns. Home: 2106 Nina Clare Rd Billings MT 59102 Office: 2512 3d Ave N Billings MT 59101 Tel (406) 252-3439

MURPHY, JERRY JOHN, b. St. Louis, Mar. 28, 1942; A.B., U. Notre Dame, 1964; J.D., St. Louis U., 1968; LL.M., Washington U., 1976. Admitted to Mo. bar, 1968, U.S. Supreme Ct. bar, 1974; asst. circuit atty. St. Louis, 1968-70; asst. U.S. atty. for Eastern dist. Mo., St. Louis, 1970-74; individual practice law, Clayton, Mo., 1974—; spl. atty. in charge St. Louis Office of Drug Abuse Law Enforcement, 1972-74; spl. cons. Spl. White House Counsel, Washington, 1974-75; spl. cons. U.S. Dept. Justice Drug Enforcement Adminstrn., 1975; instr. St. Louis U. Sch. Law, 1974—. Mem. Am., Mo., Met. St. Louis (chmn. Trial Practice Inst. 1976) bar assns., St. Louis Lawyers Assn. Recipient Spl. Act award Assn. Fed. Investigators, 1971; Narcotic Law Enforcement award U.S. Dept. Justice, 1974; award of merit St. Louis Met. Bar Assn., 1976. Home: #23 Middlesex St Brentwood MO 63144 Office: 130 S Bemiston St Suite 710 Clayton MO 63105 Tel (314) 863-5100

MURPHY, JOANNE WHARTON, b. Coshocton, Ohio, Sept. 12, 1934; A.B., Miami U., Ohio, 1956; J.D., Ohio State U., 1958. Admitted to Ohio bar, 1958, Ill. bar, 1959; asst. atty. gen., State Ohio, Columbus, 1963-65; asst. dean Coll. Law Ohio State Univ., Columbus, 1965-71, univ. ombudsman, 1973-76, adj. prof., 1973—; asso. dean, asso. prof. Sch. Law Case Western Reserve U., Cleve., 1971-73; mem. faculty U. Wis., Madison, summers 1972-74, Active Ohio Law Opportunity Fund, Cleve. Mem. Am., Ohio bar assns., Order of Coif, Phi Beta Kappa. Office: 2130 Neil Ave Columbus OH 43210 Tel (614) 422-7263

MURPHY, JOHN A., b. El Paso, Tex., Apr. 25, 1910; A.B., U. Ariz., 1932, postgrad., 1932-33; postgrad. Georgetown U., 1933-34, U. San Francisco, 1934-35. Admitted to Ariz. bar, 1937; since practiced in Phoenix, partner firm Murphy, Posner & Froimson, and predecessor firms, 1939—; dep. county atty., Maricopa County, 1937-38; asst. to U.S. Atty. Gen. Washington, 1945-48. Mem. Am., Fed., Ariz., Maricopa County Bar Assns., Am. Judicature Soc. Home: 3500 E Lincoln Dr Phoenix AZ 85018 Office: 1500 Towne House Tower Phoenix AZ 85013 Tel (602) 264-4981

MURPHY, JOHN FRANCIS, b. Portchester, N.Y., Apr. 25, 1937; B.A., Cornell U., 1959, LL.B., 1962. Admitted to D.C. bar, 1962, Kans. bar, 1969; asso. firm Winthrop, Stimson, Putnam & Roberts, N.Y.C., 1963-64; atty. Dept. of State, Washington, 1964-67; asso. firm Kirkland, Ellis, Hodson, Chaffetz & Masters, Washington, 1967-69; asso. prof. law U. Kans., 1969-72, prof., 1972-74, asso. dean, prof. law, 1975—; Afro-Asia Pub. service fellow, India, 1962-63. Legal adviser Lawrence Sierra Club, 1971-73. Mem. Am. Bar Assn., Am. Soc. Internat. Law, Internat. Law Assn., Assn. Am. Law Schs. Contbr. articles to profl. jours. Home: 2110 Owens Ln Lawrence KS 66044 Office: Sch Law U Kans Lawrence KS 66045 Tel (913) 864-4550

MURPHY, JOHN RIDGEWAY, III, b. Augusta, Ga., June 30, 1946; A.B., U. Ga., 1968, J.D., 1971. Admitted to Ga. bar, 1971; asso. firm Westmoreland, Hall, McGee & Warner, Atlanta, 1971-74; individual practice law, Atlanta, 1974—. Mem. Am., Atlanta bar assns., State Bar Ga. Home: 680 Longwood Dr NW Atlanta GA 30305 Office: 101 Marietta Tower Suite 2205 Atlanta GA 30303 Tel (404) 577-5161

MURPHY, JOHN THOMAS, JR., b. St. Louis, Aug. 17, 1917; J.D., Washington U., 1940. Admitted to Mo. bar, 1940; spl. agt. FBI, Washington, 1941-45; partner firm Murphy & Schlapprizzi, St. Louis, 1953—; pres. Group Underwriters Mut. Ins. Co., St. Louis; chmn. bd. dirs. Mound City Industries, Inc., St. Louis. Chmn. bd. dirs. Dismas Clark Found., St. Louis, 1970-76. Mem. Am., Mo., St. Louis bar assns., Lawyers Assn. St. Louis. Home: 14 Woodacre Rd Saint Louis MO 63124 Office: 1015 Locust St Saint Louis MO 63101 Tel (314) 421-0763

MURPHY, JOSEPH ANDREW, b. Pittston, Pa., Feb. 6, 1944; B.S., U. Scranton, 1965, J.D., Duquesne U., 1968. Admitted to Pa. bar, 1968; since practiced in Scranton, Pa., law clk. U.S. Dist. Ct. Middle Dist. Pa., 1968-71; asso. firm Lenahan, Dempsey & Murphy, and predecessors, 1971-74, partner, 1974—. Mem. Am., Pa., Lackawanna County bar assns. Home: 1614 Jefferson Ave Dunmore PA 18509 Office: 500 Scranton Elec Bldg Scranton PA 18503 Tel (717) 346-2097

MURPHY, JOSEPH THOMAS, b. Phila., Oct. 21, 1910; B.S. in Bus. Adminstrn., St. Joseph's Coll., 1933; LL.B., U. Pa., 1936. Admitted to Pa. bar, 1938; practiced in Phila., 1938-68; spl. asst. atty. gen. State of Pa., 1962-69; judge Phila. Municipal Ct., 1969-74, Phila. Ct. Common Pleas, 1971—. Mem. North Cath. High Sch. Alumni Assn. (dir., trustee), St. Joseph's Coll. Law Alumni (dir.), Am., Pa., Phila. bar assns., Pa., Nat. confs. state trial judges, Pa., Nat. councils juvenile ct. judges, N.Am. Judges Assn., Nat. Conf. Spl. Ct. Judges. Recipient St. Francis DeSales medal Oblates St. Francis DeSales, 1968. Home: 1206 Haworth St Philadelphia PA 19124 Office: 192 City Hall Philadelphia PA 19107 Tel (215) MU6-7926

MURPHY, MARTIN JOSEPH, b. Cleve., Feb. 28, 1905; LL.B., U. Denver, 1947; J.D. (hon.), DePaul U., 1970. Admitted to Colo. bar, 1947, U.S. Supreme Ct. bar, 1955; sr. partner firm Murphy, Morris & Susemihl, Colorado Springs, 1976—. Mem. Am. Bar Assn., Trial Lawyers Am., Phi Delta Phi. Home: Satellite Condominium Apt B-1213 411 Lakewood Circle Colorado Springs CO 80910 Office: 431 S Cascade Ave Colorado Springs CO 80903 Tel (303) 473-8823

MURPHY, MICHAEL JAMES, lawyer; b. N.Y.C., Apr. 4, 1940; B.A., Manhattan Coll., 1961; J.D., Fordham Law Sch., 1968. Admitted N.Y. bar, 1968, U.S. Dist. Ct. So. Dist. N.Y., 1970, U.S. Dist. Ct. Eastern Dist. N.Y., 1970, 2d Circuit Ct. Appeals, 1972; law clk. to U.S. Dist. Judge, So. dist. N.Y., 1968-69; asso. law firm Lord, Day & Lord, N.Y.C., 1969-76, partner, 1976—. Mem. Bar Assn., City N.Y., Bar Assn. State N.Y. Office: 25 Broadway New York City NY 10004

MURPHY, MICHAEL ROLAND, b. Denver, Aug. 6, 1947; B.A., Creighton U., 1969; J.D., U. Wyo., 1972. Admitted to Wyo. bar, 1972, Utah bar, 1973; clk. to Chief Judge David T. Lewis, U. St. Ct. Appeals, 10th Circuit, 1972-73; asso. firm Jones, Waldo, Holbrook & McDonough, Salt Lake City, 1973-76; partner firm Jones, Waldo, Holbrook & McDonough, Sale Lake City, 1977—. Mem. Utah State, Wyo. bar assns. Home: 1324 Emigration St Salt Lake City UT 84108 Office: 800 Walker Bank Bldg Salt Lake City UT 84111 Tel (801) 521-3200

MURPHY, NEALE DONEGAN, b. Norwich, Conn., Mar. 20, 1904; LL.B., Boston Coll., 1955, J.D., 1969. Admitted to R.I. bar, 1967; adminstrv. asst. to Gov. of R.I., 1935-37; U.S. marshal for Dist. R.I., 1938-47; clk. U.S. Dist. Ct. for Dist. R.I., 1947-70; individual practice law, Jamestown, R.I., 1970—; judge Jamestown Probate Ct., 1973—. Chmn. bd. trustees William H. Hall Library, Edgewood, R.I., 1968-69. Mem. R.I., Am. bar assns., Nat. Coll. Probate Judges. Home and office: Highland Dr Jamestown RI 02835 Tel (401) 423-1100

MURPHY, PATRICK NEIL, b. Wahoo, Nebr., Jan. 15, 1946; A.B., U. Nebr., 1968; J.D., Creighton U., 1972. Admitted to Nebr. bar, 1973, Iowa bar, 1973; partner Dull Law Firm, LeMars, Iowa, 1973—; asst. atty. Plymouth County (Iowa), 1973—; city atty. City of Merrill (Iowa), 1974—. Bd. dirs. Plains Area Mental Health, LeMars, 1975; mem. publicity com. Plymouth County Work Activity Center, LeMars, 1975; mem. trust com. Prairie Gold council Boy Scouts Am., Sioux City, Iowa, 1976. Mem. Am., Nebr., Iowa bar assns., Am., Iowa trial lawyers assns., Am. Judicature Soc., Iowa County Attys. Assn. Home: 420 S Greenwood Dr LeMars IA 51031 Office: 38 1st Ave NW LeMars IA 51031 Tel (712) 546-7016

MURPHY, ROBERT C., Chief judge Md. Ct. of Appeals, 1972—. Office: 361 Rowe Blvd Annapolis MD 21401*

MURPHY, RUPERT LEO, b. Byromville, Ga., July 27, 1909; LL.B., Atlanta Law Sch., 1938, LL.M., 1939. Corr., rate clk. Atlanta Freight Tariff Bur. (now So. Freight Tariff Bur.), 1925-29; asst. traffic mgr. Fulton Bag & Cotton Mills, Atlanta, 1929-42; admitted to Ga. bar, 1938; atty., traffic mgr. Ga.-Ala. Textile Traffic Assn., Atlanta, 1942-55; commr. ICC, Washington, 1955—. Past pres., chmn. Gov.'s So. Traffic League. Mem. Am., Ga. bar assns., Assn. ICC Practitioners, Am. Voc. Traffic and Transp., Nat. Indsl. Traffic League (past v.p.), S.E. Shippers Adv. Bd. (past gen. chmn.), Delta Theta Phi, Delta Nu Alpha. Home: 1400 S Joyce St Arlington VA 22202 Office: ICC 12th St and Constitution Ave Washington DC 20002 Tel (202) 275-7513

MURPHY, TERRENCE ROCHE, b. Laurium, Mich., Oct. 20, 1937; B.A., Harvard, 1959; J.D. with distinction, U. Mich., 1966. Admitted to D.C. bar, 1967, U.S. Supreme Ct. bar, 1971, U.S. Ct. Mil. Appeals bar, 1972. Trial atty. civil div. U.S. Dept. Justice, Washington, 1966-68; atty. firm Wald, Harkrader & Ross, Washington, 1968—, partner, 1972—. Mem. visitors com U. Mich. Law Sch., 1975—;

trustee Nat. Lawyers Com. Civil Rights Under Law, 1976—; chmn. D.C. Advisory Council Legal Services Corp., 1976—. Mem. D.C., Fed., Am. (chmn. trade regulation com., sec. adminstrv. law) bar assns., Am. Soc. Internat. Law, Washington Fgn. Law Soc. Author publs. in field. Home: 2934 28th St NW Washington DC 20008 Office: 1320 19th St NW Washington DC 20036

MURPHY, THOMAS LEE, b. Atlanta, Apr. 1, 1947; A.B., Ga. State U., 1969; J.D. Emory U., 1972. Admitted to Ga. bar, 1972; asso. firm Webb, Parker, Young & Ferguson, Atlanta, 1972-77; mem., dir. firm Webb, Young, Daniel & Murphy, Atlanta, 1977—; asst. dep. county atty. Fulton County (Ga.), 1975—. Tel (404) 522-8841

MURPHY, WALTER LEONARD, b. Boston, Dec. 11, 1937; B.S., Holy Cross Coll., 1959; J.D., Boston Coll., 1962. Admitted to N.H. bar, 1962; partner firm Batchelder & Murphy, Plymouth, N.H., 1964-70; individual practice law, Plymouth, 1970-72; partner firm Murphy & Deachman, Plymouth, 1972-74; judge Plymouth Dist. Ct., 1966-74; clk. N.H. Superior Ct., 1974-77; practice law, Plymouth, 1977—. Mem. N.H. (bd. govs.), Am., Grafton County (pres. 1968-70) bar assns., N.H. Superior Ct. Clks. Assn. Home: 1 Guinan Dr Plymouth NH 03264 Office: 66 Main St Plymouth NH 03264 Tel (603) 536-2300

MURPHY, WILLIAM CELESTIN, b. Chgo., Dec. 5, 1920; B.S., Harvard, 1942, LL.B., 1948. Admitted to Ill. bar, 1949; mem. firm Reid, Ochsenschlager, Murphy & Hupp, Aurora, Ill., 1948-52, partner firm, 1952—; lectr. Ill. Continuing Legal Edn. Inst.; corp. counsel City of Aurora, 1949-51. Mem. Ill., Am., Kane County (pres. 1974-75) bar assns. Office: 75 S Stolp St Aurora IL 60507 Tel (312) 892-8771

MURPHY, WILLIAM MICHAEL, b. Archbald, Pa., Jan. 9, 1913; A.B., St. Thomas Coll., 1937; LL.B., Dickinson Law Sch., 194. Admitted to Pa. bar, 1942, U.S. Dist. Ct. for Middle Dist. Pa. bar, 1942; gen. practice law, Scranton, Pa.; govt. appeal agt. SSS, 1967-76; judge advocate Lackawanna County Cath. War Vets., 1945-55. Home: 1650 Monsey Ave Scranton PA 18509 Office: 503 Mears Bldg Scranton PA 18503 Tel (717) 346-0789

MURRAY, ARCHIBALD R., b. Barbados, W.I., Aug. 25, 1933; A.B., Howard U., 1954; LL.B., Fordham U., 1960. Admitted to N.Y. State bar, 1960, So. Dist. N.Y. and Eastern Dist. N.Y., 1967; asst. dist. atty. N.Y. County, N.Y.C., 1960-62; asst. counsel to gov. N.Y., Albany, 1962-65; pvt. practice law, N.Y.C., 1965-67; cons. N.Y. Temporary State Commn. on Prep. for Constl. Conv., N.Y.C., 1966-67; counsel N.Y. State Crime Control Council, N.Y.C., 1967-68; counsel N.Y. State Office Crime Control Planning, N.Y.C., 1968-71; adminstr. N.Y. State Div. Criminal Justice, N.Y.C., 1971-72; commr. N.Y. State Div. Criminal Justice Services, N.Y.C., 1972-74; exec. dir., atty.-in-chief The Legal Aid Soc., N.Y.C., 1975—; mem. N.Y. State Council on Drug Addiction, 1965-67, N.Y. State Commn. on Revision Penal Law and Criminal Code, 1965-70, N.Y. State Interdepartmental Commn. Services to Children and Youth, 1974. Vestryman St. Philip's Episcopal Ch., 1970—, mem. standing com. Episcopal Diocese of N.Y., 1971-75, chancellor, 1975—, trustee Venture Fund, 1971—; mem. Community Service Soc., 1969-72; trustee St. Luke's Hosp. Center, 1971—; bd. dirs. 100 Black Men, 1972—. Mem. Assn. Bar of City N.Y., N.Y. State, Am. bar assns., Harlem, N.Y. County Lawyers Assns. Office: 15 Park Row 22d Floor New York City NY 10038 Tel (212) 577-3313

MURRAY, CORNELIUS DULLEA, b. Plattsburgh, N.Y., Aug. 5, 1944; A.B., Harvard, 1966; J.D., U. Mich., 1969. Admitted to N.Y. State bar, 1969, U.S. Supreme Ct. bar, 1976; law asst. appellate div., N.Y. State Supreme Ct., Albany, 1969-70; asso. firm O'Connell and Aronowitz, Albany, 1970-74, mem. firm, 1974—. Pres. Albany Child Guidance Center, 1977; v.p. Albany Jaycees, 1971. Mem. Albany County, N.Y. State, Am. bar assns., Nat. Health Lawyers Assn. Contbr. articles to legal jour.; lectr. meetings in Calif., Ill., N.Y., Ga. Home: 62-11 Woodlake Road North Albany NY 12203 Office: 100 State St Albany NY 12207 Tel (518) 462-5601

MURRAY, DANIEL FRANCIS, b. Wareham, Mass., Feb. 20, 1941; B.S., Coll. of Holy Cross, 1963; LL.B., U. Pa., 1966. Admitted to Mass. bar, 1966, U.S. Dist. Ct. for Mass., 1975; asso. firm George C. Decas, Middleboro and Wareham, Mass., 1970-74; individual practice law, Middleboro and Wareham, 1975—; asst. dist. atty. County of Plymouth (Mass.), 1973-75. Chmn. fin. com. Town of Wareham, 1975-76. Mem. Mass., Plymouth County (exec. com. 1977) bar assns. Home: RFD 1 Box 408 Great Neck Rd East Wareham MA 02538 Office: 132 N Main St Middleboro MA 02346 Tel (617) 947-4433

MURRAY, DANIEL RICHARD, b. Alexandria, La., Mar. 23, 1946; A.B., U. Notre Dame, 1967; J.D., Harvard, 1970. Admitted to Ill. bar, 1970, U.S. Supreme Ct. bar, 1974; partner firm Jenner & Block, Chgo., 1970—. Mem. Am., Ill., Chgo. (sec. devel. of law com.) bar assns. Home: 2800 N Lake Shore Dr Chicago IL 60657 Office: 1 IBM Plaza Suite 4400 Chicago IL 60611 Tel (312) 222-9350

MURRAY, DENIS LAWRENCE, b. Annapolis, Md., Aug. 10, 1942; A.B., Georgetown U., 1963, J.D., 1967. Admitted to D.C. bar, 1968, Md. bar, 1972; asst. gen. counsel Stewart's Mgmt. Corp., Washington, 1969-71; individual practice law, Washington, 1971-72; partner firm Ross, Lochte, Murray, Redding & Devlin, Bowie, Md., 1972—; atty. City of Bowie, 1972—. Bd. dirs. Bowie YMCA, 1972—, Bowie Multiple Sclorosis Soc., 1975—. Mem. Md., Prince George's County, D.C., Bowie bar assns., Md. Municipal Atty. Assn. Home: 1762 Regents Park Rd Crofton MD 21114 Office: 15518 Annapolis Rd Bowie MD 20715 Tel (301) 262-6000

MURRAY, FLORENCE KERINS, b. Oct. 21, 1916; A.B., Syracuse U., 1938; LL.B., Boston U., 1942; D.Ed. (hon.), R.I. Coll. Edn., Providence, 1956; LL.D. (hon), Bryant Coll., 1956, U. R.I., 1963, Mt. St. Josephs Coll., 1972, Providence Coll., 1974, Salve Regina Coll., 1977, others. Admitted to Mass. bar, 1942, R.I. bar, 1945, U.S. Supreme Ct. bar, 1944; partner firm Murray & Murray, Newport, R.I., 1942-56; asso. justice R.I. Superior Ct., Providence, 1956—; staff and faculty adviser Nat. Coll. State Judiciary, Reno, 1971, dir., 1975; sec. Commn. on Jud. Tenure and Discipline, 1975. Mem. Gov.'s Jud. Council, 1950-60, Gov.'s Adv. Com. on Revision Election Laws, 1950-52, Gov.'s Adv. Com. on Social Welfare, 1952, R.I. Com. on Youth and Children, R.I. Alcoholic Adv. Com., 1955-58, Gov.'s Adv. Com. on Mental Health, 1954, White House Conf. on Youth and Children, 1950, civil and polit. rights com. Pres.'s Commn. on Status Women, 1960-63, Ann. Assay Commn., 1952, Nat. Def. Adv. Com. on Women in Service, 1952-58; chmn. Newport Sch. Com., 1951-57, R.I. Com. for Humanities, 1972—, Family Ct. Study Com., 1956-58; legal adviser R.I. Girl Scouts, 1950-60; sec. R.I. Blue Shield, 1960—; vice-chmn. Nat. Blue Shield, 1968-69; mem. Boston U. Alumni Council, 1975-76; chmn. R.I. Nat. Endowment for Humanities Com.; mem. R.I. Senate, 1948-56, chmn. Spl. Legis. Com.; bd. dirs. Newport YMCA, founder, pres. Newport Girls Club, 1974-75; trustee Syracuse U.; bd. visitors Boston U. Law Sch.; mem. edn. policy and devel. com. Roger Williams Jr. Coll. Mem. Nat. (state chmn. membership com., sec. exec. com.), New Eng. (com. chmn. 1967) trial judges confs., Am. Bar Assn. (chmn. credentials com. 1972-73), Nat. Conf. State Trial Judges (chmn. credentials com. 1971-72), Am. Judicature Soc. (dir.), Am. Arbitration Assn., Kappa Beta Pi, Alpha Chi Omega. Recipient Arents Alumni award Syracuse U., 1956, Carroll award R.I. Inst. Instrn., 1956, Regina medal Salve Regina Coll., Newport, 1962, Alumni award Boston U., 1965, Outstanding Woman award Bus. and Profl. Women, 1972; mem. editorial bd. State Trial Judges Jour., 1960-64. Home: 2 Kay St Newport RI 02840 Office: 250 Benefit St Providence RI Tel (401) 277-3202

MURRAY, GEORGE A., b. Marion, Ill., Jan. 4, 1915; student So. Ill. U., 1947-49; LL.B., Cumberland U., 1953. Admitted to Mo. bar, 1955, Iowa bar, 1955; individual practice law, Cape Girardeau, Mo., 1955-60, St. Louis, 1960-62, 70—, Burlington, Iowa, 1962-70. Mem. Mo., Iowa bar assns. Home and Office: PO Box 6394 Saint Louis MO 63107

MURRAY, J. HARTLEY, b. Colorado Springs., Colo., Dec. 2, 1941; B.A., Colo. Coll., 1933; J.D., U. Colo., 1936. Admitted to Colo. bar, 1936; since practiced in Colorado Springs, partner firm Murray, Baker & Wendelken, 1936—; with JAGC, 1942-46. Pres. Colorado Springs Sch. Bd., 1953-55. Fellow Am. Coll. Trial Lawyers; mem. Am., Colo. (pres. 1972-73) bar assns., Am. Coll. Probate Counsel, Order of Coif, 1944. Home: 1706 N Prospect Colorado Springs CO 80907 Office: 301 Mining Exchange Bldg Colorado Springs CO 80903 Tel (303) 475-2440

MURRAY, JAMES CUNNINGHAM, b. Chgo., May 17, 1917; LL.B., DePaul U., 1940. Admitted to Ill. bar, 1940, U.S. Supreme Ct. bar, 1948; asst. atty. gen. State of Ill., 1946-50; regional enforcement dir. OPS, Chgo., 1950-52; asst. state's atty. Cook County (Ill.), 1952-54, 1st asst. state's atty., 1968-70; mem. 83d Congress from 3d Dist. Ill., 1954-56; partner firm Carey Tilten Murray & White, Chgo., 1956-68; judge Circuit Ct. Cook County, 1970—; alderman, Chgo., 1959-67; pres. pro tem Chgo. City Council, 1963-67, vice chmn. finance com., 1963-67; mem. Ill. Cts. Commn., 1976—. Mem. Chgo., Am. bar assns. Recipient Pacem et Terris award Quigley St. Mary's Lay Alumni, 1969, Chgo. Human Relations Commn. award, 1976. Home: 2850 S Seipp St Chicago IL 60652 Office: Daley Center Chicago IL 60602 Tel (312) 778-0415

MURRAY, JAMES JOSEPH, b. Rizal, Philippines, Oct. 14, 1938; A.B., cum laude, Tufts U., 1960; LL.B., Yale U., 1963. Admitted to N.Y. bar, 1964; law clk. to judge U.S. Dist. Ct., N.Y.C., 1963-64; asso. firm Chadbourne., Parke, Whiteside & Wolff, N.Y.C., 1964-67; asso. firm Lovejoy, Wasson, Lundgrent & Ashton, N.Y.C., 1967-71, partner, 1971—. Mem. Am., N.Y.C., N.Y. bar assns. Editor Yale Law Jour., 1962-63. Office: 250 Park Ave New York City NY 10017 Tel (212) 697-4100

MURRAY, JAMES THOMAS, JR., b. Racine, Wis., July 3, 1949; B.A., U. Wis., 1971; J.D. cume laude, Marquette U., 1974. Admitted to Wis. bar, 1974; law clk Wis. Supreme Ct., 1974-75; asso. firm Borgelt, Powell, Peterson, Frauen, Madison, Wis., 1975—. Mem. Wis. Bar Assn. Mem. Marquette Law Rev., 1972-74. Office: 828 N Broadway Milwaukee WI 53202 Tel (414) 276-3600

MURRAY, JOHN PATRICK, b. Anaconda, Mont., Jan. 27, 1931; B.S., Creighton U., 1956, J.D., 1959. Admitted to Nebr. bar, 1959, Fed. bar, 1959, Wash. bar, 1965; spl. agt. FBI, Dallas, and N.Y.C., 1959-61; mem. staff Spokane County Prosecuting Atty.'s Office, 1965-69, chief deputy, chief civil deputy, 1968-69; mem. firm Randall & Danskin, Spokane, 1969—; trust officer Old Nat. Bank, Washington, Spokane, 1961-65. Commr. Spokane County Civil Service Commn., 1969—; mem. criminal law task force Washington State Judicial Council, 1966-71. Mem. Am., Nebr., Washington, Spokane County bar assns., Estate Planning Council Spokane, Assn. Former Spl. Agts. FBI, Delta Theta Phi. Home: S 3405 Altamont St Spokane WA 99203 Office: 600 Lincoln Bldg Spokane WA 99201 Tel (509) 747-2052

MURRAY, JOHN RINGLAND, b. Oswego, N.Y., July 30, 1918; B.S. in Edn., State U. N.Y., Buffalo, 1942; LL.B., Columbia, 1947, J.D., 1969. Admitted to N.Y. bar, 1947, U.S. Dist. Ct. for No. Dist. N.Y. bar, 1947; dep. asst. atty. gen., State of N.Y., Oswego County, 1954-55; asst. dist. atty., Oswego County, N.Y., 1956-57, dist. atty., 1958-69, judge surrogate ct., 1970—. Mem. N.Y. State, Oswego County bar assns., Am. Judicature Soc., Surrogates Assn. N.Y. Home: 136 Lyon St Oswego NY 13126 Office: Court House Oswego NY 13126 Tel (315) 343-8650

MURRAY, MARSHALL HUGH, b. Eureka, Mont., Aug. 29, 1932; B.A., U. Mont., 1956, LL.B., J.D., 1956. Admitted to Mont. bar, 1956, U.S. Supreme Ct. bar, 1973; counsel ins. co., 1956-58; individual practice law, Missoula, Mont., 1958-59, Kalispell, Mont., 1959-68; partner firm Murray, Donahue & Kaufman, and predecessor, Kalispell, 1968—; dep. atty. Missoula County (Mont.), 1958-59; atty. City of Kalispell, 1961-68; spl. asst. atty. gen. State of Mont., 1972-77. Mem. Mont. Legislature, 1960-64; del. Mont. Constl. Conv., 1971-72; ruling elder, pres. bd. trustees 1st Presbyterian Ch., Kalispell; past pres. Mont. Consumer Affairs Council; mem. Flathead County (Mont.) Free Library Bd., 1973-75. Mem. State Bar Mont. (pres. 1975-76, trustee, mem. exec. bd.), N.W. Mont. Bar Assn. (past pres.), Western Trial Lawyers Assn. (Mont. gov.). Home: 239 Somerset Dr Kalispell MT 59901 Office: 240 1st Ave W Kalispell MT 59901 also PO Box 899 Kalispell MT 59901 Tel (406) 755-5700

MURRAY, PHILIP WILLIAM, b. Goshen, Ind., Sept. 5, 1939; B.S., Ind. U., 1961; LL.B., U. Mich., 1964. Admitted to Ohio bar, 1964; asso. firm Brouse & McDowell, Akron, Ohio, 1964; asst. law dir. City of Akron, 1965; asso. firm Roetzel & Andrews, Akron, 1966-71; partner firm Quine, Davis & Murray, Akron, 1971—; chmn. Little Hoover Commn. Task Force Studying County Govt., 1970. Mem. Akron, Ohio, Am. bar assns., Assn. Trial Lawyers Am. Home: 723 Palisades Dr Akron OH 44303 Office: 611 W Market St Akron OH 44303 Tel (216) 376-8111

MURRAY, RICHARD H., b. St. Paul, Sept. 20, 1936. Admitted to Minn. bar, 1961, U.S. Tax Ct. bar, 1964; asso. firm Randall, Smith & Blomquist, St. Paul, 1961-64; partner firm Oppenheimer, Wolff, Foster, Shepard & Donnelly, 1964-74; gen. counsel, prin. Touche Ross & Co., N.Y.C., 1974—; instr. William Mitchell Coll. Law, St. Paul, 1964-68. Pres. Chimera Theater Co., St. Paul, 1971-73, St. Paul Council Arts and Scis., 1973-74. Mem. Am., Minn. bar assns., Am. Judicature Soc. Home: 45 E 89th St New York City NY 10028 Office: 1633 Broadway New York City NY 10019 Tel (212) 489-1600

MURRAY, ROBERT BRUCE, b. Mpls., Apr. 3, 1927; B.A., U. Wis., 1950, LL.D., 1952. Admitted to Wis. bar, 1952, Colo. bar, 1952, U.S. Supreme Ct. bar, 1968; individual practice law, Colorado Springs, Colo., 1955-60, 67—; mem. firm Murray, Hecox and Tolley, Colorado Springs, 1960-67; hearing officer real estate commn., State of Colo., 1976—; pres. United Gold Mines Co., Condocorp Internat., Ltd. Chmn., Housing Authority of Colorado Springs, 1970-77; pres. Rocky Mountain Housing Found. Mem. El Paso County, Colo., Am. bar assns. Contbr. articles to legal jours. Home: 2607 Centre Ln Colorado Springs CO 80909 Office: 18 E Monument St Colorado Springs CO 80903 Tel (303) 634-1915

MURRAY, ROBERT YORK, b. Cambridge, Mass., Jan. 6, 1939; B.A., Georgetown U., 1961; J.D., Boston Coll., 1965. Admitted to Mass. bar, 1965, U.S. Supreme Ct. bar, 1972; asst. dist. atty. Suffolk County (Mass.), Boston, 1967-69, asst. atty. gen., chief drug div., 1969-72; asso. firm Moulton, Looney, Mazzone, Falk & Markham, Boston, 1968-72; partner firm Moulton & Looney, Boston, 1972—. Vice pres. bd. assos. Joseph P. Kennedy Meml. Hosp. for Children, Boston, 1974—; bd. dirs. Mass. Civil League, Boston, 1970—. Mem. Boston (com. civil procedure 1971—), Mass., Norfolk County, Fed. bar assns. Home: 65 Commonwealth Ave Boston MA 02116 Office: 50 Congress St Boston MA 02109 Tel (617) 742-5550

MURRAY, STEVEN WAYNE, b. Sacramento, Nov. 4, 1941; B.A., U. Calif., Los Angeles, 1963; J.D., U. So. Calif., 1967. Admitted to Calif. bar, 1968; individual practice law, Beverly Hills, Calif., 1968—, Los Angeles, 1972—. Mem. Los Angeles County, Beverly Hills bar assns. Office: 10880 Wilshire Blvd Suite 1101 Los Angeles CA 90024 Tel (213) 475-5703

MURRELL, JOHN MOORE, b. Sumter, S.C., July 27, 1897; student U. Fla., 1916-17; LL.B., Stetson U., 1919. Admitted to Fla. bar, 1919, U.S. Supreme Ct. bar, 1923; founder, partner firm Carson, Murrell & Farrington, Miami, Fla., 1921-25; partner firm Murrell & Malone, Miami, 1938-45, Murrell, Fleming & Flowers, 1945-50; individual practice law, Miami, 1950—; counsel U.S. House Jud. Com., Washington, 1933; spl. trial council City of Miami, 1942-46. Co-founder Humane Soc. Greater Miami, Bay Oaks Soroptimist Home for Aged, Miami; bd. dirs. Miami Heart Inst. Mem. Am., Fla. (v.p.) bar assns., Phi Alpha Delta (pres. alumni assn.). Home and Office: 1500 Brickell Ave Miami FL 33129 Tel (305) 377-0418

MURRELL, TURNER MEADOWS, b. Greensboro, N.C., Feb. 5, 1923; B.A., Wash. U., 1948; J.D., Washburn U., 1949. Admitted to Kans. bar, 1949, U.S. Ct. Mil. Appeals bar, 1956, U.S. Supreme Ct. bar, 1959; individual practice law, Topeka, 1949-50; judge adv. gen. USN, 1951-52; with firm Baker, Doherty & Murrell, 1952-53, Meyer, Gault, Marshall, Hawks & Murrell, 1954-61, Murrell, Scott & Quinlan, 1961-69, Murrell, Corrick, Bell & McGinnis, 1969-75, Murrell, Corrick & Coleman, 1975—; judge City of Topeka, 1953-56; chmn. bd. dirs., chmn., pres. Am. Investors Life Ins. Co., Inc., 1965—; chmn. bd. dirs. Nat. Investment Corp., Inc., 1968—, Internat. Investors Life Ins. Co., Inc., 1969—; pres. Am. Equity Fund, Inc., 1968—. Mem. Kans. Ho. of Reps., 1957-61, majority floor leader, 1959-61. Mem. Am., Kans., Topeka bar assns. Recipient Distinguished Service award City of Topeka, 1957, Young Man of Year award U.S. Jr. C. of C., 1957. Home: 421 Danbury Ln Topeka KS 66606 Office: 3301 Van Buren PO Box 5268 Topeka KS 66605 Tel (913) 266-4137

MURRY, GEORGE GORDON, b. Porterville, Calif., Oct. 3, 1912; A.B., Stanford U., 1934; J.D., Harvard, 1937. Admitted to Calif. bar, 1937; individual practice law, Gustine, Calif., 1938-70; atty. cities of Los Banos, Gustine and Newman, Calif., 1945-70; judge Merced County (Calif.) Superior Ct., 1970—. Mem. Merced County Bar Assn., Calif. Judges Assn. Office: Merced County Courts Bldg Merced CA 95340 Tel (209) 726-7364

MURRY, WILLIAM VAN, b. Colfax, La., Sept. 4, 1903; student La Salle Extension Sch. Accounting, 1934; LL.B., Cumberland U., 1936. Admitted to Miss. bar, 1937; individual practice law, Hattiesburg, Miss., 1937-73; instr. Cranston Bus. Coll., 1938. Mem. Miss. Cattle Assn. Recipient certificate of Appreciation, State Bar Assn. Home: 109 Park Hattiesburg MS 39401 Office: 204 Conner Bldg Hattiesburg MS 39401 Tel (601) 583-2680

MURTAUGH, MICHAEL KANNALLY, b. Evanston, Ill., July 12, 1944; B.A., Holy Cross Coll., 1966; J.D., U. Ill., Champaign, 1969. Admitted to Ill. bar, 1969; asso. firm Cooney & Stenn, Chgo., 1969-71, Baker & McKenzie, Chgo., 1971—. Mem. Chgo., Ill. bar assns., Chgo. Council Trial Lawyers. Office: 130 E Randolph St Chicago IL 60601 Tel (312) 565-0025

MURTAUGH, TIMOTHY JOSEPH, III, b. Evanston, Ill., Aug. 2, 1936; B.A., U. Notre Dame, 1958; J.D., U. Mich., 1961. Admitted to Ill. bar, 1962; U.S. Supreme Ct. bar, 1975; atty. Ill. Legislative Reference Bur., Springfield, 1962-63; asst. pub. defender Cook County, Ill., 1963-65; partner firm Murtaugh, Nelson & Sweet, Chgo., 1966—. Pres. Citizens Greater Chgo., 1974-75, chmn. bd., 1975—; v.p. 50th Ward Regular Democratic Orgn., 1971—; dir. North Town Community Council, 1971—. Mem. Chgo., Ill. State, Am. bar assns., Ill. Trial Lawyers Assn., Law Club Chgo. Contbr. articles to profl. jours. Home: 2700 W Morse St Chicago IL 60645 Office: 105 W Adams St Chicago IL 60603 Tel (312) 236-7268

MURTHA, JOHN STEPHEN, b. Hartford, Conn., Apr. 30, 1913; B.A., Yale, 1935, LL.B., 1938. Admitted to Conn. bar, 1938, U.S. Supreme Ct. bar, 1973; since practiced in Hartford, 1938—, partner firm Murtha Cullina Richter & Pinney, 1941—; asst. state's atty., Hartford County, 1946-51. Bd. dirs. Hartford chpt. ARC, Hartford Hosp.; trustee Hartford Rehab. Center, Boys' Clubs of Hartford; corporator St. Francis Hosp., Mt. Sinai Hosp., Inst. Living. Mem. Am., Conn., Hartford County bar assns., Am. Coll. Trial Lawyers. Home: 63 Avon Mountain Rd Avon CT 0600 Office: 101 Pearl St Hartford CT 06103 Tel (203) 549-4500

MURTHARIKA, ARTHUR PETER, b. Chola, Malawi, July 18, 1940; LL.B., London (Eng.) U., 1965; LL.M., Yale, 1966; J.S.D., 1969. Admitted to Tanzanian bar, 1970; lectr. Law U. Dar es Salaam, Tanzania, 1968-71; lectr. UN, Kampala, Uganda, summer 1969; vis. lectr. law Haile Selassie U., Ethiopia, 1970, 72; vis. prof. law Rutgers U., spring 1972; asso. prof. law Washington U., St. Louis, 1972—. Mem. Am. Soc. Internat. Law, Internat. Law Assn. Author: The Regulation of Statelessness under International and National Law, 1976; contbr. articles in field to law jours. Home: 6634 Pershing Ave St Louis MO 63130 Office: Washington U St Louis MO 63130 Tel (314) 863-0100

MUSE, LEONARD GASTON, b. Roanoke, Va., Jan. 1, 1897; B.A., Roanoke Coll., 1920; LL.B., U. Va., 1923. Admitted to Va. bar, 1923; partner firm Woods, Rogers, Muse, Walker & Thornton, Roanoke, 1923—; mem. Va. Senate, 1936-47. Pres. Va. State Bd. Edn., 1960-62; former rector bd. visitors Radford Coll., 1967-70; pres. Va. Bapt. Ch. Home; chmn. exec. com. Roanoke Coll. Mem. Roanoke (pres. 1935), Va., Am. bar assns., Am., Va., Internat. assns. ins. counsel. Home: Route 1 Box 117 Fincastle VA 24090 Office: PO Box 720 105 Franklin Rd Roanoke VA 24004 Tel (703) 342-1881

MUSGRAVE, ANNE SIGHTLER, b. Jefferson County, Ala., Aug. 15, 1890; studied law George Washington U. Admitted to D.C. bar, 1929; sr. mem. firm Musgrave and Sightler, Washington, 1930-48; individual practice law, Washington, 1948-68, Md., 1934-68. Active in various civic orgns.; past chmn. citizens com. for Prince Georges County, Nat. Reemployment Com.; past mem., chmn. Welfare Bd.; past bd. dirs. USO; chmn. George Washington Bicentennial, Laurel, Md., 1931-32. Mem. Am., D.C., Md., Prince Georges County bar assns., Am. Judicature Soc., Womens Bar Assn. D.C., Nat. Assn. Women Lawyers, Kappa Beta Phi. Contbr. articles in field to profl. jours.

MUSGRAVE, RAYMOND KENTON, b. Clearwater, Fla., Sept. 7, 1927; B.A., U. Wash., 1948; J.D., Emory U., 1954. Admitted to Ga. bar, 1953, Calif. bar, 1961; asst. gen. counsel Lockheed Aircraft Internat., Los Angeles, 1954-62; v.p. and gen. counsel Mattel, Inc., Hawthorne, Calif., 1962-72; sr. partner firm Musgrave, Welbourn & Fertman, Los Angeles, 1973-75; asst. gen. counsel Pacific Lighting Corp., Los Angeles, 1976—; dir. Orlando Bank and Trust Co. (Fla.); legal advisor LWV, Los Angeles. Vice-pres. Los Angeles S. Bay Harbor Vol. Bur.; bd. dirs. Palos Verdes Community Art Assn. Mem. Am., Calif., Inter-Am., Ga., Los Angeles County (chmn. corporate law sect. 1969-70) bar assns., Am. Judicature Soc. Home: 2717 Paseo Del Mar Palos Verdes Estates CA 90274 Office: 720 W 8th St Los Angeles CA 90017 Tel (213) 689-3265

MUSHKIN, MARTIN, b. Boston, Nov. 27, 1931; B.B.A., U. Wis., 1953; LL.B., Harvard, 1956. Admitted to N.Y. bar, 1956; 1st lt. JAGC, USAF, 1956-58; asso. firm Emile Zola Berman & A. Harold Frost, N.Y.C., 1958-60; sr. trial atty. N.Y. regional office SEC, 1960-64; practice with various firms, N.Y.C., 1964-70; partner firm Philips & Mushkin, Profl. Corp., N.Y.C., 1970—; course co-chmn. Practising Law Inst., 1975. Mem. Am., N.Y. State bar assns., Bar Assn. City N.Y. (spl. com. lawyer's responsibilities in securities transactions). Co-author: Am. Inst. C.P.A.'s Course Book on Accountants' Liability, 1977. Office: 360 Lexington Ave New York City NY 10017 Tel (212) 490-2700

MUSICK, JACK RITCHIE, b. Kingsport, Tenn., Apr. 26, 1928; A.B., Milligan Coll., 1950; LL.B., J.D., U. Tenn., 1955. Admitted to Tenn. bar, 1956; mem. firm Street, Banks, Merryman & Musick, Elizabethton, Tenn., 1956-68; judge 1st Jud. Circuit of Tenn., Elizabethton, 1968—. Mem. Am., Tenn. bar assns., Tenn. Jud. Conf., Milligan Coll. Alumni Assn. (past pres.). Home: 620 Woodland Dr Elizabethton TN 37643 Office: Ct House Elizabethton TN 37643 Tel (615) 542-5244

MUSKAL, JAMES BROWN, b. Chgo., July 28, 1938; B.M.E., U. Ill., 1960; J.D., DePaul U., 1963. Admitted to Ill. bar, 1963, U.S. Patent Office bar, 1965; asso. firm Leydig, Voit, Osann, Mayer & Holt, and predecessors, Chgo., 1962-71, mem., 1971—. Mem. Chgo. Patent Law Assn. Office: 1 IBM Plaza 4600 Chicago IL 60611 Tel (312) 822-9666

MUSKUS, EUGENE ANTHONY, b. Oak Park, Ill., Oct. 9, 1942; B.S. in Social Sci., Loyola U., Chgo., 1964; J.D., Cath. U. Am., 1968. Claims rep. Allstate Ins. Co., Hyattsville, Md., 1966-69; admitted to Md. bar, 1969; asst. state's atty. for Prince George's County, Md., 1969-72; partner firm Fisher & Walcek, Oxon Hill, Md., 1972—. Mem. coaching staff Ft. Washington (Md.) Recreation Dept., 1974—; mem. parish council St. Mary's Ch., Piscataway, Md., 1976; cubmaster Nat. Capitol area council Boy Scouts Am., Oxon Hill, 1976—. Mem. Md., Prince George's County bar assns., Nat. Dist. Attys. Assn., Fraternal Order Police. Office: 5410 Indian Head Hwy Oxon Hill MD 20021 Tel (301) 567-0700

MUSSELMAN, PETER ROGERS, b. Balt., Mar. 29, 1928; B.A., Harvard, 1949; J.D., Cleve.-Marshall Sch. Law, 1957. Admitted to Cleve. bar, 1957; v.p. Union Commerce Bank, Cleve., 1949-69, sec. bd. dirs., 1957-69; v.p. Case Western Res. U., Cleve., 1969—; pres. Univ. Circle Research Center, Cleve., 1973—; v.p. The Med. Center Co., Cleve., 1977—; dir. Westfield Growth Fund, Inc., Westfield Income Fund, Inc., Aero Distbrs., Inc. Past sec.-treas. Cleve. Clearing House Assn., Cuyahoga County Reward Commn., Cleve.; v.p. Citizens League Cleve., 1968-69; bd. dirs., treas. Cleve. Music Sch. Settlement, 1968-74, also trustee; mem. fin. com. YMCA; mem. fin. com. Fedn. Community Planning. Mem. Cleve. Bar Assn., Cleve. Soc. Security Analysts, Inst. Fin. Analysts, Cleve. Mus. Art, Western Res. Hist. Soc., Harvard, Hawken, Phillip's Exeter alumni assns. Chartered fin. analyst. Home: 11428 Cedar Rd C-7 Cleveland OH 44106 Office: 2040 Adelbert Rd Cleveland OH 44106 Tel (216) 368-4340

MUSSER, SAM FERGUSON, b. Harrisburg, Pa., July 14, 1924; B.A., St. Lawrence U., 1947; J.D., U. Va., 1950. Admitted to Pa. Supreme Ct. bar, 1950, U.S. Ct. Appeals 3d Circuit bar, 1962; individual practice law, Lancaster, Pa., 1950—; pres. Lancaster Title Abstracting Co., 1970—; pres. Conestoga Title Ins. Co., 1973—. Mem. Pa., Lancaster bar assns. Contbr. articles in field. Home: 201 S Church St Quarryville PA 17566 Office: 44 N Lime St Lancaster PA 17602 Tel (717) 397-2801

MUSSOLINE, JOHN D., b. Hazleton, Pa., Jan. 25, 1945; B.M.E., U. Fla., 1968, J.D., 1970. Admitted to Fla. bar, 1971; since practiced in Palatka, Fla., partner Walton Law Office, 1971-74, partner Walton, Mussoline & Townsend, 1974-75, Clark and Mussoline, 1975—. Mem. Putnam County Bar Assn. (legal aid chmn. 1974-75), U. Fla. Alumni Assn. (Putnam County dir.). Home: Rt 1 Box 20A East Palatka FL 32031 Office: PO Drawer V Palatka FL 32077 Tel (904) 328-2778

MUSTAKAS, GEORGE THEODORE, II, b. New Orleans, Aug. 17, 1943; B.A., La. State U., 1966; J.D., Tulane U., 1973. Admitted to La. bar, 1973; asst. atty. gen. organized crime unit La. Dept. Justice, New Orleans, 1973-76; partner firm Edwards, Porteous, and Lee, Gretna, La., 1975—; staff judge adv. 920th Weather Reconaissance Group, USAFR, Keesler AFB, Miss., 1974-77; legal advisor for res. officer assn. State of Miss. Vice pres. Gulf Coast Chpt. Res. Officers Assn.; mem. speakers bur. Gov. Carter presdl. campaign, 1976. Mem. La. State, Jefferson Parish bar assns., La. Trial Lawyers Assn., La. Dist. Attys. Assn. Office: 139 Huey P Long Ave Gretna LA 70053 Tel (504) 362-6111

MUSTO, JOSEPH JOHN, b. Pittston, Pa., Nov. 22, 1943; A.B., Kings Coll., Wilkes-Barre, Pa., 1965; J.D., Dickinson Law Sch., Carlisle, Pa., 1968. Admitted to Pa. bar, 1968; asst. dist. atty. City of Phila., 1968-69; asso. firm Bedford, Waller, Griffith, Darling & Mitchell, Wilkes-Barre, 1969-73; partner firm Griffith, Darling, Mitchell, Aponick & Musto, Wilkes-Barre, 1973-75; prin. firm Griffith, Aponick & Musto, P.C., Wilkes-Barre, 1975—; solicitor Pittston Area Sch. Dist., 1973—, Yatesville Borough, 1973—, Duryea Borough, 1975—. Mem. Luzerne County (Pa.) Govt. Study Commn., 1973-74. Mem. Am., Pa., Luzerne County bar assns., Am. Judicature Soc., Pa. Trial Lawyers Assn., Pa. Def. Inst. Home: 7 Prospect Pl Pittston PA 18640 Office: 408 Wilkes-Barre Center 39 Public Sq Wilkes-Barre PA 18701 Tel (717) 825-3495

MUTH, FREDERICK KLIEN, b. Huntington, W.Va., Jan. 11, 1947; B.B.A., Marshall U., 1969; J.D., W.Va. U., 1973. Admitted to W.Va. bar, 1973; asso. Robert W. Hensley, Bluefield, W.Va., 1973-74, partner, 1974—. Office: 301 Coal and Coke Bldg Bluefield WV 24701 Tel (304) 325-6217

MUTH, PAUL GREGORY, b. St. Louis, Mar. 12, 1912; LL.B., U. Dayton, 1935. Admitted to Ohio bar, 1935, U.S. Supreme Ct. bar, 1939; individual practice law, Vandalia, Ohio, 1935—; justice of peace Butler Twp., Montgomery County, Ohio, 1941-58; judge Municipal Ct., City of Vandalia, 1962-75; vol. fireman Butler Twp., 1938-60. Mem. Am., Ohio, Dayton bar assns. Office: 9385 N Dixie Dr Dayton OH 45414 Tel (513) 890-2232

MUTHARIKA, ARTHUR PETER, b. Cholo, Malawi, July 18, 1940; LL.B., London (Eng.) U., 1965; LL.M., Yale, 1966; J.S.D., 1969. Admitted to Tanzanian bar, 1970; lectr. Law U. Dar es Salaam, Tanzania, 1968-71; lectr. UN, Kampala, Uganda, summer 1969; vis. lectr. law Haile Selassie U., Ethiopia, 1970; vis. prof. Law Rutgers U., spring 1972; asso. prof. law Washington U., St. Louis, 1972—. Mem. Am. Soc. Internat. Law, Internat. Law Assn. Author: The Regulation of Statelessness under International and National Law, 1976; contbr. articles in field to law jours. Home: 6634 Pershing Ave MO 63130 Office: Washington U St Louis MO 63130 Tel (314) 863-0100

MUTSCHLER, JOHN GENE, b. Valley City, N.D., Feb. 8, 1928; B.S.C., U. N.D., 1950, J.D., 1953. Admitted to N.D. bar, 1953, Minn. bar, 1956; pres. John G. Mutschler & Assos., Inc., Mpls., 1958—. Mem. Minn. Bar Assn., Minn., N.D. socs. of C.P.A.'s. Office: 124 W 69th St Minneapolis MN 55435 Tel (612) 920-8703

MUTZ, GREGORY THOMAS, b. Indpls., Dec. 19, 1945; B.A., DePauw U., 1967; J.D., U. Mich., 1973. Admitted to Ill. bar 1973, U.S. Supreme Ct. bar, 1977; asso. firm Mayer, Brown & Platt, Chgo., 1973-76; corp. finance investment banker White, Weld & Co., Inc., Chgo., 1976—; gen. partner Mutz Properties, NWI Ltd.; dir. Unique Indoor Comfort Co., Iron Fireman Inc., Moncrief Inc. Mem. Am., Chgo. bar assns., Sierra Club. Office: White Weld & Co 30 W Monroe St Chicago IL 60603 Tel (312) 346-0022

MUTZEL, ROGER LOUIS, b. Lancaster, Pa., Apr. 27, 1938; B.A. in Pol. Sci., and English, Bucknell U., 1960; J.D., Temple U., 1963. Admitted to Pa. bar, 1963, Md. Ct. Appeals, 1964, U.S. Supreme Ct. bar, 1969; law clk. U.S. Dist. Ct. for Eastern Pa., 1966-68; partner firm Kassab, Cherry, Curran & Archbold, 1967—; solicitor Housing Devel. Corp. Chester (Pa.), 1970—, Delaware County Contractors Assn., 1969-73. Chmn. Delaware County br. Am. Cancer Soc., 1972. Mem. Am., Pa. trial lawyers assns. Home: 1012 Painters Crossing Chadds Ford PA 19317 Office: 214 N Jackson St Media PA 19064 Tel (215) 565-3800

MUYS, JEROME CHRISTIAN, b. N.Y.C., Sept. 7, 1932; A.B. magna cum laude in History, Princeton, 1954; LL.B., Stanford, 1957. Dep. atty. gen. Calif. Dept. Justice, San Francisco and Los Angeles, 1957-58; admitted to Calif. bar, 1958, D.C. bar, 1961; asso. firm Ely, Duncan & Bennett, and predecessor, Washington, 1958-65, partner, 1965-66; asst. gen. counsel, chief of legal staff Pub. Land Law Rev. Commn., Washington, 1966-70; vis. prof. law George Washington U., Washington, 1970-71; counsel to firm Charles F. Wheatley, Jr., Washington, 1971-73; partner firm Debevoise & Liberman, Washington, 1973—; adj. prof. internat. law of the sea George Washington U., 1972—. Officer, Battery Park Citizens' Assn., Bethesda, Md.; chmn. advisory com. Bethesda Pub. Library, 1967; mem. citizens' advisory com. to Md.-Nat. Capital Park and Planning Commn.; officer Bethesda United Methodist Church; chmn. Parents' Assn. Sidwell Friends Sch., Washington, 1972-74, trustee, 1973—. Mem. Am. Bar Assn. (mem. numerous coms. sect. on natural resources law, corp., banking, and bus. law, adminstrv. law), Internat. Law Assn. Contbr. articles in field to legal jours.; bd. editors Stanford Law Rev., 1955-57, asso. note editor, 1956-57. Home: 7501 Hampden Ln Bethesda MD 20014 Office: 806 15th St NW Suite 700 Washington DC 20005 Tel (202) 393-2080

MYDANICK, STEPHEN J., b. Bklyn., Dec. 31, 1936; B.A., Harpur Coll., 1958; LL.B., N.Y. U., 1961. Admitted to N.Y. bar, 1961; individual practice law, N.Y.C.; small claims arbitrator, N.Y.C., 1965—. Exec. v.p. Manhattan Beach Community Group. Mem. N.Y. Bar Assn., N.Y. Trial Lawyers Assn. Home: 12 Dock Ln Port Washington NY 11050 Office: 18 E 48th St New York City NY 10017 Tel (212) 371-8906

MYER, EDWARD HERMAN, III, b. Paterson, N.J., Nov. 5, 1943; B.S., U. Md., 1965, J.D., 1968. Admitted to Md. bar, 1968, D.C. bar, 1973; served to capt. JAGC, AUS, 1969-73; asso. firm Barbour & Zverina, LaPlata, Md., 1973—. Mem. Am., Charles County, D.C. bar assns., Order of Coif. Recipient Am. Jurisprudence award for domestic relations, 1968. Home: Ford Terr White Plains MD 20695 Office: 107 Saint Marys Ave LaPlata MD 20646 Tel (301) 934-2241

MYERS, ARNOLD BRIAN, b. Utica, N.Y., Jan. 6, 1940; B.A., Utica Coll. of Syracuse U., 1961; M.A., Duke, 1963; J.D., Hastings Coll. Law, 1969. Admitted to Calif. bar, 1970; asso. firm Abramson & Church, Salinas, Calif., 1970-72; mem. firm Abramson, Church & Stave, Salinas, 1972—. Mem. Am., Monterey County bar assns. Home: 109 Carmel Ave Salinas CA 93901 Office: Crocker Bank Bldg 3d Floor Salinas CA 93901 Tel (408) 758-2401

MYERS, C. BLAIN, b. New Martinsville, W.Va., July 31, 1946; B.A., Allegheny Coll., 1968; J.D., W.Va. U., 1971. Admitted to W.Va. bar, 1971; since practiced in Parkersburg, W.Va., asso. firm Malcolm Louden, 1971-73; individual practice law, 1973—; asst. pros. atty. Wood County, 1971-72, asst. city atty. Parkersburg, 1974—. Pres. Parkersburg Bicentennial Commn., 1974-76; mem. Wood County Commn. on Pornography, 1974, Little League Baseball Program, 1975-77. Mem. W.Va., Am., Wood County bar assns. Home: 1915 Foley Ave Parkersburg WV 26101 Office: 406 1/2 Market St Parkersburg WV 26101 Tel (304) 485-3678

MYERS, FREDERICK SAMES, b. Cuyahoga Falls, Ohio, Aug. 4, 1923; B.A., Case Western Res. U., 1946, LL.B., 1948. Admitted to Ohio bar, 1949, Md. bar, 1966; atty. Goodyear Aerospace Corp., Akron Ohio, 1953-61; atty. Goodyear Tire & Rubber Co., Akron, 1961-65, sec., counsel Kelly-Springfield Tire Co. subsidiary, Cumberland, Md., 1965-70, asst. counsel parent co., 1970-71, asst. sec., asst. gen. counsel, 1971-72, sec., asst. gen. counsel, 1972-73, v.p., gen. counsel, sec. 1973—; dir. Goodyear Bank, Akron. Bd. dirs. Summit County chpt. A.R.C. Served with AUS, 1943-46. Mem. Am., Ohio, Akron, Cleve. bar assns., Am. Soc. Corp. Secs.; Assn. Gen. Counsel, Delta Tau Delta. Home: 2970 Harriett Rd Cuyahoga Falls OH 44224 Office: 1144 E Market St Akron OH 44316*

MYERS, GEORGE, b. Troy, N.Y., June 30, 1902; A.B., Cornell U., 1923; J.D., Harvard U. Admitted to N.Y. State bar; v.p. O'Connel & Aronowitz, Albany, N.Y.; asst. corp. counsel City of Albany; chief atty. Office of Price Adminstrn.; city ct. judge, Albany, 1949-55. Mem. Albany County, N.Y. State bar assns. Office: 100 State St Rm 830 Albany NY 12207 Tel (518) 462-5601

MYERS, HOWARD NATHANIEL, b. Boston, Dec. 21, 1939; B.A., Ripon Coll., 1961; LL.B., U. Wis., 1964. Admitted to Wis. bar, 1966; law clk. Region 9, NLRB, Milw., 1964-66; asso. firm Schneidman & Myers, Milw., 1966-70, partner, 1970—. Mem. Am., Wis. bar assns. Home: 6243 N Berkeley Milwaukee WI 53217 Office: 735 W Wisconsin Milwaukee WI 53233 Tel (414) 271-8650

MYERS, JAMES DONALD, b. Columbia, S.C., Oct. 8, 1940; B.S. in Chem. Engring., U. S.C., 1963; J.D. cum laude, 1972. Admitted to S.C. bar, 1972, N.C. bar, 1974, U.S. Patent Office, 1976; law clk. to jr. chief judge U.S. Ct. Appeals, Richmond, Va., 1972-73; asso. firm Bell, Seltzer, Park & Gibson, Charlotte, N.C., 1973—. Mem. Am., S.C., N.C. bar assns. Mng. editor S.C. Law Rev., 1971-72. Home: 3833 Riverbend Rd Charlotte NC 28210 Office: PO Drawer 10337 Charlotte NC 28237 Tel (704) 377-1561

MYERS, JAY WALTER, b. Nescopeck, Pa., Mar. 17, 1921; A.B., Pa. State U., 1949; LL.B., Duke, 1952, J.D., 1956. Admitted to Pa. bar, 1954; practiced in Bloomsburg, Pa., 1954-72; pres. judge Pa. Ct. Common Pleas, 26th Jud. Dist., 1972—. Home: 424 Iron St Bloomsburg PA 17815 Office: Courthouse Bloomsburg PA 17815 Tel (717) 784-1991

MYERS, JEROME I., b. Phila., Nov. 26, 1895; J.D., Dickinson Sch. Law, 1919. Admitted to Pa. bar, 1919, U.S. Dist. Ct. bar Pa., 1923, U.S. 3d Ct. Appeals bar, 1937, U.S. Supreme Ct. bar, 1936; asst. mayor City of Scranton, Pa., 1920-22, city solicitor, 1934-46, dep. mayor, 1942-46; U.S. Commr., Middle Dist., Pa., 1928-42; dir., gen. counsel Green Ridge Bank (merged with Penn Security Bank & Trust Co. 1973), 1930—, pres., 1966-68. Mem. Am., Pa., Lackawanna bar assns. Elks. Home: 638 Taylor Ave Scranton PA 18510 Office: 414-415 Mears Bldg Scranton PA 18503 Tel (717) 342-3522

MYERS, JOSEPH NORWOOD, b. Indpls., July 30, 1915; A.B., Yale U., 1937; LL.B., U. Va., 1940, J.D., 1970. Admitted to Ind. bar, 1940; partner firm Myers, Northam & Myers, Indpls., 1940; gen. counsel Indpls. Legal Aid Soc., 1945-50; judge Marion County (Ind.) Municipal Ct., 1952—; pres. Indpls. Legal Aid Soc., 1954-56, dir., 1956-76; instr. in law Butler U.; writer, producer Indpls. Lawyers Gridiron Shows. Bd. mgrs. Central YMCA, Indpls.; asst. scout master troop 59 Indpls. council Boy Scouts Am.; coach Little League Baseball, Basketball, Indpls. Mem. Indpls. (v.p., bd. mgrs.), Ind. bar assns., North Am., Ind., Am. (gov.) judges assns., Yale Club of Ind. (sec. 1946-50), Indpls. Lawyers Assn. (pres. 1955-56), Delta Theta Phi. Decorated Air medal (U.S.); Croix de Guerre with palm, Medaille de la France Libere (France); Ky. col. Home: 4426 N Pennsylvania St Indianapolis IN 46205 Office: W-342 City-County Bldg Indianapolis IN 46204 Tel (317) 633-3350

MYERS, LOWELL JACK, b. Los Angeles, Jan. 26, 1930; B.S., Roosevelt U., 1951; M.B.A., U. Chgo., 1951; J.D., John Marshall Law Sch., 1956; admitted to Ill. bar, 1956; individual practice law, Chgo., 1956—. Mem. Am., Ill., Chgo. bar assns. C.P.A., Ill., D.C. Author: The Law and the Deaf, 1967; contbr. articles to legal jours. Home and Office: 1060 W North Shore Dr Chicago IL 60626 Tel (312) 875-9020

MYERS, MICHAEL JUSTIN, b. Mesa, Ariz., Nov. 2, 1943; B.S. in Econs., San Diego State U., 1965; J.D., U. Calif. at Berkeley, 1968. Admitted to Calif. bar, 1969; law clk. firm Gibson, Dunn & Crutcher, Los Angeles, 1967; asso. firm Gray, Cary, Ames & Frye, San Diego, 1968-74; sr. atty. litigation Atlantic Richfield Co., Los Angeles, 1974—; instr. Western State U., San Diego, 1974-75. Sec., Sigma Nu Meml. Scholarship Found., 1971—. Mem. Am., Calif. bar assns., Order of Coif, Phi Delta Phi. Office: 515 S Flower St Los Angeles CA 90071 Tel (213) 486-1569

MYERS, MILLER FRANKLIN, b. Aberdeen, S.D., Sept. 26, 1929; student Grinnell Coll., 1947-49; B.S. in Law, U. Minn., 1951, LL.B., 1953. Admitted to Minn. bar, 1953; exec. v.p. Dairy Queen Frozen Products of Can., Hamilton, Ont., 1954-60, pres., 1960-62; pres. Dairy Queen Nat. Devel. Co., St. Louis, 1962-65; v.p. Internat. Dairy Queen, Mpls., 1962-65, pres., 1965-70, chmn. bd., 1970-73; pres. Econo-Therm Energy Systems Corp., Mpls., 1974—. Active United Fund of Mpls., Planned Parenthood of Minn., Williams Scholarship Fund U. Minn. Mem. Am. Mgmt. Assn., Minn. Bar Assn., Young Pres's. Orgn. Home: 4810 Manitou Rd Tonka Bay MN 55331 Office: Econo-Therm Energy Systems Corp 11321 K-tel Dr Minnetonka MN 55343 Tel (612) 938-3100

MYERS, MOREY MAYER, b. Scranton, Pa., Aug. 5, 1927; A.B., Syracuse U., 1949; LL.B., Yale, 1952. Admitted to Pa. bar, 1952, U.S. Supreme Ct. bar, 1960; individual practice law, Scranton, 1952-60; mem. firm Parther, Gelb & Myers, Scranton, 1960—; asst. city solicitor Scranton, 1957-61; spl. asst. to atty. gen. Pa., 1962; chief counsel Milk Control Com. Pa., 1962-63; vis. prof. Marywood Coll. Sch. Social Work. Cons., Pres.'s Commn. on Student Unrest, 1970; chmn. Lackawanna United Fund, 1968; pres. Scranton Jewish Council, 1969-71. Mem. Am., Pa., Lackawanna bar assns. Contbr. articles in field to legal jours. Home: 1121 Myrtle St Scranton PA 18510 Office: 700 Scranton Life Bldg Scranton PA 18503 Tel (717) 342-8316

MYERS, RANDOLPH, b. Ebensburg, Pa.; A.B., St. Francis Coll., Loretto, Pa., LL.D. (hon.). Admitted to Pa. bar, U.S. Supreme Ct. bar; sr. mem. firm Myers, Taylor & Peduzzi, Ebensburg, Pa.; former bankruptcy judge U.S. Dist. Ct. for Western Dist. Pa.; dir., sr. v.p. Laurel Nat. Bank, Ebensburg; pres. Cambria Thrift Consumer Discount Co. Mem. pres's. cabinet St. Francis Coll. Mem. Am. (past pres.), Pa., Cambria County (Pa.) bar assns. Office: 213 S Center St Ebensburg PA 15931 Tel (814) 472-8190

MYERS, RAY F., b. Council Bluffs, Iowa, Aug. 22, 1920; A.B., DePauw U., 1941; LL.B., Harvard, 1948; postgrad. Stanford, 1966. Admitted to Ill. bar, 1949; with Continental Ill. Nat. Bank & Trust Co., Chgo., 1948—, exec. v.p., 1971—, corp. counsel, sec. bd. dirs., 1974—; dir. Nat. Ben Franklin Ins. Co. Sec.-treas., bd. dirs. Home for Destitute Crippled Children; trustee LaRabida Childrens Hosp. and Research Center, 1954—, pres., 1965-73; chmn. bd. regents Nat. Trust Sch., 1970-75; mem. Northwestern U. Assos.; mem. U. Chgo. Assos., mem. fund drive spl. gifts com. Mem. Am., Chgo. bar assns., Law Club, Legal Club, Chgo. Assn. Commerce and Industry, Am. Bankers Assn. (pres. trust div., dir. 1975-76), Am. Soc. Corp. Secs. Home: 1214 Brassie St Flossmoor IL 60422 Office: 231 S La Salle St Chicago IL 60693 Tel (312) 828-7490

MYERS, ROBERT DAVID, b. Springfield, Mass., Nov. 20, 1937; B.A., U. Mass., 1959; J.D., Boston U., 1962. Admitted to Ariz. bar, 1963, U.S. Dist. Ct. bar, 1963, U.S. Circuit Ct. of Appeals bar, 1964; mem. firm Harrison, Myers & Singer, P.C., Phoenix, Ariz., 1966—; mem. com. on Examinations and Admissions of the Ariz. Supreme Ct., 1970-75, chmn., 1974-75; mem. Com. on Character and Fitness of the Supreme Ct. of Ariz., 1975-77, chmn., 1975-77. Pres., Valley of the Sun chpt. City of Hope, 1965-66; active Community Orgn. for Drug Abuse Control, 1969—, pres., 1972-73; Selective Service voluntary govt. appeals agent, 1966-71; advisor to registrants, 1971—; chmn. Mayors Ad Hoc Drug Advisory Com., 1974-75; bd. dirs. Valley Big Bros., 1973—, pres., 1975. Mem. Maricopa County Bar Assn. (chmn. med.-legal liaison com. 1976—, sec. 1976-77), Am., Phoenix (pres. 1968-69), Ariz. (pres. 1970-71) trial lawyers assns., Am. Arbitration Assn., Nat. Panel of Arbitrators, Am. Judicature Soc., Am. Bd. of Trial Advocates, Western Trial Lawyers Assn. (pres. 1977), Nat. Conf. of Bar Examiners, Phoenix Assn. of Defense Counsel. Recipient Medal for Distinguished Pub. Service, Maricopa County Med. Soc., 1970, Certificate of merit, Phoenix chpt. U.S. Jaycees, 1970, Distinguished Leadership award, Am. Trial Lawyers Assn., 1971, Certificate of appreciation, Pres. of U.S., 1971; contbr. articles to legal jours. Office: 111 W Monroe St Phoenix AZ 85003 Tel (602) 252-7181

MYERS, SMITHMOORE PAUL, b. Cheyenne, Wyo., Mar. 26, 1914; B.A., Gonzaga Univ., 1936, J.D., 1939. Admitted to Wash. bar, 1940; asst. atty. gen. Wash., 1945-48; individual practice law, Seattle, 1949-55, Spokane, Wash., 1969-73; dean Gonzaga Law Sch., 1955-65, 75—, prof., 1973—; U.S. dist. atty. Eastern dist. Wash., 1966-69. Mem. Am., Wash., Spokane County (trustee) bar assns. Home: 705 S Lincoln Spokane WA 99204 Office: Gonzaga Law School 600 E Sharp Ave Spokane WA 99202 Tel (509) 328-0777

MYERS, WALLACE HASLETT, b. Worcester, Mass., Nov. 21, 1929; A.B., Clark U., 1951; J.D., Harvard, 1954; LL.M. in Taxation, Boston U., 1962. Admitted to Mass. bar, 1954, U.S. Tax Ct. bar, 1958; asso. Frank Howard, Worcester, 1957-62; mem. group law staff State Mut. Life Assurance Co. Am., 1963-67; individual practice law, Worcester, 1967—. Treas. Worcester County Republican Club; mem. Worcester Ward 10 Rep. City Com. Mem. Am., Mass., Worcester County bar assns. Home and Office: 78 1/2 Elm St Worcester MA 01609 Tel (617) 752-0855

MYERS, WHITFORD W., b. Raton, N.Mex., Aug. 8, 1920; J.D., U. Denver, 1948. Admitted to Colo. bar, 1949; since practiced in Alamosa, Colo., individual practice law, 1949-65; judge Municipal Ct., 1958-65; chief judge Colo. Dist. Ct., 12th Jud. Dist., 1965—; 1965—; rep. intermountain area to Colo. Jud. Adv. Council. Mem. Am., Colo., San Luis Valley (past pres.) bar assns., Nat. Council Juvenile Ct. Judges, Am. Judicature Soc. Office: Alamosa County Court House Alamosa CO 81101 Tel (303) 589-4996

MYERS, WILLIAM GEORGE, b. Heavener, Okla., May 12, 1924; B.S. in Physics and Chemistry, Southwestern La. Inst., 1944; M.A. in English, U. Ark., 1948; J.D., U. Mich., 1955; grad. U.S. Army Gen. Command Sch., 1949, U.S. Army Artillery Schs., 1950. Admitted to Mich. bar, 1955, Okla. bar, 1955, U.S. Ct. Mil. Appeals, 1955, U.S. Supreme Ct. bar, 1960, Ark. bar, 1971; commd. 2d lt. U.S. Army, 1949, advanced through grades to lt. col.; head Fgn. Claims Commn., Lebanon, 1958-59, Vietnam, 1963-64; command judge adv. 201st Logistical Command, Lebanon, 1958, Med. Center, Landsthul, Ger., 1959, Pine Bluff (Ark.) Arsenal, 1960-63, 4th Logistical Command, Fort Lee, Va., 1965-67, 2d Region, Air Def. Command, Richards-Gebaur AFB, Mo., 1967-70, ret., 1970; individual practice law Fayetteville, Ark., 1970—; pres. Willy-Gee, Inc., 1975—; justice of peace Washington County, Ark., 1973-76. Mem. Washington County Republican Com. Bd. dirs. Benevolent Bldg. Corp., Fayetteville, 1976—. Mem. Am., Okla., Ark., Washington County bar assns., Ret. Officers Assn., Republican Men's Club, Nat. Sojourners, Am. Legion, Ark. Boosters Club, Sigma Phi Epsilon. Decorated Bronze Star, Meritorious Service Medal; citation Lebanonese Minister of Def. Home: 764 Stone St Fayetteville AR 72701 Office: Suite 2-A Ozark Theater Bldg Fayetteville AR 72701 Tel (501) 442-6219

MYERS, WILLIAM HARBIN, b. Morton, Miss., Aug. 22, 1941; B.S. in Bus. Adminstrn., Miss. State U., 1964; J.D., U. Miss., 1969. Admitted to Miss. bar, 1969; asso. firm Bryan, Gordon, Nelson & Allen, Pascagoula, Miss., 1969-73; partner firm Gordon and Myers, Pascagoula, 1973-76, Pritchard, Myers & Gordon, 1976—. Bd. dirs. Gulf Coast YMCA, Ocean Springs, Miss., 1976—. Mem. Am., Miss. State, Jackson County (Miss.) bar assns., Am. Trial Lawyers Assn., Comml. Law League. Home: 1204 Bristol Blvd Ocean Springs MS 39564 Office: PO Drawer AA Pascagoula MS 39567 Tel (601) 769-7754 also 1200-A Washington Ave Ocean Springs MS

MYERS, WILLIAMS SIMS, JR., b. Tulsa, Feb. 6, 1924; B.S., U. Okla., 1946; J.D., Harvard, 1949. Admitted to Okla. bar, 1949, U.S. Supreme Ct. bar, 1954; asso. firm Edwin Whitney Burch, Oklahoma City, 1949-51; individual practice law, Oklahoma City, 1951-63; mem. firm Berry, Myers & Weiss, Oklahoma City, 1963-66; judge Oklahoma County Ct., 1966-67; judge 7th Jud. Dist. Okla., 1967—; with Judge Adv. Gen. Corps USAFR, 1951-76; asso. in law Oklahoma City U., 1975-76; lectr. U. Okla., 1954-55, 57-58. Bd. dirs. Oklahoma County Mental Health Assn., 1967-70; trustee Oklahoma County Law Library. Mem. Okla. (Merit awards 1968, 70, 74), Am., Oklahoma County bar assns. Recipient Brandeis award Harvard Law Sch., 1947; contbr. articles to Okla. Bar Jour. Home: 1704 Coventry Ln Oklahoma City OK 73120 Office: 807 County Courthouse Oklahoma City OK 73102

MYLES, KEVIN MILTON, b. Chgo., Oct. 17, 1948; B.A. in Liberal Arts and Scis. (Edmund Janes James scholar), U. Ill., 1970, J.D. (Theta Delta Chi scholar), 1973. Admitted to Ill. bar, 1974; asso. firm Fuqua, Fuqua & Winter, Waukegan, Ill., 1973-75, firm Snyder, Clarke, Dalziel, Holmquist & Johnson, Waukegan, 1975—; instr. debate team Lake Forest (Ill.) High Sch., 1976—. Clk. of vestry and adviser high sch. youth group Ch. of Holy Spirit, Lake Forest. Mem. Am., Lake County (Ill.) (exec. com. young lawyers sect. 1975—, vice chmn. law day com. 1976—), Ill. State bar assns., Theta Delta Chi. Home: 544 Onwentsia St Highland Park IL 60035 Office: 301 Washington St Waukegan IL 60085 Tel (312) 623-0120

MYMAN, ISRAEL, b. N.Y.C., Mar. 18, 1912; student Fordham U., 1931; LL.B., St. Lawrence U., 1934. Admitted to N.Y. bar, 1935; asst. corp. counsel City of N.Y., 1948-54; referee Unemployment Ins., N.Y. State Dept. Labor, 1975—. Home: 455 Franklin D Roosevelt Dr New York City NY 10002 Office: 299 Broadway New York City NY 10007 Tel (212) 349-1443

MYRICK, EDWARD DALTON, b. Lake Charles, La., May 28, 1944; J.D., Tulane U., 1970. Admitted to La. bar, 1970; asso. firm Anderson Leithead Scott Boudereau & Savoy, Lake Charles, 1971—. Mem. Am., La., S.W. La. (sec.-treas.) bar assns. Office: 901 Lakeshore Dr Suite 732 Lake Charles LA 70601 Tel (318) 439-2474

MYRTER, RONALD BERNARD, b. Curwensville, Pa., Sept. 4, 1927; B.S. in Commerce magna cum laude, U. Notre Dame, 1950; J.D., U. Pa., 1953. Admitted to Pa. bar, 1954, individual practice law, Clearfield, 1954-55; atty. Reliance Ins. Co., Phila., 1955-58; atty. H.J. Heinz Co., Pitts., 1958-59; atty. Ins. Co. of N. Am., Phila., 1959-66, asst. counsel, 1966-68, asst. gen. counsel, 1968-73, counsel, 1976—; counsel INA Corp., Phila., 1973-76. Mem. Am., Phila., Pa. bar assns., Pa. Def. Inst. Contbr. to legal publs. Home: 221 Foxcroft Rd Broomall PA 19008 Office: 1600 Arch St Philadelphia PA 19101 Tel (215) 241-4756

MYSE, GORDON, b. Kaukauna, Wis., June 9, 1935; B.A., Beloit Coll., 1957; LL.B., U. Mich., 1960. Admitted to Outagamie County bar, 1960; law specialist USN, 1961-64; partner firm Herrling, Hamilton & Myse, Appleton, Wis., 1964-72; judge Wis. Circuit Ct., 10th Jud. Circuit, 1972—; pres. Outagamie County (Wis.) Guidance Center, 1970; mem. Wis. Bd. Circuit Judges, 1972—; instr. Wis. Jud. Coll., summer 1976; mem. Wis. Council on Criminal Justice. Mem. ch. council Our Savior's Luth. Ch., Appleton, 1968-69; mem. Appleton Plan Commn., 1967-71; bd. dirs. Outagamie County Legal Aid Assn., Inc. Mem. Am., Wis., Outagamie County (exec. com. 1968-71) bar assns., Am. Trial Lawyers Assn., Wis. Trial Lawyers Assn. Home: 2614 N Elmwood Ct Appleton WI 54911 Office: 410 S Walnut St Appleton WI 54911 Tel (414) 739-0436

NABERS, JOSEPH LYNN, b. Brownwood, Tex., Mar. 31, 1940; B.S., Howard Payne U., 1962; J.D., Baylor U., 1967. Admitted to Tex. bar, 1967; partner firm Day & Nabers, Brownwood, 1969—; mem. Tex. Ho. of Reps., 1968—. Trustee Howard Payne U. Mem. Tex., Brownwood bar assns. Named Distinguished Alumnus, Howard Payne U., 1973. Home: 4 Quail Creek Rd Brownwood TX 76801 Office: 308 N Broadway Brownwood TX 76801 Tel (915) 646-6547

NACHMAN, M. ROLAND, JR., b. Montgomery Ala., Dec. 21, 1923; A.B. cum laude, Harvard, 1943, J.D., 1948. Admitted to Ala. bar, 1949, U.S. Supreme Court bar, 1953; asst. atty. gen. State of Ala., 1949-54; individual practice law, Montgomery, 1954-59; administrv. asst. Sen. John Sparkman, Ala., 1956; partner firm Steiner, Crum and Baker, Montgomery, 1959—; chmn. Human Rights Com. for Ala. Prison System, 1976—; permanent del. 5th Circuit Jud. Conf., 1975—; chmn. liaison com. Citizens Conference on Ala. State Courts, 1967-69; vice chmn. Permanent Study Commn. on Ala. Judicial System, 1972—; mem. Gov.'s Ethics Com. of Judiciary; mem. advisory commn. Appellate Practices for Ala. Supreme Court, 1971—; chmn. Second Citizen's Conference of Ala. State Cts., 1972-73; mem. Ala. Bd. Bar Examiners. Mem. Ala. (pres., 1973-74), Am. (mem. joint com. standards jud. discipline for judges and lawyers 1976—) bar assns., Am., Ala. law insts., Am. Judicature Soc. (dir., 1976—, recipient Herbert Lincoln Harley award) Am. Arbitration Assn., Nat. Assn. R.R. Trial Counsel. Recipient Ala. State Bar award Merit, 1974. Home: 3261 Thomas Ave Montgomery AL 36106 Office: 809 First Alabama Bank Bldg Montgomery AL 36104 Tel (205) 834-2222

NACHWALTER, GEORGE M., b. N.Y.C., July 6, 1935; B.A. in Polit. Sci., U. Miami, Coral Gables, Fla., 1957, J.D., 1960. Admitted to Fla. bar, 1960, D.C. bar, 1973; asso. firms Kellner & Lewis, Miami, Fla., 1960-61, Levine & Christie, Miami, 1961; partner firms Nachwalter & Silverstein, Miami, 1961-70, Nachwalter, Christie & Falk, Profl. Assn. and predecessor, Miami, 1970—; judge Dade County (Fla.) Municipal Ct., 1964-72. Active Boy Scouts Am.; pres. Parents for Pkwy. Children Center, Miami. Mem. Nat., Fla. (pres.) municipal judges assns., Am., Fla., Dade County, South Miami (pres.) bar assns., Am. Arbitration Assn. (arbitrator), Am. Judicature Soc., Wig and Robe Soc., Omega Delta Kappa, Tau Epsilon Rho (treas.). Recipient Roger Sorino award U. Miami, 1960. Office: 9211 Bird Rd Miami FL 33165 Tel (305) 223-2391

NACHWALTER, MICHAEL, b. N.Y.C., Aug. 31, 1940; B.S., Bucknell U., 1962; M.S., L.I. U., 1968; J.D. cum laude, U. Miami, Coral Gables, Fla., 1967; LL.M. (Stirling fellow), Yale, 1968. Admitted to Fla. bar, 1967, U.S. Supreme Ct. bar, 1972; law clk. to judge U.S. Dist. Ct. for So. Dist. Fla., 1967; pros. atty. City of South Miami, Fla., 1968-69; partner firm Kelly Black Black & Kenny, P.A., Miami, Fla., 1968—; lectr. law U. Miami, 1969-75; spl. counsel to Fla. Bar, 1973-75. Mem. exec. com. Fla. Consumer Council, 1974—. Mem. Am., Fla. (chmn. com. consumer protection 1974-75), Dade County (Fla.) (chmn. com. legal ethics), Fed. bar assns., Am. Judicature Soc., Phi Kappa Phi, Iron Arrow, Wig & Robe, Omicron Delta Kappa. Named Outstanding Graduating Sr., U. Miami Sch. Law, 1967; editor in chief U. Miami Law Rev., 1965-66. Home: 13800 SW 82d Ave Miami FL 33158 Office: 1400 du Pont Bldg Miami FL 33131 Tel (305) 358-5700

NADER, RALPH, b. Winsted, Conn., Feb. 27, 1934; A.B. magna cum laude, Princeton, 1955; LL.B. with distinction, Harvard, 1958. Admitted to Conn. bar, 1958, Mass. bar, 1959, also U.S. Supreme Ct. bar; practiced in Hartford, Conn., from 1959; lectr. history and govt. U. Hartford, 1961-63; founder Center for Responsive Law, Pub. Interest Research Group, Center for Auto Safety, Profls. for Auto Safety, Project for Corporate Responsibility; lectr. to colls. and univs.; lectr. Princeton, 1967-68. Served with AUS, 1959. Recipient Nieman Fellows, award 1965-66; named One of 10 Outstanding Young Men of Year, U.S. Jr. C. of C., 1967. Mem. Am. Bar Assn., A.A.A.S., Phi Beta Kappa. Author: Unsafe at Any Speed, 1965, rev., 1972; Beware, 1971; Working on the System: A Manual for Citizen's Access to Federal Agencies, 1972; co-author: What To Do with Your Bad Car, 1971; Action for a Change, 1972; You and Your Pension, 1973. Editor: Whistle Blowing: The Report on the Conference on Professional Responsibility, 1972; The Consumer and Corporate Accountability, 1973; co-editor Corporate Power in America, 1973; contbg. editor Ladies Home Jour., 1973—; also articles. Address: PO Box 19367 Washington DC 20036*

NADITCH, RONALD MARVIN, b. Balt., Oct. 3, 1937; B.A., Dickinson Coll., 1959; J.D., U. Md., 1962. Admitted to Md. bar, 1962; law clk. to judge Md. Ct. Appeals, 1962-63; asso. firm Goodman & Bloom, Annapolis, Md., 1964-65; asst. state's atty. Anne Arundel County (Md.), 1966—; individual practice law, Annapolis, 1965—; mem. Md. Atty. Grievance Rev. Bd., 1975—. Chmn., Annapolis Human Relations Commn., 1970-72. Mem. Am., Md. bar assns., Nat. Dist. Attys. Assn., Md. State's Attys. Assn. (dir. 1974—), Am., Md. trial lawyers assns. Contbr. articles to legal jours. Home: 12 Romar Dr Annapolis MD 21403 Office: 49 Cornhill St Annapolis MD 21401 Tel (301) 268-3434

NADLER, MYRON JAY, b. Youngstown, Ohio, July 22, 1923; student N.Mex. State Coll., 1943-44; B.S. in Econs., U. Pa., 1947; J.D. with distinction, U. Mich., 1949. Admitted to Ohio bar, 1950; partner firm Nadler, & Nadler, Youngstown, 1950—; dir. Union Nat. Bank of Youngstown; instr. law Youngstown U., 1952-59. Co-chmn. Mayor's Commn. Human Rights, Youngstown, 1957; chmn. exec. budget com. United Appeal, Youngstown, 1964-66, v.p., 1967-70; trustee Community Corp., Youngstown. Mem. Ohio Bar Assn. Found., Scribes Assn. Legal Writers, Comml. Law League Am., Ohio Bar Assn. Author: (with Saul Nadler) Nadler on Bankruptcy, 1965. Contbr. articles in field to profl. jours. Home: 2456 5th Ave Youngstown OH 44505 Office: 900 Dollar Bank Bldg Youngstown OH 44503 Tel (216) 744-0247

NAFF, JOHN MARION, JR., b. Birmingham, Ala., June 13, 1923; A.B. summa cum laude, U. Tex., Austin, 1944; J.D. magna cum laude, Harvard, 1947; B.A. first class, Oxford (Eng.) U., 1949, M.A., 1954. Admitted to Calif. bar, 1950, U.S. Supreme Ct. bar, 1970; asst. prof. law U. Tex., Austin, 1947; asso. firm Brobeck, Phleger & Harrison, San Francisco, 1949-60, partner, 1960-70; legal asst. U.S. Dist. Ct., No. Dist. Calif., San Francisco, 1970-74; supervising staff atty. U.S. Ct. Appeals 9th circuit, San Francisco, 1974—. Mem. State Bar Calif., Bar Assn. San Francisco, Am. Bar Assn., Phi Beta Kappa. Home: 640 Occidental Ave San Mateo CA 94402 Office: US Court of Appeals POB 547 San Francisco CA 94101 Tel (415) 556-7361

NAGLE, JOE, b. Middlesboro, Ky., Nov. 24, 1928; A.B., U. Ky., 1950, LL.B., 1952. Admitted to Ky. bar, 1952; spl. agt. FBI, 1958-61; asst. atty. gen. Ky., 1962-64; city atty. Middlesboro, 1968-70; commonwealth's atty. Bell County (Ky.), 1976—. Home: 815 Cirencester St Middlesboro KY 40965 Office: 2201 1/2 Cumberland Ave Middlesboro KY 40965 Tel (606) 248-2765

NAGLER, GEORGE IRVIN, b. Calgary, Alta., Dec. 11, 1936; B. Commerce, Univ. B.C., 1958; J.D., Harvard, 1969. Admitted to Calif. bar, 1970; asso. firm Greenberg & Glusker, Los Angeles, 1969-72, firm Silverberg, Rosen & Leon, Los Angeles, 1972-75, partner, 1976—. Mem. Am., Calif., Los Angeles County bar assns. Home: 1013 Loma Vista Dr Beverly Hills CA 90210 Office: 1880 Century Park East #1100 Los Angeles CA 90067 Tel (213) 277-4500

NAGY, STEPHEN ROBERT, b. Elyria, Ohio, Apr. 23, 1926; B.A., Wittenberg Coll., 1946; J.D., U. Cin., 1949; certificates Nat. Coll. State Judiciary U. Nev., 1974, 75, 76, Ohio Judicial Coll., 1977. Admitted to Ohio bar, 1950; individual practice law, Elyria, 1950-74; judge Elyria Municipal Ct., 1974—. Mem. Lorain County, Ohio State, Am. bar assns., Am. Judges Assn., Am. Jurisprudence Soc. Recipient award Ohio Supreme Ct., 1974, 75, 76. Office 327 Broad St Elyria OH 44035 Tel (216) 322-1918

NAHSTOLL, RICHARDSON WADSWORTH, b. Washington, July 8, 1918; A.B., Mich. State U., 1940; LL.B., U. Mich., 1946. Admitted to Mich. bar, 1946, Oreg. bar, 1947, U.S. Supreme Ct. bar, 1953; partner firm Eben & Nahstoll, 1947-60; partner firm Lindsay, Nahstoll, Hart & Krause, Portland, Oreg., 1960—. Mem. Oreg. (mem. bd. govs. 1962-65; pres. 1964-65), Am. (chmn. sect. legal edn. 1974-75) bar assns. Author: Ross Essay, 1964. Office: 1331 SW Broadway Portland OR 97201 Tel (503) 226-1191

NAILS, KENNETH HARRY, b. Chgo., Jan. 5, 1942; B.A., Ill. Benedictine Coll., 1963; J.D., John Marshall Law Sch., 1968. Admitted to Ill. bar, 1968; atty. Am. Mut. Ins. Alliance, Chgo., 1968-69, asst. counsel, 1969-70, asso. counsel, 1970-71, counsel, 1971-74, asst. gen. counsel, 1974-75, asso. gen. counsel, 1975-77, v.p. govt. affairs, 1977—; mem. faculty Coll. of Ins., N.Y.C., 1975—; sec. Nat. Com. Ins. Guaranty Funds, 1971-75; mem. industry adv. com. Nat. Assn. Ins. Commrs., 1969—. Pres. Clarefield Homeowners Assn., Darien, Ill., 1970—. Mem. Am. (ins. panel negligence, compensation and negligence sect.), Ill. bar assns. Office: 20 N Wacker Dr Chicago IL 60606 Tel (312) 346-5190

NAJARIAN, MELVIN KENNETH, b. Fresno, Calif., Sept. 16, 1939; B.A. in Econs., U. Calif., Los Angeles, 1961, J.D., Berkeley, 1964. Admitted to Calif. bar, 1965, D.C. bar, 1970; served to maj. JAGC, U.S. Army, 1965-69; gen. counsel Peace Corps, Washington, 1969-70; regional counsel ACTION, San Francisco, 1972-73; partner firm Haas & Najarian, San Francisco, 1973—; mem. faculty U. Md., Heidelberg, W.Ger., 1967-69; cons. to dir. ACTION, Washington, 1973—. Mem. Bar Assn. San Francisco. Recipient award of Distinction, Black Bus. Assn., 1976. Office: 451 Jackson St San Francisco CA 94111 Tel (415) 788-6330

NAKAMURA, KENNETH HISAO, b. Lihue, Hawaii, May 1, 1928; B.S., U. Hawaii, 1951; LL.B., U. Wis., 1956. Admitted to Hawaii bar, 1956, U.S. Supreme Ct. bar, 1961; dep. pros. atty. City of Honolulu, 1957-59; adminstrv. asst. to U.S. senator, 1959-62; partner firm Nakamura & Low, Honolulu, 1962—; mem. Hawaii Ho. of Reps., 1962-64. Chmn. Hawaii Republican Party, 1962-64; mem. Hawaii adv. com. U.S. Civil Rights Commn., 1962-64. Mem. Am., Hawaii bar assns., Am. Trial Lawyers Assn. Office: Suite 200 333 S Queen St Honolulu HI 96813 Tel (808) 531-1681

NAKELL, BARRY DAVID, b. Detroit, Oct. 21, 1942; student U. Calif., Los Angeles, 1960-63; LL.B., U. Ill., 1966. Admitted to Calif. bar, 1966, D.C. bar, 1974; law clk. to Hon. Roger J. Traynor, Chief Justice of Calif., San Francisco, 1966-67; asso. firm Kaplan, Livingston, Goodwin, Berkowitz & Selvin, Beverly Hills, Calif., 1967-68, firm Margolis & McTernan, Los Angeles, 1968-70; asst. prof. law U. N.C., 1970-73, asso. prof., 1973—; staff D.C. Pub. Defender Service, 1974-75. Contbr. articles to legal jours. Home: 1310 Le Clair St Chapel Hill NC 27514 Office: School of Law U NC Chapel Hill NC 27514 Tel (919) 933-5106

NAKULAK, GEORGE KALENCH, b. N.Y.C., Nov. 22, 1927; B.S., Fordham U., 1949; LL.B., N.Y. Law Sch., 1954. Admitted to N.Y. bar, 1954, N.J. bar, 1973; atty. N.Y.C. Transit Authority, 1961-75, atty.-in-charge Workmen's Compensation Bur. Office: Two World Trade Center New York City NY 10048 Tel (212) 466-6573

NAMAN, WILFORD WOLFIE, b. Waco, Tex., Mar. 6, 1887; B.A., Yale, 1908; postgrad. N.Y. U., 1910. Admitted to Tex. bar, 1911; asso. firm Naman, Howell, Smith Lee & Muldrow and predecessors, Waco, 1917-31, partner, 1931, sr. partner, 1931—; chmn. bd. dirs. State Bar Tex., 1952-53; pres., chmn. bd. dirs. KWTX Broadcasting Co., Waco, 1953-64. Chmn., Waco Charter Commn., 1976; mem. Waco Parks and Recreation Commn., 1976. Fellow Am., Tex. bar founds., Am. Coll. Trial Lawyers, Am. Coll. Probate Counsel; mem. Am., Waco-McLennan County (past pres.) bar assns., Named Outstanding Citizen, City of Waco, 1922, Outstanding Tex. Lawyer, Tex. Bar Found., 1975; Southwestern Legal Found. research fellow, 1975. Home: 3805 Castle Dr Waco TX 76710 Office: 700 Texas Center Waco TX 76701

NANCE, CECIL BOONE, JR., b. Marion, Ark., Feb. 14, 1925; LL.B., U. Ark., 1951. Admitted to Ark. bar, 1951, U.S. Supreme Ct. bar, 1963; partner firm Nance, Nance, Fleming & Wood, and predecessors, W. Memphis, Ark., 1951—; mem. Ark. Ho. of Reps., 1957-68. Mem. Am. (vice chmn. video equipment com., econ. sect. 1975-76), Ark. (chmn. jr. bar sect. 1957-58) bar assns., Am. Judicature Soc., Am., Ark. trial lawyers assns. Home: 506 Roosevelt St West Memphis AR 72301 Office: 222 N 6th St West Memphis AR 72301 Tel (501) 735-3310

NANCE, JAMES HOMER, b. Gadsden, Ala., Jan. 6, 1931; A.B., Stetson U., 1953; J.D., U. Miami, 1956. Admitted to Fla. bar, 1957; asst. state atty. Dade County, Fla., 1958; now practice in Melbourne, Fla.; lectr. continuing legal edn. Fla. Bar. Fellow Roscoe Pound Am. Trial Lawyers Found. (life); mem. Am., Brevard County, Fla. bar assns., Assn. Trial Lawyers Am., Acad. Fla. Trial Lawyers, Inner Circle Advocates. Home: 150 Poinciana St Indian Harbour Beach FL 32935 Office: 525 N Harbor City Blvd Melbourne FL 32935 Tel (305) 254-8416

NANGLE, JAMES FRANCIS, JR., b. St. Louis, July 25, 1930; B.S. in Accounting, St. Louis U., 1954, J.D., 1954. Admitted to Mo. bar, 1954, U.S. Supreme Ct. bar, 1970; individual practice law, St. Louis, 1954—; lectr. in field. Mem. Am., Mo., St. Louis bar assns., Lawyers Assn. St. Louis. Office: 408 Olive St Saint Louis MO 63102 Tel (314) 241-6116

NAPHEYS, BENJAMIN FRANKLIN, III, b. Kansas City, Mo., Apr. 17, 1936; A.B., U. Colo., 1957., J.D., U. Denver, 1964. Admitted to Colo. bar, 1964, U.S. Supreme Ct. bar, 1971; mem. firm Harden and Napheys and predecessors, Ft. Collins, Colo., 1967—; asst. county atty., Larimer County, Colo., 1968—. Chmn. Larimer County Republican Central Com., 1971-73; mem. Ft. Collins Human Relations Commn., 1973—, chmn., 1977—. Mem. Am., Colo., Larimer County (pres. 1976-77) bar assns. Home: 1817 Rangeview Dr Fort Collins CO 80521 Office: PO Box 1606 Fort Collins CO 80522 Tel (303) 482-7777

NAPHTALI, LOUIS BANNY, b. N.Y.C., June 15, 1931; B.A., Bklyn. Coll., 1952; J.D., Bklyn. Law Sch., 1958, M.L., 1961. Admitted to N.Y. bar, 1959; claim examiner Allstate Ins. Co., Bklyn., 1958-64; partner firm Armstrong, Naphtali & Schulman, Bklyn., 1959-68; asst. claims mgr. Am. Fidelity & Fire Ins. Co., Westbury, N.Y., 1964-68; asso. firm Jones, Jenkins & Warden, Bklyn., 1968-74; individual practice law, Bklyn., 1974—; adj. instr. bus. law Fashion Inst. Tech., N.Y.C. Mem. N.Y. Trail Lawyers Assn., Assn. Immigration and Naturalization Lawyers. Home: 1448 E 85th St Brooklyn NY 11236 Office: 66 Court St Brooklyn NY 11201 Tel (212) 625-1666

NAPIER, JACK RAYMOND, II, b. Breckenridge, Tex., Mar. 13, 1937; B.B.A., U. Tex., 1965, LL.B., 1965. Admitted to Tex. bar, 1965, U.S. Supreme Ct. bar, 1965; individual practice law, Dallas, 1965—. Mem. State Bar Tex., Am., Dallas bar assns., Am., Tex., Dallas trial lawyers assns., Tex. Criminal Def. Lawyers Assn. Home: 4131 Calculus Rd Dallas TX 75234 Office: Suite 808 5050 N Ervay St Dallas TX 75201 Tel (214) 748-0183

NAPOLI, JOSEPH PETER, b. Bklyn., Sept. 10, 1942; B.A., St. Johns U., 1963, J.D., 1967; LL.M., N.Y. U., 1971. Admitted to N.Y. bar, 1967; asso. firm McLaughlin, Fiscella & Gervais, N.Y.C., 1967-68; partner firm Lipsig, Napoli, Sullivan, Mollen & Liapakis, N.Y.C., 1968-76, Schneider, Kleinick, Weitz & Napoli, P.C., 1976—. Mem. Am., N.Y. State bar assns., Am. Trial Lawyers Assn., Assn. Bar City N.Y., N.Y. County Lawyers Assn., Fed. Bar Council, Am. Arbitration Assn. (med. malpractice panel). Sr. editor Trial Lawyers Quar.; contbr. articles to legal jours. Home: 20 Blackburn Ln Manhasset NY 11030 Office: 11 Park Pl New York City NY 10007 Tel (212) 962-1780

NAPPER, JAMES HAROLD, II, b. Ruston, La., Nov. 27, 1946; B.S. in Bus., La. Tech. U., 1968; J.D., La. State U., 1970. Admitted to La. bar, 1970; partner Slotwell, Brown & Sperry, Monroe, La., 1975—. Home: 2706 Crestmont St Monroe LA 71201 Office: PO Box 1591 Monroe LA 71201 Tel (318) 388-4700

NARANJO, DANIEL ALBERTO, b. San Antonio, Aug. 16, 1939; B.A., U. Tex., 1962, J.D., 1963. Admitted to San Antonio bar, 1967, U.S. Supreme Ct. bar, 1971; spl. agt. Office Special Investigations U.S. Air Force Hdqrs. Command, Washington, 1963-67; of counsel Nicholas & Barrera, Inc., San Antonio, 1968—; chmn. drug abuse program com. State Jr. Bar Tex., 1972-74, dist. dir., 1972-73, steering com. Vols. in Parole; chmn. com. to increase minority participation in bar State Bar Tex., 1975-76, grievance pros. com. 10th dist., 1976—. Bd. dirs. San Antonio Campfire Girls, Inc., 1970—, Citizens for Better Environment, San Antonio, 1974—, San Antonio Drug Abuse Central, 1973-74; mem. San Antonio Areawide Planning Adv. Com., 1976—. Mem. Am., Inter-Am., San Antonio (chmn. justice and municipal cts. com. 1972-73, dir. 1974-75, sec.-treas. 1975-76) bar assns., San Antonio Trial Lawyers Assn., Tex. Criminal Def. Lawyers Assn., San Antonio Young Lawyers Assn. (v.p. 1970-72, dir. 1972-74), Catholic Lawyers Guild (v.p. 1971, pres. 1972), Delta Theta Phi. Home: 731 Patricia San Antonio TX 78216 Office: 424 E Nueva by La Villita San Antonio TX 78205 Tel (512) 224-5811

NARDONE, CHARLES ALFRED, b. Westerly, R.I., Mar. 16, 1933; LL.B., Boston U., 1956. Admitted to R.I. bar, 1957; individual practice law, Westerly, 1958-67; partner firm Nardone Turo Liguori & Orsinger and predecessor, Westerly, 1967—. Mem. Westerly Planning Bd.; atty. Westerly Fire Dist., 1960—; mem. Westerly Municipal Conservation Commn., 1960-76. Mem. R.I., Washington County (treas. 1960-70) bar assns., R.I. Mobile Sports Fishermen (dir.). Home: Pond View Dr Westerly RI 02891 Office: 47 High St Westerly RI 02891 Tel (401) 596-0321

NARUK, HENRY JOHN, b. Middletown, Conn., May 22, 1928; B.A., Wesleyan U., Middletown, 1950; LL.B., Harvard, 1953. Admitted to Conn. bar, 1953; practiced in Hartford, 1953-54, Torrington, Conn., 1954-65; pros. atty. City Ct. of Torrington, 1954-60; corp. counsel City of Torrington, 1964-65, judge Circuit Ct., 1965-68, Ct. Common Pleas, 1968-70, Conn. Superior Ct., Middletown, 1970—; lectr. constl. law Wesleyan U., 1954; faculty advisor Nat. Coll. State Trial Judges, 1973. Corporator Farmers & Mechs. Savings Bank, Middletown, Middlesex Meml. Hosp., Rockfall Corp., Middletown. Mem. Am., Conn. bar assns. Home: 230 Ridge Rd Middletown CT 06457 Office: PO Box 660 Middletown CT 06457 Tel (203) 347-5484

NASATIR, MICHAEL DAVID, b. Los Angeles, Sept. 24, 1940; A.B., U. Calif., Los Angeles, 1962, J.D., Berkeley, 1965. Admitted to Calif. bar, 1966, U.S. Supreme Ct. bar, 1974; asst. U.S. atty., Calif., 1966-69; mem. staff San Francisco Neighborhood Legal Assistance Found., 1969; mem. firm Nasatir, Sherman & Hirsch, Beverly Hills, Calif., 1970—. Mem. Los Angeles County, Beverly Hills, Am., Fed. bar assns., Calif. Attys. for Criminal Justice, Los Angeles Criminal Cts. Bar Assn. Recipient certificate of Appreciation, Loyola U., Los Angeles, 1975. Office: 8383 Wilshire Blvd Suite 510 Beverly Hills CA 90211 Tel (213) 653-3303

NASH, DONALD DEAN, b. Portland, Oreg., Dec. 14, 1943; B.A., U. Hawaii, 1968; J.D., Harvard, 1971. Admitted to Oreg. bar, 1972; since practiced in Portland, asso. firm Winkel & Stoll, 1972-73; partner firm Nash & Margolin, 1974—. Mem. Oreg. State Bar Assn. Office: 610 SW Alder Suite 555 Portland OR 97205 Tel (503) 248-0731

NASH, PAUL LENOIR, b. Poughkeepsie, N.Y., Jan. 29, 1931; B.A., Yale Coll., 1953; LL.B., Harvard U., 1958. Admitted to N.Y. bar, 1959; asso. firm Dewey, Ballantine, Bushby, Palmer & Wood, N.Y.C., 1958-65, resident partner Brussels office, 1966-69, partner, 1966—. Mem. Am., Internat., N.Y. State bar assns., Assn. Bar City N.Y., Am. Soc. Internat. Law. Home: 4 Westminster Pl Morristown NJ 07960 Office: 140 Broadway New York City NY 10005 Tel (212) 344-8000

NASITS, ALAN C., b. El Paso, Tex., Jan. 6, 1946; B.A., U. Tex., 1968; J.D., Tex. Tech. U., 1971. Admitted to Tex. bar, 1971; staff county atty.'s office El Paso County (Tex.), 1971-76, 1st asst. atty., 1975-76; individual practice law, El Paso, 1977—. Mem. State Bar Tex. (past mem. code of criminal procedure com.), El Paso Bar Assn. Office: 604 Myrtle St El Paso TX 79901 Tel (915) 533-2484

NASON, JOHN BLAISDELL, III, b. McKeesport, Pa., Sept. 11, 1937; A.B. with distinction in Econs., Dartmouth, 1959; LL.B., U. Va., 1962. Admitted to Pa. bar, 1963; partner firm Kleinbard, Bell and Brecker, Phila., 1970—. Mem. Dartmouth Coll. Alumni Council, 1974—; trustee Com. on Equal Opportunity. Mem. Phila., Pa., Am. bar assns. Home: 1167 Norsam Rd Gladwyne PA 19035 Office: 18th floor Fidelity Bldg Philadelphia PA 19109 Tel (215) 985-1000

NASON, JOHN CHARLES, b. Victoria, Tex., Apr. 16, 1945; B.S., U. Md., 1967, J.D. cum laude, 1971. Admitted to Md. bar, 1972; asso. firm Weinberg and Green, Balt., 1972, firm Perdue, Owrutsky and Whitehead, Salisbury and Ocean City, Md., 1972—. Alt. del. Democratic Nat. Conv., 1976. Mem. Wicomico County, Md. bar assns., Order of Coif. Contbr. article to legal jours.; research editor Md. Law Rev., 1970-71. Home: 709 Burning Tree Circle Salisbury MD 21801 Office: 212 E Main St Salisbury MD 21801 Tel (301) 749-2211

NASSAU, ISIDORE, b. N.Y.C., Feb. 9, 1910; B.S., N.Y. U., 1931; LL.B., Columbia, 1934. Admitted to N.Y. bar, 1935; individual practice law, N.Y.C. Home: 639 West End Ave New York City NY 10025 Office: 11 Park Pl New York City NY 10007 Tel (212) 267-4464

NASSER, WOODROW SAM, b. Terre Haute, Ind., July 17, 1931; B.S., Ind. State U., 1957; J.D., Ind. U., 1960. Admitted to Ind. bar, 1960; individual practice law, Terre Haute, 1960-73; partner firm Nasser, Felling & Tabor, Terre Haute, 1973-76; individual practice law, Terre Haute, 1976—; counsel Eglen Hovercraft Corp., 1968-76. Chmn. Vigo County (Ind.) March of Dimes, 1961. Mem. Am. Trial Lawyers Assn., Am. Hypnotists Soc., Theta Chi, Phi Delta Phi. Home: Rural Route 12 Box 343 West Terre Haute IN 47885 Office: 1311B Ohio Blvd Terre Haute IN 47807 Tel (812) 232-1523

NASSOS, ERNEST JOHN, b. Chgo., Apr. 4, 1930; B.S., Northwestern U., 1951; M.S., U. Ill., 1952, J.D., 1955. Admitted to Ill. bar, 1955; partner firm McDermott, Will and Emery, Chgo., 1958-69; tax atty. Sears, Roebuck and Co., Chgo., 1969—. Mem. Ill. State, Chgo. bar assns., Am. Judicature Soc., Phi Alpha Delta. Home: 1346 Somerset Dr Glenview IL 60025 Office: Tax Dept Sears Roebuck and Co Sears Tower Chicago IL 60684 Tel (312) 875-9090

NAST, CHARLES COUDERT, b. Tuxedo, N.Y., July 23, 1903; B.A., Harvard U., 1925; LL.D., J.D., Columbia U., 1927. Admitted to N.Y. State bar, 1928, Fed. bar, 1928, U.S. Supreme Ct. bar, 1964; asso. firm Miller, Otis, Farr & Henderson, N.Y.C., 1927-28; asst. atty. gen. N.Y. State, 1928-29; asso. firm DeWitt, Nast, Diskin & Martini and predecessor firms, N.Y.C., 1929-37, partner, 1937-74; gen. counsel The Conde Nast Publs. Inc., N.Y.C., 1975—, dir., 1931-40, 46-69. Mem. Am., N.Y. State, N.Y. County bar assns., Assn. Bar City N.Y. Home: 501 Lexington Ave New York City NY 10017 Office: 350 Madison Ave New York City NY 10017 Tel (212) 687-0550

NATAL, SAMUEL DAVID, b. Camden, N.J., Apr. 1, 1945; B.A. in Bus. Adminstrn., Rutgers U., 1967; J.D., Villanova U., 1970. Admitted to N.J. bar, 1970, Pa. bar, 1971; asst. prosecutor Camden County, N.J., 1971-72; solicitor Voorhees (N.J.) Twp. Site Plan Com., 1972-74; solicitor Berlin Twp. (N.J.) Municipal Utilities Authority, 1973-76; asso. firm Casper and Muller, Phila., 1974-75; partner firm Lacktman and Natal, Haddonfield, N.J., 1975—. Vice-chmn., treas. So. N.J. chpt. Nat. Multiple Sclerosis Soc., Collingswood, N.J., 1974—. Mem. N.J. State, Camden County bar assns. Home: 901 Park Dr Cherry Hill NJ 08002 Office: 807 Haddon Ave Haddonfield NJ 08033 Tel (609) 428-4600

NATHAN, ANTHONY ROGER, b. Chgo., Jan. 2, 1937; B.S., DePaul U., 1959, J.D., 1964. Admitted to Ill. bar, 1964; estate tax agt. IRS, Chgo., 1964-68; individual practice law, Palatine and Niles, Ill., 1968-71; tax accountant Medidentic, Inc., Park Ridge, Ill., auditor Health and Welfare Services, Inc., Northbrook Ill., 1975-76, Fed. Energy Adminstrn., Chgo., 1976—. Bd. dirs. Juvenile Diabetes Found., 1973—. Mem. Ill. State, Chgo., Fed. bar assns., Park Ridge C. of C. Home and office: 910 Beau Dr #306 Des Plaines IL 60016 Tel (312) 593-2271

NATHAN, EDGAR J., 3D, b. N.Y.C., June 29, 1919; B.A., Williams Coll., 1941; J.D., Yale, 1947. Admitted to N.Y. bar, 1948, U.S. Supreme Ct. bar, 1955; asst. dist. atty. N.Y. County, 1947-51; asso. firm Gale Bernays Falk & Eisner, 1951-54; since practiced in N.Y.C., partner firm Gale & Falk, 1954-56, Marshall Bratter Greene Allison & Tucker, 1956-59, Karelsen Karelsen Lawrence & Nathan, 1959—; mem. N.Y. State Bd. Mediation, 1959-66; pub. mem. N.Y. State Minimum Wage Bd. for Hotel Industry, 1952-54. Mem. Am., N.Y. State, N.Y.C. bar assns., N.Y. State Dist. Attys. Assn., Am. Arbitration Assn. (nat. panel). Bd. dirs. Benjamin N. Cardozo Sch. Law, Yeshiva U., 1976—. Home: 322 Central Park W New York City NY 10025 Office: Karelsen Karelsen Lawrence & Nathan 230 Park Ave New York City NY 10017 Tel (212) 490-3535

NATHAN, JOHN EDWARD, b. N.Y.C., Dec. 3, 1942; B.E., Yale, 1964; LL.B., Yale, 1967. Admitted to N.Y. bar, 1967; partner firm Fish & Neave, N.Y.C., 1976—. Trustee Hudson Guild Settlement House, N.Y.C., 1973—. Mem. Assn. Bar City N.Y. (patent com.), Am. Bar Assn.

NATHAN, KENNETH SAWYER, SR., b. Oshkosh, Wis., Feb. 8, 1906; student U. Chgo., 1923-26; J.D. DePaul U., 1930. Admitted to Ill. bar, 1930; staff Chgo. Crime Commn., 1928-29; arbitrator Ill. Indsl. Commn., 1940-41; asst. U.S. Atty. for No. Dist. Ill., 1943-46; partner firm Nathan & Klafter, Chgo., 1954—. Mem. Am., Chgo., Ill., Fed. bar assns., Am. Judicature Soc., 7th Circuit Bar Assn., Trial Lawyers Assn., Pi Gamma Mu. Home: 119 Lockerbie Ln Wilmette IL 60091 Office: 39 S LaSalle St Chicago IL 60603 Tel (312) 726-7855

NATHAN, VINCENT MEYER, b. Tyler, Tex., Nov. 14, 1937; B.A., U. Okla., 1959; LL.B., 1961. Admitted to Okla. bar, 1961; teaching asst. Ind. U. Sch. of Law, Bloomington, 1961-63; asst. prof. U. Toledo (Ohio) Coll. of Law, 1963-66, asso. prof., 1966-69, prof., 1969—; asst. dean Coll. Law, 1966-69, asso. dean, 1969-70, dir. Council on Legal Edn. Opportunity Inst., 1969. Bd. trustees Congregation Shomer Emunim, 1975—; pres. bd. trustees Toledo Crittenton Services. Mem. Okla., Toledo Bar assns., Soc. of Am. Law. Office: University Toledo College Law Toledo OH 43606 Tel (419) 537-4176

NATHANSON, ABRAHAM LEON, b. Bklyn., Aug. 17, 1926; LL.B., Bklyn. Law Sch., 1950. Admitted to N.Y. bar, 1950; individual practice law, Bklyn., 1950—. Bd. dirs. W. Brighton Little League, Bklyn. Mem. W. County Criminal Bar Assn. (dir.), Bklyn. Bar Assn. Office: 16 Court St Brooklyn NY 11241 Tel (212) 875-2921-2

NATHANSON, NATHANIEL LOUIS, b. New Haven, Dec. 21, 1908; B.A., Yale, 1929, LL.B., 1932; S.J.D., Harvard, 1933. Admitted to Mass. bar, 1933, Ill. bar, 1946, U.S. Supreme Ct. bar, 1943; law clk. Circuit Judge Julian W. Mack, 1933-34, Supreme Ct. Justice Louis D. Brandeis, 1934-35; atty. SEC, 1935-36; asst. prof. law, Northwestern U., 1936-41, asso. prof., 1941-45, prof., 1945—, Frederic P. Vose prof., 1968—; asso. gen. counsel Office Price Adminstrn., Washington, 1942-45; Fulbright vis. lectr. law Tokyo U., 1954-55; cons. Indian Law Inst., New Delhi, 1958-59; council Adminstrv. Conf. of U.S., 1961-62; vis. research scholar Carnegie Endowment for Internat. Peace, 1964-65; vis. prof. law U. Wash., 1968-69, Ariz. State U., 1972, 74, 76. Mem. Am. Acad. Arts and Sci., Am. Soc. Internat. Law, Am. Law Inst., Am., Chgo. bar assns., Japanese Am. Soc. Legal Studies. Author: (with Carl Auerbach) Federal Regulation of Transportation, 1953; (with Louis Jaffe) Cases and Materials on Administrative Law, 1961, 68, 76. Contbr. articles in field to profl. jours. Home: 115 3d St Wilmette IL 60091 Office: 357 E Chicago Ave Chicago IL 60611 Tel (312) 649-8439

NATIONS, HOWARD LYNN, b. Dalton, Ga., Jan. 9, 1938; B.A., Fla. State U., 1963; J.D., Vanderbilt U., 1966. Admitted to Tex. bar, 1966; asso. firm Butler, Rice Cook & Knapp, Houston, 1966-71; pres. firm Nations & Cross, 1971—; v.p., dir. Ins. Corp. Am., Houston, 1972—; pres. Caplinger & Nations Galleries, Inc., Houston, 1973—, Nations Investment Corp., Houston, 1975—, NCM Trade Corp., Houston, 1975—; v.p. Delher Am. Inc., Houston, 1975—; adj. prof. law S. Tex. Coll. Law, Houston, 1967—; lectr. in field. Mem. State Bar Tex., Am., Tex. trial lawyers assns., Am., World assns. law profs., Am. Judicature Soc., Phi Alpha Delta (regional pres. 1965-66), Pi Sigma Alpha (1959-60). Contbr. articles to legal jours. Home: 811 Lovett St #28 Houston TX 77006 Office: 4600 Post Oak Pl #212 Houston TX 77027 Tel (713) 960-9690

NATIONS, MICHAEL THOMAS, b. Newnan, Ga., July 20, 1945; A.B., Duke U., 1967; J.D. cum laude Harvard, 1973. Admitted to Ga. bar, 1973; asso. firm Sutherland, Asbill & Brennan, Atlanta, 1973—. Mem. State Bar Ga. (chmn. legal aid com. younger lawyers sect. 1976—), Am., Atlanta bar assns. Home: 165 Lakeview Ave NE Atlanta GA 30305 Office: 3100 1st National Bank Tower Atlanta GA 30303 Tel (404) 658-8829

NATTER, JOHN TWOHEY, b. Schenectady, Aug. 14, 1939; B.S., U.S. Naval Acad., 1962, J.D., Cumberland Sch. Law, Samford U. 1973. Admitted to Ala. bar, 1973; mfrs. rep. Newell Equipment Co., Birmingham, Ala., 1968-70; partner firm Gorham, Natter & King, Birmingham, 1973—; lectr. U. Montevallo. Chmn. precinct Democratic party, Birmingham, 1968—. Mem. Am., Ala., Birmingham bar assns., Assn. Trial Lawyers Am. Home: 1774 Cornwall Rd Birmingham AL 35226 Office: 915 Frank Nelson Bldg Birmingham AL 35203 Tel (205) 251-9166

NATTIER, FRANK EMILE, b. St. Joseph, Mo., Sept. 2, 1915; B.S. in Fgn. Service, Georgetown U., 1937, LL.B., 1940; LL.M. in Comparative Law, N.Y. U., 1953. Admitted to D.C. bar, 1941, N.Y. State bar, 1946, U.S. Supreme Ct. bar, 1963; asso. firm Breed, Abbott & Morgan, N.Y.C., 1946-55; mem. firm Nattier & Anderson, N.Y.C., 1955-63; individual practice law, N.Y.C., 1963-70; internat. counsel Nat. Distillers and Chem. Corp., N.Y.C., 1970—; asst. and acting spl. rep. Brazil, Office Inter-Am. Affairs, also spl. asst. to U.S. Ambassador to Brazil, 1941-45. Mem. Brazilian Am. C. of C. (dir. 1968—), Pan Am. Soc. N.Y. (dir. 1975—), Assn. Bar City N.Y., Am. Bar Assn., Am. Fgn. Law Assn., Inter-Am. Bar Assn., Am. Arbitration Assn., Am. Soc. Internat. Law, Internat. Law Assn. Contbr. articles, chpts. to legal jours, textbooks. Home: 48 Spencer Ct Hartsdale NY 10530 Office: Nat Distillers & Chem Corp 99 Park Ave New York City NY 10016 Tel (212) 949-5620

NAUERT, PETER WILLIAM, b. Rockford, Ill., May 3, 1943; B.S., Marquette U., 1965; J.D., George Washington U., 1968. Admitted to D.C. bar, 1968, Ill. bar, 19—, U.S. Supreme Ct. bar, 1972; v.p., treas. Pioneer Life Ins. Co. Ill., Rockford, 1969-74, pres., 1975—. Active United Fund, Rockford, 1971—. Mem. Am., Ill., Winnebago County bar assns., Rockford C. of C. Contbr. articles to ins. jours. Home: 1531 National Ave Rockford IL 61103 Office: 127 N Wyman St Rockford IL 61101 Tel (815) 962-7731

NAUHEIM, STEPHEN ALAN, b. Washington, Nov. 17, 1942; B.S. in Accounting, U. N.C., 1964; LL.M. in Taxation, George Washington U., 1970; J.D., Georgetown U., 1967. Admitted to D.C. bar, 1968, U.S. Ct. Claims bar, 1968, U.S. Tax Ct. bar, 1971; asst. br. chief Internat. Tax br. Legis. and Regulations div., Chief Counsel's Office, IRS, 1967-71; asso. firm Surrey, Karasik & Morse, Washington, 1971-74, partner, 1975—; spl. cons. internat. tax matters U.S. Treasury Dept., 1971—; guest lectr. univs.; seminar speaker; dir. Bonabond, Inc. Mem. Internat., Am. bar assns., Internat. Fiscal Assn., World Trade Inst. (tax and fin. adv. bd.), Phi Delta Phi. Contbr. articles to profl. jours. Home: 6913 Portobello Rd McLean VA 22101 Office: 1156 15th St NW Washington DC 20005 Tel (202) 331-4008

NAVID, ROBERT ABRAHAM, b. Chgo., July 12, 1912; LL.B., John Maushall Law Sch., 1936, J.D., 1970. Admitted to Ill. bar, 1936, U.S. Supreme Ct. bar, 1970; village prosecutor Park Forest, Ill., 1958-61, magistrate, municipal justice, 1961-65. Pres. Family Counseling and Mental Health Center of South Cook County, Ill. Mem. Chgo., Ill. State, South Suburban bar assns., Am. Judicature Soc. Home: 12 Wilson Ct Park Forest IL 60466 Office: 24 Plaza Park Forest IL 60466

NAVRATIL, ROBERT NORMAN, b. N.Y.C., Dec. 27, 1928; B.A. cum laude, Maryville Coll., 1954; J.D. (scholar), U. Chgo., 1957. Admitted to Tenn. bar, 1958; partner firm Bird & Navratil, Maryville, Tenn., 1958-65, firm Bird, Navratil & Ballard, Maryville, 1966-72, firm Bird, Navratil, Ballard & Tate, Maryville, 1972-75, firm Bird, Navratil & Bird, Maryville, 1975—. Councilman, City of Maryville, 1975—; mem. Maryville Planning Commn., 1976—. Mem. Am., Tenn. (ho. of dels.), Blount County (pres.) bar assns., Blount County C. of C. (pres.). Home: 2038 Eckles Dr Maryville TN 37801 Office: 101 N Court Maryville TN 37801 Tel (615) 982-1800

NAYLOR, GEORGE LEROY, b. Bountiful, Utah, May 11, 1915; student U. Utah, 1934-36, George Washington U., 1937; J.D., U. San Francisco, 1953. Admitted to Calif. bar, 1954, Ill. bar, 1968; v.p., sec., legis. rep. Internat. Union of Mine, Mill & Smelter Workers, CIO, Utah-Nev., 1942-44; asst. mgr. So. Pacific Co., San Francisco, 1946-61; examiner, 1949-54, chief examiner, 1955; individual practice law, San Francisco, 1954—, Chgo., 1968—; carrier mem. Nat. R.R. Adjustment Bd., Chgo., 1961—; gen. counsel Can Veyor, Inc., Mountain View, Calif., 1959-64, Wiebe Mfg. Co., Inc., Hollister, Calif., 1961-66; atty. Village of Fox River Valley Gardens (Ill.), 1974-77. Mem. Am., Ill., Chgo., Calif., San Francisco bar assns. Author: Underground at Bingham Canyon, 1944; Choice Morsels in Tax and Property Law, 1966; Defending Carriers Before the NRAB and Public Law Boards, 1969. Home: 120 Center St Barrington IL 60010 Office: 220 S State St Chicago IL 60010 Tel (312) 939-2295

NAYLOR, PAUL BERTRAM, b. Tulsa, Sept. 23, 1943; B.B.A., U. Tulsa, 1964, J.D., 1967. Admitted to Okla. bar, 1968, U.S. Supreme Ct. bar, 1973; partner firm Naylor & Williams, Tulsa, 1973—. Mem. Okla., Tulsa bar assns., Okla. Trial Lawyers Assn. Office: 1701 S Boston St Tulsa OK 74119 Tel (918) 582-8000

NAZETTE, RICHARD FOLLETT, b. Eldora, Iowa, July 27, 1919; B.A., U. Iowa, 1942, J.D., 1946. Admitted to Iowa bar, 1946, U.S. Supreme Ct. bar, 1960; since practiced in Cedar Rapids, Iowa; partner firm Nazette, Hendrickson, Marner & Good, 1946—; 1st asst. atty., Linn County, Iowa, 1951-56, county atty. 1957-62; chmn. bd. dirs. United State Bank; dir. State Surety Co. Chmn. Linn County Health Center, 1968-70. Fellow Am. Bar Found.; mem. Am., Iowa State (gov. 1972-76), Linn County (pres. 1963) bar assns., Iowa County Attys. Assn (pres. 1959), Iowa Acad. Trial Lawyers (pres. 1964), Elks (exalted ruler, 1961), Optimist Internat. (v.p. 1954), Cedar Rapids Country Club (pres. 1975). Home: 2224 Country Club Pkwy SE Cedar Rapids IA 52403 Office: 200 1st St SW Cedar Rapids IA 52404 Tel (319) 364-0124

NEAHER, EDWARD RAYMOND, b. Bklyn., May 2, 1912; A.B., Notre Dame U., 1937; LL.B., Fordham U., 1943. Admitted to N.Y. bar, 1943, U.S. Supreme Ct. bar, 1960; spl. agt. FBI, 1943-45; asso. partner firm Chadbourne, Parke, Whiteside & Wolff, N.Y.C., 1945-69, U.S. atty. Eastern Dist. N.Y., Bklyn., 1969-71; judge U.S. Dist. Ct., Eastern Dist. N.Y., 1971—. Fellow Am. Coll. Trial Lawyers (jud.); mem. N.Y.C. Legal Aid Soc. (dir. 1967-69), Fordham Law Alumni Assn. (dir. 1970—), Practising Law Inst. (trustee 1976—), Am., Fed., N.Y.C. (chmn. com. fed. cts. 1966-69), N.Y. State, Bklyn. bar assns., Am. Judicature Soc., Fed. Bar Council. Home: 169 Nassau Blvd Garden City NY 11530 Office: US Courthouse 225 Cadman Plaza E Brooklyn NY 11530 Tel (212) 330-7571

NEAL, A. CURTIS, b. Nacogdoches, Tex., Nov. 25, 1922; B.B.A. in Accounting, U. Tex., 1948, LL.B., 1952. Mem. Tex. Corp., franchise tax dept. 1948-52; admitted to Tex. bar, 1951, U.S. Dist. Ct. bar for No. Dist. Tex., and So. Dist. Ill.; practiced in Amarillo, Tex., including individual practice, since 1952. Mem. exec. bd. Kids, Inc., Amarillo, 1954-65, pres., 1960; mem. exec. bd. Olsen Park PTA, Amarillo, 1955-58; exec. mem. Llano Estacade council Boy Scouts Am., 1957-62. Mem. Amarillo, Tex. bar assns., Amarillo Trial Lawyers Assn., Amarillo C. of C., Delta Theta Psi, Pi Alpha Psi. C.P.A. Home: 6205 Jameson St Amarillo TX 79106 Office: 601 Amarillo Nat Bank Bldg Amarillo TX 79101 Tel (806) 376-5327

NEAL, DAVID WILLIAM, B.A. in Polit. Sci., U. Cin., 1968; J.D., Ind. U., 1971. Admitted to Ind. bar, 1971; asso. firm Dennis, Cross, Razor, Jordan & Marshall, Muncie, Ind., 1971-75; partner firm Dunnuck, Rankin, Wyrick & Neal, Muncie, 1975—; juvenile ct. referee Delaware Circuit Ct., Delaware County, Inc. Bd. dirs. Youth Services Bur., Muncie, 1975—, Family Counseling Service, Muncie, 1976. Mem. Am., Ind., Delaware County bar assns., Am., Ind. trial lawyers assns. Spl. columnist Muncie Evening Press, 1975-76. Home: 405 S Morrison Rd Number 8 Muncie IN 47304 Office: 114 S Walnut Plaza Muncie IN 47305 Tel (317) 289-7379

NEAL, HENRY GETZEN, b. Fortson, Ga., Nov. 24, 1924; B.B.A., U. Ga., 1943, J.D., 1948. Admitted to Ga. bar, 1947; mem. firm Knox & Neal, Thomson, Ga., 1948-59; asst. atty. gen. State of Ga., Atlanta, 1959-66; exec. sec. bd. regents Univ. System of Ga., Atlanta, 1966—; dir., v.p. 1st Fed. Savs. & Loan Assn. of Thomson, 1963—; sec., dir. Dixie Wood Preserving Co., 1955-73. Mem. exec. bd. Ga.-Carolina council Boy Scouts Am., 1951-54; trustee Tift Coll., Southeastern Bapt. Theol. Sem. Mem. Am., Ga., Toombs Circuit (pres.) bar assns., U. Ga. Alumni Soc., 102d Inf. Div. Assn. Decorated Bronze Star, Purple Heart with oak leaf cluster. Home: 1242 Goodwin Rd NE Atlanta GA 30324 Office: 244 Washington St SW Room 468 Atlanta GA 30334 Tel (404) 656-2221

NEAL, JOHN SHERMAN, JR., b. Lincoln, Nebr., May 23, 1917; A.B., Franklin and Marshall Coll., 1939; LL.B., Temple U., 1948. Admitted to Pa. bar, 1949; asso. firm Dilworth, Paxson, Kalish & Green, Phila., 1949-52; partner firm Neal & Patton, Levittown, Pa., 1954—. Solicitor, Middletown Twp. Bucks County Sch. Authority, 1954—; chmn. Bucks County Hist. and Tourist Commn., 1965-75. Mem. Bucks County Bar Assn. Office: 54 Quarry Rd Levittown PA 19057 Tel (215) 946-5712

NEAL, PHIL CALDWELL, b. Chgo., July 30, 1919; A.B., Harvard, 1940, LL.B., 1943. Admitted to Calif., Ill. bars; practice in San Francisco; law clk. Justice Robert H. Jackson, 1943-45; mem. secretariat UN Conf., San Francisco, 1945; atty. Derby, Sharp, Quinby & Tweedt, 1945-46, Pillsbury, Madison & Sutro, 1946-48; asso. prof. law Stanford Law Sch., 1948-54, prof., 1954-61; prof. law U. Chgo. Law Sch., 1962—, dean 1963-75, Harry A. Bigelow prof. law, 1975—; vis. prof. Harvard Law Sch., 1957-58, Bd. dirs. Am. Bar Found., Practising Law Inst. Fellow Am. Acad. Arts and Scis. Home: 1203 E 50th St Chicago IL 60615 Office: 1111 E 60th St Chicago IL 60637*

NEAL, RICHARD CALDWELL, b. San Francisco, Apr. 10, 1947; A.B. cum laude in English, Harvard Coll., 1969; J.D., U. Calif., Berkeley, 1973. Admitted to Calif. bar, 1973; asso. firm Lawler, Felix & Hall, Los Angeles, 1973—. Mem. State Bar Calif. (disciplinary examiner 1976), Am., Los Angeles County bar assns. Tel (213) 620-0060

NEALE, J. HENRY, b. N.Y.C., July 25, 1904; B.A., Amherst Coll., 1924, LL.D. (hon.), 1974; LL.B., Harvard, 1927. Admitted to N.Y. bar, 1927, U.S. Supreme Ct. bar, 1945; asso. firm Strang & Taylor, White Plains, N.Y., 1927-31; partner firm Neale & Wilson, White Plains, 1931-36, Scarsdale, N.Y., 1936—; mem. office of gen. counsel Navy Dept., Washington, 1942-45, gen. counsel, 1945-46; counsel to Hopkins Commn., 1947. Mem. bd. edn. City of White Plains, 1935-42; chmn. ethics commn. Village of Scarsdale, 1968-75; dir. civil def. Scarsdale, 1950-53. Mem. Am. (ho. of dels. 1972—), N.Y. State (pres. 1967-68), Westchester County (pres. 1953-55) bar assns., Am. Law Inst., Am. Judicature Soc.; fellow Am. Bar Found., N.Y. State Bar Found. Home: 44 Lockwood Rd Scarsdale NY 10583 Office: Harwood Bldg Scarsdale NY 10583 Tel (914) 723-4060

NEALON, WILLIAM COOGAN, b. Pittsfield, Mass., July 19, 1931; B.S. in Chem. Engring., U. Del., 1953; J.D., Georgetown Law Sch., 1958. Admitted to Va. bar, 1958; U.S. Patent Bar, 1958, Can. Patent Bar, 1963, Mass., 1969; law clk. to judge U.S. Ct. Customs and Patent Appeals, Washington, D.C., 1956-58; 57; examiner U.S. Patent Office, 1955-56; adv. Office Naval Research Bur. Aeronautics, Washington, 1958-59; asso. firm McGrew & Edwards, Denver, 1959-62; patent counsel Harbison-Walker Refractories Co., Pitts., 1962-67; chief patent counsel, asst. sec. Am. Optical Corp., Southbridge, Mass., 1968—; dir. Med-Telectronics Milw. and Buffalo, N.Y., 1976. Mem. Am. Bar Assn., Am. Patent Law Assn., U.S. Trademark Assn., Licensing Execs. Soc., Assn. Corp. Patent Counsel. Home: Walker Pond Rd Sturbridge MA 01566 Office: 14 Mechanic St Southbridge MA 01550 Tel (617) 765-9711

NEARHOOD, WILLIAM ARTHUR, b. Toledo, Mar. 25, 1931; J.D., Ohio No. U., 1954. Admitted to Ohio bar, 1954; atty. Eaton Corp., Cleve., 1960-65, Internat. Harvester Co., Chgo., 1965-67, Darin & Armstrong Inc., Detroit, 1967-73; individual practice law, Ashland, Ohio, 1973—. Mem. Ohio State, Ashland County bar assns. Office: 124 Church St Ashland OH 44805 Tel (419) 289-1011

NEBENZAHL, BERNARD WILLIAM, b. San Francisco, Jan. 11, 1934; B.S., U. Calif., Berkeley, 1956, postgrad., 1962-63; J.D., U. Calif., San Francisco, 1966. Admitted to Calif. bar; partner firm Hurdman and Cranstoun, San Francisco, 1968—, Rudy, Rapoport & White, San Francisco, 1966-68. Bd. dirs. San Francisco Jewish Community Center, Congregation Emanu-El. Mem. San Francisco Bar Assn., State Bar Calif., Calif. Soc. C.P.A.'s (tax com.), San Francisco Estate Planning Council (dir.), Am. Inst. C.P.A.'s (fin. and estate planning subcom.). C.P.A., Calif., La. Office: Two Embarcadero Center Suite 2500 San Francisco CA 94111 Tel (415) 981-7720

NEDURIAN, VRAM, JR., b. Phila., June 14, 1923; B.S. in Econs., U. Pa., 1946; J.D., Dickinson Law Sch., 1950. Admitted to Pa. bar, 1951, U.S. Supreme Ct. bar, 1960; individual practice law, Newtown Square, Pa., 1951—; asst. dist. atty. Delaware County, Media, Pa., 1964—; solicitor Newtown Twp. Delaware County Sewer Authority, 1968—, Marple Newtown Sch. Dist., 1969—. Justice of peace, 1958-64; mem. Marple Newtown Sch. Bd., 1964-69; auditor Newtown Twp., 1952-58; dist. chmn. Boy Scouts Am., 1960-64. Mem. Am., Pa., Delaware County bar assns., Am. Arbitration Assn., Nat. Dist. Attys. Assn., Pa. Assn. Sch. Attys. Office: 3539 West Chester Pike PO Box 275 Newtown Square PA 19073 Tel (215) EL6-9292

NEELY, STUART MCALISTER, b. Harrisburg, Pa., Mar. 6, 1930; A.B., Princeton, 1951; LL.B., Harvard, 1954. Admitted to Pa. bar, 1954, D.C. bar, 1954; law clk. to Hon. Walter R. Sohn, Ct. Common Pleas, Harrisburg, Pa., 1956-57; asso. firm Schnader, Harrison, Segal & Lewis, Phila., 1958-64; partner firm Stetler & Gribbin, York, Pa., 1964-75; counsel Fed. Nat. Mortgage Assn., Phila., 1976—. Mem. Am., Pa. bar assns. Home: 288 Country Gate Rd W Valley Rd Wayne PA 19087 Office: 510 Walnut St Philadelphia PA 19106 Tel (215) 574-1400

NEESE, C.G., b. Paris, Tenn., Oct. 3, 1916; student U. Tenn., 1936; LL.B., Cumberland U., 1937. Admitted to Tenn. bar, 1938; practiced in Paris and Nashville, 1938-61; exec. asst. to gov. Tenn., 1944; adminstrn. asst. to Senator Kefauver, 1949-51; U.S. dist. judge Eastern Dist. Tenn., 1961—; past sec., gen. counsel Capitol Life Ins. Co. Tenn. Dir. primary campaigns Senator Kefauver, 1948, 54; founder, original trustee, 1st pres. Family Clinic, Nashville; trustee Tusculum Coll. Mem. Phi Delta Phi. Home: 412 Circle Heights Dr Greeneville TN 37743 Office: US Courthouse Greeneville TN 37743 Tel (615) 638-8232

NEESER, DENNIS JOHN, b. St. Cloud, Minn., May 27, 1943; B.A., St. Thomas Coll., 1965; J.D., U. Minn., 1968. Admitted to Minn. bar, 1968; spl. asst. atty. gen. State of Minn., St. Paul, 1969-71; partner firm Schneider & Neeser, Willmar, Minn., 1971—; asst. county atty. Kandiyohi County (Minn.), Willmar, 1971—; mem. teaching staff Willmar Community Jr. Coll., 1972—. Mem. Minn. State, Am. bar assns., Nat. Dist. Attys. Assn., Minn. County Attys. Assn. Contbr. to legal manual. Home: Rural Route 1 Willmar MN 56201 Office: 706 1st St Willmar MN 56201 Tel (612) 235-1902

NEFF, MARY VAUGHAN, b. Wichita, Kans., Nov. 25, 1913; A.B., U. Wichita, 1934; M.B.A., Northwestern U., 1938; J.D., John Marshall Law Sch., 1943. Admitted to Ill. bar, 1943; asst. atty. gen. State of Ill., 1943-44; asso. firm Sidley & Austin, Chgo., 1944-57; individual practice law, Chgo., 1957—. Alderman, City of Des Plaines, Ill., 1955-61. Mem. Chgo. Bar Assn. Office: 29 S LaSalle St Chicago IL 60603 Tel (312) 782-3928

NEFF, OWEN CALVIN, b. Hartville, Ohio, Sept. 4, 1918; B.A., Ohio Wesleyan U., 1940; J.D., U. Mich., 1948. Admitted to Ohio bar, 1948, U.S. Supreme Ct. bar, 1965; partner firm Snyder, Neff & Chamberlin, Cleve., 1956—; prof. Cleve. State U., 1951-71. Mem. Ohio, Am., Cleve. bar assns. Home: 175 Sterncrest Dr Moreland Hills OH 44035 Office: 410 Hanna Bldg Cleveland OH 44115 Tel (216) 696-2630

NEFF, ZEIGEL WINSTON, b. Musslefork, Mo., Apr. 17, 1916; A.B., S.W. Mo. State U., 1939; J.D., U. Mo., Columbia, 1948; LL.D., Georgetown U., 1958. Admitted to Mo. bar, 1948, U.S. Supreme Ct. bar, 1967; practiced law, 1948-51; def. counsel, atty., trial counsel, mil. judge USN, 1951-55; commr. U.S. Ct. Mil. Appeals, 1955-57; spl. asst. to judge adv. gen. U.S. Navy, 1957-58; judge Navy Ct. Mil. Rev., 1958-63; spl. asst., legal advisor to asst. dep. sec. Def., 1963-64; ret., 1964; mem. U.S. Bd. Parole (now Parole Commn.), Washington, 1964-70, acting chmn. bd., chmn. youth div., 1965-70; individual practice law, Warsaw, Mo., 1971-74; partner firm Meise, Loughlin, & Jeff, Parkville, Kansas City, Mo., 1974—; asst. atty. gen. State of Mo., 1953-54; mem. Mo. Corrections Task Force. Mem. Warsaw Truman Dam Com., 1971-74; alderman City of Warsaw, 1972-74; bd. dirs. Community Services, Inc. of North Central Mo., Sch. Criminal Justice Culver-Stockton Coll.; deacon candidate Rockhurst Coll., Kansas City, Mo., 1975—. Mem. Am. Judicature Soc., Fed. (exec. sec. Washington chpt. 1957-58), Mo. bar assns., Res. Officers Assn. (pres. Washington chpt. 1960), Bus. and Profl. Men's Assn. Decorated Navy Cross; contbr. articles to profl. jours., 1955-65. Home: 5311 NW 83d Pl Kansas City MO 64151 Office: 102 Main St Suite B Parkville MO 64152 Tel (816) 587-9110

NEGRON, RAMON CANCEL, b. Mayaguez, P.R., Jan. 25, 1937; M.F.A., U. P.R., 1960, J.D., 1968. Admitted to P.R. bar, 1968; faculty law Inter Am. U., San Juan, P.R., 1969—; legal counselor Ho. of Reps. Penal Commn., 1973-76. Mem. Am. Bar Assn. Recipient Spl. award P.R. Med. Assn., 1970, P.R. Bar Coll., 1970. Home: 304 Interamericana Rio Piedras PR 00927 Office: Dept Law Inter Am U PO Box 1293 San Juan PR 00919 Tel 765-6463

NEIDITZ, DAVID HENRY, b. Hartford, Conn., Nov. 18, 1930; A.B., Dartmouth, 1952; J.D., Harvard, 1955. Admitted to Conn. bar, 1955; individual practice law, Hartford, Conn., 1955—; mem. Conn. Ho. of Reps., 1967-75, Conn. Senate, 1975—; chmn. Conn. Senate Judiciary Com., 1975—; mem. Uniform Law Commn., 1975—. Mem. Governing bd. Council State Govts., 1974—; trustee Wadsworth Atheneum, 1957—; dir. Met. Hartford YMCA. Mem. Conn., Hartford County bar assns. Home: 33 Fulton Pl W Hartford CT 06107 Office: 1 Lewis St Hartford CT 06103 Tel (203) 527-3183

NEIL, G. EUGENE, b. Prescott, Ariz., Sept. 17, 1940; B.S. in Fin., Ariz. State U., 1963; J.D., U. Ariz., 1968. Admitted to Ariz. bar, 1968; dep. county atty. Yavapai County (Ariz.), Prescott, 1969-72, county atty., 1973-75; dep. county atty. Maricopa County (Ariz.), Phoenix, 1975—. Chmn., Cancer Drive, Prescott, 1969; bd. dirs. Boys Club, 1970-71, YMCA, 1973-75. Mem. Am. Bar Assn. Home: 312 E Deepdale Rd Phoenix AZ 85022 Office: 101 W Jefferson St Phoenix AZ 85003 Tel (602) 262-3305

NEILL, DENIS MICHAEL, b. Grand Rapids, Mich., Apr. 27, 1943; A.B. cum laude, St. Louis U., 1964; J.D. cum laude, 1967. Admitted to Mo. bar, 1967, D.C. bar, 1970, U.S. Supreme Ct. bar, 1970; atty. office of chief counsel IRS, U.S. Dept. Treasury, Newark, 1967-68; law specialist office of chief counsel U.S. Coast Guard, Washington, 1968-71; asso. firm Arcut, Fox, Kintner, Plotkin & Kehn, Washington, 1969-71; asso. firm Morgan, Lewis & Borkius, Washington, 1971-72; asst. gen. counsel U.S. Agency for Internat. Development, Washington, 1972-75, asst. adminstr., 1975-77; gen. counsel Aeromaritime Internat. Corp., Washington, 1977—. Mem. Am., D.C., Fed. bar assns., Internat. Fiscal Assn. Contbr. articles, column. to legal jours. Home: 6305 Blackwood Rd Bethesda MD 20034 Office: 1156 15th St Washington DC 20005 Tel (202) 457-7400

NEILL, KENNETH ROGER, b. Helena, Mont., Oct. 6, 1938; B.A., U. Mont., 1962, J.D., 1965. Admitted to Mont. bar, 1965; clk. Mont. Supreme Ct., 1965-66; atty. Mont. Legis. Council, Helena, 1967; partner firm Scott, Linnell, Neill & Newhall, Great Falls, Mont., 1967—. Chmn. Mont. Republican Party, 1973-75. Mem. Am., Mont. bar assns. Home: 166 Riverview Ct Great Falls MT 59404 Office: 414 Mont Bldg Great Falls MT 59403 Tel (406) 727-2200

NEILL, MARSHALL ALLEN, b. Pullman, Wash., Aug. 23, 1914; B.A. in Polit. Sci., Wash. State U., 1937; J.D., U. Idaho, 1938. Admitted to Wash. bar, 1938; individual practice law, Pullman, 1938-67; asso. justice Wash. State Supreme Ct., Olympia, 1967-72, judge U.S. Dist. Ct., Eastern Dist. Wash., Spokane, 1972—; city atty., Pullman, 1939-52; counsel to Wash. State U., 1946-67; mem. Wash. Ho. of Reps., 1949-56, Wash. Senate, 1957-67. Mem. Am. Bar Assn., Am. Judicature Soc., Inst. Jud. Adminstrn., Am. Coll. Probate Lawyers. Office: PO Box 2136 Spokane WA 99210 Tel (509) 456-6830

NEILL, ROBERT, b. Batesville, Ark., July 23, 1908; A.B., U. Mo., 1929; J.D., Harvard, 1932. Admitted to Mo. bar, 1932, U.S. Supreme Ct. bar, 1936; mem. firm Thompson, Mitchell, Thompson & Young, St. Louis, 1932-46; partner firm Thompson & Mitchell, St. Louis, 1946—; vice chmn. bd. trustees Mo. Bar, 1960—; lectr. U. Wis. Grad. Sch. Banking, 1947-54; personal counsel Adminstrn. RFC, Washington, 1953. Mem. bd. curators U. Mo., 1957-69, pres. bd., 1964-67. Mem. Am., St. Louis, Mo. bar assns., Am. Law Inst.; fellow Am. Bar Found. Home: 701 S Skinner Blvd Saint Louis MO 63105 Office: One Mercantile Center Saint Louis MO 63101 Tel (314) 231-7676

NEILL, ROBERT HAMILTON, b. Birmingham, Ala., July 13, 1934; B.S., Ala. Polytec. Inst., 1956; J.D., Birmingham Sch. Law, 1968. Admitted to Ala. bar, 1968; atty. law dept. Liberty Nat. Life Ins. Co., Birmingham, 1968—. Mem. Am., Ala., Birmingham bar assns. Home: 3104 Woodhaven Dr Birmingham AL 35243 Office: POB 2612 Birmingham AL 35202 Tel (205) 325-2739

NEILSEN, CRAIG HART, b. Logan, Utah, Aug. 30, 1941; B.S. in Polit. Sci., Utah State U., 1963; M.B.A., U. Utah, 1964; J.D., Utah Law Sch., 1967. Admitted to Idaho bar, 1967; mem. firm Parry, Robertson, Daly & Larson, Twin Falls, Idaho, 1967-68; with Neilsen & Miller Constrn. Co., Twin Falls, 1968-71, atty., partner, 1970-71; owner, atty. Neilsen & Co., Twin Falls, 1971—; officer and/or dir. Lynwood Devel. Co., Bigwood Devel. Co., Cactus Pete's, Inc. Active YMCA, United Fund. Mem. Am., Idaho, Utah bar assns., Nat., Oreg., Idaho assns. gen. contractors, Idaho C. of C., Phi Delta Phi. Contbr. articles to legal jours. Home: 803 Locust St N Twin Falls ID 83301 Office: 532 Blue Lakes Blvd N Twin Falls ID 83301 Tel (208) 733-2282

NEILSON, GEORGE WILLIAM, b. Hood River, Oreg., July 2, 1948; B.S., U. Oreg., 1970, J.D., 1973. Admitted to Oreg. bar, 1973, U.S. Dist. Ct. bar for Dist. Oreg., 1973; asso. firm Rodriguez, Neilson & Glenn, and predecessors, Madras, Oreg., 1973-75, partner, 1975—. Mem. Oreg. State Bar, Central Oreg. Bar Assn. (sec.-treas. 1975), 11th Jud. Dist. Defenders Assn. (v.p. 1976, pres. 1977). Home: 248 N Eighth St Madras OR 97741 Office: 406 5th St Madras OR 97741 Tel (503) 475-2272

NEIMAN, JOHN HAMMOND, b. Des Moines, Jan. 8, 1917; B.A., Drake U., 1939, LL.B., 1941, J.D., 1968. Admitted to Iowa bar, 1941; spl. agent FBI, 1942-46; exec. v.p., sec. Nat. Assn. Credit Mgmt., Iowa Unit, Inc., Des Moines, 1955—; mem. ethics com. Iowa Senate, 1971-74. Pres., bd. dirs. Northwest Community Hosp., Des Moines, 1973-76; chmn. Client Security and Atty. Disciplinary Commn., Iowa Supreme Ct., 1974—. Mem. Am. (ho. dels., mem. com. profl. discipline), Iowa (pres. 1967-68, award of merit 1975), Polk County (pres. 1960-61) bar assns., Am., Iowa State (dir. 1962—) bar founds., Commercial Law League Am., Comml. Bar Found., Am. Judicature Soc. Home: 3514 Wakonda Ct Des Moines IA 50321 Office: Neiman Neiman Stone & Spellman 1119 High St Des Moines IA 50309 Tel (515) 244-5284

NEIMARK, SHERIDAN, b. Youngstown, Ohio, Apr. 7, 1935; B.S. in Chem. Engring., Carnegie Inst. Tech., 1957; J.D., George Washington U., 1961. Patent examiner U.S. Patent Office, Washington, 1957-62; admitted to Va. bar, 1962, D.C. bar, 1962, U.S. Ct. Customs and Patent Appeals bar, 1963, U.S. Supreme Ct. bar, 1973; practiced in Washington, 1962—; mem. firms K. Flocks and A. Browdy, 62-68; mem. firm Browdy & Neimark, 1969—. Mem. Md. Gov.'s Planning and Adv. Council on Developmental Disabilities, 1971—, vice chmn., 1975—; mem. Montgomery County (Md.) Com. Employment Handicapped, 1972-73. Mem. Am. Bar Assn. (mem. adv. bd. developmental disabilities model legis. project 1977—), D.C. Bar, Va. State Bar, Am. Patent Law Assn. (mem. com. patent law 1965-69, chem. practice 1970—), Patent Office Soc., Nat. (nat. dir. 1973—, dir. Montgomery County chpt. 1970-72, nat. maj. award 1972), Md. (founder, dir. 1971-72) socs. autistic children. Home: 12908 Ruxton Rd Silver Spring MD 20904 Office: 1233 Munsey Bldg 1329 E St NW Washington DC 20004 Tel (202) 628-5197

NEISER, RICHARD WILLIAM, b. Covington, Ky., June 16, 1938; B.A., Centre Coll. Ky., 1960; J.D., Stetson U., 1963. Admitted to Fla. bar, 1963; with trust dept. Barnett Bank & Trust Co., St. Petersburg, Fla., 1963-64; individual practice law, 1965; asst. gen. counsel, asst. v.p. Fla. Power Corp., St. Petersburg, 1966—. Mem. St. Petersburg Bar Assn., Delta Theta Phi. Home: 1100 79th St S Saint Petersburg FL 33707 Office: PO Box 14042 Saint Petersburg FL 33733 Tel (813) 866-5784

NEISSER, PETER ALEXANDER, b. N.Y.C., Feb. 11, 1933; student U. Glenoble, France, 1950; B.A., Middlebury Coll., 1954; J.D., U. San Francisco, 1962; Certificate appelate advocacy Ariz. State U., 1977. Admitted to Ariz. bar, 1963, Fed. bar, 1963; asst. to v.p. Mutual Fund Assos., Inc., San Francisco, 1959-62; counsel Nat. Securities Inc. and Nat. Life and Casualty Ins. Co., Phoenix, 1962-64; asso. firm O'Connor, Cavanaugh, Anderson, Westover, Killingsworth & Beshears, Phoenix, 1964-66; individual practice law, Phoenix, 1966—. Vice pres. Save Our Mountains Found., 1972—; mem. exec. com. City of Phoenix Mountains Preservation Commn., 1972-74. Mem. Ariz. (mem. standing com. securities regulation 1966—, mem. environ. law sect. 1975—), Am., Maricopa County bar assns., Am., Ariz., Phoenix trial lawyers assns., Phi Alpha Delta. Contbr. articles to legal jours. Office: 1970 1st Nat Bank Plaza 100 W Washington St Phoenix AZ 85003 Tel (602) 252-1729

NELLER, RICHARD M., b. Toledo, Mar. 11, 1946; A.B., Washington U., 1968; J.D., U. Toledo, 1972. Admitted to Ohio bar, 1972, U.S. Supreme ct. bar, 1977; asso. firm Lubitsky & Lubitsky, Toledo, 1972-77; partner firm Lubitsky, Neller & Post, Toledo, 1977—. Bd. trustees Economic Opportunity Planning Assn. of Greater Toledo, Inc., 1975—. Mem. Ohio, Toledo, Lucas County bar assns. Home: 2552 Scottwood Ave Toledo OH 43610 Office: 838 National Bank Bldg Toledo OH 43604 Tel (419) 241-3535

NELLIS, JOSEPH LEON, b. Chgo., Dec. 10, 1916; B.S., Northwestern U., 1938, J.D., 1940. Admitted to Ill. bar, 1941, D.C. bar, 1947, U.S. Supreme Ct. bar, 1946; individual practice law, Washington, 1946—; asso. counsel Senate Crime Investigating (Kefauver) Com., D.C., 1950-51; spl. counsel Senate Antitrust Subcom., Washington, 1962, House of Reps. Small Bus. Com., 1957, Crime Com., 1969-70; chief counsel Ho. of Reps. Com. on Narcotics Abuse & Control, Washington; gen. counsel Council for Advancement of Psychol. Professions, 1972-76, Eleanor Roosevelt Meml. Found., 1963-67. Pres. Bethesda Chevy Chase Jewish Com., 1957-58; trustee B'nai B'rith Found., 1962—. Mem. Am., D.C. bar assns. Co-author: The Private Lives of Public Enemies, 1973; contbr. numerous articles to profl. jours. Home: 3539 Albemarle St NW Washington DC 20008 Office: Room 3260 Ho of Reps Office Bldg Annex #2 2d and D Sts SW Washington DC 20515 Tel (202) 225-1753

NELMS, ROBERT LESTER, b. Omaha, Oct. 9, 1939; B.S. in Accounting, U. So. Calif., 1965; J.D., U. Calif., Los Angeles, 1967. Admitted to Calif. bar, 1968; asso. firm Von Herzen, Catlin, Reinjohn, Los Angeles, 1968-71; individual practice law, Los Angeles, 1971—. Trustee First Presbyterian Ch., Inglewood, Calif., 1975; governing bd. Wiseburn Sch. Dist., Hawthorne, Calif. Mem. Los Angeles County Bar Assn., Lawyers Club Los Angeles. Office: 333 S Hope St Suite 3710 Los Angeles CA 90071 Tel (213) 680-9212

NELON, ROBERT DALE, b. Shawnee, Okla., Aug. 8, 1946; B.A., Northwestern U., 1968; J.D., U. Okla., 1971. Admitted to Okla. bar, 1971; law clk. Office Atty. Gen. Okla., 1966-70; asso. firm Andrews, Mosburg, Davis, Elam, Legg & Bixler, Oklahoma City, 1971, 1975—; with JAGC, USMCR, Cherry Point, N.C., 1972-74; teaching asst. Oklahoma City U. Law Sch., 1976. Mem. Am., Okla. bar assns., Am. Inst. Aeros. and Astronautics. Contbr. articles to legal jours. Home: 9101 Rolling Green St Oklahoma City OK 73132 Office: 1600 Midland Center Oklahoma City OK 73102 Tel (405) 272-9241

NELSEN, EARL ROBERT, b. Spokane, Wash., May 12, 1944; B.A. in Psychology, Eastern Wash. State Coll., 1967; J.D., U. Utah, 1972. Admitted to Wash. bar, 1972; dep. recorder Salt Lake County (Utah), 1971-72; asst. gen. counsel Western Farmers' Assn., Seattle, 1972-74; mgr. Tower Mall Properties, Vancouver, Wash., 1974—; corporate counsel, asst. sec. Weisfield's, Inc., Seattle, 1974—. Bd. dirs. Christian Ch. Conf. Grounds of Western Wash., Olympia. Mem. Wash., Seattle-King County bar assns. Home: 12400 NE 4th Pl Bellevue WA 98005 Office: 800 S Michigan St Seattle WA 98108 Tel (206) 767-2932

NELSON, CAROLYN BERRYHILL, b. Guin, Ala., June 27, 1933; B.A., Samford U., 1967, J.D., 1969. Admitted to Ala. bar, 1969; supr. mortgage loan processing and loan closing atty. City Fed. Savs. and Loan Assn., Birmingham, Ala., 1957-71; atty. firm Lange, Simpson, Robinson & Somerville, Birmingham, 1971-76; v.p., counsel Brookwood Med. Center, Inc., Birmingham, 1976—. Bd. dirs. St. Anne's Home, Inc., Birmingham, 1977—. Mem. Ala., Birmingham, Am. bar assns., Am. Soc. Hosp. Attys., Phi Alpha Delta. Home: 1200 Wickford Rd Birmingham AL 35216 Office: Brookwood Med Center Inc 2000-D Brookwood Med Center Dr Birmingham AL 35209 Tel (205) 870-5751

NELSON, DAVID ALDRICH, b. Watertown, N.Y., Aug. 14, 1932; A.B., Hamilton Coll., 1954; postgrad. (Fulbright scholar) Peterhouse, U. Cambridge (Eng.), 1954-55; LL.B., Harvard, 1958. Admitted to Ohio bar, 1958, U.S. Supreme Ct. bar, 1962; asso. firm Squire, Sanders & Dempsey, Cleve., 1958-67, mem., 1967-69, 72—; gen. counsel U.S. Post Office Dept., Washington, 1969-71, sr. asst. postmaster gen., gen. counsel, 1971; atty.-adviser Office of Gen. Counsel, Dept. Air Force, 1959-62; dir. Blount, Inc., Montgomery, Ala., 1973—, Conrad, Nelson & Co., Cleve., 1975—. Mem. Greater Cleve., Ohio State, Am., Fed. bar assns. Recipient Benjamin Franklin award U.S. Post Office Dept., 1969. Home: 2699 Wadsworth Rd Shaker Heights OH 44122 Office: 1800 Union Commerce Bldg Cleveland OH 44115 Tel (216) 696-9200

NELSON, EDWARD STANWOOD, b. Vicksburg, Miss., Sept. 12, 1928; student U. Ark.; J.D., U. Miss., 1965. Admitted to Miss. bar, 1965, Ala. bar, 1971; partner firm Bryan, Nelson, Allen, & Schroeder, Pascagoula, Biloxi, Gulfport and Hattiesburg, Miss., 1965—; partner firm Bryan, Nelson, Nettles & Cox, Mobile and Bayou La Batre, Ala., 1973—; pub. defender Jackson County (Miss.), 1965-66; city atty. Pascagoula, 1969. Mem. Jackson County, Harrison County, Miss State, Mobile County, Ala. State bar assns., Miss. Def. Lawyers Assn., Comml. Law League, Maritime Law Assn. U.S. Home: 534 Highland Woods Dr W Mobile AL 36608 Office: 1103 Jackson Ave Pascagoula MS 39567 Tel (601) 762-6631

NELSON, ELMER COLE, b. Stillwater, Okla., Nov. 26, 1926; B.B.A., Okla. U., 1952, LL.B., 1955. Admitted to Okla. bar, 1955; individual practice law, Ardmore, Okla., 1955-58, Muskogee, Okla., 1975—; county atty., Love County, Okla., 1958-61; asst. U.S. atty. Eastern Dist. Okla., 1961-66, U.S. magistrate, 1973-76; judge Municipal Ct. City Muskogee, 1969-71. Mem. Okla. Bar Assn. Home: 2419 W Okmulgee St Muskogee OK 74401 Office: Box 1842 Muskogee OK 74401 Tel (918) 682-7815

NELSON, EUGENE WALTER, b. Travis County, Tex., Oct. 19, 1914; J.D., U. Tex., 1939. Admitted to Tex. bar, 1939; asso. firm Morgan & Nelson, Austin, Tex., 1939-40; individual practice law, Austin, 1940-42; instr. Sch. Law So. Methodist U., Dallas, 1944-46; prof. bus. law U. Tex., Austin, 1946—. Mem. Tex. Bar Assn., Am. Bus. Law Assn. Author: Business Law, Text and Materials, 1958; recipient Outstanding Teaching award Standard Oil Ohio, 1967. Home: 703 Texas Ave Austin TX 78705 Office: B E B #606 U Tex Austin TX 78712 Tel (512) 471-3322

NELSON, FRED MURRAY, b. St. Louis, Aug. 12, 1922; student Westminster Coll., Fulton, Mo., 1939-41; B.A., U. Mo., 1943; J.D., U. Mich., 1945. Admitted to Mo. bar, 1945, Calif. bar, 1959, U.S. Supreme Ct. bar, 1963; asso. firms Hay & Flanagan, St. Louis, 1946-52, Robert Lund, Long Beach, Calif., 1959-61, Martin Abrams, El Monte, Calif., 1976—; partner firms Oldham & Nelson, St. Louis, 1952-58, Parks & Nelson, Long Beach, 1961-66, Kinkle Rodiger, Riverside, Calif., 1973-75; individual practice law, Long Beach, 1966-73. Mem. Am., Mo., Calif., Long Beach bar assns., Am. Trial Lawyers Assn. Recipient Green Found. award U. Mich. Moot Ct., 1945. Home and Office: 3816 Larkstone Dr Orange CA 92669 Tel (213) 433-3001

NELSON, GEORGE LEONARD, b. Salt Lake City, Aug. 27, 1897; LL.B., J.D., George Washington U.. 1922. Admitted to Utah bar, 1922, Ct. Appeals D.C. bar, 1922. U.S. Supreme Ct. bar, 1956; partner firm Romney & Nelson, Salt Lake City, 1922-71, Romney, Nelson & Cassity, Salt Lake City, 1971—; asst. county atty. Salt Lake City, 1923-25. Mem. Am., Inter-Am., Utah bar assns. Home: 900 Donner Way Apt 608 Salt Lake City UT 84108 Office: Kearns Bldg Salt Lake City UT 84101 Tel (801) 328-3261

NELSON, GILBERT FRANCIS, b. Kewanee, Ill., Aug. 5, 1905; A.B., U. Ill., 1928; J.D., U. So. Calif., 1931. Admitted to Calif. bar, 1931, U.S. Supreme Ct. bar, 1948; asst. atty. gen. State Calif., Los Angeles, 1952-60; asso. firm Johnson, Bannon, Wholwend & Johnston, Century City, Calif., 1960-65; individual practice law, Laguna Hills, Calif., 1965—. Mem. Beverly Hills (former pres.), Los Angeles bar assns., Beverly Hills Jr. C. of C. (former pres.). Home and Office: 2392 Via Mariposa St W Laguna Hills CA 92653 Tel (714) 830-7558

NELSON, GILBERT LEE, b. Princeton, N.J., Oct. 5, 1942; B.A. in Govt., Trinity Coll., 1964; J.D., Georgetown U., 1967. Admitted to N.J. bar, 1968, since practiced in New Brunswick; partner firm Teneralli, Nelson, & Shamy, 1968-73; sr. partner firm Gilbert L. Nelson, 1973—; dep. pub. defender, Middlesex County, 1969-71, asst. prosecutor, 1971-72; dir. dept. law, city atty. New Brunswick, 1975—. Mem. Charter Study Commn., New Brunswick, 1968; bd. dirs. Urban League Greater New Brunswick, 1968-69; mem. Middlesex County Econ. Opportunities Corp., 1972-74. Mem. N.J., Nat., Middlesex County, New Brunswick bar assns., Trial Lawyers Assn. Middlesex County. Home: 29 Goodale Circle New Brunswick NJ 08901 Office: 203 Livingston Ave New Brunswick NJ 08903 Tel (201) 246-4949

NELSON, GRANT STEEL, b. Mitchell, S.D., Apr. 18, 1939; B.A. magna cum laude, U. Minn., 1960, J.D. cum laude, 1963. Admitted to Minn. bar, 1963, Mo. bar, 1971; asso. firm Faegre & Benson, Mpls., 1963-64, 66-67; instr. law U. Mich., 1965-66, vis. asst. prof. law, 1969-70; asst. prof. law U. Mo., 1967-70; asso. prof. law, 1970-73, prof. law, 1973-75, Enoch H. Crowder prof. law, 1975—; vis. prof. law Brigham Young U., summer 1976. Mem. Am., Mo. bar assns., Phi Beta Kappa, Order of the Coif. Author: (with Van Hecke, Leavell) Cases and Materials on Equitable Remedies and Restitution, 1973; (with Whitman) Cases and Materials on Real Estate Finance and Development, 1976; recipient U. Mo. Law Sch. Found. Award for Meritorious Service and Achievement, 1974; contbr. articles to profl. jours. Home: 2514 Ridgefield Rd Columbia MO 65201 Office: 230 Tate Hall Univ Mo Columbia MO 65201 Tel (314) 882-8375

NELSON, HUGH FRANCIS, b. Appleton, Wis., June 21, 1927; B.S., U. Wis., 1950, LL.B., 1953. Admitted to Wis. bar, 1953; individual practice law, 1954-68; mem. firm Jury Nelson Bayorgeon & Ahrens, Appleton, 1969—. Chmn., Waverly San. Dist.; v.p. High Cliff Hist. Soc.; bd. dirs. Outagamie Pub. Defender System, Appleton Project 76 Corp., High Cliff Forest Park Assn. Mem. Am., Wis., Outagamie (past pres.), Calumet County bar assns. Home: RFD 2 Menasha WI 54952 Office: 225 N Richmond St Appleton WI 54911 Tel (414) 739-7781

NELSON, JAMES FREEMAN, b. Fairbault, Minn., Apr. 20, 1936; B.B.A., U. N.D., 1959; LL.B., William Mitchell Coll. Law, 1963. Admitted to Minn. bar, 1963, U.S. Supreme Ct. bar, 1974; asso. firm Schermer & Gensler, Mpls., 1963-64, Brink, Sobolik, Severson & Nelson, Hallock, Minn., 1964-67; partner firm Winter, Nelson and Groth, Glenwood, Minn., 1967—. Mem. Assn. Trial Lawyers Am., Glenwood C. of C. (pres. 1974). Home: Rural Route 2 Glenwood MN 56334 Office: Law Bldg Glenwood MN 56334

NELSON, JAMES JOHN, b. Mpls., Aug. 23, 1936; B.A., Augsburg Coll., 1959; J.D., William Mitchell Law Sch., 1966; postgrad. U. Minn., 1959-62, United Theol. Sem., 1976-77. Admitted to Minn. bar, 1968; individual practice law, Mpls., 1958-77; real estate adviser U.S. Postal Service, St. Paul, 1973-75; broker Custom Realty, Inc., Mpls., 1975—. Mem. Minn., Hennepin County bar assns., Minn. Evaluator's Assn. Mpls. Bd. of Realtors (sec. treas. 1975-76). Recipient awards for Cinematography, 1970-75. Home: 4717 27th Ave S Minneapolis MN 55406 Office: 4507 34th Ave S Minneapolis MN 55406 Tel (612) 729-0409

NELSON, JAMES THOMAS, b. Daytona Beach, Fla., May 29, 1917; law degree John B. Stetson U., 1941. Admitted to Fla. bar, 1941; partner firm Parkinson and Nelson, 1946-48; partner firm Schott and Nelson, 1948-52; individual practice law, 1952-64; judge 7th Judicial Circuit of Fla., Daytona Beach, 1964—; Chmn. Daytona Beach Civil Service Bd., 1952-53. Mem. Am., Fla. bar assns., Phi Alpha Delta, Daytona Beach Jaycees (pres. 1950). Home: 928 S Pennisula Dr Daytona Beach FL 32114 Office: 125 E Orange Ave Daytona Beach FL 32014 Tel (904) 258-7000

NELSON, JAMES WOODROW, b. nr. Altoona, Pa., Mar. 29, 1914; A.B., Dickinson Coll., 1935; J.D., U. Pa., 1938. Admitted to Pa. bar, 1938; law asso. to chief justice Pa. Supreme Ct., Phila., 1938-39, law clk. Supreme Ct. Pa., Phila., 1939-41; asso. firm McCoy, Brittain, Evans & Lewis, Phila., 1941-46; sr. partner firm Nelson, Campbell & Levine, Altoona, 1946—; asst. sec., dir. Boyer Bros., Inc.; v.p., dir. Condrin Oldsmobile-Cadillac, Inc. Pres. Altoona Community Chest, 1956-57, chmn. central budget com., 1957-67; mem. Altoona City Water and Sewer Authority, 1962-73; mem. Pa. Republican State Com., 1964-72, Pa. Rep. Platform Com., 1966; co-chmn. arrangements com., submission and address, Pa. Constl. Conv., 1967-68; trustee, mem. exec. com. Central Blair United Fund; trustee, bd. dirs. Community Services Pa.; bd. dirs. Blair County unit Am. Cancer Soc.; mem. nat. legacies com. UN Assn. U.S.A., 1967—; mem. Blair County Hist. Soc., Presbyn. Ch., Pa. Soc. N.Y.C. Mem. Blair County (pres. 1974-75), Pa., Phila. bar assns., Am. Arbitration Assn. (nat. panel, 1963—), Phi Beta Kappa, Order of Coif. Home: 1118 26th Ave Altoona PA 16601 Office: 309 Central Trust Bldg Altoona PA 16603 Tel (814) 944-6111

NELSON, LAWRENCE JOSEPH, b. Port Huron, Mich., May 12, 1939; B.S., Kans. State U., 1963; J.D., Washburn U., 1966. Admitted to Kans. bar, 1966, Fed. bar, 1966, Ill. bar, 1970; individual practice law, Topeka, 1966-70; municipal judge, Topeka, 1969-70; corp. counsel State Farm Ins. Co., Bloomington, Ill., 1970—; instr. bus. law Ill. State U., 1970—. Chmn. Zoning Bd. Appeals, Bloomington, 1975—. Mem. Am., Kans., Ill. bar assns., Am. Judicature Soc. Office: 1 State Farm Plaza Bloomington IL 61701 Tel (309) 662-2225

NELSON, LEONARD MARTIN, b. Rumford, Maine, Sept. 23, 1935; B.A. magna cum laude, Harvard, 1957, LL.B., 1960; Admitted to Maine bar, 1960; asso. firm Bernstein & Bernstein, Portland, Maine, 1960-62; partner firm Bernstein, Bernstein & Nelson, 1963; founding partner firm Bernstein, Shur, Sawyer & Nelson, Portland, 1974—; lectr. Law Sch. U. Maine, 1963—; chmn. exec. com. bd. dirs. Depositors Trust Co. Portland; dir. Depositors Corp. Pres. bd. trustees Portland Symphony Orch., 1963-66; chmn. Maine Arts and Humanities Commn., 1968-76; trustee Portland Pub. Library, 1971-74, Portland Soc. Art, 1975—; mem. music panel Nat. Endowment for the Arts, 1975—. Mem. Am., Maine, Cumberland County bar assns., Phi Beta Kappa. Home: 71 Carroll St Portland ME 04102 Office: 1 Monument Sq Portland ME 04111 Tel (207) 774-6291

NELSON, LESTER, b. N.Y.C., Dec. 23, 1928; B.S.S., Coll. City N.Y., 1950; LL.B., Harvard, 1953; LL.M., N.Y. U., 1959. Admitted to N.Y. bar, 1953; partner firm Miller, Montgomery & Sogi, N.Y.C., 1955—; adj. asso. prof. N.Y. Law Sch., 1973—. Pres. United Way, Harrison, N.Y.; sec., trustee Spanish Inst., N.Y.C.; sec., dir. Humane Soc. of N.Y., N.Y.C. Mem. Am., N.Y. State, New York County bar assns., Assn. Bar City N.Y. Editor Credit Manual of Commercial Laws, annual edition, 1969—; contbr. numerous articles to legal jours. Home: Pleasant Ridge Rd Harrison NY 10528 Office: 200 Park Ave New York City NY 10017 Tel (212) 687-1700

NELSON, LEWIS CLAIR, b. Logan, Utah, June 2, 1918; B.S., Utah State U., 1939; J.D., George Washington U., 1947. Admitted to D.C. bar, 1947, Utah bar, 1949, Ohio bar, 1962, N.Y. State bar, 1968; law clk. U.S. Ct. Appeals, Washington, 1947-48; asso. firm Moyle & Wanlass, Washington, 1948-51; counsel Com. Judiciary, U.S. Senate, Washington, 1951-52; partner firm Moyle, Nelson & Cotten, Washington, 1952-55; asso. counsel Champion Papers Inc., Hamilton, Ohio, 1955-65, v.p., gen. counsel, 1965-67; v.p., gen. counsel U.S. Plywood-Champion Paper, Inc., N.Y.C., 1967-72; sr. v.p. legal affairs Champion Internat. Corp., Stamford, Conn., 1972—; pub. mem. Adminstrv. Conf. U.S., Washington, 1972-74. Mem. Am. (chmn. sect. natural resource law 1968-69, del. 1970-74, mem. ethics com. 1975—), D.C., Utah, Ohio, N.Y. State bar assns., Assn. Gen. Counsel, Nat. Adv. Council, Practicing Law Inst. Home: 97 Palmers Hill Rd Stamford CT 06902 Office: 1 Landmark Sq Stamford CT 06921 Tel (203) 357-9351

NELSON, ROBERT BRUCE, b. Chgo., Feb. 21, 1935; B.A., U. Mich., 1957, J.D., 1960. Admitted to Ohio bar, 1961; with firm Jones, Day, Reavis & Pogue, Cleve., 1960—, partner, 1968—; spl. counsel to Ohio Atty. Gen., Columbus, 1973-75. Trustee Inner City Protestant Parish, Cleve., 1965—, chmn., 1971-73; trustee Children's Aid Soc., Cleve., 1970—, v.p., 1976-77. Mem. Am., Ohio bar assns., Bar Assn. Greater Cleve., Order of Coif, Phi Beta Kappa, Phi Kappa Phi, Phi Eta Sigma. Home: 3084 Van Aken Blvd Shaker Heights OH 44120 Office: 1700 Union Commerce Bldg Cleveland OH 44115

NELSON, ROBERT DOUGLAS, b. Williston, N.D., Mar. 31, 1948; B.A. cum laude, U. Calif., Los Angeles, 1970; J.D. summa cum laude, U. of Pacific, 1973. Admitted to Wash. bar, 1973; law clk. to chief judge Wash. State Ct. Appeals, div. 2, Tacoma, 1973-74; ct. commr. Wash. State Ct. Appeals, div. 2, Tacoma, 1974-75; asso. firm Davies,

Pearson, Anderson, Seinfeld, Gadbow, Hayes & Johnson, Tacoma, 1975—; adj. prof. law U. Puget Sound. 1973—. Del. Wash. State Democratic Conv., 1976. Mem. Wash. State, Am., Pierce County (Wash.) bar assns., Wash. State Trial Lawyers Assn. Editor Pacific Law Jour. Home: 4501 Garden Pl Gig Harbor WA 98335 Office: 945 Fawcett St Tacoma WA 98402 Tel (206) 383-5461

NELSON, ROBERT LOUIS, b. Dover, N.H., Aug. 10, 1931; grad. Maine Central Inst., 1949; B.A., Bates Coll., 1956; J.D., Georgetown U., 1959. Admitted to D.C. bar, 1960, U.S. Ct. Appeals bar, 1960; with U.S. Commn. Civil Rights, 1958-63; spl. asst. AID, 1963-65, program sec. Mission to Brazil, 1965-66; exec. dir. Lawyers Com. Civil Rights Under Law, 1966-70; dep. campaign mgr., treas. Muskie for Pres., 1970-72; exec. dir. Tex. Offshore Terminal Commn., 1973; sr. v.p. corp. affairs Washington Star Communications Inc., Washington, 1976—, exec. v.p., corp. counsel, 1974-76, pres. broadcast div., 1976—; dir. WLVA, Inc., Jobaro Corp., Perfin Corp., Washington Star Syndicate, First Charleston Corp.; vice chmn. Redevel. Land Agy. D.C., 1976—. Bd. dirs. Pa. Ave. Devel. Corp., Friends Nat. Zoo, Community Resources Inc., Downtown Progress; trustee Fed. City Council. Mem. Am. Bar Assn. Home: 3825 Ingomar St NW Washington DC 20015 Office: Washington Star Communications Inc 225 Virginia Ave SE Washington DC 20061 Tel (202) 484-5000

NELSON, THOMAS GEORGE, b. Idaho Falls, Idaho, Nov. 14, 1936; J.D., U. Idaho, 1962. Admitted to Idaho bar, 1962, U.S. Dist. Ct. bar, 1963; asso. firm Parry, Robertson, Daly & Larson, Twin Falls, Idaho, 1965—, partner, 1966—; mem. bd. commrs. Idaho State Bar, 1972-75, pres. 1974-75. Mem. Twin Falls City Council, 1970-73. Mem. Am., Fed. Power, Idaho bar assns., Am. Judicature Soc. Home: Route 3 Skyline Dr Twin Falls ID 83301 Office: Box 525 Twin Falls ID 83301 Tel (208) 733-3722

NELSON, WILLIAM J., b. Orangeburg, S.C., Oct. 24, 1939; B.S., Pa. Mil. Coll., 1963; J.D., Stetson U., 1968. Admitted to Fla. bar, 1968; asso. firm Bazemore & Midgley, Ft. Myers, Fla., 1968-69; partner firm Midgley & Nelson, Ft. Myers, 1969-72; judge Lee County (Fla.) Ct., 1973—; asst. pub. defender, Ft. Myers, 1969-72, hearing examiner div. youth services; legal aid atty. Mem. Lee County (Fla.), Fla., Am. bar assns. Recipient Barristers award of Merit, Stetson U., 1966. Home: 1514 Cumberland Ct Fort Myers FL 33901 Office: PO Box 2118 Fort Myers FL 33902 Tel (813) 335-2279

NELSON, WILLIAM MCKINLEY, JR., b. Toledo, Mar. 23, 1924; A.B., Yale U., 1947; J.D. Columbia U., 1949. Admitted to Ohio bar, 1949; chief def. counsel, law officer 1st Marine Div., Korea, 1952; asso. firm Spieth, Spring & Bell, Cleve., 1949-52, partner, 1953-57; asso. firm Squire, Sanders & Dempsey, Cleve., 1957-63, partner, 1964—; lectr. in field; dir. Shelby Paper Box Co. Trustee Cleve. YMCA, 1974; bd. dirs. Lakewood YMCA, 1954—, chmn., 1965-67; mem. Lakewood Charter Commn., 1950-51; co-founder Lakewood Safety Council, 1953. Mem. Cleve., Ohio State, Am. bar assns. Home: 23169 S Melrose Dr Westlake OH 44145 Office: 1800 Union Commerce Bldg Cleveland OH 44115 Tel (216) 696-9200

NEMETH, JOHN CHARLES, b. Cleve., June 24, 1945; B.A., Kent State U., 1967; J.D., Ohio State U., 1970. Admitted to Ohio bar, 1971; staff atty. Legal Aid and Pub. Defender Soc., 1971-72; partner firm Graham & Nemeth, 1972-74; individual practice law, 1974-75; partner firm Nemeth and Gantz, Columbus, Ohio, 1975—. Mem. Ohio, Columbus, Cuyahoga County bar assns., Lawyers Club Columbus, Ohio, Am. trial lawyers assns., Ohio Def. Counsel Assn. Home: 2126 Ellington Rd Columbus OH 43221 Office: 673 Mohawk St Columbus OH 43206 Tel (614) 444-6818

NEMIA, FRANK ANTHONY, b. Bklyn., Oct. 28, 1932; B.A., State U. N.Y., 1955; J.D., Syracuse U., 1957. Admitted to N.Y. State bar, 1957, U.S. Dist. Ct. bar, 1959, U.S. Supreme Ct. bar, 1961, U.S. Ct. Claims bar, 1961; partner firm Twining, Nemia, Hill & Griffen, Binghamton, N.Y., 1957—; asso. prof. law State U. N.Y., Binghamton, 1965—. Chmn., Commn. of Appraisal Adminstrv. Code, N.Y.C., 1962-64; mem. mgmt. advt. com. N.Y. State Sch. Indsl. and Labor Relations, Cornell U., 1974—; bd. dirs. State U. N.Y. at Binghamton Found., pres. 1970-72; bd. dirs. Asso. Catholic Charities, Broome County, Blue Shield Central N.Y.; pres. Broome County unit Am. Cancer Soc., 1970-74, mem. exec. com. N.Y. State div., 1970-72; pres. Diocese of Syracuse Confrat. Christian Doctrine, exec. com., 1970-72. Mem. Am. (com. on devel. law under Nat. Labor Relations Act), N.Y. State (mem. com. on labor law 1963-76, chmn. 1972-76, chmn. sec. on labor law 1976—, com. on specialization in law), Broome County bar assns., Am., N.Y. State trial lawyers assns., AAUP, Am. Bus. Law Assn., Am. Arbitration Assn. (panel arbitrators 1974—), Broome County C. of C. (recipient leadership award, 1960). Named One of Outstanding Young Men of Am., Jaycees, 1965. Contbr. articles to profl. jours. and texts. Home: 32 Lincoln Ave Binghamton NY 13905 Office: 53 Front St PO Box 1750 Binghamton NY 13902 Tel (607) 772-1700

NE MOYER, EDGAR CARROLL, b. Buffalo, June 5, 1932; B.A., U. Buffalo, 1954; J.D., N.Y. U., 1961; LL.M. (fellow), U. Wis., 1962. Admitted to N.Y. State bar, 1961, D.C. bar, 1962, U.S. Supreme Ct. bar, 1967; patrolman Buffalo Police Dept., 1958-61; gen. counsel Office Housing & Home Fin. Adminstrn., Wash., D.C., 1962-63; asso. firm David Diamond, Buffalo, 1963-66; U.S. atty. Western Dist. N.Y., 1967-69; dep. corp. counsel City Buffalo, 1969; asso. prof. Sch. Criminal Justice State U. N.Y., Albany, 1969-71; individual practice law, Buffalo, 1971-74; partner firm Boreanay, Ne Moyer & Baker, Buffalo, 1974—; clk. judge James B. Kane N.Y. State Supreme Ct., Buffalo, 1976—. Mem. Am., N.Y., Erie County bar assns., Erie County Trail Lawyers Assn. Contbr. articles Buffalo Law Review, Denver Law Jour. Office: 736 Brisbane Bldg Buffalo NY 14203 Tel (716) 854-5800

NEMTZOW, BERNARD, b. Newport, R.I., Mar. 6, 1924; A.B. magna cum laude, Brown U., 1948; J.D. cum laude, Harvard, 1951. Admitted to N.Y. bar, 1952; asso. firm Mudge, Stern, Baldwin & Todd, N.Y.C., 1951-60; counsel, asst. sec. Warner-Lambert Pharm. Co., N.J., 1960-68; v.p., gen. counsel, sec., dir. Borden, Inc., N.Y.C., 1969-74, sr. v.p., dir., 1974—. Mem. Am. Bar Assn., Bar Assn. City N.Y., Phi Beta Kappa. Home: Box 323 52 Martindale Rd Short Hills NJ 07078 Office: 277 Park Ave New York City NY 10017 Tel (212) 573-4120

NEPPLE, JAMES ANTHONY, b. Carroll, Iowa, Jan. 5, 1945; B.A., Creighton U., 1967; J.D., U. Iowa, 1970. Admitted to Iowa bar, 1970, Ill. bar, 1973; tax accountant Arthur Young & Co., Chgo., 1970; judge adv. U.S. Army, 1971-72; mem. firm Stanley Lande Coulter & Pearce, Muscatine, Iowa, 1972-75, partner, 1976—. Bd. dirs. Community Nursing Services, 1972—, pres., 1975—; bd. dirs. Friends of the Library, 1974—. Mem. Iowa Young Lawyers (exec. council), Am., Ill., Iowa bar assns. Home: 2704 Mulberry Ave Muscatine IA 52761 Office: 420 E 3d St Muscatine IA 52761 Tel (319) 263-8771

NESBIT, PHYLLIS SCHNEIDER, b. Newkirk, Okla., Sept. 21, 1919; B.S. in Chemistry, U. Ala., 1948, LL.B., 1958, J.D., 1969. Admitted to Ala. bar, 1958; asso. firm Wilters, Brantley and Nesbit and predecessor, Robertsdale, Ala., 1958-60, partner, 1960-75; partner firm Brantley and Nesbit, Robertsdale, 1975-76; judge Municipal Ct., Daphne, Ala., 1964-76, Silverhill, Ala., 1969-76; judge-elect Dist. Ct. of Baldwin County (Ala.), 1976—; county adminstr. Baldwin County, 1966-76; auditor Joint Legis. Council Ala., 1972, treas., 1972-74; city atty. City of Loxley (Ala.), 1975—. Mem. Baldwin County Bar Assn. (pres. 1967-68), Ala. Women Lawyers Assn. (pres. 1966-67), Ala. Municipal Judges Assn. (pres. 1970-72), North Am. Judges Assn., Nat. Assn. Women Lawyers, Am. Judicature Soc., Phi Alpha Delta. Home: PO Box 447 Daphne AL 36526 Office: PO Box 1138 Bay Minette AL 36507

NESBITT, JOSEPH, b. Leesburgh, Fla., Jan. 16, 1930; A.B., U. Fla., 1951; LL.B., U. Miami, 1957. Admitted to Fla. bar, 1958; law clk. to judge U.S. Dist. Ct. No. Dist. Fla., 1958-60; asst. atty. gen. State of Fla., 1960-65; gen. counsel Fla. State Bd. Examiners, 1965-69; judge 11th Jud. Circuit Ct. (Fla.), Miami, 1969—. Mem. Am. Bar Assn., Am. Judicature Soc., Phi Alpha Delta. Home: 517 Hardee Rd Coral Gables FL 33146 Office: 73 W Flagler St Miami FL 33130 Tel (305) 579-5388

NE SMITH, ALBERT NEWELL, b. Cochran, Ga., Nov. 26, 1920; grad. Middle Ga. Coll., 1941; LL.B., J.D., U. Ga., 1948. Admitted to Ga. bar, 1949; individual practice law, Cochran, 1950—. Mem. State Bar Ga. Home: PO Box 475 4 Old Chester Rd Cochran GA 31014 Office: 211 Cherry St Cochran GA 31014 Tel (912) 934-7602

NETH, SPENCER, b. Piqua, Ohio, Aug. 14, 1939; A.B., Miami U., Oxford, Ohio, 1961; J.D., Harvard, 1964, LL.M., 1966. Admitted to Ohio bar, 1964, Mass. bar, 1966; tchg. fellow, Harvard Law Sch., 1964-66; asso. firm Hale & Derr, Boston, 1966-70; asso. prof. Case Western Reserve Law Sch., 1970-73, prof., 1973—. Mem. Mass., Ohio, Am. bar assns., Soc. Am. Law Tchrs., ACLU of Greater Cleve. (legal panel). Author articles in field. Home: 2778 Derbyshire Rd Cleveland Hts OH 44106 Office: 11075 East Blvd Cleveland OH 44106 Tel (216) 368-3297

NETTERBLAD, JOHN WALTER, b. Stoughton, Wis., Apr. 1, 1934; B.B.A., U. Wis., 1957, J.D., 1960. Admitted to Wis. bar, 1960, Calif. bar, 1963; dep. dist. atty. County of San Diego, 1963-66; partner firm Higgs, Fletcher & Mack, San Diego, 1967—; treas. Defenders Program of San Diego, Inc., 1971; judge pro tem San Diego Municipal Ct., San Diego Superior Ct. Bd. dirs. Blind Recreation Center of San Diego, 1968-70, Boys and Girls Aid Soc., San Diego, 1975—. Mem. San Diego, Calif., Am. bar assns., Am. Bd. Trial Advocates, Internat. Assn. Ins. Counsel, Am. Arbitration Assn. (arbitrator). Home: 1820 Neale St San Diego CA 92103 Office: 707 Broadway Suite 1800 San Diego CA 92101 Tel (714) 236-1551

NEU, HOWARD MITCHELL, b. Chgo., Mar. 22, 1941; student U. Fla., 1958-61; B.B.A., U. Miami, 1962, J.D., 1968. Admitted to Fla. bar, 1968; mem. firms William J. Goldworn, Miami, Fla., 1968-69, Goldworn & Neu, Miami, 1969-70, Neu & Hertz, 1971-73; individual practice law, Miami, 1970-71, 73—; asso. judge, North Miami, Fla., 1971-75; instr. U. Miami, 1969-70, Miami Edn. Consortium, 1971-72, mem. N. Miami City Council, 1975—. Chmn. adv. bd. Metro Dade County Library, 1968-69; chmn. Fla. Library Devel. Council, 1971-74; bd. dirs. Abbey Hosp., Dade League of Cities. Mem. Am., Fla., Dade County bar assns., Am. Arbitration Assn., Am. Assn. Atty. C.P.A.'s. C.P.A., Fla. Home: 1860 Venice Park Dr North Miami FL 33161 Office: 1001 NE 125th St North Miami FL 33161

NEU, JOHN HOWARD, b. Sac City, Iowa, Jan. 29, 1938; A.B., Creighton U., 1960, J.D., 1966; M.A., Harvard, 1963; Ph.D. (Regents fellow), U. Nebr., 1972. Admitted to Nebr. bar, 1966, U.S. Dist. Ct. bar, 1966, 74, Calif. bar, 1974; asst. to gen. counsel Mut. Protective Ins. Co., Omaha, 1966-68; individual practice law, Omaha, 1966-70, Whittier, Calif., 1974—; asst. prof. Whittier Coll., 1971—. Mem. Am., Nebr., Calif., Los Angeles County bar assns., Am. Polit. Sci. Assn., AAUP. NDEA fellow, summer 1970; U. Nebr. Dissertation Travel fellow, 1970; Haynes Found. grantee, summer 1972; contbr. articles in field to legal jours. Home: 6217 S Greenleaf St #F Whittier CA 90601 Office: Dept Polit Sci Whittier Coll Whittier CA 90608 Tel (213) 693-0771

NEUENSCHWANDER, GORDON EARLE, b. Phila., Jan. 6, 1927; A.B., Western Res. U., 1949, LL.B., 1952. Admitted to Ohio bar, 1952, Pa. bar, 1955; atty. Nickel Plate R.R. Co., Cleve., 1953-54; asst. solicitor Pa. R.R. Co., Pitts., 1954-57; atty. Pitts. & Lake Erie R.R. Co., 1957-61, asst. gen. counsel, 1961-66, gen. counsel, 1966—, v.p., 1970—, also dir.; dir. Mahoning State Line R.R. Co.; v.p., gen. counsel Lake Erie & Eastern R.R., Youngstown & So. Ry. Co.; v.p., gen. counsel, dir. Montour R.R. Co.; gen. counsel Monongahela Ry. Co.; gen. counsel, dir. Pitts. Chartiers & Youghiogheny Ry. Co.; pres., dir. Montour Land Co. Supr. Marshall Twp. (Pa.), 1971—. Mem. Am. Pa., Allegheny County (Pa.) bar assns., Nat. Assn. R.R. Trial Counsel. Home: Meadowvue Dr RD 2 Wesford PA 15090 Office: 324 P & LE Terminal Bldg Pittsburgh PA 15219 Tel (412) 261-3201

NEUHAUSER, PAUL MICHAEL, b. N.Y.C., Dec. 18, 1933; A.B., Harvard, 1955, LL.B., 1958, LL.M., 1963. Admitted to N.Y. State bar, 1959, Iowa bar, 1968; asso. firm Simpson Thacher & Bartlett, N.Y.C., 1958-61; teaching fellow Harvard Law Sch., 1961-63; asst. prof. law, U. Iowa, 1963-66, asso. prof., 1966-69, prof., 1969—, asso. dean, 1966-72. Mem. Human Rights Commn., Iowa City, 1969-74; mem. governing bd. Episcopal Ch., 1976—. Mem. Am. (com. fed. regulation securities), Iowa (com. on corp. law) bar assns. Contbr. articles in field to profl. jours. Home: 914 Highwood St Iowa City IA 52240 Office: College of Law University of Iowa Iowa City IA 52240 Tel (319) 353-5615

NEUMANN, WILLIAM ALLEN, b. Minot, N.D., Feb. 11, 1944; B.B.A., U. N.D., 1965; J.D., Stanford, 1968. Admitted to N.D. bar, 1969; individual practice law, Bottineau, N.D., 1969—. Adv. com. N.D. State Extension Council, 1972-73, N.W. div. ARC, 1975—. Mem. Am. Bar Assn., Am. Judicature Soc. Office: 116 W 5th St Bottineau ND 58318 Tel (701) 228-3646

NEUMEISTER, KENT JUAN, b. Nebraska City, Nebr., Feb. 18, 1944; B.A., U. Nebr., 1966; J.D., Harvard U., 1969, LL.M., 1972, postgrad., 1972-73. Admitted to Mass., Nebr. bars, 1969; asso. firm Herrick, Smith, Donald, Farley & Ketchum, Boston, 1969-71; asst. prof. law Creighton U., 1973-76; asso. prof., 1976—. Mem. Am. Soc. Polit. and Legal Philosophy, Phi Beta Kappa. Home: 302 N 22d St Omaha NE 68102 Office: Creighton U Sch Law Ahmanson Law Center Omaha NE 68178 Tel (402) 449-2872

NEUSES, THOMAS PETER, b. Sheboygan, Wis., Sept. 11, 1928; B.S., Georgetown U., 1950; LL.B., U. Wis., 1953. Admitted to Wis. bar, 1953; asso. firm Federer, Grote, Hesslink & Rohde, Sheboygan, 1953-57; partner firm Federer, Grote, Ronde, Neuses & Dales, Sheboygan, 1957—. Bd. dirs. Sheboygan County Cancer Soc., 1977—. Mem. Am., Wis. Sheboygan County (pres. 1977) bar assns. Home: 233 Huron Ave Sheboygan WI 53081 Office: 607 N 8th St Sheboygan WI 53081 Tel (414) 458-5501

NEUSOM, THOMAS GEORGE, b. Detroit, Mar. 7, 1922; B.A., Detroit Inst. Tech., 1948; LL.B., Detroit Coll. Law, 1948, J.D., 1968. Admitted to Mich. bar, 1949, Calif. bar, 1949; individual practice law, Los Angeles. Mem. Los Angeles County Assessment Appeals Bd., 1964-69; pres. S. Central Area Welfare Planning Council, 1966-67; bd. dirs. Regional Welfare Planning Council, 1966-70; v.p. So. Calif. Rapid Transit Dist., bd. dirs., 1970-77. Mem. Am. Bar Assn., Langston Law Assn. Office: 1485 W Adams Blvd Los Angeles CA 90007 Tel (213) 731-1184

NEUSTEIN, ABRAHAM, b. N.Y.C.; LL.B., St. Lawrence U., 1936; M.H.L., Yeshiva U., 1948, D.H.L., 1953. Admitted to N.Y. bar, 1940, U.S. Supreme Ct. bar, 1976; ordained rabbi, 1940; rabbi Jewish Center of Brighton Beach (N.Y.), 1940—; prof. law City U. N.Y., 1971—; arbitrator N.Y.C. Civil Ct., 1972—. Mem. Bklyn. Bar Assn., Am. Bus. Law Assn., Assn. Arbitrators of Civil Ct., Rabbinical Council Am. Recipient Brotherhood Inter-Faith award, 1956. Tel (212) 332-1253

NEUTZE, DENNIS RICHARD, b. Balt., Mar. 30, 1943; B.S., U.S. Naval Acad., 1965; J.D. with honors, U. Md., 1970; M.A., Boston U., 1974; grad. Armed Forces Staff Coll., 1976. Admitted to Md. Ct. Appeals bar, 1970, U.S. Ct. Mil. Appeals bar, 1973; commd. ensign U.S. Navy Supply Corps, 1965; advanced through grades to lt. comdr. JAG Corps, 1974; staff comdr. U.S. Naval Forces, Vietnam, 1970-71; staff U.S. Naval Support Activity, Naples, Italy, 1972-74; asst. officer in charge U.S. Naval Legal Service Office, Naples, 1974-76; legal advisor Bur. Naval Personnel, Washington, 1976—. Mem. Am. Bar Assn., Inter-Am. Bar Assn., Naval Inst., Order of Coif. Home: 12708 Taustin Ln Herndon VA 22070 Office: Bureau of Naval Personnel Navy Dept Washington DC 20370 Tel (202) 692-4463

NEVILL, GUY LYLBURN, b. Rosebud, Tex., Nov. 13, 1916; LL.B., So. Meth. U., 1939. Admitted to Tex. bar, 1940; asst. atty. City of Dallas, 1946; with Dow Chem. Co., 1947—, staff counsel, Houston, 1973-74, sr. staff counsel, 1974—. Mem. Bellaire (Tex.) Zoning Bd. Appeals, 1952. Mem. Tex., Am. Houston bar assns., State Bar Tex. (natural resources council). Contbr. articles to legal jours. Home: 750 W Creekside Dr Houston TX 77024 Office: Richmond Ave Houston TX 77046 Tel (713) 623-3283

NEVILLE, HAROLD EDWARD, JR., b. Scotia, Calif., Mar. 5, 1929; B.S., Sch. Criminology, U. Calif., Berkeley, 1953; J.D., U. San Francisco, 1960. Admitted to Calif. bar; asso. firm Falk & Falk, Eureka, Calif., 1961-63, firm Sapper & Buzza, Fortuna, Calif., 1964-65; dep. dist. atty. Humboldt County (Calif.), 1963-64; partner firm Hill, Dalton & Neville, Eureka; city atty. City of Rio Dell (Calif.), 1961-72; judge Municipal Ct., Eureka, 1972—; arbitrator Am. Arbitration Assn., 1969. Office: 825 5th St Eureka CA 95501 Tel (707) 445-7231

NEVINS, FRANCIS MICHAEL, JR., b. Bayonne, N.J., Jan. 6, 1943; A.B. magna cum laude, St. Peter's Coll., 1964; J.D. cum laude, N.Y. U., 1967. Admitted to N.J. bar, 1967; atty. Middlesex County (N.J.) Legal Services Corp., 1970-71; asst. prof. law St. Louis U., 1971-74, asso. prof., 1975—. Mem. Assn. Am. Law Schs., Mystery Writers of Am., ACLU. Contbr. articles to law jours. Home: 4466 W Pine Blvd St Louis MO 63108 Office: 3642 Lindell Blvd St Louis MO 63108 Tel (314) 535-3300

NEWBERN, ST. CLAIR, III, b. Muskogee, Okla., Sept. 16, 1942; B.B.A., Tex. Christian U., 1964; LL.B., U. Tex. Austin, 1967. Admitted to Tex. bar, 1967, U.S. Supreme Ct. bar, 1972; partner firm Newbern and Hogle, Fort Worth, 1975—. Mem. Breakfast Optimist Club Fort Worth (pres. 1976—). Home:

NEWBURG, ANDRE W. G., b. Berlin, Jan. 9, 1928; A.B., Harvard U., 1949, LL.B., 1952. Admitted to N.Y. bar, 1952; mem. firm. Cleary, Gottlieb, Steen & Hamilton, 1952—, Paris, 1956-59, 74-76, Brussels, Belgium, 1960-64, N.Y.C., 1952-56, 64-74, 76—, partner, 1963—; spl. asst. 3d session Internat. Law Commn., UN, Geneva, 1951. Bd. mgrs. Hosp. for Spl. Surgery, N.Y.C., 1972—; mem. Harvard Overseers' Com. to Visit Russian Research Center, 1976—; mem. Council on Fgn. Relations, 1973—; trustee Am. Sch. Classical Studies at Athens, 1965—. Mem. Am. Assn. Internat. Commn. Jurists (dir. 1971—), Am., Internat. bar assns., Assn. Bar City N.Y., N.Y. County Lawyers Assn., Am. Soc. Internat. Law, Internat. Law and Fiscal Assn., Union Internationale des Avocats. Office: 1 State St Plaza New York City NY 10004 Tel (212) 344-0600

NEWBURG-RINN, STEVEN DAVID, b. Washington, Jan. 6, 1944; A.B. in Econs., George Washington U., 1965; J.D., U. Chgo., 1968. Admitted to Mich. bar, 1968, D.C. bar, 1969, U.S. Supreme Ct. bar, 1972; law clk. to Chief Judge Theodore Levin, U.S. Dist Ct. for Eastern Dist. Mich., 1968-69; asso. firm Fried, Frank, Harris, Shriver & Kampelman, Washington, 1969-72; sr. atty., program dir. FTC Bur. Consumer Protection, Washington, 1972—; vol. counsel D.C. Circuit Jud. Conf. Com. for Adminstr. of Justice Under Emergency Conditions, 1971-72. Mem. Am., Fed. bar assns., D.C. Bar, State Bar Mich. Home: 641 E Capitol St SE Washington DC 20003 Office: FTC Bur of Consumer Protection Washington DC 20580 Tel (202) 724-1483

NEWCOMB, DANFORTH, b. Tarrytown, N.Y., Jan. 27, 1943; B.A., U. Vt., 1965; J.D., Columbia, 1968. Admitted to N.Y. bar, 1968; asso. firm Shearman & Sterling, N.Y.C., 1968—. Mem. Am. Bar Assn., Am. Arbitration Assn. (panel of arbitrators). Office: 53 Wall St New York City NY 10005 Tel (212) 483-1000

NEWCOMB, ELLIOTT STOWELL, b. Melbourne, Fla., Dec. 13, 1942; B.A., U. Md., 1966; LL.B., U. Balt., 1969. Admitted to Md. bar, 1972; asso. firm Hoyert, Diemer, Yoho, Hooten & Mc Bride, 1971-72; individual practice law, Annapolis, Md., 1972—; instr. criminal law Anne Arundel Community Coll., 1975—. Mem. Md., Anne Arundel County bar assns. Office: 124 South St Annapolis MD 21401 Tel (301) 268-7080

NEWCOMB, JON EATHAN, b. Warsaw, Ind., Nov. 12, 1944; B.A., DePauw U., 1967; J.D., Ind. U., Bloomington, 1972. Admitted to Ind. bar, 1972, U.S. Dist. Ct. bar No. Ind., 1973; asso. R. Alexis Clarke Law Office, Bremen, Ind., 1972-76; individual practice law, Bremen, 1976—. Bd. dirs. Marshall County A.R.C. Mem. Am. Judicature Soc., Ind. Bar Assn., Bremen C. of C. (bd. dirs.). Home: 178 E Maple St Bremen IN 46506 Office: 121 N Center St Bremen IN 46506 Tel (219) 546-2091

NEWCOMER, CLARENCE CHARLES, b. Mt. Joy, Pa., Jan. 18, 1923; A.B., Franklin and Marshall Coll., 1944; LL.B., Dickinson Sch. Law, Carlisle, Pa., 1948. Admitted to Pa. bar, 1950, U.S. Supreme Ct. bar, 1962; mem. firms Rohrer, Honaman, Newcomer & Musser, Lancaster, Pa., 1957-60, Newcomer, Roda & Morgan, Lancaster, 1968-71; spl. dep. atty. gen. Pa. Dept. Justice, 1953-54; asst. dist. atty. City of Lancaster, 1960-64, 1st asst. dist. atty., 1964-68, dist. atty., 1968-72; judge U.S. Dist. Ct., Eastern Dist. Pa., 1972—. Mem. adv. council Lancaster-Lebanon council Boy Scouts Am. Mem. Am. Judicature Soc. Home: 600 Pleasure Rd Lancaster PA 17601 Office: US Courthouse Independence Mall Philadelphia PA 19106 Tel (215) 597-7847

NEWCOMER, RONALD ALLEN, b. Neptune, N.J., Feb. 21, 1943; B.S. in History and Geography, Murray State U., 1965; J.D., U. Ky., 1970. Admitted to Ky. bar, 1971; partner firm Kincaid, Wilson, Schaeffer & Hembree, Lexington, Ky., 1970—. Mem. Am., Ky., Fayette County (treas. 1976-77) bar assns. Office: Kincaid Wilson Schaeffer & Hembree 400 Central Bank Bldg Lexington KY 40507 Tel (606) 254-9371

NEWELL, HOWARD LLOYD, b. Boston, Sept. 11, 1942; B.S. in Bus. Adminstrn., Boston U., 1964, J.D., 1967. Admitted to Mass. bar, 1967; asst. prof. State U. N.Y., Albany, 1967-68; asso. firm Brown & Leighton, Boston, 1968-69; individual practice law, Boston, 1969—. Mem. Mass. (bar econs. com., chmn. subcom. trade show), Am. bar assns. Home: 982 Pleasant St Framingham MA 01701 Office: 89 State St Boston MA 02109 Tel (617) 723-3141

NEWELL, ROBERT MELVIN, b. Anacortes, Wash., Oct. 29, 1918; A.B., Stanford, 1941, J.D., 1946. Admitted to Calif. bar, 1946; partner firm Newell & Chester, Los Angeles, 1947—; prof. law Loyola U., Los Angeles, 1946-56. Mem. Am., Calif., Los Angeles County bar assns. Office: 650 S Grand Ave Los Angeles CA 90017 Tel (213) 629-1231

NEWEY, PAUL DAVIS, b. Mpls., July 4, 1914; A.A., Central YMCA Coll., Chgo., 1935; J.D., John Marshall Law Sch., 1940; A.B., Detroit Inst. Tech., 1947; diploma U.S. Treasury Dept. Law Enforcement Sch., 1943; spl. courses U.S. Govt. and Mil. Intelligence Schs., 1951-53. Admitted to Ill. bar, 1946; squad leader Bur. Census, Dept. Commerce, 1940; officer uniformed force U.S. Secret Service, 1940-42; agt. Bur. Narcotics, Treasury Dept., 1942-47; individual practice law, Chgo., 1948-51, 61-65; spl. rep. CIA, 1951-57; asst. state's atty.-investigator Cook County, Ill., 1957-58; asst. state's atty., chief investigator, chief state's atty. police, 1958-60; partner firm Adamowski, Newey & Adamowski, Chgo., 1965—; spl. investigator, Chgo., 1961—; atty. Ill. Sec. State, 1975—. Mem. Chgo. Better Bus. Bur., 1965—, Chgo. Assn. Commerce & Industry, 1965—, Wrightwood Neighbors, 1968—, Smithsonian Assos., 1965—. Mem. Am., Fed., Ill., Chgo. bar assns., Fed. Criminal Investigators Assn., U.S. Treasury Agts. Assn. (pres. 1969-70), AMVETS, Am. Judicature Soc., Am. Trial Lawyers Assn., Lawyer's Shrine Club, Internat. Assn. Chiefs of Police, Spl. Agts. Assn. Recipient Medal of Merit, named to Hall of Fame, Nat. Police Officer's Assn., 1960; recipient Merit Citation, John Marshall Law Sch., 1970; Distinguished Service award State's Atty. Cook County, 1960; Distinguished Citizens award Assyrian-Am. Welfare Council Chgo., 1970. Home: 1034 W Altgeld Ave Chicago IL 60614 Office: 11 S LaSalle St Chicago IL 60603 Tel (312) 782-1144

NEWEY, ROBERT LEROY, b. Ogden, Utah, Nov. 28, 1923; B.S., Utah State U., 1949; J.D., Stanford U., 1951. Admitted to Utah bar, 1952, U.S. Supreme Ct. bar, 1956; asso. firm Lamph & Newey (formerly Lamph, Anderson & Newey), beginning in 1954, subsequently partner; asst. dist. atty. State of Utah, 1953-69; county atty. Weber County (Utah), 1971—. Bd. regents Utah Colls. and Univs., 1977—. Mem. Am., Utah, Weber County (pres. 1970-71) bar assns., Nat. Dist. Attys. Assn. (state dir. 1975-76), Utah Assn. Prosecutors (chmn. 1974-75). Office: 2471 Grant Ave Ogden UT 84401 Tel (801) 399-5885

NEWLIN, A. CHAUNCEY, b. Cin., Aug. 8, 1905; A.B., Centre Coll., Danville, Ky., 1925, LL.D., 1958; LL.B., Columbia, 1928; D.Sc., Fla. Inst. Tech., 1975. Admitted to N.Y. bar, 1928, U.S. Supreme Ct. bar, 1935; asso. firm White & Case, N.Y.C., 1928-37, partner, 1937—. Mem. Scarsdale (N.Y.) Bd. Edn., 1947-52, pres., 1949-50; bd. dirs. Metropolitan Opera Assn., N.Y.C.; trustee Solomon R. Guggenheim Found., N.Y.C.; chmn. bd. trustees Centre Coll.; pres., dir. Marshall H. and Nellie Alworth Meml. Fund, Duluth, Minn.; v.p., dir. Jessie Smith Noyes Found., N.Y.C.; v.p., dir. The Henry L. and Grace Doherty Charitable Found., Inc., N.Y.C. Mem. Am., N.Y. State bar assns., New York County Lawyers Assn., Assn. Bar N.Y., Phi Beta Kappa, Sigma Chi. Home: 850 Park Ave apt 7C New York City NY 10021 Office: 14 Wall St New York City NY 10005 Tel (212) 732-1040

NEWMAN, ALAN LLOYD, b. Charleston, S.C., Feb. 25, 1945; B.E.E. with high honors, U. Md., 1965; J.D. with honors, George Washington U., 1969. Admitted to Md. bar, 1969, D.C. bar, 1969, Conn. bar, 1971; patent examiner U.S. Patent Office, Washington, 1965-67; asso. firm Burns, Doane, Benedict, Sweckor & Mathis, Washington, 1967-70; asso. law firm Wooster, Davis & Cifelli, Bridgeport, Conn., 1970-72; patent, in house counsel Elco Corp., Willow Grove, Pa., 1972-75; asst. gen. mgr. Malco, Amicrodot Co., Montgomeryville, Pa., 1975—. Mem. Am. Bar Assn., IEEE, Am. Patent Law Assn. Home: 19 Towerhill Rd Chalfont PA 18914 Office: 12 Progress Dr Montgomeryville PA 18936

NEWMAN, BERNARD, b. N.Y.C., Oct. 28, 1907; B.S., N.Y. U., 1928, LL.B., 1929. Admitted to N.Y. bar, 1930; asst. corp. counsel City of N.Y., 1936-42; law sec. to justice N.Y. State Supreme Ct., 1942-48, ofcl. referee Appellate Div., 1948-62; justice N.Y. State Supreme Ct., 1962; hearing officer N.Y. State Labor Relations Bd., N.Y. State Mediation Bd., 1963-65; judge Family Ct. City of N.Y., 1966-68, U.S. Customs Ct., 1968—. Chmn. N.Y. County Republican Party, 1958-62, N.Y. City Rep. Party, 1959-62; govt. appeals agt. SSS, 1941-45. Mem. Am., N.Y. State, N.Y.C. bar assns., Am. Judicature Soc., Fed. Bar Council, Nat. Legal Aid Soc., N.Y. U. Alumni Assn. (dir., recipient Alumni award 1969). Asso. editor N.Y. U. law Rev., 1927-29. Home: 25 E 9th St New York City NY 10003 Office: US Customs Ct Fed Plaza New York City NY 10007 Tel (212) 264-2800

NEWMAN, BOYD WESLEY, b. Bells, Tex., Aug. 21, 1921; B.A., Austin Coll., 1942; LL.B., U. Tex., 1948. Admitted to Tex. bar, 1948; asst. county atty. Grayson County (Tex.), 1951-56, county atty., 1966-69; individual practice law, Lewisville, Tex., 1959—; judge Lewisville Municipal Ct., 1965-72. Councilman, City of Carrollton (Tex.), 1962-66; pres. Dallas County (Tex.) League Municipalities, 1964. Mem. Carrollton C. of C. (pres. 1965). Home: 1319 San Antone St Lewisville TX 75067 Office: 130 Lewisville Center Lewisville TX 75067 Tel (214) 436-3591

NEWMAN, CHARLES ANDREW, b. Los Angeles, Mar. 18, 1949; B.A. with high honors, U. Calif., Santa Barbara, 1970; J.D., Washington U., St. Louis, 1973. Admitted to Mo. bar, 1973, U.S. Supreme Ct. bar, 1976; asso. firm Thompson & Mitchell, St. Louis, 1973—; lectr. Washington U. Sch. Law, 1976—; mem. Mo. Bar Young Lawyers Council, 1975-77. Mem. Am., Mo., Met. St. Louis (award of merit young lawyers sect.) bar assns. Home: 8164 Stratford Dr Saint Louis MO 63105 Office: 1 Mercantile Center 34th floor Saint Louis MO 63101 Tel (314) 231-7676

NEWMAN, CLINTON HARLIN, II, b. Versailles, Ky., Apr. 5, 1942; B.S., U. Ky., 1964, M.B.A., 1966, J.D., 1969. Admitted to Ky. bar, 1969; tchr. U. Ky., 1965-66; research specialist Legis. Research Commn., Frankfort, Ky., 1969-71; asst. state treas. State of Ky., Frankfort, 1972-76; sec. state State of Ky., 1975-76, asst. sec. state, 1976—. Mem. Ky. Bar Assn., Phi Delta Theta. Home: Rt 4 Box 427 Versailles KY 40383 Office: Secretary of State Room 150 State Capitol Frankfort KY 40601 Tel (502) 564-3490

NEWMAN, DALE SANFORD, b. Cleve., July 27, 1939; B.S., U. So. Calif., 1962; J.D., Southwestern U., 1966. Admitted to Calif. bar, 1967; atty. State Compensation Ins. Fund, Los Angeles, 1967-69; individual practice law, Sepulveda, Calif., 1969—; adv. com. Calif. atty. gen. Pres. Collier St. Sch. Community Adv. Council, 1975—. Mem. Calif. State, Am., Los Angeles County, San Fernando Valley bar assns. Recipient Am. Jurisprudence award Bancroft-Whitney Co., 1966. Office: 8647 Sepulveda Blvd Suite 6 Sepulveda CA 91343 Tel (213) 892-1294

NEWMAN, EDWARD, b. N.Y.C., Mar. 15, 1927; B.A., City Coll. N.Y., 1948; J.D., Bklyn. Law Sch., 1953. Admitted to N.Y. State bar, 1955; individual practice law, Carle Place, N.Y., 1955—. Mem. Am. (pres.), N.Y. State (past pres.) assns. atty.-C.P.A.'s, Am., Nassau County bar assns. Home: 28 Fern Dr E Jericho NY 11753 Office: One Old Country Rd Carle Place NY 11514 Tel (516) 741-5650

NEWMAN, FRANK CECIL, b. Eureka, Calif., July 17, 1917; A.B., Dartmouth, 1938; LL.B., U. Calif., 1941; LL.M., Columbia, 1947, J.S.D. 1953. Admitted to Calif. bar, 1942; prof. law U. Calif. at Berkeley, 1946—, Jackson H. Ralston prof. internat. law, 1947—, dean Sch. Law, 1961-66; vis. prof. law schs. Harvard, 1953-54, U. Wash., summer 1952, Salzburg Seminar in Am. Studies, Austria, summer 1954, 64, Strasbourg, France, summer 1970, 71, 75, Center Advanced Study in Behavioral Scis., 1957-58; law book editorial bd. Little, Brown & Co., 1956—; atty. OPA, N.Y.C., also Washington 1942-43, Office Gen. Counsel Navy Dept., 1943-46; cons. OPS, 1951; counsel Gov. Calif. Commn. on Unemployment Compensation, 1952; cons. GAO, 1959; bd. dirs. Fed. Home Loan Bank, San Francisco, 1962-70. Mem. exec. com., chmn. drafting com. Calif. Constn. Revision Commn., 1964-72. Mem. nat. adv. council ACLU, Amnesty U.S.A. Served from ensign to lt. USNR, 1943-46. Mem. Am. Bar Assn., Am. Soc. Internat. Law (chmn. human rights panel 1970—), Internat. Inst. Human Rights (v.p.). Author: (with Stanley S. Surrey) Newman and Surrey on Legislation, 1955. Bd. editors Human Rights Jour., Strasbourg, 1968—. Home: 53 Acacia Dr Orinda CA 94563 Office: U Calif Sch Law Berkeley CA 94720*

NEWMAN, HOWARD, b. N.Y.C., Apr. 2, 1928; B.A., Syracuse U., 1951; LL.B., Bklyn. Law Sch., 1956. Admitted to N.Y. bar, 1957; mem. firm Ginzburg Gaines Gaines DeBoissiere & Newman, S.I., N.Y. Mem. Richmond County Bar Assn., S.I. Trial Lawyers Assn. Office: 36 Richmond Terr Staten Island NY 10301 Tel (212) 447-6700

NEWMAN, JACK MILTON, b. N.Y.C., Oct. 15, 1939; A.B., U. Calif. at Los Angeles, 1961, J.D., 1965. Admitted to Calif. bar, 1966; asso. firm Arnold, Smith & Schwartz, Los Angeles, 1966-68, firm Bodle, Fogel, Julber Reinhardt & Rothschild, 1968-69; individual practice law, Los Angeles, 1969-71; partner firm Posner & Newman, Beverly Hills, Calif., 1971-76; judge Los Angeles Municipal Ct., 1976—. Counsel Los Angeles County Democratic Central Com., Calif. Dem. State Central Com., 1974-76. Mem. Calif. State Bar, Los Angeles County, Beverly Hills bar assns., Calif. Judges Assn., Municipal Ct. Judges Assn. Los Angeles County, Phi Alpha Delta. Office: 110 N Grand Ave Los Angeles CA 90048 Tel (213) 974-6111

NEWMAN, JOSEPH, b. Bklyn., Sep. 30, 1910; B.S., L.I. U., 1930; LL.B., St. Lawrence U., 1933. Admitted to N.Y. bar, 1935, U.S. Supreme Ct. bar, 1970; individual practice law, N.Y.C., 1935—. Mem. N.Y. State, Am. bar assns. Home: 1222 E 13th St Brooklyn NY 11230 Office: 401 Broadway New York City NY 10013 Tel (212) 226-7836

NEWMAN, KELLY LEE, b. Brownwood, Tex., Dec. 4, 1942; student Kilgore Coll., 1961-63; J.D., Baylor U., 1966. Admitted to Tex. bar, 1966; individual practice law, Kilgore, Tex., 1967-69; partner firm Bean, Ford, Schleier & Dickerson, Kilgore, 1969-70; partner firm Lapin, Lapin & Newman, Kilgore, 1970-71; partner firm Fenley, Bate & Newman, Lufkin, Tex., 1972—. Mem. State Bar Tex., Angelina County Bar Assn., Tex. Trial Lawyers Assn., Assn. Trial Lawyers of Am. Office: 204 E Lufkin Ave Lufkin TX 75901 Tel (713) 639-2238

NEWMAN, MIRIAM G., b. Bklyn.; B.A., Hunter Coll., 1941; LL.B., Bklyn. Law Sch., 1947, J.D., 1967. Admitted to N.Y. bar, 1947, U.S. Supreme Ct. bar; with legal dept. Mfrs. Hanover Bank (formerly Peoples Indsl. Bank), N.Y.C., 1950; partner firm Newman & Newman, N.Y.C., 1950—; mem. med. malpractice panel N.Y. Supreme Ct. Mem. Am., N.Y. Women's, Bklyn. Women's (v.p.) bar assns., Nat. Assn. Women Lawyers (officer), N.Y. County Lawyers Assn., Am. Arbitration Assn. (comml. and no-fault ins. panel), Small Claims Arbitrators Assn. (pres.), Bklyn. Lawyers Club (pres.), World Peace Through Law (com. internat. arbitration), LWV, Internat. Assn. Women Lawyers. Office: 225 W 34th St New York City NY 10001 Tel (212) 736-2113

NEWMAN, MORTON WISE, b. Evansville, Ind.; LL.B., U. Mich. Admitted to Ind. bar, 1928, Ill. bar, 1929; partner firms Newman & Salm, Evansville, 1930-52, Newman, Trockman & Flynn, Evansville, 1964-69; individual practice law, Evansville; judge Vanderburgh County (Ind.) Superior Ct., 1969—; corp. counsel City of Evansville, 1952-56; county atty. Vanderburgh County, 1969—. Bd. dirs. Evansville chpt. ARC, 1970—, Alcoholic Recovery Center, Evansville, 1971—. Mem. Evansville, Ind. bar assns., Ind. Judges Assn., Order of Coif. Mem. editorial staff Mich. Law Rev., 1928. Home: 425 S Hebron St Evansville IN 47715 Office: Civic Complex Evansville IN 47708 Tel (812) 426-5112

NEWMAN, NOEL REUBEN, b. N.Y.C., Jan. 5, 1932; A.B., Yale U., 1953; LL.B., Harvard U., 1956. Admitted to Conn. bar, 1956, U.S. Supreme Ct. bar, 1965; asso. firm Mellitz, Krentzman & Hall (now Mellitz, Krentzman & Newman), Bridgeport, Conn., 1956-66, partner, 1966—; atty. Town of Fairfield (Conn.), 1970—. Mem. Fairfield Town Meeting, 1963-67; mem. Sewer Commn., 1962-63, Bd. Fin., 1967-70. Mem. Conn., Bridgeport, Am. bar assns., Am. Trial Lawyers Assn., Am. Arbitration Assn. (panel). Home: 70 Crest Terr Fairfield CT 06432 Office: 1100 Main St Bridgeport CT 06604 Tel (203) 333-5161

NEWMAN, ROBERT WILLIAM, b. Chgo., Aug. 12, 1933; student Wright Jr. Coll., Chgo., 1951-52, U. Ill., 1952-54; LL.B., DePaul U., Chgo., 1957. Admitted to Ill. bar, 1957; mem. firm Newman, Stahl & Shadur, and predecessors, Chgo., 1959—. Mem. Ill., Chgo. bar assns., Chgo. Mortgage Attys. Assn. Office: Newman Stahl & Shadur 180 N LaSalle St Chicago IL 60601

NEWMAN, SANDERS DAVID, b. Bklyn., Nov. 28, 1930; J.D., N.Y. Law Sch., 1956. Admitted to N.Y. bar, 1956, U.S. Supreme Ct. bar, 1965, Pa. bar, 1971; mng. and trial atty. Allstate Ins. Co., Bklyn., 1956-60; asso. gen. counsel Reliance Ins. Co., Phila., 1960-63; asso. firm Otterbourg, Steindler, Houston & Rosen, N.Y.C., 1964-68; partner firm Powers & McNiff, N.Y.C., 1968-70; partner firm Blank, Rome, Klaus & Comisky, Phila., 1970—. Bd. dirs., pres. Welcome House Adoptive Parents Group Inc., Doylestown, Pa. Mem. Am., Pa., Phila. bar assns. Office: 11th Floor 4 Penn Center Plaza Philadelphia PA 19103 Tel (215) 569-3700

NEWMAN, STEPHEN AARON, b. N.Y.C., Nov. 13, 1946; B.A., Univ. Pa., 1967; J.D. cum laude, Columbia, 1970. Admitted to N.Y. bar, 1971; staff atty., dep. chief law enforcement N.Y.C. Dept. Consumer Affairs, 1970-73, chief, 1973-74; asst. prof. law N.Y. Law School, N.Y.C., 1974—; dir. Consumer Law Training Center, N.Y.C., 1975—. Mem. Jud. Screening Panel, N.Y. County, 1976; chmn. advt. com. N.Y. Regional Consumer Protection Council, 1973-74. Editor Columbia Law Review, 1968-70; contbr. articles in field to profl. jours. Office: 57 Worth St New York City NY 10013 Tel (212) 966-3500 x19

NEWMAN, STEPHEN MICHAEL, b. Buffalo, Jan. 12, 1945; A.B., Princeton, 1966; J.D., U. Mich., 1969. Admitted to N.Y. bar, 1969, Fla. bar, 1976; partner firm Hodgson, Russ, Andrews, Woods & Goodyear, Buffalo, 1969—. Bd. dirs. Jewish Center Greater Buffalo, 1974—. Mem. Am., N.Y. State, Erie County bar assns., Buffalo Life Ins. Trust and Banking Council, Estate Analysts of Western N.Y. Home: 108 Millbrook Dr Williamsville NY 14221 Office: 1800 1 M and T Plaza Buffalo NY 14203 Tel (716) 856-4000

NEWMAN, THOMAS, JR., b. Anderson, Ind., May 21, 1941; B.A., Am. U., 1965, M.A., 1970; J.D. cum laude Ind. U., 1972. Admitted to Ind. bar, 1972; asst. to Congressman J. Edward Roush, of Ind., 1959-67; legal advisor Madison County (Ind.) Police, 1972-74; asst. major atty. Ind. House of Representatives, 1975; judge, Madison County Ct., 1976, Madison County Superior Ct., 1976. Bd. dirs. Anderson Am. Revolution Bi-centennial Commn., 1976; dir. Police Athletic League. Mem. Phi Alpha Delta. Home: 334 W 8th St Anderson IN 46016 Office: Govt Center Anderson IN 46016 Tel (317) 646-9317

NEWMAN, THOMAS RUBIN, b. London, Sept. 7, 1933; B.A. cum laude, Hofstra Coll., 1957; LL.B., N.Y. U., 1960. Admitted to N.Y. bar, 1961, U.S. Supreme Ct. bar, 1964; since practiced in N.Y.C., law clk. to Asso. Judge Charles W. Froessel, N.Y. Ct. of Appeals, 1960-62; asso. firm Sabin, Bermant & Blau, and predecessor, 1963-70; partner firm Siff & Newman, 1971—; lectr. in field; mem. nat. panel arbitrators Am. Arbitration Assn., 1967—. Mem. Am., N.Y. State, N.Y.C. bar assns., Am. Law Inst., Def. Research Inst., Pi Gamma Mu. Contbr. articles in field to legal jours.; editor N.Y. U. Law Rev., 1959-60; columnist on appellate practice N.Y. Law Jour. Home: Glengary Rd Croton-on-Hudson NY 10520 Office: 233 Broadway New York City NY 10007 Tel (212) 349-3990

NEWMARK, MELVIN LESTER, b. St. Louis, Aug. 27, 1912; J.D., Washington U., St. Louis, 1936. Admitted to Mo., Fed. bars, 1936; partner firm Altman, Bremser Newmark & Altman, St. Louis, 1937-39, Newmark & Baris, 1961-75; individual practice law, St. Louis, 1940-43, 46-60, 76—; judge Olivette (Mo.) Municipal Ct., 1962-66. Mem. Mo., Met. St. Louis bar assns., Lawyers Assn. St. Louis. Named Outstanding Municipal Judge of Mo., 1966. Home: 701 Payson St Olivette MO 63132 Office: 721 Olive St Saint Louis MO 63101 Tel (314) 621-7400

NEWMARK, MICHAEL N., b. St. Louis, June 25, 1938; A.B., Washington U., 1960, J.D., 1962; LL.M. in Taxation, N.Y. U., 1963. Admitted to Mo. bar, 1962; asso. firm Newmark & Baris, 1963-64; atty. adv. U.S. Tax Ct., 1965-66; partner firm Lewis, Rice, Tucker, Allen & Chubb, St. Louis, 1966—; lectr. in tax law, Washington U. Law Sch., 1966—. Pres. St. Louis chpt. Am. Jewish Com., 1977. Mem. Bar Assn. Met. St. Louis (pres. 1975), Mo. Bar, Am. Bar Assn., Nat. Council Bar Pres.'s., Washington U. Law Alumni (pres. 1972), Washington U. Alumni (bd. govs. 1977)., Order Coif. Home: 417 Oakley Dr Clayton MO 63105 Office: 611 Olive St St Louis MO 63101 Tel (314) 231-5833

NEWMARK, MILTON MAXWELL, b. Oakland, Calif., Feb. 24, 1916; A.B., U. Calif., Berkeley, 1936, LL.B., 1947. Admitted to Calif. bar, 1941; practiced law with father, San Francisco, 1940-56; individual practice law, San Francisco, 1956-62, Lafayette, Calif., 1962—; lectr. bankruptcy State Bar of Calif. Continuing Edn. Program. Mem. Alameda County Republican Central Com., 1940-41; pres. Alameda Rep. Assembly, 1950. Mem. Am., San Francisco, Mt. Diablo bar assns. Home: 609 Terra California Dr 6 Walnut Creek CA 94595 Office: 986 Moraga Rd Lafayette CA 94549 Tel (415) 284-1404

NEWMARK, STUART, b. Bklyn., Dec. 1, 1942; B.B.A., Coll. City N.Y., 1964, J.D., 1968. Admitted to N.Y. bar, 1968; asso., partner firm Kaufman, Taylor, Kimmel & Miller, N.Y.C., 1968—; instr. Bklyn. Law Sch., 1962—. Mem. N.Y. County Lawyers Assn. Home: 1848 Cynthia Ln Merrick NY 11566 Office: 41 E 42nd St New York City NY 10017 Tel (212) MU2-2983

NEWPOL, JOSEPH JAMES, b. Boston, May 12, 1944; A.B., Boston U., 1967, J.D., 1970, LL.M., 1972. Admitted to Mass. bar, 1970; supervising tax specialist Coopers & Lybrand, Boston, 1970-75; tax atty. Gillette Co., Boston, 1975—. Mem. Am., Mass. bar assns.,

Am., Mass. socs. C.P.A.'s. Home: 32 Patricia Rd Sudbury MA 01776 Office: Gillette Co Prudential Tower Bldg Boston MA 02199 Tel (617) 421-7424

NEWSOM, BERNARD DEAN, JR., b. Berkeley, Calif., Mar. 8, 1947; B.A. in Polit. Sci., U. Calif., Santa Barbara, 1969; LL.D., U. Tex., Austin, 1973. Admitted to Tex. bar, 1972; research dir. Executives Services, Austin, 1972-73; asst. atty. gen. environ. protection Tex. Atty. Gen.'s Office, Austin, 1973—. Mem. Tex. Bar, Am., Travis County Jr. bar assns. Editor Tex. Jour. of Criminal Law, 1971-72. Ford grantee, 1971. Home: 3612 Bridle Path Austin TX 78703 Office: PO Box 12548 Capitol Station Austin TX 78711 Tel (512) 475-4143

NEWSOM, JAN LYNN REIMANN, b. Madison, Wis., Feb. 28, 1947; B.A., U. Tex., Austin, 1969, J.D., 1971. Admitted to Tex. bar, 1972; legal v.p. Nat. Compliance Co., Dallas, 1972; asso. counsel Group Hosp. Service Inc., Dallas, 1972—. Chmn. employee edn. com. Am. Cancer Soc., Dallas, 1976—; advisor on affirmative action ARC, Dallas, 1975—. Mem. Am., Tex., Dallas bar assns. Office: 2201 Main St Dallas TX 75201 Tel (214) 741-8211

NEWTON, ALEXANDER WORTHY, b. Birmingham, Ala., June 19, 1930; B.S., U. Ala., 1952, J.D., 1957. Admitted to Ala. bar, 1957, U.S. Supreme Ct. bar, 1969; partner firm Hare Wynn Newell & Newton, Birmingham, 1957—. Mem. Am., Birmingham (past mem. exec. com.), Ala. bar assns., Am., Ala. trial lawyers assns., Farrah Soc. (trustee), Internat. Soc. Barristers (past mem. bd. govs., sec.-treas., v.p.), Am. Coll. Trial Lawyers, Am. Judicature Soc. Home: 2837 Canoe Brook Ln Birmingham AL 35243 Office: 700 City Fed Bldg Birmingham AL 35203 Tel (205) 328-5330

NEWTON, ALFRED, b. Chgo., May 31, 1904; U. Ill., Urbana, 1925; LL.B., J.D., U. Mich., 1927. Admitted to Ill. bar, 1927; practiced in Chgo. Mem. Am., Ill., Chgo. bar assns., Mortgage Bankers Assn. (lectr.). Home: 1244 N Stone St Chicago IL 60610 Office: 10 S LaSalle St Chicago IL 60603 Tel (312) FR2-3247

NEWTON, AUTLEY BENJAMIN, b. Hammond, La., Mar. 25, 1936; B.A., La. State U., 1961, LL.B., 1965. Admitted to La. bar, 1965; asso. firm Hall, Raggio & Farrah, Lake Charles, La., 1965; individual practice law, Hammond, 1966-70, 1971-73; partner firm Macy, Kemp & Newton, Hammond, 1970-71; Newton & Baham, Hammond, 1973—. Del. La. Constl. Conv., 1973. Mem. Am., La., 21st Jud. Dist. (sec.-treas. 1972) bar assns., Comml. Law League, Phi Delta Phi. Recipient Am. Jurisprudence prize Joint Publishers The Annotated Reports System, 1964. Office: 105 S Cherry St Hammond LA 70404 Tel (504) 345-8660

NEWTON, BOBBY LAWRENCE, b. Creedmoor, N.C., June 13, 1935; A.B., U. N.C., Chapel Hill, 1957, J.D., 1960. Admitted to N.C. bar, 1960, U.S. Ct. Mil. Appeals, 1960; served as capt. JAGC, 1960-63; partner firm Hamrick, Doughton and Newton, Winston Salem, N.C., 1964—. Capt. United Fund, 1966-67; bd. dirs. Festival Theatre, Inc., 1967-68, 72-75; chmn. award com. Winston Salem Arts Council; chmn. spl. ad hoc com. involuntary hospitalization Forsyth County Mental Health Assn., 1972-73; bd. dirs. Winston Salem Little Theatre, 1975-77; mem. travel and conv. com., Winston Salem C. of C. Mem. Am., N.C., Forsyth County bar assns., Phi Delta Phi. Home: 1735 Meadowbrook Dr Winston-Salem NC 27104 Office: 2225 Wachovia Bldg PO Box 2759 Winston-Salem NC 27102 Tel (919) 725-0433

NEWTON, DEMETRIUS CAIPHUS, b. Fairfield, Ala., Mar. 15, 1928; B.A., Wilberforce U., 1949; J.D., Boston U., 1952. Admitted to Ala. bar, 1953, U.S. Supreme Ct. bar, 1956; sr. partner firm Newton Coar Newton & Tucker, Birmingham, Ala., 1970—; city atty. Brighton (Ala.), 1972—; judge City of Brownsville (Ala.), 1974—; adj. prof. constl. law Miles Coll. Law Sch., 1976—. Bd. dirs. Birmingham Urban League, 1975—. Mem. Am., Ala., Birmingham bar assns., NAACP (past city pres.), Am. Trial Lawyers Assn., Phi Beta Sigma. Home: 400 10th Ct W Birmingham AL 35204 Office: 2121 8th Ave N Suite 1722 Birmingham AL 35203 Tel (205) 252-9203

NEWTON, JOHN EDWARD, b. Ponca, Nebr., Apr. 4, 1904; LL.B., U. Nebr., 1926. Admitted to Nebr. bar, 1926; individual practice law, Ponca, 1926-57; county atty. Dixon County, Nebr., 1928-54; dist. judge, 1957-67; justice Nebr. Supreme Ct., Lincoln, 1967-77, ret., 1977. Mem. Am., Nebr. State bar assns. Home: Ponca NE 68770

NEXSEN, JULIAN JACOBS, b. Kingstree, S.C., Apr. 14, 1924; B.S. magna cum laude, Univ. S.C., 1948, LL.B. magna cum laude, 1950. Admitted to S.C. bar, 1950, U.S. Supreme Ct. bar, 1960; mem. firm Nexsen, Pruet, Jacobs, & Pollard, Columbia, S.C., 1950—. Mem. bd. regents Am. Coll. Probate Counsel, 1973—; mem. bd. dirs. Legal Aid Service Agency, 1975; trustee Providence Hosp., Columbia, 1970—; Richland County Pub. Library, Columbia Music Festival Assn. Mem. Am., S.C. (bd. govs. 1974—), Richland County (pres. 1974-75) bar assns., Am. Law Inst., Am. Jud. Soc., S.C. Bar Found. (past pres.), Phi Beta Kappa. Home: 2840 Sheffield Rd Columbia SC 29204 Office: First Nat Bank Bldg Columbia SC 29201 Tel (803) 771-8900

NEY, JAMES MICHAEL, b. Atlanta, Apr. 18, 1943; B.A., Furman U., 1964; J.D., U. Ga., 1966. Admitted to Ga. bar, 1966; law asst. to justice Supreme Ct. Ga., 1967-68; asso. firm Alston, Miller & Gaines, Atlanta, 1968-73, partner, 1973—; instr. John Marshall U., Atlanta, 1967-68. Deacon, Northside Dr. Bapt. Ch., Atlanta. Fellow Am. Coll. Mortgage Attys.; mem. Am., Atlanta bar assns., Am. Judicature Soc., Atlanta Lawyers Club. Spl. asso. Ga. Bar Reporter, 1967-68; editorial bd. Ga. Law Rev., 1965-66. Home: 3058 Farmington Dr Atlanta GA 30339 Office: 35 Broad St Atlanta GA 30303 Tel (404) 588-0300

NEYLAN, KATHLEEN MARY, b. Washington, Sept. 1, 1944; B.A., U. Iowa, 1966, J.D., 1967. Admitted to Iowa bar, 1967; U.S. Dist. Ct. for No. Dist. Iowa, 1969; atty. U.S. Dept. Agr., Washington, 1967; individual practice law, Elkader, Iowa, 1968—. Mem. Iowa Commn. Status Women, 1972-76; chmn. Iowa Juvenile Law Adv. Council, 1976—. Mem. Iowa Trial Lawyers Assn. (bd. govs., chmn. consumer and equal rights coms.), Iowa State (exec. council young lawyers sect., chmn. juvenile law com.), Iowa First Jud. Dist. (v.p. 1974—), Clayton County (pres., 1976—) bar assns. Office: 129 S Main Elkader IA 52043 Tel (319) 245-1561

NIBLOCK, WALTER RAYMOND, b. Little Rock, Nov. 19, 1927; B.S. in Pub. Adminstrn., U. Ark., 1951, J.D., 1953. Admitted to Ark. bar, 1953; field dir. ARC, various locations, 1953-58, chmn. Washington County chpt., 1965-67; self employed sub-gerente and dir. Industria De Pollos, S.A., Cali, Colombia, 1958-61; individual practice law, Fayetteville, Ark., 1961—. Mem. Ark. Tax Revision Study Commn., 1976. Chmn. Ark Bar Found., 1975-76. Mem. Am., Ark. (pres. 1977—), Washington County (past pres.) bar assns., Assn. Trial Lawyers Am., Ark. Trial Lawyers Assn. (pres. 1975-77), Am. Judicature Soc., Inst. Jud. Adminstrn., Delta Theta Phi. Home: 327 E Maple St Fayetteville AR 72701 Office: 20 E Mountain St Fayetteville AR 72701 Tel (501) 521-5510

NICCUM, ROBERT FREDERICK, b. Elkhart, Ind., Aug. 3, 1925; student Ohio State U., 1946-50; J.D., Cleveland-Marshall Law Sch., 1956. Admitted to Ohio bar, 1957, U.S. Supreme Ct. bar, 1962; practiced in Euclid, Ohio, 1957-69; law clk. Euclid Municipal Ct., 1959-64, judge, 1969—; asst. law dir. City of Euclid, 1964-69; lectr. bus. law Lakeland Community Coll. Mem. dist. com. Greater Cleve. Council East Shore dist. Boy Scouts Am.; pres. Euclid Council for Retarded Children, 1970—, Euclid Kiwanis Club, 1976. Mem. Cleve., Cuyahoga, Ohio State bar assns., Greater Cleve. Municipal Judges Assn. (pres. 1975), Euclid Gen. Hosp. Assn. Named Man of Year Am. Legion, 1971, Boss of Year Am. Bus. Women, 1973. Office: 545 E 222 St Euclid OH 44123 Tel (216) 731-9555

NICHOL, FRED JOSEPH, b. Sioux City, Iowa, Mar. 19, 1912; A.B., Yankton Coll., 1933; LL.B., U. S.D., 1936. Admitted to S.D. bar, 1936; mem. firm Hitchcock, Nichol & Lasegard, Mitchell, 1938-58; mem. S.D. Ho. of Reps. from Davison County, 1951-52, 57-58; state's atty. Davison County, 1947-51; circuit judge 4th Jud. Circuit S.D., 1959-65; U.S. dist. judge for S.D., 1965-66; chief judge, 1966—. Mem. exec. com. Legis. Research Council, 1951; S.D. del. Nat. Trial Judges Conv., 1962, 63, 64. Mem. sch. bd. and library bd., Mitchell, 1958-64; del. White House Conf. on Aging, 1961. Sec. S.D. del. Democratic Nat. Conv., 1956. Mem. corp. bd., also trustee Yankton Coll., 1954—. Mem. Am. Bar Assn., Am. Judicature Soc., Phi Delta Phi. Home: 1100 Tomar Rd Sioux Falls SD 57107 Office: US Court House Sioux Falls SD 57101*

NICHOLAS, EVERETT ELLISON, JR., b. Oak Park, Ill., Oct. 2, 1941; A.B., Wheaton Coll., 1963; J.D., U. Ill., 1966. Admitted to Ill. bar, 1966, Fed. Dist. Ct. of Appeals, 1972; asst. legal adviser Office of Supt. Pub. Instruction, State of Ill., 1966-70; mem. firm Robbins, Schwartz, Nicholas & Lifton, Ltd., Chgo., 1970—. Mem. dist. 90 bd. edn., River Forest, Ill., 1972-75; exec. bd. Council Sch. Attys., Nat. Assn. Sch. Bds., 1977—. Mem. Am., Ill., Chgo. bar assns., Am. Judicature Soc., Sch. Law Council (editor newsletter 1973-76, sec. 1976-77). Author: Special Education-Illinois School Law, 1977. Home: 542 Ashland River Forest IL 60305 Office: 29 S LaSalle St Chicago IL 60603 Tel (312) 332-7760

NICHOLAS, FRANK WILLIAM, b. W. Carrollton, Ohio, Nov. 12, 1898; A.B., Ohio State U., 1927, LL.B., 1927, J.D., 1967. Admitted to Ohio bar, 1927; individual practice law, 1927-35; judge Dayton (Ohio) Municipal Ct., 1935-40, Common Pleas Ct. Montgomery County (Ohio), 1941-70, Common Pleas Ct. Montgomery County and Hamilton County (Ohio), 1971—; mem. adv. council of judges Nat. Council on Crime and Delinquency, 1954-70. Mem. Am., Ohio, Dayton bar assns., Nat. Council Juvenile Ct. Judges Assn. (pres. 1958), Ohio State Juvenile Judges Assn. Home: 655 Garden Rd Dayton OH 45419 Office: 303 W 2d St Dayton OH 45402 Tel (513) 225-4191

NICHOLAS, JOHN G., b. Long Beach, L.I., Mar. 18, 1933; B.B.A., Coll. City N.Y., 1956; LL.B., St. John's U. Law Sch., 1959, J.D., 1968. Admitted to N.Y. bar, 1960; individual practice law, Flushing, N.Y., 1962—; asst. prof. bus. law Hofstra U. Del., Nat. Democratic Conv., 1974. Mem. Greek Am. Lawyers Assn. Inc. (pres.), N.Y. State Assn. Trial Lawyers, Queens County, N.Y. State bar assns. Home: 2-35 147th Pl Whitestone NY 11357 Office: 37-11 Union St Flushing NY 11354 Tel (212) 886-5200

NICHOLAS, SAMUEL JOHN, JR., b. Yazoo City, Miss., July 4, 1937; B.A., U. Miss., 1959, M.B.A., 1962; LL.B., Miss. Coll., 1966. Admitted to Miss. bar, 1966; asst. prof. econs. U. Southwestern La., Lafayette, 1962-63, Millsaps Coll., Jackson, Miss., 1963-70; individual practice law, Jackson, 1967—; also arbitrator and mediator; cons. bus. mgmt., 1963-70; exec. dir. Miss. Indsl. and Spl. Service, 1968—. Mem. Am., Fed., Miss., Hinds County bar assns., AAUP, Acad. Miss. Economists, Am. Bus. Law Assn., Am. Fin. Assn., Nat. Acad. Arbitrators, So. Econ. Assn., SW Social Sci. Assn., Am. Arbitration Assn., Am. Judicature Soc., Jackson C. of C., Sigma Delta Kappa. Home: 1650 Robert Dr Jackson MS 39211 Office: PO Box 22512 Jackson MS 39205 Tel (601) 969-3020

NICHOLLS, RICHARD HALL, b. Toronto, Ont., Can., Oct. 27, 1938; B.A. cum laude, Amherst Coll., 1960; LL.B., Stanford, 1963; LL.M. in Taxation, N.Y. U., 1964. Admitted to Calif. bar, 1964, N.Y. bar, 1965, D.C. bar, 1972; asso. firm Mudge Rose Guthrie & Alexander, N.Y.C., 1964-69, partner, 1970—. Mem. Assn. Bar City N.Y., N.Y. State Bar Assn. Home: 159 Ocean Dr W Stamford CT 06902 Office: 20 Broad St New York City NY 10005 Tel (212) 422-6767

NICHOLS, ALEXANDER LOWBER, b. Tularosa, N.Mex., Feb. 28, 1906; A.B., Haverford Coll., 1928; LL.B., U. Pa., 1931. Admitted to Del. bar, 1932, U.S. Supreme Ct. bar, 1936; partner firm Morris, Nichols, Arsht & Tunnell, Wilmington, Del., 1940-76, of counsel, 1977—. Bd. dirs. (hon.) YMCA of Wilmington and New Castle County, v.p., 1965-68; mem. budget com. United Way of Del., 1950-60, chmn., 1955-56; advisory mem. Family Service of No. Del., pres., 1952-54; mem. Episcopal Ch. Home Found.; trustee Tower Hill Sch. Assn., 1943-71; mem., former vestryman, sec. Trinity Episcopal Ch., 1973-75; mem. Wilmington Club, Country, Rotary Clubs. Mem. Del. State (chmn. com. on profl. ethics, chmn. preliminary investigatory com. of Del. Ct. on Judiciary by appointment Supreme Ct. Del.), Am. (dir. govs., 1970-73, Del. State Bar Assn. del. to Ho. of Dels., 1954-60, Del. state del. 1961-70, mem. standing com. on profl. edn., 1971-73, gavel awards com. 1974—) bar assns., Del. Legal Aid Soc. (founding, dir., sec.), Am. Bar Found, Am. Judicature Soc., World Peace Through Law Center, Phi Delta Phi. Home: 2310 W 17th St Wilmington DE 19806 Office: Wilmington Tower Box 1347 Wilmington DE 19899 Tel (302) 658-9200

NICHOLS, ANDREW LIVINGSTON, b. Newton, Mass., Jan. 8, 1936; B.A., Dartmouth, 1958; LL.B., Harvard, 1961. Admitted to Mass. bar, 1961; asso. firm Choate, Hall & Stewart, Boston, 1961-69, partner, 1969—; lectr. Mass. Continuing Legal Edn. Mem. Am., Boston bar assns. Office: 28 State St Boston MA 02109 Tel (617) 227-5020

NICHOLS, DAVID ACKART, b. Wilmington, Del., May 1, 1940; B.A., Amherst Coll., 1962; M.A. in Teaching, Wesleyan U., 1964; J.D., U. Wash., 1971. Admitted to Wash. bar, 1971; mem. firm McCush, O'Connor & Thompson, Bellingham, Wash., 1971-73, Abbott, Lant & Fleeson, 1973—. Bd. dirs. Whatcom Counseling and Psychiat. Clinic. Mem. Am., Wash State bar assns., Bellingham C. of C. (sec.). Office: 215 Mason Blvd Bellingham WA 98225

NICHOLS, EARLE MOREN, b. Princeton, Ky., July 19, 1900; LL.B., U. Ky., 1926. Admitted to Ky. bar, 1926; practice law, 1926—; asso. firm Gordon & Gordon & Moore, Madisonville, Ky., 1926-46; firm Waddill, Laffoon & Nichols, 1949-51, Nichols, Nichols, Hallyburton & Wells, Madisonville, 1952—; city atty., Madisonville, 1932-33, City of Dawson Springs, 1936-76. Mem. Ky. Bar Assn. (named sr. counsellor at law, 1976). Died Jan. 30, 1977. Home: 106 S Kentucky Ave Madisonville KY 42431

NICHOLS, FREDERICK HARRIS, b. Chgo., Jan. 31, 1936; B.A., Williams Coll., 1958; J.D., Harvard, 1961. Admitted to N.Y. State bar, 1962, U.S. Supreme Ct. bar, 1970; partner firm Cohen Swados Wright Hanifin Bradford & Brett, Buffalo, 1966—; asso. firm Cohen Swados Wright Hanifin Bradford & Brett, 1962-65. Lectr., various insts., 1967—. Bd. dirs., treas. Child and Family Services of Erie County; bd. dirs. Planned Parenthood of Buffalo. Mem. Am., N.Y. State, Erie County bar assns. Fulbright scholar Hamburg (Germany) U., 1961-62. Home: 171 Chapin Pkwy Buffalo NY 14209 Office: 70 Niagara St Buffalo NY 14202 Tel (716) 856-4600

NICHOLS, HENRY LOUIS, b. Collin County, Tex., Nov. 7, 1916; LL.B., So. Meth. U., 1940. Admitted to Tex. bar, 1939; asst. city atty. City of Dallas, 1946-51; partner firm Saner, Jack, Sallinger & Nichols, Dallas, 1951—; research fellow Southwestern Legal Fedn., 1963—. Fellow Am., Tex. bar fedns.; mem. Dallas (pres. 1963), Tex., Am. bar assns., Southwestern Legal Fedn. (dir.), Am. Judicature Soc. Home: 3904 Euclid Ave Dallas TX 75205 Office: 1200 Republic Bank Bldg Dallas TX 75201 Tel (214) 742-5464

NICHOLS, HORACE ELMO, b. Elkmont, Ala., July 16, 1912; Mus.B., Columbia, 1933, postgrad. in constnl. law, 1937-38; LL.B., Cumberland Law Sch., 1936. Admitted to Ga. bar, 1935; practice in Canton, Ga., 1938-40, Rome, Ga., 1940-48; judge Superior Ct., Rome, 1948-54; mem. Ct. Appeals Ga., 1954-66; justice Supreme Ct. Ga., Atlanta, 1966—, chief justice, 1975—. Vocal soloist World's Fair, Chgo., 1933. Mem. Sigma Alpha Epsilon, Blue Key. Home: 13 Virginia Circle Rome GA 30161 Office: 28 Jud Bldg Atlanta GA 30334*

NICHOLS, IRENE GARRETSON, b. Oklahoma City, Aug. 18, 1906; B.A., Agnes Scott Coll., 1928; student George Washington U., 1935-38; LL.B., Atlanta Law Sch., 1940; student Emory U. Law Sch., 1943. Admitted to Ga. bar, 1940; atty. War Labor Bd., Atlanta, 1942-45, Atlanta Legal Aid Soc., 1945-47, Lawyers Title Ins. Co., Atlanta, 1951-55; partner James G. Nichols Co., Atlanta, 1955—; sec. clk. U.S. Atty's office No. Dist. Ga., Atlanta, 1940-42; sec. SEC, Atlanta, 1938-42, Nat. Bituminous Coal Commn., Washington, 1937-38, FCC, Washington, 1934-37; clk. CAA, Washington, 1938, U.S. Treasury Dept., 1931-34, Ga. Power Co., Atlanta, 1928-31. Mem. State Bar Ga., AAUW, Ga. Assn. Women Lawyers (past pres.), Fed. Bar Assn. (past v.p. Atlanta). Home and Office: 933 N Highland Ave Atlanta GA 30306 Tel (404) 873-6251

NICHOLS, JACK BRITT, b. Tampa, Fla., Mar. 14, 1936; B.S. in Bus. Adminstrn., U. Fla., 1958, J.D., 1965. Admitted to Fla. bar, 1966, U.S. Dist. Ct. Middle Dist. Fla. bar, 1966, U.S. Circuit Ct. 5th Circuit bar, 1966, U.S. Supreme Ct. bar, 1971; asso. firm Gurney and Skolfield, Winter Park, Fla., 1966-68, partner, 1968-70; dir. firm Skolfield, Gilman, Cooper, Nichols, Tatich and Adams, Winter Park, 1971; v.p., dir. Skolfield, Nichols & Tatich, Orlando, Fla., 1972; pres. Nichols & Tatich, Orlando, 1975—. Bd. dirs. Orange County (Fla.) Legal Aid, 1971-72. Mem. Fla. Bar, Am., Orange County (exec. council 1972-75) bar assns., Am. Trial Lawyers Assn., Acad. Fla. Trial Lawyers, Fla. Blue Key. Recipient Am. Jurisprudence award in Evidence U. Fla. Law Sch., 1965; Distinguished Service award Winter Park Jaycees, 1971. Home: 1070 Druid Dr Maitland FL 32751 Office: PO Box 33 108 E Hillcrest St Orlando FL 32802 Tel (305) 841-8823

NICHOLS, JAMES RICHARD, b. Newton, Mass., Apr. 19, 1938; B.A. magna cum laude, Dartmouth, 1960; LL.B., Harvard, 1963. Admitted to Mass. bar, 1963; clk. Supreme Jud. Ct. Mass., 1963-64; asso. firm Herrick, Smith, Donald, Farley & Ketchum, Boston, 1964-68; asso. firm Goodwin, Procter & Hoar, Boston, 1969-76; partner firm Nichols & Pratt, Boston, 1977—; dir. Boston-Worcester Corp.; trustee pvt. and charitable trusts. Mem. Weston (Mass.) Fin. Com., 1969-74, chmn., 1973-74; trustee, sec., exec. com. Boston Mus. Sci., 1972—; trustee Civic Edn. Found., Medford, Mass., 1974—. Mem. Boston Bar Assn., Boston Security Analysts Soc., Fin. Analysts Fedn. Chartered fin. analyst. Home: 23 Wellesley St Weston MA 02193 Office: 28 State St Boston MA 02109 Tel (617) 523-6800

NICHOLS, LYLE DANIEL, b. Hattiesburg, Miss., July 25, 1942; student Gordon Mil. Coll., 1960-61; B.B.A., U. Ga., 1965; LL.B., Mercer U., 1968. Admitted to Ga. bar, 1970; mem. firm Hansell, Post, Brandon & Dorsey, Atlanta, 1968—. Mem. Atlanta Boys' Club Assistance, 1974-75. Mem. Am., Atlanta bar assns., State Bar Ga. (editor real property newsletter 1972—), Atlanta Lawyers Club, Am. Judicature Soc., Kappa Alpha Alumni Assn. (pres. 1976-77). Home: 3910 Powers Ferry Rd NW Atlanta GA 30342 Office: 3300 1st Nat Bank Tower Atlanta GA 30303 Tel (404) 581-8000

NICHOLSON, DANA, b. Mpls., Mar. 7, 1909; B.A., U. Minn., 1929, LL.B., 1931. Admitted to Minn. bar, 1931; since practiced in Mpls., asso. firm Stinchfield, Mackall, Crounse & Moore, 1931-42; partner firm Ewing, Feidt & Nicholson, 1946-52; judge Municipal Ct., 1952-59, Minn. Dist. Ct. Hennepin County, 1959—. Mem. Minn., Hennepin County bar assns., Minn. Dist. Judges' Assn. (pres. 1972-73). Home: Apt 103 5290 Villa Way Edina MN 55436 Office: 1756 Courts Tower Minneapolis MN 55487 Tel (612) 348-3223

NICHOLSON, FREDERIC ANTHONY, b. Norfolk, Va., Oct. 26, 1927; B.A., U. Va., 1950, LL.B., 1952; LL.M., N.Y. U., 1955. Admitted to Va. bar, 1953, N.Y. bar, 1953, D.C. bar, 1966; asso. firm Debevoise, Plimpton Lyons & Gates, N.Y.C., 1958-66, Hogan & Hartson, Washington, 1966-68; mem. firm Botein, Hays, Sklar & Herzberg, N.Y.C., 1968—; lectr. Georgetown Law Sch., 1967-68; adj. prof. Rutgers Law Sch., 1973—; legis. atty. IRS, 1955-59. Mem. Fed., N.Y. State bar assns., Bar Assn. City N.Y. Contbr. articles to profl. jours. Home: 68 Laurel Rd Princeton NJ 08560 Office: 200 Park Ave New York City NY 10017 Tel (212) 867-5500

NICHOLSON, HARRY DONALD, b. Jan. 16, 1935; B.A., So. Meth. U., 1957, LL.B., 1959. Admitted to Tex. bar, 1959; asst. dist. atty. Dallas County, 1961-63; 1st asst. U.S. atty. for Eastern Dist. Tex., 1963-66; owner, operator ranch, 1966-73; judge Tex. Dist. Ct., 13th Jud. Dist. of Navarro County, 1973—. Mem. adminstrv. bd. 1st Meth. Ch. Mem. State Bar Tex. Home: 2027 W Park St Corsicana TX 75110 Office: PO Box 333 Corsicana TX 75110 Tel (214) 874-8432

NICKELS, JOHN LEONARD, b. Aurora, Ill., Jan. 16, 1931; B.S., No. Ill. U., 1958; J.D., DePaul U., 1961. Admitted to Ill. bar, 1961; asso. Gates W. Clancy, Geneva, Ill., 1961-63; mem. firm Neuendorf & Nickels, Sandwich, Ill., 1963-71; individual practice law, Elburn, Ill., 1971—; village atty. Sugar Grove, Ill., 1966-70; mem. Kane County Zoning Bd. Appeals, 1967-72. Bd. trustees Waubonsee Community Coll., 1967-70. Mem. Kane County, DeKalb County, Am. bar assns., Phi Alpha Delta. Home: Route 1 Box 106K Sugar Grove IL 60554 Office: 130 N Main St Box AC Elburn IL 60119 Tel (312) 365-6441

NICKSA, WALTER C., JR., b. Hartford, Conn., Dec. 17, 1944; B.A., Yale, 1966; J.D., U. Conn., 1969. Admitted to Conn. bar, 1969; partner firm Gillespie & Nicksa, Unionville, Conn., 1972—. Mem. Hartford County, Conn., Am. bar assns. Home: 16 Hansen Rd Canton CT 06020 Office: 1783 Farmington Ave Unionville CT 06085 Tel (203) 673-3243

NICOLA, ROBERT JAMES, b. Bridgeport, Ct., Oct. 16, 1942; B.A., Franklin and Marshall Coll., 1964; J.D., U. Ct., 1967. Admitted to Ct. bar, 1967; asso. firm Damore, Jacobson & Janello, Bridgeport, 1967-68; partner firm Owens & Schine, Bridgeport, 1969—; advocate Juvenile Ct. 1st Dist. Ct., Bridgeport, 1970-75. Mem. Easton (Conn.) Conservation Commn., 1976, Ct. Indian Affairs Council, Hartford, Conn., 1973—. Mem. Ct., Bridgeport bar assns., Am. Trial Lawyers Assn., Assn. Immigration and Nat. Lawyers. Home: RFD 1 W Redding CT 06896 Office: 1100 Main St Bridgeport CT 06604 Tel (203) 334-4153

NICOLLS, KEITH KENNEDY, lawyer; b. Detroit, Feb. 2, 1922; B.S. in Mech. Engring., U. Mich., 1944, J.D., 1948. Admitted to Ill. bar, 1949; house patent counsel Goodman Mfg. Corp., Chgo., 1948-49; asso. law firm Brown, Jackson, Boettcher & Dienner, Chgo., 1949-59; asso. law firm Horton Davis McCaleb, Chgo., 1959-68; partner law firm Davis, McCaleb, Lucas & McCaleb, Lucas & Brugman, Chgo., 1968—. Village trustee, Glen Ellyn, Ill., 1962-65, village pres., 1965-69. Mem. DuPage Mayors and Mgrs. Assn. (pres. 1968-69), Patent Law Assn. Chgo., Chgo., Ill. bar assns. Home: 657 Forest Ave Glen Ellyn IL 60137 Office: 230 W Monroe St Chicago IL 60606

NIDA, ROBERT HALE, b. Los Angeles, Oct. 20, 1940; B.A., U. Calif., Santa Barbara, 1962, J.D., Los Angeles, 1965. Admitted to Calif. bar, 1966; dep. county counsel Los Angeles County, 1967-68; asso. counsel Automobile Club of So. Calif., Los Angeles, 1969-75, dir. legal div., 1975—; del. Nat. Com. on Uniform Traffic Laws, 1974—; mem. com. on motor vehicle and traffic law Transp. Research Bd. of Nat. Acad. Scis. Mem. Conf. Ins. Counsel, Los Angeles County Bar, State Bar Calif., Am. Bar Assn., Phi Alpha Delta, Delta Sigma Phi. Author: California Motor Vehicle Legislation, 1971. Office: 2601 S Figueroa St Los Angeles CA 90007 Tel (213) 746-4810

NIEBANK, CORNELIUS GEORGE, JR., b. Niagara Falls, N.Y., Oct. 21, 1925; A.B., Yale U., 1947; J.D., U. Buffalo, 1950; postgrad. Harvard U. Bus. Sch., 1969. Admitted to N.Y. bar, 1950, Ill. bar, 1953, U.S. Supreme Ct. bar, 1956; law clk. to Justice Robert H. Jackson, U.S. Supreme Ct., Washington, 1950-52; commr. U.S. Ct. Mil. Appeals, Washington, 1952-53; with Santa Fe Ry., Chgo., 1953—, v.p. law, 1976—; mem. Ill. Jud. Inquiry Bd., 1976—. Mem. Am., Ill. State, Chgo. bar assns. Home: 60 Hazel Ave Glencoe IL 60022 Office: 80 E Jackson Blvd Chicago IL 60604 Tel (312) 427-4900

NIEDERMAYER, ROY IRA, b. Washington, Mar. 28, 1947; B.A., Yale, 1969; J.D., Harvard, 1972. Admitted to Md. bar, 1972, D.C. bar, 1973; asso. firm Gordon, Feinblatt, Rothman, et al, Balt., 1972-73, Melrod, Redman & Gartlan, Washington, 1973—. Mem. Montgomery County, D.C. bar assns., Am. Trial Lawyers Assn. Office: 1801 K St NW Washington DC 20006 Tel (202) 833-3700

NIEHOFF, CARL ALBERT, b. Lehighton, Pa., July 12, 1906; A.B., Lafayette Coll., 1928; LL.B., Temple U., 1936. Admitted to Pa. bar, 1941; head dept. history Lehighton High Sch., 1928-33; supr. N.E. Pa. Nat. Defense Tng. Program, 1940-41; dir. Carbon County Civilian Defense, 1941-44; solicitor Carbon County Selective Service Bd., 1941-44; dist. atty. Carbon County, 1943-60; solicitor Carbon County Recreation Authority, Jim Thorpe, Pa., 1960-66; solicitor Lehighton Area Sch. Dist., 1943—. Mem. Am., Carbon County (chancellor 1968-69), Pa. bar assns. Recipient certificate for aid to Selective Service System, Pres. U.S., 1945. Home: 330 S 1st St Lehighton PA 18235 Office: 328 S 1st St Lehighton PA 18235 Tel (215) 377-0480

NIELSEN, ARTHUR HANSEN, b. Fairview City, Utah, Apr. 30, 1914; A.A.B., Snow Coll., 1934; J.D., U. Utah, 1937. Admitted to Utah bar, 1938, U.S. Supreme Ct. bar, 1946; law clk. Utah Supreme Ct., 1938-41; pros. atty. City of Salt Lake City, 1941-42; asst. atty. gen. State of Utah, 1942-46; individual practice law, Salt Lake City, 1941-49; sr. partner firm Nielsen, Henriod, Gottfredson, and Peck, and predecessors, Salt Lake City, 1949—; lectr. law U. Utah, 1950-69; mem. Utah Supreme Ct. Com. on Rules of Civil Procedure and Rules of Evidence, 1947—; mem. vis. com. J. Reuben Clark Law Sch., 1973; mem. adv. council Practising Law Inst., 1963-69. Mem. Salt Lake County, Am., Utah (bd. bar examiners 1949-66, chmn. 1955-66; bd. commrs. 1968-74) bar assns., Bar and Gavel Soc. Utah (hon.). Home: 2178 E 1700 S Salt Lake City UT 84108 Office: 410 Newhouse Bldg 10 Exchange Pl Salt Lake City UT 84111 Tel (801) 521-3350

NIELSEN, LOUIS B., b. Honesdale, Pa., Oct. 26, 1918; B.A., Wesleyan U., 1940; LL.D., Pa. U., 1946. Admitted to Pa. Supreme Ct. bar, 1947, Pa. Superior Ct. bar, 1948; mem. legal firms; individual practice law; dist. atty., Wayne County, Pa., 1952-63; spl. asst. atty. gen. State of Pa., 1963-64; arbitrator Am. Arbitration Assn. Key layman, mem. vestry Grace Episcopal Ch., 1952-68; mem. exec. com. Wayne County Republican Com. Mem. Pa., Am., Wayne County (v.p.) bar assns. Home: 305 16th St Honesdale PA 18431 Office: 303 10th St Honesdale PA 18431 Tel (717) 253-2105

NIEMETH, CHARLES FREDERICK, b. Lorain, Ohio, Nov. 25, 1939; B.A., Harvard, 1962; J.D., U. Mich., 1965. Admitted to Calif. bar, 1966; asso. firm O'Melveny & Myers, Los Angeles, 1965-72, partner, 1973—. Mem. Am., Los Angeles County bar assns. Office: 1800 Century Park E Los Angeles CA 90067 Tel (213) 553-6700

NIEMEYER, KENNETH EDWARD, b. Mobile, Ala., May 25, 1946; B.A., U. Va., 1969; J.D., U. Ala., 1972. Admitted to Ala. bar, 1973, Mobile County bar, 1973. With First Nat. Bank of Mobile (Ala.), 1972—, asst. trust officer, 1973-75, trust officer, 1975-76, asst. v.p., trust officer, 1976-77, v.p., trust officer, 1977—. Trustee, bd. dirs. Ala. Trust Sch.; trustee Historic Devel. Found., Greater Mobile Concerts; treas. Greater Mobile Concerts Symphony Group. Mem. Moblie, Am. bar assns., Ala. Bankers Assn. Office: 31 N Royal St Mobile AL 36621

NIENOW, HARVEY CHARLES, b. Milw., Dec. 21, 1922; B.M.E., U. Wis., 1947; J.D., Marquette U., 1950. Admitted to Wis. bar, 1950, Calif. bar, 1961; patent lawyer Cutler Hammer Co., Milw., 1950-53, BASO, Inc., Milw., 1953-57, Borg Warner Co., Santa Ana, Calif., 1957-61; mem. firm Nienow & Frater, Santa Ana, 1961—. Pres., Santa Anna-Tustin YMCA, 1967-70; v.p. Orange County Fedn. Community Chest, 1971-72; dist. chmn. Boy Scouts Am., 1973-74; bd. dirs. Santa Ana-Tustin Community Chest, 1967-71, pres., 1970-71; trustee, exec. com. Santa Ana Community Hosp., 1969-74; bd. dirs. Boys Club of Santa Ana, 1970—; mem. council Chapman Coll., 1970-74, bd. govs., 1974—. Mem. Am. (fed. practice and procedure com.), Wis., Calif., Orange County bar assns., Am. (fed. practice and procedure com.), Los Angeles patent law assns. Home: 918 River Ln Santa Ana CA 92706 Office: 888 N Main St Suite 908 Santa Ana CA 92701 Tel (714) 547-6553

NIERENBERG, GERARD IRWIN, b. N.Y.C., July 27, 1923; student N.Y. U., 1939; LL.B., St. Lawrence U., 1945. Admitted to N.Y. State bar, 1946; sr. partner firm Nierenberg, Zeif & Weinstein, N.Y.C., 1946—. Mem. Am. Bar Assn., Assn. Bar City of N.Y. Author: The Art of Negotiating, 1968; Creative Business Negotiating, 1971; How to Read A Person Like a Book, 1971; Fundamentals of Negotiating, 1973; Meta-Talk: A Guide to the Hidden Meaning of Conversation, 1973; How to Give and Receive Advice, 1975. Office: 230 Park Ave Suite 460 New York City NY 10017 Tel (212) 679-1455

NIERENGARTEN, ROGER JOSEPH, b. St. Cloud, Minn., Nov. 19, 1925; B.A., St. John's U., 1948, LL.B., Marquette U., Milw., 1951, J.D., 1968. Admitted to Minn. bar, 1951; individual practice law, St. Cloud, 1956—; atty. Stearns County (Minn.), 1962-66; spl. asst. atty. gen. State of Minn., 1972-76; adminstrv. asst. to mayor City of St. Cloud, 1954-56. Chmn. dept. edn. Minn. Cath. Conf., 1974-76. Mem. Am., Minn., Stearns County bar assns., Am., Minn. trial lawyers assns. Named one of 9 outstanding Cath. sch. bd. mems. in U.S., 1976. Home: 844 N 1st St Sartell MN 56377 Office: 501 St Germain Mall St Cloud MN 56301 Tel (612) 251-3602

NIES, HELEN WILSON, b. Birmingham, Ala., Aug. 7, 1925; B.A., U. Mich., 1946, J.D., 1948. Admitted to Mich. bar, 1948, U.S. Ct. Customs and Patent Appeals bar, 1961, D.C. bar, 1962, U.S. Supreme Ct. bar, 1962, U.S. Ct. Claims bar, 1977; atty. Office Alien Property, Dept. Justice, Washington, 1948-51; br. counsel consumer durable goods Office Price Stblzn., Washington, 1951-52; mem. firm Pattishall, McAuliffe & Hofstetter, Washington, 1961-66, partner, 1966—; mem. faculty Practising Law Inst., 1974—, Inst. Continuing Legal Edn., 1976—; mem. com. of visitors U. Mich. Law Sch., 1975—; mem. Dept. Commerce Pub. Adv. Com. for Trademark Affairs, 1976—. Pres. Mohican Hills (Md.) Civic Assn., 1960. Mem. Am. Bar Assn. (chmn. PTC sect. coms.), Bar Assn. D.C. (chmn. sect. on patent trademark and copyright law 1975-76, dir. 1976—, Outstanding Service award 1976), D.C. Bar, U.S. Trademark Assn. (chmn. lawyers adv. com. 1974-76, dir., Merit award 1976), Fed. Bar Assn., Women's Bar D.C., Nat. Assn. Women Lawyers, Am. Judicature Soc., Am. Patent Law Assn., Order of Coif, Phi Beta Kappa. Editorial bd. Patent, Trademark and Copyright Jour. Home: 6604 Rivercrest Ct Washington DC 20016 Office: 600 New Hampshire Ave Suite 470 Washington DC 20037 Tel (202) 337-4554

NIKLAS, DAVID NEIL, b. Helena, Mont., Feb. 9, 1940; B.A., Carroll Coll., 1962; LL.B., U. Mont., 1965. Admitted to Mont. bar, 1965; asso. firm Kline & Niklas, and predecessors, Helena, 1965-69, partner, 1969—. Mem. Am., 1st Jud. Dist. bar assns., State Bar Mont. Home: 121 Elmwood Ln Helena MT 59601 Office: 555 Fuller Ave Helena MT 59601 Tel (406) 442-8950

NILAND, EDWARD JOHN, JR., b. Boston, Aug. 25, 1916; J.D. cum laude, Boston Coll., 1947. Admitted to Calif. bar, 1948, U.S. Supreme Ct. bar, 1973; asso. prof. law U. Santa Clara (Calif.), 1947-52; partner firm Boccardo, Blum, Lull, Niland & Bell, San Jose, Calif., 1952—; vis. lectr. U. San Francisco Law Sch., 1948-53; lectr. continuing edn. of bar program, Calif., 1966. Bd. fellows U. Santa Clara, 1974—. Mem. Calif. Bar Assn., Assn. Trial Lawyers Am., Am. Judicature Soc., Calif. Acad. Appellate Lawyers (1st v.p. 1973-77), Calif. Trial Lawyers. Contbr. articles to legal jours. Home: 14110 Douglas Ln Saratoga CA 95070 Office: 111 W Saint John St San Jose CA 95113 Tel (408) 298-5678

NILES, PALMER ALBERT, b. Olathe, Colo., Mar. 3, 1908; B.S., U.S. Coast Guard Acad., 1929; J.D. cum laude, U. Miami (Fla.), 1952. Admitted to Fla. bar, 1952; partner firm Brigham, Black, Niles & Wright, Miami, 1952-57; partner firm Padgett, Teasley, Niles & Shaw, Coral Gables, Fla., 1957—. Fellow Am. Coll. Probate Counsel; mem. Am., Fla. Dade County, Coral Gables bar assns., Army and Navy Club (past pres.), Mil. Order of World Wars (past comdr.), Flamingo Dinner Club (past pres.). Co-author: Chpt. in Basic Practice Under Fla. Probate Code, 1976. Home: 5782 SW 50th St South Miami FL 33155 Office: 2505 Ponce de Leon Blvd Coral Gables FL 33134 Tel (305) 444-7611

NILSEN, WALTER GRAHN, b. Bklyn., Nov. 13, 1927; A.B., Columbia, 1949, Ph.D., 1956; M.S., Cornell U., 1951; J.D., Seton Hall U., 1973. Mem. tech. staff Bell Telephone Labs., 1959-69, mem. patent staff, 1969—; admitted to N.J. bar, 1973. Mem. N.J. Patent Law Assn., N.J., Am. bar assns., Sigma Xi. Home: 62 Hobart Ave Summit NJ 07901 Office: Room 3C-413 Bell Telephone Labs Murray Hill NJ 07974 Tel (201) 582-3329

NIMMER, MELVILLE BERNARD, b. Los Angeles, June 6, 1923; A.B., U. Calif., 1947; LL.B., Harvard, 1950. Admitted to Calif. bar, 1951; mem. legal dept. Paramount Pictures Corp., Los Angeles, 1951-54; partner firm Nimmer & Selvin, Beverly Hills, Calif., 1954-61; prof. law U. Calif., Los Angeles, 1961—; of counsel firm Kaplan, Livingston, Goodwin, Berkowitz & Selvin, Beverly Hills, 1961—; vice chmn. Nat. Commn. on New Tech. Uses of Copyrighted Works, 1975—. Mem. Am. Bar Assn., State Bar Calif., Soc. Am. Law Tchrs. Author: Nimmer on Copyright, 1963, rev. edit., 1977; Copyright and Other Aspects of Law Pertaining to Literary, Musical and Artistic Works, 1971; contbr. articles to legal jours. Home: 715 Malcolm Ave Los Angeles CA 90024 Office: 405 Hilgard Ave Los Angeles CA 90024 Tel (213) 825-4685

NIPPER, JOHN MICHAEL, b. Gadsden, Ala., July 8, 1944; B.S., Auburn U., 1966; J.D., U. Ala., 1969; LL.M., N.Y. U., 1970. Admitted to Ala. bar, 1969, Miss. bar, 1972; individual practice law, Grenada, Miss., 1972—; mem. Miss. Ho. of Reps., 1975—. Bd. dirs. Grenada Little Theater. Mem. Am., Ala., Miss., Grenada bar assns. Home: 1673 Martha Dr Grenada MS 38901 Office: 10 South St Grenada MS 38901 Tel (601) 226-1111

NIRO, ROBERT EUGENE, b. Newcastle, Pa., Feb. 8, 1943; B.A. in English, U. Fla., 1966; J.D., Fla. State U., 1969. Admitted to Fla. bar, 1969; adminstrv. asst. Fla. Sec. State Office, Tallahassee, 1969-71; asst. gen. counsel Fla. Div. Bond Fin. Tallahassee, 1971-76, acting gen. counsel, 1976—. Home: 1514 Seminole Dr Tallahassee FL 32301 Office: 622 Larson Bldg Tallahassee FL 32304 Tel (904) 488-4782

NISSEL, J. THOMAS, b. Balt., Dec. 29, 1930; B.A., Loyola Coll., Balt., 1952; LL.B., U. Md., 1955, J.D., 1969. Admitted to Md. bar, 1955, Fed. bar, 1955; law clk., asso. firm Weinberg & Green, Balt., 1955-56; partner firm Nissel & Thieme, 1959-63; individual practice law, Balt., 1963-71; judge Dist. Ct., 10th Dist., Ellicott City, 1971—; spl. atty. Md. State Rds. Commn., 1957-64; counsel Kennedy Hwy., 1964-66, Howard County Park Bd., 1965-66; states atty. for Howard County, 1966, county atty., 1967; asso. judge Peoples Ct. Howard County, 1970-71, chief judge, 1971. Pres., Parish Council Resurrection Ch., 1975-76, mem. council, 1976—. Mem. Am. (state co-chmn. Nat. Conf. Spl. Ct. Judges 1975-76), Md., Howard County (dir. 1976-76) bar assns., Am. Judicature Soc. Office: Dist Ct Howard County Court House 8360 Court Ave Ellicott City MD 21043 Tel (301) 465-7664

NISSEN, DAVID R., b. Provo, Utah, Mar. 7, 1932; A.B. in History, Wheaton Coll., 1954; M.A. in History, U. Ill., 1959; J.D., 1961. Admitted to Ill. bar, 1961, Calif. bar, 1962; with U.S. Dept. Justice, 1961; asst. U.S. atty., Los Angeles, 1962-65, asst. chief criminal div., 1966, chief organized crime sect., 1967-68, chief criminal div., 1969-71, spl. atty. for nat. litigation, 1971-73; mem. firm Yates & Nissen, Santa Ana, Calif., 1973—; spl. agt. CIC, Washington, 1955-57. Trustee Biola Coll., La Mirada, Calif., 1975-76. Mem. Calif. State, Ill. State, Orange County bar assns., Am. Trial Lawyers Assn. Office: 888 N Main St Santa Ana CA 92701 Tel (714) 835-3742

NISSLER, PERRY STEVENS, B.S. in Bus. Adminstrn., U. Calif., Berkeley, 1964; J.D., U. Denver, 1971. Communications Mountain Bell Co., Boulder, Colo., 1966-70, mktg. mgr., 1970-73; admitted to Colo. bar, 1972; individual practice law, Boulder, 1972-73; dep. city atty. City of Lakewood (Colo.), 1973-74; city atty. City of Littleton (Colo.), 1974—. Bd. dirs. Littleton Cultural Arts Found. Mem. Colo. Municipal League (vice chmn. sect. city attys.), Colo. Trial Lawyers Assn., Colo., Denver, Arapahoe bar assns., Littleton Friends of Library. Office: 2330 W Main St Littleton CO 80120 Tel (303) 794-7784

NITIKMAN, FRANKLIN W., b. Davenport, Iowa, Oct. 26, 1940; B.A., Northwestern U., 1963; LL.B., Yale, 1966. Admitted to Ill. bar, 1966; since practiced in Chgo., asso. firm McDermott, Will & Emery, 1966-72, partner, 1973—. Mem. Am., Ill., Chgo. Bar Assns., Chgo. Council Lawyers (treas. 1969-72), Yale Law Sch. Assn. Ill. (treas. 1972, sec. 1973, v.p. 1974, pres. 1975). Office: 111 W Monroe St Chicago IL 60603 Tel (312) 372-2000

NIX, JOHN A., b. Atlanta, May 17, 1937; B.A., Davidson Coll., 1959; LL.B., Emory U., 1964. Admitted to Ga. bar, 1964; atty. Atlanta dist. estate gift tax group IRS, 1964-67; partner firm Lokey & Bowden, Atlanta, 1967—. Counsel Lord's Day Alliance of U.S.A.; elder Central Presbyterian Ch. Mem. Am., Atlanta bar assns., Lawyers Club Atlanta, Atlanta Estate Planning Council, State Bar Ga. Home: 2985 Nancy Creek Rd NW Atlanta GA 30327 Office: 2610 1st Nat Bank Tower Atlanta GA 30303 Tel (404) 658-1034

NIXON, ELLIOTT BODLEY, b. Balt., Aug. 21, 1921; A.B., Princeton, 1942; J.D., Harvard, 1948. Admitted to N.Y. bar, 1949, U.S. Supreme Ct. bar, 1957; partner firm Burlingham Underwood & Lord, and predecessors, N.Y.C., 1956—; editor Am. Maritime Cases, Balt., 1969—. Mem. Assn. Bar City N.Y., Maritime Law Assn. U.S. Contbr. articles to encyclopaedias. Home: 420 E 23d St New York City NY 10010 Office: 1 Battery Park Plaza New York City NY 10004 Tel (212) 422-7585

NIXON, JOHN ROBERT, b. San Bernardino, Calif., Sept. 27, 1915; LL.B., Golden Gate U., 1950, J.D., 1971. Admitted to Calif. bar, 1951; individual practice law, Fresno, Calif., 1951—. Mem. Calif. Trial Lawyers Assn., Fresno County Bar Assn. Office: 1235 M St Fresno CA 93721 Tel (209) 266-8797

NIXON, LARRY SHELDON, b. Chicago Heights, Ill., Feb. 9, 1943; B.S. in Elec. Engring., U. Ill., 1965, M.S., 1966; J.D., Georgetown U., 1971. Admitted to Va. bar, 1971, D.C. bar, 1971; patent engr. Gen. Electric Co., Washington, 1966-67; patent agt. and asso. firm Cushman, Darby and Cushman, Washington, 1969-71, partner, 1972—. Mem. Am., Va., D.C. bar assns., Am. Patent Law Assn. Contbr. paper to conf., publ. Home: 6508 Lily Dhu Lane Falls Church VA 22044 Office: 1801 K St NW Washington DC 20006 Tel (202) 833-3000

NIXON, WILLIAM MICHAEL, b. N.Y.C., Sept. 8, 1946; B.A., Eastern Ky. U., 1969; J.D., U. Ky., 1972. Admitted to Ky. bar, 1973, U.S. Dist. Ct. for Eastern Dist. Ky., 1974; sr. atty. Ky. Dept. Transp., Somerset, 1973-74; asst. prof. Eastern Ky. U., Richmond, 1974—; pub. defender City of Richmond, 1974—. Mem. Am. (sect. on criminal justice), Madison County bar assns. Office: Box 688 Richmond KY 40475 Tel (606) 623-6130

NIZER, LOUIS, b. London, Eng., Feb. 6, 1902; B.A., Columbia Coll., 1922; LL.B., Columbia, 1924. Admitted to N.Y. bar; sr. partner firm Phillips, Nizer, Benjamin, Krim & Ballon, N.Y.C., Washington; gen. counsel Motion Picture Assn. Am.; exhibited paintings at Hammer Gallery, N.Y.C., Boston Mus., Permanent Art Gallery, Am. Bank & Trust Co. of Fifth Ave., N.Y.C. Mem. Am., N.Y. State bar assns., Bar Assn. City N.Y., ASCAP. Recipient Lit. Father of Year award, 1974, Golden Plate award Acad. of Achievement; author: The Implosion Conspiracy (nominee Edgar Allen Poe award 1974); The Jury Returns; My Life in Court; Commentary and Analysis of Official Warren Commission Report; What To Do With Germany; Thinking On Your Feet; Between You and Me; New Courts of Industry; contbr. articles to mags. and law periodicals. Office: 40 W 57th St New York City NY 10019 Tel (212) 977-9700

NOBLE, DAVID DEE, b. Wooster, Ohio, Oct. 28, 1941; A.B., Coll. of Wooster, 1963; LL.B., Duke U., 1966. Admitted to D.C. bar, 1967, Ohio bar, 1968; asso. Arnold Porter, Washington, 1966-68; asso. firm Critchfield, Critchfield and Johnston, Wooster, Ohio, 1966-71; individual practice law, Millersburg, Ohio, 1972—; pub. defender Wayne County, Ohio, 1973. Pres. Glenmont Council, 1972; chmn. Holmes County Dem. party, 1975—; coordinator 17th Congressional Dist. Carter for Pres., 1975-76. Mem. Am. Ohio, Holmes County bar assns., Order of Coif. Home: 3 Rustic Dr Millersburg OH 44654 Office: 4 W Jackson St Millersburg OH 44654 Tel (216) 674-6671

NOBLE, GEORGE WILLIAM, b. Sandy Ridge, Ala., Aug. 14, 1938; B.S., U. Ala., 1960, LL.B., Birmingham Sch. Law, 1965. Admitted to Ala. bar, 1965; asso. firm Speir, Robertson & Jackson, 1966-67; partner Barnett, Tingle & Noble, Birmingham, 1967—; city atty. City of Gardendale, Ala., 1968-72, mayor, 1972—; mem. Ala. Surface Mining Reclamation Commn. Mem. Am., Birmingham bar assns., Am. Trial Lawyers' Assn. Home: 129 Treasure Trial St Gardendale AL 35071 Office: 912 City Federal Bldg 2026 2d Ave N Birmingham AL 35203

NOBLE, JOHN W., b. Longview, Tex., Nov. 2, 1944; B.S., Stephen F. Austin State Coll., 1966; J.D., So. Meth. U., 1969. Admitted to Tex. bar, 1969; asso. firm Lawrence & Lawrence, Tyler, Tex., 1969-71, partner, 1971-75; partner firm Noble & Henry, Tyler, 1975—. Chmn. bd. dirs. Tex. Eastern Sch. Nursing, Tyler; bd. dirs. Med. Center Hosp., Goodwill Industries Tyler. Mem. Smith County Bar Assn. (sec. 1974), State Jr. Bar Tex. (1972-74). Tel (214) 561-1100

NOBLE, JOHN WALTER, JR., b. New Haven, Dec. 30, 1929; B.S., St. Peters Coll., 1951; J.D., Georgetown U., 1954. Admitted to D.C. bar, 1954, Ill. bar, 1964, U.S. Supreme Ct. bar, 1965; spl. agt. FBI, N.C., Kans. and Mo., 1954-59; atty. NLRB, St. Louis and Washington, 1959-63; mem. firm Vedder, Price, Kaufman & Kammholz, Chgo., 1963-64; asst. labor relations dir. Montgomery Ward Inc., Chgo., 1964-67; partner firm Noble, Sheerin & Duggan, Chgo., 1967-73, firm Friedman & Koven, Chgo., 1973—; mem. Ill. Commn. on Labor Laws, 1969—, vice chmn., 1974-76. Mem. Am., Fed., Ill. State bar assns., Am. Arbitration Assn., Pub. Employee Disputes Panel. Office: 208 S LaSalle St Chicago IL 60604 Tel (312) 8500

NOBLE, RICHARD GREEN, b. Vicksburg, Miss., Oct. 20, 1946; B.B.A., U. Miss., 1968, J.D., 1973. Admitted to Miss. bar, 1973; partner firm Lyon, Crosthwait, Terney & Noble, Indianola, Miss., 1973—; pros. atty. City of Indianola, 1975—. Mem. Am., Miss., Sunflower County (pres. 1976—) bar assns., Miss. Prosecutors Assn., Omicron Delta Kappa. Office: 100 Court St Indianola MS 38751 Tel (601) 887-3412

NOBLE, RUSSELL EDWIN, b. Kalamazoo, Oct. 31, 1923; B.A., Mich. State U., 1947; J.D., U. Mich., 1950. Admitted to Mich. bar, 1951, U.S. Supreme Ct. bar, 1958; research clk. Mich. Supreme Ct., Lansing, 1950-51; asst. pros. atty. Jackson County (Mich.), Jackson, 1952-56, pros. atty., 1957-60; partner firm Navarre & Noble, Jackson, 1960-74; judge 4th Jud. Circuit Ct., Jackson, 1974—. Jackson City commr., 1962-64. Mem. Am., Mich., Jackson County (pres. 1973-74) bar assns., Am. Judicature Soc., Greater Jackson C. of C. (pres. 1968—), Phi Alpha Delta. Home: 1728 Maybrook Rd Jackson MI 49203 Office: 312 S Jackson St Jackson MI 49201 Tel (517) 788-4365

NOCCA, JOSEPH FELIX, b. Yonkers, N.Y., Feb. 25, 1930; B.S., U. Pa., 1952; LL.D., Harvard U., 1955. Admitted to N.Y. bar, 1955; partner firm Pocari and Nocca, Yonkers, 1966-76; individual practice law, Yonkers, 1976—; asst. prof. New York Law Sch., 1957-61; commr. for the visually handicapped State of N.Y., 1975—. Mem. N.Y. State, Yonkers bar assns. Fulbright scholar, 1955; contbr. articles to legal jours. Home: 11 Highview Terr Yonkers NY 10705 Office: 20 S Broadway Yonkers NY 10701 Tel (914) YO3-2200

NOCE, DAVID DOMINIC, b. St. Louis, Feb. 29, 1944; A.B., St. Louis U., 1966; J.D., U. Mo., 1969. Admitted to Mo. bar, 1969, U.S. Dist. Ct. bar for Western Dist. Mo., 1969; legal officer U.S. Army, 1971-72; law clk. U.S. Dist. Ct. for Eastern Dist. Mo., 1972-75; asst. U.S. atty. Eastern Dist. Mo., 1975-76, U.S. magistrate, 1976—. Mem. Am. Bar Assn. Home: 7470 Stratford Ave University City MO 63130 Office: room 742 1114 Market St Saint Louis MO 63101 Tel (314) 425-6325

NOCK, GEORGE ROY, III, b. Boise, Idaho, Nov. 22, 1938; B.A., San Jose State U., 1961; J.D., Hastings Coll. Law, San Francisco, 1966. Admitted to Calif. bar, 1966, U.S. Supreme Ct. bar, 1970; dep. atty. gen. Calif., San Francisco, 1966-72; dep. dist. atty. Marin County (Calif.), 1972-74; asso. prof. law U. Puget Sound, Tacoma, 1974-77, prof., 1977—. Mem. State Bar Calif., Order of Coif. Contbr. articles to legal jours. Home: 9623 49th St W Tacoma WA 98467 Office: 8811 S Tacoma Way Tacoma WA 98499 Tel (206) 756-3327

NODELMAN, GEORGE MICHAEL, b. N.Y.C., Mar. 8, 1910; B.S.S., Coll. City N.Y., 1932; LL.B., St. John's U., Jamaica, N.Y., 1932. Admitted to N.Y. bar, 1933, U.S. Supreme Ct. bar, 1968; individual practice law, Bronx, 1933-61; house counsel Joe Norban, Inc. (Lynns Stores), N.Y.C., 1961—, v.p., 1977—. Mem. Bronx County (N.Y.) Bar Assn. Home: 425 E 72d St New York City NY 10021 Office: 601 W 26th St New York City NY 10001 Tel (212) 675-6800

NODVIN, MARVIN PHILIP, b. N.Y.C., Nov. 30, 1928; B.A., U. Ga., 1949; J.D., Emory U., 1951. Admitted to Ga., Fed. bars, 1951; individual practice law, Atlanta, 1951—. Chmn. Fulton Civil Ct. Commn.; chmn. State Ct. of Fulton County Task Force. Mem. Am., Ga., Atlanta bar assns. Office: 2410 Peachtree Cain Tower Atlanta GA 30303 Tel (404) 659-7070

NOE, GARY W., b. Austin, Tex., Dec. 25, 1946; student Tulane U.; B.A., U. Tex., Austin, 1969, J.D., 1972. Admitted to Tex. bar, 1972; asso. gen. counsel Zale Corp., Dallas, 1973—. Mem. Am., Tex., Dallas Jr. bar assns. Home: 7721 La Bolsa St Dallas TX 75248 Office: 3000 Diamond Park Dallas TX 75247 Tel (214) 634-4125

NOE, ROBERT JOHN, b. Rock Island, Ill., Mar. 1, 1939; B.A., St. Ambrose Coll., 1960; J.D., U. Notre Dame, 1963. Admitted to Ill. bar, 1963; asso. firm Wingard Schultz & Stradley, Rock Island, 1963-66; asso. firm Bozeman Neighbour Patton & Noe, Moline, Ill., 1967, partner, 1968—. Mem. Am., Ill. (assembly of dels. 1972—), Rock Island County bar assns. Pres., Jordan Cath. Sch. Bd. Edn., 1975—. Home: 1934 21st St Rock Island IL 61201 Office: 1630 Fifth Ave Moline IL 61265 Tel (309) 762-5593

NOEL, JAMES LATANE, JR., b. Pilot Point, Tex., Oct. 28, 1909; B.C.E., So. Meth. U., 1931, B.S. in Commerce, 1932, LL.B., 1937, LL.D. (hon.), 1966. Admitted to Tex. bar, 1937; budget officer Dallas County (Tex.), 1935-37, asst. dist. atty., 1937-38; asst. atty. gen. State of Tex., Austin, 1939-42, 45-46; individual practice law, Houston, 1946-61; judge U.S. Dist. So. Dist. Tex., 1961—; mem. U.S. Com. of Govt. Security, Washington, 1956-58. Bd. dirs. Parents League of Houston, Houston Symphony Soc.; mem. adminstrv. bd. St. Luke's United Methodist Ch., Houston. Mem. Am., Houston bar assns., State Bar Tex., Dist. Judges Assn. 5th Circuit. Home: 2454 Pine Valley Dr Houston TX 77019 Office: 515 Rusk Ave Houston TX 77002 Tel (713) 226-4267

NOELL, JOHN SUMMERS, JR., b. Thomaston, Ga., Sept. 22, 1941; A.B., U. Ga., 1963, J.D., 1965. Admitted to Ga. bar, 1966; partner firm Cook, Noell, Bates & Warnes, Athens, Ga., 1968—; vis. instr. trial practice U. Ga. Sch. Law, 1973-74. Mem. Athens (pres. 1976—), Western, Am. bar assns., State Bar Ga., Ga. Trial Lawyers Assn., Am. Judicature Soc. Home: 155 Skyline Way Athens GA 30601 Office: 304 E Washington St Athens GA 30601 Tel (404) 549-6111

NOHR, WILLIAM ARTHUR, b. Merrill, Wis., July 7, 1938; B.A., U. Wis., Madison, 1960, LL.B., 1964. Admitted to Wis. bar, 1964, Circuit Ct. Appeals bar, 1970; asso. firm Hoffman, Trembath & Gullickson, Wausau, Wis., 1964; mem. firm Quarles, Herriott & Clemons, Milw., 1964-69, Ebert & Ebert, Milw., 1969—. Grand Knight Pope John XXIII Council, K.C., 1973; bd. dirs. Wis. Lupus Erythematosus Soc., 1974—. Mem. Milw. Bar Assn., Am. Arbitration Assn. (arbitrator), Order of the Coif, Phi Beta Kappa. Home: 10103 N Greenview Dr Mequon WI 53092 Office: 230 W Wells Milwaukee WI 53203 Tel (414) 276-5100

NOLAN, DENNIS MICHAEL, b. Drexel Hill, Pa., Nov. 5, 1939; B.S., Villanova U., 1961; LL.J.D., 1964. Admitted to Pa. bar, 1965, U.S. Supreme Ct. bar, 1968, U.S. Dist. Ct., 1968; asso. firm John P. Trevaskis Jr., Media, Pa., 1964-68, partner, 1968—; asst. solicitor Upper Providence Township, Del. County, Pa., 1973—. Mem. Am., Pa., Delaware County Bar Assns. Home: 1031 Willowbrook Ln Media PA 19063 Office: 327 W Front St Media PA 19063 Tel (215) LO6-9100

NOLAN, HOWARD C., JR., b. Albany, N.Y., Aug. 24, 1932; B.S., Holy Cross Coll., 1954; J.D. Union U., 1957. Admitted to N.Y. bar, 1958; since practiced in Albany, N.Y., partner firm Nolan & Heller, 1961—; mem. N.Y. State Senate, 1974—. Pres., United Cerebral Palsy Assn., Capital Dist., Inc., v.p. United Cerebral Palsy Assn., N.Y., mem. finance com. United Cerebral Palsy Assns., Inc., co-chmn. United Cerebral Palsy Telethon, 1970-72; mem. Downtown Albany Unlimited (past. sec.-treas.); Albany Jr. C. of C. (past pres., past dist. pres.); dir. Pop Warner Football Northeastern N.Y.; mem. N.Y. State Mayor's Conf.; dir. Cath. Youth Orgn. Albany Diocese; trustee St. Gregory's Sch.; mem. Serra Club of Albany (past. pres.); dir. Sisters of Mercy Bd. Regents. Mem. N.Y. State Bar Assn. Home: 7 Birch Hill Rd Loudonville NY 12211 Office: 60 State St Albany NY 12207 Tel (518) 449-3100

NOLAN, JOHN BLANCHARD, b. Providence, Aug. 30, 1943; B.A., Brown U., 1965; J.D., Georgetown U., 1968. Admitted to Conn. bar, 1968; partner firm Day, Berry & Howard, Hartford. Mem. Am., Conn., Hartford County bar assns. Office: 1 Constitution Plaza Hartford CT 06103 Tel (203) 278-1330

NOLAN, JOHN EDWARD, JR., b. Mpls., July 11, 1927; B.S., U.S. Naval Acad., 1950; J.D., Georgetown U., 1955. Admitted to D.C. bar, 1955, U.S. Supreme Ct. bar, 1959, Md. bar, 1961; law clk. to Mr. Justice Clark Supreme Ct. U.S., 1955-56; adminstrv. asst. to Atty. Gen. Robert F. Kennedy, 1963-64; asso. firm Steptoe & Johnson, Washington, 1956-62, partner, 1962-63, 65—; mem. exec. Com. Lawyers Com. Civil Rights Under Law. Trustee, dir. Robert F. Kennedy Meml., 1969—. Mem. Am., D.C. (bd. govs.) bar assns., Am. Law Inst. Home: 7830 Persimmon Tree Ln Bethesda MD 20034 Office: 1250 Connecticut Ave NW Washington DC 20036 Tel (202) 223-4800

NOLAN, MICHAEL, b. Norwalk, Ohio, Jan. 5, 1943; B.S.J., Ohio U., 1965; J.D., Ohio No. U., 1969; Dr. Applied Pub. Service (hon.), Hockins Tech. Coll., 1976. Admitted to Ohio bar, 1969; asst. atty. gen., Ohio, 1969-70; asst. city solicitor, Nelsonville, Ohio, 1970-71, Athens, Ohio, 1971-72; asst. pros. atty. Athens County, 1971-72, pros. atty., Athens County, 1972-76. Mem. Am., Ohio State bar assns., Am. Ohio trial lawyers assns. Home: 700 Pleasantview Ave Nelsonville OH 45764 Office: 78 W Washington St Nelsonville OH 45764 Tel (614) 753-3943

NOLAN, PETER DAVID, b. Warwick, N.J., Dec. 10, 1942; A.B., Providence Coll., 1964; J.D., St. John's U., 1967. Admitted to R.I. bar, 1967; asso. with James F. Murphy, 1968-70; partner firm Nolan & Dailey, Coventry, R.I., 1970—; probate judge Coventry, R.I., 1968-72; town solicitor town E. Greenwich, R.I., 1970-72; probate judge Exeter, R.I., 1975, town solicitor, 1975. Mem. R.I., Am., Kent County (treas. 1974—) bar assns., Am. Trial Lawyers Assn. Home: 56 Rector St East Greenwich RI 02818 Office: 70 Main St Coventry RI 02816

NOLAN, PETER FRANCIS, b. N.Y.C., Mar. 31, 1943; B.A., Georgetown U., 1965, J.D., 1968. Admitted to D.C. bar, 1968, Calif. bar, 1972; asso. firm Pattishall, McAuliffe & Hofstetter, Washington, 1968-69; copyright examiner U.S. Copyright Office, Washington, 1969-71; atty. Walt Disney Prodns., Burbank, Calif., 1971—. Mem. Am., Los Angeles County bar assns., Copyright Soc. Los Angeles. Contbr. articles to legal jours. Office: 500 S Buena Vista St Burbank CA 91521 Tel (213) 845-3141

NOLAN, RICHARD EDWARD, b. N.Y.C., Nov. 28, 1928; A.B. cum laude, Holy Cross Coll., 1950; LL.B., Columbia U., 1957. Admitted to N.Y. bar, 1958, U.S. Supreme Ct. bar, 1962; asso. firm Davis, Polk & Wardwell, N.Y.C., 1957-65, partner, 1966—; dir. Whitbread Nolan, Inc., N.Y.C. Bd. dirs. United Neighborhood Houses of N.Y., 1970—. Mem. Am., Fed., N.Y. bar assns., Assn. Bar City N.Y., Am. Law Inst. Home: 271 Central Park W New York City NY 10024 also Bolton Landing NY 12845 Office: 1 Chase Manhattan Bank Plaza New York City NY 10005 Tel (212) 422-3400

NOLAN, RICHARD HENRY, b. Boston, Mar. 7, 1907; A.B., Holy Cross Coll., 1929; LL.B., Suffolk Law Sch., 1934. Admitted to Mass. bar, 1938; counsel Mass. Inheritance Tax Bur., Boston, 1940-62; individual practice law, Boston, 1938—; lectr. Harvard, Boston U., Boston Coll., other colls. and bar assns. Mem. Mass. Bar Assn., Greater Boston Cath. Lawyers Guild (past pres.). Author: Nolan Charts of Relationships and Degrees of Kindred, series, 1938-55; also papers. Home: 7 Lawrence Rd Weston MA 02193 Office: 4560 Prudential Tower Boston MA 02199 Tel (617) 266-1700

NOLAN, THOMAS JOSEPH, JR., b. Fresno, Calif., Mar. 10, 1945; A.A., Sacramento City Coll., 1965; B.A., Sacramento State U., 1967; J.D., U. Calif. at Davis, 1970. Admitted to Calif. bar, 1971; partner firm Flickinger Elliott & Nolan, Menlo Park, Calif., 1970-75; individual practice, Menlo Park, 1975—; mem. legal bd. ACLU, 1973—. Mem. Calif. Attys. for Criminal Justice (bd. govs.). Home: 103 Hillside Dr Woodside CT 94062 Office: 841 Menlo Ave Menlo Park CA 94025 Tel (415) 326-2980

NOLAN, VAL, JR., b. Evansville, Ind., Apr. 28, 1920; A.B., Ind. U., 1941, J.D., 1949. Admitted to Ind. bar, 1949; asst. prof. law Ind. U., Bloomington, 1949-52, asso. prof., 1952-56, prof., 1956—, acting dean, 1976; dep. U.S. Marshall, So. Dist. Ind., 1941; agt. U.S. Secret Service, White House Detail, Washington, 1942. Author: (with F.E. Horack Jr.) Land Use Control, 1955; contbr. articles to legal jours. Home: 1708 N Fee Ln Bloomington IN 47401 Office: Sch Law Indiana U Bloomington IN 47401 Tel (812) 337-7443

NOLAND, GENE ANTHONY, b. LaGrande, Oreg., Apr. 1, 1939; B.S., Eastern Oreg. Coll., 1962; J.D., Willamette U., 1964. Admitted to Oreg. bar, 1964, Calif. bar, 1967; law editor Bancroft-Whitney Co., San Francisco, 1964-72, mng. editor Calif. Jurisprudence, 1972—. Mem. Oreg., Calif. bar assns. Office: 301 Brannan St San Francisco CA 94110 Tel (415) 986-4410

NOLD, NORMAN LEE, b. Freeburg, Ill., Aug. 8, 1927; J.D., St. Louis U., 1955. Admitted to Mo. bar, 1955, Ill. bar, 1955; asso. firm Johnson & Ducey, Belleville, Ill., 1955-57; individual practice law, Freeburg, 1957—. Mem. Ill. State Bar Assn., Am. Legion (comdr. 1957), Freeburg C. of C. (treas. 1965-68). Home: 101 N Alton St Freeburg IL 62243 Office: 201 N State Freeburg IL 62243 Tel (618) 539-3175

NOLEN, K.M., b. Hemphill, Tex., Mar. 14, 1919; B.A., U. Tex., 1940, LL.B., 1946. Admitted to Tex. bar, 1946; asst. U.S. atty., So. Dist. Tex., 1947-53; asst. dist. atty., Harris County, Tex., 1953; staff law dept. Amoco Prodn. Co., Houston, 1954—. Mem. Am. Bar Assn., State Bar Tex. Home: 1617 Fannin St #2009 Houston TX 77002 Office: PO Box 3092 Houston TX 77001 Tel (713) 652-5215

NOLEN, LYNN DEAN, b. Wetumka, Okla., Sept. 16, 1940; B.A., East Central State Coll., Ada, Okla., 1961; LL.B., Okla. U., Norman, 1964. Admitted to Okla. bar, 1964, U.S. Dist. Ct. bar for Eastern Dist. Okla., 1965; individual practice law, Muskogee, Okla., 1964-69, 71—; asst. dist. atty. for Muskogee County, Okla., 1970; with JAGC, USAR, 1968-72. Mem. Muskogee County (sec. 1966), Okla., Am. bar assns. Home: 2927 Williams Ave Muskogee OK 74401 Office: 501 W Okmulgee Ave Muskogee OK 74401 Tel (918) 682-9012

NOLEN, RODNEY EARL, b. Birmingham, Ala., June 30, 1948; B.S., Auburn U., 1970; J.D., Cumberland U., 1973. Admitted to Ala. bar, 1974; partner firm Cicio & Nolen, Birmingham, 1977—. Mem. Am., Ala., Birmingham bar assns. Home: 2641 Yorkmont Dr Birmingham AL 35226 Office: 1613 2121 Bldg 8th Ave N Birmingham AL 35203 Tel (205) 322-5785

NOLTE, HENRY R., JR., b. N.Y.C., Mar. 3, 1924; B.A., Duke, 1947; LL.B., U. Pa., 1949. Admitted to N.Y. bar, 1950, Mich. bar, 1967; asso. firm Cravath, Swaine & Moore, N.Y.C., 1951-61; asso. counsel Ford Motor Co., Dearborn, Mich., 1961, asst. gen. counsel, 1964-67, 69-71, asso. gen. counsel, 1971-74, v.p., gen. counsel, 1974—; v.p., gen. counsel, sec. Philco-Ford Corp., Phila., 1961-64; v.p., gen. counsel, sec. Ford Europe, Inc., Essex, Eng., 1967-69; mem. adv. bd. Internat. and Comparative Law Center, Southwestern Legal Found., 1974. Mem. exec. com. bd. govs. Cranbrook Ednl. Community, Bloomfield Hills, Mich., 1975; pres.'s asso. Duke, 1976. Mem. Am. Judicature Soc., Am. Bar Assn. (com. on corp. law depts.), Assn. Gen. Counsel. Office: Ford Motor Co The American Rd Dearborn MI 48121 Tel (313) 323-4670

NOOJIN, RAY OSCAR, JR., b. Durham, N.C., Apr. 26, 1945; B.S. in Chemistry and English, U. Ala., 1967, J.D., 1970. Admitted to Ala. bar, 1970; jr. partner firm Sadler, Sadler, Sullivan & Sharp, Birmingham, Ala., 1970-72; partner firm Hardin, Stuart, Moncus & Noojin, Birmingham, 1972-76, Noojin, Haley & Ashford, Birmingham, 1976—. Mem. Birmingham, Ala., Am. bar assns., Ala., Am., Birmingham trial lawyers assns., Am. Judicature Soc., Bench and Bar. Editor Ala. Law Reporter. Home: 909 Greenbriar Circle Birmingham AL 35213 Office: 605 City Fed Bldg Birmingham AL 35203 Tel (205) 251-2300

NOONAN, JAMES C., b. Chgo., July 16, 1928; A.B., U. Notre Dame, 1953, M.A., 1954. Admitted to Minn. bar, 1962, U.S. Supreme Ct. bar, 1969; partner firm Firestone, Fink, Krawetz, Miley, Maas & Noonan, 1963-70, Magistad & Noonan, 1971-75; individual practice law as James C. Noonan & Assos., St. Paul, 1975—; mem. faculty Coll. St. Catherine, 1962-73. Mem. Ramsey County (Minn.), Minn., Am. bar assns. Office: 410 Minnesota Bldg Saint Paul MN 55101 Tel (612) 227-0641

NOONAN, JOHN THOMAS, JR., b. Boston, Oct. 24, 1926; B.A., Harvard, 1946, LL.B., 1954; M.A., Cath. U. Am., 1949, Ph.D., 1951; LL.D. (hon.), U. Santa Clara, 1974, U. Notre Dame, 1976. Admitted to Mass. bar, 1954, U.S. Supreme Ct. bar, 1971; mem. spl. staff NSC, 1954-55; mem. firm Herrick Smith, Boston, 1955-60; asso. prof., then prof. law U. Notre Dame, 1961-66; prof. U. Calif., Berkeley, 1966—; Holmes lectr. Harvard Law Sch., 1972 vis. prof. law So. Meth. U., 1967. Trustee Population Council, 1969-76; expert Presdl. Commn. on Population and Am. Future, 1971. Fellow Am. Acad. Arts and Scis.; mem. Am. Law Inst., Am. Bar Assn., Canon Law Soc. Am. Author: The Scholastic Analysis of Usury, 1957; Contraception, 1965; Power to Dissolve, 1972; Persons and Masks of the Law, 1976; The Antelope, 1977; editor Am. Jour. Jurisprudence, 1961-69; contbr. articles to legal jours. Office: 474 Sch of Law Boalt Hall U of Calif Berkeley CA 94720 Tel (415) 642-6646

NORDAHL, RICHARD HERMANN, b. Boston, Aug. 4, 1939; B.A., Principia Coll., 1960; J.D., Harvard, 1966. Admitted to Mo. bar, 1967; staff atty. Monsanto Co., St. Louis, 1967-69; trial atty., antitrust div. U.S. Dept. Justice, Washington, 1969-71; staff asst. White House, Washington, 1971-73; spl. asst. to Undersec. Transp., Washington, 1973; asso. firm Charles C. McCarter, St. Louis, 1973-76; individual practice law, St. Louis, 1976—. Bd. dirs. Lakeside Center Boys, St. Louis, 1976; v.p. Queeney Twp. Republican Club. Mem. W. St. Louis County C. of C., Mo., Met. St. Louis, Am. bar assns. Home: 419 Caprice Gardens Ct Ballwin MO 63011 Office: suite 212 13422 Clayton Rd Saint Louis MO 63131 Tel (314) 576-1071

NORDALE, MARY ANITA, b. Fairbanks, Alaska, Apr. 8, 1934; B.A., Gonzaga U., 1957; J.D., George Washington U., 1966. Admitted to D.C. bar, 1967, Alaska bar, 1969; staff atty. to U.S. Senator E.L. Bartlett, Washington, 1967-68; asst. U.S. atty. City of Fairbanks, 1968-69, asst. dist. atty., 1969-70; br. counsel SBA, Fairbanks, 1970-72; partner firm Jackson & Nordale, Fairbanks, 1972-74; individual practice law, Fairbanks, 1974—; spl. counsel Alaska Bar Assn. Bd. dirs. Fairbanks Rehab. Assn. Inc., 1970—; vice-chmn. Alaska Democratic Central Com., 1974—. Mem. Alaska, Am., Fed., Tanana Valley bar assns., Phi Alpha Delta. Home: PO Box 1671 Fairbanks AK 99707 Office: 601 Hughes Ave Fairbanks AK 99701 Tel (907) 456-6903

NORDHAUS, ROBERT KEITH, b. Houston, June 7, 1946; B.B.A., Tex. A. and M. U., 1968; J.D., St. Mary's U., 1971. Admitted to Tex. bar, 1971; asst. city atty. City of San Antonio, 1971-75; city atty. City of Denison (Tex.), 1975—. Mem. Am., Tex. bar assns., Tex. City Attys. Assn. Home: 802 Holland Dr Denison TX 74020 Office: 108 W Main St Denison TX 75020 Tel (214) 465-2720

NORDLING, BERNARD ERICK, b. Nekoma, Kans., June 14, 1921; student George Washington U., 1941-43; A.B. in Bus. Adminstrn., McPherson Coll., 1947; LL.B., U. Kans., 1949, J.D., 1968. Clk., FBI, Washington, 1940-43, Buenos Aires, Argentina, 1943-44; admitted to Kans. bar, 1949; practiced in Hugoton, Kan.,

1949—, partner firm Kramer, Nordling, Nordling & Fay, 1950—; city atty., Hugoton, 1951—; mem. legal com. Interstate Oil Compact Commn., 1969—; mem. supply-tech. adv. com. natural gas survey Fed. Power Commn., 1975—; mem. exec. com. Kans. Energy Adv. Council, 1976—. Trustee McPherson Coll., 1971—, mem. exec. com., coll. sec., 1975—; gov. Seward County (Kans.) Community Jr. Coll. Devel. Found., 1971—; mem. U. Kans. Devel. Com., 1976—. Mem. Am., Kans., S.W. Kans. bar assns., Am. Judicature Soc., Order of Coif, Phi Alpha Delta (pres. chpt. 1948-49). Editor U. Kans. Law Rev. sect. Kans. Bar Jour., 1949. Home: 218 N Jackson St Hugoton KS 67951 Office: 209 E 6th St Hugoton KS 67951 Tel (316) 544-4333

NORDQUIST, KENNETH LEONARD, b. Oberlin, La., Sept. 29, 1944; A.A., S. Tex. U., 1965; B.B.A., Houston U., 1967, J.D., 1969. Admitted to Tex. bar, 1969; asst. atty. gen. State of Tex., Austin, 1969-72; individual practice law, Austin, 1972-75; hearings officer Tex. Employment Commn., Austin, 1975—. Mem. Travis County Bar Assn., Internat. Assn. Personnel in Employment Security, Tex. Pub. Employees Assn., Phi Delta Psi, Phi Alpha Delta. Office: Tex Employment Commn Appeals Austin TX 78778 Tel (512) 472-6251

NORDSTROM, ROBERT JOHN, b. Cadillac, Mich., May 14, 1924; A.B. summa cum laude, Western Mich. U., 1948; J.D., U. Mich., 1949. Admitted to R.I. bar, 1949, Ohio bar, 1956; asso. firm Hinckley, Allen, Salisbury & Parsons, Providence, 1949-51; asst. prof. law Ohio State U., 1951-54, asso. prof., 1954-57, prof., 1957—, asso. dean Coll. Law, 1953-64; partner firm Porter, Stanley, Platt & Arthur, Columbus, 1973—; trustee Ohio Legal Center, 1961—. Mem. Columbus, Ohio State bar assns. Author: Introduction To Study of Law, 1958; (with Lattin) Sales and Secured Transactions, 1968; Handbook On Law Of Sales, 1970; (with Clovis) Commercial Paper, 1972; contbr. articles to legal jours. Home: 454 Village Dr Columbus OH 43214 Office: 37 W Broad St Columbus OH 43215 Tel (614) 228-1511

NORDSTROM, WILLIAM R., b. Tracy, Minn.; B.A., Gustavus Adolphus Coll., 1962; J.D., U. Minn., 1965. Admitted to Minn. bar, 1965; asso. firm Alderson, Catherwood, Austin, Minn., 1965-66; asso. firm Goulter & Nelson, Mpls., 1967-68; individual practice, Mpls., 1968—. Mgr. March of Dimes, Austin, 1967. Mem. Mower County, Hennepin County, Minn. bar assns. Office: 800 5001 W 80th St Bloomington MN 55435 Tel (612) 835-2380

NORMAN, DONALD HAMILTON, b. Hackensack, N.J., Mar. 6, 1930; B.A. summa cum laude, Rutgers U., 1952; J.D. magna cum laude, U. Miami, 1955, LL.M., 1968. Admitted to Fla. bar, 1955; asst. city atty. City of Ft. Lauderdale (Fla.), 1955-59; partner firm Ross, Norman & Cory, Ft. Lauderdale, 1959—; city atty. City of Hallandale (Fla.), 1970-72; lectr. U. Miami, 1970-74; adj. prof. Nova U., 1975—. Pres., Vis. Nurse Assn. Broward County, 1965, Harbor Inlet Assn., 1966, Ch. of the Sea, 1974-76; pres. U. Miami Broward Citizens Bd., 1975—. Mem. Am., Fla. (bd. govs. 1974—), Broward County (pres. 1964-65) bar assns. Recipient Outstanding Young Man of Ft. Lauderdale award, 1965. Home: 1924 SE 24th Ave Fort Lauderdale FL 33316 Office: 2720 E Oakland Park Blvd Fort Lauderdale FL 33306 Tel (305) 563-4358

NORMAN, GEORGE EDWARD, b. New Richmond, Wis., Oct. 2, 1936; A.B., St. Olaf Coll., 1958; J.D., U. Mich., 1961. Admitted to Wis. bar, 1961; asso. firm Doar & Knowles, New Richmond, Wis., 1961-66; partner firm Doar, Drill & Norman, New Richmond, 1967-70; partner firm Doar, Drill, Norman & Bakke, New Richmond, 1971—. Mem. Am., St. Croix Valley Bar Assns., State Bar of Wis. Office: 103 Knowles Ave New Richmond WI 54017 Tel (715) 246-2211

NORMAN, IRVING RUBIN, b. Chgo., Feb. 19, 1914; J.D., DePaul U., 1936. Admitted to Ill. bar, 1936; individual practice law, Chgo., 1936-71; judge Circuit Ct. of Cook County (Ill.), Chgo., 1971—. Mem. Am., Ill., Chgo. bar assns., Am., Ill. trial lawyers assns., Soc. Trial Lawyers (Joint award for significant contbns. to Bench and Bar). Home: 5701 N Sheridan Rd Chicago IL 60660 Office: Civic Center Chicago IL 60602 Tel (312) 443-8272

NORMAN, JOHN KUYKENDALL, b. St. Louis, Aug. 20, 1939; A.B. in Geology, U. Mo., 1962, J.D., 1964. Admitted to Mo. bar, 1964, Alaska bar, 1969, U.S. Supreme Ct. bar, 1972; with exploration dept. Skelly Oil Co., Midland, Tex. and Anchorage, 1967-69; asst. atty. gen. State of Alaska, 1969-71; mng. partner firm Cole, Hartig, Rhodes, Norman & Mahoney, Anchorage, 1971—. Mem. Greater Anchorage Area Bd. Health, 1973-75; mem. advisory bd. Alaska Div. Lands, 1976—. Mem. Am. (state chmn. com. environ. quality 1971-73), Alaska (state chmn. com. environ. law 1976—), Anchorage, Mo. bar assns., Alaska Geol. Soc. Contbr. articles to legal jours. Home: SRA 1463-F Achorage AK 99502 Office: 717 K St Suite 201 Anchorage AK 99501 Tel (907) 274-3576

NORMAN, TELFER WOODHOUSE, b. Denver, May 28, 1945; Profl. Engr., Colo. Sch. Mines, 1968; J.D., U. Coll., 1971. Admitted to Colo. bar, 1971; dep. dist. atty. Jefferson County (Colo.), 1971—. Mem. Colo., First Jud. Dist. bar assns., Colo. Dist. Attys. Assn. Home: 37 Hillside Dr Denver CO 80215 Office: Jefferson County District Attorney's Office Golden CO 80215 Tel (303) 279-6511

NORMAN, WAYNE ALBERT, JR., b. Dubuque, Iowa, Apr. 5, 1946; B.A., U. Colo., 1968; J.D. with distinction, U. Iowa, 1971. Admitted to Iowa bar, 1971, U.S. Dist. Ct. bar for So. Dist. Iowa, 1971; asso. firm Kintzinger, Kintzinger, Van Etten, Setter & King, Dubuque, 1971-73; asso. judge Iowa Dist. Ct., Dubuque, 1973-76; mem. firm Conzett, Norman & Lindahl, Dubuque, 1976—; instr. Loras Coll., 1971-72, also magistrates confs.; partner, mgr., counsel J.M. Cardinal S.A., 1971-73. Sr. warden St. John's Episcopal Ch., Dubuque; mem. Iowa State Council on Alcoholism, Iowa State Council on Juvenile Justice, Regional Health Planning Council, Regional Mental Health Bd.; pres. Regional Alcoholism Bd.; chmn. com. juvenile justice, Dubuque County, 1974-76. Mem. Iowa State, Dubuque County bar assns. Home: 410 Raymond Pl Dubuque IA 52001 Office: One Dubuque Plaza Suite 550 Dubuque IA 52001 Tel (319) 556-8552

NORMILE, C. BRUCE, b. Hannibal, Mo., Apr. 9, 1931; A.B., U. Mo., 1953, J.D., 1955. Admitted to bar, 1955; mem. firm Dulin & King, St. Louis, 1957-59; mem. firm Brown & Normile, Edina, Mo., 1960-67; judge 2nd Jud. Circuit Ct. of Mo., Edina, 1967—; spl. asst. atty. Gen. State of Mo., 1966-67; spl. judge St. Louis Ct. of Appeals, 1968-70, Mo. Supreme Ct., 1970-73, Mo. Ct. Appeals, Kansas City, 1976-77. Mem. hosp. governance com. Kirksville Osteo. Hosp., 1974—; trustee Kirksville Osteopathic Coll.; mem. bd. curators Lincoln U., Jefferson City, Mo., 1966-75, v.p., 1971-75. Mem. Am., St. Louis, Mo. bar assns., Am. Judicature Soc., Trial Judges Assn., Nat. Council Juvenile Ct. Judges, Mo. Council Juvenile Ct. Judges (pres. 1976-77). Recipient Atty.'s Gen.'s Award for Pub. Merit, 1967. Home: PO Box Edina MO 63537 Office: Knox County Ct House Edina MO 63537 Tel (815) 397-3974

NORMILE, HUBERT CLARENCE, JR., b. Phila., Apr. 12, 1943; A.B., Guilford Coll., 1965; J.D., U. Fla., 1967. Admitted to Fla. bar, 1968; asst. states atty., Titusville, Fla., 1968-69; asso. firm Storms, Pappas & Krasny, Melbourne, Fla., 1969-71; partner firm Nelson, Normile & Dettmer, Melbourne, 1971—; asst. pub. defender, 1971-73. Dir. Dist. XII Mental Health Bd., 1971—. Mem. Brevard County (dir. 1972—, treas. 1976-77, sec. 1977—, chmn. unauthorized practice of law com. 1974-76), Fla. bar assns., Phi Alpha Delta. Home: 540 Franklyn Ave Indialantic FL 32901 Office: 482 N Harbour City Blvd Melbourne FL 32935 Tel (305) 254-1776

NORRIS, ALAN EUGENE, b. Columbus, Ohio, Aug. 15, 1935; B.A. with honors, Otterbein Coll., 1957; certificate La Sorbonne, Paris, 1956; LL.B., N.Y. U., 1960. Admitted to Ohio bar, 1960; asso. firm Vorys, Sater, Seymour & Pease, Columbus, 1961-62; partner firm Metz, Bailey & Norris, Westerville, Ohio, 1962—; clk. to justice Ohio Supreme Ct., 1960-61; mem. Ohio Ho. of Reps., 1967—; pros. atty. City of Westerville, 1962-66. Mem. Westerville Zoning Bd. Appeals, 1962-66, chmn., 1966; chmn. Ohio Bicentennial Commn., 1975—. Mem. Am., Ohio, Columbus bar assns. Named Legislator of Year, Ohio Acad. Trial Lawyers, 1972, Hon. Ky. Col., 1971. Home: 58 W College Ave Westerville OH 43081 Office: 33 E Schrock Rd Westerville OH 43081 Tel (614) 882-2327

NORRIS, JERRY LEE, b. Kearney, Nebr., Dec. 6, 1941; B.S. in Bus. Adminstrn., Kearney State Coll., 1968; J.D., U. Nebr., 1971. Admitted to Nebr. bar, 1971; asso. firm Wagner and Johnson, Columbus, Nebr., 1971-74; atty. City of Columbus, 1972—; bd. govs. and instr. bus. law Platte Tech. Community Coll., Columbus, 1972—. Bd. govs. United Way, Columbus, 1976. Mem. Nebr. State Bar Assn. Home: PO Box 447 Wagner Lakes Columbus NE 68601 Office: 2424 14th St Columbus NE 68601 Tel (402) 564-3536

NORRIS, JOHN ANTHONY, b. Buffalo, Dec. 27, 1946; B.A., U. Rochester, 1968; J.D. and M.B.A. with honors, Cornell U., 1973. Fed. Comprehensive Health Planning fellow Cornell U., 1970-73; admitted to Mass. bar, 1973; asso. firm Peabody, Brown, Rowley & Storey, Boston, 1973-75; asso. firm Powers & Hall, Boston, 1975-76, partner, 1976—, mem. exec. com., 1977—; mem. clin. faculty Tufts U. Sch. Dental Medicine, 1973—; instr. Boston Coll. Law Sch., 1977—; lectr., speaker to numerous schs., assns. Mem. Am. Soc. Law and Medicine (exec. v.p.), Am., Mass. bar assns., Am. Soc. Hosp. Attys., Nat. Health Lawyers Assn., Phi Kappa Phi. Contbr. articles to legal and med. jours.; editor-in-chief Cornell Internat. Law Jour., 1972-73; editor Medicolegal News, 1973-76; editor-in-chief Am. Jour. Law and Medicine, 1973—. Home: 544 W Washington St Hanson MA 02341 Office: 30 Federal St Boston MA 02110 Tel (617) 482-6010

NORRIS, JOHN ROBINSON, b. Balt., Feb. 2, 1908; A.B., Johns Hopkins U., 1929; J.D., Harvard U., 1932. Admitted to Md. bar, 1933, U.S. Supreme Ct. bar, 1942, ICC bar, 1934; part-time field atty. Home Owners Loan Corp., Balt., 1934-41; prof. Mt. Vernon Sch. Law, Eastern U., 1935-37; asso. firm Baldwin, Jarman and Norris, Balt., 1933-43, partner, 1943-72; counsel firm Hessey & Hessey, Balt., 1972—. Mem. aviation com. C. of C. of Met. Balt., 1958-62; state chmn. fund raising Heart Assn. Md., 1957-58, trustee, 1952-55, 56-59 mem. Gov's. Study Com. on Uniform Comml. Code for Md., 1959-64; mem. ICC budget com. Assn. ICC Practitioners, 1961-66; trustee A.T. and Mary H. Blades Found., 1961—; adminstrv. bd. Grace United Meth. Ch., 1947-50, 73-76. Mem. Am., Md., Balt. City bar assns., Bar Assn. Balt. City (ct. of appeals com. 1963-64, pub. service commn. com. 1958-61, uniform comml. code com. 1954-64, grievance com. 1967-68, chmn. meml. com. 1973-74), Am. Judicature Soc., Barristers Club Balt. City, Balt. Estate Planning Counsel, Delta Upsilon. Contbr. articles to legal jours. Home: 302 Edgevale Rd Baltimore MD 21210 Office: 1311 Fidelity Bldg Baltimore MD 21201 Tel (301) 539-3300

NORRIS, MELVIN, b. Cambridge, Mass., Aug. 17, 1931; A.B., Northeastern U., 1954; J.D., Boston Coll., 1959. Admitted to Mass. bar, 1959, U.S. Supreme Ct. bar, 1965; atty. FTC, Boston, 1960-62; individual practice law, Boston, 1962-76; partner firm Norris, Kozodoy & Krasnoo, Boston, 1976—; vice chmn. Newton Crime Commn., 1966-67. Mem. Newton Bldg. Code Revision Com., 1972-73. Mem. Mass., Fed. (pres. elect Boston chpt. 1976-77) bar assns. Office: One Beacon St Boston MA 02108 Tel (617) 227-7460

NORRIS, PLEAS MILLER, b. Winona, Miss., Mar. 8, 1940; B.S., Miss. State U., 1969; postgrad. U. Miss., 1972. Admitted to Miss. bar, 1973; legal advisor, adminstrv. asst., Gov. of Miss., 1973-76. Mem. bd. United Way. Mem. Miss. Bar Assn., Jackson Young Lawyers. Recipient Outstanding Mississippian award 1975. Home: 1868 E Northside St Jackson MS 39211 Office: 413 S President St Jackson MS 39201 Tel (601) 969-1056

NORRIS, WILLIAM EDWARD, b. Chgo., Oct. 24, 1944; B.A., Roosevelt Univ., Chgo., 1966; J.D. cum laude, John Marshall, Chgo., 1969. Admitted to Ill. bar, 1969, U.S. Supreme Ct. bar, 1974; asst. pub. defender, City of Chgo., 1969-73; asst. states atty. Chgo., 1973—. Mem. Am., Ill., DuPage County bar assns. Recipient Excella Press Prize, 1969. Home: 783S Rohrer Dr Downers Grove IL 60515 Office: 5240 W James St Oak Lawn IL 60453 Tel (312) 636-0037

NORTH, WILLIAM DENSON, b. Corvallis, Oreg., Apr. 4, 1930; B.S. in Commerce and Law, U. Ill., 1952; LL.B., Harvard, 1959, J.D., 1969. Admitted to Ill. bar, 1959, U.S. Supreme Ct. bar, 1973; mem. firm Kirkland & Ellis, Chgo., 1959-66, partner, 1966—. Bd. assos. De Paul U.; mem. U. Ill. Found., Freedom to Read Found., Chgo. Mem. Am., Ill. State, Chgo. bar assns., Am. Soc. Assn. Execs., Am. Judicature Soc., Estate Planning Council, Chgo. Assn. Commerce and Industry, Legal Club Chgo., Harvard Law Sch. Assn., U. Ill. Alumni Assn. (dir.), Copyright Soc. Am. (dir.), Alpha Kappa Psi, Beta Gamma Sigma. Author: The Law—How It Affects Realtors and Member Boards, 1975. Home: 22 N Regency Dr E Arlington Heights IL 60004 Office: Suite 5600 200 E Randolph Dr Chicago IL 60601 Tel (312) 861-2056

NORTHCUTT, ROBERT RHODERIC, b. Springfield, Mo., Oct. 22, 1926; student Southwest Mo. State Coll., 1950; LL.B., U. Mo., 1954. Admitted to Mo. bar, 1954; asst. prosecuting atty., Greene County, Mo., 1955-59; individual practice law, 1959-60; hearings examiner, div. welfare, 1960-62; asst. atty. gen. State of Mo., 1962-64; atty. Mo. Hwy. Dept., 1964-68; individual practice law, 1968-70; atty. legis. branch State of Mo., 1970-72; sr. counsel, div. welfare, 1972; chief counsel Mo. Div. of Family Services, Jefferson City, 1972—. Home: Route 1 Box 74 Holts Summit MO 65043 Office: Broadway State Office Bldg Jefferson City MO 65101

NORTHROP, EDWARD SKOTTOWE, b. Chevy Chase, Md., June 12, 1911; LL.B., George Washington U., 1937. Admitted to D.C. bar, 1937, Md. bar, 1937; practiced in Montgomery County, Md., and Washington, 1937-41; partner firm Lambert, Hart & Northrop, Rockville, Md. and Washington, 1945-61; judge U.S. Dist. Ct., Dist. of Md., 1961—, chief judge, 1970—; village mgr. Village of Chevy Chase, 1933-41, atty., 1945-61; mem. Md. Senate, 1954-61, chmn. com. on taxation and fiscal affairs, 1955-58, com. on finance, 1959-61, majority leader, 1959-61. Vice chmn. Washington Met. Regional Conf. (name later changed to Met. Washington Council Govts.), chmn. legal com., 1955-61; trustee Woodberry Forest Sch. Mem. Am., Md., D.C., Montgomery County, Balt. City bar assns., Barristers, Washington Center Met. Studies, St. Cecilia Soc., Georgetown Assembly, S.R., Gate and Key, Sigma Alpha Epsilon. Recipient Distinguished Alumnus award George Washington U., 1975. Home: 4309 Wendover Rd Baltimore MD 21218 Office: US Courthouse 101 W Lombard St Suite 710 Baltimore MD 21201 Tel (301) 962-4674

NORTHROP, FILMER STUART CUCKOW, b. Janesville, Wis., Nov. 27, 1893; B.A., Beloit Coll., 1915; M.A. in Econs., Yale, 1919; M.A. in Philosophy, Harvard, 1922, Ph.D., 1924. Instr., asst. prof., asso. prof., prof. philosophy Yale, 1923-46, Sterling prof. philosophy and law, 1947-62, Sterling prof. emeritus, 1962—; vis. distinguished prof. Boston Coll. Law Sch. and Grad. Sch., 1976-77; vis. prof. U. Iowa, summer 1926, U. Mich., summer 1932, U. Va., 1931-32, U. Mex., 1949, Rollins Coll., 1960-62; sr. v.p., bd. dirs. Wenner Gren Found. for Anthrop. Research, 1947-64, hon. research fellow, 1964—; first Dyason Found. lectr. Australian Soc. Internat. Relations, univs. Melbourne, Canberra and Sydney, 1949; co-founder East-West Philosophers Confs. U. Hawaii, 1939, Natural Law Forum, U. Notre Dame; Dept. State rep. Mexican Govt., U. Mex., 1949, Govt. of Morocco-Toumliline Conf., 1957, SEATO Conf., Bangkok, 1958. Fellow AAAS; mem. Am. Philos. Assn., Am. Soc. Law Profs., Am. Acad. Polit. and Social Scis., Am. Acad. Arts and Scis. Decorated Order Aztec Eagle (Mex.); recipient Council Learned Socs. prize award, 1962; author: Science and First Principles, 1931; Meeting of East and West, 1946; Logic of Sciences and Humanities, 1947; The Taming of the Nations (Wendel Wilkie Freedom House award), 1952; Complexity of Legal and Ethical Experience, 1959; Philosophical Anthropology and Practical Politics, 1960. Home and Office: 68 Front St Exeter NH 03833 Tel (603) 778-8892

NORTON, BURNETT WILLIAM, b. Northbridge, Mass., June 3, 1925; B.S., U. R.I., 1951, M.B.A., 1967; J.D., Boston U., 1957, LL.M., 1961. Admitted to R.I. bar, 1958, Mass. bar, 1958, U.S. Patent Office, 1963, U.S. Mil. Ct. Appeals, 1964, U.S. Ct. Customs, 1965; patent atty. Leesona Corp., Warwick, R.I., 1958-65, sr. patent atty., 1965-75, patent counsel, mgr. legal operations, 1975—. Mem. Seekonk (Mass.) Bicentennial and Hist. Commn., 1975. Mem. R.I., Mass. bar assns., Naval Res. Assn., Navy Supply Corps Assn. Tel (401) 739-7100

NORTON, DAVID LAWRENCE, b. St. Paul, Oct. 28, 1945; B.A., U. Va., 1967, J.D., 1970. Admitted to Va. bar, 1970; law clk. to Justice Harry L. Carrico, justice Va. Supreme Ct., 1970-71; asso. firm Mays, Valentine, Davenport & Moore, Richmond, Va., 1971-74; v.p. First & Mchts. Corp., Richmond, 1974—. Bd. dirs. Richmond Urban League, 1975—. Mem. Am., Va., Richmond bar assns., Va. State Bar. Office: PO Box 27025 Richmond VA 23261 Tel (804) 788-2604

NORTON, GEORGE HILLMAN, b. Marietta, Ohio, Nov. 21, 1930; A.B., Brown U., 1951; J.D., Stanford, 1957. Admitted to Calif. bar, 1957; asso. firm Schofield, Hanson, Bridget, Marcus & Jenkins, San Francisco, 1957-58, Low & Ball, Menlo Park, Calif., 1958-60; partner firm Low, Ball & Norton, Menlo Park, 1961-67, Norton & Reese, Palo Alto, Calif., 1967-70, Lakin Spears, Palo Alto, 1970—. Pres., Com. for Green Foothills, Palo Alto, 1967-68. Fellow Am. Acad. Matrimonial Lawyers; mem. Am., San Mateo County, Santa Clara County, Palo Alto Area (pres. 1966-67) bar assns., Assn. Def. Counsel No. Calif., Menlo Park C. of C. (pres. 1965-66). Contbr. articles to profl. publs. Office: 285 Hamilton Ave Palo Alto CA 94301 Tel (415) 328-7000

NORTON, JOSEPH LEWIS, II, b. Shattuck, Okla., Jan. 1, 1942; B.A., U. Kans., 1964, J.D., 1967. Admitted to Kans. bar, 1967; partner firm Breyfogle, Gardner, Davis & Kreamer, Olathe, Kans., 1973—; municipal judge Spring Hill, Kans., 1967-69; prosecutor City of Olathe, 1968-72. Mem. Johnson County, Kans. bar assns., Olathe C. of C. (past dir.). Home: 308 S Stevenson St Olathe KS 66061 Office: 110 S Cherry St Olathe KS 66061 Tel (913) 782-2350

NORTON, LEWIS FRANKLIN, b. Huntington, W.Va., Sept. 26, 1930; student Ky. Mil. Inst., 1947-48; B.S., Hampden-Sydney Coll., 1952; postgrad. Marshall U., 1953; LL.B., U. Va., 1958. Admitted to W.Va. bar, 1958; claims examiner, claims supr., asst. sec., exec. v.p. Inland Mut. Ins. Co., Huntington, 1958-68, pres., 1968—. Active Cabell-Huntington chpt. ARC, United Services, Huntington Clin. Found. Mem. Cabell County, W.Va., Am. bar assns., W.Va. State Bar, Internat. Assn. Ins. Counsel, W.Va. Ins. Guaranty Assn. (chmn. 1970-74), Am. Mgmt. Soc., Huntington Claims Assn. (pres. 1966), Nat. Assn. Ind. Insurers (underwriting and assigned risk coms. 1962). Co-researcher, contbr. articles to legal publs. Home: 55 S Altamont Rd Huntington WV 25701 Office: 1017 6th Ave Huntington WV 25701 Tel (304) 523-0035

NORTON, WILLIAM BIRDSEY, b. Wilton, Iowa, Dec. 8, 1927; B.A., Drake U., 1950, J.D., 1953. Admitted to Iowa bar, 1953, U.S. Supreme Ct. bar, 1962, U.S. Dist. Ct. bar for No. Dist. Iowa, 1962, for So. Dist. Iowa, 1974; partner firm Norton & Freese, Lowden, Iowa, 1953—. Past pres. bd. United Ch. of Christ of Iowa. Mem. Am. Trial Lawyers Assn., Am., Iowa State bar assns. Home: Lowden IA 52255 Office: 508 Main St Lowden IA 52255 Tel (319) 944-5301

NORVELL, JAMES WOODROW, b. Bells, Tenn., May 4, 1913; LL.B., Memphis State U., 1937. Admitted to Tenn. bar, 1937, U.S. Dist. Ct. bar, 1938, U.S. Supreme Ct. bar, 1952; partner firm Nelson, Norvell, Wilson, McRae, Ivy & Sevier, Memphis, 1948—, sr. partner, 1952—. Mem. Memphis and Shelby County (pres. 1968-69), Tenn. (pres. 1975-76), Am. bar assns., Am. Coll. Probate Counsel (regent 1973—), Am. Judicature Soc., Am. Bar Found., Tenn. Def. Lawyers, Internat. Acad. Trial Lawyers, Judge Advs. Assn., Internat. Assn. Ins. Counsel (sec.-treas. 1969-72). Home: 765 Eaton St Memphis TN 38117 Office: 3130-100 N Main Bldg Memphis TN 38103 Tel (901) 523-2364

NORWOOD, COLVIN GAMBLE, JR., b. New Orleans, Dec. 10, 1947; B.S., Tulane U., 1969, J.D., 1972. Admitted to La. bar, 1972; asso. firm Deutsch, Kerrigan & Stiles, New Orleans, 1972-73; asso., partner, mem. firm McGlinchey, Stafford, Mintz & Hoffman, New Orleans, 1973—. Mem. La. Bar Assn. Home: 6031 Perrier St New Orleans LA 70118 Office: 4330 One Shell Sq New Orleans LA 70139 Tel (504) 586-1200

NORWOOD, DERELLE LENORE, b. Watseka, Ill., Oct. 14, 1918; B.A., State U. Iowa, 1939; J.D., Drake U., 1954. Admitted to Iowa bar, 1954, Nev. bar, 1965; practice law, Iowa, 1954-58; asso. firm Morse, Foley & Wadsworth, and predecessors, Las Vegas, 1965—. Mem. Am., Iowa State, Nev. bar assns. Home: 3704 Apache Lane Las Vegas NV 89107 Office: 302 E Carson St Las Vegas NV 89101 Tel (702) 384-6340

NOSAN, ANTHONY L., b. Cleveland, Oct. 9, 1921; LL.D., Cleveland Marshall Law Sch., 1955. Admitted to Ohio bar, 1956; individual practice law. Mem. Ohio, Cleveland, Cuyahoga bar assns. Home: 1818 E 66th Pl Cleveland OH 44103 Office: 6727 St Clair Ave Cleveland OH 44103 Tel (216) 881-4526

NOSEK, FRANCIS JOHN, JR., b. Evanston, Ill., Apr. 13, 1934; B.S., U. Idaho, 1956, J.D., 1960. Admitted to Calif. bar, 1961, U.S. Ct. Appeals 9th Circuit bar, 1961, Alaska bar, 1962; clk. firm Bell, Sanders & Tallman, Anchorage, 1960-61, asso., 1962; individual practice law, Anchorage, 1962-74; partner firm Nosek, Bradbury & Wolf, Anchorage, 1974-76; individual practice law, Anchorage, 1976—. Dir. Nat. Sci. Fair, Inc., Anchorage, 1963-64; chmn. Municipal Parks Commn., Anchorage, 1972-76. Mem. Am., Calif., Alaska, Anchorage bar assns. Staff Alaska Law Jour., 1964-68. Office: 1026 W 4th St Anchorage AK 99501 Tel (907) 274-2602

NOTESTINE, WILBUR EDMUND, b. Big Spring, Tex., Jan. 30, 1931; B.S., U. Tex., 1951, LL.B., 1954. Admitted to Tex. bar, 1954; served to 1st lt. JAGC, U.S. Army, 1955-58; atty. Shamrock Oil and Gas Corp., Amarillo, Tex., 1958-64, asst. gen. counsel, 1964-65, gen. counsel, 1965-66, v.p., 1966-67; v.p., gen. counsel Diamond Shamrock Oil & Gas Co., Amarillo, 1967—. Home: 3003 S Hughes St Amarillo TX 79109 Office: PO Box 631 Amarillo TX 79173 Tel (806) 376-4451

NOTTE, JOHN ANTHONY, JR., b. Providence, May 3, 1909; student Providence Coll., Cornell U.; A.B., J.D., Boston U.; LL.D. (hon.), U. R.I. Admitted to R.I. bar, 1935; sec. of state, R.I., 1956, lt. gov., 1958, gov., 1961-63, commr. workmens compensation div., 1975—. Dept. commdr. R.I. VFW, Mem. R.I. Bar Assn., Aurora Civic Assn. Office: 25 Canal St Providence RI Tel (401) 421-9715

NOURSE, JOHN L., b. San Francisco, Aug. 30, 1909; A.B., Stanford, 1931, J.D., 1934. Admitted to Calif. bar, 1934, U.S. Supreme Ct. bar, 1946; asso. firm Heller, Ehrman, White & McAuliffe, San Francisco, 1934-36; liquidator Ins. Commn. State of Calif., 1936-38; dep. atty. gen. State of Calif., 1938-46; individual practice law, Los Angeles, 1946-48; mem. firm Mitchell, Silberberg & Knupp, Los Angeles, 1948—; lectr. in law U. So. Calif., 1950-51. Mem. Bd. Edn. Arcadia (Calif.) Unified Sch. Dist., 1950-58; bd. trustees Arcadia Library, 1964-65. Mem. Am., Calif., Los Angeles County bar assns. Home: 1424 Via del Rey South Pasadena CA 91030 Office: 1800 Century Park E Los Angeles CA 90067 Tel (213) 553-5000

NOVACK, GERALD ALAN, b. Jersey City, July 25, 1944; B.A., Rutgers U., 1966; J.D. cum laude, Bklyn. Law Sch., 1969. Admitted to N.Y. bar, 1970; asso. firm Barrett, Smith, Schapiro Simon & Armstrong, N.Y.C., 1970-76, partner, 1976—; law clk. to asso. judge N.Y. Ct. Appeals, 1969-70. Mem. N.Y. Bar Assn., Assn. Bar City N.Y. Editor Bklyn. Law Rev., 1968-69. Office: 26 Broadway New York City NY 10004 Tel (212) 422-8180

NOVAK, HAROLD Z., b. Chgo., Apr. 3, 1915; J.D., DePaul Univ., 1939. Admitted to Ill. bar, 1939; individual practice law, Chgo., 1939-41, 1946-56; asst. to trust officer, Exchange Nat. Bank, Chgo., 1956-57, asst. trust officer, 1957-60, asst. v.p., trust officer, 1960-66, v.p., trust officer, 1966-68, sr. v.p., trust officer, 1968—; lectr. Decalogue Soc. Lawyers Continuing Legal Edn. Series, 1969, 73, Ill. Inst. Continuing Legal Edn., 1972-75, Chgo. Bar Assn. Legal Edn. Series, 1976. Pres. Land Trust Council, Ill., 1968-69; mem. bd. mgrs. Decalogue Soc. Lawyers, 1972-75; mem. Ill. Bar Assn., Chgo. Estate Planning Council, DePaul U. Estate Planning Council, Am. Jud. Soc. Contbr. articles in field to profl. jours. Home: 6944 N Kedvale Ave Lincolnwood IL 60646 Office: Exchange National Bank of Chicago LaSalle and Adams Sts Chicago IL 60690 Tel (312) 781-8180

NOVAK, PETER JOHN, b. Chgo., Apr. 16, 1939; A.B., U. Ill., 1960, LL.B., 1962. Admitted to Ill. bar, 1963, Ariz. bar, 1972; regional atty. Great Atlantic & Pacific Tea Co., Chgo., 1963-68; staff atty. to sr. atty. The Greyhound Corp., Chgo. and Phoenix, 1968-74, asst. gen. counsel, Phoenix, 1974, asst. gen. solicitor, 1976—; v.p. Greyhound Brokerage Corp., Phoenix, 1973-75. Mem. Am., Ariz., Chgo., Maricopa County bar assns., Internat. Assn. Insurance Counsels. Office: 111 W Clarendon Ave Phoenix AZ 85077 Tel (602) 248-5731

NOVAK, TABOR ROBERT, JR., b. Tampa, Fla., Sept. 28, 1944; B.A., Washington and Lee U., 1966, LL.B., 1969. Admitted to Ala. bar, 1970; asst. atty. gen., State of Ala., 1970; partner firm Ball, Ball, Duke & Matthews, Montgomery, Ala., 1971—. Dir. Montgomery Children's Center., 1975—. Mem. Am., Montgomery County bar assns., Ala. Def. Lawyers Assn., Am. Judicature Soc., Kiwanis. Home: 2286 Country Club Dr Montgomery AL 36106 Office: 200 S Lawrence St Montgomery AL 36104 Tel (205) 834-7680

NOVAK, THOMAS JAMES, b. Chgo., July 17, 1940; B.S. in Bus. Adminstrn., Marquette U., 1964; J.D., Loyola U., Chgo., 1967. Admitted to Ariz. bar, 1968, U.S. Supreme Ct. bar, 1972; estate Tax Examiner, IRS, Phoenix, 1967-68; atty. Maricopa County, Phoenix, 1968-73; commr. Superior Ct., Maricopa County, 1973—; instr. Glendale (Ariz.) Community Coll., 1971—. Mem. Ariz., Maricopa County, Am. bar assns., Am. Judicature Soc. Home: 9015 N Cobre Dr Phoenix AZ 85028 Office: 125 W Washington St Phoenix AZ 85003 Tel (602) 262-3286

NOVGROD, ISIDORE, b. N.Y.C., July 25, 1907; B.A., N.Y. U., 1939; LL.B., St. John's Coll., 1929. Admitted to N.Y. State bar, 1931; dep. asst. dist. atty. Kings County, N.Y., 1945; confidential asst. to N.Y. State and N.Y. City rent commrs., 1955-68, sr. atty., dep. chief enforcement atty., 1968-69; asst. counsel N.Y.C. Housing and Devel. Bd., 1969; law sec. N.Y. State Supreme Ct. Justice, 1969-74; individual practice law, Bklyn., 1974—. Fellow Am. Acad. Matrimonial Lawyers; mem. Am. (family law sect.), Bklyn. bar assns. Office: 16 Court St Brooklyn NY 11241 Tel (212) 855-8821

NOVICK, DAVID S., b. Madison, Wis., Oct. 2, 1911; B.A., U. Wis., 1933, J.D., 1947. Admitted to Wis. bar, 1947, U.S. Dist. Ct. bar, 1947; individual practice law, Madison, 1947-64; partner firm Novick & Wendel, Madison, 1964-72; partner firm Novick, Wendel & Center, Madison, 1972-76; mem. firm Cassidy, Wendel, Center, Upman, Madison, 1976—. Pres. Beth El Temple, Madison, 1956-58, bd. dirs., 1958—. Home: 2825-1 Century Harbor Middleton WI 53562 Office: 222 W Washington Ave Madison WI 53703 Tel (608) 251-4511

NOWAK, GEORGE PHILIP, b. New Haven, June 9, 1944; B.A., Yale U., 1966; J.D., Vanderbilt U., 1969. Admitted to Conn. bar, 1970, D.C. bar, 1971, U.S. Supreme Ct. bar, 1975; law clk. U.S. Ct. Appeals, 6th Circuit, 1969-70; asso. firm Arnold & Porter, Washington, 1970—. Spl. projects and legis. editor Vanderbilt Law Rev., 1968-69. Home: 230 8th St SE Washington DC 20003 Office: 1229 19th St NW Washington DC 20036

NOWAKOWSKI, MICHAEL NORBERT, b. Milw., Apr. 15, 1948; B.A., U. Wis., 1971, J.D., 1974. Admitted to Wis. bar, 1974, U.S. Dist. Court, 1974; individual practice law, Madison, Wis., 1974—; vol. staff atty. Madison Tenant's Union, 1976-77. Mem. bd. supervisors Dane County 6th Dist., Wis., 1975—; chmn. City of Madison Commn. Environment, 1973-77. Mem. Dane County Bar Assn., ACLU, Order of the Coif. HEW grantee, 1977—. Home: 1805 Helena St Madison WI 53704 Office: 222 S Hamilton St Madison WI 53703 Tel (608) 251-4400

NOWICKI, WALTER JOHN, b. Milw., May 26, 1898; LL.B., Marquette U., 1926. Admitted to Wis. bar, 1931; individual practice law, Milw., 1931—. Columnist local paper, 1923-25. Address: 4884 S 19th St Milwaukee WI 53221

NOWLAN, HIRAM MERRILL, JR., b. Janesville, Wis., Apr. 5, 1929; B.A., Yale, 1951; J.D., Harvard, 1954. Admitted to Wis. bar, 1954, Ga. bar, 1968; partner firm Nowlan, Mouat, Lovejoy, McGuire & Wood, Janesville, 1956-68; sec. Fuqua Industries, Inc., Atlanta, 1968—. Mem. Am., Wis., Ga., Atlanta bar assns., Am. Soc. Corp. Secs.

NOWLAND, WILLIAM SIMS, b. Miami, Fla., Aug. 5, 1941; A.B. in History and Govt., Otterbein Coll., 1963; J.D., U. Denver, 1970. Admitted to Colo. bar, 1971; individual practice law, Colorado Springs, Colo., 1971—; municipal judge City of Fountain (Colo.), 1972—. State legal counsel Colo. Jaycees, 1973. Mem. Am., Colo., El Paso County bar assns., Am. Arbitration Assn. (nat. panel 1974—). Home: 1011 Jupiter Dr Colorado Springs CO 80906 Office: suite 461 105 E Vermijo Ave Colorado Springs CO 80903 Tel (303) 471-0470

NOWLIN, JAMES ROBERTSON, b. San Antonio, Nov. 21, 1937; B.A., Trinity U., San Antonio, 1959, M.A., 1962; J.D., U. Tex., Austin, 1963. Admitted to Tex. bar, 1963; asso. firm Kelso, Locke & King, San Antonio, 1963-69; individual practice law, San Antonio, 1969—; mem. Tex. Ho. of Reps., 1967-71, 73—; instr. Am. history, govt. San Antonio Coll., 1964-67, 71-73; asso. legal counsel U.S. Senate Com. on Labor and Pub. Welfare, 1965-66. Mem. State Bar Tex., Am., San Antonio bar assns., Greater San Antonio C. of C. Office: 204 Edwards Bldg San Antonio TX 78217 Tel (512) 824-3371

NOZ, FRED, b. Phila., Aug. 21, 1928; B.A., St. John's U., N.Y.C., 1949, LL.B., 1950. Admitted to N.Y. State bar, 1950, U.S. Dist. Ct. bar for So. and Eastern Dists. N.Y., 1953, U.S. Ct. Appeals bar, 2d Circuit, 1965; with JAGC, U.S. Army, 1950-52; individual practice law, Jamaica, N.Y., 1953—. Mem. Comml. Lawyers Conf. (pres. 1972-73), Queens County (N.Y.) Bar Assn. Home: 80-15 41st Ave Elmhurst NY 11373 Office: 144-15 Hillside Ave Jamaica NY 11435 Tel (212) OL 8-7777

NUCERA, JOESPH PHILIP, b. Bridgeport, Ct., Jan. 21, 1931; B.A., Fairfield U., 1952; LL.B., Georgetown U., 1955. Admitted to Conn. bar, 1955; asst. clk. Superior Ct., Bridgeport, Conn., 1959-61; partner firm Spiegel & Nucera, Trumbull, Ct., 1951-67; individual practice law, Bridgeport, 1967—. Vice chmn. Trumbull Bd. Edn., 1961-65, Zoning and Planning Commn., Trumbull, 1973—; mem. Trumbull Town Council, 1966-67. Home: 2116 Huntington Turnpike Trumbull CT 06611 Office: 285 Golden Hill St Bridgeport CT 06604 Tel (203) 335-7393

NUERNBERG, WILLIAM RICHARD, b. Pitts., July 7, 1946; B.A. cum laude, Denison U., 1968; J.D. cum laude, U. Mich., 1971. Admitted to Pa. bar, 1971; asso. firm Eckert, Seamans, Cherin & Mellott, Pitts., 1971—. Mem. Allegheny County, Pa., Am. bar assns. Home: 16 Woodland Dr Pittsburgh PA 15228 Office: 42d floor 600 Grant St Pittsburgh PA 15219 Tel (412) 566-6000

NUERNBERGER, WILFRED WENDELL, b. Creighton, Nebr., Mar. 7, 1927; B.A. magna cum laude, Doane Coll., 1950; J.D., U. Nebr., 1952. Admitted to Nebr. bar, 1952; with firm Perry, Perry & Nuernberger, and predecessor, Lincoln, Nebr., asso., 1952-54, partner, 1954-61; judge Separate Juvenile Ct Lancaster County (Nebr.), Lincoln, 1960—; instr. U. Nebr., 1954—; chmn. task force on juvenile delinquency Nat. Adv. Commn. on Criminal Justice Standards and Goals, 1972-74; mem. Nat. Adv. Commn. Juvenile Justice and Delinquency Prevention. Past trustee Masonic Home for Boys and Girls, Fremont, Nebr.; past bd. dirs. Lincoln Council on Alcoholism; past trustee Salvation Army Bd., Lincoln; past bd. dirs. Lincoln Community Council. Mem. Nat. Council on Crime and Delinquency, Am. Bar Assn. Recipient various service awards civic orgns. Home: 2555 Woods Blvd Lincoln NE 68502 Office: County-City Bldg Lincoln NE 68508 Tel (402) 473-6367

NUGENT, CHARLES PETER, b. Oil City Pa., Sept. 6, 1906; A.B., U. Detroit, 1927; J.D., Georgetown, U., 1930. Admitted to D.C. bar, 1930, Mich. bar, 1930; individual practice law, Detroit, 1930—; resident prof. law U. Detroit, 1934-55, Mercy Coll., 1947-70. Mem. Detroit Loyalty Investigation Commn., 1942-45; pres. Detroit Rapid Transit Commn., 1951-57. Mem. Am., Mich. bar assns., Am. Judicature Assn. Moderator U. Detroit Law Jour., 1939-48. Home: 18465 Bretton Dr Detroit MI 48223 Tel (313) 961-8258

NULTY, JEROME BARRY, b. Phila., Jan. 27, 1929; B.S., U.S. Naval Acad., 1952; J.D., Temple U., 1963. Admitted to Pa. bar, 1964, U.S. Dist. Ct. for Pa., 1967, U.S. Supreme Ct. bar, 1971; elec. engr. Minn. Honeywell, Phila., 1957-59, Leeds & Northrup Corp., North Wales, Pa., 1959-63; law clk. Montgomery County (Pa.) Ct., 1964-65; asst. dist. atty., Montgomery County, 1966-69; partner firm Clemens & Nulty, Souderton, Pa., 1970—. Mem. Pa., Montgomery County bar assns. Home: Stump Hall Rd Collegeville PA 19426 Office: 510 E Broad St Souderton PA 18964 Tel (215) 723-5533

NUNNELEY, EMORY TRUFANT, b. Mt. Clemens, Mich., Sept. 16, 1908; A.B., U. Mich., 1930; LL.B., Harvard U., 1933. Admitted to N.Y. bar, 1934, D.C. bar, 1948, Minn. bar, 1955; gen. counsel CAB, 1947-55, Investors Diversified Services, Inc., 1955-60; v.p., gen. counsel N.W. Airlines, Inc., 1960-69; of counsel firm Kaler Worsley Daniel & Hollman, Washington, 1969—; chief U.S. delegation Rome Conf. on Air Law, 1952; pres. legal com. Internat. Civil Aviation Orgn., 1951-52. Mem. Am., D.C. bar assns. Home: 1952 Marthas Rd Alexandria VA 22307 Office: 710 Ring Bldg Washington DC 20036 Tel (202) 331-9100

NURICK, GILBERT, b. Hickory Corners, Pa., Nov. 23, 1906; A.B., Pa. State U., 1928; LL.B., Dickinson Sch. Law, 1931, LL.D. (hon.), 1947. Admitted to Pa. bar, 1932, U.S. Supreme Ct. bar, 1937; mem. firm McNees, Wallace & Nurick, Harrisburg, Pa., 1931-59, sr. partner, 1959—; adj. prof. law Dickinson Sch. Law, 1975—. Former pres. Tri-County United Fund, Harrisburg; pres. United Jewish Community of Harrisburg, Salem Lodge B'nai B'rith; bd. dirs. Harrisburg Polyclinic Hosp., Pa., Harrisburg chambers commerce, ARC, Family and Children's Service. Fellow Am. Bar Found.; mem. Am. Law Inst., Am. (past ho. of dels.), Pa. (past pres.), Dauphin County (past pres.), D.C. bar assns. Recipient Distinguished Alumnus award Pa. State U., 1968, Outstanding Alumnus award Dickinson Sch. Law, 1975. Author: Survey of Administrative Tribunals in Pennsylvania, 1939. Home: apt 10 Park-Scottsdale Apts Harrisburg PA 17111 Office: 100 Pine St Harrisburg PA 17108 Tel (717) 236-9341

NURICK, HERBERT RALPH, b. Harrisburg, Pa., May 23, 1940; B.A., Pa. State U., 1962; J.D., Dickinson Sch. Law, 1967. Admitted to Pa. bar, 1967; asso. firm McNees, Wallace & Nurick, Harrisburg, 1967-74, partner, 1974—. Bd. dirs. Jewish Community Center, Harrisburg, 1970-73, United Jewish Community Greater Harrisburg, 1971-72. Mem. Am., Pa. (bd. govs. 1973, ho. dels. 1973, chmn. young lawyers sect. 1973), Dauphin County bar assns., Pa. Bar Inst. (dir. 1974—), Assn. ICC Practitioners. Home: 148 Cricket Ln Camp Hill PA 17011 Office: 100 Pine St PO Box 1166 Harrisburg PA 17108 Tel (717) 236-9341

NURICK, LESTER, b. N.Y.C., Dec. 2, 1914; B.S.S., Coll. City N.Y., 1934; LL.B., Bklyn. Law Sch., 1937. Admitted to N.Y. bar, 1937; asso. firm Evans and Rees, N.Y.C., 1938-41; counsel SEC, Washington, 1941-43; counsel Internat. Finance Corp., Washington, 1956-60; chief br. internat. law Judge Adv. Gen's. Dept. U.S. Army, 1943; asso. gen. counsel IBRD and Internat. Devel. Assn., Washington, 1946—; professorial lectr. George Washington U. Law Sch., 1960—. Mem. Am. Soc. Internat. Law (exec. counsel and co-chmn. Annual Meeting for 1977). Contbr. articles to profl. jours. Office: 1818 H St NW Washington DC 20433 Tel (202) 477-2257

NUSBAUM, HERBERT STRASSBURGER, b. Clarksburg, W.Va., June 12, 1915; A.B., Duke, 1936; J.D., Harvard, 1939. Admitted to N.Y. bar, 1940, Calif. bar, 1947; mem. legal dept. Loew's, Inc., 1939-42, 46, Allied Artist Pictures Corp., 1947-1947; individual practice law, Beverly Hills, Calif., 1948-74; mem. legal dept. MGM studios, Culver City, Calif., 1974—; Juvenile Hall referee, 1970-71; instr. Glendale Coll. Law, 1973—; lectr. Continuing Edn., Bar of Calif.; mem. adv. planning com. Calif. Law Office Handbook. Mem. Hollywood Bar Assn. (pres. 1956), The Guardians, Los Angeles Copyright Soc., Acad. Motion Picture Arts and Scis., Phi Beta Kappa. Home: 2200 Duxbury Circle Los Angeles CA 90034 Office: 10202 W Washington Blvd Culver City CA 90230 Tel (213) 836-3000

NUSS, LARRY DOUGLAS, b. N.Y.C., Mar. 24, 1941; B.B.A., Washburn U., 1964, J.D., 1967. Admitted to Kans. bar, 1967, U.S. Supreme Ct. bar, 1972; partner firm Van Sickle, Nuss & Farmer, Ft. Scott, Kans., 1967—; judge Ft. Scott Municipal Ct., 1969-75. Pres. Bourbon County (Kans.) Arts Council, 1975. Mem. Kans., S.E. Kans., Bourbon County bar assns., Soc. Hosp. Attys. Recipient Distinguished Service award Ft. Scott Jaycees, 1975. Office: 11 E 1st St Fort Scott KS 66701 Tel (316) 223-0150

NUSSBAUM, AARON, b. N.Y.C., July 9, 1910; LL.B., St. John's U., 1932, LL.M., 1934. Admitted to N.Y. bar, 1934, U.S. Supreme Ct. bar, 1960; asst. dist. atty. Appeals Bur. Kings County (N.Y.), 1947-72; practice law, 1973—. Mem. Nat. Council on Crime and Delinquency, Am. Correctional Assn., Bklyn. Bar Assn., N.Y., Nat. Dist. attys. assns. Author: Second Chance—Amnesty For The First Offender, 1974. Home: 2 W End Ave Brooklyn NY 11235 Office: 16 Court St Brooklyn NY 11241 Tel (212) 237-1717

NUSSBAUM, BERNARD WILLIAM, b. N.Y.C., Mar. 23, 1937; B.A. cum laude, Columbia Coll., 1958; LL.B. magna cum laude, Harvard, 1961. Admitted to N.Y. bar, 1962; asst. U.S. atty., So. Dist. N.Y., 1962-66; partner firm Wachtell, Lipton, Rosen & Katz, N.Y.C., 1966—; lectr. law Columbia U., 1972—; sr. asso. spl. counsel House Judiciary Com., Impeachment Inquiry staff, 1974. Mem. Am., N.Y. State bar assns., Assn. of the Bar of the City of N.Y. (chmn. com. on federal cts. 1975—), Phi Beta Kappa. Note editor: Harvard Law Review, 1960-61; Harvard U. Sheldon traveling fellow, 1961-62. Home: 11 Tyler Rd Scarsdale NY 10583 Office: 299 Park Ave New York City NY 10017 Tel (212) 371-9200

NUSSBAUM, PETER DAVID, b. Bklyn., June 26, 1942; B.S., Cornell U., 1963; LL.B. cum laude, Harvard U., 1966. Admitted to N.Y. bar, 1967, Calif. bar, 1971, U.S. Supreme Ct. bar, 1976; law clk. to Hon. Irving R. Kaufman, N.Y. Second Circuit Ct., 1966-67; staff atty. Vera Inst. of Justice, N.Y.C., 1968, Center on Social Welfare, Policy and Law, N.Y.C., 1969; chief atty. Legal Aid Soc. of Alameda County, Oakland, Calif., 1971-74; partner firm Neyhart & Anderson, San Francisco, 1974—. Mem. steering com. mem. Internat. Forum of World Affairs Council. Mem. Am. Bar Assn., Bar Assn. of San Francisco, San Francisco Barristers Club (co-chmn. labor law com.), Phi Kappa Phi, Phi Eta Sigma. Articles editor Harvard Law Review, 1965-66; Fulbright scholar, U. London, 1967-68; contbr. articles to profl. publs. Office: 100 Bush St San Francisco CA 94104 Tel (415) 986-1980

NUTTER, ROBERT HEINRICH, b. Little Rock, Dec. 23, 1939; B.A. in Pharmacy, U. Fla., 1963; J.D., Stetson Coll. of Law, 1970. Admitted to Fla. bar, 1970; asst. county solicitor, Hillsborough County, Tampa, Fla., 1970-73, asst. state's atty., 1973-74, chief asst. state's atty., 1974-75; partner firm Bonanno, Nutter, Crooks & Alvarez, Tampa, 1975—; advisor Better Bus. Bur., C. of C. Tampa-Hillsborough County, 1972-75; instr. Hillsborough Community Coll., 1973-75. Vice pres. Holy Trinity Lutheran Sch. PTA, Tampa, 1974. Registered pharmacist, Fla. Mem. Hillsborough County (pres. 1976-77), Fla. State pharm. assns., Hillsborough County, Fla. bar assns. Home: 4418 Melrose Ave Tampa FL 33609 Office: 509 N Morgan St Tampa FL 33602 Tel (813) 228-8657

NUTTING, JOSEPH, b. Waterloo, Iowa, Nov. 30, 1931; A.B., State U. Iowa, 1957, J.D., 1959. Admitted to Iowa bar, 1959; partner firm Fulton, Frerichs & Nutting, Waterloo, Iowa, 1959—. Mem. bd. dirs. Waterloo Community Theatre; pres. N.E. Iowa Sports. Mem. Acad. Trial Lawyers, Iowa Bar Assn. Home: 1335 Prospect Blvd Waterloo IA 50701 Office: 616 Lafayette St Waterloo IA 50703 Tel (319) 234-7741

NYDICK, IRA, b. N.Y.C., Sept. 29, 1926; B.B.A., St. John's U., 1949; J.D., Bklyn. Law Sch., 1953; LL.M., N.Y. U., 1958. Admitted to N.Y. bar, 1953; partner firm Nydick & Ross, Melville, N.Y., 1954—; comptroller Town of Huntington (N.Y.), 1968-70; mem. Legislature Suffolk County (N.Y.), 1972-75. Mem. Suffolk County Bar Assn.,

N.Y. County Lawyers Assn., Am. Arbitration Assn. Office: 60 Broad Hollow Rd Melville NY 11746 Tel (516) 271-5400

OAKAR, JAMES LOUIS, b. Cleve., Oct. 7, 1936; B.B.A., John Carroll U., 1958; LL.B., Georgetown U., 1962. Admitted to Ohio Supreme Ct. bar, 1962, U.S. Supreme Ct. bar, 1970; asst. pros. atty. Cuyahoga County, Cleve., 1964-65; asst. U.S. atty. Dept. of Justice, Cleve., 1965-69; individual practice law, Cleve., 1969—; asst. dir. law office of prosecutor, Bedford Heights, Ohio, 1972—, Richmond Heights, Ohio, 1974—; spl. counsel to atty. gen. of Ohio, 1971—. Trustee Cath. Charities Corp.; mem. panel arbitrators Am. Arbitration Assn. Mem. Am., Ohio State, Cuyahoga County bar assns., Bar Assn. of Greater Cleve., Nat. Assn. Criminal Def. Lawyers. Home: 9617 Stoney Creek Ln Parma Heights OH 44130 Office: 1548 Standard Bldg Cleveland OH 44130 Tel (216) 861-1505

OATES, CARL EVERETTE, b. Harlingen, Tex., Apr. 8, 1931; student Schreiner Inst., Kerrville, Tex., 1948-49, Tex. A. and I. Coll., 1949-50; B.S., U.S. Naval Acad., 1955; LL.B., So. Meth. U., 1962. Admitted to Tex. bar, 1962; partner firm Akin, Gump, Strauss, Hauer & Feld, Dallas, 1962—; dir. Valley View Bank, Dallas. Chmn. advisory council Dallas Health and Sci. Museum, 1972-76, trustee, 1976; bd. dirs. Park Cities YMCA, 1973, Kiwanis Wesley Dental Center, Inc., Dallas, 1975—; deacon Highland Park Presbyn. Ch., Dallas, 1973—. Mem. Am., Tex., Dallas bar assns., Barristers, Sons of the Republic of Tex., Delta Theta Phi. Office: 2800 Republic Nat Bank Bldg Dallas TX 75201 Tel (214) 655-2734

OATES, WILLIAM JENNINGS, JR., b. Burlington, W. Va., Feb. 8, 1936; student Potomac State Coll., 1954-55, Asbury Coll., 1956; B.S. in Math., Shepherd Coll., 1960; J.D., W. Va. U., 1965. Admitted to W. Va. bar, 1965; asso. firm William H. Loy, Romney, W. Va., 1965; individual practice law, Romney, 1965-75; partner firm Oates and Saville, Romney, 1975—; pros. atty. Hampshire County (W. Va.), 1969-72; mem. W. Va. State Senate, 1972—. Treas. Hampshire County Boy Scouts Am., 1968—, dir. Potomac council, 1970—; mem. Romney Vol. Fire Co., Hampshire County Farm Bur., Romney Resource, Conservation and Devel. Corp.; del. Dem. Nat. Conv., 1976; trustee St. Stephen's Episc. Ch.; adviser Hampshire County Taxpayers Assn., Hampshire County Fair Assn.; dir. Potomac Highland Travel Council. Mem. Am., W. Va., South Branch Valley bar assns., Nat. Rifle Assn., Phi Alpha Phi. Home: 568 Sixth St Romney WV 26757 Office: 34 W Main St Romney WV 26757 Tel (304) 822-3587

O'BARR, BOBBY GENE, b. Houston, Miss., May 5, 1932; B.A., U. Miss., 1959, LL.B., 1958, J.D., 1968. Admitted to Miss. bar, 1958; practiced in Houston, Miss., 1958-59; partner firms O'Barr and O'Barr, Okolona, Miss., 1959-60, Cumbest, Cumbest O'Barr & Shaddock, Pascagoula, Miss., 1965-68, O'Barr, Hurlbert and O'Barr and predecessor, Biloxi, Miss., 1968—; adminstrv. law judge Miss. Workmen's Compensation Commn., Jackson, 1960-65; mem. Miss. Marine Resources, 1976—. Pres. Miss. Gulf Fishing Banks, Inc., Biloxi, 1974—; mem. Biloxi Port Authority, 1975—, Miss. Marine Conservation Commn., 1976—. Mem. Am., Miss. bar assns., Am. Judicature Soc., Miss. Trial Lawyer's Assn., Am. Trial Lawyer's Assn. Home: 142 Westview Dr Biloxi MS 39531 Office: 1117 W Howard Ave Biloxi MS 39533 Tel (601) 435-5536

OBENSCHAIN, SAMUEL LUTHER, JR., b. Staunton, Va., Aug. 10, 1945; B.A., U. Richmond, 1967; J.D., Washington and Lee U., 1972. Admitted to Ga. bar, 1972; asso. firm Howard & Storey, Atlanta, 1972-73; partner firm Storey & Obenschain, Atlanta, 1973—. Mem. Am., Ga., Atlanta bar assns., Atlanta Council of Younger Lawyers, Phi Alpha Delta. Home: 2415 Northside Pkwy NW Atlanta GA 30327 Office: Fulton National Bank Bldg Atlanta GA 30303 Tel (404) 522-3825

OBENSHAIN, RICHARD DUDLEY, b. Abingdon, Va., Oct. 31, 1935; B.A., Bridgewater Coll., 1956; LL.B., N.Y. U., 1959. Admitted to Va. bar, 1959, U.S. Supreme Ct. bar, 1968; asso. firm McGuire, Woods & Battle, Richmond, Va., 1960-66, partner, 1966-69; partner firm Obenshain, Hinnant, Dolbeare & Beale, Richmond, 1970—. Bd. visitors Va. Commonwealth U., 1970—; trustee Bridgewater Coll., 1976—; chmn. Republican Party Va., 1972-74, co-chmn. Rep. Nat. Com., 1974-76. Mem. Am., Va., Richmond bar assns., Am. Judicature Soc. Home: 14031 Elmstead Rd Midlothian VA 23113 Office: Obenshain Hinnant Dolbeare & Beale 1 N 5th St Richmond VA 23219 Tel (804) 643-3512

OBER, FRANK FRITZ, b. Burlington, Iowa, Sept. 14, 1937; A.B., Yale, 1959; J.D., U. Chgo., 1962. Admitted to Conn. bar, 1962, U.S. Supreme Ct. bar, 1967; asso. firm Marsh Day & Calhoun, Bridgeport, Conn., 1962-68, partner, 1968—. Vice-pres., Bridgeport Salvation Army, 1975—, pres. bd. dirs., 1971-74; dir. Health Systems Agy. of S.W. Conn., 1975—; mem. bldg. com. Fairfield (Conn.) Elementary Sch., 1974—; rep. Fairfield Rep. Town Meeting, 1968-70. Mem. Am., Conn., Bridgeport (exec. com.) bar assns., Phi Delta Phi. Home: 28 Brighton View Rd Fairfield CT 06430 Office: 955 Main St Bridgeport CT 06604 Tel (203) 368-4221

OBER, RICHARD FRANCIS, b. Balt., Feb. 13, 1915; A.B., Princeton, 1937; J.D., Harvard, 1940. Admitted to Md. bar, 1940; law clk. to U.S. Dist. Judge, Balt., 1940-41; legal officer U.S. Army Air Force, 1941-45; atty. to prin. atty. Balt. Gas & Electric Co., 1946-67; gen. counsel Fidelity & Deposit Co. Md., Balt., 1967—, v.p., 1969—, sec., 1972—; corporator Savs. Bank of Balt., 1975—; mem. Md. Corp. Law Revision Commn., 1965-67; cons. to Md. Code Revision Commn., 1974—, Md. Standing Com. on Rules of Practice and Procedure in the Cts., 1977—. Mem. Am., Md., Balt. bar assns., Am. Ins. Assn. Contbr. articles in field to legal jours. Office: Charles and Lexington Sts PO Box 1227 Baltimore MD 21203 Tel (301) 539-0800

OBERBILLIG, ROBERT CHARLES, b. Sterling, Ill., Jan. 18, 1934; B.A., Drake U., 1956, LL.B., 1958. Admitted to Iowa bar, 1958, Nebr. bar, 1960; with claims dept. Allied Mut. Ins. Co., Des Moines, 1957-60; asso. firm Abrahams, Kaslow, Story & Cassman, Omaha, 1961-65; individual practice law, Omaha, 1965-67; dir. Blackhawk County Legal Aid Soc., Waterloo, Iowa, 1967-69, Legal Aid Soc. of Polk County, Des Moines, 1969—; lectr. Law Sch., Drake U., 1972—, Law Sch. U. Wis., Madison, 1974-76, instr. Sch. Social Work, U. Iowa, 1972. Del., Christian Chs. to No. Am. Conf. on Ministry of Laity, 1966; bd. dirs., chmn. civic and community affaris dept. Omaha Area Council Chs.; commr. Nat. Study Com. on Def. Services, 1975; chmn. Nebr. adv. com. U.S. Commn. on Civil Rights; mem. Gov.'s Conf. on Human Rights; v.p. Omaha Lawyers for Fair Housing; mem. project adv. group Legal Services Program, OEO, Washington, 1968-69, 74-76; bd. dirs. Iowa Civil Liberties Union, Omaha Urban League, Omaha Area Conf. on Religion and Race, Nebr. Civil Liberties Union. Mem. Am., Nebr., Polk County bar assns., Nat. Legal Aid and Defender Assn. (dir. 1974—). Recipient First Ann. Achievement award Office Legal Services, 1968; contbr. articles to profl. jours. Home: 4010 Beaver Ave Des Moines IA 50310 Office: 102 E Grand St Des Moines IA 50309 Tel (515) 243-1193

OBERDORFER, CONRAD WALTER, b. Nuremberg, Ger., Sept. 19, 1908; J.D. cum laude, U. Munich, 1933; LL.B. magna cum laude, Northeastern U., 1939; LL.M., Harvard, 1940; came to U.S., 1934, naturalized, 1940. Admitted to Mass. bar, 1940, U.S. Supreme Ct. bar, 1953; asso. firm Herrick, Smith, Donald & Farley, Boston, 1940-41; asso. firm Choate, Hall & Stewart, Boston, 1943-50, 51-54, mem. firm, 1955—; asst. prof. law U. Wash., Seattle, 1941-43; asst. gen. counsel U.S. High Commr. for Germany, Frankfurt, 1950-51; lectr. law Northeastern U., 1945-53; vis. prof. law Harvard Law Sch., 1947; vis. lectr. govt. Harvard Grad. Sch. Pub. Adminstrn., 1947-48. Bd. dirs. Goethe Soc. New Eng., Boston, 1963—, chmn., 1971—. Mem. Order Coif. Author: (with Alfred Gleiss and Martin Hirsch) Common Market Cartel Law, 1971. Home: 150 Fletcher Rd Belmont MA 02178 Office: 28 State St Boston MA 02109 Tel (617) 227-5020

OBERDORFER, LOUIS F., b. Birmingham, Ala., Feb. 21, 1919; A.B., Dartmouth Coll., 1939; LL.B., Yale U., 1946. Admitted to Ala. bar, 1946, D.C. bar, 1949; now with firm Wilmer, Cutler & Pickering, Washington. Mem. Am., Fed., D.C. (pres. 1977—) bar assns., Ala. State Bar. Office: 1666 K St NW Washington DC 20006 Tel (202) 872-6000*

OBERHARDT, MORRIS SOLOMON, b. N.Y.C., Sept. 10, 1904; LL.B., St. Johns U., 1931, LL.M., 1932. Admitted to N.Y. bar, 1933; individual practice law, N.Y.C., 1933—. Home: 2212 Brigham St Brooklyn NY 11229 Office: 30 Vesey St New York City NY 10007 Tel (212) 732-5766

OBERST, PAUL, b. Owensboro, Ky., Apr. 22, 1914; A.B., U. Evansville, 1936; J.D., U. Ky., 1939; LL.M., U. Mich., 1941. Admitted to Ky. bar, 1938, Mo. bar, 1942; asso. firm Ryland, Stinson, Mag and Thomson, Kansas City, Mo., 1941-42; asst. prof. law U. Ky., 1946-47, prof. law, 1947—; vis. prof. U. Chgo., 1954-55; prof., dir. civil liberties program N.Y. U., 1959-61; mem. Nat. Commn. on Acad. Tenure, 1971-73. Mem. Ky. Commn. on Corrections, 1961-65; mem. Ky. Commn. on Human Rights, 1962-66, chmn., 1966-70, 73-76; trustee U. Ky., Lexington, 1963-69, 72-75. Mem. Ky., Am. bar assns., Am. Law Inst., Am. Assn. Law Schs. (exec. com. 1970-72), Am. Judicature Soc., Order of Coif, Phi Delta Phi. Contbr. articles to legal jours.; note editor Ky. Law Jours., 1938-39. Home: 829 Sherwood Dr Lexington KY 40502 Office: U of Ky Sch of Law Lexington KY 40506 Tel (606) 257-3950

OBLETZ, CLARENCE, b. Springfield, Mass., Nov. 16, 1908; B.S., U. Buffalo, 1928, LL.B., 1931. Admitted to N.Y. bar, 1932, Fla. bar, 1974; individual practice law, Buffalo, 1932-72; mem. firm Hodgson, Russ, Andrews, Woods & Goodyear, Buffalo, 1973—, Ft. Lauderdale, Fla., 1975—. Bd. dirs. Buffalo Philharmonic Orch., 1960-73, pres., 1964-65; trustee Buffalo Chamber Music Soc., 1965-73. Mem. N.Y. State, Fla., Am. bar assns. Home: 5701 White Hickory Circle Tamarac FL 33319 Office: 4000 N State Rd 7 Ft Lauderdale FL 33319 Tel (305) 484-2138

OBLINGER, WALTER L., b. Chgo., July 5, 1914; A.A., Central YMCA Coll., 1936; LL.B., Chgo.-Kent Coll. Law, 1939, J.D., 1969. Admitted to Ill. bar, 1939, U.S. Supreme Ct. bar, 1962; spl. agt. FBI, Washington, 1939-51; asso. firm Cavanaugh & Oblinger, Springfield, Ill., 1951-53; partner firm Oblinger & Oblinger, Springfield, 1953—; city atty. City of Springfield, 1963-64, corp. counsel, 1964-68; hearing officer Ill. Pollution Control Bd., 1977—. Fellow Am. Acad. Forensic Scis.; mem. Ill. State, Sangamon County bar assns., Anti-Illicit Drugs in Soc. (dir. 1973—). Home: Rural Route 1 Sherman IL 62684 Office: 520 S Sixth St Springfield IL 62701 Tel (217) 528-5131

O'BRIEN, CHARLES H., b. Orange, N.J., July 30, 1920; LL.B., Cumberland U., 1947. Admitted to Tenn. bar, 1947; individual practice law, Memphis 1948, 1951-67, Crossville, Tenn., 1967-70; dep. div. proctor Shelby County (Tenn.), 1954-58; asso. justice Tenn. Ct. Criminal Appeal, Crossville, 1970—; mem. Tenn. Ho. of Reps., 1963-65; mem. Tenn. Senate, 1965-67. Mem. Tenn. Jud. Conf. Office: 108 Hayes St Crossville TN 38555 Tel (615) 484-6641

O'BRIEN, CHILTON, b. Beaumont, Tex., Jan. 3, 1911; LL.B., U. Tex., 1936. Admitted to Tex. bar, 1936; asso., partner firm Smith, Smith & Boyd, Beaumont, 1936-40; partner firm Harkrider & O'Brien, Beaumont, 1941-49; individual practice law, Beaumont, 1949-68; partner firm O'Brien & Richards, Beaumont, 1969—; trustee Tex. Portland Cement Co., Beaumont, 1958-62; sec., dir. Gladys City Oil, Gas & Mfg. Co., Beaumont, 1941-55; dir. The Enterprise Co., Beaumont, 1953—, First Security Nat. Bank, Beaumont, 1962—; v.p., chief exec. officer Gladys City Co., Beaumont, 1970—. Chmn. City Charter Commn., 1947; pres. Beaumont Family Service, 1955; mem. Beaumont Community Council, 1958, City Planning Commn., 1962-65, City Charter Revision Com., 1972; alt. del. Democratic Nat. Conv., 1940, 52, 56; chmn. exec. com. Young Dems. of Tex., 1940. Fellow Tex. Bar Assn. Found.; mem. Am., Tex., Jefferson County bar assns., Tex. Assn. of Defense Counsel. Home: 814 22d St Beaumont TX 77706 Office: 1130 Petroleum Bldg Beaumont TX 77701 Tel (713) 832-3468

O'BRIEN, DONALD EDWARD, b. Burlington, Vt., Sept. 16, 1925; LL.B., Boston Univ., 1951. Admitted to Vt. bar, 1952; individual practice law, Burlington, Vt., 1951-57; mem. firm O'Brien & Ross, Burlington, 1957-58, Cain & O'Brien, 1958-63; superior ct. judge, Vt., 1963-66; individual practice law, Burlington, 1966—; chmn. Vt. Profl. Conduct Bd., 1973-76. Chmn. Vt. Liquor Control Bd., 1961-63, State Labor Relations Bd., 1967-76. Mem. Am., Vt. bar assns., Am. Jud. Soc. Address: 231 S Union St Burlington VT 05401 Tel (802) 863-6879

O'BRIEN, EUGENE JAMES, b. N.Y.C., July 18, 1930; B.A., St. John's U., 1952, LL.B., 1958. Admitted to N.Y. bar, 1959; partner firm Burke, Curry, Hammill & O'Brien, N.Y.C., Commack, N.Y. and Garden City, N.Y., 1960—. Mem. Nassau-Suffolk Trial Lawyers Assn. (dir.). Home: 2 Heritage Ct Ronkonkoma Long Island NY 11779 Office: 120 7th St Garden City Long Island NY 11530 Tel (516) 746-0707

OBRIEN, FRANCIS CARROLL, b. Arlington Va., June 23, 1922; B.A., Md. U., 1952; postgrad. Nat. Law Sch., 1957; LL.B., J.D., George Washington U., 1957. Admitted to D.C. bar, 1958, Md. bar, 1965, U.S. Dist. Ct., U.S. Ct. Appeals, U.S. Mil. Ct. Appeals, Superior Ct. of D.C. bars; asso. firm Swingle & Swingle, Washington, 1959-64; partner firm Swingle, Mann & Obrien, Washington, 1964-65; sr. partner firm Obrien and Clague, Hyattsville, Md., 1965—. Mem. D.C., Md., Prince Georges County (Md.) bar assns. Home: 16800 Candy Hill Rd Upper Marlboro MD 20870 Office: 4313 Hamilton St Hyattsville MD 20871 Tel (301) 927-2727

O'BRIEN, FRANCIS J., b. Bklyn., Mar. 25, 1926; B.S., Coll. of Holy Cross, 1947; LL.B., Fordham U., 1950. Admitted to N.Y. bar, 1950; now partner firm Hill, Rivkins, Carey, Loesberg & O'Brien, N.Y.C. Mem. Am. Bar Assn., Maritime Law Assn. of U.S. (1st v.p. 1976—). Office: 96 Fulton St New York City NY 10038 Tel (212) 233-6171*

O'BRIEN, FRANCIS THOMAS, b. Chgo., Aug. 3, 1904; J.D., U. Mich., 1927; postgrad. in law and commerce Northwestern U., 1927-29. Admitted to Ill. bar, 1928, Tex. bar, 1948, U.S. Supreme Ct. bar, 1942; practiced law, Chgo., 1928-43; mem. firm Wham & O'Brien, 1938-43; served to lt. comdr. USNR, 1943-46, summary and dist. judge 1st Provisional Mil. Govt. of Okinawa, mem. U.S. Mil. Commn., Ryukyu Islands; individual practice, 1946-54, 56-58, 64—; dir. USOM, Uruguay, 1954-56; spl. asst. to mng. dir. on formation Devel. Loan Fund, Washington, 1958-60; asst. dean Cornell Law Sch., Ithaca, N.Y., 1960-64. Alt. del., del. at large Republican Nat. Conv., 1952-56; co-trustee William H. Bush Trust Properties. Mem. Inter-Am., Am., Ill., Tex., Chgo., Amarillo bar assns., Law Club Chgo., Legal Club Chgo. Home: Frying Pan Ranch PO Box 326 Amarillo TX 79105 Office: 412 Petroleum Bldg Amarillo TX 79105 Tel (806) 372-3442

O'BRIEN, GERALD M., b. Grand Rapids, Minn., June 7, 1931; B.A., U. Wis., Superior, 1953, J.D., Madison, 1959. Admitted to Wis. bar, 1959; asso. firm Peickert Anderson Fisher Shannon & O'Brien and predecessor, Stevens Point, Wis., 1959-63, partner, 1963—; instr. in bus. law U. Wis., Stevens Point, 1963-72. Pres. Portage County (Wis.) United Fund, 1968, Stevens Point Serra Club, 1970, Stevens Point Plan Commn., 1970-76, Stevens Point YMCA, 1971, Cath. Bd. Edn., 1976. Mem. Am., Wis., 7th Circuit (pres.), Portage County (pres.) bar assns., Internat. Assn. Ins. Counsel, Ins. Trial Counsel Wis. Office: 1007 Ellis St Stevens Point WI 54481 Tel (715) 344-0890

O'BRIEN, JAMES EDWARD, b. Trinidad, Colo., Mar. 22, 1912; A.B., U. Calif. at Berkeley, 1932, J.D., 1935. Admitted to Calif. bar, 1935; practice in San Francisco, 1935-66; asso., partner Pillsbury, Madison & Sutro, 1935-66; v.p., dir. Standard Oil Co. Calif., San Francisco, 1966—; dir. W.P. Fuller & Co., El Portal Mining Co., Abercrombie & Fitch Co. Pres., bd. dirs. Stanford Hosp.; bd. dirs. Acad. for Ednl. Devel. N.Y., Nat. Fund for Med. Edn., Am. Enterprise Inst.; trustee Internat. and Comparative Law Center, Dallas, Southwestern Legal Found. Decorated Legion of Merit, Bronze Star; Croix de Guerre with Silver Star. Mem. San Francisco (past v.p., dir.). Internat. chambers commerce, Am. Bar Assn., Am. Soc. Internat. Law, Internat. Law Assn., Am. Law Inst. Home: 1530 Waverly St Palo Alto CA 94301 Office: 225 Bush St San Francisco CA 94104*

O'BRIEN, JOHN JOSEPH, b. Detroit, Oct. 29, 1929; Ph.B. with honors, U. Detroit, 1952, J.D., 1955; grad. Nat. Coll. Juvenile Justice, U. Nev., 1976. Admitted to Mich. bar, 1955, U.S. Supreme Ct. bar, 1959; judge Probate Ct. of Mich., Pontiac, 1975—. Trustee Camp Oakland Youth Programs, Big Bros.-Big Sisters council; councilman Village of Beverly Hills, 1973-75. Mem. Oakland County Bar Assn., State Bar Assn. of Mich., Mich. Probate and Juvenile Ct. Judges, Assn., Nat. Council Juvenile Ct. Judges, Nat. Council Crime and Delinquency, Delta Theta Phi. Home: Beverly Hills MI 48009 Office: Oakland County Courthouse Pontiac MI 48053 Tel (313) 858-0240

O'BRIEN, JOHN JOSEPH, b. Boston, July 22, 1948; A.B., Boston Coll., 1970, J.D., 1973. Admitted to Mass. bar, 1973; counsel div. water pollution control Mass. Dept. Environ. Quality Engring., Boston, 1974—, spl. counsel Mass. Pesticide Bd., Boston, 1975—. Mem. Boston, Mass., Am. (regional vice-chmn. spl. task force on state air pollution control programs, young lawyers sect. 1975, recipient citation 1975) bar assns. Contbg. author, mem. bd. editors Annual Survey Mass. Law, 1972—. Office: 3d Floor 110 Tremont St Boston MA 02108 Tel (617) 727-3855

O'BRIEN, ROBERT LEE, JR., b. Claxton, Ga., Feb. 12, 1945; A.B., Mercer U., 1967, J.D., 1973. Admitted to Ga. bar, 1973; asso. firm John D. Mattox, Jesup, Ga., 1973-74; individual practice law, Jesup, 1975-77; asst. solicitor State Ct. of Fulton County, Atlanta, 1977—. Sec.-treas. bd. trustees Wayne County (Ga.) Law Library. Mem. Am., Jesup (sec.-treas. 1975, pres. 1976) bar assns., State Bar Ga., Assn. Trial Lawyers Am., Marine Corps Res. Officers Assn. Office: Civil-Criminal Bldg Room 59 160 Pryor St SW Atlanta GA 30303 Tel (404) 572-2911

O'BRIEN, SAMUEL GREENOUGH, b. Oskaloosa, Iowa, July 11, 1920; B.A., U. Iowa, 1943, J.D., 1947. Admitted to Iowa bar, 1947; asso. firm Nyemaster, Goode, McLaughlin, Emery & O'Brien, Des Moines, 1947-52, partner, 1952—; dir. South Des Moines Nat. Bank, Inter-State Assurance Co. Chmn., Central Iowa chpt. ARC, 1969-71. Mem. Am., Iowa, Polk County bar assns. Home: 301 Tonawanda St Des Moines IA 50312 Office: Hubbell Bldg Des Moines IA 50309 Tel (515) 284-1940

O'BRIEN, THOMAS GEORGE, III, b. N.Y.C., Aug. 26, 1942; A.B. magna cum laude, U. Notre Dame, 1964; J.D., Yale, 1967. Admitted to N.Y. bar, 1967; asso. firm Carter, Ledyard & Milburn, N.Y.C., 1971—. Mem. Am., N.Y. State bar assns., Assn. Bar City N.Y. (transp. com.). Home: 333 S Irving St Ridgewood NJ 07450 Office: 2 Wall St New York City NY 10005 Tel (212) 732-3200

O'BRIEN, THOMAS J., b. N.Y.C., Jan. 8, 1939; B.S., LL.B., J.D., Fordham U. Admitted to N.Y. bar; law clerk U.S. Dist. Ct. Eastern Dist. N.Y. State, Bklyn., 1966-67; asst. U.S. atty., Eastern Dist. N.Y. State, Bklyn., 1967-68; asso. firm Skadden, Area, Slate, Meagher & Flom, N.Y.C., 1969-71; individual practice law, N.Y.C., 1971—; law instr. N.Y.C. Community Coll., Bklyn., 1966-67. Mem. N.Y. State, Nassau County bar assns. Home: 459 Foch Blvd New York City NY 11501 Office: 2 Pennsylvania Plaza New York City NY 10001 Tel (212) 947-6147

O'BRIEN, THOMAS JAMES, b. St. Paul, Oct. 12, 1923; student U. Wis., River Falls, 1941-42; B.S. in Law, William Mitchell Coll., 1947, J.D., 1949. LL.B., U. Minn. (Mpls.), 1949. Admitted to Minn., Wis. bars 1950; with O'Brien Ins. Agency, Hudson, Wis., 1940-57; individual practice law, Hudson, 1950-57; judge St. Croix County, 1957-71; individual practice law, Hudson, 1971—; reserve judge State Wis., 1971—, br. 2 Milw. County, 1975—. Co-chmn. Am. Red Cross, St. Croix County, Wis., 1946. Home: 115 7th S Hudson WI 54016 Office: 619 2d Hudson WI 54016 Tel (715) 386-5342

O'BRYAN, SAMUEL OLIVER, JR., b. Manning, S.C., Dec. 10, 1916; B.A., U. Fla., 1938, LL.B., 1940. Admitted to Fla. bar, 1940; partner firm English, McCaughan, & O'Bryan, and predecessor, Ft. Lauderdale, Fla., 1952—; dir. 1st Fed. Savs. and Loan Assn. Broward County, 1964—, chmn., 1974—. Mem. Fla., Am. bar assns. Home:

2616 N E 24th St Fort Lauderdale FL 33305 Office: 301 E Las Olas Blvd Fort Lauderdale FL 33301 Tel (305) 462-3301

OBSTFELD, HAROLD B., b. Cracow, Poland, June 17, 1946; B.A., Bklyn. Coll., 1967; J.D., Harvard, 1970; LL.M., N.Y. U., 1974. Admitted to N.Y. bar, 1971, U.S. Tax Ct. bar, 1971, U.S. Dist. Ct. bar for So. Dist. N.Y., 1971; asso. firm Lawson F. Bernstein, 1971—; adj. asst. prof. trial practice law N.Y. U. Sch. Continuing Edn., Washington Square campus, N.Y.C. Mem. Am., N.Y. State bar assns. Office: 1 Rockefeller Plaza New York City NY 10020 Tel (212) 765-1350

O'CALLAGHAN, JOHN JOSEPH, b. Boston, Aug. 19, 1941; A.B., Suffolk U., 1967; J.D., 1966; LL.M., Boston U., 1971. Admitted to Mass. bar, 1966, U.S. Dist. Ct. bar, 1968; individual practice law, South Boston, Mass., 1968—; asst. prof. govt. and econs. Suffolk U., 1970—. Mem. Mass. Bar Assn. (mem. subcom. on adminstrv. law). Office: 574 E Broadway South Boston MA 02127 Tel (617) 269-0341

O'CALLAGHAN, WILLIAM LAWRENCE, JR., b. Atlanta, Aug. 6, 1941; B.B.A., U. Ga., 1963, J.D. cum laude, 1965; LL.M. in Taxation, Georgetown U., 1968. Admitted to Ga. bar, 1965, U.S. Supreme Ct. bar, 1972; asso. firm Sutherland, Asbill & Brenna, Atlanta, 1965; capt. JAGC, U.S. Army, 1965-68; mem. firm Gambrell, Russell, Killorin, Wade & Forbes, Atlanta, 1968-74; partner firm O'Callaghan, Saunders & Stumm, Profl. Assn., Atlanta, 1974—. Mem. Am., Fed., Ga., Atlanta bar assns., Lawyers Club Atlanta, Sylvanus Morris Order Jurisprudence, Phi Beta Kappa, Phi Kappa Phi, Phi Eta Sigma, Beta Gamma Sigma. Home: 351 Green Oak Ridge Marietta GA 30067 Office: 5600 Roswell Rd Suite 360 Prado N Atlanta GA 30342 Tel (404) 252-2400

OCHS, GEORGE ARTHUR, III, b. Louisville, June 25, 1918; J.D., U. Louisville, 1969. Admitted to Ky. bar, 1941; asst. atty. Ky. Distillers Assn., Louisville, 1942-47, govt. regulations atty., 1947-67, and corporate relations dir., 1967—. Mem. Ky. Bar Assn. Home: 2427 Meadow Rd Louisville KY 40205 Office: Seagram Bldg PO Box 240 Louisville KY 40201 Tel (502) 634-1551

OCHSENSCHLAGER, IRVING JOHN, b. Aurora, Ill., Oct. 15, 1942; B.S. in Bus. Adminstrn., U. Ariz., 1965; J.D., Valparaiso U., 1968. Admitted to Ill. bar, 1968; partner firm Puckett, Barnett, Larson, Mickey, Wilson & Ochsenschlager, Aurora, 1970—; atty. City of Aurora, 1974—. Mem. Am., Ill., Kane County bar assns., Am. Arbitration Assn. Home: Route 1 Box 5 Sugar Grove IL 60554 Office: 220 E Galena Aurora IL 60507 Tel (312) 897-6921

OCKEY, RONALD JACK, b. Green River, Wyo., June 12, 1934; B.A., U. Utah, 1959; J.D., George Washington U., 1966. Admitted to Colo. bar, 1967, Utah bar, 1968, U.S. Ct. of Appeals bar, 1969; law clk. to Hon. William E. Doyle, U.S. Dist. judge, U.S. Dist. Ct. for Dist. of Colo., 1966-67; partner firm Jones, Waldo, Holbrook & McDonough, Salt Lake City, Utah, 1967—; contract negotiator NSF, Washington, D.C., 1962-66. State govtl. affairs chmn. Utah Jaycees, 1969; state del. Utah Republican State Conv., 1974-76; county del. Salt Lake County Rep. Conv., 1976. Mem. Am., Colo., Salt Lake County, Utah bar assns., Phi Delta Phi, Order of Coif. Bd. editors: George Washington Law Review, 1965-66, Utah Bar Jour., 1973—; contbr. articles to legal jours. Office: 800 Walker Bank Bldg Salt Lake City UT 84111 Tel (801) 521-3200

O'CONNELL, JAMES DANIEL, b. Highland Park, Mich., July 1, 1933; B.A., Detroit Inst. Tech., 1958; J.D., Detroit Coll. Law, 1958. Admitted to Mich. bar, 1958, U.S. Supreme Ct. bar, 1972, Fla. bar, 1972; pvt. practice law; mem. city council City of Highland Park, 1961-72, mayor pro-tem, 1965-69, council pres. pro-tem 1970, council pres., 1971-72; asso. judge Municipal Ct., Highland Park, 1974—. Recipient medal for Americanism VFW, 1971. Home: 84 Ford St Highland Park MI 48203 Office: 13818 Woodward St Highland Park MI 48203 Tel (313) 865-9289

O'CONNELL, JOHN FORSTER, b. N.Y.C., Mar. 27, 1928; A.B., Fordham U., 1948; LL.B., St. John's U., 1951. Admitted to N.Y. bar, 1953, U.S. Supreme Ct. bar, 1960; asso. firm Lord, Day & Lord, N.Y.C., 1953-71; asso. firm Burlingham, Underwood & Lord, N.Y.C., 1971-73, mem. firm, 1973—; trial and def. counsel Ct. Mil. Appeals, USCG, 1951-53; mem. panel arbitrators Am. Arbitration Assn., 1964—. Mem. Maritime Law Assn. Tel (212) 422-7585

O'CONNELL, JOHN M., JR., b. Greensburg, Pa., Oct. 3, 1939; B. Civil Engring., Villanova U., 1971; LL.B., Harvard U., 1964. Admitted to Pa. bar, U.S. Supreme Ct. bar; asso. firm Smith, Best & Horn, 1965-67; individual practice law, 1967-72; partner firm O'Connell, Silvis, & Godlewski, Greensburg, Pa., 1972—; asst. county solicitor, Westmoreland County, Pa., 1965-68, adminstr. magisterial dist. system, 1970-73. Mem. zoning hearing bd., Greensburg, 1969—; bd. trustees Jeannette Dist. Meml. Hosp., 1974—. Mem. Am., Pa., Westmoreland bar assns. Home: 8 Bayard Ave Greensburg PA 15601 Office: 126 W Pittsburgh St Greensburg PA 15601 Tel (412) 837-2275

O'CONNELL, JOSEPH JOHN, b. Yonkers, N.Y., July 5, 1918; LL.B., Fordham U., 1942. Admitted to N.Y. bar, 1942; individual practice law, Bronxville, N.Y., 1945-57, Lake Carmel, N.Y., 1957-58; editor Lawyers Coop. Pub. Co., Mt. Kisco, N.Y., 1958-62; sr. asst. editor-in-chief Matthew Bender & Co., Inc., N.Y.C., 1962—. Mem. Am., N.Y. State bar assns. Author: (with others) Bender's Forms for Civil Practice, 26 vols., 1963-76; (with Stowell Rounds) How To Save Time and Taxes, Preparing Fiduciary Income Tax Returns. Home and Office: Box 658 Carmel NY 10512 Office: Matthew Bender & Co 235 E 45th St New York City NY 10017 Tel (212) 661-5050

O'CONNELL, KENNETH JOHN, b. Bayfield, Wis., Dec. 8, 1909; LL.B., U. Wis., 1933, S.J.D., 1934. Admitted to Wis. bar, 1933, Oreg. bar, 1944; asst. atty. Wis. Tax Commn., 1934; asst. prof. law U. Oreg., 1935-40, asso. prof., 1940-44, prof., 1947-58; individual practice law, Eugene, Oreg., 1944-47; asso. justice Oreg. Supreme Ct., Salem, 1958-70, chief justice, 1970-76; chmn. Oreg. Statute Revision Council, 1950-54; vice chmn. Constl. Revision Commn. Oreg., 1961-63; lectr. in field. Mem. Am., Oreg. (Merit award 1953) bar assns., Order of the Coif, Omicron Delta Tau, Phi Delta Phi. Recipient Distinguished Service award U. Oreg., 1967, Herbert Hartley award Am. Judicature Soc. award, 1976; fellow Center for Advanced Study in Behavioral Scis., 1965-66. Contbr. articles in field to profl. jours. Home: 3393 Country Club Dr S Salem OR 97302 Office: Supreme Ct Bldg Salem OR 97310 Tel (503) 378-6006

O'CONNOR, CHARLES PATRICK, b. Boston, Sept. 29, 1940; B.S., Coll. Holy Cross, 1963; LL.B., Boston Coll., 1966. Admitted to Mass. bar 1966, D.C. bar, 1968, U.S. Supreme Ct. bar, 1974. Mem. staff Office of Gen. Counsel, NLRB, Washington, 1967-68; asso. firm Morgan, Lewis & Bockius, Washington, 1968-71, partner, 1971—; asst. majority counsel spl. election com. U.S. Ho. of Reps., 1968. Mem. Am., D.C. bar assns., Barristers. Home: 6121 Vernon Terr Alexandria VA 22307 Office: 1800 M St NW Suite 800 Washington DC 20036 Tel (202) 872-5060

O'CONNOR, DAVID FRANCIS PATRICK, b. Washington, D.C., May 3, 1946; B.A., Vanderbilt U., 1968; J.D., George Washington U., 1971. Admitted to D.C. bar, 1971; asso. firm Covington & Burling, Washington, D.C., 1971—. Mem. D.C. Bar Assn. Contbr. articles to legal jours. Office: 888 16th St NW Washington DC 20006 Tel (202) 452-6390

O'CONNOR, DENNIS MICHAEL, b. Haddon Heights, N.J., May 4, 1939; A.B., Dartmouth, 1961, M.B.A., 1962; LL.B., Harvard, 1967. Admitted to Mass. bar, 1968, N.H. bar, 1974; asso. firm Rudman, Pollock & Katz, Boston, 1967-69; partner firm Pollock, O'Connor and Jacobs, Boston and Waltham, Mass., 1970—. Mem. Am., Boston bar assns., Smaller Bus. Assn. New Eng. Contbr. articles to law jour. Home: Loon Valley Townhouses Lincoln NH 03251 Office: 470 Totten Pond Rd Waltham MA 02154 also 1 Boston Pl Boston MA 02108 Tel (617) 890-0500

O'CONNOR, EDWARD JOSEPH, b. Grand Forks, N.D., Aug. 15, 1908; LL.B., Georgetown U., 1935, LL.M., 1936. Admitted to D.C. bar, 1936, N.D. bar, 1937, Ill. bar, 1941; mem. staff Dept. Justice, Washington; mem. staff IRS, Washington, Los Angeles; mem. staff U.S. Atty's. Office, Los Angeles, anti-trust div. Dept. Justice, Los Angeles; partner firm O'Connor & O'Connor, Los Angeles; judge Calif. Superior Ct., Los Angeles. Home: 149 N Cliffwood Ave Los Angeles CA 90049 Office: 111 N Hill St Los Angeles CA 90012 Tel (213) 974-5686

O'CONNOR, FRANK DANIEL, b. N.Y.C., Dec. 20, 1909; A.B., Niagara U., 1932, LL.D. honoris causa, 1964; J.D., Bklyn. Law Sch., 1934; LL.D. (hon.), St. John's U., 1977. Admitted to N.Y. bar, 1935, U.S. Supreme Ct. bar, 1950; individual practice law, Queens County, N.Y., 1935-55; mem. N.Y. Senate, 1949-52, 54-55; dist. atty. Queens County, 1955-65; pres. N.Y.C. Council, 1966-68; justice N.Y. State Supreme Ct., 1969-76, asso. justice Appellate Div. 2d Dept., 1975-76, 76—. Mem. Queens County Bar Assn., N.Y. State Trial Lawyers Assn. Home: 8426 Charlecote Ridge Jamaica NY 11432 Office: 8811 Sutphin Blvd Jamaica NY 11435 Tel (212) 520-3755

O'CONNOR, JAMES JOHN, b. Chgo., Mar. 15, 1937; B.S., Holy Cross Coll., Worcester, Mass., 1958; M.B.A., Harvard, 1960; J.D., Georgetown U., 1963. Admitted to Ill. bar, 1964; with Commonwealth Edison Co., Chgo., 1963—, asst. v.p., 1967-70, v.p., 1970-73, exec. v.p., 1973—; dir. Talman Fed. Savings and Loan Assn. of Chgo. Bd. dirs. Chgo. Boys Club, v.p., 1970; chmn. bd. Am. Cancer Soc., Chgo., 1971-73; bd. dirs., sec. Leadership Council for Met. Open Communities, Chgo.; trustee Adler Planetarium, Chgo., Ill. Childrens Home and Aid Soc., Chgo., Field Museum Natural History, Chgo.,; bd. dirs. Lyric Opera Chgo. Mem. Am., Ill., Chgo. bar assns. Home: 9549 Monticello Ave Evanston IL 60203 Office: PO Box 767 Chicago IL 60690 Tel (312) 294-3224

O'CONNOR, JOHN JOSEPH, b. Cambridge, Mass., Aug. 29, 1910; B.B.A., Boston U., 1934; LL.B., Emory U., 1957, J.D., 1970. Admitted to Ga. bar, 1958, U.S. Supreme Ct. bar, 1965; individual practice law, Atlanta, 1958—; pres. Met. Gas Co., Atlanta, 1957-74. Bd. dirs. Cath. Social Services Inc., 1968—. Mem. Atlanta, Am. bar assns., State Bar Ga., Phi Alpha Delta, Nat. Alumni Council Boston U., Beta Gamma Sigma. Home: 360 Robin Hood Rd NE Atlanta GA 30309 Tel (404) 874-0784

O'CONNOR, JOHN PAUL, b. Evanston, Ill., Sept. 30, 1939; B.S., Xavier U., Cin., 1963; J.D., Chase Coll. Law, Cin., 1967; postgrad. Juvenile Justice Inst. U. Nev., 1969. Admitted to Ohio bar, 1967, U.S. Dist. Ct. bar for So. Dist. Ohio, 1968, U.S. 6th Circuit Ct. Appeals bar, 1968; partner firm Schuch, Grossmann & O'Connor, Cin., 1967-73; chief referee Hamilton County Juvenile Ct., 1967-73; judge Hamilton County (Ohio) Municipal Ct., 1967—; adj. prof. dept. corrections Xavier U. Mem. Am., Ohio State, Cin. bar assns. Office: Hamilton County Courthouse Cincinnati OH 45202 Tel (513) 632-8350

O'CONNOR, KATHLEEN ROSE, b. Martinez, Calif., Feb. 14, 1947; A.A., Yuba Coll., 1967; B.A., Stanford U., 1969; J.D., U. Calif. at Davis, 1972. Admitted to Calif. bar, 1973; individual practice law, Marysville, Calif., 1973-76; partner firm Evans & O'Connor, Marysville, 1976—; guest lectr. Siskiyou Coll., 1976—. Chmn. Marysville City Planning Commn., 1975-77, chmn., 1977—; bd. dirs. Yuba Coll. Found., Inc., 1976—. Mem. Sutter-Yuba Bd. Realtors, Yuba-Sutter Bar Assn. Home: 1493 Valley View Dr Yuba City CA 95991 Office: PO Box 31 Marysville CA 95901 Tel (916) 742-6988

O'CONNOR, MICHOL, b. Houston, Nov. 30, 1942; B.A., U. Tex., 1965; J.D., U. Houston, 1973. Admitted to Tex. bar, 1973; atty. 1st Ct. Civil Appeals, Houston, 1973-74; asst. dist. atty. Harris County (Tex.), 1975; asso. firm Kronzer, Abraham & Watkins, Houston, 1975—. Mem. Houston Bar Assn. (long range planning com., dir. 1977—), Houston Jr. Bar Assn. (outstanding contbn. award 1975, dir. 1974-75), Tex. Trial Lawyers Assn., Tex. Bar Assn. (adminstrn. of justice com. 1975—), Tex. Jr. Bar Assn. (chairwoman women's rights com.); contbr. articles to profl. jours. Home: 2112 Bissonnet St Houston TX 77005 Office: Kronzer Abraham & Watkins 800 Commerce St Houston TX 77002 Tel (713) 222-7211

O'CONNOR, OTIS LESLIE, b. Charleston, W.Va., July 6, 1935; A.B., Princeton, 1957; J.D., Harvard, 1963. Admitted to W.Va. bar, 1963; asso. firm Steptoe & Johnson, Charleston, 1963-69, partner, 1969—. Mem. city council Charleston, 1971-75. Mem. Am., W.Va., Kanawha County bar assns. Home: 890 Chester Rd Charleston WV 25302 Office: 608 Kanawha Valley Bldg Charleston WV 25301 Tel (304) 342-2191

O'CONNOR, SANDRA DAY, b. El Paso, Tex., Mar. 26, 1930; B.A., Stanford, 1952, LL.B., 1952. Admitted to Calif. bar, 1952, Ariz. bar, 1957; individual practice, Maryvale, Ariz., 1959-60; asst. atty. gen., Ariz., 1965-69; mem. Ariz. Senate, 1969-74; judge Superior Ct., Maricopa County, Ariz., 1974—; dir. 1st Nat Bank Ariz. Mem. Ariz. State Personnel Commn., 1967-69; trustee Stanford U., 1976—; bd. dirs. Ariz. Acad.; trustee Heard Mus., 1968-74, 76—, v.p., 1976—; bd. dirs. Phoenix Hist. Soc., Friends of Channel 8; mem. citizens adv. bd. Blood Services; adv. bd. Salvation Army. Mem. State Bar Ariz., Am. Bar Assn. Named Phoenix Woman of Year, Advt. Club, 1972; recipient award NCCJ, 1975. Home: 3651 E Denton Ln Paradise Valley AZ 85253 Office: 125 W Washington St Phoenix AZ 85003 Tel (602) 262-3892

O'CONNOR, WILLIAM JENNINGS, JR., b. Buffalo, Feb. 6, 1923; A.B., U. Toronto, 1943; LL.B., Cornell U., 1948. Admitted to N.Y. State bar, 1949; lectr. bus. law U. Buffalo, 1949-54; partner firm Penney, Penney & Buerger, Buffalo, 1955-59, firm Buerger & O'Connor, Buffalo, 1960-70, firm Phillips Lytle, Hitchcock, Blaine & Huber, Buffalo, 1970—; lectr. Practicing Law Inst., Uniform Comml. Code Inst. Mem. Erie County, N.Y. (chmn. bus. law com. 1967-68, banking, corp. and bus. law sect. 1968-69), Am. (chmn. com. on regulation of consumer credit 1974—) bar assns. Contbr. articles to legal jours. Office: 3400 Marine Midland Center Buffalo NY 14203 Tel (716) 847-8426

O'DAY, EDWIN ROBERT, b. Cleve., Feb. 18, 1926; B.A., Ohio Wesleyan U., 1950; J.D., Cleve. State U., 1954. Admitted to Ohio bar, 1954; mem. legal dept. Pickands Mather & Co., Cleve., 1950-57; v.p., treas. Lezius-Hiles Co., Cleve., 1957—; individual practice law, Cleve., 1975—. Mem. Pepper Pike Civic League, 1975—. Mem. Am., Ohio State, Greater Cleve. bar assns. Home: 31405 Creekside Dr Pepper Pike OH 44124 Office: 29525 Chagrin Blvd Suite 106 Pepper Pike OH 44124 Tel (216) 464-0443

ODDLEIFSON, PETER, b. Rochester, N.Y., Dec. 12, 1932; B.A., Yale U., 1954; LL.B., Harvard U., 1957. Admitted to N.Y. state bar, 1959; asso. firm Milbank, Tweed, Hadley & McCloy, N.Y.C., 1957-59; asso. firm Harris, Beach, Wilcox, Rubin, & Levey, Rochester, N.Y., 1959—; dir. Goulds Pumps, Inc., Seneca Falls, N.Y., 1974—. Bd. dirs. Genesee Hosp., Rochester 1970—. Mem. Monroe County, N.Y. State, Am. bar assns. Home: 166 Superior Rd Rochester NY 14618 Office: 2 State St Rochester NY 14618 Tel (716) 232-4440

ODELL, STUART IRWIN, b. Phila., Jan. 1, 1940; B.S. in Econs., 1961; LL.B., U. Miami (Fla.), 1964; LL.M., N.Y. U., 1965. Admitted to Fla. bar, 1965, Pa. bar, 1966; lectr. law N.Y. U., 1965-68, adj. asso. prof., 1968-70, adj. asst. prof., 1970-75, adj. prof., 1975—; asso. firm Morgan, Lewis & Bockius, Phila., 1966-70, partner, 1970—; lectr. Temple U., 1975; lectr. continuing legal edn. seminars. Mem. Am., Pa., Phila. bar assns. Contbr. articles to legal jours. Office: 123 S Broad St Philadelphia PA 19109 Tel (215) 491-9268

ODOM, BOB DOYLE, b. Dallas, Dec. 12, 1942; B.A., Tex. Tech. U., 1966; J.D., Baylor U., 1968; grad. Nat. Coll. Dist. Attys., Houston, 1970. Admitted to Tex. bar, 1968; asst. dist. atty. Lubbock (Tex.), 1968-69, first asst. dist. atty., 1969-73; first asst. dist. atty. Bell-Lampasas-Mills Counties (Tex.), 1973-76; partner firm Odom & Hurley, Killeen, Tex., 1976—. Mem. State Bar Tex., Bell-Lampasas-Mills County Bar Assn., Tex. Dist. and County Attys. Assn., Tex. Criminal Def. Lawyers Assn., Central Tex. Peace Officers Assn. (pres. 1975), Delta Theta Phi. Recipient Alpha Phi Omega Community Service award, 1972, Outstanding Service award, 1962. Home: 2118 Linwood Rd Temple TX 76501 Office: 303 W Rancier St Killeen TX 76541 Tel (817) 634-2621

O'DONNELL, JOHN LOGAN, b. Chgo., Mar. 6, 1914; B.A., Williams Coll., 1934; J.D., Northwestern U., 1937. Admitted to Ill. bar, 1937, N.Y. State bar, 1941; asso. firm Defrees, Buckingham, Jones & Hoffman, Chgo., 1937-38; staff atty. SEC, Washington, 1938-41; instr. Catholic U., 1938-41; asso. firm Cravath, Swaine & Moore, N.Y.C., 1941-52; partner firm Olwine, Connelly, Chase, O'Donnell & Weyher, N.Y.C., 1952—. Bd. dirs. Near East Found., N.Y.C., 1968—. Fellow Am. Coll. Trial Lawyers; mem. Am., Fed., N.Y. State, N.Y. County bar assns., Assn. Bar City N.Y. Home: 181 E 73d St New York City NY 10021 Office: 299 Park Ave New York City NY 10017 Tel (212) 688-0400

O'DONNELL, ROBERT JOHN, b. Worcester, Mass., Aug. 3, 1943; B.S. in Bus. Adminstrn., U. Calif. at Berkeley, 1965; J.D., Boston Coll. Law, 1969; certificate Coro Found., San Francisco, 1966. Admitted to Vt. bar, 1970; individual practice law Woodstock, Vt., 1970—; asso. Harvard Legal Aid Bur., 1967-68; intern San Francisco Neighborhood Legal Assistance Found., 1967; founding dir., pres. Boston Coll. Legal Assistance Bur., 1968-69. Chmn. Woodstock chpt. ARC, 1975—; mem. New Eng. Div. Adv. Council, Boston, 1975—; mem. vestry St. James Episcopal Ch., Woodstock, 1973-76. Mem. Am., Windsor County, Vt. bar assns., Am. Trial Lawyers Assn. Home: Great Maples Hartland VT 05048 Office: 5 The Green Woodstock VT 05091 Tel (802) 457-1500

O'DONOGHUE, MICHAEL JOSEPH, b. Phila., Mar. 6, 1943; A.B., St. Joseph's Coll., 1964; J.D., Villanova U., 1967; postgrad. U.S. Naval Justice Sch., 1969. Admitted to Pa. bar, 1967, U.S. Ct. Mil. Appeals, 1971; law clk. to judge Ct. of Common Pleas, Montgomery County, Pa., 1967-68; lt. JAGC, U.S. Navy, 1968-72; asso. firm Wisler, Pearlstine, Talone, Craig & Garrity, Norristown, Pa., 1972—; vice pres., gen. counsel PTI, Inc., Wayne, 1968—. Mem. Am., Pa., Montgomery County (chmn. young lawyers sect. 1975-76, bd. dirs. 1975-76, mem. young lawyers exec. com., 1976, chmn. pub. relations com. 1977—) bar assns., Montgomery County, Pa. trial lawyers assns. Office: 515 Swede St Norristown PA 19401 Tel (215) 272-8400

O'DOWD, ERIK MICHAEL, b. Tucson, Dec. 14, 1940; B.A. in Polit. Sci., Stanford U., 1962; LL.B., Georgetown U., 1965; LL.M., Harvard U., 1967. Admitted to Ariz. bar, 1966; individual practice law, Tucson, 1967-71, 74—; partner firm O'Dowd & Diamos, and predecessor, Tucson, 1971-74; lectr. U. Ariz. Coll. Law, 1967-68; chief counsel So. chpt. Ariz. Civil Liberties Union, 1968-72. Mem. Ariz. Trial Lawyers Assn., Pima County Bar Assn. Home: 3806 E Calle de Soto Tucson AZ 85716 Office: Suite 1108 Transam Bldg Tucson AZ 85701 Tel (602) 622-3595

O'DOWD, RONALD BERNARD, b. Kansas City, Mo., Oct. 18, 1944; B.B.A., U. N.Mex., 1967, J.D., 1970. Admitted to N.Mex. bar, 1971, 10th Circuit Ct. Appeals bar, 1972; sr. law clk. to U.S. dist. judge, 1970-73; atty. AEC, Albuquerque, 1973-75; atty. ERDA, Albuquerque, 1975—, bd. dirs., legal adviser Employees Fed. Credit Union, 1973—. Worker ind. gifts div. United Community Fund, 1976; gen. counsel N.Mex. Wilderness Soc., 1975—. Mem. N.Mex. State (young lawyers sect., pres. 1972-74, dir. 1974—), Am. (state chmn. com. on youth drug abuse edn. program 1972), Albuquerque (chmn. law day com. 1974) bar assns., Albuquerque Lawyers Club. Staff, Natural Resources Jour., 1968-69. Home: 8824 Horacio Pl NE Albuquerque NM 87111 Office: ERDA PO Box 5400 Albuquerque NM 87115 Tel (505) 264-7273

O'DWYER, DUNCAN WITHERBEE, b. N.Y.C., Feb. 11, 1938; B.A., Lafayette Coll., 1960; LL.B., Cornell U., 1963. Admitted to Kans. bar, 1965, N.Y. bar, 1967; partner firm Forsyth, Howe, O'Dwyer & Kenyon, Rochester, N.Y., 1969—; trial counsel Urban Renewal Agency, City of Rochester, 1972—; atty., Town of Riga, N.Y., 1968-71, Town of Murray, N.Y., 1972—; arbitrator appellate div. 4th dept. Rochester City Ct., 1972—; served as maj. Judge Adv. Gen. Corps USAR, 1975—. Clerk of session, elder Parkminster United Presbyn. Ch., Rochester, 1968-74; mem. Cornell Secondary

Schs. Com., 1968—. Mem. Am., N.Y. State, Monroe County bar assns., Cornell Club Rochester (pres. 1975-76; bd. govs. 1969-77). Home: 484 Smith Rd Pittsford NY 14534 Office: 950 Midtown Tower Rochester NY 14604 Tel (716) 325-7515

OEHLER, DANIEL JOHN, b. LaCrosse, Wis., Dec. 14, 1944; B.A., Gonzaga U., 1967; J.D., Ariz. State U., 1970. Admitted to Ariz. bar, 1971, Fed. bar, 1971; partner firm Leek & Oehler, Kingman, Ariz., 1971—. Mem. Mohave County Parks Commn., 1974—, chmn., 1975—; Democratic precinct committeeman, 1972-74; mem. Mohave County Fair Commn., 1972-74; mem. Mohave High Sch. Vocat. Adv. Com., 1972—. Mem. Am., Ariz., Mohave County (pres. 1976—) bar assns. Tel (602) 758-3521

OEHLERT, BENJAMIN HILBORN, III, b. Washington, Feb. 26, 1938; B.S. in Econs., Wharton Sch. U. Pa., 1961; LL.B., Emory U., 1963. Admitted to Ga. bar, 1963; asso. firm Heyman and Sizemore and predecessors, Atlanta, 1964-72, partner, 1972-76; of counsel to Williamson and Kermish, Atlanta, 1975-76; partner firm Oehlert, Kermish, Labovitz, Markus and Brazier, Atlanta, 1976—. Mem. Am., Ga., Atlanta bar assns., Atlanta Lawyers Club. Home: 5770 Mountain Creek Rd Atlanta GA 30328 Office: 1314 Rhodes Haverty Bldg 134 Peachtree St Atlanta GA 30303 Tel (404) 525-0457

OEHMANN, WARD HENRY, b. Washington, Mar. 9, 1911; A.B., U. Mich., 1933, J.D., 1935. Admitted to D.C. bar, 1936, Md. bar, 1958; claims examiner GAO, 1935-37; individual practice law, Chevy Chase, Md., 1937-42, 45—. Pres., Hahnemann Hosp., Washington, 1956-59. Mem. Am., Md. bar assns., D.C. Bar, Bar Assn. of D.C., Am. Judicature Soc. Home: 3203 Winnett Rd Chevy Chase MD 20015 Office: 5530 Wisconsin Ave Chevy Chase MD 20015 Tel (301) 654-4233

OERTEL, KENNETH GEORGE, lawyer, state adminstrv. ofcl.; b. N.Y.C., Feb. 27, 1943; B.A., N.Y. U., 1963, J.D., 1966. Admitted to N.Y. bar, 1970, Fla. bar, 1970; spl. agent FBI, Washington, 1967-70; asst. U.S. atty., So. Dist. Fla., 1970-72; gen. counsel State of Fla. Bd. Trustees Internal Improvement Trust Fund, Tallahassee, 1972-74; dir. State of Fla. div. Adminstrv. Hearings, Tallahassee, 1974—. Mem. The Fla. Bar, Tallahassee Bar Assn., Am. Judicature Soc. Home: Route 3 Box 441B Tallahassee FL 32303 Office: Carlton Bldg Room 530 Tallahassee FL 32304

OETTINGER, ELMER ROSENTHAL, JR., b. Wilson, N.C., Nov. 24, 1913; A.B., U. N.C., Chapel Hill, 1934, LL.B., 1939, M.A., 1952, Ph.D. in English, 1966. Admitted to N.C. bar, 1940; atty. Inst. of Govt. staff, U. N.C., 1939-41, instr., 1952-56, radio news dir., commentator ABC affiliates, Raleigh, N.C., 1948-51; lectr., 1955-60, prof., asst. dir. Inst. Gvt., 1960—; practice law, Wilson, N.C., 1941-42, 46-48; chmn., exec. sec. N.C. News Media-Adminstrn. of Justice Council, 1964—; commr. Nat. Conf. of Commrs. on Uniform State Laws, 1973—; founder-dir. ct. reporting seminars, state, local gvt. reporting seminars, 1962—; mem. Chancellor's advisory com., 1975-76. Mem. pub. affairs steering com. N.C. Dept. Pub. Instruction; v. chmn. Carolina Readers Theatre; mem. N.C. Gov.'s Com. on Safety on Hwys. Mem. Am. (legal adv. com. fair trial-free press, mem. com. media relations), N.C. bar assns., Phi Beta Kappa. Author: Copyright Law and Copying Practices, 1969; The News Media and the Courts, 1972; Fables on Life, Law & Justice, 1972; Report on Criminal Justice Information Systems and Their Effects on Access and Privacy, 1975. Editor: Popular Government mag., 1961-74. Home: 58 Oakwood Dr Chapel Hill NC 27514 Office: Inst Gvt PO Box 990 Chapel Hill NC 27514 Tel (919) 966-5381

OFFICER, PHILIP NOEL, b. Albuquerque, Sept. 7, 1938; A.A., City Coll. San Francisco, 1963; B.S., U. Calif., Berkeley, 1965, J.D., 1969. Admitted to Calif. bar, 1970; dep. dist. atty. Fresno County (Calif.), 1970-75, chief dep. dist. atty., 1975—. Sec. Appaloosa Nation Indian Guides YMCA, Clovis, Calif., 1976-77; counsel chpt. Internat. Footprinters Assn. Mem. Calif., Fresno County bar assns., Internat. Footprint Assn. Recipient certificate of Achievement Police and Prosecutors Inst., 1973. Office: 1100 Van Ness Suite 701 Fresno CA 93721 Tel (209) 488-3141

OFFNER, ERIC DELMONTE, b. Vienna, Austria, June 23, 1928; came to U.S., 1941, naturalized, 1949; B.B.A., City Coll. New York, 1949; LL.B., Cornell U., 1952. Admitted to N.Y. bar, 1952, D.C. bar, 1975; asso. firm Langner, Parry, Card & Langner, N.Y.C., 1952-57; partner firm Haseltine, Lake & Waters, N.Y.C., 1957—; professorial lectr. George Washington Law Sch., 1970-73; spl. prof. law Hofstra U., Hempstead, N.Y., 1974—. Pres., Riverdale Ethical Culture Soc., 1964-67, Riverdale Mental Health Assn., 1967-69, Ethical Culture Retirement Center, Inc., 1977—; mem. exec. com. Am. Ethical Union. Mem. U.S. Trademark Assn., Inst. Trademark Agts., Australian Patent Inst., Internat. Assn. for Protection Indsl. Property, Am. Bar Assn., Am., N.Y. (asso. editor Bull.) patent law assns. Author: International Trademark Protection, 1964, International Trademark Service, 3 vols., 1970, Vol. IV, 1972, Vol. V, 1973, Vol. VI, 1976; mem. editorial bd. Trademark Reporter, 1961-64, 69-72; editor-in-chief Cornell Law Forum, 1950-51; contbr. articles to profl. jours. Home: 5221 Arlington Ave Bronx NY 10471 Office: 122 E 42d St New York City NY Tel (212) 490-1310

O'FIEL, HUGH EDWIN, b. Beaumont, Tex., July 12, 1946; B.S., Lamar U., 1969; J.D., Baylor U., 1969. Admitted to Tex. bar, 1969; individual practice law, Beaumont, 1971—. Chmn. pub. responsibility com. Beaumont State Center for Human Devel., 1974—; pres. Optimist Club of S.E. Beaumont, 1973-74. Mem. Jefferson County Bar Assn. Home: 2165 Shady Ln Beaumont TX 77706 Office: 480 Franklin St Beaumont TX 77701 Tel (713) 833-1456

O'FLAHERTY, DANIEL FAIRFAX, b. Washington, June 26, 1925; J.D., George Washington U., 1949. Admitted to Va. bar, 1949; since practiced in Alexandria, Va., individual practice law, 1949-73; substitute judge Civil & Police Ct., 1956-67; judge Municipal Ct., 1967-70, sr. judge, 1970-74; chief judge Alexandria Gen. Dist. Ct., 1974—. Mem. Alexandria City Council, 1953-55. Mem. Va. Bar Assn., Am. Judicature Soc., Am. Judges' Assn. Home: 103 Summers Dr Alexandria VA 22301 Office: 130 N Fairfax St Alexandria VA 22314 Tel (703) 750-6380

O'FLARITY, JAMES P., b. Yazoo City, Miss., Oct. 15, 1923; B.S., Millsaps Coll., 1950; postgrad. Jackson (Miss.) Sch. Law, 1948, 53-54; J.D., U. Fla., 1965. Admitted to Miss. bar, 1954, U.S. Supreme Ct. bar, 1957, Fla. bar, 1966; asso. firm Cone, Owen, Wagner, Nugent, Johnson & McKeown, W. Balm Beach, Fla., 1966-69; individual practice law, Palm Beach and Ft. Lauderdale, Fla., 1969—. Trustee John Marshall House (nat. hon.), 1974. Fellow Am. Acad. Matrimonial Lawyers (pres. Fla. 1976—), Roscoe Pound-Am. Trial Lawyers Found.; mem. Fla. (chmn. family law sect. 1974-76, mem. exec. com. 1976—), Am. (mem. council family law sect. 1976—, editor sect. newsletter 1975-77), Palm Beach County (chmn. Circuit Ct. adv. com. 1974-77), Internat., Inter-Am., Fed. bar assns., Fla. Bar Found. (dir. 1977—, asst. sec. 1973—, chmn. projects com. 1976—), U. Fla. Law Center Council, Am. Arbitration Assn., Fla. Family Support Council Adv. Bd., Acad. Fla. Trial Lawyers, Assn. Trial Lawyers Am. (chmn. family law sect. 1971-73), Internat. Soc. Family Law, World Peace Through Law Center, Am. Judicature Soc., Am. Soc. for Legal History, Supreme Ct. Hist. Soc., SCRIBES. Contbr. articles to legal jours. Home: 908 Country Club Dr North Palm Beach FL 33408 Office: 230 Royal Palm Way Suite 216 Palm Beach FL 33480 Tel (305) 659-4666 and 201 SE 2d St Fort Lauderdale FL 33301 Tel (305) 462-4452

OGDEN, CHESTER ROBERT, b. Clarksburg, W.Va., Aug. 11, 1923; B.S., Harvard, 1946; certificate Harvard Grad. Sch. Bus. Adminstrn., 1947; LL.B., Yale, 1950. Admitted to N.Y. bar, 1952, Washington bar, 1957; asso. firm Hawkins, Delafield & Wood, N.Y.C., 1950-57, firm Preston, Thorgrimson & Horowitz, Seattle, 1957-58; v.p. R. J. Martin & Co., Spokane, Wash., 1958-63; v.p. R.J. Martin Mortgage Co., Spokane, 1958—; pres. Great Northwest Life, Spokane, 1963-64; pres., gen. counsel N. Coast Life Ins. Co., Spokane, 1965—. Mem. nat. adv. council Regional Med. Programs, HEW, 1970-74; bd. dirs. Wash. Ins. Council, 1974—. Mem. Am., Wash., Spokane County bar assns. Home: 1230 E 20th Ave Spokane WA 99203 Office: N 211 Wall St Spokane WA 99201 Tel (509) 838-4235

OGENS, RONALD LEE, b. Washington, June 5, 1942; B.S., U. Md., 1964; J.D., Am. U., 1967. Admitted to Md. bar, 1967, D.C. bar, 1968, U.S. Supreme Ct. bar, 1971; partner firm Deckelbaum, Wolpert & Ogens, Washington. Dir.-advisor Wheaton (Md.) Rescue Sqaud, 1974—. Mem. Md. State, D.C., Montgomery County bar assns., Assn. Plaintiff's Trial Attys. Home: 10308 Gainsborough Rd Potomac MD 20854 Office: 1140 Connecticut Ave Washington DC 20036 Tel (202) 223-1474

OGG, JACK L., b. Tonkawa, Okla., Sept. 27, 1920; B.A., U. Ariz., 1943, J.D., 1948. Admitted to Ariz. bar, 1948; practiced law, 1948-58; county atty. Yavapai County (Ariz.), 1954-58; judge Yavapai County Superior Ct., 1959-72, Ariz. Ct. Appeals, 1972—; chmn. Ariz. Criminal Code Commn., 1973-76. Pres. Prescott (Ariz.) United Fund, 1965. Mem. Am., Yavapai County (pres. 1955) bar assns., Am. Judicature Soc., State Bar Ariz., Ariz. Judges Assn. (pres. 1969), U. Ariz. Alumni Assn. (pres. 1962), Phi Beta Kappa. Recipient Silver Beaver award Boy Scouts Am., Freeman medal U. Ariz., 1943. Home: 1120 Copper Basin Rd Prescott AZ 86301 Office: Ct of Appeals State Capitol Phoenix AZ 85007 Tel (271) 4826

OGGEL, STEPHEN PETER, b. Monmouth, Ill., Apr. 18, 1942; B.A., Vanderbilt U., 1964; J.D., George Washington U., 1967. Admitted to D.C. bar, 1968, Calif. bar, 1970; mem. firm Sullivan, Jones & Archer, San Diego, 1974—. Office: 1400 Financial Sq San Diego CA 92101 Tel (714) 236-1611

OGILBY, BARRY RAY, b. Evansville, Ind., Jan. 19, 1947; B.S. in Geology, U. Ky., 1969; J.D., Memphis State U., 1972. Admitted to Tex. bar, 1972, Tenn. bar, 1972, Ky. bar, 1974, Calif. bar, 1977; atty. litigation Exxon Co., Houston, 1972-73, atty. mktg., Memphis, 1973-74, fed. govt. relations, Houston, 1975-76, labor and environ. law, Los Angeles, 1976—. Mem. Ky., Tenn., Tex., Houston Jr., Am. bar assns., Order of Coif. Editorial bd. Memphis State U. Law Rev., 1971-72. Home: 627 Strand Santa Monica CA 90405 Office: Suite 1251 1800 Ave of the Stars Los Angeles CA 90067 Tel (213) 552-5664

OGLE, RICHARD FERRELL, b. Birmingham, Ala., Mar. 11, 1942; B.A., U. Ala., 1964, J.D., 1968. Admitted to Ala. bar, 1968, U.S. Ct. Appeals bar, 1975; law clk. U.S. Dist. Ct., Mobile, Ala., 1968-70; asso. firm Gordon & Cleveland, Birmingham, 1970-72; partner firm Denaburg, Schoel, Meyerson & Ogle, Birmingham, 1973—. Founder, sec. Birmingham Tip-Off Club, 1973—. Mem. Am., Ala., Birmingham (pres. young lawyers sect. 1977, mem. exec. com. 1977, mem. exec. com. young lawyers sect. 1976-77) bar assns., Assn. Trial Lawyers Am., Ala. Trial Lawyers Assn., Am. Judicature Soc., Birmingham Jaycees, Farrah Law Soc., Phi Alpha Delta, Pi Kappa Alpha (nat. pres. 1976-78), Omicron Delta Kappa. Home: 2757 Cherokee Rd Birmingham AL 35216 Office: 1000 Brown-Marx Bldg Birmingham AL 35203 Tel (205) 328-5760

O'GORMAN, CORTNER BRIAN, b. Oakland, Calif., Feb. 26, 1941; B.A., Columbia, 1962; LL.B., U. Calif., Berkeley, 1965. Admitted to Calif. bar, 1966; mem. firm Eckert, O'Gorman, & McFarland, Goleta, Calif., 1966—. Mem. Calif., Santa Barbara County bar assns. Home: 5630 Via Messina Goleta CA 93017 Office: 160 N Fairview St Goleta CA 93017 Tel (805) 967-0185

O'GRADY, GERALD PATRICK, b. St. Albans, Vt., Jan. 9, 1914; A.B. magna cum laude, Tufts Coll., 1935; LL.B., Georgetown U., 1939. Admitted to D.C. bar, 1938, Calif. bar, 1971, U.S. Supreme Ct. bar, 1971; atty. CAB, Washington, 1939-41; asso. firm Whiteford, Hart, Carmody & Wilson, Washington, 1941-46; individual practice law, Washington, 1947-67; v.p. Western Air Lines, Inc., Los Angeles, 1967-72, sr. v.p., 1972—; dir. Pacific No. Airlines, Inc., 1947-67. Mem. Am., Fed., Los Angeles County bar assns., State Bar Calif., Phi Beta Kappa, Alpha Sigma Phi. Home: 7722 W 79th St Playa del Rey CA 90291 Office: 6060 Avion Dr Los Angeles CA 90009 Tel (213) 646-2377

O'GRADY, JOHN JOSEPH, III, b. N.Y.C., Mar. 21, 1933; A.B., Holy Cross Coll., Worcester, Mass., 1954; J.D., Harvard, 1957. Admitted to N.Y. bar, 1958; asso. firm Cadwalader, Wickersham & Taft, N.Y.C., 1958-66, partner, 1966—. Mem. Am., N.Y. State bar assns. Office: One Wall St New York City NY 10005 Tel (212) 785-1000

OGURAK, MELVIN, b. St. Paul, July 3, 1929; B.A. cum laude, U. Minn., 1952, B.S., 1954, J.D., 1967. Admitted to Minn. bar, 1967; asso. atty. firm Meagher, Geer, Markam & Anderson, Mpls., 1967-70; individual practice law, Mpls., 1970-73; sr. partner firm Ogurak & Striker, Mpls., 1973-75, Ogurak Law Offices, Mpls., 1975—; arbitrator Am. Arbitration Assn. Mem. Minn., Hennepin County bar assns., Minn. Trial Lawyers Assn., Assn. Trial Lawyers Am., Roscoe Pound Law Found., Phi Beta Kappa. Office: 401 2d Ave S Minneapolis MN 55401 Tel (612) 339-2731

O'HAGAN, JAMES JOSEPH, b. Chgo., Dec. 29, 1936; B.S., DePaul U., 1958, J.D., 1962. Admitted to Ill. bar, 1963; asso. firm Querrey, Harrow, Gulanick & Kennedy, Ltd., Chgo., 1958-66, partner, 1966—, mng. partner, 1971—. Mem. Am., Chgo., NW Suburban, Lake County bar assns., Ill. Trial Lawyers Assn., Trial Lawyers Club Chgo., Assn. Trial Lawyers Am. Editor: monthly abstract. Home: 2131 Manor Ln Park Ridge IL 60068 Office: 135 S LaSalle St Chicago IL 60603 Tel (312) 236-9850

O'HAIR, JOHN DENNIS, b. Detroit, Sept. 29, 1929; B.A., DePauw U., 1951; J.D., Detroit Coll. Law, 1954. Admitted to Mich. bar, 1954; asst. corp. counsel City of Detroit, 1957-65; judge Detroit Common Pleas Ct., 1965-68, Mich. Circuit Ct., 3d Jud. Circuit, 1968—; asso. prof. Detroit Coll. Law, 1961—. Mem. Detroit, Mich., Am. bar assns., Wayne County (Mich.), Mich. judges assns. Office: 1821 City County Bldg Detroit MI 48226 Tel (313) 224-5224

O'HANLON, GEORGE ALZAMORA, b. N.Y.C., Oct. 21, 1926; B.S., Columbia, 1950; J.D., Harvard, 1954. Admitted to N.Y. State bar, 1955, Ga. bar, 1973. Asso. firm Ferris, Hughes, Dorrance & Groben, Utica, N.Y., 1955-56; mem. firm Teeter, Harpending, Fox & Swartwood, Elmira, N.Y., 1956-59, Cole & O'Hanlon, Elmira, 1959-60; individual practice law, Corning, N.Y., 1970-71; partner Thomason & O'Hanlon, East Point, Ga., 1973—; town atty. Town of Big Flats, N.Y., 1958-71; urban renewal atty. City of Corning, 1970-71. Atty., Big Flats Fire Dept., 1960-71, Golden Glow Fire Dept., 1962-71; sec., Treas. Big Flats Burial Assn., 1956-71. Mem. Ga. Bar Assn. Home: 3401 Prince George St East Point GA 30344 Office: 2896 East Point St East Point GA 30344 Tel (404) 767-8254

O'HANLON, ROBERT JOSEPH, b. St. Louis, Mar. 4, 1928; J.D., St. Louis U., 1952, M.B.A., 1958; M.A. in Sociology, Crime and Delinquency, Mo. U., 1975. Admitted to Mo. bar, 1952, U.S. Supreme Ct. bar, 1956; asst. pub. defender City of St. Louis, 1954-55; asso. firm Morris A. Shenker, St. Louis, 1956-57; partner firm O'Hanlon & Daly, St. Louis, 1958-68; partner firm Lee & O'Hanlon, St. Louis, 1973—; commr. juvenile ct. St. Louis County, 1968-72. Office: 506 Olive St Saint Louis MO 63101 Tel (314) 621-2333

OHARA, JAMES FRANCIS, b. Little Rock, Sept. 5, 1948; B.A., U. Ark., Little Rock, 1970; J.D., U. Ark., Fayetteville, 1973. Admitted to Ark. bar, 1973; law clk. Pulaski County Circuit Cts., Little Rock, 1973-74; individual practice law, Little Rock, 1974—. Mem. Am., Pulaski County, Ark. bar assns., Phi Alpha Delta. Office: 1970 Union National Plaza Little Rock AR 72201 Tel (501) 372-1333

OHLMEYER, RALEIGH LAWRENCE, JR., b. Plaquemine, La., Dec. 20, 1947; B.A., La. State U., 1970; J.D., Tulane U., 1973. Admitted to La. bar, 1973; asst. dist. atty. New Orleans, 1973—, chief homicide and rape, 1976—, legal adviser to grand jury, 1976, chief armed robbery, 1975. Mem. La., Am. bar assns., La. Trial Lawyers Assn. Home: 2519 Napoleon Ave New Orleans LA 70115 Office: 2700 Tulane Ave New Orleans LA 70119 Tel (504) 822-2414

OHLRICH, ROGER CARL, b. Cleve., Sept. 15, 1938; B.B.A., U. Mich., 1961, J.D., 1964; LL.M. in Taxation, George Washington U., 1968. Admitted to D.C. bar, 1965, U.S. Supreme Ct. bar, 1968; tax law specialist IRS, Washington, 1964-67; atty., advisor U.S. Tax Ct., Washington, 1967-69; atty. Morris, Pearce, Gardner & Beitel, Washington, 1969-76; asso. firm Mays, Valentine, Davenport & Moore, Washington, 1977—; adj. prof. law Southeastern U., Potomac Law Sch. Pres. Green Acres-Glen Cove, Md. Citizens Assn., 1971; pres. Potomac Valley League of Montgomery County, Md., 1973; pres. The Little Falls Swimming Club, Inc., 1973, bd. dirs., 1971-74; bd. trustees St. Columbia's Nursery Sch., 1975—. Mem. Am. Bar Assn. (mem. taxation sec.), D.C. Bar (taxation and estates, trusts and probate divs.), Bar Assn. D.C. (mem., past chmn. taxation com.), Am. Arbitration Assn. Home: 5321 Allandale Rd Washington DC 20016 Office: 301 Barr Bldg 910 17th St NW Washington DC 20006 Tel (202) 296-4222

OHMAN, JOHN MICHAEL, b. Anaconda, Mont., Dec. 22, 1948; B.S. in Bus. Adminstrn., Creighton U., 1971, J.D., 1972. Admitted to Nebr. bar, 1973, Idaho bar, 1973; mem. firm Denman, Reeves & Ohman, Idaho Falls, Idaho, 1973—. Pres., Am. Cancer Soc., Bonneville County. Mem. Am. Bar Assn., ICC Practioners, Smithsonian Instn., Civitan Internat., Phi Alpha Delta, Omicron Delta Epsilon. Home: 190 Fieldstream Ave Idaho Falls ID 83401 Office: 690 Cambridge Dr Idaho Falls ID 83401 Tel (208) 522-2513

OHNSTAD, MARK GRANT, b. Fargo, N.D., Sept. 5, 1947; B.A. summa cum laude, Concordia Coll., 1969; J.D. cum laude, Harvard U., 1972. Admitted to Minn. bar, 1972; asso. firm Oppenheimer, Wolff, Foster, Shepard & Donnelly, St. Paul, Minn., 1972-75, Mpls., Minn., 1976—. Mem. Am., Minn., Hennepin County bar assns. Home: 1416 Cherry Hill Rd Mendota Heights MN 55118 Office: 4008 IDS Tower Minneapolis MN 55432 Tel (612) 332-6451

OJEDA, RICHARD F., b. San Antonio, Apr. 24, 1943; B.A., St. Mary's U., San Antonio, 1966, J.D., 1969. Admitted to Tex. bar, 1969; asso. firm Dilley, Ojeda, Lopez and Guzman, San Antonio, 1973—. Mem. Tex. Bar Assn., Tex. Trial Lawyers Assn., Tex. Criminal Def. Lawyers, Assn. Immigration and Naturalization Lawyers. Home: 5302 Gary Cooper St San Antonio TX 78240 Office: 1822 Tower Life Bldg San Antonio TX 78205 Tel (512) 224-7557

OKA, KENNETH, b. N.Y.C., July 31, 1916; student City Coll. N.Y., 1937; J.D., Harvard, 1940. Admitted to Fla. bar, 1940; individual practice law, Miami Beach, Fla.; justice of peace, judge small claims ct., Dade County (Fla.), 1945-57. Mayor, councilman City of Miami Beach, 1957-65. Mem. Fla., Miami Beach, Dade County bar assns. Home: 2801 Fairgreen Dr Miami Beach FL 33140 Office: 407 Lincoln Rd Miami Beach FL 33139 Tel (305) 532-6437

OKAMOTO, LILY MIYAMOTO, b. Honolulu, Dec. 1, 1932; B.B.A., U. Hawaii, 1954; LL.B., U. Mich., 1956. Admitted to Hawaii bar, 1957; law clerk Supreme Ct. of Territory of Hawaii, 1957; tax accountant Peat, Marwick, Mitchell & Co., Honolulu, 1958-60; asst. researcher Legis. Reference Bur., 1960; atty. Hawaii Ho. of Reps., 1961, 62; dep. corp. counsel City and County of Honolulu, 1962; dep. comptroller State of Hawaii, 1963-68; dep. dir. Hawaii Dept. Regulatory Agencies, 1968-70; auditor Honolulu City Council, 1970—; trustee State Employees Retirement System, 1968—; dir. First Fed. Savs. and Loan Assn. Mem. Hawaii Bar Assn., Am. Inst. C.P.A.'s, C.P.A., Hawaii. Home: 1931 Ventura St Honolulu HI 96822 Office: City Hall Honolulu HI 96813 Tel (808) 523-4785

O'KEEFE, MICHAEL PHILLIP, b. Kansas City, Mo., Feb. 20, 1947; B.A., Conception Coll., 1969; J.D. (Victor Wilson scholar), U. Mo., 1972, LL.M., 1973. Admitted to Mo. bar, 1972, U.S. Tax Ct. bar, 1976, U.S. Supreme Ct. bar, 1976; law intern Legal Aid and Defenders Soc., Kansas City, Mo., 1971; asso. firm Rosenwald & Jacob, Kansas City, 1971-76; asso. firm Hentzen, Haitbrink & Moore, Kansas City, 1976-77, partner, 1977; of counsel firm Brown and Fox, Kansas City, 1977—. Mem. Mo., Kansas City, Am. bar assns., Delta Theta Phi. Home: 7916 Gillette St Lenexa KS 66215 Office: 3100 Broadway Kansas City MO 64111 Tel (816) 753-1211

O'KEEFE, W. PATRICK, JR., b. Fox Home, Minn.; A.A., Santa Ana Coll., 1960; B.A., Calif. State U., Fullerton, 1962; J.D., U. So. Calif., 1967. Admitted to Calif. bar, 1968; loan supr. Crocker Nat. Bank, Los Angeles, 1962-67; individual practice law, Santa Ana, Calif., 1968—; founder, dir. Am. State Bank, 1963—; lectr. Continuing Edn. of Bar, 1976. Mem. Calif. Bar Assn. (corps. com. 1972—). Home: 2101 N Olive St Santa Ana CA 92706 Office: 888 N Main St Suite 1005 Santa Ana CA 92701 Tel (714) 558-1775

O'KELLEY, MADISON WILLIS, JR., b. Sandersville, Ga., May 13, 1942; B.S., U. Ala., 1964, LL.B., 1967. Admitted to Ala. bar, 1967; partner firm Pritchard, McCall & Jones, Birmingham. Mem. Birmingham, Am. bar assns., Ala. State Bar, Assn. Trial Lawyers Am. Home: 802-F Nob Hill Dr Birmingham AL 35209 Office: 831 Frank Nelson Bldg Birmingham AL 35203 Tel (205) 328-9190

O'KELLEY, NATHANIEL BOAZ, JR., b. Atlanta, Sept. 26, 1906; B.S., Stetson U., Deland, Fla., 1928, LL.B., 1932. Admitted to Fla. bar, 1932; investigator Fla. Real Estate Commn., 1935-51; municipal judge Town of Orange Park (Fla.), 1952-56, atty., 1952-56. Mem. Fla., Clay County bar assns. Home: 1448 Orange Circle S Orange Park FL 32073 Tel (904) 264-9667

OKIN, LOUIS, b. Oshipowitz, Russia, Aug. 25, 1912; came to U.S., 1912, naturalized, 1917; B.S., N.Y. U. Coll. Pure Arts and Scis., 1932; J.D., N.Y. U., 1936. Admitted to N.Y. State bar, 1936; mem. firms Sohn & Okin, 1949-60, Fisher, Okin, Gleiberman & Ezune, 1961-64, Eiber, Okin, Rafsky & Fellman, 1964-69, Okin & Rafsky, 1969-73; mem. N.Y.C. Council, 1957-61; mem. N.Y.C. Tax Commn., 1961-66; Judge Civil Ct. City N.Y., 1974—. Mem. N.Y. County Lawyers Bar Assn. Home: 75 Central Park W New York City NY 10023 Office: 111 Center St New York City NY 10017 Tel (212) 374-8010

OKINAGA, LAWRENCE SHOJI, b. Honolulu, July 20, 1941; B.A., U. Hawaii, 1963; J.D., Georgetown U., 1972. Admitted to Hawaii bar, 1972; adminstrv. asst. to mem. U.S. Ho. of Reps., Honolulu and Washington, 1964-69; asso. firm Carlsmith, Carlsmith, Wichman & Case, Honolulu, 1972, 73-76, partner, 1976—; law clk. to judge U.S. Dist. Ct., Honolulu, 1972-73. Vice pres. Moiliili Community Center, Honolulu, 1967-69, 74-76; sec. Bicentennial Hawaii Corp., 1974—; mem. citizens adv. com. Coastal Zone Mgmt., 1975—. Mem. Am., Hawaii bar assns., Am. Soc. Internat. Law, Omicron Delta Kappa. Editor-in-chief Law and Policy in Internat. Bus., 1971-72. Home: 3367 Huelani Dr Honolulu HI 96822 Office: PO Box 656 Honolulu HI 96809 Tel (808) 524-5112

OLD, THOMAS LEIGH, b. Youngstown, Ohio, Aug. 24, 1946; B.A., Mt. Union Coll., 1964; J.D., U. Cin., 1973. Admitted to Ohio bar, 1973; asso. firm Frank R. Bodor, Warren, Ohio, 1973-76; individual practice law, Warren, 1976—. Mem. Ohio State, Am., Trumbull County (Ohio) bar assns., Am. Trial Lawyers Assn. Office: 155 W Market St Warren OH 44481 Tel (216) 399-3555

O'LEARY, DANIEL VINCENT, JR., b. Bklyn., May 26, 1942; A.B. cum laude, Georgetown U., 1963; LL.B., Yale, 1966. Admitted to Ill. bar, 1967; asso. firm Wilson & McIlvaine, Chgo., 1966-74, partner, 1975—. Mem. Am., Ill. bar assns., Yale Club Chgo. Author: (with George Hale) The Public Utility Status of Total Energy Facilities, 1968, and ann. supplements. Home: 707 Park Dr Kenilworth IL 60043 Office: 135 S LaSalle St Chicago IL 60603 Tel (312) 263-1212

O'LEARY, TERRENCE V., b. St. Louis, Sept. 9, 1948; A.B., St. Louis U., 1970, J.D., 1973. Admitted to Ill. bar, 1973; asso. firm Chapman & Chapman, Granite City, Ill., 1973—. Mem. Am., Ill., Madison County, St. Clair County, Tri-City bar assns., Am., Ill. trial lawyers' assns. Office: 1406 Niedringhaus Ave Granite City IL 62040

OLENDER, JACK H., b. McKeesport, Pa., Sept. 8, 1935; A.B. summa cum laude, U. Pitts., 1957, J.D., 1960; LL.M., George Washington U., 1961. Admitted to D.C. bar, 1961, U.S. Supreme Ct. bar, 1965, Md. bar, 1966; individual practice law, Washington, 1961—. Mem. Fed., Md., D.C. (chmn. personal injury law div. 1974—) bar assns., Am. (asso. editor Torts 1965—, state committeeman for D.C. 1970-73, bd. govs. 1973-76, chmn. found. and grants com. 1975-76), Md. (gov. 1973-76) trial lawyers assns., Am. Judicature Soc., D.C. Jud. Conf., Inner Circle Advs., Assn. Plaintiffs' Trial Attys. (pres. 1969-70), World Peace Through Law Center, Am. Bd. Profl. Utility Attys., Pitts. Inst. Legal Medicine, Phi Beta Kappa. Contbr. articles to profl. jours. Office: 1725 K St NW Suite 803 Washington DC 20036 Tel (202) 296-8984

OLESON, HARVEY JAMES, b. Lemmon, S.D., May 24, 1934; B.S., S.D. State Coll., 1956; J.D., U. Mont., 1963. Admitted to Mont. bar, 1963; legal asst. Mont. Supreme Ct., 1963-64; individual practice law, Kalispell, Mont., 1965—; atty. Flathead County, Mont., 1966-73; U.S. magistrate Missoula div. Mont. dist., 1973, 75—. Mem. Mont., N.W. Mont. (past pres.) bar assns., Am., Mont. trial lawyers assns., Lawyers-Pilots Bar Assn., Nat. Dist. Attys. Assn. (past dir.), Mont. County Attys. Assn. (past pres.). Home: 1035 2d Ave E Kalispell MT 59901 Office: PO Box 1057 Kalispell MT 59901 Tel (406) 755-5063

OLINER, JACOB, b. Poland, June 20, 1913; J.D., Prague U. (Czechoslovakia), 1937; student London (Eng.) Sch. Economics, 1949-51; LL.B., N.Y. U., 1952. Admitted to N.Y. bar, 1952; lectr. law N.Y. U., 1951-58; individual practice law, N.Y.C., 1953—. Mem. N.Y. State Bar Assn., Fgn. Law Assn., Comml. Law League. Contbr. reviews, articles in field to law jours. Home: 57 Estherwood Ave Dobbs Ferry NY 10522 Office: 60 E 42d St New York City NY 10017 Tel (212) 867-7720

OLINGER, RONALD DEAN, b. Mitchell, S.D., Mar. 7, 1945; B.S., U. S.D., 1967, J.D., 1970. Admitted to S.D. bar, 1970; exec. sec. S.D. Constl. Revision Commn., 1970-72; partner firm Duncan Olinger & Srstka, Pierre, S.D., 1972—. Chmn. S.D. Racing Commn. Mem. S.D. Bar Assn. (com. on labor law), S.D. Trial Lawyers Assn., Delta Theta Phi. Home: 1120 E Broadway Pierre SD 57501 Office: 117 E Capitol St Pierre SD 57501 Tel (605) 224-8852

OLIPHANT, LAURENCE ELMER, JR., b. Indpls., Jan. 24, 1910; B.A., Northwestern U., 1931, J.D., 1934. Admitted to Ill. bar, 1934, U.S. Supreme Ct. bar, 1940, Ohio bar, 1953; gen. atty. Montgomery Ward & Co., Chgo., 1931-53; partner firm Squire, Sanders & Dempsey, Cleve., 1953—. Mem. Am., Ohio, Cuyahoga County bar assns., Bar Assn. Greater Cleve. (trustee), Def. Research Inst. (past chmn.), Internat. Assn. Ins. Counsel. Home: 2236 Harcourt Dr Cleveland OH 44106 Office: 1800 Union Commerce Bldg Cleveland OH 44115 Tel (216) 696-9200

OLIVE, BEN EUGENE, b. Weeping Water, Nebr., Nov. 3, 1935; B.A., U. Mich., 1957, LL.B., 1961. Admitted to Ohio bar, 1961; asso. firm Cowden, Pfarrer, Crew & Becker, Dayton, Ohio, 1961-66; asst. gen. counsel NCR Corp., Dayton, 1966—. Home: 7550 Normandy Lane Dayton OH 45459 Office: NCR Corp Dayton OH 45479 Tel (513) 449-2210

OLIVE, HUBERT ETHRIDGE, JR., b. Lexington, N.C., Jan. 1, 1929; B.S. in Bus. Adminstrn., U. N.C., 1951, LL.B., 1953. Admitted to N.C. bar, 1953; practiced in Lexington, 1957-70; judge 22d N.C. Dist. Ct., 1970—. Bd. dirs. Lexington Umaharic Council Boy Scouts Am. Mem. N.C. Bar Assn., N.C. Dist. Judges Assn. Home: 708 Hilltop Dr Lexington NC 27292 Office: Courthouse Lexington NC 27292 Tel (704) 246-5728

OLIVER, JOHN, III, b. Mount Holly, N.J., Sept. 8, 1927; B.A., St. Lawrence U., 1950; J.D., Cornell U., 1953. Admitted to N.Y. bar, 1953; individual practice law, Canton, N.Y., 1953—. Mem. Am., N.Y., St. Lawrence County (pres. 1976—) bar assns. Home: 23 Farmer St Canton NY 13617 Office: 30 Court St Canton NY 13617 Tel (315) 386-4595

OLIVER, JOHN LEACHMAN, b. Cape Girardeau, Mo., Nov. 26, 1916; B.A., U. Mo., 1938; LL.B., U. Va., 1941. Admitted to Mo. bar, 1941, U.S. Supreme Ct. bar, 1950; partner firm Oliver, Oliver & Jones, Cape Girardeau, 1941—; gen. counsel Mo. Utilities Co., Cape Merc. Bank & Trust Co.; pres. Mo. Bar Research, Inc., 1976—. Pres., SE Mo. council Boy Scouts Am., 1964-65, SE Mo. Hosp. Assn., 1965-67. Fellow Am. Bar Found., Am. Coll. Trial Lawyers; mem. Am. (ho. of dels. 1972-76), Mo. (pres. 1970-71), Cape Girardeau County (pres. 1956-57), Met. St. Louis bar assns. Home: 850 Alta Vista Dr Cape Girardeau MO 63701 Office: 400 Broadway Cape Girardeau MO 63701 Tel (314) 335-8278

OLIVER, JOHN PERCY, II, b. Dadeville, Ala., Dec. 3, 1942; student Am. U., 1962; A.B., Birmingham (Ala.) So. Coll., 1964; J.D., U. Ala., 1967. Admitted to Ala. bar, 1967; partner firm Oliver & Sims, and predecessors, Dadeville, 1967—; judge Ct. Common Pleas Tallapoosa County (Ala.), 1973-76. Mem. finance council Democratic party Ala., 1975—. Bd. dirs. East Tallapoosa Hosp., 1967-73; dir. Dadeville Indsl. Devel. Bd., Inc., 1968—. Mem. Am., Ala. (dir.) trial lawyers assn., Soc. Hosp. Attys. (charter), Am. Judicature Soc., Tallapoosa (sec.-treas. 1974—), Ala., Am. bar assns., Dadeville Area C. of C. (dir.), Alpha Tau Omega, Phi Alpha Delta. Home: Route 2 Summit Dr Dadeville AL 36853 Office: 109 Columbus St Dadeville AL 36853 Tel (205) 825-9296

OLIVER, JOSEPH MCDONALD, JR., b. Savannah, Ga., July 26, 1946; B.A., U. Va., 1967; J.D., U. Ga., 1970. Admitted to Ga. bar, 1970, D.C. bar, 1971, U.S. Supreme Ct. bar, 1976; asso. firm Jones, Day, Reavis & Pogue, Washington, 1971—; law clk. U.S. Ct. Claims, 1970-71. Mem. Am., Ga., D.C. bar assns. Home: 6425 31st St NW Washington DC 20015 Office: 1100 Connecticut Ave NW Washington DC 20036 Tel (202) 452-5960

OLIVER, LEWIS BENTON, JR., b. Peekskill, N.Y., Feb. 9, 1940; A.B., Harvard U., 1962; J.D., N.Y. U., 1966. Admitted to N.Y. State bar, 1967; atty. Legal Aid Soc., N.Y.C., 1967-71, 1972-76; pres. Assn. Legal Aid Attys., N.Y.C., 1971-72; atty. Prisoners Legal Services, N.Y.C., 1976—. Mem. N.Y. State Bar Assn., Assn. of Legal Aid Attys. (mem. bargaining com. 1968-75). Home: 35 Church St Nassau NY 12123 Office: 84 Holland Ave Albany NY Tel (518) 465-1545

OLIVER, MARY WILHEMINA, b. Cumberland, Md., May 4, 1919; A.B., Western Md. Coll., 1940; B.L.S., Drexel U., 1943; J.D., U. N.C., 1951. Admitted to N.C. bar, 1951; asst. circulation librarian N.J. Coll. for Women, 1943-45; asst. in law library U. Va., 1945-47; asst. librarian reference and social sci. Drake U., 1947-49; research asst. Inst. Govt., U. N.C., 1951-52, asst. law librarian, 1952-55, asst. prof. law, law librarian, 1955-59, asso. prof. law, law librarian, 1959-69, prof. law and library sci., law librarian, 1969—; cons. in field. Mem. Am. Assn. Law Libraries (pres. 1972-73, exec. bd. 1973-74), Spl. Libraries Assn., Am., N.C. bar assns., Assn. Am. Law Schs., Am. Soc. Legal History, Internat. Assn. Law Libraries, Seldon Soc., Order of Coif. Home: PO Box 733 Chapel Hill NC 27514 Office: Law Library U NC Van Hecke-Wettach Bldg 64A Chapel Hill NC 27514 Tel (919) 933-1321

OLIVER, SAMUEL WILLIAM, JR., b. Birmingham, Ala., Apr. 18, 1935; B.S., Univ. Ala., 1959; J.D., 1962. Admitted to Ala. bar, 1962; asso. firm Thomas, Taliaferro, Forman, Burr & Murray, Birmingham, 1964-66, partner, 1966—, dir. Expediter Systems, Inc., Birmingham, 1973-75, Metalplate Galvanizing, Inc., Birmingham, 1974—, Am. Design, Inc., Birmingham, 1971—; partner Med. Info. Series Co., Birmingham, 1975—. Counsel, mem. advisory bd. Jr. League, Birmingham; dir. Campfire Girls, Inc., Birmingham, 1970-72; mem. Jaycee Found., 1965-67. Mem. Am., Ala., Birmingham bar assns. Mem. Phi Alpha Delta. Home: 2913 Overton Rd Birmingham AL 35223 Office: Sixteenth Floor Bank for Savings Building Birmingham AL 35203

OLIVER, WILLIAM SETH, b. Panola, Ala., Sept. 23, 1919; B.S. in Commerce, Bus. Adminstrn., U. Ala., 1941, LL.B., 1948. Admitted to Ala. bar, 1948, Tenn. bar, 1948, N.Y. bar, 1956; individual practice law, Memphis, 1948-49; atty. Am. Petroleum Inst., N.Y.C., 1949-67; individual practice law, Panola, Ala., 1967—. Mem. Ala. State, 17th Circuit bar assns. Home and Office: PO Box 37 Panola AL 35477 Tel (205) 455-2212

OLLIFF, R(UFUS) HUDSON, b. Daytona, Fla., Aug. 24, 1926; LL.B., U. Fla., 1952, J.D., 1952. Admitted to Fla. bar, 1952, U.S. Supreme Ct. bar, 1964; practiced in Jacksonville, Fla., 1952—; chief asst. pros. atty. Duval County (Fla.) Solicitors Office, Jacksonville, 1957-63; chief asst. state atty. 4th Jud. Circuit, 1964-65; judge felony div. Duval County Criminal Ct. of Record and Circuit Ct., 1971—. Mem. Fla., Jacksonville, Am. bar assns., Am. Trial Lawyers Assn. Recipient certificate of merit Gov. Fla., 1965, Achievement award Former Pros. Attys. Duval County, 1965. Home: Jacksonville FL Office: 2d floor Duval County Courthouse Jacksonville FL 32202 Tel (904) 633-6770

OLLINGER, W. JAMES, b. Kittanning, Pa., Apr. 5, 1943; B.A., Capital U., 1966; J.D., Case-Western Res. U., 1968. Admitted to Ohio bar, 1968; partner firm Baker-Hostetler & Patterson, Cleve., 1968—; dir. Parts Assocs., Inc., Capri Advt., Inc.; lectr. Practising Law Inst. Mem. Am., Ohio bar assns., Bar Assn. Greater Cleve., Order of Coif, (lectr.); Nat. Health Lawyers Assn. Tax Inst., Internat. Found. Employee Benefit Plans, Ohio Legal Center Inst., Iowa State Tax Inst., C.L.U.'s Inst. Home: 25955 Shaker Blvd Beachwood OH 44122 Office: 1956 Union Commerce Bldg Cleveland OH 44115 Tel (216) 621-0200

OLMSTEAD, GEORGE EDWARD, b. National City, Calif., June 15, 1941; B.S. with distinction, San Diego State Coll., 1963; LL.B., Stanford, 1966. Admitted to Calif. bar, 1966, U.S. Tax Ct. bar, 1972; asso. firm Glenn & Wright, San Diego, 1966-70; partner firm Glenn, Wright, Jacobs & Schell, San Diego, 1971—. Trustee, mem. exec. com. Sr. Adult Services, Inc., San Diego, 1970-76; bd. mgmt. Fredericka Manor Retirement Facility, Chula Vista, Calif., 1970—. Mem. Am., San Diego County (chmn. probate sect. 1976) bar assns., State Bar Calif., Estate Planning Council of San Diego. Home: 8676 Cliffridge Ave La Jolla CA 92037 Office: 1434 5th Ave San Diego CA 92101 Tel (714) 234-3571

OLPIN, OWEN, b. Idaho Falls, Idaho, July 10, 1934; B.S., Brigham Young U., 1955; J.D., Columbia, 1958. Admitted to Calif. bar, 1959, Utah bar, 1971; asso. firm O'Melveny & Myers, Los Angeles, 1958-66, partner, 1966-69, 76—; vis. Rex G. Baker and Edna Heflin Baker prof. law U. Tex., 1969-70; prof. U. Utah, 1970-76, Farr Presidential Endowed Chair in environ. law, 1973-76. Pub. mem. Adminstrv. Conf. U.S., 1972—; bd. dirs. Natural Resources Def. Council, N.Y.C., Washington and Palo Alto, Calif., Center for Law in Pub. Interest, Los Angeles. Mem. Am. Bar Assn. Contbr. articles to profl. jours. Office: 611 W Sixth St Los Angeles CA 90017 Tel (213) 620-1120

OLSEN, ARNOLD, b. Butte, Mont., Dec. 17, 1916; LL.B., U. Mont., 1940, J.D., 1950. Admitted to Mont. bar, 1940, Supreme Ct. U.S. bar, 1952; atty. gen. state of Mont., 1949-57; mem. 87th to 91st Congresses; dist. judge 2d Jud. Dist. Mont., 1975—; individual practice law, Butte and Helena, Mont., 1957-61, 71-75. Mem. Am. Judicature Soc., Fed., Mont. bar assns., Phi Delta Phi. Home: Country Club Manor Apt 108 Butte MT 59701 Office: Silver Bow County Courthouse Butte MT 59701 Tel (406) 792-3442

OLSEN, CARL RANDOLPH, b. Memphis, Sept. 1, 1942; A.B., LL.B., J.D., U. Tenn. Admitted to Tenn. bar, 1967; asso. firm Rosenfield, Borod, Bogaten, Kremer, Memphis, 1967—. Pres. Friends of Memphis/Shelby County Libraries, 1974; bd. trustees Memphis/Shelby County Libraries. Mem. U. Tenn. Alumni Assn. (nat. bd. govs.). Home: 4823 Mimosa Rd Memphis TN 38128 Office: Suite 1105 67 Madison Ave Union Planters Bank Bldg Memphis TN 38128 Tel (901) 525-6361

OLSEN, CLIFFORD EUGENE, b. Morgan City, La., Dec. 6, 1944; B.S., U. Southwestern La., Lafayette, 1966; J.D., Loyola U., New Orleans, 1970. Staff accountant Voorhies, Davis & Clostio, Lafayette, 1964-66; lectr., lab. teaching asst. U. Southwestern La., 1964-66; staff accountant Peat, Marwick & Mitchell, New Orleans, 1966; tax accountant Ernst & Ernst, New Orleans, 1966-67; admitted to La. bar, 1971; tax atty. Shell Oil Co., New Orleans and Los Angeles, 1967-72; gen. counsel, sec.-treas. Euro-Pirates Internat., Inc. (Europe and S.Am.), Euro-Pirates, Ltda. (Brazil and Panama), Slater Farms, French Quarter Inn, Inc., Charles Slater Enterprises, New Orleans, 1972-74; tax and ins. mgr., counsel Diamondhead Corp., New Orleans, 1974-76; mem. firm Gegenheimer & Bienvenu, Gretna, La., 1974-77; pres. Landura Corp. La. Mem. Am., Fed., La. bar assns. Office: 2150 Westbank Expwy Oil Center Suite 324 Harvey LA 70058 Tel (504) 368-0646

OLSEN, DENNIS M., b. Blackfoot, Idaho, June 16, 1930; student Idaho State U., 1949-50; B.S with high honors, Brigham U., 1957; J.D. with honors, George Washington U., 1960. Admitted to Idaho bar, 1960; mem. legal dept. J.R. Simplot, Boise, 1960-62; mem. firm Petersen, Moss & Olsen, Idaho Falls, 1962—; mem. Idaho Commn. on Fed. Land Laws, 1969-70. Chmn. Bonneville County Young Republicans, 1962-64; chmn. Dist. 7 Idaho Young Republican League, 1964-65; precinct committeeman Bonneville County (Idaho) Rep., 1962-67; chmn. Republican Legis. Dist., 1967-72; chmn. Bonneville County Republican Central Com., 1972—; chmn. Repubican Region 7, 1974—; mem. State Rep. Exec. Com., 1974—; mem. State Rep. Exec. Com., 1974—. Mem. Idaho Trial Lawyers Assn., Assn. of Trial Lawyers of Am., Idaho Falls Lions Club (dir. Devel. Workshop), Order Coif, Phi Kappa Phi, Pi Sigma Alpha. Asso. editor: George Washington U. Law Review, 1959-60. Home: 1367 Homer St Idaho Falls ID 83401 Office: 485 E St Idaho Falls ID 83401 Tel (208) 523-4650

OLSEN, HAROLD FREMONT, b. Davenport, Wash., Oct. 17, 1920; A.B., Wash. State U., 1942, LL.B., Harvard, 1948. Admitted to Wash. bar, 1948; mem. firm Perkins, Coie, Stone, Olsen & Williams and predecessor, Seattle, 1948—. Bd. trustees mem. Seattle Golf Club; moderator Univ. Congregational Ch. Mem. Am., Wash., Seattle bar assns., Soc. Internat. Law, Am. Judicature Soc., Nat. Contract Mgmt. Assn., Aircraft Industries Assn. (chmn. legal com. 1955). Home: 8875 Overlake Dr W Bellevue WA 98004 Office: 1900 Washington Bldg Seattle WA 98101 Tel (206) 682-8770

OLSON, ALLEN I., b. Rolla, N.D., Nov. 5, 1938; LL.B., U. N.D., 1963. Served with U.S. Army Judge Adv. Gen.'s Corps, in U.S., W.Ger., 1963-67; counsel N.D. Legis. Council, 1967, asst. dir., 1968; practiced law in Bismarck, N.D., 1969-72; now atty. gen. State of N.D. Bd. dirs. Dakota Zool Soc. Mem. Nat. Assn. Attys. Gen. Office: Atty Gen's Office State Capitol Bismarck ND 58501*

OLSON, BARNEY, II, b. Chgo., Feb. 9, 1944; B.S., Miami U., Oxford, Ohio, 1966; J.D., U. Ill., 1969. Admitted to Ill. bar, 1970, U.S. Dist. Ct. bar for No. Dist. Ill., 1970; trust officer, trust dept. Continental Bank, Chgo., 1969-70; partner firm Lucas, Brown & McDonald, Galesburg, Ill., 1970-75; individual practice law, Galesburg, 1975—. Pres. Galesburg Jr. Football League, 1971—. Mem. Ill., Am., Knox County (Ill.) (v.p. 1976-77) bar assns., Am. Judicature Soc., Galesburg Jaycees. Home: 182 Brentwood Circle Oak Run Dahinda IL 61428 Office: Suite 208 Weinberg Arcade PO Box 92 Galesburg IL 61401 Tel (309) 343-8171

OLSON, CARL ERIC, b. Center Moriches, N.Y., May 19, 1914; A.B., Union Coll., 1936; J.D., Yale, 1940. Admitted to Conn. bar, 1941, N.Y. State bar, 1947; asso. firm Clark, Hall & Peck, New Haven, Conn., 1940-41; asso. firm Reid & Priest, N.Y.C., 1946-55, partner, 1956—. Bd. govs. Manhasset (N.Y.) Flower Hill Civic Assn., 1959—. Mem. Am., N.Y. State, Inter-Am., Internat. bar assns., Bar Assn. City of N.Y., Am. Soc. Internat. Law, Phi Beta Kappa. Office: 40 Wall St New York City NY 10005 Tel (212) 344-2233

OLSON, DONALD EDWARD, b. Duluth, Minn., May 24, 1922; B.S., U. Calif. at Los Angeles, 1949; LL.B., U. So. Calif., 1953. Admitted to Calif. bar, 1953; individual practice law, Culver City, Calif., 1953-60; city atty. Culver City, 1960-68, Inglewood (Calif.), 1968—. Chmn. noise regulation com. League of Calif. Model Cities, 1971-73; dist. chmn. Am. Cancer Soc., 1967, county bd. dirs., 1967. Mem. Los Angeles County, Culver City (past pres.) bar assns. Office: 1 Manchester Blvd Inglewood CA 90302 Tel (213) 649-7372

OLSON, GEORGE ALBERT, b. San Antonio, Dec. 31, 1936; B.A., U. Tex., 1958, LL.B., 1963. Admitted to Tex. bar, 1963; asso. firm Marion A. Olson (then Olson & Olson), San Antonio, 1963-65, partner, 1965-74; partner, vice chmn. bd. firm Beckmann, Stanard & Olson, 1974—; dir. Nat. Bank Ft. Sam Houston, Ft. Sam Houston BankShares, Inc., San Antonio. Hon. counsel El Patronato De La Cultura Hispano-Am., San Antonio, Humane Soc. San Antonio. Mem. Am., San Antonio (chmn. legal ethics com. 1968, vice chmn. accounting and banking liason com. 1972, chmn. entertainment com. 1964), San Antonio Jr. (pres. 1965, chmn. liason com. 1966) bar assns., Am. Judicature Soc., Tex. Assn. Bank Counsel. Office: 1200 Frost Bank Tower San Antonio TX 78205 Tel (512) 224-1871

OLSON, JOHN OLMSTEAD, b. Whitewater, Wis., July 24, 1936; B.B.A., U. Wis., 1961, LL.B., 1963. Admitted to Wis. bar, 1963; asso. firm Nikolay, Jensen & Scott, Medford, Wis., 1963-64; dist. atty. Taylor County, Wis., 1964-69; U.S. Atty. Western Dist. Wis., 1969-74; partner firm Braden & Olson, Lake Geneva, Wis., 1974—; city atty. City of Medford, 1965-69; lectr. U. Wis. Law Sch. Mem. Wis., Walworth County bar assns., Wis. Acad. Trial Lawyers Assn. Home: Route 5 Box 6 Lake Geneva WI 53147 Office: PO Box 512 Lake Geneva WI 53147 Tel (414) 248-6636

OLSON, LEONARD ALLEN, b. Youngstown, Ohio, Dec. 10, 1927; B.A., Youngstown U., 1949, LL.B., 1953. Comml. mgr. Ohio Bell Telephone Co., Youngstown, 1948-53; admitted to Ohio bar, 1953, U.S. Supreme Ct. bar, 1960; partner firm Newman, Olson & Kerr, Youngstown, 1953—; dir. Peoples Bank of Youngstown, McCartney & Sampsell, Inc., Excel Auto Glass Co., Winkle Electric Co. Chmn. Mahoning County (Ohio) for Senator Taft, 1962, 64, 70, co-chmn., 1976; bd. dirs. Goodwill Industries, Salvation Army, Youngstown. Mem. Mahoning County (trustee 1963-65), Ohio State, Am. bar assns. Home: 591 Plymouth Dr Youngstown OH 44512 Office: 1010 Union Nat Bank Bldg Youngstown OH 44503 Tel (216) 747-4404

OLSON, RALPH ELDO, b. Wenatchee, Wash., May 23, 1936; B.A., U. Wash., 1958, J.D., 1962. Admitted to Wash. bar, 1962; asst. atty. gen. State of Wash., 1962-63; mem. firm Olson & Pietig, and predecessors, Centralia, Wash., 1973—. Pres. Centralia Rotary Club, 1970-71, Centralia C. of C. 1971-72, mem. bd. Lewis County Community Concerts 1971—, chmn. Lewis County Seattle Symphony Assn. 1971-74. Mem. Wash., Am., Lewis County bar assns., Am. Adjudicature Soc., Centralia Rotary. Recipient Lewis County Distinguished Service award 1969. Home: 3316 Cooks Hill Rd Centralia WA 98531 Office: 112 W Magnolia St Centralia WA 98531 Tel (206) 736-7663

OLSON, RICHARD LEE, b. Edgerton, Wis., Feb. 12, 1931; B.S., U. Wis., 1952, LL.B., 1958; postgrad. U. Stockholm, Sweden, 1954-55. Admitted to Ohio bar, 1959, Wis. bar, 1959; asso. firm Jones, Day, Cockley & Reavis, Cleve., 1958-59; asso. firm Boardman, Suhr, Curry & Field and predecessors, Madison, Wis., 1959-61, partner, 1962—; lectr. in taxation U. Wis. Law Sch., 1962-64, lectr. Grad. Sch. Banking, 1968-71. Moderator 1st Congregational Ch., Madison, 1975-76; treas. S. Central Library System, Madison, 1975—; past pres. Dane County Easter Seal Soc. and Vol. Action Center. Mem. Am., Dane County bar assns., State Bar Wis., Am. Judicature Soc. Home: 3810 Council Crest Madison WI 53711 Office: Suite 700 131 W Wilson St Madison WI 53703 Tel (608) 257-9521

OLSON, ROBERT ARTHUR, b. Mpls., Dec. 17, 1945; student Trinity Coll., 1963-65; B.A. in Psychology, Bethel Coll., 1967; postgrad. Bethel Sem., 1967-69, St. Thomas Coll., 1969-70; J.D., U. Minn., 1973. Admitted to Minn. bar, 1973; asso. firm Bowman and Bruns, Ltd., St. Paul, 1973-76, Strommen and Assos., St. Paul, 1976—. Mem. Ramsey County, Minn., Am. bar assns. Home: 1920 Colfax St S Minneapolis MN 55403 Office: 2469 University Ave St Paul MN 55114 Tel (612) 874-0994

OLSON, THOMAS ANDREW, b. Glendive, Mont., May 30, 1938; B.S., Mont. State Coll., 1960; LL.B., U. Mont., 1963. Admitted to Mont. bar, 1963, U.S. Ct. of Appeals bar, 1977; asso. firm Landoe & Gary, Bozeman, 1967-70; county atty., Gallatin County, 1970-75; U.S. atty. Dist. Mont., Billings, 1976—; prosecutor USMC, 1963-66. Mem. Mont. Bar Assn. Home: 2031 Pryor Ln Billings MT 59103 Office: Fed Bldg Billings MT 59101 Tel (406) 657-6101

OLSON, THOMAS WILLIAM, b. Emmetsburg, Iowa, Jan. 31, 1947; A.B., Stanford U., 1968; J.D. summa cum laude, U. N.Mex., 1973. Admitted to N.Mex. bar, 1973; law clk. to Judge Oliver Seth, U.S. Ct. Appeals, 10th Circuit, Santa Fe, N.Mex., 1973-74; asso. firm Montgomery, Andrews & Hannahs, Santa Fe, 1974—; lectr. wills and trusts, U. N.Mex. at Albuquerque, 1974. Mem. N.Mex. Bar Assn., Am. Judicature Soc., Order of Coif. Editor N.Mex. Law Rev., 1972-73. Office: PO Box 2307 Santa Fe NM 87501 Tel (505) 982-3873

OLSON, WAYNE WALTER, b. Oak Park, Ill., Nov. 27, 1930; B.G.E., Morton Coll.; LL.B., DePaul U., 1953. Admitted to Ill. bar, 1953; asso. firm Damon, Hayes, White & Hoban, Chgo., 1953-56; partner firm Roger Q. White, Chgo., 1956-60; city judge, N. Riverside, Ill., 1957-64; individual practice law, Riverside, Ill., 1960-62; judge Cook County (Ill.) Circuit Ct., 1964—. Mem. Am. Bar Assn. Tel (312) 542-2900

OLSZEWSKI, PETER PAUL, b. Wilkes-Barre, Pa., May 12, 1925; A.B., Lafayette Coll., 1948; J.D., St. John's U., 1952; postgrad U. Nev., 1968, 71. Admitted to Pa. bar, 1952; counsel Parking Authority City Wilkes-Barre, Redevel. Authority; solicitor City Wilkes-Barre, 1954-62, Luzerne County, Pa., 1964-66; law clk. Judge Lewis, Ct. Common Pleas, Luzerne County, 1954; individual practice law, Wilkes-Barre, 1952-68; judge Luzerne County Ct. Common Pleas, 1968—; instr. Kings Coll., Wilkes-Barre. Vice pres. Polish Union U.S. N.Am., Wilkes-Barre, 1968; exec. bd. Penn Mountains council Boy Scouts Am., Wilkes-Barre; pres. council Kings Coll., Wilkes-Barre; chmn. bd. Catholic Youth Center, Wilkes-Barre. Mem. Wilkes-Barre Law and Library Assn., Am., Pa. bar assns., Nat., Pa. confs. state trial judges, St. John's Univ. Law Sch. Alumni (dir.). Home: 50 Old River Rd Wilkes Barre PA 18702 Office: Luzerne County Courthouse N River St Wilkes-Barre PA 18711 Tel (717) 823-6161

OLTMAN, JOHN HAROLD, b. Grand Rapids, Mich., Nov. 18, 1929; B.S. in Chem. Engring., U. Mich., 1952, J.D., 1957. Admitted to Ill. bar, 1957, Ariz. bar, 1964, Mich. bar, 1965, Fla. bar, 1968; asso. firm Mueller & Aichelle, Chgo. and Phoenix, 1957-64; asso. firm Barnes, Kisselle, Raisch & Choate, Detroit, 1964-65; partner firm Settle, Batchelder & Oltman, Detroit, 1965-67; partner firm Settle & Oltman, Detroit and Ft. Lauderdale, Fla., 1967-72; partner firm Oltman and Flynn, Ft. Lauderdale, 1972—. Mem. Am., Fla., Broward County bar assns., Am. Patent Law Assn., Am. Judicature Soc., IEEE, Fla. Engring Soc., Kiwanis (dir. Ft. Lauderdale Club 1972-74; chmn. Key Club 1970—), Phi Eta Sigma, Tau Beta Pi. Home: 2130 NE 55th St Fort Lauderdale FL 33308 Office: 915 Middle River Dr Suite 415 Fort Lauderdale FL 33304 Tel (305) 563-4814

O'MALLEY, BERNARD JOHN, b. Des Moines, Sept. 20, 1937; B.A., Creighton U., 1959, J.D., 1961. Admitted to Iowa bar, 1961; partner firm Connolly, O'Malley, Lillis & Hansen, Des Moines, 1961—; mem. Iowa Legislature, 1965-69. Fellow Am. Acad. Probate Council. Home: 2908 Ashwood Dr Des Moines IA 50322 Office: 820 Liberty Bldg Des Moines IA 50309 Tel (515) 243-8157

O'MALLEY, CORMAC KEVIN HOOKER, b. Dublin, Ireland, July 20, 1942; B.A., Harvard, 1965; J.D., Columbia, 1970. Admitted to N.Y. State bar, 1971; asso. firm Curtis, Mallet-Prevost, Colt & Mosle, N.Y.C., 1970—. Mem. Am. Bar Assn. (past chmn. African law com. sect. internat. law), Internat. Law Assn., Assn. Bar City N.Y. (arbitration com.), Am. Soc. Internat. Law (nominating com.), Am. Fgn. Law Assn. (dir.), Council Fgn. Relations. Editor: Proc. Conf. on Internat. and Interstate Regulation of Water Pollution, 1970; co-editor Current Legal Aspects of Doing Business in Black Africa, 1975. Home: 125 E 84th St New York City NY 10028 Office: 100 Wall St New York City NY 10005 Tel (212) 248-8111

O'MALLEY, JAMES, JR., b. N.Y.C., Aug. 13, 1910; A.B., Princeton U., 1932; LL.B., Harvard U., 1935. Admitted to N.Y. State bar, 1936, U.S. Supreme Ct. bar, 1970; asso. firm Root, Clark, Buckner and Ballantinee, N.Y.C., 1935-37; dep. asst. dist. atty. N.Y. County, 1938-41; served to lt. comdr. JAGC, USNR, 1941-45, in charge Navy War Crimes Office, 1945; asso. firm LeBoeuf, Lamb, Leiby & MacRae, N.Y.C., 1945-46, partner, 1947-65, sr. partner 1965—; spl. asst. to U.S. Atty. for SSS hearings, 1953-55; counsel Gov. N.Y. Adv. Com. Atomic Energy, 1956-58; dir. AGIP-USA, Inc., Pignone, Inc., Snam Progetti USA, Inc., 1968-72. Mem. N.Y. Waterfront Commn. N.Y. Harbor, 1959-61; mem. Greater N.Y. council Boy Scouts Am., 1956—. Mem. Fed. Power (pres. 1957-58), N.Y. State (chmn. atomic energy law com. 1956-63), Am. (chmn. gas and electric law com. 1955-56) bar assns., N.Y. Law Inst. (v.p. 1976—), Assn. Bar City N.Y. (exec. com. 1953-56, vice chmn. grievance com. 1964-67), Dewey Assos. (sec.-gen. 1977—), ICC Practitioners Assn., Phi Beta Kappa. Home: 131 E 69th St New York City NY 10021 Office: 140 Broadway New York City NY 10005 Tel (212) 269-1100

O'MALLEY, JESSE ROBERT, b. Brown City, Mich., Apr. 27, 1913; A.B., U. Mich., 1939, J.D., 1941. Admitted to Mich. bar, 1941, U.S. Supreme Ct. bar, 1944, Ariz. bar, 1947, Calif. bar, 1948; trial atty. anti-trust and criminal divs., Dept. Justice, 1941-49; asso. firm Cosgrove, Cramer, Diether & Rindge, Los Angeles, 1949-52; partner firm Musick, Peeler & Garrett, Los Angeles, 1952—. Trustee Jr. Statemen Found. Fellow Am. Coll. Trial Lawyers; mem. Am., Los Angeles bar assns., Am. Judicature Soc., Am. Arbitration Assn. (nat. panel), Los Angeles C. of C. Home: 2816 Sunset Hill Dr West Covina CA 91791 Office: 1 Wilshire Blvd Los Angeles CA 90017 Tel (213) 629-3322

O'MALLEY, MICHAEL EDWARD, b. Toccoa, Ga., Dec. 23, 1942; B.A., Georgetown U., 1965; J.D., Case Western Res. U., 1968. Admitted to Ohio bar, 1968; law clk. Cleve. Legal Aid Soc., 1967-68; spl. agt. FBI, N.Y.C., 1968-71; asst. county prosecutor Cuyahoga County (Ohio), Cleve., 1971-74, Putnam County (Ohio), Ottawa, 1974—; asso. firm Unverferth & Unverferth, Ottawa, Ohio, 1974—. Trustee, Putnam County Law Library, Ottawa, 1976—. Mem. Ohio (workmen's compensation com.), N.W. Ohio, Putnam County (v.p. 1977) bar assns., Nat. Dist. Attys. Assn., Soc. Former FBI Agts. Home: 157 N Walnut St Ottawa OH 45875 Office: 234 E Main St Ottawa OH 45875 Tel (419) 523-5998

O'MALLEY, ROBERT F., JR., b. South Bend, Ind., Oct. 27, 1948; B.A., U. Notre Dame, 1970; J.D., U. Fla., 1972. Admitted to Fla. bar, 1973; asso. firm Smathers & Thompson, Miami, Fla., 1973—. Mem. Dade County, Am., Fla. bar assns. Home: 16125 SW 107th Ave Miami FL 33157 Office: 1301 Alfred I DuPont Bldg Miami FL 33131 Tel (305) 379-6523

OMAN, LAFEL EARL, b. Price, Utah, May 7, 1912; J.D., U. Utah, 1936. Admitted to Utah bar, 1936, N.Mex. bar, 1947; practiced in Utah, 1937-40, in Las Cruces, N.Mex., 1947-66; judge N.Mex. Ct. Appeals, 1966-70, sr. judge, 1967-70; justice N.Mex. Supreme Ct., 1971—, chief justice, 1976—; asst. city atty. City of Las Cruces, 1958-59; city atty. Truth or Consequences, N.Mex., 1959-61; mem. N.Mex. Bd. Bar Examiners, 1964-66, N.Mex. Jud. Standards Commn., 1968-70, 71-72, N.Mex. Jud. Council, 1972-76. Mem. Am., N.Mex., Utah, Dona Ana County (pres. 1952-53), 1st Jud. Dist. bar assns., Def. Research Inst., Am. Trial Lawyers Assn., Inst. Jud. Adminstrn., Appellate Judges Conf., Nat. Legal Aid, Defender Assn., Am. Judicature Soc. (dir. 1970-74), Continuing Legal Edn. New Mex. (dir.), Conf. Chief Justices, Am. Law Inst. Recipient Herbert Harley award Am. Judicature Soc., 1974; Outstanding Service award N.Mex. State Bar, 1974, Distinguished Jud. Service award, 1974; certificate of recognition N.Mex. Jud. Conf., 1976. Home: 510 Camino Pinones Santa Fe NM 87501 Office: PO Box 848 Don Gaspar Santa Fe NM 87501 Tel (505) 827-2615

OMAN, RALPH WILEY, b. Garnett, Kans., June 5, 1897; LL.B., J.D., Washburn Coll., 1921. Admitted to Kans. bar, 1921; since practiced in Topeka, Kans.; partner firm Cosgrove, Webb & Oman, and predecessors, 1921-75, of counsel, 1975—; asst. atty. gen. Kans., 1922-23; asst. atty. Shawnee County, Kans., 1925-29; city atty. Topeka, Kans., 1937-39; mem. Kans. Supreme Ct. Nominating Com., 1962-69. Fellow Am. Coll. Trial Lawyers; mem. Am., Kans., Topeka (pres. 1947-48) bar assns. Home: 4406 Holly Ln Topeka KS 66604 Office: 1100 1st Nat Bank Tower Topeka KS 66603 Tel (913) 235-9511

OMAN, RICHARD HEER, b. Columbus, Ohio, Jan. 4, 1926; B.A., Ohio State U., 1948, LL.B., J.D., 1951. Admitted to Ohio bar, 1951; mem. legal dept. Ohio Nat. Bank, Columbus, 1951-55; partner firm Isaac Postlwaite, O'Brien & Oman, Columbus, 1955-71, Porter, Wright, Morris & Arthur and predecessor, Columbus, 1971—. Sec., exec. dir. Columbus Found., 1955—. Mem. Am., Ohio, Columbus bar assns. Home: 195 S Parkview Ave Columbus OH 43209 Office: 37 W Broad St Columbus OH 43215 Tel (614) 228-1511

O'MEARA, JOSEPH, b. Cin., Nov. 8, 1898; A.B., Xavier U., 1921; LL.B., U. Cin., 1943; LL.D., U. Notre Dame, 1969. Admitted to Ohio bar, 1921, Ind. bar, 1968; chief counsel Western & So. Life Ins. Co., Cin., 1926-40; mem. firm Merland, O'Meara, Santen & Willging, Cin., 1924-53, Dargush, Caren, Greek & King, Columbus, Ohio, 1946-53; dean, prof. law U. Notre Dame, 1952-68; mem. adv. com. appellate rules Jud. Conf. U.S.; mem. Lawyers' Com. Civil Rights under Law, Ind. Commn. Civil Rights; bd. dirs. Ind. Continuing Legal Edn. Forum. Mem. Am. Law Inst., Am., Ind. bar assns., Am. Judicature Soc. Contbr. articles to legal jours. Home: 1222 S 25th St South Bend IN 46615 Office: 108 Law Bldg Notre Dame IN 46556

O'MELVENY, GERALD RICHARD, b. Pendleton, Oreg., Sept. 1, 1913; A.B., Pomona Coll., 1935; postgrad. Harvard U., 1936-37; LL.B., U. Va., 1940, J.D., 1970. Admitted to Va. bar, 1939, Wash. bar, 1947, U.S. Supreme Ct. bar, 1973; sr. partner firms O'Melveny and Justice, Charlottesville, Va., 1939-41, O'Melveny and Cullen, Spokane, Wash., 1947-65; prof. law Gonzaga U., 1946-53; individual practice law, Spokane, 1965—; chmn. bd. Marco Corp.; dir. Western Industries, Inc., Stillwell Heating Inc., Continental Mortgage Corp., Bear Creek Yards Inc., Columbia Cabinets Corp., Nat. chmn. def. U.S. C. of C., 1967; mem. Community Action Council Bd., Spokane, 1966-69. Mem. Am., Spokane County, Wash. State (co-founder sect. family law 1949, com. chmn. 1958-59), Fed. bar assns., Judge Advs. Assn., Am. Judicature Soc., Calif. Scholarship Fedn. (hon. life), Sigma Nu Phi, Delta Sigma Rho. Decorated Bronze Star, Purple Heart; recipient Nat. award of Merit Holy Name Soc., 1960-62, Medallion Circle award Nat. Council Cath. Men, 1963; named Papal Knight of Honor, 1962. Home: S 1203 McClellan St Spokane WA 99203 Office: 1006 Paulsen Bldg Spokane WA 99201 Tel (509) 624-5308

O'MELVENY, JOHN, b. Los Angeles, Dec. 1, 1894; B.A., U. Calif., Berkeley, 1918; J.D., Harvard, 1922. Admitted to Calif. bar, 1922; asso. firm O'Melveny, Millikin, Tuller, & Macneil, Los Angeles, 1922, partner, 1923-39; sr. partner firm O'Melveny & Myers, Los Angeles, 1939-75, of counsel, 1975—. Past trustee Huntington Library and Art Gallery, San Marino, Calif.; trustee Calif. Inst. Tech., 1940-68, hon. life trustee, 1968—; adv. bd. Salvation Army, Los Angeles; bd. dirs. Barlow Hosp. Guild, Los Angeles. Mem. Calif., Los Angeles County, Century City, Am. bar assns., Nat. Legal Aid and Defenders Assn., Am. Judicature Soc., Phi Beta Kappa, Psi Upsilon. Office: 611 W 6th St Los Angeles CA 90017 Tel (213) 620-1120

OMORI, MORIO, b. Maui, Hawaii, Oct. 15, 1921; B.E., U. Hawaii, 1942, postgrad., 1943; LL.B., U. Colo., 1954. Admitted to Hawaii bar, 1954, U.S. Supreme Ct. bar, 1959; law clk. Supreme Ct. Hawaii, Honolulu, 1954-55; dep. atty. gen. Hawaii, 1955-56; individual practice law, Honolulu, 1956—; chmn. bd. Pacific Savs. and Loan Assn., Hawaii, 1970—; exec. asst. Sen. Hawaii, 1962-76. Mem. Am., Hawaii bar assns. Home: 1031 Waiiki St Honolulu HI 96821 Office: 850 Richard St Suite 602 Honolulu HI 96813 Tel (808) 533-4238

O'NEAL, FOREST HODGE, b. Rayville, La., Sept. 17, 1917; A.B., La. State U., 1938; J.D., 1940; J.S.D., Yale, 1949; S.J.D., Harvard, 1954. Admitted to La. bar, 1940, Ga. bar, 1955; asso. firm Sullivan & Cromwell, N.Y.C., 1941; asso. prof. law U. Miss., Oxford, 1945-46, prof., 1946-47; dean Mercer U. Sch. Law, Macon, Ga., 1947-56; prof. law Vanderbilt U., Nashville, 1956-59; prof. law Duke, 1959-66, dean Sch. Law, 1966-68, prof. law, 1968-76, James B. Duke prof. law, 1971-76; Alexander Madill prof. law Washington U., St. Louis, 1976—. Mem. Am., N.C. bar assns., Assn. Am. Law Schs. (exec. com. 1969-70). Author: Close Corporations: Law and Practice, 2d edit., 1971; Squeeze-Outs of Minority Shareholders: Expulsion or Oppression of Business Associates, 1975; (with Kurt F. Pantzer) The Drafting of Corporate Charters and By-Laws, 1951; (with Jordan Derwin) Expulsion or Oppression of Business Associates; Squeeze-Outs in Small Enterprises, 1961; Control Arrangements and Restrictions on Transfer of Stock, 1973; mem. bd. editors Am. Bar Assn. Jour., 1971—; editor Corporate Practice Commentator, 1959—. Home: 69 Lake Forest St Louis MO 63117 Office: Washington Sch Law St Louis MO 63130 Tel (314) 863-0100

O'NEIL, JOSEPH F., b. Boston, Jan. 29, 1929; B.S., Coll. of Holy Cross, 1950; J.D., Boston Coll., 1953. Admitted to Mass. bar, 1956, U.S. Supreme Ct. bar, 1962; Instr. immigration and nationality law Boston Coll. Law Sch., 1972—. Mem. Am. (immigration and nationality com.), Mass. (chmn. immigration and naturalization law com. 1975—) bar assns., Assn. Immigration and Nationality Lawyers (gov. 1976—, chmn. Mass.-R.I. chpt. 1974-76). Home: 104 Colwell Dr Dedham MA 02026 Office: 116 Lincoln St Boston MA 02111 Tel (617) 426-8100

O'NEIL, WILLIAM CAMPBELL, b. McKeesport, Pa., May 31, 1909; A.B., Princeton, 1932; LL.B., Harvard, 1935. Admitted to Pa. bar, 1936; asso. firm Thorp, Reed & Armstrong, Pitts., 1936-47, partner, 1947—; dir. Pitts. and Ohio Ry. Com. Trustee Shadyside Hosp., Pitts. Mem. Am., Pa., Allegheny County (Pa.) bar assns. Office: 2900 Grant Bldg Pittsburgh PA 15219 Tel (412) 288-7763

O'NEILL, C. WILLIAM, b. Marietta, Ohio, Feb. 14, 1916; A.B., Marietta Coll., 1938, L.H.D., 1953; J.D., Ohio State U., 1942; LL.D., Defiance Coll., 1953, Ohio U., 1957, W. Va. U., 1957, Miami U., Oxford Ohio, 1957, Steubenville (Ohio) Coll., 1957, Wilberforce U., 1958, Bowling Green U., 1958, Heidelberg Coll., 1958, Capital U., 1971, Bethany Coll., 1971, Dickinson Coll. Law, 1975; D.C.L., Ohio Wesleyan U., 1973; D.Pub. Service, Ohio No. U., 1973. Admitted to Ohio bar, 1942, U.S. Supreme Ct. bar; mem. firm O'Neill & O'Neill, Marietta, 1942-51; instr. polit. sci. Marietta Coll., 1949-50; prof. pub. affairs Bethany (W. Va.) Coll., 1959-60; practice in Columbus, Ohio, 1959-60; judge Supreme Ct. Ohio, 1960-70, chief justice, 1970—; prof. law Capital U. Sch. Law, 1971—; mem. Ohio Ho. of Reps. from Washington County, 1939-50; speaker of house, 1947-48, minority leader, 1949-50; atty. gen. Ohio, 1951-57; gov. Ohio, 1957-58; v.p. Nat. Center State Cts., 1977—; chmn. Nat. Conf. State Justices 1977—; Mem. Am., Ohio (Ohio Bar medal 1971), Washington County, Columbus bar assns., Am. Judicature Soc. (Herbert Hawley award 1975), Am. Legion, VFW, Soc. Benchers, Garfield Soc., Order of Coif, Phi Beta Kappa, Delta Upsilon. Named one of ten outstanding young men U.S., Jr. C. of C. U.S., 1950, Most Outstanding State Appellate Ct. Judge in U.S., Assn. Trial Lawyers Am., 1975; recipient Centennial Achievement award Ohio State U., 1970, Ohio Gov.'s award, 1972, Columbus award Columbus Area C. of C., 1974, Outstanding Jurist award Ohio Acad. Trail Lawyers, 1974, Nat. Criminal Justice award Am. Soc. for Pub. Adminstrn., 1975, Christopher Columbus award Columbus-Day U.S.A. Assn., 1975. Home: 1560 London Dr Columbus OH 43221 Office: State House Columbus OH 43215*

O'NEILL, J(AMES) WARD, b. N.Y.C., Aug. 20, 1903; A.B., Fordham U., 1924, LL.B., 1929. Admitted to N.Y. bar, 1930, U.S. Supreme Ct. bar, 1953, also other fed. cts.; law clk. Baldwin, Hutchins & Todd, N.Y.C., 1928-29; asso. firm Haight, Gardner, Poor & Havens, N.Y.C., 1930-47, partner, 1947—; lectr. N.Y. U. Practising Law Inst. Chmn., Citizens Com. for Erection High Sch., Carle Place, N.Y., 1946. Fellow Am. Coll. Trial Lawyers; mem. Am., Internat., Fed., N.Y. State bar assns., Maritime Law Assn. Recipient Law Achievement award Fordham U., 1974. Home: 304 Shore Rd Douglaston NY 11363 Office: One State St Plaza New York City NY 10009 Tel (212) 344-6800

O'NEILL, NORRIS LAWRENCE, b. Newark, May 26, 1926; student Brown U., 1946-48; LL.B., Rutgers U., 1951. Admitted to Conn. bar, 1952, N.J. bar, 1952; asso. firm Ribicoff & Kotkin, Hartford, Conn., 1952-55; individual practice law, Hartford, 1955-58; partner firm O'Neill & Steinberg, Hartford, 1958-61, firm O'Neill,

Steinberg & Lapuk, 1961-69, firm Kleinman, O'Neill, Steinberg & Lapuk, Hartford, 1969—; mem. Conn. Ho. of Reps., 1967-71; sec., dir. The Motorlease Corp., 1960—; dir. Stan Chem, Inc., 1969—. Pres. Urban League of Greater Hartford, 1963-66; bd. dirs. Greater Hartford Community Council, 1964—, pres. 1974-76; bd. dirs. United Way, Hartford, 1974-76. Mem. Am., Conn., Hartford County bar assns., Conn. Trial Lawyers Assn., Am. Arbitration Assn. Home: 17 High Farms Rd West Hartford CT 06107 Office: 99 Pratt St Hartford CT 06103 Tel (203) 547-0100

OPPEN, JAMES J., b. Berlin, Apr. 11, 1920; LL.B. cum laude, Southwestern U., 1957; came to U.S., 1923, naturalized, 1943. Admitted to Calif. bar, 1959, U.S. Supreme Ct. bar, 1968; individual practice law, Van Nuys, Calif., 1959-68, Santa Barbara, Calif., 1968—. Home: 530 Dalton Way Goleta CA 93017 Office: 10 Marine Center Bldg Santa Barbara CA 93109 Tel (805) 963-3301

OPPENBORN, HENRY LUDWIG, JR., b. Miami, Fla., Sept. 19, 1924; A.B., U. Fla., 1956; J.D., U. Miami, Coral Gables, Fla., 1960. Admitted to Fla. bar, 1960; asso. firms McDonald & McDonald, Miami, Fla., 1960-62, Lally, Miller & Hodges, Miami, 1962-67, Coughlin & Oppenborn, North Miami, Fla., 1967-72; trial counsel Metropolitan Dade County (Fla.) Transit Authority, 1972-73; county judge 11th Jud. Circuit of Fla. for Dade County, 1973—. Mem. Dade County Bar Assn. Home: 630 NE 55th St Miami FL 33137 Office: 1351 NW 12th St Miami FL 33125 Tel (305) 547-7894

OPPENHEIM, SAUL CHESTERFIELD, b. N.Y.C., Jan. 16, 1897; A.B., Columbia, 1918, A.M., 1920; J.D., U. Mich., 1926, S.J.D., 1929; LL.D., George Washington U., 1973. Admitted to Mich. bar, 1926, D.C. bar, 1935, U.S. Supreme Ct. bar, 1935; prof. law George Washington U., Washington, 1927-52, distinguished scholar and adviser Nat. Law Center, 1973—; prof. law U. Mich., 1952-65, prof. emeritus, 1965—; of counsel firm Howrey & Simon, Washington, 1966—; chmn. adv. council U.S. Mktg. Law Survey, 1938-40; co-chmn. U.S. Atty. Gen.'s Nat. Com. to Study Antitrust Laws, 1953-55. Mem. Am. (chmn. sect. antitrust law 1961-62), Fed. bar assns., AAUP (emeritus), Nat. Lawyers Club Washington (founder). Recipient Jefferson medal award N.J. Patent Law Assn., 1951, Charles F. Kettering award Patent, Trademark and Copyright Inst., George Washington U., 1957; author Cases on Trade Regulation, 1936; (with Glen E. Weston) Antitrust Law-Cases and Comments, 1970, Lawyers Robinson-Patman Act Sourcebook, 1971, Unfair Trade Practices-Cases and Comments, 1974. Home: 2440 Virginia Ave NW Washington DC 20037 Office: 1730 Pennsylvania Ave Washington DC 20006 Tel (202) 783-0800

OPPENHEIM, STEPHEN LOW, b. N.Y.C., Mar. 1, 1933; B.A. with distinction, Cornell U., 1954, LL.B. with distinction, 1956. Admitted to N.Y. State bar, 1956, Fla. bar, 1958; partner firm Oppenheim and Oppenheim, Monticello, N.Y., 1956-65, firm Oppenheim & Drew, Monticello, 1965-77, firm Oppenheim, Drew & Kane, Monticello, 1977—; v.p., dir. Legal Aid Soc. Sullivan County, 1974—. Bd. dirs. Community Gen. Hosp., Monticello, 1975—. Mem. Am., N.Y. State bar assns., N.Y., Am. trial lawyers assns., N.Y. State Assn. Library Bds. (pres. 1975-77), Am. Library Trustees Assn. (council adminstr. 1975-77), Order of Coif, Phi Beta Kappa, Phi Alpha Delta, Phi Kappa Phi. Office: PO Box 29 Monticello NY 12701 Tel (914) 794-7110

OPPENHEIMER, FRANZ MARTIN, b. Mainz, Ger., Sept. 7, 1919; B.S., U Chgo., 1942; student Universite de Granoble, France, 1938-39; LL.B. cum laude (editor Law Jour. 1945), Yale U., 1945. Research asst. com. human devel. U. Chgo., 1942-43; admitted to N.Y. bar, 1946, D.C. bar, 1955; law clk. Judge U.S. Circuit Ct. Appeals, N.Y.C., 1945-46; asso. firm Chadbourne, Wallace, Parke & Whiteside, N.Y.C., 1946-47; atty. Internat. Bank Reconstrn. and Devel., Washington, D.C., 1947-57; individual practice law, 1958—; partner firm Leva, Hawes, Symington, Martin & Oppenheimer, 1959—. Bd. dirs. Georgetown Citizens Assn., Internat. Student House; founding mem. Co. Christian Jews; trustee Inst. Empirical Econ. Research, Berlin, W. Ger., Com. 100 on Fed. City, Washington, Chatham (Va.) Hall. Mem. Am. Psychol. Assn., Am., Fed. bar assns., Am. Soc. Internat. Law (treas.), Council Fgn. Relations. Contbr. articles to legal jours. Home: 3248 O St NW Washington DC 20007 Office: 815 Connecticut Ave NW Washington DC 20006 Tel (202) 298-8020

OPPERMAN, VANCE KEITH, b. Des Moines, Jan. 8, 1943; J.D., U. Minn., 1969. Admitted to Minn. bar, 1970, ICC bar, 1975; partner firm Dohery, Rumble & Butler, St. Paul, 1969—. Mem. Minn. central com. Democratic Farm Labor Party, 1966—, mem. exec. com., 1968-70, chmn. Hennepin County (Minn.), 1968-70, del. to state convs., 1966-68, 70, 72, 74, 76. Mem. Washington County, Minn. State, Am., Fed. bar assns. Home: 421 Stagecoach Tr Afton MN 55001 Office: E-1500 1st Nat Bank Bldg Saint Paul MN 55101 Tel (612) 291-9333

O'QUINN, TRUEMAN EDGAR, b. Vernon Parish, La., May 7, 1905; J.D., U. Tex., 1932. Admitted to Tex. bar, 1932; city atty. City of Austin (Tex.), 1939-42, 46-51; served with Judge Adv. Gen. Corps U.S. Army, 1942-46, ETO, 1943-45; partner firms Hollers, O'Quinn & Crenshaw, Austin, 1952-57, O'Quinn, McDaniel & Randle, Austin, 1958-61; individual practice law, Austin, 1961-66; asso. justice Tex. Ct. Civil Appeals, 3d Supreme Jud. Dist., 1967—; lectr. U. Tex. Law Sch., 1952-53, legal advisor pres. U. Tex., 1965-67; mem. Tex. Ho. of Reps., 1931-33. Chmn. Travis County Democratic Party, 1952-66. Mem. Am., Travis County bar assns., State Bar Tex. Author: Manual for Texas Elections & Conventions of Political Parties, 1964; contbr. articles to legal publs. Home: 2300 Windsor Rd E Austin TX 78703 Office: PO Box 12547 Capitol Sta Supreme Ct Bldg Austin TX 78711 Tel (512) 475-2441

ORDOVER, ABRAHAM PHILIP, b. Far Rockaway, N.Y., Jan. 18, 1937; B.A. magna cum laude, Syracuse U., 1958; J.D., Yale, 1961. Admitted to N.Y. State bar, 1961, U.S. Supreme Ct. bar, 1965; asso. Cahill, Gordon & Reindel, N.Y.C., 1961-71; prof. law Hofstra U., Hempstead, N.Y., 1971—; mem. faculty Inst. Trial Advocacy, Cornell U., Ithaca, 1976—, vis. prof. law, 1977. Pres. Ind. Citizens N.Y., 1966. Mem. Am., N.Y. State bar assns., Am. Judicature Soc., Am. Trial Lawyers Assn., Phi Beta Kappa. Office: Law School Hofstra U Hempstead NY 11550 Tel (516) 560-3642

O'REILLY, JOHN JOSEPH, b. Bklyn., Mar. 28, 1946; B.B.A., Seton Hall U., 1968; J.D., St. John's U., 1973. Admitted to N.J. bar, 1973; jud. clk. Hon. Jacob L. Triarsi, N.J. State Ct., 1973-74; asst. dep. pub. defender Essex region, Office of Pub. Defender, State of N.J., Newark, 1974—. Mem. Am., N.J. bar assns. Office: 151 Washington St Newark NJ 07102 Tel (201) 622-2600

O'REILLY, MEL BRIAN, b. N.Y.C., Aug. 5, 1947; B.A. in Polit. Sci., Coll. of Santa Fe, 1968; J.D., U. N.Mex., 1971. Admitted to N.Mex. bar, 1971; asso. firm McCormick, Paine & Forbes, Carlsbad, N.Mex., 1971-72; asso. firm Leland Stone, Ruidoso, N.Mex., 1972-73; office resident, mgr. firm Shipley, Durrett, Conway & Sandenaw, P.C., Ruidoso, 1973—; bd. counselors Security Bank, Ruidoso. Mem. Am., Lincoln-Otero County bar assns., State Bar N.Mex., Ruidoso C. of C. (dir.). Home: Box 2295 Ruidoso NM 88345 Office: Box 3495 Hollywood Station Ruidoso NM 88345 Tel (505) 257-4678

O'REILLY, TIMOTHY PATRICK, b. San Lorenzo, Calif., Sept. 12, 1945; B.A. in Bus. Adminstrn. with honors, Ohio State U., 1967; J.D., N.Y. U., 1971. Admitted to Commonwealth of Pa. bar, 1971, U.S. Dist. Ct. bar for Eastern Dist. Pa., 1971; asso. firm Morgan, Lewis & Bockius, Phila., 1971—. Treas. com. on solid waste mgmt. East Whiteland Twp., Pa. Mem. Am. (editor com. on developing labor law sect. labor law), Pa., Phila. bar assns. Home: 5 Wood Ln Malvern PA 19355 Office: 2107 123 S Broad St Philadelphia PA 19109 Tel (215) 491-9470

ORENTLICHER, HERMAN ISRAEL, b. Brockton, Mass., Oct. 26, 1910; A.B., Harvard, 1933, J.D., 1936. Admitted to Mass. bar, 1936, D.C. bar, 1953; U.S. Supreme Ct. bar, 1940; individual practice law, Boston, 1936-37; counsel, chief briefs and opinions sect. U.S. Housing Authority, Washington, 1938-43; asst., acting gen. counsel Washington, Nat. Housing Agy., Housing and Home Finance Agy., 1944-48; asso. prof., then prof. Nat Law Center and Law Sch., George Washington U., 1949-60; asso. sec., counsel AAUP, Washington, 1960-69; asso. gen. sec., counsel, 1969-74; prof. law Emory U., 1972—; vis. prof. law Boston Coll., 1967-68; adj. prof. Va. Poly. Inst. and State U. Grad. Sch. Edn., 1972; cons. in field; spl. advisor for legisl. affairs Fed. Home Loan Bank Bd., 1974-75. Mem. Phi Beta Kappa, Phi Delta Phi. Author: Tools of the National Housing Agency, 1944; editor: (with William T. Fryer) Casebook, Legal Method and Legal System, 1968. Home: 3223-I Buford Hwy NE Atlanta GA 30329 Office: Emory U Sch Law Atlanta GA 30322 Tel (401) 329-6821

ORIEL, MAURICE, b. N.Y.C., Apr. 18, 1931; B.A., Pace Coll., 1961; J.D., N.Y. U., 1967. Admitted to N.Y. bar, 1968, also to Fed. bar; since practiced in N.Y.C., asso. Legal aid Soc., 1968-69; asso. firm Dubliner, Haydon & Straci, 1969-72; mem. N.Y. State Atty. Gen., 1972—. Mem. N.Y. County Lawyers Assn. Home: 149-05 79th Ave Flushing NY 11367 Office: 2 World Trade Center New York City NY 10047 Tel (212) 488-7557

ORINTAS, RICHARD JAMES, b. Waterbury, Conn., Mar. 2, 1942; B.S., U. Ark., 1965, J.D., 1969. Admitted to Ark. bar, 1969, U.S. Supreme Ct. bar, 1974; asso. firm Howell, Price, Howell & Barron, Little Rock, 1969-73; sr. partner firm Faubus & Orintas, Little Rock, 1973—. Mem. Ark., Pulaski bar assns., Ark., Am. trial lawyers assns., Ark. Criminal Def. Assn. Home: 2505 Wentwood St Little Rock AR 72212 Office: 810 Plaza West Bldg Little Rock AR 72205 Tel (501) 664-8550

ORKIN, LOUIS H., b. Cleve., Dec. 30, 1930; J.D., Boston U., 1954. Admitted to Ohio bar, 1954; asst. atty. gen. State of Ohio, 1957-59; asst. law dir. and pros. atty. Cleveland Heights (Ohio), 1961-64; law dir. Bedford (Ohio), 1964-73; pros. atty. Shaker Heights (Ohio), 1964—; law dir. City of Beachwood (Ohio), 1973—; acting judge Cleveland Heights Municipal Ct., 1970-73; partner firm Weiner Orkin, Abbate & Suit, Shaker Heights, Ohio, 1974—; adj. prof. municipal law Cleve. State Law Sch., 1974—. Mem. Am., Ohio, Cuyahoga County, Cleve. bar assns. Office: 20600 Chagrin Blvd Shaker Heights OH 44122 Tel (216) 561-0880

ORLINSKY, WALTER SIDNEY, b. Balt., May 19, 1938; student Johns Hopkins U., 1957-61, U. Md. Sch. Law, 1961-64. Admitted to Md. bar, 1975; tchr. state and local govt. U. Balt., 1964-65; tchr. contemporary polit. problems Free Sch., Columbia, Md., 1963-65; chmn. Nat. Conf. Local Legislators, Johns Hopkins U. Center for Met. Planning and Research, 1972-77; head cons. team Am. architects and planners Warsaw Municipal Council to West Warsaw Devel. Center, 1974-75; pres. Balt. City Council, 1971—; cons. City Council, Phoenix, Nat. League Cities; lectr. transp. policy steering com., chmn. community devel. com., mem. practitioners adv. com. U. Md. Inst. for Urban Studies. Mem. Bd. Estimates; chmn. Mayor's Task Force for Legislation in Annapolis; chmn. Balt. Bicentennial Com.; mem. Gov.'s Commn. studying reorganization state and local govt.; mem. adv. com. to state supt. schs.; mem. Gov.'s Task Force which developed legislation that established State Dept. Transp.; del. 2d Dist. Balt. to Md. Ho. of Dels., chmn. met. affairs com.; past pres. Mt. Royal Democratic Club; co-founder New Dem. Club of 2d Dist.; Young Dem. nat. committeeman, 1965; chmn. Balt. Citizens Registration Com. for Dem. Nat. Com., 1964; chmn. Citizens for Robert Kennedy, 1968; coordinator Md. Citizens for Humphrey-Muskie, 1968; state co-chmn. Citizens for Muskie, 1972; head Shriver for Pres. Com. in Md., also Shriver Nat. Polit. Adv. Com.; mem. adv. council of election ofcls. Dem. Nat. Com., 1974—; founder, past chmn. bd. Balt. Tutorial Project, Fifth Dist. Exec. Council award, 1967; bd. dirs. Balt. Mus. Art, Walters Art Gallery, Glenwood Life Center, Am. Jewish Congress, Md. and Nat. Histadrut; past co-chmn. Am. Habonim Assn., Labor Zionists Am. Mem. Acad. Polit. Sci., United Brotherhood Carpenters and Joiners Am. (hon.). Recipient Man of Year award Talmudic Acad. Alumni Assn., 1973; author: The City and the Council: Views from the Inside and Outside, 1974. Office: City Hall 100 N Holiday St Baltimore MD 21202 Tel (301) 396-4804

ORLOFF, RONALD LEONARD, b. N.Y.C., Oct. 2, 1932; B.A., Washington and Jefferson Coll., 1954; LL.B., Yale U., 1957. Admitted to Oreg. bar, 1958, Conn. bar, 1964, N.Y. State bar, 1964, Ohio bar, 1966; teaching fellow, Instr. U. Chgo., 1957-58; atty. firm Davies, Biggs, Strayer, Stoel & Boley, Portland, Oreg., 1958-63; atty. Western Elec. Co., N.Y.C., 1963-65; atty. Ohio Bell Telephone Co., Cleve., 1965-71, gen. atty., 1971—. Mem. Am., Ohio, Cleve., Oreg., Conn., N.Y. State bar assns., ACLU, Am. Judicature Soc. Home: 20676 Almar Dr Shaker Heights OH 44122 Office: Room 1429 100 Erieview Plaza Cleveland OH 44114 Tel (216) 822-7225

ORMOND, MARVIN THOMAS, b. Tuscaloosa, Ala., Jan. 4, 1919; B.A., U. Ala., 1941; LL.B., Yale, 1949. Admitted to Ala. bar, 1949, U.S. Dist. Ct. bar for No. Dist. Ala., 1949, U.S. Ct. Appeals bar, 1965; partner firm Jones, McEachin, Ormond & Fulton, Tuscaloosa, 1953—. Chmn. Salvation Army Advisory Bd. of Tuscaloosa County, 1971-72. Mem. Ala. State Bar (chmn. sect. practice and procedure 1963-65), Tuscaloosa County Bar Assn. (pres. 1965), U. Ala. Alumni Assn. (pres. Tuscaloosa chpt. 1957-58), Phi Delta Phi. Home: 1427 University Blvd Tuscaloosa AL 35401 Office: 403 First Nat Bank Bldg PO Box 2408 Tuscaloosa AL 35401 Tel (205) 349-2500

ORNSTEIN, WARREN K., b. Detroit, Jan. 8, 1928; B.A., Dartmouth, 1949; LL.B., U. Mich., 1952. Admitted to Mich. bar, 1952, Ohio bar, 1952 U.S. Supreme Ct. bar, 1960; asso. firm Guren, Merritt, Soge & Cohen, Cleve., 1954-58, partner, 1958—; dir. Cook United, Inc., 1974—. Co-chmn. lawyers div. Jewish Def. Fund, 1975; chmn. met. div. United Torch, 1960; trustee Big Bros. Cleveland, 1960-64; pres. Cleve. Dist. Golf. Assn., 1972. Mem. Am., Ohio, Cleve. Bar Assn., Phi Delta Phi. Home: 15875 Van Aren Blvd Shaker Heights OH 44122 Office: 650 Terminal Tower Cleveland OH 44113

ORODENKER, NORMAN GILBERT, b. Providence, Aug. 13, 1933; A.B., Brown U., 1955; J.D., Columbia, 1968. Admitted to R.I. bar, 1958; partner firm Levy, Goodman, Semenoff & Gorin, Providence; legal counsel Dept. Employment Security, 1960-62; chief legal counsel R.I. Depts. State Govt., 1969-72; legal counsel Registry of Motor Vehicles, 1972-74, R.I. Dept. Transp., 1974—. Mem. Am., R.I. bar assns., Phi Beta Kappa. Home: 1434 Narragansett Blvd Cranston RI 02905 Office: 40 Westminster St 15th Floor Providence RI 02903 Tel (401) 421-8030

O'RORKE, JAMES FRANCIS, JR., b. N.Y.C., Dec. 4, 1936; A.B., Princeton U., 1958; J.D., Yale, 1961. Admitted to N.Y. State bar, 1962; asso. firm Davies, Hardy & Schenck, N.Y.C., 1962-69; partner firm Davies, Hardy, Ives & Lawther, N.Y.C., 1969-72, firm Skadden, Arps, Slate, Meagher & Flom, N.Y.C., 1972—. Vice chmn. bd. trustees Mus. of the Am. Indian, Heye Found., 1977—. Mem. Am., N.Y. State bar assns., Assn. Bar City N.Y. Office: 919 Third Ave New York City NY 10022

OROSZ, RICHARD THOMAS, b. Painesville, Ohio, Dec. 26, 1942; B.S., Lake Erie Coll., 1967; J.D., Cleve. State U., 1970. Admitted to Ohio bar, 1971; individual practice law, Painesville, 1971—. Mem. corp. Lake County Mental Health Center, 1973—, dir., 1975—; bd. dirs. Lake County Family Counseling Services, 1972-73. Mem. Am., Ohio, Lake County bar assns., Lake County Law Library Assn. (sec.). Home: 261 Wickland St Painesville OH 44077 Office: 56 Liberty St Painesville OH 44077 Tel (216) 352-3324

O'ROURKE, DANIEL, b. Evanston, Ill., Mar. 22, 1947; A.B. in Econs., Coll. Holy Cross, 1969; J.D., Georgetown U., 1972. Admitted to Ill. bar, 1972; asso. firm McDermott, Will & Emery, Cgo., 1972—. Mem. Am., Chgo. bar assns. Home: 425 Birch St Winnetka IL 60093 Office: 111 W Monroe St Chicago IL 60603 Tel (312) 372-2000

O'ROURKE, DENNIS, b. Whiteclay, Nebr., Oct. 31, 1914; A.B. cum laude, Nebr. Tchrs. Coll., 1935; J.D. with distinction, George Washington U., 1939. Admitted to D.C. bar, 1939, U.S. Supreme Ct. bar, 1945, Colo. bar, 1946; auditor GAO, Washington, 1935-39; atty. U.S. Dept. Agr., Washington, 1939-45, chief basic commodity div., 1945; gen. counsel Group Health Assn., Washington, 1943; gen. counsel Holly Sugar Corp., Colorado Springs, Colo., 1945-53, v.p., 1955-63, pres., 1963-67, chmn., 1967-69, also dir.; v.p., gen. counsel Holly Oil Co., Colorado Springs, 1955-63; sr. partner firm Rouss & O'Rourke, Colorado Springs and Washington, 1972—; U.S. counsel Union Nacional de Productores de Azucar, Mexico City, 1970—; pres. Man Exec., Inc.; dir. 1st Nat. Bank Colorado Springs; dir., vice-chmn. exec. com. Colo. Public Expenditure Council; mem. bus. and industry adv. com. OECD, Paris, 1969-71; adviser U.S. dels. Internat. Sugar Confs., Geneva, 1965, Mexico City, 1959. Pres., trustee Colorado Springs Fine Arts Center, 1960-62, 67-71, 73. Mem. Am., Fed., Inter-Am., Colo., El Paso County bar assns., Order of Coif, U.S., Am. of Mexico, Am. chambers commerce, Soc. Sugar Beet Technologists. Contbr. articles to legal jours. Home: 8 Heather Dr Colorado Springs CO 80906 Office: Box 572 Colorado Springs CO 80901 Tel (303) 473-7758 also 1629 K St NW Washington DC 20006 Tel (202) 296-2639

O'ROURKE, LYLE FRANCIS, b. Oelrichs, S.D., Sept. 16, 1905; B.A., St. Mary's U., 1928; LL.B., Creighton U., 1931; LL.M., Georgetown U., 1935. Admitted to Nebr. bar, 1931, D.C. bar, 1935, N.Y. bar, 1951; spl. agt. FBI, 1932-35; partner firm MacCracken & O'Rourke, Washington, 1940-50; individual practice law, Washington, 1950-58, N.Y.C., 1955-63; partner firm DiFalco, Field, Lomenzo & O'Rourke, N.Y.C., 1963-77, firm Fried, Fragomen, Del Rey & O'Rourke, N.Y.C., 1977—. Pres. Jr. C. of C., Washington, 1938-39. Mem. Am. Bar Assn. Contbr. articles to legal jours. Office: 515 Madison Ave New York City NY 10022 Tel (212) 688-8555

O'ROURKE, THOMAS WALTER, b. Chicago Heights, Ill., Feb. 2, 1937; B.S. in Chem. Engring., Purdue U., 1959; LL.B., George Washington U., 1962. Admitted to N.Y. bar, 1963, Colo. bar, 1972; patent atty. Eastman Kodak Co., Washington, 1960-62, Rochester, N.Y., 1962-65; patent atty. Ball Corp., Boulder, Colo., 1965-72; individual practice law, Boulder, 1972-74; partner firm O'Rourke, Harris & Hill, and predecessor, Boulder and Denver, 1974-76, Boulder, Denver and Washington, 1976—; judge Eire (Colo.) Municipal Ct., 1972-74. Mem. Am., Colo., Boulder bar assns., Am. Patent Law Assn. Office: 737 29th St Boulder CO 80303 Tel (303) 444-5205

ORR, ANNE LIDE HOLLADAY, b. Orrville, Ala., Apr. 21, 1942; B.A., Auburn U., 1965; J.D., Emory U., 1973. Admitted to Ga. bar, 1973; dir. spl. projects for judge Ct. Appeals Ga., Atlanta, 1973-74; staff atty. Jud. Council Ga., Atlanta, 1974-76; partner firm Orr & Coley, Atlanta, 1976—; legal adv. Ga. Conf. Traffic Ct. Judges, 1974-76; staff atty. Traffic Ct. Com. State Bar Ga., 1974-76. Active Girl Scouts U.S.A., 1976—. Mem. State Bar Ga., Atlanta Bar Assn., Ga. Assn. Women Lawyers. Author Manual for Traffic Courts, 1976. Home: 664 Cumberland Circle NE Atlanta GA 30306 Office: 2931 N Druid Hills Rd Atlanta GA 30329

ORR, SAMUEL, b. Poland, July 11, 1890; LL.B., N.Y. U., 1912; student Office Supreme Ct. Judge Benjamin N. Cardozo. Admitted to N.Y. State bar, 1915; practiced in N.Y.C., 1916; mem. N.Y. Assembly, 1918-21; mng. atty. firm Graham & Stevenson, N.Y.C., 1915-17; dep. comptroller City of N.Y., 1938-42; magistrate City of N.Y., 1942-52; practice law, N.Y.C., to 1975. Mem. Bronx County (N.Y.) Bar Assn. Home: 3970 Hillman Ave Bronx NY 10463 Tel (212) 543-1187

ORRICK, NORWOOD BENTLEY, b. Cumberland, Md., Oct. 5, 1908; LL.B., U. Va., 1932. Admitted to Md. bar, 1933; partner firm Venable, Baetjer and Howard, Balt., 1939—; asst. atty. gen. Md., 1939-40. Mem. Bd. Library Trustees Balt. County, 1961-73, pres., 1963-67. Fellow Md. Bar Found.; mem. Am. (ho. of dels. 1967-68, 76-77), Md. (pres. 1977—), Balt. (pres. 1966-67) bar assns., Am. Judicature Soc., Order of Coif, Phi Delta Phi. Home: 7601 Club Rd Ruston MD 21204 Office: 1800 Mercantile Bank and Trust Bldg Two Hopkins Plaza Baltimore MD 21201 Tel (301) 752-6780

ORTEGA, LOTARIO DURAN, b. Gallup, N.Mex., Aug. 24, 1922; LL.B., Loyola U., Los Angeles, 1950. Admitted to N.Mex. bar, 1952; field solicitor U.S. Dept. of Interior, Albuquerque, 1959—; asst. dist. atty. McKinley County, Gallup, N.Mex., 1953-56; municipal judge City of Gallup, 1958-59. Home: 8645 Harwood Ave Albuquerque NM 87111 Office: Suite 7102 500 Gold Ave SW Albuquerque NM 87103 Tel (505) 766-2547

ORTEGA, VICTOR R., b. Santa Fe, Jan. 5, 1933; A.B., Harvard, 1954, LL.B., 1959. Admitted to N.Mex. bar, 1959, U.S. Supreme Ct. bar, 1960; asst. dist. atty. 2d Jud. Dist., Albuquerque, 1959-60; partner firm Robinson and Ortega, Albuquerque, 1960-69; U.S. atty. Dist. N.Mex., Albuquerque, 1969—; mem. N.Mex. Constl. Revision Commn., 1968-69; mem. Atty. Gen.'s Adv. Com. of U.S. Attys., 1973—, vice-chmn., 1976-77, chmn., 1977—. Mem. Albuquerque Com. on Fgn. Relations, Am., Fed. bar assns., Harvard Law Sch. Assn., Phi Beta Kappa, Sigma Xi. Home: PO Box 68 Corrales NM 87048 Office: PO Box 607 Albuquerque NM 87103 Tel (505) 766-3341

ORTH, FREDERICK JAMES, b. Terre Haute, Ind., Oct. 4, 1915; B.A., U. Wash., 1937, J.D., 1943. Admitted to Wash. bar, 1946; asso. firm Shank, Belt, Rode & Cook, Seattle, 1946-48; trial counsel Unigard Mut. Ins. Co., Seattle, 1948-50; v.p., asst. gen. counsel, 1959-60, gen. counsel dir., 1961-75, chmn. bd., 1965-75; dir. Gen. Counsel Unigard Security Ins. Co., Seattle, 1961-75, chmn. bd., 1965-75; chmn. bd., gen. counsel Cream City Mut. Ins. Co., Milw., 1965; chmn. bd. Martin Agy., Seattle, 1965-75, Jamestown Mut. Ins. Co. (N.Y.), 1970-74; dir. Unigard Olympic Life Ins. Co., Seattle, 1965-75; practice law, 1975—. Lay adviser Wash. State Hwy. Interim Com., 1959-61; mem. Wash. State adv. com. Sch. Dist. Reorgan., 1964-65; mem. Wash. State Citizens Conf. on State Legislature, 1966; trustee Downtown Seattle Devel. Assn., 1971—, pres., 1972-73; mem. Seattle Community Devel. Roundtable, 1972—, chmn., 1976; trustee Seattle Citizens Council Against Crime, 1972-75, sec., 1976; hon. consul for India for Wash., 1977. Mem. Wash., Seattle-King County, Am. bar assns., Internat. Assn. Ins. Counsel (v.p., mem. exec. com. 1963-65), Am. Coll. Trial Lawyers (state chmn. 1962). Contbr. articles to legal jours. Home: 14030 12th St NE Apt 105D Seattle WA 98125 Office: Suite 500 3d and Lenora Bldg Seattle WA 98121 Tel (206) 624-6831

ORTHUBER, GERHARD WOLFGANG, b. Berlin, Germany, May 24, 1940; B.A., St. Mary's Coll. of Calif., 1962; J.D., U. Calif., Berkeley, 1965, M.A. in Econs., Los Angeles, 1967. Admitted to Calif. bar, 1966, U.S. Supreme Ct. bar, 1973; staff mem. Youth Tng. and Employment Project, Los Angeles, 1966-67; field atty. FTC, Los Angeles, 1966-67; staff atty., exec. dir. Ventura County (Calif.) Legal Service Centers, 1966-70; mem. firm Orthuber and MacArthur, Ventura, 1970—; dir. Ventura Coll. Law, 1964—, mem. faculty, 1969-73. Mem. Ventura River Municipal Advisory Council, Ojai, Calif., 1976—. Mem. State Bar Calif., Ventura County Bar Assn. Recipient Human Rights award Mexican Am. Polit. Assn., 1969; Service award Ventura County Community Action Commn., 1975. Home: 218 N Encinal St Ojai CA 93023 Office: 26 N Fir St Ventura CA 93001 Tel (805) 648-3865

ORTIQUE, REVIUS OLIVER, JR., b. New Orleans, June 14, 1924; A.B., Dillard U., 1947; M.A., Ind. U., 1949; J.D., So. U., 1956; LL.D. (hon.), Campbell Coll., 1960; L.H.D., Ithaca Coll., 1971. Admitted to La. bar, 1956, U.S. Supreme Ct.; practice in New Orleans, 1956—. Lectr. labor law Dillard U., 1950-52; asso. gen. counsel Community Improvement Agy.; gen. counsel 8th Dist. A.M.E. Ch.; dir. United Fed. Savs. & Loan Assn., Sr. v.p. Met. Area Com.; mem. Bd. City Trust, New Orleans, New Orleans Legal Assistance Corp. Bd., Ad Hoc Com. for Devel. of Central Bus. Dist. City of New Orleans, Pres.'s Commn. on Campus Unrest, 1970. Bd. dirs. Community Relations Council, Am. Lung Assn., Antioch Coll. Law; bd. dirs. mem. exec. com. Nat. Sr. Citizens Law Center, Los Angeles, Criminal Justice Coordinating Com.; mem. exec. bd. Nat. Bar Found.; mem. exec. com. Econs. Devel. Council Greater New Orleans; trustee Health Edn. Authority of La.; trustee, mem. exec. com. Dillard U.; bd. mgmt. Flint Goodridge Hosp.; mem. adv. bd. League Women Voters Greater New Orleans; mem. men's adv. bd. YWCA. Recipient Weiss award NCCJ, 1975. Mem. Am. (del.), Nat. (exec. bd.), La. (del.) bar assns., Nat. Legal Aid and Defender Assn. (pres.), Am. Judicature Soc., Louis A. Martinet Legal Soc., World Peace Through Law Com., Blue Key, Phi Delta Kappa, Alpha Kappa Delta. Home: 4516 Annette St New Orleans LA 70122 Office: 2140 St Bernard Ave New Orleans LA 70122*

ORTON, CECIL WILLIAM, b. Maurice Iowa, June 29, 1906; student Morningside Coll., 1925-29; LL.B., LaSalle Extension U. Admitted to Neb. bar, 1937; clk. dist. ct., Dakota County, Nebr., 1935-48; practice law, South Sioux City, Neb., 1948-73; county judge, 8th Judl. Dist., Nebr., 1973—; mem. South Sioux City City Council, 1929-30; county atty. Dakota County (Neb.), 1963-71. First pres. South Sioux City C. of C., 1949; mem. South Sioux City Bd. Edn., 1953-59, atty., 1961-62. Mem. Nebr., 8th Jud. Dist. (pres. 1962), Am. bar assns., Neb. County Judges Assn., Am. Title Assn., Neb. Land Title Assn. (state pres. 1961). Home: 323 E 23d St South Sioux City NE 68776 Office: Courthouse Dakota City NE 68731 Tel (402) 494-3903

ORWIG, GEORGE EDWARD, II, b. Williamsport, Pa., Dec. 6, 1933; A.B., Dickinson Coll., 1954; J.D., Dickinson Sch. Law, 1957. Admitted to Lycoming County (Pa.) bar, 1959, Pa. Supreme Ct. bar, 1967; individual practice law, Williamsport, 1959—; solicitor Register of Wills, Recorder of Deeds and Clk. of the Orphans' Ct. of Lycoming County, Lycoming County twps., Lycoming Sanitary Com., Armstrong Twp. Zoning Hearing Bd.; legal counsel Antique Automobile Club Am., 1977—. Pres. Epilepsy Soc. of Lycoming County, Inc., 1965—; pres. Pa. div. Epilepsy Found. Am., 1974—; chmn. region III, mem. nat. bd. dirs. Epilepsy Found. Am., 1969—; mem. Pa. Developmental Disabilities Council, 1971—. Mem. Lycoming County Law Assn. (treas. 1964-74), Am., Pa. bar assns. Resource contbr. to truck history sect. of Am. Car Since 1775, 1971—. Office: 460 Market St Room 415 Williamsport PA 17701 Tel (717) 326-0657

OSANK, PAUL LEWIS, b. Cleve., Nov. 14, 1939; student Mex. City Coll., 1962; B.A., Ohio State U., 1963; J.D., Cleve. State U., 1967. Admitted to Ohio bar, 1967; partner firm Csank, Csank & Coaxum and predecessor, Cleve., 1967—; sec., gen. counsel Broadview Fin. Corp., the Broadview Savs. and Loan Co.; dir., sec., gen. counsel St. Clair Savs. Assn. Mem. Ohio, Greater Cleve. bar assns. Office: 220 Williamson Bldg Cleveland OH 44114 Tel (216) 523-1136

OSBORN, MAX NORMAN, b. Wilson, Okla., Oct. 21, 1928; B.B.A., Tex. Tech. Coll., 1950; LL.B., So. Meth. U., 1953. Admitted to Tex. bar, 1953. Served with JAGC, USAF, Wilmington, Del., 1953-55; asso. firm Turpin, Kerr, & Smith, Midland, Tex., 1955-58, partner, 1958-73; asso. justice 8th Ct. Civil Appeals, El Paso, Tex., 1973—. Mem. Am., El Paso County bar assns., State Bar Tex., Lions (dir. Midland chpt. 1969-72), Jaycees. Home: 301 Northwind El Paso TX 79912 Office: 500 City-County Bldg El Paso TX 79901 Tel (915) 543-2841

OSBORNE, EDWIN MARVIN, b. Golden City, Mo., Oct. 24, 1932; A.B., Washington U., St. Louis, 1953; LL.B., U. Calif., Los Angeles, 1960. Admitted to Calif. bar, 1960; asst. to field engring. mgr. Electro Data div. Burroughs Corp., 1956-57; research asst. Bur. Bus. and Econ. Research, U. Calif., Los Angeles, 1959-60, research asst. Sch. law, 1959-60; practice law, Ventura, Calif., 1960-73; dep. dist. atty. Ventura County (Calif.), 1960-63, chief criminal dep. dist. atty., 1963-66, chief asst. county counsel, 1966-70, county counsel, 1970-73; judge Ventura County Municipal Ct., Ventura, 1973—; chmn. Jud. Process Task Force, 1970-72; chmn. Calif. Gov.'s Select Com. Law Enforcement Problems, 1972-73; chmn. adv. com. on spl. problems in jud. process Project Safer Calif., 1974; mem. Ventura Region Criminal Justice Planning Bd., 1970-72; mem. Atty. Gen.'s Comprehensive Data System Adv. Com., 1974—; trustee Ventura County Law Library, 1970-73. Mem. Calif. Judges Assn. (criminal law and procedure com. 1974—, chmn. 1977—), Am. Bar Assn., Am. Judicature Soc., Nat. Council Crime and Delinquency, Phi Beta Kappa, Phi Eta Sigma, Eta Sigma Phi, Phi Alpha Delta. Office: Courthouse Ventura CA 93001

OSBORNE, GEORGE EDWARD, b. nr. Akron, Colo., Jun 11, 1893; A.B., U. Calif., 1916, LL.D., 1966; LL.B., Harvard, 1919, S.J.D. 1920. Admitted to Mass. bar 1919; asst. prof. law W.Va. U., 1920-21, U. Minn., 1921-23; prof. law Stanford (Calif.), 1923-58, now emeritus prof.; prof. law Hastings Coll. Law, U. Calif. at San Francisco, 1958—; dir. Commonwealth Group Mut. funds; Charles Inglis Thompson prof. U. Colo., summer 1953; acting prof. law Columbia, summer 1923, U. Chgo., summer, 1927; vis. prof. law Duke, 1931-32, U. Wash., summer, 1933, U. Calif., spring 1937, summer 1953. Chmn. railway carrier, motor carrier, lumber and timber products, clay products and other industry coms. to s set nat. minimum wage rates, 1940-43; mediator Nat. War Labor Bd., 1942-45; pub. panel mem. 1942-43, mem. President's ry. emergency bds. in engrs. and firemen's diesel manpower cases, 1949; also non-operating unions union shop case, 1952; arbitrator various labor and comml. disputes, 1946—. Mem. Phi Beta Kappa, Phi Delta Phi. Author: Cases on Property Security, 1940; Mortgages, 1951, 2d edit., 1970; Cases and Materials on Suretyship, 1956, 2d edit., 1966; Cases and Materials on Secured Transactions, 1966; co-author: American Law Property, 1952; (with Ballantine) Law Problems, 1956. Editor-in-chief Harvard Law Rev., Vol. 32. Contbr. articles and notes to legal periodicals. Home: 1021 Francisco St San Francisco CA 94109 Office: Hastings Coll Law U Calif San Francisco CA 94102

OSBORNE, HARRY KARL, JR., b. Conneaut, Ohio, Mar. 27, 1915; B.S., Mt. Union Coll., 1938; LL.B., William McKinley Sch. Law, 1950. Admitted to Ohio bar, 1951; village solicitor Malvern, Ohio, 1964-70; mem. Bd. Pub. Affairs, Minerva, Ohio, 1972—; sec. Consumers Nat. Bank, Minerva, 1965—. Home: 217 1/2 N Market St Minerva OH 44657 Office: PO Box 27 Minerva OH 44657 Tel (216) 868-5015

OSBORNE, JOHN MACK, JR., lawyer; b. Marked Tree, Ark., Sept. 22, 1921; B.A., U. Miss., 1943; LL.B., Jackson Sch. Law, 1962. Admitted to Miss. bar, 1963; chief juvenile officer Jackson (Miss.) Police Dept., 1947-72; supr. Youth Services Counselors, Region 3 Miss. Dept. Youth Services, Jackson, Miss., 1972—. Home: 724 Chickasaw Ave Jackson MS 39206 Office: 400 E Silas Brown St Jackson MS 39201

OSBORNE, RICHARD PIERCE, b. Morrilton, Ark., Sept. 5, 1946; B.S.B.A. in Accounting, Ark. Tech., 1969; J.D., Univ. Ark., Fayetteville, 1973. Admitted to Ark. bar, 1973; individual practice law, Fayetteville, 1973-75; adminstrv., legal asst. Gov. of Ark., Little Rock, 1975-76; asso. firm Niblock & Odom, Fayetteville, 1976—. Mem. Fayetteville C of C. Mem. Am., Ark., Washington County bar assns., Ark. Trial Lawyers Assn. Home: 1635 Hotz Fayetteville AR 72701 Office: 20 E Mountain PO Drawer 818 Fayetteville AR 72701 Tel (501) 521-5510

OSGOOD, ALFRED MORSE, b. Wilmette, Ill., Oct. 4, 1913; A.B., Princeton U., 1937; LL.B., Harvard, 1940. Admitted to D.C. bar, 1941; asso. firm Alvord and Alvord, Washington, 1940-41, 46-51; partner firm Lee Toomey & Kent, Washington, 1951—. Town council mem., Chevy Chase, Md., 1970-72. Mem. Am. (chmn. com. on excise and employment taxes 1973-74, 74-75), D.C. bar assns., Bar Assn. of D.C. Home: 7205 Meadow Ln Chevy Chase MD 20015 Office: 1200 18th St NW Suite 812 Washington DC 20036 Tel (202) 457-8500

OSMUNDSON, ROBERT, b. Iowa City, Jan. 9, 1919; B.A., U. Iowa, 1940, J.D., 1942. Admitted to Iowa bar, 1942; individual practice law, Iowa City, 1946-69; judge Dist. Ct. Iowa, Iowa City, 1970—. Mem. Iowa City Sch. Bd., 1949-55, pres., 1954-55. Mem. Am., Iowa bar assns. Office: Johnson County Court House Iowa City IA 52240 Tel (319) 338-7957

OSTBY, BYRON CLIFFORD, b. Superior, Wis., Aug. 17, 1924; B.S., U. Wis., 1949, J.D., 1951. Admitted to Wis. bar, 1951, U.S. Supreme Ct. bar, 1966; field sec. Wis. Med. Soc., 1951-54; individual practice law, Madison, Wis., 1954-62; exec. dir. Wis. R.R. Assn., Madison, 1962—; consul of Norway, 1967—. Mem. Wis. State Assembly, 1949-50, 51-52; bd. visitors U. Wis., 1976—. Mem. Am., Dane County bar assns., Wis. State Bar. Named Knight First Class, Royal Order of St. Olav (Norway), 1975. Home: 58 Cambridge Rd Madison WI 53704 Office: 25 W Main St Madison WI 53703 Tel (608) 257-0411

OSTERMAN, EDWARD JOHN, b. McKeesport, Pa., Oct. 2, 1931; B.A., U. Pa., 1953; LL.B., Duquesne U., 1958. Admitted to Pa. bar, 1958, Pa. Supreme Ct. bar, 1959; partner firm Eddy, Osterman & Lloyd, Pitts., 1960—; spl. atty. gen. Commonwealth of Pa., Pitts., 1963-71; solicitor White Oak Borough (Pa.), McKeesport, 1971—. Mem. adv. bd. McKeesport Area Sch. Dist., 1973. Mem. Allegheny County Bar Assn., Am. Hist. Soc. Home: 145 Victoria Dr White Oak Borough PA 15131 Office: 1430 Grant Bldg Pittsburgh PA 15219 Tel (412) 281-5336

OSTREM, DONALD LEE, b. Great Falls, Mont., Dec. 17, 1940; B.S. in Commerce, Mont. State Coll., (now Mont. State U.), 1962; LL.B., Mont. State U. (now U. Mont.), 1965, J.D., 1970. Admitted to Mont. bar, 1965, Mont. Dist. Cts. bar, 1965, Mont. Supreme Ct. bar, 1965, U.S. Dist. Ct. bar, 1965, U.S. Ct. Appeals 9th Circuit bar, 1967; partner firm Graybill, Ostrem, Warner & Crotty and predecessors, Great Falls, 1965—; city atty., Great Falls, 1970-72. Dir. St. Thomas Childrens Home, Great Falls, bd. dirs. Great Falls Library, Great Falls C. of C.; dir. Mont. League of Cities and Towns, Helena; commr. City of Great Falls, 1973—, mayor, 1976—. Mem. Am., Mont. bar assns., Am., Mont. trial lawyers assns., Am. Judicature Soc. Office: 400 1st National Bldg Great Falls MT 59401 Tel (406) 452-8579

OSTROFF, PETER IVAN, b. Washington, Dec. 15, 1942; A.B., Washington U., 1964; J.D., U. Chgo., 1967. Admitted to Ill. bar, 1967, Calif. bar, 1970; law clk. to Judge Shirley M. Hufstedler, U.S. Ct. Appeals, 9th Circuit, 1969-70; asso. firm Vedder, Price, Kaufman & Kammholz, Chgo., 1967-68; partner firm Nossaman, Krueger & Marsh, Los Angeles, 1970—; teaching fellow in law Monash U., Victoria, Australia, 1968-69. Dist. rep. Malibu (Calif.) Twp. Council, 1975—. Mem. Los Angeles County (trustee, chmn. sect. human rights), Am. (chmn. com. on litigation involving comml. transactions sect. litigation) bar assns. Office: 445 S Figueroa St Los Angeles CA 90071 Tel (213) 628-5221

OSTROWSKI, WILLIAM JOHN, b. Buffalo, Sept. 7, 1925; B.A., Canisius Coll., 1949; LL.B., Georgetown U., 1951; LL.M., George Washington U., 1952; grad. Nat. Coll. State Judiciary U. Pa., 1967, U. Nev., 1971. Admitted to N.Y. bar, 1952; law clk. firm Covington & Burling, Washington, 1952; atty. office of chief transp. Dept. Army, Washington, 1952-53; practiced in Buffalo, 1953-60; dep. corp. counsel City of Buffalo, 1956-60; judge Buffalo City Ct., 1961-76; justice N.Y. Supreme Ct., 1977—. Mem. Am., N.Y. State, Erie County (N.Y.) bar assns., Am. Judicature Soc., Am. Judges Assn. Office: Supreme Ct Chambers 77 W Eagle St Buffalo NY 14202 Tel (716) 852-1291

O'SULLIVAN, HARRY J., b. Brockton, Mass., Nov. 17, 1903; A.B., Boston Coll., 1926; LL.B., Harvard, 1929, J.D., 1974. Admitted to Mass. bar, 1929; asso. firm Chamberlain, Stone & Bosson, Boston, 1929-31, James A. Reilly, Brockton, 1931-64; individual practice law, Brockton, 1964—. Bd. dirs. Brockton Hosp., 1960-75; pres. Solanto council Boy Scouts Am., 1950-52. Mem. Mass., Plymouth County (past chmn. pub. relations com.) bar assns. Home: 293 Moraine St Brockton MA 02401 Office: 231 Main St Brockton MA 02401 Tel (617) 586-0986

OTIS, HOWARD JUDSON, b. Barron, Wis., July 9, 1918; B.S., U. Wis., 1940; postgrad., 1940-41, J.D., 1948; postgrad. U. Colo., 1953-54. Admitted to Wis. bar, 1948, U.S. Ct. Mil. Appeals bar, 1954, Colo. bar, 1967; asso. firm O.J. Falge, Ladysmith, Wis., 1948-52; atty. JAGC, USAF, 1952-68; asst. atty. gen. State of Colo., 1968; dep. dist. atty. Arapahoe County, Littleton Colo., 1969-70; judge Adams County Ct., Brighton, Colo., 1971—. Mem. Am., Wis., Colo. Adams County, Aurora bar assns., Am. Judicature Soc., Judge Advocates Assn., Colo. Assn. County Judges (mem. exec. bd., 1971, 72, 74; treas. 1975—). Office: Hall of Justice 1931 Bridge St Brighton CO 80601 Tel (303) 659-1161

OTIS, JAMES CORNISH, b. St. Paul, Mar. 23, 1912; B.A., Yale, 1934; LL.B., U. Minn., 1937. Admitted to Minn. bar, 1937; partner firm Otis, Faricy and Burger; judge Municipal Ct., St. Paul, 1948-54, Dist. Ct., St. Paul, 1954-61; asso. justice Minn. Supreme Ct., St. Paul, 1961—. Trustee Hamline U., Wilder Found. Mem. Am., Minn. bar assns., Am. Judicature Soc., Inst. Jud. Adminstrn., Minn. State Bar Found. (dir.), Am. Judges Assn. Home: 7 Crocus Hill Saint Paul MN 55102 Office: 230 State Capitol Bldg Saint Paul MN 55155 Tel (612) 296-3380

O'TOOLE, FRANCIS JOSEPH, b. Dublin, Ireland, Feb. 10, 1944; LL.B., Harvard, 1967; J.D., U. Maine, 1970. Admitted to Maine bar, 1970, D.C. bar, 1972; mem. firm Fried, Frank, Harris, Shriver & Kampelman, Washington, 1971—. Mem. Am., Maine, D.C. bar assns. Reginald Heber Smith fellow, 1970-71. Editor in chief Maine Law Rev., 1969-70; also articles. Home: 1836 Opalocka Dr McLean VA 22101 Office: 600 New Hampshire Ave Washington DC 20037 Tel (202) 965-9400

O'TOOLE, ROBERT EDWARD, b. Boston, Mar. 18, 1937; B.J., Suffolk U., 1961, J.D., 1964; J.D. (hon.), New Eng. Sch. Law, 1974. Admitted to Mass. bar, 1964, U.S. Supreme Ct. bar, 1976; partner firm O'Toole & Horrigan, Boston, 1964-66; prof. law New Eng. Sch. Law, 1966—, asst. dean, 1970-71, dean, 1971-74. Pres., Newbury St. League, Boston, 1971-74. Mem. AAUP, Am., Mass. bar assns., Am. Judicature Soc., World Assn. Law Profs., Soc. Am. Law Profs. Home: 23 Radford Ln Boston MA 02124 Office: 126 Newbury St Boston MA 02116 Tel (617) 267-9655

O'TOOLE, THOMAS WILLIAM, b. Marshalltown, Iowa, Apr. 12, 1938; B.A., U. Notre Dame, 1960; LL.B., U. Ariz., 1966. Admitted to Ariz. bar, 1966; asst. fed. pub. defender Dist. Ariz., Phoenix, 1967-76, fed. pub. defender, 1976—. Mem. Ariz. Bar Assn. Office: 230 N 1st Ave Phoenix AZ 85025 Tel (602) 261-3561

OTT, LAWRENCE L., b. Dansville, N.Y., Oct. 27, 1913; student Niagara U., 1937; LL.B., Fordham U., 1940. Admitted to N.Y. State bar, 1940; hearing man in compensation Lumberman's Mutual Casualty Co. Ill., N.Y.C., 1940-42; individual practice law, Schenectady, N.Y., 1946—; sec. treas. Mohawk Abstract Corp., 1952-72; v.p. Monroe Abstract and Title Corp., 1972—. Active Boy Scouts Am. and ARC. Mem. N.Y. State Bar Assn., N.Y State Land Title Assn., Am. Land Title Assn. Home: 256 Bradley Blvd Schenectady NY 12304 Office: 608 State St Schenectady NY 12305 Tel (518) 374-8438

OTT, ROGER DEAN, b. Alemeda, Calif., Sept. 19, 1944; B.A., Wartburg Coll., 1967; M.BA., Drake U., 1972, J.D., 1973. Admitted to Iowa bar, 1973; partner firm Noah, Smith & Ott, Charles City, Iowa, 1973—. Chmn. Floyd County Civil Service Commn.; mem. Charles City Community Drug Council, Charles City Family Counseling Coalition, Charles City Teen Tavern Bd., Charles City Community Sch. Evaluation Com. Mem. Am., Iowa State, Floyd County bar assns., Assn. Trial Lawyers Iowa. Home: 800 Third Ave Charles City IA 50616 Office: 200 N Johnson St Charles City IA 50616 Tel (515) 228-4533

OTTEN, KENNETH HARRY, b. Springfield, Ill., Mar. 17, 1918; B.S., U. Chgo., 1940; M.S., U. Okla., 1942; LL.B., U. Mich., 1954. Personnel technician Ill. CSC, Springfield, 1946-51; admitted to Ill. bar, 1955; practiced in Springfield, 1955—, individual practice law,

1955-65, partner firm Nafziger & Otten, 1965—. Chmn. Springfield Zoning Bd. Appeals, 1956-60; moderator 1st Congregation Ch., Springfield, 1972-73. Mem. Ill. State (chmn. sect. pub. utilities 1971-72), Am., Sangamon County (Ill.) (pres. 1969-70) bar assns. Home: 1215 Ivywood Dr Springfield IL 62704 Office: 916 Illinois Bldg Springfield IL 62701 Tel (217) 544-0896

OTTENHEIMER, EDWIN, b. Balt., Sept. 20, 1915; A.B., Johns Hopkins, 1936; LL.B., U. Md., 1940. Admitted to Md. bar, 1941; individual practice law, Balt., 1941-62; partner firms Hamburger, Sykes & Ottenheimer, Balt., 1962-69, Ottenheimer, Cahn & Patz, Profl. Assn. and predecessor, Balt., 1969—. Mem. Am., Md., Balt. City bar assns. Author: (with Daniel C. Joseph) Supplementary Proceedings in Maryland, 1955. Home: 7913 Long Meadow Rd Baltimore MD 21208 Office: 9th Floor Sun Life Bldg Baltimore MD 21201 Tel (301) 752-8308

OTTENHOFF, GEORGE HILLMAN, b. Temple, Tex., Sept. 2, 1944; A.B., Calvin Coll., 1966; J.D., Northwestern U., 1969. Admitted to Colo. bar, 1971; individual practice law, Alamosa, Colo., 1971—; dep. dist. atty., Alamosa, Colo., 1971-74, 76—. Bd. dirs. Valley Christian Sch. Assn., Alamosa, Sr. Citizens Center, Inc., Alamosa; mem. Alamosa County Planning Comm., 1975-76. Mem. Am., Colo., San Luis Valley bar assns. Office: 301 State Ave Alamosa CO 81101 Tel (303) 589-2577

OTTESEN, REALFF HENRY, b. Davenport, Iowa, July 10, 1941; B.A., State U. Iowa, 1963, J.D., 1965. Admitted to Iowa bar, 1965; partner firm Ottesen & Ottesen, Davenport, 1965—; asst. county atty. Scott County, Iowa, 1967—. Bd. dirs., pres. Iowa Pageant Mgmt. Corp. Mem. Am., Iowa, Scott County bar assns., Am. Trial Lawyers Assn., Assn. Trial Lawyers Iowa, Nat. Dist. Attys. Assn. Home: 2320 Salem Ct Bettendorf IA 52722 Office: 602 Davenport Bank Bldg Davenport IA 52801 Tel (319) 322-5386

OTTINGER, MARY ANN, b. Duluth, Minn., Oct. 19, 1948; B.A., Drake U., 1970, J.D., 1973. Admitted to Wash. bar, 1973; asso. firm Krutch, Lindell, Donnelly, Dempcy, Lageschulte & Judkins, Seattle, 1973-75, Peterson, Bracelin, Young & Putra, Seattle, 1975-77; individual practice law, Seattle, 1977—, instr. Seattle U., 1976. Chmn. hearing tribunal Wash. State Human Rights Commn. Mem. Am., Wash., Seattle-King County bar assns., Wash. Women Lawyers. Home: 7020 151st St NE Redmond WA 98052 Office: 224 Pioneer Bldg 600 First Ave Seattle WA 98104 Tel (206) 624-2013

OTTMAR, CLINTON RAYMOND, b. nr. Wishek, N.D., Nov. 17, 1928; Ph.B., U. N.D., 1951, J.D., 1955. Admitted to N.D. bar, 1955; asso. firm Hjellum, Weiss, Nerison & Ottmar, Jamestown, 1955-62; individual practice law, 1962-64; partner firm Ottmar & Nething, Jamestown, 1965-76, firm Ottmar & Pope, Jamestown, 1965—; states atty., Stutsman County, 1964-69; spl. asst. atty. gen. N.D., 1966—; city atty. Jamestown, 1974—. Chmn. bd. trustees N.D., Conf., United Meth. Ch.; merit badge counselor Red River Council Boy Scouts Am., 1960-73; mem. Jamestown Bd. Adjustment, 1969-74. Mem. Am., N.D. (pres. 1976, chmn. long range planning com. 1977—). Stutsman County (past pres.) bar assns., N.D. States Attys. Assn. (past sec., dir.). Home: 509 1st Ave N Jamestown ND 58401 Office: 223 1st Ave N Jamestown ND 58401 Tel (701) 252-5541

OTTO, FREDERICK POEHLER, b. Prairie du Chien, Wis., Jan. 1, 1923; Ph.B., U. Wis., 1947; J.D., 1950. Admitted to Wis. bar, 1950; dist. atty. County of Crawford (Wis.), 1967-73; title atty. Farmers Home Adminstrn., U.S. Dept. Agr. Mem. State Bar Wis., Wis. Dist. Attys. Assn. (life), Crawford County Bar Assn., Gamma Eta Gamma. Home: 322 S Minnesota St Prairie du Chien WI 53821 Office: 103 E Blackhawk Ave Prairie du Chien WI 53821 Tel (608) 326-8522

OTTO, FREDERICK SIMMONS, b. Balt., Dec. 27, 1939; B.S. in Bus., U. Colo., 1963; J.D., U. Denver, 1968. Admitted to Colo. bar, 1968; tax supr. Touche, Ross & Co., Denver, 1968-70; asso. firm Holme, Roberts & Owen, Steamboat Springs, Colo., 1971-72; v.p. Vail Assos., Inc. (Colo.), 1973—. Bd. dirs. Vail Inst., 1972-75. Mem. Colo. Soc. C.P.A.'s, Colo., Continental Divide (v.p. 1976—) bar assns. Home: PO Box 1943 Vail CO 81657 Office: PO Box 7 Vail CO 81657 Tel (303) 476-5601

OTTO, WILBUR MCCOY, b. Greenville, Pa., Oct. 11, 1936; A.B., Dickinson Coll., 1958; J.D., U. Mich., 1961. Admitted to D.C. bar, 1961, Pa. bar, 1962; asst. prof. law U.S. Mil. Acad., West Point, N.Y., 1961-65; partner firm Dickie, McCamey & Chilcote, Pitts., 1965—; lectr. Pa. Bar Inst. Mem. Am., Pa., Allegheny County bar assns., Pa. Def. Inst., Pa. Trial Lawyers Assn., Acad. Trial Lawyers Allegheny County (dir., treas.). Office: 3180 US Steel Bldg 600 Grant St Pittsburgh PA 15219 Tel (412) 281-7272

OVERBY, RICHARD JAY, b. Plentywood, Mont., Aug. 10, 1943; B.A., U. Mont., 1965, J.D., 1968. Admitted to Mont. bar, 1968; individual practice law, Plentywood, 1968-72; staff atty. Mont. Power Co., Butte, Mont., 1972-74; corporate counsel, asst. corporate sec. Cascade Natural Gas Corp., Seattle, 1974-76. Mem. Mont., NE Mont. (pres. 1977), Am. bar assns., Phi Delta Phi. Home: Rural Route 1 Plentywood MT 59254 Office: PO Box 247 Plentywood MT 59254 Tel (406) 765-2200

OVERFELT, A(RCHIE) LEE, b. Big Timber, Mont., Aug. 23, 1923; B.A., U. Mont., 1951, LL.B., 1951, J.D., 1973. Admitted to Mont. bar, 1951; practiced in Billings, Mont., since 1953, mem. firm Mouzt & Overfelt, 1953-56, individual practice law, 1956—; spl. prosecutor Custer County (Mont.), 1971, Yellowstone County (Mont.), 1973, Rosebud County (Mont.), 1975. Sec., Mont. Wildlife Fedn., 1959-61. Mem. Am., Mont. trial lawyers assns., Mont. Bar Assn., Am. Judicature Soc., Phi Alpha Delta. Home: 245 Beverly Hill Blvd Billings MT 59101 Office: 417 Petroleum Bldg Billings MT 59101 Tel (406) 252-4088

OVERHOLT, E. LLEWELLYN, JR., b. Los Angeles, Oct. 27, 1927; B.A., Occidental Coll., 1949; M.B.A., U. Calif., Berkeley, 1952; LL.B., 1956. Admitted to Calif. bar, 1957; partner firm Overholt & Overholt, Los Angeles and Anaheim, 1957-72; individual practice law, Anaheim, 1972—; Calif. inheritance tax referee Orange County (Calif.), 1968—. Trustee Anaheim City Sch. Dist., 1968—, pres., 1975-76; commr. Anaheim Parks and Recreation Commn., 1970-75, Anaheim Cultural Arts Commn., 1974-75. Mem. Am., Calif., Los Angeles, Orange County bar assns. Mng. editor Calif. Law Rev., 1955-56. Home: 651 Dwyer Dr Anaheim CA 92801 Office: 600 N Euclid St suite 560 Anaheim CA 92801 Tel (714) 776-7500

OVERHOLT, WESTON C., JR., b. Chester, Pa., May 7, 1926; A.B., Dickinson Coll., 1950, LL.B., 1953. Admitted to Pa. bar, 1954, U.S. Supreme Ct. bar, 1975; partner firm Harper, George, Buchanan & Driver, Phila., 1954—; dir. Seabrook Blanching Corp., Edenton, N.C., Bassett Steel & Tube Co., Inc., King of Prussia, Pa. Alumni trustee Dickinson Coll., 1964-71; bd. dirs. Media Youth Center (Pa.), 1965—, pres., 1974; vice chmn. Upper Providence Twp. (Pa.) Recreation Commn., 1976. Mem. Phila., Pa., Am. bar assns., Dickinson Coll. Alumni Assn. (pres. 1960-63). Named to Sports Hall of Fame Dickinson Coll., 1976. Home: 240 Timber Jump Ln Media PA 19063 Office: 1200 Western Savings Bank Bldg Philadelphia PA 19107 Tel (205) PE 5-3090

OVERMAN, GEORGE CURTIS, JR., b. Newport News, Va., Sept. 22, 1941; B.B.A., Coll. William and Mary, 1963; J.D., Coll. William and Mary, 1966. Admitted to Va. bar, 1966; asso. firm Michalos & Overman, and predecessors, Newport News, 1966-70, partner, 1970—; law rev. bd. Marshall-Wythe Sch. Law, Williamsburg; ethics com. Va. State Bar, 1973-75. Chmn. Newport News Citizen's Adv. Com., 1974-75. Mem. Newport News Bar Assn. Home: 814 Darden Dr Newport News VA 23602 Office: 6022 Jefferson Ave Newport News VA 23605 Tel (804) 244-1719

OVERSTREET, NOAH WEBSTER, JR., b. Jackson, Miss., Nov. 14, 1913; LL.B., U. Miss., 1936; grad. Army Judge Adv. Gen's. Sch., 1943. Admitted to Miss. bar, 1936; practiced in Holly Springs, Miss., 1936-40; with JAGC, U.S. Army, 1943-45; practiced in Jackson, Miss., 1945—, mem. firm Overstreet and Kuykendall and predecessors, 1969—. Fellow Am., Miss. (pres. 1964) bar founds.; mem. Am. Bar Assn., Miss. State (pres. 1967-68), Hind County (Miss.) (pres. 1954-55) bar assns. Home: 1085 Meadow Brook Jackson MS 39206 Office: PO Box 961 Deposit Guaranty Bldg Suite 1529 200 E Capitol St Jackson MS 39201 Tel (601) 948-3014

OVERTON, BEN F., Now chief justice Supreme Ct. of Fla., Tallahassee. Office: Supreme Ct Tallahassee FL 32304*

OVERTON, GEORGE WASHINGTON, b. Hinsdale, Ill., Jan. 25, 1918; A.B., Harvard, 1940; J.D., U. Chgo., 1946. Admitted to Ill. bar, 1947, U.S. Supreme Ct. bar, 1951; asso. firm Pope & Ballard, Chgo., 1946-48; partner Overton & Babcock and successors, Chgo., 1948-51; partner firm Taylor Miller Busch & Magner, Chgo., 1951-60; partner firm Overton Schwartz & Yacker Ltd. and predecessors, Chgo., 1961—. Chmn. Ill. Recreation Council, 1969-70; mem. adv. council Ill. Inst. Continuing Legal Edn., 1974—. Mem. Am., Ill., Chgo. bar assns., Assn. Bar City N.Y. (pres. 1974—), Chgo. Bar Found. Home: 1368 E 57th St Chicago IL 60637 Office: 105 W Adams St Chicago IL 60603 Tel (312) 236-6945

OVERTON, NELSON TILGHMAN, b. Newport News, Va., Feb. 7, 1928; B.A., Va. Mil. Inst., 1949; LL.B., U. Va., 1952. Admitted to Va. bar, 1952; since practiced in Hampton, Va., asso. to partner firm Montague, Cumming, Watkins & Overton, 1952-65; judge 8th Jud. Circuit Ct. Va., 1965—. Mem. Am., Va., Hampton bar assns. Office: Circuit Ct Hampton VA 23665 Tel (804) 722-6511

OVERTON, WILLIAM RAY, b. Malvern, Ark., Sept. 19, 1939; B.S. in Bus. Adminstrn., U. Ark., 1961, LL.B., 1964. Admitted to Ark. bar, 1964; partner firm Wright, Lindsey & Jennings, Little Rock, 1966—; mem. Ark. Constl. Study Commn., 1967; chmn. Ark. Gov.'s Com. for Implementing Legislation-Constl. Amendment. Fellow Internat. Acad. Trial Lawyers; mem. Am., Ark., Pulaski County bar assns., Internat. Assn. Ins. Counsel, Nat. Assn. Railroad Counsel. Home: Office: 2200 Worthen Bank Bldg Little Rock AR 72201 Tel (501) 371-0808

OVIATT, CLIFFORD REICHEL, JR., b. New Haven, May 25, 1926; B.A., Wesleyan U., 1949; LL.B., Cornell U., 1953. Admitted to N.Y. State bar, 1953, Conn. bar, 1955; asso. firm Moser, Johnson & Reiff, Rochester, N.Y., 1953-55; asso. firm Cummings & Lockwood, Stamford, Conn., 1955-61, partner, 1961-68, mng. partner, 1968—. Counsel Conn. Ready Mix Concrete Assn., dir. Conn. Bus. and Industry Assn. Rep. town meeting Town of Fairfield, 1974—, mem. fin. com., 1974—; mem. Blue Ribbon Com., Stamford, 1976; bd. trustees Outward Bound Inc., 1973—. Mem. Am., Bridgeport, Conn. (chmn. labor law sect. 1970-72) bar assns., Bridgeport C. of C., Mfrs. Assn. So. Conn. Author: Impact Of National Labor Relations Act On Health Care Institutions; Bargaining Units In The Health Care Industry. Home: 620 11 O'Clock Rd Fairfield CT 06430 Office: 855 Main St Bridgeport CT 06604 Tel (203) 366-3438

OVIATT, ROSS HANNUM, b. Huron, S.D., Apr. 14, 1918; J.D., U. S.D., 1941. Admitted to S.D. bar, 1941, U.S. Supreme Ct. bar, 1960; partner firm Loucks, Oviatt, Bradshaw, Green & Schulz, and predecessors, Watertown, S.D., 1945—; states atty. Codington County, S.D., 1951-55, S.D. Jud. Council, 1960-68, 73-74. Mem. Am. Coll. Probate Counsel (regent 1975—), Internat. Soc. Barristers, Am. Bd. Trial Advocates, Am. Judicature Soc. (bd. dirs. 1971-75), Am. Bar Assn. (bd. govs. 1968-71), State Bar S.D. (pres. 1973-74), Phi Delta Phi. Contbr. articles to profl. jours. Home: 721 1st St NW Watertown SD 57201 Office: 17 2d Ave SW Watertown SD 57201 Tel (605) 886-5812

OWEN, DAVID ROGERS, b. Honolulu, Jan. 19, 1914; B.A., U. Va., 1935, M.A., 1937, LL.B., 1939. Admitted to Md. bar, 1940, U.S. Supreme Ct. bar, 1949, U.S. Customs Ct. bar, 1965, U.S. Ct. Claims bar, 1965; asso. firm Semmes, Bowen and Semmes, Balt., 1939-49, partner, 1949—. Mem. Greater Balt. Com., 1975—. Fellow Am. Coll. Trial Lawyers; mem. Bar Assn. Balt. City, Md. State Bar Assn. (v.p. 1965-66), Maritime Law Assn. U.S. (1st v.p. 1974-76, pres. 1976—). Asso. editor Am. Maritime Cases, 1964—. Home: 8028 Thornton Rd Towson MD 21204 Office: 10 Light St Baltimore MD 21202 Tel (301) 539-5040

OWEN, FRANK, b. El Paso, Tex., Feb. 25, 1926; student Tex. Western Coll.; LL.B., U. Tex., 1951. Admitted to Tex. bar, 1951; individual practice law, El Paso; dir. Am. Bank of Commerce, 1st Nat. Bank of Fabens (Tex.). Mem. Tex. Ho. of Reps., 1950-54, Tex. State Senate, 1954-65, pres. pro-tem. Mem. Am., Tex., El Paso bar assns., Am. Judicature Soc. Home: 5508 Montoya St El Paso TX 79932 Office: 310 American Bank of Commerce Bldg El Paso TX 79901 Tel (915) 533-9753

OWEN, H. MARTYN, b. Decatur, Ill., Oct. 23, 1929; A.B., Princeton, 1951; LL.B., Harvard, 1954. Admitted to Conn. bar, 1954, U.S. Supreme Ct. bar, 1963; asso. firm Shipman & Goodwin, Hartford, Conn., 1958—, partner, 1961—; dir. Village Water Co., Simsbury, Conn., Cushman Industries, Inc., Hartford. Mem. Simsbury Zoning Bd. Appeals, 1961-67, Simsbury Zoning Commn., 1967—; sec. Capitol Region Planning Agy., 1965-66; bd. dirs. Symphony Soc. Greater Hartford, 1967-73; trustee Renbrook Sch., West Hartford, Conn., 1963-72, treas., 1964-68, pres., 1968-72, hon. life trustee, 1972—; trustee Simsbury Free Library, Hartford Grammar Sch.; corporator Inst. Living, Hartford. Mem. Am., Conn., Hartford County bar assns. Home: 44 Pinnacle Mountain Rd Simsbury CT 06070 Office: Shipman & Goodwin 799 Main St Hartford CT 06103 Tel (203) 549-4770

OWEN, JACK FLEET, b. Battle Creek, Mich., Nov. 1, 1934; B.A., Western Mich. Coll., 1952; M.A., Western Mich. U., 1962; J.D., U. Wis., 1972. Admitted to Wis. bar, 1972; investigator CSC, Chgo. region, 1962-72; atty., Waupuw, Wis., 1972-74; individual practice law, Rhinelander, Wis., 1974—. Mem. Wis., Tri-County, Fond du Lac, Dodge County bar assns. Home and Office: 126 E Davenport St Rhinelander WI 54501 Tel (715) 369-2050

OWEN, JOHN HEWITT, b. N.Y.C., Jan. 2, 1935; B.A. magna cum laude U. Notre Dame, 1956; J.D., Georgetown Law Center, 1958. Admitted to D.C. bar, 1958, N.Y. bar, 1959, U.S. Supreme Ct., 1967; individual practice law, N.Y.C., 1959-72, Cooperstown, N.Y., 1973—; pub. defender Otsego County, N.Y., 1973—. Mem. N.Y. State, Otsego County bar assns., N.Y. State Trial Lawyers Assn., N.Y. State Defenders Assn. Office: 101 Main St Cooperstown NY 13326 Tel (607) 547-8721

OWEN, NATHAN PHILIP, b. Chgo., Oct. 3, 1936; B.A. in Pub. Accounting, U. Miami (Fla.), 1957; J.D., U. Chgo., 1960. Admitted to Ill. bar, 1960; asso. firm Philip A. Winston, Chgo., 1960-61; atty. FTC, Chgo., 1961—; gen. sec. Chgo. Consumer Protection Coordinating Com., 1969-72; editor Fed. Lawyer Mag., 1962-67. Mem. Citizens Law and Order Com., Chgo. Commn. on Human Relations, 1963-68; sec., budget chmn., mem. bd. dirs. Drexel Home, Inc., 1969—. Mem. Am., Ill. State (chmn. antitrust sect. 1973-74; mem. gen. assembly 1976—), Chgo., Fed. (nat. v.p.) bar assns., Decalogue Soc., Phi Delta Phi. Home: 1030 N State St Apt 1-H Chicago IL 60610 Office: 55 E Monroe St Room 1437 Chicago IL 60603 Tel (312) 353-4435

OWEN, PHILIP CLIFFORD, b. Jacksonville, Fla., Aug. 4, 1920; J.D. with high honors, U. Fla., 1948. Admitted to Fla. bar, 1948, U.S. Dist. Ct. bar, 1948; atty. U.S. Army C.E., Jacksonville, 1950-58; asso. firm Fischette, Parrish, Owen & Held and predecessors, Jacksonville, 1958—. Mem. Jacksonville, Fla., Fed., Am. bar assns. Office: 1816 Gulf Life Tower Jacksonville FL 32207 Tel (904) 398-7036

OWEN, ROBERT HUBERT, b. Birmingham, Ala., Aug. 3, 1928; B.S., U. Ala., 1950; J.D., Birmingham Sch. Law, 1956. Admitted to Ala. bar, 1957, Ga. bar, 1965; analyst methods and procedures, supr. Ala. Power Co., Birmingham, 1952-58; asso. firm Martin, Vogtle, Balch & Bingham, Birmingham, 1958-63; asst. sec., house counsel So. Co. Services, Atlanta, 1963-69, sec., house counsel, 1969—, sec., asst. treas., The So. Co., 1969—. Rep., Atlanta area Inst. in Basic Youth Conflicts, 1971—. Mem. Am. Soc. Corp. Secs. (corporate practices com.), Am., Ala., Ga. bar assns., Delta Chi., Omicron Delta Kappa, Beta Gamma Sigma, Delta Sigma Pi, Phi Eta Sigma. Home: 6590 Bridgewood Valley Rd NW Atlanta GA 30328 Office: 64 Perimeter Center E Atlanta GA 30346 Tel (404) 393-0650

OWEN, STEPHEN FREDERICK, JR., b. Springfield, Mass., Apr. 9, 1934; B.E.E., U. Mass., 1955; grad. Westinghouse Bus. Mgmt. Program, U. Pitts., 1958-59; J.D., Cornell U., 1962; LL.M. in Taxation, Georgetown U., 1964. Admitted to D.C. bar, 1962, U.S. Supreme Ct. bar, 1966; sales engr., dir. systems dept. Westinghouse Elec. Corp., Pitts., 1957-59, N.Y.C., 1956-57; atty.-adviser div. corp. fin. SEC, Washington, 1962-64; asso. firm Loomis, Owen, Fellman & Coleman, Washington, 1964-69, partner 1969-75, sr. partner, 1975—; lectr. in field. Mem. Am. (council adminstrv. law sect. 1976—, vice chmn. food and drug com. 1974—), D.C., Fed. bar assns., Phi Delta Phi. Contbr. articles to legal jours. Home: 5610 Knollwood Rd Washington DC 20016 Office: 2020 K St NW Washington DC 20006 Tel (202) 296-5680

OWENS, ANDREW GAY, JR., b. Atlanta, Nov. 11, 1945; B.A. in Math., Morehouse Coll., 1967; J.D. U. San Francisco, 1972. Admitted to Calif. bar, 1972; asso. firm Kaplan, Livingston, Goodwin, Berkowitz & Selvin, Beverly Hills, Calif., 1972-74, Brent & Herzog, Los Angeles, 1974—; judge pro tem Los Angeles County Municipal Cts. Mem. Am. (litigation sect.), Nat., Los Angeles County, (constitutional rights, lawyer-in-the-classroom coms.), Beverly Hills (minorities and the law task force) bar assns., Assn. Bus. Trial Lawyers, Calif. Trial Lawyers Assn., Langston Law Club. Home: 6365 Green Valley Fox Hills CA 90230 Office: 1888 Century Park East Los Angeles CA 90067 Tel (213) 277-1103

OWENS, ARNOLD DEAN, b. Visalia, Calif., June 14, 1943; B.S., U. Calif., Berkeley, 1966; J.D., U. Oreg., 1969. Admitted to Oreg. bar, 1969; asso. firm O'Reilly, Anderson, Richmond & Adkins, Eugene, Oreg., 1969-71; partner firm Anderson, Richmond & Owens, Eugene, 1971-74, Owens & Loomis, Eugene, 1975—; atty. City of Coburg (Oreg.), 1971—, City of Lowell (Oreg.), 1973—; hearings officer Lane County (Oreg.), 1972—. Pres. Lane County Muscular Dystrophy Assn., Eugene, 1969-71; chmn. Eugene Human Rights Commn., 1969-71; bd. dirs. Lane County council Girl Scouts U.S. Mem. Am., Lane County, Oreg. State bar assns., Am. Judicature Soc. Contbr. continuing legal edn. articles to publs. Home: 2160 Oakmont St Eugene OR 97401 Office: 933 Pearl St Eugene OR 97401 Tel (503) 686-2807

OWENS, CHARLOTTE, b. Pippapass, Ky., Feb. 8, 1922; B.S., Eastern Ky. State Tchrs. Coll., 1942; postgrad. in law U. Ky., 1941-42; LL.B., Ind. U., 1945. Admitted to Calif. bar, 1948; individual practice law, Van Nuys, Calif., 1948-60, 62—; partner firm Barnett & Owens, Van Nuys, 1960-62. Mem. Calif. State, San Fernando Valley bar assns., So. Calif. Women Lawyers Assn. (pres. 1951-52). Office: 14411 Vanowen St Van Nuys CA 91405 Tel (213) 781-4701

OWENS, CLARK V., b. El Dorado, Kans., Sept. 24, 1915; grad. El Dorado Jr. Coll., 1936; A.B., Southwestern Coll., Winfield, Kans., 1938; J.D., Washburn U., 1947. Admitted to Kans. bar, 1947; practiced in Wichita, Kans., 1947-63, judge probate and juvenile ct., 1959-61, judge pro tem, 1957-63, referee, 1957-63; judge Sedgwick County (Kans.) Probate and Juvenile Ct., 1963-69, Sedgwick County Probate Ct., 1970-77; dist. judge 18th Jud. Dist. Kans., 1977—. Chmn. Wichita-Sedgwick County Bd. Health, 1961-63, Sedgwick County Heart Assn., Sedgwick County Leukemia Soc.; mem. Sedgwick County Health Facilities Planning Council, Kans. Gov.'s Penal Planning Council. Mem. Nat. Coll. Probate Judges Assn. (v.p.), No. Am. Judges Assn. (charter), Kans. Probate Judges Assn. (pres. 1966-67). Recipient Moundbuilder citation Southwestern Coll., 1970. Home: 1438 Lieunett St Wichita KS 67203 Office: 525 N Main St Wichita KS 67203 Tel (316) 268-7122

OWENS, FRANCIS JOSEPH, b. Chgo., Dec. 13, 1949; B.A., Loras Coll.; J.D., Northwestern U. Admitted to Wis. bar, 1974; asso. firm, Murphy, Stalper, Brenster & Desmond, Madison, Wis., 1974-76; mem. bd. govs. Young Lawyers Div. Wis. Bar Assn. Mem. Am., Dane County bar assns. Mem. Northwestern U. Law Review Staff, 1973, bd. editors, 1974. Home: 511 S Page St Stoughton WI 53589 Office: 2 E Gilman St Madison WI 53701 Tel (608) 257-7181

OWENS, HOWARD THOMAS, JR., b. Bridgeport, Conn., July 20, 1934; B.S., Holy Cross Coll., 1956; LL.B., Vanderbilt U., 1959. Admitted to Conn. bar, 1960, U.S. Supreme Ct. bar, 1966; chief asst. U.S. atty. for Conn. Dist., 1963-65; partner firm Owens & Schine, Bridgeport, 1965—; mem. Conn. Senate, 1975—. Home: 6 Pierce Ave Bridgeport CT 06604 Office: 1100 Main St Bridgeport CT 06604 Tel (203) 334-4153

OWENS, W. WROE, b. Tex., Jan. 13, 1914; J.D., U. Tex., 1938. Admitted to Tex. bar, 1938, since practiced in Austin; mem. firm Lee, Proctor & Owens, 1938, Lee, Owens & Nelson, 1939; individual practice law, 1940-42; mem. firm Owens & Krueger, 1946-51, Owens & Purser, 1951-63, Law Offices Wroe Owens, 1963-70, Owens & Blanchard, 1970-75, Law Offices Steve Harris, 1976—; spl. agt. FBI, New Orleans, 1942-45. Former bd. dirs. March of Dimes, Cerebral Palsy; nat. pres. Acacia Ednl. Found. Mem. Am., Fed., Tex., Travis County bar assns., Soc. Former Spl. Agts. FBI, Austin C. of C. (past dir. and pres.). Home: 3705 Taylors St Austin TX 78703 Office: 1206 Perry Brooks Bldg Austin TX 78701 Tel (512) 478-8100

OWENS, WILLIAM BOYD, b. Alexandria, La., Nov. 7, 1942; B.S. in Bus. Adminstrn., La. State U., 1964, J.D., 1967; LL.M., Georgetown U., 1972. Admitted to La. bar, 1967, D.C. bar, 1971, U.S. Supreme Ct. bar, 1971; asso. firm Hamel, Park, McCabe & Saunders, Washington, 1971; mem. firm Crowell, Owens & Tudor, Alexandria, La., 1972—; gen. counsel, dir. Continental Service Life & Health Ins. Co., Baton Rouge, 1972—. Treas. Kent Plantation House, 1974—; bd. dirs. Rapides United Givers Fund, 1974—. Mem. Central La. Estate Planning Council, Am., La. bar assns. Office: Box 330 Alexandria LA 71360 Tel (318) 445-1488

OWENSBY, ROGER WALKER, b. Springfield, Mo., Jan. 2, 1949; B.A. in English, SW Mo. State U., 1971; J.D., U. Mo., 1974. Admitted to Mo. bar, 1974; asso. C.B. Mayberry Law Office, Kirksville, Mo., 1974-76; asst. pros. atty. Adair County (Mo.), Kirksville, 1974-76; asst. gen. counsel Mo. Dept. Revenue, Jefferson City, 1976—. Tel (314) 751-4467

OWINGS, ALFRED JEROME, lawyer; b. Richmond, Va., Sept. 17, 1937; B.B.A., U. Notre Dame, 1960; LL.B., U. Richmond, 1965. Admitted to Va. bar, 1965; partner law firm Spinella, Spinella & Owings, Richmond, Va., 1965—. Bd. dirs. Big Brothers of Richmond, Inc., 1971-76, v.p., 1975-76; mem. Henrico County Republican Com., 1965-76. Mem. Richmond, Richmond Criminal bar assns., Notre Dame Alumni Assn. Richmond, West End Catholic Men's Assn. (pres. 1967-68). Home: Route 1 Box 94-29 Manakin Sabot VA 23102 Office: 2720 Enterprise Pkwy Richmond VA 23229

OWSLEY, PERRY LYNDON, b. Pitts., Kans., Apr. 3, 1915; student Pittsburg (Kans.) State U., 1935; LL.B., Washburn U., 1938. Admitted to Kans. bar, 1938, U.S. Circuit Ct. bar, 1950; partner firm Vance, Emery & Owsley, Belleville, Kans., 1938-42, Keller, Burnett, Owsley & Wilbert, Pittsburg, 1946-48; judge City Ct. Pittsburg, 1947-51, 38th Jud. Dist. Ct., Crawford County, Kans., 1951-55; individual practice law, Pitts., 1955-71; justice Supreme Ct. State of Kans., Topeka, 1971—; instr. law Washburn U., 1974—; chmn. State Bd. Tax Appeals, 1957-65; commr. Supreme Ct., 1966-67; spl. examiner Kans. Corp. Commn., 1968-69; mem. Bd. Law Examiners, 1968-71; chmn. Melvern Dam Commn., 1968. Mem. Am., Kans. bar assns., Washburn Law Sch. Alumni Assn., Phi Alpha Delta. Recipient Meritorious Achievement award Pittsburg State Coll., 1974. Home: 2105 Knollwood Dr Topeka KS 66611 Office: Statehouse Topeka KS 66612 Tel (913) 235-9715

OXBERGER, LEO, b. July 2, 1930; B.A., Drake U., 1954, J.D., 1957; grad. Trial Judges Coll. U. Nev., 1969, 70. Pvt. practice law, 1957-69; judge Iowa Dist. Ct., 5th Jud. Dist., 1969—; instr. law enforcement classes Area 11 Community Coll.; instr. constitutional law Drake U. Coll.; chmn. Iowa Legal Services Advisory Council. Bd. dirs. Des Moines Community Playhouse, Polk County (Iowa) Legal Aid Soc., 1968-72; chmn. Polk County Republican Central Com., 1958-62. Mem. Iowa Dist. Judges Assn. (chmn. legis com.), Am. Bar Assn. (vice chmn. com. on corrections and rehab.). Home: 662-57th St Des Moines IA 50312 Office: Polk County Courthouse Des Moines IA 50309 Tel (515) 284-6318

OXFORD, HUBERT, III, b. Beaumont, Tex., Sept. 25, 1938; B.M.E., Tex. A. and M. Coll., 1960; LL.B., U. Tex., 1963. Admitted to Tex. bar, 1963, U.S. Tax Ct. bar, 1969, U.S. Ct. Claims bar, 1975, U.S. Ct. Mil. Appeals bar, 1975, U.S. Supreme Ct. bar, 1975; clk. U.S. Dist. Ct. Eastern Dist. Tex., 1965-66; asst. dist. atty. Jefferson County (Tex.), 1966; U.S. commr. Eastern Dist. Tex., 1967-70; partner firm Benchensten, McNicholas, Oxford, Radford & Johnson, Beaumont, 1963—. Fellow Tex. Bar Found.; mem. Am. Bar Assn., Maritime Law Assn., Am. Average Adjusters. Home: 2477 Long St Beaumont TX 77702 Office: 605 San Jacinto Blvd Beaumont TX 77704 Tel (713) 833-9182

OXTOBY, ROBERT BOYNTON, b. Huron, S.D., May 8, 1921; student Ill. Coll., 1939-41; B.A., Carlton Coll., 1943; J.D., Northwestern U., 1948. Admitted to Ill. Supreme Ct. bar, 1948; partner firm VanMeter, Oxtoby & Funk, Springfield, Ill., 1949—; asst. U.S. atty., 1953-58; dir. Ill. Nat. Ins. Co., 1959—, New Hampshire Ins. Co., 1961—, Ill. Nat. Bank, 1970—. Exec. com. mem. Meml. Med. Center, Springfield, 1959—. Mem. Am., Ill. State, Sangamon County bar assns. Home: 1933 Outer Park Dr Springfield IL 62704 Office: INB Center 1 Old Capitol Plaza N PO Box 2270 Springfield IL 62705 Tel (217) 528-8491

OZAN, GERALD MARTIN, b. Cleve., May 16, 1931; B.B.A., Ohio State U., 1953; LL.D., Cleve. State U., 1960. Admitted to Ohio bar, 1960; partner firm Steiner, Stern & Ozan, Cleve., 1965—. Mem. Ohio, Cleve. bar assns. Home: 5522 Harleston Dr Lyndhurst OH 44124 Office: 813-75 Public Sq Cleveland OH 44113 Tel (216) 771-1310

OZMON, NAT P., b. Davenport, Iowa, Mar. 4, 1925; student N.Y. U., 1946-48; J.D., Northwestern U., 1954. Admitted to Ill. bar, 1954, U.S. Supreme Ct. bar, 1973; partner firm Blowitz & Ozmon, Chgo., 1954-64, Horwitz, Anesi, Ozmon, Chgo., 1964-70; owner, officer firm Horwitz, Anesi, Ozmon & Assos., Ltd., Chgo., 1970—; mem. faculty Ill. Inst. for Continuing Legal Edn., 1967—, Court Practice Inst., 1973—, Nat. Inst. Trial Advocacy, 1976—; lectr. trial practice and procedure Loyola U., Chgo., 1974-75, adj. prof. law, 1975—. Mem. Dist. 50 Bd. Edn., Harvard, Ill., 1967-72, pres., 1970-71. Mem. Am., Ill., Chgo. (librarian, bd. mgrs. 1974—) bar assns., Assn. Trial Lawyers Am. (bd. govs. 1973-75), Ill. Trial Lawyers Assn. (pres. 1969-70), Soc. Trial Lawyers (dir. 1976—), Appellate Lawyers Assn. Ill. (dir. 1973), Order Coif. Diplomate Am. Bd. Profl. Liability Attys.; contbr. articles to legal jours. Office: 188 W Randolph St Chicago IL 60601 Tel (312) 372-3822

PABST, EDMUND G., b. Chgo., Apr. 22, 1916; student U. Calif. at Berkeley; LL.D., B.S.L., Northwestern U., 1940. Admitted to Ill. bar, D.C. bar; mem. firm Leonard & Leonard, Chgo., 1940-41; lawyer FTC, D.C., 1941-42; civilian lawyer U.S. Army, 1942-43; trial atty. Office Price Adminstrn., Chgo., 1946-47; atty. Combined Ins. Co. of Am., Chgo., 1947, v.p., asst. gen. counsel, 1954-59, sec., 1959-62, exec. v.p. adminstrn., 1962-76, West German Ops., 1976—; bd. dirs., 1952—, exec. com., 1958-76; officer, bd. dirs., exec. com. Combined Am. Ins. Co., 1960-76, Combined Ins. Co. of Wis., 1953-76, Combined Life Ins. Co. of N.Y., 1971-76, Combined Opportunities. Dir. Uptown Chgo. Commn., pres., 1959-61; pres. SE Evanston Assn., 1968-70; founding mem. Dewey Community Orgn. in Evanston; bd. dirs. Citizens Civic Com. of Evanston, 1959-60; mem. Evanston Zoning Bd. Appeals, 1969—; trustee Mundelein Coll. Mem. Chgo Bar Assn. (civil rights com. 1959-70, chmn. 1966-67, ins. law com. 1947-60, chmn. 1951-52), Ill. Bar Assn., Am. Bar Assn., Health Ins. Assn. of Am. (sec. bd. dirs.), U.S. C. of C. (mem. internat. ins. advisory council), ACLU (dir. Ill. div., treas. 1969). Home: 1318 Forest St Evanston IL 60201 Office: 5050 Broadway Ave Chicago IL 60640 Tel (312) 275-8000

PACE, ROSA WHITE, b. Borger, Tex., Nov. 5, 1932; B.A., William Jewell Coll., 1953; J.D., U. Tex. Austin, 1956. Admitted to Tex. bar, 1956; since practiced in Borger; partner firm White, White & White and predecessors firms, 1956-66; individual practice law, 1966—; spl. judge, Hutchinson County, Tex., 1975. Pres. Altrusa, 1961; regent DAR, 1973-75. Mem. Am., Tex., Borger (pres. 1969-70) bar assns., Borger C. of C. Home: 513 Austin St Borger TX 79007 Office: Box 325 Borger TX 79007 Tel (806) 273-2181

PACELLA, PATRICK PAUL, b. Youngstown, Ohio, Apr. 26, 1942; B.S. in Edn., Ohio State U., 1963; J.D., U. Notre Dame, 1968. Admitted to Okla. bar, 1968, Ohio bar, 1971; patent atty. Phillips Petroleum Co., Bartlesville, Okla., 1968-70, Nat. Cash Register Corp., Dayton, Ohio, 1970-72; patent dir., spl. products, Owens-Corning Fiberglas Corp., Toledo, Ohio, 1972—. Mem. Am., Toledo Patent Law Assns., Toledo, Ohio, Okla. bar assns. Patentee in field of chemistry and fiber forming. Home: 3951 Archwood Lane Toledo OH 43614 Office: Fiberglas Tower Toledo OH 43659 Tel (419) 248-8230

PACHECO, DONALD NORMAN, b. Trinidad, Colo., Mar. 31, 1935; B.S., Univ. Denver, 1961, LL.B., 1963. Admitted to Colo. bar, 1963; deputy dist. atty. Denver, 1963-65; individual practice law, 1965-71; dist. judge, Denver, 1971-73; mem. firm Pacheco & Auer, Denver, 1971—; mem. Uniform Commn. on State Laws, 1975—. Mem. Am., Colo., Denver bar assns., Colo. Trial Lawyers Assn. Home: 18 Cherrymoor Dr Englewood CO 80110 Office: 777 Capital Life Center Denver CO 80203 Tel (303) 892-5700

PACHT, ISAAC, b. Millie, Austria, May 28, 1890; LL.B., S. Lawrence U., 1911; Admitted to Calif. bar, 1913; since practiced in Los Angeles, sr. partner firm Pacht, Ross, Warne, Bernhard & Sears, 1913—; judge Calif. Superior Ct., 1931-36; pres. Calif. State Bd. Prison Dirs., 1940-50; chmn. Calif. Commn. Criminal Law and Procedure, 1947-49; mem. Calif. State Bd. Corrections, 1945-50; chmn. Citizens Advisory Com. on Selection of Los Angeles County Jail Site, 1958; chmn. Citizens Advisory Commn. Real Estate Mgmt., 1959-63. Vice-chmn. Nat. Community Relations Advisory Council, 1966-67; chmn. Community Relations Com., 1964-67; dir. Jewish Orphans Home So. Calif., 1927— (pres. 1937-48); pres., Jewish Com. for Personal Service in State Insts., 1929-35; pres. Los Angeles Jewish Community Council, 1949-51; pres. Jewish Community Found., 1962-63, also trustee.; v.p. dir. western states region Am. Friends of Hebrew U.; trustee City of Hope, 1975. Mem. Internat. Congress Jewish Lawyers and Jurists (v.p.), mem. Am., Beverly Hills Bar assns., fellow, Am. Coll. Trial Lawyers. Home: 10401 Ashton Ave Los Angeles CA 90025 Office: 1800 Ave of the Stars Los Angeles CA 90067 Tel (213) 277-1000

PACHT, JERRY, b. Los Angeles, Jan. 24, 1922; LL.B., U. So. Calif., 1949. Admitted to Calif. 1949; individual practice law, Los Angeles, 1949-65; judge Municipal Ct., Los Angeles, 1965-66; judge Superior Ct. of Calif., Los Angeles, 1966—; lect. law, U. So. Calif.; instr. Nat. Inst. for Trial Advocacy, 1973-76. Mem. Los Angeles County Bar Assn. Recipient Trial Judge of Year, Los Angeles Trial Lawyers Assn., 1973. Home: 10218 Chrysanthemum Ln Los Angeles CA 90024 Office: 111 N Hill St Los Angeles CA 90012 Tel (213) 974-5667

PACHTER, JOHN STANLEY, b. Fort Bragg, N.C., Aug. 16, 1941; B.A., Tulane U., 1963; J.D. with honors, George Washington U., 1966, LL.M., 1970. Admitted to Va. bar, 1966, D.C. bar, 1970; served to capt. JAGC, U.S. Army, 1966-70; asso. firm vom Baur, Coburn, Simmons & Turtle, Washington, 1971-74, partner, 1974—; workshop chmn. Nat. Contract Mgmt. Assn., 1976-77; professorial lectr. engring. and applied scis. George Washington U., 1974—. Vice pres., bd. dirs. Lake Braddock Community Assn., Burke, Va., 1972-74. Mem. Am., Fed. bar assns., Nat. Contract Mgmt. Assn. Author: (with George M. Coburn) Law for Engineers, 1975. Home: 5218 Olley Ln Burke VA 22015 Office: vom Baur Coburn et al 1700 K St NW Washington DC 20006 Tel (202) 833-1420

PACKLER, ROY CARL, b. Milw., June 20, 1915; J.D., Marquette U., 1939. Admitted to Wis. bar, 1939, Fed. Ter. Hawaii, 1944; individual practice law, Milw., 1939—; served JAC Center Pacific Area 1945-46. Mem. Milw., Wis., Am. bar assns., Am. Arbitration Assn., Am., Wis. acads. trial lawyers. Office: 6616 W Bluemound Rd Milwaukee WI 53213 Tel (414) 453-5180

PACKMAN, BRUCE BARTON, b. St. Louis, Aug. 27, 1943; B.B.A. magna cum laude, U. Miami, Coral Gables, Fla., 1965, M.B.A., 1966; J.D., Washington U., St. Louis, 1969. Admitted to Fla. bar, 1970; sr. tax accountant Haskins & Sells, C.P.A's., Miami, 1969-71; individual practice law, Miami, 1971-74; partner firm Packman, Engles & Neuwahl, Miami, 1974-76, shareholder Packman & Neuwahl, P.A., 1977—. Instr. religious sch., trustee Congregation Bet Breira, Miami; active South Dade Leadership Greater Miami Jewish Fedn. Mem. Fla. Inst. C.P.A's., Fla. (vice chmn. tax sect. com. on taxation non-resident aliens and fgn. corps.), Am. bar assns., Am. Assn. Attys.-C.P.A's., Greater Miami Tax Inst. Contbr. articles to legal publs. Office: 1401 Brickell Ave Miami FL 33130 Tel (305) 358-5220

PADDOCK, JAMES WILLIAM, b. Kansas City, Mo., Aug. 15, 1928; A.B., U. Kans., 1951, J.D., 1956. Admitted to Kans. bar, 1956, U.S. Dist. Ct. bar, 1956; since practiced in Lawrence, Kans., judge Municipal Ct., 1960-63; partner firm Oyler & Paddock, 1965-72; judge Dist. Ct., 7th Jud. Dist. Kans., 1973—; lectr. U. Kans., 1959-61, 73-76. Pres., Bd. of Edn., Lawrence, 1968-70. Mem. Kans. Bar Assn., Am. Judicature Soc., Kans. Dist. Judges' Assn. Office: Judicial Bldg Lawrence KS 66044 Tel (913) 843-5722

PADGETT, CARROLL DORN, JR., b. Columbus, Ga., Oct. 16, 1947; A.B., U. Ga., 1969; J.D., U. S.C., 1972. Admitted to S.C. bar, 1972; individual practice law, Loris, S.C., 1972—; dir. CD. Mem. Am., Horry County (S.C.) bar assns., Am. Trial Lawyers Assn. Home: Route 4 PO Box 33 Loris SC 29569 Office: PO Box 792 4104 Main St Loris SC 29569 Tel (803) 357-6186 and 357-6187

PADILLA, JOSEPH CORDOVA, b. Morenci, Ariz., Oct. 6, 1902; grad. Clifton (Ariz.) High Sch., 1921. Mine cost accountant, asst. metallurgist Phelps Dodge Corp., Morenci, Ariz., 1923-32; comptroller Alianza Hispano-Americana Life Ins. Co., Tucson, 1933-35; admitted to Ariz. bar, 1936; law librarian, Spanish ct. interpreter Pima County Superior Ct., Tucson, 1936-41; head investigator GAO, San Juan, P.R., Terminal Island, Calif., 1942-43; counsel, chief title officer Tucson Title Ins. Co., 1944-66, v.p., treas., dir., 1951-66; individual part-time practice law, Tucson, 1936-42, full-time, 1966—. Dir. Ariz. Lung Assn., Tucson, 1944-76, pres., 1972-73. Mem. Ariz. Bar Assn., Land Title Assn. Ariz. (state pres. 1961-62). Home and Office: 1944 E 5th St Tucson AZ 85719 Tel (602) 623-2368

PADRICK, COMER WOODWARD, JR., b. Atlanta, Nov. 18, 1926; A.B., Emory U., 1950, J.D., 1953. Admitted to Ga. bar, 1952; asso. firm Jones, Williams, Dorsey & Kane, Atlanta, 1955-59, firm Crenshaw, Hansell, Ware, Brandon & Dorsey, Atlanta, 1959-61; partner firm Hansell, Post, Brandon & Dorsey, Atlanta, 1961—. Mem. Atlanta, Ga., Am. bar assns., Lawyers Club Atlanta, Old War Horse Lawyers Club, Am. Judicature Soc., Am. Coll. Mortgage Attys., Atlanta, DeKalb County real estate bds., Nat., Ga., Atlanta mortgage bankers assns., Nat. Home Builders Assn., Phi Beta Kappa, Phi Delta Phi, Omicron Delta Kappa. Author: Padrick on RESPA & X, 1975; pamphlets in field. Home: 3999 Beechwood Dr NW Atlanta GA 30327 Office: 3300 First Nat Bank Tower Atlanta GA 30303 Tel (404) 581-8100

PADWAY, ROBERT ALAN, b. Milw., Oct. 4, 1945; A.B., Harvard, 1967; J.D., U. Calif., Berkeley, 1970. Admitted to Calif. bar, 1970; atty. Bank Am. Corp., San Francisco, 1970-75, counsel, 1975-76, sr. counsel, 1976—. Mem. Am., Calif., San Francisco bar assns. Office: 555 California St 8th Floor San Francisco CA 94137 Tel (415) 622-6572

PAGE, DONALD ALBERT, lawyer; b. Thomaston, Ga., Oct. 13, 1930; B.S., U. Ga., 1954, LL.B., 1957, J.D., 1969. Admitted to Ga. bar, 1959; asso. law firm Parker and Daniel, Atlanta, 1959-60; pvt. practice law, Thomaston, Ga., 1960-68, 69—; partner law firm Caldwell, Bridges and Page, Thomaston, Ga., 1968-69. State rep. Gen. Assembly of Ga., 1964-65; spl. dep. ins. commr., 1970-74; spl. asst. atty. gen., Ga., 1975-77. Mem. bd. dirs. Thomaston Community Theater. Mem. Thomaston, Griffin Circuit, Ga. bar assns. Home: Mauldin Rd Thomaston GA 30286 Office: 308 S Center St Thomaston GA 30286

PAGE, JOSEPH FRENCH, III, b. Mpls., Feb. 15, 1942; A.B., Princeton, 1964; J.D., U. Mich., 1967. Admitted to Mich. bar 1968; fed. estate and gift tax examiner Detroit Dist. Office, 1967-68; served with JAGC, USAF, 1968-73; partner firm Long, Preston, Kinnaird & Avant, Detroit, 1973—. Mem. Am., Detroit bar assns., State Bar of Mich., Princeton Club of Mich. (sec. 1976-77, chmn. Alumni Schs. com. 1973). Home: 3157 Oakhill Dr Troy MI 48084 Office: 4300 City National Bank Bldg Detroit MI 48226 Tel (313) 965-9550

PAGE, MELVIN ERNEST, JR., b. Ann Arbor, Mich., June 11, 1918; B.S., Babson Inst. Bus. Adminstrn., 1948; J.D., Stetson U., 1957. Admitted to Fla. bar, 1957; individual practice law, St. Petersburg, Fla., 1957—; mayor City of Treasure Island (Fla.), 1960-62. Mem. St. Petersburg, Fla., Am. bar assns. Home: 2306 Sunset Way Saint Petersburg FL 33706 Office: 915 Tyrone Blvd N Saint Petersburg FL 33710 Tel (813) 345-1027

PAGELS, WILLIAM HERMAN, b. Milw., Mar. 12, 1930; B.S., U. Wis., 1952; J.D., 1956. Admitted to Wis. bar, 1956; mem. firm Ebert & Ebert, Milw., 1957—; village atty. Village of Whitefish Bay, Wis., 1974—. Trustee North Shore Found., 1966-67, Village of Whitefish Bay, 1966-74; chmn. North Shore Water Commn., 1970-71. Mem. Wis., Milw. bar assns., Indsl. Relations Assn. Wis. Home: 5756 N Kent Ave Milwaukee WI 53217 Office: 230 W Wells St Milwaukee WI 53203 Tel (414) 276-5100

PAGOREK, STANLEY WINFRED, b. Chgo., Apr. 19, 1947; student St. Joseph Coll., East Chgo., Ind., 1965-68; B.S. in Polit. Sci., DePaul U., 1972, J.D., 1972. Admitted to Ill. bar, 1972; individual practice law, Chgo., 1972—. Village prosecutor Village of Burnham, Ill. Mem. Am., Chgo., S. Chgo., S. Suburban bar assns., Lex Legio. Office: 717 Burnham Ave Calumet City IL 60409 Tel (312) 862-8900

PAINTER, DONALD LEE, b. Kimball, Nebr., Oct. 12, 1943; B.A., U. Wyo., 1966, J.D., 1969. Admitted to Wyo. bar, 1969; spl. asst. atty. gen. State of Wyo., Cheyenne, 1969-73; dep. county atty. Natrona County (Wyo.), 1973-75; partner firm Burk & Painter, Casper, Wyo., 1975—. Bd. dirs. Meadowlark Montessori Sch., Casper, 1975-76. Mem. Natrona County, Wyo. State bar assns., Wyo. Trial Lawyers Assn. Recipient Best Oral Argument award region 13 Nat. Moot Ct. Competition, 1969. Home: 710 E 16th St Casper WY 82601 Office: Suite A Wyoming Bldg Casper WY 82601 Tel (307) 265-6500

PAINTER, JERRY LEE, b. Great Falls, Mont., Feb. 24, 1949; B.S. in Psychology, U. Puget Sound, 1971; J.D., U. Mont., 1974. Admitted to Mont. bar, 1974; law clk. Mont. Supreme Ct., 1974-75; staff atty. Mont. Legis. Council, Helena, 1975-76, Mont. Bd. Personnel Appeals, Helena, 1976—. Mem. Am., Mont. bar assns. Office: 1417 Helena Ave Helena MT 59601 Tel (406) 449-3472

PAINTER, SAMUEL FRANKLIN, b. Lynchburg, Va., Oct. 31, 1946; B.A., U. Va., 1969; J.D., Washington and Lee U., 1972. Admitted to S.C. bar, 1972; asso. firm Nexsen, Pruet, Jacobs and Pollard, Columbia, S.C., 1972—. Mem. Richland County, Lexington County bar assns., S.C. Def. Lawyers Assn., So. Assn. Workmen's Compensation Adminstrs. (asso.), S.C. Self-Insurers Assn. (dir.). Home: 232 Woodwinds West Dr Columbia SC 29210 Office: 12th Floor 1st Nat Bank Bldg Columbia SC 29201 Tel (803) 771-8900

PAINTIN, FRANCIS ARTHUR, b. Cleve., Feb. 9, 1929; B.S. in Chem. Engring., Case Inst. Tech., 1951; J.D. with honors, George Wash. U., 1961. Admitted to Ohio bar, 1961, D.C. bar, 1962, Del. bar, 1969, U.S. Supreme Ct. bar, 1967; asso. firm Oberlin, Maky & Donnelly, Cleve., 1961-62; patent atty. legal dept. E.I. DuPont DeNemours & Co., Wilmington, Del., 1962-70, sr. patent atty., 1970—; lectr. Del. Law Sch. Widener Coll., Wilmington, 1975—. Mem. Am., Del. bar assns., Order of Coif. Home: 101 E Pembrey Dr Wilmington DE 19803 Office: Legal Dept EI DuPont DeNemours & Company Wilmington DE 19898 Tel (302) 774-2575

PAISNER, MICHAEL STEPHEN, b. Boston, Feb. 5, 1942; B.S., Northeastern U., 1966, A.S., 1967; J.D., Suffolk Law Sch., 1971. Admitted to Mass. bar, 1973; chem. buyer W.R. Grace, Cambridge, Mass., 1966-70; sr. buyer The Gillette Co., Boston, 1970-77; pres. M.S. Paisner, Inc., Needham, Mass., 1977—; lectr. bus. adminstrn. Northeastern U., 1976-77. Mem. Mass., Am. bar assns., Am. Chem. Soc. Home: 77 Leighton Rd Hyde Park MA 02136 Office: 19 Brook Rd Needham Heights MA 02194 Tel (617) 449-3466

PALACIOS, OSCAR, b. Pharr, Tex., Feb. 4, 1945; B.A., U. Tex., Austin, 1969, J.D., 1971. Admitted to Tex. bar, 1972; hearings examiner Tex. Water Quality Bd., 1972-73; individual practice law, Pharr, 1974-. Mem. State Bar Tex., Hidalgo County (Tex.) Bar Assn., Tex. Criminal Def. Lawyers Assn. Home: 1207 W Texas St San Juan TX 78589 Office: 301 N Cage St Pharr TX 78577 Tel (512) 787-9929

PALAN, PERRY, b. St. Louis, Apr. 8, 1943; B.S.E.E., Washington U., 1965; J.D., George Washington U., 1970. Admitted to Va. bar, 1970, D.C. bar, 1972; since practiced in Washington, atty. Dept. Navy, 1971; asso. firm Leitner, Palan & Martin (and predecessors), 1972-75, partner, 1976; examiner U.S. Patent & Trademark Office, 1967-71. Home: 1204 Princeton Pl Rockville MD 20850 Office: 1055 Thomas Jefferson St NW Washington DC 20007 Tel (202) 337-5900

PALERMO, ANTHONY ROBERT, b. Rochester, N.Y., Sept. 30, 1929; B.A., U. Mich., 1951; J.D., Georgetown U., 1956. Admitted to D.C. bar, 1956, N.Y. State bar, 1957, U.S. Ct. Appeals for 2d Circuit bar, 1960, U.S. Supreme Ct. bar, 1961; trial atty. U.S. Dept. Justice, Washington, 1956-58; asst. U.S. Atty. So. Dist. N.Y., N.Y.C., 1958-60; asst. U.S. Atty. Western Dist. N.Y., Rochester, 1960-61; partner firm Brennan, Centner, Palermo & Blauvelt, Rochester, 1961—; mem. character and fitness com. appellate div. N.Y. State 4th Jud. Dept. Bd. dirs. Catholic Family Center, Diocese of Rochester, 1966-72, pres., 1969-70; bd. dirs. St. Ann's Home, Rochester, 1974—, John F. Wegman Found., 1972—. Fellow Am. Coll. Trial Lawyers, Am. Bar Found; mem. Monroe County (pres. 1973), N.Y. State (ho. dels. 1973-75, 77—), Am. bar assns., Am. Judicature Soc. (dir. 1974—). Editor: Georgetown Law Jour., 1956. Home: 38 Huntington Meadow Rochester NY 14625 Office: 500 Reynolds Arcade Bldg Rochester NY 14614 Tel (716) 546-6474

PALEY, PIERCE, b. N.Y.C., Aug. 25, 1937; B.A., N.Y. U., 1957, LL.B., 1960. Admitted to N.Y. bar, 1960; individual practice law, N.Y.C., 1960—; bd. dirs. and gen. counsel Manhood Found., 1968—. Pres., Winfield Assn., Harrison, N.Y., 1974-76; bd. dirs. Harrison Day Center, Inc., 1975-76; chmn. Harrison chpt. Am. Cancer Soc., 1976—. Mem. N.Y. State Bar Assn., N.Y. State Assn. Trial Lawyers, Pan-Am. Soc. Author: Move Over, Mr. Edison, 1958; contbr. articles to legal jours. Office: 711 Third Ave New York City NY 10017 Tel (212) MU8-6500

PALIK, JAMES NELSEN, b. New Orleans, May 18, 1941; student Dartmouth Coll., 1959-63; B.S., U. Okla., 1964; J.D., U. Tulsa, 1968. Admitted to Okla. bar, 1968, N.Y. bar, 1969, U.S. Patent Office bar, 1970; asso. patent counsel Norwich Pharmacal Co. (N.Y.), 1968-70; mem. firm Ladas, Parry, von Gehr, Goldsmith & Deschamps, N.Y.C., 1970—, partner, 1976—. Mem. Am., Okla. bar assns., Am., N.Y. Patent law assns. Office: 10 Columbus Circle New York City NY 10019 Tel (212) 245-2600

PALLOT, WILLIAM LOUIS, b. Springfield, Mass., Nov. 9, 1912; LL.B., Cumberland U., 1939. Admitted to Fla. bar, 1940; practiced in Miami, Fla., 1940—, sr. partner firm Pallot, Stern, Proby & Adkins, 1948-76; of counsel firm Snyder, Young, Stern, Barrett & Tanenbaum, 1976—; chmn. Miami Nat. Bank, 1959-63; pres. Internat. Bank Miami, 1963-68, chmn., 1968-74, hon. chmn., 1974—; partner Pallot Farms, Bedford County, Tenn., 1973—; dir. Sharon Steel Corp., Pa. Engring Corp., Southeastern Pub. Service Corp., Wilson Bros. Co., NVF Co., DWG Corp., Barrington Industries, Inc., judge Municipal Ct. Coral Gables (Fla.), 1948-52; city atty. Miami and North Miami (Fla.), 1955-59. Chmn. Pub. Works Authority Miami, 1948-58, Miami Parking Authority, 1951-58; vice chmn. Dade County Planning Adv. Bd., 1961-65; exec. com. Met. Miami Municipal Bd., 1953-55, Dade County Charter Bd., 1955-57; citizens adv. bd. Fla. Meml. Coll., Biscayne Coll. Mem. Miami; chmn. Fla. regional bd. Anti-Defamation League, 1965-67; pres. Internat. Center of Fla., 1972; mem. regional export expansion council U.S. Dept. Commerce, 1971—; pres. United Way, Miami, 1973; chmn. Dade County Criminal Justice Coordinating Council, 1972—; pres. Greater Miami Bd. Internat. Trade, 1971. Mem. Am., Fla., Dade County (pres. 1965) bankers assns., Am., Fla., Dade County bar assns., Am. Inst. Banking, AIM (pres.'s council), Econ. Soc. S. Fla. (pres. 1973). Home: 9629 SW 20th Terr Miami FL 33165 Office: Inter Nat Bank Bldg Miami FL 33135 Tel (305) 547-4150

PALMBERG, EARL LAVERNE, b. Paxton, Ill., Dec. 4, 1918; B.S., U. Ill., 1941, J.D., LL.D., 1949. Admitted to Ill. bar, 1949, U.S. Supreme Ct. bar, 1954, U.S. Ct. Mil. Appeals bar, 1954; atty. U. Ill., Urbana, 1949—; comdr. Legal Flight, 9650th Air Res. Squadron, 1952-58. Mem. Champaign County, Ill. State bar assns., Nat. Assn. Coll. and Univ. Attys. (charter, chmn. constn. and by-laws com. 1961-66), Res. Officers Assn. (v.p. 1972-73), Air Force Assn. (v.p. 1965). Home: 1401 S Grove St Urbana IL 61801 Office: 258 Adminstrn Bldg Univ Ill Urbana IL 61801 Tel (217) 333-0561

PALMER, ALFRED ROINE, b. Queens, N.Y., Mar. 23, 1930; A.B., U. Miami, 1951, J.D., 1953. Admitted to Fla. bar, 1953; individual practice law, Miami, 1953—. Mem. Am., Fla., Dade County, S. Miami bar assns. Home: 7850 SW 68th Terr Miami FL 33143 Office: 7600 Red Rd Suite 217 South Miami FL 33143

PALMER, ARTHUR EDWARD, b. Emporia, Kans., Nov. 18, 1938; B.B.A., Washburn U., 1960, J.D., 1963. Admitted to Kans. bar, 1963; asst. atty. gen. State of Kans., Topeka, 1963-64; partner firm Goodell, Casey, Briman & Cogswell, Topeka, 1964—; dir. Fairlawn Plaza State Bank, Topeka. Mem. Am., Kans., Topeka bar assns. Home: 3042 Mulvane St Topeka KS 66611 Office: 215 E 8th St Topeka KS 66611 Tel (913) 233-0543

PALMER, BRUCE ALEXANDER, b. Oskaloosa, Iowa, July 11, 1927; A.B., William Penn Coll., 1949; J.D., U. Iowa, 1954. Admitted to Iowa bar, 1954, U.S. Dist. Ct. So. Dist. Iowa bar, 1966; partner firm Palmer & Palmer, Oskaloosa, 1954-63; partner firm Palmer and Stream, Oskaloosa, 1967-75; individual practice law, Oskaloosa, 1963-67, 75—; appeal agt. Selective Service, 1954-75. Pres. Mahaska County Humane Soc., 1973—. Mem. Am., Iowa, Dist. 8A, Mahaska County bar assns., Am. Judicature Soc., Delta Theta Phi. Recipient Nathan Burken Meml. award, 1954. Home: 411 S 1st St Oskaloosa IA 52577 Office: 111 1/2 High Ave E Oskaloosa IA 52577 Tel (515) 673-7589

PALMER, DOUGLAS SHAW, b. Cleve., May 16, 1921; B.A., Yale, 1942, LL.B., 1951. Admitted to N.Y. State bar, 1952, Wash. State bar, 1954; asso. firm Winthrop, Stimson, Putnam & Roberts, N.Y.C., 1951-53; asso. firm Wright, Innis, Simon & Todd, Seattle, 1954-56, partner, 1956-69; partner firm Davis, Wright, Todd, Riese & Jones, Seattle, 1969-71; individual practice law, Seattle, 1971—. Counsel Seattle Urban League, 1965-75; trustee Seattle-King County Legal Aid Bur., 1967-69; chmn. Citizens Adv. Com. Licensing and Consumer Affairs, 1971-72. Mem. Am., Wash. State bar assns. Contbr. articles to legal jours. Home: 1711 Evergreen Pl Seattle WA 98122 Office: 1218 3d Ave Suite 2200 Seattle WA 98101 Tel (206) 622-7055

PALMER, GEORGE ELLIS, b. Washington, Ind., Feb. 3, 1908; A.B., U. Mich., 1930, J.D., 1932; LL.M., Columbia, 1940. Admitted to Ind. bar, 1932; individual practice law, Indpls., 1932-39; atty., asso. gen. counsel OPA, Washington, 1942-45; asst. prof. law U. Kans., 1941-45, asso. prof. law, 1945-46; asso. prof. law U. Mich., 1946-51, prof. 1951—. Author: Cases on Trusts and Succession, 1960, 2d edit., 1968; Cases on Restitution, 1958, 2d edit., 1969; Mistake and Unjust Enrichment, 1962. Home: 2996 Provincial Dr Ann Arbor MI 48104 Office: Legal Research Bldg Ann Arbor MI 48109 Tel (313) 764-9337

PALMER, HARVARD, b. Carlinville, Ill., Sept. 17, 1914; B.A., U. Wash., 1938, J.D., 1940. Admitted to Wash. bar, 1940; individual practice law, Seattle, 1940-48; v.p. Seattle First Nat. Bank, 1948-55, head trust div., 1955-71, ret., 1971; individual practice law, Seattle, 1971—. Mem. Wash., King County, Seattle bar assns., Seattle Assn. Trust Men (past pres.), Wash. State Assn. Corp. Fiduciaries (past pres.), Estate Planning Council Seattle (past pres.), Am. Bankers Assn. (exec. com. trust div., 1967-70). Home: 9009 NW View Ave Seattle WA 98177 Office: 200 Securities Bldg Seattle WA 98101 Tel (206) 623-7500

PALMER, HAZEL, b. Climax Springs, Mo., Aug. 11, 1903; LL.B., Nat. U., 1932. Admitted to Mo. bar, 1932, practiced in Sedalia, Mo., 1932-73; asst. pros. atty. Pettis County (Mo.), 1942-55; magistrate judge, Sedalia, 1973—. Mem. adv. bd. SSS, 1942-73, Citizen's Adv. Council on Status of Woman, 1969-77; Republican nominee for U.S. senator Mo., 1958; del. Rep. Nat. Conv., 1960, 64; mem. adv. com. bd. Women's Med. Coll. Pa.; pres. Bus. and Profl. Women's Found., 1956-58. Mem. Mo., Sedalia (past pres.) bar assns., Women's Bar Assn. Mo., Nat. Assn. Women Lawyers, Bus. and Profl. Women's Club (pres. nat. fedn. 1956-58), Kappa Beta Pi, Beta Sigma Phi (internat. hon.), Nat. Lawyers Club. Named hon. Ky. Co;. Home: 901 S Vermont St Sedalia MO 65301 Office: Court House Sedalia MO 65301 Tel (816) 826-8816

PALMER, JERRY RICHARD, b. Jefferson City, Mo., Aug. 22, 1940; B.A., U. Kans., 1962, J.D., 1966. Admitted to Kans. bar, 1966; since practiced in Topeka, partner firm Fisher Patterson Sayler & Smith, 1966-70; asso. firm Fisher & Benfer, 1970-72; individual practice law, 1973-76; partner firm Stumbo, Stumbo, Palmer, McCallister & Buening, Topeka, 1977—; adj. asst. prof. law Washburn U., 1975—; pres. Topeka Legal Aid Soc., 1975. Mem. Am., Kans., Topeka bar assns., Am., Kans. (pres. 1977—) trial lawyers assns. Contbr. articles to legal jours. Home: 2700 Burlingame Rd Topeka KS 66611 Office: 2222 W 29th St Topeka KS 66611 Tel (913) 267-3410

PALMER, JOHN COWDEN, JR., b. Cedar Rapids, Iowa, July 5, 1934; B.A., Dartmouth Coll., 1956; J.D., Georgetown U., 1964. Admitted to Ill. bar, 1964; adminstrv. position with comptroller So. Ry., Washington, 1960-63; gen. atty. Santa Fe Ry., Chgo., 1964—. Mem. Conf. R.R. Freight Loss and Damage Counsel, Ill. Def. Council, Nat. Assn. R.R. Trial Counsel. Home: 423A W Briar Pl Chicago IL 60657 Office: 80 E Jackson Blvd Chicago IL 60604 Tel (312) 427-4900

PALMER, JOHN FRANCIS, b. Chester, Pa., Apr. 4, 1928; B.A., Pa. State U., 1951; LL.B., Georgetown U., 1956. Admitted to U.S. Supreme Ct. bar, 1961, Va. bar, 1956, Del. bar, 1968, Ill. bar, 1970; trial atty. U.S. Dept. Justice, Washington, 1957-62; tax counsel E.I. du Pont de Nemours & Co., Wilmington, De., 1962-69, IC Industries, Inc., Chgo., 1969—. Mem. Am., Va., Chgo. bar assns., Fed. Bar Assn. (pres. Del. chpt. 1967-68), Chgo. Assn. of Commerce and Industry, Chgo. Tax Club, Tax Execs. Inst., Execs. Club Chgo. Office: 111 E Wacker Dr Chicago IL 60601 Tel (312) 565-3062

PALMER, JOHN LEWIS, b. Milw., Nov. 22, 1921; B.A., Beloit (Wis.) Coll., 1947; J.D., U. Wis., 1949. Admitted to Wis. bar, 1949; asso. firm Whyte & Hirschboeck, Milw., 1949-56, partner, 1956-71; v.p., gen. counsel, sec. Bradley Corp., Menomonee Falls, Wis., 1971-73, exec. v.p., 1973—, also dir.; dir. Alpha Cellulose Corp., Fed.-Huber Corp., Pelton Casteel, Inc., KSM Industries, Inc., Kieckhefer Assos., Inc., Eilcar Corp. Mem. adv. com. Fox Point Bayside Sch. Dist., 1956-57; alumni trustee Beloit Coll., 1972-75. Mem. Am., Wis., Milw. bar assns., State Bar Wis. (chmn. taxation sect. 1962-63), Phi Beta Kappa, Order of Coif. Contbr. articles to legal jours.; exec. editor Wis. Law Rev., 1948-49. Home: 780 E Ravine Ln Milwaukee WI 53217 also 7939 N Tuscany Dr Tucson AZ 85704 Office: W142 N9101 Fountain Blvd Menomonee Falls WI 53051 Tel (414) 251-6000

PALMER, ORAN WALKER, b. Los Angeles, Dec. 24, 1905; student Occidental Coll., 1924-27; A.B., U. So. Calif., 1929, LL.B., 1930. Admitted to Calif. bar, 1930, U.S. Supreme Ct. bar, 1957; individual practice law, Los Angeles, 1930-31, Delano, Calif., 1931-35, Bakersfield, Calif., 1935—; dep. dist. atty. Kern County (Calif.), 1935-40, county counsel, 1941-44; partner firm Harvey Johnston Baker & Palmer, Bakersfield, 1944-66, Palmer Anderson & Strong, Bakersfield, 1966-70, Palmer & Eckert, Bakersfield, 1971-72, Palmer & Palmer, Bakersfield, 1972-73; individual practice law, Bakersfield, 1973—; city atty. Delano, 1931-35. Appeal officer SSS bd., 1952-72. Mem. Am., Calif., Kern County (past pres.) bar assns. Home: 5512 Sundale Ave Bakersfield CA 93309 Office: 110 New Stine Rd Suite B Bakersfield CA 93309 Tel (805) 831-5200

PALMER, ROBERT SIDNEY, b. Denver, Feb. 8, 1902; A.B., Colo. U., 1925, LL.B., 1927, also J.D. Admitted to Colo. bar, 1928; individual practice law; mem. Colo. Legislature, 1933; exec. dir. Colo. Mining Indsl. Bd., 1933-69, Colo. Mineral Resources Bd., 1954-61, Colo. Mining Assn.; gov. Am. Mining Congress, 1945-68; real estate broker, 1969-76; mem. Colo. Gov's. Western Mineral Advisory Council. Mem. Am. (council sect. mineral law), Colo. (council sect. mineral law 1968-69), Denver bar assns., Colo. Bd. Realtors, Mineral Law Found. Contbr. articles to profl. publs. Home: 2020 S Alton Ct Denver CO 80231 Office: 9221 E Jewell Circle Denver CO 80231 Tel (303) 755-1762

PALMER, STEPHEN, b. Lexington, Ky., Apr. 17, 1940; A.B.J., U. Ky., 1962, LL.B., 1965. Admitted to Ky. bar, 1965, U.S. Supreme Ct. bar, 1971; individual practice law, Lexington, 1965—. Pres., Manchester Center, 1972; co-leader Forum, 1975; sec. Big Bros. 1971. Mem. Ky., Fayette County bar assns. Chief editorial writer, polit. columnist The Lexington Leader, 1966-73. Home: 229 McDowell Rd Lexington KY 40502 Office: 804 Security Trust Bldg Lexington KY 40507 Tel (606) 233-0551

PALMER, WILLIAM PRESTON, b. Fall River, Mass., Apr. 29, 1897; A.B., Harvard, 1918, LL.B., 1920. Admitted to N.Y. bar, 1921, Dist. Columbia bar, 1947, U.S. Supreme Ct. bar, 1952; mem. firm Dewey, Ballantine, Bushby, Palmer & Wood and predecessor firms, N.Y.C., 1925—. Mem. N.Y. State, Am. Bar Assns., Bar Assn. City N.Y., N.Y. County Lawyers Assn., Am. Law Inst. Office: 140 Broadway New York City NY 10005

PALMESI, RALPH L., b. Carmal, N.Y., June 16, 1941; B.A., U. Conn., 1963; J.D., Georgetown U., 1966. Admitted to Conn. bar, 1966; legislative asst. to Congressman Monagan, 1966-67; asso. firm Saltman, Weiss, Weinstein & Elson, 1967-68; partner firm DePiano, Petrucelli & Palmesi, Bridgeport, Conn., 1968—; town atty. town Trumbull, Conn., 1973—. Mem. Trumbull Economic Devel. Commn., 1970-73. Mem. Conn., Bridgeport, Am. bar assns., Assn. Trial Lawyers. Home: 4296 Madison Ave Trumbull CT 06611 Office: 56 Lyon Terrace St Bridgeport CT 06604 Tel (203) 335-3187

PALMETER, NEAL DAVID, b. Elmira, N.Y., Jan. 29, 1938; B.A., Syracuse U., 1960; J.D., U. Chgo., 1963. Admitted to N.Y. State bar, 1963, U.S. Supreme Ct. bar, 1968, Washington bar, 1969; trial atty. civil div., Dept. Justice, 1966-69; asso. firm Daniels & Hovlihan and predecessors, Washington, 1969-73, partner, 1973—. Mem. Am., N.Y. State, Washington, Fed. bar assns., Am. Soc. Legal History, Am. Soc. Internat. Law. Office: 1819 H St NW Washington DC 20006 Tel (202) 293-3340

PALMIER, JOSEPH PETER, b. Brookville, Pa., July 10, 1937; A.B., Franklin and Marshall Coll., 1959; J.D., Willamette U., 1968. Admitted to Alaska bar, 1968; spl. agt. Conn. Mut. Life Ins. Co., 1959; probation parole officer State of Alaska, 1962, chmn. prisoner classification com., 1963-65; mem. faculty U. Calif. Sch. of Criminology, 1966; asst. dist. atty. State of Alaska, 1968-69; partner firm Savage, Erwin, Curran, Johnson and Palmier, Anchorage, 1969; individual practice law, Anchorage, 1969—; mem. faculty U. Alaska, 1970-73. Mem. Assn. Trial Lawyers Am., Am. Judicature Soc., Am., Alaska, Anchorage bar assns., Phi Delta Phi. Office: 731 I St Suite 108 Anchorage AK 99501 Tel (907) 279-8522

PALMIERI, EDMUND LOUIS, b. N.Y.C., May 14, 1907; A.B., Columbia U., 1926, LL.B., 1929. Admitted to N.Y. State bar, 1930; law sec. to Hon. Charles Evans Hughes at Permanent Ct. Internat. Justice, The Hague, 1929; since practiced in N.Y.C., asso. firm Hughes, Schurman & Dwight, 1929-31; asst. U.S. atty., 1931-34; asst. corp. counsel City of N.Y., 1934-37; law sec. to Mayor La Guardia, 1937-40; city magistrate, 1940-43; individual practice law, 1945-53; judge U.S. Dist. Ct., So. Dist. N.Y., 1954—; cons. Rockefeller Found., 1949. Mem. Am. Justinian Soc. Jurists, N.Y.C. Bar Assn., Phi Beta Kappa. Office: US Court House 40 Centre St New York City NY 10007 Tel (212) 791-0963

PALMIERI, JOHN ANTHONY, b. Aliquippa, Pa., June 13, 1933; B.A., Duquesne U., Pitts., 1955; LL.B., Georgetown U., 1957. Admitted to Pa. bar, 1958; legal officer Beaver County (Pa.) Juvenile Ct., 1962-64; asst. dist. atty., chief of juvenile affairs Beaver County Juvenile Affairs Dept., Aliquippa, 1964—; trial counsel, partner firm Duplaga, Tocci & Palmieri, Aliquippa, 1960—; solicitor Center Twp. Water Authority, 1960—, Center Area Sch. Dist., 1972—. Bd. dirs. Beaver County Heart Assn., United Fund, Mem. Beaver County Bar Assn., Am., Pa. (former dir. Western Pa. chpt.) trial lawyers assns. Author: Pennsylvania Juvenile Law, 1977. Office: Duplaga Tocci & Palmieri 23d and Davidson Sts Aliquippa PA 15001 Tel (412) 375-6683

PALMORE, JOHN STANLEY, JR., b. Ancon, C.Z., Aug. 6, 1917; student Western Ky. U., 1934-36; LL.B., U. Louisville, 1939. Admitted to Ky. bar, 1938; asso. firm Worsham & King, Henderson, Ky., 1939, King & Flournoy, Henderson, 1939-41; partner firm Hunt & Palmore, Henderson, 1947; individual practice law, Henderson, 1947-55; partner firm Palmore & Mitchell, Henderson, 1955-59; judge Ky. Ct. of Appeals and Supreme Ct., Frankfort, 1959—; atty. City Henderson, 1953-55, City Sebree, 1953-59, Commonwealth Ky., 5th Jud. Dist., Henderson, 1955-59. Mem. Ky. Bar Assn. Author: Palmore's Instructions to Juries. Home: Rural Route 9 Georgetown Rd Frankfort KY 40601 Office: Room 224 State Capitol Frankfort KY 40601 Tel (502) 564-6755

PALMQUIST, JAMES BENJAMIN, III, b. Medina, Ohio, Aug. 6, 1951; B.A., Baldwin-Wallace Coll., 1973; J.D., U. Louisville, 1975; postgrad. Case Western Res. U., 1975. Admitted to Ohio bar, 1976, U.S. Dist. Ct. bar No. Dist. Ohio, 1976; asso. firm Palmquist & Courtney, Medina, 1975-76; partner firm Palmquist & Palmquist, Medina, 1977—. Mem. Am., Ohio, Medina County bar assns., Am., Ohio trial lawyers assns. Home: 600 Canterbury Ln Medina OH 44256 Office: 5 Public Sq Medina OH 44256 Tel (216) 725-4935

PALUMBO, ANTHONY JOHN, b. Neptune, N.J., Apr. 24, 1946; B.S. in Accounting, Fairfield U., 1968; J.D. cum laude, U. Notre Dame, 1973. Admitted to Ariz. bar, 1973; asso. firm Jennings, Strouss & Salmon, Phoenix, 1973-77, Langerman, Begarn, Lewis, Leonard and Marks, 1977. Pres., bd. dirs. Thunderbird Sr. Little League, Phoenix, 1974, 75. Mem. Am. (sect. ins. negligence and compensation law automobile law com. 1976—), Ariz., Maricopa County bar assns., State Bar Ariz. (civil practice and procedure com. 1976—), Phoenix

Area Def. Council. Home: 12446 N Columbine Dr Phoenix AZ 85029 Office: 111 W Monroe St Phoenix AZ 85003

PANCAKE, DAVID MATTHEW, b. Huntington, W.Va., May 4, 1943; A.B., Marshall U., 1967; J.D., W.Va. U., 1971. Admitted to W.Va. bar, 1971; asso. firm Vinson, Meek & White, Huntington, 1971-72; partner firm Nelson, Hyer & Pancake, Huntington, 1972—. Bd. dirs. Friends of Cabell County (Fla.) Library, Huntington, Huntington YWCA. Mem. W.Va. State Bar, W.Va., Cabell County (sec. 1976—) bar assns., W.Va. Trial Lawyers Assn. Recipient Am. Jurisprudence award. Office: 909 Fifth Ave Huntington WV 25708 Tel (304) 525-5135

PANICHI, WILLIAM TERRY, b. Kankakee, Ill., Feb. 8, 1944; B.A., U. Ill., 1966, J.D., 1969. Admitted to Ill. bar, 1969, Calif. bar, 1975; staff asst. Speaker of Ill. House Rep., Springfield, 1970-71; pub. defender Sangamon County, Ill., 1971-72; staff asst. Ill., Senate Judiciary Com., Springfield, 1972-73; counsel Atty. Registration Commn., Springfield, 1973-74; mem. firm Ben K. Miller, Springfield, 1975—. Mem. Am., Ill. State (gen. counsel, 1973-74), Calif. State, Sangamon County bar assns. Home: 408 E Vine St Springfield IL 62703 Office: 712 S 2d St Springfield IL 62704 Tel (217) 753-1596

PANICO, JAMES PETER, b. New Haven, Apr. 14, 1936; B.S., U. Conn., 1958; J.D., U. Fla., 1967. Admitted to Fla. bar, 1967; partner Panico and Durocher, Orlando, Fla., 1967-69, Johnson and Panico, Maitland, Fla., 1969-77, James P. Panico and Assos., P.A., 1977—. Mem., Bd. Edn. Diocese Orlando, 1975-76. Mem. Am., Orange County, Seminole County bar assns., Maitland Seminole C. of C. (pres. 1976). Home: 725 Lake Sybelia Dr Maitland FL 32751 Office: 111 S Maitland Ave Maitland FL 32751 Tel (305) 647-7200

PANKEN, PETER MICHAEL, b. N.Y.C., Dec. 30, 1936; B.A. cum laude, Haverford Coll., 1957; LL.B. magna cum laude, Harvard, 1962. Admitted to N.Y. bar, 1962; asso. firm Paul, Weiss, Rifkind, Wharton & Garrison, N.Y.C., 1962-66, firm Poletti, Friedan, Prashker, Feldman & Reilly, N.Y.C., 1966-67; partner firm Parker, Chapin, Flattau & Klimpl, N.Y.C., 1967—. Mem. Am., N.Y. State (equal employment law com.) bar assns. Editor Harvard Law Rev., 1961-62. Home: 315 W 70th St New York City NY 10023 Office: 530 5th Ave New York City NY 10036 Tel (212) 986-7200

PANKOPF, ARTHUR, JR., b. Malden, Mass., Feb. 1, 1931; B.S. in Marine Transp., Mass. Maritime Acad., 1951; B.S. in Fgn. Service and Internat. Transp., Georgetown U., 1957, J.D., 1965. Admitted to Md. bar, 1965, D.C. bar, 1973, U.S. Supreme Ct. bar, 1977; eastern area mgr. Trans Ocean Van Service of Consol. Freightway, 1958-61; with U.S. Maritime Adminstrn., 1961-65; asso. firm Preston, Thorgrimson, Ellis, Holman & Fletcher, Washington, 1976—; minority counsel Com. on Mcht. Marine & Fisheries, U.S. Ho. of Reps., 1965-69; minority counsel, staff dir. Com. on Commerce, U.S. Senate, 1969-76. Home: 7819 Hampden Ln Bethesda MD 20014 Office: Suite 201 1776 F St NW Washington DC 20006 Tel (202) 331-1005

PANNIZZO, FRANK J., b. Bklyn., Jan. 1, 1939; B.A., St. Johns U., 1959, J.D., 1962; LL.M., N.Y. U., 1966. Admitted to N.Y. State bar, 1962, U.S. Dist. Ct., 1964, U.S. Ct. Appeals, 1965; asst. atty. gen. State of N.Y., 1962-67; asst. counsel N.Y.C. Dept. Marine and Aviation, 1967-69; dep. gen. counsel N.Y.C. Econ. Devel. Adminstrn., 1969-72; 1st dep. commr. N.Y.C. Dept. Ports and Terminals, 1972—. Mem. N.Y., Bklyn. bar assns. Office: New York City Dept Ports and Terminals Battery Maritime Bldg New York City NY 10004 Tel (212) 566-6612

PANOTES, WILFRIDO ELLAGA, JR., b. Camarines Norte, Philippines, June 27, 1937; Ph.B., U. Santo Tomas (Philippines), 1956, Ph.L. magna cum laude, 1957; LL.B., Ateneo de Manila (Philippines), 1962; B.A., U. Santo Tomas, 1967. Admitted to Philippines bar, 1963, N.J. bar, 1973, N.Y. State bar, 1976, U.S. Supreme Ct. bar, 1977; pvt. practice law, Philippines, 1963-65; legal officer SEC, Philippines, 1966-68; legal asst. Senate and Congress of the Philippines, 1968-72; individual practice law, Jersey City, 1973—, N.Y.C., 1976—; legal adviser Philippine Med. Assn., Philippine Nurses Assn., Bicolandia Assn., Philippine Communities Exec. Council N.Y., Fedn. Philippine Socs. N.J. Mem. Am., N.J. bar assns., N.Y. County Lawyers Assn., Nat. Assn. Immigration and Nationality Lawyers. Home: 807 Leonard Blvd New Hyde Park NY 11040 Office: 26 Journal Sq Suite 1603 Jersey City NJ 07306 also 233 Broadway New York City NY 10007 Tel (201) 963-5565

PANTZER, KURT FRIEDRICH, JR., B.A., Yale U., 1950; J.D., Harvard U., 1955. Admitted to Ind. bar, 1955; practice law, Indpls., 1955—; partner firm Royse, Travis, Hendrickson & Pantzer, 1966—, Pres. Estate Planning Council Indpls., 1977-78, Ind. Neuromuscular Research Lab., 1970—; bd. dirs. Marion County Muscular Dystrophy Found.; bd. dirs. Booth Tarkington Civic Theatre, v.p., 1977—. Mem. Indpls., Ind., Am. bar assns., Am. Coll. Probate Counsel. Home: 5827 Ravine Rd Indianapolis IN 46220 Office: 500 American Fletcher Bldg Indianapolis IN 46204 Tel (317) 632-4417

PANZER, IRVING RELLER MYRON, b. East Hampton, N.Y., Nov. 13, 1916; B.S., N.Y. U., 1937; LL.B., Harvard, 1940. Admitted to N.Y. bar, 1940, U.S. Supreme Ct. bar, 1944, D.C. bar, 1947; asso. firm Pike & Fischer, Washington, 1941; atty. SEC, Washington, D.C., 1941-43; atty. U.S. Dept. Justice, 1943; partner firm Fischer, Willis & Panzer, Washington, 1946-60; individual practice law, Washington, 1960—; adj. prof. fed. practice and procedure, Catholic U. Law Sch., 1957—; lectr. in field. Mem. Citizens Council D.C. Govt., 1963-67; mem. D.C. Commn. Arts and Humanities, 1974-76; mem. Health and Welfare Council D.C., 1963-73. Mem. Am., Fed., D.C. bar assns., D.C. Bar. Editor legal publs.; contbr. articles to profl. jours. Home: 2336 Massachusetts Ave NW Washington DC 20008 Office: 1735 DeSales St NW Washington DC 20036 Tel (202) 783-3391

PAPE, RALPH CARMEN, b. Albany, N.Y., July 15, 1937; B.S., Siena Coll., 1958; LL.B., Albany Law Sch., 1961, J.D., 1968. Admitted to N.Y. bar, 1961; individual practice law, Ravena, N.Y., 1961; commr. N.Y. State Legis. Bill Drafting Commn., 1972—; mem. Albany County Legislature, 1974—; supr., Town of Coeymans (N.Y.), 1962-73. Chmn. Coeymans Republican Com. Mem. N.Y. State, Albany County bar assns. Home: 100 Church St Coeymans NY 12045 Office: 147 Main St Ravena NY 12143 Tel (518) 756-2134

PAPER, LAWRENCE N., b. Pitts., June 29, 1932; B.B.A., U. Pitts., 1954, M.B.A., 1957; J.D., Duquesne U., 1971. Admitted to Pa. bar, 1971, U.S. Supreme Ct. bar, 1976; mem. firm Berger Kapetan & Malakoff, Pitts., 1971—; tchr. bus. law Robert Morris Coll., Pitts., 1971—. Mem. Am., Pa., Allegheny County bar assns., Res. Officers Assn., Air Force Assn., Am. Legion. Home: 574 Trotwood Ridge Rd Pittsburgh PA 15241 Office: Berger Kapetan & Malakoff 508 Law and Finance Bldg Pittsburgh PA 15219 Tel (412) 281-4200

PAPIANO, NEIL LEO, b. Salt Lake City, Nov. 25, 1933; B.A., Stanford, 1966, M.A., 1957; LL.B., Vanderbilt U., 1961. Admitted to Calif. bar, 1961; asso. firm Trippet, Yoakum & Ballantyne, Los Angeles, 1961-66, partner firm Iverson, Yoakum, Papiano & Hatch and predecessor, 1966—. Bd. dirs. Los Angeles County Welfare Planning Council, 1966-70; bd. govs. USO, 1967; bd. dirs. Calif. Alcoholism Council, 1975-76; chmn. Los Angeles Forward, 1972-74. Mem. Am., Calif., Los Angeles bar assns., Los Angeles Jaycees (pres. 1966), Los Angeles Area C. of C. (dir. 1966, 72-75). Recipient Nathan Burkan Copyright award, 1961. Office: 611 W 6th St Suite 1900 Los Angeles CA 90017 Tel (213) 687-0711

PAPKIN, ROBERT DAVID, b. New Bedford, Mass., Feb. 26, 1933; A.B., Harvard Coll., 1954; LL.B., Harvard, 1957. Admitted to Mass. bar, 1957, D.C. bar, 1964, U.S. Supreme Ct. bar, 1966; atty.-advisor Office of Gen. Counsel, U.S. Post Office Dept., Washington, 1958-59; legal asst. NLRB, Washington, 1959-61; asso. firm Cox, Langford & Brown, Washington, 1963-66, partner, 1966—. Trustee, Green Acres Sch., Rockville, Md. Mem. Bar Assn. D.C., Am., Fed., Inter-Am. bar assns. Home: 8200 Lilly Stone Dr Bethesda MD 20034 Office: 21 DuPont Circle NW Washington DC 20036

PAPOLA, JOHN ATTILIO, b. Phila., Oct. 17, 1921; B.S., LaSalle Coll., 1944; J.D., Temple U., 1948. Admitted to Pa. bar, 1952, U.S. Supreme Ct. bar, 1966; asst. dist. atty., Phila., 1952-54; mem. firm Todaro & Papola, Phila., 1955-68, Papola & Siegel, Phila., 1968-72; individual practice law, Phila., 1972—; chief counsel Acad. Notre Dame, 1964-66, Mario Lanza Inst., 1967-69. Mem. Justinian Soc., Nat. Assn. Def. Lawyers in Criminal Cases, Am. Arbitration Assn., Phi Alpha Delta. Legis. editor Temple U. Law Quar., 1948-58; author booklet on bail in Pa.; contbr. articles on juveniles to newspapers. Home: 1359 Overbrook Rd Lower Merion Greenhill Farms PA 19151 Office: 1313 One E Penn Sq Philadelphia PA 19107 Tel (215) LO3-7187

PAPPAS, STANLEY R., b. Milw., July 25, 1922; B.S., Marquette U., 1947; J.D., U. Mich., 1950. Admitted to Wis. bar, 1950; individual practice law, Milw., 1950—. Mem. Am., Wis. bar assns., Am., Wis. insts. C.P.A.'s. Office: PO Box 614 Milwaukee WI 53201 Tel (414) 224-5363

PAQUIN, WILLIAM FOREST, b. Providence, Mar. 25, 1936; B.S., Providence Coll., 1957; J.D., Boston Coll., 1964. Admitted to R.I. bar, 1964; mem. firm Noel & Orton, Providence, 1964-68; mem. firm Haronian & Paquin, Inc., Warwick, R.I., 1968—; asst. city solicitor Warwick, 1967-72; counsel manpower affairs div. R.I. Dept. Econ. Devel., 1973—. Mem. Am., R.I., Kent County bar assns., Am. Trial Lawyers Assn. Home: 42 Broadview Ave Warwick RI 02889 Office: 1719 Warwick Ave Warwick RI 02889 Tel (401) 739-9330

PARADISO, FRANCIS JOSEPH, b. Stafford, Conn., Jan. 17, 1935; B.S., Holy Cross Coll., 1956; J.D., Georgetown U., 1959. Admitted to Conn. bar, 1960; asst. prosecutor Ct. of Common Pleas State of Conn., 1963—; corporator Stafford Savs. Bank. Pres., St. Edwards Sch. Bd., Stafford, 1970-75. Mem. Am., Conn. bar assns. Home: 62 E Main St Stafford Springs CT 06076 Office: Hartford Fed Savs Bldg Stafford CT 06076 Tel (203) 684-4221

PARAS, GEORGE E., b. Sacramento, May 15, 1924; B.A., U. Calif., Berkeley, 1947; LL.B., Stanford, 1950. Admitted to Calif. bar, 1950; asso. firm Hession, Robb & Creedon, San Mateo, Calif., 1950-52; individual practice law, Sacramento, 1953-57; partner firm Rowland, Paras & Clowdus and predecessor, Sacramento, 1957-69; judge Sacramento County Superior Ct., 1970-74; justice Calif. 3d Dist. Ct. Appeal, 1974—. Mem. Conf. Calif. Judges. Home: 1681 Del Dayo Dr Carmichael CA 95608 Office: State Library and Courts Bldg Sacramento CA 95814 Tel (916) 445-4344

PARDES, RICHARD S., b. N.Y.C., Dec. 31, 1927; B.A., Bklyn. Coll., 1946; LL.B., N.Y. U., 1952. Admitted to N.Y. State bar, 1952, U.S. Supreme Ct. bar, 1960; asso. firm Tenzer, Greenblatt, Falon & Kaplan, N.Y.C., 1952-53; asso. firm Goldman & Goldman, N.Y.C., 1953-54; individual practice law, Scarsdale, N.Y., 1955—; prin. Scarsdale Funding Co., 1970—; arbitrator Small Claims Ct. Civil Ct. City N.Y., 1975—; counsel to Jewish Council of Yonkers (N.Y.), 1976—. Vice pres. Midchester Jewish Center, Yonkers, 1976. Mem. Am. Arbitration Assn. (arbitrator), Am., Westchester County, Yonkers, Bronx County bar assns. Asso. editor Advocate, 1965-73. Office: 1075 Central Park Ave Scarsdale NY 10583 Tel (914) 472-5505

PARDIECK, ROGER LEE, b. Seymour, Ind., Mar. 1, 1937; A.B., Ind. U., 1959; postgrad. Internat. Grad. Sch., U. Stockholm, Sweden; LL.B., Ind. U., 1963. Admitted to Ind. bar, 1963; spl. pros. atty. Jackson County, Ind., 1964-65; partner firm Montgomery, Elsner & Pardieck, Seymour, Ind., 1965—; bd. dirs. Fidelity Fed. Savings & Loan Assn., 1974—. Bd. dirs. Luth. Community Home, 1967—, pres., 1970-71; bd. dirs. Girls' Clubs of Am., 1967-70, Seymour C. of C., 1969-72; chmn. Indsl. Devel. Com., 1972. Mem. Ind. Trial Lawyers Assn. (bd. dirs. 1971—, pres. 1975-76), Am., Ind. State, Jackson County bar assns., The Assn. of Trial Lawyers of Am., Phi Delta Phi. Home: 925 Meadowbrook Dr Seymour IN 47274 Office: 308 W Second St Seymour IN 47274 Tel (812) 522-4109

PARELIUS, MARTIN RONALD, b. Portland, Oct. 1, 1931; B.B.A., U. Oreg., 1953; M.S., N.Y. U., 1954; LL.B., Northwestern Coll., Portland, 1962. Admitted to Oreg. bar, 1962; asst. to bus. mgr. U. Oreg. Med. Sch. (now U. Oreg. Health Sci. Center), Portland, 1961-63, dir. research services, 1963-71, bus. mgr., 1971-76, asst. v.p. for bus. services, 1977—. Mem. Oreg. Bar Assn. Home: 3814 SW Bridlemile Ln Portland OR 97221 Office: 3181 SW Sam Jackson Park Rd Portland OR 97201 Tel (503) 225-8224

PARENT, GERALD BRUNSELL, b. South Bend, Ind., Feb. 25, 1932; B.A., U. Calif., Los Angeles, 1954, LL.B., Hastings Coll. Law, San Francisco, 1959. Admitted to Calif. bar, 1960, U.S. Supreme Ct. bar, 1965; individual practice law, Santa Barbara, 1960-65; partner firms Parent & Parent, Santa Barbara, 1965-67, Hatch and Parent and predecessor, Santa Barbara, 1968—; founding dir. and sec. Bank of Montecito, Santa Barbara, 1974—. Mem. Santa Barbara County Democratic Central Com., 1960-68; mem. Santa Barbara City Airport Commn., 1962-69; pres. St. Vincent's Day Nursery, Santa Barbara, 1969, Cath. Welfare Bur., Santa Barbara, 1973. Mem. Santa Barbara County Bar Assn. (pres. 1975), Calif. Bar, Assn. Trial Lawyers Am. Home: 4343 Via Esperanza Santa Barbara CA 93110 Office: 21 E Carrillo St Santa Barbara CA 93101 Tel (805) 963-1971

PARENT, ROLAND R., b. New Bedford, Mass., Aug. 12, 1920; B.S., U. R.I., 1942; LL.B., Boston Coll., 1948, J.D., 1969. Admitted to R.I. bar, 1948, Fla. bar, 1950; individual practice law, Newport, R.I., 1948-50, Tarpon Springs, Fla., 1950-51; spl. agt. F.B.I., Ark. and Ind., 1951-53; asso. firm Smathers and Thompson, Miami, Fla., 1960-64, partner, 1964—; lectr. in field. Mem. Dade County, R.I., Am., Fla. bar assns., Maritime Law Assn. U.S., Internat. Assn. Ins. Counsel. Home: 1215 Placetas Ave Coral Gables FL 33146 Office: 1301 Alfred I DuPont Bldg Miami FL 33131 Tel (305) 379-6523

PARIS, LEONARD ALTON, b. Lynchburg, Va., Jan. 24, 1932; B.A., Richmond, 1958, J.D., 1962. Admitted to Va. bar, 1962; partner firm White, Cabell, Paris & Lowenstein, Richmond, Va., 1962—; commr. in chancery Chesterfield County (Va.), 1968; substitute judge Gen. Dist. Ct. Chesterfield County, 1972-76. Bd. dirs. Nat. Multiple Sclerosis Soc., 1974-76. Mem. Am., Va., Richmond, Chesterfield-Colonial Heights bar assns., Va. Trial Lawyers Assn., Va. Assn. Def. Attys. Home: 12201 Old Buckingham Rd Midlothian VA 23113 Office: 523 E Main St Richmond VA 23219 Tel (804) 643-9066

PARISI, PATRICK ALLEN, b. Hopkinsville, Ky., May 26, 1943; B.A., Northwestern U., Evanston, Ill., 1965; J.D., Ind. U., Bloomington, 1968. Admitted to Ill. bar, 1968; atty. trust dept. Harris Trust and Savs. Bank, Chgo., 1968-70; asso. firm Chadwell, Kayser, Ruggles, McGee, Hastings & McKinney, Chgo., 1970-73; partner firm Huges, LaForte, Achor & Parisi, Matteson, Ill., 1974-76, Achor & Parisi, Olympia Fields, Ill., 1977—; spl. asst. atty. gen. State of Ill., 1974—; hearing officer numerous high sch. bds. edn., Ill. Com. Coll. Bd. Trustee Ill. Community Coll. Dist. 515, 1969—; mem. bd. dirs. Prairie State Coll. Charitable Found. Mem. Ill., Chgo., S. Suburban bar assns. Home: 3407 Woodland Dr Olympia Fields IL 60461 Office: 21141 Governors Highway Matteson IL 60443 Tel (312) 481-1700

PARK, DANIEL JOSEPH, b. Elkin, N.C., Feb. 23, 1934; A.B., Duke, 1956, LL.B., 1959; Admitted to N.C. bar, 1959, U.S. Dist. Ct. Middle Dist. N.C., 1964; asso. Charles M. Neaves, 1959-61; individual practice law, 1961-65; partner firm Finger & Park, Elkin, 1965—; sec. Yadkin Valley Bank & Trust Co. Chmn. bd. trustees 1st United Methodist Ch.; chmn. Elkin Recreation Fund Raising Dr., Surry County Good Neighbor Council, Surry County Young Republicans. Mem. Am., N.C., 17th Dist., Surry County bar assns. Home: 157 Knollwood Dr Elkin NC 28621 Office: PO Box 557 Elkin NC 28621 Tel (919) 835-2166

PARK, JACK CURTIS, b. San Antonio, Jan. 13, 1947; B.B.A., Tex. Lutheran Coll., 1969; J.D., St. Mary's, San Antonio, 1973. Admitted to Tex. bar, 1973; asst. to v.p. U. Tex. Health Sci. Center, San Antonio, 1975—. Home: 1543 Babcock St 206 San Antonio TX 78229 Office: 7703 Floyd Curl St San Antonio TX 78284 Tel (512) 696-6708

PARK, JACK LENIS, JR., b. Athens, Ga., May 6, 1949; B.B.A., U. Ga., 1971, J.D., 1974. Admitted to Ga. bar, 1974; asso. firm Seay & Sims, Griffin, Ga., 1974—. Active Boy Scouts Am. Mem. Am., Ga. bar assns., Ga. Assn. Criminal Def. Attys. Home: Adkerson Dr Zebulon GA 30295 Office: PO Box 602 Griffin GA 30224 Tel (404) 227-2231

PARK, RICHARD CHARLES, b. Victor, Iowa, Oct. 7, 1922; B.S.C., State U. Iowa, 1944, J.D., 1947. Admitted to Iowa bar, 1947; individual practice law, Victor, 1947—. Adj. Am. Legion Post, 1948-66; treas. H.L.V. Alumni Assn.; sec. Victor Sr. Citizens Housing, Inc., 1975-76; treas. Victor Health Care Center, 1975-76. Mem. Iowa County, Iowa State, Am., 6th Jud. Dist. (sec.-treas.) bar assns. Home: 614 Main Victor IA 52347 Office: 216 Washington Victor IA 52347 Tel (319) 647-2221

PARK, WILLIAM ANTHONY, b. Blackfoot, Idaho, June 4, 1934; A.A., Boise Jr. Coll., 1954; B.A. in Polit. Sci., U. Idaho, 1958, J.D., 1963. Admitted to Idaho State bar, 1963; asso. firm Bickel and Park, 1963-64; individual practice law, Boise, 1964-69; asso. firm C.D. Suiter, Park and Suiter, Boise, 1969-71; atty. gen. State of Idaho, 1971-75; partner firm Park & Meuleman, 1975—; mem. Idaho State Land bd., 1971-75; chmn. Idaho Law Enforcement Planning Commn., 1971-75. Chmn. Idaho Bicentennial Commn., 1971—. Mem. Idaho State, Boise bar assns. Recipient Boise Jaycees Distinguished Service award, 1970. Home: 525 Warm Springs Ave Boise ID 83702 Office: 106 N 6th St Boise ID 83702 Tel (208) 336-2820

PARKER, CHARLES EDWARD, b. Santa Ana, Calif., Sept. 9, 1927; A.A., Santa Ana Coll.; J.D., Southwestern U., Los Angeles, 1957. Admitted to Calif. bar, 1958, U.S. Supreme Ct. bar, 1969; counsel First Am. Title Co., Santa Ana, 1961-65, Fed. Nat. Mortgage Assn., Washington, Los Angeles, 1968-73; prof. Sch. Law Western State U., Fullerton, Calif., 1973—. Mem. Calif. Hist. Soc., Conf. Calif. Hist. Socs., Am., Orange County, D.C. bar assns., Phi Alpha Delta. Author: Orange County, Indians to Industry, 1963. Contbr. articles to banking jours. Home: 18101 Charter Rd Villa Park CA 92667 Office: 1111 N State College Blvd Fullerton CA 92631 Tel (714) 993-7600

PARKER, FITZGERALD SALE, b. Nashville, Feb. 5, 1905; B.A., Vanderbilt U., 1925, LL.B., 1927, J.D., 1969. Admitted to Tenn. bar, 1927, U.S. Tax Ct. bar, 1973; with Nashville Trust Co., 1927, 3d Nat. Bank of Nashville (merger Nashville Trust Co. and 3d Nat. Bank of Nashville), 1966-70, trust officer, 1930-50, v.p., 1950-70; asso. firm Watkins, McGugin, McNeilly & Rowan, Nashville, 1970—. Treas. Wilkerson Hearing and Speech Center, Nashville, 1968-70; chmn. Sr. Citizen's Bd., Nashville, 1973-74. Mem. Nashville, Tenn. bar assns. Home: 420 Royal Oaks Dr Nashville TN 37205 Office: 1400 Am Trust Bldg Nashville TN 37201 Tel (615) 254-7791

PARKER, FRANK MARION, b. Asheville, N.C., Aug. 25, 1912; A.B., U. N.C., 1934, J.D., 1936. Admitted to N.C. bar, 1935; partner firm Bernard & Parker, and predecessor, Asheville, 1935-50, Parker, McGuire & Baley, and predecessor, Asheville, 1951-67; judge N.C. Ct. of Appeals, Raleigh, 1968—; mem. N.C. Senate, 1947-49. Trustee, U. N.C., 1955-63. Mem. Am., N.C. bar assns., Am. Judicature Soc., Order of Coif. Home: 244 Country Club Rd Asheville NC 28804 Office: Ruffin Bldg 1 W Morgan St Raleigh NC 27602 Tel (919) 829-4228

PARKER, GERALD CORBETT, SR., b. Hubert, N.C., Nov. 27, 1933; A.B., U. N.C., 1954; J.D., 1957. Admitted to N.C. bar, 1957; asso. firm Williams & Williams, Asheville, N.C., 1958; law clk. to N.C. Supreme Ct., 1958-59; individual practice law, Liberty, N.C., 1959—, Greensboro, N.C., 1967—; partner Parker, Rice & Myles, Wilmington, N.C., 1970—; solicitor Liberty Recorders Ct., 1959-64. Mem. Am., N.C., Randolph County, Greensboro bar assns., N.C. Acad. Trial Attys. Home: 4915 Edinborough Rd Greensboro NC 27406 Office: 214 W Friendly Ave Greensboro NC 27401 Tel (919) 273-5551

PARKER, GLENN, b. Murray, Iowa, Nov. 25, 1898; B.A., U. Wyo., 1922, J.D., 1934. Admitted to Wyo. bar, 1927, Fed. bar, 1927, U.S. Supreme Ct. bar, 1941; city atty. Laramee, Wyo., 1927-29; pros. atty. Albany County, Wyo., 1930-40; judge 2d Dist. Wyo., 1949-55, judge

Wyo. Supreme Ct., 1955-75, chief justice, 1969-71, 73-75; mem. firm Hirst and Applegate, Cheyenne, 1975—. Mem. Am., Laramie County, Wyo. bar assns., Am. Judicature Soc., Am. Law Inst. Named distinguished alumni U. Wyo., 1957; recipient Herbert Harley award Am. Judicature Soc., 1976. Office: 200 Boyd Bldg Cheyenne WY 82001 Tel (307) 632-0543

PARKER, IRVIN DURANT, b. Manning, S.C., Nov. 17, 1935; B.B.A., U. S.C., 1964, J.D., 1967. Admitted to S.C. bar, 1967; asst. atty. gen. State of S.C., 1967-72; individual practice law, Columbia, S.C., 1972-74; dir. S.C. Dept. Comsumer Affairs, Columbia, 1974—. Mem. Am., S.C., Rich County bar assns., Nat. Assn. Consumer Credit Adminstrs., Am. Conf. Uniform Consumer Credit Code States, So. Atty. Gen.'s Conf. (liaison). Contbr. articles to legal jours. Office: 2122 Devine St Columbia SC 29211 Tel (803) 758-3926

PARKER, JOHN LAWRENCE, b. Dubuque, Iowa, May 11, 1929; B.S. in Chem. Engring., U. Notre Dame, 1949, M.S. in Chem. Engring., 1950; J.D., DePaul U., 1955; M.B.A., U. Chgo., 1962. Admitted to Ill. bar, 1955, U.S. Supreme Ct. bar; mem. firm Wolfe, Hubbard et. al., Chgo., 1954-72; mem. Ill. Pollution Control Bd., Chgo., 1972; mem. firm Root & O'Keefe, Chgo., 1973-75; mem. firm Parker & Henss, Chgo., 1975-77; mem. firm John L. Parker & Assos., 1977—. Mem. Am., Ill. State, Chgo. bar assns., Am. Patent Law Assn., Patent Law Assn. Chgo. Home: 1900 Douglas St Joliet IL 60435 Office: 39 S LaSalle St Chicago IL 60603 Tel (312) 263-6560

PARKER, JOHN ROLSTON, b. Memphis, Mar. 13, 1939; B.A., Vanderbilt U., 1961, LL.B., 1964. Admitted to Tenn. bar, 1964; atty. U.S. Army C.E., Nashville, 1964-67; asso. firm Denney, Lackey & Chernau, Nashville, 1967—. Chmn. citizens adv. com. Nashville Bd. Edn., 1976—; pres. Harpeth Valley PTA, Nashville, 1972-73; chmn. fin. com. Calvary United Meth. Ch., Nashville, 1976—. Mem. Am., Tenn., Nashville bar assns., Tenn. Trial Lawyers Assn. Home: 1005 Hickory Hollow Rd Nashville TN 37221 Office: 218 3d Ave N Nashville TN 37201 Tel (615) 244-5480

PARKER, JOHN VICTOR, b. Baton Rouge, Oct. 14, 1928; B.A. in Govt., La. State U., 1949, J.D., 1952. Admitted to La. bar, 1952, U.S. Supreme Ct. bar, 1960; partner firm Parker & Parker, Baton Rouge, 1954-66, Sanders, Downing, Kean & Cazedessus, Baton Rouge, 1966—; served with JAGC, AUS, 1952-54; asst. parish atty. City of Baton Rouge, Parish of East Baton Rouge, 1956-66; spl. lectr. La. State U. Law Sch. Pres. Baton Rouge Kiwanis Club, 1976-77. Mem. Am., La. (ho. dels., gov.), Baton Rouge (pres. 1968-69) bar assns., Am. Legion, Order of Coif. Home: 5721 Hyacinth St Baton Rouge LA 70808 Office: PO Box 1588 Baton Rouge LA 70821 Tel (504) 387-0951

PARKER, LUTRELLE FLEMING, b. Newport News, Va., Mar. 10, 1924; student Cornell U. Midshipmens Sch., 1945; B.C.E., Howard U., 1946; J.D., Georgetown U., 1952. Admitted to Va. bar, 1952; examiner U.S. Patent and Trademark Office, Washington, 1948-62, asso. solicitor, 1962-70, examiner in chief, 1970-75, dep. commr. of patents and trademarks, 1975—. Chmn. Arlington County (Va.) Planning Commn., 1959-62; vice chmn. bd. trustees Arlington County Hosp.; trustee George Mason U. of Va. Mem. Va. Bar, D.C. Bar, Am. Bar Assn., Patent Office Soc. Recipient Arlington Links, Inc. Outstanding Citizens award, 1968, Presdl. Certificate of Commendation, 1970, Alpha Phi Alpha Civic award, 1972, Nat. Links, Inc. Outstanding Citizens award, 1976. Tel (703) 557-3961

PARKER, PAUL EDWARD, JR., b. Buckhannon, W.Va., Dec. 12, 1926; A.B., U. W.Va., 1949; J.D., W.Va. U., 1951. Admitted to Supreme Ct. Appeals W.Va., 1951, U.S. Ct. Appeals 4th Circuit bar, 1972; individual practice law, Fairmont, W.Va., 1951—; asst. pros. atty. Marion County (W.Va.), 1952-56, pros. atty., 1956-63; dist. atty. W.Va. Dept. Hwys., 1964—. Mem. Am., W.Va., W.Va. State bar assns., Am. Trial Lawyers Assn. Office: 807 1st National Bank Building Fairmont WV 26554 Tel (304) 366-0570

PARKER, RALPH SETH, II, b. Mpls., Jan. 5, 1933; B.S. in Law, U. Minn., 1956, J.D., 1956. Admitted to Minn. bar, 1956; mem. firm Parker & Parker, Mpls.; consul adhonorem of Peru in Mpls., 1970—. Mem. Am., Minn. State, Hennepin County (Minn.) bar assns., Consular Corps Coll., Internat. Consular Acad., Gamma Eta Gamma. Home: 1109 N Tyrol Tr Golden Valley MN 55416 Office: 838 Midland Bank Bldg Minneapolis MN 55401 Tel (612) 341-2626

PARKER, ROBERT LOWELL, b. El Paso, Tex., Jan. 29, 1920; B.A., Occidental Coll., 1941; LL.B., Loyola U., Los Angeles, 1949. Chemist, Union Oil Co. of Calif., Los Angeles, 1941-46; asso. firm James B. Christie, Pasadena, Calif., 1946-55; sr. partner firm Christie, Parker & Hale, Pasadena, 1955—. Bd. dirs. Pasadena Child Guidance Clinic, 1968-71; trustee Pasadena Rotary Found. Mem. Am., Pasadena, Los Angeles County bar assns., Am. Chem. Soc., Am. Patent Law Assn., Am. Soc. Internat. Law, Los Angeles Com. on Fgn. Relations, Internat. Patent and Trademark Assn., Licensing Execs. Soc., Pasadena C. of C. Home: 4057 Robin Hill Rd Flintridge CA 91011 Office: 201 S Lake Ave Pasadena CA 91101 Tel (213) 795-5843

PARKHURST, ARTHUR BYRON, b. Ft. Lauderdale, Fla., Sept. 6, 1933; B.S., Fla. State U., 1958; J.D., Duke U., 1961. Admitted to Fla. bar, 1961; research asst. Office of Legal Counsel Dept. of Justice, Washington, 1960; asso. firm Kelley, Tompkins & Griffin, Ft. Lauderdale, 1961-65; partner firm Parkhurst, La Hurd & Purdy, (and predecessors) Ft. Lauderdale, 1966—; city atty. City of Sunrise, Fla., 1969—. Pres. Broward County div. Children's Home Soc. of Fla., 1963-65, 66-67, mem. state bd. dirs., 1963—; bd. dirs. United Way of Broward County, 1964-65. Mem. Am., Broward County bar assns., Assn. of Trial Lawyers of Am., Broward County Trial Lawyers Assn., Broward Criminal Defense Attys., Am. Judicature Soc., Assn. of Fla. Trial Lawyers. Home: 335 Coral Way Fort Lauderdale FL 33301 Office: 1177 SE 3rd Ave Fort Lauderdale FL 33316 Tel (305) 525-3441

PARKHURST, FREDERICK W., JR., b. Boston, Aug. 12, 1928; A.B., Northeastern U., 1951, J.D., 1953; A.M., Boston U., 1955; LL.M., N.Y. U., 1968, J.S.D., 1973. Admitted to Mass. bar, 1954; individual practice law, Waltham, Mass., 1954-55; asso. prof., chmn. dept. econs., Emory and Henry Coll., Emory, Va., 1958-64; prof., chmn. dept. econs. Guilford Coll., Greensboro, N.C., 1964—; def. counsel U.S. Army Med. Corps, Tex., Korea, 1956-57. Mem. Waltham Sch. Com., 1952-55; active N.C. Democratic party; state conv. del.; bd. dirs. N.C. Right to Life, 1975-77. Mem. Mass. Bar, Am. Econ. Assn., Am. Bus. Law Assn., Assn. for Asian Studies. Ford Found. fellow, U. Pa., 1960; Duke U. fellow, 1976; contbr. articles to profl. jours. Home: 818 Larkwood Dr Greensboro NC 27410 Office: Box 8207 Guilford Coll Greensboro NC 27410 Tel (919) 292-5511

PARKHURST, TODD SHELDON, b. Evanston, Ill., Mar. 8, 1941; B.A. in Gen. Engring., U. Ill., 1963; J.D., U. Pa., 1966. Admitted to Ill. bar, 1968, U.S. Supreme Ct. bar, 1973; patent atty. firm Wolfe, Hubbard, Voit & Osann, Chgo., 1968-72, firm Olson Trexler, Wolters, Bushnell & Fosse, Ltd., Chgo., 1972—; jud. hearing officer Ill. Pollution Control Bd., 1972—. Mem. Chgo. Bar Assn., Patent Law Assn. Chgo. Contbr. articles to legal jours, popular mags. Office: 141 W Jackson Blvd #3440 Chicago IL 60604 Tel (312) HA-78082

PARKINSON, KENNETH WELLS, b. Washington, D.C., Sept. 13, 1927; A.B., George Washington U., 1950, LL.B., 1952. Admitted to D.C. bar, 1952; mem. firm Robb, Porter, Kistler and Parkinson, D.C., 1953-70; mem. firm Jackson, Campbell and Parkinson, and predecessors, D.C., 1970—, partner firm, 1977—; chmn. admissions com. and bar examiner D.C. Ct. Appeals, 1972-74; parlementarian Jud. Conf. D.C. Circuit. Pres. D.C. Crippled Children's Soc., 1976-77; chmn. Commrs. Youth Council, 1961-62. Mem. D.C. (chmn. Jr. bar sec. 1960-61), Am. bar assns., Jr. C. of C. (pres. 1958-59). Recipient Washingtonian Award as Outstanding Young Man in D.C., 1962. Home: 5417 Duvall Dr Westmoreland Hills MD 20016 Office: 1828 L St NW Washington DC 20036 Tel (202) 457-1640

PARKS, BERNARD, b. Atlanta, June 10, 1944; B.A., Morehouse Coll., 1966; J.D., Emory U., 1969; postgrad. Coll. City N.Y., 1965. Admitted to Ga. bar, 1969, U.S. Supreme Ct. bar, 1975; city govt. intern Atlanta, 1967, legis. intern, 1968; law asst. Atlanta Legal Aid Soc., Inc., 1968-69; law clk. U.S. Ct. Appeals, 1969-70; asso. firm Patterson, Parks & Franklin, and predecessors, Atlanta, 1970, partner, 1970—; chmn. bd. dirs. Opportunities Industrialization Center Atlanta, Inc., 1970—; dir. Opportunities Industrialization Center Am., 1971; pres. Met. Atlanta Council on Alcohol and Drugs, 1971-74; counsel Met. Atlanta Council on Crime and Juvenile Delinquency, 1971-72, trustee, 1976; mem. Woodrow Wilson-Martin Luther King, Jr. Fellowship Selection Com., 1975—; active YMCA, Big Bros. Atlanta; mem. Cong. Black Caucus Dinner Com., 1974-75; Mem. Am., Nat., Ga., Atlanta, Bar City bar assns., Hal Davidson Philosophy Group, NAACP, ACLU, Ga. Legal Services Program., Atlanta Council Younger Lawyers, Lawyers Com. for Civil Rights Under Law, Atlanta Legal Aid Soc., Omega Psi Phi, Phi Alpha Delta. Recipient Service award Atlanta Bd. Edn., 1974; Morehouse Coll. Distinguished Alumnus Achievement award, 1975; United Negro Coll. Fund Service award, 1976; WSB Newsmaker award, 1972; WAOK Basic Black Big Brother of Week, 1973; Outstanding Young Man of Year award Atlanta Jaycees, 1976. Office: 101 Marietta St Suite 2222 Atlanta GA 30303 Tel (404) 577-5800

PARKS, CHARLES LEVON, b. Anniston, Ala., Aug. 27, 1941; A.A., Am. U., 1963, B.A., 1964, J.D., 1967. Admitted to Ala. bar, 1967, U.S. Supreme Ct. bar; individual practice law, Anniston, 1967—; staff U.S. Senate Fgn. Relations Com., 1959-67; acting judge Calhoun County (Ala.) Juvenile Ct., 1972-76, Domestic Relations Ct., 1972-76. Mem. Calhoun County Assn. Retarded Persons, 1973—. Mem. Am., Ala., Calhoun County bar assns., Am. Trial Lawyers Assn., Delta Theta Phi. Office: 1108 Wilmer Ave Anniston AL 36201 Tel (205) 237-6645

PARKS, JOHN EMORY, b. Bridgeport, Conn., Sept. 1, 1909; LL.B. and J.D., U. Va., 1934. Admitted to Va. bar, 1933, Hawaii bar, 1937; partner with Judge Phillip L. Rice, Hawaii, 1937-38; asst. U.S. atty for Hawaii, 1939-41; asst. and acting pub. prosecutor, city and county Honolulu, 1941-46; individual practice law, Honolulu, 1946-47, 52—; judge first circuit ct. Hawaii, 1947-52; adminstr. rent control commn., Honolulu, 1942-43. Dir. Hawaii C. of C., 1951-53; dir. Civic Light Opera Assn., Honolulu, 1947-55, pres., 1947-57; dir. Hawaii Cancer Soc., 1948-59. Mem. Va., Hawaii Bar Assns. Home: 3617 Diamond Head Rd Honolulu HI 96816 Office: Suite 1114 Amfac Bldg 700 Bishop St Honolulu HI 96813 Tel (808) 524-2236

PARMET, DONALD JAY, b. N.Y.C., Aug. 12, 1931; A.B., Cornell U., 1952, J.D., 1955. Admitted to N.Y. bar, 1957, U.S. Supreme Ct. bar, 1964; asso. firm Parmet & Parmet, N.Y.C. and Jericho, N.Y., 1957-60, partner, 1960—; partner Parmet & Epstein, Jericho, N.Y., 1970-76. Trustee, counsel L.I. Profl. Nurses Assn., 1976; trustee Leukemia Soc. Am., 1972-74. Mem. N.Y., Nassau County bar assns., N.Y. County Lawyers Assn., Assn. Bankruptcy Lawyers. Home: Giffard Way Melville NY 11746 Office: 99 Jericho Turnpike Jericho NY 11753 Tel (516) 333-3377

PARNASS, EMANUEL RABIN, b. Novy Dvor, Poland, June 30, 1893; Ph.B., U. Chgo., 1915, J.D. cum laude, 1916. Admitted to Ill. bar, 1917; asso. firm D'Ancona & Pflaum, Chgo., 1916-17; partner firm Parnass & Herr, Chgo., 1919-20; capt. JAG, U.S. Army, 1920-23; individual practice law, Waukegan, Ill., 1930—; with JAGC, U.S. Army, 1941-43. Mem. Lake County (Ill.), Ill. State bar assns. Home and office: 400 Harding Ave Waukegan IL 60085 Tel (312) 662-4060

PARNELL, ALBERT HUNTER, b. Washington, Dec., 24, 1941; student U. Va.; B.A., Ark. Coll., 1965; J.D., Vanderbilt U., 1968. Admitted to Ga. bar, 1969; law clk. Nat. Aeros. Assn., 1964; tchr. George Washington High Sch., Alexandria, Va., 1965; partner firm Freeman & Hawkins, Atlanta, 1966—. Mem. Am., Atlanta bar assns., State Bar Ga., Ga. Def. Lawyers Assn. (vice pres.). Editor: Request to Charge on Georgia Law: A Compendium, 1976. Home: 228 Peachtree Hills Apt A Atlanta GA 30305 Office: 618 Fulton Federal Bldg Atlanta GA 30303

PARNELL, ANDREW WILFORD, b. Somerset, Wis., Mar. 15, 1902; B.A., St. John's U., Collegeville, Minn., 1924; LL.B., Marquette U., 1927; J.D., St. Norbert Coll., 1969. Admitted to Wis. bar, 1927; mem. firm Benton Bosser Becker & Parnell, Appleton, 1931-52; judge Wis. Circuit Ct., 10th Jud. Circuit, 1952—. Mem. Appleton Redevel. Authority, 1973-75. Mem. Wis., Am. (jour. editorial bd. 1960-65) bar assns., Nat. Conf. State Trial Judges (chmn. 1963-64). Contbr. articles to legal jours. Home: 1912 N Appleton St Appleton WI 54911 Office: Courthouse Appleton WI 54911 Tel (414) 739-6632

PARNESS, ALAN MARK, b. Bklyn., Sept. 18, 1946; B.A., Bklyn. Coll., 1967; J.D., Boston U., 1970. Admitted to N.Y. bar, 1971; atty., spl. dep. atty. gen. N.Y. State Dept. Law, N.Y.C., 1970-73; asso. firm Cadwalader, Wickersham & Taft, N.Y.C., 1973—. Mem. Am., N.Y. bar assns. Office: 1 Wall St New York City NY 10005 Tel (212) 785-1000

PARR, JACK RAMSEY, b. Dallas, May 10, 1926; B.A., U. Okla., 1949, LL.B., 1950, J.D., 1970; grad. Nat. Coll. of State Judiciary, 1966. Admitted to Okla. bar, 1950, U.S. Supreme Ct. bar, 1955, U.S. Ct. Mil. Appeals bar, 1955; practiced in Edmond, Okla., 1953-58; asst. U.S. atty. Western dist. Okla., 1958-65; judge Okla. Dist. Ct., 7th Jud. Dist., 1965—; asso. prof. law Oklahoma City U., 1966-67; mem. trial div. Ct. on The Judiciary, 1969—; comdg. officer JAGC, USNR, 1974-76; faculty adviser Nat. Coll. of State Judiciary, 1971, 72, 73. Mem. Okla., Am., Oklahoma County bar assns., Jud. Conf. Okla., Am. Judicature Soc., Judge Advs. Assn., Naval Res. Lawyers Assn., U. Okla. Coll. Law Assn. Home: 2601 NW 55th Pl Oklahoma City OK 73112 Office: 703 County Courthouse 321 Park Ave Oklahoma City OK 73102 Tel (405) 236-2727

PARRISH, BRADLEY BELL, b. Lewistown, Mont., Dec. 8, 1938; student Mont. State U., 1959-60, Coll. Alaska, 1960-61; A.B., U. Mont., 1963, J.D., 1967. Admitted to Mont. bar, 1967; dep. county atty. Fergus County (Mont.), 1967-69; individual practice law, Lewistown, 1969—. Fellow Kellogg Extension Edn. Project, 1973-75; chmn. Mont. Com. for the Humanities, 1976; mem. Mont. Ho. of Reps., 1971-72; mem. Mont. Religious Legis. Coalition. Mem. Am., Mont., Central Mont. (pres. 1975—) bar assns. Home: 103 Hillcrest Dr Lewistown MT 59457 Office: 608 Montana Bldg Lewistown MT 59457 Tel (406) 538-8733

PARRISH, JAMES DAVID, b. Statesboro, Ga., May 26, 1939; B.A., Presbyn. Coll., Clinton, S.C., 1962; J.D., Mercer U., 1971. Admitted to Fla. bar, 1971; asso. firm Howell, Kirby, Montgomery, DiAuito & Dean, Orlando, Fla., 1971-73; partner firm Hurt & Parrish, Orlando, 1973—. Mem. Fla., Am., Orange County (Fla.) bar assns., Acad. Fla. Trial Lawyers, Am. Trial Lawyers Assn. Student writing editor Mercer Law Rev., 1969-71. Home: 8553 Butternut Blvd Orlando FL 32807 Office: 1000 E Robinson St Orlando FL 32801 Tel (305) 843-1920

PARRISH, JIM, b. Great Bend, Kans., Aug. 25, 1946; B.S. in Tech. Journalism, Kans. State U., 1970; J.D. cum laude, Washburn U., 1973. Admitted to Kans. bar, 1973; individual practice law, Topeka, 1973—; mem. Kans. Ho. of Reps., 1973-74, Kans. Senate, 1974—. Mem. Kans. Trial Lawyers Assn., Topeka, Kans. bar assns. Home: 3632 S E Tomahawk Dr Topeka KS 66605 Office: 909 Topeka Ave Topeka KS 66612 Tel (913) 232-0574

PARRISH, JOHN EDWARD, b. Lebanon, Mo., June 10, 1940; B.S. in Bus. Adminstrn., Mo. U., 1962, J.D., 1965; grad. Nat. Coll. State Judiciary, U. Nev., Reno, 1974. Admitted to Mo. bar, 1962. Asso. firms Arthur Andersen & Co., St. Louis, 1965-66, Hugh Phillips, Camdenton, Mo., 1968-69; partner firm Phillips & Parrish, Camdenton, 1969-73; pros. atty. Camden County (Mo.), 1969-73; circuit judge 26th Circuit of Mo., 1973—; mem. Bd. Certified Ct. Reporter Examiners of Mo. Vice pres. Camdenton Civic Assn., 1968-72; mem. Camdenton R-3 Sch. Dist. Bd. Edn., 1973-76. Mem. Mo. Jud. Conf., Phi Delta Phi, Alpha Kappa Psi, Beta Gamma Sigma. Home: Route 2 PO Box 81E Camdenton MO 65020 Office: Camden County Courthouse Camdenton MO 65020 Tel (314) 346-5160

PARRISH, JUNE AUSTIN, b. Kansas City, Mo., June 25, 1917; A.A., Kansas City Jr. Coll., 1933; J.D., U. Mo., 1950. Admitted to Mo. bar, 1950, U.S. Supreme Ct. bar, 1958; atty. Employers Reins. Corp., Kansas City, Mo., 1950-68, asso. gen. counsel, 1968-74, gen. counsel, 1974—. Pres. Rehab. Inst. of Kansas City, 1963-65; bd. dirs. Legal Aid and Defender Soc., 1967-69, Mid-Continent council Girl Scouts U.S.A., 1973—. Mem. Am. Arbitration Assn. (nat. panel arbitrators 1975), Reins. of Am. (mem. legal com.), Am., Mo. (chmn. ins. law com.), Kansas City bar assns., Scribes, Lawyers Assn. of Kansas City. Author: (with Norman E. Risjord) Liability Insurance Cases, 1957—. Home: 41 Compton Ct Shawnee Mission KS 66208 Office: 21 W 10th St Kansas City MO 64105 Tel (816) 283-5211

PARRISH, KARL JOSEPH, b. Wilmington, Del., Oct. 5, 1927; B.A., Miami U., Oxford, Ohio, 1951; M.S., U. Pa., 1953; J.D., Temple U., 1966. Admitted to Del. bar, 1967; dir. Del. Liquor Commn., 1966-68; individual practice law, Wilmington, 1968—; chmn. New Castle County (Del.) Housing Authority, 1974-76. Pres. dist. PTA, 1972-73; bd. dirs. Children's Bur. Del. Mem. Am. Trial Lawyers, Am. Bar Assn. Home: 3211 Romilly Rd Wilmington DE 19810 Office: 1207 King St Wilmington DE 19801

PARRISH, SIDNEY HOWARD, b. Orlando, Fla., Mar. 3, 1940; B.S., Fla. State U., 1963, J.D., 1969. Admitted to Fla. bar, 1970; partner firm Troutman, Parrish & Weeks, P.A., Winter Park, Fla., 1970—; asst. city atty. City of Winter Park, 1970-72, city prosecutor, 1970-72; asst. solicitor County of Orange (Fla.), 1970-72. Trustee, deacon 1st Bapt. Ch., Orlando. Mem. Assn. Trial Lawyers Am. (med. malpractice com. 1975), Acad. Fla. Trial Lawyers, Delta Theta Phi. Office: Troutman Parrish & Weeks 427 S New York Ave Winter Park FL 32789

PARRISH, THOMAS ZANER, b. Moscow, Tex., Sept. 6, 1919; B.S., Stephen F. Austin State U., 1946; J.D., U. Tex., 1948; B.D., Southwestern Bapt. Theol. Sem., 1953. Admitted to Tex. bar, 1948; asso. firm Griffin and Morehead, Plainview, Tex., 1948-50; minister First Baptist Ch., Marietta, Okla., 1953-55; v.p., legal counsel Wayland Bapt. Coll., 1955-63; v.p. devel. Baylor U., 1963—. Bd. dirs. Heart of Tex. council Boy Scouts Am., 1970-73, pres. council, 1973, 74, 75; trustee Waco (Tex.) United Fund. Mem. State Bar Tex., Phi Delta Phi. Contbr. articles on edn. and fund raising to profl. jours. Home: 2801 Braemar St Waco TX 76710 Office: Baylor U Waco TX 76730 Tel (817) 755-2561

PARRY, RONALD RICHARD, b. Newport, Ky., May 13, 1948; B.S., Western Ky. U., 1970; J.D. (Campbell County Bar Assn. Henry J. Cook Meml. Fund scholar), U. Tenn., 1972. Admitted to Ky. bar, 1973; asso. firm Kaufmann, Johnson & Blau, Newport, 1972-77; partner firm Jolly, Johnson, Blau & Parry, Newport, 1977—; pub. defender Campbell County (Ky.), 1975—. Mem. Ky., Campbell County (v.p. 1975) bar assns., Ky., Am. trial lawyers assns., Nat. Assn. Criminal Def. Lawyers. Home: 40 Chalfonte Pl Fort Thomas KY 41075 Office: Lawyer's Bldg Newport KY 41071 Tel (606) 491-4420

PARRY, STANLEY BRIAN, b. London, Aug. 26, 1936; A.A., Los Angeles City Coll., 1957; J.D., Southwestern U., 1964. Admitted to Calif. bar, 1965; partner firm Lipton, Drizin, & Parry, Van Nuys, Calif., 1965—. Mem. Los Angeles County, San Fernando Valley bars. Office: 14332 Victory Blvd Van Nuys CA 91411 Tel (213) 786-4550

PARRY, WILLIAM HENRY, b. Bklyn., Mar. 25, 1931; B.A. cum laude, St. John's U., 1952, J.D. cum laude, 1955. Admitted to N.Y. bar, 1956, U.S. Supreme Ct bar, 1959; mem. firm S.M. and D.E. Meeker, Bklyn., 1955-56, 60—; capt. JAGC, U.S. Army, 1956-59; gen. counsel Power-Draulics, Inc., 1961-68, P.F.B. Assos., 1968—, Eastern Hydraulics, Inc., 1970-74, Q.A. Microfilm, 1974—; del. N.Y. State 10th Jud. Dist. Conv., 1965. Mem. Am., N.Y. State, Bklyn. bar assns., Savs. Bank Attys. Assn. Bklyn. Home: 3 Evelyn Ln Syosset NY 11791 Office: 1 Hanson Pl Brooklyn NY 11243 Tel (212) 783-3340

PARSELL, CHARLES VICTOR, b. Rome, N.Y., Nov. 17, 1895; A.B., Cornell U., 1917, LL.B., 1920. Admitted to N.Y. bar, 1920; partner firm Rogers & Wells, N.Y.C., 1946-74, cons., 1974—. Mem.

Am., N.Y. State bar assns., Bar Assn. City N.Y. Home: 1527 Long Hill Rd Millington NJ 07946 Tel (201) 647-0876

PARSELLS, NORMAN KING, b. Stamford, Conn., Dec. 4, 1908; B.A., Yale, 1929, LL.B., 1932. Admitted to Conn. bar, 1932, U.S. Supreme Ct. bar; mem. firm Marsh, Day & Calhoun, Bridgeport, Conn., 1932—; town counsel, Fairfield, Conn.; mem. Conn. Legislature, 1951-56, majority leader, 1955-56. Pres. YMCA of Greater Bridgeport, mem. advisory com. Mem. Bridgeport (past pres.), Conn. (past pres.), Am. bar assns. Recipient Awards C. of C., Jr. C. of C., United Way, Conn. Bar Assn. Home: 520 Hoydens Ln Fairfield CT 06430 Office: 955 Main St Bridgeport CT 06604 Tel (203) 368-4221

PARSON, DONALD PHILLIPS, b. N.Y.C., Dec. 7, 1941; B.A., Duke, 1963; J.D., Syracuse U., 1968, LL.M., N.Y. U., 1973. Admitted to N.Y. bar, 1968, U.S. Supreme Ct. bar, 1974, U.S. Ct. Appeals 2d Circuit bar, 1975; asso. firm Whitman & Ransom, N.Y.C., 1968-75, partner, 1976—; bd. visitors Syracuse U. Coll. Law. Vice chmn. Multiple Sclerosis Soc., Westchester County, N.Y. Mem. Am., N.Y. State (chmn. young lawyers sect.) bar assns. Home: 164 Pondfield Rd W Bronxville NY 10708 Office: 522 5th Ave New York City NY 10036 Tel (212) 575-5800

PARSONS, EDWARD ERNEST, b. Whittier, Calif., May 23, 1943; A.A., Fullerton Jr. Coll., 1963; B.A., U. Calif., Berkeley, 1965; J.D., U. Calif., San Francisco, 1970; M.A. in Govt., Claremont Grad. Sch., 1968. Admitted to Calif. bar, 1971; dep. dist. atty. Humboldt County, Calif., 1971—. Office: Courthouse Eureka CA 95501 Tel (707) 445-7411

PARSONS, GEORGE LAWRENCE, b. Pikeville, Ky., June 11, 1902; B.A., Morehead State U., 1953, M.A., 1957, LL.B., 1926. Admitted to Ky. bar, 1927; individual practice law, Pikeville, 1928—. Justice of peace Pike County, Ky., 1933-37. Address: Route 2 Box 259-N Pikeville KY 41501 Tel (606) 437-7015

PARSONS, JAMES BENTON, b. Kansas City, Mo., Aug. 13, 1913; B.A., James Millikin U., 1934; student U. Wis., summers, 1935-39; M.A., U. Chgo., 1946, LL.D., 1949. Successivley field agt., asst. to dean men, instr. polit. sci. Lincoln U., Jefferson City, Mo., 1934-38, acting head music dept., 1938-40; tchr. pub. schs., Greensboro, N.C., 1940-42; admitted to Ill. bar, 1949; mem. firm Gassaway, Crosson, Turner & Parsons, Chgo., 1949-51; tchr. constl. govt. John Marshall Law Sch., Chgo., 1949-51; asst. corp. counsel City of Chgo., 1949-51; asst. U.S. dist atty., 1951-60; judge superior court Cook County, Ill., 1960-61; judge U.S. Dist. Ct. No. Dist. Ill., 1961—, now chief judge. Co-chmn. Ill. Commn. N.Y. World's Fair; chmn. Chgo. Conf. Race and Religion; exec. bd. Chgo. Area council Boy Scouts Am. Bd. dirs. Trotting Charities Inc., Chgo. Urban League; turstee Lincoln Acad. Ill., Chgo. Med. Podiatry Hosp.; hon. bd. dirs. Leukemia Research Found., Inc.; nat. bd. trustees NCCJ; citizens com. U. Ill. Mem. Am., Chgo., Ill., Fed., Nat. Cook County bar assns., Ill. Acad. Criminology, N.A.A.C.P., Sigma Pi, Pi Beta Phi, Kappa Alpha Psi. Home: 2801 Martin Luther King Jr Dr Chicago IL 60616 Office: 219 S Dearborn Ave Chicago IL 60604*

PARSONS, KEITH, b. Davenport, Iowa, Apr. 28, 1912; Ph.B., U. Chgo., 1933, J.D., 1937. Admitted to Ill. bar, 1938; asso. firm Ross & Watts, 1938-42; asst. chief, later chief legal div. Chgo. Ordnance Dist., 1942-46; partner firm Milliken, Vollers & Parsons, 1946-64, Ross, Hardies, O'Keefe, Babcock & Parsons, 1965—. Mem. Hinsdale (Ill.) Bd. Edn., 1957-63, pres., 1959-63; mem. Chgo. Crime Commn., 1960—; alternate mem. Ill. Bd. Higher Edn., 1972-73; mem. citizens bd. U. Chgo., 1967—; bd. govs. Ill. State Colls. and Univs., 1970-73; trustee State Univs. Retirement System, 1972-73. Mem. Am., Ill., Chgo. (bd. mgrs. 1967-69) bar assns., Econ. Club Chgo., Law Club Chgo., Legal Club Chgo. (past pres.), Phi Beta Kappa. Home: 744 Cleveland Rd Hinsdale IL 60521 Office: One IBM Plaza Chicago IL 60611 Tel (312) 467-9300

PARSONS, RUSSELL JAMES, b. Davenport, Iowa, Dec. 16, 1918; A.B., U. Chgo., 1940, J.D., 1942. Admitted to Iowa, Ill. bars, 1942; atty. Borg-Warner Corp., Chgo., 1946-56, asst. gen. counsel, 1956-57, asst. sec., 1957-65, sec., 1965-68, asso. gen. counsel, 1968-72, v.p., gen. counsel, 1972-76, sr. v.p., 1976—. Mem. Chgo., Ill., Am. bar assns., Law Club Chgo., Legal Club Chgo., Assn. Gen. Counsel, Am. Soc. Corp. Secs. Inc. Home: 510 S Washington St Hinsdale IL 60521 Office: Borg-Warner Corp 200 S Michigan Ave Chicago IL 60604

PARTIN, CHARLES CURTIS, b. Montgomery, Ala., Jan. 9, 1946; A.B., U. Ala., 1968, J.D., 1971. Admitted to Ala. bar; law clk. to justice Ala. Supreme Ct., Montgomery, 1971-72; asso. firm Chason, Stone & Chason, Bay Minette, Ala., 1972-74, partner, 1974-76; partner firm Stone & Partin, Bay Minette, 1976—. Chmn. N. Baldwin chpt. ARC, Bay Minette, 1973-76; mem. adv. council Ret. Sr. Vol. Program, Bay Minette, 1976. Mem. Am., Baldwin County (pres. 1976-77) bar assns. Home: 1100 McConnell Ave Bay Minette AL 36507 Office: PO Box 1109 Bay Minette AL 36507 Tel (205) 937-2417

PARTIN, JOHN PATRICK, b. Macon, Mo., July 27, 1944; B.A. cum laude, Vanderbilt U., 1966; LL.D., U. Va., 1969. Admitted to Va. bar, 1969, Ga. bar, 1972; served to capt. JAGC, U.S. Army, 1969-73; partner firm Hirsch, Beil and Partin, Columbus, Ga., 1973—. Mem. Citizens Advisory Com. Community Devel., Columbus, 1975—, chmn., 1976; vestry St. Thomas Episcopal Ch., Columbus. Mem. Assn. Trial Lawyers, Am., Chattahoochee Circuit (sec.) bar assns., Columbus Lawyers Club. Home: 4836 Roxbury Dr Columbus GA 31907 Tel (404) 323-6581

PARTRIDGE, DONALD GERARD, b. Bklyn., June 4, 1913; LL.B., Fordham U., 1937; LL.M., N.Y. U., 1940. Admitted to N.Y. bar, 1940; individual practice law, Nanuet, N.Y., 1943—. Mem. N.Y., Rockland County bar assns., Catholic Lawyers Guild of Rockland County. Home: 7 Saint Anthony Ave Nanuet NY 10954 Office: 135 Main St Nanuet NY 10954 Tel (914) 623-2450

PARUSZEWSKI, CHARLES LOUIS, b. Wilmington, Del., Jan. 6, 1911; B.A., U. Del., 1933, M.A., 1934; LL.B., Temple U., 1939. Admitted to Del. bar, 1940; mem. firm Killoran & Van Brunt, Wilmington, 1940-47; individual practice law, Wilmington, 1947—; dep. atty. gen. State of Del., 1958-62, chief dep. atty. gen., 1964-68. Pres. Ampol, Wilmington, 1972. Mem. Del., Am., bar assns., Am. Judicature Soc., Nat. Dist. Attys. Assn. (dir. 1958-62, 64-68), Phi Kappa Phi. Home: 4 Tenhy Dr Perth Wilmington DE 19803 Office: 1211 King St Wilmington DE 19801 Tel (302) 655-9974

PARVIN, GARY RANDOLPH, b. Corinth, Miss., Sept. 8, 1945; B.A., Miss. State U., 1966; J.D., U. Miss., 1969. Admitted to Miss. bar, 1969; individual practice law, Starkville, Miss., 1969-76; asso. with Michael J. McCormick, Starkville, 1976—. Pres. Starkville Jaycees, 1972-73, state legal counsel, Miss., 1972-73. Mem. Am., Miss., Oktibbeha County bar assns., Miss. Trial Lawyers, Phi Eta Sigma, Kappa Sigma, Delta Theta Phi, Phi Kappa Phi. Named outstanding young man of Starkville. Office: PO Box 782 Courthouse Sq Starkville MS 39759 Tel (601) 323-5146

PASCAL, LAWRENCE JOSEPH, b. N.Y.C., Jan. 24, 1942; B.A., St. Anselm's Coll., 1964; LL.B., George Washington U., 1967. Admitted to Va. bar, 1967, D.C. bar, 1968, U.S. Supreme Ct. bar, 1971; partner firm Ashcraft, Gerel & Koonz, Alexandria, Va., 1967—; lectr. workmens compensation. Vice pres. Halloing Point Civic Assn., 1975. Mem. Am., D.C., Alexandria (Va.), N.Y. bar assns., Am., Va., trial lawyers assns., So. Assn. Workmen's Compensation Adminstrn. Contbr. articles to profl. jours. Home: 11813 River Dr Lorton VA 22079 Office: 4660 Kenmore Ave Suite 220 Alexandria VA 22304 Tel (703) 751-7400

PASCHAL, JOEL FRANCIS, b. Wake Forest, N.C., Jan. 21, 1916; B.A., Wake Forest Coll., 1935, LL.B., 1938; M.A., Princeton, 1942, Ph.D., 1948. Admitted to N.C. bar, 1938; instr. Sch. Law Wake Forest Coll., 1939-40; instr. Princeton U., 1946-47; research dir. N.C. Commn. for Improvement of Adminstrn. of Justice, 1947-48; individual practice law, Raleigh, N.C., 1949-54; vis. prof. Sch. Law Duke U., Durham, N.C., 1952-53, prof., 1954—. Mem. N.C. Bar Assn. Author: Mr. Justice Sutherland, 1951; contbr. articles to legal jours. Home: 1527 Pinecrest Rd Durham NC 27705 Office: Duke Law Sch Durham NC 27706 Tel (919) 684-3289

PASCHAL, KAY FRANCES, b. Columbia, S.C., June 7, 1943; A.B., U. S.C., Columbia, 1965, J.D., 1968, postgrad. in Pub. Adminstrn., 1973—. Admitted to S.C. bar, 1968; atty. Lexington County (S.C.) Legal Aid Service Agy., 1968-73; research asso. U. S.C. Bur. Govtl. Research and Service, Columbia, 1973-74, asst. dir. bur., 1975—; atty. Legis.-Gov's. Com. on Mental Health and Mental Retardation, 1975—. Bd. dirs. Legal Aid Service Agy., Columbia. Mem. Govtl. Research Assn., Am., S.C. (chmn. info. subcom. legisl. liaison com.), Lexington County bar assns., Nat. Inst. Municipal Law Officers, Am. Acad. Polit., Social Sci. Office: PO Box 385 Cayce SC 29033 Tel (803) 777-8156

PASCOE, WILLIAM RICHARD, b. Endicott, N.Y., May 19, 1945; B.A., U. Calif., Santa Barbara, 1967; postgrad. Oxford (Eng.) U., 1969; J.D., Harvard, 1972. Admitted to Calif. bar, 1972; congregational staff Calif. Senator, 1970; legis. aid, partner firm Landels, Ripley & Diamond, San Francisco, 1972—. Mem. Am., Calif., San Francisco bar assns. Tel (415) 788-5000

PASETTE, SALLY PHILLIPS, b. Alhambra, Calif., Mar. 25, 1945; A.B., U. Calif., Los Angeles, 1966, J.D., 1969. Admitted to Calif. bar, 1970, Ariz. bar, 1970, Wash. State bar, 1972; research asso. U. Ariz. Sch. Law, 1969-70; staff atty. Pima County (Ariz.) Legal Aid Soc., 1970-71; asso. firm Roberts Shefelman, Lawrence, Gay & Moch, Seattle, 1971-75; individual practice law, Seattle, 1975—. Mem. urban sprawl com. King County (Wash.) League of Women Voters, 1976—. Mem. Wash. State, Am., King County bar assns., Wash. State Trial Lawyers Assn., Wash. Women Lawyers. Home: 2158 E Shelby St Seattle WA 98112 Office: 650 Colman Bldg Seattle WA 98104 Tel (206) 623-1590

PASKAY, ALEXANDER L., b. Mohacs, Hungary, Nov. 5, 1922; J.D., U. Budapest, 1944; J.D. U. Miami, 1958. Admitted to Fla. bar, 1958; Research asst. U.S. Dist. Ct. So. Dist. of Fla., Miami, 1958-61; research asst. U.S. Dist. for Middle Dist. Fla., Tampa, 1961-63; bankruptcy judge U.S. Dist. Ct. Middle Dist. Fla., Tampa, 1963—; adj. prof. law Stetson U. of Law, St. Petersburg, Fla., 1973—. Mem. Nat. Conf. Bankruptcy Judges, Am., Hillsborough County Fla. bar assns., Am. Judicature Soc. Author: Handbook for Trustees and Receivers in Bankruptcy, 1973; co-author: Collier's Bankruptcy Manual. Office: 611 N Florida Ave Room 424 Tampa FL 33601 Tel (813) 228-2115

PASQUALONE, GARY LEE, b. Geneva, Ohio, July 6, 1948; A.B., Miami U., Oxford, Ohio, 1970; J.D., U. Tenn., 1973. Admitted to Ohio bar, 1974; asso. firm Robert F. Curry, Geneva, city prosecutor City of Geneva, 1975-76. Vice-pres. Ashtabula County (Ohio) Council on Alcohol and Drug Abuse. Home: 7525 Lake Shore Blvd Marion OH 44075 Office: 302 S Broadway Geneva OH 44041 Tel (216) 466-4818

PASQUARIELLO, ARTHUR A., b. Schenectady, N.Y., Apr. 14, 1945; B.A., Siena Coll., 1967; J.D., Albany Law Sch., 1972. Admitted to N.Y. State bar, 1972; mem. firm Parisi, De Lorenzo, Gordon & Pasquariello, Schenectady, 1972—. Clk., City Ct., Schenectady, 1975. Mem. N.Y. State, Schenectady County bar assns. Home: 824 Londonderry Rd Schenectady NY 12309 Office: 201 Nott Terr Schenectady NY 12307 Tel (518) 374-8494

PASS, JOSEPH J., b. McKees Rocks, Pa., June 24, 1941; B.S., Pa. State U., 1964; J.D., Duquesne U., 1967. Admitted to Pa. bar, U.S. Dist. Ct. bar, U.S. Ct. Appeals bar 3d Circuit; adminstrv. asst. to U.S. Dist. Ct. Western Dist. Pa., 1969-70; asso. firm McKay, Arch & Steele, Pitts., 1970-72; partner firm Jubelirer, Pass & Intrieri, Pitts., 1972—; served with Judge Adv. Gen. Corps AUS, 1968; dep. atty. gen. Commonwealth of Pa., 1971-72. Mem. Am., Pa., Allegheny County bar assns. Home: 106 Claridge Dr Coraopolis PA 15108 Office: Lawyers Bldg Pittsburgh PA 15219 Tel (412) 281-3850

PASSIN, ALLAN, b. N.Y.C., June 8, 1925; grad., Bklyn. Law Sch., 1950. Partner firm Passin & Williams, N.Y.C., 1950—. Mem. Am., N.Y. trial lawyers assns., N.Y. State Bar Assn., Am. Arbitration Assn. (arbitrator). Home: 33 E End Ave New York City NY 10028 Office: 521 5th Ave New York City NY 10017 Tel (212) 687-2345

PASTERNAK, N. ALFRED, b. Washington, Mar. 16, 1936; B.A., Colgate U., 1957; M.B.A., Columbia, 1959; J.D., George Washington U., 1965. Admitted to Md. bar, 1965, D.C. bar, 1965, U.S. Tax Ct. bar, 1965, U.S. Supreme Ct. bar, 1968; partner firm Pasternak & Kaufmann, Washington, 1967—; atty. corp. fin. div. SEC, 1965-66. Mem. D.C., Montgomery County, Md. State, Fed., Am. bar assns., Am. Assn. Atty.-C.P.A.'s. Home: Bethesda MD 20014 Office: 4400 Jenifer St Washington DC 20015 Tel (202) 362-4060

PASTO, JAMES HENRY, b. Memphis, Feb. 23, 1945; A.B., San Diego State U., 1967; J.D., U. San Diego, 1970. Admitted to Calif. bar, 1971; individual practice law, San Diego, 1971—; partner Pasto & Pasto, San Diego. Mem. Nat. Assn. Criminal Defense Lawyers, Calif., Am. trial lawyers assns., Assn. Am. Trial Lawyers, Calif. Attys. Criminal Justice. Home: 6420 Belle Glade Ave San Diego CA 92119 Office: 110 W C St Suite 1502 San Diego CA 92101

PASTORE, JOHN O., b. Providence, Mar. 17, 1907; LL.B., Northeastern U., 1931. Mem. R.I. Gen. Assembly, 1935; asst. atty. gen., 1937-38, 40-44; lt. gov. State of R.I., 1944-45, gov., 1945-50; mem. U.S. Senate, 1950—. Home: 91 Mountain Laurel Dr Cranston RI 02920 Office: 301 Post Office Annex Providence RI 02903 Tel (401) 421-4583

PASTORIZA, JULIO, b. Havana, Sept. 22, 1948; B.A., U. Fla., 1969; J.D., U. Miami, 1973. Admitted to Fla. bar, 1973; asso. firm Miguel A. Suarez, Miami, 1973-74; individual practice law, Miami, 1974-76; partner firm Sulli & Pastoriza, Miami, 1977—; instr. bus. law Biscayne Coll., 1972-75. Mem. Dade County Bar Assn., Cuban Am. Lawyers Assn. Home: 4230 SW 98th Ct Miami FL 33165 Office: 101 E Flagler St Miami FL 33131 Tel (305) 377-4648

PATANELLA, JAMES SAMUEL, b. Johnstown, Pa., Apr. 10, 1936; A.A. in Lib. Arts, U. Balt., 1962, J.D., 1964; M.S. in Taxation, Southeastern U., 1976. Admitted to Md. bar, 1973; asst. mgr. Pinkerton Nat. Detective Agency, Balt., 1960-62; spl. agent U.S. Dept. Defense, Washington, 1962-73; pres. Verification, Inc., 1972—; v.p., dir. Security Title & Escrow Corp., 1975—. Pres., Samuel Ogle Jr. High Sch. PTA, Bowie, Md., 1975-76. Mem. Am., Md. bar assns., Am. Judicature Soc. Home: 13413 Yorktown Dr Bowie MD 20715 Office: 9811 Mallard Dr Suite 101 Laurel MD 20811 Tel (301) 363-1117

PATCHEN, BRIAN PAUL, b. Steubenville, Ohio, Apr. 12, 1943; B.A. in Am. Culture, U. Mich., 1965, J.D., 1969. Admitted to N.Y. State bar, 1970, Fla. bar, 1973; asst. trust officer Morgan Guaranty Trust Co. N.Y., N.Y.C., 1969-71; mem. firm Kelly, Black, Black & Kenny, Miami, Fla., 1972—. Mem. Am., Fla. bar assns. Home: 7620 SW 159th Terr Miami FL 33157 Office: 1400 Alfred I duPont Bldg Miami FL 33131 Tel (305) 358-5700

PATE, CHARLES WILLIAM, b. Independence, Mo., Apr. 26, 1927; B.C.E., U. Mo., 1950; J.D., U. Tulsa, 1965. Admitted to Okla. bar, 1965; v.p. Pate Engring. Co., Tulsa, 1950-65; partner firm Frazier, Harris, Dyer, Pate & Hopper, Tulsa, 1965-74; individual practice law, Tulsa, 1974—. Mem. Okla., Tulsa County bar assns., Okla. Trial Lawyers Assn., Okla., Nat. socs. profl. engrs. Registered profl. engr., Okla. Home: 5745 S Indianapolis Ave Tulsa OK 74135 Office: 302 Center Bldg Tulsa OK 74127

PATE, GORDON RALPH, b. Buffalo, Tex., Sept. 13, 1928; B.S., Sam Houston State Tchrs. Coll., 1952; J.D., U. Tex., 1954. Admitted to Tex. bar, 1954, U.S. Supreme Ct. bar; atty. Pitts. Corning Corp.; individual practice law, Beaumont, Tex. Mem. Am., Jefferson County (dir.) bar assns., State Bar Tex. (profl. efficiency and econ. com., dist. pros. com. of state grievance com.), Tex. Assn. Def. Counsel. Home: 431 Yorktown St Beaumont TX 77707 Office: 1119 Beaumont Savs Bldg Beaumont TX 77701 Tel (713) 838-6578

PATE, JAMES LEE, JR., b. Louisville, May 8, 1942; B.A., Purdue U., 1965; J.D., U. Ky., 1968. Admitted to Ky. bar, 1969; individual practice law, Elizabethtown, Ky., 1969-73; mem. firm Pate & Richardson, Elizabethtown, 1973-75; mem. firm Pate, Richardson & Bailey, 1974-76; judge Elizabethtown City Police Ct., 1972—. Chmn. Hardin County Heart Fund, 1975-76. Mem. Delta Theta Phi. Home: 722 Sunrise Ln Elizabethtown KY 42701 Office: 123 W Dixie Ave PO Box 248 Elizabethtown KY 42701 Tel (502) 769-2379

PATE, JAMES WYNFORD, II, b. Augusta, Ga., Oct. 20, 1949; B.A., Emory U., 1971; J.D., U. Tenn., 1973. Admitted to Tenn. bar, 1974; asso. firm Winchester, Walsh, Marshall, Memphis, 1974—; asst. city atty. Germantown (Tenn.), 1976. Chmn. Greater Memphis and Shelby County Young Republicans, 1974—; mem. steering com. Shelby County Rep. Party, 1974—. Mem. Am., Tenn., Memphis, Shelby County bar assns. Recipient U.S. Law Week award U. Tenn., 1974. Home: 490 Garland St Memphis TN 38104 Office: 3200 100 N Main Bldg Memphis TN 38104 Tel (901) 526-7374

PATE, WILLIAM, b. Lubbock County, Tex., Oct. 13, 1927; B.S. with honors, Sul Ross State Coll., Alaine, Tex., 1951; M.S. with honors, U. Houston, 1953, J.D., 1970. Admitted to Tex. bar, 1970, U.S. Dist. Ct. Western Dist. Tex. bar, 1972, No. Dist. Tex., 1975, U.S. Cts. Appeals bar, 5th Circuit, 1971, 10th Circuit, 1972, U.S. Supreme Ct. bar, 1974; partner firm Kern & Pate, El Paso, 1971; individual practice law, El Paso, 1972—. Mem. citizens adv. impact study com. City of El Paso, 1973-75, El Paso Mountain com., 1975—; dir. El Paso unit Am. Cancer Soc., 1971-73; mem. El Paso Community Blood Services Adv. Council, 1975—; v.p., dir. Tex. Consumers Assn., 1973-74; mem. steering com. Council Consumer Orgns., Washington, 1974—. Mem. Am., El Paso (dir. 1974) trial lawyers assns., Am., Tex., El Paso County bar assns., Am. Assn. Petroleum Geologists, Soc. Petroleum Engrs. Office: 6044 Gateway E Suite 607 El Paso TX 79905 Tel (915) 779-2561

PATE, WILLIAM AUGUST, b. Selma, Ala., Dec. 9, 1942; B.A. in Polit. Sci., The Citadel, 1964; J.D., U. Miss., 1972. Admitted to Miss. bar, 1972; individual practice law, Gulfport, Miss., 1973—. Sec., treas. Central Harrison County Little League, 1974-75; v.p. Saucier (Miss.) Vol. Fire Dept., 1974—; sec. Saucier Jaycees, 1973-75. Mem. Am., Harrison County bar assns., Miss. State Bar, Harrison County Jr. Bar, Am., Miss. trial lawyers assns., Am. Judicature Soc., Delta Theta Phi. Home: Route 1 Box 132 Saucier MS 39574 Office: 2017 20th Ave Gulfport MS 39501 Tel (601) 864-3489

PATE, WILLIAM CRAIG, b. Coronado, Calif., Nov. 17, 1943; B.A., Whittier Coll., 1965; J.D. cum laude, U. San Diego, 1971. Admitted to Calif. bar, 1972, U.S. Dist. Ct. for So. Calif. bar, 1972, U.S. 9th Circuit Ct. Appeals bar, 1972; law clk. U.S. Ct. Appeals, 9th Circuit, 1971-72; asso. firm Legro & Rentto, San Diego, 1972-75; partner firm Rentto, Pate & Tower, San Diego, 1975—. Mem. governing bd. Coronado Unified Sch. Dist., 1977—. Mem. Am., Calif., San Diego bar assns. Home: 1144 Glorietta Blvd Coronado CA 92118 Office: 110 W A St Suite 1600 San Diego CA 92101 Tel (714) 238-1002

PATE, WILLIAM MITCHELL, b. Montezuma, Ga., Jan. 9, 1918; J.D., Emory U., 1939. Admitted to Ga. bar, 1939, U.S. Supreme Ct. bar, 1960; asso. firm Carter, Stewart & Johnson, Atlanta, 1939-41; mem. legal staff AT&T, Atlanta, 1941; atty. Atlanta NLRB, 1942-55, chief law officer, 1950-55; partner firm Nall, Sterne, Miller, Cadenhead & Dennis, Atlanta, 1955-58, Mitchell, Clarke, Pate & Anderson, Atlanta, 1958—. Mem. Am., Atlanta bar assns., State Bar Ga., Am. Judicature Soc. Contbr. articles to legal jours. Home: 605 Chestnut Hall Ln NW Atlanta GA 30327 Office: 600 Georgia Fed Savings Bldg Atlanta GA 30303 Tel (404) 577-6010

PATERNO, LOUIE ANTHONY, JR., b. Montgomery, W. Va., Feb. 6, 1943; A.B., Washington and Lee U., 1965, LL.B., 1968. Admitted to W.Va. bar, 1968; partner firm Graziani, O'Brien & Paterno,

Charleston, W.Va., 1969-70; individual practice law, Charleston, 1978—. Mem. Ho. of Dels., W.Va. Legis., 1970-74; pres. Charleston Chpt. Washington and Lee Alumni Assn. Mem. W.Va. Bar Assn. Home: 1 Grosscup Rd Charleston WV 25314 Office: Box 902 Charleston WV 25323 Tel (304) 344-3567

PATERNOSTER, FRANCIS RICHARD, b. Downsville, N.Y., July 19, 1912; A.B., Cornell U., 1934, LL.B., 1936, J.D., 1937. Admitted to N.Y. bar, 1937, U.S. Supreme Ct. bar, 1957; asso. editor Am. Law Reports, Rochester, N.Y., 1936-37; individual practice law, Walton, N.Y., 1957-73; partner firm Paternoster, Estes & O'Leary, Walton, N.Y., 1973—; estate tax atty. for Delaware County, N.Y., State of New York, 1955-58; dist. atty., Delaware County, 1958. Mem. Am., N.Y. State (del.) Delaware County (pres. 1950-54) bar assns., World Assn. Lawyers, Am., N.Y. State trial lawyers assn., Am. Judicature Soc., N.Y. State Dist. Attys. Assn. Home: 39 Gardiner Pl Walton NY 13856 Office: 28 Townsend St Walton NY 13856 Tel (607) 865-6501

PATRICK, H. HUNTER, b. Gasville, Ark., Aug. 19, 1939; B.A., U. Wyo., 1961, J.D., 1966. Admitted to Wyo. bar, 1966, Colo. bar, 1967, U.S. Supreme Ct. bar, 1974; individual practice law, Powell, Wyo., 1966—; municipal judge, Powell, 1967-68; city atty. Powell, 1969—; instr. bus. law N.W. Community Coll., 1968—. Bd. dirs. Rocky Mountain Hemophilia Found., 1967—; elder Powell Presbyterian Ch. Mem. Am., Wyo. bar assns., Wyo. Assn. of Judges (pres. 1973—), Am. Judges Assn., Am. Judicature Soc., Yellowstate Valley Estate Planning Council. Home and Office: PO Box 941 Powell WY 82435 Tel (307) 754-4012

PATRICK, JAMES PAUL, b. Lima, Ohio, Nov. 7, 1944; B.S., Bluffton Coll., 1967; J.D., Ohio No. U., 1972. Admitted to Ohio bar, 1972; individual practice law, Lima, 1972—. Bd. dirs. Marimor Workshop, 1973—. Mem. Ohio, Allen County, Auglaize County bar assns., Willis Soc. Ohio No. U. Home: 1410 Riverview Dr Lima OH 45805 Office: 209 N Main St Bldg Lima OH 45801 Tel (419) 227-3050 also 2d Floor Theatre Bldg Wapakoneta OH 45895 Tel (419) 738-3217

PATRICK, RICHARD GLEN, b. Sandpoint, Idaho, Nov. 13, 1924; student U. Idaho, 1946-49; J.D., U. Mich., 1952; grad. Nat. Coll. State Trial Judges, 1969. Admitted to Wash. bar, 1952, U.S. Dist. Ct. bar for Eastern Dist. Wash., 1953; partner firms Rodgers & Patrick, Pasco, Wash., 1953-60, Patrick & Campbell, Pasco, 1963-69; individual practice law, Pasco, 1960-63; judge Benton-Franklin County Superior Ct., 1969—; city atty. City of Pasco, 1953-63; U.S. ct. commr. for Eastern Dist. Wash., So. div., 1959-63; pres. Tri-City Estate Planning Council, 1966. Past bd. dirs. ARC, Children's Home Soc. Wash.; mem. exec. bd. Blue Mountain council Boy Scouts Am. Mem. Superior Ct. Judges Assn. (trustee), Am. Bar Assn., Nat. Assn. Juvenile Ct. Judges, Phi Beta Kappa. Office: Pub Safety Bldg Pasco WA 99301 Tel (509) 545-3528

PATRICK, RICHARD MURRAY, b. Victoria, B.C., Can., Oct. 20, 1946; B.A., Dartmouth, 1968; J.D., Washington Coll. Law, 1972. Admitted to D.C. bar, 1972, Va. bar, 1972; partner firm Lewis, Mitchell & Moore, Washington and Vienna, Va., 1972—. Mem. Am., Va., D.C. bar assns. Office: 8230 Old Courthouse Rd Vienna VA 22180 Tel (703) 790-9200

PATRICK, ROBERT WINTON, JR., b. Tifton, Ga., Jan. 11, 1940; B.A. cum laude, Fla. State U., 1961; LL.B., Yale, 1964. Admitted to Ga. bar, 1964; asso. firm Powell, Goldstein, Frazer & Murphy, Atlanta, 1964-68, partner, 1968—; spl. counsel Atlanta Crime Commn., 1967; adj. prof. law Emory U., 1972-75. Mem. Am., Ga., Atlanta bar assns. Editor-in-chief The Atlanta Lawyer, 1972-73. Home: 805 Kinloch St NW Atlanta GA 30327 Office: 1100 C & S Nat Bank Bldg 35 Broad St Atlanta GA 30303 Tel (404) 521-1900

PATRICK, WILLIAM BRADSHAW, b. Indpls., Nov. 29, 1923; A.B., The Principia, 1947; LL.B., Harvard, 1950. Admitted to Ind. bar, 1950; partner firm Patrick & Patrick, Indpls., 1950-53; individual practice law, Indpls., 1953—; gen. counsel Met. Plan Commn. Marion County and Indpls., 1955-66; dep. prosecutor Marion County, 1960-62. Mem. Indpls. Legal Aid Soc. (pres. 1963), Ind. Soc. SAR (sec. 1953-59), Lawyers Assn. Indpls., Am., Ind., Indpls., Hamilton County bar assns., Estate Planning Council Indpls. Office: 810 King Cole Bldg Indianapolis IN 46204 Tel (317) 637-2411

PATRIKIS, ERNEST THEODORE, b. Lynn, Mass., Dec. 1, 1943; B.A., U. Mass., 1965; J.D., Cornell U., 1968. Admitted to N.Y. State bar, 1969; asst. gen. counsel, asst. sec. Fed. Reserve Bank of N.Y., N.Y.C., 1968—. Mem. Assn. Bar N.Y.C., N.Y. State Bar Assn. Home: 20 E 9th St New York City NY 10003 Office: 33 Liberty St New York City NY 10045 Tel (212) 791-5022

PATTERSON, BENJAMIN RANDALL, III, b. Springfield, Ohio, Aug. 5, 1940; B.A., U. Ky., 1962; J.D., U. Fla., 1969. Admitted to Fla. bar, 1970; mng. atty. Fla. Rural Legal Services, Belle Glades, 1970-71; asst. gen. counsel Fla. Dept. Health and Rehab. Services, Tallahassee, 1971; dir. Fla. Div. Labor and Employment Opportunities, Tallahassee, 1972-74; exec. dir. Gov.'s Task Force on Workmen's Compensation, Tallahassee, 1974; individual practice law Tallahassee, Fla., 1974—; chmn. Fla. Supreme Ct. Pub. Employee's Rights Commn., 1974, mem. Fla. Prime Sponsor Advisory Council, 1974—. Mem. Fla. Bar, Am. Bar Assn. Home: 519 Short St Tallahassee FL 32303 Office: 1215 Thomasville Rd Tallahassee FL 32303 Tel (904) 224-9181

PATTERSON, BRUCE MARR, b. Los Angeles, May 14, 1939; B.S., U. Calif., Santa Barbara, 1961; LL.B., J.D., Hastings Coll. Law U. Calif., 1966. Admitted to Calif. bar, 1967; staff Orange County (Calif.) Dist. Atty.'s Office, 1967—, supr. West Municipal Ct., 1973, Juvenile Ct., 1974-76, Family Support Div., 1976—. Mem. Newport Beach (Calif.) Civil Service Commn., 1972-75; pres. Corona Highlands Property Owners Assn., 1971-74. Mem. Orange County, San Francisco bar assns., Dist. Attys. Assn. Calif., Nat. Welfare Fraud Assn., State Juvenile Officers Assn. Office: 700 Civic Center Dr Santa Ana CA 92701 Tel (714) 834-3600

PATTERSON, CHARLES DUANE, b. LaCrosse, Wis., July 16, 1932; B.A., U. Wis. at Madison, 1954, J.D., 1959. Admitted to Wis. bar, 1959; since practiced in Wausau, Wis., asso. firm Smith Pucher Tinkham & Smith, 1959-61; partner firm Tinkham Smith Bliss Patterson & Richards, 1962—; vice-chmn. Dist. 16 grievance com., 1974—. Fellow Am. Coll. Probate Counsel; mem. Am., Marathon County (chmn. ethics and grievance com. 1972-74) bar assns., State Bar Wis., Phi Beta Kappa, Order of Coif, Phi Kappa Phi. Named Outstanding Young Man, Wausau Jaycees, 1966; recipient Outstanding Optimist award, Wausau, 1975; named Man of Year, Wausau Salvation Army, 1972. Articles editor Wis. Law Rev., 1959. Home: 325 Broadway Wausau WI 54401 Office: 630 Fourth St Wausau WI 54401 Tel (715) 845-1151

PATTERSON, CLYDE C., b. Leetonia, Ohio, B.A., Ohio State U., 1935, J.D., 1938. Admitted to Ohio bar, 1938, Utah bar, 1946; now partner firm Patterson, Phillips, Gridley & Echard, Ogden, Utah; county atty. Morgan County (Utah), 1967-68. Mem. Am., Weber County bar assns., Utah State Bar (pres. 1976-77), Assn. Trial Lawyers Am., Am. Judicature Soc. Office: 427 27th St Ogden UT 84401 Tel (801) 394-7707

PATTERSON, DONALD, b. Lincoln, Nebr., Aug. 1, 1924; A.B., U. Nebr., 1947; LL.B., U. Mich., 1950. Admitted to Nebr. bar, 1950, Kans. bar, 1950; partner firms Adding, Jones & Davis, Topeka, 1950-54, Fisher Patterson Sayler & Smith, Topeka, 1955—; lectr. Washburn U. Sch. Law, 1951-52, mem. Am. Bd. Trial Advs. Fellow Am. Coll. Trial Lawyers; mem. Am., Kans., Topeka (pres. 1974-75) bar assns., Internat. Assn. Ins. Counsel, Kans. Assn. Def. Counsel (pres. 1973-74), Def. Research Inst. Home: 5119 W 25th St Topeka KS 66614 Office: 520 1st Nat Bank Tower Topeka KS 66603 Tel (913) 232-7761

PATTERSON, DUANE ALLEN, b. Lafayette, Ind., Nov. 12, 1931; B.A., DePauw U., 1953; J.D., Washington U., St. Louis, 1958. Admitted to Mo. bar, 1958, U.S. Supreme Ct. bar, 1965; atty. Union Electric Co., St. Louis, 1958-62; asst. gen. counsel Interco Inc., St. Louis, 1963-66, asst. sec., 1973, sec., 1973—, sec., dir. mem. exec. com. Internat. Shoe Co. div. Interco, St. Louis, 1966-73. Active United Way of Greater St. Louis, Arts and Edn. Council Greater St. Louis; trustee Govtl. Research Inst., St. Louis; treas., bd. dirs. Greater St. Louis council Girl Scouts U.S.A.; bd. dirs. Jr. Achievement of Mississippi Valley; bd. dirs., pres. Conv. and Visitors Bur. Greater St. Louis; chmn. bd. St. Louis County Community Chorus. Mem. Am., Mo., Met. St. Louis bar assns., Am. Soc. Corp. Secs., Sigma Chi, Phi Delta Phi. Webster Groves MO Office: Saint Louis MO

PATTERSON, DWIGHT FLEMING, JR., b. Laurens, S.C., Jan. 25, 1939; A.B., Wofford Coll., 1961; J.D., U. S.C., 1967. Admitted to S.C. bar, 1967; partner firm Perrin, Perrin & Mann, Spartanburg, S.C., 1967—. Vice chmn. Spartanburg Planning Commn.; bd. dirs. S.C. div. Am. Cancer Soc. Mem. Spartanburg County, S.C. State, Am. bar assns., Wofford Coll. Alumni Assn. (sec. bd. dirs.), Am Judicature Soc., Comml. Law League, Spartanburg Estate Planning Council (v.p.), Phi Delta Phi. Named Outstanding Young Man of Year, 1974. Home: 1275 Partridge Rd Spartanburg SC 29302 Office: PO Box 1655 Spartanburg SC 29304 Tel (803) 582-5461

PATTERSON, JOSEPH REDWINE, b. Corsicana, Tex., Apr. 16, 1927; B.A. in Philosophy, So. Methodist U., 1948, M.A. in Govt., 1951, J.D., 1954. Admitted to Tex. bar, 1954, U.S. Supreme Ct. bar, 1963; asst. dist. atty. Dallas County, 1955-56; asso. gen. counsel Traders and Gen. Ins. Co., Dallas, 1957; pres. firm Patterson, Lamberty & Kelly, Inc., 1957—. Mem. bd. mgrs. Downtown Dallas YMCA. Mem. Tex., Am., Dallas bar assns., Am. Judicature Soc. Contbr. articles to legal jours. Office: 2011 Cedar Springs Dallas TX 75201 Tel (214) 742-1156

PATTERSON, SAMUEL THORNE, JR., b. Littleton, N.C., Sept. 23, 1936; B.A., Emory and Henry Coll., 1955; LL.B., Washington & Lee U., 1964, J.D., 1970. Admitted to Va. bar, 1967; with State Farm Mutual Ins. Co., 1965-68; individual practice law, 1968—; judge Juvenile and Domestic Relations Cts. City of Petersburg (Va.), 1973—. Mem. Petersburg Bar Assn., Va. Trial Lawyers' Assn., Am. Judicature Soc., Phi Alpha Delta. Home: 1675 Berkeley Ave Petersburg VA 23803 Office: Suite 403 Community Bank Bldg Petersburg VA 23803 Tel (804) 732-7432

PATTERSON, WILLIAM NYE, b. Laurel, Miss., Jan. 3, 1936; B.S., U. So. Miss., 1958; LL.B., Jackson (Miss.) Sch. Law, 1966. Admitted to Miss. bar, 1967; individual practice law, Jackson, Miss., 1976-80; judge, dist. justice ct., Hinds County, Miss., 1973-77. Mem. N. Jackson Lawyers Club (pres. 1976). Home: 6254 Mossline Dr Jackson MS 39211 Office: 5048B N State St Jackson MS 39206 Tel (601) 362-4907

PATTERSON, WOODROW WILSON, b. Austin, Tex., Aug. 7, 1913; LL.B., U. Tex., 1936. Admitted to Tex. bar, 1936, Hawaii bar, 1944; 1st asst. dist. atty. Travis County (Tex.), 1937-40; partner firm Patterson & Patterson, Austin, 1941-73; individual practice law, Austin, 1974—; dir., gen. counsel Tex. State Bank, Austin, 1945—; chmn. bd. dirs. Univ. State Bank, Austin, 1969-73; chmn. com. legal aid Tex. State Bar, 1968-69; vis. adj. prof. Sch. Law, U. Tex., Austin, 1941—. Vice chmn. planning commn. City of Austin, 1953-54; trustee Spl. Ednl. Found., SW Tex. State U., San Marcos, 1958—. Mem. Am. Bar Assn. Home: 3419 Monte Vista Dr Austin TX 78731 Office: 1216 American Bank Tower Austin TX 78701 Tel (512) 478-4121

PATTIE, JOHN HEUSTED, b. Warren, Ohio, May 7, 1937; student St. John's Coll., Annapolis, Md., 1956-58; B.A., Calif. Western U., 1961; J.D., U. San Diego, 1965. Admitted to Calif. bar, 1966; asso. prof. bus. law and finance San Diego State U., 1965-66, prof. criminal justice adminstrn., 1973—; dep. county counsel, Imperial County, Calif., 1966-67, chief pub. defender, 1967—; individual practice law, El Centro, Calif., 1967—. Bd. trustees Central Union High Sch. Mem. Imperial County Bar Assn. (pres. 1975), Calif. Trial Lawyers Assn., Pub. Defenders Assn. Calif., Tri-County Council Criminal Justice. Office: 230 S 8th St El Centro CA 92243 Tel (714) 352-2865

PATTISHALL, BEVERLY WYCKLIFFE, b. Atlanta, May 23, 1916; B.S., Northwestern U., 1938; J.D., U. Va., 1941. Admitted to Ill. bar, 1941, D.C. bar, 1971; practiced in Chgo., 1941—; mem. firm Pattishall, McAuliffe & Hofstetter, 1969—; lectr. trademark, trade identity and unfair trade practices law Northwestern U. Sch. Law; U.S. del Diplomatic Confs. on Internat. Trademark Registration Treaty, Geneva and Vienna, 1970-73. Bd. dirs. Juvenile Protective Assn., Chgo., 1946—, pres., 1961-63; bd. dirs. Voluntary Interagy. Assn., Chgo., 1975—. Fellow Am. Coll. Trial Lawyers, Chgo. Bar Found.; mem. Internat. Patent and Trademark Assn. (pres. 1955-57, exec. com. 1955—), Am. (chmn. sect. patent, trademark and copyright law 1963-64), Internat., Ill., Chgo., D.C. bar assns., U.S. Trademark Assn. (dir. 1963-65), Legal Club Chgo., Law Club Chgo. Author: (with Hilliard) Trademarks, Trade Identity and Unfair Trade Practices, 1974; contbr. articles to legal jours. Home: 505 N Lake Shore Dr Chicago IL 60611 Office: Pattishall McAuliffe & Hofstetter Prudential Plaza Chicago IL 60601 Tel (312) 642-9518

PATTON, FRANK CALDWELL, b. McDowell County, N.C., Apr. 27, 1896; B.A., Trinity Coll. (now Duke U.), 1916, J.D., 1920. Admitted to N.C. bar, 1920; mem. firm Patton, Starnes, Thompson & Danile, and predecessors, Morganton, N.C., 1926—; asst. U.S. dist. atty. Western dist. N.C., Charlotte, 1922-32, U.S. Dist. atty., Asheville, 1932-35. Mem. Am., N.C., Burke County bar assns., Am. Coll. Trial Lawyers, N.C. State Bar. Named Man of Year, Morganton, 1961. Home: 311 W Union St Morganton NC 28655 Office: 104 S Sterling St Morganton NC 28655 Tel (704) 437-3335

PATTON, JAMES RICHARD, JR., b. Durham, N.C., Oct. 27, 1928; A.B. cum laude, U. N.C., 1948; postgrad. Yale U., Grad. Sch. Forestry, 1948; J.D., Harvard U., 1951. Admitted to D.C. bar, 1951, U.S. Supreme Ct. bar, 1963; research fellow Judge Manley O. Hudson, Harvard Law Sch., 1950-51; attache of embassy, spl. asst. to Am. ambassador, Indochina, 1951-54; with Office Nat. Estimates, Washington, 1954-55; atty. firm Covington & Burling, Washington, 1956-61; sr. partner firm Patton, Boggs & Blow, Washington, 1962—; lectr. internat. law Cornell U. Law Sch., 1963-64; dir. Lawyers Com. for Civil Rights Under Law, 1973—. Bd. dirs. Madeira Sch., Greenway, Va. Mem. Internat. Law Assn. (chmn. com. on air and sea piracy 1971), Am. Soc. Internat. Law (exec. com., treas. 1976—), Washington Inst. Fgn. Affairs, Am. Soc. Assn. Execs., Am., Inter-Am. (del. to Buenos Aires 1958) bar assns. Author: Some Tax Aspects of Equipment Leasing, 1965. Home: 456 River Bend Rd Great Falls VA 22066 Office: 1200 17th St NW Washington DC 20036 Tel (202) 223-4040

PATTON, JOHN VEVERS, b. Aberdeen, Miss., June 17, 1922; B.S., Northwestern U., 1948, LL.B., 1950, J.D., 1970. Admitted to Ill. bar, 1951, U.S. Supreme Ct. bar, 1971; partner firm McLaughlin, Patton & McLaughlin, Moline, Ill., 1954-59, firm Bozeman Neighbour, Patton & Noe, Moline, 1959—. Mem. Am. Coll. Trial Lawyers, Am., Ill., Rock Island County (pres. 1968-70) bar assns. Office: 1630 5th Ave Moline IL 61265 Tel (309) 762-5593

PATTON, ROBERT CHARLES, b. Newark, July 28, 1943; B.S., Western Mich. U., 1965; J.D., U. Ky., 1968. Admitted to Ky. bar, 1968; law clk. Ky. Ct. Appeals, 1968-69; asso. firm Benton, Benton & Luedeke, Newport, Ky., 1969—; asst. commonwealth atty. State of Ky., 17th Jud. Dist., Newport, 1969-76; asst. atty. County of Campbell, 1976—; atty. City of Silvergrove, Ky., 1972-75. Mem. Ky., Campbell County bar assns., Nat. Trial Lawyers Assn., Nat. Dist. Attys. Assn., Delta Theta Phi. Home: 172 Brentwood Pl Fort Thomas KY 41075 Office: 200 Columbia St Suite E1 Newport KY 41071 Tel (606) 261-8130

PATTON, STUART WILLIAM, b. Douglas, Ariz., Nov. 9, 1912; B.S. in Bus. Adminstrn., U. Miami, Coral Gables, Fla., 1934, J.D., 1936. Admitted to Fla. bar, 1936, U.S. Dist. Ct. bar for So. Dist. Fla., 1936, U.S. Ct. Appeals bar, 5th Circuit, 1940; asso. firm Benson & Cary, Miami, Fla., 1936-40; asst. State's atty. Dade County (Fla.), 1938; asst. U.S. atty., 1941; spl. asst. atty. gen. Lands div. Dept. Justice, 1942-45; partner firm Patton, Kanner, Segal, Zeller, LaPorte & King and predecessors, Miami, Fla., 1940—; dir. Flagship Nat. Bank of Miami, 1971—, Storer Broadcasting Co., 1972—, Delta Air Lines, Inc., Atlanta, 1972—. Charter mem. Orange Bowl Com., 1936—, pres., 1951; trustee U. Miami, 1962—, chmn. bd., 1976—; mem. Fla. Council of 100, 1973—; bd. dirs. Dade (county, Fla.) Found., 1973—. Mem. Dade County (dir. 1945-48), Fla. State, Am. bar assns. Named Hon. Consul for Southeastern Fla., Kingdom of Norway, 1972—. Home: 3211 Riviera Dr Coral Gables FL 33134 Office: 300 Northeast Airlines Bldg 150 SE Second Ave Miami FL 33131 Tel (305) 373-5761

PATTON, WARREN LOMAX, b. Berkeley, Calif., Aug. 7, 1912; B.S., Calif. Inst. Tech., 1934; student Loyola U. Calif., U. So. Calif.; J.D., Mpls. Minn. Coll. Law, 1947. Admitted to Calif. bar, 1948, U.S. Supreme Ct. bar, 1953, U.S. Patent Office bar, 1939; partner firm Fulwider, Patton, Rieber, Lee & Utecht, Los Angeles, 1938—. Mem. Los Angeles County, Wilshire, Santa Monica Bay Dist., Am. bar assns., State Bar Calif., Am. Patent Law Assn., IEEE. Office: 3435 Wilshire Blvd Suite 2400 Los Angeles CA 90010 Tel (213) 380-6800

PATTON, WAYNE GEORGE, b. St. Louis, Jan. 7, 1935; B.S. in Bus., Fla. State U., 1956; J.D., St. Louis U., 1961. Admitted to Mo. bar, 1961, U.S. Supreme Ct. bar, 1971; asso. firm Lashley, Neun & Watkins, St. Louis, 1961-69; partner firm Bild & Patton, St. Louis, 1969—; tchr. estate planning Parkway Sch. Dist., St. Louis County, 1969—. Mem. Am., Mo., St. Louis County bar assns., Bar Assn. Met. St. Louis, Lawyers Assn. St. Louis, Phi Delta Phi, Alpha Kappa Psi. Home: 9143 Fort Donelson Dr Saint Louis MO 63123 Office: 11648 Gravois Rd Saint Louis MO 63126 Tel (314) 843-7133

PATURIS, EMMANUEL MICHAEL, b. Akron, Ohio, July 12, 1933; B.S. in Bus., U. N.C., Chapel Hill, 1954, J.D. with honors, 1959, spl. student in accounting, 1959-60. Admitted to N.C. bar, 1959, D.C. bar, 1969, Va. bar, 1973; C.P.A. with firms in Charlotte and Wilmington, N.C., 1960-63; asso. firm Poyner, Geraghty, Hartsfield and Townsend, Raleigh, N.C., 1963-64; atty. Chief Counsel's Office, Washington and Richmond, Va., 1964-69; partner firm Reasoner, Davis and Vinson, Washington, 1969—. Mem. Am., D.C. bar assns., Am. Assn. Atty.-C.P.A.s, Phi Beta Kappa, Beta Gamma Sigma. Home: 2732 N Radford St Arlington VA 22207 Office: 800 17th St NW Washington DC 20006 Tel (202) 298-8100

PATZ, EDWARD FRANK, b. Balt., Aug. 25, 1932; B.S., U. Md., 1955, LL.B., 1959. Admitted to Md. bar, 1959; partner firm Ottenheimer, Cahn & Patz, and predecessors, Balt., 1959—. Bd. dirs. Md. chpt. NCCJ, 1976—, Jewish Family and Children's Service, Balt., 1969-74. Mem. Am., Md., Balt. City bar assns., Am. Judicature Soc. Home: 7917 Stevenson Rd Pikesville MD 21208 Office: 9th Floor Sun Life Bldg Baltimore MD 21201 Tel (301) 752-8308

PATZ, NATHAN, b. Balt., Apr. 5, 1905; LL.B., U. Md., 1926. Admitted to Md. bar, 1926, U.S. Ct. Claims bar, 1926, U.S. Supreme Ct. bar, 1926, U.S. Ct. Appeals bar, 4th Circuit, 1926; now individual practice law, Balt. Fellow Md. Bar Found.; mem. U. Md. Law Sch. Sch. Alumni Assn. (pres. 1969-70), U. Md. Alumni Assn., Internat. (pres. 1977—), Bar Assn. Balt. City (pres. 1976-77), Md. State, Am. bar assns. Trustee Md. Law Rev., 1976—. Office: Md Nat Bank Bldg 21st Floor Baltimore MD 21202 Tel (301) 685-6666*

PAUL, ANTHONY MARTIN, b. Cleve., Oct. 18, 1940; A.B., Bowdoin Coll., 1963; Ph.D. in Philosophy, Johns Hopkins, 1969; J.D., Yale, 1973. Admitted to Calif. bar, 1973; atty. Atlantic Richfield Co., Los Angeles, 1973—. Mem. Am., Calif. State, Los Angeles County bar assns. Office: 515 S Flower St Suite 2908 Los Angeles CA 90071 Tel (213) 486-1539

PAUL, BERNARD ARTHUR, b. Litchfield, Ill., Oct. 19, 1936; B.S., U. Ill., 1958, J.D., 1967. Admitted to Ill. bar, 1968; law clk. firm James W. Sanders, Marion, Ill., 1967-68; asst. dir. Ill. Oil Council, Chgo., 1968-69; asst. dir., staff atty. Williamson-Jackson Bi-County Legal Aid Bur., Marion, 1969-70; individual practice law, Marion, 1970—; maj. Air N.G., Springfield Capital Airport, 1965-75, Lambert St.

Louis Internat. Airport, 1975—; atty. City of Creal Springs (Ill.), 1975—. Aux. policeman City of Marion, 1974-76; deacon Zion United Ch. of Christ, Marion, 1969-71. Mem. Williamson County Bar Assn. (past pres.), Phi Alpha Delta. Recipient Outstanding Young Man Am. award, 1971, Outstanding Kiwanis Club Pres. award, 1973; named hon. Ala. Col., 1976. Home: 514 S Market St Marion IL 62959 Office: 806 W DeYoung St PO Box 31 Marion IL 62959 Tel (618) 997-4313

PAUL, JACK, b. Los Angeles, July 31, 1928; A.B., U. Calif. at Los Angeles, 1950; LL.B., Stanford, 1952; LL.M., Harvard, 1953. Admitted to Calif. bar, 1953, D.C. bar, 1953, U.S. Ct. Claims bar, 1961, U.S. Supreme Ct. bar, 1963; asso. firm Adams, Duque & Hazeltine, Los Angeles, 1953; legal officer, USAF, Wright-Patterson AFB, Ohio, 1954-56; asso. firm Beilenson & Meyer, Beverly Hills, Calif., 1956; individual practice law, Beverly Hills, 1956-65, Los Angeles, 1965-68; partner firm Paul & Gordon, Los Angeles, 1968-72, mem., 1972—. Mem. Bd. Edn., Beverly Hills, 1967-75, pres., 1970-71, 73-74; bd. dirs. Beverly Hills YMCA, 1967-75, Vista Del Mar, Los Angeles, 1971-77. Mem. Calif. State Bar, Los Angeles County, Fed., Beverly Hills, Am., Calif. State bar assns. Author: United States Government Contracts and Subcontracts, 1964. Fellow Nat. Contract Management Assn. Office: 1800 Ave of the Stars Los Angeles CA 90067 Tel (213) 879-2622

PAUL, JERRY, b. Washington, June 2, 1942; B.S., East Carolina U., 1965; J.D., U. N.C., 1968. Admitted to N.C. bar, 1968; individual practice law, Greenville, N.C., 1968-71, Durham, N.C., 1971—; mem. faculty Criminal Law Inst., U. Denver, 1976, Pub. Defender Workshop, 1976. Bd. dirs. N.C. Civil Liberties Union, 1969-70, 73-74, SCLC of N.C., 1968-74; exec. bd. Nat. Alliance Against Racist and Political Repression. Mem. Am., N.C., Fed. bar assns., Nat. Lawyers Guild. Recipient award from cast of Selma-The Life of Dr. M.L. King. Home: 616 Beechtree Ct Chapel Hill NC 27514 Office: 202 Rigsbee Ave Durham NC 27701 Tel (914) 688-4361

PAUL, LEE GILMOUR, b. Denver, July 27, 1907; A.B., Bowdoin Coll., 1929; LL.B., Harvard, 1932. Admitted to Calif. bar, 1933, U.S. Supreme Ct. bar, 1943; asso. firm Bauer Macdonald Schultheis & Pettit, Los Angeles, 1934-41; industry mem. Nat. War Labor Bd., 1942-46; partner firm Paul Hastings and Janofsky, Los Angeles, 1946—; mem. com. unauthorized practice State Bar Calif., chmn., 1968-69, Chmn. bank conf. com., 1962-71, mem. legal-med. relations com. Pres., Pasadena (Calif.) Child Guidance Clinic, 1964-65; Los Angeles Boys' Club, 1973—; chmn. Pasadena Council Alcoholism, 1966-68; trustee Boys' and Girls' Aid Soc. Los Angeles County, 1968-72. Mem. Am., Los Angeles County bar assns. Home: 1064 Armada Dr Pasadena CA 91103 Office: 555 S Flower St Los Angeles CA 90071 Tel (213) 489-4000

PAUL, RAYMOND, b. Manchuria, China, July 18, 1906; came to U.S., 1918, naturalized, 1924; student U. Berlin, 1921, Sorbonne, 1922; LL.D., Washington Square Coll., 1923, N.Y. U., 1927, Berlin U., U. Miami (Fla.), Ciudad Trijillo, India. Admitted to N.Y. State bar, 1928; individual practice law, Paris, 1935, Ger., N.Y.C.; lectr. in field. Mem. Am. Bar Assn., N.Y. Women Lawyers, Internat. Fedn. Women Lawyers, Nat. Assn. Women Lawyers. Home: 344 W 72d St New York City NY 10023 Office: 475 5th Ave New York City NY 10017 Tel (212) 532-2762

PAUL, ROBERT, b. N.Y.C., Nov. 22, 1931; B.A., N.Y. U., 1953; LL.B., Columbia, 1958. Admitted to Fla. bar, 1958, N.Y. bar, 1959; asso. firm George H. Salley, Miami, Fla., 1958-62; partner, 1962-64; sr. partner firms Landy, Paul, Morrison & White, London, 1973—, Morrison, Paul, Stillman & Beiley, N.Y.C., 1969—, Paul, Landy, Beiley & Yacos, Miami, Fla., 1964—; chmn. bd. Republic Nat. Bank of Miami, 1974—. Bd. dirs. Greater Miami Philharmonic Soc., Inc., 1976—; mem. citizens bd. U. Miami, 1977—. Mem. Dade County (Fla.), Am., Inter-Am. bar assns., Fla. Bar. Office: 200 SE First St Penthouse Greater Miami Fed Bldg Miami FL 33131 Tel (305) 358-9300

PAUL, ROBERT ALLAN, b. Albany, N.Y., Aug. 18, 1931; A.B., U. Vt., 1953; J.D., Columbia, 1956. Admitted to Vt. bar, 1957; since practiced in Burlington, Vt., asso. firm A. Pearley Feen, 1956-65, individual practice law, 1965-68, mem. firm Paul, Frank & Collins, 1968—. Bd. aldermen, Burlington, 1965-69; mem. Vt. Racing Commn., 1969-75, chmn., 1977—. Mem. Am., Vt., Chittenden County bar assns., Am. Judicature Soc. Home: 137 Crescent Rd Burlington VT 05401 Office: 135 College St Burlington VT 05401 Tel (802) 658-2311

PAUL, ROBERT DENNIS, b. Worcester, Mass., June 29, 1941; A.B. summa cum laude, Boston Coll., 1963; LL.B., Harvard, 1966; LL.M., N.Y. U., 1967. Admitted to D.C. bar, 1968, Mass. bar, 1970, U.S. Supreme Ct. bar, 1971; atty. Antitrust div. U.S. Dept. Justice, Washington, 1967-69; mem. firm Goodwin, Procter & Hoar, Boston, 1970-76, partner, 1976—; adj. prof. Western New Eng. Coll. Law Sch., 1976—. Mem. Acton (Mass.) Conservation Commn., 1975. Mem. Am., Boston bar assns. Home: 425 Great Elm Way Acton MA 01718 Office: 28 State St Boston MA 02109 Tel (617) 523-5700

PAUL, STEPHEN H., b. Indpls., June 28, 1947; B.A., Ind. U., 1969, J.D., 1972. Admitted to Ind. bar, 1972; asso. firm Baker & Daniels, Indpls., 1972—; mem. Administrv. Law Com., Ind. State Bar Assn., 1976-77. Vice pres., counsel Belle Meade Neighborhood Assn., 1976, pres., 1977. Mem. Am., Ind., Indpls. bar assns. Editor-in-chief, Ind. Law Jour.; contbr. article in field. Home: 9403 N Kenwood Ave Indianapolis IN 46260 Office: 810 Fletcher Trust Bldg Indianapolis IN 46204 Tel (317) 636-4535

PAULE, DONALD WAYNE, b. St. Louis, Jan. 9, 1943; B.S. in Engring. Sci., Washington U., 1964, J.D., 1966. Admitted to Mo. bar, 1967; asso. firm Tremayne, Lay, & Carr, Bauer & Paule, and predecessors, St. Louis, 1967-72, partner, 1973-75; individual practice law Clayton, Mo., 1975—; instr. bus. law U. Coll. Washington U., St. Louis, 1970—. Mem. St. Louis County Civil Service Commn., 1975—, chmn., 1977—; bd. dirs. West County YMCA, 1973—, Vis. Nurses Assn., 1974—. Mem. Am., St. Louis County (pres. 1975-76), Mo. bar assns., Lawyers Assn. St. Louis, Recipient Roy F. Essen Meml. award, St. Louis County Bar Assn., 1972. Home: 13293 Gateroyal St Des Peres MO 63131 Office: 120 S Central Ave Suite 949 Clayton MO 63105 Tel (314) 862-4646

PAULEY, JAMES LEROY, JR., b. Mason City, Iowa, Dec. 6, 1916; B.A., U. Iowa, 1938, J.D., 1940. Admitted to Iowa bar, 1940; individual practice law, Scranton, Iowa, 1940-42, Jefferson, Iowa, 1945-48; spl. agt. FBI, 1942-45; partner firm Hutcheon & Pauley, Jefferson, 1948-52, firm Reading, Pauley & Hutcheon, Jefferson, 1952-69, firm Reading, Pauley & Horak, Jefferson, 1969-74, firm Reading, Pauley, Horak & Ostland, Jefferson, 1974—. Bd. dirs. Jefferson Community Sch. Dist., 1954-61; mayor City of Jefferson, 1968-72. Mem. Am., Iowa State, 16th Jud. Dist. (pres. 1960-62), Greene County (pres. 1965-67) bar assns. Home: 300 Edgewood Ave Jefferson IA 50129 Tel (515) 386-4166

PAULSEN, MONRAD GOTKE, b. Clinton, Iowa, June 1, 1918; A.B., U. Chgo., 1940, J.D., 1942; J.D. (hon.) U. Freiburg (Germany), 1972. Lectr. law U. Utah, 1945-46; asst. prof. Ind. U., 1946-50, asso. prof., 1950-51; asso. prof. U. Minn., 1951-54, prof. law, 1954-56; prof. Law Sch., Columbia, 1956-68; dean, John B. Minor prof. law U. Va., Charlottesville, 1968—; Fulbright prof. U. Freiburg (Germany), 1964; vis. Am. prof. law, U. London Inst. Advanced Legal Studies, 1966; prof. law U. Göttingen (Germany), summer 1973. Mem. Wage Stblzn. Bd. Region 8, 1951-52. Author: (with S. Kadish) The Criminal Law and its Processes, 1962; (with O. Ketcham) The Juvenile Court, 1967; (with W. Adlington) Cases and Materials on Domestic Relations, 1970. Home: 1115 Hilltop Rd Charlottesville VA 22903*

PAULSON, OLIVER JEROME, b. Lostwood, N.D., Dec. 6, 1912; B.A., Intermountain Union Coll., 1935; J.D., U. Mont., 1941. Admitted to Mont. bar, 1941; adminstrv. asst. Dept. Def., Fort Dix, N.J., 1941-49; county atty. Sweet Grass County, Mont., 1950-66; asso. firm Paulson and Tulley, Big Timber, Mont., 1966—. State Moderator Mont. Conf. of United Ch. of Christ, 1970-71. Mem. Mont. County Atty.'s Assn. (pres. 1961), Park-Sweet Grass Bar Assn. (pres. 1974-76). Home: 116 5th Ave Big Timber MT 59011 Office: 201 McLeod St Big Timber MT 59011 Tel (406) 932-2147

PAULSON, RICHARD S., b. Chgo., Mar. 10, 1928; LL.B., Md. U., 1953. Admitted to Md. bar, 1953, D.C. bar, 1959; since practiced in Washington; partner firm Paulson & Humphreys and predecessors, 1969—. Pres. Jr. High Sch. PTA, Annapolis, Md., 1967-68. Mem. Am., D.C., Prince Georges County bar assns., Am. Trial Lawyers Assn., Nat. Lawyers Club, Assn. Plantiffs Trial Attys. Met. Washington, Inner Circle Advocates. Home: 606 Valleybrook Dr Silver Spring MD 20904 Office: 5272 River Rd Washington DC 20016

PAVALON, EUGENE IRVING, b. Chgo., Jan. 5, 1933; student U. Ill., 1950-53; B.S., Northwestern U., 1954, J.D., 1956. Admitted to Ill. bar, 1956, U.S. Ct. Mil. Appeals bar, 1957; served as capt. JAGC, U.S. Air Force, 1956-59; mem. legal staff Montgomery Ward Co., Chgo., 1959-62; asso. firm Louis G. Davidson, Chgo., 1962-70; mem. firm Asher, Greenfield, Goodstein, Pavalon & Segall, Chgo., 1970—; lectr. in field; instr. Ct. Practice Inst. of Chgo. Bd. dirs. Video Nursing, Inc. (name changed to Ednl. Div., Am. Jour. of Nursing Corp.), Chgo. and N.Y.C., 1970-75, Camp Channing Lawson YMCA, Chgo., 1971—. Mem. Chgo., Ill. State, Am. bar assns., Ill. Trial Lawyers Assn. (sec. 1976—), Assn. Trial Lawyers Am. (state committeeman 1975—). Editorial bd. Civil Practice before Trial, 1967, Civil Practice during Trial, 1968; contbr. articles to legal jours. Home: 365 Lincilnwood Highland Park IL 60035 Office: 228 N LaSalle St Chicago IL 60601 Tel (312) AN 3-1500

PAVIA, GEORGE M., b. Genoa, Italy, Feb. 14, 1928; B.A., Columbia U., 1948, LL.B., 1951; postgrad. U. Genoa, 1954-55. Admitted to N.Y. bar, 1951, U.S. Supreme Ct. bar, 1958; asso. firm Pavia & Harcourt, N.Y.C., 1951-55, partner, 1955—; pres., dir. Aurea Jewelry Creations, Inc.; sec. dir. Pirelli Tire Corp.; sec. Alfa Romeo, Inc., SFM Media Corp., Zanussi Corp. Mem. Am. Bar Assn., Am. Soc. Internat. Law, Consular Law Soc. Office: 63 Wall St New York City NY 10005 Tel (212) 248-5500

PAVY, HENRY GARLAND, b. Opelousas, La., Aug. 24, 1924; B.A., U. S.W. La., 1947; LL.B., La. State U., 1950. Admitted to La. bar, 1950, U.S. Dist. Ct. bar, 1951; since practiced in Opelousas, partner firm Pavy & Guilbeau, 1950-52, Andrus & Pavy, 1956-72; mem. Municipal Civil Service Bd., 1960-70. Mem. Am., La., St. Landry Parish bar assns. Home: 1009 Rose Ave Opelousas LA 70520 Office: PO Box 348 Opelousas LA 70570 Tel (318) 942-6322

PAWL, WALTER STANLEY, b. Chgo., May 13, 1894; B.S. in Mech. Engring., Armour Inst. Tech., 1921; LL.B., Washington (D.C.) Coll. Law, 1931, M.P.L., 1932. Admitted to D.C. bar, 1931, Md. bar, 1954, U.S. Supreme Ct. bar, 1936; supervisory atty.-adviser patents br. U.S. Naval Photog. Center, Washington, 1952-54; individual practice law, Adelphi, Md., 1954—; partner Helitarics, Adelphi, 1960-76, owner, dir. devel., 1976—; patent counsel Gregoire Engring. & Devel. Co., Newport, Pa., 1962—; pres., patent counsel Inventors Coop., Inc., Washington, 1969—. Mem. Fed., Am. bar assns., Am. Patent Law Assn., Sigma Nu Phi. Patentee mech. engring. field. Home and office: 2844 Powder Mill Rd Adelphi MD 20783 Tel (301) 434-5148

PAWLEY, HOWARD RUSSELL, b. Brampton, Ont., Can., Nov. 21, 1934; B.A., Man. Tchrs. Coll.; LL.B., Man. Law Sch. Called to Man. bar, 1962; individual practice law, Selkirk, 1961-69; atty. gen. Man., Winnipeg, 1973—; minister municipal affairs Man. Legislature, 1969-76; commr. No. affairs, 1971-72. Mem. Canadian, Man. bar, assns., Law Soc. Man., St. Andrews-St. Clements Agrl. Soc. (past dir.), Selkirk C. of C. (past dir.). Home: 97 Dorchester St Selkirk MB Canada Office: Room 104 Legislative Bldg Winnipeg MB R3C 0V8 Canada Tel (204) 946-7404

PAWLEY, THOMAS DÉSIRÉ, IV, b. Texarkana, Ark., Jan. 27, 1944; A.B., Harvard, 1966; J.D., St. Louis U., 1972. Admitted to Mo. bar, 1974; since practiced in Jefferson, Mo., legal asst. to dir. Mo. Dept. Corrections, 1973-74, legal counsel, 1974; asst. prof. Lincoln U., 1974-75; individual practice law, 1974—. Mem. Am., Mo. (exec. com. internat. law com.) bar assns., Mo. C. of C., AAUP, Alpha Phi Alpha. Office: 125 1/2 E High St Jefferson MO 65101 Tel (314) 634-2292

PAXTON, RALPH BRAINARD, b. Detroit Lakes, Minn., Apr. 7, 1923; student U. N.D., 1940-42, 47-49; LL.B., U. Miami, 1951, J.D., 1967. Admitted to Fla. bar, 1951; partner firm Papy, Talburt, Carruthers & Paxton, Miami, 1960-62, Talburt, Paxton & Kubicki, Miami, 1962-64; asso. firm Walton, Lantaff, Schroeder & Carson, and predecessors, Miami and W. Palm Beach, 1964-65, partner, 1965—; mem. rules com. Fla. Bar, 1976, lectr. continuing legal edn. program, 1969—. Mem. Am., Fla. (past mem. exec. council trial lawyers sect.), Dade County, Palm Beach County bar assns., Fed. Ins. Counsel, Def. Research Inst., Phi Delta Phi. Home: 4717 Juniper Ln Palm Beach Gardens FL 33410 Office: Suite 500 1675 Palm Beach Lakes Blvd Forum III West Palm Beach FL 33401

PAXTON, ROBERT CLAIR, b. Sharon, Ohio, Jan. 19, 1919; B.C.E., Ohio U., 1948; J.D., Ohio No. U., 1966. Admitted to Ohio bar, 1966; individual practice law, Caldwell, Ohio, 1966—; Noble County engr., 1970. Mem. Ohio, Noble County bar assns. Home: 518 Oaklawn Ave Caldwell OH 43724 Office: Savings and Loan Bldg Main St Caldwell OH 43724 Tel (614) 732-4413

PAXTON, SYLVIA SANDS, b. Boston, Mar. 12, 1941; A.B., Vassar Coll., 1962; J.D., Boston U., 1966. Admitted to Mass. bar, 1966, Ohio bar, 1977; advice atty. advice br. NLRB, Washington, 1966-67; asso. firm Crooks & O'Keefe, Marblehead, Mass., 1967-70; individual practice law, Marblehead, Mass., 1970-75; dir. Sands, Taylor & Wood Co., Cambridge, Mass., 1963-70. Mem. Asso. Alumnae Vassar Coll. (dir. 1972-75). Home and office: 535 Reily Rd Cincinnati OH 55215 Tel (513) 821-9593

PAYANT, VITAL ROBERT, b. Iron Mountain, Mich., June 25, 1932; B.S., Marquette U., 1954, J.D., 1956. Admitted to Wis. bar, 1956, Mich. bar, 1957; field agt. Wis. Pub. Expenditure Survey, Milw., 1956-59; individual practice law, Iron Mountain, 1959-63; atty. City Iron Mountain, 1960-63; judge Dickinson County (Mich.) Probate Ct., 1963-68, 95th Mich. Dist. Ct., Iron Mountain, 1969—; faculty Nat. Coll. State Judiciary, U. Nev. Chmn., Dickinson-Iron Mountain Mental Health Bd., 1966-73, Mich. Comm. on Aging, 1973—. Mem. Am., Dickinson County bar assns. Contbr. articles to The Judges Jour. Office: Courthouse Iron Mountain MI 49801 Tel (906) 774-0506

PAYNE, CHARLES TOM, b. Greenville, Ala., Sept. 20, 1943; grad. Huntingdon Coll., 1966, Jones Law Sch., 1971. Admitted to Ala. bar, 1972, Fed. bar, 1972; real estate appraiser Ala. State Hwy. Dept., Montgomery, 1967-71; counsel Legislative Reference Service, Montgomery, 1971-74. Bd. dirs. Montgomery Boys Club. Mem. Ala. State Bar, Trial Lawyers Am., Ala. Trial Lawyers Assn., Montgomery County Bar Assn. Home: 632 Burlington Dr Montgomery AL 36117 Office: 138 Adams Ave Montgomery AL 36104 Tel (205) 269-1391

PAYNE, DAVID MACGREGOR, b. N.Y.C., Sept. 20, 1919; B.A., Yale, 1941; LL.B., Columbia, 1948. Admitted to N.Y. bar, 1948; asso. firm Winthrop, Stimson, Putnam & Roberts, N.Y.C., 1948-55, partner, 1955—. Chmn. Zoning Bd. Appeals Pound Ridge (N.Y.), 1968-73; chmn. univ. council com. on Peabody Mus., Yale, 1971-75, v.p. univ. council, 1975-76; founding bd. govs. Assn. Yale Alumni, 1972-76; chmn. adv. council Seven Springs Farm, Mt. Kisco, N.Y., 1976—; bd. mgrs. Phoebe Griffin-Noyes Library, Old Lyme, Conn., 1976—. Mem. Am., N.Y. State bar assns., Assn. Bar City N.Y., Fgn. Bondholders Protective Council (dir.). Home: Town Woods Rd Old Lyme CT 06371 Office: Winthrop Stimson et al 40 Wall St New York City NY 10005 Tel (212) 943-0700

PAYNE, HARRY VERN, b. Lordsburg, N.Mex., Aug. 13, 1936; B.A., Brigham Young U., 1961; J.D., U. N.Mex., 1964. Admitted to N.Mex. bar, 1964; mem. firm Hannett, Hannett & Cornish, Albuquerque, 1964-68; individual practice law, 1969-70; dist. judge 2d Jud. Dist. Ct., Albuquerque, 1971—, presiding judge, 1973-74. Mem. N.Mex. Gov's. Council for Criminal Justice, Albuquerque, 1971-74; mem. Kit Carson exec. council Boy Scouts Am., Albuquerque, 1973-74. Home: 1840 Don Felipe SW Albuquerque NM 87105 Office: Bernalillo County Court House Albuquerque NM 87103*

PAYNE, ROBERT LEONARD, b. St. Louis, Jan. 12, 1942; A.B., Drury Coll., 1964; J.D., U. Mo. at Columbia, 1969. Admitted to Mo. bar, 1969; asst. pros. atty. Buchanan County, St. Joseph, Mo., 1969-71; asst. city atty. St. Joseph, 1971; mem. firm Dale, Flynn & Payne, St. Joseph, 1971-73; individual practice law, Greenfield, Mo., 1973—; pros. atty.-elect Dade County (Mo.). Bd. dirs. Dade County Meml. Hosp., Lockwood, Mo., 1975-76. Mem. Am. Bar Assn., C. of C. (sec.-treas. Greenfield 1975). Home: 505 S Allison St Greenfield MO 65661 Office: PO Box 63 Greenfield MO 65661 Tel (417) 637-2121

PAYNE, WILLIAM HOWARD, b. Norfork, Ark., Oct. 8, 1909; LL.B., Southeastern U., 1941. Admitted to Okla., D.C. bars, 1942, U.S. Supreme Ct. bar, 1947; individual practice law, Washington, 1942—; gen. counsel Cheyenne-Arapaho Indian Tribes of Okla., 1948-70, Cheyenne River Sioux Tribes S.D., 1957-72; claims atty. Cheyenne River Sioux Tribe and Fort Peck Sioux Tribe, Mont., 1957—; with JAGC, USN, 1945-46. Mem. Am. Acad. Polit. Sci., Smithsonian Assos., Nat. Press Club, Okla. Soc., Am. Legion, Okla., D.C. bar assns. Author: History of Indian Affairs Commission, 1936; Folks Say Will Rogers, 1936; Indian Laws and Treaties, 1938; Marque and Reprisal, 1957. Home: 5063 27th St N Arlington VA 22207 Office: 1086 National Press Bldg Washington DC 20045 Tel (202) 393-8268

PAYNTER, HARRY STRATTAN, II, b. New Albany, Ind., Aug. 15, 1926; A.B. in Chemistry and Biology, Ind. U., 1950; J.D., U. Louisville, 1964. Sanatarian, Clark County (Ind.) Health Dept., Jeffersonville, 1950-57; claims adjuster Meridian Mut. Ins. Co., Jeffersonville, 1957-67; admitted to Ind. bar, 1964; judge Superior Ct., Jeffersonville, 1973—; mem. Ind. Juvenile Justice Task Force, Ind. Criminal Justice Task Force. Chmn. Heart Fund, 1964-65; bd. dirs. So. Ind. Health Systems Agy., Inc. Mem. Ind. Judges Assn. (legis. com.), Ind. Correction Assn., Clark County Bar Assn., Ind. Juvenile Judges Assn., Assn. Trial Lawyers Am. Home: 1719 Jeff-Charlestown Rd Jeffersonville IN 47130 Office: Superior Ct Court House Jeffersonville IN 47130 Tel (812) 282-0045

PAYSSE, RENE SYLVAIN, b. New Orleans, Aug. 14, 1931; B.A., Tulane U., 1955, J.D., 1958. Admitted to La. bar, 1958, Fed. bar, 1958; asso., then partner firm Deutsch, Kerrigan & Stiles, New Orleans, 1958-67; partner firm Leach, Grossel-Rossi & Paysse, New Orleans, 1967—. Mem. Maritime Law Assn., Am. Bar Assn., U.S., United Kingdom assns. average adjusters, Civil Service League, Fgn. Trade Club, Internat. House, Phi Delta Phi. Office: 1540 One Shell Sq New Orleans LA 70139 Tel (504) 581-6211

PEACOCK, JAMES DANIEL, b. Moorestown, N.Y., Dec. 19, 1930; B.A., Duke U., 1952; LL.B., U. Md., 1957. Admitted to Md. bar, 1957; mem. firm Semmes, Bowen & Semmes, Towson, Md., 1957—; instr. practice ct. U. Md., 1965-69. Trustee Sheppard & Enoch Pratt Hosp.; mem. advisory council YWCA; chmn. bd. trustees Friends Sch., 1970-73. Mem. Balt. City, Balt. County, Md. State, Am. bar assns., Met. Balt. Assn. Defense Attys., Order of Coif. Home: 105 Bonnie Hill Rd Towson MD 21204 Office: 401 Washington Ave PO Box 6705 Towson MD 21204 Tel (301) 296-4400

PEARCE, LAWRENCE RAY, b. Childress, Tex., Mar. 7, 1930; A.A., Paris Jr. Coll., 1948; B.A., N. Tex. State U., 1949; postgrad. So. Meth. U., 1951-52; LL.B., U. Tex., 1958. Admitted to Tex. bar, 1958; asso. firm Turner, White, Atwood, Meer & Francis, Dallas, 1958-62, partner, 1962-63; partner firm Geary, Brice & Lewis, Dallas, 1962-68; v.p., gen. counsel Ling & Co., Inc., Dallas, 1969-70; partner firm Gardere, Porter and DeHay, Dallas, 1971—. Vestryman St. Francis Episcopal Ch., Dallas, 1962—. Mem. Dallas, Tex., Am. bar assns., Am. Judicature Soc., Order of Coif. Contbr. articles to legal jours. Home: 7703 Applecross Ln Dallas TX 75248 Office: 1700 Republic Nat Bank Bldg Dallas TX 75201 Tel (214) 741-1551

PEARL, JAMES HILDRED, b. Laredo, Tex., July 9, 1937; student Lamar Coll.; B.S., U.S. Mil. Acad., 1960; J.D., St. Mary's U., 1969. Admitted to Tex. bar, 1969, U.S. Supreme Ct. bar; asso. firm Lieck, Lieck & Leon, San Antonio, 1969-71; mem. firm Baskin, Casseb, Gilliland, Rodgers & Robertson, San Antonio, 1971-74; partner firm Casseb, Leon, Rodgers, Strong & Pearl, San Antonio, 1974—; with E.I. DuPont Co., 1966-67. Bd. dirs. county alcoholic rehab. center. Mem. Am., San Antonio bar assns., San Antonio C. of C. (task force on equal employment), Phi Delta Theta. Home: 131 Danube Dr San Antonio TX 78213 Office: 18th Floor Milam Bldg San Antonio TX 78205 Tel (512) 223-4381

PEARL, QUINN F., SR., b. Shepherdsville, Ky., Apr. 5, 1910; A.B., Western Ky. U., 1934; J.D., U. Louisville, 1973. Home: 611 Yale Dr Elizabethtown KY 42701 Office: 632 Knox Blvd Radcliff KY 40160

PEARLMAN, DONALD HERBERT, b. Portland, Oreg., Dec. 8, 1935; B.A. cum laude, Harvard, 1957; LL.B., Yale, 1960. Admitted to Oreg. bar, 1960; law clerk to Hon. John R. Ross, chief judge U.S. Dist. Ct., Carson City, Nev., 1960-61; asso. firm Keane, Harper, Pearlman & Copeland, Portland, 1962-66, partner, 1966—; instr. contract law U. Nev., 1961. Mem. Bonneville Power Adminstrn. Regional Advisory Council, Portland, 1971—. Mem. Am., Multnomah County bar assns., Oreg. State Bar. Home: 7220 SW Northvale Way Portland OR 97225 Office: 3500 First Nat Tower Portland OR 97201 Tel (503) 224-4100

PEARLMAN, RONALD ALAN, b. Hamilton, Ohio, July 10, 1940; A.B. with honors, Northwestern U., 1962, J.D. cum laude, 1965; LL.M., Georgetown U., 1967. Admitted to Mo. bar, 1965, Ill. bar, 1965, U.S. Supreme Ct. bar, 1968; atty. Office of Chief Counsel, IRS, Washington, 1965-69; asso. firm Thompson & Mitchell, St. Louis, 1969-70, partner, 1970—; instr. grad. tax program Sch. Law, Washington U., Louis, 1972—. Mem. budget and endowment fund coms. Jewish Fedn. St. Louis, 1975—, mem. leadership devel. council, 1973-75; mem. taxes and spending com. St. Louis Regional Commerce and Growth Assn., 1974—; mem. adv. com. to dir. of revenue State of Mo., 1969-73. Mem. Am. (chmn. subcom. on incorporations, com. on corp. stockholder relationships, 1974-76), Mo. (chmn. taxation com.), Met. St. Louis (mem. taxation sect., chmn., 1974-75, mem. exec. com., 1974-75) bar assns., Mid-Am. Tax Conf. (mem. planning com.), Order of Coif. Participant in ednl. seminars; contbr. articles to publs. Home: 30 Briarcliff St St Louis MO 63124 Office: One Mercantile Center St Louis MO 63101 Tel (314) 231-7676

PEARLSTEIN, PAUL DAVIS, b. Berlin, N.H., Jan. 3, 1938; A.B., U. Pa., 1959; LL.B., U. Va., 1962. Admitted to Va. bar, 1962, D.C. bar, 1963, U.S. Supreme Ct. bar, 1969; atty. advisor pub. housing adminstrn. HUD, Washington, D.C., 1964-66; constrn. and contracting mgr. Cafritz Co. and affiliated cos., Washington, 1966-68; individual practice law, Washington, 1968—; legal counsel Ben Murch Elementary Home and Sch. Assn., 1976—. Pres., HUD Toastmasters, 1966-67; Young Marrieds of the Washington Hebrew Congregation, 1969-70, Brotherhood of the Washington Hebrew Congregation, 1974-75. Mem. Am., Fed. bar assns., Va. bar, D.C. Bar, Bar Assn. of D.C. (chmn. real property law com., chmn. Speakers Bur. 1973-74, chmn. of yr. award 1977). Contbr. book revs. to legal jours., also article in real estate jour. Home: 2928 Ellicott St NW Washington DC 20008 Office: 1101 17th St NW Washington DC 20036 Tel (202) 223-5848

PEARMAN, JAMES RICHARD, b. Los Angeles, Mar. 10, 1940; A.B., Okla. Baptist U., 1963; J.D., Okla. City U., 1967. Admitted to Okla. bar, 1967; asso. firm Rhodes, Hieronymus, Holloway & Wilson, Okla. City, 1968-70; individual practice law, Tonkawa, Okla., 1971—. Pres. Tonkawa United Way, 1973; pres. Tonkawa Jaycees, 1974, Tonkawa C. of C., 1976; internat. senator Jaycees, 1976. Mem. Am. Judicature Soc., Okla. Trial Lawyers Assn. Named Kiwanian of Yr., 1971, Outstanding Young Oklahoman, 1976. Home: 215 N Jenkins St Tonkawa OK 74653 Office: 214 E Grand Tonkawa OK 74653 Tel (405) 628-2523

PEARMAN, RALPH STEWART, b. Paris, Ill., Aug. 1, 1929; B.S., U. Ill., 1951, J.D., 1953. Admitted to Ill. bar, 1953; mem. firm Massey, Anderson, Gibson & Pearman, Paris, 1953-71; states atty. Edgar County, Ill., 1960-64; circuit judge 5th Jud. Circuit Ill., Paris, 1972-76, chief judge, 1976—. Bd. dirs. Paris Youth Center. Mem. Am., Ill., Edgar County bar assns., Ill. Judges Assn., Am. Legion, C. of C., Phi Delta Phi. Home: 228 W Crawford St Paris IL 61944 Office: Courthouse Paris IL 61944 Tel (217) 463-4805

PEARSALL, JOHN WESLEY, b. Richmond, Va., Aug. 21, 1914; B.S., Randolph-Macon Coll., 1935; LL.B., U. Richmond, 1941. Admitted to Va. bar, 1940; asso. firm McGuire, Riely & Eggleston, Richmond, 1941-50, partner firm McGuire, Eggleston, Bocock & Woods, Richmond, 1950-53; gen. counsel Va.-Carolina Chem. Corp., Richmond, 1953-56; individual practice law, Richmond, 1956-60; partner firm McCaul, Grigsby & Pearsall, Richmond, 1960—; gen. counsel, dir. Estes Express Lines, Richmond, 1972—. Chpt. chmn. ARC, Chesterfield County, Va., 1944-49, campaign chmn., 1949, campaign chmn. Richmond, Henrico, and Chesterfield, Va., 1950, nat. vice chmn. fund dr., 1956, nat. gov., 1953-55; mem. budget com. Richmond Area Community Chest, 1946-47, mem. exec. com., 1947-55, trustee, 1946-50, campaign chmn., 1951, pres., 1955; pres. United Giver's Fund, 1970; v.p. Children's Aid Soc., Richmond, 1950-55, trustee, 1948-55; active Boy Scouts Am., 1953-56; mem. exec. com. Randolph-Macon Coll., 1958-76, chmn. long range plan com., 1960-76, trustee, 1955-76; mem. Chesterfield County Welfare Bd., 1951-55; trustee Sheltering Arms Hosp., Richmond, 1949—, Va. Health and Welfare Pension Fund, 1968—; bd. dirs. Jr. Achievement, 1975—. Mem. Am., Va., Richmond, Chesterfield County (pres. 1963-64) bar assns., Am. Judicature Soc., Va. State Bar Council (chmn. judicial ethics com. 1970-71), Phi Beta Kappa (pres. Richmond chpt. 1976-77), Omicron Delta Kappa. Recipient Jr. Chamber Commerce distinguished service award, 1948. Home: 7701 Riverside Dr Richmond VA 23225 Office: 320 Mutual Bldg Richmond VA 23219 Tel (804) 644-5491

PEARSALL, OTIS PRATT, b. Bklyn., Apr. 25, 1932; B.A., Yale, 1953, LL.B., 1956. Admitted to N.Y. bar, 1957, U.S. Supreme Ct. bar, 1963; asso. firm Hughes Hubbard Blair & Reed, N.Y.C., 1956-59, 60-63; partner firm Hughes Hubbard & Reed, N.Y.C., 1964—; asst. U.S. atty. So. Dist. N.Y., N.Y.C., 1959-60. Bd. govs., Bklyn. Heights Assn., 1960-67, adv. com., 1967—; trustee Soc. for Preservation of L.I. Antiquities, 1969—; L.I. Hist. Soc., 1974—. Mem. Am. Bar Assn. Office: Hughes Hubbard & Reed One Wall St New York City NY 10005 Tel (212) WH 3-6500

PEARSON, C. JUDSON, b. Battle Creek, Mich., July 2, 1919; J.D., W.Va. U., 1949. Admitted to W.Va. bar, 1949; individual practice law, St. Albans, W.Va., 1949-58; police judge City of St. Albans, 1956-58; ins. commr. State of W.Va., 1958-61; counsel Am. Life Conv., Chgo., 1961; asst. counsel Equitable Life Assurance Soc., N.Y.C., 1961-63; pres. Blue Cross Hosp. Service, Inc., also Blue Shield of So. W.Va., Inc., Charleston, 1963—; trustee Blue Cross Assn. Chgo., 1973-76; mem. adv. council W.Va. State Comprehensive Health Planning Agy., 1971-76. Mem. Assn. Life Ins. Counsel (sec.-treas. N.Y.C. 1963), W.Va. Bar Assn. Home: 1509 Quarrier St Charleston WV 25311 Office: Commerce Sq PO Box 1353 Charleston WV 25325 Tel (304) 348-6770

PEARSON, CHARLES THOMAS, JR., b. Fayetteville, Ark., Oct. 14, 1929; B.S., U. Ark., 1952, J.D., 1954; A.M., Boston U., 1963. Admitted to Ark. bar, 1954, U.S. Supreme Ct. bar, 1958; partner firm Pearson & Pearson, Fayetteville, 1954-55; served with JAGC, U.S. Navy, 1955-63; individual practice law, Fayetteville, 1963-72; sr. partner firm Pearson & Woodruff, Fayetteville, 1972—. Mem. Am., Ark., Washington County bar assns., Judge Advs. Assn., Comml. Law League, Assn. Trial Lawyers Am., Delta Theta Phi. Home: 500 E North St Fayetteville AR 72701 Office: 36 E Center St Fayetteville AR 72701 Tel (501) 521-4300

PEARSON, HENRY CLYDE, b. Ocoonita, Va., Mar. 12, 1925; LL.B., U. Richmond, 1952. Admitted to Va. bar, 1952, U.S. Supreme Ct. bar, 1958; practiced in Jonesville, Va., 1952-56, Roanoke, Va., 1961-70; asst. U.S. atty. for Western Dist. Va., 1956-61; judge Bankruptcy Ct., U.S. Western Dist. Va., 1970—; mem. Va. Ho. of Dels., 1954, 56, Va. Senate, 1968-70. Office: Fed Bldg Roanoke VA 24006 Tel (703) 982-9391

PEARSON, J. RICHMOND, b. Birmingham, Ala., Jan. 10, 1930; A.B., Morehouse U., 1955; J.D., Howard U., 1958. Admitted to Ala. bar, 1958; asst. U.S. Atty. No. Dist. of Ala., 1963-67; individual practice law, Birmingham, 1958—; mem. Ala. Senate, 1974—. Mem. Ala. Legis. Com. on State Prisons; mem. exec. bd. Ala. Goodwill Industries; bd. dirs. Ala. Youth Service; vice chmn. Ala. State Fair Authority; trustee Miles Coll. Mem. Nat., Am., Ala., Birmingham bar assns. Home: 809 Bolin St Birmingham AL 35211 Office: Citizens Fed Bldg PO Box 11135 Birmingham AL 35203 Tel (205) 252-8961

PEARSON, JAMES TILLMAN, b. Wayne County, Ga., Aug. 27, 1912; A.B., U. Fla., 1933, J.D., 1936. Admitted to Fla. bar, 1936; asso. firm Thompson and Thompson, Miami, Fla., 1936-38; partner firm Miller, Pearson and Miller, Miami, 1939-42; judge 3d Dist. Ct. Appeals State of Fla., 1958—; judge Civil Ct. Record, Dade County, Fla., 1954-58. Mem. Am., Fla., Dade County bar assns., Am. Legion, Lions, Masons, Miami Jr. C. of C. Office: 2001 SW 117th Ave Miami FL 33165 Tel (305) 552-2900

PEARSON, PHILLIP ROGER, b. Chgo., Sept. 18, 1943; B.S. in Accountancy with honors, U. Ill., 1964, J.D., 1967. Tax accountant Arthur Young & Co., Chgo., 1967; spl. agt. Office Spl. Investigations USAF, Milw., 1967-70; admitted to Ill. bar, 1968, N.Y. bar, 1972, Calif. bar, 1973; with JAGC, USAF, Patrick AFB, Fla., 1970-71; atty. Exxon Co., U.S.A., Pelham, N.Y., 1971-73, Los Angeles, 1973-76; labor counsel TRW, Inc., Redondo Beach, Calif., 1976—. Mem. Am., Los Angeles County bar assns., Calif. State Bar, Order of Coif. Office: Bldg E-2 Room 7081 One Space Park Redondo Beach CA 90278 Tel (213) 536-3743

PEARSON, RALPH JONES, b. Memphis, Jan. 22, 1919; LL.B., Memphis State U., 1941. Admitted to Tenn. bar, 1941, U.S. Supreme Ct. bar, 1954, Tex. bar, 1971; commd. 1st lt. JAG, USAF, 1947, advanced through grades to col., 1961; staff JAG, Bermuda, 1947-51; asst. staff Hdqrs. Mil. Air Transport Service, Washington, 1951-54, asst. chief legis. div. office of judge adv. gen. Hdqrs. USAF, Washington, 1954-57, dir. civil law, Hdqrs., USAF Europe, Weisbaden, Germany, 1957-61; sr. judge adv. Chanute Tech. Tng. Center, Ill., 1961-64, Lackland Mil. Tng. Center, San Antonio, 1964-68, 12th Air Force, Austin, Tex., 1968-71; ret., 1971; chief legal publs. State Bar Tex., Austin, 1971—. Mem. Am. Bar Assn., State Bar Tex. (mem. council mil. law sect. 1976—), Judge Advs. Assn. Home and Office: 4001 Greystone Dr Austin TX 78731 Tel (512) 345-1352

PEARSON, ROGER DALE, b. Crookston, Minn., Oct. 14, 1942; B.A. magna cum laude, Luther Coll., 1964; J.D. cum laude, Harvard, 1970. Admitted to N.Y. bar, 1971, U.S. Ct. Appeals 2d Circuit bar, 1975; asso. firm Cravath, Swaine & Moore, N.Y.C., 1970—. Mem. N.Y. Bar Assn. Home: 170 W End Ave New York City NY 10023 Office: 1 Chase Manhattan Plaza New York City NY 10005 Tel (212) 422-3000

PEARSON, RUSSELL ROBERTS, b. St. Paul, Dec. 6, 1926; A.B., Harvard, 1947, LL.B., 1952. Admitted to D.C. bar, 1960, Wash. bar, 1963; since practiced in Seattle, dep. pros. atty. King County, 1963-66; asso. firms Nicolai, Montgomery & Sorrel, 1967-69, Dodd, Russell, Hamlin & Coney, 1969-70, Clinton, Fleck, Glein & Brown, 1971—; fgn. service officer U.S. Dept. State, Austria and Egypt, 1952-61; contract adminstr. Boeing Co., Seattle, 1962-63. Mem. Am., Wash., Seattle-King County bar assns. Home: 3816 41st Ave NE Seattle WA 98105 Office: 2112 Third Ave Suite 500 Seattle WA 98121 Tel (206) 624-6832

PEARSON, THOMAS HOWARD, b. Clarksdale, Miss., Dec. 31, 1929; LL.B., U. Miss., 1951, J.D., 1970. Admitted to Miss. bar, 1951; individual practice law, Clarksdale, 1951—; pros. atty. Coahoma County, Miss., 1952-59, 1964-67. Mem. Coahoma County Bar Assn. (past pres. 1970). Home: Box 912 Clarksdale MS 38614 Office: 69 Delta Ave Clarksdale MS 38614 Tel (601) 627-1171

PEATROSS, WILLIAM CAMPBELL, b. Shreveport, La., Sept. 15, 1943; B.A., La. State U., 1965, J.D., 1968. Admitted to La. bar, 1968; staff atty., dir. Caddo Abstract and Title Co., Shreveport, 1968—. Pres. Caddo. Found. Exceptional Children, 1976. Fellow Am. Coll. Mortgage Attys.; mem. Am. Bar Assn. Named Legal Secs. Assn. Boss of Year, 1976. Office: PO Box 126 Shreveport LA 71161 Tel (318) 221-5266

PEAY, RICHARD VERN, b. Garfield, Utah, Mar. 19, 1923; B.S., U. Utah, 1949; LL.B., 1949, J.D., 1962. Admitted to Utah bar, 1949; asso. firm Rich & Elton, Salt Lake City, 1949-50; legal counsel Utah state hdqrs. SSS, Salt Lake City, 1951; asso. firm Nielsen & Conder, Salt Lake City, 1955-68; Utah State dir. SSS, 1969-73; ct. adminstr., Utah, 1973—; dir. Cottonwood, Inc. Mem. Am., Utah, Salt Lake County bar assns., Assn. Jud. Adminstrn., Am. Judicature Soc., Utah Fed. Exec. Assn. (pres. 1970), Nat. Conf. State Ct. Adminstrs., Ret. Officers Assn., Salt Lake City Rotary. Decorated Legion of Merit; recipient Distinguished Service Medal, SSS, 1973. Home: 2611 Hillsden Dr Salt Lake City UT 84117 Office: 250 E Broadway Suite 240 Salt Lake City UT 84111 Tel (801) 523-6371

PECCOLE, ROBERT NEIL, b. Ely, Nev., Sept. 26, 1937; B.S., U. So. Calif., 1960; LL.B., U. Calif., Hastings, 1963. Admitted to Nev. bar, 1963, U.S. Dist. Ct. Nev. bar, 1964, U.S. 9th Circuit Ct. Appeals bar, 1976, U.S. Supreme Ct. bar, 1973; since practiced in Las Vegas; asso. firm Franklin & O'Donnell, 1963-66; asst. pub. defender, 1966-69; individual practice law, 1969—; gen. counsel Clark County Bail Bond Assn., 1976—. Mem. Nev., Clark County bar assns., So. Calif. Alumni Assn., Hastings Alumni Assn., Elks., Phi Alpha Delta. Home: 600 Lacy Ln Las Vegas NV 89107 Office: 302 E Carson Suite 920 Las Vegas NV 89101 Tel (702) 382-2311

PECK, BERNARD S., b. Bridgeport, Conn., July 26, 1915; A.B., Yale, 1936, LL.B., 1939. Admitted to Conn. bar, 1939, U.S. Supreme Ct. bar, 1945; mem. firm Goldstein and Peck, Bridgeport, 1939—; judge Westport (Conn.) Municipal Ct., 1951-55. Pres., Westport YMCA, 1957-59, trustee, 1961—; pres. The Patterson Club, Inc., 1975-76. Fellow Am. Coll. Trial Lawyers, Internat. Acad. Trial Lawyers, mem. Am., Bridgeport, Conn., Westport bar assns. Home: 25 Punch Bowl Dr Westport CT 06880 Office: 955 Main St Bridgeport CT 06604 Tel (203) 334-9421

PECK, CORNELIUS JOHN, b. Calumet, Mich., Mar. 30, 1923; B.S., Harvard, 1944, certificate Bus. Sch., 1945, LL.B., 1949. Admitted to Mass. bar, 1949, U.S. Supreme Ct. bar, 1952, Wash. bar, 1954; atty. U.S. Dept. Justice, Washington, 1949-50; 1952-54; legal asst. NLRB, Washington, 1952-54; asst. prof. law U. Wash., 1954-56, asso. prof. law, 1956-58, prof. law, 1958—; vis. prof. law, U. Mich., 1973-74; chmn. Hearing Tribunal of the Wash. Bd. against Discrimination, 1969. Mem. Nat. Acad. Arbitrators, Am. Arbitration Assn., Am., Seattle-King County Bar Assns. Contbr. articles to law reviews. Home: 2340 Delmar Dr E Seattle WA 98102 Office: Sch Law Univ Wash Seattle WA 98195 Tel (206) 543-4948

PECK, DAVID WARNER, b. Crawfordsville, Ind., Dec. 3, 1902; A.B. with distinguished honors, Wabash Coll., 1922, LL.D., 1954; LL.B., Harvard, 1925; S.J.D., Suffolk U., 1952; LL.D., Union Coll., Schenectady, 1953. Admitted to N.Y. bar, 1926, U.S. Supreme Ct. bar, 1958; asst. U.S. atty. So. Dist. N.Y., 1925-28; partner firm Sullivan & Cromwell, N.Y.C., 1934-43, 58—; trustee Greenwich Savs. Bank; justice N.Y. Supreme Ct., 1943-45, asso. justice appellate div., 1st dept., 1945-47, presiding justice, 1947-57; mem. Permanent Internat. Ct. Arbitration, 1957-63; mem. task force on legal services and procedures 2d Hoover Commn., 1953-55; chmn. N.Y. State Commn. on Revision and Simplification of Constitution, 1959-61. Trustee Vincent Astor Found., Wabash Coll., N.Y. U. Law Center Found.; mem. vis. com. Ind. U. Law Sch. Fellow Inst. Jud. Adminstrn.; mem. Assn. Bar City N.Y., New York County Lawyers Assn., N.Y. State (pres. 1962), Am., Internat. bar assns., Am. Coll. Trial Lawyers, Am. Soc. Internat. Law, Am. Judicature Soc., Am. Arbitration Assn. (chmn. bd. dirs. 1965-69). Author: The Greer Case, 1955; Decision at Law, 1961. Home: 580 Park Ave New York City NY 10021 Office: 48 Wall St New York City NY 10005 Tel (212) 952-8101

PECK, JOHN W., b. Cin., June 23, 1913; A.B., Miami U., Oxford U., 1935; LL.D., U. Cin., 1938; LL.D., U. Cin. Coll. of Law, 1965, Miami U., 1966, Salmon P. Chase Coll. of Law, 1971. Admitted to Ohio bar, 1938; mem. firm Peck, Shaffer & Williams, Cin., 1935-66; exec. sec. to Ohio Gov., Columbus, 1949-50; judge Ct. of Common Pleas, Hamilton County, Ohio, 1950-51; tax commr. State of Ohio, Columbus, 1951-54; judge Ct. of Common Pleas, Hamilton County, 1954-55; justice Ohio Supreme Ct., Columbus, 1959-60; judge U.S. Dist. Ct. So. Ohio, 1961-66; judge U.S. Ct. of Appeals 6th Circuit, Cin., 1966—; mem. Jud. Conf. of U.S. Com. on Adminstrn. of Criminal Law, 1961—; lectr. Salmon P. Chase Coll. of Law, Cin., 1949-51; lectr. U. Cin. Coll. of Law, 1948-69. Trustee Miami U., 1958-59, trustee emeritus, 1975—; mem. Ohio Unemployment Commn., 1951; mem. Princeton City Sch. Dist. Bd. Edn., 1958-63, pres. bd., 1963-69; mem. vestry Christ Episcopal Ch., Glendale, Ohio, 1967-70. Mem. Fed., Ohio, Cin. bar assns. Home: 165 Magnolia Ave Glendale OH 45246 Office: 613 US Ct House & Post Office Cincinnati OH 45202 Tel (513) 684-2956

PECK, RICHARD CLEON, b. Falls City, Nebr., Sept. 16, 1917; A.B., U. Nebr., 1941, LL.B., 1942. Admitted to Nebr. bar, 1942, U.S. Dist. Ct. Nebr. bar, 1942, U.S. 8th Circuit Ct. Appeals bar, 1947; law clk. 8th Circuit Ct. Appeals, 1942; individual practice law, Plattsmouth, Nebr., 1946-56, county judge, Plattsmouth, 1948-50, county atty., 1951-56; asst. U.S. Atty., Omaha, 1956-59; clk. U.S. Dist. Ct. Nebr., Omaha, 1959-75, U.S. magistrate, 1970—. Mem. Am., Nebr., Fed. (pres. chpt. 1958) bar assns., Fed. Ct. Clks. Assn., Order Coif, Phi Delta Phi. Contbr. articles to profl. jours. Office: PO Box 457 Omaha NE 68101 Tel (402) 221-4178

PECK, RODNEY HOWARD, b. Denver, Aug. 20, 1939; A.B. cum laude, Colo. Coll., 1962; J.D., U. Denver, 1965. Admitted to Colo. bar, 1965; asso. firm Sid Pleasant, Craig, Colo., 1965-75; partner firm Pleasant, Peck and Lawrence, Craig, 1976—; mem. faculty Continuing Legal Edn. in Colo., Inc. Mem. Moffat County (Colo.) Sch. Bd., 1973—, Craig-Moffat County Police Commn., 1974-75. Mem. Am., Colo., N.W. Colo. (pres. 1967-68, 71-72) bar assns. Recipient Lawyers Title award to outstanding sr. in real estate U. Denver, 1965. Home: 833 School St Craig CO 81625 Office: PO Box 1055 Craig CO 81625 Tel (303) 824-6561

PECK, WILLIAM LLOYD, b. Joliet, Ill., Mar. 2, 1932; B.A., Carleton Coll., 1953; LL.B., U. Calif., 1961. Admitted to Calif. bar, 1962; dep. dist. atty. Ventura County (Calif.), 1962-65; partner firm Loebl, Bringgold & Peck, Ventura, 1965-75, firm Loebl, Bringgold, Peck & Parker, Ventura, 1975—. Mem. Ventura Unified Sch. Dist. Bd. Edn., 1969—, pres., 1972-73, 77; pres. Ventura Boys' Club, 1976. Mem. Ventura County Bar Assn. (sec.-treas. 1969, pres. 1972), Am., Ventura County trial lawyers assns., State Bar Calif., Am. Arbitration Assn. Home: 360 Tulane St Ventura CA 93003 Office: 2580 E Main St Ventura CA 93003 Tel (805) 648-3303

PECKAR, ROBERT S., b. N.Y.C., Apr. 30, 1946; A.B., Rutgers U., 1968; J.D., Columbia, 1971. Admitted to N.Y. bar, 1972, N.J. bar, 1972; law clk. firm Max E. Greenberg, Trayman, Harris, Cantor, Reiss & Blasky, N.Y.C., 1969-71; asso. firm Goetz & Fitzpatrick, N.Y.C., 1971-73; individual practice law, New Rochelle, N.Y., 1973—, Hackensack, N.J., 1973—. Mem. Am., N.J. bar assns., Assn. Bar City N.Y. Office: 140 Huguenot St New Rochelle NY 10801 Tel (914) 633-6300

PECKHAM, EUGENE ELIOT, b. Stamford, Conn., Aug. 11, 1940; B.A. with honors and distinction in history, Wesleyan U., 1962; J.D., Harvard, 1965. Admitted to N.Y. bar, 1965, U.S. Tax Ct. bar, 1974; asso. firm Hinman, Howard & Kattell, Binghamton, N.Y., 1965-72, partner, 1972—; vol. U.S. Peace Corps, Peru, 1966-67; adj. lectr. in accounting State U. N.Y., Binghamton, 1973-77, adj. asst. prof., 1977—. Bd. dirs. Found. of State U. N.Y., Binghamton, 1975—, v.p.,

1977; bd. dirs. Roberson Center for Arts and Scis., 1977—; mem. Broome County Local Services Commn., 1974—, Broome County Archtl. Adv. Commn., 1971-74; bd. dirs. Binghamton Girls' Club, 1970-77, pres., 1974-76, bd. mem. of yr. award, 1974; pres. Broome County Young Republican Club, 1969-70. Mem. Broome County, N.Y. State (spl. com. on availability of legal services 1973—, chmn. 1976—, subcom. on exempt orgns. tax sect.) bar assns. Home: 12 Campbell Rd Binghamton NY 13905 Office: 724 Security Mutual Bldg Binghamton NY 13901 Tel (607) 723-5341

PECKHAM, ROBERT FRANCIS, b. San Francisco, Nov. 3, 1920; A.B., Stanford, 1941, LL.B., 1945; postgrad. in Law Yale, 1941-42; LL.D., U. Santa Clara, 1973. Admitted to Calif. bar, 1945; adminstrv. asst. regional enforcement atty. Office Price Adminstrn., San Francisco, 1942-43; individual practice law, Palo Alto and Sunnyvale, Calif., 1946-48; asst. U.S. atty. No. Dist. Calif., 1948-53, chief asst. criminal div., 1952-53; mem. firm Darwin and Peckham, San Francisco, Palo Alto and Sunnyvale, Calif., 1953-59; judge Superior Ct. of Santa Clara County (Calif.), 1959-66, presiding judge, 1961-63, 65-66; judge U.S. Dist. Ct., No. Dist. Calif., 1966—, chief judge, 1976—. Trustee Foothill Coll. Dist., 1957-59, pres., 1959; bd. visitors Stanford Law Sch., 1969-75, chmn., 1971-72. Mem. Am., Fed., San Francisco, Santa Clara County bar assns., Am. Judicature Soc., Supreme Ct. Hist. Soc., Soc. Calif. Pioneers, Calif. Hist. Soc. (trustee 1974—), Stanford Law Socs. (chmn. 1974-75), Phi Beta Kappa, Phi Delta Phi. Recipient Brotherhood award Nat. Conf. Christians and Jews, 1968. Home: 101 Alma St Apt 408 Palo Alto CA 94301 Office: US Courthouse San Francisco CA 94102 Tel (415) 556-5646

PEDDER, STANLEY, b. Berkeley, Calif., Feb. 19, 1935; B.A. in Econs., U. Pacific, Stockton, Calif.; LL.B., J.D., U. Calif., Berkeley. Admitted to Calif. bar, 1961; sr. partner firm Nalott, Pedder & Stover, Lafayette, Calif.; instr. law St. Marys, Diablo Valley colls., 1965-71; pro tem judge Walnut Creek Municipal Ct. Vice pres. Lafayette C. of C., 1963. Mem. Calif., Mt. Diablo, Contra Costa County bar assns., Calif. Trial Lawyers Assn., Phi Alpha Phi. Office: PO Box 475 3445 Golden Gate Way Lafayette CA 94549 Tel (415) 283-6816

PEDEN, JAMES ALTON, JR., b. Gainesville, Fla., Apr. 24, 1944; B.A. summa cum laude, U. Miss., 1966, J.D., 1970; postgrad. (Fulbright scholar), U. Bristol (Eng.), 1966-67. Admitted to Miss. bar, 1970; asso. firm Stennett, Wilkinson & Ward, Jackson, Miss., 1970-73, partner, 1973—; staff asst. U.S. Senator John C. Stennis of Miss., 1965, Lt. Gov. William Winter of Miss., 1972-75; service officer Miss. Senate, 1972-75; capt., staff judge adv. Miss. Air N.G., 1972—. Mem. Miss. Econ. Council; bd. dirs. Community Hosp. of Jackson, 1973-75; mem. Hinds County (Miss.) Democratic Exec. Com., 1972—. Mem. Miss. Law Inst. (com. mem. 1974-76), Miss. State Bar (dir. young lawyers sect. 1973—, sec. 1976—), Am., Hinds County bar assns., Jackson Young Lawyers Assn. (sec. 1973-74, exec. com. 1974-75), Am. Judicature Soc., Phi Delta Phi, Phi Alpha Theta, Omicron Delta Kappa, Beta Theta Pi (pres. Miss. alumni assn. 1971-72), Pi Sigma Alpha, Phi Kappa Phi, Phi Eta Sigma, Eta Sigma Phi. Inst. Politics in Miss. fellow, 1971-72; contbr. articles to legal jours. Home: 507 Merigold Dr Jackson MS 39204 Office: 100 Congress St S PO Box 22627 Jackson MS 39205 Tel (601) 948-3003

PEDERSEN, DONALD BONDO, b. Mpls., Mar. 5, 1938; B.A., St. Olaf Coll., 1960; J.D., Northwestern U., 1963. Admitted to Minn. bar, 1965, U.S. Tax Ct. bar, 1970; individual practice law, Wheaton, Minn., 1965-69; asst. prof. William Mitchell Coll. Law, St. Paul, 1969-72, asso. prof., 1972-73, Capital U., Columbus, Ohio, 1973-75, prof., 1975-76; partner firm Winter, Lundquist, Sherwood, Athens & Pedersen, Wheaton, 1976—; lectr. in field. Mem. Minn. Bar Assn., Am. Judicature Soc., Comml. Law League Am., Pi Gamma Mu. Contbr. articles to profl. jours. Home: 1112 4th Ave N Wheaton MN 56296 Office: Broadway Office Bldg Wheaton MN 56296 Tel (612) 563-8244

PEDOWITZ, JAMES MORRIS, b. Bklyn., Oct. 29, 1915; B.A., N.Y. U., 1935, J.D., 1938. Admitted to N.Y. State bar, 1938, Fed. bar, 1950; 1st v.p., chief counsel Title Guarantee Co., N.Y.C., 1935—; v.p., regional counsel Pioneer Nat. Title Ins. Co., N.Y.C., 1972—. Mem. planning bd. village East Williston, L.I., N.Y., 1963-74. Mem. Nassau County, Queens County, Suffolk County, N.Y. State, Am. bar assns., Assn. Bar City N.Y., N.Y. County Lawyers Assn. Contbr. articles to legal jours. Home: 200 Dickson Circle East Williston NY 11596 Office: 120 Broadway New York City NY 10005 Tel (212) 964-1000

PEEBLES, WILLIAM LAWRENCE, b. Greenwood, Miss., Oct. 17, 1941; A.A., Miss. Delta Jr. Coll., 1961; B.S., So. Miss. U., 1964; J.D., Jackson Sch. Law, 1970. Admitted to Miss. bar, 1971; individual practice law, Hattiesburg, Miss., 1971-76; city judge Hattiesburg City Ct., 1976—. Mem. Miss. Trial Lawyers Assn., Miss. Bar Assn. Home: 806 Monterrey Lane Hattiesburg MS 39401 Office: 119 Hardy St Hattiesburg MS 39401 Tel (601) 544-6261

PEEL, ELBERT SIDNEY, JR., b. Williamston, N.C., Feb. 14, 1922; B.A. in Econs., U. N.C., 1944, LL.B., 1949. Admitted to N.C. bar, 1949; mem. firm Peel & Peel, Williamston, 1949-63; judge Superior Ct. of N.C., Williamston, 1963—; mem. N.C. Senate, 1959-61, N.C. Ho. of Reps., 1961-63. Mem. N.C. Bar Assn. Home: 906 School Dr Williamston NC 27892 Office: Martin County Ct House Williamston NC 27892 Tel (919) 792-2515

PEER, NORMAN JOSEPH, b. Orange, N.J., Sept. 9, 1936; B.A., Villanova U., 1958; LL.B., Fordham U., 1963. Admitted to N.Y. bar, 1964, N.J. bar, 1965; asso. firm Burke & Burke, Daniels, Leighton & Reid, and predecessor, N.Y.C., 1963-69, partner, 1970—; judge Atlantic Highlands (N.J.) Municipal Ct., 1972—. Bd. dirs., trustee MCOSS-Family Health-Nursing Service. Mem. Am., N.J., N.Y. State, Monmouth County (N.J.) bar assns., Am. Judges Assn. Contbr. articles to legal jours. Home: 32 Nottingham Way Little Silver NJ 07739 Office: 30 Rockefeller Plaza New York City NY 10020 Tel (212) 489-0400 also Tuller Bldg 103 E Front St Red Bank NJ 07701

PEGEON, LOUIS-PHILIPPE, Now Puisne judge Supreme Ct. of Can., Ottawa, Ont. Office: Supreme Ct Bldg Wellington St Ottawa ON K1A 0J1 Canada*

PEGRAM, JOHN BRAXTON, b. Yeadon, Pa., June 29, 1938; A.B. in Physics, Columbia, 1960; LL.B., N.Y. U., 1965. Admitted to N.Y. State bar, 1965, U.S. Supreme Ct. bar, 1971; engr. Fairchild Camera & Instrument Corp., Clifton, N.J., 1960-66; mem. firm Davis, Hoxie, Faithfull & Hapgood, N.Y.C., 1966—. Mem. Am., N.Y. State bar assns., Assn. Bar City N.Y., Am. (chmn. fed. practice and procedure com. 1974-76), N.Y. (chmn. subcom. litigation 1975-76) patent law assns., Am. Phys. Soc., IEEE, Chartered Inst. Patent Agts. (fgn. mem.). Contbr. articles to profl. jours. Office: 45 Rockefeller Plaza New York City NY 10020 Tel (212) 757-2200

PEIFFER, WILLIAM ARBA, b. Venango, Pa., July 9, 1920; B.S., Edinboro State Coll., 1941; LL.B., Dickinson Sch. Law, 1948, J.D., 1968. Admitted to Pa. bar, 1949; individual practice law, Cambridge, Pa., 1949-51, Corry, Pa., 1952—; with Pa. Dept. Revenue, Corry, 1963-64; asst. dist. atty. Erie County, Pa., 1964-66. Mayor of Corry, 1966-68. Mem. Erie County, Pa., Am. bar assns. Office: 224 Maple Ave Corry PA 16407 Tel (814) 665-2301

PEINADO, ARTHUR GILBERT, b. El Paso, Tex., Jan. 16, 1947; student Johns Hopkins U., 1964-66; A.B., U. Tex., El Paso, 1969; J.D., Harvard, 1972. Admitted to Calif. bar, 1972; mem. firm Jenkins & Perry, San Diego, 1972—; instr. U. Calif., San Diego, 1976-77. Mem. San Diego County Bar Assn. (chmn. real property sect.). Home: 4667 Niagara Ave San Diego CA 92107 Office: 1010 Second Ave Suite 2000 San Diego CA 92101 Tel (714) 239-0471

PEIREZ, LAWRENCE, b. N.Y.C., Aug. 4, 1914; LL.B., St. John's U., 1940. Admitted to N.Y. bar, 1941; individual practice law, 1951—; asst. dist. atty., Queens County, N.Y., 1950-55; dir. Viewlex, Inc., Central State Bank N.Y., Cut & Curl, Inc. Chmn. law com. Queens County Dem. Party, 1949-50; chmn. O'Connor for Gov. N.Y. State, 1966; O'Connor for Pres. N.Y.C. Council, 1965. Mem. N.Y. State, Queens County bar assns., Friars Club, B'nai B'rith (nat. chmn. civil rights div. anti-defamation league, chmn. personnel com. internat. order 1966—). Contbr. articles to legal jours. Home: 1 Bowers Ln Great Neck NY 11020 Office: 175 Great Neck Rd Great Neck NY 11021 Tel (212) 446-1616 or (516) 829-6900

PELAFAS, PETER G., b. Champaign, Ill., Dec. 17, 1928; B.A., U. Ill., 1950, LL.B., 1956, J.D., 1968. Admitted to Ill. bar, 1956; asso. firm Davidson & Pelafas, Maywood, Ill., 1957-60; individual practice law, Chgo., 1957, Bellwood, Ill., 1960, Broadview, Ill., 1964-71, River Forest, Ill., 1972—; partner firm Mosetick & Pelafas, Broadview, 1961-63. Mem. Am., Ill., West Suburban (pres. 1969), Hellenic (pres. 1973) bar assns., Delta Theta Phi (mem. Chgo. alumni senate). Home: 910 Bonnie Brae Pl River Forest IL 60305 Office: 7708 W Madison St River Forest IL 60305 Tel (312) 771-5000

PELL, RICHARD WAYNE, b. Greencastle, Ind., Apr. 12, 1941; B.A., DePauw U., 1963; LL.B., George Washington U., 1966. Admitted to Del. bar, 1966; individual practice law, Wilmington, Del., 1966-68; asst. State Pub. Defender, 1968-69; mem. firm Tybout & Redfearn, Wilmington, Del., 1969—; dep. atty. gen., 1969-70; atty. Del. Alcholic Beverage Commn., 1970; judge probate ct., Del., 1970-74; adj. prof. law Goldey Beacom Coll., 1975-76. Vice pres. New Castle County Young Republicans, 1969-70. Mem. Am. Bar Assn. (chmn. young lawyers drug abuse com. Del. 1970-74), Del. Bar Assn., Del. Valley DePauw Alumni Assn. (pres. 1970). Home: 2629 Longwood Dr Wilmington DE 19810 Office: 300 Delaware Ave Wilmington DE 19810 Tel (302) 658-6901

PELLEGRINI, FRANK LOUIS, b. St. Louis, Aug. 14, 1940; B.S., U. Notre Dame, 1962; J.D., St. Louis U., 1965; certificate in indsl. and environ. hygiene U. Cin., 1973. Admitted to Mo. bar, 1965, U.S. Supreme Ct. bar, 1971; v.p., gen. counsel Marlo Coil Co., St. Louis, 1965-66; works mgr. H.k. Porter Co., Inc., Pitts., 1966-67, gen. mgr. air conditioning group, 1968; individual oractice law, St. Louis, 1970—. Mem. St. Louis Bar Assn., St. Louis Engrs. Club, Am. Soc. Heating, Refrigeration and Air Conditioning Engrs., Am. Soc. Indsl. Hygienists. Home: 9255 Cordoba St Saint Louis MO 63126 Office: 706 Chestnut St Suite 1025 Saint Louis MO 63101 Tel (314) 241-7445

PELTIN, SHERWIN CARL, b. Milw., Aug. 2, 1929; B.B.A., U. Wis. Madison, 1950, LL.B., 1952; LL.M. in Taxation, N.Y. U., 1955; S.J.D., George Washington U., 1962. Admitted to Wis. bar, 1952, U.S. Tax Ct. bar, 1958, U.S. Ct. Claims bar, 1960; asso. firm Louis L. Meldman, Milw., 1958-62; partner firm Laikin, Swietlik & Peltin, Milw., 1962-67; mem. firm Peregrine, Marcuvitz, Cameron & Peltin, Milw., 1968—; atty.-advisor U.S. Tax Ct., Washington, 1955-58. Trustee Village of Bayside (Wis.), 1967-73. Mem. Am., Wis., Milw. bar assns., Am. Judicature Soc., Estate Counselors Forum. C.P.A., Wis. Home: 8877 N Malibu Dr Bayside WI 53217 Office: 633 W Wisconsin Ave Milwaukee WI 53203 Tel (414) 272-4833

PELTON, RUSSELL MEREDITH, JR., b. Chgo., May 14, 1938; B.A., DePauw U., 1960; J.D., U. Chgo., 1963. Admitted to Ill. bar, 1963; capt. JAGC, U.S. Air Force, 1963-66; asso. firm Peterson Ross Rall Barber & Seidel, Chgo., 1966-72, partner, 1972—. Co-founder, incorporator Chgo. Opportunities Industrialization Center, 1969, bd. dirs., gen. counsel, 1969—; chmn. Wilmette (Ill.) Sch. Bd. Caucus, 1970-71; mem. Wilmette Dist. 39 Bd. Edn., 1972—. Home: 607 9th St Wilmette IL 60091 Office: 135 S LaSalle St Chicago IL 60603 Tel (412) 263-7300

PELUSO, FRANK NICHOLAS, b. Greenwich, Conn., June 15, 1930; B.S. in Bus. Adminstrn., Boston Coll., 1952; LL.B., Fordham U., 1955, J.D., 1968. Admitted to Conn. bar, 1957, N.Y. bar, Fed. bar, 1958; partner firm Hickey & Peluso, and predecessor, Stamford and Greenwich, Conn., 1957-61; individual practice law, Stamford and Greenwich, 1961—. Mem. Am., Conn., Greenwich, Stamford bar assns., N.Y. Trial Lawyers Assn. Home: 34 Hill Rd Greenwich CT 06830 Office: 1799 Summer St Stamford CT 06905 Tel (203) 348-2000

PELZ, ROBERT LEON, b. N.Y.C., Nov. 18, 1918; B.A., Columbia, 1939, J.D., 1942. Admitted to N.Y. bar, 1942; since practiced in N.Y.C.; asso. firm Hess, Segall, Guterman, Pelz & Steiner and predecessor, 1946-53, partner, 1953—. Vice-pres., Fedn. Jewish Philanthropies N.Y., 1975-77; bd. govs. Am. Jewish Com. N.Y., 1967—. Mem. Am., N.Y. State bar assns., Assn. Bar City NY, N.Y. County Lawyers Assn. Home: 164 Brite Ave Scarsdale NY 10583 Office: 230 Park Ave New York City NY 10017 Tel (212) 689-2400

PELZER, JAMES EDWARD, b. Jamaica, N.Y., Aug. 29, 1946; B.A., U. Calif., Santa Barbara, 1967; J.D., St. John's U., 1970. Admitted to N.Y. bar, 1971, U.S. Supreme Ct. bar, 1976; law asst. appellate div. N.Y. Supreme Ct., Bklyn., 1971—. Exec. bd. Queens council Boy Scouts Am., N.Y.C., 1976—. Mem. N.Y., Bklyn. bar assns. Author: Brooklyn Heights in the Revolution, 1976. Home: 91 Dennis St Manhasset NY 11030 Office: 45 Monroe Pl Brooklyn NY 11201 Tel (212) TR 5-1300

PEMBERTON, DAVID LAWRENCE, b. Toledo, Dec. 16, 1940; B.A., Ohio State U., 1963, J.D., 1966. Admitted to Ohio bar; asso. firm George, Greek, King, McMahon & McConnaughey, Columbus, Ohio, 1966-70; partner Beery, Patterson & Pemberton, Columbus, 1970-71, Muldoon, Pemberton & Ferris, Columbus, 1972—. Sec. Pub. Utilities Commn. of Ohio, 1971-72. Mem. Ohio, Columbus bar assns., Ohio Motor Carrier Lawyers Assn., Motor Carrier Lawyers Assn. Office: 50 W Broad St Columbus OH 43215 Tel (614) 464-4103

PEMBERTON, DONALD WILLIAM, b. Nashville, Oct. 22, 1935; B.S., Memphis State U., 1957; LL.B., Vanderbilt U., 1960. Admitted to Tenn. bar, 1960; since practiced in Memphis, atty. IRS, 1960-62; asso. firm Boone, Wellford, Clark, Langschmidt & Pemberton, and predecessor, 1962-65, partner, 1965—; adj. prof. law Memphis State U., 1963—; trustee Tenn. Fed. Tax Inst.; pres. Estate Planning Council Memphis. Bd. dirs. Boys' Town, Inc. Mem. Am., Tenn. (chmn. tax sect.) bar assns. Recipient Outstanding Performance award IRS, 1962. Home: 779 Reddoch St Memphis TN 38117 Office: 2750 Commerce Sq Memphis TN 38103 Tel (901) 523-0311

PENDERGAST, WILLIAM ROSS, b. Kansas City, Mo., Oct. 1, 1931; B.S., Rockhurst Coll., 1952; J.D., Mo. U., 1957. Admitted to Mo. bar, 1957, D.C. bar, 1964; asso. firm Meyer & Smith, Kansas City, 1957-61; trial atty. FDA, Washington, 1961-64; asso. then partner firm McLean, Morton & Boustead, Washington, D.C., 1964-68; partner firm McMurray & Pendergast, Washington, 1968—. Mem. Am. Bar Assn. (chmn. com. on food and drugs, corp. and banking). Office: 1019 19th St NW Washington DC 20036 Tel (202) 833-2550

PENDERGRASS, ORVILLE DEXTER, b. Bakersfield, Mo., Dec. 26, 1910; student LaSalle Extension U., 1931-35, SW Mo. Coll., 1936-39. Admitted to Ark. bar, 1935; sch. tchr., 1935-49; individual practice law, Mountain Home, Ark., 1949—; dep. pros. atty. Baxter County, 1950-64; acting atty. City of Mountain Home, 1952-56; mem. Ark. Ho. of Reps., 1965-66. Chmn. bd., lay speaker, pres. men's club, Mountain Home Meth. Ch., also chmn. Christian social concerns com.; pres. Ark. Farm Bur. Bd., 1962-63, Baxter County (Ark.) Farm Bur., 1958-62, Baxter County Fair Assn., 1960-64. Mem. Ark., Baxter County (pres. 1955-56) bar assns. Office: 511 Main St Mountain Home AR 72653 Tel (501) 425-3419

PENDERGRASS, PHILIP PICKETT, b. Salinas, Calif., Dec. 30, 1938; A.B., Stanford, 1960; J.D., U. Calif., 1963. Admitted to Calif. bar, 1964, U.S. Supreme Ct. bar, 1970; asso. firm Jensen & Underwood, Modesto, Calif., 1965-68; partner firm Jensen & Pendergrass, Modesto, 1968-73; dep. dist. atty. Stanislaus County (Calif.), 1964-65; individual practice law, Oakdale, Calif., 1976—; adminstrv. asst. Congressman Bob Mathias, Washington, 1973-75; legis. cons. U.S. Olympic Com., 1975; polit. cons. Wis. Physicians Alliance, 1975. Mem. Republican Central Com. Stanislaus County, 1969-75, chmn., 1971-73, 77. Mem. Calif., Stanislaus County bar assns., Criminal Def. Bar of Stanislaus County. Office: 730 E F St Suite E Oakdale CA 95361 Tel (209) 847-5921

PENDLETON, DONALD MURRAY, b. Sioux City, Iowa, Mar. 30, 1914; B.A., U. Iowa, 1935, J.D., 1937. Admitted to Iowa bar, 1937; practiced in Sioux City, 1937-42, 46-65; spl. agt. FBI, 1942-46; judge Iowa Dist. Ct. for 3d Dist., 1965—; city atty. City of Sioux City, 1958-59; asst. county atty. Woodbury County (Iowa), 1941, 42, 55. Chmn. Sioux City CSC. Mem. Woodbury County, Iowa, Am. bar assns., Am. Judicature Soc., Iowa Trial Judges Assn. Home: 2215 Heights Ave Sioux City IA 51104 Office: 209 Woodbury County Courthouse Sioux City IA 51101 Tel (712) 279-6628

PENDLETON, JOHN B., b. Bronxville, N.Y., July 28, 1936; B.A., Amherst Coll., 1958; LL.B., U. Mich., 1962. Admitted to N.H. bar, 1962; now with firm Sulloway, Hollis, Godfrey & Soden, Concord, N.H.; mem. N.H. Jud. Council, 1968, vice chmn., 1972-74. Mem. Merrimack County (sec.-treas. 1965-68), N.H. (pres. 1976-77), Am. bar assns. Office: 9 Capitol St PO Box 1256 Concord NH 03301 Tel (603) 224-2341*

PENEGAR, KENNETH LAWING, b. Charlotte, N.C., May 12, 1932; B.A. in History, U. N.C., 1954; postgrad. London Sch. Econs., 1958; J.D. with honors, U. N.C., 1961; LL.M., Yale, 1962. Admitted to N.C. bar, 1961, D.C. bar, 1963; law clk. to Judge Charles Fahy, U.S. Ct. Appeals, D.C. Circuit, 1962-63; asst. prof. law U. N.C., 1963-66, asso. prof., 1966-69; asso. firm Shea & Gardner, Washington, 1969-71; prof. law, dean U. Tenn., 1971—; Ford Found. vis. prof. law Delhi U. (India), 1967-68; v.p., dir. Fed. Tax Inst. Tenn., 1973—; cons. in field. Trustee, Lawyers Com. for Civil Rights Under Law, 1976—. Mem. Am., Tenn., Knoxville bar assns., Am. Law Inst., Order of Coif, Order of Golden Fleece, Phi Kappa Phi, Omicron Delta Kappa, Phi Alpha Delta. Contbr. articles to law jours. Home: 3820 Woodhill Pl Knoxville TN 37916 Office: 1505 W Cumberland Ave Knoxville TN 37916 Tel (615) 974-2521

PENETAR, DANIEL LAWRENCE, b. Dunmore, Pa., Aug. 3, 1916; A.B., U. Scranton, 1940; LL.B., Fordham U., 1947. Admitted to Pa. bar, 1948; practiced in Scranton, 1948-72; judge Ct. of Common Pleas, Lackawanna County (Pa.), 1972—; solicitor Dunmore Borough (Pa.), 1961-71, Lackawanna County Bd. Assessors, 1967. Alt. del.-at-large Democratic Nat. Conv., Chgo., 1968. Mem. Lackawanna County, Pa. bar assns. Home: 2216 Jefferson Ave Dunmore PA 18512 Office: Ct of Common Pleas Orphans' Ct Div Courthouse Scranton PA 18503 Tel (717) 961-6748

PENIX, BILL, b. Jonesboro, Ark., Oct. 10, 1922; B.A., U. Ark., 1943, J.D., 1949. Admitted to Ark. bar 1949, U.S. Supreme Ct. bar, 1954; partner firm Penix & Penix, Jonesboro, 1949—, firm Penix, Zolper & Mixon, Jonesboro, 1976—; dep. pros. atty. Craighead County (Ark.), 1949-53. Sec., Craighead County Democratic Central Com. Mem. Ark., Craighead County bar assns. Asst. editor Ark. Law Rev. Office: Penix Zolper & Mixon McAdams Trust Bldg Jonesboro AR 72401 Tel (501) 932-7449

PENLAND, GENE BERTRAM, b. Springfield, Mo., Apr. 11, 1934; A.A., Dodge City Coll. (now Dodge City Community Jr. Coll.), 1954; B.A., U. Wichita (now Wichita State U.), 1958; LL.B., Washburn U., 1961, J.D., 1970; postgrad. Nat. Trust Sch., Northwestern U., 1967, 68. Admitted to Kans. bar, 1961, Colo. bar, 1962, Mo. bar, 1969; trust adminstr. Denver U.S. Nat. Bank, 1961-63; practiced in Salina, Kans., 1963-66, 69-71; v.p., trust officer 1st Nat. Bank & Trust Co., Salina, 1966-69, 1st Nat. Bank of Independence (Mo.), 1969; judge Saline County (Kans.) Magistrate Ct., 1971-76, Salina Municipal Ct., 1973-76, Gypsum, Kans., 1974-76, Assaria, Kans., 1975-76; asso. dist. judge, Saline County, 1976—; vis. lectr. criminal law Kans. Wesleyan U., 1973-74. Mem. Kans., Salina bar assns., Kan. Spl. Ct. Judges Assn., Phi Alpha Delta. Comments editor Washburn Law Jour., 1960-61, notes editor, 1961. Home: 1824 Page St Salina KS 67401 Office: 300 W Ash St Salina KS 67401 Tel (913) 825-4659

PENLAND, LEE STUBBS, b. Dallas; J.D. maxima cum laude, U. San Francisco, 1939. Admitted to Calif. bar, 1940, also U.S. Dist. Ct. bar, U.S. Ct. Appeals bar, U.S. Supreme Ct. bar, 1960; mem. firm Stubbs & Stubbs, San Bruno, 1942-45; asso. William A. O'Brien, San Francisco, 1947-48; research atty. Supreme Ct. Calif., 1948-53, sr. research atty., 1954-60; mem. Calif. Youth Authority Bd., 1960-68, Calif. Bd. Corrections, 1960-61; del. 4th UN Congress on Prevention Crime and Treatment of Offenders, Kyoto, Japan, 1960, Internat. Bar Assn. Council, 1960-63; mem. Internat. Conf. on Crime, Athens,

Greece, 1962; mem. Atty. Gen.'s Adv. Com. on Crime Prevention, 1957-59, Gov.'s Adv. Com. on Children and Youth, 1960; Calif. del. to White House Conf. on Children and Youth, 1960. Bd. dirs. Queens Bench Found., 1974—; dir. Skylark Residences, 1975—; past officer Am. Women for Internat. Understanding. Mem. Internat., Am., Calif., San Francisco (past dir.) bar assns., Am. Judicature Soc., Internat. Fedn. Women Lawyers, Nat. Assn. Women Lawyers (corr. sec. 1975-76, Internat. Women's Year award 1975, editor Women Lawyers Jour. 1974-76), Queens Bench (past pres.), Women's Equity Action League. Recipient Bancroft-Whitney prize U. San Francisco, 1939; Iota Tau Tau scholar, 1939; contbr. articles to profl. jours. Address: 1657 Naomi Ct Redwood City CA 94061 Tel (415) 368-9184

PENN, MARIAN ROBERTA, b. Phila., Aug. 18, 1946; B.A., Cornell U., 1968; J.D. cum laude, Harvard, 1971. Admitted to Calif. bar, 1972; atty. Monterey County (Calif.) Pub. Defender's Office, 1971-74, 75-76; staff atty. Calif. Rural Legal Assistance, Gilroy, 1976—; investigator Ralph Nader Task Force, Washington, summer 1969; staff asst. Mass. Law Reform Inst. on Dept. Agr., Boston, 1970. Mem. Monterey County Bar Assn., State Bar Calif. Home: Country Club Dr Carmel Valley CA 93924 Office: Calif Rural Legal Assistance 7872 Eigleberry St Gilroy CA Tel (408) 842-8271

PENNACCHIA, ANTHONY FRANCIS, b. Providence, May 3, 1944; B.S., Villanova U., 1965; J.D., Suffolk U., 1970. Admitted to R.I. bar, 1970, U.S. Ct. Mil. Appeals, 1971, U.S. Fed. Dist. Ct. bar, 1973; individual practice law, Providence, 1970—; lectr. Roger Williams Coll., 1972-73. Mem. R.I., Am. bar assns., Am. Judicature Soc., Am. Trial Lawyers Assn. Home: 40 Ralls Dr Cranston RI 02920 Office: 1612 Indsl Bank Bldg Providence RI 02903 Tel (401) 421-8884

PENNELL, JOHN S., b. Jackson, Mich., Jan. 7, 1916; A.B., U. Mich., 1938, J.D. cum laude, 1940. Admitted to Mich. bar, 1940, Ill. bar, 1941; partner firm McDermott, Will & Emery, Chgo., 1941—; lectr. in field. Mem. Am. (chmn. com. on partnerships of sect. taxation 1965-68; mem. council sect. taxation 1970-73, vice-chmn. 1971-73), Ill. State (exec. council on fed. taxation 1954-62, chmn. 1958-60), Chgo. (exec. council com. on fed. taxation 1970—) bar assns. Contbr. articles to legal jours. Office: 111 W Monroe St Chicago IL 60603 Tel (312) 372-2000

PENNELL, WILLIAM BROOKE, b. Mineral Ridge, Ohio, Oct. 28, 1935; A.B., Harvard U., 1957; LL.B. cum laude, U. Pa., 1961; fellow Salzburg Seminar in Am. Studies, 1965. Admitted to N.Y. State bar, 1963, Fed. bar, 1964, U.S. Ct. Claims bar, 1966, U.S. Tax Ct. bar, 1967, U.S. Supreme Ct. bar, 1967; clk. U.S. Dist. Judge Edward Weinfeld, N.Y.C., 1961-62; asso. firm Shearman & Sterling, N.Y.C., 1962-71, partner, 1971—. Bd. govs. Bklyn. Heights Assn., pres., 1969-71; chmn. bd. dirs. Willoughby House Settlement, 1972—. Mem. Assn. Bar City N.Y. (mem. fed. legis. com. 1969-72), N.Y. State Bar Assn., Fed. Bar Council. Home: 18 Cranberry St Brooklyn NY 11201 Office: 53 Wall St New York City NY 10005 Tel (212) 483-1000

PENNEY, NORMAN, b. Buffalo, Aug. 29, 1926; A.B., Yale, 1950; J.D., Cornell U., 1953. Admitted to N.Y. bar, 1953; asso. firm Penney, Penney & Buerger, Buffalo, 1953-56, partner, 1956-57; faculty Cornell U., Ithaca, N.Y., 1957—, prof. law, 1962—, dean univ. faculty, 1971-74, faculty trustee, 1974—, pres. law sch. admissions council, 1972-74; vis. prof. U. Khartoum (Sudan), 1965-66, Univs. Melbourne and Monash (Australia), 1975; cons. N.Y. State Commrs. Uniform State Laws, 1960-63, N.Y. State Law Revision Commn., 1961, 70-72; mem. U.S. del. UNCITRAL, 1970—. Mem. Am., N.Y. State, Tompkins County bar assns., Am. Law Inst., Order of Coif, Phi Kappa Phi, Phi Delta Phi. Author: (with W.E. Hogan) New York Annotations to the Uniform Commercial Code, 1961; (with Broude) Land Financing, 1970, 2d edit., 1977. Home: 216 Overlook Rd Ithaca NY 14850 Office: Cornell Law Sch Ithaca NY 14853 Tel (607) 256-3383

PENNINGTON, DAVID LOCKE, b. Phila., Jan. 25, 1931; B.S. in Econs., U. Pa., 1953; LL.B., N.Y. U., 1956. Admitted to Pa. bar, 1953, U.S. Supreme Ct. bar, 1962; law clerk Pepper, Hamilton & Scheetz, Phila., 1956, 58; house counsel Liberty Mutual Ins. Co., Phila., 1959-64; mem. firm Harvey, Pennington, Herting & Renneisen, and predecessors, Phila., 1964—; counsel Shortridge Civic Assn., 1969-72. Bd. Penn Valley Civic Assn., 1974-75. Mem. Am. (vice chmn. urban environment com. of natural resources sec.), Pa., Phila. bar assns. Home: 129 Old Gulph Rd Wynnewood PA 19096 Office: 4th Floor 7 Penn Center Plaza Philadelphia PA 19103 Tel (215) 563-4470

PENNINGTON, HARRY LUCAS, b. Wetumpka, Ala., Sept. 3, 1919; A.B., U. Ala., 1941, LL.B., 1950. Admitted to Ala. bar, 1950; individual practice law, Huntsville, Ala., 1950, 52-55; circuit solicitor 23d Jud. Circuit, Huntsville, 1951; judge 23d Jud. Circuit, Huntsville, 1955-61; mem. Ala. Ho. of Reps., 1963-70; exec. sec. to Ala. Gov. Wallace, Montgomery, Ala., 1971-75; chmn. bd. The Bank of Huntsville, Ala., 1968-76; pres. Huntsville Lumber Co., Inc., 1959—. Trustee U. N. Ala., Florence, 1968-76, Ala. A. and M. U., Huntsville, 1976—. Named Most Outstanding Mem. Ala. Ho. of Reps., 1967. Home: 6009 Macon Circle Huntsville AL 35802 Office: 809 Shoney Dr Huntsville AL 35801 Tel (205) 883-7980

PENNY, JAMES M., JR., b. Phila., Oct. 27, 1946; B.A., LaSalle Coll., 1968; J.D., Villanova U., 1971. Admitted to Pa. bar, 1971, U.S. Supreme Ct. bar, 1975; mem. staff Phila. City Solicitor, 1971-73, chief appellate and spl. litigation div., 1973—; partner firm Penny, Hinman, Bevilacqua & Guthrie, Phila., 1975—; instr. Del. Law Sch., 1974-75. Mem. consumer adv. com. to Blue Cross of Greater Phila., 1972-73. Mem. Pa., Phila. bar assns. Home: 2540 E Lehigh Ave Philadelphia PA 19125 Office: 1005 Robinson Bldg 42 S 15th St Philadelphia PA 19102 Tel (215) LO4-1537

PENNY, JOHN LAMAR, b. Pontotoc, Miss., June 20, 1916; LL.B., U. Miss., 1941. Admitted to Miss. bar, 1941; claims examiner VA, Jackson, Miss., 1946-71, ret., 1971. Mem. Phi Delta Phi. Home: 313 Wacaster St Jackson MS 39209

PENSON, EDWARD IVAN, b. N.Y.C., Feb. 5, 1937; B.S., Hofstra Coll., 1959; LL.B., Bklyn. Law Sch., 1961. Admitted to N.Y. bar, 1961; since practiced in Kings Point, N.Y., Ass. firm Demov, Morris, Levin & Shein, 1961-65, partner, 1966-71; asso. firm Dreyer & Traub, 1972; individual practice law, 1973—. Mem. Am. Bar Assn., N.Y. County Lawyers Assn. Office: 185 Great Neck Rd Great Neck NY 11021 Tel (516) 466-2313

PENTON, MARBY ROBERT, b. Gauiler, Miss., Aug. 23, 1922; student Perkinston Coll., U. So. Miss.; LL.B., 1953. Admitted to Miss. bar, 1953; individual practice law; mem. Miss. Ho. of Reps., 1962-76; with U.S. Fidelity & Guaranty Ins. Co., Pascagoula, Miss., 1952-55; claims specialist, State Farm Mutual Life Ins. Co., 1955-61; atty. Kidney Found. of Jackson County, Miss. Founder, pres. 1699 Hist. Com. Mem. Plaintiff Atty. Assn., Sch. Bd. Assn. Home: 206 Washington Ocean Springs MS 39564 Office: PO Box 506 Pascagoula MS 39553 Tel (601) 762-0802

PENWELL, J. DAVID, b. Helena, Mont., June 2, 1933; B.S., U. Mont., 1955; J.D., U. Colo., 1962. Admitted to Colo. bar, 1962, Mont. bar, 1971; city atty. Grand Lake (Colo.), 1964-69; asst. atty. gen. State of Colo., 1964-69; counsel Golden Cycle Mining, Colorado Springs, 1969, Vail Assos., Inc. (Colo.), 1970; v.p., gen. counsel Big Sky of Mont., Inc., Big Sky, 1971-74; gen. counsel, dir. Resort Condominiums Internat., Inc., Indpls., 1974—; individual practice law, Bozeman, 1974—; chmn. Resort Timeshare Council legal com., chmn. condominium com., 1972-74; co.-chmn. nat. condominium conf. Am. Land Devel. Assn., 1973-74; chmn. N.Y. Law Jour.-Real Estate Syndication Condominium Conf., 1974. Mem. Gallatin County, Am. bar assns., State Bar Mont. Contbr. articles to legal jours. Office: 420 W Mendenhall Box 1677 Bozeman MT 59715 Tel (406) 587-0693

PEPE, MICHAEL JOHN, JR., b. Phila., Dec. 10, 1937; B.A., Villanova U., 1959, LL.B., 1962. Admitted to Pa. bar, 1963; individual practice law, Phila., 1963—. Chmn. Dan Beard Dist. council Boy Scouts Am., 1970-72; supporting mem. ARC, Salvation Army Assn. Phila.; asso. mem. Friends of the Earth, UN. Assn. U.S.A.; mem. adv. com. Frankford (Pa.) Hosp., 1969—. Mem. Am., Phila., Pa. bar assns., Pa., Phila. trial lawyers assns., Assn. Trial Lawyers Am., St. Thomas Moore Soc., Justinian Soc., Am. Judicature Soc., Frankford Checker Club, Nat. Assos. Smithsonian, Am. Legion, ACLU, others. Home and office: 2603 Orthodox St Philadelphia PA 19137 Tel (215) CU8-8997

PEPINSKY, HAROLD EUGENE, b. Lawrence, Kans., Jan. 18, 1945; B.A. in Chinese Lang. and Lit., U. Mich., 1965; J.D., Harvard, 1968; Ph.D. in Sociology, U. Pa., 1972. Admitted to Ohio bar, 1968; vis. asst. prof. U. Minn., Mpls., 1970-72; asst. prof. State U. N.Y., Albany, 1972-76; asso. prof. dept. forensic studies Ind. U., Bloomington, 1976—. Mem. Am. Sociol. Assn., Acad. Criminal Justice Sci., Am. Soc. Criminology, Law and Soc. Assn., Soc. Study Social Problems. Author: Crime and Conflict: A Study of Law and Society, 1976; contbr. articles and revs. in field to profl. jours. Office: Dept Forensic Studies Sycamore Hall 302 Ind U Bloomington IN 47401 Tel (812) 337-9325

PEPPER, MORTON, b. N.Y.C., May 28, 1906; B.A., Harvard, 1927, J.D., 1930. Admitted to N.Y. State bar, 1931, U.S. Tax Ct. bar, 1931, U.S. Ct. Appeals 2d Circuit bar, 1933, U.S. Supreme Ct. bar, 1945; clk. firm Olcott, Holmes, Glass, Paul & Havens, N.Y.C., 1930, asso., 1931-33, Stern, Chalmers & McGivney, N.Y.C., 1933, Rosenberg, Goldmark & Colin, N.Y.C., 1933-36; partner Pepper & Pepper and predecessors, 1936—; founder, dir. N.Y. County Lawyers Found., Inc., 1968—; chmn. bd. dirs., dir. MFY Legal Services Inc., 1969—. Mem. Citizens Adv. Council Housing and Devel. Adminstrn., N.Y.C.; dir. Tri-Faith Housing Assn., N.Y.C., 1963-73; pres. Jewish Guild for Blind, N.Y.C., 1965-67; trustee Congregation Emanu-El, N.Y.C.; mem. exec. com. Moblzn. for Youth Inc., N.Y.C., 1965-70; com. housing and urban devel. Community Service Soc., N.Y.C., 1968—; bd. overseers Jewish Theol. Sem., N.Y.C.; dir. Nat. Accreditation Council for Agys. Serving Blind and Visually Handicapped, N.Y.C., 1970-76. Mem. Assn. Bar of City N.Y. (chmn. housing and urban devel. com. 1965-68), Am., N.Y. State bar assns., N.Y. County Lawyers Assn. (special com. on tax exemption). Home: 876 Park Ave New York City NY 10021 Office: 55 Liberty St New York City NY 10005 Tel (212) WO4-0285

PEPPERMAN, WALTER L., II, b. Phila., May 8, 1939; B.S., U. Pa., 1961, LL.B., 1967. Admitted to Del. Supreme Ct. bar, 1967, U.S. Ct. Appeals 3rd Circuit bar, 1970; asso. firm Morris, Nichols, Arsht & Tunnell, Wilmington, Del., 1967-72, partner, 1973—. Mem. Del. (chmn. med.-dental relations com. 1975—), Am. (com. on law and medicine, forum com. on health law) bar assns. Home: 104 Buck Rd Greenville DE 19807 Office: The Wilmington Tower 12th & Market Sts Wilmington DE 19801 Tel (302) 658-9200

PERAZICH, JOHN GEORGE, b. Buffalo, Mar. 20, 1941; A.B., Oberlin Coll., 1963; LL.B., George Washington U., 1967; LL.M. (E. Barrett Prettyman fellow), Georgetown U., 1969. Admitted to D.C. bar, 1967, U.S. Supreme Ct. bar, 1970; mem. staff and chief, Superior Ct. Div. Pub. Defender Service for D.C., 1969-73; partner firm Speiser, Perazich & Kolker, Washington, 1973—; asst. profl. lectr. Law Sch. George Washington U., 1971-74. Contbr. articles to legal publs. Office: 11 Dupont Circle Washington DC 20036 Tel (202) 462-3790

PERCH, BARRY J., b. New London, Conn., July 30, 1946; B.A., Tulane U., 1968, J.D., 1972. Admitted to Fla. bar, 1972; individual practice law, Ft. Myers, Fla., 1973; asso. firm Sheppard & Johnson, Ft. Myers and Lehigh, Fla., 1973-77; partner firm Sheppard & Perch, Ft. Myers and Lehigh, 1977—; abstractor, closing agt. Title Ins. Agy. of Pinellas, Inc., St. Petersburg, Fla., 1972. Mem. Fla. Bar, Am., Lee County bar assns., Am. Arbitration Assn. Home: Route 13 36 Pine Villa Ln Fort Myers FL 33901 Office: 1100 W Homestead Rd Suite D Lehigh Acres FL 33936 Tel (813) 369-3801

PERCY, JOHN HOWARD, b. Evanston, Ill., Aug. 2, 1945; B.A., Claremont Men's Coll., 1967; J.D., U. Ill., 1970; student U. Paris, 1965-66. Admitted to Mo. bar, 1970, Ill. bar, 1971; asso. firm Husch, Eppenberger, Donohue, Elson & Cornfeld, St. Louis, 1973—. Statewide mgr. lt. gubernatorial campaign Republican Party, 1972. Mem. Am., Mo., Ill., St. Clair County (Ill.), Met. St. Louis bar assns. Office: Suite 1800 100 N Broadway Saint Louis MO 63101 Tel (314) 421-4800

PERELMAN, LEWIS, b. Cleve., Feb. 26, 1931; A.B., Oberlin Coll., 1952; J.D., Harvard, 1956. Admitted to Ohio bar, 1959, U.S. Supreme Ct. bar, 1967; asso. firm Clyne, Kane, Ray and Talty, Cleve., 1959-62; partner firm Clyne and Perelman, and predecessor, Cleve., 1962-68; individual practice law, Cleve., 1969-74; atty., office of counsel Cleve. Trust Co., 1974-76, asso. counsel, 1976—. Mem. adv. council to pub. relations com. Musical Arts Assn., Cleve., 1976—. Mem. Am., Ohio State, Cuyahoga County (Ohio) bar assns., Cleve. Philos. Club. Home: 2948 Fairmount Blvd Cleveland Heights OH 44118 Office: 900 Euclid Ave Cleveland OH 44101 Tel (216) 687-5521

PERERA, LAWRENCE THACHER, b. Boston, June 23, 1935; B.A., Harvard, 1957, LL.B., 1961. Admitted to Mass. bar, 1961, U.S. Supreme Ct. bar, 1973; clk. to judge R. Ammi Cutter, Mass. Supreme Jud. Ct., Boston, 1961-62; asso. firm Palmer & Dodge, Boston, 1962-69, partner, 1969-74; judge Middlesex County (Mass.) Probate Ct., 1974—. Chmn., Boston Fin. Commn., 1971-72; overseer Peter Bent Brigham Hosp., Boston; dir. Boston Opera Assn., Inc.; v.p., dir. Back Bay Fedn. Community Devel., Inc., Boston. Fellow Am. Acad. Matrimonial Lawyers; mem. Am. Law Inst., Am., Mass., Boston bar assns. Home: 18 Marlborough St Boston MA 01116 Office: Middlesex County Probate Courthouse East Cambridge MA 02141 Tel (617) 494-4560

PERESICH, RONALD GILES, b. New Orleans, May 18, 1943; B.B.A., U. Miss., 1966, J.D., 1968. Admitted to Miss. bar, 1968, U.S. Dist. Cts. So. and No. Dists. Miss., 1968, U.S. Ct. Appeals, 5th Circuit, 1970; law clk. to Chief Justice, Miss. Supreme Ct., 1968-69; partner firm Page, Mannino & Peresich and predecessor, Biloxi, Miss., 1970—; master in changery, 1971—; pros. atty. City of Biloxi, 1974—; atty. City of Biloxi Dept. Safety and Recreation, 1974-76. Mem. Am., Miss., Harrison County, Harrison County Jr. bar assns. Office: 110 W Howard Ave Biloxi MS 39533 Tel (601) 374-2100

PEREZ, GEORGE H., b. Santa Fe, Dec. 2, 1942; B.S. in Psychology, Creighton U., 1964, J.D., 1967. Admitted to N.Mex. bar, 1968; asso. firm Montoya & Montoya, 1968-70; partner firm Sherrod & Perez, 1970-74; judge 13th Jud. Dist. of N.Mex., 1974—. Active Bernalillo (N.Mex.) Legal Aid Soc.; mem. Region III Criminal Justice Planning Commn. bd. dirs. Mem. N.Mex. Bar Assn. Home: PO Box 819 Bernalillo NM 87004 Office: PO Box 130 Bernalillo NM 87004 Tel (505) 867-2861

PEREZ, JOHN, JR., b. Rome, N.Y., July 26, 1933; B.A., U. Maine, 1955; LL.B., Syracuse U., 1963. Admitted to N.Y. bar, 1963; mem. firm Coughlin, Dermody, Ingalls & Guy, Binghamton, N.Y., 1963-64; asst. chief counsel AEC, Schenectady, 1964-74; individual practice law, Schenectady, 1975—. Mem. Schenectady County, N.Y. State bar assns., Justinian Hon. Law Soc., Phi Kappa Phi, Phi Delta Phi. Asso. editor Syracuse U. Syndicus, 1962-63. Home: 236 Mercer Ave Schenectady NY 12303 Office: 141 N Broadway St Schenectady NY 12305

PEREZ, LYNN PERKINS, b. Bunkie, La., Aug. 25, 1946; student La. State U., Alexandria, 1964-66, B.S. in Speech Edn., Baton Rouge, 1967, J.D., 1970. Admitted to La. bar, 1970; asso. firm Charles A. Riddle, Jr., Marksville, La., 1970-71; individual practice law, Moreauville, La., 1971-76, Braithwaite, La., 1977—; del. La. Constl. Conv., 1973. Mem. Avoyelles Parish (La.) Bicentennial Com., 1973-76; chmn. bd. Avoyelles chpt. ARC, 1974; del. Democratic Conv., Kansas City, Kans., 1974, N.Y.C., 1976. Mem. Am., La., Avoyelles (sec.-treas. 1970-71, v.p. 1971-72, pres. 1972-73) bar assns., Nat. Assn. Women Lawyers, La. State U. Law Alumni Assn. (treas. 1976-77, sec. 1977-78), La. Bus., Profl. Women's Clubs (chmn. Young Careerist 1976), Alpha Delta Kappa. Named Young Career Woman La. Fedn. Bus. and Profl. Women's Clubs, 1974, Young Careerist Alexandria Bus., Profl. Women's Club, 1973; recipient Freedom award Avoyelles Farm Bur., 1974. Home and office: Braithwaite LA 70040 Tel (504) 682-3111

PERINGTON, LAMONT LEE, b. Feb. 9, 1942; B.S. in Bus., Eastern Ill. U., 1965; J.D., Chgo.-Kent. Coll. Law, 1972. Admitted to Ill. bar, 1972; asso. with Gates W. Clancy, Geneva, Ill., 1972—. Mem. Ill. State, Am., Kane County bar assns. Home: 108 Logan Geneva IL 60134 Office: 428 W State St Geneva IL 60134 Tel (312) 232-4970

PERKEL, BERTRAM, b. N.Y.C., Dec. 21, 1929; B.A., N.Y. U., 1951, LL.B., 1960. Admitted to N.Y. bar, 1961; mem. firm Schulman Abarbanel Perkel & McEvoy, N.Y.C., 1967-71; individualpractice law, N.Y.C., 1974-77; mem. firm Hartman & Craven, N.Y.C., 1977—; spl. counsel Police Commr. N.Y.C., 1972-74; mem. N.Y. Gov's. Adv. Com. on Law Enforcement, 1975—. Mem. N.Y. State, Am. (co-chmn. subcom. on greivance arbitration, 1974—) bar assns. John Norton Pomeroy scholar; asso. editor N.Y. U. Law Rev., 1959-60. Office: Hartman & Craven 460 Park Ave New York City NY 10022 Tel (212) PL3-7500

PERKINS, EUGENE ORAL, b. Washington, Ind., July 2, 1923; B.S., U. Iowa, 1946; J.D., U. Colo., 1949. Admitted to Colo. bar, 1949; individual practice law, Colorado Springs, 1949-74; partner firm Perkins, Goodbee, Mason & Davis, Colorado Springs, 1974—. Chmn. fin. com. El Paso County Republican Party, 1960-68. Mem. Am., Colo., El Paso County bar assns., Colo. Cattlemen's Assn., Am., Rocky Mountain, Pikes Peak quarter horse assns., Colo. Quarter Racing Assn. (pres. 1968-70), Tau Beta Pi, Phi Alpha Delta. Home: 1900 Mesa Ave Colorado Springs CO 80906 Office: 450 Western Federal Savings Bldg Colorado Springs CO 80903 Tel (303) 633-7781

PERKINS, GEORGE FOSTER, b. Saratoga Springs, N.Y., June 14, 1917; LL.B., Albany Law Sch., Union U., 1951. Admitted to N.Y. bar, 1951; asso. law firm Butler, Kilmer, Hoey & Butler, Saratoga Springs, N.Y., 1951-53, partner, 1953-56; pvt. practice law, Saratoga Springs, N.Y., 1956—. City Judge, Saratoga Springs, N.Y., 1961-64. Mem. N.Y. State, Saratoga County bar assns., N.Y. State Magistrate's Assn. Decorated Bronze Star medal. Office: 444 Broadway Saratoga Springs NY 12866

PERKINS, GUY WHITLEY, b. Williamson, W.Va., Sept. 15, 1944; A.B., W.Va. U., 1966; J.D., 1969. Admitted to W.Va. bar, 1969; partner firm Katz, Kantor, Katz, Perkins & Cameron, Bluefield, W.Va., 1969—; ct. commr. 9th Jud. Circuit W.Va., 1974—. Co-founder, pres. Mercer County Group Home for Boys, 1970-72; pres. Mercer County Mental Health Assn., 1972-73; mem. Mercer County Democratic Exec. Com., 1972—; mem. exec. com., deacon Westminster Presbyterian Ch., 1970-73; bd. govs. Mercer County Legal Services Found., 1972-73; bd. dirs. W.Va. Assn. Mental Health, 1973-74; chmn. bd. dirs., pres. So. Highlands Community Mental Health Center, also Mercer, McDowell, Wyoming Mental Health Council, 1975—. Mem. Am., W.Va., Mercer County bar assns., Am., W.Va. trial lawyers assns., Bluefield C. of C. (dir. 1972-73). Home: 301 Ridgecrest Rd Bluefield WV 24701 Office: PO Box 727 Bluefield WV 24701 Tel (304) 327-3551

PERKINS, JAMES WOOD, b. New Bedford, Mass., Oct. 14, 1924; A.B., Harvard, 1945, J.D., 1948. Admitted to Mass. bar, 1948; engr. Sylvania Electric Products Inc., Salem, Mass., 1944-45; asso. firm Palmer & Dodge, Boston, 1948-54, partner, 1955—. Pres. Cambridge (Mass.) Civic Assn., 1962-64. Mem. Am. (chmn. sect. local govt. law 1971-72, sect. del. 1974—), Mass., Boston bar assns. Author: Tax-Exempt Financing of Community Controlled Cable Television Facilities, 1976. Home: 12 Gray Gardens E Cambridge MA 02138 Office: One Beacon St Boston MA 02108 Tel (617) 227-4400

PERKINS, ROSWELL BURCHARD, b. Boston, May 21, 1926; A.B. cum laude, Harvard U., 1945, LL.B. cum laude, 1949. Admitted to Mass. bar, 1949, N.Y. state bar 1949; asso. firm Debevoise, Plimpton & McLean, N.Y.C., 1949-53, partner firm Debevoise, Plimpton, Lyons & Gates, N.Y.C., 1957—; asst. Sec. Health Edn. and Welfare, 1954-56; counsel to Gov. state N.Y., 1959; asst. counsel Spl.

Subcom. to Investigate Organized Crime in Interstate Commerce of Senate Commerce Com., 1950; chmn. N.Y.C. Mayor's Task Force on Transportation Reorgn., 1966; mem. Pres.'s Adv. Panel on Personnel Interchange, 1968; chmn. adv. com. Medicare Adminstrn. Contracting and Subcom. HEW 1973-74. Mem. N.Y. Lawyers Com. Civil Rights, 1970-73, co-chmn. 1973-75; mem. adv. council Woodrow Wilson Sch. Pub. and Internal. Affairs Princeton U., 1967-69; chmn. bd. Sch. Am. Ballet, 1976—; dir., sec. N.Y. Urban Coalition 1967-74; trustee Pomfret Sch., 1961-76, The Brearley Sch., 1969-75; dir. Salzburg Seminar Am. Studies, 1970—. Mem. Am., N.Y. State bar assns., Assn. Bar City N.Y., Am. Arbitration Assn. (dir. 1966-71). Home: 1120 Fifth Ave New York City NY 10028 Office: 299 Park Ave New York City NY 10017 Tel (212) 752-6400

PERKINSON, DIANA MUNSEY, b. Pearisburg, Va., Apr. 13, 1947; A.B., Randolph-Macon Woman's Coll., 1969; LL.B., U. Va., 1972. Admitted to Va. bar, 1973; asso. Frank N. Perkinson, Jr., Roanoke, Va., 1972-74; partner firm Perkinson & Perkinson, Roanoke, 1974—; spl. asst. to dean U. Va. Law Sch., Charlottesville, 1971-72. Mem. Am., Va., Roanoke bar assns., Am. Trial Lawyers Assn. Named Outstanding Young Woman Am., 1975. Home: Sham Kris Farm Boones Mill VA 24065 Office: 115 W Kirk Ave Roanoke VA 24002 Tel (703) 343-2436

PERKINSON, MAURICE LEON, b. Georgetown, Ky., Mar. 18, 1932; B.B.A., U. Miami (Ohio), 1958; J.D., U. Louisville, 1963. Admitted to Ky. bar, 1963; individual practice law, LaGrange, Ky., 1963—; city atty. LaGrange, 1964-66, county atty. Oldham County (Ky.), 1972. Chmn. Oldham County chpt. ARC, 1965; pres. LaGrange PTA, Oldham County Jr. High Sch. PTA; chmn. Oldham County Dem. Party, 1972-75. Mem. Am., Ky. bar assns., Ky. Trial Lawyers Assn. Home: 400 Kentucky St LaGrange KY 40031 Office: 113 E Main St LaGrange KY 40031 Tel (502) 222-1557

PERL, ALAN FRANCIS, b. N.Y.C., May 3, 1909; A.B., Columbia U., 1929, J.D., 1931. Admitted to N.Y. bar, 1932; mem. firm Sturm & Perl, N.Y.C., 1947—; litigation atty., regional atty. NLRB, St. Louis and N.Y.C., 1937-47; labor cons. P.R. Dept. Labor, San Juan, 1947-76; lectr. Practising Law Inst., 1947-48; advisor P.R. Labor Relations Bd., 1945-75; mem. N.Y.C. Mayors Com. P.R. Affairs, 1949-55. Mem. N.Y. County Lawyers Assn. Office: Sturm & Perl 21 E 40th St New York City NY 10016 Tel (212) 685-8487

PERL, ARNOLD EDWIN, b. Beaumont, Tex., Dec. 16, 1939; B.A., U. Ill., 1961, LL.B., 1963. Admitted to Ill. bar, 1963, Tenn. bar, 1968, U.S. Supreme Ct. bar, 1967; atty. NLRB, Memphis, 1963-65, Washington, 1965-66; mem. firm McDermott Will & Emery, Chgo., 1967-68; partner firm Young & Perl, Memphis, 1969—. Mem. Am., Tenn., Memphis-Shelby County bar assns. Contbr. articles to legal jours. Home: 1265 Calais St Memphis TN 38138 Office: One Commerce Sq Suite 2380 Memphis TN 38103 Tel (901) 525-2761

PERL, ELSE SVENDSEN, b. N.Y.C., May 8, 1932; A.B., Syracuse U., 1953, LL.B., 1956. Admitted to N.Y. bar, 1956; asso. firm Marc Hermelin, N.Y.C., 1957-63; partner firm Perl & Perl, N.Y.C., 1963-68; individual practice law, N.Y.C., 1968-72, 74—; law sec. Judge Hortense Gabel, civil ct., N.Y.C., 1972-74. PTA spokesman, rep. to Bd. Edn., N.Y.C., 1969. Mem. N.Y. State Bar Assn., Nat. Orgn. for Women, Med. Soc. Jurisprudence. Home: 365 West St Harrison NY 12805 Office: 205 E 61st St New York City NY 10021 Tel (212) PL5-1090

PERLA, ROBERT, b. Bklyn., Mar. 9, 1934; B.A., N.Y. U., 1955, LL.B., 1959, J.D., 1968. Admitted to N.Y. bar, 1959; individual practice law, Bklyn., 1959—. Mem. Queens County Bar Assn. Home: 69 Birch Hill Searingtown NY 11507 Office: 1550 Myrtle Ave Brooklyn NY 11227 Tel (212) 381-6500

PERLES, JULIA, b. Bklyn., Mar. 23, 1914; LL.B., Bklyn. Coll., 1937. Admitted to N.Y. bar, 1939; partner firm Greenbaum, Wolff & Ernst, N.Y.C., 1955-70; sr. partner firm Phillips, Nizer, Benjamin, Krim & Ballon, N.Y.C., 1970—. Mem. Assn. Bar City N.Y., Am., N.Y. bar assns., N.Y. County Lawyers Assn. (chmn. spl. com. on matrimonial law 1965—). Contbr. articles in field to profl. jours. Office: 40 W 57th St New York City NY 10019 Tel (212) 977-9700

PERLIN, MARSHALL, b. N.Y.C., Aug. 23, 1920; student Rutgers U., 1939; LL.B., Columbia, 1946. Admitted to N.Y. State bar 1947, U.S. Supreme Ct. bar 1955; individual practice law, Schenectady, N.Y., 1947-50; former mem. firm Donner, Perlin & Piel, and predecessor, N.Y.C., Friedman & Perlin, N.Y.C.; individual practice, N.Y.C., 1950—. Mem. Nat. Lawyers Guild. Home: 15 W 72nd St New York City NY 10023 Office: W 44th St New York City NY 10036 Tel (212) 661-1886

PERLIN, MICHAEL LOUIS, b. Perth Amboy, N.J., Mar. 30, 1946; B.A., Rutgers U., 1966; J.D., Columbia, 1969. Admitted to N.J. bar, 1969; law clk. Superior Ct. N.J., 1969-70, appellate div., 1970-71; dep. pub. defender, Mercer County (N.J.), Trenton, 1971-74; dir. div. mental health advocacy, dep. pub. advocate State of N.J., Trenton, 1974—, acting dir. advocacy for developmentally disabled project, 1976—; adj. asst. prof. criminal justice Rider Coll., 1974—. Mem. N.J. Bar Assn. (com. on mentally handicapped, nat. patients rights com.), Mercer County Legal Aid Soc. (dir., sec.-treas. 1972-74), Am. Psychol.-Law Soc. Contbr. articles to profl. jours. Home: 122 W Farrell Ave Trenton NJ 08618 Office: 10-12 N Stockton St Trenton NJ 08625 Tel (609) 292-1780

PERLMAN, GEORGE, b. N.Y.C., Nov. 10, 1908; B.S., L.I. U., 1931; LL.B., Bklyn. Law Sch. of St. Lawrence U., 1935; J.D., Bklyn. Law Sch., 1969. Admitted to N.Y. bar, 1939; practice law, Bklyn.; atty. Social Security Adminstrn., N.Y.C., 1945-48. Author: A Practical Guide to Social Security, 1962. Home and Office: 267 Dover St Brooklyn NY 11235 Tel (212) TW1-7550

PERLMAN, JERALD LEE, b. Baton Rouge, Feb. 25, 1947; B.A., Washington and Lee U., 1969; J.D., La. State U., 1972. Admitted to La. bar, 1972; partner firm Blanchard, Walker, O'Quin & Roberts, Shreveport, La.; mem. Caddo Parish (La.) Notary Pub. Exam. Com., 1974-76. Mem. Am., La., Shreveport bar assns., Shreveport Assn. Def. Counsel (pres. 1977), Order of Coif, Phi Beta Kappa, Omicron Delta Kappa, Phi Eta Sigma. Asso. editor La. Law Rev., 1971-72. Office: PO Drawer 1126 Shreveport LA 71163 Tel (318) 221-6858

PERLMAN, MATTHEW SAUL, b. Washington, Aug. 30, 1936; A.B., Brown U., 1957; LL.B., Harvard, 1960. Admitted to D.C. and Md. bars, 1960, U.S. Supreme Ct. bar, 1964, U.S. Ct. Claims bar, 1964; atty. Office of Gen. Counsel, Dept. of Air Force, 1960-65; mem. Armed Services Bd. Contract Appeals, 1965-67; gen. counsel Pres.'s Commn. on Postal Orgn., 1967; asst. gen. counsel for operations, legal counsel Dept. Transp., Washington, 1967-69; partner firm Arent, Fox, Kintner, Plotkin & Kahn, Washington, 1969—. Pres. Civic Assn. River Falls, Inc., Potomac, Md., 1975-77. Mem. Am., Fed. bar assns. Home: 10517 Stable Ln Potomac MD 20854 Office: 1815 H St NW Washington DC 20006 Tel (202) 857-6279

PERLMAN, ROBERT G., b. Portland, Oreg., Mar. 25, 1921; LL.B., Gonzaga U., 1959, J.D., 1967; B.A., U. Wash., 1948. Admitted to Wash. bar, 1959; individual practice law, Everett, Wash., 1966—; ct. commr. Evergreen Dist., Snohomish County (Wash.), 1970-76; judge pro-tempore Everett Dist. Snohomish County, 1966-76. Mem. Wash. State Trial Lawyers Assn., Am. Judicature Soc., Comml. Law League Am. Office: 2931 Rockefeller Ave Everett WA 98201 Tel (206) 259-0281

PERLMAN, SAMUEL BORES, b. Chgo., May 5, 1904; Ph.B., U. Chgo., 1924, J.D., 1926. Admitted to Ill. bar, 1926; individual practice law, Chgo., 1926-39, 74—; sr. atty. U.S. Dept. Labor, Washington, 1939-45; chief dist. counsel Office of Price Stablzn., U.S. Govt., Chgo., 1951-53, spl. asst. U.S. atty. Chgo., 1953-54; investment counselor Shearson-Hammill Co., Chgo., 1956-74. Mem. Chgo. Bar Assn. Home: 339 Barry Ave Chicago IL 60657 Tel (312) 248-1610

PERLMUTH, WILLIAM ALAN, b. N.Y.C., Nov. 21, 1929; A.B., Wilkes Coll., 1951; LL.B., Columbia, 1953. Admitted to N.Y. State bar, 1954; asso. firm Cravath, Swaine & Moore, N.Y.C., 1955-61; partner firm Stroock & Stroock & Lavan, N.Y.C., 1962—. Trustee Aeroflex Found., N.Y.C., 1965—; dir. Harkness Ballet Found., Inc., N.Y.C., 1975—. Home: 2 Sutton Pl S New York City NY 10022 Office: 61 Broadway New York City NY 10006 Tel (212) 425-5200

PERLMUTTER, DONALD SAMSON, b. Fulton, Mo., Jan. 29, 1939; B.A., U. Mo., 1961; J.D., U. Denver, 1964. Admitted to Colo. bar, 1964; since practiced in Denver, Colo., mem. firm Fugate, Mitchem & Hoffman, 1964-65, Zall, Lutz & Zall, 1965-68, Mitchem & Perlmutter, 1968-70, Arthur & Perlmutter, 1970—. Master Columbine Lodge #147 Masons, Denver, 1976. Mem. Am., Colo., Denver bar assns., Comml. Law League of Am. Office: 3525 S Tamarac St Denver CO 80237 Tel (303) 779-1056

PERLOFF, MAYER WILLIAM, b. New Orleans, Sept. 2, 1926; B.S., U. Ala., 1949; LL.B., U. Md., 1953. Admitted to Md. bar, 1953, Ala. bar, 1957; partner firm Perloff, Reid & Briskman, Mobile, Ala., 1955—; mem. Ala. Ho. of Reps., 1966-74; mem. Ala. Senate, 1974—. Mem. Ala., Md. bar assns. Home: 3909 Radnor Ave Mobile AL 36608 Office: 257 St Anthony St Mobile AL 26603 Tel (205) 433-5412

PERLOS, ALEXANDER CHARLES, b. Bitola, Yugoslavia, July 15, 1930; B.A., Mich. State U., 1953; J.D., U. Wis., 1957. Admitted to Wis. bar, 1957, Mich. bar, 1957; individual practice law, Jackson, Mich., 1957—; pres. Perlos Corp.; circuit ct. commr., Jackson, 1959-60; pub. adminstr., Jackson County, Mich., 1961-67; mem. SBA, Jackson, 1968-69. Mem. Jackson County, Jackson, Mich., Am. bar assns., Mich., Am. trial lawyers assns., Am. Judicature Soc. Home: 5040 Brookside Dr Jackson MI 49203 Office: 302 Harris Bldg Jackson MI 49201 Tel (517) 787-4744

PERLOW, SHELDON JAMES, b. Chgo., June 10, 1945; B.S., U. Wis., 1967; grad. Northwestern U. Sch. Law, 1970. Admitted to Ill. bar, 1970; exec. v.p. R.L. Perlow Steel Corp., Chicago, 1970—. Mem. Am., Ill. State, Chgo. bar assns., Assn. Steel Distbrs. (dir.). Home: 1440 N State Pkwy Chicago IL 60610 Office: 933 E 95th St Chicago IL 60619 Tel (312) 374-6600

PERLSON, EDWARDE FREDRIC, b. Passaic, N.J., Jan. 15, 1906; B.A., U. Wis., 1930, B.A., B.L., 1933. Admitted to Wis. bar, 1933, U.S. Dist. Ct. for Eastern and Western Dists. Wis., 1933; practiced in Milw. since 1933, mng. editor, chief editorial writer Wis. Jewish Chronicle, Milw., 1949-74, editor emeritus, 1974—. Bd. dirs. Milw. Jewish Home for Aged, Jewish Vocat. Service, Jewish Family and Children's Service, Milw., Am. Friends of Hebrew U., Jerusalem, Wis. Soc. for Jewish Learning, Temple Emanu-El B'nei Jeshurun, Milw. Mem. Wis. Bar, Alpha Epsilon Pi (pres. 1930-33). Recipient Sohmer Meml. award Alpha Epsilon Pi, 1931. Home and Office: 230 W Krause Pl Milwaukee WI 53217 Tel (414) 352-6163

PERLSTEIN, GREGORY MARTIN, b. St. Louis, Dec. 20, 1948; B.A., U. Mo., Columbia, 1971; J.D., U. Mo., Kansas City, 1973. Admitted to Mo. bar, 1974; atty. Legal Aid Soc. Kansas City, 1973-75; individual practice law, Kansas City, 1975—. Mem. Am., Mo., Kansas City bar assns., Am. Trial Lawyers Assn. Contbr. to Mo. Bar Jour., 1976. Home: 9735 Benson St Overland Park KS 66212 Office: 950 Home Savings Bldg Kansas City MO 64106 Tel (816) 474-0707

PERLUSS, IRVING HARVEY, b. Los Angeles, Nov. 23, 1915; B.S. in Bus. Adminstrn., U. Calif., Los Angeles, 1937, LL.B., Berkeley, 1940. Admitted to Calif. bar, 1940, U.S. Supreme Ct. bar, 1958; tax counsel State of Calif., Sacramento, 1941-42; dep. atty. gen. State of Calif., Sacramento, 1946-49, asst. atty. gen., 1949-59; dir. Calif. Dept. Employment, Sacramento, 1959-62; judge Calif. Superior Ct., Sacramento, 1963—; justice pro tem Calif. 3d Dist. Ct. Appeal, 1972; mem. faculty Coll. Trial Judges U. Calif., Berkeley, 1969, 70. Mem. Sacramento Family Service Bd., 1968-73, Sacramento County Mental Health Adv. Bd., 1968—, Sacramento County Drug Abuse Com., 1970—. Mem. Conf. Calif. Judges (exec. com. 1975). Author: (with Julius Title) Trials, 1969; editor Calif. Law Rev., 1938-40. Office: County Courthouse Sacramento CA 95814 Tel (916) 440-5591

PERO, JEFFREY TOWNE, b. Utica, N.Y., Aug. 16, 1946; A.B., U. Notre Dame, 1968; J.D., N.Y. U., 1971. Admitted to Calif. bar, 1971; asso. firm O'Melveny & Myers, Los Angeles, 1971—. Mem. Am., Los Angeles County Bar Assn. Office: 611 W 6th St Los Angeles CA 90017 Tel (213) 620-1120

PERONE, F. FREDERICK, b. Atlantic City, May 4, 1926; B.S. in Polit. Sci., St. Joseph's Coll., 1951; LL.B., Temple U., 1955. Admitted to D.C. bar, 1955, N.J. bar, 1959; adminstrv. atty., dep. marshal U.S. Dept. Justice, 1956-57; individual practice law, Atlantic City, 1960—; sec. to speaker N.J. Gen. Assembly, 1954-55; judge Municipal Ct. Atlantic City, Northfield and Pleasantville, N.J., 1962-73; mem. Supreme Ct. com. on municipal cts., 1968-70. Mem. Fed., Atlantic County bar assns. Recipient Father Joseph F. Hogan award St. Joseph's Coll., 1964. Home: 9400 Atlantic Ave Margate City NJ 08402 Office: 1 S New York Ave Atlantic City NJ 08401 Tel (609) 344-1249

PERRY, ALAN WALTER, b. Jackson, Miss., June 27, 1947; B.B.A., U. Miss., 1969; J.D., Harvard, 1972. Admitted to Miss. bar, 1972; mem. firm Butler, Snow, O'Mara, Stevens & Cannada, Jackson, 1973—; law clk. to judge U.S. Ct. Appeals 5th Circuit, Jackson. Mem. Am., Miss. bar assns. Home: 4645 Northampton Dr Jackson MS 39211 Office: 1700 Deposit Guaranty Plaza PO Box 22567 Jackson MS 39205 Tel (601) 948-5711

PERRY, BLAIR LANE, b. Newton, Mass., Oct. 2, 1929; B.A., Williams Coll., 1951; LL.B., Harvard, 1957. Admitted to Mass. bar, 1957, U.S. Supreme Ct. bar, 1971; asso. firm Hale and Dorr, Boston, 1957-63, partner, 1963—. Mem. Am., Mass. bar assns., Am. Judicature Soc. Home: 5 Gerard Terr Lexington MA 02173 Office: 28 State St Boston MA 02109 Tel (617) 742-9100

PERRY, GREGORY MICHAEL, b. Commerce, Ga., Oct. 21, 1948; A.B., U. Ga., 1970; LL.B., Atlanta Law Sch., 1974. Admitted to Ga. bar, 1974; individual practice law, Commerce, 1974—; city atty., Commerce, 1976—, Commerce Bd. Edn., 1976—. Mem. State Bar Ga., Ga. Trial Lawyers Assn., Am. Judicature Soc., Am. Bar Assn., Delta Theta Phi. Home: 128 Clayton St Commerce GA 30529 Office: 17 State St Commerce GA 30529 Tel (404) 335-3500

PERRY, JAMES EUGENE, b. Centralia, Ill., Mar. 16, 1943; A.A., San Angelo Coll., 1963; B.A., U. Tex., 1965, J.D., 1968. Admitted to Tex. bar, 1968, U.S. Dist. Ct. for No. Tex. bar, 1976; asst. atty., Tom Green County, Tex., 1969; asst. city atty. City of San Angelo, Tex., 1969-76, city atty., 1976—. Mem. Tex., Tom Green County, Tom Green County Jr. bar assns., Tex. City Attys. Assn. Home: 1917 Raney St Apt 12 San Angelo TX 76901 Office: Box 1751 San Angelo TX 76901 Tel (915) 655-9121

PERRY, JAMES GLENN, b. Goodsprings, Ala., Jan. 16, 1926; J.D., U. Md., 1953. Admitted to Md. bar, 1952, U.S. Supreme Ct. bar, 1963; asst. safety dir. Balt. Transfer Co., 1951-53; asst. treas. Paramount Ins. Co., 1954-60; partner firm Mentzel, Perry & Murphy, Balt., 1960-62, Moncarz & Perry, Balt., 1962-74; U.S. adminstrv. law judge HEW, Greensboro, N.C., 1974—. Mem. Assn. Adminstrv. Law Judges in HEW, Am., Md. (pres. 1973-74) trial lawyers assns., Am., Md. (appeal counsel 1969), Anne Arundel County, Balt. (chmn. unauthorized practice law com. 1970) bar assns. Office: 1215 W Bessemer Ave Greensboro NC 27405 Tel (919) 378-5382

PERRY, JOSEPH SAM, b. Carbon Hill, Ala., Nov. 30, 1896; A.B., U. Ala., 1923; M.A., U. Chgo., 1925, J.D., 1927. Admitted to Ill. bar, 1927; with Legal Aid Bur., United Charities, Chgo., 1927; asso. firm Cannon & Poague, Chgo., 1928-29; asso. firm Dunbar & Rich, Chgo., 1929-33; master in chancery DuPage County, Wheaton, Ill., 1933-37; individual practice law, Wheaton, Ill., 1933-51; mem. Ill. Assembly, 1937-43; pub. adminstr. DuPage County, 1949-51; judge U.S. Dist. of Ill., Chgo., 1951—. Mem. Am., Ill., Chgo., DuPage County bar assns. Home: 683 Riford Rd Glen Ellyn IL 60137 Office: Room 2560 US Ct House 219 S Dearborn St Chicago IL 60604 Tel (312) 435-5632

PERRY, NELSON, b. Nelson County, Ky., Nov. 2, 1905; A.B., U. Louisville, 1939, LL.B., J.D., 1933; postgrad U. Chgo., 1933-34. Admitted to Ky. bar, 1933, Ill. bar, 1963; agt. FBI, 1934-48; dir. field div. Ky. Dept. Revenue, Frankfort, 1948-52; practice law, Louisville, 1952-60; trial atty. Antitrust div. U.S. Dept. Justice, Chgo., 1961-73, ret., 1973. Bd. dirs. St. Matthews (Ky.) YMCA, 1952-60, St. Matthews Library, 1955-60. Mem. Ky., Ill., Am., Louisville, Chgo. bar assns., Former FBI Agts. Soc. (chmn. local chpt. 1948-49, sec., 1950-57), Louisville C. of C. (former com. chmn.). Home: 119 Gibson Rd Louisville KY 40207 Tel (502) 896-0783

PERRY, RALPH BARTON, III, b. N.Y.C., Mar. 17, 1936; A.B., Harvard, 1958; LL.B., Stanford, 1963. Admitted to Calif. bar, 1964; partner firm Keating & Sterling, Los Angeles, 1963-68, firm Grossman, Graven & Perry, Los Angeles, 1968—. Fellow Am. Bar Found.; mem. State Bar Calif., Am., Los Angeles County bar assns., Los Angeles Lawyers Club (bd. govs. 1967—). Home: 296 Redwood Dr Pasadena CA 91105 Office: Suite 2420 One Wilshire Bldg Los Angeles CA 90017 Tel (213) 680-9770

PERRY, ROBERT JOSEPH, b. Glenford, Ohio, Nov. 19, 1932; B.A., Ohio State U., 1955, J.D., 1961. Admitted to Ohio bar, 1962; asso. firm DeVennish & Hague, Columbus, Ohio, 1962-63; asst. atty. gen. State of Ohio, Columbus, 1963-65; asso. firm Fontana, Ward, Kaps & Perry, Columbus, 1965-69, partner, 1970—; lectr. in field; vice counsul Am. Embassy, Mexico City, 1957-59. Mem. Am., Ohio, Columbus (bd. govs. 1975—) bar assns., Franklin County Trial Lawyers Assn. Home: 244 E Beck St Columbus OH 43206 Office: 50 W Broad St Columbus OH 43215 Tel (614) 224-9223

PERRY, ROGER JOHNS, b. Balt., May 4, 1930; B.A., Washington and Lee U., 1952, LL.B., 1954. Admitted to Va. State bar, 1953, W.Va. State bar, 1954. Pvt. practice law, Charles Town, W.Va., 1958-65; mem. firm Avey, Steptoe, Perry & VanMetre (and predecessor firms), Charles Town, W.Va., also Martinsburg, W.Va., 1965-70, partner, 1970—; atty., dir. Peoples Bank of Charles Town; mem. panel arbitrators, Am. Arbitration Assn., 1976—; atty. Jefferson County Firemans Assn. Mem. W.Va. House of Dels., 1969-73, mem. rules com. 1971-73, chmn. redistricting com. 1972-73; chmn. Charles Town Hist. Landmarks Commn., 1977; mem. Jefferson County Bd. Health, 1960-77; dir. Harpers Ferry Hist. Assn., 1972-77. Bd. dirs. Greater Washington Pastoral Counselling Centers, Inc. Mem. Jefferson County C. of C. (dir. 1975-77), W.Va. (mem. grievance com. Eastern dist. 1971-77), Jefferson County (pres. 1967-68) bar assns., Jefferson County Jaycees (v.p. 1961-62). Episcopalian (vestryman 1965-68). Home: The Hill Charles Town WV 25414 Office: 104 W Congress St Charles Town WV 25414

PERRY, TIMOTHY SEWELL, b. Hamlet, N.C., Feb. 28, 1947; A.B. cum laude, Princeton, 1969; LL.D., Yale, 1972. Admitted to Ga. bar, 1972; asso. firm Alston, Miller & Gaines, Atlanta, 1972—; legal aide Ga. State Senate retirement com., 1973, 74. Mem. Am., Atlanta bar assns., Ga. State Bar. Office: 1200 C&S Nat Bank Bldg Atlanta GA 30303 Tel (404) 588-0300

PERSHAN, RICHARD HENRY, b. Bklyn., Jan. 4, 1930; B.A., Yale U., 1951, LL.B., 1956. Admitted to N.Y. bar, 1956, U.S. Supreme Ct. bar, 1969, U.S. 2d Circuit Ct. Appeals bar, 1957, U.S. Dist. Cts. for Eastern and Soc. N.Y., 1957; asso. firm Davis, Polk & Wardwell, N.Y.C., 1956-60; asso. firm Finch & Schaelfer, N.Y.C., 1960-64, partner, 1965—; counsel Fine Arts Fedn., N.Y.C., 1974—; Municipal Art Soc. N.Y., 1965-70; Carnegie Hill Neighbors, Inc., 1972-76. Mem. Am., N.Y. State bar assns., Assn. Bar City N.Y., Am. Coll. Probate Counsel. Home: 1435 Lexington Ave New York City NY 10028 Office: 36 W 44th St New York City NY 10036 Tel (212) 687-3636

PERSHON, JAMES ALBERT, b. Detroit, Apr. 24, 1931; B.S. in Elec. Engring., Lawrence Inst. Tech., 1963; J.D., Catholic U. Am., 1968. Admitted to Ariz. bar, 1969, Calif. bar, 1975; elec. engr. Burroughs Corp., Detroit, 1957-68; atty. Gen. Electric Corp.,

Phoenix, 1968-70, Honeywell Info. Systems, Inc., Phoenix, 1970-74, IBM Corp., San Jose, Calif., 1974—. Mem. Ariz., Calif. bar assns., Am., Peninsula patent lawyers assns. Home: 6235 Channel Dr San Jose CA 95123 Office: 5600 Cottle Rd San Jose CA 95193 Tel (408) 256-4120

PERVIN, ABRAHAM, b. Pitts., Oct. 27, 1896; B.S., Washington and Jefferson Coll., 1918; LL.B., U. Pitts., 1920, J.D., 1968. Admitted to Pa. bar; individual practice law, Pitts. Mem. Allegheny County Bar Assn. Home: 144 N Dithridge St Pittsburgh PA 15213 Office: 416 Frick Bldg Pittsburgh PA 15219 Tel (412) 281-2487

PESCHKA, THOMAS ALAN, b. Great Bend, Kans., Oct. 15, 1931; student Coll. Holy Cross, 1949-50; B.S. in Bus. Adminstrn., U. Kans., 1953, LL.B., 1958. Admitted to Kans. bar, 1958, Mo. bar, 1960; law clk. to judge U.S. Dist. Ct., Dist. Kans., 1958-60; sec. and gen. counsel Tower Properties Co., Kansas City, Mo., 1965-74; sr. v.p., sec. and gen. counsel Commerce Bank of Kansas City, 1965—; v.p., sec. and gen. counsel Commerce Bancshares, Inc., Kansas City, 1966—. Mem. Am., Mo., Kans., Kansas City bar assns., Lawyers Assn. Kansas City. Home: 4401 Somerset Dr Prairie Village KS 66207 Office: Box 13686 720 Main St Kansas City MO 64199 Tel (816) 234-2350

PESEK, LEON FRANCIS, b. Yoakum, Tex., Sept. 17, 1928; J.D., St. Mary's U., San Antonio, 1951. Admitted to Tex. bar, 1951; county atty. Lavaca County (Tex.), 1954-58; asst. atty. gen., Austin, Tex., 1958-62; partner firm Raffaelli, Keeney & Pesek, Texarkana, Tex., 1962-66; city atty. Texarkana, 1967-71; mem. firm Hitt & Pesek, Texarkana, 1951—; atty. Cath. Women's Fraternal of Tex., Austin, 1967—. Vice chmn. Airport Authority, 1972—; atty. Texarkana Spl. Edn. Center, 1966—. Mem. Tex., NE Tex. bar assns. Home: 20 Cindywood Texarkana TX 75503 Office: 3720 Texas Bldg Texarkana TX 75501 Tel (214) 793-6571

PESHKIN, SAMUEL DAVID, b. Des Moines, Oct. 6, 1925; B.A., U. Iowa, 1948, J.D., 1951. Admitted to Iowa bar, 1951, U.S. Supreme Ct. bar, 1957; partner firm Bridges & Peshkin, Des Moines, 1951-66, Peshkin & Robinson, Des Moines, 1966—; chmn. Iowa Bd. Law Examiners, 1970-76. Fellow Am. Bar Found., Internat. Soc. Barristers; mem. Am. (bd. govs. 1973-76, ho. of dels. 1965—), Iowa (award of Merit 1974, chmn. com. continuing legal edn. 1951—, bd. govs. 1957-59), Polk County, Inter-Am., Internat., Fed. bar assns., Am. Judicature Soc., Assn. Trial Lawyers Am., Am. Law Inst. Home: 3000 Grand Ave apt 613 Des Moines IA 50312 Office: 1010 Fleming Bldg Des Moines IA 50309 Tel (515) 288-7436

PETERFREUND, HERBERT, b. Mildred, Pa., Mar. 5, 1913; A.B., Pa. State U., 1933; LL.B., Harvard, 1936; LL.M., Columbia, 1942; Admitted to N.Y. State bar, 1937; practiced in N.Y.C., 1937-41; faculty N.Y. U., 1946—, prof., 1953—, Frederick I. and Grace A. Stokes Prof. Law, 1969—; U.S. commr. Jurors So. Dist. N.Y., 1954-68; adv. com. N.Y. Jud. Conf., 1966—. Editor: Manual of N.Y. Practice, 1956; Appleton's N.Y. Practice, 1960; (with J.M. McLaughlin) Cases and Other Materials on N.Y. Practice, 3d edit., 1973; contbr. articles in field to law jours. Home: 535 E 14th St New York City NY 10009 Office: 40 Washington Sq S New York City NY 10012 Tel (212) 598-2560

PETERS, ALTON EMIL, b. Albany, N.Y., Mar. 21, 1935; A.B. cum laude, Harvard, 1955, LL.B., 1958. Admitted to N.Y. bar, 1958; asso. firm Bleakley, Platt, Schmidt & Fritz, N.Y.C., 1959-65, partner, 1965—. Dir., v.p. Am. Friends Covent Garden and Royal Ballet, N.Y.C., 1971—; chmn. council Am. Mus. Brit., Bath, 1975—, mem., 1970—; dir. English-Speaking Union U.S., N.Y.C., 1968—, exec. com., 1971—, dir. N.Y. Br., 1962—, chmn., 1972—; adv. council Episcopal Ch. Found., N.Y.C., 1964—; bd. dirs. Goodwill Industries, N.Y.C., 1965—, v.p., 1969-70, pres., 1970—; mem. overseers vis. com. dept. classics Harvard, Cambridge, Mass., 1968-73, 1975—; adv. com. Lamont Gallery, The Phillips Exeter Acad., N.H., 1970—; hon. trustee Signet Assos., Cambridge, 1973—. Mem. Am., N.Y. bar assns., Met. Opera Assn. (dir. 1968—, sec. 1974—), Met. Opera Guild, Inc. (dir. 1965—, v.p. 1968-70, first v.p. 1971-74, chmn. exec. com. 1968-70, 74—). Home: 1185 Park Ave New York City NY 10028 Office: 80 Pine St New York City NY 10005 Tel (212) RE2-2000

PETERS, BRUCE WARNER, b. Woodbury, N.J., May 8, 1943; B.A., William Penn Coll., 1966; J.D., U. Ill., 1969. Admitted to N.Y. bar, 1970; asso. firm Lines, Wilknes, Osborn & Beck, Rochester, N.Y., 1970-75; partner firm Sullivan, Peters, Burns & Holtzburg, Rochester, 1975—; town justice Penfield (N.Y.), 1973-76, town atty., 1976—; adj. faculty Rochester Inst. Tech., 1973—. Mem. Penfield Planning Bd., 1972-73. Mem. Monroe County, N.Y. State, Am. bar assns., Nat. Assn. Coll and Univ. Attys., Am. Judicature Soc. Home: 37 Wheelock Rd Penfield NY 14526 Office: One Exchange St Rochester NY 14614 Tel (716) 232-3910

PETERS, GEOFFREY WRIGHT, b. Wilmington, Del., Oct. 30, 1945; student Cornell U., 1963-64; B.A., Northwestern U., 1967; M.A., U. Denver, 1974, J.D., 1972. Admitted to Colo., Nebr. bars, 1972; individual practice law, Denver, 1972; asst. prof. law Creighton U., Omaha, 1972-75, asso. prof., 1975—; exec. dir. Inst. Bus., Law and Social Research, Omaha, 1975—; cons. Nat. Center State Cts., Washington and Mandan, N.D., Law Enforcement Asst. Adminstrn., Washington, Nat. Wiretap Commn., Washington, U.S. Civil Rights Commn., Iowa and Nebr., Nebr. Commn. Law Enforcement, Criminal Justice, Lincoln; lectr. in field. Affiliated scholar, Am. Bar Found.; chmn. Omaha Lawyers Panel-Nebr. Civil Liberties Union. Mem. Nat. Assn. Criminal Def. Attys., Am. Bar Assn., Law and Society Assn. (trustee), Assn. Am. Law Schs. (sect. chmn.), Order of St. Ives. Office: 2500 California St Omaha NE 68178 Tel (402) 449-3157

PETERS, MARVIN J., b. Chgo., Oct. 8, 1907; LL.B., DePaul U., Chgo., 1934. Admitted to Ill. bar, 1935; individual practice law, Chgo., 1935-44, 52-65; asst. corp. counsel City of Chgo., 1944-52; magistrate Circuit Ct. Cook County, Ill., 1965-71, asso. judge, 1971—. Mem. Ill. State, N.W. Suburban bar assns. Home: 643 F Burgandy Ct Elk Grove Village IL 60007 Office: Civic Center Des Plaines IL 60016 Tel (312) 296-7650

PETERS, MARY ANNE, b. Clearwater, Fla., Sept. 28, 1922; B.A., Am. U., Washington, 1965, J.D., 1967. Admitted to Va. bar, 1967, Ariz. bar, 1968, Fla. bar, 1975; individual practice law, Tucson, 1968—. Bd. dirs. Tucson Cerebral Palsy Found., 1972-75; mem. Tucson Symphony Women's Assn. Mem. Ariz., Pima and Cochise County, Va., Fla. bar assns., Am. Trial Lawyers Assn., AAUW, Alpha Gamma Delta, Alpha Delta Phi. Office: Suite 602 Transamerica Bldg 177 N Church St Tucson AZ 85701 Tel (602) 623-4334

PETERS, PETER JERROLD, b. Omaha, July 14, 1930; J.D., Creighton U., 1953. Admitted to Iowa bar, 1953, Nebr. bar. 1953; partner firms Hess, Peters, Sulhoff & Walker, and predecessors, Council Bluffs, Iowa, 1955-70, Peters, Campbell & Pearson, and predecessors, Council Bluffs, 1970—; county atty. Pottawattamie County (Iowa), 1960-61. Mem. Council Bluffs Mayor's Com. on Mass Transp.; bd. dirs. Mid-Am. council Boy Scouts Am. Mem. Am., Iowa State, S.W. Iowa, Pottawattamie County bar assns., Iowa Acad. Trial Lawyers (bd. govs. 1971—, lectr.), Council Bluffs C. of C. (Outstanding Young Man award 1964, pres. 1969-70). Home: 70 Crestwood Dr Council Bluffs IA 51501 Office: 233 Pearl St Council Bluffs IA 51501 Tel (712) 328-3157

PETERS, PHILIP GEORGE, b. Franklin, N.H., Jan. 15, 1922; B.A., U. N.H., 1943; LL.B., Boston U., 1948; LL.M., Harvard U., 1949. Admitted to N.H. bar, 1948, Mass. bar, 1948, Fed. Cts. bar, 1948; chief trial lawyer firm Wadleigh, Starr, Peters, Dunn & Kohls, Manchester, N.H., 1960-77; judge Auburn Dist. Ct. (N.H.), 1954—. Chmn. Manchester United Way; pres. Chandler Sch. PTA, YMCA. Mem. Am., N.H., Manchester bar assns., Internat. Soc. Barristers (past pres.), Internat. Acad. Trial Lawyers, Am. Trial Lawyers Assn., Internat. Ins. Counsel Assn., U.S. Judicature Soc., Judges Assn. Contbr. to Internat. Soc. Barristers Jour. Home: 191 N Gate St Manchester NH 03104 Office: 95 Market St Manchester NH 03101 Tel (603) 669-4140

PETERS, ROGER PAUL, b. N.Y.C., Feb. 6, 1905; B.A., U. Tex., 1924; J.D., N.Y. U., 1938; LL.D., U. Notre Dame, 1970. Admitted to N.Y. State bar, 1938; asso. firm Jacob Burns, N.Y.C., 1938-40; atty. chief counsel's office IRS, Washington, 1942-50; prof. law U. Notre Dame, South Bend, Ind., 1950-70, Southwestern U., Los Angeles, 1970—. Mem. Am. Bar Assn., Phi Beta Kappa. Contbr. articles in field to profl. jours. Home: 31582 Flying Cloud Dr Laguna Niguel CA 92677 Office: 675 S Westmoreland Ave Los Angeles CA 90005 Tel (213) 380-4800

PETERS, SAMUEL ANTHONY, b. N.Y.C., Oct. 25, 1934; B.A., N.Y. U., 1955; LL.B., Fordham U., 1961. Admitted to N.Y. bar, 1961, U.S. Supreme Ct. bar, 1967, Calif. bar, 1973; law clk. FCC, Washington, 1961; trial atty. U.S. Dept. Justice, Washington, 1961-68; staff counsel Lawyers Com. for Civil Rights under Law, Washington, 1968-69. litigation counsel Atlantic Richfield Co., Los Angeles, 1970-71, employee relations counsel, 1971—; Mem. personnel and tng. com. Greater Los Angeles chpt. Am. Heart Assn., 1975—. Mem. Am. Bar Assn., Langston Law Club. Mem. Fordham Law Rev., 1960-61. Home: 11471 Kensington Rd Los Alamitos CA 90720 Office: 515 S Flower St Los Angeles CA 90071 Tel (213) 486-1466

PETERSBERGER, RALPH ISAAC, b. Davenport, Iowa, Aug. 28, 1933; A.B., Harvard, 1955, J.D., 1958. Admitted to Mass. bar, 1958, D.C. bar, 1962, U.S. Supreme Ct. bar, 1962; judge adv. USAF, 1958-60; law clk. to judge U.S. Tax Ct., Washington, 1960-62; asso. firm Lee, Toomey and Kent, Washington, 1962-67, partner, 1967—. Mem. Am., Fed., D.C. bar assns. Office: 1200 18th St NW Washington DC 20036 Tel (202) 457-8514

PETERSEN, DON ROBERT, b. Salt Lake City, Mar. 17, 1937; B.S., Utah State U., 1961; J.D., U. Utah, 1964. Admitted to Utah bar, 1965; contracts adminstr. Jet Propulsion Lab., Pasadena, Calif., 1966-67; asso. then partner firm Howard, Lewis, & Petersen, and predecessors, Provo, Utah, 1967—. Treas., sec. Utah County Republican Party, 1969-74. Mem. Am., Utah, Utah County bar assns. Home: 3109 Apache Ln Provo UT 84601 Office: 120 E 300 N Provo UT 84601 Tel (801) 373-6345

PETERSEN, FRANK STANLEY, b. Elk, Calif., June 20, 1922; A.A., Santa Rosa Jr. Coll., 1948; LL.B., U. San Francisco, 1951. Admitted to Calif. bar, 1952, U.S. Dist. Ct. bar, 1952; asso. firm Preston, Falk & Johnson, Ukiah, Calif., 1952-54; individual practice law, Ukiah, 1954-60; asst. dist. atty. City of Ukiah, 1954-60; dist. atty., Mendocino County, Calif., 1960-62; mem. Calif. Senate, 1963-66; judge Superior Ct. DelNorte County, Crescent City, Calif., 1966—; judge protem 3d Dist. Ct. Appeals. Former pres. Crescent City Rotary Club. Mem. Conf. Calif. Judges. Office: Court House Crescent City CA 95531 Tel (707) 464-4139

PETERSEN, JAMES FRANKLIN, b. Omaha, July 23, 1931; B.S.B.A., U. Nebr., 1956, J.D., 1960. Admitted to Nebr. bar, 1960, Iowa bar, 1968, Alaska bar, 1972; spl. asst. atty. gen. State of Nebr., Lincoln, beginning in 1960; chief atty. Nebr. Dept. Rds., Lincoln, to 68; asst. atty. gen. State of Iowa, also spl. asst. atty. gen.; chief trial atty. Iowa Hwy. Commn., also chief counsel; asst. atty. gen. State of Alaska, Juneau, 1971-72; chief atty. Alaska Dept. Hwys., Juneau; partner firm Gregg, Fraties, Petersen, Page & Baxter, Juneau, 1972—; mem. hwy. research bd. legal affairs com. Nat. Acad. Sci. and Industry, 1970-73. Mem. Am. Trial Lawyers Assn., Am. Right-of-Way Assn. Home: PO Box 322 Juneau AK 99802 Office: 319 Seward St Juneau AK 99801 Tel (907) 586-3530

PETERSEN, NEAL LENNARD, b. San Francisco, Feb. 4, 1937; A.B., U. Calif., Berkeley, 1959; LL.B., Harvard, 1962. Admitted to Calif. bar, 1963; asst. counsel Bank of Am., San Francisco, 1962-65, asst. Washington rep., 1965-68, asst. gen. counsel, San Francisco, 1968—. Bd. dirs. Young Audiences of the Bay Area, Inc., San Francisco, 1976—. Mem. Am., Fed., San Francisco bar assns., Calif. Bankers Assn. Co-author: California Bankers Guide to Uniform Commercial Code, 1965. Home: 270 30th Ave San Francisco CA 94121 Office: Bank of Am Center PO Box 37000 San Francisco CA 94137 Tel (415) 622-2842

PETERSEN, OWEN DALE, b. Devils Lake, N.D., Feb. 15, 1944; B.S., Union Coll., 1966; J.D., U. Calif. at Los Angeles, 1969. Admitted to Calif. bar, 1970; dep. city atty. City of Torrance (Calif.), 1970-72, city prosecutor, 1972-75; partner firm Moore Capozzola & Petersen, Torrance, 1975-77; partner law offices of Owen D. Petersen, 1977—; counsel to personnel bd. City of Santa Monica (Calif.), 1972—. Mem. Calif., Los Angeles, SW Criminal Cts. (v.p.) bar assns., Torrance C. of C. Named Outstanding Young Man of Torrance, Jaycees, 1972. Office: Moore & Capozzola 21515 Hawthorne Blvd Suite 1140 Torrance CA 90503 Tel (213) 327-1515

PETERSON, ARTHUR HEROLD, b. Chgo., Aug. 8, 1939; A.B., U. Chgo., 1960; J.D., Wayne State U., 1963. Admitted to Mich. bar, 1963, Ill. bar, 1963, Alaska bar, 1973, U.S. Supreme Ct. bar, 1971; examiner Nat. Ry. Labor Conf., Chgo., 1964-66; legis. counsel Alaska State Legislature, 1966-67, revisor of statutes, 1967-73; asst. atty. gen. Alaska, 1973—; uniform law commr. Nat. Conf. Uniform State Laws, 1975—; chmn. statute revision workshop com. Nat. Legis. Conf., 1969. Bd. dirs. Alaska Civil Liberties Union, 1974—; alt. bd. dirs. Alaska Legal Services Corp., 1974—; pres. Juneau Film Soc. Mem. Alaska (chmn. statute revision subcom.), Juneau (sec.) bar assns., Phi Delta Phi. Office: Dept Law Pouch K Juneau AK 99811 Tel (907) 465-3600

PETERSON, BARRY DON, b. Wichita Falls, Tex., June 28, 1946; B.S., Tex. Tech. U., 1969; J.D., St. Mary's U., 1972. Admitted to Tex. bar, 1972; asso. firm Stokes, Carnahan & Fields, Amarillo, Tex., 1972—. Mem. Tex., Amarillo (sec.-treas. 1975-76) bar assns. Home: 2402 S Parker St Amarillo TX 79109 Office: 1002 Plaza One Amarillo TX 79101 Tel (806) 374-5317

PETERSON, CARL RUDOLF, b. Newark, Apr. 8, 1907; A.B., Princeton, 1928; LL.B., Columbia, 1931. Admitted to N.Y. State bar, 1932, D.C. bar, 1942; research asst. Columbia Law Sch., N.Y.C., 1931-33; asso. firm Hawkins, Delafield & Longfellow, N.Y.C., 1933-37; with chief counsel IRS, Washington, 1937-42, asst. head legis. and regulation div., 1941-42; partner firm Alvord & Alvord, Washington, 1942-50; mem. firm Lee, Toomey & Kent, D.C., 1950—; counsel Nat. Fin. Execs. Inst.; advisor Nat. Tax Com.; mem. ways and means com. advisory group on adminstrn. of tax laws, 1957, v. chmn. advisory group on subchpt. C, 1957-60. Mem. Am., D.C., N.Y. State bar assns., Am. Law Inst. (mem. tax advisory group), Internat. Acad. Law and Sci. Contbr. articles to profl. jours. Home: 5115 Rockwood Pkwy NW Washington DC 20016 Office: 1200 18th St NW Washington DC 20036 Tel (202) 457-8541

PETERSON, COURTLAND HARRY, b. Denver, June 28, 1930; B.A., U. Colo., 1951, LL.B., 1953; M.C.L. (Fgn. Law fellow), U. Chgo., 1959; J.D. (Fgn. Law fellow), U. Freiburg (Germany), 1963. Admitted to Colo. bar, 1953, U.S. Ct. Mil. Appeals bar, 1955; asso. firm Knight & Lesher, Denver, 1953-54; served with JAGC, USAF, 1954-56; asst. prof. law U. Colo., 1959-61, asso. prof., 1961-63, prof., 1963—, dean Sch. Law, 1974—; vis. prof. U. Calif., Los Angeles, 1965, Max Plank Inst., Hamburg, Germany, 1969, U. Tex., Austin, 1973-74. Mem. Am., Colo., Boulder County bar assns., Am. Soc. Internat. Law. Author: Die Anerkennung auslaendischer Urteile, 1964. Home: 1434 Baseline Rd Boulder CO 80302 Office: Fleming Law Bldg U of Colo Boulder CO 80302 Tel (303) 492-8047

PETERSON, DARRELL THOMAS, b. Cut Bank, Mont., Apr. 8, 1942; B.S. in Math., U. Wash., Seattle, 1964, J.D., 1967. Admitted to Wash., Mont. bars, 1967; judge advocate U.S. Air Force, Minot AFB, N.D., 1967-71; founder, partner firm Peterson, Peterson & Burns, Cut Bank, Mont., 1972—; pres. E. O. Peterson, Inc., Cut Bank, 1973—; past treas., v.p. Devel. Corp., Cut Bank. Mem. Am., Mont. bar assns., Cut Bank C. of C. Recipient Distinguished Service award Community of Cut Bank, 1975. Home: 135 2d Ave SW Cut Bank MT 59427 Office: 101 1st St SE Cut Bank MT 59427 Tel (406) 873-2231

PETERSON, DAVID LATIMER, b. Long Branch, N.J., Apr. 22, 1943; B.A. in Polit. Sci. and Portuguese, Brigham Young U., 1968; J.D., U. Okla., 1972. Admitted to Okla. bar, 1973, U.S. Dist. Ct. bar for No. Dist. Okla., 1973, 10th Circuit U.S. Ct. Appeals bar, 1975; individual practice law, Tulsa, 1973—; instr. evening div. Tulsa Jr. Coll., 1977—. Mem. Am. (mem. internat. law com. on inter-Am. law), Okla., Tulsa County bar assns., Okla. Trial Lawyers Assn., Phi Alpha Delta. Home: 8155 E 31st Ct Tulsa OK 74145 Office: Suite 424 Beacon Bldg Tulsa OK 74103 Tel (918) 582-8850

PETERSON, DAVID THOMAS, b. Mankato, Minn., May 18, 1942; B.S. in Pharmacy, U. Minn., 1966, J.D., 1971. Admitted to Minn. bar, 1971; mem. firm Blethen, Gage, Krause, Blethen, Corcoran, Berkland & Peterson, Mankato, 1971—. Bd. dirs. Mankato Rehab. Center, 1972-75, v.p., 1975-76, pres., 1976—; bd. dirs. Mankato YMCA, 1976—; trustee Schola Found., 1975—. Mem. Am., Minn., 6th Dist. bar assns.

PETERSON, DUANE MALCOLM, b. Duluth, Minn., Sept. 18, 1929; LL.B., St. Paul Coll. Law, 1953. Admitted to Minn. bar, U.S. Dist. Ct. bar, 1953; partner firm Peterson, Delano & Thompson Ltd., Winona, Minn., 1959, sr. partner, 1959—; judge Tax Ct. State of Minn., Winona, 1972—. Sec., Winona Charter Commn., 1967-70; chmn. Merit Bd. City of Winona, 1969-76. Mem. Am. (nat. com. 1975—), Minn. (pres. 1976-77) trial lawyers' assns. Home: 418 Hiawatha St Winona MN 55987 Office: 202 1st Nat Bank Bldg Winona MN 55987 Tel (507) 454-5710

PETERSON, EDWARD ADRIAN, b. St. Louis, May 19, 1941; B.S. in Bus. Adminstrn., Washington U., St. Louis, 1963; LL.B., So. Methodist U., 1966. Admitted to Tex. bar, 1966, practiced in Dallas, 1967—; asso. firm Newman & Pickering, 1967; partner firm Newman, Moore & Peterson, 1967-72, Moore, Peterson, Bauer, Williams & Musslewhite, 1972-76, Moore, Peterson, Bauer, Williams & Stollenwerck, 1977—; instr. bus. law and accounting Midwestern U., Wichita Falls, Tex., 1966-67. Chmn. bd. edn. Our Redeemer Lutheran Ch., 1974-75; bd. dirs. Luth. High Sch. Assn. Dallas, 1974—. Mem. Am., Dallas Jr. bar assns., Real Estate Fin. Execs. Assn. Contbr. articles to profl. jours. Office: 28th Floor Republic Nat Bank Tower Dallas TX 75201 Tel (214) 651-1721

PETERSON, EDWIN E., b. Hallettsville, Tex., Jan. 6, 1898; A.B., Columbia, 1929; J.D., Fordham U., 1929. Admitted to N.Y. bar, 1929; asso. firm Mitchell, Taylor, Capron & Marsh, N.Y.C., 1930-34; Davis, Polk, Sunderland & Krendl, N.Y.C., 1934-51; partner firm Lundgren, Lincoln, Peterson & McDaniel, N.Y.C., 1951-54; individual practice law, N.Y.C., 1955-69; partner firm Emmet, Martin and Martin, N.Y.C., 1969—. Vice pres., trustee Emergency Shelter, N.Y.C. Mem. Am. Bar Assn., Assn. Bar City N.Y.C., N.Y. County Lawyers Assn.

PETERSON, GREGORY ALAN, b. Mpls., Aug. 24, 1946; B.A., U. Wis., Madison, 1969, J.D., 1973. Admitted to Wis. bar, 1973; asso. firm Herrick, Hart, Duchemin & Peterson, Eau Claire, Wis., 1973-76; individual practice law, Eau Claire, 1976—; vis. asst. prof. U. Wis., Eau Claire, 1976-77. Mem. Wis., Eau Claire County bar assns. Home: 525 Lincoln Ave Eau Claire WI 54701 Office: 118 1/2 E Grand Ave Eau Claire WI 54701 Tel (715) 835-4171

PETERSON, JERRY BURNS, b. Oak Park, Ill., Aug. 18, 1928; B.S. in Chem. Engring., Purdue U., 1950; LL.B., U. Ill., 1956. Admitted to Ill. bar, 1956, Okla. bar, 1957, U.S. Patent Office bar, 1958, Tex. bar, 1971; supr. trademarks and licenses Continental Oil Co., Ponca City, Okla., 1959-66, supr. patent prosecution, 1966-69, supr. patents and trademarks, 1969-70; gen. counsel Continental Carbon Co., Houston, 1970—. Chmn. Kay County Republican Com., Ponca City, 1961-63; mem. Okla. House of Rep., 1967-69. Mem. Am. Bar Assn., Am. Patent Law Assn., Licensing Execs. Soc. Home: 1303 Country Pl Houston TX 77079 Office: 4120 Southwest Freeway Houston TX 77027 Tel (713) 623-2780

PETERSON, JOHN CHARLES, b. Wilkinsburg, Pa., Mar. 16, 1903; B.S., U. Pitts., 1926; LL.B., Yale, 1929. Admitted to Pa. bar, 1940; individual practice law; pres. Columbia Gas of Pa., Inc., Columbia Gas of N.Y., Inc., Columbia Gas of W.Va., Inc., Columbia Gas of Md., Inc., 1952-63, chmn. bd., 1963-68. Home: 1033 Portland St Pittsburgh PA 15206 Office: 431 Union Trust Bldg Pittsburgh PA 15219 Tel (412) 281-3137

PETERSON, JOHN RICHARD, b. Chgo., July 9, 1910; B.A., Northwestern U., 1932; J.D., Chgo.-Kent Coll. Law, 1935. Admitted to Ill. bar, 1935, Mass. bar, 1946, U.S. Supreme Ct. bar, 1964; counsel Continental Casualty Co., Chgo., 1940-44; gen. counsel S.J. Campbell Co., Chgo., 1944-45; asso. counsel, then gen. counsel The First Ch. of Christ Scientist, Boston, 1945—. Mem. Am., Mass., Boston bar assns., Am. Patent Law Assn. (past mem. bd. mgrs.), World Assn. Lawyers, Phi Beta Kappa, Phi Delta Phi. Office: Christian Science Center Boston MA 02115 Tel (617) 262-2300

PETERSON, KENNETH WAYNE, b. Elgin, N.D., Jan. 17, 1927; LL.B., U. N.D., 1952, J.D., 1969. Admitted to N.D. bar, 1952; atty. Fed. Land Bank, St. Paul, Minn., 1952-57; state's atty. Grant County, Carson, N.D., 1958-76; sec.-treas. Grant County Abstract Co., Carson, 1965—; city atty., Carson, 1958—; atty. Grant County State Bank, Carson, Flasher, N.D., Roosevelt Pub. Sch. Dist. 18, Carson. Mem. N.D. State, Am. bar assns., N.D. State's Atty. Assn., N.D. Title Assn., Am. Land Title Assn., Phi Delta Phi. Home and office: PO Box 345 Carson ND 58529 Tel (701) 622-3520

PETERSON, PAUL MURREY, b. Lockwood, Mo., June 5, 1897; student Westminster Coll., Fulton, Mo., 1915-17; J.D., U. Mo., Columbia, 1922. Admitted to Mo. bar, 1922; since practiced in Columbia, Mo.; prof. law U. Mo., Columbia, 1942-69, gen. counsel, 1954-69; atty. State Bar of Mo., 1936-38. Mem. Am. Judicature Soc., Nat. Assn. Coll. and Univ. Attys. (past pres.), Boone County Bar Assn. (past pres.), Am. Legion (past comdr.), Phi Alpha Delta, Order of Coif. Author: (with W. Eckardt) Possessory Estates, Future Interests and Conveyances in Missouri. Home: 200 E Parkaway Columbia MO 65201 Tel (314) 442-0968

PETERSON, PHILIP EVERETT, b. Galena, Ill., July 10, 1922; B.S., U. Ill., 1950, J.D., 1952; LL.M., Harvard, 1958. Admitted to Ill. bar, 1952, Idaho bar, 1955, U.S. Supreme Ct. bar, 1958; instr. U. Ill., Urbana, 1952; prof. law U. Idaho, Moscow, 1952—, dean, 1962-66; individual practice law, Lewiston, Idaho, 1966—. Mem. Am., Idaho, Ill. bar assns. Author law manual, articles in law revs. Home: 318 Fifth St Lewiston ID 83501 Office: University Idaho Moscow ID 83843 Tel (208) 743-0807

PETERSON, RALPH HENRY, b. Hunter, N.D., Aug. 26, 1922; B.S., U. Minn., 1945, J.D., 1947. Admitted to Minn. bar, 1947; partner firm Sturtz, Peterson, Butler & Chesterman, Albert Lea, Minn., 1947—; sec., gen. counsel Bridon Cordage, Inc., Albert Lea, 1975—; dir. Jobs, Inc., 1st Nat. Bank Albert Lea, 1st Nat. Bank of Emmons (Minn.), Edwards Mfg. Co., Olson Mfg. Co., Upin Enterprises, Inc., Upin Co., Inc., Upin Investment Co. Mem. bd. suprs. Town of Albert Lea, 1954-58; mem. Minn. State Bd. Edn., 1967-75, pres., 1971-72; mem. advisory council on fluctuating sch. enrollments State of Minn., 1974—; chmn. Freeborn County Republican Com., 1956, 57. Mem. Am. Judicature Soc., Am., Minn., Freeborn County, 10th Jud. Dist. bar assns., Albert Lea Rotary (past pres.). Home: 929 Lakeview Blvd Albert Lea MN 56007 Office: 402 S Washington Albert Lea MN 56007 Tel (507) 373-3946

PETERSON, RICHARD THOMAS, b. Anaheim, Calif., Apr. 5, 1948; B.S., U. San Francisco, 1970; J.D., U. Calif., Los Angeles, 1973; LL.M., George Washington U., 1976. Admitted to Calif. bar, 1973, U.S. Supreme Ct. bar, 1977; law clk. firm Spray, Gould and Bowers, Los Angeles, 1972-73; capt. JAGC, U.S. Army, 1974; adminstrv. law officer Pentagon, Washington, 1974—; research cons. Tech. Assistance Research Programs, Inc., Washington, 1974. Mem. Am., Calif. bar assns., U. Calif. Los Angeles Law Alumni Assn. Named Outstanding Young Man in Am. U.S. Jaycees, 1976; exec. editor U. Calif. at Los Angeles-Alaska Law Rev., 1972-73. Home: 7137 Roosevelt Ave Falls Church VA 22042 Office: 13331 Barnett Way Garden Grove CA 92643 Tel (714) 537-8034

PETERSON, RICHARD WILLIAM, b. Council Bluffs, Iowa, Sept. 29, 1925; B.A., U. Iowa, 1949, J.D., 1951; postgrad. U. Nebr., 1972—. Admitted to Iowa bar, 1951, U.S. Dist. Ct. bar for So. Dist. Iowa, 1951; practiced in Council Bluffs, 1951-76; trust officer, mgr. trust dept. 1st Nat. Bank of Council Bluffs, 1976—; U.S. commr. U.S. Dist. Ct. for So. Dist. Iowa, 1958-70, U.S. magistrate, 1970—; mem. nat. faculty Fed. Jud. Center, Washington. Mem. Council Bluffs Bd. Edn., 1958-64, pres., 1963-64; bd. dirs. Mid-Am. council Boy Scouts Am., Pottawattamie County (Iowa) chpt. ARC, Crippled Children Assn., Council Bluffs; trustee Christian Home Assn. Council Bluffs. Mem. Pottawattamie County, S.W. Iowa, Iowa, Am., Fed., Inter-Am. bar assns., Nat. Council U.S. Magistrates (1st v.p.), U. Iowa Alumni Assn. (pres. 1965-69, dir.), Phi Delta Phi, Delta Sigma Rho, Omicron Delta Kappa. Named Outstanding Young Man of Yr., Council Bluffs Jaycees, 1959. Home: 317 Burr Oak Rd Council Bluffs IA 51501 Office: 500 W Broadway Council Bluffs IA 51501 Tel (712) 322-3456

PETERSON, ROBERT MERVIN, b. Pasadena, Calif., Feb. 27, 1934; A.B., Pacific Union Coll., 1956; J.D., U. So. Calif., 1959. Admitted to Calif. bar, 1960; law clk. firm Hahn & Hahn, Pasadena, Calif., 1957-59; asso. firm Newton & Irvin, Los Angeles, 1960-65; partner firm Bunn & Peterson, Pasadena, 1965—. Bd. dirs. White Meml. Med. Center, Los Angeles, 1963—. Mem. Pasadena, Calif. bar assns., Order of Coif. Office: 251 S Lake Ave Suite 701 Pasadena CA 91101 Tel (213) 681-5621

PETERSON, ROGER FRANKLYN, b. Cedar Rapids, Iowa, June 20, 1928; B.A., Coe Coll., 1950; J.D., U. Iowa, 1956. Admitted to Iowa bar, 1956; sales supr. AT&T, Mpls., 1956-61; practiced in Waterloo, Iowa, 1961-72; judge Iowa Dist. Ct., 1st Jud. Dist., 1972—; county atty. County of Black Hawk (Iowa), 1966-67. Home: 345 Columbia Circle Waterloo IA 50701 Office: 316 E 5th St Waterloo IA 50703 Tel (319) 291-2494

PETERSON, THOMAS ANTHONY, b. Iowa City, Iowa, Dec. 2, 1947; B.A., U. Tex., 1970; J.D., U. Houston, 1973. Admitted to Tex. bar, 1973, U.S. Ct. Appeals 5th Circuit bar, 1974; asso. firm Harold Peterson, 1973-75; partner firm Peterson, Petit & Peterson, Beaumont, Tex., 1976—. Mem. State Bar Tex., Am., Jefferson County (chmn. Law Day U.S.A. com. 1977), Jefferson County Jr. (v.p. 1976-77, pres. elect 1977-78) bar assns., Am., Tex. trial lawyers assns., Assn. Trial Lawyers Am. Office: 1111 San Jacinto Bldg Orleans St at Fannin St Beaumont TX 77701 Tel (713) 838-6144

PETERSON, THOMAS LEE, b. Los Angeles, Nov. 24, 1934; B.S. in Indsl. Engring., Stanford, 1956; LL.B., George Washington U., 1961. Admitted to Calif. bar, 1962; atty. Aerojet General Corp., Azusa, Calif., 1962; Beckman Instruments, Inc., Fullerton, Calif., 1963-72; counsel ITT, Encino, Calif., 1972-76. Mem. Los Angeles Patent Law Assn. Home: 16135 St Croix St Huntington Beach CA 92649 Office: 20335 Ventura Blvd Woodland Hills CA 91364 Tel (213) 999-6000

PETERSON, WILLIAM RICHARD, b. Cadillac, Mich., Oct. 11, 1923; A.B., Albion Coll., 1945; M.A., U. Mich., 1946, J.D., 1949. Admitted to Mich. bar, 1949, Mo. bar, 1950; instr. law U. Mo., Kansas City, 1949-51; asso. firm Blackmar, Newkirk, Eager, Swanson & Midgley, Kansas City, 1950-51; individual practice law, Cadillac, 1951-54; partner firm Peterson & Wyman, Cadillac, 1955-59; judge 28th Jud. Circuit Ct., Cadillac, 1960—; pros. atty. Wexford County (Mich.), 1953-56; probate judge Wexford County, 1957-59. Mem. Am., Mich., Mo., Wexford-Missaukee bar assns., Am. Judicature Soc., Internat. Acad. Trial Judges, Mich. Judges Assn. (pres.), Mich. Assn. Professions. Author: A Guide for Fiduciaries, 1957; The View from Courthouse Hill, 1972; contbr. articles to legal jours. Home: 918 Stimson St Cadillac MI 49601 Office: Court House Cadillac MI 49601 Tel (616) 775-0129

PETIT, MICHAEL STONE, b. Beaumont, Tex., July 26, 1947; B.A., So. Meth. U., 1969; J.D., U. Tex., 1972. Admitted to Tex. bar, 1972; asso. firm Peterson, Petit & Peterson and predecessor firm, Beaumont, Tex., 1972-75, partner, 1976—. Mem. Beaumont Art Mus., 1972. Mem. Tex., Jefferson County (treas. 1976-77, dir. 1977-78), Jefferson County Jr. (pres. 1975-76) bar assns., Tex. Trial Lawyers Assn., Tex. Young Lawyers Assn. (dir. 1977-78). Home: 2315 Briarcliff Beaumont TX 77706 Office: 1111 San Jacinto Bldg Orleans at Fannin Beaumont TX 77701 Tel (713) 838-6144

PETIT-CLAIR, ALFRED JOSEPH, JR., b. Newark, Jan. 20, 1944; B.A., Rutgers U., Newark, 1966; J.D., Seton Hall U. Sch. Law, Newark, 1971. Admitted to N.J. bar, 1971, U.S. Supreme Ct. bar, 1974; wage collection hearing examiner N.J. Dept. Labor and Industry, Trenton, 1968-71; asso. firm Mandel, Wysoker, Sherman, Glassner, Weingartner & Feingold, Perth Amboy, N.J., 1971-72; individual practice law, Perth Amboy, 1972—; gen. counsel Middlesex County (N.J.) AFL-CIO Council, 1974—; mem. N.J. Supreme Ct. Com. on Admission of Fgn. Attys., 1975; vol. atty. ACLU, 1972—. Trustee Middlesex County Legal Services Corp., 1975—; mem. spl. sewerage revenue adv. com. Mayor of Perth Amboy, 1976. Mem. Am., N.J., Middlesex County bar assns., Am. Trial Lawyers Assn., Am. Judicature Soc. Home: 107 Brighton Ave Perth Amboy NJ 08861 Office: 175 Smith St Perth Amboy NJ 08861 Tel (201) 826-6460

PETKOFF, GEORGE SAMUEL, b. Helena, Ark., Dec. 12, 1936; B.S., Christian Bros. Coll., 1958; LL.B. cum laude, So. U., 1964; LL.B. (hon.), Memphis State U., 1967. Admitted to Tenn. bar, 1965 since practiced in Memphis; asso. firm Nelson, Norvell, Wilson, McRae, Ivy & Sevier and predecessors, 1965-71, partner, 1971-75; partner firm Udelsohn, Turnage, Balylock, Golden & Petkoff, 1975; individual practice law, 1976—; staff atty. City of Memphis, 1975—. Mem. Our Lady of Sorrows Sch. Bd., 1971—, pres. 1975-76; mem. Diocese Memphis Sch. Bd., 1972—, pres. 1974-75. Mem. Am., Tenn., Memphis, Shelby County bar assns., Tenn. Def. Lawyers Assn., Lawyer-Pilots Bar Assn., Fedn. Ins. Counsel. Contbr. articles in field to profl. jours. Office: 100 N Main St Memphis TN 38103 Tel (901) 523-1050

PETLEY, THOMAS CUMMINGS, b. New Rochelle, N.Y., Sept. 4, 1944; B.A., So. Methodist U., 1966; J.D., U. Houston, 1973. Admitted to Tex. bar, 1973, U.S. Dist. Ct. So. Dist. Tex. bar, 1974, 5th Circuit Ct. of Appeals bar, 1975, U.S. Dist. Ct. Eastern Dist. Tex. bar, 1976; individual practice law, Houston, 1974—. Mem. Am., Houston bar assns., Tex. Trial Lawyers Assn. Home: 11910 Steppingstone St Houston TX 77024 Office: 5417 Chaucer St Houston TX 77005 Tel (713) 526-9966

PETOCK, MICHAEL FRANCIS, b. Pottsville, Pa., Apr. 6, 1943; B.S. in Elec. Engring. with high distinction, Pa. State U., 1968; J.D. with honors, George Washington U., 1971. Admitted to Pa. bar, 1972, U.S. Supreme Ct. bar, 1976; patent agt. Gen. Electric Co., Washington, 1968-71; asso. firm Seidel, Gonda & Goldhammer, Phila., 1971-74; partner, co-founder firm Steele & Petock, Phila., 1974—. Mem. Am., Pa., Phila. bar assns., Pa. Trial Lawyers Assn., Am., Phila. patent law assns., IEEE, Order of Coif, Eta Kappa Nu, Phi Kappa Phi, Tau Beta Pi, Sigma Tau, Phi Eta Sigma. Office: 3232 IVB 1700 Market St Philadelphia PA 19103 Tel (215) 563-0500

PETRAITIS, KAREL COLETTE, b. Chgo., Apr. 4, 1945; B.A., U. Md., 1967; J.D., George Washington U., 1971; postgrad. U. Md., 1967-68, Hastings Law Sch., 1974. Admitted to Md. bar, 1972, Fed. Dist. bar for Md., 1973; law clk. Office of Law, Prince George's County, Upper Marlboro, Md., 1971-72, atty., 1972—. Active March of Dimes, 1972—; mem. Md. Adv. Com. Animal Welfare, 1976; nat. committeewoman Young Republicans, 1971—, legal counsel Md. chpt., 1973—, exec. v.p. Prince George's chpt., 1976, legal counsel Prince George's chpt., 1973—; state youth coordinator of Agnew, Mathias campaigns, 1966, 68, 77; local youth adviser for Beall, 1970, Nixon-Agnew, 1972. Mem. Am., Md., Prince George's County bar assns., Women's Bar Assn. Prince George's County, Young Alumni Assn. U. Md. (dir. 1977—), Phi Alpha Delta, Phi Alpha Theta, Pi Sigma Alpha. Recipient Distinguished Voluntary Leadership award March of Dimes, 1972; named Md. Young Republican Woman 1971-72, The Outstanding Young Republican Woman in Am., 1973-75, One of 10 Outstanding Young Women in Am., 1974. Home: 7307 Radcliffe Dr College Park MD 20740 Office: Office of Law Courthouse Upper Marlboro MD 20870 Tel (301) 952-4124

PETREE, WILLIAM HORTON, b. Winston-Salem, N.C., Nov. 4, 1920; B.S., U. N.C., 1944, J.D., 1948. Admitted to N.C. bar, 1948; partner firm Hudson, Petree, Stockton, Stockton & Robinson, Winston-Salem, 1956—. Past pres. Forsyth County Tb and Health Assn., 1953; bd. dirs. Forsyth County Heart Assn., 1959-62, Salem Coll., 1971-77, Old Salem, Inc., 1976—; chmn. Winston Salem Found., 1976—. Mem. Forsyth County (past pres.), N.C., Am. bar assns. Home: 729 Westover Ave Winston-Salem NC 27104 Office: 610 Reynolds Bldg Winston-Salem NC 27101 Tel (919) 725-2351

PETRELLA, JAMES J., b. Bayonne, N.J., July 10, 1935; A.B. cum laude, St. Peter's Coll., Jersey City, 1957; J.D., N.Y. U., 1962. Admitted to N.J. bar, 1962; law sec. to chief justice N.J. Supreme Ct., 1962-63; asso. firm Pitney, Hardin & Kipp, Newark, 1963-70; asso. counsel Gov. N.J., 1970-73; judge Municipal Ct., North Arlington, N.J., 1968-70, Bergen County (N.J.) Ct., 1973-76, N.J. Superior Ct., 1976—; atty. North Arlington Planning Bd., 1966-68, North Arlington-Lyndhurst Joint Sewer Meeting, 1966-68; prosecutor Boro of North Arlington (N.J.), 1966-68; mem. N.J. Supreme Ct. Coms., 1967-70. Mem. N.J. State (chmn. subcom. on prepaid legal services 1969-70), Bergen County (N.J.), Essex County (chmn. com. lawyer referral 1963-73, jud. selection com. 1968, judiciary com. 1968-69), West Hudson bar assns. Office: Bergen County Courthouse Hackensack NJ 07601 Tel (201) 646-3003

PETRIE, BERNARD, b. Detroit, Sept. 9, 1925; B.S., U.S. Mil. Acad., 1946; J.D., U. Mich., 1952. Admitted to N.Y. bar, 1953, Calif. bar, 1955; asso. firm Cravath, Swaine & Moore, N.Y.C., 1952-54, McCutchen, Thomas, Matthew, Griffiths & Greene, San Francisco, 1954-56; asst. U.S. atty. No. Dist. Calif., San Francisco, 1957-60; individual practice law, San Francisco, 1960—; mem. disciplinary bd. State Bar Calif., 1976—. Past treas. San Francisco Actors Workshop. Mem. Am., Fed., San Francisco (dir. 1974-76) bar assns., UN Assn. San Francisco (former pres.). Asso. editor Mich. Law Rev., 1951-52. Home: 2620 A Jackson St San Francisco CA 94115 Office: 633 Battery St San Francisco CA 94111 Tel (415) 982-4743

PETRIE, HAROLD JOHN, b. S. River, N.J., Oct. 20, 1917; B.S., Rutgers U., 1939; J.D., Georgetown U., 1947. Admitted to Wash. bar, 1948; dep. pros. atty., Yakima, 1948-52; mem. firm Robinson and Petrie, Yakima, Wash., 1952-58; mem. Wash. State Legislature, 1953-58; mem. Bd. Indsl. Ins. Appeals, Seattle, 1958-65; dir. Wash. Dept. Labor and Industries, Olympia, 1966-69; judge Ct. Appeals Div. II, Tacoma, 1969-71, chief judge, 1971-72, 75—. Mem. Am. Bar Assn., Am. Judicature Soc., Phi Beta Kappa. Office: 2000 Tacoma Mall Bldg Tacoma WA 98409 Tel (206) 593-2976

PETRINA, WILLIAM TODD, b. Jersey City, June 19, 1946; B.A. in Polit. Sci. and Philosophy, St. Peter's Coll., 1969; student U. Ariz., 1965-67; J.D., N.Y. U., 1972. Admitted to N.J. bar, 1972; law clk. to judge N.J. Superior Ct., 1972-73; asst. prosecutor, chief spl. prosecutions unit Hudson County Prosecutor's Office, Jersey City, 1973—. Mem. Am., N.J. bar assns., Nat. Assn. Dist. Attys., N.J. Prosecutors Assn. Recipient award for law enforcement N.J. Atty. Gen., 1976. Office: 595 Newark Ave Jersey City NJ 07306 Tel (201) 792-0800

PETRO, JAMES MICHAEL, b. Cleve., Oct. 25, 1948; B.A., Denison U., 1970; J.D., Case Western Res. U., 1973. Admitted to Ohio bar, 1973; spl. asst. U.S. Senator William B. Saxbe, 1972-73; asst. pros. atty. Franklin County (Ohio), Columbus, 1973-74; asst. dir. law City of Cleve., 1974; partner firm W.J., J.W., & J.M. Petro, Cleve., 1974—; prosecutor City of Rocky River (Ohio), 1976—. Mem. Am., Ohio, Greater Cleve. bar assns. Home: 235 Buckingham Rd Rocky River OH 44116 Office: 510 33 Public Sq Cleveland OH 44113 Tel (216) 621-6570

PETRO, PAUL MICHAEL, b. Donora, Pa., July 8, 1933; A.B. cum laude, U. Pitts., 1955, J.D., 1958. Admitted to Pa. bar, 1960, U.S. Supreme Ct. bar, 1966; solicitor Sheriff's Office, Washington County, Pa., 1966-68; asst. dist. atty., Washington County, Pa., 1968-73; solicitor Middle Monogahela Indsl. Devel. Assn., Inc., 1967—. Pres. Donora Borough Council, 1968. Mem. Pa., Washington County bar assns., Donora C. of C. (pres. 1967), Phi Beta Kappa, Phi Alpha Delta. Home: 13 Virginia Dr Rabe Manor Donora PA 15033 Office: 215 7th St Donora PA 15033 Tel (412) 379-9276

PETRO, SYLVESTER, b. Chgo., June 6, 1917; A.B., U. Chgo., 1943, J.D., 1945; LL.M., U. Mich., 1950. Admitted to Ill. bar, 1945, U.S. Supreme Ct. bar, 1974, U.S. Ct. of Appeals bar, 1975; individual practice law, Chgo., 1945-49; prof. law. N.Y. U., 1950-73, legal cons. N.Y.C., 1952-72; prof., dir. Inst. Labor Policy Analysis Wake Forest U. Sch. Law, Winston-Salem, N.C., 1973—. Trustee Found. Economic Edn., Irvington, N.Y., 1955—. Mem. Pont Pelerin Soc., Order of the Coif. Author: The Labor Policy of the Free Society, 1957; How the NLRB Repealed Taft-Hartley, 1958; Power Unlimited, the Corruption of Union Leadership, 1959; Sovereignty and Compulsory Public Sector Bargaining, 1974. Office: Sch Law Wake Forest U Winston-Salem NC 27106 Tel (919) 725-9790

PETROCELLI, MARIE FELICE, b. N.Y.C., July 8, 1921; student Columbia U., 1943-44, St. John's Sch. Commerce, 1944-47; LL.B., St. John's Law Sch., 1950. Admitted to N.Y. State bar, 1950, U.S. Dist. Ct. bar, 1954; individual practice law, N.Y.C., 1952—. Chairperson ann. fund drive com. St. John's Law Sch. Alumni, 1950. Mem. Bklyn., Am., N.Y. State bar assns., Catholic Lawyers Guild, N.Y. County Lawyers, Plantiff Trial Lawyers Assn., Internat. Poetry Soc. Home: 965-39th St Brooklyn NY 11219 Office: 965 39th St Brooklyn NY 11219 Tel (212) 854-5957

PETROFF, ERNEST ALEXANDER, b. Knoxville, Tenn., Sept. 1, 1945; B.S., U. Tenn., 1966, J.D., 1970. Admitted to Tenn. bar, 1970; asso. firm Baker, Worthington, Crossley & Stansberry, Huntsville, Tenn., 1970-71, partner, 1972—; asst. prof. Tenn. Tech. U., 1975-76. Mem. Am., Tenn. Bar assns., Scott County C. of C. (dir. 1972—). Contbr. articles to profl. jours. Home: PO Box 116 Huntsville TN 37756 Office: 3 Courthouse Sq Huntsville TN 37756 Tel (615) 663-2321

PETRUCELLY, JEFFREY PAUL, b. N.Y.C., Feb. 4, 1946; B.S., Coll. City N.Y., 1967; J.D., Harvard, 1972. Admitted to Mass. bar, 1972; atty. Urban Planning Aid, Cambridge, Mass., 1972-73, Neighborhood Legal Services, Lynn, Mass., 1974-75; partner firm Petrucelly and Stolzberg, Cambridge, 1976—. Mem. Mass. Bar Assn., ACLU, Mass. Lawyers Guild. Recipient Thomas Leskes award in civil rights—civil liberties Coll. City N.Y., 1967. Office: 189 Cambridge St Cambridge MA 02141 Tel (617) 661-2910

PETTAY, LEE, b. Kokomo, Ind., Mar. 8, 1945; B.A., Baldwin Wallace Coll., 1967; J.D., Ind. U., 1970. Admitted to Ind. bar, 1970, Calif. bar, 1975; asso. firm McNutt, Hurt & Blue, Martinsville, Ind., 1970-72; individual practice law, Bloomington, Ind., 1972—; dep. prosecutor Monroe County, Ind., 1972-74; city ct. judge Bloomington, Ind., 1976—. Mem. Am., Ind., Calif., Monroe County bar assns., Ind. Municipal and City Judges Assn. (pres. 1976—), Ind. Judicial Center (past bd. advisors), Am. Trial Lawyers Assn., Northside Exchange Club (bd. dirs. 1975—), Phi Alpha Delta. Home: 2441 Spicewood Ln Bloomington IN 47401 Office: 113 S College Ave Bloomington IN 47401 Tel (812) 332-3342

PETTIJOHN, BRUCE ANTHONY, b. East Orange, N.J., Mar. 1, 1920; B.S.S., Georgetown U., 1941; J.D., Fordham U., 1943; LL.M. cum laude, N.Y. U., 1951, J.S.D., 1961. Admitted to N.Y. State bar, 1943, U.S. Dist. Ct. bar for So. Dist. N.Y., 1943, U.S. Supreme Ct. bar, 1950; asso. firm Sporborg & Connolly, Port Chester, N.Y., 1945-46; partner firm Pettijohn & Pettijohn. Slingerlands, N.Y., 1946-58, sr. partner, 1948-58, counsel, 1958—; asst. atty. N.Y. State Tax Commn., 1952-53; asst. trial counsel N.Y. State Ins. Fund, 1953-58; mem. staff N.Y. State Atty. Gen.'s Office, 1958—. Recreation commr. Town of Harrison (N.Y.), 1941-58. Mem. Civil Service Attys. Bar Assn. (dir. 1972—). Home: 12 Carstead Dr Slingerlands NY 12159 Tel (518) 474-8797

PETTINE, RAYMOND JAMES, b. Providence, July 6, 1912; student Providence Coll., 1931-34; LL.B., Boston U., 1937, LL.M., 1940; LL.D., Our Lady of Porvidence Seminary, 1967. Admitted to R.I. bar, 1940, also U.S. Supreme Ct., U.S. Ct. Mil. Appeals, ICC; practiced in Providence, 1946-61; spl. counsel atty. gen. Dept. State R.I., 1948-52; asst. atty. gen. 1952-61; U.S. atty. dist. R.I., Providence, 1961-66; U.S. Dist. Court judge for R.I., 1966—, now chief judge. Vice pres., treas. Italian Collection and Reading Room Com., 1957-58; mem. R.I. Commn. to Encourage Morality in Youth, 1958-60, R.I. Family Ct. Study Commn., 1956-57. Bd. dirs., exec. com. R.I. Philharmonic Orch. Mem. R.I. Bar Assn., Italian-Am. Vets., Rrs. Officers Assn. R.I. (past pres.), NCCJ (dir.), Amvets (past judge adv. R.I.), Order Sons Italy. Home: 400 Angell St Providence RI 02906 Office: Federal Bldg Providence RI 02903*

PETTIS, RONALD EUGENE, b. Williston, N.D., Sept. 5, 1939; B.A., U. Idaho, 1961; J.D., U. Calif., Berkeley, 1969. Admitted to Calif. bar, 1970; law clk., research atty. Calif. State 4th Dist. Ct. Appeals, San Bernardino, 1969-71; asso. firm Hennigan, Butterwick & Clepper, Riverside, Calif., 1971-73; partner, 1973—. Mem. Riverside Redevel. Agy., 1972-75, chmn., 1975; bd. dirs. Riverside Press Council, 1974-76. Mem. State Bar Calif., Am., Calif., Orange County, Los Angeles County trial lawyers assns., Am. Bar Assn. Office: 4000 10th St Riverside CA 92501 Tel (714) 686-3092

PETTIT, ROGER L., b. Winfield, Kans., Dec. 14, 1946; A.B., Washburn U., 1968; J.D., Marquette Law Sch., 1974. Admitted to Wis. bar, 1974; partner firm Richmond and Pettit, Milw., 1974; asso. firm Silverstein, Hausmann and McNally, Milw., 1974-75; asso. firm Hausmann, McNally & Hupy, Milw., 1976—; instr. in law Spencerian Coll., Milw., 1974-75. Mem. Milw. County, Milw. Jr., Am., Wis. bar assns. Office: 633 W Wisconsin Ave Suite 1815 Milwaukee WI 53203 Tel (414) 271-5300

PEUGH, JAMES EDWARD, b. Rome, Ga., June 16, 1940; B.B.A., Ga. State U., 1964; LL.B. magna cum laude, Walter F. George Sch., Mercer U., 1967. Admitted to U.S. Ct. Appeals 5th Circuit bar, 1968, Ga. Supreme Ct. bar, 1969, U.S. Supreme Ct. bar; asso. firm Harris, Russell & Watkins, Macon, Ga., 1967; partner firm Gardner & Peugh, Milledgeville, Ga., 1968-72; individual practice law, Milledgeville, 1972-75; partner firm Peugh & Bradley, Milledgeville, 1975—. Mem. Am., Ga., Ocmulgee bar assns., Am. Judicature Soc., Ga. Assn. Plaintiffs Trial Attys. (asso. editor of newsletter). Editor in chief: Mercer Law Review, 19—. Office: PO Box 366 Sanford Bldg Milledgeville GA 31061 Tel (912) 452-3587

PEVEN, CHARLES LEON, b. Chgo., Mar. 18, 1934; B.A., Mich. State U., 1955; LL.B., U. Mich., 1958. Admitted to Calif. bar, 1959; dep. dist. atty. Los Angeles County, 1959-71; individual practice law, Van Nuys, Calif., 1971—. Mem. Los Angeles County, San Fernando Valley bar assns., San Fernando Valley Criminal Bar Assn. (pres. 1972-73). Office: 14407 Hamlin St Van Nuys CA 91401 Tel (213) 786-1050

PFAELZER, MORRIS, b. Phila., Apr. 12, 1913; A.B., Harvard, 1935; LL.B., U. Pa., 1938. Admitted to Pa. bar, 1939, Calif. bar, 1946, U.S. Supreme Ct. bar, 1946; partner firm Gray, Binkley, & Pfaelzer, Los Angeles, 1950-65; partner firm Pfaelzer, Robertson, Armstrong & Woodard, Los Angeles, 1966-67, partner firm Kadison, Pfaelzer, Woodard, Quinn & Rossi, Los Angeles, 1967—; lectr. law U. So. Calif., 1960-64, chmn. bd. councillors law center, 1976. Pres. Los Angeles County Bar Found., 1974-76. Mem. Am., Los Angeles County (trustee 1958-60), Pa., Phila. bar assns. Home: 230 N Carmelina Ave Los Angeles CA 90049 Office: 611 W 6th St Los Angeles CA 90017 Tel (213) 626-1251

PFALTZ, HUGO MENZEL, JR., b. Newark, Sept. 23, 1931; B.A., Hamilton Coll., 1953; LL.M., Harvard, 1960; LL.M. in Taxation, N.Y. U., 1964. Admitted to N.J. bar, 1960, Fed. Dist. Ct. N.J., 1960; asso. firm McCarter & English, Newark, 1960-62; asso. firm Bourne and Noll, Profl. Assn., Summit, N.J., 1962-74; individual practice law, Summit and Chatham, N.J., 1974—; mem. N.J. Gen. Assembly, 1966-72; del. N.J. Constl. Conv., 1966; mem. N.J. Gov's. Tax Policy Com., 1970-72. Trustee Bonnie Brae Farm for Boys, Millington, N.J., 1966-76, pres., 1973-76. Mem. Am., Essex County (N.J.), Summit (pres. 1976-77), Union County (N.J.) (trustee 1973-76), N.J. State (chmn. sect. banking law 1973-74) bar assns., Phi Beta Kappa. Editor N.J. Law Jour., 1967—. Home: 118 Prospect St Summit NJ 07901 Office: 382 Springfield Ave Summit NJ 07901 Tel (201) 273-1974

PFEFFER, MICHAEL STEPHEN, b. Maysville, Ky., May 6, 1947; B.S., Ohio State U., 1969; J.D., U. Cin., 1973. Admitted to Ohio bar, 1973; partner firm Zachman, Pfeffer & Corbin, Ripley, Ohio, 1977—; solicitor Village of Russellville, 1974-77. Mem. Ohio State, Brown County bar assns. Home: Rural Route #1 Ripley OH 45167 Office: 104 1/2 Main St Ripley OH 45167 Tel (513) 392-1142

PFEFFER, PHILIP EMMETT, b. New Orleans, Apr. 1, 1910; B.A., La. State U., 1931. Admitted to La. bar, 1946, U.S. Supreme Ct. bar, 1960; partner firm Morgan & Pfeffer, 1946-50; individual practice law, 1950-70; partner firm Pfeffer, Prieto & Williams, Covington, La., 1970—. Mem. La., St. Tammany Parish, Covington bar assns. Home: 211 S Jackson St Covington LA 70433 Office: 416 E Gibson St Covington LA 70433 Tel (504) 892-1478

PFEUFFER, ROBERT TUG, b. New Braunfels, Tex., May 15, 1937; B.A., Tex. Agrl. and Mech. U., 1959; J.D., U. Tex., 1962; postgrad. Nat. Coll. of State Judiciary, 1973, 76, Am. Acad. of Jud. Edn., 1974, Tex. Coll. of Judiciary, 1974. Admitted to Tex. bar, 1962, U.S. Supreme Ct. bar, 1964; asst. staff JAG, USAF AFB, Del., 1962-65; asso. firm Schleyer, Bartram, Reagan & Burrus, New Braunfels, 1965-70; partner firm Bartram, Reagan, Burrus & Pfeuffer, New Braunfels, 1970-73; judge 207th Dist. Ct. of Tex., New Braunfels, 1973—. Pres. New Braunfels Noon Lions Club, 1973-74; chmn. Am. Revolution Bicentennial Commn., New Braunfels, 1975-76; chmn. First United Methodist Ch. of New Braunfels, 1968; chmn. Comal County Democratic Exec. Com., 1966-73; pres. Comal County Fair Assn. Tex., 1976-77. Mem. Comal County Bar Assn. (pres. 1972), State Bar Tex. (mem. council gen. practice sect. 1970-72), Delta Theta Phi. Home: Star Route 2 Box 879 Huaco Springs Ranch New Braunfels TX 78130 Office: 206 Comal County Ct House New Braunfels TX 78130 Tel (512) 625-0881

PHARIS, FRANCIS JEAN, b. Camden, Ark., Mar. 31, 1923; B.A., La. Coll., 1946; J.D., La. State U., 1949. Admitted to La. bar, 1949; individual practice law, Pineville, La., 1949-57; dist. atty. Rapides Parish, La., 1957-65; partner firm Pharis & Pharis, Alexandria, La., 1966—. Mem. Am., La., Alexandria bar assns. Home: 100 Washington St Pineville LA 71360 Office: 831 DeSoto St Alexandria LA 71301 Tel (318) 445-8266

PHEBUS, JOSEPH WILLIAM, b. Champaign, Ill., Feb. 13, 1940; B.S. in Metal Engring., U. Ill., 1962, J.D., 1968. Admitted to Ill. bar, 1968, U.S. Supreme Ct. bar, 1975; asso. firm Phillips, Phebus, Tummelson & Bryan, Urbana, Ill., 1968-71, partner firm, 1971—; engr. Caterpillar Tractor Co., Peoria, Ill., 1965; dir., v.p., sec. Cable Communications, Inc., 1972—; dir., sec. Champaign Urbana Communications, Inc., 1972—; alderman, Urbana, 1969-71, Mayor Pro Tem, 1971. Mem. Ill. State, Champaign County bar assns., Ill. Trial Lawyers Assn., Assn. of Trial Lawyers of Am., Order of the Coif. Home: #3 Persimmon Circle Urbana IL 61801 Office: 136 W Main St Urbana IL 61801 Tel (217) 367-1144

PHELAN, JOHN JAMES, III, b. San Antonio, Feb. 16, 1942; A.B., Holy Cross Coll., 1963; J.D., Fordham U., 1966. Admitted to N.Y. State bar, 1966; trial atty. and br. chief SEC, N.Y.C., 1966-69; mem. firm Wofsey, Certilman, Haft, Snow & Becker, N.Y.C., 1968-76, Lumbard and Phelan, N.Y.C., 1977—. Trustee, Village of Ardsley (N.Y.), 1977—. Mem. Am., N.Y. State bar assns. Home: 53 Prospect Ave Ardsley NY 10502 Office: One State St Plaza New York City NY 10004 Tel (212) 422-6660

PHELAN, MARILYN ELIZABETH, b. Lubbock, Tex., July 12, 1938; B.A. with honors, Tex. Tech. U., 1959, M.B.A., 1967, D.B.A., 1971; J.D. with honors, U. Tex., 1972. Admitted to Tex. bar, 1962; individual practice law, Levelland, 1962-71; asso. prof. bus. adminstrn. Tex. Tech Univ., Lubbock, 1972-74, asso. prof. law, asso. dean Grad. Sch., 1974—. Mem. Am., Tex. bar assns., Am. Inst. C.P.A.'s, Tex. Soc. C.P.A.'s, Am. Assn. Atty. C.P.A.'s. Recipient Outstanding D.B.A. award, bus. adminstrn. faculty Tex. Tech U., 1970, Outstanding Prof. award, bus. adminstrn. Stud. Council, 1973, Am. Jurisprudence award Bancroft-Whitney, 1961; Author: Reporting Requirements for Exempt Orgns., 1976; contbr. articles to Jour. Taxation, Taxation for Lawyers, Taxation for Accountants, Taxes. Home: 1929 S Ave H Levelland TX 79336 Office: Sch Law Tex Tech U Lubbock TX 79409 Tel (806) 742-6273

PHELPS, ELBRIDGE DUFF, b. Winterset, Iowa, Dec. 15, 1911; A.B. cum laude, Jamestown Coll., 1934; J.D., U. Mich., 1937, S.J.D., 1939. Admitted to N.D. bar, 1937, Ohio bar, 1942, Okla. bar, 1952; asst. prof. bus. law U. Ill., Urbana, 1938-39; asst. prof. law U.S.D., Vermillion, 1939-40, Western Reserve U., Cleve., 1940-42; asso. firm Burgess, Fulton & Fullmer, Cleve., 1942-46; prof. law U. Okla., Norman, 1946—, David Ross Boyd prof. law, 1974—. Mem. Okla. Bar Assn., Order of the Coif. Contbr. articles in field to legal jours. Home: 512 S Lahoma St Norman OK 73069 Office: Room 324 300 Timberdell Rd Norman OK 73019 Tel (405) 325-3911

PHELPS, JAMES BARTON, b. Topeka, Apr. 27, 1917; A.B., U. Chgo., 1937; J.D., Harvard, 1940. Admitted to Calif. bar, 1940; asso. firm Morrison, Hohfeld, Foerster, Shuman & Clark, San Francisco, 1940-50; dep. dist. atty., San Francisco, 1950-52; partner firm Pelton, Gunther & Phelps, San Francisco, 1952-54; partner firm Bledsoe, Smith, Cathcart, Johnson & Phelps, San Francisco, 1954-62, Ropers, Majeski & Phelps, 1962-70; judge Municipal Ct., Palo Alto, Calif., 1970-72, Superior Ct. Santa Clara County, San Jose, 1972—. Mem. San Francisco Bar Assn. (bd. govs. 1950-52), Assn. Def. Counsel (pres. 1969-70). Office: 191 N 1st St San Jose CA 95113 Tel (408) 299-1121

PHELPS, JAMES HOWARD, b. Pocatello, Idaho, Aug. 7, 1947; student Willamette U., 1965-67; B.A., U. Oreg., 1969, J.D., 1972. Admitted to Oreg. bar, 1972; asso. firm John T. Chinnock, Madras, Oreg., 1972-74; partner firm Chinnock & Phelps, Madras, 1974-75; prin. firm James H. Phelps, Madras, 1976—; municipal judge City of Madras, 1975—. Mem. Central Oreg. Bar Assn. (pres. 1975). Office: 850 S 5th St Madras OR 97741 Tel (503) 475-2241

PHELPS, JAMES R., b. East Bernstadt, Ky., Dec. 1, 1938; A.B. with honors, U. Cin., 1960, LL.B., 1962. Admitted to Ohio bar, 1962, Ky. bar, 1965, D.C. bar, 1967, Ill. bar, 1970; trial atty. FDA, Washington, 1965-67; asst. U.S. atty. for D.C., 1967-69; asso. firm Burditt & Calkins, Chgo., 1969-70, partner, 1971-77; v.p., gen. counsel G.D. Searle & Co., Skokie, Ill., 1977—. Mem. Wheaton (Ill.) Zoning Bd., 1971-74; mem. Ill. Endangered Species Protection Bd., 1974-76. Mem. Am. (food drug and cosmetic law com., drug law subcom., asso. editor Law Notes), Ill., Ky., Fed. (food drug and cosmetic law com.), D.C. bar assns. Home: 43 Crescent Dr Glencoe IL 60020 Office: Box 1045 Skokie IL 60076 Tel (312) 982-4700

PHELPS, LOWELL DEAN, b. Chgo., July 31, 1905; B.A., U. Iowa, 1927, J.D., 1929. Admitted to Iowa bar, 1929; mem. firm Phelps & Vollertsen, Davenport, Iowa, 1935-63; judge Iowa Dist. Ct., 7th Jud. Dist., 1963—. Mem. Scott County (Iowa), State of Iowa bar assns., Iowa Dist. Ct. Judges Assn., Am. Judicature Soc. Home: 3111 Carey Ave Davenport IA 52803 Office: Courthouse 4th and Ripley Sts Davenport IA 52801 Tel (319) 326-8608

PHELPS, RICHARD JOHN, b. Centuria, Wis., Aug. 10, 1946; B.A., U. Wis., 1968, J.D., 1971. Admitted to Wis. bar, 1971; supr., staff atty. Dane County Juvenile Defender Program, Madison, Wis., 1971-73; individual practice law, Madison, 1974; exec. sec. Gov.'s Advocacy Com. for Children and Youth, Madison, 1974-75; founder, dir. Youth Policy and Law Center, Madison, 1976—; chairperson Coalition for the Revision of Wis. Children's Code, Madison, 1975-76; chmn. subcom. on children's rights Wis. Civil Liberties Union, Madison, 1976—. Mem. advisory bd. Briarpatch Runaway Center, Madison, 1970-73, Dane County Shelter Home, Madison, 1972-73. Mem. Wis. Civil Liberties Union, Wis. Bar Assn. Office: Youth Policy and Law Center 204 S Hamilton Madison WI 53703 Tel (608) 263-5533

PHELPS, W. ROBERT, JR., b. Lynchburg, Va., Nov. 30, 1924; grad. William and Mary Coll., 1951, Law Sch., 1952; grad. Jud. Coll. U. Nev., 1975, New Eng. Center for Continuing Edn., Criminal Law and Practice, 1976; Admitted to Va. bar, 1952; asst. to prosecutor Warwick, Va., 1952; individual practice law, Newport News, Va., 1952-63; partner firm Phelps & Atkinson, Newport News, 1963-69; judge Municipal Ct., Newport News, 1969-73; chief judge Va. Dist. Ct., 7th Jud. Dist., 1973—. Active U.S. Jaycees, 1952-60, Ruritan, Newport News, 1952—. Mem. Va. State Bar, Va., Am. trial lawyers assns., Va. Assn. Judges, Va. Dist. Judges Conf., William and Mary Alumnae (pres. 1964). Named Boss of Year Denbigh (Va.) Day Sch., 1968, Hon. Mayor City of Denbigh, 1971. Office: 2501 Huntington Ave Newport News VA 23607 Tel (804) 247-8811

PHILBIN, MICHAEL JAMES, b. Akron, Ohio, Mar. 10, 1946; B.A., U. Notre Dame, 1968; J.D., Vanderbilt U., 1971. Admitted to Tenn. bar, 1971; asso. firm Glasgow, Adams, Taylor & Philbin, Nashville, 1971-74, partner, 1974—. Bd. dirs. St. Mary's Orphanage, Nashville, 1977—. Mem. Nashville, Tenn., Am. bar assns., Young Lawyers Assn. (pres. Nashville sect. 1975-76), Tenn. Def. Lawyers Assn. Office: 300 James Robertson Pkwy Nashville TN 37201 Tel (615) 244-5361

PHILLIPPE, DONALD RAY, b. Cutler, Ind., Apr. 9, 1933; B.S.C., Internat. Business Coll., Ft. Wayne, Ind., 1954; B.S., Ball State U., 1959; J.D., Ind. U., 1963. Admitted to Ind. bar, 1964, U.S. Supreme Ct. bar, 1969; individual practice law, Anderson City, Ind., 1964—; judge Anderson City Ct., 1972—. Mem. Am., Ind., Madison County, Fed. bar assns., Assn. Am. Trial Lawyers. Home: 202 Mill Stream Ln Anderson IN 46011 Office: 340 W 11th St Anderson IN 46016 Tel (317) 643-0378

PHILLIPS, ANTHONY FRANCIS, b. Hartford, Conn., May 18, 1937; B.A., U. Conn., 1959; J.D., Cornell U., 1962. Admitted to N.Y. bar, 1964, U.S. Supreme Ct. bar, 1972; asso. firm Willkie Farr & Gallagher, N.Y.C., 1963-69, partner, 1969—. Mem. Am., N.Y.C., N.Y. State, N.Y. County bar assns., Phi Beta Kappa. Home: 21 Greenfield Ave Bronxville NY 10708 Office: 1 Chase Manhattan Plaza Willkie Farr & Gallagher New York City NY 10005 Tel (212) 248-1000

PHILLIPS, CARL EUGENE, b. Tifton, Ga., Apr. 28, 1917; student Ind. U. Law Sch., 1952-55, U. Ga., 1934-35; LL.B., Cumberland U., 1936; LL.B. magna cum laude, Woodrow Wilson U., 1961. Admitted to Ga. bar, 1961; commd. chief warrant officer JAGC, U.S. Army, 1946; advanced through grades to maj., 1959; ETO, 1946-49, Korea, 1950-52, Europe, 1956-59; v.p. Peabody Mfg. Co., West Point, Ga., 1972—. Chmn. United Fund, West Point; pres. West Point PTA. Mem. Ga. Bar Assn. Home: 100 Briarcliff Rd West Point GA 31833 Office: Peabody Rd West Point GA 31833 Tel (404) 645-2901

PHILLIPS, CECIL MARVIN, b. Fayette, Mo., July 19, 1946; B.A. in History with honors, U. Mo., 1968; J.D., U. Mich., 1971. Admitted to Ga. bar, 1971; since practiced in Atlanta, assoc. firm Alston, Miller & Gaines, 1971-76, partner, 1976—; prof. Law Wodrow Wilson Coll., 1972—. Mem. Am., Ga., Atlanta Bar Assns. Named one of 10 Outstanding Young People of Atlanta, 1974. Home: 865 Wesley Dr NW Atlanta GA 30305 Office: 1200 C & S Nat Bank Bldg Atlanta GA 30303 Tel (404) 588-0300

PHILLIPS, CHARLES GORHAM, b. Glen Ridge, N.J., Apr. 27, 1921; A.B., Williams Coll., 1943; J.D., Harvard, 1948. Admitted to N.Y. bar, 1949; asso. firm Cadwalader, Wickersham & Taft, N.Y.C., 1948-51; asso. firm Dewey, Ballantine, Bushby, Palmer & Wood, N.Y.C., 1951-57, partner, 1958—. Trustee Montclair (N.J.) Kimberley Acad., 1967-76, Union Congl. Ch., Montclair, 1970-74, Montclair Art Mus., 1971-76. Mem. Am., N.Y. State (chmn. sect. on banking, corp. and bus. law 1976—) bar assns., N.Y. County Lawyers Assn. (chmn. com. on corp. law 1964-67), Assn Bar City N.Y. Home: 25 Highland Ave Montclair NJ 07042 Office: 140 Broadway New York City NY 10005 Tel (212) 344-8000

PHILLIPS, DANIEL MILLER, b. Cleve., Mar. 21, 1933; student Conn. Wesleyan U., 1951-53; B.Sc., Ohio State U., 1958, LL.B., 1961. Admitted to Ohio bar, 1961; asso. firm Robison, Cenphey & O'Connell, Toledo, 1961-67, partner, 1967—. Pres. Toldeo Florence Crittenton Soc., 1971-73. Mem. Ohio, Toledo (1st v.p. 1977, exec. com.), Toledo Jr. (pres. 1972) bar assns., Ohio Def. Assn. (exec. com., pres. 1972), Fedn. Ins. Counsel, Def. Research Inst., Am. Judicature Soc. Office: 425 Libbey Owens Ford Bldg Toledo OH 43624 Tel (419) 255-3100

PHILLIPS, DAYTON EDWARD, b. Roan Mountain, Tenn., Mar. 29, 1910; LL.B., Nat. U., 1936; J.D., George Washington U., 1936. Admitted to Tenn. bar, 1935; county atty. Carter County (Tenn.), 1938-42; dist. atty. 1st Jud. Circuit of Tenn., 1942-46; mem. 80th-81st Congresses from 1st Dist. Tenn., 1946-50; judge 1st Chancery Div. Tenn., Johnson City, 1952—. Mem. Tenn. Bar Assn., Tenn. Jud. Conf. Home: 1410 Burgie St Elizabethton TN 37643 Office: Ash St Ct House Johnson City TN 37601 Tel (615) 926-2551

PHILLIPS, DONALD DALE, b. Goodland, Kans., Mar. 12, 1911; LL.B., George Washington U., 1935, J.D., 1968. Admitted to Kans. bar, 1935; pvt. practice, Colby, Kans., 1936-43; atty. City of Colby, Kans., 1940-43; U.S. magistrate, Colby, 1969—. Chmn. Northwest Kans. Ednl. Planning Commn. to establish Colby Community Coll.; mem. Colby Coll. Adv. Bd., Colby; mayor City of Colby, 1964-68. Mem. U.S. Magistrates Assn., Northwest Kans., Kans. bar assns. Office: Box 806 Colby KS 67701 Tel (913) 462-2112

PHILLIPS, DONALD LAWRENCE, b. Meadville, Pa., Aug. 13, 1935; A.B., Oberlin Coll., 1957; J.D., U. Mich., 1960. Admitted to Pa. bar, 1961; partner firm Phillips & Galanter, Pitts., 1969—. Office: 801 Lawyers Bldg Pittsburgh PA 15219 Tel (412) 281-1977

PHILLIPS, DOUGLAS CLIFFORD, b. Park City, Utah, Jan. 1, 1922; J.D., Southwestern U., 1949. Admitted to Calif. bar, 1954, U.S. Supreme Ct. bar, 1967; individual practice law, Los Angeles, 1954—; arbitrator Am. Arbitration Assn., 1963—; judge pro tem Inglewood (Calif.) Municipal Ct., 1972—; spl. agt. FBI, 1950-54. High councilor Inglewood stake Ch. of Jesus Christ of Latter Day Saints, 1964-74. Mem. Los Angeles County Bar Assn. (chmn. constl. rights com., 1967-68), Westchester (Calif.) C. of C. (past pres.), Los Angeles County Trial Lawyers Assn. Recipient citation Los Angeles City Council, 1963. Home: 1069 Camino Magenta Thousand Oaks CA 91360 Office: 5710 W Manchester Ave Suite 201 Los Angeles CA 90045 Tel (213) 776-5716

PHILLIPS, HARRY, b. Watertown, Tenn., July 28, 1909; A.B., Cumberland U., 1932, LL.B., 1933, LL.D., 1951; postgrad. George Washington U. Law Sch., 1944-45. Admitted to Tenn. bar, 1933; practiced in Watertown, 1933-37, Nashville, 1950-63; asst. atty. gen. State of Tenn., 1937-43, 46-50; served to lt. comdr. Judge Adv. Gen.'s Corps, USN, 1944-46; judge U.S. Ct. Appeals, 6th Circuit, 1963—, chief judge, 1969—; exec. sec. Tenn. Code Commn., 1953-63; mem. Tenn. Ho. of Reps., 1935-37. Mem. Am., Tenn. (award of merit 1961), Nashville, Fed. bar assns., Am. Judicature Soc. Author: Phillips Family History, 1935; Phillips Pritchard on Wills and Administration of Estates, 1955; (with others) History of the Sixth Circuit, 1976. Home: 2809 Wimbledon Rd Nashville TN 37215 Office: 648 US Courthouse Nashville TN 37203 Tel (615) 749-5447

PHILLIPS, HENRY W., b. Peru, Ill., June 2, 1923; grad. LaSalle-Peru-Oglesby (Ill.) Jr. Coll., 1943; J.D., U. Chgo., 1949. Admitted to Ill. bar, 1949; partner firm Hanley, Phillips, Traub & Ahlemeyer, and predecessors, 1949-75; individual practice law, Fairbury, Ill., 1976—. Pres., Dominy Meml. Library Bd., Fairbury; pres. Corn Belt Library System, Bloomington, Ill., 1971-72; bd. dirs. ARC. Mem. Am., Ill. (bd. govs. 1975—), Livingston County (pres. 1972) bar assns. Home and Office: Box 11 Fairbury IL 61739 Tel (815) 692-4336

PHILLIPS, JOHN ALLEN, II, b. Caddo, Okla., Oct. 27, 1911; B.A., Southeastern State U., Durant, Okla., 1934; LL.B., U. Okla., 1937. Partner firm Phillips & Stallings, Durant; city atty. City of Durant, 1953—. Mem. Okla. Bar Assn. Office: 132 N Third St Durant OK 74701 Tel (405) 924-2997

PHILLIPS, JOHN DAVISSON, b. Clarksburg, W. Va., Aug. 21, 1906; A.B., W.Va. U., 1928, LL.B., 1930; postgrad (Rhodes scholar), Oxford (Eng.) U., 1930-32. Admitted to W.Va. bar, 1932; asst. pros. atty. Ohio County, W. Va., 1937-40; partner firm Phillips, Holden, Marshall & Gardill and predecessor firms, Wheeling, W. Va., 1940—; solicitor City of Wheeling, 1942-47; mem. W. Va. State Bd. Law Examiners, 1961-75. Mem. Wheeling Park Commn., 1957—. Fellow Am. Bar Found.; mem. Am., W. Va. (pres. 1955), Ohio County bar assns., Am. Law Inst., Am. Judicature Soc. Home: Forest Hills Wheeling WV 26003 Office: 607 Bd Trade Bldg Wheeling WV 26003 Tel (304) 232-6810

PHILLIPS, JOHN MILTON, b. Kansas City, Mo., Dec. 16, 1915; A.B., U. Kans., 1937; LL.B., Harvard, 1940. Admitted to Mo. bar, 1940, U.S. Supreme Ct. bar, 1945; asso. firm Stinson, Mag, Thomson, McEvers & Fizzell, Kansas City, Mo., 1940-45, partner, 1945—; tchr. Am. Inst. Banking. Pres., Citizens Assn., 1952, Kansas City Philharmonic Assn., 1965-67; v.p. Am. Symphony Orch. League, 1965-67; bd. dirs. Greater Kansas City chpt. ARC, 1971—, chmn. legal com., 1975—; mem. soc. fellows W.R. Nelson Art Gallery. Mem. Mo. (lectr.), Am., Internat., Kansas City bar assns. Home: 311 W 99th St Kansas City MO 64114 Office: 2100 Tenmain Center Kansas City MO 64105 Tel (816) 842-8600

PHILLIPS, JOHN TAYLOR, b. Greenville, S.C., Aug. 20, 1923; A.B., Glenville State Coll., 1952; J.D., Mercer U., 1955. Admitted to Ga. bar, 1954, U.S. 5th Circuit Ct. Appeals bar, 1955, U.S. Supreme Ct. bar, 1969; practiced in Macon, Ga., 1954-64; judge State Ct. of Bibb County (Ga.), 1964—; mem. Ga. Ho. of Reps., 1959-63, Ga. Senate, 1963-64; dir. trial practice and procedure Mercer U., 1968—. Dist. lay leader United Methodist Ch., Macon dist. Mem. Macon, Ga., Am. bar assns., Jud. Council, Ga. Trial Judges Assn. (pres. 1973). Home: 1735 Winston Dr Macon GA 31206 Office: PO Box 5086 Macon GA 31208 Tel (912) 745-6871

PHILLIPS, LEONARD, b. Cin., Feb. 25, 1924; B.S., Duke U., 1945; M. Litt., U. Pitts., 1952; J.D., San Francisco Law Sch., 1962. Chemist, Dow Chem. Co., Pitts., 1949-56; chief patent engr. U. Calif. Lawrence Radiation Lab., Livermore, 1956-62; admitted to Calif. bar, 1963, U.S. Supreme Ct. bar, 1968; partner firms Fryer, Tjensvold, Phillips & Lempio, San Francisco, 1962-74, Phillips, Moore, Weissenberger, Lempio & Majestic, San Francisco, 1974—. Mem. Am. Bar Assn., Am. Chem. Soc. Office: 100 Pine St Suite 2900 San Francisco CA 94111 Tel (415) 421-2674

PHILLIPS, LLOYD MELVIN, b. Clearwater, Fla., Oct. 31, 1918; B.S., B.A., LL.B., U. Fla., 1943. Admitted to Fla. bar, 1943; individual practice law, Clearwater, 1943-59; partner firm Phillips, McFarland, Gould, Wilhelm & Wagstaff, Clearwater, 1959—; county pros. atty., 1948-53; mem. Fla. Bar Grievance Com. 6th Jud. Circuit, 1968-72, jud. nominating com., 1972-76; dir. Barnett Bank of Clearwater, N.A.; pres. Clearwater YMCA, 1965. Mem. Clearwater (pres. 1969-70), Fla., Am. bar assns., Clearwater Jaycees (pres. 1950-51). Recipient Bilgore award (Clearwater Outstanding Citizen), 1963. Home: 637 Richmond St Dunedin FL 33528 Office: 311 S Missouri Ave Clearwater FL 33516 Tel (813) 461-1111

PHILLIPS, MAURICE, b. Liverpool, Eng., June 19, 1921; B.A., N.Y. U., 1949, LL.B., 1952, Admitted to N.Y. bar, 953, Fla. bar, 1976; individual practice law, Pearl River, N.Y., 1953-59, Spring Valley, N.Y., 1959-68; partner firm Brent, Phillips, Darvoff & Davis, Nanuet, N.Y., 1969—; dir. Atlantic Micro-Film Corp., 1969-73. Chmn. community adv. bd. sewer disposal Orangetown, N.Y., 1954-56. Mem. N.Y. State, Rockland County bar assns. Office: 20 Old Turnpike Rd Nanuet NY 10954 Tel (914) 623-2800

PHILLIPS, MICHAEL MANTHEO, b. Dallas, July 12, 1945; P.B.A., U. Tex., 1968, J.D., 1969. Admitted to Tex. bar, 1969; asst. dist. atty. Harris County (Tex.), 1970-71; individual practice law, Angleton, Tex., 1971—. Office: 515 N Velasco St Angleton TX 77515 Tel (713) 849-4382

PHILLIPS, MORRIS CLAYTON, JR., b. Lexington, Miss., Aug. 17, 1944; B.B.A., U. Miss., 1966; J.D., Cumberland Sch. Law, Samford U., 1970. Admitted to Miss. bar, 1971; partner firm Wright & Phillips, Carthage, Miss., 1974—. Co-chmn. Leake County Democratic Party, 1976—. Mem. Am., Leake County (sec.-treas. 1975—), Miss. (commr. 1974-76) bar assns., Phi Alpha Delta. Recipient Am. Jurisprudence award, 1969. Home: Route 3 Carthage MS 39021 Office: 101 N Van Buren St Carthage MS 39051 Tel (601) 267-2231

PHILLIPS, RICHARD TAYLOR, b. Oxford, Miss., July 3, 1947; B.A., U. Miss., 1969, J.D., 1972. Admitted to Miss. bar, 1972; asso. firm Cliff Finch, Batesville, Miss., 1972-74; partner firm Smith & Phillips, Batesville, 1974—; judge Municipal Ct., Batesville, 1976—; dir. Panola County Fed. Savs. and Loan Assn. Mem. Fed., Am., Miss. State (dir. young lawyers sect. 1975—), Panola County (historian 1973, sec., treas. 1974, pres. 1976) bar assns., Miss. Trial Lawyers Assn. (bd. govs. 1976—, vice chmn. products liability com. 1976), Miss. Savs. and Loan League (mem. attys. sec.), Phi Kappa Phi, Delta Theta Phi. Contbr. articles to profl. jours. Home: 209 Watts St Batesville MS 38606 Office: 103 Bates St Batesville MS 38606 Tel (601) 563-4613

PHILLIPS, RONALD F., b. Houston, Nov. 25, 1934; B.S. in Gen. Bus., Abilene Christian U., 1955; J.D., U. Tex., 1965. Admitted to Tex. bar, 1965, Calif. bar, 1972, U.S. Supreme Ct. bar, 1975; corporate staff atty. McWood Corp. (merged with Occidental Petroleum Co.), Abilene, Tex., 1965-67; individual practice law, Abilene, 1967-70; adj. faculty Abilene Christian U., 1967-70; dean, prof. law Pepperdine U. Sch. Law, Anaheim, Calif., 1970—; mem. com. law sch. edn. State Bar Calif., 1970—. Active Little League; tchr. young people's Bible class Ch. of Christ, Garden Grove, Calif., Abilene and Midland, Tex. Mem. Am., Orange County bar assns. Recipient Abilene Christian U. Alumni Citation award, 1974; named Outstanding Educator Am., 1972, 75. Home: 21432 Pinetree Ln Huntington Beach CA 92646 Office: 1520 S Anaheim Blvd Anaheim CA 92805 Tel (714) 776-4490

PHILLIPS, THOMAS BERNARD, b. Kansas City, Mo., Sept. 8, 1941; B.S.B.A., Rockhurst Coll., 1964; J.D., U. Mo. at Kansas City, 1968, LL.M., 1971. Admitted to Mo. bar, 1968; asso. gen. counsel Old Am. Ins. Co., Kansas City, 1968—. Mem. Am., Mo., Kansas City bar assns., Kansas City Lawyers Assn., Am. Life Ins. Council. C.L.U. Home: 4810 McGee St Kansas City MO 64112 Office: 4900 Oak St Kansas City MO 64112 Tel (816) 753-4900

PHILLIPS, WILLIE ED, b. Mt. Holly, Ark., Mar. 6, 1945; B.A. in Psychology, U. Pacific, 1967; postgrad. in Indsl. Psychology, San Francisco State Coll., 1967-69; J.D., Hastings Coll. Law, U. Calif., San Francisco, 1972. Group counselor Peterson Juvenile Hall, Stockton, Calif, 1966-67; exec. dir. Hunters Point Tutorial Center, San Francisco, 1968-69; student coordinator legal edn. opportunity program Hastings Coll. Law, 1970-71; law clk. firm Zaks and Harris, San Francisco, 1970-72; admitted to Calif. bar, 1973; individual practice law, San Francisco, 1973—. Bd. dirs. B & B Exptl. Theatre, Inc., San Francisco, Westside Community Mental Health Center, Inc., San Francisco; mem. exec. com. Bay Area Engrng. Socs. Com. for Manpower Tng., Inc.; v.p. bd. dirs. Audrey L. Smith Devel. Center, Inc., San Francisco. Mem. Am., San Francisco bar assns., Charles Houston Law Club, Hastings Coll. Law Alumni Assn. Office: 105 Montgomery St San Francisco CA 94104 Tel (415) 788-8585

PHILLIPSON, DARRELL ERIC, b. Spokane, Wash., Apr. 7, 1947; B.A. with honors, Eastern Wash. State Coll., 1969; J.D., U. Calif. at Berkeley, 1972. Admitted to Wash. bar, 1972; staff atty. Bonjorni, Harpold & Fiori, Kent, Wash., 1971-75; sr. partner firm Wimer, Harpold, & Phillipson, Seattle, 1975—; judge pro tem. Fed. Way Dist. Ct., 1975, Aukeen Dist. Ct., 1975-77. Chmn. Kent Juvenile Ct. Conf. Com., 1974-77, counsel Kent Area Youth Activities, 1974—; counsel S.K. Youth Project, 1976—; mem. Fed. Way Adv. Bd. Mem. S. King County, King County, Wash. State bar assns. Home: 3502 S 268th St Kent WA 98031 Office: 677 Strander Blvd Seattle WA 98188 Tel (206) 248-2810

PHIPPS, HERBERT EDWARD, b. Baker County, Ga., Dec. 20, 1941; B.A. in Polit. Sci., Morehouse Coll., 1964; J.D., Case Western Reserve U., 1971. Admitted to Ga. bar, 1971; partner firm King, Phipps and Assos., Albany, Ga., 1971—. Pres. Albany Sickle Cell Found., Inc., 1972—; v.p. Albany Assn. for Retarded Citizens, 1975-76; v.p. Albany-Dougherty County Br. NAACP, 1977. Mem. State Bar of Ga., Am. Bar Assn., Ga. Trial Lawyers Assn., Assn. Trial Lawyers Am. Home: 1219 Augusta Dr Albany GA 31707 Office: 502 S Monroe St PO Box 3468 Albany GA 31706 Tel (912) 435-6149

PHOLERIC, KAREN JOY, b. Phila., Mar. 8, 1947; B.A., George Washington U., 1968; J.D., Villanova U., 1971. Admitted to Pa. bar, 1971, U.S. Supreme Ct. bar, 1975; staff atty., acting exec. dir. Delaware County (Pa.) Legal Assistance Assn., Media, 1971-73; individual practice law, Media, Pa., 1973-76; partner firm Borrebach, Pholeric, Tomlinson & Sullivan, Media, 1977—; asst. pub. defender Delaware County, 1973-77; mem. Delaware County Bd. Law Examiners, 1975—. Mem. Rose Valley (Pa.) Republican Party, 1975. Mem. Am., Pa., Delaware County bar assns. Office: 201 N Jackson St Media PA 19063 Tel (215) 565-6100

PIAZZA, FRANK ANTHONY, b. N.Y.C., Aug. 24, 1909; B.S., N.Y. U., 1931, J.D., 1933. Admitted to N.Y. State bar, 1934, U.S. Supreme Ct. bar, 1955; individual practice law, N.Y.C., 1934-46; asst. corp. counsel, N.Y.C., 1946-74; lectr. Bklyn. Coll., 1953-68. Mem. Bay Ridge Lawyers Assn., Columbian Lawyers Assn. 1st Jud. Dist. Home and Office: 112 85th St Brooklyn NY 11209

PICARDINI, JOSEPH BENJAMIN, b. Buffalo, Sept. 17, 1942; B.B.A., Cleve. State U., 1966; J.D., Cleveland-Marshall Law Sch., 1970. Admitted to Ohio bar, 1971; controller Pepsi-Cola Bottling Co., Cleve., 1970-73, Phil-Mar Corp., Euclid, Ohio, 1973—. Mem. bd. pub. affairs City of Timberlake (Ohio), 1975—. Mem. Am., Ohio, Cuyahoga County bar assns. Home: 99 East Shore Trail Timberlake OH 44094 Office: 1100 E 222nd St Euclid OH 44117 Tel (216) 531-8800

PICCIONE, JOHN J., b. Chgo., Oct. 6, 1942; B.S., U. Ill., Champaign, 1964; J.D., Loyola U., 1967. Admitted to Ill. bar, 1967; asso. firms Katz, Karacic & Helmin, Chgo., 1967-68, George F. Barrett, Chgo., 1969, Garbutt & Jacobson, Chgo., 1970; individual practice law, Wheaton, Ill., 1971—. Chmn. Wheaton Nominating Com., 1975. Mem. Ill. State, Fed., DuPage, Am. bar assns. Recipient Pres. award Wheaton Jaycees, 1974. Office: 330 S Naperville Rd Wheaton IL 60187 Tel (312) 665-5700

PICCIONE, JOSEPH JAMES, b. Lafayette, La., July 23, 1916; B.A., U. Southwestern La., 1938; LL.B./J.D., Tulane U., 1940. Admitted to La. bar, 1940; individual practice law, Lafayette, 1940-66; sr. partner firm Piccione, Piccione & Wooten, Lafayette, 1966-73. Mem. Lafayette Art Assn., 1967—, Capital Improvement Commn., 1972-76; pres. Cardinal Neuman Found., 1972-74. Mem. Am., Lafayette (past pres.), 15th Jud., La. State (bd. govs. 1972-74) bar assns., Am. Trial Lawyers Assn., Am. Judicature Soc., Internat. Platform Assn., Order of Coif. Editorial bd. Tulane Law Rev., 1939-40. Office: 115 E Main St Lafayette LA 70502 Tel (318) 234-4574

PICKELL, ROBERT JOHN, b. Montclair, N.J., June 20, 1927; A.B., U. Denver, 1952, J.D., 1956. Admitted to Colo. bar, 1956, Calif. bar, 1967; partner firm Pickell & Brown, Riverside, Calif. Mem. Am., Calif., Colo., Riverside bar assns., So. Calif. Def. Counsel, Am. Bd. Trial Attys. Office: 4075 Main St Riverside CA 92501 Tel (714) 784-0551

PICKERING, HARRY EDWARD, b. Cleve., June 9, 1919; A.B., U. Mich., 1941, J.D., 1944. Admitted to Mich. bar, 1944, Ohio bar, 1945, U.S. Supreme Ct. bar, 1967; price atty. Office Price Adminstrn., 1945-46; law clk. U.S. Dist. Ct., Cleve., 1947-49, 60-62; trial atty. antitrust div. Dept. Justice, 1949-59; asst. U.S. atty. No. Dist. Ohio, 1962-71; adminstrv. law judge Bur. Hearings and Appeals, Social Security Adminstrn., HEW, Cleve., 1971—. Chmn. Mich. Alumni Acad., 1973-74; chmn. class officers council U. Mich., 1965-66. Mem. Am., Fed. (pres. Cleve. 1957-58), 6th Circuit (v.p. 1972-73, nat. council 1972—) bar assns., Bar Assn. Greater Cleve., Fed. Adminstrv. Law Judges Conf., Nat. Dist. Attys. Assn., Barristers Soc., Nat. Wildlife Fedn., Smithsonian Assos., Soc. for Historic Preservation. Recipient Distinguished Alumnus award U. Mich., 1972. Home: 492 Dover Center Rd Bay Village OH 44140 Office: 1919 Superior Bldg Cleveland OH 44114 Tel (216) 522-4917

PICKERING, JERRALD KEITH, b. Roseville, Calif., Aug. 13, 1930; B.A., U. Pacific, 1953; J.D., U. Calif., Hastings, 1957. Admitted to Calif. bar, 1957; individual practice law, Redding, Calif., 1968—. Mem. Am., Fed., Calif., Shasta County bar assns. Contbr. articles to legal jours. Home: Millville Plains Ranch Millville CA 96062 Office: 1915 Placer St Redding CA 96001 Tel (916) 241-5811

PICKETT, ROSCOE, b. Jasper, Ga., July 3, 1920; LL.D., John Marshall Law Sch., 1947. Mem. Ga. Ho. of Reps., 1942; admitted to Ga. Supreme Ct. bar, 1947, U.S. Dist. Ct. for No. Dist. Ga. bar, 1947, U.S. 5th Circuit Ct. Appeals bar, 1950, U.S. Tax Ct. bar, 1957, U.S. Supreme Ct. bar, 1957; partner firm Pickett, Pickett & Pickett, Jasper, 1947—, Atlanta, 1976. Mem. Nat. Pub. Advisory Commn. on Econ. Devel. Mem. Atlanta, Ga., Am. bar assns., Am. Assn. Trial Lawyers (v.p. 1961). Office: 2110 Fulton Nat Bank Bldg Atlanta GA 30303 Tel (404) 688-7086

PICKLE, ROBERT DOUGLAS, b. Knoxville, Tenn., May 22, 1937; A.A., Schreiner Mil. Inst., Kerrville, Tex., 1957; B.S. in Bus. Adminstrn., U. Tenn., 1959, J.D., 1961. Admitted to Tenn. bar, 1961, Mo. bar, 1964; served to capt. U.S. Army Judge Adv. Gen. Corps, 1961-63; atty. Brown Shoe Co. Inc. (now Brown Group Inc.), St. Louis, 1963-74, asst. sec., 1969-74, sec., gen. counsel, 1974—. Mem. Am., Tenn., St. Louis County bar assns., Mo. Bar, Bar Assn. of Met. St. Louis, Am. Soc. Corporate Secs., Inc. Home: 214 Topton Way Saint Louis MO 63105 Office: Corporate Offices Brown Group Inc 8400 Maryland Ave Saint Louis MO 63105 Tel (314) 997-7500

PICKUS, ALBERT PIERRE, b. Sioux City, Iowa, Aug. 10, 1931; A.B., U. Mich., 1953; J.D., Case Western Res. U., 1958. Admitted to Iowa bar, 1958, Ohio bar, 1958; partner firm Silber, Pickus & Williams, and predecessors, Cleve., 1959-74; partner firm Squire, Sanders & Dempsey, Cleve., 1974—. Mem. U. Mich. Alumni Assn. (pres. 1973-75), Bar Assn. Greater Cleve., Iowa, Ohio, Am. bar assns. Recipient Distinguished Alumni Service award U. Mich. Alumni Assn., 1972. Office: 1800 Union Commerce Bldg Cleveland OH 44115 Tel (216) 696-9200

PICOTTE, GENE ALLEN, b. Whitehall, Mont., Oct. 11, 1924; B.S.L., Northwestern U., 1948; LL.B., Mont. State U., 1949. Admitted to Mont. bar, 1950; partner, dir. Loble, Picotte & Pauly, P.C., Helena, Mont., 1950—; sec. Mont. Advisory Com. on Civil Procedure Rules, 1960-72, chmn., 1972; mem. Mont. Ho. of Reps., 1955-56. Mem. Am., Mont. (pres. 1962-63), Lewis and Clark, 1st Jud. Dist. bar assns., Mont. Unified Bar, Am. Judicature Soc., Mont., Am. trial lawyers assns. Office: PO Box 176 833 N Main St Helena MT 59601 Tel (406) 442-0070

PIEL, WILLIAM, b. N.Y.C., Nov. 28, 1909; A.B., Princeton, 1932; LL.B., Harvard, 1935. Admitted to N.Y. bar, 1936, U.S. Supreme Ct. bar, 1941; asso. firm Sullivan & Cromwell, N.Y.C., 1936-44, partner, 1945—; cons. War Dept., 1944-45. Fellow Am. Coll. Trial Lawyers; mem. Am., N.Y. State bar assns., Am. Judicature Soc., Assn. Bar City N.Y., N.Y. County Lawyers Assn. Office: Sullivan & Cromwell 48 Wall St New York City NY 10005 Tel (212) 952-8107

PIEPER, DAROLD DEAN, b. Vallejo, Calif., Dec. 30, 1944; B.A., U. Calif., Los Angeles, 1967; J.D., U. So. Calif., 1970. Admitted to Calif. bar, 1971; asso. firm Richards, Watson, Dreyfuss & Gershon, 1970-76, partner, 1976—. Vice pres. La Canada Flintridge Coordinating Council, 1976—. Mem. Am., Calif., Los Angeles County bar assns., La Canada Flintridge C. of C. (dir. 1976—). Contbr. article to law review. Office: 333 S Hope St Los Angeles CA 90071 Tel (213) 626-8484

PIERARD, BRUCE VIRGIL, b. Marshall, Minn., Nov. 22, 1907; J.D., U. Minn., 1931. Admitted to Minn. bar, 1931; claim adjuster Indemnity Ins. Co. N.Am., Mpls., 1931-35; practice law, Fulda, Minn., 1935-37; adjuster Standard Accident Ins., Mpls., 1937-40; claim examiner Employers Mut. Casualty, Des Moines, 1940-48; practice law, Marshall, Minn., 1948-63; ct. commr. Lyon County, Marshall, 1958-62; judge Municipal Ct. Marshall, 1963-66, Probate Ct. Lyon County, Marshall, 1966-74; jud. officer Lincoln-Lyon County Ct., Marshall, 1974—; registrar of probate Lyon and Lincoln Counties, 1976—. Mem. City Council, Marshall, 1951-57. Mem. Minn. Bar Assn. Home: 232 N Hill St Marshall MN 56258 Office: Lyon County Court House Marshall MN 56258 Tel (507) 532-5401

PIERCE, ALLIN HUGH, JR., b. Bronxville, N.Y., Nov. 2, 1942; B.A., Dartmouth, 1964; J.D. Stanford, 1967. Admitted to Ill., Calif. bars, 1968; community legal counsel, Chgo., 1967-69; asso. firm Quentin L. Kopp, San Francisco, 1970; asso. firm Layman & Lempert, San Francisco, 1972-75; partner firm Massa & Pierce, San Francisco, 1975—. Office: 9 1st St Suite 700 San Francisco CA 94105 Tel (415) 495-6393

PIERCE, CHARLES INGALS, b. Chgo., Feb. 22, 1915; A.B., Princeton, 1937; LL.B., Yale, 1940. Admitted to N.Y. bar, 1942; law clk. Thomas W. Swan, U.S. Ct. Appeals 2d Circuit, 1940-41; asso. firm Davis, Polk & Wardwell, 1941-42, 46-48; asso. firm Debevoise, Plimpton, Lyons & Gates, N.Y.C., 1948-50, partner, 1950—. Mem. N.Y. State Bar Assn., Assn. Bar City N.Y., Order of Coif. Office: 299 Park Ave New York City NY 10017 Tel (212) 752-6400

PIERCE, DONALD FAY, b. Bexley, Miss., Aug. 28, 1930; B.C.S., U. Ala., 1956, J.D., 1958. Admitted to Ala. bar, 1958; law clk. to sr. U.S. Dist. judge, Mobile, Ala., 1958; partner firm Hand, Arendall, Bedsole, Greaves & Johnston, Mobile, 1959—. Mem. Ala. Def. Lawyers Assn. (pres. 1975), Def. Lawyers Assn. (exec. dir.), Def. Research Inst. (Ala. chmn.). Contbr. articles to legal jours. Home: 4452 Winnie Way Mobile AL 36608 Office: 3000 1st Nat Bank Bldg Mobile AL 36601 Tel (205) 432-5511

PIERCE, DOUGLAS FRANKLIN, b. Rogers, Tex., Aug. 26, 1924; B.B.A., U. Tex., 1949, M.B.A., 1951; LL.B., S. Tex. Coll. Law, 1956. Admitted to Tex. bar, 1956; mgr. labor relations Monsanto Chem. Co., Texas City, Tex., 1951-59; corp. dir. labor relations ACF Industries, N.Y.C., 1959-62; asst. to pres. Allied Chem. Co., Houston, 1962-68; cons. The Emerson Cons., Inc., London, 1968, Paul R. Ray & Co., Ft. Worth, 1969-72; pres. Pierce Sandford & Assos., Inc., Dallas, 1972—. Mem. Tex. Bar Assn. Home: 3901 Arlan Ln Fort Worth TX 76109 Office: Suite 4317 Republic Nat Bank Tower Dallas TX 75201 Tel (214) 651-0809

PIERCE, JOTHAM DONNELL, JR., b. Bangor, Maine, June 5, 1943; A.B., Bowdoin Coll., 1965; J.D., Harvard, 1968. Admitted to Maine bar, 1968; partner firm Pierce Atwood Scribner Allen & McKusick, Portland, Maine, 1971—. Mem. Am. (chmn. First Circuit Construction Com., Litigation Sect.), Maine State Bar Assns. Office: One Monument Square Portland ME 04111 Tel (207) 773-6411

PIERCE, NADINE, b. Ringgold, Ga., Feb. 13, 1928; LL.B., McKenzie Coll. Law, 1957. Admitted to Ga. bar, 1958, U.S. Dist. Ct. for No. Dist. Ga. bar, 1958, U.S. 5th Circuit Ct. Appeals bar, 1963, Tenn. bar, 1964, U.S. Dist. Ct. for Eastern Dist. Tenn., 1964; individual practice law, Ringgold, 1957-64. Bd. dirs. Walker-Catoosa-Dade-Chattooga Mental Health Assn., 1965-68, mem. profl. advisory bd., 1964-66; Mem. Am., Tenn, Chattanooga bar assns., State Bar Ga.,

Chattanooga Trial Lawyers Assn., Lookout Mountain Jud. Bar, Ga. Assn. Women Lawyers, Am. Inst. C.P.A.'s, Tenn. Soc. C.P.A.'s, Am. Soc. Women Accountants, Am. Womens Soc. C.P.A.'s (pres. Chattanooga chpt. 1969-70). Home: Route 4 Box 389 Ringgold GA 30736 Office: 407 High St Room G Chattanooga TN 37403 Tel (615) 267-8883

PIERCE, RICHARD HILTON, b. Westerly, R.I., May 2, 1935; A.B. cum laude, Bates Coll., 1957; J.D., N.Y. U., 1960. Admitted to R.I. bar, 1961, U.S. Dist. Ct. for R.I. bar, 1962; asso. firm Hinckley, Allen, Salisbury & Parsons, Providence, 1961-67, partner, 1967—. Councilman-at-large City of Cranston (R.I.), 1967-68; chmn. Cranston Pub. Library Trustees. Mem. R.I., Am. bar assns. Home: 74 W Blue Ridge Rd Cranston RI 02920 Office: 2200 Indsl Bank Bldg Providence RI 02903 Tel (401) 274-2000

PIERCE, WILLIAM JAMES, b. Flint, Mich., Dec. 4, 1921; A.B. in Econs., U. Mich., 1947, J.D., 1949. Admitted to Mich. bar, 1949; asst. counsel U.S. senate legis. counsel, Washington, 1949—; asso. N.Y. Law Rev. Commn., 1950—; with U. Mich., Ann Arbor, 1953—, prof. law 1958—, dir. legis. research center, 1958—, asso. dean law sch., 1971—; pres. Nat. Conf. Commrs. on Uniform State Laws, 1967-69, exec. dir., 1969—; mem. Mich. Gov.'s Commn. on Law Revision, 1975-76. Chmn. Ann Arbor Citizen's Com. on Drug Abuse, 1971. Author: Materials on Legislation, 3d edition, 1974. Home: 1505 Roxbury Rd Ann Arbor MI 48105 Office: 320 Hutchins Hall Monroe St U Mich Law Sch Ann Arbor MI 48109

PIERPOINT, POWELL, b. Phila., Apr. 30, 1922; B.A., Yale, 1944, LL.B., 1948. Admitted to N.Y. bar, 1949, U.S. Supreme Ct. bar, 1961; asso. firm Hughes Hubbard & Reed, and predecessors, N.Y.C., 1948-53, partner, 1955-61, 63—; asst. U.S. atty. So. Dist. N.Y., 1953-55; gen. counsel Dept. Army, Washington, 1961-63; v.p. N.Y. Legal Aid Soc., 1971—. Mem. N.Y.C. Bd. Ethics, 1972. Mem. Am., N.Y. State, Fed. bar assns., Am. Coll. Trial Lawyers, Assn. Bar City N.Y., N.Y. County Lawyers Assn. Office: Hughes Hubbard & Reed One Wall St New York City NY 10005 Tel (212) 943-6500

PIERSON, WILLIAM CALEY, b. Seattle, Nov. 24, 1938; B.S. in Bus. Adminstrn., U. Fla., 1961, J.D., 1967. Admitted to Fla. bar, 1968; individual practice law, Gainesville, Fla., 1970—; judge pro tempore Gainesville Municipal Ct., 1973-74. Mem. Am. Bar Assn., Phi Alpha Delta. Home: 5832 NW 33d St Gainesville FL 32605 Office: 3601 SW 2d Ave Gainesville FL 32607 Tel (904) 376-3391

PIERSON, WILLIAM THEODORE, JR., b. Washington, May 18, 1937; A.B., Cornell U., 1961; LL.B., George Washington U., 1964. Admitted to U.S. Supreme Ct. bar, 1969; asso. firm Pierson, Ball & Dowd, Washington, 1964-73, partner, 1973—. Pres. Norwood Sch. Parents Orgn., 1974-75. Mem. D.C. Bar, Bar Assn. D.C., Am., FCC bar assns., Computer Law Assn., Order of Coif. Office: 1000 Ring Bldg Washington DC 20036 Tel (202) 331-8566

PIESKI, JOHN EDWARD VICTOR, b. Blakely, Pa., Feb. 18, 1938; B.A. magna cum laude, Lehigh U., 1958; LL.D., N.Y. U., 1961. Admitted to Pa. bar, 1962; research asso. Unit Law in Psychiatry, Temple U. Med. Law Schs., Phila., 1961, 62, 63; asst. instr. govt. and constl. law Lehigh U., Bethlehem, Pa., 1958; dist. magistrate Lackawanna County (Pa.), 1970—, asst. county solicitor, 1964-66; solicitor Dickson City (Pa.) Borough, 1963-65. Mem. citizens adv. council Pa. Dept. Environ. Resources, 1971-76; mem. consumer council Pa. Dept. Agr., 1971, 72; co-chmn. Save Am's. Vital Environment. Contbr. articles to legal jours. Office: PO Box 1066 Suite 500 Dime Bank Bldg 400 Spruce St Scranton PA 18503 Tel (717) 346-7401

PIETRAFESE, JOSEPH SALVATORE, b. Cleve., Nov. 29, 1914; LL.B., J.D., Ohio State U.; Admitted to Ohio bar, 1945; referee, domestic relations ct., 1940-54; asst. county prosecutor, 1954-71. Active March Dimes, Boy Scouts Am. Mem. Ohio State, Cuyahoya, Greater Cleve. bar assns. Home: 5941 Asheroft Dr Mayfield Heights OH 44124 Office: New Ct House Lakeside Ave Cleveland OH 44113 Tel (216) 621-5000

PIETZ, COLIN DUANE, b. New London, Wis., Mar. 22, 1944; B.A. with highest honors, Wis. State U., 1966; J.D. with honors, U. Wis., 1968. Admitted to Wis. bar, 1968; served with JAG, USAF, 1968-72; asso. firm Terwilliger, Wakeen, Piehler, Conway & Klingberg, Wausau, Wis., 1972-73, partner, 1974—. Mem. Am., Wis., Marathon County bar assns., Order of Coif. Contbr. article Wis. Law Rev. Home: 5109 Von Kanel St Schofield WI 54476 Office: 401 4th St Wausau WI 54401 Tel (715) 845-2121

PIGA, STEPHEN MULRY, b. Bklyn., Apr. 9, 1929; A.B., Princeton, 1950; LL.B., Columbia, 1955. Admitted to N.J. bar, 1955, N.Y. bar, 1956; asso. firm White & Case, N.Y.C., 1955-64, partner, 1964—. Mem. Am. (former N.Y. regional chmn. employee benefit com.; lectr. nat. insts.), N.Y. State (former mem. exec. com. tax sect.; lectr.) bar assns., Assn. Bar City N.Y., N.Y. County Lawyers Assn. Home: 5 Andover Pl Fairlawn NJ 07410 Office: 14 Wall St New York City NY 10005 Tel (212) 732-1040

PIKE, GARY EUGENE, b. Culver City, Calif., May 26, 1938; A.B., Stanford, 1960, J.D., 1963. Admitted to Calif. bar, 1964; since practiced in San Diego; mem. firm Holt, Baugh, Maas, Weismantel & Pike, 1967-70, Hervey, Mitchell, Ashworth & Keeney, 1971—; mem. Calif. State Bar family law commn., 1975—. Mem. Calif. Trial Lawyers Assn., San Diego County Bar Assn. (chmn. family law 1975, lawyers reference com.). Office: 520 W Ash St Suite 200 San Diego CA 92101 Tel (714) 238-1234

PIKE, OTIS G., b. Riverhead, N.Y., Aug. 31, 1921; A.B. magna cum laude, Princeton U., 1943; J.D., Columbia U., 1948. Admitted to N.Y. bar, 1948; asso. firm Griffing & Smith, Riverhead, 1948-53; individual practice law, Riverhead, 1953-60, 74—; sr. partner firm Pike, Behringer & Hurley, Riverhead, 1960-74; justice of peace City of Riverhead, 1953-60; mem. U.S. Ho. of Reps., 1961—. Trustee Riverhead Free Library; bd. dirs. Central Suffolk Hosp., Riverhead; trustee 1st Congregational Ch., Riverhead, Mem. Suffolk County Bar Assn. Home: 132 Ostrander Ave Riverhead NY 11901 Office: 2308 Rayburn Bldg Washington DC 20515 Tel (202) 225-3826

PIKE, WILLIAM BENEDICT, b. Cleve., June 6, 1928; B.S., Kent State U., 1953; J.D., Cleve. State U., 1958. Admitted to Ohio bar, 1958, U.S. Supreme Ct. bar, 1972; judge Cuyahoga Falls (Ohio) Municipal Ct., 1973-77. Trustee, Cuyahoga Valley Community Mental Health Center.

PIKORSKY, SEYMOUR, b. Milw., Dec. 22, 1942; B.S., U. Wis., Milw., 1964; J.D., Marquette U., 1967. Admitted to Wis. bar, U.S. Dist. Ct. bar, 1967, U.S. Supreme Ct. bar, 1970, U.S. Ct. Appeals bar, 1971, U.S. Tax Ct. bar, 1973; lawyer Milw. Legal Services, 1967-74; individual practice law, Milw., 1974—; program evaluator OEO, 1974-76. Mem. nat. exec. com. Zionist Orgn. Am., pres. Milw. Dist. Zionist Orgn., 1974—. Mem. Wis. Bar Assn., Milw. Jr. Bar Assn. Home: 8150 N Seneca Rd Milwaukee WI 53217 Office: 2040 W Wisconsin Ave Milwaukee WI 53233 Tel (414) 344-9240

PILCHER, GARY LYNN, b. Youngstown, Ohio, Nov. 29, 1948; A.B., Youngstown State U., 1970; J.D., Rutgers U., 1973. Admitted to Ohio bar, 1976; asst. prof. criminal justice Youngstown State U., 1973—, also prof. Pa. State U. Shenango Valley Campus, Sharon, Pa. Mem. Acad. Criminal Justice Scis., N. Atlantic Assn. Criminal Justice Educators, Assn. Trial Lawyers Am., Am., Ohio, Mahoning County bar assns., NEA, Ohio Edn. Assn. Home: 292 Madison Ave Youngstown OH 44504 Office: 410 Wick Ave Youngstown OH 44555 Tel (216) 743-0942 also (216) 746-1851 extension 252

PILCHER, JAMES BROWNIE, b. Shreveport, La., May 19, 1929; B.S., La. State U., 1952; J.D., John Marshall Law Sch., 1955, Emory U., 1959; Admitted to Ga. bar, 1955, U.S. Supreme Ct. bar, 1963; mem. firm Arnold & Harris, Atlanta, 1955-58, Haas, Dunaway & Shelfer, Atlanta, 1958-62; individual practice law, Atlanta, 1970—; legal counsel to speaker Ga. Ho. of Reps., 1962-66; asso. city atty. City of Atlanta, 1966-70; adj. prof. law John Marshall Law Sch., 1966—. Pres., Young Democrats of Ga., 1963-64; mem. Fulton County (Ga.) Dem. Exec. Com. Mem. State Bar Ga., Am., Atlanta bar assns., Ga., Nat. criminal def. lawyers assns. Named Outstanding Young Man of Ga. in Civic Affairs, Ga. Jr. C. of C., 1960, Outstanding Young Man of Atlanta in Civic Affairs, Atlanta Jr. C. of C., 1961. Home: 434 Brentwood Dr NE Atlanta GA 30305 Office: 450 14th St NW Atlanta GA 30318 Tel (404) 892-8888

PILCHER, WALLACE HAMILTON, b. Wrens, Ga., July 24, 1934; A.B. Emory U., 1959. Admitted to Ga. bar, 1963; individual practice law, Wrens, 1963—; judge city ct., Wrens, 1974—; gen. counsel First State Bank, Wrens. Chmn. Wrens Planning Commn., 1966—; city atty., Wrens, 1966—; pres. Farmers Mut. Exchange, Wrens, 1974—. Mem. Am. Trial Lawyers Assn. Home: 128 Ellis St Wrens GA 30833 Office: 817 Estelle St Wrens GA 30833 Tel (404) 547-2581

PILKINTON, JAMES HARVEY, JR., b. Hope, Ark., Sept. 21, 1948; B.A., Hendrix Coll., 1970; J.D., U. Ark., 1973. Admitted to Ark. bar, 1973, U.S. Dist. Ct. bar for Western Dist. Ark., 1974, U.S. Ct. Appeals bar, 8th Circuit, 1975; asso. firm Pilkinton & Pilkinton and predecessor, Hope, 1973, partner, 1974—; asso. Hope City Atty's Office, 1973—. Mem. bd. deacons 1st Presbyn. Ch., Hope; v.p. Hempstead County (Ark.) unit Am. Cancer Soc., 1974-75. Mem. Am., Ark., S.W. Ark. bar assns. Home: 1019 W 15th St Hope AR 71801 Office: 116-118 E 2d St Hope AR 71801 Tel (501) 777-8871

PILLA, KENNETH JOSEPH, b. Phila., Feb. 28, 1940; B.S., Villanova U., 1961; LL.B., U. Balt., 1968. Admitted to Md. bar, 1968, U.S. Dist. Ct. bar, 1969, U.S. Supreme Ct. bar, 1974; since practiced in Balt.; dir. Housing Law Center Legal Aid Bur., Inc., 1968-75; partner firm Chartrand, Kelly & Pilla, Balt. and Annapolis, Md., 1975—. Mem. Am., Md. bar assns. Contbr. articles to profl. jours.

PILLINGER, JAMES J., b. N.Y.C., Sept. 11, 1918; LL.B., St. Johns U., 1942; LL.M., N.Y. U., 1970; B. Profl. Studies, Pace U., 1974. Admitted to N.Y. bar, 1942, U.S. Tax Ct. bar, 1944, U.S. Dist. Ct. So. Dist. N.Y., 1944, U.S. Dist. Ct. Eastern Dist. N.Y. bar, 1952, U.S. Supreme Ct. bar, 1960, U.S. 2d Circuit Ct. Appeals bar, 1973; mgr. legal research sect., editor law bull. Nat. Surety Corp., N.Y.C., 1939-42; asso. firm Bergerman & Hourwich, N.Y.C., 1942-45; partner firm Pillinger, Raiskin & Weiser, N.Y.C., 1945-61; partner firm Metnick, Pillinger & Sutera, N.Y.C., 1961-66; individual practice law, N.Y.C., 1966—; asst. prof. law Pace U., 1967-71, Baruch Coll., 1971—; mem. N.Y. State Com. on the Economy, 1974-75; legis. asst. N.Y. Gen. Assembly, 1973-74. Dir. Boys Brotherhood Republic N.Y., 1942—, pres., 1943-59; dir. Tall Oaks Civic Assn., Bayside, N.Y., 1970-74, pres., 1956-61; dir. Inst. Internat. Med. Edn., 1974—. Mem. Queens County Bar Assn. (chmn. legislation and law reform com.), N.Y. County Lawyers Assn., Northeastern Regional Bus. Law Assn., Am. Bus. Law Assn., Nat. Assn. Bus. Law Tchrs., AAUP. Contbr. articles in field to profl. jours.

PILLOTE, VERNON JOSEPH, b. Norway, Mich., Aug. 2, 1925; B.S. in Elec. Engring., U. Wis., 1945, J.D., 1949. Admitted to D.C. bar, 1952, Ill. bar, 1955; patent advisor U.S. Office Naval Research, 1950-53; mem. firm Morsbach & Pillote, Rockford, Ill., 1953—. Mem. Winnebago County, Ill. bar assns. Home: 1871 Jonquil Circle Rockford IL 61107 Office: Gas Electric Bldg Rockford IL 61101 Tel (815) 964-9312

PILLOW, ROSEMARY TORBET, b. Homer, La., Apr. 21, 1925; A.B. in Polit. Sci., La. State U., 1946; LL.B., Tulane U., 1949, J.D., 1969. Admitted to La. bar, 1950; clk. firm Breazeale, Sachse & Wilson, Baton Rouge, 1950-51; research asst. for state legis. council and state mineral bd., asst. to atty. for bd., State of La., Baton Rouge, 1952-56; right-of-way clk. firm Brown and Root, Baton Rouge, 1961-62; asst. parish atty. E. Baton Rouge Parish, 1962-71, parish clk., 1971—; notary public E. Baton Rouge Parish, 1951—. Bd. dirs. Arts and Humanities Council; mem. City-Parish Alcoholic Beverage Control Bd., Taxicab Control Bd.; bd. dirs. Baton Rouge Community Correction and Research Center, 1972-75; mem. ofcl. bd. Broadmoor United Methodist Ch.; sec. to Caucus Democratic Elected Ofcls., 1971-75; exec. bd. Baton Rouge Bicentennial Commn., 1972-75; mem. exec. com. State Bicentennial Commn.; sec. Zonta Club of Baton Rouge, 1970; mem. La. State U. Alumni Fedn., Wesleyan Service Guild, Downtown Lioness Club, Women's Aux. of La. Engring. Assn. Mem. La. State, Baton Rouge bar assns., Internat. Inst. Municipal Clks. (certified municipal clk.), La. Municipal Clks. Assn. (v.p. 1973, pres. 1974), Sec.-Treas's. Assn. (exec. bd. 1972). Home: 1401 Ashland Dr Baton Rouge LA 70806 Office: room 204 Municipal Bldg Baton Rouge LA 70801 Tel (504) 389-3123

PILLSBURY, FREDERICK STEPHEN, b. Manchester, N.H., July 25, 1919; A.B., Dartmouth Coll., 1940; LL.B., Harvard, 1946. Admitted to Mass. bar, 1947; partner firm Doherty, Wallace, Pillsbury & Murphy, Springfield, Mass., 1967—; asso. justice Superior Ct. Mass., 1965-67; trustee Springfield Instn. for Savs., 1967—. Chmn. Springfield Police Commn., 1960-62; mem. Springfield City Council, 1964-65; trustee Am. Internat. Coll., Springfield, 1967—; mem. Mass. State Lottery Commn., Braintree, 1971—. Fellow Am. Coll. Trial Lawyers, Am. Bar Found.; mem. Am., Mass. (v.p. 1963-65), Hampden County (pres. 1961-63, exec. bd. 1976—) bar assns. Office: 1387 Main St Springfield MA 01103 Tel (413) 733-3111

PINCKNEY, FRANCIS MORRIS, b. Columbia, S.C., Mar. 21, 1935; B.M.E., U. S.C., 1957; J.D. with honors, George Washington U., 1963. Admitted to N.C. bar, 1965; partner firm Richards, Shefte & Pinckney, 1963—; patent examiner U.S. Patent Office, Washington, 1959-63. Chmn. CAF Hunger Task Force, 1974-75; bd. dirs. N.C. Hunger Coalition, 1975—, chmn., 1977—; bd. dirs. Charlotte Area Fund, 1970-75. Mem. Am., N.C. 26th Jud. (exec. com.) bar assns., Patent Office Soc. Contbr. articles to legal jours. Home: 2215 Malvern Rd Charlotte NC 28207 Office: 1208 Cameron Brown Bldg Charlotte NC 28204 Tel (704) 332-8576

PINCURA, JOHN DAVID, b. Chester, Pa., May 18, 1904; B.A., Pa. State U., 1928; LL.B., Ohio State U., 1932. Admitted to Ohio bar, 1932; individual practice law, Lorain, Ohio, 1932-50; city solicitor, Lorain, 1936-50; judge Lorain County Common Pleas Ct. (Ohio), 1950—. Mem. Ohio, Lorain County, Am. bar assns., Am. Judicature Soc. Home: 1509 W Erie Ave Lorrain OH 44052 Office: Ct House Elyria OH 44035 Tel (614) 323-5776

PINDAR, GEORGE ALDRICH, b. Valdosta, Ga., May 19, 1906; LL.B., Mercer U., 1927, J.D., 1927. Admitted to Ga. bar, 1927, Tenn. bar, 1942; individual practice law, Macon, Ga., 1927-41; atty. TVA, Knoxville, 1941-44; title officer Chattanooga Title & Trust Co., 1944-45, Lawyers Title Ins. Corp., Atlanta, 1945-71; mem. firm Gershon, Ruden, Pindar & Olim, Atlanta, 1971—; instr. Mercer U., Ga. State U. Chmn. bd. dirs. Jay Hambidge Art Found., Rabun Gap, Ga., 1971—. Mem. Atlanta, Am. bar assns., Ga. State Bar, Tenn. Bar. Author: Georgia Real Estate Law, 1971; American Real Estate Law, 1976. Office: 730 Healey Bldg PO Box 2872 Atlanta GA 30301 Tel (404) 524-4991

PINE, CHARLOTTE WEIKINGER, lawyer; b. Wurzburg, Bavaria, Germany, Nov. 22, 1921; B.S., U. Md., 1943, LL.B., 1945. Admitted to Md. bar, 1946; pvt. practice law, Towson, Md., 1946—. Gen. chmn. March of Dimes, 1955-60; pres. Baltimore County chpt. Am. Cancer Soc., 1961-63; chmn. Baltimore County United Fund, 1968. Mem. Phi Delta Delta. Office: 607 Baltimore Ave Towson MD 21204

PINGEL, STEVEN RALPH, b. Los Angeles, May 23, 1944; B.S., Calif. Poly. U., 1968; J.D., U. Calif., Los Angeles, 1971. Admitted to Calif. bar, 1972; mem. firm Lemaire, Faunce & Katznelson, Los Angeles, 1973—; gen. counsel Calif. League City Employee Assns. Mem. exec. com. Calif. Republican Com., 1975-77. Mem. Am., Los Angeles County bar assns., Phi Alpha Delta. Home: 4412 Oak Ln Claremont CA 91711 Office: 2404 Wilshire Blvd Suite 700 Los Angeles CA 90057 Tel (213) 385-4433

PINKERTON, CHARLES FREDERICK, b. Salt Lake City, Mar. 7, 1940; B.A., Calif. Lutheran Coll., 1964; J.D., U. Oreg., 1967. Admitted to Nev. bar, 1968; dep. dist. atty. Washoe County, Nev., 1968-71, chief dep. dist. atty., 1971; mem. firm Goldwater, Hill, Mortimer, Sourwine, Reno, 1971-72, Goldwater, Mortimer, Sourwine & Pinkerton, 1972-75, Fahrenkopf, Mortimer, Sourwine, Mousel & Pinkerton, 1975—. Mem. Am., Washoe County bar assns., Nev. Trial Lawyers Assn., Assn. Def. Counsel, Am. Judicature Soc., Phi Delta Phi. Home: 781 Manor Dr Reno NV 89509 Office: 333 Marsh Ave Reno NV 89509 Tel (702) 323-8633

PINKERTON, JAMES DONALD, b. Chgo., May 28, 1940; B.S. in Law, Northwestern U., 1961, J.D., 1963. Admitted to Ill. bar, 1963; atty. Swift & Co., Chgo., 1963-66; atty. Household Fin. Corp., Chgo., 1966-68, asst. sec., 1968-72, sec., 1972—, asst. gen. counsel, 1974—. Trustee N. Shore Music Center, Winnetka, Ill., 1974—. Mem. Am., Ill., Chgo. bar assns., Am. Soc. Corp. Secs., Nat. Investor Relations Inst. Office: 3200 Prudential Plaza Chicago IL 60601 Tel (312) 944-7174

PINKERTON, JOHN COOPER, b. Chgo., Jan. 29, 1916; B.A., U. Fla., 1936, LL.B., 1939, J.D., 1967. Admitted to Fla. bar, 1939; founder, partner firm Kirk, Pinkerton, Sparrow, McClelland & Savary, Sarasota, Fla., 1949—; municipal judge, Sarasota, 1948-53; chmn. Fla. Milk Commn., 1964, Sarasota County (Fla.) Zoning Bd. Appeals, 1955-57. Mem. Am., Fla. (bd. govs. 1960-64), Sarasota County (pres. 1960) bar assns. Home: 1729 Cherokee Dr Sarasota FL 33579 Office: POB 3798 Sarasota FL 33578 Tel (813) 366-5700

PINKUS, MURRAY H., b. Scranton, Pa., Aug. 30, 1941; B.S., U. Pa., 1963; LL.B., 1966. Admitted to D.C. bar, 1967, Pa. bar, 1968. Asso. firm Myron A. Pinkus, Scranton, 1966-67; contract adminstr. Philco Ford, Phila., 1967-68; trust officer Girard Bank, Phila., 1968—. Office: Girard Bank One Girard Plaza Philadelphia PA 19101 Tel (215) 585-2712

PINNE, FREDERICK JOHN, III, b. Long Island City, N.Y., June 17, 1946; B.A. in English, U. Kan., 1968; J.D., U. Mo., Kansas City, 1973, LL.M. in Corp. and Comml. Law, 1976. Admitted to Mo. bar, 1973; asst. prof. law Central Mo. State U., 1973—. Home: 110 Fairview Ave Warrensburg MO 64093 Office: Central Mo State U Warrensburg MO 64093 Tel (816) 429-4767

PINOLA, FRANK LEWIS, b. Scranton, Pa., Jan. 27, 1893; student Cornell U., 1911-12; J.D., U. Pa., 1915. Admitted to Pa. bar, 1915, U.S. Supreme Ct. bar, 1922; Gowen fellow U. Pa. Law Sch., 1915-16; practiced law, Wilkes-Barre and Pittston, Pa., 1916-48; U.S. commr., 1918-35; spl. dep. gen. Pa., 1932-36; judge Ct. Common Pleas Luzerne County (Pa.), 1948-68, presiding judge, 1961-68; pres. Liberty Nat. Bank, Pittston, 1925-74; treas. Ind. Explosives Co. Pa., Scranton, 1936-69; dir. Old Republic Ins. Co., Greensburg, Pa.; Initiator, mem. com. preparing standard jury instructions Pa. Supreme Ct. Pres., Community Chest, Wilkes-Barre, 1955, Vets. Hosp. Trust Fund, 1975—; sr. v.p. Blue Cross NE Pa., 1970—; bd. dirs. King's Coll., Wilkes Coll., Wilkes-Barre. Mem. Am., Inter-Am., Internat., Pa., Luzerne County (pres. 1945-47) bar assns., Am. Judicature Soc. Home and Office: 85 James St Kingston PA 18704 Tel (717) 287-0736

PINSKY, ALBERT H., b. Erie, Pa., June 4, 1936; A.B., U. Pa., 1958; J.D., Syracuse U., 1961. Admitted to N.Y. State bar, 1962, U.S. Supreme Ct. bar, 1969; mem. firm Burkwit, Pinsky and Dandrea, Rochester, N.Y., 1964—. Mem. Monroe County, Genesee County, N.Y. State bar assns. Home: 848 Eastbrooke Ln Rochester NY 14618 Office: 16 Main St E Rochester NY 14614 Tel (716) 325-5353

PINSKY, MICHAEL S., b. Chgo., July 25, 1945; B.S., U. Ill., Champaign, 1967; J.D., DePaul U., 1971. Admitted to Ill. bar, 1971; mem. firm Levenfeld, Kanter, Baskes & Lippitz, Chgo., 1972—; conferee Internal Revenue Service, 1967-72. Mem. Am., Ill., Chgo. Bar assns. CPA. Office: 10 S LaSalle St Chicago IL 60603 Tel (312) 346-8380

PINSON, JERRY D., b. Harrison, Ark., Sept. 7, 1942; B.A., U. Ark., 1964, J.D., 1967. Admitted to Ark. bar, 1967; dep. atty. gen. State of Ark., 1967-70; individual practice law, Harrison, 1971—. Pres., United Way of Boone County (Ark.), 1974, bd. dirs., 1973; bd. dirs. Rotary Club, 1975, v.p., 1976, pres., 1977. Mem. Am., Boone County (past v.p.), Ark. bar assns., Am. Judicature Soc. Home: Skyline Dr Harrison AR 72601 Office: PO Box 1111 Harrison AR 72601 Tel (501) 365-3403

PIPERI, JAMES ALBERT, b. Galveston, Tex., July 14, 1909; pre-law student U. Tex., 1930-34; LL.B., Baylor U., 1935. Admitted to Tex. bar, 1935; partner firm Nussbaum & Piperi, Galveston, 1935-49, firm Kleinecke, Nussbaum & Piperi, Galveston, 1949-62; asst. city atty. City of Galveston, 1951-57; atty. Galveston City Civil Service Commn.; justice of the peace, Galveston, 1938-42; judge City Ct., Galveston, 1958-61; spl. county judge, 1961; judge Galveston (Tex.) Domestic Relations and Juvenile Ct., 1962—; speaker in field. Mem. Galveston County, Tex. bar assns., Tex. Judges Jud. Sect. Recipient Distinguished Service award Tex. Youth Conf., 1970, certificate of Merit K.C., 1971. Home: 7618 Beaudelaire St Galveston TX 77550 Office: County Courthouse 507 Domestic Relations Ct Galveston TX 77550 Tel (713) 762-8621

PIPPIN, DON ROGER, b. Coeburn, Va., Oct. 31, 1938; B.A., U. Va., 1960, LL.B., 1963. Admitted to Va. bar, 1963; partner firms Greear, Bowen, Mullins, Pippin & Sturgill, Norton, 1963-65, Cline, McAfee & Pippin, 1965-66; individual practice law, Norton, 1966—; dir. Farmer Exchange Bank of Coeburn; chmn. bd. Clinch Valley Manor, Inc. Chmn. adminstrv. bd. Coeburn United Methodist Ch., 1975-76. Mem. Va. State Bar, Am. Bar Assn., Calif., Va. trial lawyers assns. Office: PO Box 670 Norton VA 24273 Tel (703) 679-2030

PIPPIN, JAMES M., b. Salem, Oreg., Sept. 9, 1945; B.S., Lewis and Clark Coll., 1967; J.D., Northwestern Sch. Law, Portland, Oreg., 1971. Admitted to Oreg. bar, 1971, since practiced in Portland; asso. firm Green, Richardson, et al, 1971-73; partner firm Green, Griswold & Pippin, 1973-75, Pippin & Bocci, 1975—. Mem. Am., Oreg., Multnomah County bar assns., Am., Oreg. trial lawyers assns. Home: 2775 SW Old Orchard Rd Portland OR 97201 Office: 219 SW Stark St Bishop's House Portland OR 97204 Tel (503) 228-5201

PIRCHER, LEO JOSEPH, b. Berkeley, Jan. 4, 1933; B.S., U. Calif., Berkeley, 1954, J.D., Boalt Hall, 1957. Admitted to Calif. bar, 1958, U.S. Supreme Ct. bar, 1971; asso. firm Lawler, Felix & Hall, Los Angeles, 1957-61, partner, 1962—, sr. partner, 1966—; instr. Loyola U. Sch. Law, Los Angeles, 1959-61; author, lectr. in field. Mem. State Bar Calif., Los Angeles County, Am. bar assns., Town Hall of Calif., Phi Beta Kappa. Certified specialist in taxation law Calif. Bd. Legal Specialization. Home: 4852 Ocean View Blvd La Canada CA 91011 Office: 605 W Olympic Blvd Los Angeles CA 90015 Tel (213) 620-0060

PIRIE, JOHN CHARLES, b. Denver, Aug. 26, 1907; A.B., U. Nebr., 1929; B.A., Oxford U., 1934, M.A., 1962. Admitted to N.Y. State bar, 1936, U.S. Ct. Appeals 2d Circuit bar, 1951, D.C. Circuit bar, 1957, Md. bar, 1973; asso. firm Root, Clark, Buckner & Ballantine, N.Y.C., 1936-43; with Pan Am. World Airways, Inc., N.Y.C., 1943-71, gen. counsel, 1968-71, v.p., 1956-70, sr. v.p., 1970-71, also dir. Consol. Rail Corp. Mem. Am., N.Y., Md. bar assns., Bar Assn. City N.Y. Home: 1910 Carrollton Rd Annapolis MD 21401 Office: 220 Severn Ave Annapolis MD 21401 Tel (301) 267-8166

PIRKEY, LOUIS THOMAS, b. Fort Worth, Dec. 6, 1937; B.S. in Chem. Engring., U. Tex., 1960; J.D. with honors, George Washington U., 1964. Admitted to Tex. bar, 1964; mem. firm Arnold, White & Durkee, Houston, 1964—. Mem. Am., Houston bar assns., Am., Houston patent law assns., U.S. Trademark Assn. Home: 607 Rainwood St Houston TX 77024 Office: 2100 Transco Tower Houston TX 77056 Tel (713) 621-9100

PIROG, JOHN FRANK, b. Sioux City, Iowa, Nov. 18, 1925; B.S., Morningside Coll., 1950; LL.B., Drake U., 1952, J.D., 1968. Admitted to Iowa bar, 1952, S.D. bar, 1955; partner firm Pirog & Gates, Sioux City, 1960—. Mem. Iowa, Woodbury County bar assns., Am. Trial Lawyers Assn. Home: 2626 S Mulberry St Sioux City IA 51106 Office: 401 Davidson Bldg Sioux City IA 51101 Tel (712) 252-4339

PISCEVICH, MARGO, b. Kimberly, Nev., Apr. 6, 1947; B.S., U. Utah, 1969, J.D., 1971. Admitted to Nev. bar, 1971, U.S. Supreme Ct. bar, 1976; law clk. to justice Utah Supreme Ct., Salt Lake City, 1970; dep. atty. gen. State of Nev., Carson City, 1971-74; asso. firm Hibbs & Newton, Reno, 1974—; judge pro tem City of Reno Municipal Ct., 1974—; bd. dirs. Washoe County (Nev.) Legal Services, 1974—, chmn. bd., 1977—; legal advisor Gov.'s Commn. on Status of People, 1975-76. Mem. Am., Nev. bar assns., Am., Nev. trial lawyers assns. Office: 350 S Center St Reno NV 89501 Tel (702) 786-6868

PITCHER, STEPHEN RANDOLPH, b. Boston, May 13, 1945; B.A. in Polit. Sci. with honors, San Jose State U., 1967; J.D., Hastings Coll. Law, San Francisco, 1970. Admitted to Calif. bar, 1971, U.S. Dist. Ct. for No. Calif. bar, 1971, U.S. 9th Circuit Ct. Appeals bar, 1971; law library asst. firm Pillsbury, Madison & Sutro, San Francisco, 1967-68; field agt. legal div. San Francisco Redevel. Agency, 1968-70; editor Bancroft Whitney Co., San Francisco, 1971—; mem. Dolphin Project, San Francisco. Mem. Am. Cetacean Soc., Press Club San Francisco (sec. 1973-74, dir. 1975—), State Bar Calif., Bar Assn. San Francisco, Barristers Club. Contbr. articles to law publications. Office: 301 Brannan St San Francisco CA 94107 Tel (415) 986-4410

PITKIEWICZ, ANTHONY THOMAS, b. Fall River, Mass., May 6, 1905; LL.B., Albany Law Sch., 1926. Admitted to N.Y. State bar, 1929; individual practice law, Albany, N.Y., 1929—; town atty., spl. counsel E. Greenbush (N.Y.), 1961-71. Mem. Rensselaer County Bar Assn. Home: 239 Summit Ave Hampton Manor Rensselaer NY 12144 Office: 90 State St Albany NY 12207 Tel (518) 434-4991

PITKIN, STAN(LEY) (GARVIN), b. Mpls., May 17, 1937; B.A., San Francisco State Coll., 1960; J.D., Vanderbilt U., 1964. Admitted to Wash. bar, 1965; practiced in Bellingham, 1965-66; pros. atty. Whatcom County, 1966-69; U.S. atty. Western Dist. Wash., Seattle, 1969-76; asst. gen. counsel for hearings and appeals NOAA, Seattle, 1976—; chmn. taskforce on arrest and charging process Wash. Citizens Conf. on Crime, 1967-68; mem. Wash. Law and Justice Com., 1969-73; mem. Atty. Gen.'s Adv. Com. U.S. Attys., chmn. com. profl. proficiency, 1973-76. Pres. Whatcom County Opportunity Council, 1965-66; campaign chmn. Whatcom County March Dimes, 1967-68; organizer N.W. Air Pollution Authority 1967; mem. N.W. Wash. Health Council, 1968; mem. govt. structures com., candidate evaluation com. Seattle-King County Municipal League, 1971-76. Mem. Nat. Dist. Attys. Assn., Am., Fed. (v.p. Wash. chpt.), Wash., Whatcom County, Seattle-King County (com. drug abuse 1972-74) bar assns., Wash. Trial Lawyers Assn., Wash. Pros. Attys. Assn., Wash. Assn. Elected County Ofcls., Am. Judicature Soc., Phi Delta Phi. Named outstanding young man in Wash. State, Jaycees, 1969. Home: 13920 SE 44th Pl Bellevue WA 98006 Office: Room 23 Bldg 25 7500 Sand Point Way NE Seattle WA 98115 Tel (206) 442-0329

PITOFSKY, ROBERT, b. Paterson, N.J., Dec. 27, 1929; A.B., N.Y. U., 1951; LL.B., Columbia U., 1954. Admitted to N.Y. bar, 1956, D.C. bar, 1973; asso. firm Dewey, Ballantine, Bushby, Palmer & Wood, N.Y.C., 1957-63; prof. law N.Y. U. Law Sch., 1963-70, Georgetown U. Law Sch., 1973—; counsel firm Arnold & Porter, Washington, 1973—; counsel Am. Bar Assn. Commn. to Study FTC, 1969; dir. Bur. Consumer Protection, FTC, 1970-73; mem. Senate Intergovtl. Com. Task Force on Regulatory Reform, 1975—. Mem. Am., D.C. bar assns., Bar Assn. City N.Y. Author: (with Handler, Blake & Goldschmid) Cases and Materials on Trade Regulation, 1975. Home: 3809 Blackthorn St Chevy Chase MD 20015 Office: 1229 19th St NW Washington DC 20001 Tel (202) 872-6714

PITT, FRANK RYLANDS, b. Green Bay, Wis., Mar. 12, 1908; B.A., Columbia, 1928, LL.B., 1930; J.S.D., N.Y. U., 1934. Admitted to N.Y. bar, 1931, Ohio bar, 1949; asso. firms Bouvier & Beale, 1930-34, Wise, Shepherd & Houghton, 1934-36, Delafield, Thorne & Marsh, 1936-42, N.Y.C.; asso. prof. law U. Kans., Lawrence, 1947-48; sec., gen. counsel The DeVilbiss Co., Toledo, 1948-71; lectr., adjunct prof. law, Univ. Toledo, 1951-58, 71—. Tax collector Village Ottowa Hills, Ohio, 1968—. Mem. Am., Toledo bar assns., Nat. Spray Equipment Mfrs. Assn., Nat. Fire Protection Assn., Am. Nat. Standards Inst. Comm., Phi Alpha Delta. Recipient Distinguished Service award, Columbia, 1971. Home: 3932 W Bancroft St Toledo OH 43606 Office: Dept Law University Toledo Toledo OH 43606 Tel (419) 537-2851

PITT, GEORGE, b. Chgo., July 21, 1938; B.A., Northwestern U., 1960, J.D., 1963. Admitted to Ill. bar, 1963; asso. firm Chapman & Cutler, Chgo., 1963-67; partner firm Borge & Pitt, and predecessor, Chgo., 1968—. Mem. Am., Ill., Chgo. bar assns., Phi Delta Phi, Phi Gamma Delta. Mem. editorial staff Northwestern U. Law Rev., 1962-63. Home: 872 Burr Ave Winnetka IL 60093 Office: 120 S LaSalle St Chicago IL 60603 Tel (312) 726-6080

PITT, HARRY WARREN, b. Bklyn., June 7, 1908; student Columbia U., 1925-26; LL.B., Bklyn. Law Sch., 1929. Practice law, N.Y.C., 1931—. Mem. New York County Lawyers Assn. Office: 350 Fifth Ave New York City NY 10001 Tel (212) LO 4-4140

PITT, HARVEY LLOYD, b. Bklyn., Feb. 28, 1945; B.A., City U. N.Y., 1965; J.D., St. John's U., 1968. Admitted to N.Y. State bar, 1969, U.S. Supreme Ct. bar, 1972; atty. Office Gen. Counsel, SEC, Washington, 1968-69, legal asst. to commr., 1969, spl. counsel Office Gen. Counsel, 1970-71, editor instl. investor study, 1971, chief counsel market regulation, 1972-73, exec. asst. to chmn., 1973-75, gen. counsel, 1975—; adj. profl. lectr. George Washington U. Law Sch., 1975—, Georgetown Law Sch., 1977—. Vice pres. Glen Haven Civic Assn., 1972, pres., 1973; bd. dirs. Eldwick Homes Assn., 1974-75; adv. bd. Southwestern Legal Found., U. Calif. Securities Regulation Inst.; sustaining mem. Am. Law Inst. Mem. Am., Fed. (exec. council securities law com., recipient outstanding fed. younger lawyer award 1975) bar assns. Contbr. articles to legal publs.; recipient Equal Opportunity Employment award SEC, 1976. Home: 11204 Bedfordshire Ave Potomac MD 20854 Office: 500 N Capitol St NW Suite 707 Washington DC 20549 Tel (202) 755-1108

PITT, THOMAS ANTHONY, JR., b. W. Chester, Pa., Feb. 26, 1933; B.S. in Econs., Villanova Coll., 1954, J.D., 1961; postgrad. Nat. Coll. State Trial Judges, 1972. Admitted to Pa. bar, 1961; asst. dist. atty. Chester County, Pa., 1962-67; mem. firm Pitt & Agulnick, W. Chester, 1964-70; judge Ct. of Common Pleas, Chester County, 1970—; tchr. law Alvernia Coll., Del. Law Sch., Immaculata Coll., W. Chester State Coll. Trustee W. Chester YMCA, 1976; dir. Chester County Council Boy Scouts Am., 1976; dir. W. Chester United Fund, 1968. Mem. Pa., Chester County bar assns. Home: Church & Virginia Aves West Chester PA 19380 Office: The Ct House West Chester PA 19380 Tel (215) 431-6182

PITTENGER, WILLIAM B.C., b. Austin, Tex., Nov. 4, 1940; B.B.A. in Finance, U. Tex., 1962, LL.B., 1965. Admitted to Tex. bar; asso. firm Hochberg, Yuill & Bernstein, 1970-73, Goldberg & Alexander, 1973-75; partner Yuill & Pittenger, Dallas, 1975—. Dir. The 500, Inc., Dallas, 1976. Mem. Tex., Dallas bar assns., Dallas Estate Council. Office: Stemmons Tower West Dallas TX 75207 Tel (214) 630-5741

PITTMAN, JACK HOMER, b. Hattiesburg, Miss., May 24, 1938; B.P.A., U. Miss., 1959, J.D., 1961. Admitted to Miss. bar, 1961; partner firm Pittman & Hollimon; and predecessors, Hattiesburg, 1961—; U.S. commr., 1966-67. Mem. Am., Miss., South Central bar assns. Home: 608 S 38th Ave Hattiesburg MS 39401 Office: Suite 407 Faulkner Blvd Hattiesburg MS 39401 Tel (601) 582-4336

PITTMAN, THOMAS VIRGIL, b. Enterprise, Ala., Mar. 28, 1916; B.S. in Commerce and Bus. Adminstrn., U. Ala., 1939, LL.B., 1940. Admitted to Ala. bar, 1940; spl. agt. FBI, 1940-44; partner firm Miller & Pittman, Gadsden, Ala., 1946-51; judge Ala. Circuit Ct., 16th Jud. Circuit, 1951-66, presiding judge, 1953-66; judge U.S. Dist. Ct., Middle and So. Dists. Ala., 1966-71, chief judge So. Dist. Ala., 1971—; lectr. U. Ala. Center at Gadsden, 1948-66. Chmn. March of Dimes, Etowah County, Ala., 1949-66; vice chmn. bd. deacons 1st Baptist Ch., Gadsden, 1960's; trustee Samford U., 1975—; mem. Ala. State Bd. Edn., 1951. Mem. Etowah County Bar Assn. (pres. 1949). Office: PO Box 465 247 US Courthouse Mobile AL 36601 Tel (205) 690-2381

PITTONI, MARIO, b. N.Y.C., Aug. 13, 1906; A.B., Cornell U., 1927; LL.B., Harvard, 1930; J.D., N.Y. U., 1932. Admitted to N.Y. State bar, 1933; practiced in Mineola, 1934-38; judge Nassau County (N.Y.) Ct., 1956; justice N.Y. Supreme Ct., Mineola, 1957—; asst. U.S. atty., chief criminal div. Eastern dist., Bklyn., 1938-48; prof. Bklyn. Law Sch., 1946-57; 1st dep. commr. of commerce N.Y. State, 1955-56. Home: 51 Watts Pl Lynbrook NY 11563 Office: Supreme Ct Bldg Mineola NY 11501 Tel (516) 535-2154

PITTS, HENRY LARUE, b. McLean, Ill., Dec. 12, 1910; student Ill. State U., 1929-31; B.S., U. Ill., 1934; J.D. with honors, U. Mich., 1939. Admitted to Ill. bar, 1939; partner firm Rooks, Pitts, Fullagar & Poust, and predecessors, Chgo., 1939—; dir. Chgo. Crime Commn.; chmn. Ill. State Bd. Investment, 1970-73. Trustee Union League Found. for Boys Clubs, 1960—; mem. Episcopal Diocesan Council, 1962-65. Fellow Am. Coll. Probate Counsel, Am. Bar Found.; mem. Am. (ho. of dels. 1967-74, chmn. nat. disciplinary enforcement com. 1970-73), Ill. State (pres. 1969-70, bd. govs. 1960-71), Chgo. bar assns., Am. Judicature Soc. (dir. 1972-76), Nat. Conf. Bar Pres.'s (exec. council 1970-72), Bar Assn. 7th Fed. Circuit, Chgo. Assn. Commerce and Industry (v.p. govtl. affairs 1973-77, dir. 1973—), Order of Coif, Kappa Delta Pi. Contbr. articles to legal jours. Home: 3 S 670 Leask Ln Wheaton IL 60187 Office: 208 S LaSalle St Chicago IL 60604

PITTS, MAURICE EDWARD, b. Evansville, Ind., May 29, 1924; LL.B., Atlanta Law Sch., 1950, LL.M., 1951. Admitted to Ga. bar, 1951; with Retail Credit Co., 1946-62, Globe Life and Accident Ins. Co., 1962-66; individual practice law, Fairburn, Ga., 1963-73; partner firm James, Johnson & Pitts, Douglasville, Ga., 1973-76; partner firm Pitts & Pitts, Fairburn, 1976—. Mem. Am., Ga., Atlanta bar assns. Office: 277 N E Broad St Fairburn GA 30213

PITZNER, RICHARD WILLIAM, b. Fond du Lac, Wis., Sept. 19, 1946; B.B.A., U. Wis., 1968, M.B.A., 1969, J.D., 1972. Admitted to Wis. bar, 1972; asso. firm Murphy, Stolper, Brewster & Desmond, Madison, 1972—; instr. U. Wis., 1976; various teaching and speaking engagements. Active United Way, Madison, 1972. Mem. Am., Wis., Dane County bar assns., Am. Inst. C.P.A.'s, Wis. Soc. C.P.A.'s, Beta Gamma, Phi Eta Sigma, Beta Alpha Psi. C.P.A., Wis. Home: 613 Morningstar Ln Madison WI 53704 Office: 2 E Gilman Madison WI 53703 Tel (608) 257-7181

PIZZA, ANTHONY GEORGE, b. Toledo, Nov. 29, 1921; B. Phil., U. Toledo, 1946, LL.B., 1950. Admitted to Ohio bar, 1950; asst. pros. atty. Lucas County, (Ohio), 1951-76, pros. atty., 1976—. Mem. Toldeo Bar Assn. Home: 5810 Cresthaven St Toledo OH 43614 Office: 320 Ontario St Toledo OH 43624

PLANALP, J. ROBERT, b. Mason City, Iowa, Feb. 9, 1949; B.S., in Indsl. Relations, Creighton U., 1971, J.D., 1973. Admitted to Nebr. bar, 1973, Mont. bar, 1974; asso. firm Farnham & Moylan, Omaha, 1971-73; partner firm Landoe, Gary & Planalp, Bozeman, Mont., 1974—. Dir., Gallatin-Park Youth Guidance Home, Inc.; pres. Exchange Club Bozeman, 1976—. Mem. Am., Mont. bar assns. Office: Box 609 Bozeman MT 59715 Tel (406) 586-2335

PLANT, MARCUS LEO, b. New London, Wis., Nov. 10, 1911; A.B., Lawrence Coll., 1932, M.A., 1934; J.D., U. Mich., 1938. Admitted to Wis. bar, 1939, N.Y. bar, 1946, Mich. bar, 1949; asso. firm Miller, Mack & Fairchild, Milw., 1938-44, Cahill, Gordon, Zachry & Reindel, N.Y.C., 1944-46; prof. law, U. Mich., Ann Arbor, 1946—. Mem. Am. Bar Assn., State Bar Mich., Order of Coif, Phi Alpha Delta. Author: Cases on The Law of Torts, 1953; (with Burke Shartel) The Law of Medical Practice, 1959; (with Wex S. Malone) Cases and Materials on Workmen's Compensation, 1962; (with Wex S. Malone and Joseph Little) Cases and Materials on The Employment Relation, 1974; contbr. articles to legal jours. Home: 2311 Woodside Rd Ann Arbor MI 48104 Office: 332 Hutchins Hall Ann Arbor MI 48104 Tel (313) 764-9345

PLATT, HARRY HERMAN, b. Russia, May 8, 1902; A.B., U. Mich., 1924, J.D., 1926. Admitted to Mich. bar, 1926; mem. firm Retan, Zeleznik & Platt, Detroit, 1928-34; individual practice law, Detroit, 1934-72, Southfield, Mich., 1972—; permanent umpire Ford Motor Co.-United Auto Workers labor agreements, 1950-67; arbitrator industrial disputes; chmn. Emergency Bds., 1961, 63. Vice-pres. Orgn. for Rehabilitation and Training (ORT), N.Y.C. Mem. Nat. Acad. of Arbitrators (past pres.), Am., Detroit (former dir.) bar assns. Contbr. articles to legal jours. Home: 17546 Bircherest Dr Detroit MI 48221 Office: Suite 990 Honeywell Center 17515 W Nine Mile Rd Southfield MI 48075 Tel (313) 557-1202

PLATT, JOEL ROBERT, b. Chgo., Dec. 24, 1946; B.S., U. Ill., 1969; J.D., Georgetown U., 1974. Admitted to Ill. bar, 1974; law clk. Consumer Protection div. Office Ill. Atty. Gen., Chgo., summers 1972-73; chief counsel Ill. Gov's. Consumer Adv. Office, Chgo., 1974-76; consumer rep. FTC hearings Trade and Vocat. Sch. Regulations, Chgo., 1976; staff atty. FTC, Chgo., 1976—. Vol. legal counsel "La Gente" Community Center, Chgo., 1974-75. Office: 55 E Monroe St Suite 1437 Chicago IL 60603 Tel (312) 353-4423

PLATT, ROBERT DAY, b. Columbus, Ohio, July 15, 1933; A.B., Harvard, 1955, LL.B., 1960. Admitted to Calif. bar, 1961, Maine bar, 1970; asso. firm Berkley, Randall & Harvey, Berkeley, Calif., 1961-63; asso., partner firm Johnston, Platt, Klein & Horton, and predecessors, Oakland, Calif., 1963-69; asso. firm Preti & Flaherty, Portland, Maine, 1969-71; partner firm Lowry, Platt, Fitzhenry, Lunt & Givertz, Portland, 1971—. Mem. town council Town of Scarborough (Maine), 1972-74, chmn., 1974; pres. Found. for Blood Research, Portland, 1973—. Mem. Am., Maine, Cumberland County (Me.) (sec.-treas. 1976—) bar assns., State Bar Calif. Contbr. articles to legal jours. Office: Lowry Platt Fitzhenry Lunt Givertz PO Box 130 57 Exchange St Portland ME 04111 Tel (207) 772-8372

PLATT, STEPHEN EUGENE, b. Logansport, Ind., May 24, 1945; B.A., Valparaiso U., 1967, J.D., 1970. Admitted to Ind. bar, 1970; partner firm Virgil, Cawley & Platt, and predecessors, Elkhart, Ind., 1970-76; staff counsel Elkhart Legal Aid Soc., 1971-74; dep. prosecutor Elkhart County, 1975—. Bd. dirs. Hoosier Girls' Town, Inc., 1976—, Child Abuse and Neglect Task Force, 1975-76, Detention Center, 1976—, H.E.L.P., 1974. Mem. Am. (environ. law com. 1975—), Ind., Elkhart County, Elkhart bar assns., Phi Alpha Delta. Office: 215 S 2nd St Elkhart IN 46514 Tel (219) 294-2554

PLATTO, CHARLES, b. N.Y.C., Nov. 19, 1945; B.A., U. Pa., 1966; J.D., U. Mich., 1969; LL.M., N.Y. U., 1974. Admitted to N.Y. bar, 1970, U.S. Supreme Ct. bar, 1974, French bar as conseil juridique, 1976; Reginald Heber Smith fellow Community Legal Service Inc., Phila., 1969-71; asso. firm Cahill, Gordon & Reindel, N.Y.C., 1971-74, 76—, Paris, 1974-76. Home: 2 Berkeley Rd Scarsdale NY 10583 Office: 80 Pine St New York City NY 10005 Tel (212) 825-0100

PLAUT, NATHAN MICHAEL, b. Cin., Nov. 25, 1917; B.A., Harvard, 1939, postgrad. in law, 1946; LL.B., U. Mich., 1941. Admitted to Ohio bar, 1941, Mass. bar, 1946, N.H. bar, 1947; asso. Philip H. Faulkner, Keene, N.H., 1946-53; partner firm Faulkner, Plaut, Hanna, Zimmerman & Freund, and predecessors, Keene, 1953—. Mem. Keene Bd. Edn., 1962-65; mem. visitors com. U. Mich. Law Sch., 1962-68. Fellow Am. Coll. Probate Counsel; mem. Cheshire County (pres. 1961-62), N.H. (pres. 1971-72), Am. (ho. of dels. 1973—), Boston bar assns., Assn. Ins. Attys. (exec. council 1976—), Internat. Assn. Ins. Attys., Internat. Soc. Barristers. Home: Peg Shop Rd Kenne NH 03431 Office: 91 Court St Keene NH 03431 Tel (603) 352-3630

PLEAK, MAURICE D., b. Letts, Ind., Mar. 8, 1905; student Ind. Central Coll., 1923-24; LL.B., Ind. U., 1926. Admitted to Ind. bar, 1926, U.S. Supreme Ct. bar, 1961; individual practice law, Indpls., 1926—; dep. prosecutor Marion County, 1940-46. Mem. Lawyers

Assn. of Indpls. Office: 1001 Peoples Bank Bldg Indianapolis IN 46204 Tel (317) 632-5819

PLEASANTS, MICHAEL FRANCIS, b. Memphis, Aug. 6, 1942; B.A., Vanderbilt U., 1964; J.D., Memphis State U., 1967. Admitted to Tenn. bar, 1967; asso. firm Heiskell, Donelson, Adams, Williams & Kirsch, and predecessors, 1967-74, partner firm, 1974—. Mem. Forum for Better Memphis, 1976—; treas. Memphis Heritage Soc. Mem. Am., Memphis, Shelby County, Tenn. (lectr. seminar on criminal law for gen. practitioner 1976) bar assns., Memphis C. of C. (minority bus. assistance com.). Home: 699 Anderson Pl Memphis TN 38104 Office: Suite 2020 165 Madison Ave Memphis TN 38103 Tel (901) 525-8231

PLESKA, PHILIP LOUIS, b. Middletown, Ohio, Mar. 31, 1946; B.A., Ohio U., 1969; J.D., U. N.C., 1972. Admitted to Ohio bar, 1972, U.S. Supreme Ct. bar, 1976; asso. firm Wilmer & Wilmer, Middletown, 1972; asst. pros. atty., Warren County, Ohio, 1973-74; prosecutor City of Franklin, Ohio, 1973-75; partner firm Pleska, Fowler & Oliver, Lebanon, Ohio, 1974—; instr. real estate law, Miami U., 1976—. Mem. Am., Ohio, Warren County bar assns. Home: 3113 Columbia Rd Lebanon OH 45036 Office: 777 Columbus Ave Lebanon OH 45036

PLETCHER, GEORGE EDWIN, b. Perryton, Tex., Jan. 24, 1928; J.D., U. Notre Dame, 1951. Admitted to Tex. bar, 1951; asso. firm Helm & Jones, Houston, 1951-55; partner Helm, Pletcher, Hogan & Burrow, and predecessor, Houston, 1955—; mem. Med. Profl. Liability Study Commn. Tex. Councilman, City of Hedwig Village, 1963—. Fellow Internat. Acad. Trial Lawyers, Am. Coll. Trial Lawyers; mem. Tex. (dir. 1968-71), Houston (pres. 1975—) bar assns., Houston Legal Found. (pres. 1976—). Office: 909 Fannin St Houston TX 77002 Tel (713) 654-4464

PLETZ, FRANCIS GREGORY, b. Lakefield, Minn., Aug. 23, 1917; A.B. summa cum laude, Coll. St. Thomas, St. Paul, 1940; M.B.A. with distinction (fellow), U. Mich., 1942; J.D. magna cum laude, U. Toledo, 1950; postgrad. Stonier Sch. Banking, Rutgers U., 1956. Admitted to Ohio bar, 1950; teller 1st Nat. Bank, Lakefield, 1937-38; research asst. Bur. Bus. Research, U. Mich., 1940-41; accountant Ernst & Ernst, Detroit, summer 1941; with Toledo Trust Co., 1946—, sr. v.p., head trust dept., 1968—, sec., 1973—; dir. Alloy Founders, Inc., Throm Realty Co., C.F. Throm & Sons, Throm Supplies. Bd. trustees Toledo Soc. for Blind, 1973-76, St. Vincent Hosp., Toledo, 1976, Stranahan Charitable Found., 1968. Mem. Ohio Bankers Assn., Ohio, Lucas County, Toledo bar assns., Toledo C. of C. Clubs: Lions, Toledo, Sylvania Country (Toledo). Home: 3605 Orchard Trail Toledo OH 43606 Office: 245 Summit St Toledo OH 43603 Tel (419) 259-8146

PLEVY, ARTHUR LESTER, b. N.Y.C., May 26, 1936; student in Math., Bklyn. Coll., 1957; J.D., Bklyn. Law Sch., 1967; B.E.E., Coll. City N.Y., 1959. Admitted to N.Y. State bar, 1965, U.S. Patent Office bar, 1967, N.J. bar, 1970; engr. ITT, Nutley, N.J., 1959-61; project engr. Westex Corp., N.Y.C., 1961-65; mem. tech. staff RCA, N.Y.C., 1962-65, patent counsel, Princeton, N.J., 1965-72; individual practice law, East Brunswick, N.J., 1972—. Mem. Am., N.Y. State, N.J., Fed. bar assns., IEEE. Contbr. articles to legal jours. Patentee in electronics. Tel (201) 238-1303

PLIMPTON, FRANCIS TAYLOR PEARSONS, b. N.Y.C., Dec. 7, 1900; A.B. magna cum laude, Amherst Coll., 1922; J.D., Harvard, 1925. Admitted to N.Y. State bar, 1926; asso. firm Root, Clark, Buckner & Ballantine, N.Y.C., 1925-32, head Paris office, 1930-31; gen. solicitor Reconstrn. Finance Corp., Washington, 1932-33; partner firm Debevoise, Plimpton, Lyons & Gates, and predecessors, N.Y.C., 1933-61, 65—; ambassador, dep. U.S. rep. UN, N.Y.C., 1961-65, del. 15th-19th UN Gen. Assemblies, mem. UN adminstrv. tribunal, 1965—. Chmn., N.Y.C. Bd. Ethics, 1972—, N.Y.C. Mayor's Commn. for Distinguished Guests, 1976—. Fellow Am. Bar Found., Am. Acad. Arts and Scis.; mem. Assn. Bar City N.Y. (pres. 1968-70), Internat., Inter-Am., Am. (ho. of dels.), N.Y. State (Gold medal 1977) bar assns., Union Internationale des Avocats (v.p.), Am. Law Inst. Am. Soc. Internat. Law, Am. Br. Internat. Law Assn. Decorated chevalier Legion of Honor (France); comdr. Order of Merit (Italy); knight Order of St. John of Jerusalem; recipient Distinguished Pub. Service award New Eng. Soc. of N.Y., 1963, Fed. Bar Council, 1964, St. Nicholas Soc., 1974, Inst. on Man and Sci., 1975; Bronze medal City of N.Y., 1975; Benjamin Franklin fellow Royal Soc. Arts. Home: 131 E 66th St New York City NY 10021 Office: 299 Park Ave New York City NY 10017 Tel (212) 752-6400

PLINER, LEON MILTON, b. Shreveport, La., Sept. 30, 1924; student U. N.D., 1943; B.S. in Chem. Engring., La. State U., 1956; LL.B., Centenary Coll., 1956. Admitted to La. bar, 1956; research chem. engr. United Gas Corp., 1949-63; individual practice law, Shreveport, 1963—. Mem. Am., La., Shreveport bar assns., Am., La. trial lawyers assns. Recipient Distinguished Toastmaster award Toastmasters Internat., 1974. Home: 909 Elmwood St Shreveport LA 71104 Office: 201 Lane Bldg Shreveport LA 71101 Tel (318) 222-0728

PLOTKIN, BERNARD JOEL, b. Milw., July 4, 1934; B.B.A., U. Wis., 1956; J.D., Marquette U., 1961. Admitted to Wis. bar, 1961; since practiced in Milw., partner firm Frank, Keyes & Plotkin, 1961-64; individual practice law, 1964-66; pres. Wis. Legal Secretarial Sch., 1966-68; asst. dean bus. affairs U. Wis.-Milw. Sch. Nursing, 1968—. Mem. Wis. Bar Assn. Home: 8670 N Fielding Rd Milwaukee WI 53217 Office: U Wis Milw Sch Nursing PO Box 413 Milwaukee WI 53201 Tel (414) 963-4801

PLOTNICK, PAUL DAVID, b. Stamford, Conn., Nov. 20, 1933; A.B., U. Pa., 1955; LL.B., N.Y. U., 1962. Admitted to Conn. bar, 1962; partner firm Plotnick & Plotnick, Stamford; mem. bd. reps. City of Stamford, 1967-69; sec. traffic advisory commn., 1972-74. Mem. Conn., Am., Lawyer-Pilots' bar assns. Home: 75 Rolling Wood Dr Stamford CT 06905 Office: 671 Bedford St Stamford CT 06901 Tel (203) 324-2126

PLOURD, LEWIS ALBERT, b. Frenchville, Maine, Mar. 5, 1925; B.A., Butler U., 1949; J.D., U. So. Calif., 1957. Admitted to Calif. bar, 1957; partner firm Plourd, Blume & Scoville, El Centro, Calif., 1977—. Mem. Am., Imperial County (pres. 1959-60) bar assns., Am., Calif. trial lawyers assns., Am. Judicature Soc., Am. Arbitration Soc. Home: 1597 Elm St El Centro CA 92243 Office: 1005 State St PO Box 99 El Centro CA 92243 Tel (714) 352-3130

PLOWDEN, J. SAM, b. Atlanta, July 28, 1934; J.D., Woodrow Wilson Coll. Law, 1956, LL.M., 1957. Admitted to Ga. bar, 1958; partner firms Adams & Plowden, Atlanta, 1958-60, Plowden & Hilliard, Atlanta, 1961-63, Plowden & Travis, Atlanta, 1963-71, Plowden, Clutts & Wilson, Atlanta, 1971—. Mem. State Bar Ga. Office: 2410 Gas Light Tower 235 Peachtree St NE Atlanta GA 30303 Tel (404) 524-7505

PLUMADORE, JAN HAYWARD, b. Potsdam, N.Y., July 29, 1942; B.S., St. Lawrence U., 1964; J.D., Albany Law Sch., 1968. Admitted to N.Y. State bar, 1970; partner firm Plumadore & Plumadore, Saranac Lake, N.Y., 1970—; atty. Town of Harrietstown, N.Y., 1971—, Town of St. Armand, 1973—; mem. County Legislature, 1974—. Chmn. Franklin County Republican Party, 1976; mem. N.Y. State Olympic Commn., 1974—, Lake Placid Olympic Organizing Com., 1974—; chmn. Tri-Lakes Council Local Govt., 1975—, Assn. Adarondack County Govts. Mem. Franklin County Bar Assn. Home: Lake Kiwassa Saranac Lake NY 12983 Office: Box 91 Saranac Lake NY 12983 Tel (914) 891-0510

PLUMB, WILLIAM THOMPSON, JR., b. Rochester, N.Y., Jan. 24, 1916; A.B., U. Rochester, 1936; LL.B., Cornell U., 1939. Admitted to D.C. bar, 1945, N.Y. bar, 1939; with IRS, Washington, 1940-51, asst. head civil div. chief counsel's office, 1946-51; asso. firm Hogan & Hartson, Washington, 1951-59, partner, 1959-66, 68—; counsel firm Sutherland, Asbill & Brennan, Washington, 1966-68; cons. Commn. on Bankruptcy Laws, U.S. Treasury Dept., N.Y. Law Revision Commn.; speaker on tax subjects. Mem. Am., Fed. (authors award field of taxation 1967) bar assns. Author: Federal Tax Collection, in preparation; draftsman Fed. Tax Lien Act of 1966; contbr. articles legal jours. Home: 5214 Kenwood Ave Chevy Chase MD 20015 Office: 815 Connecticut Ave NW Washington DC 20006 Tel (202) 331-4619

PLUMLEY, ALLAN RUDOLPH, JR., b. Washington, Jan. 14, 1933; B.A., U. Va., 1955; B.S., George Washington U., 1959, J.D., 1962. Admitted to Va. bar, 1962, U.S. Supreme Ct. bar, 1970; law clk. to chief judge U.S. Dist. Ct. D.C., 1962-63; asso. firm Adams, Porter Radigan & Mays, Arlington, Va., 1963-68, partner, 1968-75, of counsel, 1975—; pres., chief exec. officer 1st Fed. Savs. & Loan Assn., Arlington, Va., 1975—, also dir.; mem. grievance and ethics com. Va. State Bar, 1972-75, mem. corp. law com., 1973-76; ct. receiver Circuit Ct. Arlington County, Va., 1965-75; dir. Fairfax County Nat. Bank; adv. dir. Va. Nat. Bank. Bd. dirs. No. Va. chpt. Am. Heart Assn., 1975—. Mem. Am., Va. State, Arlington, InterAm. bar assns., Arlington C. of C. (dir.), Delta Theta Phi. Office: 2050 Wilson Blvd Arlington VA 22216 Tel (703) 524-2100 ext 250

PLUMMER, LAWRENCE ELLSWORTH, b. Rosholt, S.D., Apr. 2, 1909; LL.B., William Mitchell Coll. Law, 1933. Admitted to Iowa bar, 1935; clk. 1st Nat. Bank, St. Paul, 1929-35; practiced in Northwood, Iowa, 1935-60; judge Iowa Dist. Ct., 2d Jud. Dist., 1960—; mayor City of Northwood, 1954-58; county atty. Worth County (Iowa), 1940-52. Mem. Am., Iowa, 2d Jud. Dist., Worth County bar assns., Iowa Dist. Court Judges Assn. (pres. 1974-75). Home: 205 Shellrock Dr Northwood IA 50459 Office: Worth County Courthouse Northwood IA 50459 Tel (515) 324-2360

PLUNKETT, CHARLES ENGLAND, b. Camden, Ark., Dec. 4, 1934; B.A., Hendrix Coll., 1956; J.D., Duke U., 1959. Admitted to Ark. bar, 1960; partner firm Streett & Plunkett, Camden, 1961-74; city atty., Camden, 1960-62; dep. pros. atty. Ouachita County (Ark.), 1960-63; judge Municipal Ct., Camden, 1965-73; chancellor 7th Chancery Dist. 1st Div. Calhoun, Columbia, Dallas, Lafayette, Ouachita, Union Counties (Ark.), 1975—. Chmn. United Fund, 1961; chmn. Easter Seals bd., 1966; chmn. County Bd. of Equalization, 1963-65. Mem. Ark., Am., Ouachita (pres. 1964-66) bar assns., Ark. Jud. Council. Home: 2230 Maul Rd Camden AR 71701 Office: PO Box 40 Ouachita County Ct House Camden AR 71701 Tel (501) 836-2796

PLYMPTON, GEORGE FRANKLIN, b. Hackensack, N.J., May 29, 1895; Litt.B., Princeton U., 1917; LL.B., J.D., Columbia, 1921. Admitted to N.J. bar, 1921; partner firm Plympton & Bentley, and predecessor, Hackensack, 1921—. Mem. N.J., Bergen County bar assns. Home: 170 Prospect Ave Hackensack NJ 07601 Tel (201) 342-6200

POAGE, WILLIAM ROBERT, b. Waco, Tex., Dec. 28, 1899; A.B., Baylor U., 1921, LL.B., 1924, LL.D., 1967, L.H.D., 1973. Admitted to Tex. bar, 1924; individual practice law, Waco, 1924-37; mem. Tex. Ho. of Reps., 1925-29, Tex. Senate, 1931-37; mem. 75th to 95th Congresses from 11th Dist. Tex.; del. Interparliamentary Union, 1947—. Author: After the Pioneers, 1969; Politics - Texas Style, 1974. Home: 600 Edgewood Ave Waco TX 78708 Office: 2107 Rayburn Bldg Washington DC 20515 Tel (202) 225-6105

POCHE, MARC BELMAR, b. New Orleans, May 1, 1934; B.A. summa cum laude, U. Santa Clara (Calif.), 1956; J.D., U. Calif., Berkeley, 1961. Admitted to Calif. bar, 1962, U.S. Supreme Ct. bar, 1968; asso. firm Ruffe & Chadwick, San Jose, Calif., 1962-64, partner, 1964-66; asso. prof. law, U. Santa Clara, 1966-70, prof. law, 1970-76; asst. to gov. of Calif., 1975—, legis. sec., 1976—; vis. prof. law U. Calif., Berkeley, 1973-74. Mem. Am., Calif., Santa Clara County bar assns. Recipient Outstanding Prof. of Yr. award, U. Santa Clara Sch. Law, 1972-73. Office: Governor's Office State Capitol Sacramento CA 95814 Tel (916) 445-3921

PODELL, JAMES J., b. Milw., Oct. 5, 1940; B.B.A., U. Mich., 1964, J.D., 1967. Admitted to Wis. Bar, 1968; asst. dist. atty. Milwaukee County, Wis., 1969-72; partner firm Podell and Podell (now Podell, Hodan & Podell), Milw., 1972—. Trustee Congregation Shalom, 1972-75, pres. Congregation Shalom Brotherhood, 1976. Fellow Am. Acad. Matrimonial Lawyers; mem. Am. (liaison family law and tax sects. 1977, chmn. family law membership com. 1977), Wis. (bd. govs. family law sect. 1977—), Milw. (chmn. speakers bur. 1973—) bar assns., Assn. Trial Lawyers Am., Defense Research Inst. Home: 400 White Oak Way Mequon WI 53092 Office: 9001 N 76th St Milwaukee WI 53223 Tel (414) 453-1710

PODOLSKI, ALFRED LAWRENCE, b. Dedham, Mass., July 23, 1924; LL.B., Boston Coll. Law, 1950; LL.D., New Eng. Sch. Law. Admitted to Mass. bar, 1951; spl. agt. FBI, 1951-52; individual practice law, Dedham, 1952-71; judge Probate Ct., Dedham, 1971-73, chief judge, 1973—; counsel Town of Dedham, 1954-71; spl. asst. atty. gen. to asst. atty. gen., Dedham, 1963-70; mem. com. on model act freeing children for adoption HEW. Mem. Am. Judicature Soc., Am., Norfolk County bar assns., Jud. Council Commonwealth of Mass., Conf. Conciliation Cts. Contbr. articles in field to legal jours. Office: 990 Washington St Dedham MA 02026 Tel (617) 326-7207

PODOLSKY, SIDNEY DAVID, b. Aurora, Ill., Sept. 5, 1905; Ph.B., U. Chgo., 1925, J.D., 1928. Admitted to Ill. bar, 1928; exec. asst. Chgo. Regional War Labor Bd., 1943-45; chief sect. wages and hours OPA, 1945-47; city atty. City of Aurora, 1950-54. Pres., YMHA Temple, Aurora, 1962, B'nai B'rith, Aurora, 1960. Mem. Ill. State, Kane County bar assns., Am. Arbitration Soc. Author: Guide to War Labor Bd. Policy, 1945. Home: 1616 Garfield St Aurora IL 60506 Office: Room 310 Keystone Bldg 30 S Stolp Ave Aurora IL 60506 Tel (312) 897-7868

POE, DOUGLAS ALLAN, b. Chgo. Heights, Ill., Nov. 14, 1942; B.A., DePauw U., 1964; J.D., Duke, 1967, LL.M., Yale, 1968. Admitted to Ill. bar, 1967, U.S. 4th Circuit Ct. Appeals bar, 1968, U.S. Dist. Ct. for No. Ill., bar, 1972, U.S. Supreme Ct. bar, 1972, U.S. 7th Circuit Ct. Appeals Bar, 1973; law clk. to Hon. Harrison L. Winter, U.S. 4th Circuit Ct. Appeals, 1968-69, to Hon. Warren E. Burger, U.S. Supreme Ct., 1969, to Hon. William J. Brennan, Jr., U.S. Supreme Ct., 1970; asso. firm Mayer, Brown & Platt, Chgo., 1970-73, partner, 1974—. Mem. Am. Bar Assn., Chgo. Council Lawyers, Order of Coif. Contbr. articles to law jours. Office: 231 S LaSalle St Chicago IL 60604 Tel (312) 782-0600

POE, H. SADLER, b. Rock Hill, S.C., Oct. 17, 1944; A.B., Princeton, 1967; LL.B., U. Va., 1971. Admitted to Ga. bar, 1971; asso. firm Alston Miller & Gaines, Atlanta, 1971-76, partner, 1976—. Mem. State Bar Ga. (past mem. securities law revision com., corporate banking and law sect.), Am., Atlanta bar assns. Contbr. articles to legal jours. Home: 793 Wellesley Dr NW Atlanta GA 30305 Office: Alston Miller & Gaines 1200 C&S Bank Bldg Atlanta GA 30303 Tel (404) 588-0300

POE, WILLIAM EDWARD, b. S. Hill, Va., Dec. 18, 1923; B.S., Wake Forest U., 1947; J.D., Harvard U., 1950. Admitted to N.C. bar, 1950; partner firm Grier, Parker, Poe, Thompson, Bernstein, Gage & Preston, Charlotte, N.C., 1953—; tax atty. Mecklenburg County, N.C., 1952-57. Precinct chmn., sec. Mecklenburg County Dem. Exec. Com., 1957-59; chmn. Charlotte-Mecklenburg County Bd. Edn., 1966-76; mem. bd. dirs. N.C. Sch. Bds. Assn., 1968-75, pres., 1969-71; trustee N.C. Baptist Children's Homes, 1959-63, Wake Forest Coll., 1963-67; pres. bd. dirs. Charlotte Christian Rehab. Center, 1976—; mem. exec. bd. Mecklenburg County Council Boy Scouts Am., 1971—; bd. dirs. Charlotte chpt. Am. Cancer Soc., 1970-76; chmn. bd. dirs. WTVI, Inc., 1976—. Mem. Am., N.C. bar assns., 26th Judicial Dist. Bar (pres. 1977), C. of C. (dir. 1971-73). So. Region Sch. Bds. Conf. (pres. 1974-75). Author: (with John F. Blair and J. Shepherd Bryan) Motor Vehicle Law in North Carolina, 1952. Named Man of Year Charlotte News, 1970. Home: 2101 Coniston Place Charlotte NC 28207 Office: 1100 Cameron Brown Bldg Charlotte NC 28204 Tel (704) 372-6730

POFFENBERGER, JOHN DWIGHT, b. Adrian, Mich., May 24, 1934; B.Indsl. Engring., Ohio State U., 1957; LL.B., George Washington U., 1961. Admitted to Ohio bar, 1961; partner firm Wood, Herron & Evans, Cin., 1961—. Mem. Am., Cin. bar assns., Cin. Patent Law Assn. Home: 5860 Miami Rd Cincinnati OH 45243 Office: 2700 Carew Tower Cincinnati OH 45202 Tel (513) 241-2324

POGOSTIN, JOSEPH MICHAEL, b. N.Y.C., Feb. 16, 1940; A.B., N.Y. U., 1961; LL.B., Boston U., 1964. Admitted to N.Y. bar, 1965; individual practice law, New Rochelle, N.Y., 1965—. Mem. N.Y. State, Westchester County, New Rochelle bar assns. Office: 560 North Ave New Rochelle NY 10801 Tel (914) 235-3654

POGREBIN, BERTRAND B., b. Bklyn., Apr. 10, 1934; A.B., Rutgers U., 1955; LL.B., Harvard, 1958. Admitted to N.Y. bar, 1959; mem. firm Rains, Pogrebin & Scher, Mineola, N.Y., 1959—; adj. asso. prof. N.Y. U. Law Sch., 1975—. Bd. dirs. Walden Sch., N.Y.C., 1976—, Pub. Edn. Assn., N.Y.C., 1975—. Mem. Am., Nassau County (N.Y.) bar assns., Indsl. Relations Research Assn. Contbr. articles to profl. jours. Home: 33 W 67th St New York City NY 10023 Office: 210 Old Country Rd Mineola NY 11501 Tel (516) 742-1470 also 110 E 59th St New York City NY 10021 Tel (212) 895-3438

POGRUND, SHERWIN IVAN, b. Chgo., Sept. 4, 1934; B.A., Roosevelt U., 1955; J.D., Northwestern U., 1957; postgrad. Oxford U. Admitted to Ill. bar; mem. firm Stone Pogrund & Korey, Chgo., 1958—, partner, 1961—; gen. counsel Profl. Remodelers Assn., 1961-77. Bd. dirs. Assn. for Family Living, 1969-71; v.p. Skokie Valley Traditional Synagogue, 1968-75. Mem. Am., Ill., Chgo. bar assns., Comml. Law League, Tau Epsilon Rho. Contbr. articles in field to mags. Office: 221 N LaSalle St Chicago IL 60601 Tel (312) 782-3675

POGSON, STEPHEN WALTER, b. N.Y.C., May 11, 1937; B.A., U. Ariz., 1958; LL.B., 1961. Admitted to Ariz. bar, 1961, U.S. Supreme Ct. bar, 1972; asso. firm Evans, Kitchel & Jenckes, Phoenix, 1962-66, partner firm, 1967—. Bd. dirs. Maricopa County Legal Aid Soc., 1975—. Mem. Am. Bar Assn., Indsl. Relations Assn., Am. Inst. Mech. Engrs., U. Ariz. Alumni Assn. (pres. Phoenix chpt. 1965-66). Home: 2108 N 9th Ave Phoenix AZ 85007 Office: 363 N 1st Ave Phoenix AZ 85003 Tel (602) 262-8866

POHL, DALE L., b. Emporia, Kans., May 10, 1936; B.S., Kans. State Tchrs. Coll., Emporia, 1958; M.P.A., U. Kans., 1959; J.D., Washburn U., 1963. Admitted to Kans. bar, 1963; partner firm Forbes and Pohl, Eureka, Kans., 1963—; city atty., Eureka, 1966—. Bd. dirs. Kans. Blue Cross, 1973—, sec., 1976-77, 2d vice chmn., 1977-78; bd. dirs. Unified Sch. Dist. # 389, 1973-77, pres., 1975-76; pres. Christ Lutheran Ch. Mem. Kans. (exec. council 1976—), SE Kans. (pres. 1972-73), Greenwood County bar assns. Contbr. articles to legal jours. Office: PO Box 528 Eureka KS 67045 Tel (316) 583-5508

POHLMAN, JAMES ERWIN, b. Iowa City, Apr. 10, 1932; A.B., Oberlin Coll., 1954; J.D., U. Mich., 1957. Admitted to Ohio bar, 1957; asso. firm Wright, Harlor, Morris & Arnold, Columbus, Ohio, 1957-62, partner, 1962—. Mem. Internat. Assn. Ins. Counsel, Am. Judicature Soc., Columbus, Ohio State, Am. bar assns. Home: 2424 Fair Ave Columbus OH 43209 Office: 37 W Broad St Columbus OH 43215 Tel (614) 224-4125

POINDEXTER, WILLIAM MERSEREAU, b. Los Angeles, June 16, 1925; B.A., Yale, 1946; J.D., U. Calif., 1949. Admitted to Calif. bar, 1952; pres. Consol. Brazing & Mfg. Co., Riverside, Calif., 1949-52; asso. firm Bledsoe, Smith & Cathcart, San Francisco, 1952-54, Robertson, Harney, Drummond & Behr, Los Angeles, 1954-57; prin. firm Poindexter & Doutre, Inc., Los Angeles, 1957—; bd. dirs. Trio Metal Stampings, Inc., 1965; sec. Prodn. Aids, Inc., 1969; sec. bd. dirs. EPD Industries, 1969-72. Fellow Am. Coll. Probate Counsel; mem. Am., Calif., Los Angeles County bar assns. Office: 1 Wilshire Blvd Los Angeles CA 90017 Tel (213) 628-8297

POINTER, JAMES EDGAR, JR., b. Gloucester County, Va., Sept. 22, 1922; B.S., Coll. William and Mary, 1943, J.D., 1949. Admitted to Va. bar, 1948; asso. firm DuVal & Pointer, Gloucester, Va., 1951-54; mem. firm Pointer & Field, Gloucester, 1958-74; individual practice law, Gloucester, 1974—; commonwealth's atty. Gloucester County, 1954-64; local counsel Va. Dept. Hwys. and Transp., 1954—; asst. sec., dir. United Va. Bank of Gloucester, 1953—. Atty. sch. bd. Gloucester County, 1954-72; sec., bd. dirs. Francis N. Sanders Nursing Home, Gloucester; chmn. adv. bd. Walter Reed Meml. Hosp., Gloucester, 1975—; trustee Riverside Hosp., Newport News, Va., 1976—. Mem. Am., Va. bar assns., Va. State Bar, Va. Trial Lawyers Assn., 13th Jud. Circuit Bar Assn. (pres. 1958—). Home and Office: Gloucester VA 23061 Tel (804) 693-2800

POJMAN, PAUL JOSEPH, b. Cleve., Aug. 22, 1917; Ph.B., John Carroll U., 1939; LL.B., Western Res. U., 1942, M.A., 1948, J.D., 1968. Admitted to Ohio bar, 1942, individual practice law, Parma, Ohio; mem. Walton Hills (Ohio) Village Council. Mem. Cleve. Bar Assn., Delta Theta Phi. Home: 17401 Egbert Rd Walton Hills OH 44146 Office: 5543 Ridge Rd Parma OH 44129 Tel (216) 884-2821

POLACEK, EDWARD, b. Chgo., June 5, 1925; B.S., Northwestern U., 1945, LL.B., 1947, J.D., 1970. Admitted to Ill. bar, 1948, U.S. Supreme Ct. bar, 1955; legal asst. firm Polacek and Lobo, Chgo., 1948-50; mem. firm Polacek, Polacek and Lobo, Chgo., 1951-63; individual practice law, Roselle, Ill., 1963—. Mem. Am., Ill., Chgo. bar assns., Tau Kappa Epsilon. Contbr. numerous articles to mags., legal jours. Office: 365 Hamstead Ct Roselle IL 60172

POLAHA, JEROME MICHAEL, b. Allentown, Pa., Feb. 21, 1940; A.A., Syracuse U., 1957; B.A., U. Nev., 1964; J.D., George Washington U., 1968. Admitted to Nev. bar, 1968; asso. firm Breen, Young, Whitehead and Hoy, Ltd., Reno, 1968-69; pub. defender Washoe County, Nev., 1969-72; partner firm Grellman, Polaha and Coffin and predecessor, Reno, 1972-76; individual practice law, Reno, 1976—; Nev. chmn. Law Day, 1970, 71-74; alt. judge Sparks (Nev.) Municipal Ct., 1970—; hearing officer Nev. State Bd. Edn., 1974—. Mem. hearing bd. sewer dist. Washoe County Health Dept., 1975—; adviser Explorer Post Nev. Area council Boy Scouts Am., 1975—; mem. No. Nev. Child Abuse Com., 1975—. Mem. Am. (Nev. chmn. young lawyers drug abuse program 1970-72), Nev., Washoe County bar assns., Nat. Assn. Criminal Def. Lawyers, Am., Nev. trial lawyers assns., Calif. Lawyers for Criminal Justice, Barristers Club of Nev. (pres. 1974-76). Home: 3220 Markridge Dr Reno NV 89509 Office: 210 S Sierra St PO Box 3556 Reno NV 89505 Tel (702) 786-5344

POLANSKY, LARRY PAUL, b. Bklyn., July 24, 1932; B.S. in Accounting, Temple U., 1958, J.D., 1973. Admitted to Pa. bar, 1973; computer systems engr. IBM Corp., Phila., 1965-67; chief dep. ct. adminstr. Phila. Common Pleas Ct., 1967-76; dep. ct. adminstr. Adminstrv. Office of Pa. Ct., Phila., 1976—; cons. Am. U. Ct. Tech. Asst. Project, 1973-76; vis. faculty Inst. Ct. Mgmt., 1971-76; faculty Temple U., 1974—; bd. dirs. Search Group, Inc., Sacramento; mem. info. task force Nat. Adv. Commn. on Criminal Justice Standards and Goals. Mem. Am., Pa., Phila. bar assns., Data Processing Mgmt. Assn. Recipient Certified Data Processor award Inst. Certification of Data Processing Profls., 1965; contbr. articles in field to profl. jours. Home: 124 Pocasset Rd Philadelphia PA 19115 Office: 1414 Three Penn Center Plaza Philadelphia PA 19102 Tel (215) LO7-3071

POLINER, BERNARD, b. Middletown, Conn., Nov. 18, 1931; B.A., U. Conn., 1954; LL.B., Boston U., 1957. Admitted to Conn. bar, 1958, Mass. bar, 1958; asso. firm Cole & Cole, Hartford, Conn., 1958—; chmn. Hartford County Med.-Legal Com., 1974-76. Chmn. Bloomfield Recreation Com., 1967-69; mem. Bloomfield Tax Rev. Bd., 1968-69; chmn. Bloomfield Zoning Bd. Appeals, 1969—. Mem. Conn., Hartford County bar assns., Am. Trial Lawyers Assn. Home: 13 Carpenter Ln Bloomfield CT 06002 Office: 1 Constitution Plaza Hartford CT 06103 Tel (203) 246-8561

POLISCHUK, GREGORY JOSEPH, b. Chester, Pa., Dec. 2, 1947; B.S. in Accounting, Boston Coll., 1969; J.D., Villanova U., 1972. Admitted to Pa. bar, 1972, U.S. Supreme Ct. bar, 1976; asso. firm Levy and Levy, Chester, 1972—; adj. prof. law Widener Coll., 1976—; dir. Essington Savs. & Loan Assn. (Pa.). Bd. dirs. Central Delaware County (Pa.) ARC, Media, 1975—. Mem. Am., Pa., Delaware County bar assns., Pa., Am. assns. trial lawyers. Home: 6 Server Ln Springfield PA 19064 Office: 710 Fidelity Bldg PO Box 737 Chester PA 19016 Tel (215) 876-3355

POLK, SYLVANUS WILLIAM, b. Purvis, Miss., Nov. 26, 1895; B.S., Miss. Coll., 1916; LL.B. cum laude, U. Miss., 1918, also J.D.; postgrad. Harvard Law Sch., 1919-20. Admitted to Miss. bar, 1918, Tenn. bar, 1922; individual practice law, Memphis, 1922-50; judge Probate Ct. of Shelby County (Tenn.), 1950—; mayor, Memphis, 1946-47; atty., Memphis, 1944-45. Mem. Memphis, Shelby County bar assns. (past pres.), Tenn., Am. bar assns., Tenn. Jud. Conf. Home: 2281 Court Ave Memphis TN 38104 Office: 122 Shelby County Ct House Memphis TN 38103 Tel (901) 528-3044

POLKING, WILLIAM GLENN, b. Carroll, Iowa, Feb. 6, 1938; B.A., Cath. U. Am., 1958, J.D., 1962. Admitted to Iowa bar, 1962, D.C. bar, 1963; individual practice law, Washington, 1962-71, Carroll, 1971—; legal adv. Nat. Conf. Catholic Charities, Washington DC 1963-67; lectr. Catholic U. Sch. Law, 1964-65; legislative atty. Citizens for Ednl. Freedom, Washington, 1969-70; lectr. Des Moines Area Community Coll., Des Moines, 1974—; county atty. Carroll County, Iowa, 1975—. Mem. Am., Iowa, Carroll County bar assns. Office: 225 E 7th St Carroll IA 51401 Tel (712) 792-1548

POLLAK, JAY MITCHELL, b. Chgo., Apr. 5, 1937; B.S., Miami U., 1959; J.D., Northwestern U., 1962. Admitted to Ill. bar, 1963, also Fed. bar; partner firm Pollak & Welsh, Chgo., 1963—; prosecutor Village of Northbrook, Ill., 1964-69. Served with U.S. Army, 1962-63. Mem. Ill., Chgo. bar assns., Zeta Beta Tau, Phi Delta Phi. Home: 846 Dundee Rd Northbrook IL 60062 Office: 150 N Wacker Dr Chicago IL 60606 Tel (312) 236-4020

POLLAK, LOUIS HEILPRIN, b. N.Y.C., Dec. 7, 1922; A.B., Harvard, 1943; LL.B., Yale, 1948. Admitted to N.Y. State bar, 1949, Conn. bar, 1956, Pa. bar, 1976; law clk. U.S. Supreme Ct. Justice Rutledge, 1948-49; asso. firm Paul, Weiss, Rifkind, Wharton & Garrison, N.Y.C., 1949-51; atty. State Dept., Washington, 1951-53; vis. lectr. Sch. Law Howard U., Washington, 1953; asst. counsel Amalgamated Clothing Workers Am., N.Y.C., 1954-55; mem. faculty Law Sch. Yale, New Haven, 1955-74, prof., 1961-65, 70-74, dean, 1965-70; prof. Law Sch. U. Pa., Phila., 1974—, dean, 1975—; vis. prof. Law Sch. U. Mich., 1961, Columbia Law Sch., 1962. Mem. New Haven Bd. Edn., 1962-68; chmn. Conn. adv. com. U.S. Civil Rights Commn., 1962-63; v.p. NAACP Legal Def. Fund, 1971—. Mem. Am. (chmn. sect. individual rights and responsibilities), Pa. bar assns., Assn. Bar City N.Y., Am. Law Inst. Author: The Constitution and the Supreme Court: A Documentary History, 1966. Home: 2225 Delancey Pl Philadelphia PA 19103 Office: 3400 Chestnut St Philadelphia PA 19174 Tel (215) 243-7481

POLLAK, STEPHEN JOHN, b. Chgo., Mar. 22, 1928; B.A., Dartmouth Coll., 1950; LL.B., Yale U., 1956. Admitted to Ill. bar, 1956, D.C. bar, 1957; asso. firm Covington & Burling, Washington, 1956-61; asst. to solicitor gen. Dept. Justice, 1961-64; dep. gen. counsel OEO, 1964-65; first asst. to asst. atty. gen. for civil rights Dept. Justice, 1965-67; adviser for nat. capital affairs to Pres., 1967; asst. atty. gen. for civil rights, 1968-69; partner firm Shea & Gardner, Washington, 1969—; chmn. jud. conf. Com. Adminstrn. Justice Under Emergency Conditions, 1971-73, dir. ALCOR, Inc., Draper & Kramer, Inc. Co-chmn. Lawyers' Com. Civil Rights under Law, 1975-77; trustee Black Student Fund, 1969—, sec., 1974-75, chmn., 1976—; pres. Housing Devel. Corp., 1976—; bd. dirs. Washington Planning and Housing Assn., 1958-67, pres., 1965-66. Mem. Am. Bar Assn., Bar Assn. D.C., D.C. Bar. (bd. govs. 1972-73, sec. 1974-75). Home: 3314 Newark St NW Washington DC 20008 Office: 734 15th St NW Washington DC 20005 Tel (202) 737-1255

POLLAN, THOMAS MILLER, b. San Antonio, Sept. 24, 1945; B.A., U. Tex., 1968, J.D., 1971. Admitted to Tex. bar, 1971; briefing atty. Tex. Supreme Ct., Austin, 1971-72; asst. atty. State of Tex., Austin, 1972—, chief ins. banking and securities div., 1976—. Mem. Am., Tex. bar assns., Phi Delta Phi. Home: 2908 Dover Pl Austin TX 78731 Office: Supreme Court Bldg Austin TX 78711 Tel (512) 475-4481

POLLARD, BILLY HOWARD, b. Minden, La., Aug. 18, 1945; B.B.A., Southwestern U., 1967; J.D., U. Tex., 1972. Admitted to Tex. bar, 1973, U.S. Dist. Ct. bar, 1973; asso. Jordan, Zwernemann, & Simmons, Houston, 1972-75, Barlow, Lacy, & Smith, Houston, 1975—. Mem. Houston Bar Assn. Home: 823 Seacliff St Houston TX 77062 Office: 17100 El Camino Real Houston TX 77058 Tel (713) 488-8800

POLLARD, OVERTON PRICE, b. Ashland, Va., Mar. 26, 1933; A.B., Washington and Lee U., 1954, J.D., 1957. Admitted to Va. bar, 1962; claims supr. Travelers Ins. Co., 1959-64; asst. atty. gen. State of Va., 1964-66, 68-70; spl. asst. Va. Supreme Ct., 1966-68; partner firm Martin Meyer & Pollard, 1970-72, Moore & Pollard, Richmond, Va., 1973—; exec. dir. Pub. Defender Commn., 1971—. Mem. Am., Va. bar assns., Va. Trial Lawyers Assn., Nat. Legal Aid and Defender Assn. Recipient Meritorious Service award Va. State Bar, 1971. Home: 7726 Sweetbriar Rd Richmond VA 23229 Office: 214 Mutual Bldg Richmond VA 23219 Tel (804) 649-7693

POLLARD, RUPERT MAURY, b. Austin, Tex., June 23, 1938; B.A., U. Tex., 1961; M.D., Southwestern Med. Sch., Dallas, 1963; J.D., So. Meth. U., 1973. Admitted to Tex. bar, 1973; individual practice law, Dallas, 1973—; asst. prof. Baylor U. Dental Coll., Dallas, 1975. Mem. State Bar Tex., Am., Dallas bar assns., Am., Tex., Dallas trial lawyers assns., Tex. Med. Assn., Dallas County Med. Soc., Am., Tex. socs. anesthesiologists. Diplomate Am. Bd. Anesthesiology. Home: 4231 Beverly Dr Dallas TX 75205 Office: 8333 Douglas St Suite 1350 Dallas TX 75225 Tel (214) 369-3600

POLLARD, THOMAS BROWN, JR., b. Nashville, July 24, 1933; A.B. in Polit. Sci., U. S.C., 1954, LL.B., 1959. Admitted to S.C. bar, 1959; asso. firm Nexsen, Pruet, Jacobs & Pollard and predecessor, Columbia, S.C., 1959-64, partner, 1964—. Mem. Am., S.C., Richland County (S.C.) bar assns. Home: Route 2 Leesville (Lake Murray) SC Office: 1200 1st Nat Bank Bldg Columbia SC 29201 Tel (803) 771-8900

POLLEY, DAVID CLELAND, b. Lead, S.D., Oct. 25, 1934; B.E.E., U. Colo., 1960, B.S. in Bus., 1960; LL.B., U. N.Mex., 1964. Admitted to Nev. bar, 1965; elec. constrn. engr. Reynolds Elec. & Engring. Co., Albuquerque and El Paso, Tex., 1960-61, house counsel, Las Vegas, Nev., 1964-67; dep. atty. gen. State of Nev., Las Vegas and Carson City, 1971-75; individual practice law, Las Vegas, 1965—. Office: 323 Las Vegas Blvd S Las Vegas NV 89101 Tel (702) 385-1125

POLLINS, JOHN WILLIAM, III, b. Greensburg, Pa., Feb. 19, 1940; A.B., U. Mich., 1961, J.D., 1964. Admitted to Pa. bar, 1964; law clk. to judge Westmoreland County (Pa.), 1964-67; partner firm Pollins & Pollins, Greensburg, 1966-71; partner firm Hammer & Pollins, Greensburg, 1972—; spl. asst. atty. gen. Commonwealth Pa., 1967-72; solicitor Greater Greensburg Indsl. Devel. Corp., Greensburg Parking Authority; mem. civil rules com. Westmoreland County Ct. Common Pleas, 1973—. Pres., mem. bd. dirs. Southwestern Pa. Lung Assn., 1976—. Mem. Westmoreland County (chmn. rules com. 1973—), Pa. bar assns., Pa. Trial Lawyers Assn. Office: 139 S Pennsylvania Ave Greensburg PA 15601 Tel (412) 834-8880

POLLITT, RICHARD MALONE, b. Allen, Md., Apr. 30, 1927; LL.B., U. Md., 1949, J.D., 1969. Admitted to Md. bar, 1949, U.S. Supreme Ct. bar, 1965; partner firm Richardson, Pollitt & Rogan and predecessors, Salisbury, Md., 1949-62; individual practice law, Salisbury, 1962-67; partner firm Pollitt, Hughes & Bahen, Salisbury, 1967-72; asso. judge First Judicial Circuit Ct. Md., 1972—, adminstrv. judge, Salisbury, 1974—; spl. asst. atty. gen. Md., 1959-72. Mem. Wicomico County, Md. State, Am. bar assns., Nat. Conf. State Trial Judges (del. 1974-77). Home: 406 Tony Tank Ln Salisbury MD 21801 Office: Court House Salisbury MD 21801 Tel (301) 742-3533

POLLOCK, JOY EILEEN, b. Phila., Aug. 3, 1943; B.A. summa cum laude, Albright Coll., 1965; J.D., U. Pa., 1968. Admitted to Pa. bar, 1968; field rep., HUD, 1968-71; asso. firm Astor & Weiss, Phila., 1974—. Mem. Am., Pa., Phila. bar assns., Women's Lawyers Assn., Henrietta Szold Hadassah, Alpha Zeta Omega (nat. pres. ladies aux. 1977—), Phi Delta Sigma. Office: 2 Penn Center Plaza Suite 720 Philadelphia PA 19102 Tel (215) LO3-1100

POLLOCK, ROBERT EVANS, b. San Francisco, Aug. 10, 1943; B.S. in Elec. Engring., U. Cin., 1966; J.D., Chase Coll., 1971. Admitted to Ohio bar, 1971; U.S. Patent Office bar, 1971, U.S. Ct. Customs and Patent Appeals bar, 1975; tech. engr. Procter & Gamble, Cin., 1966-71; patent atty., 1971-73; corp. patent counsel Dana Corp., Toledo, 1973—. Pres. Hilltoppers Civic Assn., Cin., 1973. Mem. Am., Toledo bar assns., Toledo, Am. patent law assns., Internat. Assn. Protection Indsl. Property, Licensing Execs. Soc. Home: 3438 Kirkwall Rd Toledo OH 43606 Office: 4500 Dorr Street Toledo OH 43615 Tel (419) 535-4653

POLLOWAY, JOHN MICHAEL, b. Kearny, N.J., July 13, 1944; B.S. in Math., U. Pitts., 1967; J.D., Seton Hall U., 1973. Admitted to N.J. bar, 1973; asst. prosecutor Monmouth County (N.J.), Freehold, 1973—. Mem. N.J. Bar Assn. Home: 77 Elm Ln Shrewsbury NJ 07701 Office: Monmouth County Courthouse Freehold NJ 07724 Tel (201) 431-7184

POLSTER, CARL CONRAD, b. E. St. Louis, Ill., Nov. 19, 1946; B.A., DePauw U., 1968; J.D., Washington U., St. Louis, 1971. Admitted to Mo. bar, 1971; partner Polster & Polster, St. Louis, 1971—. Mem. Mo., Met. St. Louis bar assns. Home: 1309 W Adams St Kirkwood MO 63122 Office: 763 S New Ballas Rd St Louis MO 63141 Tel (314) 872-8118

POLYDOROFF, THEODORE, b. London, June 4, 1934; B.A., U. Md., 1956; J.D., Am. U., 1958. Admitted to Va. bar, 1958, D.C. bar, 1960, U.S. Supreme Ct. bar, 1961; asso. firm Jesse, Phillips, Klinge & Kendrick, Arlington, Va., 1958-60; trial atty. ICC, 1960-65; partner firm Rea, Cross & Knebel, Washington, 1965-68; counsel firm Morgan, Lewis & Bockius, Washington, 1968-71; partner firm Ephraim & Polydoroff, Washington, 1971—; asso. professorial lectr. George Washington U., 1958-74. Mem. Am., Va., D.C. bar assns., Motor Carrier Lawyers Assn., Delta Theta Phi, Alpha Tau Omega. Author: Carrier Defenses: Acts of God The Public Enemy and The Public Authority, 1973. Home: 4904 Morning Glory Ct Rockville MD 20853 Office: 1250 Connecticut Ave NW Washington DC 20036 Tel (202) 833-1170

POMERANTZ, ABRAHAM L., b. Bklyn., Mar. 22, 1903; LL.B. cum laude, Bklyn. Law Sch., 1924. Admitted to N.Y. bar, 1924, U.S. Supreme Ct. bar, 1969; founder firm Pomerantz, Levy, Haudek & Block, N.Y.C., 1936, now sr. partner; instr. Bklyn. Law Sch., 1925; dep. chief counsel Nuremburg Trials, 1946; participant profl. seminars; mem. U.S. Supreme Ct. adv. com. on rules of practice and precedure Jud. Conf. U.S.; mem. com. on qualifications to practice before U.S. cts. 2d circuit Jud. Council. Past chmn. Fedn. Jewish Charities; past bd. dirs. New Rochelle (N.Y.) Mayor's Interracial Com. Mem. Am. Coll. Trial Lawyers, Nat. Lawyers Guild, Am. Arbitration Assn. (nat. panel arbitrators), N.Y. County Lawyers Assn., N.Y. Law Inst. Home: 146 Central Park W New York City NY 10023 Office: 295 Madison Ave New York City NY 10017 Tel (212) 532-4800

POMERANTZ, ROBERT J., b. Bklyn., Aug. 23, 1941; A.B., N.Y. U., 1963; LL.B., Bklyn. Law Sch., 1966, J.D., 1967. Admitted to N.Y. bar, 1967; asso. firm Kelner, Kelner, Stelljes & Glotzer, 1966-67, Hanner, Fitzmaurice & Onarato, 1967-71; mem. firm Goldfarb, Goldfarb & Pomerantz, Bklyn., 1971—; cons. to public co., 1973—. Mem. N.Y. State Bar Assn. Contbr. articles to legal jours. Home: 837 Ibsen St Woodmere NY 11598 Tel (212) 346-9500

POMERANTZ, SANFORD ALAN, b. Bklyn., May 22, 1941; B.A. in Psychology, L.I. U., 1962; J.D., Bklyn. Law Sch., 1968. Admitted to N.Y. bar, 1969; practice law, N.Y.C., 1969-70; asst. atty. gen. assigned Bur. Securities, State of N.Y., N.Y.C., 1970—; guest lectr. Manhattan Community Coll., 1974, N.Y. Law Sch., 1976. Mem. N.Y. State Bar Assn., L.I. U. Alumni Assn. (exec. com. 1971-73). Home: 30 Crescent Beach Rd Glen Cove NY 11542 Office: 2 World Trade Center New York City NY 10047 Tel (212) 488-2287

POMEROY, HARLAN, b. Cleve., May 7, 1923; B.S., Yale U., 1944; LL.B., Harvard U., 1948. Admitted to Conn. bar, 1949, U.S. Supreme Ct. bar, 1954, Ohio bar, 1958, D.C. bar, 1975; atty. trial sect. tax div. Dept. Justice, Washington, 1952-58; asso. firm Baker, Hostetler, & Patterson, Cleve., 1958-62, partner, 1962-75, Washington, 1975—; gen. chmn. Cleve. Tax Inst., 1971; lectr. in field. Treas. Shaker Heights (Ohio) Democratic Club, 1960-62; trustee, mem. exec. com. 1st Unitarian Ch. of Cleve., 1965-68. Mem. Ohio, Cleve., D.C., Fed., Am. bar assns. Contbr. articles to legal publs. Home: 4500 Boxwood Rd Westmoreland Hills MD 20016 Office: 818 Connecticut Ave NW Washington DC 20006 Tel (202) 857-1543

POMEROY, ROBERT CORTTIS, b. Syracuse, N.Y., Sept. 17, 1943; A.B., Hamilton Coll., 1965; LL.B. magna cum laude, Harvard, 1968. Admitted to Mass. bar, 1968; asso. firm Goodwin, Procter & Hoar, Boston, 1968-76, partner, 1977—. Mem. Boston, Am. bar assns., Phi Beta Kappa. Home: 29 Lakeview Rd Winchester MA 01890 Office: 28 State St Boston MA 02109 Tel (617) 523-5700

POMEROY, WILLIAM JEFFREY, b. Syracuse, N.Y., Sept. 3, 1946; B.A., Hamilton Coll., 1968; J.D., Cornell U., 1971. Admitted to N.Y. bar, 1972; asso. firm Fitzgerald & Taylor, Cortland, N.Y., 1972—; asst. dist. atty. Cortland County (N.Y.), 1975—. Mem. Cortland County Mental Health, Mental Retardation and Alcoholism Services Bd., 1972—, chmn., 1976. Home: 10 Anderson Dr Rd 2 Homer NY 13077 Office: 16 Tompkins St Cortland NY 13045 Tel (607) 756-7501

POMPEY, MAURICE DALE, b. South Bend, Ind., May 14, 1923; student Howard U., 1940-41, Roosevelt U., 1947; LL.B., DePaul U., 1951, J.D., 1951; grad. Nat. Coll. State Judiciary, 1975. Admitted to Ill. bar, 1951, U.S. Dist. Ct. bar for No. Dist. Ill., 1959, U.S. Ct. Mil. Appeals bar, 1975, U.S. Supreme Ct. bar, 1976; asst. corp. counsel City of Chgo., 1963; judges trial asst. Municipal Ct. of Chgo., 1963; magistrate Cook County (Ill.) Circuit Ct., 1964-70, circuit judge, 1970—. Bd. dirs. Woodlawn Chgo. Boys Club, NAACP. Mem. Am., Nat., Ill., Cook County, Chgo. bar assns. Office: 2600 S California St Chicago IL 60608

PONADER, WAYNE CARL, b. Marshfield, Wis., July 8, 1931; A.B., Ind. U., 1953, LL.B., 1956. Admitted to Ind. bar, 1956, Fla. bar, 1974; since practiced in Indpls., asso. firm Baker & Daniels, 1956-58, asso. firm Bose McKinney & Evans, 1958-60, partner firm, 1960—. Bd. dirs. Greater Indpls. Progress Com., 1968—; pres. Greater Indpls. Housing Devel. Corp., 1976—, Indpls. Housing Loan Fund, Inc., 1976—; pres. Episcopal Community Services, Inc., 1976-77. Mem. Am., Ind. Fla., Indpls. bar assns., Am. Judicature Soc., Comml. Law League, Order Coif. Home: 6536 Wyman Ct Indianapolis IN 46220 Office: 1100 First Fed Bldg Indianapolis IN 46204 Tel (317) 637-5353

PONDER, ANDREW GANT, b. Walnut Ridge, Ark., Oct. 1, 1916; B.S., U. Ark., 1939, LL.B., 1940. Admitted to Ark. bar, 1940, U.S. Supreme Ct. bar, 1944; spl. agt. FBI, Ill., Tex., Ark., Washington, 1940-49; chancery judge 8th Dist. Ark., Newport, 1951-52, 3d Jud. Dist., Newport, 1953—; chmn. Penitentiary Study Commn. State of Ark., 1967. Mem. Ark. Jud. Council (pres. 1960). Home: 1 Bowen St Newport AR 72112 Office: Court House Newport AR 72112 Tel (501) 523-2975

PONTE, GEORGE PERRY, b. New Bedford, Mass., May 24, 1905; LL.B., Boston U., 1927. Admitted to Mass. bar, 1927; mem. City Council, New Bedford, 1928-30, 1938-42, pres., 1942; mem. Mass. Ho. of Reps., 1943-44; chief legal counsel to Gov. Mass., Endicott Peabody, 1963; justice Superior Ct. of Mass., Boston, 1963-75, recall justice, 1976—. Mem. Am., Mass., Bristol County, Boston, New Bedford bar assns., Am. Judicature Soc., Am. Trial Lawyers Assn. Home and Office: 54 Mosher St South Dartmouth MA 02748 Tel (617) 992-4112

PONTIFF, PAUL EDWARD, b. N.Y.C., June 6, 1930; B.B.A., St. John's U., 1954, J.D., 1959. Admitted to N.Y. State bar, 1969; asso. firm Paul, Weiss, Rifkind, Wharton & Garrison, N.Y.C., 1950-59; tax mgr. Peat, Marwick, Mitchell & Co., C.P.A.'s, Glens Falls, N.Y., 1960-62; partner firm Caffry, Pontiff, Stewart, Rhodes & Judge, Glens Falls, 1962—. Past chmn. United Cerebral Palsy Assn. of the Tri Counties, Inc., Glen Falls, N.Y.; asst. chief Queensbury (N.Y.) Central Vol. Fire Co., 1969—; bd. visitors Wilton Developmental Center, Wilton, N.Y., 1970—. Mem. Am., Warren County, N.Y. (chmn. retirement benefits com., trustee and estates law sect. 1974-76) bar assns., Adirondack Regional C. of C. (1st v.p. Glen Falls, N.Y.). Office: 10 Harlem St Glens Falls NY 12801 Tel (518) 792-2117

PONTON, ROBERT DARRYL, b. Washington, Pa., Aug. 7, 1946; B.A., Bethany Coll., 1968; J.D., U. Pitts., 1971; M.P.A., Harvard, 1972. Admitted to Pa. bar, 1971; staff atty. Boston Legal Assistance Project, 1972; atty. U.S. Dept. Housing and Urban Devel., Pitts., 1973; gen. counsel Pa. Housing Fin. Agy., Harrisburg, 1974-75; gen. counsel Pa. Office of Adminstrn., Harrisburg, 1975; asso. firm Baskin, Boreman, Wilner, Sachs, Gondelman & Craig, Pitts., 1976—. Mem. Am., Pa., Allegheny County bar assns. Office: 10th Floor Frick Bldg Pittsburgh PA 15219 Tel (412) 562-8679

PONTZER, ROBERT FRANCIS, b. Kersey, Pa., June 13, 1904; student Pa. State Coll., 1923-24; LL.B., Georgetown U., 1928; A.B., George Washington U., 1929. Admitted to D.C. bar, 1928, Pa. bar, 1930, U.S. Supreme Ct. bar, 1954; partner firm Barbour & Pontzer, Ridgway, Pa., 1930-42, Pontzer & Pontzer, Ridgway, 1952—; pres. Ridgway Nat. Bank, 1954—. Pres. bd. trustees Elk County (Pa.) Gen. Hosp., Ridgway, 1971—. Mem. Elk County (pres. 1958—), Pa., Am. bar assns. Home: 524 Hyde Ave Ridgway PA 15853 Office: Masonic Bldg Ridgway PA 15853 Tel (814) 773-3108

POOL, J. ROSS, b. Quincy, Ill., Mar. 23, 1918; B.S., Culver-Stockton Coll., 1941; J.D., U. Tex., 1947. Admitted to Tex. bar, 1947, Ill. bar, 1960; individual practice law, Brownsville and San Antonio, Tex., 1947-58; individual practice law, asst. state's atty., Quincy, 1960-64; judge Circuit Ct., Quincy, 1964—. Mem. Am., Ill., Adams County bar assns., Am. Judicature Soc. Home: 27 Edgewood St Quincy IL 62301 Office: Ct House Quincy IL 62301 Tel (217) 223-6017

POOLE, JOHN JORDAN, b. Atlanta, May 19, 1906; Ph.B., Emory U., 1927, J.D., 1929. Admitted to Ga. bar, 1929; U.S. Dist. Ct. bar, 1930; partner firm Poole, Pearce, Cooper and Smith, Atlanta, 1934—. Mem. Ga., Atlanta bar assns. Home: 1128 Oakdale Rd NE Atlanta GA 30307 Office: Suite 310 57 Executive Park Dr South NE Atlanta GA 30329 Tel (404) 325-8196

POOLEY, BEVERLEY JOHN, b. London, Apr. 4, 1934; B.A., U. Cambridge (Eng.), 1956, LL.B., 1957, M.A., 1961; LL.M., U. Mich., 1958, S.J.D., 1961, M.L.S., 1964. Fellow Legis. Research Center U. Mich., Ann Arbor, 1958-60; lectr. U. Ghana, 1960-62; instr. U. Mich. Law Sch., 1962-63, asst. prof., 1963-66, asso. prof., 1966-70, prof., 1970—, dir. U. Mich. Law Library, 1965—. Home: 16 Geddes Heights Ann Arbor MI 48104 Office: 363 Legal Research Bldg 801 Monroe St Ann Arbor MI 48109 Tel (313) 764-9322

POORE, ADELAIDE DAVIS, b. Orlando, Fla., Apr. 22, 1937; B.A., Ohio Wesleyan U., 1959; J.D., U. S.D., 1971; D.Sc. (hon.), Jones Coll., Orlando, 1976. Admitted to Fla. bar, 1971; staff atty. Orange County Legal Aid, Orlando, 1971-72; asso. firm William O. Murrell & Assos., Orlando, 1972-73; asst. states atty. 9th Jud. Circuit Fla., Orlando, 1973—. Mem. exec. council March of Dimes, 1972—; trustee Ret. Sr. Vol. Programs, 1975—. Mem. Am., Fla., Orange County bar assns., Am. Bus. Women's Assn., Phi Delta Delta. Recipient free flow of info. award Sigma Delta Chi, 1975. Home: 333 Castilian Ct Winter Park FL 32792 Office: 1904 W Colonial Dr Orlando FL 32804 Tel (305) 841-4174

POOSER, ATKINSON EDWIN, IV, b. Lakeland, Fla., Dec. 8, 1940; B.A., Fla. State U., 1964; J.D., Mercer U., 1974. Admitted to Ga. bar, 1974, Fla. bar, 1974; mem. firm Willis, Hitt & Pooser, Warner Robbins, Ga., 1976—; pub. defender Houston County (Ga.), 1975-76. Mem. Assn. Criminal Def. Lawyers. Office: 1544 Watson Blvd Warner Robbins GA 31093 Tel (912) 923-0033

POPE, DOUGLAS VANSTONE, b. Phila., Feb. 7, 1945; A.B., Earlham Coll., 1967; J.D., U. Md., 1970; LL.M., Georgetown U., 1975. Admitted to Md. bar, 1970; atty. Western Md. R.R., Balt., 1971-73, atty. SEC, Washington, 1973-77, Washington Gas Light Co. (D.C.), 1977—; lectr. bus. law George Mason U., Fairfax, Va., No. Va. Community Coll., Annandale, 1975—. Active Balt. R.R. Community Service Orgn. Mem. Am., Md. bar assns., Am. Bus. Law Assn. Contbr. articles to legal jours. Home: 8502 Leonard Dr Silver Spring MD 20910 Office: 1100 H St NW Washington DC 20080 Tel (202) 624-6112

POPE, FRANK STARR, JR., b. Dallas, June 26, 1927; B.B.A., U. Tex. 1950, LL.B., 1952. Admitted to Tex. bar, 1952; asso. firm Frazer & Torbet, C.P.A.'s, Houston, 1952-53, Kleberg, Mobley, Lockett & Weil, Corpus Christi, Tex., 1953-61, partner, 1961—. Pres. Am. Cancer Soc., Nueces County, Tex., 1962; pres. Corpus Christi Assn. Congregations, 1967, Corpus Christi Mus., 1969, Corpus Christi chpt. NCCJ, 1972. Fellow Am. Coll. Probate Counsel; mem. Am., Tex., Nueces County (pres. 1974-75) bar assns., Am. Judicature Soc., World Assn. Lawyers. Recipient Meritorious Service award SSS, 1976. Home: 901 N Carancahua St Corpus Christi TX 78401 Office: POB 2446 Corpus Christi TX 78403 Tel (512) 884-3551

POPE, F(RED) WALLACE, JR., b. Sanford, Fla., Feb. 9, 1941; B.A., U. Fla., 1962, J.D. with honors, 1969; A.M., Boston U., 1965. Admitted to Fla. bar, 1970; research aide to judge Fla. 2d Dist. Ct. Appeal, 1970; asso. firm Trenam, Simmons, Kemker, Scharf & Barkin, Tampa, 1970-74; partner firm Johnson, Blakely, Pope & Bokor, Clearwater, Fla., 1974—. Mem. Am. (asso. editor Litigation 1973—), Clearwater (dir. 1976—), Hillsborough County (Fla.) bar assns. Antitrust editor Law Notes for the Young Lawyer, 1971-74; editor-in-chief Law Notes, 1974-75, asso. editor, 1975—; bd. editors Fla. Bar Jour., 1975—. Tel (813) 441-2440

POPE, JOHN DAWSON, III, b. Butte, Mont., May 29, 1913; student Mont. Sch. Mines, 1930-31; B.S., Mont. State U., 1933; J.D., Harvard, 1936; postgrad. Mass. Inst. Tech., 1936. Admitted to Mo. bar, 1937, U.S. Supreme Ct. bar, 1940; asst. atty. Monsanto Chem. Co., St. Louis, 1936-39; asso. firm Haynes & Koenig, St. Louis, 1939-50; partner firm Koenig & Pope, St. Louis, 1950-63; individual practice law, St. Louis, 1964-76; partner firm Pope & Fishel, St. Louis, 1977—; lectr. Washington U., 1964; mem. bd. admissions U.S. Dist. Ct. Eastern Dist. Mo., 1964-70, chmn., 1969-70. Mem. Am. Chem. Soc., AAAS, Fed., Am., Mo. bar assns., Bar Assn. Met. St. Louis, Am. Patent Law Assn., U.S. Trademark Assn. (law adv. com. 1952-54, 57-59, 63-66, 74—). Editor: American Philatelic Congress Book, 1954. Home: 55 S Gore Ave Webster Groves MO 63119 Office: 818 Olive St St Louis MO 63101 Tel (314) 241-8465

POPE, KENT SMITH, b. Harrisburg, Pa., Mar. 19, 1946; B.A., Denison U., 1968; J.D., George Washington U., 1971. Admitted to Pa. bar, 1971; partner firm Pope and Pope, Clarion, Pa., 1971—; part time prof. law. Clarion State Coll., 1976—. Mem. Am., Pa. (zone gov. young lawyers sect. 1975—; del., 1974—) bar assns. Home: 16 Barber St Clarion PA 16214 Office: 10 Grant St Clarion PA 16214 Tel (814) 226-5700

POPE, MICHAEL HOWARD, b. Springfield, Ill., Sept. 26, 1944; B.A., Tulane Univ., 1966; J.D., Duke Univ., 1973. Admitted to Ga. bar, 1973; asso. firm Sutherland, Asbill & Brannan, Atlanta, 1973-74; asso. firm Long, Aldridge, Heine, Stevens, Sumnar, Atlanta, 1974—. Mem. Am., Atlanta bar assns., State Bar Ga., Atlanta Council of Young Lawyers. Note and comment editor Duke Law Jour., 1972-73. Office: 134 Peachtree St NW Atlanta GA 30303 Tel (404) 681-3000

POPE, WILLIAM L., b. Kingstree, S.C., Mar. 4, 1933; A.B., Wofford Coll., 1954; LL.B., U. S.C., 1959. Admitted to S.C. bar, 1959; asst. atty. gen. State of S.C., 1960-65; now partner firm Robinson, McFadden, Moore & Pope, Columbia, S.C. Mem. Am., Richland County bar assns., S.C. Bar (pres. 1977-78), Am. Judicature Soc., Phi Delta Phi. Office: Jefferson Square Bldg 10th Floor PO Box 944 Columbia SC 29202 Tel (803) 779-5323

POPEJOY, THOMAS LAFAYETTE, JR., b. Albuquerque, Apr. 27, 1945; B.B.A., U. N.Mex., 1966, J.D., 1971. Admitted to N.Mex. bar, 1971; law clk. U.S. Dist. Ct., Albuquerque, 1971-72; asso. firm Sutin, Thayer & Browne, Albuquerque, 1972-76; individual practice law, Albuquerque, 1976—; adj. prof. law U. N.Mex., 1971—; mem. corrections sub-com. Gov.'s Council on Criminal Justice Planning, 1976—. Vice pres. Temporary Care Services, Albuquerque, 1975—. Mem. Am., N.Mex. bar assns., U. N.Mex. Alumni Assn. (treas., dir. Robert O. Anderson Sch. Bus. and Adminstrv. Scis. 1975—). Home: 1905 Avenida Las Campanas NW Albuquerque NM 87107 Office: 4665 Indian Sch Rd NE Albuquerque NM 87110 Tel (505) 265-6421

POPKIN, ARNOLD PAUL, b. Washington, Mar. 2, 1943; A.B., U. Md., 1965; J.D., Mt. Vernon Sch. Law, 1968. Admitted to Md. bar, 1968; asso. with Freeman & Popkin, Suitland, Md., 1970-76; individual practice law, Suitland, 1976—. Bd. dirs. Kettering Civic Fedn. Mem. Prince George's County Bar Assn. (dir., chmn. prepaid legal services plan), Suitland C. of C. (mem. coms.). Contbr. articles to newspapers. Office: 5107 Silver Hill Rd Suitland MD 20023 Tel (301) 736-5151

POPKIN, ROBERT EDWARD, b. N.Y.C., May 16, 1945; A.B., Princeton, 1967; J.D., Harvard, 1970. Admitted to N.J. bar, 1970; asso. firm McCarter and English, Newark, 1970-72; dep. atty. gen. State of N.J., Trenton, 1972—. Mem. Am., N.J., Mercer County bar assns. Office: State House Annex Trenton NJ 08625 Tel (609) 292-8554

POPKIN, WILLIAM DAVID, b. N.Y.C., Oct. 28, 1937; A.B., Harvard, 1958, LL.B., 1961; postgrad. (Fulbright fellow), India, 1961-62. Admitted to N.Y. bar, 1962, asso. firm Hess, Segall, Popkin and Guterman, N.Y.C., 1963-66; teaching fellow internat. tax program Harvard, 1966-68; asst. prof. law Ind. U., 1968-71, asso. prof., 1971-75, prof., 1975—; cons. Adminstrv. Conf. U.S. Mem. Bloomington (Ind.) Housing Authority, 1973-75. Mem. Am. Bar Assn. Author: The Deduction for Business Expenses and Losses, 1973. Home: 2000 Windsor Dr Bloomington IN 47401 Office: Ind U Sch of Law Bloomington IN 47401 Tel (812) 337-4376

POPLAR, CARL DAVID, b. Phila., Nov. 12, 1943; A.B., Syracuse U., 1964; J.D., Rutgers U., 1967. Admitted to N.J. bar, 1967, U.S. Dist. Ct. N.J. bar, 1967, U.S. SUpreme Ct. bar, 1976; atty. N.J. Dept. Community Affairs, Trenton, 1967-68; mem. Camden County (N.J.) Legal Services, 1968-69; mem. firm Stransky & Poplar, Camden, 1969-72; individual practice law, Camden, 1972—. Mem. Voorhees Township Juvenile Conf. Com., 1975—. Mem. Am., Camden County (trustee), N.J. (trustee criminal law sect., gen. counsel) bar assns., Assn. Trial Lawyers Am., N.J. Trial Lawyers Assn. (trustee). Home: 29 Chippenham Dr W Berlin NJ 08091 Office: 10 Grove St Haddonfield NJ 08033 Tel (609) 795-5560

POPOVICH, PETER STEPHEN, b. Crosby, Minn., Nov. 27, 1920; A.A., Hibbing Jr. Coll., 1940; B.A., U. Minn., 1942, B.S. in Law, 1946; J.D. (Minn. Bar Assn. scholar), St. Paul Coll. Law, 1946. Admitted to Minn. bar, 1947, U.S. Supreme Ct. bar, 1956; mem. firm Peterson, Popovich, Knutson & Flynn, and predecessors, St. Paul, 1947—; mem. Minn. Ho. of Reps., 1953-63, vice chmn. edn. com., 1955-63, appropriations com. 1955, 57; counsel various sch. dists., 1947—; chmn. planning commn. St. Mary's Point, 1970—; mem. Minn. Bd. Continuing Legal Edn., 1975—. Mem. exec. council Minn. Hist. Soc. Mem. Am., Minn., Ramsey County (Minn.) bar assns., Nat. Orgn. Legal Problems In Edn. (dir. 1975—), Minn. Council Sch. Attys. (dir. 1970—), Gamma Eta Gamma. Home: 1400 River Rd Saint Mary's Point Route 1 Lakeland MN 55043 Office: 314 Minnesota Bldg Saint Paul MN 55101 Tel (612) 222-5515

POPPER, MILTON, b. N.Y.C., Dec. 7, 1905; B.S., Columbia, 1926, LL.B., 1929. Admitted to N.Y. bar, 1930, Fed. Dist. Ct. bar, 1934; partner firm Clark & Popper, Long Beach, N.Y., 1930-34; individual practice law, Long Beach, 1934-45, 67—; partner firm Zimmerman & Popper, 1945-67; asst. and corp. counsel City of Long Beach, 1934-37. Mem. Long Beach Zoning Bd. Appeals, 1938-40; advisor to minority mems. Nassau County Bd. Suprs., 1964—; pres. City of Long Beach Sch. Bd., 1959-63. Mem. Nassau County Bar Assn. Home: 269 Franklin Blvd Long Beach NY 11561 Office: 120 W Park Ave Long Beach NY 11561 Tel (516) 432-1700

POPPLETON, ALLEN, b. Dallas, Oct. 25, 1931; A.B., U. N.C., 1953; LL.B., Yale, 1959. Admitted to Calif. bar, 1960, Ala. bar, 1964; asso. firm O'Melveny & Myers, Los Angeles, 1959-64; asso. firm Bradley, Arant, Rose & White, Birmingham, Ala., 1964-68, partner, 1969—. Mem. Am., Ala., Birmingham bar assns., Calif. State Bar, Phi Beta Kappa. Home: 3517 Mill Springs Rd Birmingham AL 35223 Office: 1500 Brown-Marx Bldg Birmingham AL 35203 Tel (205) 252-4500

PORETSKY, JOEL ALLEN, b. Bklyn., Jan. 16, 1946; B.S., Boston U., 1967; J.D. cum laude, Bklyn. Law Sch., 1971; LL.M. in Taxation, N.Y. U., 1972. Admitted to N.Y. bar, 1972, U.S. Tax Ct. bar, 1972, U.S. Supreme Ct. bar, 1975, U.S. Ct. of Appeals bar, 1975; asso. firm Fried, Frank, Harris, Shriver & Jacobson, N.Y.C., 1972—; lectr. NAACP Legal Def. Fund, Airlie House Conf. of Young Lawyers, Warrenton, Va., 1975. Mem. Am., N.Y. State bar assns. Co-author: Tax Planning in Financing and Development of Hotels, 1975. Home: 59 Cambridge Rd Great Neck NY 11023 Office: 120 Broadway New York City NY 10005 Tel (212) 964-6500

PORT, EDMUND, b. Syracuse, N.Y., Feb. 6, 1906; LL.B., Syracuse U., 1929. Admitted to N.Y. State bar, 1930, U.S. Dist. Ct. bar for No. Dist. N.Y., 1930, U.S. 2d Circuit Ct. Appeals bar, 1945; individual practice law, Syracuse, 1930-53; partner firm Michaels, Port and Cuddy and predecessor, Auburn, N.Y., 1953-64; judge U.S. Dist. Ct., No. Dist. N.Y., 1964—; asst. U.S. atty. No. Dist. N.Y., 1943-50, U.S. atty., 1951-53. Mem. Am., N.Y. State, Cayuga County bar assns., Am. Judicature Soc. Home: Townhouse 6 Standart Woods Auburn NY 13021 Office: Fed Bldg and Post Office PO Box B Auburn NY 13021 Tel (315) 252-9566

PORT, WAYNE HOWARD, b. Pitts., Feb. 9, 1947; B.S., Pa. State U., 1968; J.D., U. Pitts., 1971. Admitted to Pa. bar, 1971; asso. firm Ray, Buck, Margois, Mahoney & John, Uniontown, Pa., 1971—; spl. asst. atty. gen. Commonwealth of Pa., 1973—. Solicitor Frazier Sch. Dist., Perryopolis, Pa., 1972—. Mem. Fayette County, Pa., Am. bar assns., Phi Alpha Delta, Beta Alpha Psi. Office: 92 E Main St Uniontown PA 15401 Tel (412) 438-2544

PORTER, ARTHUR EDMUND, b. Boston, Sept. 7, 1919; B.A., Harvard, 1940, LL.B., 1942. Admitted to N.H. bar, 1942; mem. firm Porter & Hollman, 1942-46; individual practice law, Manchester, N.H., 1946-72; partner firm Porter and Hollman, Manchester, 1972—. Chmn. N.H. Library Commn. Mem. N.H., Manchester bar assns. Home: 1059 Chestnut St Manchester NH 03104 Office: 155 Myrtle St Manchester NH 03104 Tel (603) 669-4777

PORTER, CHARLES EDWARD, b. Santa Barbara, Calif., Sept. 8, 1939; A.B., U. Calif., Santa Barbara, 1961; J.D., U. Calif. Hastings Coll. Law, 1968. Admitted to Calif. bar, 1969; juvenile dep. probation officer Santa Barbara County (Calif.), 1963-65; adult dep. probation officer San Mateo County (Calif.), 1966-70; dep. dist. atty. Kings County (Calif.), 1971, Kern County, 1972-75; judge Indian Wells Justice Ct., Ridgecrest, Calif., 1975-76, E. Kern Municipal Ct., Ridgecrest, 1977—. Home: 532 Weiman St Ridgecrest CA 93555 Office: E Kern Municipal Ct Ridgecrest CA 93555 Tel (714) 375-1396 also (714) 446-2974

PORTER, CHARLES ORLANDO, b. Klamath Falls, Oreg., Apr. 4, 1919; B.A., Harvard, 1941, LL.B., 1947. Admitted to Oreg. bar, 1948, Fed. bar, 1951, U.S. Supreme Ct. bar, 1955; asst. to dir. Survey Legal Profession, Boston, 1949-51; individual practice law, Eugene, Oreg., 1951-56, 61—; mem. U.S. Congress from 4th Oreg. Dist., 1957-60, also mem. 85th-86th Congresses. Mem. Lane County, Oreg. bar assns., Am. Judicature Soc., Am., Oreg. trial lawyers assns. Author: (with A.P. Blaustein) The American Lawyer, 1954; (with R. Alexander) The Struggle for Democracy in Latin America, 1961. Home: 2680 Baker St Eugene OR 97403 Office: 96 E Broadway Suite 1 Eugene OR 97401 Tel (503) 687-2111

PORTER, FRANK E., b. 1926; B.S., LL.B., U. Wis. With Marathon div. Am. Can Co., 1955-59; legal affairs counsel Gen. Mills Co., 1959-68; v.p., sec., corp. counsel First Bank System, Inc., Mpls., 1968-74, sr. v.p., sec., gen. counsel, 1974—. Office: 1400 First Nat Bank Bldg Minneapolis MN 55480*

PORTER, HERBERT M., b. Charleroi, Pa., July 1, 1918; B.S., U. Pa., 1938; J.D., U. Calif. at Los Angeles, 1960. Admitted to Calif. bar, 1961, Fed. bar, 1961; Bd. dirs. Temple Batyahm, Mem. Los Angeles, Calif. bar assns. Author: Courtbook; The Day; Throes; contbr. articles to legal jours. Office: PO Box 248 Laguna Beach CA 92652 Tel (714) 552-1550

PORTER, JAMES DUNLOP, JR., b. Milw., Nov. 2, 1938; A.B., Yale, 1960; LL.B., Harvard, 1963. Admitted to N.Y. bar, 1964, D.C. bar, 1964; asso. firm Winthrop, Stimson, Putnam & Roberts, N.Y.C., 1963-70; asst. U.S. Atty. and chief civil div. Office of U.S. Atty. Eastern Dist. N.Y., 1970-74; partner firm Shea Gould Climenko Kramer & Casey, N.Y.C., 1974-76; chief counsel, grievances com. Assn. Bar City N.Y., 1977—. Mem. bd. govs. Bklyn. Heights Assn., 1967-72. Mem. Bklyn., D.C. bar assns., Fed. Bar Council. Contbr. articles to legal publs. Office: 36 W 44th St New York City NY 10036 Tel (212) MU2-0606

PORTER, JESSE EDWIN (RUSTY), JR., b. Helena, Ark., Nov. 29, 1948; B.S. with honors in Bus. Adminstrn., U. Ark., 1970, J.D., 1973. Admitted to Ark. bar, 1973; law clerk to Chief Justice Carleton Harris, Supreme Ct., Little Rock, 1973-74; mem. firm Shieffler, Yates & Porter, W. Helena, 1975-76; individual practice law, W. Helena, 1976—. Pres. Helena-W. Helena United Fund, 1976; v.p. W. Helena Promotional Assn., 1977. Mem. Am., Ark. bar assns., Phillips County Bar Assn. (sec.-treas.), Ark. Trial Lawyers Assn. Mem. Staff Ark. Law Review, 1972-73. Home: 127 N 5th St West Helena AR 72390 Office: 203 Plaza Ave West Helena AR 72390 Tel (501) 572-3751

PORTER, JOHN EDWARD, b. Evanston, Ill., June 1, 1935; student (scholar) Mass. Inst. Tech., 1953-54; B.S. in Bus. Adminstrn., Northwestern U., 1957; J.D. with distinction, U. Mich., 1961. Admitted to Ill. bar, 1961; atty. civil div. appellate sect. U.S. Dept. Justice, Washington, 1961-62; individual practice law, Evanston, 1962-68, 72-74; partner firm Shanesy, Hobbs, Koch, Porter & Ball, Evanston, 1968-72, Porter & Hoffman, Evanston, 1974—; state rep. 1st Legis. Dist. Ill., 1972—; dir. Legal Assistance Found. Cook County, Inc., 1967-73; mem. N. Cook County Legal Adv. Bd., 1967-73, chmn., 1967. Co-chmn. lawyers sect. United Community Services Evanston, 1965, chmn., 1967; treas. SE Evanston Assn., 1967-68, dir., 1967-69; bus. and industry chmn. Evanston March of Dimes, 1968-69; gen. counsel Cook County Young Republican Orgn., 1965, v.p. polit. affairs Niles Twp. chpt., 1966; charter mem. Evanston Rep. Workshops, 1967; co-counsel Evanston Rep. Club, 1967-70; pres. Evanston Young Rep. Club, 1968-69; precinct capt., 1968-73, mem. exec. bd. Evanston Regular Rep. Orgn., 1968—, co-chmn. 3d ward, 1968-74. Mem. Am., Ill., Chgo., N.W. Suburban bar assns., Evanston Hist. Soc. (trustee 1970-73), Evanston C. of C. (chmn. congressional action com. 1967-68). Asst. editor U. Mich. Law Rev. Home: 1124 Sheridan Rd Evanston IL 60202 Office: 360 State Nat Bank Plaza Evanston IL 60201 Tel (312) 475-0100

PORTER, JOHN ROBERTSON, b. Madison, Wis., Feb. 20, 1946; B.A., Stanford U., 1968, J.D., 1973. Admitted to Idaho bar, 1973; partner firm Peterson, Moorer & Porter, Moscow, Idaho, 1973-75; individual practice law, Moscow, 1975-77; partner firm Peterson, Chernecke & Porter, Moscow, 1977—; lectr. bus. law Washington State U., 1974—. Trustee Moscow Pub. Schs., 1974—; mem. Latah County (Idaho) Democratic Central com., Moscow, 1975—. Mem.

Idaho State Bar. Note editor Stanford Law Rev., 1972-73. Office: 113 S Main St PO Box 9247 Moscow ID 83843 Tel (208) 882-6595

PORTER, JOHN WESLEY, JR., b. Eufaula, Okla., Nov. 7, 1911; LL.B., Cumberland U., 1935; Admitted to Okla. bar, 1935, U.S. Supreme Ct. bar, 1948; practiced in Muskogee, Okla., 1935, 76—; police judge, Muskogee, 1948-53; asst. county atty. Muskogee County, 1953-61, county judge, 1961-69, judge dist. ct., 1969-76. Leader Explorer Scouts, 1959-60. Bd. dirs. Muskogee Salvation Army, 1967-69. Mem. Fed., Am., Okla. bar assns., Am., Okla. trial lawyers assns., Am. Judicature Soc., Lambda Chi Alpha. Contbr. articles to profl. jours. Home: 301 S 30th St Muskogee OK 74401

PORTER, LOUIS N., b. Bklyn., Apr. 1, 1919; LL.B., St. John's U., 1942. Admitted to N.Y. State bar, 1942; individual practice law, N.Y.C., 1950—; adj. prof. law Coll. City N.Y., 1974-75; mem. small claims panel N.Y. Civil Ct. Mem. Am. Arbitration Assn. Home: 65 Standish Dr Scarsdale NY 10583 Office: 225 Broadway New York City NY 10007 Tel (212) RE2-5480

PORTER, SAMUEL HAMILTON, b. Columbus, Ohio, July 5, 1927; B.A., Amherst Coll., 1950; J.D., Ohio State U., 1953. Admitted to Ohio bar, 1953; asso. firm Porter, Stanley, Platt & Arthur, Columbus, 1953-56, partner, 1957—. Trustee Columbus Sch. Girls, 1962-69, pres., 1968-69; trustee United Community Council, 1969-75, pres., 1973-74; mem. exec. com. bd. trustees United Way, 1973-74; trustee Gladden Community House, 1965-70. Mem. Am., Ohio (council dels. 1971-75), Columbus (gov. 1972—) bar assns. Home: 211 Preston Rd Columbus OH 43209 Office: 37 W Broad St Columbus OH 43215 Tel (614) 228-1511

PORTER, STEPHEN CALVIN, b. Dallas, May 18, 1946; B.B.A., Baylor U., 1968; J.D., So. Meth. U., 1973. Admitted to Tex. bar, 1973; partner firm McMullen & Porter, Dallas, 1973—. Mem. Tex., Dallas bar assns. Home: 6529 Burrows Ct Plano TX 75023 Office: 12700 Park Central Pl Suite 1603 Dallas TX 75251 Tel (214) 387-4844

PORTER, STEPHEN DAVIS, b. Decatur, Ill., Nov. 9, 1945; B.S. with honors, U. Ill., 1967; J.D., Duke, 1970. Admitted to Ill. bar, 1970; asst. atty. gen. State of Ill., 1970-71; asst. reporter of decisions Supreme and Appellate Cts. of Ill., Bloomington, 1971-75, reporter of decisions, 1976—. Mem. Bloomington-Normal Com. to Hire the Handicapped, 1973. Mem. Am., Ill. State, McLean County bar assns., Am. Judicature Soc. Office: Box 186 Bloomington IL 61701 Tel (309) 827-8513

PORTER, WALTER b. Lumberton, N.C., Mar. 8, 1931; A.B., U. N.C., 1953, J.D. with high honors, 1960. Admitted to N.C. bar, 1960; exec. v.p. firm Powe, Porter, Alphin & Whichard, Durham, N.C., 1973—; adj. prof. bus. law Duke U., Durham. Past bd. dirs. Family Counseling Services; bd. dirs. C. of C. (exec. com.). Mem. Am., N.C. bar assns., Order of Coif. Bd. editors N.C. Law Rev., 1959-60; recipient Chief Justice Walter Clark award, 1960, Durham Housing Industry Man of Year award, 1969; Durham Legal Secs. Assn. Boss of Year awar, 1968. Office: Suite 800 First Union Nat Bank Bldg 301 W Main St PO Box 3843 Durham NC 27702 Tel (919) 682-5654

PORTER, WILLIAM G., b. Madison, S.D., May 19, 1926; B.A., U. S.D., 1950, LL.B., 1952. Admitted to S.D. bar, 1952; now partner firm Costello, Porter, Hill, Nelson, Heisterkamp & Bushnell, Rapid City, S.D.; mem. S.D. Bd. Bar Examiners, 1968-74, chmn., 1971-74. Mem. Am., Pennington County bar assns., State Bar S.D. (pres. 1977—), Internat. Soc. Barristers, Am. Bd. Trial Advs. Office: 200 Security Bldg 704 Saint Joseph St PO Box 290 Rapid City SD 57709 Tel (605) 343-2410*

PORTER, WILLIAM JACKSON, JR., b. East Orange, N.J., Nov. 26, 1930; J.D., Woodrow Wilson Coll., 1959. Admitted to Ga. bar, 1959, U.S. Supreme Ct. bar, 1976; partner firm Owens & Porter, Norcross, Ga., 1960-72; individual practice law, Chamblee, Ga., 1972—. Mem. Am., Atlanta, Decatur-DeKalb, Gwinnett bar assns., Atlanta Lawyers Club, Am. Judicature Soc., Sigma Delta Kappa. Home: 4053 Spalding Hollow Norcross GA 30071 Office: Suite 303 2511 Carroll Ave Chamblee GA 30341 Tel (404) 458-8261

PORTERFIELD, JACK BERRY, JR., b. Birmingham, Ala., Aug. 27, 1924; student U. Richmond, 1943-47; LL.B., Washington and Lee U., 1949. Admitted to Ala. bar, 1949, since practiced in Birmingham; asso. firm Lange, Simpson, Robinson & Somerville, 1949-55; partner firm Porterfield & Scholl, 1964-67, Dunn, Porterfield, Scholl & Clark, 1967—. Mem. Am., Ala., Birmingham (pres. 1968) bar assns., Internat. Assn. Ins. Counsel, Ala. Def. Lawyers Assn. Office: Suite 1 Bldg 2 Office Park Circle Birmingham AL 35223 Tel (205) 879-9370

PORTNOY, IAN KARL, b. Phila., Aug. 27, 1943; B.A. in Sociology, U. Mich., 1965; J.D., Villanova U., 1968. Admitted to Pa. bar, 1969, D.C. bar, 1970, U.S. Supreme Ct. bar, 1973; with spl. counse)'s office Office of Edn., HEW, Washington, 1966; with counsel's office Redevel. Authority, Phila., 1967; corp. counsel Villager Industries, Inc., 1969; with firm Danzansky, Dickey, Tydings, Quint & Gordon, Washington, 1970—, partner, 1974—. Bd. dirs. Big Bros. of Nat. Capital Area, 1977-79; bd. trustees Greater Washington Ednl. Telecommunications Assn., Inc., 1977—. Mem. Am., D.C. bar assns. Contbr. articles to legal jours. Home: 5022 Allan Rd Washington DC 20016 Office: 1120 Connecticut Ave NW Washington DC 20036 Tel (202) 857-4078

POSGAY, RAYMOND JOSEPH, b. Cleve., Oct. 9, 1943; B.S., Ohio State U., 1965, J.D., 1967. Admitted to Fla. bar, 1968; v.p. Broward County Title Co., Fort Lauderdale, Fla., 1968-69; individual practice law, Fort Lauderdale, 1969—. Bd. dirs. specialized urban ministries Fort Lauderdale, United Meth. Ch., 1970-73, bd. dirs. bd. missions and ch. extension West Palm Beach dist., 1974-77, 1st v.p. com. on ch. devel. Fla. Conf., 1976—; vice chmn. adv. com. Plantation Park (Fla.) Elementary Sch., 1975-77; advisor Fort Lauderdale Goldcoasters, 1971-76, Re-Build Found., Inc., 1969—; bd. dirs. Center for Pastoral Counseling, 1974—, pres., 1975—; bd. dirs. Broward County Housing Center, 1973-74. Mem. Am., Fla., Broward County (dir. young lawyers sect. 1975-77) bar assns. Office: 1990 E Sunrise Blvd Fort Lauderdale FL 33304 Tel (305) 764-5543

POSIN, DANIEL Q., JR., b. Berkeley, Calif., May 16, 1941; B.A., U. Calif., 1963; M.A., LL.B., Yale, 1967; LL.M., N.Y. U., 1975. Staff counsel to Ralph Nader Orgn., Washington, 1967-68; lectr. econs. U. East Africa, Nairobi, Kenya, 1969-70; legis. asst. to congressman, Washington, 1971-72; admitted to Calif. bar, 1972; asso. firm Lowenthal & Lowenthal, San Francisco, 1972-73; asso. prof. law Hofstra U., Hempstead, N.Y., 1974—. Mem. Am. Bar Assn., Phi Beta Kappa. Contbg. author: Hot War on the Consumer (David Sanford editor), 1971. Office: School of Law Hofstra U Hempstead NY 11550

POSNER, DANIEL B., b. Bklyn., Oct. 28, 1917; B.A., Columbia, 1937; LL.B., Yale, 1940. Admitted to N.Y. bar, 1940; staff atty. SEC, Washington, 1940-42, N.Y.C., 1946-55; Bd. Econ. Welfare, Washington, 1942; asso. firm Fried, Frank, Harris, Shriver & Jacobson, N.Y.C., 1956-66, partner, 1967—. Mem. Am., N.Y. State bar assns., Assn. Bar City N.Y. Contbr. articles to profl. publs. Home: 29-45 169th St Flushing NY 11358 Office: 120 Broadway New York City NY 10005 Tel (212) WO4-6500

POSNER, HERBERT NELSON, b. Mt. Vernon, N.Y., Apr. 30, 1937; B.S., U. Vt., 1958; LL.B., Bklyn. Law Sch., 1961. Admitted to N.Y. bar, 1961, U.S. Dist. Ct. bar, 1964; partner firm Posner & Posner, Mt. Vernon, 1961—; counsel Mt. Vernon Urban Renewal Agy., 1975—; Sr. Citizens Housing Assn., 1975—. Mem. Am., N.Y. State, Mt. Vernon, Westchester County bar assns. Home: 3 James Dr New Rochelle NY 10804 Office: 120 E Prospect Ave Mt Vernon NY 10550 Tel (914) 668-6116

POSNER, SIDNEY HYMAN, b. N.Y.C., Oct. 4, 1902; B.S., Washington Sq. Coll., N.Y. U., 1924, J.D., N.Y. U., 1925. Admitted to N.Y. bar, 1926, U.S. Supreme Ct. bar, 1962; partner firm Paley & Posner, N.Y.C., 1927-32, Posner & Posner, Mt. Vernon, N.Y., 1932—. Mem. local draft bd. SSS, 1958-73. Mem. Am., Westchester County, Mt. Vernon bar assns. Office: 120 E Prospect Ave Mount Vernon NY 10550 Tel (914) 668-6116

POSNER, WILLIAM, b. Lithuania, July 7, 1921; B.A., Bklyn. Coll., 1948; M.A., N.Y. U., 1950; LL.B., Bklyn. Law Sch., 1961. Admitted to N.Y. bar, U.S. Custom Ct. bar, U.S. Tax Ct. bar; since practiced in N.Y.C., asso. firm David G. Oringer, 1962-63, individual practice law, 1963-65, mem. firm Posner & Kransnow, 1965—; arbitrator Small Claims dept. Civil Ct.; hearing examiner Parking Violation Bur. Bd. dirs. Adv. Bd. for Legal Assistance. Mem. Am., N.Y. County bar assns., N.Y. County Lawyers Assn., N.Y. State Trial Lawyers Assn. Office: 51 Chambers St New York City NY 10007 Tel (212) 267-5452

POSNICK, MICHAEL ALLEN, b. Mpls., June 24, 1946; B.A., U. Minn., 1968, J.D. cum laude, 1971. Admitted to Minn. bar, 1971, U.S. Dist. Ct. bar for Minn., 1971; individual practice law, Mpls., 1971—; mem. local govt. com. Minn. Housing Inst., 1973-75. Mem. Am., Minn., Hennepin County bar assns. Home and office: 2601 Princeton Ave S Minneapolis MN 55416 Tel (612) 920-4344

POSPISHIL, LLOYD LABAR, b. West Point, Nebr., May 19, 1911; B.A., U. Nebr., 1932, J.D., 1933. Admitted to Nebr. bar, 1933, U.S. Dist. Ct. bar, 1933; county atty., 1935-39, 43-51; judge Nebr. Ct. Indsl. Relations, 1961-67; mayor City of Schuyler, 1940-42; Howells city atty., 1946-68; Schuyler city atty., 1943, 58-60, 62-64; staff legal officer U.S. Navy, 1943-45; individual practice law, Schuyler, 1933—; VA service officer, 1945-75; dep. county atty., 1958—. Bd. dirs. Meml. Hosp., Inc., 1952-76; vice chmn. nat. Americanism commn. Am. Legion; pres. Schuyler C. of C. Mem. Am., Nebr. (adv. com. 1951-75, title standards com. 1967—) bar assns., Am. Title Assn., Am. Coll. Probate Counsel, Nebr. Assn. Trial Attys. (pres. 1960-61), Forty and Eight (grand cheminot 1960-61, grahd avocat 1953-54, 75—), Am. Legion (dist. comdr. 1952-54, dept. vice comdr. 1958). Office: 324 E 11th St Schuyler NE 68661 Tel (402) 362-3244

POST, JERRY CLARK, b. Fordyce, Ark., Dec. 18, 1943; B.A. in Psychology, U. Ark., 1966, J.D. with high honors (Delta Theta Phi scholar), 1972. Admitted to Ark. bar, 1972, U.S. Dist. Ct. bar for Eastern Dist. Ark., 1973; asso. firm Murphy, Blair, Post & Stroud and predecessors, Batesville, Ark., 1972-75, partner, 1976—; acting judge Batesville Municipal Ct., summer, 1975, 76; spl. prosecutor City of Batesville, 1976. Bd. dirs. Independence County (Ark.) Sheltered Workshop, 1973-76, New Start Am., Inc., criminal rehab. program, 1976-77. Mem. Am., Ark. trial lawyers assns., Ark., Am. bar assns., Delta Theta Phi. Editorial bd. U. Ark. Law Rev., 1970-72, citations editor, 1972. Office: 255 E College St Batesville AR 72501 Tel (501) 793-3821

POST, RICHARD L., b. 1920; B.A., U. Minn., 1942, J.D., 1946. Asst. sec., asst. gen. counsel Minn. Mining & Mfg. Co., 1946-69; sec., gen. counsel Honeywell, Inc., Mpls., 1969—, corp. v.p., 1971—. Office: Honeywell Inc Honeywell Plaza Minneapolis MN 55408*

POSTEN, WILLIAM SCOTT, b. East Moline, Ill., Mar. 10, 1931; J.D., William Mitchell Coll. Law, 1959. Admitted to Minn. bar, 1959; claims rep. Social Security Adminstrn., Mpls., 1960-61; asst. county atty. Hennepin County, Minn., 1961-73; judge Hennepin County Municipal Ct., 1973-76, Minn. Dist. Ct., Hennepin County, 1976—. Bd. dirs. Mpls. chpt. March of Dimes, 1970-73, Mpls. United Way, 1968-70, Mpls. Salvation Army, 1976-77. Mem. Am., Minn. State, Hennepin County bar assns., Minn. Dist. Judges Assn. Home: 4512 Park Ave S Minneapolis MN 55407 Office: 13-C Hennepin County Govt Center Minneapolis MN 55487 Tel (612) 348-4420

POSTER, ROBERT LEON, b. N.Y.C., June 24, 1940; A.B., Princeton, 1962; J.D., Harvard, 1965, L.L.M., 1966. Admitted to N.Y. State bar, 1965; since practiced in N.Y.C., asso. firm Kirlin, Campbell & Keating, 1965-71, partner, 1972-73; partner firm Gilmartin, Poster & Shafto, 1973—; arbitrator small claims div. Civil Ct. N.Y., 1976—. Mem. Assn. Bar City N.Y. (transp. law and admiralty law coms. 1973-76), Am., N.Y. State bar assns., Maritime Law Assn. U.S. Home: 40 E 88th St New York City NY 10028 Office: 26 Broadway New York City NY 10004 Tel (212) 425-3220

POSTMAN, ALAN LLOYD, b. Bklyn., July 8, 1940; B.A., N.Y. U., 1962; LL.B., Bklyn. Law Sch., 1965. Admitted to N.Y. bar, 1965, Fla. bar, 1972; asst. dist. atty. N.Y. County, 1968-73; asst. states atty., Miami, Fla., 1973-74; partner Vogler & Postman, Miami, 1975—. Office: 1 Biscayne Tower Suite 2770 Miami FL 33131 Tel (305) 358-7626

POSTOW, STUART PHILIP, b. Washington, May 22, 1947; B.S., U. Md., 1970; J.D., U. Balt., 1973. Admitted to Md. bar, 1973, D.C. bar, 1974; atty., office of gen. counsel Fed. Maritime Commn., Washington, 1973—. Mem. Am., Balt., Maritime, D.C., Md. bar assns. Home: 2445 Lyttonsville Rd No 13 Silver Spring MD 20910 Office: 1100 L St NW Washington DC 20573 Tel (202) 523-5738

POTASH, CHARLES, b. Phila., May 31, 1932; B.A., U. Pa., 1953; J.D., Temple U., 1959. Admitted to Pa. bar, 1960; law clk. Justice Benjamin R. Jones Supreme Ct. Pa., 1959-60; mem. firm Wisler, Pearlstine, Talone, Craig & Garrity, Norristown, Pa., 1961-67; partner, 1967—; solicitor Lower Merion Sch. Dist., Sch. Dist. Springfield Twp., Sch. Dist. Cheltenham Twp., Methacton Sch. Dist., Upper Perkiomen Sch. Dist., N. Penn Sch. Dist. Authority, Cheltenham Twp. Sch. Dist. Authority, Red Hill Water Authority, Upper Dublin Sch. Dist. Mem. Am.,Pa., Phila., Montgomery County (dir., 1971-75, chmn. Am. Citizenship com. 1969) bar assns. Research editor Temple Law Quar., 1958-59. Home: 712 Custis Rd Glenside PA 19038 Office: 515 Swede St Norristown PA 19401 Tel (215) 272-8400

POTASH, HOWARD KENNETH, b. Kew Gardens, N.Y., Aug. 17, 1942; A.B., Columbia Coll., 1965; J.D., N.Y. U., 1968. Admitted to Calif. bar, 1969; partner firm Mathews, Bergen, Vodicka & Potash, San Diego, 1969—. Gen. counsel, bd. dirs. Widowed to Widowed Program, Inc., 1976—. Mem. Am., San Diego County (chmn. family law legis. sub-com.) bar assns., State Bar Calif. Office: 652 Spreckels Bldg 121 Broadway St San Diego CA 92101 Tel (714) 234-8331

POTE, DORIS RUTH, A.B., Radcliffe Coll.; J.D., Suffolk U., 1967; postgrad. Harvard, 1972-73. Admitted to Mass. bar, 1967; pres. treas. Conant Littleton Co., Littleton, Mass., 1950—; registrar, asso. prof. law, Suffolk U., 1967—. Chmn. Mass. Consumers Council, 1975—; mem. Spl. Legis. Commn. on Auto Ins., 1975—; mem. rev. com. United Way, Boston, 1975. Mem. Am., Mass. bar assns., Nat. Assn. Women Lawyers, Am. Judicature, Mass. Assn. Women Lawyers (pres. 1972-73). Author: The Cemetery Industry in the United States, 1972; The Consumer Movement and the Mobile Home, 1973. Home: 46 Clinton Rd Brookline MA 02146 Office: 41 Temple St Boston MA 02114 Tel (617) 723-4700

POTH, HARRY AUGUSTUS, JR., b. Phila., Nov. 5, 1911; B.S., U. Pa., 1933, LL.B., 1936. Admitted to N.Y. bar, 1938, D.C. bar, 1948; asso. firm Reid & Priest, N.Y.C., 1937-48, partner, 1949—; advisor on electric pub. utility matters Govt. of Greece, 1953-54, Govt. of Pakistan, 1962-63; dir. Am. Utility Shares. Mem. Am., Fed., Fed. Power, N.Y. bar assns., Assn. Bar City N.Y., Am. Soc. Internat. Law, Fgn. Policy Assn. Contbr. articles in field to profl. jours.; editorial bd. U. Pa. Law Rev., 1935-36. Home: Winding Ln Greenwich CT 06830 Office: 40 Wall St New York City NY 10005 Tel (212) 344-2233

POTTER, ALLAN LESLIE, b. Corpus Christi, Tex., Apr. 27, 1947; student U. Tex., 1965-67; B.A., Baylor U., 1969, J.D., 1971. Admitted to Tex. bar, 1971, U.S. Supreme Ct. bar, 1974; law clk. Tex. 13th Ct. of Civil Appeals, 1972-73; partner firm Potter & Potter, Corpus Christi, 1973—. Mem. State Bar Tex., Am., Nueces County (chmn. com. membership 1975—) bar assns., Assn. Trial Lawyers Am., Comml. Law League Am., Nueces County Trial Lawyers, Nuces County Young Lawyers Bar, Phi Eta Sigma, Phi Alpha Delta, Alpha Epsilon Delta. Home: 4037 Pope St Corpus Christi TX 78411 Office: 516 Wilson Tower Corpus Christi TX 78401 Tel (512) 888-8203

POTTER, ALTON WILLIAM, b. Flint, Mich., May 30, 1921; B.S., Northwestern U., 1943; M.B.A., U. Chgo., 1946; J.D., U. Mich., 1949. Admitted to Ill. bar, 1950, Mich. bar, 1950; estate adminstr. 1st Nat. Bank of Chgo., 1950-51; mem. firm Holmes, Dixon, Knouff & Potter, Chgo., 1952-57, partner, 1958-67; partner firm Knouff & Ley, Chgo., 1967-73; partner firm Potter & Falk, Chgo., 1974—. Mem. Chgo. (chmn. probate practice com. 1968-69, div. chmn. trust law com. 1974-75), Ill. State, Am. bar assns., Am. Coll. Probate Counsel (Ill. state chmn. 1971-73), State Bar Mich., Law Club of City Chgo., Legal Club Chgo. Home: 2724 Wallace Dr Flossmoor IL 60422 Office: 39 S La Salle St Suite 1425 Chicago IL 60603 Tel (312) 263-2150

POTTER, C. BURTT, b. Acadia Parish, La., Dec. 21, 1908; B.A., Southwestern La. U., 1930; J.D., Baylor U. Law Sch., 1933. Admitted to Tex. bar, 1933, U.S. Supreme Ct. bar, 1965; county atty. San Patricio County (Tex.), 1935-43; atty. Fed. Works Agy., Ft. Worth, 1943-45; individual practice law, Corpus Christi, Tex., 1945-73; spl. dist. judge, 1950; partner firm Potter and Potter, Corpus Christi, 1973—. Chmn. ARC, San Patricio County, 1941-43; bd. dirs. Am. Heart Assn., Corpus Christi, 1975-77. Mem. State Bar Tex. (dir. 1950-52), Nueces County (pres. 1949-50), San Patricio County (pres. 1942-43) bar assns. Home: 420 Delaine St Corpus Christi TX 78401 Office: Potter & Potter 516 Wilson Tower Corpus Christi TX 78401 Tel (513) 888-8203

POTTER, DONALD CLINTON, b. Chgo., July 25, 1931; A.B., U. Ill., 1953, LL.B., 1958. Admitted to Ill. bar, 1959; asso. firm Clausen Miller Gorman, Caffrey & Witous, Chgo., 1962-73, partner, 1973—. Mem. Ill., Chgo., Am. bar assns. Office: 135 S LaSalle St Chicago IL 60603 Tel (312) 346-6200

POTTER, ERNEST LUTHER, JR., b. Anniston, Ala., Apr. 30, 1940; A.B., U. Ala., 1961, LL.B., 1963. Admitted to Ala. bar, 1963; asso. firm Burnham & Klinefelter, Anniston, Ala., 1963-64; asso. firm Bell, Richardson, Cleary, McLain & Tucker, Huntsville, Ala., 1964-66, partner, 1967-70; partner firm Butler & Potter, Huntsville, 1971—; instr. bus. law and polit. sci. U. Ala., Huntsville, 1965-67. Vice pres. N. Ala. Kidney Found., 1976-77; treas. Madison County Democratic Exec. Com., 1974-77. Mem. Am., Ala. (commr. 23d jud. circuit 1975—, pres. young lawyers sect. 1973), Ala. Trial Lawyers Assn. Contbr. to Marital Law in Alabama, 1976. Home: 1105 Deborah Dr Huntsville AL 35801 Office: 108 Jefferson St Huntsville AL 35804 Tel (205) 536-0096

POTTER, HOWARD HUGH, b. Valentine, Nebr., Sept. 29, 1942; B.B.A., Creighton U., 1966, J.D., 1969; M.B.A., U. Nebr., 1969. Admitted to Nebr. bar, 1969, Colo. bar, 1972; tax dept. Peat, Marwick & Mitchell, Omaha, 1969-70, Touche, Ross & Co., Denver, 1970-72; mem. firm Vaughan & Potter, Denver, 1972—. Mem. Am., Colo., Nebr. bar assns., Am. Inst. C.P.A.'s, Colo. Soc. C.P.A.'s, Nebr., Colo. real estate brokers assns. C.P.A., Colo. Home: 777 Washington St Denver CO 80203 Office: 1331 Logan St Denver CO 80203 Tel (303) 573-6434

POTTER, JOHN MICHAEL, b. Corpus Christi, Tex., Aug. 7, 1949; B.B.A., Baylor U., 1971, J.D., 1972. Admitted to Tex. bar, 1972, U.S. Supreme Ct. bar, 1976, 5th Circuit Ct. Appeals bar, 1976, U.S. Dist. Ct. bar for SW Dist. Tex.; asst. dist. atty. Nueces County (Tex.) Dist. Atty's. Office, 1972-75; research asst. Tex. Ct. Criminal Appeals, Austin, 1975—. Mem. Am., Tex., Travis County, Nueces County bar assns., Nat. Dist. Attys. Assn., Tex. County and Dist. Atty's. Assn., Tex. Criminal Def. Lawyer's Assn. Home: 911 Fall Creek Austin TX 78753 Office: Ct of Criminal Appeals Supreme Ct Bldg Austin TX 78711 Tel (512) 475-6419

POTTER, WILLIAM RICHARD, b. Austin, Tex., Oct. 13, 1933; B.B.A., U. Tex., 1955; J.D., Calif. Western Sch. Law, 1969. Admitted to Calif. bar, 1970; partner firm Procopio, Cory, Hargreaves and Savitch, San Diego, 1972-76; individual practice law, San Diego, 1976—; pres. Point Loma Tennis Club Community Corp., San Diego, 1976—. Mem. Am., San Diego County bar assns., Calif. Soc. C.P.A.'s. C.P.A., Calif.; contbr. articles to profl. jours. Office: 600 B St Suite 1850 San Diego CA 92101 Tel (714) 231-8474

POTTER, WILLIAM SAMUEL, b. Clarksburg, W.Va., Jan. 10, 1905; LL.B., U. Va., 1927. Admitted to Del. bar, 1928; asso. firm Potter Anderson & Corroon and predecessors, Wilmington, Del., 1927-30, mem. firm 1930-75, counsel, 1972—; atty. Del. Liquor Commn., 1940-43. Trustee U. Va. Law Sch. Found.; bd. visitors U. Va., 1967; mem. Dem. Nat. Com., 1956-72. Mem. Am., Del. State (pres. 1942-44) bar assns., Assn. of Bar of the City of N.Y., Phi Beta Kappa, Order of Coif, Phi Delta Phi. Co-author Del. Corporation Law Annotated, 1936. Home: 5826 Kennett Pike Wilmington DE 19807 Office: 350 Delaware Trust Bldg Wilmington DE 19801 Tel (302) 658-6771

POTTINGER, JOHN STANLEY, b. Dayton, Ohio, Feb. 13, 1940; A.B. cum laude (John Harvard hon. scholar), Harvard, 1962, LL.B., 1965; LL.D. (hon.), Lincoln U., San Francisco, 1975. Admitted to Calif. bar, 1965, U.S. Supreme Ct. bar, 1973; asso. firm Broad, Khourie & Schulz, San Francisco, 1965-69; cons., regional atty. HEW, San Francisco, 1969, dir. Office for Civil Rights, 1970-73; asst. atty. gen. Civil Rights div. Dept. Justice, Washington, 1973-77, spl. asst. to atty. gen., 1977—; pres. Pottinger and Co., Washington. Bd. dirs. Lighthouse for Blind, San Francisco, 1968. Mem. Barristers Club San Francisco. Recipient award Mexican-Am. Educators Assn., 1972, Appreciation award Nat. Assn. for Retarded Citizens, 1975; named one of 200 Future Leaders of Am., Time mag., 1974; contbr. articles to legal jours. Home: 6009 Corbin Rd Bethesda MD 20016 Office: Pottinger and Co 1730 Pennsylvania Ave Washington DC 20006 Tel (202) 638-6231

POTTS, STEPHEN DEADERICK, b. Memphis, Nov. 20, 1930; A.B. cum laude, Vanderbilt U., 1952, LL.B., 1954. Admitted to Tenn. bar, 1954, U.S. Supreme Ct. bar, 1957, D.C. bar, 1961; served with JAGC, U.S. Army, 1955-57; asso. firm Farris, Evans & Evans, Nashville, 1957-59; v.p. Cherokee Life Ins. Co., Nashville, 1959-61; asso. firm Shaw, Pittman, Potts and Trowbridge, Washington, 1961—, partner, 1968—; dir. Overseas Nat. Airways, Jamaica, N.Y. Pres., Wood Acres PTA, Bethesda, Md., 1968, Washington Area Tennis Patrons, 1969-72, Holton-Arms Sch. Fathers Club, 1976; bd. advisors Patterson Sch. Diplomacy, U. Ky., 1976—. Mem. Am., Tenn., D.C. bar assns., Phi Beta Kappa. Mem. Vanderbilt Law Rev. Home: 4410 Chalfont Pl Washington DC 20016 Office: 1800 M St NW Washington DC 20036 Tel (202) 331-4100

POU, ELIZABETH LYNNE, b. Raleigh, N.C., Aug. 9, 1946; B.A. in English, U. N.C., 1968, J.D., 1972. Admitted to Ga. bar, 1972; since practiced in Atlanta, asso. firm Powell, Goldstein, Frazer & Murphy, 1972-73, firm Nall, Miller & Cadenhead, 1973—; tchr. spl. studies Ga. State U., 1973-75. Vol. atty. YWCA Legal Assistance Clinic, 1976—; bd. dirs. Atlanta Wider Opportunities for Women, 1974-76. Mem. Am., Ga., Atlanta bar assns., Ga. State Bar (vice-chmn. pub. relations com.), Atlanta Council Younger Lawyers (dir.). Home: 867 Monroe Dr NE Atlanta GA 30308 Office: 100 Peachtree St NW Atlanta GA 30303 Tel (404) 522-2200

POUGH, W. NEWTON, b. Neeses, S.C., July 4, 1921; A.B., S.C. State Coll., 1949, J.D., 1952. Admitted to S.C. bar 1952; individual practice law, Orangeburg, S.C., 1952—; gen. counsel S.C. State Coll., Orangeburg, 1969—; dep. gen. counsel Ancient Egyptian Arabic Order Nobles of Mystic Shrines of N. and S.Am., Inc., 1972—; gen. counsel Belleville Devel. Corp., Inc., 1970, Price Hall Grand Lodge, Masons for S.C., 1964—. Chmn. bd. trustees S.C. United Methodist Ch., 1972—; vice-chmn. Orangeburg County Democratic Party, 1974-76, Orangeburg Area Mental Health Assn., 1968—. Mem. S.C. State Bar Assn., Am. Trial Lawyers Assn., Nat. Assn. Coll. and Univ. Attys. Home: Belleville Rd Orangeburg SC 29115 Office: Rene Bldg 512 Amelia St NE Orangeburg SC 29115 Tel (803) 534-1356

POULOS, JOHN WILLIAM, b. Ukiah, Calif., Jan. 7, 1937; A.B. in Econs., Stanford U., 1958; J.D., U. Calif., 1962. Admitted to Calif. bar, 1963, U.S. Supreme Ct. bar, 1970; asso. firm Gray, Carey, Ames & Frye, San Diego, Calif., 1962-64; partner firm Rawles, Nelson, Golden, Poulos & Hinkle, Ukiah, Calif., 1964-69; prof. law U. Calif., Davis, Calif., 1969—; vis. prof. law Judicial Tng. Inst., Republic of Afghanistan, 1976-77, fgn. legal advisor Ministry of Justice Republic of Afghanistan, 76-77. Bd. edn. Ukiah Unified Sch. Dist., 1967-69. Mem. Assn. Am. Law Schs., Am. Judicature Soc., Commonwealth Club Calif., Asia Soc. Fulbright-Hayes Sr. fellow, 1976-77. Author: Biography of a Homicide, 1976; Dynamics of Criminal Corrections, 1976, The Anatomy of Criminal Justice, 1976. Contbr. articles to legal jours. Home: 621 Cordova Pl Davis CA 95616 Office: Law School University of California Davis CA 95616 Tel (916) 752-2881

POUND, FRANK REESE, JR., b. Mayo, Fla., Nov. 3, 1933; B.S.J., U. Fla., 1959, LL.B., 1961. Admitted to Fla. bar, 1962, U.S. Supreme Ct. bar, 1969; asst. county solicitor Orange County (Fla.), 1962-64; atty. firm Crofter, Brewer & Holland, Titusville, Fla., 1964-66; partner firm Howell, Kirby, Montgomery & Sands, Rockledge, Fla., 1966-71; pres. firm Lovering, Pound & Lober, Rockledge, 1971—. Chmn. Titusville-Cocoa Airport Authority, 1972-76. Mem. Fla. bar, Brevard County Bar (pres. 1972-73), Phi Delta Phi. Office: 1259 S Florida Ave Rockledge FL 32958

POUND, JOHN BENNETT, b. Champaign, Ill., Nov. 17, 1946; B.A., U. N.Mex., 1968; J.D., Boston Coll., 1971. Admitted to N.Mex. bar, 1971; law clk. to judge U.S. Ct. Appeals for 10th Circuit, Santa Fe, 1971-72; asso. firm Montgomery, Federici, Andrews & Hannahs, Santa Fe, 1976—; asst. to chief bar counsel N.Mex. Supreme Ct. Disciplinary Bd., 1976—. Bd. dirs. N.Mex. Ind. Coll. Assn., 1976—, El Mirador Home for Retarded, 1976—. Mem. Am., N.Mex. (dir. young lawyers sect. 1975—), Santa Fe County bar assns. Home: 303 Don Fernando St Santa Fe NM 87501 Office: 325 Paseo de Peralta Santa Fe NM 87501 Tel (505) 982-3873

POURNARAS, STEPHEN WILLIAM, b. Providence, Nov. 22, 1919; A.B., Brown U., 1942; M.S., N.Y. U., 1951; J.D., George Washington U., 1962. Admitted to Va. bar, 1964, D.C. bar, 1965; individual practice law, McLean, Va., 1965—. Mem. Am., Va., Fairfax County bar assns., Sigma Xi. Home: 6142 Tompkins Dr McLean VA 22101 Office: 6870 Elm St McLean VA 22101 Tel (703) 356-8500

POVICH, DAVID, b. Washington, June 8, 1935; B.A., Yale, 1958; LL.B., Columbia, 1962. Admitted to D.C. bar 1962; law clk. to judge Dist. Ct. of Appeals, Washington, 1962-63; mem. firm Williams & Connolly, Washington, 1963—. Mem. D.C., Am. Bar assns., Bar Assn. of D.C., Assn. of Trial Lawyers, Barristers. Home: 3306 Rittenhouse St NW Washington DC 20015 Office: 1000 Hill Bldg Washington DC 20006 Tel (202) 331-5071

POWELL, BARBARA KEY, b. Houston, June 26, 1949; student Mt. Holyoke Coll., 1967-68; B.A., Duke, 1971; J.D., U. Houston, 1973. Admitted to Tex. bar, 1973, Okla. bar, 1975; atty. Tenneco Oil Co., Houston, 1973-74, Denver, 1974, Oklahoma City, 1974-75, Shell Oil Co., Houston, 1975—. Mem. forum 1st Presbyn. Ch. of Houston. Mem. Houston Bar Assn., Houston Jr. Bar Assn. Home: 1038 Augusta Dr Houston TX 77027 Office: PO Box 2463 One Shell Plaza Houston TX 77001 Tel (713) 220-5649

POWELL, BILLY JOE, b. Register, Ga., June 19, 1940; B.M.E., Ga. Inst. Tech., 1964; J.D., Emory U., 1967. Admitted to Ga. bar, 1968, U.S. Patent Office bar, 1968; asso. firm Newton, Hopkins & Ormsby, Atlanta, 1968-70; individual practice law, Atlanta, 1970—. Mem. Ga., Am., Atlanta bar assns., Am. Patent Law Assn., ASME. Recipient Am. Jurisprudence award Emory U., 1967. Home: 35 Park Ln NE Atlanta GA 30309 Office: 1459 Peachtree St NE Atlanta GA 30309 Tel (404) 892-8046

POWELL, EDWARD LEE, b. Mocksville, N.C., Sept. 21, 1941; A.B., U. N.C. at Chapel Hill, 1963; J.D., Wake Forest U., 1967. Admitted to N.C. bar, 1967; mem. firm Powell and Powell, Winston-Salem, N.C., 1969-74, individual practice law, Winston-Salem, 1974-75; commr. motor vehicles, N.C., 1975-77; mem. firm Yeager and Powell, Winston-Salem, 1977—; mem. N.C. Ho. of Reps., 1973-74, N.C. Bd. Transp., 1975, N.C. Council on Status of Women, 1974; lectr. continuing legal edn., N.C. Bar Assn., 1976, U.S. Motor Vehicle Law Inst., U. Colo. Law Sch., 1975,76. Mem. N.C. State Bar, N.C., Forsyth County bar assns. Home: 778 Oaklawn Ave Winston-Salem NC 27104 Office: Suite 480 NCNB Plaza Winston-Salem NC 27101 Tel (919) 722-1181

POWELL, ELIAS, b. Bialystok, Poland, Jan. 18, 1921; J.D., U. Miami, 1943. Admitted to Calif. bar, 1946, U.S. Supreme Ct. bar, 1968; individual practice law, Los Angeles, 1946-49; dep. pub. defender, Los Angeles, 1949-69; commr., judge pro tem Superior Ct. Los Angeles, 1969—. Mem. Am., Calif., Santa Monica Bay Dist., Los Angeles Criminal Cts. bar assns. Office: 111 N Grand Ave Los Angeles CA 90012 Tel (213) 974-1234

POWELL, HEDY MOEHLING, b. Huntington, W.Va., Oct. 8, 1936; B.S. in Med. Tech., Marshall U., 1968; J.D., Villanova U., 1971. Med. technologist U. Pa., 1962-67, S.S. Hope, Cartagena, Colombia, 1967, McGuire VA Hosp., Richmond, Va., 1960-62; admitted to Pa. bar, 1971; law clk. to judge U.S. Dist. Ct., Eastern Dist. Pa., 1971-73; asso. firm Pepper, Hamilton & Scheetz, Phila., 1973-76; atty. Wyeth Labs., Phila., 1976—. Mem. Philadelphia County, Pa., Am. bar assns. Editorial bd. Villanova U. Law Rev., 1971. Office: PO Box 8299 Philadelphia PA 19333 Tel (215) MU 8-4400

POWELL, JERRY TERRY, b. Campbell, Mo., Apr. 7, 1933; B.S., U. Mo., 1955, LL.D., 1958. Admitted to Mo. bar, 1958; partner firm Stinson, Mag, Thomson, McEvers & Fizzell, Kansas City, Mo., 1962—. Office: 2100 Ten Main Center Kansas City MO 64105 Tel (816) 842-8600

POWELL, JOHN BRENTNALL, JR., b. Wilmington, Del., May 2, 1937; A.B., Princeton, 1959; LL.B., U. Md., 1965. Admitted to Md. bar, 1965; clk. to judge Md. Ct. Appeals, 1965-66; asso. firm Wright & Parks and predecessor, Balt., 1966-71, partner, 1972—. Bd. dirs., exec. com. Mental Health Assn. Met. Balt., 1969-74, pres., 1971-73; bd. dirs., exec. com. Md. Assn. Mental Health, Balt., 1971-73; vestryman Emmanuel Episcopal Ch., Balt., 1971-74; bd. dirs. Florence Crittenton Services of Balt., Inc., 1976—. Mem. Am., Md. (lectr. continuing edn. programs), Balt. bar assns., Balt. Assn. Tax Counsel (chmn. program com. 1973), Balt. Estate Planning Council. Office: 6th Floor Sun Life Bldg Baltimore MD 21201 Tel (301) 539-5541

POWELL, KENNETH MANNING, b. Spartanburg, S.C., June 25, 1931; A.B., U. S.C., 1953, LL.B., 1955, J.D., 1970. Admitted to S.C. bar, 1955, Fed. bar, 1955; served as legal officer USAF, 1955-57, USAF Reserve, 1953—; individual practice law Spartanburg, 1957-75; chief judge Civil and Criminal Ct. Spartanburg County, Spartanburg, 1975—. Chmn. bd. deacons Wellford Presbyn. Ch., 1967—; del. S.C. Dem. Conv., 1975. Mem. Spartanburg County, Am. bar assns., S.C. Bar, Am., S.C. trial lawyers assns., Reserve Officers Assn., Air Force Assn. Contbr. articles to legal jours. Home: Box 184 Wellford SC 29385 Office: 112 W Daniel Morgan Ave Spartanburg SC 29301 Tel (803) 585-2260

POWELL, LEWIS FRANKLIN, JR., b. Suffolk, Va., Sept. 19, 1907; B.S., Washington and Lee U., 1929, LL.B., 1931, LL.D., 1960; LL.M., Harvard, 1932; LL.D., Hampden Sydney Coll., 1959, Coll. William and Mary, 1965, U. Fla., 1965, U. Richmond, 1970, U.S.C., 1972. Admitted to Va. bar, 1931, U.S. Supreme Ct. bar, 1937; practiced law in Richmond, 1932-71; mem. firm, Hunton, Williams, Gay, Powell and Gibson, 1937-71; asso. justice, U.S. Supreme Ct., 1971—. Chmn. bd. trustees Colonial Williamsburg Found.; chmn. spl. Charter Commn. for City of Richmond (prepared new city charter, approved in spl. election Nov. 1947); mem. Nat. Commn. on Law Enforcement and Adminstrn. Justice, 1965-67; mem. Blue Ribbon Def. Panel to study Def. Dept., 1969-70. Decorated Legion of Merit, Bronze Star (U.S.); Croix de Guerre with palms (France). Chmn. Richmond Pub. Schs. Bd., 1952-61; mem. Va. Bd. Edn., 1962-69, pres., 1968-69; mem. Va. Lee U., 1964—; hon. bencher Lincoln's Inn. Fellow Am. Bar Found. (pres. 1969-71), Am. Coll Trial Lawyers (pres. 1969-70); mem. Am. (gov., pres. 1964-65), Va., Richmond (pres. 1947-48) bar assns., Bar Assn. City N.Y., Nat. Legal Aid and Defender Assn. (v.p. 1964-65). Am. Law Inst., Soc. Cincinnati, Sons Colonial Wars, Phi Beta Kappa, Phi Delta Phi, Omicron Delta Kappa, Phi Kappa Sigma. Office: US Supreme Ct Washington DC 20543*

POWELL, MARION LESTER, b. Jacksonville, Fla., Mar. 8, 1925; student Colby Coll., Waterville, Maine, 1943-44; B.S. in Bus. Adminstrn., U. S.C., 1947, LL.B., 1949. Admitted to S.C. bar, 1949; individual practice law, Columbia, S.C., 1949; partner firm Powell & Poston, and predecessor, Aiken, S.C., 1950—; judge Municipal Ct. City of Aiken, 1955—. Mem. Am. Land Title Assn., Am., S.C. Aiken County (pres. 1976-77) bar assns. Home: 510 York St Aiken SC 29801 Office: 238 Richland Ave W Aiken SC 29801 Tel (803) 649-2513

POWELL, RALPH BURKEY, JR., b. Lake Wales, Fla., Nov. 16, 1933; B.S. in Civil Engring., Teh Citadel, 1955; J.D., U. Fla., 1959. Admitted to D.C. bar, 1970, Pa. bar, 1971; profl. engr. various firms, Warren, and Mich. and Jacksonville, Fla., 1955-69; legal counsel Gen. Bldg. Contractors Assn., Phila., 1969-72; mem. firm Harvey, Pennington, Herting & Renneisen, Phila., 1972-77, McWilliams & Sweeney, Phila., 1977—; adj. prof. law Drexel U., Phila., 1972—; lectr. continuing legal edn. pa. Bar Assn., 1976—. Mem. Am., Pa., Phila., D.C. bar assns. Office: 623 Three Penn Center Plaza Philadelphia PA 19102 Tel (215) 563-9811

POWELL, RICHARD GORDON, b. Rochester, N.Y., Jan. 7, 1918; B.S., Harvard, 1938; LL.B., Columbia, 1941. Admitted to N.Y. bar, 1941, U.S. Supreme Ct. bar, 1955; asso. firm Sullivan & Cromwell, N.Y.C., 1941-52, partner, 1952—; dir. Amicale Industries, DeLaval Separator Co., Liberian Iron Ore, Ltd., Orinoka Mills; vice chmn. bd. Colloids, Inc.; chmn. bd. Hedwin Corp., Solvay Am. Corp. Former mem. bd. mgrs. Englewood (N.J.) Community Chest; trustee, elder 1st Presbyterian Ch. Mem. Am., N.Y. State bar assns., Assn. Bar City N.Y., Am. Law Inst., N.Y. Law Inst. (pres.), Am. Soc. Internat. Law. Home: 555 Park Ave New York City NY 10021 Office: 48 Wall St New York City NY 10005 Tel (212) 952-8111

POWER, DANIEL LEO, b. Cedar Rapids, Iowa, Jan. 7, 1934; B.S., St. Louis U., 1957, J.D., 1960; LL.M., Georgetown U., 1964. Admitted to Iowa bar, 1960, Mo. bar, 1960; legis. atty. Congl. Research Service, Library of Congress, Washington, 1961; gen. counsel govt. activities subcom. House Govt. Ops. Com., U.S. Ho. of Reps., Washington, 1961-65; trial atty. tax div. U.S. Dept. Justice, Washington, 1965-71; asso. prof. law, dir. law sch. legal clinic Drake U., Des Moines, 1971-76, prof., 1976—; dir. Iowa State U. Campus Legal Services, Ames, 1972-75; dir. Drake U. Campus Legal Services, 1971-75. Bd. dirs. Polk County Legal Aid Soc., Des Moines, 1971—, Boone County (Iowa) Legal Aid, 1972—, Jasper County Legal Aid, Newton, Iowa, 1973-75. Mem. Am., Mo., Fed., Iowa, Polk County bar assns., Am. Judicature Soc., Order of Coif, Alpha Sigma Nu. Home: 3816 John Lynde Rd Des Moines IA 50312 Office: Drake U Law Sch Des Moines IA 50311 Tel (515) 271-3800

POWER, JOSEPH EDWARD, b. Peoria, Ill., Dec. 2, 1938; student Knox Coll., Galesburg, Ill., 1956-58; B.A., U. Iowa, 1960, J.D., 1964. Admitted to Iowa bar, 1964; law clk. to chief judge U.S. Dist. Ct. So. Dist. Iowa, 1964-65; mem. firm Bradshaw, Fowler, Proctor & Fairgrave, Des Moines, 1965—. Bd. dirs. Moingona council Girl Scouts U.S.A., Des Moines, 1968—, pres., 1971-74; mem. Des Moines Civil Service Commn., 1971-73; bd. dirs. Des Moines United Way, 1976—. Fellow Am. Coll. Probate Counsel; mem. Am. (com. chmn.), Iowa bar assns., Phi Delta Phi, Des Moines Estate Planners Forum. Editorial bd. Iowa Law Rev., 1964. Home: 4244 Foster Dr Des Moines IA 50312 Office: Des Moines Bldg Des Moines IA 50309 Tel (515) 243-4191

POWER, WILLIAM M., b. Doylestown, Pa., May 6, 1917; A.B., Ursinus Coll., 1939; LL.B., U. Pa., 1942. Admitted to U.S. Dist. Ct. bar for Eastern Dist. Pa., 1946, U.S. Ct. Appeals bar, 3d Circuit, 1946, U.S. Supreme Ct. bar, 1948; asso. firm Achey & Power, and predecessor, Doylestown, 1946-53, firm Power, Bowen & Valimont, Doylestown, 1959—; individual practice law, Doylestown, 1953-59; judge Bucks County Ct. Common Pleas, 1968; solicitor Controller of Bucks County, 1970-74. Mem. Am., Pa., Bucks County bar assns., Internat. Assn. Ins. Counsel, Am. Judicature Soc., Am. Trial Lawyers Assn., Fedn. Ins. Counsel, Internat. Soc. Barristers, Assn. Ins. Counsel. Office: 102 N Main St PO Box 818 Doylestown PA 18901 Tel (215) 345-7500

POWERS, DALE DAVID, b. Cleve., Feb. 8, 1931; B.S. in Bus. Adminstrn., Kent State U., 1956; J.D., Cleve. State U., 1960. Admitted to Ohio bar, 1960; agt. IRS, Cleve., 1956-59; individual practice law, Cleve., 1961—; pres. Durable Coatings Ink, Akron, Ohio, 1976—. Chmn. Mayor's Action Council Cleve., 1968; mem. ednl. concerned com. Cleve. Heights Bd. Edn., 1962; mem. Ohio State Supreme Ct. com. to draft rules juvenile ct. procedure, 1971. Mem. Cuyahoga County, Ohio State bar assns., Bar. Assn. Greater Cleve. (trustee 1974—). Home: 3881 Colony Rd South Euclid OH 44118 Office: 720 Leader Bldg Cleveland OH 44114 Tel (216) 781-3456

POWERS, DONALD EL ROY, b. Tyron, Okla., Nov. 17, 1919; B.S. in Edn., Central Okla. State Coll., 1941; LL.B., U. Okla., 1948. Admitted to Okla. bar, 1948, U.S. Supreme Ct. bar, 1954; individual practice law, Chandler, Okla., 1948; atty., Lincoln County, Okla., 1949-50; individual practice law, Chandler, 1954; judge 23d Jud. Dist., Chandler, 1955—; adminstrv. asst. Ho. of Reps., Washington, 1952-54; chmn. Supreme Ct. Spl. Study Com. on Code of Jud. Conduct, 1974; mem. Ct. of the Judiciary, Okla., 1973—; mem. Ct. Bank Review. Pres. Will Rogers council Boy Scouts Am., 1960-63. Recipient Silver Beaver award Boy Scouts Am., 1960. Mem. Am., Okla. bar assns., Am. Judicature Soc., Okla. Jud. Conf. (pres. 1968), Nat. Conf. State Trial Judges, Central State Alumni Assn. (Distinguished Former Student award 1954). Home: PO Box 524 Chandler OK 74834 Office: Court House Chandler OK 74834 Tel (405) 258-1399

POWERS, JOHN DALE, b. Baton Rouge, June 26, 1936; B.S., La. State U., 1958, J.D., 1960. Admitted to La. bar, 1960, U.S. Supreme Ct. bar, 1970; partner firm Sanders, Downing, Kean & Cazedessus, Baton Rouge, 1961—; juvenile traffic judge E. Baton Rouge Parish, 1966-74. Former pres. Legal Aid Soc. Baton Rouge, Greater Baton Rouge Safety Council, La. Arts and Sci. Center, Baton Rouge Community Concert Assn., Baton Rouge Assn. Retarded Children, Cerebral Palsy Center Greater Baton Rouge, also La., St. Joseph's Children's Home, Baton Rouge, Arts Council Baton Rouge; exec. v.p. Istrouma Area council Boy Scouts Am. Mem. Baton Rouge, La., Am., Baton Rouge Jr. bar assns., Am. Judicature Soc., Baton Rouge C. of C. (v.p.), pres.), La. State U. Alumni Assn. (past pres. local chpt.). Named Outstanding Young Man Baton Rouge, 1965, Outstanding Young Lawyer La., 1972. Home: 3730 Floyd Dr Baton Rouge LA 70808 Office: Box 1588 Baton Rouge LA 70821 Tel (504) 387-0951

POWERS, LEO JAMES, b. Waterloo, Wis., Sept. 6, 1902; J.D., Notre Dame U., 1925. Admitted to Ill. bar 1927; mgr. claims office Kemper Ins. Co., Pitts., 1925-28; mem. firm Moses, Kennedy, Stein & Bachrach, Chgo., 1928-38; reorgn. atty. SEC, Chgo., 1943-53; partner firm Powers & Boyd, Chgo., 1953-67, firm Covey, McKenney & Powers, Crystal Lake, Ill., 1967-77. Mem. Am., Ill. (named sr. counsellor 1977), Chgo., McHenry County Bar assns. Named Man of Year Notre Dame U. and Notre Dame Club McHenry County, 1971. Home: 315 Warwick Ln Crystal Lake IL 60014 Office: 88 Grant St Crystal Lake IL 60014 Tel (815) 459-0830

POWERS, WILLIAM PINKNEY, b. Birmingham, Ala., Sept. 20, 1939; A.B., Ala. Coll., 1961; J.D., U. Ala., 1964. Admitted to Ala. bar, 1964, U.S. Dist. Ct. bar for No. Dist. Ala., 1964; law clk. to C.W. Allgood, U.S. Dist. Ct., No. Dist. Ala., 1964; partner firm Gaines and Powers, Talladega, Ala., 1965-70; judge Ala. Circuit Ct., 29th Jud. Circuit, 1971—. Bd. dirs. Nat. Alumni Assn. U. Montevallo, 1963-67, 70-72, pres., 1968-69. Mem. Am., Ala., Talladega County bar assns., Am. Judicature Soc., Farrah Law Soc. Bd. editors Ala. Law Rev. Home: Route 2 Talladega AL 35160 Office: PO Box 541 Talladega AL 35160 Tel (205) 362-5721

POWLESS, KENNETH BARNETT, b. Marion, Ill., Aug. 11, 1917; B.S. in Commerce and Law, U. Ill., 1938, J.D., 1940. Admitted to Ill. bar, 1940; since practiced in Marion, Ill., individual practice law, 1951-58, 63-75; mem. firm Powless & Winters, 1946-51; mem. firm Winters, Powless & Morgan, 1958-63; partner Powless Law Office, 1975—; asst. states atty. Williamson County, 1950-51; city atty. Marion, Ill., 1951-54; spl. asst. atty. gen., 1954-58; states atty.

Williamson County, 1968-72; spl. asst. atty. gen., 1972-76. Bd. dirs. Marion Meml. Hosp., 1949-76, pres., 1956-76; lt. gov. Ill.-Eastern Iowa dist. Kiwanis Internat., 1971. Mem. Ill. State, Williamson County bar assns., Am. Soc. Hosp. Attys. Recipient Community Leaders of Am. awards News Pub. Co., 1969, 72, 75. Home: 905 N Van Buren St Marion IL 62959 Office: 108 W Jackson St Marion IL 62959 Tel (618) 993-4661

POWNALL, FREDERICK MULLEN, b. New Haven, Nov. 5, 1937; B.A., Princeton, 1959; LL.B., U. Calif., Berkeley, 1966. Admitted to Calif. bar, 1967, U.S. Supreme Ct. bar, 1973; since practiced in San Francisco, gen. counsel Calif. Bankers Assn., 1972-75; partner firm Landels, Ripley & Diamond, 1967—. Mem. Barristers Legis. Com., 1967-71, chmn. 1970-71. Office: 450 Pacific Ave San Francisco CA 94133 Tel (415) 788-5000

POWNALL, HAROLD ELLIOT, JR., b. Pasadena, Calif., July 20, 1909; student Pomona Coll., 1926-28; B.S. in Bus. Adminstrn., U. So. Calif., 1932, LL.B., 1934. Admitted to Calif. bar, 1934; individual practice law, Los Angeles, 1934-43; naturalization examiner U.S. Immigration and Naturalization Service, Los Angeles, 1943; individual practice law, Los Angeles, 1946-59; probate examiner Los Angeles County Superior Ct., 1959-61, ct. commr., 1961—. Mem. Calif. State, S.E. bar assns. Home: 965B Calle Aragon Laguna Hills CA 92653 Office: Los Angeles County Courthouse Norwalk Blvd Norwalk CA 90650 Tel (213) 773-8870

POYNER, JAMES MARION, b. Raleigh, N.C., Sept. 18, 1914; B.S. in Chem. Engring., N.C. State U., 1935, M.S. in Chem. Engring., 1937; postgrad. U. N.C. Law Sch., summer 1938; J.D., Duke, 1940. Admitted to N.C. bar, 1940; sr. partner firm Poyner, Geraghty, Hartsfield & Townsend, Raleigh, 1946—; mem. N.C. Senate, 1955-59; dir. 1st Fed. Savs. & Loan Assn., Lawyers Title of N.C., Inc., Richmond Corp., Trustee St. Mary's Episcopal Coll., Raleigh; chmn. bd. N.C. Symphony Soc.; bd. visitors Duke Law Sch. Fellow Am. Bar Found.; mem. Nat. Conf. Bar Pres's., Am. Judicature Soc. (past dir.), Am. Wake County (N.C.), N.C. (pres. 1967-68, gov.) bar assns., Raleigh C. of C. (pres. 1964-65). Home: 710 Smedes Pl Raleigh NC 27605 Office: 615 Oberlin Rd Raleigh NC 27605 Tel (919) 834-5241

POZEN, ROBERT CHARLES, b. N.Y.C., Aug. 8, 1946; A.B., Harvard, 1968; J.D., Yale, 1972, J.S.D., 1973. Admitted to N.Y. State bar, 1977; research fellow, Yale, 1972-73; asst. prof. Georgetown U., 1973-74; asst. prof. law N.Y. U., 1974-76, asso. prof., 1976—. Knox fellow, 1968-69. Mem. Phi Beta Kappa. Author: The Company State: DuPont in Delaware, 1972; Legal Choices for State Enterprises in the Third World, 1976. Contbr. articles in field to profl. jours. Home: 2A Washington Mews New York City NY 10003 Office: 40 Washington Sq S New York City NY 10012 Tel (212) 598-2557

POZEN, WALTER, b. East Orange, N.J., Oct. 17, 1933; B.A., U. Chgo., 1952, J.D., 1956. Admitted to Md. bar, 1963; asso. firm Stresser, Spiegelberg, Fried & Frank, Washington and N.Y.C., 1956-58; mem. campaign staff Harrison Williams for U.S. Senator, 1958; legis. counsel Home Rule Com., Washington, 1959-60; counsel, asso. dir. Fgn. Policy Clearing House, Washington, 1960-61; asst. to sec. Dept. Interior, 1961-67; partner Stroock & Stroock & Lavan, 1967—, head Washington office, 1967—; ofcl. rep. U.S. delegation GATT Ministerial Meeting, Geneva, 1963. Mem. Md. Gov.'s Commn. on Historic Preservation, 1968-71; mem. D.C. Bd. Elections and Ethics., 1974-75; del. Democratic Nat. Conv., 1964, counsel credentials com., 1968; counsel compliance rev. com. Dem. Nat. Com., 1974-76; mem. visiting coll. U. Chgo., 1975—. Mem. Am., Fed., D.C., Md. bar assns. Author: (with J. H. Cerf) Strategy for the Sixties, 1960; contbr. articles and book reviews to profl. jours. Home: 3806 Klingle Pl NW Washington DC 20016 Office: 1150 17th St NW Washington DC 20036 Tel (202) 293-1012 also (202) 452-9250

PRAETZEL, ROBERT PAUL, b. San Francisco, Dec. 18, 1926; B.A., U. Calif., Berkeley, 1950, LL.B., U. Calif. at San Francisco, 1953. Admitted to Calif. bar, 1954; mem. firm Myers Praetzel & Garety, Marin County, Calif., 1954—. Mem. Calif., Marin County (pres. 1974) bar assns. Office: Myers Praetzel & Garety 1615 5th Ave San Rafael CA 94901 Tel (415) 453-7121

PRAGER, DAVID, b. Ft. Scott, Kans., Oct. 30, 1918; A.B., U. Kans., 1939, J.D., 1942. Admitted to Kans. bar, 1942; since practiced in Topeka, individual practice law, 1946-59; judge Kans. Dist. Ct., 1959-71; asso. justice Kans. Supreme Ct., 1971—; lectr. in law Washburn U., 1948-68. Mem. Am., Kans., Topeka bar assns., Kans. Dist. Judges' Assn. (pres. 1968), Order of the Coif, Phi Beta Kappa, Phi Delta Phi. Home: 5130 SW 53d St Topeka KS 66610 Office: State House Topeka KS 66612 Tel (913) 354-8294

PRAGER, JEROME LEONARD, b. Dallas, Feb. 28, 1938; B.A., U. Tex., 1958, LL.B., 1960. Admitted to Tex. bar, 1960, U.S. Dist. Ct. bar for No. Dist. Tex., 1961, U.S. Ct. Appeals bar, 5th Circuit, 1962; asso. firm Hoppenstein and Prager and predecessor, Dallas, 1961-65, partner, 1965—. Bd. dirs. Jewish Family Service, Dallas, 1968—, treas., 1971-72, v.p., 1973-74; bd. dirs. Dallas Community Council, 1969-73, Jewish Welfare Fedn., Dallas, 1973—. Fellow Tex. Bar Found.; mem. State Bar Tex., Dallas, Am. bar assns., Phi Eta Sigma, Alpha Epsilon Pi (pres. local chpt. 1959-60), Phi Alpha Delta. Office: 3710 Republic Nat Bank Tower Dallas TX 75201 Tel (214) 747-4241

PRAGER, RONALD STEVEN, b. Hartford, Aug. 9, 1943; B.A., Pomona Coll., 1965; J.D., U. So. Calif., 1969. Admitted to Calif. bar, 1970; dep. dist. atty. San Diego County, 1970—. Mem. Calif., San Diego County bar assns. Office: 220 W Broadway San Diego CA 92101 Tel (714) 236-3974

PRASSEL, FRANK RICHARD, b. San Antonio, Oct. 5, 1937; B.A., Trinity U., San Antonio, 1959, M.A., 1961; LL.B., U. Tex., Austin, 1965, J.D., 1965, Ph.D., 1970. Admitted to Tex. bar, 1965; dir. law enforcement program San Antonio Coll., 1966-70; asso. prof. Calif. State U., Sacramento, 1970-71; Fulbright prof. law to Republic of China, Taipei, 1971-72; coordinator criminal justice S. F. Austin U., 1972—; spl. counsel Tex. Atty. Gen., Austin, 1967. Mem. Tex. Bar Assn. Author: The Western Peace Officer, 1972; Introduction to American Criminal Justice, 1975. Home: PO Box 957 San Antonio TX 78294 Tel (713) 569-4405

PRATHER, ALFRED VAL JEAN, b. Des Moines, Apr. 26, 1926; A.B., Bridgewater Coll., 1949; J.D., U. Va., 1952. Admitted to D.C. bar, 1952, U.S. Supreme Ct. bar, 1961; asso. firm Covington and Burling, Washington, 1952-60, partner, 1961-64; partner firm Prather Seeger Doolittle Farmer and Ewing, Washington, 1964—. Mem. DuPont Regional Scholarship Com., U. Va., 1957—. Mem. D.C., Am. bar assns., Bar Assn. D.C. Author: (with Eddie M. Harrison) No Time for Dying, 1973. Home: 4017 Harris Pl Alexandria VA 22304 Office: 1101 Sixteenth St NW Washington DC 20036 Tel (202) 296-0500

PRATHER, WATT EDMUND, b. Gooding, Idaho, Oct. 12, 1925; LL.B., U. Idaho, 1949. Admitted to Idaho bar, 1949; individual practice law, Bonners Ferry, Idaho, 1949-66; pres. Boundary Abstract & Titles Co., Bonners Ferry, 1950-65; judge Idaho 1st Jud. Dist. Ct., Coeur d'Alene, 1966—; mem. Idaho Senate, 1960-65; pros. atty. Boundary County, Idaho, 1951-56; city atty. City of Bonners Ferry, 1955-61. Mem. Idaho State, Am., 1st Jud. Dist. (pres. 1956) bar assns., Phi Alpha Delta. Office: Kootenai County Courthouse Coeur d'Alene ID 83814 Tel (208) 664-9202

PRATHER, WILLIAM CHALMERS, III, b. Toledo, Feb. 20, 1921; B.A., U. Ill., 1942, J.D., 1947. Admitted to Ill. bar, 1947; atty. First Nat. Bank of Chgo., 1947-51; asst. counsel U.S. Savs. and Loan League, Chgo., 1951-57, asso. counsel, 1957-59, gen. counsel U.S. League of Savs. Assns., Chgo., 1959—; advisor Commrs. on Uniform State Laws, 1957-58, 1974-76; ann. law lectr. continuing bus. edn. Ind. U. Bus. Sch. Mem. Am. (chmn. com. on savs. and loan com. sect. corp. banking and bus. law 1965-74), Internat. (chmn. com. on savs., bldg. socs., bus. law sect. 1974—), Chgo., Fed., Ill. bar assns., Nat. Lawyers Club, Am. Judicature Soc., Phi Delta Phi. Author: Savings Accounts, 1974; editor The Fed. Guide, 1957—, Legal Bull., 1959—. Home: 171 Green Bay Rd Winnetka IL 60093 Office: 111 E Wacker Dr Chicago IL 60601 Tel (312) 644-3100

PRATT, CHARLES A., b. Kalamazoo, Apr. 2, 1909; A.B., Howard U., 1932, J.D., 1935. Admitted to Mich. bar, 1935; individual practice law, Kalamazoo, 1935-68; judge Dist. Ct. of Mich., Kalamazoo, 1969—; trustee in bankruptcy, circuit ct. referee. Active Kalamazoo County Community Chest; Sr. Citizens, Vis. Nurses Assn. Douglas Community Center, YMCA. Mem. Kalamazoo County (past pres.), Mich. bar assns. Home: 7717 E H Ave Kalamazoo MI 49004 Office: Ct House 227 W Michigan Ave Kalamazoo MI 49006 Tel (616) 383-8710

PRATT, DESMOND FRANCIS, b. Montello, Wis., July 20, 1908; LL.B., U. Minn., 1931. Admitted to Minn. bar, 1932, Fed. Ct. bar, 1932; asso. Sweet Johnson & Sands, Mpls., 1932-34, Tryon & Everett, Mpls., 1934-35, Bryngelson Pratt & Bradley, Mpls., 1946-56, Bauers Pratt Cragg & Barnett, Mpls., 1956-58; individual practice law, Mpls., 1958—. Mem. Mpls. City Council, 1937-53; v.p., dir. Citizens League Hennepin County, 1954; com. chmn. Mpls. Aquatennial Assn., 1941. Fellow Am. Acad. Family Lawyers; mem. Am., Minn., Hennepin County bar assns. Contbr. to Family Law Handbook, 1974. Home: 5241 Richwood Dr Edina MN 55436 Office: Title Insurance Bldg Minneapolis MN 55401 Tel (612) 335-6431

PRATT, PHILIP, b. Pontiac, Mich., July 14, 1924; LL.B., U. Mich., 1950. Admitted to Mich. bar, U.S. Dist. Ct. bar, 1951; U.S. Supreme Ct. bar, 1957; asst. pros. atty. Oakland County (Mich.), 1952-53; partner firm Underwood, Pratt & Woods, Pontiac, 1953-54, Smith & Pratt, Pontiac, 1954-63; judge 6th U.S. Circuit Ct. Mich., Detroit, 1963-70, U.S. Dist. Ct., Detroit, 1970—. Mem. Am., Mich., Oakland County, Fed. bar assns., Am. Judicature Soc. Office: US Court House Detroit MI 48226 Tel (313) 226-7457

PRAY, RALPH MARBLE, III, b. San Diego, June 7, 1938; B.S., U. Redlands, 1960; J.D., U. Calif., San Francisco, 1967. Admitted to Calif. bar, 1967; asso. firm Gray, Cary, Ames & Frye, San Diego, 1967-74, partner, 1974—. Mem. Am., San Diego County bar assns., Order of Coif. Home: 1000 G Ave Coronado CA 92118 Office: 2100 Union Bank Bldg San Diego CA 92101 Tel (714) 236-1661

PRAZAK, MURIEL, b. Chgo., Dec. 6, 1926; B.A., U. Wis., 1948, LL.B., 1951. Admitted to Wis. bar, 1951; individual practice law, Clinton, Wis., 1951—. Mem. Wis., Rock County bar assns. Home: PO Box 2 Rt 1 Clinton WI 53525 Office: 213 Allen St Clinton WI 53525 Tel (608) 676-5286

PREATE, ERNEST DOMINICK, JR., b. Scranton, Pa., Nov. 22, 1940; B.S. in Econs., U. Pa., 1962, J.D., 1965. Admitted to Pa. bar, 1969; asso. firm Levy, Preate & Purcell, Scranton, 1969—; asst. dist. atty. Lackawanna County, Scranton, 1970—. Pres. Planning Council for Social Services, Lackawanna County, 1974-77; bd. United Way, Lackawanna County, Econ. Devel. Council, NE Pa. Mem. Am. Bar Assn., Pa. Bar Assn. (chmn. natural resources mgmt. subcom. of environ. law com.), Lackawanna County Bar Assn. (chmn. local criminal rules com.). Recipient Consevationalist of Yr. Award, Lackawanna County Soil Consevation Service, 1974; Sportsman of Yr. 1st Dist. Rod and Gun Club, Lackawanna County, 1974. Home: Orchard Ln Clarks Summit PA 18411 Office: 507 Linden St Scranton PA 18503 Tel (717) 346-3816

PREBLE, LAURENCE GEORGE, b. Denver, Apr. 24, 1939; engr. Colo. Sch. Mines, 1961; J.D. cum laude, Loyola U., Los Angeles, 1968. Admitted to Calif. bar, 1969; asso. firm O'Melveny & Myers, Los Angeles, 1968-75, partner, 1976—; adj. prof. law Southwestern U., 1970-75; lectr. Practicing Law Inst., 1975, 76, Calif. Continuing Edn. of Bar, 1975, 76. Vice chmn. La Canada-Flintridge Cityhood Action Com., 1975-76. Mem. Am., Los Angeles County bar assns., La-Canada-Flintridge C. of C. and Community Assn. (pres. 1974). Named Outstanding Young Man Am., 1972. Author: Usury Laws and Modern Business Transactions, 1976. Home: 863 Berkshire Ave Pasadena CA 91103 Office: 611 W Sixth St Los Angeles CA 90017 Tel (213) 620-1120

PRED, RONALD STEPHEN, b. St. Paul, Jan. 3, 1940; B.A., U. Colo., 1961; J.D., U. Denver, 1964. Admitted to Colo. bar, 1964, U.S. Dist. Ct., 1964, U.S. Ct. Appeals, 1965; partner firm McKibben, Constantine & Pred, Denver, 1969-73; individual practice law, Denver, 1973—. Co-chmn. Allied Jewish Campaign, Denver; dist. capt. Denver Democratic Party, 1971-74; vice-chmn. Denver U. Nat. Law Alumni Council. Recipient Arnold Chutchow Meml. award. Mem. Am., Colo., Denver bar assns., Am., Colo. tiral lawyers assns., Order of St. Ives, Phi Delta Phi. Office: Steele Park Bldg 50 S Steele St Denver CO 80209 Tel (303) 320-5514

PREIS, EDWIN GUSTAV, JR., b. Vicksburg, Miss., May 16, 1947; B.A., U. Southwestern La., 1969; J.D., La. State U., 1972. Admitted to La. bar, 1972; law clk. Hon. Nauman S. Scott, chief judge U.S. Dist. Ct., Western Dist. La., 1972-74; partner firm Voorhies & Labbe, Lafayette, La., 1974—. Bd. dirs. Acadiana Inservice Drug Elimination House, Inc., Lafayette, 1976—; alumni mem. faculty athletic com. U. S.W. La., 1976—. Mem. Lafayette Parish, La. State, Am. bar assns., La. Def. Counsel Assn. Home: 120 N Demanade St Lafayette LA 70503 Office: PO Box 3527 Lafayette LA 70502 Tel (318) 232-9700

PRENTICE, GEORGE B., b. Norfolk, Va., July 26, 1919; B.A., U.S. C., 1942; LL.B., Loyola U., Los Angeles, 1952. Admitted to Calif. bar, 1953; individual practice law, Ventura, Calif., 1953—. Home: 2739 Preble St Ventura CA 93003 Office: 536 E Thompson Blvd Ventura CA 93001 Tel (805) 648-3235

PRENTICE, LOIS ANNE, b. Bridgeport, Conn.; B.A. cum laude, U. Bridgeport; J.D., Columbia U. Admitted to Calif. bar, 1965; partner firm Ramsey & Prentice, Oakland, Calif., 1965; asso. firm Melvin M. Belli, San Francisco, 1965-66; individual practice law, San Francisco, 1967—. Mem. pres.'s adv. bd. and exec. com. Sonoma State Coll., 1976—. Mem. North Bay Women Lawyers (founder, pres. 1976-77), Sausalito C. of C. (dir. 1976-77), Am. Trial Lawyers Assn., Criminal Trial Lawyers No. Calif., Sausalito Environ. Action, Calif. Bar Assn. Contbr. articles to legal jours. Office: 605 Commercial St San Francisco CA 94111 Tel (415) 392-1941

PRESCOTT, STEDMAN, JR., b. Rockville, Md., Sept. 12, 1919; B.A., U. Md., 1940, LL.B., 1947, J.D., 1969. Admitted to Md. bar, 1946, U.S. Supreme Ct. bar, 1956; partner firm Staley & Prescott, Silver Springs, Md., 1946-69, firm Staley, Prescott & Ballman, Kensington, Md., 1969—; asst. atty. gen. State of Md., 1955-56, dep. atty. gen., 1957-61; counsel, dir. Montgomery Banking & Trust, 1965-69; chmn. character com. State Bar Law Examiners, Montgomery County, 1950-76; mem. adv. bd. U. Nat. Bank, 1969—. Bd. dirs., counsel Montgomery County Taxpapers League. Mem. Md., Montgomery County bar assns., Order of Coif, Delta Theta Phi. Contbr. articles to legal jours. Home: 80 Tarragon Ln Edgewater MD 21037 Office: Citizens Saving Bldg Kensington MD 20795 Tel (301) 933-1234

PRESENZA, LOUIS JAMES, b. Phila., Oct. 15, 1945; B.S., St. Joseph's Coll., 1967; J.D., Villanova U., 1970. Admitted to Pa. bar, 1971; since practiced in Phila.; law clk. Ct. of Common Pleas of Philadelphia County, 1970-71; spl. asst. atty. gen. Pa. Dept. Transp., 1971-76; gen. counsel Phila. Housing Authority, 1976—; partner firm Presenza & Di Bona, 1976—. Bd. dirs., solicitor Girard Park Civic Assn., 1972—; mem. community adv. bd. Mental Health/Mental Retardation Center, Thomas Jefferson U., 1974—. Mem. Am. Arbitration Assn., Am., Pa., Phila. bar assns. Office: Suite 1000 1315 Walnut St Philadelphia PA 19107 Tel (215) 732-5187

PRESMANES, GREGORY T., b. Atlanta, Feb. 7, 1948; B.A., Emory U., 1970, J.D., 1973. Admitted to Ga. bar, 1973; mem. firm Whitley & Presmanes, profl. corp., Atlanta. Mem. Ga., Am., Atlanta bar assns., Phi Delta Phi. Office: Suite 3308 101 Marietta St Atlanta GA 30303 Tel (404) 577-8300

PRESNAL, JAMES K., b. Tabor, Tex., July 27, 1925; B.B.A., Tex. A. and M. U., 1949; J.D., U. Tex., 1955. Admitted to Tex. bar, 1955; mem. Tex. Ho. of Reps., 1949-53; individual practice law, Austin, Tex., 1955—; chmn. bd. dirs. Republic Nat. Bank Austin, 1976—. Mem. Tex., Travis County bar assns., Tex. Soc. Assn. Execs. Office: Suite 521 First Federal Plaza Austin TX 78701 Tel (512) 474-6251

PRESSENTIN, DONALD C., b. Madison, Wis., July 22, 1923; B.S., U. Wis., 1950, LL.B., 1950. Admitted to Wis. bar, 1950; individual practice law, Monona, Wis., 1956—; municipal judge, Monona, 1968; panel arbitrators Am. Arbitration Assn. Mem. Village Bd. Monona. Mem. Wis., Dale County bar assns. Home: 5514 Goucher Ln Monona WI 53716 Office: 5011 Monona Dr Monona WI 53716 Tel (608) 222-2282

PRESSLER, HERMAN PAUL, III, b. Houston, June 4, 1930; A.B. cum laude, Princeton, 1952; J.D., U. Tex., Austin, 1957. Admitted to Tex. bar, 1957; mem. Tex. Ho. of Reps., 1957-59; asso. firm Vinson, Elkins, Searls, Connally & Smith, Houston, 1958-70; judge 133d Dist. Ct. Tex., Houston, 1970—. Home: 282 Bryn Mawr Circle Houston TX 77024 Office: 133d Dist Ct 519 Civil Courts Bldg Houston TX 77002 Tel (713) 221-6282

PRESSMAN, BARBARA WAPNER, b. Phila., Apr. 4, 1933; student Syracuse U., 1951-52, Harvard U., 1953, U. Bordeaux, 1954; A.B., Vassar Coll., 1955; postgrad U. Mich. Law Sch., 1955-57; J.D., Temple U., 1958. Admitted to Superior Ct. Pa., 1959; individual practice law, Phila., 1960-66; partner firm Pressman & Pressman, Phila., 1966-69, 73—; asso. firm Astor & Weiss, Phila., 1969-73; instr. polit. sci., econs., bus. law Temple U., 1960-68; instr. polit. sci., law Phila. Coll. Textiles and Sci., 1966-72. Candidate Pa. State Senator 17th Dist., 1976; bd. judges James A. Finnegan Fellowship Found., 1977. Home: 611 Harriton Rd Bryn Mawr PA 19010 Office: 1420 Walnut St Philadelphia PA 19102 Tel (215) 732-6750

PRESSMAN, PAUL BERNARD, b. Phila., Apr. 30, 1930; B.A., Reed Coll., 1952; J.D., U. Calif. at Los Angeles, 1958. Admitted to Calif. bar, 1959, U.S. Supreme Ct. bar, 1962; dep. atty. City of Inglewood (Calif.), 1959-60, City of Los Angeles, 1966-73; partner firm Keel & Pressman, Hawthorne, Calif., 1960-65; atty. City of Vista (Calif), 1973-77; dir. municipal legal coordination Mission Viejo Co., Calif., 1977—; prosecutor, asst. atty. City of Hawthorne, 1961-65. Mem. State Bar Calif., Am., San Diego County, No. San Diego County bar assns., Nat. Inst. Municipal Law Officers, San Diego County City Attys. Assn., Am. Arbitration Assn. (nat. panel), Phi Alpha Delta. Office: 26137 La Paz Rd Mission Viejo CA 92675 Tel (714) 837-6050

PRESTA, FRANK PAUL, b. Bronx, N.Y., May 19, 1936; B.S. in Civil Engring., Rensselaer Polytechnic Inst., 1957; J.D., Georgetown U., 1961. Admitted to Md. bar, 1963, D.C. bar, 1969, Va. bar, 1975; sr. atty. Atlantic Research Corp., Alexandria, Va., 1965-69; asso. firm Sughrue, Rothwell, Mion, Zinn & MacPeak, Washington, 1969-71; partner firm Jacobi, Lilling & Siegel, Arlington, Va., 1971—. Vice pres. Clifton (Va.) PTA, 1974; active Southwestern Youth Assn., Clifton, 1974—; bd. dirs. Dismas House, Alexandria, Va., 1977. Mem. Am. Bar Assn., U.S. Trademark Assn., Am. Patent Law Assn. Contbr. articles in field to profl. jours. Home: 12122 Beaver Creek Rd Clifton VA 22024 Office: 1755 S Jefferson Davis Hwy Alexandria VA 22202 Tel (703) 521-3330

PRESTON, GEORGE WELLING, b. Logan, Utah, Apr. 26, 1932; B.S., Utah State U., 1954, J.D., 1960. Admitted to Utah State bar, 1960; partner firm Preston, Harris, Harris & Preston, Logan, 1960—; dep. atty. Cache County, 1967—. Mem. Cache County Bar Assn. (pres. 1974-75), Am. Trial Lawyers Assn. Office: 31 Federal Ave Logan UT 84321 Tel (801) 752-3551

PRESTON, HENRY LEBARON, b. N.Y.C., Nov. 8, 1943; B.A., Yale U., 1965; J.D., U. Chgo., 1972. Admitted to Md. bar, 1972; sr. econ. analyst The Zouse Co., Columbia, Md., 1972-75; dir. fin. Gilbane Properties, Inc., Providence, R.I., 1975—. Office: 5601 Piedmont Ave Baltimore MD 21207 Tel (401) 456-5894

PRESTON, JEROME, JR., b. Staten Island, N.Y., Nov. 15, 1922; A.B., Harvard, 1947; LL.B., Yale, 1950. Admitted to Mass. bar, 1951, U.S. Dist. Ct. bar, 1952; partner firm Foley, Hoag & Eliot, Boston, 1950—; dir. Greater Boston Legal Services, Inc., 1958—; trustee Home Savs. Bank; dir. Oppenheimer Income Fund Boston, Inc. Mem.

Wellesley (Mass.) Planning Bd., 1962-70, chmn., 1966-68; bd. dirs. Cambridge Sch., Weston, Mass., 1973—, pres., 1975—; trustee Univ. Hosp., Boston, 1956—. Mem. Am., Mass., Boston (council mem. 1974-77) bar assns. Home: 10 Vane St Wellesley MA 02181 Office: 10 Post Office Sq Boston MA 02109 Tel (617) 482-1390

PRESTON, ROBERT BRUCE, b. Cleve., Feb. 24, 1926; A.B., Western Res. U., 1950, LL.B., 1952. Admitted to Ohio bar, 1952, U.S. Supreme Ct. bar, 1964; asso. firm Arter & Hadden, Cleve., 1952-63, partner, 1964—. Vice pres., trustee Citizens League of Greater Cleve., 1964-66; chmn. charter rev. commn. Cleveland Heights, 1972; mem. Cleveland Heights Housing Bd., 1976—. Mem. Greater Cleve., Ohio State, Am. bar assns., Maritime Law Assn. U.S., Nat. Assn. R.R. Trial Counsel. Home: 1210 Oakridge Dr Cleveland Heights OH 44121 Office: 1144 Union Commerce Bldg Cleveland OH 44115 Tel (216) 696-1144

PRESTON, WILBUR DAY, b. Balt., May 29, 1922; A.B., Western Md. Coll., 1942, LL.D. (hon.), 1975; LL.B., U. Md., 1949. Admitted to Md. bar, 1948; mem. firm Whiteford, Taylor, Preston, Trimble & Johnston, Balt. Trustee Western Md. Coll., chmn. bd., 1971—; trustee Assn. Independent Colls. and U.S. Fellow Am. Coll. Trial Lawyers; mem. Md. State (pres. 1975-76), Am. (mem. ho. of dels. 1972-76) bar assns., Bar Assn. Balt. City (pres. 1972-73), Order of Coif. Home: 300 Northway St Baltimore MD 21218 Office: IBM Bldg 100 E Pratt St Baltimore MD 21202 Tel (301) 752-0987

PRESTON, WILLIAM ROSS, b. Pima, Ariz., Sept. 22, 1914; student No. Ariz. U., Flagstaff, 1955; J.D., U. Ariz., Tucson, 1958. Admitted to Ariz. bar, 1959; individual practice law, Flagstaff, 1959-62; partner firm Preston, Flounoy, Flick & Challis, and predecessors, Flagstaff, 1962—; bd. govs. State Bar Ariz., 1969-72. Mem. Coconino County Bd. Health, Flagstaff, 1968-75, chmn., 1969-71; mem., chmn. Airport Adv. Commn., Flagstaff, 1972-76; bd. dirs. Grand Canyon council Boy Scouts Am., 1959-76, pres., 1968, 69; trustee Flagstaff Community Hosp., 1973-76, treas., 1974, sec., 1975, v.p., 1976; mem. Am. Arbitration Assn., Am., Coconino County (pres. 1962) bar assns. Recipient Silver Beaver award Grand Canyon council Boy Scouts Am., 1970. Home: 3300 S Pima St Flagstaff AZ 86001 Office: Arizona Bank Bldg 125 E Birch St Box E Flagstaff AZ 86001 Tel (602) 774-7386

PRETL, MICHAEL ALBERT, b. Balt., Oct. 20, 1942; A.A., St. Charles Coll., 1962; A.B., Cath. U. Am., 1964; J.D., Georgetown U., 1969. Admitted to Md. bar, 1969, D.C. bar, 1969; asso. firm Smith, Somerville & Case, Balt., 1969-76, partner, 1977—. Pres. Greater Northwood Community Council, 1974-76, NE Community Orgn., 1976-77. Mem. Am., Md. State, Balt. City bar assns. Home: 5815 Falkirk Rd Baltimore MD 21239 Office: 6th Floor 100 Light St Baltimore MD 21202 Tel (301) 727-1164

PRETTYMAN, DANIEL TRAVERS, b. Taylors Island, Md., June 27, 1919; A.B., U. Md., 1939, J.D., 1948. Admitted to Md. bar, 1948; practiced in Berlin, 1948-64; partner firm Sanford & Prettyman, 1948-49; states atty. Worcester County, 1955-64; asso. judge 1st Jud. Circuit Md., Snow Hill, 1964-75, chief judge, 1975—; mem. Gov.'s Commn. Criminal Law. Pres., Worcester County Mental Health Assn., 1962-63; bd. dirs. Heart Assn. Lower Eastern Shore, 1960-65; mem. Worcester County com. Md. Hist. Trust, 1969—. Mem. Am., Md. (exec. council 1963-64), Worcester County (pres. 1958-59) bar assns., Eastern Shore Police Assn. (pres. 1963-64), Worcester County Hist. Soc. (pres. 1962-63), Berlin C. of C. (pres. 1956-57), Am. Judicature Soc., Am. Judges Assn., Nat. Conf. State Trial Judges, Nat. Conf. Juvenile Ct. Judges, Am. Legion, Pi Sigma Alpha, Alpha Psi Omega, Alpha Tau Omega. Home: 8 Vine St Berlin MD 21811 Office: Courthouse Snow Hill MD 21863 Tel (301) 632-1616

PREUSS, RONALD STEPHEN, b. Flint, Mich., Dec. 1, 1935; A.B., U. Mo., 1957, M.A., 1963; J.D., St. Louis U., 1973. Asst. prof. English, Jr. Coll. Dist. St. Louis, 1965—; admitted to Mo. bar, 1973; partner firm Anderson, Frederick, Preuss, Eickhorst and Geissal, St. Louis, 1974—. Mem. Mo., St. Louis County, Am. bar assns., AAUP. Author: Laudamus Te and Other Poems, 1962; columnist Capital Courier, 1962-64. Co-editor Criterion, 1961-62. Home: 126 W Sarah St Saint Louis MO 63122 Office: Suite 300 222 S Meramec St Saint Louis MO 63105 Tel (314) 726-2552

PREVIANT, DAVID, b. Milw., Nov. 6, 1910; LL.B., U. Wis., Madison, 1935. Admitted to Wis. bar, 1935, Mich. bar, 1952, D.C. bar, 1961, U.S. Supreme Ct. bar, 1948, since practiced in Milw.; mem. firm Goldberg, Previant & Uelmen, and predecessors, 1936—; chief labor counsel Internat. Brotherhood Teamsters, 1958—; mem. chmn.'s task force NLRB, 1976-77. Mem. Wis. Arts Bd., 1973-75; bd. dirs. Milw. Repertory Theater, 1969-75. Mem. Am. (chmn. labor law sect. 1974-75, ho. of dels. 1976-77), Wis., Mich., D.C., Fed. bar assns., Order of Coif. Contbr. articles to legal jours. Home: 8160 N Gray Log Ln Milwaukee WI 53217 Office: 6th Floor 788 N Jefferson St Milwaukee WI 53202 Tel (414) 271-4500

PREWITT, THOMAS W., b. Lexington, Va., Jan. 29, 1937; A.B., U. N.C., Chapel Hill, 1958; LL.B., U. Miss., 1960. Admitted to Miss. bar, 1960; asso. firm Butler, Snow, O'Mara, Stevens & Caunada, Jackson, Miss., 1960—. Pres. Jackson Council on Alcoholism, U. N.C. Alumni Assn. Mem. Hinds County, Miss., Am. Bar Assns. Contbr. paper Miss. Law Inst. Home: 4636 Northampton St Jackson MS 39211 Office: Box 22567 Jackson MS 39205 Tel (601) 948-5711

PREWOZNIK, JEROME F., b. Detroit, July 15, 1934; A.B., U. Detroit, 1955; J.D., U. Mich., 1958. Admitted to Calif. bar, 1959; partner firm Gibson, Dunn & Crutcher, Los Angeles, 1968—. Mem. Am., Los Angeles County bar assns. Office: 515 S Flower St Los Angeles CA 90071 Tel (213) 488-7364

PRICE, ALFRED LEE, b. Little Rock, May 19, 1935; B.A., Hendrix Coll., 1956; LL.B., Tulane U., 1967. Admitted to La. bar, 1967, Miss. bar, 1974; office mgr., atty. Petroleum Helicopters Co., Lafayette and New Orleans, 1956-74; atty. Offshore Nav. Inc., New Orleans, 1967-74; atty., gen. counsel 1st Miss. Corp., Jackson, 1974—. Mem. La., Miss., Hinds County bar assns. Office: 700 N St Jackson MS 39205 Tel (601) 948-7550

PRICE, CLARENCE EDMUND, b. Chrisney, Ind., Mar. 28, 1913; LL.B., Ind. U., 1937. Admitted to Ind. bar, 1936; practiced in Indpls., 1937-41; trial lawyers chief counsel's office IRS, Cleve., 1945-49, counsel in charge Cleve. office, 1951-52, dist. counsel, Louisville, 1952-53, regional counsel, Cin., 1953-72; partner firm Price and Price, Dale, Ind., 1972—; lectr. law schs. Chmn. bd. trustees No. Ky. YMCA, 1956-70; elder Presbyn. Ch., Covington, Ky., 1962-70; pres. Santa Claus Sr. Citizens' Community Apts. Mem. Ind. Bar, Am. Bar Assn. Recipient Presidential citation, 1964, Albert Gallatin award Sec. of Treasury, 1972, certificate of award Chief Counsel IRS, 1972. Home: 55 Pine Dr Santa Claus IN 47579 Office: 7 E Medcalf St Dale IN 47523 Tel (812) 937-4492

PRICE, EDWARD DEAN, b. Sanger, Calif., Feb. 12, 1919; A.B., U. Calif. at Berkeley, 1947, LL.B., 1949. Admitted to Calif. bar, 1949, since practiced in Modesto, Calif.; asso. firm Price Martin and Crabtree and predecessor firms, 1949-54, partner, 1954—; chmn. bd. govs. Calif. Continuing Edn. Bar, 1971-73. Mem. Am. Bar Assn., Am. Coll. Trial Lawyers, Nat. Assn. RR Trial Counsel, State Bar Calif. (gov. 1973-76, v.p. 1975-76). Home: 1012 Wellesley Ave Modesto CA 95350 Office: PO Box 3307 Modesto CA 95353 Tel (209) 522-5231

PRICE, FRANK CHRISTIAN, b. Houston, Nov. 17, 1938; student Rice U., 1961; degree Baylor U. Law Sch., 1963. Admitted to Tex. bar, 1963; asst. dist. atty. Harris County, Tex., 1964-69; partner firm James & Price, 1969-74; judge Harris County Criminal Dist. Ct., Houston, 1974—; prof. Nat. Dist. Atty's. Coll., Houston. Pres. Post Oak Nat. Little League, Houston, also coach. Mem. Tex. Judiciary Assn., Houston Bar Assn. Home: 13143 Boheme St Houston TX 77024 Office: 301 San Jacinto St 6th Floor Houston TX 77002 Tel (713) 228-8311

PRICE, GWILYM ALEXANDER, JR., b. Pitts., July 1, 1922; student Allegheny Coll., 1940-42, LL.D., 1976; J.D., Dickinson Sch. Law, 1948, LL.D., 1972; student Nat. Coll. State Trial Judges, 1964. Asso. firm Mahlon E. Lewis, Pitts., 1949-55; admitted to Pa. Supreme Ct. bar, 1950; partner firm Gregg & Price, Pitts., 1955-63; judge Ct. of Common Pleas of Allegheny County (Pa.), 1963-74, Superior Ct. of Pa., 1974—; commr. Twp. of Mt. Lebanon (Pa.), 1960-63; faculty advisor Nat. Coll. State Trial Judges, 1970. Mem. Pa., Allegheny County bars, Pitts. Law Club. Recipient Annual award Dickinson Sch. Law, 1968. Office: 1112 Grant Bldg Pittsburgh PA 15219 Tel (412) 355-5420

PRICE, JOSEPH HUBBARD, b. Montgomery, Ala., Jan. 31, 1939; A.B., U. Ala., 1961; LL.B., Harvard, 1964; postgrad. London Sch. Econs., 1964-65. Admitted to Ala. bar, 1965, U.S. Supreme Ct. bar, 1968, D.C. bar, 1968; law clk. to U.S. Supreme Ct. Justice Hugo Black, Washington, 1967-68; asso. firm Leva, Hawes, Symington, Martin & Oppenheimer, Washington, 1968-71, partner, 1973—; v.p. Overseas Pvt. Investment Corp., 1971-73; dir. Specialized Services Inc., Superior Trucking Co. Mem. adv. com. Hugo Black Meml. Library, Ashland, Ala., 1976—, Johns Hopkins chpt. Internat. Assn. Students in Econs. and Mgmt., 1976—; bd. govs. Opportunity Funding Corp., 1976—. Mem. Am. Bar Assn., Am. Soc. Internat. Law, Phi Beta Kappa. Decorated Bronze Star; recipient Frank Knox Meml. fellowship, Harvard. Home: 4900 Brookeway Dr Bethesda MD 20016 Office: Suite 1001 815 Connecticut Ave NW Washington DC 20006 Tel (202) 298-8020

PRICE, MICHAEL GEORGE, b. Milw., Jan. 18, 1941; B.S., U. Wis., 1963, J.D., 1966. Admitted to Wis. bar, 1966; served to capt. JAGC, U.S. Army, Fort Belvoir, Va., 1967-71; asst. staff counsel, asst. grievance adminstr. State Bar Wis., Madison, 1971-77, interim exec. dir., 1977—. Mem. Am., Dane County bar assns. Home: 4625 Keating Terr Madison WI 53711 Office: 402 W Wilson St Madison WI 53703 Tel (608) 257-3838

PRICE, MILTON DAVID, JR., b. St. Paul, Nov. 20, 1927; A.B., Yale, 1950; LL.B., U. Minn., 1953. Admitted to Minn. bar, 1953; asso. Oppenheimer Law Office, St. Paul, 1953-58; individual practice law, asso. firm Gearin, Melzarek and Shiely, St. Paul, 1958—. Mem. Minn., Am., FCC bar assns. Home: 20 Nord Circle North Oaks MN 55110 Office: 500 Degree of Honor Bldg Saint Paul MN 55101 Tel (612) 227-7577

PRICE, MORTON LEWIS, b. N.Y.C., Apr. 12, 1935; B.A., Bowdoin Coll., 1956; LL.B., Yale, 1959. Admitted to N.Y. bar, 1960, Pa. bar, 1961, U.S. Ct. Appeals 2d Circuit bar, 1971, U.S. Supreme Ct. bar, 1973; law clk. Justice Herbert B. Cohen Pa. Supreme Ct., York, 1960-61; asso. firm Pomerantz, Levy, Haudek & Block, N.Y.C., 1961-63, firm Schur, Handler & Jaffin, N.Y.C., 1963-67; asso. firm Schwab & Goldberg, N.Y.C., 1967-72, partner, 1973—; atty. reporters staff N.Y. Advisory Com. on Practice and Procedure, N.Y.C., 1960; research asst. to Prof. Jack B. Weinstein, Columbia, 1960. Mem. Am. Arbitration Assn. (mem. nat. panel of arbitrators 1971—), Assn. Bar City N.Y. (chmn. com. on transp. 1976—), Am., N.Y. State bar assns. Home: 5 Peter Cooper Rd New York City NY 10010 Office: 1185 Ave of the Americas New York City NY 10036 Tel (212) 575-8150

PRICE, ROBERT EBEN, b. Waco, Tex., Jan. 13, 1931; B.A., So. Meth. U., 1952, J.D., 1954, LL.M., 1972. Admitted to Tex. bar, 1954; mem. firm Howell, Johnson, Mizell, Taylor, Price & Corrigan, Dallas, 1956—; lectr. law So. Meth. U., 1973—; served as legal officer JAGC, 1954-56, col. USAFR. Trustee Lanham Croley Found., Dallas, 1962—, St. Michael and All Angels Found., Dallas, 1972—. Fellow Am. Coll. Probate counsel; mem. Am., Dallas bar assns., State Bar Tex. (lectr. practice skills program 1974—), Phi Alpha Delta, Phi Eta Sigma, Phi Delta Theta. Editor-in-chief Southwestern Law Jour., 1953-54. Home: 4300 Arcady Ave Dallas TX 75205 Office: 2700 Republic Bank Tower Dallas TX 75201 Tel (214) 748-7511

PRICE, ROBERT STANLEY, b. Phila., Jan. 21, 1937; A.B., Kenyon Coll., 1958, LL.B. Yale, 1961. Admitted to Pa. bar, 1963; since practiced in Phila., assoc. firm Dechert, Price & Rhoads, 1961-63, atty. Smith, Kline & French, 1963-67, atty. Penn Central Co., 1967-70; counsel IU Internat. Mgmt. Corp., 1970-72; partner firm Townsend, Elliott & Munson, 1972-76; partner firm Pepper, Hamilton & Scheetz, 1977—; officer, dir. Tax Exec. Inst., Phila., 1968-72. Mem. Am., Pa., Phila. bar assns., Alpha Delta Phi (pres. 1975—). Contbr. articles in field to law Jours. Home: 1034 W Upsal St Philadelphia PA 19119 Office: 20th Floor Fidelity Bldg Philadelphia PA 19109 Tel (215) 545-1234

PRICE, THOMAS HASKETT, b. Chgo., Nov. 6, 1913; B.A., Elmhurst Coll., 1935; J.D., Chgo.—Kent Coll. Law, 1939. Admitted to Ill. bar, 1939; asst. state's atty. Du Page County (Ill.), 1939-43; asso. firm Edgar F. Thoma, Elmhurst, 1946-48; individual practice law, Elmhurst, 1948—; master in chancery, Du Page County, 1961-66; dir. Elmhurst Nat. Bank, 1949—, chmn. trust com., 1975—. Bd. dirs. Elmhurst YMCA, 1965—, Meml. Hosp., 1967—; chmn. bd. trustees Elmhurst Coll., 1971-76. Mem. Du Page County Bar Assn. (pres. 1956), Ill. State Bar Assn. Recipient Distinguished Service award Jaycees, 1970. Home: 250 E Church St Elmhurst IL 60126 Office: 105 S York St Elmhurst IL 60126 Tel (312) 832-1616

PRICE, WALTER LEE, b. Johnson City, Tenn., Mar. 14, 1914; J.D., U. Tenn., 1936. Admitted to Tenn. bar, 1936, U.S. Supreme Ct. bar, 1959; partner firm Price & Price, Johnson City, 1936-40, 45-59, Bryant Price Brandt & Jordan, Johnson City, 1959—; spl. agt. FBI, Washington, 1940-45; city atty. Johnson City, 1948-52, law dir., 1956-66; sec., dir. Johnson City Foundry & Machine Works, Inc., 1968—. Mem. Tenn. Higher Edn. Commn., 1973—; bd. dirs. People-to-People of Johnson City, Christian Home for the Aged. Fellow Am. Coll. Probate Counsel; mem. Am. Soc. Hosp. Attys., Am., Washington County (past pres.), Tenn. bar assns., Assn. Trial Lawyers Am., Law-Sci. Acad. Am., Am. Arbitration Assn. Home: 2017 Sherwood Dr Johnson City TN 37601 Office: 200 W Fairview Ave Johnson City TN 37601 Tel (615) 926-9168

PRICHARD, EDGAR ALLEN, b. Brockton, Mont., Mar. 6, 1920; student U. Tulsa, 1937-39, U. Okla., 1941; LL.B., U. Va., 1948. Admitted to Va. bar, 1947, D.C. bar, 1969, U.S. Supreme Ct. bar, 1963; partner firm McCandlish & Prichard, Fairfax, Va., 1948-61; partner firm Bauknight, Prichard, McCandlish & Williams, Fairfax, 1961-71; partner firm Boothe, Prichard & Dudley, Fairfax, 1971—. Chmn. Fairfax City Democratic Com., 1961-70; vice chmn. Va. State Bd. of Elections, 1970-74; bd. dirs. Nat. Council of Churches, 1966-72; city council mem., Fairfax, 1961-64; mayor, Fairfax, 1964-68. Mem. Christian Lawyers Guild, Am., Va., Va. State, Fairfax County (pres. 1963-64) bar assns., Am. Law Inst., Order Coif. Bd. editors: Va. Law Rev.; contbr. articles in field. Home: 3820 Chain Bridge Rd Fairfax VA 22030 Office: 4085 University Dr Fairfax VA 22030 Tel (703) 273-4600

PRICHARD, R(OBERT) I(NGRAM), III, b. Atlanta, Dec. 4, 1938; B.S., U. Ala., 1960, LL.B., 1963, J.D., 1963. Admitted to Ala. bar, 1963, Miss. bar, 1963; partner firm Stewart & Prichard, Picayune, Miss., 1963-72; judge Miss. Circuit Ct., 15th Jud. Dist., 1972—. Bd. dirs. Picayune YMCA. Mem. Am. Bar Assn., Ala. State, Miss. State bars, Picayune Jaycees (dir.). Home: 1400 5th Ave Picayune MS 39466 Office: PO Box 1075 Picayune MS 39466 Tel (601) 798-5169

PRIEST, GEORGE G., b. Denver, June 16, 1918; B.A., U. Denver, 1939, D.Law, 1972; LL.B., Westminster Law Sch. (now U. Denver), 1946. Admitted to Colo. bar, 1946; partner firm Robinson & Priest, Lakewood, Colo., 1946-50; dist. atty. 1st Jud. Dist. Colo., 1950-54; judge Colo. 1st Jud. Dist. Ct., Golden, 1960—. Vice pres. Denver Area council, regional mem. North Central Region, mem. nat. com. camping Boy Scouts Am. Mem. 1st Jud. Dist., Colo. bar assns. Home: 7492 W Cedar Circle Lakewood CO 80226 Office: Hall of Justice Golden CO 80401 Tel (303) 279-6511

PRIFTI, WILLIAM MELVIN, b. Cambridge, Mass., Feb. 13, 1926; B.S. in Bus. Adminstrn., Northeastern U., 1949; J.D., Northwestern U., 1951. Admitted to Mass. bar, 1953, U.S. Supreme Ct. bar, 1960; chief interpretative atty. Boston regional office SEC, 1955-68, chief counsel, 1968; individual practice law, Boston, 1968—; of counsel Ravech & Aronson, 1969-76; asso. firm Brown, Prifti, Leighton & Cohen, 1976—; adj. prof. law Northeastern U., 1973—. Mem. Mass., Boston, Am. bar assns., Scribes, Am. Soc. Writers on Legal Subjects. Recipient certificate of merit for superior achievement SEC, 1960; author: Securities: Public and Private Offerings, 1974. Office: 66 Long Wharf St Boston MA 02110 Tel (617) 227-9265

PRIGGE, ROBERT HAROLD, b. Great Falls, Mont., Aug. 14, 1948; B.B.A., Gonzaga U., 1970; J.D., U. Mont., 1973; LL.M. in Taxation, Boston U., 1974. Admitted to Mont. bar, 1973; mem. firm Corette, Smith & Dean, Butte, Mont., 1974-76; tax accountant Touche Ross & Co., Seattle, 1976—. Mem. Am., Mont. bar assns. Home: 10208 20th Ave NE Seattle WA 98125 Office: 2500 Financial Center Seattle WA 98161 Tel (206) 292-1800

PRIMUS, EDNA SMITH, b. Yemassee, S.C., June 27, 1944; B.A. in Polit. Sci., U. S.C., 1966, J.D., 1972. Admitted to S.C. bar, 1972, U.S. Supreme Ct. bar, 1975; instr. polit. sci. Allen U., Columbia, S.C., 1972-73; individual practice law, Columbia, 1973—; instr. law Columbia Coll., 1973; cons. S.C. Council for Human Rights, Columbia, 1973-75, mem. exec. com., 1973-74. Mem. ACLU (exec. com. 1972-75), S.C. Black Lawyers Assn. Home: 716 Pine St Columbia SC 29205 Office: 2016 1/2 Green St Columbia SC 29205 Tel (803) 799-3767

PRINCE, EDWARD MINOR, b. Washington, May 3, 1937; B.S., Yale U., 1959; LL.B., U. Va., 1962. Admitted to D.C. bar, 1963, Va. bar 1962; mem. firm Cushman, Darby & Cushman, Washington, 1963—. Mem. Va., D.C., Am. bar assns., Am. Patent Law Assn. Office: Suite 800 1801 K St NW Washington DC 20006 Tel (202) 833-3000

PRINCE, KENNETH CHARLES, b. Chgo., July 15, 1912; Ph.B., U. Chgo., 1932, J.D., 1934. Admitted to Ill. bar, 1934; since practiced in Chgo.; asso. firm Ungaro & Sherwood, 1934-43; individual practice law, 1946-47; partner firm Prince, Schoenberg, Fisher & Newman, Ltd., 1947—. Mem. Am., Fed., Ill., Chgo. (pres. 1976-77) bar assns., Comml. Law League, Law Club Chgo., Chgo. Bar Found. (bd. dirs.), Ill. Inst. Continuing Legal Edn. (adv. bd.), Decalogue Soc. Lawyers, Phi Beta Delta. Home: 1045 Hillcrest Rd Glencoe IL 60022 Office: 222 S Riverside Plaza Chicago IL 60606 Tel (312) 648-1600

PRINCI, PETER W., b. Boston, Nov. 7, 1915; LL.B. (now J.D.) Northeastern U., Boston, 1938. Admitted to Mass. bar, 1940, U.S. Supreme Ct. bar, 1949; claims adjuster, investigator The Employer's Comml. Union, 1935-42; individual practice law, Boston, 1942-71; U.S. Magistrate, Boston, 1971—; collector customs Dist. of Mass., 1961-62; counsel Town of Winthrop (Mass.), 1954-71. Selectman Town of Winthrop, 1949-51. Mem. Am., Boston, Mass. bar assns., City and Town Solicitors Assn. (past pres.), Justinian Law Soc. Mass. (past pres.). Office: 918 John W McCormack Post Office and Courthouse Boston MA 02109 Tel (617) 223-4455

PRINGLE, EDWARD ELI, b. Chgo., Apr. 12, 1914; LL.B., U. Colo., 1936, LL.D., 1976. Admitted to Colo. bar, 1936; individual practice law, Denver, 1936-57; judge Dist. Ct., Denver, 1957-61; asso. justice Colo. Supreme Ct., Denver, 1961-70, chief justice, 1970—. Mem. Am., Colo. bar assns., Am. Judicature Soc. (chmn. bd. dirs. 1974-76, Herbert Lincoln Harley award), Nat. Center for State Cts. (pres. 1977), Conf. Chief Justices (chmn. 1974-75). Home: 7865 E Mississippi St Denver CO 80231 Office: 210 State Capitol St Denver CO 80203 Tel (303) 892-2022

PRINGLE, KENNETH GEORGE, b. Minot, N.D., May 13, 1914; student Minot Tchrs. Coll., 1932-34; B.S., N.D. State U., 1936. Tchr. pub. high schs., Harvey, N.D., 1936-37; asst. scout exec. Boy Scouts Am., Albert Lea, Minn., 1937-39, scout exec., Sioux Falls, S.D., 1939-44; clk. N.D. Supreme Ct., Minot, 1946-49; admitted to N.D. bar, 1949; practiced since in Minot, partner firm Pringle & Herigstad, P.C. and predecessors, 1951-70, pres., 1970—. Bd. dirs. Minot Community Chest; elder, trustee Presbyn. Ch., Minot; active Boy Scouts Am. Mem. Ward County (N.D.) (pres. 1956), 5th Dist., N.D. State (pres. 1968-69), Northwestern Plains and Mountains (chancellor 1970-71), Am. (ho. of dels. 1971-76, bd. govs. 1974, chmn. standing com. on legal assts. 1974—) bar assns., Minot C. of C. (dir.). Recipient Silver Beaver award Boy Scouts Am., 1954, Silver Antelope award, 1967, Distinguished Eagle award, 1975; Outstanding Citizen award Minot C. of C., 1975. Home: 625 3d St SE Minot ND 58701 Office: Am Bank & Trust Bldg PO Box 1000 Minot ND 58701 Tel (701) 852-0381

PRINGLE, PAUL CHENEY, b. Summit, N.J., May 7, 1943; A.B., Dartmouth, 1965; J.D., U. Mich., 1968. Admitted to N.Y. bar, 1969, Calif. bar, 1972; asso. firm Brown, Wood, Ivey, Mitchell & Petty, and predecessors, N.Y.C., 1968-76, partner, 1976—. Mem. Am., San Francisco bar assns., N.Y. County Lawyers Assn. Home: 173 Jordan Ave San Francisco CA 94118 Office: 1 Maritime Plaza San Francisco CA 94111 Tel (415) 398-3909

PRISBREY, GRANT MCALLISTER, b. St. George, Utah, Aug. 9, 1926; B.S. in Polit. Sci., U. Utah, 1953, J.D., 1956. Admitted to Utah Supreme Ct. bar, 1956; referee Juvenile Ct. 2d Dist. State of Utah, 1956-61; chief minerals sect. Legis. Land Office, Salt Lake City, 1961-65; dep. sec. State of Utah, 1965-70; individual practice law, Salt Lake City, 1970—; reference atty. Utah State Senate, 1961; appeals writer Bur. of Land Mgmt., Washington, 1965. Mem. Utah State Bar, Phi Alpha Delta. Home: 3836 S 610 W Salt Lake City UT 84119 Office: 2155 S Main St Salt Lake City UT 84115 Tel (801) 466-0182

PRISTELSKI, JAMES STANLEY, b. Marinette, Wis., Apr. 12, 1943; B.S. in Elec. Engring., U. Wis., 1966; J.D. with Distinction, U. Iowa, 1972. Admitted to Ill. bar, 1973, U.S. Patent Trademark Office, 1974; electronic design engr. Collins Radio Co., Cedar Rapids, Ia., 1966-70; patent atty. Square D. Co., Park Ridge, Ill., 1973-75; asso. firm McWilliams & Mann, Chgo., 1975—. Mem. Am., Chgo., Ill. State bar assns., Patent Law Assn. Chgo., Arlington Heights Jaycees (dir. 1976-77, treas., 1977—), Tau Beta Pi, Eta Kappa Nu, Phi Alpha Delta. Home: 1820 N Yale Ave Arlington Heights IL 60004 Office: 53 W Jackson Blvd Suite 1215 Chicago IL 60604 Tel (312) 427-1351

PRITCHARD, LLEWELYN GEORGE, b. N.Y.C., Aug. 13, 1937; A.B. cum laude, Drew U., 1958; LL.B., Duke U., 1961. Admitted to Wash. bar, 1963; partner firm Karr, Tuttle, Koch, Campbell, Mawer & Morrow, Seattle, 1968—. Chancellor, Pacific N.W. Ann. Conf., United Meth. Ch., 1970—, also trustee; trustee Meth. Ednl. Found.; chmn. bd. trustees St. Peters United Meth. Ch., 1965-68; trustee Deaconess Childrens Home, 1970-73; bd. dirs. Planned Parenthood, 1972—; trustee U. Puget Sound, 1971—, mem. exec. com. bd. trustees, 1972—; vice chmn. bd. visitors U. Puget Sound Law Sch., 1972—; trustee Seattle Pub. Defender Corp., 1969-71; trustee Allied Arts of Seattle, 1970—, counsel to corp., 1970-73, pres., 1974—; trustee, mem. exec. com. Wesley Gardens Corp., 1967-68; trustee, mem. exec. com. Patrons of Pacific N.W. Civic, Cultural and Charitable Orgns., 1969—, sec., 1969-70, exec. v.p., 1970-72, pres., 1972-73; trustee Seattle Symphony Orch., 1972—, 2d v.p., mem. exec. com., 1975—; trustee United Arts Council, 1972-73; mem. exec. com. Choose An Effective City Council, 1968-70. Mem. Am. (exec. council sect. individual rights and responsibilities 1973—, ho. of dels. 1976—, sec. 1975-76, vice-chmn. 1976-77, chmn.-elect 1977—), Wash. (gov. King County 1975), Seattle-King County (trustee young lawyers sect. 1965-69, chmn. 1967-68) bar assns., Puget Sound Duke Alumni Assn. (pres. 1969-70). Home: 5229 140th St NE Bellevue WA 98005 Office: 2600 Sea-First Nat Bank Bldg Seattle WA 98154 Tel (206) 223-1313

PRITCHARD, WILLIAM SHELTON, JR., b. Birmingham, Ala., Dec. 24, 1924; A.B., U. Ala., 1947, LL.B., 1950. Admitted to Ala. bar, 1950; asso. firm Pritchard, McCall & Jones, Birmingham, 1950-55, partner, 1955—. Pres., U. Ala. Law Sch. Found., 1975, 76; sr. warden Ch. of the Advent, 1974; chmn. Shades Valley YMCA, 1970; bd. dirs. Met. YMCA, 1970-74, Reading Disability Found., 1967-72, March of Dimes, 1955, Speech and Hearing Found., 1976-77. Mem. Am., Ala., Birmingham (pres. 1976—) bar assns., U. Ala. Jefferson County Alumni Assn. (pres. 1958, Outstanding Alumni award 1976), Farrah Law Soc. (chmn. 1973-74), Am. Trial Lawyers Assn., Am. Coll. of Mortgage Attys., Monday Morning Quarterback Club (dir.). Home: 3805 Knollwood Ln Birmingham AL 35243 Office: 831 Frank Nelson Bldg Birmingham AL 35203 Tel (205) 328-9190

PRITCHETT, JOHN ALBERT, b. Ruffin, N.C., Oct. 7, 1896; A.B., LL.B., U. N.C., 1921, J.D., 1969. Admitted to N.C. bar, 1921; partner firm Craig & Pritchett, Windsor, N.C., 1922-28; individual practice law, Windsor, 1929-50; partner firm Pritchett, Cooke & Burch, and predecessor, 1950—; mem. council N.C. State Bar, 1941-45; mem. N.C. Senate, 1931-33; mayor City Windsor, 1937-41; mem. N.C. Ho. of Reps., 1941-43. Mem. N.C. State Bd. Edn., 1945—; trustee U. N.C., 1941-49, Z. Smith Reynolds Found., 1969—. Mem. N.C., Am. bar assns., Am. Trial Lawyers Assn., Am. Judicature Soc. Home: 301 S Queen St Windsor NC 27983 Office: 203 Dundee St Windsor NC 27983 Tel (919) 794-3161

PRITCHETT, LAFAYETTE BOW, b. Houston, Dec. 17, 1934; B.A., State U. Iowa, 1956; J.D., DePaul U., 1964. Admitted to Ill. bar, 1964, U.S. Supreme Ct. bar, 1970; asso. firm Pretzel, Stouffer, Nolan & Rooney, Chgo., 1964-69; atty. Ill. Bell Telephone Co., Chgo., 1969-72, gen. atty., 1973—. Vice chmn. Glen Ellyn (Ill.) Plan Commn., 1976-77. Mem. Am., Ill., Chgo. bar assns., Ill. Def. Counsel, Def. Research Inst. Home: 761 Hill Ave Glen Ellyn IL 60137 Office: 225 W Randolph St Chicago IL 60606 Tel (312) 727-4541

PRITIKIN, JAMES BARTON, b. Chgo., Feb. 18, 1939; B.S., U. Ill., 1961; J.D., DePaul U., 1965. Admitted to Ill. bar, 1965; partner firm Sudak, Grubman Pritikin Rosenthal & Feldman, Chgo.; instr. Chase Profl. Inst.; prosecutor Village of Harwood Heights (Ill.), 1975—. Mem. asso. bd. Mt. Sinai Hosp., Chgo.; mem. advisory bd. or profls. Central YMCA Community Coll. of YMCA Metropolitan Chgo.; chmn. Class of 1965 fundraising DePaul U. Law Sch. Mem. Am., Chgo., Ill. State, N.W. Suburban bar assns., Am. Judicature Soc., Ill. Trial Lawyers Assn., Internat. Found. Employee Benefit Plans. Home: 615 Kincaid St Highland Park IL 60035 Office: 221 N LaSalle St Chicago IL 60601 Tel (312) 372-4600

PROBASCO, GENE ARLEN, b. Creston, Iowa, May 17, 1931; student Southwestern Community Coll., 1949-51; B.S., U. Iowa, 1956, J.D., 1957. Admitted to Iowa bar, 1957; partner firm Goldberg, Mayne, Probasco, Berenstein & Yeager, Sioux City, Iowa, 1957—. Mem. Am., Iowa, Sioux City (past pres.), Woodbury County (past pres.) bar assns., Sioux City Lawyers Club (past pres.), Phi Delta Phi. Home: 4432 Perry Way Sioux City IA 51104 Office: 300 Commerce Bldg Sioux City IA 51101 Tel (712) 252-3226

PROBERT, WALTER, b. Portland, Oreg., Jan. 13, 1925; B.S., U. Oreg., 1949, J.D., 1951; J.S.D., Yale, 1957. Admitted to Oreg. Bar, 1951; individual practice law, Portland, Oreg., 1951-52; prof. Law, Case Western Res. U., 1953-59; U. Fla., 1959—; vis. prof. Law, Northwestern U., 1960-61; U. Denver, 1966-67; U. Tex., summer 1970; U. Wash., 1972-73; dir. law and social sciences program NSF, 1973-74. Mem. Com. for Protection Human Subjects. Mem. Oreg. Bar Assn., Soc. Health and Human Values, Inst. Soc. Ethics and Life Sciences, Soc. Law and Soc. Author: Law, Language & Communication, 1972; contbr. articles to profl. jours.; recipient Distinguished Teacher award, 1970. Home: 1929 NW 14th Ave Gainesville FL 32605 Office: Law Coll Univ Fla Gainesville FL 32611 Tel (904) 392-2211

PROCHASKA, SAM MAC, b. Ellsworth, Kans., Nov. 17, 1928; B.A., U. Kans., 1951, LL.B., 1953. Admitted to Kans. bar, 1953, Calif. bar, 1958; individual practice law, San Diego, 1958—. Mem. Am., San Diego County bar assns., Judge Adv. Assn., U.S. Navy League. Office: 1400 Fifth Ave Suite 3001 San Diego CA 92101 Tel (714) 233-6493

PROCTOR, DAVID GILL, b. Hartford Conn., Jan. 21, 1926; B.A., Conn. U.; LL.B., J.D., Boston U. Admitted to U.S. Fed. Ct. bar, 1959, U.S. Superior Ct. bar, 1973; state senator; judge; prosecuting atty.; individual practice law. Mem. New London, Conn. bar assns. Home: 39 Roxbury Ct Niantic CT 06357 Office: 81 Pennsylvania Ave Niantic CT 06357 Tel (203) 739-6911

PROCTOR, DAVID JAMES WILLIAM, b. Des Moines, Apr. 1, 1946; B.A., U. Iowa, 1968, J.D. (with distinction), 1971. Admitted to Iowa bar, 1971; asso. firm Bradshaw, Fowler, Proctor & Fairgrave, Des Moines, 1971-73, partner, 1974—. Mem. Am. (gas. com. pub. utility sect.), Iowa, Polk County bar assns. Home: 4822 Lakeview Dr Des Moines IA 50311 Office: Des Moines Bldg Des Moines IA 50309 Tel (515) 243-4191

PROCTOR, TERRELL WILLIAM (TERRY), b. Austin, Tex., Aug. 4, 1934; B.S. in Bus. Adminstrn., Tulsa U., 1957, postgrad., 1957-58; J.D., S. Tex. Coll. Law, 1964; diploma USAF Air U., 1958. Admitted to Tex. bar, 1963; corp. sec., office mgr. Lew Wenzel Corp., Tulsa, 1957-58; salesman Ednl. Reader Service, Inc. div. Cowles Mags. and Broadcasting Des Moines, 1958-64; dist. sales mgr. QSP, Inc. div. Reader's Digest, White Plains, N.Y., 1964-65; prin. firm T.W. Proctor & Assos., Houston, 1963—; pres., owner Proctor Supply, art and office supplies, Houston, 1967—; municipal judge, Jacinto City, Tex., 1967-71, 73-74, city sec., 1967; city atty. Lomax, Tex., 1968-70; dean Proctor's Acad. Fine Arts, 1977—. Mem. Democratic Exec. Com., Precinct 150, Houston, 1968-70. Mem. Tex., Houston, 15th Circuit, So. Dist. Tex. Fed., Greater Northshore Area, Am. bar assns., Assn. Trial Lawyers Am., Am. Judicature Soc., N.Am. Judges Assn., Houston Greater Northeast C. of C. (pres. Houston area 1970-71, 71-72), Delta Theta Phi. Contbr. articles to profl. jours. Office: 630 Uvalde Rd Houston TX 77015 Tel (713) 453-8338

PROCTOR, VENABLE BLAND, b. Victoria, Tex., Jan. 24, 1941; LL.B., U. Tex., 1964. Admitted to Tex. bar, 1964; individual practice law, Victoria, 1964—; counsel O'Connor Estate, Victoria, 1966—; dir. Victoria Bank & Trust Co. Bd. dirs. Victoria Pub. Library; advisory com. Tex. Coastal Mgmt. Program. Mem. Victoria County Bar Assn. (pres., 1969). Office: 400 Victoria Bank & Trust Bldg Victoria TX 77901 Tel (512) 575-0596

PROCTOR, WILLIAM ZINSMASTER, b. Des Moines, Nov. 30, 1902; student Drake U., 1920-22; J.D., U. Mich., 1925. Admitted to Iowa bar, 1925; mem. firm Bradshaw, Schenk & Fowler, Des Moines, 1925-35, Bradshaw, Fowler, Proctor & Fairgrave, 1935—; gen. counsel, dir. Employers Mut. Casualty Co., Employers Modern Life Co., Emcasco Ins. Co., Des Moines, Dakota Fire Ins. Co., Bismarck, N.D., Union Mut. Ins. Co. Providence; dir. emeritus Iowa-Des Moines Nat. Bank. Active Des Moines Community Chest, 1953, pres., 1956-57; pres. Des Moines United Campaign, 1956-57, Des Moines Community Services, 1957; active Roadside Settlement, 1945, pres., 1950-53; active local bd. SSS, 1942-55, chmn., 1952-55; mem. State Appeal Bd., 1955-67, chmn., 1964-67. Mem. Polk County (pres. 1945-46) Iowa (chmn. com. on corp. law 1950-61, mem. 1961—), Am. (mem. com. on corp. laws 1951-76, mem. counsel sect. corp. bank and bus. law 1963-67, chmn. com. partnerships and uninc. assns. 1965-68), Inter-Am., Internat. bar assns., Am. Judicature Soc., Fedn. Ins. Counsel, Assn. Bar City N.Y., U. Mich. Alumni Assn. (nat. dir. 1940-43). Co-author: Model Business Corporation Act Annotated, 1971. Home: 3401 Lincoln Pl Dr Des Moines IA 50312 Office: 11th Floor Des Moines Bldg Des Moines IA 50309 Tel (515) 243-4191

PROCUNIAR, PAMELA ELLEN, b. Chgo., July 3, 1942; B.A., U. Chgo., 1964; J.D., U. Pa., 1967. Legal assistance lawyer San Francisco Neighborhood Legal Assistance, 1967-68; admitted to D.C. bar, 1968, Md. bar, 1970; individual practice law, Washington, 1968-70, Md., 1970—; asso. prof. law Rutgers U., Camden, N.J. br., 1973; cons. edn., prisons, 1972—. Bd. dirs. Nat. Assn. Creative Children and Adults; mem. edn. task force Phila. Urban Coalition. Mem. Am., Md., D.C. bar assns. Recipient Alumni Sr. award U. Chgo., 1964. Contbr. book revs. to legal jours.; editorial bd. U. Pa. Law Rev., 1966-67. Home and Office: 14 Old Orchard Rd Cherry Hill NJ 08003 Tel (609) 424-5696

PROHASKA, JOSEPH RAYMOND, b. Youngstown, Ohio, July 20, 1930; B.A., Ohio State U., Columbus, 1952, J.D., 1954. Admitted to Ohio bar, 1954; with Ohio Title Corp., 1954-55; mem. firm Power, Jones & Schneider, Columbus, 1957—. Pres. Neighborhood House, Columbus, 1973. Mem. Am., Ohio, Columbus (gov. 1972-74) bar assns., Lawyers Club Columbus (pres. 1964-65), Am. Arbitration Assn. Recipient award of merit Ohio Bar Assn. Office: 100 E Broad St Columbus OH 42315 Tel (614) 221-7863

PROKOP, RUTH TIMBERLAKE, b. San Saba, Tex., May 30, 1939; B.A., George Washington U., 1961, J.D., 1965. Staff mem. Office Vice Pres. Lyndon B. Johnson, Washington, 1961-62; asst. Pres.'s Commn. on Status of Women, 1962-64; admitted to D.C. bar, also U.S. Supreme Ct. bar; legis. asst. Pres.'s Com. on Consumer Intrest, 1964-66; spl. asst. to sec. HUD, 1966-69; mem. firm Brownstein, Zeidman & Schomer, Washington, 1970-72; sr. counsel Gen. Telephone & Electronics Corp., Washington, 1972—; tax commr. D.C., 1976. Bd. govs. Womans Nat. Democratic Club, also vice-chairperson polit. action com.; bd. dirs. Nat. Com. on Household Employment. Mem. Am. (mem. council sect. sci. and tech., past chairperson privacy com.), Fed., Fed. Communications, D.C. Intergrated bar assns., George Washington U. Law Sch. Alumni Assn. (past pres.) Author: (others) A Survey of the Laws Relating to the Investment of Private Trust Funds and State Retirement Funds in Mortgage Notes, 1969. Home: 4854 Loughboro Rd NW Washington DC 20016 Office: 451 7th St SW Washington DC 20410 Tel (202) 755-7244

PRONER, A. STANLEY, b. N.Y.C., Aug. 6, 1931; B.A., U. Conn., 1954, LL.B., 1955. Admitted to N.Y. State bar, 1955, Fla. bar, 1959, U.S. Supreme Ct. bar, 1961; individual practice of law, N.Y.C., 1959—; spl. master Civil Ct. of N.Y.C., 1965. Pres. Mt. Vernon Democratic Club, 1971. Mem. N.Y. State, Bronx County bar assns., N.Y. County Lawyers Assn., N.Y. State Assn. of Trial Lawyers (dist. gov. 1970, dir. 1971), Assn. of Trial Lawyers of Am., Am. Arbitration Assn. (mem. nat. panel 1965). Office: 475 Fifth Ave New York City NY 10017 Tel (212) 686-3232

PROOST, ROBERT LEE, b. St. Louis, July 30, 1937; B.S. magna cum laude, St. Louis U., 1959; J.D., Washington U., St. Louis, 1962. Admitted to Mo. bar, 1962, Ill. bar, 1962; mem. firm Peper, Martin, Jensen, Maichel & Hetlage and predecessor firm, St. Louis, 1962—, partner, 1968—; lectr. McKendree Coll., 1963, 65, Washington U. Sch. Law, 1963-73; pres., dir. Silmasco, Inc., St. Louis, 1971—, Executype, Inc., St. Louis, 1971—. Mem. Am., Mo., Ill., Met. St. Louis (v.p. 1973, sec. 1974, pres. 1978) bar assns., Washington U. Law Alumni Assn. (pres. 1972-73, mem. alumni council 1972—), St. Louis U. Arts and Scis. Alumni Assn. (v.p. 1971), Order of Coif, Phi Delta Phi, Alpha Sigma Nu. Author: Financing the On-Going Business, 1973. Home: 319 Claymont Dr Ballwin MO 63011 Office: 24th Floor 720 Olive St St Louis MO 63101 Tel (314) 421-3850

PROPST, JOHN LEAKE, b. Winnsboro, S.C., Apr. 7, 1914; A.B., Princeton, 1935; LL.B., Duquesne U., 1940, LL.D. (hon.), 1970. Admitted to Pa. bar, 1941; mem. personal trust dept. Union Trust Co. of Pitts. (now Mellon Bank N.A.), 1936—, asst. v.p. legal div., 1950-54, v.p. trust adminstrn., 1954-70, sr. v.p. account mgmt. div., personal trust dept., 1970—. Treas., vice chmn. Urban Redevel. Authority of Pitts., 1957-71; sponsor Boys' Club Pitts.; bd. dirs. Pitts. Found.; trustee Duquesne U., Mercy Hosp., Pitts., Shadyside Hosp., Pitts. Mem. Allegheny County Bar Assn., Pa. Bankers Assn. Recipient Pro Ecclesia et Pontifice medal, Pope Paul VI, 1964; Man of Year award Pitts. Jaycees, 1973. Home: 5521 Dunmoyle St Pittsburgh PA 15217 Office: Mellon Bank Mellon Sq Pittsburgh PA 15230 Tel (412) 232-5583

PROSSER, RAYMOND JOHN, b. Chgo., Mar. 16, 1947; A.B. in Polit. Sci., Northeastern Ill. U., 1970; J.D., John Marshall Law Sch., 1974. Admitted to Ill. bar, 1974; asst. states atty. Cook County, Ill., Chgo., 1974—. Mem. Am., Ill. State, Chgo. Bar Assns. Home: 5243 W Argyle Chicago IL 60630 Office: 2600 S California St Chicago IL 60608 Tel (312) 545-1148

PROTAS, MARTIN STANLEY, b. Washington, Oct. 23, 1947; B.A., U. Md., 1970, J.D., 1972. Admitted to Md. bar, 1972, D.C. bar, 1973; mem. firm Protas, Kay, Spivok & Protas, Bethesda, Md., 1972—. V.P. Norwood Village Assn., 1976, pres., 1977. Mem. Washington, Md. State, Montgomery County, Am. bar assns., Am. Judicature Soc., Counselor Club of Montgomery County. Recipient Moot Ct. Award U. Md., 1971. Home: 1716 Chapel Hill Rd Silver Spring MD 20906 Office: 7910 Woodmont Ave Bethesda MD 20014 Tel (301) 657-3070

PROUD, RICHARD FRENCH, b. Des Moines, Jan. 19, 1922; A.B., U. Nebr., 1947; LL.B., U. Colo., 1949. Admitted to Nebr. bar, 1950; mem. firm Proud & Proud, Arapahoe, Nebr., 1950-55; atty. Mut. of Omaha, Omaha, 1955—; city atty. City of Arapahoe, 1960; county service officer Furnas (Nebr.), 1960. Bd. dirs. Nebr. Tb Assn., 1956-60. Mem. Nebr. Bar Assn., Am. Legion. Mem. Nebr. State Legislature, 1964-74, speaker, 1973, 74. Tel (402) 342-7600

PROUNIS, THEODORE OTHON, b. N.Y.C., Feb. 13, 1926; B.S., Columbia, 1949, M.S., 1950; LL.B., Fordham U., 1963. Admitted to N.Y. bar, 1964; individual practice law, N.Y.C., 1964—. Trustee, legal counsel, sec. Greek Archdiocesan Cathedral, N.Y.C., 1971—; invested archon deputatos by Ecumenical Patriarch Constantinople, 1976.

PROVENZANO, EDWARD O., b. Rochester, N.Y., Sept. 7, 1914; LL.B., Albany Law Sch., 1941. Admitted to N.Y. bar, 1941; individual practice law, 1941-67; adminstrv. judge City Ct., Rochester, N.Y., 1967-70; judge County Ct., 1970-73; judge N.Y. State Supreme Ct., Rochester, N.Y., 1973—. Mem. Monmouth County (past v.p., trustee, mem. judiciary com. 1965-66), N.Y. State, Am. bar assns. Home: 153 Seneca Pkwy Rochester NY 14613 Office: Room 436 Hall of Justice Rochester NY 14614 Tel (716) 428-5134

PROVINE, LEON EGGLESTON, b. Grenada, Miss., Feb. 6, 1924; student Northwestern U., grad. So. Law U., Memphis. Admitted to Miss. bar, 1947; county atty., Grenada County, Miss., 1948-51; individual practice law, Grenada. Mem. Miss. Bar Assn., Am. Judicature Soc. Office: Provine Bldg Grenada MS 38901 Tel (601) 226-6900

PROVINZINO, JOHN CHARLES, b. Long Prairie, Minn., Apr. 30, 1947; B.A., St. John's U., 1968; J.D., U. Minn., 1972. Admitted to Minn. bar, 1972, Fed. bar, 1972; asso. firm Murphy, Provinzino & Neils, St. Cloud, Minn., 1972-76; asso. firm Reichert, Wenner & Koch, St. Cloud, 1976—. Mem. Minn. State, Stearns, Benton bar assns., St. Cloud C. of C. Home: 5837 Pleasant Ln St Cloud MN 56301 Office: 717 1/2 St Germain St St Cloud MN 56301 Tel (612) 252-7600

PROWELL, HAROLD RICHARD, b. Steelton, Pa., Jan. 1, 1907; A.B., Princeton U., 1929; J.D., U. Pa., 1932. Admitted to Pa. bar, 1932; partner firm Prowell, Stoner & Kuhn; gen. counsel company, 1937-70; spl. counsel, dep. atty. gen. Pa. Dept. Transp. and Pub. Welfare, Harrisburg; dir., counsel Commonwealth Nat. Bank; solicitor Harrisburg-Steelton-Highspire Vocat. Tech. Sch. and Steelton-Highspire Sch. Dist. Pres., gen. counsel Pa. United Fund Inc.; pres. Community Chest, Harrisburg; mem. Pa. Gov.'s Hosp. Study Commn. Mem. Dauphin County Bar Found. (pres. 1952-53), Dauplin County (pres. 1956), Pa. (chmn. medico legal com.), Am. bar assns., Phi Beta Kappa. Contbr. articles to profl. jours. Home: 3000 Mayfred Ln Camp Hill PA 17011 Office: 408 Dauphin Bldg Harrisburg PA 17101 Tel (717) 238-1616

PROWSE, STANLEY DAWE, b. Malden, Mass., Nov. 27, 1945; B.A., Yale, 1967; M.A., Columbia, 1969; J.D., Harvard, 1973. Admitted to Ga. bar, 1973, Calif. bar, 1975; asso. firm Alston, Miller & Gaines, Atlanta, 1973-74; asso. firm Friedman, Kahan, Dysart & Fraser, San Diego, 1975—. Sec.-treas. Villa Martinique Homeowners Assn., 1976-77. Mem. Am. (chmn. sub-com. on other compensations policies, com. on compensation of lawyers, legal economics sect; mem. sect. on natural resources law, corp. law, internat. law.), Ga., Calif. bar assns. Office: Suite 1800 Financial Sq 600 B St San Diego CA 92101

PRUD'HOMME, M. EDWIN, b. Texarkana, Ark., Mar. 20, 1935; student U. Notre Dame, 1953-56, U. Tex., 1956, Dominican Coll. Tex., 1955-56; J.D., St. Mary's U., 1959; M.A. in Govt., East Tex. State U., 1971. Admitted to Tex. bar, 1959, ICC bar, 1960, U.S. Dist. Ct. Eastern Dist. Tex. bar, 1961, U.S. Supreme Ct. bar, 1965; pvt. practice, Austin, Texarkana, and Houston, Tex.; pres. Lawyers Title Texarkana, 1961-69, Prud'homme Corp., Austin, 1969-75; cons. in field of internat. trade. Active Boy Scouts Am., 1959-73. Mem. Am.,

Tex., Houston, Interam., Internat. bar assns., Am. Soc. Internat. Law, E-W Trade Council, Houston C. of C., (internat. com.), Serra Internat. Home: 14 Stillforest Houston TX 77024 Office: 1870 Pennzoil Pl South Tower Houston TX 77002 Tel (713) 237-1118

PRUITT, GARIS LAWSON, b. Chester, Pa., Oct. 2, 1942; B.A., U. Ky., 1968, J.D., 1970. Admitted to Ky. bar, 1972; since practiced in Ashland, individual practice, 1972—, partner firm Pruitt & Duvall, 1974-76, Pruitt & Dowling, 1972-74, Deiderich & Lycan, 1972-74; atty. City of Worthington (Ky.); judge pro tempore Ashland Municipal Ct.; atty. City of Russell (Ky)., 1972-74. Chmn. bus. gifts Arthritis Found., 1974-75; mem. Boyd County Bd. Elections, 1973-76; v.p. Young Republicans Boyd County, 1972. Mem. Ky., Boyd County, Greenup County bar assns., Am. Trial Lawyers Assn. Home: 141 Blackburn Ave Ashland KY 41101 Office: 320 2d Nat Bank Bldg PO Box 405 Ashland KY 41101 Tel (606) 324-3729

PRUITT, JOHN EDWIN, JR., b. Columbus, Ga., Dec. 2, 1942; B.S.Civil Engring., Va. Poly. Inst., 1964; J.D., Am. U., 1972. Engr., Va. Hwy. Dept., Richmond, 1964-65, Raymond Internat., Liberia, W.Africa, 1968; lt. C.E., U.S. Army, Vietnam, 1966-67; admitted to Va. bar, 1972, patent law bar, 1976; partner firm Rawlings & Pruitt, Fredericksburg, Va., 1972—; dir. Mine Ridge Land Co., Gen. Tire Fredericksburg, Pruitt Real Estate Co., Commonwealth Realty, Craftsman Found., Inc. Bd. dirs. Spotsylvania (Va.) Hist. Assn., 1973—, Pratt Mental Health Clinic, Fredericksburg, 1973—; mem. Spotsylvania Democratic Com., 1973—; chmn. Spotsylvania Bicentennial Com., 1975-76. Registered profl. engr., Va. Mem. Va. Soc. Civil Engrs., Nat. Soc. Profl. Engrs. Home: Rt 1 PO Box 54 Fredericksburg VA 22401 Office: 405 Amelia St Fredericksburg VA 22401 Tel (703) 373-7444

PRUITT, PRENTICE POWE, b. Gilbertown, Ala., July 7, 1916; LL.B., U. Fla., 1950, J.D. Admitted to Fla. bar, 1950, U.S. Supreme Ct. bar, 1969; judge small claims ct., Jefferson County, Fla., 1952-53; mem. firm Cooksey & Pruitt, Montiello, Fla., 1950-54; individual practice law, Montiello, 1954-65; dir. Fla. Pub. Service Commn., Tallahassee, 1965—; mem. Fla. Ho. of Reps., 1953-57, 1965-67. Mem. Fla., Tallahassee, Fla. Govt. bar assns. Home: 2233 Killarney Way Tallahassee FL 32303 Office: 700 S Adams St Tallahassee FL 32304 Tel (904) 488-7921

PRUZANSKY, JOSHUA MURDOCK, b. N.Y.C., Mar. 16, 1940; B.A., Columbia, 1960, J.D., 1965. Admitted to N.Y. bar, 1965; partner firm Scheinberg, Wolf, Lapham, DePetris & Pruzansky, Riverhead, N.Y., 1965—. Mem. N.Y. State, Suffolk County bar assns. Office: 220 Roanoke Ave Riverhead NY 11901 Tel (516) 727-5100

PRYATEL, AUGUST, b. Cleve., Sept. 20, 1913; A.B., Hiram Coll., 1936; LL.B. (J.D.), Cleve. Law Sch., 1942. Admitted to Ohio bar, 1942; asst. police prosecutor City of Cleve., 1944-49; dep. supt. ins. State of Ohio, 1949-55, supt. ins., 1955-57; judge Cleve. Municipal Ct., 1957-60, chief justice, 1960-65; judge Ct. of Common Pleas, Cuyahoga County, 1965-76, Ct. Appeals 8th Appellate Dist., 1977—. Mem. corporate bd. Cleve. Automobile Club, 1962—, trustee, 1966-72; pres. Greater Cleve. Safety Council, 1968-71; pres. adv. bd. Rose-Mary Home, Johanna Grasselli Rehab. and Edn. Center, 1971-72; trustee Suburban Community Hosp., Vols. of Am., United Cerebral Palsy Assn., Inc. of Cuyahoga County, Blue Cross of NE Ohio. Fellow Garfield Soc.; mem. Am. Judicature Soc., Ohio, Cuyahoga County, Greater Cleve. bar assns., Ohio Common Pleas Judges Assn. Recipient Pub. Service medal Griffith Found. for Ins. Edn., Ohio State U., 1956, Distinguished Service award Hiram Coll. Alumni Assn., 1967, Distinguished Service award Delta Theta Phi, 1972, Outstanding Jud. Service honor Supreme Ct. Ohio, 1974, Excellent Jud. Service honors Supreme Ct. Ohio, 1975, Superior Jud. Service honor Supreme Ct. Ohio, 1975, 76. Office: Court Appeals 8th Appellate Dist One Lakeside Cleveland OH 44113 Tel 621-3285

PRYOR, JOHN CARLISLE, b. Abingdon, Va., Oct. 3, 1883; B.A., Simpson Coll., 1907, D.C.L., 1960; J.D., U. Chgo., 1910. Admitted to Iowa bar, 1910, U.S. Supreme Ct. bar, 1930; mem. firm Pryor Riley Jones & Walsh, Burlington, Iowa, 1921—; individual practice law, Council Bluffs, Iowa, 1910-21; mem. U.S. Supreme Ct. Rules and Procedures Com.; chmn. bd. Miss. Savs. & Loan Assn. Fellow Am. Bar Found.; mem. Am. Law Inst., Iowa State Bar Assn. (pres. 1936-37, award of Merit 1960). Contbr. articles to legal jours. Home: 2009 West Ave Burlington IA 52601 Office: 321 N 3d St Burlington IA 52601 Tel (319) 754-6587

PUCCI, GERARD RICHARD, b. N.Y.C., Aug. 7, 1924; B.M.E., Va. Poly. Inst., 1944; J.D., George Washington U., 1949. Patent engr. RCA, Washington, 1946-48; tool designer Douglas Aircraft Corp., El Segundo, Calif., 1950-51; admitted to Fla. bar, 1949; patent atty. U.S. Naval Ordnance Test Sta., Pasadena, Calif., 1951-52; staff analyst N.Am. Aviation Co., Downey, Calif., 1952-54; individual practice law, Miami, Fla., 1954—; prof. aviation Miami-Dade Jr. Coll., 1966—; mem. Fla. Lawyers Title Guaranty Fund, 1956—; producer, speaker The Great Am. Adventure, radio program on Am. govt., Miami, 1962-65; mem. nat. panel arbitrators Am. Arbitration Assn., 1974—. Chmn. Coral Gables (Fla.) Planning Bd., 1959-63; mem. Coral Gables Zoning Bd., 1959-63; mem. dist. advancement com. S.Fla. council Boy Scouts Am., 1967-70. Mem. Nat. Soc. Profl. Engrs., Fla. Engring. Soc., Tau Beta Pi, Pi Tau Sigma. Recipient Old Guard award ASME, 1944, George Washington award Freedoms Found., Valley Forge, 1963; registered profl. engr., Fla.; author: Aviation Law—Fundamental Cases with Legal Checklist, 1974, rev. 3d edit., 1977. Home: 35 Menores Ave Coral Gables FL 33134 Office: 7483 Coral Way Miami FL 33155 Tel (305) 264-2177

PUCCINELLI, LEO JOHN, b. Fagnano, Italy, Sept. 8, 1921; B.A., U. Nev., 1946; J.D., U. San Francisco, 1950. Admitted to Nev. bar, 1950; partner firm Castle & Puccinelli, Elko, Nev., 1950-53; individual practice law, Elko, 1953—. Chmn. adv. bd. Nev. Youth Tng. Center, Elko, 1967—; mem. Nev. Commn. on Crime, Delinquency and Corrections, 1975—, chmn. small counties allocations com., 1975—. Mem. State Bar Nev. (bd. govs. 1967—, pres. 1976-77), Elko County Bar Assn. (pres. 1962-63), Nat. Assn. Trial Lawyers, Nev. Trial Lawyers Assn., Western States Bar Conf. (v.p. 1977-78). Home: 567 14th St Elko NV 89801 Office: 217 First National Bank Bldg Elko NV 89801 Tel (702) 738-7293

PUCCINI, ORESTE LOUIS, JR., b. Albuquerque, Jan. 10, 1944; B.A., U. N.Mex., 1966, J.D., 1969. Admitted to N.Mex. bar, 1969; staff atty. Bernalillo County (N.Mex.) Legal Aid, 1970; asso. firm Marchiondo & Berry, Albuquerque, 1970-71, firm Smiley, Albuquerque, 1971-72; partner firm Miller & Melton, Albuquerque, 1972—. Mem. Am., N.Mex. (unauthorized practice of law com.) bar assns. Tel (505) 247-4332

PUCKETT, WILLIE THOMAS, b. Estill County, Ky., Jan. 19, 1912; LL.B., Jefferson Coll., 1940. Admitted to Ky. bar, 1940; individual practice law, Louisville, 1946—. Home: 3900 Plymouth Rd Louisville KY 40207 Office: 907 S 6th St Louisville KY 40203

PUGH, GORDON ALEXANDER, b. Plaquemine, La., July 30, 1937; B.S., La. State U., 1958, J.D., 1962; postgrad. (Rotary Found. fellow) U. Edinburgh Faculty of Law, 1960-61. Admitted to La. bar, 1962; capt. JAG U.S. Army, 1962-65; asso. firm Breazeale, Sachse & Wilson, Baton Rouge, 1965-67, partner firm, 1967—; lectr., asso. prof., law La. State Law Sch., 1974—; asst. examiner Com. on Bar Admissions, Supreme Ct. of La., 1973—. Pres., bd. Lakeshore Civic Assn., Rotary Club of Baton Rouge; bd. dirs. Cancer Soc. of Greater Baton Rouge; bd. dirs., pres. Baton Rouge Speech and Hearing Found.; mem. parish council; chmn. liturgy com. Christ the King Chapel, La. State U.; mem. exec. bd., exec. com., finance v.p. Istrouma Area council Boy Scouts Am. Mem. Am., La. State (chmn. labor relations com. 1972-73), Baton Rouge (chmn. pub. relations com. 1973-74, mem. 1974-75, mem. com. on unauthorized practice of law 1975-76) bar assns. Home: 2028 E Lakeshore Dr Baton Rouge LA 70808 Office: 701 Fidelity Nat Bank Bldg PO Box 3197 Baton Rouge LA 70821 Tel (504) 387-4000

PUGH, HARRY REID, JR., b. Charters, Ky., July 27, 1911; B.S., U. Va., 1933; LL.B., Yale, 1936. Admitted to N.Y. State bar, 1937, U.S. Supreme Ct. bar, 1945; asso. Fish, Richardson & Neave (now Fish & Neave), N.Y.C., 1936-49, partner, 1950—. Mem. Am., N.Y. State bar assns., Assn. Bar City N.Y., Am., N.Y. Patent Law Assn., Am. Coll. Trial Lawyers. Home: Ridge Acres Darien CT 06820 Office: 277 Park Ave New York City NY 10017 Tel (212) 826-1050

PUGH, KEITH EMERSON, JR., b. Los Angeles, Mar. 17, 1937; student Principa Coll., 1955-58; J.D., U. So. Calif., 1962. Admitted to Calif. bar, 1962, D.C. bar, 1969, U.S. Supreme Ct. bar, 1976; dep. atty. gen. antitrust sect. State of Calif., San Francisco, 1962-65; asso. firm Broad, Busterud & Khourie, San Francisco, 1965-66, firm Joseph Alioto, San Francisco, 1966-68; asso. firm Howrey & Simon, Washington, 1968-69, partner, 1970—. Mem. Bar Assn. D.C., Am. Bar Assn., Phi Delta Phi. Home: 4301 Massachusetts Ave NW Washington DC 20016 Office: 1730 Pennsylvania Ave NW Washington DC 20006 Tel (202) 783-0800

PUGH, LARRY SAMUEL, b. Monterey Park, Calif., Apr. 7, 1944; B.A., Hanover Coll., 1966; J.D., Ind. U., 1970. Admitted to Ind. bar, 1970; individual practice law, Indpls., 1970-73; partner firm Pugh & Brown, Indpls., 1973—. Mem. Ind. State, Am., Indpls. bar assns., Ind., Am. assns. trial lawyers. Office: 8243 E Washington St Indianapolis IN 46219 Tel (317) 897-7670

PUGH, RICHARD CRAWFORD, b. Phila., Apr. 28, 1929; B.A., Dartmouth Coll., 1951; A.B. (Rhodes scholar), Oxford U., 1953; LL.B., Columbia U., 1958. Admitted to N.Y. bar, 1958, U.S. Supreme Ct. bar, 1966; asso. firm Cleary, Gottlieb, Steen & Hamilton, N.Y.C., 1958-61, partner, 1969—; prof. law Columbia U., 1961-67; dep. asst. atty. gen. Tax div. Dept. Justice, 1966-68; adj. prof. law Columbia U., 1969—. Mem. Am. Law Inst., Am., N.Y. State bar assns., Assn. Bar City N.Y., Am. Soc. Internat. Law, Internat. Fiscal Assn., Tax Forum, Council on Fgn. Relations. Author: (with W. Friedmann) Legal Aspects of Foreign Investment, 1959; (with W. Friedmann and O. Lissitzyn) International Law, 1969; (with H. Smit) Internat. Transactions in the Common Market, 1977; (with others) The Study of Federal Tax Law, 1977. Home: 68 Otter Rock Dr Greenwich CT 06830 Office: 1 State St Plaza New York City NY 10004 Tel (212) 344-0600

PUGH, ROBERT GAHAGAN, b. Shreveport, La., Aug. 25, 1924; B.S., Centenary Coll., 1946; LL.B., La. State U., 1949. Admitted to La. bar, 1949; partner firm Pugh & Nelson, Shreveport, 1967—; del. La. Constitutional Conv., 1973-74; chmn. Gov.'s Commn. Uniform Indigent System, 1975-76; chmn. Gov.'s Com. Study Capital Punishment, 1973—; La., commr. Nat. Conf. Commrs. Uniform State Laws, 1976. Mem. bd. regents State La., 1974-77; chmn. La. Indigent Defender Bd., 1976—; mem. search com. La. State U. Law Sch. Dean, 1977—; mem. La. Coordinating Council Higher Edn., 1972-73. Mem. Shreveport (pres. 1971), La. (pres. 1975-76), Am., Fed. bar assns., Am. Judicature Soc., Nat. Conf. Bar Pres. (mem. exec. council 1976-77), La. State U. Law Sch. Alumni Assn. (pres. 1977—), Mortgage Bankers Am., La. Mortgage Bankers. Author: Juvenile Laws of Louisiana, Their History and Development, 1957. Home: 5743 Lovers Ln Shreveport LA 71105 Office: 555 Commercial Nat Bank Bldg Shreveport LA 71101 Tel (318) 227-2270

PUGH, STEVEN DENT, b. Roanoke, Va., Mar. 1, 1928; B.J., U. Fla., 1953; LL.D., Cumberland Sch. Law, Birmingham, Ala., 1969. Admitted to Ala. bar, 1969; individual practice law, Birmingham, 1969—. Chmn., Citizens Opposed to Annexation, Rocky Ridge Dist., 1976—. Mem. Sigma Delta Kappa. Home: 3501 Laurel View Ln Birmingham AL 35216 Office: 512 21st St Ensley Birmingham AL 35218 Tel (205) 780-4700

PUGLIA, ROBERT KELSER, b. Westerville, Ohio, Oct. 16, 1929; B.A., Ohio State U., 1952; LL.B., U. Calif., Berkeley, 1958. Admitted to Calif. bar, 1959, U.S. Dist. Ct. bar for No. Dist. Calif., 1959, for Eastern Dist. Calif., 1969, U.S. 9th Circuit Ct. Appeals bar, 1959; dep. atty. gen. State of Calif., 1959; dep. dist. atty. Sacramento County, 1959-63, chief dept. dist. atty., 1964-69; mem. firm McDonough, Holland, Schwartz & Allen, Sacramento, 1969-71; judge Sacramento County Superior Ct., 1971-74; asso justice Calif. Ct. Appeal, 3d Dist., 1974, presiding justice, 1974—; prof. law McGeorge Coll. Law U. Pacific, 1961-69; mem. com. on criminal law and procedure Calif. State Bar, 1967-70, chmn. criminal law advisory com. for com. on legal specialization, 1971. Bd. dirs. Sacramento County Legal Aid Soc., 1966-69. Mem. Calif. Conf. Judges. Office: Room 119 Library-Cts Bldg Sacramento CA 95814 Tel (916) 322-4457

PUGLIESE, CHARLES JOHN, b. Jersey City, Apr. 23, 1942; A.B. in English Lit., Brown U., 1964; J.D., Albany Law Sch., 1968. Admitted to N.Y. bar, 1969; individual practice law, Troy, N.Y., 1969; asst. counsel N.Y. State Dept. Agr. and Markets, Albany, 1969—; atty. N.Y. State Fair, 1969—. Mem. Rensselaer County Bar Assn. Home and Office: Box 465 East Greenbush NY 12061 Tel (518) 477-7241

PULASKI, CHARLES ALEXANDER, b. Flushing, N.Y., Oct. 22, 1941; B.A., Yale, 1964, LL.B., 1967. Admitted to Conn. bar, 1967, U.S. Supreme Ct. bar, 1970, Iowa bar, 1973; law clk. U.S. Dist. Ct. Conn., 1967-68; asso. firm Tyler, Cooper, Grant, Bowerman & Keefe, New Haven, 1968-72; prof. law U. Iowa, 1972—. Office: Univ Iowa Coll Law Iowa City IA 52242 Tel (319) 353-5489

PULASKI, MICHAEL THOMAS, b. Dallas, July 18, 1945; B.M.E., La. State U., 1968, J.D., 1971, M.S. in Nuclear Engring., 1972. Admitted to La. bar, 1972, D.C. bar, 1973; asso. firm Lowenstein, Newman & Reis, Washington, 1972-73; partner firm Provosty & Sadler, Alexandria, La., 1973—. Bd. dirs. Girl Scouts of Central La., Alexandria YMCA. Mem. La. (ho. of dels.), Am., D.C. bar assns. Home: 1850 Polk St Alexandria LA 71301 Office: Box 1791 Alexandria LA 71301 Tel (318) 445-3631

PULASKI, STANLEY R., b. Balt., Feb. 21, 1901; B.S. in Commerce, DePaul U., 1926, J.D., 1929. Admitted to Ill. bar, 1930; prof. law DePaul U., Chgo., 1930-38; asst. judge Probate Ct., judge Municipal Ct., Chgo., 1950-53; asst. atty. gen. State of Ill., Chgo., 1954-61; individual practice law, Chgo., 1961—. Mem. Chgo. bar Assn., Advocates Soc. Editor, Poleamerican Law Jour., 1939-44. Home: 8757 S Baltimore Ave Chicago IL 60617 Office: 11 S LaSalle St Chicago IL 60603 Tel (312) 236-6430

PULLEY, FRANKLIN PIERCE, III, b. Ivor, Va., Dec. 6, 1919; A.B., Coll. William and Mary, 1941; postgrad. Washington and Lee U., 1945-47; LL.B. summa cum laude, Va. Coll. Commerce and Law, 1950. Admitted to Va. bar, 1950, U.S. Supreme Ct. bar, 1970; individual practice law, Waverly, Va., 1958-63, Roanoke, Va., 1954—. Instl. dir. Boy Scouts Am., 1959-60. Mem. Am., Va., Roanoke, bar assns., Va. State Bar. Home: 15 Mountain Ave Roanoke VA 24016 Office: Room 733 305 1st St Shenandoah Bldg Roanoke VA 24011 Tel (703) 342-2516

PURCELL, JEROME JAMES, b. Pottsville, Pa., Aug. 17, 1946; B.S., Ind. U., 1968; J.D., U. Pitts., 1971. Admitted to Pa. bar, 1971; asso. firm Meyer, Unkovic and Scott, Pitts., 1971-75; partner firm Shostak, Merritt and Purcell, Pitts., 1975—; asst. solicitor Brentwood Borough, Pa., 1974; mem. Fed. Pub. Defender Panel, 1975—. Mem. Allegheny County, Pa., Am. bar assns., Comml. Law League, Pa. Trial Lawyers Assn., Am. Arbitration Assn. Office: Oliver Bldg Pittsburgh PA 15222 Tel (412) 765-2666

PURCELL, JOE EDWARD, b. Warren, Ark., July 29, 1923; J.D., U. Ark., 1952. Admitted to Ark. bar, 1952, since practiced in Benton; city atty., Benton, 1955-59; municipal judge Benton-Saline County, 1959-66; state atty. gen., State of Ark., 1966-70, lt. gov., 1974—. Ark. chmn. March of Dimes, 1975-76, Ark. Am. Bicentennial, 1976; chmn. Ark. Democratic Party, 1970-72. Mem. Am., Ark., Saline County bar assns., Delta Theta Phi. Home: 604 Market St Benton AR 72015 Office: 102 W Ashley St Benton AR 72015 Tel (501) 778-1169

PURCHASE, ROBERT L., b. Bristol, Conn., Oct. 24, 1913; A.B., Union Coll., 1935, LL.B., 1939. Admitted to N.Y. bar, 1940; individual practice law, Marion, N.Y., 1940—; confdl. clk. Wayne County (N.Y.) Supreme Ct., 1942-48, 53-70; asst. dist. atty. Wayne County, 1952; town justice, mem. town bd., Marion, 1941-46. Vol. fireman, Marion; elder, trustee Marion Presbyn. Ch. Mem. N.Y. State, Wayne County bar assns. Home: 17 Union St Marion NY 14505 Office: 20 N Main St Marion NY 14505 Tel (315) 926-4244

PURDOM, THOMAS JAMES, b. Seymour, Tex., Apr. 7, 1937; B.A., Tex. Tech. U., 1962; LL.B., Georgetown Law Center, 1966. Admitted to Tex. bar, 1966; partner firms Griffith & Purdom, Lubbock, Tex., 1966-67, Garner, Vickers & Purdom and predecessors, Lubbock, 1972—; individual practice law, Lubbock, 1967; asst. dist. atty. 72d Jud. Dist., 1967-68; county atty. Lubbock County, Tex., 1968-72; speaker in field. Mem. Lubbock City-County Child Welfare Bd. Mem. Am., Tex., Lubbock County bar assns., Tex. Criminal Def. Lawyers Assn., State Bar Tex. (chmn. sect. family law). Author: Juvenile Procedures Manual, 1973. Home: 3619 55th St Lubbock TX 79413 Office: 1801 Ave Q Lubbock TX 79401 Tel (806) 747-4653

PURRINGTON, ALFRED LUTHER, III, b. Raleigh, N.C., Aug. 31, 1933; A.B., U. N.C., 1955; LL.B., Harvard, 1961. Admitted to N.C. bar, 1961; asso. partner Purrington & Culbertson, Raleigh, 1961-63; asso. Carolina Securities Corp., Raleigh, 1963-68; asst. sec., v.p. GATX/Boothe Corp., N.Y.C., 1968-70, Armco/Boothe Corp., N.Y.C., 1969-70; partner firm Purrington Hatch & McNamara, and predecessors, Raleigh, 1970—. Mem. Am., N.C., Wake County (N.C.) bar assns. Home: Route 8 Box 205 Raleigh NC 27612 Office: 605 Raleigh Bldg 5 W Hargett St Raleigh NC 27602 Tel (919) 828-7214

PURSEL, JOHN HAGERTY, b. Phillipsburg, N.J., Apr. 5, 1896; Ph.B., LaFayette Coll., Easton, Pa., 1919; grad. Harvard Law Sch., 1922. Admitted to N.J. bar, 1922; individual practice law, Newark, 1922-24, Phillipsburg, 1924—; mem. N.J. Legislature, 1929-31; prosecutor Warren County (N.J.), 1948-52; tchr. bus. law Lafayette Coll., 1945-56. Mem. Trenton (N.J.) Local Govt. Commn., 1962-67. Mem. Am., N.J., Warren County bar assns. Home: 550 Barrymore St Phillipsburg NJ 08865 Office: 100 S Main St Phillipsburg NJ 08865 Tel (201) 859-3531

PURSELL, MICHAEL DODSON, b. Pasadena, Calif., Dec. 25, 1936; B.A., U. Calif., Berkeley, 1961; J.D., U. Calif., San Francisco, 1965. Admitted to Calif. bar, 1966; atty. Orange County (Calif.) Pub. Defenders Office, 1965-72; individual practice law, Santa Ana, Calif., 1972—. Mem. Orange County Bar Assn. (dir. 1977—), Orange County Trial Lawyers Assn. (v.p.), Assn. Specialized Criminal Def. Advs. Editor: Orange County Bar Journal, 1975-77. Office: 1651 E 4th St Santa Ana CA 92701 Tel (714) 835-8855

PURSLEY, KENNETH LLOYD, b. Sandpoint, Idaho, Apr. 4, 1940; B.A., Cornell U., 1962; LL.B., U. Chgo., 1965. Admitted to Idaho bar, 1970, Ill. bar, 1965; asso. firm Hopkins, Sutter, Mulray, Davis & Cromartee, Chgo., 1965-70, Eberle, Berlin, Kading, Turnbow & Gillespie, Boise, Idaho, 1970-76, partner, 1972-76; partner firm Pursley & Underwood, 1977. Chmn., Boise City Greenbelt Com., 1974—, Statewide Study City and County Govt., 1973; mem. Boise City Design Rev. Commn., 1971-76. Vets. Meml. State Park Task Force, 1972-73. Mem. Am., Boise bar assns., Am. Judicature Soc., Order of Coif. Recipient Distinguished Service award Capitol Jaycees, Boise, 1974. Home: 1908 S Manitou St Boise ID 83706 Office: 575 N 8th St PO Box 387 Boise ID 83701 Tel (208) 342-6532

PURTLE, JOHN THOMAS, b. Greggtown, Tex., Sept. 16, 1934; A.B., U. Ark., 1957, LL.B., 1959. Admitted to Ark. bar, 1959, U.S. Supreme Ct. bar, 1967; law clk. Ark. Supreme Ct., 1959-60; asso. firm Murphy & Arnold, Batesville, Ark., 1961-63, firm Murphy, Arnold & Purtle, Batesville, 1964-65; mem. firm Bennett & Purtle, Batesville, 1966—; city atty. Batesville, 1967-75. Sec. Independence County Election Commn., 1968—. Mem. Ark., Am. bar assns., Am., Ark. trial lawyers assns., Independence County Bar Assn. Office: 150 S Third St Batesville AR 72501 Tel (501) 793-5734

PURVIN, SAUL, b. Bklyn., Oct. 23, 1916; LL.B., St. John's U., 1941. Admitted to N.Y. bar, 1942, U.S. Eastern and So. Dist. Ct. bar, 1964, U.S. Ct. Appeals bar, 1976; atty. U.S. Army, 1943-46; individual practice law, Bklyn., 1947-71; atty. U.S. Dept. Treasury, N.Y.C., 1971—. Home: 5711 Kings Hwy Brooklyn NY 11203 Office: US Treasury Box 3100 New York City NY 10008 Tel (212) 264-3132

PURVIS, GEORGE FRANK, JR., b. Rayville, La., Nov. 22, 1914; A.A., La. State U., 1932, J.D., 1935. Admitted to La. bar, 1935; individual practice law, Rayville, 1936; atty. for sec. of state, spl. asst. to atty. gen. La., 1937-41; dep. ins. commr., spl. asst. atty. gen. State of La., 1945-59; with Pan-Am. Life Ins. Co., New Orleans, 1949—, asso. gen. counsel, 1954, v.p. and asso. gen. counsel, 1955, dir., 1957, v.p. investment dept., 1959, v.p. and gen. counsel for investments, 1961, exec. v.p., 1962, pres. and chief exec. officer, 1964, chmn. bd., pres. and chief exec. officer, 1969, chmn. bd. and chief exec. officer, 1974—; dir. So. Airways, Inc., Pan—Am. de Mexico Compania de Seguros, S.A., First Nat. Bank of Commerce in New Orleans, S. Central Bell Telephone Co., First Commerce Corp.; pres. and dir. Compania de seguros Panamericana, S.A., Pan-Am. de Venezuela Compania de Seguros, C.A., Pan-Am. de Colombia Compania de Seguros de Vida, S.A., Interhemispheric Reins. Co., Seguros y Reaseguros Panamericanos, S.A.; instr. law sch. La. State U., 1946-49; lectr. U. Coll. of Tulane U., 1949-56; exec. in residence Baylor U., 1975; mem. exec. com. Health Ins. Assn. Am., 1966-70, 71-72, dir., 1965-72, chmn., 1969-71; research fellow Southwestern Legal Found., 1967—; chmn. S.S. Huebner Found. for Ins. Edn., 1977—. Bd. dirs. C. of C. of New Orleans Area, 1961-71, 73—, pres., 1970; bd. dirs. New Orleans YMCA, 1960-72, trustee, 1972—, pres., 1968-72; bd. dirs. Internat. House, 1955-71, 73—, treas., 1969, v.p., 1970-77, pres., 1977—; bd. dirs. Tb Assn. Greater New Orleans, 1961—, pres., 1967-69; trustee Gulf S. Research Inst., 1968—; dir., gen. campaign chmn. United Fund Greater New Orleans Area, 1967; state chmn. Radio Free Europe, 1967; bd. dirs. Goodwill Industries Greater New Orleans Area, 1973—; pres. Greater New Orleans Fedn. Chs., 1974-75; sr. warden St. Martin's Episcopal Ch., vestryman, mem. sch. adv. council. Mem. La., Am. bar assns., La. Law Inst., Am. Judicature Soc., Assn. Life Ins. Counsel, Fedn. Ins. Counsel, Phi Delta Phi. Named La. State U. Alumnus of Year, 1975, Boss of Year, 1975; recipient award Inst. Human Understanding, 1975, Weiss Meml. award, 1976. Home: 5501 Dayna Court New Orleans LA 70124 Office: 2400 Canal St New Orleans LA 70119 Tel (504) 821-2510

PUSATERI, LAWRENCE XAVIER, b. Oak Park, Ill., May 25, 1931; J.D. summa cum laude, De Paul U., 1953. Admitted to Ill. bar, 1953, U.S. Supreme Ct. bar, 1957; mem. JAGC U.S. Army, 1953-57; asst. state's atty. Cook County, Ill., 1957-59; asso. firm Newton, Wilhelm, Pusateri & Naborowski, and predecessor, Chgo., 1959-61, partner, 1961—; mem. Ill. Ho. of Reps., 1964-68; spl. asst. atty. gen. State of Ill., 1959-63; chmn. Ill. Crime Investigating Commn., 1964-66; chmn. Ill. Parole and Pardon Bd., 1969-70; mem. exec. com. Com. on Cts. and Justice, 1972-76; chief legal services Ill. Dept. Corrections, 1970—. Chmn. Melrose Park (Ill.) Cancer Soc., 1961-63. Fellow Am. Bar Found.; mem. Ill. State (Abraham Lincoln award for legal writing 1963, pres. 1975-76), Am. (ho. of dels.), Chgo. (bd. mgrs. 1967-68) bar assns. Named 1 of 10 Outstanding Young Men in Chgo., Chgo. Jr. Assn. Commerce and Industry 1959, 63. Home: 525 Auvergne Pl River Forest IL 60305 Office: 105 W Madison St Chicago IL 60602 Tel (312) 726-3400

PUSEY, CLARENCE EDWARD, JR., b. Rochester, N.Y., Apr. 12, 1932; A.B., U. Md., College Park, 1954, LL.B., Balt., 1956, J.D., 1969. Admitted to Md. bar, 1957, U.S. Supreme Ct. bar, 1964; asso. firm Max R. Israelson, Balt., 1957-59; individual practice law, Towson, Md., 1959—; tchr. Baltimore County Adult Edn., 1970—. Active Boy Scouts Am. Mem. Am., Md. State, Baltimore County bar assns., Am. Trial Lawyers Assn., Am. Judicature Soc. Home: 1905 York Rd PO Box 276 Timonium MD 21093 Office: Suite 803 Equitable Towson Bldg 401 Washington Ave PO Box 5515 Towson MD 21203 Tel (301) 823-7373

PUTMAN, JAMES MICHAEL, b. San Antonio, May 12, 1948; B.B.A., S.W. Tex. State U., 1969; J.D., St. Mary's U., 1972. Admitted to Tex. bar, 1972; partner firm Putman & Putman, San Antonio, 1972—. Mem. Am., Tex., San Antonio trial lawyers assns., Tex. Criminal Def. Lawyers Assn., Tex. Bar Assn. Office: 1000 Tower Life Bldg San Antonio TX 78205 Tel (512) 226-0221

PUTZELL, EDWIN JOSEPH, JR., b. Birmingham, Ala., Sept. 29, 1913; B.A., Tulane U., 1935; LL.B., Harvard U., 1938. Admitted to N.Y. bar, 1939, U.S. Supreme Ct. bar, 1945, Mo. bar, 1946; asso. firm Donovan, Leisure, Newton & Lumbard, N.Y.C. and Washington, 1937-42; asst. treas. Monsanto Co., St. Louis, 1945-46, atty., asst. sec., 1946-51, sec., 1951-77, dir. law dept., 1953-77, v.p., gen. counsel, 1963-77; partner firm Coburn, Croft, Shepherd, Herzog & Putzell, St. Louis, 1977—; dir. Mfrs. Bank & Trust Co., St. Louis. Pres., Social Planning Council, St. Louis, 1958-59, Met. Hosp. Planning Commn., 1967-69; v.p. Child Welfare League Am., N.Y.C., 1962-65; vice chmn. St. Louis County Bd. Police Commrs., 1968-72; vice chmn. bd. dirs. Ednl. TV Commn., St. Louis, 1974—; bd. dirs. St. Lukes Hosp., St. Louis, Mark Twain Summer Inst., St. Louis; vice chmn. bd. dirs. Westminster Coll., Fulton, Mo., 1977—. Mem. Am., Mo., Met. St. Louis (past chmn. corporate law dept. com.) bar assns., Gt. Plains Legal Found. Kansas City, Mo. (dir.), Am. Soc Corporate Secs. (past pres., dir.), Assn. Gen. Counsel, Am. Law Inst. Home: 9884 Copper Hill Rd Saint Louis MO 63124 Office: One Mercantile Center Saint Louis MO 63101 Tel (314) 621-8575

PUYANIC, MAXMILLION D., b. Evergreen Park, Ill., Oct. 19, 1947; B.S., B.A., Roosevelt U., Chgo., 1968; J.D., U. Miami, 1972. Admitted to Fla. bar, 1972; individual practice law, Miami, Fla., 1972—. Mem. Dade County Bar Assn. Office: 1825 S Miami Ave Miami FL 33129 Tel (305) 856-0220

PYATT, ROBERT FLEMING, b. Trenton, Mo., June 13, 1927; B.A., U. Mo., 1950, LL.B., 1953. Admitted to Mo. bar, 1953, U.S. Supreme Ct. bar, 1963; with legal dept. Phillips Petroleum Co., Bartlesville, Okla., 1953-55; asst. atty. gen. State of N.Mex., 1957-59; mem. firm Easley & Pyatt, Hobbs, N.Mex., 1959-66, firm Brown & Pyatt, Trenton, Mo., 1966-68, Frith & Pyatt, Chillicothe, Mo., 1968-74; individual practice law, Chillicothe, 1974—. Mem. Livingston County Bar Assn., Order of Coif. Bd. editors Mo. Law Rev., 1952-53. Home: 1920 Polk St Chillicothe MO 64601 Office: 822 Jackson St Chillicothe MO 64601 Tel (816) 646-2586

PYE, A. KENNETH, b. N.Y.C., Aug. 21, 1931; B.A., U. Buffalo, 1951; J.D., Georgetown U., 1953, LL.M., 1955. Admitted to D.C. bar, 1953, U.S. Ct. Mil. Appeals bar, 1953, U.S. Supreme Ct. bar, 1960, N.C. bar, 1971; prof. law Georgetown U., 1955-66, asso. dean Sch. Law, 1961-66; prof. law Duke, 1966—, dean Sch. Law, 1968-70, 73-76, chancellor, 1970-71, 76—, univ. counsel, 1971-74. Mem. Assn. Law Schs. (pres. 1976-77), Am. Law Inst., Am. Bar Assn., Order of Coif. Home: 2802 Chelsea Circle Durham NC 27707 Tel (919) 684-5824

PYFER, JOHN FREDERICK, JR., b. Lancaster, Pa., July 25, 1946; B.A., Haverford Coll., 1969; J.D., Vanderbilt U., 1972. Admitted to Pa. bar, 1972, U.S. Supreme Ct. bar, 1976; asso. firm Xakellis, Perezous & Mongiovi, Lancaster, 1972-76; partner firm Allison, Weglarz & Pyfer, Lancaster, 1976—. Mem. Am., Pa. bar assns., Am., Pa. trial lawyers assns., Nat. Assn. Criminal Def. Lawyers. Recipient Howard C. Schwab award, 1972. Contbr. articles to legal jours. Home: 1090 Richmond Rd Lancaster PA 17603 Office: 128 N Lime St Lancaster PA 17602 Tel (717) 299-7342

PYLE, RICHARD ALDEN, b. Eufaula, Okla., Apr. 16, 1931; B.A., Central State U., 1964; LL.B., Okla. U., 1966. Admitted to Okla. bar, 1966, U.S. Supreme Ct. bar, 1973, U.S. Ct. Appeals bar, 1969; individual practice law, Eufaula, 1966-69; U.S. atty. Eastern Dist. Okla., Muskogee, 1969—. Home: 302 S 5th St Eufaula OK 74432 Office: Box 1009 Muskogee OK 74401 Tel (918) 687-2543

PYLES, DIXON LEROY, b. Little Rock, Jan. 1, 1913; B.A., Millsaps Coll., 1933; LL.B., Jackson Sch. Law, 1939. Admitted to Miss. bar, 1940, U.S. Supreme Ct. bar, 1965; partner firm Tullos & Pyles, Jackson, Miss., 1940-42, Pyles & Tucker, Jackson, 1946-72, Pyles, Cupit & Maxey, and predecessors, Jackson, Miss., 1972—; instr. Jackson Sch. Law, 1970-75. Mem. Am. Bar Assn., Am. Trial Lawyers Assn. Home: 4642 Jiggetts Rd Jackson MS 39211 Office: 507 E Pearl St Jackson MS 39201 Tel (601) 354-5668

PYTELL, ROBERT HENRY, b. Detroit, Sept. 27, 1926; J.D., U. Detroit, 1951. Admitted to Mich. bar, 1952; individual practice law, Detroit; judge Grosse Pointe Farms (Mich.) Municipal Ct., 1967—. Mem. Am. Bar Assn., Am. Judicature Soc., State Bar Mich. Office: 18580 Mack St Grosse Pointe Farms MI 48236 Tel (313) 343-9200

PYTYNIA, THOMAS LEE, b. Valparaiso, Ind., Mar. 1, 1947; A.B. in History summa cum laude, Ind. U., 1969, J.D. summa cum laude, 1973. Admitted to Ind. bar, 1973; law clk. to judge U.S. Dist. Ct., No. Dist. Ind., Fort Wayne, 1973-74; asso. firm Baker & Daniels, Indpls., 1974-77; mem. legal dept. Eli Lilly & Co., Indpls., 1977—; instr. bus. law Ind. U., Bloomington, 1973. Dep. election commr. Indpls., 1974. Mem. Ind. State, Am. bar assns., Order of Coif, Phi Beta Kappa. Home: 5753 N Delaware St Indianapolis IN 46220 Office: 307 E McCarty St Indianapolis IN 46225 Tel (317) 221-2526

PYZYK, ROBERT GEORGE, b. Milw., May 21, 1950; J.D., Marquette U., 1974. Admitted to Wis. bar, 1974; intern Milwaukee County Dist. Attys. Office, 1973-74, mem. firm Niebler & Niebler, Menomonee Falls, Wis., 1974—. Mem. Milw. Jr., Milw., Am. bar assns., Am. Trial Lawyers Assn. Home: 2764 S 75th St West Allis WI 53219 Office: N95 W16975 Hwy 41 Menomonee Falls WI 53051 Tel (414) 251-5330

QUACKENBUSH, JAMES HAYES, JR., b. Columbia, S.C., May 7, 1943; B.A. in Polit. Sci., The Citadel, 1965; J.D., U. S.C., 1968. Admitted to S.C. bar, 1968; asst. atty. gen. State of S.C., 1970-72; partner firm Timberlake & Quackenbush, Columbia, 1972-74, Sanders & Quackenbush, Columbia, 1974—. Chmn., Democratic Party, City of Columbia, 1974-76; exec. dir. com. New Jud. Center and Courthouse, Richland County; chmn. Midlands Human Resources Devel. Commn., 1976. Mem. Am., S.C. (ho. of dels.), Richland County (sec., exec. com.) bar assns., S.C. Trial Lawyers Assn. Editor Richbar Newsletter, 1973—; contbr. to Water Resources Law Jour. Home: 830 Woodland Dr Columbia SC 29205 Office: Box 11252 Columbia SC 29211 Tel (803) 799-9222

QUALLEY, GEORGE THOMAS, b. Nevis, Minn., Feb. 22, 1928; B.A., Simpson Coll., 1953; B.L., Drake U., 1957, J.D., 1968. Admitted to Iowa bar, 1957, U.S. Supreme Ct. bar, 1960, D.C. bar, 1974, S.D. b r, 1976, Nebr. bar, 1976; with alien property div., then tax div. Dept. Justice, Washington, 1957-61; individual practice law, Sioux City, Iowa, Washington, Omaha and Sioux Falls, S.D., 1961—; lectr. tax seminars. Mem. Am. (taxation sect. com. on subchpt. corps.), D.C., Iowa, Nebr., S.D., Woodbury County bar assns., Iowa Accountants Assn. (hon.), Delta Theta Phi. Contbr. articles to books and jours. Office: 220 Badgerow Bldg Sioux City IA 51101 Tel (712) 255-7937

QUARANT, JACK DOMENICK, b. Indiana, Pa., Mar. 28, 1916; LL.B., U. Ill., 1952, J.D., 1968. Admitted to Ill. bar, 1952, U.S. Supreme Ct. bar, 1976; individual practice law, Elizabethtown, Ill., 1952—; asst. state atty. Pope County (Ill.), 1954-56. Mem. Am., Ill., SE Ill., Saline County bar assns., Ill. Trial Lawyers Assn. (dir. 1967—), Am. Trial Lawyers Assn. (bd. govs. 1975—), Aircraft Owners and Pilots Assn., Phi Delta Phi. Contbr. articles to legal jours. Home: Route No 1 Golconda IL 62938 Office: Box 500 Elizabethtown IL 62931 Tel (618) 285-6222

QUARLES, RALPH BANKS, b. Tuscaloosa, Ala., Aug. 24, 1944; B.A., U. Ala., 1967, J.D., 1968. Admitted to Ala. bar, 1968; with firm McQueen, Ray & Allison, Tuscaloosa, 1970-73; trust officer 1st Nat. Bank of Tuscaloosa, 1973—; lectr. U. Ala., Ala. Bankers Assn., Nat. Assn. Legal Secs. Mem. Am., Tuscaloosa County (chmn. law day com. 1974, sec.-treas. 1976-77) bar assns., Tuscaloosa Estate Planning Council (founder, past pres., mem. exec. com.). Home: 25 The Downs Tuscaloosa AL 35401 Office: 2330 University Blvd Tuscaloosa AL 35401 Tel (205) 345-5000

QUAT, LEON, b. N.Y.C., Feb. 17, 1906; B.A., Columbia, 1926, J.D., 1928. Admitted to N.Y. State bar, 1928, U.S. Supreme Ct. bar, 1940; asso. firm Rabe, Keller & Davis, Esqs., N.Y.C., 1928-36; partner firm Davis & Quat, N.Y.C., 1936—. Chmn., Great Neck (N.Y.) Forum, 1952—. Mem. N.Y. County Lawyers Assn. Book rev. editor, Columbia Law Rev., 1927-28. Home: 16 Elliot Rd Great Neck NY 11021 Office: 259 Broadway St New York City NY 10007 Tel (212) 227-8311

QUATTROCCHI, JOHN, JR., b. Providence, Oct. 15, 1913; A.B., Brown U., 1934; LL.B., Boston U., 1937. Admitted to R.I. bar, 1937, Mass. bar, 1955; asst. city solicitor Providence, 1939-41; individual practice law, Providence, 1945—; sec. state R.I., 1964; mem. U.S. Senate, 1970, 72. Candidate for mayor of Providence, 1948, 66; pres. R.I. Tennis Orgn., 1964-67. Mem. R.I., Mass. bar assns., New Eng. Law Inst. Author: Pitfalls in Marriage and Divorce, 1966. Office: 182 Mano St Providence RI 02906 Tel (401) 272-4545

QUATTROCCHI, JOHN, III, b. Providence, Nov. 24, 1942; A.B. in English, Allegheny Coll., 1964; LL.B., J.D., Boston U. Sch. Law, 1967. Admitted to R.I. bar, 1969, D.C. Court Appeals bar, 1976, U.S. Supreme Court bar, 1977; contract legal officer Dept. Air Force, 1967-68; intelligence officer USAF, 1968-70; individual practice law, Providence, 1970-76, Smithfield, R.I., 1976—; town solicitor, atty. Town of Lincoln, R.I., 1975—. Mem. Am., R.I., D.C. Court Appeals bar Assns., Am. Trial Lawyers Assn. Home: Harris Ave Lincoln RI 02865 Office: Twin Rivers Bldg 2 Douglas Pike Smithfield RI 02917 Tel (401) 231-3700

QUELLER, FRED, b. N.Y.C., July 10, 1932; B.A., City Coll. N.Y., 1954; J.D., N.Y. U., 1956. Admitted to N.Y. bar, 1956, U.S. Dist. Ct. Eastern and So. Dists. N.Y., 1958, U.S. Ct. Appeals bar, 1967, U.S. Supreme Ct. bar, 1960; individual practice law, N.Y.C., 1957-70; sr. partner firm Queller, Fisher & Block, N.Y.C., 1970—; mem. med. malpractice panel Supreme Ct. State N.Y., County N.Y.: lectr. N.Y. Acad. Trial Lawyers; mem. Compulsory Arbitration Service, 1st Jud. Dept. State N.Y.; former mem. Masters Panel, Civil Ct. City N.Y. Mem. bd. Nat. Com. for Furtherance of Jewish Edn., Bklyn., 1973—. Mem. Am., N.Y. State (dir.) trial lawyers assns., Assn. Trial Lawyers City N.Y. (dir.), Assn. Bar City N.Y., N.Y. State, Bronx County bar assns., N.Y. County Lawyers Assn., Bklyn.-Manhattan Trial Counsel Assn., Bronx Women's Bar Assn. (dir.), Jewish Lawyers Guild (dir.), Lawyers Interested in Victims' Equality (trustee). Office: 110 Wall St New York City NY 10005 Tel (212) 422-3600

QUETSCH, JAMES FRANKLIN, b. Oak Park, Ill., Nov. 13, 1933; B.A., U. Notre Dame, 1956; J.D., Chgo.-Kent Coll., 1959. Admitted to Ill. bar, 1959; asso. firm William P. Treacy, Chgo., 1959-60, firm M.A. Segarra, Chgo., 1960-62, firm Brody & Gore, Chgo., 1962-63, firm Gates Clancy, Geneva, Ill., 1963-65; partner firm Corrigan, Mackay, Quetsch & O'Reilly, Wheaton, Ill., 1965-74, firm O'Reilly & Quetsch, Wheaton, 1974-75; asso. judge 16th Jud. Circuit Ill., Geneva, 1975—. Republican committeeman City of Oak Park, 1960, Wayne Twp. (Ill.), 1966-71, Geneva, 1974-75; auditor Wayne Twp., 1966-71. Mem. Ill., Wayne County bar assns., Assn. Trial Lawyers Am. Home: 1527 Kaneville Rd Geneva IL 60134 Office: Kane County Court House Geneva IL 60134 Tel (312) 232-2400

QUICK, ALBERT THOMAS, b. Battle Creek, Mich., June 28, 1939; B.A., U. Ariz.; M.A., Central Mich. U.; J.D., Wayne State U.; LL.M., Tulane U. Admitted to Mich. bar, 1968; asst. prosecutor Calhoun County (Mich.) Prosecutor's Office, 1968; asso. firm Hatch & Hatch, Marshall, Mich., 1968-70; asst. prof. criminal justice, dir. div. criminal justice U. Maine, Augusta, 1970-74; asst. prof. law U. Louisville, 1974—; panelist numerous nat. confs. Mem. Am. Assn. Law Schs. Office: Law Sch U of Louisville Louisville KY 40208 Tel (502) 636-4207

QUIGGLE, JAMES WILLIAMS, b. D.C., Aug. 24, 1924; A.B., Princeton U., 1948; LL.B., U. Va., 1951; LL.M., Georgetown U., 1956. Admitted to D.C. bar, 1952; mem. firm Williams, Myers and Quiggle, D.C., 1951—. Mem. Am. Bar Assn. (mem. tax sec.). Contbr. articles to profl. jours. Home: 4949 Hillbrook Ln NW Washington DC 20016 Office: 888-17th St NW Washington DC 20006 Tel (202) 333-5900

QUIGLEY, JOHN BERNARD, b. St. Louis, Oct. 1, 1940; A.B., Harvard, 1962, LL.B., 1966, M.A., 1966. Admitted to Mass. bar, 1967, Ohio bar, 1973; research asso. Harvard Law Sch., 1967-69; prof. law Ohio State U. Coll. Law, Columbus, 1969—. Mem. Nat. Lawyers Guild (nat. exec. com. 1974-76). Author: Basic Laws on the Structure of the Soviet State, 1969; The Merchant Shipping Code of the USSR, 1970; The Soviet Foreign Trade Monopoly: Institutions and Laws, 1974. Office: 1659 N High St Columbus OH 43210 Tel (614) 422-1764

QUILLEN, FORD CARTER, b. Gate City, Va., Sept. 21, 1938; B.S., U. Tenn., 1961, J.D., 1966. Admitted to Va. bar, 1966; partner firm Quillen & Carter, Gate City, 1966—; former mem. 9th Dist. Ethics Com.; mem. Va. Ho. of Dels., 1970—. Mem. Va. Bar Assn. Home: Box 337 Gate City VA 24251 Tel (703) 386-7023

QUILLIAM, WILLIAM REED, JR., b. Beaumont, Tex., Jan. 21, 1929; B.A., U. Tex., 1949, B.B.A., 1951, J.D., 1953; LL.M., Harvard, 1953. Admitted to Tex. bar, 1953; since practiced in Lubbock, Tex., individual practice law, 1956-58, 60-67; trust officer Am. State Bank, 1958-59; prof. Sch. Law, Tex. Tech. U., 1968—, asso. dean, 1973—; pres. Lubbock Lands, Inc., 1966—. Mem. Tex. Ho. Reps., 1961-68. Mem. State Jr. Bar Tex. (dir. 1957-59), State Bar Tex. (estate planning com.). Recipient Outstanding Prof. award Tex. Tech. U. Sch. Law, 1971, 77; contbg. author: Texas Wills and Probate Practice, 1975; Texas Estate Administration, 1975, rev. edit., 1977; also articles. Home: 5703 Geneva Lubbock TX 79413 Office: Tex Tech Univ Sch Law Lubbock TX 79409 Tel (806) 742-6273

QUINLAN, GUY CHRISTIAN, b. Cambridge, Mass., Oct. 28, 1939; A.B., Harvard, 1960, J.D., 1963. Admitted to N.Y. bar, 1964, U.S. Dist. Ct. So. and Eastern dists. N.Y. bar, 1965, U.S. Ct. Appeals 2d Circuit bar, 1967, U.S. Supreme Ct. bar, 1969, U.S. Ct. Appeals 5th and 8th circuits bar, 1973; asso. firm Rogers & Wells, 1963-70, partner, 1970—. Mem. Am., N.Y. State bar assns. Home: 536 E 89th St New York City NY 10028 Office: 200 Park Ave New York City NY 10017 Tel (212) 972-7000

QUINLIVAN, JAMES SIMON, JR., b. New Orleans, May 13, 1926; B.B.A., Tulane U., 1949; J.D., Loyola U., 1953. Admitted to La. bar, 1953; individual practice law. Mem. La. Trial Lawyers Assn. Home: 200 Phyllis Ct River Ridge LA 70123 Office: 9537 Jefferson Hwy River Ridge LA 70123 Tel (504) 737-5563

QUINN, ALEXANDER JAMES, b. Cleve., Apr. 8, 1932; J.C.D., Lateran U., Rome, Italy, 1963; J.D., Cleve. State U., 1972. Admitted to Ohio bar, 1972; chancellor, diocese of Cleve., 1967-72, fin. sec., 1972—; dir. Midwest Bank and Trust Co., 1972—. Chaplain Anchor Club of Cleve. Mem. Cath. Lawyers Guild of Cleve. (chaplain). Author: Thoughts for Our Time, 1969; Thoughts for Sowing, 1970; Ashes from the Cathedral, 1974. Home and Office: 1027 Superior Ave Cleveland OH 44114 Tel (216) 696-6525

QUINN, ANDREW PETER, JR., b. Providence, Oct. 22, 1923; A.B., Brown U., 1945; LL.B., Yale U., 1950. Admitted to R.I. bar, 1949, Mass. bar, 1960, U.S. Dist. Ct. bar, 1951, U.S. Ct. of Appeals bar, 1952; partner firm Letts & Quinn, Providence, 1950-59; with Mass. Mut. Life Ins. Co., Springfield, 1959—, now exec. v.p., gen. counsel. Trustee, MacDuffie Sch., Baystate Med. Center. Mem. Am., Hampden County bar assns., Assn. Life Ins. Counsel, Am. Council Life Ins. (past chmn. legal sect.). Home: 306 Ellington Rd Longmeadow MA 01106 Office: 1295 State St Springfield MA 01111 Tel (413) 788-8411

QUINN, BERNARD THOMAS, b. Wilkes-Barre, Pa., Dec. 1, 1934; B.S., Villanova U., 1957, LL.B., 1960. Admitted to Pa. bar, 1962; counsel reinsurance dept. Stuyvesant Ins. Co., Allentown, Pa., 1960-63; house counsel U.S. Liability Ins. Co., King of Prussia, Pa.,

1963-68; gen. counsel, sec., dir. U.S. Investment Corp., Bethlehem, Pa., 1968—. Chmn. Lower Saucon Twp. (Pa.) Zoning Hearing Bd., 1970-76; mem. Lower Saucon Twp. Planning Commn., 1972-76. Mem. Northampton County (Pa.) Bar Assn. Home: Rural Delivery 7 Black River Rd Bethlehem PA 18015 Office: Rural Delivery 7 Black River Rd Bethlehem PA 18015 Tel (215) 866-4366 also 1030 Continental Dr King of Prussia PA (215) 688-2535

QUINN, JOHN LAWRENCE, b. Eureka, Calif., Sept. 28, 1931; B.S. in Commerce, U. Santa Clara, 1953; LL.B., Hastings Coll. Law, 1957. Admitted to Calif. bar, 1958; individual practice law, Eureka, 1958-59; dep. dist. atty. County Humboldt, Calif., 1959-64; atty. City Blue Lake, 1964-67, City Trinidad, Calif., 1965-68. Office: Suite H 730 5th St Eureka CA 95501 Tel (707) 443-8313

QUINN, JOHN RAYMOND, b. Schenectady, Dec. 29, 1935; B.A., Niagara U., 1957; LL.B., Union U., 1960. Admitted to N.Y. bar, 1961; asso. firm Leary, Fullerton, Ford & Aussicker, Schenectady, 1960-61; capt. JAGC, U.S. Army, 1962-64; individual practice law, Schenectady, 1965—; judge Schenectady City Ct., 1976—. Mem. Schenectady City Council, 1966-69, Schenectady County Bd. Reps., 1972-75; asso. counsel to N.Y. Assembly Minority, 1966-74, home rule counsel, 1975—. Mem. N.Y., Schenectady County bar assns., Am. Arbitration Assn. Home: 1644 Randolph Rd Schenectady NY 12308 Office: 157 Barrett St Schenectady NY 12305 Tel (518) 374-2640

QUINN, JOHN T., b. Phila., Mar. 29, 1930; A.B., Georgetown, 1952; J.D., Yale U., 1955; S.T.L., Catholic U., 1967. Admitted to D.C. bar, 1955; legal specialist U.S. Navy, 1956-58; mem. staff FAA, Washington, N.Y.C., 1958-62; with Diocese of Santa Rosa (Calif.), 1967-70, Diocese of San Diego, 1970—; adj. prof. law U. San Diego, 1971—. Home: PO Box 11041 San Diego CA 92111 Office: Diocesan Office PO Box 80428 San Diego CA 92138 Tel (714) 298-7711

QUINN, ROBERT COLLINS, b. Steubenville, Ohio, Mar. 10, 1937; B.A., Ohio Wesleyan U., 1960; LL.B., Ohio State Coll. Law, 1962. Admitted to Ohio bar, 1963; asso. firm Sindell, Sindell, Bourne Marcus & McElroy, Cleve., 1963, Eastman Stichter Smith & Bergman, Toledo, 1963-66; with Nationwide Ins. Cos., Columbus, Ohio, 1966—, asst. gen. counsel, 1969-72, auto ins. reform coordinator, 1972-74, legis. affairs officer, 1974-76, projects officer, 1976—. Mem. citizens adv. bd. Westerville (Ohio) Bd. Edn., 1970. Mem. Am., Ohio bar assns. Contbr. articles to legal jours. Home: 151 Walnut Ridge Ln Westerville OH 43081 Office: 246 N High St Columbus OH 43216 Tel (614) 227-7625

QUINN, THOMAS ALVORD, b. Washington, D.C., Jan. 26, 1936; B.S., Brigham Young Univ., 1959; J.D., George Washington Univ., 1963. Admitted to D.C. bar, 1964, Calif. bar, 1965, Utah bar, 1968; asso. firm Barnes, Richardson & Colburn, D.C., 1963-64; asso. firm Voegelin, Barton, Harris & Callister, Los Angeles, 1964-68; asso. firm Ray, Quinney & Nebeker, Salt Lake City, 1968-69, partner, 1969—; contract negotiator USN, 1960-63. Chmn. Utah Common Cause, 1973-74, mem. bd. dirs. Los Angeles Music Center, 1966-67; mem. Utah Govs. Council on Phys. Fitness, 1975—. Mem. Am., Utah, Calif., Salt Lake County bar assns. Contbr. articles in field to profl. jours. Home: 4193 Panorama Dr Salt Lake City UT 84117 Office: 400 Deseret Building Salt Lake City UT 84111 Tel (801) 532-1500

QUINN, TIMOTHY CHARLES, JR., b. Caro, Mich., Mar. 3, 1936; B.A., U. Mich., 1960; J.D., Columbia, 1963. Admitted to N.Y. bar, 1963; asso. firm Clark, Carr & Ellis, N.Y.C., 1963-69, firm Casey, Tyre, Wallace & Bannerman, N.Y.C., 1969-71, Arsham & Keenan, N.Y.C., 1971; asso. Conboy, Hewitt, O'Brien & Boardman, N.Y.C., 1972-74, partner, 1975—. Bd. dirs. Purchase (N.Y.) Community Chest, 1971—. Mem. Am. Bar Assn., Am. Arbitration Assn. (arbitrator N.Y.C. 1966—), Assn. City N.Y., Nat. Assn. R.R. Trial Counsel, Conf. Freight Loss and Damage Counsel, N.Y. Claims Conf. Home: 34 Pinehurst Dr Purchase NY 10577 Office: 20 Exchange Pl New York City NY 10005 Tel (212) 344-3131

QUINN, WESLEY MARION, b. Sumner County, Kans., Feb. 21, 1907; student U. N.Mex. Admitted to N.Mex. bar, 1934; partner firm Quinn and Quinn, Clovis, N.Mex., 1959-67; mem. Bd. N.Mex. State Bar Commrs., 1959-67, pres., 1965. Mem. Am., N.Mex., Curry County (pres. 1958) bar assns. Office: 123 W 4th St Clovis NM 88101 Tel (505) 762-4484

QUINN, WILLIAM FRANCIS, b. Rochester, N.Y., July 13, 1919; B.S. summa cum laude, St. Louis U., 1940; LL.B. cum laude, Harvard, 1947. Admitted to Hawaii bar, 1948, U.S. Supreme Ct. bar, 1963; partner firm Robertson, Castle & Anthony, Honolulu, 1947-57, Quinn & Moore, Honolulu, 1962-64, Jenks, Kidwell, Goodsill & Anderson, Honolulu, 1972-73, Goodsill, Anderson & Quinn, Honolulu, 1973—; gov. Ter. of Hawaii, Honolulu, 1957-59, State of Hawaii, Honolulu, 1959-62; exec. v.p. Dole Co., Honolulu, 1964-65, pres., 1965-72. Mem. Honolulu Charter Commn., 1955-56, 71-72, Hawaii Statehood Commn., 1956-57. Mem. Bar Assn. Hawaii, Am. Bar Assn., Oahu Devel. Conf. (dir. 1965—), Nat. Municipal League (v.p. N.Y.C. 1975—). Home: 1365 Laukahi St Honolulu HI 96821 Office: 1600 Castle & Cooke Bldg Financial Plaza of Pacific Honolulu HI 96813 Tel (808) 531-5066

QUIRICO, FRANCIS JOSEPH, b. Pittsfield, Mass., Feb. 18, 1911; LL.B., Northeastern U., Boston, 1932. Admitted to Mass. bar, 1932, U.S. Supreme Ct. bar, 1939; individual practice law, Pittsfield, 1932-56; justice Mass. Superior Ct., 1956-69, Mass. Supreme Ct., Boston, 1969—; city solicitor Pittsfield, 1948-52. Mem. Am., Mass., Berkshire County bar assns., Am. Law Inst., Inst. Jud. Adminstrn. Home: 1282 East St Pittsfield MA 01201 Office: 1300 Pemberton Sq Court House Boston MA 02108 Tel (617) 523-7050

QUISLING, KRISTINE MCCONACHIE, b. Oak Park, Ill., Dec. 18, 1946; B.S., U. Ill., 1968, J.D., 1971. Admitted to Ill. bar, 1971, Mich. bar 1972; asst. prosecutor Calhoun County, Marshall, Mich., 1972-74, chief asst. prosecutor, 1974-75; asst. prof. Western Mich. U., Kalamazoo, 1976. Mem. Ill., Mich. bar assns. Home and office: 7632 Ravenswood Dr Portage MI 49081 Tel (616) 327-3861

QUIST, WILLIAM WOODBURY, b. Salt Lake City, Dec. 28, 1933; A.A., Snow Coll., 1957; B.S., Utah State U., 1962; J.D., Seton Hall U., 1974. Resident structural engr., nuclear power plant, Pub. Service Electric & Gas Co., Newark, 1970-71; constrn. engr. N.J. Bell Telephone Co., Newark, 1971-75; admitted to N.J. bar, 1974; individual practice law, W. Caldwell, N.J., 1974-75; contract adminstr., Saudi Arabia, George A. Fuller Co., N.Y.C., 1976-79. Trustee, Dhahran (Saudi Arabia) Acad., 1976-78. Mem. Am., N.J., bar assns., Nat. Trial Lawyers Assn. Office: George A Fuller Co Box 95 APO New York NY 09616

RAAB, IRA J., b. N.Y.C., June 20, 1935; B.B.A., Coll. City N.Y., 1955; J.D. Bklyn. Law Sch., 1958; M.P.A., N.Y. U., 1960; M.S. in Pub. Adminstrn., L.I. U., 1961. Admitted to N.Y. State bar, 1958, U.S. Supreme Ct. bar, 1966; counsel Soc. for Prevention of Cruelty to Children, Westchester County, N.Y., 1958, N.Y.C. Dept. Correction, 1959-63; staff counsel SBA, N.Y. Regional Office, 1961-63; asst. corp. counsel, law dept. City N.Y., 1963-70; individual practice law, Lynbrook, N.Y., 1958—; gen. counsel Richmond County Soc. for Prevention of Cruelty to Children, 1970—; counsel N.Y.C. Parking and Traffic Control Agts., 1972—; judge small claims div. Civil Ct. N.Y.C., 1970—. Mem. Am. Judges Assn. (gov. N.Y., Conn. 1974—, nat. treas.), Assn. Arbitrators (past pres. 1974), Nassau County Lawyers Assn. Recipient FTC award of merit, 1974, 76. Home: 1000 Peninsula Blvd Woodmere NY 11598 Office: 8 Freer St Lynbrook NY 11563 Tel (516) 887-7400

RAAB, SHELDON, b. Bklyn., Nov. 30, 1937; A.B., Columbia, 1958; LL.B., Harvard, 1961. Admitted to N.Y. bar, 1961; dep. asst. atty. gen. State of N.Y., 1961-63, asst. atty. gen., 1963-64; asso. firm Fried, Frank, Harris, Shriver & Jacobson and predecessor firms, N.Y.C., 1964-69, partner, 1970—. Mem. N.Y. State Bar Assn., Assn. Bar City N.Y. (chmn. spl. com. on energy 1975—), Fed. Bar Council. Home: 102 Edgewood Ave Larchmont NY 10538 Office: 120 Broadway New York City NY 10005 Tel (212) 964-6500

RABALAIS, RAPHAEL JOSEPH, JR., b. New Orleans, Sept. 23, 1947; A.B. (McConnell Found. fellow), Princeton, 1968; J.D., Harvard, 1971; M.A., Mich. State U., 1974. Admitted to Mich. bar, 1972; dir. ops. Mich. State Housing Devel. Authority, Lansing, 1971-74; asst. prof. Sch. Law Loyola U., New Orleans, 1974—, faculty rep. Standing Council Academic Planning, 1975—. Mem. La. Bar Assn. (faculty rep.), Am. Assn. Law Schs. Office: Box 17 Loyola U Sch Law New Orleans LA 70118 Tel (504) 865-2278

RABB, HARRIET S., b. Houston, Sept. 12, 1941; B.A., Barnard Coll., 1963; J.D., Columbia, 1966. Admitted to N.Y. State bar, 1966, D.C. bar, 1970; asst. dean for Urban Affairs, co-dir. Employment Rights Project Columbia Law Sch., N.Y.C. Mem. N.Y. Civil Liberties Union (dir.). Author: (with Cooper, Rubin) Employment Litigation, 1976. Office: 435 W 116th St New York City NY 10027 Tel (212) 280-4292

RABB, MAXWELL M., b. Boston, Sept. 28, 1910; B.A., Harvard U., 1932, J.D., 1935; LL.D., Wilberforce Coll., 1957. Admitted to Mass. bar, 1935, N.Y. bar, 1959, U.S. Supreme Ct. bar, 1938; partner firm Rabb & Rabb, Boston, 1935-37, 46-51; adminstrv. asst. to U.S. Senator H. C. Lodge of Mass., 1937-43; legal, legis. cons. to Sec. Navy Forestal, 1946; cons. U.S. Senate Rules Com., 1952; Presdl. asst. and sec. to Cabinet, 1953-58; partner firm Stroock & Stroock & Lavan, N.Y.C., 1958—; chmn. U.S. del. to UNESCO conf., Paris, 1958; mem. Presdl. adv. panel on S. Asian Relief Assistance, 1971; mem. conciliation panel World Bank's Internat. Centre for Settlement of Investment Disputes, 1967-74, U.S. rep., 1974; mem. Coalition for Adequate Jud. Compensation, 1977; bd. dirs. legal def. league NAACP. Brandeis U. fellow. Mem. Am. Bar Assn., Am. Law Inst., Assn. Bar City N.Y., N.Y. County Lawyers Assn. Home: 145 Central Park W New York City NY 10023 Office: 61 Broadway New York City NY 10006

RABE, EDWARD ROBERT, JR., b. Chgo., Feb. 10, 1948; B.A., N. Park Coll., Chgo., 1970; J.D., Ill. Inst. Tech., Chgo.-Kent Coll. Law, 1973. Admitted to Ill. bar, also U.S. Dist. Ct. for No. Dist. Ill. bar, 1974; legal advisor, loan div. Continental Ill. Nat. Bank Trust Co., Chgo., 1974—. Mem. Am., Ill., Chgo. bar assns., Delta Theta Phi. Office: Continental Illinois National Bank 231 S La Salle St Chicago IL 60693 Tel (312) 828-4076

RABINOVITZ, BERNARD I., b. Boston, Oct. 6, 1937; B.A. with distinction, U. Ariz., 1959, LL.B., 1962. Admitted to Ariz. bar, 1962, U.S. Dist. ct. bar for Dist. Ariz., 1963, U.S. Supreme Ct. bar, 1972; practiced in Tucson, 1962-65; referee Indsl. Commn. of Ariz., 1965-69; partner firm Rabinovitz, Minker & Dix, P.C., Tucson, 1969—; spl. magistrate City of Tucson, 1969-70. Pres. Tucson Downtown Active 20-30 Club, 1972-73. Mem. Am., Pima County (Ariz.) (chmn. speakers bur.) bar assns., State Bar Ariz., Am. Trial Lawyers Assn., Phi Kappa Phi. Named Man of Year, Ariz.-Nev. Active 20-30, 1973. Home: 6911 E Rosewood St Tucson AZ 85710 Office: 808 Transamerica Bldg Tucson AZ 85701 Tel (602) 624-5526

RABKIN, SOL, b. N.Y.C., Apr. 17, 1911; B.A., Coll. City N.Y., 1934; J.D., Columbia, 1934. Admitted to N.Y. bar, 1934; atty. U.S. Dept. Labor, Washington, 1935; analyst U.S. Senate Civil Liberties Com., 1937-41; atty. immigration service U.S. Dept. Justice, Washington and N.Y.C., 1941-45, U.S. Price Control Adminstrn., Washington, 1945-47; counsel B'nai B'rith Anti-defamation League, Bklyn., 1947-71, law sec. appellate div., 1971—; gen. counsel Nat. Commn. on Aging Discrimination in Housing, 1967-70; lectr. Practicing Law Inst., 1968-72. Bd. dirs. Flatbush Rugby YMHA, Bklyn., 1968—. Mem. Am., N.Y. State bar assns., N.Y. County Lawyers Assn. Contbr. articles to legal jours. Tel (212) 522-7466

RACHANOW, GERALD MARVIN, b. Balt., Aug. 7. 1942; B.S. in Pharmacy, U. Md., 1965; J.D., U. Balt., 1972. Admitted to Md. bar, 1973; consumer safety officer FDA, 1973—; partner firm Rachanow & Wolfson, Randallstown, Md., 1975—. Mem. Balt. County Gen. Hosp. Found., Inc., 1970—. Mem. Am., Md. bar assns., Am. Soc. Pharmacy Law. Recipient Commendable Service award FDA, 1976. Home: 8817 Allenswood Rd Randallstown MD 21133 Office: 5600 Fishers Ln Rockville MD 20857 Tel (301) 443-3500

RACICOT, MARC FRANCIS, b. Thompson Falls, Mont., July 24, 1948; B.A. in English Carroll Coll., 1970; J.D., U. Mont., 1973. Admitted to Mont. bar, 1973; trial lawyer U.S. Army, Germany, 1973-76; deputy county atty. Missoula County, Missoula, Mont., 1976—. Mem. Mont. Bar Assn. Home: 2942 Juneau Dr Missoula MT 59801 Office: Office of the Atty Missoula County MT 59801 Tel (406) 543-3111

RACKMAN, MICHAEL IRWIN, b. N.Y.C., Nov. 5, 1937; B.A., Columbia, 1958, B.S., 1959, M.S., 1960; LL.B., N.Y. U., 1964. Admitted to N.Y. bar, 1965, U.S. Supreme Ct. bar, 1972; patent atty. Bell Labs., Inc., N.Y.C., 1960-65; partner firm Amster & Rothstein, N.Y.C., 1965-70, firm Gottlieb, Rackman & Reisman, N.Y.C., 1970—. Mem. N.Y., Am. patent law assns., IEEE, Phi Beta Kappa, Tau Beta Phi, Eta Kappa Nu, Order of Coif. Contbr. articles to legal jours. Home: 1710 Glenwood Rd Brooklyn NY 11320 Office: 260 Madison Ave New York City NY 10016

RACKOW, JULIAN PAUL, b. Phila., Dec. 16, 1941; A.B., Cornell U., 1963; LL.B., Harvard, 1966. Admitted to Phila. bar, 1966; asso. firm Goodis, Greenfield, Narin & Mann, Phila., 1966-69; partner firm Blank, Rome, Klaus and Comisky, Phila., 1970—. Mem. Phila., Pa. bar assns. Office: 11th floor 4 Penn Center Philadelphia PA 19103 Tel (215) LO-9-3700

RADCLIFF, WILLIAM DUDLEY, b. Columbus, Ohio, July 5, 1908; A.B., Ohio Wesleyan U., 1930; LL.B. cum laude, Ohio No. U., 1933, J.D., 1967. Admitted to Ohio bar, 1933; individual practice law, Circleville, Ohio, 1933-42; judge Common Pleas Ct., Pickaway County, Ohio, 1947-57, 4th Dist. Ct. Appeals Ohio, Circleville, 1957-63; adminstrv. dir. Supreme Ct. Ohio, Columbus, 1963—; mayor Village of Williamsport, Ohio, 1936-39; mem. Ohio Ho. of Reps., 1939-42; chmn. Nat. Conf. State Ct. Adminstrs., 1969. Fellow Ohio State Bar Found.; mem. Am., Ohio State (exec. com. 1964-67) bar assns., Am. Judicature Soc., Inst. Jud. Adminstrn. Common Pleas Judges Assn. (former chmn.). Home: 630 Ridgewood Dr Circleville OH 43113 Office: 30 E Broad St Columbus OH 43215 Tel (614) 466-2653

RADCLIFFE, GEORGE MARRIOTT, b. Balt., June 9, 1919; B.S., Princeton, 1943; LL.B., U. Md., 1949. Admitted to Md. bar, 1948, U.S. Supreme Ct. bar, 1960; mem. firm Niles, Barton & Wilmer, Balt., 1948—; faculty U. Balt. Law Sch. 1965-66. Chmn., Zoning Commission Balt. 1957-71; bd. dirs. Washington Coll., Chestertown, Md., 1976, Md. chpt. Nature Conservancy, 1976; pres. Spocott Windmill Found., 1971—; v.p. Md. Hist. Soc., 1976, pres. Grace Found., Taylor's Island, 1976, Eastern Shore Soc. Balt., 1973, Churchman's Club, Diocese of Md., 1962-64. Mem. Am., Md. State, Balt. City, Dorchester County bar assns., Internat. Assn. Ins. Counsel. Home: 312 Harper House Village of Cross Keys Baltimore MD 21210 Office: 929 N Howard St Baltimore MD 21201 Tel (301) 539-3240

RADCLIFFE, GERALD EUGENE, b. Chillicothe, Ohio, Feb. 19, 1923; B.A., Ohio U., 1948; J.D., U. Cin., 1950. Admitted to Ohio bar, 1950, U.S. Supreme Ct. bar, 1957; practiced in Chillicothe, 1950-73; judge probate and juvenile divs. Ross County (Ohio) Common Pleas Ct., 1973—; law planning officer So. Ohio Council Govts., 1969-70; asst. pros. atty. Ross County, 1966-70. Mem. Chillicothe Bd. Edn., 1968-73, pres., 1970-71; mem. Pickaway-Ross Joint Vocat. Sch. Bd. Edn., 1970-73; co-chmn. Ross County United Fund Campaign, 1972; trustee Ohio Sch. Bds. Assn.; chmn. Ross County Bldg. Commn.; mem. Chillicothe Positive Action Com.; project dir. South Central Regional Juvenile Detention Center, Ross County. Mem. Am. Judicature Soc., Nat. Dist. Attys. Assn., Am., Ohio bar assns. Recipient Outstanding Citizen of Year award Chillicothe Jr. C. of C., 1972, Outstanding Grad. award in community service Key Club of Chillicothe High Sch., 1972. Home: 5 Edgewood Ct Chillicothe OH 45601 Office: Common Pleas Ct Probate and Juvenile Divs Ross County Courthouse Chillicothe OH 45601 Tel (614) 774-1177

RADDING, RONALD STEWART, b. N.Y.C., Jan. 22, 1944; B.A. in Econs., Rutgers U., 1965; J.D., Seton Hall U., 1968. Admitted to N.J. bar, 1968; atty. legal services OEO, Newark, 1971, Perth Amboy, N.J., 1971-73, chief atty., 1972-73; asso. firm Gavin & Gavin, Union, N.J., 1973-74; atty. Patric House Legal Clinic, Jersey City, 1974—; partner firm Summerville, Radding & Campbell, Jersey City, 1976—; adj. prof. law Seton Hall U., Newark, 1975—, St. Peter's Coll., Jersey City, 1977—. Mem. N.J., Hudson County bar assns. Home: 542 Victor St Scotch Plains NJ 07076 Office: 82 Grand St Jersey City NJ 07303 Tel (201) 435-4891

RADEMAKER, WILLIAM, JR., b. Crosby, Minn., Aug. 19, 1942; B.A. in Econs., U. Wash., 1964; postgrad. Willamette U. Coll. Law, 1967-69. Asst. to Wash. State Securities Commr., Olympia, 1969-73; law clk. to Securities Adminstr., State of Wash., 1973; admitted to Wash. bar, 1973; enforcement atty. SEC, Seattle, 1973-77; in house counsel to William E. Boeing, Jr., Seattle, 1977—. Mem. Am., Wash. State, King County (Wash.) bar assns. Home: 1960 Shenandoah Dr E Seattle WA 98112 Office: 1411 4th Ave Bldg Suite 1120 Seattle WA 98101 Tel (206) 682-7760

RADENSKY, JOSEPH HAROLD, b. Los Angeles, Apr. 18, 1931; B.A. in Econs., U. Calif., Berkeley, 1953; J.D., U. Calif. Hastings Coll. Law, San Francisco, 1957. Admitted to Calif. bar, 1957, U.S. Supreme Ct. bar, 1965; clk. Melvin Belli, San Francisco, 1957, George E. Kennedy, Lynwood, Calif., 1958-59; individual practice law, Anaheim, Calif., 1959-75; partner firm Radensky & Radensky, Anaheim, 1975-76, firm Radensky, Bergstrom & Radensky, Anaheim, 1976—, adj. prof. law Western State U., 1970—; judge pro tem Orange County (Calif.) Municipal Ct., 1966—. Mem. State Bar Calif. Note and comment editor Hastings Law Jour., 1956-57; contbr. articles to legal jours. Office: 1695 Crescent Ave Suite 606 Anaheim CA 92801 Tel (714) 776-5950

RADO, PETER THOMAS, b. Berlin, Nov. 12, 1928; A.B., Harvard U., 1949, J.D., 1952, LL.M., 1953. Admitted to N.Y. bar, 1952, U.S. Supreme Ct. bar, 1971; asso. firm Ide & Haigney, N.Y.C., 1955-61, partner, 1961—. Mem. Am., N.Y. State bar assns., Assn. Bar City N.Y. Home: 25 E 86th St New York City NY 10028 Office: 41 E 42d St New York City NY 10017 Tel (212) 682-2590

RADONICH, JOHN N., b. Anaconda, Mont., Dec. 3, 1932; B.S. in Bus. Adminstrn., U. Mont., 1960, S.J.D., 1962. Admitted to Mont. bar, 1962; partner firm Boyd & Radonich, Anaconda, 1962-73, Radonich & Brolin, 1975—. Mem. Am., Mont. bar assns. Home: 905 W 3d St Anaconda MT 59711 Office: 108 E Park Ave Anaconda MT 59711 Tel (406) 563-3438

RADSCH, RICHARD THACKERAY, b. N.Y.C., Nov. 16, 1939; B.A., Yale U., 1962; J.D. cum laude, Boston U., 1972. Admitted to Mass. bar, 1972; asst. counsel John Hancock Mut. Life Ins. Co., Boston, 1972—. Mem. Am., Mass., Boston (vol. lawyers project 1977) bar assns. Recipient Am. Jurisprudence award, 1972; C.P.C.U.; C.L.U.; contbr. article to law jour. Home: 59 Dodges Row Wenham MA 01984 Office: PO Box 111 Boston MA 02117 Tel (617) 421-5097

RADZINOWICZ, LEON, b. Lodz, Poland, Aug. 15, 1906; M.A., U. Geneva, 1927; LL.D., U. Rome, 1928, U. Cracow (Poland), 1929, U. Leicester (Eng.), 1965; M.A., Cambridge (Eng.) U., 1949, LL.D., 1951. Wolfson prof. criminology U. Cambridge, 1959-73, dir. Inst. Criminology, 1960-72, fellow and vis. prof. Trinity Coll., 1948—; Walter E. Meyer research prof. law Yale, 1962-63; adj. prof. criminal law and criminology Columbia, 1966—; vis. prof. Va. Law Sch., 1968—, Rutgers U., 1970—; vis. prof. dept. sociology U. Pa., 1970—; head social def. sect. UN, N.Y.C., 1947-48; mem. Royal Commn. on Capital Punishment, 1949-53; chmn. Criminol. com. Council Europe, Strasbourg, France, 1963-70; cons. U.S. Pres's. Nat. Commn. on Violence, 1968-69. Hon. fgn. mem. Am. Acad. Arts and Scis., Australian Acad. Forensic Scis.; created knight, 1970; decorated chevalier Order of Leopold (Belgium); recipient James Barr Ames prize and medal Harvard Law Sch., 1950, Coronation medal Queen Elizabeth II, 1953, Bruce Smith Sr. award U.S. Acad. Justice Scis., 1976; Sellin Glueck award Am. Soc. Criminology, 1976; Trinity Coll.

fellow, 1948—; Yale Silliman Coll. hon. fellow, 1966—; Brit. Acad. fellow, 1973; author: History of English Criminal Law, 4 vols., 1948, 56, 68; In Search of Criminology, 1961; Ideology and Crime, 1966; editor: (with Marvin Wolfgang) Crime and Justice, 3 vols., 1971; Cambride Studies in Criminology, 33 vols., 1940. Home: Stanhope Hotel 5th Ave and 81st St New York City NY 10028 Office: Trinity Coll Cambridge England

RAE, MATTHEW SANDERSON, JR., b. Pitts., Sept. 12, 1922; A.B., Duke, 1946, LL.B., 1947. Admitted to Md. bar, 1948, Calif. bar, 1951, U.S. Supreme Ct. bar, 1967; asst. to dean Duke Sch. Law, 1947-48; asso. firm Karl F. Steinmann, Balt., 1948-49; nat. field rep. Phi Alpha Delta, Los Angeles, 1949-51; research atty. Calif. Supreme Ct., San Francisco, 1951-52; asso. firm Darling, Hall, Rae & Gute and predecessors, Los Angeles, 1953-55, partner, 1956—. Mem. Los Angeles County Republican Central Com., 1959-64, 77—; mem. Calif. Rep. Central Com., 1966—; pres. Town Hall of Calif., Los Angeles, 1975. Fellow Am. Coll. Probate Counsel; mem. Am., Los Angeles County (chmn. com. probate and trust law 1964-66), South Bay bar assns., State Bar Calif. (chmn. com. probate and trust law 1974-75), Lawyers Club of Los Angeles, Internat. Acad. Estate, Trust Law (exec. council 1974—), Legion Lex (pres. 1969-71), Phi Beta Kappa, Phi Alpha Delta (supreme justice 1972-74), Omicron Delta Kappa. Home: 600 John St Manhattan Beach CA 90266 Office: 523 W 6th St Suite 400 Los Angeles CA 90014 Tel (213) 627-8104

RAFEEDIE, EDWARD, b. Orange, N.J., Jan. 6, 1929; student Los Angeles City Coll., 1946-47, Santa Monica City Coll., 1953-54; B.S.L., U. So. Calif., 1957, J.D., 1959. Admitted to Calif. bar, 1960; legal asst. Calif. Div. Hwys., 1958-59; individual practice law, Santa Monica, 1960-69; judge Santa Monica Mcpl. Ct., 1969-71; judge Superior Ct., Van Nuys br., 1971-72, Central Dist., Los Angeles Superior Ct., 1973—; West Dist., Santa Monica, 1974—. mem. Dist. Atty.'s Adv. Council, 1968-69. Chmn., Community Service Com., 1973-74; coach Pacific Palisades YMCA Basketball, 1970-74; chmn. atty.'s div. Salvation Army, 1964, Community Chest, 1966; mem. exec. bd. Gt. Western council Boy Scouts Am., v.p., 1974-77, also chmn. Scout-O-Rama; pres., team mgr. Malibu Little League, 1973-76; chmn. Malibu Citizens Park Com., 1974-76; bd. dirs. Malibu-La Costa Property Owners Assn., Santa Monica West-Side Vols. Bur.; active Santa Monica Vets. Service League, Santa Monica YMCA, Pacific Palisades-Malibu YMCA. Mem. Calif. (del.), Santa Monica Bay Dist. (trustee 1961-69, pres. 1968), Los Angeles County bar assns., U. So. Calif. Law Alumni and Gen. Alumni assns., Legion Lex of U. So. Calif. (dir. 1975-76), Delta Theta Phi. Office: 1725 Main St Santa Monica CA 90401 Tel (213) 870-0131

RAFF, CALVIN, b. Port Washington, N.Y., Sept. 6, 1917; student St. John's U., 1939, LL.B., 1941. Admitted to N.Y. State bar, 1942, U.S. Supreme Ct. bar, 1954; mng. atty. Newmany Bisco, N.Y.C., 1942-46; mem. firm Raff & Raff, Flushing, N.Y., 1946-52, Raff & Leppel, Flushing, 1953—; govt. appeals agt. Selective Service, 1957-72; adj. prof. ins. law L.I. U. Pres. Temple Gates of Prayer, 1970-73. Mem. Queens County, N.Y. State bar assns. Home: 22-18 172 St Flushing NY 11358 Office: 135-39 Northern Blvd Flushing NY 11354 Tel (212) 359-1844

RAFF, WILLIAM FRANK, b. Goeppingen, Germany, Aug. 19, 1934; A.B. in Econs., Stanford, 1956, J.D., 1958. Admitted to Calif. bar, 1959, Hawaii bar, 1959; individual practice law, Honolulu, 1958-61, Los Angeles, 1965-71; asst. gen. counsel Equity Funding Corp. Am., Los Angeles, 1971-73; chief counsel Equity Funding Life Ins. Co., Los Angeles, 1973-76; spl. asst. to Chpt. XI receiver of THC Fin. Corp. Honolulu, 1977—. Mem. Am., Los Angeles County bar assns. Home and Office: 2134 Ridgemont Dr Los Angeles CA 90046 Tel (213) 650-1364

RAFFAELLI, JOHN DOMINICAN, b. Texarkana, Tex., Apr. 3, 1911; B.A., St. Edward's U., 1932; LL.B., U. Tex., 1936. Admitted to Tex. bar, 1936, U.S. Supreme Ct. bar, 1973; served as major, Judge Advocate Corps, U.S. Army, 1942-46; individual practice law, Texarkana, 1936—. Chmn. City Charter Com., Texarkana, 1947. Mem. Tex., Am., N.E. Tex. bar assns., Am. Judicature Soc., Tex. Trial Lawyers Assn. Home: 4101 Columbia St Texarkana TX 75503 Office: 312 W 4th St Texarkana TX 75501 Tel (214) 792-3755

RAFTERY, MICHAEL ROGER, b. Wilmar, Calif., Oct. 28, 1935; B.A., Stanford, 1957; J.D., 1962. Admitted to Calif. bar, 1963; partner firm Thompson & Colegate, Riverside, Calif., 1963-69, firm Michael R. Raftery, Riverside, 1969-75, firm Swarner & Fitzgerald, Riverside, 1975—; mem. adv. council Calif. State Atty. Gen., 1967—. Mem. State Bar of Calif. (past pres. Conf. of Barristers), Riverside County Barristers (past pres.), Am., Riverside County bar assns., Assn. Trial Lawyers Am., Calif. Trial Lawyers Assn., So. Calif. Def. Counsel. Office: 4275 Lemon St PO Box 827 Riverside CA 92502 Tel (714) 683-4242

RAGAN, GERALD EDWARD, b. Chgo., Jan. 8, 1928; B.S. in Civil Engring., Ill. Inst. Tech., 1950; J.D., Loyola U., Chgo., 1959. Admitted to Calif. bar, 1960, U.S. Supreme Ct. bar, 1960; dep. dist. atty. San Mateo County (Calif.) Dist. Atty's Office, 1961-64; partner firm Ragan & McGuire, San Mateo, Calif., 1964-71; judge Superior Ct., 1971—. Trustee Belmont (Calif.) Sch. Dist., 1965-67; candidate for State senator, 1970. Mem. Am. Bar Assn., Am., Calif., San Mateo County (pres. 1969-71) trial lawyers assns., Conf. Calif. Judges, Tau Beta Pi, Chi Epsilon. Office: Hall of Justice Redwood City CA 94063 Tel (415) 364-5600

RAGAR, THURMAN ARTHUR, b. Pine Bluff, Ark., Sept. 2, 1941; B.A., Southwestern Coll., 1964; J.D., U. Ark., 1970. Admitted to Ark. bar, 1970, U.S. Supreme Ct. bar, 1974; clk. Mo. Supreme Ct., 1970-71. Mem. Ark., Am. bar assns., Ark. Trial Lawyers Assn. Home: 252 Linden Heights Pine Bluff AR 71603 Office: 625 State St Pine Bluff AR 71601 Tel (501) 536-2555

RAGATZ, THOMAS GEORGE, b. Madison, Wis., Feb. 18, 1934; B.B.A., U. Wis., 1957, LL.B., 1961. Admitted to Wis. bar, 1961, U.S. Tax Ct. bar, 1963, U.S. Supreme Ct. bar, 1968; with Peat, Marwick, Mitchel & Co., C.P.A.'s, Mpls., 1958; instr. accounting Sch. Bus. U. Wis., 1958-60; law clk. to justice Wis. Supreme Ct., 1961-62; asso. firm Boardman, Suhr, Curry & Field, Madison, 1962-65, partner, 1965—; lectr. accounting and law Law Sch. U. Wis.; sec. State Bar Wis., 1969-70, mem. bd. govs., 1971-75, chmn. fin. com., 1975—, chmn. tax. sect.; chmn. Nat. Conf. Law Revs.; 1960-61. Bd. dirs. United Way, chmn. mgmt. study com.; chmn. Gov's. Med. Center Site Selection Com.; bd. dirs. Methodist Hosp. Found.; moderator First Congregational Ch. Mem. Wis., Dane County (sec., chmn. jud. qualification com.), Seventh Circuit, Am. bar assns., Am. Judicature Soc., Wis. Inst. C.P.A.'s, Am. Arbitration Assn., Order of Coif, Beta Gamma Sigma. Contbr. articles to legal jours.; editor-in-chief Wis. Law Rev., 1960-61. Home: 1012 Waban Hill Madison WI 53711 Office: 131 W Wilson St Madison WI 53703 Tel (608) 257-9521

RAGEN, RONALD KENT, b. Portland, Oreg., May 8, 1935; B.A., Yale, 1957; LL.B., Stanford, 1961. Admitted to Oreg. bar, 1961; asso. firm Black, Kendall, Tremaine, Boothe & Higgins, Portland, 1961-65; partner firm Rankin, Ragen, Roberts, Samson & Gallagher, Portland, 1965-76, firm Ragen & Roberts, Portland, 1976—. Mem. Oreg. Gov.'s Williamette River Greenway Com., 1969-75; Lower Willamette River Plan Rev. Com., 1975; City/County Arts Commn., 1973—. Mem. Oreg., Am., Multnomah County bar assns. Office: 3317 1st Nat Bank Tower Portland OR 97201 Tel (503) 226-3317

RAGGHIANTI, GARY THOMAS, b. San Francisco, Feb. 10, 1944; A.B., U. San Francisco, 1965, J.D., 1968. Admitted to Calif. bar, 1969, U.S. Supreme Ct. bar, 1975; dep. dist. atty. Marin County, San Rafael, Calif., 1969-71; individual practice law, San Rafael, 1971—; instr. criminal law Coll. of Marin, 1972-75. Mem. Calif., No. Calif. criminal trial lawyers assns., Marin County Bar Assn. (past dir.). Office: 1534 5th Ave San Rafael CA 94901 Tel (415) 453-9433

RAGGIO, GRIER HENRY, JR., b. Austin, Tex., Aug. 6, 1942; A.B., Harvard, 1964; J.D., Boston Coll., 1968. Admitted to Tex. bar, 1968, N.Y. State bar, 1969; adminstrv. staff City of N.Y., 1968-70; staff atty. Mobilization for Youth Legal Services, N.Y.C., 1970-71; mem. firm Norwick, Raggio & Jaffe, N.Y.C., 1971-75, Norwick, Raggio, Jaffe & Kayser, N.Y.C., 1975—. Mem. Assn. Bar City N.Y., Am., Tex., Dallas bar assns., N.Y. County Lawyers Assn. Home: 211 E 18th St New York City NY 10003 Office: 2 Pennsylvania Plaza New York City NY 10001 Tel (212) 868-7330

RAHL, JAMES ANDREW, b. Wooster, Ohio, Oct. 8, 1917; B.S., Northwestern U., 1939, J.D., 1942. Admitted to Ohio bar, 1942, Ill. bar, 1950, U.S. Supreme Ct. bar, 1962; atty. OPA, 1942-43; mem. faculty Northwestern U. Law Sch., 1946—, prof. law, 1953—, Owen L. Coon prof., 1974—, dir. research, 1966-72, dean, 1972-77; vis. prof. U. Mich. Law Sch., 1970; of counsel firm Chadwell, Kayser, Ruggles, McGee & Hastings, Chgo., 1952—, resident partner, Brussels, 1963-64; mem. faculty Salzburg Seminar Am. Studies, 1967, 72; mem. White House Task Force Antitrust Policy, 1967-68, UNCTAD Group Experts on Internat. Restrictive Trade Practices, 1973. Mem. Am. (council anti-trust sect. 1965-67), Ill., Chgo. bar assns., Chgo. Council Lawyers, Am. Law Inst., Am. Soc. Internat. Law, AAUP, Law Club Chgo. Author: (with others) Cases on Torts, 1957, 3d edit., 1977, Cases on Injuries to Relations, 1957, 3d edit., 1977; (with Schwerin) Northwestern University School of Law, A Short History, 1960; Common Market and American Antitrust, 1970; contbr. articles to legal jours. Home: 2426 Marcy Ave Evanston IL 60201 Office: 357 E Chicago Ave Chicago IL 60611 Tel (312) 649-8460

RAHM, ELINOR GAYLE, b. Warrensburg, Mo., Oct. 26, 1948; B.S. in Edn., Central Mo. State U., 1969; J.D., U. Mo., Kansas City, 1974. Admitted to Mo. bar, 1974; tchr. North Kansas City (Mo.) Pub. Schs., 1969-72; asst. prof. Central Mo. State U., Warrensburg, 1974—; partner firm Rahm, Rahm and Rahm, Warrensburg, 1976—. Mem. Mo. Bar Assn., Kappa Delta Pi. Home: Rt 4 Warrensburg MO 64093 Office: 122A Hout St Warrensburg MO 64093 Tel (816) 747-5152

RAHMAS, D. STEVE, b. Washington, Apr. 27, 1944; A.B., Columbia U., 1965, J.D., 1968. Admitted to N.Y. State bar, 1968, U.S. Supreme Ct. bar, 1976; individual practice law, Stamford, N.Y., 1968—; pres. Story House Corp., Charlotteville, N.Y., 1972-76, v.p., 1963-72. Mem. Am., N.Y. State, Delaware County, Schoharie County bar assns., Stamford, Delaware County chambers commerce. Home: Charlotteville NY 10236 Office: 7 Prospect St Stamford NY 12167 Tel (607) 652-7662

RAICHLE, FRANK G., b. Mpls., Aug. 28, 1898; LL.B., U. Buffalo, 1919; D.H.L., Canisius Coll., 1969. Admitted to N.Y. bar, 1920; counsel to com. investigating city affairs Buffalo City Council, 1937; spl. asst. to dist. atty. Erie County (N.Y.), 1938-39; lectr. U. Buffalo Law Sch., 1925-30; guest lectr. Cornell U. Law Sch.; lectr. Practicing Law Inst. Mem. Pub. Employee Relations Bd. Erie County, 1968-72; mem. N.Y. Gov.'s Com. on Compensating Victims of Automobile Accidents, 1968; regent Canisius Coll., 1966-75, regent emeritus, 1975—; bd. dirs. Erie County Soc. Prevention Cruelty to Animals. Fellow Am. Coll. Trial Lawyers (regent, past pres.), Internat. Acad. Trial Lawyers, Am., N.Y. State bar founds.; mem. Am. (com. anti-trust litigation), N.Y. State (com. fed. cts. 1969), past mem. com. criminal law, mem. numerous panels), Erie County bar assns., Assn. Bar City N.Y., Am. Law Inst., Am. Judicature Soc., U.S. Jud. Conf. (adv. com. on uniform rules of evidence for fed. cts.). Home: 88 Middlesex Rd Buffalo NY 14216 Office: 10 Lafayette Sq Buffalo NY 14203 Tel (716) 852-7587

RAILEY, CHARLOTTE LOUISE, b. Chgo., Sept. 9, 1930; B.A., Augustana Coll., Rock Island, Ill., 1952; LL.B., Columbia, 1955. Admitted to N.Y. bar, 1956, Tenn. bar, 1957, Ala. bar, 1958; asst. to prof. Columbia Law Sch., 1956; asso. firm Martin, Guenther & Tucker, Memphis, 1957, Bradley, Arant, Rose & White, Birmingham, Ala., 1958—; atty. St. Anne's Home, Inc., 1964-69. Active Birmingham Women's chpt. Freedom Found. at Valley Forge, 1974, adv. council, 1977. Mem. Am., Ala., Birmingham bar assns., Estate Planning Council of Birmingham (treas. 1975, sec. 1976, v.p. in charge programs 1977), Mortar Bd. Author: (with others) How to Administer Estates in Alabama, 1968. Office: 1500 Brown-Marx Bldg Birmingham AL 35203 Tel (205) 252-4500

RAILTON, W(ILLIAM) SCOTT, b. Newark, July 30, 1935; B.S.E.E., U. Wash., 1962; J.D., George Washington U., 1965. Admitted to Md. bar, 1966, D.C. bar, 1966; asso. firm Kemon, Palmer & Estabrook, Washington, 1966-68, partner, 1968-70; sr. trial atty. Dep. Labor, Washington, 1970-71, asst. counsel for litigation occupational safety and health, 1971-72; chief counsel U.S. Occupational Safety and Health Rev. Commn., Washington, 1972—, acting gen. counsel, 1975-76; lectr. Am. law George Washington U., 1977; law faculty Practising Law Inst., 1976—, Nat. Inst. for Occupational Safety and Health, 1977—. Regional chmn. Montgomery County (Md.) Republican Party, 1968-70; vestryman St. James Episcopal Ch., Potomac, Md., 1969-71; pres. Montgomery Square Citizens Assn., Potomac, 1970-71. Mem. Am., Md. State bar assns., Bar Assn. D.C. (vice chmn. sect. young lawyers 1971), Order of Coif. Recipient Meritorious Achievement award Dept. Labor, 1972, Occupational Service award Occupational Safety and Health Rev. Commn., 1977; author: The Examination System and the Backlog, 1965. Home: 8216 JEB Stuart Rd Potomac MD 20854 Office: 1825 K St NW Washington DC 20006 Tel (202) 634-7974

RAINES, JOHN WESLEY, b. Oceola, Ark., July 29, 1932; B.A., U. Central Ark., 1954; LL.B., U. Ark., 1968, J.D., 1969. Admitted to Ark. bar, 1968, U.S. Supreme Ct. bar, 1975; individual practice law, Little Rock. Mem. Pulaski County (Ark.) Bd. Edn., 1968—, pres., 1975—. Mem. Ark., Pulaski County bar assns. Office: PO Box 470 Little Rock AR 72201 Tel (501) 374-7436

RAINEY, JOHN DAVID, b. Freeport, Tex., Feb. 10, 1945; B.B.A., So. Meth. U., 1967, J.D., 1972. Admitted to Tex. bar, 1972; partner firm Howell, Johnson, Mizell, Taylor, Price & Corrigan, Dallas, 1973—. Bd. mgmt. Downtown YMCA, Dallas, 1973—. Mem. State Bar Tex., Dallas, Am. bar assns., Phi Alpha Delta. Home: 2522 Karla Sr Mesquite TX 75150 Office: 2700 Republic Bank Tower Dallas TX 75201 Tel (214) 748-7511

RAINS, JACK MORRIS, b. Waco, Nov. 23, 1937; B.B.A., Tex. A. and M. U., 1960; J.D., U. Houston, 1967. Spl. agt. Prudential Ins. Co. Am., Houston, 1962-67; admitted to Tex. bar, 1967, U.S. Supreme Ct. bar, 1972; asso. firm Childs, Fortenbach, Beck & Guyton, Houston, 1967-69; mng. partner Neuhaus & Taylor, Architects, Houston, 1969-71, dir., 1970—; exec. v.p., chief operating officer, sec. Diversified Design Disciplines, Houston, 1971—, also dir.; dir. 3D/Internat., N.Y.C., 1974—. Mem. Houston, Tex. State, Am. bar assns., AIA, Assn. Former Students Tex. A. and M. U. (dir. 1976—), U. Houston Law Rev. Found. (dir.), U. Houston Law Alumni Assn. (dir.), Am. Arab C. of C. (dir.). Home: 635 Knipp Rd Houston TX 77024 Office: 5051 Westheimer St Suite 1700 Houston TX 77056 Tel (713) 621-9400

RAINS, MERRITT NEAL, b. Burlington, Iowa, July 26, 1943; B.A. (hon.), U. Iowa, 1965; J.D., Northwestern U., 1968. Admitted to Ohio bar, 1968; law clk. firm Karpatkin, Ohrenstein & Karpatkin, N.Y.C., 1967; asso. firm Arter & Hadden, Cleve., 1968-76, partner, 1976—. Chmn. county govt. candidate screening com. Citizens League of Greater Cleve., 1976; trustee Cleve. Playhouse Club, 1976—. Mem. Ohio State, Am. bar assns., Bar Assn. Greater Cleve. (co-chmn. continuing legal edn. com. 1974-75, chmn. young lawyers sect., 1975-76, Meritorious Service award 1972), Ohio Defense Assn., Legal Aid Soc. of Cleve., Am. Arbitration Assn., Greater Cleve. Growth Assn., Phi Beta Kappa, Omicron Delta Kappa, Phi Delta Ph. Home: 13302 Cormere Rd Cleveland OH 44120 Office: 1144 Union Commerce Bldg Cleveland OH 44115 Tel (216) 696-1144

RAISKIN, DANIEL LEWIS, b. N.Y.C., Nov. 6, 1947; B.A., State U. of N.Y., 1968; J.D., Bklyn. Law Sch., 1971; LL.M., N.Y. U., 1972. Admitted to N.Y. bar, 1972, D.C. bar, 1975; asso. firm Briger & Assos., N.Y.C., 1972-76, partner, 1976—. Mem. Am., N.Y. bar assns. Office: 450 Park Ave New York City NY 10022 Tel (212) 371-0002

RAKOWSKY, RONALD JOHN, b. Cleve., Sept. 24, 1944; B.A., Denison U., 1966; J.D., Case Western Res. U., 1969. Admitted to Ohio bar, 1970, Fla. bar, 1971, U.S. Ct. Mil. Appeals bar, 1971, U.S. Supreme Ct. bar 1973; adminstrv. asst., instr. Law Medicine Center Case Western Res. U. Sch. Law, 1969-70; commd. capt. JAGC USAF, 1970, advanced through grades to maj., 1977; dep. staff judge adv. MacDill AFB, Fla., 1971-74; dir. mil. justice 13th Air Force, Clark AFB, Phillipines, 1974-75, Air Force Mil. Personnel Center, Randolph AFB, Tex., 1975—; instr. in bus. law U. Tampa, 1972-74. Mem. Ohio State Bar Assn. Home: 137 Thomas Edison Dr Schertz TX 78154 Tel (512) 659-1666

RALEY, FLOYD ROBERT, b. Mitchell, Ga., Feb. 10, 1935; A.B., U. Ga., 1958, LL.B., 1960. Admitted to Ga. bar, 1960; asso. firm Pierce, Ranitz & Lee, Savannah, Ga., 1960-67, Jesse W. Rush, 1962-65; partner firm Shi & Raley, 1965-73; hearing officer Ga. Dept. Agr., Macon, 1965—. Mem. Ga., Macon bar assns., Ga. Assn. Criminal Def. Lawyers, Am. Judicature Soc., Ga. Trial Lawyers Assn. Home: 144 Tatershall Ct Macon GA 31204 Office: 737 Walnut St Macon GA 31204 Tel (912) 745-1174

RALEY, JEFF FRANK, b. Ancon, Panama, May 3, 1947; B.S., U. Okla., 1969, J.D., 1972. Admitted to Okla. bar, 1972; asso. firm Gurley & McClung, Blackwell, Okla., 1972-73; partner firm Gurley, Raley & Ihrig and predecessor, Blackwell, 1973—; municipal judge, Blackwell, 1972; asst. dist. atty. Kay County, 1972-74; city atty. Blackwell, 1975—. Bd. dirs. Blackwell Jaycees, 1973-74, Western Kay County chpt. ARC, 1973-76; spl. events chmn. Blackwell United Fund Drive, 1973, chmn., 1974; county chmn. Kay County Democratic Party, 1975—. Mem. Okla. (trustee), Kay County (sec. 1972-73) bar assns., Okla. Municipal Attys. Assn. (dir. 1975—, sec.-treas. 1975—), Okla. Bar Found. (trustee). Recipient Outstanding Service award Okla. Bar Assn., 1975. Home: 154 Saralyn Dr Blackwell OK 74631 Office: 121 W Blackwell St Blackwell OK 74631 Tel (405) 363-3325

RALLI, PANDIA CONSTANTINE, b. Spring Lake, N.J., July 28, 1915; B.A., Princeton, 1937; LL.B., Harvard, 1940. Admitted to N.Y. bar, 1941; asso. firm McCanliss & Early, N.Y.C., 1940-41, Stewart & Shearer, N.Y.C., 1942-51; partner firm Carter, Ledyard & Milburn, N.Y.C., 1952—; lectr. in field. Mem. Am., N.Y. bar assns., Assn. Bar City N.Y. Home: 21 Sturgis Rd Bronxville NY 10708 Office: Carter Ledyard & Milburn 2 Wall St New York City NY 10005 Tel (212) 732-3200

RALPH, GORDON PAUL, b. Milw., Oct. 9, 1931; A.B. with honors, U. Chgo., 1951, J.D., 1954. Admitted to Ill. bar, Wis. bar, 1954, U.S. Patent Ct. bar, 1955; since practiced in Milw., asso. firm Hoffman, Cannon, McLaughlin & Herbon, 1958-61; asst. gen. counsel The Northwestern Mutual Life Ins. Co., 1961-66; v.p., corporate legal counsel Milw. Mut. Ins. Co., 1972—; div. dir. Manpower, Inc., 1966-68; pres. Modec, Inc., 1969-71. Nat. bd. trustees Laubach Literacy Inc., Syracuse, N.Y., 1965-68; pres., founder Literacy Services of Wis., 1964—. Mem. Am. Bar Assn., Am. Interprofl. Inst. (pres.), Phi Beta Kappa. Contbr. articles legal jours.; editor U. Chgo. Law Rev., 1953-54. Home: 6027 W Menomonee Dr Wauwatosa WI 53213 Office: 803 W Michigan St Milwaukee WI 53233 Tel (414) 271-0525

RALPH, RICHARD FOLSOM, b. St. Louis, July 8, 1923; B.A., Washington U., St. Louis, 1947; J.D., U. Mich., 1950. Admitted to Mo. bar, 1950, Fla. bar, 1955, U.S. Supreme Ct. bar, 1954; individual practice law, Clayton, Mo., 1950, Miami, Fla., 1955—; served with JAGC, U.S. Army, 1951-54. Mem. Am., Fla., Dade County bar assns., Maritime Law Assn U.S., Internat. Assn. Ins. Counsel, Southeastern Admiralty Law Inst., Assn. Average Adjusters U.S., Am. Judicature Soc., Propeller Club U.S. (pres. Port of Miami chpt. 1960-63). Home: 420 Aledo Coral Gables FL 33134 Office: 700 Greater Miami Fed Bldg 200 SE 1st St Miami FL 33131 Tel (305) 377-0637

RAMBO, JAMES EDMONDSON, b. Dayton, Ohio, July 26, 1923; A.B., Ohio U., 1947; LL.B., U. Cin., 1949. Admitted to Ohio bar, 1949, Fed. bar; asso. firm Coolidge, Becker Wall & Weed, Dayton, Ohio, 1949-54; asst. U.S. Atty. So. Dist. Ohio, 1954-57; asst. gen. counsel NCR Corp., Dayton, 1957-65, v.p., sec., gen. counsel, 1965—, dir., 1971—. Trustee Dayton Art Inst., 1971-75; mem. bd. U. Dayton Law Sch., 1976—. Mem. Dayton, Ohio, Am. bar assns., Assn. Gen. Counsel. Home: 1111 Oakwood Ave Dayton OH 45419 Office: NCR World Hdqrs Bldg Dayton OH 45479 Tel (512) 449-2200

RAMBO, JAMES EDWARD, JR., b. Balt., Dec. 11, 1922; A.A., Eastern Coll., Balt., 1948, B.A., 1964; LL.B., Mt. Vernon Sch. Law, 1968; J.D., U. Balt., 1970. Investigator, State of Md., Balt., 1946-55, supr. investigation, 1955-60, legal asst., 1960-63; ins. advisor U.S. Dept. Labor, Washington, 1963-76; admitted to Md. bar, 1971; individual practice law, Upper Marlboro, Balt., and Glen Burnie, Md., 1976—. Mem. Md., Am., Anne Arundel County (Md.) bar assns., Md. Trial Lawyers. Recipient Regulations for Laws incentive award Dept. Labor, 1965, 72, 75. Home: 273 Glengary Garth St Glen Burnie MD 21061 Offices: Baltimore MD also Glen Burnie MD also Upper Marlboro MD Tel (301) 766-3144

RAMEY, CARL ROBERT, b. Binghamton, N.Y., Feb. 15, 1941; A.B., Marietta Coll., 1962; M.A., Mich. State U., 1964; J.D., George Washington U., 1967. Admitted to D.C. bar, 1968, U.S. Ct. Appeals bar, D.C., 1968, 4th Circuit, 1970, 6th Circuit, 1974, U.S. Supreme Ct. bar, 1972; partner firm McKenna, Wilkinson & Kittner, Washington, 1971—. Mem. Am. Bar Assn., Fed. Communications Bar Assn. (treas. 1976-77). Recipient Nat. 1st prize ASCAP Nathan Burkan Meml. Competition, 1968; editorial staff George Washington Law Rev., 1965-67. Home: 8723 Belmart Rd Potomac MD 20854 Office: 1150 Seventeenth St NW Washington DC 20036 Tel (202) 296-1600

RAMEY, CECIL EDWARD, JR., b. Shreveport, La., Nov. 9, 1923; B.S. summa cum laude, Centenary Coll., 1943; LL.B., Yale, 1949; postgrad. Tulane U., 1950-51. Admitted to Wis. bar, 1949, La. bar, 1951; asso. firm Miller, Mack & Fairchild, Milw., 1949-50; mem. faculty Sch. Law Tulane U., New Orleans, 1950-54; asso. firm Hargrove, Guyton, Van Hook and Hargrove, Shreveport, 1954-56, partner, 1956-63; partner firm Hargrove, Guyton, Ramey and Barlow and predecessors, Shreveport, 1963—; former dir. program continuing profl. edn. Tulane Sch. Law. Trustee Centenary Coll.; bd. dirs. Shreveport-Bossier Found., Frost Found., R.W. Norton Art Found.; v.p. past chmn. Citizens Capital Improvement Com. City of Shreveport; past mem. governing bd. Shreveport YMCA; past chmn. bd. trustees Broadmoor Methodist Ch., Shreveport, past chmn. bd. stewards, tchr. couples class, certified lay speaker; past v.p. Norwela council Boy Scouts Am. Fellow Am. Coll. Probate Counsel; mem. Shreveport (mem. exec. com. 1969-71, pres. 1970), La. (gov. 1953-54, lectr. com. on continuing legal edn.), Am. bar assns., Am. Law Inst. (mem. adv. coms. for La. Law Inst., new trust, mineral codes), Centenary Alumni Assn. (pres. 1964-66), Shreveport C. of C. (v.p. 1967-69, 72-73, pres. 1974, chmn. capital improvements study com. 1967-68), Order of Coif, Phi Delta Phi. Named Shreveport's Outstanding Young Man of Year, 1956, "Mr. Shreveport", 1968; recipient Yale Law Sch. Colby Townsend Meml. award, 1948, Francis Weyland award, 1949; selected for Centenary Coll. Alumni Hall of Fame, 1970. Home: 405 Albany St Shreveport LA 71105 Office: PO Drawer B Shreveport LA 71161 Tel (318) 425-5393

RAMIREZ, JACK SWIFT, b. Memphis, July 14, 1939; B.S. in Bus. Adminstrn., U. Colo., 1962; J.D., Washburn U., 1964. Admitted to Kans. bar, 1964, Mont. bar, 1968; asso. firm Jochems, Sargent & Blaes, Wichita, Kans., 1965-68; partner firm Crowley, Haughey, Hanson, Gallagher & Toole, Billings, Mont., 1968—; mem. Mont. Ho. of Reps., 1977—. Mem. Yellowstone County (Mont.), Mont., Am. bar assns., Fedn. Ins. Counsel. Home: 4109 Rimrock Rd Billings MT 59102 Office: 500 Electric Bldg Billings MT 59101 Tel (406) 252-3441

RAMMEL, JOHN MARSHALL, b. Los Angeles, May 31. 1942; A.B., U. Notre Dame, 1963, J.D., 1964; LL.M., John Marshall Law Sch., 1971. Admitted to Ill. bar, 1964; trust officer 1st Nat. Bank of Chgo., 1966-73; asso. firm Williams, Manos, Rutstein, Goldfarb & Sharp, Chgo., 1973—. Jr. bd. Chgo. Symphony Orch., 1975—. Mem. Chgo. Bar Assn., Ill. State Bar. Office: 72 W Adams St suite 1020 Chicago IL 60603 Tel (312) 236-2084

RAMSBOTTOM, ALGERNON PETER, III, b. Ossining, N.Y., Mar. 1, 1933; B.A. magna cum laude, Patuxent Coll., 1955; J.D., Harvard, 1962. Admitted to Md. bar, 1962, D.C. bar, 1962, N.J. bar, 1964; asso. firm Oates & Fawkes, Balt., 1962-69; partner firm Pitner Pitner & Ramsbottom, Washington, 1969—. Justice of peace, Baltimore County, Md., 1963-65. Mem. Am., N.J., D.C., Md. bar assns. Home: Free State Mall Bowie MD 20715 Tel (301) 262-5200

RAMSER, JOHN FREDERICH, b. Shadyside, Ohio, May 8, 1932; A.B., Harvard U., 1954; J.D., Ohio State U., 1956. Admitted to Ohio bar, 1957, Pa. bar, 1969; counsel Wheeling Steel Corp. (W.Va.), 1959-64, asst. sec. 1964-66, asso. gen. counsel, 1966-70; asst. sec. Koppers Co., Pitts., 1974—; solicitor Powhatan Point (Ohio), 1957-59. Mem. Shadyside Sch. Bd., 1967-69. Mem. Allegheny County, Pa., Am. bar assns. Home: 1295 Heather Heights Allison Park PA 15101 Office: 1550 Koppers Bldg Pittsburgh PA 15219 Tel (412) 391-3300

RAMSEY, ALFRED PATTERSON, b. Mpls., Sept. 3, 1897; B.A., Thiel Coll., 1919, LL.D., 1964; J.D., Yale, 1922. Admitted to Minn. bar, 1922, Md. bar, 1924, U.S. Supreme Ct. bar, 1939, U.S. Circuit Ct. Appeals, 4th D.C., 1950, 3d Circuit, 1954; atty. Minn. Saint Paul and Sault Ste. Marie Railway Co., Mpls., 1922-23; asst. gen. counsel Balt. Gas and Electric Co., Balt., 1924- 48, gen. counsel, 1948-63, v.p., 1957-63, pres., 1963-66, also dir.; mem. Md. Jud. Salary and Rev. Bd., 1970. Trustee Samuel Ready Sch., Balt., 1948—, chmn., 1950-66; chmn. Vol. Council on Equal Opportunity, Inc., Balt., 1965—; vice chmn. bd. regents Morgan State U., 1975—. Mem. Am., Md. State, Balt. City bar assns., Wednesday Law Club (pres. 1940). Home: 409 Kensington Rd Baltimore MD 21229 Office: 18th floor Gas and Electric Bldg Liberty and Lexington Sts Baltimore MD 21203 Tel (301) 234-5611

RAMSEY, HORACE LIDELLE, b. Rome, Ga., Feb. 13, 1920; LL.B., John Marshall U., 1948, LL.M., 1949. Admitted to Ga. bar, 1952, U.S. Supreme Ct. bar, 1969, U.S. Tax Ct. bar, 1970; supervisory spl. agt. Office of Investigation and Inspector Gen., U.S. Dept. Agr., Atlanta, 1957-77, criminal investigator, 1977—. Mem. Ga. Bar Assn., Ga. Peace Officers Assn. Home: 101 S Division St Rome GA 30161 Tel (404) 881-4377

RAMSEY, J. KEVIN, b. Youngstown, Ohio, June 5, 1932; B.S. in Bus. Adminstrn., Youngstown U., 1954; J.D., Akron U., 1963. Admitted to Ohio bar, 1963; asst. sec., Timken Co., Canton, Ohio, 1973—. Bd. trustees Canton Welfare Fedn.; chmn. bd. trustees Ohio Valley Coll. Mem. Ohio State, Am., Stark County bar assns. Home: 706 Briar Ave NE North Canton OH 44720 Office: 1835 Dueber Ave SW Canton OH 44706 Tel (216) 453-4511

RAMSEY, JOHN ARTHUR, b. San Diego, Apr. 1, 1942; A.B., San Diego State Coll., 1965; J.D., Calif. Western U., 1969. Admitted to Colo. bar, 1969; asso. firm Henry, Cockrell, Quinn & Creighton, Denver, 1969-72; atty. Texaco, Inc., Denver, 1972-76, Chgo., 1976—; appeals agt. U.S. Selective Service, Denver, 1970-71, mem. local bd., 1972-76. Chmn. council Bethany Lutheran Ch., 1976. Home: 1059 Gartner Rd Naperville IL 60540 Office: 332 S Michigan Ave Chicago IL 60604

RAMSEY, RICHARD HEYWOOD, III, b. Dothan, Ala., June 11, 1933; B.S. in Law, U. Ala., 1955, LL.B.. 1957. Admitted to Ala. bar, 1957; individual practice law, Dothan, 1957-76. Pres. Nat. Found., Houston County, 1960-75; mem. advisory bd. Salvation Army, Dothan, 1961-76; active Dothan-Houston County Assn. Retarded Citizens. Mem. Houston County, Ala., Am. bar assns., Assn. Am. Trial Lawyers, Am. Judicature Soc. Mem. continuing legal edn. com. The Ala. Lawyers, 1969-76. Home: 404 N Cherokee Ave Dothan AL 36301 Office: POB 1825 suite 4 Town Oak Bldg Dothan AL 36301 Tel (205) 794-4154

RAMYNKE, MILDRED DAVIS, b. Morristown, S.D., Feb. 6, 1917; student S.D. State U., 1934-36; J.D., U. S.D., 1939. Admitted to S.D. bar, 1939; judge Roberts, Day and Marshall Counties (S.D.), 1958-68, County Dist. Ct., 10th Dist., Sisseton, 1968-74, 5th Jud. Circuit Ct., Sisseton, 1974—. Bd. dirs. Lake Region Mental Health, Watertown, S.D., 1965-72. Mem. S.D. Bar Assn., S.D. Judges Assn., Nat. Council Juvenile Ct. Judges. Home: Rural Route 1 Peever SD 57257 Office: Courthouse Sisseton SD 57262 Tel (605) 698-3395

RAND, EZRAEL COOKE, b. Bklyn., Jan. 8, 1942; B.S. in Econs., Bklyn. Coll., 1962; LL.B., N.Y. U., 1965. Admitted to N.Y. State bar, 1966, U.S. Dist. Ct. bar for So. Dist., 1970, for 2d Circuit Ct. Appeals, 1975; Eastern Dist., 1970, law asst. to Justice Benjamin, Appellate div. 2d dept. Supreme Ct. N.Y., 1967-69; asso. firm Weiss Rosenthal Heller Schwartzman & Lazar, N.Y.C., 1969-73, partner 1974—. Mem. Am., N.Y. State bar assns.

RAND, HARRY I., b. N.Y.C., July 27, 1912; B.S., Coll. City N.Y., 1932; J.D., N.Y. U., 1936. Admitted to N.Y. bar, 1936, D.C. bar, 1947; atty. U.S. Pub. Works Adminstrn., 1938-39, U.S. Dept. Interior, 1939-43, U.S. Dept. Justice, 1943-48; individual practice law, Washington, 1948-58; mem. firm Weisman, Celler, Allan, Spett & Scheinberg, N.Y.C., 1959-67, firm Botein, Hays, Sklar & Herzberg, N.Y.C., 1967—. Mem. N.Y.C. Bar Assn., Am. Law Inst. Home: 320 W 86th St New York City NY 10024 Office: 200 Park Ave New York City NY 10017 Tel (212) 867-5500

RANDALL, ARTHUR, b. N.Y.C., Oct. 29, 1923; B.S., N.Y. U., 1946, J.D., 1949. Admitted to N.Y. bar, 1950; asso. firm Moroze and Paulson, N.Y.C., 1950-60; dist. atty. Nassau County (N.Y.), Mineola, 1969-74, chief grand jury bur., 1963-68, chief narcotic bur., 1969-74; exec. dir. Nassau County Criminal Justice Coordinating Council, Mineola, 1975—; faculty advisor Nat. Coll. Dist. Attys., Houston, 1970; lectr. law Post Coll., 1973-74, now adj. prof.; lectr. Adelphi U. Pres. Old Bethpage Civic Assn., 1957-58, bd. dirs., 1959—. Mem. Nassau County Bar Assn., Nat. Dist. Attys. Assn., N.Y. State Dist. Attys. Assn. Recipient Achievement award Nat. Assn. Counties, 1976; co-author: Trial of Narcotic Case, 1971. Home: 14 Dover Ln Old Bethpage NY 11804 Office: 1505 Kellum Pl Mineola NY 11501 Tel (516) 535-3500

RANDALL, GARY CHARLES, b. Spokane, Wash., Dec. 13, 1939; B.S. in Accounting, U. Idaho, 1961, J.D., 1964. Admitted to Idaho bar, 1964, Wash. bar, 1967, U.S. Supreme Ct. bar, 1969; trial atty. Chief Counsel's Office, IRS, Washington, 1965-66, Seattle, 1966-70; mem. firm Lukins, Seelye & Randall, Spokane, 1970-73; asso. prof., chmn. taxation dept. Gonzaga Law Sch., Spokane, 1973—. Mem. Am. (chmn. sub-com. on taxation), Wash. bar assns. Contbr. articles to profl. jours. Home: 10024 Whitworth Dr Spokane WA 99218 Office: Gonzaga Law Sch Spokane WA 99220 Tel (509) 326-5310

RANDALL, RISHER, b. Galveston, Tex., June 6, 1929; B.A., Yale U., 1950; LL.B., U. Tex., 1953. Admitted to Tex. bar, 1953; served with Judge Adv. Gen. Corps., U.S. Army, 1953-55; partner firm Vinson, Elkins, Searls, Connaly & Smith, Houston, 1956-71; mem. staff Am. Gen. Investment Corp., Houston, 1971—. Mem. Am., Tex., Harris County, Houston bar assns. Home: 3249 Chevy Chase Houston TX 77019 Office: Box 1375 Houston TX 77001 Tel (713) 522-1111

RANDALL, WILLIAM IRVING, b. Framingham, Mass., Sept. 13, 1915; B.A., Yale, 1938; J.D., Harvard, 1941. Admitted to Mass. bar, 1941, U.S. Supreme Ct. bar, 1962. Partner firm Sheridan & Randall, Framingham, 1946-71; judge Mass. Land Ct., Boston, 1971—; selectman Town of Framingham, 1947-50; mem. Mass. Senate, 1964-70; rep. Gen. Ct. of Mass., 1951-64. Mem. Am., Mass., South Middlesex bar assns. Home: 122 Edgell Rd Framingham MA 01701 Office: Land Ct Old Courthouse Pemberton Sq Boston MA 02108 Tel (617) 227-7470

RANDERSON, ROELIF JANSEN, b. Albany, N.Y., Aug. 7, 1931; B.A., De Pauw U., 1953; J.D., Albany Law Sch., 1956; LL.M., Harvard, 1960. Admitted to N.Y. State bar, 1956, Calif. bar, 1961; asso. firm Donovan Leisure Newton & Irwin, N.Y.C., 1959-60; asso. firm Luce, Forward, Hamilton & Scripps, San Diego, 1961-68, partner, 1968—. Adviser, Jr. League San Diego, 1973-76; adv. bd. Penisula YMCA, 1976. Mem. Am., San Diego County bar assns., San Diego County Barristers Club. Home: 831 Golden Park San Diego CA 92106 Office: suite 1700 110 W A St San Diego CA 92101 Tel (714) 236-1414

RANDOL, SHERYLE LYNNE, b. Kansas City, Mo., Oct. 11, 1947; B.A., William Jewell Coll., 1970; J.D., U. Mo., 1971. Admitted to Mo. bar, 1971; asst. U.S. atty. for Mo., 1971-74; asst. regional counsel Fed. Hwy. Adminstrn., Kansas City, Mo., 1974—, mem. civil rights adv. com. for region 7, 1976—. Bd. dirs. Oak Park Counseling Center, S. Jackson County Mental Health Assn. Mem. Am., Fed., Mo., Kansas City bar assns. Home: 9205 W 72d St Shawnee Mission KS 66204 Office: 6301 Rockhill Rd Kansas City MO 64141 Tel (816) 926-5234

RANDOLPH, ARTHUR RAYMOND, JR., b. Riverside, N.J., Nov. 1, 1943; B.S., Drexel U., 1966; J.D. summa cum laude, U. Pa., 1969. Admitted to Calif. bar, 1970, U.S. Supreme Ct. bar, 1973, D.C. bar, 1973; law clk. to Judge Henry J. Friendly, U.S. Ct. Appeals, 2d Circuit, N.Y.C., 1969-70; asst. to solicitor gen. U.S. Dept. Justice, Washington, 1970-73; asso. firm Miller, Cassidy, Larroca & Lewin, Washington, 1973-75; dep. solicitor gen. U.S. Dept. Justice, Washington, 1975-77; partner firm Sharp, Randolph & Janis, Washington, 1977—; adj. prof. law Georgetown Law Center, 1974—; dir. Atty. Gen.'s Com. on Reform Fed. Jud. System, 1975—; mem. Justice Dept. Com. Fed. Rules of Evidence, 1972. Chmn., Com. Govtl. Structure, McLean, Va., 1973-74. Mem. Calif., D.C. bar assns., Am. Law Inst., Supreme Ct. Hist. Soc., Order of Coif. Recipient spl. achievement award U.S. Dept. Justice, 1971. Mng. editor U. Pa. Law Rev., 1968-69. Home: 6901 Oakridge Ave Chevy Chase MD 20015 Office: 1220 19th St NW Washington DC 20036 Tel (202) 659-2400

RANDOLPH, JOHN NEVITT, b. Casper, Wyo., July 2, 1944; B.S., U. Ala., 1966; J.D., Cumberland Sch. Law Samford U., 1968. Admitted to Ala. bar, 1968; individual practice law, Birmingham, Ala., 1968-69; asso. firm Leader, Tenenbaum & Perrine, Birmingham, 1969; partner firm Leader, Tenenbaum, Perrine & Randolph, Birmingham, 1970—. Parliamentarian and strip mining chmn. Birmingham chpt. Ala. Conservancy, 1976—. Mem. Ala. State Bar, Birmingham Bar Assn. (mem. placement com., 1973, legal referral com., 1974—), Sierra Club, Phi Delta Phi. Home: Route 1 Box 837 Leeds AL 35094 Office: 933 Bank For Savs Bldg Birmingham AL 35203 Tel (205) 251-9291

RANE, JAMES WILLIAM, b. Dothan, Ala., Sept. 15, 1946; B.S., Auburn U., 1968; J.D., Cumberland Sch. Law, 1971. Admitted to Ala. bar, 1971; law clk. McDaniel, Hall, Parson & Conerley, Birmingham, Ala., 1969-71; individual practice law, Abbeville, Ala., 1971—; judge inferior ct. Henry County, Ala., 1973-77; pres. Great So. Wood Preserving, Inc.; bd. dirs. Illa Grain Corp. Chmn., Abbeville Med. Scholarship Fund, Abbeville Med. Facility. Mem. Am., Ala., Henry County bar assns., Ala. Trial Lawyers Assn., Cordell Hull Internat. Soc., Phi Alpha Delta. Home: Alberta Dr Abbeville AL 36310 Office: PO Box 488 Abbeville AL 36310 Tel (205) 585-3464

RANEY, HOLLAMAN MARTIN, b. Greenville, Miss., Jan. 31, 1933; B.A., U. Miss., 1961, LL.B., 1961. Admitted to Miss. bar, 1961; field atty. NLRB, Memphis, 1961-63; legal asst. Miss. Chem. Corp., Yazoo City, 1963-66, atty., 1966-67, sr. atty., 1967-69, asst. gen. counsel, 1969-73, gen. counsel, 1973—. Chmn. bd. control Yazoo Library Assn., 1970-74; vice chmn. Miss. Penitentiary Bd., 1974-76. Mem. Am., Miss., Yazoo County bar assns., Yazoo County C. of C. (dir.). Home: 811 Sunset Dr Yazoo City MS 39194 Office: Box 388 Yazoo City MS 39194 Tel (601) 746-4131

RANIER, EDWARD MICHAEL, b. Jersey City, Oct. 26, 1943; B.S. in Econs., Fairleigh Dickinson U., 1965; J.D., U. Md., 1968. Admitted to Md. bar, 1968; asst. state's atty., State's Atty's. Office, Balt., 1969-74; asst. atty. gen., Office of Atty. Gen. for Md., Balt., 1974—. Mem. Am., Md. Bar Assns., Fraternal Order Police. Home: Apt 1306 302 E Joppa Rd Towson MD 21204 Office: 203 E Baltimore St Baltimore MD 21201 Tel (301) 383-6785

RANKIN, A. CLAY, III, b. Montgomery, Ala., Aug. 14, 1943; student psychology Tulane U., 1961-64; J.D., U. Ala., 1967. Admitted to Ala. bar, 1967, U.S. Supreme Ct. bar, 1971; asso. firm Hand, Arendall, Bedsole, Greaves, & Johnston, Mobile, Ala., 1967-72, partner, 1972—. Mem. bd. dirs. Mobile Hist. Devel. Found., 1974-76, Cornerstone, Inc., 1976—. Mem. Maritime Law Assn. U.S., Southeastern Admiralty Law Inst., Farrah Order of Jurisprudence. Editor-in-chief Ala. Law Rev., 1967. Home: Rt 2 Box 28 Daphne AL 36526 Office: Box 123 Mobile AL 36601 Tel (205) 432-5511

RANKIN, CHARLES EWING, b. Chester, Pa., June 17, 1918; A.B., Haverford Coll., 1939; J.D., U. Pa., 1942. Admitted to Pa. bar, 1942, U.S. Supreme Ct. bar, 1948; asso. firm Geary & Rankin, Chester, 1946-58; partner Rankin & Rankin, Chester, 1958—; mem. hearing com. disciplinary bd. Pa. Supreme Ct., 1972—; mem. Gov.'s Trial Ct. Nominating Commn. for Delaware County, 1975—. Bd. dirs. Helen Kate Furness Library, Wallingford, Pa., 1955-61; treas. Phila. Swimming Dirs. Soc., 1966-67. Mem. Am., Pa. (ho. dels.), Delaware County (pres. 1970) bar assns., Am. Coll. Probate Counsel, Order of Coif, Phi Beta Kappa. Home: 221 W Possum Hollow Rd Wallingford PA 19086 Office: 420 Ave of States Chester PA 19013 Tel (215) 876-8277

RANKIN, HENRY HOLLIS, JR., b. Mission, Tex., Jan. 11, 1915; A.A., Edinburg (Tex.) Jr. Coll. (now Pan Am. U.), 1933; LL.B., U. Tex., 1936. Admitted to Tex. bar, 1936; U.S. Supreme Ct. bar, 1955; asst. dist. atty., Hidalgo County, Tex., 1937-42; prin. firm H.H. Rankin, Jr., Mission, Edinburg, 1936-46; partner firm Rankin & Kern, Inc., and predecessors, McAllen, Tex., 1946—; city atty. City of Mission, 1937-54, 69—; judge, County Ct. at Law, Hidalgo County, 1951-53; dir. Tex. Law Enforcement Found., 1963. Dir. Tex. Hist. Found., 1969-72; mem. Tex. Hist. Commn., 1969-77; bd. trustees Mission Ind. Sch. Dist., 1964-69, pres., 1964-65. Mem. Am. (trial technique com. on ins., negligence and compensation sect.), Tex. (legal publs. com. 1972—), Hidalgo County (dir. 1973-75, pres. 1975-77) bar assns. Office: Rankin & Kern 804 Pecan St PO Box 3744 McAllen TX 78501 Tel (512) 682-2891

RANSMEIER, JOSEPH SIRERA, b. New Orleans, June 19, 1915; A.B., Oberlin Coll., 1936; A.M., Columbia, 1937, Ph.D., 1942; J.D., U. Mich., 1952. Admitted to N.H. bar, 1952; asst. prof. econs. Vanderbilt U., Nashville, 1940-42; statistician U.S. War Dept., Washington, 1945-46; asst. prof. econs. Dartmouth, 1946-52, prof., 1952; asso. firm Sulloway Hollis Godfrey & Soden, Concord, N.H., 1953-58, partner, 1958—; incorporator Concord Savs. Bank, 1967—, trustee, 1973—; dir. Concord Electric Co., 1975. Bd. visitors U. Mich. Law Sch., 1976—; incorporator Concord Hosp., 1967—, trustee, 1972—; mem. Hopkinton (N.H.) Sch. Bd., 1954-60. Mem. Am., N.H. bar assns., Am. Coll. Probate Counsel, Order of Coif, Phi Beta Kappa. Author: The Tennessee Valley Authority, 1942; also articles. Home: R F D 1 Concord NH 03301 Office: 9 Capitol St Concord NH 03301 Tel (603) 224-2341

RANSMEIER, JUDITH DUNLOP MULLIGAN, b. Bklyn., Nov. 8, 1943; B.A., Bennington Coll., 1966; J.D., Boston U., 1969. Admitted to N.H. bar, 1969; atty. Office N.H. Atty. Gen., Concord, 1969-71; asso. firm McLane, Graf, Greene, Raulerson & Middleton, Manchester, N.H., 1971-75; individual practice law, Concord, 1975—. Mem. exec. bd. League N.H. Craftsmen, Concord, 1971—; bd. dirs. Merrimack Valley Day Care Service, Concord, 1971—, pres., 1976—. Mem. N.H., Merrimack County bar assns. Home and Office: 122 Franklin St Concord NH 03301 Tel (617) 224-7847

RANSOM, DONALD EUGENE, b. Bonne Terre, Mo., July 23, 1946; B.S. in Bus. Adminstrn., S.E. Mo. State U., 1968; J.D., U. Mo., 1972. Admitted to Mo. bar, 1972; atty. St. Louis-San Francisco Ry. Co., 1972-74, gen. atty., 1974-76, asst. gen. counsel, 1976—. Mem. Am., Mo., Met. St. Louis bar assns., ICC Practicioners Assn. Office: 906 Olive St Saint Louis MO 63101 Tel (314) 241-7800

RANSOM, WALTER FREDERICK, b. Akron, Ohio, Jan. 10, 1934; B.A., U. Mich., 1956, LL.B., 1962. Admitted to Mich. bar, 1962; asst. gen. counsel Fed. Life and Casualty Co., Battle Creek, Mich., 1962-69; judge Wexford County Probate and Juvenile Cts., Cadillac, Mich., 1969—; mem. Gov.'s Commn. on Law Enforcement and Criminal Justice, 1970-72. Treas. Battle Creek Civic Theater, 1966-68; chmn. N. Central Mich. Mental Health Center Bd., 1970-73. Mem. Mich. Probate and Juvenile Ct. Judges' Assns., Nat. Council Juvenile Ct. Judges, Mich. Assn. Childrens' Agencies. Home: 419 Donnelly St Cadillac MI 49601 Office: Wexford County Court House Cadillac MI 49601 Tel (616) 775-2911

RANSON, ARTHUR JONES, III, b. Florence, S.C., Oct. 12, 1943; B.A., Eckerd Coll., 1965, postgrad. Duke, 1965-66, J.D., Vanderbilt U., 1969. Admitted to Fla. bar, 1970, U.S. Supreme Ct. bar, 1976; law clk., U.S. Dist. Ct. for Middle Dist. Tenn., 1969-70; partner firm Turnbull, Abner & Daniels, Winter Park, Fla., 1971-75; partner firm Robertson, Williams, Duane & Lewis, Orlando, Fla., 1975—; mem. law devel. com. Vanderbilt U., 1976—. Deacon, Winter Park Presbyn. Ch., 1976-79; vice-chmn. Orange County (Fla.) Dem. Exec. Com., 1975—; pres. Council of Arts and Scis. Central Fla., 1975-76; v.p. Central Fla. Civic Theatre, 1975-76; trustee Eckerd Coll., 1976-79. Mem. Am., Fla., Orange County (treas. 1976) bar assns., Acad. Fla. Trial Lawyers, Am. Judicature Soc., Assn. Trial Lawyers Am., Rotary Club, Eckerd Coll. Alumni Assn. (pres. 1974-76). Co-author: An Evaluation of Municipal Income Taxation, 1969. Home: 2719 Summerfield Rd Winter Park FL 32792 Office: 538 E Washington St Orlando FL 32801 Tel (305) 425-1606

RAPAPORT, MICHAEL SIMON, b. N.Y.C., Apr. 20, 1938; B.A., Union Coll., 1959; M.B.A., Columbia, 1964, J.D., 1964. Admitted to N.Y. bar, 1964; asso. firm Eisman, Corn, Lee, Sheftel & Block, N.Y.C., 1964-65; partner firm Rapaport Bros., White Plains, N.Y., 1965—. Mem. Assn. Bar City N.Y., Westchester County Bar Assn. Office: PO Box 272 175 Main St White Plains NY 10602 Tel (914) 428-2800

RAPEE, STUART MICHAEL, b. Rockford, Ill., May 27, 1938; B.B.A., U. Miami, 1960, J.D., 1963. Admitted to Fla. bar, 1963; asso. firm Dubbin, Schiff, Berkman & Dubbin, Miami, 1963-69; individual practice law, Miami, 1969—; v.p. Blue Lake Devel. Corp., Miami, 1963-76. Founding pres. L'Chaim Lodge B'nai B'rith, Miami Beach; dir. Keystone Point Homeowners Assn. Mem. Fla. Bar Assn. Contbr. articles in field to mag. Office: 1201 Brickell Ave Miami FL 33131 Tel (305) 358-2465

RAPER, JOHN FREDERICK, b. Mapleton, Iowa, June 13, 1913; student, Drake U., 1935; J.D., U. Wyo., 1936. Admitted to Wyo. bar, 1936; individual practice law, Sheridan, Wyo., 1936-40, 45-50, 51-53, Cheyenne, Wyo., 1961-62; U.S. atty. for Wyo., Cheyenne, 1953-61; atty. gen. State of Wyo., Cheyenne, 1962-66; judge 1st Jud. Dist. Wyo., Cheyenne, 1966-74; justice Wyo. Supreme Ct., Cheyenne, 1974—. Mem. Am., Laramie County bar assns., Wyo. State Bar, Am. Judicature Soc. Office: Supreme Ct Bldg Cheyenne WY 82001 Tel (307) 777-7557

RAPHAEL, EUGENE JOSEPH, b. N.Y.C., Dec. 21, 1900; B.A., Yale, 1922; LL.B., Columbia, 1925. Admitted to N.Y. State bar, 1926, Miss. bar, 1939; asso. firm Stein & Salant, N.Y.C., 1925-28; mem. firms Brodek, Raphael & Eisner, N.Y.C., 1928-34, Raphael & Raphael, N.Y.C., 1934-35; individual practice law, N.Y.C., 1935-39, Greenville, Miss., 1939—; U.S. bankruptcy judge No. Dist. Miss., 1970—. Bd. dirs. Hebrew Union Congregation, Greenville, 1944—, congregation pres., 1950-51; mem. exec. bd. Delta Area council Boy Scouts Am., 1952-70. Mem. Am., Washington County (Miss.) (pres. 1963) bar assns., Nat. Conf. Bankruptcy Judges (bd. govs. 1977—), Miss. State Bar, Comml. Law League Am., Am. Judicature Soc. Office: PO Box 1558 Greenville MS 38701 Tel (601) 378-2727

RAPHAEL, GERALD DAVID, b. Hamilton, Ont., Can., Jan. 24, 1943; B.A., U. San Fernando Valley, 1966, LL.B., 1968. Admitted to Calif. Supreme Ct. bar, 1969, U.S. Supreme Ct. bar, 1972; asso. firm Early, Maslach, Foran & Williams, Los Angeles, 1969-71; partner firm Sayble and Raphael, Los Angeles, 1971—. Mem. Los Angeles County Bar Assn., Los Angeles Trial Lawyers Assn. Office: Suite 300 1730 W Olympic Blvd Los Angeles CA 90015 Tel (213) 386-8870

RAPHAEL, ROBERT, b. N.Y.C., Oct. 8, 1922; B.A., U. Pitts., 1948, LL.B., 1950. Admitted to Allegheny County (Pa.) Ct. Common Pleas bar, 1950, Pa. Supreme Ct. bar, 1951, U.S. Dist. Ct. bar for Western Dist. Pa., 1954, U.S. Supreme Ct. bar, 1967, Pa. Superior Ct. bar, 1969, Pa. Commonwealth Ct. bar, 1971; individual practice law, Pitts., 1950-64; partner firm Raphael, Sheinberg & Barmen, Profl. Assn. and predecessors, 1964-68, chmn., 1968—; chmn. trial ct. nominating commn. 5th Jud. Dist. Pa., 1975—; lectr. Pa. Bar Inst. Bd. dirs. Planned Parenthood of Pitts., Inc., 1975-76. Mem. Allegheny County (pres. 1973), Pa. (chmn. sect. family law 1974-76, ho. of dels 1976), Am. (vice chmn. com. divorce law and procedures 1976, ho. of dels. 1974-76) bar assns. Office: 360 Grant Bldg Pittsburgh PA 15219 Tel (412) 471-8822

RAPHAN, BENJAMIN, b. Bklyn., Oct. 20, 1937; B.A., U. Rochester, 1959; M.B.A., Columbia, 1962, LL.B., 1962. Admitted to N.Y. bar, 1962, U.S. Tax Ct. bar, 1962; atty. SEC, Washington, 1962-65; asso. firm Tenzer Greenblatt Fallon & Kaplan, N.Y.C., 1965-70, partner, 1970—. Mem. Am. (sec. com. on programs, sect. corp. and bus. law), N.Y. State bar assns. Home: 70 Dandy Dr Cos Cob CT 06807 Office: Tenzer Greenblatt et al 100 Park Ave New York City NY 10017 Tel (212) 953-1800

RAPOPORT, LEONARD A., b. Chgo., Aug. 19, 1921; B.C.S., U. Iowa, 1941; J.D., Wm. Mitchell Coll., 1950. Admitted to Minn. bar, 1950; tech. advisor IRS, St. Paul, 1946-53; partner firm Calmenson Abramson & Co., C.P.A's, St. Paul, 1953-67; partner Alexander Grant & Co., St. Paul, 1967—. Pres., Jewish Community Center St. Paul, 1968-70, U. Minn. Hillel Found., 1965-67; chmn. Minn. State Bd. Accountancy, 1977. Mem. Minn., Ramsey City, Am. bar assns., Minn. Soc. C.P.A.'s, Am. Inst. C.P.A.'s. Contbr. articles to legal jours. Home: 1692 Highland Pkwy Saint Paul MN 55116 Office: 1710 American Nat Bank Bldg Saint Paul MN 55101 Tel (612) 222-0524

RAPP, STEPHEN KAUFMAN, b. N.Y.C., June 28, 1892; A.B., Coll. City N.Y., 1911; LL.B., Columbia U., 1914. Admitted to N.Y. bar, 1914; individual practice law, N.Y.C., 1914—; sec. Honest Ballot Assn., Inc., N.Y.C., 1918-20; arbitrator Small Claims Ct., N.Y.C., 1954-71; chmn. N.Y. County City Fusion Party, 1933. Mem. N.Y. County Lawyers Assn. (surrogate's ct. com. 1976—), N.Y. State Bar Assn. (surrogate's ct. com. 1974—). Author: Handbook of Primary Law, 1937; Handbook for Proportional Representation Canvassers, 1937. Home: 166 E 96th St New York City NY 10028 Office: 166 E 96th St New York City NY 10028 Tel (212) 348-4701

RAPPAPORT, RICHARD JEROME, b. Chgo., Aug. 13, 1943; B.S., Loyola U., Chgo., 1965, J.D. cum laude, 1967. Admitted to Ill. bar, 1967; with U.S. Dept. Justice, Chgo., 1967-69; partner firm Ross, Hardies, O'Keefe, Babcock & Parsons, Chgo., 1969—. Mem. Am., Ill., Chgo. Bar Assns., Loyola Law Alumni Assn. (pres.), Phi Sigma Tau, Alpha Sigma Nu. Home: 2945 W Farwell St Chicago IL 60645 Office: One IBM Plaza Chicago IL 60611 Tel (312) 467-9300

RAPPEPORT, JACK J., b. Bklyn., Jan. 22, 1923, B.S., Cornell U., 1948; J.D., Stetson U., 1955; LL.M., Harvard, 1956. Admitted to Fla. bar, 1957, Ariz. bar, 1968; asst. prof. law and law librarian Stetson U., 1956; asst. prof. law U. Pitts., 1958; asso. prof. law U. Ariz., 1959-62, prof. law, 1962—, asst. and counsel to pres., 1974—; individual practice law, St. Petersburg, Fla., 1957—, Tucson, 1968—; referee Tucson Juvenile Ct., 1959—; cons. juvenile ct. judge, 1959—. Mem. Ariz., Fla. bar assns., Order of the Coif. Contbr. articles to law jours. and legal texts. Home and Office: 205 N Bentley Ave Tucson AZ 85716 Tel (602) 325-6741 also (602) 795-3676

RARICK, JOSEPH FRANCIS, SR., b. Bartonville, Ill., July 6, 1921; B.A. with highest honors, U. Ill., 1943, J.D., 1948; LL.M., Columbia, 1949, J.S.D., 1956. Admitted to Ill. bar, 1948, Okla. bar, 1956; asst. prof. law U. Minn., 1949-53; asso. prof. law U. Okla., 1953-57, prof. law, 1957-67, David Ross Boyd prof. law, 1967—; cons. in field. Mem. Okla. Bar Assn., Order of the Coif, Phi Beta Kappa, Phi Kappa Phi, Phi Delta Phi. Author: The Right to Use Water in Oklahoma, 1976; contbr. articles in field to law jours. Home: 608 E Boyd Norman OK 73071 Office: 300 W Timber Dell Rd Norman OK 73019 Tel (405) 325-4011

RASH, ALAN VANCE, b. Fallbrook, Calif., Dec. 10, 1931; B.A., Tex. Western Coll., 1953; J.D., U. Tex., 1960. Admitted to Tex. bar, 1960, U.S. Supreme Ct. bar, 1972; partner firm Diamond, Rash, Leslie & Smith, El Paso, Tex., 1968—. Mem. bd. equalization City of El Paso, 1973-75; pres. Southwestern Sun Carnival Assn., 1976, pres., 1977; chmn. El Paso County Republican Party, 1963-65, 70-72. Mem. Comml. Law League Am., El Paso Trial Lawyers Assn., Am., Tex., El Paso bar assns. Home: 9137 McFall St El Paso TX 79925 Office: 1208 First City Nat Bank Bldg El Paso TX 79901

RASHBA, MALCOLM LEE, b. New Haven, Oct. 19, 1931; B.S., U. Conn., 1953, J.D., 1956. Admitted to Conn. bar, 1956; partner firm Gamm, Liebman, Rashba, Goldblatt & Greenstein, Hamden, Conn., 1958—; justice peace Town of Orange (Conn.), 1975—, mem. bd. fin., 1975—. Mem. Am., Conn., New Haven County bar assns. Office: 2405 Whitney Ave Hamden CT 06518 Tel (203) 288-6293

RASHER, STEVEN MICHAEL, b. Cleve., Aug. 19, 1948; B.S. in Bus. Adminstrn., Miami U.; J.D., U. Mich. Admitted to Ill. bar, 1973, No. Dist. Ill. Fed. Ct. bar, 1973, U.S. Ct. Appeals 7th Circuit bar, 1973; asso. firm Mayer, Brown & Platt, Chgo., 1973—. Mem. Am., Ill. State, Chgo. bar assns. Office: 231 S LaSalle St Chicago IL 60604 Tel (312) 782-0600

RASIN, GEORGE BACON, JR., b. Worton, Md., May 28, 1917; A.B., Washington Coll., Chestertown, Md., 1937; LL.B., U. Md., 1941. Admitted to Md. bar, 1941; practiced in Chestertown, 1945-50, 52-60; security officer Econ. Coop. Adminstrn., Paris, 1950-52; judge Circuit Ct. Md. 2d Jud. Circuit, Chestertown, 1960—; mem. Md. Senate, 1956-60; state's atty. for Kent County (Md.), 1955-56. Mem. Am., Md. State, 2d Jud. Circuit, Kent County bar assns. Home: 205 Valley Rd Chestertown MD 21620 Office: Courthouse Chestertown MD 21620 Tel (301) 778-4600

RASMUSSEN, PAUL ROBERT, b. Evanston, Ill., Apr. 25, 1915; B.Sc., Northwestern U., 1936; J.D., John Marshall Law Sch., 1940; postgrad. U. Ill., Urbana, 1948. Admitted to Ill. bar, 1940, U.S. Tax Ct., 1948; with trust dept. Am. Nat. Bank, Chgo., 1936-40; accountant Swisher & Co., Chgo., 1940-42, Ernst & Ernst, Chgo., 1946-49; tax counsel Crane Co., Chgo., 1949-59; counsel Abbott Labs., North Chicago, Ill., 1960-74, v.p. taxes, 1975—. Mem. Am., Chgo. bar assns., Ill. Soc. C.P.A.'s, Chgo. Tax Club (pres. 1966), Tax Execs. Inst. (pres. Chgo. chpt. 1970). Office: Abbott Labs Abbott Park North Chicago IL 60064 Tel (312) 688-3950

RASMUSSEN, SIGUN, b. Copenhagen, Dec. 21, 1910; B.A., 1936, LL.B., 1938. Admitted to Ark. bar, 1938, U.S. Dist. Ct. bar, 1946, U.S. Supreme Ct. bar, 1971; partner firm Rasmussen & Vaughn, Des Arc, Ark., 1938-42; partner firm Mallory, Rasmussen & Johnson, Hot Springs, Ark., 1946-51; individual practice law, Hot Springs, 1951-69; partner firm Rasmussen & Hogue, Hot Springs, 1969—; U.S. Magistrate Western Dist. Ark., 1971—; U.S. Commr., Western Dist. Ark., 1951-71. Mem. Am. Judges Assn., Am. Judicature Soc., Nat. Council U.S. Magistrates, Am., Ark., Garland County bar assns. Home: 1601 W Grand Ave Hot Springs AR 71901 Office: 800 Whittington Ave Hot Springs AR 71901 Tel (501) 321-2667

RASMUSSON, THOMAS, b. Lansing, Mich., Dec. 5, 1941; B.A., Mich. State U., 1963; J.D., U. Mich., 1966. Admitted to Mich. bar, 1967; law clk. to Justice H.F. Kelly, Mich. Supreme Ct., 1966-68; asst. prosecutor Ingham County (Mich.), 1968-74, chief criminal div., 1973-74, spl. prosecutor, 1974-76; individual practice law, Lansing, 1974—; mem. Lansing Model Cities Task Force on Crime and Delinquency, 1968-70; mem. ct. rules com. Mich. Supreme Ct. 1975—. Mem. Ingham County Republican Task Force on Crime, Lansing; mem. Mich. Gov.'s Task Force on Programs, Goals and Agr. Mem. Mich. State Bar, Ingham County, Am. bar assns., Am. Judicature Soc. Recipient Boss of Year award Lansing Legal Secs, 1974. Home: 610 W Ottawa St Lansing MI 48933 Office: 730 Mich Nat Tower Lansing MI 48933 Tel (517) 485-1781

RASP, JOHN CLETUS, b. St. Louis, July 8, 1942; B.S., St. Louis U., 1964, J.D. cum laude, 1967. Admitted to Mo. bar, 1967, U.S. Ct. Mil. Appeals bar, 1968, U.S. Supreme Ct. bar, 1976; trial atty., tax div. U.S. Dept. Justice, 1967-68; served with JAGC, U.S. Army, 1968-72; partner firm Peper, Martin, Jensen, Maichel and Hetlage, St. Louis, 1972—. Mem. Mo., Am. bar assns., Bar Assn. Met. St. Louis (editor St. Louis Bar Jour., 1974—, recipient award of merit Young Lawyers sect. 1976). Office: 720 Olive St Saint Louis MO 63101 Tel (314) 421-3850

RASSMAN, EMIL CHARLES, b. Indpls., July 27, 1919; B.A., Washington and Lee U., 1941; LL.B., U. Tex., 1947. Admitted to Tex. bar, 1947, U.S. Supreme Ct. bar, 1951; mem. firm Rassman, Gunter & Boldrick, Midland, Tex.; dir. Comml. Bank & Trust Co., Midland; mem. Tex. Jud. Council, 1958-61. Campaign chmn., pres. Midland County United Fund, 1956-57; chmn. Midland County chpt. ARC, 1971-73; trustee Midland Sch. Dist., 1958-61; bd. regents Tex. State U. System, 1961—, chmn., 1967-69; chmn. bd. executors Permian Basin Petroleum Mus., Library and Hall of Fame, 1973—. Fellow Am. Coll. Trial Lawyers, Am., Tex. bar founds., Am. Coll. Probate Counsel, Internat. Acad. Trial Lawyers; mem. Internat. Assn. Ins. Counsel, Fedn. Ins. Counsel, Am. Counsel Assn., State Bar Tex. (dir. 1972-75, chmn. bd. 1974-75), Midland County Bar Assn. (pres. 1960), W. Tex. C. of C. (pres. 1973-74), Tex. State C. of C. (pres. 1973-74), Phi Delta Phi, Delta Tau Delta. Home: 2405-A Wadley St Midland TX 79701 Office: 400 Midland Tower Bldg Midland TX 79701 Tel (915) 683-5656

RAST, THEODORE EDMUND, b. Atlanta, May 12, 1947; A.B., Yale U., 1969; J.D., U. Pa., 1974. Admitted to Ohio bar, 1974; asso. firm Thompson, Hine and Flory, Cleve., 1974—; lectr. Ohio Legal Center Inst., 1977. Loaned exec. Cleve. United Torch Services, 1974, team capt., 1975, div. chmn., 1976, mem. fund raising com., 1977—. Mem. Am. Bar Assn. Home: 9624 Kim Dr Chesterland OH 44026 Office: 1100 National City Bank Bldg Cleveland OH 44114 Tel (216) 241-1880

RASTETTER, RICHARD CHARLES, JR., b. Fort Dodge, Iowa, Jan. 6, 1946; B.S. in Bus. Adminstrn., Northwestern U., 1968, M.B.A., 1969; J.D. with honors, Drake U., 1972. Admitted to Iowa bar, 1972, Ind. bar, 1972; asso. firm Krieg, DeVault, Alexande & Capehart, Indpls., 1972-76; asso. firm Cline & Callahan, Indpls., 1976—; adj. prof. Ind. U., 1975. Mem. Am., Indpls., Iowa, Ind. bar assns. Office: 6284 Rucker Rd Indianapolis IN 46220 Tel (217) 257-3161

RATCLIFF, J(OHN) DONALD, b. Chillicothe, Ohio, July 28, 1915; B.S. in Bus. Adminstrn., Ohio State U., 1940, LL.B., 1942, J.D., 1967. Admitted to Ohio bar, 1942; served with JAGC, U.S. Navy, 1942-46; spl. agt. FBI, Washington, 1946-55, adminstrv. asst. to dir., 1951-54; practice law, 1955-69; judge Ross County (Ohio) Common Pleas Ct., 1969—. Gen. chmn. Community Chest, Chillicothe, 1957, pres., 1958-60, mem. budget com., bd. trustees, 1957—; active indsl. devel., 1958—. Mem. Ohio State Bar Assn. Recipient Outstanding Jud. Service award (10) Ohio Supreme Ct. Home: 642 W 5th St Chillicothe OH 45601 Office: Common Pleas Ct Gen Div Courthouse Chillicothe OH 45601 Tel (614) 774-2975

RATCLIFFE, ALLEN THOMPSON, JR., b. Beloit, Wis., Jan. 11, 1947; B.A., U. Cin., 1969; J.D., U. Denver, 1972. Admitted to Colo. bar, 1972; asso. firm Nicholas Magill, 1972-74; partner firm Ratcliffe & Chamberlin, 1974—; city atty. Steamboat Springs, Colo., 1974—; town atty. Yampa, Colo., 1974—. Mem. Criminal Justice Planning Com., Colo., 1974—. Mem. Colo., N.W., Steamboat Springs bar assns. Home: 30955 Saratoga Steamboat Springs CO 80477 Office: 928 Lincoln Ave Steamboat Springs CO 80477 also 147 W Jefferson Ave Hayden CO 81639 Tel (303) 276-3626

RATHER, GORDON SMEADE, JR., b. Little Rock, Apr. 6, 1939; B.A. cum laude, Vanderbilt U., 1961; J.D., Duke, 1968. Admitted to Ark. bar, 1968, U.S. Supreme Ct. bar, 1972; partner firm Wright, Lindsey & Jennings, Little Rock, 1968—; pres. Bar Rev. of Ark., Inc., 1969—. Mem. Ark. Territorial Restoration Commn., 1971—; bd. dirs. Pulaski County unit Am. Cancer Soc., Ark. Territorial Restoration Found. Mem. Am., Ark., Pulaski County bar assns., Am. Judicature Soc., Ark. Trial Lawyers Assn., Assn. Ins. Attys., Southeastern Admiralty Law Inst., Phi Beta Kappa. Home: 68 Robinwood Dr Little Rock AR 72207 Office: 2200 Worthen Bank Bldg Little Rock AR 72201 Tel (501) 371-0808

RATHER, JULIUS EDWARD, b. Scottsville, Ky., June 13, 1936; B.A., Western Ky. State U., 1958; LL.B., U. Ky., 1960. Admitted to Ky. bar, 1960, U.S. Supreme Ct. bar, 1971; legal asst. to Gov. Ky., 1961-63, 63-64; asso. Bert Combs, Lexington, Ky., 1964-67; partner firm Denney Morgan & Rather, Lexington, 1967—; trustee State Employees, County Employees and State Police Retirement System, 1964-68, chmn. bd., 1967-68; mem. Fayette County Legal Aid Soc., 1975—. Mem. Ky., Fayette County (Henry T. Duncan award 1976, pres. 1976) bar assns. Home: 1163 Athenia Dr Lexington KY 40504 Office: 259 W Short St Lexington KY 40507 Tel (606) 252-0824

RATHJE, S(YLVANNUS) LOUIS, b. Geneva, Ill., Nov. 1, 1939; B.A., Wheaton Coll., 1961; J.D., Northwestern U., 1964. Admitted to Ill. bar, 1964; partner firm Rathje Woodward Dyer & Burt, Wheaton, Ill., 1964—. Mem. DuPage County (Ill.), Ill., Am. bar assns. Office: 203 E Liberty Dr Wheaton IL 60187 Tel (312) 668-8500

RATHMANN, DENNIS T., b. St. Louis, Mar. 6, 1948; B.C.S., St. Louis U., 1970, J.D., 1973. Admitted to Mo. bar, 1974; individual practice law, St. Louis, 1974—. Mem. Am., St. Louis Met. bar assns. Home: 7208 Virginia St Saint Louis MO 63111 Office: 906 Olive St suite 1023 Saint Louis MO 63101 Tel (314) 241-7800

RATHVON, NATHANIEL PETER, b. Yonkers, N.Y., Apr. 23, 1921; student Yale U., 1939-41; J.D., Cornell U., 1948. Admitted to N.Y. State bar, 1949; asso. firm Milbank, Tweed, Hope and Hadley, N.Y.C., 1948-56; legal counsel Brookhaven Nat. Lab., Upton, N.Y., 1956-69; sec., gen. counsel Associated Univs. Inc., Upton, 1969—; chmn. human subjects rev. com. Brookhaven Nat. Lab., 1971—; bd. govs. Brookhaven Nat. Lab. Hosp., 1970—; mem. human subjects research subcom. VA Hosp., Northport, N.Y., 1975—. Mem. Suffolk County, Am. bar assns. Home: 141 Quaker Path Setauket NY 11733 Office: Bldg 460 Center St Upton NY 11973 Tel (516) 345-3328

RATNER, DAVID LOUIS, b. London, Sep. 2, 1931; A.B., Harvard U., 1952, LL.B., 1955. Admitted to N.Y. bar, 1955; asso. firm Sullivan & Cromwell, N.Y.C., 1955-64; asso. prof. law Cornell U., 1964-68, prof., 1968—; exec. asst. to chmn. SEC, Washington, 1966-68; chief counsel Securities Industry Study, U.S. Senate Banking Com., Washington, 1971-72; vis. prof. law Ariz. State U., 1974, Stanford U., 1974. Author: Securities Regulation, Materials for a Basic Course, 1975. Home: 125 Heights Ct Ithaca NY 14850 Office: Cornell Law Sch Ithaca NY 14853 Tel (607) 256-3672

RATNER, FRANK EPHRAIM, b. Russia, July 20, 1907; ed. Pacific Coast U. Admitted to Tenn. bar, 1939; individual practice law, Nashville. Mem. Tenn., Am., Nashville bar assns., Tenn. Trial Lawyers. Home: 6501 Harding Rd Nashville TN 37205 Office: 904 Stahlman Bldg Nashville TN 37201 Tel (615) 320-0491

RATNER, GERALD, b. Chgo., Dec. 17, 1913; Ph.B., U. Chgo., 1935, J.D. cum laude, 1937. Admitted to Ill. bar, 1937; since practiced in Chgo.; partner firm Gould & Ratner, and predecessors, 1949—; lectr. in field; officer, dir. Henry Crown & Co., The Hoffman Group, Inc., Material Service Corp., Stores Realty Corp., Sioux City and New Orleans Barge Lines, Inc. Mem. Am., Ill., Chgo. bar assns., Order of Coif, Phi Beta Kappa. Home: 900 Lake Shore Dr Chicago IL 60611 Office: 300 W Washington St Chicago IL 60606 Tel (312) 236-3003

RATNER, LEONARD GORDON, b. N.Y.C., July 10, 1916; A.B., U. Calif., Los Angeles, 1937, J.D., Berkeley, 1940; S.J.D., Harvard, 1968. Admitted to Calif. bar, 1941; law clk. to Justice Roger Traynor, Calif. Supreme Ct., 1940-42; trial judge adv. and legal officer USN, 1942-46; practiced in Los Angeles, 1946-58, asso. firm Lester William Roth, 1946-47, individual practice law, 1947-58; lectr. in law Harvard Law Sch., 1958-61; asso. prof. law U. So. Calif., 1961-64, prof., 1964—; referee Los Angeles County Juvenile Ct., 1971-72; cons. U.S. Senate Subcom. Constl. Rights, 1972-74; David Ben Gurion lectr. Hebrew U., Jerusalem, 1976. Mem. Calif., Am. (cons. com. child custody 1965-68) bar assns. Recipient award for excellence in teaching U. So. Calif. Assos., 1967; contbr. articles to profl. jours. Home: 5911 Flambeau Rd Rancho Palos Verdes CA 90274 Office: Law Center U of So Calif Los Angeles CA 90007 Tel (213) 746-2158

RAU, GEORGE HENRY, JR., b. Houston, Oct. 21, 1946; B.B.A., Tex. A. and M. U., 1969; J.D., U. Tex., 1972. Admitted to Tex. bar, 1972; asso. firm Frank W. Stevens, Angleton, Tex., 1973—. Mem. Am., Tex., Brazoria County bar assns. Home: 207 Silver Saddle Angleton TX 77515 Office: 300 N Velasco St Angleton TX 77515 Tel (713) 849-6484

RAUCCI, FRANCIS JOSEPH, b. Phila., May 17, 1936; A.B. in Polit. Sci., St. Joseph's Coll., 1958; J.D., Georgetown U., 1965. Admitted to Mont. bar, 1965, Pa. bar, 1976; individual practice law, Great Falls, Mont., 1965-68; dep. county atty. County of Cascade (Mont.), 1965-68; staff atty. Buttrey Food Stores div. Jewel Cos., Inc., Great Falls, 1968-74, v.p., asst. gen. counsel, 1974-76; v.p., sec. Acme Markets, Inc., Phila., 1976—; lectr. Coll. Great Falls, 1960-76; adj. prof. labor relations U. Mont., Missoula, 1971-76; mem. Mont. Labor Relations Bd., 1973-75, chmn., 1975-76. Mem. Mont. Citizens Com. for Improvement of Legislature, 1971; chmn. bd. trustees Mont. Sch. for Deaf and Blind, 1969-76. Mem. Am., Mont., Pa., Phila. bar assns. Home: 288 Upper Gulph Rd Radnor PA 19087 Office: Acme Markets Inc 124 N 15th St Philadelphia PA 19101 Tel (215) 568-3000

RAUCH, MARTIN WILLIAM, b. Buffalo, Jan. 20, 1934; B.S., Canisius Coll., 1956; J.D., U. Buffalo, 1959; LL.M., Georgetown U., 1961. Admitted to N.Y. bar, 1961, Fla. bar, 1971; trial lawyer Liberty Mut. Ins. Co., Buffalo, 1961-63; individual practice law, Springville, N.Y., 1963—; town atty. Concord and Sardinia (N.Y., 1961-71; sch. atty. Griffith Inst., Springville, 1961-71. Chmn., So. Erie County United Fund, 1965; arbitrator, fact finder N.Y. State Pub. Employment Relations Bd., 1968—. Mem. Am. Arbitration Assn. Home: 367 E Main St Springville NY 14141 Office: 392 E Main St Springville NY 14141 Tel (716) 592-4914

RAUH, B. MICHAEL, b. Washington, July 11, 1936; A.B., U. Mich., 1958; LL.B., U. Va., 1961; LL.M., Georgetown U., 1967. Admitted to Va. bar, 1961, D.C. bar, 1962, U.S. Supreme Ct. bar, 1967; asst. U.S. atty., Washington, 1961-64; spl. asst. OEO, Exec. Office of Pres., 1964-65; mem. firm Landis, Cohen, Singman & Rauh, Washington, 1966—. Mem. Democratic Nat. Com., 1964-65; bd. dirs. Boys' Clubs Am., 1972—. Mem. D.C., Va. bar assns., Am. Trial Lawyers Assn., Washington Urban League. Home: 3516 Sterling Ave Alexandria VA 22304 Office: 1910 Sunderland Pl NW Washington DC 20036 Tel (202) 785-2020

RAUH, JOSEPH L., JR., b. Cin., Jan. 3, 1911; B.S., Harvard U., 1932, LL.B., 1935. Admitted to Ohio bar, 1935, D.C. bar, 1947, U.S. Supreme Ct. bar, 1941; law clk. to Justice Benjamin N. Cardozo and Justice Felix Frankfurter, 1936-39; counsel to various govt. agys., 1939-42; partner firm Rauh & Levy, Washington, 1946-59, firm Rauh, Silard & Lichtman, Washington, 1959—; Washington counsel United Auto Workers, 1951-63, 66—, gen. counsel, 1963-66; gen. counsel Miners for Democracy, 1970-72; gen. counsel Leadership Conf. Civil Rights, 1964—. Mem. D.C. Bar. Home: 3625 Appleton St NW Washington DC 20008 Office: 1001 Connecticut Ave NW Washington DC 20036 Tel (202) 331-1795

RAUHAUSER, JOHN FRANKLIN, JR., b. York, Pa., Dec. 7, 1918; B.A., Ursinus Coll., 1941; LL.B., U. Pa., 1948. Admitted to bar; individual practice law, York, Pa., 1949—; solicitor York County, Pa., 1955-56, dist. atty., 1966-69. Author hist. tracts, pamphlets and booklets. Office: 104 E Market St York PA 17401 Tel (717) 854-4925

RAUSCHER, DAVID JOHN, b. St. Louis, Aug. 28, 1948; B.S., St. Benedicts Coll., Atchison, Kans., 1970; J.D., U. Mo., 1973. Admitted to Mo. bar, 1973; asso. firm Sullivan & Watkins Clayton, Mo., 1973—. Mem. St. Louis County, Met. St. Louis, Mo., Am. bar assns., Mo. Assn. Trial Lawyers, Am. Trial Lawyers Assn. Author: The Law on Defense of Driving While Intoxicated. Home: 14540 Amstel Ct Chesterfield MO 63017 Office: 130 S Bemiston St Clayton MO 63105 Tel (314) 726-6605

RAVELLA, JAMES ANTHONY, b. Niles, Ohio, Apr. 16, 1906; grad. Ohio No. U., 1928. Admitted to Ohio bar, 1928; individual practice law, Youngstown, Ohio, 1928-42, 45-50; asst. pros. atty., Warren, Ohio, 1948-49; spl. counsel, atty. gen., Ohio, 1949-50; judge Warren Municipal Ct., 1950—. Trustee YMCA, Warren; mem. exec. com. Ohio Gov.'s Traffic Safety Com. Mem. Ohio Traffic Ct. League., Ohio Municipal Judges Assn., Am., Trumbull County, Ohio bar assns. Recipient numerous award Warren Municipal Ct., certificate Ohio Dept. Hwy. Safety, 1957, 65, awards Supreme Ct. Ohio, 1975, 76. Home: 3076 Overlook Dr NE Warren OH 44483 Office: 141 South SE Warren OH 44481 Tel (216) 393-4656

RAVEN, MARK BENJAMIN, b. N.Y.C., Mar. 28, 1939; B.A., N.Y. U., 1959; LL.B., Yale, 1968. Admitted to N.Y. bar, 1969, Ariz. bar, 1970; asso. firm Fried, Frank, Shriver & Jacobson, N.Y.C., 1969-70; Reginald Heber Smith fellow Pima County (Ariz.) Legal Aid Soc., Tucson, 1970-71; partner firm Risner, Raven & Keller, Tucson, 1971—. Pres., Youth Devel., Inc., Tucson, 1976—; cons. Childbirth Edn. Assn., Tucson, 1974-76. Mem. Pima County Bar Assn., Ariz. Women's Polit. Caucus. Office: 177 N Church St Tucson AZ 85701 Tel (602) 623-3601

RAVREBY, MARK DAVID, b. Cambridge, Mass., Dec. 28, 1924; M.D., U. Iowa, 1948; J.D., Drake U., 1968. Intern, Cambridge City Hosp., 1949; resident Boston City Hosp., 1950, Des Moines VA Hosp., 1953; admitted to Iowa bar, 1968; individual practice law, Des Moines, 1968—; adj. prof. law Drake U., 1968—. Mem. AMA, Iowa State, Polk County med. assns., Am., Iowa, Polk County bar assns. Home: 1841 Ashworth St West Des Moines IA 50265 Office: 1417 Woodland St Des Moines IA 50309 Tel (515) 288-1979

RAWAIT, MARGUERITE, b. Prairie City, Ill., Oct. 16; A.B., George Washington U., 1933, J.D., 1933, LL.M., 1936; LL.D. (hon.), Baylor U., 1945. Admitted to D.C. bar, 1932, Tex. bar, 1935, U.S. Supreme Ct. bar, 1938, Va. bar, 1970; atty. IRS, Washington, 1933-64; individual practice law, Washington, 1966—; lectr. law George Washington U., 1973-75. Mem. Commn. on Status of Women, 1961-63, Citizens Adv. Council on Status of Women, 1963-69; chmn. Task Force on Family Law and on Civil and Polit. Rights of Women, 1961-69; pub. mem., also mem. coms. U.S. Commn. Internat. Women's Year. Mem. Am. (del. 1943, 45-46), Fed. (nat. pres. 1943-44), Tex., Va. bar assns., Nat. Assn. Women Lawyers (nat. pres. 1943), Internat. Fedn. Women Lawyers, AAUW, Nat. Fedn. Bus. and Profl. Women's Clubs (nat. pres. 1954-56), Zonta Internat. Recipient Alumni Achievement award George Washington U., 1965, Nat. Career Achievement award Nat. Prof. PanHellenic Assn., 1967; Potomacland Ambassador citation D.C. Bd. Trade, 1960; Nat. award Freedom's Found., 1955. Home and Office: 1600 S Joyce St Suite C-1710 Arlington VA 22202 Tel (703) 521-7385

RAWLINGS, MAURICE EDWARD, b. Onawa, Iowa, Aug. 17, 1906; student U. Iowa, 1925-27; J.D., U. S.D., 1930. Admitted to Iowa bar; practice in Sioux City, Iowa; county atty. Woodbury County (Iowa), 1935-43; dist. dir. Office Price Adminstrn., 1943-47; corp. counsel Sioux City, 1948-51; judge 4th Jud. Dist. Iowa, 1958-65; justice Iowa Supreme Ct., 1965—. Mem. Sioux City Sch. Bd., 1955-58, pres., 1957-58; bd. dirs. Good Will Industries, 1960—. Mem. Phi Gamma Delta. Recipient Distinguished Service award Woodbury County Bar Assn., 1968; named Judge of Year Iowa Lawyers Chautauqua, 1970. Home: 3433 Court St Sioux City IA 51104 Office: 608 Courthouse Sioux City IA 51101 Tel (712) 279-6610

RAY, BETH PHELPS, b. Terre Haute, Ind., Aug. 18, 1946; B.A., Rice U., 1968; J.D., Ohio State U., 1972. Admitted to Ohio bar, 1974; vis. asst. prof. legal environment of bus. Ohio State U., 1972-74, asst. prof., 1974-77; individual practice law, Columbus, Ohio, 1972—; instr. Real Estate Inst. Ohio State U., Columbus, 1974—. Mem. Am., Columbus bar assns., Women Lawyers of Franklin County, Am. Judicature Soc., Am. Bus. Women's Assn. Author: Ohio Real Estate Law Manual, 1975; contbr. to Bull. Bus. Research. Home and Office: 344 E Torrence Rd Columbus OH 43214 Tel (614) 263-4294

RAY, FRANK ALLEN, b. Lafayette, Ind., Jan. 30, 1949; A.B., Ohio State U., 1970, J.D., 1973. Admitted to Ohio bar, 1973; asst. prosecuting atty. Franklin County, Columbus, Ohio, 1973-75, chief counsel civil div., 1976—; dir. Nat. Econ. Crime Project, Nat. Dist. Attys. Assn., Washington, 1975-76; partner Ray & Dalton, Columbus, 1975—. Mem. Columbus, Ohio State, Am. Bar Assns., Nat. Dist. Attys. Assn. Named one of ten outstanding young citizens of Columbus, Jaycees, 1975. Home: 36 E Riverglen Dr Worthington OH 43085 Office: Franklin County Hall of Justice 369 S High St Columbus OH 43215 Tel (614) 462-3520

RAY, FRANK DAVID, b. Mt. Vernon, Ohio, Dec. 1, 1940; B.S. in Edn., Ohio State U., 1964, J.D., 1967. Admitted to Ohio bar, 1967, Fed. bar, 1969, U.S. Supreme Ct. bar, 1971; legal aide to Atty. Gen. Ohio, Columbus, 1965-66; bailiff Franklin County (Ohio) Probate Ct., Columbus, 1966-67; gen. referee Franklin County Probate Ct., 1967-68; asso. firm Stouffer, Wait and Ashbrook, Columbus, 1967-71; jour. clk. Ohio House Reps., 1969-71; dist. dir. SBA, Columbus, 1971—. Chmn. Central Ohio chpt. Nat. Found. March Dimes, 1974—; mem. Upper Arlington Bd. Health, 1970-75; pres. Franklin County Forum, 1970. Mem. Am., Ohio, Columbus bar assns. Recipient service award National Found. March Dimes, 1974, 75; exec. order of Ohio Commodore, 1973, Am. Jurisprudence prize, 1967. Home: 4200 Dublin Rd Columbus OH 43220 Office: 34 N High St Columbus OH 43215 Tel (614) 469-7310

RAY, GEORGE EINAR, b. Gloucester, Mass., Apr. 23, 1910; A.B., Harvard, 1932, J.D., 1935. Admitted to Mass. bar, 1935, N.Y. State bar, 1935, Tex. bar, 1949; asst. to Prof. Roswell Magill, Columbia Law Sch., 1935-36; mem. firm Cravath, de Gersdorff, Swaine and Wood, N.Y.C., 1936-38; atty. U.S. Bd. Tax Appeals, Washington, 1938-41; spl. asst. to atty. gen. U.S., tax div. Dept. Justice, 1941; prin. atty. Office Tax Legis. Counsel, U.S. Treas. Dept., 1941-42; mem. firm Hale & Dorr, Boston, 1942-44; partner firm McCulloch, Ray, Trotti, Hemphill & Meadows, Dallas, 1946—; head dept. internat. law Naval Sch. Mil. Govt., Princeton, 1944-45; chief counsel Office Army-Navy Liquidation Commr., MTO, 1945; dep. exec. dir. Office Fgn. Liquidation Commr., Dept. State, 1946; adj. prof. So. Meth. U. Law Sch., N.Y. U. Tax Inst., Practicing Law Inst.; mem. adv. group to Commr. IRS. Mem. Am., Tex., Dallas County bar assns., Southwestern Legal Found., Harvard Law Sch. Assn. Tex., Dallas Estate Council, Tex. Bar Found. Author: Incorporating the Professional Practice, 1972; (with William N. Bret, Jr.) Financial Incentives for Executives: Wealth-Building Programs and Techniques, 1975; (with Harry V. Lamon, Jr.) Fiduciary Responsibilities Under the New Pension Reform Act, 1975; contbr. articles to legal and tax jours. Home: 12615 Breckenridge St Dallas TX 75230 Office: 3000 Fidelity Union Tower Dallas TX 75201 Tel (214) 748-6151

RAY, GILBERT TERRY, b. Mansfield, Ohio, Sept. 18, 1944; B.A., Ashland Coll., 1966; M.B.A., U. Toledo, 1968; J.D. magna cum laude, Howard U., 1972. Admitted to Calif. bar, 1972; asso. firm O'Melveny & Myers, Los Angeles, 1972—; exec. dir. Nat. Conf. Law Revs., 1971-72. Bd. dirs. U. Calif. at Los Angeles Black Law Center; spl. counsel Los Angeles Bicentennial Com. Mem. Am., Nat. bar assns., Los Angeles County Bar Assn. Barristers (exec. com.). Editor-in-chief: Howard Law Jour., 1971-72. Office: 611 W 6th St Los Angeles CA 90017 Tel (213) 553-6700

RAY, H. M., b. Rienzi, Miss., Aug. 9, 1924; LL.B., U. Miss., 1949, J.D., 1968. Admitted to Miss. bar, 1949; individual practice law, 1949-61; U.S. atty. No. Dist. Miss., Oxford, 1961—; mem. exec. com. Miss. Jr. Bar, 1950-51; pros. atty. Alcorn County (Miss.), 1956-57, 58-61. Chmn., Alcorn County chpt. ARC, 1957, Alcorn County chpt. Polio Found., 1956, Corinth-Alcorn County Airport Bd., 1959-61; mem. Miss. Ho. of Reps., 1948-51; trustee Alcorn County Pub. Library, 1959-62. Fellow Miss. Bar Found. (dir.); mem. Am., Fed. (pres. Miss. chpt., recipient Distinguished Service award Miss. chpt. 1976), Miss., Lafayette County bar assns. Co-author Miss. Workmens' Compensation Act, 1948. Office: PO Box 886 Oxford MS 38655 Tel (601) 234-5907

RAY, J(AMES) ENOS, b. Ashland, Va., Feb. 11, 1913; B.A., Randolph-Macon Coll., 1934; LL.B., U. Va., 1937. Admitted to Va. bar, 1937; mem. firm Kirsh & Bayile, 1937-40; individual practice law, Richmond, Va., 1945—; mayor Town of Ashland, 1940-41, 45-50. Home: 500 Maple St Ashland VA 23005 Office: 1 N 5th St Richmond VA 23219 Tel (804) 648-3386

RAY, JAMES HARRISON, b. San Mateo, Calif., Aug. 4, 1936; A.B., Stanford U., 1959; J.D., U. Calif., Berkeley, 1964. Admitted to Calif. bar, 1965; dep. dist. atty. Santa Clara County (Calif.), 1965-66, Office of Sec., Dept. Def., 1966-69; counsel Fairchild Camera & Instrument Corp., San Francisco, 1969-71, sr. counsel, 1971—. Mem. Urban Coalition, 1971-75, steering com. World Affairs Council San Francisco, 1974-75. Mem. Am., Fed., Santa Clara bar assns., San Francisco Lawyers Assn., Phi Delta Phi. Office: 464 Ellis St Mountain View CA 94042 Tel (415) 962-4133

RAY, JOHN LAKIN, b. Charleston, W.Va., Jan. 29, 1924; B. Chem. Engring., U. Va., 1949, LL.B., 1952, J.D., 1970. Admitted to W.Va. bar, 1952; partner firm Payne, Loeb & Ray, and predecessor, Charleston, 1960—. Mem. W.Va. State Coll. Adv. Bd., 1970—, chmn., 1970-74; trustee Morris Harvey Coll., 1975—; bd. dirs. Kanawha County (W.Va.) Pub. Library, 1975—. Mem. Am., W.Va., Kanawha County bar assns. Office: 1210 One Valley Sq Charleston WV 25301 Tel (304) 342-1141

RAY, ROBERT LEWIS, b. Fayetteville, N.C., July 25, 1938; Asso. Sci., Agrl. and Tech. U., 1961; B.S., Winston-Salem (N.C.) State U., 1966; J.D., N.C. Central U., 1969; postgrad. Am. Law Inst., 1970, Northwestern U., 1971, Wake Forest U., 1975. Admitted to N.C. bar, 1969, U.S. Supreme Ct. bar, 1973; mem. firm R. Lewis Ray and Assos., Winston-Salem, 1972-75; partner firm Ray and Andrews, Winston-Salem, 1975—; justice of peace, Winston-Salem, 1964-68; mem. bd. advisors Youth Services Bur., Wake Forest U., 1972; bd. dirs. Forsyth County Econ. Devel. Corp., 1972, Alcoholism Program Forsyth County, 1971; bd. advisors Upward Bound Program, Winston Salem State U., 1972-74; legal advisor Comprehensive Health Bd., 1972-74. Mem. Am., N.C., Forsyth County, Nat. bar assns., Am. Judicature Soc., Nat. Assn. Criminal Def. Lawyers, Am. Trial Lawyers Assn., JAG Sch. Alumni Assn., Phi Alpha Delta. Home: 3325 Parrish Rd Winston-Salem NC 27105 Office: 115 New Walkertown Rd Winston-Salem NC 27105 Tel (919) 724-2893

RAY, ROY ROBERT, b. Kentuck, W.Va., Apr. 21, 1902; A.B., Centre Coll., 1924; LL.B. with distinction, U. Ky., 1928; S.J.D., U. Mich., 1930. Admitted to Ky. bar, 1928, Tex. bar, 1930, Tenn. bar, 1938; asst., then asso. prof. law So. Meth. U., 1929-37, prof. law, 1939-70, prof. emeritus, 1970—; prof. law Vanderbilt U., 1937-39; vis. prof. law U. Colo., 1931, U. Mich., 1939; Fulbright exchange prof. Seoul (Korea) Nat. U., 1966; regional counsel OPA, 1942-45, chief hearing commr., 1945-46. Mem. Nat. Acad. Arbitrators, Tex., Dallas bar assns., Southwestern Legal Found., AAUP, Order of Coif, Phi Delta Phi. Author: Condemnation Procedure, 1931; Selected Texas Statutes, 1964; (with C.T. McCormick) The Texas Law of Evidence, 1937, 2d edit. (with W.F. Young), 2 vols., 1956, and supplements; also articles. Home: 6114 Norway Rd Dallas TX 75230 Office: Sch Law So Methodist U Dallas TX 75275 Tel (214) 692-2576

RAYBURN, FRANK CHARLES, b. Library, Pa., Nov. 27, 1925; B.A., Duquesne U., 1950, LL.B., 1954. Admitted to Pa. bar, 1955; individual practice law, Pitts., 1955—; asl. asst. atty. gen. Pa., Pitts., 1958-66. Pres., Bethel (Pa.) Vol. Fire Co., chmn. Bethel Park (Pa.) Zoning Bd. Adjustment. Mem. Allegheny County Bar Assn. Home: 2516 Applegate Ave Bethel Park PA 15102 Office: 504 Grant Bldg Pittsburgh PA 15219 Tel (412) 281-6565

RAYBURN, MADISON SMARTT, b. Honey Grove, Tex., Apr. 20, 1909; student Trinity U., 1925-29; A.B., Cumberland U., 1932; LL.B., U. Ariz., 1943; postgrad. Harvard, 1944; J.D., Samford U., 1970. Admitted to Tex. bar, 1933, Tenn. bar, 1939; practiced in Slaton, Tex., 1933-39, McMinnville, Tenn., 1939-42, Houston, 1942-43, 46-53; atty. City of Slaton, 1935-38; asst. atty. Lubbock County (Tex.), 1936; chief trial atty. Harris County Atty. Office, Houston, 1953-57; judge Harris County Civil Ct. at Law No. 1, 1958-67, 80th Dist. Ct., Houston, 1967—; mayor City of Bellaire (Tex.), 1947-49, councilman, 1946-47. Mem. Tex., Houston bar assns., Am. Judicature Soc., Internat. Platform Assn., Navy League, Blue Key, Delta Theta Phi, Delta Sigma Tau. Author: Texas Law of Condemnation and Land Damage Remedies, 1960. Home: 621 Piney Point Rd Houston TX 77024 Office: Court House Houston TX 77002 Tel (713) 221-6262

RAYCROFT, LILLIAN GRACE, b. Chgo., May 10, 1930; A.B., Juniata Coll., 1950; LL.B., U. Pa., 1953. Admitted to Pa. bar, 1955; individual practice law, State College, Pa., 1964-69, 73—; asso. firm Fleming & Litke, Bellefonte, Pa., 1955-62; partner firms Litke, Gettig & Raycroft, Bellefonte, 1962-64, Jubelirer & Raycroft, State College, 1969-73; div. counsel Curtiss-Wright Corp; mem. panel Am Bd. Arbitration. Speaker Christian Women's Club of Am. Mem. Pa., Am. bar assns. Office: 740 S Atherton St State College PA 16801 Tel (814) 237-4991

RAYMER, STANLEY ADELBERT, b. Elkhart, Ind., Aug. 3, 1908; A.B., Wittenberg U., 1930; J.D., Harvard, 1933. Admitted to Ind. bar, 1933; title examiner Fed. Bank of Louisville, 1933-34; city atty. Nappanee, Ind., 1934-36; dept. pros. atty. Elkhart County, Ind., 1935-37, pros. atty., 1937-39; judge Superior Ct. 2, Elkhart, Ind., 1967-77. Pres. Pioneer Trails council Boy Scouts Am., 1955-60; bd. dirs. Elkhart Pub. Library, 1946; mem. Elkhart Park Bd., 1946-47; mem. Elkhart Sch. Bd., 1947-57, pres., 1957. Mem Am., Ind. State, Elkhart County (pres.), Elkhart (pres.) bar assns., Am. Judicature Soc. Recipient Silver Beaver award Boy Scouts Am., 1958; Golden Deeds award Elkhart Exchange Club, 1965; Outstanding Community Service award Elkhart Lions Club, 1976. Home: 3 Clarendon Dr Elkhart IN 46514 Office: 216 W High St Elkhart IN 46514 Tel (219) 293-0931

RAYMOND, GEORGE LESLIE, b. Indpls., July 1, 1943; B.S. in Psychology, Purdue U., 1966; J.D., Ind. U., 1971. Admitted to Ind. bar, 1971, U.S. Supreme Ct. bar, 1975; atty. Ind. Dept. Pub. Instruction, Indpls., 1971-73, AMAX Coal Co., Indpls., 1973—. Treas. Southport United Meth. Ch., Indpls., 1973—, 500 Festival Assos., Indpls., 1974—. Mem. Indpls., Ind., Am. bar assns. Home: 749 W Ralston Rd Indianapolis IN 46217 Office: 105 S Meridian St Indianapolis IN 46225 Tel (317) 266-2626

RAYMOND, PATRICK JOSEPH, b. Buffalo, Oct. 3, 1939; B.A., Siena Coll., 1961; LL.B., Albany Law Sch., 1964. Admitted to N.Y. bar, 1965; asst. atty. Binghamton Urban Renewal Agy., 1967-70; atty. Binghamton (N.Y.) and Broome County (N.Y.) depts. social services, 1970-73; corp. counsel City of Binghamton, 1974—. Mem. Broome County, N.Y. State bar assns. Office: City Hall Binghamton NY 13901 Tel (607) 772-7070

RAYWID, ALAN, b. Washington, Aug. 9, 1930; A.B., Duke U., 1952; LL.B., U. Mich., 1957. Admitted to Mich. bar, 1957, D.C. bar, 1957, U.S. Supreme Ct. bar, 1962; mem. admiralty and shipping sect. Civil Div., U.S. Dept. Justice, Washington, 1957-66, spl. asst. to asst. atty. gen., 1963-66; asso. firm Nixon, Mudge, Rose, Guthrie, Alexander & Mitchell, Washington, 1966-67; partner firm Cole, Zylstra & Raywid, Washington, 1967—. Chmn. Duke Alumni Adv. Admission Com., 1964-75; pres. Community Assistance, Inc., Washington, 1967-70; nat. chmn. Cable TV Campaign Humphrey-Muskie, 1968; trustee Mt. Zion Cemetery, Washington, 1975—. Mem. Am., D.C., FCC bar assns., Am. Maritime Law Assn. Office: 2011 Eye St NW Washington DC 20006 Tel (202) 659-9750

RAZOOK, RICHARD JOHN, b. West Palm Beach, Fla., July 23, 1950; B.S. in Accounting, U. N.C., 1972; J.D., U. Miami; LL.M. in Taxation, N.Y. U., 1976. Admitted to Fla bar, 1975; asso. firm Smathers & Thompson, Miami, 1976—; with Peat, Marwick, Mitchell & Co., Miami, 1973-75, N.Y.C., 1975. Mem. Am., Fla. insts. CPAs, Fla. Bd. Accountancy. Office: 1301 Alfred I DuPont Bldg Miami FL 33131 Tel (305) 379-6523

RAZZANO, PASQUALE ANGELO, b. Bklyn., Apr. 3, 1943; B.C.E., Poly. Inst. Bklyn., 1964; J.D., Georgetown U., 1969. Admitted to Va. bar, 1969, N.Y. State bar, 1970, U.S. Supreme Ct. bar, 1976; examiner U.S. Patent Office, Washington, 1966-69; mem. firm Curtis, Morris &

Safford, N.Y.C., 1969—. Mem. ASCE, Am., N.Y. State bar assns., N.Y. Patent Law Assn., Phi Delta Phi, Chi Epsilon. Home: 14 Mein Dr New City NY 10956 Office: 530 Fifth Ave New York City NY 10036 Tel (212) 682-7171

RE, EDWARD DOMENIC, b. Santa Marina, Italy, Oct. 14, 1920; B.S., St. John's U., 1941, LL.B., 1943; J.S.D., N.Y. U., 1950; Pd.D. (hon.), Aquila, Italy, 1960; LL.D., St. Mary's Coll., Notre Dame, Ind., 1968, St. John's U., 1968, Maryville Coll., Mo., 1969, N.Y. Law Sch., 1976. Admitted to N.Y. State bar, 1943; instr. law and govt. St. Johns U., 1947-48, prof. law, 1951-69, adj. prof., 1969—; prof. legal aspects of engring. Pratt Inst., 1948-49; vis. prof. Georgetown U. Sch. Law, 1962-67; spl. hearing officer Dept. Justice, 1956-61; chmn. Fgn. Claims Settlement Commn. of U.S., 1961-68; asst. sec. state ednl. and cultural affairs, 1968-69; judge U.S. Customs Ct., N.Y.C., 1969—; adj. prof. law N.Y. Law Sch., 1972—; mem. adv. com. appellate rules Jud. Conf. U.S., 1976—, mem. planning com.; faculty Fed. Appellate Judges Conf., Fed. Jud. Center, 1974—. Mem. Bd. Higher Edn. N.Y.C., 1958-69, mem. emeritus, 1969—. Mem. Am. (chmn. sect. internat. and comparative law 1965-67, del.), N.Y. State, Bklyn. bar assns., Bar City N.Y., Am. Fgn. Law Assn. (pres. 1971-73), Am. Law Inst., Fed. Bar Council (pres. 1973-74), Am. Soc. Writers Legal Subjects (pres.-elect 1976). Recipient Am. Bill of Rights citation, Morgenstern Found. Interfaith award; author: Foreign Confiscations in Anglo-American Law, 1951; (with Lester B. Orfield) Cases and Materials on International Law, rev. edit., 1965; Selected Essays on Equity, 1953; Brief Writing and Oral Argument, 4th edit., 1974; (with Zechariah Chafee, Jr.) Cases and Materials on Equity, 1967; Equity and Equitable Remedies, 1975; contbr. articles to legal jours. Home: 184 Beach 143d St Neponsit NY 11694 Office: US Customs Ct 1 Federal Plaza New York City NY 10007 Tel (212) 264-2800

REA, WILLIAM CONWAY, b. Benton, Ark., Oct. 6, 1945; B.A., U. Ark., 1968, J.D., 1970. Admitted to Ark. bar, 1970, U.S. Supreme Ct. bar, 1974; asso. firms Howell, Price, Howell & Barron, Little Rock, 1970-73, Thomas M. Bramhall, Little Rock, 1973-74; partner firm Faubus, Orintas & Rea, Little Rock, 1974-75, Moore & Rea, Little Rock, 1975—. Mem. Am., Ark. trial lawyers assns., Am. Judicature Soc., Am., Ark., Pulaski County bar assns., Phi Alpha Delta. Home: 12 Kingsbridge Way Little Rock AR 72212 Office: 1501 Spring St Little Rock AR 72202 Tel (501) 376-3322

READ, ARTHUR MARTIN, II, b. Providence, June 2, 1946; B.A., Bethany Coll., 1968; M.A., U. R.I., 1971; J.D., Boston U., 1972. Admitted to R.I. bar, 1972, U.S. Dist. Ct. bar, 1973; asso. firm Gorham & Gorham, Inc., Providence, 1972—; spl. asst. atty. gen. R.I., Providence, 1974-75; mem. legal staff Brookline (Mass.) Rent Control Bd., 1971; atty. Boston Legal Assistance Project, 1971-72; mem. R.I. Ho. of Reps., 1977—. Bd. govs. Barrington (R.I.) Boys' Choir; bd. dirs. Barrington Sr. Citizens; mem. Barrington Republican Town Com. Mem. Am., R.I. trial lawyers assns., Am., R.I. bar assns., R.I. Soc. Mayflower Descs. (counsellor), John Howland Soc. Home: 28 Belvidere Ave Barrington RI 02806 Office: Gorham & Gorham 58 Weybosset St Providence RI 02903 Tel (401) 421-7680

READ, BEVERLY C. "JOHN", b. Boston, Oct. 4, 1943; B.A., Va. Mil. Inst., 1965; J.D., Washington and Lee U., 1971. Admitted to Va. bar, 1971; asso. firm Hunton & Williams, Richmond, Va., 1971-74; partner firm Foresman, Read & Elkins, Lexington, Va., 1974-75; individual practice, Lexington, 1976—; commonwealth's atty. Lexington and Rockbridge County (Va.), 1976—. Mem. Am., Va. bar assns., Va. Trial Lawyers Assn. Named Outstanding Young Man Am., 1971. Home: 202 Paxton St Lexington VA 24450 Office: 2 E Washington St Lexington VA 24450 Tel (703) 463-7664

READ, CHARLES ARTHUR, b. Washington, Dec. 14, 1919; B.S. in Commerce, U. Va., 1941, J.D., 1947. Admitted to Va. bar, 1947, N.Y. bar, 1948, D.C. bar, 1964, U.S. Supreme Ct. bar, 1962; asso. firm Reid & Priest, N.Y.C., 1947-55, partner, 1956—; gen. counsel Pub. Power Corp., 1949-52. Trustee Am. Farm Sch., Salonica, Greece, 1969-76, U. Va. Alumni Fund and Alumni Assn., 1973—; chmn. bd. trustees Perkiomen Sch., Pennsburg, Pa., 1970—. Mem. Am., N.Y. State, D.C., Va. bar assns. Home: 162 Inwood Ave Upper Montclair NJ 07043 Office: Reid & Priest 40 Wall St New York City NY 10005 Tel (212) 344-2233

READ, FRANK THOMPSON, b. Ogden, Utah, July 16, 1938; B.S., Brigham Young U., 1960; J.D., Duke, 1963; Admitted to Minn. bar, 1963, Mo. bar, 1966, N.Y. bar, 1968, Okla. bar, 1975; asso. firm Erickson, Popham, Haik & Schnobrich, Mpls., 1964; partner firm Hansen & Hazen, St. Paul, 1964-65; atty. AT & T, Kansas City, Mo. and N.Y.C., 1965-68; asst. prof. law, asst. dean Law Sch., Duke, asso. prof., asst. dean, 1970-72, prof. law, asso. dean., 1972-73, prof., 1973-74; prof. law U. Tulsa, 1974—, dean Law Sch., 1974—. Mem. Am. Bar Assn., Am. Law Inst., Law Sch. Admissions Council (trustee 1976—), Okla. Judicial Council (chmn. 1976—). Contbr. articles to legal jours. Home: 5227 S 69 E Ave Tulsa OK 74145 Office: College of Law U Tulsa 3120 E 4 Pl Tulsa OK 74104 Tel (918) 939-6351

READY, WILLIAM EMMETT, b. Meridian, Miss., Apr. 21, 1933; B.B.A. in Accounting, U. Miss., 1954, LL.B., 1956. Admitted to Miss. bar, 1956, U.S. Supreme Ct. bar, 1967; individual practice law, Meridian, 1956—; spl. legal counsel Miss. Mental Health Bd., 1974-75; atty. Lauderdale County (Miss.) Bd. Suprs., 1975—. Mem. Miss. Comprehensive Health Planning Council, 1970-74, chmn., 1972-74; mem. Miss. Mental Health Bd., 1965—, Lauderdale County Regional Econ. Commn., 1973—; organizer, legal counsel, exec. sec., fin. chmn., govtl. liaison Region 10 Mental Health Complex, 1969—; bd. dirs. Am. Assn. Comprehensive Health Planning, 1971-73, pres., 1971-73, exec. bd., 1973—; bd. dirs. United Way, 1974—; sec. Lauderdale County Democratic Exec. Com., 1976—; mem. subcom. health resources planning, taxation and fin. steering com. Nat. Assn. Counties, 1975-77. Mem. Am. (taxation com. on adminstrv. practice), Miss. (legal aid to poor com. 1969-70), Lauderdale County (legal aid chmn., exec. bd. 1970) bar assns., Am. Judicature Soc., Am. Arbitration Assn., Miss. Assn. County Attys. (v.p., dir. 1976—), Am., Miss. trial lawyers assns., Phi Alpha Delta. Home: 1905 Apache Ridge Rd Meridian MS 39301 Office: PO Box 927 Meridian MS 39301 Tel (601) 693-6678

REAGAN, WOODROW WILSON, b. Tylertown, Miss., Aug. 9, 1912; B.S., Miss. State U., 1934; J.D. cum laude, Miss. Coll., 1964. Admitted to Miss. bar, 1964, U.S. Supreme Ct. bar, 1972; individual practice law, 1964-67; staff atty., dep. sec. State of Miss., Jackson, 1967—; participant numerous profl. seminars, symposiums. Elder, Christian Ch. (Disciples of Christ), Jackson. Mem. Miss. (uniform comml. code com.), Hind County bar assns., Am. Judicature Soc. Author numerous articles in profl. mags. and jours. Home: 1316 Kimwood Dr Jackson MS 39211 Office: Box 136 Jackson MS 39211 Tel (601) 969-6500

REAMON, WILLIAM G., b. Grand Rapids, Mich., Mar. 4, 1927; student Grand Rapids Jr. Coll., 1946-47, Aquinas Coll., Grand Rapids, 1948-51; J.D., U. Mich., 1954. Admitted to Mich. bar, 1954, U.S. Supreme Ct. bar, 1962; claims adjuster, atty. Mich. Mut. Liability Co., Grand Rapids, 1954-58; mem. firm Marcus, McCroskey, Libner, Reamon, Williams & Dilley, Grand Rapids, Battle Creek and Kalamazoo, 1958-71; pres. Reamon, Williams, Klukowski & Craft, Grand Rapids, 1972—; faculty mem. Inst. for Continuing Legal Edn., 1974-76. Kent County campaign coordinator Hart for Sen. Com., 1958; precinct del. City of Grand Rapids and Plainfield Twp., 1960—; Democratic candidate U.S. Ho. of Reps., Fifth Dist., 1960, 62, 64; chmn. Kent County Dem. Com., Fifth Congl. Dist. Dem. Com.; mem. Dem. State Central Com.; pres., bd. dirs. D.A. Blodgett Homes for Children; chmn. bd. dirs. Big Brothers of Grand Rapids; bd. dirs. Kent County div. Cath. Social Services, W.Mich. Emergency Med. Services. Mem. Am., Mich. (commr. 1969—, pres. 1976—), Grand Rapids bar assns., Am. Judicature Soc., Assn. Trial Lawyers Am. (asso. editor Jour. 1961—), Mich., Ill. trial lawyers assns. Office: 101-D Water Bldg Grand Rapids MI 49502

REAMS, BERNARD DINSMORE, JR., b. Lynchburg, Va., Aug. 17, 1943; B.A., Lynchburg Coll., 1965; M.S., Drexel U., 1966; J.D., U. Kans., 1972. Asst. prof., law librarian U. Kans., 1969-74; admitted to Kans. bar, 1973; asst. prof., law librarian Washington U., St. Louis, 1974-76, asso. prof., 1976-77, prof., 1977—, law librarian 1976—. Mem. Am. Bar Assn., Am., Southwestern (v.p. 1976-77, pres. 1978—) assns. law libraries, Order of Coif, Phi Delta Phi. Author: Law For The Businessman, 1974; (with Wilson) Segregation And the Fourteenth Amendment In the States; A Survey Of State Segregation Laws 1865-1953, 1975; (with Kettler) Historic Preservation Law: An Annotated Bibliography, 1976; Reader in Law Librarianship, 1976. Home: 2353 Hollyhead Dr Des Peres MO 63131 Office: Sch of Law Washington U St Louis MO 63130 Tel (314) 863-0100

REAMS, WILLIAM DINWIDDIE, JR., b. Culpeper, Va., Apr. 24, 1929; B.A., U. Va., 1955, LL.B., 1958. Admitted to Va. bar, 1958; individual practice law, Culpeper, 1958-73; commonwealth's atty. Culpeper County, 1960-68; judge Culpeper County Cts., 1968-70, Juvenile and Domestic Relations Dist. Cts., 16th Dist. Va., 1973—, chief judge, 1976—. Mem. Va. State Var, Nat. Council Juvenile Ct. Judges, Va. Assn. Juvenile Ct. Judges, Va. Assn. Dist. Ct. Judges, Delta Theta Phi. Home: RFD 1 PO Box 464 Culpeper VA 22701 Office: 135 W Cameron St Culpeper VA 22701 Tel (703) 825-3040

REAP, JAMES BURNETT, b. Mt. Vernon, N.Y., Oct. 17, 1930; A.B., Wesleyan U., Middletown, Conn., 1952; J.D., Harvard, 1957. Admitted to N.Y. bar, 1957, U.S. Supreme Ct. bar, 1970, U.S. Ct. Mil. Appeals, 1958, certified for gen. cts. martial JAG of Navy, 1959; partner firm Kent Hazzard Wilson Jaeger Freeman & Greer, White Plains, N.Y., 1957—; city judge White Plains, 1970—. Mem. Westchester County Bd. Suprs., 1969; comdg. officer N.Y. Naval Militia, 1973-75. Mem. Am., N.Y. State, Westchester County, White Plains bar assns. Recipient N.Y. State Conspicuous Service medal, 1975, Distinguished Citizenship award Jaycees, 1965. Office: 199 Main St White Plains NY 10601 Tel (914) 948-4700

REARDON, JOHN THOMAS, b. Quincy, Ill., Mar. 3, 1910; LL.B., St. Louis U., 1932. Admitted to Ill. bar, 1933; since practiced in Quincy, Ill., city atty., 1933-36; corp. counsel, 1936-44; state's atty. Adams County, 1944-52; judge 8th Jud. Circuit Ct., 1957-64, chief judge, 1964-76; judge Appellate Ct., 4th Jud. Dist. Ill., 1976—. Past bd. dirs. St. Mary's Hosp., Quincy Coll., Cheerful Home. Mem. Nat. Inst. Trial Advocacy (dir.), Nat. Conf. State Trial Judges (former chmn.), Am. Bar Assn. (past chmn. div. jud. adminstrn.). Home: 4143 Coachlight St Quincy IL 62301 Office: 522 Vermont St Quincy IL 62301 Tel (217) 224-7700

REASBECK, (R) REGIS, b. Meadville, Pa., Dec. 14, 1922; B.A., Allegeny Coll., Meadville, Pa., 1949, M.Ed., 1951; LL.B., U. Miami, 1954. Admitted to Fla. bar, 1954; partner firm Reasbeck and Fegers, Hollywood, Fla., 1954—; city atty., Pembroke Pines, Fla.; municipal judge, Pembroke Pines and Plantation, Fla.; gen. counsel S. Broward hosp. dist.; gen. counsel, tax assessor Broward County. Mem. Broward County Charter Rev. Bd., 1975. Mem. Nat. Assn. Arbitrators, Am. Arbitration Assn., Fla., Broward County, Hollywood bar assns., C. of C. (pres. 1950). Office: 6011 Rodman St Hollywood FL 33023 Tel (305) 983-7300

REAVIS, JOHN WALLACE, b. Falls City, Nebr., Nov. 13, 1899; LL.B., Cornell U., 1921; LL.D., Case Western Res. U., 1958. Admitted to Ohio bar, 1922, D.C. bar, 1967; asso. firm Jones, Day, Reavis & Pogue and predecessor firms, Cleve., 1921-27, partner, 1927-48, mgr. partner, 1948-75, sr. partner, 1975—. Pres. trustee Kulas Found., 1937; trustee Huntington Art and Poly. Trust, Cleve., 1952, Case Western Res. U., 1950-72. Mem. Am., Fed., Ohio, Cleve. bar assns., Am. Judicature Soc., Cornell Law Assn., Cleve. C. of C. (chmn. 1948-66), Order of Coif, Phi Kappa Phi, Phi Delta Phi. Home: 2723 Ashley Rd Shaker Heights OH 44122 Office: 1700 Union Commerce Bldg Cleveland OH 44115 Tel (216) 696-3939

REBACK, FORBES ROBINSON, b. N.Y.C., Aug. 6, 1935; B.S., Cornell U., 1958; LL.B., U. Va., 1964. Admitted to Va. bar, 1964; asso. firms Shackelford & Robertson, Orange, Va., 1964-65, Paxson, Marshall & Smith, Charlottesville, Va., 1965-67; mem. firm Richmond and Fishburne, Charlottesville, 1967-73; individual practice law, Charlottesville, 1973—; sec. Central Va. Estate Planning Council, 1976—. Pres. Blue Ridge Lung Assn., Charlottesville, 1970-73, dir., 1965—; pres. Civic League of Charlottesville and Albemarle County (Va.), 1975—. Mem. Am., Va., Charlottesville-Albemarle bar assns., Va. State Bar. Home: Hunting Ridge Farm Rt 2 Charlottesville VA 22901 Office: 230 Court Sq Charlottesville VA 22901 Tel (804) 295-1196

REBELL, MICHAEL AARON, b. Bklyn., May 4, 1943; B.A., Harvard, 1965; LL.B., Yale, 1970. Admitted to N.Y. bar, 1971, U.S. Supreme Ct. bar, 1976; asso. firm Fried, Frank, Harris, Shriver & Jacobson, N.Y.C., 1970-71; asso. dir. N.Y. Lawyer's Com. for Civil Rights Under Law, N.Y.C., 1972-73; founding partner firm Rebell & Krieger, N.Y.C. and White Plains, N.Y., 1973—; adj. asso. prof. law State U. N.Y., Purchase; speaker in field of edn. law; spl. counsel N.Y. State Assembly Edn. Com. Mem. bd. edn. Congregation Knesseth Tiffereth Israel, Port Chester, N.Y., 1975—. Mem. N.Y. State, Westchester (county, N.Y.) bar assns., Assn. Bar City N.Y. Nat. Inst. Edn. grantee, 1976-78; contbr. numerous articles to profl. jours.; research on role of cts. in edn. policy decisions. Office: 230 Park Ave New York City NY 10017 Tel (212) 532-2211

REBER, JOSEPH EDWARD, b. Butte, Mont., Aug. 9, 1940; B.A., U. Mont., 1962, J.D., 1965. Admitted to Mont. bar, 1965, U.S. Supreme Ct. bar, 1969; clk. Mont. Supreme Ct., 1965; individual practice law, Helena, Mont., 1965—; sec., treas., dir. Reber Co., 1965—; dir., officer New Finlen Hotel Co., Reber Realty & Devel. Co., Capital Co., Inc.; mng. partner Diamond Block Partnership, 1969—, Joe Reber Partnership, 1973—; gen. partner Clark Land Co., 1975—. Trustee Mont. Hist. Soc.; sec. Nat. Found., Lewis and Clark County, Mont.; mem. nat. Democratic platform com., 1976, alt. del. nat. conv., 1976; bd. dirs. Blackfeet Indian Arts Council; mem. City of Helena Redevel. Co. Mem. Am., Mont., First Judicial (pres. 1970) bar assns., Commercial Law League, Phi Delta Phi. Home: 1522 Winnie St Helena MT 59601 Office: 1645 N Montana Ave Helena MT 59601 Tel (406) 442-5100

RECHENMACHER, LEROY LEO, b. Naperville, Ill., May 28, 1912; student Iowa State Tchrs. Coll., 1932-33, John Marshall Law Sch., 1938-39; LL.B., Mt. Vernon Sch. Law, Balt., 1941; grad. Nat. Coll. State Trial Judges, 1965. Admitted to Md. bar, 1942, Ill. bar, 1946; practiced in Naperville, 1946-64; police magistrate City of Naperville, 1947-64; asso. judge Ill. Circuit Ct., 18th Jud. Circuit, 1964-70, circuit judge, 1970-73, acting chief judge, 1971-72, chief judge, 1972-73; judge Ill. Appellate Ct., 2d Dist., 1973—. Mem. Republican Precinct Com., 1947-64; chmn. Lisle Twp (Ill.) Republican Orgn., 1954-64. Mem. DuPage County (pres. 1959-60), Ill., Am. bar assns., Am. Judicature Soc., Ill. Judges Assn. (dir.). Office: 50 W Chicago Ave Naperville IL 60540 Tel (312) 355-0890

RECK, JOEL M., b. Worcester, Mass., Sept. 27, 1941; B.A., Bowdoin Coll., 1963; J.D., Harvard, 1966. Admitted to Mass. bar, 1967; partner firm Brown Rudnick Freed & Gesmer, Boston, 1974—. Trustee, Combined Jewish Philanthropies of Boston; mem. Wayland (Mass.) Growth Policy Com. Mem. Am., Mass., Boston bar assns. Home: 42 Sears Rd Wayland MA 01778 Office: 85 Devonshire St Boston MA 02109 Tel (617) 726-7800

RECTOR, LEO WESLEY, b. Mpls., Mar. 24, 1920; student N.D. State Schl. Sci., 1937-39; B.A., N.D. State Tchrs. Coll., 1945; J.D., U. Colo., 1947. Admitted to Colo. bar, 1948, U.S. Dist. Ct. bar, 1950, U.S. Supreme Ct. bar, 1959; since practiced in Colorado Springs, Colo.; dist. atty. 4th Judicial Dist., 1956-60; sr. partner firm Rector, Kane, Donley & Wills, 1960-71; sr. partner firm Rector & Retherford, 1971—. Pres. Skyway Park Civic Assn., 1961; chmn. 3d. Congressional Dist. Dem. Com., 1956-60. Mem. Am., Colo., El Paso County (pres. 1975-76), bar assns., World Assn. Lawyers, Am. Judicature Soc., Colo. Dist. Attys. Assn. (pres. 1957). Home: 2706 Andromeda Dr Colorado Springs CO 80906 Office: 228 N Cascade Ave Colorado Springs CO 80903 Tel (303) 475-2014

REDDEN, JAMES ANTHONY, b. Springfield, Mass., Mar. 13, 1929; student Boston U., 1950-52; J.D., Boston Coll., 1954. Admitted to Mass. bar, 1954, Oreg. bar, 1955; asso. firm Roberts, Kellington and Branchfield, Medford, Oreg., 1955-57; partner firm Collins, Redden, Ferris & Velure, Medford, 1957-72; state treas. State of Oreg., 1973-77; atty. gen. State of Oreg., 1977—. Mem. Oreg. State Bar, Am. Bd. Trial Advs., Oreg. Assn. Def. Counsel. Office: 100 State Office Bldg Salem OR 97310 Tel (503) 378-4400

REDDEN, LAWRENCE DREW, b. Tallassee, Ala., Dec. 16, 1922; A.B., U. Ala., 1943, LL.B., J.D., 1949. Admitted to Ala. bar, 1949, U.S. Dist. Ct. bar No. Dist. Ala., 1949, 5th U.S. Circuit Ct. Appeals bar, 1951, U.S. Supreme Ct. bar, 1968; asst. U.S. atty. No. Dist. Ala., 1949-52; partner firm Rogers, Howard, Redden & Mills, Birmingham, Ala., 1952—. Trustee Ala. Law Sch. Found., 1963—; mem. adv. bd. Cumberland Law Sch., 1975—. Fellow Am. Coll. Trial Lawyers; mem. Am., Ala. (pres. 1972-73), Birmingham (pres. 1969) bar assns., Internat. Soc. Barristers, Am. Judicature Soc. Home: 2513 Beaumont Circle Birmingham AL 35216 Office: Frank Nelson Bldg Birmingham AL 35203 Tel (205) 251-5138

REDDIN, MARY CAROLINA, b. Chgo., Sept. 7, 1947; B.A., U. Wis., 1968, J.D., 1974. Admitted to Wis. bar, 1974; staff atty. Legal Aid Soc. Milw., 1974-76; v.p., bd. dirs. C.O.P.E., Inc., Milw., 1975—. Mem. Am., Wis., Milw. Jr. bar assns. Contbr. article Info. Bull. for Wis. Legis. Council. Home: 612 N 70th St Wauwatosa WI 53213 Office: 612 N 70th St Wauwatosa WI 53213

REDDING, ROBERT WILLIAM, b. Portland, Oreg., Aug. 20, 1942; B.S., U. Oreg., 1964; J.D. cum laude, Willamette U., 1967; grad. Nat. Coll. State Judiciary, 1973. Admitted to Oreg. bar, 1967, U.S. Dist. Ct. bar for Dist. Oreg., 1967, U.S. Ct. Appeals bar, 9th Circuit, 1967; law clk. Oreg. Supreme Ct., 1967; practiced in Hillsboro, Oreg., 1968, Portland, Oreg., 1968-72; judge Oreg. Dist. Ct. for Multnomah County, 1973—; mem. faculty Nat. Coll. State Judiciary, 1974. Chmn. bd. dirs. Portland Boys Choir, 1972-73; bd. dirs. Alcohol Rehab. Assn. Oreg., 1976—. Mem. Am., Multnomah County bar assns., Oreg. Jud. Conf. (chmn. com. pub. info. 1974—, exec. com. 1976—), Oreg. Dist. Judges Assn. (exec. com. 1973—), Am. Judicature Soc., Order of the Purple, Delta Theta Phi (scholarship Key award). Editor, contbr. Willamette Law Jour., 1966-67. Home: 2988 SW Bennington Dr Portland OR 97201 Office: 1021 SW Fourth Ave Portland OR 97204 Tel (503) 248-3954

REDEKER, JAMES RUSSELL, b. Primgar, Iowa, May 28, 1941; B.A. cum laude, Central U. Iowa, 1963; M.A. in English Lit., U. Ark., 1965; J.D., U. Pa., 1968. Admitted to Pa. bar, 1968; since practiced in Phila., asso. firm White & Williams, 1968-71; asso. firm Cohen, Shapiro, Polisher, Shiekman & Cohen, and predecessor, 1971, partner, 1974—. Mem. Am., Fed., Pa., Phila. (chmn. com. child abuse, Fidelity award 1976), bar assns., Am. Judicature Soc. Author: Employer Obligations Under the Occupational, Safety and Health Act, 1971; Right of Employees to Representation During Disciplinary Interviews, 1972; Employer's Guide to the Rehabilitation Act of 1973, 1974. Home: 822 Great Springs Rd Rosemont PA 19010 Office: 12 S 12th St Philadelphia PA 19107 Tel (215) 922-1300

REDFERN, E. LEE, b. Atlanta, Oct. 21, 1942; B.B.A., U. Ga., 1964, J.D., 1967. Admitted to Ga. bar, 1966; individual practice, law, Atlanta, 1967-68; partner firm Redfern Butler & Morgan, Atlanta, 1969—. Mem. Am., Atlanta bar assns., State Bar Ga., Ga., Am. trial lawyers assns., Atlanta Lawyers Club. Office: 2000 Atlanta Gas Light Tower Atlanta GA 30303 Tel (404) 681-2000

REDFORD, MACK ANDY, b. Wendall, Idaho, July 16, 1937; B.S. in Agr. Econs., U. Ida., 1961, J.D., 1967. Ter. salesman Firestone Tire & Rubber Co., Salt Lake City, Boise, Great Falls, Mont., 1961-64; police judge, Moscow, Idaho, 1965-67; admitted to Idaho bar, 1967, since practiced in Boise; chief criminal dep., 1968-70; Idaho Atty. Gen.'s office, 1967-70, partner Webb, Johnson, Tway, Redford & Greener, 1970—. Instr., Ida. Police Acad., 1968—; chmn. Idaho Commn. for Pardons and Paroles, 1968—; mem. Gov.'s Council Criminal Justice; cons. to Idaho Supreme Court, 1971—. Mem. Police Officer Standards and Tng. Commn., 1968-69. Bd. dirs. Adults in Corrections. Alternate del. to Republican Nat. Conv., 1972. Mem. Idaho Bar Assn. (commr. 1974—, pres. 1976-77), Am. Judicature Soc., U. Idaho Alumni Assn. (exec. bd. 1971—), Justice (pres. 1966),

Phi Alpha Delta, Alpha Tau Omega. Home: 3939 Rampart Boise ID 83704 Office: Old Library Sq 815 Washington St Boise ID 83701*

REDINGTON, EDWARD SCHENCK, b. Bay Shore, N.Y., Aug. 26, 1914; B.A., Dartmouth Coll., 1936; LL.B., Yale U., 1939. Admitted to N.Y. bar, 1940; partner firm Hughes, Hubbard & Reed, N.Y.C., 1940—; dir. So. Natural Resources, Inc., So. Natural Gas Co., Birmingham, Ala. Vice pres. Bd. Edn. Bay Shore, 1950-60, chmn. Brightwaters (N.Y.) Bd. Zoning Appeals, 1950-65; bd. dirs., chmn. Southside Hosp., Bay Shore; trustee Hewlett Sch., E. Islip, N.Y., 1960-69, Allen-Chase Found., Deerfield, Mass.; bd. dirs. Episcopal Ch. Found., 1976—, mem. vestry council local ch., 1963—. Mem. Am., N.Y. bar assns., Assn. Bar City N.Y., N.Y. County Lawyers Assn. Home: 56 E Bayberry Rd Islip NY 11751 Office: 1 Wall St New York City NY 10005 Tel (212) 943-6500

REDLE, EDWARD JOSEPH, b. Sheridan, Wyo., Aug. 7, 1922; B.S., St. Louis U., 1949; LL.B., Creighton U., 1951. Admitted to Wyo. bar, 1951; municipal ct. judge, Sheridan, 1952-53; mem. Wyo. State Legis., 1953-54; county atty. Sheridan County, 1955-62; mem. firm Redle, Yonkee & Arney, Sheridan, 1962—; justice of peace, 1963-74. Mem. Sheridan County, Wyo., Am. bar assns., Am. Judicature Soc. Recipient Distinguished Service award Jr. C. of C., 1952, 53, Sheridan C. of C., 1957, Nat. Americanism Commn., Am. Legion, 1951. Home: 1050 LaClede St Sheridan WY 82801 Office: 24 S Main St Sheridan WY 82801 Tel (307) 674-7454

REDLICH, NORMAN, b. N.Y.C., Nov. 12, 1925; A.B., Williams Coll., 1947, LL.D. (hon.), 1976; LL.B., Yale, 1950; LL.M., N.Y. U., 1955. Admitted to N.Y. bar, 1951; practiced in N.Y.C., 1951-59; asso. prof. law N.Y. U., 1960-62, prof. law, 1962-74, asso. dean Sch. Law, 1974-75, dean, 1975—, editor-in-chief Tax Law Rev., 1960-66, mem. adv. com. Inst. Fed. Taxation, 1963-68; exec. asst. corp. counsel N.Y.C., 1966-68, 1st asst. corp. counsel, 1970-72, corp. counsel, 1972-74; asst. counsel Pres. Commn. on Assassination Pres. Kennedy, 1963-64. Mem. commn. on law and social action Am. Jewish Congress, 1962—; mem. Borough Pres.'s Planning Bd. Number 2, 1959-70; mem. housing com. Community Service Soc., 1962-75; counsel N.Y. Com. to Abolish Capital Punishment, 1958—. Mem. N.Y.C. Bd. Edn., 1969; mem. bd. overseers Jewish Theol. Sem., 1973—. Fellow Am. Bar Found.; mem. Assn. Bar City of N.Y. (exec. com. 1975—). Author: Professional Responsibility: A Problem Approach, 1976; contbr. articles in field. Home: 29 Washington Sq New York City NY 10011 Office: NY U Sch Law Washington Sq New York City NY 10003*

REDMAN, ROBERT ROSS, b. Yakima, Wash., Oct. 1, 1928; B.A., U. Wash., 1951, J.D., 1957. Admitted to Wash. bar, 1957; asso. firm Gavin, Robinson & Kendrick, Yakima, 1957-61; partner firm Gavin Robinson Kendrick Redman & Mays, Yakima, 1961—. Campaign chmn. United Way of Yakima County, 1975-76, pres., 1976-77. Mem. Am., Wash. State (bd. govs. 1974-77), Yakima County bar assns., U. Wash. Alumni Assn. (pres. 1973). Home: 5310 Englewood Hill Dr Yakima WA 98908 Office: 410 Miller Bldg Yakima WA 98901 Tel (509) 453-9131

REDMOND, CHARLES DANIEL, b. Columbus, Ohio, May 21, 1914; B.S. in Bus. Adminstrn., Ohio State U., 1936; LL.B., Franklin U., 1954; J.D., Capital U., 1959. Admitted to Ohio bar, 1954, U.S. Supreme Ct. bar, 1957; partner firm Volkema, Redmond & Post, Columbus, 1963-71; asso. firm Sebastian, Marsh & Redmond, Columbus, 1971—. Trustee Riverside Methodist Hosp.; trustee, pres. Wesley Glen Retirement Center. Mem. Columbus, Ohio, Am. bar assns. Home: 2857 Charing Rd Columbus OH 45221 Office: 50 W Broad St Suite 2230 Columbus OH 43215 Tel (614) 221-1661

REDMOND, CHRISTOPHER JOHN, b. Oakland, Calif., May 8, 1947; B.A., U. Kans., 1968, J.D., 1970. Admitted to Kans. bar, 1971, U.S. Supreme Ct. bar, 1974; partner firm Redmond & Redmond, Wichita, Kans., 1970—; vice chmn. bd., gen. counsel Seneca State Bank of Wichita, 1975—; pres. C & R Diversified Investments, Inc., real estate holding corp., Wichita, 1976—. Mem. com. on fund raising, Wichita chmn. Kans. Heart Assn.; bd. dirs. Am. Heart Assn. Kans. affiliate. Mem. Wichita, Kans., Am. bar assns., Kans., Am. trial lawyers assns., Comml. Law League. Recipient Service to Mankind award Kans. Heart Assn., 1976. Home: 6906 Timberon Ln Wichita KS 67208 Office: 619 W Douglas St Wichita KS 67213 Tel (316) 262-8362

REDNER, STEPHEN JOSEPH, b. N.Y.C., Feb. 21, 1947; A.A., Santa Monica City Coll., 1966; A.B. in History and Polit. Sci., U. Calif. at Los Angeles, 1968; J.D., Loyola U., Los Angeles, 1972. Admitted to Calif. bar, 1973; individual practice law, San Francisco, 1973—. Mem. Mill Valley (Calif.) Art Commn. Mem. Am., San Francisco bar assns., Calif. Trial Lawyers' Assn. Tel (415) 928-5400

REDPATH, JAMES ROBERT, b. Kansas City, Kans., Nov. 22, 1937; J.D., U. Ark., 1964. Admitted to Ark. bar, 1964, Ariz. bar, 1965, U.S. Supreme Ct. bar, 1970, U.S. Ct. Claims bar, 1972; asst. atty. gen. State of Ariz., 1965-76, asst. chief counsel civil div. dept. transp. Atty. Gen.'s Office, 1976—; guest lectr. Phoenix Coll., 1976, Ariz. Dept. Health Services, 1976. Mem. Maricopa County (Ariz.) Bar Assn., State Bar Ariz. (com. to evaluate bar exam. 1974-76, adminstrv. com. for discipline of mems. of state bar 1974-76). Recipient certificate of appreciation Am. Right of Way Assn., 1976, Ariz. Dept. Transp., 1975. Home: 902 W Catalina Dr Phoenix AZ 85013 Office: 1801 W Jefferson St 4th Floor Phoenix AZ 85007 Tel (602) 261-7291

REDSTONE, SUMNER MURRAY, b. Boston, May 27, 1923; B.A., Harvard U., 1944, LL.B., 1947. Admitted to Mass. bar, 1947, U.S. Ct. Appeals 1st Circuit bar, 1948, 8th Circuit bar, 1950, 9th Circuit bar, 1948, D.C. bar, 1951, U.S. Supreme Ct. bar, 1952; law sec. U.S. Ct. Appeals for 9th Circuit, San Francisco, 1947-48; instr. law and labor mgmt. U. San Francisco, 1947; spl. asst. U.S. Atty. Gen., Washington, 1948-51; partner firm Ford, Bergson, Adams, Borkland & Redstone, Washington, 1951-54; exec. v.p. Northeast Drive-In Theatre Corp., Boston, 1954-67, pres., 1967—. Chmn. met. div. NE Combined Jewish Philanthropies, Boston, 1963; bd. dirs. Boston Art Festival, Sidney Farber Cancer Center; pres. Theatre Owners Am., 1960-65, chmn. bd., 1966; sponsor Boston Mus. Sci.; mem. corp. New Eng. Med. Center; mem. exec. com. Am. Congress Exhibitors. Mem. Am., Boston bar assns., Harvard Law Sch. Assn., Am. Judicature Soc. Recipient William J. German Human Relations award, Am. Jewish Com. Entertainment and Communication Div., 1977; named One of 10 Outstanding Young Men, Greater Boston C. of C. Home: 98 Baldpate Hill Rd Newton Centre MA 02159 Office: 31 Saint James Ave Boston MA 02116 Tel (617) 482-5400

REED, CHARLES SEYMOUR, b. Arnold, Neb., June 4, 1896; A.B., U. Nebr., LL.B. Admitted to Nebr. bar, 1921; practice law; pres. Bank of Bellevue (Nebr.). Bd. dirs. Nebr. Goodwill Industries; founder Sod House Soc. of Nebr., Reed Community Center. Mem. Am., Nebr. bar assns., Omaha Execs. Assn. (pres.). Recipient Harlan Lewis Community award; named Boss of Year, author: Sod House Memories; Christmas In A Nebraska Soddie; The Iron Horse Came Up the South Loup Valley. Home: 501 Ridge Rd Bellevue NE 68005 Office: 2208 Hancock St Bellevue NE 68005 Tel (402) 291-6000

REED, FREDERIC CLARK, b. Casper, Wyo., Sept. 21, 1942; B.A., U. Wyo., 1965, J.D., 1967. Admitted to Wyo. bar, 1967, Colo. bar, 1967; asst. atty. gen. State of Wyo., Cheyenne, 1968-73, dep. atty. gen. criminal div., Cheyenne, 1973-75; asst. U.S. atty. Dist. of Wyo., Cheyenne, 1975—. Mem. Wyo., Laramie County bar assns. Home: 525 Dartmouth Ln Cheyenne WY 82001 Office: PO Box 668 Cheyenne WY 82001 Tel (307) 778-2220

REED, GEORGE FRANKLIN, b. Beaver, Pa., Jan. 19, 1935; B.A., Princeton, 1956; J.D., U. Pa., 1959. Admitted to Pa. bar, 1960; asso. firm Morgan, Lewis & Bockius, Phila., 1960-67; gen. counsel Pa. Ins. Dept., Harrisburg, 1967-69; ins. commr. Commonwealth of Pa., Harrisburg, 1969-71; sr. v.p. Am. Gen. Ins. Co., Houston, 1971—; pres., dir. Am. Gen. Capital Mgmt., Inc., 1976—, also officer, dir. subs. Chmn. state employees div. Tri-County United Fund, Harrisburg, 1969, bd. dirs., 1970-71. Mem. cabinet Gov. Raymond P. Shafer, 1969-71. Bd. regents Mercersburg Acad. Served with AUS, 1959-60, Pa. N.G., 1960-65. Recipient Distinguished Service award Harrisburg Jr. C. of C., 1969. Mem. Am., Tex., Pa. (chmn. young lawyers sect. 1968-69), Phila. (sec. Jr. Bar Conf. 1962-63) bar assns., Houston C. of C. (dir. 1974-75). Home: 514 Clear Spring Dr Houston TX 77079 Office: 2727 Allen Pkwy Houston TX 77019

REED, HARRY LOWE, b. Houston, Dec. 16, 1923; A.B., U. Tex., 1943, J.D., 1948. Admitted to Tex. bar, 1948; atty. Shell Oil Co., Houston, 1948-75, gen. atty. 1975—; adj. prof. S. Tex. Coll. Law, Houston, 1952—. Councilman City of Bellaire, Tex., 1953-56, mayor, 1956-57. Mem. Am., Houston bar assns., State Bar Tex., Am. Judicature Soc. Home: 5422 Dumfries St Houston TX 77096 Office: PO Box 2463 Houston TX 77001 Tel (713) 220-3405

REED, HOWARD FRANKLIN, JR., b. Niles, Ohio, Dec. 20, 1920; B.S., Temple U., 1943; LL.B., U. Pa., 1949. Admitted to Pa. bar, 1950; partner firm Reed, Gibbons & Buckley, Media, Pa., 1959-68; prothonotary Delaware County, Pa., 1953-56; judge Ct. Common Pleas, 32d Jud. Dist. Pa., Media, 1969—. Mem. exec. bd. Valley Forge council Boy Scouts Am. Mem. Am., Pa. bar assns., Pa. Trial Judges Assn. Office: Delaware County Courthouse Media PA 19063 Tel (215) 891-2135

REED, JAMES ALEXANDER, JR., b. Rochester, N.Y., Feb. 7, 1930; B.A., Amherst Coll., 1952; LL.B., Harvard, 1955. Admitted to N.Y. bar, 1958, U.S. Dist. Ct., 1960. Asso. law firm Lines, Wilkens, Osborn & Beck and predecessor Rochester, N.Y., 1958-63, partner, 1964—. Dep. town atty., Town of Pittsford, N.Y., 1976, town atty., 1977—. Mem. Monroe County, N.Y. State, Am. bar assns., Am. Judicature Soc. Home: 21 Gladbrook Rd Pittsford NY 14534 Office: 47 S Fitzhugh St Rochester NY 14614

REED, JAMES WILSON, b. Clay, W.Va., Dec. 19, 1927; A.B., W.Va. U., 1951, LL.B., J.D., 1952. Admitted to W.Va. bar, 1952; served to capt. JAGD USAFR, 1955-57; area rep. JAG, USAF, 1963; individual practice law, Clay, W.Va., 1977—; pros. atty. Clay County, W.Va., 1953-55, 68-72, 77—. Mem. W.Va., Am. bar assns., Am. Judicature Soc. Home and office: Clay WV 25043 Tel (304) 587-4862

REED, JOHN WESLEY, b. Independence, Mo., Dec. 11, 1918; A.B., William Jewell Coll., 1939; LL.B., Cornell U., 1942; LL.M., Columbia U., 1949, Jur. Sc.D., 1957. Admitted to Mo. bar, 1942, Mich. bar, 1953; with firm Stinson, Mag, Thomson, McEvers & Fizzell, Kansas City, Mo., 1942-46; asso. prof. law U. Okla., 1946-49; asso. prof., then prof. law U. Mich., 1949-64, prof. law, 1968—; prof. law, dean Law Sch., U. Colo., 1964-68; dir. Inst. Continuing Legal Edn., prof. law Wayne State U., 1968-73; vis. prof. N.Y. U., 1949, U. Chgo., 1960, Yale U., 1963-64; mem. Salzburg (Austria) Seminar Am. Studies, 1962, chmn., 1964. Pres. bd. mgrs. of ministers and missionaries benefit bd. Am. Baptist Conv., 1967-74; mem. com. visitors Judge Adv. Gen.'s Sch., U.S. Army, 1971-77. Trustee Kalamazoo Coll., 1954-64, 68-74. Mem. Colo. (bd. govs. 1964-68), Am. (council litigation sect.) bar assns., Assn. Am. Law Sch. (mem. exec. com. 1965-67), Am. Acad. Jud. Edn. (bd. govs.). Author: (with W.W. Blume) Cases and Statutes on Pleading and Joinder, 1952; (with others) Introduction to Law and Equity, 1953; Annual Advocacy Handbooks, 1963-74; also articles. Editor-in-chief Cornell Law Quar., 1941-42. Home: 3586 E Huron River Dr Ann Arbor MI 48104 Office: Hutchins Hall Ann Arbor MI 48109

REED, PAUL R., b. Wilkinsburg, Pa., Mar. 30, 1928; B.S., U. Pitts., 1950; LL.B., Georgetown U., 1953. Admitted to Del. bar, 1956; asso. firm Tunnell & Tunnell, Georgetown, Del., 1956-58; individual practice law, Georgetown, 1958—; asst. dept. atty. Gen. Sunsey County (Del.), 1958-60. Pres. Rehoboth Beach (Del.) PTA, 1966-67. Mem. Georgetown C. of C. (pres.). Office: 100 N Bedford St Georgetown DE 19947 Tel (302) 856-7326

REED, REX HOWARD, b. Joliet, Ill., Dec. 7, 1935; B.S. in Accounting, U. Ill., 1958; J.D. So. Methodist U., 1961. Admitted to Tex. bar, 1961, D.C. bar, 1965; served to capt. USAF Judge Adv. Gen., Shaw AFB, S.C., 1962-65; atty. FPC, Washington, 1965-66, NLRB, Houston, 1966-68; asso. gen. counsel U.S. Army and Air Force Exchange Service, Dallas, 1968-71; v.p., legal dir. Nat. Right to Work Legal Def. Fedn., Fairfax, Va., 1971—. Mem. Tex., Fed., Am., D.C. bar assns. Home: 1835 St Boniface St Vienna VA 22180 Office: 8316 Arlington Blvd Fairfax VA 22038 Tel (703) 573-7010

REED, ROBERT B., b. Pitts., Nov. 13, 1945; B.A., U. Fla., 1968, J.D., 1970. Admitted to Fla. bar, 1970; mem. firm Griffith & Moore, 1970-72, Reed & Smodish, Boynton Beach, Fla., 1972—; city atty., Boynton Beach 1976—, dir., legal counsel W. Boynton Beach Nat. Bank 1975—; pub. defender, Boynton Beach, 1972-73. Dir., legal counsel Greater Boynton Beach C. of C. 1972—. Mem. Palm Beach County, S. Palm Beach County bar assns., Phi Kappa Phi. Home: 160 SE 27th Ave Boynton Beach FL 33435 Office: 640 E Ocean Ave Boynton Beach FL 33435 Tel (305) 737-1995

REED, SCOTT. Now chief justice Ky. Supreme Ct., Frankfort. Office: Ky Supreme Ct Frankfort KY 40601*

REED, STANLEY FORMAN, JR., b. Maysville, Ky., Aug. 5, 1914; A.B., Yale U., 1935; LL.B., Harvard U., 1938. Admitted to N.Y. State bar, 1940; asso. firm Root, Clark, Buckner & Ballantine, N.Y.C., 1938-41; asso. firm Carter, Ledyard & Milburn, N.Y.C., 1946-66, partner, 1966—. Mem. Assn. Bar City N.Y., N.Y. State, Am. bar assns. Home: 520 E 86th St New York City NY 10028 Office: Carter Ledyard & Milburn 2 Wall St New York City NY 10005 Tel (212) 732-3200

REED, THOMAS ANDREW, b. Bklyn., Feb. 4, 1934; B.S., Fordham U., 1963; J.D., Cornell U., 1966. Admitted to N.Y. State bar, 1966; partner firm Reed & Reed, Poughkeepsie, N.Y., 1966—; town justice Town of Pleasant Valley, N.Y., 1972—; mem. Dutchess County Criminal Justice Coordinating Council. Bd. dirs. Pleasant Valley Day Care and Nursery; mem. Pleasant Valley Fire Co. Mem. N.Y. State, Dutchess County bar assns., Dutchess County, N.Y. State magistrates assns., Cornell Law Assn. Home: Meadow Ln Pleasant Valley NY 12569 Office: 75 Market St Poughkeepsie NY 12601 Tel (914) 454-4340

REED, THOMAS JAMES, b. Joliet, Ill., Jan. 1, 1940; B.A., Marquette U., 1962; J.D., U. Notre Dame, 1969. Admitted to Ind. bar, 1969; asso. firm Reller, Mendenhall, Kleinknecht & Milligan, Richmond, Ind., 1969-76; asst. prof. law Western New Eng. Coll. Sch. of Law, Springfield, Mass., 1976—; asst. city atty., Richmond, Ind., 1973. Mem. Am., Ind. bar assns., Soc. Archtl. Historians, Nat. Trust for Hist. Preservation. Drafted Ind. revised hist. preservation plan, 1974; contbr. articles on law and planning to jours. Home: 8 Drury Ln Longmeadow MA 01106 Office: Wilbraham Rd Springfield MA 01119 Tel (413) 782-6131

REEDER, BENJAMIN GARNET, b. Shinston, W.Va., Aug. 15, 1899; A.B., W.Va. U., 1921, LL.B., 1923, J.D., 1960. Admitted to W.Va. bar, 1923; individual practice law, Morgantown, W.Va., 1925—; chmn. bd. Farmers & Mchts. Bank, Morgantown, 1965-72; gen. receiver Monongalia County Circuit Ct. Chmn. bd. trustees Wesley United Methodist Ch., 1974-76; bd. dirs. Morgantown Pub. Library, 1965-76. Mem. Am., W.Va., Mongalia County bar assns. Home: 232 Wagner Rd Morgantown WV 26505 Office: PO Box 842 170 Chancery Row Morgantown WV 26505 Tel (304) 292-8488

REEF, NORMAN SIDNEY, b. Portland, Maine, Aug. 16, 1933; B.A., Boston U., 1957, LL.B., 1960. Admitted to Maine, Mass. bars, 1960, U.S. Supreme Ct. bar, 1965; asso. Lewis E. Chandler, Cambridge, Mass., 1960-62; individual practice law, Portland, 1962-63; asso. firm Bennett, Schwarz & Reef, Portland, 1964-69; partner firm Reef & Mooers, Portland, 1969—; draftsman Jury Reform Bill, 1967; mem. Gov's. Commn. Rehab., 1967; mem. Commn. Revise Ins. Laws, 1967; hearing officer Social Security Adminstrn., 1972—; instr. criminal justice dept. U. Maine, 1973—. Co-chmn. lawyers div. Heart Fund, Portland, 1963; corporator Portland Boys Club, 1968; gen. counsel Maine Democratic Party, 1974—; bd. dirs. Jewish Community Center, Portland. Mem. Am. (chmn. task force home office and budget com., pres. state committeeman 1967-68), Maine (sec., gov., v.p. 1968-70) trial lawyers assns., Am., Maine bar assns., Am. Judicature Soc. Assoc. editor Am. Trial Lawyers Assn. Law Jour., 1965. Home: 88 Hamblet Ave Portland ME 04103 Office: 482 Congress St Portland ME 04101 Tel (207) 774-6171

REEH, RICHARD LEE, b. Tulsa, Nov. 22, 1944; A.B. cum laude, Princeton U., 1967; J.D., U. Tulsa, 1972. Admitted to Okla. bar; asst. prosecutor City of Tulsa, 1973; municipal judge City of Tulsa, 1976; individual practice law, Tulsa. Mem. Tulsa Met. Area Planning Commn., 1975. Mem. Okla., Tulsa County, Am. bar assns. Home: 2324 S Cincinnati St Tulsa OK 74114 Office: 1701 S Boston Ave Tulsa OK 74119 Tel (918) 582-3405

REESE, CORRIE THOMAS, b. Jasper, Tex., May 5, 1934; B.S., Sam Houston U., 1956, J.D., U. Houston, 1966. Research technician Shell Chem. Co., Houston, 1956-63; law clk. U.S. 5th Circuit Ct. Appeals, 1964-66; asst. prof. law Baylor U., 1966-67; admitted to Tex. bar, 1967; asst. prof. law Tex. Tech. U., 1968-70, asst. dean, 1969-71, asso. prof. law, 1970-73, asso. dean, 1971-73, prof. law, 1973—, dean continuing edn. for univ complex, 1974—; asst. to pres. U. Va., 1973-74. Dist. vice-chmn. Boy Scouts Am.; mem. bd. vestry St. Christophers Episcopal Ch., mem. sch. bd. Ch. sch.; dir. Lubbock (Tex.) Theatre Center. Mem. Tex., Lubbock County bar assns., Assn. Am. Law Schs., Phi Delta Phi, Order of Coif, Order of Barons. Contbr. articles in field to legal jours. Home: 3704 64th St Lubbock TX 79413 Office: Tex Tech U Law Sch Lubbock TX 79409 Tel (806) 742-3785

REESE, JOHN HAYES, B.B.A., LL.B., So. Meth. U., 1954; LL.M. (Automotive Safety Found. fellow), George Washington U., 1965, S.J.D., 1969. Admitted to Tex. bar, 1954; asso. firm Worsham, Forsythe & Riley, Dallas, 1954-55; asst. prof. bus. adminstrn. Tex. Tech. U., Lubbock, 1959-63, asso. prof., 1963-66, asst. dean, 1960-66; asso. prof. law U. Denver, 1966-69, prof., 1969—; faculty Nat. Coll. State Judiciary, 1976-77; project dir. Center Adminstrv. Justice, Washington, 1975-76. Mem. Am. Bar Assn., State Bar Tex. Editor-in-chief Adminstrv. Law Rev., Am. Bar Assn., 1975—; contbr. articles to legal jours. Home: 6734 S Detroit Circle Littleton CO 80122 Office: U Denver Coll Law 200 W 14th Ave Denver CO 80204 Tel (303) 753-2465

REESE, NORMAN RANDOLPH, b. Portales, N. Mex., Jan. 14, 1918; student N. Mex. Mil. Inst., 1935-37; LL.B., U. Colo., 1942. Admitted to N. Mex. bar, 1942, U.S. Dist. Ct. bar for Dist. N. Mex., 1946; partner firms Reese & Reese, Roswell, N. Mex., 1942-48, Reese & Miller, Roswell, 1949-50, Reese & Snead, Roswell, 1950-51, Edwards & Reese, Hobbs, N. Mex., 1952-58, Girand, Cowan & Reese, Hobbs, 1962-68; individual practice, Hobbs, 1968-73; judge N. Mex. Dist. Ct., 5th Jud. Dist., 1973—; dist. atty. N. Mex. 5th Jud. Dist., 1949-52. Mem. Am. Judicature Soc., State Bar Assn. N. Mex., Lea County (N. Mex.) Bar Assn. Decorated Purple Heart, Air medal. Home: 1330 Cimarron St Hobbs NM 88240 Tel (505) 393-6101

REESE, THOMAS HAYDN, b. Castlegate, Utah, Jan. 19, 1920; B.S. in History, U. Utah, 1942, J.D., 1948; M.S. in Internat. Affairs, George Washington U., 1966. Admitted to Utah bar, 1949, U.S. Supreme Ct. bar, 1958; commd. capt. JAGC, U.S. Army, 1950, advanced through grades to col., 1966; faculty U.S. Army War Coll., 1965-68; exec. to JAG, 1969-71; ret., 1972; circuit exec. U.S. Ct. Appeals, 5th Circuit, La., 1972—. Mem. Am. Bar Assn., Am. Judicature Soc. Decorated Legion of Merit with 3 oak leaf clusters, Bronze Star, Air medal. Office: Suite 109 600 Camp St New Orleans LA 70130 Tel (504) 589-2730

REESER, ROBERT BENJAMIN, JR., b. Wichita, Kans., Sept. 20, 1949; B.S., U. Mo., 1971, J.D., 1974. Admitted to Mo. bar, 1974; asso. firm Crouch, Crouch, Spangler & Douglas, Harrisonville, Mo., 1974-75, partner, 1976—. Mem. Am., Cass County, Mo. bar assns., Assn. Trial Lawyers Am. Office: PO Box 280 Harrisonville MO 64701 Tel (816) 884-3238

REEVE, OLIVER JAY, b. Sumner, Iowa, Oct. 19, 1914; student U. Iowa, 1932. Admitted to Iowa bar, 1936; individual practice law, Waverly, Iowa, 1936—; county atty. Bremer County (Iowa), 1936-42. Mem. Iowa State, Bremer County bar assns., Waverly C. of C., Rotary Internat. Home: 1730 W Bremer Pkwy Waverly IA 50677 Office: suite 5 First National Bank Bldg Waverly IA 50677 Tel (319) 352-2290

REEVES, CRAWFORD DARRELL, JR., b. Decatur, Ala., Apr. 19, 1942; B.A., U. Va., 1966; J.D., U. Miss., 1968. Admitted to Miss. bar, 1968; mem. firm Sims & Sims, Columbus, Miss., 1968—; judge pro tem City of Columbus, 1975—. Mem. Miss., Lowndes County bar assns., Miss. Trial Lawyers Assn. Home: 3511 Camellia Circle St Columbus MS 39701 Office: 809 N 3rd Ave Columbus MS 39701 Tel (601) 328-2711

REEVES, DAVID ROE, b. Washington, Jan. 2, 1944; B.A., U. Denver, 1966; J.D., U. Ky., 1969. Admitted to Ky. bar, 1969, Ind. bar, 1969, Mich. bar, 1969; staff atty. Legal Aid Soc., Fort Wayne, Ind., 1969-70, staff atty. Legal Services Program, Grayson, Ky., 1970-72, dir., 1972; individual practice law, Grayson, 1972—; spl. commr. domestic relations cases Carter Circuit Ct., Grayson, 1976—. Mem. Am., Ky. State, Ind. State bar assns., Comml. Law League Am., Nat. Legal Aid and Defenders Assn., Am. Judicature Soc. Home: Rt 2 Box 60 Grayson KY 41143 Office: 1st Nat Bank Bldg Grayson KY 41143 Tel (606) 474-5541

REEVES, EUGENE EVERETT, b. Memphis, Feb. 24, 1934; student U. N. Mex., 1951-53; LL.B., U. Mo., 1956. Admitted to Mo. bar, 1956; asso. firm Ward & Reeves, Caruthersville, Mo., 1956-57, partner, 1957-70; asso. prof. law, dir. law extension U. Mo., Columbia, 1970—; spl. asst. atty. gen. State Mo., 1965-68; tchr. Mo. Assn. Realtors, 1974—; interim U.S. magistrate, 1976. Home: Route 1 Cedar Grove Blvd Columbia MO 65201 Office: 1 Tate Hall U Mo Columbia MO 65201 Tel (314) 882-7251

REEVES, GENE, b. Meridian, Miss., Feb. 27, 1930; LL.B., John Marshall U., 1964. Admitted to Ga. bar, 1964, U.S. Supreme Ct. bar, 1973; partner firm Craig & Reeves, Lawrenceville, Ga., 1964-71; individual practice law, Lawrenceville, Ga., 1971—; judge City Ct., Lawrenceville, 1969-70. Mem. Am. Bar Assn., Am. Judicature Soc. Home: 805 Scenic Hwy Lawrenceville GA 30245 Office: 131 Perry St Lawrenceville GA 30246 Tel (404) 963-5152

REEVES, ROBERT ESTILL, b. Lexington, Ky., Mar. 5, 1942; B.A., Transylvania U., 1966; J.D., U. Ky., 1969. Admitted to Ky. bar, 1969; clk. to chief justice Reed, Ky. Supreme Ct., 1969-70; asso. firm Harbison Kessinger Lisle & Bush, Lexington, 1970-74, partner, 1975—. Pres., Bluegrass Land and Nature Trust, 1975-76; chmn. citizens adv. com. Paris Pike, 1975-76; mem. Gov.'s Adv. Com. on Energy Resources, 1975-76. Mem. Fayette County Young Lawyers Assn. (past pres.), Am., Ky., Fayette bar assns., Def. Research Inst. Contbr. articles to legal jours. Office: 400 Bank of Lexington Bldg 101 E Vine St Lexington KY 40507 Tel (606) 252-3591

REEVES, ROBERT STOKES, b. Millen, Ga., Apr. 20, 1944; B.A., Emory U., 1966, J.D., 1969. Admitted to Ga. bar, 1969, U.S. Ct. Mil. Appeals bar, 1970; dep. asst. atty. gen. State of Ga., 1969-70; served with JAGC, U.S. Air Force, 1970-74; asso. firm Spivey Carlton Clark & Merrill, Swainsboro, Ga., 1974-75; partner firm Spivey & Carlton, Swainsboro, 1976—; librarian Emanuel County Law Library, 1974-76. Mem. adminstrv. bd. Swainsboro First Methodist Ch., 1975, vice-chmn., 1975—; mem. exec. com. Emanuel County council Boy Scouts Am., 1975—; pres. Emanuel County Easter Seal Soc., 1975-77. Mem. Am., Emanuel County (treas. 1974—) bar assns., State Bar Ga. Home: 2 Cowart St Swainsboro GA 30501 Office: PO Box 309 Swainsboro GA 30401 Tel (912) 237-6424

REHANEK, EDWARD WOODROW, SR., b. Westmoreland County, Pa., Jan. 21, 1921; B.A. in Sociology and Psychology magna cum laude, Kent State U., 1947; postgrad. Western Res. U. Law Sch., 1947-48; LL.B., U. San Francisco, 1951, J.D., 1959. Admitted to Calif. bar, 1955; individual practice law, Redwood City, Calif., 1955; legal officer, social service div. San Mateo County (Calif.) Dept. Pub. Health and Welfare, 1955-76. Mem. San Mateo County Civil Def. Staff, 1960-76; trustee Woodside Rd. Community Meth. Ch., Redwood City, 1965-66, bd. govs. mem. at large, 1977—. Mem. Pi Gamma Mu. Home: 2429 Ohio Ave Redwood City CA 94061 Office: 1511 Woodside Rd Redwood City CA 94061 Tel (415) 366-5865

REHM, JOHN BARTRAM, b. Paris, Nov. 23, 1930; A.B. magna cum laude, Harvard U., 1952; LL.B., Columbia U., 1955. Admitted to N.Y. bar, 1955, D.C. bar, 1969; atty.-advisor Office Legal Adviser, Dept. State, Washington, 1956-61, asst. legal adviser economic affairs, 1961-63; gen. counsel Office Pres.'s Spl. Rep. for Trade Negotiations, Washington, 1963-69; partner firm Busby, Rivkin, Sherman, Levy and Rehm, Washington, 1969-77; sr. partner firm Busby and Rehm, Washington, 1977—. Mem. Am., Fed. bar assns., Am. Soc. Internat. Law, Phi Beta Kappa. Contbr. articles to Am. Jour. Internat. Law, Jour. Maritime Law and Commerce, Columbia Jour. Transnat. Law, Law and Policy in Internat. Bus. Home: 5005 Worthington Dr Westmoreland Hills MD 20016 Office: 900 17th St NW Suite 1100 Washington DC 20006 Tel (202) 857-0700

REHNQUIST, WILLIAM HUBBS, b. Milw., Oct. 1, 1924; B.A., M.A., Stanford, 1948, LL.B., 1952; M.A., Harvard, 1949. Admitted to Ariz. bar; law clk. to former justice Robert H. Jackson, U.S. Supreme Ct., 1952-53; with firm Evans, Kitchel & Jenckes, Phoenix, 1953-55; mem. firm Ragan & Rehnquist, Phoenix, 1956-57; partner firm Cunningham, Carson & Messenger, Phoenix, 1957-60; partner firm Powers & Rehnquist, Phoenix, 1960-69; asst. atty.-gen. office of legal counsel Dept. of Justice, Washington, 1969-71; asso. justice U.S. Supreme Ct., 1971—. Mem. Nat. Conf. Commrs. Uniform State Laws, 1963-69. Mem. Fed., Am., Maricopa (Ariz.) County bar assns., State Bar Ariz., Nat. Conf. Lawyers and Realtors, Phi Beta Kappa, Order of Coif, Phi Delta Phi. Contbr. articles to law jours., nat. mags. Office: Supreme Ct US Washington DC 20543*

REIBLICH, G(EORGE) KENNETH, b. Balt., May 4, 1905; B.A. cum laude, Johns Hopkins, 1925, Ph.D. in Polit. Sci. (Univ. hon. fellow), 1928; student in Law, U. Md., 1925-28; J.D., N.Y. U., 1929; LL.M. (Univ. fellow), Columbia, 1937. Admitted to N.Y. bar, 1930, Md. bar, 1935, U.S. Supreme Ct. bar, 1952, Ariz. bar, 1968; instr. govt. N.Y. U., 1928-30; asso. firm Jenks & Rogers, N.Y.C., 1929-35; asso. in absentia, 1931-35; prof. law U. Md., 1930-63; atty. legal dept. Consol. Gas and Electric Light and Power Co. (now Balt. Gas and Electric Co.), Balt., 1944-49, cons., 1949-55; prof. U. Ariz., 1963—; exec. sec. Md. Self-Survey Commn., 1957-61. Pres. Balt. Torch Club, 1959; bd. dirs. Md. Assn. Mental Health, 1955-60; law sch. rep. Alumni Council U. Md., 1949-63. Mem. Am. Law Inst., Am. (vice chmn. state com. on adminstrv. law 1954-63), Md. State (hon. chmn. com. on Am. Law Inst. 1940-62), Balt. City (hon.), Pima County (Ariz.) bar assns., Wednesday Law Club of Balt. City (pres., hon.). Author: A Study of Judicial Administration in Maryland, 1929; Maryland Annotations to Restatement of Conflicts of Laws, 1937; Maryland Annotations to Restatement of Trusts, 1940; Baltimore City Police Commissioner's Digest of Criminal Law; Maryland State Police Digest of Laws, 1940; contbr. articles and revs. to legal publs. Home: 4661 E Don Jose Dr Tucson AZ 85718 Office: Dept Law U Ariz Tucson AZ 85721 Tel (602) 884-1041

REICH, SAMUEL JOSEPH, b. Pitts., Sept. 8, 1935; B.A., U. Pitts., 1957; LL.B., U. Pa., 1960. Admitted to Pa. bar; mem. gen. crimes sect., criminal div. U.S. Dept. Justice, 1960-61; with U.S. Atty.'s Office Western Dist. Pa., 1961-66, 1st asst. U.S. atty., 1964-66; partner firm Cooper, Schwartz, Diamond & Reich, Pitts., 1966-75; individual practice law, Pitts., 1975--; adj. prof. law Duquesne U., 1975—. Mem. Chartiers Valley Sch. Bd., 1969-75, pres., 1974-75. Mem. Allegheny County Bar Assn., Pa. Trial Lawyers Assn., Assn. Trial Lawyers in Criminal Cts. of Allegheny County (chmn. 1971), Am. Judicature Soc. Home: 59 Stancey Rd Pittsburgh PA 15220 Office: Frick Bldg Pittsburgh PA 15219 Tel (412) 391-6222

REICHEL, HAROLD I., b. Bklyn., July 28, 1931; B.A., Yeshiva U., 1952; LL.B., Bklyn. Law Sch., 1956, J.D., 1967. Admitted to N.Y. bar, 1956; asso. firm Hays St. John's Abramson & Heilbron, N.Y.C., 1955-57, firm Frank & Frank, N.Y.C., 1957-60; atty. A. A. & Hills & Co., N.Y.C., 1960-69; individual practice law, Mineola, N.Y., 1969—; gen. counsel Nat. Birchwood Corp., Mineola, 1969—. Mem. N.Y.C. Sch. Bd., 1970-73. Mem. Queens County (N.Y.), Nassau County (N.Y.) bar assns., Brandies Assn. Office: 410 E Jericho Turnpike Mineola NY 11501 Tel (516) 747-7880

REICHELDERFER, FRANK ALBERT, b. Peoria, Ill., May 30, 1919; B.S. in Accounting, U. Ill., 1940, J.D. 1793 Admitted to Ill. bar, 1943; partner firm Wilson & McIlvaine, Chgo., 1943—. Past chmn. bd. govs. Winnetka Community House (Ill.); mem. exec. council Chgo. Boy Scouts Am. Mem. Ill. (past mem. bd. govs.), Chgo. (past mem. bd. mgrs.) bar assns. Home: 1000 Pine Tree Ln Winnetka IL 60093 Office: 135 S LaSalle St Chicago IL 60603 Tel (312) 263-1212

REICHLE, VERNON EARL, b. New Ulm, Tex., Feb. 16, 1919; student U. Houston; LL.B., S. Tex. Coll. Law. Admitted to Tex. bar, 1952; with Humble Oil & Refining Co. (Exxon Co.), 1952-69; individual practice law, 1969—. Office: 1120A Vaughn Bldg Midland TX 79701 Tel (915) 683-5789

REICHMAN, FRED MARSHALL, b. St. Louis, Feb. 7, 1931; A.B., Washington U., 1955, J.D., 1955. Admitted to Mo. bar, 1955, Fed. bar, 1963; asso. firm Karol A. Korngold, St. Louis, 1957-59; partner firm Reichman, Aguirre & Wollbrink, St. Louis, 1960-66; partner firm Husch, Eppenberger, Donohue, Elson & Cornfeld, St. Louis, 1967—. Mem. Am., Mo., St. Louis Met. bar assns. Home: 6911 Columbia Pl University City MO 63130 Office: 100 N Broadway St Saint Louis MO 63102 Tel (314) 421-4800

REICIN, RONALD IAN, b. Chgo., Dec. 11, 1942; B.B.A. with high distinction, U. Mich., 1964, M.B.A., 1967, J.D. cum laude, 1967. Admitted to Ill. bar, 1967; partner firm Jenner & Block, Chgo., 1967—; mem. staff Price, Waterhouse & Co., Detroit, 1966; C.P.A., Ill. Mem. Chgo. (mem. coms. fed. taxation, 1968—, land trusts, 1974—), Ill. State, Am. (mem. sect. taxation) bar assns., Phi Kappa Phi, Beta Gamma Sigma, Beta Alpha Psi. Home: 1916 Berkeley Rd Highland Park IL 60035 Office: Jenner & Block One IBM Plaza Chicago IL 60611 Tel (312) 222-9350

REID, DALE CURTISS, b. Oklahoma City, Jan. 24, 1934; B.S., U. Calif., Los Angeles, 1955; LL.B., J.D., Stanford U., 1961; certificate Stonier Grad. Sch. Banking Rutgers U., 1972. Admitted to Calif. bar, 1961, Hawaii bar, 1962; individual practice law, Honolulu, Los Angeles, 1961-67; counsel, v.p. Bank Am., Los Angeles, 1967-73; sr. v.p., gen. counsel Lloyds Bank Calif., Los Angeles, 1973—; dir. Los Angeles Job Devel. Corps., 1973—. Mem. Calif. Bankers Assn. (seminar chmn. 1974, div. chmn. 1974-76, legal affairs com. 1976—), Am., Calif., Los Angeles County bar assns., W. Coast Corp. Bank Secs. Assn., Club: Jonathan (Los Angeles). Author: Barrister as A Banker, 1972. Home: 705 Plymouth Rd San Marino CA 91108 Office: 548 S Spring St Los Angeles CA 90013

REID, DALLAS WENDELL, b. Orleans, Ind., Aug. 16, 1907; student U. Ill., 1927-30; LL.B., Columbus U., Washington, 1937, LL.M., 1942. Asst. ticket agt. Chgo. Union Sta., Chgo., 1925-29; passenger agt. Chgo. Milw. St. Paul & Pacific R.R., Chgo., 1929-32; oil salesman Phillips Oil Co., Tulsa, 1932-33; internat. rep. Oil Workers Union AFL, 1933-34; labor expert, statis. analyst U.S. Nat. Recovery Adminstrn., Washington, 1935-36; spl. claims adjudicator U.S. R.R. Retirement Bd., Washington, 1936-38, legal adviser, 1938-42; admitted to D.C. Supreme Ct. bar, 1938, U.S. Supreme Ct. bar, 1943, Calif. Supreme Ct. bar, 1948; spl. asst. to U.S. Atty. Gen., Washington, 1942-48; mem. firms Reid, Henry & Laster, 1954-60, Reid & Maltby, 1963-67, individual practice law, San Fernando Valley, Calif., 1949—. Legal mem. adv. bd. So. Calif. Motion Picture Council, Inc. Mem. D.C. Bar Assn., Calif. State, Los Angeles County bars, Canoga Park (Calif.) C. of C. (pres. 1949-50) Delta Theta Phi (emeritus). Author: Electrical Manufacturing Industry, 1936. Home: 15232 Otsego St Sherman Oaks CA 91413 Office: 14622 Victory Blvd Van Nuys CA 91411 Tel (213) 781-6040

REID, DARCY TYSON, b. Stamford, Conn., Mar. 10, 1946; B.A., San Diego State U., 1966; J.D., Hastings Coll., 1970. Admitted to Calif. bar, 1972; individual practice law, San Francisco, 1972; atty. The Advocates Inc., San Diego, 1972; part-time legal researcher Pacific Counseling Service, San Diego, 1972-74; staff atty. VISTA at Richmond (Calif.) Legal Services Found., 1974-75; Fresno County (Calif.) Legal Services Inc., 1975—; tchr. San Diego State U., 1972-73; legal research asst. Youth for Service Project, San Francisco, 1967-68, Nat. Welfare Rights Organization, Washington, 1968, 70; legal researcher San Francisco Services, 1969-70. Mem. Law Students Civil Rights Research Council (Western adv. bd.), ACLU, Nat. Lawyers Guild, Fresno Bar Assn., Calif. Women Lawyers, State of Calif. Bar, Fresno Barristers. Home: 222 S Callisch St Apt E Fresno CA 93701 Office: 1221 Fulton Mall 505 Brix Bldg Fresno CA 93721 Tel (209) 485-9880

REID, JOHN PHILLIP, b. 1930; B.S.S., Georgetown U., 1952; LL.B., Harvard U., 1955; M.A., U. N.H., 1957; LL.M., N.Y. U., 1960, J.S.D., 1962. Admitted to N.H. bar, 1955; instr. N.Y. U., 1960-62, asst. prof. law, 1962-64, asso. prof., 1964-65, prof., 1966—. Author: Chief Justice: The Judicial World of Charles Doe, 1967; An American Judge: Marmaduke Dent, 1968; A Law of Blood: The Primitive Law of the Cherokee Nation, 1970. Office: NY U Sch of Law New York City NY 10003 Tel (212) 598-2760*

REID, RICHARD AYRES, b. Balt., Mar. 5, 1931; B.A., Yale U., 1953; LL.B., U. Va., 1956; grad. U.S. Sch. Naval Justice, 1956. Admitted to Md. bar, 1956; legal specialist U.S. Naval Reserve, 1956-59; asso. firm Royston, Mueller & McLean and predecessors, 1960-64, partner 1964—. Pres. Lida Lee Tall Sch. PTA. Fellow Am. Coll. Trial Lawyers; mem. Am., Md. State, bd. govs. 1976—), Balt. County bar assns., Dissenters Law Club, Assn. Trial Lawyers Am. Home: 4 Valley Oak Ct Timonium MD 21093 Office: 102 W Pennsylvania Ave Towson MD 21204 Tel (301) 823-1800

REID, ROBERT RAYMOND, JR., b. Evanston, Ill., Nov. 12, 1927; A.B. summa cum laude, Washington and Lee U., 1949; LL.B. cum laude, Harvard U., 1952. Admitted to Ky. bar, 1952, Ala. bar, 1955; asso. firm Bradley, Arant, Rose & White, and predecessor, Birmingham, Ala., 1954-63, partner, 1963—. Bd. dirs., past pres. Birmingham Audubon Soc., Ala. Ornithol. Soc.; bd. dirs. Ala. Zool. Soc. Mem. Am., Ala., Birmingham bar assns., Am. Judicature Soc., Phi Beta Kappa. Home: 2616 Mountain Brook Pkwy Birmingham AL 35223 Office: 1500 Brown-Marx Bldg Birmingham AL 35203 Tel (205) 252-4500

REID, RONALD L., b. Moline, Ill., Nov. 12, 1934; A.B., Emory U., 1957, LL.B., 1963. Admitted to Ga. bar, 1962; now with firm Alston, Miller & Gaines, Atlanta; adj. prof. law Emory U., 1971-75. Mem. Am., Atlanta (pres. 1976-77) bar assns., State Bar Ga., Lawyers Club of Atlanta, Bryan Honor Soc., Pi Sigma Alpha, Phi Delta Phi. Office: 1200 Citizens & So Nat Bank Bldg Atlanta GA 30303 Tel (404) 588-0300*

REID, WILLIAM A., b. Great Falls, Mont., Sept. 12, 1925; B.S. in Naval Sci. and Tactics, U. Wash., 1945; B.S. in Indsl. Engring., Mont. State U., 1948; LL.B., U. Mich., 1951. Admitted to Mont. bar, 1951, Mich. bar, 1954; asso. firm Church, Harris, Johnson & Williams, Great Falls, Mont., 1951—, now partner. Mem. Am., Mont., Cascade County (pres. 1975-76) bar assns. Home: 2769 Greenbriar Dr Rural Route 4 Great Falls MT 59405 Office: Box 1645 Great Falls MT 59403 Tel (406) 761-3000

REIDY, JOHN JOSEPH, b. Youngstown, Ohio, Mar. 8, 1905; J.D., Notre Dame U., 1927. Admitted to Ohio bar, 1928; asso. firm Joy Seth Hurd, Cleve., 1928-31; head lease and legal dept. Great A & P Tea Co., Cleve., 1931-41; individual practice law, Cleve., 1941-43; partner firm Falsgraf, Reidy, Shoup & Ault, and predecessors, Cleve., 1943-71; of counsel firm Baker, Hostetler & Patterson, Cleve., 1971—; officer, dir. various corps. Mem. Greater Cleve., Ohio, Am. bar assns. Home: 12900 Lake Ave Lakewood OH 44107 Office: 1956 Union Commerce Bldg Cleveland OH 44115 Tel (216) 621-0200

REIERSGORD, THOMAS ERWIN, b. Thief River Falls, Minn., May 9, 1932; B.S., U. Minn., 1954, J.D., 1956. Admitted to Minn. bar, 1956; asso. firm Lyman A. Brink, Hallock, Minn., 1956-58; individual practice law, Hallock, 1958-60; asst. city atty. St. Louis Park (Minn.), 1960-61; partner firm Yngue and Reiersgord, Mpls., 1961—. Mem. Minn. Bar Assn. Home: 4500 W 44th St Saint Louis Park MN 55424 Office: 6250 Wayzata Blvd Minneapolis MN 55416 Tel (612) 544-8451

REIF, LOUIS RAYMOND, b. Buffalo, N.Y., July 4, 1923; A.B., U. Buffalo, 1948; J.D., U. Mich., 1951. Admitted to N.Y. State bar, 1952; gen. atty. Nat. Fuel Gas Co., N.Y.C., 1953-58, asst. sec., 1958-60, v.p., 1960-62, sr. v.p., dir., 1962-73, pres., 1973-75, pres., chief exec. officer, 1975—; dir. Marine Midland Banks; trustee Buffalo Savs. Bank. Mem. Am. Gas Assn. (dir.), Buffalo C. of C. (dir. 1973). Home: 225 Briarhill St Williamsville NY 14221 Office: 10 Lafayette Square Buffalo NY 14203 Tel (716) 854-4360

REIFF, DAVID EDWARD, b. Oconto, Wis., Oct. 11, 1935; B.A., Wartburg Coll., 1957; J.D., Valparaiso U., 1969. Admitted to Wis. bar, 1969; with West Bend Co., 1964-66; partner firm Seroogy & Reiff, Tomahawk, Wis., 1969—; asst. city atty., Tomahawk, 1969—, mem. planning commn., 1969—; chmn. Lincoln County Civil Service Commn., 1973—. Pres. Grace Luth. Ch., Tomahawk, 1972. Mem. Am., Wis., Lincoln County (pres. 1972) bar assns. Home: 945 E Kings Rd Tomahawk WI 54487 Office: 321 W Wisconsin Tomahawk WI 54487 Tel (715) 453-2158

REIFF, WILLIAM CECIL, b. Columbus, Ga., Apr. 1, 1943; student Institut Auf Dem Rosenberg, St. Gallen, Switzerland, 1958-60, Okla. U., 1964-65; B.A., Oklahoma City U., 1967; J.D., Harvard, 1970. Admitted to Tex. bar, 1970; individual practice law, Houston, 1970—; pres. William C. Reiff & Co., real estate devel., Diversified Marine Industries. Home: 10131 Brinwood Dr Houston TX 77043 Office: 3316 Sul Ross Houston TX 77098 Tel (713) 529-4801

REIFSNIDER, GENE DAVID, b. Murphysboro, Ill., Jan. 17, 1927; LL.B., Drake U., 1951, J.D., 1968. Admitted to Iowa bar, 1951; staff Iowa Tax Dept., Des Moines, 1951-53; legal asso. Penn Mut. Ins. Co., Des Moines, 1953-56; with Bankers Life Ins. Co., Des Moines, 1956—, v.p.-mktg. services, 1956—. Vice pres. parents' bd. Drake U. Mem. Nat. Life Underwriters Assn., Am. Council Life Ins. (sub-fed. tax com.), Health Ins. Assn. Am. (ann. forum com.). Editorial bd. Estates Planners Quar., 1975—; contbr. articles to legal jours. Home: 1351 Cook Rd West Des Moines IA 50265 Office: 711 High St Des Moines IA 50307

REIGEL, JANE MARGARET, b. St. Louis, Nov. 2, 1943; B.S., U. Fla., 1968; LL.B., U. Wis., 1973. Admitted to Wis. bar; legal sec. Reigel Law Offices, DeForest, Wis., 1969-73, asso. firm, 1973—. Mem. Am., Wis., Dane County, Lawyer-Pilots bar assns., Greater Madison (Wis.) Bd. Realtors, Nat. Assn. Realtors. Home: 565 Highland Dr Windsor WI 53598 Office: Constitution Plaza DeForest WI 53532 Tel (608) 257-0083

REIHER, JAMES COLGAN, b. Racine, Wis., Aug. 3, 1944; B.S. in Bus. Northwestern U., 1966; J.D., U. Wis., 1969. Admitted to Wis. bar, 1969; staff atty. Vista Legal Aid Soc. of Mpls., 1969-70; pub. defender Legal Aid Soc. Milw., 1971-75; asso. firm Perry & First, Milw., 1976—. Mem. Wis., Milw. Jr. bar assns., Nat. Assn. Criminal Def. Lawyers, ACLU (cooperating atty.). Home: 5763 N Bay Ridge Ave Whitefish Bay WI 53217 Office: 222 E Mason St Milwaukee WI 53202 Tel (414) 272-7400

REILLY, EDWARD ARTHUR, b. Dickson City, Pa., Jan. 24, 1915; B.A., U. Scranton, 1936; LL.B., LL.D., Dickinson Sch. Law., 1939. Admitted to Pa. bar, 1940; counsel Dickson City Sch. Dist., Pa., 1950-69, Midvalley Sch. Dist., Pa., 1969—. Mem. Pa., Lackawanna bar assns. Home: 710 Main St Dickson City PA 18519 Office: 524-6 Connell Bldg Scranton PA 18503 Tel (717) 342-2751

REILLY, GERARD DENIS, b. Boston, Sept. 27, 1906; A.B., Harvard, 1927, LL.B., 1933. State House corr. for Pawtucket Times, Providence Jour., 1927-29; night copy editor Boston Traveler, 1929-30; admitted to Mass. bar, 1933, D.C. bar, 1946; asso. firm Goodwin, Procter & Hoar, Boston, 1933-34; reviewing atty. Home Owner's Loan Corp., 1934; became atty. U.S. Dept. of Labor, 1934, asst. solicitor, 1935, adminstr. Pub. Contracts Div., 1936-37, solicitor, 1937-41; mem. NLRB, 1941-46; mem. firm Reilly, Johns & Zimmerman and predecessor firms, 1946-70; asso. judge D.C. Ct. Appeals, 1970-72, chief judge, 1972-76. Lectr. constl. law Cath. U., 1946-47; counsel Senate com. on labor and pub. welfare, 1947; dir. Reed & Prince Mfg. Co., Worcester, Mass., 1963-70. Fellow Am. Bar Found.; mem. Am., D.C., Boston bar assns. Home: 3515 Lowell St Washington DC 20016 Office: 400 F St NW Washington DC 20001

REILLY, JAMES F., b. Washington, June 24, 1903; LL.B., Georgetown U. Admitted to D.C. bar, 1926; individual practice law, Washington; with JAGC, USNR, 1942-44. Mem. Am., D.C. (v.p. 1965) bar assns., Am. Coll. Trial Lawyers. Office: 821-15th St NW Washington DC 20005 Tel (202) 347-0558

REILLY, JOHN ALBERT, b. N.Y.C., Dec. 8, 1919; B.S., Coll. City N.Y., 1940; J.D., Harvard U., 1947. Admitted to Mass. bar, 1947, N.Y. bar, 1949; patent counsel Kendall Co., Boston, 1947-48; asso. firm Kenyon & Kenyon, N.Y.C., 1949-55; partner firm Kenyon & Kenyon, Reilly, Carr & Chapin, N.Y.C., 1955—. Mem. Am. Bar Assn., Assn. Bar City N.Y. (com. chmn.), N.Y. County Lawyers Assn. (chmn. patent com.), N.Y. Patent Law Assn. (v.p., bd. govs., com. chmn.), Mil. Order World Wars, City Coll. Alumni Assn. (dir.), Harvard Law Sch. Assn. Recipient Alumni Service award City Coll., 1967. Office: 59 Maiden Ln New York City NY 10038 Tel (212) 425-7200

REILLY, JOHN RICHARD, b. Dubuque, Iowa, June 4, 1928; student Loras Coll., 1946-49; B.A., State U. Iowa, 1952, J.D., 1955. Admitted to Iowa bar, 1955, D.C. bar, 1961; trial atty. antitrust div. Dept. Justice, Chgo., 1955-58; midwestern rep. Council State Govts., 1958-60; asst. to dep. atty. gen. dept. Justice, 1961-64, also chief exec. officer for U.S. Attys.; commr. FTC, 1964-67; partner firm Pierson, Ball & Dowd, Washington, D.C., 1967-72; partner firm Winston & Strawn, Washington, D.C., 1972—. Home: 12111 Stoney Creek Rd Potomac MD 20854 Office: 1730 Pennsylvania Ave NW Washington DC 20006 Tel (202) 223-8510

REILLY, LOUIS EDWARD, b. Little Falls, Minn., May 24, 1930; B.A., U. Minn., 1951; J.D., U. San Francisco, 1958. Admitted to Calif. bar, 1960; asst. gen. counsel Fed. Res. Bank of San Francisco, 1960-69, gen. counsel, 1969—. Mem. Calif., San Francisco bar assns., Phi Alpha Delta. Office: 400 Sansome St San Francisco CA 94120 Tel (415) 544-2247

REIMAN, THOMAS JAY, b. Chgo., Sept. 9, 1949; student Tulane U., 1967-68; B.A., Ga. State U., 1971; J.D. cum laude, Mercer U., 1974. Admitted to Ga. bar, 1974, N.J. bar, 1976; U.S. Dist. Ct. N.J. bar, 1976; U.S. Ct. Appeals bar, 1976; asst. area atty. long lines div. A.T. & T., Atlanta, 1974-75, atty., N.Y.C., 1975—; asst. sec. Eastern Tel. & Tel., Tranoceanic Cable Ship Co. Mem. Am., Ga., Atlanta bar assns. Contbr. articles in field to law revs. Home: 111 Hampton Dr Berkeley Heights NJ 07922 Office: AT&T Long Lines Room 3C-152 Bedminster NJ 07921 Tel (201) 234-6330

REINER, HELEN CLAIRE, b. Marshall, Ill., Apr. 2, 1917; student U. Pa., 1939-52; J.D., Temple U., 1956. Admitted to D.C. bar, 1956; sec. to regional atty. NLRB, Phila., 1938-51, sec. to regional dir., 1952-56, legal asst. to bd. mem., Washington, 1956-62, supervisory atty., bd. mem.'s staff, 1962-75, chief counsel to chmn., 1975-77, to mem., 1977—; adminstrv. asst. Regional Enforcement Commn., WSB, Phila., 1951-52. Mem. Am., Fed., D.C. bar assns., Temple U. Law Alumni Assn., Phi Alpha Delta. Mem. Moot Ct. bd. Temple U. Sch. Law, 1953-56; recipient Sarah A. Schull Meml. award, 1956. Home: 4201 Cathedral Ave NW Washington DC 20016 Office: NLRB 1717 Pennsylvania Ave NW Washington DC 20570 Tel (202) 254-9416

REINHARD, HENRY CORBEN, JR., b. Camden, N.J., Jan. 3, 1937; grad. with honors U.S. Naval Hosp. Corps Sch., 1955, U.S. Naval Clin. Lab. Sch., 1956, with distinction USAF Officer Candidate Sch., Lackland AFB, San Antonio, 1960; A.A., San Antonio Coll., 1965; B.B.A. in Econs. and Fin., U. Houston, 1969; J.D., S. Tex. Coll. Law, 1972. With USN, 1954-57; lab. technician Presbyn. Hosp., Phila., 1957; chief lab. technician Kensington Hosp., Phila., 1957-58; commd. airman 2d class USAF, 1958, advanced through grades to capt., 1966; med. lab. technician USAF Hosp., Nellis AFB and So. Nev. Meml. Hosp., Las Vegas, Nev., 1958-60; med. adminstrv. officer USAF Hosp., Randolph AFB, San Antonio, 1960-63, Thule AFB, Thule, Greenland, 1963-64; chief br. adminstrv. support div. aerospace med scis. USAF Sch. Aerospace Medicine, Brooks AFB, San Antonio, 1964-66; resigned, 1966; adminstrv. asst. to prof. medicine Baylor U. Coll. Medicine, Houston, 1966-68; adminstrv. asst. St. Luke's Episc. Hosp., Tex. Children's Hosp., Tex. Heart Inst., all in Tex. Med. Center, Houston, 1968-69, asst. adminstr., 1969-72, asso. adminstr., 1973; adminstr. Ft. Worth Children's Hosp., 1973—; admitted to Tex. bar, 1972; judge Azle (Tex.) Municipal Ct. Mem. human resources com. Tex. Heart Inst., Houston; bd. dirs. Tarrant County (Tex.) Heart Assn.; mem. regional task force on perinatal health North Central Tex. Council Govts.; mem. adv. council on health careers Tarrant County Jr. Coll.; div. chmn. United Way Campaign of Tarrant County, 1976. Mem. Am. Coll. Hosp. Adminstrs., Am., Houston, Ft. Worth-Tarrant County bar assns., State Bar Tex., Tex. Hosp. Assn. (vice chmn. council pub. edn.), Nat. Assn. Children's Hosps. and Related Instns. (trustee, chmn. council legis.), Phi Alpha Delta, Omicron Delta Epsilon. Recipient certificate of appreciation comdr. USAF Sch. Aerospace Medicine, Brooks AFB, 1966, Rhem, Hocker and Bucklin award S. Tex. Coll. Law, 1972. Home: 8612 Lake Country Dr Fort Worth TX 76179 Office: 1400 Cooper St Fort Worth TX 76104 Tel (817) 336-0732

REINHARDT, LEROY JACOB, b. Fresno, Calif., Aug. 18, 1924; B.A., Fresno State Coll., 1947; LL.B./J.D., Stanford, 1949. Admitted to Calif. bar, 1950, U.S. Supreme Ct. bar, 1973; asso. firm Crossland & Crossland, Fresno, 1950-52; individual practice law, Fresno, 1952—; dir. Garfield Water Dist., Clovis, Calif., 1961—, Internat. Water Dist., Fresno, 1951-54. Mem. Am., Calif., Fresno County (past dir.) bar assns., Am. Arbitration Assn. (panel 1963—). Home: 13155 W Shaw Ave Kerman CA 93630 Office: 1500 W Shaw Ave Fresno CA 93711 Tel (209) 226-3744

REINHART, WILLIAM JOSEPH, b. Albany, N.Y., Jan. 11, 1909; A.B., Dartmouth, 1930; LL.B., Harvard, 1933. Admitted to N.Y. bar, 1933, since practiced in N.Y.C.; partner firm Alfred E. Smith, Jr., 1937-42; asso. firm Garey & Garey, 1942-43, 47-53; partner firm Seghers & Reinhart, 1953-65; individual practice law, 1965—; of counsel firm Wikler, Gottlieb, Taylor & Howard, 1965—. Mem. Am., Fed., N.Y. bar assns., Internat. Law Assn., N.Y. County Lawyers Assn., Judge Adv. Assn., Fed. Tax Forum (pres. 1962-64), Inst. U.S. Taxation Fgn. Income (dir. 1961-67). Author: (with Paul D. Seghers) How to Do Business Abroad at the Least Tax Cost, 1955; (with Paul D. Seghers and Selwyn Nimaroff) Essentially Equivalent to a Dividend, 1960. Home: 147 Lenox Terr Maplewood NJ 07040 Office: 40 Wall St New York City NY 10005 Tel (212) 422-1080

REINITZ, ALAN HENRY, b. N.Y.C., Apr. 4, 1926; student Bklyn. Coll., 1946-49; LL.D., Bklyn Law Sch., 1952. Admitted to N.Y. State bar, 1952, U.S. Supreme Ct. bar, 1960; individual practice law, East Northport, N.Y., 1954—; lectr. in field. Mem. N.Y. State, Am., Suffolk County, Nassau County bar assns. Home: 1 Oasis Place East Northport NY 11731 Office: 514 Larkfield Rd East Northport NY 11731 Tel (516) 368-2300

REINSDORF, JERRY MICHAEL, b. Bklyn., Feb. 25, 1936; A.B., George Washington U., 1957; J.D., Northwestern U., 1960; C.P.A., U. Ill., 1959. Admitted to Ill. bar, 1960, Washington bar, 1960; atty. IRS, Chgo., 1960-64; asso. firm Chapman & Cutler, Chgo., 1964-68; partner firm Altman, Kurlander & Weiss, Chgo., 1968-74; of counsel firm Katten, Muchin, Gitles, Zavis, Pearl & Galler, Chgo., 1974—; gen. partner Carlyle Real Estate Ltd., 1971-72; chmn. The Balcor Co., 1973—; dir. Real Estate Securities & Syndication Inst., 1973—. Mem. Am., Ill., Chgo., Fed. bar assn., Order of Coif. Mng. editor Northwestern Law Rev., 1959-60. Office: 4711 Golf Rd Skokie IL 60076 Tel (312) 677-2900

REINSTADTLER, THOMAS JOHN, b. Pitts., Aug. 21, 1934; B.A., St. Vincent Coll., 1956; J.D., U. Mich., 1959. Admitted to Pa. bar; mem. firm Egler & Reinstadtler, Pitts., 1959—. Bd. dirs. Camp Fire Girls, 1971-74. Mem. Am., Pa., Allegheny County bar assns., Acad. Trial Lawyers Allegheny County (pres. 1976-77). Editor Pitts. Legal Jour. Office: 2100 Lawyers Bldg Pittsburgh PA 15219 Tel (412) 281-9810

REINSTEIN, JEROME L., b. N.Y.C., Oct. 10, 1927; B.B.A., Coll. City N.Y., 1949; LL.B., Bklyn. Law Sch., 1951, J.D., 1967; LL.M., N.Y. U., 1956. Admitted to N.Y. bar, 1951, U.S. Supreme Ct. bar, 1970; asso. firm Martin Benjamin, N.Y.C., 1951-53, Jay Leo Rothschild, N.Y.C., 1953-55; asso. firm Barron, Rice & Rockmore, N.Y.C., 1955-64, partner, 1964-70; sr. law asst. appellate div., 1st dept., N.Y. State Supreme Ct., N.Y.C., 1970-72, law sec. to justice, N.Y.C., 1972-77, dep. clk., 1977—; adj. asst. prof. law Baruch Coll., 1977—. Pres. Dist. 11 Community Sch. Bd., Bronx, N.Y., 1971-77. Mem. N.Y. State, Bronx bar assns., N.Y. County Lawyers Assn. Home: 600 W 246th St New York City NY 10471 Office: 27 Madison Ave New York City NY 10010 Tel (212) LE2-1000

REINSTEIN, TODD RUSSELL, b. Chgo., July 30, 1937; B.S. in Accounting, U. Calif., Los Angeles, 1959, J.D., 1962; postgrad. in Legal Edn., U. So. Calif., 1962-63. Admitted to U.S. Tax Ct. bar, 1963, U.S. Ct. Claims bar, 1969, Calif. bar, 1963, U.S. Supreme Ct. bar, 1975; asso. firm Bautzer, Irwin & Schwab, Beverly Hills, Calif., 1962-66; partner firm Grobe, Reinstein, Freid & Katz, Los Angeles, 1966-76; individual practice law, Los Angeles, 1976—; prof. accounting Grad. Sch. Bus. Adminstrn. Calif. State U., Northridge. Mem. Am., Los Angeles County, Beverly Hills bar assns., State Bar Calif., Beta Gamma Sigma. C.P.A., Calif.; contbr. articles to profl. pubs.; bd. editors U. Calif. at Los Angeles Law Rev., 1960-62. Office: 1880 Century Park E suite 615 Los Angeles CA 90067 Tel (213) 553-4500

REIS, CARL THEODORE, b. Indpls., Jan. 19, 1915; B.S. in Commerce and Fin., Xavier U., Cin., 1936; J.D., Ind. U., 1948. Admitted to Ind. bar, 1948, U.S. Supreme Ct. bar, 1974, ICC bar, 1948; sales mgr. Acme, Evans Co., Indpls., 1936-45; asso. firm White, Wright, Raub & Forrey, and predecessor, Indpls., 1948, partner, 1954—; dir. Kauffman Engring. Inc., Indpls., 1973—; sec., legal counsel Park Fletcher, Inc., Indpls., 1962—; dir. Edward J. Peters & Assos. Inc., Indpls. Mem. nutrition com. ARC. Mem. Ind., Indpls. bar assns., Xavier U. Alumni Assn. (nat. pres. 1967). Home: 7923 Meadowbrook Dr Indianapolis IN 46240 Office: 1000 Merchants Bank Bldg Indianapolis IN 46204

REISDORF, ROBERT ALEXANDER, b. Pitts., Aug. 26, 1924; A.B., Pa. State U., 1945; LL.B., U. Wis., 1949. Admitted to Wis. bar, 1949; individual practice law, Madison, Wis., 1949-52; loan analyst Wis. State Dept. Vets. Affairs, 1952-55; real estate specialist Pure Oil Co., Madison, 1955-57; mortgage loan mgr., treas., fin. v.p., treas. and dir. Wis. Life Ins. Co., Madison, 1957—. Mem. Dane County, Wis. bar assns. Home: 5702 Lake Mendota Dr Madison WI 53705 Office: Wisconsin Life Ins Co Box 5099 Madison WI 53705 Tel (608) 238-5841

REISLER, RAYMOND, b. Bklyn., Nov. 28, 1907; B.A., Cornell U., 1927; LL.B., Columbia, 1929, J.D., 1975. Admitted to N.Y. bar, 1929, U.S. Supreme Ct. bar, 1958; asso. and mem. firm Ruston & Snyder, Bklyn., 1930-36; individual practice law, N.Y.C. and Bklyn., 1936-67; judge Criminal Ct. City N.Y., 1967—; chief asst. counsel jud. inquiry Supreme Ct. Kings County, N.Y., 1956-57; faculty Bklyn. Law Sch., 1965-70; spl. hearing officer U.S. Dept. Justice; spl. asst. U.S. atty., hearing officer; dep. asst. atty. gen. State of N.Y.; govt. appeal agt. SSS; mem. U.S. Atty. Gen. Site Selection Com.; mem. pre-trial com. U.S. 2d Circuit Ct. Appeals; coordinator election frauds activities atty. gen. office State of N.Y. Fellow N.Y. State Bar Found.; mem. Am., N.Y. State, Bklyn. (pres.; recipient ann. service award 1975) bar assns., Fed. Bar Council, Assn. Bar City N.Y. Contbr. articles to legal jours.

REISMAN, JAMES, b. N.Y.C., Mar. 25, 1939; B.A., B.E.E., Union Coll., 1961; LL.B., N.Y. U., 1965. Admitted to N.Y. State bar, 1965; patent agt. Bell Telephone Labs., N.Y.C., 1961-65; asso. firm Amster & Rothstein, N.Y.C., 1965-70; partner firm Gottlieb, Rackman & Reisman, N.Y.C., 1970—; instr. patent bar rev. course Practising Law Inst., 1973-76. Mem. Am. Bar Assn., N.Y. Patent Law Assn., Union Coll. Alumni Assn. N.Y. (pres. 1975-77), Phi Beta Kappa, Tau Beta Pi, Sigma Xi. Office: 260 Madison Ave New York City NY 10016 Tel (212) 689-0040

REISMAN, WILLIAM MICHAEL, b. Phila., Apr. 23, 1939; B.A., Johns Hopkins, 1960; LL.B., Hebrew U. Jerusalem, 1963; Diplome en Droit Compare, Strasbourg, 1963; LL.M., Yale, 1964, J.S.D., 1965. Admitted to Conn. bar, 1964; research asso. Yale Law Sch., 1965, asso. prof., 1969-72, prof., 1972—; Fulbright scholar, The Hague, 1966-67. Mem. Am. Soc. Internat. Law, Internat. Law Assn., Council Fgn. Relations. Author: Nullity and Revision, 1971; The Art of the Possible, 1970; Puerto Rico and the International Process, 1974; Toward World Order and Human Dignity, 1976. Contbr. articles to profl. jours.; bd. editors Am. Jour. Comparative Law, 1970-76, Am. Jour. Internat. Law, 1973—, Jour. Conflict Resolution, 1974—. Home: 57 Swarthmore St Hamden CT 06517 Office: Yale Law Sch New Haven CT 06520 Tel (203) 436-8279

REISNER, EDWARD JOHN, b. Milw., Aug. 1, 1947; B.A., U. Wis., 1969, J.D., 1972. Admitted to Wis. bar, 1972; staff atty. State Bar Wis., 1972-74, legis. counsel, 1974-76; asst. dean Law Sch. U. Wis., Madison, 1976—; exec. dir. Wis. Law Alumni Assn., 1976—; legis. asst. Wis. Assembly Com. on Commerce and Consumer Affairs, 1971-72; research asst. Inst. for Environ. Studies, 1972; legal sec. advisory com. Madison Area Tech. Coll., 1974—; mem. legal assts. program bd. Lakeshore Tech. Inst., 1975—; mem. legal assts. adv. com. Vocat. Tech. Adult Edn. System, 1976—. Mem. State Bar Wis., Am. Bar Assn. Author: (with Robert Lehman) Wisconsin Probate System, 1975; contbr. articles to legal publs. Home: 4910 Paul Ave Madison WI 53711 Office: Univ Wis Law School Madison WI 53706 Tel (608) 262-7856

REISS, DANIEL, JR., b. Newark, May 16, 1941; B.A. in Econs., B.A. in English Lit., U. Miami, 1963; LL.B., Georgetown U., 1966. Admitted to D.C. bar, 1967, U.S. Supreme Ct. bar, 1972; cons. U.S. Dept. State, 1967-68; individual practice law, Washington, 1968—; pres. Constructors' Group, Ltd., 1970-73; chief legal officer Marine-Internat. Joint Venture—Sultanate of Oman, 1973-74. Mem. Am. Soc. Internat. Law, Fed. (chmn. subcom. pvt. internat. law, vice chmn. internat. law com.), Inter-Am., D.C. bar assns., Internat. Law Soc. Editor: Benedict on Admiralty, 1972. Home: 1100 22d St NW Apt 200 Washington DC 20036 Office: 1120 Connecticut Ave NW Suite 416 Washington DC 20036 Tel (202) 659-8616

REISS, MICHAEL, b. N.Y.C., Jan. 5, 1943; B.A., Harvard, 1965; LL.B., Yale, 1968. Admitted to Calif. bar, 1971; asst. prof. law center Univ. So. Calif., Los Angeles, 1968-71, asso. prof. law, 1974—; directing atty. Calif. Rural Legal Assistance, Inc., Modesto, 1971-74. Bd. dirs. Legal Aid Found. Los Angeles, 1974—. Mem. Am. Bar Assn. Office: U So Calif Law Center University Park Los Angeles CA 90007 Tel (213) 746-2187

REITER, RICHARD EDWARD, JR., b. Detroit, Dec. 18, 1946; B.S. in Bus. Adminstrn., Valparaiso U., 1968; LL.B., Atlanta Sch. Law, 1973, LL.M., 1976. Admitted to Ga. bar, 1973; individual practice law, Morrow, Ga., 1975—. Mem. Am., Clayton County bar assns., Phi Kappa Psi Alumni Assn. (dir.), Phi Kappa Psi (v.p. Ga. chpt.). Office: 2425 Lake Harbin Rd Morrow GA 30260 Tel (404) 366-5262

REITER, SUSAN KOLBRENER, b. N.Y.C., Jan. 11, 1942; B.A., Wheaton Coll., 1963; J.D., N.Y. U., 1968. Admitted to N.Y. State bar, 1968, Ill. bar, U.S. Dist. Ct. bar, 1973; counsel to Commr. Bess Myerson N.Y. Dept. Consumer Affairs, N.Y.C., 1969-70; asso. firm Overton, Schwartz & Yacker, Chgo., 1974-76; asso. counsel Bank of Am., Chgo., 1976—; lectr. U. Md., 1970-72. Mem. Chgo. Bar Assn. Office: 233 S Wacker Dr Chicago IL 60606 Tel (312) 876-7266

REITZE, ARNOLD WINIFRED, JR., b. Jersey City, Apr. 25, 1938; B.A., Fairleigh Dickinson U., 1960, J.D., Rutgers U., 1962. Admitted to N.J. bar, 1962, Ohio bar, 1969, D.C. bar, 1971; with Judge Adv. Gen. Corps, U.S. Army, 1962-63; asso. firm Stevens & Mathias, Newark, 1963; teaching asso. Ind. U., 1963-64; instr. law., U. Mich., 1964-65; asst. prof. law Case Western Res. U., 1965-67, asso. prof., 1967-69; prof. law George Washington U., 1970—, also dir. Environ. Law Program. Chmn. air conservation com. Cuyohoga County (Ohio) Tb and Respiratory Disease Assn., 1969-70. Mem. Am. (chmn. internat. law sect. environ. law com. 1971-72) D.C. bar assns., Air Pollution Control Assn. Author: Environmental Planning, Law of Land and Resources, 1974; Environmental Law, 1972; Land Acquisition for a Potomac Nat. River, Interstate Commission on the Potomac River Basin, 1973; To Have & To Hold—Land and Resources, Alaska Native Foundation, 1975; contbr. articles in field to profl. jours.; author monthly article Environment Mag., 1973—. Home: 2521 N Quebec St Arlington VA 22207 Office: Nat Law Center George Washington Univ Washington DC 20052 Tel (202) 676-6908

RELIHAN, WALTER JOSEPH, JR., univ. counsel; b. Binghamton, N.Y., Oct. 17, 1930; B.A., Cornell U., 1952, J.D., 1959. Admitted to N.Y. bar, 1959, U.S. Supreme Ct. bar, 1964; partner firm Night, Keller & Relihan, Binghamton, N.Y., 1959-67; gen. counsel N.Y. State Office of Gen. Services, Albany, N.Y., 1967-71; univ. counsel, vice chancellor for legal affairs State U. N.Y., 1971—, counsel to Research Found., State U. N.Y., 1971-76. Mem. Commn. on Architecture and Urban Design, City of Binghamton, N.Y., 1965-67. Mem. N.Y. State, Am., Broome County bar assns. Home: 46 Longwood Dr Delmar NY 12054 Office: 99 Washington Av Albany NY 12210 Tel (518) 474-7591

RELIN, LLOYD HENRY, b. Rochester, N.Y., Feb. 4, 1939; A.B., Dartmouth Coll., 1959; J.D., Yale, 1962. Admitted to N.Y. State bar, 1962; asso. firm Relin, Relin & Celona, Rochester, 1962-67, partner, 1968-73; partner firm Fix, Spindelman, Relin, LoMonaco, Turk & Himelein, Rochester, 1974-75, Relin & Goldstein, 1976—. Vice chmn. Rochester adv. council N.Y. State Div. of Human Rights, 1970-72. Mem. Am., N.Y. State, Monroe County (council banking, corp. and bus. sect. 1976—) bar assns., Comml. Law League Am. (dir. jr. mems. conf. 1969), ACLU (vice chmn., gen. counsel Genesee Valley chpt. 1968-70). Home: 9 Creek Side Rd Fairport NY 14450 Office: 1100 First Federal Plaza Rochester NY 14614 Tel (716) 325-6202

RELSON, MORRIS, b. N.Y.C., Apr. 14, 1915; B.S., City Coll. N.Y., 1935; M.A., George Washington U., 1940; J.D., N.Y. U., 1945. Admitted to N.Y. bar, 1945, U.S. Supreme Ct. bar, 1950; patent examiner U.S. Patent Office, Washington, 1937-41; patent agt. Sperry Gyroscope Co., Garden City, N.Y., 1941-45, atty., 1945-48; mem. firm Darby & Darby, 1948-49, partner, 1949—. Mem. Am. Bar Assn., Am., N.Y. (pres. 1976-77) patent law assns., IEEE. Home: 27 Tain Dr Great Neck NY 11021 Office: 405 Lexington Ave New York City NY 10017 Tel (212) OX7-7660

RELYEA, RICHARD JAMES, III, b. N.Y.C., May 23, 1940; A.B., Harvard U., 1962; LL.B., Cornell U., 1967; LL.M., N.Y. U., 1971. Admitted to N.Y. bar, 1967, Maine bar, 1971; staff trial counsel Liberty Mut. Ins. Co., Scarsdale, Bklyn. and Forest Hills, N.Y., 1967-69; asso. firm Werner, Kennedy, French, Relyea & Molloy, N.Y.C., 1969-71; asso. firm Rudman, Rudman & Carter, Bangor, Maine, 1971-73, partner, 1974-76; individual practice law, Bangor, 1977—. Mem. Hampden (Maine) Zoning Bd. Appeals, 1973—, chmn., 1976—; bd. dirs. Hampden Community Playsch., 1974—. Mem. Am., Maine State, Penobscot County (Maine) bar assns., Maine Trial Lawyers Assn. Home: PO Box 153 Hampden Highlands ME 04445 Office: PO Box 1381 6 State St Bangor ME 04401 Tel (207) 947-0188

REMBUSCH, FRANK RICHARD, b. Indpls., June 23, 1947; A.B. in Govt., U. Notre Dame, 1969; J.D., Ind. U., 1972. Admitted to Ind. bar; statute reviser, Ind. Legislative Council, 1974—, sr. legislative analyst, 1972-74, dir. Office Code Revision, 1974—. Mem. Ind. Bar Assn. Contbr. article in field; co-author Drafting Manual, Ind. Gen. Assembly, 1976. Office: 302 State House Indianapolis IN 46204 Tel (317) 269-3550

REMELMEYER, STANLEY EDWARD, b. Seattle, June 5, 1918; A.B., U. Washington, 1940; LL.B., Harvard, 1948; LL.M., U. So. Calif., 1964. Admitted to Calif. bar, 1949; individual practice law, Los Angeles, 1949-55; dept. city atty. Torrance, Calif., 1955-56; city atty., 1956—. Home: 431 Calle De Castellana Redondo Beach CA 90027 Office: 3031 Torrance Blvd Torrance CA 90503 Tel (213) 328-5310

REMINGTON, FRANCIS KIRK, b. Rochester, N.Y., Nov. 3, 1902; B.A., U. Rochester, 1923; LL.B., Harvard, 1926. Admitted to N.Y. bar, 1927; partner firm Harris, Beach, Folger, Remington, Bacon & Keating, 1931-31, firm Remington & Remington, 1931-33, firm Remington, Remington & Gifford, 1933-34, firm Remington, Remington, Gifford & Willey, Rochester, 1934-72, firm Remington, Gifford, Williams & Frey, Rochester, 1972-76, of counsel, 1976—; chief atty. Office of Price Adminstrn., 1942-43. Tel (716) 232-5225

REMINGTON, MICHAEL JOHN, b. Madison, Wis., June 5, 1945; B.S., U. Wis., 1967, J.D., 1973. Admitted to Wis. bar, 1973, U.S. Supreme Ct. bar, 1976; law clk. to chief judge U.S. Dist. Ct. for Eastern Dist. Wis., Milw., 1973-74; trial atty. criminal div. appellate sect. U.S. Dept. Justice, Washington, 1975-77; counsel Com. Judiciary U.S. Ho. of Reps., 1977—. vol. Peace Corps, Ivory Coast, 1969-71; mem. planning, mgmt. and evaluation staff, mem. final report staff Presdl. Clemency Bd., 1975. Mem. Wis. Bar Assn. (spl. liaison com. Washington), U. Wis. Law Alumni (pres. Washington), Order of Coif. Fulbright research scholar, France, 1974-75; honors program atty. Dept. Justice, 1975-77; contbr. articles to profl. publs. Tel (202) 225-3926

REMSEN, JOHN LOCKWOOD, b. New Brunswick, N.J., Apr. 5, 1928; LL.B. cum laude, U. Miami, 1953. Admitted to Fla. bar, 1953; partner firm Cromwell & Remsen, Rivera Beach, Fla., 1955—. Chmn. Palm Beach County Bd. Pub. Instruction, 1961-64; vice chmn. Palm Beach County Area Planning Bd., 1970-73; chmn. Nat. Found. Polio Telethons, Palm Beach, Fla., 1959, 60; gen. chmn. 1966 PGA Team Championship Golf Tournament, Palm Beach Gardens, Fla. Mem. The Fla. Bar (chmn. unauthorized practice of law com. 1972-75, grievance com. 1967-70, 75—), Palm Beach County Legal Aid Soc. (pres. 1958-59), Am., Palm Beach County bar assns. Home: 11960 Lake Shore Place North Palm Beach FL 33408 Office: Community Fed Bldg Riviera Beach FL 33404 Tel (305) 844-2541

REMUS, EDWARD WALTER, b. Virginia, Minn., Nov. 11, 1942; B.Chem. Engring., U. Minn., 1965; J.D., DePaul, U., 1970. Admitted to Ill. bar, 1970, U.S. Patent bar, 1970, U.S. Supreme Ct. bar, 1973—; research chem. engr. Sinclair Research Inc., Harvey, Ill., 1965-69; patent atty. Universal Oil Products, Des Plaines, Ill., 1969-71; asso. firm Allegretti, Newitt, Witcoff & McAndrews, Chgo., 1971-75, partner, 1975—. Trustee Elk Grove Twp. Sch., 1975—; v.p., counsel Elk Grove Twp. Republican Orgn., 1973—; twp. Coor. Ill. Congressman Crane, 1976; mem. plan commn. Alexian Bros. Hosp., 1976—. Mem. Am. Bar Assn., Am., Chgo. patent law assns., Am. Inst. Chem. Engrs. Home: 1037 Lincoln Ln Elk Grove Village IL 60007 Office: 125 S Wacker Dr Suite 3100 Chicago IL 60606 Tel (312) 372-2160

RENDA, CHARLES ROBERT, b. Chgo., Feb. 17, 1930; B.A., U. Ill., 1951, J.D., 1952; LL.M., Georgetown U., 1961. Admitted to Ill. bar, 1952, Calif. bar, 1959, U.S. Supreme Ct. bar, 1956; trial atty. U.S. Dept. Justice, Washington, 1955-57; asst. U.S. Atty., San Francisco, 1957-66; regional solicitor U.S. Dept. Interior, Sacramento, 1966—; spl. asst. to Asst. Atty. Gen., civil div. U.S. Dept. Justice, 1976. Mem. Am., Fed., Calif., Sacramento County bar assns., Am. Judicature Soc. Recipient Atty. Gen.'s award for Superior Performance, 1961; Meritorious Service award Dept. Interior, 1974, Spl. Achievement award, 1974. Home: 850 San Ramon Way Sacramento CA 95825 Office: 2800 Cottage Way room E-2753 Sacramento CA 95825 Tel (916) 484-4331

RENDA, THOMAS ANTHONY, b. Des Moines, Sept. 19, 1937; B.A., Loras U., 1959; J.D., Drake Law Sch., 1962. Admitted to Iowa bar, 1963; rep. Iowa State Legislature, 1964-70, asst. minority floor leader, 1969-70; judge Municipal Ct., Des Moines, 1971—. Home: 5004 SW 16th Pl Des Moines IA 50315 Office: Municipal Ct Bldg Des Moines IA 50309 Tel (515) 284-6373

RENFREW, CHARLES BYRON, b. Detroit, Oct. 31, 1928; A.B., Princeton, 1952; J.D., U. Mich., 1956. Admitted to Calif. bar, 1956; asso. firm Pillsbury, Madison & Sutro, San Francisco, 1956-65, partner, 1965-72; U.S. dist. judge No. Dist. Calif., San Francisco, 1972—; co-chmn. San Francisco Lawyers Com. for Urban Affairs, 1971-72; mem. spl. com. to propose standards for admission to practice in fed. cts. U.S. Jud. Conf., 1976—. Parish chancellor Episcopal Ch., 1968-71, sr. warden, 1973-75; mem. exec. council San Francisco Deanery, 1969-70; mem. adv. council Episc. Ch. Found., 1974—; bd. dirs. Internat. Hospitality Center, 1961-74, pres., 1967-70; bd. dirs. San Francisco Symphony Found., 1964—, pres., 1970-73; bd. dirs. Council for Civic Unity, 1968-72, pres., 1971-72; bd. dirs. Opportunity Through Ownership, 1969-72, Marin Country Day Sch., 1972-74; trustee Town Sch. for Boys, 1972—, pres., 1975—; bd. govs. San Francisco Symphony Assn., 1974—; alumni trustee Princeton, 1976—. Mem. Am., San Francisco, Calif. bar assns., Order of Coif, Phi Beta Kappa, Phi Delta Phi. Office: US Dist Ct 450 Golden Gate Ave San Francisco CA 94102 Tel (415) 556-1727

RENFRO, J. MIKE, b. Tulsa, Dec. 5, 1944; B.A., U. Okla., 1967; J.D., U. Tex., 1970. Admitted to Tex. bar, 1971; briefing atty. to judge Tex. Ct. Criminal Appeals, 1971-72; asst. county atty. Travis County (Tex.), 1972, 1st asst. county atty., 1973-75, county judge, 1975—. Bd. dirs. United Cerebral Palsy of Capital Area, Austin, Tex., 1973-74. Mem. Nat. Dist. Attys. Assn., Travis County Bar Assn., Austin Jr. Bar Assn. Home: 1300 W 51st St Austin TX 78756 Office: PO Box 1748 Austin TX 78767 Tel (512) 476-7162

RENFRO, ROBERT ROSS, b. Lents, Oreg., Nov. 28, 1911; J.D., Lewis and Clark Coll., 1940. Admitted to Oreg. bar, 1940, U.S. Supreme Ct. bar, 1955, N.H. bar, 1963, U.S. Ct. Mil. Appeals bar, 1955, Republic of Korea bar, 1959; served with JAGC, USAF, 1940-63; individual practice law, Portsmouth, N.H., 1963—. Mem. Portsmouth Planning Bd., 1965-70. Mem. Am., Oreg., N.H., Rockingham County, Portsmouth bar assns., Trial Lawyers Assn. Am., Lawyer-Pilots Assn. Home: 39 Lafayette Rd Portsmouth NH 03801 Office: 6 Market Sq Portsmouth NH 03801 Tel (603) 436-1866

RENNE, PAUL ARTHUR, b. Mpls., Nov. 2, 1930; B.A., U. Minn., 1956; LL.B., Harvard U., 1959. Admitted to D.C. bar, 1959, N.Y. bar, 1961, Calif. bar, 1964; clk. to judge U.S. Dist. Ct., Wilmington, Del., 1959-60; asso. firm Haight, Gardner, Poor & Havens, N.Y.C., 1960-61; atty. civil rights div. U.S. Dept. Justice, Washington, 1961-62; asst. U.S. atty., Washington, 1962-64; asso. firm Cooley, Gdoward, Castro, Huddleson & Tatum, San Francisco, 1964-68, partner, 1968—; asso. prof. Golden Gate Law Sch., 1968-70. Bd. dirs. San Francisco Boy's Club, 1973—. Mem. Am., Calif. State, San Francisco bar assns., Trial Attys. Am. Office: The Alcoa Bldg 20th Fl 1 Maritime Plaza San Francisco CA 94111 Tel (415) 981-5252

RENNER, DORREN LEANDER, b. Sugar Creek, Ohio, Apr. 22, 1906; A.B., Oberlin Coll., 1927; J.D., U. Mich., 1932. Admitted to Ohio bar, 1932; partner firm Smith, Renner, Hanhart, Miller & Kyler, and predecessors, New Philadelphia, Ohio, 1934—; v.p. Surety Savs. & Loan Co., Dover, Ohio, 1938—. Chmn. New Philadelphia Civil Service Commn., 1944-73. Mem. Am., Ohio Tuscarawas County bar assns. Home: 837 Oak St NW New Philadelphia OH 44663 Office: 119 W High Ave New Philadelphia OH 44663 Tel (216) 343-5585

RENNER, MICHAEL JOHN, b. Columbus, Ohio, May 11, 1947; B.A., U. Mich., 1969, J.D., 1972. Staff U.S. Congressman Marvin Esch, Ann Arbor, Mich., 1967-72; admitted to Ohio bar, 1973; asso. firm Bricker, Evatt, Barton & Eckler, Columbus, 1973—. Mem. com. lawyers Leukemia Soc.; v.p. congregation Bethany Luth. Ch. Mem. Columbus, Ohio, Am. bar assns., Assn. Trial Lawyers Am. Home: 5317 Great Oak Dr Columbus OH 43213 Office: 100 E Broad St Columbus OH 43215 Tel (614) 221-6651

RENNER, ROBERT GEORGE, b. Nevis, Minn., Apr. 2, 1923; B.A., St. John's U., Collegeville, Minn., 1946; J.D., Georgetown U., 1949. Admitted to Minn. bar, 1949, U.S. Supreme Ct. bar, 1971; asso. firm Peterson & Renner, Walker, 1953-69; U.S. atty. Dist. Minn., Mpls., 1969-77; U.S. magistrate Dist. Minn., 1977—; mem. Atty. Gen.'s Adv. Com., 1975—. Mem. Gt. Lakes Commn., 1967-69; mem. Minn. Ho. of Reps., 1957-69. Mem. Fed., Minn., Ramsey County bar assns. Home: 2115 N Rosewood Ln Roseville MN 55113

RENO, ROBERT HENKLE, b. Macomb, Ill., Mar. 24, 1917; A.B., Dartmouth, 1938; LL.B., Yale, 1941. Admitted to Ill. bar, 1946, N.H. bar, 1946; asso. firm Orr and Reno, Concord, N.H., 1946—; v.p., gen. counsel United Life & Accident Ins. Co., 1956—. Mem. N.H. Ballot Law Commn., 1950-60, Concord Sch. Bd., 1957-62; del. N.H. Constl. Conv., 1964, 74. Mem. Am., N.H. bar assns., Am. Soc. Internat. Law, Am. Judicature Soc., Fed. Tax Inst. New Eng. (exec. com.). Home: 12 Spaulding St Concord NH 03301 Office: 95 N Main St Concord NH 03301 Tel (603) 224-2381

RENO, RUSSELL RONALD, SR., b. Chgo., Oct. 23, 1904; A.B., U. Ill., 1931, J.D., 1927; LL.M., Columbia, 1940. Admitted to Ill. bar, 1927, S.D. bar, 1935; asso. firm Redmon and Redmon, Decatur, Ill., 1927-29; asst. prof. law Valparaiso U., 1931-34; asso. prof. U. S.D., 1934-36; prof. U. Md., Balt., 1936-74, prof. emeritus, 1974—; with JAGC, USAR, 1950-60; mem. S.D. Bd. Bar Examiners, 1935-36. Mem. Md. State Bar Assn., Order of Coif, Phi Beta Kappa. Author: (with others) American Law of Property, 1952. Home: 103 B Versailles Circle Baltimore MD 21204 Office: Sch Law U Md Baltimore MD 21201 Tel (301) 528-5607

RENTZ, WILLIAM CARL, II, b. Miami, Fla., July 22, 1941; student U. Fla., 1959-60; B.A., Stetson U., 1964, J.D., 1967. Admitted to Fla. bar, 1967; asso. firm Preddy, Haddad, Kutner & Hardy, Miami, 1967-70, partner, 1970-72; partner firm Rentz, McClellan & Haggard, Miami, 1972—; Dade County and S.Fla. coordinator Young Lawyer Vol. Parole Aide Program, 1971-72. Bd. dirs. S.W. Boys' Club. Mem. Am., Fla., Dade County (grievance com. 1973-74), Fed. bar assns., Assn. Trial Lawyers Am., Inner Circle Advs. Recipient certificate of appreciation for outstanding contbn. to Boys Club Am., 1973. Office: 903 Ingraham Bldg 25 SE 2d Ave Miami FL 33131 Tel (305) 371-6223

RENZ, WALTER ALBERT, b. N.Y.C., Apr. 4, 1914; A.B., Fordham U., 1934; J.D., St. John's U., 1937; M.B.A., Harvard. 1940. Admitted to N.Y. bar, 1942, U.S. Supreme Ct. bar, 1967; gen. atty. Lehigh Valley R.R., N.Y.C., 1946-54; pres., gen. counsel Am. R.R. Car Inst., N.Y.C., 1954—; gen. counsel, dir. Met. Outdoor Advt. Co., Warwick, R.I., 1970—. Chmn., R.R. Supply Group Am. Red Cross, N.Y.C., 1957-58. Mem. N.Y. State Bar Assn., Am. Soc. Assn. Execs., U.S. C. of C., Ret. Officers Assn. Home: 136 E 64th St New York City NY 10021 Office: 11 E 44th St Suite 1505 Nw York City NY 10017 Tel (212) 867-6577

RENZ, WILLIAM TOMLINSON, b. Washington, Feb. 26, 1947; B.A., Pa. State U., 1969; J.D., Dickinson Sch. Law, 1972. Admitted to Pa. bar, 1972; mem. firm Power, Bowen, & Valimont, Doylestown, Pa., 1972—; asst. JAG, USAR, 1972. Mem. Bucks County, Pa., Am. bar assns. Home: 35 Bedgate Dr Buckingham PA 18912 Office: 102 N Main St Doylestown PA 18901 Tel (215) 345-7500

RENZY, BERNARD THOMAS, III, b. Bklyn., Jan. 10, 1937; B.A., The Citadel, 1959; LL.B., U. S.C., 1963. Admitted to S.C. bar, 1963, D.C. bar, 1966, U.S. Supreme Ct. bar, 1972; reviewer IRS, Washington, 1963-69; partner firm Hamel, Park, McCabe & Saunders, Washington, 1969—; with Pub. Defender Service for D.C., 1971-72. Active Citadel Devel. Found., 1966—, Washington Tax Study Group, 1970—, McLean (Va.) Citizens' Assn., 1970—. Mem. D.C., S.C. State, Am. (chmn. ann. report commn. tax sect. 1977—), Fed. bar assns., Am. Judicature Soc., Phi Delta Phi. Mem. The Citadel Honor Ct., 1959; recipient Apostolic Benediction, Pope John XXIII, 1959, Apostolic Blessing, 1961; Outstanding Serivce award Brigadier Club of The Citadel, 1975. Home: 6201 Kellogg Dr McLean VA 22101 Office: 1776 F St NW Washington DC 20006 Tel (202) 785-1234

REPHAN, JACK, b. Little Rock, Mar. 16, 1932; B.C.S., U.Va., 1954, LL.B., 1959, J.D., 1970. Admitted to Va. bar, 1959, D.C. bar, 1961, U.S. Supreme Ct. bar, 1966; asso. firm Kanter and Kanter, Norfolk, Va., 1959-60; law clk. to judge U.S. Ct. Claims, Washington, 1960-62; asso. firm Pierson, Ball and Dowd, Washington, 1962-64; asso. firm Danzansky, Dickey, Tydings, Quint, and Gordon, Washington, 1964-69, partner, 1969—. Pres., Patrick Henry Sch. PTA, Alexandria, Va., 196B-69, Landmark Kiwanis, Alexandria, 1969-70, Seminary Ridge Civic Assn., Alexandria, 1976—. Mem. Am. (chmn. subcom. on procurement jud. remedies, sect. pub. contract law 1972-73), Va., D.C. bar assns. Contbr. article to legal publ. Home: 4008 Harris Pl Alexandria VA 22304 Office: 1120 Connecticut Ave NW Washington DC 20036 Tel (202) 857-4068

REPP, RICHARD ALLEN, b. Detroit, Aug. 12, 1939; A.B., U. Mich., 1963; J.D., Coll. William and Mary, 1968; diploma Ct. Practice Inst., 1976. Admitted to Va. bar, 1968, U.S. Supreme Ct. bar, 1976; asso. firm Hirschler, Fleischer, Weinberg, Cox & Allen, and predecessors, Richmond, Va., 1968-73, partner, 1973—; participant legal edn. programs. Bd. dirs. West of Blvd. Civic Assn., Richmond, 1973-74. Mem. Am., Va. bar assns., Lawyer-Pilots Bar Assn. Co-author: Representing Small Virginia Businesses; contbr. articles to legal, aviation jours.; asso. editor William and Mary Law Rev., 1966-68. Home: 2221 Monument Ave Richmond VA 23220 Office: 4 N 4th St Richmond VA 23219 Tel (804) 644-6041

RERKO, FREDERICK JOHN, b. Johnstown, Pa., Jan. 15, 1943; B. Chem. Engring., Ohio State U., 1965; J.D., U. Pitts., 1973. Admitted to Pa. bar, 1973; asso. firm Eckert, Seamans, Cherin & Mellott, Pitts., 1973—. Mem. Am., Pa., Allegheny County bar assns., Order of Coif. Contbr. articles to legal jours. Home: 215 Rockingham Rd Pittsburgh PA 15238 Office: 600 Grant St 42d floor Pittsburgh PA 15219 Tel (412) 566-6000

RESH, BERNARD L., lawyer; b. N.Y.C., May 9, 1926; B.B.A., Coll. City N.Y., 1948; J.D., N.Y. U., 1952, LL.M. in Taxation, 1954. Admitted to N.Y. State bar, 1953; individual practice law, 1953-67; v.p. Schwartz & Resh, N.Y.C., 1967—. Mem. N.Y. County Lawyers Assn. Office: Schwartz & Resh 150 Broadway New York City NY 10038 Tel (212) 732-6460

RESH, WARREN HARLAN, b. Winnebago, Ill., July 4, 1899; A.B. magna cum laude, U. Wis., 1921, J.D., 1928. Admitted to Wis. bar, 1928, U.S. Supreme Ct. bar, 1960; partner firm Warner, Risser & Resh, Madison, Wis., 1928-34; asst. atty. gen. Wis., Madison, 1934-66; spl. counsel State Bar Wis., 1966—. Contbr. articles in field to profl. jours.; mem. editorial staff Unauthorized Practice News, Am. Bar Assn., 1947-76. Home: 2343 W Lawn Ave Madison WI 53711 Office: 402 W Wilson St Madison WI 53703 Tel (618) 257-3838

RESNEK, FRANK MICHAEL, b. Boston, Nov. 7, 1939; A.B., Brown U., 1961; LL.B., Vanderbilt U., 1964; LL.M. in Taxation, N.Y. U., 1966. Admitted to Mass. Bar, 1966; mem. firm Tyler & Reynolds, Boston, 1966-67, Richmond, Rosen, Crosson & Resnek, Boston, 1976—; pres. Churchill Forge Inc., Newton, Mass., 1973—; counsel Med. Mobilization for Soviet Jewry, Norfolk County Bar Assn. Home: 119 Wendell Rd Newton Centre MA 02159 Office: 199 Wells Ave Newton Centre MA 02159 Tel (617) 964-0060

RESNICK, CHARLES H., b. 1924; A.B., Harvard U., 1948, LL.B., 1950. With Raytheon Co., Lexington, Mass., 1951—, sec., 1963—, gen. counsel, 1964—, v.p., 1968—. Office: 141 Spring St Lexington MA 02173*

RESNICK, FRANKLIN DELANO, b. N.Y.C., June 6, 1936; B.S., U. Fla., 1959; J.D., U. Miami, 1964. Admitted to Fla. bar, 1964, D.C. bar, 1965, Ga. bar, 1971; atty. HUD, Washington, Atlanta, 1964-70; partner firm Resnick & Lawson, Atlanta, 1970—. Mem. Am. (chmn. housing policy sub-com. real estate sect.), Fed., D.C., Ga., Fla. bar assns., Mortgage Bankers Assn. (insured loan com.), Nat. Assn. Housing Redevel. Agys., Am. Arbitration Assn., Nat. Assn. Homebuilders, Nat. Leased Housing Assn. Home: 3437 Embry Circle NE Atlanta GA 30341 Office: 101 Marietta Tower Atlanta GA 30303 Tel (404) 522-6430

RESNIK, AARON SHERMAN, b. Chgo., May 31, 1914; A.B., U. So. Calif., 1936; J.D., U. Calif., 1939. Admitted to Calif. bar, 1939; individual practice law, Los Angeles, 1939-40, 74—; with U.S. Govt., 1942-73; real estate broker, San Francisco, 1974—; lectr. law Calif. State U., Hayward, Calif., 1974—, Golden Gate U., San Francisco, 1974—; arbitrator Am. Arbitration Assn., 1974—. Mem. Fed. Bar Assn., State Bar Calif., Bar Assn. San Francisco. Recipient Gallitan award U.S. Treasury Dept., 1973. Address: 1333 Gough St San Francisco CA 94109 Tel (415) 922-1171

RESS, LEWIS M., b. N.Y.C., Sept. 30, 1930; A.B., Cornell U., 1952, LL.B., 1954, J.D., 1969. Admitted to Fla., N.Y. bars, 1956, U.S. Supreme Ct. bar, 1959; pres. firm Ress Gomez Rosenberg, Berk & Howland, P.A., North Miami, Fla. Mem. Fla., Dade County, N. Dade bar assns. Office: 1700 Sans Souci Blvd North Miami FL 33181 Tel (305) 893-5506

RESS, SAMUEL SIMON, b. Bklyn., May 6, 1912; B.B.A., Coll. City N.Y., 1933; J.D., N.Y. U., 1936. Admitted to N.Y. State bar, 1937, Mass. bar, 1950; individual practice law, N.Y.C., 1937—, W. Harwich, Mass., summers 1950—; arbitrator Civil Ct. of City N.Y., County of Bronx, 1962—; prof. law Bronx Community Coll., City U. N.Y., 1964—; practice accounting, N.Y.C., 1959—. Mem. N.Y. State Soc. C.P.A.'s, Am., Bronx County bar assns., Am. Bus. Law Assn. Editor, writer C.P.A., 1947—. Home: 3235 Cambridge Ave Bronx NY 10463 Office: 2488 Grand Concourse Bronx NY 10458 Tel (212) 933-3523

RESSEGUIE, FRANKLIN BRUNDAGE, b. South Gibson, Pa., May 28, 1921; B.A., Harper Coll., 1949; LL.B., Cornell U., 1952. Admitted to N.Y. State bar, 1954; asso. firm Pearis, Resseguie & Stone, Binghamton, N.Y., 1952-54; founder, sr. partner firm Resseguie, Powers & Richards, Binghamton, 1962; individual practice, Binghamton, 1969—; former v.p. Concepts Corp.; pres. Locator Map, Inc., Hiawatha Island Corp.; owner, developer Highland Oaks; owner Hia Island; co-owner Bell Creek Farm; dir. Inter Mission Trading, Inc., Heritage Corp. Pres., Broome County Young Republican Club, 1960; Rep. candidate for Congress, 1974. Mem. Am., N.Y. State, Broome County (civil rights com.) bar assns., N.Y. State Trial Lawyers Assn., Am. Judicature Soc. Author: (poetry) Eagle Feathers, 1973. Home: 23 Oakridge Dr Binghamton NY 13903 Office: 600 O'Neil Bldg Binghamton NY 13901 Tel (607) 723-9535

RESTEINER, HAROLD EDWARD, b. Turner, Mich., Oct. 18, 1930; J.D., Wayne State U., 1955; Admitted to Mich. bar, 1956, U.S. Supreme Ct. bar, 1962; individual practice law, Flint, Mich., 1957-64; probate judge Genesee County (Mich.), Flint, 1964—; mem. Gov.'s Crime Commn., 1972-75, Mich. Jud. Tenure Commn., 1972—. Mem. Am. Bar Assn., Am. Judicature Soc., Am. Coll. Probate Judges, Nat. Council Juvenile Ct. Judges, Mich. Probate and Juvenile Ct. Judges. Contbr. articles in field to legal jours. Home: 1114 Dyekrest Dr Flint MI 48504 Office: 919 Beach St Flint MI 48504 Tel (313) 766-8841

RETT, DONALD ALBERT, b. Newark, June 10, 1937; B.B.A. in Fin., U. Miami, 1970, J.D., 1973. Admitted to Fla. bar, 1973; law clk., atty. SEC, Miami, Fla., 1972-75; dir. Fla. Div. Securities, Tallahassee, 1975—. Mem. Am. Bar Assn., Delta Theta Phi. Office: 235 Carlton Bldg Tallahassee FL 32304 Tel (904) 488-7814

RETTBERG, PAUL ALAN, b. Chgo., June 20, 1944; B.A., DePaul U., 1966, J.D., 1970. Admitted to Ill. bar, 1970; partner firm Querrey, Harrow, Gulanick & Kennedy, Chgo., 1970—. Pres. Elk

Grove-Schaumburg Mental Health Assn., 1973-76. Mem. Chgo. Trial Lawyers Club (sec.), Ill., Chgo., Lake County bar assns. Home: 1425 Worden Way Elk Grove Village IL 60007 Office: 135 S LaSalle St Chicago IL 60603

REUBEN, JACOB, b. Chgo., July 18, 1910; student DePaul U., U. Ill., U. Chgo.; postgrad. Northwestern U.; LL.B., Chgo. Law Sch. Admitted to Ill. bar, 1943; individual practice law, Highland Park, Ill. Address: Box 223 Highland Park IL 60035

REULAND, TIMOTHY JOSEPH, b. Aurora, Ill., Aug. 5, 1948; B.A., Loyola U., Chgo., 1970; J.D., Northwestern U., 1973. Admitted to Ill. bar, 1973; asso. firm Reid, Ochsenschlager, Murphy and Hupp, Aurora, Ill., 1973—; chmn., dir. Legal Aid Bur. Kane County (Ill.), Inc., 1975-77. Mem. Am., Ill., Kane County bar assns., Am., Ill. trial lawyers assns. Exec. editor Jour. Criminal Law and Criminology Northwestern U., 1972-73. Office: 75 S Stolp St Aurora IL 60507 Tel (312) 892-8771

REUM, WALTER JOHN, b. Chgo., June 7, 1914; J.D., Chgo.-Kent Coll. Law, 1938. Admitted to Ill. bar, 1938; partner firm Reum & Casello, Chgo., 1946—; pros. atty. Village of Oak Park (Ill.), 1950-52; mem. Ill. Ho. of Reps., 1953-63. Mem. Oak Park Library Bd., 1948-50. Mem. Internat. Found. Employee Benefit Plans. Author: (with G. Mattran) Politics from the Inside Up, 1966; contbr. articles to legal jours.; named Outstanding Mem. Ill. Ho. of Reps., Ill. Press Assn., 1957. Home: 421 N East Ave Oak Park IL 60302 Office: 11 S La Salle St Chicago IL 60603 Tel (312) 372-4521

REVELLE, GEOFFREY GEORGE, b. Seattle, Apr. 23, 1947; B.A. magna cum laude, Princeton U., 1969; J.D., U. Wash., 1972. Admitted to Wash. State bar, 1972; dep. prosecutor King County (Wash.), Seattle, 1972-75; asso. firm Parks, Johnson & East, Seattle, 1975—; atty. Eastside Defender's Assn., 1975—; dir. Legal Aid to McNeil Penitentiary Inmates, 1971-72. Mem. Am., Wash. State, S. King County, Eastside bar assns., Order of Coif. Office: 506 Seattle Trust Bldg Bellevue WA 98004

REVELOS, CONSTANTINE NICHOLAS, b. Middletown, Ohio, Mar. 1, 1938; A.B., Bowdoin Coll., 1961; J.D., Duke U., 1965; LL.M., U. Calif., 1971. Admitted to Ohio bar, 1965, Mich. bar, 1975; asso. prof. law Salmon P. Chase Coll. Law, Cin., 1965-70, pres., dean, 1968-70; prof. law Detroit Coll. Law, 1971—; Mem. Am., Ohio State, Mich. State bar assns., Am. Judicature Soc., Am. Acad. of Polit. and Social Sci. Office: 136 E Elizabeth St Detroit MI 48201 Tel (313) 965-0150

REVELS, PERCY BURTON, b. McRae, Fla., Dec. 16, 1901; student U. Fla., 1924-27; LL.B., Southeastern U., 1943; LL.D., Bethune-Cookman Coll., 1966. Tchr., Putnam County, Fla., 1927-30; admitted to Fla. bar, 1930, U.S. Dist. Ct. bar, 1931; U.S. Supreme Ct. bar, 1944; individual practice law, Palatka, Fla., 1930-51; atty. Putnam County, Fla., 1933-51; judge 7th Judicial Circuit, Fla., 1951—. Trustee Bethune-Cookman Coll. Mem. Palatka Jr. C. of C., Putnam County C. of C., Hist. Soc., Am. Camellia Soc., Am., Fla., Putnam County bar assns., Internat. Bar Assn. (patron), Am. Judicature Soc., Am. Trial Judges Assn., Internat. Platform Assn., Phi Kappa Tau. Author book on Fla. civil law; editorial staff Trial Judges Jour.; contbr. articles in field to profl. jours. Home: 800 Laurel Palatka FL 32077 Office: PO Drawer 250 Palatka FL 32077 Tel (904) 328-2408

REVERCOMB, HORACE AUSTIN, JR., b. Richmond, Va., July 4, 1923; student Randolph-Macon Coll., 1940-42; Grad. of Laws, Smithdeal Massey Sch. Law, 1952. Admitted to Va. bar, 1953; practiced in King George, Va., 1956-64; judge King George and Stafford Counties Ct., 1964-73, Va. Dist. Ct., 15th Jud. Dist., 1973—, chief judge, 1975-76. Co-founder King George Fall Festival, 1959; bd. dirs. Rappahannock Area Devel. Commn., Fredericksburg, (Va.) 1961-64, Rappahannock Area Div. Alcoholism Services, 1974-75; mem. King George County Hwy. Safety Commn., 1967-75. Mem. Va. State Bar, Va. State Bar Assn., Am. Judicature Soc. Home: PO Box 133 King George VA 22485 Office: Courthouse King George VA 22485 Tel (703) 775-3573

REY, JOSEPH JOAQUIN, b. El Paso, Tex., Feb. 9, 1920; student U. Wash., 1944-45, U. Tex., El Paso, 1945-47, So. Meth. U. Law Sch., 1947-49. Admitted to Tex. bar, 1949, U.S. Supreme Ct. bar, 1961; mem. firm Norcop & Momsen, 1949-51; individual practice law, El Paso, 1951—; counsel NAACP, 1951-55; asst. city atty. City of El Paso, 1954. Mem. State Bar Tex., Inter-Am. Bar Assn., Tex. Assn. Plaintiff's Lawyers, Am. Trial Lawyers Assn. Home: 819 Driver Circle El Paso TX 79903 Office: PO Box 10187 El Paso TX 79992 Tel (915) 532-1623

REY, JOSEPH JOAQUIN, JR., b. El Paso, Tex., Apr. 2, 1939; J.D., S. Tex. Coll., 1964. Admitted to Tex. bar, 1964; individual practice law, El Paso, 1964—. Fellow Smithsonian Inst.; mem. Am., InterAm. Tex., El Paso bar assns., Jr. Bar of El Paso, Tex., El Paso trial lawyers assns., Matrix Soc., Delta Theta Phi. Office: 100 N Florence St El Paso TX 79901 Tel (915) 532-5401

REYNAUD, WILBUR WOODS, b. New Orleans, Mar. 24, 1949; B.A. in History, La. State U., 1970, J.D., 1973. Admitted to La. bar, 1973; individual practice law, Lutcher, La.; editor The News-Examiner; dir. St. James Bank and Trust Co., Lutcher, Savings Life Ins. Co., Shreveport, La. Mem. Am., La. bar assns., La. State U. Alumni Assn. (fundraising chmn. St. James Parish 1976), Phi Delta Phi. Home: 813 Main St Lutcher LA 70071 Office: 318 Texas St Lutcher LA 70071 Tel (504) 869-8566

REYNOLDS, CARL HOWARD, b. Nashville, Mich., Mar. 7, 1888; J.D., U. Mich., 1913. Admitted to Mich. bar, 1913; practice law, Lansing. Mem. Michigan Bar Assn. Home: 3008 Westchester Rd Lansing MI 48910 Office: 213 E Saint Joseph St Lansing MI 48933 Tel (517) 485-4611

REYNOLDS, CHARLES LOYD, b. Chillicothe, Tex., July 24, 1921; LL.B., So. Meth. U., 1953. Records searcher VA, Washington, 1940-43, sect. chief, Dallas, 1946-51, asst. div. chief, 1951-54; admitted to Tex. bar, 1953; practiced in Childress, Tex., 1954-64; judge Tex. Dist. Ct., 100th Jud. Dist., 1964-70; asso. justice Tex. Ct. Civil Appeals, 7th Supreme Jud. Dist., 1971—; county atty. Childress County, 1956-64; lectr. in field. Mem. Am., Childress County, 100th Jud. Dist., Am. bar assns., Am. Judicature Soc., State Bar Tex. (exec. com. jud. sect. 1968-69, 75—). Home: 3700 Huntington Dr Amarillo TX 79109 Office: Ct of Civil Appeals PO Box 9540 Amarillo TX 79105 Tel (806) 376-5323

REYNOLDS, EARL THOMAS, b. Topeka, Sept. 26, 1900; LL.B., Washburn U., 1923. Admitted to Kans. bar, 1924; individual practice law, Coffeyville, Kans., 1924—; asst. city atty., 1974—. Mem. Coffeyville Human Relations Commn., 1966—; deacon Calvary Baptist Ch. Home and Office: 405 E 5th St Coffeyville KS 67337 Tel (316) 251-3640

REYNOLDS, JAMES HAROLD, b. Dubuque, Iowa, Mar. 24, 1939; B.A., Loras Coll., 1961; J.D., U. Iowa, 1965. Admitted to Iowa bar, 1965, U.S. Supreme Ct. bar, 1973; asst. atty. Dubuque County, 1965-67; mem. firm Reynold, Kenline, Dubuque, 1967—; acting atty., Dubuque County, 1972. Bd. dirs. Aquinas Inst., chmn., 1977; bd. dirs. Dubuque Summer Festival, United Fund, Washington Neighborhood Improvement, Legal Services Iowa, Iowa Assn. Mental Health. Mem. Am., Iowa, Dubuque County bar assns., Assn. Trial Lawyers Iowa (bd. govs.). Office: 222 Fischer Bldg Dubuque IA 52001 Tel (319) 583-1768

REYNOLDS, JOHN W., b. Green Bay, Wis., Apr. 4, 1921; B.S., U. Wis., 1946, LL.B., 1949. Admitted to Wis. bar, 1949, since practiced in Green Bay; atty. gen., Wis., 1959-63; gov. State of Wis., 1963-65; U.S. dist. judge Eastern Dist. Wis., 1965—, now chief judge. Mem. Am., Wis., Brown County bar assns. Home: 4654 N Woodburn Milwaukee WI 53211 Office: Fed Bldg Milwaukee WI 53202*

REYNOLDS, R. JAMES, JR., b. Joplin, Mo., Jan. 17, 1946; B.A., Gettysburg Coll., 1967; J.D., Dickinson Sch. Law, 1971. Admitted to Pa. bar, 1971; mem. firm Fronefield, deFuria & Petrikin, Media, Pa., 1971-72, Pepper, Hamilton & Scheetz, Harrisburg, Pa., 1972—. Mem. Am., Pa., Dauphin County bar assns. Home: Rd #1 Box E 100 Etters PA 17319 Office: 10 S Market Sq Box 1181 Harrisburg PA 17108 Tel (717) 233-8483

REYNOLDS, ROBERT H., b. Magazine, Ark., Oct. 3, 1921; LL.B., Okla U., 1950. Admitted to Okla. bar, 1950, Alaska bar, 1970; asso. firm A.L. Commons, Miami, Okla., 1950; county atty., Ottawa County, Okla., 1952; individual practice law, Miami, Okla., 1954-55; asst. county atty. Oklahoma County, Oklahoma City, 1956-59; partner firm Fisher & Reynolds, Oklahoma City, 1959-67; staff asst. jud. adminstrn. sect. Am. Bar Assn., 1963-67; adminstrv. dir. cts. Alaska Ct. System, Anchorage, 1967-70; partner firm Reynolds & Tobey, Anchorage, 1971-74, firm Robinson, McCaskey, Reynolds & Frankel, Anchorage, 1975—; mem. Okla. Legislature, 1947-51. Mem. Okla., Am., Alaska bar assns., Phi Delta Phi. Contbr. articles to legal jours. Home: PO Box 1778 Anchorage AK 99510 Office: 921 W 6th Ave Anchorage AK 99501 Tel (907) 279-7431

REYNOLDS, ROBERT HUGH, b. St. Louis, Jan. 3, 1937; B.A., Yale U., 1958; J.D., Harvard U., 1964. Admitted to Ind. bar, 1964; asso. firm Barnes, Hickam, Pantzer & Boyd, Indpls., 1964-70, partner, 1971—; dir. Danners, Inc., Hawley Mfg. Corp., Mutz Corp., Raffensperger, Hughes & Co., Inc. Bd. dirs. Crossroads of Am. council Boy Scouts Am., v.p., 1971-75; bd. dirs. Family Service Assn. Indpls., sec., 1976—. Mem. Am, Ind. State, Indpls. bar assns. Editor: Comml. Real Estate Financing for Ind. Attys., 1968; co-editor Advising Indiana Businesses, 1974. Office: 1313 Merchants Bank Bldg Indianapolis IN 46204 Tel (317) 638-1313

REYNOLDS, SHEILA MAY, b. Hutchinson, Kans., Aug. 21, 1944; B.A., U. Kans., 1966, J.D., 1971. Admitted to Kans., Mo. bars, 1971; staff atty. Legal Aid Soc. Greater Kansas City (Mo.), 1971-72, Topeka Legal Aid Soc., 1973-77; legal services developer Kans. Dept. Aging, 1977—. Mem. Kans. Bar Assn. (legal aid com.), Order of Coif. Home: 1518 Western St Topeka KS 66604 Office: 2700 W 6th St Topeka KS 66606 Tel (913) 354-8531

REYNOLDS, WILLIAM BRADFORD, b. Bridgeport, Conn., June 21, 1942; B.A., Yale, 1964; LL.B., Vanderbilt U., 1967. Admitted to N.Y. State bar, 1968, D.C. bar, 1973, U.S. Supreme Ct. bar, 1971; asso. firm Sullivan & Cromwell, N.Y.C., 1967-70; asst. to Solicitor Gen., U.S. Dept. Justice, Washington, 1970-73; partner firm Shaw, Pittman, Potts & Trowbridge, Washington, 1973—. Mem. Am., D.C. bar assns., Order of Coif. Editor-in-chief Vanderbilt Law Rev. Tel (202) 331-4100

REZNECK, DANIEL ALBERT, b. Troy, N.Y., Apr. 26, 1935; B.A., Harvard U., 1956, LL.B., 1959. Admitted to N.Y. bar, 1959, D.C. bar, 1961; law clk. to Justice William J. Brennan, Jr., U.S. Supreme Ct., 1960-61; asst. U.S. atty. D.C., 1961-64; partner firm Arnold & Porter, Washington, 1964—; adj. prof. law Georgetown U., 1963—; pres. D.C. Bar, 1975-76, bd. govs., 1972—. Mem. Bar Assn. D.C., Am. Bar Assn., Am. Judicature Soc., Inst. Jud. Adminstrn. Named Young Lawyer of Year, Young Lawyers sect. Bar Assn. D.C., 1970-71; contbr. articles to legal jours. Home: 2852 Albemarle St NW Washington DC 20008 Office: 1225 19th St NW Washington DC 20036 Tel (202) 872-6776

RHEA, DAVID EDWARD, JR., b. Port Townsend, Wash., Oct. 24, 1944; B.A., U. Wash., 1966; J.D., Willamette U., 1969; grad. Nat. Coll. of State Judiciary, Reno, 1976. Admitted to Wash. bar, 1969; law clk. to chief justice Wash. State Supreme Ct., Olympia, 1969-70; dep. pros. atty. Whatcom County (Wash.), Bellingham, 1970-73; partner firm Asmundson Rhea & Atwood, Bellingham, 1973-75; dist. ct. commr. Whatcom County, 1974-75, dist. ct. judge, 1975—. Mem. Am., Wash. bar assns., Wash. Magistrates Assn. Home: 2644 W Crestline St Bellingham WA 98225 Office: Whatcom County Dist Ct 311 Grand St Bellingham WA 98225 Tel (206) 676-6770

RHEINGOLD, PAUL DAVID, b. Boston, Nov. 1, 1933; B.A., Oberlin Coll., 1955; LL.B., Harvard, 1958. Admitted to D.C. bar, 1958, Mass. bar, 1959, N.Y. bar, 1965; atty. Dept. Justice, Washington, 1958; instr. Boston U. Law-Medicine Inst., 1959-61; asst. editor-in-chief Am. Trial Lawyers Jour., 1961-63; partner firm Speiser, Shumate, Geoghan, Krause & Rheingold, N.Y.C., 1963-71; individual practice law, N.Y.C., 1971—; lectr. law and medicine Fordham Law Sch., 1972-76; counsel, trustee Mamaroneck (N.Y.) Free Library, 1975—. Mem. Am., N.Y. State bar assns., Assn. Trial Lawyers Am., N.Y. State Trial Lawyers Assn., Assn. Bar City N.Y., Phi Beta Kappa. Author: Negligence Case Techniques, 1969; Drug Liability, 1970; Environmental Law Handbook, 1971; Products Liability, 1975. Office: 200 Park Ave New York City NY 10017 Tel (212) 661-0055

RHEINSTEIN, PETER HOWARD, b. Cleve., Sept. 7, 1943; B.A. in Math with high honors, Mich. State U., 1963, M.S., 1964; M.D., Johns Hopkins, 1967; J.D., U. Md., 1973. Admitted to Md. bar, 1973; intern USPHS Hosp., San Francisco, 1967-68; resident in internal medicine USPHS Hosp., Balt., 1968-70; practice medicine specializing in internal medicine, Balt., 1970—; instr. medicine U. Md., 1970-73; med. dir. extended care facilities CHC Corp., Balt., 1972-74; dir. drug advt. div. U.S. FDA, Rockville, Md., 1974—; adj. prof. div. forensic scis. George Washington U., 1974-76; cons. in med jurisprudence. Fellow Am. Coll. Legal Medicine; mem. AMA, Am., Md., Fed. (chmn. food and drug com. 1976—) bar assns., Med. and Chirurg. Faculty Md., Balt. Med. Soc., Am. Acad. Family Physicians, Johns Hopkins Med. and Surg. Assn., Am. Coll. Health Assn., Math Assn. Am., Soc. Indsl. and Applied Math. Contbr. articles to profl. jours. Home: 621 Holly Ridge Rd Severna Park MD 21146 Office: 5600 Fishers Ln Rockville MD 20857 Tel (301) 443-3730

RHIND, JAMES THOMAS, b. Chgo., July 21, 1922; student Hamilton Coll., 1940-42; A.B. cum laude, Ohio State U., 1944; postgrad. U. Mich., 1944-45; LL.B. cum laude, Harvard, 1950. Admitted to Ill. bar, 1950; asso. firm Bell, Boyd, Lloyd, Haddad & Burns, Chgo., 1950-53, 55-58, partner, 1958—; translator U.S. Dept. War, Tokyo, 1946-47; congl. liaison officer FOA, Washington, 1954; dir. Kewaunee Sci. Equipment Corp., Statesville, N.C., VSI Corp., Pasadena, Calif., Fred. S. James & Co., Chgo., Microseal Corp., Zion, Ill., Lindberg Corp., Chgo. Trustee, Ill. Children's Home and Aid Soc., 1966—, pres., 1971-73; bd. dirs. E. J. Dalton Youth Center, 1966-69; exec. com. div. met. mission and ch. extension bd. Chgo. Presbytery, 1966-68; commr. General Assembly United Presbyn. Ch., 1963; trustee Ravinia Festival Assn., 1968—, sec. 1969-71, vice chmn. 1971-75; governing mem. The Orchestral Assn., 1971—; mem. Ill. Arts Council, 1971-75; trustee Hamilton Coll., 1974—, U. Chgo., 1975—. Mem. Am. Judicature Soc., Law Club, Legal Club, Economic Club, Commercial Club (Chgo.), Japan Am. Soc. Chgo., Sigma Phi, Phi Beta Kappa. Contbr. articles in field to profl. jours. Home: 830 Normandy Ln Glenview IL 60025 Office: 135 S LaSalle St Chicago IL 60603 Tel (312) 372-1121

RHINE, BERTRAND, b. San Francisco, Apr. 9, 1905; A.B., Stanford U., 1927; J.D., U. So. Calif., 1929. Admitted to Calif. bar, 1930, U.S. Supreme Ct. bar, 1941. Mem. Am. Bar Assn. Awarded Diplome Paul Tissandier, Fedn. Aeronautique Internat., 1959. Office: 80 S Lake Ave Suite 711 Pasadena CA 91101 Tel (213) 684-2291

RHOADS, JOSEPH, b. Wilmington, Del., July 7, 1910; B.A., Haverford Coll., 1932; J.D., U. Pa., 1936. Admitted to Pa. bar, 1936, Del. bar, 1941; asso. law firm MacCoy, Evans & Lewis, Phila., 1936-40; successively asst. sec., asst. v.p. Wilmington (Del.) Trust Co., 1940-53, v.p., 1953-75; v.p., dir. Jeflion Investment Co., Wilmington, Del., 1974—; dir. Dolphin Delaware Corp., Wilmington, 1952—; dir. Dover Tanker Corp., Wilmington, Del., 1952—; v.p., dir. Brandywine Ins. Agy., Wilmington, 1955-75. Dir., Family Service of No. Del., Wilmington, 1943-69; bd. mgrs. Wilmington Friends Sch., 1942-51. Mem. Am., Del. (sec. 1948-50) bar assns., Phi Beta Kappa. Home: 2401 Pennsylvania Av Wilmington DE 19806 Office: 1004 Wilmington Trust Bldg 100 W 10th St Wilmington DE 19801

RHODEN, THOMAS HENRY, b. New Orleans, June 16, 1944; B.S. in Physics, Millsaps Coll., 1966; J.D., U. Miss., 1970. Admitted to Miss. bar, 1970; law clk. U.S. Ct. Appeals, Ackerman, Miss., 1970-71; asso. firm Brunini, Grantham, Grower & Hewes, Jackson, Miss., 1971-74, Scott, Barbour & Scott, Jackson, 1974; partner firm Rhoden & Hetrick, Jackson, 1974—. Mem. Am., Internat., Hinds County, Miss. bar assns., Jackson Young Lawyers Assn., Miss. Savs. and Loan League (pres. attys. sect.), U.S. League Savs. Assns. (attys. com. 1977—). Home: 117 Pinehaven Dr Jackson MS 39202 Office: PO Box 2028 525 E Capitol St Jackson MS 39205 Tel (601) 969-1440

RHODES, GEORGE FRED, b. San Antonio, Aug. 2, 1925; B.S. in Elementary Edn., Tex. A. and I. U., 1950; postgrad. U. Houston Law Sch., 1950-51; LL.B., S. Tex. Sch. Law, 1954. Admitted to Tex. bar, 1954; partner firm Cole & Rhodes, Victoria, Tex., 1954-56; sr. partner firm Rhodes, Garner & Roberts, Port Lavaca, Tex., 1956—. Chmn. Calhoun County (Tex.) Democratic Exec. Com., 1956-72, Tex. Dem. Exec. Com., 1968-72; chmn. service unit Salvation Army, 1956-76; chmn. Calhoun County Hist. Commn., 1973—; bd. dirs. Tex. A. and I. U. System, 1972—, sec., 1973-77, vice-chmn., 1977—. Mem. Tex. Coastal and Marine Council, State Bar Tex., Calhoun County Bar Assn. (sec.-treas. 1969-71, pres. 1971-72). Home: Route 1 Box 80 Port Lavaca TX 77979 Office: 202 S Ann St PO Box 986 Port Lavaca TX 77979 Tel (512) 552-2971

RHODES, JOHN JACOB, III, b. Mesa, Ariz., Sept. 8, 1943; B.A., Yale, 1965; J.D., U. Ariz., 1968. Admitted to Ariz. bar, 1968, U.S. Supreme Ct. bar, 1973; asso. firm Killian, Legg and Nicholas, Mesa, 1970-74, partner, 1974-76; v.p. and legal counsel Health Maintenance Assos., Phoenix, 1977—. Mem. Mesa Bd. Edn., 1972—, clk., 1975, pres., 1976; bd. dirs., v.p., dr. chmn. Mesa United Way. Mem. Am., Ariz., Maricopa County bar assns., Mesa C. of C. (dir., pres.). Decorated Bronze Star. Office: 4747 N 22d St Phoenix AZ 85016 Tel (602) 957-9200

RHODES, KENNETH ANTHONY, b. Waverly, Pa., Aug. 8, 1930; A.B., Dickinson Coll., 1952; LL.B., Harvard U., 1955. Admitted to Pa. bar, 1956; fgn. service officer U.S. Dept. State, 1958-61; U.S. consul, Brussels, 1959-60; partner firm Oliver, Price & Rhodes, Scranton, Pa., 1961—; vis. lectr. law Keystone Jr. Coll., La Plume, Pa., 1963-64. Bd. dirs. Mus. Assn. Scranton, 1961—, pres., 1968-72; dir. Lackawanna Arts Council, Scranton, 1963-65. Mem. Am., Pa., Lackawanna County bar assns., Lackawanna Hist. Soc. (dir. 1972—). Home: Miller Rd Waverly PA 18471 Office: 1200 Scranton Nat Bank Bldg Scranton PA 18503 Tel (717) 343-6581

RHODES, RHYS DAVIES, b. Bloomington, Ind., Jan. 12, 1926; A.B., Franklin Coll. of Ind., 1950; J.D., U. Louisville, 1953. Admitted to Ind. bar, 1953; individual practice law, Paoli, Ind., 1953—; judge Paoli Town Ct., 1967-71, 75—. Mem. Ind. State, Orange County bar assns. Office: East Side Sq Paoli IN 47454 Tel (812) 723-2403

RHODES, THOMAS WILLARD, b. Lynchburg, Va., Mar. 9, 1946; A.B., Davidson Coll., 1968; LL.B., U. Va., 1971. Admitted to Va. bar, 1971, Ga. bar, 1972; asso. firm Gambrell, Russell, Killorin & Forbes, Atlanta, 1972-76, partner, 1976—. Mem. Am., Ga. bar assns. Contbr. articles to legal jours. Home: 1917 Ardmore Rd Atlanta GA 30309 Office: 4000 First Nat Bank Tower Atlanta GA 30303 Tel (404) 658-1620

RHYNE, CHARLES SYLVANUS, b. Charlotte, N.C., June 23, 1912; student Duke U., 1928-29, 32-34, LL.D., 1958; J.D., George Washington U., 1937, D.C.L., 1958; LL.D. (hon.), Loyola U., Los Angeles, 1958, Dickenson Law Sch., 1960, Ohio No. U., 1965, DePaul U., 1968, Centre Coll. Ky., 1968, U. Richmond, 1970, Howard U., 1975. Admitted to D.C. bar, 1937, U.S. Supreme Ct. bar, 1940; prof. govt. Am. U. Grad. Sch., 1945-46; prof. law George Washington U. Law Sch., 1948-54; gen. counsel Fed. Commn. on Jud. and Congl. Salaries, 1954-55; legal cons. Office of Civilian Def., Nat. Def. Adv. Commn., 1941-48; spl. cons. to Pres. U.S., 1959-60; spl. U.S. ambassador, UN high commr. for refugees and personal rep. U.S. Pres., 1971; sr. partner firm Rhyne and Rhyne, Washington; gen. counsel Nat. Inst. Municipal Law Officers, 1937—; pres. World Peace

Through Law Center, 1963—; dir. Nat. Savs. & Trust Co. Trustee Duke U., 1960—. Fellow Am. Coll. Trial Lawyers, Am. Law Library of the Middle Temple (hon.); mem. Bar Assn. D.C. (pres. 1955-56), Am. Bar Assn. (pres. 1957-58; nat. chmn. young lawyers sect. 1944-45; life mem. ho. of dels.; chmn. sect. on internat. and comparative law 1948-49; chmn. aero. law com. 1946-54, chmn. com. on Magna Carta Monument 1956-57; chmn. ho. of dels. 1956-57; chmn. spl. com. on world peace thorugh law 1958-65), Am. Bar Found. (pres. 1957-58), Am. Soc. Internat. Law (life), The Barristers, Am. Judicature Soc. (dir. 1952-57), World Assn. Lawyers (hon. pres. 1975—), Supreme Ct. Hist. Soc., Nat. Aero. Assn. (dir. 1946-48), Aero Club (trustee 1951-53), Council of Atlantic Union Com. Fed. City Council (dir. 1966-69), Nat. Lawyers Club, Nat. Press Club, Delta Theta Phi, Order of Coif, Omicron Delta Theta (hon.). Recipient Legion Lex award U. So. Calif., 1958, Grotius Peace award, 1958; Alumni Achievement award George Washington U., 1959; George Washington award Freedom Found., 1961; Pub. Service award Nat. Inst. Municipal Law Officers, 1961; C. Francis Stradford award Nat. Bar Assn., 1962; Outstanding Recognition award D.C. Bar Assn., 1965; the Gold medal Am. Bar Assn., 1966; Geroge Washington Law Achievement award, 1969; Distinguished Achievement award The Links, Inc., 1974, Nansen Ring, 1976. Author: Civil Aeronautics Act Annotated, 1939; Airports and the Courts, 1944; Labor Unions and Municipal Employee Law, 1946; Aviation Accident Law, 1947; Airport Lease and Concession Agreements, 1948; The Law of Municipal Contracts, 1952; Cases on Aviation Law, 1950; Municipal Law, 1957; International Law, 1971; Views World Leaders on Law and Peace, 1977; Justices of Internat. and Nat. Cts., 1977; The Law and Refugees, 1977; Renowned Law Givers and Great Law Documents of Humankind, 1977. contbr. monographs and articles to legal jours. Home: 1404 Langley Ln McLean VA 22101 Office: 400 Hill Bldg Washington DC 20006 Tel (202) 347-7992

RHYNE, SIDNEY WHITE, JR., b. Charlotte, N.C., Apr. 2, 1931; A.B., Roanoke Coll., 1952; LL.B., U. Pa., 1955; LL.M., Georgetown U., 1961. Admitted to Pa. bar, 1955, D.C. bar, 1957, U.S. Supreme Ct. bar, 1959; asso. firm Rhyne & Rhyne, Washington, 1957-60; partner firm Mullin, Connor & Rhyne, Washington, 1961—; lectr. Georgetown U. Law Center, Washington, 1964-70; mem. Com. on Admissions and Grievances, U.S. Ct. Appeals, 1973—; trustee D.C. Legal Aid Soc., 1968-77, pres., 1976-77. Mem. Am., D.C., Fed. Communications bar assns. Editor U. Pa. Law Rev., 1954-55. Home: 20 Oxford St Chevy Chase MD 20015 Office: 1000 Connecticut Ave Washington DC 20036 Tel (202) 659-4700

RIBICOFF, IRVING SABLE, b. New Britain, Conn., Apr. 16, 1915; B.A. summa cum laude, Williams Coll., 1936; LL.B., Yale, 1939. Admitted to Conn. bar, 1939, U.S. Dist. Ct. Conn. bar, 1944, U.S. Supreme Ct. bar, 1960, U.S. 2d Circuit Ct. Appeals bar, 1969; chief price atty. Office Price Adminstrn., Conn., 1942-44; atty. reorgn. div. SEC, 1939-41; partner firm Ribicoff & Kotkin, 1941—. Trustee Greater Hartford YMCA; bd. dirs. Hartford Jewish Fedn., 1955-58, 61-64, Symphony Soc. Greater Hartford, 1962-71, Yale Law Sch. Fund, 1967-73; mem. Grievance Com. Hartford County, 1957-61, chmn., 1960-61. Mem. Am., Conn. (chmn. fed. bench-bar com. 1967-69; chmn. specialization com. 1969-74) Hartford County, Fed. (pres. Conn. chpt., 1964-75) bar assns., Yale Law Sch. Assn. (exec. com. 1968-74; pres. Hartford and eastern Conn. chpt. 1962-63), New Eng. Law Inst. (mem. advisory council 1963-64), Order of the Coif, Phi Beta Kappa. Home: 56 Scarborough St Hartford CT 06105 Office: 799 Main St Hartford CT 06103 Tel (203) 527-0781

RIBLE, MORTON, b. Los Angeles, July 30, 1938; B.A., Princeton, 1961; J.D., Stanford, 1964; M.B.A., U. So. Calif., 1973. Admitted to Calif. bar, 1965; partner firm Darling, Mack, Hall & Call, Los Angeles, 1965-69; v.p., gen. counsel The Leisure Group, Inc., Los Angeles, 1969-76; sr. vp., gen. counsel, dir. Calif. Life Corp., Calif. Life Ins. Co., Los Angeles, 1976—. Mem. Palos Verdes Community Art Assn. (pres.), Los Angeles Jr. C. of C. (v.p.), Calif., Am., Los Angeles, San Francisco bar assns. Office: 3255 Wilshire Blvd Los Angeles CA 90010 Tel (213) 487-4310

RICCIO, WILLIS HUGH, b. Providence, Feb. 12, 1934; A.B., Brown U., 1955; LL.B., Georgetown U., 1958, LL.M., 1960, J.D., 1968. Admitted to D.C. bar, 1959, R.I. bar, 1967, U.S. Supreme Ct. bar, 1963; atty. div. corp. fin. SEC, Washington, 1958-60, trial atty. regional office, Boston, 1960-64, sr. trial atty., 1964-68, chief enforcement atty., 1968-70, spl. counsel, 1970-72, chief counsel, 1972-75, asst. regional adminstr., 1975—; lectr. securities law New Eng. Sch. Law, Boston, 1970—; guest lectr. securities law Boston Coll. Law Sch., Northeastern U. Law Sch., Boston, 1974, 75, 76. Mem. R.I. (coms. on corps. and adminstv. law), D.C. bar assns., Phi Alpha Delta. Contbr. articles to legal jours. Home: 300 River Ave Providence RI 02908 Office: SEC 150 Causeway St Boston MA 02203 Tel (617) 223-2721

RICCOBONO, XAVIER C., b. N.Y.C., Apr. 2, 1916; student Fordham U., 1936, LL.B., 1939. Admitted to N.Y. bar, 1940; individual practice law, N.Y.C., 1940-56, justice municipal ct., 1956-62, judge civil ct., 1962-67; justice Supreme Ct. N.Y., 1968-75, justice 1st dept. appellate term, 1976—. Home: 310 E 12th St New York City NY 10003 Office: 60 Centre St New York City NY 10007 Tel (212) 374-8576

RICE, DAVID GEORGE, b. Great Falls, Mont., Mar. 15, 1946; B.A., Concordia Coll., 1968; J.D., U. Mont., 1973. Admitted to Mont. bar, 1973; dept. county atty., Hill County, Mont., 1973—; mem. firm Smith & Rice, Havre, Mont., 1973—; spl. prosecutor, Havre, 1974—. Bd. dirs. Community Action Program, Havre, 1973-75; chmn. bd. edn. 1st Lutheran Ch., Havre, 1974-76; chmn. Hill County Council on Aging, Havre, 1974-76. Mem. Mont., Am. (mem. criminal law div.) bar assns., C. of C. (bd. dirs. Havre 1975-78); recipient Outstanding Law Day Program Chmn. award, Mont. Bar Assn., 1974. Home: 14 Lila Dr Havre MT 59501 Office: 129 1st St Havre MT 59501 Tel (406) 265-4364

RICE, DONALD SANDS, b. Bronxville, N.Y., Mar. 25, 1940; A.B. magna cum laude, Harvard U., 1961, LL.B. cum laude, 1964; LL.M. in Taxation, N.Y.U., 1965. Admitted to N.Y. bar, 1964, U.S. Ct. Claims, 1966; law clerk to Judge Don N. Laramore, U.S. Court of Claims, Washington, 1965-67; asso. Barrett, Smith, Schapiro, Simon & Armstorng, N.Y.C., 1967-71, partner, 1971—. Trustee Hackley Sch., Tarrytown, N.Y., 1974—. Mem. Am., N.Y.C. bar assns., Fed. Bar Council. Home: 1120 Fifth Ave New York City NY 10028 Office: Barrett Smith Schapiro Simon & Armstrong 26 Broadway New York City NY 10004 Tel (212) 422-8180

RICE, DOWNEY, b. Washington, Apr. 13, 1913; LL.B., Cath. U. Am., 1935, J.D., 1967, LL.M., 1936. Admitted to D.C. bar, 1935, Md. bar, 1955, U.S. Supreme Ct. bar, 1954; spl. agt. FBI, 1936-45; spl. asst. U.S. atty., Washington, 1948-49; asso. counsel U.S. Senate Com. on Organized Crime, 1950-51; spl. counsel preparedness subcom. U.S. Senate Armed Services Com., 1953; spl. counsel U.S. Ho. of Reps. Govt. Ops. Com., 1955, U.S. Senate Antitrust and Monopoly Com., 1957, Pa. Ho. of Reps. Com. to Investigate the Adminstrn. of Justice, 1973, Nat. Commn. for Rev. of Fed. and State Laws Relating to Wiretapping and Electronic Surveillance, 1974; cons. U.S. Senate Rackets Com., 1961; mem. firm Rice & King, Washington, 1955-65. Mem. Am., D.C. bar assns., Am. Judicature Soc. Home: 3244 Aberfoyle Pl NW Washington DC 20015 Office: 1744 R St NW Washington DC 20009 Tel (202) 232-2600

RICE, EVELYN F., b. Detroit, May 9, 1931; B.S., Mich. U., 1950; J.D., U. Calif., Berkeley, 1968. Admitted to Calif. bar, 1969; asso firm, Bernal & Rigney, Berkeley, 1969-73; partner firm, Bernal Rigney and Rice, 1972-73; individual practice law, 1973-76; lectr. Mills Coll., 1975-76. Mem. Alameda County (dir.), Berkeley-Albany (1st woman pres.) bar assns., Queens Bench Assn. Home: 115 Highland Blvd Berkeley CA 94708 2000 Center Berkeley CA 94704 Tel (415) 845-1000

RICE, GEORGE PHILIP, b. Albany, N.Y., Sept. 8, 1911; B.S., State U. N.Y., 1932, M.A., 1936; Ph.D., Cornell U., 1944; LL.B., J.D., Ind. U., 1956; postgrad. Columbia U., 1934, Heidelberg U., 1935. Admitted to Ind. bar, 1956; partner firm Tyler, Davis & Rice, 1960—; dep. prosecutor 19th Jud. Dist., Marion County, Ind., 1957-58; lectr. Ind. U. Sch. Law, 1961-63; prof. speech and law Butler U., Indpls., 1950—; gen. counsel Speech Communication Assn. Am. Mem. Ind., Fed. bar assns. Author: Law for the Public Speaker, 1958; contbr. articles to legal jours. Home and Office: 3470 N Merdian St Indianapolis IN 46208 Tel (317) 926-8532

RICE, HARRY EDGAR, b. Urbana, Ohio, Oct. 9, 1931; B.A., Miami U., Ohio, 1953; LL.B., U. Calif. at Berkeley, 1960. Admitted to Calif. bar, 1961; individual practice law, San Francisco, 1961—. Chmn. resolutions com. Marin County Republican Central Com., 1974—. Office: 1255 Post St #610 San Francisco CA 94109 Tel (415) 885-1850

RICE, JAMES B., JR., b. Kansas City, Mo., Dec. 31, 1940; B.A., U. Mo., 1962, J.D., 1965. Admitted to Mo. bar, 1965; asso. firm Rogers, Field & Gentry, Kansas City, 1967-72; mem. firm Wesner, Wesner & Rice, Sedalia, Mo., 1972-74, Rice & Romines, Sedalia, 1975—; atty. JAGC, U.S. Army, 1965-67, legal assistance officer, div. claims officer, Vietnam, 1966-67. Mem. Sedalia Police Personnel Bd., 1972-75, chmn., 1975-76; bd. dirs. Sedalia Symphony, 1975-76. Mem. Am., Kansas City, Pettis County (past pres.) bar assns., Am. Judicature Soc., Am. Assn. Trial Lawyers. Home: 2611 Plaza St Sedalia MO 65301 Office: 701 S Ohio St Sedalia MO 65301 Tel (816) 827-1631

RICE, JAMES W., b. Sparta, Wis., Oct. 19, 1924; LL.B., U. Wis., 1950; Admitted to Wis. bar, 1950; individual practice law, Sparta, 1950-64; judge County Ct. Monroe County, Sparta, 1964—; dir. Monroe County Bank, Sparta, 1960-64; faculty Nat. Coll. State Judiciary, Reno, 1975, Wis. Jud. Coll., 1972-73, 74-75; pres. Wis. Bd. Juvenile Ct. Judges, 1973; judge adv. AMVETS, 1951-52. Mem. Wis., Am. bar assns. Contbr. articles to legal jours. Home: 216 N Spring St Sparta WI 54656 Office: PO Box 165 Sparta WI 54656 Tel (608) 269-2444

RICE, JOHN CARTER, b. Clinton, Iowa, Mar. 17, 1936; A.B., State U. N.Y., Albany, 1957; LL.B., Albany Law Sch., 1960. Admitted to N.Y. bar, 1960; asso. firm Bliss & Bouck, Albany, 1960-61, DeGraff, Foy, Conway & Holt-Harris, Albany, 1961-65, partner, 1965—. Mem. Am., N.Y. State, Albany County bar assns., Justinian Soc. Office: 90 State St Albany NY 12207 Tel (518) 462-5301

RICE, JONATHAN PHILIP, b. Springfield, Mass., Apr. 17, 1940; B.A., Amherst Coll., 1962; LL.B., Yale, 1965. Admitted to Mass. bar, 1965; partner firm Appleton, Kubicek, Rice & Mitchell, Springfield, 1965—. Pres., Child and Family Service Springfield, Inc., 1975—. Mem. Am., Mass. Hampden County bar assns. Home: 30 Pleasantview Ave Longmeadow MA 01106 Office: 1387 Main St Springfield MA 01103 Tel (413) 736-6367

RICE, JULIAN C., b. Miami, Fla., Jan. 1, 1924; J.D. cum laude, Gonzaga U., 1950. Admitted to Wash. bar, 1950, Alaska bar, 1959; mem. firm Rice, Morrison & Lake, Spokane, Wash., 1950-56, Rice, Hoppner & Hedland, Fairbanks and Anchorage, 1959—; mayor City of Fairbanks, 1970-72. Mem. Am., Wash., Alaska bar assns., Am. Judicature Soc., Motor Carrier Lawyers Assn., ICC Practitioners Assn.; fellow Am. Bar Found. Home: 3026 Riverview Dr Fairbanks AK 99701 Office: 330 Wendell St PO Box 516 Fairbanks AK 99701 Tel (907) 452-1201

RICE, KENNETH BROMLEY, b. Fairbanks, Alaska, Jan. 30, 1946; B.A., Willamette U., 1968; J.D., Duke U., 1971. Admitted to N.C. bar, 1971, Iowa bar, 1971, Wash. bar, 1973; capt. USAF, 1971-72; asso. firm Bell, Ingram Johnson & Level, Everett, Wash., 1972-75; partner firm Bell, Ingram & Rice, Everett, 1975—. Mem. Am., N.C., Iowa, Wash. (pres. elect Young Lawyers sect. 1976-77) bar assns. Home: 8615 Cascadia Ave Everett WA 98204 Office: PO Box 1769 Everett WA 98206 Tel (206) 259-8125

RICE, LOUIS HENRY, b. Cleve., Dec. 30, 1944; B.A., Marquette U., 1966, J.D., 1971. Admitted to Wis. bar, 1971, Ohio bar, 1974; asso. firm Cannon McLaughlin, Milw., 1971-74, Ulmer Berne, Cleve., 1974-76; house counsel Agency Rent-A-Car, Inc., Cleve., 1976—. Recipient award labor arbitration Am. Jurisprudence, 1971. Office: 466 Northfield Rd Bedford OH 44146 Tel (216) 439-6300

RICE, PHILIP MARSHALL, b. Toledo, Dec. 28, 1931; B.C.E., U. Mich., 1954; LL.B., U. Toledo, 1961. Admitted to Ohio bar, 1961; patent atty. Owens-Ill., Inc., Toledo, 1961-71, legal counsel, 1971—, asst. sec., 1972—. Corp. mem., trustee Crestview Center of Ohio; corp. mem. Flower Hosp.; trustee YMCA Greater Toledo; asso. St. Vincent Hosp. Mem. Am., Ohio, Toledo bar assns., Am., Toledo patent law assns. Home: 2823 Barrington Dr Toledo OH 43606 Office: PO Box 1035 Toledo OH 43666 Tel (419) 242-6543

RICE, RICHARD ANTHONY, b. Waterbury, Conn., Feb. 29, 1940; Ed.B., U. Miami, 1963; J.D., Woodrow Wilson Coll. of Law, 1967. Admitted to Ga. bar, 1969; individual practice law, Atlanta, 1969—. Coach, commr. YMCA Soccer League, 1976—. Mem. Atlanta Bar Assn. (chmn. com. criminal law sec. 1976, sec. 1975-76, exec. com. 1975-76, mem. superior ct. rules com. 1974-75, vice chmn. criminal law sect. 1973-74, mem. com. Legal Aid Soc. 1972-73). Home: 3758 Cline Dr Smyrna GA 30080 Office: 1228 Fulton Nat Bank Bldg Atlanta GA 30303 Tel (404) 525-2977

RICE, ROBERT EUGENE, b. Duncan, Okla., Jan. 28, 1922; A.B., Dartmouth, 1946; LL.B., U. Mich., 1949. Admitted to Okla. bar, 1949, U.S. Supreme Ct. bar, 1953; individual practice law, Duncan, 1949-50; with Halliburton Co., Duncan, 1951—, atty., 1951-55, asst. gen. counsel, 1955-69, v.p. legal Halliburton Services Div., 1969—; mem. adv. bd. Southwestern Legal Found., Internat. and Comparative Law Center, Dallas. Mem. Stephens County (pres. 1954), Okla. (exec. council 1961-63), Am. bar assns. Office: 1015 Bois D'Arc Duncan OK 73533 Tel (405) 251-3186

RICE, ROBERT JAMES, b. Melrose, Minn., Sept. 11, 1944; A.B. in Polit. Sci., U. Wyo., 1966; M.A. in Internat. Relations, Am. U., 1967; postgrad. U. Mich., 1969; J.D., U. Wyo., 1974; postgrad. in polit. sci. and internat. law U. Fla., 1969-70. Admitted to Mont. bar, 1974; since practiced in Bozeman; individual practice law, 1974-75; partner firm Moore & Rice, 1975-76, Moore, Rice & O'Connell, 1976—. Bd. dirs. REACH, Inc. Mem. Am., Mont., Gallatin County (sec.) bar assns. NDEA fellow, 1968-71; Wyo. Law scholar, 1971-74. Home: Route 2 Box 287B Bozeman MT 59715 Office: PO Box 1288 420 W Mendenhall St Bozeman MT 59715 Tel (406) 587-5511

RICE, WILFRED CARLMOND, b. Winston-Salem, N.C., May 17, 1930; B.S., N.C. A. and T. Coll., 1955; LL.B., Wayne State U., 1959. Admitted to Mich. bar, 1960, U.S. Supreme Ct. bar, 1964; partner firm Hood, Rice & Charity, 1960-63, firm Charity & Rice, 1963-64; individual practice of law, Detroit, 1974—; dir. Wayne County Neighborhood Legal Services; legal adviser Open Door Rescue Mission. Bd. dirs. Greater New Mt. Moriah Baptist. Mem. Am., Nat., Wolverine, Detroit bar assns., Am. Trial Lawyers Assn. Office: 2436 Guardian Bldg Detroit MI 48226 Tel (313) 965-7962

RICE, WILSON A., b. Sacramento, July 15, 1946; B.A., Idaho State U., 1968; J.D., U. Calif., Berkeley, 1971. Admitted to Calif. bar, 1971, Alaska bar, 1972; staff atty. Alaska Legal Services, 1971-76; exec. dir. Trustees for Alaska, 1976—. Reginald H. Smith fellow, Anchorage, 1971-73. Bd. dirs. Alaska Conservation Found., Alaska Center for the Environment. Mem. Alaska, Calif. bar assns. Office: 1026 W 4th Ave suite 209 Anchorage AK 99501 Tel (907) 276-4244

RICH, ARTHUR DOUGLAS, b. Mattapan, Mass., Jan. 15, 1915; A.B., U. Buffalo, 1938; LL.B., Harvard U., 1940. Admitted to Mass. bar, 1941, S.C. bar, 1946; owner, mgr. Rich Plaza Shopping Center, Aiken, S.C., 1968; dir. United Fabricators, Inc., Jackson, S.C., 1965; pres. The Troy Corp., Aiken, 1968; v.p. Gabs Alinement, Inc., Aiken, 1970; mem. firm Lybrand, Rich, Cain & Simons, Aiken, 1960—. Mem. Am. Bar Assn. Recipient Silver Beaver award Boy Scouts Am., 1973. Author: Handbook of Income Tax for S.C. Home: 1114 Evans Rd Aiken SC 29801 Office: Palmetto Federal Bldg Aiken SC 29801 Tel (803) 649-4186

RICH, ELWOOD MERRELL, b. Milton, Pa., Nov. 20, 1920; B.A., Duke, 1943; J.D., U. Ill., 1946. Admitted to Calif. bar, 1947, Ill. bar, 1946; dept. dist. atty. Riverside County, Calif., 1947-51; judge Municipal Ct. of Riverside Jud. Dist., Calif., 1952-71; judge Superior Ct. of Calif., Riverside County, 1971—; dean Citrus Belt Law Sch., Riverside, 1971—. Home: 4687 Cliffside Dr Riverside CA 92506 Office: Court House 4050 Main St Riverside CA 92501 Tel (714) 787-2972

RICH, HOWARD IRA, b. N.Y.C., Jan. 28, 1930; A.B. cum laude, N.Y. U., 1951; J.D., Columbia U., 1954. Admitted to N.Y. bar, 1954, N.J. bar, 1969; asso. firm Botein, Hays, & Herzberg, N.Y.C., 1956-64, partner, 1965—; lectr. Rutgers U. Sch. Law, Newark, 1977—. Mem. Assn. Bar City N.Y., N.Y. State Bar Assn. (exec. com. tax sect. 1972-73). Home: 80 Brown Circle Paramus NJ 07652 Office: 2000 Park Ave New York City NY 10017 Tel (212) 867-5500

RICH, JACK, b. N.Y.C., Aug. 24, 1913; B.S., N.Y. U., 1933, M.A., 1936; LL.B., St. Lawrence U., 1939. Admitted to N.Y. bar, 1940; individual practice law, Bronx, N.Y., 1940—. Mem. Am., N.Y. County, Bronx County, N.Y. bar assns., Am. Judicature Soc. Home: 220 E 72d St New York City NY 10021 Office: 349 E 149th St Bronx NY 10451 Tel (212) 585-0350

RICH, JEFFREY ALAN, b. Cleve., July 10, 1945; B.A. in Polit. Sci. with distinction, Ohio State U., 1967; J.D., Cleve. State U., 1970. Admitted to Ohio bar, 1970, U.S. Supreme Ct. bar, 1973; research asst. to pres. Cleve. State U., 1970; law clk. to justice Ohio Supreme Ct., Columbus, 1970-71; asst. legis. counsel to Gov. State of Ohio, Columbus, 1971-72; asso. firm Teaford & Bernard, Columbus, 1972—; instr. Capital Law Sch., Columbus, 1973, 74. Pres., Indian Hills Residents Assn., Columbus, 1975—. Mem. Am., Ohio State, Columbus bar assns., Am., Franklin County trial lawyers assns. Editor Cleve. State Law Rev., 1969-70; contbr. articles to legal jours. Home: 6053 Rocky Rill Rd Worthington OH 43085 Office: 100 E Broad St Columbus OH 43215 Tel (614) 228-5822

RICH, JOHN TOWNSEND, b. Lansing, Mich., Mar. 10, 1943; B.A. magna cum laude, Harvard, 1965; J.D., Yale, 1969; postgrad. in jurisprudence U. Coll., Oxford, Eng., 1969-70. Admitted to N.Y. bar, 1970, D.C. bar, 1972; law clk. to Chief Judge David L. Bazelon, U.S. Ct. Appeals for D.C., 1970-71; law clk. Justice Harry A. Blackmun, U.S. Supreme Ct., 1971-72; asso. firm Shea & Gardner, Washington, 1972-76, partner, 1976—; adj. prof. law Georgetown U., 1972-75; grant reviewer Nat. Endowment for Humanities, 1975—. Mem. Am. Bar Assn., D.C. Bar (steering com. D.C. affairs div. 1976—), Bar Assn. D.C., Washington Council Lawyers, Phi Beta Kappa, Order of Coif. Editor-in-chief Yale Law Jour., 1968-69. Home: 1106 E Capitol St NE Washington DC 20002 Office: 734 15th St NW Washington DC 20005 Tel (202) 737-1255

RICH, JOSEPH THOMAS, JR., b. New Kensington, Pa., Mar. 7, 1937; A.A., Phoenix Jr. Coll., 1957; B.S., Ariz. State U., 1959; LL.B., U. Ariz., 1962. Admitted to Ariz. bar, 1962; asso. firm Minne & Sorenson, Phoenix, 1962-66; partner firm McGillicuddy & Rich, Phoenix, 1966—; commr. superior ct. County of Maricopa (Ariz.), 1973—, alt. registrar, probate div., 1974—, vol. referee, juvenile div., 1964—. Mem. Am. Bar Assn. (sect. corp. banking bus. law), State Bar Ariz. (adminstrv. law com.). Author radio courses in bus. and real estate law, Maricopa County Community Coll. Dist. Office: McGillicuddy & Rich 316 W McDowell Rd Suite 201 Phoenix AZ 85003 Tel (602) 258-8038

RICHARD, DENNIS ALAN, b. Miami Beach, Fla., May 3, 1947; A.B., U. Miami, 1969, J.D., 1972. Admitted to Fla. bar, 1972; partner firm Richard & Richard, Miami Beach, 1972—. Office: 927 Lincoln Rd Miami Beach FL 33139 Tel (305) 538-0627

RICHARD, HERSCHEL ERSKINE, JR., b. Pascagoula, Miss., July 5, 1945; B.A., Tulane U., 1967; J.D., La. State U., 1970. Admitted to La. bar, 1970; asso. firm Jones, Walker, Waechter, Portivent, Carrere

& Denegre, New Orleans, 1970-72; partner firm Cook, Clark, Egan, Yancey & King, Shreveport, La., 1972—. Mem. Am., La. Shreveport (sec.-treas.) bar assns., La. Assn. Def. Counsel (dir. 1976-77), La. Law Inst. (observer young lawyers sect.). Maritime Law Assn. U.S. Home: 622 McCormick St Shreveport LA 71104 Office: 600 Commercial Nat Bank Bldg Shreveport LA 71101 Tel (817) 221-6277

RICHARD, STANLEY BENTON, b. N.Y.C., May 8, 1918; B.S., U. Fla., 1941, J.D., 1941. Admitted to Fla. bar, 1941; asso. firm Shackleford, Farrior & Shannon, Tampa, Fla., 1941-43; partner firm Richard & Gross, Miami Beach, Fla., 1969-74; individual practice law, Miami Beach, 1945-69; partner firm Richard, Gross & Lichterman, Miami Beach, 1974—. Chmn. bd. dirs. Heart Assn. Greater Miami, 1957-59; pres. Pres.'s Council Miami Beach, 1967-68. Mem. Fla. Bar (chmn. real property, probate and trust sect. 1971-72), Miami Beach (pres. 1964), Am. bar assns. Office: 605 Lincoln Rd Miami Beach FL 33139 Tel (305) 538-6344

RICHARDS, CARLYLE EDWARD, b. Deadwood, S.D., July 21, 1935; B.A., Northwestern U., 1957; LL.B., U. S.D., 1960. Admitted to S.D. bar, 1960; law clk. to judge U.S. Dist. Ct., 1960-61; practice law, Aberdeen, S.D., 1961—. Mem. Am., S.D., Brown County bar assns., Phi Delta Phi. Home: 1619 S Dakota St Aberdeen SD 57401 Office: 207 Midwest Bldg Aberdeen SD 57401 Tel (605) 225-1295

RICHARDS, CHARLES FLEMING, JR., b. Phila., Nov. 11, 1937; B.A., Princeton, 1959; LL.B., Yale, 1962. Admitted to Del. bar, 1963; prof. law U. E. Africa, Dar es Salaam, 1962-63; dep. atty. gen. State of Del., Wilmington, 1963-64; legal sec. Commn. to Revise Del. Corp. Law, Wilmington, 1964-67; partner firm Richards, Layton & Finger, Wilmington, 1968—. Trustee, sec. Tower Hill Sch., Wilmington; chmn., pres., chief exec. officer Del. League Planned Parenthood, Wilmington, 1968-72; bd. dirs. Del. div. Am. Cancer Soc., Wilmington, Home of Merciful Rest, Wilmington; bd. dirs., sec. World Affairs Council of Wilmington. Mem. Am., Del. bar assns. Mem. editorial bd. Yale Law Jour., 1960-62. Office: 4072 Dupont Bldg Wilmington DE 19899 Tel (302) 658-6541

RICHARDS, GEORGE ALEXANDER, b. Rhinelander, Wis., Feb. 25, 1943; student U. Ariz., 1961-62; B.B.A., U. Wis., 1965; J.D., Marquette U., 1969. Admitted to Wis. bar, 1969; legal asst. to chief justice Wis. Supreme Ct., 1969-70; asso. firm Tinkham, Smith, Bliss & Patterson, and successor, Wausau, Wis., 1970-73, partner, 1973—; bd. govs. State Bar Wis., 1976—. Mem. Am., Wis., Marathon County bar assns., Alpha Sigma Nu. Editorial bd. Marquette Law Rev., 1968-69. Office: 630 4th St Wausau WI 54401 Tel (715) 845-1151

RICHARDS, JAMES JOSEPH, b. Hammond, Ind., Aug. 14, 1925; student U. San Francisco, 1947-48, Ind. U., 1948-49; LL.B., Northwestern U., 1952. Admitted to Ind. bar, 1952; individual practice law, Hammond, Ind., 1952-62; dep. pros. atty. Lake County (Ind.), 1953-55; corp. counsel City of Hammond, 1956-62; judge Superior Ct., Hammond, Ind., 1963—; chief judge Superior Ct. Lake County, 1974—; chmn. Ind. Jud. Center, 1971-76; chmn. Nat. Conf. State Trial Judges, 1974-75. Mem. Am., Ind., Hammond bar assns., Ind. Judges Assn., Am. Judicature Soc. Contbr. articles in field to legal jours. Office: 232 Russell St Hammond IN 46320 Tel (219) 931-3440

RICHARDS, JEFFERY CHARLES, b. Vancouver, B.C., Can., May 22, 1922; B. in Indsl. Engring., Rensselaer Poly. Inst., Troy, N.Y., 1944; grad. N.Y. Law Sch., 1962. Admitted to N.Y. bar, 1963; individual practice law, Poughkeepsie, N.Y., 1963—. Pres. Dutchess County (N.Y.) Bd. Health, 1974-76. Mem. N.Y. State, Dutchess County bar assns., Poughkeepsie Area C. of C. (pres. 1971). Office: 59 Academy St Poughkeepsie NY 12601 Tel (914) 471-6650

RICHARDS, JOE BRYAN, b. Colfax, Wash., June 12, 1929; B.A., U. Oreg., 1951; J.D., Willamette Coll. Law, 1954. Admitted to Oreg. bar, 1954; deputy dist. atty., Lane County, 1954-55; asso. firm Luvaas & Cobb, Eugene, Ore., 1955-57; partner firm Luvaas Cobb & Richards, Eugene, 1957-67; partner firm Luvaas, Cobb, Richards and Fraser, Eugene, 1967—; rep. Oreg. legislature, 1965-70; chmn. Oreg. Environ. Quality Commn., 1975—. Mem. Lane County, Ore., Am. bar assns. Home: 5004 Blanton Rd Eugene OR 97405 Office: 777 High St Eugene OR 97401 Tel (503) 484-9292

RICHARDS, JOHN HOWARD A., b. Paducah, Tex., Oct. 28, 1946; B.A. in Polit. Sci., N. Tex. State U., 1969; J.D., St. Mary's Law Sch., 1971. Admitted to Tex. bar, 1971; asst. atty. gen. antitrust and consumer protection div. State of Tex., 1972-77; dir. Lubbock Regional Office Tex. Atty. Gen., 1973-75, asst. chief antitrust and consumer protection div., Austin, 1975-77; asso. firm Maner, Nelson, Jones & Reaud, Lubbock, 1977—. Mem. Am. Bar Assn., State Bar Tex. (council consumer law sect. 1977—), Tex. Trial Lawyers Assn., Tex. Dist. and County Attys. Assn., Criminal Law Assn., Tex. Consumer Assn., Phi Delta Phi. Mem. staff St. Mary's Law Sch. Jour., 1971, Assn. Criminal Law Studies St. Mary's, 1971-72. Home: 4434 80th St Lubbock TX 79424 Office: PO Box 1437 1212 Texas Ave Lubbock TX 79408 Tel (806) 765-7477

RICHARDS, MARION SANDS, b. San Diego, Dec. 10, 1919; B.A., Calif. Western U., 1955; J.D., U.S. Internat. U., 1962. Admitted to Calif. bar, 1964; individual practice law, San Diego; commr. Mission Bay (Calif.) Park, 1958-64, San Diego Park and Recreation Bd., 1958-64. Mem. San Diego County Bar Assn., State Bar Calif., Am. Trial Lawyers Assn., Calif. Trial Lawyers. Home: 10688 Gabacho Ct San Diego CA 92124 Office: 1407 110 W C St San Diego CA 92101 Tel (714) 234-8679

RICHARDS, MARTIN Z., b. Boston, Apr. 5, 1943; A.B., U. Pa., 1965; J.D., Boston U., 1970; LL.M., N.Y. U., 1974. Admitted to N.Y. bar, 1970, U.S. Supreme Ct. bar, 1976; asso. firms Lynton Klein Opton & Saslow, N.Y.C., 1970-71, Pearlman & Pollack, N.Y.C., 1971-73, Lowenthal Freedman Landau Fischer & Todres, N.Y.C., 1973-74; atty. Richardson-Merrell Inc., Wilton, Conn., 1974—; adj. asst. prof. taxation Pace U., fall 1976, spring 1977. Mem. Alumni Fedn. N.Y. U., N.Y. State, Westchester bar assns. Author: (with others) Equipment Leasing as a Tax Shelter, 1976. Home: 6 Burr Farms Rd Westport CT 06880 Office: Ten Westport Rd Wilton CT 06897 Tel (203) 762-2222

RICHARDS, MAX CHARLES, b. Tucson, Feb. 5, 1938; B.S., Ariz. State U., 1960; LL.B., N.Y. U., 1963. Admitted to Ariz. bar, 1963, U.S. Supreme Ct. bar, 1973; mgmt. trainee So. Pacific Co., San Francisco, 1968, trainmaster, 1968-70; asso. firm Bilby, Shoenhair, Warnock & Dolph, Profl. Corp., Tucson, 1970-75, partner, 1975—. Den leader Cub Scouts, Tucson, 1973-76; chmn. bd. Christ United Methodist Ch., Tucson, 1971-72; bd. dirs., v.p. Tucson Youth Football, 1975-76. Mem. Am., Ariz. bar assns., Ariz. Indsl. Relations Assn., Tucson Personnel Club. Office: 9th Floor Valley National Bldg 2 E Congress St Tucson AZ 85701 Tel (602) 792-4800

RICHARDS, NORMAN BLANCHARD, b. Melrose, Mass., May 27, 1924; B.S., Bowdoin Coll., 1945; J.D., Stanford, 1951. Admitted to Calif. bar, 1951; partner firm McCutchen Doyle Brown & Enersen, San Francisco, 1951—. Fellow Am. Coll. Trial Lawyers; mem. San Francisco, Am. bar assns., Maritime Law Assn. U.S. Office: Three Embarcadero Center San Francisco CA 94111 Tel (415) 393-2000

RICHARDS, PAUL AUGUSTINE, b. Oakland, Calif., May 27, 1927; B.A., Coll. of Pacific (now U. of Pacific), 1950; J.D., U. San Francisco, 1953. Admitted to Nev. bar, 1953, U.S. Supreme Ct. bar, 1964; individual practice law, Reno, 1953-56, 69—; partner firms Richards and Swanson, Reno, 1956-62, Richards and Irish, Reno, 1962-65, Richards and Demetras, Reno, 1966-69. Gov. Ins. Attys. Legal counsel Ducks Unltd.; 1st v.p. Reno Rodeo Assn.; trustee Sierra Nev. Coll., 1971—; mem. Fed. Land Law Commn., 1974—. Mem. Nev., Washoe County (Nev.) bar assns., Reno Press Club (pres. 1976). Recipient Spl. award Sierra Nev. Coll., 1975. Office: 248 S Sierra St Reno NV 89501 Tel (702) 323-1317

RICHARDS, RALPH, b. St. Paul, June 26, 1893; B.A., U. Minn., 1915. Admitted to Fla. bar, 1927; since practiced in Clearwater, Fla., partner firm Richards, Nodine, Gilkey, Fite, Meyer & Thompson, and predecessors, 1937—, sr. partner, 1942—; municipal judge City of Clearwater, 1928-32; city atty., 1938-46; chmn. bd. Clearwater Fed. Savs. & Loan Assn., 1955—; dir. Barnett Bank, Clearwater. Chmn. bd. Pinellas County Community Found., 1969; trustee Bethune-Cookman Coll., 1960—; bd. dirs. Morton F. Plant Hosp., 1950-58. Mem. Fla. (past v.p.), Clearwater (past pres.) bar assns., Kappa Sigma. Recipient David Bilgore award for race relations Service Clubs Clearwater, 1954; Brotherhood award NCCJ, 1977; named Mr. Clearwater, Clearwater C. of C., 1976. Author: What To Do About Your Money, 1962; All About Wills, 1965; You Can't Take It With You, 1970. Home: 100 Bluff View Dr Belleair Bluffs FL 33540 Office: Richards Bldg 1235 Park St Clearwater FL 33516 Tel (813) 443-3281

RICHARDS, RICHARD, b. Cedar Rapids, Iowa, Dec. 9, 1916; A.B. cum laude, U. So. Calif., 1939, J.D., 1942; student Law Sch., Harvard, 1940. Admitted to Calif. bar, 1942; sr. partner firm Richards, Watson, Dreyfuss & Gershon, Los Angeles, 1953—. Mem. Calif. Senate, 1954-62; chmn. Los Angeles County Democratic Central Com., 1950, 52; del. Dem. Nat. Conv., 1948, 52, 60, 64; nominee for U.S. Senate, 1956, 62. Mem. Lawyers Club Los Angeles, C. of C., World Affairs Council, Los Angeles, Fed. Power bar assns. Office: 333 S Hope St 38th Floor Los Angeles CA 90071 Tel (213) 626-8484

RICHARDS, ROBERT HENRY, III, b. Phila., Jan. 26, 1938; A.B., Princeton U., 1959; LL.B., Harvard, 1962. Admitted to Del. bar, 1963, U.S. Supreme Ct. bar, 1973; dep. atty. gen. State of Del., 1963; served as judge adv. USN, 1963-66; asso. firm Richards, Layton & Finger, Wilmington, Del., 1966-68, partner, 1969—; dir. Electric Hose & Rubber Co., Wilmington. Mem. exec. com. United Way of Del. Office: 4072 DuPont Bldg Wilmington DE 19899 Tel (302) 658-6541

RICHARDSON, AMOS HAYNES, III, b. Ansonville, N.C., Jan. 14, 1922; LL.B., U. Ark., 1948; postgrad. Rutgers U., 1964. Admitted to Ark. bar, 1949; individual practice law, Little Rock, 1949—. Trustee United Methodist Ch., Little Rock, 1970—. Mem. Ark., Pulaski County bar assns., Assn. Execs. Ark., Ark. Press Assn., Ark. Broadcasters Assn., Public Relations Soc. Am., Ark. Advt. Fed. (dir., Outstanding Member award 1974), Asso. Industries Ark., Ark. C. of C., Am. Legion. Home: 1200 N Mellon Little Rock AR 72207 Office: 7100 Evergreen Rd Little Rock AR 72207 Tel (501) 666-8486

RICHARDSON, CHARLES TODD, b. Bedford, Ind., Aug. 10, 1947; A.B., Ind. U., 1969; J.D., U. Mich., 1972. Admitted to Ind. bar, 1972; asso. firm Baker & Daniels, Indpls., 1972—. Dir. Myasthenia Gravis Found., Indpls.; dir. Phi Beta Kappa Assn., Indpls. Mem. Am., Ind., Indpls., 7th Circuit bar assns. Office: 810 Fletcher Trust Bldg Indianapolis IN 46204 Tel (317) 636-4535

RICHARDSON, DOUGLAS FIELDING, b. Glendale, Calif., Mar. 17, 1929; A.B., U. Calif. at Los Angeles, 1950; J.D., Harvard, 1953. Admitted to Calif. bar, 1953; asso. firm O'Melveny & Myers, Los Angeles, 1953-68, partner, 1968—. Mem. bd. govs. Town Hall of Calif., Los Angeles, 1974—, sec., 1977—, chmn. sect. on legislation and adminstrn. of justice, 1968-70, pres. Town Hall West, 1975; bd. dirs. Hist. Soc. So. Calif., 1976—. Mem. Am., Calif., Los Angeles County bar assns., Phi Beta Kappa. Author: (with others) Drafting Agreements for the Sale of Businesses, 1971. Home: 1637 Valley View Rd Glendale CA 91202 Office: 611 W 6th St Los Angeles CA 90017 Tel (213) 620-1120

RICHARDSON, HARRY HANSBROUGH, b. Bogalusa, La., June 14, 1904; LL.B., La. State U., 1928, J.D., 1968. Admitted to La. bar, 1928, U.S. Supreme Ct. bar, 1960; practice law, Bogalusa; mem. La. Senate, 1944-52, La. Bd. Tax Appeals, 1950-52. Trustee Bogalusa Med. Center, 1956-61. Mem. Inter-Am. (sr. mem.), La., Washington Parish bar assns., Am. Judicature Soc.; Pi Kappa Alpha, Phi Delta Phi. Home: 930 Virginia Ave Bogalusa LA 70427 Office: 335 Austin St Bogalusa LA 70427 Tel (504) 732-4292

RICHARDSON, JAMES RUSSELL, b. Berea, Ky., Feb. 12, 1911; B.A., Eastern Ky. U., 1930; J.D., U. Ky., 1934; LL.M., Yale, 1955. Admitted to Ky. bar, 1935, Fla. bar, 1954; partner firm Chenault & Richardson, Richmond, Ky., 1935-40; asst. atty. gen. State of Ky., Frankfort, 1941-45; asso. prof. law Stetson U., 1949-51, U. Fla., 1951-55; individual practice law, Lexington, Ky., 1974—; prof. law U. Ky., 1957-74; mem. Com. to Revise Fla. Rules of Civil Procedure, 1950-51; of counsel firm Fowler, Rouse, Measle & Bell, Lexington, 1955-64; guest lectr. U. Ky. Med. Center, Lexington, 1964-65. Mem. Gov. Ky. Coordinating Com. on Hwy. Safety, 1964, Ky. Com. on Pathology and Forensic Medicine, 1965. Mem. AAUP, Am., Fayette County, Ky. State bar assns., Order of Coif, Delta Theta Phi. Recipient Great Tchr. award U. Ky. Alumni, 1974, Practice Ct. award U. Ky. chpt. Student Bar Assn., 1965. Author: Modern Scientific Evidence, 1974; Medico-Legal Problems, 1966; Scientific Evidence for Police Officers, 1963; Kentucky Law of Evidence, 1973; Florida Law & Procedure, 1954; contbr. articles to legal jours. Home: 763 Cottage Grove Ln Lexington KY 40502 Office: Coll of Law U Ky Lexington KY 40506 Tel (606) 258-9000

RICHARDSON, JOHN GODFREY, b. Boston, Oct. 4, 1943; B.A., U. Maine, 1966, J.D., 1969. Admitted to Maine, N.H. bars, 1969; asso. firm Michael & Wallace, Rochester, N.H., 1969-1973; partner firm Michael & Richardson, Rochester, 1973-74, Mullaney, Richardson & Cassavechia, Rochester, 1974—. Bd. dirs. Rochester Day Care Center, Dollars for Scholars, Greater Rochester Red Cross. Mem. Mullaney, Richardson and Cassavechia Profl. Assn., Strafford County Bar Assn. (sec.). Contbr. articles to Maine Law Rev. Home: 20 Tingley St Rochester NH 03867 Office: 195 N Main St Rochester NH 03867 Tel (603) 332-8216

RICHARDSON, LLOYD CLIFFORD, JR., b. Dell Rapids, S.D., Feb. 9, 1924; student U. S.D., 1942-46; B.S. in Law, U. Minn., 1949, LL.B., 1951. Admitted to S.D. bar, 1951, U.S. Supreme Ct. bar, 1972; partner firm Richardson, Groseclose, Kornmann & Wyly, Aberdeen, 1954—; solicitor C.M.St.P. & P. R.R. for N.D. and S.D., 1964. Mem. Am., S.D. (pres. 1976—) bar assns., S.D. R.R. Assn. (chmn. Aberdeen 1964), Nat. Assn. R.R. Trial Counsel, Fedn. Ins. Attys., Assn. Ins. Attys., Aberdeen C. of C. (pres. 1969). Home: 1324 N 4th St Aberdeen SD 57401 Office: PO Box 489 Aberdeen SD 57401 Tel (605) 225-6310

RICHARDSON, SCOVEL, b. Nashville, Feb. 4, 1912; A.B., U. Ill., 1934, A.M., 1936; J.D., Howard U., 1937; LL.D., Lincoln U., 1973. Admitted to Ill. bar, 1938, U.S. Supreme Ct. bar, 1943, Mo. bar, 1945; partner firm Lawrence & Richardson, Chgo., 1938-39; asso. prof. law Lincoln U., 1939-43, prof., dean Sch. Law, 1944-53; sr. atty. Office Price Adminstrn., Washington, 1943-44; mem. U.S. Bd. Parole, Washington, 1953-57, chmn. bd., 1954-57; judge U.S. Customs Ct., N.Y.C., 1957—. Trustee Nat. Council Crime and Delinquency, N.Y.C., 1957—, Howard U., 1961—, Colgate U., 1970-76; bd. dirs. Urban League of Westchester County (N.Y.), 1958—; sec. bd. govs. New Rochelle (N.Y.) Hosp., 1974—. Mem. Am. Law Inst., Am., Nat., Cook County (award of Merit 1961), Fed., Mo. bar assns., Am. Judicature Soc., Inst. Jud. Adminstrn., Bar Assn. St. Louis, Assn. Bar City N.Y., Scribes, Supreme Ct. Hist. Soc. Recipient Wisdom award of Honor Wisdom Soc., 1970, Congl. Selective Service medal, 1946, Alumni award Howard U. Bd. Trustees, 1958, Internat. Trade Service award Wall St. Synagogue, 1973; contbr. articles to legal jours. Office: One Fed Plaza New York City NY 10007 Tel (212) 264-2800

RICHARDSON, VAUGHN EDWARD, b. Willards, Md., Dec. 21, 1916; B.S., U. Md., 1938, LL.B., 1942. Admitted to Md. bar, 1946; individual practice law, Salisbury, Md., 1946—; dir. Md. Nat. Bank, Salisbury. Mem. Md. Bar Assn. Home: 716 Camden Ave Salisbury MD 21801 Office: 130 E Main St Salisbury MD 21801 Tel (301) 742-8744

RICHARDSON, WILLIAM BRUHL, b. Toledo, Oct. 28, 1912; B.B.A., U. Toledo, 1936, LL.B., J.D., 1956. Admitted to Ohio bar, 1956; dir. personnel Art Iron, Inc., Toledo, 1962—. Mem. Ohio, Toledo bar assns. Home: 4121 Barbara Dr Toledo OH 43623 Office: PO Box 964 Toledo OH 43696 Tel (419) 241-1261

RICHARDSON, WILLIAM KYLE, b. Galesburg, Ill., Dec. 6, 1913; A.B., Knox Coll., 1934; LL.B., U. Mich., 1937. Admitted to Ill. bar, 1937; circuit clk. Knox County (Ill.), 1943-66; asso. judge 9th Circuit U.S. Dist. Ct., Galesburg, 1966—. Bd. dirs. Galesburg Pub. Library, 1948—, Lions Internat., 1959-61. Mem. Am., Ill., Knox County bar assns. Home: 1635 N West St Galesburg IL 61401 Office: Courthouse Galesburg IL 61401 Tel (309) 343-3121

RICHARDSON, WILLIAM LLOYD, b. Ashland, Oreg., Jan. 10, 1932; B.A. in Polit. Sci., Coll. Idaho, 1960; J.D., U. Chgo., 1963. Admitted to Oreg. bar, 1963; law clk. Justice Rossman, Oreg. Supreme Ct., 1963-64; asso. firm Smith, Reeves & Rogers, Portland, Oreg., 1964-66; dep. dist. atty. Multnomah County (Oreg.), 1966-69; partner firm Tamblyn, Bouneff, Muller, Marshall & Richardson, Portland, 1969-71; judge Municipal Ct., Portland, 1971-72, Oreg. Dist. Ct. for Multnomah County, 1972-77, Oreg. Ct. Appeals, Salem, 1977—. Mem. Am., Oreg. State, Multnomah County bar assns., Am. Judges Assn., Am. Judicature Soc. Office: 300 State Office Bldg Salem OR 97310 Tel (503) 378-6383

RICHARDSON, WILLIAM SHAW, b. Honolulu, Dec. 22, 1919; A.B., U. Hawaii, 1941; J.D., U. Cin., 1943, LL.D., 1967. Admitted to Hawaii bar, 1946, since practiced in Honolulu; lt. gov. Hawaii, 1962-66; chief justice of Hawaii, 1966—. Chmn. Democratic Party Hawaii, 1956-62. Dir. Episcopal Diocese Honolulu. Chmn. Conf. of Chief Justices, 1972-73. Bd. dirs. Nat. Center for State Cts. Mem. Bar Assn. Hawaii (pres. 1961), Res. Officers Assn. (pres. Honolulu 1950), Am. Bar Assn. (ho. dels. 1961). Home: 3335 Loulu St Honolulu HI 96822 Office: Judiciary Bldg Honolulu HI 96813*

RICHESON, JILES DAVID, b. Ft. Worth, Aug. 4, 1944; B.B.A., U. Tex., 1966, J.D., 1969. Admitted to Tex. bar, 1969, Fla. bar, 1974; legis. asst. to U.S. Rep. Pickle, Washington, 1969-72; counsel NLRB, Fort Worth, 1972-73; partner firm Alley & Alley, Miami and Tampa, Fla., 1973—. Mem. Am., Fla., Tex., Dade County bar assns. Contbr. articles to legal jour.

RICHETTE, LISA AVERSA, b. Phila., Sept. 11, 1928; B.A., U. Pa., 1949; J.D., Yale, 1952. Instr. psychiatry and law, adminstr. study unit in psychiatry and law Yale, 1952-54; admitted to Pa. bar, 1954; asst. dist. atty., Phila., 1954-64; chief Family Ct. div. Dist. Atty.'s Office, 1956-64; vis. lectr. criminology Temple U., 1966-69, lectr. law, 1972—; lectr. jurisprudence U. Pa. grad. seminars, 1966-69; individual practice law, 1964-71; clin. prof. law Villanova U., 1970-72; judge Ct. of Common Pleas, Phila., 1971—. Chmn., Health and Welfare Council, Inc., 1966-68; vice chmn. Chancellors Commn. on Drug Abbse, 1972—; co-founder, bd. dirs. Teen-Aid, Inc.; founder, bd. dirs. Child Abuse Prevention Efforts, 1972—; pres., bd. dirs. Voyage House, Inc., 1970-72, mem. adv. bd., 1972—; bd. dirs. New Horizon Ednl. Research Inst., Inc., Architects Workshop, Phila. Child Guidance Clinic, Nat. Com. on Child Abbse, The Center-A Place to Learn; bd. commrs. Fellowship Commn. Mem. Phila. Bar Assn. Recipient Gimbel Phila. award, 1973, Fame award Phila. Friendship Fete, 1973, Humanist of Year award Phila. Ethical Soc., 1973, St. Francis award for distinguished service to youth St. Francis Boys Homes, 1973, Woman of Year award So. N.J. chpt. Nat. Cystic Fibrosis Research Found., 1974, Service to Children award Pa. Elementary Sch. Prins. Assn., 1974, Phila. Philos. Ann. award, 1974, Bridge Humanitarian award, 1974, others; author: The Throwaway Children, 1969. Home: 1918 Lombard St Philadelphia PA 19146 Office: 1503 One E Penn Sq Philadelphia PA 19107 Tel (215) MU6-7354

RICHEY, HOBART, b. Wellsburg, W.Va., Jan. 15, 1928; B.S. in Civil Engring., Va. Mil. Inst., 1951; LL.B., Harvard, 1954. Admitted to W.Va. bar, 1954, D.C. bar, 1961, Pa. bar, 1968; individual practice law, Wheeling, W.Va., 1956-59; asst. tax commr. state W.Va., Charleston, 1959-61; asso. firm Haynes & Miller, Washington, 1961-62; atty., regional counsel IRS, Pitts., 1962-67; staff asst. regional counsel, San Francisco, 1967; asst. tax counsel Koppers Co., Pitts., 1967-68, tax counsel, 1968—, asst. sec., 1972—. Chmn. community adv. council North Hills Sch. Dist., Pitts., 1972-73; co-chmn. Com. to Save Northland Pub. Library, 1976. Mem. Tax Execs. Inst. (pres. Pitts chpt. 1972-73), Am., Fed., Pa. bar assns., W.Va. Soc. C.P.A.'s, W.Va. Registered Profl. Engrs., Tax Mgmt. Adv. Bd. Office: 1550 Koppers Bldg Pittsburgh PA 15219 Tel (412) 391-3300

RICHEY, MARY ANNE, b. Shelbyville, Ind., Oct. 24, 1917; student Purdue U., 1937-40; J.D., U. Ariz., 1951. Admitted to Ariz. bar, 1951; law clk., asso. firm Scruggs, Butterfield & Rucker, Tucson, 1951-52; dep. county atty. Pima County, Ariz., 1952-54; asst. U.S. atty. Dist. Ariz., 1954-59, U.S. atty., 1960-61; partner firm Richey & Reimann, Tucson, 1962-64; judge Pima County Superior Ct., 1964-76, asso. presiding judge, 1972-76; judge U.S. Dist. Ct., Dist. Ariz., 1976—: mem. Jud. Qualification Commn., 1970-76; co-chmn. Supreme Ct. Com. to Revise Civil Jury Instructions, 1971-76; mem. Criminal Code Revision Commn., 1973-76. Pres. bd. dirs. YWCA, Tucson, 1968-69; mem. advisory bds. Salvation Army, Tucson, 1968—; mem. regional advisory bd. Am. Arbitration Assn., Tucson, 1972-76; mem. advisory bd. Big Bros. Am., Tucson, 1976—. Home: 2800 E River Rd Tucson AZ 85718 Office. US Courthouse Tucson AZ 85701 Tel (602) 792-6767

RICHMAN, GERALD FREDERICK, b. Bklyn., Apr. 30, 1941; B.Bldg. Constrn. with honors, U. Fla., 1962, LL.B., 1964, J.D., 1967; postgrad. Georgetown U. Admitted to Fla. bar, 1965, U.S. Supreme Ct. bar, 1965, U.S. Ct. Mil. Appeals bar, 1966, D.C. bar, 1967; law clk. to judge U.S. Dist. Ct., Middle Dist. Fla., 1965; with Judge Adv. Gen. Corps, U.S. Army, 1966-69; partner firm Frates Floyd Pearson Stewart Richman & Greer, Miami, Fla., 1969—; mem. Fla. Condominium Commn., 1972. Bd. dirs. Miami chpt. Anti-Defamation League. Mem. Am., Fed., Dade County (pres. 1976, dir.) bar assns., Fla. Bar (gov. young lawyers bd. 1973—), Assn. Trial Lawyers Am., Fla. Acad. Trial Lawyers, Am. Judicature Soc., Fla. Blue Key, Phi Alpha Delta, Phi Kappa Phi, Phi Eta Sigma. Exec. editor U. Fla. Law Rev., 1963-64; contbr. articles to legal jours. Office: One Biscayne Tower Suite 2500 Miami FL 33131 Tel (305) 377-0241

RICHMAN, HERSHEL JULIAN, b. Phila., Aug. 25, 1941; B.A. and B.S. in Elec. Engring., Pa. State U., 1964; J.D., Villanova U., 1967. Admitted to Pa. bar, 1967; law clk. to judge Philadelphia County Ct. of Common Pleas, 1967-68; asso. firm Klovsky, Kuby & Harris, Phila., 1968-70: spl. asst. atty. gen. Pa., mem. Pa. Environ. Pollution Strike Force, Phila., 1970-74; chief Eastern Regional Environ. Pollution Strike Force Pa., Phila., 1972-74; solicitor Bucks County (Pa.) Planning Commn., Doylestown, 1974-76; adj. prof. environ. law Drexel U., 1972—; lectr. environ. law Temple U. Sch. Law, 1975—; mem. rules com. Pa. Environ. Hearing Bd. Counsel. Bd. dirs. Allens Ln. Art Centre, Phila., 1973-76; co-chmn. land use com. Water Resources Assn. Delaware River Basin; v.p., dir. Akiba Hebrew Acad., Merion Station, Pa. Mem. Am., Pa. Phila. (chmn. com. environ. law 1975-77) bar assns., Lawyers Club of Phila. Office: 522 Swede St Norristown PA 19401

RICHMAN, JOHN M., b. N.Y.C., Nov. 9, 1927; B.A., Yale, 1949; LL.B., Harvard U., 1952. Admitted to N.Y. bar, 1953, Ill. bar, 1973; asso. firm Leve, Hecht, Hadfield & McAlpin, N.Y.C., 1952-54; atty. Kraft, Inc., 1954-63, gen. counsel Sealtest Foods div., 1963-67, asst. gen. counsel Kraft, Inc., 1967-70, v.p., gen. counsel, 1970-73, sr. v.p., gen. counsel, 1973-75, sr. v.p. adminstrn., gen. counsel, 1975—. Mem. Am. (sect. on antitrust law-consumer protection com., others), N.Y. State, N.Y.C., Ill., Chgo. bar assns., Food and Drug Law Inst., Grocery Mfrs. Am., Assn. Gen. Counsel, Northwestern Corp. Counsel Inst., Practicing Law Inst., Southwestern Legal Found. Home: 1137 Locust Rd Wilmette IL 60091 Office: Kraft Ct Glenview IL 60025 Tel (312) 998-2414

RICHMAN, LAWRENCE WILLIAM, b. Phila., Apr. 6, 1943; B.A., Pa. State U., 1964; J.D., Villanova U., 1967. Admitted to Pa. bar, 1968; house counsel Hartford Ins. Co., Phila., 1970-72; asso. firm Frank & Margolis, Phila., 1972—; served with JAG, U.S. Army, Ft. Holabird, Md., 1968-70. Football ofcl. Phila. Pub. High Schs., 1970—. Mem. Am., Phila., Pa. bar assns., Pa., Phila. trial lawyers assns. Host, Law in Your Life radio series, Phila. Home: 15 Underwood Rd Wyncote PA 19095 Office: 1315 Walnut St Philadelphia PA 19107 Tel (215) 732-3838

RICHMAN, NATHAN H., b. Catskill, N.Y., Jan. 29, 1899; student Columbia, Albany (N.Y.) Law Sch.; pupil judge John J. McManny, Albany; admitted to N.Y. State bar, 1934; individual practice law, Albany and Catskill. Mem. Albany County, Greene County bar assns. Home and Office: Number 2 Pine St Albany NY 12207 Tel (518) 436-7649

RICHMAN, RICHARD ELLIS, b. Cleve., Jan. 30, 1927; Ph.B., U. Chgo., 1947; A.B., U. Calif., Berkeley, 1950; J.D., U. Ill., 1958. Reporter, Bloomington (Ill.) Pantagraph, 1953-55, Champaign (Ill.) News-Gazette, 1956-58; admitted to Ill. bar, 1959; research coordinator Ill. Legis. Council, Springfield, 1958-61; asst. exec. dir. Ill. Bd. Econ. Devel., Springfield, 1961-63; practice law, Carbondale, Ill., 1963-65; lectr. So. Ill. U., 1963-67; state's atty. Jackson County (Ill.), 1964-71 judge 1st Jud. Circuit Ct., 1971—. Chmn. bd. reimbursement appeals Ill. Dept. Mental Health, 1964, Jackson County unit Am. Cancer Soc., 1964-66; mem. Commn. on Orgn. of Gen. Assembly of Ill., 1968-70, com. Ill. Bd. Higher Edn., 1968-69. Mem. Am., Ill. State, Jackson County bar assns., Nat. Assn. State Trial Judges, Ill. Judges Assn., Am. Judicature Soc. Home: Route 2 PO Box 257A Murphysboro IL 62966 Office: Court House Murphysboro IL 62966 Tel (618) 684-2151

RICHMAN, STEPHEN IAN, b. Cin., Mar. 26, 1933; B.S., Northwestern U., 1954; LL.B., U. Pa., 1957. Admitted to Pa. bar, 1958; asso. firm McCune & Greenlee, Washington, Pa., 1958-60; partner firm McCune, Greenlee & Richman, Washington, 1960-61, Greenlee, Richman, Derrico & Posa, Washington, 1961—. Mem. Am., Pa. bar assns. Home: 800 E Beau St Washington PA 15301 Office: Washington Trust Bldg Washington PA 15301 Tel (412) 225-7660

RICHMOND, DAVID WALKER, b. Silver Hill, W.Va., Apr. 20, 1914; LL.B., George Washington U., 1937. Admitted to D.C. bar, 1936, U.S. Supreme Ct. bar, 1941, Ill. bar, 1946, Md. bar, 1950; partner firm Miller & Chevalier, Washington, 1946—; co-chmn. Nat. Conf. Lawyers and C.P.A.'s; vice-chmn. D.C. Ct. Appeals Com. Unauthorized Practice of Law. Fellow Am. Bar Found., Am. Coll. Trial Lawyers; mem. Am. Law Inst., Am. Bar Assn. (chmn. taxation sect. 1955-57, ho. of dels. 1958-60, mem. standing com. profl. discipline). Recipient Alumni Achievement award George Washington U., 1976; contbr. articles to profl. jours. Office: 1700 Pennsylvania Ave NW Washington DC 20006 Tel (202) 393-5660

RICHMOND, EDWARD LEON, b. Boston, July 17, 1926; B.S., Boston Coll., 1948, M.A., 1949, J.D., 1959. Admitted to Mass. bar, 1959; asso. firm Ganz, Ham & Homans, Boston, 1959-67; partner firms Bloom, Deutsch, Richmond, Holtz & Drachman, Boston, 1967-71, Richmond, Kassler, Feinberg & Feuer, Boston, 1971—; arbitrator Am. Arbitration Assn.; mem. Newton (Mass.) Bd. Aldermen, 1972—. Mem. Boston Bar Assn. Office: 85 Devonshire St Boston MA 02109 Tel (617) 227-4800

RICHMOND, HERBERT BERNARD, b. Boston, Sept. 4, 1920; B.S. in Bus. Adminstrn., Boston U., 1941; M.B.A., Calif. Western U., 1965; postgrad. Blackstone Sch. Law, 1967. Admitted to Calif. bar, 1968, Fed. bar, 1968; mgmt. trainee Sears Roebuck and Co., Boston, 1946-50; controller, treas. MKM Knitting Mills, Manchester, N.H., 1952-60; mgmt. analyst Gen. Dynamics, San Diego, 1960-66; individual practice law, La Jolla, Calif., 1968—. Pres. La Jolla Shores Assn., 1974. Mem. Am., Calif., San Diego County bar assns., Am. Arbitration Assn. Home: 2915 Woodford Dr La Jolla CA 92037 Office: 1020 Prospect St La Jolla CA 92037 Tel (714) 454-0767

RICHMOND, JOHN, b. Oakland, Calif., Dec. 10, 1907; B.S., U. Calif. at Berkeley, 1928, M.S., 1934; LL.B., Oakland Coll. Law, 1942. Admitted to Calif. bar, 1946; individual practice law, Berkeley, 1946—; pres. Richmond Enterprises, Berkeley, 1928—. Mem. Am., Fed., Alameda County bar assns., Supreme Ct. Hist. Soc., Nat. Lawyers Club. Address: 1611 Bonita Ave Berkeley CA 94709 Tel (415) 841-3050

RICHMOND, LARRY JACK, b. Oskaloosa, Iowa, Aug. 19, 1939; B.A., William Penn Coll., 1961; J.D., Drake U., 1964. Admitted to Iowa bar, 1964, Ariz. bar, 1965; since practiced in Phoenix, partner firm Goodson, Richmond, Rose and Wolfram, 1965-70, firm Richmond and Wolfram, 1970-71; individual practice law, 1971—; gen. counsel Rep. party Ariz., 1969—, Young Rep. Nat. Fedn., 1967-69; Flood Control Dist. Maricopa County (Ariz.), 1968—. Vice pres. Ariz. Easter Seal Soc., 1973—, gen. counsel, 1969—; chmn. Phoenix Bd. Adjustment, 1970-73; chmn. Roosevelt Sch. Dist. Citizens Adv. Com., 1970, Mayor's Com. on Youth, 1967; campaign advisor Rep. Legis. Campaign Com., 1970—; gen. chmn. Rep. Jud. Campaign Com., 1974; chmn. Maricopa County Rep. Com. on Candidate Selection, 1976; trustee Lawyers Involved for Ariz., 1974—; dir. Salvation Army Youth and Family Center, 1967-69. Mem. Am. Trial Lawyers Assn., Am., Iowa, Ariz. Maricopa County bar assns.; Delta Theta Phi. Named Outstanding Young Man of Am., Jaycees, 1964, 1970. Home: 6040 N 41st St Paradise Valley AZ 85253 Office: Suite 2500 101 N 1st Ave Phoenix AZ 85003 Tel (602) 252-5549

RICHMOND, LYLE LEE, JR., b. Chgo., Apr. 10, 1930; B.A., Wesleyan U., 1952; LL.B., Yale, 1955. Admitted to Calif. bar, 1959, Trust Ter. Pacific Islands bar, 1970, U.S. Supreme Ct. bar, 1975, Am. Samoa bar, 1975; dep. dist. atty. Dist. Atty.'s Office, San Diego County, Calif., 1959-64; individual practice law, San Diego, 1964-70; dist. atty. Truk and Ponape Dists. Trust Ter. Pacific Islands, 1970-73, chief legal div. Atty. Gen.'s Office, 1973-75; atty. gen. Ter. Am. Samoa, 1975—. Bd. dirs. Coronado (Calif.) Hosp., 1964-65, United Community Services, Coronado, 1966-68; elder Graham Meml. Presbyn. Ch., 1966—; governing bd. Coronado Unified Sch. Dist., 1968-70. Mem. Am., San Diego County, Am. Samoa bar assns., Naval Res. Assn. Recipient resolution congratulation Congress Micronesia, 1975. Home: 132S Penicillin Ln Utelei American Samoa 96799 Office: PO Box 7 Pago Pago American Samoa 96799 Tel 633-4163

RICHMOND, PAUL JAMES, b. Middleboro, Mass., Aug. 11, 1940; B.S., Calif. State Poly. U., 1964; J.D., Boston Coll., 1968. Admitted to Calif. bar, 1969; dep. atty. gen. State of Calif., 1968-71; environ. and legis. counsel Atlantic Richfield Co., Los Angeles, 1971—. Mem. Calif. State, Am., Los Angeles County bar assns., Am. Petroleum Inst. (chmn. environ. law com. 1978—), Western Oil and Gas Assn. (legal com.). Office: 515 S Flower St Los Angeles CA 90071 Tel (213) 486-1537

RICHMOND, WILLIAM ALFRED, b. Billings, Mont., May 11, 1942; A.B., Stanford, 1965; J.D., Hastings Coll. Law, 1968. Admitted to Calif. bar, 1969; dep. dist. atty. Tulare County (Calif.), Visalia, 1969-71; asso. firm Hurlbutt, Clevenger, Long & Richmond, Visalia, 1971—. Mem. Tulare County Bar Assn., Calif. State Bar., No. Calif. Assn. Def. Counsel. Home: PO Box 36 Dry Creek Rd Lemon Cove CA 93244 Office: 701 W Center St Visalia CA 93277 Tel (209) 732-8153

RICHTER, GEORGE ROBERT, JR., b. Blue Island, Ill., July 8, 1910; A.B., U. So. Calif., 1930, LL.B., 1933. Admitted to Calif. bar, 1933, U.S. Supreme Ct. bar, 1950; since practiced in Los Angeles, asso. firm Mathes & Sheppard, 1933-35, 1936-41; mem. legal dept. Security First Nat. Bank, 1935-36; partner firm Sheppard, Millin, Richter & Hampton, 1941—; chmn. Conf. on Personal Finance Law, 1963—; mem. Calif. Commn. on Uniform State Laws, 1951-73, chmn., 1956-73; chmn. exec. com. Nat. Conf. Commrs. on Uniform State Laws, 1957-59, pres., 1959-61. Fellow Am. Bar Found.; mem. Am. (chmn. sect. corp., banking and bus. law 1962-63, chmn. com. on class actions 1973-75), Calif., Los Angeles (chmn. sect. comml. law and bankruptcy 1967-68) bar assns., Am. Law Inst. Mem. permanent editorial bd. Uniform Comml. Code, 1953—. Home: 1275 Chateau Rd Pasadena CA 91105 Office: 333 S Hope St Los Angeles CA 90071 Tel (213) 620-1780

RICHTER, HUBERT A., b. Kingston, N.Y., Jan. 4, 1924; student St. Lawrence U., 1942, 46-47, Ill. Inst. Tech., 1943-44; LL.B., Albany Law Sch., 1950. Admitted to N.Y. bar, 1950; individual practice law, Kingston, 1950-51; partner firm Richter & Werbalowsky, Kingston, 1951—; judge Kingston City Ct., 1965—; arbitrator Am. Arbitration Assn.; rep. N.E. region Nat. Conf. Spl. Ct. Judges Com., Traffic Ct. Dist. adminstr. Dist. Little League. Mem. Am., N.Y. State, Ulster County bar assns., N.Y. State Magistrates Assn. Home: 100 Harding Ave Kingston NY 12401 Office: 86 John St Kingston NY 12401 Tel (914) 338-3535

RICHTER, ROBERT CHARLES, JR., b. Ft. Worth, Jan. 10, 1948; B.A. in History and Spanish, Baylor U., 1971, J.D., 1971. Admitted to Tex. bar, 1971, U.S. Dist. Ct. bar, 1971, U.S. Supreme Ct. bar, 1975; with land dept. Shell Oil Co., New Orleans, 1971-72; individual practice law, Houston, 1972—; asst. city atty. City of Bellaire (Tex.). Mem. Am., Tex., Houston, Houston Jr. bar assns., Harris County Criminal Defense Lawyers Assn., Tex. Municipal Cts. Assn. (sec.-treas. 1976-77), Phi Alpha Delta. Home: 1305 Vassar St Houston TX 77006 Office: 7718 Bellfort St Houston TX 77061 Tel (713) 644-8011

RICKETTS, JOHN BAXTER, b. Jackson, Miss., Nov. 20, 1886; A.B., Millsaps Coll., Jackson, 1905, LL.B., 1906. Admitted to Miss. bar, 1906, S.C. bar, 1921; practiced in Jackson, Miss., 1906-20, Greenville, S.C., 1920—; mem. Miss. Legislature, one term. Mem. Am., S.C. bar assns. Office: 304 Insurance Bldg Greenville SC 29601 Tel (803) 232-7591

RICKS, ROBERT DOUGLASS, b. South Gate, Calif., July 26, 1945; B.A. in English, Calif. State U., Northridge, 1967; J.D., U. San Fernando Valley Coll. Law, 1973. Admitted to Calif. bar, 1973, U.S. Dist. Ct. bar, 1974; partner firm Ricks & Ricks, Anaheim, Calif., 1974—. Mem. Calif. Trial Lawyers Assn., Orange County Bar Assn. Office: 300 S Harbor Blvd Suite 1010 Anaheim CA 92805 Tel (714) 533-6900

RIDDEL, MARILYN ANN, b. Ashland, Ohio, Aug. 22, 1932; student cum laude, Bowling Green State U., 1949-51; B.A., La. State U., 1953; J.D., LL.B., U. Toledo, 1957. Admitted to Ohio bar, 1957, Ariz. bar, 1961; mem. firm Harold Riddel, Toledo, 1957-60, Phoenix, 1961-69; judge Maricopa County (Ariz.) Superior Ct., Phoenix, 1969—. Active Ariz. Soc. Prevention Blindness, Phoenix, Found. Blind Children, Inc., Phoenix, YMCA, Phoenix, Maricopa County Legal Aid Soc. Mem. Am., Ariz., Maricopa County bar assns., Am. Judicature Soc., Ariz. Assn. Trial Ct. Judges, Bus. and Profl. Womens Assn., DAR, Kappa Beta Pi. Home: 4519 E Cherry Lynn St Phoenix AZ 85018 Office: 125 W Washington St Phoenix AZ 85003 Tel (602) 262-3831

RIDDELL, RICHARD HARRY, b. Seattle, Nov. 29, 1916; B.A., Stanford, 1938; LL.B., Harvard, 1941. Admitted to Wash. bar, 1941, U.S. Supreme Ct. bar, 1945; partner firm Riddell, Williams, Ivie, Bullitt & Walkinshaw, and predecessors, Seattle, 1941—. Fellow Am. Coll. Trial Lawyers; mem. Am., Wash. State (pres. 1976-77), Seattle-King County (pres. 1963-64) bar assns. Home: 1620 43d Ave E Apt 11C Seattle WA 98112 Office: 4300 Seattle 1st Nat Bank Bldg Seattle WA 98154 Tel (206) 624-3600

RIDDLE, HADLEY WAYNE, b. Warrensburg, Mo., Dec. 18, 1934; B.S. in Commerce, U. Ky., 1960, J.D., 1962. Admitted to Ky. bar, 1962, U.S. Dist. Ct. Eastern Dist. Ky. bar, 1962; since practiced in Lexington, Ky.; partner firm Miller, Griffin & Marks, 1967—. Mem. Am., Ky., Fayette County, bar assns., Am. Judicature Soc., Delta Sigma Pi, Phi Alpha Delta. Home: 1609 Kensington Way Lexington KY 40511 Office: 700 Security Trust Bldg Lexington KY 40507 Tel (606) 255-6676

RIDDLE, PETER EMMONS, b. Chgo., Apr. 2, 1938; B.A., Yale U., 1960; J.D. U. Chgo., 1966. Admitted to Ill. bar, 1967, Calif. bar, 1969; mem. firm Oakes & McDonald, San Diego, 1969-72, firm McDonald, Riddle, Hecht & Worley, San Diego, 1972—; panelist Continuing Edn. of Bar, 1975, 77. Bd. mgrs. San Diego Downtown YMCA, 1975—; councilman City of Coronado, 1973-74, 76. Mem. Calif., Ill. State bar assns., San Diego County Bar Assn. (chmn. probate sect. 1974). Home: 805 Eighth St Coronado CA 92118 Office: 617 Financial Sq 600 B St San Diego CA 92101 Tel (714) 239-3444

RIDDLE, ROBERT EDWARD, b. Hagerstown, Md., Jan. 27, 1936; B.S., Wake Forest Coll., 1957, J.D., 1958. Admitted to N.C. bar, 1958, U.S. Dist. Ct. for western N.C., 1960; partner firm Willson & Riddle, 1960-62, partner firm Riddle & Briggs, 1962-65; partner firm Riddle & Shackelford, Asheville, N.C., 1968—. Pres. Centeral Service Center, YMCA. Mem. Am. Trial Lawyers Assn., N.C. Acad. Trial Lawyers, Buncombe, 28th Jud. Dist. bar assns. Home: Route 1 Brooks Branch Rd Liecester NC Office: 120 College St Asheville NC 28807 Tel (704) 258-1580

RIDDLE, SUZAN ELLEN, b. Grand Junction, Colo., Dec. 5, 1947; B.A., Tex. Tech. U., 1969, J.D., 1971. Admitted to Tex. bar, 1972; asso. firm Smith & Baker, Inc., 1971-72; law clk. to sr. judge U.S. Dist. Ct., Dallas, 1972, to judge U.S. Dist. Ct. for No. Dist. Tex., Dallas, 1972-73; asso. firm Gardere, Porter & DeHay, Dallas, 1973—; mem. devel. bd. Lakewood Bank and Trust Co., Dallas, 1977—. Deferred and planned giving task force mem. Am. Heart Assn., Dallas, 1976. Mem. Am. (tax sect.), Tex. (com. on bar jour. 1975-77) bar assns., Order of Coif. Home: 9409 Timberleaf Ln Dallas TX 75243 Office: 1700 Republic National Bank Bldg Dallas TX 75201 Tel (214) 741-1551

RIDENOUR, GARLAND QUENTIN, b. Ft. Smith, Ark., July 28, 1943; B.S. in Bus. Adminstrn., U. Ark., 1965, J.D., 1968. Admitted to Ark. bar, 1968, U.S. Supreme Ct. bar, 1973; individual practice law, Helena, Ark., 1968—; city atty. City of West Helena, 1968-73; judge West Helena Municipal Ct., 1973—. Bd. dirs. East Ark. Regional Mental Health Assn., 1970-71. Mem. Ark., Am. bar assns., Assn. Trial Lawyers Am., Ark. Trial Lawyers Assn. Home: 100 Hillsboro St Helena AR 72342 Office: 500 Pecan St Helena AR 72342 Tel (501) 338-6448

RIDER, JAMES LINCOLN, b. Newburgh, N.Y., Feb. 11, 1942; B.A., Lafayette Coll., Easton, Pa., 1963; J.D., Fordham U., 1966. Admitted to N.Y. bar, 1966, D.C. bar, 1971, Va. bar, 1973; capt. JAGC, 1967-71; mem. firm Margolius, Davis & Finkelstein, Washington, 1971—. Mem. D.C., Va. State bar assns. Tel (202) 833-3939

RIDGELY, HENRY JOHNSON, b. Camden, Del., Nov. 17. 1913; B.A., U. Del., 1935; J.D., George Washington U., 1939. Admitted to D.C. bar, 1939, Del. bar, 1940, U.S. Supreme Ct., 1943, other fed. bars; individual practice law, Dover, Del., 1940-73, sr. partner firm Ridgely & Ridgely, Dover, 1974—; dep. atty. gen. of Del. for Kent County, 1943, 47-54; atty. Kent County Levy Ct., 1947-49; chief counsel to Gov. Del., 1957-61; mem., sec. Del. Revised Code Commn., 1951-54; 1st chmn. State Pension Trustees, 1970-74. Del. Republican Nat. Conv., 1952, 56. Mem. Am. Trial Lawyers Assn.. Nat. Assn. R.R. Trial Counsel, Am. Judicature Soc., Inter-Am., Am., Del. (v.p. 1961-63, dental med. legal screening com. 1970-74, bar and bankers com. 1974—), Kent County (pres. 1968-69) bar assns., Sigma Nu. Home: Spruce Haven RD 2 Camden DE 19934 Office: 307 S State St Dover DE 19901 Tel (302) 734-5845

RIDGEWAY, ROBERT DEAN, SR., b. Hot Springs, Ark., July 27, 1925; student Henderson State Tchrs. Coll., 1946-48; LL.B., U. Ark., 1951, J.D., 1951. Admitted to Ark. bar, 1951; individual practice law, Hot Springs, 1952—; dep. pros. atty. 18th Judicial Dist., Hot Springs, 1954-60; atty. City of Hot Springs, 1961-62, municipal judge, 1963-67. Mem. Garland County (pres. 1972, exec. com. 1973—), Ark. bar assns. Office: 127 Hawthorne St Hot Springs AR 71901 Tel (501) 321-1551

RIDINGS, CRAIG ASHER, b. Bradford, Ill., Dec. 13, 1920; J.D., U. Louisville, 1943; postgrad. John B. Stetson U., 1946-47. Title examiner Louisville Title Ins. Co., 1939-42, 44-46; admitted to Ky. bar, 1947, Ill. bar, 1956; claims adjuster Am. Mut. Liability Ins. Co. of Boston, 1947-51, claims mgr., 1951-56; partner firm Yalden & Ridings, Rockford, Ill., 1956-76; individual practice law, Rockford, 1976—. Bd. dirs. Rockford chpt. Big Bros. Am., 1960-68, sec., 1965-68; bd. dirs. Ill. Bapt. State Assn., 1970-76; trustee Midwestern Bapt. Theol. Sem., 1971—, Judson Coll. Pres's. Club, 1972—; del. Democratic Nat. Conv., 1976. Mem. Winnebago County, Ky., Am. (com. ins. negligence and compensation) Ill. State (chmn. com. on unauthorized practice law 1975-76) bar assns., Am. Trial Lawyers Assn., Am. Judicature Soc. Home: 2204 Bittersweet Row Rockford IL

61108 Office: PO Box 5084 408 Camelot Tower Rockford IL 61125 Tel (815) 964-7824

RIDLEY, CLARENCE HAVERTY, b. Atlanta, June 3, 1942; B.A., Yale, 1964; M.B.A., Harvard, 1966; J.D., U. Va., 1971. Admitted to Ga. bar, 1971; mem. firm King & Spalding, Atlanta, 1971—; dir. Scofield Properties, Inc., 1973—. Mem. Atlanta Citizens' Adv. Council on Urban Devel., 1972-74; trustee St. Joseph's Village, Atlanta, 1976—; dir. Atlanta Sister Cities Program, 1975-76. Mem. Am., Atlanta bar assns., State Bar Ga., Atlanta Council Younger Lawyers (past dir.), Am. Judicature Soc. Home: 2982 Habersham Rd Atlanta GA 30305 Office: King & Spalding 2500 Trust Co Tower Atlanta GA 30303 Tel (404) 658-1450

RIDLEY, PETER STAPLETON, JR., b. Washington, Sept. 12, 1939; B.S., W.Va. State Coll., 1960; J.D. American U., 1970. Admitted to D.C. bar, 1970, U.S. Military Ct. Appeals bar, 1970; individual practice law, 1970-73; partner firm Ridley & McLean, Washington, 1973—. Mem. advisory bd. United Negro Coll. Fund, 1974—. Mem. Am., Nat., D.C. Washington bar assns. Home: 3809 13th St NE Washington DC 20017 Office: 1010 16th St NW Washington DC 20036 Tel (202) 466-3900

RIEGELMAN, HAROLD, b. Des Moines, Aug. 19, 1892; A.B., Cornell U., 1914; LL.B., Columbia, 1916, M.A., 1916. Admitted to N.Y. bar, 1916, U.S. Supreme Ct. bar, 1946; sr. partner firm Nordlinger, Reigelman, Benctar & Charney, N.Y.C., 1919-72; of counsel firm Hess, Segall, Popkin, Guterman, Pelz & Steiner, N.Y.C., 1972—; gen. counsel Citizens Budget Commn. N.Y., 1932—, Carnegie Hall Corp., 1960—; legal adviser Republic of China, 1938—; mem. adminstrv. tribunal UN, N.Y.C., 1958-59, U.S. del. to Gen. Assembly, 1959; cons. U.S. Dept. Def. and Office of Budget, 1955-56; spl. counsel U.S. Dept. Treasury, 1935; counsel State Commn. to Revise Tenement House Law, 1927-29; spl. asst. state's atty. gen. State of N.Y., 1929-30; counsel State Vets. Bonus Bur., 1948; chmn. N.Y.C. Adv. Council on Alcoholism, 1968—; del. N.Y. Constl. Conv., 1938. Mem. Am., N.Y. State, N.Y. County, N.Y.C. bar assns., Council Fgn. Relations. Decorated Bronze Star with oak leaf cluster, Silver Star; contbr. articles to legal jours. Home: 110 E 57th St New York City NY 10022 Office: 230 Park Ave New York City NY 10017 Tel (212) 689-2400

RIEGGER, WILLIAM JOSEPH, b. Benson, Minn., Mar. 14, 1924; B.S.L., U. Minn., 1949, J.D., 1950. Admitted to Minn. bar, 1951, Ariz. bar, 1951; asst. title officer Ariz. Land Title & Trust Co., Tucson, 1951-53; partner firm Riegger, Hirsch & Van Slyke, Tucson, 1953-55; asst. city atty., Tucson, 1953-54; trust officer Valley Nat. Bank, Tucson, 1956; lectr. St. Vincent Coll., Latrobe, Pa., 1957-58; prof. law U. San Francisco, 1958-66, asst. dean and prof., 1966-69, acting dean, 1969-70; asso. dean. Robert W. Harrison prof. law U. Calif. Hastings Coll. Law, San Francisco, 1971—, vice-dean, 1975—. Mem. University Club, San Francisco Probate Attys. Assn., Japanese-Am. Legal Soc., Order of Coif., Gamma Eta Gamma. Contbr. articles to profl. jours. Home: 515 Tahos Rd Orinda CA 94563 Office: 198 McAllister St San Francisco CA 94102 Tel (415) 557-1320

RIEGLE, ROY WILFORD, b. Lyons, Kans., Apr. 27, 1896; B.S. in Edn., Kans. State Tchrs. Coll., Emporia, 1946; A.B., Washburn U., 1924, A.M., 1925, LL.B., 1925, J.D., 1970. Admitted to Kans. bar, 1925, since practiced in Emporia; mem. Kans. Ho. of Reps., 1933-41, Kans. Senate, 1941-43, 53-61; probate and juvenile judge Lyon County (Kans.), 1927-33; mem. Kans. Legis. Council, 1939-41, Kans. Jud. Council, 1953-61. Mem. Kans. (various coms.), Lyon County (past pres.), 5th Jud. Dist. (past pres.) bar assns., Phi Alpha Delta. Home: 1522 Dover Rd Emporia KS 66801 Office: suite One Palace Bldg Emporia KS 66801 Tel (316) 342-0755

RIEKER, LOUIS CARL, b. Danville, Ill., Dec. 30, 1925; B.S., U. Ill., 1952; J.D., U. Colo., 1957. Admitted to Colo. bar, 1958, U.S. Supreme Ct. bar, 1976; individual practice law, Greeley, Colo., 1974—; v.p., trust officer 1st Nat. Bank, Greeley, 1957-74. Bd. dirs. Greeley Sch. Bd., 1966-72. Municipal judge, Greeley, 1975—. Mem. Am., Colo., Weld County bar assns., Phi Alpha Delta. Home: 1640 36th Ave Ct Greeley CO 80631 Office: 913 11th Ave Greeley CO 80631 Tel (303) 353-5439

RIEMER, RICHARD LEROY, b. Joliet, Ill., Mar. 7, 1925; LL.B., DePaul U., 1951. Admitted to Calif. bar, 1954, U.S. Supreme Ct. bar, 1963, U.S. Ct. Mil. Appeals bar, 1963; dep. counsel Los Angeles County (Calif.), 1954-63; asso. firm Robert K. Light, Hollywood, Calif., 1963-64; individual practice law, Santa Ana, Calif., 1964—. Mem. Am. Right of Way Assn. (internat. pres. 1975-76), State Bar Calif., Orange County Bar Assn. Office: 850 N Parton St Santa Ana CA 92701 Tel (714) 835-1551

RIESENFELD, STEFAN ALBRECHT, b. Breslau, Germany, June 8, 1908; came to U.S., 1935, naturalized, 1940; J.U.D., U. Breslau, 1932, U. Milan (Italy), 1934; LL.B., U. Calif., 1937; S.J.D., Harvard U., 1940; B.S., U. Minn., 1943; D.H.C., U. Cologne, 1970. Prof. law U. Minn., 1938-52, U. Calif. at Berkeley, 1952—, Emanuel Heller prof., 1954—; cons. bd. Econ. Warfare, 1942, UN ad hoc com. on restrictive bus. practices, 1952; mem. adv. com. Bankruptcy Rules, 1961—; vis. prof. U. Cologne, also U. Bonn (both Germany), 1956-64, U. Sydney (Australia), 1959, U. Pa., 1963, U. Auckland (N.Z.), 1968, Victoria U. (N.Z.), 1972, U. Mich., 1972. Fellow Center for Advanced Study in Behaviorial Scis., 1961-62. Mem. Am. Bar Assn., Am. Soc. Internat. Law, Internat. Law Assn., Fgn. Law Assn. Author: Protection of Fisheries Under International Law, 1943; Modern Social Legislation, 1950; California Security Transactions, 1958; Workmen's Compensation in Hawaii, 1963; Creditors' Remedies and Debtors' Protection, 1967; Practical Guide to the Uniform Commercial Code in Hawaii, 1968; Temporary Disability Insurance, 1969; contbr. articles to legal publs. Home: 1129 Amador St Berkeley CA 94707*

RIESS, DANIEL MICHAEL, b. Evanston, Ill., July 28, 1936; B.S. in Chem. Engring., Northwestern U., 1959; J.D., Georgetown U., 1967. Admitted to Ill. bar, 1968, U.S. Supreme Ct. bar, 1973, U.S. Patent Office bar, 1967; partner firm Allegretti, Newitt, Witcoff, & McAndrews, Chgo. Pres. bd. trustees Indian Trails Pub. Library Dist., Wheeling, Ill., 1976. Mem. Am., Chgo. bar assns., Am., Chgo. patent law assns., Am. Chem. Soc. Home: 625 Beverly Pl Lake Forest IL 60045 Office: 125 S Wacker Dr Chicago IL 60606 Tel (312) 372-2160

RIESS, JOHN KIMBERLY, b. Glendale, Calif., Sept. 13, 1940; B.A., Calif. State U., Long Beach, 1968; J.D., U. Calif., Los Angeles, 1971. Admitted to Calif. bar, 1972; dep. city atty. City of San Diego, 1972—; atty. San Diego Regional Employment & Tng. Consortium. Mem. Calif. Bar Assn., Naval Reserve Assn. Office: 202 C St San Diego CA 92101 Tel (714) 236-6220

RIFE, OSCAR JENNINGS, b. Wayne, W.Va., Aug. 23, 1915; student Marshall U., 1933-35, U. Ky., 1935-36; A.B. in Accounting, George Washington U., 1938, J.D. with honors, 1942. Admitted to W.Va. bar, 1946, U.S. Tax Ct. bar, 1947; clk. to Senator M.M. Neeley, Washington, 1937-41; practice law, Huntington, W.Va., 1946—; partner firm Vinson, Meek, Rife & Peoples, 1975—; instr., lectr. bus. adminstrn. dept. Marshall U., 1948-52; dir. First Huntington Nat. Bank. Trustee Huntington Galleries, 1975—. Mem. Am., W.Va. bar assns., W.Va. Tax Inst. (dir. 1967-72, pres. 1972), Phi Delta Phi. Home: 162 Woodland Dr Huntington WV 25705 Office: Suite 1000 PO Box 349 Huntington WV 25708

RIFFKIN, MITCHELL SANFORD, b. Providence, Dec. 30, 1944; B.A., U. R.I., 1966; J.D., Boston U., 1969. Admitted to R.I. bar, 1969; asso. firm Kirshenbaum & Kirshenbaum, 1969-71, Schreiber, Clingham & Gordon, 1971-73; partner firm Rosedale, Casparian and Riffkin, Providence, 1973—; pros. atty. City of Warwick (R.I.), 1972-73; bail commr. Kent County (R.I.), 1973—. Bd. dirs. New Eng. region Anti-Defamation League, Opportunities Industrialization Center R.I., R.I. Jewish Fedn., R.I. Camps Inc.; mem. R.I. Commn. on Soviet Jewry. Mem. Am. Arbitration Assn. (nat. panel), R.I. Bar Assn., Pi Sigma Alpha. Named Outstanding Young Man of Year, City of Warwick, 1976. Office: 824 Hospital Trust Bldg Providence RI 02903 Tel (401) 751-9500

RIFKIN, PAUL LOUIS, b. Asheville, N.C., June 7, 1942; B.A., U. Ga., 1964; J.D., Wake Forest U., 1967. Admitted to N.C. bar, 1969, U.S. Dist. Ct., 1973; individual practice law, Asheville, 1969—. Bd. dirs. Asheville Family Counseling Service, 1975. Mem. Am., N.C., Buncombe County bar assns., N.C. Bar. Home: 34 Marlborough Rd Asheville NC 28804 Office: 21 Page Ave Asheville NC 28801 Tel (204) 252-1333

RIFKIND, SIMON HIRSCH, b. Meretz, Russia, June 5, 1901; came to U.S., 1910, naturalized, 1924; B.S., Coll. City N.Y., 1922; LL.B., Columbia U., 1925; Litt.D., Jewish Theol. Sem., 1950; LL.D., Hofstra Coll., 1962. Admitted to N.Y. bar, 1926, Ill. bar, 1957; legis. sec. to U.S. Senator Robert F. Wagner, 1927-33; partner firm Wagner, Quillinan & Rifkind, N.Y.C., 1930-41; fed. judge So. N.Y. Dist., 1941-50; partner firm Paul, Weiss, Rifkind, Wharton & Garrison, N.Y.C., 1950—; mem. firm Stevenson, Rifkind & Wirtz, Chgo., 1957-61; dir. Revlon, Inc., Sterling Nat. Bank & Trust Co., N.Y.; Herman Phlager vis. prof. law Stanford U., 1975; spl. master Colo. River litigation U.S. Supreme Ct.; chmn. Presdl. R.R. Commn., 1961-62; mem. State Commn. Govtl. Ops. City N.Y., 1959-61; co-chmn. Pres.'s Commn. on Patent System, 1966-67; mem. mayor's mediation panel N.Y.C. tchrs. strike, 1963. Mem. Bd. Higher Edn. City N.Y., 1954-66; chmn. adminstrv. bd. Am. Jewish Com., 1953-56, chmn. exec. bd., 1956-59; former chmn. bd., now chmn. exec. com. Jewish Theol. Sem.; bd. dirs. Beth Israel Med. Center, N.Y.C., 1972—. Mem. Assn. Bar City N.Y., Am. Coll. Trial Lawyers (regent 1967-71, pres. 1976—), Phi Beta Kappa. Recipient Medal of Freedom. Home: 936 Fifth Ave New York City NY 10021 Office: 345 Park Ave New York City NY 10022 Tel (21) 644-8602

RIFMAN, AVRUM KATZ, b. Balt., Oct. 19, 1905; LL.B., U. Md., 1926. Admitted to Md. bar, 1926, U.S. Supreme Ct. bar, 1950; 1st asst., chief trial div. city solicitor office, Balt., 1943-45; individual practice law, Balt., 1945-68; police ct. magistrate So. Dist. Balt., 1951-53; asso. judge Municipal Ct. Balt., 1968-70; master in chancery Supreme Bench Balt., 1971-75, mem. firm Gallagher, Evelius & Jones, Balt., 1976—; mem. Marbury Commn., Balt., 1972, Nat. Commn. Uniform State Laws, 1957-60, Md. State Jud. Conf., 1977. Mem. Balt. Urban Coalition, 1976; commr. Jail Bd. Balt., 1973—; chmn. task force Mayor's Adv. on Crime in Balt., 1972. Mem. Balt. (chmn. grievance com. 1954-57), Am., Md. State bar assns. Home: 3412 Wabash Ave Baltimore MD 21215

RIGG, PHILIP DERMOT, b. Corpus Christi, Tex., July 6, 1943; B.A., Baylor U., 1965, LL.B., 1968. Admitted to Tex. bar, 1968; asso. firm Ralph B. Lee, Houston, 1968-73; asso. firm Hoover, Cox & Miller, Houston, 1974, partner, 1975—. Pres. bd. trustees Fort Bend Ind. Sch. Dist., Stafford, Tex. Mem. Houston, Tex., Am. bar assns. Home: 11619 Brook Meadow St Stafford TX 77477 Office: Suite 301 Post Oak Bank Bldg 2200 S Post Oak St Houston TX 77056 Tel (713) 623-4440

RIGGINS, JOHN ALFRED, JR., b. Phoenix, June 9, 1912; LL.B., U. Ariz., 1936. Admitted to Ariz. bar, 1936, U.S. Supreme Ct. bar, 1957, D.C. bar, 1969; individual practice law, Phoenix, 1936-42; partner firm Jennings, Strouss & Salmon, Phoenix, 1946—. Pres. Ariz.-Mex. Commn., 1971—; mem. exec. com. Ariz. State Univ. Found.; bd. dirs. Valley Forward Assn., Ariz. Acad. Mem. Am., Ariz., Maricopa County bar assns., Nat. Water Resources Assn., Ariz. State Reclamation Assn. Office: 111 W Monroe St Phoenix AZ 85003 Tel (602) 262-5801

RIGGS, ARTHUR JORDY, b. Nyack. N.Y., Apr. 3, 1916; A.B., Princeton, 1937; LL.B., Harvard, 1940. Admitted to Mass. bar, 1940, Tex. bar, 1943; asso. firm Warner, Stackpole, Stetson & Bradlee, Boston, 1940-41; staff mem. Solicitor's Office Dept. Labor, Washington and Dallas, 1941-42; mem. firm Johnson, Bromberg, Leeds & Riggs, Dallas, 1949—. Mem. Dallas, Am. bar assns., State Bar Tex., Phi Beta Kappa. Home: 4116 Amherst St Dallas TX 75225 Office: 211 Ervay St Dallas TX 75201 Tel (214) 748-8811

RIGGS, ARTHUR LEON, b. Kansas City, Mo.; B.C.S. in Accounting magna cum laude, Southwestern U., Los Angeles, J.D. cum laude, 1958. Admitted to Calif. bar, 1959; individual practice law, Los Angeles, 1959-64, Fullerton, Calif., 1964-68; trial atty., now house counsel Allstate Ins. Co., Los Angeles, 1970—. Mem. Calif., Los Angeles County bar assns. Home: 14752 Dunton Dr Whittier CA 90604 Office: 3450 Wilshire Blvd suite 707 Los Angeles CA 90010 Tel (213) 381-6421

RIGGS, ROGER DONALD, b. Mt. Sterling, Ky., Aug. 18, 1946; B.A., Georgetown Coll., 1968; J.D., U. Ky., 1973. Admitted to Ky. bar, 1974; partner firm Bryan, Fogle & Riggs, Mt. Sterling, 1975—; hearing officer Ky. Occupational Safety and Health Review Commn., Frankfort, Ky., 1974-75; city atty., Mt. Sterling, 1976—. Home: R 1 Maplewood Dr Mt Sterling KY 40353 Office: 10 Court St Mt Sterling KY 40353 Tel (606) 498-1442

RIGGS, THOMAS JAMES, b. Chgo., Feb. 24, 1943; B.S., Loyola U., Chgo., 1965; J.D., DePaul U., 1968. Admitted to Ill. bar; asst. state's atty. Ill., 1970-73; dep. pub. defender DuPage County (Ill.), 1973-76; gen. partner firm Loftus and Riggs, Addison, Ill., 1973—; asst. atty. Village of Addison, 1973—, City of Oak Brook Terrace (Ill.), 1973—. Mem. Ill., DuPage County (past chmn. criminal law com.) bar assns., Phi Alpha Delta. Home: 606 Myrtlewood Ln Wheaton IL 60187 Office: 8th Ave and Lake St Addison IL 60101 Tel (312) 543-3010

RIGHTER, RICHARD SCOTT, b. Topeka, Aug. 3, 1894; A.B., Washburn Coll., 1916; LL.B., Harvard, 1921. Admitted to Mo. bar, 1920, U.S. Circuit Ct. Appeals bar, 1924, U.S. Ct. Appeals bar 5th Cicuit, 1936, U.S. Supreme Ct., 1941; asso. firm Lathrop, Morrow, Fox & Moore, Kansas City, Mo., 1920-28, partner, 1928-68; partner firm Lathrop, Koontz, Righter, Clagett, Parker & Norquist, Kansas City, 1968—. Vice pres., dir. Kansas City C. of C., 1952-53; mem. 1st Jackson County (Mo.) Charter Commn., 1955; del. at large Mo. Constnl. Conv., 1943-44. Mem. Kansas City Lawyers Assn. (pres. 1946), Am., Mo. Integrated, Kansas City bar assns. Home: 805 W 51st St Kansas City MO 64112 Office: 1500 Ten Main Center Kansas City MO 64105 Tel (816) 842-0820

RIKLI, DONALD CARL, b. Highland, Ill., June 16, 1927; A.B., Ill. Coll., 1951; J.D., U. Ill., 1953. Admitted to Ill. bar, 1953, U.S. Supreme Ct. bar, 1974; individual practice law, Highland, 1953—; city atty. City of Highland, 1956-59. Fellow Am. Coll. Probate Counsel; mem. Madison County (Ill.) (pres. 1966-67), Ill. State (chmn. com. on Bill of Rights 1967-68, mem. council sect. probate and trust law 1976—), Am. (chmn. state and local bar liaison com. sect. individual rights and responsibilities 1968-70) bar assns. Author books; contbr. articles to legal publs.; bd. editors Illinois Real Property I, 1966, rev. edit., 1971; bd. editors Lawyers World, 1970-72. Home: 1312 Trenton Rd Highland IL 62249 Office: 914 Broadway Highland IL 62249 Tel (618) 654-2364

RILEY, JAMES E., b. 1926; A.B., Wesleyan U., 1949; LL.B., Yale U., 1952. Asst. counsel Office Gen. Counsel of U.S. Navy, 1953-58; counsel Collins Radio Co., 1958-62; counsel to Office Manned Space Flight, NASA, 1962-66; gen. counsel Univac div. Sperry Rand Corp., 1967-75; v.p., gen. counsel Braniff Airways Inc., Dallas, 1976—. Office: Braniff Airways Inc Exchange Park Dallas TX 75235*

RILEY, JANET MARY, b. New Orleans, Sep. 20, 1915; B.A. cum laude, Loyola U., New Orleans, 1936; B.S. in Library Sci., La. State U., 1940; J.D., Loyola U. New Orleans, 1952, LL.M. (fellow), U. Va., 1960. Tchr. Orleans (La.) Parish Schs., 1937-39; asst. info. services desk circulation dept. New Orleans Public Library, 1940-41; asst. librarian Loyola U. Library, New Orleans, 1941-43; librarian, Camp Plauche, La., 1943-45, LaGarde Gen. Hosp. New Orleans, 1945; admitted to La. bar, 1953, U.S. Supreme Ct. bar, 1960; law librarian Loyola U., New Orleans, 1945-56, instr. law, 1952-55, asst. prof. law, 1956-61, asso. prof. law, 1961-71, prof. law, 1971—, also chmn. univ. senate, mem. bd. regents., 1970-72; mem. La. Gov's. Task Force on Women and Credit, 1973—; mem. steering com. 1st Gov's. Conf. for La. Women, 1976; mem. La. Atty. Gen's. Task Force to draft a brochure on community property for marriage license applicants, 1975; mem. Orleans Parish Juvenile Ct. Adv. Com., 1971-77. Mem. La. State Bar Assn., La. State Law Inst. (council, reporter to draft proposed revision in community property and other sexually discriminatory laws 1972—), League of Women Voters, St. Thomas More Cath. Lawyers Assn., AAUP, Community Relations Council of Greater New Orleans, Blue Key, Cardinal Key, Phi Kappa Phi, Phi Alpha Delta, Beta Phi Mu. Author: Louisiana Community Property, 1972; contbr. author: Essays on the Civil Law of Obligations, 1969; Right in the Marketplace, 1975; contbr. articles in fields to legal and library sci. profl. jours. Home: 3413 Vincennes Pl New Orleans LA 70125 Office: Loyola Univ New Orleans LA 70118 Tel (504) 865-2275

RILEY, PAUL E., b. Wilmington, Ohio, Dec. 19, 1925; A.B. cum laude, Wilmington Coll., 1954; J.D., Chase Coll. Law, Cin., 1958. Admitted to Ohio bar, 1958, D.C. bar, 1971, U.S. Supreme Ct. bar, 1971; individual practice law, Wilmington, Ohio, 1958-64; partner firm Pusateri and Riley, Wilmington, 1964-67; judge probate and juvenile divs. Ct. Common Pleas, 1967-77, judge gen. div., 1977—; mem. Ohio Ho. of Reps., 1964-65. Home: 297 N Spring St Wilmington OH 45177 Office: Clinton County Courthouse Wilmington OH 45177 Tel (513) 382-2280

RILEY, RENO R., JR., b. San Antonio, Dec. 23, 1926; J.D., U. Toledo, 1952. Admitted to Ohio bar, 1952; claims atty. U.S. Fidelity & Guaranty Co., Toledo, 1952-60; individual practice law, Toledo, asst. dir. law City of Toledo, 1960-64; judge Toledo Municipal Ct., 1964-70, Lucas County (Ohio) Common Pleas Ct., Toledo, 1970—; mem. bd. dirs. Ct. Diagnostic & Treatment Center, Toledo. Chmn. sch. safety coordinating com. Toledo-Lucas County Safety Council, 1965-70. Mem. Ohio, Lucas County, Toledo bar assns., Ohio Common Pleas Judges' Assn., Am. Judicature Soc., Toledo U. Alumni Assn. (past dir.), Delta Theta Phi. Recipient Outstanding Jud. Service award Ohio Supreme Ct., 1973, Excellent Jud. Service award, 1974, 1975, 1976. Office: Lucas County Court House Toledo OH 43624 Tel (419) 259-8777

RILEY, RICHARD WILSON, b. Greenville, S.C., Jan. 2, 1933; B.A., Furman U., 1954; J.D., U. S.C., 1959. Admitted to S.C. bar, 1959; partner firm Riley & Riley, Greenville, 1960—. Mem. Furman U. Alumni Assn. (pres. 1969-71). Recipient Herbert Harley award Am. Judicature Soc., 1976. Home: 200 Sunset Dr Greenville SC 29605 Office: 218 Henrietta St Greenville SC 29601 Tel (803) 242-6624

RILEY, THOMAS ANTHONY, JR., b. W. Chester, Pa., Sept. 2, 1939; B.S. in Polit. Sci., St. Joseph's Coll., 1961; J.D., Villanova Law Sch., 1964. Admitted to Pa. Supreme Ct. bar, 1964, U.S. Supreme Ct. bar, 1971; asso. firm Rogers & O'Neill, W. Chester, 1964-66; partner firm Riley & Massey, Paoli, Pa., 1967-69, firm Lentz, Riley, Cantor, Kilgore & Massey, Paoli, 1970—, dir. Connelly Containers Inc., Phila.; mem. regional bd. Central Pa. Nat. Bank, Phila., 1972—. Mem. Nat. Alfalfa Bd., Kansas City, Mo., 1967-73, chmn., 1973-76; bd. dirs., treas. Malvern (Pa.) Retreat League, 1971—; bd. consultors Villanova (Pa.) Law Sch., 1972—. Mem. Chester County, Pa. bar assns. Home: 161 S Devon Ave Devon PA 19333 Office: 30 Darby Rd Paoli PA 19301 Tel (215) 647-3310

RILEY, TOM JOSEPH, b. Cedar Rapids, Iowa, Jan. 9, 1929; B.A., U. Iowa, 1950, J.D., 1952. Admitted to Iowa bar, 1952, U.S. Supreme Ct. bar, 1966; partner firm Simmons, Perrine, Albright & Ellwood, Cedar Rapids, 1952—; faculty Ct. Practice Inst., Chgo., 1976-77, mem. Iowa Ho. of Reps., 1960-64, Iowa Senate, 1964-68, 70-74. Pres. Linn County Mental Health Assn., 1959. Fellow Iowa Acad. Trial Lawyers; mem. Am., Iowa bar assns. Author: Response to Crisis, 1968; also articles. Home: 3610 Clark Rd SE Cedar Rapids IA 52403 Office: 1200 Mchts Nat Bank Bldg Cedar Rapids IA 52401

RILL, JAMES FRANKLIN, b. Evanston, Ill., Mar. 4, 1933; A.B., Dartmouth Coll., 1954; LL.B., Harvard U., 1959. Admitted to D.C. bar, 1959, U.S. Supreme Ct. bar, 1965; asso. firm Collier & Shannon, 1959-64; partner firm Collier, Shannon, Rill, Edwards & Scott, Washington, 1964—. Mem. D.C., Am. (chmn. subcom. on pricing practices Robinson Patman Act com. 1976—) bar assns., Am. Judicature Soc. Contbr. articles to legal jours. Home: 7305 Masters Dr

Potomac MD 20854 Office: 1055 Thomas Jefferson St NW Suite 308 Washington DC 20007 Tel (202) 337-6000

RIMM, WILLIAM RAYMOND, b. Luray, Va., Aug. 4, 1942; B.S., Va. Mil. Inst., 1964; M.A., Vanderbilt U., 1966; J.D., U. Va., 1971, M.D., 1974. Admitted to Va. bar, 1971; commd. capt. U.S. Army, 1974; intern Tripler Army Med. Center, Honolulu, 1974-75; resident in ophthalmology Walter Reed Army Med. Center, Washington, 1975—. Mem. Am. Coll. Legal Medicine, Am. Assn. Ophthalmology, Va. Bar, AMA. Office: Walter Reed Army Med Center Washington DC 20012 Tel (202) 576-3536

RIMMELS, EDWARD RICHARD, JR., b. N.Y.C., Jan. 14, 1930; A.B., Hamilton Coll., Clinton, N.Y., 1951; J.D., Columbia, 1954. Admitted to N.Y. bar, 1954, U.S. Ct. Appeals 2d Circuit bar, 1959, U.S. Supreme Ct. bar, 1971; asso. firm Breed, Abbott & Morgan, N.Y.C., 1956-58; asso. firm Mayer, Zeck & Mayer, Suffern, N.Y., 1958-59; mem. firm Montfort, Healy, McGuire & Salley, Mineola, N.Y., 1959—. Mem. N.Y., Nassau County (dir.) bar assns., Nassau-Suffolk Trial Lawyers Assn (dir.). Contbr. articles in field to profl. jours. Home: 92 Meadow St Garden City NY 11530 Office: 163 Mineola Blvd Mineola NY 11501 Tel (516) 747-4082

RINALDI, RAYMOND CLEMENT, b. Old Forge, Pa., Aug. 11, 1938; B.S., U. Scranton, 1960; LL.B., U. Md., 1963. Admitted to Pa. bar, 1965; asso. firm Gelb, Carey & Myers, 1965-67; staff Lackawanna County (Pa.) Legal Aid and Defender Assn., 1969-71; individual practice law, 1971-72; partner firm Beemer, Brier, Rinaldi & Fendrick, Scranton, Pa., 1972—; solicitor Borough of Moosic (Pa.), 1969—. Home: 3700 Parkwood Dr Moosic PA 1B507 Office: 200 Scranton Life Bldg Scranton PA 18503 Tel (717) 346-7441

RINAMAN, JAMES CURTIS, JR., b. Miami, Fla., Feb. 8, 1935; B.A., U. Fla., 1955, LL.B., 1960. Admitted to Fla. bar, 1960; asso. firm Marks, Gray, Conroy & Gibbs, Jacksonville, Fla., 1960-65, partner, 1965—, v.p., 1975—; gen. counsel Consol. City of Jacksonville, 1970-71; author, lectr. Fla. bar courses. Mem. Jacksonville Transp. Authority, 1971—; v.p., gen. counsel Jacksonville Am. Bicentennial Commn., 1974—. Mem. Am. Bar Assn., Fla. (chmn. ct. rules steering com. 1972-75, exec. council trial sect. 1971—, bd. govs. 1977—), Jacksonville (pres. 1972) bars, Assn. Ins. Attys. (pres. 1976), Internat. Assn. Ins. Attys., Def. Research Inst. (Fla. chmn. 1974—), Fla. Def. Lawyers Assn. (pres. 1973), Am. Judicature Soc., Jacksonville Area C. of C. (v.p. and gen. counsel 1974—). Recipient Distinguished Service medal, Fla. NG, 1974. Home: 3736 Rubin Rd Jacksonville FL 32217 Office: 231 E Forsyth St 4th floor PO Box 447 Jacksonville FL 32201 Tel (904) 355-6681

RING, GERARD WILLIAM, b. Wabasha, Minn., Oct. 12, 1938; B.S., Georgetown U. Sch. Fgn. Service, 1961; LL.B., U. Minn., 1964; postgrad. (Bush Leadership fellow) Harvard, 1976. Admitted to Minn. bar, 1964; practiced in Rochester, Minn., 1964-72; judge Rochester Municipal Ct., 1972, Dodge-Olmsted County (Minn.) Ct., 1972—; faculty adivser Nat. Coll. State Judiciary, 1974. Mem. sch. bd. Byron (Minn.) Ind. Sch. Dist. 531, 1969-72. Mem. Olmsted County, Minn. bar assns. Home: Route 1 Byron MN 55920 Office: Olmsted County Courthouse Rochester MN 55901 Tel (507) 285-8210

RING, JORDAN LEWIS, b. Boston, June 28, 1936; B.A., Suffolk U., 1958, LL.B. cum laude, 1960; postgrad. Harvard Grad. Sch. Law, 1960-62. Admitted to Mass. bar, 1960; partner firm Ring & Rudnick Boston, 1960—. Mem. Am., Boston bar assns., Assn. Trial Lawyers Am. Office: 55 Union St Boston MA 02108 Tel (617) 523-0250

RINGEL, HERBERT ARTHUR, b. Georgetown, S.C., Dec. 6, 1908; LL.B., U. Ga., 1930. Admitted to Ga. bar, 1930; partner firm Ringel and Ringel, Brunswick, Ga., 1930-42; atty. Brunswick Housing Authority, 1936-42; dist. atty. Glynn County (Ga.), 1937-42; partner firm Smith Cohen, Ringel, Kohler and Martin, Atlanta, 1945—; sec., gen. counsel Fidelity Fed. Savs. and Loan Assn., Atlanta, 1956—; spl. asst. U.S. atty., Atlanta, 1947-52; mem. Mayor's Com. on Crime and Delinquency, Atlanta, 1965-68. Trustee Atlanta Area Services for the Blind, 1975—; pres. Jewish Children's Services, 1969-72, Am. Jewish Com., 1964-67, Ga. Soc. Prevention Blindness, 1970-72. Mem. Am., Ga., Atlanta bar assns., Am. Judicature Soc., Internat. Assn. Ins. Counsel, Lawyers Club Atlanta, Old War Horse Lawyers Club, Optimist Club, Zeta Beta Tau. Home: 77 E Andrews Dr NW Apt 121 Atlanta GA 30342 Office: 2400 1st Nat Bank Tower Atlanta GA 30303 Tel (404) 658-1200

RINGER, ALFRED VICTOR, b. Williamsport, Ind., Nov. 10, 1903; A.B. with distinction, Ind. U., 1926, J.D., 1928. Admitted to Ind. bar, 1927; individual practice law, Williamsport, 1928—; pros. atty. Warren Circuit Ct., Ind., 1935-40; atty. Town of Williamsport, 1940-72, County of Warren (Ind.), 1953-70. Mem. Williamsport Library Bd., 1948-74; bd. dirs. Ind. Tb Assn., 1968-71. Mem. Am., Ind. (bd. mgrs. 1964-66), Seventh Circuit bar assns., Ind. Bar Found. (past pres., dir. 1971—), Am. Judicature Soc., Ind. Continuing Legal Edn. Forum (dir. 1962—), Ind. Soc. Chgo., Phi Beta Kappa. Home: 311 Lincoln St Williamsport IN 47993 Office: 110 N Monroe St Williamsport IN 47993 Tel (317) 762-2625

RINGER, BARBARA ALICE, b. Lafayette, Ind., May 29, 1925; B.A., George Washington U., 1945, M.A., 1947; J.D., Columbia, 1949. Admitted to D.C. bar, U.S. Ct. of Appeals bar, U.S. Supreme Ct. bar; copyright examiner Library of Congress, Washington, 1949-51, head, renewal and assignment sect., 1951-55, asst. chief, chief examining div., 1955-63, asst. register, 1963-72, register copyrights, 1973—; adj. prof. law Georgetown U. Law Center, 1962-72; dir. copyright div. UNESCO, Paris, 1972-73. Mem. Am., Fed., D.C. bar assns., Am. Patent Law Assn., ALA, Internat. Assn. for Protection Intellectual Property, Internat. Copyright Soc., Phi Beta Kappa, Phi Pi Epsilon, Pi Gamma Mu, Alpha Lambda Delta. Contbr. articles to profl. jours. Office: Copyright Office Library of Congress Washington DC 20540

RINGGOLD, KATHRYN EDYTHE, b. Oakland, Calif., Apr. 25, 1931; B.S., U. Calif., Berkeley; J.D., Golden Gate Law Sch., 1970. Admitted to Calif. bar, 1970; partner firm Airola & Ringgold, San Francisco, 1974—; mem. Workmen's Compensation Com., Calif. State Bar. Mem. Calif. Applicant's Attys. Assn. (pres. 1977), San Francisco Trial Lawyers Assn., Am., Calif. bar assns., Queen's Bench. Office: 995 Market St Suite 1112 San Francisco CA 94103 Tel (415) 362-7518

RINGLE, PHILIP HAMILTON, JR., b. Portland, Oreg., Mar. 23, 1931; B.A., Willamette U., 1953, J.D., 1956. Admitted to Oreg. bar, 1957; asso. firm Green, Richardson, Green & Griswold, Portland, 1958-63, Hibbard, Jacobs, Caldwell & Kincart, Oregon City, 1963-65; partner firm Misko, Njust & Ringle, Oregon City, 1965-67, Ringle & Herndon, Gladstone, Oreg., and predecessor, 1967—; municipal judge City Gladstone, 1965—. Bd. dirs. Clackamas County (Oreg.) Mental Health Assn., 1970—, Willamette View Manor, Retirement Center, 1972—, Clackamas County Criminal Justice Council, 1974—. Mem. Am., Oreg., Clackamas County, Multnomah County bar assns., Am. Trial Lawyers Assn., Oreg. State Municipal Judges Assn. (pres.). Home: 8398 Cason Rd Gladstone OR 97027 Office: 405 W Arlington St Gladstone OR 97027 Tel (503) 656-0879

RINKER, GEORGE ALBERT, b. Anderson, Ind., Dec. 9, 1919; A.B., Franklin Coll. of Ind., 1942; J.D., U. lMich., 1948. Admitted to Ind. bar, 1948, U.S. Supreme Ct. bar, 1973; individual practice law, Lafayette, Ind., 1948-50; asso. firm Stuart, Branigin, Ricks & Schilling, Lafayette, 1950-53, partner, 1953—; dir., mem. exec. com. The Lafayette Life Ins. Co., 1960—. Mem. exec. bd. Lafayette council Boy Scouts Am., 1952—, pres., 1963-64; bd. dirs., sec. Jerry E. Clegg Found., 1964—; pres. Franklin Coll. Alumni Assn., 1965-67; trustee Franklin Coll., 1967-70, 72—, treas., 1975—. Mem. Am., Ind. State, Tippecanoe County, Indpls. bar assns., Am. Judicature Soc., Am. Soc. Hosp. Attys., Am. Council Life Ins. (legal sect.), Order of Coif. Student editor Mich. Law Rev. 1947; recipient Silver Beaver award Boy Scouts Am., 1963; recipient Franklin Coll. Alumni citation, 1971. Home: 3605 Cedar Ln Lafayette IN 47904 Office: 8th floor POB 1010 Life Bldg Lafayette IN 47902 Tel (317) 423-1561

RIORDAN, HENRY PATRICK, b. N.Y.C., Apr. 2, 1924; student Fordham U., 1941-43, LL.B. cum laude, 1949; student Clarkson Coll. Tech., Potsdam, N.Y., 1943, Am. U., Biarritz, France, 1945, N.Y. U., 1946, N.Y. U. Grad. Law Sch., 1949-50. Admitted to N.Y. bar, 1949; asso. firm Townsend & Lewis, N.Y.C., 1949-50; asso. firm Cravath, Sawine & Moore, N.Y.C., 1950-60, partner, 1961—. Mem. Assn. Bar City N.Y., Am., N.Y. bar assns. Office: 1 Chase Manhattan Plaza New York City NY 10005 Tel (212) 422-3000

RIORDAN, WILLIAM F., b. Wichita, Kans., Mar. 26, 1941; B.B.A., U. N.Mex., 1965, J.D., 1968. Admitted to N.Mex. bar, 1968, U.S. Supreme Ct. bar, 1971, Tax Ct. U.S. bar, 1972; legal aid atty., Albuquerque, 1968-69; asst. atty. gen. N. Mex., 1969; asst. dist. atty. Bernolillo County (N.Mex.), 1969-72; judge 2d Jud. Dist. of N.Mex., Albuquerque, 1972—. Pres. bd. dirs. Albuquerque Hearing and Speech Center, United Way Agy. Mem. Am. Bar Assn., Am. Trial Lawyers Assn., Nat. Council of Juvenile Ct. Judges. Home: 8309 Dellwood N E Albuquerque NM 87110 Office: POB 488 Albuquerque NM 87103 Tel (505) 842-3253

RIOS, CARLOS RAMON, b. N.Y.C., Nov. 18, 1938; B.S. in Econs., U. Pa., 1960; LL.B., U. P.R., 1965. Admitted to P.R. Supreme Ct. bar, 1965, U.S. Dist. Ct. bar P.R., 1966; asso. firm Tilly & Esteves, P.R., then partner; ins. commr. Govt. of P.R., San Juan, 1973-75, atty. gen., 1975—; pres. P.R. Crime Commn., 1975. Chmn. 10th anniversary Disabled Children Assn., 1975. Mem. P.R. Bar Assn. Home: A-13 Palmasola St Torrimar Guaynabo PR 00657 Office: Office of Atty Gen San Juan PR

RIPOSANU, PAMFIL A., b. Orastie, Transylvania-Romania, Apr. 26, 1915; Licencie en Droit, Doctorate, U. Bucharest (Romania); LL.B., N.Y. Law Sch. Admitted to Bucharest bar, 1936, N.Y. bar, 1955, U.S. Supreme Ct. bar, 1975; partner firm Hoffman, Buchwald, Nadel & Hoffman, N.Y.C., 1955-60, Hennefeld & Riposanu, N.Y.C., 1960-72, Ripusanu, Leizowipt & Grae, N.Y.C., 1973-75, Riposano, Ahearn, Aballi & Diaz-Cruz, N.Y.C., 1976—; sec. gen. Presidency of Council of Ministers, Romania, 1944-45; minister-councillor in charge affairs Kingdom Romania to U.S., 1945-47. Chmn. bd. dirs. Conf. Americans Central-Eastern European Descent, N.Y.C., 1955—. Mem. Am., N.Y. bar assns., N.Y. Trial Lawyers Assn. Home: 1175 York Ave New York City NY 10021 Office: 375 Park Ave New York City NY 10022 Tel (212) PL9-9030

RISHER, JOHN ROBERT, JR., b. Washington, Sept. 23, 1938; B.S. summa cum laude, Morgan State Coll., 1960; LL.B., U. So. Calif., 1963. Admitted to Calif. bar, 1963, D.C. bar, 1967, U.S. Supreme Ct. bar, 1972; served legal officer Arty. Corps, U.S. Army, 1963-65; trial atty. fraud sect., criminal div. Dept. Justice, Washington, 1965-68; partner firm Arent, Fox, Kintner, Plotkin & Kahn, Washington, 1968-76; corp. counsel D.C. Govt., 1976—; pres. D.C. Commn. on Licensure to Practice Healing Arts, 1976—; chmn. D.C. Criminal Justice Coordinating Bd., 1976—; mem. D.C. Jud. Planning Commn., 1977—, D.C. Law Revision Commn., 1976—; mem. adv. com. on rules D.C. Superior Ct., 1975-76, adv. com. on evidence, 1975-76; chmn. D.C. Bd. Elections and Ethics Nominating Com., 1975-76. Chmn. Montgomery County Civil Liberties Union, 1970-71; mem. exec. com. Nat. Capital Area Civil Liberties Union, 1970-71; bd. dirs. D.C. Pub. Defender Service, 1975-76. Mem. Am., D.C. (exec. com. young lawyers sect. 1973-74), Fed. bar assns., Bar Assn. D.C., Nat. Inst. Municipal Law Officers, Washington Council Lawyers (exec. com. 1972-75), State Bar Assn. Calif. Home: 3311 Cleveland Ave NW Washington DC 20008 Office: Dist Bldg 14th and E Sts NW Washington DC 20004 Tel (202) 629-3858

RISSMAN, BURTON RICHARD, b. Chgo., Nov. 13, 1927; B.S., U. Ill., 1947, J.D., 1951; LL.M., N.Y. U., 1952. Admitted to Ill. bar, 1951; judge advocate USAF, 1952-53; asso. firm Schiff Hardin & Waite, Chgo., 1953-59, partner, 1959—; dir. Car X Service Systems, Inc., 1973—, Car X Muffler Shops of Ind. Inc., 1955—; mem. faculty Practicing Law Inst., 1970, 74, N.Y. Law Jour., 1973, 76. Pres. Woodridge Home Owners Assn., Highland Park, Ill., 1972-73. Mem. Am., Ill., Chgo. bar assns., Chgo. Council Lawyers, Seventh Circuit Bar Assn., Am. Judicature Soc., Order of Coif. Contbr. articles to law jours. Office: 7200 Sears Tower 233 S Wacker Dr Chicago IL 60606 Tel (312) 876-1000

RISSMAN, EMANUEL ALBERT, b. Chgo., Dec. 28, 1910; J.D., DePaul U., 1934. Admitted to Ill. bar, 1935, Calif. bar, 1949; individual practice law, Chgo., 1935-49, 51-63; asst. atty. gen. State of Ill., 1949-51; sr. partner firm Rissman & Mermall, Chgo., 1963-69; asso. judge Cook County Ct., 1969—; panel chmn. War Labor Bd., 1944-45. Bd. dirs. Portes Cancer Clinic, Chgo., 1965—. Mem. Am. (circuit chmn. 7th jud. circuit com. on cts. and community), Chgo. (chmn. com. on inquiry 1952-53), Ill. State, Calif. State, Los Angeles County bar assns., Decalogue Soc. Lawyers, Ill. Judges Assn. Office: Civic Center Chicago IL 60602 Tel (312) 443-8250

RISTAU, MARK MOODY, b. Warren, Pa., Mar. 21, 1944; B.A., Pa. Mil. Coll., 1966, Widner Coll., 1966; J.D., Case Western Res. U., 1969. Admitted to Pa. bar, 1970, D.C. bar, 1972, U.S. Supreme Ct. bar, 1973; individual practice law, Warren, Pa., 1970-75, Warren and Vancouver, B.C., Can., 1976—; pres. Autopride, Inc., San Angelo, Tex., 1975—; sr. dir. Pa. Allied Oil Producers, Vancouver, B.C., Can., 1972—; case reporter The Legal Intelligencer, 1972—. Mem. Warren County Bd. Assistance, 1970-71, chmn., 1971-72. Mem. Am. Trial Lawyers Assn., Am., Warren-Forest County bar assns. Author: So You Want a Divorce?, 1977. Home: 208 Kinzua Rd Warren PA 16365 Office: 410-411 Warren Nat Bank Bldg Warren PA 16365

RITCH, ROBERT FRANKLIN, b. Valdosta, Ga., Mar. 2, 1941; B.S. in Journalism, U. Fla., 1963, J.D., 1965. Admitted to Fla. bar, 1966, Ct. Mil. Appeals bar, 1967, U.S. Supreme Ct. bar, 1971; legal asst. to Fla. Sec. of State, Tallahassee, 1966; with Judge Adv. Gen. Corps, U.S. Army, 1967-71; with firm Jones & Ritch, Gainesville, Fla., 1976; partner, v.p. firm Ritch & Graves, Gainesville, Fla., 1976—. Mem. Fla. Bar, Fla. Defense Lawyers Assn., Am. Trial Lawyers Assn. Editor real estate sect. Manual for Para-Legals, 1976. Home: 2236 NW 19th Ave Gainesville FL 32605 Office: 711 NW 23d Ave Suites 2 and 3 Gainesville FL 32601 Tel (904) 377-2889

RITCHEY, JOHN JOSEPH, b. Mt. Vernon, Ohio, Jan. 10, 1947; B.A., Baldwin-Wallace Coll., 1969; J.D., Ohio State U., 1973. Admitted to Ohio bar, 1973; asst. atty. gen. State of Ohio, 1974—. Mem. Ohio Bar Assn. Office: 30 E Broad St Columbus OH 43215

RITCHIE, JACK, b. Forney, Tex., Nov. 13, 1921; A.A., Marshall (Tex.) Coll., 1943; J.D. with honors, U. Tex., 1946. Admitted to Tex. bar, 1946, U.S. Supreme Ct. bar, 1975; staff atty. Phillips Petroleum Co., Amarillo, Tex., 1946-74, regional chief atty., 1974—; lectr. bus. law W. Tex. State U., Amarillo Jr. Coll., 1947-74. Deacon Paramount Baptist Ch., Amarillo. Home: 3816 Ozark St Amarillo TX 79109 Office: PO Box 31690 Amarillo TX 79120 Tel (806) 374-1101

RITCHIE, JOHN, b. Norfolk, Va., Mar. 19, 1904; B.S., U. Va., 1925, LL.B., 1927; J.S.D., Yale, 1931. Admitted to Va. bar, 1927, Nebr. bar, 1927, Mo. bar, 1952, Wis. bar, 1953, Ill. bar, 1957; asso. firm Ritchie, Chase, Canady & Swenson, Omaha, 1927-28; asst. prof. law Furman U., 1928-30; asst. prof. law U. Wash., 1931-36; prof. la U. Md., 1936-37; prof. law U. Va., 1937-52; Kirby prof. law Washington U., St. Louis, 1952-53, dean, 1952-53; prof. law U. Wis., 1953-57, dean, 1953-57; Wigmore prof. law Northwestern U., 1957-72, dean, 1957-72, prof. emeritus, 1972—; prof. law U. Va., 1972-74, scholar in residence, 1974—. Bd. dirs. Am. Council on Edn., Washington, 1965-67, United Charities, Chgo., 1965-72. Fellow Am. Bar Found.; mem. Am., Va. bar assns., Assn. Am. Law Schools (pres. 1964), Judge Adv. Assn. (pres. 1952), Phi Beta Kappa, Order of Coif (pres. 1952-55). Editor: (with Neill Alford and Richard Effland) Cases and Materials on Decedents' Estates and Trusts, 4th edit., 1971. Home: 1848 Westview Rd Charlottesville VA 22903 Office: School of Law U Virginia Charlottesville VA 22901 Tel (804) 924-3914

RITCHIE, ROLAND A., b. Halifax, N.S., Can., June 19, 1910; student Trinity Coll. Sch., Port Hope, Ont., Univ. King's Coll., Halifax, Pembroke Coll., Oxford, Eng. Called to N.S. bar, 1934, created king's counsel, 1950; with firm Stewart, Smith, MacKeen & Rogers, Halifax, 1934-40; partner firm Daley, Ritchie, Black & Moriera and predecessor, Halifax, 1945-59; puisne judge Supreme Ct. of Can., 1959—. Formerly mem. bd. govs. Dalhousie U., Halifax, Univ. King's Coll. Mem. N.S. Barristers Soc. (formerly 1st v.p.), Canadian Bar Assn. Home: 177 Coltrin Rd Rockcliffe Ottawa ON Canada Office: Supreme Ct of Can Wellington St Ottawa ON K1A 0J1 Canada*

RITTENBERG, SAUL NATHAN, b. Chgo., Aug. 4, 1912; A.B., U. Calif. at Los Angeles, 1932; J.D., Northwestern U., 1935. Admitted to Calif. bar, 1935, U.S. Supreme Ct., 1943; mem. firm Loeb and Loeb, Los Angeles, 1935-43, 1946-48, partner, 1948-56, 1970—; asst. sec. Metro-Goldwyn-Mayer, Culver City, Calif., 1956-70; bd. trustees Directors Guild Am. Pension and Health & Welfare Plans, Beverly Hills, Calif., 1960-70. Bd. councillors U. So. Calif. Law Center, Los Angeles, 1972—. Mem. Am. (past chmn. sect. com.), Beverly Hills, Calif. bar assns., Los Angeles Copyright Soc., Copyright Soc. U.S.A., Am. Judicature Soc., Assn. Motion Picture and TV Producers (dir. 1956-70). Office: 10100 Santa Monica Blvd Suite 2200 Los Angeles CA 90067 Tel (213) 552-7778

RITTENOUR, JOHN THORNTON, b. Chgo., Jan. 29, 1918; B.S., Ohio State U., 1940; LL.B., Ohio No. U., 1947, J.D., 1967. Admitted to Ohio bar, 1949; individual practice law, Piketon, Ohio, 1949—; city solicitor Piketon, 1949-56; legal counsel Chesapeake & Ohio R.R. Co. and Norfolk & Western R.R. Co., 1951-77; acting county judge Pike County; dir. 1st Nat. Bank, Waverly, Ohio, 1966-77. Del. Ohio Conf. Meth. Ch., 1950-69; active United Fund, Easter Seals, ARC; trustee Shawnee State Coll., 1976—; mem. Pike County Bd. Edn., 1968-72, Pike County Bd. Mental Retardation, 1972—. Mem. Pike County, Ohio State, Am. bar assns. Address: PO Box 427 Piketon OH 45661 Tel (614) 289-2750

RITTER, ANN L., b. N.Y.C., May 20, 1933; J.D., N.Y. Law Sch., 1970; postgrad. in Law N.Y. U., 1971-72. Admitted to N.Y. bar, 1971, U.S. Supreme Ct. bar, 1975; sr. partner firm Brenhouse & Ritter, N.Y.C., 1974—. Mem. Assn. Immigration and Nationality Lawyers, Am., N.Y. State bar assns., New York County Lawyers Assn., N.Y. State Trial Lawyers Assn. Editor, N.Y. Immigration News, 1975-76. Home: 23 W 12th St New York City NY 10011 Office: The Plaza 2 W 59th St New York City NY 10019 Tel (212) PL 3-6600

RITTER, GEORGE WILLIAM, b. Vermilion, Ohio, June 30, 1886; LL.B., Baldwin U., 1907, LL.D. (hon.), 1946; LL.D. (hon.) U. Toledo, 1961. Admitted to Ohio bar, 1907, Fed. bar, 1910, U.S. Supreme Ct. bar, 1914; partner firm Kohn, Ritter, Northup & McMahon, Toledo, 1913-17; partner firm Gardner & Ritter, Toledo, Ritter, Bossel, Robinson & Marsh, Toledo; dir. law city Toledo, 1928-29. Mem. Toledo, Lucas County, Ohio State, Cleve., Am. bar assns., Assn. Bar City N.Y. Home: 4555 Forestview Dr Toledo OH 43615 Office: 240 Huron St Toledo OH 43604 Tel (419) 241-3213

RITTER, ROBERT FORCIER, b. St. Louis, Apr. 7, 1943; B.A., U. Kans., 1965; J.D., St. Louis U., 1968. Admitted to Mo. bar, 1968, U.S. Ct. Mil. Appeals bar, 1972, U.S. Supreme Ct. bar, 1972; partner firm Gray & Ritter, St. Louis, 1968—; also lectr. Mem. Lawyers Assn. St. Louis (pres. 1977-78), Am., Mo. (tort law com.), Met. St. Louis (civil cts. com.) bar assns., Am. Trial Lawyers Assn. Contbr. articles to legal jours. Home: 741 Hawbrook Rd Glendale MO 63122 Office: 1015 Locust St Suite 900 Saint Louis MO 63101 Tel (314) 241-5620

RITTER, WILLIS WILLIAM, b. Salt Lake City, Jan. 24, 1899; A.B., U. Utah; LL.B., U. Chgo., 1924; S.J.D., Harvard, 1940. Admitted to bar, Ill. 1924, D.C., 1925, Utah, 1927, practiced in Chgo. and Washington, 1924-26, Salt Lake City, 1935-49; prof. law U. Utah, 1926-50; U.S. judge Dist. of Utah, 1949—, now chief judge. Mem. Order of Coif, Phi Beta Kappa, Phi Kappa Phi. Home: Newhouse Hotel Salt Lake City UT 84101 also Thousand Springs Farm Wendell ID 83355 Office: US Courthouse 350 S Main St Salt Lake City UT 84102*

RITZEL, RICHARD STANLEY, b. N.Y.C., June 10, 1911; B.A., Holy Cross Coll., Worcester, Mass., 1932; M.A., Fordham U., 1935, LL.B., 1935. Admitted to N.Y. Supreme Ct. bar, 1935, N.Y. Ct. Appeals bar, 1952, U.S. Dist. Ct. D.C. bar, 1966; asso. firm Bernard

A Shalek, N.Y.C., 1935-36; asso. firm Mudge, Rose, Guthrie & Alexander, N.Y.C., 1936-48, partner, 1948—. Mem. Borough of Ho-Ho-Kus Council, N.J., 1948-53, chmn. fin. com., 1950-53. Mem. Assn. Bar City N.Y., N.Y. State Bar Assn., N.Y. County Lawyers Assn. Home: 23 Beechwood Rd Ho-Ho-Kus NJ 07423 Office: 20 Broad St New York City NY 10005 Tel (212) 422-6767

RITZI, WILLIAM LOUIS, b. McKees Rocks, Pa., Aug. 25, 1915; LL.B., U. So. Calif., 1939, J.D., 1941. Admitted to Calif. bar, 1941, U.S. Dist. Ct. bar for So. Dist. Calif., 1941; law clk. sr. judge U.S. Dist. Ct., So. Dist. Calif., 1941-42; asst. U.S. atty. serving as chief complaint div. U.S. Atty's Office, Los Angeles, legal advisor U.S. Grand Jury, 1942-47; chief juvenile div. Los Angeles County Dist. Atty's. Office, 1947-53, trial dep., 1950-53, calendar dep., legal advisor, 1957-63, chief Santa Monica (Calif.) Office, 1960-66, asst. dist. atty., 1966-69; judge Los Angeles Superior Ct., 1969—, supervising judge criminal cts., 1975; instr. Sch. Pub. Adminstrn. U. So. Calif., 1948-64. Mem. Los Angeles County Bar Assn. Author: Legal Aspects of Delinquency Control, 1950. Office: Dept 132 15-309 Criminal Cts Bldg 210 W Temple St Los Angeles CA 90012 Tel (213) 974-5781

RIVERA, RHONDA R., b. Phila., Mar. 9, 1938; B.A., Douglass Coll., 1959; M.Pub. Adminstrn., Syracuse U., 1960; J.D., Wayne State U., 1967. Research economist Cleve. Fed. Res. Bank, 1960-62; instr. pub. adminstrn. InterAm. U., 1962-64; admitted to Mich. bar, 1968, Ohio bar, 1976; asso. prof. econs. Hope Coll., Holland, Mich., 1968-72; asst. dean William James Coll., Allendale, Mich., 1972-74, U. Mich. Law Sch., 1974-76; asst. prof. law Ohio State U., 1976—; practice law, Grand Haven and Ann Arbor, Mich., 1968-76, Columbus, Ohio, 1976—; legal counsel Day Care Center, Ann Arbor, 1974-76. Mem. Nat. Lawyers Guild, Soc. Am. Law Tchrs. (gov. 1976-79). Recipient Uppity Woman of Year award NOW, 1975; Susan B. Anthony award U. Mich., 1976. Home: 385 E Schreyer Pl Columbus OH 43214 Office: 1659 N High St Columbus OH 43210 Tel (614) 422-2422

RIVERS, GEOFFREY ALLAN, b. Washington, Aug. 1, 1942; B.S., Ball State U., 1966; J.D., Ind. U., 1971. Admitted to Ind. bar, 1971; legal intern Marion County (Ind.) Prosecutor's Office, Indpls., 1971; dep. atty. gen. Ind., Indpls., 1972; dep. prosecutor Delaware County (Ind.), Muncie, 1973, pub. defender, 1973—; asso. firm Hampton and Quick, Muncie, 1973—. Mem. Am., Ind., Delaware County bar assns. Home: 3303 Cornwall Dr Muncie IN 47304 Office: 322 E Washington St Muncie IN 47305 Tel (317) 288-8852

RIVKIN, DONALD HERSCHEL, b. Davenport, Iowa, May 24, 1924; B.A., Yale, 1948, LL.B./J.D., 1952; B.A. in Jurisprudence (Rhodes scholar), Oxford (Eng.) U., 1950, M.A. in Jurisprudence, 1953. Admitted to N.Y. bar, 1953, U.S. Customs Ct. bar, 1964, U.S. Supreme Ct. bar, 1966, U.S. Tax Ct. bar, 1966; asso. firms Cravath, Swaine & Moore, N.Y.C., 1952-56, Solinger & Gordon, N.Y.C., 1956-59; mem. firm Rivkin Sherman and Levy and predecessors, N.Y.C., 1959—; State Dept. rep. Conf. on Internat. Conv. on Travel Agt. Contracts, Inst. Unification of Private Internat. Law, Rome, 1967; mem. working groups Dept. State adv. coms.; speaker in field. Bd. dirs., sec., counsel Operation Crossrds. Africa, N.Y.C., 1959—; mem. program and interreligious cooperation coms. Anti-Defamation League, N.Y.C., 1960—; bd. dirs., treas. Assn. Am. Rhodes Scholars, N.Y.C., 1975—. Mem. Assn. Bar City N.Y., Am. Bar Assn., Customs Bar Assn., Am. Soc. Internat. Law, Internat. Law Assn., Order of Coif, Phi Beta Kappa. Home: 16 W 77th St New York City NY 10024 Office: 750 Third Ave New York City NY 10017 Tel (212) 986-5220

RIVLIN, LEWIS ALLEN, b. N.Y.C., Oct. 15, 1929; B.A., Swarthmore Coll., 1951; LL.B. (now J.D.), Harvard U., 1957. Admitted to D.C. bar, 1957, U.S. Supreme Ct. bar, 1960; atty. patent sect. civil div. U.S. Dept. Justice, 1957-59, atty. gen. litigation sect. antitrust div., 1959-64; partner firm O'Connor, Green, Thomas, Walters & Kelly, Washington, 1964-68; partner firm Peabody, Rivlin, Lambert & Meyers, Washington, 1969—. Bd. dirs. Am. Freedom from Hunger Found., Washington, 1975—, Met. Washington Coalition for Clean Air, Washington. Mem. Am., Fed. bar assns., Bar Assn. D.C., D.C. Bar, Am. Judicature Soc. Office: 1150 Connecticut Ave NW Washington DC 20036 Tel (202) 457-1050

RIZLEY, ROBERT SEAL, b. Guymon, Okla., June 11, 1923; B.A., Okla. U., 1949; LL.B., U. Mich., 1953. Admitted to Okla. bar, 1953, U.S. Supreme Ct. bar, 1959; partner firm Martin, Logan, Moyers, Martin & Hull, Tulsa, 1956-59; U.S. atty. No. Dist. Okla., Tulsa, 1959-61; partner firm Crawford, Rizley, Prichard & Reed, Tulsa, 1962-74, Rizley, Prichard, Norman & Reed, 1974—. Pres., Tulsa Opera, Inc., 1974—. Mem. Am., Okla. bar assns., Phi Delta Phi. Home: 4710 S Yorktown Tulsa OK 74105 Office: 1100 Philtower Bldg Tulsa OK 74103 Tel (918) 583-7571

RIZZO, ANTHONY RALPH, b. Boston, Mar. 31, 1929; B.B.A., Northeastern U., Boston, 1957; J.D., Suffolk U., 1968. Admitted to Mass. bar, 1968; founder Afco Products Inc., Somerville, Mass., 1962—, chief exec. officer, v.p. subs. Yates Industries, Inc. Bd. dirs. Neighborhood Legal Services, 1971—. Mem. Mass., Somerville, Lynn, Middlesex County bar assns. Home: 19 D'Ambrosio Rd Lynn MA 01904 Office: 44 Park St Somerville MA 02143 Tel (617) 623-7723

RIZZOLO, ALLEN ALFONSO SALVATORE, b. Newark, N.J., Feb. 22, 1911; LL.B., N.J. Law Sch., 1934; J.D., Rutgers U., 1970. Admitted to N.J. bar, 1935; individual practice law, Newark, 1935-42; classification officer, adj. gen. dept., U.S. Army, 1942-46; atty. Housing Authority, Newark, 1946-75, asst. exec dir. mgmt. services, 1970-72, dir. housing, 1972-75; individual practice law, Verona, N.J., 1975—; senatorial legis. aide, State of N.J., 1968-70. Pres. bd. dirs. Boys Club Newark, 1966. Mem. Nat. Housing Conf., Nat. Assn. Housing and Redevel. Officials, AMVETS (pub. relations dir., N.J. 1946). Contbr. articles to law jours. Home and Office: 50 Fairview Ave Verona NJ 07044 Tel (201) 239-7030

ROACH, CHARLES MICHAEL, b. Canton, Ga., Mar. 17, 1948; B.A., Ga. State U., 1971; J.D., U. Ga., 1974. Admitted to Ga. bar, 1974; pvt. practice law, Canton, Ga., 1974—. Mem. Cherokee County Community Action Com., Canton, Ga., 1975-76; asst. scoutmaster Troop 817 Canton council Boy Scouts Am., 1975—. Mem. Cherokee County Realtors Assn., Canton (treas. 1976), Blue Ridge, Ga. bar assns. Home: Route 8 Lakeview Estates Canton GA 30114 Office: PO Box 677 Canton GA 30114 Tel (404) 479-1406

ROACH, JAMES TURNER, b. Silver City, N.Mex., Nov. 2, 1944; B.A., U. N.Mex., 1965, J.D., 1968. Admitted to N.Mex. bar, 1968; individual practice law, Albuquerque, 1968-72; partner firm Klecan & Roach, Profl. Assn., Albuquerque, 1972—. Mem. N.Mex., Am. bar assns. Home: 7009 Marilyn Ave NE Albuquerque NM 87109 Office: suite 1221 505 Marquette St NW Albuquerque NM 87101 Tel (505) 243-7731

ROACH, JOHN L., b. Chgo., Jan. 16, 1924; student Pa. Mil. Coll., 1943-44, DePaul U., 1945-46; J.D., Ill. Inst. Tech.-Chgo. Kent Coll. Law, 1949. Admitted to Ill. bar, 1950, U.S. Supreme Ct. bar, 1954; asst. atty. gen. Ill., 1953-57; gen. counsel. office Pub. Adminstr. Cook County, Chgo., 1969-74; individual practice law, Chgo., 1957—; lectr. law DePaul U., Chgo., 1953-73. Mem. Ill., Chgo. bar assns., Spl. Agts. Assn. Home: 7800 Augusta St River Forest IL 60305 Office: 72 W Adams St Chicago IL 60603 Tel (312) 236-2085

ROACH, MICHAEL L., b. Oak Park, Ill., Feb. 23, 1941; A.B., DePauw U., 1963; J.D., U. Ill., 1966. Admitted to Ill. bar, 1966, U.S. Supreme Ct. bar, 1976; asso. firm Hall, Meyer, Fisher, Holmberg & Snook, Waukegan, Ill., 1966-72, partner, 1972—. Mem. dist. adv. council SBA, 1973—; bd. dirs. Young Men's Fellowship, half-way house, Waukegan. Mem. Am., Ill. State, Chgo., Lake County (sec. 1974-76) bar assns. Office: 25 N County St Waukegan IL 60085 Tel (312) 244-0600

ROADMAN, ROBERT DWIGHT, b. Johnstown, Pa., Dec. 3, 1939; B.A., Yale U., 1961; J.D., George Washington U., 1966. Admitted to D.C., Va. bars, 1966; law clk. U.S. Dist. judge for D.C., 1965-67; asso. firm Danzansky, Dickey, Tydings, Quint & Gordon, Washington, 1967-72, partner, 1972—. Mem. Am., D.C. bar assns., Am. Judicature Soc., Nat. Lawyers Club, Order of Coif. Home: 3045 Normanstone Terr NW Washington DC 20008 Office: 1120 Connecticut Ave NW Washington DC 20036 Tel (202) 331-8700

ROADY, THOMAS G., JR., b. Kane, Ill., Apr. 27, 1918; A.B., U. Ill., 1940, J.D., 1948, M.A., 1949; grad. fellow Columbia, 1948-49. Admitted to Ill. bar, 1948, Tenn. bar, 1949; with JAGC, USAF Res., 1948-69; asst. prof., asso. prof., prof. U. Tenn. Coll. Law, 1949-52, prof. law, 1968-73; asso. prof., asst. dean Washington U. Sch. Law, St. Louis, 1951-52; mem. firm McDonald & Roady, Carrollton, Ill., 1952-56; prof. law Vanderbilt U., Nashville, 1956-58; asso. dean, prof. law So. Ill. U. Sch. Law, Carbondale, 1973—; vis. prof. U. Mo. Sch. Law, 1954-55; city atty. Carrollton, 1952-56; cons. Tenn. Div. Water Resources, 1963-67. Mem. Am. Bar Assn. Recipient Robert Noxon Toppan prize Columbia, 1949; author: (with Andersen) Professional Negligence, 1960; (with Covington) Selected Problems in the Law of Corporate Practice, 1960; Essays on Procedure and Evidence, 1961; contbr. articles to legal jours. Home: 1209 W Freeman St Carbondale IL 62901 Office: So Ill U Sch Law Carbondale IL 62901 Tel (618) 547-7411

ROANG, SVERRE, b. Stoughton, Wis., Jan. 17, 1915; B.A. in History and Polit. Sci., U. Wis., 1935, LL.D., 1937. Admitted to Wis. bar, 1938; asso. firm Slagg & Roang and predecessor firm, Edgerton, Wis., 1946-60; judge Rock County Ct., Br. 1, Janesville, 1960—; attended Fgn. Affairs Seminar, Cranbrook Sch. in Mich., 1957; atty. Bd. Edn., Edgerton; legal counsel, trustee Milton Coll.; U.S. del. Diplomatic Conf. on Wills, Washington, 1973; faculty Wis. Jud. Coll. Chmn., Tobacco Days Celebration, Edgerton, 1974; chmn. Acad. Selection Com. in Wis., Sen. Proxmires Acad. Selection Bd., 1956—; chmn. Camporee, Sinnissippi council Boy Scouts Am., 1970-76, organizer Bicentennial Camporee, 1976, mem. adv. bd., 1953-77, mem. exec. bd. Indian Trails council, 1951-53; treas., pres. Edgerton Bd. Edn., 1947-61; chmn. Democratic State Convs., 1953-59; co-chmn. Dollars for Dems., 1940; 1st Dist. chmn. Young Progressives, 1940; bd. dirs. Rock County Rehab. Services; trustee Albion Acad. Hist. Soc. Mem. Am., Wis., Rock County (v.p. 1959-60) bar assns., Wis. Bd. County Judges (chmn.), Wis. Bd. Juvenile Ct. Judges (sec.), Nat. Council Juvenile Ct. Judges (trustee, chmn. pub. info. com.), Am. Judicature Soc., Edgerton VFW, Judge Adv. Gen.'s Assn., Mil. Order World Wars, Fifth Army Div. Assn., Wis. Sch. Bds. Assn., Sons of Norway, Res. Officers Assn. Recipient Silver Beaver and Lamb awards Boy Scouts Am., 1959, Freedoms Found. George Washington medal, 1954, citation for editorial in Wis. Vet., 1964; author: Special Assessments in Wisconsin, 1957; editor: Wis. Vet., 1953-68. Home: 204 Bentley Pl Edgerton WI 53534 Office: 51 S Main St Courthouse Br 1 Janesville WI 53545 Tel (608) 752-7471

ROBARDS, HERBERT DAVID, b. Joplin, Mo., June 26, 1937; B.A., U. Mo., 1959, J.D., 1972. Admitted to Mo. bar, 1972; asst. atty. gen. State of Mo., 1972-74; asst. fed. pub. defender Western dist. Mo., Kansas City, 1974—. Mem. Mo. Bar Assn. Editor-in-chief U. Mo. at Kansas City Law Rev., 1971-72. Tel (816) 374-5851

ROBB, ARVIN OSWALD, b. Hanford, Wash., May 17, 1915; LL.B., U. Oreg., 1937, J.D., 1971. Admitted to Oreg. bar, 1937, Calif. bar, 1947; practiced in Baker, Oreg., 1937-42, San Jose, Calif., 1947-66; dist. atty. Baker County (Oreg.), 1940-42; served with JAGC U.S. Army, 1943-46; capt. War Crimes Trials, Japan, 1946; judge Municipal Ct., San Jose, 1966—. Office: Courthouse San Jose CA 95113 Tel (408) 299-2264

ROBB, FRANK BELFIELD, b. Washington, May 10, 1913; ed. Case Western Res. U., 1935; J.D., Cleve. Law Sch., 1945. Admitted to Ohio bar, 1945; partner firm Robb and Robb, Willoughby, Ohio, 1950-75, individual practice as Robb and Robb, Willoughby, 1975—. Mem. Cleve. Patent Law Assn., Soc. Automotive Engrs. Home: 37750 Euclid Ave Willoughby OH 44094 Office: 37750 Euclid Ave Willoughby OH 44094 Tel (216) 951-2211

ROBB, JAMES JOSEPH, b. Richland Center, Wis., June 19, 1949; B.A., U. Wis., Madison, 1971; J.D., Marquette U., 1974. Admitted to Wis. bar, 1974; partner firm Robb Law Offices, Richland Center, 1974—. Mem. State Bar Wis., Richland County (Wis.) Bar Assn. (pres. 1975-76). Lead article editor Marquette Law Rev., 1973-74. Office: 161 N Central Ave Richland Center WI 53581 Tel (608) 647-2176

ROBB, JOHN A., b. Hillsville, Pa., June 18, 1910; B.S., Duquesne U., 1933; LL.B., U. Pitts. Admitted to U.S. Ct. Appeals 3d Circuit bar, Pa. Supreme Ct. bar, U.S. Supreme Ct. bar; counsel dept. labor State of Pa., 1937, dir. workmen's compensation, 1938-39; spl. asst. solicitor City of Pitts., 1939-55; partner firm Robb, Leonard & Mulvihill, Pitts. Mem. Pa., Allegheny County (pres. 1960) bar assns., Am. Law Inst., Internat. Trial Acad., Allegheny County Trial Acad., Judicial Counsel of the 3d Circuit Ct. of Appeals. Home: 220 Orchard Dr Pittsburgh PA 15228 Office: 1212 Frick Bldg Pittsburgh PA 15219

ROBBINS, CHARLES EARL, b. Jennings, La., Nov. 6, 1922; LL.B., George Washington U., 1949. Admitted to D.C. bar, 1949; atty. War Claims Commn., Washington, 1949-54; individual practice law, Washington, 1954—. Mem. Am. Trial Lawyers Assn., Fed., D.C. bar assns. Author: Attorney's Master Guide to Expediting Top Dollar Case Settlements, 1975; contbr. article to legal jour. Office: 1086 Nat Press Bldg Washington DC 20045 Tel (202) 223-5554

ROBBINS, J. ARTHUR, b. Bklyn., Aug. 21, 1935; A.B., W.Va. Wesleyan Coll., 1958; LL.B., J.D., George Washington U., 1961. Admitted to N.Y. bar, 1962, U.S. Supreme Ct. bar, 1967; individual practice law, Bklyn.; small claims arbitrator civil ct. City of N.Y. Sec. Bergen Beach Civic Assn., Bklyn.; chmn., founder Themis Soc. Mem. N.Y. State, Bklyn., Am. Bar Assns., Brandeis Assn. (mem. bd. dirs.). Contbr. articles to legal publs. Office: 26 Court St Brooklyn NY 11242 Tel (212) 875-3511

ROBBINS, LOUIS PETERS, b. Phila., July 26, 1931; B.A., George Washington U., 1951; LL.B., Harvard U., 1954. Admitted to D.C. bar, 1957, U.S. Supreme Ct. bar, 1971; asst. corp. counsel D.C. Govt., 1957-65, prin. dep. corp. counsel, 1973—; asso. firm Grossberg, Yochelson, Brill & Fox, Washington, 1965-70; partner firm Grossberg, Yochelson, Fox & Beyda, Washington, 1971-72; chmn. D.C. Contract Appeals Bd., 1972. Mem. D.C. Bar, Fed., D.C., Am. bar assns., Am. Soc. Hosp. Attys., Nat. Assn. Coll. and Univ. Attys. Home: 2747 Unicorn Ln NW Washington DC 20015 Office: Rm 329 Dist Bldg 14th and E Sts NW Washington DC 20004 Tel (202) 629-3858

ROBBINS, MAURICE, b. Freeland, Pa., Apr. 8, 1905; LL.B., Detroit Coll. Law, 1930. Admitted to Mich. bar, 1930; individual practice law. Trustee Village of Bingham Farms, Mich., 1964-72. Mem. Mich. Bar Assn. Home: 22700 Saratoga St Southfield MI 48075 Office: 20131 James Couzens Detroit MI 48235 Tel (313) 342-5150

ROBBINS, NORMAN, b. N.Y.C., May 27, 1922; B.S., Coll. City N.Y., 1942; J.D., Georgetown U., 1950. Admitted to Washington bar, 1950, N.Y. bar, 1951, N.J. bar, 1960; br. mgr. Hearthstone Ins. Co. Am., N.Y.C., 1951-60; mem. firm Wilentz. Goldman & Spitzer, Perth Amboy, N.J., 1960-61; individual practice law, Woodbridge, N.J., 1961—. Mem. Am., N.J. State, Middlesex County, N.J. bar assns. Home: 50 Webb Dr Fords NJ 08863 Office: 568 Amboy Ave Woodbridge NJ 07095 Tel (201) 636-1600

ROBBINS, VERNON EARL, b. Balt., Aug. 16, 1921; B.A., Eastern U., 1942; J.D., U. Balt., 1959. Admitted to Md. bar, 1952; revenue agt. IRS, Balt., 1945-52; partner firm Robbins & Adams, Cambridge, Md., 1952—; individual practice law, Cambridge, 1952—. Mem. Am. Inst. C.P.A.'s, Am., N.D. bar assns., Am. Assn. Attys. and C.P.A.'s, Md. Assn. C.P.A.'s, Nat. Assn. Accountants, Am. Judicature Soc. Home: 120 Riverside Rd Cambridge MD 21613 Office: PO Box 236 Cambridge MD 21613 Tel (301) 228-0565

ROBE, EDWARD SCOTT, b. Cumberland, Ohio, July 9. 1936; A.B., Ohio U., 1959; LL.B., Duke, 1963. Admitted to Ohio bar, 1963, U.S. Supreme Ct. bar, 1968; partner firm Bridgewater & Robe, Athens, Ohio, 1965—; mem. bd. grievances and discipline Ohio Supreme Ct., 1975—. Mem. Athens County Bd. Elections, 1970—; trustee Sheltering Arms Hosp. Found. Mem. Am., Ohio (past mem. exec. com.), Athens County (past pres.) bar assns., Am. Judicature Soc. Home: 19 Roosevelt Dr Athens OH 45701 Office: Bridgewaeter & Robe 14 W Washington St Athens OH 45701 Tel (614) 593-5576

ROBERGE, WILLIAM HENRY, JR., b. Douglas, Ariz., Sept. 23, 1944; A.B., Tufts U., 1966; J.D., Georgetown U., 1969. Admitted to D.C. bar, 1969; asso. firms Smith & Pepper, Washington, 1969-72, Powell & Becker, Washington, 1972-74, Robert D. Powell, Washington, 1974-75; individual practice law, Washington, 1975-77; asso. firm Gordon & Healy, Washington, 1977—. Mem. D.C. Bar, D.C., Am., Fed. bar assns., Assn. Trial Lawyers Am. Home: 303 Currier Dr Rockville MD 20850 Office: 1821 Jefferson Pl NW Washington DC 20036 Tel (202) 785-5020

ROBERSON, GEORGE GALE, b. Gale, Ill., Dec. 12, 1903; A.B., U. Ill., 1925; J.D., Harvard U., 1929. Admitted to Ill. bar, 1930; individual practice law, Chgo., 1930-38; atty. SEC, Chgo., 1938-49; asso. firm Arvey, Hodes, Costello & Burman, and predecessors, Chgo., 1949-61, partner, 1961-75; instr. law DePaul U., Chgo., 1931-39; profl. lectr. bus. law Northwestern U., Chgo. and Evanston, 1939-75; cons., 1975—. Mem. Chgo., Ill. State, Am. bar assns., Am. Bus. Law Assn., Phi Beta Kappa. Author: (with Hodes) Law of Mobile Homes, 1957, 3d edit., 1974; (with Smith) Business Law, Uniform Commercial Code Edition, 1961, 4th edit., 1977. Home: 1112 Elmwood Ave Wilmette IL 60091 Office: Room 3800 1B0 N LaSalle St Chicago IL 60601 Tel (312) 855-5000

ROBERTI, ANTHONY, b. N.Y.C., Feb. 12, 1946; B.A., Swarthmore Coll., 1964; J.D., Boston Coll., 1971. Admitted to Pa. bar, 1972; asso. firm Martin H. Philip, Palmerton, Pa., 1972, Nanovic & McKinley, Jim Thorpe, Pa., 1973-75; individual practice law, Jim Thorpe, 1975—. Bd. dirs. Jim Thorpe YMCA, 1976—; local chpt. Arthritis Found. Mem. Pa., Carbon County (trustee 1976) bar assns. Home: 703 South St Jim Thorpe PA 18229 Office: 56 Broadway St Jim Thorpe PA 18229 Tel (717) 325-3623

ROBERTROY, MARTHA, b. Erie, Pa., Jan. 2, 1913; J.D., Woodrow Wilson Coll. Law, 1968. Admitted to Ga. bar, 1969; mem. firm Poole, Pearce, Cooper & Smith, Atlanta, 1957-69, asso. atty., 1969—. Mem. Ga. Assn. Women Lawyers (pres. 1976—), Am., Atlanta, Ga. bar assns., Ga., Nat. assns. parliamentarians. Home: 620 Peachtree St NE Atlanta GA 30308 Office: suite 310 57 Executive Park S NE Atlanta GA 30329 Tel (404) 325-8196

ROBERTS, ALBERT PHILIP, b. Bronx, N.Y., Feb. 3, 1945; B.A. in History, Siena Coll., 1966; J.D., Suffolk U., 1970. Admitted to N.Y. bar, 1971; asso. firm Russell E. Aldrich, Poughkeepsie, N.Y., 1970—. Bd. dirs. Sloper-Willen Ambulance Service, Inc., Wappingers Falls, N.Y., 1976—. Mem. N.Y., Dutchess County (N.Y.) bar assns. Home: 19 Central Ave Wappingers Falls NY 12590 Office: PO Box 3329 21 Davis Ave Poughkeepsie NY 12603 Tel (914) 454-5150

ROBERTS, B. K., b. Sopchoppy, Fla., Feb. 5, 1907; J.D., U. Fla., 1928; LL.D. (hon.), U. Miami, 1954. Admitted to Fla. bar, 1928; individual practice law, Tallahassee, 1928-49; justice Fla. Supreme Ct., 1949—, chief justice, 1953-54, 61-63, 71-72; chmn. Jud. Adminstrv. Commn., 1971-72; mem. Fla. Constl. Revision Commn., 1968-70; chmn. com. to revise jud. article Fla. Constitution, 1972; lectr. Am. appellate system St. Catherine's Coll., Oxford, Eng., summer 1974. Former pres. Fla. Heritage Found.; pres. Fla. State U. Found.; mem. bd. counselors Fla. Presbyn. Coll.; mem. awards jury Freedoms Found., 1962; mem. council advisers Fla. A. and M. U., 1975—. Fellow Am. Bar Found.; mem. Nat. Conf. Chief Justices (dep. chmn. 1972-73), Fla. Jud. Council (chmn.), Interam., Internat., Am., Fla., Tallahassee (past pres.) bar assns., Am. Law Inst., Soc. Wig and Robe, U. Miami Coll. Law, Delta Chi, Phi Alpha Delta, Alpha Kappa Psi. Recipient Distinguished Citizens's award Stetson Law Coll., 1962, also Fla. State U. Gold Key, U. Fla. Blue Key. Office: 421 Meridian Pl Tallahassee FL 32303 Tel (904) 385-3019

ROBERTS, BARRY, b. Chgo., Jan. 5, 1943; A.B., North Park Coll., 1964; J.D., U. Chgo., 1967. Admitted to D.C. bar, 1968, U.S. Supreme Ct. bar, 1971; with office of gen. counsel, ICC, Washington, 1967-70, office of gen. counsel AID, Washington, 1971-72; with firm Pope Ballard and Loos, Washington, 1972—, mem. firm, 1977—. Mem. Am., Fed., D.C. bar assns., Assn. ICC Practitioners (chmn. D.C. chpt. 1976-77). Home: 815 C St SE Washington DC 20003 Office: 888 17th St NW Washington DC 20006 Tel (202) 298-8600

ROBERTS, BENJAMIN C., b. Bklyn., Oct. 3, 1913; A.B., Bklyn. Coll., 1935; M.A. in Indsl. Relations, U. Chgo., 1936; J.D., Bklyn. Law Sch., 1948. Admitted to N.Y. bar, 1948; examiner N.Y. State Labor Relations Bd., 1941-44; mediator, arbitrator, acting gen. counsel N.Y. State Bd. Mediation, 1944-50; pub. mem. grievance bd. N.Y. State Civil Service Commn., 1958-63, pub. employees relations bd. panels, 1967—, N.Y.C. office of collective bargaining disputes and arbitration panel, 1967—; adv. arbitrator, mem. Pres.-apptd. emergency bds., 1955, 57, 58, 60; instr. extension div. sch. indsl. and labor relations Cornell U., 1948-60; mem. adv. com. N.Y. U. Conf. on Labor, 1960-68, 71—; mem. regional adv. conf. com. Region II, NLRB; mem. panels of arbitrators Fed. Mediation and Conciliation Service, Am. Arbitration Assn., N.J. and N.Y. State bds. mediation; chmn. N.Y. State Unified Ct. System Pub. Employees Employment Relations Bd., N.J. State Employment Relations Commn., Office of Collective Bargaining, City of N.Y. Mem. Nat. Acad. Arbitrators (bd. govs. 1956-59, v.p. 1960-62, chmn. N.Y. region 1960-61), Indsl. Relations Research Assn. (pres. N.Y. region 1960-61), Assn. Bar City N.Y. (com. on labor and social security legis. 1962-64, 65-66, 70-71), Am. (pub. mem. com. on labor arbitration and law of collective bargaining agreements 1967—), N.Y. State (com. on labor law, 1970-73) bar assns. Contbr. articles to legal jours. Address: 850 7th Ave New York City NY 10019 Tel (212) 541-9140

ROBERTS, BRUCE KELLER, b. Chgo., Mar. 31, 1940; B.A., Miami U., 1963; J.D. cum laude, Northwestern U., 1968. Admitted to Ill. bar, 1968; asso. firm Schuyler, Ballard & Cowen, Chgo., 1968-72, partner, 1973—. Mem. Am., Ill., Chgo. bar assns., Omicron Delta Kappa. Home: 48 Country Club Ct Palatine IL 60067 Office: 100 W Monroe St Chicago IL 60603

ROBERTS, BURTON BENNETT, b. N.Y.C., July 25, 1922; A.B., N.Y. U., 1943, LL.M., 1953; LL.B., Cornell U., 1949. Admitted to N.Y. bar, 1949, U.S. Supreme Ct. bar, 1967; asst. dist. atty. N.Y. County, N.Y.C., 1949-66; chief asst. dist. atty. Bronx County, N.Y.C., 1966-68, dist. atty., 1968-72; Justice N.Y. State Supreme Ct., N.Y.C., 1973—. Mem. Am., N.Y. State, N.Y. County, Bronx County bar assns., N.Y. State (pres. 1971-72), Nat. Dist. Attys. Assns. Home: 136 E 55th St New York City NY 10022 Office: 100 Centre St New York City NY 10013 Tel (212) 374-4782

ROBERTS, DAVID LAWRENCE, b. Mesa, Ariz., Sept. 15, 1935; B.S. in Accounting, Ariz. State U., 1960; J.D., U. Ariz., 1961. Admitted to Ariz. bar, 1961, U.S. Supreme Ct. bar, 1971; partner firm Johnson, Shelley & Roberts, Mesa, 1961—; asst. city atty. City of Mesa, 1963—. Bd. mgrs. Mesa YMCA; bd. dirs. Mesa United Way. Mem. Am., Ariz., Tri-City (past pres.) bar assns., Mesa C. of C. (dir. 1968-71). C.P.A., Ariz. Office: 48 N Macdonald St Mesa AZ 85201 Tel (602) 964-1421

ROBERTS, DAVID LEE, b. Ryan, Okla., July 2, 1934; B.S., Colo. State U., 1955; J.D., Denver U., 1959. Admitted to Colo. bar, 1959; asso. firm George A. Epperson and Donald F. McClary, Ft. Morgan, Colo., 1960-62; individual practice law, Ft. Morgan, 1962—; city atty. Ft. Morgan, 1964—; dep. dist. atty. 13th Jud. Dist., 1969—. Mem. Colo., 13th Dist. (pres.) bar assns. Office: 230 Main St Fort Morgan CO 80701 Tel (303) 867-8235

ROBERTS, DAVID RHODES, b. Mpls., July 7, 1920; A.B., Harvard, 1942, J.D., 1945. Admitted to Minn. bar, 1949; law clk. chief justice Minn. Supreme Ct., St. Paul, 1948-49; atty. Minn. Dept. Taxation, St. Paul, 1949-51; gen. atty. Bauer & Black div. Kendall Co., Chgo., 1951-53; asso. firm Sullivan, Stringer, Donnelly & Sharood, St. Paul, 1953-56, partner, 1956-58; tax counsel Mpls. Star & Tribune Co., 1958-65; gen. counsel Bush Mgmt. Co., St. Paul, Winter Park, Fla., 1962—; adj. prof. law, William Mitchell Coll. Law, St. Paul, 1953-62. Bd. dirs. St. Paul Gallery and Sch. of Art, 1955-62, St. Paul Council Arts and Scis., 1959-62; pres. Edyth Bush Charitable Found., Winter Park, 1966—. Mem. Am., Minn., Ramsey County, Hennepin County bar assns. Contbr. articles to profl. jours. Office: 1260 NW National Bank Bldg St Paul MN 55101 or 650 Barnett National Bank Bldg Winter Park FL 32789 Tel (612) 224-8118

ROBERTS, EDWIN HAYES, JR., b. Meridian, Miss., June 5, 1948; B.B.A., U. Miss., 1969, J.D., 1972. Admitted to Miss. bar, 1972; partner firm McCormick & Roberts, Oxford, Miss., 1972-74, Lamb & Roberts, Oxford, 1974-75, Roberts & Duke, Oxford, 1976—. Mem. Am., Miss., Lafayette County bar assns., Phi Alpha Delta. Office: 1115 Jackson St Oxford MS 38655 Tel (601) 234-4031

ROBERTS, FARRELL EUGENE, b. Salt Lake City, Mar. 29, 1922; B.S., U.S. Naval Acad., 1944; LL.B., U. Mich., 1949. Admitted to Mich. bar, 1949; mem. firm Dieterle & Roberts, Pontiac, Mich., 1954-66; mem. Mich. Ho. of Reps., 1956-60, Mich. Senate, 1961-66; judge Circuit Ct. Oakland County, Pontiac, 1967—. Bd. visitors U. Mich. Law Sch. Mem. Am. Judicature Soc., Mich. Trial Lawyers Assn. Office: 1200 N Telegraph Rd Pontiac MI 48053 Tel (313) 858-0355

ROBERTS, GEORGE HUNTER, b. N.Y.C., Jan. 26, 1936; B.A., Manhattan Coll., 1959; J.D., N.Y. U., 1962. Admitted to N.Y. bar, 1962, U.S. Supreme Ct. bar, 1969; partner firm Covey, Roberts & Buchanan, Katonah, N.Y., 1970—; justice Town of Lewisboro (N.Y.), 1970—; dist. atty. Katonah-Lewisboro Schs., 1975—. Chmn. Lewisboro Narcotics Guidance Council, 1971-73. Mem. Am., N.Y. State, Westchester County (chmn. real property sect. 1972-73), No. Westchester (pres. 1975-76) bar assns., Am. Judicature Soc. Office: 254 Katonah Ave Katonah NY 10536 Tel (914) 232-5161

ROBERTS, GRADY LAWRENCE, JR., b. San Antonio, Feb. 3, 1944; B.A., St. Mary's U., 1966, J.D., 1969. Admitted to Tex. bar, 1969, U.S. Ct. Mil. Appeals, 1969, U.S. Supreme Ct. bar, 1975; served with JAGC, U.S. Army, 1969-73; with Alamo Title Co., San Antonio, 1973-74; individual practice law, Pearsall, Tex., 1974—. Bd. dirs. Frio Hosp., sec., 1976; bd. dirs. Frio Pioneer Jail Mus., Pearsall Devel. Co. Mem. Tex. Criminal Def. Lawyers Assn. Recipient Am. Jurisprudence award fed. taxation, 1969, constl. law, 1969. Home: 565 Margo Dr Pearsall TX 78061 Office: 303 E Comal St Pearsall TX 78061 Tel (512) 334-2909

ROBERTS, HOWARD TOPOL, b. N.Y.C., Apr. 2, 1931; B.S., Yale U., 1953; J.D., Harvard U., 1958. Admitted to N.Y. bar, 1959; asso. firm Jacob Gruber, N.Y.C., 1959-69; counsel U.S. Banknote Corp., N.Y.C., 1969—, sec., 1976—. Mem. Am., N.Y. bar assns., N.Y. County Lawyers Assn. Home: 126 E 24th St New York City NY 10010 Office: 345 Hudson St New York City NY 10014 Tel (212) 741-8568

ROBERTS, JAMES CARLTON, b. Long Beach, Calif., Oct. 18, 1945; B.A., Claremont Men's Coll., 1968; J.D., Harvard U., 1971. Admitted to Calif. bar, 1972; asso. firm Gibson, Dunn & Crutcher, Los Angeles, 1971—. Vice chmn. legis. subcom. Los Angeles Area C. of C. Mem. Calif., Los Angeles County bar assns., Indsl. Relations Research Assn. Home: 1 Blue River St Irvine CA Office: 515 S Flower St Los Angeles CA 90071 Tel (213) 488-7342

ROBERTS, JEROME JOSEPH, b. Chgo., Nov. 11, 1943; B.B.A. with distinction, U. Mich., 1965, J.D. cum laude, 1968. Admitted to Ill. bar, 1968, U.S. Dist. Ct. bar for No. Dist. Ill., 1968, U.S. Tax Ct. bar, 1973; partner firm Jenner & Block, Chgo.; lectr. in computers and the law Northwestern U., 1970—, Chgo-Kent Coll. Law, 1974—; dir. 1st Trust & Savings Bank of Glenview (Ill.), 1st Glenview Bancorp., Inc. Mem. Chgo. Council Lawyers, Am. Bar Assn. C.P.A., Ill. Office: Suite 4400 One IBM Plaza Chicago IL 60611 Tel (312) 222-9350

ROBERTS, JOHN WALLACE, b. Stamford, Conn., Aug. 3, 1932; B.A., Yale, 1954; J.D., U. Pa., 1958. Admitted to Conn. bar, 1958, U.S. Supreme Ct. bar, 1963; trial atty., criminal div. U.S. Dept. Justice, Washington, 1958-59; law clk. to jude U.S. Dist. Ct., So. Dist. N.Y., 1961; asso. firm Ivey, Barnum & O'Mara, Greenwich, Conn., 1959-62, partner, 1962-72; partner firm Silver and Roberts, Stamford, 1972-73; prin. John W. Roberts, Stamford, 1973, Roberts & Stewart, Stamford and Greenwich, 1974—. Mem. Greenwich Town Meeting, 1967—, municipal bldg. com., 1976—, mem. Greenwich Democratic Town Com., 1976—. Mem. Am., Conn., Stamford, Greenwich bar assns., Fed. Bar Council. Editorial bd. U. Pa. Law Rev., 1956-58. Home: 242 Taconic Rd Greenwich CT 06830 Office: 1 Landmark Sq Stamford CT 06901 Tel (203) 324-6755

ROBERTS, LARRY LEE, b. Charlotte, Mich., Mar. 5, 1942; B.A., U.Md., 1970; J.D., U. Detroit, 1973. Admitted to Mich. bar, 1974; asst. prosecuting atty. Wayne County, Detroit, 1974—; chmn. legal com. Indian Village Assn. Mem. Am. (mem. criminal law sect.), Mich. (criminal law sect., mem. prosecutors appellate forum) bar assns., Nat. Dist. Attys. Assn. Home: 1431 Seminole St Detroit MI 48214 Office: 1441 St Antoine St Detroit MI 48226 Tel (313) 224-5796

ROBERTS, LARRY STEVENSON, b. Richmond, Ky., Nov. 22, 1943; B.A., U. Ky., LL.B., 1969. Admitted to Ky. bar, 1969; since practiced in Lexington, including individual practice; pub. defender, 1969-72; asst. prosecutor Office of Atty. Commonwealth of Ky., 1972—; adj. prof. law U. Ky., 1970—; police instr. Ky. Law Enforcement Council, 1975—. Mem. Nat. Dist. Attys. Assn. Home: 1278 Scoville Rd Lexington KY 40502 Office: 300 W Main St Lexington KY 40507 Tel (606) 252-3571

ROBERTS, MICHAEL JAMES, b. Salisbury, Md., Nov. 2, 1936; A.B., Duke U., 1958; J.D., Am. U., 1965. Admitted to Md. bar, 1966, D.C. bar, 1966, U.S. Supreme Ct., 1970; asso. law firm Verner, Liipfert, Bernhard & McPherson, Washington, 1965-70, partner, 1970—. Mem. D.C. Bar, Md. State Bar, Am. Bar Assn. (mem. transp. subcom. on aviation. Editor-in-Chief Am. U. Law Review, 1964-65. Home: 202 Dale Dr Silver Spring MD 20910 Office: 1660 L St NW Washington DC 20036 Tel (202) 452-7432

ROBERTS, PATRICK KENT, b. Waynesville, Mo., Feb. 9, 1948; A.B. with honors, U. Mo., Columbia, 1970, J.D., 1973; postgrad. U. Ill., Urbana, 1970-71. Employment security dep. Mo. Div. Employment Security, Columbia, 1971; admitted to Mo. bar, 1974; asst. to Senator Stuart Symington, Columbia, 1973-76; asso. firm Daniel, Clampett, Rittershouse, Dalton & Chaney, Springfield, Mo., 1976—. Mem. Mo. Bar, Am., Greene County (Mo.) bar assns., Scabbard & Blade, Phi Beta Kappa, Phi Eta Sigma. Office: PO Box 1397 SSS Park Central Towers Springfield MO 65805 Tel (417) 865-6641

ROBERTS, RANDALL LEE, b. Beeville, Tex., Nov. 3, 1946; B.A., U. Tex., 1969, J.D., 1972. Admitted to Tex. bar, 1973; mem. firm Potter, Guinn, Minton & Dickerson, Tyler, Tex., 1973—. Mem. E. Tex. Estate Planning Council, Smith County (sec. 1975-76), Tex., Am. bar assns., Smith County Jr. Bar Assn. (pres. 1976-77). Home: 3301 S Broadway Tyler TX 75701 Office: PO Box 359 Tyler TX 75701 Tel (214) 597-8311

ROBERTS, RICHARD SOLBERG, b. Blue Earth County, Minn., Dec. 4, 1926; B.A., Mankato State Coll., 1951; B.S.L., St. Paul Coll. Law, 1952, LL.B., 1954. Admitted to Minn. bar, 1954; individual practice law, Elbow Lake, Minn., 1954-67, Morris, Minn., 1967-71; judge Alexandria County Ct., Minn., 1971—. Pres. Community Meml. Hosp., Elbow Lake, 1960-64. Mem. Douglas-Grant, Minn. State, Am. bar assns. Home: Box 286 Alexandria MN 56308 Office: Douglas County Ct House Alexandria MN 65308 Tel (612) 762-2395

ROBERTS, ROBERT, JR., b. Minden, La., Sept. 20, 1903; B.A., La. State U., 1923, J.D., 1925. Admitted to La. bar, 1925, U.S. Supreme Ct. bar, 1938; mem. legal dept. Ark. Natural Gas Corp., 1934-53, chief atty., 1939-53; mem. firm Blanchard, Walker, O'Quin & Roberts, and predecessor, Shreveport, La., 1953—; dir. Ark. La. Gas Co., Md. Co., Inc., Shadyside Co., Ltd. Mem. La. State U. Found.; gov. La. Civil Service League. Mem. Am., Fed. Power, La. (ho. of dels. 1957-58), Shreveport (pres. 1962) bar assns., Order of Coif. Home: 724 Elmwood Ave Shreveport LA 71104 Office: 1st National Bank Tower Shreveport LA 71163 Tel (318) 221-6858

ROBERTS, SIDNEY I., b. Bklyn., Nov. 29, 1913; B.B.A., Coll. City N.Y., 1935; LL.B. magna cum laude, Harvard, 1938. Admitted to N.Y. State bar, 1938, U.S. Supreme Ct. bar, 1960; partner firm Roosevelt, Friedin & Littauer, N.Y.C., 1950-56, firm Anderson & Roberts, N.Y.C., 1956-57, firm Roberts & Holland, N.Y.C., 1957—; adj. prof. law, Columbia, 1971—. C.P.A., N.Y. Mem. Internat., Am., N.Y. State bar assns., Internat. Fiscal Assn., N.Y. State Soc. C.P.A.'s. Author: (with William C. Warren) U.S. Income Taxation of Foreign Corporations and Nonresident Aliens, 1966-71; (with others) Annotated Tax Forms, Practice and Procedure; contbr. articles in field to profl. jours. Home: 145 Central Park W New York City NY 10023 Office: 1301 Ave of the Americas New York City NY 10019 Tel (212) 586-5200

ROBERTS, VIRGIL PATRICK, b. Ventura, Calif., Jan. 4, 1947; A.A., Ventura Coll., 1966; B.A., U. Calif., Los Angeles, 1968; J.D., Harvard, 1972. Admitted to Calif. bar, 1972; mem. firm Pacht, Ross, & Sears, Inc., Los Angeles, 1972-76; sr. partner firm Manning, Reynolds & Roberts, Los Angeles, 1976—. Vol. counsel ACLU, Los Angeles; legal advisory com. Pub. Comm. County Govt., Los Angeles, bd. dirs. Los Angeles Legal Aid Found., 1973-76; sec. Joint Center Community Studies, Los Angeles, 1975-76; pres. Beverly Hills (Calif.) Bar Scholarship Found., 1975-76. Mem. Beverly Hills (bd. govs. 1975-76), Los Angeles bar assns., Beverly Hills Barristers Assn. (bd. govs. 1973-76), Nat. Conf. Black Lawyers, Langston Law Club (dir. 1973-75). Home: 4151 Charlene Dr Los Angeles CA 90043 Office: 1900 Ave of Stars Suite 2840 Los Angeles CA 90067 Tel (213) 277-4796

ROBERTS, WILLIAM, b. Hartford, Conn., 1937; B.A., Tufts U., 1959; LL.B., Columbia, 1962. Admitted to N.Y. bar, 1963; asst. atty. gen. dept. law N.Y. State, N.Y.C., 1963—. Home: 23 Schermerhorn St Brooklyn NY 11201 Office: 2 World Trade Center New York City NY 10047 Tel (212) 488-3375

ROBERTS, WILLIAM B., b. Detroit, Aug. 23, 1939; B.A., Mich. State U., 1961; J.D., U. Mich., 1963. Admitted to Mo. bar, 1964; mem. firm Thompson & Mitchell, St. Louis, 1963-67; atty. Monsanto Co., 1967-70; sec., asso. gen. counsel Chromalloy Am. Corp., Clayton, Mo., 1970-76, exec. v.p. law, gen. counsel, sec., 1976—; co-owner Ed Roberts Cadillac, Inc., Mansfield, Ohio. Mem. Am., Mo., St. Louis (chmn. antitrust sect. 1973) bar assns., Southwestern Legal Found. (dir. and asso. mem. Internat. and Comparative Law Center). Delta Theta Phi. Home: 1516 Chesterfield Lakes Rd Chesterfield MO 63017 Office: 120 S Central St Clayton MO 63105 Tel (314) 721-6777

ROBERTS, WILLIAM DAVID, JR., b. Refugio, Tex., June 4, 1945; B.S., Tex. A. and M. U., 1967; J.D., U. Tex., Austin, 1969. Admitted to Tex. bar, 1971; asso. firm Rhodes and Garner, Port Lavaca, Tex., 1971-74; partner firm Rhodes, Garner & Roberts, Port Lavaca, 1975—. Mem. Port Lavaca C. of C. (dir. 1975-76, pres. 1977), Tex. Jaycees (v.p. 1974), Tex., Calhoun County (pres. 1976), bar assns., Tex. Aggie Bar Assn., Phi Alpha Delta. Named Jaycee of Year, Port Lavaca, 1972. Home: Pine Village Apts #201C Port Lavaca TX 77979 Office: 202 S Ann St Port Lavaca TX 77979 Tel (512) 552-2971

ROBERTS, WILLIAM HENRY, III, b. Buffalo, June 14, 1945; A.B. cum laude, Harvard, 1967; J.D., U. Pa., 1970. Admitted to Pa. bar, 1971, U.S. Supreme Ct. bar, 1974; law clk. Ct. Common Pleas Northampton County (Pa.), 1970, U.S. Dist. Ct. Middle Dist. Pa., 1971-72; asso. firm Blank, Rome, Klaus & Comisky, Phila., 1972—. Mem. Am., Pa., Phila. bar assns. Home: 2308 Delancey Pl Philadelphia PA 19103 Office: 1100 Four Penn Center Plaza Philadelphia PA 19103 Tel (215) LO9-3700

ROBERTSHAW, JAMES, b. Greenville, Miss., May 19, 1916; B.S., Miss. State U., 1937; J.D., Harvard U., 1940, vet. certificate, 1946. Admitted to Miss. bar, 1940, U.S. Supreme Ct. bar, 1967; individual practice law, Greenville, 1940, 46—; with JAGC, U.S. Army, 1941-46; mem. firm Robertshaw & Merideth, Greenville, 1968—. Mem. Miss. Ho. of Reps., 1953-56; chmn. Airport Commn., 1967-73; chmn. Community and County Devel. Commn. Miss. Economic Council, Jackson, 1968-70; pres. Indsl. Found., Greenville, 1974. Decorated Legion of Merit, Croix de Guerre. Office: PO Drawer 1498 Greenville MS 38701 Tel (601) 378-2171

ROBERTSON, BRUCE, JR., b. San Antonio, Sept. 9, 1935; B.A., U. Tex., 1956; J.D. with highest honors, St. Mary's U., 1963. Admitted to Tex. bar, 1963; briefing atty. Tex. Supreme Ct., 1963-64; individual practice law, San Antonio, 1964—. Mem. Am., San Antonio (dir.) bar assns., State Bar Tex. (dir. sect. gen. practice), Am. Tex., San Antonio trial lawyers assns. Recipient James Norvell award Moot Ct. Competition, Charles Lieck-Fred Semaan award, 1963, award for distinguished graduating law student West Pub. Co., Am. Jurisprudence awards. Home: 626 Terrell Rd San Antonio TX 78209 Office: 1000 NBC Bldg San Antonio TX 78205 Tel (512) 225-4001

ROBERTSON, DAVID WYATT, b. Little Rock, Sept. 8, 1937; B.A., La. State U., 1960, LL.B., 1961; LL.M., Yale, 1965, S.J.D., 1968. Admitted to La. bar, 1961, D.C. bar, 1961, Tex. bar, 1976; legis. asst. to Senator Russell B. Long, Washington, 1961-62; asst. prof. law La. State U., Baton Rouge, 1962-64; lectr. law Leeds (Eng.) U., 1965-66; asso. prof. law U. Tex., Austin, 1966-68, prof., 1968—. Mem. Assn. Am. Law Schs., Soc. Am. Law Tchrs., Soc. Bartolus, Order of Coif, Omicron Delta Kappa. Author: Admiralty and Federalism, 1970; contbr. articles in field to legal jours. Office: 2500 Red River Rd Austin TX 78705 Tel (512) 471-5151

ROBERTSON, GERALD DECATUR, b. Newport News, Va., Mar. 6, 1943; B.A., Hampden Sydney Coll., 1966; J.D., Coll. William & Mary, 1969. Admitted to Va. bar, 1969, U.S. Supreme Ct. bar, 1973; asso. firm Jones, Blechman, Woltz & Kelly, Newport News, 1969-76; partner firm Atkinson & Robertson, Newport News, 1976—. Chmn. Am. Cancer Soc., Newport News, 1976. Mem. Am., Va. bar assns., Am. Arbitration Assn., Am., Va. trial lawyers assn. Home: 4 Shirley Rd Newport News VA 23601 Office: PO Box 1336 10504 Warwick Blvd Newport News VA 23601 Tel (804) 599-6300

ROBERTSON, JACK LEIGHTON, b. Condon, Oreg., Sept. 25, 1916; B.S., U.S. Naval Acad., 1938; LL.B., Stanford, 1952. Asst. to regional mgr. Pan Am. World Airways, Alaska, 1938-45, sta. mgr., San Francisco, 1946-47, sr. dispatcher, 1948-53; admitted to Calif. bar, 1952; since practiced in Menlo Park, Calif., individual practice law, 1952-62; partner firm Robertson, Alexander, Luther, Esselstein & Shiells, and predecessor, 1963—, v.p., 1970—; pres. San Mateo County (Calif.) Legal Aid Soc., 1958; bd. visitors Stanford Law Sch., 1967-70; inheritance tax referee State of Calif., 1968-76. Trustee Sequoia Union High Sch., 1969-77, Bay Area United Way, 1972—. Mem. Am., San Mateo County, Palo Alto bar assns. Office: 770 Menlo Ave Menlo Park CA 94025 Tel (415) 324-0622

ROBERTSON, JAMES, b. Cleve., May 18, 1938; A.B., Princeton U., 1959; LL.B., George Washington U., 1965. Admitted to D.C. bar, 1966, U.S. Supreme Ct. bar, 1969; asso. firm Wilmer, Cutler & Pickering, Washington, 1965-69, partner, 1973—; chief counsel Jackson (Miss.) Office, Lawyers' Com. Civil Rights Under Law, 1969-70, nat. dir., Washington, 1971-72. Mem. Am. Bar Assn. Editor-in-chief George Washington Law Rev., 1964-65. Office: 1666 K St NW Washington DC 20006 Tel (202) 872-6167

ROBERTSON, JOE THADDEUS, b. Santa Anna, Tex., Mar. 13, 1921; B.B.A., U. Tex., 1948, J.D., 1960. Admitted to Tex. bar, 1959; individual practice law, Austin, Tex., 1959—. Asst. scoutmaster Boy Scouts Am., Austin, 1964-70; vestryman Episcopal Ch., Austin, 1965-68. Mem. State Bar Tex., Travis County Bar Assn. Home: 3506 Bonnie Rd Austin TX 78703 Office: 1107 Nueces St Austin TX 78701 Tel (512) 477-8144

ROBERTSON, JOHN BERNARD, b. Cleve., Dec. 22, 1936; B.S. in Social Sci. magna cum laude, John Carroll U., 1958; LL.B. summa cum laude, U. Detroit, 1961. Admitted to Ohio bar, 1961, Mich. bar, 1962; with firm Gallagher, Sharp. Fulton, Norman & Mollison, Cleve., 1964—, partner, 1974—; lectr. law Cleve. State U., 1970-74. Mem. Am., Ohio, Greater Cleve. bar assns., Ohio Def. Assn., Def. Research Inst., Internat. Assn. Ins. Counsel. Office: Blkley Bldg Cleveland OH 44115 Tel (216) 241-5310

ROBERTSON, JONATHAN JOSEPH, b. Jackson County, Ind., July 13, 1932; B.S., Ind., 1954; J.D., Vanderbilt U., 1961. Admitted to Ind. bar, 1961, U.S. Supreme Ct. bar, 1964, Fla. bar, 1970; mem. firm Montgomery & Montgomery, Seymour, Ind., 1961-64; judge Jackson Circuit Ct., Brownstown, Ind., 1965-70, Ct. Appeals, Indpls., 1971-72; presiding judge Ct. of Appeals 1st Dist. Ct., Indpls., 1972-74, chief judge, 1975—; adj. prof. law Ind. U., Indpls., 1974—. Dir. Ind. Jud. Council. Mem. Am., Ind., Jackson County bar assns., Ind. Judges Assn., Fla. Bar Assn., Am. Judicature Soc. Contbr. articles to profl. jours. Home: RFD 2 Lake and Forest Club Brownstown IN 47220 Office: 433 State House Indianapolis IN 46204 Tel (317) 633-4925

ROBERTSON, LOUIS, b. Chevy Chase, Md., June 10, 1905; A.B., U. Mich., 1927; LL.B., George Washington U., 1929. With U.S. Patent Office, 1927-29; admitted to D.C. bar, 1929, Ill. bar, 1930; practiced in Chgo., 1930-61, Arlington Heights, Ill., 1961-77; partner firm Jones, Darbo & Robertson, 1956-61, firm Darbo, Robertson & Vandenburgh, 1961-77. Mem. Am., Chgo. bar assns., Am., Chgo. patent law assns., Michigamua, Delta Tau Delta, Phi Delta Phi. Contbr. articles to profl. jours.; originator Walker Process doctrine. Home and office: 1411 Nashua Circle Sun City Center FL 33570

ROBFOGEL, NATHAN JOSHUA, b. Rochester, N.Y., Feb. 28, 1935; B.A., Oberlin Coll., 1956; J.D., Cornell U., 1959. Admitted to N.Y. bar, 1959; asso. firm Harter, Secrest & Emery, Rochester, 1959-65, partner, 1966—. Mem. corp. United Community Chest Rochester, 1974—; treas., mem. exec. com. Jewish Community Fedn. Rochester, 1970—, bd. dirs., 1969—; bd. dirs. Rochester Area Found., 1973—; trustee Temple Beth El, 1973—; mem. exec. com. Rochester Philharmonic Orch., 1972—, bd. dirs., 1971—, chmn., 1975—; chmn. Rochester Planning Comm.; mem. Monroe County Planning Bd. Mem. Am. Judicature Soc., Am. Arbitration Assn., Am., N.Y. State, Monroe County (trustee) bar assns. Home: 5 East Blvd Rochester NY 14610 Office: 700 Midtown Tower Rochester NY 14610 Tel (716) 232-6500

ROBFOGEL, SUSAN SALITAN, b. Rochester, N.Y., Apr. 4, 1943; B.A. cum laude, Smith Coll., 1964; LL.B., Cornell U., 1967, J.D., 1970. Admitted to N.Y. bar, 1967, U.S. Supreme Ct. bar, 1971; asst. corp. counsel City of Rochester, 1967-70; asso. firm Harris, Beach and Wilcox (now Harris, Beach, Wilcox, Rubin and Levey), Rochester, 1970-74, partner, 1975—; trustee Rochester Savs. Bank, 1977—; adv. com. Cornell Law Sch., 1977—; bd. dirs. Rochester Gen. Hosp., 1972—; mem. Monroe County (N.Y.) unit Am. Cancer Soc., 1975—; mem. planning com. United Community Chest of Greater Rochester, 1976—. Mem. Am., N.Y. State, Monroe County bar assns., Am. Judicature Soc., Am. Arbitration Assn. (panel of arbitrators). Home: 5 East Blvd Rochester NY 14610 Office: 2 State St Rochester NY 14614 Tel (716) 232-4440

ROBIE, LAWRENCE A., b. Plymouth, Pa., Mar. 24, 1914; A.B., Mt. St. Mary's Coll., 1937; grad. U. Mich., 1940. Admitted Pa. bar, 1941; atty. Anti-Trust Div. U.S. Dept. Justice, 1949-52; pub. defender Fed., Pa., Supreme and Superior Cts., Pitts., 1952—. Mem. Allegheny Bar Assn. Home: 515 Demmler Dr Pittsburgh PA 15237 Office: 311 Ross St Pittsburgh PA 15219 Tel (412) 355-5825

ROBIN, EVA EFFRON, b. Patterson, N.J., Oct. 1, 1899; LL.B., N.Y. U., 1920. Admitted to N.Y. bar, Conn. bar; mem. legal firms. Mem. Am., Conn., Stamford bar assns. Home and Office: 113 Old N Stamford Rd Stamford CT 06901

ROBIN, LONNIE HANK, b. Dallas, Aug. 2, 1947; B.A., U. Tex., Austin, 1969, J.D., 1972. Admitted to Tex. bar, 1972; with Tarrant County Legal Aid Found., Ft. Worth, 1973-75; individual practice law, Ft. Worth, Tex., 1975—. Mem. Tarrant County Hosp. Dist. Consumer Advocacy Bd., 1976. Mem. State Bar Tex., Tarrant County Bar Assn., Tarrany County Young Lawyers' Assn., Comml. Law League Am. Office: 1101 Executive Plaza Fort Worth TX 76102 Tel (817) 336-7888

ROBIN, SIDNEY LEON, b. Chgo., Dec. 8, 1904; B.A., U. Ill., Urbana, 1925; J.D., U. Mich., 1927. Admitted to Ill. bar, 1927; partner firm King, Robin, Gale & Pillinger and predecessors, Chgo., 1927. Pres. Glencoe (Ill.) Sch. Bd., 1957-59; pres. Jewish Fedn. Met. Chgo., 1970-72, Jewish United Fund Met. Chgo., 1971-73. Mem. Am., Ill., Chgo. bar assns. Mem. Order of Coif, Phi Beta Kappa. Home: 70 Crescent Dr Glencoe IL 60022 Office: 135 S LaSalle St Chicago IL 60603

ROBINER, DONALD MAXWELL, b. Detroit, Feb. 4, 1935; A.B., U. Mich., 1957; J.D., Case Western Res. U., 1961. Admitted to Ohio bar, 1961, U.S. Supreme Ct. bar, 1964; with firm Gaines, Stern, Schwarzwald & Robiner, and predecessor, Cleve., 1961—, asso., 1961-67, partner, 1967-71, prin., 1971—; mem. Ohio Bd. Bar Examiners, 1974—; asst. dir. law City of Mayfield Heights (Ohio), 1961-66. Mem. community relations com. Jewish Community Fedn. Cleve., 1972—, mem. del. assembly, 1972—. Mem. Greater Cleve., Cuyahoga County, Ohio State, Am. (sect. local govt. law, legal edn. individual rights and responsibilities law) bar assns., Assn. Trial Lawyers Am., Cuyahoga County Law Dirs. Assn., Nat. Conf. Bar Examiners, Ohio Council Sch. Bd. Attys. Office: 1700 Ohio Savings Plaza 1801 E 9th St Cleveland OH 44114 Tel (216) 781-1700

ROBINS, KENNETH MICHAEL, b. Williamsport, Pa., June 19, 1944; B.S. in Econs., U. Pa., 1966; J.D. Harvard, 1969. Admitted to N.Y. State bar, 1970, Colo. bar, 1973; asso. firm Shea, Gould, Climenko & Kramer, N.Y.C., 1969-72; partner firm Brownstein Hyatt Farber & Madden, Denver, 1972—. Mem. Am., N.Y. State, N.Y.C., Colo., Denver bar assns. Home: 755 Lafayette St Denver CO 80218 Office: 1700 Lincoln Center Bldg Denver CO 80203 Tel (303) 534-6335

ROBINS, MARTIN EDWARD, b. Bklyn., May 4, 1942; A.B., Princeton, 1964; LL.B., Harvard, 1967. Admitted to N.J. bar, 1967; law sec. to Hon. Nelson K. Mintz, Chancery Div. N.J. Superior Ct., 1967-68; asso. firm Pitney, Hardin, & Kipp, Newark, 1968-70; asst. prosecutor, chief spl. prosecutions, Hudson County, N.J., 1970-74; dep. atty. gen. Office Atty. Gen., Trenton, N.J., 1974-75; exec. asst. to asst. commrs. pub. transp. N.J. Dept. Transp., Trenton, 1975—, dir. pub. transp. program devel., 1976—. Mem. Fed., N.J. bar assns. Author and editor legal articles; contbr. to Princeton Alumni Weekly. Office: 1035 Parkway Ave Trenton NJ 08625 Tel (609) 292-4161

ROBINS, MICHAEL LEWIS, b. Mpls., Aug. 23, 1930; B.S., U. Minn., 1954, LL.B., 1954, J.D., 1956. Admitted to Minn. bar, 1956, U.S. Supreme Ct. bar, 1966, Calif. bar, 1972; asso. firm Samuel, Saliterman, Mpls., 1956-57; individual practice, Mpls., 1957-58, 60-62; partner firm Fine, Robins & Simon, Mpls., 1958-60, Robins & Meshbesher, Mpls., 1962-64, Robins, Meshbesher & Kirshbaum, Mpls., 1964-66, Robins, Meshbesher, Singer & Spence, Mpls., 1966-71; mem. firm Pollock, Pollock and Fay, Los Angeles, 1972—. Mem. Am., Century City, Beverly Hills, Los Angeles County, Hennepin County, Minn., Calif. bar assns., Am. (gov. 1968-70, asso. editor jour. 1966-69), Calif., Western (gov. 1976—), Los Angeles, Minn. (gov. 1965, sec. 1966-67) trial lawyers assns., Delta Sigma Rho. Student editorial bd. Minn. Law Rev., 1955-56. Office: 1888 Century Park E #1520 Los Angeles CA 90067 Tel (213) 879-0111

ROBINSON, ALLEN BRYON, b. San Diego, Nov. 20, 1945; A.B., San Diego State U., 1967; J.D., U. Calif. at Berkeley, 1970. Admitted to Calif. bar, 1971; partner firm Foley, Foley, Jarvis, Robinson & McCardle, Hayward, Calif., 1973—; lectr. U. Md. European Div., 1971-73. Mem. So. Alameda County, Alameda County, Calif. bar assns. Office: 22300 Foothill Blvd Suite 400 Hayward CA 94541 Tel (415) 537-1333

ROBINSON, BERT K., b. Austin, Tex., Aug. 2, 1936; B.B.A., U. Tex., 1958; J.D., La. State U., 1963. Admitted to La. bar, 1963, U.S. Supreme Ct. bar, 1968, U.S. Tax Ct. bar, 1970; law clerk U.S. Dist. Ct. Eastern Dist. La., 1962-64; asso. firm Breazeale, Sachse & Wilson, Baton Rouge, 1964-66; partner firm Wray & Robinson, Baton Rouge, 1966—; sec., treas. Larry Robinson Studios, Inc., 1968-70. Mem. Am., Baton Rouge, La. (ho. of dels. 1974—), Fed. (pres. La. chpt. 1959, dir.) bar assns. Office: PO Box 3674 Baton Rouge LA 70821 Tel (504) 387-4957

ROBINSON, CALVIN RAY, b. Owensboro, Ky., Apr. 17, 1927; A.B., U. Ky., 1950, J.D., 1953; postgrad. U. Wis., 1950-51. Admitted to Ky. bar, 1953; individual practice law, Owensboro, 1953—; judge pro tempore, Daviess County, Ky., 1954-57; master commr. Daviess County Circuit Ct., 1965—. Pres. Daviess County Fish and Game Assn., 1964-66; chmn. C. of C. Civic Improvement Assn. Mem. Am., Daviess County (pres. 1965-67), Ky. bar assns., Phi Delta Phi. Home: 1909 Robin Rd Owensboro KY 42301 Office: 210 W Third St Owensboro KY 42301 Tel (502) 926-1575

ROBINSON, CALVIN S., b. Kalispell, Mont., Mar. 31, 1920; B.A., U. Mont., 1944; J.D., U. Mich., 1949. Admitted to Ill. bar, 1949, Mont. bar, 1949; asso. firm Rooks & Freeman, Chgo., 1949-50, firm Murphy, Robinson, Heckathorn & Phillips, Kalispell, 1950—. Bd. dirs. Kalispell Salvation Army, Community Fund; chmn. Kalispell Sch. Bd., 1958-64; mem. adv. council Mont. State U.; mem. Mont. Environ. Quality Council; mem. Mont. Gov.'s Commn. Revision Corporate Law; bd. visitors U. Mont. Sch. Law; adviser Mont. Unemployment Compensation Commn. Mem. Am., Ill., Mont., NW Mont. bar assns. Home: 315 Crestview St Kalispell MT 59901 Office: One Main St Kalispell MT 59901 Tel (406) 755-6644

ROBINSON, CYRIL DAVID, b. N.Y.C., July 22, 1924; LL.B., Northwestern U., 1951. Admitted to Ill. bar, 1952, U.S. Dist. Ct. bar, 1955, U.S. Supreme Ct. bar, 1958; asso. firm Cotton, Fruchtman & Watt, Chgo., 1952-55; partner firm Robinson & Fisher, Chgo., 1955-57; individual practice law, Chgo., 1957-62; instr. U. Mich. Sch. Law, Ann Arbor, 1965-66; asso. prof. law Marquette U., Milw., 1966-67; staff counsel So. Rural Research Project, Selma, Ala., 1968; asso. prof. polit. sci. Rosary Coll., River Forest, Ill., 1969-72; asso. prof. criminal justice Pa. State U., 1972—. Mem. Am. Soc. Criminology, Am. Soc. Legal History, Internat. Assn. Penal Law. Contbr. articles in field to legal jours.; mem. bd. legal publs. Northwestern U. Home: 111 Cedar Ln State College PA 16801 Office: Pa State U S-203 Human Devel Bldg University Park PA 16802 Tel (814) 865-1452

ROBINSON, DONALD CLARENCE, b. Hamilton, Mont., Mar. 16, 1941; A.B., U. Mont., 1963; J.D., George Washington U., 1967. Admitted to D.C. bar, 1967, Mont. bar, 1969; staff atty. Washington Legal Aid Agy., 1967-68; asst. U.S. atty. for Mont., 1968-69; partner firm Poore McKenzie Roth Robischon & Robinson, Butte, Mont., 1969—; pres. Mont. Legal Protection Plan, Inc. Mem. Silver Bow County (Mont.) Democratic Central Com., 1976—. Mem. Am., Mont. bar assns. Named Outstanding Young Man Am., 1973. Home: 3505 Willoughby Ave Butte MT 59701 Office: Silver Bow Block suite 400 Butte MT 59701 Tel (406) 792-0488

ROBINSON, DONALD JOE, b. Hollyridge, La., Dec. 28, 1937; B.S. in Chem. Engring., Lamar State U., 1961; J.D., Baylor U., 1967, LL.B., 1967. Admitted to Tex. bar, 1967, La. bar, 1969, Wash. bar, 1971; patent searcher U.S. Patent Office, Washington, 1961; with Penick & Ford, Ltd., Cedar Rapids, Iowa, 1961-63; project engr. Olin Mathieson Chem. Corp., W. Monroe, La., 1963-65; with Morningstar-Paisley, Inc., N.Y.C., 1965-67; individual practice law, Silsbee, Tex., 1967-69, Dallas, 1975—; environ. and gen. corporate counsel, Weyerhaeuser Co., Tacoma, Wash., 1970-72; mem. firm Stalcup, Johnson, Meyers & Miller, Dallas, 1972-73; partner firm Simon, Twombly, Held & Robinson, Dallas, 1973-75. Mem. Soc. Profl. Engrs., Am. Inst. Chem. Engrs., Delta Theta Phi. Recipient Excellence award Bancroft-Whitney Pub. Co.; Citizens Nat. Bank of Waco fellow; Waco Coca Cola Law Found. scholar; Lupton Found. scholar. Office: PO Box 29711 Dallas TX 75229 Tel (214) 241-9955

ROBINSON, E. GLENN, b. Charleston, W.Va., Jan. 1, 1924; B.S. in Bus. Adminstrn., Ohio State U., 1948; J.D., W.Va. U., 1950. Admitted to W.Va. bar, 1950, U.S. Ct. Appeals bar, 4th Circuit, 1953, U.S. Dist. Ct. bar for So. Dist. W.Va., 1952; partner firms Shannon & Robinson, Charleston, 1950-52, James, Wise, Robinson & Magnuson, Charleston, 1952-75, Love, Wise, Robinson & Woodroe, Charleston, 1976—. Pres. Children's Home Soc. of W.Va., Charleston, 1965-66. Mem. W.Va. State Bar (pres. 1972-73), Kauawha County (W.Va.) (pres. 1967-68), W.Va., Am. bar assns., Am. Coll. Trial Lawyers, Nat. Assn. R.R. Trial Counsel, Conf. of 4th Circuit, Am. Judicature Soc., Order of Coif. Home: 507 Superior Ave South Charleston WV 25303 Office: 12th floor Charleston Nat Plaza Charleston WV 25323 Tel (304) 343-4841

ROBINSON, ERNEST GORDON, JR., b. Atlanta, May 25, 1948; A.B., Mercer U., 1971; J.D., 1974. Admitted to Ga. bar, 1974; since practiced in Atlanta, asso. firm Chambers & Dismer, 1974, mem. firm Chambers & Robinson, 1975, partner firm Chambers, Siefferman, Robinson & Cooper, 1976—. Recipient Henry W. Grady Cup, Mercerian Exemplar award. Home: 4114 D'Youville Trace Atlanta GA 30341 Office: Suite 464 2200 Century Pkwy Atlanta GA 30345 Tel (404) 325-9970

ROBINSON, GERALD J., b. Balt., Dec. 1, 1931; B.A. Cornell U., 1954; LL.B., U. Md., 1956; LL.M., N.Y. U., 1963. Admitted to Md. bar, 1956, N.Y. State bar, 1958; mem. chief counsels office IRS, Washington, 1958-62; asso. firm Rabkin & Johnson, N.Y.C., 1963-68; asso. firm Carb, Luria, Glassner, Cook, & Kufeld, N.Y.C., 1968—. Mem. Am. Bar Assn. Editor: Newsletter Real Estate Tax Ideas. Home: Dogwood Ct Stamford CT 06903 Office: 529 Fifth Ave New York City NY 10017 Tel (212) 986-3131

ROBINSON, HENRY SEYMOUR, JR., b. N.Y.C., June 4, 1918; B.A., Yale, 1940; J.D., Harvard, 1943. Admitted to Conn. bar, 1947; partner firm Robinson, Robinson & Cole, Hartford, Conn., 1952—. Mem. Am., Conn., Hartford County bar assns. Home: 39 Colony Rd W Hartford CT 06117 Office: 799 Main St Hartford CT 06103 Tel (203) 278-0700

ROBINSON, JAMES KENT, b. Peru, Ill., July 15, 1927; B.S., U. Ill., 1950, J.D., 1952, postgrad., 1952-53; grad. Nat. Coll. State Trial Judges U. Nev., 1967. Admitted to Ill. bar, 1952; practiced in Ill., 1952-62; asst. state's atty. Vermilion County, Ill., 1956-59; corp. counsel City of Danville (Ill.), 1959-62; judge Vermilion County Ct., 1962-64; asso. judge Ill. Circuit Ct., 5th Jud. Circuit, 1964-70, circuit judge, 1970—; mem. Ill. Supreme Ct. Com. on Juvenile Problems, 1966-74, Ill. Supreme Ct. Com. Criminal Problems, 1975—; chmn. Ill. Gov's. Advisory Bd. on Corrections, 1968-72; instr. U. Ill. Police Tng. Inst., 1968-77; mem. faculty Nat. Coll. State Judiciary U. Nev., 1973—. Mem. Ill. State, Vermilion County, Am. bar assns. Home: 1400 Rivercrest St Danville IL 61832 Office: Vermilion County Courthouse Danville IL 61832 Tel (217) 442-3700

ROBINSON, JAMES POE, b. Grafton, W.Va., May 29, 1914; A.B., W.Va. U., 1937, J.D., 1939. Admitted to W.Va. Supreme Ct. bar, 1939; atty. U.S. C.E., 1939-42; asso. firm Stathers & Cantrall, Clarksburg, W.Va., 1942-55, partner, 1955-67; asso. firm Spilman, Thomas, Battle & Klostermeyer, Charleston, W.Va., 1967-68, partner, 1969—. Chmn. advisory bd. Salvation Army, Charleston, 1973-75; elder 1st Presbyn. Ch., Clarksburg, W.Va. Mem. Am., W.Va. (pres. 1974-75), Kanawha County (W.Va.), Harrison County (W.Va.) (pres. 1959) bar assns., W.Va. State Bar (gov. 1963-66), 4th U.S. Circuit Jud. Conf. (permanent), So. Conf. Bar Pres's. (chmn. joint com. for W.Va. Bars for 1977 conv.), Am. Judicature Soc., Res. Officers Assn. U.S. (pres. dept. W.Va.), Assn. U.S. Army, W.Va. U. Law Sch. Alumni Assn., Phi Alpha Delta. Bd. editors W.Va. U. Law Rev., 1937-39. Home: 826 Beaumont Rd Charleston WV 25314 Office: 1101 Kanawha Bank & Trust Bldg Charleston WV 25301 Tel (304) 344-4081

ROBINSON, JAMES V., b. Mexia, Tex., Apr. 17, 1927; A.A., Kilgore Jr. Coll., 1947; LL.B., U. Tex., 1951. Admitted to Tex. bar, 1951; sr. v.p., sec. Western Republic Life Ins. Co., Austin, Tex., 1953-67; sr. v.p., sec., counsel First Nat. Life Ins. Co., Houston, 1968-73, pres., 1973—; pres. First Nat. Corp., Houston, 1973-77; v.p., sec. Nat. Western Life Ins. Co., Austin, 1977—. Mem. Tex. Health Ins. Assn. (pres. 1960-61), Houston Gilbert and Sullivan Soc. (pres.), Phi Alpha Delta.

ROBINSON, JAMES WITT, b. Charlottesville, Va., Sept. 9, 1922; student Hampden-Sydney Coll., U. Va.; B.B.A., U. Miami, 1951, LL.B., 1953. Admitted to Fla. bar, 1953; asso. firm Lyle D. Holcomb, Miami, 1953-56; asso. firm Salley & Roman, Miami, 1957-58; asso. firm Smathers & Thompson, Miami, 1961-66, partner, 1967—. Mem. Dade County, Am., Fla. bar assns., Delta Theta Phi. Home: 6845 SW 144th St Miami FL 33158 Office: 1301 Alfred I DuPont Bldg Miami FL 33131 Tel (305) 379-6523

ROBINSON JOHN ROWLAND, b. N.Y.C., June 11, 1935; A.B. in History, Boston U., 1961, LL.B., 1964; postgrad. Harvard Bus. Sch., 1973. Admitted to N.Y. bar, 1965, U.S. Ct. Appeals 2d Circuit bar, 1967; asso. firm Simpson, Thacher & Bartlett, N.Y.C., 1964-66; asst. U.S. atty. So. Dist. N.Y., 1966-69; mem. strike force organized crime, 1970; partner firm Rooney & Robinson, N.Y.C., 1971-73; individual practice law, N.Y.C., 1973—. Bd. visitors Boston U. Law Sch., 1970—; trustee Harvey Sch., Katonah, N.Y., Boston U. Mem. Am., N.Y. State, Fed. bar assns. Tel (914) 967-7821

ROBINSON, LEE CHARLES, JR., b. Miami, Fla., Dec. 15, 1930; B.S. in Mech. and Indsl. Engring, U. Mich., 1952, J.D., 1954. Admitted to Fla. bar, 1955, N.Y. bar, 1955; atty. Bell Telephone Labs., N.Y.C., 1954-56; served with JAGC, USAF, Dayton, Ohio, 1956-58; asso. firm Fish & Neave, N.Y.C., 1958-73; partner firm Curtis, Morris & Safford, N.Y.C., 1973—; justice Village of Plandome (N.Y.), 1971—. Mem. Am., Fla. bar assns., N.Y. Patent Law Assn. Editor The Trademark Reporter, 1971—. Home: 25 Rockwood Rd E Plandome NY 11030 Office: 530 Fifth Ave New York City NY 10036 Tel (212) MU2-7171

ROBINSON, LUCIUS FRANKLIN, JR., b. Hartford, Conn., Oct. 3, 1895; B.A., Yale U., 1918, M.A. (hon.), 1953; LL.B., Harvard U., 1921. Admitted to Conn. bar, 1922, Fed. bar, 1926; partner firm Robinson, Robinson & Cole, Hartford, 1924—. Fellow Am. Bar Found.; mem. Hartford County (pres. 1942-44), Conn. (pres. 1956-58) bar assns. Home: 122 Main St Farmington CT 06032 Office: 799 Main St Hartford CT 06103 Tel (203) 278-0700

ROBINSON, LYLE JAMES, b. Greenville, Tenn., June 16, 1920; student Kings Coll., U. Tenn.; LL.B., Washington and Lee U., 1948, J.D. Admitted to Tenn. bar, 1950, Fla. bar, 1963; individual practice law, Kingsport, Tenn., 1950-56. sr. partner firm Bandy & Lyle, Kingsport, 1956-62; sr. partner firm Ramseur, Bradham, Lyle & Skipper, St. Petersburg, Fla., 1964—. Mem. Exec. bd. Pinellas Area Council Boy Scouts Am., 1975—; mem. advisory bd. Salvation Army, St. Petersburg, 1975—; deacon 1st Presbyn. Ch. St. Petersburg, 1965-70, elder, 1970—. Mem. St. Petersburg Bar Assn. (v.p. 1971), St. Petersburg Kiwanis (pres. 1974, 75). Home: 6801 Colony Dr S St Petersburg FL 33705 Office: 699 1st Ave N St Petersburg FL 33701 Tel (813) 895-1991

ROBINSON, NEIL CIBLEY, JR., b. Columbia, S.C., Oct. 25. 1942; B.S., Clemson U., 1966; J.D., U. S.C., 1973. Admitted to S.C. bar, 1974; asst. to dean U. S.C. Law Sch., 1972-74; law clk. to judge U.S. Dist. Ct., Aiken, S.C., 1974-76; asso. firm Grimball, Cabaniss, Vaughan & Guerard, Charleston, S.C., 1976—; pub. defender Family Ct. Richland County (S.C.), Columbia, 1973-74. Mem. Am., S.C., Charleston County, Fed. bar assns., S.C. State Bar (jud. reform com. 1975—), S.C. Trial Lawyers Assn., Am. Judicature Soc., Phi Delta Phi. Home: 44 1/2 Charlotte St Charleston SC 29403 Office: 39 Broad St Charleston SC 29402 Tel (803) 577-9440

ROBINSON, NORMAN RICHARD, b. Nokomis, Ill., May 16, 1909; LL.D., John Marshall Law Sch., 1951, J.D., 1973. Admitted to Ill. bar, 1952; individual practice law, Chgo., 1952-69; asst. atty. gen.

Ill. Consumer Fraud Div., Chgo., 1969-71; asst. state's atty. Cook County (Ill.), Consumer Complaint Div., Chgo., 1973—. Pres. Chgo. Assn. for Visually Handicapped; adv. bd. Council of Community Services, Ill. Visually Handicapped Inst. Mem. Cook County, Nat. bar assns., Am. Blind Lawyers Assn. (dir.). Recipient Blind Service Orgn. Award for Meritorious Service, 1973. Home: 7109 S Calumet Ave Chicago IL 60619 Office: 749 W 63rd St Chicago IL 60621 Tel (312) 723-1600

ROBINSON, PAUL EDWARD, b. Norton, Va., Mar. 17, 1947; B.S. in Mktg., San Diego State U., 1970; J.D., U. San Diego, 1973. Admitted to Calif. bar, 1973; dep. city atty. San Diego, 1973-76; legis. rep., San Diego, 1976—; mem. Calif. atty. gen. adv. com. on pornography, com. on organized crime and pornography; mem. League of Calif. Cities com. on employee relations. Mem. Am., San Diego County (com. on legal ethics and unlawful practice) bar assns. Office: 202 C St 8th Floor San Diego CA 92101 Tel (714) 236-6276

ROBINSON, RALPH CARLISLE, JR., b. Columbia, S.C., Aug. 27, 1935; B.S. in Bus. Adminstrn., U. S.C., 1957, J.D., 1966. Admitted to S.C. bar, 1966; law clk. to judge U.S. Dist. Ct., Columbia, 1966-67; individual practice law, Columbia, 1967-72, 73-75; partner firm Berry, Lightsey, Gibbes & Robinson, Columbia, 1972; mem. firm Lewis, Lewis & Robinson, Columbia, 1975—. Mem. Am. Judicature Soc., Am., Fed. bar assns., S.C. Trial Lawyers Assn. Home: 312 Wateree St Columbia SC 29205 Office: 3600 Forest Dr Columbia SC 29204

ROBINSON, RICHARD EARL, b. Middleton, Mich., July 31, 1916; B.A., Mich. State U., 1939; LL.B., U. Mich., 1948. Admitted to Mich. bar, 1948; practiced in Eaton Rapids, Mich., 1948-67; judge Mich. Circuit Ct., 5th Jud. Circuit, 1967—. Mem. Eaton County (Mich.), Barry County (Mich.), Mich., Am. bar assns. Home: Smithville Rd Eaton Rapids MI 48827 Office: Courthouse Charlotte MI 48813 Tel (517) 543-7500

ROBINSON, ROBERT HENRY, b. Columbia Falls, Mont., Jan. 25, 1916; B.A., U. Mont., 1940, J.D., Mont. State U., 1948; postgrad U. Hawaii, 1945-46. Admitted to Mont. bar, 1948; immigrant inspector U.S. Dept. Justice, Walla Walla, Wash., Presidio, Tex., Havre, Mont., and Cut Bank, Mont., 1940-43; instr. sch. bus. U. Mont., 1948-57; mem. firm Garlington, Lohn & Robinson, Missoula, Mont., 1954—; gen. counsel Missoula Community Hosp., 1951-75, Missoula Mercantile Co., 1948-54. Mem. Mont. Constl. Conv. Commn., 1972; chmn. Missoula County Study Commn. on Air Pollution, 1962—; mem. U. Mont. Council of 50, 1968-71. Mem. Am., Mont., Western Mont. bar assns., U. Mont. Sch. Law Alumni Assn. (past pres.), Mont. R.R. Assn. (legis. dir. 1957-73), Phi Delta Phi, Tau Kappa Alpha. Recipient Silver Beaver award, Boy Scouts Am., 1964; Missoula Distinguished Citizen award, 1963; George award, Missoula C. of C., 1976. Home: 545 E Central St Missoula MT 59801 Office: 199 W Pine St PO Box 7909 Missoula MT 59807 Tel (406) 728-1200

ROBINSON, ROBERT JOSEPH, b. Asheville, N.C., Nov. 7, 1936; B.A., Wake Forest Coll., 1958, LL.B., 1960. Admitted to N.C. bar, 1960; law clk. U.S. Dist. Judge Western Dist. N.C., 1960-61; asso. firm Uzzell & Dumont, Asheville, 1961; asst. U.S. atty. Western Dist. N.C., 1962-64; mem. firm Patla, Straus, Robinson & Moore, Asheville, 1964—. Chmn. Buncombe County Democratic Exec. Com., 1969-71; bd. dirs. Asheville Area C. of C., 1975-76, YMCA; pres. Asheville Civic Arts Council, 1970. Mem. Am., N.C., Buncombe County (pres. 1976-77, trustee 1974-76) bar assns. Home: 16 N Kensington Rd Asheville NC 28804 Office: PO Box 7625 Asheville NC 28807 Tel (704) 255-7641

ROBINSON, WILLIAM FRANKLIN, b. Hammond, Ind., Feb. 10, 1916; A.B. with high honors, Ind. U., 1942, J.D., 1944. Admitted to Ind. bar, 1944, Mich. bar, 1946, Ill. bar, 1953, Calif. bar, 1957; spl. atty. office of chief counsel IRS, Washington and Detroit, 1944-46; individual practice law, Detroit, 1946-51; asst. gen. counsel and asst. sec. Montgomery Ward & Co., Inc., Chgo., 1951-56; v.p., gen. counsel and sec. (dir.) Transam. Fin. Corp., Los Angeles, 1956—; mem. laws and regulations com. Calif. Loan and Fin. Assn., 1962—, chmn., 1968—; instr. U. Detroit Coll. Commerce and Fin., 1947-51; instr. fed. taxation Wayne U. Law Sch., Detroit, 1948-51; mem. gen. com. Conf. on Personal Fin. Law, N.Y.C., 1965—. Mem. State Bar Calif., Los Angeles County, Am. bar assns., Nat. Consumer Fin. Assn., Phi Beta Kappa. Contbr. articles to legal publs. Home: 8217 Lindante Dr Whittier CA 90603 Office: 1150 S Olive St Suite 2033 Los Angeles CA 90015 Tel (213) 742-4754

ROBINSON, WILLIAM LEWIS, b. Martin County, Ind., Feb. 16, 1932; B.A., Evansville U., 1960; M.S., No. Ill. U., 1967; J.D., John Marshall U., 1971. Admitted to Ill. bar, 1971; mem. firm Forsberg & Robinson, Forsberg Ltd., Chgo., Barrington, Des Plaines, Ill., 1975—; tchr. social studies high sch., 1960-77. Mem. Am., NW bar assns. Home: 9404 Western Des Plaines IL 60016 Office: Forsberg & Robinson Barrington IL 60010 Tel (312) 381-8740 also Forsberg Ltd Chicago IL 60602 Tel (312) FI6-6121

ROBISON, J. SHELBURN, b. Pinos Altas, N. Mex., May 27, 1894; B.S. in Mining Engring., Pa. State Coll., 1917; grad. U.S. Army Field Artillery Sch., 1922; J.D., U. San Francisco. Admitted to N. Mex. bar, Calif. bar, 1936; counsel Carmel (Calif.) Sanitary Dist., 1937-42, 46-76; counsel Pebble Beach (Calif.) Sanitary Dist., 1967-76; partner firm Robison and Whittlesey, 1946—. Pres. Carmel Unified Sch. Bd.; pres. Monterey County (Calif.) Soc. Prevention Cruelty to Animals. Mem. Am., Calif., Monterey County bar assns., Nat. Fed. Independent Bus., Tau Beta Pi. Home: Lauuen Dr Carmel CA 93921 Office: Box 1686 Ocean St and Mission St Carmel CA 93921 Tel (408) 624-3857

ROBISON, JOHN CURTIS, JR., b. Mattoon, Ill., June 16, 1943; B.A., U. Ill., 1965, J.D., 1968. Admitted to Ill. bar, 1969; asso., then mem. firm Marshall, Feiger, Robison and Quindry, Fairfield, Ill., 1969-75; individual practice law, Fairfield, 1976—. Trustee Fairfield Pub. Library, 1976. Mem. Am., Fed., Wayne County (sec.-treas.), S.E. Ill., Ill. (sect. council individual rights and responsibilities 1976-77) bar assns., Am. Judicature Soc., Nat. Assn. Criminal Def. Lawyers, Greater Fairfield Area C. of C. (dir.). Contbr. articles to Ill. Bar Jour., Loyola Univ. Chgo. Law Jour. Home: 308 W Center St Fairfield IL 62837 Office: 204 SE 3d St Fairfield IL 62837 Tel (618) 842-3726

ROBSON, EDWIN ALBERT, b. Chgo., Apr. 16, 1905; LL.B., DePaul U., 1928. Admitted to Ill. bar, 1928; mem. firm Kinne, Scovel & Robson, Chgo., 1928-45; judge Superior Ct., 1945-51, chief justice, 1950-51; judge Appellate Ct. for 1st Dist., 1951-58; judge U.S. Dist. Ct. No. Dist. Ill., 1958-70, chief judge, 1970—; organizer, chmn. Jud. Conf. Ill., 1955; chmn. adv. council to U. Ill. on short courses for practicing lawyers, 1956-59; instr. Seminar for Appellate Ct. Judges, N.Y. U., 1959; Dist. Ct. rep. for 7th Circuit to Jud. Conf. of U.S., 1966-69; dir. Coordinating Com. for Multiple Litigation of U.S. Dist. Cts.; mem. exec. com. Met. Chief Judges of U.S. Dist. Cts. Fellow Am. Bar Found.; mem. Am. (chmn. Ill. Sect. on jud. adminstrn.), Ill., Chgo. bar assns., Circuit and Superior Ct. Judges Assn. Ill., Am. Judicature Soc. (dir.), Law in Am. Soc. Found. (chmn. exec. com.). Bd. editors Manual for Complex and Multidistrict Litigation, 1968—. Home: 2418 Iroquois Rd Wilmette IL 60091 Office: 219 S Dearborn St Chicago IL 60604 Tel (312) 435-5590

ROBY, JOHN STEINER, b. Marion, Ohio, Aug. 7, 1942; B.S., Ohio State U.; J.D., Case Western Res. U. Admitted to Ohio bar, 1968, U.S. Supreme Ct. bar, 1972; spl. agt. FBI, Atlanta, 1968-69, Washington, 1969-72; v.p. Roby Krause Inc., Mansfield, Ohio, 1972—. Mem. Ohio, Am. bar assns. Home: 431 Marwood Rd Lexington OH 44904 Office: 44 Sturges Ave Mansfield OH 44907 Tel (419) 524-8411

ROBY, RONALD HAURY, b. Chgo. May 15, 1936; B.S. in Bus. Adminstrn., U. Fla., 1962; J.D., U. Miami, 1966. Admitted to Fla. bar, 1966; since practiced in Orlando, Fla.; asso. firm Magueir, Voorhis & Wells, 1966-69; individual practice law, 1969-70; partner firm Roby & Cunningham & O'Neil, and predecessors, 1971—; lectr. Fla. State Bar 1976, mem. Land Use Regulation com. Mem. Orange County, Fla., Am. bar assns. Home: 2141 Glencoe Rd Winter Park FL 32789 Office: 865 Hartford Bldg 200 E Robinson St Orlando FL 32801 Tel (305) 425-2751

ROBYN, RICHARD ALLEN, b. Kalamazoo, June 15, 1940; B.A., Kalamazoo Coll., 1962; J.D., U. Pacific, 1970. Admitted to Calif. bar, 1971; individual practice law, San Andreas, Calif., 1971-74; counsel Amador County, Calif., 1972-74; counsel, exec. officer Calaveras County, Calif., 1974—; counsel County Supvs. Assn. Calif., Sacramento, 1971-72. Mem. Calaveras County, Calif., Am. bar assns. Home: 237 California St San Andreas CA 95249 Office: Government Center San Andreas CA 95249 Tel (209) 754-4192

ROCA, PAUL MCLENNAN, b. Nebraska City, Nebr., Dec. 16, 1911; B.A., U. Ariz., 1933; J.D., George Washington U., 1941; D.Can.L. (hon.), Ch. Divinity Sch. of Pacific, 1974. Admitted to Va. bar, 1937, D.C. bar, 1940, Ariz. bar, 1941; since practiced in Phoenix, 1941—; partner firm Moore, Romley & Roca, 1942-48, Lewis & Roca, 1950—. Mem. Phoenix City Planning Commn., 1948-51; pres. Phoenix Community Council, 1950, 68, Maricopa County Legal Aid Soc., 1964; chancellor Episcopal Diocese Ariz., 1970; bd. dirs. Phoenix Community Chest, 1950-56. Mem. Am. Law Inst., Fedn. Ins. Counsel, Internat. Assn. Ins. Counsel, Assn. Life Ins. Counsel, Maricopa County Bar Assn. (past pres.) Author: The Life Insurance Law of Arizona, 1958; contbr. articles to legal jours. Home: 158 N Country Club Dr Phoenix AZ 85014 Office: 100 W Washington St Phoenix AZ 85003 Tel (602) 262-5335

ROCHE, ROBERT PAUL, b. Albany, N.Y., Feb. 2, 1937; A.B. cum laude, Coll. of Holy Cross, 1958; LL.B., Union Coll., 1961, J.D., 1968. Admitted to N.Y. State bar, 1961, Fed. Dist. Ct. bar, 1961, Tax Ct. bar, 1966; asso. firm Medwin, Tabner, & Carlson, 1961-65; partner firm Goodwin & Roche, 1965-66; partner firm Schrade, Morris & Roche, Albany, 1967-73; sr. partner firm Robert P. Roche, Albany, 1974—; trial practice judge Union Law Sch., 1970-76. Chmn. South End Catholic Consol. Sch. Bd., Albany, 1973-74; atty. Albany County, N.Y., 1974-75; trustee Maria Coll., 1976—. Mem. N.Y. State, Albany County bar assns. Contbg. editor: The Evangelist, 1966-72. Home: 20 Darnley Greene Delmar NY 12054 Office: 90 State St Albany NY 12207 Tel (518) 463-1193

ROCHELLE, WILLIAM JENNINGS, JR., b. Corsicana, Tex., Aug. 9, 1917; A.B., George Washington U., 1938, J.D., 1940. Admitted to D.C. bar, 1940, Tex. bar, 1941; partner firm Rochelle, King & Balzersen, and predecessors, Dallas, 1947—; adj. prof. law schs. So. Meth. U., U. Tex. Mem. State Bar Tex., Am. Bar Assn., Nat. Bankruptcy Conf. Lectr. insts., seminars; contbr. articles to legal jours. Office: 1435 Republic Bank Bldg Dallas TX 75201 Tel (214) 742-4171

ROCHFORD, JOHN JAMES, b. Indpls., Oct. 19, 1918; B.S. in Bus., Ind. U., 1940, LL.B., 1951, J.D., 1967. Admitted to Ind. bar, 1951, U.S. Tax Ct. bar, 1951, U.S. Supreme Ct. bar, 1957; partner firm Rochford, Blackwell and Rochford, Indpls., 1951-58, firm Raikos, Barton, Rochford and Thomas, Indpls., 1959-69; judge Marion County (Ind.) Magistrate Ct., 1957-69, Marion County Municipal Ct., 1969—. Mem. Am., Ind. State, Indpls. bar assns. Home: 4750 Washington Blvd Indianapolis IN 46205 Office: 641 City-County Bldg Indianapolis IN 46204 Tel (317) 633-3454

ROCHMAN, JEFFREY EARL, b. Chgo., May 11, 1947; B.A., U. Ill., 1968; J.D., DePaul U., 1973. Admitted to Ill. bar, 1973; asso. firm Galowich, Galowich, McSteen & Phelan, Joliet, Ill., 1973—. Bd. dirs. Easter Seal Rehab. Center Will County, 1976—. Mem. Am., Ill., Will County bar assns. Home: 1717 Taylor St Joliet IL 60435 Office: 57 N Ottawa St Joliet IL 60431 Tel (815) 727-4575

ROCK, DAVID F., b. Rochester, N.Y., Dec. 27, 1938; A.B. with honors, Syracuse U., 1960; J.D., U. Mich., 1963. Admitted to D.C. bar, 1964, Ga. bar, 1968; tax law specialist IRS, Washington, 1963-67; partner firm Haas, Holland, Levison & Gibert, 1968-75; partner firm Rock & Haley, Atlanta, 1975—; mem. So. Pension Conf.; lectr. tax insts. Bd. dirs. Voter Project, Inc.; founder, chmn. 8th Ward Civic Assn. Atlanta; co-founder, vice chmn. Atlanta Coalition on Transp. Crisis; co-founder, dir. City Wide League Neighborhoods. Mem. Am., Ga. bar assns. Contbr. articles to legal jours. Home: 370 Valley Green Dr Atlanta GA 30342 Office: Tower Pl 3340 Peachtree Rd Atlanta GA 30326 Tel (404) 231-1240

ROCK, MARK ANTHONY, b. Pitts., Nov. 17, 1943; B.S., U. Pitts., 1966; J.D., Duquesne U. Admitted to Pa. bar, 1969, Ohio bar, 1973; field atty. NLRB, 1969-73; asso. firm Gaines, Stern, Schwarzwald and Robiner, Cleve., 1973—. Mem. Am., Ohio, Cuyahoga County, Cleve. Bar Assns. Home: 16179 Windsor Dr Strongsville OH 44136 Office: 1700 Investment Plaza 1801 E 9th St Cleveland OH 44114 Tel (216) 781-1700

ROCK, RONNIE BOYD, b. Rexburg, Idaho, June 27, 1938; B.A., U. Idaho, 1963, J.D., 1969. Admitted to Idaho bar, 1965, U.S. Tax Ct. bar, 1977; partner firm Moffatt Thomas Barrett & Blanton, Boise, Idaho, 1965—. Regional pres. Nat. Cystic Fibrosis Research Found., 1974-75; v.p. Bench Optimist Club, Boise, 1975-76. Mem. Idaho Assn. Def. Counsel (sec. 1975), Am., Idaho bar assns. Home: 10085 Saranac Dr Boise ID 83705 Office: 300 1st Security Bldg PO Box 829 Boise ID 83701 Tel (208) 345-2334

ROCKAFELLOW, LEE DAVID, b. Trenton, N.J., Dec. 30, 1944; A.B. in Govt., Franklin and Marshall Coll., 1967; J.D., Suffolk U., 1973. Admitted to Pa. bar, 1973; atty. firm Cadwallader, Darlington & Clark, Morrisville, Pa., 1973—. Legal counsel Jaycees, 1975-76. Mem. Am., Pa., Bucks County bar assns., Trial Lawyers Assn. Home: 337 Magnolia Dr Levittown PA 19054 Office: 20 N Pennsylvania Ave Morrisville PA 19067 Tel (215) 295-7135

ROCKEFELLER, EDWIN S., b. Harrisburg, Pa., Sept. 10, 1927; B.A., Yale U., 1948, LL.B., 1951. Admitted to Conn. bar, 1951, D.C. bar, 1956, U.S. Supreme Ct. bar; mem. firm Bierbower & Rockefeller, Washington, 1970—; exec. asst. chmn. FTC, 1959-61; chmn. adv. bd. BNA's weekly antitrust report. Mem. Am. Bar Assn. (chmn. sect. antitrust law 1976-77). Author: Antitrust Questions and Answers, 1974; Desk Book of FTC Practice and Procedure, 2d edit., 1976. Office: 1625 K St NW Washington DC 20006 Tel (202) 347-1900

ROCKHILL, GORDON LEE, b. San Francisco, Mar. 15, 1934; B.A., U. Wash., 1960, J.D., 1962. Admitted to Calif. bar, 1963; partner firm Kerwin, LaMar, Rockhill, Lelli & Gardella, Redwood City, Calif., 1967-71; individual practice law, Redwood City, 1971-74; partner firm Rockhill & Schaiman, Redwood City, 1975—. Bd. dirs. Legal Aid Soc., 1971-72; mem. adv. bd. Canada Coll., 1974-76; human relations council Sequoia High Sch., 1974—. Mem. Am., Calif., San Mateo County (past pres.) trial lawyers assns., No. Calif. Criminal Trial Lawyers Assn. Editor-in-chief Trial & Errors, 1973-75. Home: 10 West Summit Dr Redwood City CA 94062 Office: 303 Bradford St Redwood City CA 94063 Tel (415) 364-3346

ROCKLER, WALTER JAMES, b. Mpls., Nov. 25, 1920; A.B., U. Chgo., 1940; LL.B., Harvard U., 1943. Admitted to Ill. bar, 1947, N.Y. State bar, 1951, D.C. bar, 1953, U.S. Supreme Ct. bar, 1953; partner firm Lederer, Livingston, Kahn & Adsit, Chgo., 1954-60, Pennish, Steele & Rockler, Chgo., 1962-64, Cotton, Watt, Rockler & Jones, Chgo., 1964-66, Arnold & Porter, Washington, 1966—; pros. atty. Nuremberg War Trials, Germany, 1947-49. Mem. Am., Chgo. (chmn. fed. tax sect. 1961) bar assns. Contbr. articles to legal jours. and confs. Home: 11129 Stephalee Ln Rockville MD 20852 Office: 1229 19th St NW Washington DC 20036 Tel (202) 872-6789

RODA, PETER LEONARD, b. Rochester, N.Y., Feb. 8, 1935; B.A., Amherst Coll., 1956; LL.B., Duke U., 1962. Admitted to N.C. bar, 1962; individual practice law, Asheville, 1965-73; pub. defender 28th Judicial Dist., Asheville, 1973—. Pres., Asheville Toastmasters, 1967, Asheville Jaycees, 1968. Mem. Am., N.C. bar assns. Named Asheville's Outstanding Young Man, 1968. Home: 121 Lookout Dr Asheville NC 28804 Office: 913 Courthouse Asheville NC 28801 Tel (704) 255-5131

RODDENBERY, SEABORN ANDERSON, JR., b. Tampa, Fla., May 27, 1944; B.S., U. Ga., 1967; J.D., Cumberland Sch. Law, Birmingham, Ala., 1970. Admitted to Fla. bar, 1970; asso. firm Morain & Roddenbery, Pensacola, Fla., 1971-76; individual practice law, Pensacola, 1976—; atty. Legal Aid Soc of Escambia County (Fla.), 1971—. Mem. Bapt. Hosp. Corp., Pensacola, Pensacola Human Relations Commn. Mem. Soc. Bar 1st Jud. Circuit, Escambia-Santa Rosa County, Fla., Am. bar assns. Office: 117 W Garden St suite 201 Pensacola FL 32501 Tel (904) 434-3296

RODE, JOHN KENNETH, b. Bklyn., May 29, 1935; B.S.S., Georgetown U., 1957; J.D., St. Johns U., 1970. Admitted to N.Y. State bar, 1961, So. and Eastern U.S. Dist. Ct. bars, 1965; trial atty. Allstate Ins. Co., N.Y.C., 1961-69; mem. firm O'Brien Kelly & Rode, Mineola and Riverhead, N.Y., 1969—. Mem. N.Y. State, Nassau County, Suffolk County bar assns., Nassau-Suffolk Trial Lawyers Sect. (dir.). Office: 220 Mineola Blvd Mineola NY 11501 Tel (516) 741-7707

RODELL, FRED, b. Phila., Mar. 1, 1907; A.B., Haverford (Pa.) Coll., 1926, LL.D., 1973; U. London, 1926-27; LL.B. magna cum laude, Yale, 1931, M.A. (hon.), 1939. Asst. lit. editor Century Pub. Co., N.Y.C., 1927-28; spl. legal adviser to Gov. Gifford Pinchot, Pa., 1931-33; asst. prof. law Yale, 1933-36, asso. prof., 1936-39, prof., 1939—; bd. editors, Fortune mag., N.Y.C., 1937-38; spl. feature writer Chicago Times, 1940; contbg. editor The Progressive, 1943—, Scanlan's Mag., 1969—; bd. dirs. Coop. Consumers, Inc., New Haven 1940-45, Scanlan's Literary House. Mem. staff of Pres. Hoover's Com. on Social Trends, 1930; cons. for com. of corr. Council for Democracy, 1940-42; dir. publicity, mem. consumer com. Conn. State Def. Council, 1941-43; mem. Bethany Zoning Bd., 1957-65; mem. Bethany Dem. Town Commn., 1956-64. Dem. candidate for Conn. Gen. Assembly, Bethany, 1956. Fellow Silliman Coll., Yale. Mem. Am. Arbitration Assn. (nat. panel), Phi Beta Kappa, Order Coif; hon. mem. Yale Employees, Local 142, U.C.W. Author: Fifty-Five Men: the Story of the Constitution, 1936; Woe Unto You, Lawyers, 1939; Democracy and the Third Term, 1940; Nine Men: A Political History of the Supreme Court from 1790 to 1955, 1955; Her Infinite Variety, 1966. Case and comment editor Yale Law Jour., 1930-31, now contbr. Contbr. to Life, Harper's, Reader's Digest, Saturday Rev., Look, N.Y. Times mag., Atlantic, other law revs. Home: Falls Rd Bethany CT 06525 Office: Yale U Law Sch New Haven CT 06520*

RODEN, STANLEY MICHAEL, b. Los Angeles, Nov. 1, 1941; B.A., U. Calif., 1963; LL.B., Hastings Coll., 1966. Admitted to Calif. bar, 1966; dep. dist. atty., Kings County, Calif., 1967-68, Santa Barbara County, 1968-70; individual practice law, Santa Barbara, Calif., 1970-74; district atty. Santa Barbara County, 1975—. Com. chmn. Juvenile Justice Master Plan Task Force, mem. bd. Office of Criminal Justice Planning. Mem. Calif. Dist. Attys. Assn., Barristers Club Santa Barbara, Santa Barbara, Am. bar assns. Home: 301 Oceano Apt 2-D Santa Barbara CA 93109 Office: 118 E Figueroa St Santa Barbara CA 93101 Tel (805) 963-1441

RODER, EDWARD JOHN, b. Watertown, N.Y., June 2, 1932; B.A., St. John Fisher Coll., 1976; J.D., Boston Coll., 1961. Admitted to N.Y. State bar, 1961, U.S. Supreme Ct. bar, 1965; asso. firm Yorowitch & Frank, Rochester, N.Y., 1962-63, firm Roder, Schiano & Poyzer, Rochester, 1963-66; individual practice law, Rochester, 1966-75; partner firm Roder, Missal, Trotto & Barry, Clyde and Rochester, N.Y., 1976—; asst. dist. atty. Wayne County (N.Y.), 1968-69. Mem. Wayne County Democratic Com., 1971—, v.p., 1976—; chmn. Huron town Dem. com., 1976—, mem., 1971—. Mem. Am., N.Y. State, Wayne County bar assns., N.Y. State Trial Lawyers Assn. Home: R D 1 Box 255 North Rose NY 14516 Office: 69 Glasgow St Clyde NY 14433 Tel (315) 923-2281

RODGERS, EDWARD, b. Pitts., Aug. 12, 1927; B.A., Howard U., 1949; J.D., Fla. A. and M. U., 1963. Admitted to Fla. bar, 1963; tchr. Palm Beach County (Fla.) Pub. Sch. System, 1952-60; individual practice law, W. Palm Beach, Fla., 1963-65; asst. solicitor Palm Beach County, 1965-67; judge Municipal Cts. Riviera Beach, W. Palm Beach, Fla., 1967-69; Palm Beach County Ct., 1973; adminstrv. judge, 1975—. Bd. dirs. Am. Cancer Soc., W. Palm Beach, Vis. Nurses Assn. W. Palm Beach, Dept. Minority Mental Health, W. Palm Beach, Gulf Stream council Boy Scouts Am. Mem. Nat., Fla., Palm Beach County bar assns., Am. Trial Lawyers Assn. Home: 813 S Mangonia Circle St

West Palm Beach FL 33401 Office: Room 419 Palm Beach County Courthouse West Palm Beach FL 33401 Tel (305) 837-2280

RODGERS, HENRY LEE, b. Philadelphia, Miss., Apr. 6, 1903; ed. Miss. Coll., 1920-22, Cumberland U., 1922-24; LL.B., U. Miss., 1927. Admitted to bar, 1927; partner firm Rodgers & Prisock, Louisville, 1927-42; individual practice law, 1944—; city atty. City of Louisville; dist. atty., 1946-51; judge Miss. Circuit Ct., 1951-61; justice Miss. Supreme Ct., 1961-76, presiding justice, 1976—. Mem. Miss. State Bar. Recipient letter of appreciation U. Miss. Law Center, 1976; author: Search & Seizure; Process. Home: 431 Spring St Louisville MS 39339 Office: PO Box 754 Louisville MS 39339 Tel (601) 773-9477

RODGERS, HERMAN MILLISON, b. New Castle, Pa., Sept. 10, 1916; A.B., Grove City (Pa.) Coll., 1938; LL.B., U. Pa., 1947. Admitted to Pa. bar, 1947, U.S. Supreme Ct. bar, 1971; individual practice law, Grove City, 1947-54; dist. atty. Mercer County (Pa.), 1952-54; presiding judge Ct. Common Pleas of Mercer County, 1954-66; with firm Rodgers, Marks & Perfilio, Sharon, Pa., 1966—, now sr. partner; solicitor Borough of Grove City, 1948-52, 67—. Deacon, E. Main Presbyterian Ch., Grove City. Mem. Pa., Am., Mercer County (past pres.) bar assns., Am. Judicature Soc., Pa. Council Juvenile Ct. Judges (past v.p.), Am., Pa. trial lawyers assns. Asso. editor U. Pa. Law Rev., 1940-41, 46-47. Home: 604 Woodland Ave Grove City PA 16127 Office: 81 E State St Sharon PA 16146 Tel (412) 981-8000

RODGERS, JAMES ANTHONY, b. N.Y.C., Nov. 27, 1938; B.A., Williams Coll., 1960; M.S. in Geology, Lehigh U., 1962; J.D., U. Mich., 1967. Admitted to N.Y. bar, 1968, Tex. bar, 1971; asso. firm White & Case, N.Y.C., 1967-71; counsel Exxon Corp., Houston, 1971—. Mem. Am. Bar Assn. (coal law com.), N.Y. C. of C. (past mem. tax com.). Office: Exxon Corp 800 Bell St Houston TX 77801 Tel (713) 656-6361

RODGERS, JOSEPH JAMES, b. Irvington, N.J., Jan. 18, 1947; B.A., Seton Hall U., 1968, J.D., 1973. Admitted to N.J. bar, 1973; dep. atty. gen. N.J. Div. Criminal Justice, 1973-75; asst. prosecutor Passaic County (N.J.), Paterson, 1975-77, Cape May County (N.J.), Cape May Courthouse, 1977—. Mem. Am., N.J., Passaic County bar assns., Nat. Dist. Attys. Assn. Home: 36 Foxborough Rd Ocean View NJ 08230 Office: Cape May County Court House Cape May Courthouse NJ 08210 Tel (609) 465-7111

RODI, KARL BORTON, b. Calumet, Mich., Sept. 6, 1908; A.B., Pomona Coll., 1929; J.D., Harvard, 1933. Admitted to Calif. bar, 1933, U.S. Dist. Ct. for Central div. Calif. bar, 1933, U.S. Supreme Ct. bar; asso. firm O'Melveny & Myers, Los Angeles, 1933-36; partner firm Rodi, Pettker, Galbraith, Bond & Phillips, and predecessors, Los Angeles, 1939—. Trustee Beverly Hills Unified Sch. Dist., 1963-67; commr., Beverly Hills Planning Commn., 1966-72; trustee Pomona Coll., 1973—. Office: 611 W 6th St Los Angeles CA 90017 Tel (213) 680-0823

RODIO, ORLANDO, b. Providence, May 14, 1917; A.B., Brown U., 1938; J.D., Suffolk U., 1963. Admitted to R.I. bar, 1963, U.S. Supreme Ct. bar, 1972; investigator Wage-Hour and Pub. Contracts Div., U.S. Dept. Labor, Providence, 1941-43, 46-58; field examiner, atty. NLRB, Boston, 1958-72; individual practice law, Providence, 1972—; instr. extension div. Brown U., 1966-72; legal cons. Occupational Safety div. R.I. Dept. Labor, 1973-74; instr. Providence Coll., 1975—. Chmn. No. Providence Charter Commn., 1969-70. Mem. Am., Fed., R.I. (chmn. labor com. 1975—) bar assns., Indsl. Relations Research Assn., Internat. Indsl. Relations Assn., Soc. Profls. in Dispute Resolution, Am. Arbitration Assn., Nat. Center for Dispute Resolution. Home: 439 Smithfield Rd North Providence RI 02904 Office: 1104 Industrial Bank Bldg Providence RI 02903 Tel (410) 351-2525

RODMAN, ROLAND KENT, b. Cheyenne, Wyo., June 14, 1919; B.A., U. Oreg., 1941, J.D., 1947. Admitted to Oreg. bar, 1947; individual practice law, Eugene, 1947-48; dep. dist. atty. Lane County (Oreg.), 1948-51; partner firm Rodman & Rodman, Eugene, 1953-60; judge 2d Dist. Oreg. Circuit Ct., Eugene, 1960—; justice pro tem Oreg. Supreme Ct., Eugene, 1948; lectr., U. Oreg., Eugene, 1956-58, Bd. dirs. Jr. Achievement Eugene, Oreg. Mus. Sci. and Industry, Eugene, Lane County Council Alcoholism, Lane County Community Health Council, Lane County Mental Health Center. Mem. Am., Oreg., Lane County bar assns., Am. Judicature Soc., Circuit Judges Assn. Oreg. (pres.), Phi Alpha Delta. Home: 31563 Fox Hollow St Eugene OR 97405 Office: Lane County Courthouse 8th St & Oak St Eugene OR 97401 Tel (503) 687-4257

RODMAN, WILLIAM MICHAEL, b. Washington, June 11, 1943; B.A., Northwestern U., 1964, J.D., 1968. Admitted to Ill. bar, 1968; asso. firm Tim J. Harrington, Chgo., 1968-69; legal and claims mgr. Hertz Corp., Chgo., 1969-72; partner firm Rodman & Forest, Glenview, Ill., 1972—; dir. Glenview Guaranty Savs. & Loan Assn., 1973—. Bd. dirs. Glenview C. of C., 1972—, pres., 1974-75; bd. dirs. Glenview Youth Services. Mem. Ill., NW Suburban, Am. bar assns. Home: 1703 Pickwick Ln Glenview IL 60025 Office: 950 Waukegan Rd Glenview IL 60025 Tel (312) 729-0520

RODNER, JEFFREY S., b. Yonkers, N.Y., Nov. 18, 1944; B.A., Hobart Coll., 1966; J.D., Albany Coll., 1969. Admitted to N.Y. State Apellate Div. bar, 1969; partner firm Gellert & Rodner, Yonkers, 1970—. Mem. Yonkers, Westchester County bar assns. Office: 30 S Broadway St Yonkers NY 10701 Tel (914) 969-6465

RODNERS, JAMES OTIS, b. N.Y.C., Sept. 16, 1945; student law Universidad Catolica Andres Bello; J.D., Harvard U., 1970, M.B.A., 1972. Admitted to Fed. Dist. bar, Venezuela, 1969, Mass. bar, 1972; cons. Cabot Corp.; spl. counsel Andenean Devel. Corp.; dir. Inversora Venezuela; prof. fin. law Instituto de Estudios Superiores de Administracion; prof. contracts torts Cath. U. Caracas. Mem. Am., Mass. bar assns., Am. Soc. Internat. Law, Acad. Polit. Sci. Contbr. articles to legal jours. Address: JF Kennedy Postal Station Boston MA 02114

RODOPHELE, ROBERT PAUL, b. Quincy, Mass., Feb. 15, 1948; B.S., Boston Coll., 1969, J.D., 1972. Admitted to Mass. bar, 1972; examiner City of Cambridge (Mass.) Rent Control Bd., 1973-74; asst. atty. gen. Commonwealth of Mass., Boston, 1974—. Mem. Am., Mass., Boston bar assns. Home: 24 Hamilton Ave Quincy MA 02169 Office: 1 Ashburton Pl Boston MA 02108 Tel (617) 727-2225

RODRIGUEZ, GEORGE N., SR., b. Washington, Jan. 20, 1909; student St. Mary's U., 1927-30; LL.B., U. Ariz., 1933. Admitted to Tex. bar, 1933, 9th Fed. Circuit and 5th Fed. Circuit bar, 1961, U.S. Supreme Ct. bar, 1973; individual practice law, El Paso, Tex., 1933-64; asst. atty. City El Paso, 1939-45; judge El Paso County Ct. at Law, 1964-69; dist. atty. 34th Jud. Dist., Tex., 1969; judge 168th Tex. Dist. Ct., El Paso, 1969—. Mem. NCCJ, El Paso. Mem. Am., Tex., El Paso bar assns., Am. Judicature Soc., Tex. Bar Found. Home: 401 San Saba Rd El Paso TX 79912 Office: 609 City-County Bldg El Paso TX 79901 Tel (915) 543-2810

RODRIGUEZ, RUBEN, b. Santa Fe, N.Mex., Aug. 6, 1921; J.D., U. N.Mex., 1952. Admitted to N. Mex. bar, 1952; atty. N. Mex. State Tax Commn., 1952-58; mem. staff Criminal Law Study Com., 1958-59; commr. N. Mex. State Labor Commn., 1958; atty. N. Mex. Motor Vehicle Dept., Santa Fe. Mem. N. Mex. Bar Assn. Office: 302 E Palace Ave Santa Fe NM 87501 Tel (505) 982-5521

ROE, WILLARD JOSEPH, b. Pierce County, N.D., Feb. 9, 1916; B.A., Gonzaga U., 1938, LL.B., 1940; LL.M., Cath. U. Am., 1942. Admitted to Wash. bar, 1941; practiced in Spokane, Wash., 1941-61; judge Wash. Superior Ct., Spokane, 1961—; with UNRRA, China, Europe, 1945-47; prof. constl. law and evidence Gonzaga U., 1949-62. Chmn. council on race relations NCCJ, Spokane, 1948-49; chmn. Spokane County (Wash.) Democratic Com., 1954-60; del. Dem. Nat. Conv., 1956; bd. dirs. Fairmount Meml. Park, Spokane. Mem. Wash. State Superior Ct. Judges Assn. (pres. 1976-77), Wash. State, Spokane County (pres. 1958-59) bar assns., Alpha Sigma Nu, Phi Alpha Delta. Recipient Law medal Gonzaga U., 1971; contbr. articles to legal jours. Home: 3616 West Dr Spokane WA 99204 Office: Spokane County Courthouse Spokane WA 99204 Tel (509) 456-4736

ROEDDER, WILLIAM CHAPMAN, JR., b. St. Louis, June 21, 1946; B.S., U. Ala., 1968; J.D., Samford U., 1972. Admitted to Ala. bar, 1972; law clk. to chief justice Ala. Supreme Ct., 1972-73; partner firm Hand, Arendall, Bedsole, Greaves & Johnston, Mobile, Ala., 1973—. Mem. Mobile County, Am. bar assns., Ala. State Bar, Curia Honoris, Order of Barristers, Phi Alpha Delta (pres. 1971-72). Editorial bd. Cumberland-Samford Law Rev., 1971-72. Home: 1100 Matterhorn Dr Mobile AL 36608 Office: Box 123 Mobile AL 36601 Tel (205) 432-5511

ROEHL, JOSEPH ERNEST, b. Albuquerque, Feb. 17, 1913; B.A., U. N.Mex., 1936; LL.B., U. Tex., 1946. Admitted to Tex., N.Mex. bars, 1946; law clk. judge U.S. Circuit Ct., 1946-47; asso. firm Simms, Modrall, Seymor & Simms, 1947-53; partner firm Modrall, Sperling, Roehl, Harris & Sisk, Albuquerque, 1953—; chmn. N.Mex. Supreme Ct. Com. Uniform Jury Instructions, 1961—; speaker, writer in field. Mem. Am., N.Mex. bar assns. Office: 800 Public Service Bldg Drawer 2168 Albuquerque NM 87103 Tel (505) 243-4511

ROEHRICK, JOHN PAUL, b. Faribault, Minn., May 4, 1943; B.A., Drake U., 1965, J.D., 1966. Admitted to Iowa bar, 1966; asso. firm J. Riley McManus, Des Moines, 1966-71; partner firm Comito, Roehrick & Vincent, Des Moines, 1971-76; partner firm Roehrick & Mohr, Des Moines, 1976—; instr. Des Moines Area Community Coll., 1969-71; cons. Iowa State Dept. Health, 1976; mem. profl. adv. council to Polk County (Iowa) Citizens Commn. on Corrections, 1976. Mem. Am. Bar Assn., Assn. Trial Lawyers Iowa. Author: The New Iowa Criminal Code-A Comparison, 1976. Home: 529 43d St Des Moines IA 50312 Office: 535 Insurance Exchange Bldg Des Moines IA 50309 Tel (515) 243-1403

ROEMER, CHARLES HAROLD, b. Paterson, N.J., Feb. 5, 1899; LL.B., N.Y. U., 1919. Admitted to N.J. bar, 1920, U.S. Supreme Ct. bar, 1935; city atty. City of Paterson (N.J.), 1920-23, 28-31; individual practice law, Paterson, 1920—; prof. law John Marshall Sch. Law, 1931-45. Pres. Bd. Finance, Paterson, 1948-50, Planning Commn., 1948, Indsl. Commn.; del. N.J. Constl. Conv., 1966; spl. counsel atty. gen. N.J., Soc. Establishing Useful Mfg., 1936. Mem. N.J. Bar Assn. Author: Does New Jersey Need a New Constitution?, 1930. Home: 37-27 Berdon Ave Fairlawn NJ 07410 Office: 5 Colt St 403 Paterson NJ 07505 Tel (201) 742-4680

ROEMER, HENRY C., JR., b. 1924; A.B., Harvard U., 1944; LL.B., Columbia U., 1950. Asso. firm Davis, Polk & Wardwell, 1950-58; sec., dir. R. J. Reynolds Tobacco Co., 1958-71, v.p., gen. counsel R. J. Reynolds Industries Inc., Winston-Salem, N.C., 1971—. Bd. visitors Wake Forest U. Sch. Law; mem. advisory bd. Internat. and Comparative Law Center, Southwestern Legal Found. Office: 401 N Main St Winston-Salem NC 27102*

ROESCH, JOHN THOMAS, b. Bklyn., Nov. 7, 1933; B.S., L.I. U., 1960; J.D., Bklyn. Law Sch., 1964. Admitted to N.Y. State bar, 1964; tax mgr. Pfizer Chems., N.Y.C., 1960-64; trial atty. Royal Globe Ins. Co., Mineola, N.Y., 1964-69. Pres. New E. Meadow Civic Assn., St. Raphaels Sch. Bd. Mem. N.Y. State, Am., Nassau County bar assns., Cath. Lawyers Assn., Nat. Hist. Soc., Smithsonian Soc. Home: 872 Abbott St East Meadow NY 11554 Office: 611 Newbridge Rd East Meadow NY 11554 Tel (516) 781-1719

ROESLER, ROBERT JOSEPH, b. Coffeyville, Kans., Nov. 17, 1930; B.S., Okla. City U., 1958, J.D., 1967. Admitted to Okla. bar, 1967; trust officer First Nat. Bank of Tulsa. Home: 2810 E 48th St Tulsa OK 74105 Office: Box 1 Tulsa OK 74193 Tel (918) 586-5661

ROESS, MARTIN JOHN, b. Ocala, Fla., Dec. 18, 1907; A.B., Cornell U., 1930, LL.D., 1931. Admitted to Fla. bar, 1932, D.C. bar, 1938, U.S. Supreme Ct. bar, 1935; asso. firm Rogers & Towers, Jacksonville, Fla., 1931-34; chief counsel Rental Housing div. Fed. Housing Adminstrn., Washington, 1934-38, dist. dir., Jacksonville, 1947-48; v.p., gen. counsel A. Lloyd Goode Contracting Co., Washington, 1938-46; pres. Builders Mortgage Corp., St. Petersburg, Fla., 1948-51; chmn. bd., pres. Guaranty Fed. Savs. & Loan Assn., St. Peterburg, 1962—; chmn. bd. Am. Nat. Bank, Clearwater, Fla., 1968—, Am. Bank of St. Petersburg, 1973—, N.Am., Mortgage Corp., St. Petersburg, 1955—; individual practice law, St. Petersburg, 1948—; mortgage and real estate broker; judge 6th Jud. Circuit Ct., St. Petersburg, 1967-68. Mem. Fla. Council 100, 1965—, dir., 1967-72. Mem. Cornell Law Assn., Mortgage Bankers Assn. Fla., Mortgage Bankers Assn. Am., Am., Fla. bankers assns., U.S., Fla. savs. and loan leagues, St. Petersburg Area C. of C. (dir. 1970-71, mem. com. 100 1969-70), Phi Beta Kappa, Phi Delta Phi, Sigma Alpha Epsilon. Home: 434 Park St N St Petersburg FL 33710 Office: 2100 66th St Petersburg FL 33733 Tel (813) 347-2141

ROESSLER, RICHARD MARVIN, b. St. Louis, Mo., May 26, 1939; B.S., Bus. Adminstrn., Washington U., 1962; J.D., St. Louis U., 1968. Admitted to Mo. bar, 1968, Ill. bar, 1968; mem. firm Gundlach, Lee, Eggmann, Boyle & Roessler and predecessors, Belleville, Ill., 1968—, partner, 1972—. Mem. Ill., Mo., Am., St. Clair County bar assns., Mo. Arbitration Assn. Office: 5000 W Main St Belleville IL 62223 Tel (618) 277-9000

ROESSLER, RONALD JAMES, b. Kansas City, Mo., Aug. 10, 1939; B.A., Miami U., Oxford, Ohio, 1961; J.D., U. Wis., 1964; LL.M., George Washington U., 1968. Admitted to Wis. bar, 1964, D.C. bar, 1969, W. Va. bar, 1970, Md. bar, 1973; atty. CIA, Washington, 1964-66; atty. C & P Telephone Co. Washington, 1968-72; gen. counsel v.p. Alexander & Alexander, Balt., 1972—. Active Big Bros. Am., Balt., 1967—, bd. dirs., 1967-69. Mem. Am., Md., W.Va., D.C., Wis. bar assns., Am. Judicature Soc., Omicron Delta Kappa, Phi Alpha Delta. Home: 4303 Crab Orchard Rd Glen Arm MD 21057 Office: 300 E Joppa Rd Baltimore MD 21204 Tel (301) 296-3300

ROETS, GARY LYLE, b. Milw., Oct. 9, 1942; B.S., St. Norbert Coll., 1964; J.D., Marquette U., 1968. Admitted to Wis. bar, 1968; partner firm Drury and Roets, Portage, Wis., 1968—. Mem. Wis., Columbia County (pres. 1973-74) bar assns. Home: 416 W Conant St Portage WI 53901 Office: 234 W Cook St Portage WI 53901 Tel (608) 742-4343

ROGERS, CLEETA JOHN, b. Perryville, Ark., July 24, 1930; B.A., Central State U., Edmond, Okla., 1951; J.D., Oklahoma City U., 1955. Admitted to Okla. bar, 1955; since practiced in Oklahoma City, mem. firm Rogers, Henderson & Spearman, 1955-57, Miller, Adams & Rogers, 1958-64; individual practice law, 1964-71, 73—; mem. firm Rogers, Travis & Jordan, 1971-73. Mem. Okla. Ho. of Reps., 1952-60, Okla. Senate, 1960-74; pres. Okla. Civic Music Assn., 1958-63, Oklahoma City Community Council, 1959-60. Mem. Am., Okla. bar assns., Am. Trial Lawyers Assn. Named Oklahoma City Man of Year, Oklahoma City Jr. C. of C., 1957. Home: 415 NW 18th St Oklahoma City OK 73103

ROGERS, DAN A., b. Fort Smith, Ark., Aug. 28, 1923; student U. Tulsa; J.D., U. Okla., 1950. Admitted to Okla. bar, 1950, U.S. Supreme Ct. bar, 1953; asso. firm Crouch, Rhodes and Crowe, Tulsa, 1953-60; mng. partner firm Rogers, Rogers and Jones, Tulsa, 1960—. Mem. Am., Fed., Okla., Tulsa County bar assns., Assn. Ins. Attys (exec. council), Internat. Assn. Ins. Counsel, Okla. Assn. Ins. Counsel (pres. 1975). Home: 3730 S Atlanta Pl Tulsa OK 74105 Office: 117 E 5th St Tulsa OK 74103 Tel (918) 583-5111

ROGERS, EDMUND CHENAULT, b. Louisville, June 8, 1908; B. Engring., Vanderbilt U., 1929; J.D., Georgetown U., 1933. Tchr., Wallace Sch., Nashville, 1928-29; examiner U.S. Patent Office, Washington, 1929-33; admitted to D.C. bar, 1932, Mo. bar 1935; individual practice law, Cleve., 1934; asso. firm L. C. Kingsland, St. Louis, 1935-40; partner firm Rogers, Eilers & Howell, and predecessors, St. Louis, 1941—; spl. asst. U.S. atty. gen., 1941; mem. adv. council St. Louis U. Law Sch. Bd. dirs. St. Louis Legal Aid Soc., Grace Hill House, St. Louis; lay reader local Episcopal Ch. Fellow Am. Coll. Trial Lawyers; mem. Am., Mo., St. Louis (chmn. patent sect. 1946) bar assns., Am. Patent Law Assn. (pres. 1963-64), Nat. Council Patent Law Assn. (pres. 1965). Home: 10079 Springwood Dr Ladue MO 63124 Office: suite 2162 7733 Forsyth Blvd Clayton MO 63105 Tel (314) 727-5188

ROGERS, H. JOHN, b. New Martinsville, W.Va., Apr. 22, 1940; A.B., W. Va. U., 1962; LL.B., Harvard, 1966. Admitted to W.Va. Supreme Ct. bar, 1966, U.S. Supreme Ct. bar, 1970; law clk. chief judge U.S. Dist. Ct., 1966-67; individual practice law, New Martinsville, 1967—; asst. prof. Ohio State U., 1973-74. Mem. Am., W.Va., Wetzel County bar assns., W.Va. Trial Lawyers Assn. Contbr. articles in field to profl. jours. Office: PO Box 490 New Martinsville WV 26155 Tel (304) 455-3200

ROGERS, JAMES THOMAS, b. Denver, Oct. 3, 1941; J.D., U. Wis., 1966. Admitted to Wis. bar, 1966, U.S. Supreme Ct. bar, 1973, U.S. Customs Ct., U.S. Ct. Claims, 1975, U.S. Tax Ct., 1976; chmn. Madison (Wis.) Legal Aid Soc., 1965-66; dist. atty. Lincoln County (Wis.), 1967, 69-73, 76-77; dist. atty. pro tem Oneida County (Wis.), 1972, Price County (Wis.), 1972-76; spl. city atty. City of Wausau (Wis.), 1973-74; practice law, Merrill, Wis.; chmn. judiciary com. N.E. Crime Control Commn., 1971-72. Chmn. Lincoln County Republican party, 1971-73. Mem. Lincoln County Bar Assn. (pres. 1969-70), State Bar Wis., Wis. (life), Nat. dist. attys. assns. Home: 1408 E 8th St Merrill WI 54452 Office: 120 S Mill St Merrill WI 54452 Tel (715) 536-5501

ROGERS, JOHN CHALKLEY, b. Oakland, Calif., May 29. 1944; B.A., U. Calif., 1966, J.D., 1969. Admitted to Calif. bar, 1970, Nev. bar, 1973; asso. firm Berry, Davis & McInerney, Oakland, Calif., 1970-72; individual practice law, Incline Village, Nev. and Kings Beach, Calif. Mem. adv. planning commn. Tahoe Regional Planning Agy., 1974-76, sec., bd. dirs. Lakeside Community Hosp. 1976—. Mem. Calif., Washoe County, Nev. bar assns. Home: 733 James Ln Incline Village NV 89450 Office: 785 Southwood Blvd PO Box 3508 Incline Village NV 89450 Tel (702) 831-3666 also 8645 N Lake Blvd PO Box 1335 Kings Beach CA 95719

ROGERS, JOHN D., b. Somerset, Ky., July 18, 1940; A.B., Eastern Ky. U., 1963, M.A., 1967; J.D., U. Louisville, 1972. Tchr. pub. schs., Pulaski County, Ky., 1965-66, Somerset, Ky., 1966-70; admitted to Ky. bar, 1973; partner firm Aker & Rogers, Somerset, 1974—; mem. Ky. Senate, 1976—. Mem. Am., Ky., Pulaski County bar assns. Home: 3975 Shoreline Dr Somerset KY 42501 Office: 106 W Columbia St Somerset KY 42501 Tel (606) 679-6183

ROGERS, JOSEPH MARK, b. Malvern, Ark., Apr. 9, 1943; B.A., U. Ark., 1965, LL.B., 1968. Admitted to Ark. bar, 1969; law clk. to U.S. Dist. Judge Eastern and Western Dists Ark., El Dorado, 1969-70; partner firm Hale, Fogleman & Rogers, West Memphis, Ark., 1970—; dep. prosecuting atty. Crittenden County, Ark., 1973—. Chmn. Crittenden County Heart Assn., 1971, Crittenden County Cancer Assn., 1972. Mem. Ark., N.E. Ark, Crittenden County, Am. bar assns. Home: 808 S Roselawn St West Memphis AR 72301 Office: 626 E Broadway St West Memphis AR 72301 Tel (501) 725-1900

ROGERS, LESLIE LAWTON, III, b. Mullins, S.C., Oct. 14, 1936; B.E.E., U. S.C., 1959; J.D., Georgetown U., 1967; LL.M. in Patent Law and Trade Regulations, George Washington U., 1972. Admitted to Va. bar, 1967, D.C. bar, 1967; elec. engr. Bethleham Steel, Balt., 1962-63; patent research engr. Mfr.'s Aircraft Assn., Washington, 1963-65; mgr. Washington patent ops. Bendix Corp., 1965-67; asso. firm Burns, Doane, Swecker & Mathis, Washington, 1967-69, partner, 1969—. Mem. U.S. Trademark Assn., Am., Va., D.C. bar assns., Am. Patent Law Assn. Home: 2011 Fort Dr Alexandria VA 22307 Office: 815 Connecticut Ave NW Washington DC 20006 Tel (202) 298-9185

ROGERS, ROBERT MERRITT, b. Birmingham, Ala., July 25, 1942; B.S., U. Ala., 1964; J.D., Cumberland Sch. Law Samford U., 1967. Admitted to Ala. bar, 1967; asso. firm Rogers, Howard, Redden & Mills, Birmingham, after 1967, now partner. Chmn. area Duck's

Unltd., 1965, Ala. chmn., 1966. Mem. Ala., Am. trial lawyers' assns. Office: 1033 Frank Nelson Bldg Birmingham AL 35203 Tel (205) 251-5138

ROGERS, STANLEY, b. Los Angeles, Feb. 28, 1934; A.B., Princeton U., 1956; J.D., U. Calif., Los Angeles, 1959. Admitted to Calif. bar, 1960, U.S. Supreme Ct. bar, 1974; law clk. U.S. Fed. Dist. Ct., 1959-60; asso. firm Little, Curry & Hahn, Los Angeles, 1960-62; partner firm Rogers & Harris, Los Angeles, 1962—; judge pro tem Beverly Hills (Calif.) Municipal Ct., 1968-70, Los Angeles Municipal Ct., 1975—; mem. panel Am. Arbitration Assn., 1967—. Cubmaster Westdale and Westwood Cub Scouts; trustee Los Angeles County Law Library, 1977—; dir. Westdale Home Owners Assn.; mem. Palms, Mar Vista and Del Rey Citizen Adv. Planning Com., 1973; mem. adv. councils pub. schs., 1974-77; trustee Los Angeles County Law Library, 1977—. Mem. Los Angeles County Bar Assn. Home: 661 Warner Ave Los Angeles CA 90024

ROGERS, STILLMAN DAVID, b. Nashua, N.H., Mar. 6, 1939; B.A., Harvard, 1961; J.D., Am. U., 1968. Admitted to N.H. bar, 1968; law clk. firm Keller & Heckman, Washington, 1966-67; asso. firm Faulkner, Plaut, Hanna & Zimmerman, Keene, N.H., 1968-75; with firm Olson, McMahon & Rogers, Keene, 1975—; bd. dirs. N.H. Legal Assistance, 1970-73. Mem. Keene Safety Bd. Rev., 1972-76; bd. visitors USAF Acad., 1973-76. Mem. N.H., Cheshire County (N.H.), Am. bar assns., Phi Alpha Delta. Home: RFD 2 Richmond NH 03470 Office: 39 Vernon St Keene NH 03431 Tel (603) 352-3034

ROGERS, WILLIAM DILL, b. Wilmington, Del., May 12, 1927; A.B., Princeton U., 1948; LL.B., Yale U., 1951. Admitted to D.C. bar, 1953; mem. firm Arnold & Porter, Washington, 1953—; spl. counsel, U.S. coordinator AID, 1962-65; asst. sec. for Inter-Am. Relations Dept. State, 1974-76, under sec. for economic affairs, 1976. Mem. Am. Soc. Internat. Law (pres. 1972-74), Center for Inter-Am. Relations (pres. 1965-68), Internat. Law Inst., Council on Fgn. Relations, Commn. of U.S.-Latin Am. Relations. Author: The Twilight Struggle, The Alliance for Progress and U.S.-Latin American Relations, 1967; recipient Distinguished Honor award AID, 1965. Home: 2 Jefferson Run Rd Great Falls VA 22066 Office: 1229 19th St NW Washington DC 20036 Tel (202) 872-6915

ROGERS, WILLIAM PIERCE, b. Norfolk, N.Y., June 23, 1913; A.B., Colgate U., 1934; LL.B., Cornell U., 1937. Admitted to N.Y. bar, 1937, D.C. bar, 1950; asst. dist. atty. N.Y. County, 1938-42, 46-47; counsel U.S. Senate War Investigating Com., 1947, chief counsel, 1947-48; chief counsel U.S. Senate Investigations Sub-Com. Exec. Expenditures Com., 1948-50; partner firm Dwight, Royall, Harris, Koegel & Caskey, N.Y.C. and Washington, 1950-53; dep. atty. gen. U.S., 1953-57, atty. gen., 1957-61; mem. firm Royall, Koegel, Rogers & Wells, N.Y.C. and Washington, 1961-69; U.S. sec. state, 1969-73; partner firm Rogers & Wells, N.Y.C. and Washington, 1973—; U.S. rep. 20th Gen. Assembly UN, 1967, UN Ad Hoc Com. on S. Africa, 1967; mem. Pres.'s Commn. on Crime and Adminstrn., 1965-67. Fellow Am. Bar Found.; mem. Bar Assn. City N.Y., Am., N.Y. State, D.C. bar assns., Am. Law Inst., Order of Coif, Sigma Chi. Editorial bd. Cornell Law Quar., 1935-37. Home: 7007 Glenbrook Rd Bethesda MD 20014 also 870 UN Plaza New York City NY 10017 Office: 200 Park Ave New York City NY 10017 also 1666 K St NW Washington DC 20006

ROGGE, O(ETJE) JOHN, b. Cass County, Ill., Oct. 12, 1903; A.B., U. Ill., 1922; LL.B., Harvard U., 1925, S.J.D., 1931. Admitted to Ill. bar, 1925, N.Y. bar, 1943, U.S. Tax Ct. bar, 1926; individual practice law, N.Y.C., 1947—; counsel RFC, 1934-37; spl. counsel SEC, 1937-38, asst. gen. counsel, 1938-39; asst. atty. gen. charge criminal div. U.S. Dept. Justice, 1939-40; spl. asst. to U.S. Atty. Gen., 1943-46. Mem. Am. Bar Assn., Assn. Bar City N.Y., N.Y. County Lawyers Assn., Phi Beta Kappa. Author: Our Vanishing Civil Liberties, 1949; Why Men Confess, 1959; The First and the Fifth, 1960; The Official German Report, 1961; contbg. author: Am. Jurisprudence Trials, 1965; The Rights of the Accused, 1972; contbr. articles to legal jours. Home: 44 Laurel Ledge Ct Stamford CT 06903 Office: 777 3d Ave New York City NY 10017 Tel (212) 421-6400

ROGIN, EDWARD BORIS, b. N.Y.C., May 24, 1945; B.A., U. Mich., 1967, J.D., 1970. Admitted to Calif. bar, 1971; asso. firm Orrick, Herrington, Rowley & Sutcliffe, San Francisco, 1970-76, partner, 1977—. Mem. Am., Calif., San Francisco bar assns. Office: 600 Montgomery St San Francisco CA 94111 Tel (415) 392-1122

ROGOFF, EDWIN JAY, b. Chgo., Dec. 10, 1912; student Northwestern U., 1932; J.D., DePaul U., 1936. Admitted to Ill. bar, 1936; mem. firm Rogoff & Rogoff, Chgo., 1952—; sec., treas. Lord & Rogers Ins. Agency, 1952-65; pres. Ambassador Ins. Co., Chgo., 1965—. Mem. Chgo. Bar Assn. Office: 201 N Wells St Chicago IL 60606 Tel (312) 726-3500

ROGOSHESKE, WALTER FREDERICK, b. Sauk Rapids, Minn., July 12, 1914; student St. Cloud Tchrs. Coll., 1932-33, Valparaiso U., 1933-34; B.S. in Law, U. Minn., 1937, LL.B., 1939. Admitted to Minn. bar, 1940; practiced in Sauk Rapids, 1940-50; mem. Minn. Ho. of Reps., 1943-49; judge Minn. 7th Dist. Ct., 1950-56; asso. justice Minn. Supreme Ct., 1962—; lectr. in law U. Minn., 1951-74; chmn. Mpls.-St. Paul Met. Airports Commn., 1949-50. Bd. dirs. Amicus, Inc., Mpls.; v.p. Big Bros., St. Paul. Fellow Am. Bar Found.; mem. Minn. Dist. Judges Assn. (pres. 1955-56), 7th Dist., State of Minn., Am. (council sect. criminal justice) bar assns., Am. Judicature Soc., Inst. Jud. Adminstrn., U. Minn. Law Alumni Assn. Office: State Capitol Saint Paul MN 55155

ROGOVIN, BERNARD S., b. Jersey City, Aug. 29, 1929; B.A., Bklyn. Coll., 1952; grad. Bklyn Law Sch., 1954. Admitted to N.Y. State bar, 1954; trial atty. All-State Ins. Co., 1957-58; pvt. practice, Rockville Centre, N.Y., 1958—. Vice pres. Bayswater Civic Assn., Queens, N.Y.; bd. dirs. Bayswater Jewish Center, Queens, Jewish Community Council, Queens. Mem. N.Y. State Trial Lawyers Assn., Bklyn., Nassau County, N.Y. State bar assns. Office: 100 Merrick Rd Rockville Centre NY 11570 Tel (516) 536-3344

ROGOVIN, MITCHELL, b. N.Y.C., Dec. 3, 1930; A.B., Syracuse U., 1952; LL.B., U. Va., 1954; LL.M., Georgetown U., 1960. Admitted to Va. bar, 1954, D.C. bar, 1968; chief counsel IRS, Washington, 1964-66; asst. atty. gen. Dept. Justice, Washington, 1966-69; partner firm Arnold & Porter, Washington, 1969-76, firm Rogovin, Stern & Huge, Washington, 1976—; gen. counsel Common Cause, Washington, 1970-76; spl. counsel CIA, Washington, 1975-77. Mem. Council on Fgn. Relations; dir. Nat. Legal Aid and Defenders; vice chmn. Center for Law and Social Policy; co-chmn. Council for Pub. Interest Law. Home: 4500 Klingle St NW Washington DC 20016 Office: Rogovin Stern & Huge 1730 Rhode Island Ave Washington DC 20036 Tel (202) 296-5820

ROHDE, JAMES DAVID, b. Columbia, Mo., Jan. 10, 1936; B.S. in Accounting, U. Mo., 1958; LL.B., Hastings Coll., San Francisco, 1961. Admitted to Calif. bar, 1962; individual practice law, San Francisco, 1962-63; mem. firm Low, Ball & Norton, San Francisco, 1963-64, jr. partner, 1964-67; counsel Holiday Magic Inc., San Rafael, Calif., 1967-69, Capital Funding Corp. (now Univ. Group), San Rafael, 1969-73; mem. firm Schaal, Rohde & Gamer, San Rafael, 1973—; dir. Equipment Fin. and Mgmt. Co., San Francisco, Am. Group Agys., San Rafael. Bd. dirs., gen. counsel Marin United Taxpayers, 1976. Mem. San Francisco, Calif., Marin County bar assns., Am. Bd. Trial Advocates. Home: 2 La Cuesta St Greenbrae CA 94904 Office: 4340 Redwood Hwy Suite 114 San Rafael CA 94903 Tel (417) 472-4140

ROHLEDER, L(AURENCE) HERBERT, b. Hays, Kan., Mar. 25, 1931; B.A., Washburn U., 1956, J.D., 1959; grad. Nat. Coll. State Judiciary, Reno, Nev., 1969-76. Admitted to Kans. bar, 1959; dep. treas. Ellis County (Kans.), 1949-51; partner firm Hampton, Ward and Rohleder, Great Bend, Kans., 1959-67; judge Kans. Dist. Ct., 20th Jud. Dist., Div. 2, 1967—; faculty adviser Nat. Coll. State Judiciary, 1975, 76. Active Barton County (Kans.) Jr. Coll. Endowment Assn., 1969-75. Mem. Kans. Dist. Judges Assn., Kans., S.W. Kans., Barton County (Kans.) bar assns. Author Ct. Unification Act, 1976. Home: 809 Coolidge St Great Bend KS 66530 Office: PO Box 1184 Great Bend KS 66530 Tel (316) 793-6401

ROHNER, RALPH JOHN, b. E. Orange, N.J., Aug. 10, 1938; A.B., Cath. U. Am., 1960, J.D., 1963. Admitted to Md. bar, 1964; teaching fellow Stanford, 1963-64; atty. pub. health div. HEW, 1964-65; prof. Cath. U. Am. Sch. Law, Washington, 1965—, acting dean, 1968-69, asso. dean, 1969-71; staff counsel consumer affairs subcom. U.S. Senate Banking Com., 1975-76; cons. Fed. Res. Bd., 1976—. Bd. dirs. Migrant Legal Action Program, Inc., Washington, Automobile Owners Action Council, Washington. Mem. Am. Bar Assn., Am. Judicature Soc., Am. Law Inst. Editor-in-chief Cath. U. Law Rev., 1962-63. Home: 7706 Powhatan St New Carrollton MD 20784 Office: Catholic U Sch Law Washington DC 20064 Tel (202) 635-5142

ROHWER, CLAUDE DONALD, b. Sacramento, Dec. 17, 1933; A.B., U. Calif., Berkeley, 1955, J.D., 1958. Admitted to Calif. bar, 1959; with JAGC, USAF, Nellif AFB, Nev., 1958-60; dep. atty. gen. Calif., Sacramento, 1960-61; asso. firm Downey, Brand, Seymour & Rohwer, Sacramento, 1961-64; partner Downey, Brand, Seymour & Rohwer, Sacramento, 1964-67; prof. McGeorge Sch. Law, Sacramento, 1961—. Scout master local council Boy Scouts Am., Las Vegas, 1958-60; legal advisor The Sacramento Plan, 1973-74. Mem. Sacramento, Calif., Am. bar assns., Order of Coif. Contbr. articles, chpts. to legal publs.; co-author: Contracts in a Nutshell. Home: 27 Meadowbrook Dr Davis CA 95616 Office: 3200 Fifth Ave Sacramento CA 95817 Tel (916) 449-7231

ROISMAN, ANTHONY ZELL, b. Oklahoma City, Okla., May 20, 1938; A.B. cum laude, Dartmouth Coll., 1960; LL.B., Harvard, 1963. Admitted to N.Y. State bar, 1965, D.C. bar, 1967, U.S. Supreme Ct. bar, 1968; atty. appelate sect., tax div., Dept. Justice, Washington, 1964-67; asso. firm Sullivan, Shea & Kenny, Washington, 1967-68; partner firm Roisman, Kessler & Cashdan, Washington, 1969-77; partner firm Sheldon, Harron & Roisman, Washington, 1977—; atty. Natural Resources Def. Council, 1977—. Coordinator vol. lawyers Washington Neighborhood Legal Services Program, 1968-69; mem. alumni advisory bd. Pub. Affairs, Center, Dartmouth Coll., 1974—; chmn. Citizens for Clean Energy and Carter, 1976. Mem. Am., D.C. bar assns., Americans for Democratic Action (chmn. Washington chpt. 1969-70), Lawyers Com. for Civil Rights under Law (chmn. task force on truth-in-lending regulation 1969). Office: 917 15th St NW Washington DC 20005 Tel (202) 737-5000

ROISMAN, GERALD ASHER, b. Hartford, Conn., May 12, 1937; B.A., Amherst Coll., 1959; J.D., U. Conn., 1962. Admitted to Conn. bar, 1962, U.S. Dist. Ct. for Conn., 1963, U.S. 2d Circuit Ct. Appeals bar, 1969, U.S. Supreme Ct. bar, 1977; prinicpal Gerald A. Roisman, Hartford, Conn.; spl. pros., Hartford County, 1967, justice of peace, 1962-71. Mem. bd. edn., West Hartford, 1975—. Mem. Am., Conn. Hartford County bar assns. Office: 31 Grand St Hartford CT 06106 Tel (203) 549-6700

ROKES, WILLIS PARK, b. Salt Lake City, Dec. 25, 1926; B.S., U. Utah, 1949, J.D., 1951, M.S., 1957; Ph.D., Ohio State U., 1959. Admitted to Utah bar, 1952, Nebr. bar, 1968; claims atty. Continental Agency Co., Salt Lake City, 1951-57; instr. law, ins. Ohio State U., 1957-59; asst. prof. U. Mont., 1959-61; asso. prof. U. Nebr.-Omaha, 1961-64, prof., 1964-75, regents prof., 1975—; cons. U.S. Dept. Justice. Cons. adv. com. Nat. Commn. Civil Disorders, 1967-68, Am. Inst. Property and Liability Underwriters, Ins. Inst. Am., various ins. cos. Chmn. Coalition Assns. Responsible Expressway Planning, 1970-76; mem. Omaha Mayor's Transit Users Advisory Comn., Nebr. Governor's Citizens' Advisory Group Transp., 1972-73. Mem. Utah, Nebr. bar assns., Am. Risk and Ins. Assn., Am. Soc. Chartered Life Underwriters, Am. Soc. Chartered Property and Casualty Underwriters. Author: An Analysis of Property Valuation Systems Under Eminent Domain, 1961; Human Relations In Handling Insurance Claims, 1967; No-Fault Insurance, 1971 and others; contbr. articles in field to profl. jours. Home: 9683 Meadow Dr Omaha NE 68114 Office: CBA 502-F College of Business Administration University of Nebraska Omaha NE 68101 Tel (402) 554-2546

ROLEWICK, CARL HENRY, b. Chgo., July 10, 1933; B.S., Loyola U., Chgo., 1955, J.D., 1958. Admitted to Ill. bar, 1958; practiced in Downers Grove, Ill. and Chgo., 1958-61; asst. dep. ct. adminstr. Cook County (Ill.) Ct., 1962-64; asst. dir. Adminstrv. Office of the Ill. Cts., Chgo., 1964-70, dep. dir., 1970-73; adminstr. atty. registration and disciplinary commn. Ill. Supreme Ct., 1973—; sec./reporter to numerous coms. of Ill. Jud. Conf. and Ill. Supreme Ct. Mem. Am., Ill. State (chmn. sect. on jud. adminstrn. 1968), DuPage County (Ill.) bar assns., Inst. Jud. Adminstrn., Am. Judicature Soc. Office: 203 N Wabash Ave suite 1900 Chicago IL 60601 Tel (312) 346-0690

ROLLI, JOHN MARIO ALBERT, b. New Bedford, Mass., Feb. 28, 1942; B.S., Northeastern U., 1965; J.D., Villanova U., 1968. Admitted to N.H. bar, 1968; individual practice law, Littleton, N.H., 1968—; dist. atty. Grafton County (N.H.), 1977—; mem. N.H. Gov's Commn. on Crime and Delinquency, 1975-76, N.H. Jud. Council, 1976-77; v.p. North Stratford R.R. Corp.; counsel Bethlehem (N.H.) Village Dist. Committeeman, Cub Scout Pack 230 Daniel Webster council Boy Scouts Am.; mem. Bethlehem Sch. Bd., 1975-76; treas. Bethlehem Republican Com.; bd. dirs. Littleton Indsl. Devel. Corp. Mem. Assn. Trial Lawyers Am., Am., N.H. (gov. 1973-75), Grafton County bar assns., Assn. ICC Practicioners. Bd. editors N.H. Law Weekly. Home: Mount Agassiz Bethlehem NH 03574 Office: 126 Main St Littleton NH 03561 Tel (603) 444-5221

ROLLINGS, DALE LINN, b. St. Louis, June 23, 1940; A.B., Washington U., St. Louis, 1962, J.D., 1964. Admitted to Mo. bar, 1964, U.S. Supreme Ct. bar, 1970; asso. firm Lincoln, Haseltine, Keet, Forehand & Springer, Springfield, Mo., 1964-68; asst. pros. atty. Greene County (Mo.), Springfield, 1969; asst. atty. gen. Mo., Jefferson City, 1969-71; partner firm Rollings, Gerhardt & Hazelwood, St. Charles, Mo., 1971—; lectr. bus. law SW Mo. State U., 1965-69; exec. dir. Mo. Pros. Attys. Assn., 1971-73, Internat. Order Golden Rule, 1976—. Bd. dirs. St. Joseph's Inst. for Deaf, 1974—. Mem. Mo., St. Charles County bar assns., St. Charles C. of C. Author: Estate Planning for Funeral Directors, 1976. Office: 2209 First Capitol Dr Saint Charles MO 63301 Tel (314) 946-6086

ROLLINS, OVERMAN RANDOLPH, b. Morganton, N.C., Feb. 22, 1943; B.A. in Polit. Sci., Duke, 1965, J.D., 1968. Admitted to Va. bar, 1969; asso. firm McGuire, Woods & Battle, Richmond, Va., 1968-73, partner, 1973—. Pres., Carillon Civic Assn., Richmond, 1975—; bd. dirs. Richmond Montessori Sch., 1972—, chmn. bd., 1976—; bd. dirs. Maymont Found., Richmond, 1976—. Mem. Am., Va. bar assns. Contbr. articles to legal jours. Home: 3002 Rugby Rd Richmond VA 23221 Office: 1400 Ross Bldg Richmond VA 23219 Tel (804) 644-4131

ROLLINSON, MARK, b. Chattanooga, Dec. 8, 1935; A.B. in Econs., Duke U., 1958; LL.B., George Washington U., 1962. Admitted to D.C. bar, 1964, Md. bar, 1975; asst. to trust officer Nat. Savs. and Trust Co., 1958-59; staff economist Foster Assos., 1959-60; treas., mem. exec. com. Human Scis. Research Co., McLean, Va., 1960-63; v.p. Greater Washington Investors, Inc., 1963-71; sr. partner firm Rollinson & Schaumberg, Washington, 1971—. Mem. D.C. (chmn. com. on computer-assisted legal research 1973—), Am., Internat. bar assns., Am. Mgmt. Assn., Newcomen Soc. N.Am., Nat. Assn. Accountants, Phi Alpha Delta. Home: 4701 Willard Ave Chevy Chase MD 20015 Office: 1019 19th St NW Washington DC 20036 Tel (202) 785-4200

ROLNICK, ALAN LAWRENCE, b. N.Y.C., July 2, 1940; A.B. in Polit. Sci., Bucknell U., 1962; J.D., Emory U., 1965. Admitted to Mass. bar, 1966, Ga. bar, 1971; partner firm Constangy, Brooks & Smith, Atlanta, 1971—; atty. NLRB, New Orleans and Atlanta, 1966-71. Mem. Am., Fed., Ga. bar assns. Office: 1900 Peachtree Center Bldg Atlanta GA 30303 Tel (404) 525-8622

ROLOFF, LARRY ROGER, b. Vancouver, Wash., Dec. 27, 1946; B.S., U. Oreg., 1969, J.D., 1972. Admitted to Oreg. bar, 1972; individual practice law, Eugene, Oreg., 1972—. Mem. Am., Lane County bar assns. Office: 834 Pearl St Suite 205 Eugene OR 97401 Tel (503) 686-8695

ROLPH, HENRY R., b. San Francisco, Jan. 16, 1915; A.B., Stanford U., 1936, LL.B., 1940. Admitted to Calif. Supreme Ct. bar, 1940, U.S. Fed. Ct. No. Dist. Calif., 1940, U.S. Supreme Ct. bar, 1953; asso., then partner firm Graham, James & Rolph and predecessor, San Francisco, 1940-67; judge Calif. Superior Ct., 1967—, presiding judge, 1976—; supr. City and County of San Francisco, 1956-61, acting mayor, spring and fall, 1957, summer, 1958. Sec. San Francisco Advisory Bd. Salvation Army, 1955-61; pres. Calif. Bible Soc., 1959—; chmn. No. Calif. chpt. NCCJ, 1966-68, trustee nat. bd., 1970—. Mem. Maritime Law Assn. U.S., San Francisco (chmn. admiralty com. 1967), Am. bar assns., State Bar Calif., Am. Bible Soc. (hon.), Am. Legion, VFW. Home: 2626 Lyon St San Francisco CA 94123 Office: Superior Ct of Calif Room 461 City Hall San Francisco CA 94102 Tel (415) 558-3261

ROMACK, RONALD RAY, b. Sulphur Springs, Tex., Mar. 8, 1941; A.A., Tyler Jr. Coll., 1960; B.S., E.Tex. State U., 1962; LL.B., Baylor U., 1966, J.D., 1969. Admitted to Tex. bar, 1966; asso. firm Talbert, Giessel, Barnett & Stone, Houston, 1966-68, Hill & Mathews, Houston, 1968-69; partner firm Romack & Davis, Houston, 1969-71; individual practice law, Houston, 1971—; mem. presdl. primary com. Houston Jr. Bar, 1971, com. on local regulation of land use, 1976. Mem. Am. Judicature Soc., Tex. (outstanding achievement in income taxation), Am. trial lawyers assns., Am., Tex. (outstanding award in comml. law), Houston bar assns., Delta Theta Phi. Home: 532 W 31st St Houston TX 77018 Office: 723 E 11th St Houston TX 77008 Tel (713) 868-8946

ROMANG, RICHARD EDWARD, b. Breckinridge, Okla., Jan. 20, 1912; B.A., U. Chgo., 1934; LL.B., U. Okla., 1936; certificate N.Y. U. Sch. Law, 1971, Nat. Coll. State Judiciary, U. Nev., 1972, Am. Acad. Jud. Edn., U. Colo., 1976. Admitted to Okla. bar, 1936; practiced in Oklahoma City, 1936-39, Enid, Okla., 1948-70; judge Okla. Ct. Appeals, 1971—, presiding judge, 1972, 75; mem. Okla. Ho. of Reps., 1948-60, Okla. Senate, 1960-70. Mem. Okla., Am. bar assns., Inst. Jud. Adminstrn., Phi Alpha Delta. Home: 2908 Tudor Rd Oklahoma City OK 73127 Office: 210-A State Capitol Oklahoma City OK 73105 Tel (405) 521-3751

ROMANO, CAROLE ANN, b. Worcester, Mass., Dec. 25, 1946; student Anna Maria Coll., 1964-66, Loyola U., Rome, 1966-67; A.B., Marquette U., 1968; J.D., Boston Coll., 1971. Admitted to Mass. bar, 1971, U.S. Dist. Ct. bar, 1976; asst. dist. atty. Worcester County, Mass., 1972-75, also partner firm Romano & Romano, Worcester, 1971—; vol. atty. Civil Liberties Union Mass., 1971—; legal counsel Worcester Women's Project, 1972—. Vice pres. Big Bros./Big Sisters of Worcester, 1973-76, bd. dirs., 1973—; mem. steering com. Com. to Ratify Equal Rights Amendment; bd. dirs. Urban League of Eastern Mass; adv. com. Mass. Spl. Treatment Program for Women; Mass. state coordinator Carter/Mondale 51.3 Com., 1976. Mem. Am., Mass., Worcester County bar assns., Mass. Assn. Women Lawyers, Assn. Women Lawyers of Worcester, Worcester County Law Library, Phi Alpha Theta. Office: 5 Irving St Worcester MA 01608 Tel (617) 791-8255

ROMANO, JOAN GUALTIERI, b. Rome, N.Y., Oct. 10, 1933; A.B., Sweet Briar Coll. 1955; J.D., U. Akron, 1974. Admitted to Ohio bar, 1974; clk. firm George Tzangas, Canton, Ohio, 1976; asst. prosecuting atty., Summit County, Ohio, 1976—. Mem. Akron Symphony Com., 1969-71, membership com. Akron Art Inst., 1974-75. Mem. Akron, Ohio, Am. bar assns. Home: 3037 Vincent Rd Silver Lake Village Cuyahoga Falls OH 44224 Office: 175 S Main St Akron OH 44308 Tel (216) 379-5322

ROMANOW, ROY. Now atty. gen. Province of Sask. (Can.), Regina. Office: Legislative Bldg Regina SK S4S 0B3 Canada*

ROMANYAK, JAMES ANDREW, b. Chgo., July 21, 1944; B.A., U. Ill., 1966, J.D., 1969. Admitted to Ill. bar, 1969; staff atty. Chgo. Bar Assn., 1970-71, exec. sec. Young Lawyer's sect., 1971-72, counsel spl. com. on Police/Community Relations, 1972; gen. atty. Chgo., Milw., St. Paul & Pacific RR, Chgo., 1972—. Mem. Am., Chgo., Ill. bar assns., Interstate Commerce Commn. Practioners. Office: 516 W Jackson Blvd Chicago IL 60606 Tel (312) 236-7600

ROMBAUER, MARJORIE DICK, b. Jamestown, N.D., May 11, 1927; B.A., U. Wash., 1958, J.D., 1960. Admitted to Wash. bar, 1960; prof. law U. Wash., 1960—. Mem. Scribes, Order of Coif. Author: Legal Problem Solving, 1973. Office: Condon Hall JB-20 U Wash Seattle WA 98195 Tel (206) 543-4908

ROME, LOUIS, b. Worcester, Mass., Jan. 13, 1931; A.B., Dartmouth Coll., 1953; M.S. in Social Work, Columbia U., 1955; J.D., U. Mich., 1964. Admitted to Mich. bar, 1965; asst. county prosecutor Ingham County (Mich.), 1965-66; exec. dir. Mich. Commn. on Crime and Criminal Adminstrn., 1966-70; cons. criminal justice program devel., Ann Arbor, Mich., 1970-71, 73—; staff dir. task force on community crime prevention Nat. Commn. on Criminal Justice Standards and Goals, 1971-73; dir., referee Washtenaw County (Mich.) Probate Ct. Juvenile Div., 1957-62. Active various community activities. Mem. Mich., Am. bar assns., Nat. Assn. Social Workers, Acad. Certified Social Workers, Mich. Assn. Professions. Home: 2654 Raphael Rd East Lansing MI 48823 Office: 1131 E Huron St Ann Arbor MI 48104 Tel (313) 662-2763

ROME, MORTON EUGENE, b. Balt., Sept. 9, 1913; A.B., Johns Hopkins, 1933; LL.B., Harvard, 1936. Admitted to Md. bar, 1936, U.S. Supreme Ct. bar, 1942; partner firm Rome & Rome, Balt., 1940-69; counsel firm White, Mindel, Clarke & Hill, Towson, Md., 1969—; asst. to U.S. Supreme Ct. Justice Robert H. Jackson at Nuremberg trial prosecutions, 1945-46; dir. Eutaw Savs. Bank, Balt., 1965-74; dir. local corps.; asst. state's atty. Balt. City, 1939-42. Mem. Am., Md. (v.p.), Balt. City (v.p.), Balt. County bar assns. Office: 305 W Chesapeake Ave Suite 310 Towson MD 21204 Tel (301) 828-1050

ROMEI, ADOLPH ALFONSO, b. Paterson, N.J., Aug. 2, 1929; B.S. magna cum laude, Seton Hall U., 1949; J.D., Fordham U., 1952. Admitted to D.C. bar, 1952, N.J. bar, 1952, U.S. Supreme Ct. bar, 1956; individual practice law, Paterson, N.J., 1952—; legal asst. City of Paterson, 1958-60, city atty., 1961-65; city counsel, 1965-66, 73-74; asst. counsel Passaic Valley Water Commn., 1967-70; counsel Paterson Municipal Council, 1974—; Cons. in drafting new adminstrv. code on change in form of govt. City of Paterson, 1974. Mem. Passaic County, N.J., Am. bar assns., N.J., Nat. leagues municipal attys. Office: 126 Market St Paterson NJ 07505 Tel (201) 525-1515

ROMEISER, ELLEN ROBERSON, b. Chgo., Nov. 14, 1945; B.A., Manhattanville Coll., 1967; J.D., Northwestern U., 1970. Admitted to Ill. bar, 1970; trust counsel Harris Trust and Savs. Bank, Chgo., 1971-73, 1975—. Bd. dirs. Hull House Assn. Aux., Chgo., 1976—. Mem. Chgo., (chairperson subcom. will and trust drafting techniques, trust law com. div. 1, mem., 1972-73, 1975—, chairperson 1976—), Ill. State, Am. bar assns. Home: 1423 W Fargo Ave Chicago IL 60626 Office: 111 W Monroe St Chicago IL 60603 Tel (312) 461-2671

ROMERO, FREDERIC LEE, b. Angola, Ind., Oct. 11, 1931; B.S. in Bus. Adminstrn., Tri-State Coll., 1956; J.D., Ohio No. U., 1971. Admitted to Ind. bar, 1971; individual practice law, Auburn, Ind., 1971—. Mem. Am., Ind., DeKalb County bar assns. Home: 327 E Seventh St Auburn IN 46706 Office: 307 E Ninth St Auburn IN 46706 Tel (219) 925-1932

ROMINES, KENNETH MITCHELL, b. Wilmington, N.C., Aug. 13, 1942; A.B., William Jewell Coll., 1966; J.D., U. Miss., 1968. Admitted to Miss. bar, 1968, Mo. bar, 1969, U.S. Supreme Ct. bar, 1972; law clk. Miss. Supreme Ct., 1968; asst. atty. gen. State of Mo., 1969-72; partner firm Martin, Gibson, Romines, Sedalia, Mo., 1972-74, Rice & Romines, Sedalia, 1975—. Mem. Am. Judicature Soc., Am., Fed., Mo., Miss. bar assns. Named Outstanding Young Man, U.S. Jaycees, 1971. Home: 624 W 7th St Sedalia MO 64301 Office: 701 S Ohio Ave Sedalia MO 64301 Tel (816) 827-1631

ROMINO, DOMINICK JOSEPH, b. Fairmont, W.Va., Sept. 26, 1911; A.B., W.Va. U., 1933; LL.B., J.D., U. Richmond, 1942. Admitted to W.Va. bar; individual practice law, Fairmont; asst. prosecuting atty., Marion County, W.Va., 1955-56, 1960-61. Exec. bd. Boy Scouts Am., Mountain area, 1958; vice chmn. Salvation Army exec. bd., 1976—. Mem. Marion County, W.Va., Va. bar assns., W.Va., Richmond law sch. assns.; hon. mem. McNeill Law Soc. (Richmond Law Sch.). Home: 5 Park Dr Fairmont WV 26554 Office: 313 Profl Bldg Cleveland Ave Fairmont WV 26554 Tel (304) 363-0371

ROMMEL, JOHN MARSHALL, b. Washington, Aug. 14, 1925; B.A., Am. U., 1954, J.D., 1954. Admitted to D.C. bar, 1954, U.S. Supreme Ct. bar, 1958; mem. firms Rommel, Allwine & Rommel, Washington, 1958-67, Rommel & Rommel, Washington, 1968-72, Beveridge, DeGrandi, Kline & Lunsford, 1973—. Mem. D.C., Am. bar assns., Licensing Execs. Soc., U.S. Trademark Assn. (asso.). Office: 1819 H St NW Washington DC 20006 Tel (202) 659-2811

RONEY, LARRY WRIGHT, b. Abbeville, Ala., May 14, 1936; B.S., Columbus Coll., 1969; J.D., U. Ala., 1973. Admitted to Ala. bar, 1973; individual practice law, Phenix City, Ala.; with Central of Ga. R.R., 1954-63; ins. investigator Retail Credit Co., 1963-73. Mem. adminstrv. bd. Summerville (Ala.) United Methodist Ch.; bd. dirs. Phenix City Boys' Club. Mem. Am., Ala., Russell County bar assns. Home: 1001 35th St Phenix City AL 36867 Office: 516 14th St Phenix City AL 36867 Tel (205) 297-0508

RONISH, DONALD EDWARD, b. Denton, Mont., Oct. 13, 1921; B.A., U. Mont., 1946, LL.B., 1947, J.D., 1970. Admitted to Mont. bar, 1947; individual practice law, Lewistown, Mont., 1947—; dep. atty. Fergus County (Mont.), 1949-54. Mem. Lewistown City Council, 1948-52. Mem. Mont. Bar Assn. Home: 111 Nelson Dr Lewistown MT 59457 Office: Bank Electric Bldg Lewistown MT 59457 Tel (406) 538-8212

RONSHAUSEN, ROLAND, JR., b. Chgo., Apr. 15, 1947; B.A., DePaul U., 1968, J.D., 1973. Admitted to Ill. bar, 1973; asst. to dir. transp. Outboard Marine Corp., Waukegan, Ill., 1973—. Mem. Am., Ill. State, Lake County bar assns., Assn. ICC Practitioners, Delta Nu Alpha. Office: 100 Sea Horse Dr Waukegan IL 60085 Tel (312) 689-5240

ROOD, ARNOLD CLARENCE, b. Boston, Aug. 16, 1901; S.B., Mass. Inst. Tech., 1921, S.M., 1922; LL.B., Lake Erie Sch. Law, 1928; J.D., Boston U., 1937. Admitted to Ohio bar, 1929, Mass. bar, 1932, U.S. Supreme Ct. bar, 1941, Ind. bar, 1945; metallurgist, patent atty. Una Welding, Inc., Cleve., 1922-25; asso. firm Evans & McCoy, Cleve., 1925-31; patent atty. United Shoe Machinery Corp., Boston, 1931-44, Eli Lilly & Co., Indpls., 1944-46, Polaroid Corp., Cambridge, Mass., 1946-47; individual practice law, Boston, 1947—; lectr. Boston U. Sch. Law, 1947-57. Mem., chmn. subcom. on edn. Wellesley Adv. Com.; mem. Mass. Inst. Tech. Alumni Council, 1947—. Mem. Boston Patent Law Assn. (life). Home and Office: 1848 Commonwealth Ave Brighton MA 02135

ROOF, CARL JOSEPH (JOE), b. Columbia, S.C., Jan. 10, 1938; B.S. in Bus. Adminstrn., U. S.C., 1960, J.D., 1963. Admitted to S.C. bar, 1963; individual practice law, Columbia, 1963-66; partner firm McLain, Sherrill & Wilkins, Columbia, 1966-69, Burnside & Roof, Columbia, 1969—. Mem. Am., S.C., Richland County bar assns. Home: 470 Leton Dr Columbia SC 29210 Office: Box 1516 Columbia SC 29202 Tel (803) 779-3350

ROOF, JAY BRYAN, b. Chgo., Sept. 30, 1943; B.A., U. Houston, 1965; J.D., U. Wash., 1968. Admitted to Wash. bar, 1968; dep. pros. atty. Kitsap County (Wash.), 1969; with firm Green, Roof & Krucker, and predecessor, Poulsbo, Wash., asso., 1970-71, partner, 1971—; judge Municipal Ct., Poulsbo, 1973—. Mem. Am., Wash., Kitsap County (pres. 1973-75) bar assns., Am. Judicature Soc., Am. Trial Lawyers Assn. Home: Route 1 Box 322 Poulsbo WA 98370 Office: PO Box 851 Poulsbo WA 98370 Tel (206) 779-5561

ROOK, ROGER N., b. 1928; B.S., Willamette U., LL.B., 1955. Pres., Nat. Dist. Attys. Assn. Office: Clackamas County Courthouse Oregon City OR 97045*

ROOKER, CLIFTON KEITH, b. Modesto, Calif., Nov. 5, 1937; B.A. magna cum laude, Brigham Young U., 1958; J.D. cum laude, U. Chgo., 1961. Admitted to Calif., Utah bars, 1962; asso. firm Van Cott, Bagley, Cornwall & McCarthy, Salt Lake City, 1962-66, partner, 1966-73; asso. prof. J. Reuben Clark Law Sch., Brigham Young U., Provo, Utah, 1973-75, prof., 1975—; mem. firm Martineau & Maak, Salt Lake City, 1975—; law clk. to justice Supreme Ct. Calif., 1961-62; mem. com. examiners Utah State Bar, 1967-72, chmn., 1972-73. Mem. Am., Salt Lake County bar assns., Order of Coif, Phi Kappa Phi. Contbr. articles to profl. publs.; bd. mng. editors U. Chgo. Law Rev., 1960-61. Office: Suite 1800 Beneficial Life Tower 36 S State St Salt Lake City UT 84111 Tel (801) 532-7840

ROOKS, RAYMOND NEWTON, b. Nevada, Mo., Dec. 23, 1910; B.S. cum laude, U. Ill., 1932, LL.B. cum laude, 1934. Admitted to Ill. bar, 1934; with law and claim depts. N.Am. Accident Ins. Co., Chgo., 1934-37; asso. firm Rooks, Pitts, Fullagar & Poust, and predecessors, Chgo., 1937-42, partner, 1943—. Mem. Citizens Zoning Com. Wilmette (Ill.), 1959-61, Citizens Com. on Juvenile Ct., 1961—; mem., chmn. Wilmette Plan Commn., 1963-66. Mem. Am. (del. 1955-56, 60-61), Ill., Chgo. (bd. mgrs. 1949-51, 59-63, treas. 1954-57, pres. 1961-62), 7th Fed. Circuit bar assns., Assn. ICC Practitioners, Nat. Assn. Bar Pres.'s, Am., Chgo. bar founds., Am. Judicature Soc., Am. Law Inst., Legal Club Chgo. (pres. 1958-59), Law Club Chgo. (pres. 1967-68). Home: 909 Locust Rd Wilmette IL 60091 Office: 208 S La Salle St Chicago IL 60604 Tel (312) FR2-5600

ROOS, CHARLES LOUIS, b. Richland, Wash., Aug. 30, 1947; B.S., Whitworth Coll., 1970; J.D., Willamette U., 1973. Admitted to Idaho bar, 1973; asso. firm Coughlan Imhoff & Lynch, 1973, partner to 1976; asso. firm Coulter & Ried, Boise, Idaho, 1976—. Mem. Idaho, Boise bar assns., Idaho Trial Lawyers Assn. Co-founder halfway house for state prisoners. Home: PO Box 451 Boise ID 83701 Office: PO Box 239 Boise ID 83701 Tel (208) 345-6231

ROOS, WILLIAM AUGUST, IV, b. Oceanside, N.Y., Apr. 22, 1944; B.A., Trinity Coll., Hartford, Conn., 1966; LL.B., U. Pa., 1969. Admitted to N.Y. State bar, 1970, U.S. Dist. Ct. for So. Dist. N.Y. bar, 1974; asso. firm Reynolds, Richards, LaVenture, Hadley & Davis, N.Y.C., 1969-75, partner, 1976—. Vice pres., dir. Alfred T. White, Jr. Community Center, Inc., Bklyn., 1976—. Mem. N.Y. State Bar Assn. Home: 95 Joralemon St Brooklyn NY 11201 Office: 67 Wall St New York City NY 10005 Tel (212) 422-8490

ROOSEVELT, HAVEN CLARK, b. Boston, June 5, 1940; B.A., Harvard U., 1962, LL.B., 1966. Admitted to N.Y. State bar, 1967, U.S. Supreme Ct. bar, 1973; asso. firm Cadwalader, Wickersham & Tuft, N.Y.C., 1966-75, partner, 1975—; lectr. Adelphi U., Grad. Sch. Bus. Adminstrn., 1974. Mem. Assn. Bar City N.Y., N.Y. State Bar Assn. Office: One Wall St New York City NY 10005 Tel (212) 785-1000

ROOT, DUANE G., b. Medina, N.Y., Mar. 11, 1936; B.S., State U. N.Y., 1959; J.D., U. Buffalo, 1969. Admitted to N.Y. bar, 1970; partner firm Friedman & Root, Akron, N.Y., 1971—. Home: 542 Locust St Lockport NY 14094 Office: 74 Main St Akron NY 14001 Tel (716) 542-5444

ROOT, OREN, b. N.Y.C., June 13, 1911; A.B., Princeton, 1933; LL.B., U. Va., 1936. Admitted to N.Y. State bar, 1938, U.S. Supreme Ct. bar, 1945; asso. firm Davis Polk Wardwell Gardiner & Read, N.Y.C., 1936-40; mem. firm Root Barrett Cohen Knapp & Smith, and predecessor, N.Y.C 1946-61; supt. banks N.Y. State, 1961-64; counsel Irving Trust Co., N.Y.C., 1965-72; counsel Barrett Smith Schapiro Simon & Armstrong, N.Y.C., 1972—. Bd. dirs. Vera Inst. Justice. Mem. Am. Arbitration Assn. (trustee), Am., N.Y. State bar assns., Assn. Bar City N.Y. Office: 26 Broadway New York City NY 10004 Tel (212) 422-8180

ROPER, PETER P., b. Akron, Ohio, Apr. 8, 1924; B.A., cum laude, Western Res. U., 1949, M.A., 1950; J.D., Cleve.-Marshall Law Sch., 1961. Admitted to Ohio bar, 1961; teaching fellow history Cleve. Coll., 1949-50; informational writer, chief pub. relations Ohio Hwy. Dept., 1950-53; pub. relations dir. Ohio Advt. Agy., Cleve., 1953-56; publicity and promotion mgt. Sta. WERE, Cleve., 1956-61; individual practice law, Cleve., 1961-68; exec. dir. Bar Assn. Greater Cleve., 1968—; speaker profl. confs. Chmn. Bordner Trust; former pres. Richfield Kiwanis Club, Peninsula Library Hist. Soc.; former bd. dirs. Better Bus. Bur.; former mem. gen. alumni bd. Cleve. State U.; mem. regional adv. com. Am. Arbitration Assn. Mem. Am., Ohio, Cuyahoga County, Greater Cleve. bar assns., Nat. Assn. Bar Execs. (past treas., v.p.). Home: 4840 Berkeley Dr Richfield OH 44286 Office: 118 Saint Clair Ave Cleveland OH 44114 Tel (216) 696-3525

RORSCHACH, JACK LOWELL, b. Muskogee, Okla., Sept. 20, 1909; LL.B., U. Okla., 1931, J.D., 1970. Admitted to Okla. bar, 1931, U.S. Dist. Ct. for Okla., bar, 1933, U.S. Supreme Ct. bar, 1938; individual practice law, Vinita, Okla., 1931—; gen. counsel Grand River Dam Authority, 1937-38; KAMO Electric Coop., 1948—; mem. Okla. Ho. Reps., 1939-41, Senate, 1934-38; spl. justice Okla. Supreme Ct., 1948—. Mem. Am., Okla. Craig County (pres. 1972—) bar assns., Vinita C. of C. (pres. 1964), Lions Internat. (dist. gov. for Okla. 1948-49), Phi Alpha Delta. Home: 623 S Smith St Vinita OK 74301 Office: 217 S Wilson Bldg Vinita OK 74301 Tel (918) 256-3660

ROSA, RAYMOND JAMES, b. West Springfield, Mass., Apr. 21, 1920; B.A. in Pub. Affairs, Am. Internat. Coll., 1942; LL.B., U. Mich., 1944. Admitted to Mass. bar, 1944; law clk. Mass. Supreme Jud. Ct., Boston, 1944-45; individual practice law, West Springfield, 1945—; asst. dist. atty. West dist. Mass., Springfield and Pittsfield, Mass., 1961-68. Mem. West Springfield Town Meeting, 1946-54, selectman, 1954-63; del. Democratic Nat. Conv., 1952, 56, 60. Mem. Mass., Hampden County bar assns. Home: 53 Wolcott Ave West Springfield MA 01089 Office: 10 Central St West Springfield MA 01089 Tel (413) 736-7273

ROSAN, RICHARD ADAMS, b. Bridgeport, Conn., Sept. 24, 1912; A.B., Cornell U., 1933; LL.B., Yale U., 1936. Admitted to Conn. bar, 1936, N.Y. bar, 1937, U.S. Supreme Ct. bar, 1958; asso. firm Cravath, Swaine & Moore, N.Y.C., 1936-51; with Columbia Gas System, Wilmington, Del., 1951—, gen. counsel, 195B, sec., dir., 1973—, exec. v.p., gen. counsel, sec., 1974—; dir. Electric Hose & Rubber Co. Mem. Republican Town Meeting, Greenwich, Conn., 1960-65; mem. Planning and Zoning Commn. Greenwich, 1966-69. Mem. Fed. Power (past pres.), Am. bar assns., Am. Gas Assn. (chmn. legal com.), Interstate Natural Gas Assn. (legal com.), Order of Coif, Phi Beta Kappa. Home: Duckhollow Georgetown MD 21930 Office: 20 Montchanin Rd Wilmington DE 19807 Tel (302) 429-5217

ROSAN, ROBERT J., b. N.Y.C., Nov. 13, 1931; A.B., Syracuse U., 1952; LL.B., Columbia, 1956; postgrad. Sch. Bus. N.Y. U., 1965. Admitted to N.Y. bar, 1958; with G. M. Basford Co., N.Y.C., 1960-62; v.p. Investors Funding Corp. of N.Y., N.Y.C., 1962-64; partner firm Rosan & Rosan, N.Y.C., 1964—; mem. title advisory bd. Security Title & Guarantee Corp., N.Y.C. Office: 350 Madison Ave New York City NY 10017 Tel (212) 697-1743

ROSCHE, ALFRED PAUL, JR., b. Hillsboro, Ill., July 21, 1938; B.S., U. Miami, 1963; J.D., Washington, U., St. Louis, 1963. Admitted to Mo. bar, 1963, Ill. bar, 1963; individual practice law, Hillsboro, 1963-76; farm mgr., Montgomery County, Ill., 1970-76; cattle raiser Semital and Herefords, Hillsboro, 1968-72; states atty. Montgomery County, 1968-77; EPA hearing officer State of Ill., 1973-76. Mem. Ill., Montgomery County (v.p.), St. Louis bar assns. Home: 1006 Tremont St Hillsboro IL 62049 Office: 109 S Main St Hillsboro IL 62049 Tel (217) 532-2155

ROSCHE, RICHARD PAUL, b. Balt., Apr. 2, 1928; B.S. in Accounting, U. Balt., 1955; LL.B., 1958. Admitted to Md. bar, 1959; staff atty. Harleysville Ins. Co., Towson, Md., 1965—. Pres. Reisterstown-Owings Mills (Md.) Optimist Club, 1963-64. Mem. Sigma Delta Kappa. Home: Route 1 Box 117 Dover Rd Reisterstown MD 21136 Office: 828 Dulaney Valley Rd Towson MD 21204 Tel (301) 821-1087

ROSCIA, JOHN J., b. Utica, N.Y., June 25, 1920; A.B., Cornell U., 1942, LL.B., 1947. Admitted to N.Y. bar, 1947, Calif. bar, 1951; with firm Chadbourne, Parke, Whiteside & Wolff, and predecessors, N.Y.C., 1947-55; asst. gen. counsel Rockwell Internat. Corp., Los Angeles, 1956-60, v.p., gen. counsel, 1961—. Mem. Am. Bar Assn., Phi Beta Kappa, Phi Kappa Phi, Delta Sigma Phi. Home: 1660 N Amalfi Dr Pacific Palisades CA 90272 Office: 2230 E Imperial Hwy El Segundo CA 90245*

ROSCOE, NANCY TOMERLIN, b. Bakersfield, Calif., Apr. 15, 1937; A.B., Mills Coll., 1958; LL.D., Hastings Coll. Law, 1968. Admitted to Calif. bar, 1969; individual practice law, San Francisco, 1969—. Mem. Queens Bench, Criminal Trial Lawyers Assn. No. Calif. (treas. 1975, 2d v.p. 1976), Calif. Attys. for Criminal Justice, Commonwealth Club Calif. Office: 819 Eddy St San Francisco CA 94109 Tel (415) 771-6174

ROSE, CLAYTON W., JR., b. Columbus, Ohio, Aug. 27, 1927; B.S., Ohio State U., 1950, J.D., 1952; postgrad. Nat. Coll. Juvenile Justice, 1971. Admitted to Ohio bar, 1952; asst. pros. atty. Franklin County (Ohio), 1952; partner firm Chester & Rose, Columbus, 1952-70; judge ct. common pleas Franklin County, 1971—; village solicitor Dublin (Ohio), 1962-66; advisor Syntaxis, Inc., Columbus, 1973—, Parents Without Partners, 1969—. Mem. Am., Ohio State, Columbus bar assns., Ohio Common Pleas Judges Assn., Ohio Juvenile Ct. Judges Assn., Nat. Juvenile Ct. Judges Assn., Psychology-Law Soc., Lawyers Club Columbus (v.p. 1954), Ohio Assn. Juvenile Ct. Judges (exec. com. 1971—). Home: 5075 Thornhill Ln Columbus OH 43220 Office: 50 E Mound St Columbus OH 43215 Tel (614) 462-4445

ROSE, DAVID ALLAN, b. Boston, March 24, 1906; J.D., Boston U., 1927; postgrad. Sch. Law Georgetown U., 1927. Admitted to Mass. bar, 1928, U. S. Supreme Ct. bar, 1952; asso. justice Municiple Ct. Dorchester, 1936-60; justice Superior Ct. Mass., 1960-72; justice Appeals Ct. Mass., 1972-76; counsel to firm Barron and Stadfeld; mem. Mass. Com. on Jud. Responsibility. Mem. Mass. Ho. of Reps., 1935-36; vice chmn. Human Relations Commn. Newton (Mass.); mem. Atty. Gen. Adv. Commn. Civil Rights and Civil Liberties; chmn. nat. exec. com. Anti-Defamation League. Mem. Am., Mass., Boston, Middlesex bar assns. Home: 60 Nathan Rd Newton Ctre MA 02159 Office: 18 Tremont St Boston MA 02108 Tel (617) 723-9800

ROSE, DAVID LOUIS, b. Yonkers, N.Y., Nov. 23, 1942; B.S. in Chemistry, Stevens Inst. Tech., Hoboken, N.J., 1964; J.D., Seton Hall U., Newark, 1973. Admitted to N.J. bar, 1973; research chemist CIBA Pham. Co., Summit, N.J., 1964-69; atty. patent dept. Merck & Co., Inc., Rahway, N.J., 1969—, sr. patent atty., 1975—. Middlesex County (N.J.) Municipal Committeeman, 1972—; mem. South Plainfield (N.J.) Traffic Safety Adv. Com., 1974—, chmn., 1975-76. Mem. Am., N.J. bar assns., Am., N.J. patent law assns. Home: 114 Dorset Dr South Plainfield NJ 07080 Office: 126 E Lincoln Ave Rahway NJ 07065 Tel (201) 574-4777

ROSE, DUSTIN BICKNELL, b. Coronado, Calif., Sept. 3, 1939; B.A., Parsons Coll., 1963; J.D., Calif. Western U., 1966; D.H.L., So. Calif. Bapt. Sem., 1968. Admitted to Calif. bar, 1967; partner firm H.L. and D.B. Rose, San Diego, 1968-71; sr. partne firm Rose Rockwell & Jennings, San Diego, 1971—. Chmn., Coronado (Calif.) Traffic Com., 1968-73. Mem. South Bay, San Diego County bar assns., World Council Young Men's Service Orgns. (expansion com.). Home: 3740 Riviera Dr San Diego CA 92109 Office: 1003 Isabella Ave Coronado CA 92118 Tel (714) 435-1858

ROSE, GEORGE, b. Washington, Sept. 5, 1900; A.B., Princeton U., 1922; LL.B., U. Pa., 1927. Admitted to D.C. bar, 1927, Ind. bar, 1944; individual practice law, Washington, 1927-37, Indpls., 1940—; regional atty. NLRB, Ind., 1937; tchr. labor law Ind. Law Sch., Indpls., 1950-52. Chmn., Indpls. Human Rights Commn., 1951-55. Mem.

D.C., Ind., Indpls. bar assns. Author: Understanding Labor Relations, 1962; contbr. articles to legal jours. Office: 534 Circle Tower Bldg 5 E Market St Indianapolis IN 46204 Tel (317) 637-7447

ROSE, HENRY, b. Olean, N.Y., Mar. 28, 1927; B.A., U. Buffalo, 1950, LL.B., 1951. Admitted to N.Y. bar, 1951, D.C. bar, 1953, U.S. Supreme Ct. bar, 1956; dep. asso. solicitor for labor-mgmt. laws, spl. asst. to solicitor for civil rights Dept. Labor, Washington, 1967-70, asso. solicitor for legis., legal counsel, 1970-74; gen. counsel Pension Benefit Guaranty Corp., Washington, 1974—. Mem. Am., D.C., Fed. bar assns. Home: 10691 Rain Dream Hill Columbia MD 21044 Office: 2020 K St NW Washington DC 20006 Tel (202) 254-4864

ROSE, HORACE CHAPMAN, b. Columbus, Ohio, Feb. 11, 1907; A.B., Princeton U., 1928; LL.B., Harvard U., 1931. Sec. to Justice Oliver Wendell Holmes, U.S. Supreme Ct., 1931-32; admitted to Ohio bar, 1933, D.C. bar, 1946; asso. firm Jones, Day, Cockley & Reavis and predecessor, Cleve., 1933-38; partner firm Jones, Day, Reavis & Pogue, Cleve. and Washington, 1939-42, 46-52, 56—; dir. Office Contract Settlement, Washington, 1946; asst. sec. Treasury, 1953-55, under sec., 1955-56; dir. Basic Inc., Cleve., Lear Siegler Inc., Los Angeles, Gould Inc., Chgo. Trustee Cleve. Orch., Cleve. Council World Affairs, Western Res. Acad., Episcopal Ch. Found.; trustee emeritus Princeton U. Mem. Am., Ohio, Cleve. bar assns., Am. Law Inst. (council), Phi Beta Kappa. Home: 12407 Fairhill Rd Cleveland OH 44120 also 2701 31st St NW Washington DC 20008 Office: Union Commerce Bldg Cleveland OH 44114 also 1100 Connecticut Ave NW Washington DC 20036 Tel (216) 696-3939

ROSE, IRA BERNARD, b. N.Y.C., Dec. 31, 1943; B.S. in Econs., U. Pa., 1964; J.D., U. Mich., 1967. Admitted to D.C. bar, 1967, N.Y. State bar, 1969; with SEC, Washington, 1967-68; asso. firm Phillips, Nizer, Benjamin, Krim & Ballon, N.Y.C., 1968-73, partner, 1973—; sec., dir. Imperial Industries, Inc., Hialeah, Fla., 1973—; lectr. Profl. Seminar Assos., 1976, French Soc. Security Analysts, 1974. Former mem. bd. dirs. Friends Larchmont (N.Y.) Pub. Library. Mem. Am. Bar Assn. Office: 40 W 57th St New York City NY 10019 Tel (212) 977-9700

ROSE, JAMES WEAVER, b. Lamesa, Tex., Jan. 18, 1935; B.B.A., So. Meth. U., 1957, LL.B. magna cum laude, 1960. Admitted to Tex. bar, 1960; sr. partner firm Thompson, Knights, Simmons & Bullion, Dallas. Mem. Am., Dallas bar assns. Home: 5356 Nakoma St Dallas TX 75209 Office: 2300 Republic National Bank Bldg Dallas TX 75201

ROSE, JIM WILSON, b. Laurel, Miss., Mar. 24, 1947; B.A., U. Miss., 1969, J.D., 1972. Admitted to Miss. bar, 1972; asso. firm Boyce & Holleman, Gulfport, Miss., 1972-75; partner firm McGuire & Rose, Gulfport, 1975; individual practice law, Gulfport, 1975—. Mem. Am. Bar Assn., Am., Miss. trial lawyers assns. Office: PO Box 1955 Gulfport MS 39501 Tel (601) 864-3278

ROSE, JOSEPH ROSOVSKY, b. Kanev, Kiev, Russia, July 16, 1899; Ph.B., U. Chgo., 1920, J.D., 1923; student Harvard, 1921-22; Ph.D., U. Pa., 1938. Admitted to Ill. bar, 1923, Pa. bar, 1925; examiner Pa. Pub. Service Commn., 1933-37; with U. Pa., 1937-70, prof., chmn. dept. pub. utilities, 1956-70, prof. emeritus, 1970—. Spl. counsel FCC, 1966-67; spl. dep. atty. gen., Pa., 1956-57. Author: American Wartime Transportation, 1953. Contbr. articles to profl. jours. Home: 2401 Pennsylvania Av Philadelphia PA 19130 Office: McNeil Bldg 3718 Locust St Philadelphia PA 19104 Tel (215) 684-1331

ROSE, MICHAEL I., b. Oakland, Calif., Apr. 7, 1945; A.A., Miami Dade Jr. Coll., 1964; B.B.A., U. Miami, 1967; J.D., Cumberland Sch. Law, 1970. Admitted to Fla. bar, 1971; individual practice law, Miami, 1971—. Mem. Am. Bar Assn., Am. Judicature Soc., Assn. Immigration and Nationality Lawyers. Office: 28 W Flagler St Suite 330 Miami FL 33130 Tel (305) 325-1770

ROSE, MILTON CURTISS, b. Cleve., June 5, 1904; A.B., Williams Coll., 1927; LL.B., Harvard U., 1930. Admitted to N.Y. State bar, 1932, D.C. bar, 1966; asso. firm Baldwin, Hutchins & Todd, N.Y.C., 1932-38; partner firm Baldwin, Todd & Young, N.Y.C., 1938-55; partner firm Mudge, Rdse, Guthroe & Alexander and predecessors, N.Y.C., 1955—; pres., dir. Straight Enterprises Inc., N.Y.C., Straight Improvement Co., Inc., N.Y.C. Vice pres., bd. dirs. William C. Whitney Found., 1937—; v.p., bd. dirs., sec. Mario Negri Inst. Found., 1973—; bd. dirs. Gustavus and Louise Pfeiffer Research Found., 1952—, Mary Reynolds Babcock Found., 1953—, Royal Soc. Medicine Found., 1967—; life trustee Pfeiffer Coll.; trustee Shaker Community, 1960—; trustee emeritus Simon's Rock, Inc. Mem. Assn. Bar City N.Y., Am. Bar Assn., N.Y. County Lawyers Assn., Century Assn. Home: PO Box 427 Great Barrington MA 01230 Office: 20 Broad St New York City NY 10005 Tel (212) 422-6767

ROSE, RICHARD LOOMIS, b. Long Branch, N.J., Oct. 21, 1936; A.B., Cornell U., 1958; J.D., Washington and Lee U., 1963. Admitted to N.Y. bar, 1964, Conn. bar, 1966; asso. firm Townsend & Lewis, N.Y.C., 1963-65; asso. firm Cummings & Lockwood, Stamford, Conn., 1965-71, partner, 1972—; dir., Innovative Scis., Inc., Stamford. Sec., dir. Vitam Center, Inc., Norwalk, Conn. Mem. Am., Conn., N.Y. State bar assns. Home: Deer Park Rd New Canaan CT 06840 Office: 1 Atlantic St Stamford CT 06904 Tel (203) 327-1700

ROSE, ROBERT STANLEY, b. Chgo., Dec. 23, 1921; B.B.A., Loyola U., Los Angeles, 1952, J.D., 1955. Admitted to Calif. bar, 1955, U.S. Supreme Ct. bar, 1960; dep. atty. gen. State of Calif., 1955-57; gen. counsel, dir. McCulloch Oil Corp., Los Angeles, 1958-62, also dir.; v.p., gen. counsel Occidental Petroleum Corp., Los Angeles, 1962-67, also dir.; individual practice law, Marina del Rey, Calif., 1968—; v.p., gen. counsel Hollywood Gen. Studios, Inc. dir. Auto-Control Labs, Inc., Jefferson Lake Petrochemicals of Can. Mem. Marina del Rey Bar Assn., Am. Mgmt. Assn., Am. Petroleum Inst., Am. Arbitration Assn., Council Juvenile Ct. Judges, Am. Judicature Soc., Phi Alpha Delta. Home: 4050 Via Dolce #143 Marina del Rey CA 90291 Office: 4500 Via Marina Marina del Rey CA 90291 Tel (213) 822-2061

ROSE, WILLIAM ALFRED, b. Pulaski, Tenn., Oct. 7, 1900; B.A., U. Ala., 1921, LL.B., 1923; J.D., Yale, 1924. Admitted to Ala. bar, 1923; atty. for receiver in litigation involving pub. securities U.S. Cts., 1933-37; partner firm Bradley, Arant, Rose & White and predecessors, Birmingham, 1935—. Mem. Am. (sec. legal edn. sect. 1944-48, council sect. local govt. law 3 terms), Ala., Birmingham bar assns., Assn. Bar City of N.Y., Am. Judicature Soc., Nat. Conf. Commrs. Uniform State Laws (life), Ala. Law Inst., Phi Beta Kappa, Phi Delta Phi (nat. pres. 1939-41, chief justice 1941-47). Home: 28 Country Club Blvd Birmingham AL 35203 Office: 15th Floor Brown-Marx Bldg Birmingham AL 35203 Tel (205) 252-4500

ROSEDALE, PETER K., b. Essen, Germany, July 14, 1931; A.A., Boston U., 1951, LL.B., 1954. Admitted to R.I. bar, 1955; partner firm Rosedale, Caspairan & Riffkin, Providence, 1956—; judge Providence Municipal Ct., 1962-67. Councilman City of Providence, 1959-62; mem. R.I. Ho. of Reps., 1968. Mem. R.I. Bar Assn. Home: 127 Gallatin St Providence RI 02907 Office: 824 Hospital Trust Bldg Providence RI 02903 Tel (401) 751-9500

ROSEMAN, CHARLES SANFORD, b. Jersey City, Feb. 26, 1945; B.A., Calif. State U., 1968; J.D., U. San Diego, 1971. Admitted to Calif. bar, 1972; asso. firm Greer, Popko, Miller & Foerster, San Diego, 1972-73; individual practice law, San Diego, 1973—; judge pro tem Municipal Ct. San Diego, 1974—. Bd. dirs. Big Bros., San Diego; dir. Glenaire Community Devel., San Diego. Mem. Am. Judicature Soc., Calif. Attys. for Criminal Justice, Assn. Trial Lawyers Asn., Calif., Western, Orange County, San Diego County trial lawyers assns., Am., Fed., Calif.; San Diego County bar assns., Med. Legal Bar Assn.

ROSEN, DAVID LEON, b. Pitts., Sept. 4, 1918; A.B., U. Calif., Berkeley, 1940; J.D., U. So. Calif., 1948. Admitted to Calif. bar, 1949; individual practice law Los Angeles, 1949-57; judge worker's compensation State of Calif., Los Angeles, 1957-73; presiding judge, 1973-; adj. prof. law Southwestern U., 1974—. Vice pres. Lawyers Philharmonic Soc., 1976—. Mem. Am., Los Angeles County bar assns., Am. Judicature Soc., Conf. Calif. Workers' Compensation Judges (past pres.). Home: 800 W 1st St Los Angeles CA 90012 Office: Room 4107 107 S Broadway Los Angeles CA 90012 Tel (213) 620-2730

ROSEN, DENNIS AARON, b. Chgo., June 24, 1947; B.S. in Econs., U. Pa., 1969; J.D., U. Ariz., 1972. Admitted to Ariz. bar, 1972; partner firm Thikoll, Johnston & Rosen, Tucson, 1975—. Bd. dirs. Pima Alcoholism Consortium, Tucson, 1974-77, Tucson Jewish Community Center, 1974-76. Mem. Am., Ariz. bar assns. Office: 111 S Church St Tucson AZ 85701 Tel (602) 884-9100

ROSEN, GERALD PFLAUM, b. Mpls., Dec. 8, 1912; A.B., Harvard, 1933, J.D., 1936. Admitted to Calif. bar, 1937; individual practice law, Los Angeles, 1937-41, 45-56; served to capt. JAGC, U.S. Army, 1942-45; v.p. Parkway Mfg. Corp., Pasadena, Calif., 1956-58; v.p. Am. Heritage Pub. Co., Inc., N.Y.C., 1958-65; pres. Spindrift Corp., Ft. Lauderdale, Fla., 1966-70; prof. law Loyola U., Los Angeles, 1971—; mng. dir. Vanderbilt Group of Mutual Funds, Los Angeles, 1975—. Pres. Los Angeles Tb & Health Assn., 1958, N.Y. Tb & Health Assn., 1964-65. Mem. Am., Calif., Los Angeles County bar assns. Home: 13900 Marquesas Way apt C 66 Marina Del Rey CA 90291 Office: 1440 W 9th St Los Angeles CA 90015 Tel (213) 642-2916

ROSEN, HARVEY ISRAEL, b. N.Y.C., Apr. 11, 1941; A.B., Columbia U., 1962, LL.B., 1968. Admitted to N.Y. bar, 1968; asso. firm Beekman & Bogue, N.Y.C., 1968-75, partner, 1975—. Home: 150 W 76th St New York City NY 10023 Office: 14 Wall St New York City NY 10004 Tel (212) 422-4060

ROSEN, LEON, b. N.Y.C., May 21, 1924; A.B., Coll. William and Mary, 1949; LL.B., N.Y. U., 1953. Admitted to N.Y. bar, 1954, U.S. Supreme Ct. bar, 1960; individual practice law, N.Y.C., 1955—; lectr. immigration and nationality law Practicing Law Inst. Mem. Am. Bar Assn. (adminstrv. law sect.), Assn. Immigration and Nationality Lawyers (nat. pres. 1972-73, pres. N.Y. chpt. 1967). Home: 444 E 84th St New York City NY 10028 Office: 60 E 42d St New York City NY 10017 Tel (212) 972-0870

ROSEN, MARTIN JAY, b. Bronx, N.Y., Nov. 15, 1942; B.A., Hobart Coll., 1964; LL.B., N.Y. Law Sch., 1967. Admitted to N.Y. bar, 1967, U.S. Supreme Ct. bar, 1976; law asst. Appellate Div. First Dept., N.Y.C., 1967-68; asso. firm Battle, Fowler, Stokes & Kheel, N.Y.C., 1968-69; confdl. law sec. to justice Supreme Ct. Westchester County (N.Y.), 1969-71; partner firm Kahn, Goldman & Rosen, Westchester County, 1971-75; individual practice law, White Plains, N.Y., 1975—; lectr. in field. Fellow Am. Acad. Matrimonial Lawyers; mem. Am., N.Y. State, Westchester County, Rockland County, White Plains bar assns. Contbr. articles to legal jours. Home: 4 Aberdeen Dr West Nyack NY 10994 Office: 175 Main St Suite 415 White Plains NY 10601 Tel (914) 761-6300

ROSEN, MICHAEL JOSEPH, b. Boston, Apr. 6, 1945; B.A., U. Pa., 1968; J.D., Boston U., 1971. Admitted to Mass. bar, 1971; sr. atty. Bd. Govs. FRS, Washington, 1971-74; asst. v.p., asso. counsel 1st Nat. Bank of Boston, 1974—; sec. Boston Overseas Fin. Corp., FNB Fin. Co., Invenchek Inc., FNBC Acceptance Corp.; lectr. Columbia U., 1976. Mem. Mass., Fed., Boston bar assns. Mem. Boston U. Law Rev., 1971; contbr. articles to legal jours. Office: 100 Federal St Boston MA 02159 Tel (617) 434-2872

ROSEN, MILTON W., b. Braddock, Pa., June 26, 1916; A.A., Chaffey Jr. Coll., Ontario, Calif., 1936; A.B., Pa. State Coll., 1938; J.D., U. Pa., 1941. Admitted to Pa. bar, 1941; individual practice law, Oil City, Pa., 1946-72; partner firm Rosen & Rosen, 1972—; served to capt. JAGC, U.S. Air Force, 1942-46. Mem. exec. bd. Venango County (Pa.) Indsl. Devel. Corp., 1964-77, chmn., 1972-77; mem. exec. bd. United Way, 1971-77, Salvation Army, 1972-77; bd. dirs. Oil City Hosp., 1962-73, pres., 1972-73. Mem. Am. Judicature Soc., Am., Pa., Venango County bar assns. Home: 8 Pleasant St Oil City PA 16301 Office: 17 Nat Transit Bldg Oil City PA 16301

ROSEN, MURRAY, b. N.Y.C., Mar. 1, 1924; A.B., Ind. U., 1947; M.D., U. Amsterdam (Holland), 1952; J.D., Ariz. State U., 1970. Admitted to Ariz. bar, 1971; individual practice law, Phoenix, 1971-76; cons. to tech. adv. service for attys. Mem. Am., Ariz. bar assns., Nat. Health Lawyers Assn. Am. Coll. Legal Med., Am. Med. Writers Assn. Home: 45 Meadowbrook Park Cherokee IA 51012 Tel (712) 225-5911

ROSEN, RICHARD THOMAS, b. Poughkeepsie, N.Y., Nov. 29, 1936; B.A., Columbia, 1957; J.D., Albany Law Sch., 1960. Admitted to N.Y. State bar, 1961, U.S. Supreme Ct. bar, 1964, U.S. Dist. Ct. So. Dist. N.Y. bar, 1966; practiced in Poughkeepsie, 1961—; partner firm Rosen & Rosen, 1961-62, Rosen & Tepper, 1962-66, Rosen & Cutler, 1967-68, Rosen, Cutler & Klein, 1969-73; confidential law sec. to N.Y. State Supreme Ct. justice W. Vincent Grady, 1969-75; asso. firm Guernsey, Butts & Walsh, 1975—; examiner of guardian accounts Surrogate's Ct. of Dutchess County, 1965-66. Mem. N.Y. State Bar Assn., Hudson Valley Estate Planning Council. Tel (914) 452-8200

ROSEN, ROBERT M., b. Monticello, N.Y., May 3, 1938; B.A., Syracuse U., 1961, J.D., 1962; LL.M. in Taxation, N.Y. U., 1967. Admitted to N.Y. bar, 1962, U.S. Supreme Ct. bar, 1967; partner firm Rosen & Rosen, Monticello, N.Y., 1962—; pub. defender, Sullivan County, N.Y., 1965-67, asst. county atty., 1968-69; counsel, Monticello Urban Renewal Agency, 1971, Monticello Indsl. Devel. Agency, 1974-76; village atty. Village of Monticello, 1972-76; counsel N.Y. State Assembly, 1975; estate tax atty. for Sullivan County, 1977—. Mem. Am., N.Y. (ho. dels. 1976), Sullivan County (dir. 1974-76, pres. 1975-76) bar assns., Am., N.Y. trial lawyers assns., Am. Arbitration Assn. (artitrator). Office: 265 Broadway PO Box 348 Monticello NY 12701 Tel (914) 794-7733

ROSEN, RONALD STANLEY, b. Los Angeles, July 22, 1932; A.B. cum laude, Stanford, 1954, LL.B., 1957; postgrad. (Sch. scholar) London Sch. Econs., 1953. Admitted to Calif. bar, 1958; asst. U.S. atty. So. Dist. Calif., Los Angeles, 1958-59; asso. firm Pacht, Ross, Warne & Bernhard, Los Angeles, 1959-62; partner firm Silverberg, Rosen & Leon, Los Angeles, 1962—; officer, dir. numerous corps.; chmn. Fed. Indigent Def. Com., Los Angeles, 1966-68; mem. Lawyer's Reference Com., Los Angeles, 1969-70; disciplinary referee Calif. State Bar, 1976—. Bd. dirs. Elsie DeWolfe Found.; trustee Young Musicians Found., 1973—. Mem. Am., Los Angeles County, Beverly Hills bar assns., State Bar Calif. (adminstrv. com. 1969—, chmn. 1972—), Phi Beta Kappa, Phi Delta Phi. Office: 1880 Century Park E Suite 1100 Los Angeles CA 90067 Tel (213) 277-4500

ROSEN, STANLEY WILLIAM, b. El Paso, Tex., Mar. 28, 1942; B.B.A., U. Tex. at Austin, 1963, LL.B., 1966. Admitted to Tex. bar, 1966; practiced in El Paso since, 1970, partner firms Friedman, Ehrlich & Rosen, 1970-74, Ehrlich & Rosen, 1974-76, Kern & Rosen, 1976—; lectr. State Bar Assn. Inst. on Creditor's Remedies. Bd. dirs. B'nai Zion Synagogue, El Paso, 1972-76, 3d v.p., 1976—. Mem. Am. Bar Assn., State Bar Tex., Comml. Law League. Home: 6613 La Cadena St El Paso TX 79912 Office: El Paso Nat Bank Bldg Suite 1208 El Paso TX 79901 Tel (915) 542-1659

ROSEN, STEVEN A., b. Phila., Oct. 3, 1941; B.A., U. Pa., 1963; M.A., Villanova U., 1965, J.D., 1968. Admitted to Pa. bar, 1968; asso. firm Becker, Becker & Fryman, 1968-69; asso. gen. counsel AAMCO Industries, Inc., 1969-70; gen. counsel Safeguard Industries, Inc., 1970—; partner firm Jokelson & Rosen, King of Prussia, Pa., 1972—. Mem. Am., Pa., Montgomery County bar assns., B'nai B'rith. Home: 7 Russell Pl Ambler PA 19003 Office: PO Box 323 King of Prussia PA 19406 Tel (215) 265-4000

ROSENBAUM, ARTHUR ROBERT, b. N.Y.C., Feb. 15, 1942; certificate Bernard M. Baruch. Sch. Pub. and Bus. Adminstrn., City U. N.Y.; LL.D., N.Y. Law Sch., 1965. Admitted to N.Y. State bar, 1966; partner firm Rosenbaum & Rosenbaum, N.Y.C., to 1976, Rosenbaum, Lerman & Katz, N.Y.C., 1976—. Mem. N.Y. County Bar Assn. Home: 104 New Valley Rd New City NY 10956 Office: 300 Madison Ave New York City NY 10017 Tel (212) 986-5515

ROSENBAUM, MORTIMER, b. Plainfield, N.J., Apr. 18, 1914; S.B., Mass. Inst. Tech., 1935; postgrad. Exec. Program, U. Calif., Los Angeles, 1957; J.D., U. San Diego, 1973. Engr., Gen. Dynamics Corp., San Diego, 1936-48, project engr., 1948-58, chief engr., 1958-60; exec. v.p. Gen. Dynamics Astronautics, San Diego, 1960-65; dir. aircraft Convair, San Diego, 1965-70; admitted to Calif. bar, 1973; individual practice law, San Diego, 1973—. Bd. dirs. Temple Beth Israel, San Diego; v.p., dir. Jewish Family Service, San Diego; mem. Citizen's Com. for Comprehensive Mgmt. Planning of San Diego; v.p. Beth Israel Mausoleum Corp., San Diego. Fellow Inst. Aero. and Astronautics; mem. Am., San Diego County bar assns. Home: 2104 Willow St San Diego CA 92106 Office: 1200 Third Ave San Diego CA 92101 Tel (714) 234-9101

ROSENBERG, AUGUSTA, b. Colorado Springs, Colo., Aug. 19, 1905; student U. Calif., Los Angeles, 1924-27; J.D., U. Calif., Berkeley, 1930. Admitted to Calif. bar, 1930, U.S. Dist. Ct. bar for Dist. Calif., 1931; individual practice law, Los Angeles, 1930-45, 74—; partner firm Rosenberg & Torreyson, Los Angeles, 1946-74; former lectr. U. Calif. Extension. Mem. State Bar Calif., Westwood Village Bar Assn., Westwood C. of C. (sec. 1931-60, monitoring mem.). Author: (with Wendy Stewart) Essentials of Commercial Law in California, 1936, rev. edit., 1937; former syndicated columnist Law in Everyday Life; contbr. articles to profl. and other jours. Home and office: 1423 Greenfield Ave Los Angeles CA 90025 Tel (213) 479-6449

ROSENBERG, BERNARD, b. N.Y.C., Feb. 16, 1905; J.D., N.Y. U., 1930, M.P.A., 1940. Admitted to N.Y. bar, 1931, U.S. Treasury Dept. bar, 1941, U.S. Tax Ct., 1956; asso. W. Herbert Adams, N.Y.C., 1931-33, Aaron William Levy and Adolph Feldblum, N.Y.C., 1933-41; cons., N.Y.C., 1940—. Counsel, Pub. Adminstrn. Alumni Assn., N.Y. U., 1940-41; nat. dir., com. on econ. problems Am. Jewish Congress, N.Y.C., 1941-42; sec., mem. Local Draft Bds., Bklyn., N.Y.C., 1940-49; lectr. Lincoln Lecture Series. Mem. N.Y. County Lawyers, N.Y. Criminal and Civil Cts. (v.p., dir., chmn. adminstrv. law com.) bar assns., Soc. Med. Jurisprudence, N.Y. Acad. Scis. Recipient Selective Service medal U.S. Congress, 1949; contbr. articles to legal jours. Tel (212) 927-4995

ROSENBERG, BERNARD WAYNE, b. Ambridge, Pa., Jan. 19, 1908; B.A., U. Mich., 1927, J.D., 1930. Admitted to Ohio bar, 1930, U.S. Supreme Ct. bar, 1962; individual practice law, Warren, Ohio, 1930-67; partner firm Rosenberg & Rosenberg, Warren, 1967—; asst. city solicitor Warren, 1933-37. Pres., Beth Israel Congregation, Warren, 1945-48, bd. dirs., 1933—; pres. Warren Jewish Fedn., 1949, dir., 1938—. Mem. Am., Ohio, Trumbull County (past pres.) bar assns. Home: 891 Melwood Dr NE Warren OH 44483 Office: 605 Union Savings & Trust Bldg Warren OH 44481 Tel (216) 392-0121

ROSENBERG, HERBERT, b. Chgo., Aug. 9, 1917; A.B., U. Iowa, 1937, J.D., 1939. Admitted to Iowa bar, 1939; atty. VA, Des Moines, 1946-48; individual practice law, Des Moines, 1949—. Mem. Polk County, Iowa State bar assns. Home: 2002 55th St Des Moines IA 50310 Office: 300 Key Bldg Des Moines IA 50309 Tel (515) 243-6283

ROSENBERG, HOWARD IRVING, b. Chgo., Apr. 10, 1927; A.B., Roosevelt Coll., 1949; LL.B., De Paul U., 1952. Admitted to Ill. bar, 1952, Colo. bar, 1954, U.S. Supreme Ct. bar, 1966; atty. Legal Aid Soc. Met. Denver, 1956-66, gen. counsel, 1967-73, dir., 1973—; asso. dir. research project U. Denver Coll. Law, 1966-67, adj. prof. law, 1967-73, dir. clin. edn., prof. law, 1973—; referee City and County of Denver Juvenile Ct., 1965; mem. Colo. Gov.'s Adv. Council on Legal Services, 1976—. Bd. dirs. Labors Community Agy., Inc., 1970—; mem. Denver Area Fedn. Labor Community Service Com. Mem. Am., Denver, Colo. bar assns., Am. Trial Lawyers Assn., ACLU. Mem. Order of St. Ives, 1972; recipient Outstanding Service award Legal Aid Soc. Met. Denver, 1973. Home: 330 Lafayette St Denver CO 80218 Office: 250 W 14th Ave Denver CO 80204 Tel (303) 753-3193

ROSENBERG, IRWIN ALAN, b. Yonkers, N.Y., Aug. 3, 1936; B.A., N.Y. U., 1958, J.D., 1961; Admitted to N.Y. bar, 1963; individual practice law, 1962-63; staff Legal Aid Soc., 1963-64; individual practice law, 1964-65; law asst., spl. referee Surrogates Ct., Kings County, N.Y., 1966—. Mem. Bklyn. Bar Assn. Contbr. articles to legal jours. Home: 2715 E 64th St Brooklyn NY 11234 Office: 2 Johnson St Brooklyn NY 11234 Tel (212) 643-5799

ROSENBERG, JACK, b. N.Y.C., Mar. 22, 1915; LL.B., N.Y. U., 1936; grad. Nat. Coll. Trial Judges, U. Nev., 1968. Admitted to N.Y. bar, 1937, U.S. Treasury Dept. bar, 1963; individual practice law, N.Y.C., 1937-64; judge Criminal Ct. City of N.Y., 1964—; acting judge Civil Ct. N.Y.C., 1965-66, 67, Family Ct., 1969, Supreme Ct. N.Y., 1971—; spl. dep. atty. gen., dept. law N.Y. State Election Frauds Bur.; sec. to justice City Ct., 1950, to judge Ct. Gen. Sessions, 1952-59, 60, commr. appraisals Jud. Commn. to set Appropriation Awards, 1961-62. Past trustee Park Ave. Synagogue; past co-chmn. law com. N.Y. Republican County Com.; bd. dirs., past mem. exec. com. Anti-Defamation League, bd. govs. fund raising; past bd. dirs. Flushing YM-YWHA; trustee Asso. YM-YWHA. Mem. Am. (chmn. pretrial release com. criminal law sect., mem. exec. com. Spl. Ct. Judges Conf., chmn. com. jud. conduct), N.Y. State, Fed. (past chmn. spl. com. on def. indigent persons) bar assns., Assn. Bar City N.Y. (penology com.), N.Y. County Lawyers Assn. (chmn. civil rights com.), Assn. Lawyers Criminal Cts. Manhattan (past dir.), N.Y. State Trial Lawyers Assn., N.Am. Judges Assn., Am. Arbitration Assn., N.Y. U. Law Alumni Assn. (dir.). Recipient Key Man award, 1957, Key award, 1961 both from Joint Def. Appeal, First Civic Achievement award Dist. council United Brotherhood of Carpenters and Joiners Am., 1966, certificate of honor Hebrew Home for Aged of Riverdale, 1969. Home: 401 E 89th St New York City NY 10028 Office: 851 Grand Concourse Bronx NY 10451 Tel (212) 293-8045

ROSENBERG, JOHN WAYLAND, b. Oakland, Calif., May 23, 1936; A.B., U. Calif., 1958; J.D., 1961. Admitted to Calif. bar, 1962; individual practice law, Oakland, 1962-68; partner firm Bianchi, Hoskins & Rosenberg, San Rafael, Calif., 1968—; dep. town atty. Corte Madera, 1972—; spl. counsel Town of Ross, 1975—. Mem. State Bar Calif., Alameda County, Mazin County bar assns. Home: 16 Graceland Dr San Rafael CA 94901 Office: 1000 4th St Suite 600 San Rafael CA 94901 Tel (415) 456-6020

ROSENBERG, LOUIS FRANKLIN, b. Chgo., Apr. 12, 1945; B.S., Georgetown U., 1966; J.D., U. Chgo., 1969. Admitted to Ill. Supreme Ct. bar, 1969, Ind. Supreme Ct. bar, 1971, U.S. Ct. Appeals 7th Circuit bar, 1974, U.S. Supreme Ct. bar, 1974; atty. Vermillion County (Ill.) Legal Aid Soc., Danville, 1969-70; staff atty. Legal Services Orgn. of Indpls., 1970-73; founder, exec. dir. Ind. Center on Law and Poverty, Indpls., 1973—. Mem. Ind. Bar Assn. Contbr. articles in field to profl. jours. Home: 5526 N College St Indianapolis IN 46220 Office: 129 E Market St Indianapolis IN 46204

ROSENBERG, MARSHALL LEE, b. St. Louis, Sept. 4, 1922; B.S., Washington U., St. Louis, 1943; LL.B., Columbia U., 1951, J.D., 1969. Admitted to N.Y. State bar, 1951; atty. Fed. Wage Stblzn. Bd., N.Y.C., 1951-53; asso. firm Lieberman, Katz & Aronson, N.Y.C., 1954-69; partner firm Lieberman, Aronson & Rosenberg, N.Y.C., 1970—. Office: 1501 Broadway New York City NY 10036 Tel (212) 391-4144

ROSENBERG, MILTON DAVID, b. Pitts., Mar. 8, 1924; B.A., U. Pitts, 1947; LL.B., Harvard, 1949. Admitted to Pa. bar, 1950, U.S. Dist. Ct., 1950, U.S. Ct. Appeals bar, 1956, U.S. Supreme Ct. bar, 1966; partner firm Bloom, Bloom, Rosenberg & Bloom, Washington, Pa., 1961—. Mem. Penn., Am. bar assns., Internat. Acad. Law and Sci., Pa. Trial Lawyers Assn. (dir., past pres.), Internat. Soc. Barristers, Am. Soc. Law and Medicine, Pitts. Inst. Legal Medicine, Am. Judicature Soc. Home: 29 Emerald Dr Washington PA 15301 Office: 200 Washington Trust Building Washington PA 15301 Tel (412) 225-4100

ROSENBERG, MONTAGUE MONTE, b. Jacksonville, Fla., Nov. 8, 1917; LL.B., J.D., Washington and Lee U. Admitted to Fla. bar, 1939, U.S. Supreme Ct. bar, 1975; mem. Gov.'s staff State of Fla., 1949-53; spl. counsel to Mayor of Miami Beach, Fla., gen. counsel planning bd., 1953-57; asst. city atty., Miami, 1973—; spl. counsel trial and appellate matters, 1972-73. Mem. Def. Research Inst., Fla., Dade County bar assns. (founder aux. law library 1945-67). Contbr. articles to profl. jours. Home: 5461 SW 1st St Plantation FL 33317 Office: 148 E Flagler St Miami FL 33317 Tel (305) 583-4438

ROSENBERG, PAUL EDWARD, b. Springfield, Mass., Dec. 6, 1939; B.A., U. Mass., 1961; J.D., Georgetown U., 1964. Admitted to Md. bar, 1964, D.C. bar, 1964, U.S. Supreme Ct. bar, 1969; JAG, U.S. Air Force, 1965-68; asso. firm Green Babcock & Dukes, Hyattsville, Md., 1968-70; partner firm Grene Swingle Dukes & Mann, Hyattsville, 1970-71; asso. firm Dukes Troese Mann & Wilson, Hyattsville, 1971; individual practice law, Camp Springs, Md., 1972—. Mem. exec. bd. Bowie Citizens Assn., 1969—; mem. Belair Village Adv. Com., 1975—; fin. sec./treas. Chesapeake lodge B'nai B'rith, 1972—; pres. Prince George's County Community Pool Assn., 1975—, Pointer Ridge Elementary Sch. PTA, 1975—. Mem. Am., Md., Prince Georges County bar assns. Home: 15706 Presswick Ln Bowie MD 20716 Office: Beltway Plaza 36 S 4710 Auth Pl Suite 420 Camp Springs MD 20023 Tel (301) 423-4747

ROSENBERG, RONALD, b. Phila., Oct. 2, 1933; B.S., W. Chester State U., 1955; LL.B., U. Pa., 1958. Admitted to D.C. bar, 1958, Md. bar, 1962, U.S. Supreme Ct. bar, 1964; atty. AEC, Washington, 1958-60; asso. firm Amram, Hahn and Sundlun, Washington, 1960-62, Van Arkel and Kaiser, Washington, 1962; partner firm Van Arkel, Kaiser, Gressman, Rosenberg and Driesen, Washington, 1974—; counsel Met. D.C. Congress Racial Equality, 1964-66. Mem. D.C. Bar Assn., Order of Coif, U. Pa. Law Sch. D.C. Alumni Assn. (pres.). Speaker seminars. Office: 1828 L St NW Washington DC 20036 Tel (202) 466-8400

ROSENBERG, RUTH HELEN BORSUK, b. Plainfield, N.J., Feb. 23, 1935; A.B., Douglass Coll., 1956; J.D., U. Pa., 1963. Admitted to Pa. bar, 1964, N.Y. bar, 1967, U.S. Supreme Ct. bar, 1969; law clk. Ct. Common Pleas, Phila., 1963-64; asso. firm Blank, Rudenko, Klaus & Rome, Phila., 1964-67; atty. Office Corp. Counsel City of Rochester, N.Y., 1967-68; asso. firm Nixon, Hargrave, Devans & Doyle, Rochester, 1968-74; mem. firm Nixon & Hargrave, Rochester, 1975—. Mem. Commn. Character and Fitness of Applicants for Admission to Bar. Bd. dirs. Soc. Prevention Cruelty to Children, 1976—. Mem. N.Y. State, Monroe County (dir. 1976—) bar assns., N.Y. Civil Liberties Union (v.p. 1976, dir. 1972—) Jewish Fedn. (chmn. social legislation), Phi Beta Kappa. Office: 2200 Lincoln 1st Plaza Tower Rochester NY 14604 Tel (716) 546-8000

ROSENBERG, SEYMOUR, b. N.Y.C., Sept. 8, 1931; LL.B., N.Y. U., 1955. Admitted to N.Y. State bar, 1955; mem. firm Parker Chapin & Flattau, N.Y.C., 1961-63; individual practice law, N.Y.C., 1963—. Mem. N.Y. State Bar Assn., Assn. Immigration and Naturalization Lawyers (chmn. N.Y. chpt.). Home: 96 Brookby Rd Scarsdale NY 10583 Office: 11 W 42nd St New York City NY 10036 Tel (212) 736-7251

ROSENBERG, SHELI ZYSMAN, b. N.Y.C., Feb. 2, 1942; B.A., Tufts U., 1963; J.D., Northwestern U., 1966. Admitted to Ill. bar, 1966, U.S. Tax Ct. bar, 1973; since practiced in Chgo., asso. firm Cotton, Watt, Jones, King & Bowles, 1966-71, asso. firm Schiff Hardin & Waite, 1971-73, partner, 1973—; instr. real estate fin. DePaul U., 1976; counsel Flexible Careers, Inc., Chgo., 1972—, ERA Ill., 1975--. Mem. Am., Chgo. bar assns., Chgo. Council Lawyers (pres. 1973-74, dir. 1970-76). Home: 406 Northwood Dr Glencoe IL 60022 Office: Suite 7200 233 S Wacker Dr Chicago IL 60606 Tel (312) 876-1000

ROSENBERGER, ERNST HEY, b. Hamburg, Germany, Aug. 31, 1931; B.A., Coll. City N.Y., 1955; J.D., N.Y. Law Sch., 1958; postgrad. Northwestern U., 1960; Nat. Coll. State Judiciary, 1976. Admitted to N.Y. State bar, 1958, U.S. Dist. Ct. for So. and Eastern Dist. N.Y. bars, 1960, U.S. 2d Circuit Ct. Appeals bar, 1961, U.S. Supreme Ct. bar, 1970; individual practice law, N.Y.C., 1958-72; judge Criminal Ct., City of N.Y., 1972-77; acting judge 1st dist. Supreme Ct., State of N.Y., 1973-77, justice, 1977—; adj. asso. prof. N.Y. Law Sch. 1976. Mem. Am., N.Y. State bar assns., Am. Judges Assn., Am. Judicature Soc., Nat. Soc. for Legal History, Assn. Bar City N.Y., N.Y. County Lawyers Assn. Editor: N.Y. Law Forum, 1957-58; contbr. book revs. to law jours. Home: 315 E 68th St New York City NY 10021 Office: 100 Centre St New York City NY 10013 Tel (212) 374-6216

ROSENBLATT, HENRY ROBERT, b. Boston, Jan. 8, 1930; LL.B., Boston U., 1954. Admitted to Mass. bar, 1960, U.S. Supreme Ct. bar, 1972; contractual advisor Raytheon Co., Maynard, Mass., 1958-62, Mpls. Honeywell, Brighton, Mass., 1962-64; govt. subcontract advisor, buyer Mass. Inst. Tech., Cambridge, 1964; individual practic law, Newton Centre, Mass., 1965—. Office: 603 Commonwealth Ave Newton Centre MA 02159 Tel (617) 527-4895

ROSENBLEETH, RICHARD MARVIN, b. Phila., Mar. 20, 1932; B.S. in Econs., U. Pa., 1954, J.D., 1957. Admitted to Pa. bar, 1958, U.S. Supreme Ct. bar, 1970; asst. dist. atty. City of Phila., 1958-62; asso. firm Steinberg, Steinbrook, Lavine, & Gorelick, Phila., 1962-65; partner firm Blank, Rome, Klaus & Comisky, Phila., 1965—; mem. Phila. Citizens Crime Commn. Dir. Merion (Pa.) Park Civic Assn., 1966—, pres., 1970. Mem. Am., Pa., Phila. bar assns. Home: 508 Mercer Rd Merion PA 19060 Office: 1100 4 Penn Center Plaza Philadelphia PA 19103 Tel (215) LO 9-3700

ROSENBLOOM, ALAN BRIAN, b. Newark, Oct. 7, 1948; A.B., Rutgers U., 1970, J.D., 1974. Admitted to N.J. bar, 1974; clk. to judge Superior Ct. N.J., 1974-75; asso. firm Checki, Politan & Bergman, Lyndhurst, N.J., 1975—. Mem. Phi Beta Kappa. Tel (201) 939-1550

ROSENBLOOM, DANIEL, b. N.Y.C., Feb. 11, 1930; B.A., U. Va., 1951, J.D., 1954; LL.M. in Taxation, N.Y. U., 1960. Admitted to Va. bar, 1954, N.Y. bar, 1956; asso. firm Paskus, Gordon & Hyman, N.Y.C., 1957-61; v.p., sec., counsel Phila. & Reading Corp., N.Y.C., 1962-68; v.p. corporate fin. 1st Manhattan Co., N.Y.C., 1968-71, gen. partner, 1971—. Home: 775 Park Ave New York City NY 10021 Office: 380 Madison Ave New York City NY 10017 Tel (212) 949-8032

ROSENBLOOM, H. DAVID, b. N.Y.C., May 26, 1941; A.B. summa cum laude, Princeton U., 1962; postgrad. (Fulbright scholar) U. Florence, 1962-63; J.D. magna cum laude, Harvard U., 1966. Admitted to N.Y. State bar, 1967, D.C. bar, 1968; spl. asst. to Ambassador Arthur J. Goldberg U.S. Mission to UN, 1966-67; law clk. Justice Abe Fortas, U.S. Supreme Ct., 1967-68; asso. firm Caplin & Drysdale, Washington, 1968-72, partner, 1972-77; with Dept. Treasury, Washington, 1977—; cons. Ford Found. on corp. social responsibility, 1971-72. Mem. adv. council dept. Romance lang. Princeton U. Mem. D.C. Bar, Internat. Fiscal Assn. Author: (with Bevis Longstreth) Corporate Social Responsibility and the Institutional Investor: A Report to the Ford Foundation, 1973; contbr. articles to legal jours. and papers to meetings. Home: 419 4th St SE Washington DC 20003 Office: Dept Treasury Washington DC 20036 Tel (202) 862-5060

ROSENBLOOM, NOAH SCHANFIELD, b. Mpls., Sept. 30, 1924; student Macalester Coll., 1942-43, U. Dubuque, 1943-44, U. Ill., 1944-45; B.A., U. Minn., 1948, B.S.Law, 1950, LL.B., 1952. Admitted to Minn. bar, 1953, U.S. Dist. Ct. bar for Dist. Minn., 1954, U.S. Supreme Ct. bar, 1960; partner firm Rosenbloom & Rosenbloom, Redwood Falls, Minn., 1953-63; spl. judge Municipal Ct., Redwood Falls, 1956-61; judge Minn. Dist. Ct., 5th Judicial Dist., 1963—. Mem. bd. rev. panel Minn. Fair Employment Practice Commn., 1955-62. Mem. 9th Jud. Dist., Minn. State, Am. bar assns., Am. Judicature Soc. Home: 128 Camelsback Rd New Ulm MN 56073 Office: Brown County Courthouse New Ulm MN 56073 Tel (507) 354-2014

ROSENBLUM, VICTOR GREGORY, b. N.Y.C., June 2, 1925; A.B., Columbia, 1945, LL.B., 1948; Ph.D., U. Calif., Berkeley, 1953; D.H.L., Hebrew Union Coll., 1970. Admitted to N.Y. State bar, 1949, U.S. Supreme Ct. bar, 1953, Ill. bar, 1960; staff asso. Govtl. Affairs Inst., Washington, 1952-53; asst. prof. polit. sci. U. Calif., Berkeley, 1953-57; asso. counsel, subcom. exec. legislative reorgn., com. govt. ops. U.S. Ho. of Rep., 1957-58; asso. prof. Northwestern U., Chgo., 1958-63, prof. law, polit. sci., 1963-68, 70—; pres. Reed Coll., 1968-70; Fulbright prof. U. Louvain (Belgium), 1966-67; cons. in field. Chmn. exec. com. Anti-Defamation League Chgo., 1973-76; bd. dirs. Ams. United for Life, Beth Emet Synagogue, Evanston, Ill.; chmn. Treatment Alternatives to Street Crime, 1976—. Mem. Am. Bar Assn. (chmn. sect. adminstrv. law 1977-78). Editor: (with A. Didrick Castberg) Constitutional Law: Political Roles of the Supreme Court, 1973; author: The Administrative Law Judge in the Administrative Process. Home: 2030 Orrington Ave Evanston IL 60201 Office: 357 E Chicago Ave Chicago IL Tel (312) 649-8443

ROSENFELD, ARTHUR H., b. Bklyn., May 24, 1930; exchange scholar St. Andrew's U., Fife, Scotland, 1951; A.B., Union Coll., 1952; J.D., Harvard U., 1955. Admitted to N.Y. bar, 1955; asso. firm Cox, Trainer & Shaughnessy, N.Y.C., 1957-59; asst. to pres. and gen. counsel Ronald Press Co., N.Y.C., 1959-70; exec. v.p. Warren, Gorham & Lamont, Inc., N.Y.C., 1970—, also dir.; mem. bd. advisors Council of Municipal Performance, N.Y.C. Mem. N.Y. Bar Assn., ACLU. Office: 870 7th Ave New York City NY 10019 Tel (212) 977-7450

ROSENFELD, JAY H., b. Phila., Oct. 25, 1920; B.S. in Econs., U. Pa., 1942, J.D., 1949. Admitted to Pa. bar, 1949; partner firm Rosenfeld & Weinrott, Phila., 1966—; spl. asst. atty. gen. State of Pa., 1966-70. Mem. Pa., Phila. bar assns. Home: 5814 Drexel Rd Philadelphia PA 19131 Office: 1700 Market Philadelphia PA 17903 Tel (215) LO4-1943

ROSENFELD, MARK ROBERT, b. Bklyn., May 7, 1940; B.S., U. Pa., 1962; J.D., St. John's U., 1965; LL.M. in Taxation, N.Y. U., 1969. Admitted to N.Y. bar, 1965; tax atty. Cities Service Co., N.Y.C., 1966-70; mgr. tax research Borden, Inc., N.Y.C., 1970; tax atty. Colt Industries, N.Y.C., 1970-72; v.p. Citibank, N.Y.C., 1972—, adminstr. corporate taxes Asia Pacific region, Manila, Philippines, 1976—. Mem. Am., N.Y. State bar assns. Asso. editor St. John's Law Rev., 1964-65. Home: 2147 Paraiso St Dasmarinas Village Makati Rizal Philippines Office: Citibank NA Philippines PO Box 49 Makati Comml Center Manila Philippines Tel 86-05-17

ROSENFELD, MORDECAI, b. N.Y.C., Feb. 1, 1930; A.B. (James Manning scholar, Francis Wayland scholar), Brown U., 1951; LL.B., Yale, 1954. Admitted to N.Y. bar, 1954, U.S. Supreme Ct. bar, 1958; individual practice law, N.Y.C., 1960—; adj. prof. Rutgers U. Law Sch., 1973, Rutgers U. Grad. Sch. Bus., 1972. Mem. Community Planning Bd. No. 12, Manhattan, 1972—; del. 1st Jud. Dist. Democratic Jud. Conv., 1972—. Mem. Am., N.Y. State bar assns., Fed. Bar Council of 2d Circuit, Phi Beta Kappa. Contbr. articles to legal jours. Home: 140 Cabrini Blvd New York City NY 10033 Office: 233 Broadway New York City NY 10007 Tel (212) 964-1369

ROSENFELD, MORTON M., b. St. Louis, Feb. 23, 1948; A.B. cum laude, Princeton, 1969; J.D. cum laude, U. Mich., 1972. Admitted to Calif. bar, 1972; asso. firm Agnew, Miller & Carlson, Los Angeles, 1972—. Participant Constl. Rights Found. Lawyer-in-the Classroom Program, Los Angeles. Mem. Los Angeles County Bar Assn., Constitutional Rights Found., Town Hall of Los Angeles, ACLU, Order of Coif. Note and comment editor U. Mich. Jour. of Law Reform, 1971-72. Office: 700 S Flower St Los Angeles CA 90017 Tel (213) 629-4200

ROSENGREN, CHESTER GORDON, b. Brandon, Minn., Nov. 12, 1908; M.B.A., U. Minn., 1929; LL.B., U. Mich., 1932. Admitted to Minn. bar, 1932; mem. firm Rosengren, Rufor, Hefte & Pemberton, and predecessor firms, Fergus Falls, Minn., 1932-62; judge Minn. Dist. Ct. 7th Jud. Dist., Fergus Falls, 1963-76; city atty. Fergus Falls, 1940-46; county atty. Otter Tail County (Minn.), 1956-66; Mem. Am. Coll. Trial Lawyers, Am., Minn. bar assns., Alpha Delta Phi, Phi Delta Phi. Address: 909 Mt Faith Ave Fergus Falls MN 56537 Tel (218) 736-4492

ROSENGREN, KENNETH, b. St. Paul, July 26, 1920; student Stanford; LL.B., U. Ariz., 1947. Admitted to Ariz. bar, 1947; individual practice law, Phoenix; counsel Spanish Air Base Constr. Program, Madrid, Spain, 1954-56, U.S. Navy Bur. Aeronautics, N.Y.C., 1956-59; guest lectr. Aris. State U. Diplomate Am. Bd. Trial Advocates. Mem. Am., Ariz., Maricopa County bar assns., Assn. Trial Lawyers Am., Am. Judicature Soc., Phoenix Exec. Club. Contbr. articles in field to law jours. Home: 5335 N 18th St Phoenix AZ 85016 Office: 303 Luhrs Bldg 11 W Jefferson Phoenix AZ 85003 Tel (602) 252-6561

ROSENN, KEITH SAMUEL, b. Wilkes-Barre, Pa., Dec. 9, 1938; A.B., Amherst Coll., 1960, LL.B., Yale, 1963. Admitted to Pa. bar, 1964; law clk. U.S. Ct. Appeals 2d Circuit, 1963-64; asso. firm Rosenn, Jenkins & Greenwald, Wilkes-Barre, 1964-65; asst. prof. law Ohio State U., 1965-66, prof. law., 1970—; cons. Ford Found., Rio de Janeiro, Brazil, 1966-68; vis. prof. Stanford-Chilean Law project, 1968, State U. Guanabara, Brazil, 1967, Nat. U. Paraguay, 1970. Mem. Am. Bar Assn., Am. Soc. for Study of Comparative Law (dir.), Order of Coif. Author: (with Kurst) Law and Development in Latin America, 1975. Contbr. articles in field to legal jours. Home: 3863 Woodbridge Rd Columbus OH 43220 Office: 1659 N High St Columbus OH 43210 Tel (604) 422-8563

ROSENSTEIN, JUDITH ANN, b. Newark, Oct. 7, 1944; B.A., Drew U., 1966; J.D., Rutgers U., 1969. Admitted to N.J. bar, 1970; staff atty. Essex County (N.J.) Legal Services Corp., Orange, 1969-71; sr. trial atty. Office of Pub. Defender, Jersey City, 1971—. Home: 571 Newark Ave Elizabeth NJ 07208 Office: 556 Newark Ave Jersey City NJ 07306 Tel (201) 792-6400

ROSENSTEIN, SAMUEL MURRAY, b. Frankfort, Ky., June 7, 1909; A.B., U. Ky., 1928; J.D., U. Cin., 1931; Admitted to Ohio, Ky. bars, 1931; partner firm M.M. Logan, Frankfort, 1931-33, Smith, Reed & Leary, Frankfort, 1933-48; partner firm Milliken, Handmaker & Rosenstein, Louisville, 1948-62, sr. partner, 1962-68; judge U.S. Customs Ct., Miami, Fla., 1968—; pros. atty. City Frankfort, 1933-41; acting atty. Franklin County, Ky., 1941-42; spl. counsel Commonwealth Ky., 1935-43. Mem. Ky. Bar Assn. (former sec.). Named Man of Yr., Am. Cancer Soc., 1968; recipient Gov's award, State Ky., 1967. Home: 2200 S Ocean Ln Ft Lauderdale FL 33316 Office: 51 SW 1st St Miami FL 33130 Tel (305) 350-5229

ROSENSTOCK, LOUIS ANTHONY, III, b. Petersburg, Va., July 27, 1941; B.A., Washington and Lee U., 1963; LL.B., U. Richmond, 1966, J.D., 1966. Admitted to Va. bar, 1966; capt. JAGC, U.S. Army, 1966-71; asso. firm Lavenstein & Andrews, Petersburg, Va., 1972-73, Wm. F. Binford, Prince George, Va., 1971-72; judge Petersburg (Va.) Gen. Dist. Ct., 1973-75; individual practice, Petersburg, Va., 1975—. Vice pres. Petersburg unit Am. Cancer Soc., 1976. Mem. Am., Petersburg bar assns., Va. Trial Lawyers Assn. Home: 413 Beauregard Ave Petersburg VA 23803 Office: 20 E Tabb St Petersburg VA 23803 Tel (804) 861-5114

ROSENSWEIG, ROBERT LAWRENCE, b. New Britain, Conn., Aug. 19, 1928; B.A., Yale U., 1949; LL.B., Fordham U., 1952. Admitted to Conn. bar, 1952, N.Y. bar, 1953; asso. firm Shipman & Goodwin, Hartford, Conn., 1954-57, partner, 1957—; corporator, trustee, chmn. bd. State Bank for Savs., Hartford. Corporator Hartford Hosp. Mem. Am., Conn., Hartford County bar assns. Home: 29 Westmont St West Hartford CT 06117 Office: 799 Main St Hartford CT 06103 Tel (203) 549-4770

ROSENTHAL, ALBERT JOSEPH, b. N.Y.C., Mar. 5, 1919; B.A., U. Pa., 1938; LL.B., Harvard, 1941. Admitted to N.Y. State bar, 1942, U.S. Supreme Ct. bar, 1947; law clk. to Judge Magruder, U.S. Ct. Appeals, Boston, 1941-42; spl. appellate atty. Office Price Adminstrn., Washington, 1946-47; law clk. to Judge Frankfurter, U.S. Supreme Ct., Washington, 1947-48; asst. loan officer IBRD, Washington, 1948-50; atty. Dept. Justice, Washington, 1950-52; gen. counsel Small Defense Plants Adminstrn., Washington, 1952-53; partner firm Golden, Wienshienk & Rosenthal, N.Y.C., 1953-64; prof. law

Columbia, N.Y.C., 1964—, Maurice T. Moore prof., 1974—; hearing officer N.Y. State Dept. Environ. Conservation, 1975; mem. Logan Airport Master Plan Study Team, 1975; mem. com. on environ. decision making Nat. Acad. Scis., 1975—. Mem. Am. Law Inst. Author: (with H. Korn and S. Lubman) Catastrophic Accidents in Government Programs, 1963; (with F. Grad and G. Rathjens) Environmental Control: Priorities, Policies and the Law, 1971; Federal Regulation of Campaign Finance, 1972; (with F. Grad and others) The Automobile and the Regulation of Its Impact on the Environment, 1975; contbr. articles to profl. jours. Home: 15 Oakway Scarsdale NY 10583 Office: 435 W 116th St Columbia U Law School New York City NY 10027

ROSENTHAL, ALLEN M., b. N.Y.C., Dec. 28, 1936; B.A., U. Buffalo, 1958; LL.B., Bklyn. Law Sch., 1961, LL.M., 1963. Admitted to N.Y. State bar, 1961; staff atty. Legal Aid Soc. of N.Y., 1962-64; individual practice law Bklyn. Mem. N.Y. State, Bklyn. bar assns., Comml. Lawyers Conf. (pres. 1974). Office: 186 Joralemon St Brooklyn NY 11201 Tel (212) 624-5522

ROSENTHAL, CHARLES, b. N.Y.C., Apr. 19, 1912; A.B., U. So. Calif., 1933, J.D., 1935. Admitted to Calif. bar, 1935; individual practice law, Los Angeles, 1935—; lectr. estate planning for Fidelity Lodge and City of Hope. Chancellor commdr. Knights of Phythias, Los Angels, 1942; pres., Fidelity Lodge Bnai Brith, Los Angeles, 1943; pres. men's club, dir. Beth Israel, 1955-76. Home: 366 N La Jolla Ave Los Angeles CA 90048 Office: 117 W 9th St Room 902 Los Angeles CA 90015 Tel (213) 627-5308

ROSENTHAL, DANIEL I., b. Pitts., June 3, 1914; B.A., Johns Hopkins, 1934; student Harvard, 1934-36; LL.B., U. Cin., 1937, J.D., 1968. Admitted to Ohio bar, 1937, since practiced in Springfield; spl. agt. FBI, 1941-45. Dir. Vining Broom Co., Inc. Vice pres. Ohio Bar Found. Past chmn. Clark County Jail Study Com. Mem. Am. (Ho. of Dels.), Ohio (exec. com., pres.-elect. 1974-75, pres. 1975-76), Clark County (past pres.) bar assns. Home: 500 Dover Rd Springfield OH 45504 Office: New M & M Bldg Springfield OH 45502*

ROSENTHAL, GILBERT, b. Balt., Mar. 22, 1934; B.A., U. Md., 1954, LL.B., 1957. Admitted to Md. bar, 1958, ICC bar, 1973; mem. firm Kertman & Resnick, 1958-64, Miller, Rosenthal & Laud, 1964-69; atty. Criminal Injuries Compensation Bd., Balt., 1970-72; asst. atty. gen. State of Md., Balt., 1969—. Dir. U.S. Jaycees, 1968-70; sec. Balt. Urban Coalition, 1968-70; mem. Balt. Redistricting Commn., 1965-67, Harbor Commn. Balt., 1970; mem. U.S. Council Phys. Fitness, 1967; dir. Jr. Achievement, 1967-68, Balt. Safety Commn., 1967-68, Boys Town Md., 1968-69; active Boy Scouts Am. Mem. Am., Md., Balt. City bar assns. Contbr. articles profl. jours. Home: 5405 Purlington Way Baltimore MD 21212 Office: Blaustein Bldg Baltimore MD 21201

ROSENTHAL, IRVIN HAROLD, b. N.Y.C., Nov. 22, 1927; A.B., Syracuse U., 1948; J.D., N.Y. U., 1951, LL.M. in Taxation, 1956. Admitted to N.Y. State bar, 1951; since practiced in N.Y.C., asso. firm Steckler, Frank & Gutman, 1953-60, partner, 1961-70; individual practice law, 1970-76, partner firm Rosenthal & Shays, 1977—; guest lectr. family law Albert Einstein Coll. Medicine, Bronx, Roosevelt Hosp., N.Y.C., Bklyn. Coll., N.Y. State Trial Lawyers Assn., W. Side YMCA, N.Y.C. Fellow Am. Acad. Matrimonial Lawyers; mem. Am., Nassau County bar assns., Assn. Bar City N.Y., Am. Arbitration Assn. (matrimonial and comml. panel aribtrators). Office: 500 Fifth Ave New York City NY 10036 Tel (212) 947-5566

ROSENTHAL, IRWIN MARTIN, b. Bklyn., Dec. 13, 1928; A.B. cum laude, N.Y. U., 1949; LL.B., Yale, 1952. Admitted to D.C. bar, 1953, N.Y. bar, 1954; since practiced in N.Y.C.; sec. U.S. 2d Circuit Ct. Appeals, 1952; asso. firm Goldstein, Judd & Gurfein, 1954-58; gen. counsel Security Ins. Co., New Haven, 1958; asso. firm Tenzer, Greenblatt, Fallon & Kaplan, 1958-60; partner firm Weiss, Rosenthal, Heller, Schwartzman & Lazar, 1962—; chief legal officer USAF Civil Reserve Air Fleet Program, 1952-53. Pres., founder Nat. Found. Ileitis and Colitis, Inc., 1966-77, Am. Digestive Disease Soc., N.Y.C., 1973-76; mem. N.Y. State Democratic Com., 1966-77; chmn. bd. trustees Hillcrest Jewish Center, Flushing N.Y., 1970-72; trustee Queens Speech and Hearing Center, 1968-72; Mem. Assn. Bar City N.Y., Queens County (co-chmn. corps. com.), N.Y. State, Am. (mem. banking corp. com.) bar assns., Am. Gastrointestinal Soc. Home: 81-36 192d St Jamaica Estates NY 11423 Office: 295 Madison Ave New York City NY 10017 Tel (212) 725-9200

ROSENTHAL, JEROME R., b. N.Y.C.; LL.B., N.Y. U. Admitted to N.Y. bar, 1949; individual practice law, Port Chester, N.Y., 1951—. Corp. counsel City of Port Chester, 1959-63, judge, 1971-73. Mem. N.Y. State, Westchester County bar assns. Home: 5 Bolton Pl Port Chester NY 10573 Office: 225 Westchester Ave Port Chester NY 10573 Tel (914) 937-3100

ROSENTHAL, JOSEPH MEYER, b. Bklyn., Jan. 19, 1940; A.B., Syracuse U., 1956; J.D., Harvard U., 1963; postgrad. N.Y. U. Sch. Law, 1965. Admitted to N.Y. bar, 1964, Fla. bar, 1976, U.S. Supreme Ct. bar, 1970; dep. asst. atty. gen. N.Y., 1965-66; asso. firm Lipkowitz, Plaut, Salberg & Harris, N.Y.C., 1966, Smith & Cohen, Smithtown, 1966-71; individual practice law, Smithtown, 1971-74, 77—; sr. partner firm Rosenthal & Reiss, Smithtown, 1975-77. Instl. rep. Cub Scout Pack 379, Boy Scouts Am., 1968-69, chmn. pack com., 1969-72; mem. Suffolk County (N.Y.) Democratic Com., 1966—; chmn. law com. Smithtown Dem. Com., 1973-75; coordinator Suffolk County campaign for Henry M. Jackson for Pres., 1972, N.Y. First Congressional Dist. campaign, 1976; pres. Kings Park Jewish Center, 1968-71, bd. dirs., 1966—, chmn. bd., 1975—. Mem. Am., N.Y. State, Suffolk County bar assns., N.Y. State Trial Lawyers Assn., Assn. Bar City N.Y., Navy Marine Lawyers Assn., Kings Park C. of C. (dir.). Home: 16 Landview Dr Kings Park NY 11754 Office: 91 Maple Ave Smithtown NY 11787 Tel (516) 724-8181

ROSENTHAL, JOSEPH SEMEL, b. N.Y.C., Nov. 8, 1932; B.A., N.Y. U., 1953, LL.M., 1960; LL.B., Harvard, 1958. Admitted to N.Y. bar, 1958, U.S. Supreme Ct. bar, 1966; atty. NLRB, N.Y.C., 1958-61; asso. firm Wachtel & Michaelson, N.Y.C., 1961-63; partner firm Friedlander, Gaines, Cohen, Rosenthal & Rosenberg, N.Y.C., 1963—. Mem. Am. Arbitration Assn., Am. Bar Assn. Home: 26 W Kirkwood Ave Merrick NY 11566 Office: 1140 Ave of the Americas New York City NY 10036 Tel (212) 575-9100

ROSENTHAL, MARVIN JAY, b. Rochester, N.Y., Nov. 1, 1933; B.A., Alfred U., 1955; LL.B., Cornell U., 1958, LL.D., 1969. Admitted to N.Y. State bar, 1958, D.C. bar, 1970, U.S. Supreme Ct. bar, 1970, U.S. Customs Ct. bar, U.S. Dist. Ct. bars for So., Eastern and Western Dists., U.S. Ct. Appeals bar for 2d Circuit; asso. firm Krieger & Tick, N.Y.C., 1959-63; sr. partner Fulreader & Rosenthal, Rochester, 1963—; instr. bus. law Rochester Inst. Tech., 1973—. Bd. dirs. Internat. Friendship Council, Rochester, 1964—, Pub. Broadcasting Assn., Rochester, 1970—. Mem. Am., N.Y., Monroe County (N.Y.) bar assns. Author: Congressional Investigating Committees and the Problems of Rules of Procedure, 1955. Home: 133 Dunrovin Ln Rochester NY 14618 Office: Fulreader & Rosenthal 1350 Lincoln First Tower Rochester NY 14604 Tel (716) 454-3191

ROSENTHAL, MICHAEL PHILIP, b. N.Y.C., July 21, 1936; A.B., Columbia, 1956, J.D., 1959. Admitted to N.Y. State bar, 1960, Tex. bar, 1973; asst. dir. Legis. Drafting Fund of Columbia, 1960; law clk. to judge H.R. Medina, U.S. Ct. Appeals 2d Circuit, N.Y.C., 1960-61; asso. firm Aranow, Brodsky, Bohlinger, Einhorn & Dann., N.Y.C., 1961-63; asso. firm Kaye, Scholer, Fierman, Hays and Handler, N.Y.C., 1963-64; asst. prof. law Rutgers U., Camden, N.J., 1965-67, asso. prof., 1967-68; vis. asso. prof. law U. Tex., Austin, 1967-68; prof. law, 1968—; cons. Nat. Commn. on Reform of Fed. Criminal Laws, 1968-71; cons. Canadian Fed. Commn. of Inquiry into non-med. use of drugs, Ottawa, Ont., 1971; cons. drug problems President's Commn. on Law Enforcement and Adminstrn. of Justice, 1966-67; coordinator Community Services Tex. Youth Council, Austin, 1974; mem. criminal law sect. com. on drug abuse Am. Bar Assn., 1971-73. Author: Interpretation of the Mental Health Code, 1976; contbr. articles on drug law reform to profl. jours.; guest editor Jour. Drug Issues; mem. editorial bd. Jour. of Drug Issues. Home: 3611 Laurelledge Ln Austin TX 78731 Office: 2500 Red River St U Tex Law Sch Austin TX 78705 Tel (512) 471-5151

ROSENTHAL, ROBERT, b. Mineola, N.Y., Feb. 8, 1938; A.B., Boston U., 1960, J.D., 1963. Admitted to N.Y. State bar, 1963, U.S. Supreme Ct. bar, 1971, U.S. Ct. Appeals 2d Circuit bar, 1970; legis. counsel N.Y. State Senator John D. Caemmerer, 1966; law asst. Nassau County (N.Y.) Dist. Ct., Mineola, 1967-70; asst. U.S. atty. U.S. Dept. Justice Eastern Dist. N.Y., 1970-74; individual practice law, Mineola, 1974—. Trustee Congregation Beth Sholom, Mineola, 1974—, sec., 1976—. Mem. Am., N.Y., Nassau County bar assns., Jewish Lawyers Assn. Nassau County. Home: 137 Mineola Blvd Mineola NY 11501 Office: 170 Old Country Rd Mineola NY 11501 Tel (516) 746-4898

ROSENTHAL, SIMON MILYOS, b. N.Y.C., Mar. 11, 1935; B.S. in Bus. Adminstrn. cum laude, U. So. Calif., 1957; J.D., U. Calif., Los Angeles, 1960. Admitted to Calif. bar, 1961; pub. defender Alameda County (Calif.), 1961-62; sr. asso. firm Herbert Porter, Watts, Calif., 1963; gen. rep., dep. dir. Legal Aid Soc. of Alameda County, 1964-66; dir. neighborhood legal services program Legal Aid Soc. of San Mateo County (Calif.), 1966-68, exec. dir., 1971-74; chief div. evaluation office legal service OEO, Washington, 1968-70; dep. dir. Nat. Legal Aid and Defender Assn., 1974-75; dean New Coll. of Calif. Sch. of Law, San Francisco, 1976—; cons. in field; tchr., organizer Legal Aid dirs'. seminars Cath. U. Am., 1971-75; prof. criminal law Canada Coll., Redwood City, Calif., 1973-74. Chmn. Western Legal Aid Dirs. Assn., 1971-73; mem. exec. com. Action for Legal Rights, 1971-75. Mem. San Mateo County, Am. bar assns., Calif. State Bar, Nat. Legal Aid and Defender Assn. (exec. com. 1972—, dir. 1976—). Office: PO Box 352 La Honda CA 94020 Tel (415) 747-0808

ROSENTRATER, GARY LEE, b. Greeley, Colo., Apr. 27, 1942; B.A., U. Colo., 1964, J.D., 1967. Admitted to Colo. bar, 1967; legis. atty. Legis. Research Service, Library of Congress, Washington, 1967-68; mem. firm Kreidler Durham Rosentarter & Moxley, Montrose, Colo., 1969—; municipal judge, Montrose, 1974-75. Montrose Bd. Adjustments, 1971-74. Mem. Am., Colo., 7th Jud. Dist. (past pres.) bar assns. Home: 810 S 11th St Montrose CO 81401 Office: PO Box 157 Montrose CO 81401 Tel (303) 249-3451

ROSENWALD, PETER, b. Alingsas, Sweden, Mar. 10, 1945; B.S. in Pharmacy, U. Cin., 1968; J.D., No. Ky. State Coll., 1973. Admitted to Ohio bar, 1973; staff atty. div. pub. defender Legal Aid Soc. of Cin., 1973—, supervising atty., 1975—. Mem. Cin., Ohio State, Am. bar assns., Am., Ohio trial lawyers assns., Hamilton County (Ohio) Pharm. Assn. Home: 1113 Halpin Ave Cincinnati OH 45208 Office: 222 E Central Pkwy room 308-A Cincinnati OH 45202 Tel (513) 651-3250

ROSENZWEIG, DAVID LEE, b. Pottsville, Pa., June 17, 1939; B.S., Youngstown State U., 1962; J.D., Case Western Res. U., 1968. Admitted to Ohio bar, 1968, U.S. Dist. Ct. for Nor. Dist. Ohio bar, 1969; asso. firm Squire, Sanders & Dempsey, Cleve., 1968-74; sr. v.p. adminstrn., gen. counsel Union Commerce Corp., Cleve., 1974—, also dir.; dir. Clarion Capital Corp., So. Ohio Bank, Union Capital Mgmt. Corp., Union Commerce Leasing Corp. Mem. endowment com. Jewish Community Center, Cleve., 1976. Mem. Ohio State Bar Assn., Bar Assn. Greater Cleve., Order of the Coif. Editor-in-chief Law Rev.; contbr. articles to law reviews. Office: 300 Union Commerce Bldg Cleveland OH 44115 Tel (216) 241-2100

ROSENZWEIG, JERRY, b. Mpls., Sept. 17, 1934; B.A. summa cum laude, U. Minn., 1954; LL.B., Harvard, 1957. Admitted to Minn. bar, 1957; law clk. Chief Justice Minn. Supreme Ct., 1957-59; asso. firm Wheeler, Fredrikson & Larson, Mpls., 1959-61; partner firm Halpern & Rosenzweig, Mpls., 1962-64; individual practice law, Mpls., 1965—. Mem. Am., Minn., Hennepin County bar assns., Am., Minn. trial lawyers assns., Comml. Law League of Am., Phi Beta Kappa, Delta Sigma Rho. Home: 2521 Unity Ave N Minneapolis MN 55422 Office: 1616 Park Ave Minneapolis MN 55404 Tel (612) 339-0411

ROSENZWEIG, SIMON, b. N.Y.C., Dec. 28, 1905; A.B., Cornell U., 1927, LL.B., 1929. Admitted to N.Y. State bar, 1930, U.S. Dist. Ct. bar for Eastern Dist. N.Y., 1934, for So. Dist. N.Y., 1934, U.S. Ct. Appeals bar, 2d Circuit, 1934; partner firm Tretter Rosenwein & Rosenzweig, N.Y.C., 1931-34, Rosenwein & Rosenzweig, N.Y.C., 1934-38, Tretter & Rosenzweig, N.Y.C., 1947-48; asst. counsel N.Y.C. Housing Authority, 1938-44, counsel, 1945-47; individual practice law, N.Y.C., 1948-65, 75—; dir. Mental Health Info. Service, First Jud. Dept., N.Y.C., 1965-75; lectr. on law Baruch Sch. Bus. Adminstrn., U. City N.Y. Bd. dirs. Urban League of Westchester County (N.Y.), Westchester Assn. Retarded Children, Bd. Jewish Edn., N.Y.C.; pres. Westchester Assn. Hebrew Schs., 1954-56, N.Y.C. Bd. Rev., 1974-76; mem. adv. com. on mental health N.Y. State Dept. Mental Health. Mem. Assn. Bar City N.Y., New York County Lawyers Assn., Westchester County, N.Y. State, Am. bar assns., Am. Orthopsychiat. Assn. Contbr. articles to legal jours. Home: 30 Cobb Ave White Plains NY 10606 Office: 122 E 42d St New York City NY 10017 Tel (212) OX-7-0133

ROSETA, RICHARD ALFORD, b. Seattle, Feb. 23, 1947; B.S., U. Oreg., 1969, J.D., 1972. Admitted to Oreg. bar, 1972; asso. firm Jaqua & Wheatley, and predecessors, Eugene, Oreg., 1972-75, partner, 1975—. Mem. Oreg., Am., Lane County bar assns., Oreg. Assn. Def. Counsel, Def. Research Inst. Home: 4120 Alder St Eugene OR 97405 Office: 825 E Park St Eugene OR 97401 Tel (503) 686-8485

ROSIN, RICHARD MORTON, b. Montgomery, Ala., Nov. 18, 1942; B.A. magna cum laude, Claremont Men's Coll., 1964; M.Bus. Econs., Claremont Grad. Sch., 1965; J.D., U. Calif., Berkeley, 1967. Admitted to Calif. bar, 1967, U.S. Dist. Ct. So. Dist. Calif., 1969; partner firm Greenberg, Bernhard, Weiss & Karma, Los Angeles, 1969—; lectr. bus. law U. Md. Far East div., 1968. Mem. Am., Los Angeles County bar assns., State Bar of Calif., Pi Mu Epsilon. Office: 1880 Century Park E Los Angeles CA 90067 Tel (213) 553-6111

ROSKIE, RICHARD NORMAN, b. Great Falls, Mont., July 9, 1942; B.S., Mont. State U., 1965; J.D. cum laude, Willamette U., 1969. Admitted to Oreg. bar, 1969; partner firm Black, Helterline, Beck & Rappleyea, Portland, Oreg., 1969—. Mem. Am. Bar Assn. Home: 1335 SW 66th Ave Portland OR 97225 Office: 12th Floor Bank of Calif Tower Portland OR 97205 Tel (503) 224-5560

ROSNER, JONATHAN L., b. N.Y.C., Sept. 4, 1932; B.A., Wesleyan U., 1954; J.D., N.Y. U., 1959. Admitted to N.Y. bar, 1959, U.S. Supreme Ct. bar, 1964, D.C. bar, 1976; law clk. U.S. Dist. Ct., 1959-60; asst. U.S. atty. So. Dist. N.Y., 1960-63; partner firm Rosner, Rosner & McEvoy, N.Y.C., 1963—; adj. prof. law N.Y. U., 1970—. Telethon chmn. Westchester County Muscular Dystrophy Assn., 1968, pres., 1969; bd. dirs. Maplewood Swim Club, 1971—, pres. 1974—; bd. dirs. Hartsdale Lawns Civic Assn., 1965-68; Democratic candidate for Dist. Atty. Westchester County, 1968; chmn. candidate selection com. Westchester County Dem. Com., 1976. Mem. Am. Judicature Soc., Am., N.Y. State bar assns., Assn. Bar City N.Y. N.Y. County Lawyers Assn., Fed. Bar Council, N.Y. U. Law Alumni Assn., N.Y. U. Law Rev. Alumni Assn.; contbr. articles to legal jours. Home: 33 High Ridge Rd Hartsdale NY 10530 Office: 6 E 43d St New York City NY 10017 Tel (212) 661-2150

ROSS, ALFRED JOSEPH, JR., b. N.Y.C., Nov. 21, 1938; student U. Fribourg (Switzerland), 1958-59; B.A., Georgetown U., 1960; LL.B., Harvard, 1963. Admitted to N.Y. bar, 1964; asso. firm Shearman & Sterling, N.Y.C., 1963-72, partner, 1972—. Mem. Am., N.Y., Internat. bar assns.

ROSS, BRADFORD, b. Cheyenne, Wyo., Sept. 26, 1912; student U. Va., 1928-29; student George Washington U., 1930-32, LL.B., 1936. Admitted to D.C. bar, 1936, Wyo. bar, 1939; asso. firms McNeill & McNeil, Washington, 1937-39, Lacey & Loomis, Cheyenne, 1939-41; gen. counsel FPC, Washington, 1946-53; partner firm Ross, Marsh, & Foster, Washington, 1953—. Mem. D.C. Fed., Fed. Power (pres. 1974-75), Fed. Communications, Wyo., Am. (sect. pub. utility law council 1950-55) bar assns., Am. Judicature Soc., Phi Delta Phi. Home: 3517 Tilden St NW Washington DC 20008 Office: 730 15th St NW Washington DC 20005 Tel (202) 628-2623

ROSS, CHARLES ROBERT, b. Middlebury, Vt., Feb. 24, 1920; B.A., U. Mich., 1941, M.B.A., LL.B., 1948. Admitted to Ky. bar, 1949, Vt. bar, 1954, U.S. Supreme Ct. bar, 1968; instr. Oreg. State Coll., 1948-49; with Derby Constrn. Co., Louisville, Ky., 1949-54; individual practice law, Burlington, Vt., 1954-59; chmn. Vt. Pub. Service Commn., Montpelier, 1959-61; commr. FPC, Washington, 1961-68, U.S. sect. Internat. Joint Commn. U.S. and Can., Dept. State, 1962—; cons. utility and environment, Hinesburg, Vt., 1968—; adj. prof. econs. U. Vt., 1969-74. Mem. bd. aldermen, Burlington, 1957-59; pub. mem. Adminstrv. Conf. U.S., 1971-74; adv. bd. Ford Found. Energy Policy Project, Washington, 1973-75; mem. Nat. Consumers Energy Com., 1973-74. Mem. Vt. Bar Assn. Office: PO Box F Hinesburg VT 05461 Tel (802) 482-2831

ROSS, DAVID, b. Washington, Apr. 11, 1929; student U. Md., 1948-50, LL.B., 1953. Admitted to Md. bar, 1953, U.S. Dist. Ct. bar, U.S. Ct. of Appeals bar, 1954; law clk. to Judge William L. Henderson, Ct. of Appeals, Annapolis, Md., 1953-54; practiced in Balt., 1954-68; asso. firm Ober, Williams, Grimes & Stinson, 1954-59, partner, 1960-68; asso. judge Supreme Bench of Balt. City, 1968—; asso. mem. bd. of appeals Dept. Employment Security, 1957-59. Fellow Am. Coll. Probate Counsel, Md. Bar Found.; mem. Nat. Conf. State Trial Judges, Am., Md., Balt. bar assns., Lawyers Roundtable of Balt. Home: 706 Benston Pl Baltimore MD 21210 Office: Court House Baltimore MD 21202 Tel (301) 396-5132

ROSS, DAVID P., b. Kirksville, Mo., Jan. 29, 1939; B.A., Westminster Coll., Fulton, Mo., 1961; LL.B., U. Mo., 1964. Admitted to Mo. bar, 1964; individual practice law; v.p. trust div. 1st Nat Bank of Kansas City (Mo.). Home: 6129 Larson St Kansas City MO 74133 Office: Trust Div 1st Nat Bank of Kansas City Kansas City MO

ROSS, DON CARL, JR., b. Calhoun, Ky., Sept. 1, 1927; A.B., LL.B., U. Ky., 1952. Admitted to Ky. bar, 1952, Fed. bar, 1968; claims atty. U.S. Fidelity & Guaranty Co., 1952-67; gen. counsel, dep. commr. Ky. Dept. Ins., Lexington, 1967-70; asst. v.p., counsel Ky. Central Life Ins. Co., Lexington, 1970—. Mem. Ky. Bar Assn., Phi Alpha Delta. Home: 804 Mount Vernon Dr Lexington KY 40502 Office: 200 E Main St Lexington KY 40507 Tel (606) 254-5561

ROSS, DONALD ROE, b. Orleans, Nebr., June 8, 1922; J.D., U. Nebr., 1948. Admitted to Nebr. bar, 1948; asso. firm Cook & Ross, Lexington, Nebr., 1948-53; U.S. Atty. Nebr., Omaha, 1953-56; partner firm Swarr, May, Royce, Smith, Andersen & Ross, Omaha, 1956-71; judge U.S. Circuit Ct., Omaha, 1971—. Mayor, Lexington, 1952-53. Mem. Am., Nebr., Omaha bar assns. Home: 9936 Essex Rd Omaha NE 68114 Office: PO Box 307 Omaha NE 68101 Tel (402) 221-4647

ROSS, FRANK JAMES, b. Houston, Aug. 2, 1941; B.S. in Pharmacy, Tex. So. U., 1967; J.D., U. Houston, 1973. Admitted to Tex. bar, 1973; partner firm Ross & Taylor, Houston, 1973—. Mem. Am., Tex., Houston bar assns., Tex. Criminal Def. Lawyers Assn., Tex. Jr. Bar Assn., Alpha Phi Alpha. Office: 4810 Caroline St Houston TX 77004 Tel (713) 529-3803

ROSS, HAROLD ANTHONY, b. Kent, Ohio, June 2, 1931; B.A. magna cum laude, Western Res. U., 1953; J.D., Harvard, 1956. Admitted to Ohio bar, 1956, U.S. Supreme Ct. bar, 1967; mem. firm Hornbeck, Ritter and Victory, Cleve., 1958-59; with NLRB, 8th Region, Cleve., 1959-61; mem. firm Marshman, Hornbeck, Hollington, Steadman & McLaughlin, Cleve., 1961-64; partner firm Ross & Kraushaar, and predecessors, Cleve., 1964—; gen. counsel Brotherhood Locomotive Engrs., Cleve., 1966—. Mem. Charter Rev. Commn. N. Olmsted (Ohio), 1970, 75; trustee Citizens League of Greater Cleve., 1969-75, 1976—. Mem. Am. (com. on ry. and aviation labor law), Ohio State, Cleve. bar assns. Home: 23195 Stoneybrook Dr North Olmsted OH 44070 Office: 1548 Standard Bldg Cleveland OH 44113 Tel (216) 861-1313

ROSS, HOWARD CALVIN, JR., b. Memphis, July 9, 1929; B.B.A., U. Miss., 1950; LL.B., Jackson Sch. Law, 1952. Admitted to Miss. bar, 1952, U.S. Supreme Ct. bar, 1972; with Comml. Bank & Trust Co., Jackson, Miss., 1950-52; individual practice law, Jackson, 1952—; prof. Jackson Sch. Law., 1953-63; spl. counsel City Jackson, 1966-69; asst. city pros. atty., 1971—. Mem. Am. Bar Assn. Editor Miss. Lawyer, 1953-54. Office: 300 Church Savings Bldg Jackson MS 39201 Tel (601) 948-6136

ROSS, I. ARNOLD, b. Warsaw, Poland, Feb. 14, 1897; came to U.S., 1903, naturalized, 1912; B.S., Coll. City N.Y., 1919, M.B.A., 1922; J.D., N.Y. U., 1927. Admitted to N.Y. State bar, 1928, D.C. bar, 1946, U.S. Supreme Ct. bar, 1944; individual practice law, N.Y.C., 1928-43, 46—; with Reconstrn. Fin. Corp., Washington, 1943-46; adj. prof. Baruch Coll., U. City N.Y., 1970—; mem. N.Y. State Assembly, 1934. Active Boy Scouts Am. Mem. Assn. Bar City N.Y., N.Y. County Lawyers Assn., Am. Fgn. Law Assn. (v.p. 1975—), Am., N.Y. State bar assns. C.P.A., N.Y. Contbr. articles to legal jours. Home: 815 Park Ave New York City NY 10021 Office: One State St Plaza New York City NY 10004 Tel (212) 747-1761

ROSS, JACK HAYNOR, b. Royalton, Ill., Mar. 17, 1924; B.A., U. Mo., 1948, J.D., 1950. Admitted to Mo. bar, 1950; asso. firm Mark D. Eagleton, St. Louis, 1950-53; partner firm Gross, Jones, Blumenfeld & Ross, St. Louis, 1959, firm Coleman, Ross, Carey, Goetz & Schaaf, Clayton, Mo., 1959—. Pres. bd. mgrs. Episcopal Home for Children, St. Louis, 1975—. Mem. Mo., Met. St. Louis, St. Louis County, Fed. bar assns., Assn. Trial Lawyers Am., Mo. Assn. Trial Attys. Home: 1600 Wyncliff St Saint Louis MO 63131 Office: 200 S Bemiston St Clayton MO 63105 Tel (314) 725-8000

ROSS, JAY BERNARD, b. N.Y.C., Feb. 12, 1942; B.S., U. Wis., 1964; J.D., U. Ill., 1967. Admitted to Ill. bar, 1968, U.S. Supreme Ct. bar, 1972; individual practice law, Chgo., 1971—; lectr. U. Ill. Mem. Am., Ill., Chgo. bar assns., Lawyers for the Creative Artists, Am. Assn. Psychol. Counselors, Phi Delta Phi. Staff writer Ill. Inst. Continuing Legal Edn., Chgo. Law Bull. Office: 11 S LaSalle St Chicago IL 60603 Tel (312) 372-1575

ROSS, JEAN FRANCIS, b. Colorado Springs, Colo., Jan. 1, 1931; A.B., Yale, 1953; LL.B., U. Mich., 1956. Admitted to Colo. bar, 1956; asst. atty. Bd. Water Commrs. City and County of Denver, 1956-66; mem., v.p. firm Saunders, Snyder, Ross & Dickson, Denver, 1966—; mem. Colo. Water Congress, 1959—; Bd. dirs. Bow Mar Owners, Inc., 1971-74, pres., 1973-74. Mem. Am., Colo., Denver bar assns. Barristers Soc. U. Mich., Nat. Water Resources Assn. (dir. 1975—). Contbr. articles in field to profl. jours. Office: 802 Capitol Life Center 225 E 16th Ave Denver CO 80203 Tel (303) 861-8200

ROSS, JOHN JOSEPH, III, b. St. John's, N.Y., Apr. 6, 1929; B.S., Va. Mil. Inst., 1951; LL.B., Georgetown U., 1956. Admitted to D.C. bar, 1956, U.S. Supreme Ct. bar, 1971; asso. firm Hogan & Hartson, Washington, 1956-64, partner, 1964—; mem. nat. adv. counsel Practising Law Inst., 1973—, chmn. equal employment compliance programs, 1972—; lectr. Inst. Continuing Legal Edn., Mich., 1974-75. Mem. Am. Arbitration Assn., Am., D.C., Fed. bar assns., Am. Judicature Soc., Soc. Hosp. Attys. Home: 7021 Marlan Dr Alexandria VA 22307 Office: 815 Connecticut Ave NW Washington DC 20006 Tel (202) 331-4565

ROSS, KENNETH LEVERGENE, b. Orange, Tex., Dec. 2, 1944; B.A., Southeastern La. U., 1967; J.D., La. State U., 1971. Admitted to La. bar, 1972; partner firm Seale Sledge & Ross, Hammond, La., 1974—. Mem. La. State Regional Airport Bd. Mem. La., Tangipahoa Parish bar assns. Home: PO Drawer 1120 Hammond LA 70404 Office: PO Box 1878 Hammond LA 70404 Tel (504) 345-8058

ROSS, LEMUEL HIRAM, b. Beaufort County, N.C., Feb. 4, 1909; student U. N.C.; LL.B., U. Louisville. Admitted to N.C. bar, 1936; judge Beaufort County (N.C.) Recorders Ct., 1940-42; mem. N.C. Senate, 1955, House of Reps., 1957; city atty. City of Washington (N.C.), 1951-54; county atty., Beaufort County, 1954-64. Mem. N.C. Bar Assn. Home: North Shore Washington NC 27889 Office: 206 N Market St Washington NC 27889 Tel (919) 946-3627

ROSS, MARVIN, b. N.Y.C., Nov. 4, 1927; B.S., Coll. City N.Y., 1948; J.D., N.Y. U., 1951, LL.M., 1953. Admitted to N.Y. bar, 1953; tax atty. Guggenheimer & Untermeyer, N.Y.C., 1953-57; partner firm Blum Ross Weisler Bergstein & Golden, Lawrence, N.Y., 1959—; gen. counsel Century Fed. Savs. and Loan Assn. of L.I., Cedarhurst, N.Y., 1959—, Village of Lawrence, 1975—, Village of Hewlett Neck (N.Y.), 1975—, Woodmere Fire Dist., 1975—. Mem. N.Y. State, Nassau County bar assns. Home: 173 Briarwood Crossing Lawrence NY 15559 Office: 389 Central Ave Lawrence NY 11559 Tel (516) 569-3900

ROSS, MARY COWELL, b. Oklahoma City, Oct. 1, 1910; A.B., Vassar Coll., 1932; LL.B., Memphis State U., 1938; LL.D. (hon.), U. Nebr., 1973. Admitted to Tenn. bar, 1938, D.C. bar, 1944, N.Y. bar, 1947; asso. firm Cromelin & Townsend, Washington, 1944-46, firm Royall, Koegel & Rogers, and predecessors, N.Y.C., 1946-61; individual practice law, N.Y.C., 1961—; dir. 795 Fifth Ave. Corp., 1977—. Bd. dirs. Merce Cunningham Dance Found., 1969-72, Silver Cross Day Nursery, N.Y.C., 1963-70, Central Park Community Fund, 1977—; trustee Nebr. Art Assn., 1966—; trustee U. Nebr. Found., 1966—, bd. dirs., 1974—. Mem. Am., D.C., N.Y. Women's (past pres., dir. 1957-63, 74—) bar assns., Women's Bar Assn. D.C., Nat. Assn. Women Lawyers (Distinguished Service award 1973), Bar Assn. City N.Y. Contbr. articles to Women Lawyer's Jour. Home and Office: 2 E 61st St New York City NY 10021 Tel (212) 593-3354

ROSS, RALPH HENRY, b. Victoriaville, Que., Can., Dec. 23, 1923; A.A., U. Maine, 1949; J.D., Portland U., 1951. Admitted to Maine bar, 1952, U.S. Supreme Ct. bar, 1959; clk. cts. County York, Maine, 1955-62, atty., 1962-66; asst. atty. gen., 1967; judge Maine Dist. Ct., 1968-76, chief judge, 1976—. Mem. Maine Ck. Cts. Assn. (former pres.), York (sec. 1956-64), Maine, Am. bar assns., Am. Judicature Soc., Nat. Council Juvenile Ct. Judges, Am. Judges Assn. Home: 36 June St Sanford ME 04073 Office: 73 Hammond St Bangor ME Tel (207) 947-6797

ROSS, RICHARD C., b. N.Y.C., May 5, 1927; B.A., N.Y. U., 1949, LL.B., 1950, LL.M., 1953. Admitted to N.Y. State bar, 1950; individual practice law, Mt. Vernon, N.Y., 1950—; mem. N.Y. State Gen. Assembly, 1973-76; councilman City of Mt. Vernon, 1964-65, 66-72; supr. County of Westchester (N.Y.); legis. asst. N.Y. State Assembly, 1954-63. Neighborhood commr. Hutchinson River council Boy Scouts Am., Mt. Vernon. Mem. N.Y. State, Westchester County, Mt. Vernon bar assns., YM-YWHA, Am. Legion. Contbr. articles to law revs. Home: 24 Palmer Ave Mount Vernon NY 10552 Office: 10 Fiske Pl Mount Vernon NY 10550 Tel (914) OW9-5900

ROSS, RICHARD LEE, b. St. Louis, Feb. 26, 1928; B.A., Washington U., St. Louis, 1948, J.D., 1950. Admitted to Mo. bar, 1950; v.p., sec. Banner Industkies, Inc., St. Louis, 1950-62; chmn. bd. dir. Edward K. Tryon, Inc., Phila., 1962-64; partner firm Slonim & Ross, St. Louis, 1964—; arbitrator nat. labor panel Fed. Mediation and Conciliation Service, Washington. Bd. dirs. Temple Charities and Activities Assn., St. Louis. Mem. Am. Arbitration Assn. (labor arbitrator), Am., Mo., St. Louis County bar assns., Lawyers Assn. St. Louis. Recipient Outstanding Achievement award Brotherhood Automation Workers Am., 1967; contbr. articles to Mo. Bar Jour. Home: 131 N Mosley St Creve Coeur MO 63141 Office: 111 S Meramec St Clayton MO 63105 Tel (314) 725-1060

ROSS, ROBERT D., b. Orange, N.J., Oct. 8, 1904; student Harvard U., St. John's Coll. Cambridge (Eng.) U.; law degree Northwestern U. Admitted to Ill. bar, 1931, Fla. bar, 1946; editor Fla. Supplement, Miami, 1952—. Mem. Dade County Bar Assn. Home: 8855 SW 172nd St Miami FL 33157 Office: 1129 Ingraham Bldg Miami FL 33131 Tel (305) 379-4622

ROSS, STANLEY, b. Bklyn., Jan. 20, 1924; B.B.S., Coll. City N.Y., 1949; LL.B., J.D., Bklyn. Law Sch., 1954; LL.M. in Taxation, N.Y. U., 1959. Admitted to N.Y. State bar, 1954. Home: 61-27 228th St Bayside NY 11364 Tel (212) 687-6935 also 11 Sunrise Plaza Valley Stream NY 11581 Tel (516) 872-9169

ROSS, STEPHEN, b. Bklyn., Dec. 27, 1934; A.B. cum laude, Bklyn. Coll., 1956; LL.B. cum laude, Bklyn. Law Sch., 1961. Admitted to N.Y. State bar, 1961, Fla. bar, 1964, U.S. Supreme Ct. bar, 1964; trial atty. antitrust div. U. S. Dept. Justice, N.Y.C., 1961-62; law asst. Hon. John F. Scileppi, Asso. Judge N.Y. State Ct. Appeals, N.Y.C., 1963-65; since practiced in Bklyn.; mem. firm Eisenberg & Weiss, 1965-68, partner, 1969-71; individual practice law, N.Y.C., 1971—. Bd. dirs. Enlightenment Together (drug program), Bklyn., 1972—. Mem. Am., N.Y. State, Fed., Bklyn., Fla. bar assns., Fed. Bar Council, Bklyn. Law Rev. Alumni Assn. (pres.), Bklyn. Law Sch. Alumni Assn., Philonomic Soc. Recipient Mattheson prize Bklyn. Law Sch., 1961. Author: (with Vernon Z. Crawford) Gresham's Law of Domestic Relations: The Alabama Quickie, 1961. Asso. editor Bklyn. Law Rev., 1961. Home: 380 Clinton St Brooklyn NY 11231 Office: 60 E 42nd St New York City NY 10017 Tel (212) 986-5561

ROSS, TERRY D., b. Glendale, Calif., Aug. 12, 1943; B.A., U. Calif., Santa Barbara, 1965; J.D., U. Calif., San Francisco, 1968. Admitted to Calif. bar, 1968; partner firm Gray, Cary, Ames & Frye, San Diego, 1968—; placement officer U. Calif., Hastings Coll. Law, 1967-68; active Legal Aid Soc. San Diego. Mem. Am. Arbitration Assn., Am., San Diego County (arbitration com. 1973-75), Calif. bar assns., San Diego County Barristers Assn. Contbr. articles to legal jours.; editor Hastings Law Jour., 1966-68. Home: 5172 Middleton Rd San Diego CA 92109 Office: 2100 Union Bank Bldg San Diego CA 92101

ROSS, WARREN ROBERT, b. Chgo., Apr. 30, 1921; J.D., DePaul U., 1948. Admitted to Ill. bar, 1949; since practiced in Chgo., partner firm Ross & Stamos, 1949-53, individual practice law, 1953-65, partner firm Ross, Scott & Carmody and predecessors, 1965—. Pres. Sch. Dist. 124, State of Ill., 1965-67; bd. dirs. South Chicago Community Hosp., 1971—. Mem. Ill. State, South Chgo., Chgo. bar assns., Ill. Trial Lawyers Assn. Office: 39 S LaSalle St Chicago IL 60603 Tel (312) 782-8474

ROSS, WAYNE ANTHONY, b. Milw., Feb. 25, 1943; B.S. in Bus. Adminstrn., Marquette U., 1965, J.D., 1968. Admitted to Wis. bar, 1968, Alaska bar, 1969; asst. atty. gen. State of Alaska, 1968-69; ct. trustee and standing master, family ct. div., Superior Ct. Third Jud. Dist., State of Alaska, 1969-73; asso. firm Edward J. Reasor & Assos., Anchorage, 1973—; partner firm Reasor, Miller, Ross & Griffin, Cordova, Alaska, 1973—, Reasor, Miller, Ross & McNall, Glennallen, Alaska, 1975—; instr. Anchorage Community Coll., 1973-74; mem. Supreme Ct. Com. for revision of children's rules, 1972-73. Pres. Alaska Gun Collectors Assn., 1974—, sgt. at arms, 1972-74; v.p. Alaska Right to Life, 1973-75; mem. (life) Nat. Rifle Assn., Smith & Wesson Collectors Assn.; mem. Alaska Peace Officers Assn., 1973—. Mem. Wis., Anchorage, Alaska (mem. com. on family law, 1974—; mem. law enforcement com. on alcoholism, 1971-72), Spenard (v.p., 1976), Am. (Alaska state membership chmn., mem. family law sect., 1975—) bar assns., Nat. Council Juvenile Ct. Judges (asso.). Office: 4337 Spenard Rd Achorage AK 99503 also Box 1522 Anchorage AK 99510 Tel (907) 279-2431

ROSS, WILLIAM GEORGE, b El Paso, Tex., July 10, 1941; grad. Colo. Sch. Mines, 1963; J.D., Denver U., 1971. Admitted to Colo. bar, 1971, U.S. Supreme Ct. bar, 1974; asso. firm Hayden, Ross & Sweeney and predecessor, Lakewood, Colo., 1971-74, partner, 1974—. Mem. Colo., Am. bar assns. Home: 7610 Lewis Ct Arvada CO 80005 Office: 215 S Wadsworth Blvd Lakewood CO 80226 Tel (303) 234-1600

ROSS, WILLIAM WARFIELD, b. Washington, Oct. 3, 1926; A.B., St. John's Coll., Annapolis, Md., 1948; LL.B., Yale U., 1951. Admitted to D.C. bar, 1951, U.S. Supreme Ct. bar, 1953; legal asst., exec. offices Harry S. Truman, 1952-53, Pres. Dwight D. Eisenhower, 1953; appellate sec., civil div. U.S. Dept. Justice, Washington, 1954-57; asst. to solicitor FPC, Washington, 1958-59; partner firm Wald, Harkrader & Ross, Washington, 1963—. Mem. Am. (chmn. spl. com. on revision of adminstrv. procedure act 1967-70; mem. council adminstrv. law sect. 1964-67, 70-73), Fed., Fed. Power, D.C. bar assns., Bar. Assn. D.C. (chmn. adminstrv. law sect. 1968-69; bd. govs. 1969-70). Contbr. articles to legal jours. Home: 3320 Rowland Pl NW Washington DC 20008 Office: 1320 19th St NW Washington DC 20036 Tel (202) 296-2121

ROSSER, CHARLES DANIEL, b. Birmingham, Ala., Apr. 28, 1935; B.A., Birmingham So. Coll., 1961; J.D., U. Ala., 1963. Admitted to Ala. bar, 1963; law clk. to judge U.S. Ct. of Appeals, 1963-64; asso. firm Howell T. Heflin, Tuscumbia, Ala., 1964-66; partner firm Heflin, Rosser & Munsey, and predecessor firms, Tuscumbia, 1967—. Chmn. Colbert County (Ala.) Cancer Crusade, 1970. Mem. Am., Ala., Colbert County bar assns., Assn. Trial Lawyers Am., Ala. Trial Lawyers Assn. (bd. govs. 1975-77), Am. Judicature Soc. Contbr. articles to profl. jours. Home: 103 Meadow Hill St Sheffield AL 35660 Office: 105 E 2d St Tuscumbia AL 35674 Tel (205) 383-7492

ROSSI, FAUST F., b. Rochester, N.Y., Aug. 9, 1932; B.A., U. Toronto, 1953; J.D., Cornell U., 1960. Admitted to N.Y. State bar, 1960; trial atty. tax div. U.S. Dept. Justice, Washington, 1960-62; partner firm Rossi & Rossi, Rochester, N.Y., 1962-66; asso. prof. law Cornell U., Ithaca, N.Y., 1966-70, prof., 1970—; cons. in field; mem. nat. teaching staff Bar Rev. Inc., 1973-76; prof. Nat. Inst. Trial Advocacy, 1975-76. Mem. Rochester Bd. Edn., 1965-66, v.p., 1966. Mem. Am., N.Y. State bar assns., Assn. Am. Law Schs., Soc. Am. Law Tchrs., AAUP, Order of the Coif. Office: Myron Taylor Hall Cornell Sch Law Ithaca NY 14853 Tel (607) 256-5278

ROSSIE, JOSEPH RICHARD, b. Clarksdale, Miss., Feb. 18, 1947; A.B., U. Notre Dame, 1969; J.D., U. Va., 1972. Admitted to Tenn. bar, 1972; partner firm Rosenfield, Borod, Bogatin & Kremer, Memphis, 1972—. Treas. Memphis and Shelby County Democratic Com., 1974-76; campaign mgr. Memphis, Shelby County for Carter-Mondale campaign, 1975-76. Mem. Am., Tenn. (chmn. com. for mentally disabled 1976—), Memphis, Shelby County bar assns. Office: PO Box 3070 Memphis TN 38103 Tel (901) 525-6361

ROSSMANN, ANTONIO, b. San Francisco, Apr. 25, 1941; A.B., Harvard Coll., 1963; J.D., Harvard, 1971. Admitted to Calif. bar, 1972; law clk. to Justice Tobriner, Calif. Supreme Ct., San Francisco, 1971-72; asso. firm Tuttle & Taylor, Los Angeles, 1972-75; pub. adviser Calif. Energy Resources Conservation and Devel. Commn., Sacramento, 1975-76; individual practice law, Sacramento, 1976—; spl. counsel Calif. Bus. and Transp. Agy., 1976—, County of Inyo, Calif., 1976—; lectr. U. Calif., 1977—. Mem. Am., Los Angeles County bar assns., Harvard Environ. Law Soc. (founding). Editor Harvard Law Rev., 1969-71. Home: 1429 E St Sacramento CA 95814 Office: 717 K St Sacramento CA 95814 Tel (916) 441-3770

ROSSMEISSL, JOHN ARTHUR, b. Colfax, Wash., Oct. 18, 1940; B.A., Wash. State U., 1962, LL.B., U. Chgo., 1965. Admitted to Ill. bar, 1965, Wash. bar, 1967; asso. firm Peterson, Lowry, Rall, Barber & Ross, Chgo., 1965-67; asso. firm Velikanje, Moore & Shore, Yakima, Wash., 1967-70, partner, 1970—. Bd. dirs. Mental Health Services of Yakima, 1972-76, chmn., 1975-76. Mem. Am., Ill., Wash. bar assns. Home: 2704 Brackett Ave Yakima WA 98902 Office: 303 E D St Yakima WA 98902 Tel (509) 24B-6030

ROST, RICHARD LEE, b. Cleve., Nov. 8, 1944; B.A., U. Calif., Berkeley, 1967; J.D., Hastings Coll. Law, San Francisco, 1970. Admitted to Calif. bar, 1971, Hawaii bar, 1971; dep. pub. defender Honolulu, 1970-71; asso. partner firm Padgett, Greeley & Marumoto, Honolulu, 1972-75; partner firm Padgett & Rost, Wailuku, Maui, 1975—. Mem. Am., Hawaii, Calif. bar assns., Am. Trial Lawyers Assn. Home: 562 D Piiholo Rd Makawao HI 96768 Office: 2180 Main St Wailuku HI 96793 Tel (808) 244-7905

ROSTOW, EUGENE VICTOR, b. Bklyn., Aug. 25, 1913; A.B., Yale, 1933, LL.B., 1937; LL.D., Cambridge U., 1962; LL.D., Boston U., 1976. Admitted to N.Y. State bar, 1938, U.S. Supreme Ct. bar, 1966; asso. firm Cravath, de Gersdorff, Swaine & Wood, N.Y.C., 1937-38; law faculty Yale, New Haven, 1938—, prof. law, 1944—, Sterling prof. law and pub. affairs, 1964—, dean Law Sch., 1955-65; vis. prof. U. Chgo., 1941; Pitt prof. Cambridge (Eng.) U., 1959-60; Eastman prof. Oxford (Eng.) U., 1970-71; advisor Dept. State, Washington, 1942-44, undersec. state for polit. affairs, 1966-69; secretariat UN, Geneva, Switzerland, 1949-50; chmn. Pres.'s Task Force on Communications Policy, 1967-68. Mem. Am. Law Inst., Phi Beta Kappa. Author: A National Policy for the Oil Industry, 1948; Planning for Freedom, 1959; The Sovereign Prerogative, 1962; Law, Power and the Pursuit of Peace, 1968; Peace in the Balance, 1972; The Ideal in Law, 1977; editor: Is Law Dead? 1971; contbr. articles to legal and scholarly publs. Home: 208 St Ronan St New Haven CT 06511 Office: Yale Law School New Haven CT 06520 Tel (203) 436-2234

ROSZELL, CALVERT THEODORE, b. Lexington, Ky., Mar. 30, 1924; LL.B., U. Ky., 1948. Admitted to Ky. bar, 1948; partner firm McDonald, Alford & Roszell, Lexington, 1948—; adj. prof. law Univ. Ky., 1956—; judge pro tem Fayette County Ct., 1959-64. Pres. Blue Grass council Boy Scouts Am., 1970-71; chmn. chpt. ARC, 1959-61. Mem. Am., Ky., Fayett County bar assns. Named Outstanding Young Man in Fayette County, Jr. C. of C., 1959. Home: 1840 Blairmore Ct Lexington KY 40502 Office: 156 Market St Lexington KY 40507 Tel (606) 252-8981

ROSZKOWSKI, STANLEY JULIAN, b. Boonville, N.Y., Jan. 27, 1923; B.S. in Mgmt., U. Ill., 1949, J.D., 1954. Admitted to Ill. bar, 1954, Fla. bar, 1960; sales mgr. Warren Petroleum Co., Rockford, Ill., 1954; partner firm Roszkowski, Paddock, McGreevy & Johnson, Rockford, 1955—; pres., chmn. bd. dirs. 1st State Bank, Rockford, 1963—. Bd. dirs. Sch. Hope, Rockford, 1960—; mem. Ill. Capital Devel. Bd., 1974; chmn. Rockford Fire & Police Commn., 1967-77. Mem. Am., Ill., Fla., Winnebago County (pres. 1977) bar assns., Am. Arbitration Assn., Am. Coll. Trial Lawyers, Am. Judicature Soc. Home: 2435 Cerro Vista Dr Rockford IL 61107 Office: 850 N Church Rockford IL 61107 Tel (815) 963-8451

ROTBERG, EUGENE HARVEY, b. Phila., Jan. 19, 1930; B.S., Temple U., 1951; LL.B., U. Pa., 1954; Admitted to Pa. bar, 1955, D.C. bar, 1955; with SEC, Washington, 1957-60, mem. spl. study U.S. securities market, 1960-62, chief counsel office policy research, 1963-66, asso. dir. for markets and regulation, 1966-68; treas. The World Bank, Washington, 1969—; prof. law George Washington U., 1965—. Mem. Am. Bar Assn. Recipient Distinguished Service award U.S. Govt., 1968, Distinguished Scholar award, Hofstra U., 1975; Alumnus of Yr. award Temple U., 1969. Home: 10822 Childs Ct Silver Spring MD 20901 Office: Suite E-427 1818 H St NW Washington DC 20433 Tel (202) 477-2214

ROTCHFORD, MARK DENNIS, b. Spokane, Wash., Feb. 28, 1933; LL.D., Gonzaga U., 1958, J.D., 1967. Admitted to Wash. bar, 1958; mem. firms Berkey & Retchford, Spokane, 1961-63, 75—; individual practice law, Spokane, 1959-61, 63-75. Mem. Spokane County, Wash. State, Am. bar assns., Comml. Law League Am. Office: 1215 Old Nat Bank Bldg Spokane WA 99201 Tel (509) 624-2361

ROTENBERG, ERNEST IRVING, b. Attleboro, Mass., Nov. 6, 1924; student Colby Coll., 1942; A.B., Tufts U., 1945; J.D., Boston U., 1947; student Nat. Coll. State Judiciary, Reno, 1976. Admitted to Mass. bar, 1948, U.S. Supreme Ct. bar, 1961; individual practice law, Attleboro, Mass., 1948-73; master in chancery Commonwealth Mass., 1965-70; spl. asst. atty. gen. Commonwealth Mass., 1969-73; town counsel Seekonk, Mass., 1969-73; asst. dist. atty. Mass. So. Dist., 1968-69; judge Bristol County Probate Ct., Taunton, Mass., 1972—, first judge, 1973—. Chmn. bd. trustees Southeastern Mass. U.; mem. Mass. Bd. Appeals on Motor Vehicle Liability Policies and Bonds, 1969-73; city councilman Attleboro, 1950-54. Fellow Am. Acad. Matrimonial Lawyers (bd. govs.); mem. Am., Mass., Bristol County, 4th Dist. Ct. bar assns. Contbr. articles to legal jours. Home: 45 Upland Rd Attleboro MA 02703 Office: Probate Ct Lobby 100 N Main St Attleboro MA 02703 Tel (617) 222-9140

ROTERING, NICK ANTON, b. Butte, Mont., Dec. 30, 1942; B.A., U. Mont., 1966, J.D., 1970. Admitted to Mont. bar, 1970; staff atty. Mont. Legal Services, Helena, 1970-74, Mont. Dept. Instns., Helena, 1974—. Mem. State Bar Mont. Office: 1539 11th Ave Helena MT 59601 Tel (406) 449-3930

ROTH, ANDREW IRWIN, b. N.Y.C., June 29, 1946; A.B., U. Calif. at Berkeley, 1967; J.D., Hastings Coll. Law, San Francisco, 1970. Admitted to Calif., Wash. bars, 1970; staff atty. Riverside County (Calif.) Pub. Defender's Office, 1972—; legal intern San Francisco Neighborhood Legal Assistance Found., 1968-70. Mem. Calif. Attys. for Criminal Justice. Reginald Heber Smith fellow, 1970-71. Office: Courthouse room 208 4050 Main St Riverside CA 92501 Tel (714) 787-2707

ROTH, DANIEL BENJAMIN, b. Youngstown, Ohio, Sept. 17, 1929; B.S. in Finance, Miami U., Oxford, Ohio, 1951; J.D., Case Western Res. U., Cleve., 1956. Admitted to Ohio bar, 1956, U.S. Supreme Ct. bar, 1960; partner firm Roth & Roth, Youngstown, 1956-69, Roth & Stephens, Youngstown, 1969—; dir., gen. counsel Nat. Data Processing Corp., Cin., 1961-69; chmn. bd., counsel Stony's Trucking Co., 1971-74; exec. v.p., dir., gen. counsel Toro Enterprises, Inc.; dir. Mahoning Nat. Bank, Youngstown. Admissions counsellor USAF Acad.; v.p., bd. dirs. Youngstown Jr. C. of C.; bd. dirs. Youngstown Playhouse, Rodef-Sholom Temple, McGuffey Center, Youngstown Speech and Hearing Center. Mem. Am., Ohio, Mahoning County, Lawyer Pilots bar assns., Zeta Beta Tau (nat. v.p. 1964-66), Omicron Delta Kappa, Phi Eta Sigma, Tau Epsilon Rho. Mem. Nat. Moot Ct. team Case Western Res. Law Sch., 1956; editor Case Western Res. Law Rev., 1955-56. Home: 310 Elruth Ct Girard OH 44420 Office: Union Nat Bank Youngstown OH 44503 Tel (216) 744-5211

ROTH, DAVID LOUIS, b. Bronx, N.Y., June 16, 1945; B.A., City U. N.Y., 1966; J.D., U. Fla., 1968. Admitted to Fla. bar, 1969, U.S. Supreme Ct. bar, 1972; jud. research side Fla. 4th Dist. Ct. of Appeals, Vero Beach, 1968-70; asso. firm Cone, Owen, Wagner, Nugent, Johnson & McKeown, West Palm Beach, Fla., 1970-72, partner, 1972—; U.S. Magistrate, 1971—. Mem. Am., Palm Beach County, Palm Beach County Jr. bar assns., Assn. Am. Trial Lawyers, Acad. Fla. Trial Lawyers, U.S. Magistrates Assn. Home: 4110 Washington Rd West Palm Beach FL 33405 Office: 507 N Olive Ave West Palm Beach FL 33401 Tel (305) 655-8100

ROTH, HAROLD LEW, b. Pitts., Nov. 29, 1908; A.B., U. Pitts., 1930, LL.B., 1933. Admitted to Pa., bar, 1934; now practice in Ambridge. Campaign chmn., United Fund, Ambridge, Pa.; active Beaver County fund; past pres. United Jewish Fund. Mem. Am., Pa., Beaver County bar assns. Home: 799 Ridge Rd Ambridge PA 15003 Office: 828 Merchant St Ambridge PA 15003 Tel (412) 266-6700

ROTH, JANE R., b. Phila., June 16, 1935; B.A., Smith Coll., 1956; LL.B. cum laude, Harvard, 1965. Admitted to Del. bar, 1965; asso. firm Richards, Layton & Finger, Wilmington, Del., 1965-73, mem. firm, 1973—. Pres., Del. chpt. Arthritis Found., 1972—; mem. Del. Humanities Council, 1974-76; bd. dirs. Wilmington Black Theater Ensemble, 1973—, U. Del. Library Assos., 1976—, Del. Tech. and Community Coll. Ednl. Found., 1976—; adv. bd. Coll. Marine Studies, U. Del., 1975—. Mem. Am., Del. bar assns., Harvard Law Sch. Assn. (council 1975—). Home: 2206 Old Kennett Rd Wilmington DE 19807 Office: 4072 duPont Bldg Wilmington DE 19899 Tel (302) 658-6541

ROTH, LESTER WILLIAM, b. N.Y.C., Apr. 5, 1895; LL.B., U. So. Calif., 1916. Admitted to Calif. bar, 1916; individual practice law, Los Angeles, 1916-18; partner firm Lissner, Roth & Gunter, Los Angeles, 1920-31; judge Superior Ct. Los Angeles County, 1931-36; justice pro tem Dist. Ct. of Appeals, 1934-36, justice, 1963, presiding justice, 1964—; partner firm Mitchell, Silberberg, Roth & Knupp, 1936-42, Roth & Brannen, 1942-47; v.p. Columbia Pictures Corp., Hollywood, 1947-52; individual practice law, Beverly Hills, 1952-63; dir. Standard Cabinet Works, Los Angeles, 1929—, Guaranty Union Life Ins. Co., Beverly Hills, 1940-55, City Nat. Bank of Beverly Hills, 1953—. Chmn., Mayor's Com. on Cleaning and Dyeing, 1937-38, Draft Appeal Bd., State of Calif., Los Angeles Dist., 1942-45; co-chmn. NCCJ, 1957-59; govt. appeal agt. SSS, 1962; pres. Big Bros. Assn., Los Angeles, 1921-25, B'nai B'rith, 1923-25, City of Hope, 1932-35; bd. dirs. Fed. Jewish Welfare Orgns., 1924-40; bd. dirs. Los Angeles Jewish Community Council, v.p., 1950-52; nat. v.p. Am. Jewish Com., 1951-52, nat. adv. com., 1952—; trustee Cedars of Lebanon Hosp., Los Angeles, 1929-51. Mem. Calif. (chmn. com. internal security act 1952-54, chmn. com. on photography in courtrooms 1957-59), Los Angeles (chmn. adv. com. to lawyers), Beverly Hills (pres. 1959) bar assns., Am. Coll. Trial Lawyers, Acad. Motion Picture Arts and Scis. Home: 1201 Loma Vista Dr Beverly Hills CA 90210 Office: Ct of Appeals 3580 Wilshire Blvd Los Angeles CA 90010 Tel (213) 736-2399

ROTH, NATHANIEL HAROLD, b. N.Y.C., June 29, 1921; student City Coll. N.Y., 1946-49; LL.B., Bklyn. Sch. Law, 1952. Admitted to N.J. bar, 1958, N.Y. State bar, 1971, U.S. Supreme Ct. bar, 1957; individual practice law, Lakewood, N.J., 1957—; counsel Ocean County (N.J.) Concord Ins. Co., 1965-70; judge Lakewood Municipal Ct., 1957-64, Borough S. Toms River (N.J.) Municipal Ct., 1964-67, Jackson Twp. (N.J.) Municipal Ct., 1961—; acting judge Seaside Heights, Lakehurst Borough, Point Pleasant Borough, Manchester Twp. (N.J.) Municipal Cts., 1961—. Chmn. Ocean County Mental Health Fund, 1959; active Narcotics Council Lakewood, Lakewood Downtown Redevel. Agency, 1975—; bd. dirs. NCCJ, Monmouth-Ocean County. Fellow Fed. Bar Assn.; mem. Am. Judges Assn., Am. Bar Assn. (circuit chmn. 3d, spl. cts. com.), Assn. Trial Lawyers Am. (bd. govs. local br.), N.J. Bar Assn., Ocean County Bar Assn. Named Man In News, Asbury Park Press, 1968, Boss of Yr., Ocean County Legal Secs. Assn., 19—; recipient Distinguished Service Judge award, Jackson Jaycees, 1966; contbr. article N.J. League Municipalities Mag.; originator, host traffic program radio sta. WJLK, 1969; columnist Jackson News, 1969-70. Tel (201) 363-6800

ROTH, RICHARD ALLEN, b. Belleville, Ill., Jan. 30, 1940; J.D., Washington U., St. Louis, 1963. Admitted to Mo. bar, 1963; partner firm Ziercher, Hocker, Tzinberg & Michenfelder, Clayton, Mo., 1968—. Mem. St. Louis Met. Bar Assn. Home: 563 Olive Ct Webster Grove MO 63119 Office: 130 S Bemiston St Clayton MO 63105 Tel (314) 727-5822

ROTHBERG, HARVEY JAY, b. Bklyn., Jan. 19, 1940; B.S. in Bus. Adminstrn., George Washington U., 1961, J.D., 1964. Admitted to U.S. Dist. Ct. for D.C., 1965, U.S. Ct. Appeals, 1965, Md. Ct. Appeals, 1966, Conn. bar, 1969, U.S. Supreme Ct. bar, 1968; asst. corp. counsel D.C., 1965-67; asso. firm Cole & Groner, Washington, 1967-68, asso. firm Glazer, Wechsler & Rothberg, Stamford, Conn., 1967-74; individual practice law, Stamford, 1974—. Mem. Am., Conn., Stamford bar assns., Am. Trial Lawyers Assn. Home: 11 Surrey Dr Norwalk CT 06850 Office: 760 Summer St Stamford CT 06901 Tel (203) 357-7979

ROTHBLATT, EMMA ALDEN, b. N.Y.C., Apr. 26, 1918; B.A. cum laude, Hunter Coll., 1938; M.A., Columbia, 1939; LL.B., J.D., Fordham U., 1948. Admitted to Calif. bar, 1949, N.Y. bar, 1949, U.S. Supreme Ct. bar, 1960; policewoman, detective, asst. to dir. policewomen N.Y.C. Police Dept., 1942-46; dep. commr. N.Y.C. Dept. Commerce Pub. Events, 1954-66; partner firm Rothblatt, Rothblatt, Seijas & Peskin, N.Y.C., 1966—; v.p. Darrow Investigative Services, Inc., N.Y.C. Mem. UN Com. N.Y.C.; Consular Corps Com. N.Y.C., N.Y.C. Advisory Council Alcoholism; met. bd. dirs. NCCJ. Mem. Am. Bar Assn. Decorated French Legion Honor, Italian Order Merit. Office: Rothblatt Rothblatt Seijas Peskin 232 West End Ave New York NY Tel (212) 787-7001

ROTHENBERG, SHERIBEL FLORENCE, b. Chgo., Feb. 9, 1944; A.B., Northwestern U., 1964, J.D., 1967. Admitted to Ill. bar, 1967; asso. firm Peterson, Ross, Rall, Barber & Seidel, Chgo., 1967-72; sr. trial atty. Equal Employment Opportunity Commn., Chgo., 1972—; gen. counsel Profl. Orgn. Women for Equal Rights, Chgo., 1972—. Bd. dirs. Citizens Com. for Victim Assistance, 1975—, ACLU, 1972—, 5th Ann. Conf. on Women and the Law, Austin; chmn. Ill. ACLU Women's Rights Com., 1972-74. Mem. Am., Ill. State, Chgo. bar assns., Chgo. Council Lawyers (dir. 1976—). Contbr. articles to legal publs. Office: 55 E Jackson Blvd Chicago IL 60604 Tel (312) 353-7582

ROTHENBERG, STANLEY, b. Bklyn., June 8, 1930; A.B., N.Y. U., 1950; LL.B., Harvard, 1953; LL.D., Utrecht U., Netherlands, 1954. Admitted to N.Y. bar, 1954, U.S. Supreme Ct. bar, 1960; partner firm Heit & Rothenberg, N.Y.C., 1958—; mem. nat. panel arbitrators Am. Arbitration Assn., 1965—; lectr. Practicing Law Inst., N.Y. U. Law Sch. Active, N.Y. State Com. for Children, 1970—. Mem. Am., N.Y.C. bar assns., Copyright Soc. U.S.A. (trustee, mem. exec. com. 1972-75, 76—). Fulbright scholar, 1953-54. Author: Copyright and Public Performance of Music, 1954; Copyright Law: Basic and Related Materials, 1956; Legal Protection of Literature, Art and Music, 1960; contbr. articles in field to legal jours. Home: 440 E 78th St New York City NY 10021 Office: 424 Madison Ave New York City NY 10017 Tel (212) PL5-1566

ROTHKRUG, LEONARD F., b. Bklyn., Mar. 22, 1928; B.A., Bklyn Coll., 1948, J.D., 1951. Admitted to N.Y. State bar, 1951; individual practice law, Bklyn., 1952-73, Great Neck, N.Y., 1973; lectr. zoning Inst. Design and Construction, Practicing Law Inst.; founder, chmn. Zoning Advisory Council N.Y. Mem. Bklyn., Nassau, N.Y. State Bar Assns. Home: 20 Shorecliff Pl Great Neck NY 11023 Office: 11 Grace Ave Great Neck NY 11021 Tel (516) 487-2252

ROTHMAN, BARRY KENNETH, b. N.Y.C., June 12, 1942; B.A., U. Calif., Los Angeles, 1965; J.D., Southwestern U., 1970. Admitted to Calif. bar, 1970, U.S. Dist. Ct. bar for Central Dist. Calif., 1970; gen. counsel Warner Bros. Records Co., Burbank, Calif., 1968-73; individual practice law, Hollywood, Calif., 1973—. Mem. Am., Los Angeles County bar assns., State Bar Calif. Office: suite 612 6255 Sunset Blvd Hollywood CA 90028 Tel (213) 466-8626

ROTHMAN, EDWARD, b. N.Y.C., May 17, 1911; LL.B., St. Lawrence U., 1937, LL.M., 1938; J.S.D., N.Y. Law Sch., 1955; J.D., Bklyn. Law Sch., 1967. Admitted to N.Y. State bar, 1938, U.S. Supreme Ct. bar, 1956; individual practice law, N.Y.C., 1938-71; asst. prof. law Baruch Coll. U. City N.Y., 1964-71, asso. prof., 1971-73, prof., 1974—, chmn. dept. law, 1976—. Appeals agt. U.S. Selective Service. Author: Problems in the Law of Corporations, 1963; Problems in the American Legal System, 1963; Problems in the Law of Business Organizations, 1966. Home: 3346 Bedford Ave Brooklyn NY 11210 Office: 17 Lexington Ave New York City NY 10010 Tel (212) 725-3000

ROTHMAN, HENRY ISAAC, b. Rochester, N.Y., Mar. 29, 1943; B.A., Yeshiva Coll., 1964; J.D., Cornell U., 1967. Admitted to N.Y. State bar, 1967, U.S. Supreme Ct. bar, 1974; asso. SEC, 1967-69; partner firm Booth, Lipton & Lipton, N.Y.C., 1969—. Bd. dirs. Manhattan Day Sch. Mem. N.Y., N.Y.C. bar assns. Home: 225 W 86th St New York City NY 10024 Office: 405 Park Ave New York City NY 10022 Tel (212) PL8-1700

ROTHMAN, JESSE, b. N.Y.C., Oct. 3, 1909; student Columbia, 1926-28; LL.B., St. Lawrence U., 1931. Admitted to N.Y. bar, 1935; individual practice law, N.Y.C., 1935—. Fellow Am. Acad. Matrimonial Lawyers; mem. Westchester County Bar Assn., Family Ct. Lawyers N.Y. (v.p.). Contbr. article N.Y. Daily News. Home: Doris Rd Mamaroneck NY 10543 Office: 475 Fifth Ave New York City NY 10017 Tel (212) 685-7833

ROTHMAN, STUART, b. St. Paul, Apr. 4, 1914; B.S. in Law, U. Minn., 1935, LL.B., 1937; LL.M., Harvard U., 1938, Littauer fellow Sch. Pub. Adminstrn., 1939. Admitted to Minn. bar, 1937, D.C. bar, 1955; solicitor of labor U.S. Dept. Labor, Washington, 1953-59; gen. counsel NLRB, Washington, 1959-63; mem. Constrn. Industry Stblzn. Com., 1971-74; mem. Wage Appeals Bd., U.S. Dept. Labor, Washington, 1964-76; mem. firm Rogers & Wells, Washington, 1963—. Contbr. articles in field to profl. jours. Home: 4474 Salem Ln Washington DC 20007 Office: 1666 K St NW Washington DC 20006 Tel (202) 331-7760

ROTHMAN, THOMAS MICHAEL, b. N.Y.C., June 25, 1943; B.S., State U. N.Y. at Buffalo, 1965; J.D. Georgetown U., 1968. Admitted to N.Y. State bar, 1968; atty. N.Y. State Dept. Audit and Control, Albany, 1968-70, sr. atty., 1971; mem. firm Willkie Farr & Gallagher, and predecessors, N.Y.C., 1971-76, partner, 1977—. Advisory com. on fin., 1976, treas., exec. officer Parent-Teachers-Student Assn., 1977—, Hastings-on-Hudson (N.Y.) Union Free Sch. Dist. Mem. N.Y. State, Am. bar assns., Municipal Forum of N.Y. Home: 276 Old Broadway Hastings-on-Hudson NY 10706 Office: 120 Broadway New York City NY 10005 Tel (212) 248-1000

ROTHSCHILD, ALAN FRIEND, b. Columbus, Ga., Aug. 15, 1925; B.S. in Commerce, U. Va., 1945, LL.B., 1947. Admitted to Ga. bar, 1948; partner Rosenstrauch & Rothschild, Columbus, 1948-51; asso. firm Hatcher, Stubbs, Land, Hollis & Rothschild, and predecessors, Columbus, 1951-57, partner, 1957—. Mem. adv. bd. 1st Nat. Bank, Columbus, 1965—; sec. Rothschild Co., Columbus, 1967—; dir. Rothschild Realty Co. Mem. Gov.'s Commn. on Revision Appellate Cts. Ga., 1976—; mem. bd. commrs. Med. Center, Columbus, 1958-74, chmn., 1973-74; pres. Community Counseling Center, Columbus, 1960-62; local co.-chmn. NCCJ, 1958; active Boys Club, Jr. Achievement, 1965-70, Three Arts League, 1950—; trustee Walter Alan Richards Found., 1975, St. Francis Hosp., 1956—, Springer Theatre, 1957, Brookstone Sch., 1973—; life trustee, 1st v.p. Columbus Mus. Arts and Crafts, 1965—; bd. dirs. Anne Elizabeth Shepherd Home, 1970-74; mem. bd. Health Systems Agy. Central Ga. Fellow Am. Coll. Probate Counsel; mem. Columbus Lawyers Club (past pres.), Ga., Am. bar assns., Columbus Legal Aid Soc. (bd. dirs. 1971-75, pres. 1973-74). Home: 2328 Fairway Ave Columbus GA 31906 Office: 500 Ralston Center Columbus GA 31902 Tel (404) 324-0201

ROTHSCHILD, DONALD PHILLIP, b. Dayton, Ohio, Mar. 31, 1927; A.B., U. Mich., 1950; J.D., U. Toledo, 1965; LL.M., Harvard, 1966. Admitted to Ohio bar, 1966, D.C. bar, 1970, U.S. Supreme Ct. bar, 1975; prof. law Nat. Law Center, George Washington U., D.C., 1966—; vis. prof. U. Mich. Law Sch., 1976; instr. Solicitor's Office, U.S. Dept. Labor, 1965-66; teaching fellow in law, Harvard, 1965-66; mem. advisory council on rules and procedures of practice FTC, 1970-72; arbitrator Fed. Mediation and Counciliation Service, 1969—; pres. consumer HELP. Bd. dirs. Chesapeake Found., 1967-70, Center for Correctional Justice, 1973—. Mem. Am. Arbitration Assn. (arbitrator 1969—), Fed. Bar Assn. (council on community affairs 1969-72), Nat. Legal Aid and Defender Assn., Mich., Harvard alumni assns., Phi Alpha Delta. Author: (with W. H. Anderson) Consumer Protection Text & Materials, 1973; (with W. H. Anderson) Consumer Protection Reporting Service, 1976; Collective Bargaining and Labor Arbitration, 1970. Home: 2450 Virginia Ave Washington DC 20037 Office: George Washington Univ Law Sch Washington DC 20052 Tel (202) 676-6364

ROTHSCHILD, FRANK DAVE, b. Washington, Dec. 24, 1944; B.A., Lehigh U., 1967; J.D., Georgetown U., 1970. Admitted to Washington bar, 1971, Calif. bar, 1972; law clk. U.S. Ct. Claims, Washington, 1970-71; asst. counsel NARE Life Service Co., San Francisco, 1971-72; partner firm Bunyan & Rothschild, Mill Valley, Calif., 1972—; prof. New Coll. Sch. of Law, San Francisco, 1974-75; instr. law Coll. of Marin, Kentfield, Calif., 1974—. Pres., bd. dirs. Center Point, San Rafael, Calif., 1976—. Home and Office: 415 Panoramic Hwy Mill Valley CA 94941 Tel (415) 383-6503

ROTHSCHILD, GEORGE WILLIAM, b. Chgo., Mar. 21, 1917; A.B., Harvard, 1939; J.D., U. Chgo., 1942. Admitted to Ill. bar, 1942, N.Y. State bar, 1946; asso. firm Root, Ballantine, Harlan, Bushby & Palmer, N.Y.C., 1942, 1946-49; asso. gen. counsel Econ. Coop. Adminstrn. and Mut. Security Agency, D.C., 1949-55; with GATX Corp., Chgo., 1955—, gen. counsel, 1962—, v.p., 1969—, sec., 1972—, also dir. Trustee Hull House Assn. Mem. Am., Ill., Chgo. (chmn. consumer credit remedies com. 1968-69, chmn. devel. of law com. 1970-71, chmn. urban affairs com. 1972-73) bar assns., Chgo. Council Lawyers, Order of Coif. Bd. editors U. Chgo. Law Rev. Home: 321 Hamilton St Evanston IL 60202 Office: 120 S Riverside Plaza Chicago IL 60606 Tel (312) 621-6581

ROTHSCHILD, JAMES ALLAN, b. Balt., Jan. 19, 1947; B.A., Dickinson Coll., 1969; J.D., U. Md., 1973. Admitted to Md. bar, 1973; atty. criminal div. U.S. Dept. Justice, Washington, 1973-76; asso. firm Frank, Bernstein, Conaway and Goldman, Balt., 1976—. Mem. Am., Md. bar assns. Home: 4124 Raleigh Rd Baltimore MD 21208 Office: 1300 Mercantile Bank and Trust Bldg Baltimore MD 21201 Tel (301) 547-0500

ROTHSCHILD, PETER GUY, b. Seattle, Jan. 16, 1948; B.A. with honors, Wash. State U., 1970; J.D., U. Wash., 1973. Admitted to Wash. bar, 1973; staff atty. Snohomish County (Wash.) Pub. Defenders Assn., Everett, 1973—. Mem. Am. Bar Assn., Wash. State Trial Lawyers Assn., Nat. Legal Aid and Defenders Assn. Office: Snohomish County Courthouse Everett WA 98201 Tel (206) 259-0637

ROTHSCHILD, STEVEN JAMES, b. Worcester, Mass., Mar. 23, 1944; A.B., U. Vt., 1965; J.D., Georgetown U., 1968. Admitted to D.C. bar, 1968, Del. bar, 1969; law clk. to chancellor Del. Ct. of Chancery, 1968-69; asso. firm Prickett, Ward, Burt & Sanders, Wilmington, Del., 1969-72, partner, 1972—; asso. mem. Del. Bd. Bar Examiners, 1975. Co-founder Explorers Legal post Delmarva council Boy Scouts Am., 1972; v.p., dir. Kutz Home for the Aged, Wilmington, 1972—. Mem. N.Y.C., D.C., Del. State (exec. com. 1973, corp. law com. 1973—), Am. bar assns. Home: 1207 Windon Dr Chatham Wilmington DE 19803 Office: 1310 King St Wilmington DE 19801 Tel (302) 658-5102

ROTHSTEIN, ALAN ROEL, b. N.Y.C., July 28, 1941; B.A., U. Calif. at Los Angeles, 1965; J.D., U. San Francisco, 1971. Admitted to Calif. bar, 1972; staff officer labor relations, Western region U.S. Social Security Adminstr., San Francisco, 1970-77; prin. firm Creative Mgmt. Skills, Inc., San Francisco, 1975—; cons. in field. Mem. Soc. Fed. Labor Relations Professions (pres. San Francisco chpt. 1976), Am. Arbitration Assn., Indsl. Relations Research Assn. Contbr. articles to profl. jours. Home: 332 Philip Dr Daly City CA 94015 Tel (415) 994-2645

ROTHSTEIN, ESTHER RUTH, b. South Milwaukee, Wis.; J.D., Chgo. Kent Coll. Law, 1949. Admitted to Ill. bar, 1950, U.S. Supreme Ct. bar, 1961; partner firm McCarthy & Levin, Chgo., 1955—. Mem. adv. council Degree Granting Inst., State of Ill., 1961-76; trustee Ill. Inst. Tech.; mem. adv. bd. Chgo. Kent Coll. Law; mem. vis. com. U. Chgo. Mem. Am., Fed., Ill., Chgo. (pres. elect) bar assns., Law Club, Women's Bar Assn. Ill. (pres. 1961-62), Women's Bar Assn. Ill. Found. (v.p.). Named Woman of Year, Women's Share in Pub. Service, 1976. Home: 1440 N Lake Shore Dr Chicago IL 60610 Office: 100 W Monroe St Suite 2000 Chicago IL 60603 Tel (312) 263-1155

ROTHSTEIN, GEORGE, b. N.Y.C., Mar. 28, 1900; LL.B., N.Y. U., 1922. Admitted to N.J. bar, 1922, U.S. Dist. Ct. N.J. bar, 1922; individual practice law, Union City, N.J., 1922-65, West New York, N.J., 1965—; atty. Housing Authority Twp. North Bergen, N.J., 1942-46; municipal prosecutor, 1959-71. Appeal agt. U.S. Govt. Draft Bd. #1, North Bergen, 1941-46. Mem. Hudson County Bar Assn., N. Hudson Lawyers Club. Home: 8500 Blvd E North Bergen NJ 07047 Office: 440 60th St West New York NJ 07093 Tel (201) 854-1314

ROTHSTEIN, SEYMOUR, b. Cleve., Feb. 25, 1931; B.S. in Mech. Engring., Case Inst. Tech., 1952; LL.B., George Washington U., 1958. Admitted to Ill. bar, 1962, D.C. bar, 1958; patent atty. Carrier Corp., Syracuse, N.Y., 1959-62; patent examiner U.S. Patent Office, Washington, 1955-59; partner firm Allegretti, Newitt, Witcoff & McAndrews, Chgo., 1962—. Mem. Sch. Bd. Twp. Dist. 113, Highland Park, Ill., 1973—; mem. Highland Park Plan Commn., 1975—; chmn. Deerfield Human Relations Commn., 1970-72. Mem. Chgo. Patent Law Assn. (sec. 1970, 71, dir.), Am., Chgo., 7th Circuit bar assns. Home: 495 Clavey Ct Highland Park IL 60035 Office: 125 S Wacker Dr Chicago IL 60606 Tel (312) 372-2160

ROTMAN, MICHAEL HOWARD, b. Chgo., Apr. 25, 1936; B.S.C., Roosevelt U., 1958; J.D., DePaul U., 1962. Admitted to Ill. bar, 1962, U.S. Supreme Ct. bar, 1971, U.S. Tax Ct. bar, 1962; with IRS, 1962-65; partner firm Rotman, Medansky & Flovitz, Chgo., 1976—. Mem. White House Conf. on Mentally Handicapped, 1976; mem.

Chgo. Bar probate com. Ill. Council Lawyers on Mentally Handicapped, 1975. Mem. Am., Fed., Ill., Chgo. bar assns. Tel (312) 236-2202

ROTOLO, VINCENT MARINELLO, b. Tunis, Tunisia, Aug. 6, 1907; LL.B., Fordham U., 1928; LL.M., John Marshall U., 1935; B.S., Columbia, 1937, M.A., 1939. Admitted to N.J. bar, 1929, P. R. bar, 1953; individual practice law, Hackenack, N.J., 1929-42; judge Palisades Park (N.J.) Municipal Ct., 1930-35; staff atty. NLRB, N.Y.C., Washington and San Juan, P.R., 1942-59, adminstrv. law judge, Washington, 1959-62, regional atty., San Juan, 1962-73; prof. law Inter-Am. U., San Juan, 1973—. Mem. P. R., Am., Fed. bar assns. Office: PO Box 9237 Santurce PR 00908 Tel 724-2839

ROTONDO, RALPH, b. Providence, R.I., Jan. 27, 1896; grad. Northeastern U. Admitted to bar, 1925; staff R.I. Fed. Dist. and Appeal Ct.; individual practice law; clk. claims com. R.I. Legislature, 1936-38. Mem. Am., R.I. bar assns. Home: 242 Webster Ave Providence RI 02909 Office: 640 Rhode Island Hospital Trust Bldg Providence RI 02903 Tel (401) 421-7615

ROTWEIN, ABE ARTHUR, b. N.Y.C., Mar. 19, 1915; student Jones County Jr. Coll., 1932; J.D., U. Tenn., 1937. Admitted to Tenn. bar, 1937, Miss. bar, 1941, U.S. Supreme Ct. bar, 1967; practiced in Memphis, 1937-41; practiced in Collins and Laurel, Miss., 1946, Jackson, Miss., 1947—, mem. firm Brunini & Brunini, 1948-49; individual practice law, 1949—; spl. prof. fin. Millsaps Coll. Mem. Hinds County (Miss.) Trial Lawyers Assn. (pres. 1965-66), North Jackson Lawyers Club (pres. 1975-76), Barnett Reservoir Five County C. of C. (pres. 1976). Home: 107 Sandpiper Rd Brandon MS 39042 Office: PO Box 22582 Suite 110 Rotwein Bldg Jackson MS 39205 Tel (601) 982-8937

ROTWEIN, ABRAHAM, b. Phila., Apr. 7, 1906; LL.B., Bklyn. Law Sch., 1927, LL.M., 1928. Admitted to N.Y. State bar, 1928, U.S. Supreme Ct. bar, 1954; individual practice law, N.Y.C., 1928—; prof. law Bklyn. Law Sch., 1928-62; lectr. Practising Law Inst., N.Y.C., 1945-48; arbitrator small claims ct. Civil Ct. City N.Y., 1952—. Mem. Bar Assn. City N.Y., N.Am. Judges Assn., Am. Judicature Soc., Am. Arbitration Assn. Author: Textbook on the Law of Agency, 1936, 2d edit., 1949; New York Pleading and Practice, 1950, 2d edit., 1956,; Casebook on Pleading and Practice, 2d edit., 1956; Textbook on Labor Law, 1939; Outline on Pleading and Practice, 1939; Outline on Substantive Law, 1939; contbr. articles to legal jours. Home: 241 Central Park W New York City NY 10024 Office: 19 W 44th St New York City NY 10036 Tel (212) 687-5548

ROUGEAU, RICHARD NOEL, b. Worchester, Mass., July 30, 1942; A.B., Boston Coll., 1964, J.D., 1967; postgrad. Coll. Criminal Def. Attys., 1975. Admitted to Mass. bar, 1967; staff atty. Pub. Defender Service, Washington, 1968-70; pros. atty. cities of Barnstable, Mashpee and Yarmouth, Mass., 1970-72; asso. firm Hayes & Creney, Barnstable, 1970-74; asst. counsel Town Barnstable, 1974—; asso. firm Smith & Murphy, Hyannis, Mass., 1974—; prof. Cape Cod Community Coll., West Barnstable, Mass., 1971-76. Pres., Big Brothers Cape Cod, 1972-74. Mem. Mass., Barnstable County bar assns., Am. Trial Lawyers Assn., Coll. Criminal Def. Attys. Home: 42 Stanley Way Centerville MA 02632 Office: One Winter St Hyannis MA 02601 Tel (617) 771-4230

ROUNDS, GEORGE STARR, b. Vancouver, B.C., Can., June 14, 1941; B.A., Stanford, 1963; LL.B., U. Ariz., 1966. Admitted to Ariz. bar, 1966, N.Mex. bar, 1975; partner firm Evans, Kitchel & Jenckes, Phoenix, 1972—. Mem. Ariz., Maricopa County bar assns. Office: 363 N 1st Ave Phoenix AZ 85003

ROUNDS, ROBERT CRESSEY, b. Gorham, Maine, May 9, 1896; A.B. cum laude, Bowdoin Coll., 1918; J.D., Harvard U., 1924. Admitted to Maine bar, 1924, Mass. bar, 1924, Fed. bar, 1927; practice law, Boston, 1924—, asso. firm Alger, Dean & Sullivan, 1928-30, Rounds, Cook & King, 1946—; lectr. law Boston U., 1942-47, Mass. Inst. Tech., 1947-48; co-owner Cary Tchrs. Agy., Boston, 1950-69, dir., 1969—, owner, 1969—. Incorporator, Cambridge Jr. Coll., Cambridge, Mass., 1936, trustee, 1936-75, treas., 1940-69. Mem. Middlesex County Bar Assn., Cambridge Civic Assn. Home: 31 Martin St Cambridge MA 02138 Office: 120 Boylston St Boston MA 02116 Tel (617) 542-1788

ROUNTREE, JOHN ASA, b. Birmingham, Ala., Aug. 9, 1927; A.B., U. Ala., 1949; LL.B., Harvard, 1954. Admitted to Ala., U.S. Dist. Ct. No. Dist. Ala. bars, 1954, U.S. Ct. Appeals 5th Circuit bar, 1955, N.Y. bar, 1962, U.S. Dist. Ct. So. Dist. N.Y. bar, Ct. Appeals 2d Circuit bar, 1963, U.S. Dist. Ct. Eastern Dist. N.Y. bar, 1966, U.S. Supreme Ct. bar, 1972; asso. firm Cabaniss & Johnston, Birmingham, Ala., 1954-60, partner, 1960-62; asso. firm Debevoise, Plimpton, Lyons & Gates, N.Y.C., 1962-63, partner, 1963—. Mem. Am., N.Y., Ala. bar assns., Assn. Bar City N.Y., Am. Law Inst., Am. Coll. Trial Lawyers. Home: 2 Melanie Dr Chappaqua NY 10514 Office: 299 Park Ave New York City NY 10017 Tel (212) 752-6400

ROURKE, JAMES GARRETT, b. Santa Monica, Calif., May 16, 1926; A.B., U. Calif., Berkeley, 1950, J.D., 1953. Admitted to Calif. bar, 1954; legal counsel, office of cons. tax counsel Calif. Bd. Equalization, Sacramento, 1953-54; legal counsel, div. appeals and rev. Calif. Franchise Tax Bd., 1954-55; asso. firm Holbrook, Tarr & O'Neill, Los Angeles, 1955-56; partner firms Holbrook & Rourke, Los Angeles, 1959-65, Rourke & Holbrook, Santa Ana, Calif., 1959-75, Rourke & Woodruff, Santa Ana, 1976—; planning commr. City of Santa Ana, 1958-59; city atty. City of Tustin (Calif.), 1960—. Mem. Nat. Inst. Municipal Law Officers, Am. R.R. Trial Counsel. Home: 633 Alta Vista Laguna Beach CA 92651 Office: 1055 N Main St Santa Ana CA 92701 Tel (714) 835-6212

ROUSE, GERALD EDWARD, b. Grand Island, Nebr., Jan. 19, 1944; A.B., Hastings Coll., 1968; J.D., U. Nebr., 1971; student Kearney State Coll. summer 1966, Chadron State Coll. summer 1972-74, U. Nev., summers 1972, 73, 74, 75. Admitted to Nebr. bar, 1971, Fed. bar, 1971. Mem. firm Baker & Tessendorf, Columbus, Nebr., 1971; Platte County judge, 1971-72; county judge 21st Jud. Dist., Columbus, 1972—. Chmn. Region 10 Crime Commn., 1972-73, mem. 1972—; pres. Columbus Big Brother-Big Sisters, 1974-75. Mem. Nebr. County Judges Assn. (treas. 1973—), Nat. Assn. Juvenile Judges, Nebr. Assn. Juvenile Justice. Home: 118 Lakeshore Dr Columbus NE 68601 Office: PO Box 426 Platte County Columbus NE 68601 Tel (402) 564-1311

ROUSE, JOSEPH HANWAY, b. Balt., May 3, 1943; B.E.E., U. Md., 1966, J.D., 1970. Admitted to Md. bar, 1970; asst. state's atty. Balt., 1971-72; asst. pub. defender Md., Glen Burnie, 1972—, also individual practice law, Glen Burnie, 1970—; engr. Westinghouse Electric Corp. Ocean Research and Engring. Center, 1966-71. Mem. Am., Md., Anne Arundel County bar assns., U. Md. Alumni Assn., Delta Theta Phi. Home: 22 Hatton Dr Severna Park MD 21146 Office: 106 Balto Anna Blvd NW Glen Burnie MD 21061 Tel (301) 761-8350

ROUSH, CHARLES DOW, b. Phoenix, Nov. 18, 1937; LL.B., U. Ariz., 1966. Admitted to Ariz. bar, 1966; asso. firm Lewis and Roca, Phoenix, 1966-69; partner firm Steiner and Roush, Phoenix, 1969-71; judge Ariz. Superior Ct. in Maricopa County, 1971-76, presiding criminal judge, 1973-74; partner firm Treon, Warnicke, Dann and Roush, Phoenix, 1976—; staff lectr. Nat. Coll. State Judiciary, 1975—. Mem. Am., Maricopa County (dir. 1970-71) bar assns., Am. Judicature Soc. Editor Ariz. Law Rev., 1965-66. Home: 7709 E Palm Ln Scottsdale AZ 85257 Office: Suite 2250 100 W Washington St Phoenix AZ 85003 Tel (602) 252-4895

ROUSH, DELLOYD LESTER, b. Rutland, Ohio, Mar. 12, 1923; B.B.A., Ohio State U., 1948, J.D., 1950. Admitted to Ohio bar, 1951; field claims man Nationwide Ins. Co., Columbus, Ohio, 1950-51, 55-57; job coordinator Breyfogle Indsl. Contractors, 1953-55; claim mgr., v.p. claims, asst. gen. counsel Automobile Club Ins. Co., Columbus, 1957—. Mem. Upper Arlington Civic Assn., Central Claims Exec. Assn. (pres. 1970-71), Ohio Def. Assn. (pres. 1970-71), Am., Ohio, Columbus bar assns., Am. Judicature Soc. Home: 4290 Clairmont Rd Columbus OH 43220 Office: 3590 Twin Creeks Dr Columbus OH 43204 Tel (614) 272-6951

ROUSHAR, VICTOR THOMAS, b. Torrington, Wyo., Aug. 4, 1937; B.S., U. Denver, 1961, LL.B., 1964. Admitted to Colo. bar, 1964; with firm Woodrow, Roushar, Weaver & Withers, and predecessor, Montrose, Colo., 1964—, partner, 1970—; dir., Pioneer Savs. and Loan Assn., Montrose Indsl. Devel. Corp. Mem. Am., Colo., 7th Jud. Dist. (pres.) bar assns. Home: 1022 Highland St Montrose CO 81401 Office: 144 S Uncompahgre St Montrose CO 81401 Tel (303) 249-4531

ROUTT, THOMAS HENRY, b. Grimes County, Tex., Mar. 5, 1930; J.D., Tex. So. U., 1961. Admitted to Tex. bar, 1961, U.S. Dist. Ct. bars for Dist. Cts. Tex., 1965, U.S. 5th Circuit Ct. Appeals bar, 1966, U.S. Supreme Ct. bar, 1967; individual practice in Houston, 1961-63; sr. partner firm Routt, Harper & McDonald, Houston, 1963-64; asso. firm Tillman & Hannah, Houston, 1964-65; asst. atty. gen. Office Atty. Gen. of Tex., Austin, 1965-66, asst. chief enforcement div., 1973; mng. atty. neighborhood law office Houston Legal Found., 1966-68; judge Municipal Ct. 6, Houston, 1968-72, Harris County (Tex.) Criminal Ct. at Law 6, 1973—. Bd. dirs. Riverside Gen. Hosp., Houston, Houston-Harris County chpt. ARC; bd. mgrs. South Central br. YMCA, Houston. Mem. State Bar Tex., Am., Houston, Nat. (charter mem. jud. council 1971) bar assns., Am. Judges Assn., Am. Judicature Soc., Houston Lawyers Assn. Named Citizen of Year Omega Psi Phi, 1969; recipient Community Service award Delta Sigma Theta, 1970, Distinguished Service award Frontiers Internat., 1973. Home: 3210 Prospect St Houston TX 77004 Office: 401 Caroline St Houston TX 77002 Tel (713) 228-8311

ROWAN, CLYDE C., b. Buffalo, Apr. 1, 1890; student Kans. State U., Emporia, 1912; LL.B., U. Mich., 1916. Admitted to Mont. bar, 1916, Wash. bar, 1944, U.S. Supreme Ct. bar, 1958; individual practice law, Spokane, Wash., 1944—; county pros. atty. Carbon County (Mont.), 1920-24; asst. pres. Fed. Land Bank of Spokane, 1934-44; dir. food protection U.S. Dept. Agr., four N.W. states, World War II. Chmn. Red Lodge (Mont.) Sch. Bd., 1929. Mem. Mont., Wash. bar assns. Home: 206 W 40th Ave Spokane WA 99203 Office: 920 Paulsen Bldg Spokane WA 99201 Tel (509) 624-1888

ROWAN, GERALD BURDETTE, b. Powersville, Mo., Feb. 9, 1916; A.B., N.W. Mo. State Coll., 1937; LL.B., Mo. U., 1940. Admitted to Mo. bar, 1940; mem. firms Frye and Rowan, Cape Girardeau, Mo., 1940-49, Oliver and Oliver, Cape Girardeau, 1949-59; asso. gen. counsel Kansas City Life Ins. Co., (Mo.), 1959-66, gen. counsel, 1966—, v.p., 1969, sr. v.p., 1976—, also dir.; pros. atty. Bollinger County (Mo.), 1946-49; city atty. City of Cape Girardeau, 1954-59. Bd. dirs. Mo. div. Am. Cancer Soc., 1965—, chmn., 1974-75, bd. dirs. Jackson County (Mo.) unit, 1965—, pres., 1963-65, 70-71; mem. Mo. State Park Bd., 1965—, chmn. 1969, 73; bd. dirs. Kansas City Fedn. Neighborhood Serving Agys., 1973—, pres., 1976-77. Mem. World Assn. Lawyers, Am., Kansas City bar assns., Mo. Bar, Assn. Life Ins. Counsel (compiler 12th edit. Directory of Life Ins. Lawyers 1973), Am. Life Ins. Assn., Order of Coif. Contbr. articles to legal jours.; editorial bd. Mo. Law Rev., 1938-39. Home: 209 E 67th St Kansas City MO 64113 Office: 3520 Broadway Kansas City MO 64111 Tel (816) 753-7000

ROWAN, JUSTIN MICHAEL, b. Murchison, Tex., June 15, 1920; B.S., N. Tex. State U., 1940; J.D. U. Tex., 1949. Admitted to Tex. bar, 1949, U.S. Supreme Ct. bar, 1972; exec. sec. Vet.'s Land Bd. Tex., Austin, 1949-50; chief atty. Gen. Land Office Tex., Austin, 1950-52; partner firm Justice, Justice & Rowan, Athens, Tex., 1952-55, Rowan & Davis, Tyler, Tex., 1965-72, Loftis, Rowan and Files, Tyler, 1972-76, Loftis, Rowan, Files, Clayton, Bain & Clark, Tyler, 1976—; judge ct. domestic relations, Smith County, Tex., 1972. Mem., pres. adv. bd. Mother Francis Hosp., Tyler, 1973-75; chmn. City Plan Commn., Tyler, 1965-72. Fellow Tex. Bar Found.; mem. Smith County (pres. 1971-72), Tex. bar assns. Home: 3615 Wynnwood Dr Tyler TX 75701 Office: 109 W Ferguson St Tyler TX 75702 Tel (214) 595-3573

ROWE, BENJAMEN THOMAS, b. Carrollton, Ga., Feb. 19, 1945; B.S., U. Ala., 1967, J.D., 1972. Admitted to Ala. bar, 1972; U.S. Ct. Appeals 5th Circuit bar, 1974; asso. firm Hand, Arendall, Bedsole, Greaves & Johnston, Mobile, Ala., 1972-77; partner firm McRight, Sims, Rowe & Bagwell, 1977—. Mem. Am. Bar Assn., Ala. Def. Lawyers Assn. Editor Ala. Law Rev., 1971-72. Office: PO Box 1024 Mobile AL 36601 Tel (205) 433-6961

ROWE, BRAXTON BRAGG, b. New Brockton, Ala., Mar. 13, 1911; student Troy State U., 1930-33; LL.B., U. Ala., 1942, J.D., 1969. Admitted to Ala. bar, 1942, Ala. Supreme Ct. bar, 1942; 5th Circuit Ct. Appeals bar, 1966, U.S. Supreme Ct. bar, 1972; ins. adjuster Traveler Ins. Co., Birmingham, Ala., 1942, Knoxville, Tenn., 1947; mem. firm Rowe, & Rowe, Enterprise, Ala., 1947—; atty. Coffee County, Ala., 1961—. Mem. Am. Judicare Soc., Am. Trial Lawyers Assn., Nat. Assn. Claimants and Compensation Attys., Coffee County Bar Assn. (pres. 1970-73). Office: POB 150 Enterprise AL 36330 Tel (205) 347-3401

ROWE, CHARLES WARREN, b. Knoxville, Tenn., Dec. 6, 1943; B.S. in Bus. Adminstrn., U. Ala., 1968; J.D., Cumberland Sch. Law Samford U., 1972. Admitted to Ala. bar, 1972; partner firm Rowe & Rowe, Enterprise, Ala., 1972—; judge Enterprise Recorder's Ct., 1975—. Mem. Am., Ala., Coffee County bar assns., Ala. Trial Lawyers Assn. Home: 405 Colonial Dr Enterprise AL 36330 Tel (205) 347-3401

ROWE, NANSI IRENE, b. Detroit, May 6, 1940; B.B.A., Detroit Inst. Tech., 1965; J.D., Wayne State U., 1973. Admitted to Mich. bar, 1974; tchr. Detroit Pub. Schs., 1971; exec asst. to mayor Detroit, 1974; corp. counsel law dept. dir. City of Detroit, 1975—. Bd. dirs. Homes for Black Children, 1973, United Community Services, 1977, Big Sisters, 1968. Mem. Mich., Detroit bar assns. Office: 1126 City County Bldg Detroit MI 48226 Tel (313) 224-3400

ROWE, STANLEY DAGNAL, b. Athens, Ga., Mar. 25, 1947; B.A., U. Ala., 1969, J.D., 1972; LL.M., N.Y. U., 1973. Admitted to Ala. bar, 1972, U.S. Supreme Ct. bar, 1976; asso. firm Cleary, Lee, Porter & Rowe, Huntsville, Ala., 1972—. Mem. Huntsville-Madison County C. of C., Huntsville-Madison County Indsl. Devel. Assn., Am. Judicature Soc., Farrah Law Soc., Am., Ala., Huntsville-Madison County bar assns. Contbr. articles and chpts. to legal jours. and texts. Home: 1411 Glenwood Dr SE Huntsville AL 35801 Office: 408 Franklin St Huntsville AL 35804 Tel (205) 533-1421

ROWEN, MARVIN DAVID, b. Chgo., Aug. 17, 1931; B.S., U. Calif., Los Angeles, 1953, J.D., 1956. Admitted to Calif. bar, 1957, Central Dist. 9th Circuit Fed. bar, 1957; asso. firm George I. Devor, Los Angeles, 1957; sr. trial dep. dist. atty. Los Angeles County, 1957-62; trial atty. firm Wyman Finell & Rothman, Beverly Hills, Calif., 1962-64; partner, sr. trial atty. firm Levinson, Rowen, Miller, Jacobs & Kabrins, Beverly Hills, Calif., 1964—; instr. law Los Angeles Met., Los Angeles Valley colls. Mem. exec. bd. Pacific S.W. region Anti-Defamation League of B'nai B'rith. Mem. Am., Calif., Los Angeles County, Beverly Hills bar assns., Am., Calif., Los Angeles trial lawyers assns. Office: 8601 Wilshire Blvd Beverly Hills CA 90211 Tel (213) 657-8822

ROWLAND, DAN, b. Dingus, Ky., Nov. 16, 1940; B.A., Berea Coll., 1969; J.D., U. Ky., 1971. Admitted to Ky. bar, 1972, U.S. Supreme Ct. bar, 1975; partner firm Burchett and Rowland, Martin, Ky., 1972-74; individual practice law, Prestonsburg, Ky., 1974—; pub. defender 31st Jud. Dist. Ky., Prestonsburg, 1974-76. Mem. Am., Ky., Floyd County bar assns., Am. Judicature Soc., Am. Arbitration Assn., Am., Ky. trial lawyers assns. Home: 270 Trimble Branch Rd Prestonsburg KY 41653 Office: Box 127 Prestonsburg KY 41653 Tel (606) 886-8078

ROWLAND, JAMES HENRY, JR., b. Bluefield, W.Va., Mar. 12, 1938; B.S., Ohio State U., 1960; J.D., Howard U., 1963. Admitted to Pa. bar, 1964; asst. atty. gen. State of Pa., Harrisburg, 1964-69; chief counsel Pa. Dept. Labor and Industry, Harrisburg, 1969-71; partner firm Rowland and Rowland, Harrisburg, 1964—; govt. appeals agt. Harrisburg Area Draft Bd., 1968-72. Sec. Harrisburg Boys Club, 1974-76; bd. dirs. Pa. Heart Assn., 1974-76, Center for Community Alternatives, Inc., Harrisburg, 1976; bd. mgrs. Camp Shi Kellimy of Harrisburg YMCA, 1976. Mem. Nat., Pa., Dauphin County bar assns., Nat. Conf. Black Lawyers, Am., Pa. trial lawyers assns., Omega Psi Phi (Phila. chpt. Achievement award 1969). Home: 251 Eddington Ave Harrisburg PA 17111 Office: 812 N 17th St Harrisburg PA 17103 Tel (717) 233-6787

ROWLAND, JOSEPH WESLEY, b. Wrightsville, Ga., Dec. 25, 1928; A.B., Mercer U., 1951, LL.B., 1952. Admitted to Ga. bar, 1952; practiced in Wrightsville, 1952—; judge State Ct. of Johnson County (Ga.), 1960—; county atty. Johnson County, 1970—. Mem. State Bar Ga., State Trial Judges and Solicitors Assn. Ga. Office: PO Box 227 Wrightsville GA 31096 Tel (912) 864-3371

ROWLANDS, HUBERT LLEWELLYN, b. Emporia, Kans., Oct. 17, 1920; B.A., B.S. in Edn., Emporia State Coll., 1941; J.D., U. Mich., 1948. Admitted to Mo. bar, 1948; asso. firm Dietrich, Davis, Dicus, Rowlands & Schmitt and predecessors, Kansas City, Mo., 1948-58, partner, 1958—. Protestant co-chmn. NCCJ, Kansas City, 1965-67. Mem. Lawyers Assn. Kansas City (pres. 1976-77), Am., Kansas City bar assns., Mo. Bar, Am. Judicature Soc., Order of Coif. Bd. editors Mich. Law Rev., 1948. Office: 1001 Dwight Bldg 1004 Baltimore Ave Kansas City MO 64105 Tel (816) 221-3420

ROWLEY, GEORGE HARDY, b. Greenville, Pa., May 30, 1923; student Thiel Coll., 1941-42; B.A., Yale, 1947; J.D., Harvard, 1949. Admitted to Pa. bar, 1950, U.S. Supreme Ct. bar, 1974; asst. U.S. atty. Western dist. Pa., Pitts., 1950-52; partner firm Voorhies Dilley Keck Rowley & Wallace, Greenville, 1952—; dist. mem. Gov.'s Trial Ct. Nominating Commn., 1973-75. Vice-chmn. Greenville Planning Commn., 1965-69; sec. bd. trustees Greenville Hosp., 1972—. Fellow Am. Coll. Trial Lawyers; mem. Am., Pa., Mercer County (pres.) bar assns., Am. Judicature Soc., Def. Research Inst., Pa. Def. Inst., Pa. Trial Lawyers Assn., Am. Arbitration Assn. (nat. panel). Home: 157 Plum St Greenville PA 16125 Office: 47 Clinton St Greenville PA 16125 Tel (412) 588-4800

ROWLEY, JAMES ARTHUR, b. Rockford, Ill., Mar. 12, 1934; student Ripon Coll., 1952-56; A.B., U. Wis., J.D., 1963. Admitted to Wis. bar, 1963; individual practice law, Green Lake, Wis., 1963-75, 75—. Home: Route 1 Green Lake WI 54941 Office: PO Box 565 531 Mill St Green Lake WI 54941 Tel (414) 294-3656

ROWLEY, JAMES E., b. Tarentum, Pa., Apr. 8, 1926; B.A., Washington and Jefferson Coll., 1949; LL.B., U. Pitts., 1952. Admitted to Pa. Supreme Ct. bar; partner firm Rowley, Smith, Rowley & Lewis, Aliquippa, Pa. and Ambridge, Pa., 1953-66; judge Ct. Common Pleas Beaver County (Pa.), Bever, 1966—. Bd. dirs. Aliquippa Hosp.; mem. dist. com. Logstown Council Boy Scouts Am.; elder United Presbyterian Ch. Mem. Am., Pa., Beaver County bar assns., Am. Judicature Soc., Pa. Conf. State Trial Judges. Named Man of the Year, Aliquippa Area C. of C., 1968. Office: Court House 3d St Beaver PA 15009 Tel (412) 774-5000

ROY, ROBERT SNOWDON DUNBAR, b. Mt. Kisco, N.Y., Jan. 22, 1917; B.A., Columbia, 1937; J.D., Fordham Law Sch., 1940. Admitted to N.Y. bar, 1942; asso. firm Roy & Roy, Irvington, N.Y., 1942—. Town Justice, Greenburgh, N.Y., 1948-75; trustee Irvington Sch. Bd., 1948-54. Mem. Am., N.Y., Westchester County bar assns., Westchester County Magistrates Assn. (past pres.). Office: 56 Main St Irvington NY 10533 Tel (914) 591-7722

ROYALL, CHARLES CRECY, b. Silver City, N.Mex., July 5, 1917; B.A. in Math., N.Mex. Western Coll., 1939; LL.B., U. Colo., 1942. Admitted to N.Mex. bar, 1946, Ariz. bar, 1959; asso. firm Royall & Royall, 1946-58; law clk. firm Hughes & Steward, Phoenix, 1958-59; asst. atty. gen. State of Ariz., Phoenix, 1959-64; sec., gen. mgr. and legal advisor Lake Havasu Irrigation and Drainage Dist., 1964—, Lake Havasu San. Dist., 1964—; city atty. Silver City (N.Mex.), 1946-50, 53-58; mem. N.Mex. Ho. of Reps., 1946-48, N.Mex. Senate,

1949-58. Mem. Mohave County Bar Assn. Home: 2380 N Smoketree Ave Lake Havasu City AZ 86403 Office: 1795 Civic Center Blvd Lake Havasu City AZ 86403 Tel (602) 855-2116

ROYALL, DONALD ROTH, b. Houston, June 22, 1937; B.A., Tex. A and M U., 1958; S.J.D., U. Tex., 1961. Admitted to Tex. bar, 1961, So. Dist. of Tex. bar, 1962; individual practice law, Houston, 1961-64; staff atty. Phillips Petroleum Co., Houston, 1964-66; asso. firm Fouts, Moore, Coleman & Royall, Houston, 1966-69, partner, 1969—; chmn. Family Law Advisory Commn. Tex. Bd. Legal Specialization, 1975-77; lectr. in field. Mem. Am., Houston bar assns., State Bar of Tex. (chmn. family law sect. 1977—). Office: 4600 Post Oak Pl 207 Houston TX 77027 Tel (713) 621-8444

ROYCROFT, HOWARD FRANCIS, b. Balt., Sept. 9, 1930; B.A., U. Md., 1953; LL.B., Georgetown U., 1958. Admitted to D.C. bar, 1958, Va. bar, 1958; mem. firm Hogan & Hartson, Washington, 1958-66, partner, 1966—; lectr. Howard U. Law Sch., 1973-75. Mem. Met. Washington Bd. Trade, 1968—; chmn. profl. div. United Way, 1973; bd. dirs. YMCA, 1973-76. Mem. Nat. Assn. TV Arts and Scis., Nat. Broadcasters Club, Am., FCC, D.C., Va. bar assns., Kappa Alpha, Delta Theta Phi. Home: 8703 Eaglebrook Ct Alexandria VA 22308 Office: 815 Connecticut Ave NW Washington DC 20006 Tel (202) 331-4525

ROYER, MARY KATHERINE, b. Des Moines, Nov. 19, 1946; B.A., U. Iowa, 1969; M.A., U. Mich., 1970; J.D., Northwestern U., 1973. Asst. curator human relations files U. Iowa, 1968-69; law clk. to Atty. Gen. Iowa, Des Moines, summers 1971, 72; admitted to Ohio bar, 1973; asso. firm Squire Sanders & Dempsey, Cleve., 1973-76; atty. law dept. Allied Chem. Corp., Morristown, N.J., 1976—. Mem. advisory council to Pres. U. Iowa, 1968-69; del. Iowa Republican Conv., 1972. Mem. Am. Bar Assn., Mortar Bd., Phi Beta Kappa, Alpha Lambda Delta. Office: Allied Chem Corp Law Dept PO Box 1057R Morristown NJ 07960 Tel (201) 455-2817

ROYER, WILFRIED LOUIS, b. Missoula, Mont., Jan. 14, 1941; B.S., Mont. State U., 1965; J.D., U. Mont., 1971. Admitted to Mont. bar, 1971; staff atty. Mont. Legal Services Assn., Missoula, 1971-74; partner firm Measure, Cumming & Salansky, Kalispell, Mont. 1974-76; individual practice law, Whitefish, Mont., 1976—; Mem. Am., Mont. bar assns. Home and Office: PO Box 355 Whitefish MT 59937 Tel (406) 862-5172

ROYSTER, GEORGE DURWARD, JR., b. Hartford, Conn., Aug. 28, 1941; B.A., Lafayette Coll., 1963; J.D., Washington U., 1966. Admitted to Conn. bar, 1966, U.S. Dist. Ct. bar, 1967, U.S. Supreme Ct. bar, 1973; asso. firm Halloran, Sage, Phelon & Hagarty, Hartford, 1966-72, partner, 1972—; instr. Moot Ct. program Washington U., 1965-66. Mem. Glastonbury (Conn.) Bd. Edn., 1969-75; mem. Glastonbury Town Council, 1975—. Mem. Am., Conn. (chmn. com. on trial specialization 1975), Hartford (mem. ethics com. 1976) bar assns., Am. Arbitration Assn. (panel arbitrators). Author: Insurance, 1966 (recipient Book prize Am. Jurisprudence Assn.). Office: 25 Lewis St Hartford CT 06103 Tel (203) 522-6103

ROZELL, WILLIAM BARCLAY, b. Ossining, N.Y., Mar. 30, 1943; Sc.B. in Engring., Brown U., 1965; J.D., Cornell U., 1968. Admitted to N.Y. bar, 1969, Ohio bar, 1969, Alaska bar, 1972, U.S. Supreme Ct. bar, 1976; VISTA atty. Columbus (Ohio) Met. Area Community Action Orgn., 1968-69; asso. firm White & Case, N.Y.C., 1969-72; asso. firm Faulkner, Banfield, Doogan & Holmes, Juneau, Alaska, 1972-74, partner, 1975—. Dir. Alaska Legal Services Corp., 1975—. Mem. Am., N.Y. State, Juneau, Alaska (gov.) bar assns. Contbr. articles to profl. jours. Home: 712 Main St Juneau AK 99801 Office: 311 N Franklin St Juneau AK 99801 Tel (907) 586-2210

RUANE, RICHARD EDWARD, b. Hawley, Pa., Aug. 3, 1926; B.S., Villanova U., 1950; J.D., Temple U., 1954. Admitted to Pa. bar, 1955; asso. prof. bus. law Villanova U., Pa., 1955—; individual practice law, Ardmore, Pa., 1955—. Mem. Phila. Bar Assn., Am. Bus. Law Assn. Office: 119 Coulter Ave Ardmore PA 19003 Tel (215

RUBACK, ROBERT I., b. Bklyn., May 10, 1915; B.S., St. John's U., 1936, LL.B., 1938. Admitted to N.Y. state bar, 1938, U.S. Supreme Ct. bar, 1970; individual practice law, N.Y.C., 1938-60, 1975—; partner firm Levy, Levy & Ruback, N.Y.C., 1960-75; univ. counsel Pace U., N.Y.C., 1975—, prof., chmn. taxation, 1947—. Mem. N.Y. County Lawyers Assn., Fed., Jewish bar assns. Editor St. John's U. Law Rev., 1936-38, Pace Tax Briefs, 1970—. Home: 102 Strathmore Ln Rockville Centre NY 11570 Office: 225 Broadway New York City NY 10007 Tel (212) 227-8383

RUBENFELD, LEONARD, b. Peekskill, N.Y., May 7, 1912; grad. U. Ala., 1934; LL.B., Fordham U., 1938. Admitted to N.Y. State bar, 1940; individual practice law, Peekskill and White Plains, N.Y., 1940-49; asst. atty. gen. State of N.Y., 1949; asst. dist. atty. Westchester County (N.Y.), 1949-54; sr. asst. dist. atty. City of N.Y., 1954-60, chief asst. dist. atty., 1960-62, dist. atty., 1962-68; judge Westchester County Ct., 1968-69, adminstrv. judge, 1969; justice N.Y. State Supreme Ct., White Plains, 1970—; served with JAG, AUS; dep. judge advocate gen. Jewish War Vets; panelist Practicing Law Inst. Life mem. Peekskill Vol. Fire Dept.; v.p. Peekskill Bd. Park Commrs. Mem. Am., Mt. Vernon, Westchester County, Peekskill bar assns., N.Y. State (pres. 1966), Nat. dist. attys. assns., Met. Law Enforcement Congress, County Ct., Supreme Ct. judges assns., U. Ala., Fordham Law (dir., exec., legis. coms.) alumni assns., Phi Sigma Delta. Home: 400 Nelson Ave Peekskill NY 10566 Office: 111 Grove St White Plains NY 10601 Tel (914) 682-3025

RUBENFELD, PAUL, b. Bklyn., June 27, 1928; B.S. in Accounting, N.Y. U., 1956, J.D., 1962. Admitted to N.Y. State bar, 1963, U.S. Supreme Ct. bar, 1968; individual practice law, Kew Gardens, Queens, N.Y., 1964—. Mem. Queens County, Queens County Criminal Cts., Nassau County bar assns., N.Y. State Defenders Assn., Brandeis Assn. Office: 125-10 Queens Blvd Kew Gardens NY 11415 Tel (212) 275-0200

RUBENFELD, STANLEY IRWIN, b. Queens, N.Y., Dec. 7, 1930; B.A., Columbia U., 1952, J.D. (Stone scholar), 1956. Admitted to N.Y. bar, 1956; asso. firm Shearman & Sterling, N.Y.C., 1956-65, partner, Paris, 1965-68, N.Y.C., 1968—; dir. Airco, Inc., Eleda Corp., Orbisphere Corp. Bd. dirs. Port Washington (N.Y.) Community Chest, 1973—, chmn. fund dr., 1973-74; chmn. placement com. Columbia Law Sch., 1973—; bd. dirs. Residents for a More Beautiful Port Washington, 1971—. Mem. Am., N.Y. State, N.Y.C. (tax com.) bar assns., Columbia Law Sch. (dir. 1974—), Columbia Coll. (constitution and by-laws com.) alumni assns., Tax Club, Phi Delta Phi, Tau Epsilon Phi. Rockefeller Found. grantee, 1955; editor-in-chief Columbia Law Rev., 1955-56; contbr. articles to legal jours. Home: 41 Longview Rd Port Washington NY 11050 Office: 53 Wall St New York City NY 10005 Tel (212) 483-1000

RUBENSTEIN, JEFFREY CARL, b. Chgo., Jan. 27, 1942; A.B., U. Mich., 1963, J.D., 1966; postgrad Lawyers Inst., John Marshal Law Sch., 1966-68. Admitted to Ill. bar, 1966; asso. firm Leibman, Williams, Bennett, Baird & Minow (now Sidley & Austin), 1966; asso., then prin. firm Sachnoff, Schrager, Jones & Weaver, Ltd., Chgo., 1966—; lectr. Ill. Inst. Tech., Kent Sch. Law, Practicing Law Inst. Dir. young people's div. Jewish United Fund., Chgo.; mem. nat. young leadership cabinet United Jewish Appeal, 1974—; mem. Jewish community and youth service com. Jewish Fedn. Chgo., 1974—; bd. dirs. Bur. Jewish Employment Problems, 1972—. Mem. Am., Chgo. bar assns., Chgo. Council Lawyers (chmn. ethics com.) Author/editor: Coif Law Outline Series, 1966—. Office: Suite 4700 1 IBM Plaza Chicago IL 60611 Tel (312) 644-2400

RUBERG, ROBERT EDWARD, b. Cin., Sept. 7, 1927; A.B., U. Ky., 1949, J.D., 1951. Admitted to Ky. bar, 1951; partner firm O'Hara, Ruberg, Cetrule & Osborne, Covington, Ky., 1961—; Kenton County Juvenile Ct. Judge., 1961—; atty. Kenton County Bd. Edn., 1960—. Bd. dirs. Hope Cottage, United Cerebral Palsy No. Ky., Catholic Social Service Bur.; mem. Ky. Crime Commn., 1972—, Covington Diocesan Bd. Edn., 1976—. Mem. Am. Coll. Trial Lawyers, Ky. Council Juvenile Ct. Judges (pres. 1975-76). Home: 1706 Mt Vernon Dr Fort Wright KY 41011 Office: 600 Greenup St Covington KY 41011 Tel (606) 581-3222

RUBIN, ALBERT JACK, b. Elmira, N.Y., Mar. 15, 1908; B.S., U. Pa., 1929; J.D., LL.B., Harvard, 1932. Admitted to N.Y. State bar, 1933, U.S. Dist. Ct. bar, 1934, U.S. Supreme Ct. bar, 1967; individual practice law, Rochester, N.Y., 1932-45, Penn Yan, N.Y., 1945—; lawyer Urban Renewal Penn Yan, 1970; lawyer for Village of Penn Yan, 1968-70. Mem. Yates County Bar Assn. (pres. 1951). Home: 325 Clinton St Penn Yan NY 14527 Office: 130 Main St Penn Yan NY 14527 Tel (315) 536-3833

RUBIN, ALVIN BENJAMIN, b. Alexandria, La., Mar. 13, 1920; B.S., La. State U., 1941, LL.B., 1942. Admitted to La. bar, 1942; partner firm Sanders, Miller, Downing, Rubin & Kean, Baton Rouge, 1946-66; judge U.S. Dist. Ct., Eastern Dist. La., 1966—; vis. lectr. in law La. State U., 1946—; arbitrator Fed. Mediation and Conciliation Service, 1950-66. Bd. visitors U. Chgo. Law Sch., 1972-75, U. Miami Law Sch., 1974—, Harvard Law Sch., 1975—. Mem. Am. Bar Assn. (bd. editors jour., ho. of dels. 1963-65), Am. Law Inst., Blue Key, Order of Coif. Recipient Golden Deeds award Baton Rouge State-Times, 1964, NCCJ award, 1966; author: (with McMahon) Louisiana Pleadings and Judicial Forms Annotated, 1965; (with Rubin) Louisiana Trust Handbook, 1968; contbr. numerous articles to legal jours. Office: 500 Camp St New Orleans LA 70130 Tel (504) 589-2905

RUBIN, ARNOLD E., b. Phila., Dec. 8, 1935; B.S., Drexel U., Phila., 1958; J.D., Temple Univ., 1961. Admitted to Pa. Supreme Ct. bar, 1962, U.S. Supreme Ct. bar, 1965; individual practice law, Media, Pa., 1965-77; 1st asst. public defender, Delaware County, Pa., 1966-67; mem. JAGC U.S. Army, 1965-75. Bd. dirs. Downtown Jewish Home, Phila., 1972; mem. Fedn. Jewish Agencies, 1970-76. Mem. Pa. Bar Assn. Home: 1280 Post House Ln Media PA 19063 Office: 229 N Olive St Media PA 19063 Tel (215) 565-2500

RUBIN, DONALD HARRY, b. San Diego, Apr. 24, 1944; B.A., Humboldt State Coll., 1967; J.D., U. San Diego, 1972. Admitted to Calif. bar, 1972; dep. county counsel Kern County (Calif.), Bakersfield, 1972—. Office: 1415 Truxtun Ave room 702 Bakersfield CA 93301 Tel (805) 861-2326

RUBIN, HERBERT, b. Lisbon, Conn.; A.B., Coll. City N.Y., 1938; J.D., N.Y. U., 1942. Admitted to N.Y. bar, 1942, U.S. Supreme Ct. bar, 1957; practiced in N.Y.C. since 1942, asso. firm Newman & Bisco, 1942, individual practice law, 1946-48, 50-56, partner firm Atkin & Rubin, 1948-50, sr. partner, mem. firm Herzfeld & Rubin, 1956—; mem. faculty N.Y. U. Law Sch., 1946-50, 57-64; asso. prof. law Rutgers U., 1949-57; asso. prof. constl. law L.I. U., 1964-69; mem. Adv. Council on Housing Ct., N.Y.C., 1973—; mem. N.Y. Gov's. Task Force on Jud. Reform, 1975—; mem. N.Y. Gov's. Jud. Selection Bd. for 2d Dept., 1975—; mem. N.Y. State Banking Bd., 1976—; chmn. Spl. Selection Com. for U.S. Bankruptcy Judge in N.Y., 1976, Spl. Selection Com. for U.S. Magistrates in N.Y., 1976-77. Trustee L.I. Jewish Hosp., 1974—. Mem. Am., N.Y. State (ho. of dels. 1974—), Queens County (N.Y.) (pres. 1971-72), Fed. bar assns., Assn. Bar City N.Y. Recipient Merit award United Jewish Appeal, 1961; Honor award Fedn. Jewish Philanthropies, 1960; Distinguished Service award State of Israel Bonds, 1959; Brotherhood award L.I. div. NCCJ, 1969; bd. editors N.Y. Law Jour., 1971—; editor-in-chief N.Y. U. Law Rev., 1940-41. Office: 40 Wall St New York City NY 10005 Tel (212) 344-0680

RUBIN, HOWARD MICHAEL, b. Los Angeles, Feb. 6, 1947; B.A., U. Calif., Santa Barbara, 1968; J.D., U. Calif., Los Angeles, 1971. Admitted to Calif. bar, 1972; individual practice law, Encino, Calif., 1972—; participant, speaker Los Angeles County Bar/Constl. Rights Found. Lawyer in the Classroom Program. Vice pres. Emet Young Profls., Los Angeles, 1973, pres., 1973-74, treas., 1975-76. Mem. Los Angeles County, San Fernando Valley bar assns. Mem. U. Calif., Los Angeles-Alaska Bar Rev., 1969-70. Office: 16633 Ventura Blvd Encino CA 91306 Tel (213) 990-9827

RUBIN, JAMES STEVEN, b. Los Angeles, Dec. 20, 1947; B.S. in Bus. Adminstrn., Northwestern U., 1969; J.D., U. Ill., 1973. Admitted to N.Mex. bar, 1973; econ. asst. HSB's Riksforbund, Stockholm, 1968; partner firm Mitchell, Alley & Rubin, Santa Fe, 1973—. Mem. Instl. Rev. Panel and Adv. Bd. Outreach, Santa Fe, 1976—. Mem. State Bar N.Mex., Am., 1st Jud. Dist. bar assns. Editor in chief Recent Decisions, Ill. Bar Jour., 1972-73. Office: PO Box 1932 Santa Fe NM 87501 Tel (505) 982-3512

RUBIN, MATTHEW MARTIN, b. Bronx, N.Y., Oct. 26, 1945; B.A., Trinity Coll., 1967; J.D., U. Conn., 1971; LL.M., Boston U., 1974. Admitted to Conn. bar, 1974, U.S. Dist. Ct. bar, 1976; partner firm Rubin and Rubin, Hartford, Conn., 1971—. Mem. Hartford County Bar Assn., Kiwanis (1st v.p. Hartford chpt.). Home: 44 Huntington Dr West Hartford CT 06107 Office: 36 Russ St Hartford CT 06106 Tel (203) 249-6545

RUBIN, MILES JORDAN, b. Bklyn., Sept. 17, 1929; A.B., Coll. William and Mary, 1949; LL.B., Bklyn. Law Sch., 1954. Admitted to N.Y. bar, 1954, Calif. bar, 1957, U.S. Supreme Ct. bar, 1965; legal asst. staff Judge Adv., Ft. Huachuca, Ariz., 1955-56; dep. atty. gen. State of Calif., Los Angeles, 1957-60, sr. asst. atty. gen., 1965-70; mem. firm Klinger & Rubin, Los Angeles, 1960-64; partner firm Dryden, Harrington & Swartz, Los Angeles, 1970—; lectr. Continuing Edn. of Bar Conf., 1975. Mem. Bd. of Bur. Electronic Dealer Registration, State of Calif., 1963-64. Mem. State Bar Calif. (chmn. law book com.), Am., Los Angeles County, Fed. (pres. Los Angeles chpt. 1967-68) bar assns., Assn. Bus. Trial Lawyers, Calif., Los Angeles trial lawyers assns. Office: One Wilshire Bldg Suite 703 Los Angeles CA 90017 Tel (213) 628-2184

RUBIN, MYRON L., b. Denver, Apr. 13, 1933; B.S., U. Denver, 1955, J.D., 1956; LL.M. in Taxation, N.Y. U., 1970. Admitted to Colo. bar, 1956, Calif. bar, 1959; individual practice law, Denver, 1959-69, Littleton, Colo., 1973—; tax officer trust dept. Colo. Nat. Bank, Denver, 1970-71; asso. firm Brenman, Sobol & Baum, Denver, 1971-72; instr. Arapahoe Community Coll., 1974-75. Chmn. Arapahoe Estate Planning Council, 1976. Mem. Arapahoe, Colo. bar assns., Denver Estate Planning Council, Greater Denver Tax Counsels Assn., Denver Tax Assn. Home: 350 S Krameria St Denver CO 80224 Office: 5601 S Broadway Suite 304 Littleton CO 80121 Tel (303) 795-2123

RUBIN, PETER JONATHAN, b. Bath, Maine, Apr. 10, 1945; A.B., Duke, 1967; J.D. magna cum laude, Harvard, 1970. Admitted to Maine bar, 1970, Mass. bar, 1970, U.S. Supreme Ct. bar, 1974; law clk. to judge U.S. Dist. Ct. Maine, 1970-71; partner firm Bernstein, Shur, Sawyer and Nelson, Portland, Maine, 1971—. Trustee Portland Soc. of Art, 1973-76. Mem. Maine State, Cumberland County (Maine), Am. bar assns., Am. Judicature Soc., Nat. Health Lawyers Assn. Home: 2 Cherry Circle Cape Elizabeth ME 04107 Office: One Monument Sq Portland ME 04111 Tel (207) 774-6291

RUBIN, SEYMOUR JEFFREY, b. Chgo., Apr. 6, 1914; B.A., U. Mich., 1935; LL.B. magna cum laude, Harvard, 1938, LL.M., 1939. Admitted to Ill. bar, 1939, D.C. bar, 1941; individual and asso. practice, Washington, 1948-75; prof. law Am. U., Washington, 1972—; mem. InterAm. Jud. Commn., 1974; U.S. rep. UN Commn. on Transnat. Corps., 1975; chief U.S. del. Marshall Plan Agreements, 1952; asst. adminstr. Mut. Security Adminstrn., Washington, 1952-53; gen. counsel AID, Washington, 1961-62; spl. ambassador to Bolivia, 1962; U.S. Minister to Devel. Assistance Commn., 1962-64; U.S. rep. UNCITRAL, 1968-70; chmn. adv. bd. Internat. Project, Center for Law and Social Policy, Washington, 1972. Mem. Am. Soc. Internat. Law (exec. v.p.), Council on Fgn. Relations, Am. Law Inst., Am. Bar Assn., Soc. Internat. Devel. Author: Private Foreign Investment, 1956; The Conscience of the Rich Nations — The Common Aid Effort and the Development Assistance Committee, 1966; (with others) The International Corporation, 1970; Global Companies, 1974; also articles. Recipient Sesquicentennial award U. Mich., 1967, Grand Silver medal Austria, 1967. Home: 1675 35th St NW Washington DC 20007 Office: 2223 Massachusetts Ave NW Washington DC 20008 Tel (202) 265-4313

RUBINOW, JAY ELLIOTT, b. Hartford, Conn., Feb. 27, 1912; A.B., Harvard, 1933, LL.B., 1937. Admitted to Conn. bar, 1938; practiced in Manchester, Conn., 1938-60; chief judge Circuit Ct., 1961-67; judge Conn. Superior Ct., 1967—; adminstr. Conn. Probate Ct., 1967-73. Mem. Hartford County, Conn., Am. bar assns. Tel (203) 643-5632

RUBINSON, ADOLPH ALLEN, b. Chgo., Dec. 2, 1910; Ph.B., U. Chgo., 1932, J.D. cum laude, 1934. Admitted to Ill. bar, 1934; mem. firm Adolph Allen Rubinson & Assos., Chgo., 1941-65; individual practice law, Chgo., 1965—. Bd. govs. City Club of Chgo., 1976. Mem. Chgo. Bar Assn. (chmn. atomic energy and space law com. 1964, com. sci. tech. and law 1971), Ill., Am. bar assns., U. Chgo. Law Sch. Alumni Assn. (dir. 1976). Contbr. articles to profl. jours.; asso. editor Chgo. Bar Record, 1941; legis. editor: U. Chgo. Law Rev., 1934. Home: 1002 Eastwood Rd Glencoe IL 60022 Office: One N LaSalle St Suite 1223 Chicago IL 60602 Tel (312) 782-9686

RUBINSTEIN, ALAN JAY, b. Akron, Ohio, June 13, 1941; B.A., U. Miami, 1963; J.D., U. Fla., 1965. Admitted to Fla. bar, 1965, U.S. Supreme Ct. bar, 1971; partner firm Goldberg, Rubinstein & Buckley, Ft. Myers, Fla., 1965—. Mem. Am. Bar Assn., Acad. Fla. Trial Lawyers, Assn. Trial Lawyers Am., Am. Arbitration Assn. Recipient Leadership award United Jewish Appeal, 1975. Office: 2201 Main St Fort Myers FL 33901 Tel (813) 334-1146

RUBINSTEIN, ARNOLD EDWARD, b. N.Y.C., Dec. 9, 1930; B.A., N.Y. U., 1951, LL.B., 1953. Admitted to N.Y. bar, 1955; asso. firm Jas. Maxwell Fassett, N.Y.C., 1955-56; individual practice law, N.Y.C., 1956—; arbitrator Civil Ct. City N.Y., 1975—. Mem. N.Y. County Lawyers Assn., Civil Ct. Arbitrators Assn., Am. Judges Assn. Home: 136 E 36th St New York City NY 10016 Office: 260 Madison Ave New York City NY 10016 Tel (212) 689-5470

RUBINSTEIN, LOUIS BARUCH, b. Providence, Dec. 5, 1908; B.A. with honors, Yale, 1931, LL.B., J.D., 1934. Admitted to D.C. bar, 1936, R.I. bar, 1938, U.S. Supreme Ct. bar, 1974; cons. atty. Mexican Claims Arbitration, U.S. Dept. State, Washington, 1934-39; individual practice law, Providence, 1939—; counsel to firm Zietz, Sonkin & Radin, Providence, 1948—; chief R.I. Div. Temporary Disability Ins., Providence, 1967-72; chief legal officer R.I. Dept. Employment Security, Providence, 1972—; participant legal com. Interstate Conf. Employment Security Agys., 1973-75; chmn. Legal Affairs Conf., 1973-74. Hon. life trustee Jewish Community Center R.I., Temple Emanuel, Providence; mem. legal com. Providence Charter Commn., 1939; sec. bd. dirs. Jewish Fedn. R.I., Providence, 1960—, sec., 1970-76; hon. pres. R.I. Council Jewish Nat. Fund, Providence, 1976, v.p. N.E. region, 1970—; bd. dirs. N.E. region Anti-Defamation League, 1968—. Mem. R.I. Bar Assn. (award merit 1976), Yale Club R.I. Contbr. articles to legal jours. Home: 9 Lincoln Ave Providence RI 02906 Office: 131 Wayland Ave Providence RI 02906 Tel (401) 274-1075

RUBINSTEIN, MICHAEL LEE, b. N.Y.C., Feb. 21, 1943; LL.B. with honors, Columbia, 1967. Admitted to N.Y., Alaska bars, 1967; law clk. Hon. Jay A. Rabinowitz, Asso. Justice Supreme Ct. Alaska, Fairbanks, 1967-68; asso. firm Hess, Segal, Popkin, Guterman, Pelz & Steiner, N.Y.C., 1968-70; atty. Alaska Pub. Defender Agency, Anchorage, 1970-71; partner firm Wagstaff, Rubinstein & Middleton, Anchorage, 1971-75; exec. dir. Alaska Judicial Council, Anchorage, 1975—; mem. advisory bd. Criminal Justice Center, U. Alaska; co-reporter, magistrate's advisory com. Supreme Ct. of Alaska. Commr. planning and zoning Municipality of Anchorage, 1975-76. Mem. Am. Bar Assn., Am. Soc. Criminology. Home: SRA Box 1580 H Anchorage AK 99507 Tel (907) 274-8942

RUBINTON, PETER D., b. N.Y.C., Aug. 17, 1936; A.B., U. Vt., 1958; J.D., St. John's U., 1961. Admitted to N.Y. bar, 1961, U.S. Supreme Ct. bar, 1967; asso. firm Raphael, Searles & Visch, N.Y.C., 1962-63; asso. firm Meyer & Wexler, Smithtown, N.Y., 1963-70, partner, 1970-73; partner firm Goldstein & Rubinton, Huntington,

N.Y., 1973—; arbitrator Am. Arbitration Assn., 1970—. Mem. bd. edn. Sch. Dist. #10 towns of Huntington and Smithtown, 1966-68; bd. dirs. Suffolk County Multiple Sclerosis Soc., 1974-76; chmn. atty.'s div. Suffolk County United Jewish Appeal, 1976—. Mem. Suffolk County (dir. 1976—, chmn. dist. ct. com. 1971-74, mem. judiciary com. 1975-76), N.Y. State, Am. bar assns., Nassau-Suffolk Trial Lawyers Assn. Home: 66 Flower Hill Rd Huntington NY 11743 Tel (516) 421-9051

RUBRIGHT, CHARLES RUSSELL, b. S. Bend, Ind., Jan. 29, 1947; B.S., Ind. State U., 1969; J.D., Ind. U., 1973. Admitted to Ind. bar, 1974; gen. counsel, mediator Ind. Edn. Employment Relations Bd., Indpls., 1973-74; asso. firm Bose, McKinney & Evans, Indpls., 1974—. Mem. Am., Ind., Indpls. bar assns., Soc. of Profls. in Dispute Resolution, Indsl. Relations Research Assn. Home: 6030 E 30th St Apt 1-A Indianapolis IN 46219 Office: 1100 First Federal Bldg Indianapolis IN 46204 Tel (317) 637-5353

RUBRIGHT, JAMES A., b. Phila., Dec. 17, 1946; B.A., Yale, 1969; J.D., U. of Va., 1972. Admitted to Ga. bar, 1972; asso. mem. firm King & Spalding, 1972—. Mem. Am., Atlanta, Ga., bar assns. Home: 2662 Hyde Manor Dr Atlanta GA 30327 Office: 2500 Trust Co Tower Atlanta GA 30303

RUBRIGHT, WILBUR HARRY, b. Frackville, Pa., Apr. 11, 1922; Ph.B., Dickinson Coll., 1943, J.D., 1948. Admitted to Pa. bar, 1948; individual practice law, Frackville, 1949—; legal sec. Superior Ct. Pa., 1957—; exec. sec. Pa. Self-Insurers Assn., 1966—; solicitor N. Union Twp., Butler Twp., Gordon Borough; v.p. Broad Mt. Manor. Former pres. Frackville Free Pub. Library; mem. spl. adv. com. on workmen's compensation Gov. of Pa. Mem. Am., Pa., Schuylkill County bar assns. Home: 620 Westwood Ln Frackville PA 17931 Office: Box 9 Law Bldg Frackville PA 17931 Tel (717) 874-1109

RUBTCHINSKY, IRA PAUL, b. N.Y.C., Apr. 12, 1944; B.S., State U. N.Y. at Albany, 1965; J.D., Union U., 1968. Admitted to N.Y. bar, 1968; asso. firm Tarricone, Bilgore, Weltman & Silver, and predecessor, Rochester, N.Y., 1968-73; asso. counsel N.Y. State United Tchrs., Albany, 1973—. Mem. Am., N.Y. State (sec. spl. com. on availability of legal services 1976-77) bar assns. Home: 1807 Whispering Pines Way Schenectady NY 12303 Office: New York State United Teachers 80 Wolf Rd Albany NY 12205 Tel (518) 459-5400

RUCKER, AARON EDWARD, b. Victor, Colo., Jan. 4, 1896; A.B., U. Calif., Berkeley, 1919. Admitted to Alaska bar, 1920, Calif. bar, 1928; U.S. commr., Seward, Alaska, 1920-27; claims mgr. Continental Ins. Co., Pacific Coast office, San Francisco, 1927-42; individual practice law, San Rafael, Calif., 1942—; spl. asst. atty. gen. State of Calif., 1967-68. Mem. Marin County Bar Assn. Editor: Alaska Pathfinder, monthly mag., 1919-27, Seward Daily Newspaper, 1920-27. Home: Box 428 Kentfield CA 94904 Office: 819 A St San Rafael CA 94901 Tel (415) 456-3382

RUCKER, HAROLD JAMES, b. Raducah, Ky., Dec. 8, 1921; A.B., U. Ky., 1947; J.D., 1949. Admitted to Ky. bar, 1949, Tex. bar, 1950, U.S. Supreme Ct. bar, 1957; with land dept. Shell Oil Co., Midland, Tex., 1949-50; mem. firm Perkins, German, Mims & Bell, Midland, 1951-54; asso. firm Perkins & Bezoni, Midland, 1955-56; partner firm Rucker & Rassman, Midland, 1958-60; individual practice law, Midland, 1960—; sec. Chancellor Chair Co., Master Rentals, Inc., Airline Mobile Home Park, Inc. Dir. Midland County (Tex.) Child Welfare Unit, 1957-58; pres., bd. dirs. Am. Cancer Soc., Midland, 1960-61, Midland YMCA, 1962-66; pres. SW area council YMCA, 1965-66; pres., bd. dirs. Midland Diagnostic Cancer Clinic, 1961-62; pres., bd. trustees Trinity Sch., Midland; trustee St. Andrew's (Tenn.) Sch. Mem. State Bar Tex., Midland County Bar Assn., Am. Judicature Soc., Phi Alpha Delta. Named Boss of Yr., Legal Secs. Assn., 1963; named hon. Ky. Col., 1974. Office: 716 First National Bank Bldg Midland TX 79701 Tel (915) 682-7377

RUCKER, JERRY DON, b. Dallas, Jan. 10, 1942; B.A., So. Meth. U., 1964, LL.B., 1967; curso de verano diploma Universidad Autonoma de Mexico, 1967. Admitted to Tex. bar, 1967; JAG, USN Subic Bay Philippines Law Center, 1968-70; since practiced in Dallas, with firm Akin, Gump, Strauss, Hauer & Feld, 1970-72; spl. counsel Braniff Airways, Dallas/Fort Worth Airport, 1972—; individual practice law, 1972—; gen. counsel Rucker Constrn. Co., Inc., 1974—; gen. counsel Braniff Internat. Resort Properties, 1973-74, mem. airline adv. bd. Dallas/Fort Worth Airport representing Braniff, 1972-74. Mem. City of Dallas Urban Rehab. Standards Bd., 1975-76; mem. Dallas City Planning Commn., 1976—. Mem. Tex., Dallas bar assns., Am. Arbitration Assn. Contbr. articles to legal jours. Home: 8711 Midway Rd Dallas TX 75209 Office: 635 Frito Lay Bldg Dallas TX 75245 Tel (214) 350-9076

RUDASILL, A.J., b. Clinton, Ill., Dec. 31, 1919; A.B., U. Ill., 1941, J.D., 1947. Admitted to Ill. bar, 1947; partner firm Herrick, Rudasill and Moss, Clinton, 1947—; state's atty. DeWitt County (Ill.), 1948-52. Mem. DeWitt, Ill., Am. bar assns. Home: 310 S Center St Clinton IL 61727 Office: 118 Warner Ct Clinton IL 61726 Tel (217) 935-3121

RUDD, ELDON, b. Camp Verde, Ariz., July 15, 1920; B.A. in Edn., Ariz. State U., 1947; J.D., U. Ariz., 1949. Admitted to Ariz. bar, U.S. Supreme Ct. bar; spl. agt. FBI, Pitts., Washington, Phoenix and P.R., 1950-70; asst. legal attache, Mex., Guatemala, El Salvador, Honduras, Nicaragua, Costa Rica; legal attache, Argentina; supr. Maricopa County (Ariz.), 1972-77; mem. 95th Congress from 4th Ariz. Dist., 1977—; mem. Gov's. Adv. Council Intergovtl. Relations. Bd. dirs. Ariz. Mex. Commn., Nat. Assn. Counties, western region, 1973, 74, 75; exec. bd. Ariz. Assn. Counties; ex-officio bd. mem. Scottsdale C. of C. Mem. Fed. (pres.), Ariz. State, Maricopa County, Scottsdale bar assns., Soc. Former Spl. Agts. FBI (western region v.p. 1973-74). Office: 1428 Longworth House Office Bldg Washington DC 20515

RUDDY, TIMOTHY FREDERICK, b. St. Louis, Mo., July 9, 1938; B.S., So. Ill. U., 1960; J.D., Washington U., 1963. Instr. bus. law So. Ill. U., Edwardsville, 1963-65; admitted to Mo. bar, 1963, Ind. bar, 1965; Lawyers Title Ins. Corp., 1965-66; individual practice law, Cape Girardeau, Mo., 1966—. Mem. Am., Mo., Cape Girardeau County bar assns. Home: 1222 Normal St Cape Girardeau MO 63701 Office: 226 N Sprigg St Cape Girardeau MO 63701 Tel (314) 335-0111

RUDEN, PAUL MICHAEL, b. St. Louis, Aug. 17, 1942; B.A. cum laude, Yale, 1964; J.D., Harvard, 1967. Admitted to D.C. bar, 1968, Va. bar, 1973; trial atty. CAB, Washington, 1967-69; partner firm Bowen & Ruden, Washington, 1969-70; asso. firm Wilner & Scheiner, Washington, 1971-74, partner, 1975—. Pres., Reston (Va.) Community Assn., 1972-73; chmn. Fairfax County (Va.) Com. to review commns., bds. and authorities, 1976; vice-chmn. Fairfax County Charter Study Com., 1976—. Mem. Am. Bar Assn. Recipient James Gordon Bennett Prize for Thesis, Yale, 1964; mem. panel briefing conference, Bureau Nat. Affairs, 1971. Home: 2241 Castlerock Sq Apt 22-C Reston VA 22091 Office: 2021 L St NW Washington DC 20036 Tel (202) 293-7800

RUDER, DAVID STURTEVANT, b. Wausau, Wis., May 25, 1929; B.A., Williams Coll., 1951; J.D., U. Wis., 1957. Admitted to Wis. bar, 1957, Ill. bar, 1962; asso. firm Quarles & Brady, Milw., 1957-61; prof. law Northwestern U., Chgo., 1961—, dean, 1977—; faculty U. Pa. Law Sch., 1971, Salzburg Seminar in Am. Studies, 1976; of counsel firm Schiff, Hardin & Waite, 1971-76; cons. Am. Law Inst. Fed. Securities Code Project; planning dir. Corporate Counsel Inst.; lectr. panel participant in programs conducted by Am. Law Inst., Corporate Counsel Inst., Am. Soc. Corporate Secs., Southwestern Legal Found., Fed. Bar Assn., various law schs., state bar assns. Mem. Am. (council sect. corp., banking and bus. law 1967-71), Ill., Wis., Chgo. (chmn. securities law com. 1967) bar assns., Order of Coif, Phi Beta Kappa. Editor-in-chief Wis. Law Rev., 1957; contbr. articles to profl. jours. Home: 680 Walden Rd Winnetka IL 60093 Office: 357 E Chicago Ave Chicago IL 60611 Tel (312) 649-8460

RUDES, NATHANIAL SAMSON, b. N.Y.C., Mar. 17, 1907; LL.M., Bklyn. Law Sch., 1930. Admitted to N.Y. State bar, 1934, U.S. Dist. Ct. bar, 1950; village counsel Village of Island Park (N.Y.), 1952-54, Village of Lynbrook (N.Y.), 1957-63; asso. police justice Village of Lynbrook, 1954-57. Mem. Nassau County Bar Assn. Home: 14 Crab Ave Lynbrook NY 11563 Office: 149 Broadway Lynbrook NY 11563 Tel (516) 593-7100

RUDLOFF, WILLIAM JOSEPH, b. Bonne Terre, Mo., Feb. 19, 1941; A.B., Western Ky. State Coll., 1961; postgrad. (NDEA fellow) U. Nebr., 1961-62; J.D., Vanderbilt U., 1965. Admitted to Ky. and Tenn. bars, 1965, U.S. Supreme Ct. bar, 1975; partner firm Harlin, Parker & Rudloff, Bowling Green, Ky., 1971—; U.S. Magistrate, Western Dist. Ky., 1971-75. Pres. Warren County Tb Assn., 1971-75. Mem. Am., Ky. State, Bowling Green bar assns. Home: 517 Ashmoor Dr Bowling Green KY 42101 Office: 519 E 10th St Bowling Green KY 42101 Tel (502) 842-5611

RUDSTEIN, DAVID STEWART, b. Leeds, England, Sept. 27, 1946; B.S., U. Ill., 1968, LL.M., 1975; J.D., Northwestern U., 1971. Admitted to Ill. bar, 1971; teaching asst. U. Ill. Coll. Law, 1971-72; law clerk Justice Walter V. Schaefer, Supreme Ct. Ill., Chgo., 1972-73; asst. prof. law Ill. Inst. Tech./Chgo. Kent Coll., 1973-76, asso. prof., 1976—. Mem. Soc. Am. Law Tchrs., Ill. State Bar Assn., Chgo. Council Lawyers, Order of the Coif. Office: 77 S Wacker Dr Chicago IL 60606 Tel (312) 567-5047

RUDY, ELMER CLYDE, b. Elgin, Ill., Apr. 10, 1931; B.A., Beloit (Wis.) Coll., 1953; grad. U. Mich. Law Sch., 1958. Admitted to Ill. bar, 1958; asso. firm Williams, McCarthy, Kinley, Rudy & Picha, and predecessors, Rockford, Ill., 1958-64, partner, 1965—. Bd. dirs. Booker Washington Center, Rockford, 1962-68; bd. dirs., pres., treas. Rockcrance Meml. Home for Children, Rockford, 1973—; bd dirs. Rockford Mus. Assn., 1973—. Mem. Am., Ill., Winnebago County bar assns. Home: 5024 Braewild Rd Rockford IL 61107 Office: 400 Talcott Bldg Rockford IL 61101 Tel (815) 962-7714

RUDY, JOHN FORNEY, II, b. Orlando, Fla., Aug. 25, 1938; A.B., U. N.C., 1960; LL.B., Am. U., Washington, 1963. Admitted to D.C. bar, 1964, Fla. bar, 1971; asso. firm Scrivener, Parker & Clarke, Washington, 1960-63, Williams & Wadden, Washington, 1964; served with JAGC, USAF, 1964-67; asst. U.S. atty., Washington, 1967-70, 71-74; asso. firm Wadden, Wall & Rudy, 1970-71, Macfarlane, Ferguson, Allison & Kelly, Tampa, Fla., 1974—. Dir. Civic Action Vietnam, 1966-67; polit. advisor RUN, 1966-67; v.p., mem. bd. Nat. Capital Area Boy Scouts Am., also Gulf Ridge Council, Fla., 1969-76; dir. Am. Kor-Asian Found., 1975—. Mem. Am., Fla., D.C., Fed., Hillsborough County bar assns., Asst. U.S. Attys. Assn. Recipient Silver Anvil award for outstanding performance in internat. pub. relations, U.S. Govt., 1968; contbr. articles to profl. jours. Home: 5011 Shore Crest Circle Tampa FL 33609 Office: 512 Florida Ave PO Box 1531 Tampa FL 33601 Tel (813) 223-2411

RUEBHAUSEN, OSCAR MELICK, b. N.Y.C., Aug. 28, 1912; A.B. summa cum laude, Dartmouth, 1934; LL.B., cum laude, Yale, 1937; admitted to N.Y. bar, 1938; assoc. firm Debevoise, Stevenson, Plimpton & Page, N.Y.C., 1937-42, atty. Lend Lease Adminstrn., Washington, 1942-44; gen. counsel OSRD, Washington, 1944-46; partner firm Debevoise, Plimpton, Lyons & Gates, N.Y.C., 1946—; counsel Internat. Devel. Adv. Bd., Washington, 1950-51; dir. Equitable Life Assurance Soc., U.S., Nat. Starch & Chem. Corp.; spl. advisor atomic energy to gov. N.Y. State, 1959; vice-chmn. N.Y. State adv. com. on atomic energy, 1959-62; mem. Pres's Task force on Sci. Policy, 1969-70, pres.'s Sci. Adv. Com. Panel on Chems. and Health, 1970-72; mem. commn. on Critical Choices for Am., 1973—; chmn. UN Day, N.Y. State, 1962; chmn. Spl. N.Y. Com. on Ins. Holding Cos., 1967-68, sec., dir. Fund Peaceful Atomic Devel., Inc., 1954-72; dir. Carrie Chapman Catt Meml. Fund., 1948-58; past chmn. trustees Bennington Coll.; trustee Hudson Inst., Inc., 1961-71; trustee Russell Sage Found., chmn. bd. 1965—; vice chmn. N.Y.C. Univ. Constrn. Fund, 1966-69. Mem. Am., N.Y. State bar assns., Yale Law Schl. Assn. (exec. com. and pres. 1960-62, chmn. 1962-64), Assn. Bar City N.Y., Council Fgn. Relations, Phi Beta Kappa, Sigma Phi Epsilon, Order of the Coif. Contbr. articles to profl. jours. Home: 450 E 52d St New York City NY 10022 Office: 299 Park Ave New York City NY 10017 Tel (212) 752-6400

RUECKHAUS, MELVIN DIXON, b. Red Bank, N.J., Apr. 4, 1914; B.Th., Georgetown U., 1933, J.D., 1936. Admitted to D.C. bar, 1936, N.Mex. bar, 1936; individual practice law, Albuquerque, 1936—. Home: 4138 Cor Dr Albuquerque NM 87102 Office: 319 7th St NW Albuquerque NM 87102 Tel (505) 243-1739

RUEHMANN, ALBERT CONRAD, III, b. St. Louis, June 18, 1943; B.A., Ga. State U., 1964; LL.B., U. Ga., 1967; LL.M., Harvard, 1968. Admitted to Ga. bar, 1966, Fed. bar, 1972; asso. firm Epstein & Salloway, Boston, 1968; capt. U.S. Army Judge Adv. Gen.'s Corps, Ft. Gordon, Ga., 1968-72; asso. firm Kilpatrick, Cody, Rogers, McClatchey & Reganstein, Atlanta, 1972—. Mem. Am., Ga. bar assns. Contbr. articles to legal jours. Office: 3100 Equitable Bldg 100 Peach Tree Ln Atlanta GA 30303 Tel (404) 522-3100

RUETER, BRICE FREDRIC, b. Holdrege, Nebr., Feb. 25, 1944; B.A., U. Nebr., Lincoln, 1966, J.D., 1971. Admitted to Nebr. bar, 1971; individual practice law, Wauneta, Nebr., 1971—; city atty. Wauneta, 1972—; mem. firm Hines and Hines, Benkelman, Nebr., 1972-76; v.p., dir. Midwestern Fin. Assos., Inc., Oklahoma City, 1976—. Mem. moot ct. council U. Nebr., 1970-71; pres. Wauneta Comml. Club, 1971-73. Mem. Nebr. Bar Assn., Nebr. Assn. Trial Lawyers. Home: Rueter Land and Cattle Co Wauneta NE 69045 Office: 122 Tecumseh Ave Wauneta NE 69045 Tel (308) 394-5732

RUFE, JOHN JACOB, b. Sellersville, Pa., Dec. 12, 1939; A.B., Lafayette Coll., 1962; LL.B., Duke, 1965. Admitted to Pa. bar, 1965; law clk. to Hon. Edward G. Biester, pres. judge, Ct. Common Pleas, Bucks County, Pa., 1966-68; asst. dist. atty. Bucks County, Doylestown, Pa., 1968-71; practice in Sellersville, Pa., 1965—; partner firm Rufe & Lechowicz, Sellersville. Pres. Bucks County Legal Aid Soc., 1971-72; pres. Pennridge Jaycees, 1975-76; bd. dirs. Bucks County Assn. for Retarded Children, v.p., 1977—. Mem. Pa., Bucks County (dir. 1976—) bar assns., Bucks County Estate Planning Council. Home: 509 S Fifth St Perkasie PA 18944 Office: 5 Temple Ave Sellersville PA 18960 Tel (215) 257-9268

RUFER, GERALD STEPHEN, b. Fergus Falls, Minn., Oct. 8, 1915; LL.B., U. Minn., 1940. Admitted to Minn. bar, 1940, U.S. Supreme Ct. bar, 1974; mem. firm Gillette & Meagher, Mpls., 1940-41, firm Rufer, Hefte, Pemberton, Schulze & Sorlie, Fergus Falls, 1946—; sec. Minn. Bd. Law Examiners, 1960—. Mem. Am., Minn. State bar assns., Am. Coll. Trial Lawyers, Am. Bd. Trial Advocates (advocate). Home: Rural Route 5 Fergus Falls MN 56537 Office: 110 N Mill St Fergus Falls MN 56537 Tel (218) 736-5493

RUFF, JOAN ROBERTA, b. Clay Center, Kans., Sept. 17, 1947; B.S. in Journalism, U. Kans., 1970, J.D., 1973; LL.M., N.Y. U., 1975. Admitted to Kans. bar, 1973; mem. firm Hackler, Londerholm, Speer, Vader & Austin, Olathe, Kans., 1972—. Bd. govs. Sch. Law, U. Kans., 1976—, mem. univ. devel. commn., 1977—. Mem. Am., Kans., Johnson County bar assns., Phi Alpha Delta. Home: 6601 Willow Ln Mission Hills KS 66208 Office: 201 N Cherry St Olathe KS 66061 Tel (913) 782-1000

RUFFIN, EDMUND SUMTER, III, b. Pitts., Mar. 6, 1934; A.B., Yale, 1956; LL.B., U. Va., 1961. Admitted to Pa. bar, 1962; partner firm Thorp, Reed & Armstrong, Pitts., 1970—. Mem. Allegheny County, Pa., Am. bar assns. Home: 540 Briar Cliff Rd Pittsburgh PA 15221 Office: 2900 Grant Bldg Pittsburgh PA 15219 Tel (412) 288-77S4

RUFFIN, JOHN H., JR., b. Waynesboro, Ga., Dec. 23, 1934; B.A., Morehouse Coll., 1957; LL.B., Howard U., 1960. Admitted to Ga. bar, 1961; partner firms Ruffin & Watkins, Augusta, 1961-63, Ruffin & Brown, Augusta, 1976—. Former mem. bd. Augusta Opportunities Industrialization Center; chmn. bd. Central Savannah River Area Bus. League, 1970-75; mem. adv. council Legal Services Corp. for State Ga., 1976-77; mem. Ga. adv. com. U.S. Civil Rights Commn.; v.p. Voter Edn. Project, Atlanta. Mem. Nat., Augusta bar assns., Ga. Assn. Criminal Def. Lawyers (dir. 1976-77), Ga. (pres. 1975-76), Augusta (gen. counsel) confs. Black lawyers, Nat. Lawyers Guild. Office: 1101 11th St Augusta GA 30901 Tel (404) 724-8891

RUFFIN, ROGER SHERMAN, b. San Diego, May 18, 1927; A.B. cum laude with distinction in econs., San Diego State Coll., 1950; J.D., Stanford, 1953. Admitted to Calif. bar, 1954, U.S. Supreme Ct. bar, 1972; asso. firm Luce, Forward, Kunzel & Scripps, San Diego, 1954-58; partner firm Reed, Brockway & Ruffin, San Diego, 1958-61; judge Municipal Ct., San Diego, 1961-65; judge Superior Ct., San Diego, 1965-71; partner firm Ruffin & Whalen, San Diego, 1971-75; individual practice law, San Francisco, 1975—; instr. Law Sch. U. San Diego, 19S6; lectr. philosophy dept. U. Calif., San Diego, 1967-72; lectr. Calif. Coll. Trial Judges U. Calif., Berkeley, 1968-69. Chmn. Corrections Commn. of Community Welfare Council, Law and Justice Task Force of San Diego Urban Coalition; v.p. San Diego chpt. Am. Psychology-Law Soc.; pres. San Diego Criminal Def. Lawyers Club, 1974; trustee San Diego Bail Fund and Bd. Visitors of U. San Diego Law Sch. Mem. Bar Assn. San Francisco, Calif. State Bar, Lawyers Club of San Francisco, San Diego County Bar Assn., San Diego Barristers Club, Calif. Attys. Criminal Justice. Recipient Civil Libertarian Award, San Diego Chpt. ACLU, 1971; contbr. articles to legal publs. Office: 111 Pine St Suite 1600 San Francisco CA 94111 Tel (415) 397-0860

RUFFO, PHILIP JOSEPH, b. Bklyn., Sept. 20, 1916; LL.B., Bklyn. Sch., 1947. Admitted to N.Y. bar, 1947; individual practice law, N.Y.C., 1947-62; adj. prof. law Pace U., 1973—; adj. asst. prof. law N.Y. Law Sch., 1976—; counsel N.Y.C. Labor Dept., 1962-67, acting commr. labor, 1967; gen. counsel, N.Y.C. Office Collective Bargaining, 1973; legal advisor N.Y.C. Bd. Higher Edn., 1973-74. Mem. N.J. Pub. Employment Relations Commn., N.Y. Pub. Employment Relations Bd. Mem. Bklyn. bar assn., Am. Arbitration Assn. (labor panel), N.Y. Mediation Bd., Indsl. Relations Research Assn. Contbr. articles to profl. jours. Home: 20 Harvard Ave Rockville Centre NY 11570 Office: Pace U Pace Plaza New York City NY 10038 Tel (212) 285-3349

RUGE, NEIL MARSHALL, b. Washington, Dec. 28, 1913; A.B., Stanford, 1935; J.D., U. Calif., Berkeley, 1938; postgrad. Harvard Bus. Sch., 1947. Admitted to Calif. bar, 1938, U.S. Supreme Ct. bar, 1962; asso. firm Russell & Heid, Tulare, Calif., 1939-41; adjudicator VA, San Francisco, 1946; commd. fgn. service officer Dept. State, 1947, 3d sec., Palermo, Italy and Casablanca, Morocco, 1947-52, 2d sec., 1952-59, 1st sec., 1959-68; prof. bus. law and real estate law Calif. State U., Chico, 1969—; pros. atty. Casablanca Consular Ct., 1950-53, judge, 1953-55. Mem. Fgn. Service Assn., Res. Officers Assn., Phi Beta Kappa, Phi Alpha Delta, Delta Sigma Pi. Home: 936 Bryant Ave Chico CA 95926 Office: Calif State U Chico CA 95926 Tel (916) 895-5375

RUGGIERO, DANIEL PAUL, b. Fremont, Ohio, Jan. 2, 1947; B.A., Miami U., 1969; J.D., U. Toledo, 1973. Admitted to bar, 1973, U.S. Ct. of Claims bar, 1975, U.S. Supreme Ct. bar, 1977; asst. atty. gen. Ohio, Columbus, 1973—. Mem. Am., Ohio, Columbus bar assns., Phi Alpha Delta, Theta Chi. Author: Ohio Appraisers Guide to Compensability in Eminent Domain, 1975. Home: 61 Whipple Pl Westerville OH 43081 Office: 30 E Broad St Columbus OH 43215 Tel (614) 466-2872

RUGGLES, RUDY LAMONT, b. Phila., Jan. 10, 1909; student U. Cin., 1926-27, Harvard Coll., 1927-31; Harvard scholar Geneva Sch. Internat. Studies, 1929; J.D., Boston U., 1934. Admitted to Ill. bar, 1935, U.S. Supreme Ct. bar, 1960; asso. firm Isham, Lincoln & Beale, Chgo., 1935-42; partner firm Chadwell, Kayser, Ruggles, McGee & Hastings, and predecessors, Chgo., 1946-75, of counsel, 1976—; regional atty. OPA, 1942-43; spl. counsel Navy Purchasing and Contract Termination, 1944-46. Bd. dirs., chmn. legal aid com. United Charities of Chgo., 1962-73; past chmn. lawyers div. Chgo. Crusade of Mercy; mem. citizens bd. U. Chgo., 1963—, mem. vis. com. to humanities div., 1963-74; bd. dirs. Evanston Hosp., 1965-75; trustee Newberry Library, Chgo., 1964—; bd. overseers com. to visit Harvard Coll., 1964-70, Harvard Div. Sch., 1969-75. Fellow Am. Bar Found.; mem. Am., 7th Fed. Circuit, Ill., Chgo. bar assns., Am. Judicature

Soc., Am. Soc. Internat. Law, Legal Club Chgo., Law Club Chgo. Recipient award for distinguished service to profession, community and youth of Am., Monticello Coll., 1959. Home: 1115 Mohawk Rd Wilmette IL 60091 Office: 8500 Sears Tower 233 S Wacker Dr Chicago IL 60606 Tel (312) 876-2100

RUHLY, JAMES KING, b. Detroit, Apr. 10, 1943; B.A., Mich. State U., 1965; J.D., U. Wis., 1968. Admitted to Wis. bar, 1968, U.S. Supreme Ct. bar, 1975; asso. firm Melli, Shiels, Walker & Pease and predecessors, Madison, Wis., 1968—. Mem. Am., Wis., Dane County bar assns., Wis. Sch. Attys. Assn. Home: 4210 Yuma Dr Madison WI 53711 Office: 119 Monona Ave Madison WI 53703 Tel (608) 257-4812

RUIS, RONALD HAROLD, II, b. Plant City, Fla., Mar. 9, 1946; A.B. in Polit. Sci., Duke, 1968, J.D., 1971. Admitted to N.C. bar, 1971, U.S. Supreme Ct. bar, 1976; asso. firm A.H. Borland, Durham, N.C., 1971-73; partner firm Harriss, Ruis, Mulligan, & Embree, Durham, 1973—; adj. prof. law Duke, 1973. Mem. Am., N.C. assns. trial lawyers, Am., N.C. State, 14th Jud. Dist. bar assns. Recipient Merit award The Darrow Soc., 1971. Office: PO Box 994 Durham NC 27702 Tel (919) 682-5588

RULAND, EDWIN GRANT, b. Denver, May 11, 1936; B.A., Colo. Coll., 1958; LL.B., So. Methodist U., 1961. Admitted to Colo. bar; asso. firm Groves, Dufford, Nelson & Spiecker, Denver, 1961-63; partner firm Dufford & Ruland, Denver, 1963-73; judge Colo. Ct. of Appeals, Denver, 1973—. Bd. dirs. Bridge House Rehab. Center, 1963-66; pres., bd. dirs. Hill Top House Rehab. Center, 1968; chmn. house of dels. Colo. Easter Seal Soc., 1970. Mem. Colo., Mesa County (pres. 1970), Denver bar assns. Contbr. articles in field to legal jours. Office: 2 E 14th Ave #335 Denver CO 80203 Tel (303) 861-1111

RULEY, DANIEL AVERY, JR., b. Parkersburg, W.Va., Feb. 28, 1928; A.B., W. Va. U., 1952, LL.B., 1955. Admitted to W.Va. bar, 1955; asso. firm William B. Hoff, Parkersburg, 1955-56; partner firm Hoff, Moore & Ruley, Parkersburg, 1956-70, Wilson, Ruley & Hill, Parkersburg, 1970-74, Morris & Ruley, Parkersburg, 1974—; city solicitor City of Parkersburg, 1962-65; judge W.Va. Ct. Claims, 1976—. Mem. Parkersburg Police Civil Service Commn., 1958-59; charter bd. City of Parkersburg, 1961; chmn. Wood County chpt. ARC, 1967; liaison officer U.S. Mil. Acad., 1971—. Mem. Am., W.Va., Fed., Wood County (past pres.) bar assns., W.Va. State Bar (past bd. govs.), Am. Trial Lawyers Assn., Am. Judicature Soc. Home: 2718 Riverview Dr Parkersburg WV 26101 Office: 620 Juliana St Parkersburg WV 26101 Tel (304) 422-6463

RUMBAUGH, RICHARD LEE, b. Akron, Ohio, June 25, 1941; B.S. in B.A., U. Akron, 1964, J.D., 1971. Admitted to Ohio bar, 1971; with IRS, Cleve., 1971-73; individual practice law, Salineville, Ohio, 1973-76; sr. mem. Rumbaugh & DeNicola, Salineville, 1976—. Mem. Am., Ohio, Columbiana County, Jefferson County, Fed. bar assns. Home: 9021 Avon Rd NE Salineville OH 43945 Office: 121 W Main St Salineville OH 43945 Tel (216) 679-2918

RUMRELL, RICHARD GARY, b. Tampa, Fla., Nov. 30, 1945; B.A., U. South Fla., 1967; J.D. with honors, Fla. State U., 1970. Admitted to Fla. bar, 1971, D.C. bar, 1976; congl. intern U.S. Congress, 1966; legis. intern Fla. Legislature, 1968-69; staff dir. elections com. Fla. Ho. of Reps., 1971; adminstrv. asst. Fla. State Senator Lawton Chiles of Fla., 1967; asst. state atty. 4th Jud. Circuit Fla., 1971-74; mem. firm Smathers & Thompson, Jacksonville, Fla., 1974—. Chmn. atty. div. United Way, Jacksonville, 1976; mem. Jacksonville Council Citizen Involvement; bd. dirs., sec. Mental Health Clinic, Camp Fire Girls; bd. dirs., v.p. Willing Hands, Jacksonville. Mem. Am., Jacksonville bar assns., Am. Judicature Soc. Office: 3103 Independent Sq Jacksonville FL 32202 Tel (904) 354-4030

RUNDELL, EDWARD EUGENE, b. Alexandria, La., Jan. 21, 1944; B.A., La. Poly. U., 1965, M.A., 1966; J.D., U. Tex., 1970, Ph.D., 1973. Admitted to Tex. bar, 1970, La. bar, 1974; asso. firm Stafford, Pitts & Stafford, 1974-75; partner firm Gold, Little, Simon, Weems & Bruser, Alexandria, 1976—. Mem. State Bar La., State Bar Tex., Am. Bar Assn., Def. Research Inst., La. Assn. Def. Counsel. Home: 4709 Whitehall Blvd Alexandria LA 71301 Office: 620 Murray St Alexandria LA 71301 Tel (318) 445-6471

RUNYAN, HARLEY LEE, b. Bass Lake, Ind., Feb. 25, 1932; J.D., U. Calif., Los Angeles, 1968. Admitted to Mass. bar, 1969, U.S. Supreme Ct. bar, 1969; individual practice law, Springfield, Mass., 1969—. Commr. Civic Center, Springfield, 1972-74; chmn. Republican city com., Springfield, 1973-76. Mem. Hampden County Bar Assn. Office: 95 State St Springfield MA 01103 Tel (413) 788-9173

RUPERT, JOHN EDWARD, b. Cleve., Oct. 19, 1927; A.B. in Econs., Cornell U., 1949, LL.B., 1951, J.D., 1969; grad., Sch. Savings and Loan Ind. U., 1958. Admitted to Ohio bar, 1951; with JAGC USAF, 1951-53; with Broadview Savs. and Loan Co., Cleve., 1953—, exec. v.p., sec., 1964-74, mng. officer, 1965—, pres., 1974—; pres., chief exec. officer Broadview Fin. Corp., holding co. for Broadview Savs. and Loan Co. and St. Clair Savs. Assn., also officer and/or dir. of various subsidiaries. Trustee WVIZ-TV, 1971—, Musical Arts Assn., Cleve., 1971—, Cleve. Automobile Club, 1972—; bd. dirs. West Side YMCA, Cleve., 1961—; trustee West Shore Concerts, Cleve., 1961—, pres., 1966-68; bd. dirs. Real Property Inventory of Met. Cleve., 1970—, pres., 1976; mem. Lakewood (Ohio) Bd. Edn., 1971—, pres., 1975; mem. Cornell U. Adv. Council, 1970—, pres., 1977; pres. Cleve. Interfaith Housing Corp., 1972—. Mem. Am., Cleve. bar assns., Cleve. Real Estate Bd. (affiliate 1955—), Northeastern Ohio (pres. 1971), Ohio (exec. com. 1969—, 1st v.p. 1973), U.S. (legis. com.) savings and loan leagues, Am. Savs. and Loan Inst. (pres. Cleve. chpt. 83 1963-64, nat. pres. 1970), Delta Kappa Epsilon, Phi Delta Phi. Home: 18129 W Clifton Rd Lakewood OH 44107 Office: 4221 Pearl Rd Cleveland OH 44109 Tel (216) 351-2200

RUPP, GEORGE WELLINGTON, b. Aurora, Ill., May 5, 1895; B.S. in Elec. Engring., U. Wash., 1921, E.E., 1928, LL.B., 1954, J.D., 1956. Telephone engr. Dept. Pub. Works, Washington, 1921-26, chief engr., 1926-29; cons. engr. in Seattle, and fgn. countries, 1929-31; asst. to mgr. Puget Sound Power and Light Co., 1931-35; engr. The Pactelatel Co., Seattle, 1935-49; cons. engr. fgn. countries, 1949—; admitted to Wash. State bar, 1954; individual practice law, Seattle, 1954—. Commdr. VFW, Washington State, 1942-43; chmn. Seattle-King County Municipal League coms., 1930-60; mem. State appointed vets. coms., 1952—. Fellow ASCE; mem. IEEE, Wash. State Bar Assn., Tau Beta Pi. Office: PO Box 951 Seattle WA 98111 Tel (206) 283-4131

RUPPERT, FRANCIS LAWRENCE, b. Bklyn., Feb. 23, 1933; B.S. in Mining Engring., Mo. Sch. Mines, 1959; J.D., St. Louis U., 1966. Admitted to Mo. bar, 1966, U.S. Supreme Ct. bar, 1970; real estate atty. Am. Investment Co., St. Louis, 1966; partner firm Ruppert & Schlueter, St. Louis, 1967—; instr. mil. law St. Louis U. Sch. Law, 1970—; gen. counsel Mo. chpt. ACLU, 1973—. Chmn. bd. dirs. Suicide Prevention, Inc., St. Louis, 1973-75. Mem. Am., St. Louis (chmn. mil. law com.) bar assns., Am. Inst. Mining and Metall. Engrs. Home: 47 E Sherwood St Overland MO 63114 Office: 111 S Meramec Ave Clayton MO 63105 Tel (314) 721-4333

RUSCHKY, ERIC WILLIAM, b. Wareham, Mass., June 28, 1948; B.A., Wheaton (Ill.) Coll., 1970; J.D., U. Va., 1973. Admitted to Va. bar, 1973, S.C. bar, 1974; asso. firm John Dezio, Esq., Charlottesville, Va., 1973; asso. firm Hyman. Morgan & Brown, Florence, S.C., 1973-74; asst. U.S. atty. Dist. of S.C., Columbia, 1974—; mem. mandatory continuing legal edn. study subcom. of continuing legal edn. com. S.C. Bar. Sec. Internat. Christian Leadership, Columbia, S.C., 1976—. Mem. Nat. Dist. Attys. Assn., Fed. Criminal Investigators Assn. (v.p. local chpt.), S.C. Law Enforcement Officers Assn., Christian Legal Soc. Named an Outstanding Young Man of Am., 1976. Home: 1547 Shady Ln Columbia SC 29206 Office: 151 US Courthouse Columbia SC 29201 Tel (803) 765-5483

RUSCONI, ERNEST, b. Montpelier, Vt., June 29, 1922; B.E.E., Norwich U., 1945; student Syracuse U., 1945-46; LL.B., Harvard, 1949. Admitted to Calif. bar, 1950; partner firm Rusconi Foster & Thomas, Morgan Hill, Calif., 1964—; city atty. Morgan Hill, 1956—. Mem. State Bar Calif., Am., Santa Clara County bar assns. Office: 55 W First St PO Box 98 Morgan Hill CA 95037 Tel (408) 779-2106

RUSH, BENJAMIN FRANKLIN, b. Kenova, W.Va., Mar. 4, 1915; LL.B., Jefferson Sch. Law, Louisville, 1942. Admitted to Ky. bar, 1942, Supreme Ct. U.S. bar, 1967; U.S. govt. lawyer, 1946—; dist. counsel U.S. VA, for State of W.Va., Huntington, 1975—. Mem. Fed. (past pres. Huntington chpt.), Ky. bar assns. Office: 502 8th St Huntington WV 25701 Tel (304) 529-2311

RUSH, MICHAEL DEAN, b. Camp Atterbury, Ind., Jan. 2, 1945; B.A., Hanover Coll., 1967; J.D., Valparaiso U., 1973. Admitted to Ind. bar, 1973; partner firm Roe & Rush, Columbia City, Ind., 1973—. Pres. Whitley County (Ind.) Drug Abuse Council, 1973-77; mem. Columbia City Park and Recreation Bd., 1974—. Mem. Am. (Ind. membership chmn., sect. young lawyers), Ind. State, Whitley County bar assns., Columbia City C. of C. (pres. 1976), Valparaiso U. Law Sch. Alumni Assn. (dir. 1975—), Phi Alpha Delta (Outstanding Service award 1973). Recipient Outstanding Young Man award Columbia City Jaycees, 1974. Office: 116 N Main St Columbia City IN 46725 Tel (219) 244-6600

RUSH, WAYNE FRANKLIN, b. Greenwood, S.C., Oct. 4, 1935; B.S., U. S.C., 1957, LL.B., 1964. Admitted to S.C. bar, 1964, U.S. Supreme Ct. bar, 1971; asso. firm Roberts, Jennings & Thomas, Columbia, 1964-67, partner, 1968-73; partner firm Callison, Tighe, Nauful and Rush, Columbia, 1973—. Mem. Am., Richland County, S.C. (exec. com. 1970-71) bar assns., Phi Delta Phi, Am. Judicature Soc. Mng. editor S.C. Law Rev., 1963. Home: 26 Indian Creek Trail Lands End Lexington SC 29072 Office: 1400 Pickens St Columbia SC 29202 Tel (803) 256-2371

RUSH, WILLIAM BOWMAN, b. Hartford, Conn., Sept. 30, 1934; B.A., Conn. Wesleyan U., 1956; LL.B., U. Conn., 1959. Admitted to Conn. bar, 1959; law clk. Conn. Supreme Ct., Hartford, 1959-60; partner firm Pullman Comley Bradley & Reeves, Bridgeport, Conn., 1960—. Mem. Am. Arbitration Assn., Am., Conn., Bridgeport bar assns. Editor-in-chief U. Conn. Law Rev., 1958-59. Home: 145 Jackman Ave Fairfield CT 06430 Office: 855 Main St Bridgeport CT 06604 Tel (203) 334-0112

RUSHFORTH, BERNT NELSON, b. Salt Lake City, Feb. 18, 1941; B.A., Stanford, 1964, M.A., 1966; LL.B., U. Calif. at Berkeley, 1969. Admitted to Calif. bar, 1970; U.S. Supreme Ct. bar, 1974; since practiced in Los Angeles, asso. firm O'Melveny & Myers, 1969-72; co-founder, trustee, atty. Center for Law in the Pub. Interest, 1972—. Mem. Calif., Los Angeles County bar assns. Home: Office: 10203 Santa Monica Blvd Los Angeles CA 90067 Tel (213) 879-5588

RUSIN, BRON JOHN, b. Chgo., Apr. 29, 1910; LL.B., John Marshall Law Sch., 1945, J.D., 1970. Spl. agt. intelligence unit IRS, Chgo., 1940-46; admitted to Ill. bar, 1945; individual practice law, Chgo., 1946—. Mem. Chgo. Bar Assn., Ill. Soc. C.P.A.'s Am. Inst. C.P.A.'s. C.P.A., Ill. Home: 1086 Ash St Winnetka IL 60093 Tel (312) 446-1861

RUSKIN, STEVEN A., b. N.Y.C., Nov. 5, 1945; B.A., Princeton U., 1965; J.D., Columbia U., 1968; LL.M.,. in Taxation, N.Y.U., 1973. Admitted to N.Y. bar, 1968; asso. firm Seward & Kissel, N.Y.C., 1968-71; asso. firm Cadwalader, Wickersham & Taft, N.Y.C., 1972-76, partner, 1977—. Mem. N.Y. State Bar Assn. Office: 1 Wall St New York City NY 10005

RUSS, EDMOND JOSEPH, b. Torrance, Calif., Mar. 28, 1928; A.A., El Camino Coll., 1949; B.A., U. Calif., Los Angeles, 1951, LL.D., 1954. Admitted to Calif. bar, 1955; individual practice law, Gardena, Calif., 1955—; mayor City of Gardena, 1969, 74—, city councilman, 1968-72. Named Man. of Yr., Gardena Jr. C. of C., 1964. Office: 1515 W Redondo Beach Blvd Gardena CA 90247 Tel (213) 323-8230

RUSSAKOFF, NORMAN FREDERICK, b. N.Y.C., June 23, 1945; B.A., Queens Coll., 1966; J.D., St. John's U., Bklyn., 1969. Admitted to N.Y. bar, 1970; atty. law dept. N.Y.C. Transit Authority, 1969-73; individual practice law, Bklyn., 1973-76; partner firm Russakoff & Weiss, Bklyn., 1976—. Mem. exec. bd. Westchester-Putnam council Boy Scouts Am., 1971-76, mem. council camping com., advisor to Order of Arrow, 1973-76. Mem. N.Y. State, Am. bar assns. Office: 186 Joralemon St Brooklyn NY 11201 Tel (212) 855-5020

RUSSELL, DAN M., JR., b. Magee, Miss., Mar. 15, 1913; B.A., U. Miss., 1935, LL.B., 1937. Admitted to Miss. bar, 1937; practice in Gulfport and Bay St. Louis, Miss.; U.S. judge So. Dist. Miss., 1965—, now chief judge; dir. So. Savs. & Loan Assn., Gulfport, Miss. Chmn. Hancock (Miss.) Civic Action Assn., 1964—; Democratic presdl. elector, 1964; chmn. Hancock County Election Commn., 1959-64. Mem. Miss., Hancock County (v.p. 1964-65) bar assns., Hancock County C. of C. (pres. 1946), Tau Kappa Alpha, Scribblers. Home: 321 Main St Bay Saint Louis MS 39520 Office: PO Box 1930 Gulfport MS 39502*

RUSSELL, DAVID EUGENE, b. Chicago Heights, Ill., Mar. 19, 1935; B.S. in Accounting, U. Calif. at Berkeley, 1957, LL.B., Boalt Hall, Berkeley, 1960. Admitted to Calif. Supreme Ct. bar, 1961; sr. accountant Lybrand Ross Bros. & Montgomery, San Francisco, 1960-64; asso. firm Robert C. Burnstein, Oakland, Calif., 1964-65; individual practice law, Sacramento, 1965; partner firm Russell, Jarvis, Estabrook & Dashiell, Law Corp., and predecessor, Sacramento, 1965—. Mem. Calif. Soc. C.P.A.'s, Calif., Sacramento bar assns., Comml. Law League, Nat. Assn. Chpt. XIII Trustees, Calif. State Bar (chmn. local adminstrn. com. 1972). Office: 1333 Howe Ave Suite 211 Sacramento CA 95825 Tel (916) 929-7880

RUSSELL, DAVID LYNN, b. Sapulpa, Okla., July 7, 1942; B.S., Okla. Bapt. U., 1962; J.D., Okla. U., 1965. Admitted to Okla. bar, 1965; asst. atty. gen. State of Okla., 1968-69; legal advisor to Okla. Gov., 1969-70; partner firm Jopling, Blankenship, Russell, Herrold & Leonard, Oklahoma City, 1971-72; legis. asst. to Okla. Senator Dewey Bartlett, Washington, 1973-75; U.S. atty. Western Dist. Okla., Oklahoma City, 1975-77; partner firm Benefield, Russell, Tyree & Freede, Oklahoma City, 1977—. Mem. Okla., Oklahoma County bars. Home: 2309 NW 119th Terr Oklahoma City OK 73120 Office: 2700 City Nat Bank Oklahoma City OK 73102 Tel (405) 236-1626

RUSSELL, DONALD STUART, b. Lafayette Springs, Miss., Feb. 22, 1906; A.B., U. S.C., 1925, LL.B., 1928; postgrad. U. Mich., 1929; LL.D., Wofford Coll., Lander Coll., The Citadel, U. S.C., Clemson U., C.W. Post Coll., L.I. Admitted to S.C. bar, 1929; individual practice law, Spartanburg, S.C., 1942; asst. dir. econ. stabilization Office Price Adjustment, War Dept., Washington, 1942, asst. to dir. war mobilization, 1943; dept. dir. Office War Mobilization Reconversion, Washington, 1945; asst. sec. state, Washington, 1945-47; pres. U. S.C., 1951-57; gov. State of S.C., 1963-65; mem. U.S. Senate from S.C., 1965; judge U.S. Dist. Ct., S.C., 1967-71; judge U.S. Circuit Ct. 4th Circuit, Spartanburg, 1971—; mem. Wriston Com. on Reorgn. Fgn. Service, 1954. Trustee emeritus Emory U.; trustee Converse Coll., Benedict Coll. Mem. Am., S.C. bar assns., Am. Law Inst. Home: 716 Otis Blvd Spartanburg SC 29302 Office: Fed Bldg Spartanburg SC 29304 Tel (803) 582-2167

RUSSELL, EDWIN FORTUNE, b. Rochester, N.Y., Aug. 27, 1910; B.S. in Chem. Engring., U. Mich., 1932, M.S. in Chem. Engring., 1933; J.D., N.Y. U., 1938. Cadet engr. Consol. Edison Co., N.Y.C., 1933-38, admitted to N.Y. bar, 1939; asso. firm Cullen and Dykman, Bklyn., 1939-52, partner. 1952—, counsel Village of Bronxville, N.Y., 1961-65, mayor, 1965-67. Chmn., Bronxville Bd. Zoning Appeals, 1968—. Fellow Am. Bar Found.; mem. Am., N.Y. State (chmn. ho. dels. 1975-76, pres. 1976—), Bklyn., Westchester County, Fed. Power (pres. 1955-56) bar assns., N.Y. State Bar Found. Home: 39 Park Ave Bronxville NY 10708 Office: 177 Montague St Brooklyn NY 11201 Tel (212) 855-9000

RUSSELL, FRANKLIN TAYLOR, b. Millbrook, N.Y., Mar. 18, 1936; B.A., Cornell U., 1958, M.B.A., 1960; J.D., Syracuse U., 1967. Admitted to N.Y. bar, 1969, U.S. Supreme Ct. bar, 1974; individual practice law, Syracuse, N.Y., 1967-70; asso. gen. counsel C. H. Stuart Inc., Sarah Coventry, Inc., Newark, N.Y., 1970—; dir. Arcadia Hose Co., Newark, N.Y. Pres. Finger Lakes Symphony Orch., Inc.; pres. The Newark Players Inc.; active United Fund; dir. Community Chest; mem. advisory com. Newark Developmental Center; active Wayne County Arts in Action. Mem. N.Y. State, Wayne County bar assns., Lawyers Council of Direct Selling Assn. Home: 434 Grace Ave Newark NY 14513 Office: Route 88 South Newark NY 14513 Tel (315) 331-1580

RUSSELL, HUGH EDWARD, b. Oshkosh, Wis., Sept. 13, 1924; B.S., U. Wis., 1950, LL.B., 1952. Admitted to Wis. bar, 1952; asso. firm Thompson Gruenewald & McCarty, Oshkosh, 1952-54, firm Lees & Bunge, La Crosse, Wis., 1954-56; hearing examiner State of Wis. Workman's Compensation Dept., Madison, 1956-73, dep. adminstr., 1973—. Mem. Wis., Dane County bar assns. Home: 4942 Marathon Dr Madison WI 53705 Office: 201 E Washington Ave Madison WI 53701 Tel (608) 266-1340

RUSSELL, JAMES HARLEY, b. Oak Park, Ill., Aug. 22, 1943; B.A., Ohio Wesleyan U., 1965; J.D., Ohio State U., 1969. Admitted to Ill. bar, 1970, U.S. Dist. Ct. bar, 1970; asso. firm McKenna, Storer, Rowe, White & Farrug, Chgo., 1970-75, firm Martin, Craig, Chester, & Sonnenscheim, Chgo., 1975—. Mem. Am. (mem. sect. corp. banking and bus. law), Chgo. (chmn. aviation law com.), Ill. State (council sect. on environ. law 1976-78) bar assns. Contbr. articles in field to profl. jours. Home: 41 Cedar Ln Lincolnshire IL 60015 Office: 135 S LaSalle St Chicago IL 60603 Tel (312) 236-2400

RUSSELL, JAMES HOWARD, b. South Houston, Tex., Dec. 20, 1914; B.A., U. Tex., 1935, LL.B., 1938. Admitted to Tex. bar, 1938; practiced in Beeville, Tex., 1938-39; atty. Dept. Agr., Washington and Dallas, 1939-42; served with U.S. Army, 1942-46, JAGC, 1944-46; atty. H.L. Hunt, Dallas, 1946-47; publisher Belton (Tex.) Jour., 1947-73; judge Bell County (Tex.) Ct. at Law, 1973—. Sr. warden Episcopal Ch., Belton, 1954-55. Mem. State Bar Tex. Home: 316 E 14th Ave Belton TX 76513 Office: Courthouse Belton TX 76513 Tel (817) 939-3521

RUSSELL, JOHN ST. CLAIR, JR., b. Albany, N.Y., Mar. 21, 1917; A.B., Dartmouth, 1938; LL.B., Yale, 1941. Admitted to N.Y. State bar, 1942, D.C. bar, 1965; founding partner firm Hale Russell Gray Seaman & Birkett and predecessors, N.Y.C., 1948—. Mem. Irvington (N.Y.) Zoning Bd., 1956. Mem. Am. Bar Assn., Assn. Bar City N.Y. Home: Peter Bont Rd Irvington NY 10533 Office: 122 E 42d St New York City NY 10017 Tel (212) 697-1850

RUSSELL, JOYCE MAE, b. Greensburg, Ky., Oct. 23, 1946; A.B., Western Ky. U., 1968; J.D., U. Ky., 1972. Admitted to Ky. bar, 1972; asso. firm Harlin, Parker, Lucas-English, Bowling Green, Ky., 1972-74; partner firm Cole Harned & Broderick, Bowling Green, 1974-75; corporate counsel Union Underwear Co., Inc., Bowling Green, 1975—; law clk. to judge U.S. Circuit Ct., 1972; legal aide Ky. Crime Commn., 1970-72. Mem. Am., Ky., Bowling Green bar assns., Altrusa. Home: 2319 Bellvue Dr Bowling Green KY 42101 Office: 700 Church St Bowling Green KY 42101 Tel (502) 781-6400

RUSSELL, LOUIS WYATT, b. Alto, Tex., Dec. 19, 1914; B.S., Stephen F. Austin State U., 1937; LL.B., U. Tex., 1937. Admitted to Tex. bar, 1937; asso. firm Greves & Russell, Nacogdoches, Tex., 1937-41, Stewart, Burgess & Morris, Houston, 1946-49; partner firm Keys, Russell, Seaman & Mansker, Corpus Christi, Tex., 1949—. Mem. State Bar Tex., Am., Nueces County bar assns. Office: 1917 Bank & Trust Tower Corpus Christi TX 78477 Tel (512) 884-7484

RUSSELL, PAUL GEORGE, b. Akron, Ohio, Feb. 23, 1929; A.B. in Polit. Sci. with honors, Kenyon Coll., 1950; postgrad Western Reserve U. Grad. Sch. Bus. Adminstrn., 1956; LL.B., Harvard, 1957. Admitted to N.Y. bar, 1958; asso. firm Dewey, Ballantine, Bushby, Palmer & Wood, N.Y.C., 1957-60; asst. to mng. partner E.F. Hutton & Co., N.Y.C., 1960-63, sec., 1960-63; asso. firm LeBoeuf, Lamb, Leiby & MacRae, N.Y.C., 1963-67, partner, 1967—. Mem. Am. (chmn. utility financing com. Pub. Utility sect. 1975—), N.Y., Fed. Power bar assns., Assn. Bar City NY, Beta Theta Pi, Tau Kappa Alpha. Home: 45 E 62d St New York City NY 10021 Office: 140 Broadway New York City NY 10005 Tel (212) 269-1100

RUSSELL, ROBERT GILES, b. Hot Springs, Ark., Dec. 6, 1935; B.A., Kans. U., 1960; LL.B., U. Mo., 1963. Admitted to Mo. bar, 1963; law clk. to chief judge U.S. Dist. Ct. for Western Dist. Mo., 1963-64; asso. firm Popham, Thompson, Popham, Treaty & Conway, Kansas City, Mo., 1964-68; partner firm Dixon & Russell, Warrensburg, Mo., 1968-70; judge Mo. 17th Jud. Circuit Ct., 1970—. Mem. Mo. Bar Found. (Lon Hocker award 1968), Mo., Johnson County bar assns., Mo. Trial Judges (pres.-elect). Office: Courthouse Warrensburg MO 64093 Tel (816) 747-7423

RUSSELL, ROBERT WILLIAM, b. Chgo., Apr. 7, 1923; A.B., N. Central Coll., 1943; J.D., Northwestern U., 1948. Admitted to Ill. bar, 1948; atty. Chgo. and Northwestern Transp. Co., Chgo., 1948-51, gen. atty., 1951-62, asst. gen. counsel, 1962-66, gen. solicitor, 1966-68, v.p. personnel, 1968—, v.p. labor relations, 1973—. Mem. Mt. Prospect (Ill.) Sch. Bd., 1965-67, pres., 1967. Mem. Am., Ill., Chgo. bar assns., Soc. Trial Lawyers, Law Club, Am. Mgmt. Assn., Am. Comp. Assn., Orgn. Planning Council-Conf. Bd. Home: 550 Red Barn Ln Barrington IL 60610 Office: 400 W Madison St Room 1830 Chicago IL 60606 Tel (312) 454-6400

RUSSELL, SAMUEL BROCK, b. Reading Pa., Nov. 17, 1920; A.B. in Economics, U. Mich., 1942; LL.B., U. Pa., 1948. Admitted to Pa. bar, 1949, U.S. Supreme Ct. bar, 1966; asso. firm Harold J. Ryan, Reading, Pa., 1948-57; partner firm Ryan and Russell, Reading, Pa., 1957-69; partner firm Ryan, Russell & McConaghy, Reading, 1969—; spl. asst. dist. atty. Berks County, Pa., 1964-65; mem. Pa. Labor Relations Bd., 1965. City councilman Reading, Pa., 1952-56. Mem. Berks County, Pa., Am. bar assns. Office: 304 Colonial Trust Bldg Reading PA 19601 Tel (215) 374-4859

RUSSELL, STEPHEN SPEH, b. Pitts., June 4, 1943; A.A., Hershey (Pa.) Jr. Coll., 1963; B.A., Pa. State U., 1968; J.D., Dickinson Coll., 1971. Admitted to Pa. bar, 1971; asso. firm Rhoads, Sinon & Reader, Harrisburg, Pa., 1971-72; counsel Pa. Bd. Fin. and Revenue, Harrisburg, 1972-73; field rep. Pa. Sch. Bd. Assn., Harrisburg, 1973—. Mem. Am., Pa. bar assns. Contbr. articles in field to profl. jours. Home: 231 Saint Johns Dr Camp Hill PA 17011 Office: 412 N 2d St Harrisburg PA 17101 Tel (717) 233-1642

RUSSELL, SUSAN WHITTINGTON, b. Balt., Apr. 17, 1945; B.A., Conn. Coll., 1967; J.D., Boston U., 1970. Admitted to Md. bar, 1970, U.S. Supreme Ct. bar, 1974; partner firm Sauerwein, Boyd & Decker, Balt., 1977—; dep. gen. counsel Md. State Tchrs. Assn., 1973—. Mem. 3d Dist. Citizens Com., Balt. Mem. Am., Md., Balt. bar assns. Home: 308 E Lake Ave Baltimore MD 21212 Office: 9 W Mulberry St Baltimore MD 21201 Tel (301) 727-5770

RUSSELL, T. NEWTON, b. Diamondville, Wyo., Mar. 17, 1918; B.A., Stanford, 1940, J.D., 1943. Admitted to Calif. bar. 1943; partner firm Thomas, Snell, Jamison, Russell, Williamson & Asperger, Fresno, Calif., 1943—. Bd. govs. Fresno Regional Found., 1968—; bd. dirs. Fresno Auditorium Corp., 1968—; active Fresno Art Adv. Com., 1966—. Fellow Am. Coll. Probate Counsel; mem. Fresno County Bar Assn., Am. Law Inst. Exhibited sculpture. Office: 10th Floor Fresno Towne House Fresno CA 93721 Tel (209) 442-0600

RUSSELL, TERRENCE JOSEPH, b. Jacksonville, Fla., Sept. 26, 1944; A.A., St. Leo Coll., 1964; B.A., U. Fla., 1966; J.D., Fla. State U., 1968. Admitted to Fla. bar, 1969, U.S. Supreme Ct. bar, 1975; law clerk U.S. Dist. Judge W. O. Mehrtens So. Dist. Fla., 1969; mem. firm Ruden, Barnett, McClosky, Schuster & Schmerer, Ft. Lauderdale, Fla., 1970—. Mem. Fla. (mem. sec. litigation), Am. bar assns., Acad. Fla. Trial Lawyers, Assn. Trial Lawyers Am., Gold Key (hon. leadership fraternity Fla. State U.). Home: 10841 NW 24th St Coral Springs FL 33065 Office: 900 NE 26th Ave Fort Lauderdale FL 33338 Tel (305) 565-9362

RUSSELL, THOMAS BANISTER, b. Louisville, Nov. 15, 1945; B.A., Western Ky. U.; J.D., U. Ky. Admitted to Ky. bar, 1970; partner firm Threlkeld, Whitlow & Roberts, Paducah, Ky., 1970—. Bd. dirs. Red Cross, Paducah, Market House Mus., Paducah. Mem. Ky., McCracken County (sec. 1972-73) bar assns., Ky., McCracken County (treas. 1976, 2d v.p. 1977) young lawyers assns., Assn. Trial Lawyers Am., Order of Coif. Office: PO Box 995 Paducah KY 42001 Tel (502) 443-4516

RUSSELL, WILLIAM STANTON, b. Morristown, Tenn., May 25, 1925; student Cornell U., 1943-44, Dennison U., 1944, U. N. Mex., 1944-45; J.D., U. Tenn., 1948. Admitted to Tenn. Supreme Ct. bar, 1948; claims atty. So. Fire & Casualty Co., Nashville and Shelbyville, Tenn., 1948-54; practiced in Shelbyville, 1954, 63; asst. dist. atty. 8th Jud. Circuit, 1962-63; judge 23d Jud. Circuit Tenn., 1963-69, Ct. Criminal Appeals, 1969—; mayor City of Shelbyville, 1957-61; chmn. Supreme Ct. Commn. Rules of Practice and Procedure in Criminal Cases; mem. Tenn. Jud. Council. Mem. Tenn., Am. bar assns. Reporter: Tenn. Criminal Appeals Reports, 1969-72. Home: Rt 2 Box 179 Wartrace TN 37183 Office: 402 Belmont St POB 425 Shelbyville TN 37160 Tel (615) 684-6502

RUSSIAN, STEPHEN T., b. Arlington, Mass., June 26, 1928; B.A. cum laude, Boston U., 1951, J.D. cum laude, 1953. Admitted to Mass. bar, 1953; mem. firm Stone & Glaser, Boston, 1953-54; individual practice law, Boston, 1954-57, Lexington, Mass., 1957—. Bd. dirs. ARC, Lexington Counseling Service; incorporator East Boston Savs. Bank; mem. Town Meeting, Lexington, 1957-75. Mem. Boston, Middlesex County, Central Middlesex bar assns. Home: 47 Turning Mill Rd Lexington MA 02173 Office: 24 Muzzey St Lexington MA 02173 Tel (617) 862-4181

RUSSO, ANTHONY E., b. Phillipsburg, N.J., Aug. 8, 1926; A.B., Lafayette Coll., 1948; LL.B., Rutgers U., 1952. Admitted to N.J. bar, 1953; individual practice law, Union, N.J., 1953—; asst. county atty. Union County, 1966-69, county adjuster, 1972—; municipal atty. Winfield (N.J.), 1965—; mem. governing body Union Twp., 1962—, mayor, 1974-75. Founder, past pres., bd. dirs. local civic assns. Mem. N.J., Union County, Union Twp. bar assns. Home: 23 Lancaster Rd Union NJ 07083 Office: 2000 Morris Ave Union NJ 07083 Tel (201) 688-3232

RUSSO, EDMUND PETER, b. Middletown, Conn., Apr. 23, 1923; B.A., Wesleyan U., 1947; postgrad. Stanford U. Law Sch., 1947-49; J.D., U. Miami, 1950. Admitted to Fla. bar, 1950, U.S. Supreme Ct. bar, 1956; partner firm Mayes, Sutton, Murphy & Russo, Coral Gables, Fla., 1954-62; partner Mayes & Russo, Coral Gables, 1962-69, sr. partner, 1970-74; sr. partner firm Russo, VanDoren & Allen, Coral Gables, 1974—; asso. municipal judge City of Coral Gables, 1954; field atty. Lawyers Title Guaranty Fund., Dade County, Fla., 1960—; dir. Flagship 1st Nat. Bank of Coral Gables. Mem. Am., Coral Gables, Dade County, Fla. bar assns., Phi Beta Kappa, Omicron Delta Kappa. Home: 1101 Sunset Rd Coral Gables FL 33143 Office: 4675 Ponce De Leon Blvd Coral Gables FL 33146 Tel (305) 665-0414

RUSSO, JOSEPH S., b. Hammond, La., June 26, 1931; B.S. in Accounting, La. State U., 1957, J.D., 1961. Admitted to La. bar, 1961; individual practice law, Jefferson, La., 1962—. Chmn. ARC, Jefferson Parish, 1974—, pres. Bus. and Profl. Toastmasters Club, 1965; leader Gt. Books Discussion Club, 1964-65. Mem. La. State, Jefferson bar assns. Home: 3613 Neyrey Dr Metairie LA 70002 Office: 693 Central Ave Jefferson LA 70121 Tel (504) 733-2893

RUSSO, LOUIS A., b. N.Y.C., 1911; grad. N.Y. U., 1931. Now gen. counsel Chase Manhattan Bank, N.Y.C. Home: 222 Upper Mountain Ave Upper Montclair NJ 07043 Office: Chase Manhattan Bank 1 Chase Manhattan Plaza New York City NY 10005*

RUSSO, ROY R., b. Utica, N.Y., July 26, 1936; B.A., Columbia U., 1956; LL.B. cum laude, Syracuse U., 1959. Admitted to N.Y. bar, 1959, D.C. bar, 1967, U.S. Supreme Ct. bar, 1969; atty. FCC, Washington, 1959-66; mem. firm Cohn & Marks, Washington, 1966—. Mem. St. Lawrence Parish Adv. bd., Alexandria, Va., 1969—, pres., 1973—; v.p., dir. St. Mary's Housing Corp., Alexandria, 1970—; chmn. Commn. Social Ministry, Diocese of Richmond (Va.), 1972-74; pres. bd. advs. Office Charities Diocese, Arlington, Va., 1975-77; bd. dirs. Koinonia Found., Inc., 1971—; bd. dirs. No. Va. Fair Housing, 1973—, pres., 1976—; mem. Equal Housing Opportunities Com., Met. Washington Planning and Housing Assn., 1976—; mem. Housing Task Force, Leadership Conf. Civil Rights, 1977—; mem. Community Housing Resources Bd. No. Va., 1977—. Mem. Am. Bar Assn., FCC Bar Assn., Computer Lawyers Assn., Order of Coif, Phi Alpha Delta. Home: 6528 Bowie Dr Springfield VA 22150 Office: 1920 L St NW Washington DC 20036 Tel (202) 293-3860

RUSSON, LEONARD HARRINGTON, b. American Fork, Utah, May 15, 1933; B.S., U. Utah, 1958, J.D., 1962. Admitted to Calif. bar, 1962, Utah bar, 1963; asso. firm Fitzwilliam, Memering, Stumbos & DeMers, Sacramento, 1965-66; partner firm Hanson, Wadsworth & Russon, Salt Lake City, 1966—. Mem. Am., Calif., Utah, Salt Lake County bar assns., Def. Research Inst. Assn. Home: 3604 Crestwood Dr Salt Lake City UT 84109 Office: 702 Kearns Bldg Salt Lake City UT 84101 Tel (801) 359-7611

RUSSUM, WILLIAM LANCE, b. Oakland, Calif., Dec. 24, 1941; B.A., Gonzaga U., 1963; J.D., Hastings U., 1966. Admitted to Calif. bar, 1966, Fed. Dist. Ct. bar, 1966, U.S. Ct. Appeals bar, 1966; v.p. Moffitt, James & Mendelson, Inc., Alameda, Calif.; instr. estate adminstrn. Calif. Continuing Edn. of Bar, 1975. Pres. Alameda Republican Assembly, 1968, Alameda Athletic Assn., 1970-71; mem. Alameda Recreation Commn., 1972—. Mem. State Bar Calif., Alameda County Bar Assn. Named Jaycee of Yr., One of Alameda's Five Outstand Young Men, Jaycees, 1972, other awards. Office: 2447 Santa Clara Ave Alameda CA 94501 Tel (415) 522-6900

RUST, JOSEPH CUTLER, b. Vernal, Utah, Feb. 18, 1941; B.A. in English, U. Utah, 1966, J.D., 1968. Admitted to Utah bar, 1968; asso. firm Kirton & McConkie, Salt Lake City, 1968-70; European gen. counsel Ch. of Jesus Christ of Latter Day Saints, Frankfurt, Germany, 1970-74; mem. firm Kirton, McConkie, Boyer & Boyle, Salt Lake City, 1974—. Del. Utah State Republican Conv. 1976. Mem. Utah, Salt Lake City bar assns. Contbr. articles to legal jours. Office: 336 S 3rd E Salt Lake City UT 84111 Tel (801) 521-3680

RUST, MYRON DAVIS, b. Boston, Nov. 12, 1923; student U. Maine, 1941-42; B.Marine Sci., Maine Maritime Acad., 1943; J.D., Northeastern U., 1949. Admitted to Maine bar, 1949, N.H. bar, 1957; individual practice law, York, Maine, 1949-56, Portsmouth, N.H., 1957-74, Kittery, Maine, 1974—. Mem. Maine State, N.H. State, York County (exec. com.), Rockingham County, Portsmouth City bar assns. Office: 161 State Rd Profl Bldg Kittery ME 03904 Tel (207) 439-4448

RUSTON, PAUL ARTHUR, b. Omaha, Nov. 26, 1912; grad. in pre-law U. Denver, 1934; LL.B., Westminster Law Sch., 1937. Admitted to Colo. bar, 1937; dep. dist. atty., Denver, 1941-44, dist. atty., 1946-49; regional atty. Nat. Prodn. Authority, Dept. Commerce, Colo., 1950-52; individual practice law, Denver, 1953—. Home: 7055 E Virginia Ave Denver CO 80220 Office: 714 E 18th Ave Denver CO 80203 Tel (303) 222-2709

RUTH, GERALD EUGENE, b. York, Pa., June 29, 1933; student Dickinson Coll., 1950-54; LL.B., J.D., Vanderbilt U., 1960. Admitted to Pa. bar, 1961; asso. firm Bergdoll, Dell-Alba & Noll, York, 1961-63; atty. York County Legal Aid, 1962-64; partner firm Kessler & Ruth, York, 1963-64; pub. defender, 1968, 70, 71, 72; Southeastern Pa. regional counsel Pa. Edn. Assn., 1973—; instr. comml. law Am. Banking Inst., 1965; instr. bus. law York Coll., 1963-65, 67; solicitor York County Ct., 1967-69. Former mem. York County Council Alcoholism; del. Pa. Constnl. Conv., 1967-68. Mem. Am., Pa., York County bar assns., Am., Pa. trial lawyers assns. Home: 2775 Eastwood Dr York PA 17402 Office: 120 S Duke St York PA 17403 Tel (717) 843-0097

RUTH, ROBERT J., b. Ashland, Wis., Oct. 21, 1935; J.D., U. Wis., 1963. Admitted to Wis. bar, 1963, U.S. Dist. Ct. bar, 1965, U.S. Ct. of Appeals bar, 1972, U.S. Supreme Ct. bar, 1972; with U.S. Treasury Dept., 1963; asst. dist. atty Rock County, Wis., 1964-65, corp. counsel, 1965-66, dist. atty., 1966-70; mem. firm Bolgrien & Ruth and predecessor, Beloit, Wis., 1971—; spl. prosecutor State of Wis., 1971, 76. Mem. State Council of Local Affairs and Devel., 1969-73; mem. Rock County Bd. of Suprs., 1971-73. Mem. Am., Wis., Rock County, Beloit bar assns., Am. Trial Lawyers Assn., Wis. Acad. Trial Lawyers. Home: 2227 Moccasin Trail Beloit WI 53511 Office: 542 E Grand Ave PO Box 935 Beloit WI 53511 Tel (608) 365-7702

RUTHERFORD, ALBERT GREIG, II, b. Honesdale, Pa., June 29, 1941; student Va. Mil. Inst., 1958-59; B.S., U. Scranton, 1963; J.D. (Abel Klaw scholar), Dickinson Sch. Law, Carlisle, Pa., 1966. Admitted to Pa. Supreme Ct. bar, 1966, U.S. Dist. Ct. bar for Middle Dist. Pa., 1967; partner firm Bodie & Rutherford, Honesdale, 1966—. Chmn. Honesdale Zoning Hearing Bd., 1972—; bd. dirs. Wayne County (Pa.) Meml. Hosp. Assn., 1974—. Mem. Am., Pa., Wayne County (dir.) bar assns. Named Outstanding Jaycee, Honesdale Jaycees, 1970. Home: 1416 Main St Honesdale PA 18431 Office: Courthouse Sq Honesdale PA 18431 Tel (717) 253-2500

RUTHERFORD, DANIEL RALPH, b. Chgo., Dec. 20, 1940; B.A., St. Mary's Univ., San Antonio, 1966, LL.B., 1966. Admitted to Tex. bar, 1965, U.S. Supreme Ct. bar, 1975; asso. firm Dayton Wiley, San Antonio, 1965-66; individual practice law, San Antonio, 1966—; city atty., China Grove, Tex., 1968-76. Mem. exec. com. Alamo Area council Boy Scouts Am. Mem. Am., Tex. bar assns., Tex. Assn. Trial Lawyers. Home: 3 Flintstone Ct San Antonio TX 78213 Office: 1747 Mick Williams San Antonio TX 78209 Tel (512) 828-0733

RUTHERFORD, WALTER ELLIOTT, b. N.Y.C., May 9, 1932; A.B., Brown U., 1953; LL.B., Columbia U., 1956. Admitted to N.Y. State bar, 1956; asso. firm Haight, Gardner, Poor & Havens, N.Y.C., 1960-69, partner, 1969—. Mem. Am., N.Y. State bar assn., Assn. Bar City N.Y., Fedn. Ins. Counsel, Internat. Assn. Ins. Counsel, Fed. Bar Council. Home: 34 Overlook Dr Chappaqua NY 10514 Office: One State St Plaza New York City NY 10004 Tel (212) 344-6800

RUTHMAN, REX SHIELS, b. Evanston, Ill., May 11, 1942; B.A., State U. N.Y., Albany, 1964; LL.B., Albany Law Sch., 1967. Admitted to N.Y. bar, 1967; asso. firm Carter & Conboy, Albany, N.Y., 1967-69; asso. firm Tate & Tate, Albany, 1969-74, partner, 1975—; atty. Village of Colonie (N.Y.), 1969-76. Bd. dirs. Legal Aid Soc., Albany, 1972—; counsel Albany County Com. on County Govt., 1972, Schenectady (N.Y.) Human Rights Commn., 1972-73. Mem. N.Y. State, Albany County bar assns., Fed. Bar Council. Office: 1698 Central Ave Albany NY 12205 Tel (518) 869-3531

RUTKOWSKI, JAMES ANTHONY, b. Milw., Apr. 6, 1942; B.S., Marquette U., 1964, J.D., 1966. Admitted to Wis. bar, 1966; instr. Marquette U., Milw., 1969-70, asst. instr. U. Wis. at Milw., 1969; mem. JAGC, U.S. Army, 1969-72; mem. Wis. Gen. Assembly, 1971—. Mem. Am., Milw. bar assns. Home: 10223 Kay Pkwy Hales Corners WI 53130 Office: Rm 109 N State Capitol Madison WI 53702 Tel (608) 266-8590

RUTLAND, LOUIS COOPER, b. Montgomery, Ala., Nov. 5, 1941; B.S., Auburn U., 1963; J.D., U. Ala., 1969. Admitted to Ala. bar, 1969; individual practice law, Union Springs, Ala., 1969—; city recorder Union Springs, 1969—; asst. sec. Ala. Senate, 1975—. Mem. Am., Ala. bar assns., Ala. Trial Lawyers Assn. Office: PO Box 108 Union Springs AL 36089 Tel (205) 738-4770

RUTLEDGE, IVAN CATE, b. White Pine, Tenn., Dec. 24, 1915; B.A., Carson-Newman Coll., 1934; M.A., Duke, 1940, LL.B., 1946; LL.M., Columbia, 1952. Admitted to Ga. bar, 1946, Wash. bar, 1951, Ohio bar, 1966; asst. prof. law Mercer U., Macon, Ga., 1946-47; asst. prof. law U. Wash., Seattle, 1947-51, asso. prof., 1951-53, prof., 1953-55; prof. law Ind. U., Bloomington, 1954-63; prof. law Ohio State U., Columbus, 1963-72, prof. law and pub. adminstrn., 1972—, dean, 1965-70; Fulbright lectr. U. Queensland, Brisbane, Australia, 1968; cons. to chmn. NLRB, Washington, 1962-63. Mem. Nat. Acad. Arbitrators, Am., Ohio, Columbus bar assns., Order of Coif. Editor: (with others) Labor Relations and the Law, 1965, The Developing Labor Law, 1971; contbr. articles to profl. jours. Home: 444 E Schreyer Pl Columbus OH 43214 Office: 1659 N Nigh St Columbus OH 43210 Tel (614) 422-1143

RUTLEDGE, JOHN ROBERT, b. Elizabeth, N.J., Dec. 18, 1929; B.S. cum laude, U.S. Mcht. Marine Acad., 1951; J.D., N.Y. U., 1959. Admitted to N.J. bar, 1960, U.S. Supreme Ct. bar, 1969; asso. firm John E. Selser, Manahawkin, N.J., 1959-61, Haines & Schuman, Toms River, N.J., 1961-63; v.p., gen. counsel Leisure Tech. Corp., Lakewood, N.J., 1963-71; individual practice law, Toms River, 1971—. Mem. N.J., Ocean County bar assns. Contbr. articles in field to legal jours. Home: 625 Bayside Ave Beachwood NJ 08722 Office: 236 Washington St Toms River NJ 08753 Tel (201) 244-6464

RUTTER, IRVIN C., b. N.Y.C., Nov. 8, 1909; B.A., Columbia, 1929, J.D., 1931. Admitted to N.Y. bar, 1932, Ohio bar, 1957; research asst. in law Columbia, 1931; law sec. to U.S. dist. judge for So. Dist. N.Y., 1931-34; asst. U.S. atty. So. Dist. N.Y., N.Y.C., 1934-40; spl. asst. to atty. gen. U.S., Washington, 1940-42; chief enforcement atty. OPA, N.Y.C., 1942-44, chief hearing commr., 1944-46; individual practice law, N.Y.C., 1946-56; prof. law U. Cin., 1956—; vis. prof. law Columbia, 1964; lectr. Practising Law Inst., N.Y.C.; hearing officer Ohio Civil Rights Commn. Mem. Assn. Bar City N.Y., Assn. Am. Law Schs. Author: The Facts Process, 1956; Materials on Appellate Advocacy, 1957; Materials on Legal Drafting, 1958; A Jurisprudence of Lawyers' Operations, 1961; The Trial Judge and the Judicial Process, 1963; Designing and Teaching the First-Degree Law Curriculum, 1968; Law, Language and Thinking Like a Lawyer, 1975; editor Columbia Law Rev., 1929-31; bd. editors Jour. Legal Edn.; Charles Bathgate Beck scholar, 1929; named distinguished prof. U. Cin., 1966. Home: 2930 Scioto St Cincinnati OH 45219 Office: Coll Law U Cincinnati Cincinnati OH 45221 Tel (513) 475-2661

RUTTGER, MAX JOSEPH, III, b. Litchfield, Minn., Nov. 14, 1945; B.A., Yale, 1968; J.D., Washington U., 1972. Admitted to Minn. bar, 1972; partner firm Ryan, Ryan, Ebertand Ruttger, Brainerd, Minn., 1972—. Contbr. articles to legal jours. Home: Rt 6 Box 395 Brainerd MN 56401 Office: 217 S 4th St Brainerd MN 56401 Tel (218) 829-3523

RUUD, MILLARD HARRINGTON, b. Ostrander, Minn., Jan. 7, 1917; B.S. in Law, U. Minn., 1942, LL.B., 1947. Admitted to Minn. bar, 1947, Tex. bar, 1956; asst. prof. law U. Kans., 1947-48; asso. prof., U. Tex., from 1948, subsequently prof.; asst. exec. dir. Tex. Legislative Counsel; exec. dir. Assn. Am. Law Schs., Washington, D.C., 1973—; Tex. commr., uniform state laws, 1967—; chmn. Law Sch. Admission Council, 1966-69. Mem. Tex. State, Am. bar assns., Am. Law Inst. Home: 3416 Foothill Terrace Austin TX 78731 Office: Suite 370 One Dupont Circle NW Washington DC 20036 Tel (202) 296-8851

RYAN, ATHERTON BEAL, b. Norwood, Mass., Mar. 23, 1934; B.A., U. Conn., 1956, LL.B., 1959. Admitted to Conn. bar, 1959; asso. firm George A. Downing, Manchester, Conn., 1960-64, firm King & Caldwell, Rockville, Conn., 1964-66; partner firm King, DuBeau & Ryan, Rockville, 1966—. Mem. Ellington (com.) Planning and Zoning Commn., 1962—, chmn., 1963—. Mem. Conn., Tolland County (pres. 1974-75) bar assns., Def. Research Inst. Home: 16 Virginia Dr Ellington CT 06029 Office: 38 Park St Rockville CT 06066 Tel (203) 875-3335

RYAN, DANIEL JAMES, b. Chgo., Nov. 30, 1916; B.S.C., U. Notre Dame, 1939; LL.B., Chgo.-Kent Coll. Law, 1942, J.D., 1969. Admitted to Ill. bar, 1942; asst. state's atty. for Cook County (Ill.), 1946-52; practiced in Chgo., 1952-60; judge Municipal Ct., Chgo.,

1960-63; asso. judge Cook County Circuit Ct., 1963-68, judge, 1968—. Mem. Chgo., Ill. State, Am. bar assns., Am. Judicature Soc. Home: 10345 S Seeley Ave Chicago IL 60643 Office: Civic Center Chicago IL 60602 Tel (312) 443-8084

RYAN, DAVID THOMAS, b. Torrington, Conn., Apr. 18, 1939; B.A., U. Md., 1961; J.D., Georgetown U., 1965. Admitted to Conn. bar, 1966; clk. Judge Charles House, Conn. Supreme Ct., 1965; mem. firm Cooney, Scully & Dowling, Hartford, Conn., 1966—; lectr. law U. Conn., 1975. Mem. Avon (Conn.) Charter Revision Commn., 1974-75; bd. dirs. Avon Free Pub. Library, 1975—. Mem. Conn., Hartford County bar assns., Hartford County Jr. Bar Assn. (pres. 1972), Nat. Assn. Railroad Trial Counsel. Office: 266 Pearl St Hartford CT 06103 Tel (203) 527-1141

RYAN, DENNIS PATRICK, b. Mason City, Iowa, Dec. 21, 1940; B.A., U. Ill., 1963; J.D., Northwestern U., 1966. Admitted to Ill. bar, 1966; asso., then partner firm Kirkland & Ellis, Chgo., 1966-75; partner firm Coffield, Ungaretti & Ryan, Chgo. and Waukegan, Ill., 1975-76; state's atty. Lake County (Ill.), 1976—. Trustee Village of Libertyville (Ill.), 1973-76. Mem. Lake County, Ill. State bar assns., Trial Lawyers Club Chgo. Office: County Courthouse Waukegan IL 60085 Tel (312) 689-6644

RYAN, GORDON MICHAEL, b. Rochester, Minn., Jan. 15, 1928; student Loras Coll., 1946-49; J.D., Creighton Law Sch., 1955. Admitted to Nebr. bar, 1955; asso. firm Ellick Spire Ryan & Langdon, Omaha, 1957-62, partner, 1963-67; partner firm Monen Seidle & Ryan, Omaha, 1968-71; gen. counsel and sec. Starr Broadcasting Group, Inc., New Orleans, 1971-75; partner firm McGill, Koley, Parsonage & Ryan, Omaha, 1977—; instr. med. jurisprudence Med. Sch. U. Nebr., 1963-66, bus. law, U. Nebr. at Omaha, 1964-67. Active lawyers' div. United Fund drs., 1963-67. Mem. Am., Nebr., Omaha bar assns. Office: 10010 Regency Circle Suite 300 Omaha NE 68114 Tel (402) 397-9988

RYAN, JAMES FREDERICK, b. Boston, Mar. 11, 1928; A.B., Harvard U., 1949, J.D., 1952. Admitted to Mass. bar, 1952, U.S. Supreme Ct. bar, 1957, U.S. Ct. Mil. Appeals bar, 1957; individual practice law, Boston, 1957—; atty. Mass. Crime Commn., 1963-64; spl. asst. atty. gen. Commonwealth of Mass., 1963-64; asst. corp. counsel City of Boston, 1968-73; lectr. law Suffolk Law Sch., 1958—. Mem. alumni council Roxbury Latin Sch., 1970—, pres., 1976—. Mem. Am., Mass. (chmn. Bicentennial com. 1975-76), Boston bar assns. Contbr. articles to legal jours. Home: 124 Bay State Rd Boston MA 02215 Office: 73 Tremont St Boston MA 02108 Tel (617) 523-6166

RYAN, JAMES H., b. Phila., Dec. 1, 1940; A.B., Ursinus Coll., 1963; LL.B., Harvard, 1966. Admitted to Ill. bar, 1966, U.S. Supreme Ct. bar, 1971; asso. firm McBride, Baker, Wienke & Schlosser, Chgo., 1966-72, partner, 1972—. Mem. Am., Ill., Chgo. bar assns. Home: 65 E Scott St Chicago IL 60610 Office: 110 N Wacker Dr Chicago IL 60606 Tel (312) 346-6191

RYAN, J(AMES) RICHARD, b. N.Y.C., Oct. 29, 1929; B.A., Georgetown U., 1951; J.D., Fordham U., 1954. Admitted to N.Y. State bar, 1956, since practiced in N.Y.C.; asso. firm Engel, Judge, Miller, Sterling & Reddy, 1956-62; partner firm Engel, Judge, Miller & Sterling, 1962-66, firm Kantor, Shaw & Ryan, 1966-72, firm Ryan & Silberberg, 1972—. Pres. Guiding Eyes for the Blind, Inc., N.Y.C., 1973—. Mem. Bar Assn. City of N.Y., Am. Bar Assn. Office: 200 Park Ave New York City NY 10017 Tel (212) 687-1470

RYAN, JOHN CLARENCE, b. Lebanon, Ky., Dec. 18, 1941; A.A., St. Catharine Jr. Coll., 1962; A.B., U. Ky., 1964, J.D., 1967. Admitted to Ky. bar, 1967; law clk. Ky. Ct. Appeals, Frankfort, 1967-68; partner firm Liebman and Ryan, Frankfort, 1968—; Frankfort police judge pro-tem, 1969-71; spl. asst. atty. gen. State of Ky., 1971-76; trustee Bankruptcy Ct., U.S. Dist. Ct. for Eastern Dist. Ky., 1969—. Bd. dirs. Franklin County chpt. ARC, 1973-75; mem. fin. com. Good Shepherd Ch., 1970; pres. Franklin County Young Democrats, 1971-72, dir., 1972-73. Mem. Am., Ky. (chmn. com. on unauthorized practices 1973—), Franklin County (sec., treas. 1970-71, dir. 1971-75) bar assns., Am. Judicature Soc. Named Boss of Year, Frankfort Legal Secs. Assn., 1974; recipient Frankfort Jaycees awards, 1970, 76. Home: 206 Knollwood Pl Frankfort KY 40601 Office: 403 W Main St Frankfort KY 40601 Tel (502) 223-1176

RYAN, JUAN JOSÉ, b. N.Y.C., May 2, 1929; A.B., Georgetown U., 1951, LL.B., 1959. Admitted to N.J. bar, 1960; intelligence officer CIA, Washington, 1955-59; house counsel Nationwide Ins. Co., Trenton, N.J., 1960-61; individual practice law, New Providence, N.J., 1961—. Mem. N.J. Bar Assn. (cons. bd. real property sect.). Home: 22 Pine Ct New Providence NJ 07974 Office: 1351 Springfield Ave New Providence NJ 07474 Tel (201) 464-2264

RYAN, LEONARD EAMES, b. Albion, N.Y., July 8, 1930; A.B., U. Pa., 1954; J.D., N.Y. U., 1962. Admitted to N.Y. bar, 1963, D.C. bar, 1963, U.S. Supreme Ct. bar, 1967; reporter, spl. writer on law N.Y. Times, 1962-63; asso. firm Perrell, Nielsen & Stephens, N.Y.C., 1964-66; trial atty. civil rights div. U.S. Dept. Justice, Washington, 1966-68; asst. to dir. bus. affairs CBS News, N.Y.C., 1968; program officer Office Govt. and Law, Ford Found., N.Y.C., 1968-74; individual practice law, N.Y.C., 1974—; v.p., gen. counsel W.P. Carey & Co., Inc., investment bankers, N.Y.C., 1976—; hearing examiner N.Y. State Div. Human Rights, 1976—; mem. Fed. Energy Adminstrn. natural gas transmission and distbn. adv. com.; mem. panel attys. under Criminal Justice Act of 1964, U.S. Dist. Ct. for So. N.Y.; mem. indigent defendants legal panel Supreme Ct., N.Y. County; arbitrator N.Y. Small Claims Ct.; vice chmn. bd. dirs. Community Action for Legal Services, Inc., N.Y.C. Mem. Am. Judicature Soc., Nat. Legal Aid and Defender Assn., Am. Arbitration Assn. (panel arbitrators), N.Y. State Bar Assn., Assn. Bar City N.Y., N.Y. County Lawyers Assn. Author: So You Want to Go Into Journalism, 1963; also numerous articles. Home: 32 Orange St Brooklyn NY 11201 Office: 67 Wall St New York City NY 10005 Tel (212) 943-5533 also (212) 237-1961

RYAN, LUKE FERDINAND, b. Northampton, Mass., May 20, 1908; B.A., Columbia, 1931, J.D., 1937. Admitted to N.Y. State bar, 1937, Mass. bar, 1943, U.S. Supreme Ct. bar, 1946; asso. firm Hartsell & Callahan, N.Y.C., 1937-39; partner firm Ryan & Mortenson, N.Y.C., 1939-42; individual practice law, Northampton, 1945-71; spl. justice Dist. Ct. of Hampshire, Northampton, 1960-71, presiding judge, 1971—; city solicitor City of Northampton, 1946-60; mayor, Northampton, 1951-52; past pres. Northampton Indsl. Realty Corp. Past pres. Ch. of Annunciation Holy Name Soc.; chmn. Diocesan Catholic Com. for Scouting, 1952-62; co-chmn. Hampshire County chpt. ARC campaign; chmn. fishways com. Conn. River Game-Fish Assn.; atty. Hampshire County Sportsmen Club; co-chmn. Northampton com. NCCJ; Hampshire County chmn. Passionist Monastery Retreat League; chmn. Democratic City Com., 1948-49; co-founder, bd. dirs. Florence Bus. and Civic Assn., St. Michael's Sch. Mr. and Mrs. Club; pres. Conn. Valley Club, Columbia Coll.; trustee Smiths Agrl. Sch., 1954-72. Mem. Hampshire County, Boston bar assns., Mass. Trial Lawyers Assn., Columbia Law Sch. Alumni Assn., John Boyle O'Reilly Assn. of Springfield, Ancient Order Hiberians. Recipient Dean's Lion award Columbia, St. George Cross award Nat. council Boy Scouts Am., Hampshire County. Office: Court House 15 Gothic St Northampton MA 01060 Tel (413) 584-7400

RYAN, MARTIN FREDERICK, b. Oakland, Calif., Feb. 9, 1938; A.B. in History, Stanford, 1960; J.D., U. Ariz., 1963. Admitted to Ariz. bar, 1963; asso. firm Richey & Richey, Tucson, 1963; asso. firm Ryan, Herbolich & Carragher and predecessors, Douglas, Ariz., 1963—; intern U.S. Justice Dept., 1962; city atty. City of Tombstone (Ariz.), 1964-70. Bd. dirs., Cochise Coll. Found., 1967-76, pres., 1971-74; mem. Douglas Bd. Adjustment, 1969—, chmn., 1971-74. Mem. Am., Ariz., Cochise County (pres. 1966-67) bar assns. Home: 2900 15th St Douglas AZ 85607 Office: 855 Cochise Ave Douglas AZ 85607 Tel (602) 364-7961

RYAN, PAUL MURRAY, b. Janesville, Wis., July 23, 1931; B.S., U. Wis., 1954, LL.B., 1957. Admitted to Wis. bar, 1957; asso. firm Campbell, Brennan, Steil & Ryan, S.C. and predecessor, Janesville, 1958-62, partner, 1962-69, sec.-treas., 1969—, dir., 1969—; bd. dirs. Rock County Savs. & Trust Co., 1973—. Mem. State of Wis. Ethics Com., 1974—, Probate Adv. Com. for Rock County. Vice-chmn. bd. dirs. Rock County Health Care Center, 1973—; bd. dirs. Rock Haven Retirement Home, 1973—; trustee Pinehurst Sanitarium. Mem. Am., Wis., Rock County bar assns. Home: 216 S Garfield Ave Janesville WI 53545 Office: One E Milwaukee St Janesville WI 53545 Tel (608) 756-4141

RYAN, ROBERT JOSEPH, b. Walker, Minn., Feb. 7, 1930; student Georgetown U., 1950-51; B.A., St. Johns U., 1952; LL.B., William Mitchell Coll. of Law, 1960. Admitted to Minn. bar, 1960; mem. firm Ryan, Ryan, Ebert & Ruttger, P.A., Brainerd, Minn., 1960—. Chmn., Crow Wing County Airport Commn., 1969—. Mem. Am., Minn., Ninth Judicial Dist., Crow Wing-Aitkin County (past pres.) bar assns., Minn. Trial Lawyers Assn. (dir. 1974—). Office: 217 South Fourth St Brainerd MN 56401 Tel (218) 829-3523

RYAN, ROBERT STONE, b. Worcester, Mass., Aug. 20, 1928; A.B., Princeton, 1950; LL.B., Harvard, 1956. Admitted to Pa. bar, 1957; asso. firm Drinker, Biddle & Reath, Phila., 1956-62, partner, 1962—; mem. Pa. Appellate Rules Com., 1974—. Mem. Am., Pa., Phila. bar assns. Author: Pa. Zoning, Law and Practice, 1970. Office: 1100 Phila Nat Bank Bldg Philadelphia PA 19107 Tel (215) 491-7305

RYAN, ROY FRANCIS, b. New London, Conn., Nov. 22, 1946; B.A., Yale, 1968; J.D., U. Va., 1974. Admitted to Ohio bar, 1974; asso. firm Jones Day Reavis & Pogue, Cleve., 1974—. Mem. Cleve. Tax Inst., 1975—; active United Torch Campaign, 1974—. Mem. Am., Cleve. bar assns., Order of Coif. Office: 1700 Union Commerce Bldg Cleveland OH 44115 Tel (216) 696-3939

RYAN, THOMAS FRANCIS, b. Chgo., Nov. 3, 1925; B.A. magna cum laude, St. John's Coll., Bklyn., 1948, LL.B. cum laude, 1951; LL.M., N.Y. U., 1961. Admitted to N.Y. bar, 1951, N.J. bar, 1967; staff atty. Legal Aid Soc., N.Y.C., 1951-53; asso. firm Bartels & Hartung, N.Y.C., 1953-55; firm Corcoran Kostelanetz & Gladstone, N.Y.C., 1955-64; partner firm Putney Twombly Hall & Skidmore, N.Y.C., 1964-69, firm Hess Segall Popkin Guterman Pelz & Steiner, N.Y.C., 1969—; atty. Matawan (N.J.) Zoning Bd., 1964-69, Matawan Bd. Health, 1971-76. Mem. Am., N.Y. State, N.J., Monmouth County (N.J.) bar assns., Assn. Bar City N.Y. Home: 13 Daniel Dr Matawan NJ 07747 Office: 230 Park Ave New York City NY 10017 Tel (212) 689-2400

RYAN, THOMAS LINCOLN, b. Cin., Jan. 29, 1929; B.S., Ind. U., 1951, J.D. with high distinction, 1958. Admitted to Ind. bar, 1958, U.S. Supreme Ct. bar, 1973; asso. firm Hays & Hays, Sullivan, Ind., 1958-59; asso. firm Stuart, Branigin, Ricks & Schilling, Lafayette, Ind., 1959-64, partner, 1964—. Chmn. adv. council Salvation Army, Lafayette, 1968-74; trustee Trinity United Methodist Ch., Lafayette, 1973-74. Mem. Am., Ind., Tippecanoe County bar assns. Office: PO Box 1010 The Life Bldg Lafayette IN 47902 Tel (317) 423-1561

RYAN, TICE F., JR., b. Pitts., May 24, 1918; A.B., Pa. State U., 1939; J.D., U. Pitts., 1942. Admitted to Pa. bar, 1942, U.S. Supreme Ct. bar, 1966; since practiced in Pitts., partner firm Bialas & Ryan, 1942-58, prin. firm Ryan, Newman, Geer & Goldring, 1958-68, partner firm Ryan & Bowser, 1968—; asst. JAG, USAF, 1944-46. Mem. bd. Allegheny Trails council Boy Scouts Am. 1958—, Highland Park Community Club, 1958-60. Mem. Allegheny County, Pa., Am. bar assns. Office: 1402 Grant Bldg Pittsburgh PA 15219 Tel (412) 281-0580

RYAN, WILLIAM BENEDICT, JR., b. Jacksonville, Fla., June 30, 1945; B.A. in History, U. Fla., 1967; J.D. cum laude, Stetson Coll., 1972. Admitted to Fla. bar, 1972; asso. firm Bryant, Dickens, Rumph, Franson & Miller, Jacksonville, 1972-74, partner, 1974—; instr. bus. law Fla. Jr. Coll., 1973—. Mem. Am., Fla., Jacksonville bar assns. Office: 216 American Nat Bank Bldg Jacksonville FL 32207 Tel (904) 396-4931

RYAN, WILLIAM PATRICK, b. Centralia, Ill., Jan. 23, 1924; B.A., St. Louis U., 1944; J.D., Cumberland U., 1946. Admitted to Tenn. bar, 1947, Mo. bar, 1952, Ga. bar, 1963, Ill. bar, 1969; asst. gen. counsel Standard Accident Ins. Co., Atlanta, 1952-65, Transit Casualty Co., St. Louis, 1966-69; asst. atty. gen. State of Ill., Springfield, 1969-73, spl. asst. atty. gen., 1973—; chief counsel Ill. Dept. Transp., Springfield, 1969-73; Ill. gen. counsel, v.p. St. Paul Fed. Savs. & Loan Assn., Chgo., 1973—; of counsel firm Righeimer, Righeimer & Martin, Chgo., 1973—. Mem. Am., Ill., Chgo., DuPage County, St. Louis Met. bar assns. Office: 6700 W North Ave Chicago IL 60635 Tel (312) 622-5000

RYCKMAN, JERE ARTHUR, b. Freeport, Ill., May 28, 1946; B.A., U. Ill., 1968; J.D., U. Wyo., 1971. Admitted to Wyo. bar, 1971; individual practice law, Green River, Wyo., 1971—; dep. county atty. Sweetwater County (Wyo.), 1972—; municipal judge, Green River, 1973—. Mem. Wyo., Sweetwater County bar assns. Home: 625 Hackberry St Green River WY 82935 Office: PO Box 724 Green River WY 82935 Tel (307) 875-2563

RYDALCH, LEE R., b. Tooele, Utah, Jan. 10, 1941; J.D., U. Utah, 1972. Admitted to Calif. bar, 1972; asso. firm Luce, Forward, Hamilton & Scripps, San Diego, 1972—. Com. mem. Troop 248, Boy Scouts Am., 1974—. Mem. Am. (Sherman Act com.), San Diego County bar assns., Atty's. Assn. San Diego, Order of Coif. Contbr. articles to Utah Law Rev. Office: 110 West A St Suite 1700 San Diego CA 92101 Tel (714) 236-1414

RYDER, MEYER SAMUEL, b. Chgo., Aug. 3, 1909; Ph.B., U. Chgo., 1930; J.D., John Marshall Law Sch. 1935. Admitted to Ill. Supreme Ct. bar, 1935, U.S. Supreme Ct. bar, 1949, Mich. Supreme Ct. bar, 1952; regional dir. NLRB, Cleve. and Buffalo, 1942-48; gen. counsel Internat. Assn. Machinists, Washington, 1948-51; appt. pub. mem. Nat. Wage Stabilization Bd., 1951-53; instr. to prof. indsl. relations U. Mich., 1953—; mem., chmn. numerous disputes commns. Mem. Mich. Gov's. Study Panel on Pub. Employee Labor Law, 1971-72; mem. Ann Arbor (Mich.) Mayor's Commn. on Manpower, 1974-75; mem. Mich. Civil Service Selection Commn., 1975. Mem. Mich. State, Ill. State bar assns., Nat. Acad. Arbitrators. Recipient award for Service Beyond the Call of Duty, U.S. Govt., 1944; author: Management Preparation For Collective Bargaining, 1966; contbr. numerous articles to profl. jours. Home: 2000 Longshore Dr Ann Arbor MI 48105 Office: Grad Sch of Bus Adminstrn U Mich Ann Arbor MI 48104 Tel (313) 764-1369

RYDER, RICHARD SCOTT, b. Richmond, Ind., Feb. 17, 1949; A.B. in History magna cum laude, Wittenburg U., Springfield, Ohio, 1971; J.D., Ind. U., 1974. Admitted to Mich. bar, 1975; clk. firm Reiter & Clatterbaugh, Owosso, Mich., 1974; research atty. Shiawassee County Pros. Atty's. Office, Corunna, Mich., 1974-75; asst. pros. atty. Shiawassee County (Mich.), Corunna, 1975—; instr. criminal procedure for police Lansing Community Coll., 1975. Congl. rep. to Mich. dist. conv. Am. Luth. Ch., 1976; asst. varsity soccer coach John Wesley Coll., Owosso, Mich., 1975-76. Mem. Shiawassee County Bar Assn., State Bar Mich. Named Outstanding First Year Mem., Owosso Jaycees, 1975. Office: 310 N Shiawassee St Corunna MI 48817 Tel (517) 743-5611

RYER, CHARLES WILFRED, b. Springfield, Mo., July 7, 1940; B.A., S.W. Mo. State Coll., 1962; J.D., Washington U., St. Louis, 1968; M.S., U. Oreg., 1972. Admitted to Mo. bar, 1968, Oreg. bar, 1972; law clk. Legal Aid Soc. St. Louis, 1967-68; staff atty. Legal Aid Soc. City and County St. Louis, 1968-69; interviewer Pub. Defender of Santa Clara County (Calif.), 1969-70; counselor Juvenile Ct. for Lane County (Oreg.), 1971-73, intake supr., 1973—. Mem. Oreg. State Bar, Mo. Bar. Office: 2411 Centennial Blvd Eugene OR 97401 Tel (502) 687-4110

RYMAN, ARTHUR E., JR., b. Denver, Aug. 24, 1929; B.S., Denver U., 1954, J.D., 1955; LL.M., Yale, 1959. Admitted to Colo. bar, 1956, U.S. Dist. Ct. Colo. bar, 1956, Iowa bar, 1963; individual practice law, Denver, 1956-57; asst. city and county atty. Denver, 1957-59; prof. Cumberland Law Sch., Lebanon, Tenn., 1959-60; Congl. fellow Am. Polit. Sci. Assn., Washington, 1960-61; asst., asso., then prof. law Drake U., 1961—, asso. dean clin. programs, 1975—. Mem. Ct. Practice Inst., Am. Trial Lawyers Assn., Am., Iowa, Warren County, Polk County bar assns., AAUP (past pres. Iowa conf.). Author: On Rights to Things, 1968. Contbr. articles in field to profl. jours. Office: Drake Univ Law School Des Moines IA 50311 Tel (515) 271-3851

RYNDERS, DAVID WESLEY, b. Evanston, Ill., Dec. 6, 1944; B.A. in Internat. Relations, U. Chgo., 1967; J.D., U. Fla., 1969. Admitted to Fla. bar, 1970; asso. firm Wightman, Rowe & Weidemeyer, Clearwater, Fla., 1970-71; tchr. law for the layman Pinellas County (Fla.) Sch. Bd., 1973-75; asst. county atty. Pinellas County, 1971-74, chief asst. county atty., 1974-75; county atty. Pasco County (Fla.), 1975—. Mem. Am., West Pasco, Pasco County bar assns., Fla. Assn. County Attys. Home: 30 Bowline Bend New Port Richey FL 33552 Office: PO Drawer 609 Port Richey FL 33568 Tel (813) 847-2411

RYPINSKI, RICHARD G., b. N.Y.C., Oct. 1, 1928; B.A., U. Calif., 1951, J.D., 1954. Admitted to Calif. bar, 1955; asst. chief counsel Calif. State Dept. Transp., San Diego, 1965—; mayor City of Del Mar (Calif.), 1975-76, city councilman, 1968-76; chmn. San Diego Council Govt. 1973-74. Mem. San Diego County Bar Assn., State Bar Calif. Office: 110 W C St Suite 2201 San Diego CA 92101 Tel (714) 234-8526

SAARI, DAVID JOHN, b. Virginia, Minn., Jan. 12, 1934; B.A., U. Minn., 1955, J.D., 1959. Admitted to Oreg. bar, 1962, D.C. bar, 1975; research and staff atty. League of Oreg. Cities and Bur. Municipal Research, Eugene, 1959-64; ct. exec. Circuit Ct., Portland, Oreg., 1964-67; research atty. Am. Bar Found., Chgo., 1967-68; dir. Ct. Mgmt. Study, Washington, 1968-69; dir. Ct. Mgmt. Systems, Bethesda, Md., 1970-71; dir. Center for Adminstrn. Justice, Am. U., Washington, 1971-75, asso. prof., 1973—; cons. Nat. Commn. on Causes and Prevention of Violence, 1969; asso. dir. Inst. for Advanced Studies in Justice, 1971—; cons. Ct. Mgmt. project, Cleve., 1971-74, NSF, Washington, 1973, State of Ky. Office of Jud. Planning, Frankfort, 1975-76; pres., co-founder Nat. Assn. Trial Ct. Adminstrs., 1966, 67. Mem. Am. Soc. Criminology, Oreg., D.C. bar assns., Am. Judicature Soc., Nat. Assn. Trial Ct. Adminstrs., Law and Soc. Assn. Contbr. articles in field to legal jours. Home: 7209 Exeter Rd Bethesda MD 20014 Office: Center for Adminstrn Justice American U Washington DC 20016 Tel (202) 686-2532

SABATE, ROBERT WARREN, b. Los Angeles, Mar. 9, 1931; B.S. in Geology, Tulane U., 1952, certificate in gen. commerce, 1965; M.S. in Geology, La. State U., 1957; M.B.A., Loyola U., New Orleans, 1967, J.D., 1972. With Shell Oil Co., 1957-72, sr. geologist, New Orleans; admitted to La. bar, 1972; exploration mgr. Gulf Coast region Koch Exploration Co., New Orleans, 1972—. Mem. Am., La. State bar assns., Am. Assn. Petroleum Geologists, New Orleans Geol. Soc. Recipient Scholarship-Leadership award Tulane U., 1965, Outstanding Service award Gulf Coast Assn. of Geol. Soc., 1972. Home: 6317 Barrett St New Orleans LA 70118 Tel (504) 522-9551

SABATINO, JAMES ROBERT, b. Hazleton, Pa., Sept. 28, 1927; J.D., U. Miami, 1954. Admitted to Fla. bar, 1955, U.S. Supreme Ct. bar, 1960; judge indsl. claims Fla., 1968-70; individual practice law. Republican nominee comptroller State of Fla., 1970; chmn. Fla. Boys Towns of Italy. Mem. Dade County, Am. bar assns. Office: 1100 Kane Concourse Bay Harbor Islands Miami Beach FL 33154 Tel (305) 865-9831

SABIH, DAVID S., b. Baghdad, Iraq, Dec. 31, 1935; B.S., Coll. City N.Y., 1958; M.S., U. Calif. at Los Angeles, 1961, J.D., 1973. Admitted to Calif. bar, 1973; individual practice law, Los Angeles, 1973—. Mem. Calif. Trial Lawyers Assn. Home: 3420 Castlewoods Pl Sherman Oaks CA 91403 Office: 5455 Wilshire Blvd Los Angeles CA 90036 Tel (213) 937-2100

SABIN, ARTHUR JULIUS, b. Chgo., Sept. 21, 1930; A.B. with honors, Roosevelt U., 1952; A.M., Northwestern U., 1953; J.D. with highest honors, John Marshall Law Sch., 1959. Admitted to Ill. bar, 1959; gen. counsel Frederick Chusid & Co., Chgo., 1961-71, Keystone

Chevrolet Co., Chgo., 1969—; prof. history Northeastern Ill. U., Chgo., 1962-75; asso. prof. law John Marshall Law Sch., Chgo., 1972—. Bd. edn. Niles Twp. High Schs., Skokie, Ill., 1966-67. Mem. Ill. Bar Assn., Decalogue Soc. Lawyers, Am. Jewish Hist. Assn. Contbr. articles to profl. jours. Home: 8625 Karlov St Skokie IL 60076 Office: 315 S Plymouth Ct Chicago IL 60604

SABLE, AVIN, b. Milw., Aug. 21, 1906; LL.B., Marquette U., 1929, J.D., 1965. Admitted to Wis. bar, 1929; pres. Mid-West Distbg. Co., 1940-59, A & L Sales Co., 1959-67; partner firm Kondos & Sable, Milw., 1970-73; individual practice law, 1973—. Mem. Milw., Wis. bar assns. Home: 3453 N 54th St Milwaukee WI 53216 Office: 845 N 11th St Milwaukee WI 53233 Tel (414) 271-8860

SACHS, DAVID, b. N.Y.C., Aug. 4, 1933; B.S. in Econs., U. Pa., 1954; J.D., Harvard, 1957. Admitted to N.Y. bar, 1958; asso. firm White & Case, N.Y.C., 1957-68, partner, 1968—; with JAGC, USAR, 1962-69. Mem. Am., N.Y. State (sec. tax sect. 1977) bar assns., Assn. Bar City N.Y. Author: Current Supplements, Federal Income Taxation of Banks and Financial Institutions, Semiann. Home: 2 Willow Dr Edison NJ 08817 Office: 14 Wall St New York City NY 10005 Tel (212) 732-1040

SACHS, HARRY MAURICE, JR., b. Millstone, Md., July 23, 1914; J.D., U. Balt., 1935. Admitted to Md. bar, 1936; individual practice law, Balt., 1936-40, 46-65; gen. equity master Supreme Bench Balt. City, 1965—; lectr. U. Balt., 1966—; regional rep. Am. Arbitration Assn., 1965-67. Mem. Am., Md. State bar assns., Bar Assn. of Balt. City, Am. Judicature Soc., Comml. Law League, Scribes, Nu Beta Epsilon, Phi Beta Gamma. Author: POE, Pleading and Practice, 6th edit., (Michie), vols. 1, 2, 1970, vols. 3, 4, 5, 1975. Home: Apt 315 6317 Park Hts Ave Baltimore MD 21215 Office: Court House Calvert and Lexington Sts Baltimore MD 21202 Tel (301) 396-5006

SACHS, HOWARD F(REDERIC), b. Kansas City, Mo., Sept. 13, 1925; B.A. summa cum laude, Williams Coll., 1947; J.D., Harvard, 1950. Admitted to Mo. bar, 1950; law clk. U.S. Dist. Ct., Kansas City, Mo., 1950-51; practiced in Kansas City, 1951—; mem. firm Spencer, Fane, Britt & Browne. Mem. Kansas City Commn. Human Relations, 1967-73; chmn. Jewish Community Relations Bur., 1968-71; mem. exec. com. Nat. Jewish Community Relations Adv. Council, 1968-71; pres. Urban League of Kansas City, 1957-58; co-chmn. NCCJ, Kansas City, 1958-60; chmn. Kansas City chpt. Am. Jewish Com., 1963-65; pres. Kansas City chpt. Am. Jewish Congress, 1974-77; pres. Jackson County Young Democrats, 1959-60; mem. Sch. Desegregation Task Force, Kansas City Dist., 1976—. Mem. Am., Kansas City bar assns., Mo. Bar, Phi Beta Kappa. Home: 816 W 68th Terr Kansas City MO 64113 Office: 106 W 14th St Kansas City MO 64105 Tel 474-8100

SACHS, JACK, b. N.Y.C., June 10, 1929; B.S., N.Y. U. Sch. Commerce, 1953; LL.B., Bklyn. Law Sch., 1962, J.D., 1967. Admitted to N.Y. bar, 1963, U.S. Dist. Ct. bar So. and Eastern Dists. N.Y., 1964, U.S. Ct. Appeals bar, 2d Circuit, 1973; practiced law in N.Y.C., 1963-66, 70—; legal rep., Copenhagen, 1967-70. Mem. N.Y. State, Western Hemisphere (charter) bar assns. Office: 401 Broadway New York City NY 10013 Tel (212) 431-6990

SACHS, PHILIP HELLER, b. Balt., Oct. 12, 1905; A.B., Johns Hopkins, 1925; LL.B., U. Md., 1928. Admitted to Md. bar, 1928, U.S. Supreme Ct. bar, 1960; since practiced in Balt.; partner firm Hooper, Kiefer & Cornell, 1965-73, of counsel, 1973—; chmn. Met. Transit Authority Md., 1962-67, budget and fin. com. Regional Planning Council, 1962-67; pres. Criminal Justice Commn., 1970-72; chmn. bd. Municipal and Zoning Appeals Balt., 1970—. Mem. Am., Md. State, Balt. City bar assns. Office: 343 N Charles St Baltimore MD 21201 Tel (301) 727-4700

SACHS, ROBERT SELIG, b. L.I., N.Y., Aug. 1, 1939; B.A., Ariz. State U., 1962; J.D., U. San Fernando Valley, 1971. Admitted to Calif. bar, 1972; claims adjustor Trans America Ins. Co., Los Angeles, 1964-65; law clk. San Fernando Valley Neighborhood Legal Services, Pacoima, Calif., 1968; individual practice law, Van Nuys, Calif., 1972—. Mem. Los Angeles Trial Lawyers, Los Angeles County, San Fernando Criminal bar assns., State Bar Calif. Office: 14407 Hamlin St Van Nuys CA 91401 Tel (213) 782-0022

SACHS, SIDNEY STANLEY, b. Washington, Dec. 25, 1916; B.A., Am. U., 1937; LL.B., Georgetown U., 1941. Admitted to D.C. bar, 1942, Md. bar, 1949, U.S. Supreme Ct. bar; law clk. to judge U.S. Emergency Ct. Appeals, 1943-45; asst. U.S. atty. for D.C., 1945-49; individual practice law, Washington and Chevy Chase, Md., 1949—; instr. law Am. U., 1947-52; mem. bd. Inst. Criminal Law and Procedure, Georgetown U., 1955—; mem. D.C. Jud. Conf., 1958—. Bd. govs. Citizens Communications Center; chmn. bd. Hearing, Ednl. Aid and Research Found., Inc., 1976—; bd. dirs. D.C. Assn. Mental Health, 1964-66; mem. Washington Sch. Psychiatry, 1973—. Fellow Am. Bar Found.; mem. Am. Bar Assn. (ho. of dels. 1970—, state del. 1972—). Home: 2717 Daniel Rd Chevy Chase MD 20015 Office: 1620 Eye St NW Washington DC 20006 Tel (202) 872-9090

SACK, EDWARD JACOB, b. N.Y.C., Apr. 7, 1930; A.B., Harvard, 1951, LL.B., 1954; M.Law, N.Y. U., 1959. Admitted to N.Y. bar, 1954; asso. firm Simpson Thacher & Bartlett, N.Y.C., 1954-66; atty. Am. Electric Power Service Corp., N.Y.C., 1966-69, Consol. Edison Co. of N.Y., Inc., N.Y.C., 1969—. Mem. asso. bd. regents L.I. Coll. Hosp., Bkly., 1974—. Mem. Assn. Bar City N.Y., Am. Bar Assn. Home: 125 Remsen St Brooklyn NY 11201 Office: 4 Irving Pl New York City NY 10003 Tel (212) 460-4333

SACKETT, ROBERT WILSON, b. Spencer, Iowa, Nov. 20, 1933; B.S., Iowa State U., 1957; LL.B., Drake U., 1960. Admitted to Iowa Supreme Ct. bar, 1960, U.S. Dist. Ct. for No. Dist. Iowa, 1962, U.S. Dist. Ct. for So. Dist. Iowa, 1967; with casualty claims dept. State Automobile and Casualty Underwriters, Des Moines, 1957-58, Employees Mut. Casualty Co., Des Moines, 1958-60; asso. firm Sackett, Sackett & Hemphill, and predecessors, Spencer, Iowa, 1960-63, partner, 1963—; atty. Clay County (Iowa), 1965-71; atty. cities of Spencer, Okoboji, Fostoria, Sioux Rapids, Peterson, Dickens, Greenville, Webb (all Iowa); dir. Farmers Savs. Bank, Fostoria. Mem. Am., Iowa, Clay County bar assns., Assn. Trial Lawyers Am., Assn. Trial Lawyers Iowa, Delta Theta Phi. Recipient Distinguished Service certificate Iowa County Attys. Assn., 1970. Home: Haywards Bay Okoboji IA 51355 Office: 1823 Highway Blvd Spencer IA 51301 Tel (712) 262-5564

SACKS, ALBERT MARTIN, b. N.Y.C., Aug. 15, 1920; B.B.A. magna cum laude, Coll. City N.Y., 1940; LL.B. magna cum laude, Harvard U., 1948; LL.D., York U., Toronto, Ont., Can., 1969. Admitted to D.C. bar, 1951, Mass. bar, 1957; clk. to judge U.S. Ct. Appeals, 2d Circuit, 1948-49, to Justice Felix Frankfurter, U.S. Supreme Ct., 1949-50; asso. firm Covington & Burling, Washington, 1950-52; asst. prof. law Harvard U., 1952-55, prof., 1955-69, Dane prof., 1969—, asso. dean Law Sch., 1968-71, dean, 1971—; asso. reporter Adv. Com. on Fed. Rules of Civil Procedure, 1961-66, reporter, 1966-70; dir. Mass. Adminstrv. Procedure Study Project, 1953-54; chmn. Mass. Atty. Gen.'s Adv. Com. on Civil Rights and Civil Liberties, 1966-68, Boston Mayor's Home Rule Commn., 1968-71. Mem. Am., Mass. bar assns., Am. Acad. Arts and Scis. Home: 64 Lincoln St Belmont MA 02178 Office: Dean's Office Harvard Law Sch Cambridge MA 02138 Tel (617) 495-4601

SACKS, ALEXANDER, b. N.Y.C., Nov. 11, 1909; student City Coll. N.Y., 1927-29; LL.B., Bklyn. Law Sch., 1932; postgrad. New Sch. for Social Research, 1939-40, N.Y. U. Grad. Sch. Pub. Adminstrn., 1941-42. Admitted to N.Y. bar, 1934; spl. atty. Dept. Justice, Washington and N.Y.C., 1942-47; financial cons. Supreme Hdqrs. London, on assignment by atty. gen. U.S., 1945; atty., sr. economist Office Mil. Govt., Berlin and Frankfurt, 1947-49; individual practice law, cons. economist, pub. affairs specialist, N.Y.C., 1950-71, 75—; confidential counsel N.Y. State Ct. of Claims, 1971-75. Candidate for U.S. Ho. of Reps., 23d Congl. Dist. N.Y., 1968; candidate for judge Civil Ct., 1969, 72; mem. exec. com. Bronx Republican County Com., 1969-73, counsel to chmn., 1971-73. Mem. Fed. Bar Assn., Nat. Econ. Club. Address: 888 7th Ave New York City NY 10019 Tel (212) 265-4300

SACKS, BARRY HOWARD, b. Boston, Aug. 21, 1939; B.S., Mass. Inst. Tech., 1961, M.S., 1964, Ph.D., 1967; J.D., Harvard, 1973. Asst. prof. elec. engring. U. Calif., Berkeley, 1969-70; law clk. firm Peabody, Brown, Rowley & Storey, Boston, 1972-73; admitted to Calif. bar, 1973; asso. firm Winokur, Schoenberg, Maier, Hammerman & Knudsen, San Francisco, 1973—; lectr. Golden Gate U. Grad. Sch. Taxation, 1976. Mem. Am., San Francisco bar assns., Barristers Club, Sigma Xi, Eta Kappa Nu. Fulbright scholar, 1961-62; Nat. Merit scholar, 1957-61; NSF fellow, 1967-68. Home: 940 Union St San Francisco CA 94133 Office: One California St San Francisco CA 94111 Tel (415) 392-8308

SACKS, BERNARD, b. Phila., Dec. 2, 1926; B.A., Temple U., 1949, LL.B., 1952. Admitted to Pa. bar, 1952; individual practice law, Phila., 1975—. Mem. Am., Pa., Phila. bar assns., Am. Trial Lawyers Assn. Contbr. articles to legal jours. Office: Rohm & Haas Bldg 2d Floor 6th and Market St Philadelphia PA 19106 Tel (215) 925-8200

SACKS, DAVID GREENHOOT, b. N.Y.C., Jan. 6, 1924; A.B., Columbia U., 1949, LL.B., 1948. Admitted to N.Y. bar, 1964; asso. firm Newman & Bisco, N.Y.C., 1948-51; asso. firm Simpson, Thacher & Bartlett, N.Y.C., 1952-60, partner, 1961-76; partner, mem. exec. com. Lehman Bros., N.Y.C., 1976—; spl. prof. law Hofstra U. Bd. dirs. Westchester (N.Y.) Community Health Plan, 1976, Westchester Jewish Community Services, 1971, Mamaroneck/Larchmont Student Aid Fund, 1974-75, Nat. Genetics Found., 1976—. Home: 6 Avon Rd Larchmont NY 10538 Office: 1 William St New York City NY 10004 Tel (212) 269-3700

SACKS, GARY T., b. Hartford, Conn., Dec. 31, 1941; B.S. in Bus. Adminstrn., U. Mo., 1963; J.D., Washington U., 1966. Admitted to Mo. bar, 1966, Eastern Dist. Mo. bar, 1966, 7th and 8th Circuit Cts. Appeals bar; asso. firm Goldstein and Price, St. Louis, 1966-70, mem., 1970—. Mem. planning and zoning commn. City of Olivette, Mo., 1969—. Mem. Bar Assn. City St. Louis, Am. Bar Assn., Maritime Law Assn. of Am., Order of Coif. Mem. editorial bd. Washington U. Law Quar., 1966. Home: 2 Bon Hills St Olivette MO 63132 Office: 611 Olive St Saint Louis MO 63101 Tel (314) 421-0710

SACKS, STEPHEN MICHAEL, b. Jamaica, N.Y., Apr. 12, 1942; B.S., Cornell U., 1963; LL.B., Harvard, 1966. Admitted to N.Y. bar, 1966, D.C. bar, 1968, U.S. Supreme Ct. bar, 1975; asso. firm Rosenman, Colin, Kaye, Petschek & Freund, N.Y.C., 1966-67; asso. firm Arnold & Porter, Washington, 1970-76, mem. firm, 1976—; asst. to gen. counsel Sec. of Army, 1967-70. Mem. Am. Bar Assn. Editor Harvard Law Rev. Office: 1229 19th St NW Washington DC 20036 Tel (201) 872-6681

SACKS, ZACHARY HERMAN, b. N.Y.C., Aug. 10, 1935; B.A., Yale, 1957; J.D., Columbia, 1960. Admitted to Calif. bar, 1963; trial atty. R. L. Kautz & Co., Los Angeles, 1963-65; individual practice law, Los Angeles, 1964-73; asso. firm Kendig, Stockwell & Gleason, Los Angeles, 1973—; lectr., panelist Program Bar Admittees, 1973, Symposium Workers Compensation, 1974. Certified specialist Workers Compensation Law. Mem. Calif., Los Angeles County (moderator program workers compensation law) bar assns., Workers Compensation Def. Attys. Assn. Home: 4334 Cezanne Ave Woodland Hills CA 91364 Office: Suite 302 611 S Catalina St Los Angeles CA 90005 Tel (213) 385-8087

SACORAFAS, NICK, b. Detroit, June 2, 1931; B.A., Wayne State U., 1953; J.D., Detroit Coll. Law, 1956. Admitted to Mich. bar, 1957; since practiced in Detroit; ins. adjuster State Farm Mut. Auto Ins. Co., 1956-58; asst. corp. counsel City of Detroit, 1958-74; individual practice law, 1974—. Mem. Mich. State Bar, Am. Judicature Soc., Delta Theta Phi. Contbr. articles to legal jours. Office: 4828 Kensington Detroit MI 48224 Tel (313) 882-3381

SADACCA, STEPHEN SOL, b. Bklyn., May 19, 1944; B.S. in Elec. Engring., Carnegie Inst. Tech., 1966; Bklyn. Law Sch., 1969. Admitted to Tex. bar, 1970; div. patent counsel, consumer products div. Tex. Instruments, Inc., Dallas, 1969—. Mem. Am., Tex., Tex. Jr. bar assns., Dallas-Fort Worth Patent Assn., Dallas Young Lawyers Assn. Home: 10443 Lennox Ln Dallas TX 75229 Office: Texas Instruments Inc PO Box 5474 Dallas TX 75222 Tel (214) 238-5315

SADD, GEORGE JOSEPH, b. Cleve., Aug. 3, 1941; B.S.S., John Carroll U., 1963; J.D., Western Res. U., 1967, LL.M., 1974. Admitted to Ohio bar, 1967, U.S. Supreme Ct. bar, 1972; asst. prosecutor Cuyahoga County (Ohio), 1969—, also chief appellate pros. atty., 1975—; instr. legal medicine seminar. Mem. Cleve., Ohio, Cuyahoga County bar assns. Office: Courts Tower Justice Center 1200 Ontario St Cleveland OH 44113 Tel (216) 623-7730

SADEN, GEORGE AARON, b. Brockton, Mass., Apr. 15, 1910; B.A., Yale, 1931; J.D., Harvard, 1934. Admitted to Conn. bar, 1934, Mass. bar, 1934, U.S. Supreme Ct. bar, 1937; asso. firm Goldstein and Peck, Bridgeport, Conn., 1934-42; individual practice law, Bridgeport, 1946-71; mem. firm Saden & Weiss; mem. Conn. Constl. Planning Commn., 1961-71; magistrate U.S. Dist. Ct., Conn., 1971; judge Conn. Superior Ct., 1971—; mem. Conn. Senate, 1953-54; gen. counsel Conn. Constl. Conv., 1965. Counsel, Conn. Republican Party, 1969-71. Author: Be American, 1942; contbr. articles to legal jours. Home: 5120 Park Ave Bridgeport CT 06604 Office: 1061 Main St Bridgeport CT 06604 Tel (203) 333-8102

SADLER, JAMES ALLEN, b. Boone, Tenn., Nov. 26, 1936; B.S., Delta State Coll., 1964, M.D., 1966; D.Ed., U. Miss., 1968, J.D., 1972. Admitted to Miss. bar, 1972; partner firm Bailey & Sadler, Ocean Springs, Miss., 1973—; asso. prof. La. Tech. U., 1968-70. Mem. adv. bd. Salvation Army, Jackson County, Miss., 1977—. Mem. Am., Miss., Jackson County bar assns., Phi Delta Phi. Contbr. articles to legal jours. Office: 916 Washington Ave Ocean Springs MS 39564 Tel (601) 875-8257

SADLER, LUTHER FULLER, JR., b. Jacksonville, Fla., Apr. 10, 1942; B.A. magna cum laude, Yale, 1964, LL.B., 1967. Admitted to Fla. bar, 1964; mem. firm Mahoney Hadlow & Adams, Jacksonville, 1967—. Trustee, Jacksonville Art Mus., 1975—. Mem. Am., Fla., Jacksonville bar assns., Phi Beta Kappa. Author: (with Jack H. Chambers) A Practical Guide to Bank Acquisitions and Mergers, Tax Considerations, 1976. Tel (904) 354-1100

SADLER, PHILIP MONROE, b. Silver Point, Tenn., Oct. 27, 1915; B.S., Tenn. Polytech. Inst., 1938; LL.B., U. Va., 1947. Admitted to Va. bar, 1947; partner firm Gilmer, Sadler, Ingram, Sutherland & Hutton, Palaski, Va., 1947—. Mem. Va. State Bar Council, 1971-74; v.p. Va. Bar Found., 1976—. Chmn. Pulaski County Sch. bd., 1958-68; chmn. Pulaski County Sch. Trustee Electoral bd., 1974—; mem. Pulaski County Housing Authority, 1974—. Mem. Pulaski County, Va. (chmn. com. on judiciary 1974-75; pres. 1975-76), Am. bar assns., Nat. Conf. Bar Presidents, Am. Judicature Soc., Am. Coll. Trial Lawyers, Internat. Soc. Barristers. Recipient Pulaski Citizenship award, Bus. and Profl. Women's Club, 1956; spl. merit award Pulaski County C. of C., 1955. Home: 331 Northwood Dr Pulaski VA 24301 Office: Midtown Profl Bldg PO Box 878 Pulaski VA 24301 Tel (703) 980-1360

SADLER, R. RUSSELL, b. Balt., Oct. 16, 1926; LL.B., U. Balt., 1955. Admitted to Md. bar, 1955; with State Farm Ins. Co., 1955-72, successively as claim rep., claim supt., house counsel; individual practice law, Ellicott City, Md., 1972—; asst. solicitor County Howard, 1972-75, dep. solicitor, 1975—, asso. mem. Appeals Tax Ct., 1971-72. Mem. Md., Howard County bar assns. Office: 8370 Court Ave Ellicott City MD 21043 Tel (301) 465-5366

SADOW, RICHARD ALAN, b. N.Y.C., Nov. 18, 1944; B.A., U. Cin., 1966; J.D., U. Fla., 1969. Admitted to Fla. bar, 1969; asso. firm Wicker, Smith, Pyszka, Blomquist & Davant, Miami, 1969-70; asso. firm Wolfson and Appel, Miami, 1970-73; partner firm Sadow & Lynne, Miami, 1973—. Vol. worker Kidney Found., 1975. Mem. Fla. (workman's compensation commn. 1975-76), Dade County (workman's compensation commn., 1975-76), Am. bar assns., Am. Trial Lawyers Assn., Acad. Fla. Trial Lawyers (dir. workman compensation sect. 1976-77), Am. Arbitration Assn., Delta Theta Phi. Home: 9800 SW 123d St Miami FL 33176 Office: 12550 Biscayne Blvd Miami FL 33181 Tel 895-6070

SADOWSKI, WILLIAM EDWARD, b. Springfield, Mass., Mar. 17, 1944; B.A., U. Fla., 1966, J.D., 1969. Admitted to Fla. bar, 1969, U.S. Supreme Ct. bar, 1972; mem. firm Helliwell Melrose & DeWolf, Miami, Fla., 1969-73, partner, 1973—; mem. Fla. Ho. of Reps., 1976—. Bd. dirs. Legal Services Greater Miami, 1971—; mem. Gov.'s Youth Adv. Council, 1962. Mem. Am., Fla. (Fla. constn. com. 1974—, legal aid, indigent defendant com. 1969-72), Dade County (dir. 1975—) bar assns., Am. Judicature Soc., Phi Delta Phi. Home: 6700 Brighton Pl Coconut Grove FL 33133 Office: 1400 Brickell Ave Miami FL 33131 Tel (305) 373-7571

SADOWSKY, EDWARD L., b. Bklyn., Feb. 6, 1929; A.B., N.Y. U., 1950; LL.B., Columbia, 1953. Admitted to N.Y. bar, 1953; asso. firm Gettner, Simon & Asher, N.Y.C., 1954-64; mem. firm Tenzer, Greenblatt, Fallon & Kaplan, N.Y.C., 1964—; councilman N.Y.C. 19th Dist., Queens, 1964—. Mem. N.Y., N.Y.C., Queens County, Am. bar assns., N.Y. County Lawyers Assn. Home: 13-15 160th St Beechhurst NY 11357 Office: 100 Park Ave New York City NY 10017 Tel (212) 953-1800

SADUR, STANLEY SHERMAN, b. Boston, Aug. 12, 1934; B.A. cum laude, Boston U., 1956, LL.B., 1958; postgrad. Wayne State U., 1960. Admitted to Mass. bar, 1958, Calif. bar, 1962; practiced law, Boston, 1958; atty. NLRB, Detroit, 1959-60, Los Angeles, 1960-64, trial and injunction atty., Los Angeles, 1964-67, supervisory atty., 1967-72; adminstrv. law judge Bur. Hearings and Appeals, Social Security Adminstrn., HEW, Oakland, Calif., 1972, judge in charge, 1972—. Home: 3905 Campolindo Dr Morage CA 94516 Office: Social Security Adminstrn United Calif Bank Bldg 1330 Broadway Oakland CA 94612 Tel (415) 273-7241

SAETRE, WARREN A., b. Henning, Minn., Aug. 22, 1923; B.S.; J.D., William Mitchell Coll. Law. Admitted to Minn. bar, 1951; partner firm, Warren, Minn., to 1968; U.S. Dist. Ct. judge, Thief River Falls, Minn., 1968—; county atty., Marshall County, Minn. Mem. Minn. Bar Assn., Am. Judicature Soc. Office: Dist Ct Chambers Ct House Thief River Falls MN 56701 Tel (218) 681-2811

SAFFERT, PAUL MICHAEL, b. New Ulm, Minn., May 3, 1945; B.A., Coll. St. Thomas, 1967; J.D., William Mitchell Coll., 1971. Admitted to Minn. bar, 1971; treas. Can. Am. Fin. Corp., Mpls., 1973—; treas. Canadian Am. Fin. Corp. (Can.), Mpls., 1973-76, pres. 1976—; asst. v.p. N.Am. Life & Casualty Co., Mpls., 1974-76, 2d v.p. adminstrn., 1976—. Mem. Am., Minn., Henepin County bar assns., Am. Coll. C.L.U.'s, Minn. Inst. C.P.A.'s (asso.). Home: 13312 Lakeview Dr Burnsville MN 55337 Office: 1750 Hennepin Ave Minneapolis MN 55403 Tel (612) 377-5511

SAFIR, BENJAMIN JAY, b. McKeesport, Pa., May 29, 1905; J.D., U. Mich., 1927. Admitted to Mich. bar, 1927; practice law, Detroit. Mem. Am., Mich. bar assns., Tau Epsilon Rho, Order of the Coif. Mem. editorial bd. Mich. Law Review, 1926-27. Home: 22347 Le Rhone Ave Southfield MI 48075 Office: 2600 Cadillac Tower Detroit MI 48226

SAFRAN, HUBERT MAYER, b. Salt Lake City, Dec. 25, 1930; LL.B., U. Colo., 1954. Admitted to Colo. bar, 1955; partner firm Safran & Payne, Denver, 1973—; mem. Colo. Ho. of Reps., 1965-74. Bd. dirs. Hosp. Audiences, Inc. Denver; pres. S.W. Denver Service Assn.; bd. dirs. S.W. Denver YMCA, S.W. Denver Community Center. Mem. Colo., Denver bar assns., Am., Colo. trial lawyers assns., Am. Arbitration Assn. Home: 3663 S Sheridan Blvd Denver CO 80235 Office: 1930 S Federal Blvd Denver CO 80219 Tel (303) 936-7361

SAFREN, RONALD B., b. St. Louis, May 30, 1931; A.B., U. Mo., 1956, J.D., 1959. Admitted to Mo. bar, 1964, U.S. Supreme Ct. bar, 1969; individual practice law, St. Louis, 1973—; asst. pub. defender, St. Louis, 1965-66; asst. circuit atty. St. Louis, 1966-76; adminstrv.

law judge Bur. Hearings and Appeals, Social Security Adminstrn., HEW, Milw., 1977—. Mem. Am., St. Louis Met. bar assns., Lawyers Assn., Mo. Prosecutor's Assn., Nat. Dist. Atty's Assn. Home: 2501 Wending St Milwaukee WI Office: Bur Hearings and Appeals Suite 800 735 W Wisconsin Ave Milwaukee WI 53233

SAFRIN, FRANKLIN A., b. Indpls., July 20, 1941; B.S., Ind. U., 1963, J.D., 1967. Admitted to Ind. bar, 1967; mem. firm Rocap, Rocap, Reese & Young, Indpls., 1967-77, Safrin & Reiswerg, Indpls., 1977—. Bd. dirs. Pickwick Commons Assn. Mem. Ind. U. Sch. Law Alumni Assn. (pres.). Home: 8827 Kirkham Rd Indianapolis IN 46260 Office: One Indiana Sq Suite 3160 Indianapolis IN 46204 Tel (317) 634-4321

SAGE, RAY O., b. Hays, Kans., Sept. 3, 1920; A.B., Ft. Hays State Coll., 1946; LL.B. magna cum laude, Washburn U., 1949. Admitted to Kans. bar, 1949, N.Mex. bar, 1949; individual practice law, Carlsbad, N.Mex., 1949-68, Las Cruces, N.Mex., 1968—. Mem. Nat. Assn. Coll. and Univ. Attys., N.Mex., Dona Ana County (past pres.) bar assns. Contbr. articles to legal jours. Office: PO Box 725 107 E Lohman Ave Las Cruces NM 88001 Tel (505) 523-7411

SAGE, STEPHEN SAMUEL, b. Kansas City, Mo., Mar. 22, 1927; B.S., Kans. State U., 1950; LL.B., Washburn U., 1953, J.D., 1970. Admitted to Kans. bar, 1953; county atty. Phillips County (Kans.), 1955-65; individual practice law, Phillipsburg, Kans., 1953—. Chmn. Phillips County ARC; bd. dirs. Phillips County Mental Health. Mem. N.W. Kans., Kans., Am. bar assns., Scabbard and Blade, VFW, Am. Legion, Delta Theta Phi. Home: 660 Nebraska St Phillipsburg KS 67661 Office: 620 3d St Phillipsburg KS 67661 Tel (913) 543-2022

SAGER, JOHN WILLIAM, b. N.Y.C., Aug. 27, 1946; B.A., Beloit Coll., 1968; J.D., Syracuse U., 1971. Admitted to Ohio bar, 1971; asso. firm Jones, Day, Reavis & Pogue, Cleve., 1971—. Mem. Am. Bar Assn., Bar Assn. Greater Cleve. Office: 1700 Union Commerce Bldg Cleveland OH 44115 Tel (216) 696-3939

SAGER, RODERICK COOPER, b. Washington, May 25, 1923; A.B., Syracuse U., 1948, LL.B., 1950, J.D., 1968. Admitted to N.Y. bar, 1951; asso. firm Mackenzie, Smith, Lewis, Michell & Hughes, Syracuse, N.Y., 1950-61, mem. firm, 1961-62; gen. counsel Farmers and Traders Life Ins. Co., Syracuse, 1962-66, v.p., gen. counsel, 1966-69, sr. v.p., gen. counsel, 1969-74, exec. v.p., gen. counsel, 1974—; gen. counsel Assn. of N.Y. State Life Ins. Co., N.Y.C., 1968-70. Mem. Jamesville-DeWitt (N.Y.) Central Sch. Dist. Bd. Edn., 1956-69; trustee Onondaga Community Coll., 1971-75; pres. DeWitt Community Library, 1974—. Mem. Am., N.Y. State, Onondaga County bar assns., Assn. Life Ins. Counsel. Home: 14 Lansdowne Rd DeWitt NY 13214 Office: 960 James St Box 1956 Syracuse NY 13201 Tel (315) 471-5656

SAGLE, ROBERT FRANKLIN, b. Hagerstown, Md., Dec. 8, 1930; B.A., George Washington U., 1951, J.D. with honors, 1953. Admitted to D.C. bar, 1953; capt. JAGC, USAF, 1953-56; asst. to dep. atty. gen. Dept. Justice, Washington, 1956-58, 60; asst. U.S. atty. D.C., 1958; spl. atty. Dept. Justice Task Force Organized Crime, N.Y.C. and Washington, 1958-60; legal dept. Schenley Industries, Inc., N.Y.C., 1960-62; asso. firm Cooke & Beneman, Washington, 1962-68, partner, 1968-70; partner firm Harrison, Lucey & Sagle, Washington, 1970—; counsel Bourbon Inst. N.Y.C., 1965-73. Treas., asst. sec. J. Edgar Hoover Found., 1964—; mem. task force for ballot security Republican Nat. Com., 1968, 72, co-chmn., 1976. Mem. D.C. Bar, Assn. Bar City N.Y., Bar Assn. D.C., Fed., Am. bar assns., Am. Legion, Phi Delta Phi, Sigma Chi. Editorial bd. George Washington U. Law Rev., 1952-53. Home: 5207 Bradley Blvd Bethesda MD 20014 Office: 1701 Pennsylvania Ave NW Washington DC 20006 Tel (202) 298-9030

SAHLSTROM, ELMER BERNARD, b. Seattle, Feb. 25, 1918; B.S., U. Oreg., 1945, J.D., 1947. Accountant, Haskins & Sells, N.Y.C., 1941-44; admitted to Oreg. bar, 1947, since practiced in Eugene; mem. firm Thompson & Sahlstrom, 1947-57, Sahlstrom, Lombard, Starr & Vinson, and predecessor, 1957—. Mem. Internat., Am., Oreg. bar assns., Am. Judicature Soc., Am. Trial Lawyers Assn. (pres. So. Oreg. chpt. 1973-75), Assn. Attys. and C.P.A.'s, Am. Inst. Accountants, Oreg. Soc. C.P.A.'s, Oreg. Law Sch. Alumni Assn. (pres. 1972-73), Phi Alpha Delta. Home: 715 Fair Oaks St Eugene OR 97401 Office: 915 Oak St Eugene OR 97401 Tel (503) 687-1718

ST ANTOINE, THEODORE JOSEPH, b. St. Albans, Vt., May 29, 1929; A.B., Fordham Coll., 1951; J.D., U. Mich., 1954; postgrad. (Fulbright scholar) U. London, 1957-58. Admitted to Mich. bar, 1954, Ohio bar, 1954, D.C. bar, 1959, U.S. Supreme Ct. bar, 1959; asso. firm Squire, Sanders & Dempsey, Cleve., 1954; asso. firm Woll, Mayer & St. Antoine, Washington, 1958-63, partner, 1963-65; faculty U. Mich. Law Sch., Ann Arbor, 1965—, prof. law, 1969—, dean, 1971—; labor arbitrator, 1970—; mem. pub. rev. bd. United Auto Workers, 1973—; chmn. Mich. Gov.'s Workmens Compensation Adv. Commn., 1974-75. Mem. Am., Mich. bar assns., Am. Law Inst., Indsl. Relations Research Assn., Order of Coif. Editor-in-chief Mich. Law Rev., 1953-54; co-editor Labor Relations Law: Cases and Materials, 4th edit., 1968, 5th edit., 1974. Home: 1421 Roxbury Rd Ann Arbor MI 48104 Office: U Mich Law Sch Ann Arbor MI 48109 Tel (313) 764-0514

ST CLAIR, JAMES D., b. Akron, Ohio, Apr. 14, 1920; student Augustana Coll., 1938-39; A.B., U. Ill., 1941; LL.B., Harvard U., 1944. Admitted to Mass. bar, 1947, D.C. bar, 1974, U.S. Supreme Ct. bar, 1974, Wis. bar, 1975; asso. firm Hale & Dorr, Boston, 1947-52, jr. partner, 1952-56, sr. partner, 1956-74, 74—; spl. counsel to Pres. U.S., 1974; v.p., dir. Golden Tech., Inc.; lectr. law Harvard U. Gen. counsel United Fund, Wellesley, Mass., 1966; mem. Wellesley Town Meeting, 1963-73, mem. town adv. com., 1966-69. Mem. Am., Mass., Boston bar assns., Am. Law Inst., Am. Coll. Trial Lawyers. Co-author: Assignments in Trial Practice, 1960. Home: 88 Maugus Ave Wellesley Hills MA 02181 Office: 28 State St Boston MA 02109 Tel (617) 742-9100

ST. LANDAU, NORMAN, b. Vienna, Austria, Apr. 14, 1920; student U. Lille, France, 1936-38; B.S. in Philogy, U. Ill., 1941, A.B. in Chemistry, 1941; M. in Comparative Law, N.Y. U., 1951. Admitted to D.C. bar, 1948, N.J. bar, 1964; with Pitts. Plate Glass Co., Barberton, Ohio, 1941-42; asso. firm Johnson & Johnson, New Brunswick, N.J., 1942—, patent atty., 1944-48, internat. counsel, chief trademark counsel, 1948—. Mem. Nat. Fgn. Trade Council (chmn. indsl. property com. 1975—), Pharm. Mfrs. Assn. (chmn. trademark and copyright com. 1975—), Internat. Patent and Trademark Assn. (treas. 1959—), Inter-Am. Assn. Indsl. Property (U.S. Nat. rep. 1972-77, treas., mem. exec. com. 1977—), Am. Arbitration Assn. (arbitrator 1970—), U.S. Trademark Assn. (dir. 1966-72), Am., N.Y., N.J. (pres. 1959-60) patent law assns., N.Y. Assn. Bar, Nat. Council Patent Law Assns. (past sec.), Consular Law Soc., Internat. Law Assn., D.C., N.J. bar assns. Internat. editor: Les Nouvelles, 1968—; contbr. articles to legal jours. Home: 822 E Meadow Dr Bound Brook NJ 08805 Office: PO Box 1254 New Brunswick NJ 08903 Tel (201) 524-9201

ST. MARTIN, RONALD FRANCIS, b. Attleboro, Mass., Mar. 28, 1935; B.A., Ind. U., 1957, LL.B., 1961. Admitted to Ind. bar, 1962; partner firm Reed and St. Martin, Knox, Ind., 1962-74; individual practice law, Knox, 1975—. Former pres. Calif. Twp. PTA, Base Lake Property Owners Assn. Mem. Ind., Sarke-Pulaski bar assns. Home: Rural Route 5 Box 418 Knox IN 46534 Office: 1406 S Heaton St Knox IN 46534 Tel (219) 772-6868

SAJOVEC, FRANK MICHAEL, JR., b. Cleve., Aug. 14, 1936; B.S. in Mech. Engring., Carnegie Inst. Tech., 1958; J.D., Cleve. Marshall Law Sch., 1966. Admitted to Ohio bar, 1967; patent atty. Libbey-Owens-Ford Co., Toledo, 1967-69, Eaton Corp., Cleve., 1969-75, sr. patent atty. Eaton Corp., 1975—. Mem. Am., Ohio, Cleve. bar assns., Cleve. Patent Law Assn. Office: 100 Erieview Plaza Cleveland OH 44114 Tel (216) 523-7820

SAK, ALLEN I., b. N.Y.C., Mar. 26, 1934; B.A., Alfred U., 1955; LL.B., Columbia U., 1958. Admitted to N.Y. bar, 1959, U.S. Supreme Ct. bar, 1964; asso. firms Theodore Kamens, N.Y.C., 1959, Dannenberg Hazen and Lake, N.Y.C., 1959-60, Jack Stanislaw, 1960-62; law sec. to Hon. Jack Stanislaw, 1962-66; individual practice law, Smithtown, N.Y., 1967-71, 74-76; partner firms Smith, Cohen, Sak & Warren, Smithtown, 1971-73, Baum, Skigen, Lefkowitz, Sak & Purcell, Smithtown, 1976—; dir. Suffolk Regional Off Track Betting, 1975-76, vice chmn., 1976—; dir. Suffolk County Prepaid Legal Services Corp., 1976—; mem. joint grievance com. 10th Jud. Dist., 1975—. Bd. dirs. Suffolk County ACLU, 1971-73, vice chmn., 1973. Fellow N.Y. Bar Found.; mem. Am., N.Y. State, Suffolk County (chmn. grievance com. 1968-73, dir. 1973-76, Dir's. award) bar assns. Office: 278 E Main St PO Box 648 Smithtown NY 11787 Tel (516) 265-2234

SAKER, JOSEPH MICHAEL, b. Warren, Ohio, Mar. 20, 1926; J.D., Youngstown Coll., 1955. Admitted to Ohio bar, 1955, U.S. Supreme Ct. bar, 1962; individual practice law, Warren, after 1955; now partner Saker & Saker, Warren; asst. atty. gen. Ohio, 1955-62. Mem. County Bar Assn., Ohio Assn. Attys. Gen. Home: 4801 Woodland Grove Warren OH 44483 Office: 161 Pien NE Warren OH 44481 Tel (216) 392-2589

SAKRISON, JAMES MCCALL, b. Tucson, Jan. 3, 1941; B.S., U. Ariz., 1963, LL.B., 1966. Admitted to Ariz. bar, 1966, Calif. bar, 1969; asso. firm Lesher & Scruggs, and predecessors, Tucson, 1969-70, partner, 1970-73; partner firm Slutes, Browning, Zlaket & Sakrison, and predecessors, Tucson, 1973—. Bd. mgmt. Met. YMCA, Tucson, 1970—; bd. dirs. Tucson chpt. ARC, 1971—. Mem. Calif., Ariz., Pima County (bd. dirs. 1972—), Am. bar assns. Office: 310 Transamerica Bldg Tucson AZ 85701 Tel (602) 624-6691

SAKS, RICHARD LEE, b. Newark, Jan. 10, 1944; B.A., Pa. State U., 1965, postgrad. in Pub. Adminstrn., 1965-67; J.D., Suffolk U., Boston, 1970. Admitted to N.J. bar, 1970; N.J. jud. clk., 1970-71; asso. firm Hoffman & Humphreys, Wayne, N.J., 1971-73; sr. staff atty. central ethics Adminstv. Office of Cts., Trenton, N.J., 1973-74, chief jud. edn., 1974-75, chief jud. edn. and legal research, 1975—. Mem. N.J. Bar Assn., Am. Judicature Soc., State Jud. Educators Assn. (dir., Eastern regional dir.). Recipient Am. Jurisprudence award Bancroft-Whittney Co., 1968; editorial bd. Suffolk Law Rev., 1969-70; mem., 1968-70. Office: State House Annex Trenton NJ 08625 Tel (609) 292-5286

SALATICH, PETER BLAISE, JR., b. New Orleans, Sept. 5, 1918; D.D.S., Loyola U., New Orleans, 1939, LL.B., 1962. Practice dentistry, specializing in oral surgery, New Orleans, 1940-42, 46-73, Metairie, La., 1973—; admitted to La. bar, 1962; individual practice law, Metairie, 1962—; asst. prof. oral diagnosis La. State U. Dental Sch., 1975—. Mem. La. Bar Assn., Am. Soc. Oral Surgeons, ADA. Office: 2514 Metairie Rd Metairie LA 70001 Tel (504) 833-4955

SALEH, JOHN, b. O'Donnell, Tex., June 29, 1928; B.B.A., U. Tex., 1950, J.D. with honors, 1952; postgrad. Judge Adv. Gen. Sch. U. Va., 1953. Admitted to Tex. bar, 1952, U.S. Supreme Ct. bar, 1961; asso. bd. rev. Judge Adv. Gens. Corps, U.S. Army, Washington, 1953; individual practice law, Lamesa, Tex., 1955—. Mem. Tex. Law Rev. Assn. (life), State Bar Tex., Am., Lamesa (pres. 1963-64) bar assns., Tex. Trial Lawyers Assn., Assn. Trial Lawyers Am., Order of Coif, Phi Delta Phi. Asso. editor Tex. Law Rev., 1951-52, also contbr. articles. Home: 605 Doak St O'Donnell TX 79351 Office: 502 N 1st St Lamesa TX 79331 Tel (806) 872-2171

SALEM, ALBERT MCCALL, JR., b. Washington, Apr. 3, 1939; student Georgetown U., 1956-57; A.B., U. N.C., Chapel Hill, 1960, J.D., 1963. Admitted to N.C. bar, 1963, Fla. bar, 1965, U.S. Ct. Mil. Appeals bar, 1964, U.S. Tax Ct. bar 1975, U.S. Supreme Ct. bar, 1974, U.S. Ct. Appeals bar, 1973; mem. Judge Adv. staff USAF, 1963-66; individual practice law, Tampa, Fla., 1966-70; sr. partner firm Salem, Salem, Musial, Morse and Mackenzie, P.A., Tampa, 1970—; dist. counsel Nat. Maritime Union. Mem. Am., Tampa-Hillsborough County, N.C. bar assns., Fla. Bar (unauthorized practice law com.), Fla. Acad. Trial Lawyers, Trial Judge Advs. Assn. Office: Suite 100 Salem Bldg 4600 W Kennedy Blvd Tampa FL 33609 Tel (813) 872-8424

SALERNO, CHARLES MARION, b. Clyde, N.Y., Aug. 15, 1902; LL.B., Albany Law Sch., 1925. Admitted to N.Y. State bar, 1926; individual practice law, Geneva, N.Y., 1927-34, Steuben County, Addison, N.Y., 1934—; atty. Community Nat. Bank, Addison, 1963—, dir., 1963—; atty. Village of Addison, 1936-66. Mem. Steuben County Bar Assn. Home: 29 Maple St Addison NY 14801 Office: 28 Tuscarora St Addison NY 14801 Tel (607) 359-2259

SALERNO, JOHN P., b. N.Y.C., Sept. 1, 1925; B.A., Queen Coll., 1949; LL.B., St. John's U., 1952, J.D., 1968. Admitted to N.Y. bar, 1952; asst. v.p. Am. Title Ins. Co., Bklyn., 1952-60; individual practice law, Hicksville, N.Y., 1960—. Mem. Queens City Bar Assn. Office: 560 S Broadway St Hicksville NY 11801 Tel (516) 433-7575

SALFI, DOMINICK JOSEPH, b. Phila., Aug. 29, 1937; A.A., U. Fla., 1957, B.A., 1958, J.D., 1961. Admitted to Fla. bar, 1961; practiced in Orlando, Fla., 1961-70; judge 18th Jud. Circuit Ct. Fla., 1970—; legal asst. Orange-Seminole del. to Fla. Legislature, 1967, Gov. Fla., 1968-70; state atty. Fla. 18th Jud. Circuit, 1967-69. Mem. Seminole County (Fla.) Drug Action Com.; mem. Cocoa (Fla.) Community Correctional Citizens Adv. Bd.; chief Y-Indian Guides, Altamonte Springs, Fla.; active Y-Indian Princesses, Gray-Y Football; bd. dirs. Fla. Oceanic Services Inst. Mem. Am. Bar Assn., Fla., Orange County, Seminole County bar assns., Conf. Circuit Judges (chmn. juvenile sect.), Delta Theta Phi, Delta Upsilon (pres.). Recipient Eagle Scouts award Boy Scouts Am., 1971-74, Fla. Youth Related Services Assn. award, 1974. Home: Route 1 PO Box 19 Longwood FL 32750 Office: Seminole County Courthouse Sanford FL 32771 Tel (305) 323-8030

SALIBA, WILLIAM HALEEM, b. Ozark, Ala., July 16, 1936; B.A. in Polit. Sci., U. Ala., 1958, LL.B., 1960; grad. Nat. Coll. State Judiciary, 1975. Admitted to Ala. bar, 1960, U.S. Ct. Mil. Appeals bar, 1962, U.S. Supreme Ct. bar, 1972; served with Judge Adv. Gen. Corps USAF, 1960-63; mem. firm Foreman & Brown, 1963-64; individual practice law, Mobile, Ala., 1964—; asst. city atty. City of Mobile, 1965-67; contract adminstr. Continental Motors, Mobile, 1967-68; judge Municipal Ct., Mobile, 1973—; legal adviser Mobile York Rite. Mem. Am., Mobile, Ala. bar assns., Am. Judicature Soc., Am. Judges Assn. Home: 525 Spring Park Dr Mobile AL 36608 Office: 850 Downtowner Blvd Mobile AL 36609 Tel (205) 342-0571

SALISBURY, R(OWLAND) KEITH, b. Utica, N.Y., Mar. 15, 1944; B.A., Williams Coll., Williamstown, Mass., 1966; J.D., Cornell U., 1969. Admitted to N.Y. bar, 1969; confidential law sec. to justices N.Y. State Supreme Ct., 1969-72; asso. firm Guernsey, Butts & Walsh, Poughkeepsie, N.Y., 1973-75, partner, 1975—. Bd. dirs. Hudson Valley Estate Planning Council, Poughkeepsie, 1975—. Mem. Am., N.Y. State, Dutchess County bar assns. Office: 75 Washington St Poughkeepsie NY 12601 Tel (914) 452-8200

SALISCH, VICTORIA JEAN, b. Carmel, Calif., Dec. 20, 1942; student Santa Rosa Jr. Coll., 1961-63; B.A., U. Calif., Davis, 1966; J.D., U. Pacific, 1971. Admitted to Calif. bar, 1972; legal counsel Calif. Dept. Human Resources Devel., 1971-72; dep. pub. defender Fresno County (Calif.), 1972-75; partner firm Salisch & Salisch, Fresno, 1975—; instr. McGeorge Sch. Law, U. Pacific, 1972; prof. criminal law and procedure San Joaquin Coll. Law, Fresno, 1976—; instr. bus. law Calif. State U., Fresno, 1976—. Mem. Am., Calif., Fresno County bar assns., Calif. Barristers Assn., Calif. Women Lawyers. Mem. staff Pacific Law Jour., 1969-71; Am. Jurisprudence scholar, 1969-71; Corpus Juris scholar, 1969-71. Office: 124 W Shaw Ave Suite 101 Fresno CA 93704 Tel (209) 226-9030

SALITERMAN, RICHARD ARLEN, b. Mpls., Aug. 3, 1946; B.A. summa cum laude, U. Minn., 1968, J.D., Columbia U., 1971; LL.M., N.Y. U., 1974. Admitted to Minn. bar, 1972, D.C. bar, 1973; mem. legal staff U.S. Senate Subcom. on Antitrust and Monopoly, 1971-72; acting dir., dep. dir. compliance and enforcement div. Fed. Energy Office, Region II, N.Y.C., 1974; mem. staff Presdl. Clemency Bd., Washington, 1975; individual practice law, Mpls., 1976—; adj. prof. law Hamline U., 1976—. Mem. Am., Minn., Hennepin County, D.C., bar assns., Grey Friars Soc. (pres. 1967-68), Phi Beta Kappa. Editorial staff Columbia Human Rights Law Rev., 1969-70, editorial bd., 1970-71; contbr. articles to profl. jours. Home: 11911 Live Oak Dr Minnetonka MN 55343 Office: Suite 715 First Nat Bank Bldg 120 S 6th St Minneapolis MN 55402 Tel (612) 336-2651

SALIVAR, DAVID CHARLES, b. N.Y.C., Mar. 12, 1949; B.S., U. Mo., 1971; J.D., St. Louis U., 1974. Admitted to Mo. bar, 1974; served with JAGC, USAF; mem. firm Tremaynelay, Carr & Bauer, Clayton, Mo., 1974—. Mem. St. Louis, St. Louis County, Am. bar assns. Office: suite 801 222 S Central St Clayton MO 63105 Tel (314) 863-4151

SALMON, JACOB QUINT, b. N.Y.C., Oct. 3, 1907; B.S., U. Pitts., 1928, LL.B., 1931. Admitted to Pa. bar, 1932, U.S. Supreme Ct. bar, 1960; asso. firm Moorhead & Marshall, Beaver, Pa., 1931-35; partner firm Wilson & Salmon, Beaver, 1935-70; judge Beaver County (Pa.) Common Pleas Ct., 1970—. Pres. United Cancer Council, Indpls., 1969-71, Beaver County Cancer Soc., 1963-65, Beaver County Health and Welfare Council, 1964-65; bd. dirs. Beaver County Rehab. Center, 1970—; bd. visitors U. Pitts. Sch. Law, 1970—. Fellow Am. Coll. Probate Counsel; mem. Am., Pa. (past bd. govs.), Beaver County bar assns., Am. Law Inst., Pa. Bar Inst. (dir. 1974—), Am. Judicature Soc. Home: 1005 8th Ave Beaver Falls PA 15010 Office: Courthouse Beaver PA 15009 Tel (412) 774-5000

SALMON, MAURICE LOUIS, b. Mobile, Ala., Aug. 30, 1923; B.S., U. Ala., 1943, LL.B., 1948. Admitted to Ala. bar, 1949; partner firm Watts, Salmon, Roberts, Manning & Noojin, and predecessors, Huntsville, Ala., 1950—; v.p., sec. Huntsville Indsl. Assos., 1958—; dir. Dunlop Tire & Rubber Corp.; chief counsel, dir. 1st Ala. Bank of Huntsville, 1973—; instr. U. Ala. Continuing Legal Edn., 1962. Pres. Huntsville Indsl. Expansion Com., 1968-70. Mem. Am., Ala., Huntsville-Madison County bar assns., Estate Planning Council Birmingham, Ala. C. of C. (pres. 1974-75). Home: 2201 Briarcliff Rd SE Huntsville AL 35801 Office: 200 Terry-Hutchens Bldg Huntsville AL 35801 Tel (205) 533-3500

SALO, ANN DISTLER, b. Indpls., Sept. 2, 1947; B.A., Purdue U., 1969; J.D., George Washington U., 1972; LL.M., Emory U., 1976. Admitted to Ga. bar, 1973; asso. firm Hansell, Post, Brandon & Dorsey, Atlanta, 1972—. Mem. Am., Atlanta bar assns., State Bar Ga. Office: 3300 1st Nat Bank Tower Atlanta GA 30303 Tel (404) 581-8064

SALSBERY, HAROLD FREDERICK, JR., b. Victoria, Tex., Dec. 16. 1944; B.A., U. Ky., 1970, J.D., 1973. Admitted to W.Va. bar, 1973, Ky. bar, 1973; since practiced in Parkersburg, W.Va., asso. firm Ronning & Brown, 1973-74, Burk & Bayley, 1974-75; jr. partner firm Burk & Bayley, 1975—; municipal judge City of Parkersburg, 1975—; mem. bd. Mid-Ohio Valley Mass Transit Authority, 1975—. Bd. dirs. Parkersburg YMCA, 1976—, United Fund, 1976—. Mem. Am. Bar Assn., Am. Judicature Soc. Home: 2410 Plum St Parkersburg WV 26101 Office: 415-1/2 Market St PO Box 287 Parkersburg WV 26101 Tel (304) 422-6559

SALTER, LESTER HERBERT, b. Waterbury, Conn., Apr. 26, 1918; B.S., U. Pa., 1940, LL.B., 1948. Admitted to R.I. bar, 1948, U.S. Tax Ct. bar, 1949; atty. Office Chief Counsel, IRS, Newark and Boston, 1949-53; individual practice law, Providence, 1953-57; mem. firm Salter and McGowan, Providence, 1957-70; mem. firm Salter, McGowan, Arcaro & Swartz, Providence, 1970—; lectr. Northeastern U., 1955-56; chmn. U. R.I. Fed. Tax Inst., 1972—; chmn. disciplinary bd. Supreme Ct. R.I., 1975—. Mem. Am., R.I. bar assns., Am. Judicature Soc. Asso. editor: U. Pa. Law Review, 1947-48, R.I. Bar Jour., 1961-68. Home: 75 Blackstone Blvd Providence RI 02906 Office: 1500 Industrial Bank Bldg Providence RI 02903 Tel (401) 274-0300

SALTMAN, ISRAEL H., b. Perth Amboy, N.J., Aug. 30, 1914; B.A., Rutgers U., 1936, LL.B., 1938. Admitted to N.J. bar, 1938, asso. firm Louis F. Sellye, Perth Amboy, 1947-55; spl. asst. to atty. gen. State of N.J., 1959-67; asst. counsel Middlesex County (N.J.), 1969—; dept.

judge adv. Jewish War Vets., 1968-70, 72-73, state hosp. coordinator, 1974. Mem. Perth Amboy Citizen's Adv. Com., 1962; trustee Temple Beth Mordecai, 1969—. Mem. N.J. State, Middlesex County bar assns. Home: 120 Norris Ave Metuchen NJ 08840 Office: 313 State St Perth Amboy NJ 08861 Tel (201) 826-5252

SALTONSTALL, LEVERETT, b. Chestnut Hill, Mass., Sept. 1, 1892; A.B., Harvard, 1914, LL.B., 1917; LL.D., Northeastern U., 1935, Bates Coll., 1939, Boston U., 1940, Bowdoin Coll., 1940, Amherst Coll., 1941, Williams Coll., 1941, Holy Cross Coll., 1942, Harvard, 1942, Colby Coll., 1942, Tufts Coll., 1942, De Pauw U., 1943, Clark U., 1944, Toledo U., 1945, Franklin and Marshall Coll., 1947, Trinity Coll., 1947, Coll. William and Mary, 1948, Northwestern U., 1949, Worcester Poly. Inst., 1950, Kenyon Coll., 1953, Norwich U., 1955, Brandeis U., 1958; M.S., New Bedford (Mass.) Inst. Textile and Tech., 1955, U. Mass., 1963; J.D., Portia Law Sch., 1957; D. Pub. Adminstrn., Suffolk U., 1957; D.B.A., Babson Inst., 1961; LL.D., Merrimack Coll., 1967; D.S. in Oratory, Curry Coll., 1969; Sc.D., Lowell Tech. Inst., 1968. Admitted to Mass. bar, 1919; mem. firm Gaston, Snow, Saltonstall & Hunt, 1926-28; asst. dist. atty. Middlesex County (Mass.), 1921-22; mem. Newton (Mass.) Bd. Aldermen, 1920-22; mem. Mass. Ho. of Reps., 1923-36, speaker, 1929-36; gov. Mass., 1939-44; mem. U.S. Senate, 1944-67, ret., 1967. Home: Dover MA 02030 Office: Fidelity Bldg Boston MA 02109 Tel (617) 227-8660

SALTZBURG, STEPHEN ALLAN, b. Phila., Sept. 10, 1945; A.B., Dickison Coll., 1967; J.D., U. Pa., 1970. Admitted to Calif. bar, 1971, D.C. bar, 1973, Va. bar, 1977; law clk. U.S. Dist. Ct. No. Dist. Calif., 1970-71; law clk. U.S. Supreme Ct., 1971-72; asst. prof. law U. Va., 1972-74, asso. prof. 1974—; vis. prof. U. Mich., summer 1975, U. Calif. Berkeley, 1975-76, U. Tex., summer 1977. Mem. AAUP. Author: Federal Rules Evidence Manual, 1975, supplement, 1976; A Modern Approach to Evidence, 1977; reporter Alaska Rules of Evidence. Home: 105 Smithfield Ct Charlottesville VA 22901 Office: Sch law Univ Va Charlottesville VA 22901 Tel (804) 924-3219

SALUS, SAMUEL WIEDER, II, b. Phila., July 11, 1933; grad. magna cum laude Germantown Acad., 1951; B.A., Cornell U., 1955; LL.B., U. Pa., 1960. Admitted to Phila. Cts. of Common Pleas bar, 1961, Pa. bar, 1962; law clk. Chief Judge J. Cullen Ganey Fed. Dist. Ct. Eastern Dist. Pa., 1960-61; chief pub. defender Montgomery County (Pa.), 1968—; partner firm Koch, Phelps and Salus, Norristown, Pa., 1972—. Zoning solicitor Upper Dublin Twp. Montgomery County. Mem. Pa., Montgomery bar assns., Montgomery County Trial Lawyers Assn. Office: 1 Montgomery Plaza Suite 610 Swede St and Airy St Norristown PA 19401 Tel (215) 277-2010

SALVAN, SHERWOOD ALLEN, b. N.Y.C., Dec. 2, 1942; B.B.A. in Accounting, St. Francis Coll.; M.B.A., Pace U.; J.D., N.Y. U. Admitted to N.Y. State bar, 1969; individual practice law, N.Y.C., 1972—. Mem. Am., Bronx bar assns., Am. Judicature Soc., N.Y. County Lawyers, N.Y. Trial Lawyers Assn. Contbr. articles to legal jours. Office: 501 Fifth Ave New York City NY 10017 Tel (212) MO1-0290

SALVATI, RODNEY LOUIS, b. Mt. Kisco, N.Y., Oct. 14, 1946; B.A., Syracuse U., 1968; J.D., Albany Law Sch., 1972. Admitted to N.Y. bar, 1973; individual practice law, Mt. Kisco, 1973—; dep. village atty. Village of Mt. Kisco, 1975—. Bd. dirs. Mt. Kisco Little League, 1973—; mem. Mt. Kisco Narcotics Guidance Council, 1974-75; chmn. Mt. Kisco Ethnic day Celebration, 1975. Mem. N.Y. State Bar Assn. Office: PO Box 664 8 S Moger Ave Mount Kisco NY 10549 Tel (914) 666-8478

SALVATORE, ANTHONY, b. N.Y.C., Oct. 9, 1922; LL.B., Bklyn. Law Sch., 1950; Admitted to N.Y. bar, 1951, So. Dist. bar, 1953, Eastern Dist bar, 1967; partner firm Salvatore & Sangiaori, 1951-53, Salvatore, Copertino & Tisch, 1965-72; individual practice law, 1972—; Justice of the peace Town of Brookhaven, Suffolk County, N.Y., 1960-64. Mem. Suffolk County, Am. bar assns., Family Law Com. Home: One Mill River Rd Setauket NY 11733 Office: Hillside Profl Center Route 25A East Setauket NY 11733 Tel (516) 941-4411

SALYERS, ROBERT JUSTICE, b. La Porte, Ind., July 8, 1946; B.S. in Animal Sci., Purdue U., 1968; J.D., Ind. U., 1973. Admitted to Ind. bar, 1973; tax dept. Coopers & Lybrand, Indpls., 1972-74; individual practice law, Indpls., 1974—. Bd. dirs. Greater Indpls. Assn. for Lutheran Secondary Edn., 1976--, Neo-Fight, Inc., 1976—. Mem. Am., Ind., Indpls. bar assns. Office: 614 Circle Tower Indianapolis IN 46204 Tel (317) 634-2070

SALZER, FRANK STEPHEN, b. Jersey City, Dec. 3, 1943; B.A., Seton Hall U., J.D. Admitted to N.J. bar, 1968; asso. firm Seaman and Clark, Perth Amboy, N.J., 1968-71; lawyer N.J. Mfrs. Ins. Co., Trenton, N.J., 1971—. Mem. Am., N.J., Ocean County bar assns. Home: 4 Chelsea Ct Toms River NJ Office: Box 2708 Sullivan Way Trenton NJ 08607 Tel (609) 883-1300

SALZMAN, BARRY MARK, b. Toledo, Dec. 2, 1942; B.A., U. Fla., 1964; J.D. Stetson U., 1967. Admitted to Fla. bar, 1967; mem. firm Alex D. Finch, Clearwater, Fla., 1968-69; mem. firm Fox & Burton, Clearwater, 1969-70; mem. firm Roney, Ulmer, Woodworth & Jacobs, St. Petersburg, Fla., 1970-73; judge Indsl. Claims, St. Petersburg, 1973—; adj. prof. law Stetson Coll. of Law, 1975—; asso. commr. Fla. Indsl Relations Commn., 1976. Home: 7030 Mango Ave S St Petersburg FL 33707 Office: Room 354 Fla State Office Bldg 525 Mirror Lake Dr St Petersburg FL 33701 Tel (813) 893-2321

SAMALIN, EDWIN, b. N.Y.C., Sept. 19, 1935; B.S., U. R.I., 1957; J.D., N.Y. Law Sch., 1962. Admitted to N.Y. bar, 1963; tax atty. Electric Bond & Share Co., N.Y.C., 1963-64; individual practice law, Yorktown, N.Y., 1964-69; partner firm Samalin & Shlaver, Yorktown Heights, N.Y., 1969—; instr. bus. adminstrn. Mercy Coll., Dobbs Ferry, N.Y., 1974—; mem. panel of arbitrators Am. Arbitration Assn. Accountant GAO, N.Y.C., 1956. Mem. N.Y. State, Westchester County (N.Y.) (spl. lectr.), Yorktown bar assns., N.Y. State Trial Lawyers Assn. Tel (914) 962-3808

SAMAY, Z. LANCE, b. Janoshaza, Hungary, Dec. 2, 1944; B.A., Rutgers U., 1967; J.D., Seton Hall U., 1970. Admitted to N.J. bar, 1970, U.S. Ct. Appeals for 3d Circuit, 1974, U.S. Supreme Ct. bar, 1976; law sec. appellate div. Superior Ct. N.J., 1970-71; asst. U.S. atty. for Dist. N.J., 1971-76; chief environ. protection div. Office of U.S. Atty. Fed. Dist. N.J., 1972-74, chief civil div., 1974-76; adj. prof. environ. law Seton Hall U. Sch. Law, 1973, 74, 76; trial instr. Atty. Gen.'s Advocacy Inst., 1975, 76; vice chmn. consumer affairs com. Fed. Exec. Bd., 1973-74, chmn. human resources com., 1974-75, chmn. relations with academia com., 1975-76. Mem. Am., N.J., Fed., Essex County, Morris County bar assns., Am. Judicature Soc., Seton Hall Law Alumni Assn. (adv. com. to dean 1971-72, trustee 1975-77, treas. 1975-76, pres. 1976-77). Recipient U.S. Atty. Gen's spl. commendation for outstanding service, 1973; U.S. Dept. Justice spl. achievement award for sustained superior performance, 1972, 76; co-founder notes and rewrite editor Seton Hall Law Rev., 1969-70, case notes editor, 1969. Home: 136 Kenilworth Rd Mountain Lakes NJ 07046

SAMENGA, ALFRED FRANK, b. N.Y.C., Dec. 1916; LL.B., St. John's U., Bklyn., 1941. Admitted to N.Y. State bar, 1942, U.S. Dist. Ct. for So. Dist. N.Y. bar, 1950; investigator, trial atty. Third Party Carriers, N.Y.C., 1942-51; practiced in Woodhaven, N.Y., 1951-55, Elmont, N.Y., 1955-64; judge Nassau County (N.Y.) Dist. Ct., 1965-74; acting judge Nassau County Ct., 1970-74, judge, 1975—. Merit badge counselor Nassau County council Boy Scouts Am., 1960—; panelist, lectr. civic groups; trustee Franklin Gen. Hosp., Franklin Square, N.Y., 1960—. Mem. Nassau Bar Assn., New York Workmen's Compensation Bar Assn. (v.p.), Columbian Lawyers, Cath. Lawyers (dir.), Nassau Lawyers' Assn., Am. Justinian Soc., Jurists, County Ct. Judges' Assn., Bar Assn. Nassau County. Office: 262 Old Country Rd Mineola NY 11501 Tel (516) 535-2241

SAMFORD, THOMAS DRAKE, II, b. Opelika, Ala., Mar. 4, 1934; A.B. in Politics, Princeton, 1955; J.D., U. Ala., 1961. Admitted to Ala. bar, 1961, U.S. Middle Dist. Ala. bar, 1961, 5th Circuit bar, 1961; partner firm Samford & Samford, Opelika, 1961—; judge City Ct., Opelika, 1961—. Chmn. Opelika Downtown Action Com., 1957-75; pres. Opelika C. of C., 1968, Opelika Community Chest, 1966; dir. Ala. Law Sch. Found.; mem. accounting and finance adv. bd. Auburn U. Ala. Law Inst.; mem. Ala. Citizens Task Force on Higher Edn. Mem. Am., Ala., Lee County (pres. 1965) bar assns., Farrah Law Soc., Am. Judicature Soc., Phi Beta Kappa, Phi Delta Phi, Omicron Delta Kappa. Recipient Buchanan prize in politics, 1955; named outstanding young man in Ala. Jaycees, 1967. Home: 805 Ridgewood St Opelika AL 36801 Office: Box 550 Samford Bldg Opelika AL 36801 Tel (205) 745-4654

SAMFORD, WILLIAM JAMES, II, b. Opelika, Ala., Mar. 14, 1936; A.B., U. Ala., 1957, LL.B., 1962; grad. Nat. Coll. Juvenile Justice, 1975. Admitted to Ala. bar, 1962; partner firm Samford & Samford, Opelika, 1962-75; dep. recorder City of Opelika, 1972-75; judge Lee County Dist. Ct., 1975—; lectr. Auburn U.; mem. faculty Ala. Confs. on Volunteerism, Am. Acad. Jud. Edn.; chmn. judges adv. council Ala. Dept. Youth Services, 1976; mem. Ala. Juvenile Justice Com. Bd. deacons 1st. Presbyn. Ch., Opelika, 1965; chmn. Opelika United Appeal, 1970; pres. Opelika Community Chest, 1971; bd. dirs. Youth Devel. Center, Opelika, Project Uplift, Auburn, Ala., Lee County Council for Neglected, Dependent Children. Mem. Lee County (pres. 1965), Ala., Am. bar assns., Ala. Juvenile Ct. Judges (v.p.), Nat. Council Juvenile Ct. Judges (chmn. status offenses com.). Author: Manual for Notaries Public, 1964. Home: 1125 E Collinwood Circle Opelika AL 36801 Office: Lee County Courthouse Opelika AL 36801 Tel (205) 749-3352

SAMMONS, WILLIAM EDWARD, b. Portsmouth, Ohio, Sept. 27, 1924; B.S. in Commerce, Ohio U., 1949; J.D., U. Cin., 1952. Admitted to Ohio bar, 1952, U.S. Supreme Ct. bar, 1957; individual practice law, Chillicothe, Ohio, 1952-62; judge Chillicothe Municipal Ct., 1962—. Pres., Chillicothe Exchange Club, 1966; pres. Ross County (Ohio) Conservation League, 1971. Mem. Ohio, Am., Ross County (pres., 1972) bar assns., N. Am. Judges Assn., Am. Judicature Soc., Ohio Municipal Judges Assn. (pres., 1976—), Ohio Jud. Conf. (exec. com., 1976—), Gen. J. Sill Civil War Round Table (pres. 1971-72). Home: 86 Applewood Dr Chillicothe OH 45601 Office: City Bldg Chillicothe OH 45601 Tel (614) 774-3690

SAMOL, ROBERT JOSEPH, b. Detroit, Dec. 4, 1947; B.A., Wheeling Coll., 1969; J.D., W.Va. U., 1972. Admitted to W. Va. bar, 1972; asso. firm Kahle & Kahle, Wheeling, 1972-73; asso. firm James J. Haranzo, Wheeling, 1973-75; individual practice law, Wheeling, 1975—; commr. accounts Ohio County, 1975—. Chmn. Ohio County Commn. on Crime, Delinquency and Corrections, 1974—; chmn. Wheeling Transp. Authority, 1976—. Mem. Am., Ohio County bar assns., W.Va. State Bar. Home: 1269 National Rd Wheeling WV 26003 Office: 13th St and Eoff St Wheeling WV 26003 Tel (304) 232-5940

SAMOLE, MYRON MICHAEL, b. Chgo., Nov. 29, 1943; J.D., DePaul U., 1967. Admitted to Ill. bar, 1967; individual practice law, Chgo., 1968—; exec. v.p. Fidelity Electronics, Ltd., 1970—. Pres. indsl. adv. council Prosser Vocat. High Sch., Chgo., 1974—; pres. Sutton Point Homeowners' Assn., Chgo., 1975—. Mem. Am., Chgo., Ill. bar assns., Am. Trial Lawyers' Assn., Phi Alpha Delta. Office: 5245 W Diversey Ave Chicago IL 60639 Tel (312) 637-2790

SAMOVAR, PHILLIP GERRALD, b. Los Angeles, May 30, 1942; B.A., U. Calif. at Los Angeles, 1963, LL.B., 1966. Admitted to Calif. bar, 1967, U.S. Supreme Ct. bar, 1972; dep. atty. gen. State of Calif., Los Angeles, 1966-70; corp. counsel Preferred Equities Corp., Los Angeles, 1970-71; corp. counsel, v.p. House of Fabrics, Inc., 1971—, also dir.; instr. securities regulations and anti-trust U. West Los Angeles, 1973—. Pres. Cheviot Hills Homeowners Assn., 1976—. Home: 3001 Motor Ave Los Angeles CA 90064 Office: 11250 Sherman Way Sun Valley CA 91352 Tel (213) 982-1000

SAMPLINER, THOMAS A., b. Cleve., Mar. 7, 1946; B.A., Ohio State U., 1968; J.D., U. Mich., 1971. Admitted to Ohio bar, 1971; individual practice law, 1971-73; partner firm Hermann & Hermann, Cleve., 1973—; mem. legal com. Cleve. chpt. ACLU; panel vol. Am. Arbitration Assn. Mem. Am., Ohio, Cuyahoga County bar assns., War Vets. Bar Assn. (sec.), Phi Beta Kappa, Tau Epsilon Rho (vice chancellor). Recipient awards Civil Trial Advocacy Inst., 176, Am. Arbitration Assn., 1976, Legal Aid Soc., 1974-76. Home: 13654 Fairhill Rd 101 Shaker Heights OH 44120 Office: 330 Williamson Bldg Cleveland OH 44114 Tel (216) 781-5S15

SAMPSEL, CHARLES FRANKLIN, b. Phila., May 17, 1943; B.A., Gettysburg Coll., 1965; J.D., Duke, 1968. Admitted to Pa. bar, 1969; asso. firm Begley, Carlin, Mandio, Kelton & Popkin, Bristol, Pa., 1968—; law clk. Pres. Judge Edward G. Biester, Sr., Ct. of Common Pleas of Bucks County (Pa.), 1969. Mem. Bucks County, Pa., Am. bar assns. Home: Village of Pennbrook 1117 Levittown PA 19054 Office: 120 Mill St Bristol PA 19007 Tel (215) 788-0471

SAMS, GARY MONROE, b. New Smyrna Beach, Fla., Apr. 3, 1940; B.A., Emory U., 1962; J.D., U. Fla., 1965. Admitted to Fla. bar, 1965, Ga. bar, 1966; partner firm Weekes, Candler & Sams, Decatur, Ga., 1966—. Dir. Met. Atlanta Red Cross; pres. Decatur Rotary Club, 1975-76. Mem. Am., Fla., Ga., Decatur-DeKalb bar assns., Lawyers Club of Atlanta. Home: 1204 Bellaire Dr NE Atlanta GA 30319 Office: Suite 450 One W Court Square Bldg Decatur GA 30031 Tel (404) 378-2391

SAMUELS, AARON DAVID, b. N.Y.C., Nov. 29, 1905; LL.B., St. Lawrence U., 1930. Admitted to N.Y. State bar, 1934, U.S. Dist. Ct. Eastern and So. Dists. N.Y., 1935, U.S. Supreme Ct. bar, 1954; dep. town atty., Oyster Bay, N.Y., 1950-56; dep. county atty. Nassau County, N.Y., 1956-62; chief law asst. N.Y. State Family Ct., Nassau County, 1962-75; ret., 1975. Chief U.S. appeal agt. U.S. Selective Service, 1954-71; arbitrator Am. Arbitration Assn., N.Y.C., 1965—. Mem. Am., N.Y. State, Nassau County (co-chmn. family ct. com.) bar assns., Am. Acad. Matrimonial Lawyers, Nat. Council Juvenile Ct. Judges, Nat. Reciprocal and Family Support Assn., Nat. Juvenile Ct. Services Assn. Recipient award Am. Arbitration Assn., 1968, award for service Pres. of U.S., 1959, 68, 71; author: Family Court Law and Practice in New York, 1964; contbr. articles to profl. jours. Home: 389 Fulton St Farmingdale NY 11735 Tel (516) Ch 9-4440

SAMUELS, LESLIE BERNARD, b. St. Louis, Nov. 10, 1942; B.S., U. Pa., 1960-63; LL.B. magna cum laude, Harvard, 1966. Admitted to N.Y. State bar, 1969; asso. firm Cleary, Gottlieb, Steen & Hamilton, N.Y.C., 1968-74, partner, 1975—. Mem. Carter-Mondale Transition Planning Group, Washington, 1976-77. Mem. N.Y. State Bar Assn., N.Y. County Lawyers Assn. C.P.A., Colo. Bd. editors Harvard Law Rev., 1964-66. Home: 29 Washington Sq W New York City NY 10011 Office: One State St Plaza New York City NY 10004 Tel (212) 344-0600

SAMUELS, RICHARD L., b. Chgo., Aug. 13, 1926; B.A., U. Chgo., 1944, J.D., 1950. Admitted to Ill. bar, 1950, U.S. Dist. Ct. for No. Dist. Ill. bar, 1950; practiced in Chgo., 1950-57, 61-65; asst. state's atty. juvenile div. for Cook County (Ill.), 1957-61; asso. judge Ill. Circuit Ct. of Cook County, 1968-76, circuit judge, 1976—; instr. criminal law U. Ill. Extension Div., 1962-68; adminstrv. judge Chgo. Traffic Ct., 1968-73; faculty Nat. Coll. State Judiciary; lectr. in field. Mem. Nat. Safety Council, 1971-73; mem. Ill. Sec. State's Traffic Safety Advisory Council, 1973—. Mem. Chgo., Ill. State, Am. (asst. dir. traffic ct. program 1965-68) bar assns., Am. Judicature Soc., Nat. Conf. Spl. Ct. Judges (exec. com.). Contbr. articles to legal publs. Office: Circuit Ct of Cook County Civic Center Chicago IL 60602 Tel (312) 333-7603

SAMUELS, SEYMOUR, JR., b. Nashville, Oct. 23, 1912; B.A., Vanderbilt U., 1933, J.D., 1935. Admitted to Tenn. bar, 1935; individual practice law, Nashville, 1935-40; partner firm Samuels & Allen, Nashville, 1940-42; area rent atty., dep. rent dir. OPA, Nashville, 1942-43; partner Nashville Bag & Burlap Co., 1946-59; dep. dir. law Met. Govt. Nashville, 1963-67; partner firm Hooker & Willis, Nashville, 1967; partner firm Hooker, Hooker, Willis & Samuels, Nashville, 1968; asso. firm Farris, Evans & Evans, Nashville, 1969-71; partner firm Farris, Warfield & Samuels, Nashville, 1972-74; with firm Schulman, McCarley, Hollins & Pride, Nashville, 1975, Schulman, Pride & Leroy, Nashville, 1976—. Mem. Met. Traffic and Parking Commn. Nashville, 1967-70, Met. Govt. Charter Revision Com., 1970-73, Met. Govt. Transit Authority, 1973-74; chmn. Davidson County Democratic Campaign Com. 1968; Mem. Am., Tenn., Nashville bar assns., Am. Judicature Soc., Order of Coif, Phi Beta Kappa. Contbr. articles to legal jours. Home: 4225 Harding Rd Nashville TN 37205 Office: Suite 701 501 Union St Nashville TN 37219 Tel (615) 244-6670

SAMUELS, TAYLOR WILLIAM, b. Louisville, June 14, 1940; B.S., Case Inst. Tech., 1962; J.D., Vanderbilt U., 1967. Admitted to Ky. bar, 1967, Tenn. bar, 1967; pres. Maker's Mark Distillery, Inc., Loretto, Ky. Mem. Louisville Landmarks & Preservation Commn., 1974—, chmn. Archtl. Rev. Com., Cherokee Triangle Dist., 1975—. Mem. ASCE, Ky., Am. bar assns., Distilled Spirits Council, Ky. Distillers Assn. Home: 2417 Valley Vista Rd Louisville KY 40205 Office: PO 21374 Standiford Station Louisville KY 40221 Tel (502) 368-1603

SAMUELS, THOMAS WALTER, b. Carrollton, Ill., Apr. 1, 1886; A.B., U. Ill., 1909, M.A., 1912, J.D., 1914; postgrad. Harvard, 1910-11; LL.D., Millikin U., 1966. Admitted to Ill. bar, 1914; U.S. Supreme Ct. bar. 1935; sr. partner Samuels, Miller, Schroeder, Jackson & Sly, Decatur, Ill., 1951—. Pres. bd. Macon County Tb Assn., 1918-51, bd. dirs., 1930-45; chmn. Abraham Lincoln Monument Commn. Ill., 1947; trustee Decatur, Macon County Hosp.; active Am. Bar Found., Univ. Ill. Found., Human Relations Commn. Decatur, 1963-65. Mem. Am. Bar Assn., Am. Coll. Trial Lawyers, Am. Judicature Soc., Order of Coif. Author: Discovery of Lands before Trial in Ill. Condemnation Cases, 1946; Lawyer In Action, 1974; contbr. Ill. Law Rev. Home: Decatur Club 158 W Prairie Ave Decatur IL 62525 Office: 406 Citizens Bldg Decatur IL 62525 Tel (217) 429-4325

SANBORN, DAVID WENDELL, b. D.C., June 5, 1942; B.A., Carleton Coll., 1964; M.A., U. Wis., 1966; J.D., Boston U., 1969. Admitted to Mass. bar, 1970; law clk. Sidney Sugarman Chief Judge U.S. Dist. Ct. So. Dist. N.Y., 1969-70; since practiced law in Springfield, Mass., asso. firm Brooks and Mulcahy, 1970-75, partner firm Brooks, Mulcahy & Sanborn, 1976—; town counsel, Monson, Mass., 1974—; instr. uniform comml. code Western New Eng. Coll. Law Sch., 1974-75. Mem. Am., Mass., Hampden County bar assns., ACLU. Asst. note editor Boston U. Law Review, 1968-69. Home: 34 Mattoon St Springfield MA 01105 Office: 1387 Main St Springfield MA 01103 Tel (413) 734-2156

SANBROOK, JOHN SAMUEL, b. Shanghai, China, Dec. 19, 1935; B.S., U. Santa Clara, 1956, J.D., 1959. Admitted to Calif. bar, 1960; dep. dist. atty. Imperial County (Calif.), 1960; chief asst. county atty. Santa Cruz (Calif.) County, 1960-63; county atty. Yuba County (Calif.), Marysville, 1964-65; mem. firm Rich Fuidge Marsh & Morris, Marysville, 1966—; city atty. Yuba City (Calif.), 1974—; spl. counsel City of Marysville, Redevel. Agy. Marysville. Mem. Yuba Sutter Bar Assn. (pres. 1976). Home: 965 Marlin Ct Yuba City CA 95991 Office: 1129 D St Marysville CA 95901 Tel (916) 742-7371

SANCHEZ, ERNESTO GUZMAN, b. Donna, Tex., July 17, 1945; B.B.A., Idaho State U., 1969; J.D., U. Idaho, 1972. Admitted to Idaho bar, 1973; Reginald Heber Smith fellow atty. Idaho Legal Aid Services, Caldwell, 1972-74, mng. atty., 1974—. Mem. Idaho Agrl. Labor Bd., 1973—; mem. adv. council Idaho Foster Grandparent Program. Mem. Idaho State Bar Assn. Home: 523 N Kimball St Caldwell ID 83605 Office: Idaho Legal Aid Services Box 1173 107 1/2 S Kimball St Caldwell ID 83605 Tel (208) 459-1532

SANCHEZ, MAURICE, b. Lemitar, N. Mex., May 27, 1912; B.A., U. N.Mex., 1936; B.S. in Law, Northwestern U., 1937, J.D., 1939. Admitted to N. Mex. bar, 1939; partner firm Grantham, Spann and Sanchez, Albuquerque, 1954-73; judge N.Mex. Dist. Ct., 1973—; asst. U.S. atty. N. Mex., Dept. Justice, 1944, U.S. atty., 1951; chmn. city commn., ex-officio mayor City of Albuquerque, 1954-62. Chmn. N.Mex. Unemployment Commn., 1950-53, N.Mex. Correction Commn., 1971-73. Mem. N.Mex., Am. bar assns., Am. Assn. Trial Judges, Am. Judicature Soc. Editorial bd. Northwestern Law Rev.,

1938-39. Home: 933 McDuffie Circle NE Albuquerque NM 87110 Office: PO Box 488 Bernalillo County Courthouse Albuquerque NM 87103 Tel (505) 842-3525

SANCHEZ, RAYMOND GILBERT, b. Albuquerque, Sept. 22, 1941; B.A., U. N.Mex., 1964, J.D., 1967. Admitted to N.Mex. bar, 1969; individual practice law, Albuquerque, 1970—; mem. New Mex. Ho. of Reps., chmn. House Judiciary Com., chmn. Recodification and Repeal Com., mem. Legis. Fin. Com., mem. Corp. and Bank Commn., mem. Rules and Order of Bus. Com., mem. Law Study Com. Home: 7622 Rio Grande St NW Albuquerque NM 87107 Office: 215 3d St SW PO Box 1966 Albuquerque NM 87103 Tel (50S) 247-4321

SAND, MARTIN J., b. N.Y.C., Feb. 1, 1909; A.B., Columbia, 1929; J.D., Harvard, 1932. Admitted to N.Y. bar, 1933, U.S. Supreme Ct. bar, 1948, U.S. Ct. Appeals bar, 1960, U.S. Ct. Claims bar, 1961, U.S. Ct. Mil. Appeals bar, 1961; individual practice law, N.Y.C., 1933—; asst. counsel U.S. Senate Investigation on Crime and Racketeering, 1934; v.p., dir. McDowell & Co., 1936—. Trustee Am. Fine Arts Soc., McDowell Travelling Fellowship, Cole Fund. Mem. Am., Fed., bar assns., N.Y. County Lawyers Assn., Am., N.Y. State assns. trial lawyers. Author: (with Robert Daru) Disciplinary Proceedings Arising out of the Conduct of Counsel in Criminal Cases, 1938; contbr. articles to law jours. Office: 400 Madison Ave New York City NY 10017 Tel (212) 421-3400

SANDALOW, TERRANCE, b. Chgo., Sept. 8, 1934; A.B., U. Chgo., 1954, J.D., 1957. Admitted to Ill. bar, 1958; asso. firm Ross, McGowan & O'Keefe, Chgo., 1959-61; asso. prof. law U. Minn., 1961-64, prof. law, 1964-66; prof. law U. Mich., 1966—; asst. reporter Am. Law Inst. Project on Pub. Control of Land Use, 1963-69. Mem. Mpls. Commn. on Human Relations, 1965-66. Fellow Center for Advanced Study in the Behavioral Sci., 1972-73. Author: (with F.I. Michelman) Govt. in Urban Areas, 1970; contbr. articles in field to profl. jours. Home: 1610 Shadford Rd Ann Arbor MI 48104 Office: 922 Legal Research Bldg University of Michigan Ann Arbor MI 48109 Tel (313) 764-9348

SANDBERG, JOHN STEVEN, b. Mpls., Sept. 1, 1948; A.B. in Polit. Sci. with honors, U. Mo., 1970, J.D. cum laude, 1972. Admitted to Mo. bar, 1972, Ill. bar, 1973; partner firm Coburn, Croft, Shepherd & Herzog, St. Louis, 1972—. Mem. Am., Mo., Ill., St. Clair, Met. St. Louis bar assns., Am. Judicature Soc. Adminstrv. law research grantee Am. Bar Found., 1971-72. Home: 8124 Cornell Ct Saint Louis MO 63130 Office: suite 2900 One Mercantile Center Saint Louis MO 63101 Tel (314) 621-8575

SANDBOWER, JOHN EDWARD, III, b. Cumberland, Md., Jan. 31, 1935; B.S., U. Md., 1956, LL.B., 1960. Admitted to Md. bar, 1960; law clk. firm Smith, Somerville & Case, Balt., 1958-60, asso., 1960-68, partner, 1968—; spl. asst. states atty. of Balt., 1970, 1976; lectr. in field. Mem. Bar Assn. Balt. (past pres. jr. bar), Md., Am. bar assns., Internat. Assn. Ins. Counsel. Home: 505 Patleigh Rd Baltimore MD 21228 Office: 100 Light St Baltimore MD 21202 Tel (301) 727-1164

SANDERS, BARRY ALAN, b. Phila., July 29, 1945; A.B., U. Pa., 1967; LL.B., Yale U., 1970. Admitted to Calif. bar, 1971; atty. firm Latham & Watkins, Los Angeles, 1970—. Mem. Am., Los Angeles County bar assns. Editor, Yale Law Jour. 1968-70. Home: 10100 Sunbrook Dr Beverly Hills CA 90210 Office: 555 S Flower St Los Angeles CA 90071 Tel (213) 485-1234

SANDERS, IRWIN ROBERT, b. New Orleans, Feb. 4, 1931; B.A., La. State U., Baton Rouge, 1952; J.D., Loyola U., New Orleans, 1962. Admitted to La. bar, 1962; individual practice law, Metairie, La. Sec., Council of Civic Assns. of Jefferson Parish (La.), 1975; pres. E. Lakeside Civic Assn., 1975-76. Mem. La., Jefferson Parish bar assns., New Orleans Trial Lawyers Assn., Criminal Cts. Bar Assn. (pres. 1971-72). Home: 1520 Melody Dr Metairie LA 70002 Office: 4501 I-10 Service Rd Metairie LA 70002 Tel (504) 455-5905

SANDERS, JOE WILLIAM, b. Pleasant Hill, La., May 31, 1915; B.A., La. State U., 1935, J.D., 1938. Admitted to La. bar, 1938; practiced in Many, La., 1938-42, Baton Rouge, 1946-60; judge East Baton Rouge Parish (La.) Family Ct., 1954-60; asso. justice La. Supreme Ct., 1960-73, chief justice, 1973—; mem. La. Ho. of Reps., 1940-44; group chmn. White House Conf. Children and Youth, 1960; chmn. La. Commn. on Law Enforcement and Adminstrn. Justice, 1968-70, Nat. Inst. on Crime and Delinquency, 1973, East Baton Rouge Parish Juvenile Commn., 1952-54, La. Jud. Council, 1973—; mem. exec. com. Conf. Chief Justices. Bd. dirs. Baton Rouge YMCA, 1952-55, 58-60, chmn. youth camp com., 1953-54. Mem. Nat. Council on Crime and Delinquency (council of judges 1955-76), Am. Judicature Soc., Am. Law Inst., Am., La. State bar assns., La. State U. Found., Bartolus Soc., Order of Coif, Omicron Delta Kappa, Phi Kappa Phi. Recipient award for extraordinary service to law enforcement and criminal justice Met. Crime Commn. New Orleans, 1976; contbr. articles to legal jours. Office: Supreme Ct Bldg 301 Loyola Ave New Orleans LA 70112 Tel (504) 527-5261

SANDERS, RAYMOND CARTER, JR., b. Atlanta, Sept. 12, 1942; B.B.A., U. Ga., 1965; J.D., U. San Diego, 1971. Admitted to Calif. bar, 1972; partner firm Ward & Ward & Sanders, San Diego, Calif., 1972—; arbitrator Am. Arbitration Assn., 1976. Mem. exec. com., dir. Am. Cancer Soc., 1974—; bd. dirs. San Diego Found. for Blind, 1976—. Mem. Am. Judicature Assn., Am., Calif., San Diego County bar assns., Phi Delta Phi. Home: 3738 Charles St San Diego CA 92106 Office: 530 B St San Diego CA 92101 Tel (714) 234-8541

SANDERS, RICHARD BROWNING, b. Tacoma, May 24, 1945; B.A., U. Wash., 1966, J.D., 1969. Admitted to Wash. bar, 1969, U.S. Supreme Ct. bar, 1976; asso. firm Murray Scott, McGavick and Graves, Tacoma, 1969-70, firm Caplinger & Munn, Seattle, 1970-71; individual practice law, Seattle, 1971—. Nat. committeeman Wash. Young Republican Fedn., 1971. Mem. Wash. State Trial Lawyers Assn., Libertarian Lawyers Assn. Office: 224 Dexter Ave N Seattle WA 98109 Tel (206) MA 3-6042

SANDERS, RICHARD DALE, b. Tularosa, N.Mex., Oct. 9, 1926; A.B., Stanford U., 1949, J.D., 1951. Admitted to Calif. bar, 1951; since practiced in Pittsburg, Calif., individual practice law, 1951-70; partner firm Sanders, Dodson, Hinton & May, 1970-76. Councilman, City of Pittsburg, 1958-62, mayor, 1961-62. Mem. Calif. (v.p. 1976; dir., 1970-76; fin. sec. 1973-75), Alameda-Contra Costra trial lawyers assns. Home: 86 Barrie Dr Pittsburg CA 94565 Office: 2211 Railroad Ave Pittsburg CA 94565 Tel (415) 432-3511

SANDERS, ROBERT EDWARD, b. Cin., July 29, 1947; B.A. in Eng., Eastern Ky. U., 1969, B.S. in Bus. Adminstrn., 1969; J.D., U. Cin., 1972. Admitted to Ohio bar, 1972, Ky. bar, 1972, U.S. Dist. Ct. for Ky. bar, 1972; since practiced in Covington, Ky., individual practice law, 1972-74; 1st asst. commonwealth's atty., 16th Jud. Dist. Ky., 1975—; instr. law No. Ky. U., 1974—, Thomas More Coll., 1973—. Dir. N. Ky. Community Council, 1972—; dir. Ky. Salvation Army, 1975—; dir. Old Seminary Sq., 1975—. Mem. Am., Ky., Ohio, Kenton County bar assns., Nat. Dist. Attys. Assn., Nat. Assn. Trial Lawyers, Ky. Trial Lawyers Assn., Ohid Assn. Trial Lawyers. Home: 1017 Russell Ave Covington KY 41011 Office: Suite 605 Covington-Kenton County Bldg Covington KY 41011 Tel (606) 292-2336

SANDERS, SAMUEL HENRY, III, b. Birmingham, Ala., Aug. 11, 1943; student U. Ala., 1961-64; B.A. in History, Birmingham-So. Coll., 1966; J.D., Tulane U., 1969. Admitted to Ala. bar, 1970, U.S. Dist. Ct. No. Dist. Ala. bar, 1972, U.S. Ct. Appeals 5th Circuit bar, 1974; atty. U.S. Dept. Treasury, Greensboro, N.C., 1969-72; individual practice law, Birmingham, Ala., 1972—. Mem. Big Bros. Greater Birmingham Area. Mem. Ala., Birmingham bar assns. Home: 5050 Juiata Dr Irondale AL 35210 Office: Suite 1622 2121 Bldg Birmingham AL 35203 Tel (205) 251-9384

SANDERS, WILLIAM HOBART, b. Gurley, Ala., Oct. 5, 1920; B.S., U. Ala., 1942, LL.B., 1947. Admitted to Ala. bar, 1947, Alaska bar, 1951; individual practice law, Anchorage, 1951-63; judge Superior Ct. 2d Jud. Dist. State of Alaska, Nome, 1963—; mem. Alaska Ho. of Reps., 1960-64. Mem. Am., Alaska, Northwestern bar assns., Am. Trial Lawyers Assn., Am. Legion (comdr. Alaska dept. 1959). Home and office: Box 100 Nome AK 99762 Tel (907) 443-5216

SANDERSON, REX FRANKLIN, b. Vardaman, Miss., July 19, 1939; B.B.A., U. Miss., 1961, J.D., 1970. Admitted to Miss. bar, 1970, U.S. Supreme Ct. bar, 1976; individual practice law, Southaven, Miss., 1970; partner firm Huggins & Sanderson, Southaven, 1970-71; partner firm Fox & Sanderson, Houston, Miss., 1971-74; individual practice law, Houston, 1974—; pros. atty. Chickasaw County, Houston, 1976—. Mem. Am., Miss., Chickasaw County bar assns. Home: Route 3 Box 48 Houston MS 38851 Office: Houston State Bank Bldg Houston MS 38851 Tel (601) 456-4615

SANDGREN, CLYDE DAHLMAN, b. Provo, Utah, Sept. 5, 1910; B.S., Brigham Young U., 1937; J.D., St. John's U., 1939. Admitted to N.Y. Bar, 1940, U.S. Supreme Ct. bar, 1945, Utah bar, 1947; partner firm Burroughs & Brown, N.Y.C., 1942-46; partner firm Sandgren & Blackham, Provo, Utah, 1947-54; gen. counsel Brigham Young U., Provo, 1946-75, v.p., 1961-75, spl. counsel, 1975—; partner firm Sandgren, Howard & Frazier, Provo, 1954-56. Vice chancellor Unified Ch. Sch. System, Ch. Jesus Christ Latter-day Saints, 1961-70; pres. Utah Edn. TV Found., 1960-64, Council for Utah Edn., 1953-54, Intermountain Little Symphony, 1950; mem. exec. com. Nat. Parks Council Boy Scouts Am., 1951-53. Mem. Am., Utah, Central Utah bar assns., Brigham Young U. Alumni Assn. (pres. 1947-51). Home and Office: 3535 Canyon Rd Provo UT 84601 Tel (801) 225-8600

SANDLER, CHARLES E., b. Balt., Oct. 17, 1940; B.S., U. Md., 1961; J.D., George Washington U., 1966. Admitted to Md. bar, 1966, U.S. Supreme Ct. bar, 1970; asst. mgr. Nat. Govt. Services Automotive Mfrs. Assn., Washington, 1961-69; Washington rep. Aspen Systems Corp., 1969-70; dir. dept. fed. relations Am. Petroleum Inst., Washington, 1970—. Mem. Am. Bar Assn., Sigma Delta Chi. Home: 14152 Flint Rock Rd Rockville MD 20853 Office: 2101 L St NW Washington DC 20037 Tel (202) 457-7270

SANDLER, CONRAD IVAN, b. Phila., Dec. 7, 1931; A.B. in Psychology, Temple U., 1953, J.D., 1956. Admitted to N.Y. bar, 1959; with Social Security Adminstrn., HEW, Northeastern Program Service Center, N.Y., 1956—, claims authorizer, 1956-62, reconsideration reviewer, congressional inquiries specialist, 1962-67, sect. mgr., 1967-73, sr. ops. analyst, 1973-74, group mgr., 1974-76, acting processing br. mgr., College Point, N.Y., 1976-77, quality appraisal br. mgr., 1977—. Mem. N.Y. State, Bklyn. bar assns., Phi Alpha Delta. Recipient Sara A. Shull Meml. award Sch. Law Temple U., 1956. Home: 711 Hartman Ln Far Rockaway NY 11691 Office: 96-05 Horace Harding Exp Flushing NY 11368 Tel (212) 699-6882

SANDLER, DAVID NATHANIEL, b. Lynn, Mass., June 9, 1946; B.A., U. Calif., Los Angeles, 1967; J.D., George Washington U. Nat. Law Center, 1971. Admitted to Calif. bar, 1972; atty. dept. social welfare State Calif., Sacramento, 1971-72, dep. atty. gen., San Francisco, 1972-74; mem. firm McCreadie & Sandler, Novato, Calif., 1975—. Dir., Vol. Bur. Marin County (Calif.), Inc., 1976—; nat. panel consumer arbitrators Better Bus. Bur. San Francisco, Ltd. Mem. Marin County Bar Assn. Home: 7 Estates Court San Rafael CA 94901 Office: 1127 Grant Ave Novato CA 94947 Tel (415) 892-1601

SANDLER, IRWIN EDWARD, b. Los Angeles, Dec. 17, 1932; A.B., U. Calif., Los Angeles, 1955, J.D., 1958. Admitted to Calif. bar, 1959, U.S. Dist. Ct. for Central Dist. Calif. bar, 1959; since practiced in Los Angeles, asso firm Baker, Ancel & Redmond, 1959-65, partner, 1965—. Bd. dirs. Berverlywood Homes Assn., Los Angeles, 1973—. Mem. Am., Calif., Los Angeles County (mem. com. on continuing legal edn. of the bar; constrn. law subsect.) bar assns., Calif., Los Angeles trial lawyers assns., Am. Arbitration Assn. (comml. panel). Contbr. articles to profl. jours. Office: 626 Wilshire Blvd Suite 700 Los Angeles CA 90017 Tel (213) 624-9201

SANDLER, LEONARD H., b. N.Y.C., Oct. 16, 1926; B.A., Coll. City N.Y., 1946; J.D., Columbia, 1950. Admitted to N.Y. bar, 1950; law clk. to U.S. Dist. Ct. judge, N.Y.C., 1950-51; law sec. to N.Y. Appellate Div. judge, 1951-52; asst. dist. atty. N.Y. County, 1954-63; judge Civil Ct. City N.Y.; acting justice N.Y. State Supreme Ct., N.Y.C., 1973-76, justice, 1976—. Chmn., Two Bridges Neighborhood Council; bd. dirs. Lower East Side Service Center. Mem. Bar Assn. City N.Y., Phi Beta Kappa. Recipient Toppan prize, 1948; editor Columbia Law Rev., 1948-50. Home: 39 Fifth Ave New York City NY 10003 Office: 100 Centre St New York City NY 10013 Tel (212) 374-4783

SANDLER, MARTIN LEIGH, b. Greenville, S.C., Apr. 20, 1937; B.S. in Econs., Wharton Sch. Finance U. Pa., 1958; LL.B., U. Fla, 1961. Admitted to Fla. bar, 1961, U.S. Dist. Ct. bar for So. Dist. Fla., 1961, U.S. Ct. Appeals bar, 5th Circuit, 1964; partner firm Sandler & Sandler, Miami, Fla., 1961—; spl. asst. pub. defender, Dade County, Fla., 1964; instr. in bus. law U. Miami (Fla.), 1965-67; mem. jud. nominating commn. 11th Jud. Circuit of Fla., 1974—. Mem. sustaining bd. of fellows Mt. Sinai Hosp., Miami Beach, Fla., 1964—, pres., 1975-77; trustee Mt. Sinai Med. Center, Miami Beach, 1975—. Mem. Dade County, Fla. bar assns., Comml. Law League Am. Office: 943 Ingraham Bldg 25 SE 2d Ave Miami FL 33131 Tel (305) 374-8196

SANDLER, RONALD ALLEN, b. Chgo., Dec. 10, 1940; B.S. in Indsl. Engring., U. Ill., 1962; J.D., George Washington U., 1965. Admitted to Ill. bar, U.S. Supreme Ct. bar, 1972, U.S. Patent Office bar, 1965; patent examiner U.S. Patent Office, Washington, 1963-65; patent atty. Hotpoint div. Gen. Electric Co., Chgo., 1965-67; partner firm Prangley, Dithmar, Vogel, Sandler & Stotland, Chgo., 1967-77, Boehm, Weinstein, Sandler & Mason, Chgo., 1977—. Mem. Am., Ill., Chgo. bar assns., Am., Chgo. patent lawyers assns., Order of Coif. Office: 230 W Monroe St Chicago IL 60603 Tel (312) 782-8420

SANDLIN, R. FORNEY, b. Ft. Smith, Ark., Jan. 20, 1934; B.B.A., U. Okla., 1956, LL.B., 1958. Admitted to Okla. bar, 1958, since practiced in Muskogee; mem. firm Sandlin & Payne, 1973—; asso. mem. Okla. Bd. Bar Examiners, 1976—; dir. City Bank of Muskogee; lectr. profl. seminars. Dist. commr. Boy Scouts Am., 1965-70; mem. youth program com. YMCA; bd. dirs. Salvation Army, 1968-70, Bone and Joint Hosp., Oklahoma City, 1973—; bd. dirs. Muskogee Community Nursing Service, 1964—, pres., 1964-66; trustee Bacone Coll., Muskogee, 1973-76; mem. ofcl. bd. St. Paul Methodist Ch., Muskogee, 1962—. Mem. Am., Okla. (econ. status com. 1962-63, continuing legal edn. com. 1963-66, labor law com. 1966—, corp. and banking com. 1975—), Muskogee County (sec. 1959) bar assns., Muskogee C. of C. (dir. 1966), Phi Alpha Delta. Home: 4500 Howard St Muskogee OK 74401 Office: 330 N 4th St Muskogee OK 74401 Tel (918) 683-5513

SANDOLOSKI, SANDY MOISE, b. Dallas, Nov. 30, 1921; LL.B., So. Meth. U., 1949. Admitted to Tex. bar, 1949; partner firm Weinberg, Sandoloski & McManus, and predecessor, Dallas, 1953—. Mem. Tex., Dallas bar assns. Home: 7322 Azalea St Dallas TX 75230 Office: 1800 Republic Nat Bank Tower Dallas TX 75201 Tel (214) 748-8891

SANDOVAL, RUBEN, b. El Paso, Tex., Mar. 30, 1941; grad. Tex Western Coll., 1965; grad. St. Mary's Law Sch., San Antonio, 1969. Admitted to Tex. bar, 1969, Fed. bar, 1970, Fed. Communications bar, 1971; partner firm Sandoval & Samples, San Antonio, 1971—. Mem. Am., Tex., San Antonio, Fed. Communications bar assns., Am., Tex. trial lawyers assns., Tex. Criminal Def. Lawyers Assn. Home: 8819 Oakbrook St San Antonio TX 78204 Office: 523 S Main St San Antonio TX 78204 Tel (512) 224-1061

SANDQUIST, ELROY CHARLES, JR., b. Chgo., Dec. 18, 1922; B.S., U.S. Naval Acad., 1943; J.D., Northwestern U., 1950. Admitted to Ill. Supreme Ct. bar, 1950, U.S. Supreme Ct. bar, 1971; asso. firm Peterson, Ross, Rall, Barber & Seidel, Chgo., 1950-56, sr. partner, 1961—; head civil div. Cook County (Ill.) State's Atty's. Office, 1957-60; mem. Ill. Liquor Control Commn., 1973-77; mem. Ill. Gen. Assembly, 1977—. Trustee Chgo. Temple Bldg., 1st Meth. Ch. of Chgo.; v.p., legal counsel Francis W. Parker Sch., Chgo., Lake Bluff-Chgo. Homes for Children; mem. com. pub. policy Council for Community Services in Met. Chgo.; bd. dirs., mem. finance com. Northwestern Meml. Hosp., Chgo. Mem. Chgo. (bd. mgrs. 1973-75), Ill., Am. bar assns., Northwestern U. Sch. Law Alumni Assn. (dir.), Order of Coif. Home: 353 Belden Ave Chicago IL 60614 Office: 135 S LaSalle St Chicago IL 60603 Tel (312) 263-7300

SANDROK, RICHARD WILLIAM, b. Evergreen Park, Ill., July 8, 1943; student De Paul U., 1961-63; B.A., Wheaton Coll., 1965; J.D., U. Ill., 1968. Admitted to Ill. bar, 1968; asso. firm Hinshaw, Culbertson, Moelmann, Hoban & Fuller, Chgo., 1971, Wheaton, Ill., 1972-75, partner, 1976—. Mem. Am., Ill., Chgo., Du Page bar assns., Chgo. Trial Lawyers Club. Office: 330 Naperville Rd Wheaton IL 60187 Tel (312) 653-3135

SANDS, CHARLES DALLAS, b. Wells County, Ind., July 13, 1916; B.A., Ind. U., 1939, J.D., 1941; LL.M., Columbia U., 1950. Admitted to Ind. bar, 1941, Ala. bar, 1954; prof. law U. Ala., University, 1946-54, 56—, Rutgers U., New Brunswick, N.J., 1954-56; cons. in field; conciliator Equal Employment Opportunity Commn., 1968. Chmn. Zoning Bd. Adjustment, Tuscaloosa (Ala.), 1958-74. Mem. Am. Bar Assn., Am. Judicature Soc., AAUP. Named Roscoe Pound Meml. lectr. Gujarat U., India, 1968; author: Statutes and Statutory Construction, 1972-75; contbr. articles in field to profl. jours. Home: 249 Cedarcrest St Tuscaloosa AL 35401 Office: Box 1435 University AL 35486 Tel (205) 348-5930

SANDS, DARRY GENE, b. Charleston, Ark., Jan. 4, 1947; B.S. with high honors, U. Ark., 1969; J.D., U. Kans., 1971. Admitted to Mo. bar, 1974; asso. firm Dietrich, Davis, Dicus, Rowlands, & Schmitt, Kans. City, Mo., 1974—. Mem. Am., Mo. bar assns., Lawyers Assn. Kansas City. Home: 5341 Canterbury St Shawnee Mission KS 66205 Office: 1001 Dwight Bldg 1004 Baltimore St Kansas City MO 64105

SANDS, IRA JAY, b. N.Y.C.; B.A., N.Y. U., 1941; J.D. Columbia U., 1944. Admitted to N.Y. State bar, 1944, U.S. Circuit Ct. Appeals, 1944, U.S. Dsit. Ct., 1944, Supreme Ct. bar, 1966; practice law in N.Y.C., 1944—; dir., mgr., partner First Republic Corp., 1957-66, chmn. bd., 1958-66, sec., 1960-65; dir., chmn. First Republic Underwriter, Inc., 1958-66; dir., pres. Waltham Mgmt. Inc., 1959-65; mng. partner Korvette Bldg. Assos., 1957-62, Fairfax Bldg. Assos., 1958-65, Engring. Bldg. Assos., 1958-66, Williamsbridge Assos., N.Y., 1958-65, Waltham Engring. & Research Co., Mass., 1958-62, First Republic Funding Agy., N.Y., 1961—, Atlantic Co., Fla., 1961, Marchwood Realty Co., Pa., 1961; Video Film Center Assos., N.Y.C., 1962—, DeMille Theatre Co., N.Y.C., 1962—; partner Allstate Ins. Bldg. Co., 1958, Velvex Mid-City Parking Center, 1959-65, Manhattan Parking Assos., N.Y., 1959, Imperial Sq. Co., 1960-66, Hempstead Real Estate Enterprises, N.Y., 1959, Ohio Indsl. Assos., 1961-65, Cypress Plaza Assos., Fla., 1961, Peoria (Ill.) Parking Co., 1961-66, Gulf Assos., Co., Fla., 1961-62, Pelham Park Asso., Pa., 1961; chmn. dir. First Republic Co., Inc., 1957, Triple P. Parking Corp., Ill., 1960—, Park Circle Apts., Inc., N.Y., 1960, Home Circle Apts., Inc., Pa., 1961, Beau Rivage Corp., Fla., 1961-65, Holme Realty Corp., Pa., 1962-66; gen. agt. Patriot Life Ins. Co., N.Y.C., 1959, Citizens Life Ins. Co., N.Y.C., 1962-64; chmn. exec. com., sec., dir. First Republic Corp. Am., 1961-66; chmn. exec. com., sec., dir. 1st Republic Bldg. Corp., 1962—; chmn. Tri-Mgmt. Co., 1957-64, Nat. Med. Industries, Inc., 1968-70, Health Insts. Leasing Corp., 1968-71, Am. Med. Computer Corp., 1969-71; pres. Med. Contract Supply Corp., 1968-72, 701 Realty, Inc., 1974—; gen. counsel Claredon Capital Co., 1944—; v.p. F.S. Mgmt. Corp., 1966—; dir. Sq. Mgmt. Corp., Hempstead, N.Y. Real estate cons. various pension plans; mem. N.Y. Real Estate Bd. Vice pres., Felix Schlusselberg Found., Inc.; hon. trustee Truman Library. Served to lt. AUS, 1942-45. Harlan Fiske Stone law fellow. Mem. Nat. Real Estate Club, Mchts. Club, Am. (corp. law com.). Fed. N.Y. State, Nassau County bar assns., Columbia Law Sch. Alumni Assn., Bldg. Owners and Mgrs. Assn. Mason (Shriner). Home: 973 South End St Woodmere NY 11598 Office: 515 Madison Ave New York City NY 10022

SANDS, JOHN CARLTON, b. Chgo., Aug. 16, 1929; A.B. in History, U. Ill., 1951; LL.B., John Marshall Law Sch., 1958, J.D., 1970. Admitted to Ill. bar, 1958; asso. with Irwin Wright, Chgo., 1958-66; individual practice law, Chgo., 1966—; prosecutor Village of Glenview, Ill., 1963-66. Mem. Celtic Legal Soc., Chgo., Ill., Am. Bar Assns., Chgo. Trial Lawyers Club, Am. Trial Lawyers Assn. Recipient Recognition Plaque, Village of Glenview. Office: 7 S Dearborn St Chicago IL 60603 Tel (312) 236-4980

SANDSTROM, GUSTAVE FRANK, JR., b. Grand Junction, Colo., Aug 8, 1943; B.S., U. So. Colo., 1968; J.D., U. Colo., 1971. Admitted to Colo. bar, 1971; partner firm Jenkins, O'Rouke & Sandstrom, and predecessor, Pueblo, Colo., 1971—, firm mgr., 1971—; instr. bus. law U. So. Colo., 1971-75; sec. Pueblo County Bar, 1971-72. Mem. Pueblo Regional Planning Commn., 1971—. Mem. Am., Colo. bar assns., Am., Colo. trial lawyers assns., Am. Panel Arbitrators, Am. Hosp. Lawyers Assn., Colo. Municipal Lawyers Assn. Home: 4032 Hillside Dr Pueblo CO 81008 Office: 1212 Colo Bldg Pueblo CO 81003 Tel (303) 544-8141

SANDWEG, GERARD KENNETH, JR., b. Washington, Jan. 17, 1943; B.S., St. Louis U., 1964; LL.B., U. Notre Dame, 1967. Admitted to Mo. bar, 1967; partner firm Thompson & Mitchell, St. Louis, 1967—. Mem. Am., Mo. bar assns. Home: 9 Wild Rose Dr St Louis MO 63124 Office: 1 Mercantile Center St Louis MO 63101 Tel (314) 231-7676

SANFORD, JAMES POND, b. Indpls., Aug. 23, 1947; B.S., Ind. U., 1965, J.D., 1973. Admitted to Mich. bar, 1974; mem. staff Arthur Young & Co., Bloomfield Hills, Mich., 1973-74; atty. Baker Driveaway Co., Bloomfield Hills, 1974-75; chmn. bus. law dept. Walsh Coll., 1975—; lectr. Accounting Aid Soc., Detroit, 1976. Mem. Am., Mich., Oakland bar assns., Ind. U. Alumni Assn., Phi Kappa Psi. C.P.A., Ill. Home: 2770 Lenox Troy MI 48098 Office: 3838 Livernois Troy MI 48084 Tel (313) 689-8282

SANFORD, JOHN JOSEPH, b. Providence, R.I., Sept. 24, 1944; B.S., USAF Acad., 1966; J.D. cum laude, Suffolk U., 1973. Admitted to Maine bar, 1973, Mass. bar, 1973; partner firm Harmon, Jones & Sanford, Camden, Maine, 1975—; instr. criminal law U. Maine at Augusta, 1976. Mem. Am. Bar Assn., Maine State Bar, Maine Assn. Trial Lawyers. Home: Harbor Rd Camden ME 04843 Office: 21 Elm St Camden ME 04843

SANFORD, WILLIAM C., b. Washington, Ind., Jan. 7, 1908; student U. Nev., 1926-28, LL.B., 1968; J.D., U. Calif., 1943. Admitted to Nev. bar, 1942, Calif. bar, 1943; partner firm Sanford, Sanford & McGee, Reno, 1976—; dir. Sierra Pacific Power Co. Mem. Reno Sch. Dist. #10, past chmn.; bd. dirs. U. Calif. Hastings Coll. Law, 1966—. Mem. Am., Nev., Calif. bar assns., Am. Judicature Soc. Home: 2100 Willow Tree Ln Reno NV 89509 Office: 43 N Sierra St Reno NV 89501 Tel (702) 322-9166

SANGER, HOWARD L., b. Los Angeles, May 5, 1942; B.S., U. Calif., 1964; J.D., U. Calif. at Los Angeles, 1967; LL.M., N.Y. U., 1970. Admitted to Calif. bar, 1968; partner firm Flame, Sanger, Grayson & Ginsburg, Encino, Calif., 1971—; lectr. Calif. C.P.A. Soc., Golden Gate U. Pres., San Fernando Valley Estate Planning Council. Mem. Beverly Hills Bar Assn. (sec. probate com.). Home: 19061 Tina Pl Tarzana CA 91356 Office: 16130 Ventura Blvd Encino CA 91436 Tel (213) 788-3720

SANGER, ROBERT MARSHALL, b. Arlington, Va., Jan. 7, 1949; B.A., U. Calif., Santa Barbara, 1970; J.D., U. Calif., Los Angeles, 1973. Admitted to Calif. bar, 1973, U.S. Tax Ct. bar, 1975; individual practice law, Goleta, Calif., 1973-75; sr. partner firm Sanger & Caldwell, Goleta, 1975—; judge pro tem small claims Santa Barbar-Goleta Municipal Ct., 1974—; adj. prof. law Calif. Law Inst., 1975—. Bd. dirs. Goleta Beautiful. Mem. Santa Barbara County Bar (dir.), Am. Bar Assn., Barrister's Club (dir.), Calif. Attys. for Criminal Justice. Office: 5730 Hollister Ave Suite 11 Goleta CA 93017 Tel (805) 964-6931

SANI, JOSEPH FRANCIS, b. Paterson, N.J., Feb. 26, 1902; A.B., Wilmington Coll., 1929; LL.B., LaSalle U., 1926; J.D., Cath. U. Am., 1932. Admitted to Ohio bar, 1932; city solicitor, New Philadelphia, Ohio, 1947-50; individual practice law, New Philadelphia, 1933—. Mem. Ohio Mental Health Bd., 1974—; active Boy Scouts Am.; chaplain Fraternal Order Police Assos., 1972—. Mem. Am., Ohio bar assns., Am. Judicature Soc. Home: 467 E High Ave New Philadelphia OH 44663 Office: 120 N Broadway New Philadelphia OH 44663 Tel (216) 364-5538

SANKARY, WANDA, b. Scranton, N.D., Dec. 22, 1919; LL.B., U. So. Calif., 1950. Admitted to Calif. bar, 1951; individual practice law, San Diego, Redondo Beach, Hollywood, Calif., 1951—. Mem. Calif. Assembly, 1954-55. Mem. San Diego, Hollywood bar assns. Office: 110 West C St San Diego CA 92101 Tel (714) 582-3311 also Penthouse 1741 N Ivar St Hollywood CA 90028 Tel (213) 462-0851 575 Esplanade St Redondo Beach CA 90277 Tel (213) 372-6769 and 373-1820

SANSBURY, JOHN THADDEUS, b. Danville, Ill., Oct. 2, 1929; B.S., Canisius Coll., 1951; LL.B., Fordham U., 1961, J.D., 1968. Admitted to Ohio bar, 1964, since engaged in individual practice, Columbus. Bd. dirs. Kidney Found., 1967—, treas. St. Agatha Roman Catholic Parish, 1975-76. Mem. Ohio, Columbus bar assns. Home: 2811 Wellesley Dr Columbus OH 43221 Office: 547 E Broad St Columbus OH 43215 Tel (614) 221-5395

SANT, JOHN TALBOT, b. Ann Arbor, Mich., Oct. 7, 1932; A.B., Princeton, 1954; LL.B., Harvard, 1957. Admitted to Mo. bar, 1957; asso. firm Thompson, Mitchell, Douglas & Neill, St. Louis, 1958-60; atty. McDonnell Douglas Corp., St. Louis, 1960, asst. sec., 1961, sec., 1962-69, sec., asst. gen. counsel, 1969-74, v.p., gen. counsel, sec., 1974-76, v.p., gen. counsel, 1976—. Mem. Am., Mo., St. Louis bar assns. Home: 9 Ridgewood Rd Saint Louis MO 63124 Office: PO Box 516 Saint Louis MO 63166 Tel (314) 232-8484

SANTANGELO, FRANK JOSEPH, b. Stoneham, Mass., Apr. 17, 1936; A.A., Boston U., 1960, LL.B., 1964. Admitted to Mass. bar, 1964; asso. firm Ritvo Gordon & Rosenberg, Boston, 1964-69, partner, 1969-70; partner firm Ritvo & Santangelo, Boston, 1970—. Mem. Mass., Boston bar assns. Contbr. articles to legal jours. Home: 4 Cherry Ln Braintree MA 02184 Office: 53 State St Boston MA 02109 Tel (617) 523-2328

SANTANIELLO, ANGELO GARY, b. New London, Conn., May 28, 1924; A.B., Coll. Holy Cross, Worcester, Mass., 1945; J.D., Georgetown U., 1950. Admitted to Conn. bar, 1950, U.S. Dist. Ct. bar, 1960; since practiced in New London, Conn.; individual practice law, 1950-53; partner firm Santaniello, Satti, Wilensky & Schwartz, and predecessors, 1953-65; judge Circuit Ct., 1966-71, Ct. of Common Pleas, 1971-73, Superior Ct., 1973—. Chmn. Republican Party City of New London, 1956-65. Mem. Am., Conn., New London County bar assns. Home: 25 Shirley Ln New London CT 06320 Office: Superior Ct Bldg New London CT 06320 Tel (203) 443-4245

SANTEMMA, JON NOEL, b. Oceanside, N.Y., Dec. 24, 1937; A.B., Cornell, 1960; J.D., Fordham U., 1963. Admitted to N.Y. bar, 1963, U.S. Ct. Military Appeals, 1969, U.S. Ct. of Claims, 1969, U.S. Supreme Ct., 1969; asso. firm Parnell Callahan, N.Y.C., 1963-64; asso. firm Warburton, Hyman, Deeley and Connolly, Mineola, N.Y., 1964-66; law sec. Justice Howard T. Hogan, N.Y. Supreme Ct., Mineola, 1966-71; individual practice law, Mineola, 1971-74; partner firm Santemma, Costigan and Murphy, Mineola, 1974—; lectr. Columbia Soc. Real Estate Appraisers, 1971—. Mem. N.Y. State Commn. Eminent Domain, 1972-76. Mem. Am., N.Y., N.Y.C., Suffolk County, Nassau County (v.p.) bar assns., Nassau Lawyers Assn. Recipient Outstanding Man of the Year in Law award, Long Island U., 1976. Author: Tax Certiorari Procs., Preparation of a Tax Certiorari for Trial, Acquiring Property for Public Use. Home: 47 Stillwell Ln Laurel Hollow Woodbury NY 11797 Office: 114 Old Country Rd Mineola NY 11501 Tel (516) 294-8081

SANTILLI, PAUL THOMAS, b. Columbus, Ohio, Feb. 10, 1929; B.Chem. Engring., Ohio State U., 1951, M.S., 1951; LL.B., Capital U., 1960, J.D., 1968. Chem. engr. Battelle Meml. Inst., Columbus, 1953-60, atty., 1960-63, chief corp. counsel, 1968—, v.p., 1972—; admitted to Ohio bar, 1960; chief counsel Battelle NW Labs., Richland, Wash., 1963-68; dir. Sci. Advances, Inc., Columbus, 1974—, Battelle Commons Co., Columbus, 1975—. Active Jr. Achievement of Columbus, 1972—. Mem. Columbus, Ohio State, Am. bar assns., Ohio State U. Alumni Assn., Columbus C. of C., Tau Beta Pi. Home: 1289 Fountaine Dr Columbus OH 43221 Office: 505 King Ave Columbus OH 43201 Tel (614) 424-4164

SANTO, HENRY EUGENE, b. Denver, Nov. 19, 1924; B.S. in Bus. Adminstrn., U. Denver, 1949, J.D., 1951. Admitted to Colo. bar, 1951; practiced in Denver, 1951-59; dep. dist. atty. City of Denver, 1953-57; judge City and County of Denver Municipal Ct., 1957-59, Colo. Dist. Ct., 2d Jud. Dist., 1959—; lectr. on criminal law and procedure Denver Police Acad., 1955-57; adj. prof. law U. Denver, 1964—. Mem. dist. com. Denver Area council Boy Scouts Am., 1960-67. Mem. Am., Colo., Denver bar assns., Nat. Conf. State Trial Judges, Am. Judicature Soc., Colo. Dist. Judges Assn. (exec. com. 1975-76), Order St. Ives. Recipient Community Service award as outstanding jurist, Denver, 1966; editorial bd. U. Denver Law Rev., 1950-51, Dicta, 1950-51. Office: Dist Ct City and County Bldg Denver CO 80202 Tel (303) 297-2729

SANTOS, LEONARD ERNEST, b. Caracas, Venezuela, Aug. 5, 1946; B.A., Tufts U., 1967; J.D., N.Y. U. Law Sch., 1971; postgrad. (Doughrety scholar) U. Concepcion (Chile), 1968. Admitted to Ariz. bar, 1971, D.C. bar, 1972; law clk. to Hon. Ozell M. Trask, U.S. Ct. Appeals, 9th Circuit, 1971-72; asso. firm Hogan & Hartson, Washington, 1972-76; atty. office asst. gen. counsel dept. internat. affairs Treasury Dept., Washington, 1976—. Mem. D.C., Am. bar assns. Note and comment editor N.Y. U. Jour. Internat. Law and Politics, 1969-70. Home: 911 26th St NW Washington DC 20037 Office: Treasury Dept 2014 15th and Pennsylvania Ave Washington DC 20220 Tel (202) 566-8416

SAPHIER, MICHAEL STEPHEN, b. N.Y.C., July 8, 1942; B.A., Tufts U., 1964; LL.B., J.D., N.Y. U., 1968. Admitted to N.Y. bar, 1968, Calif. bar, 1969; law clk. U.S. Dist. Ct. Eastern Dist. N.Y., 1968, U.S. Dist. Ct. Central Dist. Calif., 1969-69; asso. firm Fulop, Rolston, & Burns, Beverly Hills, Calif., 1969-71, firm Levin, Saphier, Rein, Los Angeles, 1971—. Mem. Am., Los Angeles County, Hollywood bar assns. Home: 647 Thornhill Rd Calabasas CA 91302 Office: 1900 Ave of the Stars Los Angeles CA 90067 Tel (213) 556-0100

SAPIR, ISIDORE, b. N.Y.C., Jan. 29, 1915; B.S., Coll. City N.Y., 1935; LL.B., Bklyn. Law Sch., 1938. Admitted to N.Y. bar, 1938; asso. firm Katz & Spector, N.Y.C., 1938-58, partner, 1959; individual practice law, N.Y.C., 1959-74; gen. counsel Am. Mayflower Life Ins. Co. of N.Y., N.Y.C., 1974—, also sec., dir. Democratic candidate for Family Ct. Judge Westchester County, 1968, 70, 74. Mem. Assn. Life Ins. Counsel. Home: 48 Westwind Rd Yonkers NY 10710 Office: 500 Fifth Ave New York City NY 10036 Tel (212) 221-4736

SAPORITO, JERRY LEONARD, b. New Orleans, Aug. 12, 1947; B.A., Tulane U., 1969, J.D., 1972. Admitted to La. bar, 1972; asso. firm Bernard, Micholet & Cassisa, Metairie, La., 1972—. Mem. Am., La. bar assns. Home: 1636 2d St New Orleans LA 70130 Office: 1615 Metairie Rd Metairie LA 70005 Tel (504) 834-2612

SAPP, ARMISTEAD WRIGHT, JR., b. Greensboro, N.C., Feb. 28, 1929; student N.Y. U., 1948-50, 1952-54; LL.B., U. N.C., 1957. Admitted to N.C. bar, 1957; partner firm Sapp and Sapp, Greensboro, 1957—. Chief campmaster, council commr. Gen. Greene council Boy Scouts Am., 1972—, mem. nat. council, 1976—; deacon Presbyn. Ch., Greensboro, 1976—. Mem. Internat., Am., N.C., Greensboro Dist. bar assns., Myopia Internat. Research Soc. (dir.), Internat. Platform Assn., Fgn. Policy Assn. Forum, Am. Acad. Polit. and Social Sci., Am. Judicature Soc., Am. Soc. Juvenile Ct. Judges, Am. Trial Lawyers Assn., U.S. Trademark Assn., World Assn. Lawyers, Am. Arbitration Assn. Home: 2147 Berkley Pl Greensboro NC 27403 Office: 219 W Washington St Greensboro NC 27401 Tel (919) 274-7206

SAPP, RICHARD STEWART, b. Winston-Salem, N.C., Feb. 2, 1932; B.S., U. N.C., 1954; LL.B., Wake Forest U., 1959. Admitted to N.C. bar, 1961; individual practice law, Winston-Salem, 1963—. Mem. Am., Forsyth County, N.C. State bar assns. Home: 1832 Buddinbrook Ln Winston-Salem NC 27106 Office: Reynolds Manor Shopping Center Winston-Salem NC 27106 Tel (919) 725-3875

SAPP, WALTER WILLIAM, b. Linton, Ind., Apr. 21, 1930; A.B., Harvard U., 1951; J.D., Ind. U., 1957. Admitted to Ind. bar, 1957, N.Y. bar, 1959, Colo. bar, 1967; asso. firm Cahill, Gordon & Reindel, N.Y.C., 1957-66, mem., 1966; with Colo. Interstate Corp., Colorado Springs, 1966-76, gen. counsel, 1966-76, sec., 1971-76, exec. v.p., 1975-76; sr. v.p., gen. counsel Tenneco Inc., Houston, 1976—. Mem. Am., N.Y. State bar assns., Assn. Bar City N.Y. Office: PO Box 2511 Houston TX 77001 Tel (713) 757-2731

SAPPENFIELD, ROSCOE GROVER, b. Byrneville, Ind., Nov. 21, 1892; J.D., John Marshall Law Sch., 1937; postgrad. Harvard U., 1962. Admitted to Ill. bar, 1937, U.S. Supreme Ct. bar, 1951; v.p., controller W. T. Rawleigh Co., Freeport, Ill., 1922-32; v.p., treas. Campana Corp., Batavia, Ill., 1932-37, pres., gen. counsel, 1937-60; individual practice law, Kane, DuPage, Cook counties (Ill.), 1960—; chief traveling auditor Chgo., Milw., St. Paul & Pacific R.R., Chgo., 1918-22; legal and fin. adviser to mayor, Freeport, Ill., 1924-32. Bd. dirs. Kane County (Ill.) Fair, 1955-62. Mem. Am., Ill., Chgo., Kane County bar assns., Delta Theta Phi. Home: 800 S 15th St Box 7-204 Sebring OH 44672 Office: 330 Naperville Rd Wheaton IL 60187 Tel (312) 665-8020

SAPPINGTON, WARREN ARTHUR, b. Winshester, Ill., Sept. 8, 1938; B.S., Millikin U., 1953; LL.B., U. Ill., 1956, J.D., 1968; postgrad. Ind. U., 1961-62. Admitted to Ill. bar, 1958; with Allstate Ins. Co., Decatur, Ill., 1956-58; mem. faculty Millikin U., Decatur, 1958-64, asst. prof. bus. adminstrn., 1958-64; mem. firm Record, Sappington & Healy, Decatur, 1964—; asst. atty. gen. Adolf Meyer Zone Center, Ill. Dept. Mental Health, 1969—; lectr. bus. law Millikin U., 1967—; chmn. Central Ill. Regional Law Enforcement Commn., 1971; asst. supr. Decatur Twp., Macon County Bd. Suprs., 1969—. Bd. dirs. Decatur Pub. Library, 1963-70, pres. 1966-68. Mem. Am., Ill., Decatur, Macon County bar assns., Am. Bus. Law Assn., Phi Kappa Phi. Ford Found. fellow, 1961. Home: 328 S Westlawn St Decatur IL 62522 Office: 250 N Water St Decatur IL 62523 Tel (217) 428-6629

SARASEK, PETER ANTHONY, b. Milw., May 24, 1945; B.A. magna cum laude, Cath. U. Am., 1967, M.A., 1968; J.D. cum laude, U. Wis., 1974. Admitted to Wis. bar, 1974, Ill. bar, 1974; asso. firm Wilson & McIlvaine, Chgo., 1974—. Mem. Wis., Ill., Am. bar assns., Order of Coif. Editor U. Wis. Law Rev., 1973-74. Office: 135 S LaSalle St Chicago IL 60603 Tel (312) 263-1212

SARFATY, JOSEPH, b. N.Y.C., Apr. 30, 1922; B.S., U. Calif., Los Angeles, 1949; LL.B., J.D., Loyola U., 1958. Admitted to Calif. bar, 1960, U.S. Supreme Ct. bar, 1968; mgr. western dist. Warner Bros. Pictures Distbg. Corp., Los Angeles, 1949-63; mem. firm Kurtzman & Sarfaty, Los Angeles, 1964—. Mem. Am., Los Angeles County, Beverly Hills bar assns. Home: 6537 Bothwell Rd Reseda CA 91335 Office: 1880 Century Park E Suite 218 Los Angeles CA 90067 Tel (213) 553-0355

SARGUIS, FRANCIS, b. Marseilles, France, Jan. 4, 1933; A.B., U. Calif., Berkeley, 1958; M.A., U. Calif. at Santa Barbara, 1972; J.D., U. So. Calif., 1962; LL.M., Yale, 1963. Admitted to Calif. bar, 1963, U.S. Supreme Ct. bar, 1972; dep. county counsel Santa Barbara County, Calif., 1963-66; individual practice law, Santa Barbara, 1967—; mem. Calif. Hwy. Commn., 1976—. Pres. Santa Barbara Tri-Counties chpt. UN Assn. U.S., 1970-74, mem. nat. bd. dirs., 1974—; pres. Get Oil Out, Inc., Santa Barbara, 1973-77, U.S.-China People's Friendship Assn. Mem. Calif. State Bar, Am. Soc. Internat. Law, Calif. Barristers Club (founding). Home: 101 Rametto Rd Santa Barbara CA 93108 Office: 906 Garden St Santa Barbara CA 93101 Tel (805) 963-7848

SARISOHN, FLOYD, b. Bklyn., Sept. 3, 1928; LL.B., St. John's U., 1954, J.D., 1968. Admitted to N.Y. State bar, 1954, U.S. Supreme Ct. bar, 1963; asso. firm Miller & Sarisohn, Hicksville, N.Y., 1955-61, Sarisohn & Sarisohn, Commack, N.Y., 1968-73, Belli, Sarisohn, Creditor, Carner, Thierman & Steindler, Commack, 1973-77, Sarisohn, Sarisohn, Carner, Thierman & Steindler, 1977—; justice of peace, Smithtown, N.Y., 1960-63; dist. ct. judge, Suffolk County, N.Y., 1964-67. Asso. council N.Y. State Assembly, 1976-77. Vice pres. Suffolk County council Boy Scouts Am., 1965-67; chmn. Democratic party, Smithtown, 1970-76; pres. L.I. Forum Edn., Suffolk, 1974-76. Mem. Suffolk Bar Assn., Suffolk Criminal Bar Assn., N.Y. State Trial Lawyers, Am. Trial Lawyers Assn., First Amendment Trial Lawyers Assn. Home: 8 Walter Ct Commack NY 11725 Office: 1020 Jericho Turnpike Commack NY 11725 Tel (516) 543-7667

SARKISIAN, ALBERT ELLIOT, b. Providence, Nov. 4, 1930; B.S., U. R.I., 1952; J.D., Boston U., 1956, LL.M., 1961. Admitted to R.I. bar, 1957; individual practice law, Providence, 1957—; instr. U. R.I., Kingston, 1956-58; asso. prof. law Bryant Coll., 1958-62, faculty evening div., 1958-69; coordinator Law for Laymen, U. R.I. Extension, 1972—. Bd. dirs., exec. com. R.I. Civic Chorale and Orch., 1968—. Mem. Am., R.I. bar assns. Home: 91 Barrett Ave North Providence RI 02904 Office: 409-410 Industrial Bank Bldg Providence RI 02903 Tel (401) 861-1798

SARKISIAN, BARRY P., b. Hackensack, N.J., July 9, 1948; B.S., St. Peter's Coll., Jersey City, 1969; J.D., N.Y. Law Sch., 1972. Admitted to N.J. bar, 1973; individual practice law, West New York, N.J., 1973—; prosecutor City of Union City, N.J., 1973-74, West New York, 1974—; atty. rent control bd. West New York, 1974—. Pres. West New York Beautification Com., 1971-74. Mem. Am., N.J., Hudson County bar assns., North Hudson Lawyer's Club. Office: 6135 Bergenline Ave West New York NJ 07093 Tel (201) 854-0015

SARLES, BURTON BERNARD, b. Buffalo, Jan. 18, 1927: J.D., State U. N.Y., Buffalo, 1951. Admitted to N.Y. State bar, 1951; asso. firm Lewis & Korn, Buffalo, 1951-55; partner firm Sarles & Freed, Buffalo, 1955-69, firm Sarles & Frey, Buffalo, 1970—. Mem. Erie County Bar Assn. (dir. 1965-68), N.Y. State (dist. gov. 1970-72), Erie County (pres. 1971), Am. trial lawyers. assns. Asso. editor Buffalo Law Rev., 1950-51. Office: 303 Brisbane Bldg Buffalo NY 14203 Tel (716) 853-2365

SARNOW, RAYMOND S., b. Chgo., Aug. 21, 1919; student U. Ill., 1938-39; student Northwestern U., 1940-42, J.D., 1945. Admitted to Ill. bar, 1945, U.S. Dist. Ct. bar for No. Dist. Ill., 1948, U.S. 7th Circuit Ct. Appeals bar, 1948, U.S. Supreme Ct. bar, 1948; asst. atty. gen. Ill. Atty. Gen's. Appeals Div., 1945-64, chief Appeals Div., 1963-64; magistrate Cook County Circuit Ct., 1964-71, asso. judge, 1971, judge, 1971—; pres. Magistrates Assn. Cook County, 1964-68, 70. Editor-in-chief: Ill. Law Rev., 1944-45. Office: Daley Center Chicago IL 60602 Tel (312) 443-8275

SARRAT, DONALD MICHEL, JR., b. New Orleans, Aug. 19, 1944; B.B.A., Loyola U., 1966, J.D., 1969, M.B.A., 1975. Admitted to La. bar, 1969; capt. AUS, 1969-71; controller and corp. sec. Mon-Arc Welding Supplying & Med. Specialties Inc., New Orleans, 1971—. Mem. La. State Bar Assn. Home: 217 Hector Ave Metairie LA 70005 Office: 3214 Howard Ave New Orleans LA 70113 Tel (504) 821-3700

SARSFIELD, GEORGE P., b. Vancouver, B.C., Can., Jan. 14, 1913; B.A., U. Mont., 1950, J.D., 1950. Admitted to Mont. bar, 1950, U.S. Supreme Ct. bar, 1960; individual practice law, Butte, Mont., 1950—. Mem. adv. bd. Salvation Army, 1950-76. Mem. Am., Mont. (past v.p.) bar assns., Am. Trial Lawyers Assn., U. Mont. Alumni Assn. (pres. 1964-65), Phi Delta Phi. Recipient Distinguished Service award U. Mont., 1971. Home: 2700 Floral Blvd Butte MT 59701 Office: 230 Mayer Blvd Butte MT 59701 Tel (406) 723-5413

SARTOR, DANIEL RYAN, JR., b. Vicksburg, Miss., June 2, 1932; B.A., Tulane U., 1952, LL.B., 1955. Admitted to La. bar, 1955; instr. Tulane U. Law Sch., 1955-56, asst. prof. law, 1956-57; practice law, Monroe, La., 1957—; partner firm Snellings, Breard, Sartor, Shafto & Inabnett, Monroe, 1960—. Bd. visitors Tulane U., 1974—. Mem. Am., La. bar assns., La. Law Inst. (council, sec. civil law sect.). Mem. bd. adv. editors Tulane Law Rev., 1970—. Home: 2405 Pargoud Blvd Monroe LA 71201 Office: 1503 N 19th St Monroe LA 71201 Tel (318) 387-8000

SASS, JAMES CRAIG, b. Toledo, Ohio, Dec. 1, 1947; B.A., Adrian Coll., 1969; J.D., U. Toledo, 1973. Admitted to Ohio bar, 1973, since practiced in Toledo; asso. firm Schnorf, Schnorf & Schnorf, 1973—; law clk. Ct. Common Pleas, Lucas County, Ohio, 1969-73. Mem. Am., Ohio, Toledo bar assns., Delta Theta Phi. Home: 5805 Pinecroft Dr Toledo OH 43615 Office: 503 Spitzer Bldg Toledo OH 43604 Tel (419) 242-9543

SASSER, JAMES RALPH, b. Memphis, Tenn., Sept. 30, 1936; student U. Tenn., Knoxville, 1954-55; B.A., Vanderbilt U., 1958, LL.B., 1961. Admitted to Tenn. bar, 1961; mem. U.S. Senate, 95th Congress; exec. sec. Tenn. Codes Commn., 1975-76. Bd. dirs. NCCJ, Nashville, Nashville Symphony Assn., Nashville Com. Fgn. Relations; chmn. Tenn. Dem. Party, 1973-76, v.p. Assn. State Dem. Chairmen, 1975-76. Office: US Senate Washington DC 20510 Tel (202) 224-3344

SASSONE, ROBERT LEWIS, b. Detroit, May 12, 1935; B.S. in Physics, U. Mich., 1959; J.D., Loyola U., Los Angeles, 1968. Admitted to Calif. bar, 1968, U.S. Supreme Ct. bar, 1972; asso. firm Fraser & Bogucki, Los Angeles, 1967-68; individual practice law, Santa Ana, Calif., 1968—; guest lectr. numerous colls. and univs., U.S. and abroad. Pres. Calif. Pro Life Council, 1972-73. Author: Handbook on Population, 1972, 73, 77, Handbook on Euthanasia, 1975, Release, 1975. Office: 900 N Broadway # 725 Santa Anna CA 92701 Tel (714) 547-5611

SASSOWER, DORIS LIPSON, b. N.Y.C., Sept. 25, 1932; B.A. summa cum laude, Bklyn. Coll., 1954; J.D. cum laude (Florence Allen scholar), N.Y. U., 1955. Admitted to N.Y. bar, 1955, U.S. Supreme Ct. U.S. Ct. Claims, 1961, U.S. Ct. Mil. Appeals, U.S. Customs Ct., 1969; with Legal Aid Soc., 1954; law asst. U.S. Atty's. Office, So. Dist. N.Y., 1954-55; partner firm Sassower & Sassower, N.Y.C., 1955—; law asst. to chief justice N.J. Supreme Ct., 1956-57. Dir. Internat. Inst. Women Studies, 1971, Inst. on Women's Wrongs, 1973, Exec. Woman, 1973; co-organizer Nat. Conf. Profl. and Acad. Women, 1970; founder, spl. cons. Profl. Women's Caucus, 1970. Fellow N.Y. Bar Found., Am. Acad. Matrimonial Lawyers; mem. N.Y. Women's Bar Assn. (pres. 1968-69), Bklyn. Coll. Alumni Assn. (pres. lawyers' group 1963-65), Am. (co-chmn. Nat. Conf. Lawyers and Social Workers 1973-74), Fed., N.Y. State (jud. selection com., legis. com., family law sect.), Westchester County (N.Y.), New Rochelle (N.Y.) bar assns., Assn. Bar City N.Y. (chmn. subcom. on women and legal profession and subcom. on matrimonial law reform 1971—), Assn. Feminist Consultants, Am. Arbitration Assn. (nat. panel arbitrators), N.Y. State Trial Lawyers Assn., Am. Judicature Soc., Consular Law Soc., N.Y. U. Law Alumni Assn. (dir. 1974—), Phi Beta Kappa (pres. Alumnae in N.Y. 1970-71). Recipient Distinguished Alumna award Bklyn. Coll., 1973, Distinguished Woman award Northwood Inst., Midland, Mich., 1976; named Outstanding Young Woman Am., 1969; contbr. articles to legal jours. Home: 11 Fenimore Rd New Rochelle NY 10804 Office: 200 Park Ave New York City NY 10017 Tel (212) 490-3866 also 14 Mamaroneck Ave White Plains NY 10601 Tel (914) 946-2500

SATOVSKY, ABRAHAM, b. Detroit, Oct. 15, 1907; B.S., U. Mich., 1928, J.D., 1930. Admitted to Mich. bar, 1930, U.S. Supreme Ct. bar, 1953; asso. with William H. Gallagher, Detroit, 1930-65. Pres. Nat. Fedn. Jewish Men's Clubs, 1956-58; bd. dirs. Jewish Welfare Fedn., 1960-63, Jewish Hist. Soc. Mich., 1969—; del. Jewish Community Council, 1960-77; adv. council United Synagogue Am., 1958-60. Mem. Mich., Detroit, Southfield, Am. bar assns., Am. Judicature Soc., Am. Arbitration Assn. Recipient Sem. award Jewish Theol. Sem. Am., 1952: citation merit Jewish Welfare Fedn. Detroit, 1956-58; Jerusalem award State Israel Bond Orgn., 1964. Home: 22500 Saratoga Dr Southfield MI 48075 Office: 28455 Northwestern Hwy Southfield MI 48034 Tel (313) 354-4333

SATTER, ROBERT, b. Chgo., Aug. 19, 1919; B.A., Rutgers U., 1941; LL.B., Columbia, 1947. Admitted to N.Y. bar, 1947, U.S. Supreme Ct. bar, 1950, Conn. bar, 1952; asso. firm Benjamin, Galton & Robbins, N.Y.C., 1947-52; partner firm Ritt & Satter, Hartford, Conn., 1952-61; partner firm Satter, Fleischmann & Sherbacow, Hartford, 1961-75, judge ct. common pleas, Hartford, 1975—; lectr. U. Conn. Law Sch., 1977, Yale U. coll. summer program, 1976; mem. Conn. Ho. of Reps., 1959-60, 63-66; gen. counsel Dem. Party, Conn. Legislature, 1967-75. Mem. Bd. Fin. Newington (Conn.), 1960-66; pres. Greater Hartford Community Council, 1961-63; vice-chmn. Hartford Community Renewal Team, 1960-62; chmn. bd. trustees Westledge Sch., 1974-75. Mem. Conn., Hartford County bar assns., Phi Beta Kappa. Contbr. articles to legal jours. Home: 75 Brookside Rd Newington CT 06111 Office: Court of Common Pleas 95 Washington St Hartford CT 06106 Tel (203) 547-0120

SATTERFIELD, DIXIE RUPERT, b. Princeton, Ky., Jan. 10, 1944; B.A., Murray State U., 1966; J.D., U. Ky., 1968. Admitted to Ky. bar, 1969; asso. firm Milliken & Milliken, Bowling Green, Ky., 1969-70, partner, 1971-76; partner firm Safford & Satterfield, Bowling Green, 1976—; judge pro tem City of Bowling Green, 1971—. Pres. Cumberland Trace Elementary Sch. PTA, Bowling Green. Mem. Ky., Warren County (sec. 1971, v.p. 1974, pres. 1975), Bowling Green bar assns. Office: 324 E 10th St Bowling Green KY 42101 Tel (502) 782-1340

SATTERWHITE, CHARLES FRANK, b. Lexington, Ky., Apr. 4, 1948; B.A., Transylvania Coll., 1970; J.D., U. Ky., 1973. Admitted to Ky. bar, 1973; fed.-state coordinator Ky. Dept. Labor, Occupational Safety and Health Program, Frankfort, 1974-77; individual practice law, Owenton, Ky., 1977—. Mem. Ky. Bar Assn. Home: Kelly Ct Owenton KY 40359 Office: N Thomas St Owenton KY 40359

SATTLER, JAMES MICHAEL, b. Salt Lake City, Feb. 6, 1940; B.S., U. Utah, 1962, J.D., 1966. Admitted to Hawaii bar, 1966, Calif. bar, 1973; mem. firm Anderson, Wrenn & Jenks, Honolulu, 1966-72; partner firms Jenks, Kidwell, Goodsill & Anderson, Honolulu, 1972-74, Sattler Spradlin & Brandt and predecessor, Honolulu, 1974-75; individual practice law, Honolulu, 1975—. Bd. dirs., v.p. Cloward Found. for Med. Research Honolulu, 1965—. Mem. Order of Coif, Sigma Nu, Delta Theta Phi, Phi Kappa Phi. Contbr. articles to profl. jours.; editor Utah Law Rev., 1964-66, Hawaii Bar Jour., 1967-68. Home: 1588 Hoaaina St Honolulu HI 96821 Office: 841 Bishop St Suite 2020 Honolulu HI 96813 Tel (808) 524-2914

SAUER, DOROTHY CATHERINE, b. Dubuque, Iowa, Mar. 14, 1926; student Clarke Coll., Dubuque, 1943-44. Admitted to Iowa bar, 1952, Minn. bar, 1957; individual practice law, Dubuque, 1952—. Pres., Dubuque Safety Council, 1959-60, bd. dirs., 1954—. Mem. Am., Iowa, Dubuque County (2d v.p.), Ramsey County (Minn.) bar assns., Nat. Assn. Women Lawyers. Home: Route 1 Peosta IA 52068 Office: 405 Fischer Bldg Dubuque IA 52001 Tel (319) 582-3247

SAUER, NORMAN AMBROSE, JR., b. San Francisco, Feb. 15, 1944; B.A., U. San Francisco, 1965, J.D., 1968. Admitted to Calif. bar, 1969; asso. firm Robert L. Davis, San Francisco, 1969-71; partner firm Davis & Sauer, San Francisco, 1971—. Mem. Am. Bar Assn., Assn. Trial Lawyers Am., Calif. Trial Lawyers Assn. Office: 3350 Steiner St San Francisco CA 94123 Tel (415) 567-7954

SAUER, WILLIAM JACOB, b. La Crosse, Wis., July 18, 1917; A.B., Beloit Coll., 1938; LL.B., U. Wis., 1941. Admitted to Wis. bar, 1941, U.S. Supreme Ct. bar, 1964; individual practice law, La Crosse, 1946—; asst. city atty. La Crosse, 1956-72, dep. city atty., 1973—; lectr. U. Wis. Law Sch., 1968, 70; mem. state adv. com. Wis. Uniform Comml. Code, 1968—, lectr., 1964-65. Pres. LaCrosse Symphony Orch., 1947-49. Mem. Am., Wis. State, La Crosse County (sec., 1947-49, pres., 1968-69) bar assns., Order of Coif, Phi Beta Kappa, Delta Sigma Rho. Contbr. to books, articles to legal publs. Home: 2121 Main St La Crosse WI 54601 Office: Box 904 518 State St La Crosse WI 54601 Tel (608) 782-4179

SAUERWEIN, RICHARD JOSEPH, b. Elizabeth, N.J., Oct. 30, 1929; B.S., Seton Hall U., 1951, LL.B., 1959. Admitted to N.J. bar, 1966; claims adjustor, supr. St. Paul Ins. Co., N.Y.C., 1956-66; dep. atty. gen. State N.J., Trenton, 1966-68; asso. firm John D. Leslie, Jr., Verona, N.J., 1968-70, partner, 1970-72; individual practice law, Springfield, N.J., 1972—. Vol. atty. planning bd. City of Linden (N.J.), 1973—. Mem. Am., N.J., Union County, Linden bar assns. Home: 1120 Georgian Dr Linden NJ 07036 Office: 26 Linden Ave Springfield NJ 07081 Tel (201) 467-2944

SAUL, ROLAND DALE, b. Plainview, Tex., Mar. 7, 1948; B.S., Wayland Bapt. Coll., 1970; J.D., Tex. Tech. U., 1973. Admitted to Tex. bar, 1973; asst. dist. atty. Deaf Smith County (Tex.), 1973-76; partner firm Tubb, Easterwood & Saul, Hereford, Tex., 1976—. Bd. dirs. Hereford Campfire Girls, 1973; co-chmn. fund raising com. Am. Heart Assn., 1976-77. Mem. Am., Tex., Deaf Smith County bar assns. Home: 203 Hickory St Hereford TX 79045 Office: 244 E 3d St Hereford TX 79045 Tel (806) 364-6801

SAUNDERS, CLAY NEBHUT, b. Memphis, Oct. 10, 1939; B.A., Memphis State U., 1961; J.D., U. Tenn., 1964. Admitted to Tenn. bar, 1964, U.S. 6th Circuit Ct. Appeals, 1964; mem. research and writing dept. FBI, Washington, 1961-62; law clk. U.S. Dist. Ct., Memphis, 1964-65; asst. dist. atty. gen., 13th Jud. Dist. Tenn., Memphis, 1965-68; partner firm Pittman, Clay, Morgan, Cole, Gilliland & Saunders, Memphis, 1968—. Mem. Phi Delta Phi. Home: 54 S Rose Rd Memphis TN 38111 Office: 2700 Sterick Bldg Memphis TN 38103 Tel (901) 526-6464

SAUNDERS, DELMAS FREDRICK, b. Paintsville, Ky., Nov. 8, 1941; student Georgetown Coll., 1959-62; Pharm.B., U. Ky., 1965, J.D., 1971. Admitted to Ky. bar, 1971; pharmacist Begley Drug Co., Richmond, Ky., 1965-68; law clk. Ky. Supreme Ct., 1971-72; exec. dir. Ky. Jud. Conf. and Council, 1972-73; asso. firm F. Selby Hurst, Lexington, Ky., 1973-74; partner firm Brooks, Sullivan & Saunders, Lexington, 1974-76; mem. firm Brown, Sledd & McCann, Lexington, 1976—. Mem. Ky., Fayette County bar assns. Contbr. articles in field to legal jours. Home: 1600 Fincastle Rd Lexington KY 40502 Office: 300 W Short St Lexington KY 40507 Tel (606) 254-2712

SAUNDERS, JAMES BYRON, b. Aberdeen, Miss., Feb. 10, 1908; student Tex. U., 1932. Admitted to Tex. bar, 1931; asst. atty. Smith County (Tex.), Tyler, 1932-34; judge, 1938-42; sr. partner firm Saunders, Caldwell & Schmidt, Tyler, 1957—; Chmn. Tex. Dept. Pub. Welfare, 1951-53, Tex. Bd. Ins., 1953-56. Mem. Tex. Bar Assn., Nat. Assn. Ins. Commrs. (chmn. 1956), Smith County Judges Assn. (pres. 1941). Home: 2415 Sunnybrook Dr Tyler TX 75701 Office: 345 Tyler Bank Bldg Tyler TX 75701 Tel (214) 593-0213

SAUNDERS, WILLIAM FRANCIS, b. Jersey City, Dec. 31, 1915; B.S., Washington and Lee U., 1938, LL.B., 1940. Admitted to Va. bar, 1939, N.Y. bar, 1941; asso. firm Dunnington, Bartholow & Miller, N.Y.C., 1940-48, partner, 1948—. Vice-pres., treas., trustee Valley Hosp., Ridgewood, N.J., 1968—. Mem. Am., N.Y. State, Va. bar assns., Assn. Bar City N.Y., Phi Beta Kappa, Beta Gamma Sigma, Omicron Delta Kappa, Order of Coif. Home: 520 Fairway Rd Ridgewood NJ 07450 Office: 161 E 42d St New York City NY 10017 Tel (212) 682-8811

SAUSE, JOHN WILLIAM, JR., b. Balt., Oct. 14, 1933; B.A., Williams Coll., 1955; LL.B., U. Va., 1958. Admitted to Md. bar, 1958, U.S. Supreme Ct. bar, 1966; law clk. to judge Md. Ct. Appeals, Annapolis, 1958-59; asst. state's atty. Balt., 1959-62; asso. firm Mylander & Atwater, Balt., 1962-66; asst. atty. gen. Md., Balt., 1964-66; individual practice law, Centreville, Md., 1966-75; partner firm Sause & Braden, Centreville, 1976—; legis. officer to Gov. Md., 1968-69; trial magistrate State of Md., Queen Anne's County, 1967-68, 69-71; dist. pub. defender Caroline, Cecil, Kent, Queen Anne's and Talbot counties, 1971—. Mem. Am., Md., Queen Anne's County bar assns. Home: 202 S Liberty St Centreville MD 21617 Office: 204 N Commerce St Centreville MD 21617 Tel (301) 758-0970

SAUTEBIN, BRUCE LLOYD, b. Green Bay, Wis., Nov. 9, 1948; B.A., N. Central Coll., 1970; J.D., U. Wis., 1973. Admitted to Wis. bar, 1973; partner firm Johnson, Harnisch & Sautebin, Greenwood, Wis., 1973—. Mem. Greenwood C. of C. (sec. 1974—). Home: 115 N Main St Greenwood WI 54437 Office: 209 S Main St Greenwood WI 54437 Tel (715) 267-7249

SAVAGE, BARRY EMERY, b. Jackson, Mich., Apr. 19, 1940; student Denison U., 1958-59; B.A. in Econs., U. Mich., 1962, J.D., 1965. Admitted to Ohio bar, 1965, Mich. bar, 1966; asso. firm Schlageter & Savage, Toledo, 1965-67; partner firm Boxell, Bebout, Torbet & Baker, Toledo, 1968-74; individual practice law, Toledo, 1974-76; partner firm Savage, Gibson & Yarbrough, Toledo, 1976—. Mem. State Bar Mich., Am., Toledo bar assns. Home: 2344 Eastgate St Toledo OH 43614 Office: 228 N Erie St Toledo OH 43624 Tel (419) 255-9580

SAVAGE, CLARENCE BERYL, b. Ft. Worth, July 30, 1933; LL.B., U. Tulsa, 1961. Admitted to Okla. bar, 1961; partner firm Morehead, Savage, O'Donnell, McNulty & Cleverdon, and predecessor, Tulsa, 1963—; chmn. Gov.'s Legal Com. Emergency Planning, 1967-68; chmn. Okla. Consumer Affairs Commn., 1973-75; mem. Okla. Jud. Nominating Commn., 1975-76. Mem. Am., Okla., Tulsa County bar assns., Am., Okla. (pres. 1972), Tulsa (pres. 1971) trial lawyers assns. Contbr. articles to legal jours. Home: 6002 S Joplin St Tulsa OK 74135 Office: 201 W 5th St suite 500 Tulsa OK 74103 Tel (918) 584-4716

SAVAGE, DAVID WILLIAM, b. Seattle, Nov. 14, 1944; B.A., Wash. State U., 1967; J.D., Idaho U., 1973. Admitted to Wash. bar, 1973; asso. firm Irwin, Friel & Myklebust, Pullman, Wash., 1973—. Bd. dirs. Whitman County Alcoholism Center. Mem. Am. Bar Assn., Wash., Am. trial lawyers assns. Home: Route 1 Box 79 Pullman WA 99163 Office: PO Box 604 Pullman WA 99163 Tel (509) 564-1178

SAVAGE, E. SCOTT, b. Salt Lake City, Feb. 15, 1947; J.D., U. Utah, 1972. Admitted to Utah bar, 1972; asso. firm Van Cott, Bagley, Cornwall & McCarthy, Salt Lake City, 1971-76, partner, 1976—; asso. vis. prof. environ. law U. Utah Coll. Law, 1973-75. Mem. Am., Utah, Salt Lake County bar assns., Order of Coif. Editor U. Utah Law Rev., 1970-71. Office: 141 E First South Salt Lake City UT 84111 Tel (801) 532-3333

SAVAGE, JOE CHRISTIAN, b. Oklahoma City, Nov. 2, 1939; A.B., U. Okla., 1961; LL.B., U. Ky., 1964; LL.M., Harvard, 1965. Admitted to Ky. bar, 1964; asso. firm Wallace, Turner & Trigg, Lexington, Ky., 1965-69; partner firm Turley, Savage & Moore, and predecessor, Lexington, 1969—; adj. prof. law U. Ky., 1966—, adj. prof. medicine, 1968—. Bd. dirs. Thomas Hunt Morgan Inst. Genetics, Inc., Lexington, Multiple Sclerosis Soc., 1976. Mem. Fayette County, Ky. (ho. of dels.), Am. bar assns., Ky., Am. trial lawyers assns. Named Outstanding Young Atty. in Fayette County, 1972. Home: 1212 Eldemere Rd Lexington KY 40502 Office: 134 N Limestone St Lexington KY 40507 Tel (606) 252-1705

SAVAGE, ROYCE HALSELL, b. McAlester, Okla., Mar. 31, 1904; B.A., U. Okla., 1925, LL.B., 1927. Admitted to Okla. bar, 1927, Pa. bar, 1962; asst. ins. commr. Okla., Oklahoma City, 1927-29; partner firm Monnet & Savage, Tulsa, 1929-38, Cantrell, Savage & McCloud, Oklahoma City, 1938-40; U.S. dist. judge No. Dist. Okla., 1940-61; gen. counsel Gulf Oil Corp., Pitts., 1961-69; of counsel firm Boone, Ellison & Smith, Tulsa, 1969—. Home: 2125 E 60th Ct Tulsa OK 74105 Office: 900 World Bldg Tulsa OK 74103 Tel (918) 587-0000

SAVELL, RICHARD DAVID, b. Bridgeport, Conn., Jan. 19, 1947; B.A. in Polit. Sci., Union Coll., Schenectady, 1969; J.D., Columbia, 1972. Admitted to Alaska bar, 1972, U.S. Supreme Ct. bar, 1976; asso. firm Charles E. Cole, Fairbanks, Alaska, 1972-74; partner firm Aschenbrenner & Savell, Fairbanks, 1974—; bd. dirs. Alaska Legal Services Corp., 1974—; bd. govs. Alaska State Bar, 1976—; mem. small claims rules revision com. Alaska Supreme Ct. Mem. Am., Alaska, Tanana Valley bar assns., Am. Trial Lawyers Assn. Recipient NAACP Legal Service Achievement award, 1975. Home: PO Box 2683 3.6 Mile Gilmore Trail Fairbanks AK 99701 Office: PO Drawer 72871 Suite 250 Nat Bank of Alaska Bldg 6th and Cushman Sts Fairbanks AK 99701 Tel (907) 456-5110

SAVETT, STUART HUBERT, b. Phila., Jan. 9, 1939; B.S., Temple U., 1960; LL.B., Villanova U., 1963. Admitted to Pa. bar, 1964; asso. firm Dilworth, Paxon, Kalish, Kohn & Dilks, Phila., 1963-69; partner firm Harold E. Kohn, Phila., 1969-75, Kohn, Savett, Marion & Graf, Phila., 1976—. Mem. Am., Pa., Phila. bar assns., Order of Coif. Mem. editorial bd. Villanova Law Review, 1961-62, 62-63. Home: 1605 Lombard Philadelphia PA 19146 Office: Suite 1214 1700 Market Philadelphia PA 19103 Tel (215) 665-9900

SAVITCH, LEON, b. Coatesville, Pa., Jan. 9, 1923; B.S.E., U. Pa., 1943; LL.B., Harvard, 1948. Admitted to Calif. bar, 1949; partner firm Gitelson, Coyle, Cooper & Savitch, Los Angeles, 1950-56; partner firm Buchalter, Nemer, Fields & Savitch, Los Angeles, 1957—. Commr., City of Los Angeles Pension Commn., pres., 1973-75; trustee Coro Found. Mem. State Bar Calif., Am. Judicature Soc., Am., Los Angeles County bar assns., Am. Arbitration Assn. (mem. nat. panel arbitrators 1965). Office: 700 S Flower St Suite 700 Los Angeles CA 90017 Tel (213) 626-6700

SAVITT, BEVERLY BLOCH, b. Pitts., May 12, 1926; B.S., Carnegie Inst. Tech., 1946; J.D., Boalt Hall Sch. Law U. Calif., Berkeley, 1967. Admitted to Calif. bar, 1967; practiced in San Rafael, Calif., 1968—, individual practice law, 1968, partner firms Diamond, Savitt, Mellini & Lannon, Inc. and predecessors, 1969-75, Savitt & Adams, Inc., 1976—; mem. Park Forest (Ill.) City Council, 1961-65; lectr. King Sch. Law U. Calif., Davis, 1974-75, 75-76, Continuing Edn. of Bar, 1975-77. Rich Twp. (Ill.) Democratic committeewoman, 1956-61; mem. Marin County Juvenile Justice Commn., 1972—; bd. dirs. Marin Council Civic Affairs, 1968-75. Mem. Marin County Bar Assn. (dir. 1973-75). Home: 9 Fern Ave Belvedere CA 94920 Office: 828 Mission St San Rafael CA 94901 Tel (415) 454-8980

SAVITZ, JOSEPH J., b. Wilkes-Barre, Pa., Nov. 3, 1922; B.A., Wilkes Coll., 1948; LL.B., J.D., U. Pa., 1951. Admitted to Pa. bar, 1952, U.S. Supreme Ct. bar, 1958; partner firm Rosenn, Jenkins & Greenwald, Wilkes-Barre, 1958—; nat. judge adv. Jewish War Vets., 1961-62. Trustee Wilkes Coll., 1958—, chmn., 1975—. Mem. Am., Pa., Luzerne County bar assns. Home: 744 Milford Dr Kingston PA 18704 Office: 1000 Blue Cross Bldg Wilkes-Barre PA 18711 Tel (717) 829-0511

SAWYER, ALAN FREDERICK, b. Manchester, N.H., May 15, 1906; B.B.A., Boston U., 1944; postgrad. DePauw U., 1924-25; J.D., Northeastern U., 1943. Admitted to Mass. bar, 1943; asso. firm Goodwin, Proctor & Hoar, Boston, 1943-46; individual practice law, Saugus, Mass., 1946—. Rep. Saugus Town Meeting, 1935-48; selectman Town of Saugus, 1948-51. Mem. Lynn, Essex bar assns. Home: 4 Newhall Ave Saugus MA 01906 Office: 518 Lincoln Ave Saugus MA 01906 Tel (617) 233-1920

SAWYER, C(HARLES) MURRAY, b. Concord, N.H., Feb. 2, 1906; A.B., U. N.H., 1928. Admitted to N.H. bar, 1931, U.S. Dist. Ct. bar, 1947; individual practice law, Lebanon, 1931-35, 74—, Concord, 1947-57; clk. Superior Ct. for Grafton County, 1935-47, Concord Mcpl. Ct., 1950-57, U.S. Dist. Ct. for Dist. N.H., 1957-66; probation officer Concord Mcpl. Ct., 1950-57; staff atty. Tri-County Legal Assistance, 1967-71, N.H. Legal Assistance, Lebanon, 1971-74. Mem. Woodsville Sch. Bd., 1942-48, Concord Union Sch. Dist. Sch. Bd., 1948-54; mem. N.H. Legislature, 1949, 51. Mem. N.H., Grafton County, Merrimack County bar assns. Home and office: 2 Gerrish Ct Lebanon NH 03766 Tel (603) 448-3952

SAWYER, FRANK GRANT, b. Twin Falls, Idaho, Dec. 14, 1918; B.A., U. Nev., 1941; J.D., Georgetown U., 1948; LL.B. (hon.), Linfield Coll., 1960, U. Nev., 1964. Admitted to Nev. bar, 1948, D.C. bar, 1948, U.S. Supreme Ct. bar, 1959; individual practice law, Elko,

Nev., 1948-59; dist. atty. Elko County (Nev.), 1950-58; gen. counsel Edn. Commn. of the States, 1967-69; sr. partner firm Lionel, Sawyer & Collins, Las Vegas, 1967—: gov. State of Nev., 1959-67. Chmn. Democratic State Conv., Wells, Nev., 1952, 54; rep. Nev. resolutions and platform com. Dem. Nat. Convs., 1956, 60, 64, 68, 72, 76; Dem. nat. committeeman for Nev., 1968—. Mem. Am., Nev., D.C., Elko County (pres. 1957) bar assns., Am. Judicature Soc., Nat. (dir.), Nev. (pres. 1957) dist. attys. assns. Office: 300 S 4th St Las Vegas NV 89101 Tel (702) 385-2188

SAWYER, LAURA FRANKLYNNE, b. Salisbury, N.C., July 4, 1939; B.A., Bennett Coll., 1960; J.D., U. Iowa, 1963. Admitted to N.C. bar, 1964; staff atty. Legal Aid Soc. of Forsyth County (N.C.), 1967-70, acting dir., 1970-71; partner firm Westmoreland and Sawyer, Winston-Salem, N.C., 1971—. Bd. dirs. Winston-Salem State U., 1973—; mem. planning bd. Forsyth County and City of Winston-Salem, 1973—. Mem. Forsyth County, Am. bar assns., N.C. Bar, Assn. Trial Lawyers Am., N.C. Acad. Trial Lawyers, Am. Judicature Soc., Forsyth County Criminal Def. Trial Lawyers Assn. (treas. 1976). Office: 1416 W 1st St Winston-Salem NC 27101 Tel (919) 725-3554

SAWYER, LEONARD SYLVESTER, b. Lincoln, N.H., June 14, 1925; B.A., U. N.H., 1947; LL.B., Boston U., 1950. Admitted to N.H. bar, 1950; partner firm Edes & Sawyer, Woodsville, N.H., 1954-56; individual practice law, Plymouth, N.H., 1956—; spl. justice Municipal Ct., Plymouth, 1958-65; justice Plymouth Dist. Ct., 1965—. Moderator Town of Woodstock (N.H.), 1954-58; selectman Town of Plymouth, 1963-66. Mem. Am., N.H., Grafton County (N.H.) bar assns., Am. Judicature Soc. Home: 13 Cummings St Plymouth NH 03264 Office: 79 Main St Plymouth NH 03264 Tel (603) 536-2558

SAWYER, LOREN LEE, b. Redmond, Oreg., Mar. 24, 1931; B.A., Willamette U., 1953; LL.B., U. Oreg., 1959. Admitted to Oreg. bar, 1959; individual practice law, Medford, Oreg., 1959-60; dist. judge Jackson County, 1960-68; circuit judge Jackson County, 1960—; mem. faculty Nat. Coll. State Trial Judges, Reno, Nev., 1971—. Past pres. Rogue council Campfire Girls U.S.A.; bd. dirs. Boy Scouts Am.; mem. adv. bd. So. Oreg. State Coll. Mem. Am., Oreg. bar assns., Oreg. Jud. Coll., Nat. Council Juvenile Ct. Judges. Recipient Contbn. to Safety award Medford Safety Council, 1964; named Citizen of Year, Oreg. Edn. Assn., 1972. Home: PO Box 1061 Medford OR 97501 Office: Jackson County Court House Medford OR 97501 Tel (503) 776-7045

SAWYER, SEWELL ABBOTT, b. Owatonna, Minn., Sept. 24, 1924; B.S. Law, St. Paul Coll. Law, 1952, LL.B., 1953. Admitted to Minn. bar, 1953; partner firm Sawyer, Darby and Brewer, and predecessors, Winona, Minn., 1954-69; judge Winona County Probate Ct., 1969-72, Winona County Ct., 1972—; county atty. Winona County, 1954-69. Bd. dirs. Gamehaven Area council Boy Scouts Am., 1960-65; co-founder Vol. in Ct. Services, Inc., Winona, 1971. Mem. Minn. State, 3d Jud. Dist., Winona County bar assns. Home: Rural Route 3 Pleasant Valley Winona MN 55987 Office: Courthouse Winona MN 55987 Tel (507) 452-7120

SAWYER, THOMAS BARNETT, b. San Francisco, June 21, 1912; B.A. with honors, U. Calif., Los Angeles, 1933; J.D., Harvard, 1936. Admitted to Calif. bar, 1937, U.S. Supreme Ct. bar, 1956; mem. legal dept. RCA-NBC, Hollywood, Calif., 1937-38; individual practice law, Los Angeles, 1938-40, 50-66; gen. counsel Associated Bond & Ins. Agy., Los Angeles, 1945-50; dep. dist. atty. Mendocino County (Calif.), 1966-67; dep. counsel Solano County (Calif.), 1967-69, Sonoma County (Calif.), Santa Rosa, 1969-77, ret., 1977; pvt. practice, 1977—; instr. Solano Community Coll., 1967-71, Santa Rosa Jr. Coll., 1973—. Mem. Sonoma County Bar Assn. Home: 5566 Yerba Buena Rd Santa Rosa CA 95405 Tel (707) 539-0683

SAX, LEONARD BERTROM, b. Cin., June 4, 1917; B.S.C., Northwestern U., 1939, J.D., 1942. Admitted to Ill. bar, 1942; atty. Miller Mandel & Co., Chgo., 1945-46; with Am. Buff Internat., Chgo., 1946—, pres., 1957—; chmn. bd. Ajax Hardware Corp., Los Angeles, 1968-70; pres. Fairlawn Farms, Inc., Sodus, Mich., 1962—; pres. Sax Family Found., 1958—. Mem. exec. com. Anti-defamation League Am. Jewish Com. Mem. Am., Ill., Chgo. bar assns. Contbr. articles to law revs. Office: 624 W Adams St Chicago IL 60606 Tel (312) 782-0904

SAXON, PHILIP DUNHAM, b. N.Y.C., Sept. 6, 1925; B.A., Yale U., 1946; LL.B., Harvard U., 1949. Admitted to Conn. bar, 1950, Del. bar, 1960; asso. firm Buck, McCook & Kenyon, Hartford, Conn., 1949-51; atty. Office Price Stblzn., Washington, 1951-52; jr. atty. Hercules, Inc., Wilmington, Del., 1952-54, atty., 1954-56, counsel, 1956-66, sr. counsel, 1966-68. sec., 1968—; commr. Nat. Conf. Commrs. Uniform State Laws. Trustee Wilmington Coll., Coll. Boca Raton. Mem. Am., Del. bar assns., Am. Soc. Corporate Secs., Stockholder Relations Soc. N.Y., Nat. Investor Relations Inst., Del. C. of C. (dir., mem. exec. com.). Home: Benge Rd Yorklyn DE 19736 Office: 910 Market St Wilmington DE 19899 Tel (302) 575-5122

SAYE, ALBERT BERRY, b. Rutledge, Ga., Nov. 29, 1912; A.B., U. Ga., 1934, LL.B., 1957; Ph.D., Harvard, 1941. Admitted to Ga. Ct. Appeals bar, 1957, Ga. Supreme Ct. bar, 1957, U.S. Dist. Ct. bar, 1965; prof. law U. Ga., 1957—, Richard B. Russell prof. polit. sci., 1975—; chmn. com. to revise statutes U. Ga., 1972. Mem. Ga. Bar Assn., Internat., So. polit. sci. assns. Author: (with C.J. Hilkey) Constitutional Law of Georgia, 1952; Principles of American Government, 1974; American Constitutional Law, 2d edit., 1975. Home: 190 W Lake Pl Athens GA 30601 Office: 111 Baldwin Hall U Ga Athens GA 20602 Tel (404) 542-2057

SAYPOL, IRVING HOWARD, b. N.Y.C., Sept. 3, 1905; LL.B., Bklyn. Law Sch., 1927. Admitted to N.Y. bar, 1928; examiner law dept. N.Y.C., 1927-29, asst. corp. counsel, 1929-33; counsel N.Y. State Legislature, 1934-45; chief asst. U.S. atty. So. Dist. N.Y., 1945-49, U.S. atty., 1949-51; justice 1st Jud. Dist. Supreme Ct. N.Y., N.Y.C., 1951—; co-counsel com. judiciary N.Y. State Constl. Conv., 1938. Mem. Phi Delta Phi, Omicron Delta Kappa. Home: 152 E 94th St New York City NY 10028 Office: Supreme Ct 60 Centre St New York City NY 10007 Tel (212) 374-8362

SAZAMA, THOMAS JOHN, b. Chippewa Falls, Wis., Feb. 24, 1946; B.A., U. Wis., 1968; J.D., Marquette U., 1973. Admitted to Wis. bar, 1973, U.S. Dist. Ct. Eastern and Western Dist. Wis. bar, 1973; asst. dist. atty., Chippewa County, Wis., 1973-75; partner firm Falkenberg & Sazama, Cadott, Wis., 1975—. Mem. Am., Wis., Chippewa County bar assns. Home: Route 5 Box 313 Chippewa Falls WI 54729 Office: Box 92 Cadott WI 54727 Tel (715) 289-4271

SCALERA, NICHOLAS, b. Newark, Mar. 31, 1928; B.S., U. Notre Dame, 1951; LL.B., Columbia, 1954; LL.M., N.Y. U., 1959. Admitted to N.J. bar, 1954; individual practice law, Essex County, N.J., 1956-71; judge N.J. Dist. Ct., Dist. of Essex County, 1971-72, Essex County Ct., 1972-74, Superior Ct. of N.J., 1974—. Mem. West Orange (N.J.) Bd. Edn., 1968-71. Mem. N.J., Essex County bar assns. Home: 43 Lowell Ave West Orange NJ 07052 Office: Essex County Cts Bldg Newark NJ 07102 Tel (201) 961-7270

SCALERA, RALPH FRANCIS, b. Midland, Pa., June 28, 1930; A.B., Harvard, 1952; LL.B., U. Pa., 1955. Admitted to Pa. bar, 1958; asso. firm Buchanan, Wallover & Barrickman, Beaver, Pa., 1958-59; asst. U.S. atty., Western Dist. Pa., 1959-61; partner firm Wallover, Barrickman & Scalera, Beaver, 1961-64; judge Ct. Common Pleas, Beaver County, Pa., 1964-70, pres. judge, 1966-70; partner firm Wallover, Barrickman, Scalera, Reed & Steff, Beaver, 1970-71; judge U.S. Dist. Ct. Western Dist. Pa., 1971-76; partner firm Thorp, Reed & Armstrong, Pitts., 1976—; chmn. planning council region V Pa. Crime Commn., 1969-70; chmn. Pa. Conf. on Courts, 1969; mem. Pa. Gov.'s Council on Human Services, 1968-69. Mem. bd. mgmt. Golden Triangle YMCA, 1975—; bd. dirs. McGuire Meml. Home for Retarded Children, 1964-74, Gateway Rehab. Center, 1971-74. Mem. Am., Pa., Beaver County bar assns. Home: River Rd Beaver PA 15009 Office: 2900 Grant Bldg Pittsburgh PA 15219 Tel (412) 288-2550

SCALES, ARCHIBALD HENDERSON, III, b. Norfolk, Va., June 2, 1941; A.B., Davidson Coll., 1963; LL.B., U. N.C., 1966. Admitted to N.C. bar, 1966; served to capt. JAGC, U.S. Army, 1966-70; asso. firm Craig & Brawley, Winston-Salem, N.C., 1970-72; partner firm Hall, Booker, Scales & Cleland, Winston-Salem, N.C., 1973—. Trustee, Forsyth County (N.C.) Hosp. Authority, 1976—; pres. Council on Drug Abuse, Inc., Winston-Salem, 1976; treas. Kidney Found. Forsyth County, Inc., 1974-76. Mem. Am., N.C., Forsyth County (treas., 1974-75), Forsyth Jr. bar assns., Comml. Law League Am. Home: 1315 Brookstown Ave Winston-Salem NC 27101 Office: 2111 Wachovia Bldg Winston-Salem NC 27101 Tel (919) 724-1912

SCALETTA, PHILLIP JASPER, JR., b. Sioux City, Iowa, Aug. 20, 1925; B.S., Morningside Coll., 1948; J.D., U. Iowa, 1950. Admitted to Iowa bar, 1950; U.S. Dist. Ct. bar, 1950, Ind. bar, 1966; U.S. Supreme Ct. bar, 1968; partner firm McKnight and Scaletta, Sioux City, 1950-51; field rep. Farmers Ins. Group, Sioux City, 1951-54, sr. liability examiner, Aurora, Ill., 1954-60, br. claims mgr., Ft. Wayne, Ind., 1960-66; prof. law Purdue U., West Lafayette, Ind., 1966—. Mem. West Lafayette Community Sch. Council, 1969—, Mayors Safety Com., West Lafayette, 1971—, Tippecanoe County Ct. Reform Com., 1972—, Ind. Gov.'s Commn. Individual Privacy, 1975—. Mem. Am. Arbitration Assn., Am. Bus. Law Assn. (pres.), Am. Judicature Soc., Am., Ind., Tippecanoe County bar assns., Tri State Bus. Law Assn., Midwest Bus. Adminstrn. Assn., Ind. Acad. Social Scis., Internat. Bar Assn., Computer Law Assn., Inc. Recipient Best Tchr. of Yr. award Standard Oil of Ind. Found., 1972; Outstanding Tchr. award Purdue U. Alumni Assn., 1974; author: Workbook: Business Law, Principles and Cases, 1974; contbr. numerous articles in field to profl. jours. Home: 1 Via Verde West Lafayette IN 47906 Office: 509 Krannert Bldg Purdue Univ West Lafayette IN 47906 Tel (317) 493-9026

SCALIA, ANTONIN, b. Trenton, N.J., Mar. 11, 1936; student U. Fribourg (Switzerland), 1955-56; A.B., Georgetown U., 1957; LL.B., Harvard, 1960, postgrad. (Sheldon fellow), 1961-62. Admitted to Ohio bar, 1963, Va. bar, 1970; asso. firm Jones, Day, Cockley & Reavis, Cleve., 1961-67; asso. prof. U. Va., 1967-70, prof. law, 1970-74; gen. counsel Office of Telecommunications Policy, Exec. Office of Pres., Washington, 1971-72; chmn. Adminstrv. Conf. U.S., 1972-74; asst. atty. gen., office of legal counsel U.S. Dept. Justice, 1974-77; vis. prof. Georgetown Law Center, 1977; vis. scholar Am. Enterprise Inst., 1977; prof. law U. Chgo., 1977—; cons. FCC, 1977. cons. U.S. Land Laws Revision Commn., 1968-69, U.S. CSC, 1969, 77, Va. Ct. Systems Study Commn., 1969-70; dir. Nat. Inst. Consumer Justice, 1972-73, Center for Adminstrv. Justice, 1972-74. Mem. Am. (council adminstrv. law sect. 1975—), Fed. (continuing edn. bd. 1976—) bar assns. Home: 5725 S Woodlawn Ave Chicago IL 60637 Office: Univ of Chicago Law Sch 1111 E 60th St Chicago IL 60637

SCALO, RICHARD SEBASTIAN, b. Bridgeport, Conn., May 8, 1934; B.A., Boston U., 1961; J.D., U. Conn., 1963. Admitted to Conn. bar, 1963, U.S. Supreme Ct. bar, 1970; partner firm Gordon & Scalo, Bridgeport, 1972—; pub. defender Conn. Superior Ct., 1969-71; atty. Bridgeport Housing Authority, 1971-73; lectr. internat. law; mem. State Commn. to Study Reorgn. and Unification of Cts., 1973-76. Chmn., Bridgeport Charter Revision Commn., 1975-76; mem. Conn. State Senate, 1973-74, vice-chmn. judiciary com. Mem. Bridgeport Bar Assn. Home: 5 Saint Nicholas Dr Bridgeport CT 06604 Office: 855 Main St Bridgeport CT 06604 Tel (203) 336-4881

SCANLAN, FRED T., b. Mpls., Feb. 16, 1922; B.A., U. Ariz., J.D. Admitted to Ariz. bar, 1966; mem. firm Scanlan, Schiesel & Jurkowitz, Tucson. Mem. Am., Ariz. State bar assns., Am. Trial Lawyers Assn. Home: 4742 E Montecito St Tucson AZ 85711 Office: 900 Lawyers Title Bldg Tucson AZ 85701 Tel (602) 622-3633

SCANLON, JAMES EDWARD, b. Chgo., Oct. 11, 1940; B.S. in Bus. Adminstrn., Xavier U., 1962; J.D., U. Mich., 1965. Admitted to Ill. bar, 1965; with Alexander Grant & Co., Chgo., 1965—, mgr., 1971—. Mem. Am., Ill. insts. C.P.A.'s. Home: 540 Aldine St Chicago IL 60657 Office: 600 Prudential Plaza Chicago IL 60601 Tel (312) 822-8560

SCANLON, THOMAS JOSEPH, b. Cleve., Mar. 25, 1938; B.S.S., John Carroll U., 1959; J.D., Cleve. State U., 1963. Admitted to Ohio bar, 1963, U.S. Tax Ct. bar, 1975; asso. firm Shapiro, Persky & Marken, Cleve., 1963-69; partner firm Shapiro, Persky, Marken, Scanlon & Shapiro, Cleve., and predecessors, 1969-77, firm Vanik, Monroe, Zucco, Klein & Scanlon, 1977—. Trustee DePaul Infant Home, Animal Welfare Vols., Inc.; mem. bd. advisors St. Ignatius High Sch.; active Citizens League Cleve. Mem. Am., Ohio, Greater Cleve. (Meritorious Service award 1970, 72) bar assns., Cath. Lawyers Guild, Am. Arbitration Assn. (panel arbitrators, Spl. Service award), Delta Theta Phi. Recipient spl. merit awards Cleve. State U., 1973, 74. Home: 1325 Prince Charles Ave Westlake OH 44115 Office: 1525 Leader Bldg 526 Superior Ave Cleveland OH 44114 Tel (216) 241-3737

SCANLON, THOMAS MICHAEL, b. Indpls., Apr. 20, 1909; A.B., Butler U., 1932; LL.B., Ind. U., 1935. Admitted to Ind. bar, 1935, U.S. Supreme Ct. bar, 1944; asso. firm Noel, Hickam, Boyd & Armstrong, Indpls., 1935-40; partner firm Barnes, Hickam, Pantzer & Boyd, Indpls., 1940—; sec.-treas. Ind. State Bd. Law Examiners, 1947-52. Fellow Am. Coll. Trial Lawyers, Am. Bar Found.; mem. Ind. (pres., 1955-56), Am. (chmn. sect. antitrust 1973-74, council 1966-74, ho. of dels. 1954-56, 71-72), Fed., Indpls. bar assns., Bar Assn. 7th Fed. Circuit (pres. 1956-57), Indpls. Lawyers Club (pres. 1964-65), Indpls. Lawyers Commn. (pres. 1971-73). Co-author: Preparation for Trial, 1963. Home: 9570 Copley Dr Indianapolis IN 46260 Office: 1313 Merchants Bank Bldg Indianapolis IN 46204 Tel (317) 638-1313

SCAPOLITO, GEORGE WILLIAM, b. N.Y.C., July 5, 1908; A.B., Amherst Coll., 1929; J.D., Columbia, 1932. Admitted to N.Y. State bar, 1933, U.S. Supreme Ct. bar, 1959; asso. firm Scapolito, Solinger & O'Brien and predecessors, Mt. Vernon, N.Y., 1933-44, partner, 1944-51, mng. partner, 1951-65, sr. partner, 1965—. Mem. Selective Service Local Bd. 10, Mount Vernon, N.Y., 1953-57. Mem. Westchester County, Mt. Vernon bar assns., Columbia Law Sch. Alumni Assn. Office: 100 Stevens Ave Mt Vernon NY 10550 Tel (914) 668-6200

SCARBOROUGH, CHARLES DAVIS, b. Abilene, Tex., May 5, 1941; B.A., U. Tex., Austin, 1964, J.D., 1966. Admitted to Tex. bar, 1966; asso. firm Scarborough, Black, Tarpley & Scarborough, and predecessor, Abilene, 1966-68, partner, 1968—. Vestryman St. Mark's Episcopal Ch., Abilene, 1970-72; pres. St. John's Sch. Bd., Abilene, 1974-75; chmn. Taylor County (Tex.) Democratic Com., 1976—; v.p. Tex. Art Alliance, 1976—. Mem. Abilene, Abilene Jr. (pres. 1973) bar assns., State Jr. Bar Tex. (v.p. 1975), Tex. Trial Lawyers Assn., Tex. Criminal Def. Lawyers Assn., Tex. Bar Found., Tex. Bar. Named Boss of Year Taylor County Legal Secs. Assn., 1974. Home: 1617 Woodridge St Abilene TX 79605 Office: PO Box 356 Abilene TX 79604 Tel (915) 672-8477

SCARING, STEPHEN PETER, b. N.Y.C., Oct. 13, 1941; B.A., C.W. Post Coll., 1962; J.D., Cath. U. Am., 1967. Admitted to N.Y. bar, 1968; asst. dist. atty. Nassau County (N.Y.), Mineola, 1969-77; chief Dist. Attys. Homicide Bur., 1975-77; pvt. practice, Mineola, 1977—; adj. asst. prof. grad. div. C.W. Post Coll.; adj. asst. prof. State U. N.Y., Farmingdale. Mem. Nassau Lawyers Assn., Cath. Lawyers, Nassau County Bar Assn., Nassau/Suffolk Trial Lawyers Assn. Office: 170 Old Country Rd Mineola NY 11501 Tel (516) 741-4600

SCHAAB, WILLIAM COLSON, b. Wildwood, N.J., Dec. 28, 1927; B.A., Wesleyan U., 1949, M.A., 1951; J.D., Yale, 1952. Admitted to N.Y. State bar, 1954, N.Mex. bar, 1956; asso. firm Cravath, Swaine & Moore, N.Y.C., 1952-56; partner firm Rodey, Dickason, Sloan, Akin & Robb, Albuquerque, 1959-72, v.p., dir., 1972—; lectr. U. N.Mex. Sch. Law, Albuquerque, 1965, 73-74; chmn. criminal justice system com. State Bar N.Mex., 1973-76. Mem. N.Mex. Corrections Commn., 1976—; chmn. corrections com. Met. Criminal Justice Coordinating Council, Albuquerque, 1973—. Mem. Am. Bar Assn. Spl. Blue Lake atty. Taos Pueblo, 1968-70, gen. counsel, 1971—; claims atty. Navajo Tribe, 1973—. Contbr. articles to legal jours. Home: 2222 Campbell Rd NW Albuquerque NM 87107 Office: First Plaza Albuquerque NM 87103 Tel (505) 765-5900

SCHABER, GORDON DUANE, b. Ashley, N.D., Nov. 22, 1927; A.B. with distinction, Sacramento State Coll., 1949; J.D. with honors, U. Calif., San Francisco, 1952; LL.D., McGeorge Sch. Law, 1961. Admitted to Calif. bar, 1953; partner firm Cecchettini & Schaber, Sacramento, 1953-65; lectr. McGeorge Coll Law (now Mc.George Sch. Law U. Pacific), Sacramento, 1953-56, asst. dean, 1956, dean, prof. law, 1957—; presiding judge Sacramento County Superior Ct., 1965-69; cons. establishment Sch. Law U. Puget Sound, others. Mem. Calif. Bd. Control, 1962-64; chmn. Greater Sacramento Planning Commn., 1970; cons. study jus. workload Jud. Council Calif., 1971-72; mem. Adv. Com. to Chief Justice Calif. on Superior Ct. Mgmt., 1971; cons. vehicle theft study Calif. Hwy. Patrol, 1972; panelist Sacramento Bee Crime Prevention Program, 1971—; mem. adv. com. Calif. OEO, Calif. Legal Services expt., 1972; Chmn. Sacramento County Democratic Central Com., 1960-64, mem. Dem. State Central Com., 1960-64; chmn. Dem. Central Com., Sacramento, 1960, 62, 64. Mem. Am. (chmn. membership com. sect. legal edn. and admissions to bar, 1973), Sacramento County (v.p. 1970) bar assns., State Bar Calif. (com. legal edn. 1957—, chmn. 1974-75, mem. long range adv. planning com. 1972—), Am. Judicature Soc., Order of Coif, Phi Delta Phi (hon.). Author: Contracts in a Nutshell, 1972; contbr. articles to legal jours.; named Sacramento County Young Man of Year, 1963; Trial Judge of Year, Calif. Trial Lawyers Assn., 1969. Home: 937 Piedmont Dr Sacramento CA 95822 Office: 3200 5th Ave Sacramento CA 95817 Tel (916) 449-7121

SCHACKMAN, WALTER MURRAY, b. N.Y.C., July 23, 1926; B.A., Syracuse U., J.D., 1950; LL.M., N.Y. U., 1960. Admitted to N.Y. bar, 1950; partner firm Roe & Kramer, N.Y.C., 1960-72; judge N.Y.C. Civil Ct., 1973—. Mem. Am., N.Y. State bar assns., Assn. Bar City N.Y. Home: 175 E 79th St New York City NY 10021 Office: 111 Centre St New York City NY 10013 Tel (212) 374-8102

SCHAD, LAWRENCE WILEY, b. Milw., July 3, 1945; B.A. with high honors, Denison U., 1967; J.D., U. Mich., 1970. Admitted to Ill. bar, 1970; individual practice law, Chgo., 1970—. Mem. Ill. State, Am., Chgo. (exec. bd. young lawyers sect.) bar assns., Phi Beta Kappa. Asso. editor Jour. Law Reform, 1970. Office: 180 N LaSalle St Chicago IL 60601 Tel (312) 782-9571

SCHAEFER, CHRIS ALVIN, b. Los Angeles, Apr. 1, 1943; B.A., U. So. Calif., 1965; J.D., Lincoln U., 1970. Admitted to Calif. bar, 1971; asso. firm Vallarino Costanagra & Dufficy, San Rafael, Calif., 1972-73; partner firm Dufficy, Casey, Schaefer & Ceccotti, San Rafael, 1973-76, firm Casey, Schaefer & Robertson, San Rafael, 1976—; credit officer Bank of Calif., San Francisco, 1968-70; trust officer Wells Fargo Bank, San Francisco, 1970-72. Mem. Marin County, San Francisco, Am. bar assns. Home: 40 La Cuesta St Greenbrae CA 94904 Office: 68 Mitchell Blvd San Rafael CA 94903 Tel (415) 472-7880

SCHAEFER, MICHAEL WILLIAM, b. Chgo., Feb. 22, 1944; B.A., DePaul U., 1966, J.D., 1968. Admitted to Ill. bar, 1968; asso. Tim J. Harrington, Chgo., 1968-72; partner firm Gordon, Brustin & Schaefer, 1972-77, Gordon, Schaefer, Gordon, 1977—. Mem. Ill. Bar Assn. Home: 722 S Chester St Park Ridge IL 60068 Office: 228 N LaSalle St Chicago IL 60601 Tel (312) 332-2490

SCHAEFFER, EDWARD, b. N.Y.C., May 9, 1914; B.S., St. John's Coll.; LL.B., St. John's U., 1937. Admitted to N.Y. State bar, 1938, U.S. Supreme Ct. bar, 1975; individual practice law, N.Y.C., 1938—; lectr. matrimonial law Practising Law Inst. Fellow Am. Acad. Matrimonial Lawyers (v.p., nat. bd. govs.; pres. 1973-75, bd. govs. N.Y. chpt.), mem. Am., N.Y. State (legis. com.), Bklyn. bar assns., Assn. Bar City N.Y. (family law com. 1972-75). Participator video cassette program Practising Law Inst. Home: 30 E 37th St New York City NY 10016 Office: 2 W 46th St New York City NY 10036 Tel (212) 247-4065

SCHAEFFER, MARGARET GROEFSEMA, b. Detroit, Nov. 21, 1920; A.B., U. Mich., 1943, J.D. with distinction, 1945. Admitted to Mich. bar, 1945, Calif. bar, 1949; mem. firm Markle and Markle,

Detroit, 1955-73; mem. Mich. Workmen's Compensation Appeal Bd., 1973-75; judge Mich. 47th Dist. Ct., 1975—, presiding judge, 1976—; arbitrator Am. Arbitration Assn., 1971. Trustee Farmingtown Twp. (Mich.), 1968-74; mem. Farmington Hills (Mich.) City Council, 1974-75. Mem. Am., Oakland County (Mich.) bar assns., Nat. Assn. Women Lawyers, Mich., Oakland County dist. judges assns., Women Lawyer's Assn. Mich. A gift given in recognition of significant service to Farmington community by Farmington br. AAUW to AAUW Edn. Found. Fellowships program, 1971; editor Mich. Law Rev., 1944-45. Office: 31555 W Eleven Mile Rd Farmington MI 48024 Tel (313) 477-5630

SCHAEFLER, LEON, b. N.Y.C., July 2, 1903; student N.Y. U., 1920-21; LL.B., Fordham U., 1924. Admitted to N.Y. bar, 1925, since practiced in N.Y.C.; gen. counsel Fifth Ave. Bank, N.Y.C., 1936-48; atty. Bank N.Y., 1948—; sr. partner firm Finch & Schaeffler, N.Y.C. Fellow (hon.) Am. Coll. Probate Counsel (pres. 1959-61, dir. 1957-62); mem. Fordham Law Alumni Assn. (dir. 1955-58). Contbr. articles to legal jours. Home: 36 Sutton Pl New York City NY 10022 also Chez Fleurs Elberon NJ 07740 Office: 36 W 44th St New York City NY 10036 Tel (212) 687-3636

SCHAERRER, NEIL DEAN, b. Payson, Utah, Apr. 12, 1930; B.A., Brigham Young U., 1954; J.D., U. Utah, 1959. Admitted to Utah bar, 1959; law clk. Melvin Belli, San Francisco, 1958, justices of Utah Supreme Ct., 1959-60; asst. atty. gen. State of Utah, 1960-62; mem. firm Armstrong, Rawlings, West & Schaerrer, 1964—. Mem. Utah Gov.'s Com. on Children and Youth, 1962-64. Mem. Trial Lawyers Assn. Am. Recipient Outstanding Contbn. award U. Utah Law Sch., 1959. Home: 856 E Capitol Blvd Salt Lake City UT 84103 Office: 1300 Walker Bank Bldg Salt Lake City UT 84111 Tel (801) 359-2093

SCHAFER, STEPHEN, b. Budapest, Hungary, Feb. 15, 1911; J.D., U. Budapest, 1933, Professeur Agrege, 1947. Admitted to Budapest bar, 1937; practiced in Hungary; prof. cirminal law and criminology; chmn. Prison Commn.; asst. prof. law Fla. State U., 1961-64; asso. prof. Ohio U., 1964-65; prof. Northeastern U., 1966—; pres. Supervisory Bd. Juvenile Delinquency of Hungary; mem. Law Examination Bd.; vis. prof. Tufts U., Boston U., Max Planck Inst., Germany. Mem. Internat., Am. socs. criminology, Internat. Assn. Penal Law, Am. Sociol. Assn. Author: Compensation and Restitution To Victims of Crime, 1960, rev. edit., 1970; The Victim And His Criminal, 1968, rev. edit., 1976; Theories in Criminology, 1969; Juvenile Delinquency, 1970; The Political Criminal, 1974; Introduction to Criminology, 1976; contbr. articles to legal jours. Home: 662 Washington St Baighton MA 02135 Office: Coll Criminal Justice Northeastern U Boston MA 02115 Tel (617) 437-3327

SCHAFFER, GEORGE JOHN, b. Pitts., July 1, 1907; student U. Pitts., 1946; J.D., Chgo. Kent Coll. Law, 1954; Ph.B., Northwestern U., 1959. Admitted to Ill. bar, 1955; with Bell Telephone Co. Pa., 1926-59; instr. Chgo. Kent Coll. Law, 1959, prof., 1959-63; individual practice law, Elmhurst, Ill., 1963-65; agt. in estate and gift taxes, IRS, Chgo., 1965-72, regionalist analyst, 1972-74; tchr. comml. law Coll. DuPage, Glen Ellyn, Ill., 1969-70. Mem. Ill., Chgo., DuPage County, Fed. bar assns. Address: 381 Ferndale Ave Elmhurst IL 60126 Tel (312) 833-6006

SCHAFFER, MARK DAVID, b. Phila., Jan. 6, 1941; B.S., Temple U., 1962, LL.B., 1965. Admitted to Pa. bar, 1967, U.S. Supreme Ct. bar, 1970, U.S. Ct. Appeals 3d Circuit bar, 1971; asso. firm Needleman, Needleman, Segal & Tabb, Phila., 1967-68; trial atty. Defenders Assn. Phila., 1968-69; chief atty. Fed. Ct. div. Defender Assn., Fed. Community Defender Office for Eastern Dist. Pa., Phila., 1969—; lectr. Temple U., 1975—. Mem. planning com. Jud. Conf. 3d Circuit, 1976; mem. Fed. Bench Bar Com. Mem. Pa., Phila. bar assns., Lawyers Club Phila. Home: 858 Timber Ln Dresher PA 19025 Office: Public Ledger Bldg 6th and Chestnut Sts Philadelphia PA 19106 Tel (215) WA 5-9220

SCHAIN, SEYMOUR BERNARD, b. N.Y.C., June 24, 1914; B.B.A., Coll. City N.Y., 1934; LL.B., St. Lawrence U., 1938; J.D., Bklyn. Law Sch., 1967. Admitted to N.Y. State bar, 1939; law asst. firm Zimmerman & Zimmerman, N.Y.C., 1938-39, Hetkin, Rubin & Hetkin, N.Y.C., 1939; individual practice law, N.Y.C., 1939—. Capt. election dist. Democratic party, Bronx, N.Y., 1949-60; editor-in-chief Windsor Manor Civic Assn. Bull., 1939-42. Mem. N.Y. County Lawyers Assn., Iota Theta. Author legal practice forms. Office: 51 Chambers St New York City NY 10007 Tel (212) 267-1338

SCHAIR, BURTON, b. Scituate, Mass., May 15, 1914; student Boston U. Coll. Bus. Adminstrn., 1931-33, J.D., Law Sch., 1936. Admitted to Mass. bar, 1936; partner firm Kaplan & Schair, Boston, 1936-38, Scituate, 1936-39; individual practice law, Scituate, 1939-47, Braintree, Mass., 1955-60; partner firm Schair and Duquet, Braintree, 1960-75; sr. partner firm Schair, Buquet & Gorfinkle, Braintree, 1975—; pres. S. Braintree Bd. Trade, 1948-50. Bd. dirs. Handic Kids. Mem. Plymouth County, Norfolk County, Am., Mass. bar assns., Mass., Am. trial lawyers assns., Tau Epsilon Rho. Office: 1000 Washington St Braintree MA 02184 Tel (617) 843-5030

SCHALLAU, AL, b. Williamsburg, Iowa, Jan. 23, 1942; B.A., U. Iowa, 1964; J.D., U. So. Calif., 1968. Admitted to Calif. bar, 1969; individual practice law, Los Angeles, 1969—; of counsel firm James H. Davis, Los Angeles, 1972—, firm Voorhies, Greene & O'Reilly, Los Angeles, 1973—. Mem. Los Angeles County Bar Assn., Am., Calif., Los Angeles trial lawyers assns. Home: 7900 Yorktown Ave Los Angeles CA 90045 Office: PO Box 45437 Los Angeles CA 90045 Tel (213) 641-6770 and (213) 822-9260

SCHALLER, JAMES PATRICK, b. Hazleton, Pa., July 12, 1940; B.A., King's Coll., 1965; J.D., George Washington U., 1969. Admitted to Va., D.C. bars, 1969, U.S. Supreme Ct. bar, 1972; asso. firm Jackson, Campbell & Parkinson, and predecessor, Washington, 1969-72, partner, 1972—; mem. D.C. Circuit Jud. Conf., 1975—. Mem. D.C. (chmn. young lawyers sect. 1974-75, dir. 1975-76), Am., Va. bar assns., Nat. Inst. Trial Advocacy (sec.), D.C. Def. Lawyers Assn. (sec. 1974-75, v.p. 1975-76), The Barristers, Am. Judicature Soc., Phi Delta Phi, Delta Sigma Rho, Tau Kappa Alpha. Bd. editors Dist. Lawyer, 1977; trial editor ABA Law Notes for Young Lawyers, 1974—. Home: 6120 Maiden Ln Bethesda MD 20034 Office: 1828 L St NW Suite 1111 Washington DC 20036 Tel (202) 457-1632

SCHANES, CHRISTINE ELISE, b. Jersey City, Apr. 9, 1948; B.A., U. San Diego, 1969; Ph.D., U. Notre Dame, 1975; J.D., Am. U., 1973. Admitted to Calif. bar, 1973; dep. atty. investigator Pub. Defender Office, Washington, 1969-70; law clk. Office Gen. Counsel, SBA, Washington, 1970; research asst. Inst. Studies on Justice and Social Behavior, Am. U., Washington, 1970-71; dep. atty. gen. Los Angeles, 1976—. Mem. Calif., Am., Fed. bar assns., Am. Soc. Internat. Law. Contr. Am. U. Law Rev., 1970-71. Home: 924 Rose Ave Venice CA 90291 Office: 3580 Wilshire Blvd Los Angeles CA 90010 Tel (213) 736-2351

SCHARF, ROBERT LEE, b. Chgo., May 13, 1920; J.D., Loyola U., Chgo., 1948. Various positions with FBI, Washington, Chgo., 1940-44, clk., Chgo., 1946-48, spl. agt., Birmingham, Ala., Washington, Los Angeles, 1948-73; admitted to Ill. bar, 1949, U.S. Supreme Ct. bar, 1955, Calif. bar, 1972; dep. atty. Office City Atty., City Los Angeles, 1973—; instr. Santa Monica (Calif.) Community Coll., 1975—. Mem. Los Angeles County (eminent domain com.), San Fernando Valley bar assns. Home: 18161 Karen Dr Tarzana CA 91356 Office: #1 World Way Los Angeles International Airport Los Angeles CA 90009 Tel (213) 646-3260

SCHARFF, JOSEPH LAURENT, b. New Orleans, Oct. 2, 1935; B.J., Northwestern U., 1957; J.D., Harvard U., 1964. Admitted to D.C. bar, 1965, U.S. Supreme Ct. bar, 1969; asso. and mem. firm Pierson, Ball & Dowd, Washington, 1965-73, partner, 1973—; mem. broadcast adv. com. for revision Communications Act, U.S. Ho. of Reps. Subcom. on Communications, 1977; gen. counsel Radio TV News Dirs. Assn. Mem. Am. (legal adv. com. on fair trial and free press 1973-76), D.C., Fed. Communications bar assns. Home: 12000 Turf Ln Reston VA 22091 Office: 1000 Ring Bldg Washington DC 20036 Tel (202) 331-8566

SCHARFY, G. CHARLES, b. Cleve., Nov. 26, 1916; Ph.B. magna cum laude, U. Toledo (Ohio), 1938, LL.B. cum laude, 1940, J.D., 1968. Admitted to Ohio bar, 1940; partner firm Shumaker, Loop & Kendrick, Toledo, Ohio, 1940—; dir. various corps. Mem. Am., Ohio, Toledo bar assns., Toledo Area C. of C. (trustee 1977—). Home: 2135 Hawthorn Rd Toledo OH 43606 Office: 811 Madison Ave Toledo OH 43624 Tel (419) 241-4201

SCHATZ, ALBERT G., b. Omaha, Aug. 4, 1921; A.B., Nebr. U., 1943; LL.B., Creighton U., 1948. Admitted to Nebr., U.S. Dist. Ct. bars, 1948; law clk. to Judge J. W. Woodrough, Ct. Appeals, 8th Circuit, 1948-50; partner firm Gross, Welch, Vinardi, Kauffman & Schatz, Omaha, 1950-73; judge U.S. Dist. Ct., Dist. of Nebr., 1973—. Mem. Am., Omaha, Nebr. State bar assns., Am. Coll. Trial Lawyers, Am. Judicature Soc. Home: 9929 Broadmoor Rd Omaha NE 68114 Office: PO Box 607 Omaha NE 68101 Tel (402) 221-3421

SCHATZ, ARTHUR HERSCHEL, b. Hartford, Conn., Dec. 31, 1918; A.B., Cornell U., 1940, J.D., 1942. Admitted to Conn. bar, 1942; partner firm Schatz & Schatz, Hartford, 1945—; lectr. Cornell Law Sch., 1959-73, U. Conn., 1959-70, New Eng. Law Inst., 1960-76; faculty Law Sci. Inst. U. Tex., 1956-66; del. Internat. Congress on Forensic Sci., 1960, 63, 66, 69, 72, 75, v.p., gen. counsel, 1975—; del. Congress Internat. Assn. Traffic Accident Medicine, 1963, 66, 69, 72, 75; mem. Conn. Commn. on Medicolegal Investigations, 1969—, vice chmn., 1972—. Mem. council Cornell U., 1970-77; trustee Forensic Sci. Found., 1969-72, Law Sci. Found. Am.; trustee, v.p. gen. counsel Internat. Reference Orgn. in Forensic Medicine. Fellow Law Sci. Acad. Am., Am. Acad. Forensic Scis. (chmn. jurisprudence sect. mem. exec. council 1959-71, sec.-treas. 1969-71); mem. Brit. Acad. Forensic Scis., Am. Assn. Automotive Medicine, Cornell Law Assn. (exec. com. 1958-62), Am., Conn., Hartford County bar assns., Am. Trial Lawyers Assn., New Eng. Law Inst. (exec. com. 1959-76), Soc. Med. Jurisprudence. Home: 33 Juniper Rd Bloomfield CT 06002 Office: 1 Financial Plaza Hartford CT 06103 Tel (203) 522-3234

SCHATZ, S. MICHAEL, b. Hartford, Conn., May 28, 1921; A.B., Cornell U., 1941, LL.B., 1942. Admitted to Conn. bar, 1946, N.Y. bar, 1946; sr. partner firm Schatz & Schatz, Hartford, 1956—; counsel Navy Gen. Ct. Martial Sentence Rev. Bd., 1946; gen. counsel Outdoor Advt. Assn. Conn., 1953, Conn. Veterinarian Assn., 1965, Tobacco Distbrs. Assn. Conn., 1952, Conn. State Dental Assn., 1960; partner B.L. McTeague & Co., Hartford, 1972; dir. Sage-Allen & Co., Inc., The Edward Balf Co., Dunham-Bush, Inc., The Chamers-Storck Co., Atlantic Carton Corp., The Ripley Co., Inc., Conn. Bank & Trust Co., Griese Advt. Cos. Corporator, Mt. Sinai Hosp., Hartford, St. Francis Hosp., Hartford; bd. dirs. Hartford chpt. ARC, 1960-62; pres. King Philip Jr. High Sch. PTA, 1963-64; bd. dirs. St. Francis Hosp. Assn, 1960-66, Conn. Dental Service, Inc., 1962-68, Friends Sch. Dental Medicine, U. Conn., 1970; exec. com. Cornell U. Law Sch., 1976—; corporate mem. Hartford Pub. Library, 1968. Mem. Am. (state chmn. Jr. Bar Conf. 1951, nat. chmn. state and local activities com. Jr. Bar Conf. 1953, nat. dir. conf. 1954, nat. councilman 2d circuit 1955-57), Conn. (mem. exec. com. jr. bar sect. 1950, chmn. sect. 1951, sec. assn. 1957-59), N.Y. State, Hartford County bar assns., Phi Beta Kappa, Phi Kappa Phi, Order of Coif. Editor-in-chief Cornell Law Quar., 1942. Home: 100 Norwood Rd West Hartford CT 06117 Office: One Financial Plaza Hartford CT 06103 Tel (203) 522-3234

SCHATZMAN, ARNOLD DENNIS, b. Miami, Fla., June 11, 1938; B.B.A., U. Miami, 1960, LL.B., 1964. Admitted to Fla. bar, 1964; asso. firm Aronovitz, Aronovitz & Haverfield, Miami, 1964-69; partner firm Friedman, & Britton, Miami, 1969—. Mem. Comml. Law League Am., Downtown U. Miami Athletic Fedn. (dir.), Dade County, Am. bar assns. Home: 12000 SW 88th Ave Miami FL 33156 Office: 800 SE First Nat Bank Bldg Miami FL 33131 Tel (305) 371-5192

SCHAUB, CLARENCE ROBERT, b. Huntington, W.Va., Feb. 14, 1932; student Vanderbilt U., 1949-50, Marshall U., 1953-56; J.D., W.Va. U., 1959. Admitted to W.Va. bar, 1959; law clk. to U.S. dist. judge, W.Va., 1959-60; partner firm Jenkins, Schaub, Fenstermaker & Wood, and predecessor, Huntington, 1960-76; individual practice, Huntington, 1976—; spl. asst. atty. gen. to bd. appeals W.Va. Dept. Pub. Safety, 1973-75. Charter mem. Huntington Human Relations Commn., 1973-75, chmn., 1975. Mem. Am., Fed., Lawyer-Pilots, W.Va., Cabell County (W.Va.) bar assns., W.Va. State Bar, Am. Judicature Soc. Home: 3039 Eighth St Rd Huntington WV 25701 Office: 1111 W Va Bldg Huntington WV 25701 Tel (304) 697-5711

SCHAUB, EMELIA CHRISTINA, b. Provemont, Mich., Sept. 2, 1891; J.D., Detroit Coll. Law, 1924; LL.M., U. Detroit, 1926. Admitted to Mich. bar, 1924; individual practice law, Detroit, 1924-77; pros. atty. Leelanau County (Mich.), 1937-49. Grand regent Detroit Ct. Cath. Daus. Am., 1931-32. Mem. Women Lawyers Mich., State Bar Mich. Tel (616) 256-9343

SCHAUBNUT, LAWRENCE PAUL, b. Lutcher, La., Mar. 9, 1937; B.G.S., La. State U., 1960; J.D., U. Tex., 1968. Admitted to Tex. bar, 1968; asso. firm Schaubnut & Smith, Austin, Tex., 1968—. Active Y-Indian Guides, YMCA, 1968-72. Mem. Tex., Travis County bar assns., Delta Theta Phi. Office: 2439 Bastrop Hwy PO Box 6242 Austin TX 78762 also 6154 Hwy 290 W Austin TX Tel (512) 385-2283

SCHAUER, RICHARD, b. Los Angeles, Sept. 18, 1929; B.A., Occidental Coll., 1951; J.D., U. Calif., Los Angeles, 1955. Admitted to Calif. bar, 1955; individual practice law, Los Angeles, 1955-63; judge Los Angeles Municipal Ct., 1963-65; judge Superior Ct. Calif., Los Angeles, 1965—; prof. law Loyola U., 1955-64; commr. Fair Jud. Elections Practices, 1975—. Mem. Am. (com. chmn. 1972-73), Los Angeles County bar assns., Conf. Calif. Judges (com. chmn. 1974), Order of Coif, Phi Beta Kappa, Phi Delta Phi. Editor-in-chief U. Calif. at Los Angeles Law Rev., 1954-55. Office: 111 N Hill St Los Angeles CA 90012 Tel (213) 974-5550

SCHAUFFER, HARVEY ELLIOTT, JR., b. Glassport, Pa., June 29, 1918; B.A., U. Pitts., 1938, J.D., 1942. Admitted to Pa. bar, 1943; individual practice law, Pitts., 1946-75; sr. partner firm Ludwig, Schauffler, Klein and Geddis, Attys.-Asn., Pitts., 1976—; solicitor State Capital Savs. & Loan Assn., Harrisburg, Pa.; co-counsel Pitts. chpt. DAV. Chmn. Pa. Employ the Physically Handicapped Com., 1956, mem., 1977—. Fellow Acad. Trial Lawyers of Allegheny County; mem. Am. Arbitration Assn., Pa. Trial Lawyers Assn., Assn. Trial Lawyers Am., Allegheny County, Pa. bar assns. Home: 506 Marie St Glassport PA 15045 Office: 1408 Frick Bldg Pittsburgh PA 15219 Tel (412) 281-2288

SCHAUM, MARTIN, b. Bklyn., Jan. 7, 1932; B.S.S., Coll. City N.Y., 1953; LL.B., Harvard, 1958. Admitted to N.Y. bar, 1958; counsel codes com. N.Y. State Senate, 1967-71; partner firm Naldman & Schaum, Mineola, N.Y., 1974—. Coordinator Nassau County Cancer Soc., 1968. Mem. N.Y. State, Nassau County bar assns., Harvard Law Sch. Assn. Home: 4 The Tulips Roslyn Estates NY 11576 Office: 170 Old Country Rd Mineola NY 11501 Tel (516) 742-7766

SCHAUMBERG, TOM MICHAEL, b. Amsterdam, Holland, May 29, 1938; B.A., Yale, 1960; LL.B., Harvard, 1963; postgrad. U. Frankfurt (Germany), 1963-64. Admitted to Ohio bar, 1964, D.C. bar, 1968, U.S. Supreme Ct. bar, 1972, Md. bar, 1975; atty. merger div. Bur. Restraint of Trade, FTC, 1964-67; asso. firm. Gadsby & Hannah, Washington, 1967-73, partner, 1973; partner firm Rollinson & Schaumberg, Washington, 1974—. Mem. Am., Fed., D.C. bar assns. Home: 10804 Mazwood Pl Rockville MD 20852 Office: 1019 19th St NW Suite 1300 Washington DC 20036 Tel (202) 785-4200

SCHAUPP, MELVIN ROY, b. Hart, Minn., Mar. 14, 1937; B.A., U. Minn., 1967, J.D., 1970. Admitted to Minn. bar, 1970; partner firm Angstman, Loren & Schaupp, Mora, Minn., 1973—. Mem. Am., Minn. bar assns. Home: 555 Woodland St Mora MN 55051 Office: 28 N Union St Mora MN 55051 Tel (612) 679-2872

SCHEB, JOHN MALCOLM, b. Orlando, Fla., Apr. 25, 1926; J.D., U. Fla., 1950. Admitted to Fla. bar, 1950, U.S. Supreme Ct. bar, 1966; mem. firm Wood, Scheb, Whitesell, Drymon & Warren, Sarasota, Fla., 1950-74; asso. municipal judge, Sarasota, 1957-59, city atty., 1959-70; judge 2d Dist. Ct. Appeals, Lakeland, Fla., 1975—. Pres. Sunnyland Council Boy Scouts Am., 1972-73. Mem. Sarasota County Bar Assn. (pres. 1966-67). Recipient Freedom Found. award for Bicentennial Address, 1976. Home: 2311 Hollingsworth Hill Ave Lakeland FL 33803 Office: PO Box 327 Lakeland FL 33802 Tel (813) 686-5552

SCHECHTER, DAVID ALAN, b. Providence, June 16, 1945; B.S. in Chem. Engring., U. R.I., 1967; J.D., Suffolk U., 1970. Admitted to R.I. bar, 1970, U.S. Mil. Ct. of Appeals, 1971; partner firm Schechter, Abrams & Verri, Providence, 1975—. Vice-pres. Camp Ruggles, 1975; bd. dirs. R.I. Mental Health Assn., 1973-75. Mem. Am. (chmn. sect. for comml. litigation), R.I. bar assns., Am. Trial Lawyers Assn., Comml. Law League Am. Office: 189 Governor St Providence RI 02906 Tel (401) 274-4488

SCHECHTER, THEODORE S., b. East St. Louis, Ill., Sept. 9, 1934; B.S., U. Ill., 1958; J.D., Washington U., 1958. Admitted to Mo. bar, 1958; partner firm Lake & Schechter, Clayton, Mo., 1959-75, Schechter & Zerman, Clayton, 1976—. Mem. Am., St. Louis County, Met. St. Louis bar assns., Nat. Assn. Criminal Def. Lawyers, Assn. Trial Lawyers Am. Home: 45 Granada Way Ladue MO 63124 Office: 225 S Meramec Suite 426T Clayton MO 63105 Tel (314) 727-7289

SCHEER, ROBERT JOE, b. Lima, Ohio, Apr. 12, 1944; B.S. in Bus. Adminstrn. (L.D. Ikenberry award), Manchester Coll., 1966; J.D., U. Toledo, 1969. Admitted to Ohio bar, 1969; asst. dean students U. Toledo, 1969-70; asso. firm Fuller, Henry, Hodge & Snyder, Toledo, 1970-77; mgr. equal opportunity programs Owens-Ill., Inc., 1977—. Mem. Am., Ohio, Toledo bar assns., Am. Judicature Soc., Phi Alpha Delta. Articles editor U. Toledo Law Rev., 1969. Home: 26010 W River Rd Perrysburg OH 43551 Office: PO Box 1035 405 Madison Ave Toledo OH 43666 Tel (419) 242-6543

SCHEFFLER, ALLAN J., b. N.Y.C., Apr. 15, 1941; B.A., Alfred U., 1962; LL.B., Fordham U., 1965. Admitted to N.Y. bar, 1966; asso. firm Julian Buchbinder, N.Y.C., 1965-66, Mortimer Scheffler, N.Y.C., 1966-68; partner firm Scheffler & Scheffler, New Rochelle, N.Y., 1968-73, 76—, Rubin, Bobrow, Agatuton & Scheffler, 1973-76; spl. counsel New Rochelle Consumer Affairs Com., 1970-72; dep. town atty. Bedford (N.Y.), 1976—. Co-chmn. Scarsdale (N.Y.) Cath.-Jewish Council, 1971-73, Dial Help, community telephone emergency service, 1974; founder, trustee, v.p. Temple Shaaray Tefila, Bedford; trustee Beth El Synagogue, New Rochelle, 1969-76. Mem. New Rochelle, Westchester County (publs. com.) bar assns. Home: West Circle Bedford NY 10506 Office: 271 North Ave New Rochelle NY 10801 Tel (914) 632-5800

SCHEFFLER, MARK DAVID, b. N.Y.C., Mar. 12, 1944; B.S. in Econs., U. Pa., 1966; J.D., N.Y. U., 1969. Admitted to N.Y. State bar, 1970; asso. Herman Goldman, N.Y.C., 1969-71; partner firm Scheffler & Scheffler, New Rochelle, N.Y., 1971; dep. village atty. and prosecutor Village of Larchmont (N.Y.), 1976; referee New Rochelle Small Claims Ct., 1971—; law guardian N.Y. Family Ct., 1971—. Mem. N.Y. State, Westchester County, New Rochelle bar assns. Recipient Am. Jurisprudence awards, 1968, 69. Contbr. articles to legal jours. Office: 271 North Ave room 915 New Rochelle NY 10801

SCHEFFLER, WILLIAM J., III, b. New Orleans, Apr. 13, 1942; B.S., La. State U., 1965; J.D., Loyola U. New Orleans, 1969. Admitted to La. bar; since practiced in Gretna, La., asso. firm Evans & Scheffler, and predecessors, 1969-71, partner, 1971—; asst. atty. Jefferson Parish (La.) 1973. Bd. dirs. ARC, 1970—, West Bank Boys' Club, 1972—, La. State U. Alumni Fedn., 1972—. Mem. Am., La., Jefferson Parish bar assns., Am., La. trial lawyers assns. Home: 22 Beauregard Gretna LA 70053 Office: 1100 4th St Gretna LA 70053 Tel (504) 367-9001

SCHEIMAN, JACK ISOM, b. Fort Wayne, Ind., July 8, 1933; B.S. in Bus. Adminstrn., U. Ind., 1955; LL.B., Denver U., 1958, J.D., 1970. Admitted to Colo. bar, 1958, U.S. Dist. of Colo. Ct. bar, 1958, U.S.

Ct. Appeals bar, 1958, U.S. Supreme Ct. bar, 1972; individual practice law, Denver, 1958—. Mem. Colo., Denver bar assns. Home: 400 University Blvd Denver CO 80206 Office: 666 Sherman Denver CO 80203 Tel (303) 831-7531

SCHEIN, MARVIN HERBERT, b. Balt., July 9, 1930; B.S., U. Md., 1951, LL.B., 1954; LL.M., U. Ill., 1955. Admitted to Md. bar, 1955; served with JAGC, U.S. Army, 1955-57; individual practive law, Balt., 1957—; negotiator City of Balt. Land Purchase, 1958. Mem. Nu Beta Epsilon (grand chancellor 1967-68), Beta Alpha Psi, Golden Eagle Square and Compass Club (pres. 1977). Home: 6214 Ivymount Rd Baltimore MD 21209 Office: 2001 One Charles Center Baltimore MD 21201 Tel (301) 685-7898

SCHEININ, STEVEN JOEL, b. Balt., Aug. 14, 1946; B.S., Loyola Coll., Balt., 1969; J.D., U. Balt., 1973. Admitted to Md. bar, 1973; asst. state's atty. Baltimore County (Md.), Towson, 1973—; law clk. to justice Balt. City Supreme Bench, 1971-73. Mem. Nu Beta Epsilon. Home: PO Box 10164 Towson MD 21204 Office: Court House Towson MD 21204 Tel (301) 494-3517

SCHELL, STEVEN ROSS, b. Portland, Oreg., Apr. 12, 1939; B.A. in Polit. Sci., U. Oreg., 1961, J.D., 1968; M.A. in Econs., U. Denver, 1965. Admitted to Oreg. bar, 1968; asso. firm Black, Helterline, Beck & Rappleyea, Portland, 1968-75, partner, 1975—. Mem. Oreg. Land Conservation and Devel. Commn., 1973-76, vice chmn., 1973-76. Mem. Multnomah (county, Oreg.), Oreg. State (mem. com. environ. law), Am. bar assns. Contbr. articles to environ. law publs. Home: 3708 SE Liebe St Portland OR 97202 Office: 12th floor 707 SW Washington St Portland OR 97205 Tel (503) 224-5560

SCHELL, WILLIAM BRAXTON, b. Raleigh, N.C., Feb. 24, 1924; student N.C. State U., 1942-43; B.S., U. N.C., Chapel Hill, 1948, J.D. with honors, 1951. Admitted to N.C. bar, 1951; asso. firm Smith, Moore, Smith, Schell & Hunter and predecessor, Greensboro, N.C., 1951-56, partner, 1956—; gen. counsel, dir. Texfi Industries Inc., Greensboro, Rex Plastics Inc. Vice-chmn. bd. dirs. N.C. Outward Bound. Sch., Morganton, N.C., 1975—; dir. Dillard Paper Co., Greensboro. Mem. Am. Judicature Soc., Greensboro, N.C., Am. bar assns., Order of Coif, Phi Beta Kappa, Beta Gamma Sigma, Phi Eta Sigma. Asso. editor N.C. Law Rev., 1950-51. Home: 2200 Carlisle Rd Greensboro NC 27408 Office: PO 21927 500 NCNB Bldg Greensboro NC 27420 Tel (919) 378-1450

SCHEMAHORN, CLYDE ELDON, b. LaGrange County, Ind., Aug. 27, 1906. Admitted to Ind. bar, 1939; individual practice law, LaGrange County, 1939—. Founding mem. U.S. Senatorial Club, 1977. Mem. Ind., LaGrange County bar assns. Recipient Congl. award Reps. of U.S. Congress, 1974. Office: Rural Route 5 LaGrange IN 46761 Tel (219) 463-2464

SCHENKEN, CARLTON GUSTAV, b. Washington, Dec. 22, 1903; LL.D., Georgetown U., 1925. Admitted to D.C. bar, 1925, U.S. Supreme Ct. bar, 1955, Tex. bar, 1958; asst. to pres. Jefferson Standard Life Ins. Co., Greensboro, N.C., 1936-42; spl. agt. in charge FBI, Washington, 1928-34; served with JAGC, U.S. Army, 1942-59; v.p. U.S. Auto Assn., San Antonio, 1959-69; individual practice law, San Antonio, 1969—. Office: 210 Canterbury Hill San Antonio TX 78209 Tel (512) 822-1232

SCHERER, PAUL CLARENCE, b. Evansville Ind., Mar. 5, 1926; B.B.A., Univ. Tex., 1949, LL.B., 1949. Admitted to Tex. bar, 1948; partner firm Scherer, Roberts, Slone & Gresham and predecessors, 1952—; city atty. Richmond, Tex., 1949—. Trustee Lamar Consol. Sch. Dist., 1955-76. Fellow Am. Coll. Probate Counsel. Home: 915 Foster Dr Richmond TX 77469 Office: 210 3d St Richmond TX 77469 Tel (713) 342-6163

SCHERER, ZALMAN JOSEL, b. Williamson, W.Va., Nov. 28, 1935; student W. Va. U., 1953, 55, 56; A.B., Morris Harvey Coll., 1959; postgrad. W.Va. U. Coll. Law, 1959-60; LL.B., U. Ariz., 1962. Admitted to Ariz. bar, 1963, Calif. bar, 1968; dep. dist. atty. County of San Diego, 1968—; instr. police sci. Paloma Jr. Coll. Mem. Bar Assn. Ariz., No. San Diego County Bar (past pres.), Calif., San Diego, No. San Diego dist. attys. assns. Tel (714) 236-2386

SCHERNECKER, JAMES G., b. Madison, Wis., Nov. 20, 1937; B.S. in Econs., Marquette U., 1959; J.D., U. Wis., 1965. Admitted to Wis. bar, 1966; corp. law asso. Watkins Products, Inc., Winona, Minn., 1965; asso. firm Klabacka & Schernecker, Madison, 1966-68; hearing examiner State of Wis., Madison, 1968—; vis. lectr. U. Wis. Law Sch., 1976, U. Wis. Sch. for Workers, 1974-75. Bd. dirs. Big Bros. of Dane County (Wis.), 1975—, Oreg. Pub. Schs., 1972-75. Mem. Wis. State Attys. Assn. (dir., bargaining team, 1973-75), Wis. Hearing Examiners Assn. (pres. 1973—). Home: 4585 Schneider Rd Oregon WI 53575 Office: 1 W Wilson St Madison WI 53702 Tel (608) 266-1249

SCHETTER, CARL FREDERICK, b. Mpls., May 12, 1932; B.S., Marquette U., 1954, J.D., 1959. Admitted to Wis. bar, 1959, U.S. Dist. Ct. bar, 1959, U.S. Supreme Ct. bar, 1967; individual practice law, Milw., 1959—; pres. Wis. Indsl. Promotions, Inc., 1967—; exec. dir., legal counsel Wis. Tavern Keepers Assn., Inc., 1968—. Trustee City of Shorewood, Wis., 1967-70. Mem. Am., Wis., Milwaukee County bar assns., Am. Judicature Soc., Naval Res. Lawyers Assn. Home: 6901 N Beech Tree Dr Glendale WI 53209 Office: 710 N Plankinton Ave Milwaukee WI 53203 Tel (414) 276-0560

SCHEUER, RALPH H., b. Albuquerque, Feb. 23, 1946; B.A., U. Colo., 1967; J.D., U. Va., 1970. Admitted to N.Mex. bar, 1970; sec.-treas. firm Sommer, Lawler & Scheuer, Profl. Assn., Santa Fe, 1970—; mem. State of N.Mex. Unauthorized Practice of Law Com., 1974—. Trustee Temple Beth Shalom, Santa Fe, 1970—, Orch. of Santa Fe, 1975—. Mem. State Bar N.Mex., Am. Bar Assn., Phi Alpha Delta, Pi Sigma Alpha, Phi Sigma Delta. Home: 1031 Gov Dempsey Dr Santa Fe NM 87501 Office: 213 Cathedral Pl PO Box 1984 Santa Fe NM 87501 Tel (505) 982-4676

SCHEUERMAN, THOMAS JOSEPH, b. Moline, Ill., Feb. 28, 1937; B.S. in Bus., Northwestern U., 1958; J.D., U. Iowa, 1962. Admitted to Minn. bar, 1962; profl. baseball player Yankees, Fargo, N.D., 1958; office gen. counsel Minn. Mining and Mfg. Co., St. Paul, 1962—; asst. gen. counsel, 1976—. Mem. nat. bd. dirs. Young Life, 1974—. Mem. Minn. State, Ramsey County bar assns. Home: 3077 Klondike Ave N Lake Elmo MN 55042 Office: 3M Co Box 33428 Saint Paul MN 55133 Tel (612) 733-1250

SCHEURICH, GREGORY MICHAEL, b. Chgo., Oct. 30, 1947; A.B., Loyola U., 1969, J.D. cum laude, Northwestern U., 1972. Admitted to Ill. bar, 1972, Wis. bar, 1973; staff asst. State Bar of Wis., Madison, 1972-74; asso. firm Melli, Shiels, Walker & Pease, Madison, Wis., 1974-77, Guyer, Enichen & Mayfield, Rockford, Ill., 1977—. Mem. Ill., Winnebago County bar assns., State Bar Wis. Recipient Gavel award Am. Bar Assn., 1974-75. Author: (with others) Wisconsin Law Enforcement Officers Criminal Law Handbook, 1975. Mem. editorial bd. Jour. Criminal Law, Criminology and Police Sci., 1971-72. Office: 202 Rock River Savings Bldg Rockford IL 61101 Tel (815) 965-8775

SCHIANO, CHARLES ANGELO, b. Rochester, N.Y., Feb. 12, 1934; B.A., U. Windsor; LL.B., Union U., 1959, LL.D. Admitted to N.Y. State bar, 1963; asst. Pub. Service Commn., 1960-63; individual practice law, Rochester, 1963—. Mem. Rochester City Council, 1972—; pres. Monroe County Narcotics Guidance Council, 1976—. Mem. Monroe County Bar Assn., N.Y. Trial Lawyers Assn. (pres. 1974), Rochester Lawyers (dir. 1970), Internat. Narcotic Enforcement Officers Assn., Am. Soccer League (past pres.). Named Man of Year Ecco Homo Soc.; legal editor. Home: 500 Wilder Bldg Rochester NY 19614 Office: 3562 Lake Ave Rochester NY 14612 Tel (716) 546-7150

SCHIAVO, PASCO LOUIS, b. Hazleton, Pa., June 21, 1937; B.A., Lafayette Coll., 1958; J.D., U. Pa., 1962. Admitted to Pa. bar, 1962, U.S. Dist. Ct. for Middle Dist. Pa. bar, 1965, U.S. 3d Circuit Ct. Appeals bar, 1972, U.S. Supreme Ct. bar, 1970; individual practice law, Beaver Meadows and Hazleton, Pa., 1962—; asst. dist. atty Luzerne County (Pa.), 1962-65; legal counsel Hazleton Housing Authority, 1966—; Municipal Authority Hazle Twp., 1970—, Indsl. Devel. Authority, 1972—; instr. Pa. State U., Hazleton, 1963-70; mem. disciplinary bd. Pa. Supreme Ct., 1977—. Pres. Luzerne County Commn. on Econ. Opportunity, Wilkes Barre, 1966-68. Mem. Greater Hazleton C. of C., Am., Pa., Luzerne County bar assns., Am., Pa. trial lawyers assns., Am. Judicature Soc. Contbr. articles to profl jours. Home: 139 N Vine St Hazleton PA 18201 Office: 306 Northeastern Bldg Hazleton PA 18201 Tel (717) 454-3583 also 54 Broad St Beaver Meadows PA 18216

SCHICKLER, JOHN RUSSELL, b. East Cleveland, Ohio, Aug. 1, 1917; B.A., Ohio State U., 1939, LL.B., 1941, J.D., 1967. Admitted to Ohio bar, 1941; of counsel firm Sanborn & Browfield, Columbus, Ohio, 1943-44; individual practice law, Columbus, 1943—; asst. city atty. City of Columbus, 1952; spl. state examiner investigation of Columbus Light Plant, 1952; spl. prosecutor for Urban Renewal, 1952; v.p., gen. counsel Nat. Plumbing Stores. Mem. Ohio Bar Assn. Recipient spl. commendation Columbus Better Bus. Bur., 1952. Home: 3039 Derby Rd Upper Arlington OH 43221 Office: 185 E State St Columbus OH 43215 Tel (614) 228-1891

SCHIFF, MARTIN, JR., b. Akron, Ohio, July 28, 1930; B.A. in Govt., Cornell U., 1952; J.D., Washington U., St. Louis, 1958. Admitted to Mo. bar, 1958; asso. firm Husch, Eppenberger, Donohue, Elson & Cornfeld, St. Louis, 1958-65; individual practice law, Clayton, Mo., 1965-66, Webster Groves, Mo., 1972—; partner firm Edwards & Schiff, Clayton, 1967-70, Fordyce & Mayne, Clayton, 1970-72; spl. prosecutor City of Webster Groves, 1959-61. Elder Webster Groves Presbyterian Ch., 1975—; mem. adv. com. Nipher PTA, Kirkwood, Mo. Mem. Am., Met. St. Louis, St. Louis County bar assns., Mo. Bar (bd. govs.), Mo. Assn. Trial Attys., Lawyers Assn. St. Louis, Order of Coif, Phi Delta Phi. Editor Washington U. Law Quar., 1957-58. Home: 1 Gramercy Pl Glendale MO 63122 Office: 30 Lockwood Ave Webster Groves MO 63119 Tel (314) 968-5060

SCHIFFER, LOIS JANE, b. Washington, Feb. 22, 1945; A.B., Radcliffe Coll., 1966; J.D., Harvard U., 1969. Admitted to Mass. bar, 1969, D.C. bar, 1971, U.S. Supreme Ct. bar, 1973; atty. Boston Legal Assistance Project, 1969-70; law clk. U.S. Ct. Appeals for D.C. Circuit, 1970-71; asso. firm Leva, Hawes, Symington, Martin & Oppenheimer, Washington, 1971-74; atty. Center for Law and Social Policy, Washington, 1974—; mem. screening com. Women's Legal Def. Fund., Washington, 1973-75; mem. HEW Immunization Policy Informed Consent Task Force, Washington, 1976-77; mem. D.C. Jud. Nomination Commn., 1977—. Mem. Am. Bar Assn., D.C. Bar (co-chairperson criminal law and individual rights div. 1975—), Phi Beta Kappa. Home: 4640 Brandywine St NW Washington DC 20016 Office: 1751 N St NW Washington DC 20036 Tel (202) 872-0670

SCHIFFMAN, DANIEL, b. N.Y.C., Nov. 7, 1932; B.B.A., Coll. City N.Y., 1959; J.D. (Univ. scholar), N.Y. U., 1962. Admitted to N.Y. bar, 1962, U.S. Supreme Ct. bar, 1975; pub. accountant firm Meyerson & Levine, C.P.A.'s, N.Y.C., 1959-61; asso. firm Maxwell & Diamond, N.Y.C., 1962-66; individual practice law, N.Y.C., 1966-74; partner firm Schiffman & Ellenbogen, N.Y.C., 1975—; legal sec. to Chief City Magistrate, N.Y.C., 1961-62; counsel to adminstr. Commonwealth of P.R. Econ. Devel. Adminstrn., N.Y.C., 1971-73; cons. Practising Law Inst., N.Y.C., 1963-68. Mem. Am., N.Y. State, N.Y.C. bar assns. Recipient Bancroft-Whitney prize; editorial staff N.Y. U. Law Rev. Home: 903 Park Ave New York City NY 10021 Office: 200 Park Ave New York City NY 10017 Tel (212) 682-2373

SCHILD, KITTY, b. Princeton, N.J., June 9, 1948; B.A., Rice U., 1969; J.D., U. Tex., 1972. Admitted to Tex. bar, 1972; staff atty. Tex. Legis. Council, Austin, 1972-73, El Paso (Tex.) Legal Assistance Soc., 1974-76; individual practice law, El Paso, 1976—. Bd. dirs. El Paso Rape Crisis Center, 1974-76. Mem. Am., Tex., El Paso, El Paso Women's bar assns., El Paso Trial Lawyers Assn., Coalition Women's Orgns. (1st pres. 1974-75). Home: 5900 Enterprise St El Paso TX 79912 Office: 1011 N Mesa St El Paso TX 79902 Tel (915) 544-5236

SCHILKE, NEIL WILLIAM, b. Tobias, Nebr., Jan. 30, 1934; A.B., Midland Lutheran Coll., 1958, LL.B., Coll. William and Mary, 1961. Admitted to Va. bar, 1961, Nebr. bar, 1962, Fed. bar, 1963; corp. counsel Phillips Petroleu, Idaho Falls, Idaho, 1961-62; partner firm Sidner, Svoboda, Schilke, Wiseman & Thomsen, Fremont, Nebr., 1962—; justice peace, Fremont, 1964-66; lectr. bus. law and communications law Midland Lutheran Coll., 1970—; lectr. Am. Bankers Inst., Fremont, 1964-65; dir. 1st Nat. Bank, Hooper, Nebr. Bd. dirs. Fremont YMCA, 1962—, pres., 1966-67; mem. adv. bd. Salvation Army, 1964—, chmn., 1972-73; bd. dirs. YMCA Found., 1975—; dir. Midland Cbll. Bd. Trustees, 1970—, vice chmn., 1975-77. Mem. Dodge County, Nebr., Am. bar assns., Am. Trial Lawyers Assn. Named outstanding young man City Fremont, 1966, outstanding young man State of Nebr., 1966. Contbr. articles to profl. jours. Home: 1636 E Linden St Fremont NE 68025 Office: 403 1st Nat Bank Bldg Fremont NE 68025 Tel (402) 721-7111

SCHILLER, JAMES EDWIN, b. Pendleton, Oreg., Dec. 28, 1921; B.S., U. Oreg., 1947, LL.B. (J.D.), 1949. Admitted to Idaho bar, 1949; founder partner firm Schiller, Williams & Trabert, Nampa, Idaho, 1949—; mem. Idaho Constl. Revision Commn. Mem. Am. Bar Assn., Idaho State Bar (continuing legal edn. and legis. affairs coms.), 7th Dist. (Idaho) Bar (pres.). Office: PO Box 21 Nampa ID 83651 Tel (208) 266-7809

SCHILLING, EDWIN CARLYLE, III, b. Baton Rouge, La., Apr. 5, 1943; A.B., Baylor U., 1966; J.D., La. State U., 1969. Admitted to La. bar, 1969; asst. staff judge adv. Charleston AFB, S.C., 1969-72, chief mil. justice, 1971; asso. prof. law USAF Acad., Colo., 1972-76, course dir. constl. law, 1975-76; mil. judge U.S. Air Force, 1971-72. Deacon, First So. Baptist Ch., Colorado Springs, Colo., 1974-76. Mem. Am., La. State bar assns., Order of Coif, La. State U. Law Sch. Alumni Assn. Home: 305 Cedar St Amite LA 70422 Office: Dept Law US Air Force Acad CO 80840 Tel (303) 472-3680

SCHILLING, GEORGE TOURNER, b. Bloomington, Ind., Mar. 6, 1919; A.B., Ind. U., 1940; J.D., U. Mich., 1943; M.A., Purdue U., 1977. Admitted to Ind. bar, 1946; partner firm Stuart, Branigin, Ricks & Schilling, Lafayette, Ind., 1948—. Mem. Am. Coll. of Trial Lawyers, Am. Judicature Soc., Am., Ind. (bd. mgrs. 1967-69), 7th Fed. Circuit (bd. govs.), Tippicanoe (pres. 1968-69), bar assns. Office: 8th Floor Life Bldg Lafayette IN 47902 Tel (317) 423-1561

SCHINDELAR, KATHRYN ANNE, b. Camden, N.J., Sept. 2, 1941; B.A., Syracuse U., 1964; J.D., Detroit Coll., 1968. Admitted to Mich. bar, 1969, N.J. bar, 1971, Colo. bar, 1976; individual practice law, Oakland County, Mich., 1969-76, Vail, Colo., 1976—; spl. advisor Jud. Com. Mich. Ho. of Reps., 1973. Referee, Mich. Civil Rights Comm., 1973-75. Home and office: Box 3182 Vail CO 81657 Tel (303) 476-1970

SCHINDLER, JOHN W., JR., b. Mishawaka, Ind., Apr. 25, 1922; A.B., U. Notre Dame, 1943; J.D., U. Chgo., 1948. Admitted to Ind. bar, 1948; individual practice law, Mishawaka, 1948—; mem. firm Schindler & Olson, Mishawaka, 1971—; city atty., Mishawaka, 1955. Mem. Am., Ind. (bd. mgrs., 1961-62), St. Joseph County (pres. 1960) bar assns. Home: 100 Schellinger Sq Mishawaka IN 46544 Office: 122 S Mill St Mishawaka IN 46544 Tel (219) 259-5461

SCHINMAN, HENRY LAWRENCE, B.B.A., U. Miami, 1967; J.D., U. Denver, 1969. Admitted to Fla. bar, 1970, N.J. bar, 1970; corporate counsel Boque Electric Mfg. Co., Paterson, N.J., 1970—, pres., 1975—. Mem. Am., Fla., N.J. bar assns. Home: 4 Merrywood Dr West Orange NJ 07079 Office: Boque Electric Mfg Co 100 Pennsylvania Ave Paterson NJ 07509 Tel (201) 525-2200

SCHIRALDI, BENEDICT ANTHONY, b. Bklyn., Aug. 12, 1929; B.S. in Accounting, L.I. U., 1952; J.D., Bklyn. U., 1962. Admitted to N.Y. bar, 1963; asst. chief Comml. Frauds Bur., Nassau County (N.Y.) Dist. Atty.'s Office, Mineola, 1971—. Mem. N.Y. State, Nassau County bar assns. Home: 3819 Maple St Seaford NY 11783 Office: 262 Old Country Rd Mineola NY 11501 Tel (516) 420-5064

SCHIRMEISTER, CHARLES FERDINAND, b. Jersey City, June 18, 1929; B.A., U. Mich., 1951; LL.B., Fordham U., 1956. Admitted to N.Y. State bar, 1956, U.S. Supreme Ct. bar, 1957; asst. dist. atty. New York County, 1956-61; partner firm Reid & Priest, N.Y.C., 1961—. Trustee Daytop Inc., Ocean Grove Camp Meeting Assn.; deacon Community Congl. Ch., Short Hills, N.J. Mem. New York County Lawyers Assn., Am. Bar Assn., Am. Judicature Soc. Home: 15 Beechcroft Rd Short Hills NJ 07078 Office: 40 Wall St New York City NY 10005 Tel (212) 344-2233

SCHLAFER, DALE LEHMAN, b. Detroit, Apr. 22, 1938; B.A., Amherst Coll., 1959; J.D., U. Chgo., 1962. Admitted to Ill. bar, 1962; law clk. to judge Ill. Appellate Ct., 1962-63; since practiced in Chgo., asso. firm Lee Freeman, 1963, Jacobs & McKenna, McKenna, Storer, Rowe, White & Haskell, 1963-69; individual practice law, 1970—; gen. counsel Home and Automobile Ins. Co., 1971—. Mem. Am., Chgo., Ill. State bar assns. Home: 1098 Ridgewood Dr Highland Park IL 60035 Office: 101 S Wacker Dr Chicago IL 60606 Tel (312) 236-7285

SCHLANGER, ARNOLD GEOFFREY, b. Bklyn., July 5, 1942; A.B. cum laude, U. Rochester, 1964; J.D., U. Chgo., 1967. Admitted to N.Y. bar, 1968; asso. firm Parker, Chapin, Flaftau & Klimpl, N.Y.C., 1967-70; sec., gen. counsel, dir. Nat. Spinning Co., Inc., N.Y.C., 1970—; dir. Dye Masters, Inc., Long Beach, Calif., Network Computing Corp., Charlotte, N.C. Sec., Lawyers Com. on Am. Policy Towards Viet Nam, N.Y.C., 1970—; mem. exec. bd., treas., coordinator Lawyers for McGovern, 1971-72; co-chmn. Lawyers for Ramsey Clark, N.Y.C., 1974, 76. Mem. N.Y. State Bar Assn., Lawyers Assn. Textile Industry, Am. Arbitration Assn. (panel). Home: 207 E 74th St New York City NY 10021 Office: 183 Madison Ave New York City NY 10016

SCHLANGER, JOHN, b. Kansas City, Mo., Mar. 23, 1943; B.A., Northwestern U., 1965; J.D., U. Mich., 1970. Admitted to Calif. bar, 1971; individual practice law, Los Angeles, 1971—. Treas., Valley Free Clinic, North Hollywood, Calif., 1975-76. Mem. Los Angeles County, Beverly Hills bar assns. Office: 9000 Sunset Blvd Los Angeles CA 90069 Tel (213) 278-2660

SCHLANGER, MICHAEL ASHER, b. N.Y.C., Dec. 9, 1943; A.B., Columbia, 1965; J.D., George Washington U., 1970. Admitted to D.C. bar, 1970, U.S. Supreme Ct. bar, 1974; research law librarian, Cravath, Swaine and Moore, N.Y.C., 1965-66; summer asso. firm Paul, Weiss, Rifkind, Wharton and Garrison, N.Y.C., 1969; asso. firm Covington and Burling, Washington, 1970—; staff atty. Neighborhood Legal Services Program, Washington, 1972; adj. prof. law, Am. U., Washington Coll. Law, 1973-74; guest lectr. Cath. U. Am. Sch. Law, 1972-74. Bd. dirs. Ayuda, Inc., Washington, 1977—. Mem. Order of Coif. Recipient meritorious achievement award, Neighborhood Legal Services Program, 1974. Home: 3611 39th St NW Washington DC 20016 Office: 888 16th St NW Washington DC 20006 Tel (202) 452-6184

SCHLATTER, DONALD ALLAN, b. Toledo, Aug. 25, 1929; B.S., Mass. Inst. Tech., 1951; M.I.E., LL.B., U. Toledo, 1956. Admitted to Ohio bar, 1956; with Art Iron, Inc., Toledo, 1951—, mgr. metal service div., 1954-73, pres., 1973—; ltd. individual practice law, Toledo, 1956—. Pres. Lucas County Safety Council, 1975-77, chmn. bd., 1977—; bd. mgrs. Central YMCA, 1956-62, met. bd. trustees Toledo YMCA, 1960-62, 77—. Mem. Toledo, Ohio, Am. bar assns., Am. Soc. Metals, ASTM, Steel Service Center Inst. Office: Box 964 860 Curtis St Toledo OH 43696 Tel (419) 241-1261

SCHLEGEL, FRED EUGENE, b. Indpls., July 24, 1941; B.A., Northwestern U., 1963; J.D. with distinction, U. Mich., 1966. Admitted to Ind. bar, 1966, U.S. Supreme Ct. bar, 1968; partner firm Baker & Daniels, Indpls., 1972—. Mem. Ind. Gov.'s Mansion Commn., Meridian St. Preservation Commn. Mem. Am., Ind., Indpls., 7th Circuit bar assns. Home: 5273 Illinois St Indianapolis IN 46208 Office: 810 Fletcher Trust Bldg Indianapolis IN 46204 Tel (317) 636-4535

SCHLEGEL, RAYMOND CARL, b. Reading, Pa., Oct. 26, 1929; A.B., Albright Coll., 1951; LL.B., U. Pa., 1954. Admitted to Pa. bar, 1955; partner firm Balmer, Mogel, Speidel & Roland, Reading, 1956—. Pres., YMCA of Reading and Berks County, 1974-76. Mem. Am., Pa., Berks County bar assns. Home: R D 1 Bernville PA 19605 Office: 50 N Fifth St Reading PA 19603 Tel (215) 376-1515

SCHLEHUBER, CLARENCE HAROLD, b. Peoria, Ill., Jan. 18, 1936; B.S., U. Notre Dame, 1957; J.D., William Mitchell Coll. Law, 1961. Admitted to Minn. bar, 1962, Fla. bar, 1976, Calif. bar, 1976; asso. firm West & Gowan, Rochester, Minn., 1962-68; individual practice law, Pine Island, Minn., 1969—; judge Pine Island Municipal Ct., 1969-73; spl. judge Olmsted County (Minn.) Ct., 1973—; city atty. City of Pine Island, 1962-69, sch. bd. atty., 1962—; gen. counsel Security State Bank, Pine Island, 1962—. Mem. pastoral adv. council Archbishop of St. Paul. Mem. Am., Minn., Fla., Calif. State, Goodhue County and Minn. First Dist. (pres. 1972-73) bar assns. Home and Office: PO Box 206 Pine Island MN 55963 Tel (507) 356-4436

SCHLEIT, PHILIP, b. Syracuse, N.Y., Oct. 18, 1911; B.S., Hamilton Coll., 1933; LL.B. cum laude, Syracuse U., 1936, J.D., 1970. Admitted to N.Y. bar, 1936, D.C. bar, 1947, U.S. Supreme Ct. bar, 1946; asso. Hiscock Law Firm, Syracuse, 1936-42; gen. counsel Office Civilian Def., 1943-44; chief large sect. attys. CAB, 1944-46; asso. firm Denning & Cross, Washington, 1946-47, Cummings, S, T and Cross, 1946-48; individual practice law, Washington, 1949—; partner firm Schleit & Jaycox, 1966-75; asso. prof. law Del. Law Sch. of Widener Coll., Wilmington, 1973-74. Trustee Syracuse Camp Fire Girls, 1939-42. Mem. Inter-Am., D.C. bar assns., Internat. Aviation Club. Office: Suite 425 1028 Connecticut Ave NW Washington DC 20036 Tel (202) 296-4369

SCHLESINGER, HARVEY ERWIN, b. N.Y.C., June 4, 1940; B.A., The Citadel, 1962; J.D., U. Richmond, 1965. Admitted to Va. bar, 1965, Fla. bar, 1965, U.S. Supreme Ct. bar, 1968; capt. U.S. Army Judge Adv. Gen., Ga., 1965-68; corporate counsel Seaboard Coast Line R.R. Co., Jacksonville, Fla., 1968-70; chief asst. U.S. Atty., Jacksonville, 1970-75; U.S. magistrate, middle dist. Fla., Jacksonville, 1975—; instr. law John Marshall Law Sch., Atlanta, 1967-68. Bd. dirs. Pine Castle Center for Mentally Retarded, 1970—, pres., 1972-74, chmn. bd. dirs., 1973-74, 76; trustee Pine Castle Found., 1972-76; trustee Congregation Ahavath Chesed, 1970—, treas., 1974, v.p., 1975—. Mem. Am., Va., Fla., Jacksonville, Fed. bar assns., Am. Judicature Soc. Office: 311 W Monroe St PO Box 508 Jacksonville FL 32201 Tel (904) 791-3444

SCHLESINGER, W. LOUIS, b. McKeesport, Pa., Dec. 29, 1893; law degree U. Pitts., 1914. Admitted to Pa. bar, 1916; Mem. Erie County (pres. 1933), Pa., Am. bar assns. Home: 3615 State St Erie PA 16508 Office: Suite 404 Maine Bank Bldg Erie PA 16501 Tel (814) 453-5881

SCHLESS, MICHAEL JAMES, b. Denver, Jan. 17, 1949; A.B., U. Tex., 1970, J.D., 1973. Admitted to Tex. bar, 1973; asso. firm Friday & Kazen, Austin, Tex., 1973—. Mem. adv. com. Austin Independent Sch. Dist., 1975—; mem. pub. responsibility and informed consent coms. Austin State Sch., 1976. Mem. Austin Jr. (dir. 1976—, chmn. juvenile ct. com. 1975—), Travis County bar assns., State Bar Tex. Home: 4900 Valley Oak Dr Austin TX 78731 Office: 700 San Antonio St Austin TX 78701 Tel (512) 472-9291

SCHLEUPNER, MICHAEL NICHOLAS, JR., b. Balt., Oct. 3, 1946; B.S. in History, Loyola Coll., Balt., 1968; J.D., Villanova U., 1971. Admitted to Md. bar, 1972; asso. firm Dulany & Davis, Westminster, Md., 1972-75; examiner Title Guarantee Co., Balt., 1975—. Mem. Balt., Md., Am. bar assns. Home: 3505 Brendan Ave Baltimore MD 21213 Office: Saint Paul & Lexington Sts Room 200 Baltimore MD 21202 Tel (301) 727-3700

SCHLEUSNER, CLIFFORD EDWARD, b. Saco, Mont., Feb. 15, 1918; grad. No. Mont. Coll., 1941; LL.B., U. Mont., 1951. Admitted to Mont. bar, 1951; individual practice law, Helena, Mont., 1951-52, Billings, Mont., 1953-61; asst. U.S. atty., Billings, 1961-69; dep. county atty. Yellowstone County (Mont.), 1970-75; partner firm Schleusner & Jones, Billings, 1971—. Mem. Mont., Yellowstone County bar assns. Home: 436 Crow Ln Billings MT 59101 Office: 1111 Main St Billings MT 59101

SCHLICHTER, JEROME JOSEPH, b. Belleville, Ill., Aug. 13, 1948; B.S., U. Ill., 1969; J.D., U. Calif. of Los Angeles, 1972. Admitted to Calif. bar, 1972, Ill. bar, 1973; asso. firm Levinson, Rowen & Leavy, Beverly Hills, Calif., 1972-73, firm Cohn, Carr, Korein, Kunin & Brennan, E. St. Louis, Ill., 1973—. Mem. Am., St. Louis, St. Clair County bar assns., ACLU, Ill., Calif. trial lawyers assns., Nat. Lawyers Guild. Asso. editor U. Calif. Los Angeles Law Review, 1971-72. Home: 4545 Maryland St Saint Louis MO 63108 Office: 412 Missouri Ave E Saint Louis IL 62201 Tel (618) 274-0434

SCHLIFKE, JAMES STEVEN, b. Chgo., Apr. 6, 1948; B.S. in Gen. Engring., U. Ill., 1970, J.D., 1973. Admitted to Ill. bar, 1973; atty. Ill. EPA, Springfield, Ill., 1973-74, G.D. Searle & Co., Des Plaines, Ill., 1974-77; mem. firm Stone Pogrund & Korey, Chgo., 1977—. Mem. Am., Ill., Chgo. bar assns. Home: 315 C Hawthorn St Glencoe IL 60022 Office: Suite 2800 221 N LaSalle St Chicago IL 60601 Tel (312) 782-3636

SCHLIFKIN, ROBERT STEVEN, b. Chgo., May 16, 1939; B.S., Roosevelt U., 1962; J.D., U. San Fernando Valley, 1969. Admitted to Calif. bar, 1969, U.S. Supreme Ct. bar, 1973; asso. firm Pollock, Pollock & Fay, Los Angeles, 1969—; chmn. task force I, Los Angeles County Superior Ct. Civil Trials Manual, mem. arbitration program. Mem. Am. Bar Assn., Am., Calif. (malpractice com.), Los Angeles (bd. govs. 1976-77) trial lawyers assns. Office: 1888 Century Park E Suite 1520 Los Angeles CA 90067 Tel (213) 553-3811 879-0111

SCHLOSBERG, MILES STEVEN, b. N.Y.C., June 6, 1947; A.B., Dartmouth Coll., 1968; M.B.A., Stanford U., 1972, J.D., 1972. Admitted to Alaska bar, 1972; asso. firm Nosek, Bradbury, Wolf & Scholsberg, Anchorage, 1972-73, partner, 1973-75; dir. Alaska State Div. Banking, Securities and Corps., Juneau, 1975-76; partner firm Miles S. Schlosberg, Anchorage, 1976—; chmn. bd. Brokers Title Co., Anchorage, 1976—. Mem. Alaska Bar Assn., Real Estate Securities and Syndication Inst. (dir.). Contbr. articles to legal jours. Home: 1222 U St Anchorage AK 99501 Office: 425 G St Suite 500 Anchorage AK 99501 Tel (907) 276-3125

SCHLOSSER, GEORGE MCGARRAUGH, b. Sioux Falls, S.D., Sept. 17, 1907; B.A., Yankton Coll., 1929; J.D., U. S.D., 1933. Admitted to S.D. bar, 1933, Ill. bar, 1943; practiced in Brookings, S.D., 1933-42; chief counsel Dist. Office Price Adminstrn. Office, Pierre, S.D., 1942-43; partner firm McBride, Baker, Wienke & Schlosser and predecessors, Chgo. and Oak Brook, Ill., 1943—. Pres. Village of Clarendon Hills (Ill.), 1966-70. Mem. Am., Ill., DuPage County (Ill.), Chgo. bar assns., State Bar S.D., Am. Judicature Soc. Home: 322 Harris Ave Clarendon Hills IL 60514 Office: 1211 W 22d St Oak Brook IL 60521 Tel (312) 887-8876

SCHLOTTERBECK, WALTER ALBERT, b. N.Y.C., Dec. 22, 1926; A.B., Columbia, 1949, LL.B., 1952. Admitted to N.Y. bar, 1953; with Gen. Electric Co., 1952—, dept. counsel lamp div., Cleve., 1957-60, asso. trade regulation counsel, N.Y.C., 1960-63, div. counsel component products div., Fort Wayne, Ind., 1963-67, div. counsel Housewares Div., Bridgeport, Conn., 1967-69, v.p., corp. counsel, N.Y.C., 1970-75, sec., Fairfield, Conn., 1975-76, v.p., gen. counsel, sec., Fairfield, 1976—, mem. corp. policy com., benefit plans investment com.; dir. Gen. Electric Credit Corp., 1970—. Mem. Am. Bar Assn. Home: 752 Town House Rd Fairfield CT 06430 Office: 3135 Easton Turnpike Fairfield CT 06431 Tel (203) 373-2492

SCHLOTTMAN, ELLIOTT EUGENE, b. Shreveport, La., Oct. 1, 1927; B.B.A., U. Miss., 1964, J.D., 1966. Admitted to Miss. bar, 1966, U.S. Supreme Ct. bar, 1975; practiced in Hattiesburg, Miss. Mem. S. Central Miss. Bar Assn., Sigma Chi, Phi Alpha Delta. Home: 3501 Rosewood Dr Hattiesburg MS 39401 Office: PO Box 1902 Hattiesburg MS 39401 Tel (601) 545-1700

SCHLUETER, JAMES WILLIAM, b. Cin., June 5, 1947; A.A., U. Cin., 1967, B.A., 1970; J.D., Salmon P. Chase Coll. Law No. Ky. U., 1974. Admitted to Ohio bar, 1974; ct. constable, law clk. to Judge Robert S. Kraft, Hamilton County (Ohio) Ct. Common Pleas, 1972-74; individual practice law, Cin., 1975; partner firm Schlueter, Crall & Lukey Co., Legal Profl. Assn. and predecessor, Cin., 1976, mem. firm, 1976—. Mem. Am., Cin., Ohio bar assns., Lawyer's Club Cin. Contbr. article to law rev. Office: 1553 Cedar Ave Cincinnati OH 45224 Tel (513) 591-0224

SCHMELTZER, EDWARD, b. N.Y.C., Aug. 22, 1923; B.A., Hunter Coll., 1950; M.A., Columbia U., 1951; J.D., George Washington U., 1954. Admitted to D.C. bar, 1954, U.S. Supreme Ct. bar, 1957; economist PHA, Washington, 1951-53, cons. economics, 1953-54; trial atty. Fed. Maritime Bd. Maritime Adminstrn., Washington, 1955-60, dir. bur. domestic regulations, FMC, 1961-66, mng. dir., 1966-69; partner firm Morgan, Lewis & Bockius, Washington, 1969-76, Schmeltzer, Aptaker & Sheppard, Washington, 1976—; U.S. rep., 12th Diplomatic Conf. Internat. Maritime Law, Brussels, 1967, 13th Conf., 1968. Mem. Fed., Maritime Adminstrv. bar assns. Recipient Distinguished Service award FMC, 1969. Home: 10412 Buckboard Pl Potomac MD 20854 Office: 1150 Connecticut Ave NW Suite 305 Washington DC 20036 Tel (202) 452-8711

SCHMELZER, RAYMOND WILLIAM, b. Cleve., Jan. 13, 1932; B.S., Case Western Res. U., 1953, LL.B., 1956, J.D., 1957. Admitted to Ohio bar, 1957; since practiced in Cleve., mem. firm Benesch, Friedlander, Mendelson & Coplan, 1957-65, Lambros, Calabrese, Schmelzer, Garafoli & Caterino, 1965-75, Schmelzer & Shafran, 1975—. Active United Appeal, Citizens League. Mem. Ohio, Cuyahoga County, Greater Cleve. bar assns. Home: 2751 Sherbrooke Rd Shaker Heights OH 44122 Office: 750 Prospect Ave Cleveland OH 44115 Tel (216) 781-5700

SCHMERTZ, ERIC JOSEPH, b. N.Y.C., Dec. 24, 1925; A.B., Union Coll., 1948; certificate Alliance Francaise, Paris, 1948; J.D., N.Y. U., 1954. Admitted to N.Y. State bar, 1955; prof. law Hofstra U. Sch. Law, Hempstead, N.Y., 1972—; profl. labor arbitrator; impartial chmn. City of N.Y., Uniformed Firefighters, Fire Officers; referee disciplinary cases N.Y.C. Transit Authority; contract arbitrator Gen. Electric, maj. league baseball; pub. mem. N.Y.C. Office Collective Bargaining; exec. dir. N.Y. State Bd. Mediation. Mem. Am. Arbitration Assn. (dir. labor tribunals) 1955-60), Nat. Acad. Arbitrators, N.Y. State Bar Assn. Contbr. articles to profl. jours. Home: 4550 Palisade Ave Riverdale NY 10471 Office: 122 E 42d St New York City NY 10017 also Hofstra U Sch Law Hempstead NY Tel (212) 682-6980

SCHMETTERER, JACK BAER, b. Chgo., Apr. 11, 1931; B.A., Yale, 1952, LL.B., 1955. Admitted to Ill. bar, 1955, U.S. Dist. Ct. bar, 1956; asst. U.S. atty. northern dist. Ill., Chgo., 1963-70, chief civil div., 1966-68, 1st asst. U.S. atty., 1968-70; 1st asst. state's atty. Cook County, Chgo., 1971-73; partner Gottlieb & Schwartz, Chgo., 1974—. Mem. Ill., Am., Chgo. (chmn. commn. on criminal justice, 1976—) bar assns. Contbr. articles in field to profl. jours. Home: 911 Bittersweet St Northbrook IL 60062 Office: 120 S La Salle St Chicago IL 60603 Tel (312) 726-2122

SCHMIDT, ARTHUR A., b. N.Y.C., Oct. 28, 1927; B.A., Columbia, 1949, LL.B., Georgetown U., 1952. Admitted to D.C. bar, 1952, N.Y. bar, 1952, Supreme Ct. U.S. bar, 1960, U.S. Dist. Ct. Eastern Dist. N.Y. bar, 1968, U.S. Dist. Ct. So. Dist. N.Y. bar, 1968; mem. firm Hall, Robinson & Hogan, Oyster Bay, N.Y., 1952-54; individual practice law, Huntington, N.Y., 1954-73; partner firm McLaughlin, Knight, Schmidt & Spagnoli, N.Y.C., 1973—; dep. atty. Town of Huntington, 1959-61. Chmn. fund raising Suffolk County (N.Y.) Mental Health Assn., 1958. Mem. Am., N.Y. State, Suffolk County bar assns. Home: Crane Rd Lloyd Harbor NY 11743 Office: 7 High St Huntington NY 11743 Tel (516) 423-6704

SCHMIDT, BENJAMIN, b. Louisville, Jan. 6, 1946; Sc.B., U. Louisville, 1968, J.D., 1971. Admitted to Ky. bar, 1971; individual practice law, Louisville, 1971—. Mem. Ky. Bar Assn. Home: 1505 Woodluck Ave Louisville KY 40205 Office: 835 W Jefferson St Louisville KY 40202 Tel (502) 584-0143

SCHMIDT, DOUGLAS EARL, b. Spirit Lake, Iowa, May 12, 1943; B.A., Drake U., 1965; J.D., State U. Iowa, 1968. Admitted to Iowa bar, 1968, Minn. bar, 1970; asso. firm Jurgemeyer & Eddy, Clinton, Iowa, 1968-70; partner firm Grose, Von Holtum, Von Holtum, Seiben & Schmidt, Worthington and Mpls., Minn., 1970—; mem. Minn. Supreme Ct. Com. on No Fault Ins.; lectr. in field. Mem. Am., Minn. (bd. govs.) trial lawyers assns., Am. (Merit award 1969), Minn., 13th Dist. (pres. 1974-75) bar assns. Home: 608 Ninth St Worthington MN 56187 Office: 607 Tenth St Worthington MN 56187 Tel (507) 376-4166

SCHMIDT, GLENN WALTER, b. Chgo., Oct. 1, 1917; J.D., Chgo.-Kent Coll. Law, 1947. Admitted to Ill. bar, 1942; with Continental Ill. Nat. Bank, Chgo., 1935-54, Harris Trust & Savs. Bank, Chgo., 1954-58; partner firm Kirkland & Ellis, Chgo., 1958—; lectr. in field. Mem. exec. council Lutheran Ch. Am., 1970—; chmn. Luth. Ch. Am. Found., 1962-70. Mem. Am., Ill., Chgo. bar assns., Am. Coll. Probate Counsel. Home: 6513 N Oxford Ave Chicago IL 60631 Office: 200 E Randolph Dr suite 5600 Chicago IL 60601 Tel (312) 861-2078

SCHMIDT, HILMER LOUIS, b. San Antonio, July 11, 1913; certificate St. Mary's U., 1937. Admitted to Tex. bar, 1937; asso. firm Tynan, Davis & Scherlen, San Antonio, 1937-40; mem. firm Maloney, Cook, Dozier & Schmidt, San Antonio, 1953-54; exec. dir., atty. Bexar County (Tex.) Legal Aid Assn., 1954-67, asst. dir., 1967—; asst. dist. atty. Bexar County, 1949-53. Charter mem. Alamo Heights Vol. Fire Dept., 1928-31, Hollywood Park (Tex.) Vol. Fire Dept., 1958-61; mem. Hollywood Park Zoning Bd., 1962-63; chmn. Hollywood Park Children's Recreational Com., 1962-63. Mem. Tex., San Antonio bar assns., San Antonio Trial Lawyers Assn., Am. Judicature Soc., Tex. United Community Services Assn., St. Mary's Alumnus and Oblates Assn., Hollywood Park Home Owners Assn. Recipient Distinguished Service award K.C., 1974-75. Home: 309 Mecca Dr San Antonio TX 78233 Office: 203 W Nueva St San Antonio TX 78207 Tel (512) 227-0111

SCHMIDT, JAMES WALTER, b. Xenia, Ohio, Aug. 31. 1946; B.S., Miami U., 1968; J.D., Stetson U., 1973; LL.M., U. Mo.. 1975. Admitted to Ohio, Fla. bars, 1973, U.S. Tax Ct. bar, 1971; individual practice law, Xenia, 1973—. Mem. Ohio, Fla. bar assns., Phi Alpha Delta. Home: 184 N King St Xenia OH 45385 Office: 63 1/2 E Main St Xenia OH 45385 Tel (513) 372-5330

SCHMIDT, JEROME SAMUEL, b. Detroit, Apr. 23, 1945; B.A., U. Mich., 1967; J.D., U. Wis., 1972. Admitted to Wis. bar, 1972; mem. firm Donald Eisenberg & Assos., Madison, Wis., 1972-75, firm Klein, Kueumel & Schmidt, S.C., Madison, 1975—. Mem. Wis., Dane County bar assns. Office: 301 N Hamilton St Madison WI 53701 Tel (608) 255-8199

SCHMIDT, JOHN R., b. Chgo., Nov. 14, 1943; B.A., Harvard U., 1964, J.D., 1967. Admitted to Ill. bar, 1967; asso. firm Mayer, Brown & Platt, Chgo., 1967-74, partner, 1974—; mem. Gov.'s Commn. to Revise Ill. Mental Health Code, 1973-77. Mem. Am. Bar Assn. (ho. of dels. 1973-74), Chgo. Council Lawyers (pres. 1974-76). Contbr. articles to legal jours. Home: 1350 N State Pkwy Chicago IL 60610 Office: 231 S Lasalle St Chicago IL 60604 Tel (312) 782-0600

SCHMIDT, JOSEPH THOMAS, b. Queens, N.Y., Oct. 2, 1935; B.A., St. John's U., 1957, LL.B., 1959. Admitted to N.Y. bar, 1959, U.S. Supreme Ct. bar, 1970; asst. dist. atty. Queens County (N.Y.), 1960-66; sr. atty. firm Joseph T. Schmidt, Woodhaven, N.Y., 1966—; hearing examiner N.Y.C. Parking Violations Bur., 1971—; arbitrator Am. Arbitration Assn.; hearing officer N.Y. Family Ct., 1975—. Pres. St. Thomas Apostle Parish Council. Mem. Criminal Ct., N.Y. State (citation 1966, exec. com. young lawyers sect. 1968-72), Queens County bar assns., Dist. Attys. Assn. Home: 85-53 85th St Woodhaven NY 11421 Office: 95-31 Jamaica Ave Woodhaven NY 11421 Tel (212) 441-4343

SCHMIDT, MARTHA, b. Indpls., Oct. 6, 1944; A.B., Ind. U., 1966, J.D. magna cum laude, 1972. Admitted to Ind. bar, 1972, Fla. bar, 1973; law clk. to Chief Judge Charles B. Fulton, U.S. Dist. Ct. for So. Dist. Fla., Miami, 1972-74; asso. firm Bingham Summers Welsh & Spilman, Indpls., 1974—. Mem. Am., Ind., Indpls. bar assns., The Fla. Bar. Recipient Ins. Counsel Jour. award, 1971. Office: 2700 Indiana Tower One Indiana Sq Indianapolis IN 46204 Tel (317) 635-8900

SCHMIDT, MICHAEL BRUCE, b. Corpus Christi, Tex., Sept. 22, 1948; B.B.A., U. Tex., 1970; J.D., South Tex. Coll. Law, 1973. Admitted to Tex. bar, 1973, U.S. Dist. Ct. for So. Dist. Tex. bar, 1975, U.S. 5th Circuit Ct. Appeals bar, 1975; asso. firm Pratt & Shuart, Corpus Christi, 1974-75; v.p. legal CRC Corp., Comprehensive Resources Corp., GeoDynamics Oil & Gas, Inc., 1975-76; sec., land mgr. Peninsula Resources Corp., Corpus Christi, 1976—. Sec., dir. Coastal Ben chpt. Multiple Sclerosis Soc., Corpus Christi. Mem. Am., Tex., Nueces County bar assns. Home: 315 Louise St Corpus Christi TX 78404 Office: 950 Bank & Trust Tower B & T 129 Corpus Christi TX 78477 Tel (512) 888-4224

SCHMIDT, MORTON J., b. Budapest, Hungary, Nov. 26, 1927; B.S., Marquette U., 1953, J.D., 1956. Admitted to Wis. bar, 1956; asso. firm Bendinger, Hayes & Kluwin, Milw., 1956-59; atty. Northwestern Mut. Life Ins. Co., Milw., 1960-62; partner firm Boren, Schmidt & Fleming, Cudahy, Wis., 1962-71; counsel Litton Industries, Cleve., 1971; individual practice law, Milw., 1971—. Mem. Am. Bar Assn., Maritime Law Assn., Res. Officers Assn., Assn. Commerce (pres.). Home: 5661 Forest Ct Greendale WI 53129 Office: 131 W Layton Ave Milwaukee WI 53207 Tel (414) 481-6300

SCHMIDT, RICHARD MARTEN, JR., b. Winfield, Kans., Aug. 2, 1924; A.B., U. Denver, 1945, J.D., 1948. Admitted to Colo. bar, 1948, D.C. bar, 1968, U.S. Supreme Ct. bar, 1958; dep. dist. atty., Denver, 1949-50; individual practice law, Denver, 1950-65; gen. counsel and Congressional liaison, USIA, Washington, 1965-68; partner firm Cohn and Marks, Washington, 1968—; spl. counsel U.S. Senate Agr. Investigation Com., 1959-60; instr. communications law U. Denver, 1949-62. Bd. trustees, U. Denver, 1965—, Washington Journalism Center, 1976—; advisory council program on communications and society Aspen Insts., 1976—. Mem. Denver (pres. 1963-64), Colo. (bd. govs., 1956-57, 62-65), Am. (chmn. standing com. on assn. communications, 1969-73), D.C., Fed. Communications bar assns., Bar Assn. D.C. Home: 115 5th St SE Washington DC 20003 Office: 1920 L St NW Washington DC 20036 Tel (202) 293-3860

SCHMIDT, ROBERT PAUL, b. Chgo., Oct. 28, 1941; B.A., Purdue U., 1967; J.D., U. Chgo., 1970. Admitted to Ill. bar, 1970; asso. firm Lord, Bissell & Brook, Chgo., 1970—. Mem. Ill., Am., Chgo. bar assns., Nat. Assn. R.R. Trial Counsel. Office: 115 S LaSalle St Chicago IL 60603 Tel (312) 443-0335

SCHMIDT, RONALD GENE, b. Turtle Lake, N.D., Feb. 28, 1937; B.B.A., U. N.D., 1961, J.D., 1963. Admitted to Mo. bar, 1963, N.D. bar, 1963, S.D. bar, 1966, U.S. Supreme Ct. bar, 1969, U.S. Ct. Mil. Appeals bar, 1969, U.S. Ct. Claims bar, 1969; asso. firm Lathrop Righter Gordon & Parker, Kansas City, Mo., 1963-65; partner firm Schmidt, Schroyer & Colwill, Pierre, S.D., 1970—; dir. S.D. State Legis. Research Council, 1965-70; staff dir. S.D. Constl. Revision Commn., 1968-70; mem. S.D. Commn. Intergovtl. Relations, 1968-70, Gov.'s Adv. Com. on Transp., 1965-66. Pres., Oahe YMCA, 1974—, St. Joseph Sch. Bd., 1975—; Republican committeeman Hughes County, S.D., 1974—; treas. S.D. Rep. Central Com., 1977—. Mem. S.D. (labor law com.), 6th Jud. Circuit bar assns. Home: 400 N Evans St Pierre SD 57501 Office: 120 N Euclid St Pierre SD 57501 Tel (605) 224-5813

SCHMIDT, ROY JOHN, JR., b. Bklyn., June 23, 1941; B.A., Stanford, 1963, LL.B., 1966. Admitted to Calif. bar, 1966; teaching fellow Stanford Law Sch., 1966-67; asso. firm Gibson, Dunn & Crutcher, Beverly Hills, Calif., 1967-72, partner, 1972—. Bd. dirs. Epi-Hab U.S.A., Inc., Los Angeles, Epi-Hab Los Angles, Inc. Mem.

Am., Los Angeles County, Beverly Hills (chmn. com. corps.) bar assns., Order of Coif. Articles editor Stanford Law Rev., 1965-66. Office: 9601 Wilshire Blvd suite 800 Beverly Hills CA 90210 Tel (213) 273-6990

SCHMIDT, WILLIAM LOUIS, b. Woodsfield, Ohio, Jan. 30, 1912; B.A., Ohio State U., 1934, J.D., 1937. Admitted to Ohio bar, 1937; partner firm Potts, Schmidt & Lewis, Columbus, Ohio, 1946-70, Crabbe, Brown, Jones, Potts & Schmidt, Columbus, 1970—. Mem. Am., Ohio, Columbus (pres. 1957-58) bar assns. Home: 921 Fairway Blvd Columbus OH 43213 Office: 42 E Gay St Columbus OH 43215 Tel (614) 228-5511

SCHMIER, JOSEPH, b. N.Y.C., Apr. 3, 1905; LL.B., St. John's Coll. Sch. Law, 1929. Admitted to N.Y. State bar, 1930, U.S. Dept. Justice Bd. Immigration Appeals, 1951, U.S. Dist. Ct., So. and Eastern Dists. bars, 1956, Fla. So. Dist. bar, 1960, Fla. bar, 1960, U.S. Supreme Ct. bar, 1961; individual practice law, N.Y.C., from 1930, Hallandale, Fla., 1960—. Pres. Ave N Jewish Center, Bklyn., 1935-42, Beth Torah Congregation, North Miami Beach, Fla., 1963-64, Fedn. Jewish Men's Clubs, SE region U.S., 1973-74, Men's Club, Freshmeadows Jewish Center, Flushing, L.I., 1956-58; chmn. bd. dirs. Temple Adath Yeshurun, North Miami Beach, 1959-60; mem. United Synagogue Council, Yeshiva U., 1935-37; 1st v.p. Bklyn. Jewish Community Council; mem. legal com. Queens Democratic Com., 1955-59. Mem. Fla., Miami Beach bar assns. Recipient Man of Year Award Men's Club Fla., 1973. Home: 19700 NE 22th Ave North Miami Beach FL 33139 Office: 2500 E Hallandale Beach Blvd Hallandale FL 33009 Tel (305) 945-1586

SCHMITT, EDWARD EARL, b. Kansas City, Mo., Aug. 8, 1926; B.A., Washington U., St. Louis, 1948; LL.B., U. Mo., 1951; LL.M., Columbia, 1953. Admitted to Mo. bar, 1951; mem. firm Dietrich, Tyler & Davis, Kansas City, Mo., 1954-60; partner firm Dietrich, Davis, Dicus, Rowlands & Schmitt, Kansas City, 1960—; dir. Security Investment Fund, Topeka, 1969—; mem. Mo. Cts. Modernization Commn., 1971-73. Bd. dirs. Country Club Homes Assn., pres. Stratford Gardens 1972-75. Mem. Mo. (mem. legal edn. com., chmn. 1968-71, recipient Pres.'s award 1971), Am. (mem. anti-trust and corp. com.), Kansas City (mem. legis. com.) bar assns., Am. Judicature Soc., Lawyers Assn. Kansas City (v.p. jr. sec. 1956), Kansas City C. of C., Washington U. Alumni Assn. (pres. 1957-61). Home: 1231 Huntington Rd Kansas City MO 64113 Office: 1001 Dwight Bldg 1004 Baltimore St Kansas City MO 64105 Tel (816) 221-3420

SCHMITT, JOSEPH DOUGLAS, b. South Bend, Ind., Aug. 23, 1926; B.S., U. Notre Dame, 1946; J.D., Ind. U., 1951. Admitted to Ind. bar, 1951, since practiced in South Bend. Mem. Am., Ind., St. Joseph County bar assns., Assn. Trial Lawyers Am. Home: 1152 Manchester Dr South Bend IN 46615 Offce: 301 Commerce Bldg South Bend IN 46601 Tel (219) 232-7218

SCHMITT, ROBERT FERDINAND, b. Chgo., July 26, 1934; B.A., U. Minn., M.A., 1957; J.D., William Mitchell Coll. Law, 1963. Admitted to Minn. bar, 1963, Calif. bar, 1967, Ill. bar, 1970; personnel mgr. Ralston Purina Co., Mpls., 1957-59; labor relations staff rep. Cargill, Inc., Mpls., 1959-64; asso. counsel firm Feidt & Lang, Mpls., 1964; labor relations supr. FMC-No. Ordnance div. Mpls., 1964-66; corporate asst. gen. counsel FMC Corp., San Jose, Calif., 1966-70; dir. labor relation and labor counsel N.W. Industries Inc., Chgo., 1970—. Active Boy Scouts Am., 1970-76; mem. San. Sewer Commn. Plymouth (Minn.), 1961-63. Mem. Calif. State, Ill., Am., Chgo. bar assns., Chgo. Indsl. Relations Assn. Home: 225 S Valley Rd Barrington IL 60010 Office: 6300 Sears Tower Chicago IL 60606 Tel (312) 876-7000

SCHMUCK, EDWARD JOSEPH, b. Bklyn., Sept. 11, 1909; LL.B., Fordham U., 1932. Admitted to N.Y. bar, 1933, U.S. Supreme Ct. bar, 1955; individual practice law, N.Y.C., 1933-41; gen. counsel Nat. Assn. Life Underwriters, N.Y.C., 1946-48; v.p., gen. counsel Acacia Mut. Life Ins. Co., Washington, 1948-63; partner firm Sutherland, Asbill & Brennan, Washington and Atlanta, 1963—; adj. prof. law Georgetown U., 1956-68. Mem. Am., D.C. bar assns., D.C. Bar, Assn. Life Ins. Counsel, Am. Judicature Soc. Contbr. articles to legal jours. Office: 1666 K St NW Washington DC 20006 Tel (202) 872-7800

SCHMUHL, WILLIAM JOHN, JR., b. Michigan City, Ind., July 9, 1943; B.B.A., U. Notre Dame, 1965, J.D., 1967; M.B.A., U. Chgo., 1972. Admitted to Ind. bar, 1967; asso. firm Sweeney & Sweeney, Michigan City, 1967-70; accountant Arthur Anderson & Co., Chgo., 1970-73; asst. gen. counsel 1st Bank & Trust Co., South Bend, Ind., 1973-76; chmn. dept. bus. adminstrn. and econs. St. Mary's Coll., Notre Dame, Ind., 1976—. Mem. St. Joseph County (Ind.), Ind. State, Am. bar assns. C.P.A., Ind., Ill. Home: 3522 Springbrook Dr South Bend IN 46614 Office: Saint Mary's Coll Notre Dame IN 46556 Tel (219) 284-4572

SCHMUKLER, MARTIN LAWRENCE, b. N.Y.C., Nov. 19, 1940; B.S., N.Y. U., 1965; J.D., Bklyn. Law Sch., 1968. Admitted to N.Y. bar, 1968, U.S. Dist. Ct. bar, 1971; asst. dist. atty., N.Y. County, 1968-71; partner firm Diller, Schmukler & Asness, and predecessor, N.Y.C., 1971—. Mem. Am. Bar Assn. (criminal law sect.), N.Y. County Trial Lawyers' Assn. Editor, Bklyn. Law Rev., 1966-68. Home: One Gracie Terr New York City NY 10028 Office: 345 Park Ave New York City NY 10022 Tel (212) 371-1400

SCHMUKLER, ROBERT, b. Newark, Aug. 26, 1939; B.A., Queens Coll., 1963; LL.B., N.Y. Law Sch., 1965. Admitted to N.Y. bar, 1966; individual practice law, Bklyn., 1968—; officer West Brook Ind. Div., Bklyn. Mem. N.Y. State, Kings County Criminal bar assns., N.Y. State Defenders Assn. Contbr. articles to legal jours. Office: 121 Schermerhorn St Brooklyn NY 11201 Tel (212) 834-1144

SCHMUKLER, SIDNEY, b. Bronx, N.Y., Apr. 21, 1913; LL.B., Bklyn. Law Sch., 1936. Admitted to N.Y. bar, 1943, U.S. Supreme Ct. bar, 1958, U.S. Dist. Cts. Eastern and So. Dists. N.Y.; individual practice law, Bklyn., 1943—. Chmn. Foresters dist. Boy Scouts Am. (Queens, N.Y.). Mem. Am., N.Y. State, Bklyn. bar assns., N.Y. State Trial Lawyers Assn. Office: 121 Schermerhorn St Brooklyn NY 11201 Tel (212) 834-1144

SCHNABEL, ROBERT VERNON, b. Washington, July 25, 1931; B.A., U. Va., 1953, LL.B., 1955. Admitted to D.C., Va. bars, 1955, Md. bar, 1963, U.S. Supreme Ct. bar, 1963; mem. firm Mercier, Sanders, Baker & Schnabel, P.C., Washington, 1957—. Mem. Am. Bar Assn., Bar Assn. D.C., Va. State Bar. Home: 7200 Denton Rd Bethesda MD 20014 Office: 730 15th St NW Washington DC 20005 Tel (202) 638-2241

SCHNACK, HAROLD C., b. Honolulu, Sept. 27, 1918; A.B., Stanford U., 1940, LL.B., 1947. Admitted to Hawaii bar, 1947; dep. pros. atty. City and County of Honolulu, 1948; individual practice law, Honolulu, 1948—. Mem. Phi Alpha Delta. Home: 1282 Riverside Reno NV 89503 also 4261 Panini Loop 96816 Office: Suite 301 1152 Bishop Bldg PO Box 3077 Honolulu HI 96802

SCHNAPER, LEWIS LYONS, b. Balt., June 22, 1948; B.A., U. Md., 1969, J.D., 1972. Admitted to Md. bar, 1973; asso. firm Michael Pierce, Balboa, Canal Zone, 1972, C. Daniel Held, Towson, Md., 1973; supervising atty. Alaska Legal Services, Bethel, 1973-76; prin. legal planner Office of Gov., Juneau, Alaska, 1976—. Home: Box 248 Douglas AK 99824 Office: Pouch AD Juneau AK 99811 Tel (907) 465-3512

SCHNEIDER, BARRY CHARLES, b. Bronx, N.Y., Feb. 24, 1943; B.A., State U. N.Y. Binghamton (Harpur Coll.), 1964; J.D., St. John's U., 1968. Admitted to N.Y. bar, 1968, Ariz. bar, 1972; atty. Bedford-Stuyvesant Community Legal Services Corp., N.Y.C., 1968-69; asso. firm Guzik and Boukstein, N.Y.C., 1969-71, firm Langerman, Began, Lewis, Leonard & Marks, Phoenix, 1972—. Bd. dirs. Phoenix Jewish Community Center, 1975—. Mem. Am., Ariz., Maricopa County bar assns., Am. Trial Lawyers Assn. Contbr. articles to law revs. Home: 309 W Linger Ln Phoenix AZ 85021 Office: 1400 Ariz Title Bldg Phoenix AZ 85003 Tel (602) 254-6071

SCHNEIDER, CURT THOMAS, b. Coffeyville, Kans., Oct. 12, 1943; A.A., Coffeyville Jr. Coll., 1963; B.S., Pittsburg (Kans.) State Coll., 1965; J.D., U. Kans., 1968. Admitted to Kans. bar, 1968; chief of litigation Kans. Hwy. Commn., 1968-72, Atty. Gen.'s Office, Kans., 1972-75; atty. gen. Kans., Topeka, 1975—; mem. Kans. Drug Abuse Commn., 1975. Active, Nat. Wildlife Fedn., 1974, Kans. Election Bd. Mem. Kans. U. Law Soc., Kans. U. Alumni Assn., Nat. Assn. U.S. Army, Kans. Peace Officers Assn., Kans. Commn. on Interstate Cooperation, Kans. Com. on Surety Bonds and Ins., Kans. County and Dist. Attys. Assn. (adv. council). Recipient Outstanding Alumni award Kans. State Coll., Pittsburg, 1975. Office: Statehouse Topeka KS 66612 Tel (913) 296-2215

SCHNEIDER, DAVID ANTHONY, b. Bellevue, Ky., July 22, 1938; A.B., Thomas More Coll., 1960; J.D., U. Cin., 1963. Admitted to Ohio bar, 1963, Ky. bar, 1965; with Atty. Gen. Honor Program, U.S. Dept. Justice, Washington, 1963-65; asst. atty. gen. Frankfort (Ky.), 1965-68; partner firm Ziegler & Schneider, Covington, Ky., 1968—. Bd. dirs. Ky. Heart Assn.; nat. bd. dirs. Izaak Walton League Am. Mem. Ky. Bar Assn., Am. Judicature Soc. Recipient Outstanding Young Man award Ky. Jaycees, 1970. Office: 400 Covington Trust Bldg Covington KY 41042 Tel (606) 581-4553

SCHNEIDER, FRED RICHARD, b. Velasco, Tex., Mar. 25, 1943; B.A., Drake U., 1965, J.D., 1967. Admitted to Iowa bar, 1967, U.S. Tax Ct. bar, 1970; partner firm Williams & Hart, Des Moines, 1969-73, firm Williams, Hart, Lavorato & Kirtley, W. Des Moines, 1973—; law clk. to chief judge U.S. Dist. Ct. for So. Iowa, 1967-69; dir. pre-trial release project Hawley Welfare Found., 1965-67. Bd. govs. Drake U. Law Sch., 1972—. Mem. Am., Iowa, Polk County bar assns., Am. Judicature Soc., Delta Theta Phi, Order of Coif, Phi Beta Kappa, Phi Eta Sigma. Editor-in-chief Drake Law Rev., 1966-67; contbr. articles to legal jours. Office: Suite 700 1200 35th St West Des Moines IA 50265 Tel (515) 225-1125

SCHNEIDER, FREDERICK CONRAD, III, b. New Brunswick, N.J., June 28, 1937; A.B., Princeton, 1959; J.D., Duke, 1962; M.B.A., Rutgers U., 1965. Admitted to N.J. bar, 1962, U.S. Supreme Ct. bar, 1969; individual practice law, New Brunswick, 1963-74; municipal ct. judge, East Brunswick, N.J., 1971—. Mem. Am., New Brunswick, Middlesex County, N.J. bar assns., Municipal Ct. Judges Middlesex County (sec. 1973-75, v.p. 1975—). Home: 20 Civic Center Dr East Brunswick NJ Office: 1 Jean Walling Civic Center East Brunswick NJ 08816 Mailing Address: PO Box 30 Milltown NJ 08850

SCHNEIDER, FREDERICK RICHARD, b. Milw., July 11, 1939; B.A., Luther Coll., 1961; J.D., U. Chgo., 1964. Admitted to Wis. bar, 1964, U.S. Dist. Ct. Western Dist. Wis. bar, 1966, U.S. Tax Ct. bar, 1967; asso. firm Steele, Smythe, Klos & Flynn, LaCrosse, Wis., 1964-69; asst. prof. law No. Ky. U., 1969-72, asso. prof., 1972-73, prof., 1973—, asst. dean Chase Coll. Law, 1974-76. Pres. Trinity Luth. Ch., 1974-76. Mem. Am., Wis., Cin. (profl. ethics com. 1974—) bar assns. Contbr. articles to law jours. Home: 8643 Empire Ct Cincinnati OH 45231 Office: Chase Coll Law No Ky U 1401 Dixie Hwy Covington KY 41011 Tel (606) 292-5386

SCHNEIDER, HERBERT ALAN, b. Bklyn., May 16, 1935; A.B., U. Mich., 1956; LL.B., Yale, 1959. Admitted to N.Y. bar, 1960; asso. firm Frankenthaler & Kohn, N.Y.C., 1959-60, Gordon, Brady, Caffrey & Keller, N.Y.C., 1960-62, Wikler, Gottlieb, Taylor & Howard, N.Y.C., 1962-67; partner firm Frankenthaler, Kohn & Schneider, N.Y.C., 1967—. Pres. Jewish Conciliation Bd. Am., N.Y.C., 1972—; bd. dirs. Soc. of Third St. Music Sch. Settlement, 1970-76, Jewish Family Service, N.Y.C., 1974—. Mem. Am., N.Y. State bar assns., N.Y. County Lawyers Assn. Home: 114 Walbrook Rd Scarsdale NY 10583 Office: 120 Broadway New York City NY 10005 Tel (212) 732-7400

SCHNEIDER, JON DALE, b. Camp White, Oreg., Jan. 22, 1944; B.S. in Physics, Boston Coll., 1965, J.D., 1968. Admitted to Mass. bar, 1968; partner firm Goodwin, Procter & Hoar, Boston, 1968—; panelist New Eng. Law Inst., 1974, Mass. Continuing Legal Edn., 1977. Mem. Am., Mass. bar assns., Comml. Law League Am. Office: 28 State St Boston MA 02109 Tel (617) 523-5700

SCHNEIDER, JOSEPH, b. St. Louis, Jan. 11, 1922; B.S., Washington U., St. Louis, 1948, M.S., 1950; J.D., John Marshall Law Sch., 1956. Admitted to Ill. bar, 1956, U.S. Supreme Ct. bar, 1958; partner firm Nelson, Boodell, Foster, Sugrue & Crowley and predecessor, Chgo., 1956-64; magistrate Ill. Circuit Ct. of Cook County, 1964-71, asso. judge, 1971-73, judge, 1973—; lectr. Northwestern U. Sch. of Law seminar in law and psychiatry, 1970—; chmn. Ill. Gov's. Commn. to Revise Mental Health Code, 1973—. Mem. Chgo. (chmn. com. juvenile delinquency and juvenile offenders 1956-68), Ill. (council on individual rights and responsibilities 1972-74), Am. (vice chmn. commn. on mentally disabled 1973—) bar assns., Am. Judicature Soc., Decalogue Soc., Am. Assn. Law Schs. Recipient Traffic Ct. award Am. Bar Assn., 1963; Francis J. Gerty award State of Ill-Ill. Mental Health Assn., 1972, Outstanding Service award, 1977; John Marshall Law Sch. Distinguished Alumni award, 1977. Office: Richard J Daley Center Chicago IL 60612 Tel (312) 443-8320

SCHNEIDER, LAWRENCE LEE, b. Atlanta, Apr. 16, 1946; B.A., Emory U., 1968, J.D., 1973; M.A., U. Ill., 1971. Admitted to Ga. bar, 1973; asso. firm Albert M. Horn, Atlanta, 1974-75; individual practice, 1975—. Mem. Atlanta Bar Assn., Ga. Assn. Criminal Def. Lawyers, ACLU. Home: 1444 Fairview Rd NE Atlanta GA 30306 Office: Suite 620 66 Luckie St NE Atlanta GA 30303 Tel (404) 524-6878

SCHNEIDER, LAZ LEVKOFF, b. Columbia, S.C., Mar. 15, 1939; B.A., Yale U., 1961, LL.B., 1964; LL.M., N.Y. U., 1965. Admitted to D.C., N.Y. bars, 1965, Fla. bar, 1970; asso. firm Fulton, Walter & Duncombe, N.Y.C., 1965-67, firm Rosenman, Colin, Kaye, Petschek, Freund & Emil, N.Y.C., 1967-69, firm Kronish, Lieb, Shainswit, Weiner & Hellman, N.Y.C., 1969-70; partner firm Ruden, Barnett, McClosky, Schuster & Schmerer, Ft. Lauderdale, Fla., 1970—. Mem. exec. com. Anti-Defamation League of B'nai B'rith, State of Fla., 1971—. Mem. Am., Fla., Broward County bar assns. Office: 900 NE 26th Ave Fort Lauderdale FL 33338 Tel (305) 565-9362

SCHNEIDER, LEWIS MERRILL, b. Chgo., Dec. 25, 1944; B.A., Elmhurst Coll., 1968; J.D. with honors, John Marshall U., 1973. Admitted to Ill. bar, 1973; partner firm Don & Schneider (now Kallen, Don & Schneider), Chgo., 1973—; instr. John Marshall Law Sch., 1973-74. Mem. Am., Ill., Chgo. bar assns. Contbr. articles to profl. jours. Office: Suite 350 Barrister Hall 29 S LaSalle St Chicago IL 60603 Tel (312) 236-8585

SCHNEIDER, MARJORIE LOUISE, b. Burlington, Iowa, June 29, 1923; B.S. in Law with honors, U. Ill., 1945. Admitted to Ill. bar, 1946, U.S. Dist. Ct. So. Dist. Ill. bar, 1950; asso. firm Carson and Appleman, Urbana, Ill., 1946-47, individual practice, Galesburg, Ill., 1948-76; asso. Schneider & Ward, Galesburg, 1976—; spl. asst. to atty. gen., Springfield, Ill., 1960-68. Chmn. Democratic party Knox County, 1952-56, Ill., 1954-58; mem. Dem. Nat. Com., 1955-58. Mem. Ill., Knox County bar assns. Home: 2676 Springer Rd Apt 26 Galesburg IL 61401 Office: 218-19 Weinberg Arcade Galesburg IL 61401 Tel (309) 342-6156

SCHNEIDER, MICHAEL HAYGOOD, b. San Antonio, Jan. 6, 1943; B.S., Stephen F. Austin State U., 1965; J.D., U. Houston, 1971. Admitted to Tex. bar, 1971; trial asst. Harris County (Tex.) Dist. Atty. Office, Houston, 1971-75; asso. Organized Crime Div., Chief of Consumer Fraud Div. Parks and Moss, Houston, 1975-76; gen. atty. Dresser Industries, Inc., Houston, 1976—. Bd. dirs. Concerned Teens, Inc., Houston, 1975—. Mem. Am., Houston, Houston Jr. bar assns., State Bar Tex., Nat. Dist. Attys. Assn. Home: 3618 University Blvd Houston TX 77005 Office: 601 Jefferson St Houston TX 77002 Tel (713) 784-7896

SCHNEIDER, RAYMOND WILLIAM, b. Chgo., Nov. 9, 1922; B.S. in Bus. Adminstrn., Northwestern U., 1949; LL.B., Pacific Coast U., 1961. Admitted to Calif. bar, 1962; dep. county counsel, Los Angeles County, Calif., 1962-69; county counsel of Humboldt County, Eureka, Calif., 1969—; supervising dept. probation officer, Los Angeles County, Calif., 1954-62. Chmn. steering com. Redwoods United Workshop, Eureka, 1970. Mem. County Counsel Assn. of Calif. (sec.-treas. 1976). Office: 825 W 5th St Courthouse Eureka CA 95501 Tel (707) 445-7236

SCHNEIDER, ROY BERNHARDT, JR., b. Chgo., Dec. 3, 1926; B.A., Knox Coll., 1950; J.D., Northwestern U., 1956. Admitted to Ill. bar, 1956; asso. firm Madigan & Thorsen, Chgo., 1955-57; atty. law dept. Brunswick Corp., Chgo., 1957-60, Motorola, Franklin Park, Ill., 1960-61; asst. counsel Wurlitzer Co., Chgo., 1962-63; atty. Argonne Nat. Lab. (Ill.), 1963-66; mem. firm Johnson & Colmar, Morton Grove, Ill., 1966-71; individual practice law, Morton Grove, 1971—. Mem. Chgo., Ill. State bar assns., Morton Grove C. of C. (pres. 1972, dir. 1969—). Home: 2423 N Brighton Pl Arlington Heights IL 60004 Office: 8700 Waukegan Rd Morton Grove IL 60053 Tel (312) 967-8200

SCHNEIDER, STEPHEN BRUCE, b. Wisconsin Rapids, Wis., Sept. 12, 1944; B.S., Wis. State U., Stevens Point, 1967; J.D., U. Wis., 1972. Admitted to Wis. bar, 1972; individual practice law, Madison, Wis., 1972—; chmn. bd. Capitol City Theater Corp., 1975—. Pres. Group Health Coop. S. Central Wis., 1976—. Mem. Dane County Bar Assn. Office: 222 S Hamilton St Madison WI 53703 Tel (608) 255-2893

SCHNEIDER, WILLIAM HERMAN, b. Columbus, Ohio, Apr. 11, 1925; B.E.E., Ohio State U., 1950, M.S., 1950, J.D. summa cum laude, 1952. Admitted to Ohio bar, 1953; mem. firm Power, Jones & Schneider and predecessors, Columbus, Ohio, 1953—. Chmn. Franklin County Republican Exec. Com., 1969-74; mem. state Rep. Exec. Com., 1968—; presdl. elector, 1968; mem. Upper Arlington Planning Commn., 1955-63, State Bridge Commn. Ohio, 1963-74, chmn., 1963-71; mem. bd. elections Franklin County, 1974—. Mem. Columbus, Ohio, Am. Bar Assns. Home: 2715 Wexford Rd Columbus OH 43221 Office: 100 E Broad St Columbus OH 43215 Tel (614) 221-7863

SCHNEIDERMAN, BARRY ALAN, b. Seattle, June 28, 1933; B.A., U. Wash., 1954, J.D., 1957. Admitted to Wash. bar, 1957; dep. pros. atty. King County (Wash.), 1959-61; partner firm Burns & Schneiderman, Seattle, 1961—; dir. Solkover, Davidge, Jenkins & Waugh, Inc. (formerly Seattle Advt. Agy., Inc.); col. JAGC, U.S. Army Res., 1974—. Mem. young leadership cabinet United Jewish Appeal, 1963-67; bd. dirs. Caroline Kline Galland Home, 1972—, Am. Jewish Com., 1972-75; regional bd. dirs. Anti-Defamation League, 1965—, recipient Liberty award, 1968. Mem. Am., Fed., Wash. bar assns., Am. Judicature Soc. Home: 6820 51st St NE Seattle WA 98115 Office: 2720 Bank of California Center Seattle WA 98164 Tel (206) 622-3236

SCHNEIDERMAN, IRWIN, b. N.Y.C., May 28, 1923; B.A. cum laude, Bklyn. Coll., 1943; LL.B. cum laude, Harvard, 1948. Admitted to N.Y. bar, 1949, D.C. bar, 1952, U.S. Supreme Ct. bar, 1953; asso. firm Cahill Gordon & Reindel, N.Y.C., 1948-59, partner, 1959—. Mem. Am. Bar Assn., Assn. Bar City of N.Y. Home: 203 E 72d St New York City NY 10021 Office: 80 Pine St New York City NY 10005 Tel (212) 825-0100

SCHNEIDERS, PAUL ALEXANDER, b. Evanston, Ill., Apr. 21, 1940; A.B. magna cum laude, Boston Coll., 1963; M.Teaching Arts, Harvard, 1964; LL.D. (Univ. scholar), Suffolk U., 1969. Admitted to Mass. bar, 1969; individual practice law, Canton, Mass., 1969-75; partner firm Schneiders and Flood, Canton, 1975—; mem. Mass. Ho. of Reps., 1972-74, chmn. com. jud. reform, 1972-74; instr. law Boston Coll., 1969-75; asst. dist. atty. Norfolk County (Mass.), 1973-74; pub. defender Norfolk County, 1975—. Selectman Town of Canton, 1970-73; trustee Goddard Hosp., Stoughton, Mass.; chmn. fin. com.

Ponkapoag Outdoor Recreation Center YMCA, Canton, 1975—. Mem. Am., Mass. bar assns., Mass. Legis. Assn. Author: Justice, 1972. Home, 645 Pleasant St - Canton MA 02021 Office: 2184 Washington St Canton MA 02021 Tel (617) 828-6633

SCHNESSEL, BENJAMIN SAMUEL, b. Carbondale, Pa., June 23, 1941; B.A., Muhlenberg Coll., 1963; J.D., Dickinson Sch. Law, 1966. Admitted to Pa. bar, 1966; partner firm Judd Schnessel & McDonough, Carbondale, 1966—; dir. Liberty Discount & Saving Bank, Carbondale. Vice pres. Carbondale Area YMCA; pres. Tri-County Mental Health and Mental Retardation Center, Carbondale. Mem. Pa., Lackawanna County bar assns. Office: 11-13 Park Pl Carbondale PA 18407 Tel (417) 282-1515

SCHNIDER, ROBERT ALAN, b. Flint, Mich., Nov. 18, 1945; B.A., U. Calif., Berkeley, 1967, J.D., 1970. Admitted to Calif. bar, 1971; partner firm Schnider & Schnider, Santa Monica, Calif., 1971—. Bd. dirs. Jewish Fedn. Council Los Angeles, 1974-76; pres. Jewish Family Service, Santa Monica, 1976. Mem. Am., Los Angeles County bar assns., Calif., Los Angeles County trial lawyers assns., Nat. Law Guild. Recipient Bancroft-Whitney award U. Calif., 1969. Office: 225 Santa Monica Blvd suite 408 Santa Monica CA 90401 Tel (213) 393-0124

SCHNIPPER, DON MARTIN, b. Little Rock, Jan. 17, 1939; A.B., U. Ark., 1963, J.D., 1964. Admitted to Ark. bar, 1964, U.S. Supreme Ct. bar, 1971; partner firm Wood, Smith & Schnipper, Hot Springs, Ark., 1964—; spl. asso. justice Ark. Supreme Ct., 1976—. Mem. bd. dirs. Hot Springs C. of C., 1966—, v.p., 1976-77, pres., 1977; vice chmn. bd. First United Methodist Ch., 1975-76, chmn., 1977; pres. bd. Ouachita Regional Counseling & Mental Health Center, 1970; mem. bd. Hot Springs Childrens Home. Mem. Am., Ark. (chmn. Young Lawyers sect. 1969-70, mem. ho. of dels. 1973-76, mem. exec. council 1976-79), Garland County Bar Assns., Am., Ark. Trial Lawyers Assns. Recipient Hot Springs Distinguished Service award, 1970, C. of C. Com. awards, 1966-74; named Garland County Legal Secs. Boss of Yr., 1971-72. Home: 850 Quapaw St Hot Springs AR 71901 - Office: 123 Market St Hot Springs AR 71901 Tel (501) 624-1252

SCHNUR, JACOB J., b. Chgo., Aug. 17, 1923; LL.B., DePaul U., Chgo., 1949. Admitted to Ill. bar, 1949; mem. law div. Jewel Cos., Inc., Chgo., 1955—, asst. sec., 1969-75, v.p., asst. gen. counsel, 1975—. Bd. dirs. N.W. Community Hosp. Found. Mem. Ill., Chgo. bar assns. Home: 611 S Patton Ave Arlington Heights IL 60005 Office: O Hare Plaza 5725 E River Rd Chicago IL 60631 Tel (312) 693-6000

SCHOCH, ARCH KERPER, III, b. Phila., Nov. 30, 1909; grad. Duke, 1932; J.D., U. Ala., 1934. Admitted to Ala. bar, 1934, N.C. bar, 1935, U.S. Supreme Ct. bar, 1945; individual sr. partner firm Schoch, Schoch, Schoch, and Schoch and predecessor partner, 1935—; spl. agt. FBI, 1942-45; mem. N.C. Bd. Law Examiners, 1955-69, chmn., 1967-69. Fellow Internat. Acad. Trial Lawyers (dir. 1971-77, dean 1977—), Internat. Soc. Barristers (gov. 1965-70, pres. 1969-70); mem. High Point (pres. 1952-53), N.C. (pres. 18th Jud. Dist. 1957-58), N.C. State, Fed., Am. bar assns., Am. Trial Lawyers Assn. (v.p. N.C. 1956-57). Home: 605 Westchester Dr High Point NC 27260 Office: 310 S Main St High Point NC 27260 Tel (919) 883-7151

SCHOEMAN, STEPHEN, b. N.Y.C., May 27, 1942; B.A., Colby Coll., 1964; LL.B., U. Pa., 1967; M.I.A., Columbia, 1969, certificate, 1969. Admitted to N.Y. State bar, 1970, Fla. bar, 1976; individual practice law, New Rochelle, N.Y., 1970—. Mem. N.Y. State Bar Assn. Fellow European Inst. of Columbia, 1968-69; editor, founder Criminal Law Commentator, 1972-73; patentee puppet and articulated member fastener. Office: 271 North Ave New Rochelle NY 10701 Tel (914) 576-0717

SCHOEN, EDWARD BERNARD, b. Bklyn., June 8, 1934; A.B., Princeton, 1956; LL.B., Yale, 1959. Admitted to N.Y. State bar, 1960; asso. firm Robinson, Silverman, Pearce, Aronsohn, Sand & Berman, N.Y.C., 1960-67, partner, 1967—. Mem. Assn. Bar City N.Y. Home: 1150 Park Ave New York City NY 10028 Office: 230 Park Ave New York City NY 10017 Tel (212) 687-0400

SCHOEN, LAWRENCE CARL, b. N.Y.C., Aug. 18, 1928; A.A., New Eng. Coll., 1950; LL.B., Bklyn. Law Sch., 1952. Admitted to N.Y. State bar, 1953, U.S. Dist. Ct. bar, 1954; partner firm Schoen & Getlan, and predecessors, N.Y.C., 1953—; lectr. on legal effects of dissolution of marriage. Sec., Forest Rd. Sch. PTA, Valley Stream, N.Y., 1965-67; pres. Yomen div. Grand St. Boys' Assn., 1961-66, bd. dirs. Grand St. Boys' Assn., 1966-68; pres. Valley Stream chpt. Am. Field Service, 1970-71; Nassau County Republican committeeman, 1976—. Author: Is Your Marriage Dying?, 1968; Marriage—A Human Relationship, 1969. Home: 51 Heatherfield Rd Valley Stream NY 11581 Office: 299 Broadway New York City NY 10007 Tel (212) 732-8970 also 225 Jericho Turnpike Floral Park NY 11001 Tel (516) 354-7660

SCHOEN, NOELLE L'HOMMEDIEU, b. Cambridge, Mass., Jan. 6, 1947; student Syracuse U., 1964-66; B.S. in English and Polit. Sci., U. N.Mex., 1968, J.D., 1971. Admitted to N.Mex. bar, 1973, U.S. Supreme Ct. bar, 1976; law clk. to the Navajo Tribe, 1970-71, N.Mex. Ct. Appeals, 1971-72; individual practice law, Sandoval County and Albuquerque, N.Mex., 1973—; asst. dist. atty. 13th Jud. Dist. N.Mex., 1975-76; legal adviser Navajo Tribal Prosecutor, 1970-71. Mem. N.Mex., Sandoval County Democrat party central coms., 1975—; bd. dirs. Sandoval County Legal Aid, 1974—, Energy Consumers N.Mex., Inc., 1977—, Las Placitas Assn., 1974—. Mem. U. N.Mex. Law Sch. Alumni (dir. 1977—), N.Mex. Bar Assn., Nat. Dist. Attys. Assn. Home: Star Route Box 327 Placitas NM 87043 Office: 3225 Candelaria Rd NE Albuquerque NM 87107 Tel (505) 345-7771

SCHOENBAUM, EDWARD JOHN, b. Cleve., Sept. 5, 1942; B.S., Mich. State U., 1964; J.D., Case Western Res. U., 1968; B.D., Concordia Theol. Sem., 1970, M.Div., 1974. Admitted to Ohio, Mo. bars 1968, Ill. bar, 1971; campus pastor Kans. State U., 1968-69; criminal justice planner city and county, Springfield, Ill., 1969-70; cons. Ill. Dept. Corrections, Springfield, 1970-71; mem. Gov.'s Office Human Resources, Springfield, 1971-72; asst. dir. programs and services Am. Judicature Soc., Chgo., 1972-74, dir. programs and services, 1974—; founder, pres. Attention Homes for Youth, Springfield, 1971-72; legal counsel Ill. Probation, Parole and Correctional Assn., 1971-73; founding dir. Safer Found., 1973—; vice chmn. Nat. Inst. on Crime and Delinquency Planning Commn., 1975-76, chmn., 1977—. Mem. Am., Ill., Ohio bar assns., Ill. Acad. Criminology, Nat. Council on Crime and Delinquency. Co-editor: American Courts and Justice, 1976. Home: 145 East Rd Glen Ellyn IL 60137 Tel (312) 858-6114

SCHOENEBERG, WAYNE THOMAS, b. New Orleans, Aug. 14, 1946; B.A., U. Mo., 1968, J.D., 1973. Admitted to Mo. bar, 1974, U.S. Tax Ct., 1974; asst. to dir. Law Extension, U. Mo., Columbia, 1974; partner firm Fredrick & Schoeneberg, Warrenton, Mo., 1974-75; individual practice, Warrenton, 1975-76; mem. firm George E. Sullivan, O'Fallon, Mo., 1976—. Mem. Am., Mo., St. Charles County bar assns., Am. Trial Lawyers Assn. Office: 114 Elm St O'Fallon MO 63366 Tel (314) 272-6258 also 946-7858

SCHOENFELD, HOWARD ALLEN, b. N.Y.C., Apr. 17, 1948; A.B., U. Pa., 1970; J.D., Georgetown U., 1973. Admitted to Md. bar, 1973, Wis. bar, 1976; law clk. to Hon. Digges, asso. judge, ct. appeals, Md., 1973-74; asso. firm Gordon, Feinblatt, Rothman, Hoffberger & Hollander, Balt., 1974-76; asso. firm Stepke, Kossow, Trebon & Stadtmueller, Milw., 1976—. Bd. dirs., pres. Crofton Meadows Property Regime Number One, Crofton, Md., 1974-75. Mem. Am., Wis., Md., Balt. City bar assns., Am. Judicature Soc. Office: 633 E Mason St Milwaukee WI 53202 Tel (414) 224-1000

SCHOENHALS, EDMUND L., b. Salt Lake City, Oct. 23, 1904; B.S., U. Utah, 1931, J.D., 1932. Admitted to Utah bar, 1932, U.S. Supreme Ct. bar, 1950; practiced in Salt Lake City, 1932—. Mem. Am. (com. chmn. taxation sect. 1959-70), Utah (chmn. jud. council), Salt Lake County bar assns. Home: 1100 Vista View Dr Salt Lake City UT 84108 Tel (801) 582-4391

SCHOENLAUB, FRED EDWARD, b. St. Joseph, Mo., Jan. 24, 1930; B.A., U. Mo., 1954, J.D., 1954. Admitted to Mo. bar, 1954; individual practice law, St. Joseph, Mo., 1954-63; judge 5th Circuit Ct. Mo., 1963—; asst. pros. atty. Buchanan County, 1954-57; city atty. St. Joseph, 1958-59. Active, Charter Commn., St. Joseph, 1960-61. Mem. Am., Mo., St. Joseph bar assns., Nat. Coll. State Judiciary (mem. family law faculty). Contbr. articles to legal jours. Home: 1834 Lovers Lane Terr St Joseph MO 64505 Office: Court House St Joseph MO 64501 Tel (816) 279-4890

SCHOENTAG, DAVID CHRISTIAN, b. Saugerties, N.Y., Aug. 22, 1910; B.A., Colgate U., 1932; LL.B., Syracuse U., 1935. Admitted to N.Y. bar, 1937, U.S. Ct. So. Dist. N.Y., 1941; asso. firm Wiswall, Walton, Wood & MacAffer, Kingston, N.Y., 1935-40; served with JAGC, U.S. Army, 1940-48; individual practice law, Poughkeepsie, N.Y., 1948-68; asso. firm Grandeau & Dahawski, Poughkeepsie, 1972—. Supr. Town of Beekman (N.Y.), 1957-68; exec. Dutchess County (N.Y.), 1969-72; dist. leader United Way of Dutchess County, 1972-74; mem. Dutchess County council Boy Scouts Am., 1972—; mem. N.Y. State Bridge Authority, 1974—, vice chmn., 1977. Mem. N.Y., Dutchess County bar assns. Office: 39 Market St Poughkeepsie NY 12601 Tel (914) 471-1375

SCHOENWALD, MAURICE LOUIS, b. N.Y.C., Mar. 30, 1920; B.A., N.Y. U., 1943; J.D., Case Western Res. U., 1947. Admitted to N.Y. State bar, 1947, U.S. Supreme Ct. bar, 1971; individual practice law, N.Y.C., 1947—; faculty Hofstra U., 1967-68. Fellow Am. Acad. Matrimonial Lawyers; mem. Nassau County Bar Assn., Am. Arbitration Assn. Contbr. articles on specialized securities and investment contracts to profl. jours.; licensed broker-dealer, SEC. Home: 8 Nirvana Ave Great Neck NY 11023 Office: 380 Lexington Ave New York City NY 10017 Tel (212) MO 1-3595

SCHOETTLE, FERDINAND PAUL, b. Phila., Aug. 17, 1933; B.A., Princeton, 1955; LL.D., Harvard, 1960. Law clk. Judge Learned Hand, U.S. 2d Circuit Ct. Appeals, 1960-61; admitted to Pa. bar, 1961, Minn. bar, 1976; staff Office Tax Legis. Counsel, U.S. Treasury Dept., Washington, 1961-62; asst. Sen. Joseph S. Clark, Washington, 1962-63; asso. firm Morgan, Lewis & Bockius, Phila., 1963-67; asso. prof. U. Minn., 1967-70, prof., 1970—; spl. counsel Senate Subcom. Intergovtl. Relations, 1971; vis. scholar Harvard Law Sch. Mem. Am. Bar Assn. Recipient award for Community Contbn., Ams. for Democratic Action, 1964. Author: (with Oliver Oldman) State and Local Taxes and Finance, 1974; contbr. articles to profl. jours. Office: Law Sch U Minn Minneapolis MN 55455 Tel (612) 373-2719

SCHOETTLER, ROLAND WILLIAM, JR., b. Los Angeles, Sept. 7, 1936; student Stanford, 1954-55, Loyola U., Los Angeles, 1955-59; LL.B., Southwestern U., 1964. Admitted to Calif. bar, 1965; partner firm Murchison & Cumming, Los Angeles, 1964—; instr. law Calif. Coll. Law, 1966; lectr. Calif. Continuing Edn. of Bar series, 1976; mem. com. on tort reform Los Angeles City Attys. Office; atty. spl. arbitration program Los Angeles Superior Ct.; judge pro tem Los Angeles Municipal Ct. Mem. Am. Bd. Trial Advocates, Am. Arbitration Assn., So. Calif. Def. Counsel, Los Angeles County, Wilshire (pres. 1975-76) bar assns. Office: 680 Wilshire Pl Suite 100 Los Angeles CA 90005 Tel (213) 382-7321

SCHOLL, DAVID ALLEN, b. Fountain Hill, Pa., Aug. 20, 1944; A.B., Franklin and Marshall Coll., 1966; J.D., Villanova U., 1969. Admitted to Pa. bar, 1970, U.S. Supreme Ct. bar, 1974; staff atty. consumer law reform Community Legal Services, Phila., 1969-73; exec. dir. Delaware County (Pa.) Legal Assistance Assn., Inc., Chester, 1973—. Sec., Consumers Edn. and Protective Assn., Internat., Inc.; bd. dirs. Community Assistance Project. Mem. Delaware County, Pa. bar assns. Home: 4911 Pine St Philadelphia PA 19143 Office: 410 Welsh St Chester PA 19013 Tel (215) 874-8421

SCHOLLE, LESLIE CRAIG, b. Geuda Springs, Kans., Sept. 11, 1909; B.A., U. Minn., 1932, J.D., 1932. Admitted to Minn. bar, 1932, U.S. Dist. Ct. Dist. Minn. bar, 1933, U.S. Supreme Ct. bar, 1944, U.S. Ct. Appeals 8th Circuit bar, 1961; individual practice law, St. Paul, 1932-37, Mpls., 1937-41; individual practice law, Mpls., 1946-69; partner firm Scholle & Scholle, Mpls., 1969—; municipal judge, Excelsior, Minn., 1962-64; mem. nat. panel arbitrators Am. Arbitration Assn., 1970—. Mem. Am. Judicature Soc., Am., Minn., Hennepin County bar assns. Home: 27400 Pine Bend St Shorewood MN 55331 Office: 400 2d Ave S Minneapolis MN 55401 Tel (612) 332-8581

SCHOLLE, MARK, b. Balt., June 5, 1944; B.A., U. Minn., 1966, J.D., 1969. Admitted to Minn. bar, 1969; partner firm Scholle & Scholle, Mpls., 1969—; tchr. bus. law Mpls. Vocat. Evening Sch., 1969-73. Mem. Minn., Mpls., Fed. bar assns., Am. Trial Lawyers Assn., Phi Alpha Delta. Home: 8742 Leeward Circle Eden Prairie MN 55343 Office: 804 Title Insurance Bldg Minneapolis MN 55401 Tel (612) 332-8581

SCHOLNICK, LEONARD, b. N.Y.C., Jan. 25, 1933; LL.B., N.Y. Law Sch., 1958. Admitted to N.Y. bar, 1958; spl. asst. dist. atty. Kings County (N.Y.), 1960-63; asst. corp. counsel N.Y.C., 1964-68; law sec. Supreme Ct. Kings County, 1968-72; justice 2d dept. Supreme Ct. N.Y., Bklyn., 1973—; chmn. bldg. com. N.Y.C. Council. Mem. Bklyn. Bar Assn. Office: 360 Adams St Brooklyn NY 11201 Tel (212) 643-7078

SCHOLZ, CHARLES ADAM, b. Murphysboro, Ill., Oct. 29, 1926; LL.B., Mercer U., 1949. Admitted to Ill. bar, 1950, U.S. Supreme Ct. bar, 1975; individual practice law, Quincy, Ill., 1950-69; sr. partner firm Scholz, Staff & Brickman, and predecessors, 1969—; asst. state's atty. Adams County (Ill.), 1952-56; asst. atty. gen. Ill., 1961-69. Bd. dirs. St. Mary Hosp., 1972—, Quincy Pub. Library, 1955—. Mem. Am., Ill., Adams County bar assns., Am. Jud. Soc., Am., Ill. trial lawyers assns., Comml. Law League Am. Editorial bd. Organizing and Advising Ill. Businesses. Home: 411 S 24th St Quincy IL 62301 Office: 625 Vermont St Quincy IL 62301 Tel (217) 223-3444

SCHOLZ, RICHARD F., JR., b. Sept. 15, 1928; LL.B., Mercer U. Admitted to Ill. bar; judge Adams County (Ill.) Ct., 1958-64; asso. judge Ill. Circuit Ct., 8th Jud. Circuit, 1964, judge, 1964—; mem. adv. bd. Pres.'s Com. on Juvenile Delinquency and Youth Crime; vice chmn. adv. com. Ill. Dept. Children and Family Services, 1964, chmn., 1966; vice chmn. Com. to Survey Ill. Youth Commn.; chmn. com. ct. services Jud. Conf. Ill.; mem. Com. on Uniform Rules of Circuit Cts. Ill. Bd. dirs. Adams County Community Chest and Welfare Council, Cath. Youth Orgn. Mem. Adams County, Ill. State bar assns., Ill. Judges Assn. (exec. council sect. jud. adminstrn.), Phf Alpha Delta, Kappa Sigma. Recipient Distinguished Service to Community award Internat. Assn. Machinists, Quincy, Ill., 1963, Distinguished Service award Quincy Jaycees, 1964, Distinguished Service award Ill. Jaycees, 1964. Home: 2300 Aldo Blvd Quincy IL Office: Courthouse Quincy IL 62301

SCHOMER, FRED KEITH, b. Chgo., June 21, 1939; B.A., U. Chgo., 1970, J.D., 1972. Staff atty. Beatrice Foods Co., Chgo., 1963-69, asst. gen. counsel, 1969-73, asst. gen. counsel, asst. sec., 1973-74, asst. v.p., 1974-75, exec. v.p. adminstrn. and finance internat. div., 1975—; admitted to Ill. bar, 1972. Mem. Chgo. Bar Assn. Office: 120 S LaSalle St Chicago IL 60603 Tel (312) 782-2820

SCHOONMAKER, MEYRESSA HUGHES, b. Guilford County, N.C., Jan. 7, 1940; B.A., Wake Forest U., 1960, J.D., 1968; student Free U. Berlin, 1960-61, Rutgers State U., 1962-63. Admitted to N.C. bar, 1968; asso. firm Westmoreland, Sawyer & Schoonmaker, 1968-71, partner, 1972; individual practice law, Winston-Salem, N.C., 1972—; asst. to pres. legal affairs Wake Forest U., 1975—. Trustee Forsyth County Legal Aid Soc., 1969-74; bd. dirs. Winston-Salem Family Services, Inc., 1975—, treas., 1977. Mem. Am., N.C., Forsyth County bar assns. Named Outstanding Young Woman of Year for N.C., 1972; Nat. Endowment for Humanities seminar scholar, 1977. Home: 2090 Royall Dr Winston-Salem NC 27106 Office: Taylor House 915 W 4th St Winston-Salem NC 27101 Tel (919) 722-0079

SCHORER, SHELDON, b. Nov. 2, 1948; B.A., B.H.L., Yeshiva U., 1969; J.D., N.Y. U., 1972. Admitted to N.Y. bar, 1973; asso. firm Frankle & Greenwald, N.Y.C., 1973-76; individual practice law, Bklyn., 1976—; adj. prof. bus. law, Touro Coll., N.Y.C. Mem. Am. Bar Assn., N.Y. County Lawyers Assn., Internat. Assn. Jewish Lawyers and Jurists, Com. on Law Policy and Action. Home: 107-19 70th Ave Forest Hills NY 11375 Office: 26 Court St Brooklyn NY 11242 Tel (212) 875-4776

SCHOTT, DONALD LEE, b. Cin., Sept. 20, 1936; B.A., U. Cin., 1963; J.D., Salmon P. Chase Sch. Law, 1967. Admitted to Ohio bar, 1967, U.S. Supreme Ct. bar, 1971; partner firm Schott & Blackmore, Cin., 1971-73; asst. prosecutor Municipal Ct., 1968-72; asst. prosecutor Hamilton County (Ohio), Cin., 1972-74, judge Municipal Ct., 1974—. Cluster dir. explorer scouts Dan Beard council Boy Scouts Am. Mem. Cin. Bar Assn., Am., Ohio judges assns., Am. Judicature Assn. Office: 9th St and Main St Cincinnati OH 45202 Tel (513) 632-8631

SCHOUMACHER, BRUCE HERBERT, b. Chgo., May 23, 1940; B.S., Northwestern U., 1961; M.B.A., U. Chgo., 1963, J.D., 1966. Admitted to Nebr. bar, 1966, Ill. bar, 1971; asso. firm Luebs, Tracy & Huebner, Grand Island, Nebr., 1966-67; spl. agt. USAF, Offutt AFB, Nebr. and Tanson Nhut, Vietnam, 1967-71; asso. firm McDermott, Will & Emery, Chgo., 1971-75, partner, 1976—; instr. bus. adminstrn. Bellevue (Nebr.) Coll., 1967-70; lectr. U. M., 1970-71. Mem. Am., Chgo., Nebr. bar assns. Office: 111 W Monroe Chicago IL 60603 Tel (312) 372-2000

SCHOUMAN, JAMES FREDERICK, b. Detroit, Mar. 30, 1930; A.B. with honors, Holy Cross Coll., 1952; J.D., U. Mich., 1954; M.B.A., U. Detroit, 1957. Admitted to Mich. bar, 1954, U.S. Supreme Ct. bar, U.S. Ct. Appeals 6th Circuit bar, 1974; atty. G.T.W., Detroit, 1956-67; individual practice law, Dearborn, Mich., 1967—; chmn. Mich. RR Advisory Commn., 1975; atty. Owendale-Gagetown Sch. Bd., 1976, Sheridan #5 Sch. Bd., 1976. Mem. Detroit Youth Affairs Bd., 1977. Mem. Greater Detroit Movers Assn. (exec. sec. 1966—). Home: 18534 Bretton Dr Detroit MI 48223 Office: 21925 Garrison St Dearborn MI 48124 Tel (313) 561-3548

SCHOUWEILER, BART MCCLAIN, b. Wendell, Idaho, Aug. 11, 1934; B.A., Stanford U., 1956; LL.B., Georgetown U., 1959. Admitted to Nev. bar, 1959, U.S. Supreme Ct. bar, 1971; served with JAC, USAF, 1960-63; since practiced in Reno; asst. city atty., Reno, 1963-64; mem firm Schouweiler & Schouweiler, 1965-69, U.S. Atty. Dist. Nev., 1969-72, Schouweiler & Schouweiler, 1972—; municipal judge pro tem, Reno, 1964-65; mem. Nev. State Legislature Assembly, 1966-69. Mem. Washoe County, Nev. State, Am., Fed. (pres. Nev. chpt. 1972) bar assns. Home: 835 Mt Rose St Reno NV 89509 Office: 1 E 1st St Suite 1507 Reno NV 89501 Tel (702) 322-0632

SCHOWALTER, RONALD OSCAR, b. St. Louis, July 1, 1941; B.S., U.S. Naval Acad., 1963; J.D., Washington U., St. Louis, 1972. Admitted to Mo. bar, 1972; partner firm Peper, Martin, Jensen, Maichel & Hetlage, St. Louis, 1972—; lectr. law Washington U., 1973—. Bd. alderman Crystal Lake Park, Mo. Mem. Am., Mo. bar assns., Bar Assn. Met. St. Louis, Order of Coif. Home: 2216 Cleek Ct Crystal Lake Park MO 63131 Office: 720 Olive St Saint Louis MO 63101 Tel (314) 421-3851

SCHRAG, EDWARD A., JR., b. Milw., Mar. 27, 1932; B.S. in Econs., U. Pa., 1954; J.D., Harvard, 1960. Admitted to Ohio bar, 1961; asso. firm Vorys, Sater, Seymour & Pease, Columbus, Ohio, 1961-66, partner, 1967—. Mem. Am., Ohio (corp. law com.), Columbus (securities law com.) bar assns., Columbus Area C. of C. Recipient Ohio Legal Inst. award of merit, 1968. Home: 9400 White Oak Ln Westerville OH 43081 Office: 52 E Gay St Columbus OH 43215 Tel (614) 464-6258

SCHRAM, RONALD YOUNG, b. Bklyn., June 21, 1946; B.A. with honors, U. Fla., 1968, J.D. with honors, 1970. Admitted to Fla. bar, 1971; coordinator Legal Research and Writing Program, U. Fla. Law Sch., Gainesville, 1971; individual practice law, Gainesville, 1971-73;

v.p., gen. counsel Emmer Devel. Corp., Gainesville, 1973—. Mem. Am. Bar Assn., Bar Assn. of 8th Jud. Circuit of Fla., Order of Coif, Phi Delta Phi, Phi Kappa Phi. Exec. editor U. Fla. Law Rev., 1969-70. Home: 4137 NW 33d Pl Gainesville FL 32601 Office: 2801 SW Archer Rd Gainesville FL 32608 Tel (904) 376-2444

SCHRAMM, HARVEY J., b. St. Louis, May 20, 1938; A.B., Washington U., St. Louis, 1961, J.D., 1966. Admitted to Mo. bar, 1966; asst. county counselor St. Louis County, 1966-69; individual practice law, Clayton, Mo., 1969-71; judge St. Louis County Courthouse, Clayton, 1971—. Active Am. Jewish Congress. Mem. Order of Coif. An editor Washington U. Law Rev., 1965-66. Home: 4 Chappel Ct Manchester MO 63011 Office: St Louis County Court House Clayton MO 63105 Tel (314) 889-2468

SCHRAMM, ROBERT JOHN, b. N.Y.C., Feb. 6, 1944; B.A., Fla. State U., 1966, J.D., 1969. Admitted to Fla. bar, 1969; atty. Legis. Service Bur., Tallahassee, 1969-70; atty. Fla. Dept. Ins., Tallahassee, 1970—. Scoutmaster, Suwannee River Area council Boy Scouts Am., Tallahassee, 1970—. Mem. Fla. Bar Assn., Delta Theta Phi. Home: 3512 Raymond Diehl Rd Tallahassee FL 32303 Office: PO Box 110 Tallahassee FL 32302 Tel (904) 488-7016

SCHRAUB, B.B., b. Seguin, Tex., Feb. 17, 1928; LL.B., St. Mary's U., San Antonio, 1954. Admitted to Tex. bar; judge County Ct. of Guadalupe County (Tex.), 1967-69, Tex. Dist. Ct., 25th Jud. Dist., 1971—; county judge Guadalupe County, 1969, 71; dist. atty. 25th Jud. Dist., 1971; pres. Guadalupe County Abstract Co.; dir. Nolte Nat. Bank; adv. dir. Guada-Coma Savs. and Loan Assn.; mem. legis. com. for Tex. State Judiciary, 1976-76. Commr. Seguin Pub. Housing Authority, 1966-71; mem. devel. bd. Tex. Luth. Coll. Mem. Am., Guadalupe County, South Central Tex. (pres.) bar assns., Tex. Land Title Assn. (pres. 1970-71). Recipient Membership Devel. award Lions Internat., Appreciation award, 1967; Meritorious Service award Tex. Land Title Assn., 1971. Office: County Courthouse Seguin TX 78155 Tel (512) 379-1204

SCHRECK, GORDON DALTON, b. Richmond, Va., June 6, 1943; B.A., Hampden-Sydney Coll., 1965; LL.B., U. Va., 1969. Admitted to Va. bar, 1969, S.C. bar, 1970; asso. firm Buist, Moore, Smythe & McGee, Charleston, S.C., 1969-74, partner, 1974—. Mem. Am., Va., S.C., Charleston County bar assns., Maritime Law Assn. U.S., S.C. Def. Attys Assn., Southeastern Admiralty Law Inst., Propeller Club U.S. (pres. Port of Charleston 1975-76), Charleston Lawyers Club (pres. 1977-78), Mt. Pleasant Sertoma Club (pres. 1977-78). Office: 5 Exchange St Charleston SC 29402 Tel (803) 722-8375

SCHRECKENGAST, WILLIAM OWEN, b. Greenwood, Ind., Oct. 14, 1926; LL.B., Ind. U., 1956. Claims adjuster, supr. Gulf Ins. Co., Indpls., 1950-56; admitted to Ind. bar, 1956, U.S. Supreme Ct. bar, 1971; partner firm Kitley, Schreckengast & Davis, and predecessors, Beech Grove, Ind., 1957—. Mem. Am., Ind. State (bd. mgrs. 1972-74) bar assns., Am. Judicature Soc., Ind. Def. Counsel, Def. Research Inst. Home: 3780 Fairview Rd Greenwood IN 46142 Office: 380 Main St Beech Grove IN 46107 Tel (317) 787-5389

SCHREIBER, PALMER KRESS, b. Allentown, Pa., July 27, 1940; B.A. in Econs., Brown U., 1962; LL.B., U. Pa., 1966. Admitted to Pa. bar, 1966; asso. firm Pepper, Hamilton & Sheetz, Phila., 1966-72; individual practice law, Phila. and Allentown, Pa., 1973—. Trustee, counsel Allentown Art Mus., 1970—. Mem. Phila., Lehigh County, Pa., Am. bar assns., Soc. Crippled Children and Adults (dir. 1969—), Am. Assn. Museums (trustees com. 1973—). Home: 2407 Pine St Philadelphia PA 19146 Office: 2028 Chancellor St Philadelphia PA 19103 Tel (215) 567-4900 also First Valley Bank Bldg Center Sq Allentown PA 18101 Tel (215) 432-2300

SCHREIER, PETER BATTLE, b. N.Y.C., Aug. 11, 1932; B.S., Fordham U., 1954, J.D., 1957. Admitted to N.Y. bar, 1957, U.S. Supreme Ct. bar, 1961; asso. firm Phillips, Lytle, Hitchcock, Blaine, & Huber, Buffalo, 1961-67, partner, 1967—. Bd. dirs. Heart Assn. Western N.Y., Buffalo, 1971—, chmn.-elect, 1976; trustee Buffalo & Erie County Library, 1974—. Mem. Am., N.Y. State, Erie County bar assns., Erie County Trial Lawyers Assn., Fedn. Ins. Counsel. Contbr. articles in field to legal jours. Home: 129 Meadow Rd Buffalo NY 14216 Office: 3400 Marine Midland Center Buffalo NY 14203 Tel (716) 847-8476

SCHRETTER, ALFRED EMILE, b. N.Y.C., Sept. 19, 1937; A.B., Bowdoin Coll., 1959; LL.B., Columbia, 1962. Admitted to N.Y. bar, 1963, N.J. bar, 1972, U.S. Supreme Ct. bar, 1968; asso. firm Davis, Polk & Wardwell, N.Y.C., 1962—; mem. nat. panel arbitrators Am. Arbitration Assn., 1967—. Elected mem. Common Council, Summit, N.J., 1975—; mem. zoning bd. adjustment, Summit, 1970-74, vice chmn., 1973-74. Mem. Am., N.Y. State bar assns. Home: 20 Ashland Rd Summit NJ 07901 Office: One Chase Manhattan Plaza New York City NY 10005 Tel (212) HA 2-3400

SCHREYER, WALTER KARL, b. Jersey City, May 25, 1947; B.A., Colgate U., 1969; J.D., Union U., 1972. Admitted to N.J. bar, 1973, N.Y. bar, 1974; law sec. to judge N.J. Superior Ct. Criminal Br., 1973-74; asst. prosecutor Hudson County (N.J.), 1975-77, dep. atty. gen., 1974-75. Mem. Am., N.J., N.Y., Hudson County, N.Y. County bar assns. Home: 87 A Hawthorne Ave Park Ridge NJ 07656 Office: 595 Newark Ave Jersey City NJ 07306 Tel (201) 792-0800

SCHRICKER, DAVID EDWARD, b. Davenport, Iowa, Mar. 2, 1936; B.A., Yale U., 1958; LL.B., U. Calif., Berkeley, 1964. Admitted to Calif. bar, 1965, U.S. Supreme Ct. bar, 1977; asso. firm Aiken, Kramer & Cummings, Oakland, Calif., 1965-66; dep. city atty. City of Redwood City (Calif.), 1966-67, asst. city atty., 1967-68, city atty., 1968—; port atty. Port of Redwood City, 1968—. Bd. dirs. Casa de Redwood Found., 1970—. Mem. Am., Calif., San Mateo County bar assns., Nat. Inst. Municipal Law Officers, League Calif. Cities. Office: 702 Marshall St Suite 510 Redwood City CA 94063 Tel (415) 369-6251

SCHRIMSHER, JAMES BRUCE, b. Huntsville, Ala., Jan. 22, 1949; B.S., Auburn U., 1970; J.D., U. Ala., 1973. Admitted to Ala. bar, 1973; law clk. Ala. Ct. Criminal Appeals, Montgomery, 1973-74; mem. firm Morring & Schrimsher, Huntsville, 1975—. Mem. Madison County Bar Assn., Ala. State Bar, Assn. Trial Lawyers Am. Home: 1503 Elmwood Dr Huntsville AL 35801 Office: 401 Franklin St SE Huntsville AL 35801 Tel (205) 534-0671

SCHRODER, JACK SPALDING, JR., b. Atlanta, July 10, 1948; B.A., Emory U., 1970; J.D., U. Ga., 1973. Admitted to Ga. bar, 1973; asso. firm Jones, Bird & Howell, Atlanta, 1973—. Mem. Am., Atlanta bar assns., Atlanta Council Younger Lawyers (pres. 1977—). Home: 3630 Tanglewood Dr NW Atlanta GA 30339 Office: Haas Howell Bldg Atlanta GA 30303 Tel (404) 522-2508

SCHRODER, WILLIAM HENRY, JR., b. Atlanta, Apr. 10, 1941; A.B. in Econs., U. Notre Dame, 1963; LL.B., U. Va., 1966. Admitted to Ga. bar, 1965, U.S. Supreme Ct. bar, 1972; asso. firm Troutman, Sanders, Lockerman & Ashmore, 1966-69, partner, 1969-75; partner firm Schroder, Nicholson & Meals, Atlanta, 1976—. Bd. dirs. Atlanta Jr. C. of C., 1967-68; vice chmn. Cathedral of Christ the King parish council, 1976-77. Mem. Atlanta, Am., Fed. bar assns., State Bar Ga., Assn. Trial Lawyers Am., Lawyers Club Atlanta. Recipient Am. Spirit Honor medal Ft. Benning, Ga., 1967. Home: 3094 Farmington Dr NW Atlanta GA 30339 Office: 17th Fl Cain Tower Peachtree Center Atlanta GA 30303 Tel (404) 588-0100

SCHROEDER, CHARLES FREDERICK, b. Chgo., Oct. 24, 1918; B.S., Ill. Inst. Tech., 1941, postgrad., 1943-47; J.D., DePaul U., 1950. Admitted to Ill. bar, 1951, Ohio bar, 1957; engr. AT&T, Waukegan, Ill., 1941-42; engring. mgr. U.S. Steel Co., Chgo., 1942-48; patent agt. firm Charles W. Hills, Chgo., 1948-50; patent atty. Kellogg Switchboard & Supply, Chgo., 1950-52; sr. patent atty. Owens-Corning Fiberglas Co., Toledo, 1952—. Mem. Am., Ohio, Ill., Toledo bar assns., Am., Toledo patent law assns., IEEE, Rho Epsilon, Delta Theta Phi. Patentee in field (15). Home: 2317 Valleybrook Dr Toledo OH 43615 Office: Fiberglas Tower Toledo OH 43659 Tel (419) 248-8174

SCHROEDER, EDWIN MAHER, b. New Orleans, June 25, 1937; Ph.B., Gregorian U., Rome, Italy, 1959; J.D., Tulane U., 1964; M.S., Fla. State U., 1970. Admitted to Mass. bar, 1964; teaching fellow Boston Coll. Law Sch., 1964-65; asst. prof. U. Conn. Sch. Law, West Hartford, 1965-68; asst. prof. U. Tex. Sch. Law, Austin, 1968-69, asst. law librarian, 1968-69; asst. prof. Fla. State U. Coll. Law, Tallahassee, 1969-71, asso. prof., 1971-75, prof., 1975—, law librarian 1969—. Mem. Assn. Am. Law Schs. (chmn. sect. legal research and writing 1977), Order Coif, Beta Phi Mu. Home: 2403 Perez Ave Tallahassee FL 32304 Office: Fla State U Coll Law Tallahassee FL 32306 Tel (904) 644-1004

SCHROEDER, EDWIN MELVIN, b. Chgo., Oct. 5, 1914; B.S., U. Ill., 1940; J.D., DePaul U., 1949. Admitted to Ill. bar, 1950; sec., sr. atty. Zenith Radio Corp., Chgo., 1970—. Home: 111 Park Ave Grayslake IL 60030 Office: 1000 Milwaukee Ave Glenview IL 60025 Tel (312) 391-8055

SCHROEDER, FRANCIS CHILTON, b. Detroit Lakes, Minn., Dec. 5, 1906; student U. Notre Dame, 1924-26, U. Minn., 1927; LL.B., St. Thomas Coll., 1931. Admitted to Minn. bar, 1931, U.S. Supreme Ct. bar, 1964; partner firms Schroeder & Hogan, St. Paul, 1931-34, Schroeder, Wilson, Thorwaldsen & Schroeder, and predecessors, Detroit Lakes, 1934—; judge Detroit Lakes Municipal Ct., 1960-71. Justice grand tribunal Fraternal Order of Eagles, 1972-76, chief justice, 1976—. Mem. 7th Dist., Minn., Am. bar assns., Am. Trial Lawyers Assn. Recipient Distinguished Service award as v.p. U.S. Jr. C. of C., 1937, Distinguished Service award Fraternal Order Eagles, 1957, named to Eagles Hall of Fame, 1972, Reverance for Law award, 1973. Home: Route 2 PO Box 126 Pelican Rapids MN 56572 Office: 1111 Hwy Ten E Detroit Lakes MN 56501 Tel (218) 847-9296

SCHROEDER, GERALD FRANK, b. Boise, Idaho, Sept. 13, 1939; B.A., Coll. of Idaho, 1961; J.D., Harvard, 1964. Admitted to Idaho bar, 1965; asso. firm Moffatt, Thomas, Barrett and Blanton, Boise, 1965-66; individual practice law, Boise, 1966-67; asst. U.S. atty. Dist. Idaho, 1967-69; judge Ada County (Idaho) Probate Ct., 1969-71; judge Idaho Dist. Ct., 4th Jud. Dist., Magistrates Div., 1971-75, Idaho Dist. Ct., 4th Jud. Dist., 1975—; mem. Idaho Region 2 Law Enforcement Planning Commn., 1972—, chmn., 1974-75; instr. Boise Bar Rev., 1974-76; lectr. Boise State U., 1974-75; lectr. in field; mem. faculty Nat. Coll. State Judiciary, Reno, 1975. Bd. dirs. Boise Philharmonic Orch., 1965-67, v.p., 1966; Idaho Mental Health Assn., 1969-70, Youth Tennis Found., Boise, Idaho, 1974-75. Mem. Idaho State Bar, Am. Judicature Soc., Boise Estate Planning Council. Named Lawyer of Year Boise Legal Secs. Assn., 1975; named Distinguished Citizen Idaho Statesman, 1973; author: (with Peterson) Idaho Probate Procedure, 1972; contbr. articles to legal publs. Office: Ada County Courthouse Boise ID 83701 Tel (208) 384-8906

SCHROEDER, HUBERT JAMES, b. Milw., Oct. 19, 1896; LL.B., Marquette U., Milw., 1921. Admitted to Wis. bar, 1921, Fed. Dist. Ct. bar, Milw., 1925; with Travelers Ins. Co., Milw., 1921-29; v.p., mgr. claims div. legal matters Sentry Ins. Co., Milw. and Stevens Point, Wis., 1930-61; individual practice law, Ephraim, Wis., 1961—. Mem. Wis., Door County bar assns. Home: 215 N Orchard Rd Ephraim WI 54211 Office: 215 N Orchard Rd Stevens Point WI 54211 Tel (414) 854-2085

SCHROEDER, JACK, b. Davenport, Iowa, Aug. 21, 1925; B.S., St. Ambrose Coll., 1949; J.D., Drake U., 1952. Admitted to Iowa bar, 1952; mem. Iowa Ho. of Reps., 1949-53, Iowa Senate, 1953-67, majority leader of Iowa Senate, 1957-61; pres. Gen. United Life Ins. Co., Des Moines, 1962-76, chmn., pres. Gen. United Group, Inc., Des Moines, 1967-72; dir., pres. United Security Life Co., Des Moines, 1967-72; dir. Imperial Industries, Monterey Park, Calif., 1968—, All Am. Life & Casualty Co., Chgo., 1972-76, Wilshire Ins. Co., Los Angeles, 1969-76, Hawkeye Bancorp., Des Moines, 1975—, First Fed. State Bank, Des Moines, 1971—, Iowa Lutheran Hosp., Des Moines, 1975—. Chmn. Iowa Heart Assn., 1966-67, Counsel of State Govt., 1960; mem. Pres. Eisenhower's Adv. Council on Edn., 1955; mem. Iowa Devel. Commn., 1963-67; mem. Synodical Bd. Bd. United Lutheran Ch. Mem. Am., Scott County bar assns., Am. Acad. Trial Lawyers, Am. Judicature Soc., C. of C., Delta Theta Pi. Named Outstanding Legislator, 1955; recipient Iowa Good Govt. Award, 1955. Home: 3117 Park Plaza Dr Des Moines IA 50315

SCHROEDER, JOHN (JACK) NICHOLAS, b. Lone Pine, Calif., Oct. 2, 1942; B.S. in Fin., U. San Francisco, 1964, J.D., 1968. Admitted to Nev. bar, 1969; dep. atty. gen. State of Nev., Carson City, 1970-71; asst. city atty. Reno, 1971-76; atty. No. Area Substance Abuse Council, Reno, 1974-75, Reno Internat. Airport, 1975-76; individual practice law, Reno, 1977—. Mem. Alcoholics Rehab. Assn. (trustee 1972—), Am., Nev., Washoe County bar assns., Judicature Soc. Barristers. Home: 1225 Gordon Ave Reno NV 89509 Office: One E Liberty St suite 509 Reno NV 89501 Tel (702) 329-3000

SCHROEDER, THOMAS ARNOLD, b. Chgo., May 17, 1949; B.A., Carleton Coll., 1971; J.D., Washington U., St. Louis, 1974. Admitted to Mo. bar, 1974; atty. Fed. Land Bank of St. Louis, 1974—. Mem. Met. St. Louis, Mo., Am. bar assns. Home: 6332 N Rosebury Ave Clayton MO 63105 Office: Main PO Box 491 1415 Olive St St Louis MO 63166 Tel (314) 342-3395

SCHROER, GENE ELDON, b. Randolph, Kans., Aug. 29, 1927; LL.B., Washburn U., 1957. Admitted to Kans. bar, 1957; individual practice law, Topeka, 1957-68; partner firm Jones Schroer Rice & Bryan, Topeka, 1968—. Chmn. bd. suprs. Shawnee County (Kans.) Conservation Dist., 1970—; elder Potwin Presbyterian Ch., Topeka, 1960—. Mem. Am. (bd. govs., 1st v.p. tort sect.), Kans. (past pres., bd. govs.) trial lawyers assns., Am., Kans., Topeka bar assns. Home: 223 Woodlawn St Topeka KS 66606 Office: 115 E 7th St Topeka KS 66603 Tel (913) 357-0333

SCHROTEL, JOHN THOMAS, b. Cin., Jan. 4, 1940; B.A., U. Cin., 1961; J.D., 1964. Admitted to Ohio bar, 1964, Fla. bar, 1966; mgr. Sales div. Airstream, Inc., Tampa, Fla., 1973—. Home: 8712 Hickorywood Ln Tampa FL 33615 Office: Airstream Inc Jackson Center OH 45334 Tel (813) 884-1907

SCHUBINER, S. DAVID, b. Detroit, Nov. 2, 1939; B.S., Eastern Mich. U., 1964; LL.D., Detroit Coll. Law, 1964. Admitted to Mich. bar, 1965, Calif. bar, 1973; atty. legal dept. Mfrs. Nat. Bank of Detroit, 1965-69; individual practice law, Detroit, 1969-72 Los Angeles, 1975—; dep. city atty. criminal div. City of Los Angeles, 1973-75. Office: 1221 Ocean Ave Santa Monica CA 90401 Tel (213) 393-1800

SCHUCHINSKI, LUIS, b. Havana, Cuba, Jan. 29, 1937; LL.B., Yale, 1964. Admitted to N.Y. bar, 1966, N.J. bar, 1972; asso. firm Cleary, Gottlieb, Steen & Hamilton, N.Y.C., 1964-68; acting prof. law U. Calif. at Los Angeles, 1969-70; corp. counsel CPC Internat., Englewood Cliffs, N.J., 1971—; mem. tax com. U.S. C. of C., 1974—. Mem. Assn. Bar City of N.Y., N.Y. County, Am., N.J. State, Interam. bar assns. Office: Internat Plaza Englewood Cliffs NJ 07632 Tel (201) 894-2815

SCHUCK, CARL JOSEPH, b. Phila., Nov. 21, 1915; B.S., St. Mary's Coll., Calif., 1937; postgrad. U. So. Calif., 1937-38; J.D., Georgetown U., 1941. Admitted to D.C. bar, 1940, Calif. bar, 1943, U.S. Supreme Ct. bar, 1952; atty. Dept. Justice, Washington, 1940-42, atty., alien property custodian, 1942-44; asso. firm Overton, Lyman & Prince, and predecessor, Los Angeles, 1944-47, partner, 1947—; lectr. class actions Practising Law Inst., 1973. Fellow Am. Coll. Trial Lawyers; mem. Los Angeles County (trustee 1974-76), Am. bar assns., State Bar Calif. (disciplinary bd. 1970-71), 9th Circuit Jud. Conf. (lawyer del. 1963—, chmn. lawyer-del. com. 1972, chmn. exec. com. 1977-78), Chancery Club. Contbr. articles to legal publs. Home: 62 Cottonwood Circle Rolling Hills Estates CA 90274 Office: 550 S Flower St 6th Floor Los Angeles CA 90071 Tel (213) 683-5333

SCHUDER, RAYMOND FRANCIS, b. Wickford, R.I., Dec. 27, 1926; A.B., Emory U., 1949, J.D., 1951. Admitted to Ga. bar, 1951; adminstrv. asst. tax div. trust dept. Trust Co. of Ga., Atlanta, 1951-54; asso. firm Wheeler, Robinson & Thurmond, Gainesville, Ga., 1954-59; individual practice law, Gainesville, 1959-70; partner firm Schuder & Brown, Gainesville, 1970-76, Schuder & Hartness, Gainesville, 1976—; judge Gainesville Municipal Ct., 1956-60, 72-74. Dist. supr. Upper Chattahoochee River Soil and Water Conservation Dist. Ga., 1971-74. Mem. State Bar Ga. (gov. 1966-70, chmn. com. publs. 1976—), Gainesville-Northeastern Bar Assn. (pres. 1969-70), Gainesville Estate Planning Council, Am. Judicature Soc., Phi Alpha Delta. Office: 500 Spring St Gainesville GA 30501 Tel (404) 532-0195

SCHUELLER, THOMAS GEORGE, b. Budapest, Hungary, Oct. 4, 1936; A.B., Amherst Coll., 1958; LL.B., Harvard, 1962. Admitted to N.Y. bar, 1962; asso. firm Hughes, Hubbard & Reed, N.Y.C., 1962-69, partner, 1969—. Mem. Am. Bar Assn., Assn. Bar City N.Y. Office: Hughes Hubbard & Reed One Wall St New York City NY 10005 Tel (212) 943-6500

SCHUENKE, DONALD J., b. Milw., 1929; A.B., Marquette U., 1950, law degree, 1958. Now sr. v.p. for investments, gen. counsel, sec. Northwestern Mut. Life Ins. Co., Milw. Mem. Am., Wis., Milw. bar assns., Am. Life Ins. Assn., Assn. Life Ins. Counsels, Northwestern Mut. Life Mortgage and Realty Investors (pres., trustee). Home: 7733 W Wisconsin Ave Wauwatosa WI 53213 Office: 720 E Wisconsin Ave Milwaukee WI 53202*

SCHUETTE, CHARLES ALFRED, b. Columbus, Ind., Feb. 24, 1942; B.B.A., U. Okla., 1964, J.D., 1967. Admitted to Okla. bar, 1967, Fla. bar, 1970; exec. v.p., corporate counsel Am. Devco, Inc., Miami, Fla., 1973—; v.p., corporate counsel Grand Bahama Devel. Co. Ltd., Grand Bahama Island, 1974—; partner firm Helliwell, Melrose & DeWolf, Miami. Mem. Okla., Fla., Dade County bar assns. Home: 2901 S Bayshore Dr 13-A Coconut Grove FL 33133 Office: 1401 Brickell Ave Miami FL 33131 Tel (305) 373-7571

SCHUETTE, MICHAEL, b. Manitowoc, Wis., Apr. 19, 1937; B.S., Northwestern U., 1959, J.D., 1962. Admitted to Ill. bar, 1962; asso. firm Lord, Bissell & Brook, Chgo., 1962-70, partner, 1971—. Mem. Am., Chgo. bar assns. Office: 115 S La Salle St Chicago IL 60603 Tel (312) 443-0239

SCHULBERG, JUNE SCHILIT, b. Pitts., June 16, 1929; B.A. in Polit. Sci., U. Pitts., 1965; J.D., Duquesne U., 1969. Admitted to Pa. bar, 1970, U.S. Supreme Ct. bar, 1973; atty. NLRB, 1969; asso. firms Sikov & Love, 1970-72, Berger, Kapetan & Malakoff, 1973-75; chief dep. Allegheny County (Pa.) Coroner's Office, 1970-73; individual practice law, Pitts., 1976—. Active Western Pa. Met. chpt. Anti-Defamation League. Mem. Allegheny County, Pa., Am. bar assns., Am., Pa. trial lawyers assns., Am. Arbitration Assn., Lawyers Club Allegheny County. Home: 506 Beaver Rd Edgeworth PA 15143 Office: 508 Law and Finance Bldg Pittsburgh PA 15219 Tel (412) 281-4200

SCHULDT, NICHOLAS JOHN, III, b. Jersey City, July 31, 1944; B.A., Rutgers U., 1965, J.D., 1968. Admitted to N.J. bar, 1968, D.C. bar, 1969; staff atty. Union County (N.J.) Legal Services Corp., Elizabeth, 1970-71; atty. firm Sol Rosenberg, Paterson, N.J., 1971-72, Robert S. Feder, Union City, N.J., 1972-74; asso. Julius D. Canter, Jersey City, 1974; individual practice law, Union City, 1974—; instr. landlord-tenant law Inst. Continuing Legal Edn., 1975, 76. Mem. North Hudson Lawyers Club, Am., N.J., Hudson County, Bergen County, Passaic County bar assns. Home: 105 Grand St Garfield NJ 07026 Office: 400 38th St Union City NJ 07087 Tel (201) 865-7188

SCHULHOFER, STEPHEN JOSEPH, b. N.Y.C., Aug. 20, 1942; A.B., Princeton, 1964; LL.B., Harvard, 1967. Admitted to D.C. bar, 1968, U.S. Supreme Ct. bar, 1973; law clk. to Justice Hugo L. Black, U.S. Supreme Ct., 1967-69; asso. firm Coudert Freres, Paris, 1969-72; asst. prof. law U. Pa., Phila., 1972—; alt. U.S. mem. Ct. of Arbitration, Internat. C. of C., Paris, 1971-72; reporter Speedy Trial Planning Group, U.S. Dist. Ct., Wilmington, Del., 1975—. Bd. dirs. Pa. Law and Justice Inst., Phila., 1972-74; mem. Criminal Justice Task Force, Phila. Urban Coalition, 1973—; mem. police com. Phila. Regional Planning Council, 1975—. Contbr. articles in field to profl. jours. Office: 3400 Chestnut St Philadelphia PA 19174 Tel (215) 243-6075

SCHULMAN, ALVIN HAROLD, b. N.Y.C., Aug. 26, 1930; A.B., N.Y. U., 1951; LL.B., Yale, 1954. Admitted to N.Y. State bar, 1956; asso. firm Botein, Hays, Sklar & Herzberg, N.Y.C., 1959-63, partner firm, 1964; exec. v.p., gen. counsel Marvin Josephson Assos., Inc., N.Y.C., 1974-75, pres., 1975—. Mem. Assn. Bar City of N.Y. (chmn. com. on profl., judicial ethics 1973-76, grievance com. 1976—). Home: 2 Beekman Pl New York City NY 10022 Office: 40 W 57th St New York City NY 10019 Tel (212) 556-5614

SCHULMAN, JACK MITCHEL, b. Cleve., June 21, 1942; B.A., Dartmouth Coll., 1964; LL.B., Harvard U., 1967. Admitted to Ohio bar, 1964, Calif. bar, 1975, Fla. bar, 1975; law clk. to U.S. Dist. Ct., No. Dist. Ohio, 1967-69; partner firm Schulman and Schulman, Cleve., 1969—. Mem. Am., Ohio State (chmn. com. fed. cts. and practice 1971-74), Fed., Cleve., Cuyahoga County (Ohio) bar assns., Fla. State, Calif. State bars. Recipient award for outstanding contbns. to adminstrn. of justice Ohio Municipal Judges Assn., 1974. Home: 27060 Cedar Rd Beachwood OH 44122 Office: 748 Standard Bldg Cleveland OH 44113 Tel (216) 621-0580

SCHULMAN, ROBERT EMERY, b. Chgo., Jan. 31, 1937; B.A., Northwestern U., 1958; M.A., U. Ill., 1960, Ph.D., 1962; J.D., U. Kans., 1967. Admitted to Kans. bar, 1967; dir. div. forensic psychiatry Menninger Found., Topeka, 1971—; prof. law U. Kan., 1972—; cons. children's rehab. unit U. Kans. Med. Center Child Abuse Project, 1974—, Med. Center for Fed. Prisoners, Springfield, Mo., 1974—. Sec.-treas. Kans. State Bd. Examiners Psychologists, 1976. Fellow Am. Psychol. Assn.; mem. Am., Kans. bar assns. Home: 1900 Briarwood Dr Topeka KS 66611 Office: PO Box 829 Topeka KS 66601 Tel (913) 234-9566

SCHULTE, DIANE GAIL, b. Balt., Nov. 20, 1945; B.B.A., George Washington U., 1967; J.D., U. Md., 1970; Admitted to Md. bar, 1970, U.S. Supreme Ct. bar, 1975; law clk. to judge U.S. Dist. Ct. for Md., Balt., 1970-71; asst. states atty. City of Balt., 1971-73; asst. solicitor Howard County (Md.), 1973-75; chief counsel Md. State Constl. and Pub. Law Com., Annapolis, 1975-76; individual practice law, Ellicott City, Md., 1976—. Bd. dirs. Howard County Council on Alcoholism, YMCA, United Fund., Rape Crisis Center. Mem. Md., Howard County bar assns. Office: 3685 Park Ave Ellicott City MD 21043 Tel (301) 465-8910

SCHULTE, JOHN HENRY, b. St. Petersburg, Fla., June 10, 1938; A.B., Spring Hill Coll., 1960; J.D., U. Fla., 1966. Admitted to Fla. bar, 1967, since practiced in Miami; partner firm Smathers & Thompson, 1972—. Mem. Fla. Gov.'s Council Internat. Devel., 1975; bd. dirs. Marine Council Greater Miami, 1969-76, sr. v.p., 1972-74. Mem. Am., Fla. (chmn. internat. law com. 1973-75), Inter-Am. bar assns., Internat. Law Soc., Maritime Law Assn. U.S., Ilustre Colegio de Abogados Le Lima, Peru (hon.). Home: 500 Miller Rd Coral Gables FL 33146 Office: 1301 Alfred I DuPont Bldg Miami FL 33131 Tel (305) 379-6523

SCHULTZ, EDWARD FRANCIS, b. Livingston, Mont., Mar. 28, 1946; B.S., U. Oreg., 1968; J.D., 1972. Admitted to Oreg. bar, 1972; dep. dist. atty. Lincoln County (Oreg.), 1972-73, chief dep. atty., 1973-75; dist. atty. Jefferson County (Oreg.), Madras, 1975—; instr. criminal law Linn-Benton Community Coll., 1973-74. Mem. Am., Oreg. State, Lincoln County (sec.-treas. 1974) bar assns., Central Oreg., Lincoln County (law day chmn. 1973) bars, Nat., Oreg. dist. attys. assns. Home: Route 1 Box 629M Madras OR 97741 Office: Jefferson County Courthouse Madras OR 97741 Tel (503) 475-2286

SCHULTZ, GENE PAUL, b. Elgin, Ill., Sept. 4, 1943; B.A. with honors, Northwestern U., 1965; LL.B. cum laude, Columbia, 1968. Admitted to Ill. bar, 1968, Mo. bar, 1971; asst. dist. legal officer 2d U.S. Coast Guard Dist., St. Louis, 1968-71; asst. prof. St. Louis U., 1971-74, asso. prof. law, 1974—; reporter Commn. to Draft a Modern Criminal Code, 1971-74, sec., 1974; project dir. Mo. Law Enforcement Assistance Council, 1972; cons. St. Louis Circuit Ct., 1973-74. Mem. Am., Ill., Mo., St. Louis bar assns., ACLU (dir., pres.-elect Eastern Mo. 1976-77). Contbr. articles to law jours. Home: 4392 Maryland St Louis MO 63108 Office: 3700 Lindell St Louis MO 63108 Tel (314) 535-3300

SCHULTZ, JAMES A., b. Wabasha, Minn., Feb. 24, 1943; B.A. in English, Winona State U., 1965; J.D., U. Minn., 1968. Admitted to Minn. bar, 1968, U.S. Dist. Ct. bar, 1970; with firm Flynn & Schultz, Houston, Minn., asso., 1968-70, partner, 1970-71, owner, prin., 1971—. Mem. Houston Fire Dept., Houston Vol. Ambulance Service; charter mem. Houston Devel. Corp. Mem. Am., Minn., Houston County (pres. 1976—) bar assns., Minn. Trial Lawyers Assn. (dir., chmn. criminal law sect., continuing legal edn. com.). Apptd. to Gov.'s Advisory Com. on Securities State of Minn. Home: Route 2 Houston MN 55943 Office: 111 E Cedar St Houston MN 55943 Tel (507) 896-3156

SCHULTZ, JOHN GRAHAM, b. Seward, Alaska, Nov. 19, 1938; B.A., Gonzaga U., 1962, J.D., 1963. Admitted to Wash. bar, 1963; law clk. to Robert T. Hunter, Wash. State Supreme Ct., 1963-64; asso. firm Leavy, Taber, Schultz, Bergdahl & Sweeney, Pasco, Wash., 1964—. Pres., Pasco C. of C., 1975-76. Mem. Am., Wash. State, Pasco bar assns. Home: 4321 W Irving St Pasco WA 99301 Office: 117 S 3d St Pasco WA 99301 Tel (509) 545-1434

SCHULZ, FRED EDWARD, b. Chgo., May 9, 1943; B.S. in Indsl. Mgmt. wtih distinction, Purdue U., 1965; J.D., Northwestern U., 1968. Admitted to Ill. bar, 1970, Fed. bar, 1970, U.S. Supreme Ct. bar, 1973; U.S. Peace Corps legal adviser to Congress Micronesia and to Palau Dist. Legislature, 1968-69; asso. firm Norman & Billick, Chgo., 1970-71; asso. firm Wildman, Harrold, Allen & Dixon, Chgo., 1971-76, partner, 1977—. Mem. Am., Ill., Chgo. bar assns. Home: 408 Winnetka Ave Winnetka IL 60093 Office: One IBM Plaza Chicago IL 60611 Tel (312) 222-0400

SCHULZ, KEITH DONALD, b. Burlington, Iowa, Dec. 20, 1938; B.A., U. Iowa, 1960, J.D. cum laude, 1963. Admitted to Iowa bar, 1963, Ill. bar, 1966; asso. firm Hirsch, Riepe & Wright, Burlington, 1963-64; dep. Sec. State of Iowa, 1965-66; atty. AT&T, Chgo., 1966-67; atty. Borg-Warner Corp., Chgo., 1967-72, asst. gen. counsel, 1974—; gen. counsel Borg-Warner Acceptance Corp., 1972-74; clinic chmn., v.p., dir., chmn. fin. com. Chgo. Vol. Legal Services Found. Mem. Iowa, Am., Ill., Chgo. (mem. securities law com., anti-trust law com., com. on corp. law) bar assns. Author: Guide to Filing under Article 9 of the Uniform Commercial Code, 1966; contbr. articles to profl. jours. Home: 2727 Lincoln St Evanston IL 60201 Office: 200 S Michigan Ave Chicago IL 60604 Tel (312) 663-2027

SCHULZ, ROYCE HENRY, b. Bismarck, N.D., Apr. 25, 1937; A.B., U. Calif., Berkeley, 1959, LL.B., 1962. Admitted to Calif. bar, 1963; dep. atty. gen. Calif. Dept. Justice, 1962-66; mem. firm Broad, Khourie & Schulz, San Francisco, 1966—. Mem. Am., San Francisco bar assns., State Bar Calif. Contbr. article to law jour. Home: 6212 Estates Dr Oakland CA 94611 Office: 1 California St San Francisco CA 94111 Tel (415) 986-0300

SCHUMACHER, JON LEE, b. Rochester, N.Y., Feb. 28, 1937; A.B., Princeton, 1959, J.D., U. Va., 1964. Admitted to N.Y. bar, 1964; asso. firm Nixon, Hargrave, Devans & Doyle, Rochester, 1964-72, partner, 1972—. Mem. Am., N.Y. State, Monroe County bar assns. Office: Lincoln First Tower Rochester NY 14603 Tel (716) 546-8000

SCHUMACHER, ROBERT KENT, b. Omaha, Nov. 29, 1924; B.S. in Elec. Engring., Mass. Inst. Tech., 1947; J.D., Harvard, 1950. Admitted to Okla. bar, 1952, Ill. bar, 1961; sec., patent atty., mgr. legal and patents Well Surveys, Inc., Tulsa, Okla., 1950-61; asso. firm Fitch, Even, Tabin & Luedeka, Chgo., 1961-63, partner, 1963—. Mem. Chgo., Am. bar assns., Am. Patent Law Assn., Patent Law Assn. Chgo., Sigma Xi. Home: 911 Euclid Ave Winnetka IL 60093 Office: 135 S LaSalle St Room 900 Chicago IL 60603 Tel (312) FR 2-7842

SCHUMAN, SHELDON PAUL, b. Washington, July 22, 1940; A.B., George Washington U., 1962; J.D., U. Md., 1965. Admitted to Md. bar, 1965, D.C. bar, 1966; asso. firm Keepenick, Patterson & Schuman, Bethesda, Md., 1966-69, 1970-75; asso. firm Schuman & Kane, Chartered, Bethesda, 1975—. Mem. Montgomery County (Md.) Bd. Appeals, 1973—; chmn. Montgomery County Sign Review Bd., 1968-73, Advisory Correction Com., 1967. Mem. Am., Md., Montgomery County, D.C. bar assns. Home: 8201 Lakenheath Way Potomac MD 20854 Office: 4804 Moorland Ln Bethesda MD 20014 Tel (301) 986-0200

SCHUR, GERALD SAUL, b. Chgo., Apr. 14, 1935; B.S. in Chem. Engring., Purdue U., 1957; LL.B., John Marshall Law Sch., 1963; M.P.L., Lawyers Inst., John Marshall Law Sch., 1968, J.D., 1970. Admitted to Ill. bar, 1963; patent atty. Velsicol Chem. Corp., Chgo., 1963-67; div. patent counsel SCM Corp., Skokie, Ill., 1967-71; asso. firm Arnstein, Gluck, Weitzenfeld & Minow, Chgo., 1971-75, partner, 1975—. Mem. Ill. State Bar Assn., Patent Law Assn. Chgo., Decalogue Soc. Lawyers. Office: 75th Floor Sears Tower 233 S Wacker Dr Chicago IL 60606 Tel (312) 876-7100

SCHUR, JEROME, b. Milw., May 20, 1927; B.A., U. Wis., 1948; J.D., Yale, 1951. Admitted to Wis. bar, 1951, U.S. Supreme Ct. bar, 1975; with firm Katz & Friedman, Chgo., 1951—, partner, 1961—; spl. asst. to chief judge Circuit Ct. Cook County (Ill.), 1967-68; gen. counsel Ill. Com. Fair Credit Practices, 1956-60; lectr., instr. in field. Chmn. credit legis. com. Chgo. Mayor's Com. on New Residents, 1960-67. Mem. Ill. (past chmn. workmen's compensation sect., co-editor workmen's compensation newsletter 1972—), Chgo. (past chmn. com. on indsl. commn., mem. com. labor law) bar assns., Am. Trial Lawyers Assn. (past chmn. workmen's compensation sect.), Chgo. Council Lawyers, Phi Beta Kappa. Home: 2416 Meadow Dr S Wilmette IL 60091 Office: 7 S Dearborn St Chicago IL 60603 Tel (312) 263-6330

SCHUSSLER, EDWARD GEORGE, III, b. Chgo., Oct. 12, 1943; B.A., De Pauw U., 1965; J.D., U. Ill., 1968. Admitted to Ill. bar, 1971; asst. state's atty. Champaign County (Ill.), 1968; asso. firm Gierach & Dunn., Oak Lawn, Ill., 1972-73; partner firm Gierach, Stambulis & Schussler, Oak Lawn, 1974—. Deacon, treas. All Saints Luth. Ch., Orland Park, Ill., 1973—; dir., legal counsel Orland Park C.H.I.L.D., 1976. Mem. Ill. State, Chgo. bar assns. Home: 14455 S Ridge St Orland Park IL 60462 Office: 9500 S 50th Ct Oak Lawn IL 60453 Tel (312) 424-1600

SCHUSTER, ARNOLD PAUL, b. N.Y.C., Aug. 4, 1940; A.B., Cornell U., 1962; J.D. cum laude, Columbia, 1965. Admitted to N.Y. State bar, 1965, Md. bar, 1970; asso. firm Lord, Day & Lord, N.Y.C., 1968-70; asso. firm Venable, Baetjer & Howard, Balt., 1970-75, partner firm, 1976—; counsel Commerce and Industry Combined Health Appeal, 1974—; mem. Gov.'s Commn. on Evaluation and Co-ordination of Aggressive Offender Treatment, 1976—. Pres. Mental Health Assn. Met. Balt., 1972-74. Mem. Am., N.Y. State, Md. State, Balt. City (com. profl. ethics 1975—) bar assns. Home: 5604 S Bend Rd Baltimore MD 21209 Office: 1800 Mecantile Bank and Trust Bldg 2 Hopkins Plaza Baltimore MD 21201 Tel (301) 752-6780

SCHUUR, ROBERT GEORGE, b. Kalamazoo, Dec. 5, 1931; A.B., U. Mich., 1953; LL.B., 1955. Admitted to Mich. bar. 1955, N.Y. bar, 1956; mem. firm Reid & Priest, N.Y.C., 1955-65, partner, 1965—. Mem. N.Y. State N.Y.C. bar assns. Home: 354 W 30th St New York City NY 10001 Office: 40 Wall St New York City NY 10005 Tel (212) 344-2233

SCHUYLER, DANIEL MERRICK, b. Oconomowoc, Wis., July 26, 1912; A.B. summa cum laude, Dartmouth, 1934; J.D., Northwestern U., 1937. Admitted to Ill. bar, 1937, U.S. Supreme Ct. bar, 1942, Wis. bar, 1943; tchr. constl. history Chgo. Latin Sch., 1935-37; asso. firm Schuyler & Hennessy, 1937-42, partner, 1946-48; treas., sec., controller B-W Superchargers, Inc., Milw., 1942-46; partner firm Schuyler, Richert & Stough, Chgo., 1948-58, Schuyler, Stough & Morris, Chgo., 1958-76, Schuyler, Ballard & Cowen, Chgo., 1976—; lectr. Sch. Law Northwestern U., 1946-50, asso. prof., 1950-52, prof., 1952—. Republican nominee judge Cook County Circuit Ct., 1958. Bd. dirs. United Cerebral Palsy Greater Chgo.; bd. mgrs. Mary Bartelme Home for Girls. Fellow Am. Bar Found.; Am. Coll. Probate Counsel (past pres.); mem. Chgo., Ill., Wis. bar assns., Am. Judicature Soc., Order of Coif, Phi Beta Kappa. Author: (with Homer F. Carey) Illinois Law of Future Interests, revised edition 1953; (with William M. McGovern, Jr.) Illinois Trust and Will Manual, 1970; contbr. articles to profl. jours. Home: 324 Cumnor Rd Kenilworth IL 60043 Office: 100 W Monroe St Chicago IL 60603 Tel (312) 726-8565

SCHUYLER, WILLIAM EARL, JR., b. Washington, Feb. 3, 1914; B.E.E., Cath. U. Am., 1935; J.D., Georgetown U., 1940. Admitted to D.C. bar, 1940; patent lawyer RCA, 1941-42, Sperry Gyroscope Co., 1942-44; individual practice law, Washington, 1944-51; partner firm Browne, Schuyler & Beveridge, Washingtdn, 1951-69; commr. patents U.S., Washington, 1969-71; partner firm Schuyler, Birch, Swindler, McKie & Beckett, Washington, 1971—; lectr. Practising Law Inst., N.Y.C., 1961—, also engrs. clubs, patent law assns.; spl. atty. Dept. Justice, 1955-56; prof. law Georgetown U., 1963-73; co-chmn. U.S. del. Diplomatic Conf. on Patent Cooperation Treaty, 1970; mem. U.S. del. Vienna Diplomatic Conf. on Trademark Registration Treaty, 1973. Mem. Am. (ho. dels. 1968—, sect. chmn. 1962-63), Fed., Inter-Am., D.C. bar assns., Internat. Assn. Protection Indsl. Property (internat. exec. com. 1972—), Patent and Trademark Inst. Can., IEEE, Am. Patent Law Assn., Aircraft Owners and Pilots Assn., Intellectual Property Owners (chmn. bd. 1973—), Nat. Lawyers Club. Recipient Outstanding Achievement award Cath. U. Alumni, 1970; editorial bd. Trademark Rep., 1958-61. Home: 5110 Westpath Way Sumner MD 20016 Office: 1000 Connecticut Ave NW Washington DC 20036 Tel (202) 296-5500

SCHWAB, ELMO, b. Gonzales, Tex., Jan. 17, 1937; B.A., U. Tex., 1959, LL.B., 1962. Admitted to Tex. bar, 1962, U.S. Supreme Ct. bar, 1968; mem. firm Barker, Lain, Smith & Schwab, Galveston & Hitchcock, Tex., 1968—; adj. instr. U. Tex. Med. Br. Mem. Galveston Cultural Arts Council. Mem. Am., Galveston County bar assns., State Bar Tex., Am. Judicature Soc., Am. Trial Lawyers Assn. Home: 2618 Gerol Ct Harve LaFitte Galveston TX 77550 Office: 500 First Hutchings-Sealy Bank Galveston TX 77550 Tel (713) 723-2349

SCHWABER, SANFORD SHERIDAN, b. Reading, Pa., Nov. 19, 1926; B.S. in Economics, U. Pa., 1949, J.D., 1952. Admitted to Pa. bar, 1953, Ohio bar, 1963; individual practice law, Reading, Pa., 1953-62; chief house counsel Albee Homes Inc., Niles, Ohio, 1962-73; partner firm Hanni, Tumbri & Schwaber, Youngstown, Ohio, 1973—; asst. atty. gen. State of Pa., 1955-60. Pres. B'nai B'rith, Reading, 1957-59. Mem. Ohio, Mahoning County bar assns. Recipient Outstanding Student award U. Pa., 1952. Home: 5685 Engleton Ln Girard OH 44420 Office: 219 W Boardman St Youngstown OH 44420 Tel (216) 746-6301

SCHWAM, ANDREW MARTIN, b. Detroit, May 7, 1945; B.S., McGill U., 1967; J.D., Columbia, 1970; grad. Nat. Coll. State Judiciary, 1975. Admitted to N.Y. bar, 1970, Idaho bar, 1973; asst. dist. atty. Bronx County (N.Y.), 1970-73; judge magistrates div. 2d Dist. Idaho Dist. Ct., 1974—. Home: PO Box 242 Grangeville ID 83530 Office: Idaho County Courthouse Grangeville ID 83530 Tel (208) 983-2390

SCHWANKE, K(ERMIT) DALE, b. Missoula, Mont., Mar. 29, 1943; B.S. in Bus. Adminstrn., U. Mont., 1965, J.D., 1968. Admitted to Mont. bar, 1968, U.S. Dist. Ct. bar for Dist. Mont., 1968; asso. firm Jardine, Stephenson, Blewett & Weaver, Great Falls, Mont., 1970—. Bd. dirs. Mont. Diabetes Assn., 1971—, treas., 1972-73, pres., 1973-74; bd. dirs. Great Falls Children's Receiving Home, 1973-77, v.p., 1974-75, pres., 1975-76; active lawyers' div. United Way of Cascade County (Mont.), 1975-77. Mem. Mont., Cascade County (treas. 1972), Am. bar assns., Mont. Soc. C.P.A.'s., U. Mont. Alumni Assn. (ho. of dels. 1975-77). C.P.A., Mont. Home: 4023 Ella Ave Great Falls MT 59405 Office: PO Box 2269 Great Falls MT 59403 Tel (406) 727-5000

SCHWARTZ, ALAN, b. N.Y.C., Mar. 17, 1940; B.S., Bates Coll., 1961; LL.B., Yale, 1964. Admitted to N.Y. bar, 1965; asso. firm Roseuman, Colin, Kaye, Petscher, Freund & Emil, N.Y.C., 1964-69; prof. law Ind. U., 1969—; vis. prof. U. So. Calif. Law Center, 1976-77. Mem. Assn. Am. Law Schs. (vice chmn. contracts and related comml. law sect.), Am. Bar Assn. (com. uniform comml. code.), Am. Banking Assn. Home: 1903 Chelsey Ct Bloomington IN 47401 Office: Ind U Law Sch Bloomington IN 47401 Tel (812) 337-3737

SCHWARTZ, ALAN EARL, b. Detroit, Dec. 21, 1925; B.A. with distinction, U. Mich., 1947; LL.B. magna cum laude, Harvard U., 1950. Admitted to Mich. bar, 1950; asso. firm Kelley, Drye, Warren, Clark, Carr & Ellis, N.Y.C., 1950-52; spl. asst. counsel N.Y. State Crime Commn., N.Y.C., 1951; sr. partner firm Honigman, Miller, Schwartz and Cohn, Detroit, 1952—; dir. Cunningham Drug Stores, Inc., SOS Consol. Inc., Howell Industries Inc., Handleman Co., Detroit Edison Co., Mich. Bell Telephone Co., Burroughs Corp., Pulte Home Corp., Detroitbank Corp., Detroit Bank & Trust Co., Tesoro Petroleum Corp. Bd. dirs. Detroit Renaissance, Inc., United Hosps. Detroit, Mich. Cancer Found., Jewish Welfare Fedn. Detroit. Office: 2290 First Nat Bldg Detroit MI 48226 Tel (313) 962-6700

SCHWARTZ, BERNARD, b. N.Y.C., Aug. 25, 1923; B.S.S., City Coll. N.Y., 1944, LL.B., N.Y. U., 1944; LL.M., Harvard, 1945; Ph.D., Cambridge U., 1947, LL.D., 1956; Doctorat d' Universite, Paris, 1963. Admitted to N.Y. bar, 1945; mem. faculty N.Y. U., 1947—, prof. law, 1954—, Webb prof. law, 1963—; chief counsel, staff dir. Spl. Subcom. Legis. Oversight, U.S. Ho. of Reps., 1957-58; bd. dirs. Center Adminstrv. Justice, 1973. Mem. Am. Bar Assn., Assn. Bar City N.Y. Guggenheim fellow, 1950-51. Author: Basic History of the U.S. Supreme Court, 1968; Legal Control of Government, 1972; Constitutional Law: A Textbook, 1972; The Law in America, 1974; Administrative Law, 1976. Home: 60 Sutton Pl S New York City NY 10022 Office: 40 Washington Sq S New York City NY 10012 Tel (212) 598-2559

SCHWARTZ, DAVID, b. Bklyn., Jan. 1, 1942; A.B., Harvard, 1963; J.D., Yale, 1966. Admitted to Conn. bar, 1966; asso. firm Shipman & Goodwin, Hartford, Conn., 1966-71, partner, 1971—; instr. Conn. Sch. Savs. Banking, 1967—; dir. Conn. Women's Ednl. and Legal Fund, 1975—; v.p. Legal Aid Soc. Hartford County, 1976—. Vice-chmn. Glastonbury (Conn.) Council for Human Rights, 1972-73; trustee no. Conn. chpt. Multiple Sclerosis Soc., 1972—; mem. Glastonbury Sewer Commn., 1973-75; bd. dirs. Combined Health Appeal for Bus. and Industry, Hartford, 1973—. Mem. Am., Conn. (ethics com.), Hartford County (ethics com.) bar assns. Home: 410 Three Mile Rd Glastonbury CT 06033 Office: 799 Main St Hartford CT 06103 Tel (203) 549-4770

SCHWARTZ, DENNIS LEE, b. St. Louis, Apr. 30, 1940; B.S., Millikin U., 1962; J.D., Washington U., St. Louis, 1965. Admitted to Ill. bar, 1966; since practiced in Carlinville, Ill., asso. firm Phelps & Russell, 1966-71; individual practice law, 1971-73; asso. judge 7th Circuit Ct., 1973—; asst. state's atty. Macoupin County, 1968-73. Past chmn. Macoupin County chpt. ARC. Mem. Ill. Judges Assn., Macoupin County Bar Assn. Home: 904 E 1st St N Carlinville IL 62626 Office: Macoupin County Court House Carlinville IL 62626 Tel (217) 854-3211

SCHWARTZ, EDWARD, b. Chgo., July 1, 1922; B.S., DePaul U., Chgo., 1942; M.S., Northwestern U., 1953, Ph.D. in Psychology, 1954; J.D., George Washington U., 1970. Admitted to Md. bar, 1971; research psychologist U. Calif., Los Angeles, 1954-56; counseling psychologist VA, Chgo., 56-59; supervising research psychologist VA Hosp., Hines, Ill., 1959-62; asst. chief grants mgmt. NIH, Bethesda, Md., 1962-67; chief policy and procedures Bur. Health Services, Arlington, Va., 1967-68; acting chief grants mgmt. Nat. Center Health Services Research, Hyattsville, Md., 1968-69, dir. research reports, 1969-70, health scientist adminstr., 1970-75, dir. med. malpractice info., 1975—. Mem. Rockville Sr. Citizens Commn., 1972-75. Mem. Am. Psychol. Assn., Md. Bar Assn., Md. Assn. C.P.A.'s. Office: Room 8-22 3700 East West Hwy Hyattsville MD 20782 Tel (301) 436-6938

SCHWARTZ, EDWARD ARTHUR, b. Boston, Sept. 27, 1937; A.B., Oberlin Coll., 1959; LL.B., Boston Coll., 1962; postgrad. Am. U., 1958-59, Northeastern U., 1970. Admitted to Conn. bar, 1962, Mass. bar, 1965; legal intern Office of Atty. Gen., Commonwealth of Mass.,

Boston, 1961; asso. firm Schatz & Schatz, Hartford, Conn., 1962-65, firm Cohn, Riemer & Pollack, Boston, 1965-67; gen. counsel, Digital Equipment Corp., Maynard, Mass., 1967—, sec., 1969—, v.p., 1976—. Mem. Mass., Boston bar assns. Editor Boston Coll. Indsl. and Comml. Law Rev., 1963-65, Ann. Survey of Mass. Law, 1963-65. Office: 146 Main St Maynard MA 01754 Tel (617) 897-5111

SCHWARTZ, EDWARD J., Judge, Municipal Ct. and Superior Ct., San Diego; judge U.S. Dist. Ct., So. Dist. Calif., now chief judge. Office: US District Court House San Diego CA 92101*

SCHWARTZ, GEORGE X., b. N.Y.C., Jan. 28, 1915; B.S., Temple U., 1936, LL.B., 1940. Admitted to Pa. bar, 1941; practiced in Phila., 1941—; sr. partner firm Blank, Rome, Klaus and Comisky, 1962-72; mem. Pa. Ho. of Reps., 1952-58, chmn. com. state govt. 1959-60; mem. Phila. City Council, 1960—, pres., 1972—. Mem. Phila. 34th Ward Democratic Exec. Com., Pa. Dem. Com., Dem. Nat. Com.; del. 1976 Dem. Nat. Conv.; pres. Hero Scholarship Fund of Phila.; bd. dirs. various civic instns.; mem. exec. com. Council Reform Synagogues of Greater Phila. Mem. Nat. League of Cities, Pa. Soc. of N.Y., Phila., Pa., Fed. bar assns., Temple Law Sch. Alumni Assn., Lawyers Club Phila., Crime Prevention Assn. Home: 7015 Greenhill Rd Philadelphia PA 19151 Office: 490 City Hall Philadelphia PA 19107

SCHWARTZ, HAROLD, b. Newark, July 5, 1928; B.A., N.Y. U., 1953; LL.B., Bklyn. Law Sch., 1956. Admitted to N.Y. State bar, 1957; individual practice law, Bklyn., 1957—; arbitrator Am. Arbitration Assn., 1960-76. Mem. Bklyn. Bar Assn. Office: 16 Court St Brooklyn NY 11241 Tel (212) 596-7374

SCHWARTZ, HERBERT FREDERICK, b. Bklyn., Aug. 23, 1935; B.S. in Elec. Engring., Mass. Inst. Tech., 1957; M.A. in Econs., U. Pa., 1964, LL.B. cum laude, 1964. Admitted to N.Y. State bar, 1964; asso. firm Fish & Neave, N.Y.C., 1964-72, sr. partner, 1972—; supr. mil. computer applications, cons. Philco Corp., Phila., 1959-62. Pres. Greenwich Woods North Assn., Greenwich, Conn., 1974—. Mem. Am. Bar Assn., Assn. Bar City N.Y. (trade regulation com.), Am., N.Y. (chmn. fgn. patents trademarks antitrust com.) patent law assns., IEEE, Order of Coif. Editor U. Pa. Law Rev., 1962-64; contbr. articles to legal jours. Home: Clover Pl Cos Cob CT 06807 Office: Fish & Neave 277 Park Ave New York City NY 10017 Tel (212) 826-1050

SCHWARTZ, HERMAN, b. Bklyn., Dec. 19, 1931; A.B., Harvard U., 1953, J.D., 1956. Law clk. to judge U.S. 2d Circuit Ct. Appeals, N.Y.C., 1956-57; admitted to N.Y. bar, 1957, D.C. bar, 1962; asso. firm Kaye, Scholer, Fierman, Hays & Handler, N.Y.C., 1957-59, Javits, Moore & Trubin, N.Y.C., 1960-61; asst. counsel Antitrust and Monopoly Subcom., U.S. Senate, 1961-63; prof. law State U. N.Y., Buffalo, 1963—; mem. N.Y. State Crime Control Planning Bd., 1975-76; chmn. N.Y. State Commn. Correction, 1975-76; chmn. N.Y. Gov's. Task Force Subcom. on Corrections, 1975—. Bd. dirs. Prisoners' Legal Services of N.Y., 1976—, vice chmn., 1977—. Mem. N.Y. State Bar Assn. (Criminal Justice award 1976), Soc. Am. Law Tchrs. (gov. 1975—). Recipient Medgar Evers award Buffalo chpt. NAACP, 1976; contbr. articles to law jours. and popular mags. Home: 731 Parker Blvd Kenmore NY 14223 Office: 525 O'Brian Hall State U NY at Buffalo Amherst NY 14260 Tel (716) 636-2091

SCHWARTZ, HILDA G., b. N.Y.C., Apr. 24, 1907; B.S., Washington Sq. Coll., N.Y. U.; LL.B., N.Y. U., 1929. Admitted to N.Y. bar, 1930; partner firm Schwartz & Schwartz, N.Y.C., 1938-46; head bur. estimate, sec. and trial commr. Bd. Estimate City of N.Y., 1946-51, city magistrate, 1951-58, treas., 1958-62, dir. fin., 1962-65; judge N.Y.C. Civil Ct., 1965-71; justice N.Y. Supreme Ct., 1st Jud. Dept., 1971—. Bd. dirs. Washington Sq. Outdoor Art Exhibit, N.Y.C., 1946-48; bd. mgrs. Greenwich House, N.Y.C., 1953-54. Mem. Am., N.Y. State bar assns., Assn. Bar City N.Y., N.Y. State Trial Lawyers Assn., New York County Lawyers Assn., N.Y. Women's Bar Assn. (pres. 1939-40, Distinguished Service award 1977), Assn. Supreme Ct. Justices City N.Y. (dir. 1976—). Recipient Alumni Achievement award Washington Sq. Coll., 1968, Honor awards State of Israel Bonds, 1960, Am. Jewish Congress, 1959, Women Lawyers of State of N.Y., 1951; Woman of Achievement award Fedn. Jewish Women's Orgns., 1959. Office: NY Supreme Ct 60 Centre St New York City NY 10007

SCHWARTZ, JAY, b. Racine, Wis., Feb. 25, 1934; B.S. in Indsl. and Labor Relations, Cornell U., 1955, J.D., U. Chgo., 1957. Admitted to Wis. bar, 1957, Ct. Mil. Appeals bar; served to 1st lt. JAGC, AUS, 1957-59; asst. atty. gen. State of Wis., 1959-62; asso. firm Joling & Schwartz, Kenosha, Wis., 1962-66; partner firm Schwartz & Schwarts, Racine, 1966-75; sr. partner firm Schwartz, Weber & Tofte, Racine, 1976—; mem. faculty criminal law Practising Law Inst., N.Y.C., 1970—; asst. prof. collective bargaining Carthage Coll., Kenosha, 1971-72. Mem. Am. Acad. Forensic Scis. (exec. com., past chmn. jurisprudence com.), Nat. Assn. Criminal Def. Lawyers, State Bar Wis. Contbr. articles Am. Acad. Forensic Scis. Jour. Home: 7103 3d Ave Kenosha WI 53140 Office: 704 Park Ave Racine WI 53403 Tel (414) 637-9655

SCHWARTZ, JOHN GORDON, b. Modesto, Calif., Aug. 17, 1943; B.A., Willamette U., 1965; J.D., U. Calif. at Berkeley, 1968. Admitted to Calif. bar, 1969, U.S. Supreme Ct. bar, 1974; legal research atty. Superior Ct. Calif., San Mateo County, 1969-70; mem. firm Nagle, Vale, McDowall & Cotter, San Mateo, Calif., 1970—. Mem., Am., Calif. bar assns., No. Calif. Assn. Def. Counsel. Office: 2070 Pioneer Ct San Mateo CA 94403 Tel (415) 341-8227

SCHWARTZ, JOHN ROBERT, b. Rochester, N.Y., July 9, 1944; B.S., B.A., John Carroll U., 1966; J.D., Albany Law Sch., 1969. Admitted to N.Y. bar, 1970; asso. firm Fix, Spindelman, Turk & Himelein & Schwartz, and predecessor, Rochester, 1970-73, partner, 1974—; counsel N.Y. State Senate, 1970-72; atty. Town of Ogden (N.Y.), 1972-74. Bd. dirs. Sch. Holy Childhood. Mem. Am., N.Y., Monroe County bar assns., Assn. Trial Lawyers Am., N.Y. State Trial Lawyers Assn. Home: 146 Nunda Blvd Rochester NY 14610 Office: 2 State St Rochester NY 14614

SCHWARTZ, LARRY JAY, b. Phila., May 4, 1942; B.S., Temple U., 1963, J.D., 1964; LL.M., N.Y. U., 1972. Admitted to Pa. bar, 1969; estate tax atty. IRS, Phila., 1969-70; mem. firm Pearlstine Salicin Hardiman & Robinson, Lansdale, Pa., 1972—. Mem. Am., Pa., Montgomery County, Phila. bar assns., Lansdale Jaycees. Contbr. article to Temple Law Quar. Office: 1000 N Broad St Lansdale PA 19446 Tel (215) 855-2155

SCHWARTZ, LEONARD JAY, b. San Antonio, Sept. 23, 1943; B.B.A., U. Tex., 1965, J.D., 1968. Admitted to Tex. bar, 1968, Ohio bar, 1971, U.S. Supreme Ct. bar, 1971; asso. firm Roberts & Holland, N.Y.C., 1968-70; partner firm Rigely, Schwartz & Fagan, San Antonio, 1970-71; staff counsel ACLU of Ohio, Columbus, 1971-73; partner firm Schwartz, Fisher Spater, McNamara & Marshall, Columbus, 1973-77, firm Schwartz & Fishman, Columbus, 1977—. Mem. Am., Columbus, Tex., Ohio bar assns., Am. Trial Lawyers Assn., Am. Judicature Soc., Phi Delta Phi. Home: 1428 Wakefield Ct E Columbus OH 43209 Office: 150 E Mound St PO Box 1936 Columbus OH 43216 Tel (614) 221-2600

SCHWARTZ, LESTER P., b. N.Y.C., June 28, 1919; B.S. in Accounting, N.Y. U., 1940; J.D., Bklyn. Law Sch., 1952. Tel (212) Admitted to N.Y. bar, Supreme Ct. 2d Dist., 1953, Supreme Ct. U.S. bar, 1963; individual practice law, Bklyn., 1953—. Mem. Bklyn. Bar Assn., N.J. Assn. C.P.A.'s. C.P.A., N.Y., N.J. Office: 26 Court St Brooklyn NY 11201 Tel (212) JA 2-4577

SCHWARTZ, LOIS SIEGEL, b. Bklyn., June 10, 1939; B.A., Barnard Coll., 1960; J.D., N.Y. U., 1963; postgrad. Columbia U. Grad. Sch. Polit. Sci., 1960-61. Admitted to N.Y. State bar, 1964, D.C. bar, 1966, U.S. Dist. Ct. for D.C. bar, 1966, U.S. Ct. Appeals bar for D.C. Circuit, 1966, U.S. Supreme Ct. bar, 1967; atty.-adv. Broadcast Bur. FCC, Washington, 1963-65; asso. firm Haley, Bader & Potts, Washington, 1965-70, partner, 1970-74; individual practice law, Washington, 1974—. Bd. dirs., sec. Temple Micah, 1972-74; sec. Layhill Citizens Assn., 1977—. Mem. Am., Fed. Communications (sec. 1976—), D.C. bar assns., Am. Women in Radio and TV. Home: 13007 Middlevale Ln Silver Spring MD 20906 Office: Suite 806 1225 19th St NW Washington DC 20036 Tel (202) 296-3022

SCHWARTZ, LOUIS, b. Passaic, N.J., July 21, 1912; student Dana Coll., 1929-31; LL.B., Rutgers U., 1934. Admitted to N.J. bar, 1935; individual practice law, Patterson, N.J.; judge Superior Ct. of N.J., 1976—; municipal atty. City of Totowa (N.J.), 1960-70. Mem. N.J., Passaic County bar assns. Home: 140 Hepburn Rd Clifton NJ 07012 Office: Courthouse Paterson NJ 07505 Tel (201) 525-3661

SCHWARTZ, LOUIS BROWN, b. Phila., Feb. 22, 1913; B.S. in Econs., U. Pa., 1932, J.D., 1935. Admitted to Pa. bar, 1935, U.S. Supreme Ct. bar, 1939; atty. SEC, Washington, 1935-39; chief gen. crimes and spl. projects sect. Dept. Justice, 1939-43, chief judgment and enforcement sect. antitrust div., 1945-46; also mem. inter-deptl. coms. on war crimes and status-of-forces treaties; prof. U. Pa. Law Sch., 1946—, Benjamin Franklin prof., 1964—; vis. prof. Columbia U., U. Calif., Salzburg (Austria) Seminar on Am. Studies, Cambridge (Eng.) U.; Ford vis. Am. prof. Inst. Advanced Legal Studies, U. London, 1974; mem. Atty. Gen.'s Nat. Commn. Study Antitrust Laws, 1954-55, Pa. Gov.'s Commn. Penal and Correctional Affairs, 1956-60; adv. commn. Revision Pa. Penal Code, 1963-68; mem. White House Lawyer's Com. Civil Rights Through Law, 1963—; nat. adv. council Nat. Defender Project, 1964-69; dir. Nat. Commn. Reform Fed. Criminal Laws, 1968-71; cons. State, Treasury, Justice depts. Mem. Am. Democratic Action (nat. bd.), Am. Law Inst. (adv. com. pre-arraignment code), Order of Coif. Author: Free Enterprise and Economic Organization, 1962; (with Herbert Wechsler) Model Penal Code of American Law Institute, 1962; Le Système Pénal des Etats-Unis, 1964, Law Enforcement Handbook for Police, 1970; Proposed Federal Criminal Code (with Comments and Working Papers), 1971 (with J. Flynn) Antitrust and Regulatory Alternatives, 1977. Home: 510 Woodland Terr Philadelphia PA 19104 Office: U Pa Law Sch 3400 Chestnut St Philadelphia PA 19104 Tel (215) 243-7498

SCHWARTZ, MICHAEL WILLIAM, b. N.Y.C., July 9, 1941; A.B., Harvard U., 1963, LL.B., 1967. Admitted to N.Y. bar, 1968; legis. asst. Office of Sen. Robert F. Kennedy, 1967-68; asso. firm Cleary, Gottlieb, Steen & Hamilton, N.Y.C., 1968-69; asso. prof. law N.Y. U., 1969-73; asso. firm Wachtell, Lipton, Rosen & Katz, N.Y.C., 1973—. Citizen mem. N.Y.C. Environ. Control Bd. Mem. Assn. Bar City N.Y. Office: 299 Park Ave New York City NY 10017 Tel (212) 371-9200

SCHWARTZ, MORTON LAWRENCE, b. Montreal, Que., Can., July 5, 1922 (parents Am. citizens); LL.B., Washington U., St. Louis, 1944, A.B., 1948, postgrad. in history, 1949-50, J.D., 1968. Admitted to Mo. bar, 1944, U.S. Dist. Ct. bar for Eastern Dist. Mo., 1944; rent atty. Office Price Adminstrn., St. Louis; individual practice law, Creve Coeur, Mo., 1945—. Republican candidate for U.S. Ho. of Reps., 1960, Mo. Ho. of Reps., 1966. Mem. Mo. Bar Assn. Contbr. book revs. in field to St. Louis Globe Democrat, 1960-65; editor: Missouri Creditors' Remedies, 1962, editor-in-chief, 2d rev. edit., 1967, contbr. 3d rev. edit., 1975. Home and office: 11154 Will Rogers St Creve Coeur MO 63141 Tel (314) 872-3250

SCHWARTZ, RICHARD ALAN, b. Bklyn., Dec. 8, 1943; B.S. in Advt., U. Fla., 1965; J.D., U. Miami, 1971. Admitted to Fla. bar, 1971; asso. firm Stanley Rosenblatt, Miami, Fla., 1971; partner firm Schwartz & Wayner, Miami, Fla., 1972-73; individual practice law, Miami, 1973-76; judge Dade County Ct., Miami, 1976—. Mem. Am., South Dade (founder, pres.) bar assns., Am. Arbitration Assn., South Dade C. of C. (dir. 1972-76, v.p. 1976). Office: 10700 Caribbean Blvd Suite 301 Miami FL 33189 Tel (305) 233-8822

SCHWARTZ, RONALD I., b. Detroit, Aug. 24, 1948; B.S., Mich. State U., 1970; J.D., Detroit Coll. Law, 1973. Admitted to Mich. bar, 1973; legal research asst. Detroit Coll. Law, 1971-73; closing officer Am. Title Ins. Co., 1970-73; partner firm Linden & Schwartz, Southfield, Mich., 1973-75; mem. firm Linden & Schwartz, Southfield, 1975—; active legal aid clinics RICCOD, Hearing Aid, Oakland County Legal Aid, Gateway Crisis Center. Mem. Macomb County, Oakland County, Detroit bar assns., ACLU, Am. Arbitration Assn., Soc. Profls. in Dispute Resolutions. Home: 26031 Salem St Huntington Woods MI 48070 Office: 30215 Southfield Rd 204 Southfield MI 48076 Tel (313) 646-0120

SCHWARTZ, ROY JOSEPH, b. N.Y.C., Apr. 11, 1932; B.A., N.Y. U., 1953, LL.B., 1956. Admitted to N.Y. State bar, 1956, Fla. bar, 1973, U.S. Supreme Ct. bar, 1968; asso. firm Fuchsberg & Fuchsberg, N.Y.C., 1956; individual practice law, N.Y.C., 1959—; arbitrator Compulsory Arbitration Program, Bronx County, N.Y.; indigent defendants adv. panel Appellate Div. 1st Dept.; legal advisor to registrants SSS, N.Y.C., 1965-76. Mem. Fla., N.Y. State, Bronx, Criminal Courts (Bronx County) bar assns. Home: 609 Kappock St Riverdale NY 10463 Office: 103 Park Ave New York City NY 10017 Tel (212) 687-2750

SCHWARTZ, S. DAVID, b. Ill., Nov., 1942; student Claremont Men's Coll., 1960-62; B.S., U. Calif., Santa Barbara, 1965; J.D., Hastings Coll. Law, San Francisco, 1968. Admitted to Calif. bar, 1969, U.S. Supreme Ct. bar, 1976; individual practice law, Santa Barbara. Mem. Calif., Santa Barbara County, Los Angeles County, Am., Fed. bar assns., Santa Barbara County Barristers, Los Angeles, Calif., Am. trial lawyers assns. Office: 3704 State St PO Box 30190 Santa Barbara CA 93105 Tel (805) 687-7585

SCHWARTZ, SHELDON, b. N.Y.C., Feb. 14, 1938; B.A., Hunter Coll., 1959; LL.B., N.Y. U., 1962, LL.M. in Taxation, 1963. Admitted to N.Y. State bar, 1963; asso. firm Fink, Weinberger & Levin, N.Y.C., 1963-70, firm Rosen and Reade, N.Y.C., 1970-74; individual practice law, N.Y.C., 1974—; adj. asso. prof. taxation N.Y. U., 1968—; lectr. in field. Mem. N.Y. State Bar Assn. (com. taxation), Assn. Bar City N.Y. (tax referral panel 1965—). Author: (with Daniel Berman) Tax Saving Opportunities in Real Estate Deals, 1971; contbg. editor Real Estate Review, 1971-76. Office: 295 Madison Ave New York City NY 10017 Tel (212) 889-6460

SCHWARTZ, STANLEY, JR., b. Columbus, Ohio, Apr. 8, 1921; B.A. cum laude, Ohio State U., 1942, J.D. summa cum laude, 1947. Admitted to Ohio bar, 1947; partner firm Schwartz & Schwartz, Columbus, 1947—; dir. Berkeley Bio-Engring., Inc., Hercules Trouser Co., Inc., Mediplex Inc., Am. Exec. Corp., Am. Exec. Life Ins. Co., Republic Franklin Inc.; dir., sec. Retail Mchts. Industries, Inc., ComTrac, Inc., RFI Realty Trust, Am. Realty Title Assurance Co., Republic Franklin Adv. Corp.; mem. Med. Malpractice Arbitration Panel; adj. prof. law Ohio State U. Trustee Columbus Symphony Orch., Columbus Jewish Fedn., Temple Israel Found.; mem. Devel. Com. for Greater Columbus. Mem. Columbus, Am., Ohio State bar assns., Columbus Area C. of C. (govtl. affairs com.), Order of Coif, Phi Beta Kappa. Home: 65 S Merkle Rd Columbus OH 43209 Office: 250 E Broad St Columbus OH 43215 Tel (614) 224-3168

SCHWARTZ, STEPHAN MICHAEL, b. N.Y.C., June 28, 1944; B.A., San Fernando Valley State Coll., 1966; J.D., Rutgers U., 1969. Admitted to N.J. bar, 1970; mem. Camden Regional Legal Services, Inc., Burlington, N.J., 1970—. Mem. Fed. Dist. Ct., Burlington County bar assns., ACLU. Office: 11 W Union St Burlington NJ 08016 Tel (609) 386-6660

SCHWARTZ, THEODORE ALAN, b. Phila., Apr. 25, 1945; B.A., Villanova U., 1966; J.D., Suffolk U., 1969. Admitted to Pa. bar, 1969; asso. firm Pearlstine & Salkin, Lansdale, Pa., 1969-70; asso. with Louis J. Perretti, 1970-72; asso. firm Caster & Muller, Phila., 1972-76; partner firm Mendel, Schwartz & Boer, Ltd., Phila., 1976—; instr. law Suffolk U. Law Sch., 1973—. Mem. Am., Pa., Phila. bar assns., Pa., Am. trial lawyers assn. Home: 20 Harvard Rd Norristown PA 19403 Office: 1620 Locust St Philadelphia PA 19103 Tel (215) 732-7200

SCHWARTZ, THEODORE FRANK, b. Clayton, Mo., Aug. 14, 1935; LL.B., Washington U., 1962, J.D., 1973. Admitted to Mo. bar, 1962, Calif. bar, 1974, D.C. bar, 1972, U.S. Supreme Ct. bar, 1966; partner firm Ackerman, Schiller, & Schwartz, Clayton, 1962-75; individual practice law, Clayton, 1975—. Mem. Assn. Trial Lawyers Am., Nat. Assn. Criminal Def. Lawyers, Am., Mo. bar assns., Am. Judicature Soc., Lawyers Assn. St. Louis. Home: 205 Riverbend Dr Chesterfield MO 63017 Office: 7701 Forsyth St Clayton MO 63105 Tel (314) 863-4654

SCHWARTZ, VICTOR ELLIOT, b. N.Y.C., July 3, 1940; A.B. summa cum laude, Boston U., 1962; J.D. magna cum laude, Columbia, 1965. Admitted to N.Y. bar, 1965, Ohio bar, 1974; law clk. to Hon. Charles M. Metzner, So. Dist. N.Y., 1965-67; asst. to asso. prof. law U. Cin., 1967-72, prof. law, 1972—, acting dean, 1973-74; vis. prof. U. Va. Law Sch., 1970-71; dir. Fed. Interagy. Task Force on Products Liability, 1976. Mem. Am. (chmn. faculty-liaison com. negligence, ins. and compensation sect., legal writing award 1971), Ohio bar assns., Am. Law Inst. Author: Comparative Negligence, 1974; (with Prosser and Wade) Cases and Materials on Torts, 1976. Office: U Cin Coll Law Cincinnati OH 45221 Tel (513) 475-2631

SCHWARTZ, VICTOR L., b. Phila., Mar. 23, 1939; B.A., St. John's Coll., Annapolis, Md., 1961; LL.B., Temple U., 1965. Admitted to N.Mex. bar, 1966, Pa. bar, 1967; atty. AEC, Albuquerque, 1965-67; asst. atty. gen. Commonwealth of Pa., Harrisburg, 1967-70; asst. U.S. atty. Eastern Dist. Pa., 1970-76; individual practice law, Phila., 1976—. Mem. Phila. Bar Assn., Phila. Trial Lawyers Assn., Nat. Assn. Def. Counsel, Lawyers Club. Recipient Spl. Commendation Dept. Justice. Home: 220 Locust St Philadelphia PA 19106 Office: 1521 Locust St Philadelphia PA 19102 735-2551

SCHWARTZBERG, HUGH JOEL, b. Chgo., Feb. 17, 1933; B.A. cum laude, Harvard, 1953; J.D., Yale, 1956. Admitted to Ill. bar, 1956, Conn. bar, 1957; asso. firm Ribicoff & Kotkin, Hartford, Conn., 1956-57, Lederer, Livingston, Kahn & Adsit, Chgo., 1957-62, Marks, Marks & Kaplan, Chgo., 1962-67, partner, 1967-70; partner firm Schwartzberg, Barnett & Cohen and predecessors, 1970—; lectr. Medill Grad. Sch. Journalism, Northwestern Univ., Evanston, Ill., 1976—. Acting chmn. community advisory bd. Chgo's. Joint Youth Devel. Com., 1964-67; sheriff's advisory bd. Cook County (Ill.), 1972—; chmn. U.S. Assembly Youth, Ann Arbor, Mich., 1953. Mem. Am., Ill., Chgo. (vice chmn. civil rights com.) bar assns., World Assn. Lawyers, Tau Epsilon Rho. Recipient Boylston prize, Harvard, 1953. Office: 11 S LaSalle St Chicago IL 60603 Tel (312) 726-3555

SCHWARTZMAN, HERMAN, b. Bklyn., Apr. 11, 1925; B.B.A., Coll. City N.Y., 1947; J.D., Bklyn. Law Sch., 1955. Admitted to N.Y. bar, 1955, U.S. Supreme Ct. bar, 1963; partner firm Weiss, Rosenthal, Heller, Schwartzman & Lazar, and predecessors, N.Y.C., 1956—. Trustee, Kingsbrook Jewish Med. Center, 1970—. Mem. Am., N.Y. State, N.Y.C. bar assns. Contbr. articles in field to legal jours. Office: 295 Madison Ave New York City NY 10017 Tel (212) 725-9200

SCHWARTZMAN, MARK LEE, b. Chgo., Aug. 17, 1928; B.S., U. ILL., 1950, J.D., 1952. Admitted to Ill. bar, 1952; served with JAG, USAF, 1952-54; mem. firm Wayne & Levine, Chgo., 1954-56, Rotenberg & Schwartzman, Chgo., 1956—. Mem. Am., Ill., Chgo. bar assns., Am. Trial Lawyers Assn., Phi Alpha Delta. Office: 7 S Dearborn St Room 820 Chicago IL 60603 Tel (312) RA 6-1678

SCHWARZ, RALPH J., JR., b. New Orleans, Aug. 27, 1923; B.A., Tulane U., 1941; LL.B., Columbia U., 1948. Admitted to N.Y. bar, 1949, U.S. Ct. Appeals bar for 2d Circuit, 1958, U.S. Supreme Ct. bar, 1969, 6th Circuit Ct. Appeals bar, 1973, D.C. Circuit Ct. bar, 1974, 5th Circuit Ct. bar, 1975. Mem. Assn. Bar of the City N.Y. Home: 1215 5th Ave New York City NY Office: 22 E 40th St New York City NY 10016

SCHWARZ, ROBERT JAY, b. Chgo., Feb. 22, 1931; B.S. in Chem. Engring., Ill. Inst. Tech., 1953; J.D., DePaul U., 1957; M.P.L., John Marshall Law Sch., 1962. Admitted to Ill. bar, 1957, U.S. Supreme Ct. bar, 1964; patent counsel, asst. sec. Velsicol Chem. Corp., Chgo., 1960—. Mem. Ill. State Bar Assn. (chmn. patent and trademark council), Am., Chgo. (chmn. com. taxation) patent law assns., Nat. Patent Council. Contbr. articles to Ill. State Bar Assn. Jour. Office: 341 E Ohio St Chicago IL 60611 Tel (312) 670-4543

SCHWARZBERG, HAROLD, b. N.Y.C., Jan. 4, 1905; B.A., Columbia, 1923, LL.B., 1925. Admitted to N.Y. State bar, 1926; partner firm Schwarzberg & Kittrell, N.Y.C., 1969—; lectr. Practising Law Inst., N.Y.C., 1934-61. Mem. N.Y. County Lawyers Assn. Author: (with Jule E. Stocker) Drawing Wills, 1946. Home: 1 Lincoln Plaza New York City NY 10023 Office: 217 Broadway New York City NY 10007 Tel (212) 233-4771

SCHWARZER, FRANKLIN JOHN, b. Syracuse, N.Y., Sept. 14, 1922; B.S., Williams Coll., 1945; LL.B., Syracuse U., 1951. Admitted to N.Y. State bar, 1952; partner firm Smith, Sovik, Kendrick, McAuliffe & Schwarzer, P.C., Syracuse, 1955—; village atty. Village of Cazenovia (N.Y.), 1961—. Mem. Madison County (N.Y.), Onondaga County (N.Y.), N.Y. State bar assns. Home: 66 Sullivan St Cazenovia NY 13035 Office: 200 Empire Bldg 472 S Salina St Syracuse NY 13202 Tel (315) 474-2911

SCHWARZWALDER, A(LAN) MICHAEL, b. San Diego, Oct. 30, 1943; B.A., Ohio State U., 1965, J.D., 1970. Admitted to Ohio bar, 1970; staff atty. Legal Aid Defender Soc. of Columbus (Ohio), 1970-72; partner firm Campbell, Schwarzwalder, Sanford and Baesman, and predecessor, Columbus, 1972—; mem. Ohio State Senate, 1976—. Pres. Univ. Community Assn., Columbus, 1974-76; pres. bd. dirs. North Central Community Mental Health and Retardation Services of Franklin County (Ohio), 1975-76. Mem. Columbus Bar Assn., Am. Judicature Soc. Recipient Silver Key award div. law students Am. Bar Assn., 1970. Home: 250 E 19th Ave Columbus OH 43201 Office: 40 W Gay St Columbus OH 43215 Tel (614) 224-6262

SCHWEBEL, STEPHEN MYRON, b. N.Y.C., Mar. 10, 1929; B.A. magna cum laude, Harvard, 1950; postgrad. (Frank Knox Meml. fellow) Trinity Coll., Cambridge (Eng.) U., 1950-51; LL.B., Yale, 1954. Admitted to N.Y. State bar, 1955, U.S. Supreme Ct. bar, 1965, D.C. bar, 1976; dir. UN hdqrs. office World Fedn. UN Assns., 1950-53; asso. firm White & Case, N.Y.C., 1954-59; asst. prof. law Harvard, 1959-61; asst. legal adviser for UN affairs State Dept., Washington, 1961-66, spl. asst. to asst. sec. state for internat. orgn. affairs State Dept., Washington, 1966-67, counselor on internat. law, 1973-74, dep. legal adviser, 1974—; exec. dir., exec. v.p. Am. Soc. Internat. Law, 1967-73; mem. Internat. Law Commn. of UN, 1977—; lectr. in Am. fgn. policy univs. in India for State Dept., 1952; vis. lectr. in internat. law Cambridge U., 1957; vis. prof. internat. law Australian Nat. U., 1969; prof. internat. law Johns Hopkins Sch. Advanced Internat. Studies, Washington, 1967, Edward B. Burling prof. internat. law and orgn., 1973—. Adv. bd. Center for Oceans Law and Policy, U. Va., 1975—. Mem. Washington Inst. Fgn. Affairs, Am. Law Inst., Internat. Law Assn. (Am. br. chmn. com. on charter UN exec. com. 1968-74), Am. Soc. Internat. Law (chmn. com. library 1961-62, mem. exec. council 1967—), Council Fgn. Relations, Am. Fgn. Service Assn., Inter-Am. Inst. Internat. Legal Studies (asso.), Phi Beta Kappa. Author: The Secretary-General of the United Nations, 1952; editor: The Effectiveness of International Decisions, 1971; editorial bd. Am. Jour. Internat. Law, 1967—; chmn. editorial adv. com. Internat. Legal Materials, 1967-73; mem. adv. bd. Law and Policy in Internat. Bus., 1968. Home: 1917 23d St NW Washington DC 20008 Office: Dept State Washington DC 20510

SCHWEINLE, WILLIAM EDWIN, JR., b. Houston, Feb. 8, 1942; B.S., U.S. Air Force Acad., 1963; J.D., U. Tex., 1971. Admitted to Tex. bar, 1971, U.S. Ct. Appeals fifth circuit, 1973, 10th circuit, 1975, D.C. circuit, 1973, U.S. Ct. Claims bar, 1975; with Gulf Oil Corp., Houston, 1971—, chief environ. atty., 1973—. Bd. dirs. Clear Lake City (Tex.) Civic League. Mem. Am., Houston bar assns. Office: PO Box 3725 Houston TX 77001 Tel (713) 226-3118

SCHWENN, ROBERT PAUL, b. Cullman, Ala., July 18, 1934; LL.B., U. Ala., 1960. Admitted to Ala. bar, 1960, U.S. Supreme Ct. bar, 1968; partner firm Schrader & Schwenn, and predecessor, Huntsville, Ala., 1962-64, 72-74; individual practice law, Huntsville, 1974—; asst. dist. atty. Madison County (Ala.), 1960-61; mem. Nat. Panel Consumer Arbitrators, 1976—. Alt. del. Democratic Nat. Conv., 1956; mem. exec. com. Madison County Dem. Party, 1964-68. Mem. Ala., Huntsville-Madison County bar assns. Home and Office: 5300 Whitesburg Dr SW Huntsville AL 35802 Tel (205) 881-8692

SCHWIEBERT, LLOYD ALVIN, b. Moline, Ill., June 6, 1913; A.B., Augustana Coll., 1934; J.D., State U. Iowa, 1937. Admitted to Ill. bar, 1937, Iowa bar, 1937; mem. firm Trevor & Schwiebert, Moline, 1937-47; mem. firm Kopp & Schwiebert, Moline, 1955-59; individual practice law, Moline, 1959-76; mem. firm Schwiebert & Schwiebert, Moline, 1977—; mem. inquiry panel registration and disciplinary commn. Ill. Supreme Ct., 1973-77, mem. hearing bd., 1977—. Mem. Moline Bd. of Edn., 1944-53, Augustana Coll. Bd., 1960-69. Mem. Am., Ill., Rock Island County bar assns., Moline C. of C. (v.p. 1974-76), C. of C. of Upper Rock Island County (corp. sec. 1976—), Delta Theta Pi. Co-editor-in-chief Iowa Law Review, 1936-37. Home: 2710 22 1/2 Ave Rock Island IL 61201 Office: 501 15th St Moline IL 61265 Tel (309) 762-9369

SCIBILIA, JOSEPH CHARLES, b. N.Y.C., June 28, 1935; B.A., Columbia, 1960; LL.B., St. John's U., 1963. Admitted to N.Y. State bar, 1963, U.S. Dist. Cts. Eastern and So. Dists. bars, 1966; asso. firm Doran, Gostkowski & Stienbrecher, Mineola, N.Y., 1963-66, Doran & Gostkowski, Mineola, 1967-70; partner firm Doran, Gostkowski & Scibilia, Mineola, 1970-76, Gostkowski & Scibilia, Mineola, 1976—; dir. Legal Aid Soc. Suffolk County, 1974—; mem. med. malpractice panel appellate div. 2d Dept. N.Y. Supreme Ct.; mem. panel arbitrators Am. Arbitration Assn. Mem. Am., N.Y. State, Queens County, Nassau County bar assns., Nassau-Suffolk Trial Lawyers Assn., Def. Research Inst. Office: 1539 Franklin Ave Mineola NY 11501 Tel (516) 742-4747

SCINTO, LAWRENCE FRANCIS, b. N.Y.C., Oct. 28, 1927; B.S., Worcester Poly. Inst., 1951; LL.B., St. John's U., 1956; LL.M., N.Y. U., 1958. Admitted to N.Y. bar, 1957; staff atty. AMF Corp., N.Y.C., 1957-60; asso. firm Morgan, Finnegan, Durham & Pine, N.Y.C., 1960-63; partner firm Ward, McElhannon, Brooks & Fitzpatrick, N.Y.C., 1963-71; sr. partner firm Fitzpatrick, Cella, Harper & Scinto, N.Y.C., 1971—. Mem. Am., N.Y. State, Westchester bar assns., N.Y. Patent Law Assn., N.Y. Soc. Profl. Engrs. Office: 277 Park Ave New York City NY 10017 Tel (212) 758-2400

SCISM, DANIEL REED, b. Evansville, Ind., Aug. 27, 1936; A.B., DePauw U., 1958, J.D. with distinction, Ind. U., 1965. Admitted to Ind. bar, 1965, U.S. Supreme Ct. bar, 1976; asso. firm Roberts, Ryder & Rogers, Indpls., 1965-69, partner, 1969—. Bd. dirs. Marion County Mental Health Assn., 1969-75, v.p., 1970-71; bd. dirs. Marion County chpt. Myasthenia Gravis Found., 1967-71, treas., 1970; bd. dirs. Suemma Coleman Agy., 1971-76, pres., 1973-74. Mem. Am. (mem. labor law sect., mem. com. on equal employment opportunity law 1974—), Indpls., Ind. bar assns., Ind. State C. of C. (mem. social legislation com. 1970—). Home: 11070 Winding Brook Ln Indianapolis IN 46280 Office: Suite 2020 1 Indiana Sq Indianapolis IN 46204 Tel (317) 639-5656

SCOFIELD, MILTON N., b. N.Y.C., Aug. 7, 1911; A.B., Columbia U., 1932, LL.B., 1935, J.D., 1935. Admitted to N.Y. bar, 1935; asso. N.Y.C. Law Revision Commn., 1935; chief counsel food rationing div. Office Price Adminstrn., 1942; asso. firm Stroock & Stroock, N.Y.C., 1942, 43-45; partner firm Stroock & Stroock & Lavan, N.Y.C., 1945—; cons. on rationing to U.S. Sec. War, 1943; magistrate Scarsdale (N.Y.) Police Dept., 1961-62. Mem. Am., Bar Assn., N.Y. County Law Assn., Assn. Bar of City N.Y., Phi Beta Kappa. Editor: Columbia Law Review, 1934-35. Office: 61 Broadway New York City NY 10006 Tel (212) 425-5200

SCOLARO, ANTHONY RUSSELL, b. Cedar Rapids, Iowa, Sept. 27, 1923; B.A., Coe Coll., 1948; J.D., U. Iowa, 1950. Admitted to Iowa bar, 1950; partner firm Scolaro, Glaza, Matias, Wilson and Matias, Cedar Rapids, 1950-72; asso. judge 6th Dist. Iowa Ct., Cedar Rapids, 1972—; mem. Linn County (Iowa) Bd. Suprs., 1960-70. Charter pres. Linn County Regional Planning Commn., 1960-70, Hawkeye Area Community Action Program, Linn County, Iowa. Home: 1710 Applewood Pl NE Cedar Rapids IA 52402 Office: Iowa Dist Ct 1st Ave Bridge Cedar Rapids IA 52401 Tel (319) 398-3906

SCOLES, EUGENE FRANCIS, b. Shelby, Iowa, June 12, 1921; A.B., U. Iowa, 1943, J.D., 1945; LL.M., Harvard, 1949; J.S.D., Columbia, 1955. Admitted to Iowa bar, 1945, Ill. bar, 1946; asso. Seyfarth, Shaw & Fairweather, Chgo., 1945-46; asst. prof. law Northeastern U., 1946-48, asso. prof., 1948-49; asso. prof. U. Fla., 1949-51, prof., 1951-56; vis. prof. Khartoum (Sudan) U., 1964-65; prof. U. Ill., 1958-68; prof. U. Oreg., 1968—, dean Sch. Law, 1968-74; mem. Uniform State Laws Commn. Mem. Soc. Pub. Tchrs. Law, African Law Assn., Am. Law Inst., Am. Coll. Probate Counsel, Am., Ill. State, Lane County bar assns., Assn. Am. Law Schs. (exec. com. 1976—, pres.-elect 1977), Order of Coif. Author: (with H.F. Goodrich) Conflict of Laws, 4th edit., 1964; (with R.J. Weintraub) Cases and Materials on Conflict of Laws, 2d edit., 1972; (with E.C. Halbach, Jr.) Problems and Materials on Decedents' Estates and Trusts, 2d edit. 1973; contbr. articles to profl. jours.; notes and legislation editor Iowa Law Rev., 1945; reporter Uniform Probate Code Project, 1966—; mem. joint editorial bd. Uniform Probate Code, 1972—. Office: U Oreg Sch Law Eugene OR 97403 Tel (503) 686-3848

SCORDO, JACK, b. Watertown, N.Y., Mar. 20, 1927; B.A., Union Coll., 1950; LL.B., Syracuse U., 1953. Admitted to N.Y. State bar, 1953; asst. corp. counsel City of Watertown, 1963—. Pres. Italian Am. Civic Assn., Watertown, 1963, Watertown Red and Black Football Club, Inc., Watertown, 1972-73. Mem. Jefferson County (sec. 1970), N.Y. State bar assns. Home: 226 Thompson Blvd Watertown NY 13601 Office: 209 Arsenal St Watertown NY 13601 Tel (315) 782-3770

SCOTT, ALBERT SEPTIMUS, JR., b. Chgo., Apr. 15, 1917; B.A., Stanford, 1937; J.D., Harvard, 1940. Admitted to Calif. bar, 1941, U.S. Supreme Ct. bar, 1945; clk. firm Anderson, Wrenn & Jenks, Honolulu, summer 1939; asso. firms Frank Thompson, Honolulu, 1940, Macdonald & Pettit, Los Angeles, 1941; legis. atty. Office Judge Adv. Gen. of USN, Washington, 1945-46; asso. counsel firm Erb & French, Beverly Hills, Calif., 1947; individual practice law, Claremont, Calif., 1948—; asso. in practice with son Douglas A. Scott, Claremont, 1971—. Mem. Calif., Pomona Valley, Los Angeles County bar assns. Decorated Order of Navy League medal, Treasury Silver Medal award. Office: 350 W 4th St PO Box 151 Claremont CA 91711 Tel (714) 626-1062

SCOTT, BOBBY KENNETH, b. Gravette, Ark., Oct. 6, 1933; LL.B., U. Ark., 1958. Admitted to Ark. bar, 1958; partner firm Bruno, Sarver & Scott, Ltd., Little Rock; commr. revenue State of Ark., 1969-70; legal aide to gov., 1967-69. Mem. Ark., Pulaski County bar assns. Home: 9016 Leatrice St Little Rock AR 72207 Office: Suite 444 Tower Bldg Little Rock AR 72201

SCOTT, CAROL WILD, b. Detroit, Dec. 14, 1940; B.A., U. N.C., Wilmington, 1967; J.D., U. Fla., 1970. Admitted to Fla. bar, 1970, U.S. Ct. Mil. Appeals bar, 1976; asso. Gainesville (Fla.) Legal Collective, 1971; individual practice law, Gainesville, 1972-75; civilian and staff counsel Clemency Info. Center, Indpls., 1974-75; staff counsel, Central Com. Conscientious Objectors, So. regional office, Atlanta, 1975-76; commr. U.S. Ct. Mil. Appeals, Washington, 1976—. Exec. sec. region III Drug Abuse Adv. Council, Gainesville, 1972-75. Mem. Fla. Bar, Nat. Lawyers Guild, Nat. Legal Aid and Defenders Assn. Home: 1509 Cool Spring Rd Alexandria VA 22308 Office: US Ct Mil Appeals 450 E St NW Washington DC 20442 Tel (202) 693-1901

SCOTT, JOHN BAYTOP, JR., b. Montgomery, Ala., July 21, 1930; LL.B., U. Ala., 1954. Admitted to Ala. bar, 1954; law clk. to justice Ala. Supreme Ct., 1955-56; partner firm Scott & Scott, Montgomery, 1956-64; partner firm Capell, Howard, Knabe & Cobbs, Montgomery, 1964—. Bd. dirs. Landmarks Found., Montgomery; trustee Montgomery Mus. Mem. Am., Ala., Montgomery bar assns. Home: 641 E Fairview Ave Montgomery AL 36106 Office: 57 Adams Ave Montgomery AL 36103 Tel (205) 262-1673

SCOTT, JOHN THOMSON, JR., b. Cleve., May 24, 1924; A.B., Princeton, 1948; J.D., Harvard, 1951. Admitted to Ohio bar, 1951; partner firm Squire, Sanders & Dempsey, Cleve.; dir. White Consol. Industries, Inc., Cleve. Mem. Cleve., Ohio, Am. bar assns.

SCOTT, JOHN WINFIELD, JR., b. Fayetteville, Ark., Apr. 27, 1922; B.S., Auburn U., 1943; LL.B., Harvard, 1947, LL.M., 1951. Admitted to Ala. bar, 1948, D.C. bar, 1954, N.Y. State bar, 1957; asso. firm Martin, Turner & McWhorter, Birmingham, Ala., 1947-49; faculty asst. Harvard Law Sch., 1949-51; atty. U.S. Treasury, Washington, 1951-53; asso. firm Paul, Weiss, Rifkind, Wharton & Garrison, Washington, 1953-56; asso. firm Lewis & MacDonald, N.Y.C., 1956-57, partner, 1957-62; asso. prof. taxation U. N.C., 1962-64, prof., 1964-72, Graham Kenan prof. law, 1972—. Mem. Am. Bar Assn. Contbg. editor: Mertens, Law of Federal Income Taxation, 1956. Mem. editorial bd. Tax Management, 1956-61. Contbr. articles in field to profl. jours. Home: 2308 Honeysuckle Rd Chapel Hill NC 27514 Office: School of Law Univ NC Chapel Hill NC 27514 Tel (919) 933-5106

SCOTT, JOHN WYETH (JOCK), b. Alexandria, La., June 29, 1947; B.A., Tulane U., 1969; J.D., La. State U., 1972. Admitted to La. bar, 1972; mem. firm Stafford, Randow, O'Neal & Scott, Alexandria, 1972-76; partner firm Craven and Scott, Alexandria, 1976—; mem. La. Ho. of Reps., 1976—. Bd. dirs. YMCA; asso. vestryman St. James Episcopal Ch. Mem. Am., La., Alexandria bar assns., Alexandria-Pineville C. of C. Home: 1830 Albert St Alexandria LA 71301 Office: PO Box 129 Alexandria LA 71301 Tel (318) 445-1474

SCOTT, KEITH FOSTER, b. Macomb, Ill., Feb. 19, 1911; A.B., U. Ill., 1933, LL.B., 1935. Admitted to Ill. bar, 1935; mem. firm T. M. Downing, Macomb, 1935-59; state's atty. McDonough County (Ill.), 1940-48, mast in chancery, 1948-59; judge Ill. 9th Circuit Ct., 1959-75; gen. counsel Citizens Nat. Bank of Macomb, 1976—, also dir.; past dir. Colchester Savs. and Loan Assn. Mem. Macomb Sch. Bd., 1953-59; mem. planning commn. City of Macomb. Mem. Am., Ill., McDonough County bar assns., Am. Judicature Soc. Home: 520 S Pearl St Macomb IL 61455 Office: Citizens Nat Bank Macomb IL 61455 Tel (309) 833-2789

SCOTT, LEROY, b. Washington, N.C., Oct. 20, 1909; LL.B., Wake Forest U., 1931, J.D., 1970. Admitted to U.S. Supreme Ct. bar, 1931; individual practice law, Washington, N.C.; U.S. Concilliation Commr., 1935. Chmn. council Girl Scouts U.S.A., 1967; tchr. Sunday sch. First Christian Ch., 1960-74. Mem. N.C. State Bar. Home: 202 Riverside Dr Washington NC 27889

SCOTT, MARY LOUISE, b. Ft. Worth, Oct. 15, 1932; A.B. cum laude, U. San Diego, 1955, J.D. magna cum laude, 1970; M.A., San Diego State U., 1961. Admitted to Calif. bar, 1971; tchr. San Diego Unified Sch. Dist., 1955—, curriculum writer, 1972, 73; instr. adult edn. course, 1973-74. Mem. San Diego Hist. Soc., San Diego Maritime Mus. Assn., San Diego Soc. Natural History, Save Our Heritage Orgn. Mem. Am. Bar Assn., NEA, Calif. Teachers Assn., Calif. Assn. for the Gifted, Nat. Council Teachers of English, San Diego Teachers Assn. Author: (with Arthur Polk) A Guide for Teaching You and the Law, 1973; contbr. comment to legal publ.; recipient Diocese of San Diego Citation of Honor, 1955. Office: Muirlands Jr High School 1056 Nautilus St La Jolla CA 92037 Tel (714) 459-4211

SCOTT, MICHAEL, b. N.Y.C., Oct. 11, 1930; B.A., Cornell, 1952; J.D., U. Mich., 1958; diplome Grad. Inst. Internat. Studies, Geneva, 1958-59. Admitted to Ohio bar, 1959, D.C. bar, 1971; asso. firm Squire, Sanders & Dempsey, Cleve., 1959-67, partner, 1967-74; partner firm Cox, Langford, Brown, Squire, Sanders & Dempsey, Washington, 1974—; pres. Ohio State Legal Services Assn., 1969-70. Mem. Am., Ohio, D.C., Fed. bar assns. Asso. editor U. Mich. Law Rev., 1957-58. Office: 21 Dupont Circle NW Washington DC 20036 Tel (202) 785-0200

SCOTT, NAUMAN S., chief judge U.S. Dist. Ct. Western La. Address: PO Drawer 312 Alexandria LA 71301 Tel (318) 497-6645*

SCOTT, PAUL ORION, b. Cambridge, Ohio, Nov. 4, 1948; B.A., Ohio No. U., 1970; J.D., Capital U., 1974. Admitted to Ohio, Fla. bars, 1974; asso. firm Delibera, Lyons, Koblentz & Scott, and predecessors, Columbus, Ohio, 1974-75, partner, 1976—. Mem. Am. Arbitration Assn., Am., Ohio, Franklin trial lawyers assns., Am., Ohio, Fla., Fed. bar assns. Home: 3553 Rand Ct Columbus OH 43227 Offie: 88 E Broad St Columbus OH 44215 Tel (614) 464-1600

SCOTT, PAUL TUCKER, b. Chgo., Nov. 22, 1943; B.A., U. Va., 1965; J.D., U. Richmond, 1970. Admitted to Va. bar, 1970; asso. firm Cox, Woodbridge & Smith, Fredericksburg, Va., 1970-72; partner firm Cox Woodbridge Smith & Scott, Fredericksburg, 1972—; sec., dir. Aquia Bank and Trust Co., Stafford County, Va., 1972—; sec., legal adviser to bd. dirs. Fredericksburg Country Club, 1973-77; legal counsel, dir. Hist. Fredericksburg Found., Inc.; legal counsel FHA, Spotsylvania County, Va. Dir. campaign March of Dimes, Fredericksburg, 1971. Mem. Va. Bar Assn., Va. Trial Lawyers Assn. Decorated Bronze Star with oak leaf cluster. Home: 1823 Genther Ln Fredericksburg VA 22401 Office: 620 Princess Anne St Fredericksburg VA 22401 Tel (703) 373-5300

SCOTT, SAMUEL CLARENCE, b. Columbus, S.C., June 16, 1920; LL.B., Fordham U., 1950. Admitted to N.J. bar, 1951; practiced in Jersey City, 1951-55; asso. prof. law S.C. State Coll., 1955-57; claim rep. claims dept. State Farm Ins. Co., 1960-64; asst. prosecutor Hudson County (N.J.), 1965; asst. corp. counsel Govt. of Jersey City, 1966, corp. counsel, 1972-73; judge Municipal Ct., Jersey City, 1966-72, Hudson County Juvenile and Domestic Relations Ct., 1973—. Bd. dirs. Christ Hosp., Jersey City, 1968-71, ARC, Jersey City, 1967-70, Boy Scouts Am., 1967-71, Hudson County Urban League, 1970—. Mem. Hudson County, N.J. State bar assns., Am. Trial Lawyers. Office: 595 Newark Ave Jersey City NJ 07306 Tel (201) 792-3737

SCOTT, SAMUEL SUMNEY, b. Duquesne, Pa., May 16, 1905; A.B., Princeton U., 1926; LL.B., Harvard U., 1929. Admitted to Pa. bar, 1930; sr. partner firm Scott Neely & Dunn, Pitts., 1954-69, Scott Swensen & Scott, Pitts., 1970—; dir. and gen. counsel W. Penn Motor Club, 1950-73; dir. Pa. Motor Fedn., 1953—, pres., 1962-64; pres. Stulen Machine Co., 1964—. Pres. Pitts. Hearing Soc., 1962-66; bd. dirs. Am. Hearing Soc., 1963-66, v.p., 1965-66; bd. dirs. Travelers Aid Soc., Pitts., 1965-71. Mem. Allegheny County, Pa., Am. bar assns., Am. Automobile Assn. (dir. 1963-73). Office: 2208 Lawyers Bldg Pittsburgh PA 15219 Tel (412) 281-1970

SCOTT, STEPHEN WAYNE, b. Cedar Rapids, Iowa, May 2, 1948; B.A., U. Iowa, 1970, J.D., 1973. Admitted to Iowa bar, 1973; mem. firm Kintzinger, Kintzinger, Van Etten Setter & King, Dubuque, Iowa, 1973—. Mem. Dubuque County, Iowa, Am. bar assns. Home: 653 Wilson St Dubuque IA 52001 Office: PO Box 703 Dubuque IA 52001 Tel (319) 588-0547

SCOTT, TASSO HAROLD, b. Natoma, Kans., Jan. 25, 1905; B.A., U. Colo., 1931; M.S. in Fgn. Service, Georgetown U., 1933; J.D., George Washington U., 1940. Admitted to D.C. bar, 1940, U.S. Supreme Ct. bar, 1946; atty. FTC, 1941-60; asso. commr. Indian Claims Commn., 1960-68; of counsel firm Rhyne & Rhyne, Washington, 1969-75, firm Niebell & Scott, Washington, 1976—; legis. asst. to U.S. Sen. Alva B. Adams, 1934-41. Mem. Internat., Fed., D.C. bar assns., Am. Judicature Soc., World Peace Through Law, World Assn. Judges. Home: 9615 Hillridge Dr Kensington MD 20795 Office: Suite 419 910 17th St NW Washington DC 20006 Tel (202) 659-1626

SCOTT, WILLIAM JOHN, b. Chgo., Nov. 11, 1926; student Bucknell U., 1945, U. Pa., 1946; J.D., Kent Coll. Law, Chgo., 1950. Admitted to Ill. bar, 1950; practiced in Chgo., 1950-51, 67-69; with LaSalle Nat. Bank, Chgo., 1951-53, Am. Nat. Bank & Trust Co., Chgo., 1953-58; v.p. Nat. Blvd. Bank, Chgo., 1959-62; spl. asst. U.S. atty., 1959; pres. Holiday Travel House, 1959—; treas. State of Ill., 1963-67, atty. gen., 1969—. Trustee MacMurray Coll., Jacksonville,

Ill., 1963-67. Mem. Am., Fed., Ill., Chgo. bar assn. Home: 520 S 2d St Springfield IL 62701

SCOTT, WILLIAM M., b. Great Falls, Mont., Aug. 29, 1920; B.A., U. Mont., J.D., 1943. Admitted to Mont. bar, 1943; practiced in Great Falls since 1946, sr. partner firm Scott, Linnell, Neill & Newhall; advocate Episcopal Ch., Diocese of Mont., 1973—; atty. City of Great Falls, 1947-49. Trustee, Mont. Deaconess Hosp., Great Falls, 1959-65, also pres.; chmn. Great Falls Bd. Park Commrs., 1954-58; trustee Dufresne Found., Cobb Found.; pres. bd. trustees Episcopal Ch. Meml. Found.; chmn. Cascade County (Mont.) Republicans, 1960-64; sr. warden Episcopal Ch., Great Falls, 1960; commr. City of Great Falls, 1973-77. Mem. Cascade County (pres.), Mont., Am. bar assns., Phi Delta Phi. Named Man of Year, Great Falls C. of C.; editor Mont. Law Rev. Home: 2020 3rd Ave S Great Falls MT 59401 Office: 414 Montana Bldg Great Falls MT 59401 Tel (406) 727-2200

SCOTT, WILLIAM PAUL, b. Staples, Minn., Nov. 8, 1928; A.L.A., U. Minn., 1949; B.S.L., St. Paul Coll. Law, 1952, LL.B., 1954. Admitted to Minn. bar, 1954; atty. right of way div. Minn. Hwy. Dept., St. Paul, 1945-52, civil engr. traffic and safety div., 1953-55; practice law, Arlington, Minn., 1955-61, Gaylord, Minn., 1963-67; sr. partner firm Scott Law Offices, and predecessors, Pipestone, Minn., 1967—; probate and juvenile judge Sibley County (Minn.), 1956-61; Minn. pub. examiner, 1961-63. Nat. committeeman Young Republican League, 1958-59; Sibley County Rep. chmn., 1961. Mem. Am., Minn., U.S. Supreme Ct. bar assns., Mensa, VFW, Am. Legion, Air Force Assn., Res. Officers Assn. Recipient George Washington Honor medal Freedoms Found., 1970, 72. Home: Box 704 Pipestone MN 56164 Office: Park Plaza Offices Pipestone MN 56164 Tel (507) 825-5496

SCOTT, WOODSON DENNIE, b. Bryantsville, Ky., July 19,1899; A.B., U. Ky., 1926, LL.B., 1927; postgrad. Columbia U. Law Sch., 1927-28. Admitted to Ky. bar, 1926, N.Y. State bar, 1930, U.S. Supreme Ct. bar, 1935; atty. firm Lord, Day & Lord, N.Y.C., 1928—. Mem. U.S. Olympic Com., 1968-71; mem. People to People Sports Com., 1967-77; active Ducks Unlimited, 1965-77. Mem. Am., N.Y. State, Ky. bar assns., Assn. Bar City N.Y., Nat. Rifle Assn. (pres. 1969-71). Editor: Ky. Law Jour., 1926-27. Home: 240 Foxwood Rd Stamford CT 06903 Office: 25 Broadway New York City NY 10004 Tel (212) 344-8480

SCOVEL, ALLEN LEEDOM, b. Madison, S.D., Jan. 15, 1939; B.S., U. S.D., 1961, J.D., 1965. Admitted to S.D. bar, 1965; asso. firm Gunderson, Farrar, Carrell & Aldrich, Rapid City, S.D., 1965, firm Carrell & Scovel, Rapid City, 1966-70; partner firm Costello, Porter, Hill, Nelson, Heisterkamp & Bushnell, Rapid City, 1970—; dep. states atty. Pennington County, 1967-68; prof. Nat. Coll. Bus., Rapid City, 1968-69. Lay leader 1st United Methodist Ch., 1972-75. Mem. Pennington County, Am., S.D. (related edn. com. 1976) bar assns., Delta Theta Phi. Home: 204 Berry Pine Rd Rapid City SD 57701 Office: 704 Saint Joseph St Rapid City SD 57701 Tel (605) 343-2410

SCOVILLE, DONALD LOUIS, b. Riverside, Calif., Oct. 28, 1941; B.S. in Accounting, San Diego State U., 1963, J.D., U. San Diego, 1970. Admitted to Calif. bar, 1971; partner firm Plourd, Blume & Scoville, El Centro, Calif., 1971—. Office: 1005 State St El Centro CA 92243 Tel (714) 352-3130

SCRIBNER, FRED CLARK, JR., b. Bath, Maine, Feb. 14, 1908; A.B., Dartmouth, 1930, LL.D., 1959; LL.B., Harvard, 1933; LL.D., U. Maine, 1958, Colby Coll., 1959, Bowdoin Coll., 1959, U. Vt., 1960. Admitted to Maine bar, 1933, Mass. bar, 1933, D.C. bar, 1961; asso. firm Cook, Hutchinson, Pierce and Connell, Portland, Maine, 1933-35, partner, 1935-55; partner firm Pierce, Atwood, Scribner, Allen & McKusick, Portland, 1961—; partner firm Scribner, Hall, Thornburg & Thompson, Washington, 1961—; former chmn. bd. Rockland-Rockport Lime Co., Inc., Rockland, Maine; chmn. bd. Coordinated Apparel, Ind.; dir., gen. counsel, v.p., treas. Bates Mfg. Co., Lewiston, Maine, 1946-55; gen. counsel Dept. Treasury, 1955-57, asst. sec. treasury, 1957, undersec., 1957-61; dir. Sentinel Growth Fund Inc., Sentinel Income Fund Inc., Sentinel Trustees Fund Inc., Sentinel Group Funds Inc. Mem. Am. Bd. Arbitration; mem. commr's. adv. com. on exempt orgns. IRS; chmn. ad hoc adv. group on presdl. vote for P.R.; bd. dirs. Maine Med. Center, Portland; mem. nat. council Boy Scouts Am., mem. regional exec. com.; mem. Am. Council for Nationalities; past pres. bd. trustees Bradford Coll.; trustee Cardigan Mountain Sch., Canaan, N.H.; pres. Maine Constl. Commn., 1963-64; chmn. Republican City Com., Portland, 1936-40, Maine Council Young Rep. Clubs, 1938-40; mem. Maine Rep. Com., 1940-50, chmn. exec. com. 1944-50; Rep. nat. committeeman from Maine, 1948-56; del. Rep. Nat. Conv., 1940, 44, 56, 60, 64, 68, gen. counsel arrangements com., 1956-72; counsel Rep. Nat. Com., 1952-55, 61-73; presdl. elector, 1976; mem. standing com. Diocesan Council, chancellor Diocese of Maine, Episcopal Ch.; del. Gen. Conv. Episc. Ch., 1943—. Mem. Am., Fed., Maine, Cumberland County bar assns., Am. Law Inst., Newcomen Soc. N.Am. (clk.), Phi Beta Kappa, Delta Sigma Rho, Alpha Chi Rho. Recipient Silver Beaver award Boy Scouts Am., 1948, Alexander Hamilton award, U.S. Treasury, 1961, Dartmouth Alumni Council award, 1971. Home: 335 Foreside Rd Falmouth ME 04105 Office: 10th Floor One Monument Sq Portland ME 04111 also Suite 502 1200 18th St NW Washington DC 20036 Tel (207) 773-6411

SCRIPTER, RICHARD WILLIAM, b. Detroit, Jan. 16, 1939; B.A., Western Mich. U., 1962; J.D., Wayne State U., 1967. Admitted to Mich. bar, 1968; individual practice law, Pontiac, Mich., 1968-71; partner firm Graham & Scripter, Pontiac, 1971—. Mem. Mich., Oakland County bar assns., Am., Mich. trial lawyers assns. Office: 2791 Auburn Pontiac MI 48057 Tel (313) 852-3220

SCRIVENER, FRANK EDWARD, b. Washington, May 15, 1908; A.B., George Washington U., 1931, LL.B., 1933. Admitted to D.C. bar, 1933, U.S. Supreme Ct. bar, 1942; individual practice law, Washington, 1933—; chmn. U.S. Ration Bd., 1943-45. Pres., Capitol Hill Citizens Assn., 1945-48. Mem. Bar Assn. D.C., Am. Bar Assn. Home: 4711 Quebec St NW Washington DC 20016 Office: 4400 Jenifer St NW Washington DC 20015 Tel (202) 244-0450

SCRIVENER, SAMUEL, JR., b. Washington, Feb. 14, 1905; Eng. of Mines, Lehigh U., 1926; LL.B., George Washington Univ., 1932. Admitted to U.S. Supreme Ct. bar, 1950; sr. partner firm Scrivener, Parker, Scrivener, & Clarke, Washington; chmn. exec. com., gen. counsel. Perpetual Fed. Savs. & Loan Assn., Washington. Chmn. D.C. Bd. of Zoning Appeals; pres. Washington Hosp. Center. Mem. Am., D.C. bar assns. Address: 2543 Waterside Dr NW Washington DC 20008 also Mill Point Farm Bozman MD 21612 Tel (202) 296-2950

SCROFANO, SAL GIUSEPPE, b. Augusta, Sicily, Italy, Jan. 26, 1948; B.A., U. Cin., 1970, J.D., 1974. Admitted to Ohio bar, 1974; individual practice law, Cin., 1974—. Mem. Am., Ohio, Cin. bar assns. Home: 953 Springbrook Dr Cincinnati OH 45224 Office: 1119 4th St and Walnut Bldg Cincinnati OH 45202 Tel (513) 721-2552

SCROGGS, LARRY KENNETH, b. Beebe, Ark., Oct. 8, 1941; B.A., Harding Coll., 1963; J.D., Vanderbilt U., 1971. Admitted to Tenn. bar, 1971; asso. firm Holt, Batchelor, Spicer, Gaerig & Ryan, Memphis, 1972-76, partner, 1976—; asso. firm Leo Bearman, Memphis, Tenn., 1971-72; law clk. Tenn. Pub. Service Commn., Nashville, Tenn., 1969-71. Bd. dirs. W. Tenn. Agape, Inc., Memphis, 1976—. Mem. Am., Tenn., Shelby County (Tenn.), Memphis bar assns. Office: Holt Batchelor Spicer Gaerig & Ryan 2400 100 North Main Bldg Memphis TN 38103 Tel (901) 523-1333

SCRUGGS, CHARLES HENDRICKS, III, b. Birmingham, Ala., Oct. 13, 1937; B.A., U. Fla., 1960; LL.B., U. Miss., 1964, J.D., 1964. Admitted to Miss. bar, 1964, Fla. bar, 1964; partner firm Feinberg & Scruggs, Tampa, Fla., 1964-65; asso. firm Nuccio and Taub, Tampa, 1965-67; judge Municipal Ct., Tampa, 1967-73, judge juvenile and domestic relations div. 13th Jud. Circuit Fla., 1973-74, felony div., 1974—; chmn. Hillsborough County (Fla.) Bd. Criminal Justice; mem. Hillsborough County Criminal Justice Planning Council. Charter mem. bd. trustees Tampa Women's Hosp., 1974—; bd. dirs. Tampa Big Bros., 1968-74, pres., 1969-70; dir. publicity Sta. WEDU-TV Ann. Auction, 1970-71; head usher, sec. vestry St. Andrews Episcopal Ch., Tampa. Mem. Am. (award for outstanding traffic judge 1971). Fla., Miss., Hillsborough County bar assns., Fla. Circuit Judges Conf. Recipient Distinguished Service award Tampa Jaycees, 1969, Safety certificate Allstate Ins. Co., 1971; named 1 of 10 Outstanding Young Men, Fla. Jaycees, 1970, Outstanding Fla. Municipal Judge Fla. Municipal Judges Assn., 1970. Office: care Hillsborough County Courthouse Annex Tampa FL 33602 Tel (813) 229-2030

SCRUGGS, EDWARD NEAL, b. Tuscaloosa, Ala., Jan. 29, 1923; B.S., U. Ala., 1943; LL.B., 1948. Admitted to Ala. bar, 1949; mem. firm Scruggs & Scruggs Guntersville, Ala., 1949-59; judge Circuit Ct. Marshall County, Guntersville, 1959—. Mem. Ala. Assn. Circuit Judges (pres. 1975-76). Office: PO Box 543 Guntersville AL 35976 Tel (205) 582-5731

SCUDDER, EARL HUGH, JR., b. Chgo., Aug. 26, 1942; B.S., U. Nebr., 1964, J.D., 1966. Admitted to Iowa, Nebr. bars, 1966; asso. firm Thoma Schoenthal Davis Hockenberg & Wine, 1966-67, firm Dickinson Throckmorton Parker Mannheimer & Raife, 1967-68; partner firm Nelson, Harding, Marchetti, Leonard & Tate, Lincoln, Nebr., 1968—; lectr. Drake U., Des Moines, 1966. Active U. Nebr. Found., Lincoln, Swing for Retarded, Inc., Omaha. Mem. Am., Nebr., Iowa, Lancaster County bar assns., Motor Carrier Lawyers Assn., ACLU. Office: Box 82028 Lincoln NE 68501 Tel (402) 475-6761

SCULL, DAVID LEE, b. Washington, May 10, 1943; A.B. magna cum laude, Princeton U., 1965; J.D., U. Va., 1968, M.A., 1968. Admitted to Va. bar, 1968, D.C. bar, 1969, Md. bar, 1969; asso. firm Fried, Frank, Harris, Shriver & Kampelman, Washington, 1971-74; partner firm Dobrovir, Oakes, Gebhardt, Scull, Washington, 1975—; lectr. comml. law U. Md., 1971; lectr. comparative law U. Saigon, Vietnam, 1970-71; mem. Md. Ho. of Dels. from Chevy Chase, 1975—. Mem. Am., Md., Va., D.C., Montgomery County bar assns. Home: 8717 Susanna Ln Chevy Chase MD 20015 Office: 2005 L St NW Washington DC 20036 Tel (202) 785-8919

SCULLY, JOHN MARK, b. Cape Cirardeau, Mo., Jan. 31, 1941; B.A. cum laude, S.E. Mo. State U., 1962; J.D., Washington U., St. Louis, 1966. Admitted to Mo. bar, 1966, Kans. bar, 1976; asst. pros. atty. St. Louis County, Mo., 1966-68; asst. U.S. atty. Eastern Dist. Mo., St. Louis, 1968-69; asso. firm Finch Law Firm, Cape Girardeau, 1969-73; individual practice law, Cape Girardeau, 1973-75; house counsel, v.p. Cable TV Constrn., Ltd., Chanute, Kans., 1976—; instr. S.E. Mo. U., Cape Girardeau, 1973-75; mem. Gov's. Adv. Council on Alcoholism and Drug Abuse, Cape Girardeau, 1972-75. County dir. Heart Fund Assn., Cape Girardeau, 1969-73; pres. Explorer council Boy Scouts Am., 1970-73, mem. exec. council, 1973-75; bd. dirs. Salvation Army, Cape Girardeau, 1972-75; active Sheltered Workshop, Cape Girardeau, 1969-71. Mem. Am., Mo., Kans. bar assns., Nat. Dist. Attys. Assn., Assn. Fed. Investigators, S.E. Mo. U. Alumni Assn., Phi Delta Phi. Home: 212 S Forest St Chanute KS 66720 Office: 308 E Main St Chanute KS 66720 Tel (316) 431-4160

SCURRY, RICHARDSON GANO, b. Dallas, Feb. 17, 1904; LL.B., Tex. U., 1928. Asso. firm Murphy W. Townsend, Dallas, 1928-33; individual practice law, Dallas, 1933-38, 75—; partner firm Scurry, Scurry, Hodges & Johnson, and predecessors, Dallas, 1938-75; chmn. com. on disposal of atomic energy towns AEC, 1950-52. Chmn. bd. Friends of Dallas Pub. Library, 1967-68; chmn. Commn. for Good Schs., Dallas, 1968-69. Mem. Am., Tex., Dallas (v.p. 1940) bar assns., Am. Judicature Soc., Tex. R.R. Lawyers Assn. Home: 5530 Winston Ct Dallas TX 75220 Office: 2700 Stemmons Freeway Dallas TX 75207 Tel (214) 631-7910

SEABOLD, JOHN STEWART, b. Memphis, July 1, 1943; B.B.A., U. Miss., 1965, J.D., 1968. Admitted to Miss. bar, 1968, Fla. bar, 1971; legal editor Municipal Code Corp., Tallahassee, Fla., 1969-72; atty. Fla. Dept. Commerce, Tallahassee, 1972-73; counsel Commonwealth Corp., Tallahassee, 1973-75; staff atty. The Fla. Bar, Tallahassee, 1975—; law clk. Miss. Supreme Ct., 1968. Mem. Tallahassee Bar Assn. Home: 3111 Carrib St Tallahassee FL 32303 Office: Florida Bar Tallahassee FL 32304 Tel (904) 222-5286

SEACREST, WILLIAM ALTON, b. Bethleham, Pa., July 27, 1946; A.A., U. Fla., 1966, B.S., 1968, J.D., 1971. Admitted to Fla. bar, 1971; partner firm Peterson, Carr, Harris & Seacrest, Lakeland, Fla. Bd. dirs. Girls Club Greater Lakeland, Tri-County Health Assn., Lakeland. Mem. Acad. Trial Lawyers, Am., Lakeland, 10th Jud. (sec. 1974, v.p. 1974-75, pres. 1975-76) bar assns., Polk County Trial Lawyers Assn. (sec.-treas. 1976). Home: 1632 Meadowbrook St Lakeland FL 33803 Office: 402 S Kentucky St Suite 560 Lakeland FL 33801 Tel (813) 687-8344

SEAL, JAMES LEE, b. Dayton, Ohio, July 29, 1945; B.B.A., U. Cin., 1967; J.D., Harvard, 1970. Admitted to Calif. bar, 1971, U.S. Supreme Ct. bar, 1974; asso. firm Musick, Peeler & Garrett, Los Angeles, 1971—. Mem. Calif. Barristers Assn. (v.p. 1974-76, dir. 1973-76), Am. (del. assembly young lawyers sect., 1975), Los Angeles County (superior cts. com., 1976) bar assns., Assn. Bus. Trial Lawyers. Contbr. Articles in field to legal jours. Home: 4032 Van Noord Ave Studio City CA 91604 Office: 1 Wilshire Blvd Los Angeles CA 90017 Tel (213) 629-3322

SEAMAN, JOHN GATES, b. Galveston, Tex., Mar. 9, 1919; B.A., U. Tex., 1940, LL.B., 1942. Admitted to Tex. bar, 1942; asso. firm Fountain, Cox & Gaines, Houston, 1946-51; partner firm Neel & Seaman, Corpus Christi, Tex., 1951-65, firm Keys, Russell, Seaman & Mansker, Corpus Christi, 1965—. Mem. State Bar Tex., Am., Nueces County bar assns., Am. Judicature Soc., Phi Delta Phi. Home: 618 Santa Monica St Corpus Christi TX 78411 Office: 1917 Bank and Trust Tower Corpus Christi TX 78403 Tel (512) 884-7484

SEAMAN, ROGER GEORGE, b. Chgo., May 17, 1926; J.D., John Marshall Law Sch., Chgo., 1951. Admitted to Ill. bar, 1951, U.S. Supreme Ct. bar, 1971; asst. state's atty. Cook County (Ill.), 1952-57; asst. corp. counsel City of Chgo., 1957-65; adminstrv. aide to pres. Met. San. Dist. of Chgo., 1965-73; mem. Ill. Pollution Control Bd., 1973-74; partner firm Seaman & Seaman, Chgo., 1974—; nat. judge adv. Cath. War Vets. Am., 1967-71. Pres., Young Democrats of Ill., 1962-64. Mem. Air Pollution Control Assn., Am. Pub. Works Assn., Cath. Lawyers Guild. Author: Water and Air Pollution - What Do You Control First?, 1968. Named Outstanding Young Dem., 1964. Office: 221 N LaSalle St Chicago IL 60601 Tel (312) 346-6949

SEARCY, CHRISTIAN DIETRICH, b. Jacksonville, Fla., Dec. 15, 1947; B.A., U. Va., 1970; J.D., Stetson U., 1973; grad. Hastings Coll. Trial Advocacy, 1976. Admitted to Fla. bar, 1973; asso. firm Frates, Floyd, Pearson, Stewart, Proenza & Richman, Miami, Fla., 1973-74, Howell, Kirby, Montgomery, D'Aiuto & Dean, West Palm Beach, Fla., 1974-76; partner firm Montgomery, Lytal, Reiter, Denney & Searcy, West Palm Beach, 1976—. Chmn. March of Dimes Dr., 1972. Mem. Am., Fla., Dade County, Broward County, Palm Beach County bar assns., Am. Trial Lawyers Assn., Acad. Fla. Trial Lawyers. Recipient award Bob Sikes Found., 1973. Home: 125 Dory Rd N North Palm Beach FL 33406 Office: PO Drawer 3626 West Palm Beach FL 33402

SEARLES, SIDNEY Z., b. N.Y.C., Aug. 25, 1914; student Sorbonne, Paris, 1945; B.S., St. John's U., 1934; J.D., Columbia U., 1937. Admitted to N.Y. bar, 1937; partner firm Raphael, Searles, Vischi, Scher, Glover & D'Ellia, N.Y.C., 1940—; mem. N.Y. State Commn. on Land Acquisition Law and Procedures; planning chmn. Seminar in Eminent Domain Am. Law Inst.-Am. Bar Assn., 1977-78; mem. N.Y. State Temporary Commn. Eminent Domain; examiner N.Y. State CSC; lectr. N.Y. U. Past pres. Interfaith Movement, Inc. Mem. Assn. Bar City N.Y. (chmn. spl. com. on condemnation). Contbr. articles to legal jours. and mags.; editor: Practical Guide to the Legal and Appraisal Aspects of Condemnation, 1969; Real Estate Valuation in Condemnation, 1970; recipient Arthur A. May Meml. award Am. Inst. Real Estate Appraisers, 1973. Home: 29 Woodmere Blvd Apt 4A Woodmere Long Island NY 11598 Office: 770 Lexington Ave New York City NY 10021 Tel (212) 832-7700

SEARS, BARNABAS FRANCIS, b. Webster, S.D., Nov. 13, 1902; student St. Thomas Coll., St. Paul; LL.B., Georgetown U., 1926, LL.D., 1971; LL.D., John Marshall Law Sch., 1971, William Mitchell Coll. Law, 1972. Admitted to Ill. bar, 1926; practice in Chgo., 1942—; now partner Boodell, Sears, Giambalvo, Sugrue & Crowley. Named Chicagean of Year, Chgo. Jr. C. of C., 1971. Mem. Am. (ho. dels. 1952-75, chmn. 1968-70, standing com. on fed. judiciary 1959-68), Ill. (past mem. council, chmn. sect. on jud. compensation, selection and tenure 1962—, pres. 1957-58), Kane County, Aurora, Chgo. bar assns., Soc. Trial Lawyers of Chgo., Am. Law Inst., Am. Judicature Soc., Am. Coll. Trial Lawyers (bd. regents 1961-65, pres. 1970-71; award Courageous Advocacy), Internat. Acad. Trial Lawyers. Home: 505 N Lake Shore Dr Chicago IL 60611 Office: One IBM Plaza Suite 2650 Chicago IL 60611*

SEARS, DON WALTER, b. Chillicothe, Ohio, Oct. 18, 1921; B.Sci., Ohio State U., 1946, J.D. with honors, 1948. Admitted to Ohio bar, 1949, Colo. bar, 1961; asso. firm Effler, Eastman, Stichter & Smith, Toledo, 1949-50; asst. prof. law U. Colo., 1950-52, asso. prof., 1952-55, prof., 1955—; dean sch. law, 1968-73. Bd. dirs. Colo. Urban League, 1971—. Mem. Am., Colo. (bd. govs. 1968-73), Boulder County (pres. 1970-71) bar assns., Nat. Acad. Arbitrators. Author: (with F. P. Storkee) Colorado Security Law Treatise, 1955; co-editor: The Am. Law of Mining, 1960; The Employment Relation and the Law, 1957; Labor Relations and the Law, 3rd edit., 1965; (with D. Wollett) Collective Bargaining in the Public Sector, 1972; asso. editor; The Developing Labor Law, 1971, contbr. articles to profl jours. Home: 504 Geneva Ave Boulder CO 80302 Office: U Colo Sch Law Boulder CO 80302 Tel (303) 492-7200

SEARS, JOHN PATRICK, b. Baldwinsville, N.Y., July 3, 1940; B.S., U. Notre Dame, 1960; J.D., Georgetown U., 1963. Admitted to N.Y. bar, 1963, D.C. bar, 1971, U.S. Supreme Ct. bar, 1969; clk. to judge N.Y. Ct. Appeals, 1963-65; asso. firm Nixon, Mudge, Rose, Guthrie & Alexander, N.Y.C., 1965-66; polit. adviser to Richard M. Nixon, 1965-67; exec. dir. Nixon for Pres. Com., Washington, 1967-68; dep. counsel White House, Washington, 1968-69; lectr. Kennedy Inst. Politics, Harvard U., 1969-70; partner firm Gadsby & Hannan, Washington, 1970-75; mgr. presdl. campaign Gov. Ronald Reagan, Calif., 1975-76; partner firm Baskin & Sears, Washington, 1977—. Home: 7718 Falstaff Ct McLean VA 22101 Office: 818 Connecticut Ave NW Washington DC 20006 Tel (202) 331-1174

SEARS, MARY HELEN, b. Syracuse, N.Y., Nov. 30, 1929; A.B., Cornell, 1950; J.D. with honors, George Washington U., 1960. Admitted to Va. bar, 1960, D.C. bar, 1961, U.S. Supreme Ct. bar, 1963; individual practice law, 1960-61; asso. firm Irons, Birch Swindler & McKie, Washington, 1961-69; partner firm Irons & Sears, Washington, 1969—; patent examiner, U.S. Patent Office, 1955-60. Mem. Am., D.C., Va. State bar assns., Am. Patent Law Assn., Am. Judicature Assn., Order Coif, Phi Alpha Delta. Contbr. articles in field. Home: 4654 Upton St NW Washington DC 20016 Tel (202) 466-5200

SEARS, ORETTA DIANORA, b. Cararra, Italy, Feb. 1, 1928; B.A. in English summa cum laude, Upsala Coll., 1960; J.D., U. Calif., Los Angeles, 1963. Admitted to Calif. bar, 1963, U.S. Ct. Claims bar, 1963, U.S. Supreme Ct. bar, 1966; trial atty., atty. gen's honor program, div. lands and natural resources Dept. Justice, Washington, 1963-66; lectr. in English and law Abdullahi Bayero Coll., Ahmadu Bello U., Kano, Nigeria, 1966-67; dep. dist. atty. Orange County (Calif.), 1967—, head sect. writs and appeals, 1969—. Mem. Calif. Bar, Am., Fed., Orange County bar assns., Orange County Criminal Bar Assn., Nat. Lawyers Club, D.C., Nat., Calif. dist. atty's. assns. Recipient Upsala award Phi Beta Kappa, 1960; Am. Jurisprudence prize in Bills and Notes, 1962; Best Mgr. award Orange County Govt., 1976; named Prosecutor of Month, Citizens for Decency through Law, 1974; editorial bd. U. Calif. at Los Angeles Law Rev., 1961-63. Office: PO Box 808 700 Civic Center Dr W Santa Ana CA 92701 Tel (714) 834-3616

SEASONWEIN, MILTON BERNSTEIN, b. N.Y.C., Jan. 20, 1906; A.B., Columbia, 1926, LL.B., 1929. Admitted to N.Y. bar, 1929; asso. David P. Siegel, N.Y.C., 1929-34; with Schenley Industries, Inc., N.Y.C., 1934—, gen. resident counsel and corp. sec., 1966—. Mem. Am., N.Y. State bar assns., U.S. Trademark Assn. Home: 84 Penn Rd

Scarsdale NY 10583 Office: 888 Seventh Ave New York City NY 10019 Tel (212) 957-2190

SEATON, GROVER CLEVELAND, III, b. Wilmington, N.C., Sept. 13, 1942; B.A., U. N.C., 1966; M.A., U. S.C., 1969, J.D., 1971. Admitted to S.C. bar, 1971, U.S. Supreme Ct. bar, 1975; corp. counsel S.C. Pub. Service Authority, Moncks Corner, 1971; asso. firm George Bishop, Moncks Corner, 1971-73; individual practice law, Goose Creek, S.C., 1973-75; partner firm Paul, Belk, Seaton, Howard, Charleston, S.C., 1976—. Mem. Goose Creek Mchts. Assn. (pres. 1974-76), Am., Charleston, Berkeley County bar assns., Am. Trial Lawyers Assn., Pi Sigma Alpha. Home: 207 Pandona St Goose Creek SC 29445 Office: 3370 Rivers Ave Charleston SC 29405 Tel (803) 747-3611

SEAWELL, DONALD RAY, b. Jonesboro, N.C., Aug. 1, 1912; B.A., U. of N.C., 1933, J.D., 1936. Admitted to N.C. bar, 1936, N.Y. bar, 1947; partner firm Willis & Seawell, Hickory, N.C., 1936-39; with SEC, Washington, 1939-47; partner firm Bernstein, Seawell, Kaplan & Block, N.Y.C., 1947-75; of counsel Bernstein, Seawell & Kove, N.Y.C., 1975—; chmn. bd. dirs., pres. Denver Post, Inc., Gravure West Inc., Los Angeles. Chmn., pres. Civilian-Mil. Inst., Colorado Springs, Colo.; chmn. Am. Nat. Theatre and Acad., N.Y.C., Denver Center Performing Arts, Bonfils Theatre, Denver; pres. Frederick G. Bonfils Found., Denver, Helen G. Bonfils Found., Denver. Office: The Denver Post 650 15th St Denver CO 80202 Tel (303) 297-1010

SEAY, DANIEL EDMUND, b. Watertown, Tenn., Mar. 8, 1916; student Vanderbilt U., 1938; LL.B., Cumberland U., 1953; postgrad. U. Nev., 1974, Nat. Coll. State Judiciary. Admitted to Tenn. bar, 1953, U.S. Supreme Ct. bar, 1972; Individual practice law, Lebanon, Tenn., 1953-62, 74—; gen. sessions judge Wilson County (Tenn.), 1962-74. Sec. exec. com. Wilson County Democratic Party, 1954-58. Mem. Am., Lebanon, Wilson County bar assns., Am. Judicature Soc. Home: 220 Windmill Dr Lebanon TN 37087 Office: POB 339 211 E Main St Lebanon TN 37087 Tel (615) 444-7329

SEAY, FRANK HOWELL, b. Shawnee, Okla., Sept. 5, 1938; B.A., U. Okla., 1961, LL.B., 1963. Admitted to Okla. bar, 1963; mem. firm Seay and Seay, Seminole, Okla., 1963; county atty. Seminole County, 1963-66; asst. dist. atty. 22d Jud. Dist. Okla., 1967-69; asso. dist. judge U.S. Dist. Ct. Seminole County, Wewoka, 1969-75; dist. judge 22d Jud. Dist. Okla., Wewoka, 1975—. Home: 905 Lee St Seminole OK 74868 Office: PO Box 656 Wewoka OK 74884 Tel (405) 257-2545

SEBESTA, HENRY WARREN, JR., b. Houston, Apr. 9, 1928; B.B.A., U. Tex., 1951, LL.B., 1953. Admitted to Tex. bar, 1953; atty. Continental Oil Co., Denver, 1953-55, Ft. Worth, 1955-57; gen. counsel W.E. Bakke Oil Co., San Antonio, 1957-61; individual practice law, San Antonio, 1961—; pres. Hedge Oil Co., San Antonio, 1961-76; sr. v.p. Petrolero Corp., San Antonio, 1976—, also dir.; asst. city atty. City of Terrell Hills (Tex.), 1964-67; judge Terrell Hills Municipal Ct., 1967-73; mem. exec. adv. council Equities Internat. Life Ins. Co.; mem. adv. council Nat. Right to Work Legal Def. Found., Inc.; dir. Merc. Bank & Trust Co., El Chaparral Land Devel. Co., H.R. Higgins Books, Inc., Rama, Inc., Esperanza Oil Ltd. Mem. exec. fin. com. Bexar County Republican Party, 1960-64; dist. fin. chmn. Alamo area council Boy Scouts Am., 1962-65. Mem. San Antonio (chmn. law day com., chmn. com. on unauthorized practice of law), Tex., Am. bar assns., State Bar Tex., Am. Judicature Soc., San Antonio C. of C. Home: 625 Canterbury Hill St San Antonio TX 78209 Office: 324 Milam Bldg San Antonio TX 78205 Tel (512) 224-8616

SEBORA, DAVID HOWARD, b. Junction City, Wis., Sept. 9, 1916; B.A., Ripon Coll., 1938; LL.B., U. Wis., 1945. Admitted to Wis. bar, 1940; individual practice law, Brillion, Wis., 1940-42; mem. firm Fox, Sebora and Fox, Brillion and Chilton, Wis., 1942-45; individual practice law, Chilton, 1945-55; dist. atty. Calumet County (Wis.), 1946-55; judge Calumet County Ct., 1955—. Mem. Kettle Moraine council Boy Scouts Am.; chmn. Calumet County (Wis.) Salvation Army. Mem. Calumet County, Wis. bar assns., Wis. Bd. Juvenile Ct. Judges (chmn. 1975). Office: 206 Court St Chilton WI 53014 Tel (414) 849-2361

SECREST, JAMES MILTON, b. Indpls., Aug. 7, 1935; B.S., Butler U., 1958; LL.B., Ind. U., 1962. Admitted to Ind. bar, 1962; partner firm Hilgadag, Johnson, Secrest & Murphy, 1966—. Mem. Am., Indpls., Ind., 7th Circuit bar assns., Phi Alpha Delta. Home: 1940 Huckleberry Ct Indianapolis IN 46260 Office: 1100 Circle Tower Indianapolis IN 46204 Tel (317) 638-7521

SEDAM, GLENN JAY, JR., b. Elizabeth, Pa., Jan. 27, 1937; B.A., U. Va., 1958; grad. student N.Y. U., 1960-62; J.D., Coll. William and Mary, 1969. Admitted to Va. bar, 1969, D.C. bar, 1969; asso. firm Stoptoe & Johnson, Washington, 1969-71; counsel to chmn. Republican Nat. Com., Washington 1971-72; individual practice law, Washington, 1972-73; gen counsel Com. to Re-elect Pres., 1972-73; deputy gen. counsel, Pres. Inaugural Com., 1972-73; deputy asst. sec. Congressional and Intergovernmental Affairs, U.S. Dept. Transp., Washington, 1973-74, Safety and Consumer Affairs, 1974; individual practice law, Washington and McLean, Va., 1975—; sr. partner firm Sedam & Herge Washington and McLean, Va., 1975—. Mem. various local planning coms. and task force study groups for community planning and development. Mem. Am. (council sect. internat. law), Va., D.C. bar assns. Recipient Sec. of Transp. Medal for outstanding performance of duties, 1974. Home: 907 Leigh Mill Rd Great Falls VA 22066 Office: 7600 Old Springhouse Rd McLean VA 22101 Tel (703) 821-1000

SEDERHOLM, CARL RANSOM, b. Brigham City, Utah, Jan. 27, 1928; B.S., Brigham Young U., 1953, J.D., U. Utah, 1957; LL.M., U. So. Calif., 1966. Admitted to Utah bar, 1957, Calif. bar, 1964; individual practice law, Long Beach, Calif., 1964—; dean Sch. Law, Northrop U., Inglewood, Calif., 1972—, dean of faculty, 1976—. Mem. Am., Long Beach bar assns., State Bar Calif. (com. on legal edn. 1974—, joint adv. com. on continuing edn., 1974—). Home: 3215 Warwood Rd Lakewood CA 90712 Office: 1155 West Arbor Vitae St Inglewood CA 90306 Tel (213) 641-3470

SEDGWICK, FREDERICA MAY, b. Long Beach, Calif., Dec. 11, 1932; B.A., Long Beach State Coll., 1954, M.A., 1957; M.S. in L.S., U. So. Calif., 1960; J.D., Loyola U., Los Angeles, 1970. Admitted to Calif. bar, 1971; asst. head circulation dept. U. So. Calif., 1959-61, head sci. library, 1961-63; head periodicals U. Cal. at Los Angeles, 1963-64; reference librarian Loyola U. Sch. Law, Los Angeles, 1964-70, asst. prof., asst. law librarian, 1970-74, dir. Law Library, prof., 1975—. Mem. Am., So. Calif. (sec.-treas. 1974-75, v.p. 1975-76, pres. 1976-77) assns. law libraries, Am., Calif. bar assns. Office: 1440 W 9th St Los Angeles CA 90015 Tel (213) 642-2924

SEDITA, JOSEPH J., b. Buffalo, June 19, 1918; student Millard Fillmore Coll., U. Hawaii; LL.B., U. Buffalo, 1950. Admitted to N.Y. bar, 1950; practiced law, 1950-60; judge City Ct., Buffalo, 1960-75; justice N.Y. Supreme Ct., Buffalo, 1976—. Mem. Buffalo Sewer Authority. Mem. Erie County (N.Y.) Bar Assn., Justinian Legal Soc., Assn. N.Y. State Supreme Ct. Justices. Recipient Good Citizenship award Buffalo Fire Dept.; award Buffalo Police Dept.; named Profl. Mental Health Worker of Year. Office: Erie County Hall Buffalo NY 14203 Tel (716) 852-1291

SEDIVY, EDMUND PAUL, b. Lewistown, Mont., Dec. 23, 1937; B.A., Dartmouth, 1960; LL.B., U. Mont., 1963. Admitted to Mont. bar, 1963; partner firm Morrow, Nash & Sedivy, Bozeman, Mont., 1965—. Mem. Bozeman Sch. Bd., 1974—. Mem. Mont., Am. trial lawyers assns., Gallatin County (Mont.) (pres. 1974), Mont., Am. bar assns. Home: 2205 Highland Ct Bozeman MT 59715 Office: 208 E Main St Bozeman MT 59715 Tel (406) 586-2349

SEDKY, CHERIF, b. Alexandria, Egypt, Dec. 10, 1943; A.B., Stanford, 1966; J.D., Georgetown U., 1969. Admitted to D.C. bar, 1969; asso. firm Surrey, Karasik, Green & Hill, Washington, 1969-71; asso. firm Hill, Christopher & Phillips, Washington, 1971-72, 73-75, mem., 1976—; asst. gen. counsel MCI Communications Corp., Washington, 1972-73. Mem. Am., D.C. bar assns., Phi Delta Phi. Editor: Georgetown Law Jour., 1969. Office: 1900 M St NW Washington DC 20036 Tel (202) 452-7000

SEDLER, ROBERT ALLEN, b. Pitts., Sept. 11, 1935; B.A., U. Pitts., 1956, J.D., 1959. Admitted to D.C. bar, 1959, Ky. bar, 1968, U.S. Supreme Ct. bar, 1969; asst. prof. law St. Louis U., 1961-64, asso. prof., 1964-65; asst. dean, asso. prof. law Nat. U. Ethiopia, 1963-66; asso. prof. law, U. Ky., 1966-68, prof., 1968-77; prof. law Wayne State U., Detroit, 1977—; vis. prof. law, U. Ind., summer 1971, U. Iowa, spring 1970, Washington U., spring 1976, Cornell U., 1976-77; gen. counsel Ky. Civil Liberties Union, 1971-76. Mem. Am., Ky. bar assns., Soc. Am. Law Tchrs. (bd. govs.), Order of Coif., Phi Beta Kappa. Author: The Conflict of Laws in Ethiopia, 1965; Ethiopian Civil Procedure, 1968; (with Roger C. Cramton), The Sum and Substance of the Conflict of Laws, 1977; contbr. articles to law reviews.

SEDLMAYER, GUNTER FRANK, b. Munich, Germany, May 18, 1924; B.S. cum laude, Loyola U., Chgo., 1948; J.D., Chgo. Kent Coll. Law, 1955. Admitted to Ill. bar, 1955; supr. fgn. and fed. taxes Inland Steel Co., Chgo., 1957-61; asst. sec., tax mgr. Household Fin. Corp., Chgo., 1961-76; tax dir. MSL Industries, Lincolnwood, Ill., 1977—. Mem. Am., Ill. bar assns., Tax Execs. Inst., Chgo. Tax Club. Home: 151 Reseda Ct Palatine IL 60067 Office: 7373 N Lincoln Ave Lincolnwood IL 60646 Tel (312) 777-3300

SEE, EDMUND M., b. Marrietta, Ohio, Oct. 9, 1943; B.A., Conn. Wesleyan U., 1965; J.D., Harvard, 1971. Admitted to Conn. bar, 1971; asso. firm Day, Berry & Howard, Hartford, Conn., 1971—; with Peace Corps, Gabon, Africa, 1965-67; with Neighborhood Legal Services, VISTA, Newark, 1968-69; adminstr. Hartford Vol. Legal Aid and Defender Program, 1974—. Mem. Hartford Citizens Assembly, 1974-76; pres. Hartford County Legal Aid Soc. Mem. Am., Conn., Hartford County bar assns., Phi Beta Kappa. Office: Day Berry & Howard 1 Constitution Plaza Hartford CT 06103 Tel (203) 278-1330

SEED, THOMAS FINIS, b. Springfield, Mo., Aug. 30, 1916; A.B., Kans. State Tchrs. Coll., Pittsburg, 1941; LL.B., U. Kans., 1948, J.D., 1963. Admitted to Kans. bar, 1948, U.S. Supreme Ct. bar, 1966; asso. firm William F. Pielsticker, Wichita, Kans., 1948; individual practice law, Wichita, 1949, 53-60; county atty. Sedgwick County (Kans.), 1951-53; gen. atty. VA, Wichita, 1960-77; investigator Equal Employment Opportunity Commn., Washington, 1965, Kansas City (Mo.) br., 1967. Chmn. Operation Big Count, Wichita, 1953, Wichita Territorial Centennial, 1954. Mem. Wichita, Kans., Fed. (pres. Kans. chpt.) bar assns., Nat. Lawyers Club, Phi Delta Phi. Named An Outstanding Wichitan You Should Know, KAKE radio, 1954. Home and Office: 1484 Coolidge St Wichita KS 67203 Tel (316) 265-4731

SEEFELD, GEORGE HERBERT, b. Milw., May 6, 1909; A.B. with honors, U. Wis., 1930; J.D., Harvard U., 1933. Admitted to Wis. bar, 1933, N.Y. bar, 1945, Mass. bar, 1969, U.S. Supreme Ct. bar, 1950; asso. firm Upham, Black, Russell & Richardson, Milw., 1933-44, firm Donovan, Leisure, Newton & Lumbard, N.Y.C., 1944-46, firm Davies, Hardy, Schenk & Soons, N.Y.C., 1946-51, 54-56; spl. trial counsel IRS, Dallas, 1951-53; asso. counsel Prudential Ins. Co., Newark, 1956-73; counsel to Katz & Lapointe, Pittsfield, Mass., 1973—; spl. instr. Sch. Commerce N.Y. U., 1955-56. Mem. Am. Bar Assn. (employee benefits com.). Author: (with S. Foosaner) Taxation of Life Insurance and Annuities, 1955; panelist Practising Law Inst.; contbr. articles to legal publs. Office: 29 Wendell Ave Box 572 Pittsfield MA 01201 Tel (413) 442-6939

SEEGAL, JOHN FRANKLIN, b. Newton, Mass., May 21, 1946; B.A., Harvard, 1968, J.D., 1973, M.B.A., 1973. Admitted to Calif. bar, 1973; asso. firm Orrick, Herrington, Rowley & Sutcliffe, San Francisco, 1973—. Home: 2105 Broadway San Francisco CA 94115 Tel (415) 392-1122

SEEGEL, RICHARD LAWRENCE, b. Somerville, Mass., July 13, 1937; B.A., Cornell U., 1959; LL.B., Columbia. 1964. Admitted to Mass. bar, 1964; partner firm Seegel and Seegel, Boston, 1964-69, Donahue, Seegel and Gordon, Boston, 1969-72, Lee, Muldoon, Sullivan, Seegel and Gordon, Boston, 1972—; asst. atty. gen. Mass., 1966-72. Mem. Wellesley (Mass.) Town Meeting, 1975—, mem. adv. com., 1976—. Mem. Am., Mass., Boston, Norfolk County bar assns. Office: Two Center Plaza Boston MA 02108 Tel (617) 227-7788

SEEGER, EDWIN HOWARD, b. N.Y.C., Aug. 6, 1930; B.A., Johns Hopkins U., 1951, M.A., 1953; J.D., George Washington U., 1956. Admitted to D.C. bar, 1956; asso. firm Covington & Burling, Washington, 1956-61; asst. adminstr., gen. counsel Nat. Capital Transp. Agy., Washington, 1961-64; mem. firm Prather, Seeger, Doolittle, Farmer & Ewing, Washington, 1964—. Mem. Decatur House Council, Washington, 1976—. Mem. Am. Fed. bar assns. Home: 213 S Fairfax St Alexandria VA 22314 Office: 1101 16th St NW Washington DC 20036 Tel (202) 296-0500

SEEGER, RONALD LAMOINE, b. Prairie Farm, Wis., June 10, 1930; B.A., U. Wis., 1951; J.D., U. Minn., 1956. Admitted to Minn. bar, 1956; asso. firm Michaels, Seeger & Rosenblad and predecessors, Rochester, Minn., 1956-58, partner, 1958—; counsel City of Rochester Charter Commn., 1962-74, chmn., 1971-72; dir., v.p. Legal Assistance of Minn., 1972-74; pres. Legal Assistance of Olmsted County (Minn.), 1973-75. Chmn. Gamehaven Area Boy Scout Found., Rochester, 1975-76; mem. devel. bd. St. Mary's Hosp., Rochester, 1974—. Mem. Am. (mem. house of delegates 1974—), Minn. (pres. 3d dist. 1971-72, bd. govs. 1973—), Olmsted County (pres. 1972-73) bar assns., Minn. Bar Found. (dir.). Home: 524 9th Ave SW Rochester MN 55901 Office: 228 Northwestern Bank Bldg Rochester MN 55901 Tel (507) 288-7755

SEEGERT, FREDERICK CARL, b. Milw., Apr. 10, 1925; B.A., U. Mich., 1946; J.D., U. Wis., 1950; postgrad. U. Va., 1952. Admitted to Wis. bar, 1950; individual practice law, Milw., 1950-51; JAG, U.S. Army, 1951-54; asso. firm Mueller and Seegert, Milw., 1954-66, partner, 1967—. Mem. Delafield Zoning Bd. Appeals. Mem. Am., Wis., Milw., Waukesha County bar assns. Home: 2120 Evergreen Ln Hartland WI 53029 Office: 135 W Wells St Milwaukee WI 53203 Tel (414) 276-3083

SEEHOUSEN, JOHN JOSEPH, b. Phila., Feb. 12, 1943; B.A., LaSalle Coll., 1967; J.D., Temple U., 1970. Admitted to Pa. bar, 1970; partner firm LaBrum and Doak, Phila., 1970—. Home: 321 Red Cedar Dr Levittown PA 19055 Office: 1500 Seven Penn Center Plaza Philadelphia PA 19103 Tel (215) 561-4400

SEELEY, E. VERNON, b. Boise, Idaho, Feb. 2, 1939; A.A., Boise Jr. Coll., 1959; B.A., Idaho State U., 1961; J.D., Golden Gate Law Sch., 1972. Admitted to Calif. bar, 1972; with accounting, tax, fin. depts. Del Monte Corp., San Francisco, 1961-72; tax adminstr. Rucker Corp., Oakland, Calif., 1972-73; dep. dist. atty. Stanislaus County, Modesto, Calif., 1973—. Mem. Calif., Am., Stanislaus County bar assns. Home: 3116 Williamsburg Way Modesto CA 95355 Office: Stanislaus County Courthouse PO Box 442 Modesto CA 95353 Tel (209) 526-6345

SEELEY, GLENN J., b. Wellington, Ohio, Aug. 21, 1926; B.B.A., Western Res. U., 1950; J.D., Cleve. State U., 1955. Admitted to Ohio bar, 1955, U.S. Supreme Ct. bar, 1960; mem. firm Jenson and Seeley, Avon Lake, Ohio, 1955-68; partner firm Marshman, Snyder and Seeley, Cleve., 1968—; law dir. Avon (Ohio), 1962-67. Mem. Ohio State Housing Commn. Mem. Cleve., Ohio, Am. bar assns. Named Man of Year, Lorain County, 1957. Office: One Erieview Plaza Cleveland OH 44114 Tel (216) 781-8000

SEEWALD, J. GARY, b. N.Y.C., June 27, 1946; A.B., Case Western Res. U., 1968, J.D., 1971. Admitted to Ohio bar, 1971; mem. firm Berger, Kirschenbaum & Lambros, Cleve., 1971-72; partner firm Henkin, Axner & Seewald, Cleve., 1972—. Mem. Am. Arbitration Assn. (arbitrator), Greater Cleve., Ohio, Criminal Cts. bar assns., Ohio Acad. Trial Lawyers, Am. Trial Lawyers Assn. Home: 1982 Camberly Lyndhurst OH 44124 Office: 629 Euclid Ninth Tower Cleveland OH 44115 Tel (216) 781-8288

SEFF, JAMES MICHAEL, b. N.Y.C., Jan. 27, 1941; A.B. with honors in English, U. Mich., 1963; J.D., U. Calif., 1966. Admitted to Hawaii bar, 1969, Calif. bar, 1970; legal and supply officer, USN, 1967-69; staff counsel Wine Inst., San Francisco, 1969—; mem. San Francisco Lawyers Com. Urban Affairs, 1976; dir. Jewish Family Service Agency, San Francisco, 1973—, sec., 1976—. Mem. Calif. Barristers Assn. (dir. 1976—), San Francisco Barristers' Club (dir. 1974-76, pres. 1975), Bar Assn. San Francisco (dir. 1974-75). Editor: Barristers Bailiwick, 1973-74, Conference Call, 1976; contbr. articles to legal jours. Office: 165 Post St San Francisco CA 94108 Tel (415) 986-0878

SEFTENBERG, STEPHEN LONGFELLOW, b. Oak Park, Ill., Feb. 24, 1935; A.B., Harvard, 1956, LL.B., 1959. Admitted to Ill. bar, 1959; mem. firm Wilson & McIlvaine, Chgo., 1959—. Mem. Am., Ill., Chgo. bar assns. Office: 135 S LaSalle St Room 2300 Chicago IL 60603 Tel (312) 263-1212

SEGAL, BERNARD G., B.A., U. Pa., 1928, LL.B., 1931; LL.D. (hon.), Franklin and Marshall Coll., 1953, Temple U., 1954, Dropsie U., 1966, U. Pa., 1969; J.S.D. (hon.), Suffolk U., 1969; D.H.L., Hebrew Union Coll.-Jewish Inst. Religion, 1970. Chmn. firm Schnader, Harrison, Segal and Lewis, Phila.; dep. atty. gen. Pa., 1932-35; lectr. Law Sch. U. Pa., 1931-35, 45-47; North lectr. on law Franklin and Marshall Coll., 1937-38; chmn. Commn. on Jud. and Congressional Salaries, 1953-55; charter mem. standing com. on rules of practice and procedure Jud. Conf. U.S., 1959—; co-chmn. Lawyer's Com. for Civil Rights Under Law, 1963-65; mem. Nat. Citizens Com. for Community Relations, 1964—; mem. adv. com. to U.S. Mission at UN, 1967-68; mem. Dept. State Adv. Panel on Internat. Law, 1967—; chmn. Jud. Nominating Commn., Commonwealth of Pa., 1964-65; spl. master R.R. Reorgns., U.S. Ct. Appeals, 1964—; mem. Spl. Com. on Anti-Poverty Program from Phila., 1967—; mem. Adminstrv. Conf. U.S., 1968-74, Jud. Council Pa., 1968-71, Com. to Study Workload of Supreme Ct., 1971-73, Commn. on Revision of Fed. Ct. Appellate System, 1973—; bd. dirs. Pa. Legal Services Center, 1972—; trustee Supreme Ct. Hist. Soc., 1975—; mem. Commn. on Exec., Legis. and Jud. Salaries, 1976—. Pres., chmn. bd. dirs., hon. pres. Allied Jewish Appeal; bd. dirs. Fedn. Jewish Agys. Greater Phila., Medico, Inc. div. Care, Inc., Legal Aid Soc., Phila., United Fund Greater Phila., Jewish League for Israel, Jewish Welfare Soc.; mem. adv. council Greater Phila. Movement; trustee Albert Einstein Med. Center, Jewish Publ. Soc. Am., Ency. Judaica Research Found., Margaret Chase Smith Library, Am. Friends of Hebrew U.; trustee Chapel of 4 Chaplains, Found. for Overseas Libraries of Am. Law; mem. adv. com. on pub. interest law grants Ford Found.; trustee, life mem. U. Pa.; bd. overseers U. Pa. Law Sch.; mem. joint bd. Annenberg Sch. Communications; bd. govs. Dropsie U. Mem. Am. Bar Assn. (pres. 1969-70, ho. dels. 1966—, chmn. spl. com. on lawyers in govt. 1972-74, chmn. task force on advanced jud. and legal edn., 1974—, nat. coordinator coalition on adequate jud. compensation 1975-76), Am. Bar Found. (pres. 1976—, dir.), Pa. (ho. dels. 1966-70), Phila. (past chancellor), Fed. (nat. council 1969—) bar assns., Am. Law Inst. (treas. 1955-68, 2d v.p. 1968-76, 1st v.p. 1976—), Am. Coll. Trial Lawyers (pres. 1964-65, ex officio bd. regents 1965—), Am. Judicature Soc. (chmn. bd. dirs. 1958-61, dir. 1956—), Inst. Jud. Adminstrn. (bd. fellows 1968—), Found. Fed. Bar Assn. (dir.), World Peace Through Law Center (council 1973—), Council Advancement of Legal Edn. (chmn. bd. dirs. 1972—), Council on Legal Edn. for Profl. Responsibility, Council on Legal Edn. Opportunity, U.S. Inst. Human Rights (adv. council 1972—), World Assn. Lawyers (pres. for the Americas 1976—), Nat. Conf. Bar Pres., Assn. Bar City N.Y., Fed. Communications Bar Assn., Assn. ICC Practitioners, Internat. Assn. Jewish Lawyers and Jurists, Internat. Bar Assn., Order of Coif, Delta Sigma Rho, Tau Epsilon Rho. Author: Banking and Building and Loan Law, 3 vols., 1941; editor: The Belgrade Spaceship Trial, 1972; contbr. articles to profl. jours. Office: 1719 Packard Bldg Philadelphia PA 19102 Tel (215) 491-0400

SEGAL, MARSHALL BRUCE, b. Chgo., Sept. 20, 1940; B.A., U. Calif., Los Angeles, 1961; J.D., U. Calif., Berkeley, 1965; M.D., U. Wis., 1969. Admitted to Calif. bar, 1966, Wis. bar, 1966, Ill. bar, 1970; dir. emergency medicine Little Co. of Mary Hosp., Evergreen Park, Ill., St. Bernard Hosp., Chgo.; co-dir. emergency medicine Copley

Meml. Hosp., Aurora, Ill.; asso. prof. emergency medicine U. Chgo. Hosp., Pritzker Sch. Medicine, Chgo.; cons. in field. Fellow Am. Coll. Legal Medicine (bd. govs.), Am. Acad. Forensic Scis. (exec. com.), Chgo. Acad. Law and Medicine; mem. Am., Ill., Wis., Calif., Chgo. bar assns., Chgo., Ill. State med. socs., AMA, Am. Coll. Emergency Physicians. Office: 2112 N Dayton St Chicago IL 60614 Tel (312) 327-0777

SEGAL, NORMAN MILTON, b. Elizabeth, N.J., Dec. 31, 1926; A.B., Columbia, 1949, LL.B., 1951. Admitted to N.Y. bar, 1951, D.C. bar, 1967; asso. firm Mudge Rose Guthrie & Alexander, N.Y.C., 1951-64, mem., 1964—. Mem. Assn. Bar City N.Y., Am. Bar Assn., D.C. Bar. Home: 26 Cherry St Tenafly NJ 07670 Office: 20 Broad St New York City NY 10005 Tel (212) 422-6767

SEGAL, NORMAN ROBERT, b. Phila., July 14, 1931; B.S., Temple U., 1953; J.D., U. Pa., 1959. Admitted to Pa. bar, 1959, U.S. Supreme Ct. bar, 1964; asso. firm Verlin and Goldberg, Phila., 1960-61, Abrahams and Loewenstein, Phila., 1962-63; individual practice law, Phila., 1964—. Mem. Phila. Bar Assn. Office: Suite 1009 Western Savings Fund Bldg Philadelphia PA 19107 Tel (215) KI6-6565

SEGAL, ROBERT MILTON, b. Richmond, Va., Mar. 11, 1945; B.S. in Bus. Adminstrn., U. Fla., 1968, J.D., 1971. Admitted to Fla. bar, 1971; partner firm Roth, Segal and Levine, Orlando, Fla., 1971-72; asso. firm Bornstein and Peters, Orlando, 1972-74; individual practice law, Orlando, 1974—. Mem. Orange County (Fla.), Fla. bars. Home: 771 Goldwater Ct Mastland FL 32751 Office: 125 S Court Ave Orlando FL 32801 Tel (325) 422-7152

SEGALL, LEO, b. Chgo., June 10, 1911; Ph.B., U. Chgo., 1932, J.D., 1934. Admitted to Ill. bar, 1935, U.S. Supreme Ct. bar, 1965; partner firm Asher, Greenfield, Goodstein, Pavalon and Segall, Ltd., Chgo., 1951—; dir. Internat. Found. Employee Benefit Plans, 1972-75. Bd. dirs. Home for Destitute and Crippled Children, Chgo. Mem. Am., Ill., Chgo. bar assns. Contbr. articles to legal jours. Office: 228 N LaSalle St Chicago IL 60601 Tel (312) 263-1500

SEGELSTEIN, SIDNEY, b. N.Y.C., Apr. 14, 1935; A.B. with honors, Cornell U., 1956; J.D., Harvard, 1959. Admitted to N.Y. State bar, 1960; asso. firm Goldstein & Schrank, N.Y.C., 1960-65, partner, 1965—; lectr. computer contract negotiation Brandon Systems Inst., 1975—; mem. comml. arbitration panel Am. Arbitration Assn. Mem. Am., N.Y. State bar assns., Phi Beta Kappa. Author: (with Dick H. Brandon) Data Processing Contracts: Structure, Contents and Negotiation, 1976. Home: 215 W 83rd St New York City NY 10024 Office: 99 Park Ave New York City NY 10016 Tel (212) 986-3036

SEGOR, JOSEPH CHARLES, b. N.Y.C., Dec. 23, 1935; B.B.A., U. Miami, 1957, J.D., 1960. Admitted to Fla. bar, 1960, U.S. Ct. Appeals, 1968, U.S. Supreme Ct. bar, 1974; individual practice law, Miami, Fla., 1961-66; asst. dir. Legal Services Greater Miami, Inc., 1966-67, bd. dirs., 1971—; dep. dir. Fla. Rural Legal Services, Inc., Miami, 1967-68, bd. dirs., 1969—; exec. dir., 1968-69; exec. dir. Migrant Services Found., Inc., Miami, 1969-74; mem. firm Kaplan, Dorsey, Sicking & Hessen, P.A., Miami, 1974—; mem. advisory bd. Fla. Joint Legis. Com. Migratory Labor, 1970—; bd. dirs. ACLU, Miami, 1963-66, chmn. legal panel, 1965-66; bd. dirs. Organized Migrants Community Action, Inc., Miami, 1972—, recipient Spl Merit award, 1975; mem. Fla. Advisory Com. Legal Services, 1976. Mem. Am., Fla., Dade County (Fla.) bar assns., Nat. Legal Aid Defender Assn. Office: 1951 NW 17th Ave PO Drawer 520337 Miami FL 33152 Tel (305) 325-1661

SEGREST, JERE COE, b. Dothan, Ala., Mar. 28, 1938; B.S., U. Ala., 1960, LL.B., 1962, J.D., 1969. Admitted to Ala. bar, 1962; law clk. Supreme Ct. Ala., 1962-63; partner firm Hardwick, Hause & Segrest, Dothan, 1963—; Houston County atty., 1963-74. Mem. adv. bd. Salvation Army. Mem. Am., Ala., Houston County (pres. 1968-69) bar assns., Ala. Trial Lawyers Assn. Home: 1 Camelot St Dothan AL 36301 Office: PO Box 1469 210 N Lena St Dothan AL 36301 Tel (205) 794-4144

SEGURA, LUIS M., b. Marfa, Tex., Mar. 21, 1943; B.A., St. Mary's U., San Antonio, 1964, J.D., 1968. Admitted to Tex. bar, 1968, U.S. Ct. Appeals 5th Circuit bar, 1974, also U.S. Dist. Ct.; atty. U.S. Dept. Labor, Atlanta, 1968-70; partner firm Herrera, Rocha & Segura, Inc., San Antonio, 1970-73; partner firm Segura & Jahn, Inc., San Antonio, 1973, individual practice law, San Antonio, 1973—; atty. City of Dilley (Tex.); atty. Housing Authority, Crystal City, Tex., Crystal City Housing Authority; gen. counsel Edgewood Ind. Sch. Dist., San Antonio, Dilley Ind. Sch. Dist., San Antonio. Bd. dirs. San Antonio Civil Liberties Union, San Antonio Civil Rights Litigation Center. Mem. Tex. Criminal Def. Lawyers Assn., Tex. Trial Lawyers Assn., Am. Bar Assn. San Antonio Lawyers Assn., Tex. Bar Found., Delta Theta Phi, Pi Gamma Mu. Home: 1422 E Sunshine San Antonio TX 78228 Office: 523 S Main St San Antonio TX 78204 Tel (512) 225-6191

SEHAM, MARTIN CHARLES, b. Jersey City, June 30, 1932; B.A. summa cum laude, Amherst Coll., 1954; LL.B., Harvard, 1957. Admitted to N.Y. state bar, 1957, Fed. 2d Circuit Ct. Appeals, 1959, U.S. Supreme Ct., 1963, D.C. bar, 1970, U.S. Ct. Appeals 9th circuit, 1976; asso. firm Chadbourne, Parke, Whiteside & Wolff, N.Y.C., 1957-60; asso. firm Poletti and Freidin, N.Y.C., 1960-63; partner firm Kopple & Seham, N.Y.C., 1963-66; partner firm Surrey, Karasik, Morse & Seham, N.Y.C., 1967—; legis. intern to Senator H. Lehman of N.Y., 1953; staff asst. to Senator Hubert H. Humphrey of Minn., 1954; legal asst. to subcom. constl. rights U.S. Senate Judiciary Com., 1955. Democratic committeeman Bergen County, N.Y., 1963—; bd. dirs. Urban League Bergen County, 1969-75; chmn. Bergen County Citizens for Humphrey, 1972. Mem. Am. Bar Assn., Assn. Bar City N.Y., Indsl. Relations Research Assn., Am. Arbitration Assn. Author: Federal Wage and Hour Laws, 1962; also articles in legal publs. Home: 19 Creston Ave Tenafly NJ 07670 Office: 500 Fifth Ave New York City NY 10036 Tel (212) 239-7200

SEIBEL, RICHARD DORLAND, b. Gary, Ind., Dec. 5, 1930; B.S. in Metall. Engring., Stanford, 1952, M.S. in Metall. Engring., 1953; J.D., U. Denver, 1961. Admitted to Colo. bar, 1961, Calif. bar, 1963, U.S. Patent Office bar, 1963; research metallurgist Denver Research Inst., 1955-62; asst. patent counsel N. Am. Aviation, Downey, Calif., 1962-69; partner firm Christie, Parker & Hale, Pasadena, Calif., 1969—. Mem. Am., Calif., Los Angeles bar assns., Am. Soc. Metals, Patent Law Assn. Los Angeles, Sigma Xi. Office: 201 S Lake Ave Pasadena CA 91101 Tel (213) 795-5843

SEID, RICHARD A., b. N.Y.C., Dec. 7, 1933; B.A., U. Mich., 1955; LL.B., N.Y. U., 1959. Admitted to N.Y. bar, 1960, Mass. bar, 1969, Mich. bar, 1974; asso. gen. counsel, dir. ops., OEO, N.Y.C., 1970-72; asst. prof. law U. Detroit, 1972-74; asso. prof., acting dean, 1975-76, dean, 1976—; cons. in field; spl. asst. Wayne County Prosecutor. Mem. Fair Plan Group to reform jud. campaign financing. Mem. Am., Detroit bar assns., Nat. Legal Aid Defender Assn. Home: Office: 651 E Jefferson St Detroit MI 48226

SEIDEL, FRANCIS F., III, b. Reading, Pa., Dec. 15, 1946; B.A., Gettysburg Coll., 1968; J.D., Dickinson U., 1971; B.M.S. with honors, Pitts. Inst., 1973. Admitted to Pa. bar; asso. firm Balmer, Mogel, Speidel & Roland, 1971-76; individual practice law, Sinking Spring, Pa., 1976—. Dist. commr. local council Boy Scouts Am., 1975—; pres. council St. John's Lutheran Ch., Sinking Spring, 1975-76. Mem. Berks County (chmn. naturalization com. 1974-76), Pa., Am. bar assns., Am., Pa. trial lawyers assns., Pi Lambda Sigma. Home: 445 Penn Ave Sinking Spring PA 19608 Office: 445 Penn Ave Sinking Spring PA 19608 Tel (215) 678-4004

SEIDENFELD, GLENN KENNETH, JR., b. Oceanport, N.J., Feb. 13, 1944; B.A., Northwestern U., 1966; J.D., U. Ill., 1969. Admitted to Ill. bar, Fed. bar, 1969; atty. advisor SEC, Washington, 1970-72; asso. firm McDermott, Will & Emery, Chgo., 1972-76; sec., gen. counsel Bally Mfg. Corp., Chgo. Mem. Am., Chgo. bar assns. Contbr. articles in field to profl. jours. Home: 1025 Sheridan Rd Wilmette IL 60091 Office: 2640 W Belmont Chicago IL 60618 Tel (312) 267-6060

SEIDENSTICKER, WAYDE PORTER, b. York, Pa., Feb. 27, 1938; B.S. in Bus. Adminstrn., Pa. State U., 1960, J.D., Dickinson Sch. Law, 1966. Admitted to Pa. bar, 1966; solicitor Newberry Twp. (Pa.), 1966-67, Manchester Twp. (Pa.), 1969—; East Manchester Twp. Zoning Hearing Bd., 1973-75. Chmn., York Arthritis Found., 1969. Mem. Pa., Am., York County bar assns., Am. Judicature Soc. Recipient Distinguished Service award Arthritis Found., York, 1969. Office: 55 S Queens St York PA 17403 Tel (717) 843-5105

SEIDENWURM, RICHARD LEWIS, b. N.Y.C., Feb. 1, 1941; B.A., Williams Coll., 1962; LL.B., Columbia U., 1965. Admitted to N.Y. bar, 1966, Calif. bar, 1973; asso. counsel OEO, Washington, 1965-66; asso. firm Davis Polk & Wardwell, N.Y.C., 1966-73; since practiced in San Diego, partner firm Solomon, Ward, Aguirre & Seidenwurm, and predecessors, 1973—. Mem. N.Y. State, Calif., San Diego County bar assns. Harlan Fiske Stone scholar, 1963-64. Office: Solomon Ward Aguirre & Seidenwurm 600 B St Suite 2100 San Diego CA 92101 Tel (714) 231-0303

SEIDMAN, IRVING, b. Lodz, Russia, May 29, 1901; student Pratt Inst., 1919-21, N.Y. Sch. Indsl. Arts, 1921-24, Am. Inst. Banking, Columbia, 1929-30; LL.B., St. John's U., 1928; postgrad. N.Y. U., 1932. Admitted to N.Y. State bar, 1930, U.S. Supreme Ct. bar, 1960; mem. firm Maged, Radin & Seidman, 1931—. Mem. Assn. Bar City N.Y., N.Y. Patent Law Assn., N.Y. State, Am. bar assns. Contbr. articles to legal jours.; author: Patent Office Rules and Practice, 1959. Home: 535 E 86th St New York City NY 10028 Office: 10 Columbus Circle New York City NY 10019 Tel (212) 245-2600

SEIDMAN, MICHAEL ALAN, b. Phila., June 24, 1942; B.S., Pa. State U., 1963; J.D., Temple U., 1967. Admitted to Pa. bar, 1967, U.S. Supreme Ct. bar, 1972; asst. dist. atty., Phila., 1970-74. Office: 1314 Chestnut St 12th Floor Philadelphia PA 19107 Tel (215) 732-4554

SEIDNER, EMMANUEL JOHN, b. Chgo., Dec. 6, 1909; Ph.B., Univ. Chgo., 1930, J.D., 1931. Admitted to Ill. bar, 1932; partner firm Seidner & Seidner, Chgo., 1933—. Chmn. bd. SSS, 1940-66; mem. bd. dirs. Boy Scouts Am., YMCA. Mem. Ill. (state chmn. comml. banking and bankruptcy sect. 1969-70), Chgo. bar assns. Recipient Silver Beaver award Boy Scouts Am., 1951; Presdl. citation SSS, 1967. Home: 505 N Lake Shore Dr Chicago IL 60611 Office: 10 S LaSalle St Chicago IL 60603 Tel (312) 372-1346

SEIFERT, ARTHUR JOHN, b. Chgo., Jan. 20, 1932; B.A., St. Thomas Coll., 1954; B.S.L., William Mitchell Coll. Law, 1959, J.D., 1961. Admitted to Minn. bar, 1961, Fed. Dist. Ct. Minn., 1961, Supreme Ct. U.S., 1973; asso. law firm Thomas O. Kachelmacher, Mpls., 1961-63; partner firm Bialick, Prescott & Seifert, Mpls., 1963-69; sr. partner firm Seifert, Johnson, Hall & Eide, Mpls., 1969-70; sr. partner Arthur J. Seifert, P.A., Mpls., 1970—. Mem. Am., Hennepin County, Minn. State bar assns., Am., Minn. trial lawyers assns. Home and Office: 4612 W 28th St St Louis Park MN 55416

SEIFFERT, TERRY L., b. Billings, Mont., Oct. 3, 1948; B.B.A., Mont. State U., 1970; J.D., U. Mont., 1973. Admitted to Mont. bar, 1973; asst. staff atty. Mont. Legal Services Assn., Billings, 1973-75; individual practice law, Billings, 1975—. Bd. dirs. Maternal and Infant Health Care Project, Billings, Project Tumbleweed, runaway youth program, Billings, Concern, Inc. Mem. Mont., Am. bar assns. Home: 2823 Sixth Ave N Billings MT 59101 Office: 3302 Fourth Ave N Billings MT 59101 Tel (406) 252-7503

SEIFMAN, BARRY ALLEN, b. Detroit, Mich., Oct. 14, 1946; B.A., Wayne State U., 1968, J.D. magna cum laude, 1972. Admitted to Mich. bar, 1973; partner firm Berry, Hopson, Francis, Mack, Johnson & Seifman, Detroit, 1973—; asst. city atty. Garden City (Mich.), 1973—; instr. Detroit Bus. Coll., 1976. Sec., Nat. League East Little League, Southfield, Mich., 1976-77. Mem. Am., Detroit, Oakland County bar assns., State Bar Mich. Office: 2000 Cadillac Tower Detroit MI 48226 Tel (313) 962-0525

SEIJAS, JOSEPH, b. N.Y.C., Nov. 15, 1935; B.S., N.Y. U., 1957; J.D., Bklyn. Law Sch., 1963. Admitted to N.Y. State bar, 1963, U.S. Dist. Ct. bar for So. and Eastern Dists. N.Y., 1973, U.S. Supreme Ct. bar, 1976; asso. firm Henry B. Rothblatt, Bronx, N.Y., 1963-71; partner firm Rothblatt, Rothblatt, Seijas & Peskin, Bronx, 1971—. Govt. appeals agt. SSS, 1969; mem. local bd. 19, Office U.S. Draft Bd., 1969-70. Mem. N.Y. State, Am., P.R., Inter-Am., Fed., Bronx County bar assns. Office: 191 E 161st St Bronx NY 10451 also 232 West End Ave New York City NY 10023 Tel (212) 669-1500

SEIKEL, OLIVER EDWARD, b. Akron, Ohio, July 6, 1937; B.S., Mass. Inst. Tech., 1959; J.D., U. Mich., 1962; postgrad. U. Hamburg, Ger., 1962-63. Admitted to Ohio bar, 1963; asso. firm Falsgraff, Reidy, Shoup & Ault, Cleve., 1963-68, partner, 1969-71; legal mgr. internat. ops. Midland-Ross Corp., Cleve., 1971-73; individual practice law, Cleve., 1974—; sec. Bearings, Inc., Cleve., 1974—, Midland Steel Products Co., Cleve., 1976—. Trustee Our Lady of the Wayside Home, Avon, Ohio, 1969—, Gilmour Acad., Gates Mills, Ohio, 1970—, Catholic Charities Corp., Cleve., 1975—. Mem. Am., Ohio bar assns., Bar Assn. Greater Cleve. Office: 1000 Public Square Bldg 33 Public Sq Cleveland OH 44113 Tel (216) 241-1000

SEILER, ROBERT ELDRIDGE, b. Kansas City, Kan., Dec. 5, 1912; A.B., U. Mo., 1933, LL.B., 1935. Admitted to Mo. bar, 1934; practiced in Joplin, Mo., 1935-66; city atty. of Joplin, 1950-54; judge Supreme Ct. Mo., 1967—, now chief justice. Sec. Joplin Home Rule Charter Commn., 1953-54; mem. Mo. Bd. Law Examiners, 1948-65, sec., 1950-63, pres., 1963-65. Fellow Am. Coll. Trial Lawyers; mem. Am., Jasper County, Kansas City bar assns., Am. Judicature Soc., Inst. Jud. Adminstrn., Mo. Bar, Mo. Law Sch. Alumni Assn., Nat. Conf. Bar Examiners (chmn. 1967-68). Order of Coif, Kappa Sigma. Home: 918 Laurel Rd Joplin MO 64801 Office: Supreme Ct Bldg Jefferson City MO 65101*

SEILS, WILLIAM GEORGE, b. Chgo., Aug. 9, 1935; A.B., U. Mich., 1959, J.D., 1959. Admitted to Ill. bar, 1959; partner firm Arvey, Hodes, Costello & Burman, Chgo., 1959—. Mem. Ill., Am. bar assns., Order of Coif, Tau Epsilon Rho. Contbr. articles to legal jours. Office: 180 N LaSalle St Chicago IL 60601 Tel (312) 855-5033

SEITMAN, JOHN MICHAEL, b. Bloomington, Ill., Feb. 9, 1942; B.S., U. Ill., 1964, J.D., 1966. Admitted to Calif. bar, 1966; mem. firm Scales, Patton, Ellsworth & Corbett, San Diego, 1966—. Mem. State Bar Calif., Am., San Diego County bar assns., Calif. Trial Lawyers Assn., Comml. Lawyers Group. Home: 1114 Skylark Dr La Jolla CA 92037 Office: 530 B St suite 2150 San Diego CA 92101 Tel (714) 234-9181

SEITZ, COLLINS JACQUES, b. Wilmington, Del., June 20, 1914; A.B., U. Del., 1937, LL.D., 1962; LL.B., U. Va., 1940; LL.D., Widener Coll., 1975. Admitted to Del. bar, 1940; vice chancellor Del., 1946, chancellor, 1951-66; judge U.S. Ct. Appeals, 3d Circuit, 1966—, chief judge, 1971—. Recipient James J. Hoey award, 1954; award NCCJ, 1957; Pro Ecclesia et Pontifice (papal award), 1965. Mem. Am., Del. bar assns. Home: 410 Stafford Rd Wilmington DE 19803 Office: Federal Bldg 844 King St Wilmington DE 19801*

SELANDER, RONALD DUANE, b. Mpls., Feb. 18, 1939; B.A., U. Minn., 1965, J.D., 1968. Admitted to Minn. bar, 1968; asso. firm Wurm & Selander and predecessor, Olivia, Minn., 1968-72, partner, 1972-75; individual practice law, Olivia, 1975—. Mem. Minn. State, Am. bar assns. Office: 904 1/2 W Lincoln St Olivia MN 56277 Tel (612) 523-2463

SELENBERG, CARL JOSEPH, b. New Orleans, May 29, 1945; B.A., U. Southwestern La., 1967; J.D., Tulane U., 1970. Admitted to La. bar, 1970, Fed. Dist. Ct. bar, 1970; partner firm Ortiz & Selenberg, New Orleans, 1971-74, Friedman, Ortiz & Selenberg, New Orleans, 1974-77, Orrett, Ortiz & Selenberg, 1977—; mem. faculty Tulane Sch. Social Work, 1974-76. Mem. Am., La. bar assns., Am., La. trial lawyers assns. Home: 1800 N Starrett Rd Metairie LA 70003 Office: 2100 Tulane Ave New Orleans LA 70112 Tel (504) 522-5761

SELIG, DAVID BRUCE, b. Chgo., Oct. 31, 1941; B.S. in Accounting, U. Ill., 1963; J.D., Northwestern U., 1966. Admitted to Supreme Ct. of Ill. bar, 1966, U.S. Dist. Ct. bar, 1966, U.S. Ct. of Appeals bar, 1967, U.S. Supreme Ct. bar, 1972; C.P.A., Ill.; asso. firm William J. O'Brien, Chgo., 1969-70; individual practice law, Chgo., 1968-71; asst. states atty., Cook County, Ill., 1966-68; spl. agt. in charge Ill. Bur. of Investigation, Chgo., Springfield, 1971; hearing examiner Ill. Commerce Commn., Chgo., Springfield, 1971-73; dir. Ill. Dangerous Drugs Commn., Chgo., Springfield, 1973-75; co-ordinator State Drug Abuse program, 1973-75. Rep. of Ill. State Senate to Ill. Dangerous Drugs Adv. Council, 1975—; commr. Bd. of Fire and Police Commrs., Wheeling, Ill., 1976—. Mem. Am., Ill., Chgo. bar assns., Ill. Police Assn., Ill. Soc. of CPA's. Home: 1160 Old Mill Rd Lake Forest IL 60045 Office: 61 N Milwaukee Ave Suite 200 Wheeling IL 60090 Tel (312) 537-2522

SELIGSON, AARON, b. N.Y.C., July 15, 1929; B.A., N.Y. U., 1950; LL.B., 1953. Admitted to N.Y. State bar, 1953; partner firm Seligson, Rothman & Rothman, N.Y.C., 1955—; pres. Bushnick Realty Corp., Keyport, N.J., 1958—; partner Nyack Manor Nursing Home, Valley Cottage, N.Y., Brookhaven Beach Nursing Home, Far Rockaway, N.Y., 1973—. Trustee Morris J. and Betty Kaplan Found., 1970. Mem. N.Y. Trial Lawyers Assn. Home: 35 Berkshire Rd Great Neck NY 11023 Office: 401 Broadway New York City NY 10013 Tel (212) 966-5020

SELIGSON, MAURICE VICTOR, b. Russia, Oct. 22, 1897; LL.B., Fordham U., 1922. Admitted to N.Y. State bar, 1923, U.S. Supreme Ct. bar, 1955; asso. firm Garfield & Seligson, 1925-39; individual practice law, N.Y.C., 1939—; asst. atty. gen., 1937. Mem. N.Y. County Lawyers Assn. (life). Home: 2 Herrick Dr Lawrence NY 11559 Office: 10 E 40th St New York City NY 10016 Tel (212) 683-9690

SELIKOFF, MARSHALL, b. Waterbury, Conn., Nov. 13, 1917; A.B., Albright Coll., 1939; LL.B., Rutgers U., 1949; postgrad. Nat. Coll. of Judiciary, summers, 1974, 75. Admitted to N.J. bar, 1949, U.S. Supreme Ct. bar, 1966; mem. firm John W. Taylor, Newark, 1949-55, firm Frank Zimmer, Asbury Park, N.J., 1955-60, firm Jung, Selikoff, Rathman and Dwyer, Newark, Freehold, N.J., 1960-71, firm Lane, Evans and Selikoff, Rumson, N.J., 1971-73; judge Monmouth County (N.J.), 1973-76; judge Superior Ct. of N.J., Freehold, 1976—. Mem. Supreme Ct. Rules Com. Fellow Am. Coll. Trial Lawyers; mem. N.J. (past chmn. civil procedure), Monmouth County (past pres.) bar assns., Am. Judicature Soc., N.J. Defense Assn., N.J. Trial Attys. Home: 560 N Edgemere Dr West Allenhurst NJ 07711 Office: Monmouth County Court House Freehold NJ 07728 Tel (201) 431-7098

SELL, DONALD MILLER, b. Johnstown, Pa., Nov. 12, 1925; B.S. in Chem. Engring., U. Pitts., 1948; J.D., Georgetown U., 1954. Admitted to D.C. bar, 1954, Minn. bar, 1957; individual practice law, Washington, 1954-55; asso. firm Carpenter, Kinney & Coulter, and predecessors, St. Paul, 1956-64, partner firm, 1965-67; partner firm Alexander, Sell, Steldt & DeLaHunt and predecessor, St. Paul, 1967—. Mem. Am., Minn., Ramsey, D.C. bar assns., Am., Minn. patent law assns. Office: 2501 Hudson Rd PO Box 33427 St Paul MN 55133 Tel (612) 733-1514

SELLERS, BEN ALFRED, JR., b. Galveston, Tex., Aug. 13, 1942; B.S. in Polit. Sci., Kans. State U., 1970; J.D., U. Kans., 1973. Admitted to Kans. bar, 1973; asso. firm Frank C. Norton, Salina, Kans., 1973-74; partner firm Winkley & Sellers, Salina, 1974-77, firm Sellers & Mosier, Salina, 1977—. Pres., Salina County chpt. Kans. Council on Crime and Delinquency, 1974-75; bd. dirs. Kans. Assn. Mental Health, 1974—, state treas., 1975-76; bd. dirs. Salina Jaycees, 1976—. Mem. Am., Kans., Salina bar assns. Home: 449 Regent Rd Salina KS 67401 Office: 202 W Iron Ave Salina KS 67401 Tel (913) 825-6283

SELLMER, STEPHEN MICHAEL, b. Indpls., Oct. 31, 1947; B.A., Hillsdale Coll., 1969; J.D., Indpls. Law Sch., 1973. Probation officer Municipal Ct. of Marion County (Ind.), 1971-73; admitted to Ind. bar, 1973; asso. firm Hammond Cromer & Jackson, Indpls., 1974-76;

partner firm Cartmel, Carvey, Latimer Howard & Sellmer, Indpls., 1976—; judge pro-tem Marion County Municipal and Superior Cts.; dir. Break Away, Inc., C.B. Stewart & Assos., Inc. Precinct capt. Dick Lugar Senatorial Campaign. Mem. Indpls., Ind., Am. bar assns., Am. Trial Lawyer's Assn. Home: 575 Meadowview Ln Greenwood IN 46242 Office: 9135 N Meridian St Suite C-1 Indianapolis IN 46260 Tel (317) 251-2277

SELPH, WILLIAM FRANKLIN, JR., b. Laurel, Miss., May 23, 1929; B.B.A., U. Miss., 1950, LL.B., J.D., 1954. Admitted to Miss. bar, 1954, U.S. Supreme Ct. bar, 1973; mgr. adminstrv. div. Atlantic Refining Co., Dallas, 1960-62; spl. judge youth ct., Jackson, Miss., 1971—. Mem. Hinds County, Miss., Am. bar assns., Am. Judicature Soc., Miss. Trial Lawyers Assn., Ole Miss Loyalty Found., U. Miss. Law Sch. Alumni, Phi Delta Phi (pres. 1953), Omicron Delta Kappa: recipient Phi Alpha Delta Award, 1953; hon. col. Gov.'s staff, 1964-72. Home: 5420 Runnymede Rd Jackson MS 39211 Office: Suite 1226 Capital Towers Jackson MS 39205 Tel (601) 948-3045

SELVIG, JETTIE PIERCE, b. Van Buren County, Ark., Dec. 16, 1932; LL.B., Ark. Law Sch., 1954. Admitted to Ark. bar, 1953, Calif. bar, 1961, U.S. Supreme Ct., 1969; asso. firm Belli & Choulos, San Francisco, 1961—. Treas. Calif. div. Womens Equity Action League, 1970-72, pres., 1973; active Homestead PTA, Marin Conservation League, Atty. Gen.'s Vol. Adv. Com., Mill Valley Middle Sch. Parents, Tchrs. and Students Assn.; bd. dirs. Legal Aid Soc. San Francisco, Neighborhood Legal Assistance Found. Mem. Nat. Assn. Women Lawyers (del., bus. mgr., pres. 1969-70, chairperson women in pub. service com. 1971-75), Queens Bench (dir. 1972—, treas. 1973, v.p. 1974, pres. 1975), Lawyers Club San Francisco (del.), Am., Calif., San Francisco bar assns., San Francisco Trial Lawyers Assn., Calif. Women Lawyers, Internat. Fedn. Women Lawyers, Calif. Applicants Atty. Assn. (dir. No. Calif. chpt. 1974—, v.p. 1975, pres. 1976-77), Queens Bench Found. (dir. 1974—, pres. 1974-76). Recipient certificate of honor Bd. Suprs. City and County San Francisco, 1969, Countess of Pulaski proclamation Quorum Ct. of Pulaski County, Ark., 1969, Silver Bowl of Appreciation award Girl Scouts U.S.A., 1976; honored as Hidden Heroine, San Francisco council Girl Scouts U.S.A., 1976. Home: Mill Valley CA Office: 722 Montgomery St San Francisco CA 94111 Tel (415) 981-0150

SELVIN, PAUL PHILLIP, b. Hartford, Conn., July 23, 1917; A.B. magna cum laude, Harvard, 1939; LL.B. cum laude, U. Conn., 1949. Admitted to Conn. bar, 1949, Calif. bar, 1950, U.S. Supreme Ct. bar, 1964; asso. firm Krystal & Paradis, Los Angeles, 1951-52; individual practice law, Los Angeles, 1952-58; partner firm Selvin & Weiner, P.C., and predecessors, Los Angeles, 1959—; teaching fellow, acting asst. prof. law Stanford, 1949-51; prof., lectr. Loyola U. Law Sch., Los Angeles, 1953—. Mem. State Bar Calif. (com. appellate cts.), Los Angeles, Beverly Hills bar assns., Calif. Acad. Appellate Lawyers (treas.). Office: Selvin & Weiner 1801 Ave of Stars Suite 625 Los Angeles CA 90067 Tel (213) 277-1555

SELWOOD, PIERCE TAYLOR, b. Evanston, Ill., July 31, 1939; A.B., Princeton, 1961; LL.B., Harvard, 1964. Admitted to Calif. bar, 1965; asso. firm Sheppard, Mullin, Richter & Hampton, Los Angeles, 1964-70, partner, 1971—. Mem. Am., Calif., Los Angeles County bar assns., Assn. Bus. Trial Lawyers. Contbr. articles to legal reports. Office: 333 S Hope St 48th Floor Los Angeles CA 90071 Tel (213) 620-1780

SEMAAN, FRED AMEEN, b. San Antonio, Jan. 7, 1911; student U. Tex., 1930-35, Washington Coll. Law and Nat. Law Sch., 1939-41. Admitted to Tex. bar, 1941, U.S. Supreme Ct. bar, 1957; mem. firm Schlesinger, Goodstein & Semaan, San Antonio, 1943-63, firm Goodstein & Semaan, San Antonio, 1963—. Mem. Am., San Antonio bar assns., Tex. State Bar, Am. Judicature Soc., Internat. Acad. Trial Lawyers, Tex. Criminal Def. Attys. Assn., Tex. Trial Lawyers Assn. Home: 135 W Gramercy St San Antonio TX 78212 Office: 1200 Tower Life Bldg San Antonio TX 78205 Tel (512) 223-2941

SEMENOW, ROBERT W., b. Greensburg, Pa., Dec. 6, 1897; B.S. in Econs., U. Pa., 1920; LL.B., Duquesne U., 1921; M.Litt., U. Pitts., 1937; LL.D., Rider Coll., 1961. Admitted to Pa. bar, 1921, U.S. Supreme Ct. bar, 1969; mem. faculty U. Pitts., 1920-65, prof. real estate and urban land studies, 1960-65, prof. emeritus, 1974—; individual practice law, Pitts., 1921—; dir. Pa. Real Estate Brokers License Law, 1929-35; spl. dep. atty. gen., 1940-63. Mem. Am., Pa., Pitts. bar assns., Nat. Assn. Real Estate License Law Ofcls. (exec. v.p. 1930-77), AAUP, Pa. Assn. Realtors (hon., life), Greater Pitts. Bd. Realtors (hon., life), Rho Epsilon (hon.). Author: Landlord and Tenant, 1931; Survey of Real Estate Brokers License Laws, 1936; Selected Cases in Real Estate, 1964; Questions and Answers on Real Estate, 8th edit., 1975. Home: 2217 Washington Plaza Apts Pittsburgh PA 15219 Office: 505-506 Grant Bldg Pittsburgh PA 15219 Tel (412) 261-1225

SEMENZA, LAWRENCE JOHN, b. San Francisco, Nov. 1, 1942; student Menlo Coll., 1960-62; B.A., U. Nev., 1965; J.D., U. Utah, 1968; postgrad. N.Y. U., 1968-69. Admitted to Calif. bar, 1970, Nev. bar, 1968; asso. firm Breen, Young, Whitehead & Hay, Reno, 1969-70; asst. U.S. atty. Dist. Nev., Las Vegas, 1970-75, U.S. atty., 1975—. Mem. Am., San Francisco, Washoe County, Clark County bar assns. Office: 300 Las Vegas Blvd S Las Vegas NV 89101 Tel (702) 784-5439

SEMMES, DAVID HOPKINS, b. Washington, Jan. 5, 1928; A.B. cum laude, Princeton, 1945; LL.B., LaSalle Extension U., 1956. Admitted to Md. bar, 1956, U.S. Supreme Ct. bar, 1959, D.C. bar, 1962; partner firm Semmes & Semmes, Washington, 1956-69, firm Pierson, Semmes, Crolius and Finley, Washington, 1969—; adj. prof. patent law Georgetown U., 1973-75. Mem. Am., Md., D.C. bar assns., Am. Patent Law Assn. Office: 1054 31st St NW Washington DC 20007 Tel (202) 333-4000

SEMMES, RAPHAEL, b. Washington, Jan. 10, 1921; B.A. cum laude, Princeton U., 1943; LL.B., U. Md., 1949. Admitted to Md. bar, 1949, D.C. bar, 1950; partner firm Semmes & Semmes, Washington, 1950-57, Raphael Semmes, Washington, 1957—; sec., bd. dirs. Am. Patent Law Assn., 1963-67. Bd. dirs. Nat. Capital Area council Boy Scouts Am., 1953-68, gen. counsel, 1958-63. Mem. Washington, Am. bar assns., Am. Patent Law Assn. Home: 31 Quincy St Chevy Chase MD 20015 Office: 1511 K St NW Washington DC 20005 Tel (202) 393-1510

SEMPLE, E. MICHAEL, b. Buffalo, Feb. 17, 1947; B.A., Canisius Coll., 1969; J.D., State U. N.Y., Buffalo, 1972. Admitted to N.Y. bar, 1973, Fla. bar, 1974; individual practice law, Buffalo, 1973—. Mem. Erie County (N.Y.), Fla., N.Y. State bar assns., Erie County Trial Lawyers Assn., Assn. Trial Lawyers Am. Home: 161 Willow Breeze Rd Kenmore NY 14223 Office: 785 Ellicott Square Bldg Buffalo NY 14203 Tel (716) 853-4861

SENDAK, THEODORE LORRAINE, b. Chgo., Mar. 16, 1918; A.B. cum laude in Govt., Harvard, 1940; LL.B., Valparaiso U., 1958, J.D., 1970. Admitted to Ind. bar, 1959, U.S. Supreme Ct. bar, 1969; individual practice law, Crown Point, 1959-68; atty. gen. Ind., 1969—. Mem. Nat. Assn. Attys. Gen. (vice chmn., chmn. Midwest Conf. 1970-71, pres. 1977), Am., 7th Fed. Circuit, Ind., Crown Point-Lowell bar assns. Recipient Freedoms Found. award, 1973. Home: PO Box 359 Crown Point IN 46307 Office: 219 State House Indianapolis IN 46204 Tel (317) 633-5512

SENNETT, WILLIAM CLIFFORD, b. Erie, Pa., June 1, 1930; B.A., Holy Cross Coll., Worcester, Mass., 1952; LL.B., Georgetown U., 1955. Admitted to D.C. bar, 1956, Pa. bar, 1957; partner firms Shreve Sennett & McCarthy, Erie, 1957-64, Knox Pearson & McLaughlin, Erie, 1964-67, Knox Graham McLaughlin Gornall & Sennett, Erie, 1971—; asst. atty. gen. Commonwealth of Pa., 1964-66, atty. gen., 1967-70. Mem. Pa. Bar, Am. Bar Assn., Am. Judicature Soc. Home: 6336 Red Pine Ln Erie PA 16506 Office: 23 W 10th St Erie PA 16501 Tel (814) 456-4266

SENSENBRENNER, FRANK JAMES, JR., b. Chgo., June 14, 1943; A.B., Stanford, 1965; J.D., U. Wis., 1968. Admitted to Wis. bar, 1968, U.S. Supreme Ct. bar, 1972; mem. firm McKay & Martin, Cedarburg, Wis., 1970-75; mem. Wis. Assembly, 1969-75, Wis. Senate, 1975—. Mem. Am. Bar Assn. Office: State Capitol Madison WI 53702 Tel (608) 266-1324

SENSENICH, ILA JEANNE, b. Pitts., Mar. 6, 1939; B.A., Westminster Coll., 1961; J.D., Dickinson Sch. Law, 1964. Admitted to Pa. bar, 1964, U.S. Dist. Ct. Western Dist. Pa. bar, 1965; asso firm Stewart, Beldon, Sensenich and Herrington, Pitts., 1964-70; 1st asst. pub. defender, Westmoreland County, Pa., 1970-71; U.S. magistrate, Western Dist. Pa., 1971—. Permanent trustee Dickinson Sch. Law., 1974—. Mem. Am., Pa., Allegheny and Westmoreland counties bar assns., Nat. Council Spl. Ct. Judges, Jud. Conf. Third Jud. Circuit, Nat. Council Fed. Magistrates. Recipient Alumni Achievement award Westminster Coll., 1976; contbr. articles in field to law reviews. Office: 1026 US Post Office & Courthouse Pittsburgh PA 15219 Tel (412) 644-3535

SENTELL, ROBERT PERRY, JR., b. Pinehurst, Ga., Apr. 19, 1934; diploma Mid. Ga. Coll., 1952; A.B., U. Ga., 1956, LL.B. magna cum laude, 1958; LL.M. (Ford fellow), Harvard, 1961. Admitted to Ga. bar, 1957; asst. prof. law U. Ga. Inst. Law and Govt., Athens, 1959-63, asso. prof. Sch. Law, 1964-68, prof. law, 1968—; mem. com. on law and faculties State Bar Ga., 1972-73. Active Beech Haven Baptist Ch., Athens. Mem. Blue Key, Phi Beta Kappa, Phi Kappa Phi, Phi Alpha Delta. Recipient Spl. award Mercer U. Law Rev., 1974; Distinguished Service award Ga. Municipal Assn., 1974; author books in field; contbr. articles to legal jours. Home: 495 Forest Heights Dr Athens GA 30601 Office: Law Sch Univ Ga Athens GA 30602 Tel (404) 542-7962

SENTER, DONALD ALAN, b. Everett, Washington, June 28, 1938; B.A., U. Wash., 1960, LL.B., 1964. Admitted to Wash. bar, 1965; asso. firm Bell & Ingram, Everett, 1965-68; individual practice law, Everett, 1968; partner firm Senter & Miller, Everett, 1968—. Bd. dirs. Campfire Girls. Mem. Am., Wash. bar assns. Tel (206) 259-0918

SEQUEIRA, MANUEL ALEXANDRE, JR., b. Shanghai, China, Oct. 31, 1931; B.A., U. Notre Dame, 1955, J.D., 1956. Admitted to N.Y. bar, 1957, U.S. Supreme Ct. bar, 1971; asso. firm Hill, Rivkins, Carey, Loesberg & O'Brien, N.Y.C., 1956-67, firm Lee, McCarthy & DeRosa, N.Y.C., 1967-73; partner firm DeRosa, Sequeira & Rienzo, N.Y.C., 1974—. Mem. Am., N.Y. State bar assns., Maritime Law Assn. U.S., N.Y. County Lawyers Assn., N.Y. Law Inst., Assn. Average Adjusters U.S., Am. Arbitration Assn. Home: 2168 Pondfield Ct Yorktown Heights NY 10598 Office: 102 Maiden Ln New York City NY 10005 Tel (212) 791-7450

SERGEANT, DAVID ARTHUR, b. Sioux City, Iowa, Jan. 10, 1945; B.A., St. Olaf Coll., 1967; J.D. with honors (Univ. Merit scholar), Drake U., 1970. Admitted to Iowa bar, 1970; partner firm Sergeant & Sergeant, Ft. Dodge, Iowa, 1970—; standing trustee in bankruptcy U.S. Dist. Ct. for No. Dist. Iowa, 1970—; asst. county atty. Webster County (Iowa), 1972-74. Deacon 1st Presbyn. Ch., Ft. Dodge, 1974—; mem. membership exec. com. Ft. Dodge YMCA, 1975—. Mem. Webster County, Iowa State, Am. bar assns., Am., Iowa assns. trial lawyers, Delta Theta Phi. Mem. Drake Law Rev., 1968-70, notes editor, 1969-70; editorial bd. Iowa Trial Lawyer, 1975—. Office: Suite 38 Warden Plaza Fort Dodge IA 50501 Tel (515) 576-0671

SERGEANT, WILLIAM MAC NICOLL, b. Sioux City, Iowa, Oct. 5, 1940; B.S., Iowa State U., 1961; J.D., U. Minn., 1965. Admitted to Iowa bar, 1965, Minn. bar, 1965; mem. firm Sergeant & Sergeant, profl. corp., Fort Dodge, Iowa, 1965—. Bd. dirs. First Presbyterian Ch., Fort Dodge, 1974—, Prairie Gold council Boy Scouts Am., 1975—. Mem. Am. (sect. on taxation), Iowa bar assns., Fort Dodge C. of C. (dir. 1974—). Office: Suite 38 Warden Plaza Fort Dodge IA 50501 Tel (515) 576-0671

SERGENT, STANLEY H., JR., b. Charleston, W.Va., Nov. 15, 1941; B.S. in Fin., W.Va., U., 1963, LL.B., 1966. Admitted to W.Va. bar, 1966; labor atty. FMC Corp., Charleston, 1966-69; partner firms Kaufman, Ghiz, Vealey & Sergent, Charleston, 1969-72, Hoyer and Sergent, Charleston, 1972—; panel umpire Fed. Mediation and Conciliation Service; permanent panel umpire Nat. Bituminous Coal Assn. and United Mine Workers Am. Bd. dirs. Charleston YMCA, 1974-76. Mem. Am., W.Va. bar assns., W.Va. State Bar, Am. Arbitration Assn. Home: 510 Linden Rd Charleston WV 25314 Office: 22 Capitol St Charleston WV 25301 Tel (304) 344-9821

SERHANT, JOSEPH ERVIN, b. Chgo., July 12, 1907; B.S. in Law, U. Ill., 1929; J.D., Northwestern U., 1931. Admitted to Ill. bar, 1931; city atty., City of Berwyn, Ill., 1937-70, Berwyn Twp. atty., 1945-70; chmn. bd. First Savs. of La Grange Park, Ill., 1970—. Pres. Robin Hood Ranch Assn., 1973—. Mem. Chgo. Bar Assn., Gamma Eta Gamma. Home: 18 Robin Hood Ranch Oak Brook IL 60521 Office: 6504 Cermak Rd Berwyn IL 60402 Tel (312) 654-1800

SERLIN, GERALD MARK, b. Queens, N.Y., Apr. 5, 1941; B.A., Hofstra U., 1962; LL.B., Cornell U., 1965. Admitted to N.Y. bar, 1967; claims adjuster Pacific Ins. Co., N.Y.C., 1966-68; asso. firm Irving Chapnick, N.Y.C., 1968-71; individual practice law, Mineola, N.Y., 1971—. Pres. Hedges Civic Assn., Westbury, N.Y. Mem. Nassau County (N.Y.) Bar Assn., Lawyers Interested in Victims Equity. Home: 181 Hazelwood Dr Westbury NY 11590 Office: 170 Old Country Rd Mineola NY 11501 Tel (516) 742-2915

SERMERSHEIM, MICHAEL DAVID, b. Akron, Ohio, Dec. 24, 1948; B.A., U. Akron, 1970, J.D., 1973. Admitted to Ohio bar, 1973; served with JAGC, AUS, Okinawa, 1973-76, also instr. bus. law Far East div. U. Md., 1974-76; atty./adminstr. Univ. Legal Services, U. Akron, 1976—. Mem. Cuyahoga Falls (Ohio) CSC, 1977—. Mem. Am., Ohio, Akron bar assns., Nat. Order Barristers. Nat. finalist Nat. Mock Law Office Competition, 1973. Home: 2068 25th St Cuyahoga Falls OH 44223 Office: Univ Legal Services U Akron Akron OH 44325 Tel (216) 375-7830

SERNETT, RICHARD PATRICK, b. Mason City, Iowa, Sept. 8, 1938; B.B.A., U. Iowa, 1960, J.D., 1963. Admitted to Iowa bar, 1963, Ill. bar, 1965, U.S. Dist. Ct. No. Dist. Ill. bar, 1965, U.S. Supreme Ct. bar, 1971; house counsel Scott, Foresman & Co., Glenview, Ill., 1963-70, asst. sec., house counsel, 1967-70, sec., legal officer, 1970—; mem. adv. panel on internat. copyright U.S. Dept. State, 1972-75. Mem. Am., Ill., Chgo. bar assns., Am. Patent Law Assn., Patent Law Assn. Chgo., Copyright Soc. U.S.A. (trustee 1972-75), Am. Soc. Corporate Secs. Home: 2071 Glendale Ave Northbrook IL 60062 Office: 1900 E Lake Ave Glenview IL 60025 Tel (312) 729-3000

SERVICE, ARCHIE WALTER, b. Pocatello, Idaho, Sept. 13, 1926; B.S., Stanford, 1950; LL.B., U. Idaho, 1953. Admitted to Idaho bar, 1953, U.S. Tax Ct. bar, 1956, U.S. Supreme Ct. bar, 1969; partner firm Green & Service, Pocatello, 1953-61, firm Terrell, Green, Service & Gasser, Pocatello, 1961—. Chmn. Bannock County (Idaho) Polio Dr., 1954. Mem. Am., 6th Dist. (pres. 1962) bar assns., Pocatello Estate Planning Council. Home: 33 Purdue St Pocatello ID 83201 Office: suite C 1 Center Plaza PO Box 4883 Pocatello ID 83201 Tel (208) 232-4471

SESSA, ANTHONY JOSEPH, b. Bklyn., Mar. 9, 1907; A.B., Princeton, 1929; LL.B., Harvard, 1932, also J.S.D. Admitted to N.Y. State bar, 1933; asso. firm Wingate & Cullen, Bklyn., 1933-41; partner firm Mebel & Sessa, Bklyn., 1945—; trustee Greater N.Y. Savs. Bank. Mem. N.Y.C. Youth Bd., 1947-74; trustee Meth. Hosp. of Bklyn.; bd. dirs. Bklyn. Inst. Arts and Scis. Mem. Bklyn. Bar Assn. Home: 240 Central Park S New York City NY 10019 Office: 188 Montague St Brooklyn NY 11201 Tel (212) 625-5526

SESSIONS, PAUL STANLEY, b. Ft. Wayne, Ind., May 5, 1899; B.S., Worcester Poly. Inst., 1921; J.D., Cleve. State U., 1929. Admitted to Ohio bar, 1930; mech. engr. Frank L. Sessions Cons. Engr., Cleve., 1921-29; patent atty. firm Richey & Watts, Cleve., 1929-41; partner firm Bosworth & Sessions, Cleve., 1941-73; of counsel firm Bosworth, Sessions & McCoy, Cleve., 1973—. Trustee Cleve. Zool. Soc., 1965—; pres.'s adv. com. Worcester Poly. Inst., 1970—. Mem. Am., Cleve. bar assns., Am., Cleve. patent law assns. Home: 12700 Lake Ave Apt 2707 Lakewood OH 44107 Office: 625 Nat City Bank Bldg Cleveland OH 44114 Tel (216) 781-9050

SESSIONS, WILLIAM CRIGHTON, b. Columbus, Ohio, Sept. 22, 1904; B.S., Mass. Inst. Tech., 1926; J.D., Case Western Res. U., 1930. Admitted to Ohio bar, 1930; partner firm Bosaorth, Sessions & McCoy and predecessor, Cleve., 1941—. Trustee, Cleve. Health Mus.; mem. bd. fin. advisors Cleve. YMCA; mem. corp. devel. com. Mass. Inst. Tech. Mem. Am., Cleve. bar assns., Am., Cleve. (pres. 1963-64) patent law assns., Am. Judicature Soc., Cleve. Engring. Soc., Internat. Patent and Trade Mark Assn. Home: 15710 W Shore Ct Lakewood OH 44107 Office: 625 National City Bank Bldg Cleveland OH 44114 Tel (216) 781-9050

SESTRIC, ANTHONY JAMES, b. St. Louis, June 27, 1940; B.A., Georgetown U., 1962; J.D., U. Mo., 1965. Admitted to Mo. bar, 1965, U.S. Supreme Ct. bar, 1970; clk. U.S. Dist. Ct., Eastern Mo., 1965-66; partner firm Sestric, McGhee and Miller, St. Louis, 1966-77, firm Fordyce & Mayne, St. Louis, 1977—; spl. asst. Mo. Atty. Gen., 1968; hearing officer St. Louis Met. Police Dept., 1975—. Chmn. St. Louis Air Pollution Bd. Appeals and Variance Rev., 1968-73, mem., 1966-73; mem. St. Louis Municipal Airport Commn., 1975-76; trustee Law Library Assn. St. Louis, 1975—; dist. vice chmn. St. Louis Council Boy Scouts Am., 1970-76; bd. dirs. Full Achievement, Inc., St. Louis, 1971—, Legal Aid Soc. St. Louis, 1976—. Mem. Am. (com. state chmn. 1973-76, circuit chmn. com. 1975-76), Mo. (vice chmn. council young lawyers sect. 1973-76, bd. govs. 1974-76), Met. St. Louis (sec. young lawyers sect. 1971-73, vice chmn. 1972-73, chmn. 1974-75, exec. com. 1974—) bar assns., St. Louis Lawyers Assn., Am. Judicature Soc. Contbr. articles to law jours. Home: 3967 Holly Hills Blvd St Louis MO 63116 Office: 120 S Central Ave St Louis MO 63105 Tel (314) 863-6900

SETTINO, GENEVIEVE WINIFRED, b. Ambridge, Pa., Apr. 25, 1917; B.A., Seton Hill Coll., Greensburg, Pa., 1939; M.A., Duquesne U., 1941, LL.B., 1949. Admitted to Pa. Supreme Ct. bar, 1950, U.S. Dist. Ct. bar for Western Dist. Pa., 1951; individual practice law, Ambridge, 1950—; solicitor Borough of Ambridge, 1957—, Ambridge Parking Authority, 1958—, Borough of Baden (Pa.), 1965-70; asst. pub. defender Beaver County, Pa., 1968-72, asst. dist. atty., 1970—. Mem. Beaver County (sec.), Pa., Am. bar assns., Am., Pa. trial lawyers assns. Home: 817 Melrose Ave Ambridge PA 15003 Office: 763 Merchant St Ambridge PA 15003 Tel (412) 266-4054

SETTLE, STUART WILLISTON, JR., b. Cleve., Jan. 22, 1941; B.S., U.S. Naval Acad., 1963; J.D., Harvard, 1972. Admitted to Va. bar, 1973, U.S. Supreme Ct. bar, 1976; asso. firm McGuire, Woods & Battle, Richmond, Va., 1972-74; partner firm Coates, Comess, Settle, Moore & Taylor, and predecessor, Richmond, 1974—; asst. county atty. County of Henrico (Va.), 1974-75. Mem. U.S. Naval Inst., Va., Am. bar assns., Va. State Bar, Bar Assn. City Richmond, Assn. Trial Lawyers Am. Home: 1020 W 45th St Richmond VA 23225 Office: 113 N Foushee St Richmond VA 23220 Tel (804) 643-6621

SETTLE, WILLIAM HENRY, b. Winder, Ga., June 9, 1924; J.D., Woodrow Wilson Coll. Law, 1960. Individual practice accounting, 1950-64; admitted to Ga. bar, 1962; audit dir. State of Ga., Atlanta, 1964—. Home: 1703 Timberland Rd NE Atlanta GA 30345 Office: 216 Trinity Washington Bldg Atlanta GA 30334 Tel (404) 656-2180

SETZLER, EDWARD ALLAN, b. Kansas City, Mo., Nov. 3, 1933; A.B., U. Kans., 1955, J.D., U. Wis., 1962. Admitted to Mo. bar, 1962; partner firm Spencer, Fane, Britt & Browne, Kansas City, 1962—. Mem. Am., Mo., Kansas City bar assns., Lawyers Assn. Kansas City, Estate Planning Assn. Kansas City (co-founder 1965, past bd. dirs.), Order of Coif, Phi Delta Phi (officer). Mem. editorial bd. Wis. Law Rev., 1961-62; reviewer Mo. Estate Adminstrn. Handbook. Home: 15051 Holmes St Kansas City MO 64105 Office: 1000 Power & Light Bldg Kansas City MO 64105 Tel (816) 474-8100

SETZLER, NIKKI GILES, b. Ashville, N.C., Aug. 7, 1945; B.A. in Polit. Sci., U. S.C., 1968, J.D., 1971. Admitted to S.C. bar, 1971; asso. firm Harry M. Lightsey, Jr., Columbia, S.C., 1971-73; individual practice law, W. Columbia, S.C., 1973-74; asso. firm Setzler Chewning & Scott, W. Columbia, 1977—; judge City of Cayce (S.C.), 1974-76. Atty. Town of Springdale (S.C.), 1975—; mem. S.C. Senate, 1977—. Mem. Am., S.C., Lexington County, Richland County bar assns., Am., S.C. trial lawyers assns. Home: 1309 Canary Dr West Columbia SC 29169 Office: PO Box 1036 West Columbia SC 29169 Tel (803) 796-8408

SEVEL, BERNARD JEROME, b. Balt., May 1, 1924; B.E., Johns Hopkins, 1949; LL.B., Eastern Coll., 1957; J.D., U. Balt., 1970. Admitted to Md. bar, 1958, U.S. Supreme Ct. bar, 1976; engr. Martin Co., 1954-58, head specification dept. specifications and contract negotiations, 1958-61; individual practice law, Balt., 1961—; mem. adv. com. on admiralty rules Fed. Dist. Ct., 1971—; instr. continuing legal edn. U. Md., 1977. Chmn. legal com. Temple Oheb Shalom Congregation of Balt., Inc., 1975—. Mem. Maritime Law Assn. Am., Am. Trial Lawyers Assn., Am., Md., Balt. bar assns. Home: 3305 Janellen Dr Baltimore MD 21208 Office: suite 900 1 Charles Center Baltimore MD 21201 Tel (301) 752-1960

SEVERS, GROVER LAWRENCE, b. Union Star, Ky., May 9, 1915; A.B., Adelbert Coll., 1937; LL.B., Western Reserve U., 1940. Admitted to Ohio bar, 1940, Fed. bar, 1951, U.S. Supreme Ct. bar, 1965, Fla. bar, 1972; partner firm Stevens and Severs, Elyria, Ohio, 1946-54; individual practice law, Elyria, 1955-59; partner firm Severs & Glavas, Elyria, 1960-75; partner firm Severs & Boylan, Elyria, 1975—; city atty. Oberlin, Ohio, 1958-63, 66-72. Trustee Elyria YMCA, 1949; active United Appeal, 1961. Mem. Fla., Ohio, Lorain County (pres. 1969-70) bar assns. Home: 405 W College St Oberlin OH 44074 Office: 28 Lake Ave Elyria OH 44035 Tel (216) 322-7624

SEVERSON, PETER PUTNAM, b. Phila., Jan. 22, 1935; B.A., Duke, 1957; LL.B., Stanford, 1961. Admitted to Calif. bar, 1962, Ill. bar, 1968, U.S. Supreme Ct. bar, 1969; individual practice law, San Francisco, 1962-72; counsel Ampex Corp., Redwood City, Calif., 1973-75; internat. counsel, Reading, Eng., 1975—. Mem. Am. Bar Assn. Tel (415) 367-4459

SEVIER, ERNEST YOULE, b. Sacramento, June 20, 1932; B.A., Stanford, 1954, J.D., 1956. Admitted to Calif. bar, 1956, U.S. Supreme Ct. bar, 1965; judge adv. U.S. Air Force, 1956-57; asso. firm Sedgwick, Detert, Moran & Arnold, San Francisco, 1958-62, Severson, Werson, Berke & Melchior, San Francisco, 1962-64, partner, 1964—. Mem. Am., Calif., San Francisco bar assns. Office: One Embarcadero Center 25th floor San Francisco CA 94111 Tel (415) 398-3344

SEVIER, KIRBY, b. Birmingham, Ala., Sept. 22, 1946; B.A., Birmingham-So. Coll., 1968; J.D., Vanderbilt U., 1971. Admitted to Ala. bar, 1971; law clk. to judge U.S. Dist. Ct. for No. Ala., 1971-72; asso. firm Cabaniss, Johnston, Gardner, Dumas & O'Neal, Birmingham, 1972—. Mem. Am., Ala., Birmingham bar assns., Order of Coif. Student writing editor Vanderbilt Law Rev., 1970-71; recipient best case comment award Vanderbilt Law Rev., 1970. Home: 1001 Euclid Ave Birmingham AL 35213 Office: 1900 First Nat So Nat Bldg Birmingham AL 35203 Tel (205) 252-8800

SEWARD, GEORGE CHESTER, b. Omaha, Aug. 4, 1910; B.A., U. Va., 1933, LL.B., 1936. Admitted to Va. bar, 1935, N.Y. bar, 1937, Ky. bar, 1947, also U.S. Supreme Ct. bar; with firm Shearman & Sterling, N.Y.C., 1936-53, Seward & Kissel, N.Y.C., 1953—. Trustee Benson Iron Ore Trust, Edwin Gould Found. for Children. Fellow Am. Bar Found. (chmn. model corp. acts com. 1956-65); mem. Internat. (chmn. com. on monopolies and restrictive practices 1965-68, founder, chmn. sect. bus. law 1970-74, life mem. council 1972—), Am. (chmn. sect. corp. banking bus. law 1958-59, chmn. sect. com. corp. laws 1952-58, chmn. sect. banking com. 1960-61, rep. ho. of dels. 1959-60, 63-75) bar assns., Am. Law Inst. (joint com. with Am. Bar Assn. on continuing legal edn. 1965—), Phi Beta Kappa, Phi Beta Kappa Assos. (pres. 1969-75), Cum Laude Soc., Raven Soc., Order of Coif, Theta Chi, Delta Sigma Rho. Author: Basic Corporate Practice, 1965; (with others) Model Business Corporation Act Annotated. Office: 63 Wall St New York City NY 10005

SEWARD, JOHN WESLEY, b. Albany, N.Y., Mar. 5, 1904; LL.D., Bklyn. Law Sch., 1927. Admitted to N.Y. bar, 1928, U.S. Supreme Ct. bar, 1955; mem. firm Anderson, Gasser, Ferris & Anderson, N.Y.C., 1944-71; partner firm Seward, Grant & Dickinson, N.Y.C., 1971-75, Boyd Holbrook & Seward, N.Y.C., 1976—; pres. Diaz Corp., N.Y.C., 1964—. Mem. Bar Assn. City N.Y. Tel (212) 867-8280

SEWELL, WILLIAM HARDWICK, II, b. Louisville, July 19, 1944; B.A., U. Ky., 1967, J.D., 1970. Admitted to Ky. bar, 1970; partner firm McKenzie, Woolery & Sewell, Ashland, Ky., 1972—; asst. commonwealth's atty. 32d Jud. Dist. Ky., Catlettsburg, 1974—. Republican mem. Boyd County (Ky.) Bd. Elections, 1973-74. Mem. Ky., Boyd County bar assns., So. Assn. Workmen's Compensation Adminstrs., Am. Security Council, Am. Def. Preparedness Assn., Nat. Right to Work Com., Conservative Caucus. Home: 1527 Beverly Blvd Ashland KY 41101 Office: 405 Kitchen Bldg PO Box 1554 Ashland KY 41101 Tel (606) 324-7147

SEXTON, DORRANCE, JR., b. Glen Ridge, N.J., Apr. 8, 1941; A.B., Princeton, 1963; LL.B., U. Conn., 1968. Admitted to Conn. bar, 1968; asso. firm Cummings & Lockwood, Stamford, Conn., 1968-76; prin. firm, New Canaan, Conn., 1976—. Asso. mem. Republican Town Com., Bedford, N.Y.; trustee Nat. Emphysema Found., Inc.; incorporator U. Conn. Law Sch. Found. Mem. Am., Conn. (exec. com. young lawyers sect. 1968—, chmn. 1976—) bar assns. Home: Maple Ave RFD 1 Katonah NY 10536 Office: 212 Elm St New Canaan CT 06840 Tel (203) 972-1411

SEXTON, LLOYD YOUNG, b. Smackover, Ark., Nov. 27, 1930; A.A., Jones Jr. Coll., 1950; B.S., U. So. Miss., 1952; J.D., U. Miss., 1959. Admitted to Miss. bar, 1959; individual practice law, Pascagoula, Miss., 1959—. Mem. Am., Miss., Jackson County bar assns., Miss. Trial Lawyers Assn. Home: 47 Baywood Dr Moss Point MS 39563 Office: 5006 Telephone Rd Pascagoula MS 39567 Tel (601) 769-1979

SEYKORA, JAMES EDMUND, lawyer; b. Omaha, July 17, 1946; B.A., Creighton U., 1968, J.D., 1971. Admitted to Mont. bar, 1972; asso. law firm Bert W. Kronmiller, Hardin, Mont., 1972—; county atty. Big Horn County, Mont., 1975—. Chmn. Big Horn County Festival Com., 1976. Mem. Am., Yellowstone County bar assns., State Bar of Mont. Home: 816 W Division St Hardin MT 59034 Office: 314 N Custer St Hardin MT 59034

SEYMOUR, MICHAEL JOHN, b. Chgo., Dec. 21, 1942; B.A., Duquesne U., 1964, J.D., 1967. Admitted to Pa. bar, 1967; asso. firm Mercer & Buckley, Pitts., 1967-70; partner firm Feczko & Seymour, Pitts., 1971—; asst. dist. atty. Allegheny County (Pa.), 1971-73. Mem. Am., Pa., Allegheny County (dir. young lawyers sect. 1973) bar assns. Office: 800 Lawyers Bldg Pittsburgh PA 15219 Tel (814) 261-4970

SEYMOUR, STEVEN PAUL, b. Chgo., June 27, 1946; B.A., U. Ill., 1968, J.D., 1972. Admitted to Ill. bar, 1972; individual practice law Effingham, Ill., 1973—; asst. states atty. Effingham, 1975-76. Mem. Am., Ill., Effingham County bar assns. Home: Box 103 Greenup IL 62428 Office: 109 N 4th Effingham IL 62401 Tel (217) 342-2835

SEYMOUR, WHITNEY NORTH, b. Chgo., Jan. 4, 1901; A.B., U. Wis., 1920, LL.D., 1962; LL.B., Columbia, 1923, LL.D., 1960; LL.D., Dartmouth, 1960, Duke, 1961, U. Akron, 1961, U. Man., 1961, Trinity U., 1964; D.C.L., N.Y. U., 1971. Admitted to N.Y. bar, 1924, U.S. Supreme Ct. bar, 1931; asso. firm Simpson, Thacher & Bartlett, N.Y.C., 1923—, partner, 1929-31, 33—; instr. law N.Y. U., 1924-35, Yale, 1935-43; asst. solicitor gen. U.S., 1931-33; U.S. atty. gen. com. on antitrust laws, 1953-55; pres. Legal Aid Soc., 1945-50. Mem. Am. (pres. 1960-61, Gold medal 1971), N.Y. State bar assns., Assn. Bar City N.Y. (pres. 1950-52), N.Y. County Lawyers Assn., Am. Coll. Trial Lawyers (pres. 1963-64), Lincolns Inn (hon. bencher), Law Soc. London. Recipient medals Fed. Bar Assn., 1963, Am. Arbitration Assn., 1959, St. Nicholas Soc., 1964. Home: 40 Fifth Ave New York City NY 10011 Office: One Battery Park Plaza New York City NY 10004 Tel (212) 483-9000

SFIKAS, PETER MICHAEL, b. Gary, Ind., Aug. 9, 1937; B.S., Ind. U., 1959; J.D., Northwestern U., 1962. Admitted to Ill. bar, 1962, U.S. Supreme Ct. bar, 1970; atty. Legal Aid Bur. United Charities of Chgo., 1962-63; asso. firm Peterson, Ross, Rall, Barber & Seidel, Chgo., 1963-70, partner, 1970—; prosecutor Village of LaGrange Park (Ill.), 1969-74; mem. Ill. Supreme Ct. Rules Com., 1975—; arbitrator Nat. Panel Arbitrators, 1972—; lectr. Ill. Inst. Continuing Legal Edn. Professions and Antitrust Laws, 1976. Fellow Am. Bar Found.; mem. Am. (editor in chief The Forum, 1972-76, chmn. publ. com. 1973-76), Ill. (bd. govs. 1970-76, mem. assembly 1972-76, chmn. spl. com. jud. inquiry 1976), Chgo. (editorial bd. Chgo. Bar Record 1973—) bar assns., Ill. Bar Found. (dir.), Bar Assn. 7th Fed Circuit. Recipient Maurice Weigle award Chgo. Bar Found., 1973. Contbr. articles in field to profl. jours. Home: 338 Dover St LaGrange Park IL 60525 Office: 200 E Randolph Dr Chicago IL 60601 Tel (312) 861-1400

SHADID, COY CONSTANT, b. Mangum, Okla., Aug. 21, 1914; student Okla. U., 1933-34, Tex. U., 1936-40; LL.B., So. Meth. U., 1948. Admitted to Tex. bar, 1942, Okla. bar, 1949; practice law, Altus, Okla. Mem. Altus C. of C. (pres. 1962-63), Okla., Tex., Am. bar assns., Delta Theta Phi.

SHADLE, MILO EVAN, b. Benton County, Iowa, July 25, 1923; A.B., U. Calif. at Los Angeles, 1950; LL.B., Harvard, 1953. Admitted to Calif. bar, 1954; asso. firm Schultheis & Laybourne, Los Angeles, 1953-55; partner firm Shadle, Kennedy & Pope, Los Angeles, 1956-57; individual practice law, Inglewood, Calif., 1957-60; partner firm Malloy & Shadle, Inglewood, 1960-63; individual practice law, Vista, Calif., 1963-71; partner firm Shadle, Hunt, Appelt & Hagar, Vista, 1971—. Trustee Palomar Community Coll., San Marcos, Calif., 1966—; pres. Greater San Luis Rey Area Planning and Devel. Council, 1969-70. Home: 352 Hidden Lake Ln Vista CA 92083 Office: PO Box 657 Vista CA 92083 Tel (714) 726-3837

SHAEFFER, CLINTON EDWARD, b. Fraser, Iowa, June 24, 1909; student Des Moines U., 1925-28; LL.B., Drake U., 1931, J.D., 1965. Admitted to Iowa bar, 1931; individual practice law, Des Moines, 1931-34, Marshalltown, Iowa, 1934-38; partner firm Hanzlik & Shaeffer, Cedar Rapids, Iowa, 1938-58, Shaeffer, Ackley & Kopecky, Cedar Rapids, 1958-67; judge Municipal Ct., Cedar Rapids, 1967-70, Linn County (Iowa) Juvenile Ct., 1967-70, 6th Judicial Dist., Iowa Dist. Ct., 1970—. Mem. Am., Iowa State, Linn County bar assns., Am. Judicature Soc., Iowa Dist. Ct. Judges Assn. Home: 663 Memorial Dr SE Cedar Rapids IA 52403 Office: Linn County Courthouse Cedar Rapids IA 52401 Tel (319) 398-3452

SHAEFFER, HENRY WARREN, b. Bryn Mawr, Pa., Mar. 1, 1945; B.S. cum laude, U. Pa., 1967; J.D. magna cum laude, Harvard, 1971. Admitted to Calif. bar, 1973; asso. editor Bancroft-Whitney Co., San Francisco, 1972-74, editor, 1974-76; asso. firm O'Melveny & Myers, Los Angeles, 1976—. Mem. Am., Los Angeles County bar assns. Note editor Harvard Law Rev., 1970-71. Home: 1417 N Catalina St Hollywood CA 90027 Office: 611 W 6th St Los Angeles CA 90017 Tel (213) 620-1120

SHAFER, B(ASIL) LYLE, b. Gettysburg, Ohio, Jan. 14, 1924; A.B., Harvard, 1948, postgrad. Sch. Bus. Adminstrn., 1955; J.D., Ohio State U., 1951. Admitted to Ohio bar, 1952; atty. legal dept. NCR Corp., Dayton, Ohio, 1952-59, asst. gen. counsel, 1960-65, v.p. personnel resources, 1965—; mem. adv. com. U. Dayton Law Sch.; dir. Home Savs. and Loan Assn., Dayton, Danis Industries, Inc., Dayton. Bd. dirs. United Way, Dayton, 1966-72; mem. Miami Valley council Boy Scouts Am., Dayton, 1974-75; trustee Aviation Hall of Fame, Inc., Dayton, 1971-75; v.p., dir. Jr. Achievement of Dayton, 1971-75. Mem. Am., Dayton, Ohio bar assns., Ohio Mfrs. Assn. Home: 4444 Southern Blvd Kettering OH 45429 Office: NCR World Hdqrs 1700 Patterson Blvd Dayton OH 45479 Tel (513) 449-3702

SHAFER, HUGH ALBERT MADISON, JR., b. Washington, Dec. 12, 1928; B.A., U. Md., 1951; J.D. with honors, George Washington U., 1955, LL.M., 1957. Admitted to D.C. bar, 1955, Va. bar, 1963; trial atty. anti-trust div. Dept. Justice, 1955-56; atty.-adviser to judge U.S. Tax Ct., 1956-59; asso. firm Reasoner, Davis & Davis, Washington, 1959-63; individual practice law, McLean, Va., 1963—; past pres. No. Va. Estate Planning Council. Mem. Am., Va. bar assns., Order of Coif, Omicron Delta Kappa. Home: 6804 Crutchfield St Falls Church VA 22043 Office: 6845 Elm St Suite 611 McLean VA 22101 Tel (703) 893-3380

SHAFFER, ALLEN, b. Augustaville, Pa., Dec. 7, 1925; B.A., Rickinson Coll., 1950, J.D., 1951. Admitted to Pa. bar, 1952; chief counsel Pa. Pub. Sch. Bldg. Authority, 1954-64; spl. counsel to Pa. Joint State Govt. Commn., 1968-69; individual practice law, Harrisburg and Millersburg, Pa., 1964—; arbitrator Am. Arbitration Assn. Vice pres. Muscular Dystrophy Assn. Am., 1973-76; bd. dirs. Charles P. and Margaret Polk Found., 1957—. Mem. Pa., Dauphin County bar assns. Home: 613 Lentz Ave Millersburg PA 17061 Office: 120 Market St Harrisburg PA 17101 Tel (717) 236-9511

SHAFFER, LOUIS W., b. Portsmouth, Ohio, Dec. 15, 1924; student Ohio U.; LL.B., Southwestern U. Admitted to Calif. bar, 1954. Mem. Calif., Los Angeles trial lawyers assns. Home: 4132 Crisp Canyon Rd Sherman Oaks CA 91403 Office: 800 S Robertson Blvd Los Angeles CA 90035 Tel (213) 655-8522

SHAFFER, PHILIP RAYMOND, b. Lindsborg, Kans., Feb. 6, 1942; B.A., Bethany Coll., 1966; J.D., Washburn U., 1969. Admitted to Kans. bar, 1969; partner firm Norton, Schaffer & Wasserman, Salina, Kans. Mem. Kans., Am., Saline County bar assns., Washburn Law Sch. Assn. Home: 1012 Millwood Salina KS 67401 Office: 215 S Santa Fe Salina KS 67401 Tel (913) 827-3646

SHAFTER, ALBERT JAMES, b. Carbondale, Ill., Apr. 29, 1947; B.A., So. Ill. U., 1969; J.D., U. Ill., 1972. Law intern Herman M. Adler Zone Center, Ill. Dept. Mental Health, Champaign, Ill., 1970-72; admitted to Ill. bar, 1972; partner firm Welsh, Kehart & Shafter, and predecessors, Decatur, Ill., 1972-74, partner, 1974—. Pres., Mid-Ill. March of Dimes, 1975, Macon County Legal Aid Soc., 1976; treas. Jr. Achievement Decatur, 1976; bd. dirs. Macon County Assn. for Retarded Citizens, 1972-75. Mem. Am., Ill., Decatur bar assns., Phi Beta Kappa, Phi Kappa Phi. Home: 464 Ash Ave Decatur IL 62526 Office: Suite 457 Citizens Bldg Decatur IL 62523 Tel (217) 428-4689

SHAH, INDRAWADAN KESHAVLAL, b. Mandal, Grujarat, India, Aug. 4, 1939; M.Commerce, Gujarat Univ., India, 1962, LL.M., 1967. Admitted to Ohio bar, 1974; prof. commerce Gujarat Univ., 1962-67; prof. law, N.C.B. Coll., India, 1967-71; asst. trust officer Land Title, Cleve., 1971-75; asst. v.p., asst. counsel Mellon Mfg., Cleve., 1976—. Mem. Am., Ohio, Cuyahoga County bar assns. Editor: The Lotus, 1974-76. Home: 27751 Sidney Dr #44 Euclid OH 44132 Office: Mellon National Mortgage Co 1255 Euclid Ave Euclid OH 44115 Tel (216) 696-5432

SHAIKEWITZ, RICHARD PHILIP, b. St. Louis, Mar. 6, 1938; B.S.B.A., Northwestern U., 1959; J.D., Washington U., St. Louis, 1962. Admitted to Mo. bar, 1962, Ill. bar, 1963, Fla. bar, 1963, U.S. Dist. Ct., 1963, U.S. Supreme Ct. bar, 1970; partner firm Wiseman, Shaikewitz McGivern & Wahl, Alton, Ill., 1965—. Mem. Ill. State, Mo., Fla., Madison County, Alton-Wood River bar assns., Bar Assn. St. Louis, Am., Ill. trial lawyers assns. Home: 11077 Graeser Ln Saint Louis MO 63141 Office: 620 E 3d St Alton IL 62002 Tel (618) 465-2541

SHAIN, HENRY, b. Glendale, Calif., Feb. 9, 1941; B.S., U. Calif., Berkeley, 1962; J.D., U. San Francisco, 1965. Admitted to Calif. bar, 1966; individual practice law, San Francisco, 1971-73; instr. U. Calif. extension, San Francisco, 1969-72; film critic San Mateo (Calif.) Times, 1973—. Author: Legal First Aid, 1975. Office: 400 Montgomery St San Francisco CA 94107

SHAINES, ROBERT ARTHUR, b. Newburyport, Mass., Nov. 24, 1929; student U. N.H., 1947-49; J.D. cum laude, Boston U., 1952. Admitted to Mass. bar, 1952, N.H. bar, 1954, 1st Dist. Ct. Mass., 1954, U.S. Ct. Appeals 1st Circuit bar, 1954, U.S. Dist. Ct. N.H. bar, 1955; asso. firm Lobel & Lobel, Boston, 1953-54; individual practice law, Portsmouth, N.H., 1954-56; partner firm Shaines & Brown, Portsmouth, 1956-66, Shaines, Madrigan & McEachern, Portsmouth, 1966-70, Shaines, Madrigan & McEachern, P.A., Portsmouth, 1970—; chmn. N.H. Bd. Conciliation and Arbitration, 1957—. Mayor City of Portsmouth, 1960-61. Mem. Am., N.H. (sec. 1974-76, gov. 1976), Rockingham County (pres. 1970-71) bar assns., Judge Advs. Assn., Fed. Bar Assn., Am. Trial Lawyers Assn. Office: 25 Maplewood Ave Portsmouth NH 03801 Tel (603) 436-3110

SHAKER, MITCHELL FRANCIS, b. Niles, Ohio, Jan. 3, 1922; A.B. magna cum laude, John Carroll U., 1943; J.D., Case Western Res. U., 1948. Admitted to Ohio bar, 1948; city solicitor, City of Niles, Ohio, 1949—; village solicitor, Lordstown, Ohio, 1976—. Chmn. United Appeal, 1950, 60; sec. Trumbull County Dem. Exec. Com., 1960—. Mem. Trumbull County Bar Assn. (pres. 1977-78), Order of Coif, Alpha Sigma Nu. Home: 403 Hogarth St Niles OH 44446 Office: 502-3 Niles Bank Bldg Niles OH 44446 Tel (216) 652-2762

SHAKMAN, MICHAEL LOUIS, b. Chgo., Aug. 31, 1942; A.B., U. Chgo., 1962, M.A., 1964, J.D., 1966. Admitted to Ill. bar, 1966; law clk. to justice Ill. Supreme Ct., 1966-67; asso. firm Devoe, Shadur & Krupp, Chgo., 1967-72, partner, 1972—. Pres. Hyde Park Neighborhood Club, Chgo., 1970-71. Mem. Am., Ill., Chgo. bar assns., Chgo. Council Lawyers, Am. Arbitration Assn. (arbitrator 1974—). Contbr. articles to legal jours. Home: 1473 E Park Pl Chicago IL 60637 Office: 208 S LaSalle St Chicago IL 60604 Tel (312) AN3-3700

SHALLER, WALTER STANLEY, b. Canadian, Tex., Dec. 7, 1918; B.B.A., U. Tex., 1941; J.D., So. Meth. U., 1943. Admitted to Tex. bar, 1942, U.S. Supreme Ct. bar, 1969; individual practice law, Amarillo, Tex., 1945-63, Abilene, Tex., 1970—; licensed real estate broker Tex. and Okla. Mem. Tex. Jaycees (v.p. 1953, nat. dir. 1954), chmn. March of Dimes, United Fund Div. Mem. Tex. Restaurant Assn. (dir.), Abilene Restaurant Assn. (pres.), Abilene Bar Assn. Recipient Outstanding Restaurateur award Abilene chpt. Tex. Restaurant Assn., 1973-74, Outstanding State V.P., Tex. Jaycees, 1953, Outstanding Nat. Dir. Tex. Jaycees, 1954. Home: 3118 San Miguel Abilene TX 79605 Office: PO Box 547 Buffalo Gap TX 79508 Tel (915) 692-4643

SHAMAS, RALPH DAVIS, b. Roswell, N.Mex., Oct. 30, 1948; B.B.A., U. N.Mex., 1970; J.D., U. Iowa, 1973. Admitted to Iowa bar, 1973, N.Mex. bar, 1973; partner firm Hunt & Shamas, Roswell, 1973—. State co-chmn. Law Day, 1976. Mem. Am., N.Mex. (dir. young lawyers sect. 1974-75), Iowa, Chaves County bar assns., Am. Judicature Soc. Home: 1018 Rancho Rd Roswell NM 88201 Office: 214 E 5th St Roswell NM 88201 Tel (505) 672-6221

SHAMES, HENRY JOSEPH, b. Milw., Jan. 20, 1921; A.B., U. Chgo., 1942; J.D., Harvard, 1948. Admitted to Ill. bar, 1949, Calif. bar, 1962; mem. firm Arvey, Hodes & Mantynband, 1949-61; partner firm Pacht, Ross, Warne, Bernhard & Sears, 1961-75, firm Grossman & Shames, Los Angeles, 1975—. Bd. dirs. Switzer Center, 1973—, chmn., 1966-73. Mem. Los Angeles County Bar Assn., Calif. State Bar, Assn. Bus. Trial Lawyers (v.p. 1974—, bd. govs. 1974—). Office: 5900 Wilshire Blvd Los Angeles CA 90036 Tel (213) 937-8220

SHAMPO, JAMES JOSEPH, b. Green Bay, Wis., Dec. 24, 1928; J.D., U. Wis., 1953. Admitted to Wis. bar, 1953; contract specialist Prudential Ins. Co., Newark, 1953; claim adjuster State Farm Mut. Auto Ins. Co., Bloomington, Ill., 1954-59, supt. claims, 1959-72; hearing examiner Wis. Dept. Health and Social Services, Milw., 1972—. Mem. Wis. Bar Assn. Home: 5500 W Glenbrook Rd Milwaukee WI 53223 Office: 819 N 6th St Milwaukee WI 53203 Tel (414) 224-4237

SHANAHAN, STEVEN ROBERT, b. Grand Island, Nebr., Oct. 2, 1948; B.S. in Bus. Adminstrn., U. Nebr., 1970, J.D., 1972. Admitted to Nebr. bar, 1973; commd. capt. JAGC USAF, 1973; fgn. mil. claims commr. Republic of Philippines, 1975; area def. counsel, Clark AFB,

Philippines, 1976—. Mem. Nebr. Bar Assn. Home: 1415 Alpha St North Platte NE 69101 Office: DET QD7A APO San Francisco CA 96274

SHANDORF, FRED DITTES, b. St. Paul, May 15, 1894; B.B.S., U. S.D.; LL.D., Dakota Wesleyan U. Admitted to S.D. bar, 1920; judge Mitchell (S.D.) Municipal Ct.; state's atty. Walrath County (S.D.), 1920-22; mem. Mitchell City Council. Mem. Walrath County Bar, State Bar S.D. Home: 1009 University Blvd Mitchell SD 57301

SHANK, JEROME BERNARD, b. Portland, Oreg., Oct. 17, 1920; B.A., U. Oreg., 1942; LL.B., Northwestern Coll., 1954. Admitted to Oreg. bar, 1954; partner firm Sussman, Shank, Wapnick & Caplan, Portland, 1962—; mem. debtor-creditor rights com. Oreg. State Bar, Portland, 1974-76. Trustee Congregation Beth Israel, Portland, 1965-74. Mem. Am., Oreg., Multnomah County bar assns., Phi Beta Kappa. Office: 1111 American Bank Bldg 621 SW Morrison Portland OR 97205 Tel (503) 227-1111

SHANK, WILLIAM O., b. Hamilton, Ohio, Jan. 11, 1924; A.B., Miami U., 1947; J.D., Yale, 1950. Admitted to Ohio, Ill. and U.S. Supreme Ct. bars; partner firm Shank & Briede & Spoerl, Hamilton, 1950-55; asso. firm Lord, Bissell & Brook, Chgo., 1955-58; with Chemetron Corp., Chgo., 1958—, gen. atty. and asst. sec., 1961-71, sec., gen. counsel, 1971—; dir. Midwest Carbide Corp. Mem. bus. adv. council Miami U., Oxford, Ohio, 1975—; bd. dirs. Library Internat. Relations, 1971—, Council for Community Services. Chgo., 1975—; mem. planning com. Corp. Counsel Inst., Northwestern U. Law Sch., 1969—, chmn., 1974. Mem. Chgo., Ill., Am. bar assns., Law Club Chgo., Legal Club Chgo. (past sec.-treas.), Econ. Club Chgo., Yale Law Sch. Assn. (mem. exec. com. 1970-75; pres. Ill. chpt. 1958), Phi Delta Phi. Home: 755 S Shore Dr Crystal Lake IL 60014 Office: 111 E Wacker Dr Chicago IL 60601 Tel (312) 565-5045

SHANKMAN, BERNARD, b. Russia, Mar. 2, 1908; J.D., Boston U., 1932. Admitted to D.C. bar, 1937; individual practice law, Washington, 1937—. Sec., D.C. Boxing Commn., 1967-75. Mem. D.C. Bar Assn., Assn. Trial Lawyers Am. Home: 5514 Uppingham St Chevy Chase MD 20015 Office: 1511 K St NW Suite 843 Washington DC 20005 Tel (202) 783-2838

SHANKS, HERSHEL, b. Sharon, Pa., Mar. 8, 1930; B.A., Haverford Coll., 1952; M.A., Columbia, 1953; LL.B., Harvard, 1956. Admitted to D.C. bar, 1956; atty., appellate sect., civil div. Dept. Justice, Washington, 1956-59; partner firm Glassie, Pewett, Beebe & Shanks, Washington, 1959—. Officer, exec. com. United Jewish Appeal, Washington, 1970—. Mem. D.C., Fed., Am. bar assns., Am. Judicature Soc., Nat. Lawyers Club, Bibl. Archaeology Soc. Author: The Art and Craft of Judging, 1968; City of David, 1973; contbr. articles to legal jours.; editor Bibl. Archaeology Rev. 1975—. Home: 5208 38th St NW Washington DC 20015 Office: 1737 H St NW Washington DC 20006 Tel (202) 466-4310

SHANNON, JOHN SANFORD, b. Tampa, Fla., Feb. 8, 1931; A.B., Roanoke Coll., 1952; J.D., U. Va., 1955. Admitted to Va. bar, 1955; asso. firm Hunton, Williams, Gay, Powell & Gibson, Richmond, 1955-56; solicitor Norfolk & Western Ry. Co., Roanoke, 1956-60, asst. gen. solicitor, 1960-64, gen. atty., 1964-65, gen. solicitor, 1965-68, gen. counsel, 1968-69, v.p. law, 1969—; dir. Wheeling & Lake Erie Ry. Co., Cleve., Trailer Train Co., Chgo., First Fed. Savs. & Loan Assn., Roanoke. Chancellor, Episcopal Diocese Southwestern Va.; pres. bd. trustees North Cross Sch., Roanoke; pres. Legal Aid Soc. Roanoke Valley; trustee Roanoke Coll., Salem, Va. Mem. Am., Va., Roanoke bar assns., Order of Coif, Omicron Delta Kappa, Phi Delta Phi. Editor-in-chief Va. Law Rev., 1954-55. Home: 507 Audubon Rd SW Roanoke VA 24014 Office: 8 N Jefferson St Roanoke VA 24042 Tel (703) 981-4911

SHANNON, THOMAS ALFRED, b. Milw., Jan. 2, 1932; B.S., U. Wis., 1954; J.D., U. Minn., 1961. Admitted to Minn. bar, 1962, Calif. bar, 1963, U.S. Supreme Ct. bar, 1965; asso. firm George P. Hoke, Mpls., 1961-62; atty. San Diego Unified Sch. Dist., 1962-73, dep. supt., gen. counsel, 1973-77; exec. dir. Nat. Sch. Bds. Assn., 1977—; adj. prof. law U. San Diego, 1974-77, counsel Am. Assn. Sch. Adminstrs., 1974-77; counsel Assn. Calif. Sch. Adminstrs., 1967-73; counsel Calif. State Dept. Edn.'s Project to Revise Div. 7 of Edn. Code, 1965-67; pres. San Diego County Legal Aid Soc., 1968-69; mem. Calif. Atty. Gen.'s Advisory Com., 1970-77. Mem. Am. (mem. com. on pub. edn. local govt. sect.), San Diego County (del. Calif. State Bar Conv. 1969-76), Fed. (pres. San Diego chpt. 1966) bar assns., Nat. Orgn. on Legal Problems of Edn., Council Sch. Attys., Nat. Sch. Bds. Assn. Co-author: Legal Problems in School Boards, 1966; recipient Distinguished Service award San Diego Legal Aid Soc., 1970; Recognition of Service award Council of Sch. Attys. of Nat. Sch. Bds. Assn., 1971. Home: 2126 Hartford San Diego CA 92110 Office: 1055 Thomas Jefferson St NW Washington DC 20007 Tel (202) 337-7666

SHAPERO, BERTRAM MALCOLM, b. Detroit, May 30, 1933; LL.B., U. Va., 1957, LL.D., 1970. Admitted to Mich. bar, 1969; partner firm Shapero, Shapero & Cohn, Detroit, 1969; individual practice law, Pontiac, Mich., 1970—; adminstrv. law judge Mich. Dept. Social Services, Lansing, 1974-75. Active, Citizens' Downtown Dist. Council, 1971-73, Coordinating Council for Community Redevel., 1972-73. Tel (313) 334-9525

SHAPERO, MICHAEL I., b. Cleve., Apr. 30, 1944; B.S., Ohio State U., 1966; J.D., Cleve. State U., 1970. Admitted to Ohio bar, 1971; individual practice law, Bedford Heights, Ohio, 1971—; revenue officer IRS, 1966-71. Vice pres. Bedford Heights Kiwanis Club, 1974. Mem. Am., Ohio, Greater Cleve. bar assns. Home: 22132 Westchester Rd Shaker Heights OH 44122 Office: 5333 Northfield Rd Bedford Heights OH 44146 Tel (216) 581-2300

SHAPIRA, GARY JAY, b. Erie, Pa., Nov. 10, 1940; B.A., U. Mich., 1962, J.D., 1965. Admitted to Pa. bar, 1966; partner fiem Juliante, Falcone, Shapira and Vendetti, Erie. Mem. Pa. Bar Assn., Am. Trial Lawyers Assn. Home: 118 W 42d St Erie PA 16508 Office: 713 French St Erie PA 16501

SHAPIRO, ALAN E., b. N.Y.C., Aug. 15, 1940; A.B., Tufts U., 1961; LL.B., Columbia, 1964; LL.M. in Taxation, N.Y. U., 1967. Admitted to N.Y. State bar, 1964; mem. firm Otterbourg, Steindler, Houston & Rosen, P.C., N.Y.C., 1975—. Mem. N.Y. State Bar Assn. Home: 126 Fort Hill Rd Scarsdale NY 10583 Office: 230 Park Ave New York City NY 10017 Tel (212) 679-1200

SHAPIRO, ALVIN DALE, b. N.Y.C., Apr. 30, 1930; B.J., U. Mo., 1951, LL.B., Yale, 1958. Admitted to Fla. bar, 1958, Mo. bar, 1959; partner firm Stinson, Mag, Thomson, McEvers & Fizzell, Kansas City, Mo., 1962—. Mem. Am., Mo., Fla. bar assns. Home: 816 W 52d Terr Kansas City MO 64112 Office: 2100 Ten Main Center Kansas City MO 64112 Tel (816) VI2-8600

SHAPIRO, EUGENE BERNARD, b. Chgo., Apr. 1, 1919; A.B., U. Calif., Los Angeles, 1940; postgrad. Stanford U. Grad. Sch. Bus., 1942-43; J.D., U. So. Calif., 1947. Admitted to Calif. bar, 1947, U.S. Supreme Ct. bar, 1965; individual practice law, Los Angeles and Beverly Hills, Calif., 1947-68; mem. firm, pres. Shapiro & Maguire, Beverly Hills, 1968—; mem. nat. panel arbitrators Am. Arbitration Assn., 1962—. Mem. Am. Judicature Soc., Am., Los Angeles County bar assns., Calif. Trial Lawyers Assn., Phi Kappa Phi, Nu Beta Epsilon. Home: 13455 Valleyheart Dr N Sherman Oaks CA 91423 Office: 8500 Wilshire Blvd Beverly Hills CA 90211 Tel (213) 655-5170

SHAPIRO, EUGENE L., b. N.Y.C., Nov. 26, 1947; A.B., Harpur Coll., 1968; J.D., U. Va., 1972; LL.M., N.Y. U., 1973. Admitted to N.Y. bar, 1973; asso. appellate counsel Legal Aid Soc., N.Y.C., 1974-76; asso. prof. law Memphis State U., 1976—.

SHAPIRO, FRED DAVID, b. Cleve., Nov. 10, 1926; B.A. cum laude, Ohio State U., 1949; postgrad. Columbia, 1950; LL.B., Harvard, 1954. Admitted to Ohio bar, 1954, U.S. Supreme Ct. bar, 1962; partner firm Barnett, Kent & Shapiro, Cleve., 1954-75; sr. partner firm Shapiro, Turoff & Gisser, Cleve., 1975—. Mem. Greater Cleve., Cuyahoga County (Ohio), Ohio State bar assns. Home: 19610 Lomond Blvd Shaker Heights OH 44122 Office: 1200 Standard Bldg Cleveland OH 44113 Tel (216) 241-8080

SHAPIRO, FRED RICHARD, b. Bklyn., May 13, 1935; A.A., Los Angeles City Coll., 1957; B.S., U. Calif., Los Angeles, 1959; J.D. magna cum laude, U. San Fernando Valley. With IRS, Los Angeles, 1959-68; admitted to Calif. bar, 1971; tax partner Kenneth Leventhal & Co., Los Angeles, 1972—; speaker in field. Mem. Calif. State Bar, Am. Inst. C.P.A.'s, Calif. Soc. C.P.A.'s. Home: 13531 Delano St Van Nuys CA 91401 Office: 2049 Century Park E 17th floor Los Angeles CA 90067 Tel (213) 277-0880

SHAPIRO, HADASSAH R(UTH), b. N.Y.C., June 20, 1924; B.A., Wellesley Coll., 1945; LL.B., Columbia, 1948. Admitted to N.Y. bar, 1948; asso. firm Mulligan & Jacobson, N.Y.C., 1968-73, partner, 1973—. Mem. N.Y. County Lawyers Assn., Assn. Bar City N.Y., Selden Soc. Office: 36 W 44th St New York City NY 10036 Tel (212) MU7-0096

SHAPIRO, HAROLD, b. Pereyaslov, Russia, May 1, 1906; J.D., Marquette U., 1927. Admitted to Wis. bar, 1927, Fla. bar, 1945, D.C. bar, 1960; individual practice law, Milw., 1927-43, Miami Beach, Fla., 1946—; mayor City of Miami Beach, 1953-55; mem. Miami Beach City Council, 1955-59; commentator Sta.-WINZ Radio, 1949-53, Sta.-WAHR Radio, 1955-57. Pres. Miami Beach dist. Zionist Orgn. Am., 1951-52, 63-64. Mem. Am., Fla., Dade County (Fla.), Miami Beach, Fed. bar assns., Jewish War Vets. (post comdr. 1952-53), Alpha Epsilon Pi (pres. Miami alumni club 1948-49), Tau Epsilon Rho. Author: How to Try a Summary Court-Martial Case in the Navy, 1944. Home: 2383 N Bay Rd Miami Beach FL 33140 Office: 927 Lincoln Rd suite 220 Miami Beach FL 33139 Tel (305) 538-6467

SHAPIRO, HARRY DEAN, b. Louisville, Ky., June 21, 1940; student Miami U., Oxford, Ohio, 1958-59; B.S., U. Louisville, 1962, J.D., 1964. Admitted to Ky. bar 1964, D.C. bar, 1968, Md. bar, 1970; trial atty. tax div. U.S. Dept. Justice, Washington, 1964-70; asso. firm Venable, Baetjer & Howard, Balt., 1970-75, partner 1975—. Mem. Am. (chmn. com. liens, levies and limitations tax sect. 1975—), Md., Balt. City, Ky., D.C. bar assns. Contbr. articles to profl. jours. Home: 7903 Seven Mile Ln Baltimore MD 21208 Office: 1800 Mercantile Bank and Trust Bldg 2 Hopkins Plaza Baltimore MD 21201 Tel (301) 752-6780

SHAPIRO, ISAAC, b. Tokyo, Jan. 5, 1931; A.B., Columbia, 1954, LL.B., 1956; postgrad. (Fulbright scholar), Institute de Droit Comparé, U. Paris, 1956-57. Admitted to N.Y. bar, 1957, U.S. Supreme Ct. bar, 1971; asso. firm Milbank, Tweed, Hadley & McCloy, N.Y.C., 1956-65, partner, 1966—; teaching fellow comparative law N.Y. U., 1959-61, lectr. Soviet law, 1961-67, adj. asst. prof., 1967-69, adj. asso. prof., 1969-71, 74-75; dir. Bank of Tokyo Trust Co. Mem. joint com. U.S.-Japan Cultural and Ednl. Cooperation, Washington; mem. Japan-U.S. Friendship Commn., Washington; trustee Nat. Humanities Center, Triangle Park, N.C., Japanese Ednl. Inst. N.Y. Mem. Assn. Bar City N.Y., Am., N.Y. State bar assns., Am. Soc. Internat. Law. Co-author: The Soviet Legal System, 1969; editor: The Middle East Crisis: Prospects for Peace, 1969. Office: 1 Chase Manhattan Plaza New York City NY 10005 Tel (212) 422-2660

SHAPIRO, IVAN, b. N.Y.C., Nov. 11, 1928; B.S.S., Coll. City N.Y., 1948; J.D., Harvard, 1951. Admitted to N.Y. bar, 1952; asso. and partner firm Wien, Lane & Malkin, N.Y.C., 1954-74; partner firm Greenbaum, Wolff & Ernst, N.Y.C., 1974—. Pres. Ethical Culture Soc. N.Y., 1972—; chmn. bd. govs. Ethical Culture Schs., 1976—; dir. N.Y. Civil Liberties Union, 1967—; bd. dirs. Nat. Assn. for Reform Abortion Laws., Women's Services Clinic. Mem. Assn. Bar City N.Y., N.Y. County Lawyers Assn. Co-author: Individual Responsibility and Excellence, 1974; contbr. articles to profl. jours. Home: 525 E 86th St New York City NY 10018 Office: 437 Madison Ave New York City NY 10022 Tel (212) 758-4010

SHAPIRO, J. IRWIN, b. N.Y.C., Oct. 13, 1904; B.S., N.Y. U., 1925, LL.B., 1926. Admitted to N.Y. bar, 1926, U.S. Supreme Ct. bar, 1929; asst. dist. atty. Queens County (N.Y.), 1932-51; ct. magistrate, 1951-53, judge family ct., 1954; commr. of investigation N.Y. State, 1955-57; justice City Ct., 1957-59; judge Queens County Ct., 1959-62; judge N.Y. State Supreme Ct., 1962-70; justice Appellate Div. N.Y. State, 1970—. Mem. Am., N.Y. State, Queens County bar assns., Am. Judicature Soc. Contbr. articles to legal jours.; recipient award for outstanding contbn. to Am. jurisprudence Assn. Trial Lawyers N.Y.C., 1974. Home: 165 Noye Ln Woodmere NY 11598 Office: 45 Monroe Pl Brooklyn NY 11201 Tel (212) 875-1300

SHAPIRO, JOSEPH BENJAMIN, JR., b. Augusta, Ga., Oct. 5, 1942; B.A., Emory U., 1964, J.D., 1967. Admitted to Ga. bar, 1966; partner firm Stokes & Shapiro, Atlanta, 1970—; pres. Ga. Legal Services Programs, 1975—. Mem. State Bar Ga. (exec. council younger lawyers sect. 1975—), Atlanta Lawyers Club. Asso. editor Jour. Pub. Law, 1966-67. Office: 2300 1st Nat Bank Tower Atlanta GA 30303 Tel (404) 658-9050

SHAPIRO, JOSEPH CECIL, b. Bklyn., Oct. 18, 1931; A.B., Cornell U., 1953; LL.B., Albany Law Sch., 1957. Admitted to N.Y. State bar, 1958, U.S. Supreme Ct. bar, 1964; asst. atty. gen. State of N.Y., Albany, 1958-63; asst. dist. atty. Delaware County, N.Y., 1975—. Mem. Margaretville (N.Y.) Central Sch. Bd. Edn., 1968—; trustee Four County Library Assn., Binghamton, N.Y., 1970—. Mem. Am., N.Y. State, Delaware County (sec. 1975—) bar assns. Home and office: Margaretville NY 12455 Tel (914) 586-3328

SHAPIRO, MARVIN M., b. Newark, Jan. 8, 1937; A.B., Cornell U., 1958, J.D., 1960. Admitted to N.Y. State bar, 1960; partner firm Hofheimer, Gartlir, Gottlieb & Gross, N.Y.C., 1960—. Mem. N.Y. County Lawyers Assn. Office: 100 Park Ave New York City NY 10017 Tel (212) 725-0400

SHAPIRO, MARVIN NEAL, b. Stockton, Calif., July 1, 1936; A.A., U. Calif., 1956, B.A., 1958, U.S., 1961. Admitted to Calif. bar, 1962; counsel Calif. State Compensation Ins. Fund, Los Angeles, 1962; partner firm Rose, Klein & Marias, Los Angeles, 1963—; lectr. Calif. State U., Northridge. Mem. State Bar Calif., Calif. Applicants Assn. Certified specialist worker's compensation. Office: 727 W 7th St Los Angeles CA 90017 Tel (213) 626-0571

SHAPIRO, MARVIN S., b. N.Y.C., Oct. 26, 1936; A.B., Columbia, 1957; LL.B., 1959. Admitted to D.C. bar, 1959, Calif. bar, 1962; atty. appelate sec. civil div. U.S. Dept. Justice, D.C., 1959-61; mem. firm Irell & Manella, Los Angeles, 1962—; lectr. Calif. Continuing Edn., U. So. Calif. Tax Inst., Practising Inst., U. Denver Tax Inst. Democratic nat. committeeman, Calif., 1972—; Mem. Beverly Hills (bd. govs. 1969-73), Am., Calif. bar assns., Beverly Hills Barristers (pres. 1970), Beverly Hills Law Found. (bd. govs. 1973-74). Articles editor: Columbia Law Review, 1958-59. Home: 432 N Cliffwood Ave Los Angeles CA 90049 Office: 1800 Ave of Stars Suite 900 Los Angeles CA 90067 Tel (213) 277-1010

SHAPIRO, MILTON BERNARD, b. Nyack, N.Y., Feb. 22, 1926; LL.B., N.Y. U., 1953. Admitted to N.Y. bar, 1953, U.S. Supreme Ct. Bar, 1967; individual practice law, N.Y.C., 1953-54, Spring Valley, N.Y., 1954-65, 76—; partner firm Shapiro & Reeder, Spring Valley, 1965-76. Mem. Rockland County Planning Bd., 1958-64, Rockland County Sewer Commn., 1965-69. Mem. Rockland County Bar Assn. Home: 34 Scenic Dr Suffern NY 10901 Office: 54 N Main St Spring Valley NY 10977 Tel (914) 356-3450

SHAPIRO, PAUL EDWIN, b. Phila., Apr. 25, 1941; B.A., U. Pa., 1964, J.D., 1967. Admitted to Pa. bar, 1967; asso. firm Wolf, Block, Schorr & Solis-Cohen, Phila., 1967-70; co-founder, instr., co-dir. Inst. for Paralegal Tng., Phila., 1970—; co-founder, mem. staff South St. Law Office, vol. store front law office, Phila., 1968-70; lectr. in field. Mem. young men's service com. Fedn. Jewish Agys., Phila., 1968-70. Mem. Am., Pa., Phila. bar assns. Home: 1427 Pepper Rd Rydal PA 19046

SHAPO, MARSHALL SCHAMBELAN, b. Phila., Oct. 1, 1936; A.B. summa cum laude, U. Miami (Fla.), 1958, LL.B. magna cum laude, 1964; A.M., Harvard, 1961, S.J.D., 1974. Admitted to Fla. bar, 1964, Va. bar, 1977; asst. prof. law U. Tex., Austin, 1965-67, asso. prof., 1967-69, prof., 1969-70; prof. law U. Va., Charlottesville, 1970—, Joseph M. Hartfield prof., 1976—; faculty U. Mich. Law Sch., Ann Arbor, summer 1973, U. Gottingen (Germany), summer 1976; instr. history U. Miami, 1960-61; editor, writer Miami News, 1958-59; vis. fellow Center for Socio-Legal Studies, Wolfson Coll., Oxford, Eng., 1975. Author: Tort and Compensation Law, 1976; (with P. Keeton) Products and the Consumer: Deceptive Practices, 1972; Products and the Consumer: Defective and Dangerous Products, 1970; (with P. Keeton) A Representational Theory of Consumer protection, 1974. Nat. Endowment for the Humanities sr. fellow, 1974-75; Sesquicentennial asso. U. Va., 1974-75, mem. Center for Advanced Studies, U. Va., 1976-77. Home: 100 Melissa Pl Charlottesville VA 22901 Office: U Va Sch Law Charlottesville VA 22901 Tel (804) 924-3520

SHARE, RICHARD HUDSON, b. Mpls., Sept. 6, 1938; B.S. in Accounting, U. Calif., Los Angeles, 1960; J.D., U. So. Calif., 1963. Admitted to Calif. bar, 1965, U.S. Supreme Ct. bar, 1974; sr. counsel Avco Fin. Services, Newport Beach, Calif., 1964-72; partner firm Foonberg & Frandzel, Beverly Hills, Calif., 1972—; lectr. in field. Mem. Calif. Bankers Assn., Fin. Lawyers Conf., Nat. Consumer Fin. Assn. Office: 8530 Wilshire Blvd Beverly Hills CA 90211 Tel (213) 659-2611

SHARFMAN, ROBERT JAY, b. Chgo., Mar. 23, 1936; B.S. in Commerce and Law, U. Ill., 1958; J.D., DePaul U., 1959. Admitted to Ill. bar, 1960; with Continental Ill. Nat. Bank & Trust Co., Chgo., 1960-61; individual practice law, Chgo., 1961-63; asst. atty. gen. State of Ill., Chgo., 1963-65; gen. counsel Ill. Savs. & Loan Commr., Chgo., 1965-69; mem. firm Gomberg & Sharfman, and predecessors, Chgo., 1969—. Mem. Am., Ill., Chgo. bar assns. Contbr. chpts. to profl. publs. Home: 1555 Sunnyside St Highland Park IL 60035 Office: 209 S LaSalle St Chicago IL 60430 Tel (312) 782-6194

SHARKEY, GREGORY VINCENT, b. Lakewood, N.J., Sept. 21, 1943; B.A., Washington and Lee U., 1965; J.D., Seton Hall U., 1968. Admitted to N.J. bar, 1969, Fla. bar, 1969; asst. state atty. Palm Beach County (Fla.), 1970-72; partner firm Citta, Gasser, Carluccio, Holzapfel & Sharkey, Toms River, N.J., 1972-74; individual practice law, Toms River, 1974-75; partner firm Sharkey & Sacks, Lakewood, N.J., 1975—; jud. law clk. Ocean County (N.J.), 1968-69; asst. county prosecutor Ocean County (N.J.), Toms River, 1973—. Mem. Am., N.J., Fla. bar assns., Nat. Dist. Attys. Assn. Home: 16 Pine Fork Dr Toms River NJ 08753 Office: Lakewood Plaza Lakewood NJ 08701 Tel (201) 363-5858

SHARP, ALBERT BOYD, b. Phila., Dec. 13, 1917; A.B., Princeton, 1939; J.D., U. Pa., 1946. Admitted to Pa. bar, 1947, N.J. bar, 1949, U.S. Supreme Ct. bar, 1960; asso. firm Evans, Bayard & Frick, Phila., 1947-48, firm Bleakly, Stockwell & Zink, Camden, N.J., 1949-50; individual practice law, Haddonfield, N.J., 1950—; capt. JAGC, USAR, 1947-50; instr. bus. law Rutgers U., 1950-53; solicitor Borough of Haddonfield, 1953-57, 65-73. Mem. Haddonfield Bd. Edn., 1952-57; mayor Haddonfield, 1957-65. Mem. N.J., Camden County, Phila. (asso.) bar assns. Office: 252 Kings Hwy E Haddonfield NJ 08033 Tel (609) 429-2959

SHARP, JOHN MARLON, b. Salt Lake City, May 31, 1916; LL.B., U. Utah, 1940. Admitted to Utah bar, 1948, Idaho bar, 1948; individual practice law, Idaho Falls, Idaho, 1948-59; partner firm Sharp, Anderson & Bush, Idaho Falls, 1959—; pros. atty. Bonneville County (Idaho), 1949-55. Mem. Am., Idaho State (commr. 1970-72, pres. 1973) bar assns., Idaho Falls Jr. C. of C. (pres. 1946). Office: 490 Memorial Dr Idaho Falls ID 83401 Tel (208) 522-3001

SHARP, MORELL EDWARD, b. Portland, Oreg., Sept. 12, 1920; student U. Oreg., 1939-42; LL.B., Northwestern U., 1948. Admitted to Ill. bar, 1948, Wash. bar, 1951; asst. gen. atty. law dept. Milw. R.R., Chgo., 1948-50, Seattle, 1952-56; partner firms Williams, Kinnear and

Sharp, Seattle, 1956-61, Graham, Dunn, Johnston and Rosenquist, Seattle, 1961-67; judge Wash. Superior Ct. in King County, 1967-70; justice Wash. State Supreme Ct., 1970-71; judge U.S. Dist. Ct., Western Dist. Wash., 1971—. Fellow Am. Bar Found.; mem. Am., Wash. State bar assns., Am. Judicature Soc. Bd. editors Am. Bar Assn. Jour., 1974—. Home: 9021 NE 10th St Bellevue WA 98004 Office: 410 US Courthouse Seattle WA 98104 Tel (206) 442-4424

SHARP, ROBERT EUGENE, b. Springfield, Ill., Oct. 22, 1928; A.A., Springfield Jr. Coll., 1950; B.S., Marquette U., 1953, LL.B., 1956. Admitted to Wis. bar, 1956; partner firm Foley, Capwell, Foley & Kolbe, Racine, Wis., 1962-66, Kolbe & Sharp, Racine, 1967-71, Kolbe, Sharp & Arena, Racine, 1971-73, Kolbe, Sharp & Brodek, Racine, 1974—. Pres. Council Catholic Men, Racine, 1962-64, Racine Human Relations Commn., 1964-66, Fourth of July Com. Goodwill, Racine, 1973-75. Mem. Am. Bar Assn., State Bar Wis. Named Man of the Year Scout Drum Corps, 1969. Home: 1650 College Ave Racine WI 53403 Office: 610 Main St Racine WI 53403 Tel (414) 632-1667

SHARP, ROBERT WEIMER, b. Cleve., Feb. 12, 1917; A.B., Oberlin Coll., 1939; LL.B., Harvard, 1942. Admitted to Ohio bar, 1944, since practiced in Cleve.; partner firm Gallagher, Sharp, Fulton, Norman & Mollison, and predecessors, 1958—; dir. Nat. Terminals Corp. Trustee St. Luke's Hosp. Assn., Christian Residences Found.; pres. Ohio East Area United Meth. Found., 1974—, also trustee; adv. trustee Ohio div. Am. Cancer Soc. Mem. Am., Ohio, Cleve. bar assns. Home: 3090 Fairmount Blvd Cleveland OH 44118 Office: Bulkley Bldg Cleveland OH 44115 Tel (216) 241-5310

SHARP, SUSIE MARSHALL, b. Rocky Mt., N.C., July 7, 1907; student N.C. Coll. Women, 1924-26; LL.B., U. N.C., Chapel Hill, 1929, LL.D., 1970; L.H.D., Pfeiffer Coll., 1960; LL.D., Woman's Coll. U. N.C., Greensboro, 1950, Queens Coll., 1962, Elon Coll., 1963, Wake Forest U., 1965, Catawba Coll., 1970, Duke U., 1974. Admitted to N.C. bar, 1928; partner firm Sharp & Sharp, Reidsville, N.C., 1929-49; spl. judge N.C. Superior Ct., 1949-62; asso. justice N.C. Supreme Ct., Raleigh, 1962-75, chief justice, 1975—; city atty. Town of Reidsville (N.C.), 1939-49. Mem. N.C. Constl. Commn., 1959. Mem. Am., N.C. bar assns., Am. Law Inst. Recipient Spl. Alumni award, U. N.C., Greensboro, 1975, Leadership and Service award N.C. State Grange, 1975, Spl. award N.Y. Women's Bar Assn., 1976. Home: 629 Lindsey St Reidsville NC 27320 also #26 Townehouse Apts 521 Wade Ave Raleigh NC 27605 Office: PO Box 1841 Raleigh NC 27602 Tel (919) 733-3717

SHARP, THOMAS ROGERS, b. Monte Vista, Colo., Dec. 5, 1944; B.A. magna cum laude, William Jewell Coll., Liberty, Mo., 1966; J.D. magna cum laude, U. Denver, 1969. Admitted to Colo. bar, 1969, Mo. bar, 1970; law clk. to judge U.S. Ct. Appeals, St. Louis, 1969-70; asso. firm Bryan, Cave, McPheeters & McRoberts, St. Louis, 1970, Holme, Roberts & Owen, Steamboat Springs, Colo., 1972-75; partner firm Sharp & Black, Steamboat Springs, 1975—; dir. United Bank of Steamboat Springs. Pres. Fish Creek Water and Sanitation Dist., 1974—; chmn. fin. United Methodist Ch., Steamboat Springs, 1975; bd. dirs. Yampa Valley Devel. Corp., 1974—. Mem. Am., Mo., Colo., Routt County (pres. 1975-76) bar assns. Office: Box AF Steamboat Springs CO 80477 Tel (303) 879-1572

SHARPE, DAVID JAMES, b. New Haven, Oct. 4, 1930; A.B., U. N.C., 1950; LL.B., Harvard, 1955, S.J.D., 1969. Admitted to N.C. bar, 1955, D.C. bar, 1961, U.S. Supreme Ct. bar, 1962; asst. dir. Inst. Govt., U. N.C., 1955-56; specialist U.S. AEC, Washington, 1956-57; instr. law Boston U., 1957-60; asst. prof. Law George Washington U., 1960-63, asso. prof. 1963-66, prof., 1966—. Mem. Maritime Law Assn. U.S., Am. Soc. for Legal History, Phi Delta Phi. Author: (with Murdock Head) Problems in Forensic Medicine, 1970; (with Nicholas Healy) Cases and Materials on Admiralty, 1974. Home: 4920 Flint Dr Bethesda MD 20016 Office: Nat Law Center George Washington U Washington DC 20052 Tel (202) 676-6754

SHARRATT, GLENN L., b. Oshkosh, Wis., Mar. 24, 1924; B.S., U. Wis., 1949, LL.B., 1951. Admitted to Wis. bar, 1951; regional counsel Am. Family Ins. Group, Madison, Wis., 1951-67; asso. firm Fulton, Menn & Nehs, Ltd., Appleton, Wis., 1967—. Mem. Am., Wis., Outagamie County bar assns. Office: 222 N Oneida St Appleton WI 54911 Tel (414) 731-6631

SHATTUCK, FRANK WADSWORTH, b. Birmingham, Ala., Sept. 14, 1929; A.B., DePauw U., 1951; J.D., Am. U., 1965. Adminstrv. asst. Gov.'s Office, Nev., 1960-63; admitted to Nev. bar, 1965; dep. atty. gen. Nev., 1965-66; asso. firm Adams, Reed & Bowen, Reno, 1966-67; asst. city atty. Sparks (Nev.), 1967, Reno, 1967-69; partner firm Shattuck & Van Wagoner, Reno, 1969-72; v.p., counsel Hilton Casinos, Inc., Las Vegas, 1972—. Pres. Smithridge Park Townhouse Assn., 1966-67; sec. Horizon Hill Gen. Improvement Dist., 1966-68; bd. dirs., chmn. fund raising com. Multiple Sclerosis Soc., 1967-69; chmn. dist. orgn. and extension com. Boy Scouts Am., 1970-71; chmn. legal div. United Fund, 1967, campaign chmn., 1969, dir., 1969-72, chmn. agy. relations com., 1970-71, mem. exec. com., 1971; legal counsel, bd. dirs. Reno Aces Hockey Team, 1969-72, sec., 1971-72; founder, pres. Detrap, Inc., 1971, dir., 1972; v.p. Nev. World Trade and Tourism Assn., 1974-75, pres., 1975—; mem. Paradise Twp. Adv. Council; mem. citizens adv. com. Joint Com. on Consolidation of Las Vegas and Clark County, 1975—; mem. adv. council Center for Bus. and Econ. Research, U. Nev., 1975—; vice chmn. Washoe County Democratic Central Com., 1966-68, chmn. issues com., 1970-72; chmn. Dem. State Conv., 1968; mem. Dem. State Central Com., 1968-70; candidate State Assembly, 1970; chmn. bd. dirs. Community Service Council; bd. dirs. So. Nev. Drug Abuse Council, Opportunity Village for Retarded Children, Nev. Export Council, Western Internat. Trade Group, Nev. Council on Econ. Edn., Washoe Assn. for Retarded Children, Nev. Opera Guild, 1968-69, Vis. Nurses, 1970-71, Sierra Job Council, 1969-70, Ballet West, 1969-72; trustee Reno Grand Prix, 1971, Sierra Arts Found., 1971-72. Mem. Am., Nev., Washoe County Leditor Newsletter 1966-67), Clark County bar assns. Home: 3728 Colonial Circle Las Vegas NV 89121 Office: 3000 Paradise Rd Las Vegas NV 89109 Tel (702) 732-5111

SHATTUCK, LEROY ALTUS, JR., b. Pepperell, Mass., Feb. 5, 1911; A.B., Dartmouth Coll., 1935; Ph.D., Johns Hopkins U., 1938; LL.B., Duquesne U., 1950. Admitted to Pa. bar, 1951; instr. econs. Dartmouth Coll., 1938-41; asst. prof. Carnegie Inst. Tech., 1941-42; with U.S. Steel Corp., Pitts., 1946; prof. fin. U. Pitts., 1946-73, prof. emeritus bus. adminstrn.; individual practice law, Pitts., 1951—. Mem. Pa., Allegheny County bar assns. Contbr. articles to profl. jours. Home: 107 Rockingham Ln McMurray PA 15317 Office: 155 Union Trust Bldg Pittsburgh PA 15219 Tel (412) 391-6500

SHATTUCK, WARREN LOCKE, b. Ruston, La., Nov. 6, 1908; B.A., LL.B., U. Wash., 1934; J.S.D., Yale, 1936. Admitted to Wash. bar, 1937; asst. prof. law U. Wash., Seattle, 1935-38, asso. prof., 1938-40, prof., 1940-73, prof. emeritus, 1973—; prof. Hastings Coll. Law, 1974—. Mem. Wash. State, Internat. bar assns. Editor: (with Herbert Ma) Trade and Investment in Taiwan, 1973; (with Teruo Doi) U.S.-Japanese Patent and Know-how Licensing, 1976. Home: 475 Lakeshore Dr Incline NV 89450 Office: 2030 Vallejo St San Francisco CA 94123 also 198 McAllister St San Francisco CA 94102 Tel (415) 557-2899

SHATZEN, ROBERT STANLEY, b. Detroit, Feb. 11, 1942; A.B. in Econs., Stanford, 1963, J.D., 1971, M.B.A., 1973. Admitted to Calif. bar, 1972; spl. investigations agt. Office of Insp. Gen., U.S. Air Force, 1966-71; tax mgr. Arthur Young & Co., San Francisco, 1973—. Mem. Calif. Bar Assn., Calif. Soc. C.P.A.'s, Am. Inst. C.P.A.'s. C.P.A., Calif. Home: 224 27th Ave San Mateo CA 94403 Office: Crocker Plaza Post and Montgomery Sts San Francisco CA 94104 Tel (415) 393-2700

SHAULIS, NORMAN ALBERT, b. Somerset, Pa., July 13, 1922; B.S., Temple U., 1949, J.D., 1952; grad. Nat. Coll. State Judiciary, U. Nev., 1972. Admitted to Pa. bar, 1952; partner firm Coder & Shaulis, Somerset, 1952-56; individual practice law, Somerset, 1956-64; partner firms Shaulis & Rascona, Somerset, 1964-67, Shaulis, Kimmel & Rascona, Somerset, 1967-72; judge Somerset County (Pa.) Ct. Common Pleas, 1972—; U.S. commr. for Western Dist. Pa., 1957-61; legal officer Pa. Wing CAP, 1965—. Mem. Am., Pa., Somerset County bar assns., Am. Judicature Soc., Lawyer-Pilot Bar Assn., Phi Delta Phi. Home: Hickory Hill Ln Somerset PA 15501 Office: PO Box 527 Courthouse Somerset PA 15501 Tel (814) 443-3315

SHAW, ARNOLD FRANKLIN, b. Chgo., Apr. 24, 1910; student U. Ill., 1927-29, U. Chgo., 1929-30; B.S.L., Northwestern U., 1931, postgrad., 1931-33. Admitted to Ill. bar, 1933, D.C. bar, 1952; individual practice law, Chgo., 1933-39; mfg. exec., Chgo., 1939-42, 46-48; exec. asst. to dir. Office Alien Property, U.S. Dept. Justice, Washington, 1949-50; spl. asst. to dir. OPS, Washington, 1951-52; dir. Mchts. Credit, Inc., Am. Research & Mfg. Corp. Mem. Am., Fed., D.C., Chgo. bar assns. Home: 4550 Brandywine St Washington DC 20016 Office: 503 D St NW Washington DC 20001 Tel (202) 393-4440

SHAW, BARRY NEIL, b. Newark, July 31, 1940; B.S. in Accounting, Rutgers U., 1962, J.D., 1965. Admitted to Pa. bar, 1966, N.J. bar, 1974; tax supr. Coopers & Lybrands, Phila., 1965-68; asst. v.p., corp. counsel, sec. Lincoln Bank, Phila., 1968-72; asso. firm David Berger, Profl. Assn., Phila., 1972-73; corp. counsel Waste Resources Corp., Phila., 1973-74; partner firm Dranoff & Shaw, Phila., 1974—. Mem. Am., N.J., Phila. bar assns., Am. Inst. C.P.A.'s. C.P.A., Pa. Office: 6th floor 1200 Walnut St Philadelphia PA 19107 also 546 Penn St PO Box 1006 Camden NJ 08101 Tel (215) 732-8530

SHAW, DONALD H., b. N.Y.C., June 6, 1933; B.A., St. John's Coll., 1953, LL.B., 1956. Admitted to N.Y. bar, 1956, U.S. Supreme Ct. bar, 1971; asst. U.S. atty., 1956-60; asso. firm Coudert Bros., 1960-62, firm Kantor, Shaw & Davidoff, N.Y.C., 1963—. Mem. Assn. Bar City N.Y., N.Y. State Bar Assn., Fed. Bar Council. Home: 310 W 19th St New York City NY 10011 Office: 200 Park Ave New York City NY 10017

SHAW, GORDON BICKFORD, b. Lubbock, Tex., Nov. 22, 1942; B.B.A., Tulane U., 1965, J.D., 1967. Admitted to Tex. bar, 1968; landman Atlantic Richfield Co., Dallas, 1967-68; asso. firm Blanchard, Clifford, Gilkerson & Smith, Lubbock, Tex., 1968-69; gen. counsel Square H. Industries, Inc., Dallas, 1969-71; counsel Fed. Nat. Mortgage Assn., Dallas, 1971-73; individual practice law, Corpus Christi, Tex., 1973—; partner firm Shaw, Thorpe & Stone, Corpus Christi, 1975—; instr. in field Del Mar Coll., Corpus Christi, 1974, 76; v.p., dir. Family Debt Counselors, Corpus Christi, 1974—. Mem. Goals for Dallas Com., 1968. Mem. Tex., Nueces County bar assns., Nueces County Young Lawyers Assn. Home: 5202 Moultrie St Corpus Christi TX 78413 Office: 5333 Everhart Suite 125 Corpus Christi TX 78411 Tel (512) 855-3371

SHAW, JAMES RAY, b. Leesburg, Fla., Aug. 6, 1947; B.S. in Bus. Adminstrn., U. Fla., 1970, J.D., 1972. Admitted to Fla. bar, 1972; asst. state atty. 5th Jud. Circuit, Leesburg, 1972-73; asst. atty. City of Daytona Beach (Fla.), 1973-74; indiv individual practice law, Sarasota, Fla., 1974—. Mem. Fla. Bar, Sarasota County Bar, Acad. Fla. Trial Lawyers, Beta Gamma Sigma. Office: 1922 Ringling Blvd Sarasota FL 33577 Tel (813) 366-9444

SHAW, JOHN ARTHUR, b. San Antonio, June 6, 1922; J.D., St. Louis U., 1948. Admitted to Mo. bar, 1948, U.S. Tax Ct. bar, 1953, U.S. Supreme Ct. bar, 1973; asso. firm Pollock Tenney & Dahman, St. Louis, 1948-51; legal staff St. Louis Probate Ct., 1951-53; partner firm Pollock Ward Klobasa & Shaw, St. Louis, 1953-63; asso. counsel Reliable Life Ins. Co., St. Louis, 1964-67, gen. counsel, 1967—, sr. v.p., 1969—; gen. counsel Old Reliable Fire Ins. Co., St. Louis, 1967—; pres. TRICO Service Corp., St. Louis, 1970—, Reliable Life Corp., 1974—. Sec.-treas. Tatman Found., St. Louis, 1967—; active Boy Scouts Am., 1970—. Mem. Am., Mo., Met. St. Louis bar assns., Am. Judicature Soc., Cath. Lawyers Guild St. Louis, Am. Council Life Ins., Assn. Life Ins. Counsel, Alpha Sigma Nu. Author: (with J.A. Appleman) Basic Estate Planning, 1957; editor: Missouri Probate Law and Practice, 1960. Home: 306 Luther Ln Glendale MO 63122 Office: 231 W Lockwood Ave Webster Groves MO 63119 Tel (314) 968-4900

SHAW, RICHARD ALLAN, b. Portland, Oreg., Oct. 14, 1937; B.S., U. Oreg., 1959, J.D., 1962; LL.M. in Taxation, N.Y. U., 1963. Admitted to Oreg. bar, 1962, Ariz. bar, 1967, Calif. bar, 1969, U.S. Supreme Ct. bar, 1965; faculty N.Y. U., 1962-63; served with JAGC, U.S. Army, 1963-66; asso. firm Kramer, Roche, Burch, Streich & Cracchido, Phoenix, 1966-68, Hewitt & Greaves, San Diego, 1968-71, Hewitt & Shaw, San Diego, 1972—. Chmn. Torrey Pines dist. Boy Scouts Am., 1974-76, mem. exec. bd. San Diego County council, 1974-77, v.p. council, 1977—, mem. Nat. council, 1977—; bd. dirs. Eagle Scout Alumni Assn., 1976-77. Mem. Am. (spl. adviser sect. taxation, chmn. com. on subchpt. S Corps.), San Diego County (chmn. legis. com., chmn. bus. law sect., chmn. corporation tax and partnership legis. subcom.), Fed. bar assns., Calif. State Bar (vice chmn. corp. tax com., del. state conf.), Am. Judicature Soc. Contbr. articles to legal jours.; asso. editor Fed. Bar Jour., Tax Lawyer, Oreg. Law Rev. Home: 4409 Brindisi St San Diego CA 92107 Office: 1010 2d Ave Suite 2121 San Diego CA 92101 Tel (714) 239-2121

SHAW, ROBERT ALAN, b. N.Y.C., Oct. 14, 1946; B.A., City U. N.Y., 1968, J.D., 1972. Admitted to N.Y. bar, 1973; atty. Hartford Ins. Group, 1973; individual practice law, 1973-74; asso. counsel N.Y.C. Conciliation and Appeals Bd., 1974-75; referee Adminstrv. Adjudication Bur., N.Y. State Dept. Motor Vehicles, 1975—. Democratic committeeman, Bronx County, N.Y., 1976. Mem. Am., N.Y., Bronx County bar assns., N.Y. County Lawyers Assn. Office: 2455 Sedgwick Ave Bronx NY 10468 Tel (212) 834-5515

SHAW, ROBERT BERNARD, b. Neark, N.J., Jan. 26, 1934; B.S. in Accounting, N.Y. U., 1955; LL.B., Bklyn. Law Sch., 1958, J.D., 1967. Admitted to N.Y. State bar, 1959; partner firm Shaw & Meyer, N.Y.C., 1959-64, Shaw, Issler & Rosenberg, N.Y.C., 1969-75; individual practice law, N.Y.C., 1975—; counsel com. on navigation law N.Y. State Assembly, 1969-72. Mem. N.Y. County, N.Y. State, Nassau County (past mem. matrimonial law com.) bar assns. Office: 18 E 48th St New York City NY 10017 Tel (212) 421-7070

SHAW, ROBERT LEE, b. Omaha, Sept. 27, 1919; B.A., Tulane U., 1956; LL.B., Stanford, 1959. Admitted to Calif. bar, 1959; dep. dist. atty. Ventura County (Calif.), 1959-61; partner firm Hathaway Soares Shaw & Clabauch, Ventura, Calif., 1961-66; judge Ventura Municipal Ct., 1966-70, Ventura Superior Ct., 1970—; instr. Ventura Coll. Law, 1971—. Mem. Conf. Calif. Judges, Ventura Bar Assn. (hon.), Phi Beta Kappa. Author: California Courtroom Practice and Procedure, 1976. Home: 3119 Old Coach Rd Camarillo CA 93010 Office: 501 Poli St Ventura CA 93001 Tel (805) 648-6131

SHAW, RUSSELL CLYDE, b. Cleve., Mar. 19, 1940; B.S. in Bus. Adminstrn., Ohio State U., 1962, J.D., 1965. Admitted to Ohio bar, 1965, U.S. Supreme Ct. bar, 1968; since practiced in Cleve., asso. firm Thompson, Hine and Flory, 1965, 1969-74, partner, 1974—; served to capt. JAGC, U.S. Army, 1965-69. Mem. Ohio State, Fed. bar assns., Nat. Lawyers Club. Home: 14222 Caves Rd Novelty OH 44072 Office: 1100 Nat City Bank Bldg Cleveland OH 44114 Tel (216) 241-1880

SHAWAKER, WAYNE EDWARD, b. Toledo, Oct. 7, 1903; A.B., U. Mich., 1925, J.D., 1927. Admitted to Ohio bar, 1927; sr. partner firm Shawaker & Smith, Toledo, 1967—. Pres. Toledo Bd. Edn.; chpt. chmn. Greater Toledo chpt. ARC. Mem. Toledo Bar Assn. (bd. govs.). Recipient Outstanding Alumnus award U. Mich., 1967. Home: 3211 Kenwood Blvd Toledo OH 43606 Office: 620 Security Bldg Toledo OH 43604 Tel (419) 241-3281

SHAWN, JOEL ARNOLD, b. Bklyn., Nov. 15, 1935; B.C.E., City Coll. N.Y., 1957; J.D., U. Calif., 1966. Admitted to Calif. bar, 1966, 9th Circuit Ct. Appeals bar, 1966, U.S. Dist. Ct. No. Dist. Calif., bar, 1966; with legal dept. Bechtel Corp., San Francisco, 1966-67; asso. firm Lukes & Bassoni, San Francisco, 1967-72; partner firm Kipperman, Shawn & Keker, San Francisco, 1973—. Mayor, councilman Town of Corte Madera, Calif. Mem. San Francisco Bar Assn., Criminal Trial Lawyers Assn., Am. Arbitration Assn. Office: 407 Sansome St Suite 400 San Francisco CA 94111 Tel (415) 788-2200

SHEA, DAVID MICHAEL, b. Hartford, Conn., July 1, 1922; B.A., Wesleyan U., Middletown, Conn., 1944; LL.B., Yale, 1948. Admitted to Conn. bar, 1948, U.S. Supreme Ct. bar, 1959; partner firm Bailey, Wechsler & Shea, Hartford, 1949-65; judge Conn. Superior Ct., 1966—; mem. Superior Ct. Rules Com., 1967—, mem. Appellate div., 1975—. Mem. Am., Conn., Hartford County bar assns. Office: 95 Washington St Hartford CT 06105 Tel (203) 566-3586

SHEA, EDWARD JOHN, b. North Adams, Mass., Mar. 31, 1923; B.A., Tufts Coll., 1944; LL.B., Boston Coll., 1952. Admitted to Mass. bar, 1956; asst. prof. law Tufts Coll., 1952-55; asso. prof. U. Mass., 1956-61; partner firm Callahan and Shea, and predecessors, Greenfield, Mass., 1960-74, firm Shea and Olchowski, Greenfield, 1974—; presiding justice Eastern Franklin Dist. Ct., 1974—; justice Mass. Superior Ct., 1975—. Vice pres. Mass. Arthritis Soc., 1956—; pres. Greenfield Area YMCA, 1967-71, Franklin County (Mass.) Mental Health Assn., 1961-68. Mem. Am., Mass., Franklin County bar assns., Tufts U. Alumni Assn. (pres. 1972-76), Am. Judges Assn., Am. Judicature Assn. Recipient Distinguished Service award Tufts U., 1970; named Franklin County Man of Year, Greenfield Rotary, 1973. Home: 46 Orchard St Greenfield MA 01301 Office: 173A Main St Greenfield MA 01301 Tel (413) 774-2385

SHEA, FRANCIS JEROME, b. Springfield, Mass., Jan. 8, 1934; A.B. cum laude, Holy Cross Coll., 1955; J.D., Boston Coll., 1960. Admitted to Mass. bar, 1960; U.S. Dist. Ct. bar, 1962; individual practice law, 1960—; asst. city solicitor City Chicopee (Mass.), 1962-65; gen. counsel Chicopee Falls Co-op Bank, 1962-65; corporator Community Savs. Bank, Holyoke, Mass., 1970—, Mercy Hosp., Springfield, Mass., 1970—; dir. Westover Devel. Corp. 1975—. Gen. chmn. United Fund of Chicopee, 1962; mem., founding dir. Greater Chicopee C. of C., 1966—. Mem. Mass., Hampden County, Chicopee bar assns. Home: 91 Watson St Chicopee MA 01020 Office: 99 Main St Chicopee MA 01020 Tel (413) 592-0436

SHEA, FRANCIS MICHAEL, b. Manchester, N.H., June 16, 1905; A.B., Dartmouth, 1925; LL.B., Harvard, 1928. Admitted to N.Y. bar, 1930, N.H. bar, 1930, U.S. Supreme Ct. bar, 1939, D.C. bar, 1945; asso. firm Slee, O'Brian, Hellings & Ulsh, Buffalo, 1929-33; chief opinion sect., legal div. Agrl. Adjustment Adminstrn., 1933-35; specialist legal div. SEC, 1935; gen. counsel P.R. Reconstrn. Adminstrn., 1935-36; dean, prof. law U. Buffalo, 1936-41; asst. atty. gen. U.S., 1939-45; mem. firm Shea & Gardner, Washington, 1947—; dir. Joint Conf. Legal Edn. N.Y. State, 1936-40; asso. counsel for prosecution major Axis war criminals, 1945; chmn. Atty. Gen.'s Com. on Bankruptcy Adminstrn., 1941-45; chmn. Jud. Conf. Com. Laws Pertaining to Mental Disorders, 1964-70. Mem. Am., N.Y. State, D.C. bar assns., Maritime Law Assn., Am. Law Inst., Jud. Conf. D.C. Circuit. Contbr. articles to legal jours. Home: 505 S Lee St Alexandria VA 22314 Office: 734 15th St NW Washington DC 20005 Tel (202) 737-1255

SHEA, JOHN G., b. Rochester, N.Y., Sept. 14, 1930; A.B., St. Bernard's Sem. and Coll., 1952; LL.B., Cornell U., 1956. Admitted to N.Y. bar, 1956, Pa. bar, 1967; served to 1st lt. JAGC, U.S. Army, 1957-60; counsel Gen. Electric Co., 1960-71; partner firm Shea & Shea, Bryn Mawr, Pa., 1971-73, 1976—, Drinker, Biddle & Reath, 1973-76; dir. Tri-Peg. Mem. Am., Pa., Phila., Montgomery bar assns., Main Line C. of C. (dir., exec. bd.), Order of Coif. Recipient Real Property award Cornell U.; bd. editors Cornell Law Rev. Home: 645 Radnor Valley Dr Villanova PA 19085 Office: Six Bryn Mawr Ave Bryn Mawr PA 19010 Tel (215) 527-4000

SHEA, ROBERT NASH, b. Hartford, Conn., May 3, 1932; B.A., Coll. Holy Cross, 1954; J.D., Georgetown U., 1959. Admitted to Va. bar, 1959, Conn. bar, 1960; asso. firm Schatz & Schatz, Hartford, 1960-66; individual practice law, 1966-73; partner firm Shea and Stevens, Niantic, Conn., 1974—; dir. New London Savs. and Loan Assn. Chmn., East Lyme Scholarship Assn., 1970-73; bd. dirs. Mystic Oral Sch. Mem. Am., Va., Conn. bar assns., Niantic C. of C. (pres. 1968). Home: 35 Heritage Rd East Lyme CT 06333 Office: 335 Main St Niantic CT 06357 Tel (203) 739-5466

SHEAD, WILLIAM CARROLL, b. Anderson, Tex., Mar. 23, 1927; B.S., U. Houston, 1952, M.A., 1954; J.D., S. Tex. Coll., 1959. Admitted to Tex. bar, 1959, U.S. Supreme Ct. bar, 1969; asst. city atty. Houston, 1962-63; individual practice law, Houston, 1960—. Mem. State Bar Tex., Tex. Trial Lawyers Assn., Tex. Criminal Def. Lawyers Assn., Law Sci. Acad. Editor S. Tex. Law Jour., 1958-59. Home: 202 Kolb St Pasadena TX 77502 Office: 2927 Broadway Houston TX 77017 Tel (713) 649-8944

SHEARD, KEVIN, b. N.Y.C., Jan. 30, 1916; B.A., Williams Coll., 1947; M.S., U. Wis., 1949; M.B.A., Xavier U., Cin., 1955; J.D., Loyola U., Chgo., 1959. Instr. history Williams Coll., 1947; asst. prof. bus. adminstrn. Baldwin Wallace Coll., 1955-58; instr. econs. U. Ill., 1959-64; asso. prof. bus. No. Mich. U., 1959-63; admitted to Mich. bar, 1960, Ohio bar, 1964, U.S. Supreme Ct. bar, 1965; prof. law Cleve. State U., 1963—. Mem. Marquette County (Mich.) Bar Assn. (pres. 1962). Author: Heraldry in America, 1962; (with Hugh Smith) Academic Dress & Insignia of the World's Universities, 1970; contbr. articles to legal jours. Home: 4152 W 49th St Cleveland OH 44144 Office: Cleveland State U Cleveland OH 44115 Tel (216) 687-2326

SHEARER, PARX FLETCHER, b. Red River County, Tex., Oct. 22, 1922; B.B.A., U. Tex., Austin, 1950, LL.B., 1952. Admitted to Tex. bar, 1951; individual practice law, Houston, 1952-70; partner firm Hoover, Cox & Miller, Houston, 1970—. Mem. Am., Houston bar assns. Home: 7603 Glenvista Houston TX 77061 Office: 2200 S Post Oak Rd Suite 301 Houston TX 77056 Tel (713) 623-4440

SHEARER, PAUL VICTOR, b. Columbus Junction, Iowa, Jan. 21, 1919; B.A., U. Iowa, 1940, J.D., 1942. Admitted to Iowa bar, 1942; county atty. Washington County, Iowa, 1949-51; partner firm Stewart and Shearer, Washington, Iowa, 1951—; dir. Washington Fed. Savs. and Loan Assn., 1968—. Trustee Garrett-Evangelical Theol. Sem., Evanston, Ill., 1972—; mem. Gen. Council on Ministries, United Meth. Ch., 1976—; mem. bd. fellows Sch. Religion, U. Iowa, 1973—. Mem. Am., Iowa (dist. pres. 1967-68), Washington County (pres. 1961-62) bar assns. Home: 110 E Monroe Washington IA 52353 Office: 225 W Main Washington IA 52353 Tel (319) 653-2159

SHECHTER, MORRIS, b. Los Angeles, Dec. 31, 1927; B.A. in Polit. Sci., U. Calif., Los Angeles, 1950; J.D., Southwestern U., Los Angeles, 1954. Admitted to Calif. bar, 1955; individual practice law, Long Beach and Lakewood, Calif., 1955—; judge pro tem Long Beach Municipal Ct. Bd. mgmt. YMCA, Lakewood, 1960-63. Mem. Am., Calif., Long Beach, Southeast, Los Angeles County bar assns., Calif., Los Angeles trial lawyers assns., Am. Arbitration Assn. (panel of arbitrators), Recipient Man of Year award U.S. Jaycees, 1961. Office: 5505 E Carson St #305 Lakewood CA 90713 Tel (213) 425-7491

SHEDLARZ, ROBERT JEROME, b. Bronx, N.Y., Feb. 17, 1945; B.A., N.Y. U., 1967; J.D., Notre Dame U., 1972. Asst. prof. bus. law Akron U., 1972—; admitted to Ohio bar, 1973; partner firm Kinsey & Shedlarz, Navarre, Ohio, 1974—; solicitor Village of Navarre, 1974—. Music dir. Temple Israel Religious Sch., Canton, Ohio, 1972—. Mem. Stark County (Ohio), Ohio bar assns., Stark County Law Library Assn., Am., Tri-State Regional bus. law assns., Nat. Assn. Bus. Law Tchrs. Home: 26 Basin St NW Navarre OH 44662 Office: 16 Wooster St NE Navarre OH 44662 Tel (216) 879-2719

SHEEDY, HERMAN JAMES, b. Ravenna, Ohio, June 9, 1924; A.B., Swarthmore Coll., 1948; LL.B., Harvard, 1951. Admitted to Ohio bar, 1951; asso. firm Squire, Sanders & Dempsey, Cleve., 1951-61, partner, 1961—; dir. Lubrizol Corp., Park-Ohio Industries, Harris Corp. Trustee Family Health Assn., 1961—, pres., 1973-74. Mem. Bar Assn. Greater Cleve., Am., Ohio bar assns., Phi Beta Kappa. Office: Union Commerce Bldg Cleveland OH 44115 Tel (216) 696-9200

SHEEHAN, CHARLES WINSTON, JR., b. Montgomery, Ala., Aug. 27, 1947; A.B. cum laude, U. South, 1969; J.D., U. Ala., 1972. Admitted to Ala. bar, 1972, U.S. Ct. Mil. Appeals, 1973, U.S. Supreme Ct. bar, 1976; law clk. to Richard Thompson, Tuscaloosa, Ala., 1971, legal aid clinic, Tuscaloosa, 1971; instr. bus. law John Patterson Vocat. Sch., Montgomery, Ala., 1972; asso. firm Duke, Booth, Kaufman, & Rothfeder, Montgomery, 1972; asst. judge adv., capt. JAGC, U.S. Army, Ft. Lee, Va., 1973—, def. counsel, 1973-74, chief pros. atty., 1975-76, chief mil. justice, 1976; asst. atty. gen. State of Ala., 1977—. Youth adv. Episcopal Young Churchmen Christ and Grace Episcopal Ch., Petersburg, Va., 1975-76. Mem. Am. Bar Assn., Nat. Dist. Atty.'s Assn., Farah Law Soc., Va. Crime Clinic, Phi Delta Phi, Omicron Delta Kappa, Alpha Tau Omega. Home: 2769 S Colonial Dr Montgomery AL 36111 Office: Adminstrn Bldg Office of Atty Gen Montgomery AL Tel (205) 834-5150

SHEEHAN, DENNIS MICHAEL, b. Chgo., Mar. 24, 1944; B.S. in Humanities, Loyola U., Chgo., 1966, J.D., 1969. Admitted to Ill. bar, 1969; 1st asst. state's atty., Pekin, Ill., 1970-73; felony trial asst. states atty., Springfield, Ill., 1973-75, Pekin, 1975-77; asso. firm Oltman & Morris, Pekin, 1977—. Mem. Am., Ill. bar assns. Home: 421 Haines St Pekin IL 61554 Office: Oltman & Morris Pekin IL 61554 Tel (309) 347-5586

SHEEHAN, LAWRENCE JAMES, b. San Francisco, July 23, 1932; A.B., Stanford, 1957, LL.B., 1959. Law clk. Chief Judge Charles Clark U.S. Ct. of Appeals 2d Circuit, N.Y.C., 1959-60; admitted to Calif. bar, 1960; asso. firm O'Melveny & Myers, Los Angeles, 1960-68, partner, 1969—. Mem. Los Angeles County, Calif., Fed., Am. bar assns., Order of Coif. Pres. Stanford Law Rev., 1958-59. Office: 1800 Century Park E Los Angeles CA 90067 Tel (213) 553-6700

SHEEHAN, RICHARD CHARLES, b. N.Y.C., Feb. 20, 1940; B.A., Temple U., Phila., 1967; J.D. (Alumni scholar), U. Toledo, 1970. Admitted to Pa. bar, 1970; teaching asst. social studies U. Toledo, 1968-70; instr. police sci. Penta County Community Coll., Toledo, 1970; asso. firm Duryea, Larzelere & Hepburn, Ardmore, Pa., 1970-71; asst. dist. atty. County of Montgomery (Pa.), 1972-73, asst. pub. defender, 1973-76; asso. firm Menin, Wilson & Flick, Norristown, Pa., 1973-74; individual practice law, Norristown and Audubon, Pa., 1974—; mental health rev. officer Montgomery County Ct. Common Pleas, Norristown, 1976—. Chmn. Lower Providence (Pa.) Library Com., 1974-75. Recipient Am. Jurisprudence award Outstanding Achievement Constl. Law, 1969; mem. staff U. Toledo Law Rev.; contbr. articles to legal jours. Office: 30 W Airy St Norristown PA 19401 Tel (215) 277-8380

SHEEHAN, WILLIAM FRANCIS, III, b. Balt., Mar. 11, 1947; B.A. cum laude, Yale, 1968; J.D. cum laude, U. Pa., 1971. Admitted to Washington bar, 1973, U.S. Supreme Ct. bar, 1976; law clk. Judge J. Edward Lumbard, U.S. Ct. Appeals 2d Circuit, 1971-72; asso. firm Shea and Gardner, Washington, 1972-75; asst. to solicitor gen. Dept. Justice, Washington, 1975—; cons. Commn. on Revision Fed. Ct. Appellate System, 1973-75. Editor-in-chief U. Pa. Law Rev., 1970-71. Home: 4512 Lowell St NW Washington DC 20016 Office: Dept of Justice Office of the Solicitor General Washington DC 20530 Tel (202) 739-4277

SHEEHAN, WILLIAM HAROLD, b. Childress, Tex., Mar. 6, 1928; LL.B., Baylor U., 1951. Admitted to Tex. bar, 1950; individual practice law, Friona, Tex., 1950-65; partner firm Frank D. McCown, Duman, Tex., 1965-69; partner firm Sheehan & Dubuque & Meredith, Dumas, 1969—; atty. Parmes County (Tex.), 1955-57; dist. atty. 154th Jud. Dist., 1957-61. Chmn. March of Dimes, Friona, 1954-55, Friona Community Chest, 1960-61; pres. Dumas Concert Assn., 1966-68, Dumas YMCA, 1970-72. Mem. Dumas C. of C. (pres. 1969-70), Am., Dumas, 69th Dist. bar assns., State Bar Tex. (chmn. gen. practice sect. 1972). Home: 601 Bennett Dr Dumas TX 79029 Office: 105 W 7th St Dumas TX 79029 Tel (806) 935-6451

SHEEHY, EDWARD MAUM, b. New Haven, Apr. 1, 1940; B.A., Yale, 1961; LL.B., U. Conn., 1967. Admitted to Conn. bar, 1967; asso. firm Pullman, Comley, Bradley & Reeves, Bridgeport, Conn., 1967-74, partner, 1974—. Mem. Am. Judicature Soc., Am., Conn. (past chmn. young lawyers sect., asst. sec.-treas. assn.), Bridgeport bar assns. Editor-in-chief U. Conn. Law Rev., 1966-67. Home: 7 Bunker Hill Rd Woodbridge CT 06525 Office: 855 Main St Bridgeport CT 06604 Tel (203) 334-0112

SHEEHY, JOHN JOSEPH, b. Newburgh, N.Y., July 27, 1938; B.S. cum laude, Holy Cross Coll., 1960; J.D., Boston Coll., 1963. Admitted to N.Y. State bar, 1963, U.S. Supreme Ct. bar, 1974; asst. dist. atty. N.Y. County, 1964-65; asst. counsel to Gov. State of N.Y., Albany, 1965-69; partner firm Rogers & Wells, N.Y.C., 1970-73, sr. partner, 1974—. Mem. Am., N.Y. State bar assns. Home: 5 Peter Cooper Rd apt 9C New York City NY 10010 Office: 200 Park Ave New York City NY 10017 Tel (212) 972-7020

SHEETS, GARY LEE, b. Sugar Grove, Ohio, May 15, 1944; B.B.A., Ohio U., 1969; J.D., Ariz. State U., 1972. Law clk. Greyhound Corp., Phoenix, 1971-72, atty., 1972-74; admitted to Ariz. bar, 1972, Ohio bar, 1972; asst. atty. gen. State of Ariz., counsel Ariz. Div. Securities and other state agencies, Phoenix, 1974—; vis. instr. bus. law Mesa Community Coll. Mem. Ariz. State, Maricopa County bar assns. Office: Room 200 State Capitol Phoenix AZ 85007 Tel (602) 271-3631

SHEETS, JODY GENE, b. Perryton, Tex., Dec. 19, 1946; B.A. in Polit. Sci., U. Tex., Austin, 1969, J.D., 1971. Admitted to Tex. bar, 1971; asso. firm Gassaway, Gurley & Sheets and predecessor, Borger, Tex., 1971-75, partner, 1975—. Mem. State Bar Tex., Am., Borger (pres. 1975) bar assns. Office: Suite 300 Panhandle Bank & Trust Bldg Borger TX 79007 Tel (806) 273-2857

SHEETZ, RALPH ALBERT, b. Halifax Twp., Dauphin County, Pa., June 13, 1908; Ph.B., Dickinson Coll., 1930, LL.B., U. Ala., 1933, J.D., 1969; postgrad. U. Calif., Berkeley, 1928, Sch. Law U. Mich., 1932. Admitted to Ala. bar, 1933, Pa. bar, 1934; individual practice law, Harrisburg, Pa., 1934—; solicitor Peoples Bank of Enola, Pa., 1934-75, E. Pennsboro Twp., Enola, 1934-53. Pres. E. Pennsboro Twp. PTA, Enola, 1952-53. Mem. Dauphin County, Cumberland County, Pa. bar assns. Recipient Order of Silver Trowel, 1948, York Cross of Honour, 1973. Home: 798 Valley St Enola PA 17025 Office: 6 N 3rd St Room 205 Bergner Bldg Harrisburg PA 17101 Tel (717) 238-8816

SHEFELMAN, HAROLD SAMUEL, b. N.Y.C., Apr. 15, 1898; Ph.B., Brown U., 1920, LL.D., 1965; LL.B., Yale, 1925; LL.D., Seattle Pacific Coll., 1962. Admitted to Wash. Supreme Ct. bar, 1926, U.S. Supreme Ct. bar, 1932; mem. firms Weter, Roberts & Shefelman, Seattle, 1928-50, Roberts, Shefelman, Lawrence, Gay & Moch, Seattle, 1950—; lectr. U. Wash. Law Sch., 1930-57. Regent U. Wash., 1957-75; mem. Seattle Planning Commn., 1948-71, Seattle Center Commn., 1956-71; mem. Wash. State Bd. Edn., 1951-57; pres. Pacific Sci. Center, Found., Seattle, 1969-70. Fellow Am. Bar Found.; mem. Am. (chmn. sect. municipal law 1952-54), Wash., Seattle (pres. 1937-38) bar assns., Am. Law Inst. (life), Am. Judicature Soc., Yale Law Sch. Assn. (hon. mem. exec. com.), Order of The Coif, Phi Beta Kappa. Recipient citation of honor Wash. State chpt. AIA, 1955, Distinguished Citizen award Nat. Municipal League, 1956, Outstanding Citizen award Seattle Municipal League, 1961, Others award Salvation Army, 1963, Outstanding Alumnus award Brown U., 1970. Office: 1818 IBM Bldg Seattle WA 98101 Tel (206) 622-1818

SHEFFIELD, BRYAN WILLIAM, b. London, Jan. 23, 1935; came to U.S., 1954, naturalized, 1955; B.M.E., N.Y. U., 1963, J.D., 1967. Admitted to N.Y. bar, 1968, N.J. bar, 1969; patent atty. Western Electric Co., Washington, 1963-65, N.Y.C., 1965-67, Princeton, N.J., 1967-74; patent atty. Bell Telephone Labs, Holmdel, N.J., 1974—. Committeeman Republican party Monmouth County, N.J., 1976—. Mem. Am. Bar Assn., Am., N.J., patent law assns. Home: 37 Girard St Marlboro NJ 07746 Office: Room 4B 201 Bell Labs Holmdel NJ 07733 Tel (201) 949-3190

SHEFFIELD, DAVID ALVIN, b. Shreveport, La., Aug. 3, 1927; B.A., La. Tech. U., 1953; LL.B., La. State U., 1953, J.D., 1968. Admitted to La. bar, 1953; asso. firm Gravel & Downs, Alexandria, La., 1953-55; partner firm Gravel, Humphries & Sheffield, Alexandria, 1955-56, firm Gravel, Sheffield & Fuhrer, Alexandria, 1956-65; individual practice law, Alexandria, 1965—; asst. city atty. Alexandria, 1969-73. Mem. La., Alexandria bar assns., Am., La. trial lawyers assns. Home: 511 Kimball St Alexandria LA 71301 Office: 730 Murray St Alexandria LA 71301 Tel (318) 443-0472

SHEFFIELD, FRANK ELWYN, b. Tallahassee, Jan. 4, 1946; B.S. in Mktg., Fla. State U., 1968, J.D., 1972. Admitted to Fla. bar, 1972, since practiced in Tallahassee; asso. firm J. Marshall Gifford, 1972-73, Dye & Conner, 1973; individual practice law, 1973—. Mem. Am., Fla., Tallahassee (chmn. law week com. 1975) bar assns., Tallahassee Estate Planning Council. Home: 3629 Westmorland Dr Tallahassee FL 32303 Office: Suite 229 Ellis Bldg 1311 Executive Center Dr Tallahassee FL 32301 Tel (904) 878-1161

SHEFNER, NATHAN, b. Chgo., Sept. 13, 1893. Admitted to Ill. bar, 1920, U.S. Dist. Ct. No. Dist. Ill. bar, 1921; U.S. Supreme Ct. bar, 1938; U.S. Dist. Ct. Western Dist. Mich., 1949, U.S. 7th Circuit Ct. Appeals bar, 1955; practice law, Chgo., 1920—; reporter procs. Ill. Constl. Conv., Springfield, 1920; ct. reporter Joint Senate and Ho. of Reps. com. investigating Pearl Harbor, 1946. Mem. Ill. State, Chgo. bar assns. Office: 39 S LaSalle St Chicago IL 60603 Tel (312) 263-4156

SHEFTE, DALBERT UHRIG, b. Evanston, Ill., Sept. 17, 1927; B.M.E., Northwestern U., 1949, J.D., 1952. Admitted to Ill. bar, 1952, N.C. bar, 1960, U.S. Patent Office, 1955, U.S. Supreme Ct., 1960; asso. firm Schroeder, Hofgren, Brady and Wegner, Chgo., 1954-56, Ooms and Dominick, Chgo., 1956-58, Parrott and Richards, Charlotte, N.C., 1958-62; partner firm Richards, Shefte and Pinckney, Charlotte, 1962—. Pres., Contact Telephone Counseling Service, Charlotte, 1970—; dir. Info. and Referral Service, Charlotte, 1976—; dist. com. chmn. Mecklenburg council Boy Scouts Am., 1973—; mem. Citizens Task Force on Juvenile Delinquency and the Cts., Charlotte; dir. social planning council United Community Services, Charlotte, 1977—. Mem. Am., N.C., 26th Jud. Dist. bar assns., N.C. Soc. Engrs., Charlotte Engrs. Club (pres. 1966-67). Home: 1430 Coventry Rd Charlotte NC 28211 Office: 1208 Cameron Bldg Charlotte NC 28204

SHEIDLOWER, ARNOLD M., b. N.Y.C., Oct. 14, 1934; B.B.A., Coll. City N.Y., 1954; LL.B., Columbia, 1957. Admitted to N.Y. bar, 1957; with SEC, Washington, 1959-61; asso. firm Strasser Spiegelberg, Fried & Frank, N.Y.C., 1961-65; partner firm Abrams & Sassower, and predecessors, N.Y.C., 1965—. Mem. Am., N.Y. State, Fed. bar assns. Home: 16 Arleigh Rd Great Neck NY 11021 Office: 598 Madison Ave New York City NY 10022 Tel (212) 688-4200

SHEIMAN, STUART MELVYN, b. Bridgeport, Conn., Apr. 29, 1942; B.B.A., U. Mich., 1964; J.D., Ind. U., 1969. Admitted to Conn. bar, 1969; individual practice law, Bridgeport. Mem. Am. Bar Assn., Conn. Trial Lawyers Assn. Office: 1776 North Ave Bridgeport CT 06604 Tel (203) 576-1460

SHEINBERG, LAWRENCE PHILIP, b. Bklyn., May 19, 1931; B.A., N.Y. U., 1951; LL.B., N.Y. Law Sch., 1956, LL.M., 1964. Admitted to N.Y. State bar, 1957; mem. firm Friedman & Friedman, 1957-58; counsel Gold & Lerner, 1959-65; partner firm Restaino, Fein & Sheinberg, 1966-67; individual practice law, N.Y.C., 1958—. Mgr. Boy Scouts Am., Bklyn., 1969-70; pres. Madison High Sch. Parents Assn., Bklyn., 1972-74; mem. Midway Chamber Music Group, Bklyn., 1970-73. Mem. N.Y. County Lawyers Assn., N.Y. Bar Assn., N.Y. State Trial Lawyers Assn., Am. Arbitration Assn. (active arbitrator). Home: 6 Adam Ct Highland Mills NY 10930 Office: 11 Park Pl New York City NY 10007 Tel (212) 732-0445

SHELBY, JEROME, b. N.Y.C., Mar. 17, 1930; A.B., N.Y. U., 1950; LL.B., Harvard, 1953. Admitted to D.C. bar, 1953, N.Y. bar, 1954; asso. firm Cadwalader, Wickersham & Taft, N.Y.C., 1953-63, partner firm, 1963—; sr. v.p. Marine Transport Lines, Inc., N.Y.C., 1958-76; dir., v.p. Energy Transp. Corp., N.Y.C., 1973—. Mem. Bar Assn. City of N.Y. Home: 74 Highland Ave Montclair NJ 07042 Office: One Wall St New York City NY 10005 Tel (212) 785-1000

SHELBY, RICHARD CRAIG, b. Birmingham, Ala., May 6, 1934; A.B., U. Ala., Tuscaloosa, 1957, LL.B., 1961. Admitted to Ala. bar, 1961; law clk. to justice Supreme Ct. Ala., 1961-62; practice law, Tuscaloosa, 1963—; city prosecutor City of Tuscaloosa, 1964-70; spl. asst. atty. gen. State of Ala., 1969-72; U.S. commr., western div. No. Dist. Ala., 1966-70; mem. Ala. Senate, 1970—, chmn. legis. council, 1977—, mem. bd. govs. nat. legis. council, 1974—. Recipient Distinguished Service plaque Ala. Trial Lawyers Assn., 1976. Office: 324 1st Federal Savings Bldg Tuscaloosa AL 35401 Tel (205) 345-7444

SHELL, LOUIS CALVIN, b. DeWitt, Va., Dec. 8, 1925; A.B., U. Va., 1946, LL.B., 1947. Admitted to Va. bar, 1947; asso. firm White, Hamilton & Wyche, Petersburg, Va., 1948-50; partner firm White, Hamilton, Wyche & Shell, Petersburg, 1950—. Vice mayor Petersburg City Council, 1957-60; pres. Petersburg Tb. Assn., 1951; pres. Petersburg chpt. Am. Cancer Soc., 1952; chmn. electoral bd. City of Petersburg, 1952; trustee Petersburg dist. United Methodist Ch. Fellow Am. Coll. Trial Lawyers; mem. Am., Va. State, Petersburg bar assns., Am. Judicature Soc., Va. State Bar (council 1972-75). Named Petersburg Outstanding Young Man, Jr. C. of C., 1956. Home: 1612 E Tuckahoe St Petersburg VA 23803 Office: 20 E Tabb St Petersburg VA 23803 Tel (804) 733-9010

SHELL, THURSTON ALBERT, b. Century, Fla., Aug. 27, 1930; B.B.A., U. Fla., 1952, LL.B., 1956. Admitted to Fla. bar, 1956; individual practice law, Pensacola, Fla., 1956-57; mem. firm Shell, Fleming, Davis & Menge, and predecessors, Pensacola, 1957—. Mem. Am., Escambia-Santa Rosa (pres. 1972-74) bar assns. Home: 4180 Fern Ct Pensacola FL 32503 Office: PO Box 1831 Pensacola FL 32598 Tel (904) 434-2411

SHELLEY, JAMES LAMAR, b. Joseph City, Ariz., Dec. 8, 1915; B.A. in Edn., No. Ariz. U., 1936; J.D., U. Ariz., 1949. Admitted to Ariz. bar, 1948, U.S. Supreme Ct. bar, 1954; asst. city atty., Mesa, Ariz., 1948-50, city atty., 1950—; partner firm Johnson, Shelley & Roberts and predecessor firm, Mesa, 1951—; gen. counsel League Ariz. Cities and Towns, 1957—. Mem. exec. bd. Theodore Roosevelt Council Boy Scouts Am., Phoenix, 1962—; pres. Mesa United Way, 1969-70. Mem. Nat. Inst. Municipal Law Officers (trustee), Am., Ariz., Tri-City bar assns. Home: 550 N Emerson St Mesa AZ 85201 Office: 48 N Macdonald St Mesa AZ 85201 Tel (602) 964-1421

SHELLEY, MICHAEL JOSEPH, b. Tel Aviv, Nov. 25, 1946; B.A. in English, Calif. State U., 1968; J.D., U. So. Calif., 1971. Admitted to Calif. bar, 1972; mem. firm Rose, Klein & Marias, Los Angeles, 1972—. Mem. Am., Los Angeles County bar assns., Calif. Trial Lawyers Assn. Home: 13004 Greenleaf St Studio City CA 91604 Office: 727 W 7th St Suite 850 Los Angeles CA 90017 Tel (213) 626-0571

SHELTON, DARRELL RANKIN, b. Zephyr, Tex., Aug. 15, 1913; student Howard Payne Coll., 1933-35; LL.B., Samford U., 1937, J.D., 1969. Admitted to Tex. bar, 1939, since practiced in Brownwood. Mem. Cumberland Order Jurisprudence. Home: 1219 Phillips Dr Brownwood TX 76801 Office: 101 First National Office Building Brownwood TX 76801 Tel (915) 646-7292

SHELTON, LEWIS LEONIDAS, b. Reform, Ala., Feb. 9, 1912; LL.B., Millsaps Coll., and Miss. Coll. Admitted to Miss. bar, 1940; individual practice law, Jackson, Miss. Pres. Jackson YMCA. Mem. Miss., Hinds County bar assns. Home: 261 Culberson Ave Jackson MS 39209 Office: 221 N President St Jackson MS 39201 Tel (601) 352-4661

SHELTON, LUTHER ROSSER, b. Atlanta, Feb. 19, 1914; B. Ph., Emory U., 1935, LL.B., 1936, J.D., 1970. Admitted to N.Mex. bar, 1940, Ga. bar, 1958; asso. firm Shelton & Pharr, Atlanta, 1935-36; asso. firm Hervey, Don, Hill & Hinkle, Roswell, N.M., 1939-41; individual practice law, Roswell, 1941-45; atty. Office of Price Adminstrn., Atlanta, 1945-48; staff atty., asst. gen. counsel Atlanta Legal Aid Soc., Inc., 1958—; investigator dept. pub. health, Griffin &

Macon, Ga., 1949-51. Scoutmaster Atlanta Area council Boy Scouts Am., 1954-56, explorer advisor, 1956-68. Mem. Am., N.Mex., Ga., Atlanta bar assns., Lawyers Club Atlanta, Nat. Legal Aid and Defender Assn. Contbr. articles to legal jours.; recipient Wood Badge award, 1966, spl. award for outstanding explorer advising Boy Scouts Am., 1962. Home: 1804 Roswell Rd Apt 44E Marietta GA 30062 Office: 11 Pryor St 8th Floor Atlanta GA 30303 Tel (404) 577-5260

SHELTON, SCOTT CHARLES, b. San Angelo, Tex., Dec. 14, 1946; B.A., Tex. Christian U., 1969; J.D., U. Tex., 1972. Admitted to Tex. bar, 1972; asst. city atty. Midland (Tex.), 1972-76, individual practice law, Midland, 1976—. Mem. Tex., Am., Midland County bar assns., Midland County Jr. Bar Assn. Home: 2407 Sinclair Midland TX 79701 Office: 214 N Colorado Midland TX 79701 Tel (915) 683-8861

SHEMATZ, JOHN ROBERT, JR., b. Wilmington, N.C., Aug. 11, 1942; A.B., U. Md., 1965; J.D., U. Balt., 1972. Admitted to Md. bar, 1972; tech. writer Govt. Employees Ins. Co., Chevy Chase, Md., 1973-74; atty. IRS, Balt., 1974—. Mem. Md. Bar Assn., Phi Beta Gamma. Decorated Air Medal, Vietnamese Med. Honor. Home: 1194 Ramblewood Dr Annapolis MD 21401 Tel (301) 962-3567

SHENIER, HENRY LEO, b. West New York, N.J., Feb. 25, 1902; B.S., U.S. Naval Acad., 1922; J.D., Georgetown U., 1931. Admitted to D.C. bar, 1930, Mo. bar, 1932, Ill. bar, 1945, N.Y. bar, 1947; examiner U.S. Patent Office, Washington, 1927-31; asso. firm Thomas E. Scofield, Kansas City, Mo., 1931-36, partner, 1936-41; contracting officer Bur. of Ordnance Navy Dept., Washington, 1941-45; partner firm Moore, Olson & Trexler, Chgo., 1945-46; individual practice law, N.Y.C., 1947-57; sr. partner firm Shenier & O'Connor, N.Y.C., 1958—. Mem. Am., N.Y.C. bar assns., Am. Patent Law Assn. Office: 230 Park Ave New York City NY 10017 Tel (212) 682-1986

SHENK, JOHN ALEXANDER, b. Delphos, Ohio, Nov. 9, 1906; A.B., Case Western Res. U., 1931, B.S. in Library Sci., 1932; student Judge John F. Lindemann, 1934-38. Admitted to Ohio bar, 1939, U.S. Dist. Ct. bar, No. Dist. Ohio, 1957; mem. firm Lindemann & Shenk and predecessor, Delphos, 1939-60; individual practice law, Delphos, 1960-62; sr. partner firm Shenk & Clark, Delphos, 1962—; solicitor City of Delphos, 1941-42. Mem. Delphos Pub. Library Bd., 1959-63; mem. Allen County (Ohio) Soldiers Relief Commn., 1972—. Mem. Am., Allen State, Northwestern Ohio, Allen County (chmn. probate com.), Van Wert County (Ohio) bar assns. Office: Peoples Nat Bank Bldg 202 N Main St Delphos OH 45833 Tel (419) 695-2791

SHEPARD, ALLAN GUY, b. Gardner, Mass., Dec. 18, 1922; B.S., U. Wash., 1948, J.D., 1951. Admitted to Idaho bar, 1951, U.S. Supreme Ct. bar, 1964; since practiced in Boise, Idaho; asst. atty. gen., chief counsel Idaho Dept. Hwys., 1951-56; individual practice law, 1957-61; atty. gen. State of Idaho, 1962-68; justice Idaho Supreme Ct., 1969—; mem. Idaho Ho. of Reps., 1958-62. Mem. Am. Bar Assn., Am. Judicature Soc. Office: 451 W State St Boise ID 83720 Tel (208) 384-2207

SHEPARD, CLIFFORD BISHOP, b. Jacksonville, Fla., Aug. 30, 1919; B.S.B.A., U. Fla., 1942, LL.B., 1948. Admitted to Fla. bar, 1948; practiced in Jacksonville, 1948-65; judge Duval County (Fla.) Small Claims Ct., 1965-71, Duval County Juvenile Ct., 1971-73, Fla. Circuit Ct., 4th Jud. Circuit, 1973—. Mem. Fla., Jacksonville bar assns. Home: 4233 Point La Vista Rd S Jacksonville FL 32207 Office: 330 E Bay St Jacksonville FL 32202 Tel (904) 633-6884

SHEPATIN, DAVID BURTON, b. New Haven, May 13, 1943; B.A., U. Conn., 1966; J.D., Suffolk U., 1969. Admitted to N.H. bar, 1969, Mass. bar, 1970; mem. firm Mussman & Shepatin, 1969-72; individual practice law, Littleton, N.H., 1972—; dir. Peoples Nat. Bank Littleton. Mem. N.H., Grafton County bar assns. Home: Birches Rd Sugar Hill NH Office: 12 Main St Littleton NH 03561 Tel (603) 444-2562

SHEPHERD, FRANK ANDREW, b. W. Palm Beach, Fla., Dec. 11, 1946; B.A., U. Fla., 1968; M.A., U. Mass., 1970; J.D., U. Mich., 1972. Admitted to Fla. bar, 1972, D.C. bar, 1975; asso. firm Bradford, Williams, McKay, Kimbrell, Hamann & Jennings, Miami, Fla., 1972—. Mem. Am., Fla. bar assns. Home: 5729 Marius St Coral Gables FL 33146 Office: 101 W Flagler St Miami FL 33131 Tel (305) 358-8181

SHEPHERD, WALTON, b. Wright, W.Va., Sept. 14, 1905; B.A., W.Va., U., 1930, J.D., 1931; Admitted to W.Va. bar, 1931, U.S. Supreme Ct. bar, 1942; asso. firm Blue, Dayton & Campbell, Charleston, W.Va., 1931-41; Reed, Freeman & Shepherd, Charleston, 1976—; served to maj. Judge Adv. Gen. Dept. U.S. Army, 1941-46; mem. firm Blue, Hill & Shepherd, Charleston, 1946-50, Shepherd & Hunter, Charleston, 1950-75; dep. tax commr. State of W.Va.; chief assessments and levies Capital Bldg. Charleston, 1933-35; pres. Charleston Camp Gideons Internat., 1963; elder First Presbyn. Ch., Charleston, 1968—. Mem. W.Va., Kanawha County bar assns., Phi Alpha Delta. Home: 607 Wood Rd Charleston WV 25302 Office: 212 Roane St Charleston WV 25302 Tel (304) 342-1605

SHEPPARD, ARTHUR NATHAN, b. N.Y.C., May 11, 1933; B.S. in Econs., Wharton Sch., U. Pa., 1954; J.D., Yale, 1960. Admitted to Fla. bar, 1960; asso. firm Albion & Greenfield, Miami, 1960-62; asso. firm Meyer, Weiss, Rose, Arkin, Sheppard & Shockett, Profl. Assn. and predecessor, Miami Beach, Fla., 1962-68, partner, 1968—; judge North Bay Village (Fla.) Municipal Ct., 1970-72. Bd. dirs. Dade County-Monroe Lung Assn., 1971—, v.p., 1975—; trustee Mt. Sinai Med. Center of Greater Miami, 1973—, pres. sustaining bd. fellows, 1973-75, chmn. laws com., 1976—. Mem. Fla. Bar, Dade County, Miami Beach (v.p. 1975, dir.) bar assns. Home: 1430 Stillwater Dr Miami Beach FL 33141 Office: 407 Lincoln Rd Miami Beach FL 33139 Tel (305) 538-2531

SHERAN, ROBERT JOSEPH, b. Waseca, Minn., Jan. 2, 1916; B.A., Coll. St. Thomas, St. Paul, 1936; LL.B., U. Minn., 1939. Admitted to Minn. bar, 1939; practice in Glencoe, 1939-42, Mankato, 1945-63; spl. agt. FBI, 1942-45; asso. justice Supreme Ct. Minn., 1963-70, chief justice, 1973—; mem. firm Lindquist & Vennum, Mpls., 1970-73. Mem. Minn. Bd. Law Examiners, 1956-62, 70-73; mem. Minn. Bd. Tax Appeals, 1961-63; chmn. Gov.'s Commn. on Crime Prevention and Control, 1970-73; Mem. Minn. Ho. of Reps. from Blue Earth County, 1946-50. Trustee Coll. St. Thomas, 1964-73. Fellow Am. Coll. Trial Lawyers, Internat. Acad. Trial Lawyers; mem. Am. Law Inst., Am. Judicature Soc., Inst. Jud. Adminstrn. Home: 1077 Sibley Meml Hwy Saint Paul MN 55118 Office: 230 State Capitol Saint Paul MN 55155*

SHERIDAN, JOHN EDWARD, b. Waterbury, Conn., Sept. 15, 1902; B.Sc. in Econs., U. Pa., 1925; LL.B., Temple U., 1931, LL.M., 1956, J.D., 1967. Admitted to Pa. bar, 1931, U.S. Supreme Ct. bar, 1945, D.C. bar, 1935, N.J. bar, 1935, Md. bar, 1935; dep. atty. gen. Pa. Dept. Justice, 1935-37; gen. cou,nsel Pa., N.J. Bridge Authority, 1937-38; mem. Pa. Ho. of Reps., 1938-47. Mem. Phila. Bar Assn., Lawyers Club Phila. Named Outstanding Big Bro., 1937; recipient Outstanding award Air Indsl. Coll. Armed Forces, 1957. Home and Office: 6240 Wissahickon Ave Philadelphia PA 19144

SHERIDAN, WILLIAM JOHN, JR., b. Chgo., Oct. 28, 1947; B.A., Fairfield U., 1969; J.D., U. Ill., 1972. Admitted to Ill. bar, 1972; asst. prof. Western Ill. U. Macomb, 1972-73; atty. Harris Trust and Savs. Bank, Chgo., 1973-76; mem. firm Katten, Muchin, Gitles, Zavis, Pearl & Galler, Chgo., 1976—. Mem. Chgo., Ill. State bar assns. Home: Apt 1306 2728 Hampden Ct Chicago IL 60614 Office: Suite 4100 55 E Monroe St Chicago IL 60603 Tel (312) 346-7400

SHERIFF, SEYMOUR, b. Rye, N.Y., Aug. 22, 1917; B.S., Coll. City N.Y., 1935; J.D., Yale, 1938. Admitted to N.Y. bar, 1938, D.C. bar, 1939, Md. bar, 1957; practiced law, Washington, 1938—; sr. partner firm Gardner, Morrison, Sheriff & Beddow, 1958—. Mem. Am., D.C. bar assns., Phi Beta Kappa. Home: 6910 Blaisdell Rd Bethesda MD 20034 Office: suite 1126 Woodward Bldg Washington DC 20005

SHERK, RONALD E., b. Portland, Oreg., Feb. 22, 1916; A.B., George Fox Coll., 1936; J.D., Northwestern Coll. Law, Portland, 1940. Admitted to Oreg. bar, 1940, U.S. Supreme Ct. bar, 1962; spl. agt. FBI, 1940-72; individual practice law, Oregon City, Oreg., 1972—. Mem. Internat. Assn. Chiefs of Police (asso.), Fed. (past pres. Oreg. chpt.), Oreg. bar assns. Home: 10490 SW Century Oak Dr Summerfield Tigard OR 97223 Office: Harding Bldg 511 Main St Oregon City OR 97045 Tel (503) 656-5393

SHERMAN, BERTON DALE, b. Eau Claire, Wis., Dec. 8, 1924; B.S., Wis. State Coll., Eau Claire, 1953; LL.D., U. Wis., Madison, 1953. Admitted to Wis. bar, 1953; asso. firm Sherman, Stutz & Lister, Black River Falls, Wis., 1953-55, partner, 1955—; dir. 1st Fin. Savs. & Loan Assn. of Stevens Point. Bd. dirs. Black River council Campfire Girls, 1974—. Mem. State Bar Wis., Am., Tri-County (pres. 1976) bar assns., Am. Coll. Probate Counsel. Home: 214 N 6th St Black River Falls WI 54615 Office: 104 Main St PO Box 267 Black River Falls WI 54615 Tel (715) 284-5381

SHERMAN, EDWARD HARRISON, b. Riga, Sept. 11, 1912; student Regis Coll., 1930, U. Denver, 1931-33; LL.B., U. Mich., 1937. Admitted to Colo. bar, 1937; partner firm Sherman & Morgan, and predecessors, Denver, 1966-70; lectr., cons. U. Denver, 1945-56; pub. defender County of Denver, 1966-70. State chmn. ACLU, 1955—; organizer, mem. bd. Rocky Mountain Council for Family Relations, Marriage Council of Denver, 1962; bd. dirs. Legal Aid Soc. Denver, 1958-62. Mem. Denver, Colo. bar assns., Am. Judicature Soc. Contbr. monthly articles to legal jour. Recipient Whitehead award, 1967, Adelstine award, 1970. Home: 5460 E Mansfield Ave Denver CO 80237 Office: 225 E 16th Ave Capital Life Center Denver CO 80203 Tel (303) 892-6022

SHERMAN, GARY EDWARD, b. Chgo., May 5, 1949; B.A., U. Wis., Madison, 1970, J.D. cum laude, 1973. Admitted to Wis. bar, 1973; served to lt. staff JAG, USAF, 1973; asso. firm Norlin and Spears, Washburn, Wis., 1973-74; individual practice law, Port Wing, Wis., 1974—; speaker police tng. program, 1974. Treas., Port Wing Vol. Fire Dept., S. Shore Food Buying Service; mem. Nat. Orgn. for Reform of Marijuana Laws. Mem. State Bar of Wis., Ashland-Bayfield Counties Bar Assn. (sec. treas.). Home and Office: Port Wing WI 54865 Tel (715) 774-3693

SHERMAN, HARRY ALAN, b. Pitts., Oct. 28, 1906; B.A., U. Pitts., 1929, LL.B., 1932, J.D., 1960. Admitted to Pa. bar, 1933; individual practice law, Pitts., 1933—; dean Labor Relations Inst., 1945-54; spl. counsel Atty. Gen. of Pa., 1951-54; regent Internat. Acad. Law and Sci., 1965-68. Chmn. Americans Battling Communism, 1944—. Mem. Am., Pa., Allegheny County bar assns., Am. Trial Lawyers Assn. (nat. chmn. rivers and lakes sect. admiralty div. 1966-67). Editor Pa. Republican, 1944-60; contbg. editor Lex et Scientia, 1965-68. Home: 4311 University Dr Coral Gables FL 33146 Office: 1709 Blvd of the Allies Pittsburgh PA 15219 Tel (412) 471-7777

SHERMAN, JOHN WARRINGTON, b. Balt., July 1, 1918; J.D., U. Balt., 1938. Admitted to Md. bar, 1939, N.Y. bar, 1956, Ill. bar, 1961; atty. income tax div. State of Md., Annapolis, 1939-42, 46-47, Standard Oil Co. Ind. and affiliates, Balt., 1947-55, N.Y.C., 1955-61, Chgo., 1961—. Mem. Am., Chgo. bar assns., Patent Law Assn. Chgo., U.S. Trademark Assn. (v.p. 1976-77), Internat. Assn. Protection of Indsl. Property. Contbr. articles to profl. jours. Office: 200 E Randolph Dr Suite 2106 Chicago IL 60601 Tel (312) 856-7924

SHERMAN, MARTIN PETER, b. N.Y.C., May 2, 1940; B.A., U. Calif., Los Angeles, 1961; J.D., U. Chgo., 1964; LL.M., U. So. Calif., 1969. Admitted to Calif. bar, 1965, Pa. bar, 1972; law clk. to judge Appellate Dept., Los Angeles Superior Ct., 1964-65; dep. county counsel Los Angeles County, 1965-66; asst. regional counsel OEO, San Francisco, 1966-67; with legal dept. Atlantic Richfield Co., Los Angeles, 1969-73, Phila., 1972-73; asso. counsel legal dept. Ampex Corp., Redwood City, Calif., 1973—. Mem. Am. Bar Assn., Calif. Trial Lawyers Assn. Home: 1131 Stanley Way Palo Alto CA 94303 Office: 401 Broadway Redwood City CA 94063 Tel (415) 367-4457

SHERMAN, MAX, b. Newark, Mar. 1, 1914; LL.B., Rutgers U., 1937. Admitted to N.J. bar, 1938, U.S. Supreme Ct. bar, 1945; partner firm Max Sherman, and predecessors, Springfield, N.J.; counsel Twp. Springfield, 1952-58; judge Municipal Ct. Springfield, 1963-72; counsel Crestmont Savs. and Loan Assn., Maplewood, N.J., 1966—; title atty. Commonwealth Land Title Ins. Co., Chelsea Title & Guaranty Co., Lawyers Title Ins. Co., N.J. Realty Title Ins. Co., Am. Title Ins. Co., Chgo. Title Ins. Co., Prudential Ins. Co. Am., Howard Savs. Bank, Investors Savs. and Loan Assn.; treas. Sherwood Devel. Corp., dir. Short Hills Nat. Bank, Springfield State Bank. Mem. Am., N.J., Union County bar assns. Office: 26 Linden Ave Springfield NJ 07081

SHERMAN, PETER RICHARD, b. South Bend, Ind., Apr. 14, 1939; B.S. with distinction, Ind. U., 1961; LL.B., Georgetown U., 1964, LL.M., 1966. Admitted to D.C. bar, 1965, U.S. Supreme Ct. bar, 1968; law clk. to Judge U.S. Dist. Ct. for D.C., 1964-65; E. Barrett Prettyman fellow in trial practice D.C. Ct. System, 1965-66; partner firm Kuder, Sherman, Fox, Meehan & Curtin, Washington, 1968—; adj. prof. law Am. U., 1977. Mem. D.C. Bar Assn. Contbr. articles to legal jours. Office: 1900 M St NW Washington DC 20036 Tel (202) 331-7120

SHERMAN, WILLIAM FARRAR, b. Little Rock, Sept. 12, 1937; B.A. in History and Govt., U. Ark., 1960; LL.B., U. Va., 1964. Admitted to Ark. bar, 1964; asst. U.S. atty. Eastern Dist. Ark., 1966-69; commr. Ark. Securities Dept., Little Rock, 1969-71; partner firm Jacoway & Sherman, Little Rock, 1971—; mem. Ark. Ho. of Reps., 1974—. Committeeman, Pulaski County (Ark.) Democratic Party, 1972-74, presdl. campaign coordinator, 1972; bd. stewards First United Methodist Ch., Little Rock. Fellow Ark. Bar Found.; mem. Am., Ark., Pulaski County bar assns. Home: 450 Midland St Little Rock AR 72205 Office: 504 Pyramid Life Bldg Little Rock AR 72201 Tel (501) 372-3148

SHERMOEN, JEROME WILLIAM, b. Fargo, N.D., Jan. 22, 1927; student N.D. State U., Fargo; Ph.B., J.D., U. N.D. Admitted to N.D. bar, 1952, Minn. bar, 1968; partner firms Barnett, Bergeson, Whittlesey, Shermoen & Paneratz, Fargo, 1953-60, Lanier, Knox & Shermoen, Fargo, 1960-68, Furuseth & Shermoen, International Falls, Minn., 1968-69, Shermoen & Shermoen, International Falls, 1976—; individual practice law, International Falls, 1969-76; citv atty., cities of South International Falls, Minn., Big Falls, Minn., Island View, Minn.; dir. Internat. State Bank of International Falls. Mem. Am., Minn., 15th Dist. (pres. 1976—), Koochiehing (pres. 1976—) bar assns., Order of Coif. Office: 406 5th Ave International Falls MN 56649 Tel (218) 283-4494

SHERNOFF, WILLIAM MARTIN, b. Chgo., Oct. 26, 1937; J.D., U. Wis., 1962. Admitted to Calif. bar, 1966; individual practice law, Claremont, Calif., 1967—; lectr. seminars in field. Mem. Am., Calif. (bd. govs.) trial lawyers assns. Contbr. articles to legal jours. Named Trial Lawyer of Year, Los Angeles, 1975. Office: 666 S Indian Hill St Claremont CA 91711 Tel (714) 632-4935

SHERR, RONALD HERBERT, b. Phila., Dec. 10, 1929; B.S., Temple U., 1951, LL.B., 1956. Admitted to Pa. bar, 1957; partner firms Detweiler, Sherr & Hughes, Phila., 1957-71, Wright, Spencer, Manning & Sagendorph, Norristown, Pa., 1971-74, Spencer, Sherr & Moses, Norristown, 1974—; lectr. Pa. Bar Inst.; solicitor Upper Moreland Twp. (Pa.) Sch., Dist. and Upper Moreland Twp. Sch. Dist. Authority, 1974—. Mem. Am., Pa., Phila., Montgomery County bar assns., Def. Research Inst., Pa. Def. Inst., Assn. Def. Counsel, Montgomery County Trial Lawyers Assn. Office: 107 E Main St Norristown PA 19401 Tel (205) 279-5300

SHERRILL, JOSEPH NEWTON, JR., b. Wichita Falls, Tex., Aug. 1, 1929; B.S. in Marine Transp., Mass. Inst. Tech., 1952; J.D., Harvard U., 1955. Admitted to Tex. bar, 1955; partner firm Sherrill, Pace & Rogers, and predecessors, Wichita Falls, 1955-71; chmn. bd. dirs. Sherrill, Pace, Rogers, Crosnoe & Morrison, 1971—; chmn. bd. dirs. Wichita Clutch Co., Inc., Wilson Mfg. Co., Inc., 1st Fed. Savs. Loan Assn. Wichita Falls; sec. Moran Bros., Inc.; dir. 1st Nat. Bank, Byers, Tex. Chmn. bd. trustees Trinity U., 1973-76; trustee Midwestern State U. Found., Inc.; nat. vice chmn. Harvard Law Sch. Fund; trustee, pres. Wichita Falls Mus. Art Center. Lectr. Oil Gas Taxation Inst. Southwestern Legal Found. So. Meth. U. Law Sch., 1968. Office: PO Drawer 5008 Wichita Falls TX 76307 Tel (817) 322-3145

SHERROD, RANDALL LAVERN, b. Beaver, Okla., May 9, 1948; B.A., Tex. Tech. U., 1970, J.D., 1973. Admitted to Tex. bar, 1973; asst. atty. City of Amarillo, Tex., 1973; asst. criminal dist. atty. Randall County (Tex.), 1974, criminal dist. atty., 1975—. Mem. Nat. Dist. Attys. Assn., Tex. Dist. and County Atty's Assn., Am., Amarillo trial lawyers assns., Amarillo Jr. Bar Assn. Home: 1501 Brookhaven St Canyon TX 79015 Office: Randall County Courthouse Canyon TX 79015 Tel (806) 655-2188

SHERRY, ARTHUR HARNETT, b. Berkeley, Calif., Mar. 10, 1908; A.B., St. Mary's Coll., 1929; J.D., U. Calif., 1932. Admitted to Calif. bar, 1932, U.S. Supreme Ct. bar, 1952; atty. Alameda County (Calif.) Legal Aid Soc., 1932-33; dep. and asst. dist. atty., Alameda County, 1933-51; asst. chief counsel Calif. Crime Study Commn. on Organized Crime, 1950-52; chief asst. atty. gen. State of Calif., 1951-53; Walter Perry Johnson Prof. law, prof. criminology U. Calif., Berkeley, 1953-75; prof. law Hastings Coll. Law, U. Calif., San Francisco, 1975; project dir. Survey of Criminal Justice in U.S., Am. Bar Found., 1954-58, 75—; dir. Calif. Penal Code Revision Project, 1964-69. Mem. Am., Calif., Alameda bar assns., Am. Law Inst., Assn. de Droit Penal, Calif. Peace Officers Assn., Am. Justice Inst. (dir.). Contbr. articles to law jours. Home: 319 El Cerrito Ave Piedmont CA 94611 Office: Hastings Coll Law U Calif 198 McAllister St San Francisco CA 94102 Tel (415) 557-2692

SHERRY, EDWARD NORMAN, b. Schenectady, Aug. 25, 1920; B.E.E., Syracuse U., 1943; LL.B., Yale, 1948. Admitted to N.Y. bar, 1952; U.S. Ct. Appeals 3d Circuit bar, 1953, 2d Circuit bar, 1968, 5th Circuit bar, 1971, U.S. Supreme Ct. bar, 1965; asso. firm Dewey, Ballantine, Bushby, Palmer & Wood, N.Y.C., 1950-58, mem., 1958—. Mem. Am. Judicature Soc., Am., N.Y. bar assns., Assn. Bar City N.Y. Home: 360 Stanwich Rd Greenwich CT 06830 Office: 140 Broadway New York City NY 10005 Tel (212) 344-8000

SHERRY, JOHN SEBASTIAN, b. Homestead, Pa., Apr. 18, 1946; B.A., U. Dayton, 1968; J.D., Duquesne U., 1971. Admitted to Pa. Supreme Ct. bar, 1972, U.S. Supreme Ct. bar, 1975; staff atty. Travelers Ins. Co., Pitts., 1972—; individual practice law, Library, Pa., 1973—; arbitrator Am. Arbitration Assn. Candidate for Pa. Ho. of Reps., 1976. Mem. Allegheny County (Pa.) Pa., Am. bar assns., Pa. Trial Lawyers Assn., Assn. Trial Lawyers Am. Home: 1916 Riggs Rd Library PA 15129 Office: 1050 Chatham Center Office Bldg Pittsburgh PA 15219 Tel (412) 566-2121

SHERRY, METTERY I., b. New Orleans, Oct. 2, 1936; B.S., Loyola U., 1958, J.D., 1961. Admitted to La. bar, 1961; law clk. Civil Dist. Ct., New Orleans, 1961-62; asso. firm Cobb & Wright, New Orleans, 1962-67; individual practice law, New Orleans, 1967-69; mem. firm Sherry & Villarrubia, Metairie, La., 1969—. Pres. Pontchartrain Shores Civic Assn., 1973-74; chmn. LaFreniere Park Adv. Bd., 1973-75; mem. Vets. Blvd. Bus. Assn. Mem. Jefferson Bar Assn., Delta Theta Phi. Home: 4513 Folse Dr Metairie LA 70002 Office: suite 104 1900 Veterans Blvd Metairie LA 70005 Tel (504) 837-2533

SHERTZER, GEORGE E., b. 1928; B.A., Yale U.; LL.B., Columbia U. Admitted to N.Y. bar, 1957; asso. firm Winthrop. Stimson, Putnam & Roberts, until 1959; asst. counsel Gen. Telephone & Electronics Corp., Stamford, Conn., 1959-66, gen. atty. Gen. Telephone & Electronics Service Corp., 1966-69, v.p., gen. atty., 1969-72, corp. v.p., gen. counsel, 1972-76, sr. v.p., gen. counsel, 1976—. Office: Gen Telephone & Electronics Corp One Stamford Forum Stamford CT 06904*

SHERVHEIM, LLOYD OLIVER, b. Kensington, Minn., June 22, 1928; student Gustavus Adolphus Coll., 1948-50, U. Minn., 1952; B.S., Minn. Coll. Law, 1956; LL.B., William Mitchell Coll. Law, 1959, J.D., 1958. Asst. to corp. sec. Investors Diversified Services, Inc., Mpls., 1952-59; admitted to Minn. bar, 1959; legal counsel Investors

Syndicate Life Ins. Co., Mpls., 1959-66; gen. counsel Western Life Ins. Co., St. Paul, 1966-72; corp. sec. The St. Paul Cos., Inc., 1969—, chief legal officer, 1972—, also dir. various bus. cos.; mem. Lake Elmo (Minn.) Council, 1970—; chmn. Congl. contact subcom. Minn. Health Ins. Com., 1970-72. Chmn. troop 98 Arrowhead council Boy Scouts Am., 1961-66, Cub Scouts pack 98, 1957-61; chmn. bd. trustees Christ Luth. Ch., Lake Elmo, 1974-75; mem. Met. Open Space Adv. Bd., 1972-73, chmn. protection open space task force, 1972-73. Mem. Am., Fed. (v.p. planning Minn. chpt. 1976—), Hennepin County (Minn.), Minn. State, Ramsey County (Minn.) bar assns., Am. Judicature Soc., Am. Life Conv. (Minn. v.p. 1969-71), Am. Soc. Corporate Secs., Assn. Life Ins. Counsel, Corp. Counsel Assn. Minn. (dir.), Ins. Fedn. Minn. (dir.), Twin City Life and Health Claim Assn. (pres. 1967-68), Hennepin and Ramsey County Citizen's League, Delta Theta Phi. Home: 3065 Klondike Ave N Lake Elmo MN 55042 Office: 385 Washington St Saint Paul MN 55102 Tel (612) 221-7671

SHERWIN, ROBERT VEIT, b. N.Y.C., May 2, 1919; B.A., Columbia, 1940, J.D., 1943. Admitted to N.Y. bar, 1948; individual practice law, N.Y.C., 1948—; adj. lectr. Borough Manhattan Community Coll., Bklyn. Coll. Fellow Soc. Sci. Study of Sex, Am. Acad. Matrimonial Lawyers; mem. Soc. Med. Jurisprudence. Author: Sex and the Statutory Law, 1949; Photography and the Law, 1957; Compatible Divorce, 1969. Contbr. articles in field to legal jours. Home: 401 E 86th St New York City NY 10028 Office: 12 E 41st St New York City NY 10017 Tel (212) LE2-2525

SHERWOOD, ARTHUR MORLEY, b. Buffalo, Oct. 3, 1939; B.A. cum laude, Harvard, 1961; J.D., U. Mich., 1964. Admitted to N.Y. bar, 1967, Mich. bar, 1965; law clk. U.S. Dist. Judge Ralph M. Freeman, Detroit, 1964-66; asso. firm Phillips, Lytle, Hitchcock, Blaine & Huber, Buffalo, 1966-70, partner, 1971—. Dir., sec. Episc. Ch. Home of Western N.Y., 1969—; vestryman Trinity Ch., Buffalo, 1972-74; bd. dirs. Compass House, Buffalo, 1972—. Mem. Am., N.Y., Erie County bar assns., Analytical Psychology Soc. Western N.Y. (pres. 1976—). Asst. editor U. Mich. Law Rev., 1963-64. Contbr. articles to legal jours. Home: 3770 Windover Dr Hamburg NY 14075 Office: 3400 Marine Midland Center Buffalo NY 14203 Tel (716) 847-8492

SHERWOOD, DONALD S., b. Honolulu, July 3, 1928; B.A., Bklyn. Coll.; LL.B., Columbia, 1953. Admitted to N.Y. State bar, 1953, U.S. Supreme Ct. bar, 1958; individual practice law, N.Y.C. Mem. Am., N.Y. trial lawyers assns. Tel (212) 966-7271

SHERWOOD, SAMUEL, b. Denver, Apr. 29, 1908; B.A., U. Calif., Los Angeles, 1930; J.D., U. Calif. at Berkeley, 1933. Admitted to Calif. bar, 1930, Hawaii bar, 1935; asso. firm Kemp & Stainback, Honolulu, 1935-38; individual practice law, Honolulu, 1938-54, Los Angeles, 1955—; judge Workers' Compensation Appeals Ct., Los Angeles, Long Beach and Inglewood, Calif., 1960-75; with JAGC, U.S. Army, 1941-45. Mem. State Bar Calif., Hawaii Bar Assn. Home and Office: 1015 Casiano Rd Los Angeles CA 90049 Tel (213) 476-2374

SHERWOOD, SAMUEL ISAIAH, b. St. Louis, Aug. 10, 1911; LL.B., George Washington U., 1941, J.D., 1968. Admitted to D.C. bar, 1947, U.S. Supreme Ct. bar, 1952, Md. bar, 1954; individual practice law, Washington, 1948—; gen. counsel Big Bros. Nat. Capital Area, Washington, 1973—. Mem. Am., D.C. (chmn. civil service law com. 1968-72), Prince Georges County bar assns. Home: 8500 New Hampshire Ave Silver Spring MD 20903 Office: 910 17th St NW Washington DC 20006 Tel (202) 296-4272

SHERWOOD, WILLIAM EDWARD, b. Nyack, N.Y., July 26, 1940; B.A., Syracuse U., 1962; J.D., N.Y. Law Sch., 1970. Admitted to N.Y. bar, 1971; asso. firm Freund & Donnelly, Spring Valley, N.Y., 1970-71; partner firm Freund & Sherwood, Spring Valley, 1972—; asst. dist. atty. Rockland County (N.Y.), 1974-75. Office: 501 S Main St PO Box 358 Spring Valley NY 10977 Tel (914) 356-0488

SHEVIN, ROBERT LEWIS, b. Miami, Fla., Jan. 19, 1934; B.A., U. Fla., 1955; J.D. magna cum laude, U. Miami, 1957. Admitted to Fla. bar, 1957; partner firm Shevin, Goodman & Holtzman, 1957-67; partner firm Shevin & Shevin, Fla., 1967-70; mem. Fla. House of Reps. 1963-65; mem. Fla. State Senate, 1965-70; atty. gen. State of Fla., 1970—; chmn. Fla. Legislature's Select Com. to Investigate Organized Crime and Law Enforcement; chmn. Intermin Com. on Crime and Law Enforcement; chmn. Legislature's Interim Study Com. on Urban Affairs, chmn. Legislature's Interim Study Com. on Urban Affairs, chmn. subcom. on jurisprudence; chmn. Help Stop Crime Program subcom. Gov.'s Council on Criminal Justice. Recipient Allen Morris award, 1969; named One of 10 Most Valuable Members of Fla. Legislature, Capital Press Corps, 1965; recipient Futherance of Justice award Fla. Pros. Attys. Assn; Conservationist of Year awards Fla. Wildlife Fedn., 1973, Audubon Soc., 1974. Mem. Am. Bar Assn., Fla. Bar, Jud. Council Fla. Home: 2000 N Meridian Rd Tallahassee FL 32303 Office: Capitol Tallahassee FL 32304*

SHEWARD, RICHARD SIDNEY, b. Jackson, Ohio, May 21, 1944; B.B.A., Ohio U., 1967; J.D., Capital U., 1974. Admitted to Ohio bar, 1974; trial atty. Office of Pros. Atty., Franklin County (Ohio), 1974—; with JAGC, U.S. Army Res., 1968—. Mem. Am., Ohio, Columbus bar assns. Tel (614) 462-3555

SHIELD, THEODORE PETER, b. Akra, N.D., May 23, 1920; LL.B., U. So. Calif., 1948. Admitted to Calif. State bar, 1949; dep. dist. atty. County of Los Angeles, 1949-53; practiced in Los Angeles since 1953, mem. firms, sr. partner firm Betts, Ely & Loomis, 1953-62, Betts & Loomis, 1962-69, Loomis, Shield & Smith, 1969, Shield & Smith, 1969—; judge pro tem Los Angeles County Superior Ct., South Bay Jud. Dist.; arbitrator Los Angeles Attys. Spl. Arbitration Plan. Fellow Internat. Acad. Trial Lawyers; mem. Los Angeles County, Am. bar assns., Calif. State Bar, Assn. So. Calif. Def. Counsel, Am. Judicature Soc., Assn. Dep. Dist. Attys., Def. Research Inst. (dir. and mem. exec. com. 1973-76), Internat. Assn. Ins. Counsel (mem. exec. com. 1970-74, pres. 1974-75), Am. Bd. Trial Advs. (Trial Lawyer of the Year 1974). Hdme: 4646 Sugarhill Dr Rolling Hills Estates CA 90274 Office: 1200 Wilshire Blvd Los Angeles CA 90017 Tel (213) 482-3010

SHIELDS, CHARLIE DEWITT, b. Center, Miss., Mar. 26, 1909; student Am. Law Sch., Chgo., 1929-30. Admitted to Miss. bar, 1930; individual practice law, Meridian, Miss., 1930; partner firm Shields and Denton, Meridian, 1932-33, firm Shields and Gipson, Meridian, 1934-35, Shields and Hughes, Meridian, 1935-36, firm Shields, McDonald and Thomas, Meridian, 1936-38, firm Shields, Harwell and Woodall, Meridian, 1945-58, firm Jones, Shields and Woodall, Meridian, 1976—; pres. First Savings and Loan Assn., Meridian, Bankers Trust Savings and Loan Assn., Meridian. Mem. exec. com. Democratic Party, 1930—; past trustee Clark Coll., Newton, Miss. Mem. Miss., Lauderdale County bar assns. Home: 2715 28th St Meridian MS 39301 Tel (601) 693-1343

SHIELDS, DAVID WILLIAM, JR., b. Rensselaer, Ind., Jan. 12, 1899; LL.B., Vanderbilt U., 1922. Admitted to Tenn. bar, 1920; supt. county schs., Tenn., 1925-32; mem. Tenn. Ho. of Reps., 1943-45; county judge, Tenn., 1950-58. Mem. sch. bd., 1925-32; county hwy. commr., Tenn., 1947-50. Mem. Am., Tenn. bar assns. Home: Route 4 Manchester TN 37355 Tel (615) 728-3664

SHIELDS, FLOYD FRANCIS, b. Wathena, Kans., Sept. 9, 1901; A.B., U. Kans., 1925; J.D., Washburn U., 1932. Admitted to Kans. bar, 1932, Ill. bar, 1938, U.S. Supreme Ct. bar, 1940, Mo. bar, 1953; asso. firm Colmery, McClure, Funk, Letourneau & Wilkinson, Topeka, and predecessors, 1938—; spl. counsel Kans. Corp. Commn., Topeka, 1933-37; gen. counsel Gen. Expressways, Inc. (formerly Keeshin Freight Lines, Inc.), Chgo., 1937-43, 46-51; dir. Gen. Transport Govt. Iran, 1943-45; transp. specialist Office Inter-Am. Affairs, Washington and S.Am., 1945; gen. counsel Water Dist. 1, Johnson County, Kans., 1954-76. Mem. Am., Kans., Ill. bar assns., Mo. Bar Integrated, Am. Judicature Soc., Phi Alpha Delta. Home: 5325 W 60th Terr Mission KS 66205 Office: 5822 Reeds Rd PO Box 68 Shawnee Mission KS 66201 Tel (913) 432-3622

SHIELDS, GAIL ELDON, b. Urbana, Ill., Sept. 27, 1947; B.A., U. Colo., 1969; J.D., U. Denver, 1972. Admitted to Colo. bar, 1973, U.S. Supreme Ct. bar; asst. county atty. Jefferson County (Colo.), Golden, 1973—. Mem. Am., Colo. bar assns., Colo. Trial Lawyers Assn. Home: 389 Cypress St Broomfield CO 80020 Office: 1700 Arapahoe St Golden CO 80419 Tel (303) 279-6511 ext 262

SHIELDS, GEORGE TERKEL, b. Seattle, May 6, 1928; B.A., Whitman Coll., Walla Walla, 1950; J.D., Columbia, 1953. Admitted to Wash. bar, 1953; partner law firms, Spokane, 1957-64, individual practice law, 1964-69; judge Superior Ct. Wash. for Spokane County, 1969—; instr. community property and contracts Gonzaga U., Spokane, 1961-66; mem. Wash. Tech. Adv. Com. on Corrections to Law and Justice Planning Com., 1971-74. Sec. standing com. Episcopal Diocese Spokane, 1967-68; mem. diocesan council, 1968-71, del. gen. convs., 1970, 73, 76; jr., now sr. warden Cathedral St. John Evangelist, 1962—; mem. Gov. Wash. Task Force Jail Improvement, 1972-73; pres. Greater Spokane Music and Allied Arts Festival Assn., 1963-65; active Spokane United Crusade, 1967-68; mem. steering com. White House Conf. Children and Youth, 1969-71; regional chmn. Gov. Wash. Conf. Libraries, 1968; pres. trustees Spokane YWCA, 1967-68. Mem. Am., Wash. (chmn. com. real property, probate and trusts 1962-65), Spokane County (hon.) bar assns., Superior Ct. Judges Assn. (trustee 1973, 74, chmn., editor Judges Criminal Procedure Benchbook Project 1974—), Wash. Jud. Council, Whitman Coll. Alumni Assn. (pres. 1969-71), Phi Beta Kappa (pres. Indland Empire chpt. 1966), Beta Theta Pi (v.p. 1967-70). Chmn. editorial bd. CLE Community Property Desk Book Project, 1973—. Home: 726 W 21st Ave Spokane WA 99203 Office: County Courthouse Spokane WA 99201 Tel (509) 456-4707

SHIELDS, REED FRANKLIN, b. Ridgefield, Conn., Jan. 13, 1921; student Butler U., 1938-41; LL.B., N.Y. U., 1950. Admitted to Conn. bar, 1950; individual practice law, Ridgefield, 1950-76; mem. firm Weinstein Shields, Schaffer, Hirsch and Lev, Ridgefield and Norwalk, Conn., 1976—; judge Conn. Probate Ct., Dist. 68, 1955-75; corp. counsel Town of Ridgefield, 1951-55; chmn. exec. com. Probate Assembly State of Conn., 1960-68; chmn. Ridgefield Pension Commn., 1965-75. Incorporator Ridgefield Boys' Club; bd. dirs. Ridgefield Community Center, 1952-55, also incorporator. Mem. Nat. Coll. Probate Judges, Phi Delta Phi. Home: 34 Gallows Hill Rd Redding CT 06896 Office: 470 Main St Ridgefield CT 06877 Tel (203) 438-9691

SHIELDS, WILLIAM HENRY, b. Walland, Tenn., Apr. 11, 1929; B.A., Maryville Coll., 1950; J.D., U. Tenn., 1953. Admitted to Tenn. bar, 1953, Fla. bar, 1963; individual practice law, Maryville, Tenn., 1955-63; partner firm Pavese, Shields, Garner, Haverfield & Kluttz, Ft. Myers, Fla., 1964—; dir. S. Fla. Migrant Legal Services, Lee County Legal Aid Soc., 1966-69. Mem. Lee County Port Advisory, Lee County Indsl. Devel. Authority; mem. jud. nominating com. 2d Dist. Ct. Appeal. Mem. Fla. Bar (chmn. com. on specialization 1970-76), Am., Lee County bar assns., Assn. Trial Lawyers Am., Acad. Fla. Trial Lawyers. Contbr. articles in field to profl. jours. Home: 1399 Whiskey Creek Dr Fort Myers FL 33901 Office: PO Drawer 1507 Fort Myers FL 33902 Tel (813) 334-2195

SHIELL, LYALL GUTHRIE, JR., b. New Orleans, Aug. 26, 1920; B.A., Tulane U., 1942, LL.B., 1949. Admitted to La. bar, 1949, U.S. Supreme Ct. bar, 1974; individual practice law, New Orleans, 1949—. Mem. La. State Bar Assn. Office: 2757 Tulane Ave New Orleans LA 70119 Tel (504) 822-0579

SHIFFMAN, SIDNEY J., b. Bklyn., Sept. 5, 1924; student City Coll. N.Y., 1942, St. John's U., 1948; LL.B., Bklyn. Law Sch., 1951; LL.M., N.Y. U., 1955. Admitted to N.Y. State, Fed. bars, 1951; individual practice law, N.Y.C., Bklyn., 1951-69; motor vehicle referee Utica Northern Dist., N.Y., 1969—. Home: 17 Court Knolle New Hartford NY 13413 Office: State Office Bldg Utica NY 13501 Tel (315) 797-6120

SHILLINGBURG, JAMES EDWARD, b. Gallup, N.Mex., Apr. 21, 1936; A.B., Stanford U., 1958; LL.B., Harvard, 1961. Admitted to D.C. bar, 1961, N.Y. bar, 1969, N.J. bar, 1973; law clk. U.S. Dist. Ct., 1961-62; spl. asst. to asst. atty. gen., 1968-69; appellate atty., tax div. U.S. Dept. Justice, Washington, 1963-68; asso. firm Lord, Day & Lord, N.Y.C., 1969-72, partner, 1972—. Mem. Am., N.Y. State, N.J., D.C. bar assns., Assn. Bar City N.Y. Home: Summit NJ Office: 25 Broadway New York City NY 10004

SHIMM, MELVIN GERALD, b. N.Y.C., Jan. 30, 1926; A.B., Columbia, 1947; LL.B., Yale, 1950. Admitted to N.Y. bar, 1950; asso. firm Cahill, Gordon, Zachry & Reindel, N.Y.C., 1950-51; atty. Wage Stablzn. Bd., Washington, 1951-52; Bigelow fellow U. Chgo., 1952-53; asst. prof. law Duke, 1953-56, asso. prof., 1956-59, prof., 1959—; sr. legal cons. Brookings Inst., 1965-67; dir. Orientation Program in Am. Law, Assn. Am. Law Schs., 1968-70; res. advisor Walter E. Meyer Research Inst. Law, 1963-65. Chmn., Durham (N.C.) Zoning Bd. Adjustment, 1966-70. Editor: Law and Contemporary Problems, 1955-61, 74-76, Jour. Legal Edn., 1955-63. Home: 2429 Wrightwood Ave Durham NC 27705 Office: Sch Law Duke U Durham NC 27706 Tel (919) 684-5687

SHIMOFF, PAUL MARTIN, b. San Francisco, Nov. 1, 1947; A.B. in Econs., U. Calif., Los Angeles, 1969, J.D., 1972. Admitted to Calif. bar, 1972, U.S. Dist. Ct. bar No. and Central Dists. Calif., 1972, U.S. Ct. Appeals bar for 9th Circuit, 1973, U.S. Ct. Claims bar, 1973, U.S. Tax Ct. bar, 1973; mem. firm Surr & Hellyer, San Bernardino, Calif., 1972—; lectr. estate planning Calif. State U., Los Angeles, 1976. Chmn. San Bernardino-Riverside Law in a Free Soc., 1975-76. Mem. Am. (taxation subcom. on civil and criminal penalties), Calif. (taxation subcom. on gift and inheritance tax), San Bernardino (chmn. continuing edn. of bar) bar assns. Tel (714) 884-4707

SHINABERRY, RICHARD ALLEN, b. Toledo, June 7, 1940; B.B.A., U. Toledo, 1966; J.D., 1972; M.B.A. (Robert G. Rodkey fellow), U. Mich., 1967. Admitted to Ohio bar, 1973; mem. firm Friedman, Adler, Goldberg & Rosen, Toledo, 1973-76, Rosen, Shinaberry, Jacobi & Moore, Toledo, 1976—; with fin. dept. Chrysler Corp., Detroit, 1967-69, Nat. Bank of Detroit, 1969, Questor Corp., Toledo, 1969-72. Founder, gen. counsel Conn. Point Inc. (Home for Runaway Children), Toledo, 1976—; 1st v.p., trustee Toledo Golden Gloves Assn., Inc., 1975—. Mem. Am., Ohio State, Toledo bar assns. Recipient Pacemaker award U. Toledo, 1967. Home: 509 Dussel Dr Maumee OH 43537 Office: 260 Spitzer Bldg Toledo OH 43603 Tel (419) 255-1504

SHINDER, SOLOMON, b. N.Y.C., Sept. 1, 1929; B.B.A., Coll. City N.Y., 1949; LL.B., Bklyn, Law Sch., 1953. Admitted to N.Y. State bar, 1954; individual practice law, Rochester, N.Y., 1956-64; partner firm Goldman and Shinder, Rochester, 1964—. Mem. Am., Monroe County bar assns., Am. Soc. Legal History. Home: 337 Avalon Dr Rochester NY 14618 Office: 911 Wilder Bldg Rochester NY 14614 Tel (716) 546-5445

SHINE, DONALD PATRICK, b. St. Louis, Jan. 28, 1923; B.S. in Commerce magna cum laude, St. Louis U., 1948, J.D. magna cum laude, 1956. Admitted to Mo. bar, 1956; asst. v.p. Boatmens Nat. Bank, St. Louis, 1952-67; v.p. St. Louis County Nat. Bank, Clayton, Mo., 1967-73; v.p., sec. Plant Facilities and Engring., Inc., St. Louis, 1974—; mem. Econ. Adv. Com. State Mo., 1974—; mem. St. Louis County Welfare Commn. (pres. 1974—); mem. St. Louis County Child Welfare Adv. Commn., 1974—. Mem. Riverview Gardens Sch. Bd., pres., 1961-64. Mem. Met. St. Louis, St. Louis County bar assns., Alpha Sigma Nu. Home and Office: 6 Club Grounds So Dr Florissant MO 63033 Tel (314) 831-2442

SHINN, MELVIN Y., b. Honolulu, Mar. 20, 1940; B.S., U. Hawaii, 1962; J.D., U. Nebr., 1966. Admitted to Nebr., Hawaii bars, 1966; legal aid U.S. Senator H.L. Fong, Washington, dep. corp. counsel City and County of Honolulu; gen. counsel Honolulu Redevel. Agy., dep. mng. dir., mng. dir.; chief clk. Senate Judiciary, Hawaii State Legis., Honolulu, 1970-74; individual practice law, Honolulu, 1970—; counsel Hawaii Legis. Senate Pres., Honolulu, 1974—. Mem. Am., Hawaii bar assns. Office: 33 S King St Suite 223 Honolulu HI 96813 Tel (808) 533-6294

SHIOMOS, THOMAS NICHOLAS, b. Phila., Feb. 16, 1921; B.A., Temple U., 1950, LL.B., 1953. Admitted to Pa. bar, 1954; asst. dist. atty. Philadelphia County, 1955-65, criminal trial commr., 1965-67, dep. ct. adminstr., 1968-69; adminstr. Municipal Ct., 1969-71; judge Philadelphia County Ct. of Common Pleas, 1971—. Office: 469 City Hall Philadelphia PA 19107 Tel (215) MU6-7338

SHIPMAN, MARK SAMUEL, b. Hartford, Apr. 16, 1937; B.A., U. Conn., 1959, LL.B., 1962. Admitted to Conn. bar, 1962, U.S. Supreme Ct. bar, 1973; asso. firm Schatz & Schatz, Hartford, 1962-64, partner, 1967—; partner Iosco & Shipman, Newington, Conn., 1964-67; prosecutor 15th Circuit Ct. Conn., 1964-66; town atty., Newington, 1975—. Town councilman, Newington, 1966-67, 73-74; mem. Newington Charter Revision Commn., 1969-75, chmn., 1969, 72, 75; bd. dirs. Greater Hartford Transit Dist., 1973—, vice chmn., 1975—. Fellow Am. Acad. Forensic Scis. (sec. jurisprudence sect. 1974, chmn. 1975); mem. Am., Conn., Hartford County bar assns., Am., Conn. trial lawyers assns., Nat. Inst. Municipal Legal Officers. Home: 71 Rosewood Dr Newington CT 06111 Office: One Financial Plaza Hartford CT 06103 Tel (203) 522-3234

SHIPMAN, RONALD PERRY, b. Lafayette, Ind., Feb. 12, 1934; B.A., Wabash Coll., 1956; J.D., Golden Gate U., 1967. Admitted to Ind. bar, 1970, U.S. Patent Office bar, 1962; practice in Mountain View and Fremont, Calif., 1962-70, Oxford, Ind., 1970-73; judge Benton Circuit (Ind.) Ct., 1973—. Office: Courthouse Fowler IN 47944 Tel (317) 884-0370

SHIPP, LEE, b. Cass County, Tex., Dec. 16, 1924; A.A., Kilgore Coll., 1944; J.D., Notre Dame U., 1948. Admitted to Tex. bar, 1948; partner firm Hutchison & Shipp, Dallas, 1954-63, firm Shipp & Crooks, Dallas, 1964-72; individual practice law, Dallas, 1972—. Mem. Am., Tex. bar assns., Am. Judicature Soc. Home: 4224 Stanford St Dallas TX 75225 Office: 1020 Republic Bank Tower Dallas TX 75201 Tel (214) 742-8757

SHIRA, WILLIAM ALVIA, III, b. Washington, Feb. 15, 1942; B.A., Kenyon Coll., 1964; J.D., Western Res. U., 1967. Admitted to Ohio bar, 1967; served with Judge Adv. Gen.'s Corps, USAF, 1968-74; asst. pros. atty. Greene County (Ohio), 1974-75; asso. firm James F. Gill, Fairborn, Ohio, 1975-76; individual practice law, Fairborn, 1976—. Mem. Am., Ohio, Greene County, Dayton bar assns., Air Force Assn. Author U.S. State Dept.-Def. Dept. study Turkish taxes. Home: 432 Silvercrest Terr Dayton OH 45440 Office: 1 1/2 S Central Ave Fairborn OH 45324 Tel (513) 878-3900

SHIREY, DANIEL RAY, b. Buffalo, Oct. 4, 1942; B.S. in Metall. Engring., Ohio State U., 1966, J.D., 1968, M.S., 1969; M.B.A., Jacksonville State U., 1973; postgrad. Loyola U., Chgo., 1976—. Admitted to Ohio bar, 1969, U.S. Ct. Mil. Appeals bar, 1969, D.C. bar, 1973; served with JAGC, 1969-73; partner firm McGrath & Shirey, Columbus, Ohio, 1973-76; of counsel Hoffman Law Offices, River Grove, Ill., 1977—. Mem. Worthington (Ohio) Bicentennial Celebration Com., 1974-75; tech. adv., counsel Aviation Safety Inst. Mem. Am., Ohio State, Columbus, D.C. bar assns., AMA. Author: Real Estate Investment: The Anatomy of a Syndicate, 1973. Office: Hoffman Law Offices 8945 W Grand Ave River Grove IL 60171 Tel (312) 453-9009

SHIRLEY, JOHN RAY, b. Norton, Kans., Dec. 6, 1944; B.S. in Accounting, Kans. State U., 1968; J.D., Washburn U. Admitted to Kans. bar, 1973; asso. firm Wallace, Brantley, & Shirley and predecessor, Scott City, Kans., 1973-75, partner, 1975—; city atty. Scott City, 1975—; dep. atty., Scott County, 1974—. Mem. Am., Kanas., bar assns., Kans. Trial Lawyers Assn. Office: 325 Main St Scott City KS 67871 Tel (316) 872-5291

SHOEMAKER, DANIEL WEYBRIGHT, b. Harrisburg, Pa., Mar. 20, 1931; B.S., Millersville State Coll., 1952; J.D., George Washington U., 1956. Admitted to D.C. bar, 1956, Pa. bar, 1957; individual practice law, York, Pa., 1957—, partner firm Shoemaker & Thompson,

York, 1971—; legal aid Bar Assn., 1959; dist. atty. York County, 1961-65; del. Constl. Conv. Pa., 1967-68. Home: RD 1 Felton PA 17322 Office: 103 E Market St York PA 17401 Tel (717) 848-5888

SHOEMAKER, JAMES RICHARD, b. Lincoln, Ill., June 10, 1943; B.S., Bradley U., 1965, B.S., 1966; J.D., U. Ill, 1972. Admitted to Ill. bar, 1972; asso. firm Sype & Kalivoda, Rockford, Ill., 1972, firm Kalivoda, Turner and Shoemaker, Rockford, 1972-76; partner firm Turner & Shoemaker, Rockford, 1977—. Mem. Am. Arbitration Assn. (arbitrator 1976), Winnebago County, Ill. State, Am. bar assns. Home: 1713 Hancock St Rockford IL 61103 Office: 510 N Church St Rockford IL 61103 Tel (815) 964-8211

SHOFFNER, ROBERT LEE, JR., b. Burlington, N.C., May 9, 1942; B.S. in Bus. Adminstrn., U. N.C., 1964, J.D., 1967. Admitted to N.C. bar, 1967, U.S. Dist. Ct., Eastern Dist. N.C., 1972; pvt. practice law, Kinston, N.C., 1970, Grifton, N.C., 1971; partner law firm Williamson, Shoffner & Herrin (and predecessor firms), Greenville, N.C., 1971—. Mem. N.C., Pitt County, bar assns., N.C. Acad. Trial Lawyers, Am. Lawyers Assn., Beta Gamma Sigma. Office: 210 S Washington St Greenville NC 27834

SHOFNER, JIM DALE, b. Tulsa, Sept. 12, 1943; B.S., Okla. State U., 1965; J.D., Tulsa U., 1967. Admitted to Okla. bar, 1968; partner firm Shofner & Perrault, Tulsa, 1974—. Mem. Am., Okla., Tulsa bar assns., Okla. Young Lawyers Conf., Okla. Trial Lawyers Assn. Office: 4143 E 31st Pl Tulsa OK 74135 Tel (918) 749-8891

SHOLES, DAVID HENRY, b. Providence, June 1, 1943; A.B., Brown U., 1965; J.D., Boston U., 1968. Admitted to R.I. bar, 1968, Mass. bar, 1968, U.S. Tax Ct. bar, 1973; individual practice law, 1969-72; sr. partner firm Sholes & Sholes, Providence and Warwick, R.I., 1972—; lectr. U. R.I. Providence Extension Div., 1971-73; mem. R.I. State Senate. Mem. Cranston (R.I.) Traffic Safety Commn., 1975-76. Mem. R.I. Bar Assn., Phi Alpha Delta. Home: 310 Norwood Ave Cranston RI 02905 Office: 40 Westminster St Providence RI 02903 Tel (401) 751-4410

SHONKWILER, JOHN PAYSON, b. Decatur, Ill., Apr. 5, 1933; B.A., U. Ill., 1955; J.D., Northwestern U., 1962. Admitted to Ill. bar, 1962; partner firm Shonkwiler & Shonkwiler, Monticello, Ill., 1962-65; magistrate 6th Jud. Circuit, Decatur, 1965-71; asso. judge, Decatur, 1971-72; presiding circuit judge, Piatt County (Ill.), 1972—. Mem. Ill., Piatt County bar assns., Trial Judges' Assn., Am. Judicature Soc., Asso. Judges' Assn. (pres. 1970-71, coordinating com. 1970—). Am. Acad. Jud. Edn. scholar, 1970. Home: 510 E McClelland St Monticello IL 61856 Office: Courtroom 1 Piatt County Court House Monticello IL 61856 Tel (217) 762-5861

SHOOP, JOHN ESPER, b. Darby, Pa., June 6, 1943; B.A., Kent State U., 1968; J.D., Cleve. State U., 1971. Admitted to Ohio bar, 1971; legal intern div. estate and gift tax IRS, Cleve., 1969; legal intern, law clk. Lake County (Ohio) Cts. of Common Pleas, 1970-71; practiced in Painesville, Ohio, 1971—; asst. pros. atty. Lake County, 1971-73, pros. atty., 1977—; pub. defender Lake and Geauga Counties, 1973-75; mem. Painesville City Council, 1975. Bd. dirs. Lake County Free Clinic, Sheltered Industries, Sr. Citizens Council, Lake County, Dan Beard Dist. council Boy Scouts Am., Cath. Youth Orgn. Advisory Bd., Lake and Geneva counties. Mem. Lake, Geauga, Ohio State, Am. bar assns., Nat. Dist. Atty.'s Assn. Recipient award for community action Gov. Ohio, 1974, award for service to humanity above self interest Lake County Prosecutor, 1974. Office: room B-321 New Market Mall PO Box 673 Painesville OH 44077 Tel (216) 357-5577

SHOOSMITH, JOHN FRANCIS, JR., b. Rahway, N.J., Jan. 22, 1948; B.A., Seton Hall U., 1970, J.D., 1973. Admitted to N.J. bar, 1973, U.S. Supreme Ct. bar, 1977; dep. atty. gen. State of N.J., Trenton, 1973—. Mem. Am., N.J., Middlesex County, Mercer County bar assns., Assn. Trial Lawyers Am. Home: 14-11 Hunters Glen Dr Plainsboro NJ 08536 Office: State House Annex Trenton NJ 08625 Tel (609) 292-8560

SHORE, MARVEL, b. Los Angeles, Nov. 21, 1915; A.B., San Francisco State U., 1942; J.D., Hastings Coll., 1945. Admitted to Calif. bar, 1945, U.S. Supreme Ct. bar, 1952, Immigration Appeals bar, 1950; individual practice law, Los Angeles, Sacramento and San Francisco, 1945-72; judge HEW, Oakland, Calif., 1972—. Mem. Calif. State Bar, Fed., San Francisco bar assns. Home: 1177 California St San Francisco CA 94108 Office: Suite 930 1330 Broadway St Oakland CA 94612 Tel (415) 273-7695

SHORR, DAVID IRWIN, b. Boston, Apr. 20, 1945; B.S. in Bus. Adminstrn., U. R.I., 1966; J.D., Suffolk U., 1969. Admitted to Mass. bar, 1970, U.S. Dist. Ct. bar for Dist. Mass., 1970; individual practice law, Framingham, Mass., 1970—. Bd. dirs. Temple Israel Brotherhood, Natick, Mass., 1975—. Mem. Mass., Middlesex, South Middlesex, Boston bar assns., Comml. Law League Am. Home: 25 Cherry Rd Framingham MA 01701 Office: 24 Union Ave Framingham MA 01701 Tel (617) 879-4412

SHORT, JOEL BRADLEY, b. Birmingham, Ala., Dec. 27, 1941; B.A., U. Colo., 1963, J.D., 1966. Admitted to Kans. bar, 1966, U.S. Supreme Ct. bar, 1976; partner firm Short & Short, Ft. Scott, Kans., 1966—. Mem. Ft. Scott City Commn., 1975-76; trustee Ft. Scott Community Coll., 1972-75. Mem. Am., Kans., Bourbon County bar assns., Kans. Trial Lawyers Assn. (bd. govs. 1975-76, state treas. 1976-77). Recipient Outstanding Young Man award U.S. Jaycees, 1973. Home: 10211 Foster Overland Park KS 66212 Office: 401 Capitol Fed Bldg 95th and Noll Overland Park KS 66212 Tel (316) 223-0530

SHORTELL, THOMAS JOHN, b. Hartford, Conn., Mar. 8, 1942; A.B., Trinity Coll., 1964; LL.B., Cath. U. Am., 1967. Admitted to Conn. bar, 1967; asso. firm Adinolf, Kelly & Spellacy, Hartford, 1967-70, partner firm Updike, Kelly & Spellacy, Hartford, 1971—; U.S. Govt. appeals agt., 1968-70. Mem. Hartford County, Conn. State bar assns. Home: 141 Westerly Terr Hartford CT 06105 Office: 1 Constitution Plaza Hartford CT 06103 Tel (203) 547-1120

SHREVE, CHARLES UPTON, III, b. Detroit, Mar. 24, 1898; A.B., Harvard, 1919, J.D., 1921; spl. courses U. Paris, 1945; postgrad. Wayne State U., 1963. Admitted to Mich. bar, 1921; partner firm Yerkes, Goddard, McClintock and Shreve, Detroit, 1921-33; asso. firm Frank Murphy, Detroit, 1933-46; individual practice law, Detroit, 1946—; mgr. Trembley Lodge, Detroit, 1946—; v.p., gen. counsel, dir. Manestee Music Camp, 1964; legal counsel Mich. Ret. Officers Assn., 1968; Mem. Freedom Festival Com., Detroit, 1959. Mem. Mich., Detroit bar assns., Am. Judicature Soc., Amvets., Am. Legion, VFW, DAV, Judge Advs. Gen Assn., Res. Officers Assn., Mil. Order World Wars (state comdr. 1961), Mil. Nat. Trial Lawyers Assn., Am. Bd. Arbitrators, Internat. Platform Assn., Detroit C. of C. Decorated Croix de Guerre, French Fgn. Legion Medal, Medal de Blesse (France), King Peter Medal of Honor (Yugoslavia). Home and Office: 1040 Iroquois St Detroit MI 48214

SHREVES, HOWARD BRUCE, b. Chgo., May 2, 1943; A.B. in History, Holy Cross Coll., Worcester, Mass., 1965; J.D., Georgetown U., 1969. Admitted to S.D. bar, 1969, La. bar, 1972, U.S. Ct. Mil. Appeals bar, 1970; legal asst., office of dep. atty. gen. and criminal div. Dept. Justice, Washington, 1966-69; with JAGC, U.S. Army, 1969-73; asso. firm Deutsch, Kenrigan & Stiles, New Orleans, 1973-75, partner, 1976—. Mem. La. State, New Orleans, Fed., Am. bar assns., New Orleans Assn. Def. Counsel. Home: 88 Tern St New Orleans LA 70124 Office: 4700 One Shell Sq New Orleans LA 70139 Tel (504) 581-5141

SHRIGLEY, ALFRED ROLFE, b. Boston, June 6, 1914; A.B., Harvard, 1936; LL.B., Boston U., 1940. Admitted to Mass. bar, 1940; individual practice law, Boston, 1940—; partner firm Richardson & Tyler, Boston, 1974—; asst. dist. atty. Plymouth County, (Mass.), 1968-74; vice-consul Republic Panama, 1940-64, Mexico, 1940-50; counsel Hingham, Mass., 1955—; mem. Mass. Home Rule Commn., 1961-62, Mass. Commn. Criminal Law, 1967-68; rep. Mass. Gen. Ct., 1961-68. Home: 153 Summer St Hingham MA 02043 Office: 84 State St Boston MA 02109 Tel (617) 523-0800

SHRINSKY, JASON LEE, b. Pitts., June 15, 1937; B.A., U. Pitts., 1959; J.D., George Washington U., 1962. Admitted to Va. bar, 1963, D.C. bar, 1964; law clk. trainee FCC, Washington, 1961-62, gen. atty., complaints and compliance div., 1963, atty. advisor, 1964; asso. firm Grove, Paglin, Jaskowitz, Sells, Gilliam & Putbrese, Washington, 1964-66; asso. offices of Arthur Stambler, Washington, 1967-69; partner firm Stambler & Shrinsky, Washington, 1969—. Co-chmn. D.C. chpt. U.S. Sports for Israel Com. Mem. Nat. Broadcasters Club (pres. 1973-74), Am., Fed. Communications (treas. 1974-75, mem. exec. com. 1975-76), Va., D.C. bar assns. Contbr. articles to jours. N.Mex., Mo., Colo. broadcasters assns. Home: 9812 Glenolden Dr Potomac MD 20854 Office: 1120 Connecticut Ave NW Suite 270 Washington DC 20036 Tel (202) 872-0010

SHRIVER, DONALD LAURENCE, b. Chgo., Sept. 10, 1942; A.B., Knox Coll., 1964; J.D., Washington U., St. Louis, 1967. Admitted to Mo. bar, 1967, Ill. bar, 1968; served as capt. JAGC, U.S. Army, 1967-71; partner firm Downey, Yalden, Shriver & Yalden, and predecessors, Rockford, Ill., 1971—; asst. pub. defender Winnebago County (Ill.), Rockford, 1973-76. Bd. dirs. Community Coordinated Child Care Assn., 1974—, v.p., 1975; bd. dirs. YMCA Men, 1976—, treas. 1976-77. Mem. Am., Ill., Winnebago County (past sec., past v.p., now pres. young lawyer's sect.) bar assns. Home: 208 Paris Ave Rockford IL 61107 Office: 401 W State St Rockford IL 61101 Tel (815) 963-4895

SHUFORD, JERRY LEE, b. Valdese, N.C., Oct. 18, 1936; B.A., San Francisco State U., 1963; J.D., Southwestern U., Los Angeles, 1970. Admitted to Calif. bar, 1970; revenue officer IRS, Los Angeles, 1965-66; investigator U.S. CSC, 1966-70; asso. firm Butterworth & Waller, Los Angeles, 1970-71; partner firm Shuford & Shuford, Indio, Calif., 1971—; atty. City of Coachella (Calif.), 1975—. Bd. dirs. United Way, Coachella Valley, 1973-75, pres., 1975. Mem. Calif. State Bar, Desert, Riverside County bar assns., Calif. Criminal Justice Bar, Calif. Trial Lawyes Assn. Office: PO Drawer XXX Indio CA 92201 Tel (714) 347-0731

SHUFORD, PAUL MASON, b. Richmond, Va., July 2, 1922; B.S., Washington and Lee U., 1943; J.D., 1948. Admitted to Va. bar, 1948; instr. Washington and Lee Law Sch., 1948; partner firm Wicker, Baker & Shuford, Richmond, 1958, firm Wallerstein, Goode, Dobbins & Shuford, Richmond, 1958-72; sr. v.p., sr. trust officer Central Nat. Bank of Richmond, 1972-73; corporate v.p. Central Nat. Corp., Richmond, 1974; individual practice law, Richmond, 1975—; instr. U. Richmond, 1975—; dir., counsel Nat. Tobacco Festival, 1950—. Trustee The Collegiate Schs., Richmond, 1975—. Mem. Am. Judicature Soc., Am. (Silver Gavel award for editorial column Richmond News Leader 1958-60), Va., Richmond (pres. 1972) bar assns. Office: Suite 418 Mutual Bldg Richmond VA 23219 Tel (804) 648-4434

SHULA, ROBERT JOSEPH, b. South Bend, Ind., Dec. 10, 1936; B.S., Ind. U., 1958; J.D., 1961. Admitted to Ind. bar, 1961, U.S. Customs Ct. bar, 1967; served with Judge Advocate Gen. Staff, U.S. Air Force, 1961-65; partner firm Bingham, Summers, Welsh & Spilman, Indpls., 1965—; pres. Meridian Women's Clinic, Inc., Indpls., 1973—; v.p. 5th Season Travel, Inc., Indpls., 1975—. Trustee Indpls. Mus. Art, 1974—, pres. Oriental Art Soc., 1974—; bd. dirs. Ind. Civil Liberties Union, 1970-75, Flanner House, Indpls., 1975—. Mem. Am., Ind., Indpls. bar assns., Am., Ind. trial lawyers assns., Bar Assn. 7th Fed. Circuit, Am. Soc. Appraisers. Home: 4137 N Meridian St Indianapolis IN 46208 Office: 1 Indiana Sq 2700 Indiana Tower Indianapolis IN 46204 Tel (317) 635-8900

SHULL, ROBERT ALAN, b. Phila., May 27, 1947; B.A., Coll. Emporia, 1969; J.D., Rutgers U., 1972. Admitted to Ariz., N.J., U.S. Dist. Ct. for Ariz. bars, 1973, U.S. 9th Circuit Ct. Appeals bar, 1974; asso. firm Strong and Pugh, Phoenix, 1973-75, partner, 1975—. Mem. Am., Maricopa County bar assns., State Bar Ariz. Office: 2701 N 7th Ave Phoenix AZ 85007 Tel (602) 263-9759

SHULL, WILLIAM EDGAR, JR., b. Quincy, Ill., Aug. 8, 1947; B.A., Wichita State U., 1968; postgrad. U. Utah, 1969; J.D., U. Mo., 1972. Admitted to Mo. bar, 1972, U.S. 8th Circuit Ct. Appeals bar, 1972, U.S. 10th Circuit Ct. Appeals bar, 1975, U.S. Supreme Ct. bar, 1975, U.S. 5th Circuit Ct. Appeals, 1977; asso. firm Duncan & Russell, Kansas City, Mo., 1972-76; partner firm Gettig, Coulson and Shull, Kansas City, Mo., 1976—; asst. instr. law U. Mo., 1974—. Mem. Am., Mo., Clay County, Kansas City bar assns., Phi Alpha Delta. Home: 527 NE 98th Pl Kansas City MO 64155 Office: 2601 Kendallwood Pkwy Kansas City MO 64119 Tel (816) 455-2525

SHULMAN, ADLEY MARN, b. Los Angeles, Aug. 28, 1931; A.A., U. Calif., Los Angeles, 1951, A.B. with highest honors, 1953, J.D., 1958. Admitted to Calif. bar, 1958, U.S. Supreme Ct. bar, 1967; partner firm Shulman and Shulman, Beverly Hills, Calif., 1958—; tchr. Law for the Layman, Los Angeles, Centinela Valley, S. Bay, El Segundo adult schs., 1971—; awarded lifetime credential adult edn., 1970. Vice pres. Pacific SW bd. Anti-Defamation League, 1970-73, mem. exec. com., chmn. urban affairs com., 1968-69; v.p., founding dir. Neighbors Unlimited; mem. commn. on law and legis. of community relations com. Jewish Fedn. Council, 1971—; mem. joint commn. social action United Synagogue Am., 1963-66; active Community Apex, Block Party Neighbors. Mem. Calif., Los Angeles County, Beverly Hills (chmn. del. to Calif. Bar Conf. of Dels., 1973, del. 1970—, mem. bd. govs. 1973-76, chmn. referral service 1976—) bar assns., Order of Coif, Phi Beta Kappa. Co-recipient Human Relations award Los Angeles City Human Relations Bur., 1970; contbr. articles to legal publs. Office: 485 S Robertson Blvd Beverly Hills CA 90211 Tel (213) 272-8741

SHULMAN, CORINNE S., b. Mpls., Apr. 12, 1931; A.A., U. Calif., Los Angeles, 1950, B.A., 1952, J.D., 1956. Admitted to Calif. bar, 1957, U.S. Supreme Ct. bar, 1967; individual practice law, Beverly Hills, Calif., 1957-58; partner firm Shulman and Shulman, Beverly Hills, 1958—; mem. panel of arbitrators Am. Arbitration Assn., 1973—. Vice pres. LWV of Beverly Hills, 1961-63; mem. regional adv. bd. Pacific S.W. region Anti-Defamation League, 1964—; founding dir. Neighbors Unltd., Los Angeles. Mem. Calif. State Bar, Los Angeles County, Beverly Hills bar assns., Los Angeles Trial Lawyers Assn., Phi Beta Kappa. Co-recipient 1st ann. Human Relations award City of Los Angeles, 1970; contbr. articles to legal jours. Office: 485 S Robertson Blvd Beverly Hills CA 90211 Tel (213) 272-8741

SHULMAN, HARVEY JAY, b. N.Y.C., Apr. 23, 1949; B.S. in Physics, U. Md., 1969; J.D., U. Mich., 1972. Admitted to Md. bar, 1972, D.C. bar, 1977; law clk. to chief judge U.S. Ct. Appeals for 1st Circuit, Portland, Maine, 1972-73; staff atty. Media Access Project, Washington, 1973-75, exec. dir., 1975—; cons. toxic substances U.S. Senate Subcom. on Environment, 1971. Mem. D.C. Bar Assn., Order of Coif, Phi Beta Kappa, Phi Kappa Phi, Sigma Pi Sigma, Phi Eta Sigma. Home: 1106 N Illinois St Arlington VA 22205 Office: 1609 Connecticut Ave NW Washington DC 20036 Tel (202) 232-4300

SHULMAN, JAMES HAROLD, b. Hartford, Conn., Apr. 5, 1946; A.B., George Washington U., 1968, J.D., 1971. Admitted to Conn. bar, 1971, D.C. bar, 1972, U.S. Supreme Ct. bar, 1974; aide to Sen. Abraham Ribicoff, Washington, 1965-71; asso. firm Ribicoff & Kotkin, Hartford, 1971-75, partner, 1975—. Trustee Watkinson Sch., Hartford, 1968—. Mem. Am., Conn., Hartford County bar assns. Mem. editorial staff George Washington Law Rev., 1969-71. Office: 799 Main St Hartford CT 06103 Tel (203) 527-0781

SHULMAN, WARREN SCOTT, b. St. Petersburg, Fla., Oct. 8, 1942; B.B.A., U. Ga., 1964, J.D., 1966. Admitted to Ga. bar, 1965; asso. firm Shulman & Alembik, Atlanta, 1966-67; staff officer CIA, Washington, 1967-72; asso. firm Shulman, Bauer, Deitch, Raines & Hester, and predecessors, Atlanta, 1972-73, partner, 1973—; dir. Colonial Equities, Inc., G & S Investment Co., Inc., Atlanta. Trustee Congregation Beth Jacob, Atlanta, 1977—; mem. Atlanta C. of C. Internat. Task Force, 1975—; mem. Atlanta Jewish Welfare Fedn., fund raising com., 1975; bd. dirs. Hebrew Acad. Atlanta, mem. bldg. fund com., 1974-75. Mem. Am., Ga., Atlanta bar assns., Phi Kappa Phi, Am. Soc. Writers on Legal Subjects. Co-author: Georgia Practice and Procedure, 4th edit., 1975; contbr. articles to legal jours. Home: 2941 Cravey Dr Dr Atlanta GA 30345 Office: 1500 Peachtree Center Harris Tower Atlanta GA 30303 Tel (404) 588-1500

SHULTS, DAVID ARNOLD, b. Hornell, N.Y., Oct. 25, 1943; A.B., Princeton, 1965; J.D., Cornell U., 1968; M.B.A., U. Rochester, 1972. Admitted to N.Y. State bar, 1969; partner firm Shults & Shults, Hornell, 1969—; dir. Steuben Trust Co. Bd. dirs. Bethesda Community Hosp., 1972—, Hornell YMCA, 1974—. Mem. Am., N.Y., Hornell, Steuben County bar assns. Home: 66 Maple St Hornell NY 14843 Office: 9 Seneca St Hornell NY 14843 Tel (607) 324-1104

SHULTS, ROBERT LUTHER, JR., b. Pine Bluff, Ark., Oct. 25, 1925; B.S. cum laude, La. State U., 1950; LL.B. cum laude, Harvard, 1953. Admitted to Ark. bar, 1953; partner firm Wright, Lindsey, Jennings, Lester & Shults, Little Rock, Ark., 1953-65, firm Lester and Shults, Little Rock, 1965—. Trustee Ark. Blue Cross-Blue Shield, Inc. Chmn. Winthrop Rockefeller Found., 1974—; trustee U. Ark., 1970—, chmn. bd., 1976—; chmn. Little Rock Great Decisions Program, 1962; chmn. Pulaski County Econ. Opportunity Agy., 1965-66. Mem. Ark. (chmn. legal edn. council, 1963-66, chmn. exec. com., 1968-69), Am., Pulaski County (pres., 1971-72) bar assns., Am. Judicature Soc. Home: 11 Glenridge Rd Little Rock AR 72207 Office: 2000 Worthen Bank Bldg Little Rock AR 72201 Tel (501) 375-2301

SHULTZ, AUDREY FLITCH, b. Ponca City, Okla., Oct. 31, 1896; A.B., U. Okla., 1917, M.A., 1918, J.D., 1967. Admitted to Okla. bar, 1968; individual practice law, Norman, Okla., 1968—; mem. advisory bd. Norman Exchange Bank, 1970-72. Mem. trustees' law com. Presbyn. Ch., 1973-76; mem. sch. bd., Norman, 1938-42; chmn. Cleve. County March of Dimes, 1938; mem. Norman Civic Improvement Council, 1970-76; mem. local and state bd. League Women Voters. Mem. Okla., 10th Circuit Ct. Appeals, Am. Bar Assns., Phi Beta Kappa, Kappa Beta Pi. Recipient Okla. Law Sch. Merit award, 1967, U. Okla. 50 year service award, 1967, Ednl. Found. honor award, AAUW, 1964, named nat. life mem., 1976. Home and Office: 412 W Main St Norman OK 73069 Tel (405) 321-9739

SHULTZ, DONALD RICHARD, b. Mitchell, S.D., Sept. 14, 1930; LL.B., U. S.D., 1954. Admitted to S.D. bar, 1954, U.S. Supreme Ct. bar; mem. firm Lynn Jackson Shultz Ireland & Lebrun, Rapid City, S.D., 1954—. Mem. Am. Bd. Trial Advs., Internat. Soc. Barristers. Office: PO Box 1377 Rapid City SD 57709 Tel (605) 342-2592

SHULTZ, JOHN DAVID, b. Hollywood, Calif., Oct. 9, 1939; student Harvard, 1960-61; A.B., U. Ariz., 1964; J.D., U. Calif., Berkeley, 1967. Admitted to N.Y. bar, 1968; asso. firm Cadwalader, Wickersham & Taft, N.Y.C., 1968—; sec., counsel Copy Tech., Inc., 1971-73. Trustee Shore Acres Point Corp., Mamaroneck, N.Y., St. Thomas Ch., N.Y.C. Mem. Am., N.Y. State bar assns., Assn. Bar City N.Y. Office: One Wall St New York City NY 10005 Tel (212) 785-1000

SHULTZ, W.O., II, b. Paint Rock, Tex., June 8, 1926; B.S. in Chem. Engring., U. Tex., 1950, J.D., 1958. Admitted to Tex. bar, 1957, U.S. Dist. Ct. bar for Western Tex., 1960, U.S. Dist. Ct. bar for No. Tex., 1967, U.S. Supreme Ct. bar, 1964, U.S. Dist. Ct. bar for So. Tex., 1970, U.S. 5th Circuit Ct. Appeals bar, 1970; asst. atty. gen., State of Tex., 1958-73; atty., U. Tex. System, 1972-76, asso. gen. counsel, 1976—. Mem. Tex., Travis County bar assns., Supreme Ct. Hist. Soc. Office: 201 W 7th St Austin TX 78701 Tel (512) 471-7565

SHUMAKER, THOMAS ALLEN, b. Akron, Ohio, Sept. 1, 1946; B.A., U. Akron, 1968, J.D., 1973. Admitted to Ohio bar, 1974; bus. analyst corporate planning and research Goodyear Tire & Rubber Co., Akron, 1967-73, 74-76; sr. staff mgmt. control Goodyear Internat. Corp., 1973-74; partner firm Emershaw, Brown, Eshelman & Shumaker, Akron, 1974—. Mem. Am., Ohio, Akron bar assns. Office: 27 S Forge St Akron OH 44304 Tel (216) 376-4122

SHUMAN, JOHN RIDGELY, b. Balt., June 3, 1946; B.S. with honors in Accounting, N.Y. U., 1968; J.D., Stetson U., 1971. Admitted to Fla. bar, 1971; asso. firm Goldner, Marger, Davis & Rightmyer, St. Petersburg, Fla., 1971-72; individual practice law, St. Petersburg, 1972-75, Clearwater, Fla., 1975—. Mem. Comml. Law League Am., Conf. on Personal Fin. Law, Nat. Consumer Fin. Assn., Lawyers Title Guaranty Fund, Fla. Bar (chmn. creditors' rights and credit regulation com. Corp., Banking and Bus. Law Sect. 1976-77), Am. Bar Assn., Beta Alpha Psi. Author article Florida's New Replevin Law-A Constitutional Accomodation, The Florida Bar Jour., 1976. Office: Suite 205 Arbor Office Center 1321 US Hwy 19 S Clearwater FL 33516 Tel (813) 531-5858

SHUMAN, JOSEPH DUFF, b. Pitts., Dec. 27, 1942; B.A., Yale, 1964; LL.B., Harvard, 1967. Admitted to Pa. bar, 1967; asso. firm Thorp, Reed & Armstrong, Pitts., 1967-73; partner firm Thorp, Reed & Armstrong, Pitts., 1974—. Bd. dirs. Planned Parenthood Center of Pitts., 1971-74. Mem. Allegheny County (mem. pub. relations com.), Am. (mem. sec. of corp. banking, bus. law), Pa. bar assns. Home: 3333 Ivanhoe Rd Pittsburgh PA 15241 Office: 2900 Grant Bldg Pittsburgh PA 15219 Tel (412) 288-7723

SHUMAR, PETER HUGHES, b. Detroit, Jan. 27, 1946; B.B.A., U. Mich., 1968; J.D., Wayne State U., 1971. Admitted to Mich. bar, 1971, U.S. Supreme Ct. bar, 1976; asso. firm Liberson, Fink, Feiler, Crystal & Burdick, Detroit, 1971-73; individual practice law, partner firm Shumar & Murphy, Marquette and Munising, Mich., 1973—; adj. prof. No. Mich. U., Marquette, 1975—. Mem. Am. Arbitration Assn., Am. Judicature Soc., Mich. Assn. Professions, ACLU (chmn. Mich. chpt.). Office: 151 Rock St Marquette MI 49855 Tel (906) 228-8316

SHUMATE, JACK DAVID, b. Louisville, Mar. 13, 1936; B.S. in Chem. Engring., Rose-Hulman Inst. Tech., 1957; J.D., Salmon P. Chase Coll. Law, 1962; postgrad. Southwestern Legal Inst., 1974. Admitted to Ohio bar, 1962, Mich. bar, 1974; sr. asst. city prosecutor Columbus (Ohio), 1963-67; chief legal service Dept. Urban Affairs, State of Ohio, 1967-71; asso. firm Brownfield, Kosydar, Bowen, Bally & Sturtz, Columbus, 1971-72; staff atty. May Dept. Stores Co., St. Louis, 1972-73; atty. Consumers Power Co., Jackson, Mich., 1973—. Mem. Mich. Oil and Gas Assn., Jackson County, Mich. bar assns. Author: New Concepts for Ohio Homes, 1968; GEM Plan, 1970. Home: 3888 Kirkwood St Jackson MI 49203 Office: 212 W Michigan St Jackson MI 49201 Tel (517) 788-1255

SHUMWAY, JAMES MCBRIDE, b. Edinburg, Ill., Aug. 6, 1921; B.S. in Mgmt. and Econs., U. Ill., 1946; J.D., Stanford, 1951. Admitted to Calif. bar, 1952; county counsel Solano County, Calif., 1956-67; individual practice law, Fairfield, Calif., 1969—; chmn. State Calif. Alcoholic Beverage Control Appeals Bd., 1968-72; mem. Calif. Unemployment Ins. Appeals Bd., 1968; asst. adminstr. Health and Welfare Agy. State Calif., 1967-68. Mem. Fairfield Planning Commn., 1956-63, chmn., 1958-63. Mem. Solano County Bar Assn. (dir. 1961), Legal Aid. Soc. Solano County (pres. 1960-62), Nat. Assn. County Ofcls., Fairfield-Suisan C. of C. (dir. 1956-58), Dist. Atty's Assn. Calif. (1st v.p. 1966-67, mem. exec. bd. 1962-67), Nat. Assn. County Civil Atty.'s (dir. 1966-67), Phi Delta Phi. Office: Suites 303 and 304 1545 N Texas St Fairfield CA 94533 Tel (707) 425-3232

SHUPING, C(LARENCE) LEROY, JR., b. Greensboro, N.C., Jan. 11, 1920; B.S. in Commerce, U. N.C., 1941, J.D., 1947. Admitted to N.C. bar, 1947, U.S. Ct. Appeals 4th Circuit bar, 1959; spl. agt. FBI, 1942 43; mem. firm. Shuping and Shuping, Greensboro, 1947—. Chmn. N.C. Med. Liaison Com. for Vet. Affairs, 1953-56; chmn. bd. trustees, bd. stewards Christ Methodist Ch., Greensboro, 1956-59; mem. GuilfordDemocratic Exec. Com., 1956 58. Mem. N.C. State Bar, N.C., Greensboro bar assns., Am. Legion (N.C. state comdr. 1952-53, N.C. state judge adv. 1951-52, 75—), Phi Alpha Delta. Recipient Certificate Appreciation, Sec. War, 1945; Certificate of Appreciation, N.C. State Dem. Exec. Com., 1966; Citations of Appreciation, Am. Legion, 1967, 70, 76. Home: 610 Whittier Dr Greensboro NC 27403 Office: 430 W Friendly Ave PO Drawer 239 Greensboro NC 27402 Tel (919) 274-1521

SHUR, GEORGE MICHAEL, b. Portland, Maine, Nov. 10, 1942; A.B., Colby Coll., 1964; J.D., Boston U., 1968. Admitted to Maine bar, 1968; partner firm Bernstein, Shur, Sawyer & Nelson, Portland, 1968—; corporator Portland Savs. Bank, 1970—. Bd. dirs. Portland Players, Inc., 1969—, pres., 1972-74; corporator Portland Boys Club, 1976—, bd. dirs., 1977—; trustee N. Yarmouth Acad., 1969—, sec., 1972—; bd. dirs. Portland Jewish Community Center, 1969-72, Portland chpt. ARC, 1969-73; mem. budget com. Portland United Way, 1972-76. Mem. Nat. Assn. Coll. and Univ. Attys. (exec. bd. 1974—, nat. membership chmn. 1972-76), Am., Maine, Cumberland County bar assns., Assn. Trial Lawyers Am., Nat. Orgn. Legal Problems Edn., Maine Sch. Mgmt. Assn. Author: Legal Liability of Faculty, 1976. Office: One Monument Sq Portland ME 04111 Tel (207) 774-6291

SHURE, H. WILLIAM, b. New Haven, Apr. 5, 1940; A.B., Dartmouth, 1961; LL.B., U. Va., 1964. Admitted to Conn. bar; asso. firm Sachs, Sachs, & Sachs, New Haven, 1964, 67-71, partner, 1971-76; partner firm DiSesa, Hogan & Shure, New Haven, 1976—; asst. minority counsel select com. on presdl. campaign activities U.S. Senate, 1973; chief counsel, staff dir. Conn. Legislature Sub-com. to Investigate Leasing Practices, 1974; cons. counsel U.S. Senate Com. on Govt. Ops. subcom. on fed. spending practices, efficiency and open govt. Bd. dirs., mem. exec. com. New Haven Jewish Fedn.; co-chmn. New Haven Jewish Fedn. Community Relations Com.; sec., dir. Congregation B'Nai Jacob, Woodbridge, Conn.; v.p. Conn. Jewish Community Relations Com.; mem. exec. com. Nat. Jewish Community Advisory Council; vice chmn. Conn. Regional B'nai B'rith Anti-Defamation League; staff asst., area rep. for Senator Lowell P. Weicker, Jr., 1971—. Mem. New Haven County (exec. com.), Conn., Am. bar assns., Am. Trial Lawyers Assn. Recipient Torch of Liberty award New Haven div. Anti-Defamation League of B'nai B'rith, 1976. Home: 9 Cassway Rd Woodbridge CT 06525 Office: 246 Church St New Haven CT 06510 Tel (203) 787-4191

SHUSS, J. LOGAN, b. Larned, Kans., Nov. 28, 1915; A.B., U. Kans.,J.D., 1940. Admitted to Kans. bar, 1940, U.S. Dist. Ct. bar for Dist. Kans., 1947; asso. Earl Bohannon, Parsons, Kans., 1940-41; partner firm Bohannon & Shuss, Parsons, 1946-52; county atty. Labette County, Kans., 1947-51; city atty. City of Altamont (Kans.), 1965-70. Mem. Parsons Police Bd., Parsons Recreation Commn.; bd. dirs. Parsons YWCA. Mem. Kans., Am., SE Kans. bar assns. Home: 1230 Morgan Ave Parsons KS 67357 Office: 70 Parsons Plaza Parsons KS 67357 Tel (316) 421-1670

SHUTER, BRUCE DONALD, b. N.Y.C., Feb. 20, 1940; B.A., Alfred U., 1961; J.D., N.Y. U., 1964. Admitted to N.Y. bar, 1965, Pa. bar, 1971; staff atty. Fed. Res. Bd., Washington, 1964-68; chief counsel Securities Credit Control, 1968-70; asso. firm Drinker, Biddle & Reath, Phila., 1970-73, partner, 1973—. Mem. Am., Fed., Pa., Phila. bar assns. Recipient Bancrof-Whitney prize for Legal Excellence, 1964; contbr. articles in field to profl. jours. Home: 6342 N 6th St Philadelphia PA 19126 Office: 1100 National Bank Bldg Broad & Chestnut St Philadelphia PA 19107 Tel (215) 491-7317

SHUTLER, K. EUGENE, b. Wichita, Kans., Mar. 27, 1938; A.B., U. Pa., 1960; LL.B., Yale, 1963. Admitted to Pa. bar, 1966, Calif. bar, 1971; asso. firm Stradley, Ronon, Stevens & Young, Phila., 1965-68; v.p. Shareholders Mgmt. Co., Los Angeles, 1968-72; v.p., gen. counsel Republic Corp., Los Angeles, 1972—; dir. Const. Rights Found., 1975—. Mem. urgent issues adv. bd. Yale Law Sch., 1976—; v.p. So. Calif. Squash Racquets Assn., 1975—. Mem. Am., Calif., Pa., Beverly Hills, Phila. bar assns. Home: 16801 Severo Pl Encino CA 91316 Office: 1900 Ave of the Stars Los Angeles CA 90067 Tel (213) 553-3900

SHUTTER, STEVEN GARY, b. Bklyn., June 8, 1944; A.B., Tufts U., 1966; J.D., N.Y. U., 1969. Admitted to N.Y. bar, 1970, Fla. bar, 1973, U.S. Supreme Ct. bar, 1976; atty. VISTA, Denver, 1969-70; trial atty. CAB, Washington, 1970-72; asso. firm J. Leonard Fleet, Hollywood, Fla., 1972-73; partner firm Berger and Shutter, Pembroke Pines, Fla., 1973—; city prosecutor, Pembroke Pines, 1973—; gen. counsel, pres. Epilepsy Found. Broward County (Fla.), 1974-76. Vice pres. United Taxpayers Assn., Pembroke Pines, 1974-75. Mem. Am., Fla., Broward County bar assns., Fla. Acad. Trial Lawyers. Office: 1900 N University Dr Pembroke Pines FL 33024 Tel (305) 962-9622

SHUTTLEWORTH, KENNETH ROBERT, b. Wilmington, Del., Nov. 16, 1940; B.S., Memphis State U., 1965, J.D., 1968. Admitted to Tenn. bar, 1968; asso. firm Goff Winchester & Walsh, 1968-70, firm Nelsen Norvell Wilson McRae Ivy & Sevier, 1970-74; partner firm Chiezza & Shuttleworth, Memphis, 1974—; sec., treas. Fin. Courier Service, Inc., 1972—. Pres. Citizens Police Community Relations com., Memphis; sec. Memphis House, Inc.; sr. warden Holy Trinity Episcopal Ch., Memphis; bd. dirs. Trezevant Episc. Ch. Home, Memphis. Mem. Memphis-Shelby County (pres. young lawyers sect. 1975, dir.), Am. (chmn. drug abuse com.), Tenn. (chmn. drug abuse com.) bar assns. Home: 1510 Peabody Ave Memphis TN 38114 Office: 161 Jefferson Ave suite 1100 Memphis TN 38103 Tel (901) 521-0550

SHWERGOLD, MARCEL, b. Antwerp, Belgium, May 29, 1939; B.S. cum laude, N.Y. U., 1959; J.D. cum laude, Harvard, 1962. Admitted to Supreme Ct. N.Y. bar, 1963; asso. firm Shea Gallop Climenko & Gould, N.Y.C., 1962-69; v.p., gen. counsel Lyntex Corp., N.Y.C., 1969; partner firm Weiss Rosenthal Heller Schwartzman & Lazar, N.Y.C., 1970-76; partner firm Milman & Shwergold, N.Y.C., 1977—. Mem. Am., N.Y. State bar assns., Assn. Bar City N.Y. Home: 201 E 28th St New York City NY 10016 Office: 711 3d Ave New York City NY 10017 Tel (212) 697-2880

SHY, PAUL RUSSELL, b. Breckenridge, Mo., May 13, 1923; J.D., U. Mo., 1950. Admitted to Mo. bar, 1950, U.S. Dist. Ct. bar, 1950, U.S. Ct. of Appeals bar, 1953, U.S. Supreme Ct. bar, 1956; individual practice law, Chillicothe, Mo., 1952-53; asst. U.S. atty., Kansas City, Mo., 1953-58; sec., gen. counsel, sr. v.p. Commerce Trust Co., Kansas City, Mo., 1958-71; partner firm Raymond, West & Shy, Kansas City, 1971—. Mem. Legal Aid Soc. (pres. 1968-69), Am. (state membership chmn. 1967-72), Mo. (dir. 1970-76) bar assns. Office: 911 Main St 2300 Commerce Tower Kansas City MO 64105 Tel (816) 421-1170

SHYER, HERBERT PAUL, b. Los Angeles, Apr. 29, 1930; B.A., U. Calif. at Los Angeles, 1950, M.A., 1952; LL.B., Harvard U., 1956. Admitted to N.Y. bar, 1957, Fed. bar, 1958; asso. firm Cleary, Gottlieb, Steen & Hamilton, N.Y.C., 1957-67; asso. counsel Equitable Life Assurance Soc. U.S., N.Y.C., 1967-69, asso. gen. solicitor, 1969-70, 2d v.p., asso. gen. solicitor, 1970, v.p., asso. gen. solicitor, 1970-73, v.p., dep. to gen. counsel, 1973-75, sr. v.p., gen. counsel, 1975—. Mem. Assn. Bar City N.Y., N.Y. State, Am. bar assns., N.Y. County Lawyers Assn. Home: 304 W 81st St New York City NY 10024 Office: 1285 Ave of Americas New York City NY 10019 Tel (212) 554-3971

SIBAL, ABNER WOODRUFF, b. N.Y.C., Apr. 11, 1921; A.B., Wesleyan U., Middletown, Conn., 1943; LL.B., St. Johns U., 1949. Admitted to Conn. bar, 1949, D.C. bar, 1965; partner firm Sibal, Hefferan & Rimer, Norwalk and Wilton, Conn., 1952-70, Gadsby & Hannah, Washington, 1970-74; pros. atty. Norwalk City Ct., 1951-55; corp. counsel City of Norwalk, 1959-60; gen. counsel Equal Employment Opportunity Commn., Washington, 1975—; chmn. Conn. Commn. on Corp. Law, 1959. Chmn., Norwalk-Wilton chpt. ARC, 1954-56; mem. 87th and 88th Congresses from 4th Dist. Conn.; mem. Conn. Senate, 1956-60, minority leader, 1959-60; bd. dirs. Norwalk C. of C., 1954-57. Mem. Am. Bar Assn. Home: 6431 Quincy Pl Falls Church VA 22042 Office: 2401 E St NW Washington DC 20506 Tel (202) 634-6400

SIBERT, LILYAN GOODE, b. Heerlen, The Netherlands, Jan. 31, 1946; B.A., U. Houston, 1968, J.D., 1970. Admitted to Tex. bar, 1971, D.C. bar, 1976; staff atty. GSA, Washington, 1971-72; staff atty. Tenn. Gas Transmission, Houston, 1972-76, asso. gen. atty., 1976—. Mem. Am., Tex., Tex. Jr., Houston, Houston Jr., Fed., Fed. Power, D.C. bar assns., Am. Judicature Soc., Order of Barons, Kappa Beta Pi. Home: 7630 White Fir Dr Houston TX 77088 Office: PO Box 2511 Houston TX 77001 Tel (713) 757-3379

SIBLEY, HORACE HOLDEN, b. Phila., Oct. 13, 1939; B.A., Vanderbilt U., 1961; LL.B., U. Ga., 1963; M.B.A., Ga. State U., 1971. Admitted to Ga. Supreme Ct. bar, 1964, U.S. Supreme Ct. bar, 1974; partner firm King & Spalding, Atlanta, 1968—. Elder Trinity Presbyn. Ch., Atlanta, 1969-73; mem. exec. com., vice chmn., dir. Butler St. YMCA, Atlanta, 1970—; mem. exec. com., dir. Goodwill Industries of Atlanta, Inc., 1974—; advisory trustee Henrietta Egleston Hosp. for Children, Inc., Atlanta, 1974—; bd. dirs. United Way of Metropolitan Atlanta, Inc., 1976—. Research Atlanta, 1976—; participant Leadership Atlanta. Mem. Atlanta, Ga., Am. bar assns., s., Corp. Counsel Assn. (dir.), Blue Key, Phi Kappa Phi, Omicron Delta Kappa. Home: 2894 Arden Rd NW Atlanta GA 30327 Office: 2500 Trust Co Tower Atlanta GA 30303

SICKLES, CARLTON RALPH, b. Hamden, Conn., June 15, 1921; B.S. cum laude, Georgetown Coll., 1943, J.D., 1948. Admitted to D.C. bar, 1949, Md. bar, 1955; asst. gen. counsel United Mine Workers of Am. Welfare and Retirement Fund, 1949-51; individual practice law, Washington and Md., 1952-59; partner firm Sickles & Sickles, Washington, 1959-63; adj. prof. Georgetown U. Law Sch., 1960-67; partner firm Sickles, Goldberg & Sickles, Washington, 1967-71; individual practice law, Md. and D.C., 1971—; del. Md. Ho. of Dels., 1955-62; mem. 88th-89th Congresses at large rep. from Md., 1963-67; bd. dirs. D.C. Metropolitan Area Transit Authority, 1967-73, alt. dir., 1975—; commr. Md. State Planning Commn., 1969—. Mem. Am., D.C., Fed., Md. State, Prince George County bar assns. Home: 7111 Kempton Rd Lanham MD 20801 Office: 1003 K St Washington DC 20001 Tel (202) 393-2860

SICULA, PAUL EDWARD, b. Milw., Jan. 31, 1939; B.S., U. Wis., 1962, LL.B., 1964. Admitted to Wis. bar, 1964; asso. firm I.D. Gaines, Milw., 1964-65, firm Riggins, Sicula & Race, Milw., 1965-66; partner firm Atinsky, Kahn & Sicula, Milw., 1966—. Mem. Wis. Assembly, 1966-76. Mem. Milw., Wis. bar assns., Wis., Am. (state committeeman) trial lawyers assns., Wis. Acad. Trial Lawyers (dir.), Lawyers for Migrant Workers. Research editor Wis. Law Rev., 1963-64. Home: 2951 N 53rd St Milwaukee WI 53210 Office: 212 W Wisconsin Ave Milwaukee WI 53203 Tel (414) 273-4950

SIDAMON-ERISTOFF, CONSTANTINE, b. N.Y.C., June 28, 1930; B.S. in Geol. Engring., Princeton U., 1952; LL.B., Columbia U., 1957. Admitted to N.Y. State bar, 1958; law clk. and asso. firm Kelley, Drye & Warren, N.Y.C., 1957-64; individual practice law, N.Y.C., 1964-65; asst. to mayor N.Y.C., 1966, hwy. commr., 1967, adminstr. N.Y.C. Transp. Adminstrn., 1968-73; individual practice law, N.Y.C., 1974—; mem. bd. dirs. Met. Transp. Authority, 1974—; chmn. subcom. mass transit, com. transp. law Transp. Research Bd., Washington, 1976—. Trustee Carnegie Hall, N.Y.C., 1966—, Phipps Houses, N.Y.C., 1974—, Caramoor Center Music and the Arts, Katonah, N.Y., 1961—; dir. Mid-Hudson Pattern Progress, Poughkeepsie, N.Y., 1974—; mem. policy bd. N.Y. State Legis. Inst., 1976—; del. Republican Nat. Conv., Kansas City, Mo., 1976. Mem. Assn. Bar City N.Y., Orange County, N.Y. County lawyers assns., Am., N.Y. State bar assns., Am. Inst. Mining, Metall. and Petroleum Engrs., Phi Delta Phi. Home: 120 East End Ave New York City NY 10028 Office: 36 W 44th St Suite 812 New York City NY 10036 Tel (212) 661-2820

SIDES, JACK DAVIS, JR., b. Dallas, Sept. 18, 1939; B.B.A., U. Tex., Austin, 1962, J.D. with honors, 1963. Admitted to Tex. bar, 1963; asso. firm Jackson, Walker, Winstead, Cantwell & Miller, Dallas, 1963-68; partner firm White, McElroy, White, Sides & Rector, Dallas, 1968—; judge moot ct. competition and mock trials So. Meth. U., 1969-72. Active Am. Cancer Soc., 1968-74, Dallas YMCA, 1972-75, Am. Heart Assn., 1972-74. Mem. Dallas (ethics com. 1973—), Tex., Am. bar assns., Dallas Assn. Def. Counsel (sec. 1972-73), Tex. Assn. Def. Counsel, Phi Delta Phi. Editor Tex. Law Rev., 1962-63. Office: 2505 Republic Bank Tower Dallas TX 75201 Tel (214) 748-0961

SIDES, JOHN HOWARD, b. Fredericktown, Mo., July 2, 1933; A.B., U. Mo., 1960, J.D., 1962. Admitted to Mo. bar, 1962; asst. pros. atty. Scott County (Mo.), 1962-64; judge Scott County Probate Ct., 1964—. Mem. Mo., Scott County bar assns., Mo. Assn. Probate and Magistrate Judges, Sikeston C. of C. (past dir.). Home: 605 Park Ave Sikeston MO 63801 Office: Courthouse Benton MO 63736 Tel (314) 545-3511

SIDOR, WALTER JOHN, SR., b. Hartford, Conn., Nov. 17, 1911; student Clark U., 1928-30; B.S., Trinity Coll., Hartford, 1932; LL.B., Duke, 1935. Admitted to Conn. bar, 1935; partner firm Kosicki & Sidor, 1935-39; asst. clk. Hartford City Police Ct., 1939-41, clk., 1941-42, prosecutor, 1942-43, judge, 1943-45; judge Conn. Ct. of Common Pleas, 1953-65, Conn. Superior Ct., 1966—; mem. Conn. State Bar Examining Com., 1966-69; mem. select com. Nat. Conf. Bar Examiners, 1969-70; mem. Conn. Adult Probation Commn., 1972-75, Conn. Parole Evaluation Commn., 1974-76. Chmn. Wethersfield (conn.) Sch. Bldg. Com., 1951-53; mem. Wethersfield Com. to Draft New Charter, 1953; corporator St. Francis Hosp., Hartford. Mem. Hartford County, Conn., Am. bar assns., Am. Judicature Soc. Home: 1554 Asylum Ave West Hartford CT 06117 Office: 95 Washington St Hartford CT 06106 Tel (203) 566-4704

SIEBEN, HARRY ALBERT, JR., b. Hastings, Minn., Nov. 24, 1943; B.A., Winona (Minn.) State Coll., 1965; J.D., U. Minn., 1968. Admitted to Minn. bar, 1968; partner firm Grose, Von Holtum, Von Holtum, Sieben & Schmidt, Ltd., Mpls., 1968—. Mem. Minn. Ho. of Reps., 1971—. Mem. Am., Minn., Hennepin County bar assns., Am. Trial Lawyers Assn. Home: 90 Valley Ln Hastings MN 55033 Office: 4940 Viking Dr Suite 558 Minneapolis MN 55435 Tel (612) 835-2575

SIEFFERMAN, FLOYD EARL, JR., b. Cin., Mar. 12, 1932; B.S., U.S. Mil. Acad., 1954; LL.B., Emory U., 1960, J.D., 1971. Admitted to Ga. bar, 1959, U.S. Supreme Ct. bar, 1970; asso. firm Gambrell, Harland, Russell, Moye & Richardson, Atlanta, 1959-65, partner, 1965-66; partner firm Long & Siefferman, Atlanta, 1966-75, firm Chambers, Siefferman, Robinson & Cooper, 1976—. Mem. Am., Ga., Atlanta bar assns., Lawyers Club Atlanta, Am. Judicature Soc., Am., Ga. assns. trial lawyers. Contbr. articles to legal jours. Home: 475 Mount Vernon Hwy Atlanta GA 30327 Office: suite 464 2200 Century Pkwy NE Atlanta GA 30345 Tel (404) 325-9970

SIEGAN, BERNARD HERBERT, b. Chgo., July 28, 1924; student Herzl Jr. Coll., Chgo., 1943, 46, Carnegie Inst. Tech., 1943, Roosevelt Coll., 1946-47; J.D., U. Chgo., 1949. Admitted to Ill. bar, 1950; asso. firm Rosenberg, Stein & Rosenberg, Chgo., 1950-52; partner firm Siegan & Karlin, Chgo., 1952-73; pres., sec., partner cos. engaged in real estate and real estate devel., 1955-70; research fellow law and econs. U. Chgo., 1968-69; adj. prof. law U. San Diego, 1973-74, prof., 1974-75, Distinguished prof., 1975—; weekly columnist Freedom Newspapers, 1973—; chmn. Conf. On Taking Issue, San Diego, 1975; chmn. adv. com. Conf. on Rights of the Regulated, Coronado, Calif., 1976. Mem. Am., Chgo. bar assns. Recipient Monk's Meml. award Inst. for Human Studies, 1972, award CEEED Orgn., 1975; author: Land Use Without Zoning, 1972, Other People's Property, 1976; editor: Planning Without Prices, 1977; Interaction of Economics and Law, 1977; contbr. articles to legal jours.; research fellow Urban Land Inst., 1976. Home: 6005 Camino de la Costa La Jolla CA 92037 Office: U San Diego Sch Law Alcala Park San Diego CA 92110 Tel (714) 291-6480

SIEGEL, ARNE, b. N.Y.C., July 1, 1929; B.B.A., Coll. City N.Y., 1950; J.D., Harvard, 1953. Admitted to N.Y. bar, 1953, N.J. bar, 1970; partner firm Siegel & Katz, N.Y.C., 1957-64; asso. firm O'Connor & Farber, N.Y.C., 1964-67; accountant M. Sternlieb & Co., Hackensack, N.J., 1967-71; individual practice law, Englewood, N.J., 1971—; pub. defender Borough of Cresskill (N.J.), 1975—. Mem. Bar Assn. City N.Y., N.Y. State, N.J. State, Bergen County (N.J.) bar assns., Beta Gamma Sigma, Beta Alpha Psi. C.P.A., N.J., N.Y. Home: 29 New St Cresskill NJ 07626 Office: 155 N Dean St Englewood NJ 07631 Tel (201) 568-3386

SIEGEL, ARTHUR EDGAR, b. Cin., Dec. 29, 1930; A.B., Harvard, 1952; LL.B., U. Cin., 1955, J.D., 1970. Admitted to Ohio bar, 1955, U.S. Ct. Appeals (6th Circuit), 1956, (3rd Circuit), 1975; since practiced in Cin., asso. firm Magrish & Magrish, 1955-57; counsel Wilson Freight Co., 1958—; pres. Travel A-GoGo, 1970-73. Mem.

Cin. Lawyers Club, Am. Trial Lawyers Assn., Ohio Bar Assn. Home: 7724 Sagamore Dr Cincinnati OH 45236 Office: 3636 Follett Ave Cincinnati OH 45223 Tel (513) 681-5600

SIEGEL, BELLE FLAXMAN, b. Elizabeth, N.J., May 18, 1904; B.A., U. Mich., 1927; M.S. in Social and Econ. Research, Simmons Coll., 1929; LL.B., U. San Francisco, 1946. Insp. div. women in industry N.Y. state Dept. Labor, N.Y.C., 1931-36, supr. div. homework, 1936-40; admitted to Calif. bar, 1946; adjudicator claims VA, San Francisco, 1946; asso. firm Sugarman & Bernheim, San Francisco, 1948; individual practice law, San Francisco, 1946-50, Los Angeles, 1950—. Mem. Los Angeles County Bar. Office: Suite 757 727 W Seventh St Los Angeles CA 90017 Tel (213) 626-6120

SIEGEL, JAY SANFORD, b. N.Y.C., Aug. 14, 1929; A.B., N.Y. U., 1950, LL.B., 1954. Admitted to N.Y. bar, 1955, Conn. bar, 1956, D.C. bar, 1971; asso. firm Pelgrift, Dodd, Blumenfeld & Nair, Hartford, Conn., 1957-59, firm Danaher, Lewis & Tamoney, Hartford, 1959-60; individual practice law, Hartford, 1960-69; partner firm Siegel, O'Connor & Kainen, Hartford, 1970—; spl. counsel to gov. Conn., 1970-74; mem. U.S. Senate from Conn., 1959-69. Mem. Am. (chmn. labor relations law sect. 1977-78), Conn. (chmn. labor law sect. 1961-63) bar assns., Indsl. Relations Research Assn. Contbr. articles to legal jours. Office: 60 Washington St Hartford CT 06106 Tel (203) 547-0550 also 1747 Pennsylvania Ave Washington DC 20006 Tel (202) 833-2545

SIEGEL, JERRY LAWRENCE, b. Fayetteville, Ark., Dec. 6, 1946; B.A., Stanford, 1968; M.S., London Sch. Econs., 1970; J.D., Yale, 1972. Admitted to Calif. bar, 1972, N.Y. bar, 1975; law clk. U.S. Dist. judge for No. Dist. Calif., 1972-73, U.S. Supreme Ct., Washington, 1973-74; asst. U.S. atty. for So. Dist. N.Y., N.Y.C., 1974—. Articles editor Yale Law Jour., 1971-72. Home: 176 E 64th St New York City NY 10021 Office: 1 Saint Andrews Plaza New York City NY 10007 Tel (212) 791-0041

SIEGEL, MARTIN JAY, b. N.Y.C., Apr. 12, 1942; B.A. in Econs., Mich. State U., 1963; J.D., Bklyn. Law Sch., 1966. Admitted to N.Y. bar, 1967, Calif. bar, 1974, D.C. bar, 1974, U.S. Supreme Ct. bar, 1970; student asst. U.S. Atty.'s Office, Eastern Dist. N.Y., Bklyn., 1965-66, Legal Aid Soc., N.Y.C., 1969-71; individual practice law, Heidelberg, W.Ger., 1971-72, N.Y.C., 1972—; arbitrator Am. Arbitration Assn., 1973—, Bronx Civil Ct., 1973—, N.Y.C. Small Claims Ct., 1973—; hearing examiner Parking Violations Bur., 1974—. Jr. chmn. United Jewish Appeal, 1974-75. Mem. Am., N.Y. State bar assns., Am. Judges Assn. Home: Apt 1209 3419 Irwin Ave Riverdale NY 10463 Office: 7th floor 1140 Ave of Americas New York City NY 10036 Tel (212) 869-0930

SIEGEL, MARVIN H., b. Pitts., Oct. 11, 1934; B.B.A., U. Miami (Fla.), 1956, J.D., 1962. Admitted to Fla. bar, 1962; accountant Roth & Gottlieb, Miami, 1955-61; asst. controller Jackson Meml. Hosp., Miami, 1961-65; asso. dean for fin. and hosp. affairs Sch. Medicine U. Miami, 1965—; nat. chmn. Group on Bus. Affairs, Am. Med. Colls., 1973-74; mem. Data Devel. Liaison Commn., Assn. Am. Med. Colls.; mem. Fla. Kidney Disease Bd., 1971-72. Mem. Am., Fla. bar assns., Am. Soc. Hosp. Attys. Contbr. articles to profl. jours. Home: 10331 SW 119th St Miami FL 33156 Office: U Miami Sch Medicine PO Box 520875 Biscayne Annex Miami FL 33152 Tel (305) 547-6601

SIEGEL, MARVIN SELCER, b. Fargo, N.D., Apr. 10, 1936; B.A., U. Mich., 1958; J.D., Stanford U., 1961. Admitted to Calif. bar, 1962; asso. David B. Gold, San Francisco, 1961-63, firm Holmdahl & Fletcher, Oakland, Calif., 1963-64; partner firm Longstreth & Siegel, Menlo Park, Calif., 1964-75, firm Jorgenson Cosgrove & Siegel, Menlo Park, 1975—; pres. Legal Aid Soc. San Mateo County, 1973-75. Chmn. Menlo Park Library Comn., 1975—. Mem. Am., San Mateo County (past chmn. legal services com.), Palo Alto Area (past chmn. legal services com.) bar assns. Home: 1806 Edgewood Ln Menlo Park CA 94025 Office: 1100 Alma St Suite 210 Menlo Park CA 94025 Tel (415) 323-7711

SIEGEL, MAYER, b. N.Y.C., Sept. 29, 1936; B.B.A. magna cum laude, Coll. City N.Y., 1956; LL.B. cum laude, N.Y. U., 1961, LL.M., 1964. Admitted to N.Y. bar, 1961, U.S. Tax Ct. bar, 1965; asso. firm Fried, Frank, Harris, Shriver & Jacobson, N.Y.C., 1961-74, partner, 1974—. Mem. N.Y. State Bar Assn. Contbr. articles to legal jours. Home: 2820 Ocean Pkwy Brooklyn NY 11235 Office: 120 Broadway New York City NY 10005 Tel (212) 964-6500

SIEGEL, NORMAN IRA, b. Bklyn., Oct. 26, 1941; B.A., Colgate U., 1963; J.D. cum laude, Union U., 1966. Admitted to N.Y. bar, 1977; partner firm Abelove, Siegel, Abelove & Hester, Utica, N.Y., 1967—; dir. Associated Laundries of Am., Inc., 1965—, Associated Linen Services, Inc., 1973—; chmn. bd. Foster Paper Co., 1968—. Mem. Utica Sch. Bd., 1973-74. Mem. Oneida County (N.Y.), N.Y. State bar assns., Justinian Soc. Editorial bd. Albany Law Sch. Law Rev., 1964-66. Home: 2505 Edgewood Rd Utica NY 13501 Office: 124 Bleecker St Utica NY 13501 Tel (315) 724-8101

SIEGENDORF, ARDEN MICHAEL, b. Miami Beach, Fla., Oct. 13, 1938; student U. Fla., 1956-57; B.B.A., U. Miami, 1960, J.D., 1963. Admitted to Fla. bar, 1963; spl. asst. atty. gen. Fla., 1963; research aide to Judge Mallory Horton, Fla. 3d Dist. Ct. of Appeals, 1963-64; legal counsel Dade County Ho. of Dels., Fla. Legislature, 1965-67; asst. atty. gen. charge S.Fla. Office, 1965-71; commr. City of Miami, 1971; judge Dade County Ct., 1971-74; judge Circuit Ct., 11th Jud. Circuit, Miami, 1974—; asso. justice Fla. Supreme Ct., 1974; v.p. Fla. Conf. County Ct. Judges, 1974; instr. Miami-Dade Community Coll., 1976-77; lectr. Nat. Coll. State Judiciary, 1977. Vice chmn. Fla. regional bd. Anti-Defamation League of B'nai B'rith, 1975; chmn. adv. bd. Comprehensive Offender Rehab. Program, 1974; mem. jud. com. planning Fla.'s Bicentennial Celebration, 1975; mem. Democratic Exec. Com., 1970; pres. Young Dem. Clubs of Dade County, 1967, of Fla., 1970. Mem. U. Miami Law Sch. Alumni Assn. (past pres.), Iron Arrow, Wig and Robe, Omicron Delta Kappa. Recipient Outstanding Young Man of Miami award Miami Jr. C. of C., 1973; Ky. Col. Author: Review and Sentence Fla. Rules of Criminal Procedure Handbook, 1968. Home: 2951 S Bayshore Dr Miami FL 33133 Office: 73 W Flagler St Miami FL 33130 Tel (305) 579-5366

SIEGFRIED, ARTHUR PAUL, b. Long Branch, N.J., Apr. 28, 1935; student, U. Pa., 1958; law degree, Seton Hall U., 1962. Admitted to N.J. bar, 1963, U.S. Supreme Ct. bar, 1968; asso. firm Klatsky, Himelman & Siegfried, Red Bank, N.J., 1963-72; individual practice law, Red Bank, 1972—; municipal ct. judge, Fair Haven, N.J., Atlantic Highlands, N.J., Shrewsbury, N.J.; acting municipal ct. judge various cities, Monmouth County, N.J., 1969—. Mem. N.J. State Bar Assn., Monmouth County Municipal Ct. Judges Assn. (pres.). Office: 188 E Bergen Pl Red Bank NJ 07701 Tel (201) 842-8200

SIEGFRIED, DAVID C., b. N.Y.C., Feb. 15, 1942; A.B., Princeton U., 1964; J.D., Harvard, 1967. Admitted to N.Y. State bar, 1970; asso. firm Milbank, Tweed, Hadley & McCloy, N.Y.C., 1968-76, partner, 1977—. Vice chmn. N.Y. Legal Aid Soc. Assos. and Young Lawyers Fund Raising Campaign, 1973-75, co-chmn., 1976; mem. Christian edn. com. Community Congl. Ch., Short Hills, N.J., 1976. Mem. Am., N.Y. State bar assns., Princeton Class of 1964 (pres. 1969-74, mem. class council 1974—), Friends of Princeton Track (v.p. 1976). Home: 12 Taylor Rd Short Hills NJ 07078 Office: 1 Chase Manhattan Plaza New York City NY 10005 Tel (212) 422-2660

SIEMER, DEANNE C., b. Buffalo, Dec. 25, 1940; B.A., George Washington U., 1962; LL.B., Harvard U., 1968. Examiner, Office of Mgmt. and Budget, Exec. Office of Pres., Washington, 1964-65; partner firm Wilmer, Cutler & Pickering, Washington, 1976-77; now gen. counsel Dept. Def., The Pentagon; mem. exec. com. Washington Lawyers Com. for Civil Rights Under Law, 1970-77; mem. bd. overseers vis. com. to Law Sch., Harvard U., 1970-76; faculty mem. State U.N.Y., Buffalo, 1973-75, Nat. Inst. for Trial Advocacy, 1974-77. Mem. D.C., Am. bar assns., Phi Beta Kappa. Office: 3E 980 Dept of Def The Pentagon Washington DC 20301

SIGELBAUM, HARVEY CHARLES, b. Newark, Jan. 13, 1937; student Rutgers U., 1956-57; A.B., U. Miami, 1958; J.D., Bklyn. Law Sch., 1962. Admitted to N.Y. bar, 1963, U.S. Supreme Ct. bar, 1968; claims adminstr., atty. Consol. Mut. Ins. Co., Bklyn., 1958-65; individual practice law, N.Y.C., 1963-69; atty. Am. Consumer Ins. Co., N.Y.C., 1965-67; atty. Urban Community Ins. Co., N.Y.C., 1967, exec. v.p., 1969-70, pres., 1970—, also dir.; partner firm Sigelbaum & Rosenberg, N.Y.C., 1969—; adj. asso. prof. Coll. of Ins., 1970—; lectr. in field. Bd. dirs., exec. com. Consumer Assembly of N.Y., 1971—; chmn. consumers adv. council N.Y. State Ins. Dept., 1972—; bd. dirs. Coop. League of U.S.A., Washington, 1972—, mem. exec. com., 1976; trustee, exec. com. Rochdale Inst., 1973—; mem. adv. council N.Y.C. Dept. Consumer Affairs, 1975—; mem. jud. selection panel Com. To Reform Jud. Selection, N.Y.C., 1972; mem. central com. Internat. Coop. Alliance. Mem. Am. Arbitration Assn. (panel 1975), Ins. Soc. N.Y. (lectr. 1976), Am., N.Y., Queens County bar assns., N.Y. County Lawyers Assn., Def. Research Inst., Fedn. Ins. Counsel, Ins. Soc. N.Y. Contbr. articles to profl. publs. Home: 340 W 28th St New York City NY 10001 Office: 309 W 23d St New York City NY 10011 Tel (212) 691-8400

SIGLER, WILLIAM MCLEMORE, b. Hattiesburg, Miss., Nov. 1, 1946; B.S.B.A. in Finance, U. So. Miss., 1970; J.D., U. Miss., 1973; postgrad. Am. Inst. Banking, 1970-71. Admitted to U.S. Dist. Ct. for No. and So. Dist. Miss., 1973, U.S. Tax Ct., 1975, U.S. Supreme Ct., 1975; mem. firms Schlottman & Sigler, 1974, Rogers, Morris, Fair, Schlottman & Sigler, 1974-75; individual practice law, Hattiesburg, 1975—; dep. sherrif Forrest County, Miss., 1973—; asst. to dist. atty. 12th Jud. Dist., 1973; mem. narcotics unit Hattiesburg Police Dept., 1973; mem. JAGC Miss. N.G. Supt. Sunday sch., mem. bd. deacons Bay St. Presbyn. Ch., Hattiesburg. Mem. Hattiesburg C. of C., Am., Miss., South Central Miss. (chmn. com. sheriff's relations 1974-75, sec. sect. young lawyers) bar assns., Assn. Trial Lawyers Am., Miss. Trial Lawyers Assn., U. So. Miss. Alumni Assn. (pres. Lafayette County chpt. 1972-73). Home: 202 Patton Ave Hattiesburg MS 39401 Office: 111 E Front St Hattiesburg MS 39401 Tel (601) 544-7961

SIGMAN, LOUIS EDWARD, b. Chgo., Mar. 3, 1944; B.A., U. Wis., 1966; J.D., Northwestern U., 1969. Admitted to Ill. bar, 1969, U.S. Dist. Ct. No. Dist. Ill. bar, 1969; asso. firm Shulman and Baum, Ltd., Chgo., 1970—. Mem. Am., Ill., Chgo. bar assns. Home: 3033 N Sheridan Rd Chicago IL 60657 Office: 39 S LaSalle St Chicago IL 60603 Tel (312) 236-4316

SIGMAN, MICHAEL, b. N.Y.C., May 3, 1935; A.B., Morris Harvey Coll.; J.D., Am. U. Admitted to Fla. bar, 1966; mem. firm Sigman & Sigman, Fla., 1966-68, Sigman and Cohen, 1970-72, Sigman, Cohen, Marks and Stone, 1972-74; individual practice law, 1968-70, Orlando, Fla., 1974—. Mem. Fla., Orange County bar assns. Home: Box 463A Longwood FL 32750 Office: Suite 1515 CNA Tower Orlando FL 32801 Tel (305) 843-7333

SIGMON, RICHARD ROLAND, b. Roanoke, Va., Nov. 30, 1924; J.D., U. Md., 1957; LL.M., George Washington U., 1959. Admitted to Md. bar, 1957, U.S. Supreme Ct. bar, 1961, D.C. bar, 1966; atty., advisor ICC, Washington, 1957-59; atty., asst. gen. counsel Am. Trucking Assn., Inc., Washington, 1959-65; asso. firm Rice, Carpenter and Carraway, Washington, 1965-69, mem., 1969—; asst. sec. Nat. Freight Claim Council, 1954-57; lectr. in transp. Southeastern U., Washington, 1964-66; instr. freight claims and claim prevention Md. Motor Truck Assn. Mem. Am. Bar Assn., Assn. ICC Practitioners (pres., chmn. exec. commn. 1968-69), Motor Carrier Lawyers Assn., Am. Judicature Soc., Selden Soc., Am. Soc. Legal History, Am. Arbitration Assn. (nat. panel), Supreme Ct. Hist. Soc. Editor: Miller's Law of Freight Loss, 1974; contbr. articles to legal jours. Home: 7401 New Hampshire Ave Hyattsville MD 20783 Office: 1111 E St NW Washington DC 20004 Tel (202) 737-7173

SIGNORE, STEPHEN ROMEO, JR., b. Ambler, Pa., Dec. 2, 1944; A.B., U. Pa., 1966; J.D., Duquesne U., 1969. Admitted to Pa. bar, 1970, U.S. Supreme Ct. bar, 1975; law clk. Hon. J. William Ditter, Jr., U.S. Dist. Ct. Eastern Dist. Pa., 1969-71; asso. firm Brunner, Conver & Glackin, Lansdale, Pa., 1971-73; mem. firm Narducci & Signore, Norristown, Pa., 1973—; instr. part time real estate dept. Temple U., 1973—; instr. part time bus. law, Montgomery County Community Coll., 1973—; asst. pub. defender Montgomery County part time, 1972—. Mem. bd. dirs. N. Pa. YMCA, 1971—; treas. Ambler Jaycees, 1972. Mem. Am., Pa., Montgomery County bar assns., Assn. Trial Lawyers Am., Pa., Montgomery County trial lawyers assns. Home: 66 Davis Rd Ambler PA 19002 Office: Suite 608 One Montgomery Plaza Norristown PA 19401 Tel (215) 275-2230

SIGNORELLI, ERNEST LEONARD, b. N.Y.C., June 19, 1924; B.A., Washington Sq. Coll., N.Y. U., 1948, J.D., Sch. Law, 1948, LL.M., 1953; grad. Nat. Coll. State Trial Judges, U. N.C., 1968. Admitted to N.Y. bar, 1949, U.S. Supreme Ct. bar, 1960; individual practice law, N.Y.C., 1949-54, Copiague, N.Y., 1954-63; judge Ct. of Spl. Sessions, Babylon, N.Y., 1960-63, Suffolk County (N.Y.) Dist. Ct., 1964-69, Suffolk County Ct., 1970-75; judge Suffolk County Surrogate Ct., 1976—; asst. dist. atty. for Suffolk County, 1957-59. Founder Babylon Youth Council, Inc. Mem. Am., N.Y. State, Suffolk County bar assns., Suffolk County Criminal Bar Assn., Police Assn. Suffolk County, Columbian (founder), Babylon Town lawyers assns., N.Y. State, Suffolk County magistrates assn., County Judges Assn., Surrogates Assn. Office: Surrogate's Ct County Center Riverhead NY 11901 Tel (516) 727-4700

SIKES, ALFRED CALVIN, b. Cape Girardeau, Mo., Dec. 16, 1939; B.A., Westminster Coll., 1961; J.D., U. Mo., 1964. Admitted to Mo. bar, 1964; asso. firm Allen, Woolsey & Fisher, Springfield, Mo., 1964-68; asst. atty. gen. Attys. Gens. Office, Jefferson City, Mo., 1969-72; exec. dir. Mo. Transition Govt., Jefferson City, 1972-73; dir. Mo. Dept. Community Affairs, Jefferson City, 1973-74, Mo. Dept. Consumer Affairs, Regulation and Licensing, Jefferson City, 1974—; legal counsel Jr. Chamber Internat., 1971-72; partner Radiozark Enterprises. Campaign mgr., John Danforth for U.S. Senate, 1970, Gov. Christopher S. Bond, Mo., 1972; polit. cons. Nebr. Republican gubernatorial candidate; mem. Mo. Organized Crime Task Force, 1970-71. Mem. Mo. Bar Assn. Home: 2454 E Greenwood Ave Springfield MO 65804 Office: 505 Missouri Blvd Jefferson City MO 65101 Tel (314) 751-3946

SILBER, DAVID JAY EDWARD, b. Poughkeepsie, N.Y., Sept. 2, 1944; B.A., Hobart Coll., 1966; J.D., Albany Law Sch., 1969. Admitted to N.Y. bar, 1969, U.S. Supreme Ct. bar, 1974; partner firm Silber & Silber, Poughkeepsie, 1969-74, 77—; sr. atty. mental health info. service N.Y. State Appellate Div., Poughkeepsie, 1974-77; lectr. psychiat./legal problems. Bd. dirs. Dutchess County Arts Council, 1976—; mem. Pleasant Valley (N.Y.) Zoning Bd. Appeals, 1975—. Mem. Am., N.Y. State, Dutchess County bar assns., N.Y. Trial Lawyers Assn. Office: 11 Cannon St Poughkeepsie NY 12601 Tel (914) 454-3940

SILBERBERG, PHILIP ERWIN, b. N.Y.C., June 15, 1927; B.C.E., Cornell, 1948; LL.B., Harvard, 1951. Admitted to N.Y. State bar, 1951, U.S. Supreme Ct. bar, 1968; atty. Port of N.Y. Authority, 1951-55; atty. Columbia Broadcasting System, Inc., 1955-61, sr. atty., 1961-67, asst. gen. atty., 1967-68; v.p., gen. counsel Visual Electronics Corp., N.Y.C., 1968-70; individual practice law, N.Y.C., 1970-71; partner firm Ryan & Silberberg, N.Y.C., 1971—. Chmn. Council of Greenburgh (N.Y.) Civic Assns., 1957-63; dir.-at-large Nat. Fedn. Settlements and Neighborhood Centers, N.Y.C., 1974—. Mem. N.Y. State, White Plains bar assns., N.Y. County Lawyers Assn. (com. state legislation 1954-60, 71—, patent, trademarks and copyrights 1972—). Home: 72 Hartsdale Ave White Plains NY 10605 Office: 200 Park Ave New York City NY 10017 Tel (212) 687-1470

SILBERG, JAY ELIOT, b. N.Y.C., Apr. 5, 1941; B.A., Amherst Coll., 1963; LL.B., Harvard, 1966. Admitted to N.J. bar, 1966, Dist. Columbia bar, 1968; atty. Office Gen. Counsel, AEC, 1966-69; asso. firm Shaw, Pittman, Potts & Trowbridge, Washington, 1969-73, partner, 1973—. Home: 6600 Braeburn Pkwy Bethesda MD 20034 Office: 1800 M St NW Washington DC 20036 Tel (202) 331-4100

SILBERMAN, JAY WILLARD, b. Chgo., July 15, 1938; B.S.B.A., Northwestern U., 1960; J.D., De Paul U., 1966. Tax and audit statistician Price, Waterhouse & Co., Chgo., 1960-62; admitted to Ill. bar, 1966; partner firm Silberman and Gershon, Ltd., Chgo., 1974—; dir. numerous cos. Chmn. Deerfield (Ill.) campaign dr. United Fund, 1973; mem. Dist. Caucus, Sch. Bd., Deerfield. Mem. Chgo. Bar Assn. (mem. lawyer reference and probate practice coms.), Beta Alpha Psi, Delta Sigma Pi. Recipient Am. Jurisprudence prize Joint Pubs. Annotated Reports System, 1964, award of appreciation De Paul U. Coll. Law, 1975. Office: Suite 2225 One N LaSalle St Chicago IL 60602 Tel (312) 726-2400

SILBERMAN, NATHAN B., b. Stamford, Conn., Aug. 8, 1902; Ph.B., Brown U., 1924; J.D., N.Y. U., 1928. Admitted to Conn. bar, 1929; individual practice law, Stamford, 1929; prosecutor Stamford City Ct., 1960. Chmn. Multiple Sclerosis Soc. Stamford, 1965; pres. Stamford Jewish Center, 1962. Mem. Stamford Bar Assn. (pres. 1960). Home: 1241 High Ridge Rd Stamford CT 06903 Office: 109 Atlantic St Stamford CT 06901 Tel (203) 324-9231

SILBERMAN, PAUL, b. Balt., June 12, 1932; B.S., U. Balt., 1955, LL.B., 1960. Admitted to Md. bar, 1960; asso. George McManus, Balt., 1962-66; atty. Balt. VA, 1966-76; asst. dist. counsel VA, Balt., 1976—. Home: 4270 Labyrinth Rd Baltimore MD 21215 Office: 216 Federal Bldg Baltimore MD 21201 Tel (301) 358-6269

SILER, EUGENE EDWARD, JR., b. Williamsburg, Ky., Oct. 19, 1936; B.A. cum laude, Vanderbilt U., 1958; LL.B., U. Va., 1963; LL.M., Georgetown U., 1964. Admitted to Ky. bar, 1963, Va. bar, 1963, D.C. bar, 1963; legal intern, E. Barrett Prettyman fellow Georgetown U., Washington, 1963-64; asso. firm Eugene Siler, Sr. Williamsburg, Ky., 1964-70; U.S. atty. for Eastern Dist. Ky., Dept. Justice, Lexington, 1970-75; judge U.S. Dist. Ct. for Eastern and Western Dists. Ky., 1975—; county atty. Whitley County, Ky., 1965-70. Mem. Regional Mental Health Bd., London, Ky., 1966-70. Mem. Fed., Am. bar assns. Recipient Freedom's Found. medal, 1968; contbr. articles to legal publs. Home: 820 Walnut St Williamsburg KY 40769 Office: Fed Courthouse Barr St PO Box 1689 Lexington KY 40501 Tel (606) 252-2312

SILETS, HARVEY MARVIN, b. Chgo., Aug. 25, 1931; B.Sc. cum laude, DePaul U., 1952; J.D., U. Mich., 1955. Asst. advance tng. program IRS, U. Mich., 1952-53; admitted to Ill. bar, 1955, N.Y. bar, 1956, U.S. Supreme Ct. bar, 1959; asso. firm Paul Weiss Rifkind Wharton & Garrison, N.Y.C., 1955-56; partner firm Harris Burman & Silets, Chgo., 1962—; asst. U.S. atty. No. Dist. Ill., 1958-60, chief tax atty. U.S. Atty's Office, 1960-62; lectr. law John Marshall Law Sch., 1962-66; gen. counsel Nat. Treasury Employees Union, Chgo. Mem. Chgo., Am., Fed. (dir.; chmn. judicial com. 1971—, fed. rules com. 1972—, treas. 1974, sec. 1975, v.p. 1976, pres. elect 1977—) bar assns., Bar Assn. 7th Fed. Circuit (chmn. com. criminal law and procedure 1972—). Office: 7 S Dearborn St Chicago IL 60603 Tel (312) 236-2994

SILLIMAN, BENJAMIN DEWAYNE, b. Ardmore, Okla., Sept. 10, 1895; B.A., Coe Coll., 1917; LL.B., State U. Iowa, 1923. Admitted to Iowa bar, 1923; individual practice law, Cedar Rapids, Iowa, 1927—; mem. firm Silliman & Gray, Cedar Rapids, 1938-52, Silliman Gray & Stapleton, Cedar Rapids, 1952—; assigned by Judge Adv. Gen. to Nuremberg trials, 1945. Trustee Coe Coll.; past pres. Iowa, Cedar Rapids Community Chest. Mem. Linn County Bar Assn. (past pres.), Phi Delta Phi. Office: 807 American Bldg Cedar Rapids IA 52401 Tel 364-1535

SILLIMAN, JOHN EDDY, b. Bronxville, N.Y., Mar. 9, 1934; B.A., Yale, 1956; LL.B., Columbia U., 1959. Admitted to Conn. bar, 1959, Hawaii Fed. bar, 1962, U.S. Supreme Ct. bar, 1967; law clk. Justice Howard W. Alcorn, Conn. Supreme Ct., Hartford, 1963-64; asso. firm Murtha, Cullina, Richter & Pinney, Hartford, Conn., 1964-68, partner, 1969—. Pres. Conn. Halfway House, Hartford, 1971-74. Mem. Hartford County, Conn., Am. bar assns. Home: 126 Mountain Rd W Hartford CT 06107 Office: 101 Pearl St PO Box 3197 Hartford CT 06103 Tel (203) 549-4500

SILLMAN, JUSTIN, b. Columbus, O., Dec. 25, 1902; LL.B., Ohio State U., 1925, J.D. cum laude, 1970. Admitted to Ohio bar, 1925; partner firm Garek & Sillman, Columbus, 1925-32, 65-71, C.C.

Crabbe, Garek & Sillman, 1932-65; individual practice law, Columbus, 1972—. Mem. Columbus, Ohio State bar assns., Order of Coif. Home: 2715 Floribunda Dr Columbus OH 43209 Office: 88 E Broad St Columbus OH 43215 Tel (614) 221-6629

SILVA, MILTON RAYMOND, b. Fall River, Mass., June 16, 1923; Ph.B., Providence Coll., 1946; J.D., Suffolk U., 1952. Admitted to Mass. bar, 1953; asso. firm Horvitz & Horvitz, Fall River, 1953-58; individual practice law, Fall River, 1958-60; partner firm Silva & Logozzo, Fall River, 1960-70; judge 2d Dist. Bristol County Ct., 1971—. Chmn. Fall River Bd. Police, 1954-58, 64-68; rep. Mass. Gen. Ct., 1960-64. Mem. Mass. Bar, Am. Bar Assn. Home: 1550 Gardners Neck Rd Swansea MA 02777 Office: 45 Rock St Fall River MA 02720 Tel (617) 679-8161

SILVEIRA, RONALD ANTHONY, b. San Rafael, Calif., Aug. 28, 1948; A.B., U. San Francisco, 1970, J.D., 1973. Admitted to Calif. bar, 1973; individual practice law, San Rafael, 1973—. Mem. Calif. Hist. Soc., U. San Francisco Alumni Assn., U. San Francisco Law Soc., Phi Alpha Delta. Office: 140 Blackstone Dr San Rafael CA 94903 Tel (415) 479-7837

SILVER, CHARLES JACOB, b. Bklyn., Feb. 13, 1921; A.B., St. John's U., 1947; LL.B., N.Y. Law Sch., 1949. Admitted to N.Y. State bar, 1950, Calif. bar, 1971; individual practice law, N.Y.C., 1950-55; atty. Allstate Ins. Co. N.J., Murray Hill, 1955-67; casualty and legal claim dir. Countrywide Ins. Group, Los Angeles, 1967-68; asst. v.p. claims, liability and legal claim mgr. Transam. Ins. Co., Los Angeles, 1969—. Dep. atty. gen. election frauds div., N.Y. State, 1950, 51, 52; judge adv. Am. Legion N.J., 1955-60; v.p., trustee Lions Internat. N.J., 1957-59. Mem. Am., Calif. State, Los Angeles County bar assns. Home: 23238 Bigler St Woodland Hills CA 91364 Office: 1150 S Olive St Suite 2110 Los Angeles CA 90015 Tel (213) 742-4277

SILVER, GRAY, JR., b. Martinsburg, W.Va., Mar. 22, 1912; A.B., W.Va. U., 1935; LL.B., W.Va. Coll. Law, 1937. Admitted to W.Va. bar, 1937; practiced in Martinsburg, W.Va., 1937-60; judge 23d Jud. Circuit Ct. of W.Va., 1961-76; city atty. City of Martinsburg, 1950-60; mem. W.Va. Supreme Ct. Com. on Standard Jury Instrns., Criminal Div., 1963-76; mem. vis. com. W.Va. U. Coll. Law, 1958-60. Trustee City Hosp., Martinsburg, 1939—, pres., 1956-58. Mem. W.Va. Jud. Assn. (pres. 1966-67), Am., W.Va. bar assns., W.Va. State Bar (vice chmn. com. on legal ethics 1956-57, gov. 1957-60), Nat., W.Va. councils juvenile ct. judges, W.Va. Law Sch. Assn. (life; bd. govs., pres. 1973-74), Beta Theta Pi. Home: 501 S Queen St Martinsburg WV 25401 Office: Berkeley County Courthouse Martinsburg WV 25401 Tel (304) 263-3521

SILVER, HARRY, b. Phila., March 3, 1932; B.S. in Bus. Adminstrn., St. Joseph's Coll., 1955; LL.B., Temple U., 1959; postgrad. Georgetown, 1956, also Drexel Inst. Admitted to Pa. bar, 1960; sr. officer firm Silver, Miller & Silver, Phila. Bd. dirs. Union Fire Assn., St. Joseph's Coll., Bala-Narberth Lions. Mem. Am., Phila. bar assns., Internat. Bus. Bar, Trial Lawyers Assn., Comml. Law League, Am. Med-Law Soc. Hon. mem. Hahnemann Med. Coll. Alumni. Home: 209 Bryn Mawr Ave Bala Cynwyd PA 19004 Office: 1707 Rittenhouse Sq Philadelphia PA 19103 Tel (215) 735-5731

SILVER, MURRAY MENDEL, b. Savannah, Ga., Oct. 15, 1929; LL.B., U. Ga., 1953. Admitted to Ga. bar, 1953, U.S. Supreme Ct. bar, 1974; individual practice law, Atlanta, 1953-72; mem. firm Silver, Zevin, Sewell & Turner, Atlanta, 1972—; gen. counsel Ga. Dept. Labor, 1967-70, adv. counsel, 1971—. Mem. Ga., Am. bar assns., Am. Judicature Soc. Office: 100 Colony Sq Suite 1700 Atlanta GA 30309 Tel (404) 892-8150

SILVER, RALPH DAVID, b. Chgo., Apr. 19, 1924; B.S., U. Chgo., 1943; C.P.A., U. Ill., 1948; J.D., DePaul U., 1952. Admitted to Ill. bar, 1952; since practiced in Chgo., staff accountant David Himmelblau & Co., 1946-48; agt. IRS, 1948-51; mem. firm Lawrence J. West & Assos., 1952-55; chief fin. exec. Barton Brands, Ltd., 1955—. Vice-chmn. Glencoe Caucus Com., 1973-75; bd. dirs. Max and Minnie Reich Found., The Silver Found. Mem. Am., Chgo. bar assns., Am. Soc. C.P.A.'s. Home: 1124 Old Elm Ln Glencoe IL 60022 Office: 200 S Michigan Ave Chicago IL 60602

SILVER, ROBERT DICKINSON, b. Cleve., Oct. 25, 1934; B.A., U. Chgo., 1957; J.D., U. Calif. at Los Angeles, 1966. Admitted to Calif. bar, 1966; asso. firm Barnes et al, Ventura, Calif., 1966-69, partner, 1970-71; individual practice law, Ventura, 1971—; gen. counsel World U. in Ojai (Calif.), 1974—. Mem. Am., Calif., Ventura County (chmn. tax. sect.) bar assns. Office: 21 S California St suite 205 PO Box 1455 Ventura CA 93001 Tel (805) 648-2891

SILVER, SAMUEL IRVING, b. West Blocton, Ala., Sept. 5, 1913; student U. Fla., 1931-33; LL.B., U. Miami, Coral Gables, Fla., 1937, J.D., 1937; grad. Nat. Coll. State Judiciary, 1973, Am. Acad. Jud. Edn., 1976. Admitted to Fla. bar, 1937, U.S. Supreme Ct. bar, 1958; mem. firm Silver, Kaplan, Dietz & Lasky, Miami, Fla., 1937-49, firm Pallot, Silver, Pallot, Proby & Adkins, Miami, 1950-72; judge West Miami (Fla.) Municipal Ct., 1949-58, asso. judge, 1958-72; judge Fla. Circuit Ct., 11th Jud. Circuit, 1972—; sec., gen. counsel, dir. Inter Nat. Bank of Miami, 1963-72; chmn. Fla. adv. council Am. Arbitration Assn. Vice chmn. Coral Gables Zoning Bd., 1961-63; trustee Dade County Sch. Bd., 1955-57; pres. South Fla. Inter-Profl. Council, 1967-69. Mem. Dade County (Fla.) (pres. 1964-65), Am. bar assns., Am. Arbitration Assn. (dir.), Fla. Bar (gov. 1966-74, exec. com. 1972-73); hon. mem. Soc. Wig and Robe, Iron Arrow, Phi Alpha Delta. Home: 90 Edgewater Dr apt 614 Coral Gables FL 33133 Office: 1110 Courthouse 73 W Flagler St Miami FL 33130 Tel (305) 579-5426

SILVERBERG, HERBERT MYRON, b. Phila., Jan. 24, 1939; B.A., U. Pa., 1961, J.D., 1968. Admitted to D.C. bar, 1968; assoc. firm Covington & Burling, Washington, 1968-72; chief mental health div. Pub. Defender Service D.C., Washington, 1972-74; dir. Am. Bar Assn. Commn. on the Mentally Disabled, Washington, 1974-76; asso. prof. lectr. law and forensic sci. George Washington U., 1973-76; research asso. U. N.Mex. Law Sch., Albuquerque, 1976—; mem. Mental Health Rules Advisory Com., D.C. Superior Ct., 1973-76; cons. HEW. Mem. Charles County (Md.) Mental Health Com., and Drug Abuse Com., 1969-73. Mem. D.C. Bar Assn. Author: Protecting the Legal Rights of the Mentally Handicapped, 1975; contbr. article in field to law jours. Home: 1019 Bishop's Lodge Rd Santa Fe NM 87501 Office: U of N Mex Law Sch Albuquerque NM 87131

SILVERBERG, JOSEPH HELLER, b. Milw., Dec. 21, 1929; B.S., U. Wis., 1952, LL.D., 1954. Admitted to Wis. bar, 1954; asso. atty. Maurice B. Pasch, Madison, Wis., 1954-55; atty. Manpower Inc. of Madison, 1957—. Pres. Madison Central YMCA, 1975. Mem. State Bar Wis., Nat., Wis. assns. temporary services, Nat. Employment Assn. (dir. 1969-73), Wis. Assn. Employment Agys. (pres. 1968). Home: 4905 Holiday Dr Madison WI 53711 Office: PO Box 911 115 E Main St Madison WI 53701 Tel (608) 257-1057

SILVERBERG, LEWIS HENRY, b. Los Angeles, Nov. 1, 1934; B.A., Pomona Coll., 1955; J.D., U. Calif. at Los Angeles, 1958. Admitted to Calif. bar, 1959; partner firm Fredman, Karpinski, Silverberg & Shenas, San Diego, 1961-65, Fredman & Silverberg, 1965-71, Fredman, Silverberg & Lewis, Inc., 1971—; inheritance tax referee for State of Calif., 1971—; dir. San Diego County Bldg. Contractors, 1975-76. Bd. dirs. Inst. Burn Medicine, 1972-75; pres. San Diego exec. council City of Hope, 1975-76; mem. alumni council Pomona Coll., 1971-75. Mem. Calif., San Diego County Bar Assns. Home: 9430 Loren Dr LaMesa CA 92041 Office: 3252 5th Ave San Diego CA 92103 Tel (714) 291-3434

SILVERBERG, MICHAEL JOEL, b. Rochester, N.Y., Aug. 12, 1932; B.A., U. Rochester, 1954; LL.B., Columbia, 1957; postgrad. (Fulbright scholar), U. Strasbourg (France), 1958-59. Admitted to N.Y. bar, 1958, U.S. Supreme Ct. bar, 1967; instr. Columbia Law Sch., 1957-58; asso. firm Phillips, Nizer, Benjamin, Krim, & Ballon, N.Y.C., 1960-67, partner, 1967—. Active Miss. Vol. Service, Lawyers Com. for Civil Rights Under Law, 1965; mem. N.Y.C. exec. bd. Am. Jewish Com., 1970—, mem. nat. exec. council, 1971—. Mem. Am., N.Y. State bar assns., Assn. Bar City N.Y. Office: 40 W 57th St New York City NY 10019 Tel (212) 977-9700

SILVERBERG, NATHAN SHANON, b. Warsaw, Poland, Sept. 9, 1900; came to U.S., 1905; LL.B., U. Buffalo, 1925. Admitted to N.Y. bar, 1926, U.S. Supreme Ct. bar, 1951; partner firm Silverberg, Silverberg, Yood & Sellers, Buffalo. Mem. Am., Erie County bar assns. Office: 615 Brisbane Bldg Buffalo NY 14203 Tel (716) 854-6495

SILVERBERG, SHELDON, b. N.Y.C., Apr. 19, 1929; LL.B., Brooklyn Law Sch., 1951. Admitted to N.Y. bar, 1951, U.S. Dist. Ct. for So. Dist. N.Y. bar, 1954, U.S. Dist. Ct. for Eastern Dist. N.Y. bar, 1955, U.S. Ct. Appeal for 2d Circuit, 1959; asso. firm Schwartz & Stoll, N.Y.C., 1951-54; asso. firm Ruben Schwartz, N.Y.C., 1954-66, partner firm Ruben Schwartz & Silverberg, N.Y.C., 1966—. Counsel Jewish Community Council Oceanside, N.Y., 1975—, pres., 1977—. Trustee Temple Avodah, Oceanside, 1973-75. Mem. N.Y. County Lawyers Assn., Decorum Credit Club (sec.), Manhattan Credit Group (treas.). Office: 450 7th Ave New York City NY 10001 Tel (212) 695-3550

SILVERBLATT, ARTHUR, b. Wilkes-Barre, Pa., July 27, 1910; A.B. cum laude, Harvard, 1930, J.D., 1933. Admitted to Pa. bar, 1934, U.S. Dist. Ct., 1934; individual practice law, Wilkes-Barre, 1933-50; partner firm Silverblatt & Townend, Wilkes-Barre, 1950—; asst. dist. atty. Luzerne County (Pa.), 1939-49, 1st asst. dist. atty., 1955-59; dir. Northeastern Bank of Pa. Pres. Wyoming Valley United Fund, 1963-64; chmn. Luzerne County Bicentennial Commn; bd. dirs. Osterhout Free Library, Children's Service Center. Fellow Am. Bar Found.; mem. Am., Pa., Luzerne County (pres. 1970-71) bar assns., Pa. Def. Inst. Recipient certificate of recognition NCCJ, 1964, award Pa. Mental Health, Inc., 1966. Home: 192 James St Kingston PA 18704 Office: United Penn Bldg Wilkes Barre PA 18701 Tel (717) 823-5181

SILVERMAN, ALBERT ALAN, b. Copenhagen, Oct. 14, 1908; J.D., Loyola U., Chgo., 1940. Admitted to Ill. bar, 1940, Wis. bar, 1959, U.S. Supreme Ct. bar, 1960; chmn., pres., chief counsel Vilter Mfg. Corp., Milw., 1945—. Mem. Wis. Devel. Authority, 1969-70, Milw. City Devel. Com., 1965-70. Mem. Am., Wis., Milw., Ill., Chgo. bar assns., Heating, Refrigerating and Air Conditioning Engrs., Master Brewers Assn. Am., Milw. Assn. Commerce, Zool. Soc. Milw. County. Named Man of Year, Milw. chpt. Unico Nat., 1967; recipient Francis J. Mooney-St. Thomas More award Loyola U. Sch. Law, Chgo., 1974, Community Relations award Milw. Police Chief, 1974. Office: 2217 S 1st St Milwaukee WI 53207 Tel (414) 744-0111

SILVERMAN, BENNET HUGH, b. Bklyn., Oct. 6, 1938; A.B., Columbia, 1959; J.D., 1962. Admitted to N.Y. bar, 1963, U.S. Supreme Ct. bar, 1967, U.S. Customs Ct., 1970, U.S. Ct. of Mil. Appeals, 1967; partner firm Katz, Wittenberg, Levine & Silverman, N.Y.C., 1963—. Mem. Internat., Am., N.Y., N.Y.C. bar assns. Home: 105 Manor Dr White Plains NY 10603 Office: 370 Lexington Ave New York City NY 10017 Tel (212) 725-1616

SILVERMAN, BRIAN CHARLES, b. Chgo., Aug. 2, 1943; B.A., Roosevelt U., 1969; J.D., DePaul U., 1971. Admitted to Ill. bar, 1971, Mass. bar, 1972; with Cook County (Ill.) Pub. Defender's Office, Chgo., 1972—, supr. Felony Trial div., 1976—; faculty Nat. Coll. Criminal Def. Lawyers and Pub. Defenders, Houston, 1977. Pres., Walpole Point Homeowners Assn., 1975-76. Mem. Ill., Am. bar assns., Decalogue Soc. Home: 2020 N Larrabee St Chicago IL 60614 Office: 1500 Maybrook Dr Maywood IL 60153

SILVERMAN, GEORGE B., b. Maywood, Ill., Nov. 26, 1924; B.S., U. Ill., 1948; J.D., Chgo. Kent Coll. Law, 1969. Admitted to Ill. bar, 1969; pres. Silverwood Ins. Agy., Oak Park, Ill., 1957-63; gen. counsel, sec. Heritage Ins. Group, Lincolnwood, Ill., 1961—; partner firm Udoni, Silverman, Connelly & Gaines, Chgo., 1972—. Mem. Chgo., Ill. bar assns., Maywood C. of C. (chmn. 1963-66). Office: 221 N La Salle Chicago IL 60601 Tel (312) 332-5240

SILVERMAN, LEON, b. N.Y.C., June 9, 1921; B.A., Bklyn. Coll., 1942; LL.B., Yale, 1948; postgrad. London Sch. Econs., 1948-49. Admitted to N.Y. bar, 1949; asso. firm Riegelman, Strasser, Schwartz & Spiegelberg, N.Y.C., 1949-53; asst. U.S. atty. So. Dist. N.Y., 1953-55, asst. dep. atty. gen. Dept. Justice, Washington, 1958-59; partner firm Fried, Frank, Harris, Shriver & Jacobson, N.Y.C., 1960—; counsel N.Y. Gov.'s Com. to Rev. N.Y. Laws and Procedure in the Area of Human Rights, 1967-68, Com. to Rev. Legis. and Jud. Salaries, 1972-73; mem. adv. com. on criminal rules to com. on rules of practice and procedure Jud. Conf. U.S.; pres. N.Y. Legal Aid Soc., 1970-72, dir., 1966—. Fellow Am. Coll. Trial Lawyers; mem. Am. Law Inst., Practising Law Inst. (trustee), Assn. Bar City N.Y. (exec. com.), N.Y. State, Fed., Am. bar assns., Fed. Bar Council. Home: 16 Oak Dr Great Neck NY 11021 Office: 120 Broadway New York City NY 10005 Tel (212) 964-6500

SILVERMAN, OWEN ALEXANDER, b. Pitts., Sept. 25, 1935; student U. Pitts., 1953-55; B.S., U. Calif., Los Angeles, 1957, LL.B., 1960, J.D., 1968; postgrad. U. So. Calif., 1961-63. Civic salesman Greater Pitts. C. of C., 1953-55; rep. Joseph Struhl Co., Pitts., 1954-55; salesman Innes div. Genesco, Los Angeles, 1956-60; accountant Berdner Tempkin Ziskin Matzher & Kahn, C.P.A.'s., Los Angeles, 1957, Lefkowitz Burke Parker & Freedman, C.P.A.'s., Los Angeles, 1957, Leonard Jacobson, C.P.A., Los Angeles, 1957, Alexander Grant & Co., Los Angeles, 1960; admitted to Calif. bar, 1961, U.S. Supreme Ct. bar, 1972; dep. dist. atty. County of Los Angeles, 1961-62; asso. firm LeRoy Center, Redondo Beach, Calif., 1962-64; sr. partner firm Owen A. Silverman, and predecessor, Lawndale, Calif., 1964-72, Torrance, Calif., 1973—, pres., 1973—; arbitrator Am. Arbitration Assn., 1964—; judge pro tempore South Bay Municipal Ct., Torrance, 1966. Mem. Assn. Trial Lawyers Am., Calif., Los Angeles and Orange County trial lawyers assns., Los Angeles County, South Bay bar assns., Dist. Attys. Assn., U. Calif. Los Angeles Alumni Assn., Phi Alpha Delta. Office: 23224 Crenshaw Blvd Torrance CA 90505 Tel (213) 420-3990

SILVERMAN, RAMON ALVIN, b. Savannah, Ga., June 24, 1931; J.D., U. Ga., 1954. Admitted to Ga. bar, 1955, Fed. bar, 1958; partner firm Silverman & Silverman, Savannah, 1955-66; chief condemnation Savannah Dist. C.E., Savannah, 1966-75; partner firm Neiman & Silverman, Savannah, 1975—. Mem. Fed., Ga., Savannah bar assns., Comml. Law League Am., Ga. Trial Lawyers Assn. Home: 4653 Cumberland Dr Savannah GA 31045 Office: PO Box 9711 5 Bull St Savannah GA 31402 Tel (912) 234-3421

SILVERMAN, REBECCA AXELROD, b. Lutsk, Russia, Nov. 20, 1903; came to U.S., 1906, naturalized, 1912; A.B., N.Y. State Tchrs. Coll., 1924; LL.B., Albany Law Sch. Union U., 1928, J.D., 1968. Admitted to N.Y. State bar, 1928; partner firm Silverman & Silverman, Glen Falls, N.Y., 1930—. Mem. Zoning Bd. Appeals Glens Falls, 1966—, Youth Council Glens Falls, 1958—. Home: 14 Cunningham Ave Glens Falls NY 12801 Office: 110 Glen St Glens Falls NY 12801 Tel (518) 792-1722

SILVERMAN, RONALD I., b. Big Spring, Tex., Aug. 30, 1939; B.A., U. Calif., Los Angeles, 1961, J.D., 1966. Admitted to Calif. bar, 1967; corporate atty. firm O'Melveny & Myers, Los Angeles, 1966-69; corp. real estate atty. firm Aaronson, Weil & Friedman, Los Angeles, 1969-71; real estate atty. firm Cox, Castle, Nicholson & Weekes, Los Angeles, 1973-76; dir. N.Am. ops. Pacific Hotels & Devel. Ltd., London, 1971-73. Bd. dirs. Humanistic Law Inst. Mem. Am., Los Angeles County bar assns., Assn. Real Estate Attys., Am. Land Devel. Assn. (condominium com.). Office: Suite 2800 2049 Century Park East Los Angeles CA 90067 Tel (213) 277-4222

SILVERS, BERNARD ARNOLD, b. Bklyn., July 19, 1929; B.A., U. Calif., Los Angeles, 1954; J.D., Loyola U., Los Angeles, 1967. Accountant, various C.P.A. firm, Los Angeles, 1960-67; admitted to Calif. bar, 1967; asso. firm Olincy & Olincy, Westwood, Calif., 1967-71; individual practice law, Beverly Hills, Calif., 1971—. Mem. Calif., Los Angeles, Beverly Hills bar assns. Recipient Am. Jurisprudence prize in code pleading. Tel (213) 655-2816

SILVERSTEIN, CARL J., b. N.Y.C., Nov. 18, 1928; B.A., Syracuse U., 1950; LL.B., Bklyn. Law Sch., 1958, J.D., 1967. Admitted to N.Y. bar, 1958; asso. firm Turetzky, Cohen & Rosen, Monticello, N.Y., 1959-63; partner firm Cohen & Silverstein, Monticello, 1963—; asst. dist. atty. Sullivan County (N.Y.), 1964-71. Pres., Jewish Community Center, Monticello, 1964-65, Temple Sholom, Monticello, 1972-74; chmn. Village of Monticello Neighborhood Youth Facility, 1975-76. Mem. N.Y. State, Sullivan County bar assns., N.Y. State Trial Lawyers Assn. Office: 250 Broadway PO Box 552 Monticello NY 12701 Tel (914) 794-5533

SILVERSTEIN, LOUIS ARTHUR, b. Ansonia, Conn., Jan. 18, 1921; B.A., Yale, 1941, LL.B., 1948. Admitted to Conn. bar, 1948; asso. firm Herman D. Silberberg, Ansonia, 1948-55; partner Silberberg & Silverstein, Ansonia, 1955-69; individual practice law, Ansonia, 1969—; judge City Ct. Ansonia, 1955-59. Mem. Am., Conn., Valley bar assns., Comml. Law League Am., Conn. Trial Lawyers Assn. Office: 252 Main St Ansonia CT 06401 Tel (203) 734-5439

SIMBURG, MELVYN JAY, b. San Francisco, June 15, 1946; A.B., U. Calif., Berkeley, 1968; J.D., Columbia, 1972, M. Internat. Affairs, 1972. Admitted to Wash. bar, 1972; asso. firm Perkins, Coie, Stone, Olsen & Williams, Seattle, 1972-76; adj. prof. Law Sch. U. Puget Sound, Tacoma, 1972-74; individual practice law, Seattle, 1974—. Pres., Leschi Improvement Council, Seattle; active Seattle Film Soc., Seattle Art Museum. Mem. Seattle-King County, Wash., Am. bar assns., World Trade Club Seattle, World Affairs Council Seattle. Contbr. Columbia Jour. Law and Social Home: 235 Lake Dell Ave Seattle WA 98122 Office: suite 220 Grand Central on Park St Seattle WA 98104 Tel (206) 622-6150

SIMEONE, JOSEPH JOHN, b. Quincy, Ill., Oct. 8, 1921; J.D., Washington U., St. Louis, 1946; B.S., St. Louis U., 1953; LL.M., U. Mich., 1956, S.J.D., 1962. Admitted to Mo. bar, 1946, Ill. bar, 1946; asst. prof. law St. Louis U., 1947-50, asso. prof., 1950-57, prof., 19S7-71; judge Mo. Ct. Appeals, St. Louis Dist., 1972—. Mem. Mo. Bar, Bar Assn. Met. St. Louis. Recipient Smithson award Mo. Bar, 1976. Home: 405 Newport St Webster Groves MO 63119 Office: Civil Cts Bldg 12th and Market Sts Saint Louis MO 63101 Tel (314) 453-4609

SIMHAUSER, WALTER JAMES, b. Bloomington, Ill., May 1, 1918; student Ill. Wesleyan U., 1936-38, Iowa State U., 1939; LL.B., Lincoln Coll. Law, 1948. Admitted to Ill. bar, 1948; city atty. Springfield (Ill.), 1969-72; individual practice law, Springfield, 1949—. Mem. Assn. Trial Lawyers Am., Ill. Trial Lawyers Assn., Am., Ill. State, Sangamon County bar assns. Home: 1208 S MacArthur Blvd Springfield IL 62704 Office: 522 E Monroe St Springfield IL 62701 Tel (217) 528-5627

SIMMONDS, JAMES HENRY, b. Lynchburg, Va., Apr. 19, 1905; B.S., U. Va., 1927, LL.B. (now J.D.), 1930; LL.M., Columbia U., 1931. Admitted to Va. bar, 1929, N.Y. bar, 1932, D.C. bar, 1933; asso. firm Root, Clark, Buckner & Ballantine, N.Y.C., 1931-33; asst. commonwealth atty. Arlington County (Va.), 1933-39; partner firm Simmonds, Coleburn, Towner, Carman & Evans, Arlington, Va., 1939—. Fellow Am. Coll. Trial Lawyers, Am. Bar Found.; mem. Am., Va., Arlington County (pres. 1948) bar assns., Va. State Bar (pres. 1958-59), Order of Coif, Phi Beta Kappa, Phi Delta Phi. Asso. editor: Va. Law Review, 1929-30. Home: 3615 N 27th St Arlington VA 22207 Office: 1500 N Courthouse Rd Arlington VA 22201 Tel (703) 525-7700

SIMMONS, HOWARD K., b. Providence, R.I., May 29, 1902; LL.B., Boston U., 1924. Admitted to R.I. Bar, 1925, U.S. Dist. Ct. for R.I. bar, 1926; asso. firm Walling and Walling, Providence, 1925-29; individual practice law, Providence, 1929—. Mem. R.I. Integrated Bar, R.I. Bar Assn., Am. Trial Lawyers Assn., R.I. Def. Attys. Assn. Home and office: 31 Tanglewood Dr East Providence RI 02915 Tel (401) 433-1420

SIMMONS, J. EARL, JR., b. Phila., Dec. 19, 1932; A.B., St. Joseph's Coll., 1954; J.D., U. Pa., 1957. Admitted to Pa. bar, 1958; individual practice law, Phila., 1958-68; judge Phila. Municipal Ct., 1968—. Mem. Phila., Pa., Am. bar assns., Pa. Conf. of State Trial Judges, Am. Judicature Soc., Am. Judges Assn. Office: 518 City Hall Philadelphia PA 19107 Tel (215) 686-7906

SIMMONS, JUDSON HAWK, b. Atlanta, Feb. 20, 1946; B.S., U. Nottingham (Eng.) and Washington and Lee U., 1969; J.D., U. Ga., 1972; certificate Parker Sch. of Fgn. and Comparative Law, Columbia, 1976. Admitted to Ga. bar, 1973; law clk, to judge 5th Circuit Ct. of Appeals, Miami, Fla., 1972-73; asso. firm Kilpatrick, Cody, Rogers, McClatchey & Regenstein, Atlanta, 1973—; asso. in law Columbia, 1975—. Mem. Am., Ga., Atlanta bar assns., Am. Assn. Law Sch. Profs. Contbr. articles to profl. jours. Office: 3100 Equitable Bldg 100 Peachtree St Atlanta GA 30303 Tel (404) 522-3100

SIMMONS, LAWRENCE JAMES, b. Kaysville, Utah, Mar. 24, 1910; J.D., U. Utah, 1933. Admitted to Utah bar, 1936, U.S. Dist. Ct. bar for D.C., 1938, U.S. Supreme Ct. bar, 1947; individual practice law, Washington, 1938—. Mem. D.C., Utah bar assns. Home: 4852 Bayard Blvd Crestview MD 20016 Office: 1120 19th St NW Washington DC 20036 Tel (202) 833-9230

SIMMONS, LOUIS F., JR., b. 1930; LL.B., U. Detroit, 1958. Pres., Detroit Bar Assn., 1977—. Office: 2163 Guardian Bldg Detroit MI 48226*

SIMMONS, MAX E., b. Monon, Ind., May 29, 1942; B.S. in Bus., Ind. U.; J.D., U. Louisville. Admitted to Ky. bar, 1972; law clk. Jefferson (Ky.) Circuit Ct., 1970-72; individual practice law, Louisville, 1972—. Mem. Ky., Am., Louisville bar assns. Home: 9822 Vieux Carre Dr Louisville KY 40223 Office: 140 Chenweth Ln Louisville KY 40207 Tel (502) 897-1123

SIMMONS, RAYMOND HEDELIUS, b. San Francisco, Sept. 27, 1930; student City Coll. San Francisco, 1948-50; A.A., U. Calif., Berkeley, 1952; J.D., U. San Francisco, 1955. Admitted to Calif. bar, 1955; individual practice law, San Francisco, 1956-58; asso. firm Stave and Bryan, Salinas, Calif., 1958-59; dep. dist. atty. Monterey County (Calif.), 1960-62; asso. firm Thomás, Muller & Pia, Salinas, 1962-64; partner firm Muller, Pia & Simmons, Salinas, 1964-74; judge Municipal Ct., Salinas Jud. Dist., 1974—; instr. police officers' tng. course in criminal law Hartnell Coll., Salinas, 1961-65; instr. criminal law and procedure to Hwy. Patrol Officers, Salinas, 1969. Mem. Monterey County Water Recreation Adv. Commn., 1962-66; head Monterey County March of Dimes Campaign, 1962, Salinas YMCA Fund Dr., 1971; bd. dirs. Savawork Enterprises, 1970-72; lay adv. bd. Palma High Sch., 1973-74; mem. com. Calif. Rodeo Assn., 1959-74. Mem. State Bar Calif. (exec. council conf. of barristers 1960-64), Monterey County Bar Assn. (sec. 1966-67). Office: Monterey County Courthouse Salinas CA 93901 Tel (408) 424-8611

SIMMONS, ROBERT LEE, b. Charlevoix, Mich., June 30, 1927; A.B. in Philosophy, U. Mich., 1949; J.D. cum laude, Cleve. State U., 1957; grad. Nat. Coll. State Trial Judges, 1966. Admitted to Ohio bar, 1957, Calif. bar, 1974; atty. Lambros & Simmons, Painesville, Ohio, 1957-65; judge Lake County (Ohio) Common Pleas Ct., 1965-70, 75-76; asso. prof. law Cleve. State U., 1970-72; asso. prof. U. San Diego, 1972-74, prof., 1976—; law dir. City of Mentor (Ohio), 1970-72, City of Eastlake (Ohio), 1975. Bd. dirs. Lake County Center for Alcoholism and Drug Abuse, 1972-76. Mem. San Diego County, Ohio State, Calif. bar assns. Author: Winning to the Court, 1971; Winning Before Trial, 1973. Office: U San Diego Sch Law Alcala Park San Diego CA 92119 Tel (714) 291-6480

SIMMONS, SHERWIN PALMER, b. Bowling Green, Ky., Jan. 19, 1931; A.B., Columbia U., 1952, LL.B., 1954, J.D., 1969. Admitted to Tenn. bar, 1954, Fla. bar, 1957; partner firm Fowler, White, Collins, Gillen, Humkey & Trenam, Tampa, Fla., 1956-69; partner firm Trenam, Simmons, Kemker, Scharf & Barkin, Tampa, 1970—; atty. advisor U.S. Tax Ct., Washington, 1954-56. Gov., Central Fla. dist. Sertoma Internat., 1966-67, Dist. Gov.'s award, 1967; trustee Hillsborough County Soc. Crippled Children & Adults, 1956-65, pres., 1960-61; treas. Hillsborough County Pub. Edn. Study Commn., 1965-66; mem. adv. bd. Salvation Army, 1959-62, 64-66, sec., 1960-61. Fellow Am. Coll. Probate Counsel, Am. Bar Found.; mem. Am. (vice chmn. adminstrn. taxation sect. 1972-75, chmn., 1975-76), Fed. bar assns., Fla. Bar (chmn. taxation sect. 1964-65), Am. Law Inst., Am. Judicature Soc., So. Fed. Tax Inst. (trustee; pres. 1974, chmn. 1975), Internat. Acad. Estate and Trust Law. Author: Federal Taxation of Life Insurance, 1966; contbr. articles profl. jours. Home: 3010 Samara Dr Tampa FL 33618 Office: First Florida Tower PO Box 1102 Tampa FL 33602 Tel (813) 223-7474

SIMMONS, THOMAS EVERETT, b. Grand Forks, N.D., July 15, 1937; B.S., U. S.D., 1960, LL.B., 1961. Admitted to S.D. bar, 1961; partner firm Bangs, McCullen, Butler, Foye & Simmons, Rapid City, S.D., 1961—. Mem. Am., Pennington County (pres. 1974) bar assns., Fedn. Ins. Counsel, S.D. Bd. Bar Examiners (chmn. 1976). Home: 209 S Berry Pine Rd Rapid City SD 57701 Office: 818 Saint Joe St Rapid City SD 57701 Tel (605) 343-1040

SIMMS, ARTHUR EDWARD, JR., b. Cainey Springs, Tenn., Dec. 16, 1920; LL.B., Cumberland U., 1945; J.D., Samford U., 1969. Admitted to Tenn. bar, 1945; claim specialist Tenn. Dept. Vet. Affairs, Nashville, 1945-51; judge Ct. Gen. Sessions, Lincoln County, Tenn., 1951-52; partner firm Simms & Simms, Fayetteville, Tenn., 1952—. Mem. Fayetteville (Tenn.) Bd. Zoning Appeals, 1967-69. Mem. Fayetteville, Lincoln County, Tenn. (ho. of dels. 1974-76) bar assns. Home: Huntsville Hwy Fayetteville TN 37334 Office: 101 N Main Ave Fayetteville TN 37334

SIMMS, CHARLES WILLIAM, b. Balt., Sept. 29, 1944; A.A., Catonsville Community Coll., 1964; J.D., U. Balt., 1967. Admitted to Md. bar, 1972, U.S. Dist. Ct. bar, 1974, U.S. Supreme Ct. bar, 1976; staff atty. Amoco Oil Co., Balt., 1973-76; asso. firm Arnold, Beauchemin & Huber, Balt., 1976-77; asst. corporate counsel EASCO Corp., Balt., 1977—. Mem. Md. Bar Assn. Home: 10076 Century Dr Ellicott City MD 21043 Office: 21st Floor Arlington Fed Bldg 201 N Charles St Baltimore MD 21201

SIMMS, JOHN GOVAN, b. Barnwell, S.C., Jan. 21, 1899; LL.B., U. S.C., 1919. Admitted to S.C. bar, 1919, Fla. bar, 1927; practiced in Barnwell, 1919-23; atty. prohibition unit IRS, Washington, 1923-25, rent atty., until 1947; individual practice law, Orlando, Fla., 1925-37, Miami, Fla., 1937-42, 47—. Mem. Fla. Bar. Office: 18005 SW 157th Ave Miami FL 33187 Tel (305) 235-2178

SIMMS, MICHAEL ALAN, b. Cleve., Mar. 29, 1948; B.A. in Econs., Ohio State U., 1970; J.D. magna cum laude, Capital U., 1973. Admitted to Ohio bar, 1973, U.S. Dist. Ct. for No. Ohio bar, 1973, U.S. 6th Circuit Ct. Appeals bar, 1975; legal intern atty. gen.'s office, State of Ohio, 1972-73; partner firm Banaceau, Brown & Hausler, Cleve., 1973—; instr. Ohio Para-legal Inst., Cleve., 1974—. Mem. Am., Ohio State, Cleve. bar assns., Comml. Law League, K.P., Phi Alpha Delta. Home: 4050 Linnell Rd South Euclid OH 44121 Office: 1501 Euclid Ave Suite 730 Cleveland OH 44115 Tel (216) 696-3111

SIMOLA, TED ORESTE, b. Trinidad, Colo., May 4, 1940; B.S., U. Wyo., 1964, J.D., 1966. Admitted to Iowa bar, 1966, Wyo. bar, 1967; asst. atty. Laramie County (Wyo.), Cheyenne, 1967-70, prosecuting atty., 1967—, dep. atty., 1971—. Bd. dirs. Cheyenne Community Action Program; bd. advisors bus. coll. Laramie Community Coll., Cheyenne. Mem. Am. Wyo., Iowa bar assns. Office: 1912 Capitol Ave Cheyenne WY 82001 Tel (307) 632-6468

SIMON, ERNEST DANIEL, b. Chgo., Feb. 8, 1935; B.A., U. Ill., 1956; J.D., Northwestern U., 1960. Admitted to Ill. bar, 1960; asso. firms Horka & Lindell, Chgo., 1960-63, Arthur B. Sacks, Chgo., 1963-64; partner firm Loundy & Simon, Chgo., 1964-69; asso. firm Greenbaum & Browne, Chgo., 1969—. Office: 180 N LaSalle St Chicago IL 60601 Tel (312) 782-8300

SIMON, H. LEON, b. Aurora, Ill., Mar. 21, 1938; B.S., Ariz. State Coll., 1961; J.D., U. Ill., 1967. Admitted to Ill. bar, 1967, Nev. bar, 1968; atty. State Securities Commn., Springfield, Ill., 1967; dep. pub. defender Clark County (Nev.), 1968-69, juvenile referee, 1969-72, dep. dist. atty., 1972-72, chief dep. dist. atty., 1975—. Chmn., Anti-Defamation League, Springfield, 1967. Mem. Ill., Nev. bar assns. Office: 200 E Carson Las Vegas NV 89101 Tel (702) 386-4011

SIMON, HERMANN ERNST, b. Frankfurt-on-Main, Germany, Oct. 11, 1900; LL.D., U. Frankfurt-Main, 1924, N.Y. U., 1941. Admitted to N.Y. bar, 1943; partner firms Loewenthal, Rheinstein and Simon, Frankfurt-on-Main, 1926-33, Fried, Frank, Harris, Shriver and Jacobson, N.Y.C., 1947—. Mem. Assn. Bar City N.Y., New York County Lawyers Assn., Am., Internat. bar assns. Office: 120 Broadway New York City NY 10005 Tel (212) 964-6500

SIMON, H(UEY) PAUL, b. Lafayette, La., Oct. 19, 1923; B.S., U. Southwestern La., 1943; J.D., Tulane U., 1947. Admitted to La. bar, 1947, U.S. Ct. Appeals 5th Circuit bar, 1957, U.S. Supreme Ct. bar, 1968; asst. prof. advanced accounting U. Southwestern La., 1944-45; principal Haskins & Sells, C.P.A.'s, New Orleans, 1945-57; sr. partner firm Deutsch, Kerrigan & Stiles, New Orleans, 1957—. Mem. Am. Judicature Soc., New Orleans Assn. Notaries, Am. Assn. Atty. C.P.A.'s, Am. Inst. C.P.A.'s, Soc. La. C.P.A.'s, Am., Inter-Am., Internat., La., New Orleans bar assns. Mem. editorial bd. Tulane Law Review, 1945-47; asso. editor The Louisiana C.P.A., 1956-60. Home: 6075 Canal Blvd New Orleans LA 70124 Office: 4700 One Shell Square New Orleans LA 70139 Tel (504) 581-5141

SIMON, J. MINOS, b. Kaplan, La., Feb. 27, 1922; LL.B., La. State U., 1946. Admitted to La. bar, 1946, U.S. Supreme Ct. bar, 1960; individual practice law, Lafayette, La., 1946—. Mem. La. Bar Assn., La., Am. trial lawyers assns. Office: 1408 Pinhook Rd Lafayette LA 70501 Tel (318) 234-3263

SIMON, LAWRENCE PAUL, JR., b. New Iberia, La., Dec. 1, 1943; B.A. in Philosophy (cum laude), Notre Dame Sem. New Orleans, 1965; B.A. in Theology (magna cum laude), Cath. U. of Louvain (Belgium), 1967; J.D., Tulane U., 1972. Admitted to La. bar, 1972, Fed. bar, 1975; asso. prof. philosophy, theology Loyola U. of South, New Orleans, 1968; asso. firm Liskow & Lewis, Lafayette, La., 1972-75; partner firm Liskow & Lewis, Lafayette, 1976—. Mem. Lafayette Parish 15th Jud. Dist. (sec. 1975-76), La. (sec. young lawyers sect. 1976-77, sect. pres. elect 1977-78, bd. dirs. Young Lawyers Council 1975-76), Am. bar assns. Fellow Inst. Politics, New Orleans. Recipient Morrison award Tulane Law rev., 1972. Office: PO Box 52008 Lafayette LA 70505 Tel (318) 232-7424

SIMON, MARILYN, b. N.Y.C., Dec. 22, 1941; B.A., Bklyn. Coll., 1963; J.D., Seton Hall U., 1971. Asst. advt. mgr. Elizabeth Arden Sales Corp., N.Y.C., 1963-64; office mgr. Joseph E. Murray & Assos., San Francisco, 1964-67; v.p. in charge sales Battani, Ltd., N.Y.C., 1967-75; admitted to N.Y. bar, 1971, also fed. bars So. and Eastern dists. N.Y.; law clk. to Bankruptcy Judge Roy Babitt, So. Dist. N.Y., 1975; asso. firm Leinwand, Maron, Hendler & Krause, N.Y.C., 1975-76, Phillips, Nizer, Benjamin, Krim & Ballon, N.Y.C., 1976—. Mem. Am., N.Y. State bar assns. Home: 500 E 77th St New York City NY 10021 Office: 40 W 57th St New York City NY 10019 Tel (212) 977-9700

SIMON, MICHAEL K., b. Phila., Nov. 2, 1946; B.A. magna cum laude, Tufts U., 1968; J.D., U. Pa., 1971. Admitted to Pa. bar; law clk. to judge U.S. Dist. Ct. Eastern Dist. Pa., 1971-72; asso. with David Berger, Phila., 1972—. Mem. Am., Pa., Phila. bar assns. Home: 602 S Washington Sq Philadelphia PA 19106 Office: 1622 Locust St Philadelphia PA 19103 Tel (215) 732-8000

SIMON, SHERWIN O., b. Chgo., Mar. 6, 1915; ed. Northwestern U., Evanston, Ill., U. Ill.; LL.B., J.D., Chgo. Kent Coll. Law, 1941. Admitted to Ill. bar, 1941; partner firm Simon & DeMars, Chgo., 1946. Mem. Chgo. Bar Assn. Home: 3935 Jarvis St Lincolnwood IL 60645 Office: 100 W Monroe St Chicago IL 60603 Tel (312) 782-0172

SIMON, STANLEY C., b. Memphis, May 6, 1926; B.S. cum laude, N.Y. U., 1954; LL.B., U. Tenn., 1948. Admitted to Tenn. bar, 1947, Tex. bar, 1957, U.S. Supreme Ct. bar, 1953; tax accountant Lybrand Ross Bros. & Montgomery, N.Y.C., 1953-56, tax mgr., Dallas, 1956-61; mem. firm Atwell Grayson & Atwell, Dallas, 1961-69, Grayson & Simon, Dallas, 1969-73, Simon & Twombly, Dallas, 1974—; lectr. So. Meth. U. Sch. Law, 1969-74. Mem. Am., Dallas bar assns., State Bar Tex., Internat. Fiscal Assn., Internat. Tax Assn. Dallas, Profit Sharing Council Am. C.P.A., Tenn., Tex. Office: Suite 202 Two Turtle Creek Village Dallas TX 75219 Tel (214) 526-2590

SIMONDS, ALBERT RHETT, JR., b. Charleston, S.C., Feb. 5, 1943; B.A., U. N.C., 1965; J.D., U. Pa., 1968. Admitted to S.C. bar, 1969, D.C. bar, 1971; asst. counsel U.S. House Armed Services Investigating Subcom., Washington, 1969-70; asso. firm Debevoise & Liberman, Washington, 1970-74, partner, 1975—. Mem. Am., D.C., S.C., Fed. Power (treas. 1973—) bar assns. Home: 624 S Lee St Alexandria VA 22314 Office: 806 15th St NW Washington DC 20005 Tel (202) 393-2080

SIMONE, MARTIN MASSIMO, b. New Haven, Sept. 26, 1946; B.A. in History, Loyola U., Los Angeles, 1968, J.D., 1971. Admitted to Calif. bar, 1972; law clk., personal research atty. Judge Campbell M. Lucas, Los Angeles Superior Ct., 1972-74; asso. firm Schwartz, Steinsapir & Dohrmann, Los Angeles, 1974—. Mem. local sch. adv. bd., 1973-75. Mem. Los Angeles County, Calif., Am. bar assns., Lawyer's Club Los Angeles, Am. Judicature Soc. Contbr. article to Strikes, Stoppages and Boycotts, 1977. Home: 13120 Constable Granada Hills CA 91344 Office: 2049 Century Park E Suite 1900 Los Angeles CA 90067 Tel (213) 277-4400

SIMONEAUX, FRANK PAUL, b. Napoleonville, La., Oct. 30, 1933; student Nicholls State Coll., 1952-54; B.A. in Govt., La. State U., 1956, LL.B., 1961. Admitted to La. bar, 1961; asso. firm Breazeale, Sachse & Wilson, Baton Rouge, 1963-67, partner, 1967—; mem. La. Ho. of Reps., 1972—; mem. La. Legis. Council; lt. col. JAGC, La. NG, 1956—; participant Eagleton Inst. Politics, Rutgers U., 1974, State Dept. Conf., Washington, 1975. Pres. InterCivic Council, Baton Rouge, 1973. Mem. East Baton Rouge Parish, La. State, Am. bar assns., Council for a Better La., La. Law Inst., Baton Rouge C. of C. Home: 5921 Forsythia Ave Baton Rouge LA 70808 Office: PO Box 3197 Baton Rouge LA 70821 Tel (504) 387-4000

SIMONET, WILLIAM FLOYD, b. Orlando, Fla., July 12, 1932; B.A. (hon.), Weslyan U., 1954; J.D. with high honors, U. Fla., 1958. Admitted to Fla. bar, 1958; asso. firm Walton, Lantaff, Schroeder, Adkins, Carson & Wahl, Miami, Fla., 1958-61, Akerman, Senterfitt, Eidson & Mesmer, Orlando, 1961-62; partner firm Gray, Gray & Simonet, Orlando, 1962-68, Fishback, Davis, Dominick & Simonet, Orlando, 1971—; individual practice law, Orlando, 1968-71; chmn. relationship com. Orange County Lawyers and Realtors. Mem. Orange County, Fla., Am. bar assns., Orlando Area C. of C. (dir. 1975, chmn. of year 1973). Home: Route 4 Box 513 Orlando FL 32807 Office: 170 E Washington St Orlando FL 32801 Tel (305) 425-2786

SIMONS, CHARLES EARL, JR., b. Johnston, S.C., Aug. 17, 1916; A.B., U. S.C., 1937, LL.B. cum laude, 1939. Admitted to S.C. bar, 1939; mem. firm Lybrand, Simons and Rich, Aiken, S.C., 1939-64; judge U.S. Dist. Ct. S.C., Aiken, 1964—; mem. S.C. Ho. of Reps., 1942, 47-48, 1961-64, mem. ways and means com., 1947-48, 61-64; mem. S.C. Constl. Revision Com., 1948; del. U.S. Jud. Conf., 1973—. Mem. Am., S.C. (bd. discipline and grievance 1958-61) bar assns., Phi Beta Kappa. Recipient Algernon Sidney Sullivan award, 1937, 64. Home: 910 Valley Green Dr SW Aiken SC 29801 Office: US Court House Aiken SC 29801 Tel (803) 648-6896

SIMONS, JAMES MARCUS, b. Cleburne, Tex., May 6, 1939; LL.B., U. Tex., 1965. Admitted to Tex. bar, 1964, U.S. Supreme Ct. bar, 1970; asst. city atty., Pasadena, Tex., 1965-66; with Office of Inspection, U.S. OEO, Washington, 1966-68, mem. firm Simons, Cunningham, Coleman, Nelson & Howard, Austin, Tex., 1968—. Mem. Travis County, Fed. bar assns., State Bar Tex. Home: 804 Theresa Austin TX 78703 Office: 501 W 12th Austin TX 78701 Tel (512) 478-9332

SIMONS, MORTON LEONARD, b. Windsor, Ont., Can., Aug. 9, 1928; B.A., U. Mich., 1950, J.D., 1952. Admitted to N.Y. State bar, 1953, U.S. Supreme Ct. bar, 1958; asst. counsel N.Y. Pub. Service Commn., Albany, 1952-57; counsel Gas. Distbrs. Info. Service, D.C., 1957-61; partner firm Simons & Simons, D.C., 1962—; advisor Inst. for Pub. Interest Representation Georgetown U. Law Center, 1971—; pub. mem. Nat. Gas Survey, 1975—. Mem. Am. (mem. com. on law library of Congress), Fed. Power (chmn. com. on liaison with adminstrv. law judges) bar assns., Order Coif, Phi Beta Kappa, Phi Kappa Phi, Phi Eta Sigma. Bd. editors Mich. Law Review, 1951-52. Home: 3850 Tunlaw Rd NW Washington DC 20007 Office: 1629 K St NW Washington DC 20006 Tel (202) 293-1819

SIMONS, RICHARD DUNCAN, b. Niagara Falls, N.Y., Mar. 23, 1927; A.B., Colgate U., 1949; LL.B., U. Mich., 1952. Admitted to N.Y. bar, 1952; individual practice law, Rome, N.Y.; asst. corp. counsel City of Rome, 1955-58, corp. counsel, 1960-63; justice N.Y. Supreme Ct., 5th Dist., 1964—; asso. justice Appellate Div., 3d Dept., 1971-73, 4th Dept., 1973—. Mem. Rome, Oneida County (N.Y.), N.Y. State, Am. bar assns. Home: 1410 N George St Rome NY 13440 Office: Courthouse North James St Rome NY 13440 Tel (315) 336-6140

SIMONS, SHELDON MARVIN, b. Bklyn., Oct. 16, 1927; B.S., U. Miami, 1948; J.D., 1951; M.S. in Health Law, U. Pitts., 1972. Admitted to Fla. bar, 1951, N.Y. bar, 1952; partner firm Simons, Simons & Simons, Miami, Fla., 1951-73; individual practice law, Miami, 1973—; adj. prof. Fla. Internat. U., Miami; lectr. U. Pitts., 1971-72; instr. Miami Dade Jr. Coll., 1973. Mem. hosp. services task force Comprehensive Health Planning Council S. Fla., Miami, 1973-75. Mem. Am. Arbitration Assn., Am. Soc. Hosp. Attys., Fla. Assn. Hosp. Attys. (past pres.), Nat. Health Lawyers Assn., Fla. Bar Assn. Contbr. articles to med. and legal jours. Columnist health law Medico. Home: 4808 Granada Blvd Coral Gables FL 33146 Office: 3661 S Miami Ave Suite 507 Miami FL 33133 Tel (305) 856-9350

SIMONS, WILLIAM BRADFORD, b. Dodgeville, Wis., June 24, 1949; B.A. cum laude, Carleton Coll., 1967; M.A. cum laude in Russian Lang. and Lit., Norwich U., 1974; J.D., U. Wis. at Madison, 1974. Admitted to Wis. bar, 1974; fgn. service staff officer USIA, Soviet Union, 1975; mem. staff Documentation Bur. E. European Law, U. Leiden Law Sch. (Netherlands), 1976—. Mem. Am. Bar Assn., Am. Assn. Advancement Slavic Studies, Am. Soc. Internat. Law. Asst. editor Rev. Socialist Law, 1976—; contbr. articles to legal jours. Home: 448 Prairie Ave Fond du Lac WI 54935 Office: Documentation Bureau for East European Law Rapenburg 82 Leiden The Netherlands

SIMONS, WILLIAM WALTER, b. N.Y.C., Mar. 13, 1928; B.A., Washington Sq. Coll., N.Y. U., 1950; J.D., N.Y. U., 1954. Admitted to N.Y. bar, 1954, Mass. bar, 1960, U.S. Supreme Ct. bar, 1961; asso. firm Moses & Singer, N.Y.C., 1954-60, Albert Silverman, Pittsfield, Mass., 1960-62; individual practice law, Pittsfield, 1962-70; partner firm Simons & Cook, Pittsfield, 1970—; asst. dist. atty. Western Dist. Mass., 1968-72; mem. hearing com. Mass. Bd. Bar Overseers, 1975—. Mem. Mass., N.Y. State, Berkshire (pres. 1972-73) bar assns., Am. Trial Lawyers Assn. Home: 43 Commonwealth Ave Pittsfield MA 01201 Office: 28 North St Pittsfield MA 01201 Tel (413) 499-0316

SIMPKINS, LLOYD LEWIS, b. Mt. Vernon, Md., June 6, 1920; B.S. in Agr., U. Md., 1947, LL.B., 1952, J.D., 1969. Admitted to Md. bar, 1952; individual practice law, Princess Anne, Md., 1952-71; judge Dist. Ct. of Md., 1971-75, Md. 1st Jud. Circuit, 1975—; mem. Md. Ho. of Dels., 1950-58; asst. Gov. of Md., 1958-61; sec. State of Md., 1961-67. Home: Route 1 Princess Anne MD 21853 Office: Courthouse Princess Anne MD 21853 Tel (301) 651-1630

SIMPKINS, LOY MURL, b. Carter, Okla., Apr. 13, 1936; B.S. cum laude, Southwestern State Coll., Weatherford, Okla., 1955; J.D., U. Okla., 1958. Admitted to Okla. bar, 1958, Tex. bar, 1967, U.S. Supreme Ct. bar, 1971; practiced in Elk City, Okla., 1958-65; asst. prof. law Baylor U., 1965-68, asso. prof., 1968-69, prof., 1969—. Mem. Nat. Council Family Relations (affiliate), Okla. Bar Assn., State Bar Tex. Author: Cases on Domestic Relations, 1967, rev. edits., 1970, 75; (with McSwain and Norvell) Cases and Materials for Texas Land Practice, 1967; Marriage Counseling for Texas?, 1969; (with McSwain and Wendorf) Cases and Materials on Trust and Probate Administration, 1971; Texas Family Law, 5 vols., 1976. Home: 1016 Hummingbird Ln Waco TX 76710 Office: Baylor U Sch of Law Waco TX 76703 Tel (817) 755-3611

SIMPSON, ALDO J., b. Millersburg, Ind., Aug. 4, 1892; J.D., Valparaiso Ind., 1914. Admitted to Ind. bar, 1914; mem. firm Vail & Simpson, Goshen, Ind., 1920-27; mem. firm Vail, Simpson & Firestone, Goshen, 1928; individual practice law, Goshen, 1919-32, 76—; judge Elkhart Circuit Ct., Goshen, 1932-76; chmn. bd. dirs. Salem Bank & Trust; dep. pros. atty., Goshen, 1917-22, city atty., 1926-30. Precinct committeeman Republican com., 1951; Rep. county chmn., Elkhart County, 1922-29; Rep. city chmn., Goshen, 1925-29. Mem. Elkhart County, Goshen, Ind. State bar assns., Am. Judicature Soc., Assn. of Trial Lawyers of Am., Ind. Judges Assn. Recipient Silver Beaver award Boy Scouts Am., Others award Salvation Army. Home: 414 S 6th St Goshen IN 46526 Office: Shoots Bldg Goshen IN 46526 Tel (119) 533-7598

SIMPSON, DANIEL REID, b. Glen Alpine, N.C., Feb. 20, 1927; B.S., Wake Forest U., 1949, LL.B., 1951. Admitted to N.C. bar, 1951. Partner, Simpson, Baker & Aycock, and predecessor, Morganton, N.C., 1952—; mem. N.C. Legislature, 1957-61, 63. Mem. Am., N.C. trial lawyers assns., Am., N.C. bar assns. Home: Church St Glen Alpine NC 28628 Office: 204 E McDowell St PO Drawer 1329 Morganton NC 28655 Tel (704) 437-9744

SIMPSON, GEORGE BROWN, b. Providence, Ky., Sept. 24, 1929; A.B., Western Ky. U., 1951; J.D., U. Ky., 1954. Admitted to Ky. bar, 1954; with JAGC, USAF, 1954-56; individual practice law, Sturgis, Ky., 1957—; city atty. Sturgis, 1957-71; mem. Ky. Workmen's Compensation Bd., 1972-76, hearing officer, 1977—; mem. Ky. Bd. Claims, 1972-76. Mem. Union County LKy.) Library Bd., 1966-70. Mem. Ky. Bar Assn., So., Internat. assns. compensation adminstrs. Home and Office: 514 1/2 Adams St Sturgis KY 42459 Tel (502) 333-5337

SIMPSON, GORDON, b. Gilmor, Tex., Oct. 30, 1894; B.A., U. Tex., 1915, J.D., 1919. Admitted to Tex. bar, 1919, U.S. Supreme Ct. bar, 1942; mem. Tex. Ho. of Reps., 1923-27; judge 7th Jud. Dist., Tex., 1930; asso. justice Tex. Supreme Ct., 1945-49; gen. counsel Gen. Am. Oil Co., Dallas, 1949-55, pres., 1955-60; of counsel firm Thompson, Knight, Simmons and Bullion, Dallas, 1960—; chmn. Dept. Army Commn. for rev. of war crime cases tried at Dachau, Germany, 1948; pres. Tex. Civil Jud. Council, 1955-56. Chmn. Tex. Presbyterian Found., 1953-57, 62-66; ruling elder Highland Park Presbyn. Ch., Dallas. Fellow Am. Bar Found.; mem. State Bar Tex. (pres. 1941-42), Judge Advs. Assn. (pres. 1955-56), Am. Law Inst. (life), Internat., Am., Dallas, Smith County bar assns., Ind. Petroleum Assn. Am. (life, pres. 1958-59), Phi Alpha Delta. Home: 4409 Belclaire Dallas TX 75205 Office: 2300 Republic Bank Bldg Dallas TX 75201 Tel (214) 655-7580

SIMPSON, HARRELL ABNER, b. Evening Shade, Ark., Feb. 19, 1913; student Ark. Tech. U., 1933; LL.B., U. Ark., 1938; grad. Nat. Coll. State Trial Judges, U. N.C., 1968. Admitted to Ark. bar, 1938, U.S. Supreme Ct. bar, 1952; individual practice law, Pocahontas, Ark., 1939-54; judge Ark. 16th Circuit Ct., 1955—; dep. pros. atty. Randolph County (Ark.) and 16th Jud. Circuit Ark., 1939-44; pros. atty. 16th Circuit Ark., 1945-48; mem. Ark. Criminal Code Revision; mem. Com. for Promulgation Ark. Model Criminal Instructions. Mem. Little League Commn., Pocahontas, 1953-54; cub scout master Pocahontas council Boy Scouts Am., 1952-53; chmn. Randolph County March of Dimes, 1945-46. Mem. Am., Ark., Randolph-Lawrence bar assns., Ark. Jud. Council (pres. 1972-73), Am. Judges Assn., Am. Judicature Soc. Adviser, cons. Arkansas Law Enforcement Officer's Criminal Procedure Manual, 1969-70. Home: 511 Pine St Pocahontas AR 72455 Office: Circuit Judge's Office Courthouse Pocahontas AR 72455 Tel (501) 892-3144

SIMPSON, JOHN PAUL, b. Durham, N.C., Nov. 14, 1945; B.A., Wake Forest U., 1968, J.D., 1972. Admitted to N.C. bar, 1972, U.S. Supreme Ct. bar, 1975; partner firm Bennett, McConkey & Simpson, Morehead City, N.C., 1972-76; individual practice law, Morehead City, 1976—. Mem. N.C. Water Safety Council, 1975—; mem. task force N.C. Developmental Disabilities Council, 1975-76; pres. Carteret County Concerned Citizens, 1974-75. Mem. Am., Carteret County, N.C. bar assns. Home: 222 Larkin St Morehead City NC 28557 Office: 710 Arendell St Morehead City NC 28557

SIMPSON, JOHN WHITE, b. Pitts., Sept. 29, 1922; B.A., U. Rochester, 1944; LL.B., Harvard, 1948. Admitted to Ill. bar, 1949, D.C. bar, 1950, Calif. bar, 1953; with CAB, 1949-51; dir. law dept. Western Air Lines, Inc., 1953-67; partner firm Koteen & Burt, Washington, 1967—. Mem. Am., Fed., D.C. bar assns. Home: 3617 Ridgeway Terr Falls Church VA 22044 Office: 1150 Connecticut Ave NW Washington DC 20036 Tel (202) 467-5700

SIMPSON, LAURENCE PACKER, b. Marinette, Wis., June 29, 1895; LL.B., U. Ill., 1922, LL.M., 1928; J.D., Yale, 1930. Admitted to Ill. bar, 1922, practiced in Chgo., Laguna Hills, Calif.; prof. law N.Y. U. 1968-72, Loyola Law Sch., Los Angeles, 1972—. Author: Simpson on Suretyship, 1942; Cases on Suretyship, 1950; Cases on Contracts, 1956; Simpson on Contracts, 1965. Home: 471A Calle Cadiz Laguna Hills CA 92653 Tel (714) 837-8815

SIMS, LARRY ULMAN, b. Moundville, Ala., Sept. 3, 1941; A.B., U. Ala., 1962, LL.B., 1965. Admitted to Ala. bar, 1965, U.S. Supreme Ct. bar, 1966; partner firm Hand, Arendall, Bedsole, Greaves & Johnston, Mobile, Ala., 1965-77, Coale, Helmsing, Lyons & Sims, Mobile, 1977—; chief asst. dist. atty. Mobile County, 1970. Mem. Am., Ala., Mobile bar assns., Farrah Order Jurisprudence, Bench and Bar Hon. Soc. (pres.), Phi Alpha Delta. Comments editor Ala. Law Rev. Home: 410 Austill Pl Mobile AL 36608 Office: 2750 1st National Bank Bldg Mobile AL 36601 Tel (205) 432-5521

SIMS, M(ARION) JACK, b. North Little Rock, Ark., Mar. 5, 1929; B.S., LL.B., 1958; J.D., 1969. Admitted to Ark. bar, 1958, U.S. Supreme Ct. bar, 1971; since practiced in Little Rock, asso. firm Pope Pratt & Shamburger, 1959-66; partner firm Eubanks Hood & Sims, 1966; individual practice law, 1966—; research analyst Ark. Legis. Council, 1958-59. Mem. Am., Ark., Pulaski County bar assns., Am. Trial Lawyers Assn. Home: 5701 Alta Vista Dr North Little Rock AR 72118 Office: Union Life Bldg Suite 701 Little Rock AR 72201 Tel (501) 374-9992

SIMS, MARSHALL RICHARD, b. Atlanta, June 8, 1939; A.B., Mercer U., 1961; LL.B., Walter F. George Sch. Law, 1963. Admitted to Ga. bar, 1962, U.S. Supreme Ct. bar, 1967; asso. firm Jones, Spark, Benton & Cock, Macon, Ga., 1962-63; asst. atty. gen. State of Ga., 1965-68; partner firm Seay & Sims, Griffin, Ga., 1969—. Mem. Am., Ga., Griffin bar assns., Am. Judicature Soc. Home: 840 E College Griffin GA 30223 Office: 222 Meriwether Griffin GA 30223 Tel (404) 227-2231

SIMS, THOMAS ELWOOD, b. Independence, Mo., Dec. 15, 19 31; B.B.A., U. Kansas City, 1957, LL.B., 1961; ed. U. Utah, 1972, U. Nev., 1973, Hastings Coll. Law, U. Calif., San Francisco, 1975. Admitted to Mo. bar, 1961; claim rep. State Farm Mut. Ins. Co., Kansas City, 1959-61; asso. firm Rogers, Field & Gentry, 1961-68; partner firm Rogers, Field, Gentry, Benjamin & Robertson, 1968-70; judge Municipal Ct. Kansas City, 1970—; rep. for Clay County, charter mem. N.W. Mo. Law Enforcement Assistance Council, 1969-70; vice chmn. Clay County Juvenile Ct. Assistance Com., 1970; faculty Nat. Coll. State Judiciary, U. Nev., summers 1974-75, Am. Judicature Soc.-Vt. Citizens Conf., 1976; mem. state-wide jud. planning com. Mo. Supreme Ct., 1977. Elder, 1st Presbyn. Ch., North Kansas City, 1971; instl. rep. Troop 179 Boy Scouts Am., 1972, advancement chmn., troop com. chmn. Kansas City Area council, 1975; pres. S.W. Clay Republican Assn., 1969-70; chmn. bd. dirs. Sober House, Inc., 1971-73; chmn. bd. Regional Center for Criminal Justice, 1971; treas., bd. dirs. Mo. Inst. for Justice, Inc., 1973, pres., 1976; mem. Cts. Task Force, Mo. Action Plan for Pub. Safety, 1975; bd. dirs. Alternative Opportunities, Inc., 1975, Spl. Offenders Counsel, 1976; sec. bd. dirs. U. Mo. at Kansas City Law Found., 1974-76. Mem. Am., Mo., Clay County, Kansas City (chmn. municipal cts. com. 1966-69) bar assns., Mo. Municipal and Magistrate Judges Assn. (trustee 1976), Am. Judges Assn., Am. Judicature Soc. (dir.), U. Mo. at Kansas City Alumni Assn. (pres., dir. 1967, chmn., past pres. council 1968-69, Service award 1974), U. Mo. Alumni Alliance (founder, dir.), Phi Alpha Delta (del. Nat. Conf. 1970), Omicron Delta Kappa, Legion of Honor, DeMolay. Home: 126 NE 43d St Kansas City MO 64116 Office: 1101 Locust St Kansas City MO 64106 Tel (816) 474-4040

SINCLAIR, IVAN BENJAMIN, b. Pitts., June 19, 1933; B.A., Pa. State U., 1955, LL.B., Dickinson Sch. Law, 1958. Admitted to Pa. bar, 1959, U.S. Supreme Ct. bar, 1964; partner firm Harvey, Pugh & Sinclair, Media, Pa., 1959—. Pres. Citizens Council of Delaware County, 1971-74; chmn. Good Govt. Coalition, 1973-75; chmn. Young Republicans of Pa., 1966-68; chmn. Com. to Rebuild the G.O.P., 1974—. Mem. Pa. (bd. govs. 1966-67, chmn. young lawyers sect. 1966-67; chmn. unauthorized practice com. 1972-75), Delaware County (chmn. young lawyers sect. 1963-64; chmn. criminal corrections com. 1974-75) bar assns. Home: 1221 Robin Hill Rose Tree Rd Media PA 19063 Office: Court House Sq N Media PA 19063 Tel (215) 565-0700

SINCLAIR, JAMES JOHN, b. Helena, Mont., June 3, 1934; LL.B., U. Mont., 1960. Admitted to Mont. bar, 1960; partner firm Berger, Anderson, Sinclair & Murphy, Billings, Mont., 1960—. Mem. Am., Mont. bar assns., Am. Trial Lawyers Assn. Home: 1929 Lyndale Billings MT 59101 Office: 2512 3rd Ave N Billings MT 59103 Tel (406) 252-3439

SINCLAIR, KENT, JR., b. San Diego, July 8, 1946; A.B. cum laude, U. Calif., 1968, J.D., 1971; diplomate Nat. Inst. Trial Advocacy, 1973. Admitted to Calif. bar, 1972, N.Y. State bar, 1973. Law clk. to chief judge U.S. Ct. Appeals for 9th Circuit, 1971-72; chief screening atty. U.S. Ct. Appeals for 9th Circuit, San Francisco, 1972; asso. firm Shearman & Sterling, N.Y.C., 1972-76; U.S. magistrate U.S. Dist. Ct. So. Dist. of N.Y., N.Y.C., 1976—; adj. prof. Fordham U. Sch. Law, 1973—; faculty mem. Practicing Law Inst. Trial Advocacy Program, 1976; faculty mem. and team leader Nat. Inst. for Trial Advocacy, Regional Trial Tng. Inst. Mem. Am. Judges Assn., Am., N.Y. State (sec. fed. cts. com. 1976-78) bar assns., Assn. Bar City N.Y. (young lawyers com. chmn. 1977-79), Nat. Conf. Spl. Ct. Judges (chmn. discovery com. 1977—), Nat. Council U.S. Magistrates (dir. 1977—). Author: Problems and Materials on Trial Advocacy, 1977; chief note and comment editor Calif. Law Rev., 1970-71. Home: 336 Central Park W Apt 3B New York City NY 10025 Office: US Courthouse Foley Sq New York City NY 10007 Tel (212) 791-0751

SINDT, RUSSELL JOHN, b. Holdrege, Nebr., Feb. 21, 1947; B.S., U. Nebr., Lincoln, 1968, J.D., 1971. Admitted to Nebr. bar, 1971, Colo. bar, 1971; legal counselor Nebr. Dept. Natural Resources, Lincoln, 1971; dep. city atty. City of Lakewood (Colo.), 1972-75, chief dep. atty., civil sect., 1974-75; individual practice law, Lakewood, 1975—; city atty., Golden, Colo., 1977—. Mem. Nebr., Colo., Jefferson County (Colo.) bar assns., Colo. Trial Lawyers Assn. Office: 1485 Holland St Lakewood CO 80215 Tel (303) 237-9508

SINESIO, RONALD VAL, b. Youngstown, Ohio, Jan. 6, 1949; A.B., Mt. Union Coll., 1971; J.D., Ohio No. U., 1974. Admitted to Ohio bar, 1974; mem. firm Schubert and Sinesio, Warren, Ohio, 1977—. Bd. dirs. March of Dimes, chmn. Walk-a-Thon, 1977. Mem. Am., Trumbull County bar assns. Office: 269 Seneca St Warren OH 44481 Tel (216) 399-4424

SINGER, ALVIN IRA, b. Highland Park, Ill., Oct. 12, 1931; B.A., DePauw U., 1953; J.D., Northwestern U., 1956. Admitted to Ill. bar, 1956, U.S. Supreme Ct. bar, 1960; asso. firm Singer, Singer & Singer and predecessors, Highland Park, 1956-58, partner, 1958-71; asso. judge Ill. 19th Jud. Circuit Ct., 1971—; justice of the peace, Lake County (Ill.), 1961-63; magistrate Ill. 19th Jud. Circuit Ct., 1964-65. Mem. Am., Ill. State (chmn. com. traffic laws and cts. 1968), Lake County (gov. 1958-72), Chgo. bar assns., Am. Judicature Soc., Ill. Judges Assn., Phi Delta Phi. Author: Lake County Magistrates Manual, 1964; Magistrates Manual for the 2d Appellate Court District, 1969; contbr. articles to legal publs. Office: Courthouse Waukegan IL 60085 Tel (312) 689-6600

SINGER, ANDREW WARREN, b. Chgo., Feb. 1, 1942; B.S. in Econs., U. Pa., 1963; LL.B. cum laude, Harvard, 1966. Admitted to D.C. bar, 1967; atty., advisor to judge U.S. Tax Ct., Washington, 1966-68; asso. firm Covington & Burling, Washington, 1968-75, partner, 1975—; lectr. Nat. Law Center, George Washington U., 1974—. Mem. Am. Bar Assn. (chmn. subcom. for liaison with U.S. Tax Ct.). Home: 10313 Holly Hill Pl Potomac MD 20854 Office: 888 16th St NW Washington DC 20006 Tel (202) 452-6064

SINGER, ARTHUR HENRY, b. N.Y.C., May 5, 1923; B.S. cum laude, N.Y. U., 1947; LL.B., Bklyn. Law Sch., 1950, J.D., 1967. Admitted to N.Y. bar, 1950, Nev. bar, 1971; partner firm Singer & Singer, N.Y.C., 1950-57; individual practice law, N.Y.C., 1957-59; controller Sinclair Mills, N.Y.C., 1959-60; accountant Robert A. Weiner, N.Y.C., 1960-61; tax mgr. Klein & Ziegler, N.Y.C., 1961-64; tax mgr. Smith, Rohmiller, Swenson & Clark, Bakersfield, Calif., 1965-66; practice accounting, Bakersfield, 1966-69; tax mgr. Elmer Fox & Co., Las Vegas, 1969-73; pres. Singer Profl. Corp., Las Vegas, 1973—; trustee Nev. C.P.A. Found. for Edn. and Research, 1971-73, vice chmn., 1972-73, instr. numerous courses, 1977—. Vice pres. Bay Terr., Queens (N.Y.) Community Council, 1955-56; mgr. Little League, 1957-63; treas. United Jewish Appeal, 1966; 1st v.p. Bakersfield Cultural Council, 1967-68; scoutmaster, cubmaster Boy Scouts Am. Mem. Nev., Clark County (chmn. continuing edn. com. 1977) bar assns., Nev. (mem. taxation com. 1975-77, moderator TV income tax panel 1976, 77), Calif., N.Y. State socs. C.P.A.'s. Contbr. articles to profl. publs. Home: 3044 Plaza St Las Vegas NV 89121 Office: 120 E Flamingo St Suite 371 Las Vegas NV 89109 Tel (702) 732-4501

SINGER, BARRY HAAS, b. N.Y.C., Mar. 10, 1931; B.A., Amherst Coll., 1952; J.D., Columbia, 1955. Admitted to N.Y. State bar, 1955, U.S. Supreme Ct. bar, 1972; mem. staff N.Y. State Commn. on the Cts., N.Y.C., 1955; asso. firm, Greenbaum, Wolff & Ernst, N.Y.C., 1956-57, firm Ehrich, Stock, Valicenti, Leighton & Holland, N.Y.C., 1958-61; partner firm Milton Pollack, N.Y.C., Pollack & Singer, and predecessors, 1967-75; partner firm Lowenthal, Landau, Fischer & Singer, N.Y.C., 1976; asso. counsel to speaker N.Y. State Assembly, Albany, 1967. Mem. Scarsdale (N.Y.) Bowl Com., 1975—; pres. Scarsdale Town Club, 1975-76; v.p. Hamilton Madison House, 1958-67, dir., 1958-67; trustee Jewish Bd. of Guardians, 1964—; trustee Mid-Westchester, YM & YWHA, 1965—, v.p., 1966-72. Mem. Am., N.Y. State Bar assns., Assn. Bar City N.Y., Maritime Law Assn. U.S. Home: 40 Crossway Scarsdale NY 10583 Office: 250 Park Ave New York City NY 10017 Tel (212) 986-1116

SINGER, EDWIN MCMAHON, b. N.Y.C., July 13, 1911; A.B., Columbia, 1934, postgrad. 1936-37; J.D., Fordham U., 1936. Admitted to N.Y. bar, 1937; individual practice law, N.Y.C., 1937—. Mem. Am. Bar Assn., Assn. Bar City N.Y., Guild Catholic Lawyers. Home: 1020 Park Ave New York City NY 10028 Office: 666 Fifth Ave New York City NY 10019 Tel (212) 246-5800

SINGER, ESTHER C., b. Chgo., Mar. 4, 1908; J.D., DePaul U., 1928. Admitted to Ill. bar, 1928; partner firm Singer & Singer, Highland Park, Ill., 1930—. Mem. Ill., Lake County bar assns. Address: 1980 Sheridan Rd Highland Park IL 60035 Tel (312) 432-4070

SINGER, HERBERT JAY, b. Chgo., Apr. 12, 1941; B.S. in Gen. Engring, U. Ill., 1963; J.D., Loyola U., Chgo., 1966. Admitted to Ill. bar, 1967, U.S. Supreme Ct. bar, 1970, U.S. Patent and Trademark Office, 1967; asso. firm Silverman & Cass, Chgo., 1967-70, mem. firm, 1970—. Mem. Am., Ill., Chgo. bar assns., Am. Patent Law Assn., U.S. Trademark Assn., Internat. Assn. Young Lawyers, Patent Law Assn. Chgo. (bd. mgrs. 1976-77, sec. 1976-77). Home: 3740 Radcliffe Dr Northbrook IL 60062 Office: 105 W Adams St Chicago IL 60603 Tel (312) 726-6006

SINGER, HOWARD J., b. N.Y.C., Jan. 6, 1943; B.S. in Advt. and Mktg., U. Fla., 1965; J.D., U. Miami, Coral Gables, Fla., 1972. Admitted to Fla. bar, 1972; group dir. Burger King Corp., Miami, Fla., 1967-75, v.p. real estate and constrn., 1975-77; group v.p. Church's Fried Chicken, Inc., San Antonio, 1977—. Mem. Dade County (Fla.), Fla. bars. Contbr. articles to real estate jours. Home: 3711 Hunters Point San Antonio TX 78230 Office: 355A Spencers Lane San Antonio TX 78201 Tel (512) 735-9392

SINGER, LINDA R., lawyer; b. Boston, May 2, 1941; A.B. magna cum laude, Radcliffe Coll., 1963; J.D. summa cum laude, George Washington U., 1968. Admitted to D.C. bar, 1968; asso. firm Kurzman & Goldfarb, Washington, 1968-71; partner firm Goldfarb, Singer & Austern, and predecessor, Washington, 1971—; vis. lectr. Stanford, U. Calif. at Los Angeles law schs., 1975; exec. dir. Center for Community Justice, 1971—. Mem. Am., D.C. (steering com. Div. IV 1976—) bar assns., Am. Arbitration Assn. (dir. 1974—), Women's Legal Def. Fund, Washington Council Lawyers, Nat. Council on Crime and Delinquency. Author: (with Ronald Goldfarb) After Conviction: A Review of the American Correction System, 1973; contbr. articles to legal jours. Office: 918 16th St NW Washington DC 20006

SINGER, NORMAN J., b. Boston, Aug. 1, 1938; B.S. in Econs., U. Pa., 1960; J.D., Boston U., 1964; S.J.D., Harvard, 1975. Admitted to Mass. bar, 1964, Ala. bar, 1974; asst. prof. law Haile Sellassie I U., Addis Ababa, Ethiopia, 1964-68, vis. scholar, 1970; research fellow Yale, 1967-70; prof. law and anthropology U. Ala., 1971—; vis. scholar Inst. Comparative Law, Belgrade, Yugoslavia, 1975-76; cons. in field. Mem. Am. Sociol. Assn., Am. Anthropol. Assn., Soc. Am. Law Tchrs., Ala. Acad. Sci. Contbr. articles to legal publs. Office: U Ala Sch Law PO Box 1435 University AL 35486 Tel (205) 348-5930

SINGER, ROBERT NEIL, b. Albuquerque, May 1, 1942; B.A., U. N.Mex., 1964; J.D., Cath. U., 1968. Admitted to N.Mex. bar, 1968; asst. dist. atty. N.Mex. 2d Jud. Dist., 1968-69; asso. mem. firm Montoya & Montoya, Albuquerque, 1969-70; partner firm Coors, Singer & Broullire, Albuquerque, 1970—; spl. asst. atty. gen. state of N. Mex., 1969, 75; adj. prof. criminal law U. Albuquerque, 1973-75; asso. prof. law U. N.Mex., 1975; instr. N.Mex. Bar Rev., 1975-76. Mem. law enforcement com. Met. Criminal Justice Coordinating Council, Albuquerque, 1975-76. Mem. Am., N.Mex., Albuquerque bar assns., N.Mex. Trial Lawyers Assn., Delta Theta Phi, Inst. Legal Research (past pres.). Home: 7501 El Morro Rd NE Albuquerque NM 87109 Office: Suite 1100 Am Bank of Commerce Bldg 200 Lomas NW Albuquerque NM 87102 (505) 243-3547

SINGER, SHELVIN, b. Chgo., Apr. 9, 1931; B.S., No. Ill. U., 1954; M.A., U. Ill., 1960; J.D., DePaul U., 1960. Admitted to Ill. bar, 1960, U.S. Supreme ct. bar, 1966; partner firm Dietrich & Singer, DeKalb, Ill., 1960-61; atty. SEC, Chgo., 1961-64; asst. pub. defender Cook County (Ill.), 1964-67, spl. asst. to pub. defender, 1967-73; asst. prof. bus. law No. Ill. U., 1960-61; prof. law Ill. Inst. Tech./Chgo.-Kent Coll. Law, 1967—; chmn. Ill. Def. Project, 1970—; chmn. bd. Cook County Criminal Def. Consortium, 1975—; dir. fed. grant for indigent def. systems analysis, 1974-76. Bd. dirs., mem. exec. com. Nat. Legal Aid and Defender Assn., 1973—. Fellow Nat. Coll. Criminal Def. Lawyers and Pub. Defenders (regent 1974—); mem. Am., Ill., Chgo. bar assns. Recipient award of Merit, Cook County Pub. Defender, 1966, Ill. Pub. Def. Assn. award, 1973. Editor: Public Defender Source Book, 1976. Contbr. articles to legal jours. Office: 77 S Wacker Dr Chicago IL 60606 Tel (312) 567-5049

SINGER, STEVEN DAVID, b. Worcester, Mass., Dec. 25, 1946; A.B., Syracuse U., 1969; J.D., Boston U., 1972; LL.M., N.Y. U., 1973. Admitted to Mass. bar, 1972; partner firms Singer & Grantham,

Boston, 1974, Perlow & Singer, Boston, 1976—; asso. firm Siegel, Prager & Wishnow, Boston, 1974-75. Home: 58 Beacon St Boston MA 02108 Office: One Center Plaza Boston MA 02108 Tel (617) 742-3250

SINGLETON, EUSTACE BYRON, b. Lufkin, Tex., Oct. 3, 1909; A.B., U. Tex., 1933, LL.B., 1933, J.D., 1933. Admitted to Tex. bar, 1933, U.S. Supreme Ct. bar, 1941, U.S. Ct. Claims bar, 1952, U.S. Ct. Customs and Patent Appeals bar, 1956, U.S. Bd. Immigration Appeals bar, 1947; partner firm Underwood, Strickland & Singleton, Amarillo, Tex., 1933-38, firm Monning & Singleton, Amarillo, 1939-49, firm Singleton & Trulove, Amarillo, 1950-60; individual practice law Amarillo, 1960—; dep. adminstr. War Savs. Staff, Washington, 1939-43; nat. committeeman War Fin. Com., Dallas, 1943-46; city atty. Amarillo, 1941-48; U.S. conciliation commr. and referee in bankruptcy, 1933-40. Mem. nat. bd. govs. Arthritis Found., 1960-70; bd. dirs. Edna Gladney Home, Fort Worth, 1942-56; dir. ARC, Amarillo Panhandle area, 1938-46. Mem. Tex. Jr. (pres. 1938-40), Amarillo, Am., Fed. bar assns., State Bar Tex., Am. Judicature Soc., Amarillo Trial Lawyers Assn. Home: 2405 Lipscomb St Amarillo TX 79109 Office: 1408 Am Nat Bank Bldg Amarillo TX 79101 Tel (806) 372-2222

SINGLETON, JOHN VIRGIL, JR., b. Kaufman, Tex., Mar. 20, 1918; B.A., U. Tex., 1942. Admitted to Tex. bar, 1942; practiced in Houston, 1946-66; mem. firm Fulbright & Jaworski, 1953-57; partner firm Barrow, Bland, Rehmet & Singleton, and predecessors, 1953-66; judge U.S. Dist. Ct., So. Dist. Tex., Houston, 1966—; pres. Houston Jr. Bar Assn., 1952-53; co-chmn. 5th Circuit Dist. Judges Div. Jud. Conf., 1969, chmn., 1970; mem. Tex. Depository Bd., 1963-66. Co-chmn. Harris County Lyndon B. Johnson for Pres. Com., 1960-61; del.-at-large Democratic Nat. Conv., 1956, 60, 64; regional coordinator Dem. party Lyndon B. Johnson-Hubert Humphrey Campaign for Pres., 1964. Mem. Am., Houston (v.p. 1956-57, editor Houston Lawyer 1954-55), Tex. (chmn. grievance com. for Harris County 1963-66, dir. 1966) bar assns., U. Tex. Ex-Students Assn. (life mem., pres. Houston 1961-62, mem.-at-large exec. council), Cowboys, Delta Tau Delta, Phi Alpha Delta. Home: 221 Sage Rd Houston TX 77056 Office: 515 Rusk Ave Houston TX 77002

SINGLEY, FREDERICK JACOB, JR., b. Balt., July 10, 1912; A.B., Johns Hopkins U., 1933; LL.B., U. Md., 1936. Admitted to Md. bar, 1936; asso. firm Hinkley, Burger and Singley (later Hinkley and Singley), Balt., 1936-40, partner 1940-67; asso. judge Md. Ct. Appeals, Annapolis, 1967—. Mem., Am., Md. bar founds., Am., Md., Balt. bar assns., Am. Law Inst., Am. Judicature Soc., Order of Coif, Phi Beta Kappa. Office: Courts of Appeal Bldg Annapolis MD 21401 Tel (301) 267-5341

SINYKIN, GORDON, b. Madison, Wis., June 18, 1910; B.A., U. Wis., 1931, LL.B., 1933. Admitted to Wis. bar, 1933, U.S. Supreme Ct. bar, 1961; practiced law, Madison, 1933-35, 32-42, 45—; partner firm LaFollette, Sinykin, Anderson & Munson and predecessors, 1945—; exec. counsel to gov. Wis., 1935-38; spl. counsel State of Wis., 1935-38, Wis. Ins. Dept., 1962-65; mem. com. on ins. laws revision Wis. Legis. Council, 1966—; lectr. U. Wis. Law Sch., 1950-52. Mem. Madison Mayor's Commn. on Human Rights, 1958-63; bd. dirs. Community Welfare Council, 1957-66, pres., 1961-63; bd. dirs. United Community Chest, 1965-69, v.p., 1968-69; bd. dirs. Health Planning Council, 1967-68; bd. dirs. Methodist Hosp., 1969—, chmn. bd., 1975—. Fellow Am. Bar Found.; mem. Am. (ho. dels. 1975—), Dane County (pres. 1956-57) bar assns., State Bar Wis. (bd. govs. 1957-60), Am. Law Inst., Wis. Bar Found. (pres., dir.), Order of Coif, Phi Beta Kappa, Phi Kappa Phi, Phi Eta Sigma. Editor-in-chief: Wis. Law Rev., 1932-33. Home: 721 Seneca Pl Madison WI 53711 Office: 222 W Washington Ave Madison WI 53703 Tel (608) 257-3911

SIPARI, ORAZIO, b. Cleve., May 3, 1917; B.S. in Bus. Adminstrn., Ohio State U., 1941, J.D., 1948. Admitted to Ohio bar, 1948, Ind. bar, 1950; with Sonio Petroleum Co., Evansville, Ind., 1948-50; asso. firm Ortmeyer, Bamberger, Ortmeyer & Foreman, firm Leanza, Longano & Farina; atty.-in-charge SEC, Cleve., 1958—. Mem. Lyndhorst (Ohio) CSC, 1971—. Recipient award of Merit, Ohio Bar Assn., 1966; contbr. articles to legal jours. Home: 1918 Caronia Dr Lyndhurst OH 44124 Office: Room 899 Federal Office Building 1240 E 9th St Cleve OH 44199 Tel (216) 522-4060

SIPE, JAMES ROTHGEB, b. Harrisonburg, Va., July 19, 1931; B.A., U. Richmond, 1955; LL.B., U. Va., 1958. Admitted to Va. bar, 1958; atty. Rockingham County and City of Harrisonburg, 1960-68; partner firm Conrad, Litten, Sipe & Miller, Harrisonburg, 1968—. Pres. Rockingham Library Assn., 1976. Mem. Va., Harrisonburg-Rockingham bar assns. Office: 218 E Market St Harrisonburg VA 22801 Tel (703) 434-5353

SIRICA, JOHN J., b. 1904; LL.B., Georgetown U., 1926; hon. degrees Coll. New Rochelle (N.Y.), Brown U., New Eng. Sch. Law, Fairfield U., City U. N.Y. Former mem. firm Hogan & Hartson, Washington; judge U.S. Dist. Ct. for D.C. 1957—. chief Judge, 1971-74; adj. prof. law Georgetown U. Law Center. Mem. Am. Bar Assn., Bar Assn. D.C. (hon.). Phi Alpha Delta. Office: US Ct House Washington DC 20001*

SIRILLA, GEORGE M., b. Fayette, Pa., May 1, 1929; B.M.E., Rensselaer Poly. Inst., 1952; LL.B., Georgetown U., 1956, J.D., 1967. Admitted to D.C., Va. bars, 1956, U.S. Supreme Ct. bar, 1960; asso. firm Cushman, Darby & Cushman, Washington, 1956-60, partner, 1960—; vis. lectr. patent law Cath. U. Am., 1960. Mem. Am. Patent Law Assn., Am., D.C. (sec. patent sect. 1960, chmn. Amicus Briefs com. patent sect. 1977), bar assns., Tau Beta Pi, Pi Tau Sigma, Phi Delta Phi. Home: 6524 Windermere Circle Bethesda MD 20852 Office: 1801 K St NW Washington DC 20006 Tel (202) 833-3000

SIRKIN, JOSHUA ALLEN, b. Miami Beach, Fla., Mar. 16, 1939; B.A., U. N.C.; J.D., Stetson U. Admitted to Fla. bar, 1963; asso. firm Harris & Sirkin, and predecessor, Miami, Fla., 1963-66, partner, 1966—; guest lectr. U. Miami Law Sch., 1974. Mem. Dade County (Fla.), Fla., Am. bar assns., Phi Alpha Delta (pres. 1962-63). Recipient Distinguished Pres. award Optimists Internat., 1970, Man of Year award Nor-Isle Optimist Club Inc., 1970. Home: 5765 SW 119th St Miami FL 33156 Office: Dade Fed Bldg 21 NE First Ave Miami FL 33131 Tel (305) 358-1455

SIRMONS, DON THORNTON, b. St. Petersburg, Fla., Aug. 4, 1948; B.A., U. Fla., 1970, J.D., 1973. Admitted to Fla. bar, 1973; partner firm McCauley and Sirmons, Panama City, Fla., 1974-77; asso. judge Panama City Municipal Ct., 1975-76, Springfield (Fla.) Municipal Ct., 1975-76; county judge Bay Cts., Fla., 1977—. Mem. adv. bd. St. Andrews Bay Center for Retarded Citizens, Lynn Haven, Fla., 1975-77; mem. human rights advocacy com. dist. II, Fla. Dept. Health and Rehab. Services, 1976—. Mem. Bay County (Fla.) Bar Assn. Office: 3503 E 3d St Panama City FL 32401 Tel (904) 769-0276

SISEMORE, L. ORTH, b. Ft. Klamath, Oreg., Mar. 8, 1905; B.A., U. Wash., 1929, LL.B., 1931. Admitted to Oreg. bar, 1931; dist. atty. Klamath County (Oreg.), from 1936; circuit judge Klamath County, 1965-75. Mem. Am., Oreg. bar assns. Office: 540 Main St Klamath Falls OR 97601 Tel (503) 882-7228

SISK, PHILIP LAURENCE, b. Lynn, Mass., Oct. 25, 1913; A.B., Coll. Holy Cross, 1935; J.D., Boston Coll., 1938. Admitted to Mass. bar, 1938, Fed. bar, 1946; individual practice law, Lynn, 1938—. Mem. bd. overseers, 1974—; trustee Mass. Com. Continuing Legal Edn., Inc.; mem. sch. com. city Lynn, 1939-51. Fellow Am. Coll. Trial Lawyers (state chmn. 1969-70), Am., Mass. bar founds. (pres. 1960-62); mem. Lynn, Mass. (pres. 1968-70), Am. (del.) bar assns. Defense Research Inst. (Mass. chmn. 1965-68), Mass. Assn. Defense Counsel (pres. 1966), Internat. Assn. Ins. Counsel, Am. Judicature Soc. (dir. 1976—). Home: Flint St Marblehead MA 01945 Office: 38 Exchange St Lynn MA 01901 Tel (617) 593-0110

SISK, ROBERT JOSEPH, b. Hartford, Conn., Nov. 8, 1928; A.B., Dartmouth Coll., 1950; LL.B., Yale U., 1956. Admitted to N.Y. State bar, 1957, U.S. Supreme Ct. bar, 1963; asso. firm Hughes, Hubbard & Reed, N.Y.C., 1956-63, partner firm, 1964—; dir. Allied Artists Industries, 1967—; mem. exec. com. 1975—; dir. Allen-Bradley Co., 1973—. Fellow Am. Coll. Trial Lawyers; mem. Assn. Bar City N.Y. Home: 123 Drum Hill Rd Wilton CT 06897 Office: 1 Wall St New York City NY 10005 Tel (212) 943-6500

SISKIN, MYRON W., b. Bronx, N.Y., Apr. 2, 1931; B.S. in Accounting, N.Y. U., 1952, LL.B., 1955, LL.M. in Tax Law, 1961. Admitted to N.Y. bar, 1957; legal aid N.Y. U., 1954-55; individual practice law, pvt. practice accounting, N.Y.C., 1957—. Pres. Lido Homes Civic Assn., Lido Beach, N.Y., 1965. Mem. New York County Lawyers Assn., N.Y. State C.P.A. Soc. C.P.A. Tel (212) 683-1658

SITES, JAMES PHILIP, b. Detroit, Sept. 17, 1948; Examen Philosophicum in Polit. Sci., U. Oslo, 1969; B.A. in Polit. Sci., Haverford Coll., 1970; J.D., Georgetown U., 1973. Admitted to Md. bar, 1973, D.C. bar, 1974; law clk. firm Amram, Hahn & Sandground, Washington, 1971-72, to Hon. James C. Morton, Jr., sr. asso. judge Md. Ct. Spl. Appeals, 1974-75, to Hon. Orman W. Ketcham, D.C. Superior Ct., 1975-76; naturalization examiner U.S. Immigration and Naturalization Service, Chevy Chase, Md., 1976—; law enforcement ranger U.S. Nat. Park Service, Glacier Nat. Park, summers, 1971-76. Mem. Am., Md. State bar assns., Am. Judicature Soc., D.C. Bar, World Peace Through Law Center, Conservative Caucus, Young Republicans, Am.-Scandinavian Found. Contbr. articles on Norway to Nat. Observer, 1968-69. Home and Office: 6401 Kennedy Dr Chevy Chase MD 20015 Tel (301) 654-4790

SITLER, ROSS EDWARD, b. Dodge City, Kans., Nov. 11, 1926; B.S., U. Calif., Los Angeles, 1957; J.D., U. San Fernando, 1971. Admitted to Calif. bar, 1972; adminstrv. asst. Union Oil Corp., Los Angeles, 1958-60, Hagy & Hagy, Inc., Century City, Calif., 1960-65; owner, operator Find-All Employment Agy., 1965-69. Advisor to handicapped Valley Coll.; Easter Seal chmn. San Fernando Valley, 1964; comdr. Army and Navy Legion of Valor, 1963; mem. Los Angeles Urban Planning Commn., 1974-75. Mem. San Fernando Criminal, San Fernando Valley, Los Angeles County bar assns., Calif. Trial Lawyers Assn., DAV (life). Decorated D.S.C., Purple Heart. Home: 9636 Aqueduct Ave Sepulveda CA 93143 Office: 8155 Van Nuys Blvd 360 Panorama City CA 91402 Tel (313) 994-9414

SITTE, KLAUS DIETRICH, b. Drantum, Germany, Aug. 7, 1947; B.A., Gustavus Adolphus, St. Peter, Minn., 1969; J.D., U. Mont., 1972. Admitted to Mont. bar, 1972; law clk. Mont. Supreme Ct., 1972-73; asst. staff atty. Mont. Legal Services Assn., Missoula, 1973-74, staff atty., 1974—. Mem. Am., Mont. bar assns., Am. Judicature Soc., Phi Delta Phi. Home: 430 Blaine Missoula MT 59801 Office: 127 E Main Missoula MT 59801 Tel (406) 543-8343

SKAKLES, GREG J., b. Anaconda, Mont., Oct. 13, 1947; B.A., Carroll Coll., 1969; J.D. with honors, U. Mont., 1972. Admitted to Mont. bar, 1972; mem. McKeon Law Firm, Anaconda, 1972-75; individual practice, Anaconda, 1975—. Mem. Mont., Am. bar assns., Mont., Am. trial lawyers assns. Home: 311 E 6th St Anaconda MT 59711 Office: 117 Main St Anaconda MT 59711 Tel (406) 563-6700

SKALNIK, CHARLES, b. Medford, Okla., Apr. 22, 1895; LL.B., Okla. U., 1925. Admitted to Okla. bar, 1924, U.S. Tax Ct. bar, 1944; individual practice law, Tulsa, 1925—; instr. Tulsa Law Sch., Tulsa U., 1925-47. Chmn., Tulsa County Bd. Adjustment, 1968-70. Mem. Phi Delta Phi, Lambda Chi. Office: Suite 324 Court Arcade Bldg Tulsa OK 74103 Tel (918) 583-8503

SKEES, WILLIAM LEONARD, JR., b. Indpls., Jan. 26, 1947; B.A., Ball State U., 1969; J.D. magna cum laude, Ind. U., Bloomington, 1971. Admitted to Ind. bar, 1971; law clerk Hon. Jesse E. Eschbach, U.S. Dist. Judge for No. Dist. Ind., Ft. Wayne, 1971-72; asso. firm Ice, Miller, Donadio & Ryan, Indpls., 1971—; bd. visitors Ind. U. Sch. of Law. Mem. Am., Ind., Indpls. bar assns., Order Coif. Bd. editors Ind. Law Jour., 1970-71; contbr. articles to legal jours. Home: 5247 Luzzane Dr Indianapolis IN 46220 Office: 111 Monument Circle Indianapolis IN 46204 Tel (317) 635-1213

SKELLY, JOSEPH GORDON, b. Oil City, Pa., June 2, 1935; B.S., U. Notre Dame, 1957; J.D., Villanova U., 1962. Admitted to Pa. Supreme Ct. bar, 1963, U.S. Supreme Ct. bar, 1968, Pa. Superior Ct. bar, 1971, Pa. Commonwealth Ct. bar, 1970; asso. firm Breene, Frame & Magee, Oil City, 1963-67; asst. counsel Pa. Cath. Conf., Harrisburg, Pa., 1967-68; partner firm Ball & Skelly, Harrisburg, 1968—. Bd. dirs. Alcoholism Services, Inc., Harrisburg, 1973—; mem. exec. bd. Keystone Area council Boy Scouts Am. Mem. Am., Pa., Dauphin County bar assns., Pa. Trial Lawyers Assn. Home: 232 Poplar Ave New Cumberland PA 17070 Office: 127 State St Harrisburg PA 17101 Tel (717) 233-7902

SKELTON, DARRELL JEAN, b. Pratt, Kans., May 4, 1924; student U. Florence (Italy), 1945; B.S., B.A., U. Denver, 1950; LL.B., 1952. Admitted to Colo. bar, 1952, U.S. Supreme Ct. bar, 1957; partner firm Tilly & Skelton, Denver, 1952-65; individual practice law, Lakewood, Colo., 1965-69; partner firm Skelton & Miller, Wheat Ridge, Colo., 1970-74, Skelton, Matassa & Dean, Wheat Ridge, 1974-75, Skelton, O'Dell & Oviatt, Wheat Ridge, 1976—. Mem. Colo. State Legislature, 1964-65; chmn. Colo. Recreation Trails Com., 1972-74, Jefferson County Open Space Com., 1973-75. Mem. Colo., Denver, 1st Judicial bar assns. Home: 16826 W 57th Ave Golden CO 80401 Office: 4380 Harlan St Wheat Ridge CO 80033 Tel (303) 423-0166

SKELTON, MARVIN LEE, b. Dallas, Nov. 13, 1924; B.S., So. Meth. U., 1948, LL.B., 1950. Admitted to Tex. bar, 1950; with land dept. Texaco, Tex., N.Mex., Colo., Utah, Ariz., 1950-55; atty. legal dept. Atlantic Richfield Co., Dallas, 1955-63, regional atty., Houston, 1963—. Mem. Am., Tex., Houston bar assns., Soc. World War I Aero Historians, Am. Aviation Hist. Soc., Phi Alpha Delta. Home: 6207 Rutherglenn St Houston TX 77096 Office: 1900 Saint James PL Houston TX 77056 Tel (713) 965-6155

SKENYON, JOHN MICHAEL, b. Providence, May 10, 1947; B.S., Cath. U. Am., 1969, J.D., 1973. Admitted to R.I. bar, 1973, Conn. bar, 1974; elec. engr. Singer-Link Co., Silver Spring, Md., 1969-70; mem. firm Wooster, Davis & Cifelli, Bridgeport, Conn., 1973-77, firm Fish & Richardson, Providence, 1977—; law clk. to R.I. Dept. Pub. Defender, 1971-72. Mem. Am., Conn., R.I., Bridgeport bar assns., Am., Conn. patent law assns., Assn. Trial Lawyers Am. Bd. editors Conn. Bar Jour. Home: Wake Robin Apt 311 Washington Hwy Lincoln RI 02865 Office: 636 Indsl Bank Bldg Providence RI 02903 Tel (401) 831-5090

SKERRY, DAVID PAUL, b. Medford, Mass., Apr. 14, 1942; B.S., Boston U., 1965; J.D., Boston Coll., 1968. Admitted to Mass. bar, 1968, U.S. Supreme Ct. bar, 1971, U.S. Ct. Appeals bar, 1970; sr. tax specialist Arthur Andersen & Co., C.P.A.'s, Boston, 1968-70; partner firm Skerry, Campbell & Hennessey, Medford, 1970—; vis. lectr. bus. law Boston U., 1969-72, Boston State Coll., 1975—. Mem. sch. com. City of Medford, 1969-72; mem. Medford City Council, 1972—. Mem. Am., Mass., Middlesex County bar assns., Am. Arbitration Assn. Home: 20 Wyman St Medford MA 02155 Office: 5 High St Medford MA 02155 Tel (617) 391-7000

SKIBELL, CARL ALBERT, b. N.Y.C., Apr. 11, 1932; B.B.A., U. Tex., 1953; J.D., So. Methodist U., 1958. Admitted to Tex. bar, 1957, U.S. Supreme Ct. bar, 1965; partner firm Skibell & Blicker, Dallas, 1958-65; individual practice law, Dallas, 1965-72, 75—; partner firm Skibell, Russ & Adams, Dallas, 1972-75; judge City of Farmers Branch, Tex., 1962—; dir. Goals Inc. Mem. Am., Tex. bar assns., Am. Judges Assn., Am. Judicature Soc., Tex. Municipal Ct. Judges Assn. Home: 13823 Tanglewood St Dallas TX 75234 Office: 2700 Mercantile Bank Bldg Dallas TX 75201 Tel (214) 758-6652

SKIDD, THOMAS PATRICK, JR., b. Norwalk, Conn., July 2, 1936; B.A., Georgetown U., 1958; LL.D., Yale, 1961. Admitted to Conn. bar, 1961, U.S. Supreme Ct. bar, 1963; asso. firm Cummings & Lockwood, Stamford, Conn., 1961-70, partner, 1970—; dir. Conn. Attys. Title Guaranty Fund, 1974—. Bd. dirs. Stamford Red Cross, 1967-71; dirs. Stamford United Fund, 1974-75. Mem. Conn., Stamford bar assns. Office: 1 Atlantic St Stamford CT 06904 Tel (203) 327-1700

SKINNER, JOHN GODMAN, b. Washington, May 26, 1942; A.B., Georgetown U., 1964, J.D. with honors, 1967. Admitted to Ga. bar, 1968; asso. firm Smith, Currie & Hancock, Atlanta, 1967—. Mem. Am., Ga., Atlanta bar assns. Prodn. editor George Washington U. Law Rev., 1966-67. Home: 4273 Blackland Way NE Marietta GA 30067 Office: 1400 Fulton Nat Bank Bldg Atlanta GA 30303 Tel (404) 512-3800

SKINNER, LEMOINE, III, b. St. Louis, July 15, 1944; B.A., Princeton, 1966; J.D., Hastings Coll. Law, 1972. Admitted to Calif., Mo. bars, 1973; asso. firm Hullverson, Hallverson & Frank, St. Louis, 1973-75, Pettit, Evers & Martin, San Francisco, 1975—. Mem. Am. Bar Assn., Thurston Soc., Order of Coif. Tel (415) 434-4000

SKINNER, SAMUEL K., b. Chgo., June 10, 1938; B.S. in Accounting, U. Ill., Urbana, 1960; J.D., DePaul U., 1966. Computer sales rep. IBM, Chgo., 1961-68; admitted to Ill. bar, 1966; individual practice law, 1966-68; asst. U.S. atty. Office U.S. Atty. No. Dist. Ill., 1968-75, dep. chief criminal div., 1970-71, chief div. spl. investigations, 1971-75, 1st asst. U.S. atty, 1971-75, U.S. atty., 1975-77; mem. firm Sidley & Austin, Chgo., 1977—; mem. Interdepartmental Policy Com. for Rev. of Central States Teamsters Pension and Welfare Funds; mem. U.S. Dept. Justice White Collar Crime Com.; mem. Atty. Gen's. U.S. Attys'. Advisory Com.; instr. trial practice John Marshall Law Sch. Recipient Dept. Justice Outstanding Service award U.S. Atty. Gen., 1972, 74; named 1 of 10 Outstanding Citizens of Chgo., Chgo. Jr. Assn. Commerce and Industry, 1974. Home: 670 E Old Elm Rd Lake Forest IL 60045 Office: Sidley & Austin 1 First Nat Plaza Chicago IL 60603

SKINNER, TRUMAN ARNOLD, b. Greenwood, Ark., Aug. 13, 1936; B.S., U. Fla., 1958, LL.B., 1964. Admitted to Fla. bar, 1965; partner firm Helliwell, Melrose & DeWolf, Miami, Fla., 1965—; dir. U.A. Columbia Cablevision Co., dir., sec. Am. Bankers Ins. Co. Fla.; dir. Miami Nat. Bank. Mem. Met. Dade County (Fla.) Charter Rev. Bd., 1968-69. Mem. Am., Dade County bar assns., Am. Judicature Soc. Office: 1401 Brickell Ave 9th floor Miami FL 33131 Tel (305) 373-7571

SKLAR, JERRY, b. N.Y.C., Nov. 2, 1929; B.B.A., Coll. City N.Y., 1950; J.D., Bklyn. Law Sch., 1967, LL.B., 1953. Admitted to N.Y. bar, 1954; individual practice law, N.Y.C., 1954—; lectr. Bklyn. Coll., 1956-68. Mem. Queens County Rep. Com., 1970-73. Mem. N.Y. Bar Assn., N.Y. Soc. C.P.A.'s, Assn. Attys.-C.P.A.'s, C.P.A., N.Y. Contbr. articles in field to profl. jours. Home: 137-48 71st Ave Flushing NY 11367 Office: 60 E 42d St New York City NY 10017 Tel (212) MU 7-4972

SKLAR, WILFORD NATHANIEL, b. Salt Lake City, Dec. 13, 1916; B.S., U. Pitts., 1942; J.D., Southwestern Sch. Law, 1955. Admitted to Calif. bar, 1960; claims rep. Allstate Ins. Co., Riverside, San Bernardino, Calif., 1956-60; individual practice law, Riverside, 1960—; owner Camera Exchange Inc., Pitts. Mem. human relations com. City of Riverside, 1965-68; chmn. Anti-Defamation League Riverside County, 1960—; bd. dirs. Watkins House, U. Calif., Riverside, Family Services Riverside County; mem. Riverside Transp. Com., Riverside Downtown Devel. Program. Co-pub. Workmens Compensation Handbook, 1962-65, 68, 71. Office: 4353 Main St Suite 101 103 Law Bldg PO Box 1245 Riverside CA 92502 Tel (714) 683-1454

SKOLLER, CHARLES EDWARD, b. N.Y.C., July 26, 1932; B.A., Bklyn. Coll., 1957; LL.B., Bklyn. Law Sch., 1959, J.D., 1967. Admitted to N.Y. bar, 1960; asso. firm Breitkoff Singer & Breitkoff, Jamaica, N.Y., 1962; asst. dist. atty. Queens County (N.Y.), 1962-66; individual practice law, Queens, N.Y., 1966-70; partner firm Weinstein Skoller & Kaye, and predecessor, Forest Hills, N.Y., 1970—. Mem. Queens Asst. Dist. Attys. Assn. (pres.), Queens County Criminal Cts. Bar Assn., Queens County Bar Assn. Office: 118-21 Queens Blvd Forest Hills NY 11375 Tel (212) 793-6200

SKOLNICK, S. HAROLD, b. Woonsocket, R.I., June 17, 1915; A.B. cum laude Amherst Coll., 1936; J.D., Boston U., 1940. Admitted to R.I. bar, 1940, U.S. Supreme Ct. bar, 1946, D.C. bar, 1947, Fla. bar,

1952; atty. War Dept., Washington, 1940-42; asst. gen. counsel, asst. chief legal dept. Office Chief Ordnance Dept. Army, Washington, 1947-50; asso. firm Francis I. McCanna, Providence, 1951-52; partner firm French & Skolnick, Miami, 1953-60; individual practice law, Miami, 1961—. Mem. Am., R.I., D.C., Dade County bar assns., Am. Judicature Soc., Am. Acad. Polit. and Social Scis., Am. Defense Preparedness Assn. Office: Suite 1119 AI duPont Bldg 169 E Flagler St Miami FL 33131 Tel (305) 371-7587

SKOPIL, OTTO RICHARD, JR., b. Portland, Oreg., June 3, 1919; B.A. in Econs., Willamette U., 1941, LL.B., 1946. Admitted to Oreg. bar, 1946, U.S. Supreme Ct. bar, 1967; practiced in Salem, Oreg., 1946-72; judge U.S. Dist. Ct., Portland, 1972—. Trustee Willamette U., 1969-71; mem. Oreg. Commn. on Staffing Standards of Oreg. Mental Hosps., 1969-70; bd. dirs. Internat. Christian Leadership. Mem. Oreg. State Bar (gov.), Marion County (Oreg.) Bar Assn. Home: 1 Goya St Lake Oswego OR 97034 Office: 702 US Courthouse Portland OR 97205 Tel (503) 221-3543

SKOUSEN, RICHARD EARL, b. Phoenix, Sept. 3, 1935; B.S., Brigham Young U., 1959; J.D., U. Ariz., 1962. Admitted to Ariz. bar, 1962; partner firm Skousen, McLaws, & Skousen, Mesa, Ariz., 1962—. Chmn. Mesa Parks and Recreation Bd., 1976—; bishop Ch. of Jesus Christ of Latter Day Saints, 1975—; bd. dirs. Southside Dist. Hosp., Mesa; mem. adv. bd. Desert Samaritan Hosp., Mesa, 1973—. Mem. Am., Ariz. trial lawyers assns., Am., Ariz., Tri-City (past pres.) bar assns., Order of Coif. Home: 2059 E Hackamore St Mesa AZ 85203 Office: 20 E Main St suite 700 Mesa AZ 85201 Tel (602) 833-8800

SKULINA, THOMAS RAYMOND, b. Cleve., Sept. 14, 1933; A.B., John Carroll U., 1951-55; J.D., Case-Western Res. U., 1959; LL.M., 1962. Admitted to Ohio bar, 1959, U.S. Supreme Ct. bar, 1964; asso. firm Leanza, Bernard, & Longano, Cleve., 1959-60; asst. gen. atty. Consol. Rail Corp., Cleve., 1960—; partner firm Skulina & Stringer, Cleve., 1967-73; income tax adminstr., fed. fund coordinator City of Warrensville Heights, Ohio, 1970—. Mem. Am., Ohio, Cuyahoga, Greater Cleve. bar assns., Am. Acad. Trial Attys., Ill., Ohio trial lawyers assn. Contbr. articles to legal jours. Home: 5870 Cable Ave Cleveland OH 44127 Office: 420 Standard Bldg Cleveland OH 44113 Tel (216) 696-2240

SKUPA, WILLIAM STANLEY, b. Portland, Oreg., Feb. 28, 1945; B.S. in Bus. Adminstrn., Nev. So. U., 1967; J.D., U. Calif., Los Angeles, 1970. Admitted to Nev. bar, 1970; dep. dist. atty. Clark County (Nev.), 1971-72; asso. firm Morse, Foley & Wadsworth, Las Vegas, 1972-75; partner firm Skupa & Mainor, Las Vegas, 1975—. Mem. Am., Nev., Clark County bar assns., Am. Trial Lawyers Assn. Office: 302 E Carson St Las Vegas NV 89101 385-2557

SKUTT, VESTOR JOSEPH, b. Deadwood, S.D., Feb. 24, 1902; LL.B., Creighton U., 1923, LL.D., 1971; LL.D., U. Nebr. at Omaha, 1958, U. Nebr. Coll. Medicine, 1964. Admitted to Nebr. bar, 1923, Tex. bar, 1923; individual practice law, Omaha, 1923-24; mem. legal dept. Mut. Benefit Health and Accident Assn. (now Mut. of Omaha), 1924-30, v.p., 1947-48, exec. v.p., 1948-49, pres., 1949-64, chmn. bd. dirs., chief exec. officer, 1953—, also dir.; v.p. United Benefit Life Ins. Co., Omaha, 1936-49, chmn. bd., 1963—; pres. Companion Life Ins. Co., N.Y.C., 1949-63, chmn. bd. dirs., 1963—; chmn. bd. Mut. of Omaha Fund Mgmt. Co., 1968—. Gen. chmn. United War and Community Chest Campaign, Omaha, 1945; nat. crusade chmn. Am. Cancer Soc., 1967; founding pres. Nebr. Wildlife Fedn., 1970-72; chmn. Jr. Achievement Omaha, 1974; bd. dirs. World Rehab. Fund, Inc., numerous other civic activities. Mem. Am. Bar Assn., Assn. Life Ins. Counsel, Nat. Alliance Businessmen (chmn. 1976-77), Ins. Econs. Soc. Am. (exec. com.), Fedn. Ins. Counsel (Man of Year 1971), Delta Theta Phi. Recipient Nebraskan of Year award Nebr. Broadcasters Assn., 1964; Golden Sword of Hope award Am. Cancer Soc., 1966; Nat. Distinguished Service award United Negro Coll. Fund, 1975; Golden Plate award Am. Acad. Achievement, 1976; others. Home: 400 N 62d St Omaha NE 68132 Office: Dodge at 33d St Omaha NE 68131 Tel (402) 342-7600

SKWIERAWSKI, MICHAEL JOSEPH, b. Milw., Oct. 19, 1942; B.S. in Accounting, Marquette U., 1964; J.D., Georgetown U., 1967. Admitted to Wis. bar, 1967; asso. firm Bernstein, Wessel & Lewis, Milw., 1967-70; asst. dist. atty., Milw. County, Wis., 1970-73; asso. firm Shneidman & Myers, Milw., 1973-76; asso. firm Purtell, Purcell, Wilmot & Burroughs, Milw., 1976—; chief atty. organized crime div. Milw. County, 1972-73; spl. asst. U.S. atty., eastern dist. Wis., 1972-73; ct. commr., Milw. County, 1976—. Mem. Am., Wis. trial lawyers assns., Wis., Milw. Jr. bar assns. Home: 5030 W Washington Blvd Milwaukee WI 53208 Tel (414) 272-8550

SKYDELL, NORMAN BARUCH, b. N.Y.C., May 20, 1944; A.B., Columbia, 1965; J.D., U. Pa., 1968. Admitted to N.Y. bar, 1968; asso. firm Kass, Goodkind, Wechster & Gerstein, N.Y.C., 1969-72, mem., 1973—. Mem. Am. Bar Assn. Home: 180 W End Ave New York City NY 10023 Office: 122 E 42d St New York City NY 10017 Tel (212) 490-2332

SLACK, HARRY ALLEN, b. Atlanta, Ill., July 15, 1900; LL.B., Ill. Wesleyan U., 1924. Admitted to Oreg. bar, 1931; practiced in Coquille, Oreg. Mem. Oreg. State Bar (bd. govs. 1961-64), Am., Oreg. bar assns. Home: 110 Gould St Coquille OR 97423 Office: 222 E 2d St Coquille OR 97423

SLADE, HERBERT THOMAS, b. Syracuse, N.Y., Aug. 10, 1915; A.B., Hamilton Coll., 1937; LL.B., Syracuse U., 1940; grad. with honors Ins. Inst. Am., 1960. Admitted to N.Y. bar, 1941, U.S. Supreme Ct. bar; asso. firm Smith, Sovik, Levine & Richardson, Syracuse, 1946-49; exec. atty. Frank H. Hiscock Legal Aid. Soc., Syracuse, 1950-55, bd. dirs., 1957—; regional claims atty. Nationwide Mut. Ins. Co., Syracuse, 1955—; guest lectr. Syracuse U. Coll. Law, instr. law and social work Univ. Coll., 1951-52; mem. arbitration panel Am. Arbitration Assn. Mem. Onondaga County (N.Y.) Council Social Agys., 1951-57, Camillus (N.Y.) Narcotics Guidance Council, 1971-74. Mem. Am., N.Y. State, N.Y., Onondaga County (1st v.p. 1974) bar assns., Soc. C.P.C.U.'s. Contbr. articles to profl. publs. Home: 18 Richlee Dr Camillus NY 13031 Office: 110 Elwood-Davis Rd North Syracuse NY 13212 Tel (315) 451-4660

SLADE, TOM BOG, b. Columbus, Ga., Mar. 19, 1920; Ph.B., Emory U., 1941, J.D., 1944. Admitted to Ga. bar, 1943, U.S. Supreme Ct. bar, 1950; asso. firm Swift, Pease, Davidson & Chapman, Columbus, 1944-49, partner, 1949-71; partner firm Page, Scrantom, Harris, McGlamry & Chapman, Columbus, 1971—. Chmn., Com. for a Greater Community, Columbus, 1967. Mem. Ga. State Bar, Am., Chattahoochee (pres. 1960) bar assns., Columbus Lawyers Club (pres. 1956), Am. Judicature Soc. Editorial bd. Emory U. Law Rev., 1942-44. Home: 2866 Techwood Dr Columbus GA 31902 Office: 1043 Third Ave PO Box 1199 Columbus GA 31902 Tel (404) 324-0251

SLADKUS, HARVEY IRA, b. Bklyn., Mar. 5, 1929; A.B., Syracuse U., 1950; J.D., N.Y. U., 1961. Admitted to N.Y. bar, 1962, U.S. Supreme Ct. bar, 1967; asso. firm Morris Ploscowe, N.Y.C., 1961-66; individual practice law, N.Y.C., 1966-67; partner firm Dweck & Sladkus, N.Y.C., 1968—; lectr. in field. Mem. Am., N.Y., N.Y.C. bar assns., Am. Arbitration Assn. (panel arbitrators), Am. Acad. Matrimonial Lawyers (bd. govs. local chpt. 1970-73, 75—, chmn. com. family ct. and family law, 1973-75). Contbr. articles N.Y. Law Jour.; author profl. presentations. Office: 666 5th Ave New York City NY 10019 Tel (212) 246-6666

SLAFF, GEORGE, b. Passaic, N.J., May 22, 1906; A.B., Harvard, 1926; J.D., Stanford, 1929. Admitted to N.Y. bar, 1930, Calif. bar, 1947; asso. firm William A. Hyman, N.Y.C., 1930-31; partner firm Slaff & Sass, N.Y.C., 1932-38; spl. counsel City of Louisville (ky.), 1935-37; prin. atty. pub. utility div. SEC, Washington, 1938-39; sr. atty., chief counsel Fed. Power Commn., Washington, 1938-42, 45; field dir. ARC, Eng., 1942, asst. to delegate, Algiers, N. Africa, 1942-43, dir. food supply, Italy, France, 1943-45; chief counsel Fed. Power Commn., Washington, 1945-46; counsel Samuel Goldwyn Prodns., Los Angeles, 1946-68; sr. partner firm Slaff, Mosk & Rudman, Los Angeles, 1965—. Bd. dirs., treas. Permanent Charities Com. Entertainment Industry, Los Angeles, 1955—; mem. Beverly Hills (Calif.) City Council, 1966—, mayor, 1968-69, 75-76. Mem. Am., Los Angeles County, Beverly Hills bar assns. Contbr. articles in field to profl. jours. and mags. Home: 712 Whittier Dr Beverly Hills CA 90210 Office: Suite 825 9200 Sunset Blvd Los Angeles CA 90069 Tel (213) 275-5351

SLAGLE, RICHARD LYNN, b. Hot Springs, Ark., Sept. 30, 1944; B.A. with distinction, Henderson State U., 1966; J.D. with honors, U. Ark., 1969. Admitted to Ark. bar, 1969; partner firm Anderson & Slagle, Hot Springs, 1969-72, firm Wootton, Land & Mathews, Hot Springs, 1972—. Mem. Am., Ark. (ho. of dels. 1976—), Garland County bar assns., Phi Alpha Delta. Note editor Ark. Law Rev., 1968-69. Office: First National Bank Bldg Hot Springs AR 71901 Tel (501) 623-2593

SLATER, HERBERT JEROME, b. N.Y.C., Jan. 18, 1928; A.B., L.I. U., 1949; J.D., Bklyn. Law Sch., 1952. Admitted to N.Y. bar, 1954, U.S. Supreme Ct. bar, 1954; asso. firm Jerome Edelman, Bklyn., 1953-57; individual practice law, Bklyn., 1957—. Mem. N.Y. State, Bklyn. bar assns., Am., N.Y. State (trustee 1975-76) trial lawyers assns., Lawyers Interested in Victims' Equality (trustee 1975-76). Home: 1663 E 29th St Brooklyn NY 11229 Office: 26 Court St Brooklyn NY 11242 Tel (212) 625-6624

SLATTERY, JAMES P., b. Bklyn., July 18, 1942; B.A., St. John's Coll., 1963, J.D., 1966. Admitted to N.Y. bar, 1969, U.S. Supreme Ct. bar, 1973, U.S. Ct. Appeals bar, 1975; asso. firm Cullen & Dykman, Bklyn., 1969—. Mem. Am., N.Y. State, Bklyn. bar assns., Real Property Tax Assessment Bar Assn. Office: 177 Montague St Brooklyn NY 11201 Tel (212) 855-9000

SLAUGHTER, ARTHUR PHILIP, b. Rosita, Coahuila, Mex., May 3, 1941; B.A., Rice U., 1963; J.D., U. Houston, 1970. Admitted to Tex. bar, 1967; corporate counsel Big Three Industries, Inc., Houston, 1967—. Bd. dirs. The Design Collaborative, Inc., 1977—. Mem. Am. Bar Assn. Home: 2600 Ridgewood Houston TX 77006 Office: 3535 W 12th St Houston TX 77008 Tel (713) 864-7701

SLAUGHTER, CONSTANCE IONA, b. Jackson, Miss., June 18, 1946; B.A., Tougaloo Coll., 1967; J.D., U. Miss., 1970; ISSP diploma Harvard U., 1966. Admitted to Miss. bar, 1970, U.S. Supreme Ct. bar, 1974; staff atty. Lawyers Com for Civil Rights Under Law, Jackson, 1970-72; individual practice law, Forest, Miss., 1972—; exec. dir. So. Legal Rights Assn., Forest, 1972—; instr. law Tougaloo Coll., 1970-72, 75-77, Quincy cons., 1974-75; bd. dirs. Central Miss. Legal Services, Inc., Jackson, 1972—, N. Miss. Rural Legal Services, Oxford, 1969—. Mem. Forest Zoning Bd., 1974—; mem. council St. Michael's Parish, 1977. Mem. Am., Nat., Miss., Magnolia, Scott County bar assns., Nat. Conf. Black Lawyers, Am. Judicature Soc., Delta Found., Inc. Recipient Woman of Year award Greyhound Corp. and Jackson Adv., 1972; Civil Libertarian award Elks, 1971; named Outstanding Mississippian, 1973; Ms. Mag. Found Woman, 1973, Outstanding Young Woman Am., 1976; author: The Status of Mississippi Homemakers, 1977. Office: 568 Jones St PO Box 88 Forest MS 39074 Tel (601) 469-4982

SLAUGHTER, LOGAN ALLEN, b. Fort Benning, Ga., Feb. 11, 1942; B.A., U. Miss., 1964; J.D., U. Ark., 1971. Admitted to Ark. bar, 1971, Tex. bar, 1973; asso. firm Rose, Barron, Nash, Williamson, Carrol & Clay, Little Rock, 1971-73; atty. office dist. counsel VA, Houston, 1973—; guest lectr. Tex. Woman's U. Sch. Nursing, 1975—. Mem. Am., Fed., Tex. bar assns. Contbr. articles in field to profl. jours. Home: 10223 Chatterton Houston TX 77043 Office: 2515 Murworth Houston TX 77043 Tel (713) 226-4127

SLAVICK, BETTY SHEILA MINTZ, b. Chgo., Dec. 24, 1917; Ph.B., Marquette U., 1938, LL.B., 1940. Admitted to Wis. bar, 1940; since practiced in Milw.; claims adjuster U.S. F. & G. Ins., 1961-71; with Goetz & Haessler Agy., 1971-72; with U.S. Govt., 1973-74; vol. atty. Legal Aid Soc. Milw., 1960-61; adVisor Jewish Family Service. Mem. LWV (legal com., 1975—). Mem. Kappa Beta Pi. Home: 5444 N Iroquois Milwaukee WI 53217 Tel (414) 228-2834

SLAVIN, SHERMAN RALPH, b. Watertown, N.Y., Jan. 16, 1922; B.A., Harvard, 1942, LL.B., 1949. Admitted to Conn. bar, 1949; individual practice law, Watertown, Conn., 1951—; atty. Town of Watertown, 1965-68, 71-72. Mem. Watertown Bd. Edn., 1952-61; trustee Watertown Library, 1965-68. Mem. Waterbury, Litchfield County, Am. bar assns. Home: 55 Woolson St Watertown CT 06795 Office: 700 Main St Watertown CT 06795 Tel (203) 274-6719

SLAVITT, EARL BENTON, b. Chgo., Sept. 12, 1939; B.S. in Econs., U. Pa., 1961, J.D., 1964. Admitted to Ill. bar, 1964, U.S. Supreme Ct. bar, 1971; since practiced in Chgo.; asso. firm Wisch, Crane & Kravets, 1964-66, Ressman & Tishler, 1966-69; asso. firm Levy and Erens, 1969-73, partner, 1973—; lectr. bus. law Walton Sch. Commerce, Chgo., 1967-69; lectr. John Marshall Law Sch., Chgo., 1968-69. Mem. Ill., Am., Chgo. bar assns., Chgo. Council Lawyers. Contbr. articles to legal jours. Home: 405 Darrow Ave Evanston IL 60202 Office: 208 S LaSalle St Chicago IL 60604 Tel (312) 368-9500

SLAVITT, SAMUEL S., b. N.Y.C., Feb. 11, 1906; student Yale U., 1923-25; B.S., N.Y. U., 1930, LL.B., 1929. Admitted to N.Y. bar, 1930; individual practice law, White Plains, N.Y., 1931—; confdl. law sec. to asso. justice N.Y. Supreme Ct., 1951-63. Mem. N.Y. State, Westchester County (chmn. com. on appellate cts.), White Plains (past pres.) bar assns. Home: 61 Smith Ave White Plains NY 10605 Office: 199 Main St White Plains NY 10601 Tel (914) 949-6732

SLAWSON, WILLIAM DAVID, b. Grand Rapids, Mich., June 2, 1931; B.A., Amherst Coll., 1953; M.A., Princeton, 1954; LL.B., Harvard, 1959. Admitted to Colo., bar, 1959; asso. firm Davis, Granham & Stubbs, Denver, 1959-64, partner, 1964-65; atty.-advisor Office of Legal Counsel, Dept. Justice, Washington, 1965-67; prof. law U. So. Calif., Los Angeles, 1967—; vis. prof. law U. Pa., 1972-73, Stanford, summer 1973; gen. counsel Price Commn., Washington, 1971-72; asst. counsel Pres.'s Commn. on Assasination of Pres. John F. Kennedy (Warren Commn.), 1964. Contbr. law review articles to profl. jours. Office: U So Calif Univ Park Los Angeles CA 90007 Tel (213) 746-2185

SLAYNE, BRIAN G., b. Mineola, N.Y., Mar. 26, 1940; B.A., Fairfield U., 1961; J.D., St. John's U., 1969. Admitted to N.Y. bar, 1969; asso. firm Thacher, Proffitt & Wood, N.Y.C., 1969-73, partner, 1973—; adj. asst. prof. law St. John's U. Mem. Am., N.Y. State bar assns., Assn. Bar City N.Y. Home: 247 Doremus Ave Ridgewood NJ 07450 Office: 40 Wall St New York City NY 10005 Tel (212) 483-5927

SLEDD, HERBERT DAVIS, b. Paris, Ky., Mar. 19, 1925; student U. Ky., 1946-48; J.D., Chgo.-Kent Coll. Law, 1952. Admitted to Ky. bar, 1952, U.S. Supreme Ct., 1963; practiced in Lexington, 1952—; mem. firm Brown, Sledd & McCann, 1956—; asst. atty. Fayette County (Ky.), Lexington, 1960-64. Chmn. adminstrv. bd. Disciples of Christ Central Christian Ch., 1959-60, chmn. congregation, 1966-70, elder; vice chmn. dist. com. Blue Grass council Boy Scouts Am., 1956-58; mem. Ky. Statute Revision Commn., 1965-68; bd. dirs. United Cerebral Palsy of Blue Grass; chmn. bd. govs. Lexington unit Shriners Hosps. for Crippled Children; trustee Lexington Theol. Sem., 1959—, chmn. bd., 1966-69. Fellow Am. Coll. Trial Lawyers, Am. Bar Found., Am. Law Inst.; mem. Am. (ho. of dels., bd. govs., sec. 1975—), Ky. (past pres. Younger Lawyer's Conf., pres. 1965-66, named Outstanding Lawyer 1959, bd. govs. 1958-69), Fayette County (gov. 1955-61, pres. 1958) bar assns., Ky. Bar Found. (pres. 1964-70), Ky. Peace Officers Council (chmn. 1967-68), Lexington C. of C. (pres. 1974), U. Ky. Alumni Assn., Spindletop Hall. Home: 1617 Richmond Rd Lexington KY 40502 Office: 300 W Short St Lexington KY 40507 Tel (606) 254-2712

SLEIK, THOMAS SCOTT, b. LaCrosse, Wis., Feb. 24, 1947; B.S., Marquette U., 1969, J.D., 1971. Admitted to Wis. bar, 1971; asso. firm Hale Skemp Hanson Schnurrer & Skemp, LaCrosse, 1971-75, partner, 1975—. Mem. LaCrosse Area Bd. of Edn., 1973—, v.p., 1975; mem. exec. bd. Gateway Area council Boy Scouts Am., 1974—, treas., 1976; mem. LaCrosse Area Conv. and Visitors Bur., 1974—. Mem. Am., Wis., LaCrosse County bar assns. Home: 4082 Glenhaven Dr LaCrosse WI 54601 Office: 515 State Bank Bldg LaCrosse WI 54601 Tel (608) 784-3540

SLEMMER, CARL WEBER, JR., b. Camden, N.J., Mar. 28, 1923; B.S., Muhlenberg Coll., 1948; J.D., Temple U., 1963. Personnel asst. Heyden Chem. Corp., Princeton, N.J., 1948-49; with RCA, Camden, N.J., 1950-55; with Allied Chem. Corp., 1955-67, mgr. employee relations, gen. chem. div., Morristown, N.J., 1965-66, mgr. indsl. relations Idaho Nuclear Corp. subs., Idaho Falls, 1966-67; dir. employee relations ESB Inc., Phila., 1967—; admitted to N.J. bar, 1972, Pa. bar, 1972, Fla. bar, 1974. Mem. U. Pa. Labor Council. Mem. Am., N.J., Fla. bar assns., Indsl. Relations Assn. Phila., Phi Delta Phi. Office: ESB Inc Rising Sun and Adams Aves Philadelphia PA 19120 Tel (215) FI 2-8000

SLEPPIN, SOL HERMAN, b. Minsk, Russia, Sept. 20, 1903; student N.Y. U., 1920-24, LL.B., 1924. Admitted to N.Y. State bar, 1926; partner firm Cohen & Sleppin, N.Y.C., 1926-34; individual practice law, N.Y.C., 1934-41, 49—; partner firm Sleppin & Sleppin, N.Y.C., 1941-49; police judge Village of Saddle Rock, N.Y., 1951-59; hearing examiner N.Y.C. Parking Violations Bur., 1970—; arbitrator City Ct. of City of N.Y., 1970—. Trustee, Jewish Centre for UN, 1965—, treas., 1968-74, v.p., 1974—. Mem. N.Y. County Lawyers Assn. Home: 411 E 57th St New York City NY 10022 Office: 400 Madison Ave New York City NY 10017 Tel (212) 355-5622

SLICHTER, DONALD ALLEN, b. Milw., Feb. 18, 1932; A.B., Princeton, 1954; J.D., U. Mich., 1961. Admitted to Calif. bar, 1962; asso. firm Orrick, Herrington, Rowley & Sutcliffe, San Francisco, 1961-67, partner, 1968—. Mem. Am., San Francisco bar assns., State Bar Calif. Home: 82 Jordan Ave San Francisco CA 94118 Office: 600 Montgomery St San Francisco CA 94111 Tel (415) 392-1122

SLICK, JANET MARIE, b. Long Beach, Calif., Aug. 7, 1947; J.D., Pepperdine U., 1972. Admitted to Calif. bar, 1973; U.S. Dist. Ct. for Central Calif. bar, 1974; partner firm Slick & Slick, Long Beach, 1973—. Mem. State Bar Calif., Long Beach Bar Assn. Office: 440 Redondo Suite 201 Long Beach CA 90814 Tel (213) 434-1354

SLOAN, DAVID WARREN, b. N.Y.C., Oct. 15, 1937; B.A., Columbia, 1959, LL.B., 1962. Admitted to N.Y. bar, 1962, U.S. Dist. Ct. bar, S. Dist. N.Y., 1963; asso. firm Parker, Duryee, Zunino, Malone & Carter, N.Y.C., 1962-68, partner, 1969—. Office: 1 E 44th St New York City NY 10017 Tel (212) 573-9330

SLOAN, DONNIE ROBERT, JR., b. Nashville, July 24, 1946; B. Indsl. Engring., Ga. Inst. Tech., 1968; J.D. cum laude, U. Ga., 1971; LL.M., Harvard, 1975. Admitted to Ga. bar, 1971; corp. counsel Southwire Co., Carrollton, Ga., 1971-74, mng. atty., 1974; asso. firm Hyatt & Rhoads, Atlanta, 1975—; instr. legal research, research asst. U. Ga., Athens, 1970-71. Mem. Am. Bar Assn., State Bar Ga., Am. Judicature Soc., Ga. Assn. Paraplegics, Phi Kappa Phi. Home: 4399 Tree Haven Dr Atlanta GA 30342 Office: 2200 Peachtree Center Harris Tower Atlanta GA 30303 Tel (404) 659-6600

SLOAN, EUGENE, b. Powhatan, Ark., Sept. 15, 1892; A.B., Ark. Coll., Batesville, 1912; LL.B., Vanderbilt U., Nashville, 1915. Admitted to Ark. bar, 1915; since practiced in Jonesboro; mem. firm Lamb, Caraway & Wheatley, 1915-17, Lamb, Furney & Sloane, 1916-17, Sloan & Sloan, 1917-77; city atty. City of Jonesboro, 1918-22; pres., dir. Fed. Land Bank Assn. for Craighead and Greene Counties, 1924-62. Mem. Am., Ark., Craighead bar assns. Home: State Hwy 18 PO Box 267 Jonesboro AR 72401 Office: 215 Jefferson St Jonesboro AR 72401 Tel (506) 932-2671

SLOAN, F(RANK) BLAINE, b. Geneva, Nebr., Jan. 3, 1920; A.B. with high distinction, U. Nebr., 1942, LL.B. cum laude, 1946; LL.M. in Internat. Law, Columbia, 1947. Admitted to Nebr. bar, 1946, N.Y. bar, 1947; law clk. firm Sloans, Keenan & Corbitt, Geneva, 1936-42; asst. to spl. counsel Intergovtl. Com. for Refugees, N.Y.C., 1947;

mem. office legal affairs staff UN Secretariat, N.Y.C., 1948—, gen. counsel UN Relief and Works Agy. for Palestine Refugees, Beirut, 1958-60, dep. dir. office of legal counsel, 1964-66, dir. gen. legal div., 1966—; rep. of sec.-gen. sessions of Commn. on Internat. Trade Law, 1969-76, on legal subcom. on Peaceful Uses of Outer Space, 1969-77; legal adviser UN Conf. on Human Environment, Stockholm, 1972, Security Council Sessions in Africa, 1972, in Latin Am., 1973; mem. sec.-gen's del. to Internat. Conf. on Vietnam, Paris, 1973. Mem. Am. Soc. Internat. Law, Am. Acad. Polit. and Social Sci., Order of Coif, Phi Beta Kappa. Decorated Air medal; recipient appellate ct. competition award Nebr. Law Sch., 1946; contbr. articles to legal publs.; editor Nebr. Law Rev., 1942-43. Home: 23 Hall Rd Briarcliff Manor NY 10510 Office: Office of Legal Affairs Gen Legal Div UN New York City NY 10017 Tel (212) 754-5348

SLOAN, JAMES LOUIS, b. Ft. Smith, Ark., July 30, 1917; A.B., Subiaco Coll., 1947; LL.B., U. Ark., 1950, J.D., 1969; LL.M., N.Y. U., 1952; certificate of completion JAG Sch., U.S. Army, Charlottesville, Va., 1965, Indsl. Coll. Armed Forces, Washington, 1972. Admitted to Ark. bar, 1950, U.S. Supreme Ct. bar, 1954; individual practice law, Little Rock, 1953—; instr. law, Ohio No. Coll. Law, Ada, 1950-51; instr., teaching fellow N.Y. U. Law Sch., N.Y.C., 1951-52; asst. atty. gen. and chief asst. atty. gen. State of Ark., Little Rock, 1953-56; instr. law, Ark. Law Sch., Little Rock, 1953-66; spl. atty. Ark. Legis. Council, Bur. Research, Little Rock, 1957, 59, 61, 63, 65 sessions Ark. Gen. Assembly. Mem. Ark., Pulaski County Bar Assns., Ark. Criminal Def. Lawyers Assn., Phi Alpha Delta, Omicron Delta Kappa. Contbr. articles to legal publs. Home: 5401 Southwood Rd Little Rock AR 72205 Office: 1100 Worthen Bank Bldg Little Rock AR 72201 Tel (501) 372-2497

SLOAN, JAMES WENDELL, b. Hoxie, Kans., Dec. 30, 1927; A.B., Washburn U., 1950, J.D., 1952. Admitted to Kans. bar, 1952; partner firm Sloan, Listrom, Eisenbarth, Sloan & Glassman, Topeka, 1952—; asst. atty. Shawnee County, Kans., 1960-62. Chmn. Shawnee County Democratic Central Com., 1961-66; pres. Topeka Civic Theatre, 1955-56. Mem. Am., Kans., Topeka bar assns. Home: 349 Woodbury Ct N Topeka KS 66606 Office: 714 Capitol Fed Bldg Topeka KS 66603 Tel (913) 357-6311

SLOAN, JEROME S., b. Detroit, Feb. 24, 1930; B.A., U. Chgo., 1953, J.D., 1956; LL.M., Yale, 1966; docteur en droit Université d'Aix, (France), 1962. Admitted to Ill. bar, 1956, Mich. bar, 1958, N.Y. bar, 1959, D.C. bar, 1960, French bar, 1961; partner firm Grant, Green, Sidman, & Shelly, Detroit, 1959-63; asso. prof. law Temple U., 1966-72, prof., 1972—; adviser select senate com. on campaign practices, 1974. Mem. Inter-Am. Bar Assn., Am. Soc. Arts and Letters. Author: Status and Process in the American Law. Contbr. articles to legal jours. Office: Temple U Law Sch Philadelphia PA 19122 Tel (412) 787-7830

SLOAN, SHELDON HAROLD, b. Mpls., Dec. 25, 1935; B.S. in Bus. Adminstrn., U. Calif., Los Angeles, 1958; J.D., U. So. Calif., 1961. Admitted to Calif. bar, 1962, U.S. Supreme Ct. bar, 1973; atty. civil div. U.S. Dept. Justice, Washington, 1962-63; partner firm Brown & Brown, Los Angeles, 1963-73; judge Los Angeles Jud. Dist., 1973-76; partner firm Brown & Brown, Los Angeles, 1976—; mem. Calif. Bd. Profl. Engrs., 1972-73; staff Calif. Judges Coll., 1975. Bd. dirs. Community TV So. Calif., 1973. Mem. Los Angeles County, Calif., Am. Bar assns. Office: 10100 Santa Monica Blvd Suite 2080 Los Angeles CA 90067

SLOAN, WILLIAM TROY, b. Memphis, Aug. 12, 1947; B.B.A., U. Miss., 1969, J.D., 1972. Admitted to Miss. bar, 1972; sales agt. Greater Bus. and Indsl. Devel. Corp., 1969; bank examiner Miss. Dept. Bank Supervision, 1969-70; asso. firm Omar D. Craig, Oxford, Miss., 1972-74; individual practice law, Oxford, 1974—; dir. Farm Fish Inc. Mem. Oxford City Planning Commn., 1975—. Mem. Am., Lafayette County (officer) bar assns., Miss. State Bar, Am., Miss. trial lawyers assns., Oxford Eating Club, Delta Theta Phi. Home: 911 S Lamar St Oxford MS 38655 Office: 102 1/2 S Lamar St Oxford MS 38655 Tel (601) 234-1667

SLOANE, EDWARD FREDERICK, b. Gettysburg, Pa., Aug. 11, 1926; A.B., George Washington U., 1950, LL.B., 1951. Admitted to D.C. bar, 1951, Va. bar, 1977, U.S. Dist. Ct. for D.C., 1951, U.S. Ct. Appeals bar, 1952, U.S. Supreme Ct. bar, 1961; atty. Office of Gen. Counsel, Fed. Home Loan Bank Bd., Washington, 1951-68, asst. gen. counsel, 1960-63, asso. gen. counsel, 1963-68; partner firm Sloane & Muldoon, Washington, 1968-73, Sloane & Rogal, Washington, 1973—; mem. Adminstrv. Conf. of U.S., 1960-61. Pres., Hope Lutheran Ch., Annandale, Va., 1965. Member D.C., Va., Fed. bar assns. Office: Suite 517 1225 Connecticut Ave NW Washington DC 20036 Tel (202) 659-2133

SLOANE, IRA P., b. Bklyn., Feb. 4, 1939; B.A., C.W. Post Coll., 1960; LL.B., N.Y. U., 1964. Admitted to N.Y. State bar, 1964; law sec. to judge N.Y. State Ct. Appeals, 1964-66; exec. asst. to senator, Washington, 1967; asso. firm Pratt, Caemmerer & Cleary, Mineola, N.Y., 1968-69; asso. spl. counsel Suffolk County Bd. Suprs., 1970; mem. firm Greshin, Sloane & Ziegler, Smithtown, N.Y., 1970—; instr. law N.Y. Law Sch., 1966. Bd. dirs. Civil Liberties Union Suffolk County. Mem. Am., N.Y. State, Nassau County bar assns. Editor-in-chief N.Y. Law Forum, 1963. Office: 12 Bank Ave Smithtown NY 11787 Tel (516) 265-2550

SLONIM, ARTHUR H., b. St. Louis, June 21, 1927; A.B., Washington U., St. Louis, 1948, LL.B., 1950, J.D., 1968. Admitted to Mo. bar, 1950, Fed. bar, 1956, U.S. Supreme Ct. bar, 1956, U.S. Ct. Appeals bar, 1971; asso. firm Frey and Korngold, St. Louis, 1950-52; commissioned officer Judge Advocate Gen.'s U.S. Air Force, 1952-54; individual practice law, St. Louis, 1954-60; partner firm Friedman and Slonim, Mo., 1960-61; individual practice law, Mo., 1962-67; partner firm Slonim and Ross, 1967—; instr. real estate law Washington U., St. Louis, 1964-71. Mem. Planning Commn. University City, Mo., 1959-62, also chmn.; bd. dirs. Shaare Zedek Synagogue, University City. Mem. Am., St. Louis County bar assns., Bar. Assn. Met. St. Louis, Lawyers Assn. St. Louis. Contbr. articles to legal jours. Home: 9439 Old Bonhomme Rd St Louis County MO 63132 Office: 111 S Meramec Ave Suite 506 Meramec Bldg Clayton MO 63105 Tel (314) 725-1060

SLOSS, DAVID ALAN, b. Fayetteville, N.C., Oct. 17, 1945; B.A., Tufts U., 1967; J.D., Columbia 1970. Admitted to N.Y. bar, 1971; asso. firm Olslan, Grundman & Frome, N.Y.C., 1970-75, partner, 1976—. Mem. N.Y. State, Am. bar assns. Home: 299 W 12th St New York City NY 10014 Office: Olslan Grundman & Frome 90 Park Ave New York City NY 10016

SLOTNICK, MICHAEL COTLER, b. Utica, N.Y., Apr. 30, 1935; B.A. Magna Cum Laude, U. Miami, 1957, J.D. Cum Laude, 1960. Admitted to Fla. bar, 1960, U.S. Ct. Appeals 5th Circuit bar, 1961; asso. firm Bolles & Prunty, Miami, Fla., 1962-65; partner firm Prunty, Olsen & Slotnick, Miami, 1965-70; asso. firm Pallot, Poppell, Goodman & Shapo, Miami, 1970-73; partner firm Pallot, Poppell, Goodman & Slotnick, Miami, 1973—. Chmn. Kendale Elementary Sch. Citizens Adv. com., Miami, 1975-76; pres. Kendale Home Owners Assn., Miami, 1970-72, Temple Zion, 1972-74. Mem. Fla. Bar, Am., Dade County bar assns. Contbr. articles to U. Miami Law Rev., books. Home: 10340 SW 96th Terr Miami FL 33176 Office: 1504 Alfred I duPont Bldg Miami FL 33131 Tel (305) 371-2723

SLOUGH, JOHN EDWARD, b. Phila., May 29, 1942; B.A. in Polit. Sci., Calif. State U., 1965; J.D., U. Calif., Hastings Coll. Law, 1972; LL.M., U. London, 1973. Admitted to Calif. bar, 1973, Fla. bar, 1975, Md. bar, 1975, D.C. bar, 1976, U.S. Supreme Ct. bar, 1976; atty. Bank of Am., San Francisco, 1973-74; asst. corp. counsel Easco Corp., Balt., 1975-76; v.p., gen. counsel Snelling and Snelling, Inc., Sarasota, Fla., 1976—. Mem. Am., Calif., D.C., Fla., Md. bar assns., Bar Assn. Balt. Home: 7331 Biltmore Dr Sarasota FL 33581 Office: Snelling and Snelling 4000 S Tamiami Trail Sarasota FL 33579 Tel (813) 922-9616

SLOVENKO, RALPH, b. New Orleans, Nov. 4, 1927; B.E., Tulane U., 1948, LL.B., 1953, M.A., 1960, Ph.D., 1965; postgrad. (Fulbright scholar) U. Aix-en-Provence (France), 1954-55. Admitted to La. bar, 1953, Kans. bar, 1965, Mich. bar, 1976; prof. law Tulane U., 1954-64; sr. asst. dist. atty., New Orleans, 1964-65; prof. law and psychiatry U. Kans., 1965-67, also Menninger Found., Topeka, 1965-67; asso. firm Mouton, Roy, Carmouche & Hailey, New Orleans, 1967-69; prof. Wayne State U., 1969—; vis. prof. law U. Republic South Africa, Durban, Cape Town, Witwatersrand, and Port Elizabeth, 1976. Bd. dirs. SIECUS (Sex Info. and Edn. Council U.S.), N.Y.C. Fellow Am. Psychiat. Assn. (Guttmacher award 1973); mem. Am. Orthopsychiat. Assn. (dir.), Law-Psychology Soc., So. Soc. Philosophy, Psychology, Am. Psychology-Law Soc. (dir.), Am. Acad. Psychoanalysis (sci. asso.), Am. Acad. Psychiatry and law (asso. editor jour. 1972—). Author books, including: Psychotherapy, Confidentiality and Privileged Communication, 1966; Psychiatry and Law, 1973; editor books, including: Sexual Behavior and the law, 1965; (with J. Knight) Motivations in Play, Games and Sports, 1967; contbr. numerous articles to law, psychiatry and philosophy jours.; editor Am. Lecture Series in Behavioral Sci. and Law, 1964—. Office: Wayne State U Law Sch Detroit MI 48202 Tel (313) 577-3963

SLOVER, GEORGE, JR., b. Bryn Mawr, Pa., Dec. 15, 1926; A.B., U. Tenn., 1945; LL.B., Harvard, 1949. Admitted to Tex. bar, 1950; asso. firm Johnson, Bromberg, Leeds & Riggs, Dallas, 1949-58, partner, 1958—. Mem. Am. Law Inst. Office: 1500 211 N Ervay St Dallas TX 75201 Tel (214) 748-8811

SLOVER, WILLIAM LEWIS, b. Washington, D.C., Aug. 15, 1937; A.B., Yale U., 1959, LL.B., Columbia U., 1962. Admitted to D.C. bar, 1962; partner firm Slover & Loftus, Washington, 1962—. Home: 9460 River Rd Potomac MD 20854 Office: 1224 17th St NW Washington DC 20036 Tel (202) 347-7170

SLUNT, JOSEPH BERNARD, b. Balt., Dec. 13, 1940; B.S. in Transp., U. Balt., 1962, LL.B., 1965. Admitted to Md. bar, 1966; trial atty. bur. hearing counsel FMC, Washington, 1970—. Pres. Gum Springs Farm Citizens Assn., 1974-75; v.p. Fairland PTA, 1976-77, Epiphany Lutheran Ch., 1974-76, White Oak Citizens Coalition, 1977—. Home: 14317 Sturtevant Rd Silver Spring MD 20904 Office: 1100 L St NW Washington DC 20573 Tel (202) 523-5783

SLUTZKY, LORENCE HARLEY, b. Chgo., Jan. 27, 1946; B.S., So. Ill. U., 1968; J.D., John Marshall U., 1972; postgrad. U. Exeter (Eng.) 1971. Admitted to Ill. bar, 1972, Fla. bar, 1973, U.S. Supreme Ct. bar, 1976; law clk. U.S. Dist. Ct. No. Dist. Ill., Chgo., 1972-73; asst. states atty. Civil Actions Bur. Cook County (Ill.) States Atty's. Office, 1973-76, spl. asst. state's atty., 1976—; mem. firm Robbins, Schwartz, Nicholas, Lifton, Ltd., Chgo., 1976—. Vol. atty. Creative Arts, Chgo. Mem. Am., Fla., Ill., Chgo. bar assns., Am. Arbitrations Assn. (comml. panel). Contbr. articles to legal jours. Home: 423 W Grant Pl Chicago IL 60614 Office: 29 S LaSalle St Chicago IL 60602 Tel (312) 332-7760

SLY, RICHARD ALLEN, b. Vancouver, Wash., June 14, 1935; student Portland State Coll., 1953-55; B.B.A., U. Oreg., 1957; J.D., Willamette U., 1963. Admitted to Oreg. bar, 1963, U.S. Supreme Ct. bar, 1971; asso. firm Black & Apicella, Portland, Org., 1963-65; dep. dist. atty. Multnomah County (Oreg.), Beaverton, 1969-73; asst. atty. gen. State of Oreg., 1973; asso. firm Bouneff, Muller & Marshall, Portland, 1974-75; partner firm Bloom, Chaivoe, Ruben, Marandas & Berg, Portland, 1975—; law clk. State Indsl. Accident Commn., Oreg., 1962-63; judge pro tempore Multnomah County Dist. Ct., 1975—; mem. lawyer placement com. Oreg. State Bar, 1967, com. for procedure and practice, 1971-73. Sec. bd. Greek Orthodox Community Oreg.; bd. dirs. Washington County Comprehensive Health Planning Council, Comprehensive Health Planning Assn. Portland Met. Area. Mem. Oreg., Multnomah County bar assns., Am., Oreg. trial lawyers assns. Asso. editor Willamette Coll. Law Jour., 1963; contbr. articles to legal jours. Home: 4626 SW 35th Pl Portland OR 97221 Office: 1600 SW 4th Ave Portland OR 97201 Tel (503) 221-1135

SMALKIN, FREDERIC NELSON, b. Balt., May 21, 1946; B.A., Johns Hopkins, 1968; J.D., U. Md., 1971; postgrad. JAG Sch., 1972. Admitted to Md. bar, 1972, U.S. Supreme Ct. bar, 1975; law clk. to chief judge U.S. Dist. Ct. for Md., 1971-72; commd. 2d lt. JAGC, U.S. Army, 1968, advanced through grades to capt., 1970; asst. to gen. counsel, hdqrs. Dept. Army, Washington, 1974-76; Res., 1976; U.S. magistrate for Dist. Md., 1976—. Mem. Am., Fed., Md. State bar assns., Am. Judicature Soc., Order of Coif, Phi Beta Kappa. Office: 244 US Courthouse 101 W Lombard St Baltimore MD 21201 Tel (301) 962-3840

SMALL, BENJAMIN FRANCIS, III, b. Indpls., Apr. 10, 1947; A.B., Ind. U., 1969, J.D. cum laude, 1972. Admitted to Ind. bar, 1972; asso. firm Bingham, Summers, Welsh and Spilman, Indpls., 1972—. Named Outstanding Young Man Am., Jaycees. Mem. Ind., Indpls., Am. bar assns. Contbr. spl. report to Indpls. C. of C., 1975. Home: 6206 N Meridian St Indianapolis IN 46260 Office: 2700 Indiana Bank Tower Indianapolis IN 46204 Tel (317) 635-8900

SMALL, GUS H., JR., b. Macon, Ga., Mar. 17, 1943; A.B., Emory U., 1965; J.D. cum laude, Mercer U., 1969. Admitted to Ga. bar, 1970, U.S. Dist. Ct. No. Dist. Ga. bar, 1971, U.S. Circuit Ct. Appeals 5th Circuit bar, 1972, U.S. Supreme Ct., 1977; atty. U.S. Army, 1969-71; asso. firm Zusmann, Sikes, Pritchard & Cohen, Atlanta, 1971-75, partner, 1975—; adj. prof. bankruptcy law Mercer U., 1976—. Mem. Atlanta (chmn. sect. bankruptcy), Ga., Am. bar assns., Southeastern Bankruptcy Law Inst. (dir.). Contbr. articles profl. jours. Office: 1795 Peachtree Rd NE Atlanta GA 30309 Tel (404) 897-7027

SMALL, JAMES MICHAEL, b. Shreveport, La., Dec. 3, 1945; student La. Poly. Inst., 1963-66; J.D., La. State U., 1969. Admitted to La. bar, 1969; asso. firm Stafford & Pitts, Alexandria, 1969-70, Gravel, Roy & Burnes, Alexandria, 1970—; mem. Gov.'s Commn. on Uniform Indigent Def. System, La. Adv. Council to Legal Services Corp.; lectr. La. Bar Assn., 1976; mem. La. Indigent Defender Bd. Mem. Am., La., Alexandria (exec. com. 1975—, chmn. criminal law com. 1975—) bar assns., La. Trial Lawyers Assn. (exec. com.), Nat. Assn. Criminal Def. Lawyers, Order of Coif, Phi Alpha Delta, Phi Kappa Phi. Editor criminal law sect. La. Trial Lawyers Brief, 1974-76; editor La. Law Rev., 1967-69. Home: 4141 Jackson St Apt 202 Alexandria LA 71301 Office: 711 Washington St Alexandria LA 71301 Tel (318) 487-4501

SMALL, JONATHAN ANDREW, b. N.Y.C., Dec. 26, 1942; student U. Paris, 1962-63; B.A., Brown U., 1964; LL.B., Harvard, 1967; M.A., Fletcher Sch. of Law and Diplomacy, 1968; LL.M., N.Y. U., 1974. Admitted to N.Y. State bar, 1967; law clk. for judge of U.S. Ct. Appeals for 2d circuit, 1968-69; asso. firm Debevoise, Plimpton, Lyons & Gates, N.Y.C., 1969-75, partner, 1976—; cons. Spl. Task Force on N.Y. Taxation, 1976. Mem. Am., N.Y. State bar assns., Phi Beta Kappa. Home: 1025 Fifth Ave New York City NY 10028 Office: 299 Park Ave New York City NY 10017

SMALL, MENDEL, b. Kansas City, Mo., Feb. 14, 1933; A.A., Kansas City Jr. Coll., 1952; B.A., U. Kans., 1954; J.D., Harvard, 1958. Admitted to Mo. bar, 1958; asso. firm Terte, Levi and Etal, Kansas City, 1958-61, Brenner, Ewing, Lockwood & O'Neal, Kansas City, 1961-62; individual practice law, Kansas City, 1962-71; partner firm Spencer, Fane, Britt & Browne, Kansas City, 1971—. Dir. Congregation Beth Shalom, Kansas City. Mem. Am., Mo., Kansas City bar assns., Am. Judicature Soc., Lawyers Assn. Home: 11223 Walnut St Kansas City MO 64114 Office: 106 W 14th St Kansas City MO 64105 Tel (816) 474-8100

SMALL, WILLIAM HARDIN, b. Petersburg, Ill., Jan. 19, 1918; B.Edn., Ill. State U., 1939; J.D., U. Ill., 1948. Admitted to Ill. bar, 1948, Ind. bar, 1960, U.S. Supreme Ct. bar, 1973; asst. state's atty., Knox County, Ill., 1948-52, state's atty, 1952-56; partner firm Small & Henning, Galesburg, Ill., 1956-58; corp. atty. Central Soya Co., Ft. Wayne, Ind., 1958—; mayor, Galesburg, 1957-58; atty. Fort Wayne (Ind.) Bicentennial Commn., 1975-76. Vice pres. Ill. Municipal League, 1958; mem. Ind. Gov's. Economy Program Task Force, Indpls., 1969. Mem. Am. Bar Assn., Phi Alpha Delta. Author: Labor Relations Counselor, 1970-71; Guide to FTC Rules for Mail Order Merchandisers, 1976. Home: 206 N Seminole Circle Fort Wayne IN 46807 Office: 1300 Fort Wayne Nat Bank Bldg Fort Wayne IN 46802 Tel (219) 422-8541

SMART, TERRY DANIEL, b. Scottsboro, Ala., Sept. 24, 1946; B.S., U. Ala., 1968; J.D., Memphis State U., 1972. Admitted to Tenn. bar, 1972; partner firm Dobbs, Gatti & Smart, Memphis, 1974—. Mem. Tenn. Bar Assn., Tenn. Trial Lawyers Assn. Staff mem. Memphis State U. Law Rev., 1971-72; contbr. articles to legal jours. Home: 6161 Chinaberry St Memphis TN 38138 Office: 100 North Main Bldg suite 3300 Memphis TN 38103 Tel (901) 527-6336

SMART, VAN WESLEY, b. Riverside, Calif., Nov. 24, 1907; B.S., U. Calif., 1929, LL.B., Golden Gate Coll. Law, 1935. Admitted to Calif. bar, 1937, D.C. bar, 1972; insp. FDA, San Francisco, 1937-42, asst. to chief Western dist., 1946-50, litigation officer, Washington, 1950-61, dep. dir. div. regulatory mgmt., 1961-64, chief drug, device and cosmetic br., 1964-70; individual practice law, Carmel, Calif., 1970—. Mem. Am., Monterey County bar assns., Ret. Officers Assn. Recipient certificate of appreciation HEW, 1966; award of merit FDA, 1966. Address: 26123 Atherton Dr Carmel CA 93921 Tel (408) 624-5598

SMATHERS, GEORGE A., b. Atlantic City, Nov. 14, 1913; A.B., U. Fla., 1937, LL.B., 1938. Partner firm Walter Dunigan, 1938; asst. U.S. dist. atty. in charge, Miami, from 1940; asso. firm Smathers, Thompson, Maxwell & Dyer, Miami; partner firm Smathers and Thompson, Miami, 1969—; asst. to atty. gen. for prosecution of war fraud cases, 1945-46; mem. 80th and 81st Congresses from 4th Fla. Dist., 1947-51, U.S. Senate from Fla., 1951-69. Mem. Am., D.C., Fla., Dade County (v.p.) bar assns. Home: Key Biscayne Hotel Key Biscayne FL 33043 Office: 1301 Alfred I DuPont Bldg Miami FL 33131

SMEE, KENNETH HARRY, b. Battle Creek, Mich., Feb. 19, 1936; B.A., Valparaiso U., 1958; J.D., U. Ky., 1960. Admitted to Ky. bar, 1960, Fed. Dist. Ct. bar, 1968; chief law clk. Ct. Appeals Ky., 1960-67; partner firm Anggelis & Vimont, Lexington, Ky., 1968-75; individual practice law, Lexington, 1975—; legal officer Civil Air Patrol. Mem. Ky., Fayette County bar assns. Home: 514 Grantchester Rd Lexington KY 40505 Office: PO Box 1629 Lexington KY 40501 Tel (606) 255-4492

SMETHURST, RAYMOND STEVENS, JR., b. Washington, Nov. 21, 1935; B. Metall. Engring., Cornell U., 1958; J.D., George Washington U., 1961. Admitted to Md. bar, 1961; mem. firm Adkins, Potts & Smethurst, Salibury, Md., 1961—; spl. labor relations cons. Nat. Transp. Agy., 1962-63; city atty. Pocomoke City (Md.), 1967—; asst. judge People's Ct. Wicomico County (Md.), Salisbury, 1969-70; counsel Wicomico County Housing Authority, Salisbury, 1967-75; asst. mem. Md. State Bd. Law Examiners, 1966-68; mem. atty. grievance commn. Md. Bar, 1975—; gen. counsel Salisbury Jr. C. of C., 1968. Mem. Am., Fed., Wicomico, Md. State bar assns., Order of Coif. Asso. editor George Washington Law Rev., 1960-61. Home: Rt 1 Riverside Rd Eden MD 21822 Office: One Plaza E Salisbury MD 21801 Tel (301) 749-0161

SMILEY, MARTHA ELLEN, b. Mission, Tex., Sept. 27, 1947; B.A., Baylor U., 1969; J.D., U. Tex., 1972. Admitted to Tex. bar, 1972; staff atty. Law Research Corp., Austin, 1972-73; asst. atty. gen. State of Tex., Austin, 1973—, chief tax div., 1976. Mem. adv. bd. KTBC-TV, Austin, 1975-76; commr. Austin Commn. Status Women, 1975—; dir. Austin Women's Center, 1975—; steering com. Austin Urban League Interest Group, 1976; chmn. Tex. Women's Polit. Caucus, 1975-76. Mem. Travis County Bar Assn., Phi Alpha Delta. Named Outstanding Young Woman Austin, Austin Am. Statesman newspaper, 1976. Office: Box 12548 Capitol Station Austin TX 78711 Tel (512) 475-4721

SMITH, ALLAN KELLOGG, b. Hartford, Conn., Aug. 17, 1888; A.B., Trinity Coll., Hartford, 1911, LL.D. (hon.), 1968; LL.B., Harvard, 1914. Admitted to Conn. bar, 1914; asst. U.S. atty., Conn., 1917-23, U.S. atty., 1924-25; partner firm Day, Berry & Howard, Hartford, 1923—. Mem. Am. Bar Assn. Home: 89 Sunset Farm Rd West Hartford CT 06107 Office: One Constitution Plaza Hartford CT 06103 Tel (203) 278-1330

SMITH, ARTHUR DWIGHT, JR., b. Logan, Utah, Nov. 6, 1942; B.S., Utah State U., 1965; J.D., George Washington U., 1968. Admitted to D.C. bar, 1968; trial atty. Lands and Natural Resources Div., U.S. Dept. Justice, 1968-73; asso. prof. law U. Idaho, 1973-77, prof., 1977—. Home: 403 N Polk St Moscow ID 83843 Office: Coll Law Moscow ID 83843 Tel (208) 885-7077

SMITH, ARTHUR LEE, b. Davenport, Iowa, Dec. 19, 1941; B.A., Augustana Coll., 1964; M.A., Am. U., 1968; J.D., Washington U., 1971. Admitted to Mo. bar, 1971; partner firm Peper, Martin, Jensen, Maichel & Hetlage, St. Louis, 1976—. Mem. Am., Mo. bar assns., Bar Assn. St. Louis, Am. Arbitration Assn., Commercial Arbitration Panel, Order of Coif. Office: 720 Olive St Saint Louis MO 63101 Tel (314) 421-3850

SMITH, BENJAMIN HARRISON, b. Lakeland, Ga., Feb. 27, 1923; LL.B., Cumberland U., 1947. Admitted to Ga. bar, 1947; practiced in Waycross, Ga., 1947—; judge State Ct. of Ware County (Ga.), 1958—. Mem. Am., Ga. trial lawyers assns., Waycross Bar Assn. (pres.). Home: 1707 Oconee Rd Waycross GA 31501 Office: 107 Albany Ave Waycross GA 31501

SMITH, BRUCE EDWIN, b. Hays, Kans., Feb. 6, 1936; B.A., U. Kans., 1958; J.D., U. Oreg., 1965. Admitted to Oreg. bar, 1965; mem. firm Brophy, Wilson & Duhaime, Medford, Oreg., 1965-70, firm Young, Horn, Cass & Scott, Eugene, Oreg., 1971—; supr. clin. program U. Oreg. Law Sch., 1972-74, vis. lectr. in law, 1974. Mem. Eugene Zoning Bd. Appeals, 1971-74. Mem. Oreg., Am. bar assns., Assn. Trial Lawyers Am., Oreg. Council Sch. Attys. (v.p. 1976-77). Editor Oreg. Law Rev., 1964-65. Home: 965 Sherwood Pl Eugene OR 97401 Office: 101 E Broadway Suite 200 Eugene OR 97401 Tel (503) 687-1515

SMITH, BYRON OWEN, b. Mitchell, S.D., July 28, 1916; A.B., Stanford, 1937, J.D., 1940. Admitted to Calif. bar, 1940; asso. firm Stephens, Jones, Inch & La Fever, Los Angeles, 1940-41; partner firm Stephens, Jones, La Fever & Smith, Los Angeles, 1945-76, Adams, Duque & Hazeltine, Los Angeles, 1977—; spl. asst. to atty. gen. U.S., 1946-50. Fellow Am. Coll. Probate Counsel; mem. Am., Calif. bar assns., Phi Delta Phi. Home: 765 Canterbury Rd San Marino CA 91108 Office: 523 W 6th St Los Angeles CA 90014 Tel (213) 620-1240

SMITH, CARL THURMAN, b. Hannibal, Mo., Dec. 31, 1915; B.S., Anderson Coll., 1949; J.D., Ind. U., 1953. Admitted to Ind. bar, 1953, U.S. Dist. Ct. bar, 1964, U.S. Supreme Ct. bar, 1969; individual practice law, Anderson, Ind., 1954-58; judge Municipal Ct., Anderson, 1956-58, Circuit Ct., 1959—; mem. Jud. Study Com. on Judges' Benchbook; mem. Legis. Com. on Post-conviction Relief, 1975-76. Pres., Anderson Urban League, 1961-65; pres. Anderson Salvation Army, 1965-69; bd. dirs. Madison County Mental Health Assn., Center for Mental Health; pres. Anderson Assn. Chs., 1969-73. Mem. Ind. Judges' Assn. Home: 2319 Starlight Dr Anderson IN 46012 Office: 16 E 9th St Anderson IN 46016 Tel (317) 646-9358

SMITH, CARLETON WRIGHT, b. Concord, N.H., Sept. 12, 1936; B.A., Wilkes Coll., 1966; J.D., U. Tenn., Knoxville, 1968. Admitted to Tenn. bar, 1970; law clk. U.S. Dist. Ct. Eastern Dist. Tenn., Greenville, 1968-73; partner firm Burkhard and Smith, Greenville, 1973—; instr. labor law Tusculum Coll., 1975—. Chmn. profl. sect. United Fund, Greenville, Tenn., 1973-75. Mem. Am., Tenn., Greene County bar assns., Tenn. Trial Lawyers Assn. (bd. govs. 1975-77). Home: 1528 Kevin Ln Greenville TN 37743 Office: 103 E Church St Greenville TN 37743 Tel (615) 639-8168

SMITH, CHARLES DURYEA, IV, b. Alfred, N.Y., Nov. 4, 1941; A.B., Oberlin Coll., 1964; M.A., Washington U., St. Louis, 1967; J.D., Boston U., 1972. Admitted to Mass. bar, 1973, U.S. Ct. Appeals 1st Circuit bar, 1975; vol. Peace Corps, Ethiopia, 1964-66; area supr. Am. Field Service, N.Y.C., 1967-69; manpower devel. specialist Dept. Labor, 1971-73; staff atty. Boston U. Sch. of Law Center for Criminal Justice, 1973—; lectr. Boston U. Met. Coll., 1974—. Mem. Am., Mass., Boston bar assns., African Law Assn. Am. Co-author: Right to Counsel in Criminal Cases: The Mandate of Argersinger v. Hamlin, 1976. Home: 472 Putnam Ave Cambridge MA 02139 Office: 209 Bay State Rd Boston MA 02215 Tel (617) 353-3021

SMITH, CHARLES EMORY, b. Quincy, Fla., Oct. 14, 1934; B.S. in Accounting, Central State Coll., 1961; J.D., Howard U., 1965. Admitted to D.C. bar, 1970; agt. IRS, Washington, 1961-62; atty. Port of N.Y. Authority, 1965-66; legis. analyst Xerox Corp., 1966-67; atty. Office Econ. Opportunity, Washington, 1967-69; asso. dir. Pres's. Adv. Council on Minority Bus. Enterprises, Washington, 1969-71; pres. The Quincy Co., Inc., Washington, 1970—; partner firm Boasberg, Hewes, Klores, Smith and Kass, Washington, 1971-73; sr. partner firm Charles E. Smith, Washington, 1973—; prrf. bus. law Howard U., 1967-70, Fed. City Coll., 1970—; exec. dir. Urban Bus. Edn. Assn., 1971; pres. The Lincoln-Douglass Travel Agy., Inc. Bd. dirs. Suburban Md. Econ. Devel. Corp. Mem. Nat. (exec. dir., gen. counsel 1974-75), Am., D.C. bar assns., Nat. Congress Community Econ. Developers, Unified Bar Assn. D.C. Author: Attorney's Handbook for Minority Economic Development, 1973. Home: 1401 Blair Mill Rd Silver Spring MD 20910 Office: 1328 New York Ave NW Washington DC 20005 Tel (202) 393-0240

SMITH, CHARLES FORSTER, b. Rhinelander, Wis., July 16, 1918; B.A., U. Wis., 1941, LL.D., 1948. Admitted to Wis. bar, 1948; asso. firm Tinkham, Smith, Bliss, Patterson and Richards, Wausau, Wis., 1948-51, partner, 1951—; mem. Wausau City Council, 1950-60; mem. Wis. Senate, 1963-67, chmn. Senate Caucus, 1964-67. Mem. Marathon County (Wis.) Bd., 1950-60, chmn., 1957-58; past pres. Cancer Soc., Marathon County; mem. Wis. Natural Beauty Council, 1965-74; bd. dirs. Wausau YMCA, Easter Seals, Marathon County. Mem. Internat. Assn. Ins. Counsel, Marathon County Bar Assn. (pres. 1965-66), Am., Wis. bar assns. Home: 910 Fulton St Wausau WI 54401 Office: 630 Fourth St Wausau WI 54401 Tel (715) 845-1151

SMITH, CHARLES JOHN, b. Moline, Ill., Apr. 9, 1918; LL.B., U. Ill., 1942. Admitted to Ill. bar, 1942; practiced in Moline, 1946-64, 77—, Orion, Ill., 1959-64, 77—; judge City Ct., Moline, 1954-64, Ill. Circuit Ct., 14th Jud. Circuit, 1964-76. Mem. Rock Island County (Ill.) Bar Assn. Home: 2719 13 Street Ct Moline IL 61265 Office: 2719 13th St Ct Moline IL 61265 Tel (309) 762-6185

SMITH, CHARLES LEE, b. Seattle, Nov. 17, 1945; B.A., U. Chgo., 1968; J.D., U. Wash., 1973. Admitted to Wash. bar, 1973; pub. defender, Seattle, 1973; atty. Legis. Transp. Commn., 1974; individual practice law, Seattle, 1974—; judge pro-tem Seattle Municipal Ct., 1975—. Bd. dirs. Ballard Community Schs., 1974—. Mem. Am., Wash. State, Seattle-King County bar assns. Author: Fight That Ticket, 1976. Office: Colman Bldg 811 First Ave Seattle WA 98104 Tel (206) 622-1160

SMITH, CHARLES MICHAEL, b. San Francisco, June 26, 1932; B.S., U. Santa Clara, 1954; LL.B., U. San Francisco, 1959. Admitted to Calif. bar, 1960; dep. dist. atty. Alameda County (Calif.), Oakland, 1960-62; asso. firm Campbell, Custer, Warburton & Britton, 1962-67; partner firm Campbell, Warburton, Britton, Fitzsimmons & Smith, San Jose, 1967—; chmn. med.-legal liaison com. Mem. Am., Calif. (lectr.), Santa Clara County (lectr., trustee) bar assns., No. Calif. Def. Assn. (dir. 1977—). Office: 8th Floor 1st Nat Bank Bldg San Jose CA 95113 Tel (408) 295-7701

SMITH, CHARLOTTE GROESBEECK, b. San Antonio, July 23, 1918; student San Antonio Jr. Coll., 1934-36; B.A., U. Tex., 1940, J.D., 1940. Admitted to Tex. bar, 1940, U.S. Dist. Ct. bar for So. Dist. Tex., 1943; asso. firm Kelly & Looney, Edinburg, Tex., 1941-44; tchr. Army Edn. Center, Ft. Clayton and Albrook AFB Edn. Service, C.Z., and Div. Schs., Balboa, C.Z., 1961-63, San Antonio, 1965-67; mem. firm Smith, Smith & Mealy, Kingsland, also Llano, Tex., 1967—; pres. Llano County Title Co., Inc., Kingsland, Tex., 1974—. Vice pres. Lackland PTA, San Antonio, 1965-66. Mem. Nat. Assn. Women Lawyers, Am. Judicature Soc., Bus. and Profl. Women's Club (pres. McAllen, Tex., chpt. 1942-43), Bertram C. of C., Mortar Bd., Phi Mu (past chpt. pres.), Phi Theta Kappa, Pi Lambda Theta, Kappa Beta Pi (province dir. 1942-43). Home: PO Box 96 Buchanan Dam TX 78609 Office: PO Box 446 Kingsland TX 78609 Tel (915) 388-4545

SMITH, CHESTERFIELD H., b. Arcadia, Fla., July 28, 1917; J.D., U. Fla., 1948, LL.D. (hon.), 1972; LL.D. (hon.), John B. Stetson U., 1972, Suffolk U., 1973, Norwich U., 1973, Akron U., 1973; L.H.D. (hon.), St. Leo Coll., 1974; D.C.L. (hon.), Jacksonville U., 1975. Admitted to Fla. bar; asso. firm Treadwell & Treadwell, Arcadia, 1948-50, Holland & Knight, Bartow, Bradenton, Lakeland, Tallahassee and Tampa, 1950—; chmn. Fla. Constl. Revision Commn., 1965-67, Gov. Askew's Citizens for Jud. Reform, 1972; mem. Fed. Jud. Nominating Commn. Fla., 1975—, Fed. Commn. on Exec., Legis. and Jud. Salaries, 1976—; hon. co-chmn. Resource Center for Consumers Legal Services, 1975—; city commr., Bartow, 1955, city atty., 1956-59; trustee Inst. Ct. Mgmt., 1970-72; trustee Legis 50, Center for Legis. Improvement, 1970—, treas., mem. exec. com., 1976—. Trustee U. Fla. Law Center Assn., Wesleyan Coll., Macon, Ga.; mem. exec. com. Lawyers Com. for Civil Rights Under Law; mem. council Council for Pub. Interest Law; mem. adv. com. National St. Law Inst. High Sch.; mem. council U. Fla.; bd. advisers Center for Govtl. Responsibility, U. Fla. Coll. Law. Fellow Am. Coll. Trial Lawyers, Internat. Acad. Trial Lawyers, Am., Fla. bar founds.; mem. Am. (pres. 1973-74, bd. govs. 1969-70, 72-75, del. 1966—, membership chmn. Fla. 1965-66), Fla. (pres. 1964-65, bd. govs. 1958-63, exec. com. 1959-64), 10th Jud. Circuit (pres. 1956-57) bar assns., Nat. Legal Aid and Defender Assn. (chmn. nat. membership com. 1969-70, dir. 1971—, Arthur von Briesen award 1974), Am. Judicature Soc. (exec. com. 1969-72, dir. 1965-72, Herbert Lincoln Harley award 1973), Nat. Conf. Bar Pres.'s (pres. 1968-69, exec. com. 1965-70), Am. Law Inst., Scribes, Assn. Bar City N.Y., Inst. Jud. Adminstrn., Order of Coif, Fla. Blue Key, Phi Beta Kappa, Phi Kappa Phi, Phi Delta Phi, Alpha Tau Omega. Recipient Distinguished Floridian award Fla. C. of C., 1969, Golden Plate award Am. Acad. Achievement, 1975, Pres.'s Spl. award Nat. Bar Assn., 1975; named Fla. Patriot, Bicentennial Commn. Fla., 1975. Home: 1710 Mariposa Ave Bartow FL 33830 Office: 92 Lake Wire Dr Lakeland FL 33802 Tel (813) 682-1161

SMITH, CLATER WEBB, JR., b. Balt., Dec. 14, 1931; B.A., U. Va., 1954, LL.B., 1957; Admitted to Md. bar, 1958; asso. firm Smith, Somerville & Case, Balt., 1958-64; partner firm Shoemaker & Smith, Frederick, Md., 1964—; county atty., Frederick County, Md., 1970, asst. atty. gen., 1970—. Sec., United Givers Fund, Frederick, 1965-75. Office: 124 N Court St Frederick MD 21701 Tel (301) 663-8100

SMITH, CLAUDE CARROLL, b. Shelburn, Ind., Nov. 14, 1888; B.S., Central Normal Coll. of Ind., 1911; B.A., Swarthmore Coll., 1914, LL.D., 1957; LL.B., U. Pa., 1917. Admitted to Pa. bar, 1917; U.S. Supreme Ct. bar, 1938; asso. firm Duane, Morris & Heckscher, Phila., 1917-23, partner, 1923—. Mem. Am., Pa., Phila. bar assns. Tel (215) 854-6315

SMITH, CLAUDE RICHARD, b. Birmingham, Ala., Nov. 30, 1942; B.A., U. Ala., 1964; J.D., Samford U., 1967; postgrad. Loyola U., 1970-72. Admitted to Ala. bar, 1967, La. bar, 1972; sr. atty. Fed. Land Bank of New Orleans, 1969—; treas. Tri-Banks Employees Credit Union, 1972-74, pres., 1975-76, currently v.p., also dir. Vol. La. Coalition for Handicapped Children, New Orleans; bd. govs. Suburban Villas Civic Assn., Metairie, La.; deacon, bd. trustees Meml. Baptist Ch., Metairie. Mem. Am., Jefferson Parish, Ala., La. State bar assns. Notary Pub., Orleans Parish, La. Home: 4317 Troy St Metairie LA 70001 Office: 860 Saint Charles Ave New Orleans LA 70130 Tel (504) 586-8101

SMITH, DANIEL CLAYTON, b. Spokane, Wash., Mar. 9, 1916; A.B., U. Chgo., 1937, J.D., 1940. Admitted to Ill. bar, 1940, Wash. state bar, 1953; tchr. U. Chgo. Law Sch., 1940-41; individual practice law, Chgo., 1941-50; asst. gen. counsel Weyerhaeuser Co., Tacoma, 1950-61, gen. counsel, 1961-69, v.p., 1969-75; v.p., gen. counsel FMC Corp., Chgo., 1976—. Mem. Am., Chgo. bar assns., Am. Arbitration Assn. (panel arbitrators), Assn. Gen. Counsel, Order Coif, Phi Beta Kappa. Home: 990 N Lake Shore Dr Apt 26-E Chicago IL 60611 Office: FMC Corp 200 E Randolph Dr Chicago IL 60601 Tel (312) 861-6022

SMITH, DANIEL CLIFFORD, b. Cin., Aug. 9, 1936; B.S., Ariz. State U., 1960; postgrad. George Washington U., 1961-62; J.D., Am. U., 1965. Admitted to D.C. bar, 1966, Va. bar, 1967, U.S. Supreme Ct. bar, 1969, U.S. Ct. Mil. Appeals bar, 1966, U.S. Tax Ct. bar, 1966; asso. firm Alpern & Feissner, Washington, 1966; atty. FTC, Washington, 1966-70; asso., partner firm Arent, Fox, Kintner, Plotkin & Kahn, Washington, 1970—; gen. counsel Optimist Club of Chantilly (Va.), 1970—. Mem. D.C. Bar, Bar Assn. D.C. (dir.), Va. State Bar, Va. Trial Lawyers Assn., Am., Fed. bar assns., Assn. Trial Lawyers Am., Am. Judicature Soc., Supreme Ct. Hist. Soc., Nat. Lawyers Club, Delta Theta Phi. Home: 11900 Ledgerock Ct Potomac MD 20854 Office: 1815 H St NW Washington DC 20006 Tel (202) 857-6050

SMITH, DANIEL HARRISON, JR., b. Chgo., Apr. 27, 1933; B.A., Howard U., 1959, J.D., 1967. Admitted to Ill. bar, 1971, U.S. Supreme Ct. bar, 1975; individual practice law, Chgo., 1971—. Mem. Am., Ill., Cook County, Chgo., Nat. bar assns., Am. Judicature Soc., Am. Arbitration Assn. Home: 6955 S Bennett Ave Chicago IL 60649 Office: 19 S LaSalle St Chicago IL 60603 Tel (312) 726-1630

SMITH, DAVID H., b. N.Y.C., Sept. 20, 1938; A.B., Colgate U., 1960; J.D., Columbia, 1965. Admitted to N.Y. State bar, 1965, Calif. bar, 1971; sr. atty. SEC, N.Y.C. and Washington, 1965-69; asso. atty. Coudert Bros., N.Y.C., 1969-70, Tuckman and Phillips, San Francisco, 1970-71; partner firm Louis O. Kelso, Inc., San Francisco, 1971-75, firm Smith & Hartman, San Francisco and Los Angeles, 1975—; sec. Bangert, Dawes, Reade, Davis & Thom, Inc., Cybermed Corp. Bd. dirs. Telegraph Hill Dwellers Assn., 1972-76; pres. and sec. Small Yacht Racing Assn. of San Francisco Bay. Mem. Am., Calif., San Francisco bar assns. Office: Smith and Hartman One Maritime Plaza San Francisco CA 94111 Tel (415) 421-7007

SMITH, DAVID LEE, b. Waco, Tex., Oct. 18, 1935; B.A., East Tex. State U., 1957; J.D., U. Tex., 1962. Admitted to Tex. bar, 1962; asst. city atty. City of Abilene (Tex.), 1962-63; judge Abilene Municipal Ct., 1963-65; asso. firm Brooks, Jones & Gordon, Abilene, 1963-65; partner firm Spann, Perry & Smith, and predecessors, Corpus Christi, Tex., 1965—; legal adviser Pastoral Counseling Center, Corpus Christi, 1974—. Sr. warden All Saints Episcopal Ch., Corpus Christi, 1976. Mem. Nueces County, Tex. bar assns., Am., Tex. trial lawyers assns. Home: 601 Gulf Shore Pl Corpus Christi TX 78411 Office: 900 Wilson Bldg Corpus Christi TX 78401 Tel (512) 884-8221

SMITH, DAVID POST, b. Oshkosh, Wis., July 9, 1920; B.S., U. Wis., 1949, J.D., 1960. Admitted to Wis. bar, 1960, Ohio bar, 1961; atty. dept. engring. Republic Steel Corp., 1960-62; asso. firm Harold Craney, Bloomington, Wis., 1962-63; partner firm Stovekin & Smith, Bloomington, 1963; individual practice law, Boscobel, Wis., 1963—. Mem. Grant County Bar Assn., State Bar Wis. Home: 925 1/2 Wisconsin Ave Boscobel WI 53805 Office: Box 68 905 Wisconsin Ave Boscobel WI 53805 Tel (608) 375-4129

SMITH, DEAN CONRAD, b. Seattle, Sept. 5, 1929; student Whitman Coll., 1947-48; B.S., U. Wash., 1951, LL.B., 1952. Admitted to Wash. bar, 1952; asso. firm George T. Mickell, Seattle, 1952; with Judge Adv. Gen. Corps, U.S. Army, 1953-54; dep. pros. atty. Yakima County, Wash., 1955-56; partner firm Smith & Smith, Wapato, Wash., 1957-69; U.S. atty. Eastern Dist. Wash., 1969-77; partner firm Hemovich, Smith & Nappi, Spokane, Wash., 1977—; mem. Atty. Gen.'s Adv. Commn., 1973—, chmn., 1973-74; adj. prof. Gonzaga U. Sch. Law, 1973-74; mem. faculty Spokane (Wash.) Bar Rev. Course, 1974—; vis. lectr. Asian and Far East Inst. for Law Enforcement, Tokyo, 1974; mem. rules com. 9th Circuit Jud. Conf., 1971-77. Mem. Wash. Republican Com., 1966-68; chmn. Yakima County Republican Central Com., 1968-69. Mem. Am., Wash. State, Spokane County, Yakima County, Fed. bar assns., Am. Trial Lawyers Assn. Home: W 1907 Riverside Spokane WA 99206 Office: 510 Lincoln Bldg Spokane WA 99710 Tel (509) 624-3233

SMITH, DEAN ELBERT, b. Ravenna, Ohio, Apr. 20, 1933; B.B.A., U. Akron, 1954, J.D., 1972. Comml. mgr. Ohio Bell Telephone Co., Akron, Ohio, 1954-76; admitted to Ohio bar, 1972; individual practice law, Akron, 1973—. Mem. Am., Ohio, Akron bar assns., Akron C. of C. (dir. 1962). Home: 1604 Kingsley Ave Akron OH 44313 Office: 1650 W Market St Akron OH 44313 Tel (216) 867-9224

SMITH, DEANN DUFF, b. Springfield, Mo., Mar. 8, 1941; B.A., LindenWood Coll., 1963; J.D., Stanford, 1966. Admitted to Mo. bar, 1967; asst. atty. gen. State of Mo., Jefferson City, 1967-68; with NLRB, St. Louis, 1969; judge, ex officio magistrate Texas County (Mo.) Probate Ct., 1970—. Mem. Texas County Mental Health Bd., 1975—; mem. Regional Adv. Council on Drugs and Alcohol Abuse, 1976. Mem. Mo., Texas County bar assns., Mo. Assn. Probate, Magistrate Judges (dir. 1974-76). Office: Texas County Courthouse Houston MO 65483 Tel (417) 967-3663

SMITH, DONALD BITZER, b. Doylestown, Pa., Nov. 4, 1913; A.B., Pa. State U., 1934; LL.B., Temple U., 1937. Admitted to Pa. bar, 1938; sr. partner firm Donald B. Smith and Assos., Perkasie, Pa., 1937—. Mem. Pa., Bucks County (pres. 1956) bar assns. Office: 311 N 7th St Perkasie PA 18944 Tel (215) 257-3666

SMITH, DONALD ERVIN, b. New Lothrop, Mich., Apr. 28, 1921; A.B., U. Mich., 1942, LL.B., 1946. Admitted to Mich bar, 1946; individual practice law, Owosso, Mich., 1946-58, Ann Arbor, Mich., 1958—; cons. to Labor Com. U.S. Senate, 1956—; pros. atty., Shiawassee County, Mich., 1950-54; state senator 15th dist., Mich., 1954-58. Mem. Mich. Bar Assn. Office: PO Box 55 Coronna MI 48817 Tel (517) 743-5926

SMITH, DONALD LEE, b. Clinton, N.C., Mar. 25, 1939; J.D., Wake Forest U., 1964. Admitted to N.C. bar, 1964; asso. city atty. City of Raleigh (N.C.), 1965-69, city atty., 1969-71; partner firm Ball, Coley & Smith, Raleigh, 1971-73; judge N.C. Superior Ct., 1973—. Mem. Am., N.C., N.C. State, Wake County (N.C.) bar assns. Home: 1248 Donaldson Dr Cary NC 27511 Office: Wake County Courthouse Raleigh NC 27602 Tel (919) 733-2823

SMITH, DONALD PUTNEY, JR., b. Wyandotte, Mich., Aug. 12, 1931; B.S., U. Denver, 1955, J.D., 1956; grad. Nat. Coll. State Trial Judges, 1965, Appellate Judges' Seminar, N.Y. U., 1974. Admitted to Colo. Supreme Ct. bar, 1956; U.S. Supreme Ct. bar, 1969; mem. firm Myrick, Smith, Criswell & Branney, Englewood, Colo., 1956-64; judge Colo. Dist. Ct., 18th Jud. Dist., 1964-71, chief judge, 1968; judge Colo. Ct. Appeals, 1971—; asst. atty. gen. State of Colo., 1959-60, spl. asst. atty. gen., 1961; city atty. City of Sheridan (Colo.), 1960-64; asst. city atty. City of Englewood, 1960-64; mem. regional criminal justice planning council, 1968-70; faculty adviser Nat. Coll. State Trial Judges, 1969; lectr. in field; instr. Inst. for Ct. Mgmt., 1977; mem. state personnel bd. rev. Colo. Jud. System, 1968-70; mem. Colo. Jud. Planning Council, 1976—. Mem. Colo. Hwy. Safety Council, 1964-65; pres. Inter-Faith Task Force for Community Services, Arapahoe County, Colo., 1966-69; chmn. Arapahoe County Inst. Community Devel.; mem. exec. bd. Denver area council Boy Scouts Am.; del. 1st Internat. Conf. Appellate Magistrates, Manila, Phillipines, 1977. Mem. Am., Colo. (bd. govs. 1976—), Arapahoe County bar assns., Am. Judicature Soc., Phi Delta Phi (magister Brewer Inn 1956). Recipient Distinguished Service award Littleton (Colo.) Jr. C. of C., 1965; named Pub. Servant of Year Littleton Ind. Newspaper, 1974. Home: 3303 E Costilla Ave Littleton CO 80122 Office: Colo Ct of Appeals State Judicial Bldg 2 E 14th Ave Denver CO 80203 Tel (303) 861-1111

SMITH, DONALD STUART, b. N.Y.C., Nov. 23, 1928; A.B., Lafayette Coll., 1952; J.D., Fordham U., 1955. Admitted to D.C. bar, 1955; trial atty. U.S. Dept. Justice, Washington, 1955-58; asst. U.S. atty., Washington, 1958-72; judge Superior Ct. of D.C., 1972—; instr. criminal law Prince Georges Community Coll., Largo, Md., 1976-77. Mem. Am., D.C. bar assns. Office: Superior Court Bldg Washington DC 20001 Tel (202) 727-1490

SMITH, DONALD W., b. San Francisco, Sept. 18, 1923; student U. Calif., Berkeley; J.D., U. San Francisco, 1951. Admitted to Calif. bar, 1953; partner firm Linley Duffy and Smith, El Cajon, Calif., 1956-62; judge 1962—; acting city atty. City of La Mesa (Calif.), 1958-59; asst. city atty. City of El Cajon, 1959-62. Mem. Calif. Conf. Judges, Calif. State Bar (chmn. com. on law books 1975—). Office: 110 E Lexington St El Cajon CA 92020 Tel (714) 442-9861

SMITH, DOUGLAS MAGRUDER, b. Newport News, Va., Aug. 21, 1929; B.A., Washington & Lee U., 1951, J.D., 1953. Admitted to Va. bar, 1952; since practiced in Newport News, asso. firm Hall, Martin & Smith, and predecessors, 1953-56, partner, 1956-61; judge Corp. Ct., reorganized as 7th Jud. Circuit Ct., 1961—. Past pres. Peninsula Boys' Club; past pres. bd. dirs. YMCA; trustee United Methodist Children's Home. Mem. Va. Jud. Conf. (exec. com. 1972-73), Am., Newport News bar assns. Contbr. articles in field to legal jours. Home: 9 Club Terr Newport News VA 23606 Office: 2501 Huntington Ave Newport News VA 23607 Tel (804) 247-1561

SMITH, DOUGLAS OMAR, JR., b. Birmingham, Ala., Feb. 2, 1935; B.S., B.A., U. Ark., 1956, LL.B., Yale U., 1959. Admitted to Ark. bar, 1959, U.S. Supreme Ct. bar, 1971; asso. firm Warner Warner & Ragon, Fort Smith, Ark., 1959-60; partner Warner & Smith, Fort Smith, 1961—; dir. United Fed. Savs. and Loan, 1970—, pres., 1973—. Dir. Ft. Smith Sch. Bd., 1971—, pres., 1972-73; mem. Ark. State Health Coordinating Council, 1971—, chmn., 1971-73; dir. Bost Sch. Limited Children, 1966-69, pres., 1968-69; bd. dirs. Ft. Smith Girls Club, 1975—, Western Ark. Counseling and Guidance Center, 1975—; Western Ark. Health Systems Agy., 1975—; mem. Juvenile Services Commn., 1974. Fellow Am. Coll. Trial Lawyers, Ark. Bar Found. (dir. 1973-75); mem. Sebastian County (pres. 1967), Ark. (mem. house dels. 1972-76, exec. council, 1972-75) Am. bar assns., Internat. Assn. Ins. Counsel, Am. Judicature Soc. Home: 13 Berry Hill Fort Smith AR 72903 Office: 214 N 6th St Fort Smith AR 72902

SMITH, DOYLE JACKSON, JR., b. Chillicothe, Mo., May 26, 1938; B.A., Vanderbilt U., 1959; J.D., Harvard, 1962. Admitted to Tenn. bar, 1962, U.S. Supreme Ct. bar, 1972; partner firm Dann, Blackburn & Smith, Memphis, 1970—; mem. Tenn. Legislature, 1964-68. Bd. dirs. Memphis Heart Assn., Memphis and Shelby County Safety Council, 1965-67, Front St. Theater, 1965-70; mem. legal div. Shelby United Neighbors, 1968-76. Mem. Am., Tenn., Memphis and Shelby County bar assns., W. Tenn. Sportsman's Assn., W. Tenn. Hist. Soc., Tenn. Geneal. Soc. Home: 843 Thistledown Dr Memphis TN 38117 Office: 140 Jefferson Memphis TN 38103 Tel (901) 525-0212

SMITH, EDGAR EUGENE, b. Cin., May 23, 1935; B.A., David Lipscomb Coll., 1956; J.D., Vanderbilt U., 1959. Admitted to Tenn. bar, 1959, Fla. bar, 1959, Ala. bar, 1962; served to capt. Judge Adv. Gens. Corps U.S. Army, 1959-62; partner firm Humphrey, Lutz & Smith, Huntsville, Ala., 1962-73, Humphrey & Smith, Huntsville, 1973—. Chmn., bd. dirs. Madison Acad., Huntsville, 1967—; bd. dirs. David Lipscomb Coll., 1968—. Mem. Huntsville-Madison County, Am. bar assns., Assn. Trial Lawyers Am., Ala. Trial Lawyers Assn., David Lipscomb Coll. Nat. Alumni Assn. (pres. 1967-68). Home: 2216 Harris Rd Huntsville AL 35810 Office: 509 Madison St Huntsville AL 35801 Tel (205) 533-1116

SMITH, EDWARD DEWITT, b. Kankakee, Ill., Dec. 17, 1943; B.S. in Zoology, Chemistry, Eastern Ill. U., 1965; B.S. in Pharmacy, U. Ill. Med. Center, Chgo., 1968; J.D. with honors, John Marshall Law Sch., 1974. Admitted to Ill. bar, 1974; pharmacist Ryan Pharmacies, Kankakee, 1970-74, part-time, 1977—; pros. atty. Kankakee County (Ill.) State's Atty.'s office, 1974-76, asst. pub. defender Kankakee County, 1976; partner firm Smith & O'Connor, Kankakee, 1976—. Alderman, City of Kankakee. Mem. Ill. State, Kankakee Valley, Chgo. bar assns., Ill., Kankakee Valley Pharm. Assns. Tel (815) 933-6686

SMITH, EDWARD LAWRENCE, b. N.Y.C., Aug. 9, 1910; A.B., Colgate U., 1931; LL.B., Harvard, 1934. Admitted to Conn. bar, 1935, N.Y. bar, 1936; asso. firm Burlingham Underwood & Lord, and predecessors, 1935-42; with Dept. Justice, 1942-54; partner firm Kirlin Campbell & Keating, N.Y.C., 1954—; spl. asst. to U.S. atty. gen., atty. in charge admiralty and shipping sect., N.Y. office, 1943-53. Mem. Maritime Law Assn. U.S. Home: Wagon Wheel Trail Westport CT 06880 Office: 120 Broadway New York City NY 10005 Tel (212) 732-5520

SMITH, EDWARD SAMUEL, b. Birmingham, Ala., Mar. 27, 1919; student Ala. Poly. Inst., 1936-38; A.B., U. Va., 1941, J.D., 1947. Admitted to Va. bar, 1947, D.C. bar, 1948, U.S. Supreme Ct. bar, 1951, Md. bar, 1953; asso. firm Blair, Korner, Doyle & Appel, Washington, 1947-49, partner, 1949-54; partner firm Blair, Korner, Doyle & Worth, Washington, 1954-61; chief trial sect., tax div., U.S. Dept. Justice, Washington, 1961, asst. for civil trials, 1961-63; partner firm Piper & Marbury, Balt., 1963—, sr. partner tax dept., 1963—, mng. partner, 1971-74. Trustee St. Andrew's Soc. of Washington, pres., 1956-58. Mem. Am. (spl. advisor com. on IRS regional meetings, tax sect., chmn. com. on tax litigation, sect. litigation), Md. (chmn. sect. taxation, 1971-72), Balt. City, Fed., D.C., Va. Bar Assns., Balt. Assn. Tax Counsel, Judicial Conf. of Fourth Circuit (permanent), Nat. Tax Assn.-Tax Inst. Am. Contbr. articles to publs.; speaker insts. Home: 101 Longwood Rd Baltimore MD 21210 Office: 2000 First Maryland Bldg Baltimore MD 21201 Tel (301) 539-2530

SMITH, EDWIN DUDLEY, b. Far Rockaway, N.Y., Oct. 4, 1936; B.S. in Math., U. Kans., 1960, J.D., 1963. Admitted to Kans. bar, 1963, U.S. Supreme Ct. bar, 1972; partner firm Fisher, Patterson, Sayler & Smith, Topeka, 1963—. Mem. Am., Kans., Topeka bar assns., Am. Judicature Soc., Internat. Assn. Ins. Counsel, Kans. Assn. Def. Counsel. Home: 1918 Arrowhead Rd Topeka KS 66604 Office: 520 1st Nat Bank Tower Topeka KS 66603 Tel (913) 232-7761

SMITH, EDWIN RUSSELL, b. Willacoochee, Ga., Sept. 29, 1917; student U. Ga.; LL.B., Atlanta Law Sch., 1941. Admitted to Ga. bar, 1942; partner firm Grantham & Smith, Douglas, Ga., 1949-52; individual practice law, Douglas, 1953—; spl. master Waycross (Ga.) Jud. Circuit Ct., 1962—; solicitor Ga. State Ct. of Coffee County, 1972-74, judge, 1974-76; judge Douglas Recorder's Ct., 1976—. Pres. Coffee County Indsl. Corp., 1952-66; chmn. Douglas, Coffee County Indsl. Authority, 1960-66; chmn. ofcl. bd. 1st Meth. Ch., 1958-60, 61-62, 64-66. Mem. Waycross Circuit Bar Assn. (sec.-treas. 1953-56), State Bar Ga., Am. Judicature Soc., Waycross Circuit Bar, Douglas-Coffee County C. of C. (hon. life 1968—), Douglas Bar Assn. Named Man of Year Coffee County, 1959. Home: 821 N Daughtrey Ave Douglas GA 31533 Office: 303 N Peterson Ave Douglas GA 31533 Tel (912) 384-5799

SMITH, EDWIN STEEVES, b. Rochester, Minn., June 24, 1938; B.A., Carleton Coll., Northfield, Minn., 1960; grad. U. Minn. Law Sch., 1963; certificate Nat. Trust Sch., Northwestern U., 1964. Admitted to S.D. bar, 1963; trust officer Aberdeen (S.D.) Nat. Bank, 1963-65; partner firm Tinan, Carlson, Padrnos & Smith, Mitchell, S.D., 1965—; dep. states atty. Davison County (S.D.), 1968-75. Pres. S.D. Children's Aid, Mitchell, 1970-71; pres. bd. trustees Meth. Hosp., Mitchell, 1971—; com. mem. S.D. Ethics Commn., 1975—; state chmn. S.D. Republican Central Com., 1973-75, state committeeman, 1972-73, 77—. Mem. Am. (chmn. state membership 1972-73), S.D. (chmn. young lawyers sect. 1971-72) bar assns., State Bar S.D., Kiwanis (past pres.). Contbr. articles to mags. Home: 1020 Chalkstone Dr Mitchell SD 57301 Office: Box 488 204 Johnson Bldg Mitchell SD 57201 Tel (605) 996-5542

SMITH, ELBERT SIDNEY, b. Springfield, Ill., Oct. 27, 1911; J.D., U. Ala., 1936. Admitted to Ill. bar, 1936; individual practice law, Decatur, Ill., 1936-42; mem. firm Redmon, Smith & Hull, Decatur, 1942-58; mem. firm Downing, Smith, Jorgensen & Uhl, Decatur, 1958—; mem. Ill. Senate, 1948-56; auditor State of Ill., 1956-60. Vice-pres. 6th Ill. Constl. Conv., 1970. Mem. Am., Ill. bar assns., Am. Judicature Soc. Home: 510 Seigel St Decatur IL 62522 Office: Box 149 249 N Franklin St Decatur IL 62525 Tel (217) 429-2391

SMITH, ELZY J., b. Artesia, Miss., June 6, 1929; B.C.S., Southeastern U., 1951; J.D., U. Miss., 1960. Admitted to Miss. bar, 1960, U.S. Ct. Appeals bar, 5th Circuit, 1970; municipal judge, 1968-69; now partner firm Sullivan, Smith, Hunt & Vickery, Clarksdale, Miss. Fellow Miss. Bar Found.; mem. Am., Coahoma County (sec.-treas. 1964-66, pres. 1970-71) bar assns., Miss. State Bar (pres. 1977—), Miss. Def. Lawyers Assn., Def. Research Inst., Inc., Phi Delta Phi, Phi Kappa Phi. Editorial staff Miss. Law Jour., 1958-59. Office: 123 Court St PO Box 1196 Clarksdale MS 38614 Tel (601) 627-5251*

SMITH, ERNEST EDGAR, b. Gonzales, Tex., Sept. 8, 1936; B.A. summa cum laude, So. Meth. U., 1958; postgrad. (Rotary Found. fellow), U. London, 1958-59; LL.B. magna cum laude, Harvard, 1962. Admitted to Tex. bar, 1962; law clk. to judge U.S. Ct. Appeals Fifth Jud. Circuit, New Orleans, 1962-63; asst. prof. U. Tex. Law Sch., 1963-65, asso. prof., 1965-68, prof., 1968—, dean, 1974—; mem. Interstate Oil Compact Commn., State Bar Tex., 1963—. Mem. pres.'s adv. com. academic goverance U. Tex., Austin. Recipient Teaching Excellence award Tex. Law Sch., 1966; author: (with M.K. Woodward) Texas Probate and Decedents Estates, 1971; (with Huie and Woodward) Cases and Materials on Oil and Gas, 1972; contbr. articles to legal jours.; editor Harvard Law Rev., 1960-62; editorial adv. bd. Community Property Jour., 1975—. Home: 1400 Winsted Ln Austin TX 78703 Office: 2500 Red River Austin TX 78705 Tel (512) 471-1621

SMITH, EULYSE MCCOWN, b. Faulkner, Miss., Oct. 31, 1918; LL.B., U. Tex., 1942, J.D. Admitted to Tex. bar, 1942, Tenn. bar, 1944; individual practice law, Memphis. Mem. Tex., Memphis-Shelby County, Tenn., Am. bar assns. Office: 208 Adams St Memphis TN 38103 Tel (901) 526-5026

SMITH, EVERET FOY, b. Lexington, N.C., Sept. 15, 1913; B. Chem. Engring., N.C. State U., 1939; J.D., Loyola U., 1950. Admitted to Ill. bar, 1950, Ind. bar, 1961; chem. engr. Comml. Solvents Corp., Terre Haute, Ind., 1939-45; patent trainee, 1945-46; patent agt., atty. Standard Oil Co., Chgo., 1946-56; patent atty. Internat. Minerals & Chem. Corp., Skokie, Ill., 1956-58, patent counsel, 1958-60; patent atty. Eli Lilly and Co., Indpls., 1960-66, patent counsel, 1966-75, sr. patent counsel, 1975—. Mem. Am. Chem. Soc., Am., Ind. State (past chmn. patent sect.), Indpls. bar assns., Internat. Patent and Trademark Assn. Home: 3926 Glenview Dr Indianapolis IN 46240 Office: 307 E McCarty St Indianapolis IN 46206 Tel (317) 261-3186

SMITH, EVERETT HENSEL, b. Dallas, Aug. 11, 1915; B.A., Austin Coll., 1937; J.D., U. Tex., 1941. Admitted to Tex. bar, 1941, Miss. bar, 1953; asst. staff judge adv. U.S. Air Force, 1946-55, mem. bd. rev., Washington, 1955-59; staff judge adv., pres. fgn. claims commn. Caribbean Air Command, C.Z., 1959-63; chief mil. justice Lackland Mil. Tng. Center, San Antonio, 1963-67; sr. partner firm Smith Smith & Mealy, Kingsland and Llano, Tex., 1967—; atty. City of Granite Shoals (Tex.), 1968-75, City of Bertram (Tex.), 1972—; sec. Llano County Title Co., Inc., Kingsland, 1974—. Mem. Am., Hill Country bar assns., Kingsland C. of C. (past dir.). Author: Specified Articles of the Uniform Code of Military Justice, 1966. Home: PO Box 96 Buchanan Dam TX 78609 Office: PO Box 446 Kingsland TX 78639 also 102 W Sandstone St Llano TX 78643 Tel (915) 388-4545

SMITH, FARRELL DEE, b. Corpus Christi, Tex., July 27, 1916; B.B.A., U. Tex., 1936, LL.B., 1940. Admitted to Tex. bar, 1940, U.S. Dist. Ct. for So. Tex., 1940, U.S. Supreme Ct. bar, 1955; individual practice law, Corpus Christi, 1940—; mayor City of Corpus Christi, 1955-59; pres. City-County Child Welfare Bd., 1952. Mem. Tejas Commn., S. Tex. AAU; v.p. Corpus Christi Central Bus. Dist. Assn. Mem. Am., Tex., Nueces County bar assns. Home: 2757 Ocean Dr Corpus Christi TX 78404 Office: 425 Schatzel St Corpus Christi TX 78401 Tel (512) 882-9439

SMITH, FREDERICK DOUGLAS, b. Ellsworth, Kans., Mar. 29, 1917; A.B., U. Iowa, 1940; LL.B., Hastings Coll. Law, U. Calif., 1954. Admitted to Calif. bar, 1956, U.S. Supreme Ct. bar, 1974; individual practice law, San Francisco, 1956—; pub. defender City and County of San Francisco; lectr. Continuing Edn. of Bar, 1972, 75. Bd. dirs. San Francisco Neighborhood Legal Found., 1965-67, Hunter's Point Defenders, 1968-76, Inst. Criminal Justice, 1971-76, No. Calif. Service League, 1973-76; mem. jud. com. San Francisco Bar Assn. Mem. No. Calif. Trial Lawyers Assn., Calif. Pub. Defenders Assn., San Francisco Lawyers Club, No. Calif. Lawyers Guild. Recipient award of Merit, State Dept. Edn., 1975. Home: 535 Los Palmos Dr San Francisco CA 94127 Office: 850 Bryant St Room 205 San Francisco CA 94103 Tel (415) 553-1671

SMITH, GARY POOLE, b. Florence, Ala., July 14, 1933; B.A., Univ. Mo., 19S4; LL.B., Univ. Ala., 1960. Admitted to Ala. bar, 1960; legal asst. bd. govs. FRS, Washington, 1960-61; trial atty. Tax Div., U.S. Dept. Justice, Washington, 1961-66; with firm Johnston & Shares, Birmingham, Ala., 1966-72; partner firm Najjar, Najjar, Vincent & Smith, Birmingham, 1972—. Mem. Am., Ala., Birmingham bar assns. Home: 648 Paden Dr Birmingham AL 35226 Office: 1030 Brown Marx Building Birmingham AL 35203 Tel (205) 252-2116

SMITH, GARY RANDALL, b. Ft. Smith, Ark., Oct. 16, 1944; A.B., U. Ky., 1967, J.D., 1969; LL.M., N.Y. U., 1970. Admitted to Ky. bar, 1969, Ga. bar, 1970, Fla. bar, 1969; asso. firm Powell, Goldstein, Frazer & Murphy, Atlanta, 1970-72; asst. prof. law Emory U., Atlanta, 1972-75, asso. prof., 1975—, asst. dean, 1975—; mem. Gov.'s Legal Advisory Council on Workmen's Compensation, Atlanta, 1974—; Bd. dirs., pres., mem. exec. com. Druid Hills Civic Assn. Mem. Am., Fla., Ga., Ky., Atlanta (mem. med. legal com. 1974—), bar assns., Am. Trial Lawyers Assn. Contbr. articles to profl. jours. Home: 1733 Ponce de Leon Atlanta GA 30307 Office: Emory Univ Sch Law Atlanta GA 30322 Tel (404) 329-6828

SMITH, GARY WAYNE, b. Atlanta, Feb. 28, 1949; B.A. in History and Social Studies, Stetson U., Deland, Fla., 1971, J.D., Coll. Law, St. Petersburg, Fla., 1974. Admitted to Fla., Ga. bars, 1974; individual practice law, Atlanta, 1974—. Music dir. Virginia Ave. Baptist Ch., Atlanta, 1974—. Mem. Atlanta, Ga., Am. bar assns., Am. Trial Lawyers Assn., Ga. Assn. Criminal Def. Lawyers, Phi Alpha Delta. Key recipient Lambda Chi Alpha, 1971; recipient Freshman Moot Ct. award Stetson U. Coll. Law, 1972, Alumni award Stetson U., 1973. Home: 1042 Viscount Ct Avondale Estates GA 30002 Office: Suite 1402 Atlanta Center 250 Piedmont Ave NE Atlanta GA 30308 Tel (400) 588-0333

SMITH, GAVIN HARRIS, b. Houston, Dec. 5, 1945; B.B.A., U. Tex., Austin, 1970, J.D., 1971. Admitted to Tex. bar, 1971; Briefing atty. 1st Ct. Civil Appeals, Houston, 1971-72; mem. legal dept. Tenneco Inc., Houston, 1972—. Mem. Am., Tex., Houston bar assns., Alpha Tau Omega (chmn. bd. dirs.) Home: 2503 Watertown Mall Houston TX 77057 Office: PO Box 2511 Houston TX 77001 Tel (713) 757-3150

SMITH, GEOFFREY RICHARD WAGNER, b. San Francisco, May 26, 1945; A.B., Stanford, 1967, J.D., 1970. Admitted to Calif. bar, 1971, D.C. bar, 1971, U.S. Supreme Ct. bar, 1975; asso. firm Covington and Burling, Washington, 1970—; cons. Nat. Commn. on Marijuana and Drug Abuse, 1971-72. Bd. dirs. Washington Area Council on Alcoholism and Drug Abuse, 1976—, Washington Ballet, 1976—. Mem. State Bar Calif., D.C., Am. bar assns. Contbr. article to legal rev. Home: 2459 P St NW Washington DC 20007 Office: 888 16th St NW Washington DC 20036 Tel (202) 452-6302

SMITH, GEORGE EDWIN, b. Lewiston, Utah, May 3, 1933; B.A., State U. Iowa, 1955; J.D., U. Colo., 1966. Admitted to Colo. bar, 1966; asso. firm Evans Phelps & Shepherd, Pueblo, Colo., 1966-67; individual practice law, Pueblo and Alamosa, Colo., 1967-74; partner firm Smith & Selby, Alamosa, 1975—. Pres., Alamosa Sch. Bd., 1975—; bd. dirs. San Luis Valley Nutrition Program for the Elderly, 1973—, San Luis Valley Vocat. Sch., 1976—. Mem. Colo., San Luis Valley bar assns. Home: 206 13th St Alamosa CO 81101 Office: 422 4th St PO Box 1322 Alamosa CO 81101 Tel (303) 589-6757

SMITH, GEORGE EMMETT, b. Glens Falls, N.Y., Aug. 2, 1928; B.S. in Econs., Fordham U., 1953, J.D., 1956; M.A. in Econs., N.Y. U., 1959. Admitted to N.Y. State bar, 1956; atty. Union Carbide Corp., N.Y.C., 1956-67; asst. sec., asst. gen. counsel Xerox Corp., Stamford, Conn., 1967-75; sr. v.p., gen. counsel LTV Corp., Dallas, 1975—. Mem. Am., N.Y. State, Dallas bar assns., State Bar Tex. Home: 10048 Hollow Way Dallas TX 75229 Office: PO Box 5003 Dallas TX 75222

SMITH, GEORGE MAYNARD, b. Cairo, Ga., Oct. 5, 1907; A.B., Mercer U., 1929. Admitted to Ga. bar, 1933, D.C. bar, 1967; pros. atty. Cairo-Grady County (Ga.), 1935-39; spl. asst. atty. gen. Francis Biddle, 1942-44; sr. partner firm Smith, Currie & Hancock, Atlanta, 1950—. Industry mem. Nat. Wage Stabilization Bd., 1951. Mem. Am. Bar Assn., Lawyers Club. Home: 3900 Randall Ridge Rd NW Atlanta GA 30327 Office: 2600 Peachtree Center Harris Tower 233 Peachtree St NE Atlanta GA 30303 Tel (404) 521-3800

SMITH, GERALD MONROE, b. St. Louis, Apr. 8, 1931; B.J., U. Mo., 1952; J.D. with distinction, U. Mich., 1958. Admitted to Mo. bar, 1958, since practiced in St. Louis; asst. U.S. atty. Eastern Dist. Mo., 1959; asso. firm Coburn, Croft & Cook and successors, 1959-63; asso. firm Guilfoil, Symington, Petzall & Smith and predecessors, 1963-66, partner, 1966-69; commr. St. Louis Ct. of Appeals, 1969-71; judge Mo. Ct. of Appeals, St. Louis Dist., 1971—, chief judge, 1975-76. Mem. Am., Mo. bar assns., St. Louis Lawyers' Assn., Order of the Coif. Home: 416 Luther Ct Glendale MO 63122 Office: 12th and Market Sts Civil Ct Bldg St Louis MO 63101 Tel (314) 453-4605

SMITH, GLENN LEWIS, b. Des Moines, Feb. 27, 1944; B.A., Drake U., 1965, J.D., 1968. Admitted to Iowa bar, 1968, U.S. Dist. Ct. bar, 1969; law clk. Iowa Supreme Ct., 1968-69; asso. Polk County Legal Aid Soc., 1969; partner firm Duncan, Jones, Riley & Finley, Des Moines, 1970—. Bd. dirs. Greater Des Moines Montessori Assn., Inc., 1972—. Mem. Am., Iowa, Polk County bar assns., Am., Iowa trial lawyers assns. Home: 2839 Ridge Rd Des Moines IA 50311 Office: Equitable Bldg Des Moines IA 50309 Tel (515) 288-0145

SMITH, GORDON L., b. Virginia, Minn., Mar. 27, 1919; LL.B., St. Paul Coll. Law, 1951. Admitted to Minn. bar, 1951; claims mgr. St. Paul Fire & Marine Ins. Co., 1946—. Mem. Minn. State Bar Assn. Office: 30 E Marie St West Saint Paul MN 55165 Tel (612) 455-6600

SMITH, GREGORY BUTLER, b. Muncie, Ind., June 20, 1946; A.B., Ind. U., 1968; J.D., 1971. Admitted to Ind. bar, 1971; dep. pros. atty. Delaware County, Ind., 1971-72; partner firm Smith & Smith, Muncie, 1971—. Mem. adminstrv. bd. High St. Methodist Ch., Muncie, 1975—; bd. dirs. Muncie Meals on Wheels, 1973—; pres. Delaware County Young Republicans Club, 1976-77. Mem. Am., Ind., Muncie bar assns., Young Lawyers Assn. Muncie, Ind. Trial Lawyers Assn. Office: 201 N High St Muncie IN 47305

SMITH, HAMILTON, b. N.Y.C., Feb. 11, 1926; B.A., Yale, 1947; J.D., U. Mich., 1950. Admitted to N.Y. State bar, 1951, Ill. bar, 1952, U.S. Supreme Ct. bar, 1971; asso. firm Fish, Richardson & Neave, N.Y.C., 1950-52; asso. firm McDermott, Will & Emery, Chgo., 1952-60, partner, 1960—. Mem. Am., Ill. State, Chgo. bar assns. Home: 840 Wagner Rd Glenview IL 60025 Office: 111 W Monroe St Chicago IL 60603 Tel (312) 372-2000

SMITH, HARMON TOMPKINS, JR., b. Atlanta, Mar. 20, 1942; B.B.A., U. Ga., 1964, LL.B., 1967. Admitted to Ga. bar, 1967; asso. firm James I. Parker, Cedartown, Ga., 1967-69; partner firm Norton Smith and Majors, Gainesville, Ga., 1969-71, Smith and Millikan, Gainesville, 1971-74, Smith and Bell, Gainesville, 1976—; judge, Recorders Ct., Dawsonville, Ga.; trustee, U.S. Bankruptcy Ct., Gainesville div. No. Dist. Ga. Office: 380 Green St NE PO Box 1276 Gainesville GA 30501

SMITH, HAROLD STANHOPE, b. Arcadia, Fla., Aug. 27, 1917; A.A., U. Fla., 1946, LL.B., 1948; J.D., 1967; M.A., George Washington U., 1964. Admitted to Fla. bar, 1948, U.S. Supreme Ct. bar, 1957, Korean bar, 1953, practiced in Arcadia, 1948, Everglades, Fla., 1948-51, Naples, Fla., 1953-64; county atty. Collier County (Fla.), 1948-61, pros. atty., 1948-51, sch. bd. atty., 1948-63; judge City Ct., Naples, Fla., 1953-64; chief judge 20th Jud. Circuit Ct., 1970-74; mem. Jud. Qualifications Commn., 1974—.

SMITH, HAROLD TELIAFERRO, JR., b. Miami, Fla., Apr. 10, 1947; B.S. in Mathematics, Fla. A. and M. U., 1968; J.D., U. Miami, 1973. Admitted to Fla. bar, 1973; asst. pub. defender County of Dade (Fla.), 1973-76, asst. county atty., 1976—. Bd. dirs. Coconut Grove Family Clinic, Miami. Mem. Nat., Fla. bar assns., Kappa Alpha Psi (dir.). Office: Dade County Court House Room 1626 Miami FL 33130 Tel (305) 579-5151

SMITH, HENRY J., b. N.Y.C., Jan. 2, 1919; A.B., Fordham U., 1940; LL.B., Harvard U., 1947. Admitted to N.Y. bar, 1948; now with firm McCarthy, Fingar, Donovan & Glatthaar, White Plains, N.Y.; treas. Legal Aid of Westchester (N.Y.), 1962-72, dir. 1964-72, mem. exec. com. 1968-72; spl. counsel Town of Greenburgh, 1963-69, City of White Plains, 1967—, City of New Rochelle (N.Y.), 1969. Bd. dirs. Welserv OEO, 1968-72. Fellow Am. Bar Found.; mem. White Plains (dir. 1957-66), Westchester County (pres. 1963-65, dirs. council 1965—), N.Y. State (exec. com. 1972—, pres. 1977—), Am. bar assns., Am. Judicature Soc. Office: 175 Main St White Plains NY 10601 Tel (914) 946-3700*

SMITH, HERBERT HERMAN, b. Syracuse, N.Y., Mar. 12, 1906; A.B., Syracuse U., 1928; J.D., 1930. Admitted to N.Y. bar, 1931; asso. firm Clerk, Hiscock, Williams and Cowie, Syracuse, 1930-34; individual practice law, Waverly, N.Y., 1935-59; asst. atty. gen. State of N.Y., Albany, 1959-68; exec. dir. and counsel N.Y. State Assn. of Counties, 1968—; justice of peace Waverly, 1938-42; dist. atty. Tioga County (N.Y.), 1943-55; atty. Village of Waverly, 1944-54, Waverly Sch. Dist., 1940-58. Pres., Waverly Bd. Trade, 1940. Mem. N.Y. State, Tioga County (pres. 1943-45) bar assns., Am. Soc. Assn. Execs. Home: 42 Juniper Dr Clifton Park NY 12065 Office: 150 State St Albany NY 12207 Tel (518) 465-1473

SMITH, HERMAN TALLIFERRIO, b. Fulton, Ark., Oct. 6, 1915; B.A., Prairie View U., 1937; J.D., Southwestern U., 1954. Co-owner Smith & Rand Service Center & Pub. Service Cab Co., Texarkana, Tex., 1938-42; owner Four Way Laundry, Los Angeles, 1946-55; admitted to Calif. bar, 1956; individual practice law, Los Angeles, 1956—; atty. Legal Def. Fund, Watts NAACP, 1965; chmn. Los Angeles chpt. NAACP, 1965-69. Republican nominee 55th Assembly Dist. State Calif., 1958, 23rd Congressional Dist., 1962; mem. Los Angeles County Jud. Procedures Commn., 1962—. Mem. Calif. State Bar Assn., Prairie View Alumni Assn., Nat. Conf. Black Lawyers, ACLU. Co-author: California Politics and Policies, 1965. Recipient Pub. Service awards Los Angeles County, 1969, Merit awards State Legis. Rules Com., 1969, Watts Branch NAACP, 1965, 76, Los Angeles br., 1966. Office: 8918 S Broadway Los Angeles CA 90003 Tel (213) 750-7854

SMITH, HORACE, JR., b. Orangeburg, S.C., Nov. 22, 1942; B.A., Fla. State U., 1964; J.D., Samford U., 1967. Admitted to Fla. bar, 1967, U.S. Supreme Ct. bar, 1971; since practiced in Daytona Beach, Fla.; partner firm Dunn & Smith, Smith, 1967; individual practice law, 1967-76; partner firm Dunn, Upchurch, Smith and Doyle, 1976; chief asst. state's atty. 7th Jud. Circuit, Fla., 1969-77; partner firm Dunn, Bernardini, Smith & Burnett, 1977—; city atty. City of Bunnell, Fla., 1976—; instr. criminal law Daytona Beach Community Coll., 1976—; spl. state's atty. Polk and Breward Counties. Bd. dirs. United Child Care, Inc., Daytona Beach, 1976—; bd. visitors Embry Riddle Aero. Inst. Mem. Fla. (com. on criminal rules), Volusia County (pres.), Am. bar assns., Nat. Dist. Attys. Assn., Fla. Prosecuting Attys. Assn., Acad. Trial Lawyers, Liaison of Circuit Judges' Conf. (chmn. jud. poll and ct. coms.). Home: 314 Riverside Dr Ormond Beach FL 32074 Office: 444 Seabreeze Suite 800 Daytona Beach FL Tel (904) 258-1222

SMITH, HORTON, b. Seattle, June 1, 1925; B.A., U. Wash., 1947, LL.B., 1950, J.D., 1968; grad. Nat. State Trial Judges course U. Nev., 1971. Admitted to Wash. bar, 1951, U.S. Supreme Ct. bar, 1962; asso. firm Elvidge, Watt, Veblen & Tewell, Seattle, 1954-58; sr. partner firm Smith, Lindell, Krutch, Carr & Poliak, Seattle, 1958-64; commr. King County (Wash.) Superior Ct., 1964-69; sr. partner firm Smith, Lind. Thom & Mussehl, Seattle, 1969; judge King County Superior Ct., Seattle, 1969—. Exec. bd. Chief Seattle council Boy Scouts Am.; pres. SEADRUNAR Drug Treatment Center, Seattle, 1971-73. Mem. Am. Bar Assn. (state jud. del. 1974—), Am. Judicature Soc., Superior Ct. Judges Assn., Nat. Assn. State Trial Judges. Contbr. articles to legal jours. Office: Superior Court Seattle WA 98104 Tel (206) 344-4055

SMITH, HOWARD SAMUEL, b. Los Angeles, Jan. 13, 1932; B.S. with great distinction, Stanford, 1953; LL.B., Harvard, Admitted to Calif. bar, 1958, U.S. Supreme Ct. bar, 1964; since practiced in Los Angeles, law clk. U.S. Dist. Ct., 1957-58; asso. firm Mitchell, Silberberg & Knupp, 1958, now partner. Mem. western regional bd. United Way Los Angeles, 1975—, vice-chmn., 1976—; mem. Los Angeles chpt. Am. Jewish Com., vice-chmn., 1976—. Mem. Am., Calif., Los Angeles County bar assns. Home: 1715 Westridge Rd Los Angeles CA 90049 Office: 1800 Century Park E Los Angeles CA 90067 Tel (213) 553-5000

SMITH, HUGH ROBERTS HOVAL, b. Chgo., Nov. 24, 1916; A.B., Yale, 1939, LL.B., 1942. Admitted to D.C. bar, 1946, Md. bar, 1960; asso. firm Wilmer and Broun, Washington, 1946-50, partner, 1950-62; partner firm Wilmer, Cutler and Pickering, Washington, 1962—. Mem. Am. Bar Found., Am., D.C. bar assns. Home: 6803 Meadow Ln Chevy Chase MD 20015 Office: 1666 K St NW Washington DC 20006 Tel (202) 872-6020

SMITH, JAMES ALBERT, b. St. Louis, Oct. 29, 1923; A.B., U. Redlands, 1949; J.D., Hastings Coll. Law, U. Calif., 1952; postgrad. Oxford (Eng.) U., 1973, 74, Hague (Netherlands) Acad. Internat. Law, 1974, 75. Admitted to Calif. bar, 1953; chief trial dep. dist. atty. County of San Bernardino (Calif.), 1956-57; individual practice law, Redlands, Calif., 1958—. Mem. Am., Inter-Am., San Bernardino County (pres. 1967-68) bar assns., Am. Soc. Internat. Law, State Bar Calif. (pres. conf. barristers 1959). Home: Office: 130 W Vine St Redlands CA 92373 Tel (714) 793-3333

SMITH, JAMES ALBERT, b. Starks, La., Sept. 5, 1921; J.D., La. State U., 1950. Admitted to La. bar, 1950; partner firm Smith & Wise, Lake Charles, 1950—; asst. dist. atty. Calcasieu Parish, La., 1955-60. Chmn. Calcasieu-Cameron Polio Dr., 1955, Calcasieu-Cameron Heart Fund Dr., 1967. Mem. Am., La. State, S.W. La. bar assns. Home: 4313 Essex St Lake Charles LA 70601 Office: 1117 Kirkman St PO Box 1706 Lake Charles LA 70601 Tel (318) 439-2413

SMITH, JAMES BRADLEY, b. East St. Louis, Ill., July 11, 1945; B.B.A., Tex. A. and M. U., 1969; J.D., U. Tex., 1972. Admitted to Tex. bar, 1972; gen. counsel Tex. Senate Affairs Com., Austin, 1973; asst. dist. atty. Brazos County (Tex.), Bryan, 1974-76; judge Brazos County Ct.-at-Law, 1976—. Chmn., Brazos Valley chpt. March of Dimes, 1975. Mem. Brazos County Bar Assn., Tex. Dist. and County Attys. Assn., State Bar Tex. Home: 1007 E 29th St Bryan TX 77801 Office: Brazos County Courthouse Bryan TX 77801 Tel (713) 822-7373

SMITH, JAMES CLOUDIS, b. Jacksonville, Fla., May 25, 1940; B.S., Fla. State U., 1962; J.D., Stetson U., 1967. Admitted to Fla. bar, 1967; partner firm Dale & Stevens, Ft. Lauderdale, Fla., 1967-68, Smith, Young & Blue, Tallahassee, 1972—; exec. asst. Fla. Sec. of State, Tallahassee, 1968-69, dep. sec. of state, 1969-71; sec. asst. Fla. Lt. Gov., Tallahassee, 1971; dep. sec. Fla. Dept. Commerce, Tallahassee, 1971; sr. staff asst. to Gov. Fla., Tallahassee, 1971-72; chmn. Fla. Gov's. Task Force on Mobile Homes. Mgr. Fla. Gov. Reubin Askew's Reelection Campaign, 1974; trustee Fla. State U. Found., Inc.; mem. council advisers, pres's. fund for excellence Fla. State U.; mem. Fla. Council of 100; bd. overseers Stetson Coll. Law. Mem. Leon County (Fla.), Broward County (Fla.), Tallahassee, Fla., Am. bar assns., Am. Judicature Soc., Tallahassee Area C. of C. (steering com.), Fla. State U. Alumni Assn. (pres.). Recipient Walter Mann award Stetson U. Coll. Law, 1967. Home: 1720 Tarpon Dr Tallahassee FL 32303 Office: PO Box 1833 Tallahassee FL 32302 Tel (904) 222-7206

SMITH, JAMES GEORGE RHINEHARDT, b. Williamsport, Pa., Apr. 17, 1936; B.B.A., Baylor U., 1957; J.D., 1966. Admitted to Tex. bar, 1965, U.S. Supreme Ct. bar, 1969; partner firm Barker, Lain, Smith & Schwab, Galveston, Tex., 1965—; trust officer 1st Hutchings-Sealy Bank, 1962-65; agt. IRS, U.S. Treasury, Houston, 1959-62. Asso. state chmn. Nat. Found. March of Dimes, 1974—, chmn. Galveston County, 1976—; treas. Performing Arts Com., Galveston, 1970—. Mem. Am., Tex. bar assns., Galveston Estate Planning Council, Nat. Assn. Estate Planning Councils. Names Outstanding Citizen of Yr., Galveston Jaycees, 1970. Home: 2501 Beluche Galveston TX 77550 Office: 2200 Market St Suite 500 Galveston TX 77550 Tel (713) 765-9353

SMITH, JAMES OTIS, b. Boston, Dec. 17, 1909; A.B., DePauw U., 1933; LL.B., Northeastern U., 1938, J.D., 1971. Admitted to Mass. bar, 1943; asso. firm Abbott, Carr Turner & Smith, Boston, 1944, partner, to 1973; individual practice law, Melrose, Mass., 1973—. Admitted to Boston, Middlesex bar assns., Am. Judicature Soc. Home: 177 Essex St Saugus MA 01906 Office: 723 Main St Melrose MA 02176 Tel (617) 665-6454

SMITH, JAMES ROBERT, b. Waycross, Ga., Feb. 9, 1928; LL.B., U. Ga., 1953. Admitted to Ga. bar; individual practice law, Colquitt, Ga.; solicitor Ga. State Ct., 1953-56; mem. Ga. Ho. of Reps., 1960-62. Home: Route 2 PO Box 282A Colquitt GA 31737 Office: 100 Grow St Colquitt GA 31737 Tel (912) 758-2784

SMITH, JAMES T., b. Atlanta, Jan. 8, 1925; B.S., U. Ga., 1948; LL.B., Atlanta Law Sch., 1950, LL.M., 1951. Admitted to Ga. bar, 1950. U.S. Supreme Ct. bar, 1956; claims examiner Kemper Ins. Co., 1948-51; claims mgr. Standard Accident Ins. Co., Atlanta, 1951-56; gen. counsel Martin A. Hayes & Co., Nashville, Tenn., 1956-62; gen. atty. VA, Atlanta, 1962—. Pres. Vinings, Civic Club, Atlanta, 1974-75; pres. Middle Tenn. U. Ga. Alumni, 1960-62; pres. Sertoma Club of Nashville, 1960. Mem. Am., Ga., Fed. bar assns. Named Sertoman of Year, 1960. Home: 3680 Tanglewood Dr NW Atlanta GA 30339 Office: 730 Peachtree St NW Atlanta GA 30308 Tel (404) 526-2721

SMITH, JAMES WALKER, b. Jacksonville, Fla., Aug. 28, 1941; B.A., Stetson U., 1963; J.D., 1966. Admitted to Fla. bar, 1966; asso. firm Howell, Kirby, D'Aiuto & Dean, 1968-69; partner firm Hoffman, Hendry, Smith, Stoner & Schoder, Daytona Beach, Fla., 1969—. Mem. Am. Arbitration Assn. Office: 605 S Ridgewood Ave Daytona Beach FL 32014 Tel (904) 255-0505

SMITH, JEFFERSON VERNE, JR., b. Greenville, S.C., Oct. 10, 1948; B.A. magna cum laude, Furman U., 1970; J.D. magna cum laude, U. S.C., 1974. Admitted to S.C. bar, 1973; asso. firm Carter & Philpot, Greenville, 1974-75; partner firm Carter, Philpot, Johnson & Smith, Greenville, 1975—; municipal judge City of Greer (S.C.), 1974-77. Mem. Am. Bar Assn. Home: Route 2 Hwy 14 Greer SC 29605 Office: 123 Broadus Ave Greenville SC 29601 Tel (803) 242-3566

SMITH, JEFFREY MICHAEL, b. Mpls., July 9, 1947; B.A. summa cum laude, U. Minn., 1970, J.D. magna cum laude, 1973; student U. Malaya, Kuala Lumpur, Malaysia, 1967-68. Admitted to Ga. bar, 1973; asso. firm Powell, Goldstein, Frazer & Murphy, Atlanta, 1973-76; partner firm Rogers & Hardin, Atlanta, 1976—; adj. prof. profl. liability Emory U. Sch. Law, 1976—; lectr. in law Duke U. Sch. Law, 1976—, Vanderbilt U. Sch. Law, 1977—. Mem. Am., Atlanta bar assns., State Bar Ga. (chmn. legal ethics com., younger lawyers sect. 1977—), Minn. Sch. Law Alumni Assn. (dir. 1976—), Order of Coif, Phi Beta Kappa. Mem. Minn. Law Rev., 1971-73, pres., 1972-73; cons. editor, mem. adv. bd. Profl. Liability Reporter, 1977—. Home: 1556 Anita Pl NE Atlanta GA 30306 Office: Suite 3200 101 Marietta Tower Atlanta GA 30303 Tel (404) 522-4700

SMITH, JOHN BUNDY, b. Berwyn, Ill., Sept. 10, 1939; A.A., Morton Jr. Coll., 1959; B.S., Fla. So. Coll., 1961; J.D., Northwestern U., 1964; postgrad. John Marshall Sch. Law, 1964-65. Admitted to Ill. bar, 1964, Fla. bar, 1970; asst. counsel Personnel Pool of Am., Inc., Chgo., 1965-70, Ft. Lauderdale, Fla., 1970—, gen. counsel, 1972—, sec., 1967—, also dir.; organizing dir. Nat. Assn. Temporary Services, Inc., Washington, 1966. Mem. Fla., Ill. bar assns., Nat. Health Lawyer's Assn., Phi Alpha Delta, Sigma Phi Epsilon, Omicron Delta Kappa, Delta Sigma Pi. Home: 5321 SW 9th St Plantation FL 33317 Office: 521 S Andrews Ave Fort Lauderdale FL 33301 Tel (305) 581-2154

SMITH, JOHN FRANCIS, III, b. White Plains, N.Y., Sept. 24, 1941; A.B., Princeton, 1963; LL.B., Yale, 1970. Admitted to Pa. bar, 1970; asso. firm Dilworth, Paxson, Kalish & Levy, Phila., 1970-75, partner, 1975—. Mem. exec. com. Employment Discrimination Referral Project, Phila., 1971-74. Pres. Society Hill Civic Assn., 1975-76, Phila. Chamber Ensemble, 1977. Mem. Am., Pa., Phila. bar assns. Home: 329 S Lawrence St Philadelphia PA 19106 Office: 2600 Fidelity Bldg Philadelphia PA 19109

SMITH, JOHN KERWIN, b. Oakland, Calif., Oct. 18, 1926; B.A., Stanford, 1949; LL.B., Hastings Coll. Law U. Calif., San Francisco, 1954. Admitted to Calif. bar, 1955, U.S. Supreme Ct. bar, 1961; partner firm Haley, Schenone, Birchfield & Smith, Hayward, Calif., 1954—. Mem. Hayward Parks Commn., 1957; mem. Hayward City Council, 1959-66, mayor, 1966-70; chmn. Alameda County Mayors Conf., 1968; chmn. revenue taxation com. League Calif. Cities, 1968; pres. div. League Calif. Cities, 1969. Mem. Am., Calif., Alameda County bar assns., Am. Judicature Soc. Office: 1331 B St PO Box 450 Hayward CA 94543 Tel (415) 538-6400

SMITH, JOHN KIRKLAND, JR., b. Columbia, S.C., Jan. 8, 1924; B.S., J.D., U. S.C., 1955. Admitted to S.C. bar, 1955, U.S. Supreme Ct. bar, 1960; examiner U.S. Patent Office, Washington, 1955-60, classifications atty., 1960; individual practice law, Columbia, 1960—. Mem. Phi Delta Phi. Address: 861 Arbutus Dr Columbia SC 29205

SMITH, JULIAN CLAUD, JR., b. Los Angeles, Oct. 25, 1935; B.S., Calif. Poly. Inst., 1957; J.D., U. Utah, 1971. Admitted to Nev. bar, 1970, U.S. Supreme Ct. bar, 1974; dep. atty. gen. State of Nev., Carson City, 1971-74; individual practice law, Carson City, 1971—. Mem. Carson City Bicentennial Commn., 1976; mem. Winnemucca (Nev.) City Council, 1967-68; trustee Rocky Mountain Law Found. Mem. State Bar Nev. Home: 4630 Garnet Way Carson City NV 89701 Office: 502 N Division St Carson City NV 89701 Tel (702) 883-3206

SMITH, JULIUS NORMAN, b. Paterson, N.J., Nov. 1, 1906; Ph.B., Yale, 1929, LL.B., 1931. Admitted to Conn. bar; asst. town counsel, Conn., 1935, 45; pros. atty. Fairfield (Conn.) Municipal Ct., 1951-54; judge probate dist. Fairfield, 1955-59; individual practice law, Bridgeport, Conn. Pres., Internat. Inst. Bridgeport, Inc., 1942-45, pres. Family Service Soc. Fairfield, 1958-61, sec., 1960-61, chmn., 1962-66; mem. Grievance Com. Fairfield County. Mem. Am., Conn., Bridgeport bar assns. Home: 1980 Stratfield Rd Fairfield CT 06430 Office: 955 Main St Bridgeport CT 06603 Tel (203) 367-1125

SMITH, K. CLAY, b. New Orleans, Aug. 29, 1937; B.B.A., Notre Dame U., 1960; LL.B., Georgetown U., 1964, J.D., 1964. Admitted to Ind. bar, 1964; spl. agt. FBI, 1964-67; asso. firm Kightlinger Young Gray & DeTrude, Indpls., 1967-72; pres. Underwood Machinery Transport, Inc., Indpls., 1972—. Chmn. Indpls. License Bd., 1974—. Mem. Ind., Indpls. bar assns., Ind. Motor Truck Assn. (chmn. bd.). Contbr. editorials to Transp. Engr. Office: 940 W Troy Ave Indianapolis IN 46225

SMITH, KEN MCFARLANE, b. Kokomo, Ind., Feb. 12, 1927; B.S., Ind. U., 1948, LL.B., 1950, J.D., 1967. Admitted to Ind. bar, 1950, Va. bar, 1954, U.S. Ct. Mil. Appeals, 1952, U.S. Supreme Ct. bar, 1958; individual practice law, Arlington, Va., 1954—; partner firm Kinney & Smith, Arlington, 1960—, mng. partner, 1973—; asst. pub. defender State of Ind., 1950; asst. commonwealth atty. State of Va., 1955-59, head civil litigation sect., 1956-59; asst. commr. accounts Arlington County (Va.), 1960—; substitute judge Arlington Gen. Dist. Ct., 1961—; instr. appellate ct. procedure Ind. U., 1950; tchr. bus. law U. Va., 1957; chmn. bd. Bank of Arlington, 1970-73; dir. Hamilton Bank & Trust Co., 1971. Bd. dirs. Arlington Corps Salvation Army, 1961-66, chmn. bd., 1963-66; del. Interservice Club Council Arlington County, 1962-64, v.p., 1963, pres., 1964; chmn. explorer program Boy Scouts Am., 1971-73; mem. adv. bd. Council Ind. Colls. Va., 1972-74; mem. Va. Adv. Legis. Council, 1958-66; bd. mgrs. YMCA, 1959-61, vice chmn., 1960-61; chmn. No. Va. Heart Assn. Fund Drive, 1962; vice chmn. Sch. Bond Commn., 1968; bd. dirs. Alcoholics Rehab. Inc., 1965-68, mem. adv. bd., 1968-72; bd. assos. U. Richmond, 1973, trustee, 1974—. Mem. Am., Ind., Arlington County bar assns., Va. Commonwealth Attys. Assn. Home: 4056 N 27th Rd Arlington VA 22207 Office: 2007 N 15th St PO Box 749 Arlington VA 22216 Tel (703) 525-4000

SMITH, KENNETH MCRAE, b. San Diego, May 10, 1928; LL.B., Stanford, 1950, J.D., 1952; grad. Calif. Coll. for Judiciary, 1969, Nat. Coll. Trial Judges, 1973. Admitted to Calif. bar, 1952; asso. firm Parker Stanbury Reese & McGee, Santa Ana, Calif., 1952-63; partner firm Guy and Smith, Newport Beach, Calif., 1962-68; judge West Orange County (Calif.) Municipal Ct., 1968—. Mem. Am. Bar Assn., Conf. Calif. Judges, Phi Alpha Delta. Recipient Humanitarian award Jewish War Vets., 1975. Office: 8143 13th St Westminster CA 92683 Tel (714) 896-7175

SMITH, KIRK, b. Cogswell, N.D., Feb. 5, 1930; Ph.B., U. N.D., 1956, J.D., 1957. Admitted to N.D. bar, U.S. Dist. Ct. bar, U.S. Ct. of Appeals bar, 1957; law clk. 8th Circuit Ct. of Appeals, Fargo, N.D., 1957-58; partner firm Bangert, Bangert & Smith, Enderlin, N.D., 1958-59, Arnason & Smith, Grand Forks, N.D., 1959-63; justice Municipal Ct. Grand Forks, 1960-61, County Ct., Grand Forks, 1961-63; judge County Ct. with increased jurisdiction, Grand Forks, 1963-77, Dist. Ct. for 1st Jud. Dist., Grand Forks, 1977—; mem. various legal coms., task forces. Mem. Am., N.D. bar assns. Contbr. articles in field to legal jours. Office: Court House Grand Forks ND 58201 Tel (701) 775-2571

SMITH, LARRY ALFRED, b. Hattisburg, Miss., July 16, 1948; B.B.A., U. Miss., 1970, J.D., 1973. Admitted to Miss. bar, 1973; asso. firm Megehee, Brown & Williams, Pascagoula, Miss., 1973—. Bd. dirs. Jackson County (Miss.) Boys Club, 1974-76; chmn. Pascagoula Elections Com., 1976—. Mem. Jackson County (pres. young lawyers sect. 1975-76, pres. sr. sect. 1976-77), Am., Miss. bar assns. Office: POB 787 Pascagoula MS 39567 Tel (601) 762-2271

SMITH, LARRY GLENN, b. Montgomery, Ala., Aug. 6, 1924; student U. Ala., 1942-43, 46-48; LL.B., U. Fla., 1949. Admitted to Fla. bar, 1949, U.S. Supreme Ct. bar, 1970; individual practice law, Panama City, Fla., 1949; asso. firm Mathis & Mathis, Panama City, 1953-57; asst. state's atty. 14th Jud. Circuit of Fla., 1953-57; research asst. Fla. Supreme Ct., 1958-60; partner firms Baker, Baker & Smith, Orlando, Fla., 1960-64, Isler, Welch, Smith, Higby & Brown, Panama City, 1964-72; judge Fla. Circuit Ct., 14th Jud. Circuit, 1973—; mem. Fla. Bd. Bar Examiners, 1967-72, vice chmn., 1972. Pres. Bay County (Fla.) Library Assn., 1957-58; mem. Panama City Airport Bd., 1955-58. Mem. Fla. Bar, Am. Bar Assn., Am. Judicature Soc., Fla. Conf. Circuit Judges (chmn. com. pub. info. and press relations). Office: Bay County Courthouse Panama City FL 32401 Tel (904) 763-4018

SMITH, LAWRENCE A., JR., b. Rockford, Ill., Sept. 25, 1936; B.S., U. Ill., 1958, J.D., 1961. Admitted to Ill. bar, 1961; partner firm Smith, Smith, & Smith, Savanna, Ill., 1961-75; city atty. Savanna, 1961-65; asso. circuit judge, Mt. Carroll, Ill., 1975—. Trustee Savanna Twp. Library, 1964-70. Mem. Am., Ill. State bar assns. Home: RFD 2 Savanna IL 61074 Office: Carroll County Ct House Mt Carroll IL 61053 Tel (815) 244-7085

SMITH, LAWRENCE AARON, b. Bklyn., Aug. 2, 1938; B.B.A., Hofstra Coll., 1960; LL.B., Bklyn. Law Sch., 1962. Admitted to N.Y. bar, 1963; individual practice law, N.Y.C., 1963—. Office: 277 Broadway New York City NY 10007 Tel (212) 227-3102

SMITH, LAWRENCE SHANNON, b. Dallas, Oct. 6, 1943; B.A., U. Tex., 1965, J.D., 1970. Admitted to Tex. bar, 1970, U.S. Supreme Ct. bar, 1974; partner firm Small, Craig & Werkenthin, Austin, Tex., 1970—. Mem. Am. Bar Assn., State Bar Tex. Office: 2600 Austin Nat Bank Tower Austin TX 78701 Tel (512) 472-8355

SMITH, LEO EMMET, b. Chgo., Jan. 6, 1927; J.D., DePaul U., 1950. Admitted to Ill. bar, 1950; asso. with law firm, also engaged in pvt. industry, 1950-54; asst. states atty. Cook County, Ill., 1954-57; asst. counsel Traffic Inst., Northwestern U., Evanston, Ill., 1957-60; asst. exec. sec. Comml. Law League Am., Chgo., 1960-61, exec. dir., editor Comml. Law Jour., 1961—. Mem. Am., Ill. bar assns., World Assn. Lawyers. Contbr. articles to legal jours. Home: 1104 S Knight St Park Ridge IL 60068 Office: 222 W Adams St Chicago IL 60606 Tel (312) 236-4942

SMITH, LEON EDWARD, JR., b. Great Bend, Kans., May 30, 1937; A.A., Parsons (Kans.) Jr. Coll., 1957; B.S. in Archtl. Engring., Kans. State U., 1960; J.D., Washburn U., 1966. Admitted to Kans. bar, 1966, Idaho bar, 1969; atty. engr., contract sect. E.I. duPont de Nemours, Wilmington, Del., 1966-67; v.p., gen. mgr. Rex Furniture Co. (Ga.), 1967-68; partner firm Smith & Beeks, Twin Falls, Idaho, 1968—; county atty. Twin Falls County (Idaho), 1970-72; prof. design engr. Burgwin & Matin Cons. Engrs., Denver, Topeka, Kansas City, Mo., 1963-66. Councilman, zoning commr. City of Twin Falls, 1973. Mem. ASCE, Am., Idaho trial lawyers assns., Kans., Idaho, 5th Jud. Dist. bar assns. Registered profl. engr., Kans., Idaho, Del. Home: 671 Monte Vista Dr Twin Falls ID 83301 Office: 210 6th Ave E PO Box 508 Twin Falls ID 83301 Tel (208) 733-6684

SMITH, LESLIE CLARK, b. Balt., July 15, 1941; B.A., Vanderbilt U., 1962; J.D. with high distinction, U. Ky., 1971; LL.M., U. Western Australia, 1976. Admitted to N.Mex. bar, 1971, U.S. Supreme Ct. bar, 1975; partner firm Buhler, Smith, Fitch & Stout, Truth or Consequences, N.Mex., 1971-75; asst. prof. law U. Western Australia, 1975; individual practice law, Truth or Consequences, 1976—. Chmn., Fine Arts Soc., 1974, Continuing Edn. Com., Truth or Consequences, 1976. Mem. Am., N.Mex. bar assns., Order of Coif. Contbr. articles to legal jours. Office: PO Box 409 Truth or Consequences NM 87901 Tel (505) 894-7116

SMITH, LYMAN H., b. Naples, N.Y., Jan. 10, 1918; A.B., Cornell U., 1940, LL.B., 1942. Admitted to N.Y. State bar, 1946, U.S. Supreme Ct. bar, 1964, U.S. Ct. of Claims, 1964, U.S. Treasury Dept. bar, 1951, U.S. Dist. Ct. bar, Western Dist., 1947; individual practice law, Penn Yan, N.Y., 1946-64; dist. atty. Yates County, N.Y., 1948-63; judge Surrogate and Family Ct., Yates County, 1965-73; justice Supreme Ct., 7th Jud. Dist. N.Y., 1973—. Chmn. Criminal Jury Instrns. Com., N.Y., 1976—. Lay reader Episcopal Ch. of U.S.A., 1954; pres. Yates County Community Chest, 1950-51, Penn Yan Rotary Club, 1957, Yates County Hist. and Geneal. Soc., 1959-60; chmn. Yates County Civil War Centennial Commn., 1961; bd. dirs. Family Counseling Service of Fingerlakes, Soldiers and Sailors Hosp., Penn Yan; trustee Garrett Meml. Chapel, Bluff Point, N.Y., Nundawaga Soc. Mem. Am., N.Y. State, Yates County (pres. 1959) bar assns., County Judges Assn. N.Y. (v.p. 1973), Surrogates Assn. N.Y. State, Family Ct., Supreme Ct. (chmn. com. on criminal jury instrns.) judges assns. N.Y., Internat. Assn. Probate Judges (life), Nat. Council Juvenile Ct. Judges, Phi Delta Phi. Home: RD 3 Dundee NY 14837 Office: Supreme Ct Chambers Penn Yan NY 14527 Tel (607) 243-8883

SMITH, MARK ALLAN, b. Long Beach, Calif., Apr. 17, 1945; B.S., Western State U., 1969, J.D., 1971. Admitted to Calif. bar, 1972, U.S. Fed. Ct. bar, 1972, U.S. Supreme Ct. bar, 1976, U.S. Tax Ct., 1977; owner multi-atty. law firm, Laguna Niguel, Calif., 1972—; judge pro tem, Orange County, Calif., 1973—. Mem. Am., Calif., Orange County bar assns., Calif. (sustaining), Orange County trial lawyers assns., J. Rueben Clark Law Soc. Office: 30001 Crown Valley Pkwy Suite H Laguna Niguel CA 92677 Tel (714) 831-2080

SMITH, MARK CRAIG, b. New Hampton, Iowa, Mar. 25, 1948; B.S. in Math. Notre Dame U., 1970; J.D. (hon.), Drake U., 1973. Admitted to Iowa bar, 1973, U.S. Tax Ct. bar, 1973; partner firm Stamatelos, Payton & Smith, W. Des Moines, 1973-74, Stamatelos & Smith, West Des Moines, 1974—; asst. to U.S. atty. So. Dist. Iowa, 1972-73. Mem. Am., Iowa, Polk County bar assns., Am., Iowa assns. trial lawyers, Phi Alpha Delta. Notes editor Drake Law Rev., 1972-73. Home: 4700 Western Hills Dr West Des Moines IA 50265 Office: 930 Grand Ave West Des Moines IA 50265 Tel (515) 223-1631

SMITH, MARTIN ALLEN, b. Chgo., Dec. 11, 1934; B.S. in Law, Northwestern U., 1955, J.D., 1957. Admitted to Ill. bar, 1957, U.S. Supreme Ct. bar, 1957; asso. Smith & Munson, Chgo., 1957-59; individual practice law, Chgo., 1959—. Mem. Am. Trial Lawyers Assn., Am., Ill., Chgo. (past chmn. lawyers reference com.), bar assns., Tau Epsilon Rho. Home: 505 N Lake Shore Dr Chicago IL 60611 Office: 10 S LaSalle St Chicago IL 60603

SMITH, MARVIN HUGH, b. Federalsburg, Md., Aug. 10, 1916; A.B., Washington Coll., Chestertown, Md., 1937; LL.B., U. Md., 1941. Admitted to Md. bar, 1941; practiced in Denton, Md., 1946-68; asso. judge Md. Ct. Appeals, 1968—; mem. Commn. to Revise Criminal Law of Md., 1952; asst. atty. gen. State of Md., 1953-55; chmn. bd. trustees Client's Security Trust Fund of Bar of Md., 1966-68; del. Md. Constl. Conv., 1967. Mem. Caroline County (Md.) Bd. Edn., 1951-53, pres., 1952-53; mem. exec. bd. Del-Mar-Va Area council Boy Scouts Am., 1967—, v.p., 1969-71, pres., 1971-73. Mem. Am., Md. (gov. 1957-58, 68-69) Caroline County bar assns. Recipient Silver Beaver award Boy Scouts Am., 1968, Distinguished Eagle Scout award, 1975. Home: 318 Maple Ave Federalsburg MD 21632 Office: PO Box 309 Denton MD 21629 Tel (301) 479-2693

SMITH, MAX W., b. Lenox, Iowa, July 27, 1937; B.A., Drake U., 1965, J.D., 1965. Admitted to Iowa bar, 1965, U.S. Dist. Ct. bar So. Dist. Iowa, 1966; friend of ct., Polk County, Iowa, 1966-72; dir. bur. collections Iowa Dept. Social Services, Des Moines, 1972—; mem. spl. child support adv. com. HEW, 1975. Mem. Am., Iowa, Polk County bar assns., Am. Pub. Welfare Assn., Nat. Reciprocal and Family Support Enforcement Assn. (pres. 1975-76, now dir.). Home: 2917 SE 10th St Des Moines IA 50315 Office: Lucas State Office Bldg Des Moines IA 50319 Tel (515) 281-5767

SMITH, MAXINE STEWARD, b. Delaware County, Okla., Jan. 25, 1921; student U. Calif. Extension, 1962-65, Ariz. State U., Tempe, 1939-40, 40-41; LL.B., LaSalle Extension U., 1961. Admitted to Calif. bar, 1962; individual practice law, San Diego, 1962-65; staff atty. Legal Aid Soc. of San Diego, Inc., 1965-72; dep. dist. atty. child support div., San Bernardino County, Calif., 1973; individual practice law, San Diego, 1974—; tchr. adult edn. real estate law San Diego City Schs., 1962-64. Trustee Crossroads Found., 1971—. Mem. San Diego County Bar Assn., Am. Judicature Soc., Calif. Women Lawyers, Order Fifinella, Ninety-Nines, Inc., Nat. Aero. Assn., Aircraft Owners and Pilots Assn., Phi Alpha Delta. Office: 1007 5th Ave 1124-3 San Diego CA 92101 Tel (714) 232-3777

SMITH, MILAN DALE, JR., b. Pendleton, Oreg., May 19, 1942; B.A. cum laude, Brigham Young U., 1966; J.D. (Nat. Honor scholar), U. Chgo., 1969. Admitted to Calif. bar, 1970, D.C. bar, 1972, U.S. Supreme Ct. bar, 1977; asso. firm O'Melveny & Myers, Los Angeles, 1969-72; partner firm Smith & Hilbig, Torrance, Calif., 1972—; mem. Hinton Moot Ct. Com., 1968-69. Pres. Informed Voters League, Torrance, 1975—; vice chmn. bd. Ettie Lee Homes for Youth. Mem. Los Angeles, Am. (coordinator real estate syndicate subcom. 1973-75) bar assns. Office: 21515 Hawthorne Blvd Suite 1290 Torrance CA 90503 Tel (213) 542-7361

SMITH, NATALIE GINGELL, b. Pontiac, Mich., July 20, 1942; B.A., Smith Coll., Northampton, Mass., 1964; J.D., U. Mich., 1967. Admitted to Wash. bar, 1967, Ariz. bar, 1970, Wis. bar, 1973; individual practice law, Sells, Ariz., 1970-72; asso. firm Perry & First, Milw., 1973-74; unemployment hearing examiner State of Wis., Madison, 1975-76; individual practice law Madison, 1976—. Chairperson Madison Broadbard Telecommunications Regulatory Bd., 1974—. Home: 1214 Brookwood St Madison WI 53711 Office: 302 E Washington St Suite 209 Madison WI 53703 Tel (608) 255-9769

SMITH, NOAH MACK, b. Clintwood, Va., Sept. 1, 1927; B.B.A., George Washington U., 1964; J.D., Georgetown U., 1971. Admitted to Va. bar, 1971; sr. planning and procedures analyst intelligence div. IRS, Washington, 1970—; adj. prof. Coll. Pub. Affairs, Am. U., 1975—. Mem. Fed. Criminal Investigators Assn. (nat. committeeman). Recipient spl. achievement award IRS, 1973. Home: 7120 Sea Cliff Rd McLean VA 22101 Office: 1111 Constitution Ave NW Washington DC 20024 Tel (202) 566-3098

SMITH, NORMAN, b. Atlanta, Feb. 1, 1947; A.B., U. Ga., 1968, J.D., 1972. Admitted to Ga. bar, 1972, U.S. Dist. Ct. No. Dist. Ga. bar, 1973; asso. firm Vaughn, Barksdale & Nation, Convers, Ga., 1972-75; individual practice law, Barnesville, Ga., 1975—; atty. Lamar County, Ga., First Nat. Bank of Barnesville, So. Railway, Mem. State Bar Ga., Am. Bar Assn. Club: Rotary. Home: Harrell Cir Barnesville GA 30204 Office: 342 College Dr Barnesville GA 30204 Tel (404) 358-3282

SMITH, NORMAN T., b. Akron, Ohio, Nov. 23, 1935; B.S., Ohio State U., 1957; M.B.A., Case-Western Res. U., 1959; LL.B., U. Mich., 1963. Admitted to Ohio bar, 1963; partner firm Wright, Harlor, Morris & Arnold, Columbus, Ohio, 1963-77, Porter, Wright, Morris & Arthur, Columbus, 1977—; exec. dir. Ohio Title Ins. Rating Bur., 1972—; asso. counsel Columbus Bd. Realtors. Sr. warden St. Mark's Episcopal Ch., Upper Arlington, Ohio, 1970-73. Mem. Am., Ohio (vice-chmn. bd. govs. real property sect.), Columbus (past chmn. real property com.) bar assns., Am., Ohio (pres. 1975-76) land title assns., Ohio Bar Found. Contbr. articles to legal jours. Office: 37 W Broad St Columbus OH 43215 Tel (614) 224-4125

SMITH, PAUL GORDON, b. Chanute, Kans., Jan. 3, 1936; B.S., U. Ala., 1958, J.D., 1962. With comml. loan dept. 1st Nat. Bank of Birmingham (Ala.), 1958; asst. U.S. Dist. Judge for Western Dist. Ala., Birmingham, 1962-63; admitted to Ala. bar, 1962; partner firm Huie Fernambuco Stewart & Smith, Birmingham, 1963—. Bd. mgrs. YMCA, Birmingham, 1975—. Mem. Birmingham, Ala., Am. bar assns., Ala. Trial Lawyers Assn., Ala. Def. Lawyers Assn. Contbr. articles to legal jours. Office: Suite 825 1st Ala Bank Bldg Birmingham AL 35203 Tel (205) 251-1193

SMITH, PHILIP NEURATH, JR., b. Washington, Sept. 12, 1942; B.S., U. Md., 1964; LL.B., George Washington U., 1967. Admitted to D.C. bar, 1968; fin. analyst SEC, Washington, 1965-68, atty., 1968-70; asso. firm Lawler, Kent & Eisenberg, and predecessors, Washington, 1970-75, partner, 1975—. Mem. Am., Fed., D.C. bar assns. Home: 4517 Butterworth Pl NW Washington DC 20016 Office: 1156 15th St NW Washington DC 20005 Tel (202) 293-2240

SMITH, R. GRAEME, b. Akron, Ohio, Apr. 24, 1925; B.A., Franklin and Marshall Coll., 1946; LL.B., Yale, 1950. Admitted to Conn. bar, 1950, U.S. Supreme Ct. bar, 1959, Fla. bar, 1966; asso. firm Alcorn, Bakerwell & Alcorn, Hartford, Conn., 1950-53, partner, 1954-75, counsel, 1975—; law clk. jud. com. Conn. Gen. Assembly, 1950; sec. 1st Conn. Bancorp., 1970-75. Trustee Franklin and Marshall Coll., 1959-69. Mem. Hartford County, Conn., Fla., Am. bar assns., Am. Judicature Soc. Office: One American Row Hartford CT 06103 Tel (203) 522-1216

SMITH, RALPH CLARENCE, JR., b. Bainbridge, Ga., Dec. 29, 1936; B.B.A., U. Ga., 1963, LL.B., 1963. Admitted to Ga. bar, 1964; since practiced in Bainbridge, asso. firm Miller & Kirbo, 1964-65; partner firm Smith & Cato, 1965-69; individual practice law, 1970-74; partner firm Smith & Perry, 1975—; aide to Ga. State Senate floor leader, 1965; dir. 1st Port City Bank. Mem. Am., Ga., Bainbridge-Decatur County (pres.) bar assns., Bainbridge-Decatur Jr. and Sr. Chambers Commerce, Club: Lions. Home: Lake Douglas Rd Bainbridge GA 31717 Office: PO Box 542 Bainbridge GA 31717 Tel (912) 246-2271

SMITH, RALPH HARRY, JR., b. Pitts., Sept. 16, 1928; B.A., U. Pitts., 1949, J.D., 1952. Admitted to Pa. bar, 1953; since practiced in Pitts., individual practice law, 1953-60; judge Allegheny County Ct., 1960-61, Allegheny County Ct. of Common Pleas, 1961—. Past bd. dirs. St. John's Gen. Hosp., Pitts. Mem. Am., Pa., Allegheny County bar assns., Order of Coif. Contbr. articles in field to legal jours.; editorial staff U. Pitts. Law Rev., 1950-52. Home: 102 Gail Dr Pittsburgh PA 15237 Office: 708 City-County Bldg Pittsburgh PA 15219 Tel (412) 355-5446

SMITH, REES R(OLAND), b. Chgo., Aug. 16, 1929; B.S. in Chemistry and Police Sci., Mich. State U., 1952; J.D., Woodrow Wilson Coll. Law, 1961. Admitted to Ga. bar, 1962; since practiced in Atlanta, individual practice law, 1965—; microanalyst Ga. State Crime Lab., 1957-65. Mem. Ga. Assn. Criminal Def. Lawyers, State Bar Ga., (vice chmn. criminal law sect. chmn., 1973, sec.-treas. 1974-76, pres. 1977—), Atlanta Bar Assn. (chmn. Criminal law sect. 1975, treas. 1976). Office: 1724 Fulton Nat Bldg Atlanta GA 30303 Tel (404) 523-2936

SMITH, RICHARD B., b. Lancaster, Pa., July 9, 1928; B.A., Yale, 1949; LL.B., U. Pa., 1953. Admitted to N.Y. State bar, 1955, U.S. Supreme Ct. bar, 1972; asso. firm Hodges, Reavis, McGrath, Pantaleoni & Downey, N.Y.C., 1953-55; atty. W. R. Grace Co., N.Y.C., 1955-57; asso. firm Reavis & McGrath, N.Y.C., 1957-63, partner, 1963-67; commr. SEC, Washington, 1967-71; partner firm Davis, Polk & Wardwell, N.Y.C., 1971—. Trustee, N.Y.C. Citizens Budget Commn., 1976—; mem. council Adminstrv. Conf. U.S., 1971-74. Mem. Am. (vice chmn. commn. on law and the economy 1976—), N.Y. State bar assns., Assn. Bar City N.Y., Am. Judicature Soc., Am. Law Inst. (adviser Fed. Securities Code). Office: 1 Chase Manhattan Plaza New York City NY 10005 Tel (212) 422-3400

SMITH, RICHARD CLARK, b. Jefferson, Wis., Oct. 10, 1914; LL.B., U. Wis., 1938. Admitted to Wis. bar, 1938, Ill. bar, 1944; partner firm Mistele & Smith, Jefferson, 1938-42, 45-60; atty. law dept. Montgomery Ward, Chgo., 1944-45; individual practice law, Jefferson, 1960—; v.p. and gen. counsel Farmers & Mchts. Bank of Jefferson, 1970—. Mem. Am., Jefferson County bar assns., State Bar Wis. Home: 332 E Linden Dr Jefferson WI 53549 Office: 108 S Main St Jefferson WI 53549 Tel (414) 674-3233

SMITH, RICHARD JOYCE, b. Hartford, Conn., July 28, 1903; B.A., Catholic U. Am., 1924; LL.B., Yale, 1927; LL.D., Am. Internat. U., 1970. Admitted to Conn. bar, 1927, N.Y. bar, 1933, U.S. Supreme Ct. bar, 1944; asst. prof., asso. prof. law Yale Law Sch., New Haven, 1927-33; partner firm Whitman & Ransom, N.Y.C., 1934—; chief counsel U.S. Senate Com. on Petroleum Resources, 1944-45; trustee N.Y., N.H. & H. R.R., 1961—, Avis, Inc., 1975—; Social Sci. Research Council fellow, London, Dublin, Ireland, 1929-30. Mem. Conn. State Bd. Pardons, 1937-43; Conn. State Bd. Edn., 1951-56; Nat. Citizens Com. for Pub. Schs., 1951-56; del. Democratic Nat. Conv., 1940. Mem. Am., N.Y. State, Conn. bar assns., Assn. Bar City N.Y. Home: 139 Main St Southport CT 06490 Office: Whitman & Ransom 522 Fifth Ave New York City NY 10036 Tel (212) 575-5800

SMITH, RICHARD THEODORE, b. Atlanta, Oct. 28, 1946; B.B.A., Ga. State U., 1970; J.D., Emory U., 1973. Admitted to Ga. bar, 1974; asso. firm Hansell, Post, Brandon & Dorsey, Atlanta, 1974—. Mem. Am., Ga. bar assns. Home: 8120 Tynecastle Dr Atlanta GA 30346 Office: 47 Perimeter Center East NE Atlanta GA 30346 Tel (404) 581-8400

SMITH, ROBERT BUCHMAN, b. Pitts., Mar. 3, 1945; B.A., U. Pitts., 1967, J.D., 1971. Admitted to bar, 1972; asst. city solicitor City of Pitts. Law Dept. trial div., 1971—; partner firm Lebovitz, Lebovitz & Kwall, Profl. Assn., Pitts., 1973—; mem. faculty Allegheny County (Pa.) Community Coll., 1971-73; lectr. Regional Personnel Services Center Southwestern Pa. Econ. Devel. Dist., Pitts., 1973—. Mem. Allegheny County, Pa. bar assns., Pa., Western Pa. trial lawyers assns. Home: 6825 Penham Pl Pittsburgh PA 15208 Office: 319 City-County Bldg Pittsburgh PA 15219 Tel (412) 255-2003

SMITH, ROBERT DIXON, b. Arlington, Mass., Aug. 23, 1943; A.B., Northeastern U., Boston, 1966; J.D., Boston U., 1970. Admitted to Mass. bar, 1970; individual practice law, Arlington, 1970—; atty., cons. Municipal Cons., Inc., Canton, Mass., 1971-74; legal cons. Mass. Spl. Commn. on Needs of the Handicapped, Boston, 1974-75. Mem. Am., Mass. bar assns., Nat. Health Lawyers Assn. Office: 52 Wyman Terr Arlington MA 02174 Tel (617) 648-3512

SMITH, ROBERT JACKSON BATES, JR., b. Augusta, Ga., Nov. 9, 1941; B.B.A., U. Ga. at Athens, 1963, LL.B., 1965. Admitted to Ga. bar, 1965; partner firm Yow, Lee & Smith, Augusta, 1966-67, firm Allgood & Childs, Augusta, 1968-69; U.S. atty. So. Dist. Ga., Augusta, 1969—; instr. law Augusta Coll., 1966-69. Legal counsel, mem. exec. com. Richmond County (Ga.) Republican Party, 1967-68; bd. dirs. Easter Seals Soc., Augusta, 1965-69, 1st v.p., 1967-68. Mem. Fed., Am., Ga. State, Augusta bar assns., Augusta Trial Lawyers Assn. Named Outstanding Young Man Richmond County, 1969. Home: 1138 Glenn Ave Augusta GA 30904 Office: PO Box 2017 Augusta GA 30903 Tel (404) 724-0517

SMITH, ROBERT JAMES, b. Richmond, Va., Dec. 9, 1924; A.B., Washington and Lee U., 1948, J.D., 1950. Admitted to Va. bar, 1951; partner firm Smith, Norwood and Shepherd, and predecessors, Richmond, 1951-71; individual practice law, Richmond, 1971—; substitute judge Domestic Relations Dist. Ct., Henrico County, Va., 1974—; legal advisor, bd. dirs. Bapt. Home Ladies, Richmond. Mem. Henrico County Democratic Com. Mem. Am., Richmond bar assns., Va. Trial Lawyers Assn. Office: Suite 724 Mutual Bldg Richmond VA 23229 Tel (804) 649-0716

SMITH, ROBERT JOHN, b. Waupaca, Wis., Jan. 20, 1944; B.S. in Civil Engring., U. Wis., 1967, J.D. cum laude, 1974. Admitted to Wis. bar, 1974, U.S. Dist. Ct. for Western Wis. bar, 1974; asst. prof. engring. U. Wis., 1974—. Treas. Nakoma Area Neighborhood Assn., Madison, 1976. Mem., Am., Wis., Dane County bar assn., ASCE, Nat., Wis. socs. profl. engrs., Nat. Constrn. Industry Panel, Am. Arbitration Assn. Registered profl. engr., Wis.; recipient Achievement award Sec. Navy, 1971; contbr. articles to profl. jours. Home: 4017 Cherokee Dr Madison WI 53711 Office: 432 N Lake St Room 725 Madison WI 53706 Tel (608) 262-2061

SMITH, R(OBERT) MARLIN, b. South Bend, Ind., June 29, 1929; B.A., Carleton Coll., 1951; J.D., U. Chgo., 1956. Admitted to Ill. bar, 1956, U.S. Supreme Ct. bar, 1975; asso. firm Ross, Hardies, O'Keefe, Babcock & Parsons, Chgo., 1956-65, partner, 1966—; spl. counsel Village of Mt. Prospect (Ill.), 1966—; village atty., corp. counsel Village of Bolingbrook (Ill.), 1967—; adj. prof. Coll. Urban Scis. U. Ill. at Chgo., 1974—; dir. Chgo. Lawyers Com. for Civil Rights Under Law. Mem. Chgo. (chmn. com. on local govt. 1972-73), Ill. (chmn. com. on local govt. of law sect. council 1976—), Am. bar assns., Nat. Inst. Municipal Law Officers, Legal Club Chgo., Am. Inst. Planners (affiliate), Am. Soc. Planning Ofcls., Lambda Alpha, Author: (with others) A Guide for County Zoning Administration, 1965, A Guide to Municipal Zoning Administration, 1972; contbr. articles to profl. publs. Home: 2329 Pioneer Rd Evanston IL 60201 Office: Suite 3100 One IBM Plaza Chicago IL 60611 Tel (312) 467-9300

SMITH, ROBERT SELLERS, b. Samson, Ala., July 31, 1931; B.S., U. Va., 1953, LL.B., 1958. Admitted to Ala. bar, 1959; partner firm Smith, Huckaby & Graves, Huntsville, Ala., 1963—; counsel U.S. Senate Commn. on Labor and Pub. Welfare, 1961-63. Pres. Legal Aid Soc. of Madison County (Ala.), 1971-76. Mem. Ala., Am., Internat. bar assns. Author: Alabama Legal Forms Annotated, 1967; Modern Office Forms for Lawyers, 1969; Alabama Law for the Layman, 1975. Home: 6004 Macon Ct Huntsville AL 35801 Office: suite 50 Central Bank Bldg Huntsville AL 35801 Tel (205) 533-5040

SMITH, ROGER DAVIS, b. Yonkers, N.Y., May 21, 1923; S.B., Mass. Inst. Tech., 1948; LL.B., Yale, 1953. Admitted to N.Y. bar, 1953, U.S. Tax Ct. bar, 1954; asso. firm Carter, Ledyard & Milburn, N.Y.C., 1953-66; partner firm Jackson & Nash (formerly Jackson, Nash, Brophy, Barringer & Brooks), N.Y.C., 1966—. Mem. Am., N.Y. State bar assns., Assn. Bar City N.Y. Home: 454 Route 32 N New Paltz NY 12561 Office: 330 Madison Ave New York City NY 10017 Tel (212) 949-0662

SMITH, RONALD WILLIAM, b. Great Falls, Mont., June 30, 1936; LL.B., La Salle U., 1968. Admitted to Mont. bar, 1967; individual practice law, 1967-73; mem. firm Smith & Rice, Havre, Mont., 1973—; city atty. Chester (Mont.), 1968-71; town atty. Hingham (Mont.), 1973—; dep. county atty. Hill County (Mont.), 1968-69; county atty. Liberty County (Mont.), 1969. Bd. dirs. Havre Day Care Center, Bear Paw Youth Guidance Home. Mem. Mont. Bar Assn., Mont. Trial Lawyers, Nat. Dist. Atty. Assn., Montana County Atty. Assn. Home: PO Box 128 Havre MT 59501 Office: Ryan Bldg Havre MT 59501 Tel (406) 265-4369

SMITH, ROY LEE, b. Columbus, Ga., Apr. 22, 1901; LL.B., U. Ala., 1924. Admitted to Ala. bar, 1924; partner firm Smith & Smith, Phenix City, Ala.; dir. Phenix Girard Bank, 1927—; pres. 1st Fed. Savings and Loan Assn. of Russell County (Ala.), 1936-72, chmn. bd., 1972—; mem. Ala. Bar Commn., 1949-65. Mem. bd. pensions and homes for ministers Ala.-West Fla. Conf. United Meth. Ch., 1970—. Mem. Russell County C. of C. Ldir. Phenix City chpt. 1965-75), Assn. U.S. Army (pres. Columbus-Phenix City-Ft. Benning chpt. 1969-70). Office: PO Box 519 Corner 14th St and 3d Ave Phenix City AL 36867 Tel (205) 298-7886

SMITH, RUSSELL, JR., b. Fairfield, Iowa, Mar. 4, 1911; B.A. cum laude, Parsons Coll., 1933; J.D., U. Iowa, 1936. Admitted to Iowa bar, 1936, Mo. bar, 1973; practiced in Fairfield, 1936-37; supr. Iowa State Tax Commn., Des Moines, 1937-40; claims atty. Hartford Ins. Group, Des Moines, 1940-46, Kansas City, Mo., 1946-74; judge Mo. Probate Ct., Van Buren, 1974-76. Mem. Mo. Bar Assn. Home: Rt 2 Van Buren MO 63965 Tel (314) 323-8312

SMITH, RUSSELL BRYAN, b. Ft. Worth, Nov. 1, 1936; B.B.A., So. Meth. U., 1959, J.D., 1962. Admitted to Tex. bar, 1962; partner firm Woodruff & Smith, and predecessors, Dallas, 1962-75; individual practice law, Dallas, 1975—. Mem. Dallas City Council, 1971-73; dep. mayor pro tem City of Dallas, 1973-75; pres. All Sports Assn., 1975-76. Mem. Am., Tex., Dallas bar assns., Am. Judicature Soc., Am., Tex. trial lawyers assns., Am. Bd. Trial Advocates, Dallas Assn. Trial Lawyers, Dallas Estate Council, Phi Alpha Delta. Named Outstanding Young Man, Dallas Jr. C. of C., 1967, One of Five Outstanding Young Texans, Tex. Jaycees, 1972, Outstanding Man in Dallas, Dallas Roosters, 1975. Home: 6323 Danbury Ln Dallas TX 75214 Office: 211 N Ervay Bldg 1800 Dallas TX 75201 Tel (214) 745-1771

SMITH, RUSSELL EVANS, b. Butte, Mont., Nov. 16, 1908; LL.B. cum laude, U. Mont., 1931. Admitted to Mont. bar, 1931; marshal, law clk., Mont. Supreme Ct., 1931-33; practiced in Cut Bank, Mont., 1933-35, Missoula, Mont., 1935-42, 45-66; counsel for Mont., OPA, 1942-43; judge U.S. Dist. Ct. for Mont., 1966—, now chief judge. Lectr. U. Mont. Law Sch. Mem. Mont. Bd. Bar Examiners. Mem. Mont. Bar Assn. (past pres. 1956), Alpha Tau Omega, Phi Delta Phi. Home: 529 Evankelly Rd Missoula MT 59801 Office: US Post Office Bldg Missoula MT 59801*

SMITH, SAMUEL FRANK, JR., b. Memphis, Dec. 17, 1940; B.A., Southwestern U., Memphis, 1963; J.D., Memphis State U., 1973. Admitted to Ky. bar, 1974, Fed. Ct. Western Dist. Ky. bar, 1974; asst. v.p. Union Planters Nat. Bank, Memphis, 1965-73. Mem. Bowling Green Bar Assn. Home: 1519 Sherwood Dr Bowling Green KY 42101 Office: 431 E 10th St Bowling Green KY 42101 Tel (502) 843-6506

SMITH, SAMUEL STUART, b. Harrisburg, Pa., Nov. 18, 1936; B.B.A., U. Miami (Fla.), 1958, J.D., 1960. Admitted to Fla. bar, 1960; asso. firm Smith, Mandler, Smith, Werner, & Jacobowitz, Profl. Assn., Miami Beach, Fla., beginning in 1960, subsequently partner and mng. officer; instr. law U. Miami, 1972—. Vice-pres. Jewish Family & Childrens Service, Inc., Miami. Fellow, Am. Coll. Probate Counsel; mem. Am., Fla. (gov. 1974—) Miami Beach bar assns. Contbr. articles to legal jours. Home: 7965 SW 142nd St Miami FL 33158 Office: 407 Lincoln Rd Miami Beach FL 33139 Tel (305) 534-8271

SMITH, SELMA MOIDEL, b. Warren, Ohio, Apr. 3, 1919; student Los Angeles City Coll., 1936-37, U. Calif., 1937-39, U. So. Calif., 1939-41; J.D., Pacific Coast U., 1942. Admitted to Calif. bar, 1943, U.S. Supreme Ct. bar, 1958; mem. firm Moidel, Moidel, Moidel & Smith, Los Angeles, 1943—. Mem. Internat. Fedn. Women Lawyers, World Peace Through Law Center, Inter-Am., Am., Los Angeles bar assns., State Bar Calif., Council Bar Assns. Los Angeles County, Lawyers Club Los Angeles, Nat. Assn. Women Lawyers, Nat. Assn. Composers U.S.A. Office: 408 South Spring St Los Angeles CA 90013 Tel (213) MA 8-8271

SMITH, SPENCER BERNE, b. Syracuse, N.Y., July 7, 1940; A.B. in History, Coll. of Wooster (Ohio), 1962; J.D., Duke, 1965. Admitted to Pa. bar, 1965; asso. firm McNees, Wallace & Nurick, Harrisburg, Pa., 1965-70, partner, 1970—. Bd. dirs. Girls Club of Harrisburg; ruling elder Camp Hill (Pa.) Presbyterian Ch.; campaign exec. United Way, Harrisburg. Mem. Am., Pa., Dauphin County bar assns., Motor Carrier Lawyers Assn., Phi Beta Kappa. Home: 2306 Logan St Camp Hill PA 17011 Office: 100 Pine St PO Box 1166 Harrisburg PA 17108 Tel (717) 236-9341

SMITH, SPENCER LANIER, b. Lakeland, Fla., Sept. 25, 1938; B.A. in History, Trinity Coll., Hartford, Conn., 1960; J.D., U. Chgo., 1963. Admitted to Fla. bar, 1963, D.C. bar, 1964; asso. firm Arnold & Porter, Washington, 1963-64; counsel, editor U.S. Senate Subcom. on Constl. Rights, 1964-66; sr. research atty. Jud. Conf. for D.C., 1967; legis. counsel NIMH, Bethesda, Md., 1968; dir. Fla. Rural Legal Services, Miami, 1968-71; atty. Navajo Legal Services, Window Rock, Ariz., 1971-72; partner firm Smith & Smith, Miami, 1972—; instr. in law U. Miami, 1975-76; atty., dir., chief pilot Smith Freighting, Ltd. Mem. Fla. Bar. Home and Office: 4420 SW 62d Ave Miami FL 33155 Tel (305) 665-7658

SMITH, STEPHEN KENDALL, b. Burlington, Vt., May 31, 1941; A.B. with distinction and honors Ind. U., 1964; B.A., Oxford (Eng.) U., 1966, M.A., 1971; J.D., Columbia U., 1972. Admitted to Ind. bar, 1972; asso. firm Barnes, Hickam, Pantzer & Boyd, Indianapolis, 1972—. Fund raiser United Fund, 1976—, Indpls. Jr. Achievement, 1976—. Mem. Assn. Am. Rhodes Scholars, Am., 7th Circuit, Ind., Indpls. bar assns., Indpls. Com. on Fgn. Relations. Home: 4414 N Meridian St Indianapolis IN 46208 Office: 1313 Merchants Bank Bldg Indianapolis IN 46204 Tel (317) 638-1313

SMITH, STEVEN LEE, b. Hamilton, Ohio, Sept. 13, 1946; B.S., Ball State U., 1968; J.D., Ohio State U., 1972. Admitted to Ohio bar, 1973; asso. firm Eugene L. Matan, Columbus, 1973-75; partner firm Matan, Rinehart & Smith, Columbus, 1975—. Treas. Winchester (Ohio) Village Civic Assn., 1976—. Mem. Am., Ohio State, Columbus bar assns., Ohio Acad. Trial Lawyers, Am. Trial Lawyers Assn., Comml. League Am. Office: 16 E Broad St Columbus OH 43215 Tel (614) 228-2678

SMITH, SUMNER HERBERT, b. Everett, Mass., Aug. 28, 1923; LL.B., Suffolk Coll., 1950. Admitted to Mass. bar, 1952; individual practice law, Lynn, Mass., 1952—. Office: 180 Market St Lynn MA 01903 Tel (617) 598-0711

SMITH, TEMPLETON, b. Pitts., Aug. 19, 1919; B.A., Harvard, 1940, postgrad. indsl. adminstrn., 1943, LL.B., 1947, J.D., 1968. Admitted to Pa. bar, 1948, U.S. Supreme Ct. bar, 1953; asso. firm Rose, Eichenauer, Stewart & Rose, Pitts., 1948-49; counsel law dept. Koppers Co. Inc., Pitts., 1949—, asst. sec., 1961—. Mem. Mt. Lebanon (Pa.) Parking Authority, 1954-61; chmn. Mt. Lebanon Bd. Adjustment, 1961-76, Mt. Lebanon Home Rule Study Commn., 1972-74. Mem. Am., Pa., Allegheny County bar assns. Home: 776 Valleyview Rd Pittsburgh PA 15243 Office: 1550 Koppers Bldg Pittsburgh PA 15219 Tel (412) 391-3300

SMITH, THOMAS RAMSAUR, JR., b. Charlotte, N.C., Feb. 12, 1938; A.B., Princeton U., 1960; LL.B., U. Va., 1963. Admitted to Va. bar, 1963, N.Y. bar, 1964; asso. firm Brown, Wood, Ivey, Mitchell & Petty, N.Y.C., 1963-70, partner, 1971—. Mem. Am. Bar Assn., Assn. Bar City N.Y. Home: 12 Masterton Rd Bronxville NY 10708 Office: 1 Liberty Plaza New York City NY 10006 Tel (212) 349-7500

SMITH, TIMOTHY RANDOLPH, b. Meridian, Miss., July 7, 1945; B.A. in Polit. Sci., U. Miss., 1967, J.D., 1969. Admitted to Miss. bar, 1969; law clk. to chief justice Miss. Supreme Ct., 1969-70; drafting atty. Miss. Ho. Reps., 1970-71; mem. Gov.'s Staff, 1971-72; spl. projects coordinator Miss. Research and Devel. Center, 1971-72; mem. firm Heidelberg, Woodliff & Franks, Jackson, Miss., 1972—; mem. adv. com. Hinds County Youth Ct., 1973-74. Pres. Greater Jackson Area Community Orgn. Drug Abuse Control, 1972-73; mem. nat. governing bd. Common Cause; former mem. ethics study com. Miss. Legislature. Fellow Inst. Politics in Miss.; mem. Am., Miss., Hinds County bar assns., Miss. Law Inst., Miss. Econ. Council, Jackson Young Lawyers, Am. Judicature Soc., Miss. Claims Assn., Phi Delta Phi. Home: 1717 Hillview Dr Jackson MS 39211 Office: suite 1030 Capital Towers Jackson MS 39201 Tel (601) 948-3800

SMITH, TOXEY HALL, JR., b. Pearl River County, Miss., July 31, 1938; B.A., U. Miss., 1960, LL.B., 1962, J.D., 1967. Admitted to Miss. bar, 1962; asst. dist. atty., Lafayette County, Miss., 1962; spl. agt. FBI, 1962-65; individual practice law, Wiggins and Ocean Springs, Miss., 1965—; judge Juvenile Ct., Stone County, Miss., 1975—. Mem. Am., Miss., Stone County bar assns., Am., Miss. trial lawyers assns. Office: PO Drawer 8 Wiggins MS 39577 Tel (601) 928-3222 also PO Box 836 Ocean Springs MS 39564 Tel (601) 875-1231

SMITH, TRUMAN HENRY, JR., b. Paris, Ark., Sept. 12, 1937; B.S.B.A., U. Ark., 1960, J.D., 1969. Admitted to Ark. bar, 1969; asso. firm Niblock, Hipp & Gibson, Fayetteville, Ark., 1969-71; individual practice law, Fayetteville, 1971—; city prosecutor Fayetteville, 1972-75. Mem. Ark. (ho. of dels. 1972-75), Washington City, Am. bar assns., Am. Trial Lawyers Assn. Office: 112 South East St Fayetteville AR 72701 Tel (501) 521-7000

SMITH, TURNER TALIAFERRO, JR., b. Washington, Dec. 16, 1940; B.A., Princeton U., 1962; LL.B., Harvard U., 1968. Admitted to Va. bar, 1968; asso. firm Hunton, Williams, Gay, Powell & Gibson, Richmond, Va., 1968-75; partner firm Hunton & Williams, Richmond, 1975—. Mem. Richmond, Va., Am. (mem. spl. com. atomic energy law 1974-76, chmn. environ. controls com. corp., banking and bus. law sect. 1973—) bar assns. Contbr. articles to legal jours. Home: 215 Gun Club Rd Richmond VA 23221 Office: 707 E Main St PO Box 1535 Richmond VA 23212 Tel (804) 788-8200

SMITH, VANCE CLIO, b. Springfield, Ill., June 22, 1916; B.A., U. Toronto, 1938; J.D., Harvard, 1941. Admitted to Ill. bar, 1941; asso. firm Damon, Hayes, White & Hoban, Chgo., 1946-51, partner, 1949-51; asst. gen. counsel Nat. Tea Co., Chgo., 1951-57; asst. corp. counsel Lubermen's Mut. Casualty Co., Chgo., 1957-76; asst. sec. Kemper Corp., Long Grove, Ill., 1967-76; sec., dir. Tower Fin. Corp., Chgo., 1972-76, Am. Underwriting Corp., Chgo., 1972-76, Nat. Agts. Service Co., Chgo., 1972-76. Mem. Northfield (Ill.) Zoning Bd. Appeals, 1969-70. Mem. Chgo. Bar Assn., Chgo. Legal Club, Harvard Law Sch. Assn., Kappa Sigma. Home: 1879 Grove Dr Northfield IL 60093

SMITH, W. KELLY, b. Lakeland, Fla., Oct. 10, 1936; B.Chem. Engring., U. Fla., 1959, M.S. in Engring., 1961, J.D., 1966. Admitted to Fla. bar, 1966; process engr. Rayonier, Inc., Ga., N.Y.C. and Seattle, 1960-64; asso. firm Holland & Knight, Lakeland, 1966-69; asst. state prosecutor Orange County (Fla.), Orlando, 1967-70; partner firm Helliwell, Melrose & DeWolf, Orlando, 1970-73, W. Kelly Smith, Orlando, 1973—. Chmn. pollution control bd. Reedy Creek Improvement Dist., Walt Disney World, Fla., 1972—. Mem. Am., Fla., Orange County bar assns. Contbr. articles to profl. publs. Home: 405 Melanie Way Maitland FL 32751 Office: Suite 700 Hartford Bldg 200 E Robinson St Orlando FL 32801 Tel (305) 425-4521

SMITH, WALKER WILLIAM, b. Topeka, Oct. 6, 1920; B.A., Washburn U., 1942, LL.B., 1948. Admitted to Kans. bar, 1948, Okla. bar, 1952, Tex. bar, 1958; practiced in Russell, Kans., 1948-50, Wichita, Kans., 1950-52; atty. Stanolind Oil & Gas Co., Oklahoma City, 1952-54; atty. Am. Petrofina Corp., Dallas, 1954—, sec., 1970—. Mem. Tex. Bar Assn. Home: 3805 Princess Ln Dallas TX 75229 Office: PO Box 2159 Dallas TX 75221 Tel (214) 750-2813

SMITH, WAYNE VINCENT ROBERT, b. Guelph, Ont., Can., Dec. 11, 1943; A.B., U. Waterloo, Ont., 1965; J.D., U. Tex., 1968. Admitted to Tex. bar, 1970, Calif. bar, 1972; law clk. for Judge Wayne Justice, Tyler, Tex., 1968-70; asso. Welby K. Parish, Gilmer, Tex., 1970-71; individual practice law, Lafayette, Calif., 1973—; legal counsel Calif. Jaycees, 1975-76. Mem. Calif., Mt. Diablo, Tex. bar assns. Contbr. articles to legal jours. Office: 987 Moraga Rd Lafayette CA 94549 Tel (415) 284-1944

SMITH, WILLIAM ALFRED, b. Richmond, Va., Feb. 4, 1931; A.B. cum laude, Va. Union U., 1955; J.D., Howard U., 1958. Admitted to Va. bar, 1958; asso. firm W. Hale Thompson, 1958-59; individual practice law, Hampton, Va., 1959-69; sec., exec. v.p. Movon Corp., Hampton, 1969-73; partner firm Walker, Smith, Felton & Scott, Newport News, Va., 1973—; cons. U.S. Commn. on Civil Rights, 1959-60. Pres. Citizens Boys' Club, Hampton, 1970-72, pres. Hampton Citizens Orgn., 1967. Mem. Am., Peninsula, Old Dominion bar assns. Recipient Kappa Alpha Psi Frat. award, 1969. Home: 33 Azalea Dr Hampton VA 23669 Office: 1715 25th St Newport News VA 23607 Tel (804) 244-0171

SMITH, WILLIAM B., b. St. Louis, Nov. 5, 1941; B.B.A., U. Notre Dame; J.D., St. Louis U. Admitted to Mo. bar, 1966, U.S. Supreme Ct. bar, 1970; served with Judge Adv. Gen. Corps U.S. Army, 1966-70; asso. firm Whalen, O'Connor & Collins, St. Louis, 1970-72, Dubail, Judge, Kilker & Maier, St. Louis, 1972—. Bd. dirs. Greenbriar Hills Property Owners Assn., St. Louis, 1973-74. Mem. Am., Mo. bar assns. Home: 12341 Creekhaven St Des Peres MO 63131 Office: One Mercantile Center Suite 3210 St Louis MO 63101 Tel (314) 241-4261

SMITH, WILLIAM BENJAMIN, b. Rockford, Ill., Sept. 18, 1948; B.A., Tulane U., 1970; student Nottingham (Eng.) U., 1968-69; J.D., U. Calif. San Francisco, 1973. Admitted to Calif. bar, 1973; since practiced in San Francisco, asso. firm Hoberg, Finger, Brown & Abramson, 1973-75, firm Abramson & Bianco, 1975—; lectr. U. Calif. Hastings Coll. Law, 1975—. Mem. Calif., San Francisco bar assns., Calif. Trial Lawyers Assn., Barristers Club, Queens Bench, Phi Beta Kappa. Home: 887 Camino Ricardo Moraga CA 94556 Office: 44 Montgomery St San Francisco CA 94102 Tel (415) 421-7995

SMITH, WILLIAM CHARLES, b. Batavia, N.Y., June 9, 1930; A.B., U. Buffalo, 1952; LL.B., Harvard, 1955. Admitted to Maine bar, 1955, D.C. bar, 1962; asso. firm Hutchinson, Pierce, Atwood & Allen, Portland, Maine, 1955-57, partner, 1958-59; atty. office tax legis. counsel U.S. Dept. Treasury, Washington, 1959-61; partner firm Pierce, Atwood, Scribner, Allen & McKusick, Portland, 1961—; dir. Sanborn's Motor Express, Inc., Portland; mem. exec. com. Fed. Tax Inst. New Eng. Vice chmn. budget com. United Community Services, 1966-68, chmn., 1968-70, mem. nat. budget and consultation com., 1969-71; mem. Area 5 Mental Health Adv. Bd., 1972-74; bd. dirs. Portland Goodwill, 1967-69, United Community Services, 1968-74, 75—, Portland Widows' Wood Soc., 1962—; trustee Portland Regional Opportunity Program, 1967-68, Fryeburg Acad., 1976—. Mem. Am., Maine, Cumberland County bar assns., Am. Law Inst. Home: 28 Orchard St Portland ME 04102 Office: One Monument Square Portland ME 04101 Tel (207) 773-6411

SMITH, WILLIAM FRENCH, b. Wilton, N.H., Aug. 26, 1917; A.B. summa cum laude, U. Calif., Los Angeles, 1939; LL.B., Harvard, 1942. Admitted to Calif. bar, 1942; sr. partner firm Gibson, Dunn & Crutcher, Los Angeles, 1946—; dir. Pacific Lighting Corp., Los Angeles, 1967—, Pacific T & T Co., San Francisco, 1969—, Pacific Mut. Life Ins. Co., Los Angeles, 1970—, Crocker Nat. Bank Crocker Nat. Corp., San Francisco, 1971—, Jorgensen Steel Corp., Los Angeles, 1974—. Trustee Claremont Men's Coll., 1967—, Henry E. Huntington Library and Art Gallery, San Marino, Calif., 1971—, Cate Sch., Carpinteria, Calif., 1971—; nat. trustee Nat. Symphony Orch., Washington, 1975—; bd. dirs. Los Angeles World Affairs Council, 1970—, pres. 1975—; bd. dirs. Partnership for the Arts in Calif., Inc., San Francisco, 1971—; bd. dirs. Center Theatre Group, Los Angeles Music Center, 1970—, v.p., 1973—; mem. U.S. Advisory Commn. on Internat. Ednl. and Cultural Affairs, Washington, 1971—; mem. Panel on Internat. Info., Edn. and Cultural Relations, Washington, 1974—; del. East-West Center for Cultural and Tech. Interchange, Hawaii, 1975—; mem. Los Angeles Mayor's Ad Hoc Com. on City Finances, 1975—; bd. dirs. Calif. Found. for Commerce and Edn., 1975—; mem. exec. com. Calif. Roundtable, 1976—. Fellow Am. Bar Found.; mem. State Bar Calif. (chmn. disciplinary appeals bd., 1968), Am., Los Angeles County (chmn. com. on adminstrv. agys.) bar assns., Am. Law Inst., Am. Judicature Soc., Harvard Law Sch. Assn. of So. Calif. (nat. v.p. and chmn. 1962-64), Calif. C. of C. (dir. 1963—, pres. 1974-75). Office: 515 S Flower St Los Angeles CA 90071 488-7236

SMITH, WILLIAM JENNINGS, b. Spurgeon, Mo., Oct. 14, 1908; student Trinity U., 1930, U. Tex., 1931, U. N.Mex., 1932; LL.B., Stamford U., 1937. Admitted to Ark. bar, 1937, U.S. Supreme Ct. bar, 1940; atty., asst. gen. atty. Mo. Pacific R.R. Co. Ark., Little Rock, 1946-63, gen. atty., 1963-74; partner firm Smith, Williams, Friday, Eldredge & Clark, and predecessors, Little Rock, 1946-74, of counsel, 1974—; legis. advisor Carl E. Bailey Gov. Ark., 1939, Gov. Homer M. Atkins, 1941, Gov. Francis Cherry, 1953-54; legis. advisor, mem. Ark. Workmen's Compensation Commn., 1940-45; exec. sec. Ark. Gov. Ben Laney, 1945-46, personal counsel, 1947-48, Gov. Orval E. Faubus, 1957-67; asso. justice Ark. Supreme Ct., 1958; prof. med. jurisprudence Med. Sch. U. Ark., Little Rock, 1946-66; chmn. bd. dirs. Fed. Home Loan Bank Little Rock, 1965-73. Vice pres., dir. Ark. State Fair, Little Rock, 1950—. Fellow Am. Assn. Trial Lawyers; mem. Am., Ark. (chmn. exec. com. 1955), Pulaski County bar assns., Little Rock C. of C. (pres. 1971). Recipient Lawyers-Citizen award Ark. Bar Assn. and Found., 1975, Distinguished Service award Coll. Med. U. Ark., 1976; contbr. article Ark. Law Rev. Home: 1421 N University St apt N-325 Little Rock AR 72207 Office: First National Bldg Little Rock AR 72201 Tel (501) 376-2011

SMITH, WILLIAM L., JR., b. Melrose Park, Ill., May 24, 1946; B.A., Iowa U., 1968, J.D., 1971. Admitted to Ill. bar, 1971; asso. firm Lewis Overbeck & Furman, Chgo., 1971-73; partner firm Hollobow & Taslitz, Chgo., 1974—; gen. counsel Friendship Village of Schaumburg (Ill.), 1974—. Mem. Am., Ill., Chgo. bar assns. Home: 199 Olmsted St Riverside IL 60546 Office: 29 S LaSalle St Chicago IL 60603 Tel (312) 782-8444

SMITH, WILLIAM LANCASTER, b. Lebanon, Ky., June 14, 1923; LL.B., U. Notre Dame, 1950. Admitted to Ind., Ky., U.S. Supreme Ct. bars, 1950, Tex. bar, 1953; individual practice law, Dallas, 1953—. Mem. Am., Tex., Dallas, Ind., Ky. bar assns., Notre Dame Alumni Assn. (nat. pres. 1965). Home: 4511 Nashwood Ln Dallas TX 75234 Office: 211 N Ervay St Suite 803 Dallas TX 75201 Tel (214) 747-1546

SMITH, WILLIAM W., b. Birmingham, Ala., Aug. 28, 1941; B.S., Auburn U., 1963; J.D., Cumberland Sch. Law Samford U., 1966. Admitted to Ala. bar, 1966, U.S. Supreme Ct. bar, 1971; partner firm Hogan, Smith & Alspaugh, Birmingham, 1967—; with Judge Adv. Gen. Corps USAR, 1966-74. Mem. Ala. Trial Lawyers Assn. (sec. treas. 1970-74, v.p. No. dist. 1975—), Assn. Trial Lawyers Am. (Ala. chmn. sect. environ. law), Birmingham Plaintiff Lawyers Assn., Birmingham Bar Assn. Recipient certificate of appreciation United Handicap Industries of Am., 1975. Home: 3765 Locksley Dr Mountain Brook AL 35223 Office: 1201 10 City Fed Bldg Birmingham AL 35203 Tel (205) 324-5635

SMITH, WILLIAM WAYNE, b. Booneville, Miss., Oct. 15, 1942; student Northeast Miss. Jr. Coll., 1970-72, Miss. State U., 1972-75; J.D., Jackson Sch. Law, 1971. Admitted to Miss. bar, 1971; accountant Miss. Hosp. and Med. Service (Blue Cross/Blue Shield), Jackson, 1966-69; claims rep. Miss. Farm Bur. Ins. Cos., Jackson, 1969-73; mem. firm Cunningham, Smith & Ferrell, Booneville, 1973—; instr. para-legal tng. Northeast Miss. Jr. Coll., 1975—. Mem. Am., Miss., Prentiss County bar assns., Miss., Am. trial lawyers assns. Home: 300 Parkwood Grove Rd Booneville MS 38829 Office: 110 1/2 N Main St Booneville MS 38829 Tel (601) 728-5361

SMITH, WILLIE TESREAU, JR., b. Sumter, S.C., Jan. 17, 1920; A.B., Johnson C. Smith U., 1948, J.D., S.C. State Coll., 1954. Admitted to S.C. bar, 1954, U.S. Supreme Ct. bar, 1960; individual practice law, Greenville, S.C., 1954-67; sr. atty. Legal Services Agy. Greenville County (S.C.) Inc., 1967-73, exec. dir., 1973-77; family ct. judge 13th Judicial Circuit S.C., 1977—; mem. law sch. bd. S.C. State Bar, 1975—. Active Greenville County Redevel. Authority, 1972-74; trustee Sch. Dist. Greenville County, 1974-76. Mem. Am., Nat., Greenville County bar assns., Greater Greenville C. of C. (co-chmn. community relations com. 1963-73). Home: 601 Jacob Rd Greenville SC 29605

SMITH, WREDE HOWARD, JR., b. Sioux City, Iowa, May 11, 1949; B.A., De Pauw U., 1971; J.D., Northwestern U., 1974. Admitted to Wis. bar, 1974, U.S. Dist. Ct. for Western Dist. Wis. bar, 1974; asso. firm Ross & Stevens, Madison, Wis., 1974—. Mem. Am., State of Wis., Dane County bar assns. Office: One South Pinckney St Madison WI 53703 Tel (608) 257-5353

SMITHERMAN, DAVID EWART, b. Liberty Hill, La., Feb. 21, 1897; B.A., La. State U., 1920, J.D., 1922. Admitted to La. bar, 1922; since practiced in Shreveport; partner Smitherman, Tucker & Mason, 1922-31, Smitherman, Smitherman, Lunn, Hussey & Chastain, and predecessors, 1931—; dir. Home Fed. Savs. and Loan Assn. Shreveport; atty. La. Dept. Pub. Works, 1941-42. Mem. Am., La., Shreveport bar assns., Am. Judicature Soc. Home: 4320 Richmond Ave Shreveport LA 71106 Office: 717 Commercial Nat Bank Shreveport LA 71101 Tel (318) 227-1990

SMITHERS, FRANCIS SYDNEY, b. Rhinebeck, N.Y., Mar. 23, 1942; B.S., U. Pa., 1964; J.D., Boston U., 1970. Admitted to Mass. bar, 1970; law clk. to judge Land Ct., 1970-71; mem. firm Cain, Hibbard & Myers, Pittsfield, Mass., 1971—. Bd. dirs. Berkshire Center for Families and Children, Inc., v.p., 1975—. Mem. Am., Mass., Berkshire bar assns. Office: 184 North St Pittsfield MA 01201 Tel (413) 443-4771

SMITHERS, JOHN WESTWOOD, b. Richmond, Va., June 14, 1909; B.S., U. Richmond, 1935, LL.B., 1932; postgrad. (research fellow) Harvard, 1935-36. Admitted to Va. bar, 1932, U.S. Supreme Ct. bar, 1965; instr. law, U. Richmond, 1932-35, prof. law, 1936-64, adj. prof. law, 1970—; partner firm Wells, Smithers & Bradshaw, Richmond, 1964-69; mem. city council, Richmond, 1960-64. Mem. Am., Va., Va. State, Richmond bar assns., Va. (exec. dir. 1962-77), Richmond trial lawyers assns., Am. Soc. Assn. Execs., Newcomen Soc. N.Am., Am. Law Inst. (life), Phi Alpha Delta (supreme marshal, supreme vice-justice, 1950-54), Omicron Delta Kappa. Contbr. articles to law revs. Home: 5403 Ditchley Rd Richmond VA 23226 Office: Suite 722 Mutual Bldg 909 E Main St Richmond VA 23219 Tel (804) 643-7616

SMITHSON, EDWIN JOHN, b. Donora, Pa., Sept. 21, 1922; student U. Ill., 1943, U. Ala., 1943, Temple U., 1940-41, Jesus Coll. Oxford (Eng.) U., 1945; A.B., U. Pitts., 1947; J.D., Chase Coll. Sch. Law, 1968. Admitted to Ohio bar, 1968; individual practice law, Dayton, Ohio, 1968—; research asso. logistics mgmt. Ohio State U., 1968-71; prof. procurement law Air Force Inst. Tech., Wright-Patterson AFB, Ohio, 1971—. Mem. Am., Ohio, Fed. bar assns., Am. Trial Lawyers Assn. Author: (with others) Government Contract Law, 1968-71, 72—. Office: 3980 Philadelphia Dr Dayton OH 45405 Tel (513) 277-7711

SMODISH, MICHAEL P., b. N.Y.C., Apr. 22, 1945; B.A., U. Fla., 1967, J.D., 1969. Admitted to Fla. bar, 1969; asso. firm Friedman & Britton, Fort Lauderdale, Fla., 1969-72, Sobo & Wellens, Fort Lauderdale, 1972; partner firm Reed & Smodish, Boynton Beach, Fla., 1973—; asst. atty. City of Boynton Beach, 1976. Mem. Am. Bar Assn., Fla. Bar.

SMOLKA, PETER HENRY, b. Prague, Czechoslovakia, Nov. 28, 1919; B.S. in Chem. Engring., Mass. Inst. Tech., 1941, M.S., 1942; LL.D., Rutgers U., 1949. Admitted to D.C. bar, 1950, U.S. Supreme Ct. bar, 1953; research engr. Gt. Lakes Carbon Corp., Morton Grove, Ill., 1942-46; patent atty. Esso Research and Engring. Co., N.Y.C., Elizabeth, N.J., Washington, 1946-57, licensing atty., Elizabeth, 1957-61; partner firm Burns Doane Swecker and Mathis, Washington, 1961—; mem. study mission on licensing in eastern Europe, U.S. Dept. Commerce, summer 1976. Mem. Am., D.C. bar assns., Am. Patent Law Assn., Internat. Patent and Trademark Assn., Licensing Execs. Soc., Am. Chem. Soc. Contributing author chpts.: International Licensing Agreements, 1965. Home: 6233 Radcliff Rd Alexandria VA 22307 Office: 815 Connecticut Ave NW Washington DC 20006 Tel (202) 298-9185

SMOOT, THURLOW BERGEN, b. Glendive, Mont., Dec. 30, 1910; student U. Mont., 1929; J.D., U. Colo., 1933; Admitted to Mont. bar, 1933, Ohio bar, 1934; trial and appellate atty., trial examiner NLRB, Cleve., 1937-47; individual practice law, Cleve., 1947—. Mem. Am. (chmn. sect. on labor relations law 1966-67), Ohio, Greater Cleveland, Cuyahoga County bar assns. Contbr. articles to legal jours. Home: 12700 Lake Ave Lakewood OH 44107 Office: 2141 Illuminating Bldg Cleveland OH 44113 Tel (216) 781-1930

SMUCK, JOHN CARL, b. Washington, Dec. 19, 1937; B.A., U. Va., 1959; J.D., Harvard, 1962. Admitted to D.C. bar, 1963, U.S. Ct. Mil. Appeals bar, 1964, U.S. Ct. Claims bar, 1967, U.S. Supreme Ct. bar, 1970; asso. firm Cross, Murphy & Smith, Washington, 1966-67, mem. firm, 1976—; asso. firm Ballard & Beasley, Washington, 1967-76. Mem. Am. Bar Assn., Bar Assn. D.C. Office: 1128 16th St NW Washington DC 20036 Tel (202) 393-8668

SMUTNY, MICHAEL SHERIDAN, b. Chgo., Jan. 26, 1939; B.A., Cornell Coll. (Iowa), 1961; J.D., U. Minn., 1964. Admitted to Minn. bar, 1964; individual practice law, Adams, Minn., 1964-65; mem. firm Frogner, Smutny & Plowman, Harmony, Minn., 1965—, partner firm, 1966—; vol. advisor Harmony Library Bd., city atty., 1968—; chmn. Fillmore County Youth and Law Program, 1972—; pres. Harmony Devel. Corp., 1971-73. Sec.-treas. Fillmore County Handicapped Services, Inc., 1975—; fin. chmn. Fillmore County Republican Com., 1969-71, conv. chmn., 1970. Mem. Am. Bar Assn., Minn. Bar Assn. (bd. govs. 1975—, ethics com. 1976, v.p. 10th dist. 1976-77, pres. 10th dist. 1977), Fillmore County Bar Assn. (pres. 1973-76), Harmony Jaycees (pres. 1973-74), Civic and Commerce Assn. (sec. 1967-69). Home: 515 3d St SE Harmony MN 55939 Office: 32 Main Ave Harmony MN 55939 Tel (507) 886-2324

SMYTH, JOSEPH A., b. Upper Darby, Pa., Apr. 7, 1945; B.A. in Govt., U. Notre Dame, 1967; J.D., Villanova U., 1971. Admitted to Pa. bar; law clk. Montgomery County (Pa.) Ct. Common Pleas, 1971-72; asst. dist. atty. Montgomery County, 1972-73; individual practice law, Norristown, Pa., 1973—; 1st asst. county solicitor Montgomery County, 1973—; instr. criminal law Montgomery County Community Coll.; solicitor E. Norriton Twp. Zoning Hearing Bd. Mem. Am., Pa., Montgomery County bar assns., Pa. Trial Lawyers Assn. Office: 516 DeKalb St Norristown PA 19404 Tel (215) 272-5373

SNAVELY, JOHN THOMAS, II, b. N.Y.C., Nov. 23, 1940; B.S., B.A., Clemson U., 1962; M.S.W., U. Mich., 1969; J.D., U. Tulsa, 1967. Admitted to Pa. bar, 1971; field youth counselor div. state homes and schs. Okla. Dept. Pub. Welfare, 1964-65, Tulsa dist. dir. Okla. Juvenile Parole and Aftercare Service, 1965-67; grad. research asst. Inst. Labor and Indsl. Relations, Ann Arbor, Mich., 1968-69; regional exec. dir. S. Central regional planning council Pa. Gov.'s Justice Commn., Harrisburg, 1969-71; exec. dir. Phila. regional planning council, 1971-74, exec. dir. Pa. Gov.'s Justice Commn., Harrisburg, 1974-75; individual practice law, Phila., 1975—; lectr. criminal justice planning Rutgers U., Camden, N.J., 1975—; mem. and reporter speedy trial planning group U.S. Dist. Ct. for Eastern Pa., 1975—. Mem. com. on community tensions Phila. Fellowship Commn.; mem. com. community devel. fund Phila. Health and Welfare Council; past mem. Citizens Com. Phila. City Charter Revision; past mem. exec. com. Nat. Assn. Urban Criminal Justice Planning Adminstrs. Mem. Am., Pa., Phila. bar assns., Am. Acad. Polit. and Social Sci., Am. Soc. Pub. Adminstrn. Office: 1710 Spruce St Philadelphia PA 19103 Tel (215) 546-4229

SNEAD, WILLIAM E., b. Frederick, Okla., Oct. 21, 1937; B.A., U. N.Mex., 1959, J.D., 1961. Admitted to N.Mex. bar, 1961; partner firm Ortega and Snead, Albuquerque; asst. atty. gen. State of N.Mex., 1961-62; adj. prof. law U. N.Mex., 1971; mem. bd. advisors Ct. Practice Inst., 1973-77. Mem. Albuquerque Met. Parks and Recreation Advisory Bd., 1962-68, chmn., 1967; mem. Save the Volcanoes Assn.; mem. City of Albuquerque Ad Hoc Com. Environment, 1971-72; bd. dirs. Mountain Valley Assn., 1971-72. Mem. Albuquerque Bar Assn. (dir. 1970—, pres. 1973-74), State Bar N.Mex. (chmn. state bar assn. on environ. control 1969—, vice chmn. com. to revise rules of evidence, 1973—), Albuquerque Lawyers Club, Assn. Trial Lawyers Am., N.Mex. Trial Lawyers Assn. (pres. 1976—), Phi Sigma Alpha, Tau Kappa Alpha. Asst. editor Natural Resources Jour., 1960-61. Home: 4148 Dietz Farm Circle NW Albuquerque NM Office: 201 Twelfth St NW PO Box 2226 Albuquerque NM 87103 Tel (505) 842-8177

SNEDEKER, LARRY HAYMES, b. Springfield, Mo., Sept. 28, 1946; B.A., Drury Coll., 1968; J.D., Vanderbilt U., 1971. Admitted to Tenn. bar, 1971; met. atty. Met. Govt. of Nashville and Davidson County, 1971-76, legal counsel met. council, 1976—. Mem. Nashville, Tenn., Am. bar assns. Office: 1714 Parkway Towers 404 James Robertson Pkwy Nashville TN 37219 Tel (615) 242-6493

SNEED, ARNOLD RANKIN, b. Huntsville, Ala., May 5, 1945; B.A., U. Ala., 1967; J.D., Samford U., 1972. Admitted to Ala. bar, 1973; partner firm Lammons Bell & Sneed, Huntsville, 1974—; legal dept. Fed. Res. Bank Atlanta, 1970, 71. Mem. Am., Ala. bar assns. Home: Route 5 Box 57 Huntsville AL 35811 Office: 132 W Holmes St Huntsville AL 35801 Tel (205) 533-2410

SNEED, EARL, b. Tulsa, Jan. 19, 1913; A.B., U. Okla., 1934, LL.B., 1937; LL.M., Columbia U., 1948, S.J.D., 1961. Admitted to Okla. bar, 1937, U.S. Supreme Ct. bar, 1961; individual practice law, Tulsa, 1937-39; sec. civic, aviation and legis. depts. Tulsa C. of C., 1940-41; vis. asso. prof. law U. Okla., 1945-46, asso. prof., 1946-48, prof., 1948-65, acting dean Coll. Law, 1949-50, dean, 1950-65; of counsel firm Crowe, Dunlevy, Thweatt, Swinford, Johnson & Burdick, Oklahoma City; pres. Liberty Nat. Corp., Oklahoma City, 1970-76; vice chmn. bd. Liberty Nat. Bank & Trust, 1970-76; pres. Sneed Oil Co.; dir. CAP Corp., owner, operator farms in Cleveland and Pottawatomie counties, Okla.; dir. Law and Banking Program, Sch. Banking of South, La. State U., Baton Rouge. mem. vestry All Souls Episcopal Ch., Oklahoma City, jr. warden, 1975, sr. warden, 1976; chmn. Gov. Bellman's Com. on Jud. Reform, Gov. Bartlett's Com. on Ethics in Govt., Gov. Bartlett's Com. to Fin. Okla. Bus. Devel. Corp. form Pvt. Sources, Jud. Council Okla., 1953-65; mem. Gov. Murray's Okla. Crime Study Commn.; treas. Okla. Acad. for State Goals; nat. v.p., chmn. devel. com. Nat. Municipal League, 1971-76; pres. Okla. Municipal League, 1964-65; chmn. Central Okla. Transp. and Parking Authority, 1966—, Okla. Advs. for Arts, 1976; past pres., chmn. bd., life mem. bd. Oklahoma City Symphony; past pres. Okla. Heart Assn., Cleveland County Cancer Assn.; v.p. Oklahoma City Ballet Soc., Inc.; adv. dir. Okla. Med. Research Found.; v.p., mem. exec. com. Okla. Health Scis. Found.; bd. dirs., mem. exec. com. U. Okla. Research Inst.; bd. dirs. Am. Heart Assn., 1969-73, United Appeal Oklahoma City; trustee Froniters of Sci. Found., Okla. Art Center, U. Okla. Devel. Authority; mem. adv. bd. Salvation Army. Fellow Am. Bar Found. (chmn. Okla. 1973-74); mem. Am., Okla. (past com. chmn., trustee Okla. Bar Found. 1966-72), Oklahoma County (bd. govs. 1975—), Cleveland County (past pres.) bar assns., Am. Judicature Soc. (past dir., Herbert Harley award), Order of Coif, Phi Beta Kappa, Beta Gamma Sigma, Phi Delta Phi, Beta Theta Pi (past nat. v.p., scholarship commr.). Recipient Distinguished Service award U. Okla., 1972; editor Oklahoma Practice Methods Book, 1965; contbr. articles to legal jours. Home: 1707 Drury Ln Oklahoma City OK 73116 Office: 1700 Liberty Tower Oklahoma City OK 73102 Tel (405) 232-0661

SNEED, JAMES LYNDE, b. Tulsa, June 24, 1938; A.B. cum laude, Harvard, 1960; J.D., U. Okla., 1963. Admitted to Okla. bar, 1963; partner firm Conner, Winters, Randolph & Bellaine, Tulsa, 1962-69; pres., dir. firm Sneed, Lang, Trotter & Adams, Tulsa, 1970—; trustee Okla. Bar Found., 1976—. Trustee Hillcrest Med. Center, Tulsa, 1975—; bd. dirs. Okla. Grand River Dam Authority, 1976—. Mem. Am., Okla. (chmn. bus., banking and corp. sect. 1971, mem. securities regulation com. 1971, vice chmn. 1975—), Tulsa County (exec. com. 1972) bar assns., Am. Judicature Soc., Tulsa Estate Planning Forum. Contbr. articles to legal jours. Home: 2264 S Terwilleger St Tulsa OK 74114 Office: 411 Thurston Nat Bldg Tulsa OK 74103 Tel (918) 583-3145

SNELL, MURRELL WATKINS, b. Phenix, Va., May 8, 1904; student Randolph Macon Men's Coll., Ashland, Va., 1925-27; LL.B., Cumberland U., 1928; J.D., Samford U., 1969. Admitted to Tenn. bar, 1928, since practiced in Elizabethton; city atty., Elizabethton, 1937-43, city judge, 1948-52, city councilman, 1969-74, vice mayor, 1971-73; sessions judge Carter County (Tenn.), 1943-47, 74—; atty. Elizabethton Power Bd., 1962-74; atty. gen. 1st Jud. Dist. Tenn., 1947-48, judge Criminal Ct., 1957-58. Former chmn., sec. Carter County Election Commn.; mem. adminstrv. bd., steward, chmn. council on ministries 1st United Methodist Ch. Mem. Tenn., Carter County bar assns. Home: 201 Donna Ave Elizabethton TN 37643 Office: Carter County Court House Elizabethton TN 37643 Tel (615) 542-6442

SNELL, RICHARD, b. Phoenix, Nov. 26, 1930; B.A., Stanford, 1952, J.D., 1954. Admitted to Ariz. bar, 1954; asso. firm Snell & Wilmer, Phoenix, 1956-61, partner, 1961—; dir. Ariz. Pub. Service Co., Phoenix, 1975—. Mem. Am., Ariz., Maricopa County (Ariz.) bar assns. Home: 4515 N Dromedary Rd Phoenix AZ 85018 Office: 3100 Valley Center Bldg Phoenix AZ 85073 Tel (602) 257-7249

SNELL, SEWARD B., b. Chgo., July 3, 1922; B.S. in Bus. Adminstrn., Northwestern U., 1944; M.A., Columbia, 1947; J.D., Harvard, 1948. Mem. Conn. bar, 1949, Mass. bar, 1953; individual practice law, Windsor, Conn., 1949-51; atty. Northeastern Gas Transmission Co., Springfield, Mass., 1951-58; atty. Tenn. Gas Transmission Co., Houston, 1958-63, asst. sec., 1963-66; asst. sec. Tenneco, Inc., Houston, 1966—; adj. prof. law S. Tex. Coll. Law, 1972—. Mem. state bars Conn., Mass., Am. Soc. Corp. Secs. Contbr. articles to legal jours. Home: 3 Hedwig Green Houston TX 77024 Office: 1010 Milam St Houston TX 77024 Tel (713) 757-4093

SNELL, WILLIAM N., b. Nevada City, Calif., Feb. 23, 1916; A.B., Stanford U., 1937, J.D., 1940. Admitted to Calif. bar, 1940; asso. firm McCutchen, Olney, Mannon & Greene, San Francisco, 1940-41; partner firm Thomas, Snell, Jamison, Russell, Williamson & Asperger, and predecessors, Fresno, Calif., 1942—. Mem. Am., Fresno County bar assns., State Bar Calif., Am. Law Inst., Am. Judicature Soc., Assn. Trial Lawyers Am., Order of Coif, Delta Theta Phi. Home: 7475 N Valentine Ave Fresno CA 93711 Office: 10th Floor Fresno's Towne House Fresno CA 93721 Tel (209) 442-0600

SNELLINGS, GEORGE MARION, JR., b. Monroe, La., Apr. 28, 1910; A.B., Princeton U., 1929; LL.B., Harvard U., 1932; M.C.L., Tulane U., 1933. Admitted to La. bar, 1933, U.S. Supreme Ct. bar, 1944; asso. prof. law Tulane U., 1933-35; mem. firm Hudson, Potts, Bernstein & Snellings, Monroe, 1935-42; Snellings, Beard, Sartor, Shafto & Inabnett, Monroe, 46—; mem. legal staff War Prodn. Bd., Washington, 1942-44; legal aide to Chief Naval Communications, Washington, 1944-46; dir. Delta Air Lines, Inc.; chmn. bd. Central Bank, Monroe. Bd. regents U. of South. Fellow Am. Coll. Trial Lawyers; mem. Am., La. State bar assns. Home: 101 Country Club Rd Monroe LA 71201 Office: 1503 N 19th St PO Box 6134 Monroe LA 71203 Tel (318) 387-8000

SNEPP, FRANK WARREN, JR., b. Memphis, Aug. 4, 1919; A.B., Columbia, 1940, postgrad. in Law, 1940-41; J.D., Duke, 1948. Admitted to N.C. bar, 1948; mem. firm Ervin, Horack, Snepp & McCartha, Charlotte, N.C., 1948-67; resident judge Superior Ct. of N.C., 26th Jud. Dist., 1967—; mem. N.C. Ho. of Reps., 1957-60; mem. N.C. Commn. on State Govt., 1959-60; chmn. N.C. Jail Study Commn., 1967-68; mem. N.C. Corrections Commn. Mem. N.C. Bar Assn., Am. Judicature Soc., Order of Coif, Phi Beta Kappa. Home: 3752 Larkston Dr Charlotte NC 28211 Office: Mecklenburg County Courthouse Charlotte NC 28202 Tel (704) 374-2734

SNIDER, RICHARD EUGENE, b. Bloomfield, Mo., Oct. 4, 1933; A.B., SE Mo. State U., 1956; LL.B., U. Mo., Columbia, 1958. Admitted to Mo. bar, 1958; individual practice law, Cape Girardeau, Mo., 1958—; pros. atty. Cape Girardeau County, Mo., 1959-60, asst. pros. atty., 1962-68; adminstrv. asst. to U.S. Congressman Burlison, 1968-70. Mem. Jr. C. of C., 1958-65, C. of C., 1965-70; pres. bd. dirs. E. Mo. Community Action Agency, 1970-73; vice chmn. Cape Girardeau Housing Authority, 1968-72; resource person for Church Soc. for Coll. Work Seminar, 1974, NAACP legal fund, ACLU. Mem. Mo. Bar Assn., Coll. Criminal Trial Lawyers, Acad. Trial Advocacy, Am. Trial Lawyers Assn. Hon. col. of Mo., 1964-72; contbr. article to legal jour. Home: 539 S Pacific St Cape Girardeau MO 63701 Office: 14 N Pacific St Cape Girardeau MO 63701 Tel (314) 334-2815

SNIDOW, JOHN CHAPMAN, JR., b. Woodbay, W.Va., July 19, 1916; LL.B., Washington and Lee U., 1940, J.D., 1976. Admitted to Va. bar, 1939; individual practice law, Christiansburg, Va., 1940-56, 69-74; partner firm Snidow and Devore, Christiansburg, 1956-69, 74—; judge Gen. Dist. Ct., 27th Jud. Dist. Va., 1974—. Home: Little Circle Blacksburg VA 24060 Office: PO Box 508 Christiansburg VA 24073 Tel (703) 382-2661

SNITOW, MARTIN S., b. Bklyn., Feb. 10, 1947; B.A., Queens Coll., 1966; LL.B., Yale, 1969. Admitted to N.Y. State bar, 1969, U.S. Supreme Ct. bar, 1973; since practiced in N.Y.C., asso. firm Arsham & Keenan, 1973—; asst. corp. counsel Consumer Protection div. N.Y.C. Law Dept., 1969-73. Mem. Assn. Bar City of N.Y., N.Y. County Lawyers Assn. Home: 300 E 33rd St New York City NY 10016 Office: 277 Park Ave New York City NY 10017 Tel (212) 759-1000

SNITZER, EDWARD LOUIS, b. Phila., Oct. 1, 1931; B.S., Temple U., 1952; LL.B., U. Pa., 1955. Admitted to Pa. bar, 1956, U.S. Supreme Ct. bar, 1970; dep. legal dir. Phila. Redevel. Authority, 1958-65; asso. firm Mesirov, Gelman, Jaffe & Cramer, Phila., 1966-69, partner, 1969-72, of counsel, 1972—; mem. faculty Temple U. Law Sch., 1964-72. Active Settlement Music Sch., Phila., 1960—; trustee Rodeph Shalom Synagogue, Phila., 1973—. Mem. Phila., Pa., Am. bar assns. Author: Pennsylvania Eminent Domain Law Practice, 1965; contbr. articles to legal jours.; NRC research grantee, 1968. Office: Fidelity Bldg 15th Floor Philadelphia PA 19109 Tel (215) 893-5062

SNODDY, JOHN EDWIN, b. Pasadena, Calif., Sept. 26, 1917; B.A., Whitman Coll., Walla Walla, Wash., 1939; J.D., U. Calif., 1942. Admitted to Calif. bar, 1942, Wash. bar, 1945; mem. firm Graves, Kizer, and Graves, Spokane, 1945-54; partner firm Brown & Snoddy, Spokane, 1954-64; individual practice law, Spokane, 1964—; tchr. Spokane Falls Community Coll. Chmn. edn. com. City of Spokane. Mem. Calif., Washington State, Spokane County (pres. 1968-69) bar assns. Home: W1107 12th St Spokane WA 99204 Office: 1001 Old Nat Bank Bldg Spokane WA 99201 Tel (509) 624-0166

SNODGRASS, JOHN DAVID, b. Scottsboro, Ala., Mar. 27, 1938; B.S. in Commerce and Bus. Adminstrn., U. Ala., 1960, LL.B., 1962. Admitted to Ala. bar, 1962; asso. firm Ford, Caldwell, Ford and Payne, Huntsville, Ala., 1963-66; mem. Ala. Legislature, 1968; judge 23rd Jud. Circuit, Huntsville, 1968-72, presiding judge, 1973—; instr. U. Ala., Huntsville, 1974-75; mem. permanent study commn. jud. system Ala., Ala. Adv. Commn. on Jud. Article, State-Fed. Jud. Council of Ala. Bd. dirs. Huntsville Indsl. Expansion Commn., 1970-74, Christmas Charities. Mem. World Peace Through Law, Ala. Assn. Circuit Judges (sec.-treas. 1971-73), Ala., Am. (jud. adminstrn. div., appellate judges conf. joint com. on tech. 1975-76) bar assns., Nat. Conf. State Trial Judges (del. 1969-76, exec. com. 1973-76). Recipient Good Govt. award Madison County, Huntsville Jaycees, 1968-69; grad. Nat. Coll. State Judiciary, 1969, postgrad., 1974. Home: 718 DeSota Rd Huntsville AL 35801 Office: Madison County Courthouse Huntsville AL 35801 Tel (205) 536-5911

SNOOK, JEFFREY LYNN, b. Derry Twp., Mifflen County, Pa., July 28, 1947; B.A., Dickinson Coll., 1969, J.D. cum laude, 1972. Admitted to Pa. bar, 1972; asso. firm Brugler & Levin, Lewistown, Pa., 1973—. Mem. Am., Pa., Mifflen County (sec.-treas. 1975—) bar assns., Am., Pa. trial lawyers assns. Office: PO Box 752 10 S Wayne St Lewistown PA 17044 Tel (717) 248-4971

SNOUFFER, WILLIAM CAMPBELL, b. Fort Monmouth, N.J., Oct. 14, 1939; A.B., Antioch Coll., 1962; J.D., U. Chgo., 1965. Admitted to Oreg. bar, 1965; law clk. to justice Oreg. Supreme Ct., 1965-66; dep. dist. atty. Multnomah County, Oreg., 1966-68; asso. firm Lindsay, Nahstoll, Hart, Duncan, Dafoe & Krause, Portland, Oreg., 1968-72; prof. law Lewis and Clark Law Sch., 1972-76; judge Dist. Ct., Multnomah County, Oreg., 1976—. Trustee Met. Pub. Defender, Portland, 1972-76; mem. exec. bd. ACLU of Oreg., 1974-76; exec. sec. Oreg. Jud. Fitness Commn., 1975-76. Mem. Oreg. State Bar, Am., Multnomah County bar assns., Am. Assn. Law Schs. Author: Criminal Justice Standards in Oregon, 1975; co-editor: Oregon Criminal Law, 1974; contbr. articles to legal jours. Office: Multnomah County Courthouse Portland OR 97204 Tel (503) 248-3511

SNOW, CARLTON JAMES, b. Lynchburg, Va., Dec. 26, 1939; A.B., Taylor U., 1962; M.Div., Fuller Theol. Sem., 1965; M.A., U. Wis., 1966, J.D., 1969. Admitted to Oreg. bar; asst. prof. Sch. Law Loyola U., Los Angeles, asst. prof. Coll. Law Willamette U., Salem, Oreg., asso. prof., asso. dean. Mem. Am. Arbitration Assn., Am. Bar Assn., Soc. Profls. Dispute Resolution. Home: 1030 Schurman St Salem OR 97302 Office: Winter and Ferry Sts Salem OR 97301 Tel (503) 370-6380

SNOW, GERALD TAYLOR, b. Kansas City, Mo., Apr. 17, 1944; B.A., Stanford, 1969; J.D., Harvard, 1972; LL.M. in Taxation, N.Y. U., 1976. Admitted to Calif. bar, 1972, Utah bar, 1973, U.S. Tax Ct. bar, 1975; asso. firm Ray, Quinney & Nebeker, Salt Lake City, 1972—; clk. Boston Legal Assistance Project, 1971. Mem. Am., Utah (editor newsletter young lawyers sect. 1974-75, exec. com. sect. 1973-75), Salt Lake County bar assns. Office: Deseret Bldg suite 400 79 S Main St Salt Lake City UT 84111 Tel (801) 532-1500

SNOW, H. EDWARD, b. Natick, Mass., Apr. 25, 1914; LL.B., Suffolk U., 1936. Admitted to Mass. bar, 1936; individual practice law, Natick, 1936—; presiding judge Mass. Dist. Ct., Natick, 1954-75, ret., 1975; mem. Mass. Ho. of Reps., 1939-43, 46-54, chmn. com. on judiciary, 1947-52, com. on legal affairs, 1941-44. Mem. Am., Mass., South Middlesex bar assns. Home and Office: 15 Travis Rd Natick MA 01760 Tel (617) 653-5161

SNOW, RODNEY GORDON, b. Santa Monica, Calif., Sept. 26, 1943; B.S. in History, U. Utah, 1969, J.D. (Walker Bank and Trust scholar), 1971. Admitted to Utah bar, 1971; research asst. Am. Bar Assn.'s Spl. Com. on Standards of Jud. Conduct, U. Utah Coll. Law, 1969-70; law clk. U.S. Atty.'s Office, Dist. Utah, 1970-71, asst. U.S. atty., 1973-76; atty.-adviser office gen. counsel div. air quality and radiation EPA, Washington, 1971-73; fellow U. Utah Law Sch., 1973-75; asso. firm Clyde and Pratt, Salt Lake City, 1976—. Mem. Washington Council of Lawyers, Am. Bar Assn., Am. Judicature Soc. Named Outstanding Asst. U.S. Atty. for Utah, U.S. Dept. Justice, 1976. Home: 7603 Silver Fork Dr Salt Lake City UT 84121 Office: 351 S State St Salt Lake City UT 84101 Tel (801) 524-5689

SNOW, RONALD LOUIS, b. Franklin, N.H., Aug. 3, 1935; B.A., Dartmouth, 1958; LL.B., Yale, 1961. Admitted to N.H. bar, 1961; partner firm Orr & Reno, Concord, N.H., 1966—. Former pres. Concord YMCA; chmn. drug abuse program Daniel Webster council Boy Scouts Am.; chmn. N.H. Ballot Law Commn. Mem. Am., N.H. bar assns. Recipient Outstanding Citizen award Concord C. of C., 1970, named Man of Year, 1972. Office: 95 N Main St Concord NH 03301 Tel (603) 224-2381

SNOW, TOWER CHARLES, JR., b. Boston, Oct. 28, 1947; A.B. cum laude, Dartmouth, 1969; J.D., U. Calif., Berkeley, 1973; grad. Nat. Inst. Trial Advocacy, 1974. Admitted to Calif. bar, 1973, 9th Circuit bar, 1973, U.S. Dist. Ct. No. Dist. Calif., 1973; asso. firm Orrick, Herrington, Rowley & Sutcliffe, San Francisco, 1973—. Mem. Bar Assn. San Francisco, Barristers Club. Home: 5906 Bruns Ct Oakland CA 94611 Office: 600 Montgomery St San Francisco CA 94111 Tel (415) 392-1122

SNOW, VERNON LAVARD, b. Salina, Utah, Sept. 18, 1927; B.S. in Accounting, U. Utah, 1949, J.D., 1957. Admitted to Utah bar, 1957, Calif. bar, 1964, Alaska bar, 1967; asso. firm Eks, Ayn & Anderson, Salt Lake City, 1957-59; atty. Regional Counsel's Office Western Region, San Francisco, 1959-67; asst. atty. gen. State of Alaska, 1967-69; partner firm Debenham & Snow, Anchorage, 1972-74; partner firm Gallagher, Cranston & Snow, Anchorage, 1974-75, sec.-treas., 1975—; dep. commr. of revenue State of Alaska, 1969-70. Mem. Am., Calif., Utah, Alaska bar assns. Office: 310 K St 500 Anchorage AK 99504 Tel (907) 276-1994

SNYDER, BERNARD A., b. Eddyville, Nebr., Mar. 19, 1910; J.D., Loyola U., Chgo., 1939. Admitted to Ill. bar, 1939; bookkeeper First Nat. Bank, Chgo., 1927-29, Am. Radiator Co., Chgo., 1929-31; corr. N.Y. Life Ins. Co., Chgo., 1931, salesman, 1931-33; clk. Scurlock Kontanerette Corp., Chgo., 1933-36; real estate mgr. Chgo. Mortgage Investment Co., 1936-42; asso. firm Sonnenschein, Berkson, Lautman, Levinson & Morse, Chgo., 1942-43; partner firm DiGrazia & Snyder, Summit, Ill., 1946-65; partner firm Pokorny & Snyder, La Grange, Ill., 1966—. Mem. Chgo., West Suburban, South Suburban Bar Assns., Phi Alpha Delta. Office: 100 W Plainfield Rd La Grange IL 60525 Tel (312) 354-7877

SNYDER, FARRY MARTIN, b. London, Ky., Oct. 22, 1941; B.S. in Economics and Bus. Adminstrn., Georgetown (Ky.) Coll., 1963; J.D., U. Ky., 1966. Admitted to Ky. bar, 1966; financial aid dir., coor. fed. programs, legal counsel, adj. prof. law, Georgetown Coll., 1966-68; asst. coor., program budget planning U. Ky. at Lexington, 1968-70; asst. budget dir. U. Ky. System, 1970-73; asso. dir., legal counsel Ky. Council Pub. Higher Edn., 1973-75, exec. asst., legal counsel, 1975-76, interim exec. dir., 1976, exec. dir., 1976—. Mem. vestry Good Shepherd Episcopalian Ch., Lexington; mem. bd. dirs. Central Ky. Youth Symphony, Lexington, Mem. Ky., Am. bar assns. Home: 712 Fairway Dr Lexington KY 40502 Office: 8th Floor Capital Plaza Tower Frankfort KY 40601

SNYDER, GEORGE WALTER KING, JR., b. Chgo., July 8, 1940; A.B., Harvard, 1962, J.D., 1966. Admitted to Ill. bar, 1967, U.S. Dist. Ct. bar for No. Dist. Ill., 1967, for Dist. Oreg., 1974, Oreg. bar, 1971; asso. firms Wilson & McIlvaine, Chgo., 1966-71, Hardy, Buttler, McEwen, Weiss & Newman, Portland, Oreg., 1971-72; counsel, asst. to lobbyist for City of Portland, 1973; individual practice law, Portland, 1973—; alt. participant Oreg. State Bar program of legal service to Oreg. Legislature, 1975. Democratic precinct committeeman, 1974-76; chmn. housing com. Raleigh Hills-Garden Home Community Planning Orgn., Washington County, Oreg., 1975. Mem. Oreg. Stat Bar, Multnomah County, Ill. State bar assns. Home: 1830 NE 11th St Portland OR 97212 Office: 2207 NE Broadway Portland OR 97232 Tel (503) 287-4850

SNYDER, HARRY GROSS, b. Davenport, Iowa, Feb. 11, 1938; B.S., U. Wis., 1961; J.D., Marquette U., 1964. Admitted to Wis. bar, 1964, U.S. Supreme Ct. bar, 1971; served with JAGC, U.S. Air Force, 1964-67; asst. dist. atty. Waukesha County (Wis.), 1968-69; asso. firm Herro, Snyder, Chapman & Snyder, Oconomowoc, Wis., 1969—; mem. Wis. Ho. of Reps., 1975—. Mem. Wis., Waukesha County, Milw. bar assns., Am. Judicature Soc., Oconomowoc Area C. of C. (pres. 1974-75), Res. Officers Assn. (staff judge adv. 1970-72; v.p. air force sect. 1975-76). Home: 331 E Summit Ave Oconomowco WI 53066 Office: 156 E Wisconsin Ave Oconomowoc WI 53066 Tel (414) 567-8770

SNYDER, HARRY LAMBRIGHT, Charleston, W.Va., Nov. 12, 1927; B.A., W.Va. U., 1948, LL.B., 1950. Admitted to W.Va. bar, 1950; asso. firm Mohler, Peters & Snyder, Charleston, 1950-56; mem. legal dept. United Fuel Gas Co., Charleston, 1956-71; mem. law dept. Columbia Gas Transmission Corp., Charleston, 1971—; mem. W.Va. Ho. of Del., 1953-55, chief clk. judiciary com., 1955. Bd. dirs. United Way, Charleston, 1965-67, 74—; bd. dirs. Community Council of Kanawha County, Charleston, 1960-69, 74—, pres., 1965-67. Mem. Am., W.Va., Kanawha County bar assns., Order of Coif, Phi Beta Kappa. Note editor W.Va. Law Rev., 1949-50. Office: PO Box 1273 Charleston WV 25325 Tel (304) 346-0951

SNYDER, KEITH SPURLING, b. Caldwell County, N.C., June 17, 1933; B.A., U. N.C., 1955, LL.B., 1958. Admitted to N.C. bar, 1958; individual practice law, Lenoir, N.C., 1958-66; judge N.C. Dist. Ct., 25th Dist., 1966-69; U.S. atty. Western Dist. N.C., Asheville, 1969—. Trustee, Mars Hill Coll. Mem. Phi Alpha Delta. Recipient Distinguished Service award Lenoir (N.C.) Jr. C. of C., 1966. Office: PO Box 132 Asheville NC 28802 Tel (704) 258-2850

SNYDER, LESLIE CROCKER, b. N.Y.C., Mar. 8, 1942; A.B., Radcliffe Coll., 1962; certificate Harvard Bus. Sch., 1963; J.D., Case Western Res. U., 1966. Admitted to Ohio bar, 1966, N.Y. State bar, 1967; asso. firm Kaye, Scholer, Fierman, Hayes & Handler, N.Y.C., 1966-68; chief trial bur., sex crimes N.Y. County Dist. Atty.'s Office, N.Y.C., 1968-76; chief trials Office of Spl. N.Y. State Prosecutor, spl. asst. atty. gen., N.Y.C., 1976—; mem. Mayor's Task Force on Rape. Mem. Assn. Bar City N.Y. (sex and law coms.), Am., N.Y. State, N.Y. Women's bar assns. Recipient Mademoiselle award Women of Achievement for 1974. Home: 850 Park Ave New York City NY 10021 Office: 2 World Trade Center New York City NY 10047 Tel (212) 466-1250

SNYDER, LESTER B., b. Boston, Mar. 19, 1928; B.S., Syracuse U., 1951; J.D., Boston U., 1956; LL.M., Columbia, 1961. Admitted to Mass. bar, 1956, Conn. bar, 1965, U.S. Supreme Ct. bar, 1969; prof. law U. Conn. Sch. Law, W. Hartford, 1957—; prof.-in-residence, tax div. Dept. Justice, Washington, 1969-70; vis. prof. law N.Y. U., 1972-73; chmn. Conn. State Elections Commn., 1974-76; with CBS News Channel 3 TV, Hartford, 1975-76. Mem. Conn. Task Force on Income Maintenance, 1976. Mem. Am., Conn. (chmn. law revision com. 1966-67) bar assns., Tax Club Hartford. Recipient Outstanding Service award Sec. State Conn., 1976; contbr. articles to legal jours.; editor-in-chief Jour. Real Estate Taxation, 1973—. Home: 30 Candlewood Dr West Hartford CT 06117 Office: U Conn Sch Law West Hartford CT 06117 Tel (203) 523-4841

SNYDER, MARION GENE, b. Louisville, Jan. 26, 1928; LL.B. cum laude, Jefferson Sch. Law, 1950; J.D. cum laude, U. Louisville, 1969. Admitted to Ky. bar, 1950, D.C. bar, 1970; individual practice law, Louisville, 1950—; city atty., Jeffersontown, Ky., 1953-57; magistrate 1st dist. Jefferson County, 1957-61; mem. 88th Congress from 3d Ky. Dist., 90th-95th Congresses from 4th Ky. Dist., mem. Pub. Works com., Merchant Marine com. Vice pres. Ky. Magistrates and Commrs., 1958; v.p. Jeffersontown Civic Center, 1953-54. Mem. Am., D.C., Ky. bar assns., Nat., Ky., Louisville bds. realtors, Ky. Farm Bur. Home: 8405 Old Brownsboro Rd Louisville KY 40222 Office: 140 Chenoweth Ln Louisville KY 40207 Tel (502) 897-1123

SNYDER, MICHAEL, b. Oakland, Calif., Nov. 5, 1939; B.A., Calif. State U. at Hayward, 1965; J.D., U. Calif. Hastings Coll. Law, San Francisco, 1968. Admitted to Calif. bar, 1969; dep. dist. atty. San Bernardino County (Calif.), 1969-71; mem. firm Staiger, Yank, Mollinelli & Preston, San Francisco, 1971—; referee juvenile ct. Alameda County (Calif.) Superior Ct., 1975—. Mem. Am. Arbitration Assn. (panel of arbitrators), Mensa. Home: 15730 Via Sorrento San Lorenzo CA 94580 Office: 100 Van Ness Ave San Francisco CA 94102 Tel (415) 565-2988

SNYDER, PATRICK LEE, b. Oconomowoc, Wis., Oct. 20, 1935; B.C.S., U. Notre Dame, 1957; LL.B., Marquette U., 1960. Admitted to Wis. bar, 1960, U.S. Supreme Ct. bar, 1965; partner firm Herro, Snyder, Chapman & Snyder, Oconomowoc, 1960—; city atty. Oconomowoc, 1963—. Past chmn. Oconomowoc Area Cancer Crusade. Mem. Wis., Waukesha County (pres.) bar assns. Home: 203 N Maple Terr Oconomowoc WI 53066 Office: 156 E Wisconsin Ave Oconomowoc WI 53066 Tel (414) 567-6916

SNYDER, WILLIAM EDWARD, b. Evanston, Ill., Nov. 3, 1944; B.S., Northwestern U., 1966, J.D., 1969. Admitted to Ill. bar, 1969; law clk. Hon. Julius Hoffman, U.S. Dist. Ct. No. Dist. Ill., 1969-71; asso. firm Chadwell, Kayser, Ruggles, McGee & Hastings, Chgo., 1971—. Mem. Am., Chgo., Ill. State bar Assns. Home: 400 E Randolph St #2919 Chicago IL 60601 Office: 135 S La Salle St Chicago IL 60603 Tel (312) 726-2545

SNYDER, WILLIAM FIRTH, b. Amsterdam, N.Y., Sept. 17, 1922; B.A. magna cum laude, Harvard U., 1943; J.D., U. Mich., 1949. Admitted to Mich. bar, 1949, Ohio bar, 1950; asso. firm Marshman, Hollington & Steadman (now Marshman, Hornbeck, Hollington, Steadman & McLaughlin), 1949-60, partner, 1960-68; sr. partner firm Marshman, Snyder & Seely (now Marshman, Snyder, Seely, Corrigan & Isaac), Cleve., 1968—; mem. bd. commns. on discrepancies and grievances Supreme Ct. Ohio, 1970-76, chmn., 1977. Chmn. bd. trustees Cuyahoga County (Ohio) Hosps.; sec. bd. trustees Shaker Med. Center Hosp., 1955—. Mem. Order of Coif. Office: 1 Erieview Plaza Cleveland OH 44114 Tel (216) 781-8000

SOAPE, G. DEAN, b. Carthage, Tex., Mar. 30, 1933; student Panola Jr. Coll., 1952; B.B.A. in Accounting, Stephen F. Austin State U., 1954; LL.B., U. Houston, 1959. Admitted to Tex. bar, 1959; with Peat, Marwick, Mitchell & Co., Houston, 1954-59; individual practice law, Houston, 1960-71; mem. firm Soape, Foster & Hall, 1972—. Office: 1541 So Nat Bank Bldg Houston TX 77002 Tel (214) 693-3450

SOARES, ROBERT JOSEPH, b. Hanford, Calif., Oct. 2, 1931; B.S., U. Calif., Berkeley, 1953, J.J.D., Boalt Hall, 1958. Admitted to Calif. bar, 1959; dep. dist. atty. Ventura County, Calif., 1959-62; partner firm Hathaway Soares & Shaw, Ventura, Calif., 1962-69; judge Municipal Ct., Ventura, 1969—. Mem. Calif. State Bar, Conf. Calif. Judges (dir. 1975—). Office: 501 Poli St Ventura CA 93001 Tel (805) 648-6131

SOBEL, ALAN PHILIP, b. Chgo., Oct. 6, 1943; B.A., U. Ill., 1966; J.D., DePaul U., 1969. Admitted to Ill. bar, 1969; since practiced law in Chgo., asso. firm Marks, Marks & Kaplan, 1969-72, Lieberman, Levy Baron & Stone, 1972-76, individual practice law, 1976—. Mem. Chgo., Ill., Am. bar assns., Nu Beta Epsilon. Comment editor DePaul Law Review, 1968; book review editor, 1968; editor-in-chief The Summons, 1968. Home: 7724 Lowell St Skokie IL 60076 Office: 33 N LaSalle St Chicago IL 60602 Tel (312) 236-8110

SOBELOFF, JONATHAN, b. N.Y.C., Sept. 29, 1934; A.B. with high distinction, U. Mich., 1955; J.D. magna cum laude, Harvard U., 1958. Admitted to Mich. bar, 1958, D.C. bar, 1965; individual practice law, Detroit, 1958-62; staff Office of Tax Legis. Counsel, U.S. Dept. Treasruy, 1962-64; individual practice law, Washington, 1964-66; prof. law Georgetown U., Washington, 1966—; faculty adviser The Tax Lawyer, 1972-74, 77—. Mem. Am., Law Inst., Internat. Fiscal Assn., Nat. Tax Assn.-Tax Inst. Am., Assn. Am. Law Schs. (com. on continuing legal edn.), Am. Bar Assn. (chmn. tax sect. com. on tax accounting problems 1972-73), Fed. Bar Assn. (dep. chmn. taxation com. 1971-72). Author: Tax and Business Organization Aspect of Small Business, 4th edit., 1974; contbr. articles to legal jours. Home: 6720 Brigadoon Dr Bethesda MD 20034 Office: Georgetown U Law Center 600 New Jersey Ave NW Washington DC 20001 Tel (202) 624-8349

SOBLE, H. DAVID, b. Rochester, N.Y., Nov. 15, 1946; B.A., Syracuse U., 1968; J.D., U. Chgo., 1971. Admitted to Calif. bar, 1972, D.C. bar, 1973; asso. firm Loeb & Loeb, Los Angeles, 1971-72; legis. asst. to congressman, Washington, 1972—; pres. Tax Cons., Inc., Alexandria, Va., 1973—. Office: 2404 Rayburn House Office Bldg Washington DC 20515 Tel (202) 225-6234

SOBOTA, RAYMOND JOHN, b. N.Y.C., Feb. 7, 1928; A.B., U. Notre Dame, 1949; LL.B., Georgetown U., 1951. Admitted to D.C. bar, 1952, Pa. bar, 1953, U.S. Supreme Ct. bar, 1960; partner firm Cardoni, Coslett, Cappellini, Sobota & Diccone, Wilkes-Barre, Pa., 1972—; asst. solicitor Luzerne County (Pa.), 1967; solicitor Wyoming Valley San. Authority, 1969. Bd. dirs. Pa. Lung Assn. Mem. Am., Luzerne County (bd. censors 1970-71) bar assns., Am. Arbitration Assn. (panel arbitrators 1975—), Am. Trial Lawyers Assn., Lawyers Pilots Bar Assn. Home: 1814 Wyoming Ave Forty Fort PA 18704 Office: 515 United Penn Bank Wilkes-Barre PA 18701 Tel (717) 822-8163

SODARO, DEAN JOSEPH, b. Oak Park, Ill., May 6, 1927; B.S., Union Coll., Schenectady, N.Y., 1949; J.D., Chgo.-Kent Coll., 1953. Admitted to Ill. Supreme Ct. bar, 1953, U.S. Dist. Ct. bar, 1954, U.S. Ct. of Appeals bar, 1956; individual practice law, Chgo., 1953-72; lectr. law Chgo. Kent Coll., 1958-72, prof., 1972—; legal advisor Sheriff of Cook County (Ill.), 1966-70; arbitrator Am. Arbitration Assn., 1970-76. Pres., founder Oak Park-River Forest Boys Football Club, 1968-72; assessor Oak Park Twp., 1974—. Mem. Ill. State Bar Assn. Contbr. articles in field to profl. jours. Home: 535 N Marion St Oak Park IL 60302 Office: 77 S Wacker Dr Chicago IL 60606 Tel (312) 567-5000

SODEN, HAROLD ROBERT, b. Cohoes, N.Y., Nov. 16, 1908; B.S., Colgate U.; LL.B., Union U., 1933. Admitted to N.Y. bar, 1934; asso. firm Leary & Fullerton, Saratoga Springs, N.Y., 1933-36, R.C. Prime Assos., Lake Placid, N.Y., 1936-39; individual practice law, Lake Placid, 1939-61; dist. atty. Essex County (N.Y.), 1939-48; justice Supreme Ct., Lake Placid, 1961—. Supr., Town of N. Elba (N.Y.), 1949-60. Home: 58 Mirror Lake Dr Placid NY 12946 Office: 66 Mirror Lake Dr Lake Placid NY 12946 Tel (518) 523-2585

SODERSTROM, ROBERT SCOTT, b. Chgo., June 5, 1944; A.B., Kenyon Coll., Gambier, Ohio, 1966; J.D., Loyola U., Chgo., 1969. Admitted to Ill. bar, 1969; asso. firm McKenna, Storer, Rowe, White & Farrug, Chgo., 1969-75, partner, 1975—. Mem. Am., Ill., Chgo. bar assns., Trial Lawyers Club Chgo., Ill. Appellate Lawyers Assn., Def. Research Inst., Ill. Def. Council. Home: 619 Wagner Rd Glenview IL 60025 Office: 135 S LaSalle St Chicago IL 60603 Tel (312) 332-0913

SOFAER, ABRAHAM DAVID, b. Bombay, India, May 6, 1938; B.A. in History magna cum laude, Yeshiva Coll., 1962; LL.B. (Root-Tilden scholar) cum laude, N.Y. U., 1965. Admitted to N.Y. bar, 1965; law clk. U.S. Ct. Appeals, D.C., 1965-66; U.S. Supreme Ct., Washington, 1966-67; asst. U.S. atty. So. Dist. N.Y., N.Y.C., 1967-69; prof. law Columbia, 1969—. Bd. dirs. MFY Legal Services, Citizens Union. Mem. Am. Bar Assn. Author: War Foreign Affairs and Constitutional Power: The Origins, 1976; contbr. articles to legal jours. Office: Dept Law Columbia Univ 435 W 116th St New York City NY 10027 Tel (212) 280-5086

SOFFAR, CHARLES EDWARD, b. Houston, June 22, 1948; B.A. in Polit. Sci., 1970, J.D. (Childs, Fortenbach, Beck & Guyton scholar), Bates Coll., 1972. Admitted to Tex. bar, 1972; drafting clk. Tex. Probate System, State Bar Tex., Houston, 1972; asst. city atty. City of Houston, 1973; individual practice law, Houston, 1974—; vol. in parole State Bar Tex., Houston, 1975. Mem. Tex. Trial Lawyers Assn., State Bar Tex., Am., Houston bar assns., Houston Jr. Bar Assn. Home: 2221 Westcreek Ln apt 18-F Houston TX 77027 Office: 2421 San Felipe St Houston TX 77019 Tel (713) 522-0771

SOHM, KEITH ELIPHET, b. Burley, Idaho, July 26, 1923; J.D., U. Utah, 1952. Admitted to Utah bar, 1952, U.S. Supreme Ct. bar, 1962; atty. Utah Pub. Service Commn., Salt Lake City, 1952-68, dir. transp. and hearing examiners, 1968-74; adminstrv. law judge Utah Indsl. Commn., Salt Lake City, 1975—; individual practice law, Salt Lake City, 1952-76. Active Great Salt Lake council Boy Scouts Am. Home: 2057 Lincoln Ln Salt Lake City UT 84117 Office: 350 E 5th S Salt Lake City UT 84111 Tel (801) 533-6411

SOHN, LOUIS BRUNO, b. Lwow, Poland, Mar. 1, 1914; LL.M., Diplomatic Sc.M., John Casimir U., 1935; LL.M., Harvard U., 1940, S.J.D., 1958; came to U.S., 1939, naturalized, 1943. Asst. to Judge M. O. Hudson, 1941-48; research fellow Harvard Law Sch., 1946-47, lectr. law, 1947-51, asst. prof. law, 1951-53, John Harvey Gregory lectr. in world orgn., 1951—, prof. law, 1953-61, Bemis prof. internat.

law, 1961—; cons. ACDA, 1960-70, Office Internat. Security Affairs, Dept. Def., 1963-70; asst. to del. Permanent Ct. Internat. Justice, San Francisco Conf. UN, 1945; exec. sec. legal subcom. on atomic energy Carnegie Endowment for Internat. Peace, 1946; asst. reporter on progressive devel. internat. law Am. and Canadian bar assns., 1947-48; cons. UN secretariat, 1948, 69, legal officer, 1950-51; counselor internat. law Dept. State, 1970-71; U.S. del. to UN Law of Sea Conf., 1974—. Recipient World Peace Hero award World Federalists of Can., 1974. Mem. Am. Soc. Internat. Law (exec. council 1954-57, v.p. 1965-66), World Parliament Assn. (legal adviser 1954-64), Internat. Law Assn. (v.p. Am. br.), Am. Law Inst., Am. Bar Assn., Fedn. Am. Scientists (vice chmn. 1963, mem. council 1964-65, 68-69), Commn. Study Orgn. Peace (chmn. 1968—). Author: Cases on World Law, 1950; Cases on United Nations Law, 1956, 2d edit., 1967: (with G. Clark) World Peace Through World Law, 1958, 3d edit., 1966; Basic Documents of African Regional Organizations, 4 vols., 1971-72; International Protection of Human Rights (with T. Buergenthal), 1973. Editor devel. internat. law Am. Bar Assn. Jour., 1947-50; bd. editors Am. Jour. Internat. Law, 1958—. Home: 780 Boylston St Boston MA 02199 Office: Harvard Law Sch Cambridge MA 02138

SOISSON, WILLIAM HENRY, b. Connellsville, Pa., May 18, 1911; B.A., Georgetown U., 1932, J.D., 1935. Admitted to Pa. bar, 1936, U.S. Dist. Ct. for Western dist. Pa., 1937; spl. counsel Dept. Banking, State of Pa., 1936-40; gen. counsel Connellsville Housing Authority, 1949-76, Sch. Dist., 1955-57, Area Sch. Dist., 1966-74, Municipal Authority, 1949-76, Area Sch. Authority, 1967-76, Twp., 1946-50, 63-76, Bullskin Twp. Sch. Dist., 1947-66, Saltlick Twp., Pa., 1963-74, North Fayette Vocat.-Tech. Sch. Dist., 1970-74. Chmn. Connellsville Planning Commn., 1946-66; trustee Carnegie Free Library, Connellsville, 1954—, pres., 1975—. Mem. Pa. Sch. Solicitors Assn., Pa. (ho. of dels. 1973-76), Fayette County (pres. 1972) bar assns. Address: PO Box 802 Connellsville PA 15425

SOKARIS, PETER G., b. Albany, N.Y., May 13, 1938; B.A. Amherst Coll., 1961; J.D. Western New Eng. Coll., 1970. Admitted to N.Y. State bar, 1972; individual practice law, Albany, N.Y., 1972—. Home: 542 Myrtle Ave Albany NY 12208 Office: 100 State St Albany NY 12207 Tel (518) 463-6693

SOKOLOWSKI, STANLEY WILLIAM, b. Newark, Oct. 28, 1924; B.Metall.Engring., Rensselaer Poly. Inst., 1949; M.B.A., Rutgers U., 1962; J.D., Seton Hall U., 1969. Metall. engr. Bendex Corp., Teterboro and Red Bank, N.J., 1952-68; admitted to N.J. bar, 1970, U.S. Patent Office bar, 1972, Fla. bar, 1974; atty. Legal Services Orgn., Asbury Park, N.J., 1970-71; patent atty. Ingersoll Rand Corp., Princeton, N.J., 1971-73; individual practice law, Matawan, N.J., 1973—. Mem. Matawan Borough Council, 1969-72. Mem. Monmouth County Bar Assn. Home and Office: 70 Ravine Dr Matawan NJ 07747 Tel (201) 566-9075

SOLBERG, DARRYL OTTO, b. Mankato, Minn., Nov. 10, 1945; B.A., St. Olaf Coll., 1967; J.D., U. Chgo., 1973. Admitted to Calif. bar, 1972; partner firm McDonald, Riddle, Hecht & Worley, San Diego, 1973—. Mem. Phi Beta Kappa. Office: 617 Financial Sq 600 B St San Diego CA 92101 Tel (714) 239-3444

SOLBERT, PETER OMAR ABERNATHY, b. Copenhagen, Mar. 9, 1919; B.A., Yale, 1941; J.D., Harvard, 1948. Admitted to N.Y. bar, 1949, U.S. Supreme Ct. bar, 1952; asso. firm Davis Polk & Wardwill, N.Y.C., 1948-57, partner, 1957—; dep. asst. sec. def. Internat. Security Affairs, 1963-65. Mem. Internat., Am. bar assns., Internat. Law Assn., Am. Fgn. Law Assn., Am. Soc. Internat. Law, N.Y. State Bar, Bar Assn. City N.Y. Home: 2 Sutton Pl New York City NY 10022 Office: 1 Chase Manhattan Plaza New York City NY 10005 Tel (212) HA 2-3400

SOLDWEDEL, FRED WILMOT, b. Pekin, Ill., Oct. 15, 1931; B.S., Northwestern U., 1953; LL.B., Stanford U., 1958; LL.M. in Taxation, U. So. Calif., 1962. Admitted to Calif. bar, 1958, Ill. bar, 1961, U.S. Supreme Ct. bar, 1967; asso. firm Boyle, Atwill, Mardian & Stearns, Pasadena, Calif., 1958-64; mng. partner firm Parker, Berg, Soldwedel & Palermo, Pasadena, 1964—. Bd. dirs. Pasadena Tournament of Roses Assn., Pasadena Symphony, San Gabriel council Boy Scouts Am. past pres. San Marino Community Council; pres. So. Calif. Presbyn. Homes; Monte Vista Grove Homes; trustee, deacon, elder San Marino Community Ch.; sec. Pasadena Cardiovascular Research Found. Mem. Am., Pasadena (treas.), Los Angeles County bar assns., Pasadena C. of C. (pres.), Naval Res. Assn., Los Angeles World Affairs Council, Northwestern, Stanford U., U. So. Calif. alumni assns. Phi Delta Phi. Office: 234 E Colorado Blvd Pasadena CA 91101 Tel (213) 793-5196

SOLE, EMMETT CARY, b. Lake Charles, La., Aug. 10, 1943; J.D., La. State U., 1968. Admitted to La. bar; law clerk 2d Circuit Ct. Appeal, La., 1968-69; asso. firm Stockwell, St. Dizier, Sievert & Viccellio, Lake Charles, from 1969; partner firm Stockwell, Sievert, Viccellio, Clements & Shaddock, Lake Charles, 1972—. Mem. Lake Charles Planning & Zoning Commn., 1975, Democratic State Central Com., La., 1975. Mem. La. Bar Assn. (mem. Ho. Dels.), La. Law Inst. (jr.), La. State Bar Assn. (young lawyers sec., dist. rep. to council), Phi Alpha Delta. Home: 2417 Gardenia St Lake Charles LA 70601 Office: PO Box 2900 Lake Charles LA 70601 Tel (318) 436-9491

SOLEM, WILLIAM MARTIN, b. Harve, Mont., Aug. 21, 1943; B.B.A., U. Mont., 1965, J.D., 1968. Admitted to Mont. bar, 1968; partner firm Burns, Solem & Mackenzie, Chinook, Mont., 1968—; atty. Blaine County (Mont.), 1971—; dir. Security State Bank, Harlem, Mont., Western Bank N.A., Chinook. Bd. dirs. Lloyd Sweet Ednl. Found., 1971—. Mem. Am., Mont. bar assns., Nat. Dist. Attys. Assn., Chinook C. of C. Home: 1125 Pennsylvania Ave Chinook MT 59523 Office: 408 Ohio St Chinook MT 59523 Tel (406) 357-3150

SOLENDER, ELLEN KARELSEN, b. N.Y.C., Sept. 4, 1923; A.B., Oberlin Coll., 1944; J.D., So. Meth. U., 1971. Admitted to Tex. bar, 1971; instr. So. Meth. U. Sch. Law, Dallas, 1971-74, asst. prof., 1974—. Vice chmn. Fund Solicitation Bd., City of Dallas, 1973—. Mem. Dallas, Tex., Am. bar assns., Scribes. Asso. editor Southwestern Law Jour., 1970-71. Home: 9131 Devonshire St Dallas TX 75209 Office: Southern Methodist U Sch Law Dallas TX 75275 Tel (214) 692-2580

SOLERWITZ, JACK BERNARD, b. N.Y.C., Feb. 16, 1937; B.A. in English, Adelphi U., 1958; M.S. in Ednl. Adminstrn., Hofstra U., 1960; LL.B., J.D., Fordham U., 1964. Admitted to N.Y. bar, 1965, U.S. Ct. Mil. Appeals bar, 1969, U.S. Supreme Ct. bar, 1969, D.C. bar, 1976; individual practice law, Mineola, N.Y., 1969—. Mem. Am., Nassau County, Suffolk County, N.Y. State, Fed. bar assns., N.Y. State Trial Lawyers Assn., Fed. Bar Council, Jewish Lawyers Assn. Nassau County. Home: 141 Chichester Rd Huntington NY 11743 Office: 170 Old Country Rd Suite 310 Mineola NY 11501 Tel (516) 742-4300

SOLEY, JUDITH LESLIE, b. Columbia, Mo., July 14, 1945; A.B., U. Calif., Los Angeles, 1967; J.D., Boalt Hall, U. Calif., Berkeley, 1970. Admitted to Calif. bar, 1971; asso. firm Parichan, Krebs, Renberg & Eldridge, Fresno, Calif., 1970-72; asso. firm Gallagher, Levis & Soley, Fresno, 1972-74; partner firm Gallagher, Soley & Gollmer, Fresno, 1974—; mem. bd. dirs. Fresno County Legal Services, 1973—, pres., 1975; chmn. Atty. Reference Service, 1976-77; mem. com. on legal reference service, state bar legal services sect., 1976-77. Mem. Fresno Community Council, 1971-72; mem. Calif. Criminal Justice Commn. Fresno County, 1974—; mem. mayor's com. to employ the handicapped, 1975-77. Mem. Calif. (chmn. women's rights com., 1976), Am. Trial Lawyers Assns., Calif., Am., Fresno County (dir., 1972-75) Bar Assns., Fresno County Barristers (dir. 1971-73, 75-76). Office: 830 T W Patterson Bldg Fresno CA 93721 Tel (209) 237-6668

SOLIEN, WILLIAM ALDON, b. Stoughton, Wis., June 14, 1921; B.A., U. Wis., 1945, J.D., 1947. Admitted to Wis. bar, 1947, Fla. bar, 1966; individual practice law, 1947—; affiliated Bank N.Mex., Albuquerque, 1961-63, Lighthouse Point Bank (Fla.), 1963-72. Mem. Fla. Bar, State Bar of Wis., N. Broward Bar Assn., Trial Lawyers Assn., Wis. Law Alumni Assn., Phi Delta Phi. Home: 2329 NE 25th St Lighthouse Point FL 33064 Office: 2261 NE 36th St Lighthousg Point FL 33064 Tel (305) 785-1450

SOLIS, CARLOS, b. Managua, Nicaragua, May 15, 1945; A.B., U. San Francisco, 1967, J.D., 1969. Admitted to Calif. bar, 1970, U.S. Supreme Ct. bar, 1973; asso. firm Kindel & Anderson, Los Angeles, 1969-76, partner, 1976—. Bd. dirs. Los Angeles Jr. C. of C., 1976-77, Internat. Student Center, Los Angeles, 1976-77. Mem. Los Angeles County (chmn. law schs. com., 1975-77), Am. bar assns., State Bar Calif., Am. Trial Lawyers Assn., Phi Delta Phi (province award Grad. of Year 1969), Alpha Sigma Nu, Pi Sigma Alpha, McAuliffe Law Honor Soc. Contbr. articles to legal publs. Home: 405 La Mirada Ave San Marino CA 91108 Office: Kindel & Anderson 26th floor 555 S Flower St Los Angeles CA 90071 Tel (213) 680-2222

SOLLEE, WILLIAM LAWRENCE, b. Jacksonville, Fla., June 25, 1942; B.B.A. magna cum laude, U. Fla., 1964, J.D. cum laude, 1966. Admitted to Fla. bar, 1966, D.C. bar, 1967; partner firm Ivins, Phillips & Barker, Washington, 1972—. Mem. Am., Fla., D.C. bar assns. Contbr. articles to legal jours. Office: 1700 Pennsylvania Ave NW Washington DC 20006 Tel (202) 393-7600

SOLMSON, WILLIAM S., b. St. Louis, Nov. 18, 1942; B.S. in Commerce, Washington and Lee U., 1964; J.D., Vanderbilt U., 1967. Admitted to Tenn. bar; mem. firm Canada, Russell & Turner, Memphis, 1967-74, partner, 1974—; instr. bus. law Memphis State U., 1967-69. Bd. dirs. Memphis Boys' Town, 1973—, v.p., 1975—. Office: 1213 Union Planters Bank Bldg Memphis TN 38103 Tel (901) 521-1111

SOLOMON, BENJAMIN B., b. Phila., June 18, 1909; B.S., Temple U., 1931; LL.B., U. Pa., 1933. Admitted to Pa. bar, 1938; asst. atty. gen. Commonwealth of Pa., also chief counsel Pa. Game Commn., Harrisburg, 1967—; individual practice law, Phila., 1938—. Pres. Middle Atlantic region Nat. Fedn. Jewish Men's Clubs. Mem. Phila. Bar Assn., Pa. Trial Lawyers Assn. Home: 1742 E Washington Ln Philadelphia PA 19138 Office: suite 1644 Suburban Station Bldg 1617 John F Kennedy Blvd Philadelphia PA 19103 Tel (215) 561-2555

SOLOMON, GERALD RAY, b. Uniontown, Pa., Feb. 26, 1942; B.A., U. Pitts., 1965; J.D., Temple U., 1968. Admitted to Pa. bar, 1968; asso. firm Margolis & Margolis, Uniontown, 1968-69; individual practice law, Uniontown, 1969-76; mem. firm Solomon & Davis, Uniontown, 1977—; asst. dist. atty., Fayette County, Pa., 1969-72, 1st. asst. dist. atty., 1974—; solicitor Fayette County Housing Authority, Uniontown, 1974—; solicitor, controller Fayette County, 1972—; solicitor Brough of Masontown, Pa., 1970—, Jefferson Twp., 1969—, German Twp., 1970—, Fayette County Assn. Retarded Children, 1973-75; mem. Pa. Bd. Exam. Pub. Accountants, 1972-75. Mem. Pres.'s Council Youth Opportunity, Washington, D.C., 1969; co-chmn. Call of Hope, Uniontown, 1970; regional chmn. Heart Fund, Fayette County, 1973-75. Mem. Am., Pa., Fayette County bar assns., Am., Pa. trial lawyers assns., Nat. Dist. Attys. Assn. Home: 511 N Water St Masontown PA 15461 Office: 99 E Main St Uniontown PA 15401 Tel (412) 437-2793

SOLOMON, JONATHAN, b. New Castle, Pa., Nov. 19, 1946; B.A. cum laude, Washington and Jefferson Coll., 1967; J.D., Northwestern U., 1970. Admitted to Pa. bar, 1970, U.S. Supreme Ct. bar, 1976; partner firm Solomon & Solomon, New Castle, 1970—; solicitor New Castle Area Sch. Dist., 1970—, Taylor Twp., 1973—, Wilmington Twp., 1975—, Little Beaver Twp., 1975—. Bd. dirs. New Castle Playhouse, 1972-74; pres. Lawrence County (Pa.) Vis. Nurses Assn., New Castle, 1975—. Mem. Pa., Lawrence County (sec.) bar assns. Home and Office: 421 E Moody Ave New Castle PA 16101 Tel (412) 654-9941

SOLOMON, MICHAEL BRUCE, b. Chgo., Nov. 8, 1945; B.A., U. Miami, 1967, J.D., 1970. Admitted to Fla. bar, 1970; asso. firm Theodore M. Trushin, Miami Beach, Fla., 1970—. Ombudsman, Dade County, Democratic and Republican nat. convs., 1972. Mem. Am. Trial Lawyers Assn., Phi Delta Phi. Recipient Am. Jurisprudence award in bus. assns., 1969. Home: 5775 Collins Ave Miami Beach FL 33140 Office: 420 Lincoln Rd Suite 600 Miami Beach FL 33139 Tel (305) 532-4801

SOLOMON, PHILIP F., b. Warsaw, Poland, Feb. 28, 1921; B.A., Bklyn. Coll., 1938; LL.B., St. John's U., Bklyn., 1943. Admitted to N.Y. bar, 1944; individual practice law, N.Y.C., 1944-51; sr. partner firm Solomon & Solomon, N.Y.C., 1951—; lectr. in field. Mem. Am. Acad. Matrimonial Lawyers (nat. pres. 1975—, pres. N.Y. State chpt. 1965-68, pres. emeritus 1969—), New York County Lawyers Assn. (chmn. family ct. com. 1968-75, gov.), N.Y. State (chmn. legis. com. sect. family law 1966-69), Am. (vice chmn. com. on membership sect. family law), Queens County (N.Y.) bar assns. Home: 99-12 65th Rd Forest Hills NY 11375 Office: 350 Fifth Ave New York City NY 10001 Tel (212) 695-0031

SOLOMON, RICHARD ALLAN, b. N.Y.C., July 29, 1917; A.B., Harvard U., 1939; LL.B., Yale U., 1942. Admitted to N.Y. bar 1942, D.C. bar 1969, U.S. Supreme Ct. bar, 1947; atty. Washington, 1942-58, asst. gen. counsel, 1951-58; chief litigation sect. Antitrust div. Dept. fo Justice, Washingotn, 1958-62; gen. counsel FPC, Washington, 1962-69; partner firm Wilner & Scheiner, Washington, 1969—. Mem. Am., Fed. (mem. exec. com. 1976—), D.C. bar assns., Yale Law Sch. Assn. of Washington (pres. 1960), Fed. Energy Bar Assn. (exec. com. 1976—). Recipient Tom Clark award 1964. Home: 6805 Delaware St Chevy Chase MD 20015 Office: 2021 L St NW Washington DC 20036 Tel (202) 293-7800

SOLOVAY, NORMAN, b. N.Y.C., Sept. 4, 1930; A.B., Cornell U., 1951; LL.B., Columbia, 1957. Admitted to N.Y. State bar, 1958; mem. firm Rasenman Goldmark Colin & Kaye; partner firm Holtzmann Wise & Shepard, N.Y.C., 1972—; law sec. to judge N.Y. Ct. Appeals, 1965-66. Mem. Assn. Bar City N.Y. (com. on adminstrv. law 1966-69), Am. Bar Assn. (chmn. housing and urban devel. com. 1971-72), Phi Alpha Delta. Editor: The Business Break-Up, 1973; (with Peter Ehrenhaft) Corporate Aspects of the Business Break-Up, 1974. Home: 28 Narrow Rocks Rd Westport CT 06880 Office: 30 Broad St 47th floor New York City NY 10004 Tel (212) 747-5500

SOLOVEITZIK, HAROLD B., b. Westerly, R.I., Sept. 29, 1913; B.S., U. R.I., 1935; LL.B., Boston U., 1938. Admitted to R.I. bar, 1938; now in individual practice law, Westerly; town solicitor Town of Richmond, 1947-54, Town of New Shoreham, 1961-68; atty. Shelter Harbor Fire Dist., 1948—, Weekapaug Fire Dist., 1950-75; appeal agt. SSS, 1948—. Mem. Washington County (pres. 1959-61), R.I. (pres. 1976-77), Am. bar assns., Assn. Trial Lawyers Am. Office: 2 Elm St Westerly RI 02891 Tel (401) 596-4358*

SOLSBERY, ALEX DEAN, b. San Saba, Tex., Aug. 28, 1921; LL.B., Baylor U., 1949, J.D., 1969. Admitted to Tex. bar, 1954, N.Mex. bar, 1959; individual practice law, Roswell, N.Mex., 1959—. Mem. N.Mex., Tex. bar assns. Office: PO Box 801 Roswell NM 88201 Tel (505) 622-0505

SOMERMEYER, HERBERT FREDERICK, b. Balaton, Minn., Nov. 27, 1928; B.S. in Elec. Engring., Iowa State U., 1950; LL.B. cum laude, William Mitchell Coll. Law, 1957. Admitted to Minn. bar, 1957, Colo. bar, 1972, U.S. Patent Office bar, 1958; asso. firm Carlsen & Carlsen, Mpls., 1957-59; mgr. patent dept. Univac, St. Paul, 1959-63; staff atty. Sperry Rand Corp., 1963-65; patent atty. Mueller & Aichele, Phoenix, 1965-69; patent atty. IBM Corp., Boulder, Colo., 1969-71, sr. patent atty., 1971-74, cons. patent atty., 1975—. Mem. Colo. bar assns., Am. Patent Law Assn., IEEE. Office: IBM Corp PO Box 1900 Boulder CO 89302 Tel (303) 447-5383

SOMMER, BERNARD, b. Bklyn., May 23, 1922; student Bklyn. Coll., 1939-41, Syracuse U., 1943-44; LL.B. cum laude, Bklyn. Law Sch., 1947. Admitted to N.Y. bar, 1947; asso. firm Cox & Calie, N.Y.C., 1947; partner firm Keyles & Sommer, Bklyn., 1948-61; sr. dep. Nassau County, N.Y., 1963-65; sr. partner firm Koeppel Sommer Lesnick & Martone and predecessors, Mineola, N.Y., 1966—; dir. dept. real estate Nassau County, N.Y., 1962. Pres. Munson Lawns Civic Assn., W. Hempstead, N.Y., 1951-54. Mem. N.Y. State (lectr.), Nassau County (lectr.), Suffolk County (lectr.), Am. bar assns., Columbia Soc. Real Estate Appraisers. Contbr. articles to legal publs. Home: 224 Peach Tree Dr East Norwich NY 11732 Office: 220 Old Country Rd Mineola NY 11501 Tel (516) 747-6300

SOMMER, GERALD IRA, b. N.Y.C., June 20, 1944; B.A. in Econs., Am. U., 1966; J.D., George Washington U., 1969. Admitted to D.C. and Md. bars, 1970; legal intern organizing dept. AFL-CIO, 1969-70; staff counsel Am. Fedn. Govt. Employees, 1970-73; legal asst. to internat. pres. Service Employees Internat. Union, Washington, 1973—. Mem. Am., D.C. bar assns. Home: 1205 Kathryn Rd Silver Spring MD 20904 Office: 2020 K St NW Washington DC 20006 Tel (202) 452-8750

SOMMER, MURRAY I., b. N.Y.C., Nov. 26, 1920; B.S., Coll. City N.Y., 1942; LL.B., Columbia, 1947. Admitted to N.Y. bar, 1948, U.S. Supreme Ct. bar, 1953; asso. firm Bogart & Lonergan, N.Y.C., 1948-56, Charles Gold, N.Y.C., 1957; partner firm Sommer & Sklar, N.Y.C., 1958—; adj. asst. prof. Bklyn. Coll. Pharmacy, 1969-72. Mem. N.Y. County Lawyers Assn. Office: 30 Vesey St New York City NY 10007 Tel (212) 962-2790

SOMMER, ROBERT GEORGE, b. N.Y.C., July 4, 1928; LL.B., U. Fla., 1950, J.D., 1967; grad. U.S. Army Command and Gen. Staff Coll., 1971. Admitted to Fla. bar, 1950, U.S. Supreme Ct. bar, 1963, U.S. Ct. Mil. Appeals, 1963; real property officer Bur. Land Mgmt., U.S. Dept. Interior, Ter. Alaska, 1953-55; partner firm Sommer, Frank & Weston, Miami, Fla., 1955-60; individual practice law, Miami, 1960—; capt. Delta Air Lines, Miami, 1960—. Col., aviation staff officer Office of Chief Army Res., Washington. Mem. Air Line Pilots Assn., Soc. Am. Mil. Engrs., Res. Officers Assn. U.S., U.S. Army Aviation Assn. Office: Box 786 Tamiami Sta Miami FL 33144 Tel (305) 264-7113

SOMMERFELD, ALAN EDWARD, b. Mpls., Jan. 8, 1947; B.A. in Govt., Mont. State U., 1970; J.D., U. Minn., 1973. Admitted to Mont. bar, 1973; officer JAGC, U.S. Army, Okinawa, Japan, 1974-76, chief mil. justice and claims, 1976, assigned Ft. Carson, Colo., 1977—. Recipient Kanshagyo citation Govt. of Japan. Office: Office Staff JAGC Fort Carson CO 80913 Tel (303) 579-5361

SOMMERS, JAMES RICHARD, b. Milw., Apr. 22, 1948; B.S., Met.E., Purdue U., 1970; J.D., U. Wis., 1973. Admitted to Wis. bar, 1973; asso. firm Hunter, Tikalsky & Steimel, Waukesha, Wis., 1973—. Bd. dirs. Waukesha Tng. Center, 1974—, Vis. Nurses Assn., 1977—. Mem. Waukesha County Bar Assn. (chmn. law for layman program 1974-76, chmn. fee arbitration com.), Tau Beta Pi. Home: 405 S Hartwell Ave Waukesha WI 53186 Office: 253 South St Waukesha WI 53186 Tel (414) 547-6211

SOMSEN, HENRY NORTHROP, b. New Ulm, Minn., Aug. 12, 1909; B.A., U. Minn., 1932, J.D., 1934. Admitted to Minn. bar, 1934; partner firm Somsen, Dempsey, Johnson & Somsen, New Ulm, 1934-40; partner firm Somsen & Dempsey, New Ulm, 1940-46; partner firm Somsen & Somsen, New Ulm, 1946-55; individual practice, New Ulm, 1955-64; partner Somsen & Dempsey, New Ulm, 1964-71; partner firm Somsen, Dempsey & Schade, New Ulm, 1971—. Trustee Minn. State Parks Found., 1967-77; bd. dirs. Minn. Council State Parks, 1956—, pres., 1974-75; pres. New Ulm Community Concert Assn., 1947—; bd. dirs. Union Hosp., 1959-77, Highland Homes, 1970—, New Ulm Meml. Found., 1958—; bd. dirs. New Ulm Industries, Inc., 1952—, pres., 1968—; bd. dirs. New Ulm Industries Found., 1953—, pres., 1968—; mem. City Charter Commn., 1940, 51, pres., 66. Mem. Am., Minn. State bar assns., Am. Judicature Soc., Am. Arbitration Assn. (panel arbitrators 1967—). Mem. bd. editors U. Minn. Law Review, 1932-33. Home: 29 Camelsback Rd New Ulm MN 56073 Office: State Bond Bldg New Ulm MN 56073 Tel (507) 354-2161

SONBERG, MICHAEL ROBERT, b. Bklyn., N.Y., Oct. 17, 1947; A.B., Queens Coll., 1968; J.D., Harvard, 1971. Admitted to N.Y. State bar, 1972, U.S. Ct. Appeals bar, 1975; asso. firm Weiss Rosenthal

Heller Schwartzman & Lazar, N.Y.C., 1971—. Mem. Am., N.Y. State bar assns., Assn. Bar City of N.Y. Home: 201 E 28 St New York City NY 10016 Office: 295 Madison Ave New York City NY 10017 Tel (212) 725-9200

SONDERICKER, WILLIAM F., b. N.Y.C., Sep. 14, 1924; B.S., N.Y. U., 1948; LL.B., Cath. U. Am., 1952. Admitted to N.Y. bar, 1953, U.S. Supreme Ct. bar, 1963; since practiced in N.Y.C., asso. firm Olwine, Connelly, Chase, O'Donnell & Weyher, and predecessor firm, 1952-62, partner, 1962—. Mem. Am. Arbitration Assn. (arbitrator), Assn. Bar City N.Y., N.Y. State Bar Assn., Am. Inst. Mining, Metall. and Petroleum Engrs. Author: The Law Is On Your Side, 1957; contbr. articles in fields to profl. jours. Home: 850 Park Ave New York City NY 10021 Office: 299 Park Ave New York City NY 10017 Tel (212) 688-0400

SONNENSCHEIN, HUGO, b. Chgo., Feb. 22, 1917; B.A., Lake Forest Coll., 1944; LL.B., U. Va., 1941, J.D., 1944; LL.M., John Marshall Coll. Law, 1945. Admitted to Ill. bar, 1942; asso. firm Wilson and McIlvaine, Chgo., 1944-45, individual practice law, Chgo., 1946-54; partner firm Martin, Craig, Chester and Sonnenschein, Chgo., 1954—; asst. U.S. atty., Chgo., 1945-46; asst. to chief justice Municipal Ct. of Chgo., 1956-57; editor Chgo. Bar Record, 1950-66. Pres., trustee Library of Internat. Relations, 1966-69; trustee Lake Forest Coll., 1969—; pres., trustee Modern Poetry Assn., 1976—. Mem. Am., Ill., Chgo. bar assns., Judge Advocates Assn., Selden Soc., Assn. Art Historians, Phi Beta Kappa, Delta Upsilon, Delta Sigma Rho. Asso. editor Fed. Bar Jour., 1945-47, Am. Bankruptcy Review, 1946-49. Home: 809 Lincoln Ave Winnetka IL 60093 Office: 115 S La Salle St Chicago IL 60603 Tel (312) 368-9700

SORG, GERARD REGIS, b. St. Marys, Pa., Apr. 6, 1947; B.A. in Econs., St. Vincent Coll., 1969; J.D., Duquesne U., 1972. Admitted to Pa. bar, 1972; pub. defender Elk County (Pa.), 1974-75; partner firm Trambley & Sorg, St. Marys, 1975—; mental health rev. officer Elk, Cameron, Mckean and Potter counties, 1976—. Adviser, Jr. Achievement, St. Marys, 1975. Mem. Pa. Bar Assn. Home: 436 Charles St Saint Marys PA 15857 Office: 9 Railroad St Saint Marys PA 15857 Tel (814) 781-3412

SORG, HERBERT PETER, b. St. Marys, Pa., Dec. 19, 1911; student St. Vincent Coll., 1927-31; LL.B., Duquesne U., 1935. Admitted to Pa. bar, 1935; practiced in St. Mary's, Pa., 1935-55; judge U.S. Dist. Ct. for Pa., Pitts., 1955—, now sr. judge. Mem. Pa. Ho. of Reps., 1940-53, majority whip, 1945-47, majority leader, 1947, speaker, 1947-53. Mem. Pa. Bar Assn., Am. Judicature Soc. Home: 110 Crescent Dr Pittsburgh PA 15228 Office: Room 803 US Courthouse Pittsburgh PA 15219*

SORGENFREI, ROBERT L., b. Elkhart Twp., Ind., Sept. 25, 1919; LL.B., Ind. U., Indpls., 1953. Admitted to Ind. bar, 1953, Calif. bar, 1963; trial lawyer VA, Indpls., 1953-57; estate tax examiner, IRS, Indpls., 1957-62; trust counsel Security Pacific Nat. Bank, Los Angeles, 1962—; lectr. U. So. Calif., 1973. Mem. Los Angeles County, Am. bar assns., Am. Bankers Assn. Home: 2140 El Molino Pl San Marino CA 91108 Office: 333 S Hope St Los Angeles CA 90051 Tel (213) 613-7272

SORIANO, NICHOLAS M., b. White Plains, N.Y., Dec. 11, 1942; A.B., Boston Coll., 1964; LL.D., Fordham U., 1967. Admitted to N.Y. bar, 1967; mem. joint legis. com. Banking Law N.Y.C. and Albany, 1967-70; individual practice law, Armonk, N.Y., 1967-72, White Plains, N.Y., 1972—; mem. Ad Hoc Adv. Group on Indemnification Ins., 1968. Mem. N.Y., Westchester County, No. Westchester bar assns., N.Y. County Lawyers Assn. Author: Handling Your House Closing: A Practical Guide, 1974. Office: 2 Bryant Ave White Plains NY 10605 Tel (914) WH 9-9040

SORKIN, LAURENCE TRUMAN, b. Bklyn., Oct. 20, 1942; A.B., Brown U., 1964; LL.B., Yale, 1967; LL.M. (Fulbright scholar 1967-68), London Sch. Econs. and Polit. Sci., 1968. Admitted to N.Y. State bar, 1968, D.C. bar, 1972; asso. firm Cahill, Gordon & Reindel, N.Y.C., 1969-75, partner, 1975—; law clk. Judge J. Joseph Smith, U.S. Ct. Appeals, 2d Circuit, 1968-69. Mem. Assn. Bar City N.Y. (com. trade regulation 1974—), Phi Beta Kappa. Home: 101 Central Park W New York City NY 10023 Office: 80 Pine St New York City NY 10005 Tel (212) 825-0100

SORKIN, NATHANIEL, b. N.Y.C., Jan. 10, 1912; LL.B. cum laude, St. John's U., 1935. Admitted to N.Y. bar, 1936; individual practice law, N.Y.C., 1936-41, 1951-55; law sec. to justice N.Y.C. Municipal Ct., 1941-46; law asst. to commr. investigation, N.Y.C., 1946-47; dep. commr. investigation, 1947-51; commr. Temporary City Housing Rent Comm., N.Y.C., 1948-50; justice N.Y.C. Municipal Ct., 1955-62; judge N.Y.C. Civil Ct., 1962—; acting justice N.Y. State Supreme Ct., N.Y.C., 1971, 1975; referee N.Y.C. Small Claims Ct., 1954-55; mem. Dept. Com. Ct. Adminstrn., 1st dept., N.Y.C., 1974—. Mem., Mayor's Adv. Com. Handicapped, N.Y.C., 1968-73; exec. bd. Greater N.Y. councils Boy Scouts Am., chmn. Scouting for Handicapped, N.Y.C.; mem. N.Y. bd. Anti-Defamation League, N.Y.C. Mem. Am., N.Y., N.Y.C. bar assns., N.Y. County Lawyers Assn., Am. Judicature Soc. Recipient Key award Philonomic Council, 1935, award, U.S. Treasury, 1945.

SORKIN, SAUL, b. N.Y.C., June 24, 1925; A.B., Bklyn. Coll., 1948; J.D., Harvard, 1951. Admitted to N.Y. State bar, 9951, U.S. Supreme Ct. bar, 1961; dep. asst. Atty. Gen., N.Y., 1951-54; mem. firm Newman, Aronson & Neumann, N.Y.C., 1954-55; individual practice law, N.Y.C., 1955-65, 72—; partner firm Sorkin & Berger, N.Y.C., 1965-72; hearing officer Blue Cross and hosps., 1972—. Mem. N.Y. State Bar Assn. (mem. sub-com. on marine ins.), Assn. of Bar of City of N.Y. (mem. com. on transp.), Queens County Bar Assn., Maritime Law Assn. of U.S. Author: How to Recover for Loss or Damage to Goods in Transit, 1976; contbr. articles to profl. jours. Home: 5 Orchard Rd Great Neck NY 11021 Office: 225 W 34th St New York City NY 10001 Tel (212) 695-2660

SORLING, CARL AXEL, b. Moline, Ill., Sept. 13, 1896; LL.B., U. Mich., 1921, J.D., 1922. Admitted to Ill. bar, 1922; partner firm Sorling, Northrup, Hanna, Cullen and Cochran, Springfield, Ill. Mem. Am., Ill. State, Chgo., Sangamon County bar assns. Home: 1711 Illini Rd Springfield IL 62704 Office: 820 Illinois Bldg Springfield IL 62701 Tel (217) 544-1144

SOSLAND, KARL Z., b. Springfield, Mass., Apr. 3, 1933; B.A., U. Conn., 1955; LL.B., Columbia, 1959. Admitted to N.J. bar, 1960; asso. firm Robert Gruen, Hackensack, N.J., 1960-64; partner firm Gruen & Sosland, Hackensack, 1964-65; partner firm Scangarella & Sosland, Pompton Plains, N.J., 1965-70; individual practice law, Pompton Plains, 1970—; atty. bd. adjustment City of Norwood, N.J., 1965-74; municipal atty. Pequannock Twp., N.J., 1971—; judge Municipal Ct. of Pompton Lakes, 1976—. Mem. Fairlawn (N.J.) Bd. Edn., 1964-66; pres. Kinnelon, N.J. Bd. Edn., 1971. Mem. Am., N.J., Morris County bar assns. Office: 434 Blvd at Route 23 Pompton Plains NJ 07444 Tel (201) 839-6770

SOSNOV, AMY WIENER, b. Atlantic City, Aug. 9, 1943; B.A., Temple U., 1970; J.D., Villanova U., 1973. Admitted to Pa. bar, 1973; asso. firm Sosnov & Sosnov, Norristown, Pa., 1973-74, partner, 1974—; founder Consumer Edn. Project, 1974, Woman's Legal Resource Group, 1974; pres. Neighborhood Meals on Wheels, 1975—. Mem. Nat. Assn. Women Lawyers, Am. Bar Assn. Home: 251 W DeKalb Pike King of Prussia PA 19406 Office: 540 Swede St Norristown PA 19401 Tel (215) 279-8700

SOSNOV, STEVEN ROBERT, b. Phila., June 10, 1942; B.S., Temple U., 1963; J.D., N.Y. U., 1966. Admitted to N.Y. State bar, 1966, D.C. bar, 1967, Pa. bar, 1970; trial atty. civil div. customs sect. U.S. Dept. Justice, N.Y.C., 1966-69; asst. atty. gen. Pa. Dept. Justice, Phila., 1971-72; sr. partner firm Sosnov & Sosnov, Norristown, Pa., 1972—. Mem. Am. Arbitration Assn. (arbitrator), Am., Fed., Pa., Montgomery, Inter-Am. bar assns., Assn. Customs Bar. Office: 540 Swede St Norristown PA 19401 Tel (215) 279-8700

SOULE, LEWIS FRANKLIN, b. Lawrence, Mass., Aug. 11, 1924; B.A., Harvard, 1949, LL.B., 1953. Admitted to Mass. bar, 1953, N.H. bar, 1955; mem. legal staff Liberty Mut. Ins. Co., Boston, 1953-55; partner firm Sayer & Soule, Salem, N.H., 1955-57, Devine & Millimet, Manchester, N.H., 1957-50; individual practice law, Salem, from 1959; partner firm Soule, Leslie & Bronstein, Salem, 1959—; dir. Rockingham County Trust Co., Salem Broadcasting Co., Inc. (WVNH). Selectman City of Salem, 1958-61; del. N.H. Constnl. Conv., 1964; alt. del. Republican Nat. Conv., 1964. Mem. Am., N.H., Rockingham County (pres. 1969) bar assns. Home: 127 Main St Salem NH 03079 Office: 88 N Broadway Salem NH 03079 Tel (603) 898-9776

SOUTEE, STEPHEN RICHARD, b. Marionville, Mo., Mar. 3, 1947; B.S., Southwest Mo. State U., 1969; J.D., Oklahoma City U., 1973. Admitted to Mo. bar, 1973; individual practice law, Crane, Mo. 1973—. Mem. Am. Trial Lawyers Assn., Am., Mo., 39th Jud. Circuit bar assns. Home: 23 Washington St Marionville MO 65705 Office: PO Box L Marionville MO 65705 Tel (417) 463-7117

SOUTER, DAVID HACKETT, b. Melrose, Mass., Sept. 17, 1939; A.B., Harvard, 1961, LL.B., 1966; postgrad. (Rhodes scholar) Oxford U., 1963. Admitted to N.H. bar, 1966, U.S. Supreme Ct. bar, 1970; asso. firm Orr & Reno, Concord, 1966-68; asst. atty. gen. N.H., Concord, 1968-71, dep. atty. gen., 1971-76, atty. gen., 1976—. Trustee, Concord Hosp., N.H. Hist. Soc. Mem. N.H. Bar Assn., Phi Beta Kappa. Office: State House Annex Concord NH 03301 Tel (603) 271-3655

SOUTHARD, RICHARD CHARLES, b. Lockport, N.Y., Nov. 16, 1932; A.B., Syracuse U., 1954; J.D., Cornell U., 1957. Admitted to N.Y. State bar, 1957; U.S. Supreme Ct. bar, 1968; asso. firm Fogle, Andrews and Pusateri, Lockport, 1957; served as capt. JAG Dept., USAF, 1958-60; asso. firm Chester & Grove, Lockport, 1961; partner firm Harris and Southard, Lockport, 1962—; asst. county atty. Niagara County (N.Y.), 1962, county atty., 1964-65; atty. Town of Wilson, 1962—; corp. counsel, Lockport, 1976—; counsel Niagara County Water Dist., 1974—. Chmn. Eastern Niagara County chpt. ARC, 1965-66, fund chmn., N.Y., 1966, fund chmn. Buffalo div., 1976—, mem. Nat. Conv. Resolutions Com., 1967, nat. conv. orgn. com., 1977. Mem. Am., Niagara County, Lockport City (pres. chmn. grievance com.) bar assns., Nat. Inst. Municipal Law Officers. Recipient Distinguished Service award Lockport Jaycees, 1966. Home: 827 Willow St Lockport NY 14094 Office: 300 Bewley Bldg Lockport NY 14094 Tel (716) 433-6794

SOUTHGATE, JAMES CHANDLER, b. Syracuse, N.Y., Mar. 5, 1944; B.A., N.Y. U., 1968, J.D., 1971. Admitted to N.Y. bar, 1972; asso. firm Cravath, Swaine & Moore, N.Y.C., 1971—. Mem. Am., N.Y. State bar assns. Office: 1 Chase Manhattan Plaza 57th Floor New York City NY 10005 Tel (212) 422-3000

SOUTTER, THOMAS DOUGLAS, b. N.Y.C., Nov. 1, 1934; B.A., U. Va., 1955, LL.B., 1962. Admitted to N.Y. bar, 1963, R.I. bar, 1969; atty. firm Breed Abbott & Morgan, N.Y.C., 1962-68, with Textron Inc., Providence, 1968—, v.p., gen. counsel, 1973—. Mem. Am., Internat., R.I. bar assns. Office: 40 Westminster St Providence RI 02903 Tel (401) 421-2800

SOVEREIGN, KENNETH LESTER, b. Sartell, Minn., Feb. 20, 1919; B.S., U. Minn., 1942, postgrad., 1946-47; J.D., William Mitchell Coll. Law, 1955; Advanced Mgmt. Program, Harvard, 1964. Admitted to Minn. bar, 1955; personnel dir., safety dir. Waldorf Paper Products Co., St. Paul, 1953-60, corp. indsl. relations dir. Hoerner Waldorf Corp., 1966-68, v.p. indsl. relations, 1968-70, v.p. indsl. relations, sr. atty., 1971-73, v.p., sr. atty., 1973—; apprenticeship tng. rep. State of Minn., 1947-49, asst. labor conciliator, 1949-53, mem. indsl relations exec. council, occupational safety and health rev. bd., mem. indsl. relations adv. council U. Minn.; lectr. U. Minn., St. Thomas Coll. Past chmn. employees div. United Fund, 1958, 75; bd. dirs. Tri-Lakes Assn., 1955—; past chmn. E. Oakdale Zoning Com., 1960-64; active St. Paul Employer's Assn., 1968-73, pres., 1973-75; chmn. charter commn., Lake Elmo, 1974—. Mem. Am., Minn. (labor law sec., environ. law sec.) assns., St. Paul Personnel Dirs., Minn. Assn. Commerce and Industry (occupational safety com.). Recipient Bolton award Paper Industry, 1965; fellow Soc. for Advancement Mgmt., 1971; contbr. articles to jours. Home: 4415 Olson Lake Trail N Lake Elmo MN 55042 Office: Box 3260 St Paul MN 55165 Tel (612) 641-4660

SOVERN, MICHAEL IRA, b. N.Y.C., Dec. 1, 1931; A.B. summa cum laude, Columbia, 1953, LL.B., 1955. Admitted to N.Y. State bar, 1956, U.S. Supreme Ct. bar, 1973, U.S. 2d Circuit Ct. Appeals bar, 1974; asst. prof. law U. Minn., 1955-56, asso. prof., 1956-58; vis. asst. prof. law Columbia, 1957-58, asso. prof., 1958-60, prof., 1960—, dean faculty law, 1970—; spl. counsel to Gov. N.J., 1974—; cons., mediator in field. Fellow AAAS; mem. Am. Law Inst., Am. Bar Assn., Assn. Bar City N.Y. (library com.), N.Y. State Bar Assn. (com. on legal edn. and admission to bar), Soc. Profls. in Dispute Resolution, Nat. Acad. Arbitrators. Author-moderator: Due Process for the Accused, WNBC, N.Y.C., 1965-66; author: Legal Restraints on Discrimination in Employment, 1966; co-author: Cases and Materials on Law and Poverty, 1973; contbr. articles to law reviews.

SOWALD, BEATRICE KRONICK, b. Amsterdam, N.Y., May 29, 1927; B.A., Ohio State U., 1948, J.D., 1966. Admitted to Ohio bar, 1966; staff atty. Columbus (Ohio) Legal Aid and Defender Soc., 1967—, supervising atty. family unit, 1972—. Mem. Gov.'s Task Force on Credit for Women, 1974-75. Mem. Ohio, Columbus (family law com.) bar assns., Women Lawyers of Frankli County. Home: 125 Eastmoor Blvd Columbus OH 43209 Office: 241 S High St Columbus OH 43215 Tel (614) 224-8374

SOYBEL, ARTHUR, b. N.Y.C., June 16, 1925; B.A. in Polit. Sci., U. N.C. at Chapel Hill, 1947; Mus.B., Manhattan Sch. Music, 1950; J.D., N.Y. Law Sch., 1954. Admitted to N.Y. bar, 1955; partner firm Nearing, Soybel & Prigal, N.Y.C., 1968—; gen. counsel Found. for Religion and Mental Health, Inc., Briarcliff Manor, N.Y., 1971—. Mem. Assn. Bar City N.Y., N.Y. State Bar Assn. Office: 36 W 44th St New York City NY 10036 Tel (212) 687-5544

SPACE, THEODORE MAXWELL, b. Binghamton, N.Y., Apr. 3, 1938; A.B., Harvard, 1960; LL.B., Yale, 1966. Admitted to Conn. bar, 1966, U.S. Supreme Ct., 1969; asso. firm Shipman & Goodwin, Hartford, Conn., 1966-71, partner, 1971—. Mem. Bloomfield (Conn.) Bd. Edn., 1973-75, chmn., 1975—; mem. Bloomfield Human Relations Commn., 1973-75; dir. Citizens' Scholarship Found. Bloomfield, 1973—; corporator Hartford Pub. Library; mem. Bloomfield Democratic Town Com., 1976—. Mem. Am., Conn., Hartford County bar assns. Home: 59 Prospect St Bloomfield CT 06002 Office: 799 Main St Hartford CT 06103 Tel (203) 549-4770

SPAETH, EDMUND BENJAMIN, JR., b. Washington, June 10, 1920; A.B. magna cum laude, Harvard, 1942, LL.B., 1948. Admitted to Pa. bar, 1949; judge Ct. of Common Pleas, Phila., 1964-73, Superior Ct. of Pa., 1973—; lectr. law of evidence U. Pa. Law Sch. Chmn. bd. trustees Bryn Mawr Coll., bd. dirs. Diagnostic and Rehab. Center. Mem. Am., Pa., Phila. bar assns., Am. Law Inst., Am. Judicature Soc., Order of Coif, Phi Beta Kappa. Home: 635 Westview St Philadelphia PA 19119 Office: Room 558 City Hall Philadelphia PA 19107 Tel (215) 686-7797

SPAHR, KENNETH GORDON, b. Akron, Ohio, Oct. 18, 1939; B.A., Kent State U., 1970; J.D., U. Akron, 1974. Admitted to Ohio bar, 1974; staff atty. to Sumit County Legal Defender, Akron, 1973-75; legal adviser to Cuyahoga Falls (Ohio) Police, 1975-77, also individual practice law, Akron, 1974—; instr. criminal justice studies Kent State U., also Lakeland Community Coll., 1970-72; instr. Summit County Sheriff's Acad. Mem. Am., Ohio, Akron bar assns., Internat. Assn. Chiefs of Police, Barristers Club Cuyahoga Falls, Assn. Trial Lawyers Am. Home: 600 Yager Rd Clinton OH 44216 Office: 3232 S Main St Akron OH 44319 Tel (216) 644-5341

SPAIN, DONALD FREDRICK, b. Warren, Ohio, Aug. 27, 1945; B.S., Ohio State U., 1968; J.D., U. Ky., 1971. Admitted to Fla. bar, 1971; asst. state atty. major crimes div. Dade County (Fla.), 1972-77; mem. firm Pollack, Rosenfeld, Spain & Cullen, Miami, Fla., 1977—. Mem. Fla. Bar Assn. Home: 4600 San Anaro Dr Coral Gables FL 33146 Tel (305) 642-9996

SPAIN, JOHN RICHARD, b. Warren, Ohio, Oct. 24, 1919; J.D., Youngstown State U., 1954. Admitted to Ohio bar, 1954; partner firm Spain & Spain, Warren, 1954-73, v.p., 1973—; pros. atty. City of Warren, 1955-57; acting judge Warren Municipal Ct., 1971-76. Mem. Comml. Law League, Ohio, Trumbull County (pres. 1975-76) bar assns. Home: 380 Quarry Ln Warren OH 44483 Office: 137 E Market St Warren OH 44482 Tel (216) 399-7557

SPAK, MICHAEL IRWIN, b. Chgo., Dec. 20, 1936; B.S., DePaul U., 1958, J.D., 1961; LL.M., Northwestern U., 1962. Admitted to Ill., Mich. bars, 1961, Mo. bar, 1962; prof. law DePaul U., 1969-74, Chgo.-Kent Coll. Law, 1974—; staff judge adv. U.S. Army, 1963-69; profl. reporter Uniform Comml. Code Com., Ill. Jud. Conf. Mem. Am., Ill., Chgo., St. Louis, Fed. bar assns., State Bar Mich., Judge Advs. Assn. Contbr. articles in field to profl. jours. Home: 1143 N Smith Rd Palatine IL 60067 Office: 77 S Wacker Dr Chicago IL 60606

SPALDING, FRANCIS ODIORNE, b. Chgo., July 31, 1929; B.A., Yale, 1950; J.D., Northwestern U., 1964. Admitted to Ill. bar, 1964; asso. firm Isham, Lincoln & Beale, Chgo., 1964-65; asst. prof., asst. dean Northwestern U., 1965-68, asso. prof. law, 1968-71, prof. law, 1971—, asso. dean, 1972—; dir. Legal Assistance Found. Chgo., 1972-76. Mem. Am. Law Inst., Chgo. Council Lawyers, Am., Ill. State, Chgo. bar assns. Contbr. articles to legal jours. Home: 1000 N State St Chicago IL 60610 Office: 357 E Chicago Ave Chicago IL 60611 Tel (312) 649-8440

SPANGLER, JAMES C., b. Chgo., Nov. 11, 1924; Ph.B., Marquette U., 1946, LL.B. (now J.D.), 1949. Admitted to Wis. bar, 1949, Ill. bar, 1950; asso. firm Geary & Stagman, Chgo., 1949-53; spl. asst. to States Atty. of Cook County (Ill.), 1953-56; master in chancery Circuit Ct. of Cook County, 1954-66; spl. asst. atty. gen. State of Ill., 1966-67; partner firm Kennery, Golan, Morris, Spangler & Greenberg, Chgo., 1968—; Mem. Bd. Appeals of Cook County, 1956-66. Mem. Am., Wis., Ill., Chgo. bar assns., Ill. Trial Lawyers Assn. Home: 914 Bonnie Brae St River Forest IL 60305 Office: 120 S LaSalle St Chicago IL 60603 Tel (312) 263-2300

SPANN, HANS RUDOLPH, b. Berlin, May 6, 1901; came to U.S., 1904, naturalized, 1909; LL.B., St. Johns Coll., 1930; LL.M., St. Johns U., 1935. Admitted to N.Y. State bar, 1936; real estate broker, 1926-27; purchase dir. N.Y.C. Bd. Edn., 1956-63, dep. supt. sch. supplies, 1963-68; asso. firm Willing & Reid, Mt. Vernon, N.Y., 1968—. Mem. Fairlawn (N.J.) Borough Youth Council, 1942; v.p. Fairlawn Elementary Sch. PTA, 1939; pres. Fairlawn Vol. Assn. Fire Co., 1938-39. Home: 160 S Middletown Rd Pearl River NY 10965 Office: Chemical Bank Bldg 22 West 1st St Mount Vernon NY 10550 Tel (914) 664-3500

SPANN, ROBERT FRANK, b. Nashville, Jan. 8, 1932; B.S., George Peabody Coll., 1955; J.D., YMCA Law Sch., 1966. Admitted to Tenn. bar, 1967; individual practice law, Nashville, 1969—. Mem. Tenn., Nashville bar assns. Home: 436 Rolling Mill Rd Old Hickory TN 37138 Office: 325 Plus Park Blvd Nashville TN 37217 Tel (615) 244-3601

SPANN, WILLIAM BOWMAN, b. Savannah, Ga., June 10, 1912; A.B., Emory U., 1932, LL.D., 1973; LL.B., Harvard, 1935. Admitted to Ga. bar, 1935, U.S. Supreme Ct. bar, 1960; practice law, Atlanta, 1935—; asso. firm Alston, Foster, Moise & Sibley, 1935-41; partner firm Alston, Miller & Gaines, and predecessors, 1942—; prof. Woodrow Wilson Coll. Law, 1947—; chmn. adv. bd. Fulton County Juvenile Ct., 1953-63; dir., trustee Pres.'s Lawyers Com. Civil Rights Under Law, 1963—; commr., mem. exec. com. Uniform State Laws, 1965—; dir. Atlanta Legal Aid Soc.; trustee Atlanta Lawyers Found. Trustee Loridans Found. Fellow Am. Bar Found., Am. Coll. Trial Lawyers; mem. Internat., Inter-Am., Fed., Am. (gov. 1961-64, mem. ho. of dels. 1954—, chmn. ho. of dels. 1970-72, life mem., nat. pres. 1977—), Ga., Atlanta bar assns., Am. Judicature Soc., Am. Law Inst.,

Atlanta Lawyers Club (past pres.), Phi Beta Kappa, Tau Kappa Alpha, Delta Tau Delta. Mem. editorial bd. Am. Bar Jour., 1976—. Home: 3415 Habersham Rd NW Atlanta GA 30305 Office: Citizens and Southern National Bank Bldg Atlanta GA 30303 Tel (404) 588-0300

SPANNAUS, WARREN RICHARD, b. St. Paul, Dec. 5, 1930; B.B.A., U. Minn., 1958, J.D., 1963. Admitted to Minn. bar, 1963; spl. asst. atty. gen. State of Minn., 1963-65; mem. staff U.S. Sen. Walter F. Mondale of Minn., 1965-66, campaign dir. Sen. Mondale, 1966; chmn. Democratic-Farmer-Labor Party of Minn., 1967-69; practiced law, Mpls., 1969-71; atty. gen. State of Minn., St. Paul, 1971—. Bd. dirs. United Cerebral Palsy of Greater St. Paul Inc., Sch. for Social Devel., Mpls. Mem. Am., Minn., Hennepin County, Ramsey County bar assns., Nat. Assn. Attys. Gen., Midwest Assn. Attys. Gen. (past chmn.), Am. Judicature Soc. Home: 2619 Robbins St Minneapolis MN 55410 Office: 102 State Capitol Saint Paul MN 55155

SPARGER, AUDREY YVONNE, b. Shawnee, Okla., Oct. 27, 1930; B.S., Southwestern Mo. U., 1953; postgrad. Georgetown U., 1955-58; J.D., Okla. U. of Law, 1959. Admitted to Okla. bar, 1959; practiced in Oklahoma City, 1960-65; asst. atty. gen. State of Okla., 1971-73; judge Okla. Indsl. Ct., Oklahoma City, 1973—; asso. prof. law Oklahoma City U., 1976—. Mem. Internat. Assn. Accident Bds. and Commns. (pres. Western region 1974-75). Recipient award Hospitality Club, 1974. Home: 1716 Deason Dr Edmond OK 73034 Office: PO Box 53483 Oklahoma City OK 73105 Tel (405) 521-3661

SPARGER, KEVIN WAYNE, b. Lafayette, Ind., Mar. 5, 1948; B.S., Ind. U., 1970, J.D., 1973. Admitted to Ind. bar, 1973, Ga. bar, 1974; asso. firm Oliver & Duckworth, Jonesboro, Ga., 1973-76; partner firm Oliver, Duckworth, & Sparger, Jonesboro, Ga., 1977—. Mem. Ind., Ga., Clayton County bar assns., Ind., Ga. real estate assns. Home: 3190 Rhonda Dr Jonesboro GA 30236 Office: 146 N McDonough St Jonesboro GA 30237

SPARGO, THOMAS JAMES, b. Rome, N.Y., Apr. 27, 1943; A.B., St. Bernard's Sem., 1965; J.D., Syracuse Law Sch., 1971. Admitted to N.Y. bar, 1972; asso. firm Koblenz and Koblenz, Albany, N.Y., 1972—; law asst. Appellate Div. 3rd dept., 1971-72; N.Y. State Council Retail Merchants, 1972-73; ct. attendant to adminstrv. judge to 3rd Jud. Dist., 1975; counsel to N.Y. Republican State Com., 1973—; dir. Spargo Wire Co., 1972. Asst. town atty. Town of Guilderland, N.Y., 1973; pres. Friends Guilderland Free Library. Mem. Guilderland C. of C. (pres.). Contbr. article to legal jour. Home: 8 Hiawatha Dr Guilderland NY 12084 Office: 90 State St Albany NY 12207 Tel (518) 462-4242

SPARKS, GALEN M., b. Dallas, Nov. 14, 1939; A.B. in Polit. Sci. and History, Vanderbilt U., 1962; J.D., So. Meth. U., 1968. Admitted to Tex. bar, 1968; asst. city atty. City of Dallas, 1968—. Mem. Tex., Dallas Bars, Air Pollution Control Assn., Nat. Mil. Intelligence Assn., Assn. U.S. Army, Phi Alpha Delta. Office: 504 Municipal Bldg Dallas TX 75201 Tel (214) 748-9711 Ext 294

SPARKS, GUY, b. Holt, Ala., Aug. 10, 1927; A.B., U. Ala., 1948, LL.B., J.D., 1950. Admitted to Ala. bar, 1950, U.S. Supreme Ct. bar, 1960; individual practice law, Anniston, Ala., 1950—; spl. asst. atty. gen. State of Ala., 1957-63; chief counsel Ala. Revenue Dept., Montgomery, 1959-61; commr. revenue State of Ala., 1961-63. Vice pres. Ala. Edn. Authority, 1961-63; mem. Ala. Planning and Indsl. Devel. Bd., 1961-63; mem. Ala. Pub. Sch. Corp., 1961-63. Mem. Am., Ala., Calhoun County bar assns. Recipient 75th Anniversary Distinguished Service award Ala. State Council of Machinists, 1963. Office: 409 Commercial Bank Bldg Anniston AL 36201 Tel (205) 237-5711

SPARKS, JACK, b. Austin, Tex., Aug. 22, 1911; B.B.A., U. Tex., 1932; LL.B., 1938. Admitted to Tex. bar, 1938, U.S. Supreme Ct. bar, 1972; atty. Gen. Land Office, Tex., Austin, 1940-42; judge Travis County, Tex., 1946-48; individual practice law, Austin, 1948-67; asst. atty. gen., Tex., 1967—. Mem. Tex., Travis County bar assns., Tex. Bar Found., Tex. Assn. Def. Lawyers. Home: 2602 Oakdale Ct Austin TX 78703 Office: Supreme Court Building Austin TX 78711 Tel (512) 475-3131

SPARKS, JAMES DILLING, b. Monroe, La., June 6, 1910; LL.B., Washington and Lee U., 1932, J.D., 1965. Admitted to Va. bar, 1932, La. bar, 1933. Individual practice law 1933—; served to lt. comdr. USNR, 1941-45; mem. La. State Senate, 1952-60. Mem. Am., La., Monroe, 4th Dist. (pres. 1948) bar assns., Monroe Navy League (pres. 1973-74), Bayou Desiard Country Club. Home: 2104 Island Dr Monroe LA 71201 Office: 1401 Royal Ave Monroe LA 71201 Tel (318) 388-1440

SPARKS, JAMES ROBERT, b. Greenville, Ga., May 25, 1918; A.B. cum laude, Mercer U., 1941, J.D., 1947. Admitted to Ga. bar, 1946, U.S. Supreme Ct. bar, 1958; individual practice law, Greenville, 1947-54; asst. U.S. atty. No. Dist. Ga., 1954-63, asst. dist. atty. Atlanta Jud. Circuit, 1963-69, atty. in charge Organized Crime Strike Force, U.S. Dept. Justice, Atlanta, 1969-75; asst. dir. Pros. Atty. Council Ga., 1975—; col. JAGC, USAR. Pres. Greenville Civitan Club; chmn. Community Chest and ARC; scoutmaster Boy Scouts Am., 1950-52. Mem. Ga., Atlanta, Fed., Am. bar assns., Ga. Peace Officers Assn., Nat. Dist. Attys. Assn., Ft. McPherson Officers Club, Atlanta Lawyers Club. Recipient award appreciation Ga. Police Acad.; author: Search and Seizure Manual for Police Officers, 1964; Court Authorized Wiretapping, 1976. Home: 2479 Peachtree Rd NE Apt 715 Atlanta GA 30305 Office: Suite 380 GAE Bldg 3951 Snapfinger Pkwy Decatur GA 30035 Tel (404) 289-6278

SPARKS, JOHN O., b. Woodward, Okla., Apr. 7, 1939; B.A., U. Okla., 1961, J.D., 1966. Admitted to Okla. bar, 1966; asst. dist. atty. Woodward County (Okla.), Woodward, 1967-68; asst. dist. atty. Oklahoma County, Oklahoma City, 1968-69; asst. U.S. atty. Western Dist. Okla., Oklahoma City, 1969-70; mem. firm Boatman, Rizley & Sparks, Woodward, 1970-74, firm Rizley, Sparks & Fetzer, Woodward, 1975, firm Rizley & Sparks, Woodward, 1976; individual practice law, Woodward, 1977—. Chmn. Woodward County Republicans, 1972-74. Mem. Am., Oklahoma County, Woodward County bar assns., Phi Alpha Delta. Home: 3611 Cedar Ridge Ln Woodward OK 73801 Office: PO Box 968 Woodward OK 73801 Tel (405) 256-8647

SPARKS, MEREDITH PLEASANT, b. Palestine, Ill., Dec. 9, 1905; A.B. with distinction, Ind. U., 1927, M.A., 1928; Ph.D., U. Ill., 1936; LL.B., J.D., Rutgers U., 1958. Tchr. high sch. chemistry, Rochester, Ind., 1928-29; with patent dept. E.I. duPont de Nemours & Co., Niagara Falls, N.Y., 1929-34; with Northan Warren, N.Y.C., 1939, Am. Cyanamid, Bound Brook, N.J., 1941-45; admitted to Fla. bar, 1958, Ct. Customs and Patent Appeals, 1965, U.S. Supreme Ct. bar, 1973; individual practice law, Westfield, N.J., 1958-68, Miami, Fla., 1966—. Mem. nat. bd. Med. Coll. Pa., 1977. Mem. Am., Dade County, Internat. bar assns., Nat. Assn. Women Lawyers (SE regional dir. 1973—), AAUW (legis. chmn. Miami br. 1973-75), N.J. Internat. Patent and Trademark Assn., Am. Chem. Soc. Author: Sodium, 1934; contbr. articles to Am. Chem. Soc. Jour.; patentee in field of chemistry. Home: 5129 Granada Blvd Coral Gables FL 33146 Office: 834 Alfred I duPont Bldg 169 E Flagler St Miami FL 33131 Tel (305) 374-8418

SPARKS, SAMMY DOYLE, b. Roswell, N.Mex., Oct. 24, 1944; student Kilgore Jr. Coll., 1963-64; B.S., Sul Ross State U., 1967; J.D., U. Tex., 1970. Admitted to Tex. bar, 1970; partner firm Webb, Stokes & Sparks, San Angelo, Tex., 1972—. Mem. Tom Green County Bar Assn., Am., Tex. trial lawyers assns. Home: 2941 Sierra Circle San Angelo TX 76901 Office: PO Box 1271 San Angelo TX 76901 Tel (915) 653-6866

SPARROW, GEORGE NORTH, JR., b. San Juan, P.R., Sept. 7, 1941; A.S. in Forestry, Abraham Baldwin Coll., 1963; B.S. in Forestry, U. Ga., 1966; J.D., Mercer U., 1969. Admitted to Ga. bar, 1970; staff atty. Ga. Constl. Revision Commn., 1969; partner firm Archer, Sparrow, Barnes, Barron & Wallhausen, and predecessors, East Point, Ga., 1970—; city atty. City of E. Point, 1973—. Mem. State Bar Ga. (co-chmn. local govt. com. younger lawyers sect. 1973-74), Ga. Municipal Assn. (legis. com. city atty's. sect. 1975-76), Am., Atlanta bar assns., Atlanta Council Younger Lawyers. Office: 3401 Whipple Ave Suite 254 East Point GA 30344 Tel (404) 763-3401

SPARROW, JOHN PRENTISS, b. Cambridge, Mass., July 19, 1915; A.B., Harvard, 1938; LL.B., 1941. Admitted to Mass. bar, 1946, Calif. bar, 1947, U.S. Supreme Ct. bar, 1955; law clk. Ropes & Gray, Boston, summer 1940; asso. firm McCutchen, Thomas, Matthew, Griffiths, & Greene, San Francisco, 1946-47; dep. dist. atty. Alameda County (Calif.), 1947-53; asso. firm Johnson & Stanton, San Francisco, 1953-54; asst. U.S. atty., San Francisco, 1954-55; asso. counsel bd. regents U. Calif. at Berkeley, 1956-72; judge Superior Ct. of Calif., Oakland, 1971—; instr. law U. San Francisco, 1947-52, Golden Gate U., 1953-55, San Francisco Law Sch., 1954—; trustee San Francisco Law Sch. Author: (with others) California Condemnation Practice, 1960. Office: 1225 Fallon St Oakland CA 94612 Tel (415) 874-6184

SPARVERO, LOUIS JAMES, b. Pitts., Nov. 4, 1920; B.S. in Physics and Engring., U. Pitts., 1940; postgrad. Bowdoin Coll., Mass. Inst. Tech., 1944-45; J.D., Duquesne U., 1954. Asst. physicist Gulf Research & Devel. Co., 1940-41; contract adminstr. Office of Naval Research, 1946-55; admitted to Pa. bar, 1955, U.S. Supreme Ct. bar, 1960; individual practice law, Allegheny County, Pa., 1955—; judge Pa. Ct. Common Pleas, 5th Jud. Dist., 1973—; regional dir. Pa. Labor Relations Bd., 1963-68; mem. Pa. Pub. Utility Commn., 1968-73. Mem. Am., Pa. Allegheny County, Fed. bar assns., Am. Judges Assn., Am. Judicature Soc. Home: 8013 Lawrence Dr Bethel Park PA 15102 Office: City-County Bldg Pittsburg PA 15219 Tel (412) 833-3617

SPATUZZA, GEORGE JOHN, b. Ragusa, Italy, Nov. 4, 1896; came to U.S., 1908; LL.B., Northwestern U., 1917, J.D., 1970. Admitted to Ill. bar, 1918; individual practice law, Chgo., 1918-55; sr. partner firm Spatuzza Yedor & Buckley, Chgo., 1955-60, Spatuzza & Spatuzza, 1960—. Mem. Ill. Bar Assn., Justinian Soc. Lawyers (co-founder 1921, pres. 1925). Decorated knight Crown of Italy, Star of Solidarity, commenda and grand officer Order Star of Solidarity (Italy). Home: 300 S Austin Blvd Oak Park IL 60304 Office: 221 N LaSalle St Chicago IL 60601

SPAULDING, CHARLES CLINTON, JR., b. Durham, N.C., Nov. 10, 1907; A.B., Clark U., 1930; LL.B., St. John's U., 1935, J.D., 1968. Admitted to N.C. bar, 1946; spl. rep., asst. to treas., atty., asst. treas., counsel, gen. counsel, v.p., gen. counsel and dir. N.C. Mut. Life Ins. Co., Durham, 1936-73, dir., 1973—; partner firm Pearson, Malone, Johnson, DeJarmon and Spaulding, Durham, 1973—; dir. Mechanics & Farmers Bank, Mut. Savs. & Loan Assn., Durham; former legal services cons. OEO, D.C.; former chmn. Citizens Adv. Com. Workable Program HUD. Former bd. dirs. N.C. office Am. Cancer Soc.; bd. dirs. N.C. Cancer Inst., Lumberton; trustee, corp. sec. St. Augustine's Coll., Raleigh, N.C. Mem. Nat. Bar Found., Am. (former subcom. chmn. taxation sect.), Nat. (recipient C. Francis Stratford award 1973) bar assns., N.C. Assn. Black Lawyers, G.H. White Bar Assn. (v.p.), Assn. Life Ins. Counsel (emeritus). Office: 112 1/2 W Parrish St Durham NC 27702 Tel (919) 682-5407

SPAULDING, LARRY DEAN, b. Muscatine, Iowa, June 22, 1941; B.A., U. No. Iowa, 1967; J.D., Drake U., 1907. Admitted to Iowa bar, 1970; asso. firm Bradshaw, Fowler, Proctor & Fairgrave, Des Moines, 1970-73, partner, 1973—. Mem. Am., Iowa, Polk County bar assns., Iowa Acad. Trial Lawyers, Assn. Iowa Def. Counsel, Am. Trial Lawyers Assn. Home: 3101 Guthrie Ave Des Moines IA 50314 Office: Bradshaw Fowler Proctor & Fairgrave 11th floor Des Moines Bldg Des Moines IA 50309 Tel (515) 243-4191

SPEAR, H. DYKE N., b. New London, Conn., Feb. 26, 1935; B.A., Trinity Coll., Hartford, Conn., 1957; J.D., U. Conn., 1960. Admitted to Conn. bar, 1960, U.S. Dist. Ct. bar, 1968, U.S. Ct. of Appeals bar, 1969, U.S. Supreme Ct. bar, 1971; since practiced in Hartford, individual practice law, 1961—; lectr. in field Manchester Community Coll., 1966, Greater Hartford Community Coll., 1968. Mem. W. Hartford Conservation Commn., 1971-75, W. Hartford Republican Town Com., 1972-76, Greater Hartford Sports & Recreation Council, 1975—. Mem. Conn., Hartford County bar assns. Home: 181 Ridgewood Rd W Hartford CT 06107 Office: 10 Trumbull St Hartford CT 06103 Tel (203) 522-0341

SPEAR, WILLIS EARL, b. Moss, Tenn., Mar. 5, 1920; student Cumberland U., 1939-41, LL.B., 1944; J.D., Samford U., 1969. Admitted to Tenn. bar, 1944, U.S. Dist. Ct. bar, for Middle Dist. Tenn., 1973; mem. firm Maley & Spear, Celina, Tenn., 1944-46; individual practice law, Celina, 1946—; judge Clay County (Tenn.) Ct. of Gen. Sessions, 1950-58, 66—, Clay County Ct. Common Pleas, 1973—; mayor, city judge City of Celina, 1961-63; govt. appeal agt., legal advisor Tenn. Selective Service Bd. for Clay County, 1944—. Chmn. Clay County Democratic Primary Election Commn., 1952-56, Clay County Democratic Exec. Com., 1961-65; tchr. adult men's Sunday Sch. Celina 1st Bapt. Ch. Home and Office: PO Box 6 Pub Square Celina TN 38551 Tel (615) 243-2352

SPEARS, ADRIAN ANTHONY, b. Darlington, S.C., July 8, 1910; student The Citadel, 1927, U. N.C., 1928; LL.B., U. S.C., 1934, J.D., 1971. Admitted to S.C. bar, 1934, Tex. bar, 1937; individual practice law, Darlington, 1934-36, San Antonio, 1937-61; spl. Tex. Dist. judge, 1951; U.S. dist. judge Western Dist. Tex., San Antonio, 1961-62, chief judge, 1962—; del. 5th Circuit Jud. Conf., 1955-58; mem. Jud. Conf. of U.S. Com. on Adminstrn. Criminal Law; faculty Seminar for Newly Apptd. Judges; bd. dirs. Fed. Jud. Center, 1971-75; mem. Com. to Consider Standards for Admission to Practice in Fed. Ct., 1976. Chmn. bd. adjustment City of Alamo Heights, 1947-49; chmn. Charter Revision Com., City of San Antonio, 1949; del. Nat. Democratic Convs., 1952, 56, 60; mem. Tex. Dem. Exec. Com., 1950-52; trustee Our Lady of Lakes U. Mem. Am., Fed. (dir. San Antonio chpt.), Tex., S.C., San Antonio (pres. 1959-60) bar assns., Fifth Circuit Dist. Judges Assn. (pres.), Pi Kappa Phi, Phi Delta Phi, Omicron Delta Kappa. Recipient Rosewood Gavel award St. Marys U. Law Sch., 1971. Home: 9004 Wickfield St San Antonio TX 78217 Office: 655 E Durango Blvd San Antonio TX 78206 Tel (512) 229-6565

SPEARS, ROBERT FIELDS, b. Tulsa, Aug. 1, 1943; B.B.A., Tex. Technol. Coll., 1965; J.D. with honors, U. Tex., 1968. Admitted to Tex. bar, 1968; asso. firm Rain Harrell Emery Young & Doke, Dallas, 1968-73, partner, 1974—. Mem. Am., Tex., Dallas bar assns., Order of Coif, Chancellors, Phi Delta Phi. Asso. editor Tex. Law Rev., 1967-68. Office: 4200 Republic Nat Bank Tower Dallas TX 75201 Tel (214) 742-1021

SPECCHIO, MICHAEL RONALD, b. Huntington, N.Y., Aug. 27, 1942; A.A., U. San Francisco, 1962; J.D., U. Pacific, 1970. Admitted to Nev. bar, 1971; chief trial dep. Washoe County (Nev.) Pub. Defender, 1973-75; admitted to U.S. Dist. Cts. 9-10th circuits, U.S. Ct. Claims; practice law, 1975—. Mem. Nev. Trial Lawyers Assn., Assn. Trial Lawyers Am., Nat. Dist. Atty's. Assn., Nat. Assn. Criminal Def. Lawyers, Fed., Am. bar assns., Am. Judicature Soc., Am. Notarial Soc. Recipient certificates of achievement Inst. Narcotics and Drug Abuse, 1974, Police and Pros. Inst., 1973, Am. Jurisprudence award Bancroft-Whitney, 1970. Office: Suite 311 195 S Sierra St PO Box 588 Reno NV 89501 Tel (702) 323-4922

SPECK, FLETCHER ALLEN, b. Kansas City, Mo., Aug. 17, 1946; B.A., U. Kans., 1969; J.D., U. Mo., Kansas City, 1972. Admitted to Mo. bar, 1972, asso. firm Spencer, Fane, Britt & Browne, Kansas City, 1972—. Mem. legal panel Western Mo. dist. ACLU, 1974—; mem. alumni council Pembroke Country Day Sch., Kansas City, Mo., 1975—. Mem. Am., Kansas City bar assns., Lawyers Assn. Kansas City. Mem. sr. staff, contbr. U. Mo. Kansas City Law Rev., 1970-72; cases and statutes editor The Urban Lawyer, 1971-72. Home: 6911 Rockhill Rd Kansas City MO 64113 Office: 106 W 14th St Kansas City MO 64105 Tel (816) 474-8100

SPECTOR, ABRAHAM, b. Bklyn., Feb. 18, 1929; B.A., L.I. U., 1955; LL.B., Bklyn. Law Sch., 1951, LL.M., 1952. Admitted to N.Y. bar, 1951, U.S. Supreme Ct. bar, 1956; served with JAGC, U.S. Army, 1952-54; individual practice law, Bklyn., 1954-75; partner firm Held Spector & Sternberg, N.Y.C., 1975—; atty. of record, gen. counsel Country Wide Ins. Co., N.Y.C., 1975—; master N.Y.C. Civil Ct.; arbitrator N.Y.C. Small Claims Ct., Am. Arbitration Assn.; hearing examiner N.Y.C. Bd. Edn. Mem. Am., Bklyn. bar assns., Am., N.Y. State trial lawyers assns. Office: 75 Maiden Ln New York City NY Tel (212) 425-0512

SPECTOR, BENNETT ALAN, b. N.Y.C., Jan. 4, 1946; B.S. in Bus. Adminstrn., U. Fla., 1968, J.D., 1972. Admitted to Fla. bar, 1972, Calif. bar, 1976; with Ernst & Ernst, 1968-69; asso. firm Friedman, Britton & Stettin, Miami, 1972-75; mem. firm Plotkin & Saltzburg, Los Angeles, 1976—. Mem. Am., Dade County, Beverly Hills bar assns. Office: 10960 Wilshire Blvd Suite 1220 Los Angeles CA 90024 Tel (213) 477-5567

SPECTOR, EDWARD SAUL, b. Buffalo, Dec. 22, 1926; LL.B., U. Buffalo, 1951. Admitted to N.Y. bar, 1951, Fed. bar, 1959; individual practice law, Buffalo, 1951-56; partner firm Spector and Troy, Buffalo, 1956—; atty. Kennore (N.Y.) Village, 1971-75; N.Y. estate tax atty. Erie and Wyoming counties, 1975—. Mem. adv. cabinet Supt. Schs., Kenmore-Town of Tonawanda, 1971—. Mem. N.Y. State, Erie County bar assns. Editorial bd. U. Buffalo Law Rev., 1951. Home: 123 Irving Terr Town Tonawanda NY 14223 Office: 390 Ellicott Square Bldg Buffalo NY 14203 Tel (716) 853-6226

SPECTOR, MARTIN WOLF, b. Phila., Apr. 28, 1938; B.A., Pa. State U., 1959; LL.B., U. Pa., 1962. Admitted to Pa. bar, 1962; law clk., 1962-63; asso. firm Wolf Block & Schorr & Solis-Cohen, 1963-67; asst. counsel, now v.p. ARA Services, Inc., Phila., 1967—. Mem. Com. of Seventy, 1971—, vice-chmn. Mem. Phila., Pa. bar assns., Food Service and Lodging Inst., Nat. Restaurant Assn. Home: 517 Mercer Rd Merion PA 19066 Office: 6th and Walnut Sts Philadelphia PA 19106

SPECTOR, RICHARD LEWIS, b. San Francisco, Mar. 2, 1945; A.B., U. Calif., Berkeley, 1968. Admitted to Calif., U.S. Dist. Ct. for No. Dist. Calif., U.S. 9th Circuit Ct. Appeals bars, 1973; now practice in Belmont, Calif.

SPECTOR, ROBERT MELVYN, b. Boston, Mar. 5, 1926; A.B., Boston U., 1948, M.A., 1949, M.Ed., 1950, Ph.D., 1961; LL.B., Boston Coll., 1959, J.D., 1969. Master, Boston Latin Sch., 1956-63; admitted to Mass. bar, 1960, U.S. Supreme Ct. bar, 1969; asst. prof. constl. history Worcester State Coll., 1963-66, asso. prof., 1966-69, prof., 1969—; sr. lectr. Univ. Coll. Northeastern U., 1960—; dir. Center for Study Constl. Govt., Worcester, 1972—. Mem. Am. Soc. Legal History. Recipient Harry E. Pratt Meml. award Ill. State Hist. Soc., 1976; contbr. articles to hist. and ednl. jours. Home: 7 Old Wood Rd Framingham MA 01701 Office: Worcester State Coll 486 Chandler St Worcester MA 01602 Tel (617) 752-7700

SPECTOR, SYDNEY M., b. N.Y.C., Apr. 17, 1910; B.A., Lehigh U., 1931; J.D., N.Y.U., 1936; grad. Army Indsl. Coll. Admitted to N.Y. State bar, 1937, U.S. Supreme Ct. bar, 1959; mem. firm Rosenblatt & Jaffe, N.Y.C., 1935-39; partner firm Davidson, Spector & Levy, N.Y.C., 1946-48; v.p., exec. dir. Legal Aid Soc., Westchester County, White Plains, N.Y., 1965—; mem. N.Y. State Crime Control Bd., 1968—. Mem. Am., N.Y. State, Westchester N.Y. County bar assns., N.Y. County Lawyers Assn. Home: 63 Bayne Pl White Plains NY 10605 Office: 1 North Broadway White Plains NY 10601 Tel (914) 682-0277

SPEECE, JOSEPH MORRIS, b. Anderson, Ind., Jan. 30, 1942; B.S. in Indsl. Mgmt., Purdue U., 1965; J.D., Ind. U., 1968. Admitted to Ind. bar, 1968; corp. atty. Nat. Home Acceptance Corp., Lafayette, Ind., 1968, Ind. Refrigerator Lines Co., Muncie, 1970-72; partner firm Wilson and Speece, Muncie, 1972—; asst. prof. fin. and mgmt. Ball State U., Muncie, 1973. Mem. Delaware County (Ind.), Ind. State, Am. bar assns., Assn. Comml. Law League. Home: 916 Warwick Rd Muncie IN 47302 Office: 110 E Washington St Muncie IN 47305 Tel (317) 282-2274

SPEER, ALFRED ALTEN, b. St. Louis, Apr. 12, 1931; A.B., J.D., Washington U., St. Louis, 1957. Admitted to Mo. bar, 1957; partner firm Speer, Herzog & Ponfil, and predecessors, St. Louis, 1969-75; individual practice law, St. Louis, 1975—; pres. Mid-Am. Great Plains Fin. Corp., 1969—, chmn. bd., 1974—; chmn. bd. Mid-Am. Ins. Co., 1970-76, dir., 1966-76; chmn. bd. Century Oil & Gas Corp., 1974—; lectr.; mem. Mo. Ho. of Reps., 1961-66; co-chmn. Mo. Commn. to Reapportion the Senate, 1971; mem. tech. and adv. rev. com. St. Louis County Planning Commn., 1966-72; mem. Local Govt. Commn. Mo., 1957-66. Bd. dirs. Laurel Haven Sch. Exceptional Children, 1969—, chmn., 1977—. Mem. Am., Mo., Lawyer-Pilots, St. Louis bar assns., Am. Mgmt. Assn., Soc. Advancement Mgmt., Phi Delta Phi. Home: 840 Alexandra St Glendale MO 63122 Office: 7733 Forsyth Blvd Suite 1854 Saint Louis MO 63105 Tel (314) 862-8500

SPEER, WILSON EDWARD, b. Kansas City, Mo., Nov. 14, 1929; A.B., U. Kans., 1952, LL.B., 1954. Admitted to Kans. bar, 1954; partner firm Hackler, Londerholm, Speer, Vader & Austin, Olathe, Kans., 1957—. Mem. Johnson County Charter Commn., 1975-76. Mem. Am., Kans., Johnson County (pres. 1975-76) bar assns. Home: 9301 Mackey Dr Overland Park KS 66212 Office: 201 N Cherry St PO Box 1 Olathe KS 66061 Tel (913) 782-1000

SPEERS, AUSTIN BURGESS, b. Kansas City, Mo., Sept. 14, 1920; J.D., U. Mo., Kansas City, 1952. Admitted to Mo. bar, 1952, U.S. Supreme Ct. bar, 1961; partner firm Speers & Slyter, and predecessors, Kansas City, 1958—; spl. asst. atty. gen. State of Mo., 1967-69; asst. county counselor Jackson County (Mo.), 1969-73. Adviser Parents Without Partners, Kansas City, 1966—. Mem. Am., Kansas City, Mo. bar assns., Am., Mo. trial lawyers assns. Recipient Law-Med. award U. Mo., Kansas City, 1951. Home: 607 Huntington Rd Kansas City MO 64113 Office: 826 Commerce Tower 911 Main St Kansas City MO 64105 Tel (816) 221-7612

SPEERT, BERRYL ALAN, b. Balt., Feb. 5, 1938; B.S. in Econs., U. Pa., 1959; J.D., U. Md., 1964. Bailiff, Judge Reuben Oppenheimer, Supreme Bench Balt. City, 1962-63; law clk. to chief judge U.S. Dist. Ct. for Md., 1963-64; admitted to Md. bar, 1964; asso. firm Frank, Bernstein, Conaway & Goldman, Balt., 1964-70, partner, 1970—. Mem. Am., Md. State, Balt. City bar assns. Contbr. articles to legal publs. Home: 2109 Southcliff Dr Baltimore MD 21209 Office: 1300 Mercantile Bank & Trust Bldg Baltimore MD 21201 Tel (301) 547-0500

SPEISER, STUART MARSHALL, b. N.Y.C., June 4, 1923; LL.B., Columbia, 1948. Admitted to N.Y. bar, 1948, D.C. bar, 1971; partner firm Speiser & Krause, N.Y.C. and Washington, 1950—; mem. com. on internat. aviation law World Peace Through Law Center, 1964—. Mem. Am. Inst. Aeros. and Astronautics (asso.), Am. Trial Lawyers Assn. (asso. editor aviation law 1957—, chmn. aviation law sect. 1955-64), N.Y.C. (past mem. aeros. com.), N.Y. County, N.Y. State, Am. bar assns., Bklyn.-Manhattan Trial Counsel Assn., Fed. Bar Council (com. on aero. law), Lawyer-Pilots Assn. (past dir.), Am. Soc. Internat. Law; fellow Internat. Acad. Law and Sci., Internat. Soc. Barristers (dir.). Author: Recovery for Wrongful Death, 1966, 2d edit., 1975; Lawyers' Economic Handbook, 1969; Attorneys' Fees, 1973; Res Ipsa Loquitor, 1973; A Piece of the Action, 1977; also other books, articles. Named Hon. Atty. Gen. of La., 1958. Office: 1507 Pan Am Bldg 200 Park Ave New York City NY 10017 Tel (212) 661-0011

SPELL, CARROL LEE, b. Indian Bayou, La., Nov. 4, 1925; B.A., Southwestern La. Inst., 1948; LL.B., La. State U., 1952, J.D., 1968. Admitted to La. bar, 1952; individual practice law, Abbeville, La., 1952-62; sr. dist. judge 15th Jud. Dist. Ct., Parishes of Acadia, Lafayette and Vermilion, 1962—; atty. to assist Inheritance Tax Collector, Abbeville, 1952-56; city atty. Towns of Erath and Delcambre, 1954-62. Mem. Am., La., 15th Jud. Dist., Vermilion bar assns., Nat. Judicature Soc., Abbeville C. of C. (dir. 1954-60). Home: 103 E Valcourt St Abbeville LA 70510 Office: PO Box 69 Abbeville LA 70510 Tel (318) 893-4000

SPELLACY, LEO MICHAEL, b. Cleve., Nov. 15, 1934; B.S. in Govt., Georgetown U., 1956; LL.B., Case Western Res. U., 1959. Admitted to Ohio bar, 1959; asst. pros. atty. County of Cuyahoga (Ohio), 1960-68; judge Cuyahoga County Ct. of Common Pleas, 1969—, presiding judge, 1975—; mem. criminal justice co-ordinating council Cuyahoga County Ct. Mgmt. Project; bd. advisors Cuyahoga Regional Info. System. Trustee St. John Hosp., Cleve.; regent St. Ignatius High Sch., Cleve. Mem. Ohio State Bar Assn. Recipient award for Jud. Service Supreme Ct. Ohio, 1972, 73, 74, 75, 76. Office: Courthouse 1 Lakeside Ave Cleveland OH 44113 Tel (216) 621-5800

SPELMAN, JAMES CHARLTON, b. Chgo., July 4, 1933; B.A., Mich. State U., 1954; J.D., U. Ill., 1961. Admitted to Ill. bar, 1961; asso. firm Andrews & Peterson, 1961-65; partner firm Andrews, Peterson & Spelman, 1965-69; partner firm Neilsen, Sumberg & Spelman, Rockford, Ill., 1969-70, firm Sumberg & Spelman, Rockford, 1970-72, firm Pedderson, Menzimer, Conde, Stoner, Ferolie, Spelman & Killoren, Rockford, 1972-76; pres. firm James C. Spelman & Assos., P.C., Rockford, 1976—. Chmn. Rockford Planning Commn., 1974-75; bd. dirs. Goldie Floberg Center for Children, Rockford. Mem. Ill., Winnebago County bar assns. Office: 321 W State St Rockford IL 61101 Tel (815) 965-9100

SPENCE, ROBERT ATWELL, b. Kinston, N.C., Apr. 28, 1922; B.S. in Commerce, U. N.C., 1943, LL.B., 1948. Admitted to N.C. bar, 1948; mem. firm Wood and Spence, Smithfield, N.C., 1955-62; individual practice law, Smithfield, 1962-76; mem. firm Spence & Spence, Smithfield, 1976—; counsel S.C.L. Ry., So. Ry., Nationwide Ins. Co., U.S.F & G Great Am. Ins. Co.; city atty. Smithfield; commr. uniform state laws. Mem. N.C., Am. bar assns., N.C. Acad. Trial Lawyers, Johnston County Bar (pres.). Home: 611 E Church St Smithfield NC 27577 Office: Courthouse Sq PO Box 1335 Smithfield NC 27577 Tel (919) 934-7181

SPENCE, WISHART FLETT, B.A. in Polit. Sci., U. Toronto (Ont., Can.), 1925; postgrad. Osgoode Hall Sch. Law, Toronto; LL.M., Harvard U., 1929; LL.D., York U., 1974. Called to Ont. bar, 1928; with firm Starr, Spence & Hall till 1934, then partner firm Spence, Spence & Shoemaker; justice Supreme Ct. of Ont., 1950-63, Supreme Ct. of Can., 1963—; chmn. Royal Commn. on Coastal Trade, 1955—. Recipient Gold medal Osgoode Hall Sch. Law. Office: Supreme Ct of Canada Wellington St Ottawa ON K1A OJ1 Canada*

SPENCER, CLIFFORD MORRIS, JR., b. Birmingham, Ala., July 9, 1940; B.A., U. Ala., 1962, J.D., 1964. Admitted to Ala. bar, 1964; partner firm Pritchard, McCall & Jones, Birmingham, 1971—; instr. mil. law ROTC Advanced Cadets, Samford U., 1976; spl. asst. atty. gen. State of Ala. Bd. mgmt. Downtown YMCA, Birmingham; deacon Ind. Presbyterian Ch., Birmingham, also mem. sch. bd. Mem. Am., Ala., Birmingham bar assns. Home: 124 Greenbriar Ln Birmingham AL 35213 Office: 831 Frank Nelson Bldg Birmingham AL 35203 Tel (205) 328-9190

SPENCER, DALE RAY, b. Pocatello, Idaho, Oct. 21, 1925; B.J., U. Mo., 1948, M.A., 1955, J.D., 1968. Prof. communications law U. Mo., Columbia, 1950—; admitted to Mo. bar, 1969; individual practice law, Columbia, 1969—; cons., lectr. in field. Bd. dirs. Wonderland Camp for Handicapped Children, Rocky Mount, Mo., 1973—. Mem. Mo., Am. bar assns., Investigative Reporters and Editors, Am. Newspaper Pubs. Assn. (7-man press-bar com. 1976—), Mo. Faculty in Higher Edn. (pres. 1976), Sigma Delta Chi. Recipient Joyce Swan Distinguished Faculty award U. Mo. Sch. Journalism, 1967; author: Law for the Newsman, 1971, rev. 3d edit., 1975; contbr. articles to profl. publs. Home: 917 La Grange St Columbia MO 65201 Office: Sch Journalism U Mo Columbia MO 65201 Tel (314) 882-7436

SPENCER, GEORGE HENRY, b. Vienna, Austria, June 21, 1928; B.E., Yale, 1948; J.D., Cornell U., 1952. Admitted to N.Y. bar, 1952, D.C. bar, 1959; examiner U.S. Patent Office, Washington, 1952-54; individual practice law, N.Y.C. and Washington, 1954-62; served with JAGC U.S. Army Res., 1956-62; partner firm Spencer and Kaye, Washington, 1962—; mem. nat. panel arbitrators Am. Arbitration Assn. Mem. Am., Lawyer-Pilots bar assns., Am. Patent Law Assn., Judge Advocates Assn. Lectr. ad hoc World Trade Inst., German Patent Assns. Office: 1920 L St NW Washington DC 20036 Tel (202) 659-9720

SPENCER, HARRY ARTHUR, b. Bishops Walton, Eng., Sept. 16, 1903; A.B., U. Nebr., 1929, LL.B. cum laude, 1930, J.D., 1969. Admitted to Nebr. bar, 1929; practiced in Lincoln, Nebr., 1929-44; judge Lancaster County (Nebr.) Ct., 1945-51, Nebr. Dist. Ct., 3d Jud. Dist., 1951-61; asso. justice Nebr. Supreme Ct., 1961—; lectr. U. Nebr. Law Sch., 1942-62. Pres. Lincoln Council Chs., 1957. Mem. Am. (chmn. appellate judges conf. 1971-72, ho. of dels. 1973—), Nebr. State (exec. bd.), Lincoln (pres. 1946) bar assns., Am. Judicature Soc. Recipient Good Govt. award Lincoln Jr. C. of C., 1958. Home: 1500 Crestview Dr Lincoln NE 68506 Office: State Capitol Bldg Lincoln NE 68509 Tel (402) 432-4578

SPENCER, JAMES OWEN, JR., b. Demopolis, Ala., June 22, 1937; B.S., U. Ala.; 1959, LL.B., 1965. Admitted to Ala. bar, 1965, U.S. Supreme Ct. bar, 1972; asso. firm Davies, Williams & Wallace, Birmingham, Ala., 1965-69; asso. firm Balch, Bingham, Baker, Hawthorne, Williams & Ward, and predecessor, Birmingham, 1969, partner, 1970—; mem. panel Am. Arbitration Assn. Mem. Jefferson County (Ala.) Republican Exec. Com., 1970-72. Mem. Birmingham (pres. sect. young lawyers 1971), Ala. State, Am. bar assns., Ala. Def. Lawyers Assn. Home: 19 Crestview Circle Birmingham AL 35213 Office: PO Box 306 Birmingham AL 35201 Tel (205) 251-8100

SPENCER, MERRITT ELMAN, b. Shattuck, Okla., June 17, 1940; B.A., Abilene Christian Coll., 1961; J.D., South Tex. Coll. Law, 1967. Admitted to Tex. bar, 1967; with CSC, 1963-67; asso. firm Brackeen and Pennington, 1968-73; individual practice law, Tomball, Tex., 1973—. Home: Stagecoach St Magnolia TX Office: 28107 Hwy 149 Tomball TX 77375 Tel (713) 351-4994

SPENCER, RICHARD CHARLES, b. N.Y.C., May 2, 1943; B.A., Syracuse U., 1964; M.A., U. N.H., 1965; J.D., State U. N.Y. at Buffalo, 1968. Admitted to Calif. bar, 1969; clk. U.S. Dist. Ct., Central Dist., Calif., 1968-69; dep. dist. atty., Los Angeles Dist. Atty. Office, 1969-70; partner firm Baker, Ancel & Redmond, Los Angeles, 1970—. Mem. Los Angeles County, Am. bar assns., Los Angeles, Calif. trial lawyers assns., Assn. Trial Lawyers Am. Spl. projects editor, contbr. article Buffalo Law Rev., 1967-68. Recipient Am. Jurisprudence Book award, 1968, Lawyers Coop. award, 1968, Fed. Bar Assn. award, 1968. Office: 26626 Wilshire Blvd Suite 700 Los Angeles CA 90017 Tel (213) 624-9201

SPENCER, ROCK THOMAS, SR., b. Troy, N.Y., Dec. 28, 1929; A.B., N.Y. State Coll. Tchrs, 1951; J.D. magna cum laude, Mercer U., 1957. Admitted to Ga. bar, 1956; asso. firm Westmoreland & Thornton, Macon, Ga., 1957-59; since practiced in Warner Robins, Ga., partner firm Wisse & Spencer, 1959-62; individual practice law, 1962-64; partner firm Spencer, Smith & Williams, and predecessors, 1964-74; adminstrv. law judge State Bd. Workmen's Compensation, 1974-76; 1st solicitor State Ct. Houston County (Ga.), 1965-66; city atty. Warner Robins, 1959-62, 1976—. Chmn., Houston County Speech & Hearing Center, 1963—; pres. Houston County United Givers Fund, 1965-65; dist. chmn. Boy Scouts Am., 1968; mem. bd. consultors Sacred Heart Parish, Warner Robins, 1971-73. Mem. Houston Circuit (past pres.), Ga. State (bd. govs.) bar assns., Am. Judicature Soc. Contbr. articles in field to legal jours. Home: 296 N Lakeshore Dr Warner Robins GA 91093 Office: Suite 4A Robins Fed Credit Union Bldg Warner Robins GA 31093 Tel (912) 923-5891

SPENCER, SAMUEL, b. Washington, Dec. 8, 1910; B.A., Harvard U., 1932, J.D., 1935. Admitted to N.Y. bar, 1937, D.C. bar, 1938, U.S. Supreme Ct. bar, 1950; asso. firm Shearman & Sterling, N.Y.C., 1935-37, firm Covington, Burling, Rublee, Acheson & Shorb, Washington, 1937-40, 45-47; partner firm Spencer, Whalen & Graham, and predecessors, Washington, 1947—; pres. Bd. Commrs. D.C., 1953-56; dir. Riggs Nat. Bank, C.N.O. & T.P. Ry. Co., Tenn. Ry. Co. Pres., Washington Hosp. Center, 1958-60, bd. dirs., 1958-65; sr. warden St. John's Ch., Washington, 1974—. Mem. Am., D.C. bar assns., Am. Judicature Soc., Phi Beta Kappa. Home: 4814 Dexter St NW Washington DC 20007 Office: 2000 Massachusetts Ave NW Washington DC 20036 Tel (202) 785-1220

SPENCER, THAXTER PARKS, b. Boston, June 25, 1921; A.B., Harvard, 1943, LL.B., 1949. Admitted to Mass. bar, 1949; with New Eng. Mut. Life Ins. Co., Boston, 1949—, asso. counsel, 1964-67, asst. sec., 1967, counsel, 1967-68, v.p., 1968—, sec., 1974—. Bd. dirs., sec. New Eng. Hosp., Dimock Community Center. Mem. Am., Mass. bar assns., Assn. Life Ins. Counsel. Co-editor: Federal Taxation of Insured Pension Plans, 1973—. Home: 147 W Canton St Boston MA 02118 Office: 501 Boylston St Boston MA 02117 Tel (617) 266-3700

SPENCER, VAINO HASSAN, b. Los Angeles, July 22, 1920; A.A. summa cum laude, Los Angeles City Coll., 1949; LL.B., Southwestern Sch. Law, 1952. Admitted to Calif. bar, 1952; practiced in Los Angeles, 1952-61; judge Los Angeles Superior Ct., 1976—, Los Angeles Municipal Ct., 1961-76; mem. adv. bd. Calif. Joint Legis. Com. Legal Equality, 1973—; mem. exec. com. Los Angeles Jud. Dist. Municipal Ct., 1974-75. Mem. Women Lawyers' Assn. (Ernestine Stahlhut award 1974), Black Women Lawyers, Los Angeles Bar Assn., Calif. Conf. Judges. Recipient Trailblazer award Nat. Negro Women, 1962, Most Distinguished Alumna award Los Angeles City Coll., 1966. Office: 111 N Hill St Los Angeles CA 90012 Tel (213) 974-5582

SPENGLER, SILAS, b. Neenah, Wis., Oct. 20, 1930; B.A., Yale, 1953; LL.B., U. Pa., 1960. Admitted to N.Y. bar, 1962; asso. firm Simpson, Thacher & Bartlett, N.Y.C., 1960-64; partner firm Spengler, Carlson, Gubar, Churchill & Brodsky, N.Y.C., 1964—; dir. Velcro Industries N.V., PBA, Inc. Trustee Sheltering Arms Child Services, St. Christopher/Jennie Clarkson Child Services. Office: 280 Park Ave New York NY 10017 Tel (212) 682-4444

SPERBER, DAVID SOL, b. N.Y.C., July 28, 1939; A.B., Univ. Calif., Los Angeles, 1961; LL.B., 1964. Admitted to Calif. bar, 1965, U.S. Supreme Ct. bar, 1973; dep. atty. gen. State of Calif., 1964-68; individual practice law, 1968—. Mem. Fed. Indigent Def. Panel, Los Angeles, 1969-76; active The Hear Center; asso. chmn. United Jewish Welfare Fund. Mem. Los Angeles County bar assn., San Fernando Valley Criminal Bar Assn., Los Angeles Trial Lawyers Assn., Lawyers Club Speakers Bur. Recipient Am. Legion Citizenship award. Office: 2501 W 3d St Los Angeles CA 90057 Tel (213) 380-3200

SPERBER, PHILIP, b. N.Y.C., Feb. 29, 1944; B.S. in Elec. Engring., N.J. Inst. Tech., 1965; J.D., U. Md., 1969. Admitted to Md. bar, 1970, D.C. bar, 1970, U.S. Ct. Customs and Patent Appeals bar, 1971, U.S. Supreme Ct. bar, 1976; asst. to pres. NJE Corp., Kenilworth, N.J., 1965-66; partner firm Blair, Olcutt & Sperber, Washington, examiner U.S. Dept. Commerce, Washington, 1966-68; partner firm Blair, Olcutt & Sperber, Washington, 1968-71; v.p. counsel, officer Cavitron Corp., N.Y.C., 1971—; v.p., dir. Ultrasonic Industry Assn., Inc., New Rochelle, N.Y., 1974-77; chief instr. Am. Negotiating Inst., 1976—; U.S. del. Internat. Electro-tech. Commn., 1976-77. Dir. N.J. Jaycees, 1966; mem. econ. devel. council Met. Washington Bd. Trade, 1967; pres. Runnymede Hills Civic Assn., 1972-73; judge Am. Arbitration Assn., 1974—. Mem. Am. (chmn. corp. banking and bus. law commn.), N.Y. State, N.J. (dir. food, drug and cosmetic sect.) bar assns., IEEE (sr.), Assn. Advancement Med. Instrumentation. Recipient commendation Am. Law Inst., 1976; named outstanding U.S. Jaycee, 1966; author: Intellectual Property Management: Law-Business-Strategy, 1974; Negotiating in Day-to-Day Business, 1976. Contbr. articles to profl. and tech. jours. Home: 149 Reynolds Ave Whippany NJ 07981 Office: Cavitron Corp 1290 Ave of the Americas New York City NY 10019 Tel (212) 977-8444

SPERLI, RALPH DOMINIC, b. Cleve., June 2, 1939; B.A., Baldwin Wallace Coll., 1961; J.D., Western Res. U., 1964. Admitted to Ohio bar, 1964; asst. county prosecuter Cuyahoga County (Ohio), 1965-73; mem. firm Dempsey, Giuliani, Sperli, McMahon & Longo, Cleve., 1973—. Mem. Charter Rev. Commn. City of Parma Heights (Ohio), 1972. Mem. Cleve., Ohio, Cuyahoga County (fed. rules com.), Cuyahoga County Criminal (pres.-elect) bar assns., Nat. Assn. Criminal Def. Lawyers (trustee). Home: 21274 Kenwood Ave Rocky River OH 44116 Office 410 Leader Bldg Cleveland OH 44114 Tel (216) 241-0520

SPERO, MORTON BERTRAM, b. N.Y.C., Dec. 6, 1920; B.A., U. Va., 1942, LL.B., 1946. Admitted to Va. bar, 1946, U.S. Supreme Ct. bar, 1961; mem. legal staff of chmn. NLRB, Washington, 1946-48; individual practice law, Petersburg, Va., 1948-70; sr. partner firm Spero and Levinson, Petersburg, 1970-75, Spero and Diehl, Petersburg, 1975—. Chmn. United Fund, Petersburg, 1960; pres. dist. 4 Va. Council on Social Welfare, 1966, Southside Va. Sheltered Workshop, Petersburg, 1965, Congregation Brith Achim, Petersburg, 1973. Mem. Am., Va., Petersburg (sec. 1963-65) bar assns., Am., Va. (v.p. 1972) trial lawyers assns., Va. State Bar (gov. sect. criminal law 1970-74, chmn. bd. govs. 1973), Rotary Club, Civitan Club (hon.), Elks (exalted ruler 1968), B'nai B'rith (pres. 1951, 59, named Outstanding Mem. Petersburg lodge 1966). Recipient Service to Law Enforcement award Petersburg Police Dept., 1965. Home: 13 Woodmere Point Apts Petersburg VA 23803 Office: Suite 203 The Community Bank Bldg Petersburg VA 23803 Tel (804) 733-0151

SPEVACK, SAMUEL, b. Russia. 1903; student City Coll. N.Y.; LL.B., Bklyn. Law Sch., 1923, LL.M. cum laude, 1924. Admitted to N.Y. bar, 1926; individual practice law, Bklyn. Mem. Bklyn., Met. bar assns. Home: 35 Prospect Park W Brooklyn NY 11215 Office: 66 Court St Room 1704 Brooklyn NY 11201 Tel (212) MA 4-2455

SPEZIALE, JOHN ALBERT, b. Winsted, Conn., Nov. 21, 1922; B.A., Duke, 1943, J.D., 1947. Admitted to Conn. bar, 1948; clerk judiciary com. Conn. Gen. Assembly, 1949; dir. Torrington (Conn.) Civil Def., 1951-52; fed. atty. Office of Price Stablzn., 1951-52; sr. partner firm Speziale and Lefebre, Torrington, mem. firm Speziale, Mettling, Lefebre & Burns, Torrington, 1958-61; city atty. Torrington, 1957-59; state treas. Conn., 1959-61; judge Torrington Municipal Ct., 1949-51; judge Conn. Ct. Common Pleas, 1961-65; judge Conn. Superior Ct., 1965—, presiding judge Appellate Div. Superior Ct. (Conn.), Litchfield, 1975—; mem. Conn. State Jud. Council, 1955-59; co-chmn. Conn. Justice Commn., 1976—; mem. Conn. Commn. on Adult Probation, 1976—. Mem. Am., Litchfield County, Conn. bar assns., Nat. Conf. State Trial Judges (exec. com.). Home: 278 Wind Tree Torrington CT 06790 Office: Ct House Litchfield CT 06759 Tel (203) 567-5438

SPIEGEL, ALBERT ALEXANDER, b. McKeesport, Pa., Mar. 9, 1916; B.A., U. Pitts., 1937; J.D., Harvard, 1940. Admitted to Calif. bar, 1946; individual practice law, Los Angeles, 1949—; sec., dir. Beaumont Meadows, Inc. Gen. chmn. United Jewish Welfare Fund, Los Angeles, 1966-67; pres. Jewish Fedn. Council Greater Los Angeles, 1971-72, also bd. dirs.; pres. Jewish Community Found.; past pres. Beth Shalom Temple, Santa Monica, Jewish Community Council of Bay Cities, Santa Monica Bay Zionist Dist., Jewish Community Center, Bay Cities, Crescent Bay Lodge 1028 B'nai B'rith; mem. nat. campaign cabinet United Jewish Appeal; bd. dirs. Am. Jewish Joint Distbn. Com., United HIAS Service; trustee Santa Monica Hosp., Inst. for Jewish Policy Planning and Research of Synagogue Council Am., Jewish Publ. Soc. Am.; mem. exec. com. Am. Israel Pub. Affairs Com.; bd. overseers Jewish Theol. Sem. Am., Hebrew Union Coll. Calif.; chmn. bd. govs. U. Judaism; bd. govs. U.S.-Israel Binational Sci. Found.; mem. nat. governing council Am. Assn. for Jewish Edn. Mem. Santa Monica Bay Area Bar Assn. (past pres.). Home: 807 N Elm Dr Beverly Hills CA 90210 Office: 641 N Sepulveda Blvd Los Angeles CA 90049 Tel (213) 476-1251

SPIEGEL, SAMUEL A., b. N.Y.C.; LL.B., St. John's U., 1936. Admitted to N.Y. State bar, 1937, U.S. Supreme Ct. bar; asso. firm Spiegel & Davis, N.Y.C., 1956-62; judge Civil Ct., N.Y.C., 1962-66; justice N.Y. State Supreme Ct., N.Y.C., 1966-76, asst. adminstrv. judge, 1971-76; surrogate N.Y. County, 1976—; instr. law USN, 1943-46; adj. prof. constl. and criminal law Pace U. Mem. N.Y. State Assembly, 1956-62; chmn. Sch. Bd. 3, N.Y.C., 1960-62; pres. Stuyvesant Polyclinic Hosp., 1953; v.p., bd. dirs. Grand St. Settlement House; bd. dirs. Young Mens Philanthropic League. Mem. Am., N.Y. bar assns., New York County Lawyers Assn., Am. Judicature Soc., Am. Legion, St. John's Law Sch. (past pres.), Seward Park High Sch. (Hall of Fame) alumni assns. Recipient Chief Justice Harlan Fiske

Stone Meml. award Assn. Trial Lawyers City of New York, 1975, numerous service awards; named Alumnus of Year, Seward Park High Sch., 1960. Home: 577 Grand St New York City NY Office: 31 Chambers St New York City NY 10007 Tel (212) 374-4500

SPIER, ALAN ROBERT, b. New Haven, Feb. 4, 1939; A.B., Harvard, 1960, J.D., 1964. Admitted to Conn. bar, 1964; asso. firm Robinson, Robinson & Cole, Hartford, Conn., 1964-70, partner, 1970—. Mem. Am., Conn., Hartford County bar assns. Office: 799 Main St Hartford CT 06103 Tel (203) 278-0700

SPIES, EMERSON GEORGE, b. Akron, N.Y., Nov. 6, 1914; A.B., Hobart Coll., 1936, LL.D., 1966; B.A. Juris, Oxford (Eng.) U., 1938, B.C.L., 1939. Admitted to N.Y. State bar, 1940, Va. bar, 1946; tutorial fellow U. Chgo., 1939-41; asso. firm Mudge, Stern, Williams, Tucker, N.Y.C., 1941-43; capt. JAGC, AUS, 1943-46; asst. prof. law U. Va., 1946-47, asso. prof., 1947-49, prof., 1950-70, Hartfield prof. law 1970—, dean Sch. Law, 1976—; vis. prof. Australian Nat. U., 1964; mem. test council Pres's. Law Sch. Admissions Council, 1964-67. Trustee Hobart and William Smith Coll., 1970-74. Mem. N.Y. State, Va. bar assns., Order Coif, Phi Beta Kappa. Home: The Barn Northfield Rd Charlottesville VA 22901 Office: U of Va Sch of Law Charlottesville VA 22904 Tel (804) 924-7343

SPIES, FRANK STADLER, b. Adrian, Mich., Aug. 7, 1939; B.B.A., U. Mich., 1961, LL.B., 1964. Admitted to Mich. bar, 1964; asso. firm Schmidt, Smith, Howlett & Halliday, Grand Rapids, 1964-66; chief enforcement div. Grand Rapids City Atty.'s Office, 1966-69; first asst. U.S. Atty.'s Office for Western Dist. Mich., Grand Rapids, 1969-74, U.S. atty., 1974—. Mem. Am., Fed., Mich., Grand Rapids bar assns. Home: 2122 Tenway Dr SE East Grand Rapids MI 49506 Office: 544 Fed Bldg Grand Rapids MI 49503 Tel (616) 456-2404

SPIES, FREDERIC KESSLER, b. Pottstown, Pa., June 8, 1926; A.B., Dickinson Coll., 1950, J.D., 1952; LL.M., N.Y. U., 1956. Admitted to Pa. bar, 1952, Ark. bar, 1961; asst. prof. Dickinson Law Sch., Carlisle, Pa., 1953-56; prof. law U. Ark., Fayetteville, 1956-76; prof. Law Sch., U. Ark. at Little Rock, also prof. legal medicine Coll. Medicine, 1976—. Fellow Am. Acad. Forensic Scis.; Mem. Am., Pa., Berks County, Ark., Pulaski County bar assns., AAUP. Recipient Distinguished Teaching and Research award U. Ark. Alumni, 1974, Spl. award Meritorious Service, Ark. Bar Assn., 1966. Home: 27 Hayfield Rd Little Rock AR 72207 Office: 400 W Markham St Little Rock AR 72201 Tel (501) 375-6444

SPIES, PHILIP LAWRENCE, b. Chgo., Apr. 7, 1942; B.S., Purdue U., 1965; J.D., So. Meth. U., 1970. Admitted to Tex. bar, 1970, U.S. 5th Circuit Ct. Appeals bar, 1972, No. (1972), Eastern (1973), Western (1973), and So. (1976) U.S. Dist. Ct. of Tex. bars, No. (1973) and So. (1976) U.S. Dist. Ct. of Okla. bars; legal cons. Tex. State Health Dept., Austin, 1970-74; individual practice law, Austin, 1975—. Mem. Am., Travis County bar assns., State Bar Tex., Tex. Trial Lawyers, Assn. Trial Lawyers Am. Home: 3905 Petra Path Austin TX 78731 Office: The One Highland Center Bldg Suite 551 Austin TX 78752 Tel (512) 459-3339

SPILKER, H. LARRY, b. Salt Lake City, Mar. 7, 1933; B.S., U. Utah, 1965, J.D., 1968. Admitted to Idaho bar, 1968; atty. Idaho Nuclear Corp., and Aerojet Nuclear Co., Idaho Falls, 1968-74; gen. counsel, asst. sec. Aerojet Nuclear Co., 1974-76; gen. counsel, asst. sec. EG&G Idaho, Inc., Idaho Falls, 1976—. Mem. Am. Bar Assn., ERDA Contractor Attys. Orgn. Home: Route 1 Box 83D Idaho Falls ID 83401 Office: PO Box 1625 Idaho Falls ID 83401 Tel (208) 522-6640

SPILLER, PAUL HARVEY, b. Wilmington, Del., Aug. 22, 1948; B.A., U. Del., 1970; J.D., John Marshall Law Sch., 1973. Admitted to Del. bar, 1973; asso. mem. firm Kimmel, Spiller & Bradley, Wilmington, 1973—. Mem. Del., Am. bar assns., Del. Trial Lawyers Assn. Office: 401 Market Tower Bldg 9th and Market Sts Wilmington DE 19801 Tel (302) 571-0800

SPINA, ANTHONY FERDINAND, b. Chgo., Aug. 15, 1937; B.S. in Social Sci., Loyola U., Chgo., 1959; J.D., De Paul U., 1962. Admitted to Ill. bar, 1962; asso. firm Epton, Scott, McCarthy & Bohling, Chgo., 1962-64; individual practice law, Elmwood Park, Ill., 1964—; atty. for Leyden Twp., 1969—, for Village of Rosemont, 1971; counsel, pres., dir. for Cook County Twp. ofcls., 1975—. Dir. Edgebrook C. of C.; auditor-trustee St. Rocco Soc. Simbario; cons. Elmwood Park Village Bd. and various Cook County Twps.; mem. Elmwood Park Bldg. Code Planning Commn. bd. appeals. Mem. Ill. State Bar, Chgo., Am. Bar Assns., Am. Judicature Soc., Nat. Honor Soc. Secondary Schs., Loyola Deans Key, Blue Key, Justinian Soc. of Lawyers, Pi Gamma Mu, Delta Theta Phi. Recipient housing awards Loyola U., 1965, 71, 76, award of appreciation Cook County Twp. Ofcls. representing 30 Cook County Twps., 1974, K.C. Certificate of merit; drafted Elmwood Park bldg. code., 1975. Office: 7610 W North Ave Elmwood Park IL 60035 Tel (312) 453-0372

SPINA, FRANCIS XAVIER, b. Pittsfield, Mass., Nov. 13, 1946; B.A., Amherst Coll., 1968; J.D., Boston Coll., 1971. Admitted to Mass. bar, 1971, Fed. bar, 1972; mng. atty. Springfield (Mass.) office Western Mass. Legal Services, Inc., 1972-74; individual practice law, Pittsfield, 1974-76; asso. firm Reder & Whalen, Pittsfield, 1976—; asst. city solicitor, Pittsfield, 1975—. Mem. Mass., Berkshire bar assns. Home: 115 Pomeroy Ave Pittsfield MA 01201 Office: Reder & Whalen 31 Wendell Ave Pittsfield MA 01201 Tel (413) 448-8271

SPINA, NICHOLAS M., b. Chgo., Mar. 14, 1946; B.S., Loyola U., 1967; J.D., Chgo.-Kent Coll. Law, 1971. Admitted to Ill. bar, 1971; asst. states atty. Cook County (Ill.), 1971—; asst. gen. counsel Dominick's Finer Foods, Ill., 1972-73; partner firm Kwiatt, Silverman & Spina, 1975-75, firm Spina and Barton, Chgo., 1975—. Campaign mgr. Com. to Elect Judge Adam N. Stillo Circuit Ct. Judge, 1977. Mem. Chgo., Ill. State, Am. bar assns., Justinian Soc. Lawyers. Loyola U. Merit scholar, 1966-67. Office: 221 N LaSalle St Chicago IL 60601

SPINDELMAN, NORMAN MELVIN, b. Rochester, N.Y., July 31, 1928; B.S., U. Mich., 1950, J.D., 1952. Admitted to N.Y. bar, 1953, U.S. Dist. Ct. Western N.Y., 1955, No. N.Y., 1955, U.S. Supreme Ct. bar, 1956, U.S. Ct. Appeals, 1956; asso. firm Fix, Spindelman, Turk & Himelein, Rochester, N.Y., 1953-59, partner, 1959—. Home: 229 Corwin Rd Rochester NY 14610 Office: 500 Crossroads Bldg 2 State St Rochester NY 14610

SPINDLER, JAMES WALTER, b. Middletown, Ohio, Feb. 24, 1939; B.A., Cornell U., 1961; LL.B., Harvard, 1964. Admitted to Ohio bar, 1964, Mass. bar, 1968; with JAGC, USMC, 1964-68; asso. firm Hale and Dorr, Boston, 1968-73, partner, 1973—. Lincoln (Mass.) town rep. to Subregion Intertown Liaison Com., 1969-75; mem. Lincoln Sch. Com., 1977—. Mem. Am., Mass., Boston bar assns. Translator: (with Harold J. Berman) Soviet Criminal Law and Procedure, 1966, rev. edit., 1972. Home: Weston Rd Lincoln MA 01773 Office: 28 State St Boston MA 02109 Tel (617) 742-9100

SPINNEY, LEON LESLIE, b. N. Berwick, Maine, Aug. 19, 1903; A.B., Bowdoin Coll., 1926; J.D., Boston U., 1929. Admitted to Maine bar, 1929; municipal judge, Brunswick, Maine, 1942-60; partner firm Spinney & Dolloff, Brunswick, 1962-70, sr. partner, 1970—; incorporator Brunswick Savs. Instn., Brunswick. Mem. Cumberland, Sagadalwoc, Maine bar assns. Home: 37 Elm St Topsham ME 04086 Office: 172 Maine St Brunswick ME 04011 Tel (207) 725-5842

SPINNEY, RICHARD BARRY, b. N.Y.C., Sept. 21, 1946; A.B., Roanoke Coll., 1968; J.D., Albany Law Sch., 1971. Admitted to N.Y. bar, 1972; individual practice law, Stamford, N.Y., 1972—. Asst. counsel on election law N.Y. State Joint Legis. Ct., 1972; atty. Town of Roxbury (N.Y.), Charlotte Valley Central Sch. Dist., Gilboa Conesville Central Sch. Dist., 1975—. Mem. Am., N.Y. State, Delaware County bar assns. Home: 31 Lake St Stamford NY 12167 Office: 74 Main St Stamford NY 12167 Tel (607) 652-3443

SPIRN, STUART DOUGLAS, b. Manchester, N.H., Sept. 27, 1945; A.B. in History, Coll. William and Mary, 1967, J.D., 1970. Admitted to Va. bar, 1970; served as capt. JAGC, U.S. Army, 1970-73; cts. program adminstr. Office Gov. Va. Div. Justice and Crime Prevention, Richmond, 1973-75, courts system counsel, 1975—; individual practice law, Williamsburg, Va., 1975—; cons. Nat. Manpower Survey, Am. Inst. Research, Am. Acad. Jud. Edn., Nat. Center for State Cts. Trustee Norge (Va.) Civic Assn.; mem. James City-County (Va.) Social Service Bd. Mem. Am., Va., Fed. bar assns., Va. Trial Lawyers Assn., Am. Soc. Internat. Law, Am. Judicature Soc. Va. State, Fed. prosecutors assns. Contbr. articles to legal jours. Office: Francis St at Blair St Williamsburg VA 23185

SPITLER, DANIEL MERRILL, JR., b. Cape Girardeau, Mo., Sept. 29, 1939; B.A., Central Meth. Coll., 1963; J.D., Cumberland Sch. Law, 1969. Admitted to Mo., Ala. bars, 1969; asso. firm C. H. Erskine Smith, 1969-73; individual practice law, Birmingham, Ala., 1973—; instr. law Miles Coll., 1974—. Mem. Birmingham Regional Planning Commn. Mem. Am., Ala. bar assns., Birmingham Home Builders Assn., Birmingham Mortgage Assn. Recipient Most Dedicated Investigator award Miles Coll., 1976. Home: 1840 Chandcroft Circle Pelham AL 35124 Office: 1970 Chandalar South Office Park Pelham AL 35124 Tel (205) 663-6912

SPITZ, GERALD JOSEPH, b. Ridley Park, Pa., June 23, 1941; B.A., Pa. Mil. Coll., 1963; J.D., Dickinson Sch. Law, 1966. Admitted to Pa. bar; asso. firm Chadwick, Petrikin, Ginsburg & Wellman, Pa., 1969-70, Fronefield, deFuria & Petrikin, Pa., 1970-75; individual practice law, Media, Pa., 1975—; asst. dist. atty. Delaware County (Pa.), 1976—. Bd. dirs. SE Pa. br. ARC, 1976—. Mem. Am., Delaware County bar assns. Home: 901 10th Ave Prospect Park PA 19076 Office: 117 N Olive St Media PA 19073 Tel (215) 565-3000

SPITZ, MICHAEL BARRY, b. Boston, Dec. 19, 1938; B.B.A., U. Mass., 1960; LL.B. cum laude, Boston Coll., 1963. Admitted to Mass. bar, 1963, U.S. Dist. Ct. bar, 1965; asso. firm Rittenberg & Rittenberg, Boston, 1963-66, Lyne, Woodworth & Evarts, Boston, 1966-68; corp. counsel Friendly Ice Cream Corp., Wilbraham, Mass., 1968—. Mem. Boston, Hampden County bar assns. Mem. editorial staff Boston Coll. Indsl. and Comml. Law Rev. Home: 73 Farmington Ave Longmeadow MA 01106 Office: 1855 Boston Rd Wilbraham MA 01095 Tel (413) 543-2400

SPITZER, ALEXANDER, b. N.Y.C., Apr. 14, 1946; B.S. in Bus. Adminstrn., U. Fla., 1967, J.D., 1969; LL.M. in Taxation, N.Y. U., 1970. Admitted to Fla. bar, 1969, N.Y. bar, 1974; staff Internat. Bur. Fiscal Documentation, Amsterdam, Holland, 1970-72; internat. tax analyst GAF Corp., N.Y.C., 1972-73; asso. tax counsel Gulf and Western Industries, Inc., N.Y.C., 1973—. Mem. Am. Bar Assn. Editor in chief European Taxation, 1971-72; editor Taxation of Companies in Europe, 1970-72, Value Added Taxation in Europe, 1970-72. Home: 30 E 9th St New York City NY 10003 Office: 1 Gulf and Western Plaza New York City NY 10023 Tel (212) 333-4427

SPIVACK, GORDON BERNARD, b. New Haven, June 15, 1929; A.B., philos. orations honors with exceptional distinction, Yale, 1950, LL.B. magna cum laude, 1955. Admitted to Conn. bar, 1955, N.Y. bar, 1970, U.S. Supreme Ct. bar, 1962; atty., antitrust div. U.S. Dept. Justice, Washington, 1955-61, asst. chief, 1961-64, chief field ops., 1964-65, dir. ops., 1965-67, cons. to asst. atty. gen., 1968; partner firm Lord, Day and Lord, N.Y.C., 1970—; vis. lectr. law Yale, 1970—, asso. prof. law, 1967-70. Mem. N.Y. State Bar Assn., Bar Assn. City N.Y. Office: 25 Broadway New York City NY 10004 Tel (212) 344-8480

SPIVACK, JOHN MICHAEL, b. N.Y.C., June 22, 1942; B.A., Columbia, 1964; J.D., U. of Fla., 1967, M.A.T., 1973, LL.M., N.Y. U., 1968. Admitted to Fla. bar, 1967, Ga. bar, 1969, Pa. bar, 1971; mem. firm Smith, Currie, & Hancock, Atlanta, 1968-70; mem. firm Handler, Gerber & Widmer, Harrisburg, Pa., 1970-71; grad. instr. U. Fla.; 1972—. Mem. Am., Pa., Fla. bar assns., State Bar Ga., Am. Acad. Polit. and Social Sci., Am. Hist. Assn., Orgn. Am. Historians, Phi Kappa Phi. Recipient West Pub. Co. Labor Law award. Home: 504-11 SW 34 St Gainesville FL 32607

SPIVAK, PETER BEECHING, b. Phila., Jan. 9, 1933; B.A., Ohio Wesleyan U., 1954; J.D., Northwestern U., 1957. Admitted to Mich. bar, 1958, U.S. Supreme Ct. bar, 1962; asst. U.S. atty. Eastern Dist. Mich., 1958-60; law clk. to judge U.S. Dist. Ct. Eastern Dist. Mich., 1960-62; mem. firms Dyer, Meek, Ruegsesser and Bullard, Detroit, 1960-62, Spivak and James, Detroit, 1962-63, Penton, Nederlander, Tracy & Dodge, Detroit, 1963-64; chmn. Mich. Pub. Service Commn., 1964-68; judge Wayne County (Mich.) Common Pleas Ct., 1968-72, presiding judge, 1971; judge Wayne County 3d Jud. Circuit Ct., 1972—; pub. adminstr. Wayne County, 1963-64. Trustee, mem. exec. com. New Detroit, Inc., 1971—. Mem. exec. com., dir. Music Hall Center for Performing Arts, Detroit, 1972—, chmn. bd., 1972-74; trustee Detroit City Theatre, U. Wash. Inst. for Study Contemporary Social Problems; bd. dirs. Detroit Pub. Library Film Council, 1973—; active Detroit Inst. Arts, NAACP. Mem. Detroit, Mich., Am. bar assns. Contbr. articles to legal publs., book revs. to Detroit Free Press. Office: 403 Old County Bldg 600 Randolph St Detroit MI 48226 Tel (313) 224-5225

SPIVEY, JOHN B., b. Adrian, Ga., Jan. 29, 1897; pvt. study law, 1915. Admitted to Ga. bar, 1915; asso. firm Price & Spivey, Swainsboro, Ga., 1919-57; Spivey and Carlton, Swainsboro, 1957—; judge superior ct., Middle Judicial Circuit, Ga., 1966; mem. Ga. House Reps., 1929-37; mem. Ga. Senate, 1937-41, pres., 1937-41. Mem. Emanuel County (chmn. 1972-76), Middle Circuit, Ga., Am. bar assns., Am. Judicature Soc. Home: 328 W Main St Swainsboro GA 30401 Office: City Hall Bldg Swainsboro GA 30401 Tel (912) 237-2121

SPIZER, SAM WALLACE, b. Montreal, Que., Can., June 16, 1907; student U. Calif., Los Angeles, 1927; J.D., Southwestern Sch. Law, 1930; came to U.S., 1907, naturalized, 931930. Admitted to Calif. bar, 1930; individual practice law, Huntington Park, Calif., 1930-60; judge Huntington Park Municipal Ct., 1960-77. Chmn. U. Calif., Los Angeles Scholarship Com. Mem. Municipal Cts. Judges Assn. Los Angeles County (chmn. 1969-70).

SPIZZ, HARVEY WARREN, b. Bklyn., Apr. 7, 1943; A.B., Columbia Coll., 1964; J.D. U. Miami, 1967. Admitted to Fla. bar, 1967, N.Y. bar, 1968; counsel U.S. Small Bus. Adminstrn., 1967-68; staff atty. Hunts Point (N.Y.) Legal Services, 1968-71; sr. staff atty. Community Action for Legal Services, N.Y.C., 1971, exec. dir. law clinic Hofstra U., 1971-73, asst. prof. law, 1973-76; partner firm Spizz & Gans, Mineola, N.Y., 1976—. Mem. Nassau County Bar Assn. Home: 41 Devon Rd Great Neck NY 11023 Office: 114 Old Country Rd Mineola NY 11501 Tel (516) 747-8877

SPIZZIRRI, RICHARD DOMINIC, b. Oak Park, Ill., Feb. 21, 1933; A.B. magna cum laude, Brown U., 1955; LL.B. cum laude, Harvard, 1958. Admitted to N.Y. bar, 1959; asso. firm Davis Pohk & Wardwell, N.Y.C., 1958-67, mem. firm, 1958—. Trustee Juilliard Sch., N.Y.C., 1967—. Mem. Bar Assn. City N.Y., Am. Bar Assn. Office: 1 Chase Manhattan Plaza New York City NY 10005 Tel (212) 422-3400

SPOJA, WILLIAM ALOYSIUS, JR., b. Lewistown, Mont., Aug. 29, 1930; A.B., Coll. of Great Falls, 1952; J.D., U. Mont., 1969. Admitted to Mont. bar, 1969; individual practice law, Lewistown, Mont., 1969—; Fergus County atty., 1969—. Mem. Mont. State Bd. Health and Environ. Scis., 1975—, Lewistown city-county planning bd. Mem. Mont. County Attys. Assn., Mont., Am. bar assns. Office: 3d and Broadway Sts Lewistown MT 59457 Tel (406) 538-8127

SPONG, WILLIAM BELSER, JR., b. Portsmouth, Va., Sept. 29, 1920; LL.B., U. Va., 1947; LL.D. (hon.), Hampden- Sydney Coll., 1968; postgrad. U. Edinburgh (Scotland), 1947-48. Admitted to Va. bar, 1947; practiced in Portsmouth, Va., 1948-76; partner firm Cooper, Spong and Davis, 1956-67, 75-76; gen. counsel Commn. on Orgn. of Govt. for Conduct of Fgn. Policy, Washington, 1973-75; dean Marshall-Wythe Sch. Law, Coll. William and Mary, Williamsburg, Va., 1976—, lectr., 1948-49; mem. Va. Ho. of Dels., 1954-56, Va. Senate, 1956-66; mem. U.S. Senate from Va., 1966-73; vis. scholar U. Va. Sch. Law, 1973, Woodrow Wilson Internat. Center, 1973; adj. prof. U. Richmond Sch. Law, 1974-76; Cutler lectr. Marshall-Wythe Sch. Law, 1974-76; chmn. Va. Commn. on Pub. Edn., 1958-62. Fellow Am. Bar Found.; mem. Am., Va. (pres. 1976), Portsmouth bar assns., Va. State Bar (exec. com. 1960-64), Am. Judicature Soc., Order of Coif, Pi Kappa Alpha, Phi Alpha Delta, Omicron Delta Kappa. Home: 111 Montague Circle Williamsburg VA 23185 Office: Marshall-Wythe Sch Law Coll William and Mary Williamsburg VA 23185 Tel (804) 253-4304

SPOONER, MARK JORDAN, b. Norfolk, Va., Nov. 11, 1945; A.B., Georgetown U., 1967; J.D., U. Va., 1970. Admitted to D.C. bar, 1970, Va. bar, 1970; asso. firm Arnold and Porter, Washington, 1970—. Mem. Am., D.C., Va. State bar assns. Office: 1229 19th St NW Washington DC 20036 Tel (202) 872-6931

SPOONT, MAXWELL BECK, b. Pitts., Mar. 19, 1930; A.B. cum laude, Syracuse U., 1950; LL.B. magna cum laude, Syracuse U., 1957, J.D., 1968. Admitted to N.Y. bar, 1957, U.S. Ct. of Claims bar, 1964, U.S. Supreme Ct. bar, 1964; partner firm Twining & Fischer, Binghamton, N.Y., 1962-70; spl. asst. atty. gen. Oneida County (N.Y.) Investigation, 1959-62; asst. atty. gen. State of N.Y. Dept. Law, 1970-74; spl. asst. atty. gen acting in superseder of Wyo. County Dist. Atty., 1971-73; acting dep. atty. gen. State of N.Y. Dept. Law, 1974—; atty. (honor law grad. recruitment program), Office of Alien Property, Dept. Justice, Washington, 1957-59. Mem. Am., N.Y. State, Broome County bar assns., Order of Coif, Phi Kappa Phi, Justinian Hon. Law Soc. Home: 78 Aldrich Ave Binghamton NY 13903 Office: Empire State Plaza Agency Bldg 1 9th floor Albany NY 12223 Tel (518) 474-1620

SPOTTS, EDWARD O., b. Duquesne, Pa., Apr. 24, 1903; B.S., U. Pitts., 1924, LL.B., 1927. Admitted to Pa. bar, 1927; practice law, Pitts., 1927—; asso. firm Spotts, Gill and Morrow; dep. atty. gen. of Pa., 1932-35; asst. county solicitor Allegheny County, Pa., 1935-36. Mem. Am., Pa., Allegheny County bar assns., Am. Trial Lawyers Assn. (bd. govs. 1957, state v.p. 1955-58, pres. Western Pa. chpt. 1962), Acad. Trial Lawyers of Allegheny County. Author: The Great Auto Insurance Fraud, 1970; The Plaintiff Rests, 1971; Autobiography of a Trial Lawyer, 1976; asso. editor Am. Trial Lawyers Assn. Law Jour., 1953-72. Home: 1014 Cambridge St Natrona Heights PA 15065 Office: Frick Bldg Pittsburgh PA 15219

SPRADLIN, THOMAS RICHARD, b. Pauls Valley, Okla., June 9, 1937; A.A. with distinction, Ggorge Washington U., 1958, B.A. with distinction, 1959, J.D. with honors, 1963. Admitted to Va. bar, 1963, U.S. Supreme Ct. bar, 1967; clk. FBI, Washington, 1955-56; asst. to U.S. Senator A.S. Mike Monroney, Washington, 1956-63; asso. firm Clifford, Warnke, Glass, McIlwain & Finney, Washington, 1967-72, partner, 1973—; dir. Univ. Assos., Inc., Washington; pres. Applied Practical Tng., Inc., Arlington, Va. Mem. Am., Fed., D.C., Va. bar assns., Order of Coif, Phi Beta Kappa, Pi Gamma Mu, Delta Sigma Rho, The Lamar Soc. Asso. editor George Washington Law Rev., 1961-62. Home: 1425 4th St SW Washington DC 20024 Office: 815 Connecticut Ave NW Washington DC 20006 Tel (202) 298-8686

SPRAGENS, ROBERT MCMURTRY, JR., b. Lexington, Ky., Dec. 28, 1944; B.A., U. Louisville, 1966; J.D., U. Ky., 1969. Admitted to Ky. bar, 1969; partner firm Spragens & Smith, Lebanon, Ky., 1969—; city atty. City of Lebanon, 1973-75; asst. commonwealth's atty., 11th Judicial Dist. Ky., 1976—. Bd. dirs. Mary Immaculate Hosp., 1974—. Mem. Am., Ky., Marion County bar assns., Am. Trial Lawyers' Assn. Home: Star Route Lebanon KY 40033 Office: 15 Court Sq Lebanon KY 40033 Tel (502) 692-3141

SPRAGUE, THOMAS CHARLES, b. Berwyn, Ill., Dec. 27, 1941; A.B., Kenyon Coll., 1964; J.D. with honors, Chgo.-Kent Coll. Law, 1971. Admitted to Ill. bar, 1971; partner firm Borkenhagen & Sprague, LaGrange, Ill., 1971—. Bd. dirs. LaGrange Area United Fund, 1976—, LaGrange Kiwanis Club; trustee Lyons Township. Mem. Am., Ill., W. Suburban bar assns. Office: 521 S LaGrange Rd LaGrange IL 60525 Tel (312) 352-9400

SPRATLING, RONALD NILE, JR., b. Murray, Utah, Sept. 30, 1932; B.S. in Law, U. Utah, 1957, J.D., 1959. Admitted to Utah bar, 1959; asst. atty. gen. State of Utah, Salt Lake City, 1958-62; pres. Holladay Lumber & Hardware Co., Salt Lake City, 1970-76; pres. Holladay Bank & Trust Co., Salt Lake City, 1974-76; pres. Holladay Thrift & Loan Co., Salt Lake City, 1976—. Mem., original incorporator Holladay Rotary Club, 1960-76. Mem. Am. Trial Lawyers, Am., Utah State, Salt Lake County bar assns. Home: 4115 Gary Rd Salt Lake City UT 84117 Office: 4735 Highland Dr Salt Lake City UT 84117 Tel (801) 278-6744

SPRAY, JOSEPH LAURENCE, b. Los Angeles, Nov. 22, 1927; student Lake Forest Coll., 1945-46; student U. Calif., Berkeley, 1946-51, J.D., Hastings Coll. Law, San Francisco, 1951. Admitted to Calif. bar, 1952, U.S. Dist. Ct. bar for Central Dist. Calif., 1952; asso. firm Spray-Gould & Bowers, Los Angeles, 1952-56, partner, 1956-66; partner firm Archbald Zelezny & Spray, Santa Barbara, 1966—. Diplomate Am. Bd. Trial Advocates (pres. 1960). Fellow Internat. Acad. Trial Lawyers; mem. State Bar Calif. (pro tem mem. disciplinary bd. 1975—, chmn. adminstrv. com. 1971-74), Am. Bar Assn., Internat. Assn. Ins. Counsel, Assn. So. Calif. Def. Counsel (dir. 1964-65, 70-71), Legion Lex. Home: 4083 Cuervo St Santa Barbara CA 93110 Office: 3888 State St Santa Barbara CA 93105 Tel (805) 687-7721

SPRING, LIONEL MYRON, b. N.Y.C., Mar. 13, 1928; B.S., N.Y. U., 1949, LL.B., 1953. Admitted to N.Y. bar, 1955; partner firm Deutsch & Spring, N.Y.C., 1961—; small claims judge Civil Ct., N.Y. County. Mem. N.Y.C. Bar Assn., Am. Arbitration Assn. Home: 6 Canterbury Rd S Harrison NY 10528 Office: 300 Madison Ave New York City NY 10017 Tel (212) 661-0722

SPRING, RAYMOND LEWIS, b. Warsaw, N.Y., Aug. 5, 1932; A.B., Washburn U., Topeka, 1957, J.D., 1959. Admitted to Kans. bar, 1960, U.S. Ct. Appeals bar 10th Circuit, 1960; asso. firm Crane, Martin, Claussen & Ashworth, Topeka, 1959-65; Workmen's Compensation examiner State of Kans., 1961-62; asst. prof. law Washburn U., 1965-68, asso. prof., 1968-70, asso. prof., acting dean, 1970-71, prof., dean, 1971—; mem. cts. subcom. Kan. Gov.'s Com. on Criminal Adminstrn., 1970—. Bd. dirs. Topeka Welfare Planning Council, 1964-66; chmn. Shawnee County Young Republicans, 1962-64; bd. dirs. Shawnee Council Campfire Girls, Inc., 1965-68; leader edn. div. Topeka United Fund, 1972; deacon Central Congregational Ch., 1972-74. Mem. Am., Kans., Topeka bar assns., Barristers, Delta Theta Phi. Author: (with Ryan) Vernon's Kansas Criminal Code Annotated, 1971, Vernon's Kansas Code of Criminal Procedure, 1973. Home: 1616 Jewell St Topeka KS 66604 Office: 1700 College St Topeka KS 66621 Tel (913) 295-6600

SPRING, STEPHEN ROYSTON, b. Rochester, N.Y., July 15, 1945; B.A., Gettysburg Coll., 1967; J.D., Albany Law Sch., Union U., 1970. Admitted to N.Y. bar, 1971, U.S. Dist. Ct. bar No. Dist. N.Y., 1971; asso. firm Maynard, O'Connor & Smith, Albany, 1971—. Mem. N.Y. State, Albany County bar assns., Capital Dist. Trial Lawyers Assn. Home: 32 Mayfair Dr Slingerlands NY 12159 Office: 90 State St Albany NY 12207 Tel (518) 465-3553

SPRINGER, JAMES VAN RODEN, b. N.Y.C., July 9, 1934; A.B., Harvard U., 1955, LL.B., 1961. Admitted to N.Y. bar, 1962, D.C. bar, 1962, U.S. Supreme Ct. bar, 1968; law clk. to chief judge U.S. Ct. of Appeals 2d Circuit, N.Y.C., 1961-62; asso. firm Covington & Burling, Washington, 1962-67; asst. legal adviser Dept. State, Washington, 1967-68; dep. solicitor gen. Dept. Justice, 1968-71; asso. firm Dickstein, Shapiro & Morin, and predecessors, Washington, 1971, partner, 1972—. Mem. Am., D.C. bar assns. Pres. Harvard Law Rev. 1960-61. Home: 3017 44th Pl NW Washington DC 20016 Office: 2101 L St NW Washington DC 20037 Tel (202) 785-9700

SPRINKLE, THOMAS W., b. Wilmington, Ohio, Aug. 11, 1914; B.S., Wilmington Coll., 1951; LL.B., U. Cin., 1954, J.D., 1954. Ret. lt. col. USAF; admitted to Ohio bar, 1954, practiced in Wilmington, 1954-77; judge probate and juvenile div. Ct. of Common Pleas, Clinton County, Ohio, 1977—. Mem. Ohio, Ohio State, Clinton County Bar Assns. Home: 709 N South St Wilmington OH 45177 Office: PO Box 543 Wilmington OH 45177 Tel (513) 382-2401

SPRITZER, RALPH SIMON, b. N.Y.C., Apr. 27, 1917; B.S., Columbia, 1937, LL.B., 1940. Admitted to N.Y. bar, 1941, U.S. Supreme Ct. bar, 1950; atty. U.S. Dept. Justice, 1946-62; gen. counsel FPC, Washington, 1961-62; dep. solicitor gen. U.S. Dept. Justice, Washington, 1962-68; prof. law U. Pa., 1968—; cons. Adminstrv. Conf. U.S. Govt., 1970—, Ford Found., 1972—; Pa. Gov.'s Justice Commn. 1972-75; spl. counsel Fed. Election Commn., 1975-76. Mem. Am. Law Inst. Recipient Tom C. Clark award Fed. Bar Assn., 1968; Superior Service award U.S. Dept. Justice, 1960. Home: 2117 Pine Philadelphia PA 19103 Office: U Pa Law School 3400 Chestnut St Philadelphia PA 19104 Tel (215) 243-5638

SPRIZZO, JOHN EMILIO, b. Bklyn., Dec. 23, 1934; B.A., St. John's Coll., 1956, LL.B., 1959. Admitted to N.Y. bar, 1960; staff U.S. Dept. Justice, Washington, 1959-63; asst. U.S. atty. So. dist. N.Y., 1963-68, chief appellate atty., 1964-65, asst. chief criminal div., 1966-68; asso. prof. Fordham U. Law Sch., 1968-72; partner firm Curtis Mallet Prevost Colt & Mosler, N.Y.C., 1972—; mem. Knapp Commn. on Police Corruption, 1971-72. Office: 100 Wall St Room 1500 New York City NY 10005

SPROUL, HARVEY LEONARD, b. Williamsburg, Ky., Oct. 8, 1933; B.S., U. Tenn., 1955, J.D., 1957. Admitted to Tenn. bar, 1957, U.S. Ct. Mil. Appeals bar, 1958, U.S. Supreme Ct. bar, 1960; partner firms Dannel & Sproul, and predecessor, Lenoir City, Tenn., 1961-65, Sproul & Russell, Lenoir City, 1968-70, Sproul & Bailey, Lenoir City, 1971-73; individual practice law, Lenoir City, 1966-67, 74—; judge Loudon County (Tenn.) Ct., 1966-74. Chmn. Tellico Area Planning Council, 1967-74, East Tenn. Law Enforcement Adv. Com., 1974-75; vice chmn. Tenn. Adv. Com. for Local Planning, 1971-74; chmn. bd. Mid-East Community Action Agy., 1972-75; dir. Overlook Mental Health Center, 1973-74. Mem. Am., Tenn., Loudon County (pres. 1968) bar assns., Am., Tenn. trial lawyers assns., Tenn. County Judges Assn. (v.p. 1972-74), Lenoir City C. of C. (dir.), Phi Delta Phi, Delta Sigma Phi. Recipient Distinguished Service award Lenoir City, 1962; named Outstanding Young Man in Tenn. by Tenn. Jaycees, 1966. Office: 109 W Broadway Lenoir City TN 37771 Tel (615) 986-8054

SPROUL, MASON MILLER, b. Staunton, Va., Feb. 15, 1940; A.B., Yale U., 1962; LL.B., U. Va., 1966, J.D., 1970. Admitted to Va., W.Va. bars, 1966; partner firm Sanders and Sproul, Princeton, W.Va., 1966-67; individual practice law, Staunton, Va., 1968—; counsel Family Revival Fellowship. Dir. Staunton-Augusta (Va.) Mental Health Assn., 1968-73. Mem. Va. State Bar, Staunton Augusta, Am. bar assns., W.Va. State Bar. Office: Court Sq May Bldg Staunton VA 24401 Tel (703) 885-5146

SPROUSE, HARLOW LEE, b. Vega, Tex., Mar. 19, 1931; B.A., N. Tex. State U., 1956; J.D., U. Tex., Austin, 1960. Admitted to Tex. bar, 1960; partner firm Underwood, Wilson, Sutton, Berry, Stein & Johnson, Amarillo, Tex., 1960—; dir. 13th Bar Dist. State Bar Tex., 1975—; dir. Law Focused Edn., Inc., 1976—. Fellow Tex. Bar Found.; mem. Am., Tex., Amarillo (pres. 1972-73) bar assns. Home: 5003 Tawney St Amarillo TX 79106 Office: Amarillo National Bank Bldg Amarillo TX 79101 Tel (806) 376-5613

SPROW, HOWARD THOMAS, b. Atlantic City, N.J., Dec. 4, 1919; A.B. cum laude, Colgate U., 1942; J.D., Columbia, 1945. Admitted to N.Y. bar, 1946; mem. firm Brown, Wood, Fuller, Caldwell & Ivey, N.Y.C., 1945-70, partner, 1954-70; gen. counsel, v.p. corporate and pub. affairs, sec. Merrill Lynch, Pierce, Fenner & Smith, Inc., N.Y.C., 1970-76, Merrill Lynch & Co., Inc., 1973-76; partner firm Rogers & Wells, N.Y.C., 1977—; chmn. SEC adv. com. on broker/dealer compliance, 1972-74; chmn. advisory panel N.Y. Law Revision Commn. to Recodify N.Y. State Ins. Law, 1976—. Adj. prof. law Fordham U. Trustee, St. Lawrence U., Canton, N.Y.; trustee, vice chmn. bd. Westminster Choir Coll., Princeton, N.J. Mem. Am., N.Y. State bar assns., Assn. Bar City N.Y., N.Y. County Lawyers Assn., Am. Fgn. Lawyers Assn., Am. Judicature Soc. Mem. editorial bd. Columbia Law Rev., 1943-45. Home: 32 Fair St Cooperstown NY 13326 Office: 200 Park Ave New York City NY 10017 Tel (212) 972-3960

SPROWL, CHARLES RIGGS, b. Lansing, Mich., Aug. 22, 1910; A.B., U. Mich., 1932; J.D., 1934. Admitted to Ill. bar, 1935; partner firm Taylor, Miller, Magner, Sprowl, & Hutchings, Chgo., 1945—; dir. Paul F. Beich Co., Western Transp. Co., Busch and Schmitt, Inc., Simmons Engring. Corp., A. H. Ross & Sons Co., Petersen Aluminum Corp. Mem. bd. edn. New Trier Twp. High Sch., 1959-65, pres., 1963-65; bd. dirs. Glencoe (Ill.) Pub. Library, 1953-65, pres., 1955-56; bd. dirs. Cradle Soc., Evanston, Ill.; trustee Highland Park Hosp., 1959-69; bd. dirs. Juvenile Protective Assn., 1943-53; bd. dirs., Northwestern U. Settlement Assn., 1963—, pres., 1963-70; mem. Glencoe Zoning Bd. Appeals, 1956-76, chmn., 1966-76. Mem. Chgo., Ill., Am. bar assns., Am. Coll. Trial Lawyers, Soc. Trial Lawyers, Law Club Chgo. (pres. 1969-70), Legal Club (pres. 1953-54). Home: 558 Washington Ave Glencoe IL 60022 Office: 120 S LaSalle St Chicago IL 60603 Tel (312) 782-6070

SPROWL, JAMES ALEXANDER, b. Evanston, Ill., May 18, 1941; B.S.E.E., U. Mich., 1964, B.S. in Engring. Physics, 1964, J.D. cum laude, 1967. Admitted to Ill. bar, 1967; asso. firm Mason, Kolehmainen, Rathburn & Wyss, Chgo., 1967-72, partner, 1972-74; research atty. Am. Bar Found., Chgo., 1974—; lectr. law Northwestern U., 1970—, Chgo.-Kent Sch. Law, Ill. Inst. Tech., 1974—; vis. asso. prof. law U. Ill., spring 1977; dir. Ill. Bar Automated Research, Inc., Chgo., 1974—. Mem. Am., Ill. State, Chgo. bar assns., Chgo. Patent Law Assn., IEEE. Author: A Manual for Computer-Assisted Legal Research, 1976. Contbr. articles to law revs. Home: 825 Lincoln St Evanston IL 60201 Office: Am Bar Found 1155 E 60th St Chicago IL 60637 Tel (312) 667-4700

SPRUILL, JOSEPH E., JR., b. Washington County, Va., July 21, 1931; B.A., U. Richmond, 1955, LL.B., 1958. Admitted to Va. bar, 1958; now partner firm Lewis and Spruill, Tappahannock, Va.; commonwealth atty. Essex County (Va.), 1963-74. Mem. Am., Va., No. Neck (pres, 1974) bar assns., Va. State Bar (council, legal ethics com. 1971-75, pres. 1976-77), McNeill Law Soc., Delta Theta Phi, Omicron Delta Kappa. Office: 315 Cross St Tattahannock VA 22560 Tel (804) 443-3373*

SPRUNG, ARNOLD, b. N.Y.C., Apr. 18, 1926; A.B. in Physics, Dartmouth, 1947; J.D., Columbia, 1950. Admitted to N.Y. State bar, 1950, U.S. Supreme Ct. bar, 1971; mem. firm Burgess, Dinklage & Sprung, N.Y.C., 1950, sr. partner, 1973—. Mem. Am. Bar Assn., N.Y. County Lawyers Assn., N.Y., Am. patent law assns. Home: 339 Cedar Dr W Briarcliff Manor NY 10510 Office: 600 Third Ave New York City NY 10016

SPRUNG, MURRAY, b. N.Y.C., Aug. 9, 1903; LL.B., St. Johns U., 1928, LL.M., 1931. Admitted to N.Y. bar, 1930, U.S. Ct. Mil. Appeals, 1951, Supreme Ct. Japan, 1952, U.S. Supreme Ct. bar, 1956; individual practice law, N.Y.C., 1930-50; partner firm Bushell & Sprung, Tokyo, 1950-65; individual practice law, N.Y.C., 1965—; prosecutor Pacific War Crimes Trials, U.S. Army, 1946-47; hon. pres. Kyoto (Japan) Jr. Coll. Fgn. Langs., 1951-55. Vice-chmn. Japanese Am. Citizens League, 1949—; pres. Am. Camp Assn. N.Y., 1941-43; counsel Vets. Bur. N.Y. Urban League 1972—. Mem. Assn. Bar City N.Y., Am. Bar Assn. Dai-Ichi Bengoshi Kai, Internat. Legal Soc. Named Man of Yr. Japanese-Am. Citizens League (N.Y. Chpt.), 1975; recipient service award St. Johns U. Sch. Law. Home: 225 W 86th St New York City NY 10024 Office: 485 Fifth Ave New York City NY 10017 Tel (212) 682-7779

SPRUNK, JAMES A., b. 1919; student U. Toledo; LL.B., U. Mich., 1949. With firm Fuller, Seney, Henry & Hodge, 1949-68; v.p., gen. counsel Owens-Illinois, Inc., Toledo, 1968—. Office: PO Box 1035 Toledo OH 43666*

SPURLIN, ROBERT EVANS, b. Richmond, Ky., Apr. 28, 1938; B.A., Eastern Ky. U., 1964; J.D., U. Ky., 1966. Admitted to Ky. bar, 1967; real estate broker, auctioneer, Richmond, 1960-66; legal and legis. asst. to Lt. Gov. Wendall H. Ford, Frankfort, Ky., 1967-70; commr. pub. service, Frankfort, 1972-76, tchr. comml. law and bus. law Eastern Ky. U., 1970. Mem. Am., Ky., Madison County bar assns. Recipient Certificate of Appreciation City of Richmond, 1972; Citation of Appreciation Richmond Am. Legion, 1974; named Madison County's Outstanding Young Man, 1973. Home: Millstone Dr Richmond KY 40475 Office: 214 N Third St Richmond KY 40475 Tel (606) 623-7406

SPURLOCK, JOE CLARENCE MARLIN, b. Throckmorton, Tex., Aug. 31, 1910; B.A., U. Tex., Austin, 1933, LL.B., 1933. Admitted to Tex. bar, 1933, U.S. Supreme Ct. bar, 1964; partner firm Spurlock & Schattman, Ft. Worth, 1947-69; judge Tex. Dist. Ct., 96th Dist., Ft. Worth, 1969-75; asso. justice Tex. Ct. Civil Appeals, 2d Supreme Jud. Dist., 1975—. Mem. State Bar Tex., Am., Fed. bar assns. Home: 5030 Norma St Fort Worth TX 76103 Office: Ct of Civil Appeals Civil Cts Bldg Fort Worth TX 76102 Tel (817) 334-1166

SPURLOCK, OLIVER MAXWELL, b. Chgo., Feb. 28, 1945; B.A., U. Ill., Chgo., 1969; law degree; Admitted to Ill. bar, 1974; asst. state's atty., Cook County, Ill., 1973-75; asso. firm Ewell, Graham, McCormick and Ross, Chgo., 1975—; lectr. Ill. Inst. Tech., Chgo., Kent Coll. Mem. Cook County Bar Assn. Contbr. articles to profl. jours. Home: 822 E 52d St Chicago IL 60615 Office: 180 N LaSalle St Suite 1212 Chicago IL 60601 Tel (312) 263-2664

SQUADRON, HOWARD M., b. N.Y.C., Sept. 5, 1926; A.B. in History with honors, Coll. City N.Y., 1946; LL.B., Columbia U., 1947. Admitted to N.Y. bar, 1948; mem. faculty Law Sch. U. Chgo., 1947-48; asso. firm Stroock Stroock & Lavan, N.Y.C., 1948-50; staff counsel Am. Jewish Congress, N.Y.C., 1950-52; asso. firm Phillips, Nizer, Benjamin & Krim, N.Y.C., 1952-54; partner firm Squadron, Gartenberg, Ellenoff & Plesent, and predecessors, N.Y.C., 1954—. Chmn., N.Y. Met. council Am. Jewish Congress, 1961-64, chmn. gov. council, 1968-76; chmn. ad hoc com. City U. N.Y., 1970-72; chmn. exec. com. Found. for Am. Dance, 1968—; organizer, chmn. bd. dirs. Dance Theatre Found., 1972-74; 55th St. Dance Theatre Found., 1976—; bd. dirs., exec. com. N.Y. Found. for Arts, 1971—; bd. dirs. Creative Artists Program Service, 1972—. Mem. Am., N.Y. State bar assns., Bar Assn. City N.Y., Interracial Council Bus. Opportunity (founding dir.), N.Y. Civil Liberties Union. Editor Columbia Law Rev., 1946-47. Home: 4930 Goodridge Ave Riverdale NY 10471 Office: 551 Fifth Ave New York City NY 10017 Tel (212) 661-6500

SRENASKI, STEVEN PAUL, b. Green Bay, Wis., Nov. 17, 1948; B.A., Lawrence U., 1971; J.D., U. Wis., 1974. Admitted Wis. bar, 1974; partngr law firm Smith, Harlow & Srenaski, Manitowoc, Wis., 1974—. Active Wis. Heart Assn., 1975—. Mem. Wis., Manitowoc County, Am. bar assns., MENSA, Manitowoc Lions Club. Office: 927 S 8th St Manitowoc WI 54220 Tel (414) 682-6181

SRULOWITZ, MARVIN, b. N.Y.C., Dec. 16, 1948; A.A., B.A., Yeshiva U., 1969; J.D., N.Y. U., 1972. Admitted to N.Y. bar, 1973, U.S. Dist. Ct. bar for Eastern and So. dists. N.Y., 1973, U.S. Ct. Appeals bar, 2d Circuit, 1974, U.S. Customs Ct. bar, 1976, U.S. Supreme Ct. bar, 1976; asso. firm Delson & Gordon, N.Y.C., 1972—. Mem. Am., N.Y. State bar assns., N.Y. County Lawyers Assn., Am. Arbitration Assn. Home: 20 Jeffrey Pl Monsey NY 10952 Office: 230 Park Ave New York City NY 10017 Tel (212) 686-8030

STACEY, MICHAEL LEIGH, b. Detroit, Apr. 8, 1922; B.S., Wayne State U., 1947, LL.B., 1950. Admitted to Mich. bar, 1951; partner firm Nussbaum & Stacey, Detroit, 1951-71; judge 3d Jud. Circuit Ct. of Mich., Detroit, 1971—. Office: 1501 City-County Bldg Two Woodward Ave Detroit MI 48226 Tel (313) 224-5210

STACHEWICZ, RAYMOND ANTHONY, b. Cleve., Aug. 23, 1926; B.S., John Carroll U., 1952; LL.B., Cleve. Marshall Coll., 1956, J.D., 1968. Individual practice law, Cleve., 1956—. Mayor City of Garfield Heights (Ohio), 1970-76. Mem. Ohio, Cleve. bar assns., Am. Arbitration Assn. Home: 5660 Andover Blvd Garfield Heights OH 44125 Office: 5251 Turney Rd Garfield Heights OH 44125 Tel (216) 587-3500

STACK, PAUL FRANCIS, b. Chgo., July 21, 1946; B.S., U. Ariz. at Tucson, 1968; J.D., Georgetown U., 1971. Admitted to Ill. bar, 1971, U.S. Supreme Ct. bar, 1975, U.S. Tax Ct. bar, 1974; law clk. to U.S. dist. judge, Chgo., 1971-72; asst. U.S. Atty. No. Dist. Ill., Chgo., 1972-75; asso. firm Katten, Muchin, Gitles, Zavis, Pearl & Galler, Chgo., 1975-76; partner firm Stack & Filpi, 1976—. Mem. Chgo., Am. bar assns., Bohemian Lawyers Assn. Chgo. Home: 238 N Delaplaine Rd Riverside IL 60546 Office: Suite 954 135 S La Salle St Chicago IL 60603 Tel (312) 782-0690

STACKHOUSE, PETER KING, b. Lakewood, Ohio, May 19, 1944; B.A., Colgate U., 1966; student London Sch. Econs., 1965-66; LL.B., U. Va., 1969. Admitted to Va. bar, 1969; spl. agt. FBI, 1969-71; asso. firm Tolbert, Lewis & FitzGerald, Arlington, Va., 1972-74; mem. firm Tolbert, Smith, FitzGerald & Ramsey, Arlington, 1974—. Mem. Va., Am. bar assns., Va. State Bar. Office: 2300 S 9th St Arlington VA 22204 Tel (703) 521-5252

STACKLER, EDWARD KORNFIELD, b. Chgo., July 21, 1908; Ph.B., U. Chgo., 1931, J.D., 1933. Admitted to Ill. bar, 1933, since practiced in Chgo.; pres. Security Guards, Inc., Mark IV Security Service. Mem. Am., Inter-Am., Ill., Chgo. bar assns., Decalogue Soc., Am. Judicature Soc., Ill. Trial Lawyers Assn. Office: Suite 4050 875 N Michigan Blvd Chicago IL 60611 Tel (312) 337-6663

STACKLER, RONALD ERROL, b. Chgo., July 30, 1937; B.A. magna cum laude, Yale, 1959; J.D., U. Chgo., 1962. Admitted to Ill. bar, 1962, Calif. bar, 1969; practiced in Chgo., 1962-68, Los Angeles, 1969-73; asst. to chmn. Baker Industries, Beverly Hills, Calif., 1966-69; v.p. Internat. Industries, Inc., Beverly Hills, 1969-71, Heitman Mortgage Co., Los Angeles, 1971-72; gen. counsel Dept. Revenue, State of Ill., Springfield, 1973; asst. dir. ins. State of Ill., Springfield, 1973-74, dir. registration and edn., 1974-77; mem. firm Spivack and Lasky, Chgo., 1976—. Mem. Ill. Dangerous Drugs Adv. Bd., Natural History and Conservation Bd., Comprehensive State Health Planning Bd., State Univ. Retirement Bd., Vocat. Rehab. Bd., State Mus. Bd., Inter-Govt. Energy Task Force. Named Man of Yr. in Ins. Industry, Israel Bond Orgn., 1973; recipient citation Jewish Nat. Fund Chgo., 1976. Home: 70 E Walton Chicago IL 60611 Office: 69 W Washington Chicago IL 60602 Tel (312) 372-1700

STACY, CHARLES BRECKNOCK, b. Charleston, W.Va., Sept. 2, 1924; B.S., Yale U., 1948, LL.B., 1951. Admitted to W.Va. bar, 1951, U.S. Supreme Ct. bar, 1976; asso. firm Spilman, Thomas, Battle & Klostermeyer, Charleston, W.Va., 1951-58, partner, 1958—; pres. W.Va. Tax Inst., 1959-60. Bd. dirs. Charleston Symphony Orch., Inc., 1960-70, pres., 1962-63; trustee The Greater Kanawha Valley Found., 1968-72, chmn., 1970-72; bd. dirs. Community Council Kanawha Valley, Inc., 1971—, pres., 1975—; bd. dirs. United Way Kanawha Valley, Inc., 1973—, mem. exec. com. 1975—. Mem. Kanawha County, W.Va., Am. (chmn. com. legis. recommendations, sect. taxation 1975—) bar assns., W.Va. State Bar. Contbr. articles to legal jours. Home: 1560 Thomas Circle Charleston WV 25314 Office: 1101 Kanawha Banking & Trust Bldg Charleston WV 25301 Tel (304) 344-4081

STADTMAUER, DAVID, b. N.Y.C., Dec. 16, 1934; B.A., Yeshiva U., 1956; LL.B., N.Y. U., 1960. Admitted to N.Y. State bar, 1961; partner firm Fuss, Geller & Stadtmauer, N.Y.C., 1964-65; law sec. to justice of N.Y. Supreme Ct., N.Y.C., 1965-72; commr. N.Y.C. Civil Service Commn., 1972-74; judge Civil Ct., N.Y.C., 1974—; arbitrator in spl. arbitration procs. Civil Ct., 1965-68. Mem. Borough of Manhattan Community Bd., 1965-74. Mem. Assn. Bar City of N.Y., N.Y. County Lawyers Assn. Home: 140 Cabrini Blvd New York City NY 10033 Office: 111 Centre St New York City NY 10013 Tel (212) 374-8442

STAED, ROBERT EMMET, b. St. Louis, July 17, 1914; LL.D., St. Louis U., 1948. Admitted to Mo. bar, 1948; individual practice law, St. Louis, 1948—; city atty. City of Kirkwood (Mo.), 1970-76, City of Florissant (Mo.), 1977—; partner firm Kappel, Neill, Staed & Wolff. Mem. Kirkwood City Council, 1960-70. Mem. Am., Mo., St. Louis bar assns. Home: 1411 Northlin Dr Kirkwood MO 63122 Office: 706 Chestnut St Saint Louis MO 63101 Tel (314) 241-3355

STAFFORD, CHARLES FREDERICK, b. Burlington, Wash., June 24, 1918; B.A. with honors in Polit. Sci., Whitman Coll., 1940, LL.D., 1956; LL.B., Yale, 1946. Admitted to Wash. bar, 1947; chief dep. pros. atty., Skagit County, Wash., 1947-52; judge Superior Ct. of Skagit and Island Counties, 1952-69; mem. Wash. Ct. Appeals, 1969-70; justice Wash. Supreme Ct., 1970—; chief justice, 1975—; mem. faculty Nat. Coll. State Trial Judges, summers, 1968, 69. Mem. Wash. Bench-Bar-Press Com., 1964—; mem. adv. com. Supreme Ct. Pub. Defender Demonstration Project; chmn. Com. on Juvenile Justice, Wash. Little White House Conf. Mem. exec. bd. Mt. Baker area council Boy Scouts Am., 1965-70, Tumwater Area council, 1970-73. Trustee Wash. State Capital Mus., 1975—. Mem. Wash. State, Am. bar assns., Am. Judicature Soc., Am. Law Inst. Phi Beta Kappa, Delta Sigma Rho, Beta Theta Pi. Contbr. articles to legal jours. Home: 2016 Clairemont Circle Olympia WA 98502 Office: Wash Supreme Ct Temple of Justice Olympia WA 98504*

STAFFORD, CHESTER JEFFERSON, b. Pearisburg, Va., Apr. 20, 1939; B.A., Coll. William and Mary, 1961; LL.B., U. Va., 1964. Admitted to Va. bar, 1964; partner firm Dillow & Stafford, and predecessor, Pearisburg, 1964—; mem. Va. Ho. of Dels., 1971—. Chmn. cancer drive, Giles County, Va., 1967; pres. Giles County United Fund, 1973. Mem. Va., Giles County bar assns. Office: Dillow & Stafford Pearisburg VA 24134 Tel (703) 921-3411

STAFFORD, ROBERT AYER, b. Honolulu, Dec. 6, 1918; B.A., U. Hawaii, 1939; LL.B., Yale, 1942. Admitted to D.C. bar, 1942, Hawaii bar, 1942, Calif. bar, 1957; sr. partner firm Stafford, Buxbaum & Chakmak, Claremont, Calif., 1957—. Pres. Calif. Sch. Bds. Assn., 1973; trustee Scripps Coll., Claremont, 1969—; chmn. Calif. Equal Ednl. Opportunities Commn., 1975-77. Mem. Am., Calif., Hawaiian, Pomona Valley bar assns., Calif. Trial Lawyers Assn. Home: 362 W 12th St Claremont CA 91711 Office: 414 Yale Ave Claremont CA 91711 Tel (714) 626-1224

STAFSHOLT, JON, b. St. Paul, Apr. 17, 1943; A.A., Calif. Lutheran Coll., 1963; B.A., U. Mo., 1965, B.Journalism, 1965; J.D., U. Minn., 1971. Admitted to Minn. bar, 1972; partner firm Stafsholt and Helseth, Elbow Lake, Minn., 1972—. Pres. Elbow Lake Civic and Commerce Assn., 1972-73. Mem. Minn. State (bd. govs. 1975—), 16th Dist. (pres. 1974-75), Am. bar assns., Am. Arbitration Assn. Home: Elbow Lake MN 56531 Office: Elbow Lake MN 56531 Tel (218) 685-4452

STAHL, CHARLES EUGENE, b. Washington, Sept. 23, 1944; A.B., Notre Dame U., 1967; J.D., Northwestern U., 1971. Advisor urban life Chgo. Com. on Urban Opportunity, 1967-68; staff Community Relations Service, U.S. Dept. of Justice, Washington and Chgo., 1969-71; asso. firm Newman & Hess, Chgo., 1972-74; partner firm Newman, Hess & Stahl, Chgo., 1974-75, firm Newman, Stahl & Shadur, Chgo., 1976—. Mem. Am., Ill., Chgo., Cook County bar assns. Contbr. articles in field to profl. jours. Office: 180 N LaSalle St Chicago IL 60601 Tel (312) 263-4200

STAHL, E. THOMAS, b. Balt., Apr. 19, 1920; J.D., U. Md., 1948. Admitted to Md. bar, 1948; individual practice law, Balt., 1948—. Mem. Md., Balt. bar assns. Home: 5005 Falls Rd Terr Baltimore MD 21210 Office: 1220 Fidelity Bldg Charles and Lexington Sts Baltimore MD 21201 Tel (301) 685-4558

STAHLA, EDWARD ALAN, b. Kimball, Nebr., Feb. 17, 1943; B.A. in Polit. Sci., U. Wyo., 1965, J.D., 1968. Admitted to Nebr., Wyo. bars, 1968, Alaska bar, 1969; partner George L. Gucker, Ketchikan, Alaska, 1969-70; city atty. Ketchikan, 1970-77; partner firm Christianson, Royce & Stahla, Sitka, 1977—. Program leader Jr. Achievement, 1970. Mem. Alaska (bd. govs. 1972—, sec. 1973, pres. 1975—), Nebr., Wyo. bar assns., Nat. Inst. Municipal Attys. (state rep. 1975). Home: PO Box 2165 Sitka AK 99835 Office: PO Box 4 Sitka AK 99835 Tel (907) 747-6681

STAIB, MARK EDWARD, b. Tiffin, Ohio, Jan. 31, 1948; A.B. magna cum laude, John Carroll U., 1970; J.D., U. Va., 1973. Admitted to Ohio bar, 1973; asso. firm Hahn, Loeser, Freedheim, Dean and Wellman, Cleve., 1973—. Mem. Bar Assn. Greater Cleve. Certified civil trial adv., Cuyahoga County Bar Assn. Office: 800 National City E 6th Bldg Cleveland OH 44114 Tel (216) 621-0150

STAIR, HUNTER DOUGLAS, b. Detroit, Feb. 7, 1929; B.A., Wesleyan U., 1951; J.D., Detroit Coll. Law, 1955. Admitted to Mich. bar, 1955, U.S. Supreme Ct. bar, 1973; mem. firm Lungerhausen & Stair, Mt. Clemens, Mich., 1955-67; judge Municipal Ct., Mt. Clemens, 1968; judge 41st Dist. Ct., 1968-71; judge Macomb County Circuit Ct., Mt. Clemens, 1971—. Commr. Mt. Clemens, 1959; mayor pro tem, Mt. Clemens, 1961-63; mem. Macomb County Bd. Suprs., 1963-67. Mem. Macomb County Bar Assn., N.Am. Judges Assn., Am. Judicature Soc. Home: 85 S Wilson Blvd Mount Clemens MI 48043 Office: Macomb County Ct Bldg Mount Clemens MI 48043 Tel (313) 465-1211

STALEY, AUSTIN LEANDER, b. Pitts., Dec. 30, 1902; LL.B., Duquesne U., 1928; J.D., St. Vincent Coll., 1963. Admitted to Pa. bar, 1928; asst. city solicitor City of Pitts., 1934; dep. atty. gen. State of Pa., 1935, dir. workmen's compensation, 1936, dep. sec. labor and industry, 1937-38; judge U.S. Ct. Appeals, 3d circuit, 1950—, chief judge, 1966-68, U.S. sr. circuit judge, 1968—. Mem. Am., Pa., Allegheny County bar assns., Am. Law Inst. Home: Quail Hill Ln Fox Chapel PA 15238 Office: 725 US Post Office and Courthouse Pittsburgh PA 15219 Tel (412) 644-3550

STALEY, HUGH ARTHUR, b. Shelby County, Ohio, Mar. 28, 1900; J.D., Ohio No. U., 1926. Admitted to Ohio bar, 1926; partner firm Spidel, Staley, Hole & Hanes and predecessors, Greenville, Ohio, 1950—; pros. atty., Darke County, Ohio, 1937-41. Trustee, Ohio No. U., 1965-72; chmn. Darke County Polio Fund, 1947-54. Mem. Am., Ohio, Darke County (Ohio) bar assns. Office: Spidel Staley Hole & Hanes 210-212 Weaver Bldg Greenville OH 45331 Tel (513) 548-1157

STALEY, JOSEPH HARDIN, JR., b. Tyler, Tex., May 23, 1937; B.A., Yale, 1959; LL.B., Tex. U., 1964. Admitted to Tex. bar, 1964; mem. firm Locke, Purnell, Boren, Laney & Neely, Dallas, 1964—; counsel Banking and Currency Com., U.S. Senate, Washington, 1968-69; mem. nat. adv. council SBA, 1971—; mem. constl. revision com. Tex., 1974. Bd. dirs. Dallas Soc. Crippled Children, 1973-76, Dallas YMCA, 1975—. Mem. Am., Tex., Dallas bar assns., Phi Alpha Delta. Home: 4445 Rheims Pl Dallas TX 75209 Office: 3600 Republic Bank Tower Dallas TX 75201

STALEY, THOMAS LEE, b. Indpls., Apr. 25, 1946; B.B.A., N. Tex. State U., 1968; J.D., U. Tex., 1971. Admitted to Tex. bar, 1971, Okla. bar, 1972; asso. area counsel HUD, Oklahoma City, 1971-73; asst. counsel USLIFE Real Estate Services Corp., Dallas, 1973-75; vice pres., counsel Murray Fin. Corp., Dallas, 1976—. Mem. Am., Tex., Okla., Dallas bar assns. Address: 1010 W Mockingbird Ln PO Box 47791 Dallas TX 75247 Tel (214) 630-7070

STALLARD, CARL ELDON, b. Lawrence, Kans., Jan. 13, 1929; B.S. in Bus., U. Kans., 1951, LL.B., 1956. Admitted to Mo. bar, 1956, Kans. bar, 1956, S.C. bar, 1965, Ohio bar, 1971; v.p. Traders Nat. Bank, Kansas City, Mo., 1959-63; sr. v.p. trust dept. 1st Nat. Bank of S.C., Columbia, 1963-71; exec. v.p. 1st Trust Co. of Ohio, Columbus, 1971—. Pres., Columbus Assn. for the Performing Arts, 1975-77; bd. dirs. Cancer Clinic, Columbus, 1976-77. Mem. Ohio Bankers Assn. (mem. exec. com. trust div. 1975-77), Columbia Estate Planning Council (past pres.), Am. Bar Assn. (vice chmn. significant legis. com.), S.C. Bank Trust Assn. (pres. 1965-66). Home: 4648 Stonehaven Dr Columbus OH 43220 Office: 100 E Broad St PO Box 1205 Columbus OH 43216 Tel (614) 461-5892

STAMM, ALAN, b. Galesburg, Ill., Nov. 22, 1931; student Universidad Nacional de Mexico, summer 1950; A.B., Yale, 1952; J.D., Harvard, 1957. Admitted to Calif. bar, 1957, U.S. Supreme Ct., 1963; asso. firm Thelen, Marrin, Johnson & Bridges, San Francisco, 1957-60; staff atty. Litton Industries, Inc., Beverly Hills, Calif., 1960-66, asst. sec., 1963-66; sec., gen. counsel Internat. Rectifier Corp., Los Angeles, 1966-69, v.p., 1968-69; v.p., gen. counsel Republic Corp., Los Angeles, 1969-71, also dir., 1970-71; v.p., gen. counsel Saturday Rev. Industries, N.Y.C., 1971-72; v.p., gen. counsel Mattel, Inc., Hawthorne, Calif., 1972-74, staff cons., 1974-75; of counsel firm Long & Levit, Los Angeles, 1975—; dir. Synestructics, Inc. Trustee Center for Law in the Pub. Interest. Mem. Am., Fed., Calif., San Francisco, Los Angeles bar assns., Am. Jewish Com., Harvard Law Sch. Assn., Los Angeles World Affairs Council, Am. Arbitration Assn. (nat. panel of arbitrators), NAACP, UN Assn. U.S.A., World Peace Through Law Center, Sierra Club, Phi Beta Kappa. Home: 1613 Manning Ave unit B-2 Los Angeles CA 90024 Office: 1900 Ave of the Stars suite 1800 Los Angeles CA 90067 Tel (213) 879-1222

STAMM, CHARLES H., III, b. 1938; A.B., Princeton U., 1960; J.D., Yale U., 1963. Atty., Conn. Gen. Life Ins. Co., Hartford, 1963-67, asst. counsel, 1967-70, asso. counsel, 1970, gen. counsel, 1970—, sec., 1974—. Office: Conn Gen Life Ins Co Hartford CT 06152*

STAMM, FRED R., b. Milw., May 8, 1913; B.S., Marquette U., 1933, LL.B., 1935. Admitted to Wis. bar, 1935; individual practice law, Markesan, Wis., 1935—; atty. Village of Marquette, 1954—, Village of Kingston, Markesan Sch. Bd., 1967—, Green Lake Sanitary Dist., 1968—. Mem. Wis., Green Lake County bar assns. Home: 531 N Margaret St Markesan WI 53946 Office: 36 S Bridge St Markesan WI 53946 Tel (414) 398-2900

STAMM, KENNETH RUSSELL, b. Fort Wayne, Ind., Apr. 26, 1944; A.B., Ind. U., 1968, J.D., 1972. Admitted to Ind. bar, 1972; intern Marion County (Ind.) Prosecutor's Office, Indpls., 1971-72, dep., 1972; asso. firm Webb & Webb, Noblesville, Ind., 1972-73; analyst Ind. Legis. Council, Indpls., 1973; asso. firm Nisenbaum & Brown, Indpls., 1974-76; dep. atty. gen. Indpls., 1976—; individual practice law, Indpls., 1972—. Mem. Am., Ind. State, Indpls. bar assns., Phi Alpha Delta. Home: 5323 Rosslyn Ave Indianapolis IN 46220 Office: Atty Gen's Office Statehouse Indianapolis IN 46220 Tel (317) 633-4654

STAMMER, WILLIAM B., b. N.Y.C., Feb. 14, 1941; A.B., N.Y. U., J.D., LL.M.. Admitted to N.Y. bar, 1964, U.S. Supreme Ct. bar, 1970; with firm Gasperini, Koch & Savage, N.Y.C., 1966-70; with Internat. Playtex, Inc., N.Y.C., 1970—. Mem. Am. bar assn., Assn. Bar City N.Y. Home: 35 Monroe Pl Brooklyn Heights NY 11201 Office: 888 7th St New York City NY 10019

STAMOS, JOHN JAMES, b. Chgo., Jan. 30, 1924; LL.B., DePaul U. Admitted to Ill. bar, 1949; asst. corp. counsel City of Chgo., 1950-53; asst. state's atty. Cook County, Chgo., 1953-66, state's atty., 1966-68; judge Appellate Ct. of Ill., Chgo., 1968—; mem. Ill. Cts. Commn., 1974—. Recipient Nat. Dist. Attys. Assn. award, 1968; Ill. State Attys. award, 1968; Liberty Bell award Fed. Bar Assn. No. Dist. Ill., 1968. Home: 2400 Colony Ct Northbrook IL 60062 Office: Civic Center Chicago IL 60602 Tel (312) 793-5462

STAMP, FREDERICK PFARR, JR., b. Wheeling, W.Va., July 24, 1934; B.A., Washington and Lee U., 1956; LL.B., U. Richmond, 1959. Admitted to Va. bar, 1959, W.Va. bar, 1960; assoc. firm Schmidt, Laas, & Schrader, Wheeling, 1960-63; partner firm Schmidt, Laas, Schrader & Miller, Wheeling, 1963-74; partner firm Schrader, Miller, Stamp & Recht, Wheeling, 1974-76, Schrader, Stamp & Recht, 1977—; dir. Security Nat. Bank & Trust Co. Mem. W.Va. State Legislature, 1966-70, W.Va Bd. Regents, 1971—. Mem. Am., W.Va., Ohio County bar assns., Assn. Am. Trial Lawyers. Home: 32 Williamsburg Wheeling WV 26003 Office: 816 Central Union Bldg Wheeling WV 26003 Tel (304) 233-3390

STAMP, NEAL ROGER, b. Watkins Glen, N.Y., Sept. 19, 1918; A.B., Cornell U., 1940, J.D., 1942. Admitted to N.Y. bar, 1943; individual practice law, Rochester, N.Y., 1946-47; asst. sec. corp., asso. legal counsel Cornell U., Ithaca, N.Y., 1947-59, sec. corp., asso. legal counsel, 1959-62, sec. corp., 1959—, univ. counsel, 1962—; lectr. Practising Law Inst.; dir. aero. lab., research found.; dir. First Nat. Bank & Trust Co., Ithaca. Trustee, Tompkins County Meml. Hosp., 1959-66, pres., 1961-62. Mem. Am., N.Y. State, Tompkins County bar assns., Assn. Bar City N.Y., Nat. Assn. Coll. and Univ. Attys. (pres. 1976—). Home: 205 N Sunset Dr Ithaca NY 14850 Office: 500 Day Hall Cornell U Ithaca NY 14853 Tel (607) 256-5124

STAMPER, RUSSELL WRIGHT, b. Buffalo, Sept. 26, 1944; B.S., State U. N.Y. at Buffalo, 1967; J.D., U. Buffalo, 1973. Admitted to Wis. bar, 1973; atty. Legal Aid Soc. of Milw., 1973-76; individual practice law, Milw., 1976—; part-time instr. Milw. Area Tech. Coll. Mem. Wis., Milw., Milw. Jr. bar assns., Wis. Council on Criminal Justice. Home: 3129 N 51st Blvd Milwaukee WI 53216 Office: 600 W Walnut St Milwaukee WI 53212 Tel (414) 562-9232

STANCZAK, DAVID LOREN, b. Waukegan, Ill., Dec. 2, 1945; B.A. in Polit. Sci., U. Ill., 1967, J.D., 1971. Admitted to Ill. bar, 1971; corp. counsel City of Bloomington (Ill.), 1971—. Bd. dirs. McLean County Assn. Mental Health. Mem. Am., Ill., McLean County bar assns., Nat. Inst. Municipal Law Officers. Home: 1201 N State St Bloomington IL 61701 Office: 109 E Olive St Bloomington IL 61701 Tel (309) 828-7361

STANCZYK, BENJAMIN CONRAD, b. Detroit, Apr. 4, 1915; A.B., Wayne State U., 1936; J.D., U. Mich., 1939. Admitted to Mich. bar, 1939, U.S. Dist. Ct. bar for Eastern Dist. Mich., 1939, U.S. 10th Circuit Ct. Appeals bar, 1944, U.S. 6th Circuit Ct. Appeals bar, 1947; asso. firms Schudlich Ude & Jefferson, Detroit, 1939-42, Dann, Atlas & Tilchen, Detroit, 1946-48; asst. pros. atty. Wayne County (Mich.), 1949-57; judge Detroit Common Pleas Ct., 1957-75; vis. judge Mich. Ct. System, 1975—. Judge adv. Disabled Am. Vets. of Mich., 1964-71; pres., organizer Tri-County Dental Health Council, Detroit, 1969; pres. advisory bds. Vols. Am., 1977—. Mem. Am. Bar Assn. (Mich. chmn. com. on spl. cts.), Mich. State Bar, Delta Sigma Rho, Pi Sigma Alpha. Home: 4151 Courville St Detroit MI 48224 Tel (313) 371-7430

STANDER, IRVIN, b. N.Y.C., Dec. 6, 1906; B.S. in Edn., U. Pa., 1927, LL.B., 1929. Admitted to Pa. bar, 1929; individual practice law, Phila., 1929—; spl. asst. atty. gen. Pa. Dept. Justice, 1935-40; adminstr. zoning com. Phila. City Council, 1952-55; dep. atty. gen. Pa. Dept. Justice, 1955-63; workmen's compensation referee Pa. Dept. Labor and Industry, 1972—; chmn. Phila. Dist. Compensation Referees bd., 1974-76. Pres. Greater West Oak Lane Community Council, 1962-64; bd. dirs., pres. Neighborhood Centre, 1964-67; mem. adv. bd. Hebrew Sunday Sch. Soc., 1945—. Mem. Am., Pa., Phila. bar assns. Recipient Humanitarian award Phila. Assn. for Retarded Citizens, 1975; Humanitarian of the Year award Half-Century Sq. Club, 1976; other community service awards; contbr. articles in field to profl. jours. Home: 8220 Thouron Ave Philadelphia PA 19150 Office: 916 One E Penn Sq Philadelphia PA 19107 Tel (215) 563-9901

STANFIELD, ANDREW LOUIS, b. East Point, Ga., Jan. 31, 1917; A.B., Emory U., 1942; LL.B., Atlanta U., 1950, LL.M., 1951. Admitted to Ga. bar, 1950, U.S. Supreme Ct. bar, 1973; individual practice law, Atlanta; mem. East Point City Council, 1950-57; recorder City of East Point, 1957-60. Mem. Am., Atlanta bar assns. Home: 2277 N Main St East Point GA 30344 Office: 2301 National Bank Georgia Bldg Atlanta GA 30303 Tel (404) 524-2878

STANG, THOMAS ANDERSEN, b. Seattle, Mar. 12, 1935; B.A., U. Wash., 1956, LL.B., 1962. Admitted to Wash. bar, 1962; dep. prosecutor, asst. chief criminal dep. King County (Wash.), 1962-67; individual practice law, Seattle, 1967—; judge pro tem Seattle Municipal Ct., 1967—. Hon. consul of Norway for Wash. and Idaho, 1967—. Mem. Wash., Seattle, King County bar assns. Home: 4245 NE 89th Seattle WA 98115 Office: 806 Joseph Vance Bldg Seattle WA 98101 Tel (206) 623-3957

STANGER, ROLAND JONATHAN, b. Detroit, Oct. 7, 1910; A.B., U. Mich., 1931, J.D., 1934. Admitted to N.Y. bar, 1935; asso. firm Mudge, Stern, Williams and Tucker, N.Y.C., 1934-39; instr. law Western Res. U., 1939-40; asst. prof. law Ohio State U., 1940-46, asso. prof., 1946-54, prof., 1954-71; prof. law Ind. U., 1971—; Bd. Econ. Warfare, Fgn. Econ. Adminstrn., 1942-46; dep. fgn. trade adminstr. Fgn. Trade Adminstrn., Govt. Greece, 1947-48; chair internat. law Naval War Coll., 1958-59; prof. pub. internat. law Haile Sellasie U, Ethiopia, 1965-67. Mem. Order of Coif, Phi Beta Kappa. Home: 508 S Lincoln Bloomington IN 47401 Office: Sch Law Ind U Bloomington IN 47401 Tel (812) 337-8736

STANIFORTH, ROBERT OLIVER, b. Pueblo, Colo., Oct. 30, 1916; A.B., U. Colo., 1939, postgrad. in polit. sci., 1939-41; postgrad. in polit. sci. U. Calif., Berkeley, summer 1940-41; LL.B., U. So. Calif., 1945. Admitted to Calif. bar, 1945; law clk. to fed. judge William Healy, 1945, to Chief Justice Phil Gibson, Supreme Ct. of Calif., 1946; individual practice law, San Diego, 1946-48; partner firm Swing, Scharnikow & Staniforth, San Diego, 1948-59; judge Municipal Ct., San Diego, 1959-63, San Diego Superior Ct., 1963-76; asso. justice 4th Dist. Calif. Ct. of Appeal, 1976—; lectr. law San Diego State U., 1948-65, U. Calif., Los Angeles, 1965-70; adj. prof. law U. San Diego, 1965-70. Mem. Calif. Judges Assn. (dir. exec. bd. 1974-76). Office: State Bldg San Diego CA 92101 Tel (714) 236-7265

STANISCI, THOMAS WILLIAM, b. Bklyn., Nov. 16, 1928; B.A., St. John's Coll., 1949, J.D., 1953. Admitted to N.Y. State bar, 1953; library asst. N.Y. County Lawyer's Assn., N.Y.C., 1949-50, 52-53; asso. firm DiBlasi, Marasco & Simone, White Plains, N.Y., 1954-60, firm Simone, Brant & Stanisci, White Plains, 1960-66, firm Shayne, Dachs, Weiss, Kolbrener, Stanisci & Harwood, Mineola, N.Y., 1966—; instr. adult edn. ins. law, 1955-57; lectr. Practicing Law Inst., 1973-74; instr., lectr. Am. Mgmt. Assn., 1974; guest instr. Adelphi U., 1975. Mem. Am. Arbitration Assn. (arbitrator 1970—), Am., Nassau-Suffolk trial lawyers assns., Columbian Lawyers Assn., Nassau County Bar Assn. Author: Malpractice—Reading a Hospital Record, 1973; An Analysis of a Hospital Record, 1976. Home: 27 Treeview Dr Melville NY 11746 Office: 1501 Franklin Ave Mineola NY 11501 Tel (516) 747-1100

STANLEY, ARTHUR JEHU, JR., b. Lincoln County, Kans., Mar. 21, 1901; LL.B., U. Mo. at Kansas City, 1928. Admitted to Mo. bar, 1927, Kans. bar, 1928; partner firm Stanley, Stanley, Schroeder, Weeks & Thomas, and predecessors, Kansas City, Kans., 1928-58; county atty., Wyandotte, Kans., 1935-41; judge U.S. Dist. Ct. Kans., Kansas City, 1958-60, chief judge, 1961-71, sr. judge, 1971—; mem. Kans. State Senate, 1941; mem. Jud. Conf. U.S., 1967-70, chmn. com. on operation of jury system, 1973—; mem. Jud. Conf. U.S. Bicentennial Com., 1975—. Fellow Am. Bar Found.; mem. Am., Kans., Leavenworth County bar assns., Am. Judicature Soc. Contbr. articles to legal jours. Home: 501 N Esplanade Leavenworth KS 66048 Office: Fed Bldg Leavenworth KS 66048 Tel (913) 682-8450

STANLEY, JACK W., b. Vancouver, Wash., July 6, 1914; B.A., U. Wash., Seattle, 1937; LL.B., Willamette U., 1949, J.D., 1970. Admitted to Oreg. bar, 1949; v.p. Pacific Title Ins. Co., Salem, Oreg., 1955-62; pres. Pioneer Title Co. of Lane County, Eugene, Oreg., 1962-69, Willamette Valley Title Co., Salem, 1970-76. Mem. Oreg. Land Title Assn. (pres. 1959-60), Phi Delta Phi. Office: 318 Church St NE PO Box 825 Salem OR 97308 Tel (503) 581-0555

STANLEY, JOHN WILLIAM, JR., b. Concord, N.H., Mar. 17, 1922; A.B., Bowdoin Coll., 1948; LL.B., Boston U., 1951. Admitted to N.H. bar, 1951; partner firm Stanley, Tardif, Shapiro, Concord, 1951—; county atty. Merrimack County (N.H.), 1955-60; corporator Concord Savs. Bank; ret. lt. col. JAGC, U.S. Air Force. Pres. Concord Youth Hockey Assn., 1971-73; v.p. Babe Ruth Baseball League, Concord. Mem. Merrimack County, N.H., Am. bar assns. Home: 127 Mountain Rd Concord NH 03301 Office: 41 Centre St Concord NH 03301 Tel (603) 225-6627

STANLEY, JUSTIN ARMSTRONG, b. Leesburg, Ind., Jan. 2, 1911; A.B., Dartmouth, 1933, A.M. (hon.), 1952; LL.B., Columbia, 1937; LL.D., John Marshall Law Sch., 1975, Suffolk U., 1976. Admitted to Ill. bar, 1937; mem. firm Isham, Lincoln & Beale, Chgo., 1937-66;

mem. firm Mayer, Brown & Platt, Chgo., 1967—; co-chmn. Joint Chgo., Ill. State Bar Assns. Com. to review disciplinary procedures in Ill., 1971-73; chmn. disciplinary com. Ill. Supreme Ct., 1973-75; asst. prof. law Chgo. Kent Coll., 1938-43; v.p. Dartmouth 1952-54. Trustee Rush-Presbyn. St. Luke's Med. Center, Chgo., 1955—; bd. dirs. Ill. Children's Home and Aid Soc., Chgo., 1958-64; trustee Wells Coll., 1960-69, Rockford Coll., 1962-70; bd. visitors Columbia Law Sch., 1953—; vis. com. U. Chgo. Law Sch., 1972-75. Fellow Am. Coll. Trial Lawyers, Am. Bar Found.; mem. Am. (pres. 1976—, chmn. pub. utilities sect. 1970-71, chmn. spl. com. on youth edn. for citizenship 1973-75), Chgo. (pres. 1967-68) bar assns., Ill., Fed. Power bar assns., Am. Law Inst., Am. Judicature Soc. Office: 231 S LaSalle St Chicago IL 60604 Tel (312) 782-0600

STANLEY, WILLIAM ELBERT, JR., b. Wilmington, N.C., Apr. 9, 1943; B.B.A., U. N.C., 1965, J.D., 1969. Admitted to N.C. bar, 1969; treas. W.E. Stanley Pension Planning Co., Inc., Greensboro, N.C., 1970—. Home: 407 Elmwood Dr Greensboro NC 27408 Office: 1009 W Market St Greensboro NC 27403

STANLEY, WILLIAM PAUL, b. Chgo., Aug. 29, 1947; B.S. in Bus. Adminstrn., U. Dayton, 1969; J.D., U. Cin., 1972. Admitted to Ind. bar, 1972; individual practice law, South Bend, Ind., 1972—; dep. city atty. City of South Bend, 1974-75; judge U. Notre Dame Law Sch. Practice Ct., 1975, 76; mem. St. Joseph County (Ind.) Criminal Com. Mem. St. Joseph County Bar Assn. (pres. sect. young lawyers 1976). Office: 315 N Main St South Bend IN 46601 Tel (219) 288-8381

STANSBURY, PHILIP ROGER, b. Milw., May 7, 1931; A.B., Haverford Coll., 1953; J.D., Harvard U., 1956. Asso. firm Covington & Burling, Washington, 1958-66, partner, 1966—. Mem. Am. Bar Assn., Am. Soc. Internat. Law. Office: 888 16th St NW Washington DC 20006 Tel (202) 452-6074

STANSKY, LYMAN, b. N.Y.C., July 18, 1900; A.B., Cornell U., 1920; J.D., Fordham U., 1922. Admitted to N.Y. bar, 1922, U.S. Supreme Ct. bar, 1941; individual practice law, N.Y.C., 1922—; mem. panel Am. Arbitration Assn., 1953—; spl. master N.Y. Supreme Ct.; counsel Art and Antique Dealers League Am. Bd. dirs. Harlem Assertion of Rights, 1973—. Mem. N.Y. County Lawyers Assn. (dir. 1965-71, mem. com. law, psychology and psychiatry 1973—, com. law reform 1971—, com. profl. ethics 1973—, com. on judiciary 1977—). Contbr. articles to legal publs.; mem. Cornell Law Quar. Home: 25 Sutton Pl S New York City NY 10022 Office: 667 Madison Ave New York City NY 10021 Tel (212) PL 3-9755

STANTON, FRED RANDOLPH, b. Andalusia, Ala., July 17, 1924; B.A., Emory U., 1948; LL.B., U. Fla., 1951, J.D., 1967. Admitted to Fla. bar, 1951; asso. firm Copeland, Therrel, Baisden & Peterson, Miami Beach Fla., 1952-55, partner firm Therrel, Baisden, Stanton, Stillman, Brown & Wood, and predecessors, Miami Beach, Fla., 1955—. Pres. United Cerebral Palsy Assn. of Miami, 1971-73, vice chmn. bd., 1973-77; mem. Miami Beach Kiwanis Club, 1953—, pres., 1961, lt. gov. 16th Div. Fla. dist. Kiwanis Internat., 1966; mem. com. United Fund Dr. Dade County, 1970-77. Mem. Am. Judicature Soc., Nat. Legal Aid and Defender Assn., Dade County (chmn. legal ethics com. 1969-71, dir., 1970-73), Dade County, Miami Beach, Fla. (profl. ethics com. 1972—) Am. bar assns., Phi Delta Phi. Home: 6125 S W 120th St Miami FL 33156 Office: 1111 Lincoln Rd Mall Miami Beach FL 33139 Tel (305) 672-1921

STANTON, MARK LYLE, b. Elizabeth, N.J., Nov. 8, 1935; A.B., Columbia U., 1957; LL.B., U. Va., 1960. Admitted to Va. bar, 1960, N.J. bar, 1961, U.S. Supreme Ct. bar, 1966; partner firm Dorn and Stanton, Dunellen, N.J., 1963-65, Stanton & Recht, Piscataway, N.J., 1967-73, firm Stanton and Stadtmauer, Piscataway, 1976—; atty. Piscataway Twp. (N.J.) Zoning Bd., 1962-65, Piscataway Twp. Planning Bd., 1962-64, Piscataway Twp. Bd. Health, 1963-67; municipal prosecutor North Plainfield (N.J.), 1964-65. Mem. Am., N.J., Middlesex County (pres. 1973) bar assns. Home: 575 Easton Ave Somerset NJ 08873 Office: 491 S Washington Ave Piscataway NJ 08854

STANTON, NILE, b. Indpls., Aug. 27, 1944; B.S., Ball State U., 1965, M.A., 1969; J.D., Ind. U., 1973. Admitted to Ind. bar, 1973; partner firm Stanton, Boyle Hyatt & Reuben, Indpls., 1974—; exec. dir. Indpls. Lawyers Commn., 1972-74. Bd. dirs. P.A.C.E., Indpls., 1976-77. Mem. Nat. Assn. Criminal Def. Lawyers, Am. Judicature Soc., Am. Trial Lawyers Assn., Am., Ind. State (ho. of dels. 1975—, exec. council criminal justice sect. 1976-77), Indpls. bar assns., Delta Sigma Rho-Tau Kappa Alpha, Pi Gamma Mu. Co-author: Indiana Criminal Law Sourcebook, 1974; editorial bd. Ind. Law Rev., 1972-73; named Hon. Lifer, Ind. State Prison, 1975. Office: 1444 Consolidated Bldg Indianapolis IN 46204 Tel (317) 634-2200

STANZIANI, JOSEPH HENRY, b. Phila., Nov. 9, 1930; B.A., Hobart Coll., Geneva, N.Y., 1952; LL.B., U. Pa., 1955; grad. Nat. Coll. State Trial Judges, 1973. Admitted to Pa. bar, 1955, U.S. Ct. Appeals 3d Circuit bar, 1958; asso. firm Rawle & Henderson, Phila., 1958-61, Waters, Fleer, Cooper & Gallager, Norristown, Pa., 1962-71; judge Montgomery County (Pa.) Common Pleas Ct., 1971—; dir. Pa. Bar Inst., 1970-75; sec. Montgomery County Jud. Conf., 1972—. Mem. Am., Pa., Montgomery bar assns., Pa. Conf. State Trial Judges, Nat. Council Juvenile Judges, Phi Beta Kappa. Recipient alumni citation Hobart Coll., 1973. Home: 2056 Woodland Rd Abington PA 19001 Office: Montgomery County Courthouse Norristown PA 19404 Tel (215) 275-5000

STAPP, JERRY LEE, b. Bessemer, Ala., Oct. 12, 1928; B.A., U. Ala., 1954, J.D., 1954, postgrad., 1954. Admitted to Ala. bar, U.S. Dist. Ct. bar; partner firms Lipscomb, Brobston, Jones & Brobston, Bessemer, 1954-61, Stapp & Nice, Birmingham, Ala., 1961-63, Cloud, Berry, Ables & Stapp, Huntsville, Ala., 1966-68; individual practice law, Huntsville, 1968—; adminstrv. asst. to U.S. Senator Lister Hill, 1956-58; pres. Local Govt. Study Commn., 1971-73. Active Huntsville Indsl. Devel. Assn., Huntsville Better Bus. Bur.; state v.p. Young Democrats of Ala., 1960-62; bd. dirs. of Aid Retarded Citizens Assn., Civitan Care. Mem. Huntsville-Madison County, Bessemer, Ala., Am. bar assns., Ala., Am. trial lawyers assns., Am. Judicature Soc., Farrah Law Soc., Huntsville-Madison County C. of C. Author Local Govt. Study Commn. report; author, draftsman fed., Ala. legislation. Home: 7818 Benton St Huntsville AL 35802 Office: 407 Franklin St Huntsville AL 35801 Tel (205) 536-3375

STAR, SOLOMON EMANUEL, b. N.Y.C., June 3, 1910; student N.Y. U., 1926-28, LL.B., 1931. Admitted to N.Y. bar, 1932, U.S. Supreme Ct. bar, 1972; asso. firm McManus, Ernst & Ernst, N.Y.C., 1931-46; partner McManus & Ernst, 1946—. Chmn. municipal town govt. Town Club Scarsdale, 1969-71. Mem. Assn. Bar City N.Y., N.Y. County Lawyers Assn. (chmn. com. on unlawful practice of law, 1968-72, treas. 1972—). Contbr. articles in field to profl. jours. Office: 350 Madison Ave New York City NY 10017 Tel (212) MU5-3933

STARGATT, BRUCE MARVIN, b. N.Y.C., July 8, 1930; B.A., U. Vt., 1951; LL.B., Yale, 1954. Admitted to N.Y. bar, 1955, Del. bar, 1955; D.C. bar, 1956, U.S. Supreme Ct. bar, 1971; asso. firm Young, Conway, Stargatt & Taylor and predecessors, Wilmington, Del., 1956-59, partner, 1959—; legal officer USAF, Dover AFB, Dover, Del., 1954-56; chmn. Gov.'s Com. for Revision of Del. Criminal Laws, 1965-67. Fellow Am. Coll. Trial Lawyers; mem. Am., Del. bar assns. Recipient Good Govt. citation Com. of 39, 1969. Office: 1401 Market Tower Wilmington DE 19899 Tel (302) 571-6614

STARGEL, JOSEPH HOYT, JR., b. Gainesville, Ga., Apr. 18, 1927; LL.B., Atlanta Law Sch., 1956, LL.M., 1957. Admitted to Ga. bar, 1967; mayor City of Gainesville, 1971-72; city commr., Gainesville, 1967-76; adminstrv. law judge Ga. State Bd. Workmen's Compensation, Gainesville, 1976—. Mem. Gainesville, Northeastern, Ga., Am. bar assns. Home: 2519 Club Dr Gainesville GA 30501 Office: 311 Green St Gainesville GA 30501 Tel (404) 532-5204

STARK, ARTHUR B., b. N.Y.C., Apr. 3, 1926; A.B., U. Miami (Fla.), 1948, LL.B., 1951, J.D., 1968. Admitted to Fla. bar, 1951, U.S. Supreme Ct. bar; partner firm Koeppel, Stark & Newmark, Miami, Fla., 1968—; asst. pub. defender Dade County (Fla.), 1957-69; counsel Dade County del. to spl. session Fla. Legislature on Reapportionment, 1963. Mem. Am., Fla., Dade County bar assns., Fla. Acad. Trial Lawyers, Fla. Criminal Def. Attys. Assn. (pres. 1968-69), Nat. Assn. Def. Lawyers in Criminal Cases. Home: 700 Biltmore Way Coral Gables FL Office: 11 35 Dupont Bldg Miami FL 33131 Tel (305) 374-5355

STARK, JOHN CHALEY, b. Indpls., Jan. 2, 1935; A.B., DePauw U., 1955; J.D. with highest distinction (Wendell Willkie Law scholar), Ind. U., 1964. Admitted to Ind. bar, 1964, U.S. Supreme Ct. bar, 1969; v.p., treas. D.C. Stark Co., Inc., Indpls., 1957-60; investment analyst Am. United Life Ins. Co., Indpls., 1960-63; law clk., mem. firm Baker & Daniels, Indpls., 1963-65; partner firm Henderson & Stark, Indpls., 1965-70, firm Wooden, Stark, McLaughlin & Sterner, Indpls. 1970—; dir. Astro Broaching Corp., B & H Tool and Machine Corp., Jackson's Realty & Builders Co., Inc., Turtle Creek Convalescent Centers Inc. Coach basketball and football Jordan YMCA, Indpls., 1968-71, 1973—; mem. planning com. Washington Twp. Schs., Marion County, Ind., 1973; bd. dirs. Ft. Myers (Fla.) Community Hosp., Inc., 1972—; bd. mgmt. Jordan YMCA, 1970-73; mem. adminstrv. bd. Methodist Ch., 1968—. Mem. Am., Ind. (bd. mgrs. 1969-70) bar assns., Ind. Young Lawyers (pres. 1970), Order of Coif, Ind. U. Law Sch. Alumni Assn. (treas. 1968, dir. 1967-70), Phi Kappa Psi (trustee and treas. found. 1974—), Alpha Phi Omega, Phi Delta Phi. Home: 6865 Fox Lake S Dr Indianapolis IN 46278 Office: 1100 Merchants Bank Bldg Indianapolis IN 46204

STARK, MAURICE EDMUND, b. Ft. Dodge, Iowa, Sept. 22, 1921; B.S.C., U. Iowa, 1942, J.D., 1949. Admitted to Iowa bar, 1949; U.S. Dist. Ct. bar, 1950, Tax Ct. bar, 1951, Ct. of Appeals bar, 1956; law clerk U.S. Dist. Judge Henry N. Graven, Iowa, 1949-50; spl. atty. Criminal Div. Dept. of Justice, Washington, 1951; trial atty. Office of Chief Counsel Internal Revenue Service, N.Y.C., 1951, 53-55; mem. firm Stark, Crumley & Jacobs, Ft. Dodge, Iowa, 1955—; mem. Midwest Region Liaison Com. with Internal Revenue Service, 1962-71; mem. adv. group Commr. of Internal Revenue, 1969-70; mem. Fed. Tax Liaison Com. in Iowa, 1968—. Pres., Community Nursing Service, Ft. Dodge, 1958-59, Ft. Dodge C. of C., 1961-62. Mem. Am., Webster County (pres. 1976), Iowa State (chmn. com. on taxation 1967-69) bar assns., Beta Gamma Sigma, Order of Artus, Omicron Delta Kappa, Delta Theta Phi. Recipient Meritorious Pub. Service award, Commr. of Internal Revenue, 1971; notes editor Iowa Law Rev., 1948-49. Home: 701 Crest Ave Fort Dodge IA 50501 Office: M-22 Warden Plaza Fort Dodge IA 50501 Tel (515) 576-7558

STARK, RICHARD ALVIN, b. Ann Arbor, Mich., Apr. 6, 1921; A.B., DePauw U., 1943; M.B.A., Harvard, 1947; LL.B., Ind. U., 1948. Admitted to Ind. bar, 1948, N.Y. bar, 1949; asso. firm Milbank, Tweed, Hadley & McCloy, N.Y.C., 1948-57, partner, 1957—. Mem. Am. (corp. law com., securities law com.), N.Y. State (corp. law com.) bar assns. Office: 1 Chase Manhattan Plaza New York City NY 10005 Tel (212) HA2-2660

STARK, THOMAS MICHAEL, b. Riverhead, N.Y., Feb. 13, 1925; B.S., Holy Cross Coll., 1945; LL.B., Harvard, 1949. Admitted to N.Y. State bar, 1950; individual practice law, Riverhead, 1949-62; judge County Ct. Suffolk County (N.Y.), 1963-68; justice Supreme Ct. State of N.Y., Riverhead, 1969—; justice of peace, Riverhead, 1956-57. Mem. Riverhead Bd. Edn., 1959-62; vice chmn. N.Y. State Office of Ct. Adminstrn. Com. on Criminal Jury Instructions, 1975—. Mem. Suffolk County, N.Y. State, Am. bar assns., N.Y. State Trial Judges Assn. (criminal law chmn. bench book com. 1970-75). Home: Bay Woods Aquebogue NY 11931 Office: Suffolk County Courthouse Riverhead NY 11901 Tel (516) 727-4700

STARKEY, LAWRENCE VINCENT, b. Greenville, S.C., Dec. 12, 1936; B.S., Clemson U., 1957; J.D., LL.B., U. S.C., 1959; M.P.A., Syracuse U., 1971. Admitted to S.C. bar, 1959, Ga. bar, 1965; atty. IRS, Washington, 1959-63, Atlanta, 1963-71, chief estate and gift tax sect., 1971-74; asso. firm Starkey, Benham & Bedford, Atlanta, 1974-76. Pres., Clemson U. Alumni Assn., 1973-74, Atlantic Coast Conf. Club of Atlanta, 1976. Mem. Ga. Bar Assn., Atlanta Estate Planning Council. Speaker insts. and seminars. Home: 1025 Riverbend Dr N W Atlanta GA 30339 Office: suite 210 6600 Powers Ferry Rd N W Atlanta GA 30339 Tel (404) 256-2438

STARNES, JAMES WRIGHT, b. E. St. Louis, Ill., Apr. 3, 1933; student St. Louis U., 1951-53; LL.B., Washington U., St. Louis, 1957. Admitted to Mo. bar, 1957, Ill. bar, 1957; asso. firm Stinson, Mag, Thomson, McEvers & Fizzell, Kansas City, Mo., 1957-60, partner, 1960—. Partner Mid-Continent Properties Co., 1959—, Monticello Land Co., 1973—; sec. Packaging Products Corp., Mission, Kans. Bd. dirs. H.E.E.D., Kansas City, Mo., 1965-73, pres., 1966-67; bd. dirs. Kansas City Halfway House Found., exec. com., 1966-69, pres., 1966; bd. dirs. Joan Davis Sch. for Spl. Edn., 1972—, v.p., 1972-73, pres. elect 1975-76; bd. dirs. Mo. Assn. Mental Health, 1968-69; bd. dirs. Kansas City Assn. Mental Health, 1966—, pres., 1969-70. Mem. Am., Kansas City bar assns., Mo. Bar, Kansas City Lawyers Assn. Mem. advisory bd. Washington U. Law Review, 1957—. Home: 20901 Pebble Ln Lenexa KS 66220 Office: 2100 Ten Main Center Kansas City MO 64105 Tel (816) 842-8600

STARR, HAROLD PAGE, b. Phila., June 17, 1932; B.S. in Physics, Yale, 1954; LL.B., Harvard, 1961. Admitted to Pa. bar, 1962; asso. firm Pepper, Hamilton & Scheetz, Phila., 1961-69, partner, 1969—; sec. Selby, Battersby & Co., Phila. Fin. sec. Friends of Phila. Museum of Art, 1974—. Mem. Phila., Pa., Am. bar assns. Office: 123 S Broad St Philadelphia PA 19109 Tel (215) 545-1234

STARR, ISADORE RAYMOND, b. Vitebsk, Russia, June 15, 1901; came to U.S., 1911, naturalized, 1922; A.B., Detroit City Coll., 1921; D.C.L., LL.B., Detroit Coll. Law, 1923. Admitted to Mich. bar, 1923, U.S. Supreme Ct. bar, 1960, practice law, Detroit; legal adviser Selective Service Bds., World War II, Korean War. Election commr. Detroit, 1929-42; pres. Russian War Relief, 1945; del. Am. Jewish Conf., 1947; pres. Congregation Lubavitcher Center, Detroit, 1977—; mem. and del. Detroit Jewish Community Council, 1945—. Mem. Mich., Detroit bar assns. Home: 22150 Church Rd Oak Park MI 48237 Office: 3715 Cadillac Tower Detroit MI 48226 Tel (313) 963-0050

STARRETT, LOYD MILFORD, b. St. Louis, Aug. 13, 1933; A.B., Harvard, 1953, LL.B., 1958. Admitted to Mass. bar, 1959, 1st Circuit bar, 1959, U.S. Dist. Ct. Mass., 1960, U.S. Supreme Ct. bar, 1965, 5th Circuit bar, 1973; law clk. firm Covington & Burling, Washington, 1957, Cahill, Gordon, Reindel & Ohl, N.Y.C., 1958, to Chief Judge Calvert Magruder U.S. Ct. Appeals for 1st Circuit, Boston, 1958-59; asso. firm Foley, Hoag & Eliot, Boston, 1959-63, partner, 1963—; mem. teaching team trial advocacy workshop Harvard Law Sch., 1975, 76, 77; dir. Park Mobile, Inc., A.W. Hastings & Co., Inc. First v.p. Cape Ann Interfaith Commn., Gloucester, Mass., 1970-72, treas., 1972—; bd. dirs. Rockport (Mass.) Joint Youth Fellowship, 1969—, coordinator, 1967-69, exec. dir., 1969-71, treas., 1971—; moderator Town of Rockport, 1975—; mem. Rockport Zoning Bd. Appeals. Mem. Am., Mass., Boston bar assns., Am. Soc. Hosp. Attys., Am. Judicature Soc., Assn. ICC Practitioners, Mass. Moderators Assn., Am., Mass. assns. trial lawyers. Home: 23 Granite St Rockport MA 01966 Office: 10 Post Office Sq Boston MA 02109 Tel (617) 482-1390

STASSEN, JOHN HENRY, b. Joliet, Ill., Mar. 22, 1943; B.S., Northwestern U., 1965; J.D., Harvard, 1968. Admitted to Ill. bar, 1968, U.S. Ct. Mil. Appeals bar, 1969, U.S. Supreme Ct. bar, 1972; partner firm Kirkland & Ellis, Chgo., 1968-69, 73—; lt. JAGC, U.S. Navy, 1969-72; sec. Bd. of Trade Clearing Corp., Chgo., 1975—. Mem. Am., Ill., Chgo. bar assns. Contbr. articles to legal jours. Office: 200 E Randolph Dr Chicago IL 60601 Tel (312) 861-2238

STATHAS, CHARLES JOHN, b. Milw., Mar. 23, 1931; B.B.A., U. Wis., 1953, J.D., 1958. Admitted to Wis. bar, 1958; atty. Nat. Bank Detroit, 1958-61; asst. v.p., legal counsel U. Wis., 1961-71, sr. legal counsel, 1971—, asst. trust officer Bd. Regents, 1971—; v.p. Wis. U. Bldg. Corp., 1962—. Mem. Legal Aid Soc. Madison, 1956-58; mem. budget com. United Way Dane County, 1972-74; bd. dirs. Wis. Ballet Co., 1973-74. Mem. Dane County Bar Assn., State Bar Wis., Nat. Assn. Coll. U. Attys., Phi Delta Phi. Contbr. articles to legal jours. Home: 110 Carillon Dr Madison WI 53705 Office: 1220 Linden Dr Madison WI 53706 Tel (608) 262-6166

STATLAND, EDWARD MORRIS, b. Washington, Aug. 20, 1932; A.B., George Washington U., 1954, J.D. with honors, 1959. Admitted to D.C. bar, 1959, Md. bar, 1959, U.S. Supreme Ct. bar, 1964; asst. corp. counsel D.C., 1960-62; partner firm Statland & Zaslav, Washington and Montgomery County, Md. Mem. D.C. Bar, D.C., Montgomery County, Md. State, Am. bar assns., Assn. Plaintiff's Trial Attys., Am. Judicature Soc. Home: 6 Windermere Ct Rockville MD 20852 Office: 1101 17th St NW Washington DC 20036 Tel (202) 296-0555

STATLER, JOHN CONWAY, b. Rockwood, Pa., May 9, 1920; A.B., Lincoln Meml. U., 1941; LL.B., U. Mich., 1948. Admitted to Md. bar, 1948, Colo. bar, 1949; partner firm Todd & Statler, Lamar, Colo., 1949-57; individual practice law, Lamar, 1957-71; judge Colo. Dist. Ct. 15th Jud. Dist., 1971—; city atty. City of Lamar, 1954-56; town atty. Town of Holly (Colo.), 1955-71; asst. dist. atty. Colo. 15th Jud. Dist., 1956-71; chmn. Colo. Commn. on Judicial Qualifications, 1975-76. Fellow Internat. Soc. Barristers (jud.); mem. Am., S.E. Colo., Colo. (v.p. 1968) bar assns. Home: 1204 S 7th St Lamar CO 81052 Office: PO Box 1214 Lamar CO 81052 Tel (303) 336-7424

STATON, ROBERT EMMETT, b. Suffolk, Va., July 11, 1946; B.A., Presbyn. Coll., Clinton, S.C., 1968; J.D., U. S.C., 1971. Admitted to S.C. bar, 1971; mem. firm Barnes, Austin & Ellison, Columbia, S.C., 1971—. Bd. dirs. Richland County (S.C.) Cancer Assn., 1976—. Mem. Am., S.C., Richland County bar assns., S.C. Def. Attys. Assn., Columbia Young Lawyers Club. Home: 3103 Travis Ct Columbia SC 29204 Office: PO Box 11929 Columbia SC 29211 Tel (803) 799-1111

STAUBER, RONALD JOSEPH, b. Toledo, Nov. 8, 1940; B.B.A., U. Toledo, 1962; J.D., Ohio State U., 1965. Admitted to Calif. bar, 1967, U.S. Dist. Ct. Central Dist. Calif., 1967, U.S. Supreme Ct. bar, 1972; corps. counsel dept. investment div. of corps. State of Calif., Los Angeles, 1965-67; partner firm Blacker & Stauber, Beverly Hills, Calif., 1967—. Bd. dirs. Jewish Free Loan. Mem. Beverly Hills (mem. corps. com., real estate com.), Los Angeles County (bus. and corp. sect.), Am. (corps., banking and bus. law sect.) bar assns. Home: 508 N Sierra Dr Beverly Hills CA 90210 Office: 421 S Beverly Dr Beverly Hills CA 90212 Tel (213) 879-1295

STAUDER, MICHAEL HENRY, b. St. Louis County, Mo., Nov. 20, 1944; B.S. in Bus. Adminstrn., Christian Bros. Coll., Memphis, 1966; J.D., U. Miss. at Oxford, 1969. Admitted to Miss. bar, 1969, Fla. bar, 1972; spl. agt. FBI, Washington, 1969-72; sr. partner firm Gamot & Stauder, West Palm Beach, Fla., 1972—; city prosecutor Pahokee (Fla.), 1972-76, atty. bd. commrs. Pahokee Housing Authority, 1972—. Mem. Palm Beach County, Miss., Am. bar assns., Soc. Former Agts. FBI, Am. Trial Lawyers Assn., Acad. Fla. Trial Lawyers, Fla. Bar Assn. Registered real estate salesman, Fla. Office: 811 N Olive Ave Suite 200 West Palm Beach FL 33401 Tel (305) 655-9266

STAUSS, EDWARD FRANK, JR., b. New Orleans, Dec. 12, 1915; student engring. Tulane U., 1931-34, LL.B., 1937; postgrad. in bus. Harvard U., 1960. Admitted to La. bar, 1937; titleman Humble Oil and Refining Co., 1937-39; v.p. Stauss & Haas, Inc., New Orleans, 1939-41; asso. firm May & Carrere, New Orleans, 1945-51; atty. Freeport Minerals Co., New Orleans, 1951—; asst. sec., 1953-57, asst. v.p., asst. sec., 1957-70, v.p., asst. sec., 1970—. Pres. New Orleans Bur. Govtl. Research, 1963-65, Pub. Affairs Research Council La., 1971-73; mem. vestry Trinity Episcopal Ch., New Orleans, 1967-71. Mem. Am., La. bar assns., Am. Judicature Soc. Home: 1423 Valence St New Orleans LA 70115 Office: PO Box 61520 New Orleans LA 70161 Tel (504) 568-4234

STAVINS, RICHARD LEE, b. Urbana, Ill., Sept. 26, 1943; B.S. in Journalism, Northwestern U., 1965, J.D. cum laude, 1968. Admitted to Ill. bar, 1968, U.S. Dist. Ct. bar, 1969, U.S. Ct. Appeals bar, 1969, U.S. Supreme Ct. bar, 1971; asso. firm Dorfman, DeKoven, & Cohen, Chgo., 1968-70; mem. firm Blumenthal, Schwartz & Stavins, Chgo., 1970—. Mem. Am., Ill. State, Chgo. bar assns., Am. Trial Lawyers Assn., Phi Alpha Delta, Sigma Delta Chi. Ford Found. fellow, 1967. Office: 105 W Madison St Chicago IL 60602 Tel (312) FR 2-3566

STEAKLEY, ZOLLIE COFFER, JR., b. Rotan, Tex., Aug. 29, 1908; B.A., Hardin-Simmons U., 1929, LL.D., 1959; J.D., U. Tex., 1932; LL.D., U. Corpus Christi, 1958. Admitted to Tex. bar, 1932; practiced in Sweetwater, Tex., 1932-39, Austin, Tex., 1946-57; asst. atty. gen. State of Tex., 1939-42, 46, sec. of state, 1957-61; justice Tex. Supreme Ct., 1961—. Home: 3302 Mount Bonnell Dr Austin TX 78731 Office: PO Box 12248 Capitol Sta Austin TX 78711 Tel (512) 475-2621

STECHEL, IRA BROOK, b. N.Y.C., Sept. 23, 1947; B.A. magna cum laude, Coll. City N.Y., 1969; J.D., Cornell U., 1972; LL.M. in Taxation, N.Y. U., 1976. Admitted to N.Y. State bar, 1973; U.S. Supreme Ct. bar, 1976; law intern Office Dist. Atty. N.Y. County, N.Y.C., 1971; asso. atty. firm Burns Jackson Miller Summit & Jacoby, N.Y.C., 1972—. Mem. Am., N.Y. State bar assns., Assn. Bar City N.Y., Phi Beta Kappa. Note editor Cornell Jour. Internat. Law, 1971-72; contbr. articles to legal jours. Office: 445 Park Ave New York City NY 10022 Tel (212) 980-3200

STECKLER, WILLIAM ELWOOD, b. Mt. Vernon, Ind., Oct. 18, 1913; LL.B., Ind. Law Sch., 1936, J.D., 1937; LL.D., Wittenberg U., Springfield, Ohio, 1958; H.H.D., Ind. Central Coll., 1969. Admitted to Ind. bar, 1936, practiced in Indpls., 1937-50, mem. firm Key & Steckler; pub. counselor Ind. Pub. Service Commn., 1949-50; judge U.S. Dist. Ct. So. Dist. Ind., 1950—, now chief judge; mem. adj. faculty Ind. U. Law Sch. Mem. Ind. Election Bd., 1946-48; chmn. speakers bur. Democratic State Central Com., 1948. Recipient Man of Year award Indpls. Law Sch., 1970. Mem. Am., Fed., Ind., Indpls. bar assns., Am. Judicature Soc. Nat. Lawyers Club, Jud. Conf. U.S. (pretrial com. judges study group 1956-65, trial practice and technique com. 1965-69, operation of jury system com. 1969-75), Am. Legion, Order of Coif, Sigma Delta Kappa. Home: RFD 2 Box 149 I Trafalgar IN 46181 Office: Fed Bldg Indianapolis IN 46204*

STEDMAN, RICHARD RALPH, b. Columbus, Ohio, July 18, 1936; B.S. in Bus. Adminstrn., Ohio State U., 1958, J.D. (Mershon fellow), 1964. Admitted to Ohio bar, 1964; asso. firm Vorys, Sater, Seymour & Pease, Columbus, 1964-70, partner, 1970—; lectr. in field. Trustee Columbus Cancer Clinic. Mem. Ohio, Columbus bar assns. C.P.A., Ohio; editor-in-chief Ohio State Law Jour., 1963-64; contbr. articles to profl. jours. Home: 2665 Lane Rd Columbus OH 43220 Office: 52 E Gay St Columbus OH 43215 Tel (614) 464-6224

STEED, ROBERT LEE, b. Augusta, Ga., Nov. 20, 1936; A.B., Mercer U., 1958, LL.B., 1961. Admitted to Ga. bar, 1961; law clk. Supreme Ct. of Ga., 1961-62; asso. firm King & Spaulding, Atlanta, 1962-66, partner, 1967—. Trustee Mercer U., 1972-76; chmn. bd. visitors Mercer Law Sch., 1968-70. Mem. Ga. (pres. young lawyers sect. 1968, gov. 1968), Am., Atlanta bar assns., Lawyers Clubs of Atlanta, Old War Horse Lawyers Club; pres. Mercer Law Sch. Alumni Assn., 1969. Home: 1058 Namench Dr NW Atlanta GA 30327 Office: 2500 Trust Co Tower Atlanta GA 30303 Tel (404) 572-4600

STEEFEL, ROBERT DAVID, b. Rochester, N.Y., May 5, 1901; A.B., Harvard Coll., 1922, LL.B., 1924. Admitted to N.Y. bar, 1925, U.S. Supreme Ct. bar, 1933; asso. firm Stroock, Stroock & Lavan, N.Y.C., 1924-36, partner, 1937—; gov. Real Estate Bd. N.Y., also chmn. new legislation com.; trustee Title Guarantee Co. Appeal agent N.Y.C. Draft Bd.; mem. Mayor's Spl. Task Force on Child Abuse, N.Y.C., 1968-74. Mem. Bar Assn. City N.Y., N.Y. County Lawyers Assn. Home: 1125 Park Ave New York City NY 10028 Office: 61 Broadway St New York City NY 10006 Tel (212) 425-5200

STEEL, LEWIS M., b. N.Y.C., Apr. 25, 1937; B.A., Harvard, 1958; LL.B., N.Y. Law Sch., 1963. Admitted to N.Y. bar, 1963, Calif. bar, 1973; asso. counsel NAACP, N.Y.C., 1964-68; partner firm diSuvero, Meyers, Oberman & Steel, N.Y.C., 1970-72, Eisner, Levy, Steel & Bellman, N.Y.C., 1973—. Contbr. article N.Y. Times Mag. Office: 351 Broadway New York City NY 10013

STEEL, RICHARD, b. N.Y.C., Dec. 2, 1903; B.S., Hamilton Coll., 1925, LL.B., N.Y. U., 1928. Admitted to N.Y. State bar, 1928, U.S. Supreme Ct. bar, 1937; individual practice law, N.Y.C., 1928—. Mem. Am., N.Y. State, N.Y. County bar assns., Assn. Bar City N.Y. Home: 305 E 86th St New York City NY 10028 Office: 61 Broadway New York City NY 10006 Tel (212) 269-6845

STEEL, WILLIAM CARLTON, b. Cincinnati, Iowa, Feb. 6, 1916; A.B., Grinnell Coll., 1938; LL.B., Harvard, 1941. Admitted to N.Y. bar, 1942, Fla. bar, 1946; asso. firm Steel, Hector & Davis and predecessors, Miami, Fla., 1946-50, partner, 1951—. Fellow Am. Coll. Trial Lawyers, Am. Bar Found. Mem. Internat., Am. (ho. of dels. 1962-68), Inter-Am., Dade County (pres. 1961-62) bar assns., Fla. Bar, Am. Soc. Internat. Law, Am. Judicature Soc., S. Fla. Inter-profl. Council (pres. 1963-64). Home: 177 Ocean Lane Dr Key Biscayne FL 33149 Office: 1400 S E 1st Nat Bank Bldg Miami FL 33131 Tel (305) 577-2816

STEELE, ALLEN MULHERRIN, b. Franklin, Tenn., July 8, 1917; student Davidson Coll, 1935-36; B.A., Vanderbilt U., 1939, LL.B., 1941. Admitted to Tenn. bar, 1941; asso. firm Manier & Crouch, Nashville, 1941, 1945; atty. Life & Casualty Ins. Co., Nashville, 1946-53, v.p. gen., counsel, 1955-66, exec. v.p., gen. counsel, 1966-70, pres. 1970—. Pres. Nashville ARC, 1953-54, Salvation Army 1958-59; campaign chmn. United Giver Fund 1962-63. Mem. Am., Tenn., Nashville bar assns., Assn. Life Ins. Counsel, Nashville C. of C. (pres. 1972), Phi Delta Phi. Home: 1001 Overton Lea Rd Nashville TN 37220 Office: Life and Casualty Tower Nashville TN 37219 Tel (615) 254-6406

STEELE, BRENT ELLIS, b. Indpls., Aug. 25, 1947; B.S., Ind. U., 1969, J.D., 1972. Admitted to Ind. bar, 1972; partner firm Steele, Steele & Steele, Bedford, Ind., 1972—; pub. defender Lawrence County (Ind.), 1975-76. Chmn. Older Am. Services' Area 15; commr., pack leader Cub Scouts; mem. adv. bd. Salvation Army. Mem. Lawrence County, Ind. State bar assns., Criminal Def. Bar Assn. Home: Rural Route 13 PO Box 560 Bedford IN 47421 Office: Bedford Nat Bank Bldg Bedford IN 47421

STEELE, CLIFFORD J., b. Bklyn., July 7, 1945; student L.I. U., 1962-66; J.D., U. Buffalo, 1969. Admitted to N.Y. State bar, 1970, Fed. bar, 1970, U.S. Supreme Ct. bar, 1974; asso. firm Miserendino, Krull & Foley, Buffalo, 1968-74; individual practice law, Buffalo, 1974—. Mem. Am., Erie County, N.Y. State bar assns., N.Y. State, Erie County trial lawyers assns., Am. Arbitration Assn. Home: 33 Presidents Walk Williamsville NY 14221 Office: 69 Delaware Ave Suite 1100 Buffalo NY 14202 Tel (716) 856-3000

STEELE, ROBERT LEE, b. Cleve., Aug. 10, 1930; B.A., Ohio Wesleyan U., 1951; M.A. in Edn., Western Reserve U., 1952, LL.B., 1955. Admitted to Ohio bar, 1955; partner firm Steele and Steele, Cleve., 1955-70; individual practice law, Cleve., 1970—; pros. atty. City of Euclid, Ohio, 1957-68; law dir. Village of Willoughby Hills, Ohio, 1966-67; judge Euclid Municipal Ct., 1968-69. Home: 8691 Lake Forest Trail Chagrin Falls OH 44022 Office: 800 Engineers Bldg Cleveland OH 44114 Tel (216) 543-5314

STEEN, MELVIN CLIFFORD, b. Mpls., Feb. 16, 1907; J.D., U. Minn., 1929. Admitted to Minn. bar, 1931, N.Y. bar, 1931, D.C. bar, 1947; asso. firm Root, Clark, Buckner & Ballantine, N.Y.C., 1929-45, partner, 1944-45; partner firm Cleary, Gottlieb, Steen & Hamilton, N.Y.C., 1946—; dir. Astra Pharm. Products, Inc., MITE Corp., Fairchild Industries, Inc., Nabisco-Astra Nutrition Devel. Corp., Astra Nutrition (U.S.A.), Inc. Bd. dirs. Legal Aid Soc. N.Y., Sherman Fairchild Found. Mem. Internat. Law Assn., Am., N.Y. State bar assns., Assn. Bar City N.Y., N.Y. County Lawyers Assn., Order of Coif, Delta Theta Phi. Decorated chevalier Legion d'Honneur; recipient Outstanding Achievement award U. Minn., 1975. Home: 5 Hampshire Circle Bronxville NY 10708 Office: One State St Plaza New York City NY 10004 Tel (212) 344-0600

STEENSLAND, JAMES LEROY, b. Blanchardville, Wis., May 17, 1906; LL.B., U. Wis., 1933. Admitted to Wis. bar, 1933; individual practice law; atty. Wis. Div. Motor Vehicles, Mem. parks bd. Home: 906 Mohican Pass Madison WI 53711 Tel (608) 274-1209

STEERE, PETER KORMANN, b. Marquette, Mich., Sept. 15, 1929; B.A., Haverford Coll., 1951; J.D., U. Wash., 1957. Admitted to Wash. bar, 1958, U.S. Supreme Ct. bar, 1971; asst. corp. counsel City of Seattle, 1957-61; legal adviser Seattle World Fair, 1961-62; practiced in Seattle, 1962-72; judge Wash. Superior Ct., King County, 1972—. Mem. Wash. State Judges, World Assn. Judges. Home: 2333-43d St E Seattle WA 98112 Office: W813 King County Courthouse Seattle WA 98104 Tel (206) 344-4065

STEGER, WILLIAM MERRITT, b. Dallas, Aug. 22, 1920; B.S., Baylor U., 1938-41; LL.B., So. Meth. U., 1950. Admitted to Tex. bar, 1951; practiced in Longview, Tex., 1951-53, Tyler, Tex., 1959-70; U.S. atty. Eastern Dist. Tex., 1953-59; judge U.S. Dist. Ct., Eastern Dist. Tex., 1970—. Mem. State Bar Tex. Office: PO Box 3684 US Courthouse and Fed Bldg Beaumont TX 77704 Tel (713) 838-0271

STEGMAN, CLEMENT ALBERT, JR., b. Chgo., Mar. 2, 1938; B.S.C., Loyola U., 1961, J.D., 1968. Admitted to Ill. bar, 1968; trust officer Continental Ill. Nat. Bank & Trust Co. of Chgo., 1972—. Mem. Chgo. Bar Assn., Phi Alpha Delta, Beta Alpha Psi. Home: 460 Mill Valley Rd Palatine IL 60067 Office: 231 S LaSalle St Chicago IL 60693 Tel (312) 828-3672

STEGMEIER, JAMES LLOYD, b. Columbus, Ohio, Aug. 28, 1922; B.A., Ohio State U., 1946, LL.B., 1948, J.D., 1967. Admitted to Ohio bar, 1949, U.S. Dist. Ct. bar for So. Dist. Ohio, 1950; atty. examiner Ohio Dept. Hwys., Columbus, 1949-52; chief condemnation atty. Ohio Turnpike Commn., Columbus, 1952-56; legis. counsel Ohio Dept. Transp., Columbus, 1957—; mem. Grandview Heights (Ohio) City Council, 1947-51. Mem. Ohio Bar Assn., Am. Assn. State Hwy. Ofcls. (25 Yr. Distinguished Service award 1975, chmn. com. legal affairs 1975—), Am. Assn. State Hwy. and Transp. Ofcls. Contbr. articles to transp., legal jours. Home: 4065 Saturn Rd Columbus OH 43220 Office: 25 S Front St Columbus OH 43215 Tel (614) 466-8480

STEHL, EDWARD, III, b. Pitts., June 28, 1921; A.B., George Washington U., 1948, J.D., 1950. Admitted to Va. bar, 1951; mem. firm Blanton, Mason & Stehl, Bowling Green, Va., 1951-55, Mason & Stehl, Bowling Green, 1955-58; individual practice law, Bowling Green, 1958—; judge Caroline County Ct., Va., 1958-69. Mem. Am., Va. bar assns., Am., Va. trial lawyers assns., Order of Coif. Office: Box 116 Court House Ln Bowling Green VA 22427 Tel (804) 633-5222

STEIL, GEORGE KENNETH, b. Darlington, Wis., Dec. 16, 1924; J.D., U. Wis., 1950. Admitted to Wis. bar, 1950, U.S. Tax Ct., 1971; asso. J.G. McWilliams, Janesville, 1950-53; partner firm McWilliams & Steil, Janesville, 1954-60, Campbell, Brennan, Steil & Ryan, 1960-76; pres. Brennan, Steil, Ryan, Basting & MacDougall, Janesville, 1977—; instr. U. Wis. Law Sch., 1968-74, lectr., asso. dir. gen. practice course, 1974. Mem. Am., Wis. (chmn. legal edn. and bar admissions com. 1969-76, pres. elect 1976—), Rock County bar assns., Janesville Area C. of C. (pres. 1970-71). Home: 431 Apache Dr Janesville WI 53545 Office: 1 E Milwaukee St Janesville WI 53545 Tel (608) 756-4141

STEIMANN, URBAN JOSEPH, b. Sherburn, Minn., Sept. 16, 1908; B.A., Coll. of St. Thomas, 1930; LL.B., Minn. Coll. of Law, 1934; J.D., William Mitchell Coll. Law, 1969. Admitted to Minn. bar, 1935; individual practice law, Faribault, 1937-69; judge Dist. Ct., 3rd Jud. Dist. State of Minn., 1969—; commr. Rice County Ct., 1938-43; village atty., Morristown and Nerstrand, Minn., 1939-69; acting atty., Rice County, 1943-46; city atty., Faribault, 1947-48; atty., Rice County, 1948-59. Bd. dirs. Faribault Civic Music Assn., 1954-64, Faribault Area United Fund, 1958-66, Archdiocesan Bur. Catholic Charities, 1960-64, Faribault Art Center, 1960-68; bd. dirs. Rice County Dist. One Hosp., 1960-65, gen. counsel, 1965-69. Mem. Am., Minn., 5th Dist. bar assns., Minn. Dist. Judges' Assn. (dir.), Am. Judicature Soc., Am. Trial Lawyers' Assn. Recipient Distinguished Service medal Roman Catholic Archdiocese of St. Paul and Mpls., 1959; Distinguished Service award Faribault Jr. C. of C., 1971. Home: 827 SW 8th Ave Faribault MN 55021 Office: PO Box 467 Rice County Court House Faribault MN 55021 Tel (507) 334-7729

STEIN, ABE LEWIS, b. Eveleth, Minn., Sept. 5, 1903; B.A., U. Wis., 1927; LL.B., Harvard, 1930. Admitted to Ill. bar, 1931, D.C. bar, 1968; individual practice law, Chgo., 1931-42; atty. FCC, N.Y.C. and Washington, 1934-36, 44-47; asst. atty. gen. State of Ill., Chgo., 1937-40; atty. Office of Price Adminstrn., Washington, 1942-44; gen. practice law, Washington, 1947—. Mem. Am., FCC, D.C. bar assns. Home: 1600 S Joyce St Arlington VA 22202 Office: 1329 E St NW Washington DC 20004 Tel (202) 737-7944

STEIN, ADRIENNE, b. N.Y.C., Nov. 15, 1924; B.B.A., City U. N.Y., 1944; J.D., Pacific Coast U., 1967. Admitted to Calif. bar, 1967; asso. firm Gottlieb, Gottlieb & Stein, and predecessor, Long Beach, Calif., 1967-73, partner, 1974—; mem. faculty Pacific Coast U. Sch. Law. Pres., dir. Long Beach Jewish Community Center; bd. dirs. Long Beach Jewish Community Fedn.; mem. region 3 agy. relations and priorities com. United Way. Mem. Calif., Los Angeles County, Long Beach bar assns., ACLU. Home: 3815 Gaviota St Long Beach CA 90807 Office: 675 E Wardlow Rd Long Beach CA 90807 Tel (213) 424-0427

STEIN, DAVID JOHN, b. Ft. Dodge, Iowa, June 12, 1941; B.A., Buena Vista Coll., 1963; J.D., Drake U., 1967. Admitted to Iowa bar, 1967, U.S. Ct. Appeals bar, 1968; mem. firm Montgomery & Stein, Spirit Lake, Iowa, 1967-70; individual practice law, Milford, Iowa, 1970—; county atty. Dickinson County (Iowa), 1969-70. Pres. E. Okoboji Improvement, Spirit Lake, 1973; mem. Arnolds Park (Iowa) Sch. Bd., 1974-75. Mem. Am., Iowa, Dickinson County bar assns. Home: 1201 J Ave Milford IA 51351 Office: 926 Okoboji Ave Milford IA 51351 Tel (712) 338-4741

STEIN, DONALD STANLEY, b. Canton, Ohio, May 16, 1931; B.S., Kent State U., 1956; J.D., Cleveland Marshall Law Sch., 1961. Admitted to Ohio bar, 1961; individual practice law, Cleve., 1962-68; mem. firm Kalk and Valore, Cleve., 1968—; asst. dir. law City of Cleve., 1968. Pres., Brith Emith Temple Brotherhood, Pepper Pike, Ohio; chmn. com. Greater Cleve. council Boy Scouts Am., Beachwood, Ohio, 1974—; active Citizens League of Greater Cleve., 1974—; trustee Courage Center, Inc., Cleve. Mem. Am., Ohio State, Greater Cleve., Cuyahoga County, War Vets. (pres. 1968) bar assns. Home: 23205 Ranch Rd Beachwood OH 44122 Office: Suite 300 1717 Illuminating Bldg Cleveland OH 44113 Tel (216) 241-0484

STEIN, ERIC, b. Holice, Czechoslovakia, July 8, 1913; J.U.D., Charles U., Prague, Czechoslovakia, 1937; J.D., U. Mich., 1942. Admitted to Ill. bar, 1946, D.C. bar, 1953; practiced in Prague, 1937; acting dep. dir. Office UN Polit. Affairs, Dept. State, Washington, 1955, adviser U.S. del. UN Gen. Assembly, N.Y.C., 1947-55; asso. prof. law U. Mich., 1956-58, prof. internat. law and orgn., 1958-76, H.E. Yntema prof. law, 1976—, co-dir. internat. legal studies, 1958—; vis. prof. Stanford, 1956, 77, Law Faculties, Stockholm, Uppsala and Lund, Sweden, 1969, U. London Inst. Advanced Legal Studies, 1975; mem. adv. panel, bur. European affairs State Dept., 1966-73, cons., 1966-73. Mem. Am. Bar Assn., Internat. Law Assn., Council Fgn. Relations, Am. Soc. Internat. Law (exec. council 1954-57, bd. rev. and devel. 1965-67, 70-75), Brit. Inst. Internat. and Comparative Law. Author: (with others) American Enterprise in the European Common Market—A Legal Profile, vols. 1 and 2, 1960; (with H. K. Jacobson) Diplomats, Scientists and Politicians: The United States and the Nuclear Test Ban Negotiations, 1966; Harmonization of European Company Law—National Reform and Transnational Coordination, 1971; Impact of New Weapons Technology on International Law, 1971; (with Peter Hay, Michel Waelbroeck) European Community Law and Institutions in Perspective, 1976. Editor: (with Peter Hay) Law and Institutions in the Atlantic Area: Readings, Cases and Problems, 1967. Home: 2649 Heather Way Ann Arbor MI 48104 Office: 918 Legal Research Bldg U Mich Law Sch Ann Arbor MI 48109 Tel (313) 764-0541

STEIN, GARY EDWARD, b. Columbus, Ohio, Sept. 11, 1949; B.A., Capital U., 1971, J.D., 1974; postgrad. Ohio State U., 1976. Admitted to Ohio bar, 1974, Fla. bar, 1975; gen. counsel, exec. asst. to adminstr. Ohio Bur. Employment Services, Columbus, 1975—; part-time practice law, Columbus, 1976—; solicitor New Lexington (Ohio), 1977—. Mem. Am., Ohio, Fla., Columbus (corp. com. 1976—) bar assns. Home: 1101-A Iron Gate Ln Columbus OH 43213 Office: 50 W Broad St Columbus OH 43215 Tel (614) 221-7762

STEIN, HARRY BINDER, b. Fayetteville, N.C., May 20, 1914; A.B., U. N.C., 1935, J.D., 1937. Admitted to N.C. bar, 1938, U.S. Supreme Ct. bar, 1971; individual practice law, Fayetteville, 1938—; city atty. City of Fayetteville, 1966-72. Mem. Fayetteville Pub. Works Commn., 1956—; chmn. Fayetteville Sch. Bd., 1970—; trustee Fayetteville Tech. Inst., 1972—. Mem. Am., N.C. State, Cumberland County bar assns. Author: Legacy, 1954.

STEIN, JACOB A., b. Washington, Mar. 15, 1925; LL.B., George Washington U., 1948. Admitted to D.C. bar, 1948, Md. bar, 1956; partner firm Stein, Mitchell & Mezines, Washington, 1972—; chmn. spl. com. U.S. Dist. Ct. for D.C. to Revise Rules of Court, 1973; mem. civil rules adv. com. Superior Ct. D.C., 1970—; mem. com. Grievances and Admissions U.S. Ct. Appeals D.C., 1970-74; chmn. D.C. Ct. Appeals Com. Admissions, 1972; lectr. in field, Fellow Am. Coll. Trial Lawyers; mem. Am., Md. bar assns., Am. Trial Lawyers Assn., Assn. Plantiff's Trial Attys. Met. Washington (pres. 1959-60), Internat. Acad. Trial Lawyers. Author: District of Columbia Tort Casefinder, 1967; Closing Argument, 1969; Cross Examination of Defendant's Physician Witness, 1973; Trial Handbook for Maryland Lawyers, 1972; Damages and Recovery, 1972; Legal Spectator, 1976. Home: 5000 Garfield St NW Washington DC 20016 Office: 1800 M St NW Washington DC 20036 Tel (202) 737-7777

STEIN, MELVYN BERNARD, b. Los Angeles, Sept. 12, 1941; B.B.A., Calif. Western U., 1962, J.D., 1965. Admitted to Calif. bar, 1966; individual practice law San Diego, 1966-70; partner firm Ellman & Stein, San Diego, 1970—; asst. prof. law San Diego Community Coll., 1977. Bd. dirs. San Diego Imperial council Girl Scouts U.S.A., 1973—. Mem. Am., San Diego County (speakers bur. 1973—), Calif. bar assns., San Diego Trial Lawyers Assn. Office: 110 West C St Suite 1811 San Diego CA 92101 Tel (714) 239-9327

STEIN, MICHAEL G., b. Chgo., Aug. 11, 1913; LL.B., DePaul U., 1936. Admitted to Ill. bar, 1936, U.S. Supreme Ct. bar; asso. firm Silverstein & Levin, Chgo., 1936-42; corp. counsel City of Chgo., 1942-75; individual practice law. Local chmn. ARC; mem. speakers com. U.S. Savings Bonds; mem. bd. govs. State of Israel Bonds. Office: 134 N LaSalle St Chicago IL 60602 Tel (312) 782-4194

STEIN, RAYMOND HAROLD, b. Balt., Dec. 27, 1946; A.B. in Edn., U. N.C., 1969; J.D., Cumberland Law Sch., 1973. Admitted to Ga. bar, 1973; partner firm Zachary & Stein, Atlanta. Mem. Atlanta, Am. bar assns. Office: 6025 Roswell Rd Suite 420 Atlanta GA 30328 Tel (404) 256-5225

STEIN, ROBERT ALLEN, b. Mpls., Sept. 16, 1938; B.S. Law, U. Minn., 1960, J.D. summa cum laude, 1961. Admitted to Wis. bar, 1961, Minn. bar, 1967; asso. firm Foley, Sammond & Lardner, Milw., 1961-64; prof. Law Sch. Univ. Minn., Mpls., 1964—, asso. dean, 1976—; of counsel firm Mullin, Weinberg & Daly, Mpls., 1970—; vis. prof. U. Calif., Los Angeles, 1969-70, U. Chgo., 1975-76; commr. uniform state laws Minn., 1973—; acad. fellow Am. Coll. Probate Counsel, 1975; vis. scholar Am. Bar Found., Chgo., 1975-76. Mem. Am., Minn. (exec. council probate and trust law sect. 1972—), Hennepin County bar assns. Author: Stein on Probate, 1976; contbr. articles to Real Property, Probate & Trust Jour., Bench and Bar of Minn. Home: 6005 Manchester Dr Minneapolis MN 55422 Office: Law School University of Minnesota Minneapolis MN 55455 Tel (612) 373-5212

STEIN, STANLEY MICHAEL, b. Passaic, N.J., Dec. 2, 1942; B.A., U. Pitts., 1964; J.D., Duquesne U., 1971. Admitted to Pa. bar, 1971; asso. firm Feldstein, Bloom & Grinberg, Pitts., 1971-74; partner firm Feldstein, Bloom, Grindberg, Stein & McKee, Pitts., 1974—; asst. exec. dir. Allegheny County Bar Assn., 1967-71; solicitor Allegheny County Coroner, 1976—. Dir. ACLU, 1971-72, United Mental Health of Allegheny County, 1975—. Mem. Am., Allegheny County bar assns. Book editor Duquesne Law Review. Home: 5668

Darlington Rd Pittsburgh PA 15217 Office: 707 Law Finance Bldg Pittsburgh PA 15210 Tel (412) 471-0677

STEINBERG, ABRAM, b. Poland, Mar. 25, 1924; A.B., Coll. City N.Y., 1947; LL.B., U. Pa., 1949. Admitted to N.Y. bar, 1950, U.S. Supreme Ct. bar, 1955; partner firm Steinberg and Kennedy, Suffern, N.Y., 1956—; village atty. Village of Pomona (N.Y.), 1967—, Suffern (N.Y.), 1956-71. Mem. N.Y. State, Rockland County (N.Y.) bar assns. Office: 233 Lafayette Ave Suffern NY 10901 Tel (914) 357-1154

STEINBERG, ALAN J., b. St. Louis, Feb. 28, 1941; B.S. in Bus. Adminstrn., U. Mo., 1963; J.D., St. Louis U., 1967; LL.M., Washington U., 1975. Admitted to Mo. bar, 1967; asso. firm Gleick and Steinberg, St. Louis, 1967-69; asso. and partner firm Lashly, Caruthers, Rava, Hyndman & Rutherford, St. Louis, 1969-74; individual practice law, St. Louis, 1974-76; mem. firm Steinberg and Crotzer, Clayton, Mo., 1976—; instr. for Peat Marwick Mitchell & Co., C.P.A.'s, 1974; instr. Meramec Community Coll., 1975—, Mo. Bar, 1975—. Senator, Jr. Chamber Internat., 1971. Mem. Am., Mo. bar assns., Bar Assn. Met. St. Louis. Home: 11943 Emerald Green St Creve Coeur MO 63141 Office: 120 S Central Ave suite 434 Clayton MO 63105 Tel (314) 727-9400

STEINBERG, HOWARD E., b. N.Y.C., Nov. 19, 1944; A.B., U. Pa., 1965; J.D., Georgetown U., 1969. Admitted to N.Y. bar, 1970, since practiced in N.Y.C.; partner firm Dewey, Ballantine, Bushby, Palmer & Wood, N.Y.C., 1977—. Mem. Am., N.Y. State bar assns., Assn. Bar City N.Y. Office: 140 Broadway New York City NY 10005 Tel (212) 344-8000

STEINBERG, JACK, b. Seattle, Jan. 6, 1915; B.A., U. Wash., 1936, J.D., 1938. Admitted to Wash. bar, 1938; partner firm Steinberg and Steinberg, Seattle; judge pro tem Seattle Municipal Ct., 1952; mem. Wash. Gov's. Commn. Status of Women, 1964-65. Mem. Wash., Kings County, Seattle bar assns., Am. Judicature Soc. Home: 6826 43d Ave NE Seattle WA 98115 Office: 1210 Joseph Vance Bldg Seattle WA 98101 Tel (206) 622-5510

STEINBERG, JEROME LEONARD, b. Bronx, N.Y., Sept. 1, 1930; B.B.A., City Coll. N.Y., 1952; LL.B., J.D., Bklyn. Law Sch., 1955. Admitted to N.Y. bar, 1955, U.S. Dist. Ct. bar, 1957; individual practice law, Bklyn., 1955-60; atty. N.Y.C. Housing Authority, 1960-65; law sec. to judge Civil Ct., 1965-70; judge Civil Ct. City of N.Y., 1970—. Mem. Assn. Civil Ct. Judges, N.Y.C., Kings County law secs. assns. (pres. county assn. 1966-70), v.p. city assn. 1967-70). Home: 524 Lorimer St Brooklyn NY 11414 Office: 15 Willoughby St Brooklyn NY 11201 Tel (212) 643-3324

STEINBERG, JOSEPH LAWRENCE, b. N.Y.C., Oct. 6, 1928; B.A., Bklyn. Coll., 1950; LL.B., Columbia, 1953. Admitted to Conn. bar, 1953; individual practice law, Hartford, Conn., 1955-58; partner firm Kleinman, O'Neill, Steinberg & Lapuk, Hartford, 1958—; mem. adj. faculty dept. English U. Hartford, 1968—, U. Conn. Sch. Social Work, 1976—; moderator weekly news program Conn. Pub. TV, 1969—; family psychotherapist Bristol Hosp., 1974-76, Hartford Hosp., 1975—; leader divorce workshop U. Mich., Child and Family Service Soc., Wheeler Clinic, Greater Hartford Community Coll., Bristol Hosp., 1976—. Bd. dirs. Hartford Family Services Soc., Inst. Bioenergetic Analysis of New Haven. Mem. Am. Bar Assn. (co-chmn. com. family and marriage counseling sect. family law). Author: The Principles of Supplemental Real Estate Financing, 1967; Real Estate Sales Contracts, 1970; Campers' Favorite Campgrounds, 1974; The Therapeutic Potential of the Divorce Process, 1976. Home: 210 Terry Rd Hartford CT 06105 Office: 99 Pratt St Hartford CT 06103 Tel (203) 547-0100

STEINBERG, LAWRENCE EDWARD, b. Dallas, Nov. 25, 1935; B.B.A., U. Tex., 1958; LL.D., So. Meth. U., 1960. Admitted to Tex. bar, 1960, U.S. Supreme Ct. bar, 1964; practice law, Dallas, 1960—; partner firm Steinberg, Luerssen & Vogelson, 1971—. Mem. Dallas Urban Rehab. Standards Bd., 1975-76; regional bd. chmn., mem. nat. law com. Anti-Defamation League B'nai B'rith. Mem. Am., Tex., Dallas bar assns. Mem. editorial bd. Southwestern Law Jour., 1959-60. Home: 7308 Glendora St Dallas TX 75230 Office: 2200 Fidelity Union Tower Dallas TX 75201 Tel (214) 748-9312

STEINBERG, PAUL BURTON, b. Bklyn., Mar. 21, 1940; B.B.A. cum laude, U. Miami, 1961; J.D., Stetson U., 1963. Admitted to Fla. bar, 1963, D.C. bar, 1965; individual practice law, Miami Beach, Fla., 1963-71, 76—; partner firm Steinberg & Morton, Miami Beach, 1972-73, Steinberg & Neustein, Miami Beach, 1973-76, Steinberg & Sorota, 1976—; mem. Fla. Ho. of Reps., 1972—. Mem. Fla., D.C., Dade County bar assns., Stetson Lawyers Assn. (dir.). Recipient Golden Apple award Dade County Edn. Assn., 1969. Office: 505 Lincoln Rd Miami Beach FL 33139 Tel (305) 538-2344

STEINBERG, QUENTIN, b. Seattle, May 23, 1945; B.A., U. Wash., 1967, J.D., 1971. Admitted to Wash. bar, 1971; partner firm Steinberg & Steinberg, Seattle, 1971—. Mem. Am. Bar Assn., Wash. State Trial Lawyers Assn. Home: 10033 41st Ave NE Seattle WA 98125 Office: 1210 Joseph Vance Bldg Seattle WA 98101 Tel (206) 622-5510

STEINBERG, ROBERT PHILIP, b. Danville, Ill., Apr. 4, 1931; B.A., DePauw U., 1953; LL.B. (Root-Tilden scholar), N.Y. U., 1956. Admitted to N.Y. bar, 1956, Pa. bar, 1959; asso. firm Shearman & Sterling, N.Y.C., 1956; asso. firm Drinker Biddle & Reath, Phila., 1958-65, partner, 1965—. Trustee 1st Presbyn. Ch., Phila., 1963-66; bd. dirs. The Lighthouse, Phila., 1966-70. Mem. Am., Pa., Phila. bar assns., Judicature Soc. Editor-in-chief N.Y. U. Law Rev., 1955-56. Home: 3815 Oak Rd Philadelphia PA 19129 Office: 1100 Philadelphia National Bank Bldg Philadelphia PA 19129 Tel (215) 491-7293

STEINBERG, SIGMUND H., b. Alliance, N.J., Mar. 4, 1900; A.B., U. Pa., 1921, LL.B., 1924. Admitted to Pa. bar, 1924, U.S. Supreme Ct. bar 1934; asso. firm Wolf, Block, Schorr & Solis-Cohen, 1924-28; partner firm Steinberg, Greenstein, Gorelick & Price, and predecessors, Phila., 1931—. Pres. Germantown Jewish Center, 1950-52. Mem. Am., Pa., Phila. bar assns., Phila. Lawyers Assn., B'nai Brith, Am. Jewish Congress, Zionist Orgn. Am., Am. Legion. Editor U. Pa. Law Review 1923-24. Office: 1339 Chestnut St Suite 818 Philadelphia PA 19107 Tel (215) 564-3880

STEINBERGER, HUGH MARION, b. Balt., Mar. 12, 1920; B.S. in Commerce, U. Va., 1941; LL.B., George Washington U., 1950. Admitted to D.C. bar, 1950, U.S. Supreme Ct. bar, 1961; mem. firm Grubbs and Steinberger, Washington, 1951-65; gen. counsel Jacobs Transfer, Inc., Washington, 1954-65; pres. Staff Builders of Washington, Inc., 1965—, Tri-State Services, Inc., Washington, 1976—; pres. D.C. Trucking Assn., 1962-64, Met. Washington Temporary Services Assn., 1966-67; v.p. Am. Parcel Assos., 1962-63; guest lectr. U. Md. Adult Edn. Center. Pres. Ft. Gaines Citizens Assn., 1960; sec., treas. Touchdown Club of Washington, 1977. Mem. D.C. Bar Assn., Staff Builders Franchisee Counseling Assn. (sec., treas.). Home: 4701 Willard Ave Chevy Chase MD 20015 Office: 1000 Connecticut Ave NW Washington DC 20036 Tel (202) 293-2285

STEINBRECHER, FRANCIS JOHN, b. Joliet, Ill., May 27, 1908; B.S. in Commerce, Loyola U., Chgo., 1932, J.D., 1936. Admitted to Ill. bar, 1936, ICC bar, 1948; atty. Atchison, Topeka and Santa Fe Ry. Co., Chgo., 1942-50, commerce atty., 1950-64, asst. gen. atty., 1964-73; individual practice law, Chgo., 1973—. Mem. ICC Practitioners Assn. Home: 1237 W Farwell Ave Chicago IL 60626 Office: 224 S Michigan Ave Chicago IL 60604 Tel (312) HA 7-8870

STEINBRONN, RICHARD EUGENE, b. Chgo., Oct. 16, 1941; B.A., St. John's U., 1963; LL.B., Notre Dame U., 1966. Admitted to Ind. bar, 1966; partner firm Thornburg, McGill, Deahl, Harman, Carey & Murray, Elkhart, Ind., 1973—. Pres. Jr. Achievement of Elkhart County, Inc., 1975-76. Mem. Ind. State Bar (mem. trial lawyers' sec.). Home: 1214 E Jackson Blvd Elkhart IN 46514 Office: 305 First Nat Bank Bldg Elkhart IN 46514 Tel (219) 293-0681

STEINER, ERWIN HUGO, b. Milw., Oct. 12, 1943; B.S., U. Wis., 1966, J.D., 1969. Admitted to Wis. bar, 1969, U.S. Dist. Ct. bar for Western Dist. Wis., 1970, Eastern Dist. Wis., 1971; asst. prof. law U. Wis.-Eau Claire, 1972—; individual practice law, Eau Claire, 1973—; dep. corp. counsel Eau Claire County, 1973-76; adviser U. Wis.-Eau Claire Legal Aids Bd.; mem. Eau Claire County Bd. Realtors. Mem. State Bar Wis. Named Boss of Year Chippewa chpt. Am. Bus. Women's Assn., 1975. Office: 12 1/2 S Barstow St Eau Claire WI 54701 Tel (715) 835-2033

STEINER, FREDERICK KARL, JR., b. Prescott, Ariz., Mar. 10, 1927; B.A., Stanford, 1950, J.D., 1952. Admitted to Ariz. bar, 1952, U.S. Supreme Ct. bar, 1976; asso. firm Snell & Wilmer, Phoenix, 1952-65, partner, 1965—. Bd. dirs. Epi-Hab Phoenix, Inc., 1958—, pres., 1960-62; bd. dirs. Ariz. Tb and Respiratory Disease Assn., 1961-63, pres., 1962-63; mem. Phoenix Citizens Bond Adv. Com., 1970—; mem. exec. com. Phoenix Mountains Preservation Com., 1972—. Mem. Am. Law Inst., Stanford Alumnae, Delta Theta Phi. Contbr. articles to Ariz. Law Rev., Ariz. Weekly Gazette. Home: 2915 E Sherran Ln Phoenix AZ 85016 Office: 3100 Valley Center Phoenix AZ 85073 Tel (602) 257-7228

STEINER, H(AROLD) WALTER, b. Trenton, N.J., Jan. 3, 1912; B.A., U. So. Calif., LL.D., 1936. Admitted to Calif. bar, 1936, U.S. Supreme Ct. bar, 1945; served with JAGC, U.S. Army, 1944-47; partner firm McKinney, Steiner & Baxter, Santa Ana, Calif., 1953-63; dep. dist. atty. Orange County (Calif.), 1950-53; judge Orange County Municipal Ct., 1963-66, Orange County Superior Ct., 1966—. Mem. Santa Ana City Planning Commn., 1960-61; inheritance tax appraiser State of Calif., 1961-63. Mem. Am., Orange County bar assns., Calif. State Bar. Office: Courthouse Civic Center Santa Ana CA 92701 Tel (714) 834-4694

STEINER, JOHN STEPHEN, b. St. Louis, Nov. 21, 1945; B.A., U. Mo., 1967, M.A., 1968; J.D., Tulane U., 1971. Admitted to Mo. bar, 1971, La. bar, 1971, U.S. Supreme Ct. bar, 1975; law clk. to U.S. dist. judge for Eastern La., 1971-72; asso. firm Armstrong, Teasdale, Kramer & Vaughan, St. Louis, 1972-76; partner firm Riezman and Blitz, 1977—; gen. counsel Jr. Achievement of Mississippi Valley, Inc., 1975—, Mo. Republican Finance Com., 1975—. Mem. Ladue (Mo.) Planning and Zoning Commn., 1976—. Mem. Am., Mo., La. St. Louis Met. bar assns. Home: 64 Fair Oaks Rd Ladue MO 63124 Office: 120 S Central St Suite 1028 Clayton MO 63105 Tel (314) 727-0101

STEINHARDT, ARNOLD HERMAN, b. Wilkes Barre, Pa., Mar. 19, 1926; student Pa. State U., 1943-45; B.S. in Bus., Temple U., 1947; J.D., U. Pa., 1950. Admitted to Pa. bar, 1950, U.S. Supreme Ct. bar, 1971; individual practice law, Hazleton, Pa., 1950—; prin. examiner Pa. Ins. Dept., 1956-57; U.S. Commr. Middle Dist Pa., 1960-64. Former vol. counsel Soc. for Prevention of Cruelty to Animals, Inc., Hazleton; commr. Anthracite council Boy Scouts Am.; tchr. Beth Israel Temple Sunday Sch., Hazleton. Mem. Luzerne County Bar Assn. Home and Office: 161 S Laurel St Hazleton PA 18201 Tel (717) 454-2351

STEINHAUS, RICHARD ZEKE, b. N.Y.C., Dec. 27, 1927; B.S., N.Y. U., 1951; J.D., Bklyn. Law Sch., 1955; D.H.L., N.Y. Coll. Podiatric Medicine, 1974; Admitted to N.Y. bar, 1956, D.C. bar, 1961; individual practice law, N.Y.C., 1956-65, partner firm Blinder & Steinhaus, N.Y.C., 1965-73, Steinhaus & Hochhauser, N.Y.C., 1973-76; individual practice law, Tarrytown and Albany, N.Y., 1976—; acting village judge, Dobbs Ferry, N.Y., 1965-66; vis. lectr. Ithaca Coll. Sch. of Communications, 1973. Mem. Am., N.Y., Internat., Westchester bar assns., Assn. Bar City N.Y., N.Y. Magistrates Assn. Contbr. articles to profl. jours. Home: 33 Saranac St Dobbs Ferry NY 10522 Office: 80 S Broadway Tarrytown NY 10591 Tel (914) 631-1400 also 150 State St Albany NY 12207 Tel (518) 463-8911

STEINHILPER, FRANK ABBOTT, b. Bayonne, N.J., July 9, 1919; B.S., Pa. State U., 1940; LL.D., Fordham U., 1944. Admitted to N.Y. State bar, 1944, Mass. bar, 1968; patent agt. Merck & Co., Rahway, N.J., 1940-44, Hercules, Inc., Wilmington, Del., 1946-50; v.p. Xerox Corp., Rochester, N.Y., 1950-67; partner firm Rosen & Steinhilper, Chestnut Hill, Mass., 1968—; chmn. bd. Jaccard Corp., Buffalo, 1960—, Ferronics, Inc., 1968—, Housing Systems, Inc., 1969—. Mem. Am., Mass. bar assns., Am. Patent Law Assn., Am. Chem. Soc. Home: Stonehedge Lincoln MA 01773 Office: 200 Boylston St Chestnut Hill MA 02167 Tel (617) 332-7900

STEINHOUSE, CARL L., b. N.Y.C., July 18, 1931; B.S., N.Y. U., 1952; LL.B., Bklyn. Law Sch., 1959. Admitted to N.Y. bar, 1959, Ohio bar, 1971; trial atty. N.Y. Office, antitrust div. U.S. Dept. Justice, 1959-73, Hawaii Office, 1961-65, asst. chief Cleve. Office, 1965-66, chief, 1966-73; asso. firm Jones, Day, Reavis & Pogue, Cleve., 1973-74, partner, 1974—. Trustee Pepper Pike Civic League, 1973-76. Mem. Am. Bar Assn. (vice chmn. criminal subcom. antitrust sect. 1975—), N.Y. County Lawyers Assn. Recipient numerous awards Dept. Justice; contbr. articles to profl. publs. Home: 28599 S Woodland St Pepper Pike OH 44124 Office: 1700 Union Commerce Bldg Cleveland OH 44115 Tel (216) 696-3939

STEINMARK, ALVIN LEON, b. Greeley, Colo., Jan. 8, 1935; J.D., U. Colo., 1959. Admitted to Colo. bar, 1959; individual practice law, Greeley, 1959—. Mem. Am., Colo., Weld County bar assns. Home: 1922 20th St Rd Greeley CO 80631 Office: Suite 500 Greeley Nat Plaza Greeley CO 80631 Tel (303) 356-6464

STEINMETZ, DONALD WALTER, b. Milw., Sept. 19, 1924; B.A., U. Wis., 1949, J.D., 1951. Admitted to Wis. bar, 1951; individual practice law, Milw., 1951-58; 1st asst. dist. atty. City of Milw., 1958-65; asst. atty. gen. State of Wis., 1965-66; judge Milwaukee County (Wis.) Ct., 1966—; mem. Chief Judge Study Com., Fin. Reporting Com., Study Com. for TV and Radio Coverage in Courtroom. Pres. Sunday Morning Breakfast Club, South div. High Sch. Old Timers, Milw. W Club. Mem. Am., Wis. bar assns., Am. Judicature Soc. Office: 901 N 9th St Milwaukee WI 53233 Tel (414) 278-4523

STELLMON, WILLIAM ANDREW, b. Winchester, Idaho, May 2, 1933; B.S., U. Idaho, 1959, LL.B., 1960. Admitted to Idaho bar, 1960, U.S. Supreme Ct. bar, 1970; partner firm Ware, Stellmon & O'Connel, Lewiston, Idaho, 1960—; atty. City of Lewiston, 1970-74; dep. prosecutor Nez Perce County (Idaho), 1974. Bd. dirs. Lewiston Boys' Club, 1965—, Lewiston Vis. Nurses Assn., 1968-74, Lewis-Clark Legal Services, Inc., 1969-72, Nez Perce County Econ. Devel. Council, 1965-66. Mem. Am., Idaho bar assns., Def. Research Inst. Home: 1122 10th Ave Lewiston ID 83501 Office: 1219 Idaho St Lewiston ID 83501 Tel (208) 743-1516

STEM, WILLIAM ROBERT, b. Warren County, N.J., Aug. 17, 1915; B.A., George Washington U., 1939; LL.B., Rutgers U., 1947; postgrad. Howard U. Admitted to N.J. bar, 1949; U.S. Supreme Ct. bar, 1956; individual practice law, Frenchtown, N.J., 1949—; prosecutor Hunterdon County, N.J., 1963-68; judge N.J. Municipal Ct., 1951-59; v.p. Union Nat. Bank, Frenchtown, 1955-59; advisory bd. The Hunterdon County Nat. Bank, Flemington, N.J., 1959—. Treas. Frenchtown Service of Salvation Army, Hunterdon County, 1952—. Mem. N.J. State Bar Assn. (mem. com. on law enforcement 1976), Hunterdon County, Warren County, Am. bar assns., Delta Theta Phi. Home: R D #3 Box 421 Milford NJ 08848 Office: 49 Bridge St Frenchtown NJ 08825 Tel (201) 996-4241

STEMBER, ABRAHAM, b. N.Y.C.; LL.B., St. John's U., 1935; LL.M., 1936. Admitted to N.Y. bar, 1936, U.S. Ct. Mil. Appeals, 1951; partner firm Ferreri and Stember; individual practice law, Bklyn.; chief counsel excise com. N.Y. State Assembly. Mem. Bklyn. Bar Assn. Home: 720 E 32d St Brooklyn NY 11200 Office: 66 Court St Brooklyn NY 11201 Tel (212) TR5-0678

STEMBRIDGE, GEORGE MORTON, JR., b. Milledgeville, Ga., May 8, 1946; B.B.A., U. Ga., 1968; J.D., Mercer U., 1971. Admitted to Ga. bar, 1971, Fifth Circuit Ct. Appeals, 1976, Supreme Ct. U.S., 1976; asso. firm Christopher & Feutral, Griffin, Ga., 1971-72; partner firm Christopher & Stembridge, Griffin, 1972; individual practice law, Milledgeville, 1972—; atty. Baldwin County Hosp. Authority, 1973—. Mem. Am., Baldwin County, Ocmulgee Circuit bar assns., State Bar Ga., Bar Assn. Middle Dist. Ga., Ga. Soc. Hosp. Attys., Am. Soc. Hosp. Attys., Phi Kappa Phi, Beta Alpha Psi, Beta Gamma Sigma, Scabbard and Blade. Office: 102 Sanford Bldg Milledgeville GA 31061 Tel (912) 452-7143

STEMPLER, JACK LEON, b. Newark, Oct. 30, 1920; B.A., Montclair State Coll., 1943; LL.B., Cornell U., 1948. Admitted to N.Y. bar, 1949, D.C. bar, 1949; atty. Com. Uniform Code Mil. Justice, Dept. Def., Washington, 1948-49, atty. adviser Legis. div., 1949-50, asst. counsel Munitions Bd., 1950-53, counsel Armgd Forces Housing Agy., 1952-54, Advanced Research Projects Agy., 1958-65, asst. gen. counsel logistics, 1953-65, asst. to sec. def. for legis. affairs, 1965-70; gen. counsel Dept. Air Force, Washington, 1970-77; asst. to Sec. Def. for legis. affairs, 1977—. Mem. Fed., D.C. bar assns., Cornell Law Sch. Assn., Montclair State Alumni Assn. Recipient Outstanding Civilian Performance award Dept. Def., 1959, Distinguished Civilian Service award, 1965, with Bronze palms, 1969, 70, Exceptional Civilian Service awards USAF, 1973, 75, 77. Home: 4701 Newcomb Pl Alexandria VA 22304 Office: Pentagon Washington DC 20301 Tel (202) 697-6210

STEPHENS, ALBERT LEE, JR., b. Los Angeles, Feb. 19, 1913; A.B. cum laude, U. So. Cal., 1936; LL.B., 1938. Admitted to Calif. bar, 1939, U. S. Supreme Ct. bar, 1944; practice law, 1939-59; judge Superior Ct. Los Angeles, 1959-61, U.S. Dist. Ct. Central Calif., Los Angeles, 1961—, now chief judge. Chmn. bd. coun-Dist. Calif., Los Angeles, 1961—. Chmn. bd. councillors Sch. Internat. Relations. U. So. Calif. Mem. Am., Los Angeles (trustee 1955-57, 59-61) bar assns., Am. Judicature Soc., World Affairs Council, Chancery Club (pres. 1960-61), Town Hall Los Angeles, Nat. Lawyers Club, Phi Kappa Tau, Phi Alpha Delta, Pi Sigma Alpha, Blackstonian (pres.), Skull and Scales (v.p.). Home: 232 S June St Los Angeles CA 90004 Office: 312 N Spring St Los Angeles CA 90012*

STEPHENS, CHARLES RAYMOND, b. Thomasville, Ala., Sept. 17, 1942; B.S., U. Ala., 1965, M.A., 1968, J.D., 1974. Admitted to Ala. bar, 1974; asso. firm Bankhead, Petree & Savage, Jasper, Ala., 1974; mem. firm Bankhead, Savage & Stephens, Jasper, 1975—. Mem. adv. com. for community devel., Jasper, 1975; bd. dirs. Goodwill Industries, Jasper, 1976—; pres. Civitan Club, Jasper, 1976. Mem. Ala., Walker County bar assns. Home: 106 Shererwood St Jasper AL 35501 Office: 311 W 18th St Jasper AL 35501 Tel (205) 384-4574

STEPHENS, E. EDWARD, b. Phoenix, B.C., Can., Dec. 6, 1907; B.S., U. Calif., Berkeley, 1933; LL.B., George Washington U., 1938; LL.M., Georgetown U., 1946. Admitted to D.C. bar, 1938, U.S. Supreme Ct. bar, 1945; practiced in Washington, 1947—; of counsel firm Shipley, Smoak & Akerman, 1974—; syndicated newspaper columnist Counsel for the Taxpayer, 1969—; founder Tax Practice Inst., Washington, 1948, Phila., 1954, Balt., 1954, dir., chief lectr., Washington, 1948-57, Phila., 1954-57, Balt., 1954-57; professorial lectr. in tax law George Washington U., 1949-51. Bd. dirs. Animal Welfare League Alexandria (Va.), 1959-64. Recipient George Washington U. Alumni Achievement award, 1946; contbr. articles to legal jours. Home: 908 Darton Dr Alexandria VA 22308 Office: 1108 National Press Bldg Washington DC 20045 Tel (202) 783-1647

STEPHENS, GEORGE EDWARD, JR., b. Lawrence, Kans., Mar. 26, 1936; student U. Colo., 1954-59; LL.B., Stanford, 1962. Admitted to Calif. bar, 1963; law clk. to judge U.S. Dist. Ct. for Central Calif., 1962-64; partner firms Pollock & Palmer, Los Angeles, 1964-69, Gates, Morris, Merrell & Stephens, Los Angeles, 1969-72, Paul, Hastings, Janofsky & Walker, Los Angeles, 1972—. Fellow Am. Coll. Probate Counsel, Internat. Acad. Probate and Trust Law, Am. Bar Found.; mem. Los Angeles County, Am. bar assns., State Bar Calif., Chancery Club. Office: 555 S Flower St 22d floor Los Angeles CA 90071 Tel (213) 489-4000

STEPHENS, JAMES WARREN, JR., b. Newport News, Va., Feb. 14, 1924; B.A., U. Va., 1949, LL.B., 1951. Admitted to Va. bar, 1950; asso. firm Montague, Ferguson & Holt, Newport News, 1951-55; partner firm Ferguson, Yates & Stephens, Newport News, 1955-62; individual practice law, Newport News, 1962-67; partner firm

Stephens & Wentworth, Newport News, 1967—; dir. Dominion Nat. Bank of the Peninsula, 1972—. Commr., Newport News Redevel. and Housing Authority, 1969-70; pres. United Way of Va. Peninsula, 1970-71; trustee St. Paul's Coll., Lawrenceville, Va., 1976—; vice-chancellor Episcopal Diocese of So. Va., 1977—. Mem. Am. (Va. chmn. com. def. indigent persons 1965-68), Va., Newport News (pres. 1969) bar assns. Home: 116 Longwood Dr Newport News VA 23606 Office: 2600 Washington Ave PO Box 252 Newport News VA 23607 Tel (804) 244-1463

STEPHENS, JOHN EARL, b. Lakeland, Fla., Aug. 25, 1944; B.B.A., Loyola U., New Orleans, 1966, J.D., 1969. Admitted to La. bar, 1969, Fla. bar, 1970; partner firm Gustafson, Caldwell, Stephens & Ferris, Fort Lauderdale, Fla., 1971—; city atty. Sea Ranch Lakes (Fla.), 1975—. Mem. Am., Broward County trial lawyers assns. Office: 1415 E Sunrise Blvd Fort Lauderdale FL 33304

STEPHENS, JOHN WILLIAM, b. Davenport, Iowa, May 23, 1944; A.B., San Diego State U., 1966; J.D., U. Calif., Los Angeles, 1969. Admitted to Calif. bar, 1970; asso. Greene & Pancer, Santa Monica, Calif., 1970-71; individual practice law La Jolla, Calif., 1971—; lectr. U. Calif., San Diego extension, La Jolla, 1976. Pres. ACLU San Diego and Imperial Counties (Calif.), 1976, chmn. ACLU legal panel, 1974-75. Mem. Nat. Lawyers Guild (past chpt. pres.), San Diego County Bar Assn. Office: 836 Prospect St La Jolla CA 92037 Tel (714) 459-0234

STEPHENS, JOSEPH TAYLOR, b. New Albany, Miss., Feb. 19, 1939; B.B.A., U. Miss., 1961, J.D., 1969. Admitted to Miss. bar, 1969; asso. firm Henley, Lotterhos & Bennett, Jackson, Miss., from 1969, subsequently partner. Coach, YMCA Baseball, 1976; bd. dirs. Jackson Indigent Defender, Inc., 1975—. Mem. Am., Miss., Hinds County bar assns., Oil and Gas Lawyers Assn. (pres. 1974-75). Home: 5207 Suffolk Circle Jackson MS 39211 Office: 990 Deposit Guaranty Plaza Jackson MS 39205 Tel (601) 948-5131

STEPHENS, RICHARD GLENN, b. Chgo., May 1, 1926; B.E.E., Purdue U., 1948; J.D., George Washington U., 1953. Admitted to D.C. bar, 1953, N.Y. State bar, 1957; patent counsel Link Aviation, Inc., Binghamton, N.Y., 1953-56; individual practice law, Binghamton, 1957—; v.p. Character Recognition Corp., 1963-70. Mem. Am., N.Y. State, Broome County bar assns., Am. Patent Law Assn. Home: 3141 Hickory Ln Binghamton NY 13903 Office: 318 Security Mutual Life Bldg Binghamton NY 13901 Tel (607) 723-8295

STEPHENS, RICHARD WILLIAM, b. Kinston, N.C., July 2, 1944; B.A., Tulane U., 1966; J.D., U. Ga., 1969. Admitted to Ga. bar, 1970; law clk. to judge U.S. Ct. Claims, Washington, 1969-70; asso. firm Kilpatrick, Cody, Rogers, McClatchey & Regenstein, Atlanta, 1970-73; partner firm Varner & Stephens, Atlanta, 1973—. Mem. Am., Ga., Atlanta bar assns. Home: 1934 Colland Dr NW Atlanta GA 30318 Office: 2020 Gas Light Tower Atlanta GA 30303 Tel (404) 577-6370

STEPHENS, ROBERT F., Now atty. gen. State of Ky., Frankfort. Office: State Capitol Frankfort KY 40601*

STEPHENS, ROBERT LEONARD, JR., b. Bellingham, Wash., Nov. 14, 1943; B.A. in History, U. Wash., 1967; J.D., Syracuse U., 1970. Admitted to Mont. bar, 1970; mem. firm Sandall, Moses & Cavan, Billings, Mont., 1970-71; individual practice law, Billings, 1971-76; mem. firm Calton & Stephens, Ltd., Billings, 1976—; staff legal advisor ACLU of Mont., 1971-74. Mem. Yellowstone County Zoning Bd., 1974, Mayor's Ad Hoc Com., 1973. Mem. Yellowstone County, Mont., Am. bar assns., Mont., Am. trial lawyers assns., Mont. Criminal Def. Lawyers Assn. (v.p., dir.), Am. Judicature Soc. Home: 246 Ave B Billings MT 59101 Office: 206 N 29th St Suite 226 Billings MT 59101 Tel (206) 245-6182

STEPHENSON, DONLEY RANDALL, b. Abilene, Tex., Feb. 15, 1944; B.A., Tex. Tech. Coll., 1966; J.D., U. Tex., 1969. Admitted to Tex. bar, 1969; served to capt. JAGC, U.S. Army, 1969-73; asst. dist. atty. Dallas, 1973—; asso. firm Anderson, Smith, Null & Stofer, Victoria, Tex., 1973—. Bd. dirs. Boys' Club Victoria; active United Way. Mem. Victoria County Jr. Bar Assn. (pres.), Victoria County Bar Assn. Office: Box 1969 Victoria TX 77901 Tel (512) 573-9191

STEPHENSON, JAMES BENNETT, b. Greenup, Ky., Jan. 6, 1916; A.B., U. Ky., 1938, LL.B., 1951. Admitted to Ky. bar, 1939, U.S. Supreme Ct. bar, 1950; individual practice law, Pikeville, Ky., 1940-S7; judge Circuit Ct., Div. I, Pike County, Ky., 1957-72; justice Ky. Supreme Ct., Frankfort, 1972—. Mem. Ky. Bar Assn., Phi Delta Phi. Home: 108 Walnut Dr Pikeville KY 41501 Office: 239 New State Capitol Frankfort KY 40601 Tel (502) 564-6910

STEPHENSON, JOHN DEUEL, JR., b. Great Falls, Mont., Oct. 25, 1934; B.A., Yale, 1956; LL.B., Harvard, 1960. Admitted to Mont. bar, 1960; asso. firm Jardine, Stephenson, Blewett and Weaver, Great Falls, 1960-67, partner 1968—. Trustee Great Falls Pub. Sch. Dist., 1970-76; bd. dirs. United Way of Cascade County, 1974—; bd. dirs., v.p. Paris Gibson Sq., 1976—; pres. N. Mont. chpt. Arthritis Found., 1962-63. Mem. Am., Mont., Cascade County bar assns. Home: 200 3d Ave North Great Falls MT 59401 Office: 700 First National Bank Bldg Great Falls MT 59401 Tel (406) 727-5000

STEPHENSON, RANDALL LEE, b. Des Moines, Dec. 28, 1948; B.A., U. Iowa, 1971; J.D., Fla. State U., 1973. Admitted to Iowa bar, 1974; asso. firm Beck, Pappajohn & Shriver, Mason City, Iowa, 1974—. Bd. dirs., legal advisor Jaycees, 1974—; bd. dirs. Jr. Achievement, 1975—, ARC, 1975—, Mason City United Way, 1977—. Mem. Am., Iowa (jr. bridge-the-gap com. mem. 1975), Cerro Gordo County (sec. 1977) bar assns. Home: 211 Parkridge Dr Mason City IA 50401 Office: 800 Brick and Tile Bldg Mason City IA 50401 Tel (515) 423-4264

STEPHENSON, ROY LAVERNE, b. Spirit Lake, Iowa, Mar. 14, 1917; B.A., State U. Iowa, 1938; J.D., 1940; LL.D., Parsons Coll., 1963. Admitted to Iowa bar, 1940; asso. firm Oliver P. Bennett, Mapleton, Iowa, 1940-41; served with U.S. Army, 1941-46, def. counsel, ETO, 1942-44; asso. firm Fountain, Bridges, Lundy & Stephenson, Des Moines, 1946-53; U.S. atty. for So. Dist. Iowa, 1953-60; judge U.S. Dist. Ct., So. Dist. Iowa, 1960-71, chief judge, 1962-71; judge U.S. Ct. Appeals, 8th Circuit, 1971—; mem. budget com. Jud. Council U.S., 1969-75. Mem. Iowa Gov.'s Ann. Prayer Breakfast Com., 1961-75; trustee Sch. Religion U. Iowa, 1962—; chmn. Polk County Republican Central Com., 1951-53. Mem. Am., Iowa, Polk County bar assns., Am. Judicature Soc., Order of Coif. Decorated Silver Star, Bronze Star; recipient Legal Clinic award Drake U., 1975. Home: 4202 Muskogee St Des Moines IA 50309 Office: 301 US Courthouse Des Moines IA 50309 Tel (515) 284-4515

STERLE, JOSEPH ANTHONY, b. Tyler, Tex., Dec. 6, 1942; B.A., U. Tex., 1970, J.D., 1973. Admitted to Tex. bar, 1973; asst. city atty. Texarkana (Tex.), 1974-76. Mem. N.E. Tex., Bowie County, Texarkana, Am. bar assns. Home: 10 Pine Ridge Circle Texarkana TX 75501 Office: 407 Texas Blvd Texarkana TX 75501 Tel (214) 793-4926

STERLING, THOMAS EVERETT, b. State College, Pa., Aug. 3, 1922; B.E.E., U. Cin., 1944; B.S., Mass. Inst. Tech., 1949; J.D., George Washington U., 1954. Admitted to Pa. bar, 1961, D.C. bar, 1961, N.Y. bar, 1956; prof., atty. Pa. State U., State College, 1958-65; individual practice law, State College, 1965—. Mem. Am., Pa. bar assns. Home: 215 Circle Dr State College PA 16801 Office: Box 14 State College PA 16801 Tel (814) 238-9455

STERN, DAVID G., A.B., Harvard U., 1968, J.D., 1971. Admitted to Mass. bar, 1971; asso. firm Choate, Hall & Stewart, Boston, 1971-76; asso. firm Brown, Rudnick, Freed & Gesmer, Boston, 1976—. Mem. Boston, Mass., Am. bar assns. Office: 85 Devonshire St Boston MA 02109 Tel (617) 726-7800

STERN, GEOFFREY, b. Columbus, Ohio, Nov. 29, 1942; B.A. cum laude, Ohio State U., 1965, J.D. summa cum laude, 1968. Admitted to Ohio bar, 1968; asso. firm Alexander, Ebinger, Holschuh, Fisher & McAlister, Columbus, 1968-72; asso. firm Folkerth, Calhoun, Webster, Maurer & O'Brien, Columbus, 1972, partner, 1973—. Guest lectr. Grad. Sch. Mgmt. U. Rochester. Mem. City Council, Bexley, Ohio, 1973—. Mem. Am., Ohio, Columbus (chmn. publications com. 1973-75, mem. profl. ethics com. 1975—) bar assns., Am. Judicature Soc., Order Coif, Phi Beta Kappa. Contbr. articles to legal jours. Home: 167 S Stanwood Rd Columbus OH 43209 Office: 230 E Town St Columbus OH 43215 Tel (614) 228-2945

STERN, GERALD, b. N.Y.C., Apr. 15, 1935; B.A., Bklyn. Coll., 1958; J.D., Syracuse U., 1963; LL.M., N.Y. U., 1970. Admitted to N.Y. bar, 1963, U.S. Supreme Ct. bar, 1966; asst. dist. atty. New York County, 1963-65; legal dir. OEO, Syracuse, 1965; staff atty. Pres.'s Commn. on Law Enforcement and Adminstrn. Justice, Washington, 1965-67; asst. corp. counsel N.Y.C. Corp. Counsel's Office, 1967-68; asst. dir. Adminstrn. of Cts., First Dept., N.Y. State, 1968-70, dep. dir., 1970-72, dir., 1972-74; adminstr. State Commn. on Jud. Conduct, N.Y.C., 1974—; instr. polit. sci. Queens Coll., 1970; asst. adj. prof. Lehman Coll., 1971-74; cons. Law Enforcement Study Center, Washington U., St. Louis, N.Y. State Commn. on Revision of Constn., Legis. Drafting Project, Columbia U. Mem. Gov.'s Adv. Council on Alcoholism, 1969-71. Mem. Am. (chmn. com. on alcoholism and drug reform 1969-74), N.Y. State bar assns., Assn. Bar City N.Y., Order of Coif. Mem. law rev. bd. Syracuse Law Sch., 1962-63; contbr. articles to legal jours. Home: 20 Coralyn Ave White Plains NY 10605 Office: 801 2d Ave New York City NY 10017 Tel (212) 949-8888

STERN, GERALD M., b. Chgo., Apr. 5, 1937; B.S. in Economics, U. Pa., 1958; LL.B., Harvard, 1961. Admitted to D.C. bar, 1961, U.S. Supreme Ct. bar, 1971; trial atty., Civil Rts. Div., U.S. Dept. Justice, 1961-64; asso. firm Arnold & Porter, Wash. D.C., 1964-68, partner, 1969-76; founding partner firm Rogovin, Stern & Huge, Wash. D.C., 1976—. Mem. Am. Bar Assn., Assn. Trial Lawyers of Am., Authors League of Am. Author: The Buffalo Creek Disaster, 1976; co-author: Southern Justice, 1965. Office: 1730 Rhode Island NW Washington DC 20036 Tel (202) 296-5820

STERN, HENRY HIRSH, b. St. Louis, Apr. 10, 1903; B.S. in Econs., U. Pa., 1923; J.D., Washington U., 1926. Admitted to Mo. bar; partner firm Stern & Burnett, 1925-35, Burnett, Stern & Liberman, 1935-66, Baron, Stern & Liberman, 1966-70, Susman, Stern, Agatstein & Heifetz, Clayton, Mo., 1970—; asst. atty. gen. State of Mo., 1930-31. Mem. Am., Mo., St. Louis bar assns. Home: 6310 Waterman Ave Saint Louis MO 63130 Office: 7733 Forsyth Blvd Clayton MO 63105 Tel (314) 862-0900

STERN, HENRY LOUIS, b. Essen, Germany, Jan. 2, 1924; Ph.B. with gen. honors, U. Chgo., 1947, J.D., 1950. Admitted to Ill. bar, 1950, N.Y. bar, 1956, Calif. bar, 1964; atty.-adviser SEC, Chgo. and Washington, 1950-55; individual practice law, N.Y.C., 1955-57; gen. counsel Holly Corp., N.Y.C. and Azusa, Calif., 1957-67, sec., 1960-67; asso. firm Mitchell, Silberberg & Knupp, Los Angeles, 1967-69, partner, 1970—; lectr. Practising Law Inst. Mem. Los Angeles County (chmn. sect. bus. and corps. law 1974-75), Am. (com. fed. regulation securities, 1972—) bar assns., State Bar Calif. Asso. editor: U. Chgo. Law Rev., 1949-50. Office: 1800 Century Park E Los Angeles CA 90067 Tel (213) 553-5000

STERN, HERBERT JAY, b. N.Y.C., Nov. 8, 1936; B.A., Hobart Coll., 1958, LL.D. (hon.), 1974; J.D. (Ford Found. scholar), U. Chgo., 1961; LL.D. (hon.), Seton Hall Coll., 1973; L.H.D. (hon.), Newark State Coll., 1973; D.C.L. (hon.), Bloomfield Coll., 1973; Litt.D. (hon.), Montclair State Coll., 1973. Admitted to N.Y. State bar, 1961, N.J. bar, 1971; asst. dist. atty. New York County, 1962-65; trial atty. organized crime and racketeering sect. Dept. Justice, 1965-69; chief asst. U.S. atty. Dist. of N.J., Newark, 1969-70, U.S. atty., 1971-74, U.S. dist. judge, 1974—. Trustee, Chilton Hosp.; mem. adv. com. U. Chgo. Law Sch. Mem. Am., N.J., Fed. (past pres. Newark chpt.), Essex County bar assns., Am. Judicature Soc., Phi Alpha Delta. Named One of America's 10 Outstanding Young Men, U.S. Jr. C. of C., 1971. Office: US Post Office and Courthouse Newark NJ 07101 Tel (201) 645-6340

STERN, HERBERT LYMAN, JR., b. Chgo., Apr. 10, 1915; A.B., Yale U., 1936, LL.B., 1939. Admitted to Ill. bar, 1939; asso. firm Gottlieb & Schwartz, Chgo., 1939-48, partner, 1948—; chmn. bd. T C Mfg. Co., Evanston, Ill.; sec.-treas. La Mere Industries, Inc., Walworth, Wis., 1960—, Marland Environ. Systems, Inc., Walworth, 1974—. Sec., bd. dirs. Found. for Hearing and Speech Rehab., Chgo., 1950—; chmn. Lake County (Ill.) Democratic Central Com., Waukegan, 1968—. Mem. Am., Ill., Chgo., Lake County bar assns. Home: 1128 Green Bay Rd Highland Park IL 60035 Office: 120 S La Salle St Suite 1500 Chicago IL 60603 Tel (312) 726-2122

STERN, HOWARD SANFORD, b. Cleve., Jan. 21, 1929; B.Sc. in Bus. Adminstrn., Ohio State U., 1950; LL.B., Case Western Res. U., 1956, J.D., 1965. Admitted to Ohio bar, 1956; asso. firm Sindell & Sindell, Cleve., 1953-58; partner firm Steiner, Stern & Ozan, Cleve., 1959—; acting judge Bedford (Ohio) Municipal Ct., 1963-67; pros. atty. City of Warrensville Heights (Ohio), 1967—. Trustee Warrensville Twp., 1961-64. Mem. Ohio State, Greater Cleve. bar assns., Cuyahoga County (Ohio) Law Dirs. Assn. Home: 165 Sterncrest Dr Chagrin Falls OH 44022 Office: suite 813 75 Public Square Cleveland OH 44113 Tel (216) 771-1310

STERN, LYNNE ROTHSCHILD, b. New Orleans, Feb. 1, 1947; B.A., U. Mich., 1968; J.D., Columbia, 1971. Admitted to La. bar, 1971; law clk. Hon. F.J.R. Heebe, U.S. Dist. Judge Eastern Div. La., 1972; asso. firm Nelson & Nelson, New Orleans, 1972-73, partner, 1973-74; asst. prof. Loyola U. Law Sch., New Orleans, 1974-76, lectr., 1977—; arbitration panelist U.S. Steelworkers and Am. Can Co., 1975. Home: 2226 Chestnut St New Orleans LA 70130 Office: Loyola Law Sch New Orleans LA 70130 Tel (504) 866-5471

STERN, RALPH DAVID, b. Longview, Tex., June 20, 1943; A.B., Bucknell U., 1963; J.D., U. Chgo., 1966. Admitted to Ill. bar, 1967, D.C. bar, 1967, Calif. bar, 1971, U.S. Supreme Ct. bar, 1970; law clk. Ill. Appellate Ct., Chgo., 1966-67; asso. firm Sidney Kleinman, Chgo., 1967-68; asso. firm Ressman & Tischler, Chgo., 1968-69; asst. schs. atty. San Diego City Schs., 1971-73, schs. atty., 1973—; exec. asst. Orange County (Calif.) Bd. Suprs., Santa Ana, 1970-71. 1st v.p. Legal Aid Soc. San Diego, Inc., 1975, pres., 1976. Mem. Am., Calif., San Diego County bar assns., Nat. Orgn. on Legal Problems of Edn., Nat. Sch. Bd. Assn. Council of Sch. Attys. Contbr. articles to profl. jours. Office: 4100 Normal St San Diego CA 92103 Tel (714) 293-8450

STERN, SAMUEL ALAN, b. Phila., Jan. 21, 1929; A.B., U. Pa., 1949; LL.B., Harvard, 1952. Admitted to Mass. bar, 1952, D.C. bar, 1958; asso. firm Cox, Langford, Stoddard & Cutler, Washington, 1956-62; partner firm Wilmer, Cutler & Pickering, Washington, 1962—; vis. prof. law Harvard, 1976; dir. Inst. Internat. and Fgn. Trade Law, Georgetown U., 1971—; pres.'s council Tulane U., 1976—; asst. counsel Warren Commn., 1974; cons. Nat. Adv. Commn. on Selective Service, 1966; cons. UN, 1974—. Mem. Am. Law Inst., Am. Soc. Internat. Law, Am., D.C. bar assns. Contbr. articles to legal jours. Home: 3626 Prospect St NW Washington DC 20007 Office: 1666 K St NW Washington DC 20006 Tel (202) 872-6414

STERN, STEVEN TERRY, b. Phila., Jan. 7, 1944; B.A., U. Pa., 1965; J.D., Temple U., 1968. Admitted to Pa. bar, 1968; asso. firm Mesirov, Gelman, Jaffe & Cramer, Phila., 1968-70, 72-74; adminstrv. dir. Israel Securities Authority, Jerusalem, Israel, 1971; asst. legal adviser State Revenue Adminstrn., Ministry of Finance, Israel, 1971-72; partner firm Jacobsen & Stern, Norristown, Pa., 1974—; faculty Inst. Paralegal Tng., Phila., 1975—. Mem. cabinet New Leadership for Israel Bonds, Phila., 1974—; mem. speakers bur. United Way of Southeastern Pa., 1976—. Mem. Trial Lawyers of Montgomery County, Phila., Pa., Montgomery County bar assns., Assn. for Jewish Children (dir.). Author: Introduction to Civil Litigation, 1977. Office: 325 Swede St Norristown PA 19401 Tel (215) 275-7567

STERNHAGEN, WILLIAM GEORGE, b. Havre, Mont., July 11, 1929; B.A. in Bus., Carroll Coll., 1958; LL.B., J.D., U. Mont., 1961. Admitted to Mont. bar, 1961; atty., City of Glasgow, Mont., 1961-64; partner firm Hoffman & Sternhagen, Glasgow, 1962-64; U.S. commr., 1963-64; asst. atty. gen. for State of Mont., Helena, 1965-67; partner firm Loble, Picotte, Loble, Pauly & Sternhagen, Helena, 1967-74; individual practice law, Helena, 1974; legal counsel The Anaconda Co., Helena, 1974-75, dir. office of govtl. affairs, 1975—; hearing examiner Mont. Aero. Commn., 1969; mem. Constl. Conv. Commn., Helena, 1971; mem. State Judicial Nominating Commn., 1973, 74, 75, 76; trustee State Bar of Mont., 1975-76; mem. Employment Advisory Council mem., 1975-76; bd. dirs. Mont. Taxpayers Assn., Helena, 1975-76; sec. Judge Lester H. Loble Found., 1975-76. Mem. Am., 1st Judicial Dist. bar assns., Am., Mont. trial lawyers assns., Common Cause. Decorated D.F.C., Air medal; recipient Kiwanis Service to Youth award, 1972; inducted into Carroll Coll. Football Hall of Fame, 1975. Home: 2031 Broadway St Helena MT 59601 Office: 1625 Eleventh Ave Helena MT 59601 Tel (406) 443-5810

STERNKE, MYRL BRANDT, b. Brookfield, Mo., Mar. 23, 1923; LL.B., U. Mo., 1949. Admitted to Mo. bar, 1948; individual practice law, Palmyra, Mo., 1950—; chmn. bd., dir. Palmyra State Bank. Mem. Palmyra Bd. Pub. Works, 1964-68. Mem. Mo. Bar Assn., Palmyra C. of C. (pres. 1960). Home: 304 W Jefferson St Palmyra MO 64361 Office: 204a S Main St Palmyra MO 63461 Tel (314) 769-2588

STERNSCHEIN, JOSEPH, b. N.Y.C., Sept. 4, 1934; LL.B., Bklyn. Law Sch., 1959. Admitted to N.Y. bar, 1960. Mem. Queens Bar Assn. Office: 40-41 75th St Elmhurst NY 11373 Tel (212) 478-9300

STERRETT, ROBERT WENDELL, JR., b. Atlanta, Jan. 7, 1944; B.A., U. Ga., 1966, J.D., 1969. Admitted to Ga. bar, 1969, Fla. bar, 1970; law clk. U.S. dist. Ct., Tampa, Fla., 1969-71; atty. So. Bell Telephone and Telegraph Co., Atlanta, 1971—. Mem. Willing Hands, Jacksonville, Fla., 1971-72; Tech.-Ga. Devel. Fund., 1975-76. Mem. Am., Ga. (anti-trust sects.), Fla., Atlanta bar assns., Ga. State bar (vice-chmn. public info. com. young lawyer's sect., 1974-75, chmn. 1975—), Corp. Counsel Assn. Greater Atlanta. Contbr. articles to law revs. Home: 367 Jade Cove Dr Roswell GA 30075 Office: 1245 Hurt Bldg Atlanta GA 30303 Tel (404) 529-8043

STETSON, ROBERT CRAWFORD, b. Phoenix, Sept. 26, 1934; A.B., Stanford, 1956, LL.B., 1958. Admitted to Calif. bar, 1959; atty. Honolulu Oil Corp., 1958-61; v.p., gen. counsel Consol. Freightways, Menlo Park, Calif., 1961—. Mem. Am., Calif. bar assns., Motor Carrier Lawyers Assn. Office: 175 Linfield Dr Menlo Park CA 94025 Tel (415) 326-1700

STEUBEN, NORTON LESLIE, b. Milw., Feb. 14, 1936; B.A., U. Mich., 1958, J.D. with distinction, 1961. Admitted to N.Y. bar, 1962, Colo. bar, 1975; asso. firm Hogson, Russ, Andrews, Woods & Goodyear, Buffalo, 1961-65, partner, 1966-68; lectr. State U. N.Y. Buffalo, 1961-68; asst. prof. law U. Colo., 1968-70, asso. prof., 1970-74, prof., 1974—; faculty U.S. C. of C., Inst. for Orgn. Mgmt., Boulder, Colo., 1971, Am. Law Inst.-Am. Bar Assn. Continuing Profl. Edn., 1976—; officer Buffalo-Niagara Indsl. Devel. Corp., 1963-68; Opportunities Devel. Corp., Buffalo, 1966-68. Mem. Boulder (Colo.) Human Rights Commn., 1969-72, chmn., 1972-74; mem. Boulder Landlord-Tenant Com., 1973-74; trustee Boulder Open Space Bd., 1976—. Mem. Am., N.Y. State, Colo., Boulder County bar assns., AAUP, Order of Coif, Tau Epsilon Rho. Author: Cases and Materials on Real Estate Planning, 1974; Teacher's Manual for Cases and Materials on Real Estate Planning, 1974; contbr. articles to profl. jours.; recipient award for distinguished service to the community Buffalo Area C. of C., 1966; John W. Reed award, 1970; U. Colo. award for excellence in teaching, 1972. Home: 845 8th St Boulder CO 80302 Office: 418 Fleming Law Bldg U Colo Boulder CO 80309 Tel (303) 492-7963

STEVENS, ETHAN KNOWLTON, b. Detroit, May 19, 1906; A.B., Cornell U., 1927; LL.B., J.D., U. Mich., 1929. Admitted to Mich. bar, 1929, N.Mex. bar, 1947; individual practice law, Detroit, 1929-41; mem. firm Bulkley, Ledyard, Dickinson & Wright, Detroit, 1942-43, Clark, Klein, Brucker & Waples, Detroit, 1944-45, Krebbiel & Stevens, Clayton, N.Mex., 1946-53; individual practice law, Clayton,

1953—; asst. dist. atty. Union County (N.Mex.), 1953-54, 1961-62; city atty. Clayton, 1961-68; asst. atty. gen. State of N.Mex., 1969, 71; contract pub. defender Clayton, 1975—. Mem. N.Mex. State, Am. bar assns. Home: 23 N Third Ave Clayton NM 88415 Office: 111 Walnut St Box 336 Clayton NM 88415 Tel (505) 374-9322

STEVENS, GERALD M., b. Detroit, May 31, 1930; B.S. in Forestry, Mich. State U., 1951; J.D., U. Detroit, 1957. Admitted to Mich. bar, 1958; mem. legal div. Bd. Wayne County (Mich.) Rd. Commrs., 1955-61; asso. firm Langs, Molyneaux & Armstrong, Detroit, 1961-65; individual practice law, Owosso, Mich., 1965—; pros. atty. Shiawassee County (Mich.), 1968-72; atty. Nardin Park Methodist Ch.; tchr. John Wesley Coll., Lansing (Mich.) Community Coll.; mem. Region V Crime Commn. Mem. com. on candidates Civic Searchlight, Taylor Twp. Sch. Bd., Bd. Canvassers; bd. dirs. YMCA, Community Concert, Inc., Shiawassee County unit Am. Cancer Soc.; pres. Owosso Day Care Center; pres., dir. Lung Assn. Genesee Valley. Mem. Am., Mich. (council mem. young lawyers sect.), Detroit, Shiawassee County bar assns. Home: 800 N State Rd Owosso MI 48867 Office: 319 E Main St Owosso MI 48867 Tel (517) 725-5161

STEVENS, HAROLD A., b. John's Island, S.C., Oct. 19, 1907; B.A., Benedict Coll., 1930, LL.D. (hon.); LL.B., Boston Coll. Law, 1936, LL.D. (hon.); LL.D. (hon.) Fordham U., Creighton U., Manhattan Coll., Morgan State Coll., Villanova U., Notre Dame U., St. Johns U., Yeshiva U., Holy Cross Coll. Admitted to Mass. bar, 1936, N.Y. bar, 1938, S.C. bar, 1940, U.S. Supreme Ct. bar, 1943; mem. firm Andrews & Stevens, N.Y.C., 1938-42, Dyett & Stevens, 1942-48, Brandenburg & Stevens, 1948-50; judge Ct. of Gen. Sessions, N.Y.C., 1951-55; justice N.Y. Supreme Ct., 1955-58, justice Appellate Div., First Dept., 1958-69, presiding judge Appellate Div., 1969—; judge N.Y. State Ct. of Appeals, 1974; instr. labor law Assn. Cath. Trade Unionists, N.Y.C., 1938-42, 47-50; spl. counsel Pres.'s Com. Fair Employment Practices, 1942-43; counsel Brotherhood of Sleeping Car Porters and Provisional Com. to Organize Colored Locomotive Firemen. Bd. dirs., past pres. Cath. Interracial Council N.Y.; archdiocesan bd. govs. CYO, U.S. Cath. Hist. Soc.; mem. N.Y. State Assembly, 1947-50; bd. dirs. Council on Religion and Internat. Affairs, Acad. Polit. Sci., Nat. Center for State Cts., Grand St. Boys' Assn.; trustee Inner-City Scholarship Fund, Inc., Law Center Found., N.Y. U. Law Sch., Benedict Coll., William Nelson Cromwell Found., Grand St. Boys' Found.; fellow Boston Coll. Law Sch.; mem. pres.'s council Boston Coll. Mem. Am., Nat., N.Y. State (plaque 1974) bar assns., Bar Assn. City N.Y., Guild Cath. Lawyers (citation 1974), Harlem, County lawyers assns., Am. Judicature Soc., Assn. Supreme Ct. Justices N.Y., Am. Soc. Internat. Law, Order of Coif, Phi Beta Sigma (Achievement award 1951). Recipient Thomas More medal Boston Coll. Law Sch. Alumni Assn., 1974, Distinguished Jurist award N.Y. U. Law Sch. Alumni Assn., 1975, Gold medal award CYO Club of Champions, 1975. Office: 27 Madison Ave Appellate Div Court House New York City NY 10010 Tel (212) 532-1000

STEVENS, HENRY LEONIDAS, III, b. Warsaw, N.C., May 12, 1923; B.A., U. N.C., 1947; LL.B., Wake Forest Coll., 1951, J.D., 1970. Admitted to N.C. bar, 1951; partner firm Bealsey & Stevens, Kenensville, N.C., 1951—. Mem. Duplin County, N.C. State, Am. bar assns. Home: 701 Forrest Rd Warsaw NC 28398 Office: PO Box 26 Courthouse Sq Kenansville NC 28349 Tel (919) 296-2676

STEVENS, JOHN PAUL, b. Chgo., Apr. 20, 1920; A.B., U. Chgo., 1941; J.D. magna cum laude, Northwestern U., 1947. Admitted to Ill. bar, 1949; law clk. to Asso. Justice Wiley Rutledge, Supreme Ct. of U.S., 1947-48; asso. firm Poppenhusen, Johnston, Thompson & Raymond, Chgo., 1948-52; asso. counsel Subcom. on Study of Monopoly Power, Jud. Com., U.S. Ho. of Reps., 1951; partner firm Rothschild, Stevens, Barry & Myers, Chgo., 1952-70; U.S. circuit judge U.S. Ct. of Appeals for 7th Circuit, Chgo., 1970-75; asso. justice Supreme Ct. of U.S., Washington, 1975—; lectr. Northwestern Sch. Law, 1950-54, U. Chgo. Law Sch., 1954-58. Mem. Am., Fed., Ill., Chgo. bar assns., Am. Law Inst., Order of Coif, Phi Beta Kappa, Psi Upsilon, Phi Delta Phi. Contbr. chpt. to Mr. Justice, 1956, also articles to profl. publs. Office: US Supreme Ct Bldg 1 1st St NE Washington DC 20543 Tel (202) 393-1640

STEVENS, JOHN SHORTER, b. Asheville, N.C., May 30, 1933; A.B. in Econs., U. N.C., Chapel Hill, 1956, LL.D., 1961. Admitted to N.C. bar, 1961; partner firm Redmond, Stevens, Loftin & Currie, Asheville, 1961—; mem. N.C. Gen. Assembly, 1969, 71, 73, 75, chmn. judiciary com., 1973, rules com., 1975; dir. Bank of Asheville. Pres. bd. dirs. Meml. Mission Hosp., Asheville. Mem. N.C. Bar Assn. (gov.), Phi Beta Kappa. Home: 83 Forest Rd Asheville NC 28803 Office: suite 610 Gennett Bldg Asheville NC 28807

STEVENS, JOSEPH EDWARD, JR., b. Kansas City, Mo., June 23, 1928; B.A., Yale U., 1949; J.D., U. Mich., 1952. Admitted to Mo. bar, 1952; asst. to dist. legal officer USN 11th Naval Dist. Legal Office, San Diego, 1953-55; asso. firm Lombardi, McLean, Slagle & Bernard, Kansas City, Mo., 1955-56; asso. firm Lathrop, Koontz, Righter, Clagett, Parker & Norquist, and predecessor, Kansas City, 1956-62, partner, 1962—; counsel Kansas City Bd. Election Commrs., 1973-77; chmn. Mo. adv. council Legal Services Corp., 1976—; mem. Mo. Compensation Commn., 1977—. Co-chmn. bd. Kansas City Chamber Choir, 1973-75; adv. trustee Kansas City Philharmonic, 1976—; chmn. adminstrv. bd., trustee Central United Meth. Ch., Kansas City. Mem. Mo. Bar (bd. govs. 1975—), Am., Kansas City bar assns., Lawyers Assn. Kansas City, Am. Judicature Soc. Recipient Lon O. Hocker Meml. Trial Lawyer award Mo. Bar Found., 1962; contbg. author Missouri Civil Trial Practice. Home: 425 W 55th St Kansas City MO 64113 Office: 1500 Ten Main Center Kansas City MO 64105 Tel (816) 842-0820

STEVENS, JOSEPH JOSHUA, JR., b. Mobile, Ala., Mar. 13, 1940; B.S., Millsaps Coll., 1962; postgrad. Miss. State U., 1962-63; J.D., U. Miss., 1966. Admitted to Miss. bar, 1966; mem. firm Tubb, Stevens & Morrison, West Point, Miss., 1966—; pros. atty., West Point, 1967-71. Pres. Clay County Community Chest, West Point; trustee First United Methodist Ch., West Point. Mem. Am., Miss., Clay County bar assns., Miss. State Bar, Miss. Def. Attys. Assn., West Point C. of C. (pres. 1975). Office: 220 Court St PO Box 324 West Point MS 39773 Tel (601) 494-2611

STEVENS, PAULINE MARY, b. Toledo, Feb. 28, 1947; A.B., Vassar Coll., 1969; J.D., U. Pa., 1972. Admitted to Calif. bar, 1973; teaching fellow Law Sch., U. Pa., 1971-72; counsel Bank of Am. Nat. Trust and Savs. Assn., Los Angeles, 1972—. Mem. Women's Bar Assn. Los Angeles, Los Angeles Fin. Lawyers Conf. Mem. program com. for Calif. Banker's Assn. Bank Counsel Seminar, 1976; contbr. article to legal publ. Office: 555 S Flower Suite 900 Los Angeles CA 90071 Tel (213) 683-2541

STEVENS, RICHARD JAMES, b. Chgo., Jan. 11, 1915; A.B., U. Chgo., 1936, J.D., 1938. Admitted to Ill. bar, 1938; partner firm Askow & Stevens, 1940-66, firm Tenney, Bently, Guthrie & Howell, 1966-71, firm Todhunter and Stevens, 1971—. Pres. Chgo. Meml. Assn., 1965—. Mem. Chgo. (bd. mgrs. 1943), Ill. bar assns. Home: 5032 Blackstone St Chicago IL 60615 Office: Room 2111 135 S LaSalle St Chicago IL 60603 Tel (312) 782-3656

STEVENS, RICHARD O., b. Manila, Nov. 22, 1943; B.S., U. San Francisco, 1965, J.D., 1968. Admitted to Calif. bar, 1969, U.S. Supreme Ct. bar, 1972; staff judge adv. U.S. Army Courts-Martial, Vietnam, 1970; dep. pub. defender, San Francisco, 1971-72; asso. firm Raymond E. Bright, San Francisco, 1972-73; individual practice law, San Francisco, 1973-74; partner firm Stevens & Stevens, San Francisco, 1974—. Mem. Calif. Pub. Defenders Assn., Criminal Trial Lawyers Assn. Home: 155 21st Ave San Francisco CA 94121 Office: Sheldon Building Suite 715 #9 First St at Market San Francisco CA 94105 Tel (415) 495-3824

STEVENS, ROBERT WILSON, b. Portland, Oreg., Dec. 17, 1912; A.B., DePauw U., 1934; LL.B., Columbia, 1937. Admitted to Ohio bar, 1938; asso. firm Jones, Day, Reavis & Pogue, and predecessors, Cleve., 1937-49, partner 1948—. Mem. Cleve., Ohio bar assns. Office: 1700 Union Commerce Bldg Cleveland OH 44115 Tel (216) 696-3939

STEVENS, WILLIAM JAMES, b. Chgo., Jan. 26, 1940; B.A., U. Chgo., 1962; J.D., Chgo. Kent Coll. Law, 1966. Admitted to Ill. bar, 1966, U.S. Supreme Ct., 1972. Asso. firm Tenney and Bentley, Chgo., 1966-70; partner firm Foss Schuman & Drake, Chgo., 1970—. Mem. legal com. ACLU, 1969-71. Mem. Chgo., Ill. bar assns., Chgo. Council Lawyers. Home: 5739 S Maryland St Chicago IL 60637 Office: 11 S LaSalle St Chicago IL 60603 Tel (312) 782-2610

STEVENSON, DONALD JAY, b. Nashville, Nov. 6, 1944; B.A., U. Tex., Arlington, 1966; J.D., So. Meth. U., 1973. Admitted to Tex. bar, 1973; asso. firm Parnass, Cline & Hill, Irving, Tex., 1973-74, Welz, Anderson & Peters, Dallas, 1974; partner firm Grant, Stevenson & Franklin, Dallas, 1975—; judge Coppell (Tex.) Municipal Ct., 1973—. Active legal aid com. Tarrant County, Tex., 1975-76. Mem. Dallas, Ft. Worth-Tarrant County bar assns. Home: 911 Moorhead Ct Arlington TX 76014 Office: 3131 Turtle Creek St Dallas TX 75219 Tel (214) 521-5830

STEVENSON, JOHN REESE, b. Chgo., Oct. 24, 1921; A.B., Princeton, 1942; LL.B., Columbia, 1949, Dr.Jur.Sc., 1952. Admitted to N.Y. bar, 1949, U.S. Supreme Ct. bar, 1964; with firm Sullivan & Cromwell, N.Y.C., 1950—, mem. 1956-69, 75—, of counsel, 1973—; legal adviser with rank of asst. sec. U.S. Dept. State, 1969-72; ambassador, spl. rep. of Pres., Law of the Sea Conf., 1973-75; U.S. mem. Permanent Ct. of Arbitration, The Hague, 1969—; U.S. rep. Internat. Ct. Justice, Namibia (S.W. Africa) case, 1970; dir. Adela Investment Co., Daiwa Bank Trust Co. Trustee Andrew W. Mellon Found., Rockefeller U., Nat. Gallery of Art; bd. dirs. Acad. Polit. Sci., Fgn. Policy Assn. Fellow Am. Bar Assn. (hon.); mem. Am. Soc. Internat. Law (pres. 1966-68), N.Y. State (chmn. com. on internat. law 1963-65), Inter-Am. bar assns., Internat. Law Assn., Institut de Droit Internat., Assn. Bar City N.Y. (chmn. com. on internat. law 1958-61), Am. Arbitration Assn. (chmn. internat. sect. law com. 1973—), Council on Fgn. Relations, Am. Law Inst. Author: The Chilean Popular Front, 1942. Contbr. articles in field to legal jours. Home: 620 Park Ave New York City NY 10021 Office: 48 Wall St New York City NY 10005 Tel (212) 952-8063

STEVENSON, NICHOLAS, b. Vancouver, B.C., Can., July 10, 1921; B.B.A., Clark U., 1949; LL.B., Northwestern U., 1956. Admitted to Ill. bar, 1956; mem. firm Mandel, Lipton & Stevenson, Ltd. and predecessors, 1957—. Bd. dirs. Chgo. Child Care Soc., North Shore Mental Health Clinic, Family Counseling Service, Glencoe; bd. dirs. Child Care Assn. Ill., recipient Friends of Children award 1973. Recipient Vol. Service award, Afro-Am. Family and Community Services. Mem. Chgo. Bar Assn. (adoption com.). Home: 770 Bluff St Glencoe IL 60022 Office: 10 S LaSalle St Chicago IL 60603 Tel (312) 236-7081

STEVENSON, NOEL C., b. Sacramento, Dec. 24, 1907; J.D., Pacific Coast U., 1943. Admitted to Calif. bar, 1944, U.S. Supreme Ct. bar, 1951; individual practice law, Sacramento and Los Angeles; dist. atty. Sutter County, Calif., 1951-54. Mem. State Bar Calif., U.S. Supreme Ct. Hist. Soc. Author: Search and Research, 1951, rev. edit., 1973; How to Build a More Lucrative Law Practice, 1967; Successful Cross Examination Strategy, 1971; editor: The Genealogical Reader, 1958; contbr. articles to legal, hist. jours. Office: 2303 Bancroft Ave Los Angeles CA 90039 Tel (213) 662-4497

STEVENSON, RUSSELL BENNETT, JR., b. Balt., Oct. 28, 1941; B.S., in Mech. Engring., Cornell U., 1964; J.D., Harvard, 1969. Admitted to D.C. bar, 1970, U.S. Supreme Ct. bar, 1976; asso. firm Surrey, Karasik, Greene & Hill, Washington, 1970-71; asso. prof. law Nat. Law Center, George Washington U., Washington, 1971-75, prof., 1975—; Fulbright lectr., France, 1977; asso. editor and spl. projects dir. Environ. Law Inst., 1971. Cons. mayor's commn. on indsl. and comml. devel., Washington, 1973; mem., vol. atty. ACLU, 1970—; exec. com. Lawyers Com. for Civil Rights Under Law, 1972-74. Mem. D.C., Am. bar assns., Am. Soc. Internat. Law, Washington Council Lawyers (interim pres., exec. com.). Contbr. articles to legal publs. Office: Nat Law Center George Washington Univ Washington DC 20052 Tel (202) 676-7483

STEVER, DONALD WINFRED, JR., b. Altoona, Pa., Jan. 25, 1944; B.A. cum laude, Lehigh U., 1965; J.D., U. Pa., 1968. Admitted to Conn. bar, 1968, N.H. bar, 1969, Fed. bar, 1970, U.S. Ct. Appeals bar, 1972, U.S. Supreme Ct. bar, 1973; mem. staff law dept. Aetna Life & Casualty, Hartford, Conn., 1968-69; atty. adminstrv. div. Office Atty. Gen., Concord, N.H., 1969-72; asst. atty. gen. Chief Environ. Protection Div. Office Atty. Gen. 1972-77; vis. prof. environ. studies Dartmouth Coll., Hanover, N.H., 1977—. Mem. N.H., Am. bar assns. Home: 104 S Main St Hanover NH 03755 Office: Carpenter Hall Dartmouth Coll Hanover NH 03755 Tel (603) 646-2838

STEWART, ALLAN FORBES, b. Kansas City, Kans., Nov. 14, 1947; B.A. in Polit. Sci., U. Mo., St. Louis, 1969; J.D., St. Louis U., 1972. Admitted to Mo. bar, 1973, U.S. Supreme Ct. bar, 1976; mng. atty. Legal Aid Soc. St. Louis County, Clayton, Mo., 1973-76; partner firm Braun, Newman & Stewart, Clayton, 1976—. Mem. Am., St. Louis County bar assns., Bar Assn. Met. St. Louis (chmn. juvenile law sect.), Lawyers Assn. St. Louis. Contbr. to Mo. Family Law Handbook, 2d edit., 1976. Home: 7311 Hoover St Saint Louis MO 63117 Office: 150 N Meramec St Clayton MO 63105 Tel (314) 862-0309

STEWART, BRUCE FOULDS, b. Detroit, Dec. 1, 1934; B.S., Menlo Coll. 1956; M.B.A., U. So. Calif., 1958; J.D., U. Santa Clara, 1969. Research and devel. adminstr. Lockheed Missiles & Space Corp., Sunnyvale, Calif., 1958-66, 67-70; planning specialist Philco-Ford Co., Palo Alto, Calif., 1966-67; admitted to Calif. bar, 1971, U.S. Supreme Ct. bar, 1974; practiced in Palo Alto, 1971-76; legal counsel Sacramento Savs. (Calif.), 1976—; participant Hastings-Am. Trial Lawyers 1st Nat. Coll. Advocacy. Mem. Am., Santa Clara County, Palo Alto, Sacramento County bar assns. Home: 4985 Arboleda Dr Fair Oaks CA 95628 Office: 5th and L Sts Sacramento CA 95804 Tel (916) 444-8555

STEWART, CHARLES LYMAN, b. Norwich, Conn., Sep. 6, 1924; B.A. magna cum laude, Amherst Coll., 1950; LL.B., Yale, 1954. Admitted to N.Y. bar, 1954; since practiced in N.Y.C., asso. firm Donovan, Leisure Newton & Irvine, 1954-56; asst. U.S. atty. Eastern Dist. N.Y., 1956-59; asso. firm Dunnington, Bartholow & Miller, N.Y.C., 1959-61, partner, 1961—; dir. Beekman Estate, 1973—, Tiffany & Co., 1975—. Bd. dirs. Sheltering Arms Children's Service, 1973—. Mem. Am., N.Y. State, Fed. bar assns., Fed. Bar Council. Home: 80 East End Ave New York City NY 10028 Office: 161 E 42nd St New York City NY 10017 Tel (212) 682-8811

STEWART, CHARLES THORP, b. Edgewood, Pa., Feb. 14, 1918; B.A., Cornell U., 1940; J.D., Yale, 1943. Admitted to N.Y. bar, 1943, since practiced in N.Y.C.; asso. firm Cravath, Swaine & Moore, 1943-45, 46-55; asst. sec., asst. gen. atty. R.H. Macy & Co., Inc., 1955-56, sec., gen. atty., 1956-60; sec., gen. counsel J.C. Penney Co., Inc., 1960-69, v.p., dir., 1967—, gen. counsel, dir. pub. affairs, 1969—, sr. v.p., 1974—; with Office Gen. Counsel, Dept. Navy, 1945-46, counsel Office Naval Research, 1946, spl. asst. to gen. counsel, 1946; dir. Inmont Corp. Bd. dirs., vice chmn. YMCA Greater New York; chmn. exec. com. bd. trustees Cornell U. Fellow Am. Bar Found.; mem. Am. Bar Assn., Assn. Bar City N.Y., Am. Law Inst., U.S. C. of C. (dir. 1971-77). Home: 135 E 71st St New York City NY 10021 Office: 1301 Ave of Americas New York City NY 10019 Tel (212) 957-6502

STEWART, DANIEL LEWIS, b. N.Y.C., Sept. 25, 1937; B.A., U. Calif., Los Angeles, 1958; J.D., Harvard, 1961; B.Litt., U. Oxford (England), 1963; Ph.D., U. Wis., 1967. Admitted to Calif. bar, 1962, U.S. Supreme Ct. bar, 1970; overseas fellow, vis. prof. Internat. Legal Center, Santiago, Chile, 1967-69; asso. firm Gang, Tyre & Brown, Los Angeles, 1970; chief environ. law sect. Nat. Legal Program Health Problems of Poor, Los Angeles, 1970-71; prof. law Loyola Law Sch., Los Angeles, 1971—. Mem. South Coast Air Quality Mgmt. Hearing Bd., 1977—. Mem. Calif. Bar Assn., Univ. Calif., Los Angeles, Univ. Wis., Harvard alumni assns., Phi Beta Kappa. Fulbright scholar, Chile, 1963-64; author: El Derecho de Aguas en Chile, 1970.

STEWART, DENNIS JOE, b. Leon, Iowa, Dec. 26, 1934; B.A., U. Nebr., 1960; postgrad. Princeton, 1960-61; M.A., Kans. State Coll., 1962; J.D., U. Mo., 1965. Admitted to Kans. bar, 1968, Mo. bar, 1969; law clerk to Hon. William H. Becker, chief judge U.S. Dist. Ct., Kansas City, Mo., 1968-71; asst. gen. counsel U. Mo., 1971-72; asst. prof. law Washburn Municipal U., 1972-73; U.S. magistrate Western Dist. Mo., Springfield, 1973—; dir., supr. Washburn Legal Clinic, 1971-72. Mem. Am., Kans., Mo., Greene County bar assns. Asso. editor U. Mo. at Kansas City Law Review, 1967-68; draftsman Manual for Complex Litigation, 1972—. Contbr. articles to legal jours. Home: 2846 E Ridgeview Circle Springfield MO 65804 Office: Box 590 Jewell Station Springfield MO 65804 Tel (417) 865-8361

STEWART, DUNCAN JAMES, b. Amsterdam, N.Y., Apr. 24, 1939; B.A., Cornell U., 1961, LL.B., 1964. Admitted to N.Y. bar, 1964; asso. firm Willkie Farr Gallagher Walton & FitzGibbon, N.Y.C., 1964-65; asso. firm Willkie Farr & Gallagher, N.Y.C., 1967-72, partner, 1972—. Mem. Am., N.Y. State bar assns., Assn. Bar City N.Y. Office: 1 Chase Manhattan Plaza New York City NY 10005 Tel (212) 248-1000

STEWART, FREDERICK GEORGE, b. Los Angeles, Jan. 17, 1942; A.A., Glendale Coll., 1961; B.S., Calif. State U., Northridge, 1964; J.D., U. Calif., Los Angeles, 1967. Admitted to Calif. bar, 1968; dep. dist. atty. Office of Dist. Atty., County of Los Angeles, 1969—. Office: 210 W Temple St Room 18000 Los Angeles CA 90012 Tel (213) 974-3511

STEWART, HOMER FRANCIS, b. Little Rock, Mar. 26, 1915; B.S. in Bus. Adminstrn., U. Tenn., 1940, J.D., 1941. Admitted to Tenn. bar, 1941; individual practice law, 1947-56; partner firm Watkins, McGugin Stewart McMeilly & Finch, Nashville, 1956-70; individual practice law, Nashville, 1971-72; partner firm Stewart, Este & Donnell, and predecessor, Nashville, 1973—. Mem. alumni adv. com. U. Tenn. Coll. Law, 1972—. Mem. Nashville, Tenn., Am., Fed. bar assns., Am. Judicature Soc., Fedn. Ins. Counsel, Internat. Assn. Ins. Counsel, Def. Research Inst., Def. Lawyers Assn., World Assn. Lawyers, World Peace Through Law Assn. Office: 14th Floor Third Nat Bank Bldg Nashville TN 37219 Tel (615) 244-6538

STEWART, ISAAC DANIEL, JR., b. Salt Lake City, Nov. 21, 1932; B.A. magna cum laude, U. Utah, 1959, J.D., 1962. Admitted to Utah bar, 1962; clk. Utah Supreme Ct., Salt Lake City, 1962; atty. antitrust div. U.S. Dept. Justice, Washington, 1962-65; asst. prof. law U. Utah, 1965-68, asso. prof., 1968-70; mng. partner Jones, Waldo & McDonough, Salt Lake City, 1970—; chmn. law and poverty com. Utah State Bar, 1966-68; commr. Utah Bd. Oil, Gas and Mining, 1976—. Chmn., Utah Gov.'s Com. Legal Rights Children, 1965-66. Mem. Am., Utah, Salt Lake County bar assns., Am. Judicature Soc., ACLU (nat. dir., dir. Utah chpt., pres. 1967), Order of Coif, Phi Beta Kappa, Phi Kappa Phi. Recipient Elbert D. Thomas award U. Utah, 1959; editor-in-chief Utah Law Rev., 1961-62; contbr. articles to profl. publs. Office: 175 S Main St 800 Walker Bank Bldg Salt Lake City UT 84111 Tel (801) 521-3200

STEWART, JACKSON MACDOWELL, JR., b. Phila., June 19, 1946; B.A., Lycoming Coll., 1968; J.D., Temple U., 1971. Admitted to Pa. bar, 1971; asso. firm ReDavid, Orlowsky & Natale, Media, Pa., 1971-74; partner firm Natale, Zetusky & Stewart, Media, 1974-75; asst. dist. atty. Delaware County, Pa., 1975—; asst. solicitor Borough of Upland, Delaware County, 1974. Active Nat. Hemophilia Fund Dr., Broomall, Pa., 1973; active March of Dimes Crusade, Delaware County, 1975. Mem. Nat., Pa. (asso.) dist. attys. assns., Pa., Delaware County bar assns. Office: 216 W Front St Media PA 19063 Tel (215) LO6-9200

STEWART, JOHN ALAN, b. Dallas, May 12, 1947; B.B.A., U. Tex., Arlington, 1969; J.D., Tex. Tech. U., 1971. Admitted to Tex. bar, 1972; individual practice law, Irving, Tex., 1972-74; asso. firm Blankenship & Potts, Dallas, 1974—. Democratic candidate for Tex. Ho. of Reps., 1976. Mem. Am., Dallas, Tex., Irving bar assns. Home:

PO Box 1505 Irving TX 75060 Office: Suite 720 8111 Preston Rd Dallas TX 75225 Tel (214) 691-3400

STEWART, MURRAY BAKER, b. Muskogee, Okla., May 16, 1931; B.A., U. Okla., 1953, LL.B., 1955; postgrad. in Taxation, Georgetown Law Sch., 1958-59. Admitted to Okla. bar, 1955, U.S. Supreme Ct. bar, 1958, U.S. Ct. Mil. Appeals bar, 1958; partner firm Stewart & Stewart, Tulsa and Muskogee, Okla., 1955, 62-72; asst. v.p. First Nat. Bank and Trust Co. of Tulsa, 1959-62; mem. firm Hutchins, Stewart, Stewart & Elmore, Tulsa, 1972—. Mem. Am., Okla., Tulsa bar assns., Phi Delta Phi. Contbr. articles to legal jours. Office: 4021 S Harvard Ave Tulsa OK 74129 Tel (918) 749-4411

STEWART, POTTER, b. Jackson, Mich., Jan. 23, 1915; B.A. cum laude, Yale, 1937, LL.B. cum laude, 1941; postgrad. (Henry fellow) Cambridge (Eng.) U., 1937-38. Admitted to Ohio bar, 1941, N.Y. bar, 1942; asso. firm Debevoise, Stevenson, Plimpton, & Page, N.Y.C., 1941-42, 45-47; partner firm Dinsmore, Shohl, Coates & Deupree, Cin., 1947-50, 1951-54; judge U.S. Ct. Appeals, 6th Circuit, 1954-58; justice U.S. Supreme Ct., 1958—; mem. Cin. City Council, 1950-53; vice mayor City of Cin., 1952-53; mem. com. on ct. adminstrn. Jud. Conf. U.S., 1955-58. Mem. White House Conf. on Edn., 1954-55. Home: 5236 Palisade Ln NW Washington DC 20016 Office: 1 First St NE Washington DC 20543 Tel (202) 393-1640

STEWART, RAYMOND C., b. Martins Ferry, Ohio, Apr. 11, 1936; B.S. in Chemistry, Ohio State U., 1958; M.S., U. Calif. at Berkeley, 1960; J.D., Georgetown U., 1968. Admitted to Va. bar, 1968, D.C. bar, 1968; patent examiner U.S. Patent Office, Washington, 1960-62; asst. editor Am. Chem. Soc., Washington, 1962-64; patent agt. firm Dicke & Craig, Washington, 1964-68; partner firm Craig, Antonelli, Stewart & Hill, Washington, 1968-71; partner firm Stewart & Kolasch, Ltd., Falls Church, Va., 1971-75, Birch, Stewart, Kolasch & Birch, Falls Church, 1975—. Mem. Am. Bar Assn., U.S. Trademark Assn., Am. Chem. Soc., Patent Lawyers Club D.C. (pres. 1972-73), Internat. Patent and Trademark Assn., Am. Patent Law Assn., Va. State Bar (gov. patent sect. 1977—). Office: 301 N Washington St Falls Church VA 22046 Tel (703) 241-1300

STEWART, SAMUEL BRADFORD, b. Chattanooga, Oct. 5, 1908; B.A. with honors in Polit. Sci., U. Va., 1927; J.D., Columbia, 1930. Admitted to N.Y. bar, 1931, Calif. bar, 1947; asso. firm Cravath, deGersdorff, Swaine & Wood, N.Y.C., 1930-39; partner firm Blake, Voorhees & Stewart, N.Y.C., 1939-47; gen. counsel Bank Am., San Francisco, 1947-67, exec. v.p., 1959-67, sr. adminstrv. officer, 1967-70, sr. vice chmn., 1970-73, chmn. gen. trust com., 1970—; sr. vice chmn. Bank Am. Corp. Pres., United Bay Area Crusade, San Francisco, 1956-57; pres. Sponsor San Francisco Performing Arts Center, 1973—; chmn. Salk Inst. Biol. Studies, La Jolla, Calif., 1974—. Mem. Am., San Francisco (v.p., dir. 1967) bar assns. Editor, The Business Lawyer, 1960. Home: 2288 Broadway San Francisco CA 94115 Office: care Bank of America Box 37000 San Francisco CA 94137 Tel (415) 622-2217

STEWART, STANLEY KIRK, b. Hanover, Ill., July 29, 1942; B.A., U. Chgo., 1965; J.D., Chgo.-Kent Coll. Law, 1972. Admitted to Ill. bar, 1973; confidential asst. to dep. dir. GSA, Washington, 1973-74; partner firm Shimeall, Stewart and Brendemuhl, Chgo., 1974—. Exec. sec. Ill. Racing Bd., 1972-73. Mem. Am., Chgo. bar assns., Am. Mgmt. Assn. Office: 180 N LaSalle St Chicago IL 60601 Tel (312) 236-5690

STEWART, THOMAS BYRD, b. Seattle, Jan. 1, 1919; B.A., U. Wash., 1941; M.A., Johns Hopkins, 1947; LL.B., Yale, 1950. Admitted to Alaska bar, 1951; law clk. U.S. Dist. Ct., Alaska, 1950-51; asst. Atty. Gen. Terr. of Alaska, 1951-54; mem. Alaska Ter. Legislature, 1955-56; individual practice law, Juneau, Alaska, 1956-61; mem. Alaska Senate, 1959-61; adminstrv. dir. Alaska Ct. System, 1961-66; judge Superior Ct. of Alaska, Juneau, 1966—, presiding judge 1st Jud. Dist., 1967—; exec. officer Alaska Statehood Com., 1955-56; sec. Alaska Constl. Conv., 1955-56. Pres. Alaska Heart Assn.; dir. Am. Heart Assn., 1960-70; chmn. S.E. Alaska Democratic Com.; mem. state Dem. Com., 1954-60. Mem. Alaska, Am. bar assns., Am. Judicature Soc., Nat. Conf. Juvenile Ct. Judges. Home: 925 Calhoun Ave Juneau AK 99801 Office: State Ct Bldg Pouch U Juneau AK 99811 Tel (907) 465-3420

STEWART, WILLIAM CLAYTON, JR., b. Middletown, Ohio, Dec. 30, 1929; B.A., Miami U., Oxford, Ohio, 1951; J.D., U. Cin., 1953. Admitted to Ohio bar, 1953, Calif. bar, 1959, U.S. Supreme Ct. bar, 1967; chief major contracts, legal advisor Ryan Aero. Co., San Diego, 1955-64; gen. counsel, asst. sec. Hitco, Gardena, Calif., 1964-70; asst. gen. counsel Cubic Corp., San Diego, 1970—; sr. partner firm Stewart & Has-Ellison, La Mesa, Calif., 1970—; sec. Western Ordnance & Hydraulics, Inc., San Diego, 1974—. Mem. Calif., San Diego County bar assns., San Diego Trial Lawyers Assn. Office: 7950 Wetherly St La Mesa CA 92041 Tel (714) 461-3438

STEYER, ROY HENRY, b. Bklyn., July 1, 1918; A.B., Cornell U., 1938; LL.B. cum laude Yale U., 1941. Admitted to N.Y. state bar, 1941, U.S. Supreme Ct. bar, 1955, Fed. bar, 1947; mem. firm Sullivan & Cromwell, N.Y.C., 1941-42, 46—, partner 1953—. Trustee N.Y.C. Sch. Volunteer Program, Inc., 1974—. Mem. Am. Coll. Trial Lawyers, Am. (chmn. com. antitrust problems in internat. law 1959-62), N.Y. State, Internat. bar assns., Assn. Bar City N.Y., N.Y. County Lawyers Assn. (dir. 1972—), Am. Judicature Soc., N.Y. Law Inst., Order Coif, Phi Beta Kappa, Phi Kappa Phi. Home: 112 E 74th St New York NY 10021 Office: 48 Wall St New York NY 10005 Tel (212) 952-8180

STICHTER, JOHN ALAN, b. Toledo, Jan. 13, 1934; B.S., Northwestern U., 1955; LL.B., U. Mich., 1960. Admitted to N.Y. bar, 1961, U.S. Supreme Ct. bar, 1977; asso. firm Donovan, Leisure, Newton & Irvine, N.Y.C., 1960-64, 67-71; asst. U.S. atty. criminal div. U.S. Atty. Office, So. Dist. N.Y., 1964-67; asso. firm Dunnington, Bartholow & Miller, N.Y.C., 1971, partner, 1971—. Mem. Am., N.Y. State bar assns., Assn. Bar City N.Y., Fed. Bar Council. Home: 444 E 86th St New York City NY 10028 Office: 161 E 42d St New York City NY 10017 Tel (212) 682-8811

STICKLAND, JOSEPH TIM, b. Tampa, Fla., Aug. 17, 1939; A.B. in Econs., Duke, 1962; LL.D., Emory U., 1966. Admitted to Fla. bar, 1967; individual practice law, Lakeland, Fla., 1967-73; asst. county solicitor County of Polk (Fla.), 1968-69; judge Municipal Ct., St. Leo, Fla., 1969-70; city atty. City of Mulberry (Fla.), 1970-72; prosecutor Mulberry Municipal Ct., 1970-72, Lakeland Municipal Ct., 1970-71; judge Lakeland Municipal Ct., 1971-72, Polk County Ct., 1972-76; circuit judge, 1977—; adminstrv. Judge, 1975-76; mem. bicentennial com. of bar and judiciary Fla. Supreme Ct., 1975-76. Chmn. Polk County March of Dimes, 1969; bd. dirs. Lakeland YMCA, 1970-72. Mem. Lakeland, Fla., 10th Jud. Circuit, Am. bar assns., Acad. Fla. Trial Lawyers, Am. Judicature Soc., Delta Theta Phi, Theta Chi, Kappa Kappa Psi. Recipient Outstanding Young Man award Lakeland Jaycees, 1972, Jud. Services award Lakeland Police Benefit Assn., 1972, citation for jud. adminstrn. excellence Lakeland City Commn. Office: PO Box 2286 Polk County Courthouse Bartow FL 33830 Tel (813) 533-0411

STICKLAND, PHIL DOWELL, b. Abilene, Tex., Oct. 17, 1941; B.A., U. Tex., Austin, 1963, J.D., 1966; postgrad. Southwestern Bapt. Theol. Sem., Ft. Worth, 1966-67. Admitted to Tex. bar, 1966; asso. firm Irby and McConnico, Ft. Worth, 1967; asso. dir. Christian Life Commn. Bapt. Gen. Conv. of Tex., Dallas, 1968—. Bd. dirs. Tex. Safety Assn., Austin, Tex. United Community Services, Austin, Interracial Bapt. Inst., Dallas, Community Council of Greater Dallas. Author: (with Wm. S. Garmon) How to Fight the Drug Menace, 1970; (with James M. Dunn, Ben E. Loring, Jr.) Endangered Species, 1976. Office: 208 Baptist Bldg Dallas TX 75201 Tel (214) 741-1991

STIDHAM, MICHAEL ALLEN, b. Blue Diamond, Ky., Apr. 17, 1948; A.A., Lees Jr. Coll., 1968; A.B., U. Ky., 1970, J.D., 1972. Admitted to Ky. bar, 1973; partner firm Miller, Stidham & McGrath, Jackson, Ky., 1973—; asst. atty., 39th Judicial Dist., Ky., 1974-76; public defender Breathitt and Wolfe Counties (Ky.), 1976—. Chmn. Disaster Relief Fund Breathitt and Lee Counties, 1975—. Mem. Ky., Am. Bar Assns. Home: Box 732 Jackson KY 41339 Office: 1132Y2 Main St Jackson KY 41339 Tel (606) 666-5401

STIEFEL, ERNEST CHARLES, b. Mannheim, Ger., Oct. 29, 1907. Admitted to Ger. bar, 1932, French license, 1936, Brit. bar, 1937, N.Y. State bar, 1946; counsel Condert Bros., N.Y.C.; sr. analyst OSS, State Dept., U.S. Mil. Govt., Washington, 1941-45; adj. prof. law N.Y. Law Sch. Mem. Am. Bar Assn., Fgn. Law Assn., N.Y. County Lawyers Assn. Author: German Commercial Law; Doing Business in Germany. Home: 200 East End Ave New York City NY 10028 Office: 200 Park Ave New York City NY 10017 Tel (212) 973-8884

STIEN, BARRY GENE, b. Hartford, Conn., Oct. 8, 1944; A.B., Temple U., 1966; J.D., George Washington U., 1969. Admitted to D.C. bar, 1970, U.S. Supreme Ct. bar, 1973; trial atty., div. civil rights Dept. Justice, Washington, 1969-71; asso. firm Benson, Stien and Braunstein, and predecessors, Washington, 1971-72, partner, 1972—. Mem. Am. Bar Assn., Assn. Trial Lawyers Am., Bar Assn. D.C., Am. Soc. Law and Medicine, Assn. Plaintiffs Trial Attys. D.C., Phi Alpha Delta. Home: 1709 Crestview Dr Potomac MD 20854 Office: Benson Stein & Braunstein 653 Washington Bldg Washington DC 20005 Tel (202) 393-8500

STIER, JUDE LAWRENCE, b. N.Y.C., Nov. 7, 1927; B.A., Syracuse U., 1949; J.D., Harvard, 1952. Admitted to N.Y. State bar, 1952; partner firm Garber & Stier, Liberty, N.Y., 1953-58, Stier & Cohen, 1962-74; individual practice law, Liberty, 1958-62, 74—; village justice, 1970—; town justice Town of Liberty, 1968; asst. county atty. Sullivan County, 1961. Councilman, Town of Liberty, 1962-68; trustee Congregation Ahavath Israel, Liberty, 1955-73; trustee Community Gen. Hosp. of Sullivan County, 1965—, pres. bd., 1975—. Mem. Am., N.Y. State, Sullivan County (pres. 1974-75) bar assns. Tel (914) 292-8020

STILES, NED BERRY, b. Mayslick, Ky., Aug. 7, 1932; A.B., Miami (Ohio) U., 1953; LL.B., U. Cin., 1958. Admitted to Ohio bar, 1958, N.Y. bar, 1962; atty. SEC, Washington, 1958-61, with office of gen. counsel, 1960-61; asso. firm Cleary, Gottlieb, Steen & Hamilton, N.Y.C., 1961-67, partner, 1968—. Trustee West Side Montessori Sch., N.Y.C., 1975. Mem. Assn. Bar City N.Y., Internat. Bar Assn. Co-author: The Silent Partners - Institutional Investors and Corporate Control, 1965; contbr. articles to law jours. Office: 1 State St Plaza New York City NY 10004 Tel (212) 344-0600

STILES, WILLIAM NEIL, b. Portland, Oreg., Mar. 28, 1938; B.A., Yale, 1960, LL.B., 1963. Admitted to Calif. bar, 1964, Oreg. bar, 1965; law clk. U.S. Ct. of Appeals, Ninth Circuit, Los Angeles, 1963-64; asso. firm Miller, Anderson, Nash, Yerke & Wiener, Portland, 1964-71; asso. firm Sussman, Shank, Wapnick & Caplan, Portland, 1972—, partner, 1975—. Active City of Beaverton Housing Task Force; mem. debtor-creditor rights com. Oreg. State Bar. Mem. Multnomah County Bar Assn. Contbr. articles to legal jours. Home: 6055 SW 130th St Beaverton OR 97005 Office: 1111 American Bank Bldg Portland OR 97205 Tel (503) 227-1111

STILLER, SHALE DAVID, b. Rochester, N.Y., Feb. 23, 1935; B.A., Hamilton Coll., 1954; LL.B., Yale U., 1957; M.L.A., Johns Hopkins U., 1977. Admitted to Md. bar, 1957; law clk. Md. Ct. Appeals, 1957-58; with firm Frank, Bernstein, Coraway & Goldman, Balt., 1959—, partner, 1963—; instr. U. Md. Law Sch., 1963—; mem. Gov.'s Commn. to Revise Md. Code, 1971—. Trustee Park Sch., 1975—; pres. Balt. chpt. Am. Jewish Com., 1969-71; pres. Jewish Family and Children's Service, 1972-74; bd. dirs. Assn. Jewish Charities of Balt., 1971—. Mem. Am., Md. State bar assns., Md. Bar Found., Am. Law Inst., Am. Coll. Probate Counsel, Order of Coif. Contbr. articles to profl. jours. Home: 1406 Mason St Baltimore MD 21217 Office: 1300 Mercantile Bank & Trust Bldg Baltimore MD 21201 Tel (301) 547-0500

STILLMAN, NINA GIDDEN, b. N.Y.C., Apr. 3, 1948; A.B. with distinction, Smith Coll., 1970; J.D. cum laude, Northwestern U., 1973. Admitted to Ill. bar, 1973, U.S. Dist. Ct. bar, 1973, U.S. Ct. Appeals, 1974; asso. firm Vedder, Price, Kaufman & Kammholz, Chgo., N.Y.C., Washington, 1973—. Mem. jr. governing bd. Chgo. Symphony Orch., 1975—; bd. dirs., legal advisor to Planned Parenthood Assn., Chgo. area, 1976—; chmn. juvenile justice com. Chgo. Council Lawyers, 1975; pres. Smith Coll. Club of Chgo., 1972-74. Mem. Am., Chgo. bar assns., Execs. Club Chgo., Phi Beta Kappa, Order of the Coif. Office: 115 S LaSalle St Chicago IL 60603 Tel (312) 781 2237

STILLWELL, PARKS, b. Hannibal, Mo., Apr. 3, 1918; LL.B., Washington U., St. Louis, 1941, J.D., 1968. Admitted to Mo. bar, 1941, Calif. bar, 1946; partner firm Miller, Beck & Stillwell, San Fernando, Calif., 1946-51; judge Municipal Ct., Los Angeles Jud. Dist., 1952-61, Calif. Superior Ct. for County of Los Angeles, 1961—. Home: 1714 Heather Ridge Dr Glendale CA 91207 Office: 111 N Hill St Los Angeles CA 90012 Tel (213) 974-5641

STILLWELL, WALTER BROOKS, III, b. Whitehall, Wis., July 30, 1946; B.A. cum laude, Wake Forest U., 1968; J.D., U. Ga., 1971. Admitted to Ga. bar, 1971; asso. firm Hunter, Houlihan, Maclean, Exley, Dunn & Connerat, Savannah, Ga., 1971-73, mem., 1974—. Alderman, City of Savannah, 1974—; mem. Gov.'s Adv. Council on Coastal Zone Mgmt., from 1976; mem. Greater Savannah Conv. and Visitors Council; trustee Historic Savannah Found., Inc., 1975—. Mem. Am., Savannah bar assns., State Bar Ga. Office: PO Box 9848 Savannah GA 31402 Tel (912) 236-0261

STIMMEL, FREDERICK CYRIL, b. Chattanooga, Sept. 24, 1922; B.S., Babson Inst. Bus. Adminstrn., 1949; LL.B., Albany Law Sch., 1953. Admitted to N.Y. bar, 1954, U.S. Supreme Ct., 1967; asso. firm Wiswall, Wood, Walton & MacAffer, Albany, N.Y., 1954-60, individual practice law, Albany, 1960-64; counsel N.Y. State Bar Assn., Albany, 1964—; spl. asst. gen. State of N.Y., Albany, 1971-76; mem. paralegal adv. com. Schenectady County (N.Y.) Community Coll., 1975—. Mem. Am., N.Y. State bar assns., Nat. Orgn. Bar Counsel (past pres.). Office: 1 Elk St Albany NY 12207 Tel (518) 445-1211

STINSON, JOSEPH MORRIS, b. Tylertown, Miss., Nov. 25, 1940; B.S., Miss. Coll., 1961; J.D., Jackson Sch. Law, 1970. Admitted to Miss. bar, 1970, U.S. Supreme Ct. bar, 1974; individual practice law, Tylertown, 1972—. Mem. Am., Miss., Tri-County bar assns., Assn. Trial Lawyers Am., Miss. Trial Lawyers Assn., Walthall County C. of C. (pres. 1975), Walthall County Jaycees (pres. 1967). Office: 1108 Beulah St Tylertown MS 39667 Tel (601) 876-5121

STIPHER, KARL JOSEPH, b. Indpls., Oct. 23, 1912; B.S., Butler U., 1935; student Harvard Law Sch., 1935-36; LL.B., Ind. U., 1938. Admitted to Ind. bar, 1938; asso. firm Gilhom & Gillom, Indpls., 1938-45; dep. atty. gen. Ind., 1945-47; asso. firm Baker & Daniels, Indpls., 1948-50, partner, 1950—. Mem. Ind. Civil Code Study Commn., 1968-71; bd. dirs. Cath. Social Services, Alcoholic Rehab. Center, Our Lady Grace Acad., Brebeuf Prep. Sch.; pres., bd. dirs. Domestic Relations Counseling Service; bd. visitors Ind. U. Law Sch. Mem. Am., Ind. (pres. 1975-76), Indpls. (pres. 1973), 7th Fed. Circuit Ct. (pres. 1968-69), Inter-Am., Internat. bar assns., Am. Law Inst., Am. Bar Found., Am. Coll. Trial Lawyers, Ind. Soc. Chgo., Nat. Assn. R.R. Trial Counsel. Home: 7111 Fremont Ct Indianapolis IN 46256 Office: Fletcher Trust Bldg Indianapolis IN 46204 Tel (317) 636-4535

STIPP, CHRISTIAN FREDERICK, b. Carrollton, Mo., Aug. 24, 1916; A.B., Mo. Valley Coll., 1939. Admitted to Mo. bar, 1947; since practiced in Carrollton, Mo., partner firm Stipp and Thomas, and predecessors, 1947—. Mem. Carrollton Bd. Edn.; bd. dirs. Carroll County (Mo.) Meml. Hosp. Mem. Am. Mo., Carroll County (pres. 1973-75) bar assns. Home: Route 4 Carrollton MO 64633 Office: 2 N Main St Carrollton MO 64633 Tel (816) 542-0910

STIRLING, EDWIN TILLMAN, b. Washington, Nov. 5, 1927; B.S., George Washington U., 1951, J.D., 1953. Admitted to D.C. bar, 1954, U.S. Supreme Ct. bar, 1958, Md. bar, 1960; law clk. to judge U.S. Circuit Ct. Appeals, Washington, 1953-54; asst. U.S. atty., Washington, 1954-58; asso. firm Welch, Mott & Morgan, Washington, 1958-64; partner firm Reasoner, Davis & Vinson, Washington, 1965—. Pres. Wood Acres Citizens Assn., 1956; dir. Hillcrest Children's Center, 1968-74; trustee Washington City Orphan Asylum, 1975—; bd. govs. Children's Hosp. Nat. Med. Center, 1976—, St. Albans Sch., 1976—; bd. govs. Norwood Sch., 1965-76, chmn. 1972-76. Mem. D.C., Md. bar assns. Home: 7012 Beechwood Dr Chevy Chase MD 20014 Office: 725 15th St NW Washington DC 20005

STIRLING, THOMAS LUKE, JR., b. Holyoke, Mass., July 13, 1941; A.B., Cornell U., 1964, J.D., 1969. Admitted to Hawaii bar, 1970; asso. firm Ashford & Wriston, Honolulu, 1970-73; partner firm Kelso, Spencer, Snyder & Stirling, Honolulu, 1973—; mem. Hawaii Family Ct. Rules Com. Pres. Vol. Info. and Referral Service, Honolulu, 1974; chmn. Cornell Alumni Secondary Schs. Com. of Hawaii, 1971—. Mem. Am. (chmn. meetings com. sect. young lawyers 1974), Hawaii State (pres. sect. young lawyers 1975, asst. sec. 1976) bar assns., Hawaii Estate Planning Council, Am. Judicature Soc., Common Cause. Decorated Bronze Star; recipient award for Distinguished Vol. Service, Aloha United Way, 1975. Home: 984 Koae St Honolulu HI 96816 Office: suite 1800 745 Fort St Honolulu HI 96813 Tel (808) 524-5183

STITELER, EDWARD SIMPSON, b. Rockwood, Pa., Nov. 1, 1922; B.A., Yale U., 1947; J.D., Dickinson Sch. Law, 1956. Admitted to Pa. bar, 1957, U.S. Supreme Ct. bar, 1967; asso. firm Smith, Best and Horn, Greensburg, Pa., 1956-63; individual practice law, Greensburg, 1963-66; asst. counsel West Penn Power Co., Greensburg, 1966-69, chief counsel, 1969—; workmen's compensation referee Commonwealth of Pa., 1963-66. Mem. planning commn. City of Greensburg, 1960-64; mem. Westmoreland County (Pa.) Fed. Housing Authority, 1965-73. Mem. Am., Pa., Westmoreland County bar assns. Home: 524 N Maple Ave Greensburg PA 15601 Office: 700 Cabin Hill Dr Greensburg PA 15601 Tel (412) 837-3000

STITT, LEMOINE DONALDSON, b. Chgo., Sept. 24, 1925; Ph.B., U. Chgo., 1945, J.D., 1949. Admitted to Ill. bar, 1949; justice of peace Palatine Twp., Ill., 1957-63; magistrate Circuit Ct. of Cook County (Ill.), 1964-65; mem. firm Johnson, Zahler, Campbell & Stitt, Chgo., 1960-65; mem. firm Stitt, Kearns & Szala, Palatine, Ill., 1965-71; mem. firm Stitt, Moore, Kearns & Szala, Arlington Heights, Ill., 1971-76; mem. firm Stitt, Moore & Szala, Arlington Heights, 1976—. Mem. Am. (family law sect.), Ill., Chgo. (matrimonial com. 1971—), Lake County bar assns., Am. Judicature Soc., Am. Matrimonial Acad. Office: 102 S Arlington Heights Rd Arlington Heights IL 60005 Tel (312) 255-6500

STITTLEBURG, PHILIP CHARLES, b. Reedsburg, Wis., Nov. 17, 1947; B.A., U. Wis., 1969, J.D., 1972. Admitted to Wis. bar, 1972, Fed. Ct. bar for Eastern and Western Dists. Wis.; asso. firm R.D. Endicott and Assos., LaFarge, Wis., 1972-77; partner firm Jenkins and Stittleburg, LaFarge, 1977—; asst. dist. atty. Vernon County, Wis., 1974—. Mem. Vernon County, Bar Assn., Assn. Trial Lawyers Am., Wis. Sheriff's and Dep. Sheriff's Assn. Home: Box 808 LaFarge WI 54639 Office: Box 808 LaFarge WI 54639 Tel (608) 625-2185

STOCK, EDWARD KENDALL, b. Washington, Sept. 8, 1936; B.A., Am. U., 1961; J.D., Marshall Whyth Sch. Law, Coll. William and Mary, 1964. Admitted to Va. bar, 1965; partner firm Schantz, Stock, Marshall & Wade, McLean and Leesburg, Va., 1970—; mem. grievance com. 10th dist., chmn. com. to study malpractice ins. Va. State Bar. Mem. Loudoun County (Va.) Open Space Com.; spl. edn. adv. com. Loudoun County, chmn., 1977; alumni bd. Marshall Whyth Sch. Law. Mem. Va. (mem. com. on legal ethics and profl. responsibility), Fairfax County, Loudoun County bar assns., Va. Trial Lawyers Assn. Home: Rt 2 Box 95 Leesburg VA 22075 Office: PO Box 328 McLean VA 22101 Tel (703) 790-1522 also PO Box 779 Leesburg VA 22075 Tel (703) 777-1663

STOCK, SHELDON KENT, b. St. Louis, Feb. 15, 1941; B.S. in Bus. Adminstrn., Washington U., St. Louis, 1962, J.D., 1964. Admitted to Mo. bar, 1964, U.S. Supreme Ct. bar, 1971; trial and def. counsel USMC, 1965-67; asst. county counsellor St. Louis County, 1968; individual practice law, St. Louis, 1969-72; partner firm Brackman, Copeland, Oetting, Copeland, Walther & Schmidt, Clayton, Mo.,

1973—. Vice chmn. Decent Lit. Commn. St. Louis County; mem. Inter-Govtl. Relations Commn. St. Louis County. Mem. Mo., St. Louis County (sec. 1976), North St. Louis County (past pres.), Met. St. Louis bar assns. Recipient Roy F. Essen award as outstanding young lawyer of year St. Louis County Bar Assn., 1974. Home: 7120 Wydown Blvd Clayton MO 63105 Office: Suite 600 130 S Bemiston Ave Clayton MO 63105 Tel (314) 863-7500

STOCKELL, HENRY COOPER, JR., b. Washington, Apr. 3, 1920; student George Washington U., 1938-39; J.D., Am. U., 1947. Admitted to D.C. bar, 1947, Fla. bar, 1955, Ga. bar, 1962; individual practice law, Washington, 1947-52; atty. Office Regional Counsel, Jacksonville, Fla., 1954-56, asst. regional counsel, 1956-58, regional counsel S.E. Region, Atlanta, 1958-76; dep. gen. counsel Dept. Treasury, Washington, 1976—; served to maj. Judge Adv. Gen. Corps, AUS, 1942-46. Mem. Am., Fed., Fla., Ga., D.C. bar assns., Judge Advs. Assn. Contbr. articles to profl. publs. Home: 9211 Bailey Ln Fairfax VA 22030 Office: 3308 Main Treasury Bldg 15th and Pennsylvania Ave Washington DC 20220 Tel (202) 566-2977

STOCKEY, WILLIAM EUGENE, b. Pitts., July 18, 1946; B.S., Duquesne U., 1968, J.D., 1972. Admitted to Pa. bar, 1972, N.Y. bar, 1974, Calif. bar, 1974, Tex. bar, 1975, N.J. bar, 1976, Ohio bar, 1974; law clk. U.S. Dist. Ct. for Western Pa., 1969-71; partner firm Lewis & Stockey, Pitts., 1972—. Bd. dirs. Baldwin-Whitehall Sch. Dist., Pitts., 1975—. Mem. Am., Allegheny County bar assns., Pa. Assn. Trial Lawyers. Home: 4615 W Brightview Dr Pittsburgh PA 15227 Office: 907 Plaza Bldg Pittsburgh PA 15219 Tel (412) 391-0818

STOCKHAM, RONALD LEE, b. Trenton, N.J., Apr. 14, 1942; B.A., U. Pa., 1964; J.D., Temple U., 1968. Admitted to Pa. Supreme Ct. bar, 1968, Pa. Superior Ct. bar, 1968, U.S. Supreme Ct. bar, 1972; asso. firm Stuckert, Yates & Krewson, Newtown, Pa., 1968-72; sr. mem. firm Stockham & Donahue, and predecessor, Morrisville, Pa., 1972—; asst. dist. atty. Bucks County (Pa.), Doylestown, 1971-73. Dir. Pennbury Soc., Inc., Morrisville, Free Library Assn., Morrisville Hist. Soc., Morrisville Rotary Club; com. chmn. Bucks County Friends of Scouting, 1970. Chmn. Lower Bucks County Secondary Sch. com. of U. Pa. Mem. Am., Pa., Bucks County bar assns. Tel (215) 736-0031

STOCKMAN, LEWIS JOSEPH, b. N.Y.C., July 26, 1934; A.B., Princeton, 1956; J.D., Harvard, 1959. Admitted to N.Y. bar, 1960; sec. to Hon. James T. Hallinan of N.Y. Supreme Ct., 1962; mem. firm Hart & Hume, N.Y.C., 1965—. Bd. dirs. Am. Cancer Soc., Queens, N.Y. Mem. Am., N.Y. (chmn. constrn. and surety div. ins. sect. 1975-76), Queens County bar assns. Office: 10 E 40th St New York City NY 10016 Tel (212) 686-0920

STOCKMAN, WALTER, b. N.Y.C., Sept. 10, 1918; LL.B., Bklyn. Law Sch., 1951. Admitted to Fla. bar, 1966; U.S. Supreme Ct., 1970; commd. U.S. Air Force, 1942, advanced through grades to lt. col., 1966; chief U.S. Mil. Procurement and Contract Termination, Los Angeles, 1967-68; ret., 1968; gen. counsel The Blackhawk Group, Delray Beach, Fla., 1969-72. Mem. Brevard County Bar Assn. Home: 5200 Ocean Beach Blvd apt 221 Cocoa Beach FL 32931 Office: 1325 N Atlantic Ave PO Box 855 Cocoa Beach FL 32931

STOCKTON, JAMES MARION, b. Pontotoc, Miss., Sept. 20, 1907; LL.B., Miss. Coll., Clinton, 1941. Admitted to Miss., fed. bars, 1940; pros. atty. City of Jackson (Miss.), 1941-43; spl. agt. FBI, 1943-69, ret., 1969; individual practice law, Como, Miss., 1969—. Mem. Miss. State, Pamola County (Miss.) bar assns. Home: Rt 1 PO Box 59 Como MS 38619 Office: Harmontown Rd Rt 1 Como MS 38619 Tel (601) 526-5040

STOCKTON, RALPH MADISON, JR., b. Winston-Salem, N.C., June 22, 1927; B.S. with honors, U. N.C., 1948, J.D., 1950. Admitted to D.C. bar, 1950, N.C. bar, 1950, U.S. Supreme Ct. bar, 1973; partner firm Hudson, Petree, Stockton, Stockton & Robinson, Winston-Salem, 1956—; lectr. Nat. Inst. for Trial Advocacy, U. Colo., 1973. Vice chmn. bd. trustees Winston-Salem State U. Fellow Am. Coll. Trial Lawyers, Am. Bar Found; mem. Am., N.C. (bd. govs. 1957-60, chmn. appellate rules study com. 1973—, pres. 1976-77), Forsyth County (past pres.) bar assns., Forsyth County Legal Aid Soc. (pres. 1969), Fourth Circuit Jud. Conf., Internat. Assn. Ins. Counsel, Am. Judicature Soc. (dir.), Order of Coif, Law Alumni Assn. U. N.C., Phi Delta Phi. Editor: N.C. Law Rev. Home: 2696 Reynolds Dr Winston-Salem NC 27104 Office: 610 Reynolds Bldg Winston-Salem NC 27101 Tel (919) 725-2351

STOCKWELL, OLIVER PERKINS, b. East Baton Rouge Parish, La., Aug. 11, 1907; LL.B., La. State U., 1932. Admitted to La. bar, 1932; partner firm Stockwell, St. Dizier, Sievert & Viccellio, and predecessor, Lake Charles, 1933-75; sr. partner firm Stockwell, Sievert, Viccellio, Clements & Shaddock, Lake Charles, 1975—; dir. Lakeside Nat. Bank, Lake Charles; research fellow S.W. Legal Found., Dallas, 1967—. Pres. La. Assn. Young Mens Bus. Clubs, 1935, Council for a Better La., 1972; bd. dirs. Pub. Research Council La., YMCA, La. State U. Found.; chmn. bd. suprs. La. State U. Fellow Am. Bar Found., Am. Coll. Trial Lawyers, Am. Coll. Probate Counsel; mem. Internat. Assn. Ins. Counsel, World Assn. Lawyers of World Peace Through Law Center, Internat., Inter-Am., Am. (former mem. ho. of dels.), La. (pres. 1962), S.W. La. (pres. 1942) bar assns., Jud. Council, Am. Counsel Assn. (dir.), Fedn. Ins. Counsel, Am., La. (pres.) law insts., Am. Judicature Soc., Comml. Law League, Mid Continent Oil and Gas Assn., La. State U. Law Sch. Alumni (pres. 1956), Lake Charles C. of C. (pres. 1949), Order of Coif, Lambda Chi Alpha, Omicron Delta Kappa. Home: 205 Shell Beach Dr Lake Charles LA 70601 Office: PO Box 2900 One Lakeside Plaza Lake Charles LA 70601 Tel (318) 436-9491

STODDART, JOHN BERGMAN, JR., b. Malvern, Iowa, Apr. 6, 1919; A.B., U. Nebr., 1941; LL.B., U. Mich., 1946. Admitted to Ill. bar, 1947, N.J. bar, 1960, U.S. Supreme Ct. bar, 1953; asso. firm Brown, Hay & Stephens, Springfield, Ill., 1947-53; asst. state's atty. Sangamon County (Ill.), 1949-51; U.S. atty. So. Dist. Ill., 1953-58; with Prudential Ins. Co. Am., Newark, 1958—, sr. v.p., gen. counsel, 1969—. Chmn. United Way campaign, Newark, 1972; chmn. bd. trustees Overlook Hosp., Summit, N.J., 1972-74. Fellow Inst. Jud. Adminstrn.; mem. Am. Bar Found., Am. (sec. sect. corp. banking and bus. law, vice chmn. 1977-78), Ill., N.J., Essex County bar assns., Fed. Bar Council, Am. Judicature Soc. Home: 45 North Rd Short Hills NJ 07078 Office: Prudential Plaza Newark NJ 07101 Tel (201) 877-6200

STOFFER, THOMAS LAWRENCE, b. Homeworth, Ohio, Dec. 21, 1922; A.B., Ashland Coll., 1946; J.D., Case Western Res. U., 1948. Admitted to Ohio bar, 1948; adjuster Nationwide Mut. Ins. Co., Cleve., 1949-51, claims atty., New Haven and Canton, Ohio, 1951-71, regional claims atty., Canton, 1971—. Pres. nat. mission bd. Brethren Ch., 1974-76; bd. trustees Ashland Coll., 1966—, vice chmn., 1974—. Mem. Soc. Chartered Property and Casualty Underwriters, Ohio, Stark County bar assns., Delta Theta Phi; contributing author: The Ophthalmologist's Office: Planning and Practice, 1975. Home: 332 47th St NW Canton OH 44709 Office: 1014 N Market Ave Box 8379 Canton OH 44711 Tel (216) 456-0551

STOHLER, ZANE EDWARD, b. New Castle, Ind., Oct. 1, 1926; B.S. in Bus., Ind. U., 1948, LL.B., 1950. Admitted to Ind. bar, 1950, U.S. Dist. Ct. bar for So. Dist. Ind., 1950; pros. atty. Randolph County (Ind.), 1953-62; partner firm Mendenhall, Hunter, & Stohler, Winchester, Ind., 1955-66; judge Randolph County Circuit Ct., 1967—; city atty. City of Winchester, 1964-66. Pres. Eastern Ind. Mental Health Services, Inc., 1970-72. Mem. Ind. Council Juvenile Ct. Judges (sec.), Order of Coif. Tel (317) 584-7231

STOKES, ARCH YOW, b. Atlanta, Sept. 2, 1946; B.A., Emory U., 1967; J.D., 1970. Admitted to Ga. bar, 1970, U.S. Ct. Mil. Appeals, 1971; dep. asst. atty. gen. State of Ga., 1970; atty., mil. judge U.S. Marine Corps, 1971-73; asso. firm Branch & Swann, Atlanta, 1973-75, partner, 1976—; counsel, bd. dirs. Ga. Hospitality and Travel Assn., 1977—; instr. law Ga. State U., 1974—. Mem. Am., Atlanta (editor Atlanta Lawyer 1974—) bar assns., State Bar Ga., Lawyers Club Atlanta, Ga. C. of C., Sigma Alpha Epsilon, Phi Delta Phi, Omicron Delta Kappa. Author: The Wage and Hour Law Guidebook for Hotels, Motels and Restaurants, 1976; The Equal Opportunity Law Guidebook for Hotels, Motels, Restaurants and Institutions, 1977; mng. editor Emory Law Jour., 1969-70. Home: 3127 Mountain Creek Circle Roswell GA 30075 Office: 3400 Peachtree Rd Atlanta GA 30326 Tel (404) 262-1243

STOKES, CARL NICHOLAS, b. Memphis, Jan. 26, 1907; LL.B., U. Memphis, 1934. Admitted to Tenn. bar, 1934; asso. firm Norvell & Monteverde, 1934-38; clk. City Ct. Memphis (Tenn.), 1938-42, Criminal Cts. Shelby County (Tenn.), 1946-50; judge Traffic Ct., Memphis, 1950-52; asso. firm Shea & Pierotti, Memphis, 1952-62; v.p., gen. counsel Allen & O'Hara, Inc., Memphis, 1962-72; counsel firm McDonald, Kuhn, Smith, Gandy, Miller & Tait, Memphis, 1972-76; partner firm Stokes, Kimbrough, Grusin & Kizer, P.C., Memphis, 1976—; mem. Estate Planning Council Memphis; dir. 1st Fed. Savs. & Loan Assn. Chmn. advisory bd. Salvation Army, Memphis; trustee Shrine Sch. Handicapped Children, Inc. Mem. Am., Memphis, Shelby County bar assns. Home: 2237 Massey Rd Memphis TN 38138 Office: 2612 Clark Tower Memphis TN 38137 Tel (901) 767-7750

STOKES, DON, b. Dallas, Feb. 10, 1941; B.B.A., So. Meth. U., 1963, J.D., 1965. Admitted to Tex. bar, 1965, U.S. Supreme Ct. bar, 1969, U.S. Dist. Ct. bar for Eastern Dist. Tex., 1970; spl. agt. FBI, Portland, Oreg., also Chgo., 1966-69; 1st asst. criminal dist. atty. Harrison County (Tex.), 1969-71; county judge Harrison County, 1973—; judge Harrison County Juvenile Ct., 1973—; chmn. Harrison County Juvenile Center Adv. Bd., 1975—. Pres. Harrison County Cancer Soc., 1970; bd. dirs. Marshall (Tex.) Urban Renewal Agy., 1972-73, East Tex. Council Govts., 1973—, East Tex. Human Devel. Corp., 1973—; v.p. Red River Valley Assn., 1973—; trustee 1st United Meth. Ch., Marshall, 1976—. Mem. State Bar Tex., Am., N.E. Tex., Harrison County (pres. 1975-76) bar assns., Soc. Former Spl. Agts. FBI, Order of Woolsack. Recipient Blalock award Marshall Jaycees, 1973. Home: 700 Bergstrom Pl Marshall TX 75670 Office: Harrison County Courthouse Marshall TX 75670 Tel (214) 935-7872

STOKES, JOHN REYNOLDS, JR., b. Loma Linda, Calif., Aug. 13, 1917; B.A., U. Calif., Berkeley, 1946, LL.B., 1948. Admitted to Calif. bar, 1948; partner firm Stokes, Steeves, Calligan & Warren, and predecessors, Arcata, Calif.; city atty. City of Arcata, 1950-73. Chmn. Humboldt County (Calif.) Democratic Central Com., 1954-64. Home: Star Route Blue Lake CA 95525 Office: 381 Bayside Rd Arcata CA 95521 Tel (707) 822-1771

STOKES, LOUIS, b. Cleve., Feb. 23, 1925; student Western Res. U., 1946-48; J.D., Cleve. Marshall Law Sch., 1953; LL.D. (hon.), Wilberforce U., 1969. Admitted to Ohio bar, 1953; since practiced in Cleve.; chief trial counsel firm Stokes, Charcter, Perry, Whitehead, Young & Davidson; mem. 91st, 93d-95th Congresses from 21st Ohio Dist., mem. Appropriations com., Budget com.; guest lectr., 1960—. Mem. adv. council African-Am. Inst. Internat.; bd. dirs. Karamu House; trustee Martin Luther King, Jr. Center Social Change, Forest City Hosp., Cleve. State U.; vice chmn. bd. trustees St. Paul A.M.E. Zion Ch.; mem. exec. com. Cuyahoga County Democratic Party, Ohio State Dem. Party; chmn. King/Kennedy Assassination Com. Fellow Ohio State Bar Assn.; mem. NAACP (v.p. Cleve. br. 1965-66, chmn. legal redress com. 1960-65, recipient Distinguished Service award), Am., Cuyahoga County (chmn. criminal courts com. 1964-68, past trustee), Cleve. bar assns., Urban League, Citizens League, Am. Legion, John Harlan Law Club, ACLU, Kappa Alpha Psi. Office: 2455 Rayburn House Office Bldg Washington DC 20515 Tel (202) 225-7032

STOKES, PAUL MASON, b. Miami Beach, Fla., July 16, 1946; B.A. magna cum laude, Duke U., 1968; J.D., U. Chgo., 1971. Admitted to Fla. bar, 1971; law clk. to judge U.S. Dist. Ct., So. Dist. N.Y., N.Y.C. 1971-72; asso. firm Smathers & Thompson, Miami, Fla., 1972—; pub. defender City of Miami Springs, Fla., 1973-74, pub. defender City of Hialeah, Fla., 1974-76. Mem. Dade County, Am., Fla. bar assns., Dade County Def. Bar Assn., Nat. Assn. R.R. Trial Counsel, Order Coif, Phi Beta Kappa. Recipient William T. LaPrade prize for hist. writing Duke U., 1968. Office: 1301 Alfred I DuPont Bldg Miami FL 33131 Tel (305) 379-6523

STOKES, ROBERT GLENN, b. Lake Wales, Fla., Sept. 28, 1935; LL.B., Stetson U., 1962. Admitted to Fla. bar, 1963; legal asst. Fla. Sec. State, 1962-63; asst. atty. gen., Tallahassee, Fla., 1963-66; asst. pub. defender 10th Circuit, Barton, Fla., 1966-67; judge Lakeland (Fla.) City Ct., 1967-68, Fla. 10th Circuit Ct., 1973—. Office: County Courthouse Bartow FL 33830 Tel (813) 533-0411

STOKKE, ALLAN H., b. Minot, N.D., Sept. 2, 1940; A.B., Concordia Coll., 1962; J.D., U. Chgo., 1965. Admitted to Calif. bar, 1966, U.S. Supreme Ct. bar, 1975; dep. dist. atty. Orange County (Calif.), 1966-68; partner firm Cohen, Stokke, Owen & Davis, Santa Ana, Calif., 1968—; judge pro tem Orange County Superior Ct., 1970-75, Central Orange County Municipal Ct.; commr. Santa Ana (Calif.) Citizens Crime Commn. Mem. Calif. State Bar, Orange County Bar Assn. Author: (with others) Concepts of Criminal Law, 1976. Tel (714) 835-1205

STOLARIK, ROBERT JOSEPH, b. Williston Park, N.Y., Aug. 8, 1929; A.B., St. Peter's Coll., 1951; J.D., Fordham U., 1956. Admitted to N.Y. State bar, 1957, U.S. Ct. of Mil. Appeals bar, 1976, U.S. Supreme Ct. bar, 1967; individual practice law, Rockland County, N.Y., 1956-69; judge Family Ct., 1969-74, County Ct., 1974—; asst. county atty., 1959-60; asst. dist. atty., 1960-65; municipal atty. Villages of Suffern and Sloatsburg, 1965-68. Mem. advisory bd. Rockland County Council Boy Scouts Am. Mem. Rockland County Bar Assn., Catholic Lawyers' Guild Rockland County, Rockland County Magistrates Assn., County Ct. Judges' Assn. N.Y. State, Navy-Marine Corps Res. Lawyers' Assn., Marine Corps League; Res. Officers Assn. U.S. Home: 1 Provost Dr Suffern NY 10901 Office: Court House Main St New City NY 10956 Tel (914) 638-0500

STOLBA, NORMAN E., b. Cedar Rapids, Iowa, Mar. 23, 1918; B.A., U. Calif., Los Angeles, 1948; J.D., Loyola U., Los Angeles, 1958. Admitted to Calif. bar, 1959; asso. firm Craig, Weller and Laugharn, Los Angeles, 1959-61; individual practice law, Los Angeles, San Bernardino, Calif., Canyon Lake, Calif., Torrance, Calif., 1961—; instr. debtor creditor law LaVerne (Calif.) Coll., 1965. Mem. Calif., Southwest Los Angeles, Harbor bar assns. Office: 3465 W Torrance Blvd Torrance CA 90505 Tel (213) 370-4555

STOLL, NORMAN ROBERT, b. Washington, Dec. 16, 1942; B.S. cum laude, U. Wis., 1964; LL.B., Harvard, 1968. Admitted to Oreg. bar, 1969; individual practice law, Portland, Oreg., 1969—; lectr. Portland State U., 1970-73; mem. Multnomah County (Oreg.) Chief Criminal Ct. Adv. Com., 1971-75. Mem. Am. (antitrust pvt. litigation monograph com. 1976-77), Oreg. bar assns., ACLU, Am., Oreg. (sec., treas. 1975-76) trial lawyers assns., Oreg. Assn. Criminal Def. Counsel (pres. 1971-73). Contbr. articles to legal jours. Office: 610 SW Alder St Portland OR 97205 Tel (503) 227-1601

STOLLER, HERBERT, b. Balt., Apr. 1, 1929; B.S., U. Wis., 1949; LL.B., Harvard, 1952; LL.M. in Taxation, N.Y. U., 1960. Admitted to N.Y. State bar, 1953; asso. firm Cleary, Gottlieb, Friendly & Hamilton, N.Y.C., 1953-58; asso. firm Curtis, Mallet-Prevost, Colt & Mosle, N.Y.C., 1959-62; partner firm, 1962—; law sec. Hon. Harrie B. Chase, U.S. Ct. Appeals for 2d Circuit, 1952-53. Mem. Am., N.Y. State bar assns., Assn. Bar City N.Y. Editor Harvard Law Rev., 1950-52. Home: 1120 Fifth Ave New York City NY 10028 Office: 100 Wall St New York City NY 10005 Tel (212) 248-8111

STOLTZ, ALLISON JOHN, JR., b. Sacramento, Aug. 8, 1923; LL.B., Southwestern U., 1954. Admitted to Calif. bar, 1964; partner firm Parker Stanbury McGee & Babcock, Los Angeles. Office: 315 W 9th St Los Angeles CA 90015

STOLTZ, HENRY CLIFF, b. Olney, Ill., Nov. 21, 1929; B.S., U. Mich., 1958; J.D., U. Ky., 1972. Admitted to Ky. bar, 1973; individual practice law, London, Ky., 1973—; domestic relations commr. Laurel and Knox Counties (Ky.), 1976-77. Mem. Ky., Am., Laurel County bar assns. Home: Rt 6 Box 413 London KY 40741 Office: PO Box 716 London KY 40741 Tel (606) 864-6242

STOLTZ, JOHN ROBERT, b. Milw., Aug. 4, 1944; A.B., U. Notre Dame, 1966; J.D., Marquette U., 1969. Admitted to Wis. bar, 1969, U.S. Supreme Ct. bar, 1976; law clk. Milwaukee County (Wis.) Circuit Ct., 1967; claims service rep. Milw. Mut. Ins. Co., 1967-69, subrogation atty., 1969-71; asso. firm Callahan & Arnold, Columbus, Wis., 1971—. Bd. dirs. Ryan-Powell-Carroll Scholarship Fund, U. Notre Dame, 1968—. Mem. Columbia County (pres. 1974-76), Wis., Am., Dodge County (Wis.) bar assns., Internat. Platform Assn., Am. Judicature Soc. Home: 308 Fairway Dr Columbus WI 53925 Office: 159 S Ludington St Columbus WI 53925 Tel (414) 623-2330

STOLTZ, ROBERT JOHN, b. Milw., Sept. 6, 1912; LL.B., Marquette U., 1935. Admitted to Wis. bar, 1935; partner firm Schloemer, Stoltz & Merriam, and predecessor, West Bend, Wis., 1935-60; judge Washington County (Wis.) Ct., 1960-76; chief judge 6th Jud. Dist. Ct., 1976—; mem. faculty Wis. Jud. Coll., 1969-71, Nat. Coll. State Judiciary, Reno, Nev., 1975; dir., v.p. State Bank of Newburg (Wis.); chmn. bd. dirs. Germantown Mut. Ins. Co.; dir. West Bend Savs. & Loan Assn. Clk., West Bend Sch. Dist., 1947-59. lMem. Am., Wis., Washington County bar assns., Wis. State Bd. Criminal Ct. Judges (chmn. 1974-75), Wis. State Bd. County Ct. Judges. Office: Court House PO Box 518 West Bend WI 53095 Tel (414) 334-3779

STONE, BEN HARRY, b. Gulfport, Miss., Jan. 18, 1935; B.B.A., Tulane U., 1957; J.D., U. Miss., 1961, Admitted to Miss. bar, 1961; asso. firm Brunini, Grantham, Grower & Hewes, Jackson, Miss., 1961-62; partner firm Eaton, Cottrell, Galloway & Lang, Gulfport, 1962—; mem. Miss. Senate, 1968—; mem. adv. council Miss.-Ala. Sea Grant, 1976—; mem. bd. govs. Council State Govts. Mem. Am., Harrison County (pres. 1968) bar assns. Editorial bd. Miss. Law Jour., 1960-61. Office 2300 14th St Gulfport MS 39501 Tel (601) 864-2682

STONE, BERTRAM ALLEN, b. Chgo., Nov. 14, 1915; LL.B., Chgo. Kent Coll. Law, 1938, J.D., 1969. Admitted to Ill. bar, 1938; sr. partner firm Stone, Pogrund & Korey, Chgo., 1961—; gen. counsel Chgo. Electroplaters Inst., Ill., Ind. and Wis., 1961—; gen. counsel Febrics Salesman's Club Chgo., 1961—. Mem. Ill. State, Chgo. bar assns., Decalogue Soc. Lawyers. Contbr. legal articles to Nat. Assn. Metal Finishers publ. Home: 329 Sunset Dr Wilmette IL 60091 Office: 221 N La Salle St Chicago IL 60601 Tel (312) 782-3636

STONE, DONALD MARTIN, b. Los Angeles, Apr. 14, 1943; B.A., U. Calif. at Los Angeles, 1966, M.A., 1967; J.D., Loyola U., 1971. Admitted to Calif. bar, 1972; asso. firm Kirtland & Packard, Los Angeles, 1972-75; mem. firm Staitman & Snyder, Los Angeles, 1975—. Mem. Los Angeles County Bar Assn. Home: 1930 Karen St Burbank CA 91504 Office: 15910 Ventura Blvd #1501 Encino CA 91436 Tel (213) 872-3530

STONE, DOUGLAS CLYDE, b. McGehee, Ark., Dec. 16, 1922; student Columbia, summer 1945; LL.B., U. Miss., 1947. Admitted to Miss. bar, 1947; asso. firm Stone, Graham, Segrest & Johnson, and predecessors, Columbus, Miss., 1947—, sr. partner, 1976—. Mem. Miss. Employment Security Commn., 1952-56, chmn., 1965-72; mem. Miss. Jr. Coll. Commn., 1964-70; mem. nat. council USO, 1970-77; community dir. Bank of Miss., West Point. Mem. Miss. Bar Found., Am., Miss., Lowndes County (pres. 1968) bar assns., Am. Judicature Soc., Comml. Law League Am., Miss. trial lawyers assns., Miss. Def. Lawyers Assn., Kappa Alpha (exec. council 1965-77). Home: 1202 11th Ave N Columbus MS 39701 Office: PO Box 166 Commercial Dispatch Bldg Columbus MS 39701 Tel (601) 328-5021

STONE, EDWIN CHESTER, b. Bassett, Va., Feb. 28, 1939; B.A., Bridgewater Coll., 1961; LL.B., U. Va., 1964. Admitted to Va. bar, 1964; asso. firm Dalton, Stone & Clay, Radford, Va., 1964-75; partner firm Davis & Stone, Radford, 1975—; dir. First & Mchts. Nat. Bank, Radford. Bd. dirs. Radford Coll. Found., 1973-75; pres., bd. dirs. St. Albans Psychiat. Hosp., Radford, 1975. Mem. Montgomery-Floyd-Radford, Va., Am. bar assns. Home: 27 Fieldale Dr Radford VA 24141 Office: W End Profl Bldg Radford VA 24141 Tel (703) 639-9081

STONE, EDWIN STANTON, JR., b. Beaumont, Tex., Nov. 1, 1908; LL.B., Houston Law Sch., 1938; M.A., Sussex Coll. Tech., 1976. Admitted to Tex. bar, 1939; individual practice law, Freeport, Tex., 1939-50; mem. firm Stone & Davis, Freeport, 1950-65, Stone, Davis & Stovall, Freeport, 1965-68; individual practice law, Sour Lake, Tex., 1968—; mem. Tex. Legislature, 1953-57, chmn. revenue and taxation com., 1955-57; exec. asst. atty. gen. Tex., 1963-65. Chmn. Brazos River Harbor Nav. Dist. Tex., 1947-52; vol. counselor VA Drug Abuse Program, 1974-75. Mem. State Bar Tex., Am. Judicature Soc. Recipient merit award VA. Home and office: Box 609 Sour Lake TX 77659 Tel (713) 287-3511

STONE, GEORGE SHERWOOD, b. N.Y.C., Mar. 15, 1943; B.A., Brown U., 1965; M.A., Am. U. Sch. Internat. Service, 1968; J.D., N.Y. U., 1971, LL.M., 1975. Fgn. service officer Dept. State, Washington, 1966-67; admitted to N.Y. bar, 1971; asst. dist. atty. Bronx County (N.Y.), 1971-75; partner firm Stone, Silverson & Finn, N.Y.C., 1975—. Mem. Am., N.Y. State bar assns., Order of Coif. Office: Stone Silverson & Finn 400 Madison Ave New York City NY 10017 Tel (212) PL 2-5353

STONE, IRWIN JOSEPH, b. Malden, Mass., Jan. 15, 1934; B.S., U. R.I., 1955; J.D., Boston U., 1957. Admitted to Fla. bar, 1958; individual practice law, Miami, Fla., 1958—. Dep. gov. Area III Fla. chpt. Civitan Internat. Office: 2770 SW 27th Ave Miami FL 33133 Tel (305) 446-5727

STONE, JAMES DORSEY, b. Balt., June 15, 1940; B.S. in Econs., U. Pa., 1962; LL.B., U. Md., 1966. Admitted to Md. bar, 1966; trust officer 1st Nat. Bank of Md., Balt., 1969-72; partner firm White, Mindel, Clarke & Hill, Towson, Md., 1972—; sec. Evapco, Inc. Mem. Am., Md. bar assns., Balt. Estate Planning Council. Home: 7108 Bellona Ave Baltimore MD 21212 Office: 305 W Chesapeake Ave Towson MD 21204 Tel (301) 828-1050

STONE, JOSEPH MARSHALL, b. Charleston, W.Va., June 30, 1945; A.B., W.Va. U., 1967, J.D., 1970. Admitted to W.Va. bar, 1970; clk. U.S. Dist. Ct., Huntington, W.Va., 1970-71; asst. prof. Marshall U., Huntington, 1971—, dir. advising and M.B.A. advisor, 1974-76, faculty advisor Alpha Kappa Psi, Lambda Chi Alpha, 1972—, adv. com. Student Legal Services, 1973—. Chmn. Huntington Consumer Protection Adv. Bd. 1975—. Mem. Am., W.Va. bar Assns., Am. Judicature Soc., Am. Bus. Law Assn., Nat. Assn. Bus. Law Tchrs., Am. Psychology Law Soc., ACLU, AAUP, Alpha Kappa Psi, Phi Alpha Delta. Recipient Am. Jurisprudence award for contracts, 1968, Tchr. of Yr. award Marshall U., 1974. Home: 102 Kay Crest Dr #2 Huntington WV 25705 Office: Marshall U Coll Bus Huntington WV 25701 Tel (304) 696-2442

STONE, JOSEPH MORRIS, b. N.Y.C., Mar. 5, 1917; B.Social Sci., Coll. City N.Y., 1936; LL.B., Bklyn. Coll., 1939, J.D., 1972. Admitted to N.Y. bar, 1939, D.C. bar, 1955, U.S. Supreme Ct. bar, 1945; prosecutor Nuremberg War Crimes Trials, 1946-48; spl. asst. to Solicitor of Labor, Dept. Labor, 1950-53; individual practice law, Washington, 1955—; spl. counsel U.S. Senate Labor Com., 1957. Mem. Am., D.C. bar assns., Nat. Acad. Arbitrators. Author: The Construction Worker under Federal Wage Laws, 1959. Home: 6816 Meadow Ln Chevy Chase MD 20005 Office: 1030 15th St NW Washington DC 20015 Tel (202) 737-7068

STONE, LAURENCE HENRY, b. Saco, Maine, Apr. 9, 1921; B.S., Bowdoin Coll., 1943; M.A., Harvard U., 1947; LL.B., Yale U., 1950. Admitted to Mass. bar, 1951; asso. firm Withington, Cross, Park & McCann, Boston, 1950-51; with Fed. Res. Bank Boston, 1951—, v.p., gen. counsel. Mem. Planning Bd. Wellesley (Mass.), 1963-73, chmn., 1971-72; mem. Town Meeting Wellesley, 1957—. Home: 90 Fairbanks Ave Wellesley MA 02181 Office: 30 Pearl St Boston MA 02106 Tel (617) 426-7100

STONE, LAWRENCE MAURICE, b. Malden, Mass., Mar. 25, 1931; A.B. magna cum laude, Harvard, 1953, J.D., 1956. Admitted to Mass. bar, 1956, Calif. bar, 1958; tax legis. counsel U.S. Treasury Dept., 1964-66; prof. law U. Calif. Berkeley, 1966—; of counsel firm Irell and Manella, Century City, Calif, 1966—. Office: Sch Law U Calif Berkeley CA 94720 Tel (415) 642-7249

STONE, MURRAY, b. Richmond, N.Y., Jan. 28, 1938; B.A., Okla. U., 1961; J.D., Washington U., St. Louis, 1965. Admitted to Mo. bar, 1966, U.S. Supreme Ct. bar; asso. firm Librach & Heller, 1966; partner firm Harper & Stone, 1967-71; individual practice law, St. Louis, 1971—; mem. Mo. Ho. of Reps., 1972-76, vice chmn. criminal procedure com. Mem. Mo. Bar Assn., Nat. Assn. Criminal Def. Lawyers. Home: 12561 Ladue Lake Ct Saint Louis MO 63141 Office: 722 Chestnut St Saint Louis MO 63101 Tel (314) 231-2020

STONE, NICHOLAS RADE, b. Pitts., Oct. 4, 1919; B.S. in Chemistry, U. Pitts., J.D. Admitted to Pa. bar, 1949, U.S. Supreme Ct. bar; partner firm Stone & Silvestri, firm Stone & Raynovich; individual practice law, Pitts.; solicitor City Pitts., Vernona Boro and Wilmeroing Boro (Pa.); asst. dist. atty.; atty. Serb Nat. Fedn., Pitts., Nat. Slovak Soc., Pitts. Pres., Brashear Assn., Pitts., S. Side Community Council, Pitts. Mem. Allegheny County, Pa., Am. trial lawyers assns., S. Side C. of C. (pres.). Home: 5525 Beacon St Pittsburg PA 15217 Office: 409 Plaza Bldg Pittsburg PA 15219 Tel (412) 391-3782

STONE, NORBORNE CLARKE, JR., b. Mobile, Ala., Feb. 28, 1925; LL.B., U. Ala., 1947. Admitted to Ala. bar, 1947; sr. partner firm Stone & Partin, Bay Minette, Ala., 1947—; mem. Jud. Inquiry Commn., State Ala., 1975—. Chmn. local chpt. ARC, 1949-53. Mem. Ala. Bar Assn. (bd. commrs. 1971—). Home: 701 Mixon Bay Minette AL 36507 Office: 200 Second Bay Minette AL 36507 Tel (205) 937-2417

STONE, OLIVER ELLIS, b. Burlington, Vt., June 29, 1917; B.A., Wesleyan U., 1939; LL.B., Harvard, 1942. Admitted to Mass. bar, 1946, D.C. bar, 1952, U.S. Supreme Ct. bar, 1951; atty. Nat. Service Bd. for Religious Objectors, Washington, 1945-46; legal officer Intergovernmental Com. for Refugees, Internat. Refugee Orgn., Washington, 1946-52; individual practice law, Washington, 1952—. Mem. Am., D.C. bar assns. Office: 821 15th St Washington DC 20005 Tel (202) NA8-2765

STONE, RICHARD B., b. Chgo., Mar. 24, 1935; B.S., Northwestern U., 1957; LL.B., DePaul U., 1961. Admitted to Ill. bar, 1961; partner firm Altschuler, Melvoin & Glasser, Chgo. Mem. Am. Inst. C.P.A.'s, Ill. Soc. C.P.A.'s, Ill., Chgo. bar assns. Home: 3000 N Sheridan Rd Chicago IL 60657 Office: 69 W Washington St Chicago IL 60602 Tel (312) 326-9500

STONE, ROBERT CLARK, b. Upper Montclair, N.J., Aug. 25, 1916; B.S., U. Ky., 1939, J.D., 1941. Admitted to Ky. bar, 1940; atty. legal sect. Ky. Dept. Revenue, Frankfort, 1942-43; spl. agt. FBI, Detroit, Buffalo, Washington, Los Angeles, Louisville and Frankfort, 1943-66; commr. bur. tng. Ky. Dept. Justice, Richmond, 1966—; asso. prof. Coll. Law Enforcement, Eastern Ky. U., Richmond, 1975—; mem. Ky. Crime Comm. Dist. chmn. San Fernando Valley council Boy Scouts Am., 1955. Mem. Ky., Madison County bar assns., Ky. Peace Officers Assn. (dir.), Internat. Assn. Chiefs Police, Am. Judicature Soc., Internat. Narcotic Officers Enforcement Assn. Home: 318 Summit Ave Richmond KY 40475 Office: Box 608 EKU Richmond KY 40475 Tel (606) 622-2756

STONE, ROBERT DELMAR, b. Lakewood, Ohio, May 17, 1922; A.B., Hamilton Coll., 1944; LL.B., Columbia U., 1948, J.D., 1969. Admitted to N.Y. State bar, 1949; partner firm Pearis, Resseguie & Stone, Binghamton, N.Y., 1952-58; exec. dept. sec. of state N.Y. State Dept. State, Albany, 1959-60; dep. commr. gen. services N.Y. State Office Gen. Services, Albany, 1960-66; appointments officer to gov. State of N.Y., Albany, 1967; counsel and dep. commr. legal affairs N.Y. State Edn. Dept., Albany, 1968—. Pres., Albany YMCA, 1974, bd. dirs., 1966-74; chmn. bd. dirs. Binghamton YWCA, 1958. Mem. Am., N.Y. State, Broome County bar assns. Home: 198 Westchester Dr S Delmar NY 12054 Office: State Edn Bldg Washington Ave Albany NY 12234 Tel (518) 474-6400

STONE, SAMUEL CLIFFORD, b. El Dorado, Kans., Oct. 2, 1942; B.A., U. Kans., 1963; J.D., U. Tulsa, 1966. Admitted to Kans. bar, 1966, Okla. bar, 1966; asso. firm Ungerman, Grabel, Ungerman & Letter, Tulsa, Okla., 1966-68; asst. atty. City of Tulsa, 1968-72; individual practice law, Tulsa. Chmn. fin. and taxation subcom. Tulsa City-County Growth Strategy Task Force, 1976—. Mem. Am., Kans., Okla., Tulsa County bar assns. Office: 800 Thurston National Bldg Tulsa OK 74103 Tel (918) 583-1178

STONE, SOLON JONES, b. Balt., Dec. 15, 1910; B.S. in Elec. Engring., Va. Mil. Inst., 1933; LL.B., Harvard, 1937. Admitted to N.Y. bar, 1938; asso. firm Little & Burt, 1937-42; asst. personnel dir. Gen. Motors Corp., 1942-45; asso. firm Kenefick, Cooke, Mitchell, Bass & Letchworth, 1945-49, partner Kenefick firm and successor firm Phillips, Lytle, Hitchcock, Blaine & Hubor, Buffalo, 1949—; mem. Gov.'s Workmen's Compensation Rev. Com., 1961-62, Workmen's Compensation Bd. Adv. Com., 1960—. Mem., twice chmn. Western N.Y. Heart Assn.; chmn. N.Y. State Heart Assembly, 1968-70; del. Am. Heart Assn., 1967-70; trustee St. Mary's Sch. for Deaf; former mem. Legal Aid Soc. Fellow Am., N.Y. bar founds.; mem. Bar Assn. Erie County (v.p. 1974-75, pres. 1975-76), Am., N.Y. State (ho. of dels. 1974—, chmn. spl. com. on 4th dept. grievance plan 1974-75, mem. com. on assn. action program 1976—), Erie County Bar Found. (past trustee), Buffalo C. of C. Recipient Edmund Campion Soc. Man of Year award; Am. Heart Assn. Distinguished Service award; contbr. articles to legal jours. Home: 20 High Ct Snyder NY 14226 Office: 3400 Marine Midland Center Buffalo NY 14203 Tel (716) 847-8478

STONE, WILLIAM ALLEN, b. Porterville, Calif., July 24, 1939; A.B., Stanford, 1961, J.D., 1964. Admitted to Calif. bar, 1965; since practiced in Bakersfield, Calif., with firm Mack, Bianco, Means, Mack & Stone, and predecessor, asso., 1965-70, partner, 1970-71; judge Bakersfield Municipal Ct., 1971—. Mem. Calif. Judges Assn., Am. Judicature Soc. Home: 6200 Pembroke Ave Bakersfield CA 93308 Office: 1415 Truxtun Ave Bakersfield CA 93301 Tel (805) 861-2411

STONER, MICHAEL ALAN, b. Newport, R.I., Mar. 15, 1944; B.A., Duke, 1966; J.D., Emory U., 1969. Admitted to Ga. bar, 1969, U.S. Mil. Ct. Appeals bar, 1971, U.S. Dist. Ct. bar, 1975; served with Judge Adv. Gen. Corps, U.S. Army, 1970-73; asso. firm Peek, Arnold, Whaley & Cate, Atlanta, 1974; partner firm Zagoria & Stoner, Atlanta, 1974—. Mem. Am., Ga. bar Assns. Home: 1048 Avon Breeze Ct Stone Mountain GA 30083 Office: Suite 1000 Gas Light Tower 235 Peachtree St NE Atlanta GA 30303 Tel (404) 681-0611

STONER, RICHARD BURKETT, b. Ladoga, Ind., May 15, 1920; B.S., Ind. U., 1941; J.D., Harvard, 1947. Admitted to Ind. bar, 1947; with Cummins Engine Co., Inc., Columbus, Ind., 1947—, exec. v.p., corp. gen. mgr., 1966-69, vice chmn., 1969—, also dir.; vice chmn., dir. Cummins Engine Found.; pres., dir. Irwin-Sweeney-Miller Found.; dir. Kirloskar Cummins Ltd., Am. Fletcher Nat. Bank and Trust Co., Pub. Service Ind., Am. Fletcher Bank (Suisse) Switzerland, Am. United Life Ins. Co. Trustee Ind. U.; chmn. Ind. Forum, Inc. Mem. Ind. State C. of C. (dir.), Machinery Allied Products Inst. (exec. com.). Home: 2770 Franklin Dr Columbus IN 47201 Office: 301 Washington St Columbus IN 47201 Tel (812) 379-5451

STOPPELS, ALLEN DALE, b. Hull, Iowa, Dec. 25, 1924; A.B., Hope Coll., 1947; J.D., U. Mich., 1950. Admitted to Mich. bar, 1951; asst. pros. atty. Kent County (Mich.), 1953-58; judge Probate Ct. Kent County, 1959—. Trustee Hope Coll., 1962-75, hon. trustee, 1975—. Mem. Am. Bar Assn., Am. Judicature Soc., Nat. Coll. Probate Judges, Nat. Juvenile Ct. Judges Assn., Mich. Probate Judges Assn. (pres. 1973-74). Home: 2150 E Shiawassee Dr SE Grand Rapids MI 49506 Office: Room 401 Hall of Justice Grand Rapids MI 49502 Tel (616) 774-3634

STORCH, IRVING RONALD, b. N.Y.C., Oct. 4, 1918; B.S., N.Y. U., 1938; LL.B., Harvard U., 1941. Admitted to N.Y. state bar, 1941, Fed. bar, 1949, U.S. Tax Ct. bar, 1974; atty. U.S. Dept. Interior, Washington, D.C., 1941-42; atty. U.S. Dept. Justice, Washington, D.C., 1943-45; partner firm Lowell & Storch, N.Y.C., 1946-47; individual practice law, N.Y.C., 1969—; partner firm Schwartz, Weissberger, Leichter & Storch, N.Y.C., 1964-69. Village tax assessor Village of Westbury, N.Y., 1975-76. Mem. N.Y. County Lawyers Assn. Home: 880 Pepperidge Rd Westbury NY 11590 Office: 120 Broadway St New York City NY 10005 Tel (212) 732-2570

STOREY, ROBERT DAVIS, b. Tuskegee, Ala., Mar. 28, 1936; A.B., Harvard, 1958; J.D., Western Res. U., 1964. Admitted to Ohio bar, 1964; atty. E. Ohio Gas Co., Cleve., 1964-66; asst. dir. Legal Aid Soc. of Cleve., 1966-67; asso. firm Burke, Haber and Berick, Cleve., 1967-70, partner, 1971—. Trustee Phillips Exeter Acad., 1968—, Cleve. State U., 1971—; v.p. Asso. Harvard Alumni, 1974-77; steering com. Nat. Urban Coalition, 1976—. Mem. Bar Assn. Greater Cleve. Named to Top Ten Young Men of Year, City of Cleve., 1967. Home: 2385 Coventry Rd Cleveland Heights OH 44118 Office: 1500 Central Nat Bank Bldg Cleveland OH 44114 Tel (216) 771-2700

STOREY, WILLIAM MARION, b. Savannah, Ga., Aug. 16, 1924; A.B., U. N.C., 1947, J.D., 1950. Admitted to N.C. bar, 1950, U.S. Supreme Ct. bar, 1960; individual practice law, Raleigh, N.C., 1950-55; mem., atty. N.C. Bd. Pharmacy, 1950-55; guest lectr. U. N.C. Sch. Pharmacy, 1952-53; sec., treas. N.C. Bar Assn. Found., Raleigh, 1960—. Mem. Am. Judicature Soc., Assn. Continuing Legal Edn. Adminstrs. (exec. com. 1960-64), Nat. Assn. Bar Execs. (exec. com. 1956-59), N.C. Bar Assn. (exec. v.p., treas. 1955—, Judge John J. Parker award 1971). Home: 701 Yarmouth Rd Raleigh NC 27607 Office: 1025 Wade Ave Raleigh NC 27605 Tel (919) 828-0561

STOREY, WOODROW WILSON, b. Mt. Rainier, Md., Dec. 12, 1912; J.D., Am. U., 1937, LL.M., 1938. Admitted to D.C. bar, 1937, Md. bar, 1945, Va. bar, 1969, U.S. Supreme Ct. bar, 1944; with GAO, Washington, 1937-40; comptroller Dept. Def., Washington, 1946060; v.p. Martin Marietta Co., Balt., 1960-67, Vitro Corp., N.Y.C., 1967-68; individual practice law, Washington, Arlington and Alexandria, Va., 1968—. Mem. Am., Md., Va., Fed. bar assns., Assn. U.S. Army, Am. Def. Preparedness Asssn. Home: 1002 S Riverside Dr Indialantic FL 32903 Office: 632 N Washington St Alexandria VA 22314 Tel (703) 836-6800

STORK, WILLIAM CAUGHMAN, b. Columbia, S.C., Nov. 2, 1943; B.S. in Banking and Fin., U. S.C., 1966, J.D., 1969. Admitted to S.C. bar, 1969, U.S. Dist. Ct. for S.C., 1969, U.S. 4th Circuit Ct. Appeals bar, 1974; law clk., S.C. Supreme Ct., 1969; atty. U.S. Army, 1969-71; asso. firm Barnes, Austin & Ellison, Columbia, 1972-73, partner, 1974—. Mem. Am., S.C. bar, Richland County bar assns. Contbr. articles to legal jours. Home: 3113 Longleaf Rd Columbia SC 29205 Office: Suite 1718 Bankers Trust Tower Columbia SC 29211 Tel (803) 799-1111

STORM, DONALD FRANKLIN, b. Gays, Ill., May 18, 1929; B.S., U. Ill., 1951, J.D., 1953. Admitted to Ill. bar, 1953; mem. firm Craig & Craig, Mt. Vernon, Ill., 1956-57; asst. to legal counsel U. Ill., Urbana, 1957-59; tax atty. Lincoln Nat. Life Ins. Co., Ft. Wayne, Ind., 1959-64; asst. gen. counsel Ill. Agrl. Assn. Bloomington, 1964-69; asst. v.p., tax counsel State Farm Cos., Bloomington, 1969—. Mem. Lexington (Ill.) Sch. Bd., 1971-74. Mem. Am., Ill., McLean County bar assns. Co-author: Law for the Veterinarian and Livestock Owner, 1959. Home: Timber Ridge Lexington IL 61753 Office: One State Farm Plaza Bloomington IL 61701 Tel (309) 662-2559

STORM, E. MACBURNEY, b. Greenwich, Conn., Apr. 1, 1932; B.A., Cornell, 1953, J.D., 1960. Admitted to Conn. bar, 1960, N.Y. bar, 1961; asso. firm Stewart, Schantz & Kenning, Rochester, N.Y., 1961-64; asso. firm Moser, Johnson & Reif, Rochester, 1964-65; asst. trust officer Security Trust Co. of Rochester, 1965-67, trust officer and asst. v.p., 1967-76, v.p., 1976—; justice Town of Ogden, N.Y., 1967-71. Mem. Monroe County Estate Planning Group, Monroe County Bar Assn., Am. Inst. Banking, N.Y. Magistrates Assn., Nat. Ski Patrol Assn. Office: 1 East Ave Rochester NY 14638 Tel (716) 262-4548

STORM, MARY ELIZABETH, b. Frederick, Md., Jan. 11, 1940; student St. John's Coll., Annapolis, 1958-60; B.A., Hood Coll., 1962; J.D., George Washington U., 1966. Admitted to Md. bar, 1967; mem. firm Storm & Storm, Frederick and Emmitsburg, Md., 1967—; instr. estate planning Frederick Community Coll., 1969-70, mem. adv. com. asso. degree nursing program, 1970—, recorder, 1970-72. Mem. Md. Comprehensive Health Planning Council, 1971—, vice chmn., 1975—; vice chmn. Md. Health Coordinating Council, 1977—; mem. Health Systems Agy. W. Md., 1976—; 2d v.p. Md. Young Democrats, 1961; bd. dirs. sec. Girl Scout council Central Md., 1972-73, Frederick Orgn. for Rehab., 1970-71, Mem. Nat. Assn. Women Lawyers (del. Md. 1969-73), Frederick County (rec. sec. 1971—), Am., Md. (council com. family and juvenile law 1968-70) bar assns., Am. Assn. Comprehensive Health Planning (dir. 1976—), Phi Delta Delta. Home: 321 S Market St Frederickton MD 21701 Office: 114 A W Church St Frederickton MD 21701 Tel (301) 662-8266

STORMO, LLOYD HERMAN, b. Watertown, S.D., Apr. 28, 1908; LL.B., U. S.D., 1933, J.D., 1933; student U. Denver. Admitted to S.D. bar, 1933, Colo. bar, 1940; practice law, S.D., 1933-40, Denver, 1940—; state's atty. 11th Jud. Dist. S.D., 1934-38; partner firm Gould & Stormo, Denver. Mem. Am. Bar Assn., Am. Trial Lawyers Assn., Phi Delta Phi. Home: Brooks Towers 1020 15th St Denver CO 80202 Office: 2520 Lincoln Center 1660 Lincoln St Denver CO 80203 Tel (303) 892-5511

STORMS, CLIFFORD BEEKMAN, b. Mount Vernon, N.Y., July 18, 1932; B.A., Amherst Coll., 1954; LL.B., Yale, 1957. Admitted to N.Y. bar, 1957; asso. atty. firm Breed, Abbott & Morgan, N.Y.C., 1957-64; with CPC Internat. Inc., Englewood Cliffs, N.J., 1964—, asst. gen. counsel, 1968-73, v.p. legal affairs, 1973-75, v.p., gen. counsel, 1975—; trustee Food and Drug Law Inst., 1976—. Pres. Edgemont Civic Assn., Scarsdale, N.Y., 1964-66. Mem. Am., N.Y. State bar assns. Assn. Bar City N.Y., Assn. Gen. Counsel, Phi Beta Kappa. Home: 11 Serenity Ln Cos Cob CT 06807 Office: CPC Internat Inc International Plaza Englewood Cliffs NJ 07632 Tel (201) 894-2714

STORRS, RALPH EUGENE, b. Amarillo, Tex., Sept. 11, 1945; B.B.A., W. Tex. State U., 1968; J.D., U. Tex., 1971. Admitted to Tex. bar, 1972; asso. firm Small, Craig and Werkthin, Austin, Tex., 1971; dist. atty. Potter County (Tex.), Amarillo, 1972-74; partner firm Fairweather, Hale & Storrs, Amarillo, 1974-75, firm Busby and Storrs, Amarillo, 1975—. Mem. Am., Tex. bar assns., Tex., Amarillo trial lawyers assns. Home: 3515 Huntington St Amarillo TX 79109 Office: 110 E 5th St Amarillo TX 79101 Tel (806) 372-5793

STORRS, RICHARD S., b. Orange, N.J., May 9, 1910; A.B., Yale, 1932; LL.B., Harvard, 1935. Admitted to N.Y. bar, 1936; asso. firm Sullivan & Cromwell, N.Y.C., 1935-45, mem. firm, 1945—; dir. Transatlantic Fund, Inc., Panhandle Eastern Pipe Line Co., Trunkline Gas Co., De Vegh Mut. Fund, Inc., Mass Mut. Income Investors Inc. Trustee Village of Cove Neck. Mem. Am., N.Y. State, N.Y.C. bar assns., Phi Beta Kappa, Alpha Delta Phi, Elihu. Home: Cove Neck Rd Oyster Bay NY 11771 Office: Sullivan & Cromwell 48 Wall St New York City NY 10005 Tel (212) 952-8024

STOTT, JOHN MICHAEL, b. Reading, Pa., July 4, 1947; B.A., Gettysburg Coll., 1969; J.D., Dickinson Sch. Law, 1972. Admitted to Pa. bar, 1972; asso. firm Austin, Speicher, Boland, Connor & Giorgi, Reading, 1972—; solicitor Reading Sch. Dist., 1976—, Muhlenberg Vocat. Tech. Sch., 1976—. Bd. dirs. Olivet Boys' Club, 1975. Mem. Pa., Berks County bar assns., Pa. Trial Lawyers Assn. Home: 923 Hamilton Pl Wyomissing PA 19610 Office: 44 N Sixth St Reading PA 19601 Tel (215) 374-8211

STOTTER, JAMES, II, b. Cleve., Oct. 12, 1929; B.A., Yale, 1951, LL.B., 1954; postgrad. U. So. Calif. Law Sch., 1958-60. Admitted to D.C. bar, 1954, Calif. bar, 1955, Ct. Mil. Appeals bar, 1956, U.S. Supreme Ct. bar, 1961; judge advocate officer USAF, NATO observer for Dept. State, 1954-57; asst. U.S. atty. Dept. Justice, Los Angeles, 1957-59, asst. chief civil div. U.S. Atty.'s Office, Los Angeles, 1967—; mem. firms, Los Angeles and Beverly Hills, Calif., 1959-67; panel arbitrator Am. Arbitration Assn., 1960—; hearing officer reconscientious objectors Dept. Justice, 1971-74; prof. law Calif. Coll. Law, Los Angeles, 1969-73; Mem. alumni adv. council Loomis Sch., Windsor, Conn.; mem. So. Calif. admissions adv. com. Yale. Mem. Am., Fed., Calif., D.C. bar assns., Los Angeles Lawyers Club. Recipient Spl. Merit award Dept. Justice, 1971, spl. commendation citation Drug Enforcement Adminstrn., 1976. Home: 201 S Carmelina Ave Los Angeles CA 90049 Office: Suite 1135 US Courthouse 312 N Spring St Los Angeles CA 90012 Tel (213) 688-2449

STOUDENMIRE, STERLING FRANKLIN, JR., b. Sumter, S.C., May 20, 1915; A.B., Furman U., 1937; LL.B., J.D., George Washington U., 1941. Admitted to D.C. bar, 1941, S.C. bar, 1940, Ala. bar, 1955, U.S. Supreme Ct. bar, 1947; individual practice law, Washington, 1941-53, Mobile, Ala., 1971—; gen. counsel Waterman S.S. Corp., Mobile, 1953-71. Mem. Am., Ala., S.C., Maritime Bar Assns., Maritime Adminstrv. Bar Assn., Soc. Former Spl. Agts. FBI, Phi Delta Phi. Home: 4251 Wilkinson Way Mobile AL 36608 Office: 316 International Trade Center Mobile AL 36602 Tel (205) 432-9709

STOUT, DAVID ALLYN, b. Scranton, Pa., June 16, 1947; B.A., U. Cin., 1970; J.D., No. Ky. Coll., 1974. Admitted to Ohio bar, 1974; law clk. Hamilton County (Ohio) Common Pleas Ct., 1970-74; dir. pvt. complaint unit City Prosecutor's Office, Cin., 1974; asst. pros. atty. Hamilton County, Cin., 1975—. Active Republican Club, Hamilton County, Lincoln Park Baptist Ch., Cin. Mem. Nat. Reform Assn. (Pitts.), Ohio State, Cin. bar assns., Phi Alpha Delta, Alpha Phi Omega. Home: 7775 Cella Dr Cincinnati OH 45239 Office: Room 420 1000 Main St Cincinnati OH 45202 Tel (513) 632-8359

STOUT, JAMES ALLEN, b. Iowa City, Iowa, July 19, 1938; B.B.A., U. Iowa, 1960; J.D., Drake U., 1963. Admitted to Iowa bar, 1963, N. Mex. bar, 1970; asso. firm Wisdom, Sullivan, & Golden, Des Moines, 1962-66; capt. JAGC, U.S. Air Force, 1963-66; atty. office of chief counsel AEC, Albuquerque, 1966-73; counsel Rocky Flats area office ERDA, Golden, Colo., 1973—. Mem. Order of Coif. Office: PO Box 928 Golden CO 80401 Tel (303) 497-2025

STOUT, KOEHLER SHERIDAN, b. Deer Lodge, Mont., Sept. 1, 1922; B.S. in Mining Engring., Mont. Sch. Mines, 1948, M.S. in Geol. Engring., 1949. Admitted to Mont. bar, 1958; mine capt. Warren Foundry & Pipe Corp., Dover, N.J., 1951-52; prof. engring. sci. Mont. Coll. Mining Sci. and Tech., Butte, 1952—, chmn. engring. div., 1966—, acting dean academic affairs, 1975—; chmn., mem. Mont. Bd. Profl. Engring. and Land Surveyors, 1967-72. Bd. dirs., pres. World Mus. Mining, 1970-75. Mem. Am., Mont. bar assns., Nat. Soc. Profl. Engrs., Am. Inst. Mining, Metall. and Petroleum Engrs., Mont. Mining Assn. (past pres., dir. 1972—). Contbr. articles on mining engring. and law to publs. Home: 1327 W Granite St Butte MT 59701 Tel (406) 792-8321

STOVALL, JAMES TRUMAN, III, b. Montgomery, Ala., Nov. 6, 1937; A.B., U. Ala., 1959, J.D., 1960; postgrad. Hague Acad. Internat. Law, 1965. Admitted to Ala. bar, 1960, U.S. Ct. Mil. Appeals bar, 1961, D.C. bar, 1968, U.S. Supreme Ct. bar, 1968; served to maj. JAGC, AUS, 1961-68; asso. firm Clifford, Glass, McIlwain & Finney, Washington, 1968-73, partner, 1973—; instr. bus. law U. Md., Korea, 1961-62, Germany, 1964-66. Bd. dirs. Am. Indian Lawyer Tng. Project, 1975—, Washington Lawyers Project, Robert F. Kennedy Meml., 1970-74. Mem. Bar Assn. D.C., Am., Fed. bar assns., Farrah Law Soc. Home: 6206 Winston Dr Bethesda MD 20034 Office: 815 Connecticut Ave NW Washington DC 20006 Tel (202) 298-8686

STOWELL, WILLIAM RICHARD, b. Chgo., Oct. 10, 1939; B.S. in Psychology, Quincy (Ill.) Coll., 1961; J.D., U. Akron, 1967. Admitted to Ill. bar, 1968; atty. firm Hunter & Hutmacher, Quincy, 1969, William F. Nissen, Quincy, 1969-71; individual practice law, Quincy, 1971—; atty. City of Quincy, 1969; asst. atty. gen. State of Ill., 1972—. Mem. Ill., Adams County bar assns., Ill. Jaycees. Home: 2020 Oak St Quincy IL 62301 Office: 429 Hampshire St Quincy IL 62301 Tel (217) 222-1442

STRACENER, NEALON, b. Kipling, La., June 29, 1916; B.A. in Journalism, La. State U., 1942, J.D., 1948. Admitted to La. bar, 1947, U.S. Supreme Ct. bar, 1958; practiced in Baton Rouge, 1947—; founder, pres., atty. Guaranty Fed. Savs. & Loan Assn., 1957—; field counsel Fed. Nat. Mortgage Assn., 1956-61; area counsel VA, 1957—; policy issuing agt. Am. Title Ins. Co., 1971—; gen. counsel Republican State Central Com. of La. Del. Rep. Nat. Convs., 1959, 60; chmn. 6th dist. Rep. Exec. Com. East Baton Rouge Parish; deacon 1st Bapt. Ch., Baton Rouge. Mem. Am., La. State, Eaton Baton Rouge bar assns., Am. Judicature Soc., Am. Coll. Mortgage Attys., Theta Xi, Sigma Delta Chi. Editor La. Republican, 1952-62. Home: 9461 Woodbine Dr Baton Rouge LA 70815 Office: 3155 Weller Ave Baton Rouge LA 70805 Tel (504) 356-2491

STRACKS, ROBERT JEFFREY, b. Woodmere, N.Y. May 30, 1943; student Wash. U., 1960-62; A.B. with distinction, U. Mich., 1964; LL.B. magna cum laude, Harvard, 1967. Admitted to Ill. bar, 1967; asso. firm Sonnenschein, Carlin Nath & Rosenthal, Chgo., 1967-74; v.p., counsel Wauterlek & Brown, Inc., Chgo., 1974—. Mem. Chgo. Council Lawyers, Am., Ill., Chgo. bar assns. Editorial bd. Harvard Law Rev., 1965-67. Home: 913 Greenwood Ave Winnetka IL 60093 Office: 300 W Washington St Chicago IL 60606 Tel (312) 641-3300

STRADER, CHARLES J., b. Portland, Oreg., May 1, 1928; B.S., U. Oreg., 1950; LL.B., Northwestern Coll., Portland, 1960. Admitted to Oreg. bar, 1960; partner firm Hicks, Tongue, Dale & Strader, Portland, 1961-67; partner firm Black, Helterline, Beck & Rappleyea, Portland, 1968—. Mem. Am., Oreg. State, Multnoman County bar assns., Am. Trial Lawyers Assn. Office: Bank of California Tower Portland OR 97205 Tel (503) 224-5560

STRADER, JAMES DAVID, b. Pitts., June 30, 1940; B.A. in Econs., Mich. State U., 1962; J.D., U. Pitts., 1965. Admitted to Pa. bar, 1966, W.Va. bar, 1972; asso. firm Peacock, Keller & Yohe, Washington, Pa., 1967-68; atty. U.S. Steel Corp., Pitts., 1968-76, gen. atty. workers' compensation and casualty, 1977—. Commr. Twp. of Mt. Lebanon (Pa.), 1974—; mem. Democratic Nat. Platform Com., 1976; deacon Presbyn. Ch. Mem. Allegheny County (Pa.), Pa., Am. (vice chmn. com. on workmen's compensation and employer's liability law) bar assns. Home: 445 Old Farm Rd Mount Lebanon PA 15228 Office: 600 Grant St Pittsburgh PA 15230 Tel (412) 433-2960

STRANAHAN, DUANE, JR., b. Toledo, Mar. 9, 1930; student Princeton, 1951; M.A., Columbia, 1953; J.D., U. Mich., 1962. Admitted to Ohio bar, 1962; asso. firm Marshall, Melhorn, Cole, Hummer and Spiter, Toledo, 1967, partner, 1967—; dir. Grumman Am. Aviation Corp., Toledo Trust Co., NW Ohio Bancshares, Shadow Valley Devel. Corp., Parrish Power Products; partner Winwell Exploration Co., Hydro Carbon Exploration and Devel. Co. Bd. dirs. Mich. Council Trout Unltd., United Toledo Com., Toledo Mus. Art, Med. Coll. Ohio, ARC, Community Chest, Toledo Humane Soc., trustee Toledo Hosp. Endowment. Office: 14th floor National Bank Bldg Toledo OH 43604 Tel (419) 243-4200

STRAND, ALFRED BENJAMIN, JR., b. Knoxville, Feb. 13, 1940; B.A., Carson-Newman Coll., 1962; B.S., U. Tenn., 1964; J.D., Cumberland Sch. Law Samford U., 1967. Admitted to Tenn. bar, 1967; asso. firm Joe H. Felknor, Dandridge, Tenn., 1967-71; individual practice law, Dandridge, 1971-75; partner firm Strand & Goddard, Dandridge, 1976—; circuit judge 2d Jud. Dist. Part 2, 1975-76; asso. prof. bus. adminstrn. Carson-Newman Coll., 1967-71. Pres. Dandridge Jaycees, also state protocol officer, 1968-69, senator, 1975. Mem. Am., Tenn., Jefferson County (pres. 1976—) bar assns., Tenn. Trial Lawyers Assn., Tenn. Def. Lawyers Assn., Alpha Kappa Psi, Phi Alpha Delta. Home: Oakwood Dr Dandridge TN 37725 Office: Legal Center Gay St Dandridge TN 37725 Tel (615) 397-3413

STRAND, PAUL DAVID, b. La Porte, Ind., Feb. 7, 1931; B.A., Upper Iowa U., 1951; postgrad. U. Minn., 1953; J.D., Drake U., 1957. Admitted to Iowa bar, 1957; tchr. St. Ansgar (Iowa) Community Sch. Dist., 1951; ins. adjuster, casualty claims Hawkeye Security Ins. Co., Des Moines, 1956-57; tchr. Luther Coll., Decorah, Iowa, 1957; sec., treas. Mac Masters, Inc., Decorah, 1960—; dir. Security Bank & Trust Co., Decorah, 1972-73; pros. atty. Winneshiek County (Iowa), Decorah, 1958-64; sr. partner firm Strand, Anderson, Radwenz & Larson, Decorah. Pres. bd. dirs. Area One Vocat. Sch., Calmer, Iowa, 1974—. Mem. Winneshiek County (pres. 1959-61) Iowa (spl. mem. com. adminstrv. law 1970-76), Am. bar assns., Decorah C. of C. Home: Rural Route Decorah IA 52101 Office: 112 W Main St Decorah IA 52101 Tel (319) 382-2959

STRAND, ROGER GORDON, b. Peekskill, N.Y., Apr. 28, 1934; A.B., Hamilton Coll., 1955; LL.B., Cornell U., 1961; grad. Nat. Coll. State Trial Judges, 1968. Admitted to Ariz. bar, 1961; asso. firm Fennemore, Craig, Allen & McClennen, Phoenix, 1961-67; judge Superior Ct., Phoenix, 1967—. Bd. dirs. Central Ariz. Arthritis Found., chmn., 1964-65. Mem. Am., Ariz., Maricopa County bar assns., Ariz. Judges Assn., Aircraft Owners and Pilots Assn., Phi Delta Phi, Sigma Phi. Home: 5825 N 3d Ave Phoenix AZ 85013 Office: Superior Ct Bldg Phoenix AZ 85003 Tel (602) 262-3921

STRANDNESS, ODIN JOHN, b. Churches Ferry, N.D., May 5, 1904; B.A., U. N.D., 1928, J.D., 1934; postgrad. U. Wis., 1934-35. Admitted to N.D. bar, 1933; individual practice law, Fargo, N.D., 1935—; asst. state's atty. Cass County (N.D.), 1936-48; judge Municipal Ct., Fargo, 1956-72; magistrate U.S. Dist. Ct., 1971-76. Active Boy Scouts Am.; pres. bd. dirs. N.D. Ho. of Mercy, Fargo, 1940-52; supt. 1st Luth. Ch. Sunday Sch., Fargo, 1950-69, active ch. bds. Mem. Cass County, N.D. bar assns. Recipient Baden Powell award Boy Scouts Am., 1971. Home and Office: 2305 9 1/2 St N Fargo ND 58102 Tel (701) 235-4012

STRANGE, GEORGE JOHN, b. Loogootee, Ind., Nov. 12, 1945; A.B. with highest distinction, Ind. U., 1966; J.D. cum laude, Harvard, 1969. Admitted to Wis. bar, 1969, U.S. Supreme Ct., Tex. bars, 1973; asso. firm Foley & Lardner, Milw., 1969-73; asso. firm Stalcup, Johnson, Meyers & Miller, Dallas, 1973—; instr. real estate Tex. A. and M. U., 1975. Mem. Wis., Tex., Dallas bar assns. Contbr. articles to legal jours. Home: 5740 Caruth Haven Apt 241 Dallas TX 75206

STRANIERE, ROBERT ALAN, b. N.Y.C., Mar. 28, 1941; B.A. cum laude, Wagner Coll., 1962; J.D., N.Y. U., 1965, LL.M., 1969. Admitted to N.Y. bar, 1966; asso. firm Marchi and Ahearn, S.I., 1966; asst. corp. counsel City of N.Y., 1966-68, asst. legis. rep., 1968-69; individual practice law, S.I., 1968-75; partner firm Marchi, Straniere & Meyers, P.C., S.I., N.Y.C., 1975—; counsel to N.Y. State Senator John J. Marchi, 1970. Chmn. community bd. 2, S.I., 1971; treas. Iron Hills Civic Assn., S.I., 1976—. Mem. Richmond County, N.Y. State bar assns., Assn. Bar City N.Y. Office: 358 Saint Marks Pl Staten Island NY 10301 Tel (212) 273-4848

STRANKMAN, GARY ELVIN, b. Shelton, Wash., Mar. 23, 1941; B.A., U. Wash., 1963; J.D., U. Calif., 1966; M.A., San Francisco State U., 1968; grad. Nat. Coll. Dist. Atty's., Houston, 1973. Admitted to Calif. bar, 1967; staff atty. Contra Costa Legal Services Found., Richmond, Calif., 1968; dep. dist. atty. Contra Costa County (Calif.), 1968-74, asst. dist. atty., 1974—; lectr. criminal justice dept. Contra Costa Coll., 1971—, No. Calif. Police Acad., Los Medanos Coll., Pittsburgh, Calif., 1971—. Mem. Richmond Bar Assn., Calif. Dist. Atty's. Assn., Contra Costa Peace Officers Assn. Office: 100 37th St Richmond CA 94805 Tel (415) 233-7060

STRASHEIM, JERROLD LEE, b. Lincoln, Nebr., Sept. 25, 1931; B.S., U. Nebr., 1955; LL.B. cum laude, 1957. Admitted to Nebr. bar, 1957; law clk. to U.S. Dist. Judge Robert VanPelt, Lincoln, 1957-58; asso. firm Mason, Knudsen, Dickeson, Berkheimer, Lincoln, 1958-62; bankruptcy judge U.S. Dist. Ct. for Nebr., Omaha, 1962-73; lectr. Law Sch. Creighton U., Omaha, 1965-75; minority counsel U.S. Sen. Subcom. on Improvement in Jud. Machinery, 1959-60; pres. Omaha-Council Bluffs Legal Aid Soc., 1975-76; mem. bd. dirs. Omaha Legal Aid Soc., 1974-76. Mem. Omaha, Nebr., Am. bar assns. Contbr. articles to legal jours. Office: 1400 One First National Center Omaha NE 68102 Tel (402) 346-3600

STRASSBURGER, EUGENE BONN, b. Pitts., Sept. 23, 1886; A.B., Harvard, 1908, LL.B., 1910; LL.D., Duquesne U., 1930. Admitted to Pa. bar, 1910, U.S. Supreme Ct. bar, 1913; partner firm Wilima H. Lemon, Pitts., 1910-19, Strassburger & McKenna, Pitts., 1919—; prof. negotiable instruments Duquesne U., 1920-42; standing master bd. governance Supreme Ct. Pa.; chmn. law library com. Allegheny County Cts.; chmn. orphans' ct. rules com. Allegheny County. Trustee, sec. Maurice and Laura Falk Found. Mem. Am. Law Inst. (exec. com., council), Am. Judicature Soc., Am., Pa., Allegheny County bar assns., Harvard Law Sch. Alumni Assn. (council, v.p.), Harvard Law Sch. Assn. Western Pa. (pres. 1951-52). Author: Special Problems in Negotiable Instrument Law, 1940. Home: 6515 Beacon St Pittsburgh PA 15217 Office: Grant Bldg Pittsburgh PA 15219 Tel (412) 281-5423

STRASSHOFER, ROLAND HENRY, JR., b. Cleve., May 21, 1924; A.B., Case Western Res. U., 1948, J.D., 1950. Admitted to Ohio bar, 1950, U.S. Supreme Ct. bar, 1957; atty. SEC, 1950-52; asso. firm Pennell, Carlson & Rees, Cleve., 1953-63; partner firm Brown & Strasshofer, Cleve., 1963-67, Ford, Whitney & Haase, Cleve., 1970-75, Bremer, Thompson, Morhard, Coyne & Strasshofer, 1976—; dir. Anderson-Bolds, Inc.; mem. nat. labor panels Fed. Mediation and Conciliation Service, Am. Arbitration Assn. Republican candidate Ohio Legislature, 1958; trustee Hillcrest Hosp., Mayfield Heights, Ohio, 1967—, pres., 1967-69; pres. Cleve. Singers Club, 1962-64; vestryman Christ Ch., 1975—. Mem. Am. Coll. Legal Medicine, Am. Soc. Hosp. Attys., Am., Fed., Ohio bar assns., Bar Assn. Greater Cleve. (trustee), Phi Delta Phi. Home: 2865 Coleridge Rd Cleveland OH 44118 Office: 2100 East Ohio Bldg Cleveland OH 44114 Tel (216) 781-9191

STRATEMEIER, EDWARD HENRY, III, b. Kansas City, Mo., Feb. 26, 1949; B.A., Kans. U., 1971; J.D., U. Mo. at Kansas City, 1973. Admitted to Mo. bar, 1974; asso. firm Niewald, Risjord & Waldeck, Kansas City, Mo., 1974-75; individual practice law, Kansas City, Mo., 1975-76; asst. corporate counsel Russell Stover Candies, Kansas City, Mo., 1976—. Mem. Mo., Kansas City bar assns., Phi Alpha Delta. Home: 3018 W 73d Terr Prairie Village KS 66208 Office: 1004 Baltimore Ave Kansas City MO 64105 Tel (816) 842-9240

STRATTON, HENRY DAVIS, b. Pikeville, Ky., Aug. 9, 1925; student Pikeville Coll., 1943, 46-47, Asbury Coll., 1943; LL.B., U. Louisville, 1950. Admitted to Ky. bar, 1950, U.S. Supreme Ct. bar, 1956; partner firm Stratton, Mays & Hays, and predecessors, Pikeville, 1950—; chmn. Ky. Fed. Jud. Selection Commn., 1977—; v.p., pres., dir. Citizens Bank of Pikeville, 1960—. Bd. dirs. Meth. Hosp. of Ky.; trustee Pikeville Coll., 1974—, Clients Security Fund, 1972-75; bd. regents Eastern Ky. U., 1970—. Mem. Am., Ky. (ho. of dels. 1955-56, bd. govs. 1966—, chmn. jud. selection com. 1970-75, pres. 1974-75, 76—), Pike County bar assns., Am. Assn. Trial Lawyers, Ky. Bar Found. (pres. 1973-75), Nat. Conf. Uniform State Laws (commr. 1974—). Home: 110 Cedar Dr Pikeville KY 41501 Office: 2d St Pikeville KY 41501 Tel (606) 437-7308

STRATTON, WAYNE THOMAS, b. Topeka, Dec. 16, 1933; A.B., Washburn U., 1955, J.D., 1958. Admitted to Kans. bar, 1958, U.S. Dist. Ct. Kans. bar, 1958, U.S. Supreme Ct. bar, 1969; asso. firm Ascough, Bausch, Johnson & Stratton, Topeka, 1960-61; asso. firm Goodell, Casey, Briman & Cogswell, and predecessors, 1961-63, partner, 1963—; adj. asso. prof. law Washburn U., 1968—. Mem. Topeka Bd. Edn., 1973—, pres., 1976. Mem. Am., Kans., Topeka bar assn., Kans. Assn. Def. Counsel, Am. Soc. Hosp. Attys., Internat. Assn. Ins. Counsel, Am. Judicature Soc. Home: 1719 Village Dr Topeka KS 66604 Office: 215 W 8th St Topeka KS 66603 Tel (913) 233-0593

STRAUB, CHESTER JOHN, b. Bklyn., May 12, 1937; B.A., St. Peter's Coll., 1958; LL.D., U. Va., 1961. Admitted to N.Y. State bar, 1962, Fed. Ct. So. and Eastern Dists. N.Y. bar, 1963, U.S. Ct. Appeals, 1967; asso. firm Willkie, Farr & Gallagher, N.Y.C., 1963-71, partner, 1971—; dir. Bklyn. Legal Services Corp. Vice chmn. Bklyn. Community Dist. Planning Bd.; finance chmn. Eastern Dist. com. Boy Scouts Am.; trustee Greenpoint YMCA; mem. N.Y. State Senate, 1973-75, N.Y. State Assembly, 1967-72; mem. Democratic Nat. Com.; vice chmn. N.Y.C. Dem. Com. Mem. Am., N.Y. State, Bklyn. bar assns., Assn. Bar City N.Y. Office: 1 Chase Manhattan Plaza New York City NY 10005 Tel (212) 248-1000

STRAUCH, IRVING MERRELL, b. Memphis, May 26, 1914; certificate U. Chgo., 1935; LL.B., U. Tenn., 1935, J.D., 1937. Admitted to Tenn. bar, 1937; asst. city atty., Memphis, 1938-41; prof. So. Law U., Memphis, 1938-64; individual practice law, Memphis, 1937-65; judge U.S. Circuit Ct., Memphis, 1965—. Mem. Bd. Commrs. for Promotion of Uniformity of Legis., 1968—; mem. Am. Uniform Law Commn. Formulated No-fault Auto Ins. Mem. Am. (law and medicine com.), Tenn., Memphis, Shelby County bar assns. Home: 75 S Rose Rd Memphis TN 38117 Office: Shelby County Ct House 140 Adams St Memphis TN 38103 Tel (901) 528-3022

STRAUS, KARL HERMAN, b. Mannheim, Ger., Feb. 7, 1921; LL.B., N.Y. U., 1950. Admitted to N.Y. bar, 1951, N.C. bar, 1953, U.S. Tax Ct., 1955; asst. to gen. supt. Ecusta Paper Corp., Pisgah Forest, N.C., 1938-43; investigator intelligence div. U.S. Treasury Dept., 1944-45; mem. firm Patla, Straus, Robinson & Moore, Asheville, N.C., 1953—; gen. counsel, dir. Sky City Stores, Inc.; dir. Mills Mfg. Corp., Western region Wachovia Bank & Trust Co. Pres., Federated Jewish Charities of Asheville, 1962-63; chmn. Heart Fund., Asheville, 1966-67; bd. dirs. Asheville Civic Arts Council, 1966-68, Asheville Baseball Club, 1968-70; Asheville-Buncombe County Community Relations Council, 1970-76; mem. Asheville-Buncombe County Sinking Fund Commn., 1968—; trustee Meml. Mission Hosp., Asheville, 1963-70, U. N.C., Asheville, 1975—. Mem. Am., N.C., Buncombe County (pres. 1970-71) bar assns. Home: 38 Lotus Pl Asheville NC 28804 Office: Gannett Bldg Asheville NC 28807 Tel (704) 255-7641

STRAUSER, ROBERT WAYNE, b. Little Rock, Aug. 28, 1943; B.A., Davidson Coll., 1965; postgrad. Vanderbilt U. Sch. Law, 1965-66; J.D., U. Tex. at Austin, 1968. Admitted to Tex. bar, 1968, U.S. Ct. Mil. Appeals bar, 1975; staff atty. Tex. Legis. Council, Austin, 1969-72; chief counsel jud. com. Tex. Ho. of Reps., Austin, 1972-73, judiciary com. Constl. Conv. Tex., 1974; exec. dir. Tex. Assn. Taxpayers, Austin, 1974—; lt. comdr. JAGC, U.S. Navy Res., 1971—. Mem. Am. Bar Assn., Naval Res. Assn., Am. Soc. Assn. Execs., Tex. Soc. Assn. Execs. Author: Franchising Litigation and Legislation, 1971. Home: 3204 Greenlee Dr Austin TX 78703 Office: 809 Southwest Tower 7th and Brazos sts Austin TX 78701 Tel (512) 472-8838

STRAUSS, BARRY MARK, b. N.Y.C., Feb. 7, 1942; B.S. in Commerce, N.Y. U., 1963, J.D., 1966; M.B.A., St. John's U., 1972. Admitted to N.Y. State bar, 1968; tax mgr. Price Waterhouse & Co., N.Y.C., 1968-72; tax atty. Lehman Bros. Inc., N.Y.C., 1972—; auditor Edelson Miller Ellin & Rosenblatt, N.Y.C., 1966-68. Active Boy Scouts Am., 1975—. Mem. N.Y. State Bar Assn., Am. Inst. C.P.A.'s, Bklyn. C. of C. Home: 25 Yale Ave Hewlett NY 11557 Office: One William St New York City NY 10004 Tel (212) 269-3700

STRAUSS, BENTON CHARLES, b. Chgo., Mar. 20, 1947; B.A., U. Ill., 1968; J.D., Loyola U., 1972. Admitted to Ill. bar, 1972; trust officer Am. Nat. Bank and Trust Co., Chgo., 1972-74; asso. firm Katten, Muchin, Gitles, Zavis, Pearl and Galler, Chgo., 1974—; instr. med. jurisprudence Chgo. Coll. Osteo. Medicine, Chgo., 1974—; cons. Nat. Bd. Examiners for Osteo. Physicians and Surgeons, Inc., 1975; cons. The Bus. Week Letter, 1976. Mem. Chgo. Bar Assn. (trust law com. 1975—, editor Young Lawyers Jour. 1974-75, com. on evaluation of candidates (jud. screening) 1976—, officer young lawyers sect. 1975-76), Ill., Am. bar assns. Home: 1842 Sunset Rd Highland Park IL 60035 Office: 55 E Monroe St Chicago IL 60603 Tel (312) 346-7400

STRAUSS, HENRY JAMES, b. Hallettsville, Tex., July 15, 1924; B.A., U. Tex., Austin, 1951, J.D., 1957; grad. U. Minn. Juvenile Ct. Judges Inst., 1967, Nat. Council Juvenile Ct. Judges Summer Coll. U. Colo., 1968. Med. technician hosps. labs., 1945-55; chemist, toxicologist Tex. Dept. Pub. Safety Lab., 1956-57; admitted to Tex. bar, 1957, practiced in Abilene, 1957—; asst. county atty. Taylor County (Tex.), 1961, county atty., 1962; judge Taylor County Ct. at Law, 1963, Taylor County Ct. of Domestic Relations, 1963—. Mem.

adv. bd. Abilene Girls Home, Marbridge House, Abilene, Pastoral Care and Counseling, Abilene; bd. dirs. Abilene Council on Alcholism, Inc.; v.p. trustees Anson James Meml. Med. Soc. Mem. State Bar Tex. (mem. family law council 1976—, mem. exec. com. jud. sect. 1976—), Abilene Bar Assn. Office: Taylor County Courthouse Abilene TX 79602 Tel (915) 677-1711

STRAUSS, PETER LESTER, b. N.Y.C., Feb. 26, 1940; A.B., Harvard, 1961; LL.B., Yale, 1964. Admitted to D.C. bar, 1965; fed. jud. clerkships, 1964-66; lectr. law Haile Sellassie I U., Addis Ababa, Ethiopia, 1966-68; asst. to solicitor gen. Dept. Justice, Washington, 1968-71; prof. law Columbia, 1971-75, 77—; gen. counsel U.S. Nuclear Regulatory Commn., Washington, 1975-77; chmn. com. on agy. decisional processes Adminstrv. Conf. U.S., 1976-77. Mem. Am. Bar Assn., Assn. Bar City N.Y. Editor: Fetha Negast, The Law of the Kings, 1968; contbr. articles to profl. jours. Home: 6417 Tone Dr Bethesda MD 20034 Office: Columbia Univ Law School New York City NY 10027 Tel (212) 280-2640

STREATER, HAROLD STOCKMAN, b. Winona, Minn., Feb. 4, 1917; A.B., Dartmouth, 1938; J.D., U. Mich., 1941. Admitted to Minn. bar, 1941; partner firm Streater, Murphy, Brosnahan & Langford, Winona, 1949—; city atty. City of Winona, 1951-61. Mem. Minn., Am. bar assns., Am. Coll. Probate Counsel. Office: 64 E 4th St Winona MN 55987 Tel (507) 454-2925

STREETER, HALFORD IVAN, b. Detroit, May 24, 1909; A.A., Port Huron Jr. Coll., 1929; B.A. with distinction, U. Mich., 1931, J.D., 1933. Admitted to Mich. bar, 1933; practiced in Port Huron, 1933-55; judge Mich. Circuit Ct., 31st Jud. Circuit, 1956—. Bd. dirs. St. Clair County Assn. Retarded Children, 1952—, Mich. Assn. Retarded Children, 1956—. Mem. St. Clair County (pres. 1940), Mich. State bar assns., Mich. Judges Assn., Mich. Forest Assn. Home: 2736 Strawberry Ln Port Huron MI 48060 Office: 234 County-City Bldg Port Huron MI 48060 Tel (313) 984-4434

STREIGHTOFF, FRANK DOAN, b. Muncie, Ind., Jan. 11, 1918; B.S. in Biology, Calif. Inst. Tech., 1940; M.S. in Botany, Butler U., 1956, B.S. in Bus., 1960, M.B.A., 1963; J.D., Ind. U., Indpls., 1970. Admitted to Ind. bar, 1970; lab. technician Allison div. Gen. Motors Corp., Speedway, Ind., 1941; biochemist biol. research div. Eli Lilly and Co., Indpls., 1942-70, patent technician, 1971-73, patent atty. fgn. patent dept., 1973—. Mem. bicentennial com., community devel. com. City of Franklin (Ind.), 1976. Mem. Ind. Bar Assn., Am. Patent Law Assn., Am. Chem. Soc., Am. Soc. Microbiology, Nat. Registry Microbiologists, Ind. Acad. Sci. Home: 250 N Home Ave Franklin IN 46131 Office: 307 E McCarty St Indianapolis IN 46206 Tel (317) 261-3385

STREIT, THOMAS JOHN, b. Aurora, Ill., Aug. 3, 1940; A.B., Marquette U., 1962; LL.B., U. Mich., 1965. Admitted to Ill. bar, 1965; asso. firm Lord, Bissell & Brook, Chgo., 1965-67; partner firm Dreyer, Foote & Streit Assos., Aurora, 1967—. Mem. Am., Kane County, Ill. bar assns. Home: 2361 Tanglewood Dr Aurora IL 60506 Office: 900 N Lake St Aurora IL 60506 Tel (312) 897-8764

STREKALL, STEPHEN JOHN, b. Helena, Mont., June 3, 1924; B.A. in Bus. Adminstrn., U. Mont., 1946, B.A. in Law, 1947, LL.B., 1948. Admitted to Mont. bar, 1948; accountant Price Waterhouse & Co., N.Y.C., 1948-49; asst. office mgr. Stanley H. Arkeright Inc., Billings, Mont., 1949-50; mgr. P. & R. Service Co., Billings, 1950-56; v.p. Empire Sand & Gravel Co., Billings, 1954-59; title officer Abstract Guaranty Co., 1959-73; mgr. 1st Am. Title & Escrow of Billings, 1973—; sec.-treas. Granite Const. Co., Billings, 1969-72. Mem. Mont., Yellowstone bar assns. Home: 2821 Terrace Dr Billings MT 59102 Office: 1216 16th St W Alpine Village N Suite 21 Billings MT 59102 Tel (406) 248-7877

STRICKLAND, EDWIN ANSEL, b. Birmingham, Ala., Apr. 5, 1939; B.S., U. Ala., 1961, LL.B., 1964. Admitted to Ala. bar, 1964; since practiced in Birmingham; served with JAGC, U.S. Army, 1964-67; partner firm Wingo, Bibb, Foster, Conwell & Strickland, 1967-76; county atty. Jefferson County (Ala.), 1976—. Mem. Am., Ala., Birmingham bar assns., Assn. R.R. Trial Counsel, Am. Soc. Hosp. Attys., Ala. Def. Lawyers Assn. Home: 3801 12th Ct S Birmingham AL 35222 Office: Room 213 Jefferson County Ct House Birmingham AL 35203 Tel (205) 325-5688

STRICKLAND, HOWARD JEROME, b. Port St. Joe, Fla., Feb. 8, 1940; student Auburn U., 1958-61; LL.B., Mercer U., 1964. Admitted to Ga. bar, 1963; asso. firm Shi & Raley, Macon, Ga., 1964-65, partner, 1965-66; asst. solicitor gen. Macon Jud. Circuit, 1966-68; asso. firm Jones, Cork, Miller & Benton, Macon, 1968-70, partner, 1970—; chmn. younger lawyers sect. Moot Ct. Competition, 1969; instr. Inst. Continuing Legal Edn., 1973, 74, 76. Chmn. Bibb County (Ga.) Young Republicans, 1965; mem. Bibb County Rep. Com., 1974—; bd. dirs. Macon Salvation Army, 1974—. Mem. Am., Macon bar assns., Am. Judicature Soc., State Bar Ga. (bd. govs. 1976—). Home: 7339 Wesley's Walk Macon GA 31204 Office: 500 1st Nat Bank Bldg Macon GA 31201 Tel (912) 745-2821

STRICKMAN, LEONARD PAUL, b. Bklyn., Apr. 14, 1942; A.B., U. Rochester, 1963; LL.B., Yale, 1966. Admitted to N.Y. bar, 1967, U.S. Supreme Ct. bar, 1972; asst. prof. law Boston U., 1966-68, asso. prof., 1968-70; minority counsel U.S. Senate Select Com. on Equal Ednl. Opportunity, 1970-72; asso. prof. Boston Coll., Newton Centre, Mass., 1972—; cons. Senate Com. on Labor and Pub. Welfare, 1973-75; mem. Mass. Health Facilities Appeals Bd., 1975—. Mem. Assn. Am. Law Schs. (Boston Coll. Law Sch. del. ho. of reps.). Office: 885 Centre St Newton Centre MA 02159 Tel (617) 969-0100

STRINGER, PHILIP, b. St. Paul, June 9, 1899; B.A., Yale, 1921; LL.B., Minn. Coll., 1923. Admitted to Minn. bar, 1923; partner firm O'Brien, Horn & Stringer, St. Paul, 1923-50, firm Stringer, Donnelly, Allen & Sharood, St. Paul, 1950-72, firm Stringer, Donnelly, Courtney, Cowie & Rohleder, St. Paul, 1972—. Chmn. St. Paul Charter Commn., 1948-68. Mem. Ramsey County (past pres.), Minn. State, Am. bar assns. Home: 716 Goodrich Ave Saint Paul MN 55105 Office: 1200 Northwestern Bank Bldg Saint Paul MN 55101 Tel (612) 227-7784

STRITEHOFF, JOHN CARROLL, JR., b. N.Y.C., July 4, 1928; B.A., Rutgers U., 1954, LL.B., 1957. Admitted to N.J. bar, 1958, U.S. Supreme Ct. bar, 1965; asso. firm Milmed and Rosen, Union City, N.J., 1958-61; individual practice law, Union City, 1961-66, Blairstown, N.J., 1966—; city prosecutor Weehawken (N.J.), 1960-66; judge N. Warren (N.J.) Municipal Ct., 1967—. Mem. N.J., Warren County (v.p.) bar assns. Home: R D 2 Blairstown NJ 07825 Office: Main St Blairstown NJ 07825 Tel (201) 362-6134

STROBAUGH, TERENCE PHILIP, b. Altoona, Pa., May 1, 1936; B.S. in Chemistry, St. Francis Coll., Loretto, Pa., 1960; M.S. in Chemistry, Villanova U., 1967; J.D., Temple U., 1972. Research chemist Merck Sharp & Dohme Research Labs., West Point, Pa., 1960-67; mem. patent dept. Merck & Co. Inc., West Point, 1967-73; admitted to Pa. bar, 1973; atty. Rohm & Haas Co., Phila., 1973—. Mem. Towamencin Twp. (Pa.) Bd. Suprs., 1976—. Mem. Pa. Bar Assn., Am., Phila. patent law assns.

STROBEL, MARTIN JACK, b. Bklyn., July 4, 1940; B.A., Columbia, 1962; J.D., Cleveland Marshall Law Sch., 1966. Admitted to Ohio bar, 1966; counsel Def. Supply Agy., Cleve., 1966-68, staff atty., 1968-69, mgr. contracts, 1969-70, gen. counsel, asst. sec. Dana Corp., Toledo, 1970-76, v.p., gen. counsel, 1976—. Mem. Fed., Am., Ohio, Toledo bar assns., Pub. Affairs Council, Machinery and Allied Products Inst. Office: PO Box 1000 Toledo OH 43601 Tel (419) 535-4650

STROBRIDGE, MAURICE EARL, b. Newark, N.Y., Feb. 2, 1925; A.B., Syracuse U., 1949; J.D., Albany Law Sch., 1952. Admitted to N.Y. bar, 1952, U.S. Supreme Ct. bar, 1958; asso. firm Nixon, Hargrave, Devans & Dey, Rochester, N.Y., 1952-54; partner firm Strobridge & Biddle, Newark, 1954-60; individual practice law, Newark, 1960—; town atty. Town of Macedon (N.Y.), 1957—; dist. atty. Wayne County, N.Y., 1962-65; village atty. Village of Newark, 1971—. Bd. dirs., v.p. Newark-Wayne Community Hosp., Inc., 1966-72. Mem. Am., N.Y. State, Wayne County bar assns. Home: 403 Grace Ave Newark NY 14513 Office: 605 Mason St Newark NY 14513 Tel (315) 331-0730

STRODE, JOSEPH ARLIN, b. DeWitt, Ark., Mar. 5, 1946; B.S. in Elec. Engring., U. Ark., 1969; J.D., So. Meth. U., 1972. Admitted to Ark. bar, 1972; elec. engr. Tex. Instruments, Inc., Dallas, 1969-70, mem. patent staff, 1970-72; asso. firm Bridges, Young, Matthews & Davis, Pine Bluff, Ark., 1972-74, partner, 1975—. Pres. Jefferson Wildlife Assn., 1974-76; bd. dirs. United Way Jefferson County, 1975—. Mem. Am., Ark., Jefferson County bar assns., Order of Coif. Home: 3112 Boone St Pine Bluff AR 71603 Office: 315 E 8th St Pine Bluff AR 71611 Tel (501) 534-5532

STRODE, WILLIAM CLAY, b. Kenosha, Wis., Sept. 26, 1929; B.A., U. Chgo., 1950; J.D., Stetson U., 1958. Admitted to Fla. bar, 1958, U.S. Dist. Ct. bar, 1959, 5th Circuit Ct. bar, 1965; asso. firm C. L. McKaig, Sarasota, Fla., 1959-63; partner firm Strode, Hereford & Taylor, and predecessors, Sarasota, 1964—; asst. state atty. 12th Jud. Circuit Fla., Sarasota, 1963-70; city atty. City of Sarasota, 1970—; chmn. Sarasota County Charter Rev. Bd., 1970. Bd. dirs. Ringling Mus. Member's Council, 1974-76, trustee mus., 1976—. Office: 46 N Washington Blvd Sarasota FL 33577

STROHECKER, ALBERT JACOB, III, b. Reading, Pa., Feb. 27, 1946; B.A. in Polit. Sci., U. Pa., 1968; J.D., Boston U., 1971. Admitted to Pa. bar, 1971; asso. firm Balmer, Mogel, Speidel & Roland, Reading, 1971-75; asst. atty. gen., hearing examiner, counsel to liquidation div. Commonwealth Pa. Ins. Dept., Harrisburg, 1975—; trial counsel Pa. N.G., 1976—. Home: 4907 Bretney Dr Harrisburg PA 17112 Office: Room 411 Finance Bldg Harrisburg PA 17120 Tel (717) 783-8862

STROM, LOUIS JOHN, b. Omaha, Jan. 6, 1925; B.M.E., U. Nebr., 1950; J.D., Creighton U., 1959. Admitted to Nebr. bar, U.S. Patent Ct. bar, 1967; cons. No. Natural Gas Co., Omaha, 1959-64; asso. H. Robert Henderson, 1964-67; partner firm Henderson, Strom & Sturm, Omaha, 1967—; lectr. law Creighton U., 1968—. Mem. Am., Nebr., Omaha bar assns. Home: 3022 S 106th St Omaha NE 68124 Office: 990 Woodmen Tower Omaha NE 68102 Tel (402) 342-1797

STROMBERG, ARNOLD FERDINAND, b. St. Paul, June 3, 1909; student U. Minn., 1936-40; LL.B., St. Paul Coll. Law, 1950. Admitted to Minn. bar, 1950; mem. firm Faricy Burger Moore & Costello, St. Paul, 1951-60; individual practice law, St. Paul, 1960—. Mem. Minn., Ramsey County (Minn.), Am. bar assns., Phi Beta Gamma. Home: 1507 Duluth St Saint Paul MN 55106 Office: 1507 Duluth St Saint Paul MN 55106 Tel (612) 776-5571

STROMBERG, ROSS ERNEST, b. Arcata, Calif., May 5, 1940; A.B., Humboldt State U., 1962; LL.B., U. Calif. at Berkeley, 1965. Admitted to Calif. bar, 1966; asso. firm Hanson, Bridgett & Marcus and predecessor, San Francisco, 1965-70, partner 1970—. Bd. dirs. East Bay Found. for Health Careers Edn., 1975—. Mem. Am. Soc. Hosp. Attys. (pres. elect 1977-78, bd. dirs. 1973—), San Francisco Bar Assn., Am. Judicature Soc. Home: 475 Boynton Ave Berkeley CA 94707 Office: One Kearny St San Francisco CA 94108 Tel (415) 781-5500

STROMER, DUANE LEE, b. Glenvil, Neb., Sept. 9, 1935; B.C.E., Rensselaer Poly. Inst., 1959; J.D., U. Denver, 1966. Admitted to Colo. bar, 1966, Neb. bar, 1966; house counsel Kans.-Nebr. Natural Gas Co. Inc., 1966-71; partner firm Conway, Connolly & Stromer, Hastings, Nebr., 1971-74; partner, head trial sect. firm Nelson, Harding, Madehetti, Leonard & Tate, Lincoln, Nebr., 1974—; city atty. City of Hastings, 1971-74. Mem. Nebr., Am. bar assns. Tel (402) 475-6761

STRONG, DEWITT JOHN, b. Rice Lake, Wis., Aug. 28, 1946; B.S., U. Wis., Madison, 1968, J.D., 1971. Admitted to Wis. bar, 1971; mem. firm Klein, Kuemmel & Schmidt, S.C., Madison, Wis. Mem. Am., Dane County bar assns., State Bar Wis., Mensa. Office: 301 N Hamilton St Madison WI 53703 Tel (608) 255-8199

STRONG, JACK BOYNTON, b. Carthage, Tex., Feb. 18, 1930; B.A., U. Tex., 1950, J.D., 1952. Admitted to Tex. bar, 1952; mem. firm Roberts, Harbour, Smith, Harris, French & Ritter, Longview, Tex., 1973—; mem. Tex. Senate, 1963-71. Home: 605 Noel Dr Longview TX 75601 Office: 404 N Green St Longview TX 75601 Tel (214) 757-4001

STRONG, WILLIAM KENDRICK, b. Madison, Wis., Aug. 8, 1935; B.A., Beloit Coll., 1957; J.D., U. Mich., 1960. Admitted to Ariz. bar, 1961; asso. firm Tognoni, Parsons & Gooding, Phoenix, 1961-64; partner firm Tognoni & Pugh, Phoenix, 1965-71; prin. firm Strong and Pugh, Phoenix, 1972—; faculty asso. Ariz. State U., 1971—. Mem. Am., Maricopa County bar assns., Assn. Trial Lawyers. Home: 7729 N 4th Ave Phoenix AZ 85021 Office: 2701 N 7th St Phoenix AZ 85007 Tel (602) 263-9759

STROTHER, GEORGE BEAUREGARD, IV, b. Duluth, Minn., Apr. 20, 1949; B.A., in Economics, Carleton Coll., 1971; J.D., U. Wis., 1974. Admitted to Wis. bar, 1974; since practiced in Madison, Wis., hearing examiner State of Wis., 1975; law clk. to Judge Norris Maloney, Dane County Circuit Ct., 1975-76; staff atty. Dane County Legal Services, Inc., 1976—. Mem. Wis. State, Dane County (mem. legal aid com.) bar assns. Home: 105 N Yellowstone Dr Madison WI 53705 Office: 16 N Carroll St Madison WI 53703 Tel (608) 262-0626

STROUD, JOHN FRED, JR., b. Hope, Ark., Oct. 3, 1931; student Hendrix Coll., 1949-51, Syracuse U., 1951-52; B.A., U. Ark., 1959, LL.B., 1960. Admitted to Ark. bar, 1959, U.S. Supreme Ct. bar, 1963; mem. firm Smith, Stroud, McClerkin, Conway & Dunn and predecessors, Texarkana, Ark., 1959—; atty. City of Texarkana, 1961-62; legis. asst. to U.S. senator John L. McClellan, 1962-63; spl. justice Ark. Supreme Ct.; chmn. Ark. Bar Found., 1975. Chmn. Texarkana Airport Authority, 1969; chmn. Texarkana Indsl. Found. com., 1974-75; campaign chmn. Texarkana United Way, 1977. Mem. Texarkana C of C (pres. 1969), Miller County (pres. 1968), Am., Ark., SW Ark., Texarkana bar assns., Am. Coll. Probate Counsel, Red River Valley Assn. (v.p. 1974-75). Recipient Silver Beaver award Caddo Area council Boy Scouts Am., 1974; Exceptional Accomplishment award Ark. State C. of C., 1973; named Texarkana's Oustanding Young Man, Texarkana Jaycees, 1966. Home: 208 Georgian Terr Texarkana AR 75502 Office: State Line Plaza Suite 6 Texarkana AR 75502 Tel (501) 773-5651

STROUPE, ODES LAWRENCE, JR., b. Charlotte, N.C., Mar. 10, 1946; B.A. in Polit. Sci., N.C. State U., 1968; J.D. with honors, U. N.C., Chapel Hill, 1971. Admitted to N.C. bar, 1971; asso. firm Joyner & Howison, Raleigh, N.C., 1971-76, partner, 1976—. Mem. Am. (sect. anti-trust law), N.C., Wake County (chmn. young lawyers sect. 1974-76, dir. 1974-77) bar assns. Bd. editors, contbr. articles N.C. Law Rev. Home: 1029 Cedarhurst Dr Raleigh NC 27609 Office: 906 Wachovia Bldg Raleigh NC 27609 Tel (919) 828-9371

STROUSE, HARRY DUNLAP, JR., b. Rochester, N.Y., Oct. 21, 1923; student Miami U., Oxford, Ohio, 1941-42, 45-47; LL.B., U. Mich., 1950, J.D., 1950. Admitted to Ill. bar, 1950; 1st asst. state's atty. Lake County (Ill.), 1956; asst. U.S. atty No. Dist. Ill., 1956-58; police magistrate 4th Jud. Div. of Lake County, 1960-63; practiced in Waukegan, Ill., 1958-66; asso. judge Circuit Ct., 1966-68; judge Ill. Circuit Ct., 19th Jud. Circuit, 1968—, chief judge, 1974—; mem. faculty Ill. Jud. Conf., 1968, 71, 73; trial judge U. Ill. Law Sch. Office: 312 Courthouse Waukegan IL 60085 Tel (312) 689-6322

STROUSE, JOHN FRANKLYN, JR., b. N.Y.C., Oct. 29, 1930; A.B., Manhattan Coll., 1952; LL.B., Fordham U., 1955. Admitted to N.Y. bar, 1955, Mass. bar, 1971; trial atty. firm Burke & Mahoney, Burlington, Mass., 1971—. Mem. Fin. Com. Town of Westboro, 1974-76, 76-79. Mem. Mass., Worcester County bar assns. Home: 5 Valley Brook Rd Westboro MA 01581 Office: 31 Burlington Mall Rd Burlington MA 01803 Tel (617) 273-1270

STROUT, ARTHUR EDWARDS, b. Rockland, Maine, Sept. 6, 1935; A.B., Bowdoin Coll., 1957; LL.B., Harvard, 1960. Admitted to Maine bar, 1960, D.C. bar, 1964; law clk. U.S. Ct. Appeals 9th Circuit, 1960-61; trial lawyer tax div. U.S. Dept. Justice, 1961-64; partner firm Strout, Payson, Pellicani & Cloutier, Rockland, 1968—. Trustee Penobscot Bay Med. Center, 1973—. Mem. Maine Bar Assn. Office: 7 Masonic St Box 248 Rockland ME 04841 Tel (207) 594-8470

STRUBBE, THOMAS RUDOLPH, b. Ft. Wayne, Ind., Mar. 30, 1940; B.S., Ind. U., 1962; J.D., Tulane U., 1965. Admitted to Ind. bar, 1965, Ill. bar, 1969; mem. legal dept. The Lincoln Nat. Life Ins. Co., Ft. Wayne, 1965-68, asst. counsel, 1967-68; mem. legal dept. Washington Nat. Corp., Evanston, 1968—, v.p., gen. counsel, sec., 1974—. Bd. dirs. Epilepsy, Found. Am., 1975—; mem. bd. Christian Outreach, Glencoe Union Ch., 1974—. Mem. Am. Bar Assn., Assn. Life Ins. Counsel, Am. Soc. Corp. Secs. Home: 230 Fairview Rd Glencoe IL 60022 Office: 1630 Chicago Ave Evanston IL 60201 Tel (312) 866-3025

STRUCKMEYER, FRED CHRISTIAN, JR., b. Phoenix, Jan. 4, 1912; LL.B., U. Ariz., 1936. Admitted to Ariz. bar, 1936; practiced in Phoenix, 1936-39, 46-50; dep. county atty. Maricopa County (Ariz.), 1939-42; spl. legal adviser Maricopa County Pub. Schs., 1946-50; trial judge Maricopa County Superior Ct., 1950-55; justice Ariz. Supreme Ct., 1955—, chief justice, 1960, 61, 66, 71. Recipient Charles D. Poston award Urban League, 1955, award of Distinguished Service Greater Phoenix Council for Civic Unity, 1955, 75th Anniversary medallion of Merit U. Ariz., 1960, Distinguished Citizen award U. Ariz. Alumni Assn., 1975. Home: 7151 N 3d St Phoenix AZ 85020 Office: 213 S-W Wing State Capitol Bldg Phoenix AZ 85007 Tel (602) 271-4532

STRUK, THEODORE O., b. Pitts., Aug. 21, 1932; B.A., Pa. State U., 1954; LL.B., U. Pa., 1957. Admitted to Pa. bar, U.S. Supreme Ct. bar, 1966; atty., house counsel staff Philco Corp., 1957; adminstrv. asst. to U.S. Dist. Ct., 1958-61; asso. firm Griggs, Moreland, Blair & Douglas, Pitts., 1961-62; asso. firm Dickie, McCamey & Chilcote, Pitts., 1962, now partner. Mem. Am., Pa., Allegheny County bar assns., Fedn. Ins. Counsel, Phi Beta Kappa. Home: 113 Siebert Rd Pittsburgh PA 15237 Tel (412) 281-7272

STRUNCK, JAMES EMMETT, b. Chgo., Jan. 4, 1920; B.S., U. Ill., 1948; J.D., Chgo-Kent Coll. Law, 1950; grad. Nat. Coll. State Judiciary U. Nev., Reno, 1972. Admitted to Ill. bar, 1950, U.S. Ct. Mil. Appeals bar, 1958; served with Judge Adv. Gen. Corps USAF, 1951-53; asst. corp. counsel in charge aviation and contracts dept. law City of Chgo., 1953-69; legal staff officer Ill. Air N.G., 1953-70; asso. judge Circuit Ct. of Cook County (Ill.), 1970, judge, 1971—; mem. Ill. Senate, 1958-62; mem. jet aircraft noise panel Exec. Office of Pres., 1966; chmn. com. on aviation law Nat. Inst. Municipal Law Officers, 1966-70; mem. Ill. Constl. Conv., 1969-70; mem. com. planning and goals World Peace Through Law Center. Mem. World Assn. Lawyers (founding), World Assn. Judges, Am., Fed., Ill. State, Chgo. bar assns., Am. Judicature Soc. Contbr. articles to legal jours. Office: Criminal Ct of Cook County 26th and S California Ave Chicago IL 60608 Tel (312) 542-3171

STRUNK, JOHN ANDREW, b. Scranton, Pa., Mar. 17, 1927; B.E., E. Stroudsburg State Coll., 1950; J.D., Temple U., 1954. Admitted to Pa. bar, 1969; estate tax atty. IRS, Phila., Scranton, Pa., 1955—. Mem. Pa., Lackawanna County bar assns. Home: 3 Cross Dr Scranton PA 18505 Office: 125 N Washington Ave Scranton PA 18503 Tel (717) 344-7111

STRUVE, LARRY D., b. Los Angeles, Oct. 30, 1942; B.A., U. Nev., 1964; M.A., Tufts U., 1965; J.D., U. Calif., 1968. Admitted to Nev. bar, 1968; asso. firm Wait & Shamberger, Reno, 1969-71; dep. dist. atty. Washoe County (Nev.), 1971-74, chief civil dep. dist. atty., 1975—; mem. Nev. Pub. Works Bd., 1973—. Bd. dirs. ARC, 1971-72. Mem., Am., Nev., Washoe County bar assns., Nat. Dist. Attys. Assn., Am. Judicature Soc., U. Nev. Alumni Assn. (pres. 1973-74), Phi Alpha Delta. Recipient Community Service award United Way, 1971;

contbr. articles to legal jours. Office: PO Box 2008 Reno NV 89505 Tel (702) 785-5670

STUART, GARY LESTER, b. Gallup, N.Mex., Oct. 8, 1939; B.S., U. Ariz., 1965, J.D., 1967. Admitted to Ariz. bar, 1967; partner firm Jennings, Strouss & Salmon, Phoenix, 1967—; mem., chmn. ethics com. State Bar Ariz. Vice pres. bd. dirs. Moon Valley Homeowners Assn., Phoenix, 1974—; bd. visitors U. Ariz., 1974—. Mem. Am. Bar Assn., Am. Arbitration Assn., Am. Judicature Soc., State Bar Ariz., Phoenix Assn. Def. Counsel, Def. Research Inst., Am. Bd. Trial Advs. Author, editor Ariz. Law Rev., 1964-67. Home: 618 W Moon Valley Dr Phoenix AZ 85023 Office: 111 W Monroe Phoenix AZ 85003 Tel (602) 262-5895

STUART, HARVEY, b. N.Y.C., Aug. 20, 1929; A.B., U. Mich., 1950; J.D., N.Y. U., 1965. Admitted to N.Y. bar, 1965, N.J. bar, 1973; mem. law dept. CBS, N.Y.C., 1965-66; individual practice law, N.Y.C., 1966-67, N.Y.C. and Oceanport, N.J., 1973-75; asso. firm Jack S. Hoffinger, N.Y.C., 1968; mem. firms Hoffinger & Stuart, N.Y.C., 1969-73, Stuart & Zavin, N.Y.C., 1976—; arbitrator small claims div. Civil Ct. of N.Y.C., 1972—. Mem. N.J., N.Y. State bar assns., Bar Assn. City N.Y., Assn. Arbitrators, Order of Coif. Mem. staff N.Y. U. Law Rev., 1963-65. Home: 33 Wardell Circle Oceanport NJ 07757 Office: 60 E 42d St New York NY 10017 Tel (212) 661-5380

STUART, JOHN MARBERGER, b. N.Y.C., Apr. 3, 1927; A.B., Columbia, 1948, J.D., 1951. Admitted to N.Y. bar, 1951, U.S. Supreme Ct. bar, 1955; asso. firm Reid & Priest, N.Y.C., 1951-64, partner, 1965—. Mem. Am. Bar Assn., N.Y. County Lawyers Assn. Home: 31 Westgate Blvd Plandome NY 11030 Office: 40 Wall St New York City NY 10005 Tel (212) 344-2233

STUART, ROBERT ALLAN, b. Sheridan, Wyo., Mar. 11, 1917; student U. Wyo., 1934-35; A.B., U. Mich., 1938, J.D., 1941. Admitted to Wyo. bar, 1941, Ill. bar, 1941, U.S. Supreme Ct. bar, 1950; asso. firm Brown, Hay & Stephens, Springfield, Ill., 1941-56, partner, 1956—; gen. counsel Ill. Assn. Park Dists., 1954—; prof. law Lincoln Coll. Law, Springfield, 1948-52. Pres. Springfield Park Bd., 1954-75; pres. Boys Farm Found., Springfield, 1964-66; chmn. Lincoln Home Dist., Boy Scouts Am., 1948-74; mem. council bd. Abraham Lincoln Council, 1948-74; mem. Springfield Regional Plan Commn., 1968-74; bd. dirs. Springfield Auditorium Authority, 1965-70; mem. Youth Commn. Springfield YMCA, 1948-65; mem. Gov.'s Torts Law Commn., 1960-64, Gov.'s Adv. Council to Dept. Local Govt. Affairs, 1968-73; trustee Nat. Recreation and Park Assn., 1968—; bd. dirs. Nat. Recreation Found., 1975—; mem. nat. council Boy Scouts Am., 1960-74; mem. com. of visitors U. Mich. Law Sch., 1967—. Mem. Sangamon County, Ill., Wyo. State, Am. (nat. sec., v.p. Jr. Bar Conf. 1950-53) bar assns., Met. Bar Assn. St. Louis. Author legal and legislative notes col. Illinois Parks and Recreation Mag., 1954—. Home: 2100 Wiggins Ave Springfield IL 62704 Office: 700 1st Nat Bank Bldg Springfield IL 62701 Tel (217) 544-8491

STUBBLEFIELD, DWIGHT LYMAN, b. Amarillo, Tex., Feb. 6, 1941; B.B.A., So. Meth. U., 1963, J.D., 1966. Admitted to Tex. bar, 1966; partner firm Clayton & Stubblefield, Amarillo, 1968—. Mem. Am., Tex., Amarillo (past chmn. legal aid com.) bar assns., Am. Dairy Goat Assn. (dir., pres.). Home: 6809 Green Haven Rd Amarillo TX 79110 Office: 2506 W 45th St Amarillo TX 79109 Tel (806) 355-4441

STUBBS, MILLARD FRANCIS, b. Glennville, Ga., Mar. 4, 1943; B.A. in Polit. Sci., Economics, Ga. So. Coll., 1966; J.D., Mercer U., 1969. Admitted to Ga. bar, 1970; individual practice law, Reidsville, Ga., 1970—; mem. legal com. environ. defense fund Sierra Club, Nat. Wildlife Fedn., 1972—; pub. defender Atlantic Jud. Circuit Ga., 1973; judge Municipal Ct., Collins, Ga., 1975—; city atty., Reidsville, 1976; atty. Hosp. Authority, Reidsville Housing Authority. Mem. Am., Ga. bar assns., Ga. Trial Lawyers' Assn., Am. Judicature Soc. Home: Route 1 Box 92 Collins GA 30421 Office: PO Box 325 Brazell St Reidsville GA 30453 Tel (912) 557-4781

STUBBS, ROBERT SHERWOOD, II, b. St. Louis, Nov. 11, 1922; A.B., Univ. Ala., 1942; J.D. with distinction, George Washington U., 1952. Admitted to D.C. bar, 1952, Ala., 1952, Hawaii, 1957, Ga. bar, 1968; prof. law, Emory U., Atlanta, 1963-73, adj. prof., 1976; exec. asst. atty. gen., Ga. State Law Dept., Atlanta, 1973—. Mem. Decatur-DeKalb Bar Assn., Atlanta Lawyers Club, Am. Judicature Soc. Home: 2599-B Pilgrim Way NE Atlanta GA 30345 Office: 132 State Judicial Building Atlanta GA 30334 Tel (404) 656-3305

STUBENBERG, JAMES ARTHUR, b. Honolulu, Mar. 9, 1944; B.B.A., So. Meth. U., 1966; J.D., Loyola U., Los Angeles, 1970. Admitted to Hawaii bar, 1970; partner firm Stubenberg, Shigemura, Roney & Gniffke, Honolulu, 1974—. Mem. Am., Hawaii bar assns. Home: 995 Kalapaki St Honolulu HI 96821 Office: Ten Marin St Honolulu HI 96817 Tel (808) 524-0933

STUCKI, HANS ULRICH, b. Spiez, Switzerland, Apr. 29, 1948; B.A., Ohio State U., 1970; J.D., U. Notre Dame, 1974. Admitted to Ohio bar, 1974; asso. firm Buckingham, Doolittle & Burroughs, Akron, Ohio, 1974—. Home: 1056 Endicott Akron OH 44313 Office: 1 Cascade Plaza Akron OH 44313 Tel (216) 376-5300

STUDDARD, KENNETH EARL, b. O'Donnell, Tex., Aug. 10, 1931; B.B.A., U. Tex., 1954, LL.B., 1957. Admitted to Tex. bar, 1957; accountant, partner Phillips, Sheffield, Hopson, Lewis & Luther, Houston, 1957-63, Haskins & Sells (merger Phillips, Sheffield, Hopson, Lewis & Luther and Haskins & Sells), Houston, 1963-77, N.Y.C., 1977—. Pres., dir. Florence Crittenton Services, Houston, 1972-77. Mem. State Bar Tex., Am. Inst. C.P.A.'s, Tex. Soc. C.P.A.'s (gen. chmn. 10th tax inst. 1963), Houston Estate and Fin. Forum (dir. 1969-74), Houston Bus. and Estate Planning Council (pres. 1974). Office: 1114 Ave of Americas New York City NY 10036 Tel (212) 422-9600

STUDER, DONALD EDWARD, b. Cleve., Sept. 3, 1930; B.S. with honors, U. Fla., 1963; J.D. magna cum laude, U. San Diego, 1968. Admitted to Calif. bar, 1969, U.S. Supreme Ct. bar, 1972; individual practice law, San Diego, 1969-71, 73—; asso. firm Brundage Williams & Zellmann, San Diego, 1971-72. Mem. San Diego Bar Assn., Indsl. Relations Research Assn. San Diego, Phi Kappa Phi, Sigma Pi Sigma, Sigma Tau Sigma, Phi Delta Phi. Asso. editor U. San Diego Law Rev., 1967-68. Home: 15812 Lime Grove Rd Poway CA 92064 Office: 4161 Home Ave San Diego CA 92105 Tel (714) 263-6661

STUDHOLME, JOSEPH GRAY, b. Smethport, Pa., Dec. 30, 1914; B.A., U. Wis., 1937; J.D., U. Denver, 1957. Admitted to Colo. bar, 1957; mem. firm McDougal & Studholme, and predecessors, 1959-63, firm Rogers, McLain & Studholme, 1963-70; municipal judge City of Lakewood (Colo.), 1970—. Chmn. Lakewood Park and Recreation Dist. Bd., 1965-69. Mem. Am., Colo., Denver bar assns., Am. Judges Assn. Home: 110 S Yukon St Lakewood CO 80226 Office: 44 Union Blvd Lakewood CO 80228 Tel (303) 234-8636

STUMBERG, IONE STEELE (MRS. GEORGE WILFRED STUMBERG), b. Franklin, Tex., Sept. 25, 1902; B.A., Baylor Coll., 1922, LL.B., U. Tex., Austin, 1937. Admitted to Tex. bar, 1937; research asst. Law Sch. U. Tex., 1964-67; com. revision Texas Penal Code, 1968-69; briefing atty. Tex. Supreme Ct., 1942-43; atty. Tex. State Senate, 1969—. Home: 1201 Gaston Ave Austin TX 78703 Office: Room G-28 State Capitol Austin TX 78701 Tel (512) 472-3249 also 475-3083

STUMP, GARY LEE, b. Paris, Ky., Jan. 22, 1944; B.S. in Social Welfare, Fla. State U., 1966, J.D., 1969. Admitted to Fla. bar, 1969; partner Whittaker, Pyle & Stump, Orlando and Oviedo, Fla. Mem. Orange County, Seminole County bar assns., Delta Tau Kappa. Office: 130 Marks St Orlando FL 32803 Tel (305) 425-2583

STUPAR, BRANKO, b. Washington, Pa., Nov. 24, 1922; B.A., Muskingum Coll., 1947; student Ohio Wesleyan Coll., 1943-44; J.D., Am. U., 1951. Admitted to D.C. bar, 1951, Md. bar, 1961, U.S. Supreme Ct., 1975; atty. FHA, Washington, 1954; partner firm Faulkner, Shands, Stupar & Tucker, Washington, 1954—. Republican nominee Ho. of Reps., 26th Dist. Pa., 1954. Mem. Am., Fed., D.C., Md. bar assns., Counsellors D.C. Home: 9115 Harrington Dr Potomac MD 20854 Office: 910 16th St NW Washington DC 20006 Tel (202) 466-8585

STURGES, WILLIAM SIMS, b. Le Mars, Iowa, Oct. 31, 1927; B.S., U. Nebr., 1951, J.D., 1953. Admitted to Iowa bar, 1953; partner firm Sturges & Sturges, Le Mars, 1953—; atty. Plymouth County (Iowa), 1955-72. Sec., Le Mars Ind. Sch. Dist., 1957-64. Mem. Phi Delta Phi. Home: 35 9th St SW Le Mars IA 51031 Office: 16 2d St SE Le Mars IA 51031 Tel (712) 546-7861

STURGIS, JOHN WILLIAM, b. Portland, Maine, Apr. 16, 1909; B.A., U. Maine, 1931; J.D., Harvard, 1934. Admitted to Maine bar, 1934, U.S. Supreme Ct. bar, 1976; individual practice law, Portland, 1934—. Mayor City of Portland, 1970, mem. City Council, 1968-77; mem. Portland Sch. Com., 1946-67. Mem. Cumberland County, Maine bar assns. Home: 88 Mackworth St Portland ME 04103 Office: 415 Congress St Portland ME 04111 Tel (207) 772-2876

STURM, MICHAEL OWEN, b. Fairbury, Nebr., Nov. 8, 1943; B.S., Iowa State U., 1966; J.D., Cath. U. Am., 1973. Admitted to Va. bar, 1973, Iowa bar, 1974; patent examiner U.S. Patent Office, Washington, 1966-71; patent advisor U.S. Office Naval Research, Arlington, Va., 1971-73; asso. firm Henderson & Strom, Des Moines, 1973-75; partner firm Henderson, Strom & Sturm, Des Moines, 1976—. Mem. Am., Iowa bar assns., Am., Iowa (treas. 1976) patent law assns., Patent Office Soc. (asso.). Recipient Spl. Achievement award Office Naval Research, 1972; contbr. articles to profl. jours. Home: Rt 2 Winterset IA 50273 Office: 1213 Savings and Loan Bldg Des Moines IA 50309 Tel (515) 288-9589

STURTZ, LAURENCE EDWARD, b. Rockville Centre, N.Y., Dec. 31, 1942; B.A. in Econs., Ohio State U., 1964, J.D., 1967. Admitted to Ohio bar, 1967, U.S. Supreme Ct. bar, 1972; asso. firm Brownfield, Kosydar, Folk, Yearling & Dilenschneider, Columbus, Ohio, 1967-70; partner firm Brownfield, Kosydar, Bowen, Bally & Sturtz, Columbus, 1971—; dir., gen. counsel Hosp. Audiences, Inc., Columbus; gen. counsel Columbus chpt. Am. Youth Hostels; spl. counsel Ohio Soc. Crippled Children and Adults. Mem. Am., Ohio, Columbus bar assns., Ohio Assn. Trial Lawyers, First Amendment, Am., Franklin County trial lawyers assns. Home: 4540 Helston Ct Columbus OH 43215 Office: 140 E Town St Columbus OH 43215 Tel (614) 221-5834

STURTZ, WILLIAM ROSENBERG, b. Albert Lea, Minn., Apr. 7, 1925; B.A., U. Mich., 1948, J.D., 1951; grad. Nat. Coll. Juvenile Justice, 1971, Nat. Coll. State Judiciary, 1974 (both U. Nev.). Admitted to Minn. bar, 1951; since practiced in Albert Lea; mem. firm Meighen, Knudson, Sturtz & Peterson, 1951-59, Sturtz, Peterson, Sturtz & Butler, 1959-69; judge Probate and Juvenile Ct. Freeborn County, Albert Lea, 1969-72; judge County Ct. (Freeborn), Albert Lea, 1972—; instr. Lea Coll., 1967-72. Mem. Freeborn County, Minn. bar assns., Minn. State Judges Assn., Nat. Council Juvenile Ct. Judges. Home: 209 Ridge Rd Albert Lea MN 56007 Office: Court House Albert Lea MN 56007 Tel (507) 373-0624

STUTH, HARRY PETER, JR., b. Corpus Christi, Tex., Dec. 26, 1929; B.A., St. Mary's U., San Antonio, 1951; J.D., 1952. Admitted to Tex. bar, 1952; individual practice law Corpus Christi, 1952-64; pres. Fin. Advisors, Dallas, 1970—. Mem. Tex., Dallas bar assns., Soc. Casualty and Property Underwriters. Home: 3778 Brookhaven Club Dr Dallas TX 75234 Tel (214) 247-2207

STUTSMAN, CARL ALLEN, JR., b. Los Angeles, Oct. 13, 1913; A.B., U. So. Calif., 1934, LL.B., 1937. Admitted to Calif. bar, 1937, U.S. Supreme Ct. bar, 1943, Mass. bar, 1944; chief atty. Bd. Econ. Warfare, Washington, 1942-44; sr. atty., office chief counsel IRS, Washington, 1944-46; mem. firms Overton Lyman & Plumb, 1946-50, Hill Farrer & Burrill, 1950—; individual practice law, Los Angeles, 1937-43. Bd. dirs. Los Angeles Town Hall. Mem. Am. (bd. tax sect.), Los Angeles bar assns., Am. Arbitration Assn., Internat. Fiscal Assn. Office: 3400 Union Bank Sq Los Angeles CA 90071 Tel (213) 620-0460

SUBRANNI, ROBERT PETER, b. Phila., Aug. 8, 1940; A.B., Rutgers U., 1962; J.D., Villanova U., 1965. Admitted to N.J. bar, 1966; dep. atty. gen. N.J., 1966-67; asst. pros. atty. Atlantic County (N.J.), 1967; acting dir. Cape Atlantic Legal Services, 1968-69; individual practice law, Atlantic City, 1969—; asso. prof. bus. law Atlantic Community Coll., 1970—; legal counsel N.J. Jaycees, 1974-76; counsel Shore Meml. Hosp. Nursing Assn., Inc. Mem. Am., Atlantic County, N.J. bar assns., Am. Trial Lawyers Assn., Am. Judicature Soc. Recipient Presidential Keyman award N.J. Jaycees, 1975. Home and Office: 1624 Pacific Ave Atlantic City NJ 08401 Tel (609) 348-2524

SUCHMAN, STEWART RICHARD, b. N.Y.C., May 18, 1942; B.A., U. Calif., Los Angeles, 1966; J.D., Hastings Coll. Law, 1969. Admitted to Calif. bar, 1970; atty. Calif. Dept. Corps., San Francisco, 1970-71; partner firm Oster, Millard & Suchman, Santa Ana, Calif., 1971—. Mem. Calif., Orange County bar assns., Bar Assn. San Francisco. Office: 444 W 10th St Santa Ana CA 92701 Tel (714) 543-8477

SUCHOZA, JOSEPH ARNOLD, b. Pottstown, Pa., Nov. 23, 1928; B.A., Ursinus Coll., 1950; LL.B., U. Pa., 1953. Admitted to Pa. bar, 1954; individual practice law, Pottstown, 1956-61; asso. firm O'Donnell, Weiss, Mattei, Koury & Suchoza, Pottstown, 1961—; solicitor Pottstown Sch. Dist., 1963-65, Pottstown Borough Authority, 1972-73; councilman Borough of Pottstown, 1958-60. Sec. Police Pension Fund Com., 1960-65; mayor Borough of Pottstown, 1966-70; mem. Brandywine Battlefield Commn., 1977—. Mem. Pa., Montgomery bar assns., Montgomery County Trial Lawyers Assn. Recipient Robert S. Trucksess prize, 1950; named Jaycee Young Man of Year, 1961. Home: 938 Spruce St Pottstown PA 19464 Office: 41 High St Pottstown PA 19464

SUDARSKY, REUBEN, b. Russia, Feb. 11, 1903; B.C.S., N.Y. U., 1924, LL.B., 1927. Admitted to Conn. bar, 1928; partner firm Sudarsky & Sudarsky, Hartford, Conn., 1933—. Mem. Am., Conn., Hartford County bar assns. Home: 47 Hillsboro Dr West Hartford CT 06107 Office: 1 Constitution Plaza Hartford CT 06103 Tel (203) 525-3467

SUDWEEKS, JAY DEAN, b. Fort Peck, Mont., June 10, 1940; A.A., Ricks Coll., 1960; B.S., Brigham Young U., 1966; J.D., U. Utah, 1969. Admitted to Idaho bar, 1969, U.S. Supreme Ct. bar, 1973; partner firm May May Sudweeks & Fuller, Twin Falls, Idaho, 1969—. Bd. dirs. United Way. Mem. Am. Bar Assn., Idaho Trial Lawyers Assn. (pres. 5th jud. dist. 1975-76, chmn. consumer protection com. 1976—). Office: 516 2d St E PO Box 105 Twin Falls ID 83301 Tel (208) 733-7180

SUFRIN, MURRAY N., b. Camden, N.J., Apr. 12, 1941; B.A., U. Pa., 1963; J.D., Rutgers U., 1966. Admitted to N.J. bar, 1966; individual practice law, to 1974; partner firm Sufrina & Hermon, Cherry Hill, N.J., 1974—. Pres., Big Bros. of Camden County, 1969. Mem. Am., Camden County, N.J. bar assns. Home: 54 Trowbridge Ln Clementon NJ 08021 Office: Suite 619 One Cherry Hill St Cherry Hill NJ 08002 Tel (609) 667-6200

SUGAR, PHILIP JOHN, b. Oakland, Calif., Jan. 4, 1946; B.A., Calif. State U., Sacramento, 1969; J.D., U. Calif., San Francisco, 1973. Admitted to Calif. bar, 1973; spl. liaison Calif. State Bar coms., 1972; investigator Hal Lipset Investigations, San Francisco, 1972-73; dep. city atty. City of Los Angeles, 1974—. Mem. Am., Calif., Los Angeles County bar assns., Calif., Los Angeles County barristers assns. Recipient Spl. Merit award Moot Ct., 1973; editor Sacramento State Hornet, 1968-69. Office: 1700 City Hall E 200 N Main St Los Angeles CA 90012 Tel (213) 485-3627

SUGARMAN, JULIAN JOSEPH, b. Buffalo, Oct. 8, 1932; B.A., U. Buffalo, 1954, LL.B., 1957, J.D., 1957. Admitted to N.Y. bar, 1957, U.S. Supreme Ct. bar, 1975; individual practice law, Buffalo, 1958—. Mem. Erie County, N.Y. State bar assns. Recipient award Bur. Nat. Affairs. Home: 124 Saint Johns Pl Town of Tonawanda NY 14223 Office: 422 Niagara Falls Blvd Buffalo NY 14223 Tel (716) 837-3164

SUGARMAN, MYRON GEORGE, b. San Francisco, Nov. 7, 1942; B.S., U. Calif., Berkeley, 1964, J.D., 1967. Admitted to Calif. bar, 1967; with JAGC, U.S. Army, 1968-71; partner firm Cooley, Godward, Castro, Huddleson & Tatum, San Francisco. Mem. Am., Fed. bar assns., Order of Coif, Phi Beta Kappa. Editorial bd. Calif. Law Rev., 1966-67. Office: 1 Maritime Plaza San Francisco CA 94111 Tel (415) 981-5252

SUGARMAN, PAUL R., b. Boston, Dec. 14, 1931; A.A., Boston U., 1951, J.D. cum laude, 1954. Admitted to Mass. bar, 1954, U.S. Ct. Mil. Appeals bar, 1955. U.S. Supreme Ct. bar, 1965; served with Judge Adv. Gen. Corps, U.S. Army, 1955-58; now partner firm Fink, Sugarman & Sugarman, Boston; mem. Mass. Atty. Gen's. Hwy. Law Study Commn., 1965. Fellow Am. Coll. Trial Lawyers; mem. Am., Mass. (pres. 1976-77), Boston bar assns., Assn. Trial Lawyers Am. (gov. 1966-68, pres. Mass. chpt. 1968-70). Recipient Law Week award Boston U., 1954; asso. editor Boston U. Law Rev., 1952-54. Office: 101 Tremont St Boston MA 02108 Tel (617) 542-1000*

SUGARMAN, ROBERT ALAN, b. Hartford, Conn., May 31, 1947; B.A., George Washington U., 1969; J.D., U. Va., 1972. Admitted to Fla. bar, 1972; asso. firm Kaplan, Dorsey, Sicking & Hessen, P.A., Miami, Fla., 1972—; spl. prof. Inst. for Labor Research and Studies, Fla. Internat. U., Miami, 1974-76. Mem. Am. Bar Assn., Internat. Found. of Employee Benefit Plans. Office: PO Drawer 520337 1951 NW 17th Ave Miami FL 33152 Tel (305) 325-1661

SUGGS, JOHN THOMAS, b. Denison, Tex., Dec. 22, 1904; B.B.A., J.D., U. Tex., 1927. Admitted to Tex. bar, 1927, U.S. Supreme Ct. bar, 1931; asso. firm Denison & Dallas, 1927-38; dist. judge Grayson and Collin Counties, Tex., 1938-44; gen. counsel, v.p., pres., chmn. bd. Tex. & Pacific Ry. Co., Dallas, 1944-69; now gen. practice law, Dallas; dir. Denison State Nat. Bank, 1st Nat. Bank of Van Alstyne (Tex.); lectr., instr. So. Meth. U., 1969-76; dist. judge Grayson and Collin Counties, Tex., 1938-44. Fellow Tex. Bar Found.; mem. Am., Tex., Dallas bar assns., Mexican Acad. Internat. Law. Contbr. articles to profl. jours. Home: 4206 Fairfax St Dallas TX 75205 Office: 3033 1st International Bldg Dallas TX 75270 Tel (214) 741-1166

SUIT, MARVIN WILSON, b. Maysville, Ky., July 13, 1933; B.S., U. Ky., 1955, LL.B., 1957, J.D., 1970. Admitted to Ky. bar, 1957, U.D. Dist. Ct. Eastern Dist. Ky. bar, 1959; practiced in Flemingsburg, Ky., 1957—; asso. firm McIntire, McIntire & Suit, 1959-64; individual practice law, 1964-74; partner firm Suit, McCartney & Price and predecessor, 1975—; police judge, 1959-75; master commr. Fleming Circuit Ct., 1960-75; atty. Fleming County, 1975-77; spl. circuit judge, 19th Jud. Dist., 1970-75. Chmn. Fleming County chpt. ARC, 1959—; trustee United Methodist Ch., Flemingsburg, 1974—. Mem. Ky., Fleming County bar assns., Phi Delta Phi. Recipient Ky. Bar Assn. award for Writing, 1957. Home: 440 Chappel Ln Flemingsburg KY 41041 Office: 108 E Water St Flemingsburg KY 41041 Tel (606) 845-7131

SUKO, LONNY RAY, b. Spokane, Wash., Oct. 12, 1943; B.A. with distinction, Wash. State U., 1965; J.D., U. Idaho, 1968. Admitted to Wash. bar, 1968, U.S. Dist. Ct. bar for Eastern Dist. Wash., 1969; law clk. to Hon. Charles L. Powell, chief judge U.S. Dist. Ct. for Eastern Dist. Wash., 1968-69; asso. firm Lyon, Beaulaurier, Aaron, Weigand & Suko and predecessor, Yakima, Wash., 1969-72, partner, 1972—; U.S. magistrate Eastern Dist. Wash., 1971—. Mem. Yakima County Bar Assn. (sec. 1971), Phi Beta Kappa, Pi Sigma Alpha, Phi Kappa Phi, Phi Alpha Delta. Office: PO Box 1689 201 E Lincoln Ave Yakima WA 98907 Tel (509) 248-7220

SULKEN, HERMAN, b. N.Y.C., July 22, 1909; B.A., Lehigh U., 1930; LL.B., Harvard, 1933. Admitted to N.Y. State bar, 1934, U.S. Dist. Ct. bar, 1965, U.S. Supreme Ct. bar, 1970; practiced in N.Y.C., 1934—; asso. firm Seligsberg & Lewis, 1934-36; partner firm Sulken & Horowitz, 1936-38; individual practice law, 1938—; acting judge Kings Point (N.Y.), 1975. Mem. planning bd., Kings Point, 1970-75;

pres. Kings Point Civic Assn., 1971-73; trustee Temple Beth-El, pres. Men's Club. Mem. Fed. Bar Council, Harvard Law Sch. Alumni Assn., Harvard Club, Engineers Country Club. Contbr. articles in field to profl. jours. Home: 12 Briar Ln Kings Point NY 11024 Office: 310 Madison Ave New York City NY 10017 Tel (212) OX7-0674

SULLIVAN, ALLAN E., b. New Glasgow, N.S., Can., June 23, 1932; B.A., Dalhousie U., Halifax, N.S., 1954, LL.B., 1956. Called to N.S. bar, 1956; formerly with firm Sullivan, Smith, Cameron and Bourdreau; apptd. Minister Welfare and Mines, Minister under the Water Act, 1970-72; atty. gen. Province of N.S., 1972—; dir. Sydney Steel Corp. Bd. dirs. Bairncroft Child-Care Inst. Mem. N.S. Barristers Soc., Cape Breton, Canadian barristers assns. Home: 53 Lynnbrook Dr Sydney River NS Canada Office: PO Box 7 Halifax NS B3J 2L6 Canada*

SULLIVAN, BOB LEWIS, b. Lubbock, Tex., Oct. 9, 1947; A.A., Schreiner Inst., 1968; B.B.A., Baylor U., 1972, J.D., 1972. Admitted to Tex. bar, 1972; mem. legal aid staff, Waco, Tex., 1972-73; asso. firm George Thompson & Assos., Ft. Worth, 1973-75; individual practice law, Ft. Worth, 1975—. Pres. Tarrant County Services for Hearing Impaired, 1975-76; sec. Parole Aid Steering Com. Tex., 1973-74; mem. com. on law Haltom-Richland Area C. of C., 1976; mem. exec. com. Miss Deaf Tex. Pageant, 1976, 78; life mem. Tarrant County Assn. for Hearing Impaired Children for Tarrant County, Tex. Soc. Interpreters for the Deaf; Sunday sch. tchr., Ft. Worth. Mem. State Bar Tex., Am., N.E. Tarrant County bar assns., Tarrant County Young Lawyers Assn., Tarrant County Criminal Def. Lawyers Assn., Phi Delta Phi (clk.), Phi Theta Kappa. Recipient Frank B. Tirey Criminal Law award, 1972, certificates of appreciation Ft. Worth Silent Club, 1975, Gov. Tex. for work on Parole Aid Com., 1973, Most Distinguished Person award Ft. Worth Assn. of the Deaf, 1977. Home: 5720 Ammons St Fort Worth TX 76117 Office: 1315 Brookside Bldg Hurst TX 76053 Tel (817) 282-9183

SULLIVAN, BRUCE RANDALL, b. Albany, N.Y., Aug. 5, 1911; B.A., Colgate U., 1935; LL.B., Union U., 1938, J.D., 1968. Admitted to N.Y. State bar, 1938; sr. partner firm Ainsworth Sullivan Tracy & Knauf, Albany, 1938—; mem. deptl. com. for ct. adminstrn. 3d Jud. Dept., State of N.Y., 1961—. Trustee, Albany Law Sch., Union U. Fellow Am. Coll. Trial Lawyers; mem. Albany County Bar, Am., N.Y. State bar assns., N.Y. State Trial Lawyers Assn., Capital Dist. Trial Lawyers Assn., Internat. Assn. Ins. Counsel, Am. Arbitration Assn. (panel). Home: 5 Tudor Rd Albany NY 12203 Office: Ainsworth Sullivan Tracy & Knauf 75 State St Albany NY 12207 Tel (518) 434-4171

SULLIVAN, CHARLES WILLIAM, b. Silver Spring, Md., Dec. 4, 1942; A.B., Boston Coll., 1964, J.D., 1967; LL.M., Harvard, 1970. Admitted to Mass. bar, 1967, N.Y. bar, 1970, U.S. Supreme Ct. bar, 1972; asso. firm Sullivan & Cromwell, N.Y.C., 1970—; dir. New Eng. Patriots Football Club, Inc., 1972—, v.p., 1977—; gen. counsel, treas., dir. Graphco Am. Charts, Inc., 1974—; mem. exec. com. Nat. Football League, 1975—, mem. ethics com., 1976—; dir. Nat. Football League Films, Inc., Nat. Football League Properties, Inc.; chmn. exec. com. Nat. Football League Mgmt. Council, 1977—. Vice chmn. com. young lawyers N.Y. Legal Aid Soc., N.Y.C., 1971-75; bd. dirs. Found. for Children with Learning Disabilities, 1977—. Mem. Am., N.Y. State bar assns., Bar Assn. City N.Y., Am. Judicature Soc., Am. Soc. Internat. Law. Home: 59 W 12th St New York City NY 10011 Office: 48 Wall St New York City NY 10005 Tel (212) 952-8281

SULLIVAN, DONALD JEROME, b. N.Y.C., July 18, 1929; B.A., Iona Coll., 1951; J.D., Bklyn. Law Sch., 1954. Admitted to N.Y. State bar, 1955, U.S. Supreme Ct. bar, 1960; individual practice law, N.Y.C., 1955-65; judge N.Y.C. Civil Ct., 1966-69, N.Y. State Supreme Ct., Bronx, 1970—; mem. N.Y. State Assembly, 1960-65. Mem. N.Y.C., Bronx bar assns., Assn. Bar City N.Y. Recipient Loftus award in law Iona Coll., 1966, Law award VFW, 1970. Office: 851 Grand Concourse Bronx NY 10451 Tel (212) CY3-8000

SULLIVAN, ELDON BISBEE, b. Washington, June 30, 1904; A.B., Yale U.; J.D., Cornell U. Admitted to N.Y. bar, 1959; partner firm Winner, Sullivan & Delaney, Elmira, N.Y., 1959—. Mem. Am., N.Y. State, Chemung County, Steuben County bar assns. Home: 110 High Rd Corning NY 14830 Office: 110 Baldwin St Elmira NY 14901 Tel (607) 734-8144

SULLIVAN, ERIC P., b. N.Y.C., June 11, 1937; B.S., Georgetown U., 1959; LL.B., Fordham U., 1963. Admitted to N.Y. bar, 1963, U.S. Supreme Ct. bar, 1970; asso. firm Olwine, Connelly, Chase, O'Donnell & Weyher, N.Y.C., 1963-66, Walsh & Frisch, N.Y.C., 1966-70, partner, 1971—. Mem. Am., N.Y. State, N.Y.C. bar assns. Office: Walsh & Frisch 250 Park Ave New York City NY 10017 Tel (212) 687-6100

SULLIVAN, JAMES ANDERSON, b. Wabash, Ind., July 1, 1925; A.B., Ind. U., 1952, J.D. (John H. Edwards fellow), 1954. Asso. firm Gibson, Dunn & Crutcher, Los Angeles, 1954-56; admitted to Calif. bar, 1955, U.S. Supreme Ct. bar, 1963; mem. corp. legal staff Hughes Aircraft Co., Culver City, Calif., 1956-58, div. counsel, El Segundo, Calif., 1958-63, aerospace group counsel, Culver City, 1963-65; of counsel firm Sweeney, Cozy & Deidrich, Torrance, Calif., 1965-72; partner firm Buck, Sullivan, Gavendo & Bavetta, Redondo Beach, Calif., 1973-75; individual practice law, Redondo Beach, 1975—; mem. panel arbitrators Am. Arbitration Assn., 1966—, Fed. Mediation and Conciliation Service, Washington, 1966—. Pres. South Bay Estate Planning Council, Redondo Beach, 1967-68. Mem. State Bar Calif., Los Angeles County, South Bay Dist., Am. bar assns., Ind. Law Club (sec. 1953), Order of Coif, Phi Beta Kappa, Phi Eta Sigma (treas.), Phi Delta Phi (chpt. historian 1953, Grad. of Year 1954). Recipient Hastings award Ind. U., 1952; sr. asso. editor Ind. Law Jour., 1953-54. Home: 43 Margate Sq Palos Verdes Estates CA 90274 Office: 1650 Pacific Coast Hwy suite 212 Redondo Beach CA 90277 Tel (213) 373-7709

SULLIVAN, JAMES JOSEPH, JR., b. Boston, Feb. 9, 1926; A.B., Harvard, 1947, LL.B., 1951. Admitted to Mass. bar, 1952, U.S. Dist. Ct. bar Dist. Mass., 1953, U.S. Ct. Appeals bar 1st Circuit, 1953, 5th Circuit, 1974; asst. U.S. atty. Mass., 1953-56; partner firm DiMento & Sullivan, Boston, 1956—; asst. dist. atty., chief fraud div. Suffolk County, Mass., 1957-60; corp. counsel City of Boston, 1966-67. Chmn. Boston Real Property Bd., 1960-66. Mem. Mass., Boston bar assns., Mass. Trial Lawyers Assn., Nat. Assn. Def. Lawyers in Criminal Cases. Office: 100 State St Boston MA 02109 Tel (617) 523-5253

SULLIVAN, JAMES MORTIMER, JR., b. Potsdam, N.Y., Mar. 21, 1922; A.B. in Govt., St. Lawrence U., 1943; postgrad. Am. U., 1943; LL.B., Harvard, 1949. Admitted to N.Y. bar, 1949; partner firm Bond, Schoeneck & King, Syracuse, N.Y., 1949-69, 76—; U.S. atty. No. Dist. N.Y., Syracuse and Albany, 1969-76; Nat. Inst. Pub. Affairs intern assigned fgn. liaison dept. Lend Lease Adminstrn., Washington, 1943; acting house counsel Oneida Ltd. (N.Y.), 1962. Active Community Chest, ARC, YMCA. Mem. Am. (N.Y. liaison rep. com. on evaluation disciplinary enforcement), Fed., N.Y. State (chmn. grievance com., mem. membership com. banking law sect.), Onondaga County (past pres., dir., chmn. grievance and profl. ethics com., mem. unauthorized practice law com.) bar assns., Fed. Exec. Assn. Central N.Y. (past pres.), Am. Arbitration Assn. (nat. panel arbitrators), N.Y. State Fair Trial Free Press Conf., Harvard Law Sch. Alumni Assn. Upstate N.Y., St. Lawrence U. Alumni Assn. (past pres., chmn. fund drs. Central N.Y.). Home: 104 Winterton Dr Fayetteville NY 13066 Office: One Lincoln Center Syracuse NY 13202 Tel (315) 422-0121

SULLIVAN, JAMES O'KEEFE, b. Great Falls, Mont., Sept. 5, 1922; A.B., Western Mich. U., 1944; J.D., Georgetown U., 1949. Admitted to D.C. bar, 1949, Calif. bar, 1953, N.D. bar, 1954, Conn. bar, 1964; trial atty. antitrust div. U.S. Dept. Justice, San Francisco, 1949-54; partner firm Sullivan, Jones & Archer, San Diego, San Francisco and Los Angeles, 1967—. Fellow Am. Coll. Trial Lawyers; mem. San Diego County, Am. bar assns. Home: 2308 King Arthur Ct La Jolla CA 92037 Office: 14th Floor 600 B St San Diego CA 92101 Tel (714) 236-1611

SULLIVAN, JAMES PATRICK, b. Augusta, Ga., Mar. 17, 1944; B.A. Fordham U., 1965, J.D., N.Y. U., 1968. Admitted to N.Y. State bar, 1969, asst. corp. counsel City N.Y., 1968-70, asso. Simpson, Thacher & Bartlett, N.Y.C., 1970-73, asso. counsel Warner Communications Inc., N.Y.C., 1973—. Mem. Community Sch. Dist. # 13, Bklyn., 1970-72, vice-chmn. Community Planning Bd., # 3, Bklyn. 1975—. Mem. Am., N.Y.C. (mem. municipal affairs com.) bar assns., Bedford-Stuyvesant Lawyers Assn. Office: 75 Rockefeller Plaza New York City NY 10019 Tel (212) 484-6517

SULLIVAN, JAMES ROBERT, b. Rochester, N.Y., Oct. 10, 1938; B.A., Weidner Coll., 1960; LL.B., Albany Law Sch., 1963, J.D., 1968. Admitted to N.Y. State bar, 1963, U.S. Supreme Ct. bar, 1967; partner firm Lamb, Webster, Walz, Donovan & Sullivan, Rochester, 1965—; town atty. Town of Wheatland, N.Y., 1968-71, 72-76. Active United Fund, 1965-66. Mem. Am., N.Y. State, Monroe County bar assns., Transp. Club, Rochester C. of C. Office: Suite 700 19 W Main St Rochester NY 14614 Tel (716) 325-2150

SULLIVAN, JAMES VINCENT, b. N.Y.C., Oct. 18, 1913; A.B., Fordham U., 1935; LL.B., 1939, J.D., 1939; J.S.D., Bklyn. Law Sch., 1954. Admitted to N.Y. State bar, 1940; asso. firm Clark & Baldwin, N.Y.C., 1940-42; individual practice law, N.Y.C., 1946—; legal asst. N.Y. State Bd. Law Examiners, 1941-75; faculty Baruch Coll., U. City N.Y., 1946—, prof. law, 1972—, chmn. dept. law, 1970-76, prof. emeritus, 1977—. Mem. N.Y. State Bar Assn., AAUP, Am. Bus. Law Assn. Author: Law of Real Estate Transactions, 1956; Materials in Law of Business Contracts, 1964; Law of Business Corporations, 1969. Home: 205 E 72d St New York City NY 10021 Office: 17 Lexington Ave New York City NY 10010 Tel (212) 725-3008

SULLIVAN, JEREMIAH P., JR., b. Boston, Dec. 20, 1947; A.B., Stonehill Coll., 1969; J.D., Boston Coll. Law, 1972. Admitted to Mass. bar, 1972, N.H. bar, 1972; deputy clk. Nashua (N.H.) Dist. Ct., 1972-73; asst. dist. atty. Suffolk County, Boston, 1973—; lectr. law enforcement Boston State Coll. Mem., Mass. N.H. bar assns. Office: Pemberton Square Courthouse Boston MA 02108 Tel (617) 723-9700

SULLIVAN, JOHN FRANCIS, b. Omaha, Apr. 25, 1914; student No. Ariz. U., 1932-35; LL.B. (J.D.), Georgetown U., 1939. Admitted to Ariz. bar, 1940, U.S. Supreme Ct. bar, 1966; mem. firm Sullivan & Sullivan, Phoenix, 1940-42, Langmade & Sullivan, 1946-60; dep. county atty. Maricopa County (Ariz.), 1942; mem. firm Sullivan, Mahoney & Tang, and predecessors, Phoenix, 1965; reporter of decisions Supreme Ct. Ariz., 1946-47, judge pro tempore Superior Ct., 1973. Commr. housing authority City of Phoenix, 1950-52, chmn. Urban Renewal Commn., 1957-59, councilman city council, 1952-56; mem. Employment Security Commn. Ariz., 1966-67. Office: Sullivan Mahoney & Tang 11 W Jefferson St Phoenix AZ 85003 Tel (602) 254-8861

SULLIVAN, JOHN JOSEPH, b. Sparta, Wis., Jan. 27, 1903; LL.B., Marquette U., 1925. Admitted to Wis. bar; partner firm Laughlin, McCarthy and Sullivan, 1925-28; partner firm Sullivan and Taugher, 1928-48; individual practice law, Wauwatosa, Wis., 1948—; sec. Wauwatosa Bd. of Appeals. Mem. Milw. Bar Assn. Contbr. articles in field to profl. jours. Home and office: 605 N 76th St Wauwatosa WI 53213 Tel (414) 258-9149

SULLIVAN, JOHN L., b. Elk City, Okla., July 24, 1917; B.S., So. Meth. U., 1939, J.D., 1947. Admitted to Tex. bar, 1947; atty., mgr. City of Beeville (Tex.), 1948-51; mgr. City of Alice (Tex.), 1951-56, mgr. City of Clearwater (Fla.), 1956; v.p., gen. mgr. Chiles Drilling Co., Alice, 1957-67; individual practice law, Corpus Christi, Tex., 1967—. Mem. Alice Planning Commn., 1958-62; dir., pres. Alice Water Authority, 1959-67. Mem. Tex., Nueces County bar assns. Office: Guaranty Bank Plaza Corpus Christi TX 78401

SULLIVAN, JOHN LAWRENCE, b. Manchester, N.H., June 16, 1899; A.B., Dartmouth U., 1921; LL.B., Harvard U., 1924; LL.D., Duquesne U., 1943, U. N.H., 1949, Loyola U., 1949. Admitted to N.H. bar 1923, U.S. Supreme Ct. bar, 1935, D.C. bar, 1949, U.S. Ct. Claims bar, 1958; asst. to commr. IRS Washington, 1939-40, asst. Sec. of Treasury, Washington, 1940-44; asst. Sec. of Navy for air, 1945-46, Undersec. of Navy, 1946-47, Sec. of Navy, 1947-49; sr. partner firm Sullivan, Beauregard, Clarkson, Moss & Brown, and predecessors, Washington, 1945—; partner firm Sullivan & Wynot, and predecessors, Washington, 1930—. Home: 4871 Glenbrook Rd NW Washington DC 20016 Office: 1800 M St NW Washington DC 20036 Tel (202) 785-8000

SULLIVAN, JOHN THIELEN, b. Detroit, Jan. 18, 1932; B.A., U. Notre Dame, 1954; LL.B., Yale, 1957. Admitted to N.Y. State bar, 1958; asso. firm Cadwalader, Wickersham & Taft, N.Y.C., 1958-61, Cole & Deitz, N.Y.C., 1964-65, partner, 1966-70, Hawkins, Delafield & Wood, N.Y.C., 1970—; staff atty., br. chief SEC, N.Y.C., 1962-64; lectr. in field. Mem. N.Y. State Bar Assn., Assn. Bar City N.Y. Home: 131 E 66th St New York City NY 10021 Office: 67 Wall St New York City NY 10005 Tel (212) 952-4843

SULLIVAN, JOSEPH ANDREW, b. Detroit, Dec. 22, 1919; B.S., U. Detroit, 1946, LL.B., 1948. Admitted to Mich. bar, 1948, U.S. Supreme Ct. bar, 1957; partner firm Hand, Sullivan, Hull & Kiefer, Detroit, 1948-50; asst. pros. atty. Detroit, 1949-55, asst. atty. gen., 1955-57, dep. atty. gen. 1957-58; judge Mich. 3d Jud. Circuit Ct., 1958—, chief judge, 1967-74; counsel firm Bodman, Longley, Bogle, Armstrong & Dahling, Detroit, 1976—; instr. Law Sch. U. Detroit; faculty adviser Nat. Coll. Judges, Reno; lectr. in field; former pres. Nat. Conf. Met. Cts.; mem. bd. dirs. Nat. Center State Cts.; participant Mich. Drafting Comm. Criminal Code Revision. Mem. com. visitors Inst. Ct. Mgmt., Denver, 1971-73. Mem. Am. (com. rep.), Mich., Detroit bar assns., Am. Judicature Soc., Inst. Jud. Adminstrn., U. Detroit Law Alumni (past pres.). Home: 1161 Bishop St Grosse Pointe Park MI 48230 Office: Mfrs Bank Tower 100 Renaissance Center Detroit MI 48243 Tel (313) 259-7777

SULLIVAN, JOSEPH CHARLES, b. N.Y.C., Feb. 6, 1927; B.E.E., Manhattan Coll., 1950; LL.B., St. John's U., 1954; LL.M., N.Y. U., 1958. Admitted to N.Y. bar, 1955, U.S. Dist. Ct. bar for So. Dist. N.Y.), 1956, U.S. Dist. Ct. bar for Eastern Dist. N.Y., 1956, U.S. Dist. Ct. bar (for No. Dist. N.Y.), 1960, U.S. Ct. Appeals bar, 1960 U.S. Ct. Customs and Patent Appeals bar, 1963, U.S. Supreme Ct. bar, 1976; design engr. Sperry Corp., Long Island City, N.Y., 1950-54; atty. Control Instrument Co. subs. Burroughs Corp., Bklyn., 1954-55; asso. firm Kane, Dalsimer, Kane, Sullivan and Kurucz, N.Y.C., 1955-60, partner, 1960—; lectr. Practicing Law Inst., 1960—; arbitrator Am. Arbitration Assn., 1964—. Active Garden City (N.Y.) Athletic Assn., Boy Scouts Am., Little League, 1961—; L.I. Soccer League, 1972—. Mem. IEEE, Assn. Bar City N.Y., Am., N.Y. State bar assns., Am., N.Y. patent law assns. Registered U.S. Patent Office, 1957. Contbr. articles in field to profl. jours. Home: 82 Eton Rd Garden City N 420 Lexington Ave New York City NY 10017 Tel (212) 687-6000

SULLIVAN, JOSEPH PATRICK, b. Bronx, N.Y., Mar. 17, 1931; B.A., St. John's Coll., N.Y.C., 1952, LL.B., 1957. Admitted to N.Y. bar, 1957; claims adjuster Allstate Ins. Co., N.Y.C., 1957-58; asso. firm Mendes & Mount, N.Y.C., 1958-62; individual practice law, N.Y.C., 1962-64; law sec. to justice N.Y. State Supreme Ct. 1st Jud. Dist., 1965-68; judge Civil Ct., N.Y.C., 1969-72; justice N.Y. State Supreme Ct., 1973—. Mem. Am., N.Y. State, Bronx County (N.Y.) bar assns., Assn. Bar City N.Y. Office: 851 Grand Concourse Bronx NY 10415 Tel (212) CY 3-8000

SULLIVAN, LAWRENCE ANTHONY, b. Flushing, N.Y., May 27, 1923; B.A. with distinction, U. Calif. at Los Angeles, 1948; J.D. magna cum laude, Harvard, 1951. Admitted to Mass. bar, 1952; law clk. 1st Circuit U.S. Ct. Appeals, 1951-52; asso. Foley, Hoag & Eliot, Boston, 1952-55, 1957-60, partner, 1960-67; acting prof. law U. Calif. at Berkeley, 1955-57, prof. 1967—; mem. governing bd. Earl Warren Legal Inst., 1970-75, Nat. Housing and Econ. Devel. Law Project, 1971-76; mem. acad. planning com. U. Calif. at Berkeley, 1968-72, chmn. 1970-72, mem. budget com., 1974—, chmn. 1976—. Dir., vice-chmn. Commonwealth Orgn. Dem. (Mass.), 1964-67. Mem. Am. Bar Assn., Assn. Am. Law Schs., Inst. Advanced Legal Studies of London (Eng.) U. Author: Handbook on the Law of Antitrust, 1977; contbr. articles in field to profl. jours. Home: 2737 Claremont Blvd Berkeley CA 94705 Office: Sch Law Boalt Hall Univ Calif Berkeley CA 94720 Tel (415) 642-5451

SULLIVAN, LEONARD JUSTIN, b. New Orleans, Nov. 3, 1935; B.B.A., Tulane U., 1958; J.D., Loyola U., 1965. Admitted to La. bar, 1965, Tex. bar, 1970; tax atty. Shell Oil Co., Houston, 1972—. Mem. Customs Bar Assn. Contbr. article to publ. Home: 14819 Chadbourne Dr Houston TX 77079 Office: 1500 Old Spanish Trail Houston TX 77025 Tel (713) 795-3201

SULLIVAN, MARK ANTHONY, JR., b. Jersey City, Dec. 11, 1946; A.B., Georgetown U., 1968; J.D., Rutgers U., 1973. Admitted to N.J. bar, 1973; law clk. appellate div. N.J. Superior Ct., 1973-74; dep. atty. gen. State of N.J., 1974—. Mem. Am., N.J., Hudson County (N.J.) bar assns., Phi Alpha Delta. Recipient Internat. Acad. Trial Lawyers award, 1973. Home: 57-10 Fox Run Dr Plainsboro NJ 08536 Office: 25 Scotch Rd Trenton NJ 08625 Tel (609) 292-8147

SULLIVAN, MARTIN FRANCIS, JR., b. Louisville, Aug. 24, 1930; B.S., U. Louisville, 1958, LL.B., 1960. Admitted to Ky. bar, 1960; asst. dist. dir. HEW, Ky., 1958-65; first asst. county atty. Jefferson County (Ky.), 1965-70; individual practice law, Louisville, 1970—; served as lt. col. JAGC, USAR, 1964-77; mem. Louisville and Jefferson County Human Relations Commn., 1970-74. Mem. Louisville, Ky. bar assns. Home: 3714 Hillsboro Rd Louisville KY 40207 Office: Butchertown Legal Arts Bldg 1675 Story Ave Louisville KY 40206 Tel (502) 587-0145 also 587-0228

SULLIVAN, MICHAEL DEAN, b. Chgo., Feb. 16, 1940; B.B.A. cum laude, U. Notre Dame, 1962, J.D., 1965. Admitted to Ill. bar, 1965; law clerk Hon. Roger J. Kiley, U.S. Ct. Appeals, 7th Circuit, Chgo., 1965-66; mem. firm Jenner & Block, Chgo., 1967-74; gen. atty. Chgo. Milw. Corp., gen. atty., corporate counsel Chgo., Milw., St. Paul and Pacific R.R. Co., Chgo., 1974—. Mem. Am. (adj. mem. tax sec., com. employee benefits), Chgo. (fed. taxation and employee benefits coms.), Ill. State (corp. and securities com.) bar assns., Chgo. Assn. Commerce and Industry (fed. revenue and expenditures com.). Mng. editor Notre Dame Law Review, 1964-65. Home: 739 Park River Forest IL 60305 Office: 516 W Jackson Blvd Chicago IL 60606 Tel (312) 236-7600

SULLIVAN, MICHAEL THOMAS, b. Milw., July 18, 1924; B.A., Marquette U., 1945, J.D., 1948; LL.M. in Taxation, John Marshall Law Sch., 1972; grad. Nat. Coll. for State Judiciary, U. Nev., 1974, 76. Admitted to Wis. bar, 1948; practiced in Milw., 1948-51, West Allis, Wis., 1951-53; judge Br. 2, Circuit Ct. for State of Wis., 1953-63; judge probate div. Milwaukee County (Wis.) Ct., 1963-77, chief judge, 1975—, sr. judge in probate, 1970—. Chmn. exec. com. Project Turnaround; exec. com. Commn. on Family Resources; sec.-treas. Milwaukee County Orphans' Bd. Mem. Wis., Milw., bar assns., Am. Judicature Soc. Contbr. articles to legal jours. Home: 5200 S Tuckaway St Greenfield WI 53221 Office: 901 N 9th St Milwaukee WI 53233 Tel (414) 278-5112

SULLIVAN, PETER BLAND, b. West Hartford, Conn., June 1, 1923; A.B., Holy Cross Coll., Mass., 1945; J.D., Boston Coll., 1949. Admitted to Conn. bar, 1949, U.S. Supreme Ct. bar, 1957; asso. firm Hoppin, Carey & Powell, Hartford, Conn., 1949-53, partner, 1953—; mayor City of West Hartford, 1961-63; counsel Conn. Gov. John D. Lodge, 1953-55; asst. atty. gen. State of Conn., 1955-57. Mem. Hartford County, Conn., Am. bar assns. Home: 18 Farm Hill Rd West Hartford CT 06107 Office: 266 Pearl St Hartford CT 06103 Tel (203) 249-6891

SULLIVAN, RAYMOND HENRY, b. Lynn, Mass., Jan. 21, 1924; A.B., Boston Coll., 1949; J.D., Suffolk U., 1955. Admitted to Mass. bar, 1955, Fed. bar, 1959, U.S. Supreme Ct. bar, 1976; individual practice law, Lynn, Mass., 1955—; asst. solicitor City of Lynn, 1969—. Mem. council City of Lynn, 1952-57. Mem. Lynn, Essex County bar assns., City Solicitors and Town Counsels Assn. Office: 180 Broadway St Lynn MA 01904 Tel (617) 598-6420

SULLIVAN, ROBERT EDWIN, b. Helena, Mont., Aug. 1, 1917; A.B., U. Notre Dame, 1940, J.D., 1946; LL.D., Carroll Coll., 1965. Admitted to Mont. bar, 1942, Ohio bar, 1946, N.D. bar, 1952; individual practice law, Ohio, 1946-47; prof. law U. Notre Dame, South Bend, Ind., 1947-54; prof. law U. Mont., 1954—, dean Law Sch., 1955—; dir. 1st Trust Co.; dir. Continuing Legal Edn., Mont. Mem. Mont. Nat. Conf. on Uniform State Laws, 1957—, v.p., 1970-71; chmn. Gov.'s Com. Revise Marriage and Divorce Laws; co-chmn. Gov.'s Com. to Revise Mont. Corp. Law; mem. adv. com. Ind. Dept. Conservation, 1953-54; mem. Rocky Mountain Mineral Found. Mem. Am., Mont. bar assns., Am. Judicature Soc. (dir.). Recipient Borromeo award Carroll Coll., 1961; author handbooks; contbr. articles to profl. jours.; editor newsletter sec. Mineral and Natural Resources Law, 1967-70. Home: 112 Hillcrest Dr Missoula MT 59801 Office: Sch Law U Mont Missoula MT 59801 Tel (406) 243-4311

SULLIVAN, ROBERT LINCOLN, JR., b. Hanford, Calif., Oct. 16, 1942; B.S., U. Calif., Berkeley, 1964; J.D., U. San Francisco, 1967. Admitted to Calif. bar, 1968; asso. firm Pillsbury, Madison & Sutro, San Francisco, 1967-69; asso. firm Tuckman & Phillips, San Francisco, 1969-71; partner firm Crossland, Crossland, Caswell & Bell, Fresno, Calif., 1971—. Mem. Bar Assn. San Francisco (chmn. law day 1970), Fresno County, Am. bar assns., Phi Kappa Psi (pres. 1963-64), McAuliffe Honor Soc. Recipient Faculty award Academic Excellence U. San Francisco Sch. Law, 1967. Editor-in-chief U. San Francisco Law Rev., 1966-67. Office: 1100 Guarantee Savings Bldg Fresno CA 93721 Tel (209) 233-6641

SULLIVAN, ROGER KENT, b. Wichita, Kans., July 4, 1945; B.S., U. Kans., 1967, J.D., 1971. Admitted to Kans. bar, 1971; asso. firm Payne & Jones, Olathe, Kans., 1971—; municipal judge City of Prairie Village (Kans.), 1974—. Mem. Am., Kans., Johnson County bar assns., Am. Trial Lawyers Assn. Tel (913) 782-2500

SULLIVAN, ROGER MICHAEL, b. Rochester, N.Y., Dec. 27, 1930; B.A. magna cum laude, Marist Coll., Poughkeepsie, N.Y., 1965; LL.B. (Jaffin fellow), Columbia, 1968. Admitted to Conn. bar, 1968, D.C. bar, 1968; asso. firm Wiggin & Dana, New Haven, 1968-72; asso. firm Kilpatrick, Kahl & Josephson, Branford, Conn., 1972-73, partner, 1973—. Mem. Am., Conn. bar assns., Am. Trial Lawyers Assn. Office: 175 Montowese St Branford CT 06405 Tel (203) 488-7217

SULLIVAN, TERENCE ANTHONY, b. Willmantic, Conn., Feb. 24, 1938; B.A., U. Conn., 1963, M.A., 1965, J.D., 1971. Admitted to Conn. bar, 1971; pub. defender State of Conn., Manchester, 1971-74; asst. prof. Wethersfield Sch. Law, Hartford, Conn., 1974-75; asst. prof. bus. law U. Conn., Storrs, 1975—. Mem. Willington (Conn.) Bd. Fin., 1975—. Mem. Am. Bus. Law Assn., Am., Conn., Tolland City bar assns. Home: 11 Ridgewood Rd Willington CT 06279 Office: U Conn Stors CT 06279 Tel (203) 429-4907

SULLIVAN, THOMAS FRANCIS, b. Springfield, Mass., Aug. 8, 1938; B.S., U. Conn., 1962; J.D., Washburn U., 1972. Admitted to Kans. bar, 1972; asso. firm Weeks, Thomas, Lysaught, Bingham, Mustain, Kansas City, Kans., 1972-76; asso. firm McDonald, Chambers & Dykes, Overland Park, Kans., 1976—; city prosecutor, Fairway, Kans., 1972-74. Mem. Am., Kans., Kansas City, Wyandotte and Johnson counties bar assns., Washburn Law Sch. Alumni Assn., Am., Kans. trial lawyers assns., Am. Jurisprudence Assn. Home: 815 W 60th Terr Kansas City MO 64113 Office: Cloverleaf Bldg #5 Overland Park KS 66201 Tel (913) 384-5454

SULLIVAN, THOMAS PATRICK, b. Evanston, Ill., Mar. 23, 1930; student Loras Coll., 1947-49; LL.B., cum laude, Loyola U., Chgo., 1952. Admitted to Ill. bar, 1952; asso. firm Jenner & Block, Chgo., 1954-62, partner, 1963—; speaker legal seminars. Fellow Am. Coll. Trial Lawyers; mem. Am., Ill., 7th Circuit, Chgo. bar assns., Am. Law Inst., Am. Judicature Soc. Recipient medal of Excellence, Loyola U. Law Sch., 1965, Ill. Pub. Defender Assn. award, 1972; contbr. articles to profl. publs. Office: One IBM Plaza Chicago IL 60611 Tel (312) 222-9350

SULLIVAN, WILLIAM A., JR., b. Warren, Ohio, Aug. 8, 1939; B.A., Trinity Coll., 1961; LL.B., Columbia U., 1964. Admitted to Ohio bar, 1964; asso. firm Dennison & McGeough; 1964-65; asso. firm Evans, Gentithes's Meermams, 1965-70; exec. dir., gen. counsel Mahoning-Trumbull Council Govts., Youngstown, 1970-73; pres. Western Reserve Econ. Devel. Agy., Niles, Ohio, 1973—; dir. Nat. Council Urban Econ. Devel., 1971. Councilman-at-large, Warren, Ohio, 1966-67; v.p. Mahoning Valley Regional Mass Transit Authority, 1968-70; chmn. Ohio Environ. Protection Agy. Citizens Council, 1973-74. Mem. Trumbull County, Ohio, Am. bar assns. Office: 918 Youngstown Rd Suite B Niles OH 44446 Tel (216) 545-4333

SULLIVAN, WILLIAM C., b. St. Louis, Aug. 26, 1928; J.D. cum laude, St. Louis U., 1952. Admitted to Mo. bar, 1952, Kans. bar, 1964, U.S. Supreme Ct. bar, 1971; atty., gen. solicitor Southwestern Bell Telephone Co., St. Louis, 1956-75, gen. solicitor, 1975—; served to capt. JAGC, USAF, 1952-55. Mem. citizens adv. council Parkway Sch. Dist., St. Louis, 1971-73. Mem. Am., Mo., Kans., Met. St. Louis bar assns. Contbr. articles to legal jours. Office: 1010 Pine St Saint Louis MO 63101 Tel (314) 247-4995

SULLIVAN, WILLIAM CLINTON, b. Birmingham, Ala., Sept. 3, 1926; LL.B., U. Ala., 1949. Admitted to Ala. bar, 1949; practiced in Talladega, Ala., 1949-58; judge Ala. 29th Jud. Circuit Ct., 1958—; mayor Town of Lincoln (Ala.), 1952-58; vice chmn. Ala. Pattern Jury Instruction Com., 1967—. Mem. Talladega County Bar Assn. (pres. 1956-57), Ala., Am. bar assns., Ala. Assn. Circuit Judges (pres. 1974-75). Home: Lincoln AL 35096 Office: Jud Bldg Talladega AL 35160 Tel (205) 362-2030

SULLIVAN, ZANE KEETS, b. Glendive, Mont., May 7; B.A. in Psychology, Mont. State U., 1968; J.D., U. Mont., 1972. Admitted to Mont. bar, 1972; partner firm Jordan, Sullivan & Baldassin, Missoula, Mont., 1972—. Mem. Am., Mont., Western Mont. bar assns., Missoula Young Lawyers, Legal Soc., Missoula C. of C. (v.p., dir.), Phi Delta Phi. Recipient Law Day award Mont. Bar Assn., 1974; certificate of appreciation Hellgate High Sch. Home: 1225 Vicki Dr Missoula MT 59806 Office: Box 1035 201 E Broadway Missoula MT 59807 Tel (406) 543-8351

SULLY, IRA BENNETT, b. Columbus, Ohio, June 3, 1947; A.B. cum laude, Ohio State U., 1969, J.D. summa cum laude, 1974. Admitted to Ohio bar, 1974; asso. firm Schottenstein, Garel, Swedlow & Zox, Columbus, Ohio, 1974—. Mem. Columbus, Ohio, Am. bar assns. Contbr. articles to legal jours. Home: 305 E Sycamore St Columbus OH 43206 Office: 250 E Broad St Columbus OH 43215 Tel (614) 221-3211

SULZBERGER, CARL LEWIS, b. East Orange, N.J., July 12, 1939; B.S. in Elec. Engring., Newark Coll. Engring., 1962, M.S.E.E., 1966; J.D., Rutgers U., Newark, 1973. Elec. engr. Pub. Service Electric and Gas Co., Newark, 1962-73, atty. law dept., 1973—; admitted to N.J. bar, 1973, U.S. Dist. Ct. bar for Dist. N.J., 1973; corp. atty. Garden State Underground Plant Location Service, Inc., Iselin, N.J., 1974—. Mem. Livingston Twp. Zoning Bd. Adjustment, 1969—; pres. congregation Grace Luth. Ch., Livingston, 1976; bd. mgrs. Luth. Home, Jersey City, 1976-77. Mem. IEEE, Am. Bar Assn., Tau Beta Pi, Eta Kappa Nu. Recipient Keyser-Snell award in personnel relations Newark Coll. Engring., 1962, Distinguished Service award Livingston Jaycees, 1969; co-recipient Englebrecht Outstanding Scholarship award Rutgers Law Sch., 1973. Home: 60 Mounthaven Dr Livingston NJ 07039 Office: 80 Park Pl Newark NJ 07101 Tel (201) 624-4618

SUMIDA, GERALD AQUINAS, b. Hilo, Hawaii, June 19, 1944; A.B. Summa cum Laude, Princeton, 1966, certificate Woodrow Wilson Sch. Pub. and Internat. Affairs, 1966; J.D., Yale, 1969. Admitted to Hawaii Supreme Ct. bar, 1970, U.S. Dist. Ct., 1970, U.S. Ct. Appeals 9th Circuit bar, 1970; research asso. Center of Internat. Studies Princeton, 1969; asso. firm Carlsmith, Carlsmith, Wichman and Case, Honolulu, 1970-76, partner, 1976—. Bd. dirs. Legal Aid Soc. Hawaii, Honolulu, 1974; chmn. Hawaii Commn. on the Year 2000, Honolulu, 1975—; mem. exec. com. Honolulu Community Media Council, 1976; bd. govs. Pacific and Asian Affairs Council, Honolulu, 1976—; bd. dirs., sec. Hawaii Correctional Legal Services, Inc., Honolulu, 1976; bd. dirs. Indo-Pacific Soc., Honolulu, 1976—. Mem. Am., Hawaii State bar assns., Am. Soc. Internat. Law, Am. Judicature Soc., Phi Beta Kappa. Recipient T. Woodrow Wilson award, Am. Whig-Cliosophic Soc., 1966. Contbr. articles in field to profl. jours. and books. Homee 1130 Wilder Ave Honolulu HI 96822 Office: PO Box 656 Honolulu HI 96809 Tel (808) 524-5112

SUMINSKI, JOHN HENRY, b. Newark, May 22, 1947; B.A., Seton Hall U., 1969; J.D., U. Notre Dame, 1972. Admitted to N.J. bar, 1972; law sec. to judge U.S. Dist. Ct., N.J., 1972-77; asst. U.S. atty. City of Newark, 1973—. Mem. N.J. Bar Assn. Recipient Spl. Achievement award Dept. Justice, 1974, Spl. Commendation award U.S. Atty. Gen., 1975. Home: 16 Valley Stream Circle St Morris Plains NJ 07950 Office: 970 Broad St Newark NJ 07101 Tel (201) 645-2363

SUMMER, ALBIOUN F., b. Pelahatchie, Miss., Nov. 2, 1921; diploma Hinds Jr. Coll., 1942; student U. Miss. Sch. Law, 1946-47; LL.B., Jackson Sch. Law, 1950. Admitted to Miss. bar; town atty. Town of Pelahatchie, 1950-51; mem. Miss. Bd. Vets. Affairs, 1957; exec. asst., legal adviser to Gov. Miss., 1958, chief asst., legal adviser, 1968-69; chancery judge Miss. 5th Dist., 1958-61; atty. gen. State of Miss., 1969—. Mem. So. Attys. Gen. Assn. (past chmn., mem. nat. exec. com. 1971), Nat. Assn. Attys. Gen. (pres. 1975-76), Phi Delta Theta, Beta Theta Pi. Office: Office of Atty Gen Gartin Justice Bldg PO Box 220 Jackson MS 39205

SUMMER, BERNARD, B.S., N.Y. U., 1932, J.D., 1935. Admitted to N.Y. bar, 1936, U.S. Supreme Ct. bar, 1966; mem. firm Bronstein, Summer & Ansell, Mineola, N.Y., 1974-77; individual practice law, Garden City, N.Y.; dep. county atty. Nassau County, N.Y., 1964-67; adminstr. office legal services Nassau County Dept. Social Services, 1967-71. Pres. Walthoffer Community Assn., North Bellmore, N.Y., 1964-65. Fellow Am. Acad. Matrimonial Lawyers; mem. Nassau County Bar Assn., Nassau County Lawyers Assn. Home: 2103 Jacqueline Ave North Bellmore NY 11710 Office: 1399 Franklin Ave Garden City NY 11530 Tel (516) 747-4455

SUMMERS, ALFRED HUGH, b. Palestine, Tex., May 21, 1945; B.A. in Physics, Austin Coll., 1967; student Keesler Tng. Center, 1970; J.D., U. Houston, 1973. Admitted to Tex. bar, 1973; individual practice law, Palestine, 1973—, v.p., campaign mgr. Palestine United Way, 1975—; dist. chmn. Boy Scouts Am., Palestine, 1976. Mem. State Bar Tex., Anderson County (v.p. 1976-77), Am. bar assns., Tex. Criminal Def. Lawyers Assn. Home: 921 N Cedar St Palestine TX 75801 Office: PO Box 1399 Palestine TX 75801 Tel (214) 729-2128

SUMMERS, NORMAN FRANCIS, b. Balt., Sept. 6, 1926; LL.B., U. Balt., 1956, J.D., 1956. Admitted to Md. bar, 1956, U.S. Supreme Ct. bar, 1961; claims adjuster U.S. F. & G. Co., Balt., 1954-56; individual practice law, Balt., 1956—; trial magistrate Baltimore County (Md.), 1966-69. Mem. Unsatisfied Claim and Judgement Fund Bd., 1969. Mem. Am., Md. bar assns., Trial Lawyers Assn. Home: 4505 Ridge Ave Baltimore MD 21227 Office: suite B 4715 Leeds Ave Baltimore MD 21227 Tel (301) 247-0200

SUMMERS, PEGGY, b. Arnegard, N.D., May 8, 1931; B.S., Van Norman U., 1964, LL.B., 1966, J.D., 1966. Admitted to Calif. bar, 1967; individual practice law, Lone Pine, Calif., 1967—; pub. defender Inyo County (Calif.), 1967-68. Mem. State Bar Calif., Fed., Inyo County bar assns., Lawyer-Pilots Bar Assn., Women Lawyers Assn. Recipient award of Merit, Bancroft Whitney, 1966, commendation Am. Arbitration Assn., 1968. Home: 1091 S Main St Lone Pine CA 93545 Office: 101 N Main St Lone Pine CA 93545 Tel (714) 876-5561

SUMMERS, ROBERT B., b. San Antonio, July 28, 1939; B.B.A., U. Tex., 1962; LL.B., U. Houston, 1967. Admitted to Tex. bar, 1966, U.S. Dist. Ct. bar Western Dist. Tex., 1972; individual practice law. Mem. Tex. Assn. Def. Counsel. Editorial bd. U. Houston Law Rev. Home: 3007 S Valley View St San Antonio TX 78217 Office: 1910 Tower Life Bldg San Antonio TX 78205 Tel (512) 224-5406

SUMMERS, RONALD JAMES, b. Cranston, R.I., Oct. 19, 1930; B.A., Syracuse U., 1952, J.D., 1957. Admitted to N.Y. bar, 1958; partner law firm Sullivan, Gough, Skipworth, Summers & Smith, Rochester, N.Y., 1959—. Justice, Town of Perinton, N.Y., 1960—. Mem. Internat. Assn. Ins. Counsel, Am. Arbitration Assn. (arbitrator), Am., N.Y. State, Monroe County bar assns., N.Y. State Magistrates Assn. Home: 18 Mt Rise St Fairport NY 14450 Office: 1020 Reynolds Arcade Bldg Rochester NY 14614

SUMMERVILLE, ERIC ALEXANDER, b. Caldwell, N.J., Feb. 10, 1942; B.A., Kenyon Coll., 1964; LL.B., Rutgers U., 1967. Admitted to N.J. bar, 1967, U.S. Supreme Ct. bar, 1973; staff atty. Newark Legal Services Project, 1970-72; dir. Rutgers Legal Aid Clinic, 1972-73, Patrick House Legal Clinic, Jersey City, 1973—; partner firm Summerville, Rudding & Campbell, Jersey City, 1976—; adj. prof. Seton Hall Law Sch., 1974—. Mem. Am., N.J., Hudson County bar assns. Home: 13 Wells Ct Bloomfield NJ 07003 Office: 80-82 Grand St Jersey City NJ 07302 Tel (201) 451-6000

SUMSION, RICHARD GLEN, b. Salt Lake City, Jan. 6, 1931; B.S., Brigham Young U., 1955; J.D., U. Utah, 1961. Admitted to Utah bar, 1961; partner firm Hansen & Sumsion, Salt Lake City, 1962-63, Hansen, Sumsion, Madsen & Randquist, Salt Lake City, 1963-66, Henriksen Murdock & Sumsion, Salt Lake City, 1966-69; adminstrv. law judge Utah State Indsl. Commn., Salt Lake City, 1969—. Mem. Internat. Assn. Indsl. Accident Bds. and Commns. (past conv. chmn.). Home: 3275 Joyce Dr Salt Lake City UT 84109 Office: 350 E 5th S St Salt Lake City UT 84111 Tel (801) 533-6411

SUNDAHL, JOHN ALAN, b. Bismarck, N.D., Aug. 1, 1948; B.A., U. Wyo., 1970; J.D., 1972. Admitted to Wyo. bar, 1972, U.S. Supreme Ct. bar, 1976; partner firm Godfrey and Sundahl, Cheyenne, Wyo., 1974—. Chmn., Cheyenne Fire Dept. Civil Service Commn., 1976—. Mem. Am., Wyo. bar assns., Cheyenne C. of C. Home: PO Box 4002 Cheyenne WY 82001 Office: PO Box 328 Cheyenne WY 82001 Tel (307) 632-6421

SUNDELL, LANNY SELVIN, b. Eureka, Calif., Nov. 9, 1945; B.A., Calif. State U., 1967; J.D., U. Calif. at Davis, 1970. Admitted to Calif. bar, 1971, U.S. Supreme Ct. bar, 1974; staff atty. Calif. Rural Legal Assistance, Gilroy, 1971-72; staff atty. Stanislaus County Legal Assistance, Inc., Modesto, Calif., 1972-75, directing atty., 1975—. Pres., Comprehensive Health Planning Council of Stanislaus County, 1974-75. Mem. State Bar Calif., Am., Stanislaus County bar assns., Nat. Legal Aid and Defender Assn. Author: Protecting Your Home From Creditors: The Filing of a Declaration of Homestead, 1974; Bankruptcy, 1974; You Can Use the Name of Your Choice! California Law on Name Usage, Name Change and Birth Certificates, 1975; Tenant Handbook: A Practical Guide to Dealing with Landlords, 3d edit., 1976. Office: 925 J St PO Box 3291 Modesto CA 95353 Tel (209) 524-6212

SUNDEN, GARY RICHARD, b. Portland, Maine, Dec. 16, 1940; B.A., Dickinson Coll., 1962; J.D., N.Y. U., 1966, LL.M., 1968. Admitted to N.Y. State bar, 1966; staff Legal Aid Soc., N.Y.C., 1967-68; individual practice law, N.Y.C., 1968—. Office: 401 Broadway New York City NY 10013 Tel (212) 925-4848

SUNDERLAND, THOMAS ELBERT, b. Ann Arbor, Mich., Apr. 28, 1907; A.B., U. Mich., 1928; J.D., U. Calif., Berkeley, 1930; postgrad. Harvard Bus. Sch., 1948. Admitted to Mich. bar, 1930, N.Y. bar, 1933, U.S. Supreme Ct. bar, 1948, Ill. bar, 1949, Mass. bar, 1962, D.C. bar, 1962, Ariz. bar, 1969; asso. firm Cadwalader, Wickersham & Taft, N.Y.C., 1931-33, firm Milbank, Tweed, Hope & Webb, N.Y.C., 1933-35, firm Townley, Updike & Carter, N.Y.C., 1935-40; gen. counsel Pan Am. Petroleum & Transport Co., Am. Oil Co. and affiliates, N.Y.C., 1940-48, gen. counsel, dir., mem. exec. com., 1946-56; v.p., dir., gen. counsel, mem. exec. com. Standard Oil Co. (Ind.), Chgo., 1948-60; pres. United Fruit Co., Boston, 1959-65, chmn., 1965-69; partner firm Snell & Wilmer, Phoenix, 1969—; dir. N.C.R. Corp., 1960—, Johns-Manville Corp., 1960-76, Liberty Mut. Ins. Co., 1960-69, 1st Nat. Bank Boston, 1959-69, Bd. dirs., mem. exec. com. United Fund Boston, 1960-68; mem. corp. Museum Sci. Boston, 1960-69; v.p., bd. dirs. Phoenix Symphony Assn., 1973—; trustee Boston Hosp. for Women, 1960—; bd. dirs. Boys' and Girls' Camps, Inc., Boston, 1964-68, Morgan Meml., Inc., 1965-69, Soc. Prevention of Blindness, 1950-60; nat. trustee Lake Forest (Ill.) Coll., Phoenix (Ariz.) Country Day Sch.; mem. corp., exec. com. Winsor Sch., Boston; mem. corp. Northeastern U., Boston; mem. vis com. law schs. Harvard, U. Mich., U. Chgo., Stanford. Mem. Am. Law Inst., Am. Bar Assn. (chmn. antitrust sect. 1956-58), Assn. Bar. City N.Y., Assn. Gen. Counsel, Council Fgn. Relations, Council Latin Am. (dir., exec. com.). Recipient Nat. Bus. Leadership award U. Mich., 1965, Outstanding Achievement award, 1970. Home: 5840 E Starlight Way Scottsdale AZ 85253 Office: 3100 Valley Center 201 N Central Ave Phoenix AZ 85073 Tel (602) 257-7262

SUNLEAF, ROGER WENDELL, b. Bellevue, Iowa, May 26, 1938; B.A., U. Iowa, 1959, J.D., 1963. Admitted to Iowa bar, 1963; asso. firm McFarlin & McFarlin, Montezuma, Iowa, 1964-66; partner firm McNeil & Sunleaf, Montezuma, 1966—; city atty. City of Montezuma, 1965—. Chmn. Poweshiek County Republican Party, 1972-74. Mem. Iowa State, Poweshiek County Bar assns., Iowa Municipal Attys. Assn., Assn. of Trial Lawyers of Am., Iowa Trial Lawyers Assn. (bd. dirs. 1976—). Home: 906 E Washington St Montezuma IA 50171 Office: 105 N 4th St Montezuma IA 50171 Tel (515) 623-5604

SUPINA, GERALD JOSEPH, b. Ionia, Mich., July 1, 1941; B.Arch., U. Detroit, 1965; J.D., Detroit Coll. Law, 1970. Admitted to Mich. bar, 1970; individual practice law, 1970—, Portland, Mich., 1971—; city atty. City of Portland, 1974—. Pres. Portland Jaycees, 1975; mem. bd. Portland C. of C., 1972-74. Mem. Am., Ionia-Montcalm bar assns., Comml. Law League. Home: 850 Kent St Portland MI 48875 Office: 242 Kent St Portland MI 48875 Tel (517) 647-7227

SURAN, ROBERT HERMAN, b. Milw., Oct. 14, 1934; B.S., U. Wis., 1956, J.D., 1959. Admitted to Wis. bar, 1959; individual practice law, Milw., 1959-71; partner firm Suran & Suran, Brown Deer, Wis., 1971—. Mem. bd. appeals City of Glendale (Wis.). Mem. Am. Trial Lawyers Assn. Office: 6051 W Brown Deer Rd Brown Deer WI 53223 Tel (414) 354-4140

SURETT, COREY HOWARD, b. Newark, Aug. 10, 1940; B.A., Rutgers U., 1962; J.D., Suffolk U., 1971. Admitted to Mass. bar, 1971; dir. Boston Area Office, wage and hour div. U.S. Dept. Labor, 1974—, asst. area dir., 1971-74. Mem. Mass., Fed. bar assns. Office: 100 Summer St Room 1522 Boston MA 02110 Tel (617) 223-6751

SURLES, OLIVER STEVENS, b. Dunn, N.C., Feb. 15, 1941; A.A., Campbell Coll., 1961; B.A., U. N.C., 1964; J.D., Wake Forest U., 1972. Admitted to N.C. bar, 1972; asso. firm Weeks & Muse, Tarboro, N.C., 1972-74; partner Weeks, Muse & Surles, Tarboro, 1974—. Mem. N.C., Nash-Edgecombe (sec., treas. 1976-77), 7th Jud. Dist. (sec., treas. 1974-76) bar assns., U.S. Jr. C. of C. (parliamentarian Tarboro chpt. 1974-75). Home: 1506 Speight Ave Tarboro NC 27886 Office: 211 E Pitt St Tarboro NC 27886 Tel (919) 823-3925

SUROVIK, BOB JOE, b. Glen Rose, Tex., Oct. 27, 1936; B.B.A. in Accounting, Tex. A. and M. Coll., 1958; LL.B., U. Tex., 1961. Admitted to Tex. bar, 1961; instr. in bus. law U. Tex. Sch. Bus., 1960-61; partner firm McMahon, Smart, Wilson, Surovik & Suttle, Abilene, Tex., 1963—. Pres. Abilene State Sch. Vol. Council, 1970-72; bd. dirs. Chisholm Trail council Boy Scouts Am., 1973—. Mem. State Bar Tex. (chmn. dist. 17 grievance com. 1972-73), Abilene Bar Assn., Abilene C. of C. (dir. 1975—, v.p. 1977). Named Outstanding Young Lawyer Tex. Jr. Bar, 1973, Abilene Jr. Bar, 1973. Home: 2025 Brookhaven Ave Abilene TX 79605 Office: PO Box 1440 Abilene TX 79604 Tel (915) 677-9138

SURREY, WALTER STERLING, b. Denver, July 24, 1915; s. Samuel and Pauline (Sterling) S.; student Coll. City N.Y., 1932-34; B.S., U. Va., 1936; LL.B., Yale U., 1939. Admitted to N.Y. bar, 1939, D.C. bar, 1950, U.S. Supreme Ct. bar, 1955; atty. Dept. Justice, Washington, 1940-41; research asst. Randolph Paul, Lord, Day & Lord, N.Y., 1939-40; atty. Bd. Econ. Warfare, Washington, 1941-43; attached charge econ. warfare Am. Legation, Stockholm, 1943-45; chief div. econ. security controls Dept. State, Washington, 1945-47, asst. legal adviser, 1947-50, cons., 1950-52; cons. ECA, 1948-59; now sr. partner firm Surrey, Karasik & Morse, Washington; professorial lectr. law George Washington U. Law Sch., 1962-63; adj. prof. Fletcher Sch. Law and Diplomacy, Tufts U., Boston, 1965—; trustee, vice chmn. Central Aguirre Co.; dir. Envirotech Corp. Mem. U.S. del. negotiating on German external assets Switzerland, Sweden, Spain and Portugal, 1945-46; U.S. mem. spl. com. on German property Inter-Am. Econ. and Social Council; mem., acting chmn. Nat. Conf. Internat. Econ. and Social Devel., 1963-65; bd. dirs., gen counsel, ex-officio mem. exec. com. Nat. Council for U.S.-China Trade; gen. counsel. mem. Iran-U.S. Bus. Council. Mem. U.S. C. of C. (internat. com.), Am. Soc. Internat. Law (pres. 1976—), Am. Law Inst., Nat. Planning Assn. (dir., gen. counsel). Editor: Law Governing International Business Transactions; contbr. articles to legal jours. Home: 5171 Manning Pl NW Washington DC 20016 Office: 1156 15th St NW Washington DC 20005 Tel (202) 331-4000

SUSMAN, MINNIE ELIZABETH, b. Butler, Pa., Jan. 2, 1909; B.A., U. Pitts., 1929, LL.B., 1932. Admitted to Pa. Bar, 1932, U.S. Supreme Ct. bar; individual practice law, Butler, 1932-46; chmn. dept. edn. Greater Pitts. Guild for the Blind, 1961-72. Mem. AAUW (past pres.), Nat. Council Jewish Women. Address: 5819 Ferree St Pittsburgh PA 15217

SUSSMAN, CARL B., b. Chgo., Dec. 25, 1913; J.D., Ill. Inst. Tech. Admitted to Ill. bar, 1937; individual practice law, Chgo., 1937-71; U.S. magistrate No. Dist. Ill., 1971—; mem. Ill. Parole and Pardon Bd., 1965-69; mem. bd. dirs. Chgo. House of Correction, 1965-69, Cook County Dept. Corrections, 1969-71. Hon. trustee Cancer Prevention Center, Inc., 1972—. Mem. Chgo. Bar Assn. (chmn. assn. meetings), Decalogue Soc. Lawyers (Distinguished Service award 1950). Contbr. articles to legal jours. Tel (312) 435-5640

SUSSMAN, F. RICHARD, b. N.Y.C., Feb. 20, 1932; A.B., Clark U., 1953; LL.B., Columbia, 1956. Admitted to N.Y. bar, 1956, U.S. Dist. Ct. (So. and Eastern N.Y.) bar, 1958, U.S. Ct. Appeals (2d circuit) bar, 1958; since practiced in N.Y.C.; asso. firm Fish & Fox, 1956-57, Wikler, Gottleib, Stuart, Taylor & Long, 1958-62; partner Schultz, Frank & Sussman, 1963-65; partner Sussman & McGrath, 1966-68; individual practice law, 1969—; pres. Inland Devel. Corp., N.Y.C., 1969-73. Mem. Columbia Univ. Law Sch. Alumni Assn., Internat. Council Shopping Centers, Green Farms Assn. (Westport, Conn., pres). Home: 12 Arrowhead Rd Westport CT 06880 Office: 60 E 42d St New York City NY 10017 Tel (212) 867-8780

SUSSMAN, GILBERT, b. N.Y.C., June 23, 1905; B.A., U. Oreg., 1925; LL.B., Columbia, 1929. Admitted to Conn. bar, 1933, Oreg. bar, 1944; mem. research staff and faculty Yale Law Sch., 1929-34; sr. atty. Agrl. Adjustment Adminstrn., Washington, 1934-35, Nat. Recovery Adminstrn., Washington, 1935; regional atty. U.S. Resettlement Adminstrn., Portland, Oreg., 1935-36, U.S. Dept. Agr., Portland, 1937-43; asst. gen. counsel Bonneville Power Adminstrn., Portland, 1943-45; individual practice law, Portland, 1945—; partner firm Sussman, Shank, Wapnick & Caplan, and predecessors, Portland, 1957—. Bd. dirs. Portland Center Hearing Speech, 1953-58, v.p., 1956-58; bd. dirs. Community Council, Portland, 1955-62, v.p., 1960-62; bd. dirs. Jewish Welfare Fedn., 1956-62, 71-76, sec., 1961-63; bd. dirs. United Good Neighbors, 1962-65, 66—; bd. dirs. Oreg. United Appeal, 1971-75, chmn. budget panels, 1970-73. Mem. Oreg. State Bar, Multnomah County Bar Assn., Comml. Law League Am. Contbr. articles to legal jours. Office: 1111 American Bank Bldg Portland OR Tel (503) 227-1111

SUSSMAN, JEROME J., b. Bklyn., May 28, 1936; A.B., Princeton, 1956; LL.B., Harvard, 1959. Admitted to N.Y. State bar, 1959, Calif. bar, 1971; asso. firm McLaughlin & Stern, N.Y.C., 1959-60, Gartenberg & Ellenoff, N.Y.C., 1960-63; asso. Jesse Moss, N.Y.C., 1963-65; atty. Columbia Pictures Corp., N.Y.C., 1965-68; asso. firm Golenbock & Barell, N.Y.C., 1968-70; atty. Am. Internat. Pictures, Inc., Beverly Hills, Calif., 1970-72, asso. gen. counsel, asst. sec., 1972-75, corporate sec., 1975-76; distbn. counsel Twentieth Century-Fox Film Corp., Los Angeles, 1976—. Mem. Calif., N.Y., Beverly Hills, Los Angeles bar assns., Los Angeles Copyright Soc. Contbr. articles to legal jours. Office: 10201 W Pico Blvd Los Angeles CA 90035 Tel (213) 277-2211

SUSSMAN, LOUIS, b. Jersey City, Aug. 2, 1908; B.C.S., N.Y. U., 1933, LL.B., John Marshall Law Sch., 1937. Admitted to N.J. bar, 1936; prin. firm Louis Sussman & Co., Jersey City, 1937—. C.P.A., N.J., N.Y. Office: 26 Journal Square Jersey City NJ 07306 Tel (201) 653-0930 also 9273 Collins Ave Surfside FL 33154

SUSSMAN, ROSS ABBOTT, b. Mpls., Nov. 13, 1933; B.S. in Law, U. Minn., 1955; LL.B., 1957. Admitted to Minn. bar, 1957; individual practice, Mpls., 1957—; lectr. Hamline U., St. Paul, 1976. Bd. dirs. Friends of Mpls. Pub. Library, 1966—, pres. 1969. Mem. Hennepin County, Minn. bar assns. Contbr. articles to legal jours. Home: 2743 Dean Pkwy Minneapolis MN 55416 Office: 430 Oak Grove on the Park Minneapolis MN 55403 Tel (612) 870-7733

SUSTER, RONALD JOSEPH, b. Cleve., Oct. 31, 1942; B.A., Western Reserve U., 1964; J.D., Case Western Reserve U., 1967. Admitted to Ohio bar, 1967, Fla. bar, 1975; asst. law dir. City of Cleve., 1967; asst. county prosecutor Cuyahoga County, Ohio, 1968-71; asst. atty. gen. State of Ohio, 1971-76; dir. law Highland Heights, Ohio, 1976; individual practice law, Cleve., 1968—. Mem. Cleve. Acad. Trial Lawyers, Am. Trial Lawyers, Am., Cleve. bar assns. Office: 1027 E 185th St Cleveland OH 44119 Tel (216) 531-2666

SUTHERLAND, ALFRED DELLOYD, b. Fond du Lac, Wis., Feb. 28, 1891; A.B., Ripon Coll., 1913; LL.D., Harvard, 1917. Admitted to Wis. bar, 1919, U.S. Supreme Ct. bar, 1945, other fed. cts.; individual practice law, Fond du Lac, Wis., 1918—; U.S. commr. Eastern dist. Wis., 1919-28; dir. pub. welfare Wis. Bd. dirs. Fond du Lac Pub. Welfare Assn., YMCA. Mem. Am. Bar Assn. (50 yr. mem.), Am. Jud. Soc. (50 yr. sustaining mem.), Res. Officers Assn. (pres. 1926), Izaak Walton League Am. (past dir., nat. v.p., hon. pres. 1957), Fond du Lac C. of C. (pres. 1925-26), Theta Sigma Tau, Pi Delta Kappa. Recipient Outstanding Work in Conservation award NASH Motor Co., 1954, Broughton award 1951, LaBudde award, 1966, Outstanding Work in Conservation award Ripon Coll., 1971; author: 60 Years Afield and Observations on Conservation, also articles. Office: 104 S Main St Fond du Lac WI 54935 Tel (414) 921-1610

SUTHERLAND, MATTHEW ROZELIUS, b. New Orleans, Feb. 7, 1919; B.A., Tulane U., 1947, J.D., 1949. Admitted to La. bar, 1949; law clk., La. Supreme Ct., 1949-52; counsel Pan-Am. Life Ins. Co., New Orleans, 1952-57, asst. gen. counsel, 1957-62, gen. counsel 1962—, 2nd. v.p., 1967-75, v.p., 1975—; alt. dir. Pan-Am. de Venezuela, 1966-71; Pan Am. de Guatemala, 1967—; Pan-Am. de Colombia, 1974—. Del. La. Constl. Conv., 1973; mem. La. Sch. Bds. Assn., pres. 1960; Nat. Sch. Bds. Assn., dir., 1958-61; pres. Orleans Parish Sch. Bd., 1959, 63, 66. Mem. Am., La., New Orleans bar assns., Assn. Life Ins. Counsel, Am. Judicature Soc., Am. Life Ins. Assn., Health Ins. Assn., Am., La. Insurers Conf., Phi Beta Kappa. Contbr. papers to law jours. Home: 2743 Gallinghouse St New Orleans LA 70114 Office: 2400 Canal St New Orleans LA 70119 Tel (504) 821-2510

SUTHERLUND, DAVID ARVID, b. Stevens Point, Wis., July 20, 1929; B.A., U. Portland, Oreg., 1952; J.D., U. N.Mex., 1957; postgrad. U. Wis., 1957. Admitted to D.C. bar, U.S. Supreme Ct. bar, 1961; with ICC, Washington, 1957-58; atty. office of gen. counsel Am. Trucking Assns., Washington, 1958-62; asso. firm Morgan, Lewis & Bockius, Washington, Phila., 1962-66, partner, 1966-72; of counsel firm Turney & Turney, Washington, 1972-75; partner firm Fulbright & Jaworski, Washington, 1975—. Mem. Am. (pub. utilities and adminstrv. law sects.), Fed. (sec. rules and procedural methods sect., mem. adminstrv. law com.) bar assns., Motor Carrier Lawyers Assn. (sec., 1963-65), Am. Arbitration Assn., Nat. Lawyers Club, Lawyers Club N.Y.C., Bar Assn. D.C., Am. Judicature Soc., Assn. Trial Attys. Am., ICC Practitioners Assn. Founder, chmn. bd. govs. Transp. Law Jour. Home: 2130 Bancroft Pl NW Washington DC 20008 Office: 1150 Connecticut Ave NW Washington DC 20036 Tel (202) 452-6847

SUTLEY, PHILLIP MCKAY, b. Balt., Jan. 10, 1941; A.B., Johns Hopkins, 1962; LL.B., U. Balt., 1967. Admitted to Md. bar, 1967; individual practice law, Balt., 1967-74; partner firm Sutley & Marr, Balt., 1974—; mem. Tydings Commn. to Study Prosecutorial Function, 1974-75. Mem. Am., Md., Balt. City bar assns. Office: Fidelity Bldg Baltimore MD 21201 Tel (301) 727-2040

SUTTENBERG, JOEL PAUL, b. Cambridge, Mass., July 25, 1944; B.A., Yale U., 1966; J.D., Boston U., 1969. Admitted to Mass. bar, 1969, Fed. bar, 1974; mem. Mass. Defenders Com., 1969-70; dep. asst. atty. gen. Civil Rights and Civil Liberties Div., 1971-74; asso. firm Cohn, Riemer & Pollack, Boston, 1974-75; partner firm Cherwin & Glazier, Boston, 1975—; dir. Eagle Ridge Coal Co., Village Mall, Inc. Vice pres. mens' assos. Hebrew Rehab. Center for Aged, Roslindale, Mass.; mem. urban affairs com. Am. Jewish Com. Mem. Mass., Boston bar assns. Home: 5 Radcliffe Rd Weston MA Office: 141 Milk St Boston MA 02109 Tel (617) 482-2777

SUTTER, WILLIAM GEORGE, JR., b. Pitts., Jan. 5, 1941; B.A., Allegheny Coll., 1962; LL.B., Duquesne U., 1965. Admitted to Pa. bar, 1965, U.S. Ct. Appeals 3d Circuit bar, 1965, U.S. Supreme Ct. bar, 1970; asso. firm Thorp, Reed & Armstrong, Pitts., 1965; asso. firm Egler, McGregor & Reinstadtler, Pitts., 1966-69; gen. counsel Urban Redevel. Authority of Pitts., 1969-71; mng. partner firm Sutter & Sutter, Pitts., 1969—; counsel Pa. Assn. of Housing and Redevel. Agencies, 1967-73. Mem. Swissvale Area Schs. Bd. Edn. Mem. Am. Arbitration Assn., Allegheny County Bar Assn. Home: Trevanian Ave Pittsburgh PA 15218 Office: 443 Blvd of Allies Pittsburgh PA 15219 Tel (412) 261-3773

SUTTLE, STEPHEN HUNGATE, b. Uvalde, Tex., Mar. 17, 1940; B.A., Washington and Lee U., 1962; J.D., U. Tex., 1965. Admitted to Tex. bar, 1965, U.S. Supreme Ct. bar, 1972; briefing atty. to judge U.S. Dist. Ct. No. Dist. Tex., 1965-67; partner firm McMahon, Smart, Wilson, Surovik & Suttle, Abilene, Tex., 1967-70; mem. Tex. Commn. on Jail Standards. Budget com. United Way; bd. dirs., sec., pres. Boys Clubs Abilene; bd. dirs., chmn. Citizens for Better Govt.; bd. dirs. Community Action Program, Abilene Fine Arts Mus., Abilene Community Theater, Allegro Dance Club; vestryman Ch. of Heavenly Rest, Episcopal. Mem. Am. (chmn. achievement award com., mem. explorer law com. young lawyers sect.), Tex. (chmn. dist. grievance com., mem. merit award com., spl. com. on disruption trials, selection, compensation and tenure of state judges com.), Abilene (sec.-treas., dir., chmn. constn. and by-laws revision com., mem. admissions to bar com.) bar assns., Abilene C. of C. (mem. Jobs 70 com., dir. Operation Mainstream). Home: 1405 Woodland Trail Abilene TX 79605 Office: Box 1440 Abilene TX 79604 Tel (915) 677-9138

SUTTLE, THOMAS HENRY, JR., b. Jackson, Miss., Aug. 12, 1941; B.A., Miss. State U., 1963; J.D., U. Miss., 1971. Admitted to Miss. bar, 1971; asso. firm Daniel, Coker, Horton, Bell & Dukes, Jackson, 1971-75, partner, 1975—. Mem. Am., Miss., Hinds County bar assns., Jackson Young Lawyers Assn. Office: 405 Tombigbee St PO Box 1084 Jackson MS 39205 Tel (601) 352-7607

SUTTON, BARRETT BOULWARE, b. Forsyth, Ga., July 6, 1927; A.B., Vanderbilt U., 1949, LL.B., 1950. Admitted to Tenn. bar, 1950; with Life & Casualty Ins. Co. of Tenn., Nashville, 1950—, gen. counsel, 1970—, sr. v.p., 1972—, also dir. and mem. exec. com. Pres. Nashville Council Community Services, 1968-70; vice chmn. Nashville United Way Campaign, 1975; elder Presbyn. Ch., Nashville. Mem. Assn. Life Ins. Counsel, Order of Coif, Phi Beta Kappa. Home: 750 Greeley Dr Nashville TN 37205 Office: Life and Casualty Tower Nashville TN 37219 Tel (615) 254-1511

SUTTON, JOHN F., JR., b. Alpine, Tex., Jan. 26, 1918; J.D., U. Tex., 1941. Admitted to Tex. bar, 1941; asso. firm Brooks, Napier, Brown & Matthews, San Antonio, 1941-42; spl. agt. FBI, Washington, 1942-45; asso. firm Matthews, Nowlin, Macfarlane & Barrett, San Antonio, 1945-48; partner firm Kerr, Gayer & Sutton, San Angelo, Tex., 1948-51, Sutton, Steib & Barr, San Angelo, 1951-57; prof. law U. Tex., Austin, 1957-69, William Benjamin Wynne prof. in law, 1969—. Mem. Am. (co-draftsman code profl. responsibility), Travis County bar assns., State Bar Tex. Author: (with McCormick, Elliott and Sutton) Cases and Materials on Evidence, 1971. Home: Route 1 Box 36C Buda TX 78610 Office: 2500 Red River St Austin TX 78705 Tel (512) 471-5151

SUTTON, JOHN PAUL, b. Youngstown, Ohio, July 24, 1934; B.A., U. Va., 1956; J.D., George Washington U., 1963. Admitted to Va. bar, 1964, Calif. bar, 1965; patent examiner U.S. Patent Office, Washington, 1956, 59-62; tech. advisor U.S. Ct. Customs and Patent Appeals, Washington, 1962-64; asso. firm Flehr, Hohbach, Test, Albritton & Herbert, San Francisco, 1964-68, Limbach, Limbach & Sutton, San Francisco, 1969—; lectr. Practicing Law Inst., N.Y.C., 1968, San Francisco, 1969, Southwestern Legal Found., Dallas, 1970, Continuing Edn. of Bar Calif., 1971, 75, U. Calif. at Berkeley Sch. Law, 1975. Mem. Bar Assn. San Francisco, Calif. (pres. 1974-75), San Francisco (pres.) patent law assns. Contbr. articles to legal jours. Home: 2421 Pierce St San Francisco CA 94115 Office: 3000 Ferry Bldg San Francisco CA 94111 Tel (415) 433-4150

SUTTON, RICHARD IKE, b. Honolulu, Apr. 5, 1917; A.B., Stanford, 1937, LL.D., 1950, J.D., 1951. Admitted to Hawaii bar, 1950; law clk. Fed. Ct., 1950-52; asso. firm Sutton & Sutton, 1952-62, fed. judge, Wake Island, 1970-74. Del. Hawaii Constnl. Conv., 1968; mem. Hawaii Legislature, 1974—. Mem. Am., Fed. (pres. Hawaii chpt. 1973-74), Hawaii (pres. 1974) bar assns. Home: 3539 Kahawalu St Honolulu HI 96817 Office: State Capitol Room 420 Honolulu HI 96813 Tel (808) 595-3366

SVETANICS, MILTON FRANK, JR., b. St. Louis, July 1, 1937; B.S., St. Louis U., 1960, J.D., 1967. Admitted to Mo. bar, 1967; atty. Gen. Am. Life Ins. Co., St. Louis, 1967—, now asst. gen. counsel; spl. asst. atty. gen. State of Mo., 1968. Alderman, St. Louis, 1969—; mem. St. Louis City Planning Commn., 1972, Community Sch. Council; mem. exec. bd. United Way; v.p. St. Louis Health and Welfare Council, 1972-74. Mem. Nat. Assn. Securities Dealers (chmn. dist. bus. conduct com.), St. Louis Bar Assn. (chmn. municipal law com. 1973-75). Recipient Community Betterment award, 1971; named Outstanding Young Man, St. Louis Jr. C. of C., 1972. Home: 1007 Veronica St Saint Louis MO 63147 Office: 1501 Locust St Saint Louis MO 63174 Tel (314) 231-1700

SWACKER, FRANK WARREN, b. N.Y.C., May 18, 1922; B.A., Union Coll., Schenectady, 1947; J.D., U. Va., 1949; LL.B. in Internat. Law, N.Y. U., 1961. Admitted to Va. bar, 1948, N.Y. bar, 1950, Supreme Ct. U.S. bar, 1952, Ohio bar, 1962, Wis. bar, 1969; individual practice law, N.Y.C., 1949-54, 64-68; atty. Caltex Petroleum Corp., N.Y.C., 1955-60, Marathon Oil Co., Ohio, 1961-63; internat. counsel Allis-Chalmers Corp., Milw., 1968-77; pvt. practice law, Washington, 1977—. spl. asst. dep. atty. gen. State of N.Y., 1950; govtl. adviser U.S., P.I., Algeria; lectr. Ohio No. U., 1962, N.Y. World Trade Inst., 1976; mem. panel experts Am. Arbitration Assn. Mem. World Peace Through Law, Am. Soc. Internat. Law, Am. Fgn. Law Assn., Assn. Bar City N.Y., Am., Va., Wis. bar assns. Co-editor, contbr. Business and Legal Aspects of Latin American Trade and Investment, 1977; contbr. articles to legal jours. Office: 55-20 N 10th St Arlington VA 22205 Tel (703) 241-1239

SWAIM, CHARLES HALL, b. Delta, Colo., Dec. 31, 1939; Geophys. Engr., Colo. Sch. Mines, 1961; J.D., N.Y. U., 1964. Admitted to Colo. bar, 1964, Tex. bar, 1965, Mass. bar, 1971; mem. legal staff Tex. Instruments, Inc., Dallas, 1964-65, asst. counsel, 1967-71; jr. partner firm Hale and Dorr, Boston, 1974—. Mem. Am., Mass. bar assns. Office: 28 State St Boston MA 02109 Tel (617) 742-9100

SWAIN, DONALD HUGHES, b. Norwood, Ohio, Aug. 24, 1931; A.B., U. Cin., 1953, J.D., 1955. Admitted to Ohio bar, 1955; individual practice law, Cin., 1957-66; partner firm Bauer, Swain & Morelli, Cin., 1966-68; sr. asso. firm Swain & Hardin, Cin., 1969—; judge adv. USAF, McConnel AFB, Wichita, Kans., 1955-57; asst. atty. gen. State of Ohio, Cin., 1959-63; solicitor Village of Addyston (Ohio), 1964-65; spl. counsel Cin. City Solicitor, 1963; mem. Ohio Ho. of Reps., 1954. Bd. dirs. Hamilton County (Ohio) Agrl. Soc., 1970—, v.p., 1972—; bd. dirs. Cancer Control Council Greater Cin., 1969—; bd. dirs. Cancer Family Care, Cin., 1971—, sec., 1971-73, treas., 1975—. Mem. Am., Ohio, Cin. bar assns. Recipient citations for achievement by Cin. City Mgr. and Ohio Atty. Gen., 1961. Home: 5314 Elmcrest Ln Cincinnati OH 45242 Office: Suite 408 1501 Madison Rd Cincinnati OH 45206 Tel (513) 221-8000

SWAIN, ROBERT STRINGFIELD, b. Asheville, N.C., July 25, 1921; LL.B., U. N.C., 1949. Admitted to N.C. bar, 1949; individual practice, Asheville, 1949-55; U.S. commr. Asheville, 1951-54; dist. solicitor Buncombe and Madison Counties (N.C.), 1956-67; partner firm Swain, Leake & Stevenson, Asheville, 1967—; mem. N.C. Senate, 1977—. Mem. N.C., Buncombe County (treas. 1950-53, trustee 1954-57) bar assns., N.C. Assn. Trial Lawyers. Recipient Outstanding Service award Jaycees, 1958. Home: Route 5 Box 1112 Asheville NC 28803 Office: 301 Northwestern Bank Asheville NC 28801 Tel (704) 253-8374

SWAN, SCOTT HUGH, b. Anaconda, Mont., Jan. 28, 1943; B.A., Coll. William and Mary, 1965, J.D., 1969. Admitted to Va. bar, 1969; asso. firm May Garrett & Miller, Richmond, Va., 1969-70, firm Bremner Byrne & Baber, Richmond, 1970-75; dep. commonwealth's atty. City of Richmond, 1975—. Mem. Am., Va., Richmond bar assns. Office: Courts Bldg Richmond VA 23219 Tel (804) 780-8045

SWANBERG, ROBERT FRANCIS, b. Butte, Mont., Aug. 27, 1915; LL.B., U. Mont., 1940. Admitted to Mont. bar, 1938; individual practice law, Missoula, Mont., 1939-42; atty. office of solicitor U.S. Dept. Labor, Mpls., 1942, county atty. Missoula County, Mont., 1946-50; spl. asst. U.S. Atty., Helena, Mont., 1951-52; chmn. Mont. Indsl. Accident Bd., Helena, 1953-69; partner firm Rankin & Acher & Robert F. Swanberg, Helena, 1969—. Mem. State Bar of Mont. Office: 316 Fuller Ave Helena MT 59601 Tel (406) 442-8450

SWANN, EUGENE MERWYN, b. Phila., Aug. 1, 1934; B.S., Temple U., 1957; M.A., U. Mass., 1959; LL.B., U. Calif., Berkeley, 1962. Admitted to Calif. bar, 1963, U.S. Supreme Ct. bar, 1968; dep. dist. atty. Contra Costa County (Calif.), 1963-67; exec. dir. Contra Costa Legal Services, Richmond, Calif., 1967—; lectr. econs. U. Calif., Berkeley, 1967—, Stanford Grad. Sch. Bus., 1972—. Mem. Am., Contra Costa, Calif. bar assns., Charles Huston Law Club. Named Outstanding Legal Services Atty. in Nation Nat. Legal Aid Pub. Defender Assn., 1972. Home: 43 Donald Dr Orinda CA 94563 Office: 332-10th St Richmond CA 94801 Tel (415) 233-9954

SWANSON, CARL AUGUST, JR., b. Dekalb, Ill., Mar. 1, 1918; B.S., Northwestern U., 1941, J.D., 1947. Admitted to Ill. bar, 1948; practiced in Dekalb, 1950-63; city atty. City of Dekalb, 1953-56; states' atty. County of Dekalb, 1956-63; asso. judge 16th Circuit, Ill. Circuit Ct., 1963-70, judge, 1970—. Mem. Ill., Dekalb County bar assns. Home: 437 College Ave Dekalb IL 60115 Office: Courthouse Sycamore IL 60178 Tel (815) 895-9161

SWANSON, DAVID WARREN, b. Fairmont, Minn., Mar. 20, 1932; A.B., Augustana Coll., Rock Island, Ill., 1953; J.D., U. Mich., 1956. Admitted to Mich. bar, 1956, N.Y. bar, 1958; asso. firm White & Case, N.Y.C., 1956-66, partner, 1967—, adminstrv. partner, 1974—. Trustee Henry M. Blackmer Found., Inc., 1967—; mem. vis. com. U. Mich. Law Sch., 1974—. Mem. Am., N.Y. State bar assns., Assn. Bar City N.Y. Home: 57 Undercliff Rd Montclair NJ 07042 Office: 14 Wall St New York City NY 10005 Tel (212) 732-1040

SWANSON, HARRY BROOKS, b. Reno, June 4, 1928; A.B., U. Nev., 1950; LL.B., U. Calif., San Francisco, 1953. Admitted to Nev. bar, 1953; asst. city atty. Reno, 1953-54; JAG, USAF, 1954-56; mem. firm Swanson, Swanson & Capurro, and predecessors, Reno, 1956—; guest lectr. Hastings Coll. Law, U. Calif., San Francisco, 1956-68;

mem. Nev. State Legis., 1958-64; mem. bd. govs. Hastings Coll. Law Alumni Assn., 1970-74. Mem. Am., Washoe County, Nev. State bar assns., Assn. Trial Lawyers Am. Editor Nev. State Bar Jour., 1956-62; Nev. editor Trusts and Estates, 1963-71; contbr. articles to legal jours. Home: 2001 Sierra Sage Ln Reno NV 89509 Office: Box 2417 Reno NV 89505 Tel (702) 329-8686

SWANSON, MAYNARD FRANCIS, JR., b. Moline, Ill., Aug. 25, 1935; A.B., Grinnell Coll., 1957; J.D., Duke, Durham, N.C., 1960. Admitted to Fla. bar, 1960; dep. clk. 6th Circuit Ct., Clearwater, Fla., 1960; asso. firm James M. Stephens, Tarpon Springs, Fla., 1961-62; individual practice law, Clearwater, 1962-73; judge Pinellas County Ct., St. Petersburg, Fla., 1973—, City of Tarpon Springs, 1961; tchr. law Pinellas County Adult Edn., 1963-67. Mem. Am., Clearwater bar assns., Fla. Bar, Pinellas Trial Lawyers Assn., Am. Judicature Soc., ACLU. Home: 782 Village Lake Terr Saint Petersburg FL 33715 Office: 150 5th St N Saint Petersburg FL 33701 Tel (813) 898-4161

SWANSON, RALPH JOHN, b. Red Oak, Iowa, Nov. 22, 1920; B.A., State U. Iowa, 1947, J.D., 1948. Admitted to Iowa bar, 1948, U.S. Supreme Ct. bar, 1965. Individual practice law, Red Oak, 1948—; sr. partner firm Swanson, Boeye & Bloom, Red Oak, 1970—; county atty. Montgomery County (Iowa), 1951-55; dir. Blue-Cross of Iowa, 1967—. Bd. dirs. Red Oak Indsl. Found.; trustee Murphy Meml. Hosp., Red Oak, 1949—. Mem. Am., Iowa State, SW Iowa (pres.) bar assns., Red Oak C. of C., (pres. 1951-52). Contbr. articles to law jours. Home: 1119 Boundary St Red Oak IA 51566 Office: 209 Coolbaugh St Red Oak IA 51566 Tel (712) 623-2554

SWANSON, WILLIAM FREDIN, JR., b. Phila., Sept. 10, 1928; B.A., U. Pitts., 1950; J.D., Harvard, 1953. Admitted to Pa. bar, 1954; atty. Moorhead & Knox, Pitts., 1953-58; asst. counsel PPG Industries, Pitts., 1959-67; asst. gen. counsel Rockwell-Standard Corp., Pitts., 1967, asst. gen. counsel comml. products group N.Am. Rockwell Corp. (merger with N.Am. Aviation, Inc.), 1967-68, gen. counsel comml. products group, 1968-71, staff v.p., asso. gen. counsel, 1971-75, (name changed to Rockwell Internat. Corp. 1973), sec., staff v.p., asso. gen. counsel, 1975—. Mem. parents council Wake Forest U., 1975—. Mem. Am. Soc. Corp. Secs., Am., Pa., Allegheny County bar assns., U. Pitts. Alumni Council (v.p. 1966-68). Home: 358 Braddsley Dr Pittsburgh PA 15235 Office: 600 Grant St Pittsburgh PA 15219 Tel (412) 565-2902

SWARTS, JAMES LAW, b. Kansas City, Mo., Dec. 15, 1946; B.A., U. Mo., 1968, J.D., 1971. Admitted to Mo. bar, 1972; asso. firm Jack C. Terry, Independence, Mo., 1972—; part-time asst. to Jackson County (Mo.) Pub. Adminstr., 1976—; law clk. for Circuit Ct. Judge Laurence R. Smith, 1971-72. Mem. Eastern Jackson County Bar Assn. Home: 2003 Pembroke Crescent W Independence MO 64057 Office: 554 S Ash St Independence MO 64053 Tel (816) 254-6070

SWARTS, KEM WINTHROP, b. Lincoln, Nebr., Apr. 8, 1946; B.A., U. Nebr., 1968, J.D., 1971. Admitted to Nebr. bar, 1971; asso. firm Maupin, Dent, Kay, Satterfield, Girard and Scritsmier, North Platte, Nebr., 1971-72; partner firm Olds and Swarts, Wayne, Nebr., 1973—. Bd. dirs. Wayne Community Chest, 1973—, pres., 1975—; elder United Presbyterian Ch. Wayne, 1976—; bd. regents alt. U. Nebr., Lincoln. Mem. Am., Nebr. bar assns., North Platte Jaycees (sec. 1971-72), Phi Delta Phi. Office: 223 Main St Wayne NE 68787 Tel (402) 375-3585

SWARTZ, ALAN LEONARD, b. Providence, May 6, 1935; B.S., Boston U., 1957, J.D., 1959; LL.M., N.Y. U., 1960. Admitted to R.I. bar, 1959, Mass. bar, 1960, U.S. Tax Ct. bar, 1961, U.S. Supreme Ct. bar, 1970; atty., office chief counsel IRS, 1960-65; partner firm Arcaro & Swartz, Providence, 1965-70, firm Salter, McGowan, Arcaro & Swartz, Inc., Providence, 1970—; Kenneson fellow, instr. N.Y. U. Sch. Law, 1959-60. Mem. Am., R.I. bar assns. Sr. editor Boston U. Law Rev., 1958-59. Contbr. articles to legal jours. Home: 10 Dorset Rd Pawtucket RI 02860 Office: 1500 Indsl Bank Bldg Providence RI 02903 Tel (401) 274-0300

SWARTZ, BARBARA ELLEN, b. Bridgeport, Conn., July 23, 1945; B.A., Temple U., 1966; M.A., U. Mich., 1967; J.D., N.Y. U., 1971. Admitted to N.Y. bar, 1971, U.S. Dist. Ct. bar, 1975, U.S. Ct. Appeals bar, 1976; Reginald Heber Smith Poverty Law fellow Law Reform Unit Camden (N.J.) Regional Legal Services, 1972-73; asst. clin. prof. N.Y. U. Law Sch., N.Y.C., 1973—; dir. Bedford Hills Women's Prison Project, 1973—; mem. bd. dirs. Washington Sq. Legal Services, 1974—; cons. on project on Bedford Hills, N.Y. Council on Humanities. Bd. dirs. Project Green Hope, 1975—. Mem. Nat. Lawyers Guild, N.Y. County Lawyers Assn. (com. on crime and penology). Author: Making the Law Work for You: A Prisoner's Guide, 1976. Office: 80 5th Ave Rm 1502 New York City NY 10011 Tel (212) 924-3200

SWARTZ, JOHN DEXTER, b. N.Y.C., Feb. 22, 1907; B.S., Colby Coll., 1929; J.D., Harvard U., 1933. Admitted to N.Y. bar, 1934, D.C. bar, 1962, U.S. Supreme Ct. bar, 1951; individual practice law, N.Y.C., 1934-41; spl. atty. criminal div. U.S. Dept. Justice, Washington, 1941-44, trial atty. antitrust div., N.Y.C., 1944-46, spl. asst. to Atty. Gen., N.Y.C., 1946-53, asst. chief antitrust div., N.Y.C., 1953-67; partner firm Swartz, Stark, Amron & Haberman, N.Y.C., 1967—. Mem. Assn. Bar City N.Y., Am., N.Y. State bar assns. Office: 1133 Ave of Americas New York City NY 10036 Tel (212) 765-6930

SWARTZ, KENNETH ARTHUR, b. July 25, 1926; B.A., Iowa Wesleyan Coll., 1951; J.D., Ill. U., 1953. Admitted to Ill. bar, 1953, Fed. Dist. Ct. bar, 1954; asso. firm, Gann, Secord, Stead & McIntosh, Chgo., 1953-57; partner firm, Brawseke and Swartz, Morton Grove, Ill., 1964; individual practice law, 1964—; dir. numerous corps. Mem. Chgo., Ill. bar assns. Recipient Distinguished Service award Iowa Wesleyan Coll. Alumni Assn., 1965. Home: 1214 Overlook Dr Golf IL 60029 also 5945 Dempster St Morton Grove IL 60053 Tel (312) 267-1535

SWARTZ, LEE CARTER, b. Harrisburg, Pa., July 20, 1936; B.S., Albright Coll., 1958; J.D., Dickinson Sch. Law, Carlisle, Pa., 1961. Admitted to Pa. bar, 1962, U.S. Supreme Ct. bar, 1966; mem. firm H. Joseph, Harrisburg, 1962-69; partner firm Hepford, Zimmerman & Swartz, Harrisburg, 1970—; writer, course planner Pa. Continuing Legal Edn.; vis. lectr. Dickinson Sch. Law. Pres., Police Athletic League of Greater Harrisburg, 1969-74. Mem. Am., Pa., Dauphin County (treas. 1974—) bar assns., Am. Judicature Soc., Am., Pa. (pres. 1977—, editor The Barrister) assns. trial lawyers, Pitts. Inst. Legal Medicine, Pa. Bar Inst. (pres. 1975-76). Home: 919 Wilhelm Rd Harrisburg PA 17111 Office: 111 N Front St PO Box 889 Harrisburg PA 17108 Tel (717) 234-4121

SWARTZ, ROBERT P., b. Paterson, N.J., Sept. 7, 1934; B.A., Rutgers U., 1956, J.D., 1958. Admitted to N.J. bar, 1958, U.S. Supreme Ct. bar, 1963; with Allstate Ins. Co., 1960-62; individual practice law, 1962-70; asst. sec.-counsel Paterson Bd. Edn., 1967—; city counsel City of Paterson, 1967. Mem. N.J., Passaic County bar assns., N.J. Assn. Sch. Attys., Nat. Orgn. Legal Problems of Edn. Home: 3 Ridge Terr Paterson NJ 07514 Office: 33 Church St Paterson NJ 07505 Tel (201) 271-1440

SWATEK, WILLIAM EDWARD, b. Kingsport, Tenn., Jan. 6, 1940; student Spring Hill Coll., 1958-62; LL.B., Cumberland U., 1966. Admitted to Ala. bar, 1969; individual practice law, Birmingham, Ala., 1969-72, Pelham, Ala., 1972—; judge City of Pelham, 1972-76, City of Montevallo, Ala., 1972-77. Mem. Am., Birmingham bar assns., Am. Trial Lawyers Assn. Office: PO Box 825 Alabaster AL 35007 Tel (205) 663-0905

SWAUN, JOHN WESLEY, b. New Haven, June 20, 1939; B.B.A., U. Miami, 1961, J.D., 1966. Admitted to Fla. bar, 1966, U.S. Tax Ct. bar, 1967, U.S. Ct. Claims bar, 1969; with IRS, Washington, 1966-69; individual practice law, Miami, Fla., 1969—. Mem. Am., Fla. bar assns., Delta Theta Phi. C.P.A., Fla. Home: 19160 SW 132d Ave Miami FL 33177 Office: 1497 NW 7th St Miami FL 33125 Tel (305) 642-0722

SWEARINGER, RONALD EARLE, b. Mpls., Sept. 24, 1926; B.A., U. Wash., 1950; J.D., U. So. Calif., 1958. Admitted to Calif. bar, 1958, U.S. Ct. Mil. Appeals bar, 1962; individual practice law, Hollywood, Calif., 1959-72; judge Municipal Ct. Hollywood, 1972-74, Los Angeles Superior Ct., 1974—; prof. law Northrop U., 1973—. Mem. Calif., Los Angeles County bar assns. Office: 111 N Hill St Los Angeles CA 90014 Tel (213) 974-5599

SWEAT, NOAH S., JR., b. Corinth, Miss., Oct. 2, 1922; B.C.S., U. Miss., 1946, J.D., 1949; LL.M., George Washington U., 1952; postgrad. Acad. Internat. Law, The Hague, Holland, 1952, U. Paris Faculté de Droit, 1952-53, Nat. Coll. State Judiciary U. Colo., 1964. Admitted to Miss. bar, 1949; practiced in Corinth, 1949-50, 53-54; asst. clk. U.S. Ho. of Reps. Com. on Vet. Affairs, 1950-52; dist. atty. 1st Jud. Dist. Miss., 1955-62; judge Miss. Circuit Ct., 1st Jud. Dist., 1962-70; adj. prof. law U. Miss., 1968-70, prof., 1970—; mem. Miss. Ho. of Reps., 1948-52; pros. atty. Alcorn County (Miss.), 1953-54; founder U. Miss. Law Center Miss. Jud. Coll., Intern Program. Bd. dirs. Miss. Criminal Justice Inst., 1970—. Mem. Am. Judicature Soc. (dir. 1972-76), Am., Miss. (chmn. coms.) bar assns., Conf. Miss. Judges (chmn. jud. seminar com. 1966-70), Omega Delta Kappa. Author: (with others) Mississippi Circuit Court Practice, 1969; named to U. Miss. Hall of Fame. Office: Law Sch U Miss University MS 38677 Tel (601) 232-7361

SWEDMARK, GAYLE SMITH, b. Folkston, Ga., Sept. 16, 1940; student Fla. State U., 1957-59, Western Wash. Coll., 1961-62; LL.B., U. Iowa, 1964. Admitted to Iowa bar, 1964, Fla. bar, 1965; research asst. to Honorable Wallace Sturgis, Dist. Ct. Appeal, 1st Dist. Fla., 1964-65; staff counsel Fla. State Rd. Dept., Tallahassee, 1966; asso. firm Parker, Foster, Madigan, Tallahassee, 1967-70; partner firm Madigan, Parker, Gatlin, Truett & Swedmark, Tallahassee, 1970—. Mem. Fla., Tallahassee (dir. 1971, 76) bar assns. Mem. bd. editors Iowa Law Review, 1964. Home: 2913 Lakeshore Dr Tallahassee FL 32303 Office: 318 N Monroe St Tallahassee FL 32302 Tel (904) 222-3730

SWEEN, JIM R., b. Ft. Dodge, Iowa, Sept. 18, 1943; B.A., U. Iowa, 1967, J.D., 1969. Admitted to Iowa bar, 1969; asso. firm Lundy, Butler, Wilson & Hall, Eldora, Iowa, 1969-74; individual practice law, Eldora, 1974—; atty. Hardin County, Eldora, 1975—. Pres., Eldora Area Community Betterment Council, 1975—. Mem. Am., Iowa, Hardin County (pres. 1976—), Dist. 2B bar assns., Iowa Assn. Trial Lawyers, Iowa County Atty. Assn., Nat. Dist. Atty. Assn. Home: 1509 14th Ave Eldora IA 50627 Office: 1233 14th Ave Eldora IA 50627 Tel (515) 858-5461

SWEENEY, DAVID BRIAN, b. Seattle, June 23, 1941; A.B. magna cum laude, Yale, 1963; LL.B., Harvard, 1967. Admitted to Wash. bar, 1968; asso. firm Roberts, Shefelman, Lawrence, Gay & Moch, Seattle, 1968-75, partner, 1976—. Mem. Seattle-King County, Wash. State, Am. bar assns., Estate Planning Council Seattle. Home: 2311 43rd Ave E Seattle WA 98112 Office: 1818 IBM Bldg Seattle WA 98101 Tel (206) 622-1818

SWEENEY, GEORGE THOMAS, b. Denver, Dec. 26, 1929; B.A., Colo. Coll., 1949; LL.B., U. Denver, 1953. Admitted to Colo. bar, 1953, U.S. Supreme Ct. bar, 1955; partner firm Hayden, Ross & Sweeney, Lakewood, Colo., 1957—; chmn. bd. Aurora Nat. Bank, Montbello State Bank, Adams County Bank, Bank of Applewood. Pres. Mercy Hosp., Denver. Mem. Colo., 1st Jud. Dist. bar assns. Home: 15361 W 26th Ave Golden CO 80401 Office: 215 S Wadsworth St Lakewood CO 80226 Tel (303) 234-1600

SWEENEY, JOSEPH CONRAD, b. Boston, Mar. 11, 1933; A.B., Harvard U., 1954; J.D., Boston U., 1957; LL.M., Columbia U., 1963. Admitted to Mass. bar, 1957; served with JAGC, U.S. Navy, 1958-62; asso. firm Haight, Gardner, Poor & Havens, N.Y.C., 1963-66; prof. law Fordham U. Sch. Law, N.Y.C., 1966—; vis. Emory S. Land prof. mcht. marine affairs U.S. Naval War Coll., Newport, R.I., 1972-73; U.S. rep. UN Commn. Internat. Trade Law, Mcht. Shipping Legis., 1970—; U.S. rep. UN Conf. Trade and Devel. Internat. Shipping Legis., 1976—. Mem. Maritime Law Assn. U.S., Am. Soc. Internat. Law, Internat. Law Assn., Am., Mass. bar assns. Editor Internat. Project Finance. 1976; contbr. articles to legal jours. Home: One Lincoln Plaza New York City NY 10023 Office: Fordham U Sch Law Lincoln Center New York City NY 10023 Tel (212) 956-6643

SWEENEY, JOSEPH MODESTE, b. Phila., Sept. 6, 1920; Baccalaureat, U. Grenoble (France), 1938, Licence en Droit, 1945; LL.B., Harvard, 1948; Dr. honoris causa, U. Lyon (France), 1969. Admitted to D.C. bar, 1948, U.S. Supreme Ct. bar, 1953; with Legal Adviser's Office, State Dept., 1948-56; from asso. prof. to prof. law, dir. Inst. Comparative Law, N.Y. U. Law Sch., 1956-68; dean Tulane U. Law Sch., 1968—. Mem. Am. Law Inst., Am. Soc. Internat. Law. Author papers in field. Home: 6028 Pitt St New Orleans LA 70118*

SWEENEY, LAVERNE, b. Parkersburg, W.Va., Feb. 25, 1947; A.B., W.Va. U., 1969, J.D., 1973. Admitted to W.Va. bar, 1973; individual practice law, Grafton, W.Va., 1973—. Bd. dirs. Legal Aid Soc., Morgantown, W.Va., 1973-76, YMCA, Grafton, 1973—. Mem. Am. Bar Assn., Am., W.Va. trial lawyers assns. Home: 710 Maple Ave Grafton WV 26354 Office: 207 W Main St Grafton WV 26354 Tel (304) 265-0948

SWEET, CHARLES GREENLEAF, b. Lewiston, Maine, Aug. 5, 1918; A.B., Pa. State U., 1939; LL.B., Harvard, 1946. Admitted to D.C. bar, 1947, Pa. bar, 1947; practiced in Washington County, Pa., 1947-63; judge Washington County Ct. Common Pleas, 1963—, presiding judge, 1964—. Del. Democratic nat. conv., 1952. Office: Courthouse Washington PA 15301 Tel (412) 225-1121

SWEET, DAVID J., b. Jersey City, Feb. 11, 1938; A.B., Princeton, 1958; LL.B., Harvard, 1961. Admitted to N.Y. State bar, 1962; asso. firm Clark, Carr & Ellis, N.Y.C., 1962-68, Aranow, Brodsky, Bohlinger, Benetar & Einhorn, N.Y.C., 1968-69, partner, 1970—; counsel Com. on Housing, N.Y. State Assembly, 1977—. Mem. exec. bd. N.Y. chpt. Am. Jewish Com., 1972—; trustee Jewish Bd. Guardians, 1977—. Mem. Am., N.Y. State bar assns., N.Y. County Lawyers Assn., Assn. Bar City N.Y., Phi Beta Kappa. Home: 110 East End Ave New York City NY 10028 Office: 469 Fifth Ave New York City NY 10017 Tel (212) 889-1470

SWEET, HOWARD ALAN, b. Madison, Wis., June 6, 1945; A.B., U. Wis., 1967; J.D., Harvard, 1970. Admitted to Wis. bar, 1970; asso. firm LaFollette, Sinykin, Anderson & Munson, Madison, 1970-73, partner, 1973—. Bd. dirs. Madison Kiddie Camp, Inc., 1974—. Mem. Wis., Dane County bar assns. Home: 506 W Shore Dr Madison WI 53715 Office: 222 W Washington Ave Madison WI 53715 Tel (608) 257-3911

SWEETRING, SYLVESTER JOHN, b. Quincy, Ill., July 5, 1904; student U. Chgo., 1923-28. Admitted to Utah bar, 1929; individual practice law, Price, Utah, 1929-40, 51—; commr. Utah State Bar, 1933-36; judge Municipal Ct. Price, 1940-51. Mem. Am., Eastern Utah, Utah bar assns., Delta Theta Phi. Home: 340 N 2d St E Price UT 84501 Office: 23 S Carbon Ave Price UT 84501 Tel (801) 637-1460

SWEIGERT, WILLIAM T., A.B., LL.B., U. San Francisco. Admitted to Calif. bar; practiced in San Francisco; asst. to Earl Warren, atty. gen. State of Calif., chief asst.; chief sec. to Earl Warren, Gov. Calif.; judge San Francisco Municipal Ct., 1949; judge Calif. Superior Ct., presiding judge criminal div.; judge U.S. Dist. Ct., No. Dist. Calif., 1959—, sr. judge, 1973—; lectr. in law U. San Francisco; panel lectr. Continuing Edn. of Bar; chmn. U.S. Dist. Ct. Rules Com. Recipient St. Thomas More award U. San Francisco, 1967. Office: 450 Golden Gate Ave San Francisco CA 94102

SWENSEN, JAN CLOVIS, b. Pitts., July 16, 1937; B.S., U. Pitts., 1959, J.D., 1962. Admitted to Pa. bar, 1963, U.S. Ct. Customs and Patent Appeals bar, 1965, U.S. Supreme Ct. bar, 1974; asso. firm Brandt, Riester, Brant & Malone, Pitts., 1965-66; partner firm Scott, Swensen & Scott, Pitts., 1966—. Dir. Edgewood (Pa.) Sch. Dist., 1975—; senator Jr. Chamber Internat. Senate, Pitts. Mem. Am., Pa., Allegheny County bar assns. Recipient Outstanding Civic Contribution for Conservation award Allegheny Conservation Dist., 1973. Home: 421 Locust St Pittsburgh PA 15218 Office: 2208 Lawyers Bldg Forbes Ave Pittsburgh PA 15219 Tel (412) 281-1970

SWENSON, KURT MCFARLAND, b. Rome, N.Y., Feb. 11, 1945; B.A. in Bus. Adminstrn., Colby Coll., Waterville, Maine, 1967; J.D., Boston Coll., 1970. Admitted to N.H. bar, 1970; law clk. to judge U.S. Dist. Ct. N.H., Concord, 1970-71; asso. firm Wiggen & Nourie, Manchester, N.H., 1971-73, partner, 1974—; dir. John Swenson Granite Co., Inc., Concord. Selectman Town of Hopkinton (N.H.), 1974—. Mem. Am., N.H. (chmn. com. on citizens' rights 1972-74) bar assns. Editor Boston Coll. Indsl. and Comml. Law Rev., 1970. Office: 875 Elm St Manchester NH 03101 Tel (603) 669-2211

SWENSON, ROBERT W., b. Hendricks, Minn., Mar. 4, 1919; B.S.L., U. Minn., 1940, J.D., 1942. Admitted to N.Y. bar, 1943; legal dept. CBS, N.Y.C., 1942-43; asso. firm Davis, Polk, Wardwell Sunderland & Kiendl, N.Y.C., 1943-46; asso. prof. law Drake U., Des Moines, 1946-48, prof., 1948-53; prof. law U. Utah, 1953—. Instr. summer sessions Stanford, N.Y. U., U. Minn., U. Iowa, U. Tex., Washington U. Co-author six textbooks, law rev. articles. Home: 1381 Butler Ave Salt Lake City UT 84102 Office: Coll Law U Utah Salt Lake City UT 84112 Tel (801) 581-7338

SWETT, ALBERT HERSEY, b. Medina, N.Y., Feb. 18, 1923; B.Engring., Yale U., 1944; LL.B., Harvard U., 1949. Admitted to N.Y. bar, 1949; asso. firm Harris, Beach & Wilcox, Rochester, N.Y., 1949-56, mem. firm, 1957-66; v.p., gen. counsel Xerox Corp., Stamford, Conn., 1966-75, Coca-Cola Co., 1975—. Served with USNR, 1942-46. Mem. Am., N.Y. State bar assns., Assn. Bar City N.Y., Assn. Gen. Counsel, Tau Beta Pi. Address: 310 North Ave NW Atlanta GA 30313

SWETT, STUART HAMILTON, b. Ellsworth, Maine, June 18, 1935; A.B., Claremont Men's Coll., 1956; postgrad. Hastings Coll. Law, 1959-61; J.D., Lincoln U., 1963. Admitted to Calif. bar, 1964, U.S. Supreme Ct. bar, 1968; claims investigator and adjuster Hartford Fire Ins. Group, Oakland, Calif. and Allstate Ins. Co., San Diego, 1961-64; dep. city atty. City of San Diego, 1964-70, chief criminal dep. city atty., 1970—. Bd. dirs. Episcopal Diocese of San Diego; chief layreader, vestryman and clk. of vestry Christ Episc. Ch., Coronado; chmn. bd. Episc. Community Service; pres. Agy. Pres's. Council United Way of San Diego; bd. dirs. United Way of San Diego; pres. San Diego Chpt. Claremont Men's Coll. Alumni Assn. Mem. State Bar Calif., San Diego County Bar Assn. (chmn. municipal ct. com., past chmn. ins. com.), Phi Delta Phi. Home: 1460 3rd St Coronado CA 92118 Office: Office of City Atty City Adminstrn Bldg 202 C St San Diego CA 92101 Tel (714) 236-6240

SWIFT, DOUGLAS MCKEAN, JR., b. San Diego, July 9, 1937; A.B., Princeton, 1959; J.D., U. Va., 1965. Admitted to Va. bar, 1965; since practiced in Winchester, Va., asso. firm Kuykendall & Whiting, 1965-71, partner, 1971; individual practice, 1971-75; partner firm Williams & Swift, 1975—. Mem. Am., Va., Winchester-Frederick County (past v.p.) bar assns., Am. Judicature Soc. Office: 36 S Cameron St PO Box 242 Winchester VA 22601 Tel (703) 662-0003

SWIFT, EUGENE CLINTON, JR., b. Providence, Sept. 8, 1945; A.B. cum laude, Brown U., 1967; J.D., U. Pa., 1971. Admitted to Pa. bar, 1971; asso. counsel Phila. Nat. Bank, 1972-75; resident counsel, sec. MDC Corp. and subs., Cherry Hill, N.J., 1975—. Mem. Am., Pa. bar assns., Comml. Law League, Nat. Assn. Comml. Fin. Attys. Editor U. Pa. Law Rev., 1970-71. Home: 711 Old Lancaster Rd Bryn Mawr PA 19010 Office: 26 Springdale Rd Cherry Hill NJ 08003 Tel (609) 424-3344

SWIFT, RICHARD ERNEST, b. Palestine, Tex., Feb. 1, 1928; A.B., U. Tex., 1949, LL.B., 1951. Admitted to Tex. bar, 1951; county atty. Anderson County (Tex.), 1957-62; individual practice law, Palestine,

1962—. Home: Route 5 Box 355 Palestine TX 75801 Office: 700 N Sycamore St Palestine TX 75801 Tel (214) 729-5144

SWIFT, WILLIAM BROCK, b. Lake Charles, La., Mar. 22, 1947; B.S., La. State U., 1970, J.D., 1972. Admitted to La. Supreme Ct. bar, 1972; U.S. Ct. Appeals 5th Circuit bar, 1973, U.S. Supreme Ct. bar, 1976; partner firm Jones, Patin, Harper, Tete & Wetherill, Lake Charles, 1974—. Mem. Am., S.W. La. bar assns., La., S.W. La. assns. def. counsel. Home: 2606 Park Dr Lake Charles LA 70601 Office: PO Box 910 Lake Charles LA 70601 Tel (318) 439-8315

SWIGERT, WILLIAM THERON, b. Oak Park, Ill., May 24, 1936; B.S., Fla. State U., 1958; J.D., U. Fla., 1961. Admitted to Fla. bar, 1961, U.S. Dist. Ct. bar, 1961, U.S. Supreme Ct. bar, 1965, Tax Ct. of U.S. bar, 1969; practiced in Ocala, 1961-73; partner firm Ayres, Swigert, Cluster, Tucker & Curry, 1963-73; atty. City of Belleview, 1963-70; city prosecutor, Ocala, 1969-70; judge Marion County Ct., 1973-74; circuit judge Fifth Jud. Circuit Fla., Ocala, 1974—. Pres., Methodist Mens Club, 1967-71; mem. adminstrv. bd. First United Meth. Ch.; chmn. Sunshine Christmas Festival, 1963-64, Multiple Sclerosis Drive, 1970-73; mayor, Ocala, 1970-75; pres. Ocala Jr. C. of C., 1963-64, Distinguished Service award, 1965, legal counsel, 1969-71, Good Govt. award, 1973, also bd. dirs.; pres. 8th St. Elementary PTA, 1965-66; Cub Scout leader, bd. dirs. Boy Scouts Am.; dir. CD, Ocala. Mem. Am., Fla., Marion County (pres. 1969) bar assns., Am. Judicature Soc., Ocala-Marion County C. of C., Com. of 100, U. Fla. Alumni Assn., Fla. Sheriffs Assn. (hon. life), Phi Alpha Delta. Recipient certificates of appreciation Ocala Chess Club, 1972, Boy Scouts Am., 1972, VFW, 1972-73. Home: 2033 SE 15 Ln Ocala FL 32670 Office: Marion County Courthouse PO Box 1506 Ocala FL 32670 Tel (904) 732-3170

SWIMMER, DAVID R., b. St. Louis, Nov. 20, 1947; B.S. in Biology, St. Louis U., 1969, J.D., 1972. Diplomate, Center for Trial and Appellate Advocacy, Hastings Coll., 1976; admitted to Mo. bar, 1973; with St. Louis County Counselor's office, 1972-73; trial asso. J.B. Carter & Assos., St. Louis, 1973-74; partner firm Steiner, Fenlon & Swimmer, Clayton, Mo., 1974; municipal judge, Breckenridge Hills, Mo., 1975, Parkdale, Mo., 1976—. Mem. Am., Mo. bar assns., Bar Assn. Met. St. Louis, Am. Trial Lawyers Assn., Vol. Parole Assn. (Merit award). Office: 8003 Forsyth St Suite 220 Clayton MO 63105 Tel (314) 721-4378

SWINDLER, WILLIAM FINLEY, b. St. Louis, Oct. 24, 1913; A.B., Washington U., 1935; M.A., U. Mo., 1936, Ph.D., 1942; LL.B., U. Nebr., 1958. Admitted to Nebr. bar, 1958, D.C. bar, 1959, U.S. Supreme Ct. bar, 1961, Va. bar, 1968; dean Sch. Journalism U. Nebr., Lincoln, 1946-56; John Marshall prof. law Coll. William and Mary, Williamsburg, Va., 1958—; vis. distinguished prof. law U. Okla., 1974; gen. counsel Va. Com. on Constl. Revision, 1969-70; research dir. Va. Ct. System Study Com., 1970-71. Mem. Am., Nebr., D.C. bar assns., Am. Law Inst., Supreme Ct. Hist. Soc. (chmn. advisory bd.), Order of Coif. Author: Magna Carta: Legend and Legacy, 1965; Court and Constitution in the 20th Century, Vols. I-III, 1969, 70, 74; Sources and Documents of U.S. Constitutions, Vols. I-X, 1973-76. Home: 20 Cole Ln Williamsburg VA 23185 Office: Coll William and Mary Williamsburg VA 23185 Tel (804) 253-4305

SWIRE, JAMES BENNETT, b. Bklyn., July 10, 1942; A.B., Princeton U., 1963; LL.B., Harvard U., 1966. Admitted to N.Y. bar, 1967, D.C. bar, 1976; asso. firm Rogers, Hoge & Hills, N.Y.C., 1966-73, partner, 1974—; guest lectr. Seton Hall Law Sch., 1977. Mem. Assn. Bar City N.Y. (chmn. com. medicine and law 1977—), Am., N.Y. bar assns. Office: 90 Park Ave New York City NY 10016 Tel (212) 953-9200

SWIRE, MARVIN SIDNEY W., b. Portland, Oreg., Dec. 2, 1912; J.D., Northwestern Coll. Law, 1934. Admitted to Oreg. bar, 1934; asso. firm Coan, Rosenberg & Swire, Portland, 1945-60; asso. firm Rosenberg, Swire & Riebe, Portland, 1960—; mem. Oreg. Bd. Bar Examiners, 1953-57, chmn., 1957. Mem. Am., Oreg. bar assns. Home: 2840 SW 103 Portland OR 97225 Office: 921 S W Washington Portland OR 97205 Tel (503) 227-5691

SWOBE, CHESTER COE, b. Reno, May 23, 1929; B.S., U. Nev., 1954; LL.B., U. Denver, 1958. Admitted to Nev. bar, 1959; asst. U.S. atty. Dept. Justice, Reno, 1960-62; asso. firm Sidney W. Robinson, Reno, 1963-66; individual practice law, Reno, 1967—; mem. Nev. Assembly, 1960-66, minority floor leader, 1965-66; mem. Nev. Senate, 1966-75, minority floor leader, 1969-70, chmn. Washoe County del., 1971-73. Exec. bd. Nev. area council Boy Scouts Am.; bd. dirs. Salvation Army, Reno. Mem. Sigma Nu Alumni Assn. Named Young Man of Year, Reno Jr. C. of C., 1963, Outstanding Alumni, U. Nev. Alumni Assn., 1968. Home: 1495 Belford Rd Reno NV 89509 Office: Suite 903 One E First St Reno NV 89501 Tel (702) 322-2154

SWOPE, JOHN FRANKLIN, b. Mt. Kisco, N.Y., June 21, 1938; B.A., Amherst Coll., 1960; LL.B., Yale, 1963. Admitted to N.H. bar, 1963; with United Life and Accident Ins. Co., Concord, N.H., 1963—, pres., 1974—; pres. Ins. Info. Office of N.H.; dir. ULAICO Equity Services, Inc., Hampshire Funding Inc. Trustee N.H. Higher Edn. Asst. Found., Concord; mem. Concord Zoning Bd. of Adjustment. Mem. Am., N.H., Merrimack County bar assns., Assn. Life Ins. Counsel, N.H. Life and Health Ins. Guaranty Assn. (chmn.), Am. Life Ins. Assn. (v.p.). C.L.U. Home: Long Pond Rd Concord NH 03301 Office: 1 Granite Pl Concord NH 03301 Tel (603) 224-7741

SYKORA, CYRIL WILLIAM, b. Breckenridge, Minn., Aug. 8, 1913; student N.D. State Sch. Sci., 1931-33; LL.B. magna cum laude, William Mitchell Coll. Law, 1938; post grad. Nat. Coll. State Trial Judges, 1968, 72, Am. Acad. Jud. Edn., 1974, 75, 76. Admitted to Minn. bar, 1938; practiced in Mpls., 1938-42, 46-58; referee Minn. Juvenile Ct., 4th Jud. Dist., 1958-63; judge Hennepin County (Minn.) Municipal Ct., 1963—, chief judge, 1971-72; instr. William Mitchell Coll. Law, 1938-42, 46-58, asst. dean, 1946-58; mem. criminal justice adv. com. Minn. Gov.'s Commn. on Crime, 1968-72. Mem. Hennepin County Assn. Mental Health, 1961-68; bd. advisors Assumption Sem., 1965-71; mem. bd. edn. Archdiocese of St. Paul-Mpls., 1971-72. Mem. Am., Minn. (chmn. com. traffic law enforcement 1969-71), Hennepin County bar assns., Am. Judges Assn., Am. Judicature Soc., Minn. County Judges Assn., Minn. Municipal Judges Assn., Citizen's League of Hennepin County (founding). Originated concept of non-crime traffic violation laws, 1971. Office: 9-C Hennepin County Govt Center Minneapolis MN 55487 Tel (612) 348-2898

SYLVESTER, JOSEPH H., b. Derby, Conn., Feb. 21, 1929; B.A., Northwestern U., 1950; J.D., Boston Coll., 1953. Admitted to Mass. bar, 1953, Conn. bar, 1955, U.S. Supreme Ct. bar, 1973; claims adjustor Travelers Ins. Co., Waterbury, Conn., 1953-54; atty. Lycoming div. Avco Mfg. Corp., Stratford, Conn., 1954-55; partner firm Cohen, Sylvester & Micci, and predecessor, Shelton, Conn., 1958—; city atty. Shelton, 1955-58, judge city ct., 1958-60; asst. pros. 5th Circuit Ct., Ansonia, Conn., 1961-70, chief pros., 1971—. Mem. Am., Conn., Valley bar assns., Am. Arbitration Assn. Recipient Outstanding Young Man of Year award Jaycees, Shelton, 1960; Golden Deeds award Exchange Club, 1970. Home: 30 Meadowbrook Dr Shelton CT 06484 Office: 433 Howe Ave Shelton CT 06484 Tel (203) 735-3364

SYNNESTVEDT, JOHN TAFEL, b. Bryn Athyn, Pa., July 2, 1926; B.S. in Mech. Engring., Cornell U., 1948; J.D., U. Pa., 1952. Admitted to Pa. bar, 1953; asso. firm Synnestvedt & Lechner, Phila., 1952-63, partner, 1963—. Mem. Phila., Am. bar assns., Phila. Patent Law Assn., Licensing Execs. Soc. Home: 736 Fetters Mill Rd Huntingdon Valley PA 19006 Office: 12 S Twelfth St Philadelphia PA 19107 Tel (215) 923-4466

SYRING, WILLIAM JOSEPH, b. Toledo, Apr. 29, 1918; A.B., Notre Dame U., 1940, LL.B., J.D., 1942; LL.M., Cath. U., 1948. Admitted to Ohio bar, 1942, D.C. bar, 1948; mem. legal staff FPC, Washington, 1943, 48; with U.S. Dept. Treasury, Washington, 1942-43; individual practice law, Toledo, 1950—. Trustee Model Cities Program, 1969-72; co-chmn. Ohio Cath. Conf., 1960-62; pres. Toledo Diocesan Council Cath. Men, 1960-61. Mem. Am., Ohio State, Lucas County, Toledo bar assns., Ohio, Am. Trial Lawyers Assns., Toledo Plaintiffs Trial Lawyers Assn. (pres. 1967). Decorated Bronze Star. Office: Room 414 706 Madison Ave Toledo OH 43624 Tel (419) 255-0896

SYSAK, RONALD FRANCIS, b. Scranton, Pa., Mar. 29, 1938; A.A., Paul Smith Jr. Coll., 1957; B.A., Fairleigh Dickinson U., 1959; LL.B., N.Y. Law Sch., 1964; postgrad. law Georgetown U., 1966. Admitted to N.Y. State bar, 1965, Utah bar, 1972; staff atty. FCC, Washington, 1965-66; trial atty. NLRB, Denver, 1966-71; partner firm Prince, Yeates, Ward & Geldzahler, Salt Lake City, 1970—. Mem. Am. Bar Assn. (labor law sect.). Office: 455 S 3d East Salt Lake City UT 84111 Tel (801) 521-3760

SZABAD, GEORGE MICHAEL, b. Gorki, Russia, Feb. 21, 1917; B.S., Columbia U., 1937, LL.B., 1939. Admitted to N.Y. State bar, 1940, U.S. Supreme Ct. bar, 1944, D.C. bar, 1947; asso. firm Oseas & Pepper, N.Y.C., 1939-40; asso. counsel to trustees Asso. Gas & Electric Co., 1940-42; with Dept. Labor, 1942-47, chief, appelate sect. Officer of Solicitor, 1944-45; asso. firm Blum, Haimoff, Gersen, Lipson & Szabad, and predecessors, N.Y.C., 1947-49, partner, 1949—; dir., sr. v.p., sec. Burndy Corp., Norwalk, Conn., 1954—; pres. TelAutograph Corp., N.Y.C., 1953-54; dir. York Research Corp.; head econs. sect. Dept. State, 1945-46. Trustee Town of Scarsdale (N.Y.), 1973—, mayor, 1977—; pres. dist. bd. edn., 1960-62; pres. Scarsdale Town Club, 1966-67; bd. govs. Am. Jewish Com., 1964—, mem. exec. com., 1973-76, chmn. nat. edn. com., 1963-70, chmn. com. orgn., 1972-76. Mem. Am., N.Y. State bar assns., Bar Assn. City N.Y., Fed. Bar Assn. N.Y., Consular Law Soc. (past treas.). Author legal articles. Home: 16 Continental Rd Scarsdale NY 10583 Office: Burndy Corp Richards Ave Norwalk CT 06856 Tel (203) 838-4444

SZABO, JOSEPH MATHIAS, b. Budapest, Hungary, July 19, 1921; J.D. summa cum laude, U. Budapest, 1944; J.D., Boston Coll., 1961. Admitted to Budapest bar, 1952, Mass. bar, 1963; law clk. Budapest Cts., 1948-52; corp. atty. State Corp., Budapest, 1952-54; practiced in Budapest, 1954-56; clk. State St. Bank & Trust Co., Boston, 1957-58; law clk. firm Rittenberg & Rittenberg, Boston, 1961-63; individual practice in Boston 1963—; lectr. in law New Eng. Law Sch.; arbitrator Am. Arbitration Assn. Mem. Mass., Boston bar assns., Comml. Law League. Office: 100 State St Boston MA 02109 Tel (617) 523-0728

SZAFRAN, JAMES JOSEPH, b. Oil City, Pa., June 15, 1947; B.A., Pa. State U., 1969; J.D., U. Pitts., 1972. Admitted to Pa. bar, 1972; law clk. to presiding judge Beaver County (Pa.), 1972-73; asso. firm Max P. Gabreski, Oil City, 1973-74; asst. trust officer NW Pa. Bank Trust Co., Oil City, 1974—; trust officer Planters Nat. Bank & Trust Co., Rocky Mount, N.C., 1976—. Mem. Am., Venango County (Pa.) bar assns. Office: Planters National Bank Trust Co 131 N Church St Rocky Mount NC 27801 Tel (919) 977-3111

SZOLOSI, MICHAEL ROY, b. Toledo, Nov. 30, 1944; B.A., U. Toledo, 1966; J.D., Ohio State U., 1968. Admitted to Ohio bar, 1969; asst. atty. gen. State of Ohio, Columbus, 1971-75, spl. litigation sect. chief, 1975-76, 1st asst. atty. gen., 1976—; atty. adviser Washington, 1969-71, research atty. Legis. Reference Bur., 1969. Mem. Am., Ohio bar assns. Home: 2692 Andover Rd Columbus OH 43221 Office: 30 E Broad St Columbus OH 43215 Tel (614) 466-2885

TAAFFE, THOMAS JAMES, b. White Plains, N.Y., July 31, 1937; B.A., Butler U., 1963; J.D., Georgetown U., 1968. Admitted to Wash. bar, 1969; law clk. to judge King County (Wash.) Superior Ct., 1969-70; asso. firm Barker, Day & Taylor, Seattle, 1970-74; individual practice law, Seattle, 1974—. Mem. Seattle Municipal League, 1971—; trustee Ruth Sch. for Girls, 1973—, treas., 1975, pres., 1976. Mem. Wash. State Bar Assn., Wash. State Trial Lawyers Assn. Office: 417 SW 152d St Seattle WA 98166 Tel (206) 242-4900

TABAC, WILLIAM LOUIS, b. Cleve., Oct. 4, 1940; B.A., Case Western Res. U., 1962; J.D., George Washington U., 1966. Legis. asst. Senator Stephen M. Young of Ohio, Washington, 1965-66; asst. to commr. IRS, Washington, 1966-67; admitted to Va. bar, 1967, Ohio bar, 1975; law clk. to judge U.S. Ct. Appeals for 6th Circuit, Cin., 1968-69; asst. prof. law Cleve. State U., 1969-72, asso. prof., 1972-74, prof., 1975—, asst. dean Sch. Law, 1972-75; producer, moderator You and The Law, Sta. WHK-AM, Sta. WMMS-FM, Sta. WCSB-FM (all Cleve.), Sta. WLNO-FM, London, Ohio; mem. domestic relations ct. study com. Fedn. for Community Planning, Cuyahoga County, Ohio, 1976—. Mem. Va. State, Cleve., Ohio State bar assns. Contbr. articles to legal jours.; editor George Washington U. Law Rev.; recipient Twyla M. Conway award Pub. Service Broadcasting, 1976. Office: 1026 Law Coll Bldg Cleve State U Cleveland OH 44115 Tel (216) 687-2350

TABIN, JULIUS, b. Chgo., Nov. 8, 1919; B.A., U. Chgo., 1940, Ph.D. in Physics, 1946; LL.B., Harvard, 1949. Admitted to D.C. bar, 1949, Calif. bar, 1949, Ill. bar, 1950; physicist metall. lab. U. Chgo., 1943-44; physicist Los Alamos (N.Mex.) Sci. Lab., 1944-45; physicist Argonne Nat. Lab., AEC, Chgo., 1946; staff mem., group supr. Inst. Nuclear Studies Mass. Inst. Tech., 1946-49; patent examiner U.S. Patent Office, Washington, 1949-50; asso. firm Fitch, Even, Tabin & Luedeka, Chgo., 1950-52, mem., 1952—; lectr. U. Chgo., 1959. Mem. Am., D.C., Ill. State, Chgo. bar assns., State Bar Calif., Patent Law Assn. Chgo. Home: 162 Park Ave Glencoe IL 60022 Office: 135 S LaSalle St Chicago IL 60603 Tel (312) 372-7842

TABIN, SEYMOUR, b. Chgo., May 6, 1918; B.A., U. Chgo., 1938, J.D., cum laude, 1940. Admitted to Ill. bar, 1940, U.S. Supreme Ct. bar, 1950; partner firm Froelich, Grossman, Teton and Tabin, Chgo., 1950—; dir. Bank of Highland Park (Ill.), Bank of Elk Grove (Ill.). Mem. Ill., Chgo. bar assns., Phi Beta Kappa, Order of Coif. Home: 1148 Lincoln Ave Highland Park IL 60035 Office: 120 S LaSalle St Chicago IL 60603 Tel (312) 726-2122

TABOR, AUGUSTUS HARLAN, b. Terre Haute, Ind., Jan. 25, 1948; B.S., B.A. cum laude, Ind. State U., 1970, J.D. cum laude, 1974. Admitted to Ind. bar, 1974; partner firm Felling & Tabor, Terre Haute, 1974—; cooperating atty. Ind., ACLU. Mem. Am., Ind. bar assns. Recipient Am. Jurisprudence award for Excellent Achievement in Criminal Law. Home: 25 Van Buren Blvd Terre Haute IN 47807 Office: 103 S 3rd St Terre Haute IN 47807 Tel (812) 238-1408

TACHNA, RUTH CANDACE, b. N.Y.C., Feb. 24, 1914; B.A., Cornell U., 1934, LL.B. cum laude, Bklyn. Law Sch., 1937. Admitted to N.Y. bar, 1938, U.S. Supreme Ct. bar, 1956; law sec. to judge Kross, N.Y.C., 1938-40; individual practice law, N.Y.C., 1940-60; founding atty. Westchester County (N.Y.) Legal Aid Soc., White Plains, N.Y., 1961-64; partner firm Tachna & Krassner, White Plains, 1964—; atty. civil def. dept. Town of Harrison (N.Y.), 1953-54. Mem. Westchester County Criminal Ct. Bar Assn. (treas. 1969-72), N.Y. County Lawyers Assn. (legis. com. 1972-74). Mng. editor Matthew Bender, 1968—; contbr. articles to legal jours.; editor Bklyn. Law Rev. Office: 2 William St White Plains NY 10601 Tel (914) WH8-5550

TACKETT, CHARLES M., b. Prestonsburg, Ky., Apr. 5, 1929; LL.B., U. Ky. Admitted to Ky. bar, 1952; practiced in Lexington, Ky., 1955-72; judge Circuit Ct., 1972—; asst. commonwealth atty. Commonwealth of Ky., 1970-72. Mem. Ky. Bar, Am. Bar Assn. Home: 316 Taylor Dr Lexington KY 40505 Office: Fayette County Courthouse 2d floor Lexington KY 40507 Tel (606) 255-9325

TAFT, PETER RAWSON, b. Cin., Mar. 3, 1936; B.A., Yale, 1958, LL.B., 1961. Admitted to D.C. bar, 1963, Calif. bar, 1969; law clk. to judge U.S. Ct. Appeals, Montgomery, Ala., 1961-62; law clk. to Chief Justice, U.S. Supreme Ct., Washington, 1962-63; asso. firm Williams & Connolly, Washington, 1963-67, partner, 1967-68; partner firm Munger, Tolles & Rickershauser, Los Angeles, 1969-75, 77—; asst. atty. gen. land and natural resources div. U.S. Dept. Justice, Washington, 1975-77. Mem. D.C., Calif., Am. (council litigation sect. 1976-77) bar assns., Phi Beta Kappa. Recipient matriculation prize Yale, 1954, Gordon Brown prize, 1958. Home: 2700 Neilson Way Santa Monica CA 90405 Office: 606 S Hill St Los Angeles CA 90014 Tel (213) 626-1491

TAFT, ROBERT STEPHEN, b. N.Y.C., Nov. 1, 1934; B.A., Dartmouth, 1956; LL.B., Columbia, 1959; LL.M., N.Y. Law Sch., 1960. Admitted to N.Y. bar, 1959, since practiced in N.Y.C.; asso. firm Reid & Priest, 1960-66, Denis B. Madura, 1967; partner firm Hatfield, Brady & Taft, 1968—; trustee Practicing Law Inst. Found., 1970—; prof. N.Y. Law Sch. 1973—. Bd. dirs. Odyssey House 1970—. Mem. Am., N.Y. State, bar assns. tax columnist N.Y. Law Jour., 1971—; contbr. articles to legal jours. Home: 85 Nassau Dr Great Neck NY 11021 Office: 277 Park Ave New York City NY 10017 Tel (212) 826-2155

TAFT, SETH CHASE, b. Cin., Dec. 31, 1922; A.B., Yale, 1943, LL.B., 1948. Admitted to Ohio bar, 1948; asso. firm Jones, Day, Reavis & Pogue, Cleve., 1948-59, partner, 1959—; dir. Technicare, Cole Nat. Corp., Capital Nat. Bank, Cleve. County commr. Cuyahoga County (Ohio), 1971—. past pres. Citizens League, Govtl. Research Inst., Cleve. Guidance Center for Disturbed Children, Community Action Against Addiction; now pres. No. Ohio Areawide Coordinating Agency, Yale Univ. Council. Mem. Cleve., Cuyahoga County, Ohio, Am. bar assns. Home: 6 Pepper Ridge Rd Cleveland OH 44124 Office: 1700 Union Commerce Bldg Cleveland OH 44115 Tel (216) 696-3939

TAFT, SHELDON ASHLEY, b. Cleve., Mar. 2, 1937; B.A., Amherst Coll., 1959; LL.B., Harvard, 1962. Admitted to Ohio bar, 1962; asso. firm Vorys, Sater, Seymour & Pease, Columbus, 1965-69, 71-73, partner, 1973—; asst. atty. gen., chief legal counsel Pub. Utilities Commn. Ohio, Columbus, 1969-71. Republican candidate for Supreme Ct. Ohio, 1974. Mem. Am. (pub. utilities sect.), Ohio (pub. utilities sect.), Columbus bar assns., Assn. ICC Practitioners. Home: 317 Stanbery Ave Bexley OH 43209 Office: 52 E Gay St Columbus OH 43215 Tel (614) 464-6308

TAFT, THURMAN WILLIAM, b. Provo, Utah, Oct. 31, 1908; A.B., U. Utah, 1931; J.D., George Washington U., 1936. Admitted to D.C. bar, 1936, Utah bar, 1937; asst. gen. counsel Inst. Inter Am. Affairs, Washington, 1944-49; asst. county atty. Salt Lake County, Utah, 1951-58; individual practice law, Salt Lake City, 1951-61; U.S. atty. Dist. of Utah, Salt Lake City, 1961-69; chmn. Utah Bd. Drugs, 1971-72. Chmn. Utah Citizens Council on Liquor Control, 1973-74, 76—. Mem. Am., Fed., Utah, Salt Lake County bar assns., Salt Lake City Legal Aid Assn. (past pres.). Home: 1129 Stansbury Way Salt Lake City UT 84108 Office: 500 Kennecott Bldg Salt Lake City UT 84133 Tel (801) 521-4135

TAFT, WILLIAM LEE, b. Monroe, Mich., Mar. 27, 1918; A.B., U. Mich., 1939, LL.B., 1942. Admitted to Mich. bar, 1942; individual practice law, Monroe, 1946-68; judge U.S. Dist. Ct., Monroe, 1969-70, 75—; atty. Port of Monroe, 1954-68, City of Monroe, 1964, 65, 68; circuit ct. commr. Monroe County, 1950-68. Mem. Monroe Bd. Edn., 1950-62. Mem. Trial Lawyers Assn., Dist. Judges Assn. Mem. Mich. State Bar Jour. Home: 1596 Riverview St Monroe MI 48161 Office: 106 E 1st St Monroe MI 48161 Tel (313) 243-6900

TAGGART, DONALD REBER, b. Norristown, Pa., Feb. 1, 1909; LL.B., Rutgers, 1931. Admitted to N.J. bar, 1932, U.S. Supreme Ct. bar, 1957; pres. Donald R. Taggart, P.A., Haddonfield, N.J., 1972—; counsel bd. trustees First Presbyterian Ch., Haddonfield, 1970-76. Mem. Am., N.J., Camden County bar assns., Am. Trial Lawyers Assn., Am. Arbitration Assn., Am. Judicature Soc. Office: 27 Kings Hwy E Haddonfield NJ 08033 Tel (609) 795-0505

TAGGART, JOHN YEATMAN, b. Decatur, Ill., Mar. 9, 1932; B.S. in Bus. Adminstrn. cum laude, Ohio State U., 1953; J.D. summa cum laude, 1959; LL.M., N.Y. U., 1964. Admitted to N.Y. State bar, 1960, U.S. Tax Ct. bar, 1960, U.S. Supreme Ct. bar, 1964, U.S. Customs Ct. bar, 1974; asso. firm White & Case, N.Y.C., 1959-63; atty., adviser Office Tax Legis. Counsel, U.S. Treasury Dept., Washington, 1963-66; counsel firm Windels & Marx, and predecessors, N.Y.C., 1966-73, partner, 1973—; asso. prof. to prof. law N.Y. U., N.Y.C., 1966-76; lectr. in field. Mem. Am., N.Y. State, N.Y.C. bar assns., Taxation with Representation Assn. (nat. com.), Tax Analysts and Advs. Assn. (legal activities policy bd.). Contbr. articles to legal jours.; editor-in-chief

Tax Law Rev., 1966-71. Home: 200 6th Ave New York City NY 10013 Office: 51 W 51st St New York City NY 10019 Tel (212) 977-9600

TAGGART, LESLIE DAVIDSON, b. Glasgow, Scotland, Aug. 8, 1910; A.B., Columbia, 1931, LL.B., 1934. Admitted to N.Y. bar, 1934; sr. partner firm Watson, Leavenworth, Kelton & Taggart, N.Y.C., 1934—. Mem. Am. Coll. Trial Lawyers, Am. Patent Law Assn., U.S. Trademark Assn. Home: 2 Melwood Ln Westport CT 06880 Office: 100 Park Ave New York City NY 10017 Tel (212) MU3-4221

TAIT, COLIN C., b. N.Y.C., June 17, 1932; B.A., Cornell U., 1954; LL.B., Yale, 1959. Admitted to Conn. bar, 1959, U.S. Supreme Ct. bar, 1962; mem. firm Robinson, Robinson & Cole, Hartford, Conn., 1959-64, partner, 1965-66; asso. prof. U. Conn. Law Sch., W. Hartford, 1966-69, prof., 1969—, asso. dean, 1975—. Trustee Westminster Sch., Simsbury, Conn.; mem. Conn. Power Facility Evaluation Council, 1975—. Mem. Conn. Bar Assn., Order of Coif. Contbr. to Yale Law Jour. Home: R F D #4 Winsted CT 06098 Office: Greater Hartford Campus U Conn West Hartford CT 06117 Tel (203) 583-4841

TAIT, EDWARD THOMAS, b. Indiana, Pa., Apr. 9, 1920; B.S., U. Pitts., 1942, J.D., 1949. Admitted to Pa. bar, 1949, D.C. bar, 1960, U.S. Supreme Ct. bar, 1953; law clk. Pa. Superior Ct., 1949-50, Ct. Appeals 3d Circuit, 1951; with Trust Dept. Pitts. Nat. Bank, 1950-51; asso. firm Kountz, Fry & Meyer, Pitts., 1951-53; exec. dir. and exec. asst. to chmn. SEC, Washington, 1953-55; spl. asst. to Pres. Eisenhower, Washington, 1955-56; commr. FTC, Washington, 1956-60; partner firm Whitlock, Markey & Tait, Washington, 1960-69; partner-in-charge firm Reed Smith Shaw & McClay, Washington, 1970—; mem. FTC Adv. Com., BNA ATRR Adv. Bd. Sr. warden Christ Ch., Pitts., 1950-53; vestryman St. John's Ch., Lafayette Square, Washington; trustee St. John's Child Devel. Center, Washington. Mem. Am., Pa., Allegheny County bar assns., Order of Coif, Phi Alpha Delta. Home: 26 Kalorama Circle NW Washington DC 20008 Office: 1150 Connecticut Ave Washington DC 20036 Tel (202) 457-6191

TAIT, ROBERT EDGAR, b. Lima, Ohio, Sept. 3, 1946; B.A. cum laude, Kenyon Coll., 1968; J.D. cum laude, U. Mich., 1973. Admitted to Ohio bar, 1973; asso. firm Vorys, Sater, Seymour & Pease, Columbus, Ohio, 1973—. Mem. Columbus, Ohio, Am. bar assns., Nat. Def. Assn., Ohio Self Insurers Assn. Home: 1462 Northam Rd Upper Arlington OH 43221 Office: 52 E Gay St Columbus OH 43215 Tel (614) 464-6400

TAKEYAMA, ROY Y., b. Maui, Hawaii, Jan. 25, 1928; B.B.A., Bradley U., 1951; M.Ed., U. Ill., 1952; J.D., U. Mich., 1962. Admitted to Hawaii bar, 1962; individual practice law; pres. Rand H. Inc., Yuki's, Inc.; v.p. Evelyn Wood Reading Dynamics Inst. Hawaii, Inc. Sec. bd. regents U. Hawaii, Mem. Am., Hawaii bar assns. Office: Bishop Insurance Bldg Suite 223 Honolulu HI 96813 Tel (808) 533-6294

TALBOT, EARL ARMOUR, b. Chgo., Jan. 23, 1939; A.B., Wabash Coll., 1961; J.D., U. Ill., 1964. Admitted to Ill. bar, 1964; with Chgo. Title and Trust Co., 1964-67; asso. firm Kirkland & Ellis, Chgo., 1967-73, partner, 1973—; advisor to drafting coms. land transactions and condominium acts Conf. of Commrs. on Uniform State Laws. Mem. Chgo., Ill., Am. (chmn. title ins. com. sect. real property) bar assns., Chgo. Council Lawyers, Am. Land Title Assn. (asso.), Ill. Land Title Assn. (hon.). Home: 631 W Surf St Chicago IL 60657 Office: 200 E Randolph Dr Suite 5600 Chicago IL 60601 Tel (312) 861-2168

TALBOTT, FRANK, III, b. Danville, Va., Mar. 26, 1929; B.A., U. Va., 1951, LL.B., 1953. Admitted to Va. bar, 1952; served as 1st lt. JAGC, U.S. Army, 1953-56; asso. firm Meade, Talbott & Tate, Danville, Va., 1956-59; partner firm Talbott, Wheatley & Talbott, Danville, 1959-66; asst. gen. counsel Dan River Inc., Danville, 1966-68, v.p., gen. counsel, 1968-76; partner firm Clement, Wheatley, Winston, Talbott & Majors, Danville, 1977—. Vice chmn. Danville Sch. Bd., 1964-70; bd. dirs. United Fund Danville, 1959-63; trustee Va. Student Aid Found., 1963-68. Mem. Am. Judicature Soc., Am., Va. (v.p. 1965-66, exec. com. 1967-70), Danville (pres. 1965-66) bar assns., Phi Alpha Delta. Home: 420 Maple Ln Danville VA 24541 Office: Suite 400 Masonic Bldg Danville VA 24541 Tel (804) 793-8221

TALBOTT, MARVIN S., b. Winner, S.D., Mar. 20, 1923; B.S. in Commerce, U. Ky., 1948; J.D., U. S.D., 1950. Admitted to S.D. bar, 1950; individual practice law, Winner, 1950-51; spl. agt. FBI, 1951-52; county judge Tripp County, S.D., 1952-54; state's atty. Tripp County, 1955-58, county judge, 1960-68, dist. county judge, 1969-74, judge Circuit Ct., 1975—. Mem. Am., S.D., 6th Jud. Circuit bar assns., Phi Alpha Delta. Home: 246 W 5th St Winner SD 57580 Office: PO Box 70 Winner SD 57580 Tel (605) 842-3856

TALBOY, GARNER GARRETT, b. Wessington, S.D., June 17, 1909; student Whitman Coll., 1927-29, U. Oreg., 1929-30; LL.B., Northwestern Sch. Law, Lewis and Clark U., 1933. Admitted to Oreg. bar, 1933; practiced in Portland, 1933-42, 46-74; judge Municipal Ct., King City, Oreg., 1974—; chmn. Tualatin (Oreg.) Fire Dist. Civil Service Commn. Bd. dirs. King City Civic Assn., 1970-73. Mem. Oreg. State Bar, Northwestern Coll. Law Alumni, Delta Theta Phi. Contbr. numerous articles on law to local ins. jours. Home: 16565 SW King Charles St King City Tigard OR 97223 Office: 15390 SW 116th St King City OR 97223 Tel (503) 639-6795

TALIAFERRO, BRUCE OWEN, b. Kansas City, Mo., Feb. 13, 1947; B.A., U. Ark., 1969; J.D., U. Tulsa, 1971. Admitted to Okla. bar, 1972; staff atty. Tulsa County (Okla.) Legal Aid Soc., 1971-72; asso. firm Dennis J. Downing & Assos., Tulsa, 1972—; capt. JAGC, USAFR, 1972—. Mem. Am., Tulsa County bar assns., Am. Judicature Soc. Home: 5678 S Utica Ave Tulsa OK 74105 Office: 606 Mid-Continent Bldg Tulsa OK 74103 Tel (918) 585-1235

TALIAFERRO, HENRY BEAUFORD, b. Shawnee, Okla., Jan. 12, 1932; B.A. with distinction, U. Okla., 1954, J.D., 1956. Admitted to Okla. bar, 1956, U.S. Supreme Ct. bar, 1966, D.C. bar, 1969; asso., partner firm Monnet, Hayes & Bullis, Oklahoma City, 1956-66; exec. dir. OEO Legal Services Program, Oklahoma County, 1966-67; dir. congressional relations, acting exec. dir. Pres.'s Nat. Advisory Commn. Civil Disorders, 1967-68; asso. solicitor for Indian Affairs, Dept. Interior, D.C., 1968-69; partner firm Casey, Lane & Mittendorf, D.C., 1971— candidate U.S. Ho. of Reps., Okla., 1966; cons. establishment of legal services programs to OEO, 1966-67. Panel on Am. Family, Acad. for Ednl. Devel., 1976—; fin. com. Democratic Nat. Com., 1971—; mem. Fairfax County Planning Commn., Fairfax County, Va., 1973; mem. corp. The Madeira Sch., Greenway, Va., 1973—. Mem. D.C., Okla., Am., Fed. Power bar assns., Phi Beta Kappa, Phi Alpha Delta. Co-author: Report of National Advisory Commission on Civil Disorders, 1968; contbr. articles to profl. jours. Home: 1325 Merrie Ridge Rd McLean VA 22101 Office: 815 Connecticut Ave NW Washington DC 20006 Tel (202) 785-4949

TALKINGTON, ROBERT VAN, b. Dallas, Aug. 23, 1929; A.A., Tyler Jr. Coll., 1949; B.S., U. Kans., 1951, LL.B., 1954. Admitted to Kans. bar, 1954; individual practice law, Iola, Kans., 1954-61; partner firm Conderman & Talkington, Iola, 1961—; county atty. Allen County (Kans.), 1957-63; city atty. City of LaHarpe (Kans.), 1965-69, City of Moran; atty. Allen County Community Jr. Coll. Trustee Iola Pub. Library, 1962-70; mem. Kans. Ho. of Reps., 1969-73; mem. Kans. Senate, 1973—, v.p., 1977—. Mem. Allen County, Kans., Am. bar assns., Assn. Ins. Attys. Home: 20 W Buchanan St Iola KS 66749 Office: 20 N Washington St PO Box 725 Iola KS 66749 Tel (316) 365-5125

TALLANT, DAVID, JR., b. Oak Park, Ill., Mar. 16, 1931; A.B., Claremont Mens Coll., 1953; J.D., Duke, 1956. Admitted to Ill. bar, 1956; asso. firm Chapman & Cutler, Chgo., 1956-65, partner, 1965—. Mem. Am., Ill., Chgo. bar assns.

TALLANT, DAVID ARTHUR, b. National City, Calif., Sept. 11, 1940; B.A., Loma Linda U., 1962; J.D., U. So. Calif., 1966. Admitted to Calif. bar, 1967; asso. firms Burke West, Ridgecrest, Calif., 1967, Rust, Hoffman & Mills, Sacramento, 1968-70; individual practice law, Sacramento, 1971—. Mem. Calif., Am., Sacramento County bar assns. Office: PO Box 254808 Sacramento CA 94825 Tel (916) 488-7300

TALLEY-MORRIS, NEVA BENNETT, b. Judsonia, Ark., Aug. 12, 1909; B.A., Ouachita Bapt. U., 1930; M.Ed., U. Tex., Austin, 1938, postgrad., summers 1939-41; postgrad. Am. Bar Inst., 1966-68, 70. Tchr. high sch., White County, Ark., 1930-37, prin. high sch., 1937-42; ordnance insp. U.S. Govt., 1942-45; intern C.C. Talley Law Offices, North Little Rock, Ark., 1945-47; admitted to Ark. bar, 1947, U.S. Dist. Ct. bar Eastern Dist. Ark., 1947, U.S. Supreme Ct. bar, 1950; practice law, Little Rock, 1947—. Bd. dirs. Pulaski County (Ark.) Legal Aid Bur., 1968-71; mem. Ark. Council on Children and Youth, 1948-75, chmn., 1952-54. Fellow Am. Acad. Matrimonial Lawyers (bd. govs. 1970—), Ark. Bar Found. (Spl. award for Distinguished Service to Legal Profession 1970); mem. Am. (chmn. com. family law long range planning 1975—, chmn. family law sect. 1969-70, mem. standing com. 1973—, mem. ho. of dels. 1970-74), Ark. (ho. of dels. 1973-76) bar assns., Nat. (pres. 1956-57, Annual Service award 1961), Ark. (pres. 1950-52) assns. women lawyers, World Assn. Lawyers, Am. Judicature Soc., Pulaski County (Ark.) Bar, Phi Alpha Delta (hon. life Garland chpt.). Named Countess of Pulaski, Pulaski County Ct., 1968; recipient Outstanding Achievement award Ark. Assn. Women Lawyers, 1969; author: Family Law Practice and Procedure, 1973; Appellate Civil Practice and Procedure, 1975; bd. editors: Domestic Relations Manual, 1976. Home: 101 N State St Little Rock AR 72201 Office: 722 W Markham St Little Rock AR 72201 Tel (501) 372-2756

TALLMAN, ROBERT GEORGE, b. Allentown, Pa., Oct. 19, 1930; B.A., Miami U., Oxford, Ohio, 1952; LL.B., U. Va., 1954. Admitted to Pa. bar, 1954; partner firm Butz, Hudders & Tallman, Allentown, 1962—; dir. Arbogast & Bastian, Inc., Jordan Mut. Ins. Co., Allentown Pneumatic Gun Co., Charles L. Bell Co. Trustee Cedar Crest Coll., 1968—, Swain Sch., Inc., 1969—, Wiley House, 1966-71. Office: Butz Hudders & Tallman 740 Hamilton Mall Allentown PA 18101 Tel (215) 439-1451

TALLON, DANIEL B., b. Albany, N.Y., Jan. 29, 1927; B.A., St. Bernardine of Siena Coll., 1950; LL.B., Union U., 1955; J.D., Albany Law Sch., 1968. Asso. firm Ainsworth & Sullivan, Albany, N.Y., 1953-54, Carusone & Carusone, Glens Falls, N.Y., 1954-49; partner firm Carusone & Tallon, Glens Falls, 1959-70; individual practice law, Glens Falls, 1970—; adminstrv. assigned counsel Warren County, N.Y., 1960-68. Chmn. Glens Falls UN Commn., 1954-58; mem. Glens Falls Planning Bd., 1955-58, Glens Falls Zoning Bd. Appeals, 1958-60, Warren County Planning Commn., 1960-63. Mem. Am., N.Y. State, Warren County bar assns., N.Y. State Defenders Assn., Am. Arbitration Assn., Am., N.Y. State trial lawyers assns. Mem. staff Albany Law Sch. Rev., 1952-53. Home: 2 Yorkshire Dr Queensbury NY 12801 Office: 171 Ridge St Glens Falls NY 12801 Tel (518) 793-4401

TALLY, EMMETT MURCHISON, JR., b. Tavares, Fla., Mar. 23, 1912; LL.B., U. Fla., 1937, J.D., 1967. Admitted to Fla. bar, 1937; individual practice law, Tavares, 1935-45; individual practice law, Mt. Dora, Fla., 1970—. Chmn. planning commn. Central Fla. Diocese Episcopal Ch., 1976. Home: 936 Fairview Ave Mount Dora FL 32757 Office: PO Box 378 Mount Dora FL 32757 Tel (904) 383-7121

TALLY, LOU, b. San Antonio, Oct., 15, 1947; B.A. in Polit. Sci., U. Fla., 1969, J.D., 1972. Admitted to Fla. bar, 1972; asst. states atty. 5th Jud. Circuit, Fla., 1972—; partner firm Tally, Moore & Tally, Mount Dora, Fla., 1973—; mem. Fla. Bar Subcom. Juvenile Ct. Procedure, 1973-75. Pres. United Appeal Lake County, 1977; trustee Bay St. Players Community Theater, 1975—; chmn. Lake County Democratic Exec. Com., 1975-76, Mem. Fla., Am., Lake County bar assns., Fla. Pros. Attys. Assn., Nat. Dist. Attys. Assn., Fla. Theater Conf. Recipient Pres.'s award Young Dem. Clubs Fla., 1974. Home: Box 897 Mount Dora FL 32757 Office: Box 378 Mount Dora FL 32757 Tel (904) 383-7121

TAMISIEA, HUGH JUSTIN, b. Missouri Valley, Iowa, Sept. 23, 1898; B.A. with high distinction, State U. Iowa, 1922, J.D., 1924. Admitted to Iowa bar, 1924; partner firm Tamisiea & Tamisiea, Missouri Valley, 1924-70; firm Tamisiea, Tamisiea & Smith, Missouri Valley, 1970—; atty. City of Missouri Valley; drainage atty. Des Moines; corp. counsel, dir. census Southwestern Iowa; asst. state's atty. Des Moines. Mem. Iowa Gen. Assembly, 1931-32; mem. Missouri Valley Bd. Edn., 1937-42, pres., 1942-48, sec., 1948-55. Mem. Am., Iowa bar assns., SW Iowa Bar, Harrison County Bar. Contbr. articles to legal jours. Home: 207 N Third St Missouri Valley IA 51555 Office: PO Box 219 413 E Erie St Missouri Valley IA 51555 Tel (712) 642-2226

TAMM, EDWARD ALLEN, b. St. Paul, Apr. 21, 1906; student Carroll Coll., 1923-24, LL.D., 1974; student U. Mo., 1924-27; LL.B., Georgetown U., 1930, LL.D., 1965; J.S.D. (hon.), Suffolk U., 1971. Admitted to Minn. bar, 1943, D.C. bar, 1972, U.S. Supreme Ct. bar, 1947; exec. FBI, Washington, 1930-48; judge U.S. Dist. Ct., Washington, 1948-65, U.S. Ct. Appeals, D.C. Circuit, 1965—; chief judge U.S. Temporary Emergency Ct. Appeals, Washington, 1972—. Mem. Am., Fed., D.C. bar assns., Am. Law Inst., Am. Judicature Soc. Contbr. articles to legal jours. Office: US Courthouse US Court Appeals Washington DC 20001 Tel (202) 426-7000

TANENBAUM, MELVYN, b. Bklyn., Jan. 20, 1935; B.S., N.Y. U., 1955, J.D., 1957. Admitted to N.Y. bar, 1958, U.S. Supreme Ct. bar, 1963; asso. firm David L. Glickman, Huntington, N.Y., 1958-62; asst. counsel, psl. counsel Suffolk County Water Authority, Oakdale, N.Y., 1959-63; individual practice law, Huntington, 1963-74; spl. dep. N.Y. State Atty. Gen. in the Election Fraud Bur., 1963-71; asst. county atty., counsel bd. elections Suffolk County, 1971-73, judge County Ct., 1974—. Mem. Huntington Jewish Center. Mem. Am., N.Y. State, Suffolk County bar assns., County Judges Assn. N.Y. (legis. com., com. on nominations), Am., N.Y. trial lawyers assns. Home: 7 High St Huntington NY 11743 Office: 23 Greene St Huntington NY 11743 Tel (516) 673-8400

TANG, THOMAS, b. Phoenix, Jan. 11, 1922; B.S., U. Santa Clara, 1947, also postgrad. Law Sch.; LL.B. with distinction, U. Ariz., 1950. Admitted to Ariz. bar, 1950, Calif. bar, 1951; dep. county atty. Maricopa County, Ariz., 1953-57; asst. atty. gen. State of Ariz., 1957-58; judge Ariz. Superior Ct., 1963-70; now mem. firm Sullivan, Mahoney and Tang, Phoenix. Councilman, City of Phoenix, 1960-62, vice-mayor, 1962. Mem. State Bar Ariz. (gov. 1971—, pres. 1977—), Nat. Council Juvenile Ct. Judges, Alpha Sigma Nu, Phi Delta Phi. Office: 403 Luhrs Bldg 11 W Jefferson St Phoenix AZ 85003 Tel (602) 254-8861

TANKERSLEY, IRVIN LEE, b. Norwich, Norfolk, Eng., Apr. 2, 1945; B.B.A., Memphis State U., 1967; J.D., Tulane U., 1972. Admitted to Tenn. bar, 1972; individual practice law, Memphis, 1972—; gen. counsel Shelby County (Tenn.) Welfare Dept., 1972-73; asst. prof. bus. law Memphis State U., 1973—. Mem. Am., Memphis-Shelby County, Tenn. bar assns. Home: 6019 Southampton St Memphis TN 38138 Office: 1101 1st Am Bank Bldg Memphis TN 38103 Tel (901) 526-0241

TANKSLEY, JEPTHA CHARLES, b. Banks County, Ga., Dec. 18, 1920; B.S., U.S. Mil. Acad., 1943; LL.B., Emory U., 1949; B.B.A., Ga. State U., 1952. Admitted to Ga. bar, 1949; mem. firm Branch & Branch, Atlanta, 1949-52; asst. trial solicitor gen., Fulton Superior Ct., Atlanta, 1952-56; judge Superior Ct. Atlanta Jud. Circuit, 1957-76; chief judge Fulton Superior Ct., Atlanta Jud. Circuit, 1976—. Dir. Met. Atlanta Assn. for the Blind. Mem. Am., Atlanta, Ga. (treas. 1964-71) bar assns., Council Superior Judges of Ga. (sec., treas. 1967-70), Lawyers Club of Atlanta, Am. Judicature Soc., West Point Soc. of Atlanta (dir.), Assn. of U.S. Army (past pres. Atlanta chpt.), Mil. Order of World Wars (comdr. Atlanta chpt.), N. Ga. Coll., Emory U. Law Sch., Ga. State U. alumni assns. Recipient numerous awards. Home: 3440 Paces Forest Rd NW Atlanta GA 30327 Office: 711 Fulton County Ct House 136 Pryor St SW Atlanta GA 30303 Tel (404) 572-2901

TANKSLEY, RAYMOND RICHARD, JR., b. Spokane, Wash., June 9, 1931; J.D., Gonzaga U., 1955. Admitted to Wash. bar, 1955; since practiced in Spokane; individual practice law, 1957-76; partner firm Tanksley, Richard, Padden, Derr & Carroll, 1976—. Mem. Republican State Com. Spokane County, 1968-72. Mem. Wash. State Bar Assn., Wash. State, Am. trial lawyers assns. Home: 2418 S Manito Blvd Spokane WA 99203 Office: 404 Great Western Bldg Spokane WA 99201 Tel (509) 624-4343

TANNENWALD, PETER, b. Washington, Apr. 8, 1943; A.B., Brown U., 1964; LL.B., Harvard U., 1967. Admitted to D.C. bar, 1968, U.S. Supreme Ct. bar, 1972; asso. firm Arent, Fox, Kintner, Plotkin & Kahn, Washington, 1967-74, partner, 1975—. Mem. Am., Fed., D.C., Fed. Communications bar assns., Harvard Law Sch. Assn. D.C. (v.p.). Office: 1815 H St NW Washington DC 20006 Tel (202) 857-6024

TANNER, JOHN JERRY, b. Tulsa, Mar. 30, 1930; B.S., Okla. State U., 1951; LL.B., U. Tulsa, 1957. Admitted to Okla. bar, 1957; with land dept. Sunray D-X Oil Co., Tulsa, 1957-60; asst. county atty. Tulsa County, 1960-67; individual practice law, Tulsa, 1967—. Mem. Okla., Tulsa County bar assns., Okla. Trial Lawyers Assn., Sigma Nu. Office: 2404 Fourth Nat Bank Bldg Tulsa OK 74119 Tel (918) 582-4161

TANNEY, MARK I., b. Bklyn., Sept. 1, 1942; B.A., Hofstra U., 1963; M.S., L.I. U., 1969; J.D., Bklyn. Law Sch., 1972. Admitted to N.Y., N.J. bars, 1973, U.S. Supreme Ct. bar, 1976; asso. firm Burger Lavallee & Lewis, Carle Place, N.Y., 1973, firm Weisman Celler Spett Modlin & Wertheimer, N.Y.C, 1974; individual practice law, N.Y.C. and Westwood, N.J., 1975—; of counsel Moore & Wohl, N.Y.C., 1974—. Alumni recruitment Hofstra U., 1976—; trustee River Dell Regional Bd. Edn., 1975-78. Mem. N.J. Sch. Bds. Assn., N.J. Edn. Assn., Am., Bergen County, N.J., N.Y. State bar assns., N.Y. County Lawyers Assn. Office: 99 Kinderkamack Rd Westwood NJ 07675 also 230 Park Ave New York City NY 10017 Tel (201) 666-0700

TANNEY, WILLIAM JAMES, b. Washington, Dec. 28, 1925; J.D., Am. U., 1952. Admitted to Va. bar, 1950, Fla. bar, 1953; asso. firm Jessee, Phillips, Clinge & Kendrick, Arlington, Va., 1950-51; mem. firm Gowler, White, Gillen, Yancey & Humphkey, Tampa, Fla., 1953-54, Wightman, Rowe & Tanney, Clearwater, Fla., 1954-64, Tanney & Forde, 1964—. Pres., Belleair Civic Assn., 1956-57. Mem. Am., Fla. (chmn. trial lawyers sect.) bar assns., Clearwater Bar Assn., Acad. Fla. Trial Lawyers (dir. 1965-67), Clearwater C. of C. Home: PO Box 1256 Clearwater FL 33517 Office: 631 Chestnut St Clearwater FL 33516 Tel (813) 446-5967

TANSEY, JOHN TERRY, b. Cin., Nov. 15, 1940; A.B., U. Cin., 1962; LL.B., George Washington U., 1965. Admitted to D.C. bar, 1966, U.S. Supreme Ct. bar, 1971; law clk. Hon. Oliver Gasch, U.S. Dist. Ct., D.C., Washington, 1965-66; staff atty. office of dep. atty. gen. U.S. Dept. Justice, Washington, 1967-70; partner firm Martin, Whitfield, Thaler and Bebchick, Washington, 1970—. Mem. staff D.C. Crime Commn., 1967-68, D.C. Commn. on Adminstrn. of Justice under emergency conditions, 1968-69. Mem. D.C. (treas. Young Lawyers Sect., 1970-71), Am. bar assns., Order of Coif. Home: 9239 Georgetown Pike Great Falls VA 22066 Office: 1701 Pennsylvania Ave NW Washington DC 20006 Tel (202) 298-6350

TANSEY, THOMAS JAMES, b. Boston, Oct. 4, 1939; B.S. in Biochemistry, U. Wis., 1968; J.D., U. Miami, Coral Gables, Fla., 1972. Admitted to Fla. bar, 1972; individual practice law, Ft. Lauderdale, Fla., 1972—; arbitrator Am. Arbitration Assn. Mem. Am., Broward County (Fla.) bar assns. Office: 2430 W Oakland Park Blvd Fort Lauderdale FL 33311 Tel (305) 733-0374

TAPHORN, JOSEPH BERNARD, b. Beckemeyer, Ill., Oct. 9, 1921; B.S. in Agr., U. Ill., 1943; B.S. in Engring., George Washington U., 1949, LL.B., 1950. Admitted to N.Y. bar, 1952, D.C. bar, 1961; atty. Pollard and Johnston, N.Y.C., 1950-52; atty. IBM Corp., Armonk, N.Y., 1952—, patent examiner, 1946-49, clasifier, 1949-50. Pres. Huntley Civic Assn., Eastchester, N.Y., 1958-59, Jr. Challengers

Ski Club, Poughkeepsie, N.Y., 1968-69. Mem. Am., N.Y. State, Dutchess County, D.C. bar assns., N.Y. Patent Law Assn. Home: 8 Scenic Dr Poughkeepsie NY 12603 Office: Old Orchard Rd Armonk NY 10504 Tel (914) 765-3527

TAPLEY, JAMES LEROY, b. Greenville, Miss., July 10, 1923; A.B., U. N.C., 1947, J.D., 1950. Admitted to N.C. bar, 1951, D.C. bar, 1961; atty. So. Ry. Co., Washington, 1953—, v.p. law, 1975—. Mem. Am. Bar Assn., Assn. ICC Practitioners. Home: 7007 Beechwood Dr Chevy Chase MD 20015 Office: PO Box 1808 920 15th St NW Washington DC 20013 Tel (202) 628-4460

TAPLIN, MARTIN WILLIAM, b. Chgo., Mar. 20, 1938; B.B.A., U. Miami, 1960; J.D., Stetson U., 1963. Admitted to Fla. bar, 1964; individual practice law, Miami Beach, Fla., 1963—; chief real estate cons. First Mortgage Investors, Miami Beach, 1974—. Mem. Miami Beach C. of C., S. Beach Redevel. Task Force, Fla. Bar, Am., Miami Beach bar assns. Office: 801 Arthur Godfrey Rd Miami Beach FL 33140 Tel (305) 532-7361

TAPPEN, DAVID MUIR, b. N.Y.C., Nov. 7, 1925; A.B., Princeton, 1947; LL.B., Columbia, 1950. Admitted to N.Y. bar, 1950, D.C. bar, 1963; asso. firm Satterlee & Stephens, N.Y.C., 1950—, partner 1961—. Mem. Bar Assn. D.C. Home: 1185 Park Ave New York City NY 10028 Office: 277 Park Ave New York City NY 10017 Tel (212) 826-6200

TAPSCOTT, LEO JOSEPH, b. Des Moines, Apr. 12, 1920; student Notre Dame U.; J.D., Drake U., 1949. Admitted to Iowa bar, 1949; atty. State of Iowa, 1949-51, Polk County Iowa, 1955-56; individual practice law, Des Moines, 1951-54, 57—; with legal dept. Iowa Employment Security, 1949-51. Mem. Polk County, Iowa bar assns. Home: Rural Route 10 W Des Moines IA 50309 Office: 310 Rey Bldg Des Moines IA 50309 Tel (515) 288-3295

TARANTINO, LOUIS GERALD, JR., b. Bridgeport, Conn., Sept. 7, 1934; B.A., U. Pa., 1955, LL.B., 1958. Admitted to Conn. bar, 1958, N.Y. state bar, 1960; asso. firm Beekman & Bogue, N.Y.C., 1959-67, partner 1968-76; dir. Mohawk Valley Community Corp., Herkimer, N.Y., 1976—, Fill-R-Up-Systems, Inc., Ft. Lauderdale, Fla., 1972—; Knapp Foundry Co., Guilford, Conn., 1969—; Dolphin Inc., Wilmington, Del., 1962—. Trustee, St. Anthony Ednl. Found., N.Y.C., 1971—, pres., 1976—; trustee Gepeto Charitable Trust, Southampton, N.Y., 1968—. Mem. Conn., N.Y. State bar assns., Bar Assn. City N.Y. Address: 113 Herrick Rd Southampton NY 11968 Tel (516) 283-6860

TARASI, LOUIS MICHAEL, JR., b. Cheswick, Pa., Sept. 9, 1931; B.A., Miami U. (Ohio), 1954; J.D., U. Pa., 1959. Admitted to Pa. bar, 1960; asso. firm Burgwin, Ruffin, Perry, Pohl & Springer, Pitts., 1959-65, partner, 1965-68; sr. partner Conte, Courtney & Tarasi, Pitts., 1968—; lectr. in field. Mem. St. Vincent DePaul Penal Com., Pitts., St. Thomas More Soc., Pitts. Mem. Am., Pa., Allegheny County bar assns., Western Pa. (pres. 1975), Pa. (sec., 1976—, parliamentarian, 1975, v.p. 1977) trial lawyers assns. Editor, Barrister, 1974—. Home: 940 Beaver St Sewickley PA 15143 Office: 1825 Grant Bldg Pittsburgh PA 15219 Tel (412) 391-7135

TARBOX, JAMES CUSHMAN, b. Monticello, Minn., Mar. 4, 1902; B.A., U. Minn., 1922; LL.B. magna cum laude, St. Paul Coll. Law, 1926; J.D. magna cum laude, William Mitchell Coll. Law, 1969. Admitted to Minn. bar, 1926, U.S. Supreme Ct. bar, 1970; individual practice law, St. Paul. Mem. Am., Minn. bar assns., Am. Judicature Soc. Home: 1649 Birchwood Rd Saint Paul MN 55119 Office: W-972 First Nat Bank Bldg Saint Paul MN 55101 Tel (612) 227-8321

TARGAN, DONALD GILMORE, b. Atlantic City, Apr. 7, 1933; B.A., Am. U., 1959; J.D., 1961. Admitted to N.J. bar, 1962; individual practice law, Atlantic City, 1962-66; spl. disaster counsel SBA, Atlantic City, 1962-63; asst. U.S. atty. Camden (N.J.), 1966-69; individual practice law, Atlantic City, 1969—. Mem. Am., N.J., Atlantic County bar assns., Atlantic City Jaycees. Contbr. articles to legal jours. Home: Longport Ocean Plaza Apts Longport NJ 08403 Office: 1 S New York Ave Atlantic NJ 08401 Tel (609) 348-1106

TARKINGTON, CARLTON BRUCE, b. Nashville, June 2, 1936; B.A., George Peabody Coll. for Tchrs., 1959; LL.B., Vanderbilt U., 1963, J.D., 1963. Admitted to Tenn. bar, 1963; individual practice law, Nashville, 1963—; Tenn. rep. West Pub. Co., 1963—; mem. Met. County Council, 1963-67. Mem. Davidson County (Tenn.) Democratic Exec. Com., 1960; chmn. bd. trustees Nashville Presbytery Cumberland Presbyn. Ch. Mem. Tenn. Bar Assn., Tenn. Trial Lawyers Assn. Home and Office: 204 Olive Branch Rd Nashville TN 37205 Tel (615) 352-4162

TARKOFF, MICHAEL HARRIS, b. Phila., Oct. 3, 1946; B.A., U. Miami, 1968, J.D., 1971. Admitted to Fla. bar, 1973, U.S. Supreme Ct. bar, 1976; asst. pub. defender Miami (Fla.) Pub. Defender's Office, 1973—; guest lectr. U. Miami Sch. Law. Mem. Dade County Democratic Exec. Com., 1970-72; pres. Young Dems. of Dade County (Fla.), 1971, trustee, 1973-75. Mem. Fla. Bar (trial lawyers sect.), Fla. Criminal Def. Lawyers Assn. Recipient Am. Jurisprudence award Lawyers Co-op. Pub. Co., 1970, Internat. Acad. Trial Lawyers award, 1971. Office: 1351 NW 12th St Room 800 Miami FL 33125 Tel (305) 547-7709

TARLOCK, ANTHONY DAN, b. Oakland, Calif., June 2, 1940; A.B., Stanford, 1963, LL.B., 1965. Admitted to Calif. bar, 1965; asst. prof. law U. Ky., 1966-68; asst. prof. Ind. U., 1968-70, asso. prof., 1970-72, prof., 1972—. Chmn. Bloomington (Ind.) City Plan Commn., 1971-73. Author: (with Charles J. Meyers) Water Resource Management, 1971; (with Eva and John Hanks) Environmental Law And Policy, 1974. Home: 1108 S High St Bloomington IN 47401 Office: Sch of Law Ind U Bloomington IN 47401 Tel (812) 337-6455

TARLOW, ARTHUR LEE, b. Portland, Oreg., Mar. 15, 1942; student Whitman Coll., 1960-62; B.S. in Law, U. Oreg., 1963, J.D., 1966; grad. career prosecutor course Nat. Coll. Dist. Attys., 1970; A.A.S., Portland Community Coll., 1973. Admitted to Oreg. Supreme Ct. bar, 1966, U.S. Supreme Ct. bar, 1971, U.S. Ct. Claims, 1976; dep. dist. atty. Office Multnomah County (Oreg.) Dist. Atty., 1969-71; shareholder firm Bolliger, Hampton & Tarlow, P.C., Beaverton, Oreg., 1971—; instr. Portland Community Coll., 1971-73. Pres. Washington County (Oreg.) Pub. Affairs Forum, 1974-75, dir., 1975—; trustee Met. Pub. Defender Corp., 1974—. Mem. Oreg. State, Washington County bar assns., Nat. Counter Intelligence Corps Assn., Beaverton Area C. of C. (dir. 1975—), Phi Delta Phi, Beta Theta Pi. Home: 5210 SW 18th Dr Portland OR 97201 Office: 4240 SW Cedar Hills Blvd Beaverton OR 97005 Tel (503) 641-7171

TARNAY, ROBERT STEVENS, b. N.Y.C., May 13, 1913; A.B., U. Mich., 1934; J.D. with distinction, George Washington U., 1938. Admitted to D.C. bar, 1938, Conn. bar, 1938; spl. asst. to U.S. Atty. Gen., Dept. Justice, Washington and Honolulu, 1938-45; individual practice law, Washington, 1945—. Mem. D.C., Conn. bar assns., Phi Alpha Delta. Editor-in-chief Washington Banktrends, 1965—. Home: RTE 1 Box 88 F Newburg MD 20664 Office: 734 15th St NW Suite 503 Washington DC 20005 Tel (202) 347-0243

TARNOFF, JEROME, b. Bklyn., June 22, 1931; A.B., Syracuse U., 1952; J.D., Columbia, 1957. Admitted to N.Y. bar, 1957, U.S. Ct. Appeals 2d Circuit bar, 1961; partner firm Sheldon, Tarnoff & Murphy and predecessor firms, N.Y.C., 1957—; counsel N.Y. City Indsl. Devel. Agy., 1974—. Chmn. policy com. N.Y. County Dem. Party, 1975—; mem. Community Planning Bd., 1966-75; trustee Grand St. Settlement, Asso. Y's N.Y. Mem. Assn. Bar City N.Y., Am. Arbitration Assn. (nat. panel arbitrators), Phi Alpha Delta. Recipient Distinguished Service award NAACP, 1975. Home: 535 E 86th St New York City NY 10028 Office: 292 Madison Ave New York City NY 10017 Tel (212) 683-8844

TARNOW, HERMAN HARRIS, b. N.Y.C., June 16, 1943; B.A., Bklyn. Coll., 1964; J.D., Syracuse U., 1967. Admitted to N.Y. bar, 1968, U.S. Supreme Ct. bar, 1975; asso. firm Friedman & Friedman, N.Y.C., 1968-72; legal cons. N.Y.C. Police Dept., 1972-74; prin. firm Tarnow & Assos., N.Y.C., 1974—; lectr. in field at European seminars and symposiums, 1975. Mem. N.Y. State Bar Assn. (chmn. criminal justice sect., mem. ethics com.), Attys. Counsel for Criminal Justice (pres.). Recipient Judge B. Schwartz award Syracuse U., 1967; award Onondaga County (N.Y.) Bar Assn., 1967; Wohl Meml. scholar, 1966-67. Home: 344 E 51st St New York City NY 10022 Office: 501 Madison Ave New York City NY 10022 Tel (212) 355-3977

TAROFF, LESTER PAUL, b. Phila., Nov. 7, 1945; B.A., L.I. U., 1968; J.D., Bklyn. Law Sch., 1971. Admitted to N.Y. bar, 1972; mem. firm Ross, Suchoff, Taroff & Jason, N.Y.C., 1972—. Mem. Am., N.Y. State bar assns., N.Y. County Lawyers Assn., Comml. Law League Am. Home: 42 Hawthorne St Mount Sinai NY 11766 Office: 261 Broadway New York City NY 10007 Tel (212) 349-1668

TAROLLI, THOMAS LOUIS, b. Coalport, Pa., May 29, 1935; B.S., U. Pitts., 1957; LL.B., George Washington U., 1961. Admitted to Ohio bar, 1961, U.S. Circuit Patent Office bar, 1969; partner firm Yount, Tarolli & Weinshenker, Cleve., 1971—. Office: 1111 Leader Bldg Cleveland OH 44114 Tel (216) 621-2234

TARPEY, JAMES KENNETH, b. N.Y.C., Sept. 28, 1943; B.B.A., St. John's U., 1965; J.D., Fordham U., 1968. Admitted to N.Y. bar, 1971, Colo. bar, 1972; spl. agent FBI, Denver, 1969-70, Chgo., 1970, Washington, 1970, N.Y.C., 1970-72; asst. atty. gen. State of Colo., Denver, 1972-75; hearings examiner Colo. Pub. Utilities Commn., Denver, 1975-77; individual practice law, Denver, 1977—. Mem. Am. (pub. utility law sect., adminstrv. law sect.), Colo. (mem. adminstrv. law com.) bar assns. Home: 3870 S Helena St Aurora CO 80013 Office: 1100 Republic Bldg 1612 Tremont Pl Denver CO 80202 Tel (303) 222-4758

TARPEY, LEO MICHAEL, JR., b. Evanston, Ill., Jan. 5, 1934; B.S., Loyola U., Chgo., 1955, J.D., 1957. Admitted to Ill. bar, 1958, U.S. Dist. Ct. No. Dist. Ill. bar, 1960; asso. firm Lord, Bissell & Brook, Chgo., 1958-59; asso. firm Geo. F. Barrett, Chgo., 1959-63; partner firm Doyle & Tarpey, Chgo., 1963-76; partner firm Pretzel, Stouffer, Nolan & Rooney, Chgo., 1976—. Pres. River Forest Jr. High Sch. PTA, 1976-77; area chmn. Community Fund, 1973-74. Mem. Am., Ill. State bar assns., Soc. Trial Lawyers, Ill. Def. Counsel. Home: 942 Keystone River Forest IL 60305 Office: 100 W Monroe Chicago IL Tel (312) FI6-1973

TARPY, THOMAS MICHAEL, b. Columbus, Ohio, Jan. 4, 1945; A.B., John Carroll U., 1966; J.D., Ohio State U., 1969. Admitted to Ohio bar, 1969; partner firm Vorys, Sater, Seymour & Pease, Columbus, 1969—. Mem. Columbus Area Leadership Program, 1976-77. Mem. Am., Ohio, Columbus (chmn. law insts. com. 1973-76) bar assns., Phi Delta Phi. Home: 1716 Doone Rd Columbus OH 43221 Office: 52 E Gay St Columbus OH 43215 Tel (614) 464-6209

TARRANT, RICHARD JOSEPH, b. Jersey City, Dec. 11, 1897; A.B., Fordham U., 1919, LL.B., 1924; A.M., St. Peters Coll., Jersey City, 1922. Admitted to N.J. bar, 1924, D.C. bar, 1969, Md. bar, 1969, U.S. Supreme Ct. bar, 1967; asst. state mgr. Home Owner Loan Coop. N.J., 1933-42; supervising atty., alien property custodian City of N.Y., 1942-44; state dir. for N.J., Office Price Adminstrn., 1944-47; atty. FCC, Washington, 1957-67. Mem. Am., Md., D.C., Hudson County (N.J.) bar assns. Home and Office: 7801 Hampden Ln Bethesda MD 20014 Tel (301) 656-8455

TARRANT, RICHARD THOMAS, b. San Francisco, Feb. 21, 1940; B.A., Ariz. State U., 1962; LL.B., U. San Francisco, 1963. Admitted to Calif. bar, 1964; staff atty. Dept. Water Resources, State of Calif., Sacramento, 1964-65; asso. firm Nelson, Boyd, MacDonald & Tarrant, San Rafael, Calif., 1965-67, partner, 1967—; dep. city atty. City of San Rafael, 1965-70. Mem. Calif., Marin County bar assns. Home: 42 Los Ranchitos #1 San Rafael CA 94903 Office: 1000 4th St Suite 375 San Rafael CA 94901 Tel (415) 453-0534

TARRICONE, CARL CHRISTOPHER, b. Rochester, N.Y., Sept. 26, 1918; LL.B., U. Buffalo, 1946. Admitted to N.Y. State bar; partner frim Tarricone, Bilgore, Weltman, Silver & Albert, Rochester, 1965—; dir., sec. Naum Bros., Inc., Rochester, 1956—. Active PTA, Boy Scouts Am. Mem. Nat. Tool Die Precision Machinery Assn. Home: 115 Candy Ln Rochester NY 14615 Office: 100 Powers Bldg Rochester NY 14614 Tel (716) 232-7170

TARTA, STEVEN W., b. Paterson, N.J., Jan. 9, 1947; B.A., Alfred U., 1968; J.D., John Marshall Law Sch., 1971; postgrad. Hague Acad. Internat. Law (Netherlands), 1970. Admitted to N.J. bar, 1972; jud. clk. to judges Superior Ct., Ocean County, N.J., 1971-72; asst. county prosecutor Passaic County (N.J.), 1972-73; individual practice law, Hawthorne, N.J., 1973—. Mem. Passaic County, N.J. bar assns., Nat. Dist. Attys. Assn., Am. Soc. Law and Medicine. Home: 208 Washington Ave Hawthorne NJ 07506 Office: 274 Lafayette Ave Hawthorne NJ 07506 Tel (201) 427-7072

TARTER, STANLEY MARVIN, b. Somerset, Ky., Apr. 13, 1927; B.S. in Indsl. Chemistry, U. Ky., 1950; J.D., U. Cin., 1956. Admitted to N.C. bar, 1957, Fla. bar, 1969, Mo. bar, 1976; atty. Am. Enka Corp., Asheville, N.C., 1956-58; atty. Monsanto Co., St. Louis, 1958—. Home: 31 Chapel Hill St Louis MO 63131 Office: 800 N Lindbergh Blvd St Louis MO 63166 Tel (314) 694-3121

TASOFF, LLOYD ARTHUR, b. N.Y.C., Aug. 25, 1915; B.S., Coll. City N.Y., 1935; J.D., Bklyn. Law Sch., 1938. Admitted to N.Y. bar, 1938, Calif. bar, 1949, U.S. Supreme Ct. bar, 1960; with U.S. Dept. Justice, 1941-47; individual practice law, Los Angeles, 1948—. Mem. Assn. Immigration and Nationalization Lawyers, Los Angeles County Bar Assn., Lawyers Club Los Angeles. Office: Suite 1220 Wilshire West Plaza 10880 Wilshire Blvd Los Angeles CA 90024 Tel (213) 474-2545

TATAR, LEONARD BLAIR, b. Houston, Nov. 24, 1935; B.A., U. Tex., 1958; J.D., U. Houston, 1961; postgrad. in taxation, Georgetown U., 1964-65. Admitted to Tex. bar, 1961, U.S. Supreme Ct. bar, 1964; mem. firm Aaron Goldfarb, Houston, 1961-64; trial atty. U.S. Dept. Justice, Washington, Fort Worth, 1964-69; individual practice law, Houston, 1969—; faculty Practicing Law Inst.; mem. Tex. bar com.; lectr. U. Houston and Tex. peer skills course. Mem. Am. Bar Assn. (mem. tax sec.), Tex. Bar Assn. (mem. peer com., tax sec.), Houston Bar Assn. (mem. continuing legal edn. com.). Author: The Texas Lawyer—Why and How to Incorporate, 1969. Office: 905 River Oaks Bank Tower Houston TX 77019 Tel (713) 526-8821

TATE, ALBERT, JR., b. Opelousas, La., Sept. 23, 1920; student Yale, 1937-38, LL.B., 1947; student La. State U., 1938-39, certificate, 1948; B.A., George Washington U., 1941. Admitted to La. bar, 1948; practiced in Ville Platte, La., 1948-54; judge La. Ct. Appeals, 1st Circuit, 1954-60; presiding judge La. Ct. Appeals, 3d Circuit, 1960-70; asso. justice La. Supreme Ct., 1958, 70—; mem. faculty Inst. Jud. Adminstrn. N.Y. U., 1965—, appellate judges seminar U. Ala., 1966, 68, 69, U. Nev., 1967; prof. law La. State U., 1967-68; mem. Adv. Council for Appellate Justice, 1971-75; del. La. Constl. Conv., 1973-74. Active Evangeline Area council Boy Scouts Am., 1948—, dist. chmn., 1949-50; chmn. La. Commn. on Aging, 1956-59; mem. La. Gov.'s Commn. on Rehab. and Corrections, 1970-74; bd. dirs. La. State U. Found. Mem. Am. (chmn. exec. com. Appellate Judges Conf. 1966-76, rep. adv. council Nat. Center for State Cts., Washington, 1971-72), La. bar assns., Am. Judicature Soc. (dir. 1969-73), Am. Bar Found. (vice chmn. study adminstrn. appellate cts. 1970-76), La. Conf. Ct. Appeal Judges (pres. 1967-70), Delta Kappa Epsilon. Recipient Nat. Jud. award of merit Am. Trial Lawyers Assn., 1972; author: Cases and Materials, Louisiana Civil Procedure, 1968, 2d. rev. edit., 1975; Treatises for Judges: A Selected Bibliography, 1971; contbr. articles to legal jours. Home: 410 W Wilson St Ville Platte LA 70586 Office: 301 Loyola Ave New Orleans LA 70112 Tel (504) 527-5361

TATE, FREDERICK GEORGE, b. Boston, Feb. 9, 1925; A.B. magna cum laude, Brown U., 1951; LL.B., Harvard, 1954. Admitted to N.Y. bar, 1955; asso. firm Rogers & Wells, and predecessors, N.Y.C., 1954-67, partner, 1968—; dir. Fairmount Chem. Co., Inc., Newark; dir., sec. Rising Paper Co., Housatonic, Mass. Mem. Am. Arbitration Assn. (mem. comml. panel), Assn. Bar City N.Y., Am. Bar Assn., Phi Beta Kappa. Home: 27 Darwood Pl Mt Vernon NY 10553 Office: 200 Park Ave New York NY 10017 Tel (212) 972-3994

TATE, HAROLD SIMMONS, JR., b. Taylors, S.C., Sept. 19, 1930; A.B. cum laude, Harvard, 1951, J.D., 1956; postgrad. Clemson U., 1953. Admitted to S.C. bar, 1956; partner firm Boyd, Knowlton, Tate & Finlay, Columbia, S.C., 1962—. Mem. admission and scholarship com. Harvard, 1961—; trustee Columbia Hist. Found., 1971-75, Richland County (S.C.) Pub. Library, Columbia, 1973—. Mem. Am. Law Inst., Am. Judicature Soc., Am., S.C., Richland County bar assns. Contbr. articles, book revs. to profl. jours. Home: 15 Gibbes Ct Columbia SC 29201 Office: 1250 SCN Center Columbia SC 29201 Tel (803) 779-3080

TATE, JOHN HENRY, II, b. El Paso, Tex., Jan. 14, 1943; B.S., U.S. Mil. Acad., 1964; J.D., U. Tex., 1972. Admitted to Tex. bar, 1972; asso. firm Oppenheimer, Rosenberg, Kelleher & Wheatley, San Antonio, 1972—; chmn. legal research bd. U. Tex. Law Sch., 1971-72, also teaching quizmaster; lectr., panelist seminars in field. Bd. dirs. Community Guidance Center, San Antonio. Mem. Comml. Law League Am., San Antonio, Am., Tex. bar assns. Home: 603 Olmos Dr E San Antonio TX 78212 Office: suite 620 711 Navarro St San Antonio TX 78205 Tel (512) 224-7581

TATE, JOSEPH TEMPLE, b. Dale, Ill., Aug. 12, 1899; LL.B., Washington U., St. Louis, 1923. Admitted to Mo. bar, 1923; practiced in Union, Mo., 1923-53; judge Mo. Circuit Ct., 20th Jud. Circuit, 1953—; pros. atty. Gasconade County (Mo.); city atty. City of Belle (Mo.), City of Bland (Mo.), City of Owensville (Mo.), Rosebud (Mo.), Gerald (Mo.). Home: 201 Wally St Union MO 63084 Office: Courthouse Union MO 63084 Tel (314) 583-2687

TATE, MILTON YORK, JR., b. Giddings, Tex., May 14, 1939; B.B.A., U. Tex., 1960, J.D., 1963. Admitted to Tex. bar, 1963; partner firm Moorman & Tate, Brenham, Tex., 1966—. Pres. Brenham Indsl. Found., Inc., 1973-76; bd. dirs. Lower Colo. River Authority, 1975—. Mem. Am. Bar Assn. Tel (713) 836-5664

TATE, PATRICK HARALSON, b. Oxnard, Calif., Mar. 31, 1946; B.S., Jacksonville State U., 1968; J.D., Cumberland Sch. Law, Sanford U., 1971. Admitted to Ala. bar, 1971; individual practice law, Ft. Payne, Ala., 1973—; county atty. DeKalb County (Ala.), 1975—. Mem. Ala., DeKalb County bar assns., Ala. Municipal Judges Assn. Home: 257 Forest Ave Fort Payne AL 35967 Office: 115 First St Fort Payne AL 35967 Tel (205) 845-1047

TATE, RALPH RICHARDS, JR., b. Oakland, Calif., Mar. 11, 1941; B.S. in Accounting, U. Utah, 1965, J.D., 1968. Admitted to Utah bar, 1968, U.S. Tax Ct. bar, 1968; asso. firm Nielsen, Conder, Hanson & Henriod, Salt Lake City, 1968-72; partner firm Henriksen, Fairbourn and Tate, Salt Lake City, 1972—; mem. legal staff Utah Legislature, 1973. Mem. Salt Lake County Bar Assn. Home: 4335 Vallejo Dr Salt Lake City UT 84117 Office: 320 S 5th St E Salt Lake City UT 84102 Tel (801) 521-4145

TATE, ROBERT GREYE, b. Birmingham, Ala., Mar. 9, 1932; B.A., U. Ala., 1953, LL.B., 1957. Admitted to Ala. bar, 1957, U.S. Supreme Ct. bar, 1972; mem. firm Thomas Taliaferro Forman Burr & Murray, Birmingham, 1957—. Deacon, Shades Valley Presbyterian Ch., Birmingham, 1962-65, 67-70, elder, 1970-73, 75—; treas. Birmingham Audubon Soc., 1973—; pres. Ala. Wildflower Soc., 1975—. Mem. Birmingham Bar Assn. (past treas.), Ala. Def. Lawyers Assn. Office: 1600 Bank for Savings Bldg Birmingham AL 35203 Tel (205) 251-3000

TATUM, FRANK DONOVAN, JR., b. Los Angeles, July 10, 1920; A.B. in Engring., Stanford, 1942, J.D., 1950; B.C.L., Oxford (Eng.) U., 1949. Admitted to Calif. bar, 1950, since practiced in San Francisco; asso. firm Cooley, Godward, Castro, Huddleson & Tatum, 1950-58, partner, 1958—. Mem. San Francisco Mayor's Fiscal Adv. Com.;

mem., sec. Calif. and S.W. Dist. Coms. for Selection Rhodes Scholars; mem. Calif. Com. for Selection Fulbright Scholars; bd. dirs. United Bay Area Crusade, Mental Health Assn., St. Elisabeth's Infant Hosp., Legal Aid Soc., Youth Law Center. Mem. Am., San Francisco (jud. search com.) bar assns., State Bar Calif., Phi Beta Kappa, Order of Coif, Tau Beta Pi. Rhodes scholar, 1947. Home: 3377 Washington St San Francisco CA 94118 Office: 1 Maritime Plaza suite 2000 San Francisco CA 94111 Tel (415) 981-5252

TAURO, G. JOSEPH, b. Lynn, Mass., Jan. 10, 1906; student Coll. Bus. Adminstrn. Boston U., 1923-23, J.D., Law Sch., 1927, LL.D., 1964; LL.D., Suffolk U., 1969, U. Mass., 1970. Admitted to Mass. bar, 1927; practiced in Lynn, 1927-61; judge Mass. Superior Ct., 1961-62, chief justice, 1962-70; chief justice Supreme Jud. Ct. of Mass., 1970-76, ret., 1976; prof. law Boston U., 1976—; chmn. bd. Security Nat. Bank, Lynn, 1976—; chief legal counsel Mass. Gov., 1960-61. Pres., Boston U. Law Sch. Alumni, 1955-56. Mem. Am. Bar Assn., Am. Law Inst. Home: One Cliff Rd Swampscott MA 01907 Office: Boston U Sch Law 765 Commonwealth Ave Boston MA 02215 Tel (617) 353-2789

TAUSSIG, JOSEPH MAURICE, b. Chgo., June 10; student U. Wis., 1922-24; B.S., J.D., 1929. Admitted to Ill. bar, 1929; asso. firm Kirkland, Fleming, Green & Martin, Chgo., 1929-44; individual practice law, Chgo., 1945—. Mem. Am., Chgo., Ill. State, Fed. bar assns. Home: 3260 Lake Shore Dr Chicago IL 60657 Office: 5 S Wabash Ave Chicago IL 60603 Tel (312) 726-0316

TAUZER, STEPHEN MICHAEL, b. Woodland, Calif., Aug. 23, 1945; B.A., U. San Francisco, 1967; J.D., U. Calif., Davis, 1970. Admitted to Calif. bar, 1971; pub. defender Kern County, Calif., 1971-75, dist. atty., 1975—. Mem. Kern County Bar Assn. Office: 1415 Truxton Ave Bakersfield CA 93301 Tel (805) 861-2423

TAVOLACCI, CARL ERCOLE, b. Bklyn., Nov. 9, 1912; LL.B., St. John's Law Sch., 1935, LL.M., 1936. Admitted to N.Y. State bar, 1936, U.S. Supreme Ct. bar, 1957; practice law, Bklyn., 1936—, mem. firm Tavolacci & De Matteo, 1945-68. Pres. Iron Hills Civic Assn., 1973-74. Mem. N.Y. State Bar Assn., N.Y. State Trial Lawyers, Bay Ridge Lawyers Assn. (pres. 1972), Am. Legion (comdr. Bath Beach chpt. 1951). Office: 8510 18th Ave Brooklyn NY 11214 Tel (212) 232-5000

TAYLOR, BOYD DAVID, b. Temple, Tex., Nov. 24, 1932; B.A., U. Tex., 1952, LL.B., 1955. Admitted to Tex. bar, 1955, W.Va. bar, 1968, Mass. bar, 1973; with Cabot Corp., 1958—, gen. mgr. LNG Projects, Boston, 1971-72, asst. to pres., 1972-74, v.p., gen. mgr. div. oil and gas, Pampa, Tex., 1974—; dir. Citizens Bank & Trust Co., Pampa. Pres. Pampa C. of C., 1975-76; trustee Lovett Meml. Library, Pampa; bd. dirs. Tex. Research League, Austin. Mem. Tex., W.Va., Mass., Am. bar assns., Ind. Petroleum Assn. Am. (dir.), Panhandle Producers, Royalty Owners Assn. Home: 1901 N Russell Pampa TX 79065 Office: POB 1101 Pampa TX 79065 Tel (806) 669-2581

TAYLOR, CARROLL STRIBLING, b. Port Chester, N.Y., Jan. 14, 1944; B.A. in History, Yale, 1965; J.D., U. Calif., Boalt Hall, 1968. Admitted to Calif. bar, 1969, Hawaii bar, 1969; researcher Legis. Reference Bur., Honolulu, 1968-70; reporter Hawaii Probate Code Revision Project, Honolulu, 1970-71; asso. firm Chun Kerr & Dodd, Honolulu, 1971-75; partner firm Hamilton & Taylor, Honolulu, 1975—. Mem. Hawaii (exec. com. 1973—), Calif., Am. bar assns. Home: 46-429 Hololio St Kaneohe HI 96744 Office: Suite 1402 841 Bishop St Honolulu HI 96813 Tel (808) 524-3824

TAYLOR, CARSON GITT, b. Lancaster, Pa., Jan. 14, 1946; B.A., Amherst Coll., 1967; J.D., Duke, 1970. Admitted to Calif. bar, 1971, U.S. Dist. Ct. Central Dist. Calif. bar, 1971, U.S. Ct. Appeals 9th Circuit bar, 1973; asso. firm Taylor, Roth & Grant, Los Angeles. Mem. Nat. Lawyers Guild. Home: 11842 1/2 Washington Pl Los Angeles CA 90066 Office: 619 S Bonnie Brae St Los Angeles CA 90057 Tel (213) 484-8280

TAYLOR, CHARLES REEVES, b. Keyser, W.Va., Dec. 7, 1934; A.A., Potomac State Coll., 1954; A.B., W.Va. U., 1956, J.D., 1958. Admitted to W.Va. bar, 1958, Fed. bar, 1961, U.S. Supreme Ct. bar, 1973; individual practice law, Keyser, W.Va., 1966-76; pros. atty., Mineral County, W.Va., 1961-65; U.S. commr. Fed. Jud. System, No. Dist. W.Va., Keyser, 1966-71; chief judge 21st Jud. Circuit W.Va., 1977—. Trustee Burlington United Methodist Home Children and Youth, Inc., 1967—. Mem. W.Va. (v.p. 2d congl. dist. 1960), Am. bar assns., W.Va. State Bar, W.Va. Jud. Assn., Phi Alpha Delta, C. of C. Home: 1390 Lynmar St Keyser WV 26726 Office: PO Drawer T Keyser WV 26726 Tel (304) 788-5150

TAYLOR, CLARENCE BUFORD, b. Pineville, Ky., Jan. 16, 1937; B.A., Ohio State U., 1959, LL.B., 1962, J.D., 1962; grad. basic and career courses Judge Adv. Gen.'s Sch., Charlottesville, Va., 1963, 71. Admitted to Ohio bar, 1962, U.S. Ct. Mil. Appeals bar, 1963; with JAGC, 1963-69; supr. field attys. VA, Cleve., 1969-72; chief asst. to U.S. atty. No. Dist. Ohio, Cleve., 1972—. Mem. Ohio State Bar Assn., Cleve. Lawyers Assn., Alpha Phi Alpha. Home: 8572 Usher Rd Olmsted Township OH 44138 Office: 400 US Courthouse Cleveland OH 44114 Tel (216) 522-4393

TAYLOR, CLARENCE WILSON, b. Pitts., Mar. 21, 1917; B.A., U. Del., 1938; LL.B., Yale, 1941. Admitted to N.Y. bar, 1942, Del. bar, 1947; adminstrv. asst. Austin Co., N.Y.C., 1941-43; legal asst. to v.p. Dravo Corp., Wilmington, Del., 1943-46; asso. firm Hastings, Stockly, Walz and Wise, 1946-54; partner firm Hastings, Lynch and Taylor, 1954-59, Hastings, Taylor and Willard, Wilmington, 1959—; asst. atty. Levy Ct. of New Castle County (Del.), 1951-52, chief atty., 1958-66; dep. atty. gen. State of Del., 1953-55; county atty. New Castle County, 1967-72; judge Del. Superior Ct., 1972—. Bd. dirs. Wilmington Sr. Center, Inc., 1959-73; mem. Supreme Ct. Adv. Com. on Litigation Ethical Problems, Com. on Opinions of Supreme Ct.; mem. Republican State Platform and Legis. Drafting Coms. of Del.; vestryman Immanuel Episcopal Ch., Wilmington. Mem. Del., Am. bar assns., Phi Kappa Phi. Home: 2310 W 11th St Wilmington DE 19805 Office: Superior Ct Pub Bldg 10th and King Sts Wilmington DE 19801 Tel (302) 571-2374

TAYLOR, CLINTON ODELL, b. Dallas, Oct. 14, 1943; B.A., U. Tex., 1966; J.D., U. Ark., 1969. Admitted to Ark. bar, 1970, U.S. Dist. Ct. bar, 1970; partner firm Murphy, Carlisle & Taylor, Fayetteville, Ark., 1970-76; individual practice law, Fayetteville, 1976—. Mem. Am., Ark., Washington County (Ark.) bar assns., Ark. Trial Lawyers Assn., Phi Alpha Delta. Office: 14 1/2 E Center St Fayetteville AR 72701 Tel (501) 521-2424

TAYLOR, DYER JUSTICE, b. Columbia, S.C., Sept. 25, 1922; student Johns Hopkins, 1942, U. N.C., 1946-48; J.D., George Washington U., 1951; grad. Nat. Coll. State Judiciary, U. Nev., 1972, 74. Admitted to U.S. Dist. Ct. bar for D.C., 1951, U.S. Ct. Appeals bar, D.C. Circuit, 1951, U.S. Ct. Mil. Appeals bar, 1954, U.S. Ct. Claims bar, 1955, U.S. Supreme Ct. bar, 1955; asso. firm Ballard & Beasley, Washington, 1951-55; trial atty. Justice Dept., Washington, 1955-57, asst. U.S. atty. for D.C., 1957-58; jr. partner firm Laskey & Laskey, Washington, 1958-60; asst. solicitor Interior Dept., Washington, 1960-61; hearing examiner ICC, Washington, 1961-63; trial examiner FPC, Washington, 1963-70; asso. judge D.C. Superior Ct., 1970—; pres. Fed. Trial Examiners Conf. (now called Fed. Adminstrv. Law Judges Conf.), 1970. Chmn. municipal affairs Beverly Hills Citizens Assn., Alexandria, Va., 1958. Mem. Am., Fed., D.C. bar assns., Fed. Adminstrv. Law Judges Conf. Recipient certificate of distinction Alumni Assn. of Central High Sch., 1971, Scholarship certificate Delta Theta Phi, 1951. Home: 1946 Creek Crossing Rd Vienna VA 22180 Office: 613 G St NW Washington DC 20001 Tel (202) 727-1466

TAYLOR, E. TED, b. Fayette, Ala., June 3, 1940; B.S., U. Ala., 1962, J.D., 1966. Admitted to Ala. bar, 1966; law clerk firm deGraffenried, deGraffenried & deGraffenried, Tuscaloosa, Ala., 1964-66; asso. firm Hamilton, Denniston, Butler & Riddick, Mobile, Ala., 1966-67; partner firm McDowell & Taylor, Prattville, Ala., 1967-74; individual practice law, Prattville, 1974—. Bd. dirs. Prattville YMCA, Prattville Gen. Hosp., Autauga County (Ala.) Am. Cancer Soc., Autauga County United Way. Mem. Prattville C. of C., Autauga County 19th Jud. Circuit (pres. 1973), Ala., Am. bar assns., Am. Judicature Soc., Ala., Am. trial lawyers assns., Farrah Law Soc., U. Ala. Nat. Alumni Assn. (v.p. 1972). Named Outstanding Young Man of Autauga County, 1971, one of ten Outstanding Young Men Ala., 1971. Office: 114 E Main St Prattville AL 36067 Tel (205) 365-2221

TAYLOR, EDWARD FORT, b. Oxford, N.C., Jan. 13, 1906; student U. S.C., 1925-27; LL.B., U. N.C., 1930. Admitted to N.C. bar, 1929; practiced in Oxford, 1930—, individual practice law, 1930-34, 47-52, 69—, mem. firms Parham and Taylor, 1934-47, Hicks and Taylor, 1952-69; atty. Granville County (N.C.) Bd. Edn., 1936-72; county atty. Granville County, 1940-44, 69-73; solicitor Granville County Recorder's Ct., 1948-56; atty. City of Oxford, 1940-43, Granville County Alcoholic Beverage Control Bd., 1969-73. Trustee Granville County Library, 1950—, chmn., 1953-58; chmn. Granville County Democratic Exec. Com., 1946-70. Mem. Granville County, N.C. bar assns., N.C. State Bar. Home: 214 Gilliam St Oxford NC 27565 Office: Planters Nat Bank Bldg Hillsboro St Oxford NC 27565 Tel (919) 693-8300

TAYLOR, EDWARD MCKINLEY, JR., b. Dayton, Ohio, Apr. 19, 1928; J.D. with distinction, Ohio No. U., 1951. Admitted to Ohio bar, 1951, U.S. Supreme Ct. bar, 1971, U.S. Ct. Mil. Appeals bar, 1973; partner firm Taylor & Taylor, Dayton, 1957—; asst. city atty. Dayton, 1957—; col. JAGC, U.S. Air Force Res., 1957—. Mem. Am, Ohio, Dayton bar assns., Judge Adv. Assn. Home: 7417 N Main St Dayton OH 45415 Office: Municipal Bldg Dayton OH 45415 Tel (513) 225-5022

TAYLOR, EDWIN DRUMMOND, b. Detroit, Oct. 13, 1920; A.B., U. Miami, 1949, J.D., 1952. Admitted to Fla. bar, 1952, N.C. bar, 1972; individual practice law, Miami, Fla., 1952-65; staff atty. Dade County (Fla.) Legal Aid Soc., 1965-69; asst. prof. Appalachian State U., 1969-72; individual practice law, Banner Elk, N.C., 1972—. Home: RTE 5 Box 351 AA Boone NC 28607 Office: Box 82 Banner Elk NC 28604

TAYLOR, EDWIN ERNEST, b. Balt., Mar. 2, 1920; certificate U. Md., 1952, St. Johns Coll., 1959; A.A., Eastern Coll. Commerce and Law, 1960; certificate Mich. State U., 1961; LL.B., Mt. Vernon Sch. Law, 1964; diploma U. So. Calif., 1967; J.D., U. Balt., 1970. Law enforcement officer Balt. City Police Dept., 1944-69, dir. personnel div., 1966-67, dir. youth div., 1967-68, col.-chief criminal investigation div., 1968-69; admitted to Md. bar, 1968; individual practice law, Balt., 1970—; legal counsel Mcpl. Employees Credit Union, Balt. Vice pres. Boys Town Homes of Md., 1966—. Mem. Am., Fed. (bd. govs. Balt. chpt., chmn. law observance com.), Md., Balt. bar assns., Internat. Assn. Chiefs of Police, U. Balt. Alumni Assn. Recipient Outstanding Citizen award Gov. Md., 1968, Achievement award Met. Civic Assn., 1964, Md. Senate resolution for police services to Balt., 1970, Balt. City Council resolution, 1970, also numerous commendations Police Dept.; named Alumnus of Year, Eastern Coll. Commerce and Law, 1968. Office: Suite 900 One Charles Center Baltimore MD 21201 Tel (301) 539-8231 also suite 300 Loyola Fed Bldg Towson MD 21204 Tel (301) 296-3366

TAYLOR, EVERETT BAILEY, b. Montgomery County, Ohio, Oct. 8, 1899; B.S., Dartmouth, 1921; LL.B., Yale, 1925, J.D., 1971. Admitted to N.Y. bar, 1928, Idaho bar, 1941; with Travelers Ins. Co., Hartford, Conn., 1926-28, First Nat. City Bank, N.Y.C., 1928-40; individual practice law, Sun Valley, Idaho, 1941—; asst. sec. Idaho State Senate, 1961, 63, 65. Mem. Idaho Senate, 1964; councilman City of Sun Valley, 1967-72, pres., 1970-72; trustee Sun Valley Hosp., 1967-72. Mem. Am., N.Y., Idaho bar assns., Am. Judicature Soc. Home and Office: Sun Valley Inn Sun Valley ID 83353 Tel (208) 622-4111 also PO Box 901 Hailey ID 83333 Tel (208) 788-4062

TAYLOR, FLOYD WENTWORTH, b. Ft. Stockton, Tex., Aug. 6, 1943; student Grinnell Coll., 1961-62; B.A., U. Okla., 1965, J.D., 1968. Admitted to Okla. bar, 1968; legal intern legal div. Okla. Hwy. Dept., Oklahoma City, 1967-68, trial atty., 1969-70; gen. counsel Okla. Dept. Transp., Oklahoma City, 1970—. Mem. Oklahoma City Jr. C. of C., Phi Delta Phi. Contbr. article to legal jour. Office: 200 NE 21st St Oklahoma City OK 73107 Tel (405) 521-2630

TAYLOR, GEORGE HAL, b. Provo, Utah, May 15, 1915; B.A., U. Utah, 1940, J.D., 1942. Admitted to Utah bar, 1942; since practiced in Salt Lake City; counsel Utah State Tax Commn., 1946-50; asst. atty. gen. Utah, 1951-52; dep. county atty., 1952-53; partner firm Moffat, Iverson, & Taylor, 1966-72; judge Dist. Ct., 1973—. Mem. Am., Utah bar assns. Home: 1620 Sherman Ave Salt Lake City UT 84105 Office: 240 E 4th St S Salt Lake City UT 84111 Tel (801) 328-7359

TAYLOR, HARRY EARL, JR., b. Honolulu, Dec. 14, 1921; student U. Hawaii, 1941; A.A., Sacramento Jr. Coll., 1942; B.A., George Washington U., 1948, LL.B., 1949, J.D., 1949. Admitted to D.C. bar, 1949, Md. bar, 1955, U.S. Supreme Ct. bar, 1953; sr. partner firm Taylor & Waldron, Washington, 1950-69, firm Taylor & Smith, Upper Marlboro, Md., 1970-76, firm Taylor, Smith & Parker, Brandywine, Md., 1976—. Mem. Md. Ho. of Dels., 1950-54; del. Md. Constl. Conv., 1967; chmn. Prince Georges County (Md.) Bd. License Commrs., 1966; mem. Prince George's County Property Tax Assessment Appeal Bd., 1976. Mem. Am., Md., Washington, Prince George's County bar assns., Am. Trial Lawyers Assn., Assn. to Advance Ethical Hypnosis, Delta Theta Phi. Home: Route 2 Box 262 Brandywine MD 20613 Office: Route 2 Box 262 Brandywine MD 20613 Tel (301) 372-8887

TAYLOR, HERBERT H., JR., b. Tarboro, N.C., Sept. 7, 1911; A.B., U. N.C., 1932, J.D., 1935. Admitted to N.C. bar, 1935; judge Edgecombe County (N.C.) Recorder's Ct., 1940-42, 46-57; now partner firm Taylor, Brinson & Aycock, Tarboro; atty. Town of Tarboro, 1947—, Edgecombe County, N.C., 1957—; gen. counsel Carolina Tel. & Tel. Co., 1957—; chmn. N.C. Vets. Commn., 1950-56. Mem. 7th Jud. Dist., N.C. (gov. 1969—, pres. 1977—), Am. bar assns., N.C. State Bar, Am. Judicature Soc., Phi Beta Kappa, Phi Delta Phi. Editorial staff N.C. Law Rev., 1934-35. Office: 210 E Saint James St PO Drawer 308 Tarboro NC 27886 Tel (919) 823-8108*

TAYLOR, HERMAN LAMON, b. Knox County, Ill., Jan. 18, 1902; A.B. magna cum laude, Knox Coll., 1926; J.D. cum laude, U. Chgo., 1932. Admitted to Ill. bar, 1933; asso. firm McCulloch & McCulloch, Chgo., 1933-41; partner firm Essington, McKibbin, Beebe & Pratt, Chgo., 1941-69; partner firm McCulloch, Veatch & Taylor, Chgo., 1969—; dir., gen. counsel Church Fedn. Greater Chgo.; dir. gen. counsel Electric Assn., Chgo. Chmn., Flossmoor (Ill.) Zoning Bd., 1961-73; mem. Flossmoor Plan Commn., 1962-73. Mem. Am., Ill., Chgo. bar assns., Am. Judicature Soc. Named Knox Coll. Alumnus of Year, 1971; recipient Electric Assn. award, 1975. Home: 1610 Brassie Ave Flossmoor IL 60422 Office: 72 W Adams St Chicago IL 60603 Tel (312) CE6-2386

TAYLOR, HOBART, JR., b. Texarkana, Tex., Dec. 17, 1920; A.B., Prairie View (Tex.) State Coll., 1939; A.M., Howard U., 1941; J.D., U. Mich., 1943; L.H.D., Agrl. and Tech. Coll. N.C.; LL.D., Pacific U., Shaw U., Knoxville Coll. Admitted to Mich. bar, 1944, D.C. bar, 1968; research asst. Mich. Supreme Ct., 1944-45; jr. partner firm Bledsoe & Taylor, Detroit, 1945-48; asst. pros. atty. Wayne County (Mich.), 1949-50, corp. counsel, 1951-61; sr. mem. firm Taylor, Patrick, Bailer & Lee, Detroit, 1958-61; spl. counsel Pres.'s Com. Equal Employment Opportunity, 1961-62, exec. vice chmn., 1962-65; spl. asst. to Vice Pres. U.S., 1963; asso. counsel to Pres. Johnson, 1964-65; dir. Export-Import Bank U.S., 1965-68; partner firm Dawson, Riddell, Taylor, Davis & Holroyd, and predecessors, Washington, 1968—; dir. Aetna Life and Casualty Co., Urban Nat. Corp., Gt. Atlantic and Pacific Tea Co., Westinghouse Electric Corp., Standard Oil Co. (Ohio). Bd. govs. ARC, Washington; vice chmn. bd. trustees Wolf Trap Found. for Performing Arts, Washington. Mem. Fed., Inter-Am., Am., Mich., D.C. bar assns. Home: 4200 Massachusetts Ave NW Washington DC 20016 Office: Washington Bldg NW Washington DC 20005 Tel (202) 393-6900

TAYLOR, HOWARD DONE, b. Payson, Utah, June 27, 1909; B.S., Brigham Young U., 1931; J.D., George Washington U., 1937. Admitted to D.C. bar, 1937, Mass. bar, 1961, N.Y. state bar, 1965; with IRS, 1939-65, asst. regional commr., Boston, 1955-61, regional commr. N. Atlantic Region, N.Y.C., 1961-65; partner firm Wikler, Gottlieb, Taylor, & Howard, N.Y.C., 1965-76. Mem. N.Y. State, Fed. bar assns., Assn. Bar City N.Y. Contbr. articles to legal jours. Home: 2756 Edgewood Provo UT 84601 Tel (801) 374-6529

TAYLOR, HOWARD HARPER, b. Detroit, June 5, 1926; B.A., Stanford U., 1949, LL.B., 1951. Admitted to Calif. bar, 1952; asso. firm Wright, Thomas, Dorman & Fox, San Diego, from 1951; trust dept. atty. 1st Nat. Bank, San Diego, from 1952; individual practice law, San Diego, 1953—; chmn. San Diego Adv. Council, 1967-71. Mem. Calif., San Diego County bar assns. Am. Arbitration Assn. (arbitrator 1967—). Home: 980 Scott St San Diego CA 92106 Office: Suite 1700 Security Pacific Plaza Bldg 1200 3d Ave San Diego CA 92101 Tel (714) 239-0239

TAYLOR, HUBERT LEE, b. Jasper, Ala., Mar. 30, 1943; A.B. in History, U. Ala., 1965; B.S. in Bus., 1964, LL.B., 1967. Admitted to Ala. bar, 1967, since practiced in Gadsden; county atty. Walker County (Ala.), 1970; city atty., Gadsden, 1971-73; mem. Ala. Ho. of Reps., 1974—, selected as most outstanding orator, 1976. Ordained deacon United Methodist Ch. Mem. Am., Etowah, Ala. bar assns. Home: 2714 Hazel St Gadsden AL 35901 Office: 823 Forrest Ave Gadsden AL 35901 Tel (205) 547-3641

TAYLOR, JOE CLINTON, b. Durant, Okla., Mar. 28, 1942; B.A. in Polit. Sci., Okla. State U., 1965, J.D., 1968. Admitted to Okla. bar, 1968; mem. firm Primrose, Norman, Okla., 1968; spl. judge Bryan County (Okla.), Durant, 1969-72, asso. judge, 1972-76; dist. judge and chief judge 19th Dist. Ct. Okla., Durant, 1976—. Chmn. bd. dirs. Bryan County Youth Shelter, Inc., 1976—; task force chmn. CROP Hunger Walk, 1976. Mem. Okla. Bar Assn., Okla. Jud. Conf., Delta Theta Phi. Home: 424 W Olive St Durant OK 74701 Office: Bryan County Court House Durant OK 74701 Tel (405) 924-3450

TAYLOR, JOHN AXEL, b. Van Nuys, Calif., Apr. 20, 1934; B.S., U. Calif., Los Angeles, 1956; J.D., Stetson U., 1962. Admitted to Fla. bar, 1962, D.C. bar, 1964, Nev. bar, 1965, U.S. Supreme Ct. bar, 1972; with IRS, 1962-64; law clk. to Clark County Dist. Atty. and George Abbott, Minden, 1964-65; asso. firm Sullivan & Taylor, Las Vegas, Nev., 1965-67, Dorsey & Taylor, Las Vegas, 1967-68, Morse & Graves, Las Vegas, 1968-69; individual practice law, Las Vegas, 1970-71; prin. Taylor Profl. Corp., Las Vegas, 1971—. Past co-chmn. Billy Graham Premiere Com., Las Vegas; pres. Las Vegas camp Gideons Internat., 1976; sec. Calif.-Nev. Gideon State Assn., 1970-73, mem. state cabinet, 1971-76; Clark County Republican vice-chmn., 1970-71, conv. chmn., 1968; bd. dirs., past sec. Internat. Edn. Found.; sec. bd. trustees Faith Communications Corp.; pres. bd. trustees Las Vegas Rescue Mission; trustee Mel Tari Evangelistic Assn. Mem. Fed. (past local pres.), Am. bar assns., Am. Trial Lawyers Assn., Am. Judicature Soc., Christian Legal Soc., Delta Theta Phi. Elected to Intercollegiate Sailing Hall of Fame, 1973. Office: 300 E Fremont St Suite 105 Las Vegas NV 89101 Tel (702) 384-5514

TAYLOR, JOHN FISHER, b. Center, Tex., Mar. 12, 1918; student U. Tex. Austin, 1935-37; LL.B., Samford U., 1938; postgrad. Washington and Lee U., 1945. Admitted to Tex. bar, 1944, U.S. Dist. Ct. C.Z. bar, 1947, U.S. Dist. for Eastern Tex. Dist. Ct. bar, 1950; U.S. Ct. Mil. Appeals bar, 1961, U.S. Supreme Ct. bar, 1961; commd. U.S. Army, 1940, advanced through grades to col. USAAF, 1961; with Dept. Def., 1962-72; individual practice law, San Antonio, 1972—. Mem. Tex. Bar assn. Decorated D.F.C., Air medal with eleven oak leaf clusters. Home and office: 7515 Buckskin Ln San Antonio TX 78227 Tel (512) 674-3471

TAYLOR, JOHN FRANKLIN, b. Pinedale, Ariz., Apr. 4, 1930; B.A., Ariz. State U., 1958; LL.B., U. Ariz., 1961. Admitted to Ariz. bar, 1961, Fed. bar, 1961; asso. firm Taylor & Porter, Snowflake, Ariz., 1961; individual practice law, Snowflake, 1962-63, atty. Navajo County, Ariz., 1964-75; judge Superior Ct., Ariz., Holbrook, 1975—; mem. Ariz. Criminal Code Commn., 1973-75. Mem. adv. com. Grand

Canyon Council Boy Scouts Am., 1967-77. Mem. Apache-Navajo Bar Assn. (pres. 1974-75). Home: PO Box 398 Snowflake AZ 85937 Office: Navajo County Complex Holbrook AZ 86025 Tel (602) 524-6161

TAYLOR, KEITH ELMER, b. Oakley, Idaho, Apr. 5, 1928; B.S., M.S., Utah State U., 1951; J.D., Stanford, 1954. Admitted to Calif. bar, 1954, Utah bar, 1955, U.S. Supreme Ct. bar, 1960; mem. firm Parson, Behle & Latimer, Salt Lake City, 1955-71, pres., 1971—. Mem. Am., Salt Lake County bar assns. Home: 821 16th Ave Salt Lake City UT 84103 Office: 79 S State St Salt Lake City UT 84147 Tel (801) 532-1234

TAYLOR, LARRY DELANO, b. Montgomery, W.Va., Nov. 16, 1934; B.A., W. Va. U., 1956, LL.B., 1962. Admitted to W.Va. bar, 1962; atty., legal dept. W.Va. Dept. Hwys., Charleston, 1962; asst. contract adminstr. FMC, South Charleston, W.Va., 1963-64; asst. atty. gen. State of W.Va., 1964-70; individual practice law, Charleston, 1970—. Pres. Little League Baseball, 1971, St. Agnes Grade Sch. PTA, 1970 (both Charleston). Mem. W.Va., Kanawha County bar assns., Phi Alpha Delta. Home: 1800 Roundhill Rd Apt 1904 Charleston WV 25314 Office: 1331 Charleston National Plaza Charleston WV 25301 Tel (304) 346-0563

TAYLOR, LARRY LEE, b. Ft. Benning, Ga., July 13, 1944; B.A., Miami U., Oxford, Ohio, 1966; J.D., U. Ga., 1970. Admitted to Ga. bar, 1970; asso. firm Young & Dicus, Columbus, Ga., 1970-71; partner firm Young, Ford & Taylor, Columbus, 1971-74; individual practice law, Columbus, 1974—; dir. Columbus Legal Aid, 1972—. Mem. Muscogee County (Ga.) Bd. Voter Registrars, 1973-75, 76—. Mem. Am., Chattahoochee Circuit (pres. 1975-76) bar assns., State Bar Ga., Ga. Trial Lawyers Assn., Columbus Lawyers Club. Home: 4 Kingswood Ct Columbus GA 31907 Office: 820 Second Ave Columbus GA 31901 Tel (404) 324-4391

TAYLOR, LELAND BARIDON, b. Poughkeepsie, N.Y., July 5, 1920; B.S., Syracuse U., 1942, J.D., 1948. Admitted to N.Y. bar, 1948; partner firm Fitzgerald & Taylor, Cortland, N.Y., 1948—; judge City of Cortland, 1952-57; v.p. First Nat. Bank of Dryden. Pres. Cortland Meml. Hosp., Cortland Free Library. Fellow Am. Bar Found.; mem. Am., N.Y. (v.p. 1975-77), Cortland County bar assns. Named Jaycee Young Man of Year for Cortland County and N.Y. State. Office: 16 Tompkins St Cortland NY 13045 Tel (607) 756-7501

TAYLOR, MARY JOAN (MRS. EDWARD MCKINLEY TAYLOR), b. Kenton, Ohio, Dec. 24, 1926; A.B.A., St. Mary of Springs Coll., 1945; J.D. with high distinction, Ohio No. U., 1951; postgrad. U. Wyo., 1954-56. Law librarian Franklin U., 1948-49; admitted to Ohio Supreme Ct. bar, 1951, U.S. Supreme Ct. bar, 1971; asso. firm Cessna, McMahon Taylor, Kenton, Ohio, 1951-52; asso. firm Titus T. Mitchell, Wichita Falls, Tex., 1953; partner firm Taylor & Taylor, Dayton, Ohio, 1957—. Mem. Dayton, Ohio bar assns., Dayton Bus. and Profl. Women's Club, Kappa Beta Pi. Home and Office: 7417 N Main St Dayton OH 45415 Tel (513) 278-2723

TAYLOR, MAURICE GLENN, JR., b. Charleston, W.Va., Sept. 15, 1942; B.S. in Bus. Adminstrn., W.Va. U., 1964, LL.B., 1967. Admitted to W.Va. bar, 1967; asst. pros. atty., Kanawha County (W.Va.), 1967; law clk. U.S. Dist. Ct., Huntington, W.Va., 1967-69; asso. firm Campbell, Woods Bagley Emerson McNeer and Herndon, Huntington, 1969-71; individual practice law, Huntington, 1971—; U.S. magistrate, Huntington, 1971—. Pres., bd. dirs. Appalachian Craftsmen, Inc. Mem. W.Va. State, Cabell County bar assns. Home: 1822 Wiltshire Blvd Huntington WV 25701 Office: 731 5th Ave Huntington WV 25701 Tel (304) 529-1211

TAYLOR, MUIRISON KEITH, b. Taylorville, Ill., Nov. 7, 1906; B.S., Dartmouth, 1928; J.D., San Francisco Law Sch., 1937. Admitted to Calif. bar, 1938, U.S. Supreme Ct. bar, 1962; asso. firm Pelton & Gunther, San Francisco, 1965—; individual practice law, Corte Madera, Calif., 1962—. Trustee Larkspur-Corte Madera Sch. Dist., 1950-63. Mem. Marin Bar Assn., Am. Arbitration Assn. Home: 5 Mariner Green Dr Corte Madera CA 94925 Office: 5710 Paradise Dr Corte Madera CA 94925 also 114 Sansome St San Francisco CA 94104 Tel (415) 392-2770 and 924-7227

TAYLOR, NELSON WHITFORD, III, b. Beaufort, N.C., Aug. 17, 1928; student The Citadel, 1945-47; A.B. in Polit. Sci., U. N.C., 1949, J.D., 1955. Admitted to N.C. bar, 1955; asso. firm Tally, Tally and Taylor, Fayetteville, N.C., 1955-57, partner, 1957-65; individual practice law, Beaufort, 1965-72; partner firm Taylor & Marquardt, Beaufort, 1972-75, Morehead City, N.C., 1975—. Chmn. Cumberland County chpt. ARC, 1961-64; chancellor Diocese E. Carolina, 1973-76, mem. exec. com., 1976-77. Mem. Am., N.C. bar assns., Am. Trial Lawyers Assn., N.C. Acad. Trial Lawyers, Carteret County, 3d Jud. Dist. bar assns. Home: 2001 Shepard St Morehead City NC 28557 Office: 610 Arendell St Morehead City NC 28557 Tel (919) 726-0001

TAYLOR, PAUL, b. Hoboken, N.J., May 22, 1938; B.A., St. Lawrence U., 1961, LL.B., 1965; LL.M., U. Mich., 1966. Admitted to N.Y. bar, 1966, U.S. Supreme Ct. bar, 1969; asst. mng. clk. Dewey, Ballantine, Bushby, Palmer and Wood, N.Y.C., 1963-66; atty. Hartford Ins. Group, N.Y.C., 1966-67; supervising atty. Broome Legal Assistance Corp., Binghamton, N.Y., 1967-70; individual practice law, Newark Valley, N.Y., 1970—; treas. Tioga Amateur Repeater, Inc., 1974-76. Pres., Tioga County (N.Y.) chpt. March of Dimes, 1972-73; lay reader Episcopal Ch., 1972-74. Home: Box 139 Newark Valley NY 13811 Office: RD 1 Newark Valley NY 13811 Tel (607) 754-5418

TAYLOR, RAYMOND EDWARD, b. Hydro, Okla., Aug. 24, 1943; B.A., St. Marys U., 1966, J.D., 1969; grad. JAG Sch., U. Va., 1969. Admitted to Tex. bar, 1969, U.S. Ct. Mil. Appeals bar, 1969, U.S. Dist. Ct. bar, 1973, U.S. Supreme Ct. bar, 1976; fed. commr. for Vietnam, 1970; chief def. counsel Brook Army Med. Center, Ft. Sam Houston, Tex., 1971-72, chief of mil. assistance, 1971; of counsel firm Ribak Mead & Maddox, San Antonio, 1977—; house counsel San Antonio Free Clinic. Fund raiser Arthritis Found., 1976-77. Mem. Am., Tex., San Antonio bar assns., Tex., San Antonio trial lawyers assns., San Antonio Young Lawyers Assn. Research fellow Am. Bar Assn., 1968-69. Home: 2827 Chisholm Trail San Antonio TX 78217 Office: 630 GECU Exec Bldg 6061 NW Expy San Antonio TX 78201 Tel (512) 734-6608

TAYLOR, REESE HALE, JR., b. Los Angeles, May 6, 1928; A.B. with distinction, Stanford, 1949; LL.B., Cornell U., 1952. Admitted to Calif. bar, 1954, Nev. bar, 1966; asso. firm Gibson, Dunn & Crutcher, Los Angeles, 1952-58; individual practice law, Los Angeles, 1959-61, Beverly Hills, Calif., 1961-65; asso. firm Wiener, Goldwater & Galatz, Las Vegas, Nev., 1966-67; chmn. Pub. Service Commn. Nev., 1967-71; partner firm Laxalt, Berry & Allison, Carson City, Nev., 1971—; vice chmn. Nev. Tax Commn., 1967-69. Mem. Carson City Republican Central Com., 1971—, Nev. del., mem. platform com., Rep. Nat. Conv., 1976; chmn. Nev. Citizens for Reagan, 1976; pres. Lake Glen Manor Homeowners' Assn., 1972-74. Mem. Am. Bar Assn., Am. Judicature Soc., Phi Gamma Delta, Phi Delta Phi. Contbr. articles to legal jours. Office: 402 N Division St Box 646 Carson City NV 89701 Tel (702) 882-0202

TAYLOR, ROBERT GORDON, b. Texarkana, Tex., Sept. 23, 1944; B.S. in Bus. Adminstrn., U. Ark., 1966, J.D., 1969. Admitted to Ark. bar, 1969, Tex. bar, 1971, U.S. Supreme Ct. bar, 1976; served to 1st lt. JAGC, U.S. Army, 1969-71; since practiced in Houston, mem. firm Butler, Binion, Rice, Cook, & Knapp, 1971-76, Boswell, O'Toole, Davis & Pickering, 1976—; mem. Harris County Fee Arbitration Com., 1976—. Mem. Am., Tex., Ark., Houston, Houston Jr. bar assns., Am. Assn. Hosp. Lawyers. Office: 2400 Two Shell Plaza Houston TX 77002 Tel (713) 225-1801

TAYLOR, ROBERT GROVER, b. Sacramento, Oct. 26, 1923; student Wheaton Coll., 1941-43, Harvard, 1944, Mass. Inst. Tech., 1945; A.B., Stanford, 1947, J.D., 1949. Admitted to Calif. bar, 1949, D.C. bar, 1974; asso. firm Crimmins, Kent, Draper & Bradley, San Francisco, 1950-51; mem. firm Tuttle & Taylor Inc., Los Angeles, 1951—; panelist Practicing Law Inst.; chmn. coms., Nat. Council Farmer Coops., 1967—; pres. Constitutional Rights Found., 1976—. Trustee Fuller Theol. Sem., 1957-63; bd. visitors Stanford Sch. Law, 1971-74. Mem. Am., Calif., Los Angeles bar assns., Order Coif, Phi Beta Kappa. Contbr. articles to legal jours.; note editor Stanford Law Rev., 1947-49. Home: 3116 Elvido Dr Bel Air CA 90049 Office: 609 S Grand Ave Los Angeles CA 90017 Tel (213) 683-0600

TAYLOR, ROBERT JOSEPH, b. Sewickley, Pa., Mar. 27, 1945; B.A., U. Pitts., 1967, J.D., 1970. Admitted to Pa. bar, 1971, U.S. Dist. Ct. bar, 1973. Individual practice law, Ambridge, Pa., 1972—. Mem. Am. Bar Assn., Pa. Trial Lawyers Assn. Office: 337 Merchant St Ambridge PA 15003 Tel (412) 266-2370

TAYLOR, ROBERT LOVE, b. Embreeville, Tenn., Dec. 20, 1899; Ph.B., Milligan Coll., 1921; LL.B., Yale, 1924. Admitted to Tenn. bar, 1923; mem. firm Cox, Taylor, Epps, Miller & Wilson, Johnson City, Tenn. and Kingsport, Tenn., 1924-49; judge U.S. Dist. Ct. Tenn., Knoxville, 1949—. Trustee Milligan Coll. Mem. Com. on Trial Practice and Technique, Corby Ct. (Yale chpt.), Jud. Conf. U.S., Order of Coif, Phi Delta Phi. Home: 3567 Talahi Dr Knoxville TN 37919 Office: Federal Bldg Knoxville TN 37901 Tel (615) 523-8933

TAYLOR, RONALD LEWIS, b. Los Angeles, Oct. 14, 1942; A.A., Cerritos Coll., 1966; A.B., U. Calif., Riverside, 1968; J.D., U. Calif., Davis, 1971. Admitted to Calif. bar, 1972, U.S. Ct. Appeals 9th Circuit, 1974, U.S. Dist. Ct. Central and So. Dists., 1974, U.S. Supreme Ct., 1977; Reginald Heber Smith Nat. Poverty Law fellow Merced (Calif.) Legal Services Assn., 1971-73; dir. litigation Community Legal Services of Riverside (Calif.), 1973-75, exec. dir. Inland Counties Legal Services, 1976—; trainer Nat. Legal Services, 1974—; judge pro tem Riverside Municipal Ct. Bd. dirs. Box Springs Mountains Conservation Assn., Riverside, 1973—, Western Center Law and Poverty, 1977—; pres. Merced County Tenant Rights Assn., 1972-73. Mem. Calif. Trial Lawyers Assn., State Bar Calif. (legal services sect.), Riverside County Bar Assn. Home: 6081 Del Ray Ct Riverside CA 92506 Office: 3616 Main St Mission Inn Rotunda Suite 405 Riverside CA 92501 Tel (714) 784-1020

TAYLOR, RONALD LOUIS, b. Memphis, July 18, 1942; B.A. magna cum laude, Miss. State U., 1964; J.D., U. Miss., 1970. Admitted to Miss. bar, 1970, U.S. Supreme Ct. bar, 1976; asso. firm B.G. Perry, Southaven, Miss., 1970-71; partner firm Perry & Taylor, Southaven, 1971-73, Perry, Taylor & Whitwell, 1973-75, Taylor, Whitwell & McClure, 1975—; city atty. Memphis and Newport, Miss., 1972-77; municipal judge City of Horn Lake (Miss.), 1975-77. Vice chmn. Southaven Library Bd., 1973-76. Mem. Am., Miss. (bd. commrs. 1974-75), DeSoto County bar assns., Am., Miss. trial lawyers assns., Miss. Prosecutors Assn., Miss. Jud. Coll., Southaven-Horn Lake Area C. of C. (dir.), Phi Kappa Phi, Delta Theta Phi. Tel (601) 342-1300

TAYLOR, RUSSELL BENTON, b. Eskridge, Kans., May 16, 1925; B.S., U. Kans., 1949, J.D., 1951. Admitted to Kans. bar, 1951; individual practice law, Eskridge, Kans., 1951—; mayor City Eskridge, 1959; pres. Eskridge State Bank, 1958-69, chmn. bd., 1969—. Home and office: Box 128 Eskridge KS 66423 Tel (913) 449-2639

TAYLOR, SAMUEL, b. Boston, Nov. 5, 1906; A.B. magna cum laude, Harvard, 1927, LL.B., 1930. Admitted to Mass. bar, 1930, Calif. bar, 1932; law clk. to Supreme Jud. Ct. Mass., Boston, 1930-31; asso. firm Brobeck, Phleger & Harrison, San Francisco, 1931-33; atty. Fed. Emergency Adminstrn. Pub. Works, Washington, 1933-35, regional counsel, 1935-39; atty. IRS, Washington, 1939-40, regional counsel IRS, Los Angeles, 1940-43; asso. firm Heller, Ehrman, White & McAuliffe, San Francisco, 1943-45; sr. partner firm Taylor & Schwartz, San Francisco, 1945-58, firm Taylor & Winokur, and successors, San Francisco, 1958-75, Taylor & Faust, San Francisco, 1975—. Mem. Am., San Francisco bar assns., State Bar Calif., Am. Law Inst. Home: 312 Coleridge Ave Palo Alto CA 94301 Office: One California St suite 2550 San Francisco CA 94111 Tel (415) 421-9535

TAYLOR, VINCENT FRANK, b. Flatonia, Tex., Nov. 9, 1915; B.A., U. Tex., 1938, J.D., 1941. Admitted to Tex. bar, 1941; U.S. Supreme Ct. bar, 1952; asso. firm Byrd, Davis & Eisenberg, Austin, Tex., 1959-62; asst. atty. gen., Tex., 1950-72; prof. law St. Mary's U., San Antonio, Tex., 1973—; atty. State Ins. Receiver, 1954-58, Interstate River Compact Commn., Tex., State Pollution Control Agencies, Tex.; city atty. city of Smithville, Tex., 1948-56. Mem. Am., San Antonio bar assns. Author: Environmental Law, Case Book; (fiction) Rustters Hill, Tempest Valley; David Crockett; contbr. articles on water and environ. law to profl. jours. Home: Silcer Creek Ranch Fitzhugh Rd Austin TX 78736 Office: 1 Camino Santa Maria Sch Law St Mary's U San Antonio TX 78284 Tel (512) 436-3425

TAYLOR, WILLIAM BARRETT, IV, b. Arlington, Va., Dec. 15, 1945; B.S., Fla. State U., 1968, J.D., 1972. Admitted to Fla. bar, 1972, U.S. Dist. Ct. bar for Middle Dist. Fla., 1972, U.S. Ct. Appeals bar 5th Circuit, 1974; asso. firm MacFarlane Ferguson Allison & Kelly, Tampa, Fla., 1972—. Trustee Carrollwood Recreation Dist., Tampa; bd. govs. Friends of the Library, Tampa. Mem. Am., Fla. bar assns. Office: 512 N Florida Ave Tampa FL 33601 Tel (813) 223-2411

TAYMAN, BARRY DAVID, b. Balt., Feb. 22, 1943; A.A., U. Balt., 1964, LL.B., 1968. Admitted to Md. bar, 1971; asso. firm Reuben Caplan, Balt., 1971-72; field atty. VA Regional Office, Balt., 1972-74; atty. advisor U.S. Army Claims Service Office of JAG, Ft. Meade, Md., 1974—. Mem. Md., Fed. bar assns. Home: 9713 Tulsemere Rd Randallstown MD 21133 Office: US Army Claims Service Fort Meade MD 20755

TEAGNO, JOSEPH ROBERT, b. Shaker Heights, Ohio, Oct. 2, 1916; B.M.E., Tri-State U., 1939; LL.D., 1976; J.D., Wayne State U., Detroit, 1943. Admitted to Mich. bar, 1945, Ohio bar, 1949; gen. patent counsel Eaton Crop., Cleve., 1957—. Mem. Republican Fin. Com. N.E. Ohio. Mem. U.S. Trademark Assn., Assn. Corporate Counsel, Licensing Execs. Soc., Pacific Indsl. Property Assn., Am., Mich., Ohio, Cleve. bar assns., Am., Cleve. (pres. 1961-62) patent law assns., Soc. Automotive Engrs., NAM. Home: 23401 Bryden Rd Shaker Heights OH 44122 Office: 100 Erieview Plaza Cleveland OH 44114 Tel (216) 523-5110

TEASS, HORACE ARGYLE, b. Bedford County, Va., Aug. 27, 1901; B.S. in Commerce, U. Va., 1924, M.S. in Economics, 1925, LL.B., 1929, J.D., 1970; Admitted to Va. bar, 1929, N.Y. bar, 1931; asso. firm Robb, Clark and Bennett, N.Y.C., 1929-34, partner 1934-37; partner firm Robb and Teass, N.Y.C., 1938-40; individual practice law, N.Y.C., 1940—; gen. counsel, chmn. bd. dirs. McNab, Inc., Mt. Vernon, N.Y., 1974—; gen. counsel, dir. John B. Moore Corp., South Amboy, N.J., 1955—; gen. counsel, dir. IDD Inc., 1958-71. Pres. Jackson Heights Forum, Jackson Heights, N.Y., 1942-43; dir. Music Research Found., Inc., 1945-65. Mem. Am., N.Y. State, N.Y. County bar assns., U. Va. Alumni Assn. (pres. N.Y. chpt. 1950-51), Order of Coif, Phi Beta Kappa (past pres. N.Y. alumni chpt.), Phi Alpha Delta (justice N.Y. alumni chpt., 1950-51). Contbr. articles to law jours. Home: 4 Sussex Ave Bronxville NY 10708 Office: 11 Broadway New York NY 10004 Tel (212) 422-4750

TEAZE, ROBERT STEWART, b. Toyko, Japan, Sept. 26, 1925 (parents Am. citizens); A.B., Dartmouth Coll., 1949; LL.B., Hastings Coll. Law, 1958. Admitted to Calif. bar, 1959; dep. city atty. San Diego, 1959-61, chief dep. city atty., 1961-66, asst. dep. city atty., 1966—. Mem. San Diego County, Calif. bar assns., Phi Alpha Delta. Home: 6111 Romany Dr San Diego CA 92120 Office: City Administration Building Community Concourse San Diego CA 92101 Tel (714) 236-6220

TEBBE, CARL GRAHAM, JR., b. Wichita, Kans., June 13, 1935; B.A., Yale, 1957; LL.B., U. Calif., Berkeley, 1963. Admitted to Calif. bar, 1964, D.C. bar, 1975; asso. firm Tuttle & Taylor (name changed to Tuttle & Taylor, 1969), Los Angeles, 1963-68, partner, 1969, mem., 1969-70, 71—; asst. dean Sch. Law U. Calif., Berkeley, 1970-71. Bd. dirs. Boalt Hall Alumni Assn., 1965-74, 76—. Mem. Am., Los Angeles County bar assns., State Bar Calif., Order of Coif. Article editor Calif. Law Rev., 1962-63. Office: 609 S Grand Ave Los Angeles CA 90017 Tel (213) 683-0600

TEBELIUS, JOHN JAMES, b. Harvey, N.D., Sept. 20, 1911; LL.B., U. Minn., 1937. Admitted to N.D. bar, 1937; individual practice law, Harvey, 1940—; state's atty. County of Wells, N.D., 1943-54; atty. City of Harvey, 1959-67. Mem. Greater N.D. Assn., Am. Bar Assn., State Bar Assn. N.D., Am. Judicature Soc. Home: 905 Allen Ave Harvey ND 58341 Office: 1012 Lincoln Ave Harvey ND 58341 Tel (701) 324-2540

TEDARDS, WILLIAM PRICE, JR., b. Greenville, S.C., May 21, 1942; B.A., Washington and Lee U., 1964, LL.B., 1967. Admitted to D.C. bar, 1968; trial atty. div. mergers Bur. Restraint of Trade, FTC, Washington, 1967-70; sr. asso. antitrust dept. firm Breed, Abbott & Morgan, N.Y.C., 1970-72; sr. asso., partner firm Nicholson & Carter, Washington, 1972—. Mem. Am., D.C., Fed. bar assns. Recipient commendation for superior service FTC, 1970; editor Merger Case Digest, 1976. Home: 2114 O St Washington DC 20037 Office: 21 Dupont Circle NW Washington DC 20036 Tel (202) 785-5050

TEGLAND, LEIGHTON B., b. Windom, Minn., Mar. 9, 1947; B.S., Calif. Western U., 1969; J.D., U. So. Calif., 1972. Admitted to Calif. bar, 1972; field rep. for Senator W. Craig Biddle, State of Calif., Riverside, 1972-73; asso. firm Thompson & Colegate, Riverside, 1972—. Mem. Citizens Univ. Com., 1973—. Mem. Am., Riverside County bar assns., Riverside County Barrister Assn. (pres. 1975-76), So. Calif. Def. Assn., Phi Alpha Delta. Home: 5242 Glenhaven Riverside CA 92506 Office: 3737 Main Suite 600 Riverside CA 92502 Tel (714) 682-5550

TEICHBERG, ARTHUR JAY, b. N.Y.C., Aug. 3, 1934; B.S., N.Y. U., 1955, J.D., 1958. Admitted to N.Y. bar, 1959; individual practice law, N.Y.C., 1963—; guest speaker in field on radio and TV. Mem. N.Y. State, New York County bar assns. Office: 370 Lexington Ave New York City NY 10017 Tel (212) 725-8544

TEITELBAUM, HUBERT IRVING, b. Pitts., July 2, 1915; A.B., U. Pitts., 1937, J.D., 1940. Admitted to Pa. bar, 1940; spl. agt. FBI, 1940-43; with Mil. Govt. Germany, 1946-49; practiced in Pitts., 1949-55, 61-71; 1st asst. U.S. atty. Western Dist. Pa., 1955-58, U.S. atty., 1958-61; judge U.S. Dist. Ct., Western Dist. Pa., 1971—; faculty fellow U. Pitts. Sch. Law, 1970. Trustee Montefiore Hosp., Pitts., Woodville State Hosp., Carnegie, Pa. Mem. Am. Law Inst., Am. Judicature Soc., Acad. Trial Lawyers Allegheny County (Pa.), Trial Lawyers Assn. Western Pa., Am., Fed., Pa. Allegheny County bar assns., Nat., Allegheny County lawyers clubs, Order of Coif. Home: 4913 Wallingford St Pittsburgh PA 15213 Office: 1036 US Post Office and Courthouse Pittsburgh PA 15219 Tel (412) 644-3524

TEITLER, SAMUEL L., b. N.Y.C., Apr. 6, 1906; LL.B., St. Lawrence U., 1927. Admitted to N.Y. bar, 1929; partner firm Newman, Hauser & Teitler, N.Y.C., 1931-63, firm Teitler & Teitler, N.Y.C., 1964—; pres. Lepel High Frequency Labs, Inc., Maspeth, N.Y., 1942-46, chmn. bd., 1946—; dir., gen. counsel World Airways Inc., Oakland, Calif., vice chmn., 1971—; vice chmn., sec., dir. Worldamerica Investors Corp., Oakland, 1971—. Pres. Kew Gardens Community Council, 1954-57. Mem. Am. Bar Assn., N.Y. County Lawyers Assn., Am. Soc. Metals, Assn. Mfg. Engrs., Am. Arbitration Assn. Office: 140 Broadway New York City NY 10005 Tel (212) 344-3440

TEJA, G. DAVE, b. Auburn, Calif., May 27, 1934; B.A., Sacramento State Coll., 1955; J.D., U. San Francisco, 1958; M.Pub. Adminstrn., Golden Gate U., 1977. Admitted to Calif. bar, 1961; U.S. Supreme Ct. bar, 1971; individual practice law, Yuba City, Calif., 1961-62, 75-76; co-pub. defender Yuba County (Calif.), 1961-62; dep. dist. atty. Sutter County (Calif.), 1962; dist. atty., pub. adminstr. Sutter County, 1963-74; asso. prof. criminal justice Calif. State U., Sacramento, 1974-76; judge Sutter County Municipal Ct., 1976—. Mem. Am. Judicature Soc., Phi Alpha Delta. Home: 1558 Dave Pl Yuba City CA 95991 Office: Courthouse Annex PO Box 1580 Yuba City CA 95991 Tel (916) 673-6831

TELEPAS, GEORGE PETER, b. Kingston, N.Y., Nov. 20, 1935; B.S., U. Fla., 1960; J.D., U. Miami, 1965. Admitted to Fla. bar, 1965; with firm Williams & Jabara, Coral Gables, Fla., 1967, Preddy, Haddad, Kutner & Hardy, Miami, Fla., 1965-66; prin. firm George P. Telepas, P.A., Miami, 1968—. Mem. Am., Fla., Dade County bar assns., Am., Fla. trial lawyers assns. Home: 16010 Kingsmoor Way Miami Lakes FL 33014 Office: 1933 SW 27th Ave Miami FL 33145 Tel (305) 856-9000

TELL, ARTHUR CHARLES, b. Evanston, Ill., May 9, 1937; A.B., Dartmouth, 1961; J.D., Ohio State U., 1963. Admitted to Ohio bar, 1964, U.S. Supreme Ct. bar, 1974; partner firm George, Greek, King, McMahon & McConn, Columbus, Ohio, 1970—. Mem. Am., Ohio, Columbus bar assns., Am. Judicature Soc., Motor Carriers Lawyers Assn. (lectr. confs. 1972, 75, 77). Office: 100 E Broad St Columbus OH 43215 Tel (614) 228-1541

TEMKIN, MARTIN MISCHA, b. Providence, Mar. 28, 1929; A.B., Brown U., 1950; J.D., Boston U., 1953. Admitted to Mass. bar, R.I. bar, 1953, U.S. Dist. Ct. bar, 1955, U.S. Tax Ct. bar, 1962; partner firm Temkin, Merolla & Zurier, Providence, 1962—; legal counsel tax div. City of Providence, 1958-75; mem. corporate bd. People's Savs. Bank. Trustee Miriam Hosp.; v.p., bd. trustees Jewish Home for Aged of R.I.; bd. dirs. R.I. Summer Opera Assn., Friends R.I. Sch. for Deaf; former pres. Urban League of R.I., Hebrew Free Loan Assn. Mem. Am., Mass., R.I. bar assns. Home: 80 Posneganset Ave Warwick RI 02888 Office: 40 Westminster St 20th Floor Providence RI 02903 Tel (401) 751-2400

TEMPLAR, HENRY GEORGE, b. Cowley County, Kans., Oct. 18, 1904; LL.B., Washburn U., 1927, J.D., 1971, LL.D., 1973. Admitted to Kans. bar, 1927; partner firms Renn & Templar, Arkansas City, Kans., 1928-39, Templar, Wright & Templar, and predecessors, Arkansas City, 1946-53, 55-62; U.S. atty. for Dist. Kans., 1953-54; judge U.S. Dist. Ct., Dist. Kans., 1962-74, sr. judge, 1974—; mem. Kans. Ho. of Reps., 1933-41, Kans. Senate, 1945-53; mem. Kans. Jud. Council, 1939-41, 45-49, 53. Mem. Topeka, Kans. State bar assns. Home: 207 N 2d St Arkansas City KS 67005 Office: US Courthouse and Fed Bldg Topeka KS 66683 Tel (913) 295-2738

TEMPLAR, TED MAC, b. Arkansas City, Kans., Sept. 27, 1929; student Cowley County Community Coll., 1949; B.B.A., Washburn U., 1951, J.D., 1954. Admitted to Kans. bar, 1954; individual practice law; judge Arkansas City (Kans.) Ct., 1969-73; mem. Kans. Ho. of Reps., 1972-77. Pres. bd. dirs. Cherokee Strip Living Museum, 1965—. Mem. Am., Kans., Cowley County bar assns., Arkansas City Area C. of C., Kappa Sigma, Delta Theta Phi. Home: 2128 Edgemont St Arkansas City KS 67005 Office: 121 W Fifth Ave Arkansas City KS 67005 Tel (316) 442-1700

TEMPLE, DOUGLAS, b. E. Syracuse, N.Y., Sep. 20, 1919; B.A., Syracuse U., 1941, LL.B., 1944. Admitted to N.Y. bar, 1944; asso. firm Andrews, McBride, Abend & Pomeroy, Syracuse, 1944-48; individual practice law, E. Syracuse, 1948—; atty. N.Y. Pub. Schs., 1961—, Village of E. Syracuse, 1968-72. Mem. Onandaga County Bar Assn. Home: 16 Pebble Hill Dr S Dewitt NY 13212 Office: 218 W Manlius St East Syracuse NY 13257 Tel (315) 437-2684

TEMPLE, LARRY EUGENE, b. Plainview, Tex., Dec. 26, 1935; B.B.A., U. Tex., Austin, 1957, LL.B., 1959. Admitted to Tex. bar, 1959; asso. firm Powell, Rauhut, McGinnis, Reavley & Lochridge, Austin, 1960-63; adminstrv. asst. to Gov. John Connally, Tex., 1963-64, exec. asst., 1964-67; spl. counsel to Pres. of U.S., Washington, 1967-69; individual practice law, Austin, 1969—; mem. adv. council to Grad. Sch. Social Work, U. Tex., 1969—, chmn., 1972-74. Mem. Nat. Democratic Policy Com., 1969-72. Mem. State Jr. Bar Tex. (chmn. 1967), Am., Austin Jr. (pres. 1962-63) bar assns. Home: 2606 Escondido Cove Austin TX 78703 Office: POB 261 Austin TX 78767 Tel (512) 477-4467

TEMPLEMAN, JOHN ALDEN, b. Urbana, Ill., Jan. 26, 1945; A.B., U. Calif., Berkeley, 1966, J.D., 1969. Admitted to Calif. bar, 1970, N.Mex. bar, 1972; mem. firm Sutin, Thayer & Browne, Albuquerque, 1971-72; counsel N.Mex. Dept. Edn., 1973-76; mem. firm Glascock, McKim & Heed, Gallup, N.Mex., 1976; firm W. Peter McAtee & Assos., Albuquerque, 1977—. Mem. Calif., N.Mex. bar assns. Home: 600 Encino Pl NE Albuquerque NM 87102 Office: 2125 Wyoming NE Albuquerque NM 87112 Tel (505) 293-1330

TEMPLETON, HOWARD WALLACE, b. Hoxie, Ark., Mar. 21, 1938; B.S., Ark. State U., 1963; J.D., U. Ark., 1966. Admitted to Ark. bar, 1966; asso. firm Brown, Compton & Prewett, El Dorado, Ark., 1966-68; partner firm Lady & Templeton, Jonesboro, Ark., 1968-69, Seay & Templeton, Jonesboro, 1969-76, Seay, Templeton & Bristow, Jonesboro, 1976-77; judge 12th Chancery Circuit Ark., Jonesboro, 1977—. Bd. dirs. YMCA Jonesboro. Mem. Am., Ark., Craighead County bar assns. Home: 1406 Redbud Circle Jonesboro AR 72401 Office: PO Box 1404 Jonesboro AR 72401 Tel (501) 932-1655

TENGI, FRANK ROBERT, b. Garfield, N.J., Aug. 11, 1920; B.S. in Bus. and Pub. Adminstrn., Georgetown U., 1946; LL.D., Fordham U., 1951. Admitted to N.Y. State bar, 1955, U.S. Supreme Ct. bar, 1967, U.S. Ct. Claims bar, 1967, U.S. Dist. Ct. So. Dist. N.Y. bar, 1967, U.S. Dist. Ct. Eastern Dist. N.Y., 1967, Tax Ct. U.S. bar, 1968; asst. sec. Am. Internat. Aviation Agy., Inc., N.Y.C., 1961-69, asst. treas., 1969-75; asso. firm Lee, Mulderig & Celentano, N.Y.C., 1965-70; asst. sec. Am. Internat. Underwriters Corp., N.Y.C., 1965—, Am. Internat. Underwriters Assn., N.Y.C., 1965—, Starr Tech. Risks Agy., Inc., N.Y.C., 1967—, C.V. Starr & Co., Inc., N.Y.C., 1965—; treas. The Starr Found., N.Y.C., 1970—; asst. comptroller taxation Am. Internat. Group, Inc., N.Y.C., 1971—. Mem. N.Y. County Lawyers Assn., Tax Exec. Inst., U.S. C. of C., Soc. Ins. Accountants. Home: 969 Mayfair Way Plainfield NJ 07060 Office: 102 Maiden Ln New York City NY 10005 Tel (212) 791-7643

TENNANT, JOHN SELDEN, b. Saginaw, Mich., Feb. 3, 1906; B.A., U. Mich., 1928, J.D., 1931; LL.D., Central Mich. U., 1968. Admitted to N.Y. bar, 1933, Supreme Ct. U.S. bar, 1969; asso. firm White & Case, N.Y.C., 1932-47, partner, 1948-76, of counsel, 1977—; gen. counsel U.S. Steel Corp., 1955-71. Mem. Internat. Legal Aid Assn. (pres. 1964-74, now v.p., dir.), Nat. Legal Aid and Defender Assn. (v.p. 1956-71), Am., N.Y. State, Internat., Inter-Am. bar assns., Assn. Bar City N.Y., N.Y. County Lawyers Assn., Order of Coif, Delta Theta Phi. Recipient Outstanding Achievement award U. Mich., 1967, Sesqui-Centennial award, 1967, Arthur V. Briesen award Nat. Legal Aid, 1965. Home: 220 Hobart Ave Summit NJ 07901 Office: 14 Wall St New York City NY 10005 Tel (212) 732-1040

TENNANT, THOMAS MICHAEL, b. Anniston, Ala., July 23, 1948; B.S., Auburn U., 1970; J.D., Mercer U., 1973. Admitted to Ga. bar, 1973; partner firm Webb, Fowler & Tanner, Lawrenceville, Ga. Vice chmn. Gwinnett County Heart Unit, 1975-76, bd. dirs., 1976—. Mem. Gwinnett County Bar Assn. (v.p. 1976-77), State Bar Ga. (dir. younger lawyers sect. 1977-78, 9th Congl. dist. rep. to exec. council 1977—, chmn. lawyer ethics com. 1976-77), Phi Delta Phi. Home: 167 King Arthur Dr Lawrenceville GA 30245 Office: 234 Luckie St SW Lawrenceville GA 30245 Tel (404) 963-3423

TENNESSEN, ROBERT JOSEPH, b. Adrian, Minn., Aug. 24, 1939; B.A. in Economics, U. Minn., 1965, J.D., 1968. Admitted to Minn. bar, 1968, Fed. bar, 1968; asso. firm Peterson, Engbe Engberg & Peterson and predecessors, Minn., 1968-75; asso. firm Grose, Von Holtum, Von Holtum, Sieben & Schmidt, Ltd., Mpls., 1975—. Mem. Minn. State Senate, chmn. commerce com., 1971—; mem. Fed. Privacy Protection Study Commn. of the U.S. Senate, 1975—. Mem. Hennepin County, Minn., Am. bar assns. Office: 4940 Viking Dr Suite 558 Minneapolis MN 55435 Tel (612) 835-2575

TENNEY, HAROLD FRANK, b. Decatur, Ill., Feb. 2, 1933; B.S., U. Ill., 1956, LL.B., 1957. Admitted to Ill. bar, 1957; since practiced in Decatur; partner firm Hull, Tenney & Campbell, 1957-64; partner firm Armstrong, Winters, Prince, Tenney, Featherston & Johnson, 1964-76; individual practice law, 1976—. Mem. Am., Ill., Macon County bar assns., Am. Judicature Soc. Home: 257 S Glencoe Decatur IL 62522 Office: 1264 Citizens Bldg Decatur IL 62525 Tel (217) 423-1800

TEPLE, EDWIN RUSSELL, b. Bloomsburg, Pa., June 20, 1913; A.B., Ohio No. U., 1933; J.D., Ohio State U., 1936. Admitted to Ohio bar, 1936; legal staff Social Security Bd., Washington, 1936-39, CAB, Washington, 1939-41; asst. regional atty. FSA, Cleve., 1941-43; regional atty. War Manpower Commn., Cleve., 1943-44; asst. regional atty. HEW, Cleve., 1946-52; individual practice law, Cleve. and Willoughby, Ohio, 1953—; labor arbitrator, 1957—; lectr. law faculty Case Western Res. U., 1952—; pres. Century Fed. Credit Union, Cleve., 1950-56. Pres. bd. dirs. Sunny Lane Sch., Willoughby, 1956-61, Consumers League of Ohio, 1960-71; bd. dirs. Nat. Consumers League, 1961-73; elder First Presbyterian Ch. of Willoughby. Mem. Nat. Acad. Arbitrators (chmn. Ohio 1964, 66, 72, bd. govs. 1972-75, chmn. com. on devel. of arbitrators 1976—), Am. Arbitration Assn. (chmn. regional council Cleve. 1969-72), Internat. Soc. Labor Law and Social Security (treas. Geneva 1966—), Am. (pub. chmn. internat. labor law com. labor relations law sect. 1974—), Ohio State, Lake County bar assns., Labor Law Group. Author: Arbitration as a Method of Dispute Settlement; contbr. articles to legal jours. Home: 7093 S Ln R D 3 Willoughby OH 44094 Office: 38052 Euclid Ave Willoughby OH 44094 Tel (216) 942-4252

TEPPER, ROBERT ISAAC, b. Long Branch, N.J., Feb. 26, 1939; A.B., Ohio Wesleyan U., 1961; J.D., Cleve. Marshall Law Sch., 1965. Admitted to Vt. bar, 1968; law clk. Vt. Legal Aid, Rutland, Vt., 1967, atty., 1968; individual practice law, Rutland, 1968-69, 75—; state's atty. Rutland County, 1969-75; instr. Castleton State Coll., 1973-76, Champlain State Coll., 1974—; lectr. various law enforcement orgns. Chmn. Rutland Town Republican com., 1972, del. Vt. Rep. conv., 1972. Mem. Vt., Rutland County bar assns., Vt. State's Atty.'s Assn. (fin. com. chmn. 1971). Home: 75 Susan Ln Rutland VT 05701 Office: 82 Merchants Row Rutland VT 05701 Tel (802) 775-4361

TEPPER, ROBERT RONALD, b. Chgo., June 26, 1945; B.A., U. Mich., 1966, J.D. cum laude, 1969. Admitted to Ill. bar, 1969; served as VISTA vol., N.Y.C., E. St. Louis, 1969-71; asso. firm Rosenthal and Schanfield, Chgo., 1971-76, mem., 1976—. Mem. Chgo. Bar Assn. Home: 1137 Country Ln Deerfield IL 60015 Office: 55 E Monroe St Chicago IL 60603 Tel (312) 236-5622

TERESI, JOSEPH CHARLES, b. Albany, N.Y., Dec. 5, 1946; B.S. in Accounting cum laude, Boston Coll., 1968; J.D., Albany Law Sch., 1971. Admitted to N.Y. bar, 1972; asso. with Paul T. Devane, Albany, 1972-73; asso. firm Ainsworth, Sullivan, Tracy & Knauf, Albany, 1973—; asst. pub. defender Albany County (N.Y.), 1972—. Mem. Am., N.Y. State, Albany County bar assns. Home: 42 Nathaniel Blvd Delmar NY 12054 Office: 75 State St Albany NY 12207 Tel (518) 434-4171

TERET, STEPHEN PAUL, b. N.Y.C., Mar. 28, 1945; B.A., St. Lawrence U., 1966; J.D., Bklyn. Law Sch., 1969. Admitted to N.Y. bar, 1969; staff atty. Harlem Assn. of Rights, Inc., N.Y.C., 1969-70; mem. firm Brandt & Laughlin, Westfield, N.Y., 1970—. Trustee Chautauqua-Cattaraugus Library System; bd. dirs. Chautauqua Legal Services, Inc., Westfield United Fund. Mem. N.Y., No. Chautauqua (pres. 1977) bar assns., Am. Trial Lawyers Assn., Am. Soc. Law and Medicine. Contbr. articles in field to profl. jours. Home: 11 Cottage St Westfield NY 14787 Office: 158 E Main St Westfield NY 14787 Tel (716) 326-3174

TERLIZZI, RAYMOND THOMAS, b. Chgo., Mar. 12, 1935; B.S. in Commerce, U. Notre Dame, 1956; LL.B., U. Calif., Berkeley, 1964. Admitted to Ariz. bar, 1965; partner firm Kipps, Franklin & Terlizzi, and predecessors, Tucson, 1966-69; U.S. magistrate, Tucson, 1971—. Mem. State Bar Ariz., Am., Pima County bar assns. Office: 424 US Courthouse Tucson AZ 85701 Tel (602) 792-6348

TEROS, JAMES THEODORE, b. Rock Island, Ill., Feb. 18, 1945; A.B., Augustana Coll., 1967; J.D., Valparaiso U., 1972. Admitted to Ill. bar, 1973; chief appellate div. Rock Island County State's Atty. office; asst. state's atty., chief criminal div., Rock Island County, Rock Island. Mem. Ill. Bar Assn. Home: 3909 14th Ave Rock Island IL 61201 Office: 1504 3d Ave Rock Island IL 61201

TERRELL, ALLEN MCKAY, JR., b. Atlanta, Aug. 5, 1943; LL.B., Harvard, 1968. Admitted to N.Y. bar, 1969, Del. bar, 1970; asso. firm Hale, Russell & Stentzel, N.Y.C., 1968-70; asso. firm Richards, Layton & Finger, Wilmington, Del., 1970—; dir. SODAT-Del., Inc., Wilmington, 1970-76. Bd. dirs. Wilmington YMCA, 1975—; trustee Wilmington Med. Center, 1976—, Woodlawn Trustees, Inc., 1976—, Wilmington Friends Sch., 1976—. Mem. Am., Del. bar assns. Home: 198 Brecks Ln Wilmington DE 19899 Office: 4072 duPont Bldg Wilmington DE 19801 Tel (302) 658-6541

TERRELL, BUFORD CARL, b. Lubbock, Tex., May 27, 1940; B.A., Tex. Tech. U., 1965, J.D., 1969. Admitted to Tex. bar, 1970, U.S. Dist. Ct. No. Dist. Tex. bar, 1970, Ct. Appeals 5th Circuit bar, 1972; individual practice law, Lubbock, 1970—. Chancellor St. Christopher's Episcopal Ch. Mem. Am. Psychology-Law Assn., State Bar Tex., Phi Alpha Delta. Home: 5602 16th Pl Lubbock TX 79416 Office: 2227 34th St Lubbock TX 79411 Tel (806) 747-4445

TERRELL, JAMES EDWARD, b. Evansville, Ind., Jan. 17, 1941; A.B., Yale, 1963; LL.B., Harvard, 1966. Admitted to Ind. bar, 1966, Calif. bar, 1969, N.Y. bar, 1970; asso. firm Lord, Day & Lord, N.Y.C., 1970-72; v.p., sr. counsel energy products group TRW, Inc., Los Angeles, 1972—. Mem. Am., Calif. bar assns. Office: TRW Inc 9841 Airport Blvd Los Angeles CA 90045 Tel (213) 535-0655

TERRERI, FRANK JOHN, b. New Castle, Pa., Apr. 25, 1922; B.S., Youngstown U., 1951; J.D., Western State U., Fullerton, Calif., 1971. Admitted to Calif. bar, 1972; asso. firm Thomas Moore & Assos., Los Angeles, 1973-74; partner firm Stroschein & Terreri, Santa Ana, Calif., 1974-75, Terreri & Pozzi, Santa Ana, 1975—; mem. claims staff Allstate Ins. Co., Santa Ana, 1963-73. Mem. Am. Bar Assn., Orange County Trial Lawyers Assn., Assn. So. Calif. Def. Counsel, Am. Arbitration Assn. (apptd. arbitrator), Phi Alpha Delta. Home: 400 S Flower St #88 Orange CA 92668 Office: 1651 E 4th St #225 Santa Ana CA 92701 Tel (714) 558-0322

TERRIS, BRUCE JEROME, b. Detroit, Aug. 3, 1933; A.B. summa cum laude, Harvard U., 1954, LL.B. magna cum laude, 1957. Admitted to D.C. bar, 1957, U.S. Supreme Ct. bar, 1960; atty. Internal Security Div., Dept. Justice, 1957-58, personal asst. to solicitor gen., 1958-59, asst. to solicitor gen., 1959-65, cons. community relations service, 1967; co-chmn. Nat. Conf. on Law and Poverty, Dept. Justice and OEO, 1965; asst. dir. Nat. Crime Commn., Washington, 1965-67; cons. Rand Corp., Santa Monica, Calif., 1967; cons. Univ. Research Corp., Washington, 1967-69, asst. to v.p. for D.C., 1967-68; vis. prof. law Cath. U., 1967-68; exec. dir. Anacostia Assistance Corp., Washington, 1968-69; co-founder, sr. atty. Center for Law and Social Policy, Washington, 1969-70; practice law, Washington, 1970—; advisor to Ad Hoc Select Com. on Outer Continental Shelf, U.S. Ho. of Reps., 1975-76, 77—. Mem. campaign staff Senator Robert Kennedy, 1968; co-founder, pres. Better Homes Inc., Washington, 1961-65; co-organizer 1500 Block Club, Washington, 1961-66; co-founder, bd. dirs. Housing Devel. Corp., Washington, 1965—, Community Action, 1965-70; active Coalition of Conscience, 1965-66; founding mem., bd. dirs. Capital E. Found., Washington, 1967-69; chmn. D.C. Democratic Central Com., 1968-72; pres., bd. dirs. Project Share, 1968-72; bd. dirs. D.C. Home Rule Com., 1968-74, Anacostia Citizens and Mchts. Assn., 1970-71, Consumers United Group, Inc., 1973-76; mem. D.C. Met. Self-Determination Steering Com., 1971-74; mem. vis. commn. Architecture Sch., Howard U., 1972; bd. dirs., sec. D.C. Devel. Corp., 1974—, Model City Devel. Corp., 1974—, Council for Pub. Interest Law, 1976—. Mem. D.C. Bar Assn. Article editor Harvard Law Rev., 1956-57; hon. fellow U. Pa. Law Sch., 1977; contbr. articles to legal jours. Home: 1855 Shepherd St NW Washington DC 20011 Office: 1526 18th St NW Washington DC 20036 Tel (201) 332-1882

TERRY, DON HILTON, b. Pasadena, Calif., Dec. 22, 1928; grad. magna cum laude, Southwestern U., 1958. Admitted to Calif. bar, 1959; police officer City of Pasadena, 1951-59; individual practice law, Pasadena, 1959—; lectr. continuing edn. of bar, criminal law. Committeeman Pasadena Tournament Roses, 1960—. Mem. State Bar Calif., Los Angeles County, Pasadena, Criminal Cts. bar assns., Calif. Attys. for Criminal Justice, Nat. Assn. Defense Attys. in Criminal Cases. Office: 234 E Colorado St Suite 222 Pasadena CA 91101 Tel (213) 796-4371

TERRY, ELMER LYNN, b. Orem, Utah, Sept. 15, 1912; B.S., U. Utah, 1937, LL.B., 1938, J.D., 1967. Admitted to Utah bar, 1938; dep. atty. Utah County, 1939-66; individual practice law, Provo, Utah, 1966—; examiner Utah State Bar, 1962-68; instr. sociology Brigham Young U., Provo, 1970—. Mem. Utah County Bar Assn. (past pres.), Phi Beta Kappa, Phi Kappa Phi, Order of Coif. Home: 1219 Elm Ave Provo UT 84601 Tel (801) 373-3255

TERSCHLUSE, VAL, b. Union, Mo., Oct. 5, 1926; J.D., St. Louis U., 1951. Admitted to Mo. bar, 1951; practice law, Clayton, Mo. Mem. Am., Mo., St. Louis, St. Louis County bar assns., Greater St. Louis Claims Assn., Lawyers Assn. Home: 1982 Karlin Dr Town and Country MO 63131 Office: 7733 Forsyth Blvd Suite 950 Clayton MO 63105 Tel (314) 726-2525

TERWILLIGER, WALTER THOMAS, b. Wausau, Wis., May 10, 1945; B.A., Northwestern U., 1967; J.D., U. Wis., 1970. Admitted to Wis. bar, 1970, U.S. Ct. Mil. Appeals, 1972; mem. firm Terwilliger, Wakeen, Piehler, Conway & Klingberg, Wausau, 1970—; served with Judge Adv. Gen.'s Corps, U.S. Army, 1968-74; active Madison Legal Aid Soc., 1969. Adviser to registrant's selective service bd., 1972-75; bd. dirs. Wausau chpt. ARC, 1976—. Mem. Am., Wis., Marathon County bar assns., C. of C. (numerous coms.). Home: 3133 N Ninth St Wausau WI 54401 Office: 401 4th St Wausau WI 54401 Tel (715) 845-2121

TERZIAN, BERJ ANDREW, b. N.Y.C., Sept. 24, 1931; B.S., City Coll. N.Y., 1958; LL.B., Bklyn. U., 1962, J.D., 1967. Admitted to N.Y. bar, 1962, U.S. Patent Office bar, 1961, U.S. Supreme Ct. bar, 1974; law clerk, asso. firm Eyre, Mann & Lucas, N.Y.C., 1958-68; asso., mem. firm Pennie & Edmonds, N.Y.C., 1968—. Mem. Am., N.Y. State, N.Y.C. bar assns., N.Y. Patent Law Assn. Office: 330 Madison Ave New York City NY 10017 Tel (212) 986-8686

TESAR, RUDOLPH, b. Omaha, Sept. 2, 1907; B.A., Creighton U., 1929, LL.B., 1929. Admitted to Nebr. bar, 1930; mem. Nebr. legislature, 1931-35; county atty., dep. Douglas County, Nebr., 1936-41; individual practice law, Omaha, 1941-64; judge Dist. Ct. of Nebr., Omaha, 1964—. Mem. Park and Recreation Com., Omaha, 1935-45; mem. Stadium Com., Omaha, 1942-45. Mem. Am., Nebr., Douglas County bar assns. Contbr. articles to profl. jours. Home: 11916 Jackson Rd Omaha NE 68154 Office: Douglas County Hall Justice Omaha NE 68102 Tel (402) 444-7015

TESCHNER, PAUL AUGUST, JR., b. Green Bay, Wis., June 20, 1925; student U. Wis., 1943-44; B.B.A., Northwestern U., 1949; J.D. with distinction, Ind. U. Bloomington Sch. Law, 1953. Admitted to Ind. bar, 1953, Ill. bar, 1954; teaching asso. Northwestern U. Sch. Law, 1953-54; asso. firm Pope & Ballard, Chgo., 1954-58, partner, 1958-72; sr. partner firm Teschner & Teschner, Chgo., 1972-75; chief exec. officer Teschner P.C., Chgo., 1975—; instr. tax, bus. and constitutional law Elmhurst Coll., 1960-73; adj. prof. legal ethics Ind. U. Bloomington Sch. Law, 1975-76. Sec. Hinsdale (Ill.) Zoning Bd. Appeals, 1966—; mem. Ill. Master Plan Com. on Legal Edn., 1968-69. Mem. Ill. State (assembly del. 1972—), Chgo., Am. bar assns., World Assn. Lawyers (founding life), Order of Coif. Contbr. numerous articles to legal jours.; note editor Ind. Law Jour., 1950-53. Home: 316 E 6th St Hinsdale IL 60521 Office: 39 S LaSalle St Chicago IL 60603 Tel (312) 332-0346

TESORO, GEORGE ALFRED, b. Rome, Feb. 6, 1904; J.D., U. Rome, 1925, D. Polit. Sci., 1929, Ph.D. in Taxation, 1930. Admitted to D.C. bar, 1948, U.S. Supreme Ct. bar, 1965; individual practice law, Rome, 1927-38; instr. taxation U. Rome, 1930-35; asso. prof. pub. fin. and taxation U. Bari (Italy), 1935-38; news editor radio sta. WOV, N.Y.C., 1941-42; lectr. econs. Lawrence Coll., Appleton, Wis., 1942; vis. prof., lectr. adj. prof. econs. Am. U., Washington, 1942-55; cons.

Bd. Econs. Warfare, Washington, 1943; economist chief sect. Fgn. Econ. Adminstrn., Office Fgn. Liquidation, 1944-46; economist, dep. econ. adviser, econ. adviser div. econ. devel. and Office Western European Affairs, Dept. State, 1946-55; sr. econ. officer, counselor U.S. Mission, Geneva, 1956-65; counsel firm Cox, Lanford and Brown, Washington, 1965-69, Coudert Bros., Washington, 1969—; dir. Ferrero U.S.A., Inc., Castelli Furniture, Inc., Castelli Industries, Inc., Impregilo U.S.A., Inc., Ambienti Design, Inc., Bencor Corp. of Am. Chmn. bd. trustees Am. U. Rome, 1976—. Mem. Am., Fed. bar assns., Bar. D.C., Am. Soc. Internat. Law, Washington Fgn. Law Soc., Am. Fgn. Service Assn. Author: La Psicologia Della Testimonianza, 1929; Le Penalita' delle Imposte Dirette, 1930, Principii di Diritto Tributario, 1938; founder, editor Italan Journal Fiscal Law, 1937-38; decorated commdr. Merito della Repubblica, 1971. Home: 4000 Massachusetts Ave NW Washington DC 20016 Office: 1 Farragut Sq S Washington DC 20006 Tel (202) 783-3010

TESSAR, JOSEPH HENRY, b. N.Y.C., Apr. 15, 1925; LL.B., Boston U., 1952. Admitted to R.I. bar, 1954, U.S. Supreme Ct. bar, 1960; individual practice law, East Providence, R.I., 1954—; judge probate ct., City of East Providence, 1970-71. Mem. Boston U. Law Sch. Alumni Assn., R.I. Bar Assn., Nat., Internat. assns. probate judges, Am. Judicature Soc., New Eng. Land Title Assn., Mass. Conveyance's Assn. Home and Office: 91 Winslow St East Providence RI 02915 Tel (401) 433-1310

TESSEL, STANLEY, b. Bklyn., Nov. 9, 1929; LL.B., Bklyn. Law Sch., 1952. Admitted to N.Y. bar, 1952, U.S. Supreme Ct. bar, 1957; partner firm Turkewitz & Tessel, Bklyn., 1955-72, Kramer, Dillof & Tessel, N.Y.C., 1972—. Mem. N.Y. State Trial Lawyers Assn. (lectr. on med. malpractice), N.Y. County Lawyers Assn., Practicing Law Inst. Office: 233 Broadway New York City NY 10007 Tel (212) 267-4177

TESSEM, LEIF FRANCIS, b. Joliet, Ill., July 15, 1942; B.A., San Diego State U., 1964; J.D., Calif. Western U., 1968. Admitted to Calif. bar, 1969, U.S. Supreme Ct. bar; partner firm Tessem Espinoza & Manning, San Diego, 1976—. Trustee, Anderson Found. Mem. Criminal Def. Lawyers Club San Diego, Calif., San Diego bar assns., Phi Delta Phi. Tel (714) 231-1905

TESTA, RICHARD JOSEPH, b. Marlboro, Mass., Apr. 21, 1939; B.A. cum laude, Assumption Coll., Worcester, Mass., 1959; LL.B., Harvard, 1962. Admitted to Mass. bar, 1962, U.S. Supreme Ct. bar, 1967; atty. firm Gaston, Snow, Motley & Holt, Boston, 1962-73; partner firm Testa, Hurwitz & Thibeault, Boston, 1973—; dir. Teradyne, Inc. Bd. dirs. Assumption Coll.; mem. Wayland (Mass.) Zoning Bd. of Appeals. Mem. Am., Boston bar assns. Home: 6 Longfellow Rd Wayland MA 01778 Office: 100 Federal St Boston MA 02110 Tel (617) 956-4500

TETON, ALFRED B., b. Poland, Dec. 25, 1914; A.B. (Reynolds fellow 1934-36), U. Chgo., 1935, J.D. cum laude, 1936; LL.M., Yale, 1942. Admitted to Ill. bar, 1936, U.S. Supreme Ct. bar, 1941; asst. to Fed. Master in Chancery, 1936-38; spl. asst. to Atty. Gen., sr. atty. U.S. Dept. Justice, 1939-42; partner firm Froelich, Grossman, Teton & Tabin, Chgo., 1946-76, Froelich, Grossman & Teton, 1976—; v.p., gen. counsel West Towns Bus Co.; served to capt. JAGC, USAAF, 1944-46. Vice pres. Highland Park (Ill.) Ref. Temple, 1960; pres. B'nai B'rith Lodge; Chgo. pres., nat. v.p. Am. Technion Soc. Mem. Am., Fed., Chgo. bar assns., Phi Beta Kappa, Order of Coif. Sterling fellow Yale, 1938-39; contbr. articles to profl. jours. Home: 188 Harbor St Glencoe IL 60022 Office: 120 S LaSalle St Chicago IL 60603 Tel (312) 236-2454

TETREAULT, GEORGE ANTONIO, JR., b. Holland, Mass., Feb. 26, 1931; B.S., Northeastern U., 1952; LL.B., Western New Eng. Coll., 1960. Admitted to Mass. bar, 1963; individual practice law, Palmer, Mass., 1963—; mem. firm Skvirsky Danziger Tetreault & Schubert, Springfield, Mass., 1975—; clk. Dist. Ct. Western Worcester (Mass.), 1965-66; atty. VA, Buffalo, 1971-72. Office: 697 N Main St Palmer MA 01069 Tel (413) 283-5336

TEVENI, FRANK MEDINA, b. Houston, Aug. 18, 1925; B.B.A., St. Mary's U., San Antonio, 1953, LL.B., 1958, J.D., 1970. Admitted to Tex. bar, 1958, since practiced in San Antonio; sr. partner firm Teveni, Mach & Clarke, San Antonio, 1975—; legal adviser Religious Order of Mary Immaculate, 1965—. Bd. dirs. Barrio Betterment Corp., San Antonio, 1975—. Mem. Tex. Bar Assn., Phi Delta Phi, Kappa Pi Sigma. Home: 118 Jesus St San Antonio TX 78207 Office: Suite 401 San Antonio Savings Bldg San Antonio TX 78205 Tel (512) 226-0851

THABES, JOHN ALLEN, b. Brainerd, Minn., Feb. 25, 1933; student U. Minn., 1952-55; B.S. in Law, St. Paul Coll. Law, 1957; LL.B., William Mitchell Coll. Law, 1960. Admitted to Minn. bar, 1960, Fla. bar, 1961; asso. firm Nolan, Alderman & Holden, Brainerd, 1960-61; asso. firm Saunders, Curtis, Ginestra & Gore, Ft. Lauderdale, Fla., 1961-67, partner, 1967—, dir., 1969—, pres., 1974—. Mem. Broward County (Fla.), Aitkin-Crow Wing County (Minn.), Minn. State bar assns., Fla. Bar (appellate rules com. 1975—), Assn. Trial Lawyers Am., Acad. Fla. Trial Lawyers (dir. 1966-76, parliamentarian 1969-71, treas. 1971-72, sec. 1972-73, pres.-elect 1973-74, pres. 1974-76), Broward County Trial Lawyers Assn. (sec. 1966-67, 1st v.p. 1969, pres. 1970, bd. govs. 1973-74, 1974-75, 1975-76). Home: 23 Castle Harbor Isle Fort Lauderdale FL 33308 Office: PO Box 4078 Fort Lauderdale FL 33338 Tel (305) 525-0531

THACKER, JESS WILDER, b. Brooksville, Fla., Apr. 20, 1914; A.B., Fla. State U., 1935; M.A., U. Mich., 1940; J.D., U. Fla., 1948. Admitted to Fla. bar, 1948; partner firm Thacker & Thacker, Kissimmee, Fla.; partner firm Wilder & Thacker, Clearwater, Fla., 1966—; prof. bus. law St. Petersburg Jr. Coll., Clearwater, 1967—. Mayor, commr. City of Kissimmee, 1969-70; trustee 1st United Methodist Ch. Kissimmee and Clearwater. Mem. Am. Bar Assn., Clearwater, Fla. bars. Home: 1454 S Hercules Ave Clearwater FL 33516 Office: PO Box 1808 Clearwater FL 33517 Tel (813) 446-3074

THACKER, LESTER LEE, b. Litchfield, Ill., Nov. 26, 1938; B.S., Eastern Ill. U., 1963; J.D., DePaul U., Chgo., 1969. Admitted to Ill. bar, 1969; asso. firm Bissonette, Nutting & Wallace, Kankakee, Ill., 1969-72; partner firm Bissonnette, Nutting, Thacker & Sacks, Kankakee, 1972—; dir. Azzarelli Constrn. Co. of Ill. and Fla. Vice pres., dir. United Parents for Exceptional Children, 1974-75; legacy chmn. Kankakee County Nat. Found. March of Dimes, 1970-74; counsel, mem. commn. Kankakee County Housing Authority, 1972—, Kankakee Community Devel. Agy., 1976—. Mem. Am., Ill., Kankakee County bar assns. Recipient Am. Jurisprudence prize Bancroft-Whitney Co. Office: 312 S Schuyler Ave Kankakee IL 60901 Tel (815) 933-6637

THAL, STEVEN HENRY, b. N.Y.C., Nov. 16, 1942; B.A. in Econs., U. Mich., 1964, J.D., 1967; postgrad. (Fulbright scholar 1967, Ford Found. scholar 1967) U. Tubingen (W.Ger.), 1967-68. Admitted to N.Y. bar, 1968; asso. firms Donovan Leisure Newton & Irvine, N.Y.C., 1968-69, Handler, Kleiman & Sukenik, N.Y.C., 1969-72; partner firm Thal & Youtt, N.Y.C., 1972—. Mem. N.Y. State Bar Assn., Assn. Bar City N.Y. Contbr. articles to legal jours. Office: 919 Third Ave New York City NY 10022 Tel (212) 751-3300

THALER, MARTIN S., b. Bklyn., Mar. 22, 1932; B.B.A., Coll. City N.Y., 1953; LL.B., Yale U., 1958. Admitted to D.C. bar, 1958; law clerk Judge Luther W. Youngdahl, U.S. Dist. Court, Washington, D.C., 1958-60; lectr. law George Washington U., 1959-60; individual practice law, Washington, D.C., 1960—; adjunct prof. commercial law Georgetown U. Law Center, 1971—. Trustee Glenelg Country Sch., Glenelg, Maryland, 1963-71, sec., 1964-71, counsel, 1963—; trustee Washington Theatre Club, Inc., D.C., 1963-73, v.p., 1966-69, pres., 1969-72. Mem. Am., Federal, D.C. Bar Assns., D.C. Bar Assn. Office: 1701 Pennsylvania Ave NW Washington DC 20006 Tel (202) 298-6350

THALHOFER, JOSEPH JOHN, b. Klamath Falls, Oreg., Apr. 4, 1924; A.B., Harvard, 1950, J.D., 1952. Admitted to Oreg. bar, 1952; dep. dist. atty. Klamath County (Oreg.), 1952-53; asso. firm Cunning & Brewster, Redmond, Oreg., 1954-56; judge Deschutes County (Oreg.) Dist. Ct., 1957—. Pres., Deschutes United Fund, 1959; active Modoc Area council Boy Scouts Am. Mem. Am. Bar Assn., Am. Judicature Soc., Dist. Judges Assn. Oreg. (pres. 1962). Recipient Silver Beaver award Boy Scouts Am., 1966. Home: 2530 NE 8th St Bend OR 97701 Office: Courthouse Bend OR 97701 Tel (503) 382-4000

THATCH, WILLIAM R., b. Lovell, Wyo., July 31, 1927; B.S., U. Wyo., 1950, LL.B., 1952. Admitted to Fed. bar, 1973; solicitor's office, Indian div. Dept. Interior, Washington, 1956-57; atty. City of Lovell, 1960-61; dep. atty. Big Horn County (Wyo.), Lovell, 1959-60; individual practice law, Lovell, 1958—; justice of peace,xpeace, Lovell. Home: 464 E 3rd St Lovell WY 82431 Office: Hyart Bldg Lovell WY 82431 Tel (307) 548-7315

THATCHER, DICKINSON, b. Huntington Beach, Calif., May 26, 1919; B.S., U. Calif. at Los Angeles, 1941; J.D., Stanford U., 1948; LL.M. in Taxation, U. So. Calif., 1962; postgrad. N.Y. U., 1943-44, U. Paris, 1945-46. Admitted to Calif. bar, 1948, U.S. Tax Ct. bar, 1954, U.S. Supreme Ct. bar, 1954, U.S. Ct. Claims bar, 1956; dep. city atty., Los Angeles, 1948-51; credit atty. Union Oil Co. Calif., Los Angeles, 1951-54; trial atty. tax div. Dept. Justice, Washington, 1954-56; asst. U.S. Atty. Los Angeles, 1956-57; individual practice law, N. Hollywood, Calif., 1959-72, Van Nuys, Calif., 1957-59, 72-77. Mem. Am., Los Angeles County (chmn. council affiliated bar pres.'s 1968-70), San Fernando Valley (pres. 1966) bar assns. Contbr. articles to legal jours. Office: 14540 Haynes St Suite 109 Van Nuys CA 91411 Tel (213) 786-6500

THAYER, LUCIUS HARRISON, b. Boston, Oct. 13, 1927; A.B. cum laude, Amherst Coll., 1949; J.D. magna cum laude, Harvard, 1952. Admitted to N.Y. bar, 1953, Mass. bar, 1961; law clk. to Hon. Augustus N. Hand, judge U.S. Ct. Appeals, 2d Circuit, 1952-53; asso. firm Davis Polk Wardwell Sunderland & Kiendl, N.Y.C., 1953-55; atty. adviser Dept. Justice, Washington, 1955-56; asso. firm Patterson, Belknap & Webb, N.Y.C., 1956-60; asso. firm Hale and Dorr, Boston, 1961-62, partner, 1962—; asst. treas., clk. dir. Exolon Co., Tonawanda, N.Y., 1958—; clk., dir. Control Logic, Inc., Natick, Mass., 1958—; asst. pres., clk., dir. Sherwood Investors, Inc., Boston, 1963—. Chmn. N.Y.C. Young Republicans, 1958; bd. dirs. Am. Congl. Assn., 1967—, 1st v.p., 1974—. Mem. Am., Mass., Boston bar assns., Phi Beta Kappa. Editor: Harvard Law Rev., 1950-52. Home: 15 Circuit Rd Chestnut Hill MA 02167 Office: 28 State St Boston MA 02109 Tel (617) 742-9100

THEBERGE, LEONARD JOSEPH, b. Oceanside, N.Y., May 17, 1935; B.A., Columbia U., 1957; certificate U. Paris, 1954; LL.B., N.Y. Law Sch., 1960; M.A., U. Oxford, 1968. Admitted to N.Y. bar, 1961, D.C. bar, 1962, Mass. bar, 1969, Mich. bar, 1972; asst. U.S. atty. Eastern Dist. N.Y., 1963-66; atty. FTC, Washington, 1961-62; internat. counsel Upjohn Co., Kalamazoo, Mich., 1969-72; vice. pres. corp. services Rohr Industries, San Diego, 1972-74; pres. Nat. Legal Center for Pub. Interest, 1975—. Chmn. Kalamazoo Hist. Commn., 1971-72; bd. dirs. St. Peters Coll., Oxford Found., 1969—, U.S. Inst. Study Conflict, 1974. Fellow Royal Econ. Soc.; mem. Am., Fed., Internat. bar assns., Mid-Am. (dir. 1976), Southeastern (dir. 1976—), Great Plains (dir., 1976;), Mountain States (dir. 1977), Mid-Atlantic (dir. 1977) legal founds., Oxford Soc., Columbia Coll. Assn., Mich. Hist. Soc., Natural Hist. Soc. San Diego (chmn. 1973-75), San Diego Hist. Soc. (1973—). Editor: The Internat. Lawyer, 1969; Current Legal Aspects of Doing Business in Europe, 1971; Multinational Corporation Checklist for Foreign Subsidiaries, 1975. Home: 5801 Huntington Pkwy Bethesda MD 20014

THEISS, WILLIAM ROBERT, b. Oakland, Calif., Aug. 31, 1933; B.A., Valparaiso U., 1955, LL.B., 1957; LL.M., Yale, 1959. Admitted to Ill. bar, 1958; asso. firm Kirkland & Ellis, Chgo., 1959-65, partner, 1965—. Bd. dirs. Legal Assistance Found. Chgo., 1973—, v.p., 1976—. Contbr. articles to profl. jours. Office: 200 E Randolph St Chicago IL 60601 Tel (312) 861-2170

THELIN, CALVIN BLAINE, b. Oak Park, Ill., Sept. 8, 1929; A.B., Colgate U., 1951; student Stanford U., 1956-57; J.D., Northwestern U., 1957. Admitted to Ill. bar, 1958, ICC bar, 1964, U.S. Tax Ct., 1976; partner firm Goldsmith, Dyer, Thelin, Schiller & Dickson, Aurora, Ill., 1958—; asst. atty. gen., 1960-61; city atty. Aurora, 1961-64; spl. asst. atty. gen. Ill., 1970—; gen. atty. Aurora Redevel. Commn., 1974—; gen. atty. Aurora Met. Exposition, Auditorium and Office Bldg. Authority, 1974. Pres. United Community Services, 1970. Mem. Am., Ill., Kane County bar assns., Greater Aurora C. of C. (pres. 1965-67). Home: Box 643R Route 1 Batavia IL 60510 Office: 104 E Downer Pl Aurora IL 60504

THELIN, HOWARD JAMES, b. Los Angeles, Feb. 7, 1921; A.B., U. Calif., Los Angeles, 1946; LL.B., U. So. Calif., 1949. Admitted to Calif. bar, 1950; individual practice law, Glendale, Calif., 1950-52, 53-63; partner firm Thelin and Rainville, Glendale, 1952-53, Thelin, Yates and Morris, Glendale, 1963-66; judge Municipal Ct., Los Angeles Jud. Dist., 1966-76, Calif. Superior Ct. Los Angeles County, 1976—; mem. Calif. Assembly, 1957-66. Mem. Conf. Calif. Judges (sec.-treas. 1972-73, exec. bd. 1973-74), Lawyers Club of Los Angeles, Los Angeles County Bar Assn. Legion Lex. Recipient Rominger award Am. Legion Press Assn., 1953, Freedom Found. award for essay, 1955. Home: 632 Robin Glen Dr Glendale CA 91202 Office: 111 N Hill St Los Angeles CA 90012 Tel (213) 974-5689

THERIEAU, EUGENE ERNEST, JR., b. Riverside, Calif., May 23, 1929; A.B. in Econs., U. San Diego, 1974, J.D., 1967. Admitted to Calif. bar, 1968; dep. dist. atty. County of San Diego, 1969-70; partner firm Phillips, Therieau, and Sciaretta, San Diego, 1970-73, firm Therieau and Genochio, San Diego, 1973—; dean Cabrillo Pacific U. Coll. Law, San Diego, 1973—. Mem. San Diego Jr. C. of C. (v.p. 1973), San Diego County Bar Assn., Calif. Trial Lawyers Assn. Office: 4900 Mercury St San Diego CA 92111 Tel (714) 560-8663

THERRIEN, RICHARD FERNAND, b. Goffstown, N.H., Mar. 1, 1940; A.B., St. Anselm's Coll., 1962; J.D., Suffolk U., 1970. Admitted to Mass. bar, 1970, N.H. bar, 1970; asst. atty. gen. Atty. Gen.'s Office, Concord, N.H., 1970-72; individual practice law, Manchester, N.H., 1972—. Legis. counsel, Manchester, 1973-75; legal counsel N.H. Jaycees. Mem. ACLU. Recipient Pres.'s award of Honor, N.H. Jaycees, 1976. Home: 24 Notre Dame Ave Allenstown NH 03275 Office: 69 W Merrimack St Manchester NH 03101

THEVOS, JOHN GEORGE, b. N.Y.C., Mar. 16, 1912; A.B., N.Y. U., 1935, LL.B., 1937. Admitted to N.J. bar, 1939; partner firm Azar & Thevos, Paterson, N.J., 1939-40; partner firm Saros & Thevos, Newark, 1941-51; partner firm Shavick, Thevos, Stern, Schotz & Steiger, Paterson, 1958-68; individual practice, Paterson, 1973—; asst. U.S. atty. for Dist. of N.J., 1951-53; dep. atty. gen. State of N.J., 1954-55; adminstrv. dir. N.J. Dept. Law and Pub. Safety, 1955-58; prosecutor Passaic County (N.J.), 1958-70, spl. asst. county counsel, 1972—. Commr. Paterson Bd. Health, 1938-40; mem. Paterson Bd. Edn., 1949-53. Mem. Am., N.J., Passaic County bar assns. Home: 384 E 37th St Paterson NJ 07504 Office: 140 Market St Paterson NJ 07505 Tel (201) 278-6828

THIBEAULT, GEORGE W., b. Cambridge, Mass., Sept. 21, 1941; B.S. Northeastern U., 1964; M.B.A., Boston Coll., 1966, J.D., 1969. Admitted to Mass. bar, 1969; since practiced in Boston, asso. Gaston, Snow & Ely, Bartlett, 1969-73; partner firm Testa, Hurwitz & Thibeault, 1973—. Mem. Am., Mass. bar assns., Am. Arbitration Assn. Home: 114 Indian Pipe Ln Concord MA 01742 Office: 100 Federal St Boston MA 02110 Tel (617) 956-4500

THIBODEAU, JOSEPH HENRY, b. Grosse Pointe Woods, Mich., Nov. 21, 1941; A.B. in History, Coll. of Holy Cross, Worcester, Mass., 1963; J.D. cum laude, U. Detroit, 1966. Admitted to Mich. bar, 1966, U.S. Supreme Ct. bar, 1970, Colo. bar, 1971, U.S. Tax Ct., 1972; refund trial atty. tax div. Dept. Justice, Washington, 1966-69; legal advisor to Gov. William G. Milliken, State of Mich., Lansing, 1969-71; pvt. practice law, Denver, 1972-74; partner firm Nelson, Harding, Marchetti, Leonard & Tate, Denver, 1974—. Mem. Mich., Colo., Denver Am. bar assns., Greater Denver Tax Counsels Assn., Denver Tax Assn., Denver, Rocky Mountain estate planning councils. Contbr. articles to legal jours. Office: 1600 Broadway Suite 2310 Denver CO 80202 Tel (303) 893-6868

THIEBLOT, ROBERT JEAN, b. Teaneck, N.J., Apr. 7, 1933; A.B., Princeton, 1955; LL.B., Harvard, 1960. Admitted to Md. bar, 1960; asso. firm Rollins, Smalkin, Weston & Andrew, Balt., 1960-64; partner firm Allen, Thieblot & Alexander, and predecessors, Balt., 1964—; lectr. law Eastern Coll., Balt., 1964-70, U. Balt., 1970-76. Commr., Hist. and Archtl. Preservation Balt., 1969-73; mem. Commn. to Rev. Annotated Code Md., 1975—; mem. Balt. Bd. Sch. Commrs., 1971-72. Mem. Am., Md. State bar assns., Md. Hist. Trust (chmn. Balt. City com. 1975). Home: 1508 Park Ave Baltimore MD 21217 Office: 910 Keyser Bldg Baltimore MD 21202 Tel 837-1140

THIEMAN, FREDERICK PAUL, JR., b. Tulsa, May 28, 1926; B.A., LL.B., U. Tulsa; Individual practice law, Tulsa, 1952-59; partner firm Crowe & Thieman, Tulsa, 1960—. Bd. dirs., counsel Magic Empire council Girl Scouts U.S.A., 1956-64; bd. dirs. Okla. Angus Assn. Mem. Okla., Am., Tulsa County bar assns. Home: 3215 E 61st St Tulsa OK 74136 Office: 5800 E Skelly Dr Tulsa OK 74135 Tel (918) 622-4222

THIEME, PHILIP RHAMY, b. Ft. Wayne, Ind., Sept. 30, 1935; B.S., Ind. U., 1959; J.D., U. Miami (Fla.), 1966. Admitted to Ind. bar, 1966, Fla. bar, 1966; asso. firm Hoffman, Moppert & Solomon, Ft. Wayne, 1966-70; judge Allen County (Ind.) Superior Ct., 1971—. Home: 5110 Tacoma Ave Fort Wayne IN 46807 Office: Courthouse Fort Wayne IN 46802 Tel (219) 423-7055

THIEME, RAYMOND GEORGE, b. Balt., Nov. 17, 1930; A.B., Loyola Coll., 1952; J.D., U. Md., 1956. Admitted to Md. bar, 1956; asst. states atty. Anne Arundel County (Md.), 1966-70, dep. states atty., 1970-71, states atty., 1971-73; judge Dist. Ct. Md., Annapolis, 1973—. Home: 1796 Chesapeake Place Pasadena MD 21122 Office: Dist Ct Md PO Box 843 Annapolis MD 21404 Tel (301) 224-1731

THIERMAN, JOSEPH F., b. N.Y.C., July 13, 1929; B.A., N.Y. U., 1952; J.D., St. John's U., 1954. Admitted to N.Y. State bar, 1955; individual practice law, N.Y.C., 1955-68; partner firm Sarisohn, Thierman, Sarisohn, Steindler, Hicksville, N.Y., 1968-74, Belli, Sarisohn, Creditor, Carner, Thierman & Steindler, Jericho, N.Y., 1974—. Mem. Nassau County, Queens County bar assns., Nassau Lawyers Assn. Tel (516) 543-7667

THIGPEN, CHARLES ALLEN, b. Greensboro, Ala., Dec. 7, 1941; B.S., U. Ala., 1965, J.D., 1972. Admitted to Ala. bar, 1972; asso. firm Dishuck & Dishuck, Tuscaloosa, Ala., 1972-73; partner firm Tucker, Gray & Thigpen, Tuscaloosa, 1973-76, Burke & Thigpen, Greensboro, Ala., 1976—; counsel Ala. Press Assn.; spl. asst. atty. gen. State of Ala. Pres., Tuscaloosa County Mental Health Assn.; pres. bd. dirs. Univ. Community Coop., Tuscaloosa; mem. adv. com. Indian Rivers Mental Health Center, Tuscaloosa; mem. rev. of human rights com. Ridgecrest Children's Center, Tuscaloosa. Mem. Am., Ala., Tuscaloosa County bar assns., Am. Trial Lawyers Assn., Farrah Law Soc. Office: 1113 Main St Greensboro AL 36744 Tel (205) 758-5591

THIGPEN, JIMMY EARL, b. Corpus Christi, Tex., Dec. 30, 1947; B.B.A. in Accounting, U. Houston, 1970; J.D., S. Tex. Coll. Law, 1973. Admitted to Tex. bar, 1973; mem. firm Flood, Linzy & Thigpen, Temple, Tex., 1976—. Loaned exec. Temple United Way, 1974—. Mem. Am. Bar Assn., SW Legal Found., Jaycees (dir. Temple 1974-77, v.p. 1977—), Temple C. of C. (mem. indsl. relations com. 1975-76, chmn. 1976-77), SW Football Ofcls. Assn., Delta Theta Phi. Home: 4510 Spanish Oak St Temple TX 76501 Office: 100 W Adams St Temple TX 76501 Tel (817) 773-1663

THIGPEN, RICHARD ASHLEY, b. Birmingham, Ala., Mar. 22, 1943; A.B., U. Ala., 1965, M.A., 1965, J.D., 1968; LL.M., with highest honors, Yale, 1969. Admitted to Ala. bar, 1968; dir. men's activities, U. Ala., 1967-68, asst. counsel, 1969-70, lectr. law, 1969-73, asst. prof. law, 1973-75, prof. law, 1975—, exec. asst. to pres., 1970-74, exec. v.p., 1974—; acting chief exec. officer, 1974—; chmn.

univ. fin. com., 197-72. Mem. Tuscaloosa (Ala.) Community Devel. Bd. 1975, Tuscaloosa Mental Health Md., 1974, Tuscaloosa Council on Arts and Humanities, 1976, Ala. Commn. on Handicapped, 1976. Mem. Nat. Assn. Coll. and Univ. Attys., Am. Assn. Univ. Adminstrs., Soc. Am. Law Tchrs., Am., Ala. bar assns., Order of Coif, Phi Alpha Theta, Pi Sigma Alpha, Omicron Delta Kappa (faculty adviser 1969-70), Phi Delta Phi. Recipient Spl. Leadership commendation Ala. State Legis., 1976. Home: 39 The Downs Tuscaloosa AL 35401 Office: Box B U Ala University AL 35486 Tel (205) 348-5100

THINNES, THOMAS ARTHUR, b. Selma, Ind., Dec. 29, 1939; student Miami U., Oxford, Ohio, 1959-60, U. Cin., 1960-62; B.S., Ariz. State U., Phoenix, 1963; LL.B., U. Ariz., Tucson, 1966. Admitted to Ariz. bar, 1966; pub. defender Maricopa County (Ariz.), Phoenix, 1966-68; mem. firm Thinnes & Lindholm, Phoenix, 1969-71; partner firm Flynn Kimerer Thinnes & Derrick, Phoenix, 1971—. Mem. Ariz., Am. assns. trial lawyers, Am., Maricopa County bar assns., State Bar Ariz., Nat. Assn. Criminal Def. Lawyers. Office: 100 W Washington St #1950 Phoenix AZ 85003 Tel (602) 254-6511

THIRKELL, EDWARD DONALD, b. San Mateo, Calif., June 4, 1940; A.B. in Econs., U. Calif., Berkeley, 1962, J.D., 1966. Admitted to Calif. bar, 1970; dept. dist. atty., tng. coordinator San Mateo County Dist. Atty.'s Office, Redwood City, Calif., 1970-76; partner firm Thirkell, Pierpoint & Kemp, San Mateo, 1976—. Mem. Am., San Mateo bar assns., Calif. Dist. Attys. Assn. Editor Due Process Jour. Home: 2108 Howard Ave San Carlos CA 94070 Office: 181 2d Ave Suite 625 San Mateo CA 94401 Tel (415) 348-1016

THODE, EVERETT WAYNE, b. Broadlands, Ill., Apr. 30, 1920; B.S., U. Ill., 1943; LL.B., U. Tex., 1950; S.J.D., Harvard, 1964. Admitted to Tex. bar, 1950, Utah bar, 1969; briefing clk. Tex. Supreme Ct., Austin, 1950; asst. atty. gen. State of Tex., Austin, 1951-52; asso. Ralph Yarborough, Austin, 1952-55; asso. prof. U. Tex. Law Sch., Austin, 1955-59, prof., 1959-67; prof. law U. Utah, Salt Lake City, 1967—. Mem. Am. (reporter spl. com. on standards of jud. conduct 1969-72), Utah, Tex. bar assns., Am. Law Inst., Am. Judicature Soc. Author: (with others) Torts, Cases and Materials, 1968, 2d edit., 1977; Injuries to Relations, 1968, 2d edit., 1977; (with Mazor and Lebowitz) Introduction to the Study of Law, 1970; also articles. Home: 470 S 13th St E Salt Lake City UT 84102 Office: U Utah Law Sch Salt Lake City UT 84112 Tel (801) 581-7993

THOM, CHARLES RICHARD, b. Storrs, Conn., Apr. 17, 1913; B.A., George Washington U., 1934, LL.B., 1936. Admitted to N.Y. bar, 1937; practiced in Port Jefferson, N.Y., 1937-59, partner firm Thom & Boylan, 1946-59; police commr. Suffolk County, 1959-62; judge Family Ct. Suffolk County, 1962-68; justice N.Y. State Supreme Ct., Riverhead, 1969—; asst. dist. atty. Suffolk County, 1952-56, chief asst. dist. atty., 1957-59. Mem. N.Y. State, Suffolk County bar assns., Assn. N.Y. State Supreme Ct. Justices, Phi Alpha Delta. Home: 125 Bleeker St Port Jefferson NY 11777 Office: Court House Griffing Ave Riverhead NY 11901 Tel (516) 727-4700

THOMAJAN, ROBERT, b. N.Y.C., May 4, 1941; B.S., N.Y. U., 1962; J.D., St. John's U., 1965. Admitted to N.Y. State bar, 1965; asso. firm Nixon, Mudge, Rose, Guthrie, Alexander & Mitchell, N.Y.C., 1965-68; mem. firm Milgrim, Thomajan & Jacobs, N.Y.C., 1968—; arbitrator Civil Ct., City of N.Y., 1975—. Mem. Assn. Bar City N.Y. (com. on admiralty), N.Y. State, Am. bar assns., N.Y. State Trial Lawyers Assn., Maritime Law Assn. U.S. Office: 25 Broadway New York City NY 10004 Tel (212) 952-9292

THOMAN, MARK, b. Cin., Apr. 28, 1935; B.A., Yale, 1956; LL.B., Harvard, 1959. Admitted to N.Y. State bar, 1960; asso. firm Lord, Day & Lord, N.Y.C., 1960-66, partner, 1966—; dir. Stokely Van Camp Corp., Cadbury Schweppes USA. Mem. Am., N.Y. City bar assns. Office: 25 Broadway New York City NY 10004 Tel (212) 344-8480

THOMAS, ANDREW JOHNSTON, b. Birmingham, Ala., Sept. 1, 1897; A.B., U. Richmond, 1918; LL.B., U. Ala., 1920; LL.B., Columbia U., 1922. Admitted to Ala. bar, 1920, U.S. Supreme Ct. bar, 1955; mem. firm Thomas, Taliaferro, Forman, Burr & Murray, Birmingham, 1964—; mem. adv. bd. Cumberland Sch. Law, Samford U., Birmingham, 1962—. Mem. Am., Ala., Birmingham (pres. 1934-35) bar assns., Am. Coll. Trial Lawyers, Am. Judicature Soc., Am. Legion, Phi Delta Phi, Phi Gamma Delta. Office: 1600 Bank for Savs Bldg Birmingham AL 35203 Tel (205) 251-3000

THOMAS, DANIEL HOLCOMBE, b. Prattville, Ala., Aug. 25, 1906; LL.B., U. Ala., 1928. Admitted to Ala. bar, 1928; practice in Mobile, 1929-51; asst. solicitor Mobile County, 1932-39; U.S. dist. judge for So. Dist. Ala., Mobile, 1951—. Vice pres., mem. exec. bd. Mobile Area council Boy Scouts Am., 1961-66, pres., 1967-68; trustee Ala. Dept. Archives and History. Mem. Am. Bar Assn., Phi Delta Theta, Phi Delta Phi. Home: 13 Dogwood Circle Mobile AL 36608 Office: US Court House and Customs House Mobile AL 36602 Tel (205) 690-2816

THOMAS, DAVID (DEA), b. Madison County, Ala., Feb. 26, 1937; A.B., U. Ala., 1958, LL.B., 1961, J.D., 1961. Admitted to Ala. bar, 1961; asst. dist. atty. 23d Jud. Circuit, Ala., 1961-65, dist. atty., 1965-69; individual practice law, Huntsville, Ala., 1969—. Pres., Huntsville Jaycees, 1963; bd. dirs. Huntsville Indsl. Expansion Com., 1963-64; bd. dirs. C. of C., 1963-64; chmn. Madison County Cancer Soc., 1963; bd. dirs. Sertoma Club, 1965; mem. Madison County Democratic Exec. Com., 1964-68. Mem. Am., Madison County bar assns., Am., Ala. trial lawyers assns., Am. Judicature Soc., Ala. Criminal Def. Lawyers Assn. Recipient Mr. Lawman award Madison County Sheriff's Dept., 1965; senatorship Jaycees Internat., 1975. Home: Apt 215 417 Julia St Huntsville AL 35805 Office: 103 Central Bank Bldg Huntsville AL 35801 Tel (205) 536-0732

THOMAS, DONALD SCOTT, b. Bogata, Tex., June 10, 1920; LL.B., U. Tex., 1944. Admitted to Tex. bar, 1944; asso. firm Clark, Thomas, Winters & Shapiro, and predecessors, Austin, Tex., 1944-50, partner, 1950-58, sr. partner, 1958—. Fellow Am. Coll. Trial Lawyers. Home: 3901 Balcones Dr Austin TX 78731 Office: Capital Nat Bank Bldg PO Box 1148 Austin TX 78767 Tel (512) 472-8442

THOMAS, E. MARSHALL, b. Ft. Madison, Iowa, Mar. 17, 1907; B.A., U. Iowa, 1930, J.D., 1932. Admitted to Iowa bar, 1932; asso. O.H. Allbee, Marshalltown, Iowa, 1932-33; mem. legal dept. Fed. Land Bank, Omaha, 1933-34; asso. firm Smith & O'Connor, Dubuque, Iowa, 1934-43; with firm O'Connor, Thomas, Wright, Hammer, Bertsch & Norby, and predecessors, Dubuque, 1943—, of counsel, 1973—; mem. Iowa Bd. Bar Examiners, 1953-61; chmn. Nat. Conf. Bar Examiners, 1954-55. Pres. Dubuque Community Chest, 1941; trustee The Finley Hosp., Dubuque, 1954-65, pres., 1963-64. Fellow Am. Bar Found.; mem. Dubuque County, Iowa (com. uniform jury instructions 1956-63, chmn. 1963—), Am., Inter-Am. bar assns., Fedn. Ins. Counsel (v.p. 1953-54), Am. Coll. Probate Counsel, Am. Coll. Trial Lawyers, Iowa Def. Counsel Assn., Iowa Acad. Trial Lawyers, Am. Judicature Soc., Order of Coif. Home: 1940 Coates St Dubuque IA 52001 Office: 200 Dubuque Bldg Dubuque IA 52001 Tel (319) 582-3601

THOMAS, EARL JOHN, b. Long Beach, Calif., Aug. 1, 1939; B.A., U. Washington, 1961, LL.B., 1964. Admitted to Calif. bar, 1965; asso. firm Archer, Zamloch Esq., Torrance, Calif., 1969-70; individual practice law, San Diego, Calif., 1970-73; partner firm Thomas & Witt, San Diego, 1973—. Prof. law Western State U., 1972—; bd. hearing officer for bd. suprs. taxicab appeals, San Diego, 1974—. Mem. Calif., San Diego bar assns., Def. Bar Assn. (exec. com.), San Diego Trial Lawyers Assn. Home: 4745 Lomitas Dr San Diego CA 92116 Office: 5114 El Cajon Blvd Room 7 San Diego CA 92115 Tel (714) 287-0051

THOMAS, EDWARD OSCAR, b. Balt., Oct. 24, 1917; B.A., Johns Hopkins U., 1940; J.D., U. Md., 1948. Admitted to Md. bar, 1947; asso. firm Harley, Wheltle & Victor, Balt., 1948-55; individual practice law, Balt., 1955-57, Snow Hill, Md., 1957-71; judge Dist. Ct. Md., Snow Hill, 1971—. Mem. Am., Md., Worcester bar assns. (pres. county chpt. 1965-66; v.p. state chpt. 1966-67, bd. govs. 1972-73), Worcester County Hist. Soc. (pres. 1966-68). Home: 209 W Federal St Snow Hill MD 21863 Office: Box 100 Dist Ct Md Snow Hill MD 21863 Tel (301) 632-2525

THOMAS, ELIOT BURNHAM, b. Boston, Dec. 23, 1912; A.B., Dartmouth, 1934; J.D., Harvard, 1940. Admitted to Pa. bar, 1941; since practiced in Phila.; atty. Rohm & Haas Co., 1941-42; asso. firm Drinker, Biddle & Reath, 1943-52, partner, 1952—; dir. Mack Printing Co. Mem. Am. Law Inst., Am., Pa., Phila. bar assns. Author: Federal Securities Act Handbook. Home: 220 Locust St Apt 29-B Philadelphia PA 19106 Office: 1100 Pa Nat Bank Bldg Broad and Chestnut Sts Philadelphia PA 19107 Tel (215) 491-7283

THOMAS, ELLEN KEATING, b. New London, Conn., Nov. 22, 1932; B.A., Oberlin Coll., 1955; J.D. cum laude, Ind. U., 1973. Admitted to Ind. bar, 1973, U.S. Supreme Ct. bar, 1976; partner firm Thomas & Craft, Bloomington, Ind., 1973—; adj. asst. prof. law Ind. U., 1974—; v.p. Monroe County (Ind.) Council, 1974-76; county atty., Monroe County, 1977—. Bd. dirs. Ind. Civil Liberties Union, 1972-76. Mem. Am., Ind. State, Monroe County, Fed. bar assns., So. Ind. Estate Planning Council. Office: 103 1/2 N College Ave Bloomington IN 47401 Tel (812) 339-4411

THOMAS, EUGENE BRAY, JR., b. Middletown, Conn., Sept. 23, 1921; student Dartmouth Coll.; A.B., Wesleyan U., 1943; LL.B., U. Va., 1949. Admitted to D.C. bar, 1950, Supreme Ct. U.S. bar; partner firm Kilpatrick, Ballard & Beasley, 1950-58; asso. firm LeBoeuf, Lamb, Lieby & MacRae, Washington, 1959-61, partner, 1962—. Mem. Am. Bar Assn., Bar Assn. D.C. Home: 6828 Melody Ln Bethesda MD 20014 Office: 1757 N St NW Washington DC 20036 Tel (202) 457-7500

THOMAS, EUGENE C., b. Idaho Falls, Idaho, Feb. 8, 1931; A.B., Columbia U., 1952, J.D., 1954. Admitted to Idaho Supreme Ct. bar, 1954, U.S. Ct. Appeals 9th Circuit bar, 1958, U.S. Supreme Ct. bar, 1970; sr. partner firm Moffatt, Thomas, Barrett & Blanton, Boise, Idaho. Dir. United Fund, Boise; pres., chmn. bd. dirs. St. Luke's Hosp., Ltd., Boise, Mountain States Tumor Inst., Boise. Mem. Am., Boise bar assns., Idaho State Bar. Home: 4515 Hillcrest Dr Boise ID 83705 Office: PO Box 829 Boise ID 83701 Tel (208) 345-2334

THOMAS, GRACE WILKEY, b. Birmingham, Ala., Mar. 9, 1910; student U. Ga. Extension, Atlanta, 1947-48; LL.B., Atlanta Law Sch., 1946, LL.M., 1948. Auditor, GAO, Atlanta, 1943-46; admitted to Ga. bar, 1947, U.S. Supreme Ct. bar, 1955; asso. firm Barrett & Hayes, Atlanta, 1949-54; individual practice law, Atlanta, 1954—; candidate for Gov. Ga., 1954, 62, Ga. Ct. Appeals Judge, 1974. Fellow Roscoe Pound Found. (hon.); mem. Ga., Nat. (exec. bd., state del., chmn. annual meetings) assns. women lawyers, Am., Ga., Atlanta bar assns., Am., Ga. trial lawyers assns., Ga. Assn. Criminal Trial Lawyers. Home: 1982 Westminster Way NE Atlanta GA 30307 Office: 20 Marietta St NW Atlanta GA 30303 Tel (404) 688-3028

THOMAS, HAROLD ARTHUR, b. Boston, Oct. 23, 1915; B.B.A., Boston U., 1941. Admitted to Tex. bar, 1950; individual practice law, Corpus Christi, Tex., 1950-70; judge Ct. of Domestic Relations Nueces County (Tex.), Corpus Christi, 1971—. Mem. Bldg. Standards Bd., Housing Bd. of Appeals, 1968-70. Mem. Am., Tex. bar assns. Contbr. articles in field to profl. jours. Home: 530 Belleview St Corpus Christi TX 78412 Office: County Ct House Corpus Christi TX 78401 Tel (512) 883-7454

THOMAS, HOWARD BERKELEY, b. Berkeley, Calif., Apr. 26, 1912; B.A., U. Calif., 1933, J.D., 1936. Admitted to Calif. bar, 1936, U.S. Supreme Ct. bar, 1968; partner firm Thomas, Snell, Jamison, Russell, Williamson & Asperger, Fresno, Calif., 1940—. Mem. Am., Fresno County bar assns., Calif. State Bar, Phi Beta Kappa, Order of Coif, Delta Theta Phi, Pi Sigma Alpha. Home: 4821 N Wishon St Fresno CA 93704 Office: Fresno's To Townehouse Fresno CA 93721 Tel (209) 442-0600

THOMAS, JAMES BURNHAM, b. Boise, Idaho, Feb. 20, 1944; B.A., Yale U., 1965, J.D., U. Calif., 1968. Admitted to Calif. bar, 1968; asso. firm Wolf, Cummins & Dubin, Beverly Hills, Calif., 1969; tax cons. Computax Corp., El Segundo, Calif., 1970—. Mem. Calif., Los Angeles County, Am. bar assns. Office: 601 Nash St El Segundo CA 90245 Tel (213) 772-2502

THOMAS, JAMES GALE, b. Cedar Rapids, Iowa, Feb. 24, 1940; B.S., Iowa State U., 1962; J.D., Drake U. Admitted to Iowa bar, 1972; tchr. Central City (Iowa) Schs., 1962-67; prison adminstr. Iowa State Men's Reformatory, Anamosa, 1967-69; counselor Men's Halfway House, Des Moines, Iowa, 1969-72; with Larry Cormey Law Firm, Anamosa, 1972—. Mem. Iowa (young lawyers), Jones County bar assns., Iowa Trial Lawyers Assn., Iowa State Edn. Assn. Home: 306 N Ford St Anamosa IA 52205 Office: 102 N Ford St Anamosa IA 52205 Tel (319) 462-4346

THOMAS, JOHN JOSEPH, b. Pine Grove, Pa., Dec. 10, 1932; A.B., U. Nebr., 1954; J.D., U. Wash., 1959. Admitted to Wash. bar, 1959, Ind. bar, 1968; asso. firm Guttormsen, Schelfield, Wilits & Ager, Seattle, 1959-61; mgr. legal dept. Sweden Freezer Mfg. Co., Seattle, 1961-67; house counsel Arvin Industries, Inc., Columbus, Ind., 1967-71, v.p., sec., 1971—, gen. counsel, 1976—. Mem. Am., Ind. bar assns. Office: 1531 E 13th St Columbus IN 47201 Tel (812) 379-3912

THOMAS, JOHN WATIES, b. Columbia, S.C., Aug. 29, 1917; A.B., U. N.C., 1939; J.D., U. S.C., 1941. Admitted to S.C. bar, 1941; partner firm Thomas, Cain & Lumpkin, Columbia, 1945-52, firm Thomas & Lumpkin, Columbia, 1952-55, firm Roberts, Jennings, Thomas & Lumpkin, Columbia, 1956-61, firm Roberts, Jennings & Thomas, Columbua, 1962-76, firm Dial, Jennings, Windham, Thomas & Roberts, Columbia, 1976—; mem. Nat. Conf. Commrs. on Uniform State Laws, 1951—. Mem. Am., S.C. (chmn. exec. com. 1959-60), Richland County bar assns., Internat. Assn. Ins. Counsel, Am. Judicature Soc. Home: 3600 Chateau Dr Columbia SC 29204 Office: 707 Barringer Bldg PO Box 1792 Columbia SC 29202 Tel (803) 799-9888

THOMAS, JOSEPH ALLAN, b. Los Angeles, Aug. 12, 1929; B.S., U. So. Calif., 1954, J.D., 1957. Admitted to Calif. bar, 1958; individual practice law, Downey, Calif., 1958-60; mem. corp. legal staff Pacific Mut. Life Ins. Co., Newport Beach, Calif., 1960—, 2d v.p., 1975—. Bd. dirs., counsel Downey Tng. Center for Retarded Children, 1960-71; bd. govs. South Coast YMCA, 1974—; bd. dirs. Laguna Niguel Homeowners Assn. Mem. Calif., Orange County bar assns. Home: 23741 Paseo del Campo Laguna Niguel CA 92677 Office: 700 Newport Center Dr Newport Beach CA 92663 Tel (714) 640-3321

THOMAS, LUCIA THEODOSIA, b. Cheyenne, Wyo., Mar. 10, 1917; B.A., Xavier U., New Orleans, 1936; LL.B., Terrell Law Sch., 1940; LL.M., John Marshall Law Sch., 1942, M.Patent Law, 1943. Admitted to D.C. bar, 1940, Ill. bar, 1942, U.S. Supreme Ct. bar, 1944; asso. firms George A. Barker, Washington, 1938-41, Richard E. Westbrooks, Chgo., 1941-42, Prescott Burroughs Taylor & Carey, Chgo., 1942-43; atty. Office Price Adminstrn., Chgo., 1943-47; partner firm Crockett & Thomas, Chgo., 1948-56; claims examiner Social Security Adminstrn., Chgo., 1956-57; asst. state's atty. Cook County (Ill.) Juvenile Ct., 1957-61, 65-69; individual practice law, Chgo., 1961-65; asst. to judge Cook County Juvenile Ct., 1969-73; law clk. to justice Ill. Appellate Ct. 1st Dist., Chgo., 1973-74; asst. corp. counsel City of Chgo., 1974—. Bd. dirs. Beatrice Youth Service, Chgo., 1961-76; mem. St. Anselm Sch. Bd., Chgo., 1969-72; mem. adv. bd. King Urban Progress Center, Chgo., 1973-76. Mem. Am., Chgo., Ill., Cook County (Richard Westbrooks award 1969), Fed., Internat., Nat., Latin-Am. bar assn., Women's Bar Assn. Ill., Internat. Fedn. Women Lawyers, Nat. Assn. Women Lawyers, Cath. Lawyers Guild. Recipient medal of Merit Knights of St. Peter Claver, 1971, spl. award Delta Sigma Theta, 1976. Home: 5035 Drexel Blvd Townhouse B Chicago IL 60615 Office: room 511 City Hall Chicago IL 60602 Tel (312) 744-7764

THOMAS, MASON PAGE, JR., b. Charlotte, N.C., Jan. 21, 1928; B.S. in Commerce, U. N.C., 1949, J.D., 1951; postgrad. U. Chgo., 1952-53. Admitted to N.C. bar, 1951; caseworker Child Welfare Dept., Gaston, Orange and Guilford Counties, N.C., 1952-57; counselor-solicitor Gaston (N.C.) County Domestic Relations and Juvenile Ct., Gastonia, N.C., 1957-59; judge, Wake County (N.C.) Domestic Relations and Juvenile Ct., Raleigh, N.C., 1959-64; dir. Nash Edgecombe Economic Devel. Corp., Rocky Mount, N.C., 1964-65; prof. law and govt. U. N.C., 1965—. Bd. dirs. N.C. Art Soc., 1975—; mem. advisory bd. N.C. Museum Hist., 1975—. Mem. N.C. State, N.C., Am. bar assns., Nat. Council on Crime and Delinquency, Nat. Council Juvenile Ct. Judges. Author: Training for Juvenile Court Judges, 1965; (with L. Lynn Hogue) Kids and Cops, Law Enforcement Services for Children in North Carolina, 1974; contbr. articles in field to profl. publications and texts. Home: 501 E North St Chapel Hill NC 27514 Office: PO Box 990 Chapel Hill NC 27514 Tel (919) 966-5381

THOMAS, MELVIN CARROLL, JR., b. Balt., May 26, 1944; B.A., Franklin and Marshall Coll., 1966; J.D., Northwestern U., 1969; LL.M., Georgetown U., 1973. Admitted to D.C. bar, 1970, Md. bar, 1970. Staff chief counsel's office IRS, Washington, 1969-73; asso. firm Hunton & Williams, Washington, 1973-76; staff Joint Com. on Internal Revenue Taxation, Washington, 1976—. Mem. Md., D.C. bar assns. Home: 217 Mill Harbor Dr Arnold MD 21012 Office: 5210 Dirksen Office Bldg Washington DC Tel (202) 224-5561

THOMAS, OWEN KENNETH, b. Muncie, Ind., Jan. 23, 1935; B.Pharmacy, Ohio No. U., 1957; J.D., Chgo.-Kent Coll. Law, 1970. Admitted to Ill. bar, 1970; partner firm Joelson & Thomas, Harvey, Ill., 1972—. Home: 301 E Corning St Peotone IL 60468 Office: 169 E 154th St Harvey IL 60426 Tel (312) 333-6810

THOMAS, PAUL RICHARD, b. Meadville, Pa., Aug. 13, 1920; A.B., Cornell U., 1942; LL.B., Dickinson Sch. Law, 1948; grad. Nat. Coll. Judiciary, 1964. Admitted to Pa. bar, 1948; asst. dist. atty. Crawford County (Pa.), 1949-55, dist. atty., 1955-63; pres. judge Crawford County Ct. of Common Pleas, 1964—. Bd. dirs. West Crawford United Fund, 1970-76; corporator Meadville (Pa.) City Hosp. Mem. Am. Bar Assn., Am. Judicature Assn., Pa. Conf. Trial Judges (pres. 1970-72). Home: 738 Chestnut St Meadville PA 16335 Office: Courthouse Meadville PA 16335 Tel (814) 336-1151

THOMAS, PETER WINTHROP, b. N.Y.C., Dec. 19, 1929; A.B., Rutgers U., 1951, LL.B., 1953. Admitted to N.J. bar, 1953; practiced in Newark, 1953-71, Morristown, 1971-73; asst. counsel Morris County, N.J., 1963-73; judge N.J. Superior Ct., Newark, 1973—; mem. N.J. Gen. Assembly, 1968-72, N.J. Senate, 1971-73, asst. majority leader, 1973; counsel Kinnelon Borough Council, 1965-73, Passaic Twp. Planning Bd., 1970-73; instr. bus. law Rutgers U., New Brunswick, N.J., 1955-60; guest lectr. N.J. Inst. Continuing Legal Edn., 1964-67; dir. Midlantic Nat. Bank, Morristown. Chmn. fund dr. Newark United Appeals, 1960, Newark Area YM-YWCA, 1960-70; chmn. Morris County Republican Com., 1965-68; trustee Morris Area Arts Council, All Souls Hosp., Morristown; bd. dirs. Glen Kirk Sch., Morristown. Mem. Am., N.J., Morris County bar assns., Rutgers U. Assn. of Morris County (pres. 1960-61). Recipient Distinguished Service award Chatham (N.J.) Jaycees, 1964, Outstanding Rep. Serving Morris County award, 1966. Home: 25 Rowan Rd Chatham NJ 07928 Office: Essex County Courthouse Newark NJ 07102 Tel (201) 961-7235

THOMAS, RICHARD MARVEL, b. Greenwich, Conn., May 29, 1929; B.S. in Engring., U.S. Coast Guard Acad., 1951; J.D. with honors, George Washington U., 1959. Admitted to D.C. bar, 1959, Mo. bar, 1970; commd. ensign USCG, 1951, advanced through grades to capt., 1972; chief br. rules of rd. USCG Hdqrs., Washington, 1962-67; comdg. officer USCG Durable, Galveston, Tex., 1967-69; dist. legal officer 2d Coast Guard Dist., St. Louis, 1969-73; sr. gen. ct.-martial mil. judge, Washington, 1973—. Mem. St. Louis Bar Assn., Maritime Law Assn., U.S. Naval Inst., Phi Delta Phi. Home: 6 Chalfont Ct Washington DC 20016 Office: care Commandant (G-L-5) USCG Washington DC 20590 Tel (202) 426-1616

THOMAS, RICHARD VAN, b. Superior, Wyo., Oct. 11, 1932; B.S. in Bus. Adminstrn., U. Wyo., 1954, LL.B., 1956; LL.M. in Taxation, N.Y. U., 1961. Admitted to Wyo. Supreme Ct. bar, 1956, U.S.

Supreme Ct. bar, 1960, U.S. 10th Circuit Ct. Appeals bar, 1960, U.S. Dist. Ct. bar for Dist. Wyo., 1959, U.S. Ct. Mil. Appeals bar, 1960; teaching fellow N.Y. U. Sch. Law, 1956-57; served with JAGC, USAF, 1957-60; law clk. Hon. John C. Pickett, judge U.S. 10th Circuit Ct. Appeals, 1960-63; asso. firm Hirst, Applegate, Cheyenne, Wyo., 1963-64; partner firm Hirst, Applegate and Thomas, 1964-69; U.S. atty. for Dist. Wyo., 1969-74; justice Wyo. Supreme Ct., 1974—. Pres. Laramie County (Wyo.) United Way, 1972, mem. bd. trustees, 1973-74, chmn., 1973, chmn. combined fed. campaign, 1974; bd. dirs. Goodwill Industries of Wyo., Inc., 1974-77; chmn. Cheyenne dist. Boy Scouts Am., 1977; mem. exec. com. Cheyenne (Wyo.) Crusade for Christ, 1974; chancellor Episcopal Diocese of Wyo. Mem. Wyo. State Bar, Am., Laramie County bar assns., Phi Kappa Phi, Omicron Delta Kappa, Sigma Nu. Named Civil Servant of Yr., Cheyenne Assn. Govt. Employees, 1973, Boss of Yr., Indian Paintbrush chpt. Nat. Secs. Assn., 1974. Home: 941 Shoshoni St Cheyenne WY 82001 Office: Supreme Ct Bldg Cheyenne WY 82001 Tel (307) 777-7573

THOMAS, RITCHIE TUCKER, b. Cleve., Aug. 12, 1936; B.A., Cornell U., 1959; J.D., Case Western Res. U., Cleve., 1964. Admitted to Ohio bar, 1964, D.C. bar, 1971; atty. Office of Gen. Counsel, U.S. Internal Trade Commn., Washington, 1964-67; asso. atty. firm Squire, Sanders & Dempsey, Cleve., 1967-69; partner firm Cox, Langford & Brown, Washington, 1969—. Bd. dirs., exec. com. Meridian House Internat., Washington, 1976—. Mem. Fed. Bar Assn., Bar Assn. D.C., Order of Coif. Office: 21 Dupont Circle NW Washington DC 20036 Tel (202) 785-0200

THOMAS, STEPHEN MASON, b. Asheville, N.C., Sept. 22, 1945; B.A., U. N.C., Chapel Hill, 1967, J.D., 1970. Admitted to N.C. bar, 1970; asso. firm Patrick, Harper & Dixon, Hickory, N.C., 1971-76, partner, 1976—. Mem. Am., N.C., Catawba County bar assns., Am. Judicature Soc. Office: 225 4th St NW Hickory NC 28601 Tel (704) 322-7741

THOMAS, (TAYLOR) ALFRED, b. Eureka, Calif., Feb. 27, 1910; A.B., Calif. State U., Fresno, 1933; LL.B., J.D., San Francisco Law Sch., 1942. Admitted to Calif. bar, 1943; individual practice law, Fresno, 1947—; mem. pub. appeals rev. bd. City of Fresno, 1948-58. Mem. Fresno County Democratic Central Com., 1950—; bd. overseers Calif. Sch. Profl. Psychology, 1974—. Mem. Am., Calif., Fresno County (past pres.) bar assns., Calif. Trial Lawyers, Fresno Plaintiff's Lawyers. Home: 825 E Hampton Way Fresno CA 93704 Office: 3042 Tulare St Fresno CA 93721 Tel (209) 237-7173

THOMAS, WAYNE ELVIN, b. Silverton, Tex., Feb. 16, 1928; B.A., W. Tex. State U., 1947; J.D., U. Tex., Austin, 1951. Admitted to Tex. bar, 1951; partner firm Thomas & Burdett, Hereford, Tex., 1951—. Dist. committeeman Boy Scouts Am., 1954-56; chmn. United Fund, 1963-64, Indsl. Devel. Commn., 1967-68; pres., dir. Deaf Smith County, 1954-67; chmn. coordinating bd. Tex. Coll. and Univ. Systems, 1969—. Fellow Am. Coll. Probate Counsel; mem. Am. Judicature Soc., Tex. Bar Found., Am. Bar Assn., Order of Coif, Delta Theta Phi. Home: 206 Sunset Dr Hereford TX 79045 Office: PO Box 1917 Hereford TX 79045 Tel (806) 364-5700

THOMAS, WILLIAM GRIFFITH, b. Washington, Nov. 1, 1939; student Williams Coll., 1957-59; J.D., U. Richmond, 1963. Admitted to Va. bar, 1963; partner firm Thomas & Sewell, Alexandria, Va., 1963—; mem. Nat. Conf. Commrs. on Uniform State Laws, 1963-70, 74—; co-counsel Va. Code Commn., 1964-66; counsel Va. Election Law Study Commn., 1968-70; mem. Va. Condominium Study Commn., 1973-74, Va. Condominium Adv. Com., 1975—. Sec. Va. Democratic Party, 1968-70, chmn., 1970-72. Mem. Am., Va., Alexandria bar assns. Recipient Distinguished Service award Alexandria Jaycees, 1969. Home: 318 N Quaker Ln Alexandria VA 22304 Office: 607 Prince St PO Box 820 Alexandria VA 22313 Tel (703) 836-8400

THOMASON, CHARLES TOLIVER, b. Randolph County, Ala., Mar. 28, 1910; student Jacksonville State U., 1929-31; grad. Birmingham (Ala.) Sch. Law, 1935. Admitted to Ala. bar, 1935; individual practice law, Birmingham, 1935-36, Anniston, Ala., 1936—; municipal judge, Anniston, 1946-50; mem. Ala. Ho. of Reps. from Calhoun County, 1950-54. Del., Democratic Nat. Conv., 1956. Mem. Ala., Calhoun County bar assns. Home: 907 Isabell Ave Anniston AL 36201 Office: PO Box 441 Anniston AL 36201 Tel (205) 236-3671

THOMASON, JOHN JOSEPH, b. St. Louis, Mo., July 28, 1929; student Southwestern Coll., Memphis, 1947-49; LL.B., U. Tenn., 1952; postgrad. Judge Advocate Gen. Sch., U. Va., 1953. Admitted to Tenn. bar, 1952, U.S. Supreme Ct. bar, 1971; partner firm Nelson, Norvell, Wilson & Thomason, Memphis, 1957-67, Thomason, Crawford & Hendrix, 1967—. Chmn., Tenn. Appellate Ct. Nominating Commn., 1971—. Pres., Memphis Arts Council, 1971-73; pres. Boys Club of Memphis, 1975-77. Fellow Am. Bar Found.; mem. Am. (ho. of dels. 1966-67, 74-76), Tenn., Memphis and Shelby County (Law Day award 1967) bar assns. Editor: How to Find the Courthouse, 1975. Home: 1584 Carr Ave Memphis TN 38104 Office: 100 N Main Bldg Suite 2518 Memphis TN 38103 Tel (901) 525-8721

THOMPSON, BILLY LEE, b. Longleaf, La., Apr. 1, 1925; B.B.A., Stephen F. Austin State Coll., 1949; LL.B., S.Tex. Coll. Law, 1952. Admitted to Tex. bar, 1953; partner firm Musslewhite & Thompson, 1953-56; county atty., Angelina County, Tex., 1957-60; individual practice law, Lufkin, Tex., 1960—. Home: Route 1 Box 210C Pollok TX 75969 Office: PO Box 301 123 Calder Sq Lufkin TX 75901 Tel (713) 634-4118

THOMPSON, BRUCE ARTHUR, b. Enderlin, N.D., Oct. 28, 1925; B.A., U. Calif. at Berkeley, 1949, J.D., 1953. Admitted to Calif. bar, 1954, U.S. Supreme Ct. bar, 1971; dep. dist. atty. Ventura County, Calif., 1954-57, asst. dist. atty., 1957-61, dist. atty., 1961-62; partner firm Gustafson, Thompson & Cohen, Oxnard, Calif., 1962-66; individual practice law, Ventura, Calif., 1966-68; partner firm Thompson & Laing and predecessors, Ventura, 1968—; sec., El Roblar Corp., Ojai, Calif., 1965—; instr. Ventura Coll., 1973-76; mem. and chmn. Ventura County Air Pollution Control Dist. Hearing Bd., 1969—; mem. disciplinary bd. State Bar of Calif., 1976— city atty., Ojai, 1977—. Mem. real estate edn. adv. com. Ventura Coll., 1972—. Mem. State Bar Calif., Ventura County Bar Assn. (pres. 1966), Am. Judicature Soc., Phi Alpha Delta. Contbr. articles to legal jours. Home: 940 Spring St Oak View CA 93022 Office: 374 Poli St PO Box 968 Ventura CA 93001 Tel (805) 648-2527

THOMPSON, CHARLES WILLIAM SYDNOR, b. Balt., Feb. 18, 1924; student St. Andrews U., Scotland, 1945; A.B., Syracuse U., 1947; J.D., Harvard, 1950; postgrad. London Sch. Econs., 1951. Admitted to N.Y. bar, 1952, N.C. bar, 1946; asso. firm Davis, Polk, Wardwell, N.Y.C., 1951-54; partner firm Grier, Parker, Poe, Thompson, Bernstein, Gage & Preston, Charlotte, N.C., 1954—; vice-recorder, City of Charlotte, 1959-61. Mem. community facilities Com., Charlotte and Mecklenburg County, 1969-72, vice-chmn. 1969-70; bd. dirs. Charlotte Symphony Orchestra Soc., 1957-71, pres. 1958-61; bd. dirs. Charlotte Opera Assn., 1966—, pres. 1971-75. Mem. Planned Parenthood Assn. Greater Charlotte (dir. 1969-73; pres. 1971-72), Harvard Law Sch. Assn. N.C. (sec. treas. 1956-76, pres. 1976), Am., N.C., 26th Jud. Dist. bar assns. Contbr. articles to law reviews. Home: 1622 Brandon Rd Charlotte NC 28207 Office: 1100 Cameron Brown Bldg Charlotte NC 28204 Tel (704) 372-6730

THOMPSON, CLIFFORD EDWIN, b. Dawsonville, Ga., June 18, 1918; student Berry Coll., Ga. State U., So. Bus. U., Mercer Extension, Internat. Corr. Schs.; LL.B., Woodrow Wilson Coll. Law, 1959. Admitted to Ga. bar, 1960; individual practice law, Marietta, Ga. Mem. Cobb County Rep. Exec. Com., 1966-70, 75-76. Mem. Am. Judicature Soc., Am. Trial Lawyers Assn. Recipient Bancroft-Whitley award, 1959. Home: 2711 Beverly Dr NE Marietta GA 30066 Office: 142 S Park Sq Marietta GA 30060 Tel (404) 422-8870

THOMPSON, EDWARD P., b. Ann Arbor, Mich., June 8, 1946; B.A., Kalamazoo Coll., 1968; J.D., U. Mich., 1970. Admitted to Oreg. bar, 1971; prof. bus. law Lane Community Coll., Eugene, Oreg., 1972-76; partner firm Young Horn Cass & Scott, Eugene, 1976—. Bd. dirs. Western Rivers council Girl Scouts U.S.A., 1971—. Mem. Am., Oreg. (chmn. com. on corp. and partnership law), Lane County bar assns. Office: 101 E Broadway Suite 200 Eugene OR 97401 Tel (503) 687-1515

THOMPSON, ELLIS WOODY, b. Port Heches, Tex., Oct. 18, 1922; LL.B., Tulane U., 1950. Admitted to La. bar, 1950; judge City Ct. for Calcasieu Parish Ward Four, Sulphur, La., 1954—. Mem. Am. Judicature Soc., La. City Judges Assn. (v.p.), La. Juvenile Judges Assn. (pres.), Phi Delta Phi. Home: 2500 Roxton St Sulphur LA 70663 Office: PO Box 288 Sulphur LA 70663 Tel (318) 527-6388

THOMPSON, FRANK ROBERT, b. Manilla, Iowa, Jan. 15, 1916; B.A., U. Iowa, 1939, J.D., 1941. Admitted to Iowa bar, 1941; individual practice law, Stuart, Iowa, 1941-45; partner firm Batschelet & Thompson, Guthrie Center, Iowa, 1945—; county atty., Guthrie County, 1943-48, 1963-64; mem. Iowa Ho. of Reps., 1953-57. Mem. Iowa State, Guthrie County bar assns. Home: 103 N 12th St Guthrie Center IA 50115 Office: 107 N 5th St Guthrie Center IA 50115 Tel (515) 747-2231

THOMPSON, FREDERICK THOMAS, b. North Adams, Mass., Nov. 18, 1940; B.A., Ottawa U., 1962; J.D., Washburn Law Sch., 1966. Admitted to Kans. bar, 1966, Mass. bar, 1972, U.S. Supreme Ct. Bar, 1972; asst. gen. counsel Kans. Corp. Commn., Topeka, 1966; asso. firm Rooney and Rooney, Topeka, 1966-67; counsel Sprague Electric Co., North Adams, 1967-75, v.p. corp. relations, 1975—. Vice pres. bd. dirs. Williamstown Boys' club, 1969—; mem. YMCA bldg. coms. Topeka and North Adams.; bd. dirs. Topeka Jaycees, 1966; trustee Mass. Community Coll., 1969—; mem. N. Berkshire Indsl. Devel. Commn. Mem. Am., Kans., Mass. bar assns., Elec. Ind. Assn. (chmn. labor relations com.), Electronic Industries Assn., Industrial Relations Council (mem. exec. com.), Nat. Elec. Mfrs. Assn. (mem. indsl. relations council), N. Berkshire C. of C. Contbr., asso. editor: The Developing Labor Law, 1970-76. Named Jaycee of the Month, 1966. Home: 85 Cobble View Rd Williamstown MA 01267 Office: 87 Marshall St North Adams MA 01247 Tel (413) 664-4411

THOMPSON, HARRISON COFFIN, JR., b. Daytona Beach, Fla., Apr. 27, 1925; A.B., John B. Stetson U., 1948, LL.B., 1949. Admitted to Fla. bar, 1949, U.S. Supreme Ct. bar, 1960; practice law, Daytona Beach, 1949-51; atty. Office Price Stblzn., Washington, 1951-53; trial atty. NLRB, Ft. Worth, 1953-57, supervising atty., 1957-60; partner firm Shackleford, Farrior, Stallings & Evans, Tampa, Fla., 1960—. Mem. Am., Fla. (mem. labor relations com. 1957—, chmn. 1963-64), Hillsborough County bar assns., Greater Tampa C. of C. Home: 660 Poinsettia Rd Belleair FL 33516 Office: PO Box 3324 Tampa FL 33601 Tel (813) 228-7621

THOMPSON, HOLLIS, b. Lodi, Wis., Nov. 4, 1942; B.A., U. Wis., 1964, J.D., 1972. Admitted to Wis. bar, 1972; asso. firm Tarrant, Mattka & Robertson, Blair, Wis., 1972; individual practice law, New Lisbon, Wis., 1973—; asst. dist. atty. Trempealeau County, Wis., 1972; city atty. City of New Lisbon, 1973—, village atty. Village of Camp Douglas, Wis., 1976—. Pres., New Lisbon Promotional Orgn., 1975—, dir., 1975—; mem. Blair City Plan, 1972. Mem. Am., Juneau County bar assns., State Bar Wis. Home: 223 E Park St New Lisbon WI 53950 Office: 107 S Monroe St New Lisbon WI 53950 Tel (608) 562-3680

THOMPSON, J. CHARLES, b. Los Angeles, Sept. 19, 1939; J.D., U. Denver, 1966. Admitted to Colo. bar, 1967, Nev. bar, 1967; mem. firm Weiner, Goldwater & Waldman, Las Vegas, 1967-75; judge Dist. Ct. Nev., Las Vegas, 1975—; lectr. bus. law U. Nev. Mem. exec. bd. dirs. S. Nev. Drug Abuse Council; bd. S. Nev. Children's Behavioral Service, Nev. Mental Hygiene and Mental Retardation. Mem. Am. Bar Assn., State Bar Nev., Am. Arbitration Assn. Office: 200 E Carson St Dept 1 Clark County Courthouse Las Vegas NV 89101 Tel (702) 386-4011

THOMPSON, J. ROY, JR., b. D.C., Sept. 26, 1911; B.S., Okla. State U., 1933; J.D., George Washington U., 1941. Admitted to D.C. bar, 1941, Md. bar, 1952, Okla. bar, 1941; mem. firm Thompson, McGrail & O'Donnell, Washington, 1964-75, Thompson, Larson, McGrail & O'Donnell, Washington, 1975-76, Thompson, Larson, McGrail, O'Donnell & Harding, Washington, 1977—. Fellow Am. Coll. Trial Lawyers (chmn. D.C. 1975-76); mem. D.C., Montgomery County, Md., Okla., Fed., Am., Internat. bar assns., Internat. Assn. Ins. Counsel. Home: 5214 Portsmouth Rd Bethesda MD 20016 Office: 730 15th St Washington DC 20005 also 414 Hungerford Dr Rockville MD 20850 Tel (202) 628-2244

THOMPSON, JAMES HENRY, b. Knoxville, Tenn., July 13, 1937; B.S. in Bus. Adminstrn., U. Fla., 1965; J.D., Fla. State U., 1969. Admitted to Fla. bar, 1969; with Legis. Reference Bur., State of Fla., Tallahassee, 1969; asso. firm Wood, Scheb, Whitesell, Drymon & Warren, Sarasota, Fla., 1969-71; individual practice law, Englewood, Fla., 1971—; city atty. City of North Port (Fla.), 1971-75. Mem. Sarasota County, Fla., Am. (com. on death taxes) bar assns. Phi Alpha Delta. Office: 260 Dearborn Ave Englewood FL 33533 Tel (813) 474-5502

THOMPSON, JAMES JOSEPH, JR., b. Butler, Ala., Oct. 7, 1942; B.S., Auburn U.; J.D., Cumberland Sch. Law. Admitted to Ala. bar; partner firm Hare, Wynn, Newell & Newton, Birmingham, Ala. Mem. Am., Ala., Birmingham bar assns., Am. Judicature Soc., Am. Trial Lawyers Assn. Contbr. articles to legal jours. Home: 3768 River Ridge Circle Birmingham AL 35223 Office: 700 City Fed Bldg Birmingham AL 35203 Tel (205) 328-5330

THOMPSON, JAMES ROGER, b. Alma, Ga., Oct. 6, 1932; B.A., Emory U., 1960, J.D., 1962. Admitted to Ga. bar, 1962; since practiced in Atlanta, individual practice law, 1962-65, asst. dist. atty., 1965-71; chief magistrate U.S. Magistrate's Ct. No. Dist. Ga., 1971-74, individual practice law, 1974—; vice-chmn. Gov.'s Commn. on Organized Crime, 1969; chmn. So. Regional Intelligence Conf., 1967-70; private sector rep. Speedy Trial Com., No. Dist. Ga., 1975—; faculty U. Ga. Inst. Continuing Legal Edn., 1967-68; lectr. State Ga. Police Acad., 1965-70; tng. asso. Atlanta Police Dept., 1965-70. Mem. Ga. Bar Assn., Ga. Assn. Criminal Def. Lawyers, Nat. Assn. Criminal Def. Lawyers, Atlanta Lawyers Club. Home: 2584 Leslie Dr Atlanta GA 30345 Office: 2403 Nat Bank of Ga Bldg Atlanta GA 30303 Tel (404) 688-0440

THOMPSON, JAMES STINSON, b. Grundy, Va., Nov. 22, 1936; LL.B., U. Tenn., 1960, J.D., 1960. Admitted to Va. bar, 1961, Tenn. bar, 1964; asso. firm M. M. Long, St. Paul, Va., 1961-64; partner firm Finnell, Thompson, Scott & Logan, Cleveland, Tenn., 1964—. Bd. dirs. Cleveland Boys Club. Mem. Tenn. (ho. of dels.), Bradley County (Tenn.), Am. bar assns., Tenn., Am. trial lawyers assns. Home: 3616 Belmont Circle Cleveland TN 37311 Office: 213 1/2 Broad St Cleveland TN 37311 Tel (615) 472-3391

THOMPSON, JAMES WILLIAM, b. Dallas, Oct. 22, 1936; B.S. in Bus. Adminstrn., U. Mont., 1958, J.D., 1962. Admitted to Mont. bar, 1962; asso. firm Cooke, Moulton, Bellingham & Longo, Billings, Mont., 1962-64; asso. firm Felt, Speare & Thompson and predecessor, Billings, 1964-65, partner, 1965-72; partner firm McNamer, Thompson & Cashmore, Billings, 1973—; city atty. City of Billings, 1964-66; mem. Yellowstone County (Mont.) Legal Services Bd., 1969-70. Bd. dirs. Billings Community Action Program (now Dist. 7 Human Resources Devel. Council), 1968—, v.p., 1968-70, pres., 1970-75; bd. dirs. United Way, Billings, 1973—. Mem. Yellowstone County, Am. bar assns., State Bar Mont. (mem. continuing legal edn. com.), Billings and Mont. Soc. C.P.A.'s. Home: 123 Lewis Ave Billings MT 59101 Office: 620 Midland Bank Bldg Billings MT 59101 Tel (406) 252-5678

THOMPSON, JIMMY EUGENE, b. Clarendon, Tex., Mar. 1, 1922; B.A., U. Tex., 1942, LL.B., 1947. Admitted to Tex. bar, 1947; briefing atty. Tex. Supreme Ct., Austin, 1947-48; staff atty. Phillips Petroleum Co., Amarillo, 1948-49; individual practice law, Pampa, Tex., 1949—. Pres., Pampa Fine Arts Commn., 1969. Mem. State Bar Tex. (past dir.). Home: 1912 Dogwood St Pampa TX 79065 Office: 260A Hughes Bldg Pampa TX 79065 Tel (806) 665-8408

THOMPSON, JOHN PAUL, b. Washington, June 15, 1920; B.A., George Washington U., 1942; J.D., U. Denver, 1950. Admitted to Colo. bar, 1950, U.S. Supreme Ct. bar, 1956; individual practice law, Denver, 1950-54, 59—; mem. Colo. Pub. Utilities Commn., 1954-59; pres. Western Conf. Pub. Service Commns., 1958-59; lectr. U. Denver Coll. Law, 1951-53, 59-60. Mem. Transp. Law Inst. (chmn. 1967-69), Motor Carrier Lawyers Assn. (exec. com. 1970-71), Colo. Bar Assn. Home: 5151 E Vassar Ave Denver CO 80222 Office: 450 Capitol Life Center E 16th Ave at Grant St Denver CO 80203 Tel (303) 861-8046

THOMPSON, JOHN WILSON, JR., b. Buffalo, Apr. 29, 1946; B.A., U. Pitts., 1968, J.D., 1971. Admitted to Pa. bar, 1971; partner firm Shoemaker & Thompson, York, Pa., 1973—; city solicitor City of York, 1973—; solicitor Hopewell Twp. (Pa.) Zoning Bd., 1973—; solicitor Dallastown Area (Pa.) Sch. Dist., 1974—. Mem. exec. com. York County Republican Com., 1976—. Mem. Am., York County (med. legal liaison), Pa. bar assns., Am. Trial Lawyers Assn. Office: 103 E Market St York PA 17401 Tel (717) 843-9957

THOMPSON, JON EDWARD, b. Albuquerque, June 19, 1942; A.B., U. Ill., 1965, J.D., 1968. Admitted to Ill. bar, 1968; partner firm Chadwell Kayser Ruggles McGee & Hastings, Chgo., 1968-76; sr. atty. Kraft Inc., Glenview, Ill., 1976—. Mem. Am., Chgo., Ill. bar assns. Home: 11 Sweetwood Ct Indian Head Park IL 60525 Office: Kraft Inc Kraft Ct Glenview IL 60025 Tel (312) 998-2000

THOMPSON, KELLY DAVID, b. Bowling Green, Ky., Apr. 24, 1948; B.A., Western Ky. U., 1969; J.D., U. Ky., 1972. Admitted to Ky. bar, 1972; trial atty. Ky. Dept. Transp., 1972-73; law clk. Ky. Ct. Appeals, 1973-74; individual practice law, Bowling Green, 1974—. Mem. Ky., Am. bar assns., Am. Judicature Soc., Delta Tau Delta, Phi Kappa Phi. Home: 436 Glenn Lily St Bowling Green KY 42101 Office: 410 E 11th St PO Box 275 Bowling Green KY 42101 Tel (502) 781-7890

THOMPSON, LAWRENCE LOWELL, b. Washington, Aug. 23, 1945; A.B. cum laude, Harvard, 1967; J.D., U. Va., 1972. Admitted to Fla. bar, 1973, Ga. bar, 1973; law clk. to judge U.S. Ct. Appeals 5th Circuit, 1972-73; asso. firm Huie, Ware, Sterne, Brown & Ide, Atlanta, 1973—. Mem. State Bar Ga. (chmn. mental health com., young lawyers sect. 1975-76). Bd. dirs. Met. Atlanta Council on Alcohol and Drugs, 1974—; NW Unitarian Ch., 1974—. Notes editor Va. Law Rev., 1971-72. Office: 1200 Standard Fed Savings Bldg Atlanta GA 30303 Tel (404) 522-8700

THOMPSON, LOUIS ALVIS, b. Pembroke, Ga., Nov. 24, 1922; LL.B., U. Ga., 1949, M.B.A., 1951. Admitted to Ga. bar, 1949; instr. Armstrong State Coll., Savannah, Ga., 1951-58; asso. firm O'Brien & Spillane, Savannah, 1951-54; individual practice law, Savannah, 1954-65; partner firm Thompson & Benken, Savannah, 1965—; chmn. Ga. State Bd. Accountancy. Mem. Am., Ga. (pres.) assns. Attys.-C.P.A.'s, Am. Bar Assn., Am. Inst. C.P.A.'s, Ga. Assn. C.P.A.'s (v.p.), Savannah State Planning Council. C.P.A., Ga. Home: 4118 Amsterdam Circle Savannah GA 31405 Office: Box 8126 Savannah GA 31402 Tel (912) 233-1196

THOMPSON, MARK BAIRD, III, b. E. Orange, N.J., Mar. 18, 1938; B.A., U. N.Mex., 1961, J.D., 1965. Admitted to N.Mex. bar, 1967; law clk. N.Mex. Ct. Appeals, Santa Fe, 1966-67; individual practice law, Las Cruces, N.Mex., 1967-69, Albuquerque, 1972-73; asst. atty. gen. State of N.Mex., Santa Fe, 1969-70; asst. U.S. atty., Albuquerque, 1971; staff atty. Inst. Pub. Law U. N.Mex., 1973-76; asso. firm Modrall, Sperling, Roehl, Harris & Sisk, Albuquerque, 1976—; lectr. canon law Episcopal Sem. of the SW, Austin, Tex., 1975-76. Mem. Am., N.Mex. bar assns. Contbr. articles to legal jours. Office: Pub Service Bldg 8th Floor Albuquerque NM 87101 Tel (505) 243-4511

THOMPSON, MARTTIE LOUIS, b. Meridian, Miss., July 5, 1930; B.S., U. Toledo, 1954; postgrad. St. John's U., 1955-57. Admitted to N.Y. bar; asso. dir., house counsel Ft. Greene Community Corp., Bklyn., 1966-68; mng. atty. MFY Legal Services, N.Y.C., 1968-70, exec. dir., 1970-71; gen. counsel, exec. dir. Community Action for Legal Services, Inc., N.Y.C., 1971—. Mem. Nat. Legal Aid and Defender Assn. (exec. com.), Housing Adv. Council, Citizens Union (planning bd.), N.Y. State bar Assn., N.Y. County Lawyers Assn., Assn. Bar. City N.Y. (spl. com. on criminal justice). Author: Minority Opportunities in Law for Blacks, Puerto Ricans and Chicanos, 1974. Home: 401 N Arlington Ave East Orange NJ 07017 Office: 335 Broadway New York City NY 10013 Tel (212) 966-6600

THOMPSON, NEIL DANIEL, b. Calexico, Calif., Feb. 21, 1935; A.B., U. Calif. at Los Angeles, 1957; Ph.D., Columbia, 1963; LL.B., Harvard, 1963. Admitted to N.Y. State bar, 1963, U.S. Supreme Ct. bar, 1973; asso. firm Justice Maxwell Fassett, N.Y.C., 1964-65, Doman & Ablondi, N.Y.C., 1965-69, Pollack & Kaminsky, and predecessors, N.Y.C., 1969—. Fellow Am. Soc. Genealogists; mem. N.Y. County Lawyers Assn., Am. Soc. Internat. Law, Internat. Law Assn., Phi Beta Kappa. Home: 380 Riverside Dr New York City NY 10025 Office: 61 Broadway New York City NY 10025 Tel (212) 952-0330

THOMPSON, PETER NICHOLAS, b. Dayton, Ohio, Nov. 28, 1946; A.B., DePauw U., 1969; J.D., U. Mich., 1972. Admitted to Minn. bar, 1973; law clk. to judge U.S. Dist. Ct., Mpls., 1973-74; asso. prof. law William Mitchell Coll. of Law, St. Paul, Minn., 1974—; reporter Minn. Supreme Ct. Advisory Com. for Uniform Rules of Evidence, 1975—. Mem. Minn. Fair Trial Free Press Council, Minn. Bar Assn. Home: 15520 Holdridge Rd E Wayzata MN 55391 Office: 875 Summit Ave St Paul MN 55105 Tel (612) 227-9171

THOMPSON, PORTER, b. Berlin, N.H., Aug. 1, 1904; B.S. Bowdoin Coll., 1926; LL.B., Harvard, 1929. Admitted to Maine bar, 1929, Mass. bar, 1929; asso. firm Warner Stackpole Bradlee & Cabot, Boston, 1929-31; partner firm Perkins Thompson Hinckley & Veddy, Portland, Maine, 1934-73, of counsel, 1973—; dir. Canal Nat. Bank, 1953—. Mem. Am., Maine, Cumberland County (Maine) bar assns. Decorated Legion of Merit. Home: 65 Waites Landing Rd Falmouth ME 04105 Office: 1 Canal Plaza PO Box 426 Portland ME 04112 Tel (207) 774-2635

THOMPSON, RALPH EVERETT, b. Alpharetta, Ga., Sept. 3, 1923; student So. Bus. U., 1941-42; LL.B., Woodrow Wilson Coll., 1965. Admitted to Ga. bar, 1965, Fed. bar, 1965; officer traffic dept. Ga. R.R., Atlanta and West Point R.R., Western Ry. Ala., Atlanta, 1942-73; mgr. commerce, atty. So. Freight Assn., Atlanta, 1973—. Mem. Am. Bar Assn., State Bar Ga., Assn. ICC Practitioners. Home: 2340 Hopewell Rd Alpharetta GA 30201 Office: 151 Ellis St NE Atlanta GA 30303 Tel (404) 659-6266

THOMPSON, ROBERT DODD, b. Lewes, Del., July 27, 1924; B.A., U. Md., 1951, LL.B., 1953. Admitted to Md. bar, 1953, Del. bar, 1956; individual practice law, Georgetown, Del., 1957-62, 74; judge Family Ct., Georgetown, 1962-74, chief judge, 1974—. Mem. Am., Del. bar assns., Nat. Council Juvenile Ct. Judges, Am. Judicature Soc. Home: 99 Lynnhaven Dr Woodbrook St Dover DE 19901 Office: Family Ct Bldg Georgetown DE 19947 Tel (302) 856-S442

THOMPSON, ROBERT THOMAS, b. Pontiac, Ill., Jan. 25, 1930; A.B., Emory U., 1950, J.D. with honors, 1952. Admitted to Ga. bar, 1951, S.C. bar, 1964, D.C. bar, 1973, U.S. Supreme Ct. bar; asso. firm Wilson, Branch, Barwick & Vandiver, Atlanta, 1952-64, partner, 1957-64, sr. partner firm Thompson, Ogletree and Deakins, Greenville, S.C., Atlanta, Washington, 1964-77; sr. partner firm Thompson, Mann & Hutson, 1977—; mem. Emory U. Law Sch. Council; mem. Chmn's. Task Force NLRB, 1974—. Mem. Ga. State Indsl. Relations Com.; chmn. Task Force on Pub. Employer Labor Relations, Greater Greenville; Mem. NLRB Chmn.'s Task Force Procedure, 1976-77. Mem. ofcl. bd., fin. commn., Methodist Ch., 1965-70. Mem. Am. (labor law sect., adminstrv. law sect., co-chmn. adminstrv. law judge sub-com., practice and procedure com.), Fed., D.C., Atlanta (sec., treas., 1961), S.C., Greenville County bar assns., Am. Judicature Soc., State Bar Ga. (pres. younger lawyers sect., mem. bd. govs.), Lawyers Club of Atlanta, Soc. Hosp. Attys., Am. Hosp. Assn., C. of C. U.S. (dir. 1970—, chmn. labor relations com., treas. 1977—); Emory U. Alumni Council. Mgmt. advisor to U.S. delegation, ILO Conf., Switzerland, 1970; lectr. labor-mgmt. relations labor law, equal employment and safety in employment. Home: 519 McDaniel Ave Greenville SC 29605 Office: Suite 2222 Daniel Bldg Greenville SC 29602 Tel (803) 242-3200

THOMPSON, SMITH, b. Los Angeles, Feb. 26, 1926; B.S. in Fgn. Service, Georgetown U., 1950; J.D., U. Va., 1953. Admitted to Ill. bar, 1953, D.C. bar, 1953; since practiced in Chgo., asso. firm Winston & Strawn, 1953-56, Crowell & Liebman, 1956-58, individual practice, 1958-65; partner firm Springer & Thompson, 1958-69; asst. gen. atty. Teletype Corp. (Bell System), 1969-71; Midwest atty. Western Electric Co., 1971—. Mem. Chgo. Bar Assn. Contbr. articles to legal jours. Office: 514 Greenwood Ave Kenilworth IL 60043 Tel (312) 494-6780

THOMPSON, VAN, JR., b. Albuquerque, Oct. 27, 1933; student So. Meth. U., 1953-55; J.D., U. Tex., 1959. Admitted to Tex. bar, 1959; briefing atty. Supreme Ct. Tex., Austin, 1959; asso. with Ewell H. Muse, Jr., Austin, 1960-63; asst. atty. gen. Tex., Austin, 1971-72; asso. firm Booth & Lloyd, Austin, 1973; individual practice law, Austin, 1964-70, 74—. Mem. bd. aldermen City of Rollingwood, Tex., 1962-63, bd. dirs. Western Hills Little League, 1963; bd. dirs. Austin Aqua Festival, 1971-72. Mem. Travis County Bar Assn., Tex., Am. trial lawyers assns., Phi Delta Phi. Home: 3003 Willowood Circle Austin TX 78703 Office: 1202 Perry-Brooks Bldg Austin TX 78701 Tel (512) 474-6866

THOMPSON, VICTOR BRUCE, b. Oklahoma City, Apr. 12, 1947; B.S. in Econs., U. Pa., 1969; J.D., U. Tulsa, 1973. Admitted to Okla. bar, 1974; minority staff counsel U.S. Senate Com. on Budget, 1975; v.p., gen. counsel Utica Bankshares Corp., 1975-77; mem. firm Malloy, Thompson & Malloy, Tulsa, 1977—. Mem. Am., Okla. bar assns. Mem. U. Tulsa Law Rev. Home: 3814 S Wheeling St Tulsa OK 74105 Office: 1924 S Utica St Suite 810 Tulsa OK 74104 Tel (918) 747-3491

THOMPSON, WALTER WRIGHT, b. Bentonia, Miss., Apr. 14, 1946; B.S., U. Miss., 1968, J.D., 1971. Admitted to Miss. bar, 1971; partner firm Luckett, Luckett, Luckett & Thompson, Clarksdale, Miss. Chmn. No. Dist. Miss., Delta Area council Explorer Scouts, 1975—; chmn. County Red Cross Profls., 1974; vestryman Episcopal Ch., 1975—. Mem. Miss. State Bar Assn. (com. parolee assistance 1972), Clarksdale C. of C. (chmn. merit award com. 1974). Home: 40 John St Clarksdale MS 38614 Office: 143 Yazoo Ave Clarksdale MS 38614

THOMPSON, WESLEY HOWARD, b. N.Y., May 3, 1917; B.A., Union Coll., 1938; LL.B., Albany Law Sch., 1941, J.D., 1968. Admitted to N.Y. bar, 1942, Del. bar, 1946; individual practice law, Georgetown, Del.; referee Unemployment Compensation Commn. Pres. Active Young Republicans of Del. Mem. Del., Sussex County bar assns. Home: 36 Park Ave Rehoboth Beach DE 19971 Office: Thompson Bldg The Circle Georgetown DE 19947 Tel (302) 856-7216

THOMPSON, WILLARD DONALD, b. La Grange, Ga., July 24, 1943; B.S. in Edn., U. Ga., 1967, J.D., 1970. Admitted to Ga. bar, 1970; asst. dist. atty. Macon (Ga.) Jud. Circuit, 1971—, first asst. dist. atty., 1975—; dir. Prosecutorial Clinic, Mercer U. Sch. Law, 1972-74; bd. dirs. Middle Ga. Council on Drugs, 1972-76; adv. com. Macon Jr. Coll. Criminal Justice, 1974—. Mem. pack. com. Cub Scouts Am., 1975; active State Crime Commn. Criminal Justice Planning Task Force, 1975; mem. Macon-Bibb Criminal Justice Standards and Goals Steering Com., chmn. Prosecution Task Force, 1976. Mem. Am., Ga., Macon bar assns., Nat., Ga. dist. attys. assns. Home: 674 Woodridge Dr Macon GA 31204 Office: 300 Bibb County Courthouse Macon GA 31201 Tel (912) 745-6871

THOMPSON, WILLIAM ALEXANDER, b. Ft. Worth, May 31, 1928; LL.B., U. Ala., 1952. Admitted to Ala. bar, 1952; partner firm Donaldson and Thompson, Birmingham, Ala., 1954-62; asst. city atty. City of Birmingham Law Dept., 1962-74; judge 10th Jud. Circuit Ct. of Ala. Mem. Birmingham, Ala. bar assns., Circuit Judge Assn. Home: 700 Staffordshire Dr Birmingham AL 35226 Office: 411 Courthouse Birmingham AL 35203 Tel (205) 325-5753

THOMPSON, WILLIAM JOSEPH, b. Portland, Maine, Sept. 27, 1911; B.A., Marshall U., 1933; J.D., W.Va. U., 1940; LL.D., W.Va. State Coll., 1965. Admitted to W.Va. bar, 1940; asso. firm Townsend & Townsend, Charleston, W.Va., 1940-50; judge Intermediate Ct., Charleston, 1950-66; individual practice law, St. Albans, W.Va., 1967-76; ret., 1977; mem. adv. council judges Nat. Council Crime and Delinquency, 1953-66, trustee council, to 1966; chmn. W.Va. Gov.'s Com. Crime and Delinquency, 1967-69. Past pres. Action for Appalachian Youth. Mem. W.Va. State Bar, Am. Legion. Named West Virginian of Year, Gazette-Mail, 1958; recipient Hannah G. Solomon award Charleston chpt. Nat. Council Jewish Women, 1966. Home: 315 Dewey Dr Saint Albans WV 25177

THOMS, WILLIAM EDWARD, b. Bridgeport, Conn., Nov. 22, 1940; B.A., Colgate U., 1961; J.D., Yale, 1964; M.Civil Law, Tulane U., 1971. Admitted to D.C. bar, 1966, La. bar, 1969, N.D. bar, 1974; adminstrv. aide Conn. State Labor Council, Hamden, 1964-65; atty. ICC, Washington, 1966-67; asst. prof. law Loyola U., New Orleans, 1967-70, Chgo.-Kent Coll. Law, Ill. Inst. Tech., 1970-72; vis. asso. prof. law Mercer U., Macon, Ga., 1972-73, Western New Eng. Coll., Springfield, Mass., summer 1973; asso. prof. U. N.D., Grand Forks, 1973—; research asso. transp. law N.D. State U., Fargo, 1974—; atty. La. Legis. Council, Baton Rouge, summers 1969, 70. Mem. N.D. Bar Assn. Author: Reprieve for the Iron Horse, 1973, Travelers and Tonnage, 1975, Are Railroad Strikes Obsolete?, 1975, Amtrak in North Dakota—The First Five Years, 1975. Home: 415 18th Ave S Grand Forks ND 58201 Office: Law School U North Dakota Grand Forks ND 58202 Tel (701) 777-2961

THOMSEN, HELGE, b. Tyler, Minn., June 10, 1919; A.A., Grandview Coll., 1939; B.S., St. Paul Coll. Law, 1941, LL.B., 1946. Admitted to Minn. bar, 1943, U.S. Supreme Ct. bar, 1948; spl. agt. supr. FBI, various locations, 1942-53; individual practice law, Mpls., 1954-72; partner firm Thomsen, Nybeck, Zeck, Herbst & Johnson, Mpls., 1972—. Mem. Minn. State Bar Assn. Office: 7250 France Ave S Edina MN 55435 Tel (612) 835-7000

THOMSEN, ROSZEL CATHCART, b. Balt., Aug. 17, 1900; A.B., Johns Hopkins, 1919; LL.B., U. Md., 1922. Admitted to Md. bar, 1922; practiced in Balt.; asso. firm Clark, Thomsen & Smith, and predecessor, 1922-27, partner, 1927-54; judge U.S. Dist. Ct., 1954—, chief judge, 1955-70; mem. numerous coms. Jud. Conf. U.S., chmn. standing com. on rules of practice and procedure, 1973—; sec. Md. State Bd. Law Examiners, 1943-44. Pres., Balt. Bd. Sch. Commrs., 1944-54; trustee Goucher Coll., 1936—, chmn. bd., 1954-67; v.p. Balt. Council Social Agys., 1943-46. Mem. Am., Md., Balt. bar assns., Am. Law Inst. Editor: Classified Index Md. Motor Vehicle Cases, 2d edit., 1935. Home: 118 Enfield Rd Baltimore MD 21212 Office: 710 US Court House 101 W Lombard St Baltimore MD 21201 Tel (301) 685-3522

THOMSON, EDWARD NAPIER, b. Pitts., Aug. 20, 1936; A.B., Reed Coll., 1958; J.D., U. Chgo., 1961. Admitted to Calif. bar, 1963; individual practice law, San Francisco, Sausalito, Calif., 1963—. Vol. legal advisor Marin County (Calif.) Planned Parenthood, 1969—; bd. dirs. Berkeley (Calif.) Center Human Interaction, 1968—. Home: 2 Palmer Ct Tiburon CA 94920 Office: 2300 Bridgeway Sausalito CA 94965 Tel (415) 332-2670

THOMSON, PAUL RICE, JR., b. Syracuse, N.Y., Dec. 28, 1941; B.A. in History, Va. Mil. Inst., 1963; J.D., Washington and Lee U., 1966. Admitted to Va. bar, 1966, Ct. Mil. Appeals bar, 1967; judge adv. USMC, 1966-69; asso. firm Clement, Wheatley, Winston & Ingram, Danville, Va., 1969-71; asst. U.S. atty. Western Dist. Va., Roanoke, 1971-75, U.S. atty., 1975—; pres. Roanoke Valley Law Enforcement Council, 1975-76; mem. Bd. Conciliation and Arbitration Panel, Richmond (Va.) Diocese; dir. Found. for Prepaid Legal Services of Va.; mem. Fed.-State Law Enforcement Council, 1975—. Vice pres. Danville Jr. C. of C., 1971. Mem. Va. Bar Assn., Assn. Trial Lawyers Am. Recipient Spl. Achievement award Dept. Justice, 1974. Office: Poff Fed Bldg Franklin Rd and 2d St Roanoke VA 24008 Tel (703) 982-6250

THOMSON, WILLIAM EDWARD, JR., b. Sharon, Pa., Oct. 1, 1935; B.S. in Chem. Engring., Bucknell U., 1957; J.D., Georgetown U., 1963. Admitted to Va. bar, 1963, Ohio bar, 1964, Calif. bar, 1970; asso. firm Oberlin, Maky, Donnelly & Renner, Cleve., 1963-69; partner firm Lyon & Lyon, Los Angeles, 1969—; examiner U.S. Patent Office, Washington, 1959-62. Mem. Pasadena (Calif.) Parks and Recreation Commn., 1976—, Pasadena Tournament of Roses Assn., 1974—; pres. Pasadena SW Little League, 1974-76; Pasadena YMCA Bd. Mgmt., 1974—; trustee Intervarsity Christian Fellowship, 1971—. Mem. Am., Los Angeles County bar assns., State Bar Calif., Va. State Bar, Christian Legal Soc. Recipient Constl. Law award Am. Jurisprudence Assn., 1961, Hon. Service award PTA, Pasadena, 1974. Home: 940 Arden Rd Pasadena CA 91106 Office: 800 Wilshire Blvd Los Angeles CA 90017 Tel (213) 489-1600

THOMSON, WILLIAM HILLS, b. Chgo., Nov. 6, 1942; B.A., U. Ill., 1964, J.D., 1966. Admitted to Ill. bar, 1967; asst. trust officer Pullman Bank and Trust Co., Chgo., 1967-69; asst. counsel Wurlitzer Co., Chgo., 1969-74, corp. counsel, 1974-76; staff atty., corp. law dept., AMA, Chgo., 1976-77; asst. v.p., trust officer First Nat. Bank Blue Island (Ill.), 1977—. Mem. Chgo., Am. bar assns. Office: 13057 S Western Ave Blue Island IL 60406 Tel (312) 385-2200

THORDSEN, HERMAN, b. N.Y.C., June 23, 1933; A.B., San Jose State Coll., 1962; J.D., Loyola U., Los Angeles, 1972. Admitted to Calif. bar, 1972, Fed. Ct. bar Central Dist. Calif., 1972, 9th Circuit Ct. Appeals bar, 1972, U.S. Tax Ct. bar, 1974, U.S. Customs Ct. bar, 1976, U.S. Supreme Ct. bar, 1976; individual practice law, Los Angeles, 1972—; judge pro tem Los Angeles Municipal Ct. Div. 96, 1975—; speaker. Mem. Am., Beverly Hills, Los Angeles County, Criminal Cts., Juvenile Cts., Century City bar assns., Lawyers Club Calif. (gov. 1976). Office: 1901 Ave of the Stars Suite 1045 Los Angeles CA 90067 Tel (213) 277-1800

THOREEN, GERALD LEONARD, b. Mpls., Mar. 11, 1933; B.S.L., U. Minn., 1955, LL.B., 1957. Admitted to Minn. bar, 1957; asso. firm Palmer and Palmer, Mpls., 1959-63; trust officer St. Cloud (Minn.) Nat. Bank and Trust Co., 1963-65; asso. firm Hughes, Hughes, Thoreen & Sullivan, and predecessors, St. Cloud, 1965-69, partner, 1970—; lectr. bus. law St. John's U., Collegeville, Minn., 1966-67; bd. dirs., chmn. Stearns-Benton Counties Law Library, St. Cloud, 1970—. Bd. dirs., past pres. St. Cloud Pub. Library, 1966-70, 73-77; bd. dirs. Great River Regional Library, St. Cloud, 1969-71, also pres.; mem. sch. bd., vice chmn. Cathedral High Sch., 1975—. Mem. Am., Minn. (past chmn. probate and trust law sect., mem. council), Stearns, Sherburne, Benton, Mille Lacs County bar assns. Office: 808 Saint Germain St Saint Cloud MN 56301 Tel (612) 251-5474

THORN, JAMES READ, b. East Orange, N.J., Nov. 8, 1918; J.D., St. Mary's U., 1950. Admitted to Tex. bar, 1950, U.S. Ct. Mil. Appeals bar, 1957; chief appellate counsel U.S. Air Force, Washington, 1966-70, sr. mil. judge, 1970-72; asso. firm James F. Gardner, San Antonio, 1972-74; criminal justice coordinator Alamo Area Council of Govts., San Antonio, 1974—. Mem. Nat. Assn. Criminal Justice Planners, San Antonio Bar Assn., Phi Delta Phi. Home: 11615 Raindrop Dr San Antonio TX 78216 Office: Three America's Bldg San Antonio TX 78205 Tel (512) 225-5201

THORNBURG, FREDERICK FLETCHER, b. South Bend, Ind., Feb. 10, 1940; A.B., DePauw U., 1963; postgrad U. Notre Dame, 1965; J.D. magna cum laude, Ind. U., 1968. Admitted to Ind. bar, 1968, U.S. Tax Ct. bar, 1970, U.S. Supreme Ct. bar, 1971; law clk. to judge U.S. Ct. Appeals 7th Circuit, Chgo., 1968-69; partner firm Thornburg, McGill, Deahl, Harman, Carey & Murray, South Bend, 1969—; lectr. St. Mary's Coll., 1975—. Past pres. Jr. C. of C., also NAB Adv. council. Bd. dirs. Michiana Pub. Broadcasting Corp., South Bend, Met. South Bend YMCA, Civic Center Found., South Bend, Merry Lea Environ. Center, Wolflake, Ind. Mem. Am., Ind. State bar assns., Order of Coif, Phi Delta Phi, Alpha Delta Sigma. Recipient Am. Jurisprudence Criminal Law award, 1966; asso. editor in chief Indiana Law Jour., 1967-68; contbr. articles to legal jours. Office: First Bank Bldg South Bend IN 46601 Tel (219) 233-1171

THORNBURG, HARRY B., b. Anderson, Ind., June 14, 1915; student Anderson Coll.; LL.B., U. Miami, Fla., 1955. Admitted to Ind. bar, 1955, U.S. Supreme Ct. bar; individual practice law, Anderson, 19—. Mem. Madison County Bar Assn., Tau Epsilon Rho. Home: 612 Country Club Ln Anderson IN 46012 Office: 2 W 8th St Anderson IN 46016 Tel (317) 644-1333

THORNBURGH, RICHARD LEWIS, b. Pitts., June 16, 1932; B.Engring., Yale, 1954; LL.B., U. Pitts., 1957; LL.D., Washington and Jefferson Coll., 1976. Admitted to Pa. bar, 1958, U.S. Supreme Ct. bar, 1965; staff counsel Aluminum Co. Am., Pitts., 1957-59; asso. firm Kirkpatrick, Lochart, Johnson & Hutchison, Pitts., 1959-69, partner, 77—; U.S. atty. for Western Pa., Pitts., 1969-75; asst. atty. gen. criminal div. U.S. Dept. Justice, Washington, 1975-77. Mem. Pa. Constl. Conv., 1967-68; mem. mens adv. bd. Home Crippled Children, Pitts., 1966-75; mem. Home Rule Charter Adv. Com., Pitts., 1969; chmn. adv. regional planning council, Pa. Gov.'s Justice Commn., 1969-73. Fellow Am. Bar Found.; mem. Allegheny County, Pa., Am. bar assns., Am. Judicature Soc. Named man of year in law Pitts. Jaycees, 1970, Pitts. Man of Year, 1976; recipient medallion Fed. Drug Enforcement Adminstrn., 1973. Contbr. articles to profl. jours. Home: 412 S Linden Ave Pittsburgh PA 15208 Office: 1500 Oliver Bldg Pittsburgh PA 15222 Tel (412) 355-6550

THORNE, CARL FRANK, b. Luling, Tex., Nov. 15, 1940; B.S. in Petroleum Engring., U. Tex., 1962; J.D., Baylor U., 1967. Admitted to Tex. bar, 1967; pres. Sedco Internat., S.A., Tehran, Iran, 1974—. Office: 1901 N Akard St Dallas TX 75201 Tel (214) 748-9281

THORNE, SAMUEL EDMUND, b. N.Y.C., Oct. 14, 1907; A.B., Coll. City N.Y., 1927; LL.B., Harvard, 1930; M.A. Yale, 1948; Litt.D., Wesleyan U., 1957; LL.D. (hon.), U. Cambridge, 1969. Asst. asso. prof. law Northwestern U., 1933-41; asso. prof. law Yale, 1945-48, prof. law, 1948-55, Simeon E. Baldwin prof. legal history, 1955-56; prof. legal history Harvard, 1956-73, Charles Stebbins Fairchild prof. legal history, 1973—. Vis. prof. legal history Cambridge U., 1951-52, Maitland lectr., 1959. Henry E. Huntington Library fellow, 1937-39; Guggenheim fellow, 1948, 51, 57. Fellow Am. Acad. Arts and Scis., Mediaeval Acad. Am., Brit. Acad., Soc. Antiquaries (London), Societá Italiana di storia del diritto; mem. Mass., Royal hist. socs., Am. Philos. Soc., Bibliog. Soc. London, Selden Soc., Am. Soc. Legal History (pres.), Pipe Roll Soc., Soc. Pub. Tchrs. Law. Editor: A Discourse Upon Statutes, 1942; Prerogativa Regis, 1949; Readings and Moots at the Inns of Court in the Fifteenth Century, 1954. Editor, translator Bracton, On the Laws and Customs of England, 1968. Home: 3 Berkeley Pl Cambridge MA 02138*

THORNE, WILLIAM ALBERT, b. Chgo., Feb. 20, 1924; J.D., Valparaiso U., 1949. Admitted to Ind. bar, 1949, U.S. Supreme Ct. bar, 1960; asso. firm Thorne and Yoder, Elkhart, Ind., 1963-69, partner firm Thorne, Yoder and Grodnik, Elkhart, 1969—. Pres. Elkhart Bd. Parks and Recreation, 1965-73, Elkhart Water Works Bd., 1975—; organizer, pres. Elkhart County Assn. Mental Health; bd. dirs., pres. Adult and Child Guidance Clinic, Elkhart, 1957-60; bd. dirs. United Way of Elkhart County, 1964-65. Mem. Am. Arbitration Assn. (arbitrator), Am., Ind. State, Elkhart County, Elkhart City (pres. 1973-74), Seventh Circuit Fed. bar assns. Mem. editorial com. Uniform Comml. Code forms Ind. Continuing Legal Edn. Forum, 1974, participant seminar, 1974. Office: 228 W High St Elkhart IN 46514 Tel (219) 294-7473

THORNER, DAVID ALBERT, b. Santa Monica, Calif., Mar. 16, 1948; A.B., Coll. of Idaho, 1969; J.D., U. Wash., 1972. Admitted to Wash. bar, 1972, U.S. Supreme Ct. bar, 1976; asso. firm Tankoff, Dauber & Shaw, Yakima, Wash., 1973-74, Smith, Scott & Hanson, Yakima, 1974-75; partner firm Weeks, Buren, Thorner & Dietzen, Yakima, 1975—; legal officer USAR, 1972. Bd. dirs. Yakima/Kittitas Work Release Program, 1974—. Mem. Am., Wash. State bar assns.,

Am. Trial Lawyers Assn., Wash. State Trial Lawyers. Office: 417 E Chestnut Ave Yakima WA 98907 Tel (509) 248-5311

THORNTON, GERALD DEWAYNE, b. Sioux City, Iowa, Aug. 16, 1924; B.A., U. Iowa, 1949, J.D., 1951. Admitted to Iowa bar, 1951; counsel Meredith Corp., Des Moines, 1951-65, gen. counsel, 1965-76, asst. sec., 1965, sec., 1966, v.p. adminstrv. services, 1968-76, v.p., adminstrv. services, sec., dir., 1976—. Mem. Am., Iowa, Polk County bar assns., Greater Des Moines C. of C. (past pres.), C. of C. U.S. (mem. panel on privacy 1976—). Home: 3908 Adams Des Moines IA 50310 Office: 1716 Locust St Des Moines IA 50336 Tel (515) 284-9397

THORNTON, J. DENNIS, b. Waterloo, Iowa, Sept. 17, 1949; B.A., U. Notre Dame, 1971; J.D., Marquette U., 1974. Admitted to Wis. bar, 1974; individual practice law, Milw., 1974-76; partner firm Goldman & Thornton, Milw., 1976—. Mem. Am., Milw. bar assns., State Bar Wis. Office: 623 N 2d St Milwaukee WI 53203 Tel (404) 276-2623

THORNTON, ROBERT YENNEY, b. Portland, Oreg., Jan. 28, 1910; A.B., Stanford, 1932; J.D., George Washington U., 1937. Admitted to D.C., Oreg. bars, 1937; research asst. Legis. Reference Service U.S. Congress, Washington, 1935-37; law clk. U.S. Ct. Appeals, Washington, 1938; individual practice law, Medford and Tillamook, Oreg., 1938-53, Salem, Oreg., 1969-71; atty. gen. State Oreg., Salem, 1953-69; asso. judge Oreg. Ct. Appeals, Salem, 1971—; mem. Oreg. Ho. of Reps., 1951-53. Bd. dirs. Cascade Area council Boy Scouts Am., 1965-75, Salem Boys' Club, 1965-75. Mem. Am., Marion County bar assns., Am. Judicature Soc. Contbr. articles to legal jours.; decorated Order Sacred Treasure 3d class (Japan); recipient awards Portland State U. student body, 1959, Japanese Am. Citizens League, 1975, Oreg. Dist. Attys. Assn., others. Home: 2895 Alvarado Terr S Salem OR 97302 Office: State Office Bldg Salem OR 97310 Tel (503) 378-6380

THORP, WILLIAM LEWIS, b. Rocky Mount, N.C., Feb. 2, 1925; student U. N.C., 1946-51, LL.B., 1951. Admitted to N.C. bar, 1951, U.S. Dist. Ct. bar for Eastern Dist. N.C., 1951, U.S. Ct. Appeals bar, 4th Circuit, 1955; practiced law in Rocky Mount, 1951—; partner firms Thorp & Thorp, 1951-59, Thorp, Spruill, Thorp, Trotter & Biggs, 1959-63, Thorp & Etheridge, 1965-76, Thorp & Anderson, 1976—, individual practice law, 1963-65. Mem. N.C. advisory com. U.S. Commn. on Civil Rights, 1954-58; mem. Rocky Mount City Council, 1964-68. Fellow Internat. Acad. Trial Lawyers, N.C. Acad. Trial Lawyers (pres. 1974-77); mem. N.C. (chmn. com. delivery legal services to poor 1973-76, gov. 1974-77), Am. bar assns., N.C. State Bar, Internat. Soc. Barristers, Assn. Trial Lawyers Am. Author: Thorp's North Carolina Trial Practice Forms, 1975. Home: 230 S Grace St Rocky Mount NC 27801 Office: 1605 W Thomas St PO Box 32 Rocky Mount NC 27801 Tel (919) 446-8118

THORPE, DAVID WATTS, b. Bradenton, Fla., Mar. 7, 1946; B.A., U. South Fla., 1968; J.D., Fla. State U., 1971. Admitted to Fla. bar, 1972; atty. Hills County, Pampa, Fla., 1971-73; state's atty. 13th Jud. Circuit Fla., Tampa, 1973-74. Mem. Am., Fla., Hills County bar assns. Recipient certificate for Pub. Service, Hills County, 1973. Office: 100 Shell Point Rd Number 1 POB 356 Ruskin FL 33570 Tel (813) 645-6440

THORPE, PHILIP CUTLER, b. Lansing, Mich., May 11, 1932; B.A., Mich. State U., 1954; J.D. with honors, U. Mich., 1959. Law clk. to judge U.S. Dist. Ct. for Western Dist. Mich., Grand Rapids, 1959-61; admitted to Mich. bar, 1960, Ind. bar, 1974; asso. firm Luyendyk, Hainer, Hillman, Karr & Dutcher, Grand Rapids, 1961-64; instr. law U. Mich., 1964-65; asst. prof. law U. N.C., Chapel Hill, 1965-67; asst. prof., asst. dean Sch. Law, Ind. U., 1967-70, asso. prof., 1970—. Mem. Am., Ind., Monroe County bar assns., State Bar Mich., Am. Judicature Soc., AAUP. Contbr. articles, books revs. to legal jours. Office: Ind U Sch of Law Bloomington IN 47401 Tel (812) 337-3942

THORSEN, RICHARD PIERCE, b. Evanston, Ill., May 12, 1945; B.S. in Bus. Adminstrn., Northwestern U., 1967, J.D., 1971. Admitted to Ill. bar, 1971; loan officer James Talcott Co., Chgo., 1971-72; credit analyst Continental Bank, Chgo., 1972-73; asst. v.p. Hyde Park Bank, Chgo., 1973-75; v.p. Water Tower Bank, Chgo., 1975-76; v.p. Pioneer Bank, Chgo., 1976—; instr. dept. accounting Am. Inst. Banking, 1974—, in bus. law Northwestern U., 1975—. Mem. Chgo., Ill., Am. bar assns. Columnist Chgo. Daily Law Bull. Office: 4000 W North Ave Chicago IL 60639 Tel (312) 772-8600

THORSNES, MICHAEL TOD, b. La Jolla, Calif., Jan. 3, 1943; A.B., San Diego State U., 1965; J.D., U. San Diego, 1968. Admitted to Calif. bar, 1969; partner firm Higgs, Fletcher & Mack, San Diego, 1968—; adj. prof. law U. San Diego, 1975; guest lectr. Calif. Western Sch. Law, 1972-74. Bd. visitors U. San Diego Sch. Law. Mem. Am., San Diego County bar assns. Office: 1800 Home Tower 707 Broadway San Diego CA 92112 Tel (714) 236-1551

THORSON, JOHN OLIVER, b. Minot, N.D., Sept. 20, 1906; student Minot State Tchrs. Coll., 1924-29; LL.B., U. N.D., 1932, J.D., 1968. Admitted to N.D. bar, 1932; individual practice law, Minot, 1932-34; with FERA, 1934-35; mem. N.D. Pub. Welfare Bd., 1935-42; agt. IRS, 1945-47; city atty. McClusky, N.D., 1947-53, 58-72; states atty. Sheridan County, N.D., 1953-57, 61-67; individual practice law, McClusky, 1947—. Vice pres. N.D. Central Hwy. Assn., 1968. Bd. dirs. 1st Dist. Health Unit, 1947—; bd. dirs. S. Central Health Planning Council, 1972-75; dir. Med. Health Center, McClusky, N.D., 1956-77, pres., 1964-77. Mem. Am. Bar Assn., State Bar Assn. N.D. Recipient Founders programe award Lions, 1974; Quent Gonser award outstanding service to boy scouts, 1955. Mem. staff N.D. Law Review, 1931. Home: 421 N Manden St Bismarck ND 58501 Tel (701) 258-8833

THRASHER, ELWIN ROLAND, JR., b. Woodville, Tex., Oct. 22, 1943; B.A., U. Fla., 1965, J.D., 1967. Admitted to Fla. bar, 1967, U.S. Dist. Ct. bar No. Dist. Fla., 1973, U.S. Ct. Appeals bar 5th Circuit, 1975; asst. staff judge adv. Amarillo (Tex.) AFB, 1968; asst. staff judge adv. USAF Acad., Colorado Springs, 1969-70; staff judge adv. Zaragoza Air Base, Spain, 1970-73; asso. firm Jim L. Dye & Assos., Tallahassee, Fla., 1973-74; partner firm Dye & Thrasher, Tallahassee, 1974—; mil. judge U.S. Air Force, 1970-73; speaker Fla. Bar Continuing Legal Edn. Course, 1976. Mem. Am., Fla., Tallahassee bar assns., Phi Alpha Delta. Author: Legal Guide, 1970. Home: 3943 Leane Dr Tallahassee FL 32303 Office: 1120 Thomasville Rd Tallahassee FL 32303 Tel (904) 224-1205

THRASHER, HENRY GRADY, III, b. Toccoa, Ga., Oct. 20, 1942; B.S., Ga. Inst. Tech., 1964; J.D., Emory U., 1968. Admitted to Ga. bar, 1968; trial atty. div. corp. fin. SEC, Washington, 1968-69; asso. firm Peek, Whaley & Haldi, Atlanta, 1969-73; partner firm Spearman & Thrasher, and predecessors, Atlanta, 1973—. Mem. Am., Ga., Atlanta bar assns. Office: 2430 Tower Pl 3340 Peachtree Rd NE Atlanta GA 30326

THROCKMORTON, ALMA ROBERT, b. Los Angeles, July 14, 1933; B.A., Brigham Young U., 1958; J.D., U. So. Calif., 1961. Admitted to Calif. bar, 1962; asst. U.S. atty. Central Dist., Calif., Los Angeles, 1962-64; partner firm Munns, Kofford, Hoffman, Hunt & Throckmorton, Pasadena, Calif., 1969—; lectr. sch. pharmacy U. So. Calif., Los Angeles. Trustee Bd. Edn. Monrovia Unified Sch. Dist., 1968-69; mem. bd. appeals Monrovia, 1973-75. Mem. Los Angeles County Bar Assn. Home: 1128 Teresita Circle Monrovia CA 91016 Office: 199 N Lake Ave Suite 300 Pasadena CA 91101 Tel (213) 795-9733

THROOP, JOHN SCYSTER, JR., b. Water Valley, Miss., Dec. 19, 1918; B.S. in Polit. Sci., Davidson Coll., 1940; LL.B., U. Miss., 1947, J.D., 1968. Admitted to Miss. bar, 1947, U.S. Dist. Ct. bar, 1947, U.S. Supreme Ct. bar, 1956; individual practice law, Water Valley, 1947—; served as maj. JAGC, U.S. Army, 1951-52. Pres., Water Valley Jr. C. of C., 1948-49, 49-50, Water Valley Rotary Club, 1965; mem. Miss. State Senate, 1954-55. Mem. Am., Miss. bar assns., Miss. Assn. of Trial Lawyers, Phi Alpha Delta, Phi Gamma Delta. Named Water Valley Outstanding Young Man of Year, 1948. Home: 535 Airways Dr Water Valley MS 38965 Office: Edgar Professional Bldg Water Valley MS 38965 Tel (601) 473-2351

THROWER, RANDOLPH WILLIAM, b. Tampa, Fla., Sept. 5, 1913; Ph.B., Emory U., 1934, J.D., 1936. Admitted to Ga. bar, 1935, D.C. bar, 1951; asso. firm Sutherland, Asbill & Brennan, Atlanta and Washington, 1936-42, 46-47, partner, 1947-69, 71—; spl. agt. FBI, 1942-44; commr. IRS, Washington, 1969-71; mem. Met. Atlanta Crime Commn., 1972—; mem. pub. rev. bd. Arthur Andersen & Co., 1974—. Trustee Emory U., 1972—; trustee Wesleyan Coll., chmn., 1972—; mem. governing bd. Woodward Acad., College Park, Ga. Fellow Am. Bar Found.; mem. Am. (chmn. sect. taxation 1961-63, ho. of dels. 1964-66, 74—, chmn. spl. com. to survey legal needs 1971—), Atlanta (pres. 1958-59) bar assns., Atlanta Lawyers Club (pres. 1954), Atlanta Legal Aid Soc. (pres. 1953), Am. Law Inst. Home: 2240 Woodward Way NW Atlanta GA 30305 Office: 3100 1st Nat Bank Tower Atlanta GA 30303 Tel (404) 658-8711

THRUN, ROBERT, b. Eagle River, Wis., July 1, 1913; B.A., U. Wis., 1936; J.D., Harvard, 1939. Admitted to N.Y. bar, 1940; mem. firm Reavis & McGrath, N.Y.C., 1946—; counsel, sec. Ringling Bros.-Barnum & Bailey Combined Shows, Inc., 1952-67, dir., gen. counsel, 1971—; gen. counsel, v.p., exec. com., dir. U.S. Com. for UNICEF, 1954—; village atty. Village of Croton-on-Hudson (N.Y.), 1959-60, 61-67; trustee, sec. Sotterley Mansion Found., 1962—; gen. counsel Pulitzer Pub. Co., 1971—, also dir. Mem. Am. Bar Assn., Assn. Bar City N.Y. Home: Finney Farm Rd Croton-on-Hudson NY 10520 Office: Reavis & McGrath 345 Park Ave New York City NY 10022 Tel (212) 752-6830

THUET, PAUL ANTHONY, JR., b. S. St. Paul, Nov. 13, 1916; B.S.L., U. Minn., 1937, J.D., 1939. Admitted to Minn. bar, 1939; atty. City of S. St. Paul, 1947-49; enforcement dir. Office of Price Stabilization, St. Paul, 1951-52; acting municipal judge S. St. Paul, 1952-58; partner firm Thuet, Collins, Simonson & O'Connell, S. St. Paul, 1947-75; partner firm Thuet & Collins, S. St. Paul, 1976—; mem. Minn. Senate, 1958-66, minority leader, 1963-66. Mem. Nat. Soc. State Legislatiors, Am., Minn. (bd. govs. 1956-60) bar assns. Office: 833 Southview Blvd South Saint Paul MN 55075 Tel (612) 451-6411

THUNE, RICHARD MASON, b. Salem, Mass., Aug. 24, 1947; B.A., U. Pa., 1969; postgrad. Mansfield Coll., Oxford U., 1969; J.D., Boston U., 1972. Admitted to N.Y. State bar, 1973; Conn. bar, 1974; asso. firm Reynolds, Richards, LaVenture, Hadley & Davis, N.Y.C., 1972—; vol. N.Y.C. Legal Aid Soc., 1973—. Fund raiser Greenwich Health Assn., 1976—. Mem. Am., Conn. bar assns. Home: 147 Round Hill Rd Greenwich CT 06830 Office: 67 Wall St New York City NY 10005 Tel (212) 422-8490

THURMAN, RUTH FLEET, b. St. Petersburg, Fla., Sept. 27, 1929; A.A., St. Petersburg Jr. Coll., 1949; B.A., Smith Coll., 1951; LL.B., Stetson U., 1963, J.D., 1967. Admitted to Fla. bar, 1963; practiced in St. Petersburg, 1964-75, partner firm Collins, Hallett, Ford & Thurman, 1969-75; asst. prof. law Stetson U., St. Petersburg, 1975, now asso. prof., also dir. continuing legal edn., 1975—; asst. to state atty. for Pinellas and Pasco Counties (Fla.), 1967-68; mem. Fla. Bd. Bar Examiners, 1973-75. Bd. dirs. Civic Music Assn., St. Petersburg, sec., 1969-70; bd. dirs. South Pinellas chpt. ARC, 1967-72, Fla. West Coast Ednl. TV, 1967—. Mem. Fla. Assn. Women Lawyers (pres. 1969-70), St. Petersburg Bar Assn. (sec. 1970-71), St. Petersburg Legal Aid Soc. (dir. 1965-67), Jr. League St. Petersburg. Home: 2411 Brevard Rd NE Saint Petersburg FL 33704 Office: Stetson U Coll Law 1401 61st St Saint Petersburg FL 33707

THURMAN, SAMUEL DAVID, b. Washington, Dec. 7, 1913; A.B., U. Utah, 1935; J.D., Stanford, 1939. Admitted to Utah bar, 1940, Calif. bar, 1946, U.S. Supreme Ct. bar, 1950; partner firm Irvine, Skeen & Thurman, Salt Lake City, 1939-42; prof. law Stanford, 1942-62; dean, prof. law U. Utah, Salt Lake City, 1962-75, Distinguished prof. law, 1975—; vis. prof. law U. Mich., 1949, N.Y. U., 1955; Marion Rice Kirkwood prof. law Stanford, 1961-62; dir. Nat. Legal Services Corp., Washington, 197S—; mem. Calif. Law Revision Commn., 1954-59; dir. Council on Legal Edn. for Profl. Responsibility, 1969-73. Fellow Am. Bar Found.; mem. Am. Law Inst., Am. Bar Assn. (council on legal edn. 1965—), Order of Coif (nat. pres. 1977—), Phi Beta Kappa. Author: (with others) Cases on the Legal Profession, 1970; (with others) The Study of Federal Tax Law, 1976; contbr. articles in field to legal jours.; editorial bd. Foundation Press, 1962—. Home: 875 Donner Way Salt Lake City UT 84108 Office: Coll Law U Utah Salt Lake City UT 84112 Tel (801) 581-8711

THURMAN, WINN MONROE, b. Kansas City, Mo., May 23, 1929; A.B., William Jewell Coll., 1949; J.D., U. Mo., 1952. Admitted to Mo. bar, 1952, U.S. Supreme Ct. bar, 1968; enlisted in U.S. Marine Corps, 1952, commd. 2d lt., 1953, designated JAGC, 1969, advanced through grades to lt. col., 1968; dep. staff judge adv. 5th Marine Div., Camp Pendleton, Calif., 1966-67, Mil. judge, 1968-70; exec. officer 3d bn. 1st Marine Div., Vietnam, 1967-68; staff judge adv., Quantico, Va., 1970-72, 2d Marine Aircraft Wing, Cherry Point, N.C., 1972-74; ret., 1976; partner firm Shirkey & Thurman, Kansas City, 1976—; trial observer to Japanese Cts., 1974-75. Mem. Mo. Bar, Nat. Contract Adminstr. Assn., Phi Delta Phi. Decorated Legion of Merit, Bronze Star with 2 gold stars, Purple Heart (U.S.); Cross of Gallantry (Vietnam); recipient citation Japanese Ministry of Justice, 1975, Japanese Def. Facility Adminstrn. Bur., 1975. Home: 7509 W 98th Terr Overland Park KS 66212 Office: 1014 Argyle Bldg Kansas City MO 64106 Tel (816) 842-3030

THURMOND, GEORGE MURAT, b. Del Rio, Tex., Oct. 22, 1930; B.A., U. South, 1952; LL.B., J.D., U. Tex., 1955. Admitted to Tex. bar, 1955; partner Montague & Thurmond, Del Rio, 1958-69; judge Tex. Dist. Ct., 63d Dist., Del Rio, 1970—; mem. Tex. Ho. of Reps., 1955-58. Mem. Am., Tex., Border Dist., Val Verde County bar assns. Home and Office: Box 1195 Del Rio TX 78840 Tel (512) 775-3741

THURSTON, MORRIS ASHCROFT, b. Logan, Utah, May 25, 1943; B.A., Brigham Young U., 1967; J.D., Harvard, 1970. Admitted to Calif. bar, 1971; asso. firm Latham & Watkins, Los Angeles, 1970—. Mem. Am., Los Angeles County (co-editor trial lawyers sect. newsletter 1976—) bar assns., State Bar Calif., Assn. Bus. Trial Lawyers. Home: 1564 N Pacific Ave Glendale CA 91202 Office: 555 S Flower St Los Angeles CA 90071 Tel (213) 485-1234

THURSTON, PHILLIP BURNETT, b. N.Y.C., Sept. 9, 1908; A.B., Columbia U., 1928, LL.B., 1930. Admitted to N.Y. bar, 1931, mng. partner firm Everett, Walker and Thurston and Walker, Thurston and Garrahan, N.Y.C., 1932-37; sec. N.Y.C. Planning Commn., 1938-45; city magistrate, N.Y.C., 1945-54; justice Domestic Relations Ct. City N.Y., 1954-62; judge Family Ct. State N.Y., 1962—. Active Boy Scouts Am.; bd. dirs. Fedn. Protestant Welfare Agys. N.Y.C., YMCA Greater N.Y.C., 1934—. Mem. Am. Bar Assn. (vice chmn. family law judges com. 1971-73), Soc. Med. Jurisprudence. Contbr. articles to profl. jours.; recipient Silver Beaver award for Distinguished Service to Boyhood, Nat. Council Boy Scouts Am., 1962. Home: Apt 810 Windsor Tower 5 Tudor City Pl New York City NY 10017 Office: 60 Lafayette St New York City NY 10013 Tel (212) 374-8985

TIBBS, DON VAUGHN, b. Manti, Utah, Nov. 14, 1924; J.D., U. Utah, 1949. Admitted to Utah bar; past asso. Larson Lewis Law Office; past mem. firm Tibbs & Tervort, Manti; past pub. defender Sevier County (Utah); past county atty. Sanpete County (Utah); past Utah State Bar Commr.; now judge Utah 6th Jud. Dist. Ct. Past chmn. Nat. Found. March of Dimes, ARC, Am. Field Service; high councilman Manti Stake Latter Day Saints Ch. Mem. Am., Utah, So. Utah (past pres.) bar assns., Utah Prosecutors Assn. (past pres.), Am. Trial Lawyers Assn., Utah Dist. Judges Assn. (past pres.), Utah Jud. Council. Home: 380 E Union St Manti UT 84642 Office: Sanpete Courthouse Manti UT 84642 Tel (801) 835-2121

TICE, JOHN EDWARD, b. Los Angeles, May 4, 1925; B.A., U. So. Calif., 1945; J.D., Calif. Western U., 1972. Admitted to Calif. bar, 1972; individual practice law, San Diego, 1970—. Mem. Am. Bar Assn., Phi Beta Kappa. Office: 519 Broadway San Diego CA 92101 Tel (714) 232-1718

TICHY, GEORGE JOSEPH, b. Astoria, Oreg., May 27, 1918; B.S., U. Oreg., 1940, J.D., 1940; postgrad. Washington and Lee U., 1946. Admitted to Wash. bar, 1940, Oreg. bar, 1940, U.S. Supreme Ct. bar, 1949, 9th Circuit Ct. Appeals bar, 1949, U.S. Dist. Ct. Western Wash. bar, 1941, Eastern Wash., 1953, D.C. Ct. Appeals bar, 1967; dep. city atty. Longview, Wash., 1941-42; municipal judge, Longview, 1942-43; disputes hearing officer Nat. War Labor Bd., 1943-44; individual practice law, Longview, 1940-43, Spokane, Wash., 1946—; mgr., gen. counsel, sec. Timber Products Mfrs. (Assn.), Spokane, 1946—; mgr., counsel, sec.-treas. Roosevelt Lake Log Owners Assn., Inc., 1949—; U.S. employer del. 1st, 2d tripartite tech. meeting World Timber Industry to ILO, UN, Geneva, 1958, 73, advisor to dels. World Woodworking Industries, Geneva, 1967, del. to 2d meeting ILO, UN, 1975; lectr. labor law Gonzaga U., Spokane, 1950-52. Mem. Oreg. State, Wash. State, Spokane County bar assns., Am. Bar Assn. (mem. labor, internat. labor law sects.), Phi Alpha Delta. Home: Windsong Dr Liberty Lake WA 99019 Office: Timber Products Bldg 951 E 3d Ave Spokane WA 99202 Tel (509) 535-4646

TIEMANN, ANNA LYNN, b. Seguin, Tex., Oct. 18, 1940; B.S., Tex. Luth. Coll., 1964; postgrad St. Mary's Law Sch., 1964-65. Admitted to Tex. bar, 1972; sec. firm Dibrell, Tiemann & Irvine and predecessor firms, Seguin, 1960-65, briefing clk., 1966-71, asso., 1972-74, partner, 1975—. Mem. Am. Bar Assn., Assn. Trial Lawyers Am., State Bar Tex. (mem. Bar-Press conf. 1975—). Tex. Trial Lawyers Assn., Tri-County Bar Assn. S. Central Tex. Home: Box 533 Seguin TX 78155 Office: 207 S Camp St Seguin TX 78155 Tel (512) 379-2896

TIERNEY, GERALD MILES, JR., b. Battle Creek, Mich., Jan. 21, 1947; A.B., Princeton U., 1968; J.D., U. Va., 1973. Admitted to Va. bar, 1973, N.Y. bar, 1974; asso. firm Lord, Day & Lord, N.Y.C., 1973—. Asst. sec. Downtown-Lower Manhattan Assn., 1975—. Mem. Assn. Bar City N.Y. Office: 25 Broadway New York City NY 10004 Tel (212) 344-8480

TIERNEY, JAMES PATRICK, b. Kansas City, Mo., Apr. 30, 1927; B.S., Rockhurst Coll., 1948; postgrad. Oxford U., 1948; LL.B., Harvard, 1951. Admitted to Mo. bar, 1951; partner firm Lathrop, Koontz, Clagett, Parker & Norquist, Kansas City, Mo., 1951—. Chmn. Fair Housing Commn. Kansas City, 1968. Mem. Mo., Am., Kansas City bar assns. Office: 1500 Ten Main Center Kansas City MO 64105 Tel (816) 842-0820

TIERNEY, JOHN JOSEPH, b. Nassau City, N.Y., Feb. 9, 1941; B.A., Manhattan Coll., 1963; J.D., St. John's U., 1966. Admitted to N.Y. bar, 1969; individual practice law, Port Jefferson Station, N.Y., 1970—; partner firm Tierney & Tierney, Port Jefferson Station, 1974—. Mem. N.Y. State, Nassau and Suffolk counties bar assns. Office: 409 Route 112 Port Jefferson Station NY 11776 Tel (516) 928-1853

TIERNEY, KEVIN HUGH, b. Bristol, Eng., Sept. 22, 1942; B.A., Cambridge (Eng.) U., 1964, M.A., 1968, LL.B., 1965; LL.M., Yale, 1967. Called to English bar, 1966; asso. firm Donovan, Leisure, Newton & Irvine N.Y.C., 1969-70; asso. prof. law Wayne State U., 1971-75, prof. 1975—; mem. nat. adv. council Center for Adminstrn. of Justice, 1972—; reporter Mich. Standard Jury Instrn. Com., 1975—. Mem. Honourable Soc. Lincoln's Inn (Eng.). Author: Courtroom Testimony, a Policeman's Guide, 1970; How to be a Witness, 1971; contbr. articles to profl. jours. Office: Law Sch Wayne State U Detroit MI 48202 Tel (313) 577-3975

TIERNEY, MICHAEL PATRICK, b. Port Chester, N.Y., Feb. 18, 1944; B.A., Manhattan Coll., 1966; J.D., Columbia, 1969. Admitted to N.Y. State bar, 1969, 2d circuit U.S. Ct. Appeals bar, 1970, U.S. Supreme Ct. bar, 1975; asso. firm Cahill Gordon & Reindel, N.Y.C., 1969—. Mem. Am., N.Y. State bar assns. Office: 80 Pine St New York City NY 10005 Tel (212) 825-0100

TIERNEY, WILLIAM JOHN, b. N.Y.C., June 18, 1913; A.B., John Marshall Coll., 1932-34; LL.B., John Marshall Law Sch., 1934-37. Admitted to N.J. bar, 1940; asso. firm George P. Moser, Union City, N.J., 1935-59; individual practice law, Union City, 1959—; asst. corp. counsel, Union City, 1945-73, prosecutor, 1952-59; mem. State Assembly, N.J. 1942-46. Mem. Am., N.J., Hudson County bar assns., North Hudson Lawyers Club. Home: 28 Merritt Dr Oradell NJ 07649 Office: 4315 Bergenline Ave Union City NJ Tel (201) 864-5603

TIESEN, FRANK GUY, b. Freeman, S.D., Nov. 8, 1940; A.A., El Camino Coll., 1961; B.A., San Jose State U., 1963; J.D., Calif. Western U., 1967. Admitted to Calif. bar, 1967; asso. firm Andreasen, Gore, Grosse, & Wright, Oceanside, Calif., 1968-71, Richard D. Ring, Vista, Calif., 1971-73; individual practice law, Vista, 1973—; dep. dist. atty. Ventura County (Calif.), 1968. Mem. Vista Park & Recreation Commn., 1971-74; bd. dirs., v.p. Vista Irrigation Dist., 1974—; bd. dirs., v.p. Bueno Colo. Municipal Water Dist., 1977—. Mem. Calif., San Diego County, No. San Diego County (v.p. no. county assn. 1973) bar assns. Contbr. articles in field to profl. jours. Office: 142 Jefferson St Vista CA 92083

TIFFANY, GEORGE OLIVER, b. Durango, Colo., Oct. 24, 1903; student Stanford, 1921-23, Ariz. U., 1924-25, Colo. U. Law Sch., summer 1926; LL.B., Northwestern U., 1928, LL.M., 1929; certificate Nat. Inst. Comml. and Orgn. Execs., summer 1928. Admitted to Ill. bar, 1928, U.S. Supreme Ct. bar, 1938, Conn. bar, 1940; practiced in Chgo., 1929-32; trial lawyer Legal Aid Bur., Chgo., 1933-35; atty. Home Owners Loan Corp., Chgo., 1933-35; gen. counsel Evaporated Milk Assn., Chgo., 1935-39; gen. counsel Nestlé/Unilac Group of Cos., Stamford, Conn., 1939-69; trustee Swiss Reinsurance Co., Zurich and dir. of affiliated and associated cos. in U.S., Stamford, Conn., 1948-76. Chmn. Stamford chpt. ARC, 1963-66; chmn. tax com. Conn. Regional Export Expansion Council, U.S. Dept. Commerce, Hartford, Conn., 1964-74. Mem. Chgo., Conn., Am., Stamford, Fed. bar assns., Am. Judicature Soc., Phi Alpha Delta. Recipient Dairy Ambassador citation Dairy Industries Soc., Internat., 1956. Office: 508 Ridgeway Center PO Box 3518 Ridgeway Sta Stamford CT 06905 Tel (203) 348-4006

TIGHE, EDWARD MARSH, b. Dallas, Tex., Mar. 23, 1922; LL.B., South Tex. Coll. Law, 1951. Admitted to Tex. bar, 1951; since practiced in Dallas. Mem. vestry Ch. Assention, Dallas, 1960-61; capt. Heart Fund Dallas, 1973—. Mem. Tex. Bar Assn. Home: 5336 Ridgelawn St Dallas TX 75214 Office: 4539 N Central Expressway Dallas TX 75205 Tel (214) 522-1483

TIGHT, DEXTER CORWIN, b. San Francisco, Sept. 14, 1924; A.B., Denison U., 1948; J.D., Yale, 1951. Admitted to Calif. bar, 1951; asso. firm Pillsbury, Madison & Sutro, San Francisco, 1953-60; gen. atty. W.P. Fuller Paint Co., San Francisco, 1960-62; gen. atty. Schlage Lock Co., San Francisco, 1962-68, gen. counsel, 1968-76, v.p. corp. devel., 1968-74, v.p., 1974-76; dir. govt. and pub. affairs Crown Zellerbach Corp., 1976—; dir. Pacific Coast Holdings, Shaw-Clayton Plastics. Exec. bd. San Francisco council Boy Scouts Am.; commr. San Francisco Juvenile Delinquency Commn., 1970-72; bd. dirs. San Francisco Boys Club, 1973—, Bayview Hunters Point Coll., No. Calif. NAACP Legal Def. Fund; asso. Golden Gate U. Mem. Am., Calif., San Francisco bar assns., Phi Beta Kappa. Home: 2744 Steiner St San Francisco CA 94123 Office: 1 Bush St San Francisco CA 94104 Tel (415) 823-5562

TILBURY, ROGER, b. Guthrie, Okla., July 30, 1925; B.S. (Battenfeld scholar), U. So. Calif., 1945; LL.B., J.D., U. Kans., 1949; postgrad. Oxford U., 1949; LL.M., Columbia, 1951. Admitted to Mo. bar, 1950, Oreg. bar, 1953, U.S. Supreme Ct. bar, 1964; asso. firm Rogers, Field & Gentry, Kansas City, Mo., 1950-53, firm Stern, Reiter & Day, Portland, Oreg., 1953-56; partner firm Roth & Tilbury, Portland, 1956-58; individual practice law, Portland, 1958—; circuit judge pro tem., Oreg., 1972—; sec. Barrington Properties, Inc.; arbitrator, mediator, fact finder, Portland, 1973—; mem. nat. panel arbitrators U.S. Mediation and Conciliation Service. Mem. Greenpeace Found., Save the Redwoods League, E. African Wildlife League, Animal Defender League. Mem. Oreg. Bar Assn., Internat. Soc. Barristers. Home: 9310 NW Cornell Rd Portland OR 97229 Office: 1123 SW Yamhill St Portland OR 97205 Tel (503) 223-6291

TILL, PAUL HENRY, b. Jamaica, N.Y., Dec. 28, 1942; B.A., Adelphi U., 1964; J.D., Bklyn. Law Sch., 1967. Admitted to N.Y. bar, 1967, N.J. bar, 1969; asso. counsel The Chase Manhattan Bank, N.Y.C., 1968-72; asso. firm Snevily, Ely & Williams, Westfield, N.J., 1972-74; asst. counsel Sterling Nat. Bank & Trust Co., New York, N.J., 1974-75; counsel First Nat. State Bank, Edison, N.J., 1976-77; First Jersey Nat. Bank, Jersey City, 1977—. Mem. N.Y. County Lawyers Assn. Author: Military Awards of the Empire State, 1972. Home: 60 Gill Ln Iselin NJ 08830 Office: 2 Montgomery St Jersey City NJ 07302 Tel (201) 547-7661

TILLEMANS, PAUL JOHN, b. Marshall, Minn., Jan. 25, 1946; B.A. in Psychology, St. Thomas Coll., 1969; J.D., U. Notre Dame, 1972. Admitted to Ind. bar, 1972; asst. v.p., trust officer 1st Nat. Bank of Mishawaka (Ind.), 1972—. Mem. Am., Ind., St. Joseph bar assns., South Bend Estate Planning Council. Home: 821 Golfview Ln South Bend IN 46617 Office: 101 Lincolnway E Mishawaka IN 46544 Tel (219) 259-3711

TILLER, LAUREL LEE, b. Morton, Wash., Jan. 11, 1938; B.A., Willamette U., 1960; J.D., U. Wash., 1963. Admitted to Wash. bar, 1963; asst. atty. gen. State Wash., Olympia, 1963-65; partner firm Dysant, Moore, Tiller & Murray, Centralia, Wash., 1965—; judge Centralia Municipal Ct., 1968—. Office: Rock & Pine Sts Centralia WA 98531 Tel (206) 736-9301

TILLERS, PETER, b. Riga, Latvia, July 4, 1943; A.B., Yale, 1966; J.D., Harvard, 1969, LL.M., 1972. Admitted to Calif. bar, 1970; asso. firm Mitchell, Silberber & Knupp, Los Angeles, 1969-70; instr. law U. Wis., 1970-71; asst. prof. U. Puget Sound, 1972-74, asso. prof., 1974-76; vis. asso. prof. Boston Coll., 1975-76; fellow law and humanities Harvard U., 1976-77; asso. prof. Rutgers U., Camden, N.J., 1977—. Mem. Am. Soc. Legal History. Office: 5th and Pennsylvania Sts Camden NJ 08102

TILLEY, NORWOOD CARLTON, JR., b. Rock Hill, S.C., Dec. 16, 1943; B.S., Wake Forest U., 1966, J.D., 1969. Admitted to N.C. bar, 1969; law clk. to chief U.S. dist. judge, 1969-71; asst. U.S. atty. Middle Dist. N.C., Greensboro, 1971-74, U.S. atty., 1974-77; mem. firm Osteen Adams & Tilley, Greensboro, 1977—. Mem. Am., N.C. bar assns. Home: 1106 Montpelier Dr Greensboro NC 27410 Office: PO Box 2489 Greensboro NC 27402 Tel (919) 274-2949

TILLISCH, MICHAEL RAVN, JR., b. Des Moines, Mar. 15, 1923; B.S., U. Wis., 1948, LL.B., 1950. Admitted to Wis. bar, 1950; Nebr. bar, 1958; with Employers Ins. of Wausau (Wis.), 1950—, claim mgr., Omaha, 1958-60, regional claim mgr., Los Angeles, 1960-66, regional v.p., 1966—. Dist. fin. chmn. Samoset council Boy Scouts Am., Wausau, 1968; pres. Franklin Sch. PTA, Wausau, 1969-71; pres. United Way of Marathon County (Wis.), 1975-77; bd. dirs. Trees for Tomorrow, 1975—. Mem. Wausau Area C. of C. (dir.), U. Wis. Alumni Assn. (pres. 1971-72), State Bar Wis., Marathon County Bar Assn., Wis. Mfrs. and Commerce. Home: 2 North Hill Rd Wausau WI 54401 Office: 2000 Westwood Dr Wausau WI 54401 Tel (715) 842-6056

TILLMAN, WHEELER MELLETTE, b. Charleston, S.C., Aug. 25, 1941; B.A., U. of South, 1963; J.D., U. S.C., 1966. Admitted to S.C. bar, 1966; served to capt. as asst. Staff Judge Adv. USAF, Vandenberg AFB, 1966-69; individual practice law, Charleston Heights, S.C., 1969-75; partner firm Tillman & Rivers, North Charleston, 1975—; mem. S.C. House of Reps., 1973—. Mem. Am., S.C., Charleston County bar assns. Office: PO Box 4295 Charleston Heights SC 29405 Tel (803) 554-9171

TILTON, CHARLES NORRIS, b. Jensen Beach, Fla., Feb. 9, 1925; J.D., U. Fla., 1950. Admitted to Fla. bar, 1950, La. bar, 1963; partner firm Scott & Tilton, Jensen Beach, Fla., 1968-75; pres. C. Norris Tilton, Jensen Beach, 1975—. Asst. scout master, Gulf Stream council Boy Scouts Am., 1958-73, com. chmn. Troop 811, 1973—. Mem. Martin County Bar Assn. (sec. treas. 1974, v.p. 1975, pres. 1976). Home: 2126 River Court Jensen Beach FL 33457 Office: 1936 NE Ricou Rd Jensen Beach FL 33457 Tel (305) 334-3305

TILTON, DENNIS STUART, b. Milw., Feb. 22, 1945; B.A. in English, San Diego State U., 1966; J.D., U. Calif. Hastings Coll. of Law, 1970; M.A. in Edn., U. Redlands, 1971. Admitted to Wis. bar, 1970, Calif. bar, 1972; individual practice law, Milw., 1971-72; instr. sch. law U. Redlands (Calif.), summer 1973; instr. indsl. law and English, Riverside (Calif.) City Coll., 1973—; dep. dist. atty. Superior Ct. Trial Dept., County of San Bernardino, Calif., 1973—; high sch. tchr. Palm Springs (Calif.) High Sch., 1970-71; tchr. Moreno Valley High Sch., Sunnymead, Calif., 1972-73. Cons. on edn. and law U.S. Senate Com. on Judiciary, 1974. Mem. Am., Calif., Wis., San Bernardino County bar assns., Am. Arbitration Assn., U. Calif.-Hastings Coll. Law, U. Redlands, San Diego State alumni assns., Phi Delta Phi. Contbr. poems and articles to mags. and profl. jours. Home: 336 E Sunset Dr N Redlands CA 92373 Office: 351 N Arrowhead Ave San Bernardino CA 92415 Tel (714) 383-2461

TILTON, EDWIN ODIN, b. Worcester, Mass., Aug. 2, 1915; A.B., Harvard, 1936; LL.B., Yale, 1940. Admitted to N.Y. bar, 1941; mem. firm Hodgson, Russ, Andrews, Woods & Goodyear, Buffalo, N.Y., 1946—. Mem. Assn. Bar of City N.Y., Am., N.Y. State (mem. com. corp. law, banking, corp. and commercial law section), Erie County bar assns. Office: 1800 One M & T Plaza Buffalo NY 14203 Tel (716) 856-4000

TIMBERG, SIGMUND, b. Antwerp, Belgium, Mar. 5, 1911; B.A., Columbia, 1930, M.A., 1930, LL.B., 1933. Admitted to N.Y. bar, 1935, U.S. Supreme Ct. bar, 1940, D.C. bar, 1954; asso. firm Straus & Kenyon, N.Y.C., 1933; sr. atty. office of solicitor Dept. Agr., Washington, 1933-38, SEC, 1938-42; chief div. indsl. organ. Bd. Econ. Warfare and Fgn. Econ. Adminstrn., Washington, 1942-44; spl. asst. to atty. gen., chief sect. judgments and judgment enforcement antitrust div. Dept. Justice, Washington, 1944-52; sec. UN Ad Hoc Com. on Restrictive Bus. Practices, N.Y.C., 1952-54; individual practice, Washington, 1954—; prof. Georgetown U. Law Sch., 1951-53, Parker Sch. of Fgn. and Comparative Law Columbia, 1967—. Mem. Am. Law Inst., Am. (chmn. internat. trade com. antitrust sect.), D.C., N.Y. State, Fed., Internat. (vice chmn. restrictive bus. practices com.) bar assns., Internat. Law Assn., Am. Fgn. Law Assn., Am. Patent Law Assn., Assn. Bar City N.Y., Washington Fgn. Law Soc. (past pres.), Am. Soc. Internat. Law, Copyright Soc. Am. (past trustee). Contbr. numerous articles to legal jours.; editor Columbia Law Rev., 1931-33. Home: 3519 Porter St NW Washington DC 20016 Office: 815 15th St NW Washington DC 20005 Tel (202) 393-1074

TIMBERLAKE, HAROLD KENAN, b. Chattanooga, Oct. 9, 1935; B.A., U. of the South, 1958; LL.B., Vanderbilt U., 1961, J.D., 1969. Admitted to Ala. bar, 1962; asso. firm Page & Williams, Huntsville, Ala., 1962-63; partner firm Beck and Timberlake, Huntsville, 1963-68, firm Timberlake & Werdehoff, Huntsville, 1973-76; individual practice law, Huntsville, 1976—. Mem. Am. Judicature Soc., Ala. Trial Lawyers Assn., Assn. Trial Lawyers Am., Huntsville-Madison County Bar Assn. Home: 5702 Tannahill Circle Huntsville AL 35802 Office: 106 South Side Sq Huntsville AL 35801 Tel (205) 539-3496

TIMLIN, ROBERT JAMES, b. Buffalo, July 26, 1932; A.B. cum laude, Georgetown U., 1954, J.D., 1959, LL.M., 1964. Admitted to Ill. bar, 1959, D.C. bar, 1960, Calif. bar, 1965; mem. legal dept. Pa. R.R., Chgo., 1959-60; asso. firm Douglas, Obear & Campbell, Washington, 1960-61; spl. atty. criminal div. U.S. Dept. Justice, Washington, 1961-64; asst. U.S. atty. Central and So. Dists. Calif., Los Angeles, 1964-66; asso. firm Hennigan, Ryneal & Butterwick, Riverside, Calif., 1966-67; atty. City of Corona (Calif.), 1967-70, 71-76; individual practice law, Riverside, 1970-71, 74-76; owner, officer firm Hunt, Palladino and Timlin, Riverside, 1971-74; judge municipal ct. Corona Jud. Dist., 1976—; instr. torts Citrus Belt Law Sch., Riverside, 1976—; atty. City of Norco (Calif.), 1971-72, 74-76. Mem. Calif. Judges Assn., Am. Judicature Soc., Am. Bar Assn., Phi Alpha Delta. Recipient Spl. award Riverside County Heart Assn., 1968; Spl. citation Riverside County Comprehensive Health Planning Assn., 1970. Home: 659 W Hacienda Dr Corona CA 91720 Office: 505 S Buena Vista Ave Corona CA 91720 Tel (714) 737-5689

TIMMERMAN, GEORGE BELL, JR., b. Anderson, S.C., Aug. 11, 1912; student The Citadel, 1930-34, LL.D., 1950; LL.B., U. S.C., 1937, J.D., 1970. Admitted to S.C. bar, 1937; asso. firm George Bell Timmerman, Lexington, S.C., 1937-42; individual practice law, Lexington, 1942, 46-55, 59-67; lt. gov. State S.C., 1947-55, gov., 1955-59; judge S.C. 11th Jud. Circuit Ct., 1967—; asst. chief trial atty. Santee-Cooper Authority, Charleston, S.C., 1941. Mem. S.C. Bar, Am. Bar Assn., Am. Judicature Soc. Home: PO Box 6 Batesburg SC 29006 Office: PO Box 337 Lexington SC 29072 Tel (803) 359-2371

TINKER, JOEL DOUGLAS, b. Van Nuys, Calif., July 15, 1934; B.S., U. Tex., 1957, LL.B., 1963. Admitted to Tex. bar; briefing atty. Tex. Ct. Criminal Appeals, Austin, 1963-64; asst. dist. atty. Nueces County (Tex.), 1964-68; individual practice law, Corpus Christi, Tex., 1968—; speaker in field. Mem. Tex., Nueces County bar assns., Tex. Criminal Def. Attys. Assn. (dir.), Contbr. articles to legal jours. Home: 1010 Furman St Corpus Christi TX 78401 Office: 801 Lipan St Corpus Christi TX 78403 Tel (512) 882-4378

TINKHAM, RICHARD PERRY, b. Atlanta, Mar. 19, 1917; B.A., U. Wis., 1938, LL.B., 1940. Admitted to Wis. bar, 1940, U.S. Supreme Ct. bar, 1955; atty., office atty. gen. State Wis., Madison, 1940; clk. to judge Circuit Ct. Appeals, 7th Circuit, Chgo., 1940-41; partner firm Tinkham, Smith, Bliss, Patterson & Richards, Wausau, Wis., 1946—; pres. Wis. State Bar, 1968-69. Chmn. Marathon County (Wis.) Republican Party, 1950-54. Fellow Am. Coll. Trial Lawyers, Am. Bar Found.; mem. Am., Wis. bar assns., Order of Coif, Wausau Area C. of C. (pres. 1961-62). Notes editor U. Wis. Law Rev., 1939-40. Home: 910 13th St Wausau WI 54401 Office: 630 4th St Wausau WI 54401 Tel (715) 845-1151

TINNELL, ROBERT WAYNE, b. Minden, La., Oct. 10, 1937; A.A., Del Mar Coll., 1957; B.B.A., U. Tex., 1961, J.D., 1963. Admitted to Tex. bar, 1963; staff atty. El Paso Natural Gas Co., 1963-66, atty. Office of Gen. Counsel, 1966-68; individual practice law, El Paso, 1968—. Bd. dirs. Am. Heart Assn., El Paso, 1966-69; chmn. Citizens Environ. Council, 1975-76. Mem. Tex., El Paso bar assns., El Paso Trial Lawyers Assn., Phi Alpha Delta. Home: 4473 Eleanor St El Paso TX 79922 Office: 609 First National Bldg 109 N Oregon St El Paso TX 79901 Tel (915) 532-6381

TINNELLY, JOSEPH THOMAS, b. Albany, N.Y., Feb. 12, 1912; A.B., St. Joseph's Coll., 1934; certificate in theology St. Vincent's Seminary, 1939; J.D., St. John's U., 1942; LL.M., Harvard, 1943; J.S.D., Columbia, 1957. Ordained priest, Roman Catholic Ch., 1939; admitted to N.Y. bar, 1942, U.S. Supreme Ct. bar, 1962; faculty Sch. Law, St. John's U., 1947-59, dean, 1952-59, counsel Congregation of the Mission, 1959—, coordinator self study program, 1965-69, spl. counsel bd. trustees, 1965-69; gen. cons. Daughters of Charity of St. Vincent dePaul, NE province, Albany, 1959—, cons. to govt., Paris, 1972, Rome, 1974; chmn., counsel com. law sch. deans to advise N.Y. State Ct. Appeals on Rules for admission to the bar, 1954; chmn. Bklyn and N.Y. State Bar assns. to revise code of ethics, 1957. Mem. Am., N.Y. State, Bklyn. bar assns., Diocesan Attys. Assn., Cath. Lawyers Guild, Nat. Assn. Coll. and Univ. Attys., Phi Delta Phi. Author: Part-Time Legal Education, a Study of Night Law Schools, 1957; founder, editor The Cath. Lawyer, 1955-59; contbr. articles to legal jours. Home and Office: DePaul Provincial House 96 Menands Rd Albany NY 12204 Tel (518) 462-5593

TINTNER, LEONARD, b. Wilkes-Barre, Pa., June 3, 1930; B.A., Dickinson Coll., 1956, J.D., 1959. Admitted to Pa. bar, 1960; asso. firm Compton, Handler, Berman & Boswell, Harrisburg, Pa., 1959-65; partner firm Berman, Boswell, Snyder & Tintner, Harrisburg, 1965—; solicitor, recorder of deeds Dauphin County, Pa., 1964-72, spl. county solicitor, labor, 1973—; instr. Harrisburg Area Community Coll., 1971-74. Vice pres. Tri-County Welfare, Harrisburg; bd. dirs. Tri-County United Way, Harrisburg; active Jewish Community Center, Harrisburg, Harrisburg Citizens' Adv. Com., Dauphin County Child Care Service, Capitol Area Blue Cross, Harrisburg. Mem. Dauphin County (sec. 1964-73, pres. 1976—, del. 1972—), Pa. bar assns. Tel (717) 236-9377

TIPPY, ROGER W(ILLIAM), b. Urbana, Ill., Nov. 27, 1940; B.A., Stanford, 1962; LL.B., Yale, 1965. Admitted to D.C. bar, 1966, Mass. bar, 1970, Mont. bar, 1974; research asso. Conservation Found., Washington, 1965-67; counsel New Eng. River Basins Commn., Boston, 1968-71; asst. atty. gen. Commonwealth of Mass., Boston, 1971-73; staff atty. Mont. Legis. Council, Helena, 1973-77; vis. lectr. Northeastern U. Sch. Law, 1971-73; sec. adminstrv. code com. Mont. Legislature, 1975—. Mem. Am. Bar Assn., State Bar Mont. Contbr. articles to legal jours. Home: 804 Breckenridge St Helena MT 59601 Tel (406) 443-3677

TIPTON, VIRGIL RAY, b. Ada, Okla., Nov. 30, 1940; B.A., East Central State Coll., 1963; J.D., Okla. U., 1973. Admitted to Okla. bar, 1973; individual practice law, Pauls Valley, Okla., 1973—; city atty. Pauls Valley, 1975—. Home: 1605 S Walnut Pauls Valley OK 73075 Office: 101 S Willow Pauls Valley OK 73075 Tel (405) 238-6323

TIRANA, BARDYL RIFAT, b. Geneva, Dec. 16, 1937; A.B., Princeton, 1959; LL.B., Columbia, 1962. Admitted to D.C. bar, 1962, U.S. Supreme Ct. bar, 1974; trial atty. admiralty and shipping sect. U.S. Dept. Justice, Washington, 1962-64; asso. firm Amram, Hahn & Sundlun, Washington, 1965-68, partner, 1969-72; partner firm Sundlun, Tirana & Scher, Washington, 1972—. Mem. at large D.C. Bd. Edn., 1970-74; co-chairperson 1977 Inaugural Com. Mem. D.C. Bar Assn., Maritime Law Assn. Home: 3550 Tilden St NW Washington DC 20008 Office: Watergate 600 Bldg Washington DC 20037 Tel (202) 337-6800

TISINGER, DAVID HARVEY, b. Carrollton, Ga., May 8, 1937; B.S., Ga. Inst. Tech., 1958; J.D., U. Ga., 1963. Admitted to Ga. bar, 1962; partner firm Tisinger, Tisinger & Vance, Carrollton, 1963—; chmn. bd. dirs. Carrollton State Bank; instr. U. Ga., 1963. Mem. bd. regents Univ. System Ga., 1972—. Mem. Am., Ga. (exec. com. young lawyers sect., 1965-68) bar assns., Trial Attys. Am., Phi Beta Kappa. Office: 202 Tanner St Carrollton GA 30117 Tel (404) 832-3505

TISINGER, DAVID LOVING, b. Rose Hill, Tex., Mar. 21, 1915; B.A., Tex. A. and M. U., 1935; postgrad. Fordham U., 1935-36; LL.B., U. Tex., 1939. Admitted to Tex. bar, 1938, U.S. Supreme Ct. bar, 1971; lectr. law U. Tex., 1942-46; partner firm Hollers & Tisinger, Austin, Tex., 1942-46; partner firm Tisinger & Sloan, Austin, 1950-58; individual practice, Austin, 1958—. Bd. dirs. Legal Aid Clinic, 1942-45. Mem. State Bar of Tex., Tex. Aggie (mem. nominating com. 1975-76, chmn. 1976-77), Travis County (pres. 1956) bar assns. Asst. editor: Tex. Law Rev., 1937-39. Office: 206 First National Life Bldg Austin TX 78701 Tel (512) 478-0790

TITOLO, JOACHIM, b. Phila., May 7, 1910; LL.B., St. John's U., 1937, LL.M. in Internat. Law, 1938. Admitted to N.Y. bar, 1937; asst. dist. atty., N.Y., 1938-47; partner firm Titolo, Brulia and Werther, N.Y.C., 1948-50; exec. asst. U.S. atty. So. Dist. N.Y., 1950-52; dep. dist. dir. Office Price Stblzn., 1952-54; directing atty. firm Joseph Dean Edwards, N.Y.C., 1960-62; asst. counsel N.Y. State Crime Commn., 1963-65; asst. corp. counsel City of N.Y., 1965-71; individual practice law, Port Jervis, Hawaii, 1971—. Trustee, Queensbury Pub. Library, 1960-65. Mem. N.Y. State Bar Assn. 17 Office: 41 Sussex St Port Jervis HI 96743 Tel (814) 856-5166

TITONE, VITO JOSEPH, b. N.Y.C., July 5, 1929; B.A., N.Y. U., 1951; J.D., St. John's U., 1956. Admitted to N.Y. bar, 1957; partner firm Maltese & Titone, N.Y.C., 1958-68; justice N.Y. State Supreme Ct., 1969-76; asso. justice 2d dept. Appelate Div., 1976—; adj. prof. St. John's U., City U. N.Y.; counsel to pres. pro tem N.Y. State Senate, 1965, Judiciary Commn. N.Y. Constl. Conv., 1966; bd. dirs. criminal justice program St. John's U. Mem. Am., N.Y. State, Richmond County bar assns., Supreme Ct. Justices Assn., Justinian Soc. Home: 1 Duncan Rd Staten Island NY 10301 Office: Staten Island Chambers County Courthouse Saint George SI NY 10301 Tel (212) 390-5358

TITTSWORTH, CLAYTON MAGNESS, b. Tampa, Fla., Nov. 8, 1920; student U. Tampa, 1939-42; LL.B., Stetson Law Sch., 1951. Admitted to Fla. bar, 1951; partner firm Tittsworth & Tittsworth, Tampa, 1951-65, Brandon, Fla., 1964—. Mem. Hillsborough County (Fla.), Fla., Am. bar assns. Office: 111 E Brandon Blvd Brandon FL 33511 Tel (813) 689-7141

TITUS, HERBERT WILLIAM, b. Baker, Oreg., Oct. 17, 1937; B.A., U. Oreg., 1959; LL.B., Harvard, 1962. Admitted to Oreg. bar, 1962; trial atty. U.S. Dept. Justice, Washington and Kansas City, Mo., 1962-64; asst. prof. law U. Okla., Norman, 1964-66; asso. prof. law U. Oreg., Eugene, 1966-70, prof., 1970—; vis. prof. law U. Colo., 1970-71. Home: 3238 Edandale Ln Eugene OR 97405 Office: Law Sch U Oreg Eugene OR 97403 Tel (503) 686-3880

TITUS, LEWIS ROBERT, JR., b. Los Angeles, Mar. 27, 1942; B.A., U. So. Calif., 1968; J.D., Loyola U., Los Angeles, 1973. Admitted to Calif. bar, 1973; legal advisor Los Angeles County Sheriff's Dept., 1963-76; individual practice law, Altadena, Calif., 1976—. Mem. Calif. Law Enforcement Legal Advisors (v.p.). Tel (213) 798-3782

TITUS, REX BURDETTE, b. Weiser, Idaho, July 8, 1917; LL.B., U. Mo., 1940. Admitted to Mo. bar, 1940; individual practice law, Joplin, Mo., 1940-66; judge Mo. Ct. of Appeals, Springfield, 1966—. Mem. Am., Mo., Jasper County bar assns. Office: PO Box 1956 SSS Springfield MO 65805 Tel (417) 869-0485

TOAL, JEAN HOEFER, b. Columbia, S.C., Aug. 11, 1943; B.A., Agnes Scott Coll., 1965; J.D., U. S.C., 1968. Admitted to S.C. bar, 1968, U.S. Dist. Ct. bar S.C., 1968, U.S. Ct. Appeals 4th Circuit bar, 1969; asso. firm Haynsworth, Perry, Bryant, Marion & Johnstone, Greenville, S.C., 1968-70; asso. firm Belser, Belser, Baker & Barwick, Columbia, 1970-72; partner Belser, Baker, Belser, Barwick & Toal, Columbia, 1973—. Treas. Opportunities Industrialization Center S.C., 1971—; mem. S.C. Human Affairs Commn., 1972-74; rep. S.C. Legislature, 1974—, mem. judiciary com., 1974—, mem. rules com., 1977—. Mem. Am., S.C., Richland County bar assns., S.C. Def. Lawyers, Am. Judicature Soc. Author: S.C. Uniform Consumer Credit Code. Home: 2418 Wheat St Columbia SC 29205 Office: PO Box 11848 Columbia SC 29211 Tel (803) 799-9091

TOBIN, HAROLD WILLIAM, b. San Francisco, Apr. 7, 1922; student U. San Francisco, 1940, J.D., 1946. Admitted to Calif. bar, 1949; U.S. atty. War Crimes trials, Manila, Philippines, 1946-48, 51; asso. firm Hone & Lobree, San Francisco, 1949-51; asso. with Ben L. McKinley, 1951-53; partner firm Jacobsen & Tobin, San Francisco, 1953-57, Tobin & Ranson, San Francisco, 1957-67, individual practice law, San Francisco, 1970-71, Antioch, Calif., 1971—. Mem. San Francisco Republican County Central Com., 1949-51, 70-71; sec. Bay Area Rapid Transit Citizens Adv. Group, San Francisco, 1972-74; mem. Police Commn., Antioch, 1977—; bd. dirs. 120 Fellowship, Oakland, Calif., numerous chs., schs. in San Francisco area. Mem. Am. (award 1956), Contra Costa County (Calif.) bar assns., State Bar Calif. (pres. conf. of barristers 1957-58), Bar Assn. San Francisco (past dir.), Am. Trial Lawyers Assn., Barristers Club San Francisco (past pres.). Home: 1227 Putnam St Antioch CA 94509 Office: 2901 Lone Tree Way Suite C Antioch CA 94509 Tel (415) 757-9400

TOBIN, JOHN WHITEFIELD, b. Vinton, Iowa, June 23, 1895; student State U. Iowa, 1913-17. Admitted to Iowa bar, 1917; partner firm Tobin, Tobin & Tobin, Vinton, 1919-46, Tobin, Bordewick, Fischer & Fischer, and predecessors, Vinton, 1946—; judge Dist. Ct. Iowa, 1954-70; mem. Iowa Jud. Nominating Commn., 1971—. Nat. pres. Izaak Walton League Am., 1952-53. Mem. Am., Iowa, Benton County bar assns., Judicature Soc. Home: 1003 1st Ave Vinton IA 52349 Office: 110 E 4th St Vinton IA 52349 Tel (319) 472-2353

TOBIN, MICHAEL J., b. N.Y.C., Feb. 10, 1940; B.A., Providence Coll., 1961; J.D., St. John's U., 1965. Admitted to N.Y. bar, 1966; asso. firm Lines, Wilkens, Osborn & Beck, Rochester, N.Y., 1968-74, partner, 1974—. Mem. Monroe County (N.Y.) Legislature 24th Dist., Rochester, 1976—. Mem. Am., N.Y. bar assns. Office: 47 S Fitzhugh St Rochester NY 14614 Tel (716) 454-6480

TOBIN, RICHARD JOHN, b. Boston, Aug. 1, 1934; B.S., Boston Coll., 1956, LL.B., 1962. Admitted to Mass. bar, 1963, Conn. bar, 1967; asst. corp. counsel City of Boston, 1964-67; asst. gen. counsel New Haven Redevel. Agy., 1967-68; partner firm Commings & Lockwood, Stamford, Conn., 1968—. Mem. Stamford Conservation Commn., 1970-73; chmn. Stamford Transit Dist., 1973—. Mem. Conn., Stamford (1st v.p.) bar assns. Home: 389 Ocean Dr West Stamford CT 06902 Office: 1 Atlantic St Stamford CT 06901 Tel (203) 327-1700

TOBIN, ROBERT PERCY, b. Gilbert, Ill., Oct. 3, 1904; B.S., U. Ill., LL.B., 1929. Admitted to Ill. bar, 1929; various positions including adjuster, supr., claims mgr., legal dept. Zurich Ins. Co., Chgo., 1929-57; partner firm McBreen & Tobin, Chgo., 1957-75, McBreen, Tobin & Jacobson, Chgo., 1975—. Home: One Oak Brook Club Dr B-106 Oak Brook IL 60521 Office: 20 N Wacker Dr Room 1370 Chicago IL 60606 Tel (312) 332-6405

TOBIN, STANLEY ELLIOT, b. Boston, Sept. 13, 1930; s. B.A. cum laude, Harvard, 1953; LL.B., Yale, 1958. Admitted to Calif. bar, 1959, U.S. Supreme Ct. bar, 1963; partner firm Hill, Farrer & Burrill, Los Angeles, 1959—; annual guest lectr. Stanford Law Sch., 1961-76, vis. lectr., 1976; cons. in field. Mem. Calif. Gov.'s Adv. Council on Intergovt. Personnel Act. Mem. Am. Bar Assn., Harvard Club of So. Calif. (pres. 1970-71), Yale Law Sch. Alumni Assn., Boston Latin Sch. Alumni Assn. of Western States (pres. 1974-76). Contbr. articles to legal jours. Office: Union Bank Square 445 S Figueroa St Los Angeles CA 90071 Tel (13) 620-0460

TOBOLOWSKY, HERMINE DALKOWITZ, b. San Antonio, Jan. 13, 1921; student Incarnate Word Coll., 1937-38, U. San Antonio, 1939-40; LL.B., U. Tex., 1943. Admitted to Tex. bar, 1943; asso. firm Lang, Byrd, Cross & Ladon, San Antonio, 1943-47; individual practice law, San Antonio, 1947-51, Dallas, 1951—. Mem. speaker's adv. com. Tex. Ho. of Reps, 1970; mem. Nat. Health Adv. Council, 1966-69; Tex. state chmn. ratification Equal Rights Amendment, 1972; pres. Minnie L. Maffett Fund, 1976. Mem. Tex. Fedn. Bus. and Profl. Women's Club, Nat. Assn. Women Lawyers, Am., Tex. bar assns. Contbr. articles to legal jours.; named Tex. Woman of Year Tex. Women's Polit. Caucus, 1975. Home and Office: 6247 Desco St Dallas TX 75225

TOCKER, PAUL H., b. N.Y.C., Dec. 13, 1938; B.B.A., U. Miami, Coral Gables, Fla., 1960; J.D., Bklyn. Law Sch., 1965. Admitted to N.Y. bar, 1966; partner firm Borst Smith & Tocker, Schenectady, 1972—; law guardian Family Ct.; arbitrator Am. Arbitration Assn., Schenectady County Arbitration Procedure. Bd. dirs. Schenectady Boys' Club, Schenectady YMCA; v.p. B'nai B'rith, 1976-77. Mem. Am., Schenectady County, N.Y. State bar assns., Def. Research Inst., Schenectady C. of C., Schenectady County Hist. Soc. Office: 18 Jay St Schenectady NY 12305 Tel (518) 374-9151

TOCKMAN, GERALD, b. St. Louis, Sept. 29, 1937; B.A., Washington U., St. Louis, 1958, J.D., 1960. Admitted to Mo., Ill. bars, 1960, D.C. bar, 1971, U.S. Supreme Ct. bar, 1976; individual practice law, St. Louis, 1960—. Mem. Am., Mo., Ill., St. Louis bar assns., Am. Trial Lawyers Assn. Contbr. articles to legal jours. Office: 706 Chestnut St Suite 1010 Saint Louis MO 63101 Tel (314) 241-8909

TODD, DENNIS FOUSHEE, b. Sacramento, Jan. 12, 1937; B.S., Oreg. State U., 1959; LL.B., U. Calif., Berkeley, 1966. Admitted to Oreg. bar, 1967; since practiced in Portland, asso. firm Davies, Biggs, Strayer, Stoel & Boley, 1966-68; partner firm Smith, Todd & Ball, 1968—; mem. bd. dirs. Oreg. Selective Service Lawyers Panel, 1970. Bd. dirs. Tri-County chpt. March of Dimes, 1969-76, chmn. bd. 1975, mem. nat. council, 1975-76. Mem. Am. (state and local taxation com.), Oreg., Multnomah County bar assns., Am. Heritage Assn. (dir., exec. com. 1973—). Office: 400 Oregon Nat Bldg Portland OR 97205 Tel (503) 228-6375

TODD, HENRY CUNNINGHAM, b. San Francisco, Aug. 14, 1913; A.B., U. Calif., 1934, LL.B. (now J.D.), 1937. Admitted to Calif. bar, 1938, Ohio bar, 1946, U.S. Supreme Ct. bar, 1960; partner firm Todd & Todd, San Francisco, 1938-66, Gavin McNab, Schmulowitz, Sommer Aiken and Todd, San Francisco, 1966-69, Sommer and Todd, San Francisco, 1969-70, Erskine, Tulley, Boyd and Todd, San Francisco, 1970-72; individual practice law, San Francisco, 1972—; gen. counsel Bank of Canton Calif., 1967—, also dir.; guest lectr. U. San Francisco Labor Mgmt. Sch.; impartial labor arbitrator, 1954—. Mem. San Francisco Bar Found. (trustee 1977), Calif., San Francisco bar assns., Lawyers Club (pres. 1967), Hastings Coll. Alumni Assn. (pres. 1972-73), Atty. Probate Assn. (pres. 1977). Home: 351 Sherwood Way Menlo Park CA 94025 Office: Suite 502 625 Market St San Francisco CA 94105 Tel (415) 362-0520

TODD, JAMES DALE, b. Scotts Hill, Tenn., May 20, 1943; B.S., Lambuth Coll., 1965; M.Combined Scis., U. Miss., 1968; J.D., Memphis State U., 1972. Admitted to Tenn. bar, 1972, U.S. Supreme Ct. bar, 1975; asso. firm Waldrop, Hall, Tomlin, & Farmer, Jackson, Tenn., 1972-76, partner, 1976—. Bd. dirs. Jackson Boys' Club, 1975-76. Mem. Jackson-Madison County (sec.-treas. 1973-74), Tenn. bar assns., Jackson C. of C. (chmn. subcom. Goals for Jackson 1976). Home: 128 Mimosa Dr Jackson TN 38301 Office: 106 S Liberty St Jackson TN 38301 Tel (901) 427-2648

TODD, JOHN JOSEPH, b. South Saint Paul, Minn., Mar. 16, 1927; student St. Thomas Coll., 1944, 46-47; B.S. in Law, U. Minn., 1949, LL.B., 1950. Admitted to Minn. bar, 1951; practiced in South Saint Paul, 1951-72; judge Minn. Tax Ct., 1956-72; asso. justice Minn. Supreme Ct., 1972—. Chmn. Minn. Fair Trial-Free Press Council. Mem. Am., Minn. State (gov.), 1st Dist. (pres. 1960-61) bar assns., Minn. Trial Lawyers Assn. Home: 6659 Argenta Trail W Inver Grove Heights MN 55075 Office: Minn Supreme Ct State Capitol Saint Paul MN 55155 Tel (612) 296-2153

TODD, THOMAS NATHANIEL, b. Demapolis, Ala., Sept. 24, 1938; B.A. in Polit. Sci., So. U., Baton Rouge, 1959, J.D. magna cum laude, 1963. Admitted to La. bar, 1963, U.S. Ct. Mil. Appeals, 1965, Ill. bar, 1967, U.S. 7th Circuit Ct. Appeals bar, 1968, U.S. Dist. Ct. of No. Ill. bar, 1970, U.S. Supreme Ct. bar, 1971; atty. office of solicitor U.S. Dept. Labor, Washington, 1963-64; served with JAGC, U.S. Army, 1964-67; U.S. atty., Chgo., 1967-70; asst. prof. law, asst. dir. center for urban affairs Northwestern U., 1970-74; partner firm Tucker, Watson, Butler & Todd, Chgo., 1974—; dir. midwest task force for commn. report Search and Destroy, Black Panthers and Police, 1973; guest speaker in field. Pres. Chgo. chpt. So. Christian Leadership Conf., 1971; exec. v.p. Operation P.U.S.H., 1971-73. Mem. Chgo. Com. United Negro Coll. Fund, Ill. Black Legis. Clearing House (mem. adv. bd.), Com. for a Black Mayor Chgo., So. Univ. Alumni Assn., So. Univ. Found. Recipient Leadership citation Council for Met. Open Communities, 1970; certificate of achievement Kappa Alpha Psi, 1971, Afro-Am. Policemen's League, Chgo., 1971; Activist award SCLC, 1971; 7th award Independent Democratic Orgn., Chgo., 1971; Achievement award Men's Fedn., So. U., 1972; Harambee award Power, Inc., 1972; Outstanding Achievement award Nat. Consumer Info. Center, Washington, 1974; Black Excellence award P.U.S.H. Expo, 1974; Ark. Traveler award, Little Rock, 1975, Nat. Edn. award Phi Beta Sigma, Detroit, 1975; Appreciation award Chgo. chpt. Grambling Alumni Assn., 1975; Meritorious award Nat. Conf. Black Polit. Scientists, 1976; contbr. articles to pop. and profl. jours. Office: 1 N LaSalle St Suite 2525 Chicago IL 60602 Tel (312) 332-5751

TOHILL, ANTHONY BERNARD, b. Holbrook, N.Y., Nov. 20, 1942; J.D., State U. N.Y., 1970. Admitted to N.Y. bar, 1971, U.S. Supreme Ct. bar, 1975; law clk. to judge U.S. Dist. Ct., Buffalo, 1970-72; partner firm Tooker, Tooker & Esseks, Riverhead, N.Y., 1973—. Mem. N.Y., Suffolk County bar assns. Home: Baiting Hollow Calverton NY 11933 Office: 108 E Main St Riverhead NY 11901 Tel (516) 727-3277

TOKAIRIN, BERT SHIRO, b. Honolulu, Apr. 1, 1926; B.S., U. Hawaii, 1953; LL.B., U. Wis., 1955. Admitted to Hawaii bar, 1958; pub. prosecutor, Honolulu, 1955-64; individual practice of law, Honolulu, 1964—. Mem. Am., Hawaii bar assns., Am. Judicature Soc., Assn. of Trial Lawyers, Honolulu Japanese Jr. C. of C. (past pres.), Honolulu Japanese C. of C. (1st v.p., dir.). Home: 3536 Pinao St Honolulu HI 96822 Office: 700 Bishop St Honolulu HI 96813 Tel (808) 521-2951

TOLBERT, FRANK EDWARD, b. Bloomington, Ind., Dec. 20, 1928; A.B., Ind. U., 1952, LL.B., 1955. Admitted to Ind. bar, 1955; partner firm Miller, Tolbert, Hirschauer & Wildman, and predecessors, Logansport, Ind., 1955—. Pres. bd. trustees United Methodist Ch., Logansport, 1965-70; pres. Logansport YMCA-YWCA, 1968-71, Friends of Library, 1960—. Mem. Am., Ind. (ho. of dels. 1965—, bd. mgrs. 1970-72), Cass County (past pres.) bar assns., Am., Ind. trial lawyers assns. Home: 2600 E Broadway Logansport IN 46947 Office: 216 4th St Logansport IN 46947 Tel (219) 753-3195

TOLEDO, JOSE VICTOR, b. Arecibo, P.R., Aug. 14, 1931; B.A., U. Fla., 1950; B.L., U. P.R., 1955. Admitted to P.R. bar, Fed. bar, 1956; judge U.S. Dist. Ct., Dist. P.R., 1970—, now chief judge; asst. U.S. atty., Dist. P.R., 1960-61; partner firm Rivera Zayas, Rivera Cestero & Rua, San Juan, P.R., 1961-63, Segurola, Romero & Toledo, 1963-67, Toledo & Cordova, 1967-70; Mem., sec. P.R., Civil Rights Commn., 1969-70; chmn. municipal grievances com., San Juan, 1969-70. Home: 1917 Platanillo St Santa Maria San Juan PR 00927 Office: care US Courthouse Old San Juan PR 00904*

TOLES, EDWARD B., b. Columbus, Ga., Sept. 17, 1909; A.B., U. Ill., 1932; J.D., Loyola U., 1936. Admitted to Ill. bar, 1936, U.S. Supreme Ct. bar, 1960; individual practice law, Chgo., 1936-69; asst. atty. U.S. Housing Authority, D.C., 1939-40; asst. gen. counsel, corr., Chgo. Daily Defender, 1943-45; judge U.S. Bankruptcy Ct., No. Dist. of Ill., Chgo., 1969—. Mem. Nat. (com. on judiciary 1960-69), Am. (vice chmn. civil rights, responsibilities com. 1975-76), Fed., Chgo. (bd. mgrs. 1969-70), Cook County (past pres.), 7th Circuit bar assns., Am. Judicature Soc., Nat. Conf. Bankruptcy Judges, World Peace Through Law Center. Recipient numerous awards; contbr. articles to profl. jours.; editor Cook County Bar News, 1961-63; columnist Bench and Bar, Nat. Bar Assn. Bull., 1969-75. Home: 4800 Chicago Beach Dr Chicago IL 60615 Office: 219 S Dearborn St Chicago IL 60604 Tel (312) 435-5648

TOLL, MAYNARD JOY, b. Los Angeles, Sept 11, 1906; A.B., U. Calif. at Berkeley, 1927; LL.B. magna cum laude, Harvard, 1930; LL.D., Occidental Coll., 1963, Northrop U., 1975. Admitted to Calif. bar, 1930, since practiced in Los Angeles; partner firm O'Melveny & Myers, 1940—. Dir. Copley Press, Inc., Cyprus Mines Corp., Western Fed. Savs. & Loan Assn., Earle M. Jorgensen Co., Russell Reynold Assos. Inc. Chmn. Los Angeles Community Chest campaign, 1953; trustee Los Angeles City Bd. Edn., 1944-49, pres., 1947-48. Former trustee Los Angeles County Bar Found., Los Angeles County Mus. Art; trustee Hollywood Turf Club Asso. Charities, John R. and Dora Haynes Found., Hosp. Good Samaritan; bd. dirs. Automobile Club So. Cal., 1970—, v.p., 1971-73, chmn. bd., 1973-75; bd. dirs. Am. Automobile Assn., 1972-74; mem. exec. council Nat. Conf. Bar Presidents, 1968-70; bd. dirs. Council Legal Edn. Profl. Responsibility, 1973—, Council on Founds. Fellow Am. Coll. Probate Counsel, Am. Bar Found. (dir., pres. 1974-76); mem. Am., Los Angeles County (pres. 1963) bar assns., Inst. Jud. Adminstrn., Nat. Legal Aid and Defender Assn. (pres. 1966-70), State Bar Calif., Am. Judicature Soc. (chmn. bd. dirs. 1972-74), Calif. Alumni Assn. (past pres.). Home: 414 S Irving Blvd Los Angeles CA 90020 Office: 611 W 6th St Los Angeles CA 90017

TOLL, SEYMOUR I., b. Phila., Feb. 19, 1925; B.A., Yale, 1948, LL.B., 1951. Admitted to N.Y. State bar, 1953, Pa. bar, 1956; law clk. to judge U.S. Dist. Ct. So. Dist. N.Y., 1951-52; asso. firm Hartman & Craven, N.Y.C., 1952-55; asso. and mem. firm Richter, Lord, Toll & Cavanaugh, Phila., 1955-65, 69; individual practice law, Phila., 1965-68, 1969-74; mem. firm Toll & Ebby, Phila., 1975—. Pres. Phila. Citizens' Council on City Planning, 1967-69; pub. dir., exec. com. Phila. Housing Devel. Corp., 1967-72. Mem. Phila., Pa., Am., Fed. bar assns., Phi Beta Kappa. Author: Zoned American, 1969; contbr. articles to legal jours.; editor The Retainer, 1972-73. Home: 453 Conshohocken State Rd Bala-Cynwyd PA 19004 Office: Toll & Eby Suite 2040 1845 Walnut St Philadelphia PA 19103 Tel (215) 567-5770

TOLLE, NORMAN LOUIS, b. Bklyn., Jan. 31, 1948; B.A., State U. N.Y., 1969; J.D., N.Y. U., 1972. Admitted to N.Y. bar, 1973; asso. U.S. Equitable Life Assurance Soc., N.Y.C., 1972-73, atty., 1973-75, asst. counsel, 1975—. Mem. Assn. Bar City N.Y., N.Y. State Bar Assn., N.Y. County Lawyers Assn. Office: Equitable Life Assurance Soc 1285 Ave of the Americas New York City NY 10019 Tel (212) 554-2256

TOMAR, RICHARD THOMAS, b. Camden, N.J., Mar. 4, 1945; A.B., Columbia U., 1967; J.D., U. Pa., 1970. Admitted to D.C. bar, 1971, N.J. bar, 1971, Md. bar, 1976; asso. firm Denning and Wohlstetter, Washington, 1971; individual practice law, Washington, 1971; atty., cons. Rail Services Planning Office, Office Pub. Counsel, ICC, Washington, 1976-77. Mem. Superior Ct. Trial Lawyers Assn. (press officer 1974-75, legal officer 1976—), Assn. Trial Lawyers Am., D.C. Bar Assn. Office: 1775 K St NW Washington DC 20006 Tel (202) 293-7100

TOMASCHOFF, ERWIN ABRAHAM, b. Vienna, Austria, Dec. 31, 1931; A.B. with distinction, George Washington U., 1957; M.B.A., U. Chgo., 1958, J.D. with distinction, 1961. Admitted to Ill. bar, 1961, U.S. Supreme Ct. bar, 1970; instr. law U. Chgo. Law Sch., 1961; asso. firm Mayer, Brown & Platt, Chgo., 1961-66, partner firm 1967—. Mem. Am., Ill. State (chmn. subcom. secured transactions 1966-69), Chgo. (chmn. comml. code com. 1975-76) bar assns., Phi Beta Kappa, Order of Coif. Office: 231 S LaSalle St Chicago IL 60604 Tel (312) 782-0600

TOMASIN, JOHN, b. Detroit, May 28, 1924; J.D., Rutgers U., 1950. Admitted to N.J. bar, 1950, U.S. Supreme Ct. bar, 1956; individual practice law, Union City, N.J.; judge West New York, N.J., 1960-71; town atty., West New York, 1971-75; dept. county counsel Hudson County, N.J., 1975—; town atty., Guttenberg, N.J., 1954—. Mem. Hudson County, N.J. State, Am. bar assns., North Hudson Lawyers Club (pres. 1966), Disabled Am. Vets. (N.J. State judge adv. 1954—). Home: 112A 56th St West New York NJ 07093 Office: 4800 Kennedy Blvd Union City NJ 07087 Tel (201) 863-1821

TOMASULO, NICHOLAS ANGELO, b. N.Y.C., Oct. 18, 1907; A.B., Coll. City N.Y., 1930; LL.B., Columbia, 1933. Admitted to N.Y. bar, 1933; individual practice law, N.Y.C., 1933-39; dep. collector internal revenue and revenue agt., N.Y.C., 1939-43; atty. Office Chief Counsel, IRS, Washington, 1943-59; atty., legis. counsel staff Joint Com. Internal Revenue, U.S. Congress, Washington, 1959-73; prof. Wayne State U. Law Sch., Detroit, 1973—. Mem. Fed., Am. bar assns. Contbr. articles, addresses to legal jours. and meetings. Home: 1010 Stafford Pl Detroit MI 48207 Office: Room 370 Wayne State Univ Law Sch Detroit MI 48202 Tel (313) 577-9362

TOMCZAK, ANTHONY CASIMIR, b. Chgo., Jan. 17, 1910; A.B., Loyola U., Chgo., 1931; J.D., Northwestern U., 1934. Admitted to Ill. bar, 1934, Calif. bar, 1944, U.S. Supreme Ct. bar, 1970; individual practice law, Chgo., 1934-43, Los Angeles, 1954-57; trial atty. Nat. Automobile and Casualty Ins. Co., Los Angeles, 1944, gen. mgr. claims and legal dept., 1945-46; gen. counsel Colonial Ins. Co., Los Angeles, 1947-53; presiding workers' compensation judge San Diego Dist., 1957—. Mem. Am., San Diego County bar assns., Am. Judicature Soc., State Bar Calif., Thomas More Soc. of San Diego, Compensation Ins. Attys. Assn. (pres. 1950), So. Calif. Conf. of Workers' Compensation Judges (pres. 1964). Home: 1039-A Coast Blvd La Jolla CA 92037 Office: 1350 Front St San Diego CA 92101 Tel (714) 236-7321

TOMLINSON, HERBERT WESTON, b. Upland, Pa., Feb. 11, 1930; B.S., Pa. State U., 1952, postgrad., 1956-57; J.D., Dickinson Sch. Law, 1960; postgrad. Temple U., 1969-73. Admitted to Pa. bar, 1961, U.S. Supreme Ct. bar, 1968; since practiced in Media, Pa.; individual practice law, 1961—; exec. dir. Legal Services Program

Delaware County (Pa.), 1966-68; pub. defender Delaware County, 1971-75; prof. bus. law Pa. State U., 1969-75, Widence Coll., 1971-76; prof. polit. sci. Delaware County Community Coll., 1971-75. Pres. Delaware County Community Concert Assn., 1970; auditor Burough of Media, 1975—; nat. dir. U.S. Jaycees, 1966; Rep. candidate for U.S. Congress, 1976; bd. dirs., legal counsel Community Arts Center, 1976—; pres. Historic Delaware County Found., 1970. Mem. Am., Pa., Delaware County bar assns., Am. Arbitration Assn., AAUP, Pa. Trial Lawyers Assn., Assn. Trial Lawyers Am., Nat. Assn. Securities Dealers, Delaware County Real Estate Bd., Am. Legion (comdr. 1969). Home: 320 N Providence Rd Media PA 19063 Office: 8 W Front St Media PA 19063 Tel (215) LO6-9097

TOMLINSON, ROBERT JOHN, b. Detroit, May 4, 1936; B.A., U. Mich., 1958; J.D. Wayne State U., 1961. Admitted to Mich. bar, 1959, Wash. bar, 1972; internat. counsel Parke-Davis & Co., Detroit, 1962-67; asso. firm Heritier & Abbott, Detroit, 1968; asso. counsel Mich. Consol. Gas Co., Detroit, 1969-70; v.p.-legal Wash. Natural Gas Co., Seattle, 1971—; asso. prof. law Wayne State U., 1964-68, U. Wash., 1972—. Mem. Wash. State, Seattle-King County, Am. bar assns. Home: 8533 SE 76th Pl Mercer Island WA 98040 Office: PO Box 1869 815 Mercer St Seattle WA 98111 Tel (206) 622-6767

TOMLJANOVICH, ESTHER MOELLERING, b. Galt, Iowa, Nov. 1, 1931; LL.B., William Mitchell Coll. Law, 1955. Admitted to Minn. bar, 1955; asst. revisor statues State of Minn., 1955-66, revisor of statutes, 1974-77; judge 10th Jud. Dist. Ct., Stillwater, Minn., 1977—; individual practice law, Lake Elmo, Minn., 1969-74. Mem. Bd. Edn., North St. Paul-Maplewood Schs., 1971-73; mem. Lake Elmo (Minn.) Planning Commn., 1969-73. Mem. Minn. Bar Assn., Bus. and Profl. Women's Assn. Office: Court House Stillwater MN 55155

TONACHEL, PIERRE ANTOINE, b. S.I., N.Y., July 11, 1931; A.B., Cornell U., 1952; J.D., Columbia, 1955. Admitted to N.Y. State bar, 1956, U.S. Supreme Ct. bar, 1967; asso. firm Patterson, Belknap & Webb, N.Y.C., 1956-61, Spear & Hill, N.Y.C., 1961-64; partner firm Upham, Meeker & Weithorn, N.Y.C., 1964-76, Baer, Marks & Upham, N.Y.C., 1976—; cons. Price Commn., Washington, 1972. Mem. Am., Fed. bar assns., Assn. Bar City N.Y. Home: 26 Bethune St New York City NY 10014 Office: 405 Lexington Ave New York City NY 10017 Tel (212) 344-1700

TONDEL, LAWRENCE CHAPMAN, b. N.Y.C., Apr. 9, 1946; A.B. with honors, Wesleyan U., 1968; J.D., U. Mich., 1971. Admitted to N.Y. State bar, 1972; asso. firm Brown, Wood, Ivey, Mitchell & Petty, N.Y.C., 1971—. Mem. N.Y. State, Am. bar assns., Assn. Bar City N.Y. Office: 1 Liberty Plaza New York City NY 10006 Tel (212) 349-7500

TONDRO, TERRY JAY, b. Santa Monica, Calif., May 7, 1938; A.B., Cornell U., 1961; LL.B., N.Y. U., 1967; M.Phil., Yale, 1973. Atty., Gen. Counsel's Office OEO, Washington, 1967-68; admitted to N.Y. bar, 1968; asso. firm Paul, Weiss, Goldberg, Rifkind, Wharton & Garrison, N.Y.C., 1968-69; asso. prof. law U. Conn. Sch. Law, West Hartford, 1973—; cons. on hist. preservation law Hartford (Conn.) Architecture Conservancy, 1975—. Mem. regional planning commn. Capitol Region Council Govts., Hartford, 1974—, vice chmn., 1975—; trustee Conn. Trust for Hist. Preservation, 1975—. Mem. N.Y., Conn. bar assns., Nat. Trust for Hist. Preservation. Author: Design Controls for Neighborhood Conservation, 1976. Office: 1800 Asylum Ave West Hartford CT 06117 Tel (203) 523-4841

TONDRYK, VINCENT W., JR., b. Chgo., July 21, 1917; B.S., DePaul U., 1939, J.D., 1941. Admitted to Ill. bar, 1941, Ind. bar, 1942; judge Circuit Ct. Cook County (Ill.), 1965—. Mem. Am., Ill., Chgo. bar assns., Advocates Soc. (Ill.), Nat. Advocates Soc. Home: 6800 N Jean Ave Chicago IL 60646 Office: Chicago Civic Center Chicago IL 60602 Tel (312) 443-5500

TONE, PHILIP WILLIS, b. Chgo., Apr. 9, 1923; B.A., U. Iowa, 1943, J.D., 1948; grad. fellow Yale Law Sch., 1948. Law clk. Justice Wiley Rutledge, Supreme Ct. U.S., 1948-49; admitted to Iowa bar, 1948, Ill. bar, 1950, D.C. bar, 1950; asso. firm Covington & Burling, Washington, 1949-50; asso., partner firm Jenner & Block, Chgo., 1950-72; judge U.S. Dist. Ct. for No. Dist. Ill., 1972-74, U.S. Ct. of Appeals for 7th Circuit, Chgo., 1974—; spl. counsel Nat. Commn. on Causes and Prevention Violence, 1968-69; sec., chmn. Ill. Supreme Ct. Rules Com., 1963-71. Jud. fellow Am. Coll. Trial Lawyers; mem. Am., Ill. (bd. govs. 1960-64), Chgo. (bd. mgrs., librarian 1966-69) bar assns., Am. Law Inst., Ill. Soc. Trial Lawyers, Am. Judicature Soc., Law Club Chgo., Legal Club Chgo. Author: (with Albert E. Jenner, Jr.) Historical and Practice Notes, Ill. Civil Practice Act and Supreme Court Rules, 1956, 68; contbr. articles to legal jours. Office: 219 S Dearborn St Chicago IL 60604 Tel (312) 435-5806

TONRY, RICHARD ALVIN, b. New Orleans, June 25, 1935; A.B. with honors in Edn., Springhill Coll., 1960, M.A. with honors in Philosophy, 1962; postgrad. (NDEA fellow) Georgetown U., 1961; J.D., Loyola U., 1967. Admitted to La. bar, 1967; sr. partner firm Tonry, Mumphrey & D'Antonio, Chalmette, La., 1967—. State rep. dist. 103, 1976—; chmn. Heart Fund, 1971-73; mem. New Orleans council Boy Scouts Am. Mem. La., Am., Fed. bar assns., La. Trial Lawyers Assn. Office: 9061 W Judge Perez Dr Chalmette LA 70043 Tel (504) 271-0472

TOOHILL, JOSEPH VINCENT, b. Wapella, Ill., Jan. 22, 1908; B.D., St. Louis U., 1931. Admitted to Ill. bar, 1931; individual practice law Canton, Ill., Farmington, Ill.; pres. Bank of Farmington, 1946-67, chmn. bd. dirs., 1967—. Mem. Ill. Bar Assn. Office: 74 E Fort St Farmington IL 61531 Tel (309) 245-2463

TOOKER, ROBERT LUCE, b. Riverhead, N.Y., June 21, 1929; B.A., Amherst Coll., 1951; LL.B., Yale, 1958. Admitted to N.Y. bar, 1958, U.S. Dist. Ct. bar, 1965, U.S. Supreme Ct. bar, 1967; partner firm Tooker, Tooker & Esseks, Riverhead, 1958—; dir. Suffolk County Nat. Bank; spl. atty. Town of Riverhead, 1960-64, pres., 1966-68, dir., 1964-71; mem. Central Suffolk Hosp. Assn., 1959-76. Mem. Suffolk County (dir. 1971-74), Am., N.Y. State bar assns. Home: 3 Waterview Ct Riverhead NY 11901 Office: 108 E Main St Riverhead NY 11901 Tel (516) 727-3277

TOOLE, BRUCE RYAN, b. Missoula, Mont., June 21, 1924; J.D., U. Mont., 1949. Admitted to Mont. bar, 1950, U.S. Dist. Ct. for Mont. bar, 1951, U.S. 9th Circuit Ct. Appeals bar, 1952; individual practice law, Missoula, 1950; dep. county atty., Missoula County (Mont.), 1952; asso. firm Crowley, Haughey, Hanson, Gallagher & Toole, Billings, Mont., 1951-59, partner, 1959—; mem. Gov.'s Advisory Council on Workmen's Compensation, State of Mont., 1972-74; bd. visitors U. Mont. Law Sch., 1971—. Sec. No. Rockies Regional Cancer Center, 1974—. Fellow Am. Coll. Trial Lawyers; mem. Internat. Assn. Ins. Counsel, Assn. Ins. Attys., Am. Yellowstone County (pres. 1973) bar assns., State Bar Mont. (trustee 1974-75, pres. 1977—). Home: 3019 Glacier Dr Billings MT 59102 Office: 500 Electric Bldg Billings MT 59101 Tel (406) 252-3441

TOOLE, EDWARD CHARLES, JR., b. Abington, Pa., May 31, 1937; B.S. in Indsl. Mgmt., LaSalle Coll., 1959; J.D., Villanova U., 1967. Admitted to Pa. bar, 1967, U.S. Supreme Ct. bar, 1970; clk. to Judge John Morgan Davis, U.S. Dist. Ct. Eastern Dist. Pa., 1967-69; asso. firm Clark, Ladner, Fortenbaugh & Young, Phila., 1969-73; partner firm Clark, Ladner, Fortenbaugh & Young, Phila., 1974—. Mem. Phila., Pa., Am. (pub. utility law and bus. and commerce sects.) bar assns. Office: 1700 Widener Bldg 1339 Chestnut St Philadelphia PA 19107 Tel (215) 564-5300

TOOLEY, JOHN FRANCIS, JR., b. New Orleans, Aug. 2, 1930; B.A., Tulane U., 1956, LL.B., 1958. Admitted to La. bar, 1958; partner firm Briere, Tooley & Stephenson, New Orleans, 1958-61; partner firm Deutsch, Kerrigan & Stiles, New Orleans, 1961-72; partner firm John F. Tooley, Jr. & Assos., Gretna, La., 1973—. Past pres. Terrytown Civic Assn., Gretna, 1964-65; officer La. State Fireman's Assn.; past pres. Terrytown Vol. Fire Dept., 1970-72. Mem. Am., La. State, Jefferson Parish bar assns., La. Trial Lawyers Assn., Am. Judicature Soc., Civil Service League, La. Dist. Attys. Assn., La. Assn. Def. Counsel. Home: 2164 Guardian Ave Gretna LA 70053 Office: 418 Wright Ave Gretna LA 70053 Tel (504) 367-9935

TOOMEY, DANIEL EDWARD, b. Bklyn., Sept. 17, 1942; A.B. in Econs., St. Peter's Coll., Jersey City; J.D., Georgetown U. Admitted to D.C. bar, 1968, U.S. Supreme Ct. bar, 1973; law clk. D.C. Ct. Appeals, 1967-68; asst. U.S. atty. for D.C., 1968-72; asso. firm Sachs, Greenebaum & Tayler, Washington, 1972-74, partner, 1974—. Mem. Am. Bar Assn., D.C. Bar Assn. (vice chmn. young lawyers sect. 1975-76). Assn. U.S. Attys. Assn. for D.C. Home: 3222 Pickwick Ln Chevy Chase MD 20015 Office: 1620 Eye St NW Washington DC 20006 Tel (202) 872-9090

TOOMEY, DAVID JOHN, b. Waterbury, Conn., Aug. 10, 1937; B.S. in Physics, Fairfield U., 1959; LL.B., Fordham U., 1963. Admitted to N.Y. bar, 1964, U.S. Supreme Ct. bar, 1967; partner firm Pennie & Edmonds, N.Y.C., 1969—. Commr., Montclair (N.J.) Redevel. Agy., 1975—. Mem. Am. Bar Assn., N.Y. Patent Law Assn. Office: 330 Madison Ave New York City NY 10017 Tel (212) 986-8686

TOOMEY, JOHN MARTIN, b. Lewiston, Maine, Sept. 8, 1932; A.B., Bates Coll., 1954; J.D., U. Mich., 1960. Admitted to Mich. bar, 1961, U.S. Supreme Ct. bar, 1967; partner firm Dulgeroff & Toomey, Ann Arbor, Mich., 1961-67; individual practice law, Ann Arbor, 1967-69; partner firm Toomey & Francis, Ann Arbor, 1969-71, Toomey & Hamilton, Ann Arbor, 1971-72; individual practice law, Ann Arbor, 1972-75; partner firm Toomey & Stewart, Ann Arbor, 1975—. Mem. Mich., Washtenaw County bar assns. Office: 210 E Huron St Suite C Ann Arbor MI 48108 Tel (313) 769-2130

TOOMEY, PAUL REED, b. Iowa City, Iowa, July 1, 1936; B.A., U. Miami, 1958; J.D., Harvard U., 1961. Admitted to Fla. bar, 1962, Calif. bar, 1971; asso. firm Scott, McCarthy, Steel, Hector & Davis, Miami, Fla., 1963-68; chief tax div. Office Atty. Gen. Fla., Tallahassee, 1968-69; corp. counsel Lockheed Aircraft Corp., Burbank, Calif., 1969-76; Mem. Am., Fla., Calif., Los Angeles County bar assns. Home: 2840 Gulf Dr Sanibel Island FL 33957 Tel (813) 472-2411

TOON, CASSIUS HARRY, b. Johnson City, Tenn., May 11, 1938; A.B., W.Va. Wesleyan Coll., 1962; J.D., W.Va. U., 1969. Admitted to W.Va. bar, 1969, U.S. Supreme Ct. bar, 1974; staff atty., chief hearing examiner, counsel Gas Pipeline Safety div. Pub. Service Commn. of W.Va., 1969-74; v.p. govt. affairs W.Va. Mfrs. Assn., Charleston, 1974—. Mem. Am. Bar Assn., W.Va. State Bar. Home: 2919 Noyes Ave Charleston WV 25304 Office: Suite 730 Charleston National Plaza Charleston WV 25301 Tel (304) 342-2123

TOOTHMAN, JAMES EDWARD, b. Oakland, Calif., Mar. 25, 1946; B.S., U. San Francisco, 1968; M.B.A., U. Santa Clara, 1969, J.D., 1972. Admitted to Calif. bar, 1973; since practiced in San Jose; asso. firm Donovan, Smith, Anderson & Toothman and predecessor firms, 1973-74, partner, 1975-76; partner firm Toothman, Whitaker, Sprinkles & Sinseri, 1976—. Bd. dirs. Santa Clara County Children's Home Soc., 1975, Santa Clara County Heart Assn., 1976. Mem. Calif., Santa Clara County bar assns. Home: 17321 Valley Oak Dr Monte Sereno CA 95113 Office: 2 N 2d St San Jose CA 95113 Tel (408) 275-6020

TORBET, JOHN RANDOLPH, b. New River, N.C., Nov. 5, 1943; B.A., U. Colo., 1965, J.D., 1968. Admitted Colo. bar, 1968, U.S. Supreme Ct. bar, 1972; partner firm Evans, Peterson, Torbet & Briggs, Colorado Springs, Colo., 1969-75; individual practice law Colorado Springs, 1975—; municipal judge City of Fountain (Colo.), 1972—; instr. police sci. and hotel law El Paso Community Coll., Colorado Springs, 1971-73. Vol. probation counsellor Colorado Springs Municipal Ct., 1972, El Paso County Dist. Ct., 1971. Mem. Am., Colo., El Paso County bar assns., Colo. Trial Lawyers Assn., Colo. Municipal Judges Assn. (dir. 1976—). Recipient certificate of merit for probation vol. 4th judicial dist. El Paso County Dist. Ct., 1971. Office: 105 E Vermijo Ave Suite 461 Colorado Springs CO 80930

TORGERSON, KENNETH ALFRED, b. Mpls., Nov. 15, 1941; B.A., Dartmouth, 1963; J.D., Northwestern U., 1966. Admitted to Ohio bar, 1966; asso. firm Baker, Hostetler & Patterson, Cleve., 1966-74, partner, 1975—; with JAGC, U.S. Army, 1967-70. Mem. Am., Ohio, Cleve. bar assns. Office: 1956 Union Commerce Bldg Cleveland OH 44115 Tel (216) 621-0200

TORII, DENNIS ROGER, b. Chgo., Apr. 3, 1944; B.A., Northeastern Ill. U., 1966; J.D., Chgo.-Kent Coll. Law, 1971. Admitted to Ill. bar, 1971, U.S. Supreme Ct. bar, 1975; partner firm Lanzillotti, Storto, Torii and Russo, Berwyn, Ill., 1976—. Mem. Am., Ill., Chgo., West Suburban, DuPage County bar assns., Delta Theta Phi. Office: 3415 S Harlem Ave Berwyn IL 60402

TORKELSON, WILLIAM EDWARD, b. Madison, Wis., Oct. 23, 1908; Ph.B. in Econs., U. Wis., 1930, LL.B., 1933, J.D., 1966. Admitted to Wis. bar, 1933, U.S. Supreme Ct. bar, 1950; asso. firm Richmond Jackman Wilkie & Toebaas, Madison, 1932-44; asst. atty. gen. state of Wis., 1944-49; chief counsel Pub. Service Commn. of Wis., 1949-74; ret., 1974; mem. legal adv. com. Nat. Power Survey, 1963-64. Mem. Am., Dane County, Fed. Power bar assns. Recipient certificate of pub. service FPC, 1964. Home: 4157 Manitou Way Madison WI 53711

TORMEY, THOMAS JAMES, b. Grundy Center, Iowa, Jan. 24, 1925; B.A., B.S., U. Ariz., 1953, J.D., 1956. Admitted to Ariz. bar, 1956, U.S. Supreme Ct., 1960; partner firm Gatewood & Greenway, Tucson, 1956-59; asst. city atty., Tucson, 1959-61; prof., law librarian U. Ariz., 1961—. Author: (with C.M. Smith) Summary of Arizona Community Property Law, 1964. Home: 811 E E 1st St Tucson AZ 85719 Office: U Ariz Tucson AZ 85721 Tel (602) 884-1547

TORNQUIST, LEROY JOHN, b. Chgo., Apr. 2, 1940; B.S., Northwestern U., 1962, J.D., 1965. Admitted to Ill. bar, 1965; asso. firm King, Robin, Gale & Pillinger, Chgo., 1966-71, of counsel, 1971-76; asso. dean, dir. trial advocacy Loyola U. Sch. Law, 1976—; pres. Ct. Practice Inst., 1974. Mem. Cook County (Ill.) Bd. Sch. Trustees, Chgo., 1971-76; alderman City of Park Ridge (Ill.), 1971-75. Mem. Ill., Chgo., Am. bar assns. Home: 410 S Fairview St Park Ridge IL 60068 Office: 41 E Pearson St Chicago IL 60603 Tel (312) 670-2933

TORO, AMALIA MARIA, b. Hartford, Conn., Nov. 6, 1920; B.A., U. Conn., 1942; J.D., Yale, 1944. Admitted to Conn. bar, 1944; asso. firm Wiggin and Dana, New Haven, 1944-46; atty. Office Sec. State, Conn., 1946-75; individual practice law, Hartford, 1975—. Mem. Ford Found. Com. on Voting and Election Systems, 1971-72; mem. State Employees's Retirement Commn., 1957-75; mem. Conn. Gov.'s Commn. Employment of the Handicapped, 1973—. Mem. Conn. Assn. Municipal Attys. (past pres.), Conn. State Employees Assn. (Outstanding State Employee award 1973), Greater Hartford U. Conn. Alumni Assn., Conn. Bar Assn., Bus. and Profl. Women's Club. (Woman of Year award 1969). Recipient AMITA (Am.-Italian) award, 1970, Italian-Am. Gold Medal award, 1975. Home: 17 Clarkridge Rd Wethersfield CT 06109 Office: 234 Pearl St Hartford CT 06103 Tel (203) 522-0173

TORO, EUGENE FRANCIS, b. Providence, July 9, 1933; A.B., Providence Coll., 1955; J.D., Boston U., 1959. Admitted to R.I. bar, 1959, U.S. Supreme Ct. bar, 1965; asst. pub. defender State of R.I., 1961-74; pres. firm Toro Law Assos., Providence, 1971—; mem. R.I. Gov.'s Commn. on Criminal Responsibility of Mentally Ill, 1969—; lectr. law Providence Coll., 1970-71, Roger Williams Coll., 1969. Bd. dirs. Sophia Little Home, Cranston, R.I., 1961-74, sec., 1970-73. Fellow Am. Coll. Trial Lawyers; mem. Am., R.I. (chmn. criminal law sect. 1976—), R.I. Def. bar assns., Am. Trial Lawyers Assn. (chmn. criminal law sect. 1973—), Justinian Soc. Home: 400 Varnum Dr Warwick RI 02818 Office: 1808 Industrial Bank Bldg Providence RI 02903 Tel (401) 351-7752

TORREGROSSA, JOSEPH ANTHONY, b. Bklyn., Sept. 23, 1944; A.B. summa cum laude, Villanova U., 1966, J.D. magna cum laude, 1969. Admitted to N.Y. bar, 1969, Pa. bar, 1970, U.S. Supreme Ct. bar, 1975; law clk. U.S. Dist. Ct. for Eastern Pa., 1969-71; asso. firm Morgan, Lewis & Bockius, Phila., 1971—. Bd. dirs. Prisoner's Rights Council, Phila., 1970—. Mem. Am., Pa., Phila. bar assns. Contbr. articles to law revs. Home: 315 Riverview Rd Swarthmore PA 19081 Office: 2100 Fidelity Bldg Philadelphia PA 19109 Tel (215) 491-9620

TORTORELLA, ANTHONY NATALE, b. Boston, Dec. 12, 1946; B.S. magna cum laude, Boston Coll., 1967, J.D., 1971; LL.M. in Taxation, N.Y. U., 1974. Admitted to Mass. bar, 1971, U.S. Tax Ct., 1973, U.S. Ct. Claims, 1974, U.S. Supreme Ct. bar, 1974; law clk. to judge U.S. Ct. Claims, Washington, 1974-76; adj. asst. prof. Bentley Coll., Waltham, Mass., 1977—. Mem. Am., Boston bar assns., Beta Gamma Sigma, Mensa. Office: 93 Langley Rd Boston MA 02135 Tel (617) 254-8090

TOSCANO, JOHN P., JR., b. Westerly, R.I., July 18, 1937; A.B., Providence Coll., 1959; J.D. cum laude, New Eng. Law Sch., Boston, 1963. Admitted to Mass. bar, 1964, R.I. bar, 1965, U.S. Supreme Ct. bar, 1969; individual practice law, Westerly, R.I., 1965—; mem. Pub. Defender's Office State of R.I., 1968-74; asst. pub. defender, probate judge, Hopkinton, R.I., 1972-74; asst. town solicitor, Town of Charlestown, 1976-77, town solicitor, probate judge, 1977—. Mem. R.I., Mass., Washington County Bar Assns. Home: 28 Newton Ave Westerly RI 02891 also 473 Atlantic Ave Misquamicut RI 02891 Office: 23 Canal St Westerly RI 02891 Tel (401) 596-1233

TOTTEN, RANDOLPH FOWLER, b. Washington, June 20, 1943; B.A., Yale U., 1965; LL.B., U. Va., 1968. Admitted to Va. bar, 1968; clk. Va. Supreme Ct., 1968-69; asso. firm Hunton & Williams, Richmond, Va., 1969—. Trustee Ch. Schs. Diocese of Va., 1974—. Mem. Am., Va., Richmond bar assns. Office: 707 E Main St Richmond VA 23219 Tel (804) 788-8281

TOWE, THOMAS EDWARD, b. Cherokee, Iowa, June 25, 1937; B.A., Earlham Coll., 1959, U. Paris, 1956; LL.B. with honors, U. Mont., 1962; LL.M., Georgetown U., 1965; postgrad. U. Mich., 1965—. Admitted to Mont. bar, 1962; capt. JAGC, 1962-65; practiced law, Billings, Mont., 1967—; mem. Mont. Ho. of Reps., 1971, 73-74; mem. Mont. Senate, 1975—, chmn. judiciary com., 1975, chmn. state adminstrn. com., 1977, mem. consumer counsel com. Former mem. bd. dirs. Mont. Consumer Affairs Council; bd. dirs. Rimrock Guidance Found., Dist. Youth Guidance Home of Billings, Concern, Inc., Regional Community Services for Developmentally Disabled; adv. com. Mont. Crime Control Bd. Mem. Mont., Yellowstone County bar assns., Billings C. of C. Contbr. articles to legal jours. Home: 2640 Burlington Ave Billings MT 59102 Office: 2525 6th Ave N Billings MT 59101 Tel (406) 248-7337

TOWER, PHILIP CLARK, b. Phoenix, Feb. 2, 1945; B.A., Princeton U., 1966; J.D., U. Ariz., 1969. Admitted to Ariz. bar, 1969, Calif. bar, 1972; served with Judge Adv. Gen. Corps U.S. Marine Corps, 1969-72; asso. firm Evans, Kitchel & Jenckes, Phoenix, 1973-76; mem. firm McLoone, Theobald & Galbut, Phoenix, 1976—. Bd. dirs. Phoenix YMCA, 1974—; chmn. law explorers task force Theodore Roosevelt Council Boy Scouts Am. Office: 2627 E Thomas Rd Suite 2A Phoenix AZ 85016 Tel (602) 957-1810

TOWER, TIMOTHY WARD, b. Petaluma, Calif., July 29, 1945; B.A., U. Calif., Davis, 1967; J.D., U. Calif., Berkeley, 1970. Admitted to Calif. bar, 1971; clk. firm Gray, Cary, Ames & Fry, San Diego, 1970, asso., 1971-76; partner firm Rentto, Pate & Tower, San Diego, 1976—. Adviser to Explorer Post, Boy Scouts Am., 1975—; mem. youth activities com. San Diego Jaycees, 1975. Mem. Am., Calif., San Diego County bar assns. Recipient Am. Jurisprudence awards U. Calif., 1967-68; research editor Calif. Law Rev., 1969-70. Office: 1600 Bank of California Plaza 110 W A St San Diego CA 92101 Tel (714) 238-1002

TOWEY, EDWARD BERNARD, b. Denver, July 16, 1931; B.S., Georgetown U., 1953; LL.B., U. Colo., 1956. Admitted to Colo. bar, 1957, U.S. Supreme Ct. bar, 1971; asso. firm Davis, Graham & Stubbs, Denver, 1956-61; asst. dist. atty. 17th Jud. Dist., Colo., 1961-67; dep.

pub. defender, 1968; sr. partner firm Towey & Zak, Denver, 1961—. Democratic precinct com. chmn. Jefferson County, Colo., 1968-72. Fellow Am. Coll. Trial Lawyers; mem. Colo., Adams County bar assns., Am., Colo. trial lawyers assns., Order of Coif. Contbg. author: Neuropsychological Testing in Organic Brain Dysfunction; contbr. articles to Rocky Mountain Law Rev. Home: 11480 W 27th Pl Lakewood CO 80215 Office: 1701 W 72d Ave Suite 210 Denver CO 80221 Tel (303) 428-7411

TOWNE, VERNON WEST, b. Rosalia, Wash., Sept. 22, 1910; A.B., Wash. State U., 1932; J.D., U. Wash., 1937. Admitted to Wash. bar, 1937; asst. librarian Supreme Ct. Law Library, Olympia, Wash., 1937-38; practice law, Rosalia, 1938-40, Seattle, 1945-61; reporter Supreme Ct. Wash., Olympia, 1941-45; judge Municipal Ct. Seattle, 1961—; lectr. Grad. Sch. U. Wash., 1968—. Trustee, Univ. Presbyn. Ch. Found., Presbyn. Ministries, Inc. Mem. Am. (First Place awards for improvements in ct. procedures 1962-65, 68), Wash., Whitman County (pres. 1939-40), Seattle bar assns., Am. Judicature Soc., N.Am. Judges Assn., Sigma Alpha Epsilon, Phi Kappa Phi, Alpha Sigma Rho. Author: Washington Practice Methods, 1956, rev. edit., 1976. Home: 10514 11th St NW Seattle WA 98177 Office: 111 Pub Safety Bldg Seattle WA 98104 Tel (206) 625-2701

TOWNSEND, EDWIN CLAY, b. Parsons, Tenn., Nov. 22, 1924; LL.B., Cumberland U., 1947; A.B., 1948; J.D., Samford U., Birmingham, Ala., 1969. Admitted to Tenn. bar, 1947, U.S. Dist. Ct. bar, 1949; individual practice law, Parsons, Tenn., 1947—; sr. partner firm Townsend & Townsend; pub. Parsons News Leader, 1952-63; pres. Parsons Land Title Co. Inc., Townsend Enterprises Inc., Parsons East Inc., TLT Corp.; v.p., dir. Decatur Land Corp.; dir. Parsons Printing Corp. Mem. Am., Tenn. (bd. govs. 1972-75, ho. dels.), 22d Judicial Circuit (past pres.), Five County bar assns., Am. Judicature Soc., Tenn. Trial Lawyers Assn., Tenn. Def. Lawyers Assn. Home: Perryville Hwy Parsons TN 38363 Office: 111 W 2d St Parsons TN 38363 Tel (901) 847-3111

TOWNSEND, HAROLD LEE, b. Fayetteville, N.C., July 13, 1922; B.A., Wake Forest U.; J.D., U. Va. Admitted to Va. bar, 1948; atty. Commonwealth of Va., 1960-64; individual practice law, Emporia, Va., 1948—. Mayor of Emporia, 1960-64; mem. Emporia Airport Commn., 1958-73. Mem. Va., Am. trial lawyers assns., Am. Judicature Soc., Am. Soc. Law and Medicine. Named Man of Year, Boy Scouts Am., 1972, 73, 47. Home: 802 Brunswick Ave Emporia VA 23847 Office: 300 S Main St Emporia VA 23847 Tel (804) 634-6111

TOWNSEND, RICHARD CRAIG, b. LaCrosse, Wis., Apr. 11, 1945; B.S. in Accounting, U. Ill., 1967, J.D., 1971. Admitted to Ill. bar, 1971; tax supr. Touche Ross & Co., Chgo., 1971—; financial asst. Ogilvie for Gov., 1972. Mem. exec. com. Ill. Rep. Tom MacNamara, 1974, 76. Mem. Ill., Am. bar assns., Ill. Soc. C.P.A.'s, Am. Inst. C.P.A.'s. Contbr. articles to profl. jours. Home: 201 E Chestnut St Chicago IL 60611 Office: 111 E Wacker Chicago IL 60601 Tel (312) 644-8900

TOWSE, SETH, b. White Plains, N.Y., Nov. 15, 1934; A.B., Dartmouth, 1960; J.D., Cornell U., 1963. Admitted to N.Y. bar, 1965; law apprentice N.Y. State Dept. Law, Albany, 1963-65, dep. asst. atty. gen., 1965, asst. atty. gen., 1965-67; asso. firm DeGraff, Foy, Conway & Holt-Harris, Albany, 1967-69; individual practice law, Albany, 1969—; asst. counsel Civil Service Employees Assn., 1967-69; counsel N.Y. State Police Benevolent Assn., 1969-72; mem. fact-finding panel N.Y. State Pub. Employment Relations Bd., 1973—. Trustee Albany Acad., 1972-75. Mem. Am., N.Y. State, Albany County bar assns., Cornell Law Assn., Dartmouth Club of Eastern N.Y. (sec.-treas. 1973—). Home and Office: 8 Marian Ln Albany NY 12211 Tel (518) 436-7857

TOY, C. HENRY, b. Wilmington, Del., June 12, 1945; B.A., Tufts U., 1967; J.D., U. Denver, 1970. Admitted to Colo. bar, 1971; clk. David B. Richeson, 1968-71; individual practice law, Lakewood, Colo., 1972—. Home: PO Box 585 Pinecliffe CO 80471 Office: 7314 W Colfax Ave Lakewood CO 80215 Tel (303) 232-2838

TRABISH, STEVEN EDWARD, b. Chgo., Aug. 20, 1945; B.A., U. Calif. at Los Angeles, 1967; J.D., Loyola U., 1970. Admitted to Calif. bar, 1971; asso. firm Flint & MacKay, Los Angeles, 1970-71, Miller, Clearwaters & Trabish, Los Angeles, 1972-75, Trabish, Caplan & Peterson, Marina del Rey, Calif., 1976—. Mem. Am., Los Angeles, Marina del Rey (past pres.) bar assns., St. Thomas More Law Assn. Office: 4676 Admiralty Way Suite 902 Marina del Rey CA 90291 Tel (213) 822-2818

TRABUE, KENNETH ELLSWORTH, b. Alton, Ill., Aug. 13, 1933; B.S. in Indsl. Econs., Purdue U., 1956; J.D., Ind. U., 1961. Admitted to Ind. bar, 1961, Va. bar, 1962; multiple line adjuster St. Paul Fire and Marine Ins. Co., Indpls., 1956-61, claims mgr., Roanoke, Va., 1962-64; asso. firm Hunter, Fox & Fox, Roanoke, 1965-66; partner firm Hunter, Fox & Trabue, Roanoke, 1967-77; judge 23d Jud. Circuit Va., 1977—; faculty mem. Va. Western Community Coll., 1972-75. Pres., Cave Spring Jaycees, 1964-65; group chmn. legal sect. United Fund of Roanoke Valley, 1970, chmn. profl. div., 1971, chmn. services div., 1972; pres. Hunting Hills Homeowners Assn., 1975-76. Mem. Am., Va., Roanoke (dir. 1970-73) bar assns., Va. State Bar, Va. Trial Lawyers Assn. (pres. 1976-77), Def. Research Inst., Va. Assn. Def. Attys. (sixth dist. v.p. 1971). Home: 5207 Archer Dr SW Roanoke VA 24014 Office: PO Box 211 Roanoke VA 24003 Tel (703) 981-2437

TRACI, DONALD PHILIP, b. Cleve., Mar. 13, 1927; B.S. cum laude, Coll. of Holy Cross, Worcester, Mass., 1955; J.D. magna cum laude, Cleve. State U., 1955. Admitted to Ohio bar, 1955, U.S. Supreme Ct. bar,; partner firm Spangenberg, Shibley, Traci & Lancione, Cleve.; lectr. in field. Fellow Internat. Acad. Trial Lawyers; mem. Am., Ohio Greater Cleve., Cuyahoga County bar assns., Assn. Trial Lawyers Am., Ohio, Cleve. acads. trial lawyers, Am. Judicature Assn., Catholic Lawyers Guild. Home: 10416 Lake Ave Cleveland OH 44102 Office: 1500 National City Bank Bldg Cleveland OH 44114 Tel (216) 696-3232

TRACT, E. JAY, b. Phila., June 5, 1947; B.S., LaSalle Coll., Phila., 1969; J.D., Villanova U., 1972. Admitted to Pa. bar, 1972; law clk. to Hon. Joseph L. McGlynn, Ct. Common Pleas, Phila., 1972-73; partner firm Hoopes and Tract, and predecessor, Reading, Pa., 1973—. Mem. Nat. Jury Project, ACLU. Office: 212 N 6th St Reading PA 19603 Tel (215) 376-7411

TRACY, EARL WALTER, JR., b. San Antonio, Jan. 2, 1923; student Tex. A. and M. U., 1940-43, Syracuse U., 1943-44, San Antonio Coll., 1948-49; B.S. in Petroleum Engring., 1950; LL.B., St. Mary's U., 1957, J.D., 1967. Admitted to Tex. bar, 1957, U.S. Supreme Ct. bar, 1971; resevoir engr. Petroleum Service Co., San Antonio, 1949-60; partner firm Tracy & Cook, San Antonio, 1960—; municipal judge Olmas Park (Tex.), 1965—. Mem. Tex., San Antonio bar assns., Cosmo Club. Contbr. articles to legal jours. Home: 6800 Moss Oak San Antonio TX 78229 Office: 1 Park 10 East suite 149 San Antonio TX 78213 Tel (512) 736-2868

TRAEGER, EDGAR ALFRED, b. Sumner, Iowa, Apr. 10, 1901; grad. Cedar Rapids (Iowa) Bus. Coll., 1918; tchr.'s tng. Coe Coll., 1920; grad. corr. course in law LaSalle Extension, U. Chgo., 1932; read law with Judge M.M. Cooney, West Union, Iowa, 1930-32. Admitted to Iowa bar, 1932; tchr. country sch., 1920-22; farmer, 1922-26; clk. Dist. Ct. Fayette County (Iowa), 1927-34, county atty., 1935-36; practice law, West Union, 1934—; partner Traeger & Koempel, 1948—; mayor City of West Union, 1938-50. Chief, West Union CD; chmn. Fayette County Republican Central Com. Mem. Fayette County, Iowa bar assns. Home: 504 N Vine St West Union IA 52175 Office: 103 N Vine St West Union IA 52175 Tel (319) 422-3859

TRAFFORD, PERRY D., JR., b. N.Y.C., Aug. 3, 1903; J.D., Harvard U. Admitted to N.Y. bar, 1934; partner firm Ferris, Bangs, Davis, Trafford & Suz, and predecessors, N.Y.C. Trustee, N.Y. Infirmary, Bermuda Biol. Sta. for Research. Mem. Am., N.Y.C., Westchester, No. Westchester bar assns. Home: 430 Harris Rd Bedford Hills NY 10507 Office: 74 Trinity Pl New York City NY 10006

TRAGER, DAVID GERSHON, b. Mt. Vernon, N.Y., Dec. 23, 1937; A.B., Columbia, 1959; LL.B., Harvard, 1962. Admitted to N.Y. bar, 1963, U.S. Ct. Appeals, 1963, U.S. Dist. Ct., 1964; asso. firm Emile Zola Berman & A. Harold Frost, N.Y.C., 1963-65; asst. corp. counsel City of N.Y., Appeals Div., 1967; law clk. Judge Kenneth B. Keating, N.Y. Ct. Appeals, 1968-69; asst. U.S. atty., chief appeals div. Eastern N.Y., 1970-72; prof. law Bklyn. Law Sch., 1972-74; chmn. Bklyn. Citizens Ind., Non-Partisan Jud. Screening Panel, 1973; U.S. atty. Eastern Dist. N.Y., 1974—. Mem. Am. Bar Assn., Assn. Bar City N.Y. Office: 225 Cadman Plaza E Brooklyn NY 11201 Tel (212) 330-7060

TRAGESSER, ROGER CHARLES, b. San Diego, Nov. 19, 1938; B.A., U. Portland, 1962; M.S. in Psychology, Portland State U., 1969; J.D. cum laude, Lewis and Clark Coll., 1973. Admitted to Oreg. bar, 1973; asso. firm Lovett, Stiner & Fasano, Portland, 1973-76; corp. counsel Pay Less Drug Stores N.W. Inc., Beaverton, Oreg., 1976—; instr. Mt. Hood Community Coll. Mem. Am., Oreg. State bar assns., Am. Trial Lawyers Assn., Delta Theta Phi. Recipient Am. Jurisprudence awards Amjor Pub. Co., 1970. Home: 11855 SW Pearson Ct Beaverton OR 97005 Office: 10605 SW Allen Blvd Beaverton OR 97005 Tel (503) 641-5151

TRAINOR, CHARLES ST. CLAIR, b. Albany, P.E.I., Can., Dec. 8, 1901; B.A. cum laude, St. Dunstan's U., 1923. Called to P.E.I. bar, 1927, created king's counsel, 1938; appt. judge Kings County Ct., 1942, Queens County Ct., 1949; justice Supreme Ct. of P.E.I., 1967—, chief justice, 1970—; chmn. P.E.I. Pub. Utilities Commn., 1946-67, P.E.I. Vets. Land Act Advisory Bd., from inception to 1967; clk. P.E.I. Legis. Assembly, 10 yrs. Bd. mgrs. Kings County Meml. Hsop., Charlottetown (P.E.I.) Sch. Bd.; pres. P.E.I. div. Canadian Red Cross Soc.; chmn. bd. govs. U. P.E.I., 1969—. Office: PEI Supreme Ct Charlottetown PE Canada*

TRAMMELL, DAN DERYL, b. Lamesa, Tex., Sept. 18, 1945; B.B.A., Tex. Tech. U., 1969; J.D., U. Tex., 1972. Admitted to Tex. bar, 1972; asst. county dist. atty. Denton County, Tex., 1972-74; judge Denton County Ct., 1975—. Bd. dirs. Emily Fowler Pub. Library, Denton, 1975—, Denton County Mental Health Assn., 1975—, Denton United Way, 1975—. Mem. State Bar Tex., Denton County Bar Assn., County Judges and Commrs. Assn. Tex., Denton C. of C. (bd. dirs. 1975—). Home: 1217 Austin St Denton TX 76201 Office: Denton County Courthouse Denton TX 76201 Tel (817) 387-1212

TRAMMELL, GEORGE WARD, III, b. Long Beach, Calif., Aug. 26, 1936; B.S. in Fin., U. So. Calif., 1958, J.D., 1962. Admitted to Calif. bar, 1963; dep. dist. atty. Los Angeles County, 1963-71; judge Municipal Ct. Los Angeles, 1971—; cts. cons. Am. Bar Assn., 1968-70. Mem. Am., Los Angeles County bar assns., Conf. Calif. Judges, Am. Judicature Soc. Office: 110 N Grand Ave Los Angeles CA 90012 Tel (213) 974-6015

TRAMONTINE, JOHN O., b. Iron Mountain, Mich., Sept. 21, 1932; B.S. in Chem. Engring., U. Notre Dame, 1955; LL.B., N.Y. U., 1960. Admitted to N.Y. bar, 1960, Ill. bar, 1963, U.S. Supreme Ct. bar, 1970; asso. firm Arthur Dry Kalish Taylor & Wood, N.Y.C., 1958-62, asso. firm Wolf Hubbard Voit & Osann, Chgo., 1962-63; asso. firm Fish & Neave, N.Y.C., 1963-69, partner, 1970—; patent examiner U.S. Patent Office, Washington, 1956-58. Mem. Am. Bar Assn., Assn. Bar City N.Y. (chmn. patents com. 1974—), N.Y. Patent Law Assn. Office: Fish & Neave 277 Park Ave New York City NY 10017 Tel (212) 826-1050

TRAPANI, JOHN, b. Venice, Italy, Aug. 23, 1929; Dottore in Giurisprudenza, U. Rome, 1951; LL.B., St. John's U., 1959. Admitted to N.Y. bar, 1961, Calif. bar, 1965, U.S. Supreme Ct. bar, 1971; asst. law librarian St. John's U., 1956-59, Supreme Ct. Library, Bklyn., 1959-62; asst. fgn. law librarian Los Angeles County Law Library, 1962-65; dep. prosecutor City of Pasadena (Calif.), 1966-68; dep. pub. defender County of Los Angeles, 1968; staff atty. Pasadena Legal Aid Soc., 1968-71; directing atty. Stanislaus County (Calif.) Legal Assistance, Modesto, 1971-72; sr. atty. Los Angeles Legal Aid, 1972-73; dir. litigation Los Angeles Center Law and Justice, 1973-74; asso. prof. law Pepperdine U., 1974-77. Mem. Internat., Inter-Am., Am., Calif., N.Y., Los Angeles County bar assns., World Assn. Lawyers, Am. Soc. Internat. Law, Am. Soc. Legal History, Am. Trial Lawyers Assn. Home: 404 S 6th St Alhambra CA 91801 Office: 317 W Main St suite 219 Alhambra CA 91801 Tel (213) 282-8439

TRASK, GEORGE GRAHAM, b. Wilmington, N.C., Sept. 3, 1940; student U. Vienna (Austria), 1961; B.A., Davidson Coll., 1962; J.D., Harvard U., 1967. Admitted to S.C. bar, 1968, Ga. bar, 1969; spl. asst. Nat. Adv. Commn. on Civil Disorders, Washington, 1967; asso. firm King & Spalding, Atlanta, 1968-69; individual practice law, Beaufort, S.C., 1970-71; asso. firm Jones, Bird & Howell, Atlanta, 1971-72, partner, 1973-75; partner firm Huie, Ware, Sterne, Brown & Ide, Atlanta, 1976-77; chmn. bd. 1st Carolina Bank, Beaufort, 1969—, also pres., 1977—; pres. Beaufort Broadcasting Co., Inc., 1975-77. Asso. vestryman St. Luke's Episcopal Ch., Atlanta, 1972-75; mem. Leadership Atlanta, 1975-76. Mem. Atlanta, Ga., S.C., Am. bar assns., Atlanta Lawyers Club. Home: 3104 Roberta Dr NW Atlanta GA 30327 Office: PO Box 230 Beaufort SC 29902

TRASK, OZELL MILLER, b. Wakita, Okla., July 4, 1909; A.B. magna cum laude, Washburn Coll., 1931; LL.B., Harvard, 1934. Admitted to Mo., Kans. bars, 1934, Ariz. bar, 1940, D.C. bar, 1965; partner firm Jennings, Strouss, Salmon & Trask, Phoenix, 1942-69; judge U.S. Ct. Appeals, 9th Circuit, Phoenix, 1969—; chief counsel Ariz. Interstate Stream Comm., 1960-69. Bd. dirs. Phoenix Met. YMCA; bd. dirs., past pres. Ariz. State Cancer Soc.; bd. dirs. Am. Cancer Soc.; trustee Phoenix Art Museum, 1968-69; gen. chmn. NCCJ. Mem. Am., Ariz., Maricopa County bar assns., Am. Judicature Soc. Office: 7469 Federal Bldg Phoenix AZ 85025

TRAUTMAN, HERMAN LOUIS, b. Columbus, Ind., Sept. 26, 1911; B.A., Ind. U., 1946, LL.B., 1937, J.D., 1946; postgrad. N.Y. U., 1953; Ford Found. fellow Harvard Law Sch., 1954-55. Admitted to Ind. bar, 1937, Tenn. bar, 1952; practiced in Evansville, Ind., 1937-43; pres. Crescent Coal Co., Evansville, 1941-43; asso. prof. naval sci. U. Va., Charlottesville, 1944-46; prof. law U. Ala., Tuscaloosa, 1946-49, Vanderbilt U., Nashville, 1949—; vis. prof. law N.Y. U., 1955, U. Mich., 1963-64. Chmn. bd. trustees West End United Methodist Ch., Nashville. Mem. Am. Law Inst. (life), Nat. Conf. Jud. Adminstrn., Am. (chmn. subcom. on income taxation of estates and trusts 1961-76), Tenn. (hon., chmn. sect. on real property, probate and trust law 1958-59), Nashville bar assns., Nashville Estate Planning Council, Order of Coif, Scribes. Contbr. articles in field to books and legal jours. Home: 5100 Stanford Dr Nashville TN 37215 Office: Vanderbilt Law Sch Bldg Nashville TN 37240 Tel (615) 322-2810

TRAVER, COURTLAND LEE, b. New Haven, Sept. 20, 1935; B.A., U. Conn., 1957; LL.B., Georgetown U., 1966. Admitted to Va. bar, 1967, D.C. bar, 1966; law clk. to chief judge D.C. Superior Ct., 1966-67, to judge U.S. Ct. Appeals D.C., 1967-68; partner firm Boothe, Prichard and Dudley, Fairfax, Va., 1968—. Mem. Am., Va. bar assns. Home: 1005 Congress Ln McLean VA 22101 Office: 4085 University Dr Fairfax VA 22030 Tel (703) 273-4600

TRAVIS, JAY A., III, b. McComb, Miss., June 8, 1940; B.B.A., U. Miss., 1962, J.D., 1965. Admitted to Miss. bar, 1965; asso. firm Thompson, Alexander & Crews, Jackson, Miss., 1967-69; partner firm Butler, Snow, O'Mara, Stevens & Cannada, Jackson, 1969—; mem. bd. bar commrs. Miss. State Bar, 1975-77. Mem. Miss. State Bar (2d v.p. 1976-77, pres. young lawyers sect. 1975-76), Am. Bar Assn. (nat. exec. com. young lawyers sect.), Hinds County Bar, Estate Planning Council Miss. (pres. 1975-76), Miss. Law Inst. (chmn. 1974), Phi Delta Phi. Office: PO Box 22567 1700 Deposit Guaranty Plaza Jackson MS 39205 Tel (601) 948-5711

TRAVIS, RONALD CARL, b. Punxsutawney, Pa., June 11, 1944; B.S., Lycoming Coll., 1967; LL.D., Dickinson Sch. Law, 1970. Admitted to Pa. bar, 1971; law clk. to chief justice Pa. Supreme Ct., 1970-71; asso. firm Candor, Youngman, Gibson & Gault, Williamsport, Pa., 1971-74, partner firm, 1975—; asst. city solicitor City of Williamsport, 1974—; instr. law Williamsport Sch. of Commerce, 1972-75; mem. rules com. U.S. Dist. Ct. for Middle Dist. Pa., 1973—. Mem. Lycoming County Pub. Relations Com., 1973—. Mem. Am., Pa., Lycoming County bar assns., Assn. Trial Lawyers Am. Home: 1509 Elmira St Williamsport PA 17701 Office: 23 W 3d St Williamsport PA 17701 Tel (717) 322-6144

TRAVIS, WILLIAM JOHN, b. St. Louis, Jan. 11, 1947; B.A. cum laude, U. Pa., 1968; J.D., U. Mich., 1973. Admitted to Mo. bar, 1973; asso. firm Armstrong, Teasdale, Kramer & Vaughan, St. Louis, 1973—. Mem. Am., Mo., St. Louis bar assns. Home: 7069 Westmoreland Dr St Louis MO 63130 Office: 611 Olive Suite 1950 St Louis MO 63101 Tel (314) 621-5070

TRAXLER, WILLIAM BYRD, b. Greenville, S.C., July 10, 1912; student The Citadel, 1929-30; student U. Tex., 1930-32; J.D., George Washington U., 1940. Admitted to D.C. bar, 1940, S.C. bar, 1940, U.S. Circuit Ct. Appeals D.C. bar, 1940, U.S. 4th Circuit Ct. Appeals bar, 1960; partner firm Hinson, Traxler and Hamer, Greenville, S.C., 1950-58; partner firm Rainey, Fant, Traxler and Horton, Greenville, 1958-60; individual practice law, Greenville, 1960—. Bd. dirs. Visiting Nurse Assn., Greenville, 1957-59; United Way, Greenville, 1976; chmn. taxation com., vice-chmn. bd. health, Greenville, 1960-70. Mem. S.C., Greenville County (pres. 1976) bar assns., Phillis Wheatly Assn., Torch Club (pres. 1956), Greenville C. of C., George Washington Law Assn., Law Sci. Acad., Phi Alpha Delta. Named Chmn. of Yr., Greenville C. of C., 1967. Alumni Achievement Award, George Washington U., 1946; author: Military Government in Germany, 1960; Political Third Parties, 1968; History of the Fourteenth Amendment, 1974; The Jury Numbers Game, 1976. Home: 100 Trail's End Greenville SC 29607 Office: 606 E North St Greenville SC 29603 Tel (803) 233-1661

TRAYLOR, ORBA FOREST, b. Providence, Ky., June 16, 1910; B.A., Western Ky. U., 1930; M.A., U. Ky., 1932, Ph.D., 1948; J.D., Northwestern U., 1936. Admitted to Ky. bar, 1941; head dept. econs. Ashland (Ky.) Coll., 1935-36; asso. prof. econs. and sociology Western Ky. U., 1938-40; asst. prof. econs. and bus. U. Denver, 1946-47, U. Mo., 1947-50; specialist Econ. Cooperation Adminstrn., Greece and Turkey, 1950-53; pub. fin. expert UN, Egypt, 1954-56; fin. commr. State of Ky., 1958-60; dir. econ. affairs office of high commr. Ryukyus, 1960-65; prof. econs. and public adminstrn. U. Ala., 1965-75; prof. pub. adminstrn. San Diego State U., 1975-76, Western Ky. U., 1976—. Mem. Am., Ky. bar assns., Am., So. econ. assns., Am. Soc. for Pub. Adminstrn., Nat. Tax Assn., Tax Inst. Am., Beta Gamma Sigma, Delta Sigma Pi. Mem. editorial bd. Pub. Adminstrn. Review, 1973-76; contbr. articles to profl. publs. Home: 6820 Criner Rd SE Huntsville AL 35802 Office: Western Ky U Coll Bus and Pub Affairs Bowling Green KY 42101 Tel (502) 745-3893

TRAYLOR, WILLIAM HUGH, b. Washington, Ind., June 24, 1921; B.S. in Chem. Engring., Purdue U., 1942; J.D., Ind. U., 1950. Admitted to Ind. bar, 1950, Ga. bar, 1967, Pa. bar, 1973; gen. counsel Indpls. Legal Aid Soc., 1951-53; asso. firm Johnson & Weaver, Indpls., 1953-67; asst. prof. Emory U., Atlanta, 1967-71; prof. Sch. Law Temple U., Phila., 1971—, vice dean, 1974—; pres. Legal Services Orgn. Indpls., 1965-67. Bd. dirs. YMCA Indpls., 1960-67. Mem. Am., Phila. bar assns., Order of Coif. Author manual on evidence for dist. justices. Office: Sch Law Temple U Philadelphia PA 19122 Tel (215) 787-1924

TRAYNER, RONALD GEORGE, b. Los Angeles, Dec. 6, 1942; A.B., Occidental Coll., 1964; J.D., Stanford, 1967. Admitted to Calif. bar, 1968; asso. firm Musick Peeler & Garrett, Los Angeles, 1968-72, partner, 1973—. Mem. State Bar Calif., Am., Los Angeles County bar assns. Office: Musick Peeler & Garrett One Wilshire Blvd Los Angeles CA 90017 Tel (213) 629-3322

TRAYNOR, JOHN THOMAS, b. Devils Lake, N.D., Nov. 19, 1926; student U.S. Naval Acad., 1945-46; B.A., U. N.D., 1949, J.D., 1951. Admitted to N.D. bar, 1951, U.S. Dist. Ct. bar, 1951, U.S. Ct. of

Appeals bar, 1955, U.S. Tax Ct. bar, 1976; mem. firm Traynor & Rutten and predecessors, Devils Lake, 1951-72; city magistrate, Devils Lake, 1952-62; county justice, Ramsey County, N.D., 1962-72. Chmn., Home Rule Charter Commn., Devils Lake, 1976—; bd. dirs. Lake Region Community Concert Assn.; bd. dirs. Lake Region Jr. Coll. Theatre Guild; chmn. bd trustees N.D. Elks Assn. Fellow Am. Coll. of Probate Counsel; mem. Am., N.D., Lake Region bar assns., Internat. Soc. of Barristers and World Peace Through Law Assn. Recipient U. of N.D. Sioux award, 1969, Distinguished Service award, State of N.D., 1953. Home: 601 12th Ave Devils Lake ND 58301 Office: 509 Fifth St Devils Lake ND 58301 Tel (701) 662-4077

TRAYNOR, MICHAEL, b. Oakland, Calif., Oct. 25, 1934; B.A., U. Calif., Berkeley, 1955; J.D., Harvard, 1960. Admitted to Calif. bar, 1961, U.S. Supreme Ct. bar, 1966; dep. atty. gen. State of Calif., San Francisco, 1961-63; spl. counsel Calif. Senate Com. on Local Govt., Sacramento, 1963; asso. firm Cooley, Godward, Castro, Huddleson & Tatum, San Francisco, 1963-69, partner, 1969—; vice chmn. San Francisco Spl. Cts. Com., 1971-75; mem. Joint Commn. on Fair Jud. Election Practices, 1976—; acting and vice chmn. San Francisco Neighborhood Legal Assistance Found., 1967. Trustee Head-Royce Schs., Oakland, 1974—, Sierra Club Legal Def. Fund, 1974—, Lawyers' Com. for Civil Rights Under Law, 1976—. Mem. Am. Law Inst., Am. Bar Assn., Am. Judicature Soc., Calif. State Bar, Bar Assn. San Francisco, (pres. 1973), Lawyers Club of San Francisco. Contbr. articles to legal jours. Home: 3131 Eton Ave Berkeley CA 94705 Office: 20th Floor Alcoa Bldg One Maritime Plaza San Francisco CA 94111 Tel (415) 981-5252

TREACY, THOMAS BERNARD, b. N.Y.C., Dec. 26, 1928; B.S., Fordham U., 1950, J.D., 1954. Admitted to N.Y. State bar, 1955, U.S. Supreme Ct. bar, 1960; asso. firm Nevius, Brett & Kellogg, N.Y.C., 1955-56; asso. firm Nevius, Jarvis & Pilz, N.Y.C., 1956-64, partner, 1964-65; asso. partner firm Jarvis, Pilz, Buckley & Treacy, and predecessors, N.Y.C., 1966—. Mem. N.Y. County Lawyers Assn., Soc. Am. Mil. Engrs., ASCE, N.Y. State, Fed., Am. (chmn. liason com. N.Y. State pub. contract sect. 1976—) bar assns. Home: 330 Muttontown Rd Syosset NY 11790 Office: 115 Broadway New York City NY 10006 Tel (212) 227-8150

TREADWAY, WILLIAM EUGENE, b. Bloomington, Ind., Dec. 20, 1901; A.B., Ind. U., 1924; J.D., George Washington U., 1927; S.J.D., U. Mich., 1933. Admitted to Ind. bar, 1927, Kans. bar, 1942; individual practice law, Spencer, Ind., 1927-41, Indpls., 1939-41; served to lt. col. Judge Adv. Gen.'s Corps, U.S. Army, 1941-45; gen. atty. Santa Fe Ry., Topeka, Kans., 1945-71; vis. prof. law Washburn U., Topeka, 1971—; pros. atty. Owen County, Ind., 1927-29; mem. Ind. Ho. of Reps., 1934-39. Mem. Am., Kans., Topeka bar assns., Delta Theta Phi. Author: General Corporation Code vol. of Kansas Statutes Annotated, 1975. Contbr. articles to legal jours. Home: 3500 Avalon Ln Topeka KS 66604 Office: Washburn U Law School Topeka KS 66621 Tel (913) 295-6660

TREANOR, WALTER GLADSTONE, b. N.Y.C., Feb. 19, 1922; B.A., Principia Coll., 1943; J.D., Washington U., St. Louis, 1949. Admitted to Mo. bar, 1949, Calif. bar, 1959, U.S. Supreme Ct. bar, 1964; staff atty. Fanchon & Marco, Inc., St. Louis, 1949-51; commerce atty. Mo. Pacific R.R., St. Louis, 1951-58; with Western Pacific R.R., San Francisco, 1958—, gen. counsel, 1970, v.p. law, 1973—; city atty. St. Ann, Mo., 1951-56, Breckenridge Hills, Mo., 1956-58; civil service commr. Contra Costa County, Calif., 1966—, pres., 1968-72. Bd. trustees Acalanes Union High Sch. Dist., 1965-70, pres., 1966. Mem. Calif. State Bar, Assn. ICC Practitioners, Nat. Assn. R.R. Trial Lawyers. Named Man of Yr., Orinda, Calif., 1965. Home: 5 Keith Dr Orinda CA 94563 Office: 526 Mission St San Francisco CA 94105 Tel (415) 982-2100

TREAT, WILLIAM WARDWELL, b. Boston, May 23, 1918; A.B., U. Maine, 1940; M.B.A., Harvard, 1947. Admitted to Maine bar, 1945, N.H. bar, 1949, U.S. Supreme Ct. bar, 1955; judge N.H. Probate Ct., Exeter, 1958—; pres., chmn. bd. Hampton Nat. Bank, 1958—; faculty Nat. Center for State Judiciary, Reno, 1975—; chmn. N.H. Jud. Council, 1976; adv. bd. Nat. Center for State Cts., 1973—; pres. Nat. Coll. Probate Judges, 1968—. Bd. dirs., v.p. Hundred Club of N.H. Mem. Am. Law Inst., N.H., Am. bar assns. Author: Treat on Probate, 3 vols., 1968; Local Justice in the Granite State, 1961; contbr. articles to profl. jours. Home: PO Box 498 Hampton NH 03842 Office: 100 Winnacunnet Rd Hampton NH 03842 Tel (603) 926-6311

TREBACH, ARNOLD SHEPARD, b. Lowell, Mass., May 15, 1928; A.A., Calvin Coolidge Coll., 1948; J.D., New Eng. Sch. Law, 1951; M.A., Princeton, 1957, Ph.D., 1958. Admitted to Ma. bar, 1951; prof. Center for Adminstrn. of Justice, Am. U., 1972—, dir. Inst. on Drugs, Crime and Justice, 1974—; chief adminstrn. of justice sect. U.S. Commn. on Civil Rights, Washington, 1960-63; adminstr. Nat. Defender Project Am. Bar Center, 1963-64; chmn. ann. meeting program Am. Soc. Criminology, Toronto, Ont., Can., 1975. Author: The Rationing of Justice, 1964; contbr. articles to legal jours. Office: Center for Adminstrn Justice Am U Massachusetts and Nebraska Ave NW Washington DC 20016 Tel (202) 606-2534

TRECKELO, RICHARD MICHELE, b. Elkhart, Ind., Oct. 22, 1926; A.B., U. Mich., 1951, J.D., 1953. Admitted to Ind. bar, 1953; partner firm Thornburg, McGill, Deahl, Harman, Carey & Murray, Elkhart and South Bend, Ind., 1971—. Pres., bd. dirs. Elkhart Legal Aid Services, 1972-74; v.p., bd. dirs. Family Counseling Services, 1966-72. Mem. Am., Ind. (ho. of dels. 1967-70), Elkhart County, Elkhart (pres. 1975) bar assns. Office: 305 1st Nat Bank Bldg Elkhart IN 46514 Tel (219) 293-0681

TREDINNICK, ROBERT WESLEY, b. Kearny, N.J., Aug. 20, 1923; B.A., Ursinus Coll., Collegeville, Pa., 1943; LL.B., Temple U., 1950. Admitted to Pa. Supreme, Superior and Trial Cts. bar, 1950; partner firm Smillie, Bean, Davis & Tredinnick, Norristown, Pa., 1955-65, Bean, DeAngelis, Tredinnick & Giangnilio, Norristown, 1965-70; judge Court of Common Pleas 38th Judicial Dist., Pa., 1970—. Bd. dirs., pres. No. Pa. br. ARC, Lansdale, 1964-65; pres. N. Penn Hosp., Lansdale, Pa., 1971-72. Mem. Am., Pa., Montgomery (pres. 1968) bar assns. Home: 56 Oak Dr Lansdale PA 19446 Office: Court House Norristown PA 19404 Tel (215) 275-5000

TREECE, JAMES LYLE, b. Colorado Springs, Colo., Feb. 6, 1925; A.S., Mesa Coll.; student U.S. Naval Acad., 1944-46, Colo. State U., 1943; J.D., U. Colo., 1949; postgrad. U. No. Colo., 1977. Admitted to Colo. bar, 1952; asso. firm Yegge, Hall Treece & Evans, and predecessors, Denver, 1951-58, partner, 1958-69; U.S. atty. Dist. Colo., 1969-77; partner firm Ellison & Treece, Denver, 1977—; judge Greenwood (Colo.) Municipal Ct., 1968-69; guest lectr. in field. Chmn. Colo. Bd. Pub. Welfare, 1963-68, Colo. Bd. Social Services, 1968-69; mem. Colo. Gov's. Com. on Health and Med. Services, 1965-69. Mem. Am., Colo. (chmn. trial sect., bd. govs. 1967-69), Denver (v.p. 1966-67, trustee 1963-66), Fed. (v.p. 1974-75, pres. 1975-76) bar assns. Recipient S.E. Denver Pacemaker award University Park News, 1967, Community Leaders award News Pub. Co., 1968. Tel (303) 825-6264

TREIMAN, ALBERT HYMAN, b. N.Y.C., Apr. 28, 1916; B.A., City Coll. N.Y., 1937; J.D., St. John's U., 1939, J.S.D., 1940. Admitted to N.Y. State bar, 1939, U.S. Dist. Ct. bar, 1942, U.S. Supreme Ct. bar, 1947, U.S. Ct. Appeals, 1956, Tax Ct. U.S., 1966; individual practice law, Plainview, N.Y., 1939—. Mem. Am., N.Y. State, Nassau County bar assns., N.Y. State Defenders League, Jewish Bar Assn. Office: 465 S Oyster Bay Rd Plainview NY 11803 Tel (516) 938-2288

TREMBLATT, JOHN YAGER, b. Washington, Oct. 2, 1945; B.A., U. Calif. at Berkeley; J.D., U. Calif. at Los Angeles. Admitted to Calif. bar, 1971; staff juvenile law project, 1971; partner firm Somers Kallen Grant & Tremblatt, 1971-76; individual practice law, San Diego, 1976—; tchr. immigration law Calif. State U. at San Diego, 1975. Mem. San Diego Bar Assn. Organized East Los Angeles Free Clinic Draft Mil. Counseling Center. Office: 2150 First Ave San Diego CA 92101 Tel (714) 234-8273

TREMBLAY, ELIE GERALD, b. Nashua, N.H., Oct. 4, 1922; B.A., U. Va., 1949, LL.B., 1951. Admitted to Va. bar; partner firm Tremblay & Smith, Charlottesville, Va., 1962—. Bd. dirs. Salvation Army, Charlottesville, 1970—. Mem. Charlottesville-Albemarle (pres. 1975-76), Am., Va. bar assns., Va. State Bar, Va. (pres. 1975-76), Am. assns. trial lawyers. Home: Broomley Rd Flordon Charlottesville VA 22901 Office: 105-109 E High St Charlottesville VA 22901 Tel (804) 977-4455

TREMBLAY, LUCIEN, b. Montreal, Que., Can., Mar. 25, 1912; B.A., Sem. Philosophy, Montreal, 1933; LL.M., U. Montreal, 1936, LL.D., 1944, hon. LL.D., 1965; LL.D., Laval U., 1963. Called to bar Que., 1936; individual practice law, Montreal, 1936-61; prof. civil procedure U. Montreal, 1949-59; chief justice Province Que., 1961-77; supernumerary judge Ct. Appeal Que., 1977—; chancellor U. Montreal, 1967-70. Mem. Can. Bar Assn. Home: Habitat 67 Cite Du Havre Montreal PQ H3C 3R6 Canada Office: Court House Montreal PQ H2Y 1B6 Canada Tel (514) 873-3146

TREMONT, T. PAUL, b. N.Y.C., Aug. 20, 1933; B.S., Fairfield U., 1955; J.D., Georgetown U., 1957. Admitted to D.C., Conn. bars, 1957; individual practice law, Bridgeport, Conn., 1959—. Mem. Am., Conn. (past chmn. com. on adminstrn. of civil justice) bar assns., Conn. Trial Lawyers Assn. (past pres.). Editorial bd. Georgetown Law Jour., 1957; contbr. articles to legal jours. Office: 64 Lyon Terr Bridgeport CT 06604 Tel (203) 335-5141

TRENAM, JOHN JAMES, b. Evanston, Wyo., July 13, 1912; student U. Utah, 1931-33; B.S., Georgetown U., 1940, LL.B., 1944. Admitted to D.C. bar, 1944, Fla. bar, 1948; atty., office chief counsel IRS, 1945-47; partner firm Fowler, White, Gillen, Humkey & Trenam, Tampa, Fla., 1948-69, firm Trenam, Simmons, Kemker, Scharf & Barkin, Tampa, 1970—; vis. prof. law Stetson U., St. Petersburg, Fla., 1953-73. Mem. Am., Fla. (bd. govs. 1963-69) bar assns. Home: 914 S Sterling Ave Tampa FL 33609 Office: 2600 1st Financial Tower Tampa FL 33602 Tel (813) 223-7474

TRENNEPOHL, DONALD L., b. Anderson, Ind., May 20, 1921; B.S. in Bus. Adminstrn., Ind. U., 1948, J.D., 1951. Admitted to Ind. bar, 1951; since practiced in Angola, Ind., judge, 1952-58, pros. atty. Steuben County, 1959-62; partner firm Wood & Trennepohl, then firm Trennepohl, Berger, & Shoop; prof. Tri-State U. Bd. dirs. Steuben County Hosp., Angola Library. Mem. Ind. State, Steuben County bar assns. Home: 802 S Washington St Angola IN 46703 Office: Tri-State U Angola IN 46703 Tel (219) 665-3141

TREPEL, ANTHONY J., b. N.Y.C., Aug. 25, 1932; student U. Calif., Los Angeles; B.A., Ariz. State U., 1954; LL.B., Stanford U., 1961. Admitted to Calif. bar, 1962; now partner firm Trepel & Clark, San Jose, Calif. Mem. Am., Palo Alto, Santa Clara County (pres. 1976) bar assns., State Bar Calif. Office: Suite 622 101 Park Center Plaza San Jose CA 95113 Tel (408) 275-0501

TREVETT, THOMAS NEIL, b. Rochester, N.Y., Mar. 14, 1942; B.S., St. John Fisher Coll., 1964; J.D., Albany Law Sch., 1967. Admitted to N.Y. State bar, 1967; since practiced in Rochester, asso. firm Thomas H. Meagher, 1967-68, asso. firm Sullivan, Gough, Skipworth, Summers and Smith, 1968-72, partner, 1972—; town atty. Ontario (N.Y.), 1972-74; chmn. Wayne County Charter Commn., Lyons, N.Y., 1976-77. Mem. N.Y. State, Monroe and Wayne counties bar assns., Am. Trial Lawyers Assn. Home: 7656 Roder Pkwy Ontario NY 14519 Office: 1020 Reynolds Arcade Bldg Rochester NY 14614 Tel (716) 454-2181

TREWEEK, SALLY ANN, b. Allentown, Pa., May 27, 1942; A.B., Conn. Coll., 1964; J.D., U. So. Calif., 1973. Admitted to Calif. bar, 1973; asso. firm O'Melveny & Myers, Los Angeles, 1973—. Mem. Women Lawyers of Los Angeles (dir.), Los Angeles County, Am. bar assns. Contbr. article to legal publ. Office: 611 W Sixth St Suite 3700 Los Angeles CA 90017 Tel (213) 620-1120

TREXLER, RICHARD R., b. Mpls., Feb. 14, 1906; B.M.E., U. Minn., 1927; LL.B., J.D., Georgetown U., 1971. Admitted to D.C. bar, 1930, Ill. bar, 1935; examiner U.S. Patent Office, Washington, 1927-34; mem. firm Olson, Trexler, Walters, Bushnell & Fosse, and predecessors, Chgo., 1934—. Mem. Am., Chgo. bar assns., Am., Chgo. (pres. 1969) patent law assns. Home: 9509 Lawndale Evanston IL 60203 Office: 141 W Jackson Blvd Chicago IL 60604 Tel (312) 427-8082

TRIAS-MONGE, JOSE, b. San Juan, P.R., May 5, 1920; B.A., U. P.R., 1940; M.A., Harvard U., 1943, LL.B., 1944; J.S.D., Yale U., 1947. Admitted to P.R. bar, 1945; first asst. atty. gen., P.R., 1949, atty. gen., 1953-57; individual practice law, San Juan, 1957-74; chief justice Supreme Ct. P.R., 1974—; faculty U. P.R. Law Sch., 1947—; mem. Constl. Conv. P.R., 1951-52; U.S. rep. to Caribbean Commn., 1954-60, Inter-Am. Juridical Com., OAS, 1966-67; mem. Gov.'s Commn. for Reform Jud. System P.R. Vice pres. Festival Casals, Inc., 1957-69, 73-74; trustee U. P.R., 1962-67. Mem. Am., P.R. bar assns. Contbr. articles to profl. jours. Office: PO Box 2392 San Juan PR 00903 Tel (809) 723-3550

TRIBE, LAURENCE H., b. 1941; A.B. summa cum laude, Harvard U., 1962, J.D. magna cum laude, 1966. Admitted to Calif. bar, 1966; law clk. to justice Calif. Supreme Ct., 1966-67, Justice Stewart, U.S. Supreme Ct., 1967-68; asst. prof. law Harvard U., 1968-71, prof., 1972—, research asso. program on tech. and sci., 1969-72; exec. dir. tech. assessment panel Nat. Acad. Scis., Washington, 1968-69; mem. advisory com. on tech. and values Nat. Sci. Fedn.-Nat. Endowment for Humanities, 1973-75. Mem. N.Y.C. Bar Assn., Phi Beta Kappa. Author: (with others) Technology—Processes of Assessment and Choice, 1969; (with L. Jaffe) Environmental Protection, 1971; Channeling Technology Through Law, 1973; When Values Conflict, 1975; American Constitutional Law, 1977. Office: Law Sch Harvard U Cambridge MA 02138

TRICKEL, WILLIAM, JR., b. Chambersburg, Pa., Feb. 12, 1937; B.A., U. Fla., 1960, J.D., 1963. Admitted to Fla. bar, 1963; partner firm Leonhardt, Trickel, Leigh & Gibson, Orlando, Fla.; chmn. 9th Jud. Nominating Commn., 1973—; asso. judge Orlando Municipal Ct., 1970-76; adj. instr. Allied Legal Services Fla. Technol. U., 1976—. Pres. Legal Aid of Orange County, Inc., 1971-72. Mem. Am., Fla. (chmn. jud. com. 1972-74), Orange County (pres. 1971-72) bar assns., Am. Judicature Soc., Soc. Am. Hosp. Attys., Council Bar Assn. Presidents (chmn. 1973-74). Home: Rt 1 Box 81 Matiland FL 32751 Office: 39 W Pine St Orlando FL 32801 Tel (305) 422-5154

TRIEBSCH, ROBERT ERNEST, b. San Francisco, Jan. 4, 1939; A.B., U. Calif. at Davis, 1960; LL.B., U. Calif. at Berkeley, 1963. Admitted to Calif. bar, 1966; partner firm Muller, Pia & Simmons, Salinas, Calif., 1967-74; individual practice law, Turlock, Calif., 1974—. Bd. dirs. Statesman of Stanislaus State Coll., 1976—. Mem. Turlock C. of C. (dir. 1975—, v.p. 1975-76), Calif., Monterey County (dir. 1970-71, treas. 1970), Stanislaus County bar assns., Calif. Conf. Barristers (dir. 1972-75, editor Conf. Call, 1973-74). Office: 261 N Palm St Turlock CA 95380 Tel (209) 632-9964

TRIFARI, NORMA MARIE, b. Bklyn., May 7, 1912; B.A., Adelphi Coll., 1934; LL.B., Fordham U., 1939. Admitted to N.Y. bar, 1940, R.I. bar, 1942; individual practice law, Providence, 1942—; atty. R.I. Legal Aid, 1942-43; rationing atty. Office of Price Adminstrn., 1945-46. Mem. R.I. Bar Assn. Home: 3 Lee Ann Dr Barrington RI 02806 Office: 1231 Indsl Bank Bldg Providence RI 02903 Tel (401) 421-1283

TRIGUEIRO, GARY LOUIS, b. Fallon, Nev., Sept. 17, 1947; B.S. in Bus. Adminstrn., U. Nev., 1969; J.D., U. Calif., Berkeley, 1972. Admitted to Calif. bar, 1972, Oreg. bar, 1976; tax supr. Touche Ross & Co., San Francisco, 1972-75, Salem, Oreg., 1975—. Mem. Oreg. Soc. C.P.A.'s. C.P.A., Calif., Oreg. Home: 1486 Joplin St S Salem OR 97302 Office: PO Box 867 Salem OR 97308 Tel (503) 581-2431

TRIMBLE, ROBERT LYNN, b. Dallas, Jan. 31, 1940; B.A., So. Meth. U., 1961, LL.B. cum laude, 1964. Admitted to Tex. bar, 1964; trial atty. tax div. Dept. of Justice, 1964-68; partner firm Tyler & Trimble, Dallas, 1969-73, Winstead, McGuire, Sechrest & Trimble, Dallas, 1973—. Mem. Am., Dallas bar assns. Office: 1700 Mercantile Dallas Bldg Dallas TX 75201 Tel (214) 742-1700

TRIMBLE, STEPHEN ASBURY, b. Washington, July 25, 1933; A.B., U. N.C., 1955; LL.B., Georgetown U., 1961. Admitted to D.C. bar, 1961, U.S. Supreme Ct. bar, 1965; law clk. to judge U.S. Dist. Ct., Washington, 1960-62; asst. corp. counsel for D.C., 1962; mem. firm Hamilton & Hamilton, Washington, 1962—, partner, 1966—; mem. Jud. Conf. for D.C. Circuit, 1972-77, Jud. Conf. for D.C. Cts., 1976-77; mem. grievance com. U.S. Dist. Ct. for D.C.; sec. John Carroll Soc., Washington, 1975-76. Mem. Bar Assn. D.C. (dir. 1971-73, sec. 1973-74, pres. elect 1975), Am. Bar Assn. (ho. of dels.), Nat. Assn. R.R. Trial Counsel (v.p. 1973-76, dir. 1970-73), Nat. Conf. Bar Pres.'s, Nat. Assn. Coll. and Univ. Attys., D.C. Def. Lawyers Assn. (v.p. 1974), Lawyers Club D.C., Def. Research Inst., Barristers Club (sec. 1971), Counsellors Club (pres. 1973), Phi Delta Theta. Contbr. articles to legal jours. Home: 3215 Van Hazen St NW Washington DC 20015 Office: 600 Union Trust Bldg Washington DC 20005

TRIMBLE, THOMAS JAMES, b. Carters Creek, Tenn., Sept. 3, 1931; B.A., David Lipscomb Coll., 1953; J.D., Vanderbilt U., 1956; LL.M., N.Y. U., 1959. Admitted to Tenn. bar, 1956, Ariz. bar, 1961, D.C. bar, 1963, Tenth Circuit Ct. Appeals, 1971, Ninth Circuit Ct. Appeals, 1975, U.S. Supreme Ct. bar, 1972; teaching fellow N.Y. U., 1956-57; judge adv. USAF, 1957-60; asso. firm Jennings, Strouss & Salmon, Phoenix, 1961-62, partner, 1962—. Bd. dirs. Big Sisters Ariz., 1970-76, pres., 1975; bd. dirs. Sunnydale Childrens Home, 1965-75; arbitrator Am. Arbitration Assn. Mem. Am., Fed., Ariz., Maricopa County bar assns., Order of Coif. Mng. editor Vanderbilt Law Rev., 1956; editorial bd. Ariz. Bar Jour., 1975—. Home: 4800 E Clearwater Pkwy Paradise Valley AZ 85253 Office: 111 W Monroe St Phoenix AZ 85003 Tel (602) 262-5911

TRINNAMAN, JOHN ELLIS, b. Salt Lake City, Aug. 17, 1942; B.A., Columbia, 1964, M.B.A., 1966; J.D., U. Va., 1969. Admitted to Calif. bar, 1970; asso. firm Paul, Hastings & Janofsky, Los Angeles, 1969—. Mem. Am., Los Angeles County (editor probate and trust sect. newsletter) bar assns., Order of Coif. Treas., mng. bd. editors U. Va. Law Rev., 1968-69. Home: 740 S Hudson St Pasadena CA 91106 Office: 555 S Flower St Los Angeles CA 90071 Tel (213) 489-4000

TRIPLETT, ELLSWORTH C., b. Waterloo, Ind., Sept. 12, 1924; LL.B., Ind. U., 1951. Admitted to Ind. bar, 1951, Ariz. bar, 1956, U.S. Ct. Mil. Appeals bar, 1959; U.S. Supreme Ct. bar, 1962; hearing officer Indsl. Commn. Ariz., Phoenix, 1975—; staff judge adv. U.S. Air Force, 1953-74, advanced through grades to col., 1965. Mem. State Bar Ariz., Res. Officers Assn. Home: PO Box 33236 Phoenix AZ 85067 Office: 1601 W Jefferson St Phoenix AZ 85067 Tel (602) 271-5421

TRIPLETT, GEORGE RAPHAEL, b. Cheat Bridge, W.Va., Sept. 13, 1935; diploma Shenandoah Coll., 1955; B.S., Davis and Elkins Coll., 1956; Menkemeller grantee Washington and Lee U. Sch. Law, 1956-59; J.D. (Bd. Govs. scholar), W.Va. U., 1962; postgrad. Nat. Coll. State Trial Judges, 1968, 70, U. N.C., 1968, U. Nev., 1970, 72. Tchr. math. Harrison County (W.Va.) Bd. Edn., Clarksburg, 1959; agt. State Farm Ins. Co., Coalton, W.Va., 1959-60; tchr. Randolph County (W.Va.) Bd. Edn., Elkins, 1959-60; dep. assessor Monongalia County (W.Va.), Morgantown, 1961; admitted to W.Va. bar, 1962; legal asst. W.Va. state auditor and securities commr., 1962, W.Va. securities and corp. commr. and state auditor, 1962; adminstrv. asst. to state auditor, 1963-64; asso. James C. Reed, Charleston, 1964; asst. U.S. dist. atty. No. Dist. W.Va., 1964-68; judge 20th Jud. Circuit Ct. W.Va., 1968—; resource discussion leader Internat. Conf. Ct. Vols., Detroit, 1970; lectr. Davis and Elkins Coll., W.Va. Wesleyan Coll., Indiana U. of Pa., W.Va. U. Coll. Law, 1972-75. Mem. Am. (vice-chmn. forest resources, mem. coal com.), W.Va., Randolph County bar assns., Am. Judicature Soc., W.Va. Jud. Assn. (chmn. jud. edn. com. 1972-75, mental health com. 1974-75, chmn. Seminar Program 1972-77), W.Va. Juvenile Judges Assn., Nat. Council Juvenile Ct. Judges, Fraternal Order Police (asso.), Nat. Conf. State Trial Judges (jud. environment com., jud. decision making in environ. law), Phi Alpha Delta. Contbr. articles to legal jours. Home: PO Box 1513 Elkins WV 26241 Office: 48 1/2 Randolph Ave Elkins WV 26241

TRIPP, NORMAN DENSMORE, b. Binghamton, N.Y., Apr. 11, 1938; A.B., U. Miami, 1962; LL.B., J.D. magna cum laude, Cleve. State U., 1967. Admitted to U.S. Supreme Ct. bar, 1973, Fla. bar, 1967, Ohio bar, 1967; asso. firm Watson Hubert & Davis, Fort Lauderdale, Fla., 1968-70; partner firm Tripp and Niles, Fort Lauderdale, 1970-77, firm Tripp and Conklin, Fort Lauderdale, 1977—; asst. state atty. State of Fla., 1970-72. Pres., Children's Home Soc., S.E. region Fla., 1976-77; pres. Vis. Nurses Assn. Broward County (Fla.), 1976-77. Mem. Am. Bar Assn., Fla. Bar, Broward County Bar, Am., Fla., Broward County trial lawyers assns. Office: 2000 E Oakland Park Blvd PO Box 11402 Fort Lauderdale FL 33339

TROGAN, NICHOLAS RICHARD, III, b. Saginaw, Mich., May 31, 1943; A.B., Central Mich. U., 1966; J.D., U. Notre Dame, 1969. Admitted to Mich. bar, 1969; asso. Joseph J. Trogan, Saginaw, 1969; asso. firm Doozan, Scorsone, Trogan & Trogan, Saginaw, 1970; individual practice law, Saginaw, 1971—; spl. asst. atty. gen. Lansing, Mich., 1971—. Mem. Mich. State Bar Assn., Mich. Trial Lawyers Assn., Assn. Trial Lawyers of Am. Office: 7628 Gratiot Rd Saginaw MI 48603 Tel (517) 781-2060

TROM, C. STANLEY, b. Pasadena, Calif., Aug. 23, 1940; B.A., Pacific Lutheran Coll., 1962; J.D., U. Calif., San Francisco, 1965. Admitted to Calif. bar, 1966; dep. dist. atty. Ventura (Calif.) County, 1965-73, dist. atty., 1973—. Mem. Calif. Bar Assn. Office: 501 Poli St Ventura CA 93001 Tel (805) 648-6131

TRONE, DOANE GEORGE, b. Browning, Ill., Feb. 28, 1905; LL.B., Lincoln Coll. Law, Springfield, Ill., 1942. Admitted to Ill. bar, 1942; master in chancery Schuyler County (Ill.) Circuit Ct., 1949-58; county clk. Schuyler County, 1934-42; asst. atty. gen. Schuyler and Brown Counties, Ill., 1960-68. Mem. Am., Ill. bar assns. Home: 626 W Lafayette St Rushville IL 62681 Office: 114 N Congress St Rushville IL 62681 Tel (217) 332-3127

TROOBOFF, PETER DENNIS, b. Balt., June 22, 1942; A.B. cum laude, Columbia U., 1964; student Institut d'Etudes Europeennes, Paris, 1962-63; LL.B. cum laude, Harvard U., 1967; LL.M., London Sch. Econs., 1968; diploma cum laude Hague Acad. Internat. Law, 1968. Admitted to N.Y. State bar, 1968, D.C. bar, 1970; research asst. Harvard Law Sch., Cambridge, 1968-69; intern econ. and bus. affairs div. Office Legal Adviser, U.S. Dept. State, 1966; asst. to exec. editor for "The "The Advocates," WGBH-TV, Boston, 1969; dir. English-speaking seminars Hague Acad. Internat. Law, 1972; lectr. in internat. orgns. U. Va. Sch. Law, Charlottesville, 1973; asso. firm Covington & Burling, Washington, 1969-75, partner, 1975—. Mem. Council Fgn. Relations, Am. Soc. Internat. Law (exec. council 1970-73), Am. Bar Assn., Internat. Law Assn. Contbr. articles to legal jours. Office: 888 16th St NW Washington DC 20006 Tel (202) 452-6098

TROOST, FRANK WILLIAM, b. Joliet, Ill., June 8, 1916; B.S. in Bus. Adminstrn., U. So. Calif., 1937, LL.B., 1939. Admitted to Calif. bar, 1939; practiced law, 1939-65; judge Municipal Ct., Culver City, Calif., 1965—. Mem. U. So. Calif. Law Alumni Assn. (pres. 1961), Calif. Judges Assn. (past v.p.), SW Los Angeles Bar Assn. (past pres.). Office: 4130 Overland St Culver City CA 90230 Tel (213) 837-1251

TROP, MICHAEL LESLIE, b. Bronx, N.Y., July 13, 1947; B.A., Queens Coll., 1969; J.D., N.Y. U., 1972, LL.M., 1976. Admitted to Fla. bar, 1972, N.Y. bar, 1973; asso. firm Moss, Wels & Marcus, N.Y.C., 1972-75; asso. firm Schwartz, Nash, Heckerling, Tescher & Morgenstern, Miami, 1976—. Mem. Am., N.Y. State bar assns., Fla. Bar, Phi Beta Kappa. Office: 1401 Brickell Ave Miami FL 33131 Tel (305) 358-1544

TROPP, ROBERT ALAN, b. Tampa, Fla., Jan. 20, 1946; A.B., Mercer U., 1967; LL.B., S.Tex. Coll. Law, 1971. Admitted to Fla. bar, 1972; asst. state's atty. 13th Jud. Circuit Fla., Hillsborough County, 1971-73; asst. city atty. Tampa, 1974; asso. firm Barrs, Melendi & Williamson, Tampa, 1975-76; individual practice law, Tampa, 1976—. Mem. Hillsborough County Bar Assn. Home: 4141 Bayshore Blvd Tampa FL 33611 Office: 100 E Twiggs St Tampa FL 33602 Tel (813) 225-1611

TROTT, BERNARD LEROY, b. Kearney, Nebr., Oct. 29, 1923; A.B., Nebr. Wesleyan U., 1947; J.D. with distinction, U. Mich., 1949. Admitted to Mo. bar, 1949, U.S. Supreme Ct. bar, 1954, Colo. bar, 1955; asso. firm Warrick, Brewer and Lamkin, Kansas City, Mo., 1949-54; individual practice law, Colorado Springs, 1955-61; partner firm Trott and Kunstle, Colorado Springs, 1961-68, firm Trott, Kunstle and Hughes, Colorado Springs, 1968—; dir. Western Nat. Bank, Mountain States Pipe and Supply Co. City councilman, Mission, Kans., 1953, 54; trustee Broadmoor Community Ch., 1966-72, chmn., 1971-72; pres. El Paso County chpt. Am. Cancer Soc., 1968-69; chmn. Cancer Crusade, 1967-68. Mem. El Paso County (pres. 1972, 73), Colo., Am. bar assns. Home: 23 Broadmoor Ave Colorado Springs CO 80906 Office: 321 First National Bank Bldg Colorado Springs CO 80903 Tel (303) 636-5123

TROTTA, ROBERT DAVID, b. Waterbury, Conn., Aug. 17, 1937; B.A., Hobart Coll., 1962; J.D., Syracuse U., 1965. Admitted to N.Y. State bar, 1966, U.S. Supreme Ct. bar, 1974; partner firm Davis & Trotta, Millerton, N.Y., 1967—; first dep. pub. defender Dutchess County (N.Y.), 1967—; atty. Town of Northeast (N.Y.), 1973—; sch. atty. NE Central Sch. Dist., 1973—. Mem. Dutchess County Charter Rev. Com., 1975-76; exec. council Boy Scouts Am., 1975—; trustee Millerton Free Library, 1973—. Mem. N.Y. State, Dutchess County bar assns., N.Y. State Trial Lawyers Assn. Home: Rt 199 Millerton NY 12546 Office: Dutchess Ave Millerton NY 12546 Tel (518) 789-4656

TROTTI, ROBERT SWIFT, b. Brookeland, Tex., Feb. 11, 1917; B.B.A., U. Tex., 1948, LL.B., 1950. Admitted to Tex. bar, 1949, U.S. Supreme Ct. bar, 1954; chief corp. div. Office of Sec. State of Tex., 1950-52, acting Asst. Sec. State, 1952-53; first asst. atty. gen. Tex., 1953-55; mem. firm Blakley & Walker, Dallas, 1955-61, McCulloch, Ray, Trotti, Hemphill & Meadows, Dallas, 1961—; chmn. revision of corp. laws com. State Bar Tex. Mem. Am., Tex., Dallas bar assns., Phi Alpha Delta, Dallas C. of C. Home: 6146 Yorkshire Dr Dallas TX 75230 Office: 3000 Fidelity Union Tower Dallas TX 75201 Tel (214) 748-6151

TROUT, WILLIAM JOHN, b. Des Moines, Nov. 5, 1937; student Iowa State U., 1955, Marquette U., 1957-59; LL.B., Drake U., 1962, J.D., 1968. Admitted to Iowa bar, 1962, U.S. Supreme Ct. bar, 1976; legal counsel Iowa Legis. Research Bur., 1962-63; partner firm Coppola, Trout, Taha & Gazzo, and predecessors, Des Moines, 1963—. Mem. Iowa, Polk County bar assns. Home: 1700 Casady Dr Des Moines IA 50315 Office: 400 Plymouth Bldg Des Moines IA 50307 Tel (515) 244-3197

TROUTMAN, CHARLES HENRY, III, b. Wooster, Ohio, Mar. 25, 1944; B.A. in Anthropology, Wheaton (Ill.) Coll., 1966; J.D., Am. U., Washington, 1969; M. Comparative Law, So. Meth. U., 1970. Admitted to D.C. bar, 1969, Ill. bar, 1969, Trust Ter. of Pacific Islands, 1972, Guam bar, 1973, U.S. Supreme Ct. bar, 1976; asst. atty. gen. Guam, 1970-74; partner firm Trotman, Troutman & Assos., Guam, 1974-75; atty. gen. Guam, 1975-77; chmn. Territorial Crime Commn., 1975-77; mem. Jud. Council Guam, 1975-77. Mem. Am., Ill., Fed. bar assns., Am. Soc. Internat. Law, Christian Legal Soc. Recipient Washington Law Reporter award Am. U. Law Sch., 1970, Am. Jurisprudence award So. Meth. U., 1970. Office: PO Box 455 Agana GU 96910 Tel (Guam) 477-9861

TROUTMAN, HENRY BATTEY, b. Rome, Ga., June 15, 1886; student U. Ga., 1905-06, 08-09. Admitted to Ga. bar, 1910, since practiced in Atlanta; mem. firm Troutman, Sanders, Lockerman & Ashmore and predecessors firms, Atlanta, 1930—; mem. Fulton County Civil Service Bd., World War II; mem. bd. Office Price Adminstrn., World War II; mem. aldermanic bd. City of Atlanta, 1962-64, mem. sch. bd., 1920-21. Mem. Am., Ga., Atlanta bar assns. Home: 1118 W Wesley Rd NW Atlanta GA 30327 Office: 1500 Candler Bldg Atlanta GA 30303 Tel (404) 658-8000

TROUTMAN, HOLMES RUSSELL, b. Beckley, W.Va., July 27, 1933; B.A., Marshall Coll., 1955; LL.B., U. Miami, 1958. Admitted to Fla. bar, 1958; mem. firm Akerman, Turnbull, Senterfitt & Edison, Orlando, Fla., 1958-62, Fishback, Davis, Dominick & Troutman, Orlando, 1962-69; individual practice law, Winter Park, Fla., 1969-70; partner firm Troutman, Parrish & Weeks, and predecessor, Winter Park, 1970—; city atty. Winter Park, 1968-72, city prosecutor, 1970-72; legal adviser Orange-Seminole Legis. Del., 1966. Mem. Am., Fla. (bd. govs. 1972—, pres. 1977—), Orange County (pres. 1968-69) bar assns., Acad. Fla. Trial Lawyers (dir. 1968-72), Legal Aid Soc. (pres. 1968-70). Recipient Good Govt. award Orlando Jr. C. of C., 1969; contbr. articles to legal jours. Home: 1600 Barcelona Way Winter Park FL 32789 Office: 222 W Comstock St Suite 200 Winter Park FL 32789 Tel (305) 647-2277

TROWBRIDGE, CYRUS PFEIFFER, b. Ottawa, Ill., Aug. 24, 1928; B.A., Denison U., 1950; J.D., U. Va., 1953. Admitted to Va. bar, 1952, Fla. bar, 1956; individual practice law, Stuart, Fla., 1956-60; judge 19th Circuit Ct. Fla., Stuart, 1960—. Mem. Martin County Bar Assn., Scribes, Order of Coif, Mensa, Intertel. Editor-in-chief Va. Law Rev., 1952-53. Office: PO Box 445 Stuart FL 33494 Tel (305) 283-6760

TROXELL, DANA CHASE, b. Montclair, N.J., Mar. 27, 1930; A.B., Harvard, 1951; LL.B., U. Va., 1956; LL.M. in Taxation, N.Y. U., 1962. Admitted to N.Y. bar, 1957, N.J. bar, 1972; asso. firm Dewey, Ballantine, Bushby, Palmer & Wood, N.Y.C., 1956-60; asso. firm Olwine, Connelly, Chase, O'Donnell & Weyher, N.Y.C., 1960-64; asso. firm Perkins, Daniels & McCormack, N.Y.C., 1964-66, partner, 1966-74; partner firm Burke & Burke, Daniels, Leighton & Reid, N.Y.C., 1975—. Mem. Am., N.J. bar assns., Tax Mgmt. Estate Advisory Bd. Home: 44 Windermere Terr Short Hills NJ 07078 Office: 30 Rockefeller Plaza New York City NY 10020 Tel (212) 489-0400

TROY, ANTHONY FRANCIS, b. Hartford, Conn., Apr. 16, 1941; B.A. in Govt., St. Michaels Coll., 1963; LL.B., U. Richmond, 1966. Admitted to Va. bar, 1966, D.C. bar, 1972, U.S. Supreme Ct. bar, 1970; asst. atty. gen. Va., 1966-72; asso. firm Colson & Shapiro, Washington, N.Y.C. and Boston, 1972-74; dep. atty. gen. State of Va., 1974-75, chief dep. atty. gen., 1975-77, atty. gen., 1977—; mem. Va. Crime Commn., Va. Council Criminal Justice; counsel to Electricity Cost Commn., Senate Privileges and Elections subcom. on Redistricting, Jt. Coms. of Privileges and Elections on Campaign Funding and Financing. Past pres. Cheaterfield Young Dems.; bd. dirs., trustee Buford Acad. Mem. Am., Va., Richmond bar assns., Nat. Assn. Attys. Gen., Phi Delta Phi. Home: 2841 Earlswood Rd Midlothian VA 23113 Office: 1101 E Broad St Richmond VA 23219 Tel (804) 786-2071

TROY, BRIGITTA BALOS, b. N.Y.C., July 13, 1940; A.B., Radcliffe Coll., 1961; J.D., U. So. Calif., 1969. Admitted to Calif. bar, 1970; partner firm Kandel & Troy, Los Angeles, 1970-76; asst. exec. dir., gen. counsel Los Angeles County Bar Assn., 1976—. Mem. risk mgmt. adv. com. Los Angeles County, 1975-76. Mem. Am., Calif., Los Angeles County bar assns. Office: 606 S Olive St suite 1212 Los Angeles CA 90014 Tel (213) 624-8571

TRUCKS, JAMES FRANK, b. Birmingham, Ala., May 14, 1945; A.B. magna cum laude, Birmingham So. Coll., 1964; J.D. magna cum laude, Cumberland Sch. Law, 1968; LL.M. in Taxation, Washington U., St. Louis, 1969. Admitted to Ala. bar, 1968, U.S. Tax Ct. bar, 1969, U.S. Supreme Ct. bar, 1975; asso. firm Lange, Simpson, Robinson & Somerville, Birmingham, 1969-72, partner, 1973-76; gen. counsel Sci. Games Devel. Corp., Atlanta, 1977—. Chmn. med. clinic bd. City of Birmingham, 1973-76. Mem. Ala. State Bar, Birmingham, Am. bar assns., Phi Beta Kappa. Office: 2625 Cumberland Pkwy NW Atlanta GA 30339 Tel (404) 433-1822

TRUE, BOBBY KNOX, b. Georgetown, Ky., Nov. 1, 1934; B.A., Georgetown Coll., 1955; LL.B., U. Ky., 1959. Admitted to Ky. bar, 1959; pvt. practice law, Bedford, Ky., 1959—; county atty., Trimble County, Ky., 1962-74; dir. Bedford Loan & Deposit Bank, 1970—. Chmn., Trimble County Democratic Party, 1972—. Mem. Ky., Am. bar assns. Club: Bedford Rotary (pres. 1963-64). Home: Bedford KY 40006 Office: Main St Bedford KY 40006

TRUITT, ROBERT RALPH, JR., b. Chaves County, N. Mex., Jan. 21, 1948; student Odessa Coll., 1969; B.A., also B.B.A., Southwestern U., 1970; J.D., U. Tex., 1973. Admitted to Tex. bar, 1973, U.S. Ct. Appeals Fifth Circuit, 1976, Dist. Ct. Western Tex., 1977; asso. firm Turpin, Smith & Dyer, Midland, Tex., 1973-77; individual practice law, Midland, 1977—. Mem. Midland County, Am. bar assns., State Bar Tex., Midland County Jr. Bar Assn., Pi Gamma Mu. Recipient Student Achievement award Wall St. Jour., 1970; staff Am. Jour. Criminal Law, 1972-73. Home: 2601 N A St Apt #104 Midland TX 79701 Office: 300 First Nat Bank Bldg Midland TX 79701 Tel (915) 682-2525

TRULOCK, CHARLES R., JR., b. Orlando, Fla., Mar. 11, 1940; B.S., U. Tampa, 1962; J.D., Fla. State U., 1968. Admitted to Fla. bar, 1969; asso. firm James M. Russ, 1968-70; pros. atty. Orange County (Fla.), 1970-72; individual practice law, Orlando, Fla., 1972—. Mem. Am., Fla. bar assns. Home: PO Box 2932 Orlando FL 32802 Office: 302 First Federal Bldg 109 E Church St Orlando FL 32801 Tel (305) 841-9051

TRUMAN, CATHARINE TURK, b. Candor, N.Y., Sept. 6, 1915; A.B., Syracuse U., 1936, postgrad., 1936-38. Admitted to N.Y. State bar, 1951, No. Dist. of N.Y. bar, 1951; mem. firm Turk and Boldman, Owego, N.Y., 1951-64, firm Turk, Truman, Bishop and Simpson, Owego, 1965—. Mem. Estate Planning Council of So. N.Y., Am., N.Y. (exec. com. young lawyers sect. 1952-54), Tioga County (pres. 1956) bar assns. Home: Box 290 RD 3 Owego NY 13827 Office: 29 Lake St Owego NY 13827 Tel (607) 687-0567

TRUMBULL, TERRY ALAN, b. Berkeley, Calif., Nov. 5, 1945; B.A. in Econs., U. Calif., 1967; J.D., Georgetown U., 1970; LL.M., George Washington U., 1973. Admitted to D.C. bar, 1971, Calif. bar, 1973, U.S. Supreme Ct. bar, 1975; sr. staff mem. Inst. Pub. Adminstrn., Washington, 1970-71; legal adviser to dep. asst. adminstr. for planning and evaluation EPA, Washington, 1972-73; counsel regulatory affairs Nuclear Energy div. Gen. Electric Co., San Jose, Calif., 1973—; adviser to gubernatorial candidate Jerry Brown, 1973-74. Chmn. Santa Clara County (Calif.) People for a Golden Gate Nat. Recreation Area, 1974-76; co-chmn. Brown for Gov.; Santa Clara County, 1974; mem. Santa Clara County Planning Commn., 1976—; mem. Family Planning Interagency Commn., Santa Clara, Calif., 1977—; mem. Joint Transp. Planning Com., Santa Clara County, 1976—. Mem. Calif., D.C. bar assns. Contbr. articles in field to profl. jours. Home: 1514 Bird Ave San Jose CA 95125 Office: Mail Code 602 175 Curtner St San Jose CA 95125 Tel (408) 297-3000

TRUSTY, FRANK O., II, b. Jackson, Ky., July 2, 1939; J.D., U. Ky., 1963; postgrad. in chemistry No. Ky. Coll., 1974-75. Admitted to Ky. bar, 1964; asso., partner firm Hughes, Clark & Ziegler and predecessors, Covington, Ky., 1964-72; asst. Commonwealth's atty. Kenton County, Ky., 1972-76; Commonwealth's atty. 16th Jud. Dist., Covington, Ky., 1976—; instr. polit. sci. U. Ky. Community Coll., Covington, 1966-68, Thomas More Coll., Edgewood, Ky., 1972—; criminal law city atty., city prosecutor Crescent Springs, Ky., 1963-75; city prosecutor, Ft. Mitchell, Ky., 1967-69. Vice pres. Covington Kenton County Jaycees; chmn. bd. Hope Cottage; dist. chmn. Boy Scouts Am.; mem. comprehensive care bd. No. Ky. Mental Health; bd. dirs. No. Ky. Community Center. Mem. Nat. Dist. Attys. Assn. (mem. victim/witness com.), Ky., Kenton County (past pres.) bar assns., Ky. Commonwealth Attys. Assn. Named outstanding young man of Kenton County, 1973. Home: 147 Williamsburg St Fort Mitchell KY 41017 Office: City County Bldg 303 Court St Covington KY 41011 Tel (606) 292-2336

TRYBULSKI, WALTER JACOB, b. North Walpole, N.H., Nov. 19, 1905; LL.B., Northeastern U., Springfield, Mass., 1942, J.D., 1942. Admitted to Mass. bar, 1943; since practiced in Chicopee; alderman City of Chicopee, 1934-40, treas., 1940-48, mayor, 1952-56. Commr. Mass. Indsl. Accident Bd., 1962-69. Mem. Am., Mass., Hampden County (Mass.), Chicopee (pres. 1974) bar assns., Am. Trial Lawyers Assn. Home and office: 14 Carlton Ave Chicopee MA 01020 Tel (413) 592-1832

TRYGSTAD, LAWRENCE BENSON, b. Holton, Mich., Mar. 22, 1937; B.A., U. Mich., 1959; J.D., U. So. Calif., 1967. Admitted to Calif. bar, 1968; tchr. Am. history and govt. Los Angeles Unified Sch. Dist., 1959-68, asst. vice prin., 1965-68, pres. faculty assn., 1965-66, 67-68; legal counsel Calif. Tchrs. Assn., Los Angeles, 1968-71; partner firm Trygstad & Odell, Los Angeles, 1971—; instr. tchr. negotiation U. Calif., Northridge; panelist TV show Law and the Teacher. Bd. dirs. George Washington Carver Found., Los Angeles. Mem. State Bar Calif., Am., Los Angeles County bar assns., Calif., Los Angeles trial lawyers assns., Nat. Assn. Tchr. Attys., Phi Alpha Delta. Author publs. for tchrs. orgns. Home: 4209 Aleman Dr Tarzana CA 91356 Office: 1800 Century Park E #517 Los Angeles CA 90067

TRYNIN, CHARLES HARRISON, b. N.Y.C., Aug. 17, 1905; B.S. cum laude, Harvard, 1926, LL.B. (now J.D.), 1929. Admitted to N.Y. bar, 1930, U.S. Supreme Ct. bar, 1965; asso. firm Ernst, Gale, Bernays, & Falk, N.Y.C., 1930-35; asso. with Maurice Smith, N.Y.C., 1935-58; individual practice law, N.Y.C., 1935—. Mem. Am. Bar City N.Y., N.Y. County Lawyers Assn. Home: 2 5th Ave New York City NY 10011 Office: 230 Park Ave New York City NY 10017 Tel (212) 986-3855

TSCHIRHART, DANIEL LEE, b. Ruth, Mich., Apr. 25, 1941; B.A., U. Detroit, 1965; J.D., Detroit Coll. Law, 1969. Admitted to Mich. bar, 1970; asst. prosecutor County of Ingham (Mich.), 1970-74; judge Mich. 54-B Dist. Ct., 1974—. Mem. Am., Mich., Ingham County bar assns., Mich. Dist. Judges Assn. Office: 410 Abbott Rd East Lansing MI 48823 Tel (517) 337-1731

TSENIN, KSENIA (KAY), b. Shanghai, China, Jan. 10, 1947; student San Francisco State U., 1965-70; J.D., U. San Francisco, 1973. Admitted to Calif. bar, 1973; partner firm Ilyin & Tsenin, San Francisco, 1976—; cons. Queens Bench Found., San Francisco, 1976; asst. legal coordinator Calif. NOW, Inc., 1975—; founder Marin Abused Women's Services. Mem. San Francisco Bar Assn., Calif., N. Bay women lawyers assns., NOW (pres. Marin County chpt. 1975-76). Office: 1136 Clement St San Francisco CA 94118 Tel (415) 387-5779

TUAL, BLANCHARD EVERETT, b. Memphis, Mar. 12, 1945; B.A., U. Fla., 1967; J.D., U. Tenn., 1970. Admitted to Tenn. bar, 1970; partner firm Tual, Gordon, Tual & Riley, Memphis, 1970—. Bd. dirs. Barksdale Boys Club, 1975—, Am. Cancer Soc., 1975—; staff fund raising drive LeMoyne Owens Coll., 1972-75. Mem. Am., Tenn., Memphis-Shelby bar assns., Memphis-Shelby Young Lawyers (pres. 1977—). Home: 2700 Lombardy Memphis TN 38111 Office: 1041 Sterick Bldg Memphis TN 38103 Tel (901) 525-6665

TUCKER, BILLY DYKES, b. Ft. Worth, Feb. 27, 1924; student Tex. Tech. U., 1941-46; LL.B., Tex. U., 1949. Admitted to Tex. bar, 1949; asst. dist. atty. Lubbock (Tex.), 1950-52; partner firm Howard, Tucker & Waller, Lubbock, 1952-72; individual practice law, Lubbock, 1972—. Trustee Lubbock Ind. Sch. Dist., 1968-72, pres., 1972-74. Mem. Lubbock County Bar Assn., State Bar Tex. Office: 1703 Ave K Lubbock TX 79401 Tel (806) 762-4344

TUCKER, BOWEN HAYWARD, b. Providence, Apr. 13, 1938; A.B. in Math., Brown U., 1959; J.D., U. Mich., 1962. Admitted to R.I. bar, 1963, Ill. bar, 1967, U.S. Supreme Ct. bar, 1970; asso. firm Hinckley, Allen, Salisbury & Parsons, Providence, 1962-66; atty. Caterpillar Tractor Co., Peoria, Ill., 1966-72, sr. atty., 1972; counsel FMC Corp., Chgo., 1972—. Mem. com. on rights of minors Ill. Commn. on Children, 1974—; sec. Ill. div. ACLU, 1975—. Mem. Am., R.I., Ill., Chgo. (chmn. com. juvenile law 1976-77) bar assns., Engine Mfrs. Assn. (chmn. legal com. 1972), Constrn. Industry Mfrs. Assn. (exec. com. lawyers' council 1972, 75—, vice chmn. 1977), Machinery and Allied Products Inst. (products liability council 1974—), Phi Alpha Delta. Home: 107 W Noyes St Arlington Heights IL 60005 Office: 200 E Randolph Dr Suite 6700 Chicago IL 60601 Tel (312) 861-5940

TUCKER, CHARLES FREDERICK, b. Lynn, Mass., May 22, 1941; B.A., Yale, 1963, J.D., 1966. Admitted to Conn. bar, 1966, N.H. bar, 1971; regional planner Central Naugatuck Valley Planning Agy., Waterbury, Conn., 1966-70; planning dir. Southeastern N.H. Regional Planning Commn., Exeter, N.H., 1971—; adj. prof. U. N.H., 1970—; vis. lectr. Shoals Marine Labs., 1975—. Mem. commn. overseers Strawberry Banke Inc., 1973—, chmn., 1975-77; mem. N.H. Planners Assn., 1971—, mem. exec. com., 1974-77. Contbr. articles in field to profl. jours. Home: 16 Epping Rd Exeter NH 03833 Office: 3 Water St Exeter NH 03833 Tel (603) 778-0586

TUCKER, DAVEY LEWIS, b. Jacksonville, Fla., May 23, 1943; B.A., Miss. State U., 1965; J.D., U. Miss., 1968. Admitted to Miss. bar, 1968; individual practice law, Jackson, Miss., 1968—; prof. bus. law Miss. Coll., Clinton, 1969-72. Mem. Miss., Hinds County bar assns., Miss., Am., Hinds County trial lawyers assns., Delta Theta. Home: 5512 Ridgewood Rd Jackson MS 39211 Office: 118 S President St Jackson MS 39201 Tel (601) 948-4870

TUCKER, DON EUGENE, b. Rockbridge, Ohio, Feb. 3, 1928; B.A., Aurora Coll., 1951; LL.B., Yale, 1956. Admitted to Ohio bar, 1956; asso. firm Manchester, Bennett, Powers & Ullman, Youngstown, Ohio, 1956-63, partner firm, 1963-72, counsel, 1972—; gen. counsel Comml. Shearing, Inc., Youngstown, 1972-75, v.p., gen. counsel, 1975—; dir. Union Nat. Bank, Youngstown. Mem. Am., Ohio, Mahoning County (past pres., psat trustee) bar assns., Greater Youngstown C. of C. (dir. 1973—). Home: 6838 Tanglewood Dr Youngstown OH 44512 Office: 1775 Logan Ave Youngstown OH 44505 Tel (216) 746-8011

TUCKER, FRANK GEORGE EDWIN, b. Grand Junction, Colo., Feb. 15, 1941; B.S., U. Colo., 1964, J.D., 1967. Admitted to Colo. bar, 1967; staff atty. to U.S. Park Service, Dept. Interior, Washington, 1967-68; legis. counsel Nat. Assn. Electric Cos., Washington, 1968-70; staff Office of Gen. Counsel, EPA, 1970-71; partner firm Tucker & Tucker, Glenwood Springs, Colo., 1971-72; dist. atty. Pitkin, Garfield and Rio Blanco counties (Colo.), 1972—; atty. adviser White House Hist. Soc., 1967-70. Mem. Am., Colo., 9th Jud. Dist. bar assns., Am. Trial Lawyers Assn., Nat., Colo. (dir.) dist. attys. assns. Home: 301 Rockledge Dr Glenwood Springs CO 81601 Office: Court House Annex Glenwood Springs CO 81601 Tel (303) 945-8635

TUCKER, JACK WILLIFORD, b. Gardena, Calif., Oct. 31, 1926; J.D., U. So. Calif., 1951. Admitted to Calif. bar, 1952, U.S. Ct. of Mil. Appeals bar, 1953; served to lt. JAGC, U.S. Army, Washington, 1952-53; house counsel Republic Indemnity Ins. Co., Los Angeles, 1954-56; individual practice law, Los Angeles, 1956—; instr. Met. Community Coll., Los Angeles, 1958-72. Mem. Am., Los Angeles County, SW Los Angeles bar assns., Los Angeles Trial Lawyers Assn. Office: 4818 Lincoln Blvd Marina del Rey CA 90291 Tel (213) 823-5466

TUCKER, JAMES GUY, b. Oklahoma City, June 13, 1943; B.A. in Govt., Harvard, 1964; J.D., U. Ark., Fayetteville, 1968. Admitted to Ark. bar, 1968; asso. firm Rose, Barron, Nash, Williamson, Carroll & Clay, Little Rock, 1968-70; pros. atty. 6th Jud. Dist. Ark., Pulaski and Perry Counties, 1971-72; atty. gen. Ark., Little Rock, 1973—. Teaching fellow Am. U. and Internat. Coll., Beirut, Lebanon, 1966; free lance war corr. Republic Vietnam, 1965, 67. Vice pres. Ouachita area Girl Scout Council, 1971-72. Bd. dirs. Ark. chpt. Am. Civil Liberties Union, 1968-70, Medcore Found., Inc., 1968—; chmn. Shorter Coll. Scholarship Com., 1969; mem. deferred gifts adv. com. Am. U., Beirut, 1971—; chmn. Ark. Criminal Justice and Hwy. Safety Information Safety. Named Ark. Young Man of Yr., 1972. Mem. Am., Ark., Pulaski County bar assns., Ark. Pros. Atty.'s Assn., Nat. Dist. Atty.'s Assn., Am. Judicature Soc., Nat. Assn. Attys. Gen., Phi Alpha Delta, Sigma Alpha Epsilon (Rush chmn., treas. 1963-64). Author: Arkansas Men at War, 1968. Home: 7 White Oak Lane Little Rock AR 72207 Office: Justice Bldg Little Rock AR 72201*

TUCKER, JAMES L., b. Big Stone Gap, Va., July 1, 1941; A.B., Coll. William and Mary, 1963, B.C.L., 1966. Admitted to Va. bar, 1966; asso. firm Carneal, Smith & Athey, Williamsburg, Va., 1967-68, firm Gilmer, Sadler, Ingram, Thomas & Sutherland, Pulaski, Va., 1969-70; individual practice law, Pulaski, 1970—. Mem. Va. State Bar, Am., Pulaski County bar assns., Phi Beta Kappa. Contbr. articles to legal publs. Home: 320 Maple St Dublin VA 24084 Office: 28 W Main St Box 849 Pulaski VA 24301 Tel (703) 980-6066

TUCKER, JAMES WILFRED, b. Cullman, Ala., Feb. 17, 1931; B.S. in Commerce and Bus. Adminstrn., U. Ala., 1953, LL.B., 1955. Admitted to Ala. bar, 1955; individual practice law, Cullman, 1955—; city judge, Cullman, 1959-62, Hanceville, Ala., 1957-60; county solicitor Cullman County (Ala.), 1962-70. Mem. Ala. Trial Lawyers Assn. Home: 1317 Beth NW Cullman AL 35055 Office: 111B Downtown Plaza Cullman AL 35055 Tel (205) 734-4462

TUCKER, JOHN HELLUMS, JR., b. Pine Bluff, Ark., Feb. 25, 1891; A.B., Washington and Lee U., 1910, LL.D., 1958; LL.B., La. State U., 1920, LL.D., 1956; LL.D., Tulane U., 1959, Loyola U., 1966; D.L.H., Centenary Coll., 1972. Admitted to La. bar, 1920, U.S. Supreme Ct. bar, 1930; individual practice law, Shreveport, La., 1920; mem. firm James E. Smitherman, Shreveport, 1920-32, firm Tucker, Martin, Holder, Jeter, and Jackson, Shreveport, 1932—; pres. La. State Law Inst., Baton Rouge, 1938-65, chmn., 1966—; mem. Supreme Ct. com. on profl. ethics and grievances, 1928-34; past lectr. civil law Tulane U., Loyola U. Mem. Shreveport, La., Am. bar assns., Phi Beta Kappa, Phi Delta Phi, Order Coif. Contbr. articles to legal jours. Home: 906 McCormick Blvd Shreveport LA 71104 Office: 1300 Beck Bldg Shreveport LA 71101 Tel (318) 425-7764

TUCKER, MARY ANN, b. Fargo, N.D., Jan. 20, 1938; B.S., N.D. State U., 1961; M.S., Iowa State U., 1965; J.D., Ind. U., 1973. Admitted to Ind. bar, 1973; patent atty. Eli Lilly and Co., Indpls., 1973—. Sec. bd. visitors Ind. U. Indpls. Law Sch., 1974—. Mem. Ind., Indpls. bar assns., Internat. Patent and Trademark Assn., Indpls. Law Sch. Alumni Assn. (dir.), Phi Alpha Delta, Sigma Xi, Phi Kappa Phi. Contbr. articles to legal publs. Home: 61 Ridgeway Dr Brownsburg IN 46112 Office: 307 E Mc Carty St Indianapolis IN 46206 Tel (317) 261-3425

TUCKER, ROBERT ALAN, b. Memphis, Nov. 30, 1933; B.B.A., Memphis State U., 1959, J.D., 1965. Admitted to Tenn. bar, 1965; partner firm Gipson & Tucker, Memphis, 1965—. Mem. Am. Bar Assn., Tenn. Trial Lawyers, Nat. Hist. Soc., Nat. Audubon Soc., Delta Theta Phi. Office: Suite 1104 Exchange Bldg Memphis TN 38103 Tel (901) 525-6331

TUCKER, ROBERT KENNETH, b. Benton Harbor, Mich., Jan. 25, 1942; B.B.A., Western Mich. U., 1964, M.B.A., 1967; J.D., U. Fla., 1968. Admitted to Fla. bar, 1969; asso. firm Bradford, Williams, McKay, Kimbrell, Hamann & Jennings, Miami, Fla., 1969—. Mem. Dade County (Fla.), Fla., Am. bar assns., Dade County Def. Bar Assn., Def. Research Inst., Phi Delta Phi. Home: 1133 Andora Ave Coral Gables FL 33146 Office: 101 E Flagler St Miami FL 33131 Tel (305) 358-8181

TUCKER, RONALD CREIGHTON, b. Anderson, Ind., May 24, 1946; A.B., Purdue U., 1968; J.D., Ind. U., 1973. Admitted to Ind. bar, 1974; individual practice law, Anderson, 1974—; mem. Madison County Community Legal Services Corp., Inc. Bd. dirs. Madison County Dramatic Players, Anderson Exchange Club. Mem. Am., Ind. State, Madison County bar assns. Home: 1625 Lynnwood Dr Anderson IN 46012 Office: 6 W 8th St Anderson IN 46016 Tel (317) 643-8428

TUCKER, SAMUEL LEE, b. McComb, Miss., Nov. 1, 1944; B.A., Millsaps Coll., 1966; student Miss. State U., 1967; J.D., U. Miss., 1971. Admitted to Miss. bar, 1971, Fed. bar, 1971; legislative draftsman Miss. Ho. Reps., 1971-76, sr. legal asst., counsel judiciary com., 1976—. Mem. Miss. State, Hinds County bar assns., Jackson Young Lawyers. Office: Room 206 New Capitol Bldg Jackson MS 39216 Tel (601) 354-6184

TUCKER, STEFAN FRANKLIN, b. Detroit, Dec. 31, 1938; A.Bus., Flint Jr. Community Coll., 1958; B.B.A., U. Mich., 1960, J.D., 1963. Admitted to D.C. bar, 1964, U.S. Ct. Claims bar, 1964, U.S. Tax Ct. bar, 1964; clk. to judge U.S. Tax Ct., Washington, 1963-64; asso., then partner firm Arent, Fox, Kintner, Plotkin & Kahn, Washington, 1964-74, firm Tucker, Flyer, Sanger, Reider & Lewis, Washington, 1975—; speaker in field; professorial lectr. law George Washington U., 1970—; mem. nat. com. U. Mich. Law Sch. Fund, 1972—. Mem. Am. (points to remember editor Tax Lawyer 1966-72, vice chmn. com. real estate tax problems sect. taxes 1975-77, chmn. real estate com.), Fed., D.C. bar assns.; contbr. articles to legal jours.; editorial bd. Taxation for Lawyers, 1972—; mem. adv. bd. Bur. Nat. Affairs Housing and Devel. Reporter, 1973-76; editorial adv. bd. Jour. Real Estate Taxation, 1975—. Office: 1730 Massachusetts Ave NW Washington DC 20036 Tel (202) 452-8600

TUCKER, STEPHEN THOMAS, b. Berkeley, Calif., Sept. 30, 1939; student Pacific U.; B.S., Willamette U., 1962, J.D., 1965. Admitted to Calif. bar, 1966; dep. dist. atty. Alameda County (Calif.), 1966-68, asso. firm Eliassen & Postel, San Francisco, 1968-69; partner firm Dunivan, Wies, Murphy & Tucker, Hayward, 1969-70; dep. dist. atty. Sonoma County (Calif.), 1970—; lectr. Santa Rosa Jr. Coll., 1974—; guest lectr. Los Guillicos Crime Justice Center. Active Boy Scouts Am. Mem. Calif., Sonoma County bar assns., Redwood Empire Trial Lawyers Assn., Calif. Dist. Attys. Assn., Calif. Family Support Council. Home: 915 Helena Ave Santa Rosa CA 95404 Office: PO Box 1556 Santa Rosa CA 95402 Tel (707) 527-2641

TUCKER, STEVEN LEE, b. Albuquerque, July 31, 1947; B.A., St. John's Coll., 1969; J.D., U. Denver, 1972. Admitted to Colo. bar, 1972, N.Mex. bar, 1972; law clk. to judge 10th Circuit Ct. of Appeals, 1972-73; asso. firm Watson, Stillinger & Lunt, Santa Fe, 1973-75, Jones, Gallegos, Snead & Wertheim, Santa Fe, 1975—. Mem. Am., First Jud. Dist. bar assns. Articles editor Denver Law Jour., 1971-72. Home: 433 Delgado Pl Santa Fe NM 87501 Office: PO Box 2228 Santa Fe NM 97501 Tel (505) 982-2691

TUCKER, WARREN AUSTIN, b. Muskegon, Mich., Oct. 28, 1929; B.A., Pa. State U., 1954; LL.D., Fordham U., 1958. Admitted to N.Y. bar, 1958, Alaska bar, 1962; partner firm Buckalew & Tucker, 1964-69; judge Alaska Dist. Ct., 1969—; mem. Commn. on Jud. Qualifications. Mem. Am., Alaska bar assns. Tel (907) 274-8611

TUDOR, CHARLES DORSEY, b. Webb City, Mo., May 11, 1917; A.B., U. Mo., Columbia, 1938, LL.B., 1940. Admitted to Mo. bar, 1940; individual practice law, Joplin, Mo., 1940—; asst. pros. atty. Jasper County (Mo.), 1951-52, 65-66. Mem. Joplin Pub. Bd., 1963-71, 73—, pres., 1973—; pres. Mo. Library Trustees Assn., 1970-71. Mem. Mo., Jasper County bar assns., Mo., Am. library assns. Home: 2932 E 17th St Joplin MO 64801 Office: 708 Frisco Bldg Joplin MO 64801 Tel (417) 623-2901

TUDOR, JOHN MARTIN, b. Kenton, Ohio, Jan. 2, 1937; B.A., Ohio State U., 1959; LL.B., Duke U., 1962. Admitted to Ohio bar, 1962, U.S. Supreme Ct. bar, 1973; asso. firm Squire, Sanders & Dempsey, Cleve., 1962-65; individual practice law, Kenton, 1965-69; partner firm Mahon, Tudor & Van Dyne, Kenton, 1969—, firm Tudor, Cloud & Cesner, Columbus, Ohio, 1972—; adj. prof. law Ohio No. U., 1964-67. Mem. Ohio State, Hardin County (past pres.) bar assns., Hardin County Hist. and Archtl. Soc. (founder), Phi Delta Phi. Home: 411 Cecelia St Kenton OH 43326 Office: 8 E Broad St Columbus OH 43215 Tel (614) 228-8787 also Ahlefeld Bldg Pub Sq Kenton OH 43326 Tel (419) 673-1292

TUELL, DAVID RIPLY, JR., b. Seattle, Feb. 9, 1936; B.A., U. Wash., 1957, J.D., 1959. Admitted to Wash. bar, 1960; tax analyst Nalleys Inc., Tacoma, 1959-60; partner firm Albert, Andrews, Worswick & Tuell, Tacoma, 1960-64, firm Tuell & Anderson, 1967-74, firm Tuell, Anderson & Hudson, Tacoma, 1975—; individual practice, Tacoma, 1964-67. Mem. Tacoma Sch. Bd., 1965—, pres., 1970, 74. Mem. Am., Wash. bar assns., Am. Contract Bridge League (life master), Am. Bowling Congress (Tacoma masters champion; dir. Western conf. 1970—, pres. 1975-76). Home: 1013 Laurel Ct Tacoma WA 98466 Office: 1457 S Union St Tacoma WA 98405 Tel (206) 749-0070

TUETING, WILLIAM FRANCIS, b. Fargo, N.D., Aug. 29, 1942; student Carleton Coll., 1960-63; B.S., Columbia, 1965, LL.B., 1968. Admitted to N.Y. bar, 1969; asso. firm Simpson Thacher & Bartlett, N.Y.C., 1968-73, Spengler Carlson Guber Churchill & Brodsky, N.Y.C., 1973—. Mem. Assn. Bar City N.Y., Council of N.Y. Law Assos. (chmn. steering com. 1974-76), Am., N.Y. State bar assns. Office: 280 Park Ave New York City NY 10017 Tel (212) 682-4444

TUJO, JOHN ALBERT, b. Windsor, Ont., Can., Aug. 2, 1937; B.B.A., U. Portland, 1959; J.D., Lewis and Clark Northwestern Coll. Law, 1964. Admitted to Oreg. bar, 1965; individual practice law, Portland, Oreg.; prof. bus. law U. Portland, Portland State U. Mem. Multnomah County (Oreg.) Bar, Am. Trial Lawyers Assn., Alpha Kappa Psi. Office: 927 Boise Cascade Bldg Portland OR 97201 Tel (503) 224-5260

TUKE, MARGARET ELIZABETH, b. Indpls., Dec. 10, 1947; A.B., Ind. U., 1968, J.D., 1971. Admitted to Ind. bar, 1971; atty. Ind. Civil Rights Commn., 1976—; dep. city atty. Bloomington (Ind.), 1972-74; individual practice law, Bloomington, 1974-75; chief investigator Bloomington Human Rights Commn., 1972-75; dep. juvenile probation officer Bloomington, 1970-71; legal adv. panel Bloomington Human Rights Commn., 1975-76, commr., chmn. bylaws com., 1977—. Mem. Monroe County Democratic Central Com., 1972-76; precinct vice-committeeman Dem. Party, 1972-74, committeeman, 1974-76, del. state conv., 1974. Mem. Am. Bar Assn. Tel (812) 339-7532

TULISANO, RICHARD DON, b. Hartford, Conn., Nov. 7, 1939; B.A. in Sociology, U. Conn., grad. Law Sch., 1969. Admitted to Conn. bar, 1969; asso. firm Pizzella & Pizzella, 1969-71, firm Pizzella, Nassau & Tulisano, Newington, Conn., 1971-73; individual practice law, Rocky Hill, Conn., 1973—; mem. Conn. Gen. Assembly, 1975-76, 77—. Mem. Am. Judicature Soc., Am. Acad. Polit. and Social Sci., Conn., Hartford County, New Britain bar assns. Recipient Jurisprudence Book prize, 1969; Corpus Juris Secundum award, 1969. Home: 11 Sunny Crest Dr Rocky Hill CT 06067 Office: 2606 Main St Rocky Hill CT 06067 Tel (203) 563-9305

TULL, JOHN ANDERSON, b. Denver, Sept. 1, 1943; A.B., Williams Coll., 1965; LL.B., Yale, 1970. Admitted to Ariz. bar, 1971, U.S. Supreme Ct. bar, 1975; Reginald Heber Smith fellow Pima County Legal Aid, Tucson, 1970-72, staff atty., 1972-74, exec. dir., 1974—; chmn. Ariz. statewide legal services project, 1975-76. Mem. Pima County Bar Assn. Home: 2125 N Silverbell Rd Tucson AZ 85705 Office: 377 S Meyer Ave Tucson AZ 85701 Tel (602) 623-9461

TULL, WILLIAM FREED, b. Sellersville, Pa., Apr. 30, 1934; student Pa. State U., 1952; A.B., Ursinus Coll., 1956; J.D., U. N. Mex., 1965. Admitted to Alaska bar, 1968; staff atty. Alaska State Housing Authority, 1968-70; individual practice law, Palmer, Alaska, 1970-76; partner firm Tull & Luffberry, Palmer, 1976—; real estate broker, 1970—; pres. 1st Alaska Corp., 1973—. Mem. Alaska (dir. 1976—), Palmer (dir. 1971—) chambers commerce, Alaska Bar Assn. Home: Star Route A Box 6 Palmer AK 99645 Office: PO Box 896 Palmer AK 99645 Tel (907) 745-3206

TULLOS, EUGENE COURSEY, b. Raleigh, Miss., Jan. 21, 1942; B.S., Miss. Coll., Clinton, 1964; J.D., U. Miss., 1966. Admitted to Miss. bar, 1966; partner firm Tullos & Tullos, Raleigh, Miss., 1966—. Mem. Am., Miss. bar assns., Am., Miss. trial lawyers assns. Home and office: PO Box 74 Raleigh MS 39153 Tel (601) 782-4242

TUMOLA, THOMAS JOSEPH, b. Newtown Square, Pa., Jan. 18, 1941; B.S. in Econs., Villanova U., 1962, J.D., 1966; postgrad. in taxation Temple U. Law Sch., 1970-72. Admitted to Pa. bar, 1967, U.S. Tax Ct. bar, 1971; law clk. to Judge Harry E. Kalodner, U.S. Ct. Appeals, 3d Circuit, Phila., 1966-68; asso. firm Clark, Ladner, Fortenbaugh & Young, Phila., 1968-73, partner, 1974—. Mem. Phila., Pa., Am. Fed. bar assns., Gamma Phi. Mem. Villanova Law Rev., 1964-66. Home: 807 Bowman Ave Wynnewood PA 19106 Office: 1700 Widener Bldg 1339 Chestnut St Philadelphia PA 19107 Tel (215) LO4-5300

TUMOLO, JOHN ANTHONY, b. Pitts., Feb. 3, 1945; B.A., Duquesne U., 1967, J.D., 1970. Admitted to Pa. bar, 1970; asso. firm Larsen Murray & O'Neill, Pitts., 1970-73; partner firm Murray O'Neill & Tumolo, 1973—. Mem. Big Bros. of Allegheny County, Pitts., 1972—. Mem. Am., Pa., Allegheny County bar assns., Am. Trial Lawyers Assn. Home: 6624 Jackson St Pittsburgh PA 15206 Office: 316 4th Ave Pittsburgh PA 15222 Tel (412) 281-3344

TUNG, KO-YUNG, b. Peking, China, Feb. 20, 1947, came to U.S., 1964, naturalized, 1977; B.A., Harvard U., 1969, J.D. magna cum laude, 1973. Admitted to N.Y. bar, 1973; asso. firm Debevoise, Plimpton, Lyons & Gates, N.Y.C., 1973-76; partner firm Tung & Drabkin, N.Y.C., 1976—; adj. asst. prof. law N.Y. U. Sch. Law, 1975—. Participating atty. Community Law Offices, N.Y.C., 1973—; vol. atty. Vol. Urban Cons. Group, N.Y.C., 1973—, Chinatown Planning Council, N.Y.C., 1973—. Mem. Am., N.Y. State bar assns., Assn. Bar City N.Y., Am. Soc. Internat. Law, Japanese Am. Soc. Legal Studies, Japan Soc., China Inst. Am., Phi Beta Kappa. Fellow faculty law Tokyo U., 1971-72. Editor: Harvard Internat. Law Jour., 1970-73. contbr. articles to profl. jours. Home: 27 E 94th St New York City NY 10028 Office: 299 Park Ave New York City NY 10017 Tel (212) 751-0566

TUNICK, ANDREW J., b. N.Y.C., July 10, 1943; B.A., Colgate U., 1964; LL.B., Columbia, 1967. Admitted to N.Y. bar, 1968; partner firm Phillips, Nizer, Benjamin, Krim & Ballon, N.Y.C., 1968—. Home: 345 E 73d St New York City NY 10021 Office: 40 W 57th St New York City NY 10019 Tel (212) 977-9700

TUNNELL, JAMES MILLER, JR., b. Frankford, Del., June 17, 1910; B.A., Princeton, 1932; B.A. in Jurisprudence (Rhodes scholar), Oxford (Eng.) U., 1934, B.C.L., 1935. Admitted to Del. bar, 1936; partner firms Tunnell & Tunnell, Georgetown, Del., 1936-51, 54-58, Morris, Nichols, Arsht & Tunnell, Wilmington, Del., 1958—; asso. justice Del. Supreme Ct., 1951-54; pres. Sussex Trust Co., 1947-51; dir. Wilmington Trust Co., Delmarva Power & Light Co. Trustee, dir. U. Del.; bd. dirs. Hist. Soc. Del.; trustee Princeton Theol. Sem., Am. Bar Found. Fellow Am. Coll. Trial Lawyers; mem. Del., Sussex County (Del.) (pres. 1955-58), Am. bar assns., Am. Judicature Soc., World Peace Through Law Com. Office: Morris Nichols Arsht & Tunnell Wilmington Tower 12th and Market Sts Wilmington DE 19899 Tel (302) 658-9200

TUNSTILL, GARLAND ALBERT, b. Cisco, Tex., Nov. 16, 1901; LL.B., Cumberland U., 1923. Admitted to Tex. bar, 1923; individual practice law, Fort Worth and Houston. Mem. State Bar Tex. Recipient certificate for over 50 years service to community, state and nation, State Bar of Tex., 1974. Home and Office: 7420 Haywood Dr Houston TX 77023 Tel (713) 926-9011

TUPPER, KENT PHILLIP, b. Huron, S.D., July 24, 1931; B.A., U. Minn., 1956; J.D., William Mitchell Coll. Law, 1963. Admitted to Minn. bar, 1963, U.S. Supreme Ct. bar, 1971; partner Tupper & Rosenbower, Mpls., 1963-67; dir. legal services Leech Lake Indian Reservation, Minn., 1967-69, chmn. bd. dirs., 1970—; partner firm Tupper, Smith & Seck, Ltd., Walker, Minn., 1969—; bd. dirs. Legal Assistance Minn., 1975—. Chmn. collections Salvation Army, Walker, 1974—; chmn. Shingobee Township Democratic Farm Labor Party, 1972-77; del. Minn. Democratic Party Convention, 1972. Mem. Minn. 15th Dist. bar assns., Assn. Trial Lawyers Am. Home: PO Box 146 Walker NM 56484 Office: PO Box 160 Walker MN 56484 Tel (218) 547-1711

TURELLI, RICHARD DANIEL, b. Denver, May 30, 1935; B.S., Regis Coll., 1957; LL.B., U. Denver, 1963. Admitted to Colo. bar, 1963; mem. firm Turelli & Towner, Westminster, Colo., 1963-64; law clk. to justice Colo. Supreme Ct., 1964-65; dep. dist. atty. Adams County (Colo.), Brighton, 1965; chief clk. Colo. Supreme Ct., Denver, 1965—; instr. law Arapahoe Community Coll., Littleton, Colo.,

1971-73. Vol. youth probation counsellor, Adams County; bd. dirs. Listen Found. Porter's Hosp., 1975—. Home: 6495 W Leawood Dr Littleton CO 80123 Office: 210 State Capitol Denver CO 80203 Tel (303) 892-2066

TURK, JAMES CLINTON, b. Roanoke, Va., May 3, 1923; A.B. in Econs., Roanoke Coll., Salem, Va., 1949; LL.B., Washington and Lee U., Lexington, Va., 1952, J.D., 1972. Admitted to Va. bar, 1952; partner firm Dalton, Poff, Turk & Stone, Radford, Va., 1952-72; judge U.S. Dist. Ct., Western Dist. Va., Roanoke, 1972-73, chief judge, 1973—; mem. Va. Senate, 1959-72. Pres., Radford C. of C., 1956-57. Mem. Am., Va. bar assns., Am. Judicature Soc., Am. Coll. Trial Lawyers. Home: 1002 Walker Dr Radford VA 24141 Office: Profl Bldg PO Box 2796 Roanoke VA 24141 Tel (703) 982-6216

TURK, S. MAYNARD, b. Roanoke County, Va., Oct. 14, 1925; B.A. in Econs., Roanoke Coll., 1949; LL.B., Washington and Lee U., 1952. Admitted to Va. bar, 1951, Del. bar, 1961, U.S. Patent and Trademark office bar, 1975; with Hercules Inc., 1954—, sr. counsel, Wilmington, Del., 1966-70, sr. patent counsel, 1970-72, dir. patent dept., 1972-76, gen. counsel, 1976—. Mem. Republican Policy Advisory Com., State of Del.; mem. A.I. duPont Sch. Dist. Bd. Edn., Wilmington, 1976—; bd. visitors Radford Coll., 1971—, rector, 1972-75; chmn. law alumni fund Washington and Lee U.; bd. dirs. Del. Nature Edn. Soc.; dep. chmn. Boys' Club Capital Fund Dr., Wilmington. Mem. Assn. Gen. Counsel, Am. Bar Assn., Phila. Patent Law Assn., Mfg. Chemists Assn. (legal advisory com.), Southwestern Legal Found. (advisory bd.), Licensing Execs. Soc., N.A.M., Am. Judicature Soc., Nat. Security Indsl. Assn. Home: PO Box 3958 3917 Heather Dr Greenville DE 19807 Office: 910 Market St Wilmington DE 19899 Tel (302) 575-7000

TURKAL, DONAL LLOYD, b. Detroit, Aug. 14, 1924; J.D., George Washington U., 1950. Admitted to D.C. bar, 1950, Va. bar, 1956, Mo. bar, 1970; examiner Interstate Commerce Commn., Washington, 1950-55; asst. gen. atty. Seaboard Coast Line R.R., Richmond, Va., 1956-59, gen. atty., 1959-67, asst. gen. solicitor, 1967-69; asst. gen. counsel St. Louis-San Francisco Ry. Co., St. Louis, 1969-73, asso. gen. counsel, 1973—. Mem. Am., Mo. bar assns., Assn. Interstate Commerce Commn. Practitioners. Office: St Louis San Francisco Ry Suite 1023 906 Olive St St Louis MO 63101 Tel (314) 241-7800

TURLEY, ROBERT JOE, b. Mt. Sterling, Ky., Dec. 6, 1926; LL.B., U. Ky., 1949. Admitted to Ky. bar, 1949, U.S. Supreme Ct. bar, 1959; partner firm Turley, Savage & Moore, and predecessors, Lexington, Ky., 1949—; spl. counsel City of Lexington, 1970-72; spl. counsel Ky. Bd. Edn., 1975—; gen. counsel Shriners Hosps. for Crippled Children, U.S., Can., Mex., 1976—. Mem. Am., Ky., Fayette County bar assns., Assn. Trial Lawyers Am. Office: 134 N Limestone St Lexington KY 40507 Tel (606) 252-1705

TURLINGTON, EDGAR LAWRENCE, JR., b. Richmond, Va., Sept. 23, 1932; B.A., U. Richmond, 1954, LL.B., 1959. Admitted to Va. bar, 1959, U.S. Supreme Ct. bar, 1965; partner firm White, Cabell, Paris & Lowenstein, and predecessors, Richmond, 1959—. Instr. domestic relations J. Sargeant Reynolds Community Coll., 1975-76. Mem. Va. State Bar (mem. 3d dist. com. 1974-77), Am., Va., Richmond bar assns., Va., Richmond trial lawyers assns. Home: 104 Portland Pl Richmond VA 23221 Office: 523 E Main St Richmond VA 23219 Tel (804) 643-9066

TURNER, CECIL LEON, b. Wichita, Kans., Oct. 3, 1941; A.A., Pueblo Jr. Coll., 1962; B.A., U. Colo., 1964; J.D., Colo. U., 1967. Admitted to Colo. bar, 1967, Fed. bar, 1967; individual practice law, Pueblo, Colo., 1967; asst. city atty., Pueblo, 1967, dep. dist. atty., 1968, chief dep. dist. atty., 1969, asst. dist. atty., 1972—. Mem. Colo., Pueblo bar assns., Colo. Dist. Attys. Assn. (dir.). Home: 92 Fordham Cirlce Pueblo CO 81005 Office: 10th St and Main St Pueblo CO 81003 Tel (303) 544-0077

TURNER, E. DEANE, b. Auburn, N.Y., Aug., 4, 1928; A.B., Princeton, 1950, LL.B., Harvard, 1953. Admitted to N.Y. State bar, 1953; asso. firm Dewey, Ballantine, Bushby, Palmer & Wood and predecessor firms, N.Y.C., 1953-63, partner, 1963—. Mem. Am., N.Y. State bar assns., N.Y. County Lawyers Assn., Assn. Bar City N.Y. Home: 1120 Fifth Ave New York City NY 10028 Office: 140 Broadway New York City NY 10005 Tel (212) 344-8000

TURNER, ERNEST RAYMOND, b. Hopedale, Mass., July 4, 1912; LL.D., Northeastern U., 1938, postgrad., 1939-41. Admitted to Mass. bar, 1942, U.S. Supreme Ct. bar, 1960; asso. firm Ellis, Title, Turner, Francesconi & McBride, Rogers, Alden, Turner, Burgess, & Capella, Springfield, Mass., 1947—; lectr. in field. Mem. Sixteen Acres Civic League, pres. 1964-65, legal counsel 1956-63; legal counsel Springfield Power Squadron, 1970-77. Mem. Hampden, Mass. (mem. real estate com. 1975) Am. (mem. real estate com. 1972-77) bar assns. Conveyancers Assn. Home: 212 Prynnwood Rd Longmeadow MA 01106 Office: 31 Elm St Springfield MA 01103 Tel (413) 781-2470

TURNER, HENRY REDMAN, III, b. Louisville, Apr. 23, 1933; B.A., Emory Coll., 1954; LL.B., Yale, 1957. Admitted to N.Y. bar, 1971; dir. corp. planning Harper & Row Pubs., N.Y.C., 1968-69; v.p. circulation McCall Pub. Co., N.Y.C., 1969-76, Book Digest Co., Inc., N.Y.C., 1976-77; pres. Am. Family Pubs., N.Y.C., 1977—; dir. Select Mags., Inc., 1973-76. Mem. Mag. Pubs. Assn. (chmn. circulation com. 1975-77), Putnam County Hist. Soc. (v.p. 1974-76). Contbr. articles to legal jours. Home: Old Fishkill Rd Cold Spring NY 10516 Office: 641 Lexington Ave New York City NY 10022 Tel (212) 935-4731

TURNER, JAMES HENRY, b. Atlanta, Dec. 16, 1918; B.A., U. Fla., 1940; J.D., Stetson U., 1969. Admitted to Fla. bar, 1969, U.S. Supreme Ct. bar, 1972; individual practice law, St. Petersburg, Fla., 1969—; pres. firm J. Henry Turner, St. Petersburg, 1973—. Mem. Am., Fed., Fla. bar assns., Delta Theta Phi, Nu Beta Epsilon. Contbr. articles to legal jours. Home: 1201 Seville Ln NE St Petersburg FL 33704 Office: Suite 511 3151 3d Ave N St Petersburg FL 33713 Tel (813) 898-6735

TURNER, JAMES KIBBE, b. Long Beach, Calif., Oct. 11, 1928; B.S., U. So. Calif., 1951; LL.B., Loyola U., Los Angeles, 1954. Admitted to Calif. bar, 1955; dep. dist. atty. County of Orange (Calif.), 1958-59, 67-69; practiced in Corona del Mar, Calif., 1959-67; judge Municipal Ct., West Orange County Jud. Dist., 1969-71, County of Orange Superior Ct., 1971—. Mem. Phi Delta Phi. Office: County Courthouse 700 Civic Center Dr Santa Ana CA 92701 Tel (714) 834-3226

TURNER, JEROME, b. Memphis, Feb. 18, 1942; B.A., Washington and Lee U., 1964, LL.B., 1966. Admitted to Tenn. bar, 1966, U.S. Supreme Ct. bar, 1972; clk. to Hon. Robert M. McRae, U.S. Dist. Ct. for Western Dist. Tenn., 1966-67; asso. firm Canada, Russell & Turner, Memphis, 1967-73, partner, 1974—. Mem. Am., Tenn., Memphis-Shelby County bar assns., Order of Coif, Phi Delta Phi, Omicron Delta Kappa. Editor: Washington and Lee Law Rev., 1965. Office: 12th floor Union Planters Bank Bldg Memphis TN 38103 Tel (901) 521-1111

TURNER, LUCIUS DON, b. Belleville, Ill., Mar. 12, 1911; B.A., U. Ill., 1932; J.D., St. Louis U., 1935. Admitted to Ill. bar, 1935, Mo. bar, 1936, Okla. bar, 1953; individual practice law, Belleville, 1935-37; Ill. atty. for Fed. Land Bank, 1938; mem. firm Jones, Grant, Sebat & Turner, Mt. Vernon, Ill., 1939-41; legal counsel Sohio Petroleum Co., St. Louis, 1941-50; exec. v.p. Rinehart Oil News Co., Dallas, 1950-53; gen. counsel Nat. Tank Co. (name changed to CENATCO), Tulsa, 1953-73; legal cons. Combustion Engring., Tulsa, 1973—. Bd. dirs. Tulsa YMCA, 1957-69, pres., 1962; trustee Children's Med. Center, 1972-76, pres., 1974; bd. dirs. Kidney Found. of Okla.-So. Kans., 1969-73; mem. Okla. Council Econ. Edn., 1965-73, Okla. Petroleum Council, 1963-73, Asso. Industries Okla., 1963-73; mem. Tulsa Community Mental Health Bd., 1973—, chmn., 1977—. Mem. Midcontinent Oil and Gas Assn. (exec. com. Kans.-Okla. div. 1961-73), Am. Arbitration Assn. (panel), Ill., Okla., Tulsa County bar assns., Tulsa Mfrs. Club (pres. 1965), Met. C. of C. (legal counsel 1960-70, pres. 1970). Home: 5681 S Delaware Pl Tulsa OK 74105 Tel (918) 582-5864

TURNER, RICHARD CLARK, b. Avoca, Iowa, Sept. 30, 1927; B.A., State U. Iowa, 1950, J.D., 1953. Admitted to Iowa bar, 1953; partner Turner & Turner, Avoca, 1953-54; asst. county atty., 1954-56; practice law, Council Bluffs, Iowa, 1956-67; atty. gen. State of Iowa, Des Moines, 1966—. Town clk., Avoca, 1953-60; mem. Iowa Senate, 1961-65. Mem. Am., Iowa, S.W. Iowa, Polk County, Pottawattamie County bar assns., Am. Trial Lawyers Assn., Iowa Acad. Trial Lawyers, Am. Judicature Soc., Nat. Assn. Attys. Gen., Am. Legion, 40 and 8. Home: 1054 21st St West Des Moines IA 50265 Office: State Capitol Bldg Des Moines IA 50318*

TURNER, RICHARD LAZEAR, b. Huntington, W.Va., Feb. 22; B.A., Yale, 1948, LL.B., 1951. Admitted to N.Y. bar, 1952; asso., then partner firm Nixon, Hargrave, Devans & Dey, Rochester, N.Y., 1951-62; dir. Schlegel Mfg. Co. (now Schlegel Corp.), Rochester, 1958—, chmn. bd., 1962—, chief exec. officer, 1964—, pres., 1972—; dir. Marine Midland Bank, Rochester, Genesee Brewing Co., Rochester, Fasco Industries, Boca Raton, Fla. Bd. dirs. Indsl. Mgmt. Council, Rochester, chmn. Hochstein Sch. Music, Rochester; trustee Genesee Country Mus., Mumford, N.Y., Wells Coll., Aurora, N.Y., Hillside Children's Center, Rochester. Office: 1555 Jefferson Rd PO Box 197 Rochester NY 14601 Tel (716) 244-1000

TURNER, ROGER FELIX, b. Milton, Mass., Mar. 3, 1901; LL.B., Suffolk U., 1926, LL.M., 1962, J.D., 1968; postgrad. Episcopal Theol. Sem., Cambridge, Mass., 1966-69. Admitted to Mass. bar, 1926; individual practice law, Milton, Mass., Walpole, Mass.; pres. Milton Co., Inc. Pres. N.E. chpt. U.S. Olympians. Mem. Mass., Boston bar assns. Author: edges, 1973; contbr. articles to legal and theol. jours. Home and Office: 397 Elm St Walpole MA 02091 Tel (617) 668-0698

TURNER, STEPHEN MILLER, b. Omaha, Mar. 13, 1939; B.S., William Jewell Coll., 1961; J.D., U. Iowa, 1965; M.Comparative Law, U. Chgo., 1966; postgrad. U. Paris, 1966. Admitted to Iowa bar, 1964, Ohio bar, 1968, D.C. bar, 1975; asst. U.S. atty., No. Dist. Iowa, Sioux City, 1966-68, U.S. atty., 1967-68; asso. firm Squire, Sanders & Dempsey, Cleve., 1968-74, partner, 1974—, resident partner, Brussels, 1975—; partner firm Cox, Langford & Brown, Washington, 1974—; sr. staff asso. Presdl. Council on Exec. Reorgn., 1969-70. Home: 68 Ave Emile Duray 1050 Brussels Belgium Office: 165 Ave Louise 1050 Brussels Belgium Tel (02) 648-1717

TURNER, THOMAS FRANCIS, b. Bklyn., June 9, 1918; B.B.A., Manhattan Coll., 1940; LL.B., Fordham U., 1948. Admitted to N.Y. bar, 1949; mem. firm Turner & Balistreri, N.Y.C., Garden City and Mineola, N.Y. Mem. Queens, N.Y.C., Nassau County bar assns., N.Y. County Lawyers Assn. Office: 286 Old Country Rd Mineola NY 11501 Tel (516) 747-3220

TURNER, VERNON MAGRUDER, b. Ennis, Tex., Nov. 6, 1922; LL.B., Baylor U., 1947, J.D., 1969; LL.M., U. Houston, 1955. Admitted to Tex. bar, 1947; individual practice law, Cisco, Tex., 1948-49; atty. Texaco Inc., Houston, 1949-50; served as 1st lt. Judge Adv. Gen. Corps, U.S. Army, 1950-52; div. atty. Midstates Oil Corp., Houston, 1952-55; atty. Tenneco Oil Co., Houston, 1955-64, asst. gen. atty., 1964-66, gen. atty., 1966-70, sr. v.p., gen. counsel, 1970—. Mem. Cypress-Fairbanks Ind. Sch. Dist. Bd. Edn., Houston, 1966-75, v.p., 1971-73, pres., 1973-75. Mem. Am., Tex. (v.p. corp. counsel sect. 1975-76) Houston bar assns. Home: 10819 Glenway St Houston TX 77070 Office: PO Box 2511 Houston TX 77001 Tel (713) 757-3293

TURNIER, WILLIAM JOHN, b. Jersey City, N.J., Dec. 10, 1939; B.S., Fordham U., 1963; M.A., Pa. State U., 1967; LL.B., U. Va., 1968. Admitted to N.Y. State bar, 1969; asso. firm Cravath, Swaine & Moore, N.Y.C., 1968-73; asso. prof. law U. N.C., Chapel Hill, N.C., 1973—. Mem. N.Y. State Bar Assn., Order of the Coif, Phi Beta Kappa, Phi Alpha Theta. Contbr. articles in field to legal jours. Office: Sch of Law U NC Chapel Hill NC 27514 Tel (919) 933-5106

TUROFF, JACK NEWTON, b. Cleve., Dec. 8, 1933; B.B.A., Ohio State U., 1955, J.D., 1960. Admitted to Ohio bar, 1960, U.S. Supreme Ct. bar, 1969; individual practice law, Cleve., 1960; with office of atty. gen. State of Ohio, Cleve., 1961-64; asso. firm Dudnik, Komito, Nurenburg, Plevin, Dempsey and Jacobson, Cleve., 1964-65; mem. firm Turoff and Turoff, Cleve., 1965—. Sec., Orthodox Jewish Children's Assn.; bd. dirs. Jewish Big Bros. Assn. Mem. Assn. Trial Lawyers Am., Ohio State, Cuyahoga County, Greater Cleve. bar assns. Home: 23372 Wendover Dr Beachwood OH 44122 Office: 620 Leader Bldg Cleveland OH 44114 Tel (216) 781-0150

TUROFF, JOHN LOUIS, b. Petersburg, Alaska, July 27, 1928; B.A., Vanderbilt U., 1952, J.D., 1953. Asso. firm Smith, Field, Doremus and Ringel, 1956-59; partner firm Murphy, McFarland and Turoff, Atlanta, 1960-71; partner firm Brookins and Turoff, Atlanta, 1971—; judge pro hac vice Civil Ct. Fulton County, Ga., 1962. Trustee Oglethorpe U., 1974—. Mem. Am., Atlanta bar assns., State Bar of Ga., Atlanta Estate Planning Council, Atlanta Vanderbilt Alumni Assn. (pres. 1966-67), Phi Delta Phi. Tel (404) 659-2880

TUROFF, ROBERT SANFORD, b. Cleve., Aug. 12, 1937; B.B.A., Kent State U., 1959; J.D., Cleve. Marshall Law Sch., 1963. Admitted to Ohio bar, 1963, U.S. Supreme Ct. bar, 1969; field agt. Audit Div., IRS, 1961-65; asst. U.S. Atty. No. Dist. Ohio, 1965-69; partner firm Turoff & Turoff, Cleve., 1969—. Trustee Jewish Big Brother Assn., Cleve., Temple on the Heights, Cleve. Mem. Ohio State, Fed., Cuyahoga County bar assns., Bar Assn. Greater Cleve. Office: 620 Leader Bldg Cleveland OH 44114 Tel (216) 781-0150

TUROSKY, EDWARD A., b. Farrell, Pa., Jan. 3, 1924; B.A., U. Pitts., 1949, LL.B./J.D., 1952. Admitted to Pa. bar, 1953; solicitor Farrell Area Sch. Dist., 1954—, Farrell Area Sch. Dist. Municipal Authority, 1959—; bus. mgr. Farrell Area Sch. Dist., 1971—. Mem. Farrell Bd. Adjustments, 1956—, Farrell Human Relations Commn.; mem. Mercer County Bd. Viewers, 1971—. Mem. Pa., Mercer County bar assns., Assn. Ednl. Negotiators. Home: 1708 Shady Dr Farrell PA 16121 Office: 1031 Roemer Blvd Farrell PA 16121 Tel (412) 347-1960

TURRELL, JAMES JOEL, b. Wilkes-Barre, Pa., Mar. 29, 1943; A.B., U. Pa., 1965, LL.B., 1968. Admitted to Pa. bar, 1969; individual practice law, Tunkhannock, Pa., 1969-75; partner firm Farr, Davis & Turrell, Tunkhannock, 1976—; solicitor Tunkhannock Sch. Dist., 1970—, Sullivan County, Pa., 1972-76; asst. dist. atty. Wyoming County, Pa., 1976—. Bd. dirs. Wyoming County United Fund, 1969—, Wyoming County Cancer Soc., 1969-75; treas. Wyoming County Mental Health Assn., 1972-75. Mem. Wyoming County, Pa., Am. bar assns. Office: 7 Marion St Tunkhannock PA 18657 Tel (717) 836-3185

TURRENTINE, LOWELL, b. Liberty, N.Y., Sept. 28, 1895; A.B., Princeton, 1917, LL.B., 1922; S.J.D., Harvard, 1929. Admitted to Ohio bar, 1922, N.Y. bar, 1926, Calif. bar, 1929; asso. firm Squire, Sanders & Dempsey, 1922-25, firm Clark, Buckner & Howland, N.Y.C., 1926-28; asso. prof. law Stanford, 1929-31, prof., 1931-61, Kirkwood prof. emeritus, 1961—; vis. prof. law Tulane U., 1963-65, U. So. Calif., La. State U. Mem. Am., Palo Alto Area bar assns., State Bar Calif. Author: Cases and Text on Wills and Adminstration, 1962; contbr. articles to legal jours. Home: 850 Webster St 815 Palo Alto CA 95301

TURRI, JOSEPH A., b. Seneca Falls, N.Y., July 24, 1943; B.A. cum laude, U. Buffalo, 1965; J.D., Cornell U., 1970. Admitted to N.Y. State bar, 1971, U.S. Supreme Ct. bar, 1974; asso. firm Harris, Beach, Wilcox, Rubin & Levey, Rochester, N.Y., 1970—. Treas., chief fiscal officer Gift of Privacy, Rochester, 1973-77. Mem. N.Y. State, Monroe County bar assns. Tel (716) 232-4440

TURTLE, ROBERT HENRY, b. N.Y.C., Mar. 23, 1938; B.S., Queens Coll., 1958; LL.B., Columbia, 1962. Admitted to N.Y. State bar, 1962, D.C. bar, 1964, Calif. bar, 1976; asso. firm Paul, Weiss, Rifkind, Wharton & Garrison, N.Y.C., 1962-63; mem. Office of Gen. Counsel, Dept. Air Force, Washington, 1963-65, spl. asst., asst. sec., 1965; spl. asst., asst. sec. program coordination HEW, Washington, 1966; partner firm Vom Baur, Coburn, Simmons & Turtle, Washington, 1967—; chmn. bd. Inst. for Resource Mgmt. Inc., 1970—; cons. in field. Mem. Mayor's Council on Youth Opportunity, Washington, 1971-72; mem. Nat. Commn. for Protection of Human Subjects of Biomed. and Behavioral Research, 1974—; bd. dirs. Library Theatre Inc., Washington, 1971-73. Mem. Am. (chmn. com. on civil rights and responsibilities 1972-74), Fed., N.Y. State, Calif. bar assns., Bar Assn. D.C., Assn. Bar City N.Y. Office: 1700 K St NW Suite 1101 Washington DC 20006 Tel (202) 833-1420

TURVILLE, EDWARD ARCHIBALD, b. Phila., Aug. 14, 1914; student St. Petersburg Jr. Coll., 1933-34; B.A., Washington & Lee U., 1936; LL.B., George Washington U., 1940. Admitted to Fla. bar, 1941, Washington bar, 1941; mem. firm McClure & Turville, St. Petersburg, Fla., 1946—. Mem. Am., St. Petersburg (past pres.), Fla. Sch. Bd. Attys. Assn. (past pres.). Home: 648 Myrtle Way S Saint Petersburg FL 33705 Office: 112 6th St N Saint Petersburg FL 33701 Tel (813) 822-4785

TUSAN, THOMAS JAMES, b. Sanger, Calif., June 6, 1946; B.A., Fresno State Coll., 1968; J.D., Hastings Coll. Law U. Calif., 1972. Admitted to Calif. bar, 1972; legal counsel Calif. Compensation Ins. Fund, Fresno, 1973-74; asso. firm Ferrari & Cole, Fresno, 1974—. Mem. Fresno County Barristers (pres. 1976), Fresno State Alumni Assn. (dir. 1973-75). Office: PO Box 391 Fresno CA 93708 Tel (209) 486-5580

TUSTIN, KAREN KLEIV, b. Bremerton, Wash., Dec. 9, 1942; B.A., Stanford, 1964, LL.B., 1968. Admitted to Calif. bar, 1970; asso. firm Hillyer & Irwin, San Diego, 1970-73; dep. pub. defender El Dorado County, Calif., 1974—. Mem. Placerville (Calif.) Planning Commn., 1974—, vice chmn., 1977, mem. citizens adv. com. to prepare gen. plan, 1974-75, v.p. talent bank, 1975-76, pres., 1976-77. Mem. Am., Calif., El Dorado County bar assns., AAUW, Order of Coif, Phi Beta Kappa. Office: 3003 Bedford Ave Placerville CA 95667 Tel (916) 626-2441

TUTEUR, ROBERT I., b. Newark, Jan. 25, 1946; B.S. in Economics, U. Pa., 1968; J.D., Temple U., 1972, LL.M., 1975. Admitted to Pa. bar, 1972, also U.S. Dist. Ct. Eastern Dist. Pa.; asso. firm Daniel Sherman, Phila., 1972-73; mem. firm Eilberg, Corson, Getson & Abramson, Phila., 1973—. Mem. Am., Phila. (mem. sect. taxation) bar assns. Office: 1300 One E Penn Sq Philadelphia PA 19107 Tel (215) LO4-3030

TUTHILL, HOWARD SHAW, b. Marlboro, N.Y., Sept. 30, 1918; B.S. in Commerce, U. Va., 1939, LL.B., 1941. Admitted to N.Y. bar, 1941, Conn. bar, 1951; asso. firm Davis, Polk & Wardwell, N.Y.C., 1941-50; partner firm Cummings & Lockwood, Stamford, Conn., 1951—; mem. trust bd. 1st Nat. City Bank, N.Y.C., 1971-73; dir. Advance Investors Corp., 1974-76; dir. McGraw-Hill, Inc., 1975—. Chmn. Helen M. de Kay Found., 1970—. 1970. Mem. Am. Coll. Probate Counsel, Conn. State, Stamford bar assn. Editor-in-chief Va. Law Rev., 1940-41. Home: 81 Inwood Rd Darien CT 06820 Office: 1 Atlantic St Stamford CT 06904 Tel (203) 327-1700

TUTHILL, JAMES PEIRCE, b. Montclair, N.J., July 3, 1947; B.A., Rockford Coll., 1969; J.D., Northwestern U., 1972. Admitted to Ill. bar, 1972; asso. firm Schuyler, Ballard & Cowen, Chgo., 1972—. Mem. Ill., Chgo. bar assns., Nat. Health Lawyers Assn. Editor Jour. Criminal Law, 1972. Home: 600 N McClurg Ct Chicago IL 60611 Office: 100 W Monroe St Chicago IL 60603 Tel (312) 726-8565

TUTT, LOUISE THOMPSON, b. Centerville, Iowa, Nov. 10, 1937; B.A. in English, U. Ariz., 1963, J.D., 1969. Admitted to Calif. bar, 1972, U.S. Dist. Ct. for So. Calif. bar, 1972, Mo. bar, 1976; individual practice law, La Jolla, Calif., San Diego, 1972-75; clk. firm Graham, Paden, Welch, Martin & Albano, 1976. Bd. dirs. La Jolla Sinfonia, 1975. Mem. Calif., Mo., Kansas City bar assns. Contbr. articles to popular mag. Home: 1207 W 25th St Terr Independence MO 64052

TUTTLE, EDWARD EUGENE, b. Los Angeles, Oct. 28, 1907; B.S., Calif. Inst. Tech., 1928; J.D., U. So. Calif., 1931. Admitted to Calif. bar, 1931, U.S. Supreme Ct. bar, 1936, D.C. bar, 1974; asso. firm Farrand & Slosson, Los Angeles, 1931-41; sr. partner firm Tuttle & Taylor and predecessor firm, Los Angeles, 1941—; pres. Essick Investment Co., Los Angeles, 1951—; dir. Ameron, Inc. Pres. Welfare Planning Council, Los Angeles region, 1960-62; bd. dirs. Los Angeles World Affairs Council; trustee Pomona Coll., 1963—, vice chmn. bd., 1975—; trustee Orthopaedic Hosp., Los Angeles, 1963—, Claremont Univ. Center, 1976—. Mem. State Bar Calif., Mchts. and Mfrs. Assn. (dir.). Office: 609 S Grand Ave Los Angeles CA 90017 Tel (213) 683-0600

TUTWILER, CHARLES ANDERSON, b. Lexington, Va., June 16, 1903; LL.B., Washington and Lee U., 1924, J.D., 1969. Admitted to Va. bar, 1924, W.Va. bar, 1924; asso. firm Tutwiler, Crockett & LaCaria and predecessors, Welch, W.Va., 1924-30, partner, 1930—; v.p. W.Va. Bd. Law Examiners, 1963—; gen. receiver Circuit Ct. McDowell County, 1930—; dir. McDowell County Nat. Bank, Welch, So. Ins. Agy., Welch. Mem. Salvation Army Adv. Bd., 1956—. Mem. W.Va. (pres. 1973-74), McDowell County, Am., W.Va. State (pres. 1956-57) bar assns. Home: Southwood Addition Welch WV 24801 Office: 145 McDowell St Welch WV 24801 Tel (304) 436-3135

TVEDT, JOSEPH ARNOLD, b. Cocoa Beach, Fla., Jan. 21, 1944; B.A. in Chemistry, Ariz. State U., 1968, J.D., 1971. Admitted to Ariz. Supreme Ct., 1971, U.S. Dist. Ct. bar, 1971; asst. city atty., Phoenix, 1972—. Mem. Ariz., Maricopa County bar assns., Nat. Dist. Attys. Assn. (del. exec. prosecutor course at Nat. Coll. Dist. Attys., 1975). Office: 620 W Washington St Rm 434 Phoenix AZ 85003 Tel (602) 262-6461

TWEHUES, PAUL HENRY, JR., b. Stillwater, Okla., July 17, 1943; B.A., U. Cin., 1970, J.D., 1973. Admitted to Ky. bar, U.S. Dist. Ct. bar, 1973; asso. firm William Threlkeld, Williamston, Ky., 1973-75; individual practice law, Newport, Ky., 1975—; city atty. city of Silver Grove (Ky.), 1973—; bd. dirs. Campbell County (Ky.) Pub. Defender Service; atty. bd. ethics Ky. Gen. Assembly, 1974—. Bd. dirs. Sr. Citizens of No. Ky., 1975—. Mem. Am. Bar Assn. (mem. family law sect.). Office: Suite 301 Campbell Towers Newport KY 41071 Tel (606) 491-5844

TWIGHT, CHARLOTTE AUGUSTA, b. N.Y.C., Mar. 7, 1944; B.A. summa cum laude, Calif. State U. at Fresno, 1965; J.D., U. Wash., 1973; postgrad., 1965-66. Admitted to Wash. bar, 1973; lectr. dept. bus., govt. and soc. U. Wash., Seattle, 1975—; speaker in field. Computer programmer/analyst Naval Command Systems Support Activity, Washington, 1966-70. Mem. Wash. Bar Assn. Author: America's Emerging Fascist Economy, 1975. Contbr. articles to legal jours. Exec. editor Wash. Law Rev., 1972-73. Office: PO Box 15185 Seattle WA 98115 Tel (206) 525-3611

TWISS, RICHARD SPENCER, b. Seattle, Dec. 2, 1944; B.A., U. Wash., 1967; J.D., Harvard, 1970. Admitted to Wash. bar, 1970; mem. firm Perkins, Coie, Stone, Olsen & Williams, Seattle, 1970—. Mem. Am., Wash., Seattle-King County bar assns. Home: 942 20th St E Seattle WA 98112 Office: 1900 Washington Bldg Seattle WA 98101 Tel (206) 682-8770

TWIST, CHARLES RUSSELL, b. Los Angeles, July 8, 1943; B.A., U. Chgo., 1966; J.D., U. Iowa, 1970. Admitted to Iowa bar, 1970, Ill. bar, 1976; asst. staff dir. dept. profl. standards Am. Bar Assn., 1971-72, staff dir., 1972—, staff dir. com. on ethics and profl. responsibility, 1971—, com. on law lists, 1972—; supr. coms. on fed. limitations on atty.'s fees, unauthorized practice of law, and law book pub. practices, 1971—. Mem. U. Chgo. Alumni Cabinet, 1974-76. Mem. Am., Iowa bar assns. Home: 175 E Delaware Pl Chicago IL 60611 Office: 1115 E 60th St Chicago IL 60637 Tel (312) 947-3890

TWOHIG, ROBERT RAYMOND, JR., b. Huntington, W.Va., Nov. 15, 1943; A.B., Marshall U., 1966; J.D., Ohio State U., 1969. Admitted to Ohio bar, 1969, D.C. bar, 1970; mem. law faculty Ohio State U., Columbus, 1971-73; partner firm Handelman & Twohig, Columbus, 1973—. Mem. Nat. Lawyers Guild, Columbus, Ohio bar assns. Home: 186 E 11th Ave Columbus OH 43201 Office: 186 E 11th Ave Columbus OH 43201 Tel (614) 294-1636

TYDINGS, JOSEPH DAVIES, b. Asheville, N.C., May 4, 1928; grad. McDonogh (Md.) Sch., 1946; B.A., U. Md., 1951, LL.B., 1953 LL.D. (hon.), C.W. Post Coll., 1967, Parsons Coll., 1967. Admitted to Md. bar, 1952; asso. firm Tydings, Sauerwein, Benson & Boyd, Balt., 1955-57; partner firm Tydings & Rosenberg, Balt., 1958-61; U.S. atty. Dist. Md., 1961-64; U.S. senator from Md., 1965-71; partner firm Danzansky, Dickey, Tydings, Quint & Gordon, Washington, 1971—; of counsel Tydings & Rosenberg, Balt.; spl. counsel UN Fund for Population Activities, 1971—. Del., Internat. Penal Conf., Bellagio, Italy, 1963, Interpol Conf., Helsinki, 1963, Mexican-U.S. Interparliamentary Conf., Mexico City, 1965, Council Intergovtl. Com. for European Migration, Geneva, 1966, NATO Assembly, Brussels, 1968, Atlantic Conf., P.R., 1970; bd. regents U. Md., 1974—; trustee McDonogh (Md.) Sch., 1974—; mem. Md. Ho. of Dels. from Hartford Country, 1955-61; campaign mgr. for John F. Kennedy in Md. Primary, 1960. Cited as outstanding legislator Md. Press Corr., 1961; named One of 10 Outstanding Young Men, Balt. Jr. Assn. Commerce, 1962; recipient August Volmer award Am. Soc. Criminology, 1969; Nat. Brotherhood citation Washington chpt. NCCJ, 1970; Margaret Sanger award for distinguished pub. service Planned Parenthood-World Population. Mem. Am., Fed., D.C., Md., Balt., Harford County, Balt. Jr. (pres. 1960) bar assns. Author: Born to Starve, 1970. Home: Oakington Havre de Grace MD 21078 Office: 1120 Connecticut Ave Washington DC 20036 Tel (202) 331-8700

TYE, JOSEPH CLAIRE, b. Griswold, Iowa, Jan. 2, 1904; student Grinnell Coll., 1921; LL.B., U. S.D., 1926, J.D., 1926. Admitted to S.D. and Nebr. bars, 1926; city atty. Kearney (Nebr.), 1932-38, mayor, 1941-45. Chmn. Buffalo County Rep. Com. Fellow Am. Coll. Trial Lawyers; mem. Nebr. State (pres. 1959-60), Buffalo County bar assns., Assn. Ins. Attys., Kearney C. of C. (past pres.), Phi Delta Phi. Home: 1026 W 22d St Kearney NE 68847 Office: 1419 Central Ave Kearney NE 68847 Tel (308) 237-3155

TYE, WILLIAM RANDALL, b. Atlanta, July 18, 1946; A.B. in Polit. Sci., U. Ga., 1968, J.D., 1971. Admitted to Ga. bar, 1972, U.S. Supreme Ct., 1976; asso. firm Sanders, Hester, Holley, Askin & Dye, Augusta, Ga., 1971-72, Troutman, Sanders, Lockerman & Ashmore, Atlanta, 1972—; legal intern FCC, D.C., 1970. Mem. Ga., Atlanta bar assns., Motor Carrier Lawyers Assn. Home: 5985 Riverwood Dr Atlanta GA 30328 Office: 1400 Candler Bldg Atlanta GA 30303 Tel (404) 658-8112

TYGRETT, HOWARD VOLNEY, JR., b. Lake Charles, La., Jan. 12, 1940; B.A., Williams Coll., 1961; LL.B., So. Meth. U., 1964. Admitted to Tex. bar, 1964; gen. atty. U.S. Securities and Exchange Commn., Fort Worth, 1964-65; law clk. chief judge Joe E. Estes, U.S. Dist. Ct., N. Dist. Tex., Dallas, 1965-67; individual practice law, Dallas, 1967—. Mem. Am., Dallas bar assns. Home: 8530 Jourdan Way Dallas TX 75225 Office: 715 Preston State Bank Bldg Dallas TX 75225 Tel (214) 369-3201

TYKULSKER, LEON H., b. Morristown, N.J., Sept. 24, 1919; B.A., Cornell U., 1940, M.A., 1941; LL.B., Columbia, 1950. Admitted to N.Y. bar, 1950; law clk. to U.S. dist. judge for So. N.Y., 1950-51; asso. firm Guggenheimer & Untermyer, N.Y.C., 1952-64, partner, 1964—. Mem. Assn. Bar City N.Y., N.Y. State Bar Assn. Editor Columbia Law Rev., 1948-50. Office: Guggenheimer & Untermyer 80 Pine St New York City NY 10005 Tel (212) 344-2040

TYLER, BRUCE DAVID, b. Rockville, Conn., Feb. 14, 1943; B.B.A., U. Notre Dame, 1964; J.D., St. John's U., 1971. Admitted to N.Y. State bar, 1972, U.S. Supreme Ct. bar, 1976; atty. Merrill Lynch & Co., N.Y.C., 1970-72, Drexel Burnham Lambert, Inc., N.Y.C., 1972—. Mem. Am., N.Y. State, N.Y. County (com. on securities and regulation) bar assns. Home: 77 Morewood Oaks Port Washington NY 11050 Office: 60 Broad St New York City NY 10004 Tel (212) 480-6112

TYLER, DONALD WILLIAM, b. Columbia, S.C., Dec. 20, 1944; A.B., Davidson (N.C.) Coll., 1967; J.D., U. S.C., 1970. Admitted to S.C. bar, 1970, U.S. Dist. Ct. S.C., 1971, U.S. Ct. Appeals 4th Circuit, 1973; asso. firm King & Brooks, Columbia, 1970-72; asso. firm Kermit S. King, Columbia, 1972—. Mem. Am., S.C., Richland County (chmn. family law sect. 1974-75) bar assns., Am., S.C. (sec. 1973-75) trial lawyers assn. Home: 2429 Feather Run Trail West Columbia SC 29169 Office: 1330 Laurel St Columbia SC 29201 Tel (803) 779-4997

TYLER, GEORGE GRAYSON, b. Bellaire, Ohio, June 10, 1906; A.B., Hamilton Coll., 1927; J.D., Columbia, 1931, LL.M., 1933. Admitted to N.Y. bar, 1932, U.S. Tax Ct. bar, 1935, U.S. Supreme Ct. bar, 1937, U.S. Ct. of Claims bar, 1953; asso. firm Barry, Wainwright, Thacher & Symmers, N.Y.C., 1931-33; with U.S. Agrl. Adjustment Adminstrn. and U.S. Treasury Dept., 1933-34; asso. firm Cravath, Swaine & Moore, N.Y.C., 1934—, partner, 1946—; trustee Tax Found., Inc., N.Y.C., mem. bd. visitors Columbia U. Sch. Law. Fellow Am. Bar Found., N.Y. State Bar Found.; mem. Am. (Ross Essay prize 1936), N.Y. State bar assns., Assn. Bar City N.Y., Am. Judicature Soc. Contbr. articles to legal jours. Home: 1080 Fifth Ave New York City NY 10028 Office: Cravath Swaine & Moore 1 Chase Manhattan Plaza New York City NY 10005 Tel (212) 422-3000

TYLER, HAROLD RUSSELL, JR., b. Utica, N.Y., May 14, 1922; A.B., Princeton, 1942; LL.B., Columbia, 1949. Admitted to N.Y. bar, 1950; asso. firm Casey, Lane & Mittendorf, N.Y.C., 1952-53; asst. U.S. atty. So. Dist. N.Y., 1953-55; mem. firm Gilbert, Sefall & Young, N.Y.C., 1955-59, 61-62; asst. atty. gen. U.S., Washington, 1959-61; U.S. dist. judge So. Dist. N.Y., 1962-75; dep. atty. gen. U.S., Washington, 1975-77; mem. firm Patterson, Belknap, Webb & Tyler, N.Y.C., 1977—. Adj. prof. law N.Y. U. Law Sch., 1966-75; vis. prof. Inst. Criminology, Cambridge U., 1968. Mem. Waterfront Commn. N.Y. Harbor, 1961-62; vice chmn. Adminstrv. Conf. U.S., 1975-77. Home: Indian Hill Rd Bedford NY 10506 Office: 30 Rockefeller Plaza New York City NY 10020 Tel (212) 541-4000

TYLER, JOEL JEFFREY, b. Balti, Romania, July 28, 1921; student Ind. U., 1939-41; B.A., N.Y. U., 1943; LL.B., Fordham U., 1946. Admitted to N.Y. bar, 1949; practiced in N.Y.C., 1944-47; atty. law dept. Allied Chem. & Dye Corp. (now Allied Chem. Corp.), N.Y.C., 1947-50; individual practice law, N.Y.C., 1951-66; spl. asst. atty. gen. State of N.Y., 1956-57; sec. N.Y. Workmen's Compensation Bd., 1960-61; commr. of licenses City of N.Y., 1966-68; judge N.Y.C. Criminal Ct., 1968—; acting justice N.Y. Supreme Ct., 1976—. Mem. Bar Assn. City N.Y., Bronx, Am. bar assns., Am. Judicature Soc. Office: 100 Centre St New York City NY 10013 Tel (212) CY3-8000

TYNER, E. DAVID, b. Ocala, Fla., Mar. 16, 1941; B.A., Stetson U., 1963, J.D. with honors, 1967. Admitted to Fla. bar, 1967; partner firm Sumner Tyner & McKnight, Dade City, Fla., 1968—; pros. atty. Pasco County (Fla.), 1969-72. Bd. dirs. Dade City Little Theatre. Mem. Fla. Bar (grievance com. 6th jud. circuit), Pasco County (past pres.), Am. bar assns., Am. Trial Lawyers Assn. Home: 251 Hwy 579 Dade City FL 33525 Office: 106 S 16th St Dade City FL 33525 Tel (904) 567-5658

TYSON, JOHN CAIUS, III, b. Montgomery, Ala., Oct. 7, 1926; B.S., U. Ala., 1948, LL.B., 1951. Admitted to Ala. bar, 1951; practiced in Montgomery, 1951-60; asso. firm Jones, Murray & Stewart, 1951; individual practice, 1951-56; asso. firm Tyson & Wampold, 1956-60; asst. atty. gen. State of Ala., Montgomery, 1959-71; asso. judge Ala. Ct. Criminal Appeals, 1972-76, presiding judge, 1976—; lectr. U. Ala., 1960-70. Bd. dirs. Montgomery YMCA, Soc. Pioneers of Montgomery. Mem. Am. Judicature Soc., Am., Ala., Montgomery County (exec. com. 1963) bar assns. Contbr. articles to legal jours. Home: 3114 Jasmine Rd Montgomery AL 36111 Office: Room 306 Judicial Bldg Montgomery AL 36101

TYSON, RICHARD EUGENE, b. Parkersburg, W.Va., Oct. 1, 1926; A.B. in Govt., Ind. U., 1949; J.D., W.Va. U., 1952. Admitted to W.Va. bar, 1952; asso. firm J. J. N. Quinlan, Huntington, W.Va., 1952-56; partner firm Parsons, Baker & Tyson, Huntington, 1959-60, firm Tyson & Albright, and predecessors, Huntington, 1960-68; individual practice law, Huntington, 1968—; asst. atty. City of Huntington, 1953-54, municipal ct. judge, 1957-63; asst. pros. atty. Cabell County (W.Va.), Huntington, 1969. Mem. lay adv. bd. St. Mary's Hosp., Huntington; counselor Tri-State Area council Boy Scouts Am., Huntington. Mem. W.Va. State Bar, Am., Cabell County, W.Va. bar assns., Am. Assn. Hosp. Attys., W.Va. Alumni Assn., Ind. U. Alumni Assn., Marshall U. Found., Phi Alpha Delta. Home: 136 Larkspur Dr Huntington WV 25705 Office: Suite 302 Kelly Harfield Bldg 704 4th Ave Huntington WV 25714 Tel (304) 529-2593

TYSON, ROY KNOX, b. Houston, May 30, 1942; B.A., Southwestern U., Georgetown, Tex., 1964; J.D., So. Meth. U., 1971. Admitted to Tex. bar, 1971, U.S. Tax Ct. bar, 1972; asso. firm Sorrell Anderson & Sorrell, Corpus Christi, Tex., 1971-73, firm Touchstone Bernays & Johnston, Dallas, 1973-76; atty. and counsel Southwestern Bell Telephone Co., Dallas, 1976—. Mem. Am., Dallas (unauthorized practice of law com.) bar assns., State Bar Tex., Phi Delta Phi. Recipient Law Enforcement Assistance award U.S. Dept. Justice, 1969. Home: 4500 Rheims Pl Dallas TX 75205 Office: 308 S Akard St suite 2010 PO Box 5521 Dallas TX 75222 Tel (214) 748-2900

UBINGER, JOHN WALTER, JR., b. Pitts., Jan. 31, 1949; B.B.A. cum laude, Ohio U., 1970; J.D., U. Notre Dame, 1973. Admitted to Pa. bar, 1973; asso. firm Eckert, Seamans, Cherin & Mellott, Pitts., 1973—. Mem. Am., Pa., Allegheny County bar assns. Office: 42nd floor 600 Grant St Pittsburgh PA 15219 Tel (412) 566-6000

UDRIS, JURIS, b. Riga, Latvia, Aug. 15, 1932; B.A., Rutgers U., 1956; LL.B., Harvard U., 1959. Admitted to Mass. bar, 1959; partner firm Goodwin, Procter & Hoar, Boston, 1959—; mem. Mass. Land Records Commn. Mem. Weston Zoning Bd. Appeals. Mem. Greater Boston C. of C., Am., Mass. bar assns. Home: 256 Simon Willard Rd Concord MA 01742 Office: 28 State St Boston MA 02109 Tel (617) 523-5700

UELMEN, GERALD FRANCIS, b. Greendale, Wis., Oct. 8, 1940; B.A., Loyola U., Los Angeles, 1962; J.D., Georgetown U., 1965, LL.M., 1966. Admitted to D.C. bar, 1966, Calif. bar, 1967, U.S. Supreme Ct. bar, 1974; asst. U.S. atty., Los Angeles, 1966-70, chief spl. prosecutions div., 1970; prof. law Loyola U. Sch. Law, Los Angeles, 1970—, asso. dean, 1973-75; cons. RAND Corp., 1974—; adj. prof. Nat. Inst. Trial Advocacy, 1974-75. Mem. Am., Los Angeles County, Fed. bar assns., Calif. Attys. for Criminal Justice. Author: (with Victor G. Haddox) Drug Abuse and the Law, 1974. Office: 1440 W 9th St Los Angeles CA 90015 Tel (213) 642-2939

UFBERG, MURRAY, b. Danville, Pa., July 30, 1943; A.B., Bucknell U., 1964; J.D., Duquesne U., 1968. Admitted to Pa. bar, 1968, U.S. Dist. Ct. Middle Dist. Pa. bar, 1969; partner firm Roseun, Jenkins & Greenwald, Wilkes-Barre, Pa., 1973—. Former pres. B'nai B'rith; mem. bd. Ecumenical Enterprises, Inc. Mem. Pa., Luzerne County bar assns., Pa. Trial Lawyers Assn. Home: 644 Charles Ave Kingston PA 18704 Office: Blue Cross Bldg Wilkes-Barre PA 18711 Tel (717) 829-0511

UFFORD, CHARLES WILBUR, JR., b. Princeton, N.J., July 8, 1931; B.A. cum laude (Francis H. Burr scholar), Harvard, 1953; student (Lionel de Jersey Harvard Studentship) Emmanuel Coll., Cambridge (Eng.) U., 1953-54; LL.B., Harvard, 1959. Admitted to N.Y. bar, 1961; since practiced in N.Y.C., asso. firm Riggs, Ferris & Geer, 1959-61; asso. firm Jackson, Nash, Brophy, Barringer & Brooks, 1961-69, partner, 1969—. Pres., Met. Squash Racquets Assn. N.Y.C., 1965-67; bd. dirs. U.S. Squash Racquets Assn., 1971-73; trustee Nat. Squash Racquets Ednl. Found., Princeton, N.Y.C., 1972—. Fellow Am. Coll. Probate Counsel; mem. Am. (chmn. subcom. taxation sect. 1975—), N.Y. State (exec. com. sect. trusts and estates law 1976—, chmn. com. on taxation gifts, estates and trusts 1975-76) bar assns., Assn. Bar City N.Y. Contbr. articles in field to legal jours. Home: 150 Mercer St Princeton NJ 08540 Office: 330 Madison Ave New York City NY 10017 Tel (212) 949-0665

UFHOLZ, L. TERRENCE, b. Cleve., Mar. 16, 1949; B.S. in Mgmt., U. Akron, 1971, J.D., 1974. Admitted to Ohio bar, 1974; asso. firm Alpeter, Diefenbach, Davies, Koerber & Nostwich, Akron, 1974-76; partner firm Koerber, Nostwich & Ufholz Co., Akron, Ohio, 1976—. Mem. Ohio, Akron bar assns. Office: 711 Centran Bldg Akron OH 44308 Tel (216) 762-0303

UHL, SIMON KREBS, b. Somerset, Pa., Feb. 22, 1903; A.B., Princeton, 1926; LL.B., U. Pitts., 1934. Admitted to Pa. bar, 1935; individual practice law, Somerset, 1935—; dir. Somerset Trust Co., 1948—. Pres., Somerset County Tb Soc., 1948-56; bd. dirs. Children's Aid Soc., 1950-59; mem. Pa. Milk Control Commn., 1956-63, chmn., 1960-63; pres. bd. trustees Somerset State Hosp., 1973—; mem. ch. council Trinity Lutheran Ch., Somerset, 1972-75. Mem. Pa., Somerset County bar assns. Decorated Bronze Star. Home: RFD 1 Somerset PA 15501 Office: 118 W Main St Somerset PA 15501 Tel (814) 445-5123

UHLENHOPP, HARVEY HAROLD, b. Butler County Iowa, June 23, 1915; A.B., Grinnell Coll., 1936, LL.D., 1973; J.D., U. Iowa, 1939. Admitted to U.S. Dist. Ct. bar, Dist. of Iowa, 1939, Iowa bar, 1939, U.S. 8th Circuit Ct. of Appeals bar, 1941; partner firm Uhlenhopp & Uhlenhopp, Hampton, Iowa, 1939-53; judge Dist. Ct. Iowa, 1953-70; justice Iowa Supreme Ct., 1970—; mem. Iowa Ho. of Reps., 1951-52. Mem. Iowa, Am. bar assns., Am. Judicature Soc. (dir. 1966-70), Inst. Jud. Adminstrn., Am. Law Inst., Iowa Dist. Ct. Judges Assn. (pres. 1968-69). Contbr. articles to profl. publs. Home: 815 4th Ave SE Hampton IA 50441 Office: PO Box 341 Hampton IA 50441 Tel (515) 456-3592

UHLIR, GEORGE CLEIGH, b. Knox County, Nebr., Sept. 30, 1894; LL.B., Valparaiso U., 1917, J.D. (hon.), 1970; postgrad. U. Nebr., 1919. Admitted to Nebr. bar, 1919, S.D. bar, 1920; individual practice law, Chamberlain, S.D., 1919-21, Kimball, S.D., 1921-28, Kokomo, Ind., 1928—; govt. appeal agt. Howard County (Ind.), 1940-69. Chmn. bd. cemetery regents, Kokomo. Mem. Howard County, Ind. State, Am. bar assns. Home: 715 E Walnut St Kokomo IN 46901 Office: 528-530 Armstrong Landon Bldg Kokomo IN 46901 Tel (317) 457-1936

UKISHIMA, DANIEL SHO, b. Honolulu, Oct. 27, 1944; B.B.A., Gonzaga U., 1966, J.D., 1970. Admitted to Hawaii bar, 1970; dep. atty. gen. State of Hawaii, Honolulu, 1970-72; partner firm Rice, Lee & Wong, Honolulu, 1972-73; individual practice law, Honolulu, 1973-74; partner firm Ukishima & Matsubara, Honolulu, 1974—; chmn. Hawaii Criminal Injuries Compensation Commn., 1975—. Chmn. bd. dirs. Keiki Korners, Inc., 1975—. Mem. Am., Hawaii bar assns., Phi Alpha Delta. Office: Suite 1748 190 S King St Honolulu HI 96813 Tel (808) 536-1835

ULIBARRI, JOE THOMAS, b. Pueblo, Colo., July 31, 1943; A.A., Pueblo Jr. Coll., 1963; B.A., So. Colo. State Coll., 1965; J.D., U. Denver, 1970. Admitted to Colo. bar, 1971; staff atty. Pueblo County Legal Services, Inc., 1971-73, Mexican Am. Legal Def. & Edn. Fund, Denver, 1973-74; since practiced in Pueblo, individual practice law, 1974; regional asst. atty. gen. State of Colo., Pueblo, 1974—; instr. U. So. Colo., 1973; mem. nominating com. Colo. Supreme Ct., 1974, Gov.'s Ethics Com., 1974. Active Chicano Democratic Caucus, Pueblo, 1974—; treas. Pueblo Regional Planning Commn., 1975—. Mem. Colo., Pueblo County bar assns. Home: 209 Melrose Ave Pueblo CO 81004 Office: 701 Court St Pueblo CO 81003

ULLMAN, SAMUEL CHARLES, b. Washington, Dec. 29, 1943; B.A. cum laude, U. Fla., 1965, J.D., 1967; LL.M., U. Miami, 1975. Admitted to Fla. bar, 1968, D.C. bar, 1968; atty. adviser U.S. Tax Ct., Washington, 1968-69; mem. firm Smathers & Thompson, Miami, 1970—; adj. prof. U. Miami Sch. Law, Coral Gables, Fla., 1976—. Mem. Dade County, Am., D.C., Fla. (chmn. tax sect. 1977—), bar assns., Delta Theta Phi. Home: 2333 Brickell Ave Apt 1115 Miami FL 33129 Office: 1301 Alfred I Dupont Bldg Miami FL 33131 Tel (305) 379-6523

ULLOM, MARC FREDRIC, b. Akron, Ohio, Aug. 11, 1947; B.A. in Polit. Sci., U. Akron, 1968, J.D., 1972. Sr. indsl. engr. B.F. Goodrich Co., Akron, 1968-72; admitted to Ohio bar, 1972; chief legal adviser to Ohio Auditor, Columbus, 1972-76; chief dep. clk. of cts. for Summit County, Ohio, 1976—. Mem. Columbus, Am. bar assns., Pi Sigma Alpha. Home: 149 Hayes Ave Cuyahoga Falls OH 44221 Office: 209 S High St Akron OH 44308 Tel (216) 379-5456

ULLRICH, THOMAS WILLIAM, b. Washington, D.C., May 23, 1945; B.A., Coll. of William and Mary, 1967; J.D., Stetson Coll., 1970. Intern, NASA Legal Office, Cape Kennedy, Fla., 1969; admitted to Fla. bar, 1970, D.C. bar, 1971, Va. bar, 1971; clerk to Hon. Andrew M. Hood chief judge D.C. Ct. of Appeals, 1970-71; individual practice law, Washington and Va., 1971—. Mem. Am., Fed., Va., Fla. bar assns., D.C. Unified Bar. Recipient awards for Constl. law, Trusts and Labor law, Am. Jurisprudence, 1968, 69; George C. Dayton award, 1970. Home: 5616 Glenwood Dr Alexandria VA 22310 Office: 1625 K St NW Washington DC 20006 Tel (202) 347-5179

ULLSTROM, L. BERWYN, b. Memphis, Nebr., Sept. 18, 1919; student Scottsbluff Coll., 1937-40; B.S. in Math and Sci., U. Mich., 1946; J.D., U. Denver, 1948. Admitted to Colo. bar, 1948, U.S. 10th Circuit Ct. Appeals bar, 1949, U.S. Supreme Ct. bar, 1954, U.S. 5th Circuit Ct. Appeals bar, 1968; individual practice law, Denver, 1948-51, 61—; instr. aviation law U. Denver, 1948-51; atty. Civil Aero. Adminstrn., Ft. Worth and Washington, 1951-54; asso. gen. counsel Fed. Civil Def. Adminstrn., Battle Creek, Mich., 1954-56; exec. asst. dir. OCDM, Exec. Office of Pres., 1958-61; observer joint task force 7, Pacific Thermonuclear Operation Redwing, 1956. Mem. Aircraft Owners and Pilots Assn., Lawyer-Pilots Bar Assn., Am., Colo., Denver bar assns., Am., Colo. trial lawyers assns., Toastmasters, Denver Jr. Bar Assn. (chmn. 1950), Phi Delta Phi.

ULRICH, RICHARD HENRY, b. St. Louis, May 7, 1943; B.A., Grinnell Coll., 1965; J.D., U. Mo., 1968. Admitted to Mo. bar, 1968; asso. firm Shifrin, Treiman, Bamburg & Dempsey, and successors, St. Louis, 1968-74, partner, 1974—. Asso. adviser legal explorer posts Boy Scouts Am., 1973-75. Mem. Am., Met. St. Louis, Mo. bar assns. Home: 368 Dungate St Chesterfield MO 63017 Office: 11 S Meramec St Suite 1350 Clayton MO 63105 Tel (314) 862-3232

ULRICH, ROBERT G., b. Evanston, Ill., May 6, 1935; LL.B., Marquette U., 1960. Admitted to Ill. bar, Wis. bar; law clk. to fed. dist. judge, Milw., 1961-62; atty., S.C. Johnson & Son, Inc., Racine, Wis., 1962-65, Motorola Inc., Franklin Park, Ill., 1965-68; atty. Jewel Cos. Inc., Melrose Park, Ill., 1968-75, asst. gen. counsel, 1971-75; v.p., gen. counsel Great Atlantic & Pacific Tea Co., Inc., Montvale, N.J., 1975—. Home: 500 Weymouth Dr Wyckoff NJ 07481 Office: 2 Paragon Dr Montvale NJ 07645 Tel (201) 573-9700

ULTERINO, EUGENE DENNIS, b. Rochester, N.Y., Aug. 19, 1941; B.A. with honors, U. Rochester, 1963; LL.B., Georgetown U., 1966. Admitted to N.Y. bar, 1966; clk. to judge N.Y. State Ct. Appeals, Albany, 1966-68; asso. firm Nixon, Hargrave, Devans & Doyle, Rochester, 1968-75, partner, 1976—. Mem. Am. Bar Assn., Am. Hosp. Lawyers Assn. Home: 347 Hillside Ave Rochester NY 14610 Office: Lincoln First Tower Rochester NY 14603 Tel (716) 546-8000

UMIN, STEVEN MICHAEL, b. N.Y.C., Jan. 28, 1939; B.A. summa cul laude, Yale U., 1959, LL.B. cumlaude, 1964; postgrad. (Rhodes scholar) Oxford U., 1959-61. Admitted to D.C. bar, 1967; law clk. to chief justice Calif. Supreme Ct., San Francisco, 1964-65, to Asso. Justice Potter Stewart, U.S. Supreme Ct., Washington 1965-66; counsel U.S. Senate Subcom. Improvements in Jud. Machinery, 1966-67; adj. prof. civil procedure, criminal procedure, criminal law Georgetown U., 1970-75; partner firm Williams & Connolly, Washington, 1975—. Home: 129 4th St SE Washington DC 20003 Office: 839 17th St NW Suite 1000 Washington DC 20006 Tel (202) 331-5047

UMSTATTD, MAC, b. Matoaka, W.Va., Mar. 11, 1922; B.A., U. Tex., 1948, J.D., 1947. Admitted to Tex. bar, 1947, U.S. Supreme Ct. bar, 1957; asso. Dan Moody, Austin, Tex., 1948-50; staff judge adv. U.S. Air Force, 1950-53; atty., asst. gen. counsel Lower Colorado River Authority, Austin, 1950-58, gen. counsel, 1958—. Pres., Austin Young Men's Bus. League, 1952. Mem. Am., Travis County (coms.) bar assns., Tex. Water Conservation Assn. (legal com. 1971—), Gulf Intracoastal Canal Assn., Phi Beta Kappa, Phi Alpha Delta, Pi Kappa Alpha. Editor Tex. Law Rev., 1946-47. Home: 2903 Richard Ln Austin TX 78703 Office: PO Box 220 Austin TX 78767 Tel (512) 474-5931

UNDERHILL, WILLIAM AMORY, b. Basinger, Fla., Feb. 21, 1910; LL.B., Stetson U., 1936, LL.D., 1969. Admitted to Fla. bar, 1936, D.C. bar, 1952, U.S. Supreme Ct. bar, 1946; practiced in DeLand, Fla., 1936-42; pros. atty. Volusia County (Fla.), 1940-42; with Dept. Justice, Washington, 1946-52, acting asst. atty. gen., 1950-51, 1st asst. to dep. atty. gen., 1951, acting dept. atty. gen., antitrust div., 1951, atty. asst. atty. gen. in charge lands and natural resources div., 1951-52; individual practice law, DeLand and Washington, 1952—. Asso. dir. Young Democrats Am., 1946; trustee Stetson U., 1977—; bd. overseers Stetson U. Law Sch., 1965—, chmn., 1977—; bd. dirs. Law Center Found., St. Petersburg (Fla.) Inc., pres., 1971-77; trustee St. Leo Coll., 1968—; trustee Bert Fish Testamentary Trust, DeLand, 1968—, pres. bd., 1977—. Mem. DeLand (pres. 1938), Fla. State (v.p. 1939) jr. Chambers Commerce, Fla. C. of C., D.C. Bar, Am., Fed., Fla., Volusia County bar assns., Stetson U. Alumni Assn. (pres. 1971), Phi Alpha Delta, Pi Kappa Phi, Theta Alpha Phi. Recipient George Washington Honor medal award Freedoms Found. of Valley Forge, 1970; Ben C. Willard award Stetson Lawyer Assn., 1970; C.H.I.E.F. award Ind. Colls. and Univs. Fla., 1974; Distinguished Alumni award Stetson U., 1974; William Amory Underhill award established in his honor Stetson U., 1974. Home: 145 N Garfield Ave DeLand FL 32720 Office: PO Box 66 DeLand FL 32702 Tel (904) 734-2147 also 1625 K St NW Washington DC 20006 Tel (202) 737-7888

UNDERWOOD, ROBERT CHARLES, b. Gardner, Ill., Oct. 27, 1915; A.B., Ill. Wesleyan U., 1937; J.D., U. Ill., Champaign, 1939; LL.D., Loyola U., Chgo., 1969, Ill. Wesleyan U., 1970, Eureka Coll., 1970. Admitted to Ill. bar, 1939; practiced in Bloomington, Ill., 1939-46; city atty. City of Normal (Ill.), 1939-46; asst. state's atty. McLean County (Ill.), 1942-46; judge McLean County Ct., 1946-62; justice Ill. Supreme Ct., 1962—, chief justice, 1969-75. Active Meth. Ch. of Normal; vice chmn. Ill. Commn. on Children; chmn. Bd. Higher Edn. Com. to Survey Legal Edn. Needs in Ill., 1968. Fellow Pa. Mason Juvenile Ct. Inst.; mem. Am. Law Inst., McLean County, Ill. (award of merit 1975), Am. (chmn. bd. elections) bar assns., Am. Judicature Soc. (dir.), Inst. Jud. Adminstrn., Ill. County and Probate Judges Assn. (pres. 1951-52), Sigma Delta Kappa. Recipient Distinguished Service award U.S. Jr. C. of C., 1948, Good Govt. award, 1953; citation for pub. service Ill. Welfare Assn., 1960, Outstanding Citizen award Normal C. of C., 1962, certificate of outstanding achievement U. Ill. Coll. Law, 1969; contbr. articles to legal jours. Home: 11 Kent Dr Normal IL 61761 Office: Supreme Ct Bldg Springfield IL 62706 Tel (217) 782-7864 also 300 Peoples Bank Bldg Bloomington IL 61701

UNDERWOOD, THOMAS BRYAN, JR., b. Chillicothe, Ohio, Mar. 28, 1932; B.A., Coll. of Wooster, 1954; J.D., Ohio State Univ., 1956. Admitted to Ohio bar, 1957; partner firm Day, Ketterer, Raley, Wright & Rybolt, Canton, Ohio, 1960-70; asso. prof. law, asso. dean, Indiana Univ., Bloomington, 1970—. Mem. Am., Indiana bar assns., Order of Coif, Phi Alpha Delta. Contbr. articles in field to profl. jours. Home: 3209 E 10th St Apt 7N Bloomington IN 47401 Office: School of Law Indiana University Bloomington IN 47401 Tel (812) 337-5361

UNDERWOOD, TOM RUST, b. Lexington, Ky., Oct. 11, 1926; LL.B., U. Ky., 1950. Admitted to Ky. bar, 1950. Mem. Ky., Fayette County bar assns. Office: 507 Security Trust Bldg Lexington KY 40507 Tel (606) 255-6609

UNGARO, GERARD M., b. Chgo., Aug. 27, 1893; ed. Northwestern U. Admitted to Ill. bar, 1919; individual practice law, Chgo. Mem. Chgo., Ill., Am. bar assns. Home and Office: 471 Sunset Rd Winnetka IL 60093 Tel (312) 446-2613

UNGEMACH, CHARLES JOHNSON, b. Denver, Jan. 16, 1930; B.S. in Physics Engring., B.S. in Bus., U. Colo., 1954; J.D., William Mitchell Coll. Law, 1959. Admitted to Minn. bar, 1959, U.S. Dist. Ct. bar, 1959; engr. Honeywell Inc., Mpls., 1954-56, atty. Honeywell patent law office, 1956—, patent counsel Aerospace & Def. Group, 1967-75, Photographic Products div., 1975—. Mem. Minn. Patent Law Assn. (past pres.), Aerospace Industries Assn. (past vice chmn. patent com.). Contbr. articles in field to profl. jours. Home: 3216 Rankin Rd Minneapolis MN 55418 Office: Honeywell Plaza Minneapolis MN 55408 Tel (612) 870-6409

UNGEMAH, DONALD WAYNE, b. Passaic, N.J., Oct. 3, 1943; B.S., Wilkes Coll., 1965; J.D., Villanova U., 1968. Admitted to N.J. bar, 1969; individual practice law, Atlantic City, 1970-74; dir. N.J. Div. Workers Compensation, Trenton, 1974-76; asso. firm Horn, Weinstein, Kaplan and Goldberg, Atlantic City, 1976—. Treas. N.J. Transp. Exposition, Inc., Atlantic City. Mem. N.J., Atlantic County bar assns., Mainland C. of C. Home: 2305 Wabash Ave Northfield NJ 08225 Office: 1301 Atlantic Ave Atlantic City NJ 08401 Tel (609) 348-4515

UNGER, HAROLD M., b. N.Y.C., July 7, 1944; A.B., Brown U., 1966; J.D., Boston U., 1969. Admitted to N.Y. bar, 1971; pres. Internat. Pension Systems, Ltd., N.Y.C.; v.p., gen. counsel Pension Concepts, N.Y.C., cons. pension design and adminstrn. Mem. Am. Soc. Pension Actuaries (asso.), N.Y. State, Am. bar assns. Office: 40 W 57th St New York City NY 10019 Tel (212) 765-2000

UNGER, MARTIN PAUL, b. Bklyn., Oct. 18, 1939; B.A., Alfred U., 1960; J.D. cum laude, N.Y. U., 1964; LL.M., Bklyn. Law Sch., 1967. Admitted to N.Y. bar, 1964, U.S. Supreme Ct. bar, 1975; since practiced in N.Y.C.; law clk. to judge U.S. Dist. Ct., Eastern Dist. N.Y., 1964-66; asso. firm Christy, Bauman, Frey & Christy, 1966-67, firm Skadden, Arps, Slate, Meagher & Flom, 1967-71; partner firm Beekman & Bogue, 1971—. Mem. Am. Bar Assn., Assn. Bar City N.Y. (fed. cts. com. 1971-73, civil cts. com. 1973-76), Order of Coif. Contbr. articles to legal jours. Home: 2196 Brighton Way Merrick NY 11566 Office: 5 Hanover Sq New York City NY 10004 Tel (212) 422-4060

UNION, MARVIN LOUIS, b. Cleve., Oct. 29, 1944; B.E.E., Case Inst. Tech., 1966; J.D., Case Western Res. U., 1969. Admitted to Ohio bar, 1969; with Yount and Tarolli, Cleve., 1967-70; sr. patent atty. Eaton Corp., Cleve., 1970—. Chmn. Chester Twp. Bd. Zoning Appeals, 1971—. Mem. Am., Ohio, Cleve. bar assns., Cleve. Patent Law Assn. Home: 12983 Lynn Dr Chesterland OH 44026 Office: 100 Erieview Plaza Cleveland OH 44114 Tel (216) 523-5114

UNTI, STEVEN FRANCIS, b. Seattle, Oct. 3, 1948; B.S., Washington and Lee U., 1970; J.D., Cornell U., 1973. Admitted to Ga. bar, 1973; asso. firm Mitchell Clarke Pate & Anderson, Atlanta, 1973—. Mem. State Bar Ga., Am., Atlanta bar assns. Office: Suite 600 Ga Fed Savs Bldg Atlanta GA 30303 Tel (404) 577-6010

UNVERZAGT, GEORGE WILLIAM, b. Hinsdale, Ill., Jan. 18, 1931; A.B., Elmhurst Coll., 1953; J.D., U. Chicago, 1959. Admitted to Ill. bar, 1959, U.S. Supreme Ct. bar, 1970; staff atty. Burlington Lines, Inc., Chgo., 1959-61; asso. firm Charley Popejoy, Glen Ellyn, Ill., 1961-63; partner firm Popejoy, Bowman, Unverzagt & Nelson, Wheaton, Ill., 1963-68, firm Bowman, Unverzagt & Teschner, Wheaton, 1968-70; judge Circuit Ct., Wheaton, 1970-75, chief judge, 1975—; village atty. Willowbrook (Ill.), 1963-65, Villa Park (Ill.), 1965-70, Wayne (Ill.), 1967-70, Oak Brook (Ill.), 1968-70. Alderman, City of Elmhurst, 1961-62. Mem. Am., Ill., DuPage County bar assns., Ill. Judges Assn. (dir.), Am. Judicature Soc., Ill. Jud. Conf. (mem. exec. com. 1975—). Home: 410 S Illinois Ave Villa Park IL 60181 Office: Court House Reber St at Liberty Dr Wheaton IL 60187 Tel (312) 682-7300

UPDIKE, CHARLES BRUCE, b. N.Y.C., June 10, 1939; A.B., Amherst Coll., 1961; M.A., George Washington U., 1964; LL.B., Harvard, 1967. Admitted to N.Y. State bar, 1968; law sec. to judge U.S. Dist. Ct., So. Dist. N.Y., asst. U.S. atty., 1968-72; asso. firm Debevoise, Plimpton, Lyons & Gates, N.Y.C., 1972-76; mem. firm Williamson & Schoeman, N.Y.C., 1976—. Mem. Am., N.Y. State bar assns., Assn. Bar City N.Y., Fed. Bar Council. Tel (212) 661-5030

UPRICHARD, JAMES EDWARD, JR., b. Cleve., Aug. 16, 1942; B.A., St. Francis Coll., 1965; J.D., Cath. U., 1970; student Brief Writing Inst., George Washington U., 1972. Admitted to Ohio bar, 1970, U.S. Supreme Ct. bar, 1973; individual practice law, Cleve., 1970-71; asst. atty. gen., Columbus, Ohio, 1971-76. Mem. Ohio, Cleve., Columbus, Cuyahoga County bar assns. Home: 5143 Schuylkill St Columbus OH 43220 Office: State Office Tower 30 W Broad St Columbus OH 43215 Tel (614) 466-3232

URBOM, WARREN KEITH, b. Atlanta, Nebr., Dec. 17, 1925; A.B. with highest distinction, Nebr. Wesleyan U., 1950; J.D. with distinction, U. Mich., 1953. Admitted to Nebr. bar, 1953; asso. firm Baylor, Evnen, Baylor, Urbom & Curtiss and predecessors, Lincoln, Nebr., 1953-58, partner, 1959-70; U.S. dist. judge, Lincoln, 1970-72, chief judge, 1972—; mem. Nebr. Supreme Ct. Com. on Practice and Procedure, 1965—. Mem. Am., Nebr., Lincoln bar assns., Jud. Conf. (subcom. fed. jurisdiction). Home: 4510 Van Dorn St Lincoln NE 68506 Office: 586 US Courthouse Lincoln NE 68501 Tel (402) 471-5231

URIBE, JORGE ALBERTO, b. Bogota, Colombia, Sept. 1, 1942; A.B., Columbia, 1964; J.D., U. Calif., 1967. Admitted to Calif. bar, 1967; asso. firm Kadison, Pfaelzer, Woodard, Quinn & Rossi, Los Angeles, 1967-71, partner, 1971—. Mem. Am., Los Angeles County bar assns., Thurston Soc., Order of Coif. Recipient Am. Jurisprudence Prize for Excellence, 1967. Office: 611 W 6th St 23rd floor Los Angeles CA 90017 Tel (213) 626-1251

URION, PAUL BATCHELLER, b. Chgo., Dec. 29, 1916; A.B., Dartmouth, 1938; J.D., U. Va., 1941. Admitted to N.H. bar, 1942, Va. bar, 1948, U.S. Supreme Ct. bar, 1972; served as capt. JAG, 1943-46; city solicitor, Rochester, N.H., 1949-55, 60-70, 71—; individual practice law, Rochester, 1948—; mem. N.H. Jud. Council, 1975—. Trustee Nasson Coll., 1976—, Spaulding Youth Center, 1963-68, 71-74. Mem. Am., N.H. (sec. jr. bar. conf. 1949), Va., Strafford County (pres. 1971-72) bar assns. Recipient Silver Beaver award Boy Scouts Am., 1962. Home: 27 Broad St Rochester NH 03867 Office: 69 S Main St Rochester NH 03867 Tel (603) 332-1420

URIS, ALAN M., b. N.Y.C., Apr. 4, 1934; B.A., Dartmouth, 1955; LL.B., N.Y. U., 1958. Admitted to N.Y. bar, 1959, Vt. bar, 1970; individual practice law, Queens, N.Y., 1960-70; staff Assemblyman Joseph Lisa, Flushing, N.Y., 1965-70; counsel various legis. coms. State Vt., 1970; partner firm Uris & Hutton, 1971-76; individual practice law, Waitsfield, Vt., 1976—; atty. Town of Warren (Vt.), 1970—, Waitsfield br. Howard Bank. Mem. Vt., Washington County bar assns. Home: RFD Warren VT 05674 Office: Box 25 Waitsfield VT 05673 Tel (802) 496-2267

URQUHART, CHARLES FOX, III, b. Franklin, Va., Aug. 9, 1942; B.A., Washington and Lee U., 1964, J.D., 1970. Admitted to Va. bar, 1970; mem. trust dept. Wachovia Bank & Trust Co., Winston-Salem, N.C., 1970-71; individual practice law, Courtland, Va., 1971—; commr. in chancery, Southampton County, Va., 1973—. Dist. exec. commr. Boy Scouts Am., 1974—; lt. Courtland Vol. Fire Dept., 1972—; pres. Franklin Little Theatre, 1975-76; trustee Ridley Found. 1971—. Mem. SAR, SCV, Order Stars and Bars, Southampton Hist. Soc., Naval Res. Assn., Am. Legion, Res. Officers Assn. Home and Office: Box 85 Courtland VA 23837 Tel (804) 653-2046

URSERY, FREDERICK STANLEY, b. Pine Bluff, Ark., Mar. 5, 1942; A.B. cum laude, Vanderbilt U., 1964; LL.B., Columbia, 1967. Admitted to Ark. bar, 1967; asso. firm Friday, Eldredge & Clark, Little Rock, 1969-74, partner, 1974—; exec. sec. com. on jury instructions-criminal Ark. Supreme Ct., 1971—. Bd. stewards First Methodist Ch., Little Rock, 1975—. Mem. Ark. (mem. ho. of dels.), Am. bar assns., Ark. Bar Found. (dir.). Home: 2804 N Taylor St Little Rock AR 72207 Office: First Nat Bldg 20th floor Little Rock AR 72201 Tel (501) 376-2011

URSO, JOHN R., b. Detroit, May 6, 1943; B.A., U. Mich., 1965; J.D., Wayne State U., 1968. Admitted to Mich. bar, 1968; asso. prof. law U. Detroit; judge Municipal Ct., Grosse Point Park, Mich. Home: 789 Westchester St Grosse Pointe Park MI 48230 Office: 15115 E Jefferson St Grosse Pointe Park MI 48230 Tel (313) 822-3535

USSERY, ALBERT TRAVIS, b. Gulfport, Miss., Mar. 12, 1928; A.B., Washington U., St. Louis, 1950; LL.B., U. N.Mex., 1951, J.D., 1968; LL.M., Georgetown U., 1955. Admitted to N.Mex. bar, 1951; partner firm Gallagher & Ussery, Albuquerque, 1951-53, Threet, Ussery & Threet, Albuquerque, 1957-60, McRae, Ussery, Mims, Ortega & Kitts, Albuquerque, 1964-65, Ussery, Burciaga & Parrish, Albuquerque, 1969—; individual practice law, Albuquerque, 1955-57, 61-63, 66-69; chmn. bd. Am. Bank of Commerce, 1966-70, Rio Grand Valley Bank, 1972—; 1st lt. JAGC, U.S. Army, 1953-55; instr. mil. law U. N.Mex., 1956, corp. fin., 1956-57, bus. law, 1960-61; spl. counsel on water law City of Albuquerque, 1956-66. Mem. State Bar N.Mex., Am., Albuquerque, Fed. bar assns., Albuquerque Lawyers Club. Home: Rio Grande Blvd at Eakes Rd NW Albuquerque NM 87107 Office: 200 Rio Grande Valley Bank Bldg 501 Tijeras Blvd NW PO Box 487 Albuquerque NM 87103 Tel (505) 247-0145

UTCHEN, THEODORE MORRIS, b. St. Paul, June 25, 1929; B.A., U. Kans., 1950; J.D. with distinction, U. Mich., 1958, LL.M., 1959. Admitted to Kans. bar, 1958, Mich. bar, 1958, Mo. bar, 1959, Ill. bar, 1974; asso. firm Brewer & Myers, Kansas City, Mo., 1959-60, firm John C. Frank, Wichita, Kans., 1960-61; trust officer Bank of Okla., Tulsa, 1961-64; trust officer No. Trust Co., Chgo., 1964-68; house counsel Miami Corp., Chgo., 1968—. Mem. Am., Ill. State bar assns., Order of Coif, Phi Beta Kappa. Office: 410 N Michigan Ave Chicago IL 60611 Tel (312) 644-6720

UTTER, ROBERT FRENCH, b. Seattle, June 19, 1930; B.S., U. Wash., 1952, LL.B., 1954. Admitted to Wash. bar, 1954; law clerk Wash. Supreme Ct., 1954-55; deputy prosecuting atty. King County (Wash.), 1955-57; individual practice law, Seattle, 1957-59; ct. commr. King County Superior Ct., 1959-64; judge King County Court, 1964-69, Wash. Ct. Appeals, 1969-71; state supreme ct. justice, Wash., 1971—, acting chief justice, 1977-78; lectr. U. Wash. Law Sch., Seattle U. Past pres., co-founder Seattle Big Brothers Assn., 1965-67, Job Therapy, Inc., 1963-71; chmn. gov.'s com Community Based Corrections, 1971-72. Recipient Man of Year award, Seattle Jr. C. of C., 1964; Outstanding Alumnus award Linfield Coll., 1973. Author: Selection and Retention, 1973. Home: 3013 Sherwood Dr Olympia WA 98501 Office: Temple of Justice Olympia WA 98504

UTTERBACK, PRISCILLA WOOTEN, b. Holly Springs, Miss., Dec. 10, 1902; B.A., Southeastern State Tchrs. Coll., 1924. Admitted to Okla. bar, 1929; asso. firm Utterback & Utterback and predecessors, Durant, Okla., 1930-32, partner, 1932-50; individual practice law, Durant, 1950—. Life mem. Okla. Soc. Crippled Children, Oklahoma City, Okla. Hist. Soc.; active Five Civilized Tribes Mus., Muskogee, Okla., Okla. Heritage Assn., Oklahoma City; trustee Robert Lee Williams Pub. Library, Durant, Highland Cemetery, Oklahoma City; past v.p. Okla. League Young Democrats. Fellow Am. Coll. Probate Counsel; mem. Am., Okla., Bryan County (former pres.) bar assns., Nat., Okla. (past v.p.) assns. women lawyers, Am. Judicature Soc. Home: 409 N 4th St Durant OK 74701 Office: Utterback Bldg Box 126 Durant OK 74701 Tel (405) 924-4185

UVENA, FRANK JOHN, b. Ernest, Pa., Feb. 2, 1934; A.B., Ohio U., 1959; LL.B., Ohio State U., 1963. Admitted to Ill. bar, 1963, U.S. Supreme Ct. bar, 1971; asso. firm McDermott, Will & Emery, Chgo., 1963-68; atty. R.R. Donnelley & Sons Co., Chgo., 1968-72, gen. atty., 1972-75, v.p., gen. counsel, 1975—. Mem. Chgo. Crime Commn. Mem. Am., Chgo., Ill. bar assns., Practising Law Inst. Office: 2223 Martin Luther King Dr Chicago IL 60616 Tel (312) 326-8000

UVILLER, H. RICHARD, b. N.Y.C., July 3, 1929; B.A., Harvard, 1951; LL.B., Yale, 1953. Admitted to N.Y. State bar, 1954, U.S. Supreme Ct. bar; with office of legal counsel U.S. Dept. Justice, Washington, 1953-54; with dist. atty.'s office N.Y. County, N.Y.C., 1954-68; prof. Columbia Law Sch., N.Y.C., 1968—. Mem. Assn. Bar City N.Y., Am. Law Inst. Author: Casebook, The Processes of Criminal Justice, 1974; contbr. articles to legal jours. Home: 51 Fifth Ave New York City NY 10003 Office: 435 W 116th St New York City NY 10027 Tel (212) 280-4160

VADER, JAY H., b. Kansas City, Kans., Oct. 10, 1948; B.S., Kans. State U., 1970; J.D., Washburn U., 1973. Admitted to Kans. bar, 1973, U.S. Dist. Ct. bar for Dist. Kans., 1973; legal intern Pub. Defender's Office, Topeka, 1973; partner firm Maurin, Vader & Sheeley and predecessors, Kansas City, Kans., 1974—; judge pro tempore Edwardsville (Kans.) Municipal Ct., 1976; juvenile judge pro tempore Wyandotte County (Kans.) Juvenile Ct., 1976. Mem. Kans., Wynodette County, Am. bar assns., Kans. Trial Lawyers Assn., Assn. Trial Lawyers Am. Home: 1301 N 25th St Kansas City KS 66102 Office: 845 Armstrong St Kansas City KS 66101 Tel (913) 371-8383

VAFIADES, LEWIS V., b. Hermon, Maine, Mar. 25, 1919; A.B., Bowdoin Coll., 1942; LL.B., Boston U., 1950. Admitted to Mass. bar, 1950, Maine bar, 1950; now partner firm Vafiades, Brountas & Kominsky, Bangor, Maine; bd. dirs. Bowdoin Alumni Fund, 1963-68, chmn., 1964-65, 67-68; mem. Bowdoin Alumni Council, 1968-72; overseer Bowdoin Coll., 1973—; pres. Pine Tree Legal Assistance, Inc. for Maine, 1969-70. Mem. Am., Maine State (pres. 1976), Penobscot County (pres. 1962-63) bar assns., Maine Trial Lawyers Assn. (pres. 1970-74), Assn. Trial Lawyers Am. (nat. committeeman 1970-72). Office: Vafiades Brountas & Kominsky One Merchants Plaza Bangor ME 04401 Tel (207) 947-6915*

VAGUE, HAROLD RAYMOND, b. Ellsworth, Kans., Mar. 1, 1920; B.A., U. Colo., 1942, LL.B., 1949. Admitted to Colo. bar, 1949, U.S. Supreme Ct. bar, 1962; commd. U.S. Air Force, 1946, advanced through grades to maj. gen., 1973; mem. JAGC, 1950—, asst. Judge Adv. Gen., 1971-73, Judge Adv. Gen., 1973—. Mem. Am., Fed. bar assns., Judge Adv. Assn. Home: 86 Westover Ave Bolling AFB DC 20336 Office: HQ USAF/JA Washington DC 20314 Tel (202) 693-5700

VAIL, JOHN JOSEPH, b. South Amboy, N.J., Dec. 26, 1929; B.S. in Liberal Arts, Seton Hall U., 1951; LL.B., Notre Dame U., 1956. Admitted to N.J. bar, 1957; law clk. Gilhooley, Yauch & Fagan, Newark, 1956-57; asso. firm Foley & Manzione, Iselin, N.J., 1957-59; individual practice law, South Amboy, 1960—; atty. Sayreville Zoning Bd., 1961-63; judge Sayreville Municipal Ct., 1963-66; municipal prosecutor, South Amboy, 1974-75; counsel Squibb and Titanox Employees Fed. Credit Union, New Brunswick, N.J. Mem. Am., N.J. State, Middlesex County bar assns., Am. Judicature Soc. Home: 9 Lani St Sayreville NJ 08879 Office: 121 N Broadway St South Amboy NJ 08879 Tel (201) 721-2430

VAIL, JOHN THOMAS, b. South Amboy, N.J., June 22, 1932; A.B., Georgetown U., 1954, LL.B., 1961. Admitted to Hawaii bar, 1962; partner firm Ueuha, Vail & Luna, Wailuku, Hawaii, 1966-75; individual practice law, Wailuku, 1975—. Home: Kekaulike Ave Kula Maui HI 96817 Office: 1972 Wells St Wailuku HI 96793 Tel (808) 244-7621

VAIL, RUSSELL OLUS, b. Satanta, Kans., Jan. 28, 1941; B.A., Southwestern Coll., Winfield, Kans., 1963; J.D., Am. U., 1966. Admitted to Mich. bar, 1973; legis. asst. to Congressman Robert Dole (Republican, Kans.), Washington, 1964; sr. field claim rep. State Farm Mut. Auto Ins. Co., Falls Church, Va., 1965-67; spl. agt. FBI, Albany, N.Y., Detroit, 1967-71; staff atty. Ford Motor Co. Office Gen. Counsel, Dearborn, Mich., 1971-74; individual practice law, Brighton, Mich., 1974—. Mem. Am., Livingston County (Mich.) bar assns., Assn. Trial Lawyers Am. Recipient Dean's award Am. U., 1966. Office: 9947 E Grand River Ave Brighton MI 48116 Tel (313) 229-5252

VALDERAS, HAROLD LOUIS, b. N.Y.C., Dec. 17, 1923; B.B.A., So. Meth. U., 1950, J.D., 1954; postgrad. Am. Acad. Judicial Edn. U. Ala., 1973, Nat. Coll. State Judiciary U. Nev., 1976. Admitted to Tex. bar, 1954, U.S. Dist. Ct. bar, 1954, U.S. Supreme Ct. bar, 1958; individual practice law, Ft. Worth, 1955-71; served with JAGC, USAAF; judge Municipal Cts., Ft. Worth, 1971-72, chief judge, 1972-77; dist. judge 233d Judicial Dist. Tex., 1977—; Internat. dir. Internat. Good Neighbor Council, Monteray, Mex., 1972-74; chmn. Tarrant County (Tex.) Heart Assn., 1974; bd. dirs. Tarrant County United Way, Casa Manana Musicals, N. Tex. Arthritis Found., Met. YMCA, NCCJ, Cath. Social Services, St. Theresa's Home; advisory bd. Big Bros. of Tarrant County. alt. del. Democratic Nat. Conv., Kansas City, 1974. Mem. State Bar Tex. (vice chmn. sect. municipal judges), Fed. Bar (pres. Ft. Worth chpt. 1960), Tarrant County Criminal (dir. 1974), Ft. Worth-Tarrant County, Am. bar assns., Judge Advocates Assn. Named Good Neighbor of Year Internat. Good Neighbor Council, 1972; recipient numerous awards for profl. and civic activities. Office: 233d Judicial Dist Tex Civil Cts Bldg Fort Worth TX 76102 Tel (817) 334-1794

VALEGO, EDWARD F., b. Chicopee, Mass., Sept. 14, 1917; J.D., Boston U., 1948. Admitted to Mass. bar, 1951; dir. rent control City Chicopee, 1954-55, asst. city solicitor, 1966-72; prosecutor Dist. Ct. Chicopee, 1960-66. Mem. Chicopee Bar Assn. Office: 10 Center St Chicopee MA 01013 Tel (413) 592-1845

VALENT, HENRY, b. Watkins Glen, N.Y., July 21, 1915; A.B., Cornell U., 1936, LL.B., 1938. Admitted to N.Y. bar, 1938; individual practice law, Watkins Glen, 1938-41, 46—; dir. Nat. Bank and Trust Co., Hi Speed Check weighter Co. Sec. Watkins Glen Youth Center, Inc.; dir. Schuyler Hosp., Sullivan Trail council Boy Scouts Am. Mem. Schuyler County, N.Y. State, Am. bar assns. Author: Road Racing at Watkins Glen. Home: RD 2 Watkins Glen NY 14891 Office: Glen National Bank Bldg Franklin St Watkins Glen NY 14891 Tel (607) 535-2771

VALENTINE, GARRISON NORTON, b. N.Y.C., Apr. 7, 1929; B.A., Yale, 1950, LL.B., 1964. Admitted to Conn. bar, 1964; partner firm Hoppin, Carey & Powell, Hartford, Conn., 1964—. Dir. Middlesex County Extension Council, 1967-75; chmn. Old Saybrook (Conn.) Conservation Commn., 1968-75; dir. Conn. Assn. Conservation Commns., 1965-68; trustee Hammonasset Sch., 1974—. Mem. Am., Conn., Hartford County bar assns. Contbr. articles to legal jours. Home: Otter Cove Old Saybrook CT 06475 Office: 266 Pearl St Hartford CT 06103 Tel (203) 249-6891

VALENTINE, RICHARD CLARK, b. Evanston, Ill., May 15, 1928; B.B.A., Lake Forest Coll., 1951; LL.D., Chgo.-Kent Coll., 1956. Admitted to Ill. Supreme Ct. bar, 1956; asso. firm Lord, Bissell & Brook, 1956-67, partner, 1968—. Mem. Am., Ill., Chgo. bar assns., Soc. Trial Lawyers, Ill. Def. Counsel, Internat. Assn. Ins. Counsel, Def. Research Inst. Contbr. articles in field to profl. jours. Home: 2620 Lincoln St Evanston IL 60201 Office: 115 S LaSalle St Chicago IL 60603 Tel (312) 443-0212

VALLELY, JAMES LEO, b. Boston, June 19, 1913; LL.B., Northeastern U., 1936. Admitted to Mass. bar, 1937; asst. corp. counsel Boston, 1941-50, spl. atty. gen., 1952; counsel to Gov. of Mass., 1957; presiding justice Barnstable (Mass.) Dist. Ct., 1957-58; asso. justice Mass. Superior Ct., Boston, 1958—; mem., vice chmn. Mass. Jud. Counsel, 1972-76; mem. Mass. Ho. of Reps., 1939-42. Mem. Boston, Mass. bar assns. Home: 128 Chestnut St Newton MA 02165 Office: New Ct House Boston MA 02108

VALLONE, PETER FORTUNATE, b. N.Y.C., Dec. 13, 1934; B.S.S., Fordham Coll., 1956, LL.B., 1959. Admitted to N.Y. State bar, 1960; law clk. firm Dewey-Ballantine, Bushby, Palmer & Wood, N.Y.C., 1959-60; spl. asst. N.Y. State Atty. Gen.'s Office, N.Y.C., 1960; mem. firm Weinberg & Jacobowitz, Far Rockaway, N.Y., 1961-62, Vallone & Calabrese, Long Island City, N.Y., 1962—; mem. N.Y.C. City Council, 1973—. Sec., bd. dirs. Boys Club, Queens, N.Y., 1967—; mem. community planning bd. Queens County, N.Y., 1973; exec. chmn. Astoria Civic Assn., Long Island City, 1967—; moderator commentators Immaculate Conception Ch.; vol. counsel Community Sch. Bd. 30. Mem. Queens County, N.Y. State, Am. bar assns., Columbian Lawyers Assn., N.Y. State Trial Lawyers Assn., Queens County Criminal Bar Assn., Catholic Lawyers Guild of Queens County (past pres., dir.). Recipient George W. Bacon award Fordham Law Sch., 1959; N.Y.C. Community Service citation, 1972-73. Home: 18-33 21st Dr Long Island City NY 11105 Office: 22-55 31st St Long Island City NY 11105 Tel (212) 274-0909

VAN AKEN, WILLIAM RUSSELL, b. Shaker Heights, Ohio, Dec. 1, 1912; B.S., Lafayette Coll., 1934; LL.B., Case Western Reserve U., 1937. Admitted to Ohio bar, 1938; mem. firm Pennell, Carlson & Rees, Cleve., 1943-49; mem. firm Van Aken, Bond, Withers & Ashman, and predecessors, Cleve., 1949—; chmn. bd. Ohio Bar Automated Research Corp., 1975—; trustee Ohio Legal Center Inst., 1971-77; v.p., dir. Ohio Bar Title Ins. Co.; mem. Ohio Legislature, 1943-44, 47-48; mem. Shaker Heights City Council, 1951-55. Mem. Am., Ohio State (pres. 1958-59), Greater Cleve. bar assns., Am., Ohio State (pres. 1972-77) bar founds., Am. Judicature Soc. Author: (with R. L. Hauser) Ohio Practice Real Estate, 1964; contbg. editor Baldwin's Ohio Legal Forms, 1962. Recipient Ohio Bar medal, 1975. Home: 22299 Douglas Rd Shaker Heights OH 44122 Office: 1028 Nat City Bank Bldg Cleveland OH 44114 Tel (216) 781-4680

VAN ALLEN, WILLIAM KENT, b. Albion, N.Y., July 30, 1914; A.B., Hamilton Coll., 1935; LL.B., Harvard, 1938. Admitted to N.Y. bar, 1938, D.C. bar, 1939, U.S. Supreme Ct. bar, 1946, N.C. bar, 1951, U.S. Ct. Claims bar, 1946, U.S. Tax Ct. bar, 1939, FCC bar, 1939, ICC bar, 1940; with firm Hanson, Lovett & Dale, Washington, 1938-41, 46-50; partner firm Moore and Van Allen, and predecessor, Charlotte, N.C., 1950—. Trustee Mint Mus. Art, 1976—, Spastics Hosp., 1952-59; chmn. Mecklenburg County (N.C.) Bd. Pub. Welfare, 1957-59; chmn. bd. mgrs. Charlotte Country Day Sch., 1959-61; bd. dirs. N.C. Found. Commerce and Industry, 1965-73. Mem. Am. Arbitration Assn. (chmn. area adv. council 1967-76), Am., N.C. bar assns., Am. Judicature Soc., Jud. Conf. 4th Circuit, Phi Beta Kappa. Home: 265 Cherokee Rd Charlotte NC 28207 Office: 3000 NCNB Plaza Charlotte NC 28280 Tel (704) 374-1300

VAN ANTWERP, DANIEL JANSE, b. Detroit, Jan. 4, 1935; A.B., Sacred Heart Sem., 1956; J.D., U. Detroit, 1965; certificate Nat. Coll. State Trial Judges, 1972. Adminstrv. asst. Chrysler Corp., 1958-60; budget analyst, circuit ct. probation officer Wayne County, 1961-66; admitted to Mich. bar, 1966; supervising atty. Rouse, Selby, Dickinson, Shaw & Pike, Detroit, 1966-69; recorder's ct. judge City of Detroit, 1966; circuit and recorders judge Mich. Supreme Ct., 1970; judge Ct. Common Pleas Wayne County, 1971—, presiding judge, 1976. Bd. dirs. Univ. Dist. Community Assn., Fitzgerald Community Council. Mem. Am. Judicature Soc., Mich., Detroit bar assns., Nat. Council Crime and Delinquency, Delta Theta Phi. Author: Bail Bond Manual, 1967; Subrogation Procedure, 1968. Home: 18625 Muirland St Detroit MI 48221 Office: City-County Bldg Detroit MI 48226 Tel (313) 224-5498

VAN BRUNT, BERGEN HOUSTON, b. Frankfort, Ind., Nov. 27, 1911; LL.B., U. Utah, 1933, Ind. U., 1936. Admitted to Ind. bar, 1937, Calif. bar, 1945; claims atty. Md. Casualty Ins. Co., 1936-39, Ohio Casualty Ins. Co., 1939-40, mgr. claim dept. Detroit, 1940-42, San Francisco, 1945-46; partner firm Jackson & Van Brunt, San Francisco, 1946-52; individual practice law, San Francisco, 1953—. Mem. Personnel Bd. Millbrae (Calif.), 1962-67. Mem. Am. Bd. Trial Advs., San Francisco, Calif. trial attys. assns., Am. Trial Lawyers Assn., Lawyers Club San Francisco. Home: 1220 Cardigan Rd Hillsborough CA 94010 Office: 1255 Post St #740 San Francisco CA 94109 Tel (415) 771-1240

VAN BUREN, PAUL BARTLETT, b. Mpls., Oct. 9, 1938; B.A. magna cum laude, U. S.D., 1960; J.D., Stanford, 1964; Rhodes scholar Oxford (Eng.) U., 1960-61. Admitted to S.D. bar, 1964, Calif. bar, 1965; asso. firm May Boe & Johnson (now May Johnson & Burke), Sioux Falls, S.D., 1964-66; legal counsel Pacific Coast div. Owens-Corning Fiberglas Corp., Santa Clara, Calif., 1966-68; dept. counsel nuclear energy mktg. dept. Gen. Electric Co., San Jose, Calif., 1968—. Past chmn. Santa Clara County Young Republicans; bd. dirs. San Jose Theatre Guild. Contbr. articles to legal jours. Office: General Electric Co 175 Curtner Ave San Jose CA 95125 Tel (408) 925-1081

VANCE, ANDREW PETER, b. Detroit, Jan. 23, 1925; A.B. cum laude, Harvard U., 1948, LL.B., 1952. Admitted to D.C. bar, 1952, N.Y. bar, 1976, U.S. Tax Ct. bar, 1957, U.S. Ct. Customs and Patent Appeals, 1962; trial atty. gen. litigation sect., civil div. Dept. Justice, Washington, 1953-62, chief customs sect., Washington and N.Y.C., 1962-76; partner firm Barnes, Richardson & Colburn, N.Y.C., 1976—. Mem. Fed. Bus. Assn. N.Y. (pres. 1975-76), Am. Bar Assn., Assn. Bar City N.Y., Assn. Customs Bar. Recipient Atty. Gen's Distinguished Service award, 1975, Superior Performance award Civil Div., 1975, Distinguished Service award, 1972, 68, 70, 74, spl. citation Dept. Treasury, 1976. Home: 11 Old Army Rd Scarsdale NY 10583 Office: 475 Park Ave S New York City NY 10016 Tel (212) 725-0200

VANCE, ANTHONY CHARLES, b. Erie, Pa., Oct. 4, 1931; B.S., Pa. State U., 1954; J.D., George Washington U., 1960; LL.M., Georgetown U., 1962. Admitted to Va. bar, 1960, D.C. bar, 1960; asso. firm Turney & Turney, Washington, 1960-63, partner, 196367; partner firm Major, Sage, Vance, & King, Alexandria, Va., 1968-70, Croft, Dail & Vance, 1971-76; individual practice law, Washington, 1976—; lt. col. JAGC, USAF, 1960—. Mem. Va., D.C., Am. bar assns., Motor Carrier Lawyers Assn., ICC Practitioners Assn., Phi Alpha Delta. Bd. editors Law Rev. George Washington U., 1958-59. Office: 1300 Old Chain Bridge Rd McLean VA 22101 Tel (703) 821-1305

VANCE, CHARLES, b. Parsons, Kans., Oct. 16, 1904; LL.B., Washburn U., 1928. Admitted to Kans. bar, 1928; partner firm Vance, Hobble, Neubauer, Nordlin, Sharp & McQueen, and predecessors, Liberal, Kans., 1929—; mem. Kans. Jud. Council, 1945-46; mem. Kans. Ho. of Reps., 1941-46. Fellow Am. Coll. Trial Lawyers, Am. Coll. Probate Counsel; mem. Kans., Am. bar assns. Asst. editor Hatchers Kans. Digest, 1929. Home: 211 Cornell St Liberal KS 67901 Office: PO Drawer I Liberal KS 67901 Tel (316) 624-2548

VANCE, CYRUS ROBERTS, b. Clarksburg, W.Va., Mar. 27, 1917; student Kent Sch.; B.A., Yale, 1939, LL.B., 1942; LL.D., Marshall U., 1963, Trinity Coll., Hartford, Conn., 1966, Yale, 1968, W.Va. U., 1969, Brandeis U., 1971. Admitted to N.Y. bar, 1947, U.S. Supreme Ct. bar, 1960; asst. to pres. Mead Corp., 1946-47; with Simpson Thacher & Bartlett, N.Y.C., 1947-56, partner, 1956-61, 67—; sec. state U.S., 1977—; gen. counsel Dept. Def., 1961-62; sec. of army, 1962-63; dep. sec. def., 1964-67; spl. rep. of the Pres., Cyprus, 1967, Korea, 1968; U.S. negotiator Paris Peace Conf. on Vietnam, 1968-69. Spl. counsel, preparedness investigating subcom. Senate Armed Services Com., 1957-60; cons. counsel spl. Com. on Space and Astronautics, U.S. Senate, 1958; chmn. com. on adjudication of claims Adminstrv. Conf. of U.S.; mem. Com. to Investigate Alleged Police Corruption in N.Y.C., 1970-72. Dir. IBM, Pan Am. World Airways, One William St. Fund, N.Y. Times Co. Bd. dirs., chmn. bd. Union Settlement Assn., Inc., 1953-61; trustee Yale, Urban Inst., N.Y. Presbyn. Hosp.; chmn. trustees Rockefeller Found., 1975—. Recipient Medal of Freedom, 1969. Fellow Am. Coll. Trial Lawyers; mem. Am. Bar Assn., Assn. Bar City N.Y. Office: Dept State 2201 C St NW Washington DC 20520*

VANCE, JAMES, b. Cleve., May 20, 1930; B.A., Baldwin Wallace Coll., Berea, Ohio; J.D., Marshall Coll. Admitted to Ohio bar, 1960; asst. treas. Republic Steel Corp., Cleve., 1965-68; treas. Addressograph-Multigraph Corp., Cleve., 1968-72; v.p. fin. Cin. Milacron Inc., 1972—. Mem. Am., Ohio bar assns., Am. Mgmt. Assn., Fin. Execs. Inst., Nat. Machine Tool Builders, Machinery and Allied Products Inst. Home: 6600 Wyman Ln Cincinnati OH 45243 Office: 4701 Marburg Ave Cincinnati OH 45209 Tel (513) 841-8546

VANCE, VERNE WIDNEY, JR., b. Omaha, Mar. 10, 1932; B.A., Harvard U., 1954, J.D., 1957. Admitted to D.C. bar, 1957, Mass. bar, 1964; law clk. to U.S. dist. judge, Mass., 1957-58; asso. firm Covington & Burling, Washington, 1958-60; atty. adv. Devel. Loan Fund, Washington, 1960-61; legal counsel AID, Washington, 1961-63; asso. firm Foley, Hoag & Eliot, Boston, 1963-67, partner 1967—; lectr. law Boston U., 1964-66. Mem. Mass. Adv. Council Edn., 1969-75, chmn. 1975; pres. UN Assn. Greater Boston, 1965-66, treas. 1974—; bd. dirs. Internat. Students Assn. Greater Boston, 1964-66; dir., clk. Cultural Edn. Collaborative, 1976—. Editor: Harvard Law Rev., 1955-57; contbr. articles to legal jours. Home: 101 Old Orchard Rd Chestnut Hill MA 02167 Office: 10 Post Office Sq Boston MA 02109 Tel (617) 482-1390

VANCE, WILLIAM GILTNER, b. Atlanta, Jan. 23, 1938; A.B. in Econs., Emory U., 1959; LL.B., U. Va., 1963. Admitted to Ga. bar, 1963; asso. firm Kilpatrick, Rogers, McClatchey and Regenstein, Atlanta, 1963-67; partner Troutman, Sanders Lockerman & Ashmore and predecessor, Atlanta, 1968—; counsel com. on law and order Met. Altanta Commn. on Crime and Juvenile Delinquency, 1964-66. Mem. Atlanta, Ga., Am. bar assns., Lawyers Club of Atlanta, Order of Coif. Home: 570 Londonberry Rd Atlanta GA 30327 Office: 1400 Candler Bldg Atlanta GA 30303 Tel (404) 658-8113

VAN CLEAVE, ROBERT BRINK, b. Kansas City, Mo., Dec. 21, 1944; B.A., Kans. U., 1966, J.D., 1970. Admitted to Kans. bar, 1970; research atty. Kans. Supreme Ct., Topeka, 1970-71; securities commr. State of Kans., 1971; mem. firm McAnany, Van Cleave & Phillips, P.A. Mem. Kans., Johnson County bar assns. Office: 4140 W 71st St Prairie Village KS 66208 Tel (913) 831-4040

VAN DALEN, CORNELIUS GERARD, b. Quincy, Mass. Nov. 27, 1921; student Am. Inst. Banking, N.Y.C., 1939-40; B.A., Tulane U., 1951, J.D., 1955. Admitted to La. bar, 1955, U.S. Ct. Appeals 5th Circuit bar, 1959; clk. firm Deutsch, Kerrigan & Stiles, New Orleans, 1953-55, asso., 1955-58, partner, 1958—; dir. Southeastern Admiralty Law Inst. Bd. dirs. Community Relations Council, New Orleans, 1967—. Mem. Am., La., New Orleans, Fed., Inter-Am. bar assns., Maritime Law Assn. U.S., Phi Alpha Delta, Phi Beta Kappa. Recipient W. Publishing Co. Contracts award, 1955. Home: 5724 Berkley Dr New Orleans LA 70114 Office: 4700 1 Shell Sq New Orleans LA 70139 Tel (504) 581-5141

VAN DE BOGART, JAMES AARON, b. Oak Park, Ill., Nov. 4, 1927; B.S. in Polit. Sci., U. Wis., 1952, J.D., 1963. Admitted to Wis. bar, 1963, since practiced in Whitewater; partner firm Soffa & Van De Bogart, 1963-67; individual practice law, 1967-68; asso. prof. law U. Wis. Whitewater, 1968—. Councilman City of Whitewater, 1970-73; pres. 1st English Lutheran Ch., 1969; chairperson Luth. Campus Ministry, U. Wis.-Whitewater, 1976. Mem. Am., Wis., Walworth County bar assns. Am. Bus. Law Assn., U.S. Marine Corps League (judge adv. 1976—), Phi Delta Phi. Home and Office: 130 S Prince Whitewater WI 53190 Tel (414) 473-5568

VANDEGRIFT, LUCIAN BICKFORD, b. Woodland, Calif., June 18, 1926; B.A., U. Calif., Berkeley, 1950, J.D., Boalt Hall, 1953. Admitted to Calif. bar, 1954; dep. atty. gen. State of Calif., Sacramento, 1954-59; dep. dist. atty. Butte County, Calif., 1959-60, asst. dist. atty., 1960-62, dist. atty., 1962-68; asst. sec. Calif. Health and Welfare Agy., Sacramento, 1968-70, sec. Human Relations Agy. Health and Welfare Agy., 1970-71; judge Calif. Superior Ct. for County of Butte, 1971—. Mem. Calif. Bar Assn., Am. Judicature Soc. Recipient Calif. Mental Health-Mental Retardation Program award Gov. Calif., 1965. Office: 1 Court St Oroville CA 95965 Tel (916) 534-4611

VANDENBURGH, EDWARD CLINTON, III, b. Chgo., Sept. 27, 1915; B.S., Ia. State U., 1937; LL.B., Duke U., 1940; M.P.L., John Marshall Law Sch., 1947. Admitted to Iowa bar, 1940, Ill. bar, 1946; partner law firm Darbo, Robertson & Vandenburgh, Arlington Heights, Ill., 1961—; adj. prof. John Marshall Law Sch., 1959—. Mem. Am. (chmn. patent, trademark and copyright sect. 1976-77), Ill. bar assns., Am. Patent Law Assn., Patent Law Assn. Chgo. Author: Trademark Law & Procedure, 1959, 1968; co-author: The Encyclopedia of Patent Practice and Invention Management, 1964;

contbr. articles to profl. jours. Home: 31 Elizabeth Ln Barrington IL 60010 Office: 15 N Arlington Heights Rd Arlington Heights IL 60004

VANDERHOEF, JERRY M., b. Hornell, N.Y., Apr. 5, 1937; A.B., Mercer U., 1959, J.D., 1962. Admitted to Ala. bar, 1963; practiced in Tuscumbia, Ala., 1963-66; judge Colbert County (Ala.) Ct., 1966-77, Ala. Dist. Ct. for Colbert County, 1977—; mem. adv. com. on juvenile practice and procedure Ala. Supreme Ct. Bd. dirs. Ala. Dept. Youth Services. Mem. Am., Ala. bar assns., Am. Judicature Soc., Nat. Council Juvenile Ct. Judges, Nat. Council on Crime and Delinquency. Home: 1103 Catalpa St Tuscumbia AL 35674 Office: Colbert County Courthouse Tuscumbia AL 35674 Tel (205) 383-6721

VANDERSTAR, JOHN, b. Jersey City, Sept. 17, 1933; B.S., Princeton U., 1954; LL.B., Harvard U., 1961. Admitted to D.C. bar, 1961, U.S. Supreme Ct. bar, 1967; asso. firm Covington & Burling, Washington, 1961-70, partner, 1970—; adj. prof. Georgetown Law Sch., 1971-75. Mem. Am. Bar Assn., ACLU (exec. bd. 1971—, chmn. 1976—). Office: 888 16th St NW Washington DC 20006

VAN DERVEER, JOSEPH WILLIAM, JR., b. Tuscaloosa, Ala., Mar. 31, 1946; B.S., U. Ala., 1970; J.D., Vanderbilt U., 1973. Admitted to Tenn. bar, 1974; asso. firm Boult, Cummings, Conners & Berry, Nashville, 1975—; counsel Salvation Army, Nashville. Fund raiser Tenn. Bot. Gardens, Nashville; solicitor Am. Cancer Assn., Nashville; fund raiser Cumberland Mus., Nashville, Mem. Am., Tenn., Nashville bar assns. Office: First American Center Nashville TN 37238 Tel (615) 244-2582

VANDER VENNET, GEORGE WILLIAM, JR., b. Davenport, Iowa, July 20, 1937; B.A. cum laude, U. Notre Dame, 1959, LL.B., 1962. Admitted to Iowa bar, 1962, Ill. bar, 1962; asso. G.W. Vander Vennet, Sr., Davenport, 1962-63; with trust dept. 1st Nat. Bank of Chgo., 1963—, v.p., 1970—, head personal trust unit, 1970-72, mgr. new enterprises div., 1973—; dir. Am. Rubber and Plastics Corp., LaPorte, Ind., 1974—. Pres. St. Francis Xavier Sch. Bd., Wilmette, Ill., 1973—; mem. Bus. Men for Loyola U. Chgo., 1976—. Mem. Ill., Chgo. bar assns. Home: 915 Ashland St Wilmette IL 60091 Office: One First Nat Plaza Chicago IL 60670 Tel (312) 732-4290

VAN DER VOORT, ROBERT, b. Crafton, Pa., Apr. 15, 1909; B.S., Guilford Coll., 1929; M.A., Haverford Coll., 1930; J.D., U. Pitts., 19—. Admitted to Pa. bar, 1935, U.S. Supreme Ct. bar, 1934; 1st asst. dist. atty., Allegheny County, Pa., 1948-52; solicitor Moon Twp., Pa., 1947-59; judge Allegheny County Ct. Common Pleas, Pitts., 1959-73, Superior Appellate Ct., Pitts., 1974—. Corp. bd. dirs. N. Hills Passavant Hosp., Pitts. Mem. Am., Pa., Allegheny County bar assns. Home: 1524 Robertson Dr Pittsburgh PA 15237 Office: 1115 Grant Bldg Pittsburgh PA 15219 Tel (412) 355-5432

VANDERVRIES, JOHN NICHOLAS, b. Lawrence, Kans., June 10, 1916; A.B., Wabash Coll., 1937; J.D., Northwestern U., 1940. Admitted to Ill. bar, 1940, U.S. Supreme Ct. bar, 1959 1959; partner firm Chapman & Cutler, Chgo., 1940—; served to 1st lt. JAGC, U.S. Army, 1944-46. Pres. Village of Northfield (Ill.), 1947-50; chmn. Zoning Bd. Appeals Highland Park (Ill.), 1952-65. Mem. Chgo., Ill., Am. bar assns., Nat. Assn. Water Cos. Home: 309 Warwick Towers Lakes Barrington IL 60010 Office: 111 W Monroe St Chicago IL 60603 Tel (312) 726-6130

VANDIVORT, WILLIAM CLAYTON, b. Cape Girardeau, Mo., June 2, 1947; B.A., Westminster Coll., 1969; J.D., Georgetown U., 1972. Admitted to Mo. bar, 1972, Ill. bar, 1973; asso. firm Greenfield, Davidson, Mandelstamm & Voorhees, St. Louis, 1972-74, Hux & Green, Sikeston, Mo., 1974-77; individual practice law, Sikeston, 1977—. Mem. Bar Assn. Met. St. Louis, Am., Ill., Mo. bar assns., Omicron Delta Kappa, Phi Alpha Theta. Editor: Georgetown Law Jour., 1971-72. Home: 104 Autumn Dr Sikeston MO 63801 Tel (314) 471-8278

VAN DOMELEN, HAROLD EDWARD, b. Shelby, Mich., Aug. 2, 1915; LL.B., Hope Coll., 1938; LL.D., U. Mich., 1941. Admitted to Mich. bar, 1941; practiced in Hart, Mich., 1946-60; pros. atty. Oceana County (Mich.), 1946-60; judge 27th Mich. Circuit, 1960—. Office: County Bldg Hart MI 49420 Tel (616) 873-3977

VAN DOREN, GERALD RAY, b. New London, Wis., Nov. 21, 1908; B.S. in Law, Princeton U., 1931; J.D., Northwestern U., 1933. Admitted to Ill. bar, 1934, Fla. bar, 1971; mem. firm Isham Lincoln & Beale, Chgo., 1934-43, Joslyn, Parker, Van Doren & Kell, Woodstock, Ill., 1946-51, Russo, Van Doren & Allen, Coral Gables, Fla., 1969—. Home: 8800 SW 184th Terr Miami FL 33157 Office: 4685 Ponce de Leon Blvd Coral Gables FL 33146 Tel (305) 665-0414

VAN DORN, WALTER GOFF, b. Orange, N.J., Sept. 15, 1933; A.B., Dartmouth, 1955; LL.B., Harvard, 1960; postgrad. tax program Boston U. Admitted to Mass. bar, 1961; asso. firm Rackemann, Sawyer & Brewster, Boston, 1960-64, partner firm, 1965—; lectr. law Boston U., 1969—; lectr. Fed. Tax Inst. of New Eng., New Eng. Law Inst., Colby Coll. Tax Inst., Mass. Continuing Legal Edn., Inc., N.H. Bar Assn., Grad. Realtors' Inst. Mem. Am., Boston (taxation sect., steering com.) bar assns. Home: 236 Beacon St Boston MA 02116 Office: 28 State St 28th Floor Boston MA 02109 Tel (617) 523-3550

VAN EEPOEL, AUGUST MICHAEL, b. N.Y.C., May 30, 1948; B.S.B.A. in Accounting with honors, U. Fla., 1970, J.D. with honors, 1972. Admitted to Fla. bar, 1973; asso. firm Trenam, Simmons, Kemker, Scharf & Barkin, Tampa, Fla., 1973—; bd. dirs. Law, Inc., Tampa, 1975-76. Mem. parish council Sacred Heart Ch., Tampa, 1974—. Mem. Fla. Bar (exec. council tax sect. 1975—). C.P.A., Fla.; exec. editor U. Fla. Law Rev., 1972; Internat. Law Appellate Moot Ct. U. Fla., 1971-72. Office: 2600 First Financial Tower PO Box 1102 Tampa FL 33602 Tel (813) 223-7474

VAN EPPS, RUTH EDITH HANSEN, b. Manitowoc, Wis., Sept. 1, 1906. Admitted to Wis. bar, 1936; partner firm Kelley; Wyseman, Muchin & Hansen, Manitowoc, 1936-45; individual practice law, Weyauwega, Wis., 1945-63, sr. partner Van Epps, Gull and Werth, Weyauwega, 1963—. Active Girl Scouts U.S.A., 1926-73, chmn. fund drive, 1960-73. Mem. Am., Wis., Waupaca County bar assns., Weyauwega C. of C. Home: Orchard Hill Weyauwega WI 54983 Office: 108 W Main Weyauwega WI 54983 Tel (414) 867-2156

VANESKA, ROBERT JOHN, b. Milw., Feb. 14, 1925; B.A., Carroll Coll., 1950; LL.B., U. Wis., 1954. Admitted to Wis. bar, 1954; individual practice law, Madison, Wis., 1954-60, Menomonee Falls, Wis., 1969—; mem. firm Tilg & Koch, Milw., 1960-64, John McLario, Menomonee Falls, 1964-69. Mem. Wis. Bar Assn., Wis. Brokers Assn. Contbr. articles to law and bldg. jours. Office: N88 W 17015 Main St Menomonee Falls WI 53051 Tel (414) 255-1588

VAN GEMERT, ROBERT J., b. 1922; A.B., U. Calif., 1948, LL.B., Boalt Hall Sch. Law, 1950. With Safeway Stores, Inc., Oakland, Calif., 1951—, asst. sec., 1964-65, asst. gen. counsel, 1965-68, v.p., sec., gen. counsel, 1968—. Office: 201 4th St Oakland CA 94660*

VAN GERPEN, EARL J., b. Avon, S.D., Nov. 11, 1931; B.S. in Bus. Adminstrn., U. S.D., 1953; LL.B., Harvard U., 1956. Admitted to Ga. bar, 1957; since practiced in Atlanta, asso. firm Nall, Miller, Cadenhead & Dennis, 1957-61, firm Powell, Goldstein, Frazer & Murphy, 1961-63; partner firm O'Kelley, Hopkins & Van Gerpen, 1963-70, firm Van Gerpen & Bovis, 1970—; dir., program chmn. Sandy Springs Bus. Assn., 1970-72. Mem. Am., Atlanta (chmn. sub-com. on fees and govtl. relations of real estate sect. 1976—), Decatur-DeKalb Counties bar assns., State Bar Ga., Lawyers Club Atlanta, Ga. Def. Lawyers Assn., Def. Research Inst. Home: 5550 Cross Gate Ct NW Atlanta GA 30327 Office: Suite 350 53 Perimeter Center E Atlanta GA 30346 Tel (404) 394-5600

VAN GESTEL, ALLAN, b. Boston, Dec. 3, 1935; B.A., Colby Coll. 1957; LL.B., Boston U., 1961. Admitted to Mass. bar, 1961, U.S. Supreme Ct. bar, 1972; asso. firm Goodwin Procter & Hoar, Boston, 1961-70, partner, 1970—; spl. counsel Boston Fin. Commn., 1974. Mem. Scituate (Mass.) Bd. Zoning Appeals, 1970, Scituate Planning Bd., 1972. Mem. Boston, Mass., Am. bar assns. Editorial bd. Boston U. Law Rev., 1960-61. Home: 88 Beacon St Boston MA 02108 Office: 28 State St Boston MA 02109 Tel (617) 523-5700

VAN HOOMISSEN, GEORGE ALBERT, b. Portland, Oreg., Mar. 7, 1930; B.A., U. Portland, 1951; J.D., Georgetown U., 1955, LL.M., 1957. Admitted to D.C. bar, 1955, Oreg. bar, 1956, Tex. bar, 1972; dep. dist. atty. Multnomah County (Oreg.), 1957-59, dist. atty., 1962-70; dean Nat. Coll. Dist. Attys., prof. law U. Houston, 1970-73; judge Oreg. Circuit Ct., 4th Jud. Dist., dept. 11, 1973—; practiced in Portland, 1969-72; mem. Oreg. Ho. of Reps., 1959-62. Mem. Am. Bar Assn. Office: 1021 SW 4th Ave Portland OR 97204 Tel (503) 248-3082

VAN IDEN, BYRON DOUGLAS, b. Cleve., Feb. 17, 1942; B.B.A., Western Res. U., 1975; J.D., Cleve. State U., 1972. Admitted to Ohio bar, 1972; individual practice law, Cleve., 1972—. Mem. Ohio, Cuyahoga County bar assns. Office: 3800 Payne Ave Cleveland OH 44114 Tel (216) 391-6998

VAN KESSEL, GORDON HOWARD, b. Los Angeles, June 16, 1939; A.B., U. Calif., 1962, J.D., 1965. Admitted to Calif. bar, 1965; law clk. to judge Calif. Supreme Ct., 1965-66; asso. firm Feldman, Waldman & Kline, San Francisco, 1966-67; asst. pub. defender Alameda County, Calif., 1967-70; staff lawyer San Francisco Lawyers' Com. for Urban Affairs, 1970-71; prof. law Hastings Coll. of Law, San Francisco, 1971—, dir. Criminal Justice Clinic, 1971—. Mem. Calif. Bar Assn. Producer videotape series on criminal law practice; author: California Criminal Law Practice Training Syllabus and Reference Manual, 1976. Office: Hastings College of Law 198 McAllister St San Francisco CA 94102 Tel (415) 557-2468

VAN LOAN, EUGENE MERRITT, III, b. Ft. Benning, Ga., Nov. 23, 1942; A.B., Yale, 1964; LL.B., Harvard, 1967. Admitted to N.H. bar, 1967, U.S. Tax Ct. bar, U.S. Supreme Ct. bar, U.S. Ct. Custom and Patent Appeals bar, 1971; served to capt. JAGC, U.S. Army, 1967-71; asso. firm Wadleigh, Starr, Peters, Dunn & Kohls, Manchester, N.H., 1971-75, partner, 1975—. Counsel, N.H. Pres. Ford Com., 1976; v.p. N.H. Easter Seal Soc., 1975-76; pres. Greater Manchester Mental Health Center, 1975-76, Bedford Hist. Soc., 1975-76, Bedford Dollars for Scholars, 1972-76. Mem. N.H., Manchester bar assns. Contbr. articles to legal jours. Home: Chandler Rd Bedford NH 03102 Office: 95 Market St Manchester NH 03101 Tel (603) 669-4140

VAN LUVANEE, JOHN ARTHUR, b. Doylestown, Pa., Feb. 18, 1947; B.A., Kalamazoo Coll., 1969; J.D., U. Mich., 1972. Admitted to Pa. bar, 1972; asso. firm Eastburn and Gray, Doylestown, 1972—. Mem. Bucks County, Pa., Am. bar assns. Home: 404 Merion Dr Newtown PA 18940 Office: 60 N Main St Doylestown PA 18901 Tel (215) 345-7000

VAN METER, DONALD EDWARD, b. Kansas City, Mo., Sept. 7, 1937; B.S., U. Okla., 1960, J.D., 1972. Admitted to Okla. bar, 1972; individual practice law, Lawton, Okla., 1972—; asst. dist. atty. Comanche County, Okla., 1972. Mem. Norman (Okla.) Human Relations Commn., 1970-72; mem. Lawton City Council, 1974-76; chmn. Comanche County Republican Com., 1972-77; unit commr. Black Beaver council Boy Scouts Am., 1976—. Mem. Am., Okla., Comanche County bar assns., Okla. Trial Lawyers Assn. Editor: (with Mark Ashton) Oklahoma Bar Association Desk Manual, 1976. Office: 626 D Ave Lawton OK 73501 Tel (405) 248-2383

VANMETER, LYNN HARRISON, b. Lincoln, Ill., June 19, 1924; LL.B., So. Meth. U., 1954. Admitted to Tex. bar, 1954; counsel Trinity Universal Ins. Co., Dallas, 1959-64; individual practice law, Dallas, 1964—. Mem. Tex. State Bar. Office: 2323 Fidelity Union Dallas TX 75201 Tel (214) 748-0809

VAN NATTA, GEORGE G., b. St. Helens, Oreg., Jan. 19, 1907; LL.B., Willamette U., 1929. Admitted to Oreg. bar, 1928; individual practice law, St. Helens, 1928-64; sr. partner firm Van Natta & Petersen, St. Helens, 1964—. Home: Route 1 Box 560 Rainier OR 97048 Office: Gray Bldg Saint Helens OR 97051 Tel (503) 397-0513

VAN NATTA, ROBERT PAUL, b. Hillsboro, Oreg., July 6, 1945; B.A., Willamette U., 1966, J.D., 1970. Admitted to Oreg. bar, 1970; partner firm Van Natta & Petersen, St. Helens, Oreg., 1970—. Mem. citizens planning adv. com. Mist-berkinfeld, 1975—. Mem. Oreg. State, Am., Columbia County (Oreg.) bar assns., Oreg. Small Woodlands Assn., Associated Oreg. Loggers, Inc. Feature editor Willamette Lawyer, 1969-70; editor Van Natta's Workmen's Compensation Reporter, 1968-77. Home: Route 1 PO Box 560 Rainier OR 97048 Office: 222 S First St Saint Helens OR 97051 Tel (503) 397-4091

VANNEMAN, EDGAR, JR., b. El Paso, Ill., Aug. 24, 1919; B.S., Northwestern U., 1941, J.D., 1947. Admitted to Ill. bar, 1947; asso. firm Campbell, Clark & Miller, Chgo., 1947-49; asst. gen. solicitor Chgo. & Northwestern Ry. Co., Chgo., 1949-62; gen. atty. Brunswick Corp., Chgo., 1962—; alderman City of Evanston (Ill.), 1957-65, mem. sch. bd., 1965-70, commr. NE park dist., 1967-70, mayor, 1970-77. Mem. Am., Ill. (assembly 1972—; bd. govs. 1968-70), Chgo. bar assns., Law Club Chgo., Soc. Trial Lawyers. Home: 715 Monticello Pl Evanston IL 60201 Office: 1 Brunswick Plaza Skokie IL 60076 Tel (312) 982-6000

VAN NESS, JEREMY DALE, b. Detroit, Mar. 19, 1943; B.A., Wayne State U., 1965, J.D., 1968. Admitted to Ill. bar, 1970, Calif. bar, 1976; real estate counsel Continental Ill. Nat. Bank and Trust Co., Chgo., 1970-72; gen. counsel Ill. Housing Devel. Authority, Chgo., 1972—, acting dir., 1977; gen. counsel Larwin Group, Encino, Calif., 1977—; gen. counsel Chgo. Women in Broadcasting. Mem. exec. com. Chgo. Met. chpt. Nat. Assn. Housing and Redevel. Ofcls. Mem. Am., Ill., Chgo. bar assns. Home: Santa Monica CA Office: 16255 Ventura Blvd Encino CA 91436 Tel (213) 986-8890

VAN NOY, ALLAN CAMERON, b. Oakland, Calif., Apr. 4, 1938; B.S., U. Calif., 1962; J.D., San Francisco Law Sch., 1968. Admitted to Calif. bar, 1970; with Travelers Ins. Co., Oakland, 1964—. Bd. dirs. Salinas Pop Warner Little League Baseball, 1973-75, Salinas Babe Ruth, 1973—, Salinas United Way, 1974-75, Salinas Jaycees, 1974-75. Home: 310 San Miguel Ave Salinas CA 93901 Office: 21 W Alisal St Salinas CA 93901

VAN NUYS, FRANCIS, b. Kansas City, Mo., Apr. 13, 1912; student Park Coll., 1929-31; A.B. magna cum laude, Harvard, 1933, LL.B. magna cum laude, 1936. Admitted to N.Y. bar, 1939; mem. staff Cravath, de Gersdorff, Swaine & Wood, N.Y.C., 1936-40; mem. legal staff of trustees Asso. Gas & Electric Corp., 1940-42; with Bethlehem Steel Corp. (Pa.), 1942—, asso. gen. counsel, 1963-67, dir. law dept., 1965-67, v.p. law and gen. counsel, 1967—. Mem. Am., N.Y. State, Pa., Northampton County, bar assns., Am. Law Inst., Am. Iron and Steel Inst., Phi Beta Kappa. Editor Harvard Law Rev., 1935-36. Home: 2424 N Main St Bethlehem PA 18017 Office: Martin Tower Bethlehem PA 18016*

VAN ORMAN, CHANDLER LEE, b. Oak Park, Ill., Jan. 15, 1941; A.B., U. N.C., 1963; LL.B., U. Va., 1966. Admitted to Va. bar, 1966, D.C. bar, 1966, U.S. Supreme Ct. bar, 1972; atty. FTC, Washington, 1966-67; asso. firm Wheeler & Wheeler, Washington, 1967-73, partner, 1973—. Vice chmn. Nat. Debutante Cotillion, Washington, 1968; vice chmn. fund raising com. Children's Hosp., Washington, 1969-70; mem. Lawyers Taskforce on Election Law Violations, 1972. Mem. D.C. Bar Assn., Motor Carrier Lawyers Assn. Home: 5201 Norway Dr Chevy Chase MD 20015 Office: 704 Southern Bldg Washington DC 20005 Tel (202) 347-7117

VAN OVERBEEK, THELMA TAYLOR, b. San Francisco, Jan. 28, 1918; B.S., U. Calif. at Berkeley, 1939; J.D., U. Pacific, 1967. Admitted to Tex. bar, 1968; asso. firm Cofer, Dillon & Giesenschlag, Bryan, Tex., 1969-71; mem. firm Cofer & van Overbeek, Inc., Bryan, 1972—. Mem. Brazos County Bar Assn. (pres. 1976-77), Am., Tex. State bar assns. Home: 3615 Sunnybrook Ln Bryan TX 77801 Office: 200 E 33d St Bryan TX 77801 Tel (713) 822-7575

VAN PATTEN, CHARLES ADAMS, b. Mount Vernon, N.Y., Jan. 29, 1907; B.A., Yale, 1929, J.D., 1932. Admitted to N.Y. bar, 1934, U.S. Supreme Ct. bar, U.S. Tax Ct. bar, other fed. bars; partner firm Dimmock, Snyder & Van Patten, N.Y.C., 1941-73; of counsel Soons & Soons, 1973—. Mem. Holland Soc. N.Y., (trustee 1961-69, 73—, sec. 1961-69). Mem. Am. Bar Assn., Bar Assn. City N.Y. Named knight comdr. Order of Merit Republic Ecuador, 1950. Home: 1220 Park Ave New York City NY 10028 Office: 230 Park Ave New York City NY 10017 Tel (212) 889-9180

VAN PELT, ROBERT, b. Gosper County, Nebr., Sept. 9, 1897; A.B., Doane Coll., 1920, LL.D., 1959; LL.B., U. Nebr., 1922; L.H.D., Westmar Coll., 1960. Admitted to Nebr. bar, 1922; practiced in Lincoln, Nebr., 1922-57; judge U.S. Dist. Ct. for Nebr., 1957-70, sr. judge, 1970—; asst. U.S. Atty., 1930-34; lectr. Nebr. Law Coll., 1946-57. Del., Republican Nat. Conv., 1940, 44, 48; trustee Doane Coll., 1928-68. Mem. Am. Coll. Trial Lawyers, Am. Coll. Probate Counsel (adv. com. jud. conduct 1969—), Phi Sigma Kappa, Phi Delta Phi. Home: 2323 Woodscrest St Lincoln NE 68502 Office: Fed Bldg Lincoln NE 68508

VANSLYKE, PAUL, b. Dallas, Mar. 13, 1942; B.E.E., U. Tex. 1964; J.D., So. Meth. U., 1968. Admitted to Tex. bar, 1968, D.C. bar, 1969, U.S. Supreme Ct. bar, 1971; mem. patent dept. Mobil Oil Corp., Dallas, 1964-69; asso. firm Arnold, White & Durkee, Houston, 1969-73, partner, 1973—; adj. prof. law S. Tex. Coll. Law, 1972—; lectr. in field. Mem. Am., Houston, Houston Jr. (dir. 1976), Tex. Jr. (dir. 1973-74) bar assns., Houston, Am. patent law assns. Home: 171 Plantation Houston TX 77024 Office: 2100 Transco Tower Houston TX 77056 Tel (713) 621-9100

VAN SOELEN, ESTHER SMITH, b. Clovis, N.Mex., Apr. 4, 1928; A.A., Cottey Jr. Coll. for Women, 1945-47; B.A., LL.B., U. Okla., 1947-51. Admitted to N.Mex. bar, 1951; partner firm, Smith & Smith, Clovis, 1951-61; individual practice law, Clovis, 1961—; instr. bus. law Clovis Community Coll. Mem. State Bar N.Mex., Curry County, Am. bar assns. Named Boss of Year Clovis Legal Secs. Assn., 1976. Office: 409 Pile St PO Drawer 1080 Clovis NM 88101 Tel (505) 763-4428

VAN TATENHOVE, LESTER, b. Holland, Mich., Sept. 25, 1914; A.B., Hope Coll., Holland, Mich., 1936; LL.B., Harvard, 1939. Admitted to Calif. bar, 1940; individual practice law, Santa Ana, Calif., 1940-61; judge, Orange County Superior Ct., Santa Ana, 1961—; instr. law Sch. Law, Western State U., Anaheim, Calif., 1968-76. Chmn. Orange County Democratic Central Com., 1953-61; del. to nat. Dem. conv., 1956-60. Mem. Conf. Calif. Judges. Home: 2227 N Rosewood St Santa Ana CA 92706 Office: Orange County Courthouse 700 Civic Center Dr W Santa Ana CA 92701 Tel (714) 834-3734

VAN VALKENBURG, FRED ROBERT, b. Denver, May 3, 1948; B.B.A., Gonzaga U., 1970; J.D., U. Mont., 1973. Admitted to Mont. bar, 1973; asst. city atty., Missoula, Mont., 1973-75; individual practice law, Missoula, 1975; mem. firm Smith, Connor, & Van Valkenburg, Missoula, 1976—; pub. defender Missoula County, Mont., 1975—. Mem. Mont. Criminal Def. Lawyers Assn. Office: 211 W Front St Missoula MT 59801 Tel (406) 543-8222

VAN VEEN, HENRY GEORGE, b. N.Y.C., Nov. 14, 1903; B.S., N.Y. U., 1926; LL.B., 1929. Admitted to N.Y. State bar, 1929, U.S. Supreme Ct. bar, 1933; clk., asso. Hays St. John & Buckley and sucessor firms, 1928-35; asso. John Finnerty, N.Y.C., 1936-38; asso. firm Joseph Cassidy, 1928-42; mem. firm Fanning, Kaplan & Van Veen, N.Y.C., 1947-49; mem. firm Kaplan & Van Veen, N.Y.C., 1949-51; mem. firm Bronstein & Van Veen and successor firms, N.Y.C., 1948-76; of counsel firm Bronstein, Van Veen & Bronstein, N.Y.C., 1976—; asso. gen. counsel, congl. liaison office Office Price Control, 1942-47; congl. liaison officer, cons. Office Housing Expediter, 1947-51. Vice chmn. N.Y. law com. N.Y. Republican Com., 1936-40; del. N.Y. State Rep. convs., 1936-42. Mem. N.Y. County Lawyers Assn., Fed. Bar Assn. Recipient Silver Beaver award

Boy Scouts Am. Home: 44 Amherst Rd Port Washington NY 11050 Office: 400 Madison Ave New York City NY 10017 Tel (212) 688-8224

VAN VLEET, WILLIAM BENJAMIN, JR., b. Milw., Dec. 4, 1924; student Lawrence Coll., 1943-44; J.D., Marquette U., 1948. Admitted to Wis. bar, 1948, Ill. bar, 1950; gen. counsel George Rogers Clark Mut. Casualty Co., Rockford, Ill., 1948-59; gen. counsel Pioneer Life Ins. Co. of Ill., Rockford, 1955—, exec. v.p., gen. counsel, dir., 1968—. Mem. council of adminstrn. Boylan Central Cath. High Sch., Rockford, 1965-72; mem. Rockford Diocesan Bd. Edn., 1970—; mem. exec. com. Nat. Assn. Bds. Edn., 1972—, v.p., 1972-74, pres., 1974-76; bd. dirs. Nat. Cath. Edn. Assn., 1975—; mem. lay adv. bd. St. Anthony's Hosp., Rockford, 1977—. Contbr. articles to Cath. edn. jours. Home: 811 Coolidge Pl Rockford IL 61107 Office: 127 N Wyman St Rockford IL 61101 Tel (815) 987-5023

VAN VLIERBERGEN, BRIAN RICHARD, b. Chgo., Aug. 27, 1937; B.S. in Psychology, Loyola U., 1959; J.D., John Marshall Law Sch., 1965. Admitted to Ill. bar, 1965; legal counsel Health Care Service Corp., Chgo., 1965-71, sec., 1971—, v.p., 1971—; sec. Ft. Dearborn Life Ins. Co., Chgo.; dir. Health Maintenance Orgn. Ill., Inc., Chgo. Mem. St. Francis Xavier Sch. Bd., Wilmette, Ill., 1972-75. Mem. Am., Ill. State (sec. ins. com. 1973-75), Chgo. bar assns., Inter-American Fedn. Lawyers, Am. Mgmt. Assn. Office: 233 N Michigan Ave Chicago IL 60601 Tel (312) 661-4826

VAN VOORHIS, JOHN, b. Rochester, N.Y., June 14, 1897; A.B., Yale, 1919; LL.D., Hobart Coll., 1953, Union U., Albany, N.Y., 1954, U. Rochester, 1958, N.Y. Law Sch., 1966, Bklyn. Law Sch., 1967. Admitted to N.Y. bar, 1922; practiced in Rochester, 1922-36; justice N.Y. Supreme Ct., 7th Jud. Dist., 1937-53, asso. justice appellate div., 1st Jud. Dept., 1947-53; asso. judge N.Y. State Ct. Appeals, Albany, 1953-67; mem. firm Branch, Van Voorhis, Turner & Wise, Rochester and N.Y.C., 1967-76, firm Van Voorhis & Van Voorhis, Rochester and N.Y.C., 1976—. Fellow Am., N.Y. bar founds., Phi Beta Kappa Assos.; mem. Am., N.Y. State (spl. award 1973), N.Y.C., Monroe County (N.Y.) bar assns., Phi Beta Kappa. Home: 714 Rock Beach Rd Rochester NY 14617 Office: 1 Graves St Rochester NY 14614 Tel (716) 232-4221 also 120 Broadway Room 3017 New York City NY 10005 Tel (212) 962-0330

VAN WAGONER, ROBERT LOUIS, b. Detroit, June 4, 1936; B.S., Northwestern U., 1958; J.D., Calif. Western U., 1966. Admitted to Nev. bar, 1967; law clk. Nev. Supreme Ct., Carson City, 1966-67; asst. city atty. City of Reno, 1967-68, city atty., 1971—; asso. firm Richard E. Fray, Reno, 1969-70; mem. firm Shattuck & Van Wagoner, Reno, 1970-71; mem. Nev. Crime Commn., 1971—. Bd. dirs. Multiple Sclerosis Soc., 1970—, chmn. bd., 1973-74; bd. dirs. Washoe Assn. Retarded Children, 1972-73; adv. bd. dirs. Ret. Sr. Vol. Program, 1973—. Mem. Am., Nev., Washoe County bar assns., Am., Nev. trial lawyers assns., Nat. Inst. Municipal Law Officers (chmn. city/state relations com. 1973—), Am. Judicature Soc., Barristers Club Reno, Phi Delta Phi. Named Outstanding Legal Counsel, Nev. State Prison Jaycees, 1975. Admitted to U.S. Supreme Ct. bar, 1973. Office: 490 S Center St Reno NV 89505 Tel (702) 785-2056

VANYO, JAMES PATRICK, b. Wheeling, W.Va., Jan. 29, 1928; B.S. in Mech. Engring., W.Va. U., 1952; J.D., Chase Law Coll., 1959; M.A., U. Calif., Los Angeles, 1966, Ph.D., 1969. Admitted to Ohio bar, 1959, U.S. Patent bar, 1959, Calif. bar, 1961. Asst. to pres. Remanco Inc., Santa Monica, Calif., 1959-61; proposal and contract specialist Marquardt Corp., Van Nuys, Calif., 1961-63; long range planning analyst Litton Industries Co., Woodland Hills, Calif., 1968-70; asso. prof. law, tech. and systems, U. Calif., Santa Barbara, 1970—; lectr. in field. Mem. Ohio, Calif. bar assns. Contbr. articles to legal and engring. jours.; editorial bd. Jour. Environ. Systems, 1973—. Office: Dept of Mech and Environ Engring U of Calif Santa Barbara CA 93106 Tel (805) 961-2904

VARDAMAN, HUGH MERRILL, b. Anniston, Ala., Feb. 24, 1944; B.A., U. Ala., 1966; J.D., Cumberland Sch. Law, 1969. Admitted to Ala. bar, 1970; partner firm Merrill, Merrill & Vardaman, Anniston, 1970—. acting atty. City of Anniston, 1971, asst. recorder, 1975-76, pub. defender, 1976; recorder City of Weaver, 1973-76. Mem. Am., Calhoun County, Ala. bar assns., Anniston Exchange Club (pres. 1974), Phi Alpha Delta. Home: 14 Mont Camille St Anniston AL 36201 Office: PO Box 1498 Anniston AL 36202 Tel (205) 237-1601

VARDAMAN, JOHN WESLEY, b. Montgomery, Ala., June 22, 1915; B.A., U. Ala., 1936, LL.B., 1938. Admitted to Ala. bar, 1938, Fifth Circuit Ct. of Appeals bar, 1945, U.S. Supreme Ct. bar, 1956; individual practice law, Montgomery, Ala., 1938-39; asst. atty. gen. Ala., 1939-43; mem. firm Merrill, Merrill & Vardaman, and successors, Anniston, Ala., 1943—. Pres. Anniston Exchange Club, 1950; chmn. bd. trustees Dist. IV TB Hosp., 1958; chmn. bd. trustees Anniston Country Club, 1945-76. Mem. Am., Ala. (past pres. jr. sect; pres. 1961-62), Calhoun County, (past pres.) bar assns. Office: PO Box 1498 Commercial National Bank Bldg Anniston AL 36202 Tel (205) 237-1601

VARGAS, ERNEST ARTHUR, b. Lima, Peru, Sept. 7, 1938; B.A., U. Calif., Los Angeles, 1961; J.D., Loyola U., Los Angeles, 1964. Admitted to Calif. bar, 1965, U.S. Ct. Mil. Appeals bar, 1965; asso. firm Oliver, Good & Sloan, Los Angeles, 1965-68; partner firm Oliver, Sloan, Vargas, Shaffer, & Lindvig, Los Angeles, 1968—; tchr. Loyola U. Sch. Law, 1963-64. Dist. chmn. Los Angeles Area council Boy Scouts Am., 1966-68. Mem. Am., Calif. State, Los Angeles County bar assns., Am., Calif., Los Angeles trial lawyers assns., Am. Arbitration Assn., U. Calif. Alumni Assn., Loyola Alumni Assn., Phi Delta Phi. Office: 611 W 6th St Suite 3300 Los Angeles CA 90017 Tel (213) 624-4201

VARNER, KINCH MORGAN, III, b. Union Springs, Ala., June 7, 1941; A.B., Princeton, 1963; LL.B., Duke, 1966. Admitted to Ala. bar, 1966, Ga. bar, 1970; individual practice law, Auburn, Ala., 1966-67, Atlanta, 1971-73; asso. firm Kilpatrick, Cody, Rogers, McClatchey & Regenstein, Atlanta, 1969-71; partner firm Varner & Stephens, Atlanta, 1973—. Mem. Ala., Am., Atlanta bar assns., State Bar Ga., Am. Judicature Soc., Omicron Delta Kappa. Home: 3647 Cloudland Dr NW Atlanta GA 30327 Office: 2020 Gas Light Tower Atlanta GA 30303 Tel (404) 577-6370

VARTAN, LEO RICHARD, b. Kearny, N.J., Nov. 16, 1942; B.A., W.Va. Wesleyan Coll., 1965; J.D., John Marshall Law Sch., 1968. Admitted to N.Y. bar, 1969; asst. dep. pub. defender Essex County (N.J.), 1970; prosecutor Hudson County, Kearny, 1970, asst. prosecutor, 1970-73, judge, 1973—. Mem. Hudson County Juvenile Aid Com. Mem. N.J., Am., Hudson County, W. Hudson bar assns. Named Outstanding Young Am. in Law (N.J.), Pres.'s Com. on Outstanding Young Ams., 1974-75. Home: 54 Hamilton Kearny NJ 07032 Office: 591 Summit Ave Jersey City NJ 07306 Tel (201) 792-7143

VARTANIAN, WALTER GREGORY, b. Boston, Mar. 5, 1935; B.A., Boston U., 1956, J.D., 1959. Admitted to Mass. bar, 1959, U.S. Dist. Ct. bar, 1961, U.S. Ct. Appeals bar, 1964, U.S. Supreme Ct. bar, 1965; individual practice law, Cambridge, Mass., 1959-68, Boston, 1968—. Mem. Mass., Boston, Cambridge-Arlington-Belmont (treas.) bar assns., Mass. Conveyancers Assn., Assn. Immigration and Nationality Lawyers (sec. Mass. chpt.). Sr. editor Law Rev., 1958-59. Home: 92 Clark St Belmont MA 02178 Office: 79 Milk St Boston MA 02109 Tel (617) 542-8964

VASSALLO, DANIEL CHRISTOPHER, b. N.Y.C., June 15, 1934; J.D., St. John's U. Admitted to N.Y. bar, 1960; mem. firm Curtis, Hart & Zaklukiewitz, Merrick, N.Y. Mem. Nassau County Bar Assn., Nassau-Suffolk Trial Lawyers Assn. Home: The Fairway Oak Beach NY 11702 Office: 1835 Merrick Ave Merrick NY 11566

VASTI, THOMAS FRANCIS, JR., b. Jamaica, N.Y., Sept. 13, 1935; B.S., Loyola U., 1963; LL.B., Bklyn. U., 1958, J.D., 1967. Admitted to N.Y. bar, 1958, U.S. Tax Ct., 1968; individual practice law, Pleasant Valley, N.Y., 1967—; instr. Dutchess Community Coll. Bd. dirs. Arlington Central Sch., Poughkeepsie, N.Y., 1964-72; town justice Pleasant Valley, 1968-75; town councilman Town of Pleasant Valley, 1968-75. Mem. N.Y. State, Dutchess County bar assns., N.Y. State Assn. Magistrates, Pleasant Valley C. of C. Home: Lakeshore Dr Pleasant Valley NY 12569 Office: Main St Route 44 Pleasant Valley NY 12569 Tel (914) 635-8866

VATER, ROBERT WILLIAM, b. Enid, Okla., Aug. 29, 1932; B.B.A., U. Okla., 1954, J.D., 1957. Admitted to Okla. bar, 1957, Ark. bar, 1961, Ala. bar, 1970; atty. Apco Oil Corp., 1958-61; individual practice law, Ft. Smith, Ark., 1961-69, Anchorage, 1969-71; partner firm Martin, Vater & Snyder, Fort Smith, 1971—. Mem. Am., Okla., Ark. (chmn. mineral law sect. 1968-69, 73-74) bar assns., Ark. Oil and Gas Inst. (co-chmn. 1968, 74), mem. Am. Assn. Petroleum Landmen (asso.). Office: 505 First National Bank Bldg Fort Smith AR 72901 Tel (501) 782-4028

VATSURES, PETER THOMAS, b. Delaware, Ohio, Apr. 15, 1927; B.S., Ohio State U., 1953, J.D., 1953. Admitted to Ohio bar, 1954; mem. Gen. Tax Hearing Bd., State Ohio Dept. Taxation, 1954-57; individual practice law, Delaware, 1957-60; judge Delaware Municipal Ct., 1960-65; partner firm Marriott & Vatsures, Delaware, 1966—. Mem. Mayor Delaware 2000 Com., 1977—; pres. Delaware County Tb and Health Assn., 1968-69; pres. Delaware County Traffic Safety Council, 1963-64. Mem. Ohio State, Delaware County (pres. 1962-63) bar assns., Phi Delta Phi. Home: 170 Hillside Dr Delaware OH 43015 Office: 15 W Central Ave Delaware OH 43015 Tel (614) 363-1259

VAUGHN, GLENN C., b. Danville, Va., Nov. 4, 1944; A.B., Hampden Sydney Coll., 1966; J.D., Dickinson Sch. Law, 1969. Admitted to Pa. bar, 1970; asso. firm Liverant, Senft & Cohen, York, Pa., 1969-72; mem. firm Carn & Vaughn, York, 1973—; asst. pub. defender, 1973-75; solicitor to prothonotary York County, 1976—. Vice pres. York City Sch. Bd., 1975—; mem. York City Zoning Bd. Adjustment, 1973-75. Mem. Am., Pa., York County bar assns. Office: 22 S Beaver St York PA 17401 Tel (717) 845-9687

VAUGHN, JAMES CARLETON, JR., b. Augusta, Ga., July 24, 1942; B.B.A., U. Ga., 1964, J.D., 1966; LL.M., So. Meth. U., 1971. Admitted to Ga. bar, 1965; asso. firm Sanders, Thurmond, Hester, Jolles & McElmurray, Augusta, 1966; capt. U.S. Army Judge Adv. Gen.'s Corp., Worms, Germany, 1966-70; partner firm Fulcher, Hagler, Harper & Reed, Augusta, 1971-75; individual practice law, Augusta, 1975—. Deacon Reid Meml. Presbyn. Ch., Augusta, 1973—; v.p. YMCA Augusta, 1975—. Mem. Am., Augusta bar assns., State Bar Ga. Home: 753 McClure Dr Augusta GA 30909 Office: 1104 Georgia Railroad Bank Bldg Augusta GA 30902 Tel (404) 722-4443

VAUGHN, JOHN VINCENT, b. N.Y.C., Jan. 26, 1931; B.B.A., Manhattan Coll., 1953; LL.B., St. John's U., N.Y.C., 1960. Admitted to N.Y. State bar, 1960, U.S. Dist. Ct. bars for Eastern Dist. N.Y., 1963, for So. Dist. N.Y., 1963, U.S. Supreme Ct. bar, 1965; practiced in Nassau and Suffolk counties, N.Y., 1960-69; judge Suffolk County (N.Y.) Dist. Ct., 1969—; justice of the peace Town of Babylon (N.Y.), 1965; dist. del. N.Y. State Constl. Conv., 1967; acting judge Suffolk County Ct., 1973, 74. Mem. Suffolk County Bar Assn. Home: 70 Easton St Lindenhurst NY 11757 Office: Suffolk County Dist Ct Veterans Memorial Hwy Hauppauge NY 11787 Tel (516) 979-2000

VAUGHN, MICHAEL EDWARD, b. Hendersonville, N.C., May 20, 1946; A.B. in History, U. N.C., Chapel Hill, 1968, J.D., 1971. Admitted to N.C. bar, 1971; law clk. N.C. Ct. Appeals, 1971-72; partner firm Vaughn & Gray, Asheville, N.C., 1972; chief asst. pub. defender Buncombe County, N.C., 1973; chmn. dept. paralegal studies Southwestern Tech. Inst., Sylva, N.C., 1974-75; individual practice law, Asheville, 1975—. Mem. Am., N.C. bar assns., N.C. Acad. Trial Lawyers. Home: 410 Lakeshore Dr Asheville NC 28802 Office: 114 Miles Bldg Asheville NC 28801 Tel (704) 255-8085

VAUGHN, NORMAN, b. Alabama City, Ala., June 13, 1932; A.B. in Journalism, U. Ga., 1966; J.D. summa cum laude, John Marshall U., Atlanta, 1973. Admitted to Ga. bar, 1973; individual practice law, Cornelia, Ga., 1973—; sr. right-of-way agt. Ford, Bacon & Davis Constrn. Co., 1974-76; land agt. Shell Pipe Line Corp., 1976—. Mem. Am. Bar Assn., Am. Right of Way Assn. Recipient Corpus Juris Sr. award, Am. Jurisprudence awards. Home: 2016 Main St apt 2114 Houston TX 77002 Office: PO Box 153 Cornelia GA 30531 Tel (404) 778-2914

VAUGHN, OSCAR NORMAN, b. Alabama City, Ala., June 13, 1932; A.B.J., U. Ga., 1966; J.D. summa cum laude, John Marshall U., Atlanta, 1973. Admitted to Ga. bar, 1973; individual practice law, Cornelia, Ga., 1973—; sr. right of way agt. Ford Bacon & Davis Constrn. Corp., Monroe, La., 1974-76; land agt. Shell Pipe Line Corp., Houston and Anaheim, Calif., 1976—. Mem. Am. Bar Assn., Am. Right of Way Assn. Home: 1259 N Alamo St Anaheim CA 92801 Tel (714) 991-9200

VAUX, DONALD JOSEPH, b. Seattle, June 8, 1946; B.A. in Polit. Sci., Seattle U., 1968; J.D., Gonzaga U., Spokane, 1973. Admitted to Wash. bar, 1973, U.S. Dist. Ct. bar Eastern Dist. Wash., 1973, U.S. Dist. Ct. bar Western Dist. Wash., 1976; individual practice law, Spokane, 1973—; pres. Wash. Bur. Collections, Inc., 1975, Credit Research Bur., Inc., 1976. Mem. Wash., Spokane County bar assns. Home: E 620 Ermina St Spokane WA 99207 Office: 703 N Monroe St Spokane WA 99201 Tel (509) 328-1770

VEARY, RAYMOND PAUL, JR., b. Acushnet, Mass., Aug. 6, 1947; B.A., Norwich U., 1969; J.D., Boston Coll., 1972. Admitted to Mass. bar, 1973, R.I. bar, 1973, also Fed. bar; staff atty. R.I. Inmate Legal Assistance Program, Cranston, 1973-74; partner firm Xifaras, Pina, Lantz & Veary, New Bedford, Mass., 1976—; counsel New Bedford Fed. and State Tenants' Assn., 1974-76; asso. legal counsel Mass. Jaycees; dir. Onboard Legal Services, Inc., New Bedford, 1974-76. Commr. New Bedford Housing Authority; bd. dirs. South End Peoples Council. Mem. Mass., New Bedford bar assns., ACLU, New Bedford Preservation Soc. Recipient Brownfield Meml. award New Bedford Jaycees, 1974, Appollo award Tau Kappa Epsilon, 1974. Office: 401 County St New Bedford MA 02741 Tel (617) 993-1781

VEGA, BENJAMIN URBIZO, b. La Ceiba, Honduras, Jan. 18, 1916; A.B., U. So. Calif., 1938, Postgrad., 1939-40; LL.B., Pacific Coast U. Law, 1941. Admitted to Calif. bar, 1947, U.S. Supreme Ct. bar, 1958, U.S. Dist. Ct. So. dist., 1947; asso. firm Anderson, McPharlin & Connors, Los Angeles, 1947-48, firm Newman & Newman, Los Angeles, 1948-51; dep. dist. atty. County of Los Angeles, 1951-66; judge Los Angeles County Municipal Ct., East Los Angeles Jud. Dist., 1966—. Mem. Calif. Gov.'s Adv. Com. on Children and Youth, 1968; bd. dirs. Los Angeles-Mexico City Sister City Com. Mem. Conf. Calif. Judges, Municipal Ct. Judges' Assn. Los Angeles County, Am. Judicature Soc. Recipient award for outstanding services as judge Mayor of Los Angeles, 1973, Distinguished Pub. Service award Dist. Atty. Los Angeles County, 1973. Office: 4837 E 3d St Los Angeles CA 90022 Tel (213) 264-4200

VELARDI, CHARLES HENRY, b. N.Y.C., Aug. 31, 1928; B.S., Coll. City N.Y., 1950; LL.B., St. John's U., 1953. Admitted to N.Y. bar, 1953, U.S. Supreme Ct. bar, 1967; individual practice law, Brewster, N.Y., 1960—; town atty. Town of Southeast, Putnam County, N.Y., 1954-75; mem. grievance com. 9th Jud. Dist. for Appellate Div., 2d Dept. State of N.Y., 1974—. Trustee Brewster Central Sch., 1958-61. Mem. Am., N.Y. State, Putnam County (pres. 1974-75), Lawyers-Pilots bar assns. Address: Rt 6 Brewster NY 10509 Tel (914) 279-4000

VELELLA, GUY JOHN, b. N.Y.C., Sept. 25, 1944; B.A., St. John's U., Bklyn., 1967; J.D., Suffolk U., 1970. Admitted to N.Y. bar, 1971; law sec. to justice N.Y. Supreme Ct., 1971-72; partner firm Velella Velella & Basso, Bronx, N.Y., 1973—; mem. N.Y. State Assembly, 1973—. Mem. Columbian Assn. State Employees (dir.), Columbian Lawyers Assn., Pelham Bay Taxpayers and Civic Assn., Am., Bronx, N.Y. State bar assns., Columbus-ESCA Alliance Inc., Phi Alpha Delta. Recipient Outstanding Legislator award Columbia Assn. Civil Service Employees, 1973, Fidelis Juri award Supreme Ct. Officers, 1974, Outstanding Service award Throggs Nesh Assn. for Retarded, 1976, Youth Service award Bronx YMCA, 1975. Office: 2113 Williamsbridge Rd Bronx NY 10461 Tel (212) 931-1220

VELEZ, ARNALDO, b. Baire, Cuba, July 17, 1949; B.A., U. Miami (Fla.), 1969, J.D., 1972. Admitted to Fla. bar, 1972; partner firm Taylor, Brion, Buker & Greene, Miami, Fla., 1972—. Mem. Am. Trial Lawyers Assn., Am. Bar Assn., Acad. Fla. Trial Lawyers, Cuban-Am. Bar Assn. Office: 1451 Brickell Ave Miami FL 33131 Tel (305) 379-9303

VELIE, FRANKLIN BELL, b. N.Y.C., July 28, 1942; A.B., Harvard, 1965, LL.B., 1968. Admitted to N.Y. State bar, 1969; asso. firm Lord, Day & Lord, N.Y.C., 1968-71; asst. U.S. atty. So. Dist. N.Y., 1971-75, asst. chief criminal div., 1974-75; partner firm Gordon, Hurwitz, Butowsky, Baker, Weitzen & Shalov, N.Y.C., 1975—. Mem. Assn. Bar City N.Y., N.Y. State Bar Assn., N.Y. County Lawyers Assn. Home: 7 Locust Cove Ln Kings Point NY 11024 Office: 299 Park Ave New York City NY 10017 Tel (212) 486-1550

VELIKANJE, EMILE FREDERICK, b. Yakima, Wash., Apr. 3, 1912; student Yakima Valley Jr. Coll., 1932, U. Wash., 1935. Admitted to Wash. bar, 1936, U.S. Supreme Ct. bar, 1958; partner firm Velikanje Moore and Shore and predecessors, Yakima, Wash., 1936—. Dir. Yakima C. of C.; pres. Yakima Knife & Fork, 1961-62, Yakima Community Concerts, 1958-61; dir. War Fund Drive, 1943-44. Fellow Am. Bar Found., Am. Coll. Probate Counsel (regent 1970—, mem. exec. bd. 1972—, treas. 1976—); mem. Yakima County (pres. 1948-49), Wash. State (lectr.; gov. 1956-59, pres. 1971-72), Am. (lectr.; del. 1965-71) bar assns. Mem. editorial bd. Probate Notes, 1974—. Home: 8711 Hawthorne Dr Yakima WA 98908 Office: 303 E D St Yakima WA 98901 Tel (509) 248-6030

VELIKANJE, GEORGE F., b. Yakima, Wash., May 16, 1940; B.A. in Law, U. Wash., 1963, LL.B., 1965. Admitted to Wash. bar, 1965; law clk. Ryan, Askren, Carlson, Bush & Swanson, Seattle, 1964-65; asso. firm Velikanje, Moore & Shore, and predecessors, Yakima, 1965-66, partner, 1967—. Bd. dirs. Yakima Area Arboretum, 1967-75, pres., 1975—; bd. dirs. United Way of Yakima County, 1973—; dir. Yakima County Allied Arts Council, 1973—; vice chmn. Yakima Sch. Dist. Operation and Maintenance Levy Dr., 1973-74, chmn., 1974-75. Mem. Am., Wash. (chmn. com. on legal asst. 1975-76, chmn. seminar law office mgmt. and econs. 1971), Yakima County (sec. 1967-68) bar assns., Greater Yakima C. of C. (dir. 1970-73, pres. 1976-77). Home: 217 N 22d Ave Yakima WA 98902 Office: 303 E D St Yakima WA 98901 Tel (509) 248-6030

VELURE, LYLE CARL, b. Coos Bay, Oreg., Jan. 2, 1941; B.S. in Econs., U. Oreg., 1963, J.D., 1966. Admitted to Oreg. bar, 1966; asso. firm Collins, Velure & Heysell, and predecessors, Medford, 1966-68, partner, 1968—; participant Pub. Employee Relations Bd. State Oreg., 1973-75. Active budget com. Sch. Dist. 549C, Medford, 1973-76. Mem. Oreg. Assn. Def. Counsel, Am. Assn. Trial Lawyers. Contbr. handbook; papers presented profl. assns. Office: 328 Central Ave Medford OR 97501 Tel (503) 779-4333

VENABLE, GILBERT TUCKERMAN, b. Pitts., Mar. 30, 1942; B.A., Cornell U., 1964; J.D., U. Pitts., 1967. Admitted to Pa. bar, 1968, Ariz. bar, 1975; law clk. to chief judge U.S. Ct. of Appeals, Phila., 1967-68; exec. dir. Pitts. chpt. ACLU, 1968-70; asst. prof., asst. dean Coll. Law, Ariz. State U., Tempe, 1970-76; partner firm Venable, Rice, Lee and Capra, Phoenix, 1976—; staff atty. Children's Def. Fund, Cambridge, Mass., 1973-74; cons. U.S. Forest Service, Tempe, 1973-76; dir. Legal Resources Inst., Tempe, 1972-73. Mem. exec. com. Allegheny County Council on Civil Rights, Pitts., 1968-70; pres. Ariz. Civil Liberties Union, 1971-73. Mem. U. Pitts. Law Sch. Alumni Assn. (award 1967), Assn. Trial Lawyers (award 1967), Order of Coif. Comment editor U. Pitts. Law Rev., 1966-67. Home: 2173 E Howe St Tempe AZ 85281 Office: Suite 2060 Ariz Bank Bldg 101 N 1st Ave Phoenix AZ 85003 Tel (602) 257-0336

VENTANTONIO, JAMES B., b. Orange, N.J., Jan. 5, 1940; B.A. in Sociology, Seton Hall U., 1961, J.D., 1964. Admitted to N.J. bar, 1965, Fed. Dist. Ct. N.J. bar, 1965, U.S. Ct. Mil. Appeals bar, 1965, U.S. Supreme Ct. bar, 1968; served to maj. JAGC, U.S. Army, 1969;

sr. staff atty. Newark Legal Services, 1969-70; dir. Somerset-Sussex Legal Services, N.J., 1970-74; asso. prof., dir. clin. edn. programs Seton Hall Law Center, 1974—. Vice chmn. law revision com. N.J. Mental Health Planning Com., 1975; bd. dirs. Nat. Legal Aid and Defender Assn., 1973—; apptd. by Gov. to N.J. Adv. Council Legal Services, 1975; bd. dirs. Action for Legal Rights, 1973-74. Mem. Am., N.J. (mem. gen. council, chmn. standing com. availability Legal services) bar assns. Office: 1095 Raymond Blvd Newark NJ 07102 Tel (201) 642-0810

VENTRESS, JOSEPH LE ROY, b. N.Y.C., Dec. 15, 1924; student U. Florence (Italy), 1945; A.B., U. So. Calif., 1949, J.D., 1951. Admitted to Calif. bar, 1951; partner firm Labowe & Ventress, Los Angeles, 1953—; legal advisor Consulate Gen. Italy, 1956—. Pres. Italian Resource Center, U. Calif., Los Angeles; founder Patrons of Italian Culture; pres. Dante Alighieri Soc., 1964-65; nat. expansion dir. UNICO Nat., a Nat. Service Orgn., 1966-68. Mem. State Bar Calif., Los Angeles County Bar Assn. Editor Italy Is mag.; decorated comdr. Italian Republic; lectr. on Italian history and lit.; contbr. articles on Italy-U.S. relations to newspapers and mags. Office: 1229 W First St Los Angeles CA 90026 Tel (213) 624-7335

VERGON, FREDERICK PORTER, JR., b. Mesa, Ariz., June 12, 1944; B.A., Denison U., 1966; J.D., Case Western Res. U., 1969. Admitted to Ohio bar, 1969; mem. firm Mc Neal, Schick & Archibald, Cleve., 1969—. Mem. Ohio Def. Assn., Am., Ohio, Greater Cleve. bar assns., Phi Delta Phi. Contbr. articles to legal jours. Home: 3306 Maynard Rd Shaker Heights OH 44122 Office: 520 Williamson Bldg Cleveland OH 44114

VERHAAREN, HAROLD CARL, b. Salt Lake City, Apr. 11, 1938; J.D., U. Utah, 1965. Admitted to Utah bar, 1965; partner firm Verhaaren & Meservy, and predecessors, Salt Lake City, 1965—; law clk. to justice Utah Supreme Ct., 1964-65; mem. una Chmn., Salt Lake Mount Olympus Planning Dist., 1969—; area chmn. sustaining membership enrollment Boy Scouts Am., 1975, 76. Mem. Am., Utah, Salt Lake County bar assns., Am. Judicature Soc., Mountain States Pension Conf., Phi Eta Sigma, Phi Kappa Phi. Office: 466 E 500 S Suite 100 Salt Lake City UT 84111 Tel (801) 322-5555

VERNIS, FRANK CARL, JR., b. McKeesport, Pa., Nov. 6, 1927; student U. Pitts., 1948, U. Tampa, 1949; J.D., U. Miami, 1953. Admitted to Fla. bar, 1953; individual practice law, Miami, Fla., 1953-70; sr. partner firm Vernis & Bowling, Coconut Grove, Fla., 1970—. Mem. Fla., Dade County bar assns. Office: 2951 S Bayshore Dr Coconut Grove FL 33133 Tel (305) 442-8142

VERON, JUANEITA MARIE, b. South Gate, Calif., Nov. 1, 1925; B.A., U. So. Calif., 1947, J.D., 1950. Admitted to Calif. bar, 1951; individual practice law, Huntington Park, Calif., 1951-53, 58-71; partner firm Armstorng & Veron, Huntington Park, 1953-58, Armstrong, Veron & Wilbur, Downey, Calif., 1971-77; judge Los Angeles Municipal Court, 1977—. Mem. Calif., Los Angeles County bars, Assn. Calif. Judiciary, Legion Lex, Phi Delta Delta. Tel (213) 974-6111

VERRILL, CHARLES OWEN, JR., b. Biddeford, Maine, Sept. 30, 1937; A.B., Tufts U., 1959; J.D., Duke U., 1962. Admitted to D.C. bar, 1962; since practiced in Washington, asso. firm Weaver & Glossie, 1962-64, Barco, Cook, Patton & Blow, 1964-66, partner firm Patton, Boggs & Blow, 1967—. Mem. Am. (chmn. com. on comml. treaties 1967-71), Fed., FCC bar assns., Bar Assn. D.C., Duke U. Law Alumni (council 1972-75). Home: 8205 Dunsinane Ct McLean VA 22101 Office: 1200 17th St NW Washington DC 20036 Tel (202) 223-4040

VERRILL, RALPH THOMAS, b. N.Y.C., Mar. 8, 1937; B.A., Columbia U., 1958; LL.B., N.Y. U., 1964. Admitted to N.Y. bar, 1965; prin. atty., law dept. Port Authority of N.Y. and N.J., N.Y.C., 1968—. Mem. Am., N.Y. State, N.Y. County bar assns. Home: 13 Leghorn Ct Huntington NY 11746 Office: 1 World Trade Center New York City NY 10048

VESCELUS, JOHN WILLIAM, b. Elkhart, Ind., May 6, 1921; student Ind. U., 1939-42; A.B., Wheaton Coll., 1947; J.D., Ill. Inst. Tech., 1951; postgrad. Northwestern U., 1947. Admitted to Ill. bar, 1951; individual practice law, Ill., 1951-54; partner firm Vescelus & Douglas, West Chicago, Ill., 1954-56, firm Vescelus, Perry & Pollard, and predecessors, 1956—; trust officer West Chicago State Bank; city atty. West Chicago, 1955-57. Mem. Am., Ill. DuPage County bar assns., Am. Judicature Soc. Office: 330 Naperville Rd Wheaton IL 60187 Tel (312) 665-2500

VESTAL, ALLAN DELKER, b. Indpls., Nov. 26, 1920; A.B., DePauw U., 1943; LL.B., Yale, 1949. Admitted to Iowa bar, 1949; instr. law U. Iowa, Iowa City, 1949-50, asst. prof., 1950-53, asso. prof., 1953-57, prof., 1957-67, Murray prof., 1967-72, Carver prof., 1972—; vis. prof. Texas Tech. U., Lubbock, summer 1974, U. Tenn., Knoxville, 1975, U. N.C., Chapel Hill, 1976. Mem. Johnson County Regional Planning Commn., 1965—. Mem. Nat. Conf. Commrs. on Uniform State Laws, Order of Coif (v.p.). Author: Res Judicata/Preclusion, 1969, Iowa Practice, 1974. Home: 1704 Glendale St Iowa City IA 52240 Office: College of Law U Iowa Iowa City IA 52242 Tel (319) 353-4394

VETRI, DOMINICK RICHARD, b. Passaic, N.J., Oct. 9, 1938; B.S.M.E., N.J. Inst. Tech., 1960; J.D., U. Pa., 1964. Admitted to N.J. bar, 1965; law clk. Hon. Harold Kolovsky, Assignment Judge Passaic County, 1964-65; asso. firm Meyner & Wiley, Newark, 1965-67; asst. prof. law U. Oreg., 1967-71, asso. prof., 1971-74, prof., 1974—. Bd. dirs. Lane County (Oreg.) Legal Aid Service, Inc., 1971—. Mem. Am., N.J. State, Lane County bar assns., Am. Assn. Law Schs., ACLU (dir. Oreg. chpt. 1973-74). Author: (with Frank Lacy) Oregon Minor Court Judges' Manual, 1972; (with Fredric Merrill) Problems & Materials on Federal Courts & Procedure, 1974; Educating the Lawyer: Clinical Experience as an Integral Part of Legal Education; Product Liability: The Developing Framework for Analysis; Product Liability: The Prima Facie Case. Home: Route 1 PO Box 55M Brownsville OR 97327 Office: U of Oreg Sch of Law Eugene OR 97403 Tel (503) 686-3868

VIALL, WILTON SHELLEY, III, b. Cin., Apr. 6, 1948; B.A. cum laude, U. Wash., 1970, J.D. (William W. Wallace scholar), 1973. Admitted to Wash. bar, 1973; asso. firm Curran, Kleweno, Johnson & Curran, Kent. Wash., 1972-75; individual practice law, Seattle, 1975—; instr. Highline Community Coll., Midway, Wash., 1976—. Mem. Wash., Seattle-King County bar assns., Phi Beta Kappa, Phi Alpha Theta. Home: 20601 SW 2d St Seattle WA 98168 Office: 501 3d Ave Seattle WA 98104 Tel (206) 623-0967

VICKERY, BYRON LAMAR, b. Columbus, Ohio, Apr. 26, 1937; B.A. in Polit. Sci., Ohio State U., 1959, LL.B., 1964. Admitted to Ohio bar, 1965, Mich. bar, 1965; asst. counsel Dow Chem. Co., 1965-67; gen. counsel F & R Lazarus div. Federated Dept. Stores, 1967-72; individual practice law, Columbus, 1972—. Home: 44 W Jeffrey Pl Columbus OH 43214 Tel (614) 224-8166

VICKORY, CHARLES BRANSON, JR., b. Greensboro, N.C., Jan. 8, 1929; A.B., Guilford Coll., 1954; LL.B., Wake Forest Coll., 1957. Admitted to N.C. bar, 1957, U.S. Supreme Ct. bar, 1966, U.S. Tax Ct. bar, 1972; claims authorizer Social Security Adminstrn., Birmingham, Ala., 1957-60; atty. Estate Tax IRS, Greensboro, 1960-62, 69-70, Asheville, N.C., 1962-69; partner firm Connor & Vickory, Mt. Olive, N.C., 1970-72, firm Whitley & Vickory, Mt. Olive, 1972-76; individual practice law, Mt. Olive, 1977—. Mem. Am., Fed., N.C., Wayne County (pres. 1976-77) bar assns., N.C. Acad. Trial Lawyers. Tel (919) 658-2610

VICTOR, EDWARD GARY, b. Cleve., July 7, 1940; B.S., U. Ill., 1962; M.B.A., Northwestern U., 1963, J.D., 1968. Admitted to Calif. bar, 1969; asso. firm Irell & Manella, Los Angeles, 1968-74, partner, 1974—; lectr., writer U. So. Calif. Tax Inst., 1972, 76. Mem. State Bar Calif., Los Angeles Bar Assn., Order of Coif. Editor Northwestern U. Law Rev., 1967-68. Home: 134 N Carmelina St Los Angeles CA 90049 Office: 1800 Ave of the Stars Los Angeles CA 90067 Tel (213) 277-1010

VICTOR, WILLIAM HENRY, b. Akron, Ohio, Feb. 26, 1913; A.B., U. Akron, 1934; LL.B., Western Res. U., 1937. Admitted to Ohio bar, 1937; asso. firm Beery, Underwood, Ryder & Kroeger, Akron, 1937-46; asst. pros. atty. Summit County (Ohio), 1946-50; municipal judge, Akron, 1950-59; judge, Summit County Ct. Common Pleas, 1959-71; judge Ct. of Appeals, Akron, 1971—. Mem. Am., Ohio, Akron bar assns. Home: 431 Orlando Ave Akron OH 44320 Office: Summit County Court House Akron OH 44308 Tel (216) 379-5750

VICTORSON, LARRY, b. Detroit, Jan. 31, 1943; B.A., Wayne State U., 1964; J.D., U. Mich., 1967. Admitted to Mich. bar, 1968, Tex. bar, 1968, U.S. Supreme Ct., 1972; asst. dist. atty. County of El Paso (Tex.), 1968-72; spl. atty. Dept. Justice, Washington, 1972; individual practice law, El Paso, 1972—. Mem. Young Lawyers Assn., Tex. Trial Lawyers Assn., Tex. Criminal Def. Lawyers Assn., El Paso Criminal Def. Lawyers Assn., El Paso Bar Assn. (chmn. com. criminal law 1974). Office: 600 Myrtle St El Paso TX 79901 Tel (915) 542-0761

VICTORY, JEFFREY PAUL, b. Shreveport, La., Jan. 29, 1946; B.A., Centenary Coll., 1967; J.D., Tulane U., 1971. Admitted to La. bar, 1971; asso. firm Tucker, Martin, Holder, Jeter & Jackson, Shreveport, 1971—, partner, 1977—. Mem. Shreveport (v.p. sect. young lawyers 1976, pres.-elect 1977—), La., Am. bar assns., La. Law Inst. (mem. jr. bd. 1977—). Recipient award for knowledge and assistance in developing arbitration program Shreveport Better Bus. Bur., 1975. Office: 1300 Beck Bldg Shreveport LA 71101 Tel (318) 425-7764

VIDEAN, JAMES MORGAN, b. Flint, Mich., June 3, 1927; B.A., Ohio State U., 19S0, J.D., 1952. Admitted to Ohio bar, 1952, Ariz. bar, 1964, U.S. Dist. (Ariz.) Ct. bar, 1965, U.S. 9th Circuit Ct. Appeals bar, 1973; asst. atty. gen. Ohio, 1952-58; partner firm Videan & Dixon, Columbus, Ohio, 1958-62; research analyst Supreme Ct. Ariz., Phoenix, 1964-66; partner firm Renaud, Cook & Videan, Phoenix, 1966—. Mem. Ariz. Bar Assn., Def. Research Inst., Ariz. Bd. Trial Advocates. Office: 11 W Jefferson Phoenix AZ 85003 Tel (602) 253-5101

VIELE, TERRY JAMES, b. Norfolk, Va., June 15, 1943; A.B., U. Calif. at Berkeley, 1965; J.D., U. Calif. at San Francisco, 1971. Admitted to Calif. bar, 1972; partner firm Whipple & Viele, Ventura, Calif., 1973—. Mem. Calif., Ventura County bar assns., Ventura County Family Law Assn., Ventura County Trial Lawyers Assn. Office: 542 Poli St Ventura CA 93001 Tel (805) 643-8658

VIETH, G. DUANE, b. Omaha, Sept. 20, 1923; B.A., U. Iowa, 1947, J.D., 1949. Admitted to Iowa, D.C. bars, 1950, U.S. Supreme Ct. bar, 1955; partner firm Arnold & Porter, Washington, 1949—; trustee Mortgage Investors Washington, 1970—; mem. com. admissions and grievances U.S. Ct. Appeals D.C. Circuit, 1973—. Trustee Fed. City Council, 1972—, Landon Sch. Boys, 1973—, Iowa Law Sch. Found., 1971—. Mem. Am., D.C., Iowa bar assns., Order of Coif, Omicron Delta Kappa. Home: 3717 Cardiff Rd Chevy Chase MD 20015 Office: 1229 19th St NW Washington DC 20036 Tel (202) 872-6901

VIETS, HAMILTON PARKER, b. Fond du Lac, Wis., May 5, 1917; B.A., U. Wis., 1940, J.D., 1941. Admitted to Wis. bar, 1941; tax accountant Sentry Ins. Co., Stevens Point, Wis., 1949-66, asso. counsel, 1966-74, asst. gen. counsel, 1974—; sec. Sentry Fund, Inc., Sentry Equity Services, 1969. Bd. suprs. Portage County, Wis., 1964-72; bd. dir. Stevens Point Pub. Library, 1968—; mem. N. Central Wis. Regional Planning Commn., 1974—. Mem. Am., Wis., Portage County (pres. 1968) bar assns. Home: Route 1 Box 176-V Amherst WI 54406 Office: 1421 Strongs Ave Stevens Point WI 54481 Tel (715) 344-2345

VIEUX, ERNEST MERLE, b. Greensburg, Kans., Nov. 22, 1913; Tchrs. certificate Emporia State Tchrs. Coll., 1935; LL.B., U. Tex., 1941. Admitted to Tex. bar, 1941, Kans. bar, 1942, U.S. Supreme Ct. bar, 1971; practiced in Meade, Kans., 1946-55, Dodge City, 1975—; county atty. Meade County (Kans.), 1946-55; judge Kans. Dist. Ct., 16th (formerly 31st) Jud. Dist., 1955-75. Mem. ofcl. bd. United Methodist Ch., Meade, Dodge City, Kans. Mem. Dodge City, S.W. Kans., Am. bar assns., Bar Assn. State Kans. Home: 505 Annette St Dodge City KS 67801 Office: Civic Plaza 2016 1st Ave Dodge City KS 67801 Tel (316) 225-0771

VILLIOTTE, RICHARD BLAISE, b. Brighton, Mass., Feb. 19, 1943; B.A., Boston Coll., 1964; J.D., New Eng. Sch. Law, 1968. Admitted to Mass. bar, 1969; atty. legal dept. Md. Casualty Co., Boston, 1968-74; individual practice law, Revere, Mass., 1969—; mental health legal advisor Suffolk County, 1975—; election commr. City of Revere, 1974—; instr. bus. law Newbury Jr. Coll., Boston, 1975—. Mem. Mass., Boston, Chelsea-Revere bar assns. Case note editor New Eng. Sch. Law Jour., 1966-68. Home: 255 Revere St Revere MA 02151 Office: 94 Central Ave PO Box 33 Revere MA 02151 Tel (617) 289-5865

VIMONT, RICHARD ELGIN, b. Lexington, Ky., Aug. 3, 1936; B.S. in Commerce, U. Ky., 1958, J.D., 1960. Admitted to Ky. bar, 1960, U.S. Dist. Ct. Eastern Dist. Ky. bar, 1960, U.S. Supreme Ct. bar, 1965; asso. firm Denney & Landrum, Lexington, 1960-61, Brown, Sledd & McCann, Lexington, 1961-62; partner firm Anggelis, Vimont & Bunch and predecessors, Lexington, 1963—; asst. commonwealth atty., Ky., 1974-75; vis. prof. Transylvania U., 1965. Mem. Lexington City Commn., 1972-73, Ky. Crime Commn., 1973-74. Mem. Am. Bar Assn. Home: 1412 Lookout Circle Lexington KY 40502 Office: 111 Church St PO Box 2086 Lexington KY 40501 Tel (606) 252-2202

VINCENT, RICHARD LEE, b. Pine Bluff, Ark., Dec. 21, 1942; B.S., Samford U., 1968, J.D., 1968. Admitted to Ala. bar, 1968; asso. firm Najjar & Najjar, Birmingham, Ala., 1968-71, partner, 1971—. Mem. Am., Ala. bar assns., Ala. Trial Lawyers Assn., Ala. Criminal Def. Lawyers Assn., Phi Alpha Delta (pres. Birmingham Alumni chpt. 1971). Home: 3433 Coventry Dr Birmingham AL 35224 Office: 1030 Brown Marx Bldg Birmingham AL 35203

VINCENTI, SHELDON ARNOLD, b. Ogden, Utah, Sept. 4, 1938; A.B., Harvard, 1960, J.D., 1963. Admitted to Utah bar, 1963; probation officer 1st Dist. Juvenile Ct., Ogden, 1963; individual practice law, Ogden; pros. atty. City Ogden, 1966-68; partner firm Lowe and Vincenti, Ogden; city atty. S. Ogden, 1968-70; atty. City of Pleasant View, Utah, 1970; legis. asst. U.S. Rep. McKay of Utah, 1971-72, adminstrv. asst., 1973; asso. prof. Coll. Law U. Idaho, Moscow, 1973—, asso. dean, 1974—. Pres. bd. dirs. Family Counseling Service, Ogden, 1970; bd. dirs. United Fund No. Utah, Ogden, 1970; mem. State Central Com. Utah Democratic Party, chmn. Weber County (Utah) Dem. Party, 1969-70; bd. dirs. U. Idaho Community Devel. Center. Home: 517 E B St Moscow ID 83843 Office: University Idaho College Law Moscow ID 83843 Tel (208) 885-6422

VINE, LEO, b. Providence, Aug. 7, 1930; A.B., Brown U., 1952; J.D., Harvard, 1955. Admitted to Conn. bar, 1955, U.S. Supreme Ct. bar, 1972; asso. firm Yudkin & Yudkin, Derby, Conn., 1957-59; individual practice law, Shelton, Conn., 1959-69; partner firm Vine & Welch, Shelton, 1969-77, Winnick, Vine & Welsh, 1977—; corp. counsel City of Shelton, 1964-67, 69. Mem. Valley Bar Assn. (pres. 1966), Phi Beta Kappa. Named Young Man of year, Jaycees, 1961. Home: 3 Rimmon Hill Rd Woodbridge CT 06525 Office: 70 Platt Rd Shelton CT 06484 Tel (203) 929-6351

VINING, GEORGE JOSEPH, b. Fulton, Mo., Mar. 3, 1938; B.A., Yale, 1959; B.A., Cambridge (Eng.), 1961, M.A., 1970; J.D., Harvard, 1964; Admitted to D.C. bar, 1965; staff office of criminal justice Dep. Atty. Gen.'s Office, Dept. Justice, Washington, 1964-65; asst. to exec. dir. Nat. Crime Commn., Washington, 1965-66; asso. firm Covington & Burling, Washington, 1966-69; asst. prof. law U. Mich., Ann Arbor, 1969-72, asso. prof., 1972-74, prof., 1974—; research asso. law Clare Hall, Cambridge, 1973; cons. in field. Hearing officer credentials com. Democratic Nat. Conv., 1972. Mem. Am. Bar Assn., D.C. Bar, Am. Friends of Cambridge U. (sec. 1969—). Contbr. articles to legal jours. Home: 1503 Morton Ave Ann Arbor MI 48104 Office: Law School U of Mich 337 Hutchins Hall Ann Arbor MI 48104 Tel (313) 763-2288

VINSON, CHARLES EVERETT, b. El Paso, Tex., Apr. 8, 1947; B.S., U. Tex., 1970, M.S., 1971, J.D., 1973. Admitted to Tex. bar, 1974; legal asst., grand jury bailiff Dist. Attys. Office, Travis County, Tex., 1972-73; asso. firm Collins, Langford & Pine, El Paso, 1974—. Mem. El Paso Bar Assn., El Paso Young Lawyers Assn., El Paso Jaycees (dir.). Home: 6552 Fiesta St El Paso TX 79912 Office: 1100 Bassett Tower El Paso TX 79901 Tel (915) 533-6955

VINSON, FRED MOORE, JR., b. Louisa, Ky., Apr. 3, 1925; A.B., Washington and Lee U., 1948, LL.B., 1951, LL.D., 1968. Admitted to D.C. bar, 1951; asso. firm James M. Earnest, 1951-54, Reasoner & Davis, Washington, 1954-63; partner firm Reasoner, Davis & Vinson, Washington, 1963-65, 69—; asst. atty. gen. criminal div. Dept. Justice, Washington, 1965-69; chmn. bd. trustees D.C. Pub. Defender Service, 1976—; mem. D.C. Circuit Jud. Conf., 1960—; chmn. com. admissions and grievances U.S. Ct. Appeals for D.C. Circuit, 1974—; gen. counsel Inaugural Com., 1961; mem. Adminstrv. Conf. U.S., 1963-65. Fellow Am. Bar Found.; mem. Am. (ho. dels. 1971-75), Fed., D.C. (pres. 1971-72, bd. govs.) bar assns., Phi Beta Kappa, Order of Coif. Home: 5310 Carvel Rd Washington DC 20016 Office: 800 17th St NW Washington DC 20006 Tel (202) 298-8100

VINSON, LANCE CHRISTOPHER, b. Long Beach, Calif., May 3, 1943; B.A., Claremont Men's Coll., 1964; J.D., Loyola U., Los Angeles, 1967. Admitted to Calif. bar, 1967, Ill. bar, 1973; law clk., asso. firm Knapp, Gill, Hibbert & Stevens, Los Angeles, 1967-68; judge adv. U.S. Navy, Newport, R.I., Brunswick, Maine and San Juan, P.R., 1968-72; enforcement atty. U.S. EPA, Chgo., 1972-73, chief case devel. unit, 1973-75, chief case devel. sect. air enforcement br., 1975-76, chief enforcement and legal support br., Denver, 1976—; panelist environ. law seminars Am. Bar Assn., 1976; lectr. in field. Active, Am. Diabetes Assn., Deerfield, Ill., 1973-76. Recipient Am. Jurisprudence Prize in Evidence, 1967. Office: 1860 Lincoln St Denver CO 80295 Tel (303) 837-2361 also 837-4812

VIOLANTE, MICHAEL JOSEPH, b. Niagara Falls, N.Y., July 17, 1945; B.S. in Econs., Boston Coll., 1967; J.D., Suffolk U., 1970. Admitted to N.Y. bar, 1971; asso. firm Minicucci & Halpin, Niagara Falls, 1970-73; individual practice law, Niagara Falls, 1973—; asst. pub. defender Niagara County, 1971-75. Mem. Western N.Y., Am., Niagara Falls (past treas.), Niagara County, N.Y. County bar assns., Am. Trial Lawyers Assn. Home: 1006 85th St Niagara Falls NY 14303 Office: 803 Division Ave Niagara Falls NY 14305 Tel (716) 282-0447

VIRDEH, ABRAHAM, b. Kermanshah, Iran, Aug. 3, 1930; B.S., U. Calif. at Berkeley, 1958, Med. Tech., U. Calif. at San Francisco, 1960; J.D., Lincoln U., San Francisco, 1970. Admitted to Calif. bar, 1971; asso. firm Levy & Van Bourg, San Francisco, 1971-72, firm Eugene C. Treaster, Sacramento, 1972-73; individual practice law, Eureka, Calif., 1973—; environ. health & safety coordinator City and County of San Francisco, 1969-70. Mem. Am., Calif. bar assns., Calif. Trial Lawyers Assn., Calif. Applicant Attys. Assn. (bd. govs.). Home: 3666 J St Eureka CA 95501 Office: 819 7th St PO Box 1029 Eureka CA 95501 Tel (707) 443-8691

VIRGA, MICHAEL JAMES, b. Sacramento, Jan. 11, 1932; B.A., U. Santa Clara, 1953, LL.B., 1958. Admitted to Calif. bar, 1959; trial atty. Dist. Atty.'s Office Sacramento, 1959-62; city prosecutor City of Sacramento, 1962-64; partner firm Virga, Fields & Klein, Sacramento, 1964-70; judge Sacramento Municipal Ct., 1970-74, Sacramento Superior Ct., 1974—. Office: Courthouse Sacramento CA 95814

VISCONTI, GIRARD ROCCO, b. Providence, Sept. 27, 1941; A.B., Providence Coll., 1965; J.D., Suffolk U., 1968. Admitted to R.I., Mass. bars, 1968; partner firm Abedon & Visconti, Ltd., Providence; exec. sec., gen. counsel R.I. Subcontractors Assn., Providence, 1970—. Bd. dirs. R.I. Civic Chorale, Providence. Mem. Am. Subcontractors Assn. (legal adv. com.), Am. Arbitration Assn. (panel), Am., R.I. bar assns.,

Assn. Trial Lawyers Am. Office: 1025 Industrial Bank Bldg Providence RI 02903 Tel (401) 331-3563

VITACCO, GUY R., b. Bklyn., July 5, 1930; B.A., St. John's U., 1952; LL.B., N.Y. Law Sch., 1957. Admitted to N.Y. bar, 1958, U.S. Supreme Ct. bar, 1965; individual practice law, Elmhurst, N.Y., 1958—; asst. dist. atty. Queens County, N.Y., 1960-64; counsel N.Y.C. com. N.Y. State Senate, 1965, 66. Bd. dirs. St. John's Hosp. of Queens. Mem. Columbian Lawyers Assn. Queens (program chmn., past pres.), Am. Arbitration Assn., Queens County Bar Assn. (com. on civil ct., com. legal edn., judiciary com.). Named Man of Year, Glendale chpt. Unico Nat., 1966. Office: 87-10 Queens Blvd Elmhurst NY 11373 Tel (212) 898-5060

VITAL, RICHARD LESTER, b. New Orleans, Oct. 22, 1942; A.B., Marshall U., 1964; J.D., W.Va. U., 1967. Admitted to W.Va. bar, 1967; asst. city atty. Huntington (W.Va.), 1967-71; city atty. Barboursville (W.Va.), 1974-75; partner firm Broh & Vital, Huntington, 1970—. Mem. Am., W.Va. bar assns., W.Va. State Bar, Cabell County Bar. Office: 664 Main St Barboursville WV 25504 Tel (304) 736-3437

VITALIE, CARL LYNN, b. Clinton, Ind., Aug. 31, 1937; D. Pharmacy, U. So. Calif., 1961, J.D., 1965. Admitted to Va. bar, 1966, Calif. bar, 1967; pharmacist, So. Calif., 1961-65; staff atty. Am. Pharm. Assn., Washington, 1965-66; staff pharmacist Sav-On Drugs, Inc., Marina del Rey, Calif., 1966-69, asst. dir. indsl. and pub. relations, 1969-71, dir. pharmacies, 1971-74, v.p. pharmacy ops., 1974—; lectr. pharmacy law and ethics U. So. Calif., 1968-70; mem. Calif. Bd. Pharmacy, 1968-76; U.S. liaison sec. Internat. Pharm. Students Fedn., 1959-62. Mem. Am., Va., Calif. bar assns., Am., Calif. pharm. assns., Am. Mgmt. Assn., Nat. Assn. Bds. of Pharmacy, Delta Theta Phi, Phi Delta Chi. Licensed pharmacist, Calif., Nev., Tex.; author: Establishment and Maintenance of Membership Standards in Professional Societies of Pharmacists, 1967. Office: 418 Lincoln Blvd Marina del Rey CA 90291 Tel (213) 870-1291

VITEK, REGINALD ALVIN, b. Bakersfield, Calif., Apr. 23, 1942; A.B., San Diego State Coll., 1964; J.D., U. Calif. at Los Angeles, 1967. Admitted to Calif. bar, 1967; mem. firm Seltzer, Caplan, Wilkins & McMahon, San Diego, 1967—. Mem. Am. (Calif. co-chmn. com. on litigation involving comml. trans. litigation sect.), Calif., San Diego County bar assns., Calif., San Diego trial lawyers assns. Home: 4919 Longview El Cajon CA 92020 Office: 3003 4th Ave San Diego CA 92103 Tel (714) 291-3003

VITELLO, DANIEL P., b. Italy, June 29, 1904; LL.B., J.D., Rutgers U., 1929. Admitted to N.J. bar, 1931; individual practice law, Newark, Red Bank and Oceanport, N.J. Mem. Monmouth County Bar Assn. Home and Office: 1312 Eatontown Blvd Oceanport NJ 07757 Tel (201) 542-2474

VITKO, JOHN PETER, b. Virginia, Minn., Sept. 7, 1931; A.A., Virginia (Minn.) Jr. Coll., 1951; B.S., U. Minn., 1953, J.D., 1955. Admitted to Minn. bar, 1955, U.S. Dist. Ct. bar, 1955, U.S. Circuit Ct. Appeals 8th Circuit bar, 1958; partner firm Blomquist, Vitko, Neimeyer & Mooney, St. Paul, 1955-75; partner firm Dorsey, Windhorst, Hannaford, Whitney and Halladay, St. Paul, 1975—; dir. The Splty. Mfg. Co., St. Paul, Caldwell Phillips, Inc., St. Paul. Pres. Viking Growth Fund., Mpls., 1962-63; asst. campaign chmn. ARC, St. Paul, 1965; bd. dirs. William Boss Found., St. Paul, 1968—; pres. Internat. Assn. Torch Clubs, 1969-70. Mem. Am., Minn., Ramsey County bar assns. Home: 45 Island Rd North Oaks MN 55110 Office: W 1468 1st National Bank Bldg Saint Paul MN 55101 Tel (612) 227-8017

VITT, GEOFFREY JUDD, b. N.Y.C., Oct. 30, 1946; B.A., George Washington U., 1969, J.D., 1972. Admitted to Va. bar, 1972, U.S. Supreme Ct., 1976; asso. firm Cohen & Rosenblum, Alexandria, Va., 1972-74; partner firm Cohen & Vitt, Alexandria, 1974—. Mem. Am. Trial Lawyers Assn., Va. State Bar. Office: 320 King St Alexandria VA 22313 Tel (703) 836-2121

VITTEK, JOSEPH FRANCIS, JR., b. Balt., May 8, 1940; B.S., Mass. Inst. Tech., 1962; J.D., Suffolk U., 1971; LL.M., Harvard, 1973. Admitted to Mass. bar, 1971, N.H. bar, 1977; asso. dir. Flight Transp. Lab., Mass. Inst. Tech., Cambridge, 1970-74, asst. prof. aeros. and astronautics, 1974-76; prof. law, dir. research Franklin Pierce Law Center, Concord, N.H., 1976—; individual practice law, Cambridge, Mass., 1971-77, Northfield, N.H., 1977—; v.p., clk. Found. for the Future, Cambridge, 1975—. Mem. Newton Transp. Planning Bd., 1972-73. Mem. Am. Bar Assn. Recipient NASA Apollo Achievement award. Home: Hodgdon Rd Northfield NH 03276 Office: Franklin Pierce Law Center Concord NH 03301 Tel (603) 228-1541

VITTI, LOUIS PETER, b. Pitts., Dec. 27, 1940; B.A., Duquesne U., 1963, J.D., 1968. Admitted to Pa. bar, 1969; law clk. to Charles N. Caputo, Pitts., 1968-69, Judge David B. Fawcett, Jr., 1969; asso. firm Stone & Raynovich, Pitts., 1969-71; v.p. corp. Ryan & Bowser, Pitts., 1971-76; partner firm Markovitz & Vitti, Pitts., 1977—; counsel, Associated Trades and Crafts Union, 1970; hearing examiner Pa. Labor Relations Bd., 1971-73; spl. counsel State of Ohio, 1971—; Pa. commr. Profl. and Occupational Affairs, 1973-75. Bd. alumni Duquesne U., 1974—; instr. staff St. Susanna's, 1976—; chmn. Corpus Christi Joing Sch. Bd. Mem. Pa., Allegheny County bar assns., Western Pa. Trial Lawyers Assn. Named Pa. Man of Year, Italian Am. Press Radio Assn., 1974; asso. editor Juris Newspaper, 1968. Home: 167 McKenzie St Pittsburgh PA 15235 Office: 505 Manor Bldg Pittsburgh PA 15219 Tel (412) 281-1725

VITTITOW, ROBERT COURTLAND, b. DeWitt, Ark., Dec. 24, 1940; B.A. in History, U. Ark., Monticello, 1962; LL.B., Tulane U., 1966. Admitted to Ark. bar, 1966, U.S. Supreme Ct. bar, 1971; partner firm Huey & Vittitow, Warren, Ark., 1967—; municipal judge City of Warren, 1970; juvenile referee Bradley County, Ark., 1973-76; mem. continuing edn. com. Ark. Juvenile Justice Inst.; mem. juvenile justice task force Gov.'s Ounce of Prevention Com. Bd. dirs. Bradley County C. of C., 1975-77, Delta Counseling and Guidance Service, 1975-76. Mem. Ark. Trial Lawyers Assn., Ark. Bar assn. Home: 215 Power St Warren AR 71671 Office: 103 S Myrtle St Warren AR 71671 Tel (501) 226-2675

VIVENZIO, ANTHONY DAVID, b. Lawrence, Mass., May 30, 1947; B.S. in Bus. Adminstrn., Boston U., 1968, J.D., 1972. Admitted to Mass. bar, 1972, Wash. bar, 1973, U.S. Dist. Ct. bar, 1976; VISTA atty. Grant-Adams County Legal Services, Moses Lake, Wash., 1973; trial lawyer Mass. Defenders Com., Boston and New Bedford, 1973-74; dir., founder Olympic Legal Services, Port Angeles and Port Townsend, Wash., 1974-76; staff atty. Seattle-King County (Wash.) Youth Law Office, 1976—; instr. law Peninsula Coll., Port Townsend, 1975. Mem. Mass., Wash. bar assns., Wash. Assn. Legal Services Projects, Wash. Defenders Assn., Nat. Legal Aid and Defender Assn. Legal Services Corp. grantee, 1974-76. Home: 3445 E Spruce St Seattle WA 98122 Office: 1511 E Alder St Seattle WA 98122

VLADECK, JUDITH POMARLEN, b. Norfolk, Va., Aug. 1, 1923; B.A., Hunter Coll., 1945; LL.B. (now J.D.), Columbia, 1947. Admitted to N.Y. bar, 1947, U.S. Supreme Ct. bar, 1962, U.S. Army Ct. of Mil. Rev., 1971; asso. firm Condrad & Smith, N.Y.C., 1947-51; individual practice law, N.Y.C., 1951-57; mem. firm Vladeck, Elias, Vladeck & Lewis, N.Y.C., 1957—; cooperating atty. Workers Def. League; counsel to City U. N.Y. Women's Coalition; tchr., lectr. Practising Law Inst., Cornell U. Bd. dirs. N.Y. Civil Liberties Union, 1963-68. Mem. Am., N.Y. bar assns. Editor: (with Stephen C. Vladeck) Collective Bargaining in Higher Education - The Developing Law, 1975. Home: 115 Central Park W New York City NY 10023 Office: 1501 Broadway New York City NY 10036 Tel (212) 354-8330

VLADECK, STEPHEN CHARNEY, b. N.Y.C., Apr. 29, 1920; B.A., N.Y. U., 1941; LL.B., J.D., Columbia, 1947. Admitted to N.Y. bar, 1948, U.S. Supreme Ct. bar, 1952; sr. partner firm Vladeck, Elias, Vladeck & Lewis, and predecessors, N.Y.C., 1949—. Mem. Am., N.Y. State bar assns., N.Y. County Lawyers Assn., Westchester County Lawyers Assn., Bar City N.Y., Fed. Bar Counsel. Co-editor: Collective Bargaining in Higher Education, 1976. Home: 115 Central Park W New York City NY 10023 Office: 1501 Broadway New York City NY 10036

VLAICH, MILDRED ANN JOVANOVICH, b. Detroit, Oct. 16, 1922; B.A., Wayne State U., 1944, LL.B., 1946, J.D., 1946. Admitted to Mich. bar, 1947; asst. state prosecutor for Macomb County (Mich.), 1949-52; partner firm Vlaich & Orris, Center, Line, Mich., 1952-74; judge Oakland County (Mich.) Dist. Ct., 52d Dist., 3d Div., 1975—; supr. Macomb County, 1963-66. Mem. Macomb County Child Guidance Clinic, 1964-66. Mem. Am. Bar Assn., Mich. State Bar (arbitrator grievance com. 1972-74), Law Study Soc., Mich. Dist. Judges Assn., Am. Judges Assn., Nat. Assn. Women Lawyers, Women Lawyers Mich., AAUW, Phi Alpha Delta. Recipient Pub. Service award Wayne State U., 1976. Office: 52d Dist/3d Div Dist Ct 530 Pine St Rochester MI 48063 Tel (313) 651-2400

VOBACH, WILLIAM HERMAN, b. Chgo., Dec. 25, 1929; A.B. magna cum laude, Oberlin Coll., 1951; J.D., U. Mich., 1954. Admitted to Mich. bar, 1954, Ind. bar, 1955; asso. firm Baker & Daniels, Indpls., 1954-55; asso. firm Locke, Reynolds, Boyd & Weisell, Indpls., 1955-63, partner, 1963-69, sr. partner, 1969—; arbitrator Am. Arbitration Assn., 1970—; mem. Marion County (Ind.) Variance Appeals Bd., 1976. Ward chmn., Lawrence Twp., Marion County Republican Party, 1972—. Mem. Am., Ind., Indpls. (treas. 1964, 65) bar assns., Internat. Assn. Ins. Counsel. Office: Suite 2120 One Indiana Sq Indianapolis IN 46204 Tel (317) 639-5534

VOCE, MARY FRANCES, b. Flint, Mich., Feb. 4, 1944; B.A., U. Mich., 1966; LL.B., U. Va., 1969; LL.M., N.Y. U., 1975. Admitted to N.Y. bar, 1970; asso. firm Breed Abbott & Morgan, N.Y.C., 1969—. Mem. Assn. Bar City N.Y., N.Y. State Bar Assn., Council N.Y. Law Assos. Home: 40 Fifth Ave New York City NY 10011 Office: 1 Chase Manhattan Plaza New York City NY 10005 Tel (212) 676-0800

VOGEL, CHARLES JOSEPH, b. Otter Tail County, Minn., Sept. 20, 1898; LL.B., J.D., U. Minn., 1923. Admitted to Minn. bar, 1923, N.D. bar, 1924; mem. firm Lewis & Bach, Minot, N.D., 1923-24; individual practice law, Fargo, N.D., 1925-34; mem. firm Vogel & Vogel, Fargo, 1934-36, firm Thorp, Wattam & Vogel, Fargo, 1937-41; judge U.S. Dist. Ct., N.D., 1941-55; judge U.S. 8th Circuit Ct., Fargo, 1954—, chief judge U.S. Ct. Appeals, 1965-67, sr. judge, 1967—. Bd. govs. Neuropsychiat. Inst., Fargo; chancellor Episcopal Ch., Diocese of N.D., 1946-65. Mem. Am. Bar Assn., Order of Coif, Phi Alpha Delta. Home: 1701 10th St S Fargo ND 58102 Office: PO Box 3006 Fargo ND 58102 Tel (701) 235-8736

VOGEL, DAVID AGNEW, b. New Castle, Ind., Dec. 27, 1925; B.S. in Chem. Engring., Purdue U., 1945, M.S., 1948; LL.B., Chgo.-Kent Coll. Law, 1951; postgrad. John Marshall Law Sch., 1953-54; M.B.A., Ill. Inst. Tech., 1977. Admitted to Ill. bar, 1951, U.S. Supreme Ct. bar, 1957; asso. firm Moore, Olson & Trexler, Chgo., 1951-53, firm Moore, Prangley & Clayton, Chgo., 1953-54; partner firm Prangley, Clayton & Vogel, Chgo., 1954-57, Smith, Baird & Clayton, Chgo., 1957-58, Prangley, Baird, Clayton, Miller & Vogel, Chgo., 1958-69, Prangley, Dithmar, Vogel, Sandler & Stotland, and predecessor, Chgo., 1969-77, Vogel, Dithmar, Stotland, Stratman & Levy, 1977—; partner Gurnee Apts. (Ill.), 1969—, Big Oaks Assos., Gurnee, 1970—; dir., sec. Gravi-Mechanics Co.; dir., treas. H.S.V. Corp., 1970-73; dir. Acoustic Fiber Sound Systems. Vice pres. Young Republican Orgn. Ill., 1953-55; trustee Chgo.-Kent Coll. Law, 1967-69, chmn. adv. bd., 1971—; trustee Kendall Coll., 1970—, vice chmn., 1971—. Fellow AAAS; mem. Am., Ill. trial lawyers assns., Am. Chem. Soc., Am., Ill., Chgo. bar assns., Am., Chgo. patent law assns., Am. Agrl. Econs. Assn., Sigma Xi, Tau Beta Pi, Omega Chi Epsilon, Phi Lambda Upsilon, Tau Kappa Epsilon, Phi Alpha Delta. Home: 1136 Long Valley Rd Glenview IL 60025 Office: 105 W Adams St Chicago IL 60603 Tel (312) FR2-2552

VOGEL, JOHN HENRY, b. Milw., Feb. 20, 1944; B.S. cum laude, Princeton, 1965; J.D., U. Mich., 1968. Admitted to N.Y. bar, 1970, D.C. bar, 1972, U.S. Supreme Ct. bar, 1973; asso. firm Lord, Day & Lord, N.Y.C., 1969-71; asso. firm Patton, Boggs & Blow, Washington, 1971-77, partner, 1977—; stagiaire European Econ. Community, Brussels, 1968-69. Mem. Bar Assn. City N.Y., Am., Internat. bar assns., Phi Delta Phi. Home: 9213 Farnsworth Dr Potomac MD 20854 Office: 1200 17th St NW Washington DC 20036 Tel (202) 223-4040

VOGEL, ROBERT, b. Coleharbor, N.D., Dec. 6, 1918; B.S., U. N.D., 1939; LL.B., Mpls. Coll. Law, 1942. Admitted to N.D. bar, 1943; practiced law in Garrison, N.D., 1943-54; state's atty. McLean County, N.D., 1948-54; U.S. atty., Fargo, 1954-61; mem. firm Vogel, Bair & Brown, Mandan, N.D., 1961-73; judge N.D. Supreme Ct., Bismarck, 1973—. Sec., Nonpartisan League State Exec. Com., 1952. Mem. N.D. Parole Bd., 1966-73. Fellow Am. Bar Found.; mem. Internat. Soc. Barristers, Am. Coll. Trial Lawyers. Home: 1201 Monte Dr Mandan ND 58554 Office: State Capitol Bismarck ND 58501 Tel (701) 224-2221

VOGEL, (THOMAS) WORTHINGTON, b. Oakland, Calif., Feb. 9, 1939; B.A., U. Calif., 1961; J.D., U. San Diego, 1969. Admitted to Calif., bar; comdr. JAGC, U.S. Navy Res., 1977—; asso. firm Vogel, Martin, Schwartz & Jacobs, San Jose, Calif., 197072; with Dist. Atty.'s Office, County of Fresno (Calif.), 1972—, team leader sexual assult unit, 1976—, team chief felony trial, 1975—; instr. Humphrey's Coll. Law, 1972-75, Fresno City Coll., 1976—. Mem. adv. bd. Fresno County Rape Counseling, 1976-77. Mem. Calif. Dsit. Atty.'s Assn., Phi Alpha Delta. Office: 1100 Van Ness St Fresno CA 93721 Tel (209) 488-3160

VOGEL, WILLIAM WHITTEN, b. Merion, Pa., Oct. 28, 1926; B.A., Haverford Coll., 1950; LL.B., U. Pa., 1953. Admitted to Pa. bar, 1955; asso. firm Wisler, Pearlstine, Talone & Gerber, Norristown, Pa., 1954-66; commr. Lower Merion Twp., 1958-64, Montgomery County (Pa.), Norristown, 1964-66; judge Ct. Common Pleas 38th Jud. Dist., Norristown, 1966—. Home: 315 Kent Rd Wynnewood PA 19096 Office: Court House Norristown PA 19404 Tel (215) 275-5000

VOHS, ROBERT ALLEN, b. Downey, Calif., Feb. 13, 1943; B.S. in Edn., Kans. State Tchrs. Coll., 1964; J.D., Washburn U., Topeka, Kans., 1969. Admitted to Kans. Supreme Ct. bar, 1969, U.S. Dist. Ct. bar for Dist. Kans., 1969, U.S. Ct. Appeals bar, 10th Circuit, 1970; law clk. to Hon. D.C. Hill, judge U.S. Ct. Appeals, 10th Circuit, 1969-71; asso. firms Wunsch & Wunsch, Kingman, Kans., 1971-73, Ralph Foster, Wichita, Kans., 1973—. Mem. Am., Kans., Wichita bar assns. Office: 201 N Market St PO Box 208 Wichita KS 67201 Tel (316) 263-0156

VOIGT, HARRY HOLMES, b. Louisville, Oct. 6, 1931; A.B., Miami U., Oxford, Ohio, 1953; LL.B., N.Y. U., 1956. Admitted to N.Y. bar, 1956, D.C. bar, 1956; asso. firm Cravath, Swaine & Moore, N.Y.C., 1956-57, 1960-69; partner firm LeBoeuf, Lamb, Leiby & MacRae, Washington, 1972—; asst. to chmn. FPC, Washington, 1970-72; mem. Adminstrv. Conf. U.S., 1974—. Mem. Am., Fed. Power, Fed., D.C. bar assns., Bar Assn. City N.Y. Office: 1757 N St NW Washington DC 20036 Tel (202) 457-7500

VOLINKATY, RICHARD ALVIN, b. New Ulm, Minn., Oct. 7, 1945; B.A. in Polit. Sci., Coll. St. Thomas, 1967; J.D., U. Mont., 1970. Admitted to Mont. bar, 1970, U.S. Dist. Ct. bar for Dist. Mont., 1970; legal intern Mont. Atty. Gen., Helena, 1969; atty. litigation unit Mont. Legal Services, Helena, 1970; staff atty. Missoula-Mineral County (Mont.) Legal Services, 1971-73; individual practice law, Missoula, 1973—; judge Missoula City Ct., 1973; speaker in field; participant nat. TV news programs. Mem. Am., Mont. bar assns., Am. Judicature Soc., Phi Delta Phi. Home: 618 Brooks St Missoula MT 59801 Office: 601 Western Bank Bldg Missoula MT 59801 Tel (406) 728-6691

VOLKER, DALE MARTIN, b. Lancaster, N.Y., Aug. 2, 1940; B.A., Canisius Coll., 1963; LL.B., State U. N.Y. at Buffalo, 1966. Admitted to N.Y. State bar, 1967; partner firm Volker & Murphy, 1967-72; individual practice law, Lancaster, 1972—; mem. Depew (N.Y.) Police Dept., 1963-72; mem. N.Y. State Assembly, 1972, N.Y. State Senate, 1975—. Chmn. Catholic Charities appeal St. Augustine's Parish, Depew; chmn. Depew United Fund Appeal. Mem. N.Y. State, Erie County bar assns., Canisius Alumni Assn. (past v.p.), Jr. C. of C. Named Outstanding Citizen, Depew Police Dept., 1977. Home: 31 Darwin Dr Depew NY 14043 Office: 63 Central Ave Lancaster NY 14086 Tel (716) 685-4805

VOLLMER, THOMAS EDWARD, b. Syracuse, N.Y., Jan. 27, 1942; B.A. in Math., U. Notre Dame, 1963; J.D., Harvard, 1966. Admitted to N.Y. bar, 1966; asso. firm Dewey, Ballantine, Bushby, Palmer & Wood, N.Y.C., 1969-76; asst. sec., gen. atty. Barnes Group, Inc., Bristol, Conn., 1976—; served as legal officer USNR, 1966-69. Mem. Am., N.Y. State bar assns. Office: 18 Main St Bristol CT 06010 Tel (203) 583-1331

VOLNER, JILL WINE, b. Chgo., May 5, 1943; B.S., U. Ill., 1964; J.D., Columbia U., 1968; LL.D. (hon.), Hood Coll., 1975. Admitted to N.Y. state bar, 1969, U.S. Supreme Ct. bar, 1974, D.C. bar, 1976; trial atty. U.S. Dept. Justice, Washington, 1969-73; asst. spl. prosecutor Watergate Spl. Prosecutor's Office, Washington, 1973-75; lectr. law Columbia U. Sch. Law, 1975, 76; asso. firm Fried, Frank, Harris, Shriver & Kampelman, Washington, 1975-77; gen. counsel U.S. Army, Washington, 1977—. Mem. D.C., Supreme Ct., Fed. bar assns., Nat. Women's Polit. Caucus. Recipient award for sustained superior performance U.S. Dept. Justice, 1972, meritorious award, 1973. Office: The Pentagon Washington DC 20310 Tel (202) 697-9235

VOLPE, EDWARD LESLIE, b. Canon City, Colo., Aug. 19, 1944; B.A., U. Colo., 1966, J.D., 1969. Admitted to Colo. bar, 1969; law clk. judge James K. Groves, Supreme Ct. State Colo., Denver, 1969-70; asso. firm William H. Erickson, Denver, 1970-71; asso., then partner firm Morrato, Gueck and Colantuno, Denver, 1971-72; individual practice law, Denver, 1972—. Mem. Denver, Colo., Am. bar assns., Order of Coif. Asso. editor U. Colo. Law Rev., 1968-69. Office: 1025 Capitol Life Center 16th & Grant Sts Denver CO 80203 Tel (303) 534-5121

VOLPE, MICHAEL JOSEPH, b. Schenectady, Jan. 7, 1944; A.B., Syracuse U., 1965, LL.B. (now J.D.) summa cum laude, 1967. Admitted to N.Y. bar, 1967; law asst. Appellate div. Supreme Ct. 3d Jud. Dept., Albany, N.Y., 1967, asst. dep. clk., 1970-72, dep. clk., chief law asst., 1972—; asso. firm Chernin & Gold, Binghamton, N.Y., 1968-70; asst. atty. Town of Rotterdam (N.Y.), 1971-74, atty., 1974-75. Bd. dirs. Rotterdam Boys' Club, 1972—; co-chmn. Schenectady County Cancer Crusade, 1975. Mem. N.Y., Schenectady County bar assns., Order of Coif, Phi Kappa Phi. Home: 31 Old Fort Ave Schenectady NY 12306 Office: Justice Bldg Empire State Plaza Albany NY 12223 Tel (518) 474-3632

VOLPERT, RICHARD SIDNEY, b. Cambridge, Mass., Feb. 16, 1935; B.A., Amherst Coll., 1956; LL.B., Columbia, 1959. Admitted to Calif. bar, 1960; asso. firm O'Melveny & Myers, Los Angeles, 1959-67, partner, 1967—. Sec., Los Angeles County Natural History Mus. Found., 1976, trustee, 1974—; bd. councilors U. So. Calif. Law Center, 1976—; bd. dirs., asst. sec. Jewish Fedn. Council Los Angeles, 1976—; bd. dirs., gov. U. Judaism, Los Angeles. Mem. Am., Los Angeles County (trustee 1968-70) bar assns., Calif. State Bar (editor jour. 1972-73), Los Angeles (editor jour. 1965-67, chmn. sect. real property 1974-75) bars. Home: 4001 Stansbury Ave Sherman Oaks CA 91423 Office: 611 W 6th St suite 3700 Los Angeles CA 90017 Tel (213) 620-1120

VOMBAUR, FRANCIS, b. Riverton, N.J., Sept. 17, 1908; B.A., Amherst Coll., 1929; LL.B., Harvard U., 1932. Admitted to N.Y. bar, 1934, U.S. Supreme Ct. bar, 1939, D.C. bar, 1948, Ill. bar, 1952; asso. firm Milbank, Tweed & Hope, N.Y.C., 1933-42; regional counsel for Am. and Panama, coordinator of Inter-Am. affairs Office of Coordinator of Inter-Am. Affairs, Emergency Office of Pres., 1942-46; individual practice law, Washington, 1946-53; gen. counsel Dept. Navy, Washington, 1953-60; partner firm Hensel & vom Baur, and successors, Washington, 1960-62, vom Baur, Coburn, Simmons & Turtle, Washington, 1962—; chmn. coordinating com. on model procurement code Am. Bar Assn., 1972—. Chmn. Republican Fin.

Com. D.C., 1975—. Mem. Fed. Bar Assn. (chmn. com. evaluation and long range planning 1976—, Exceptionally Distinguished Service award 1972). Author profl. pamphlets; contbr. articles to legal jours.; author: Federal Administrative Law, 2 vols., 1942; editor: Navy Contract Law, 2d edit., 1959. Office: 1700 K St NW Suite 1101 Washington DC 20006 Tel (202) 833-1420

VON BEROLDINGEN, DOROTHY, b. Chgo.; student Northwestern U.; A.A., U. Calif.; LL.B., U. San Francisco Sch. Law, 1954; J.D., San Francisco Law Sch., 1968. Admitted to Calif. bar, 1955; individual practice law, San Francisco, 1955—; mem. gov's. commn. on law of pre-emption, 1966-67; v.p. Econ. Opportunity Council, 1964-66; chmn. lawyers' com. San Francisco Bd. Suprs., 1972—. Mem. Civil Service Commn., City and County San Francisco, 1964-66; mem. San Francisco Bd. Suprs., 1966—, chmn. fin. com., 1968-76, chmn. planning and devel. ct., 1966-68; bd. dirs. Golden Gate Bridge, 1976—. Mem. State Bar Calif., Am. Bar Assn., San Francisco Lawyers Club, Queen's Bench, St. Thomas More Soc., Order of the Woolsack. Office: Ghirardelli Sq 900 Northpoint Chocolate Bldg 4th floor San Francisco CA 94109 Tel (415) 441-1211

VON BLUM, WARREN PAUL, b. Phila., Mar. 30, 1943; A.B., San Diego State U., 1964; J.D., U. Calif. at Berkeley, 1967. Admitted to Calif. bar, 1969; faculty dept. rhetoric U. Calif. at Berkeley, 1968-72, div. interdisciplinary and gen. studies, 1972—, vice-chmn. div., 1974—; lectr. U. Calif. at Davis Sch. Law, 1975. Mem. Calif. Bar Assn. Author: The Art of Social Conscience, 1976; also articles. Recipient Distinguished Teaching award U. Calif. at Berkeley, 1974. Home: 1801 Vine St Berkeley CA 94703 Office: Div Interdisciplinary and Gen Studies 301 Campbell Hall U Calif Berkeley CA 94720 Tel (415) 642-5640

VON CONRAD, GUNTER HEINRICH, b. Cologne, Germany, Nov. 18, 1934; ed. U. Bonn (W.Ger.), 1955-56, U. Cologne (W.Ger.), 1959-63; M.C.L., George Washington U., 1965. Admitted to D.C. bar, 1965, U.S. Customs Ct. bar, 1967, U.S. Supreme Ct. bar, 1969; grad. law clk. firm Arent, Fox, Kintner, Plotkin & Kahn, Washington, 1963-65, asso. firm 1963-67; asso. firm Barnes, Richardson & Colburn, N.Y.C., Chgo., Washington, 1967-74, partner, 1974—; adj. prof. law Georgetown U., 1971, Mem. council German Luthern Ch., Washington; chmn. Council Internat. Law and Fgn. Trade, 1970-73. Mem. D.C., Fed. bar assns. Recipient Distinguished Service award, 1971, Exceptionally Distinguished Service award, 1972 (both Fed. Bar Assn.); columnist Washington Jour., 1974—. Home: 5804 Greentree Rd Bethesda MD 20034 Office: 1819 H St NW Washington DC 20006 Tel (202) 659-8404

VON DER HEYDT, JAMES ARNOLD, b. Miles City, Mont., July 15, 1919; A.B., Albion (Mich.) Coll., 1942; J.D., Northwestern, 1951. Admitted to Alaska bar, 1951; pvt. law practice, Nome, 1953-59; judge superior ct., Juneau, Alaska, 1959-66; U.S. dist. judge, Alaska, 1966—, now chief judge; U.S. commr., Nome, Alaska, 1951—; U.S. atty. div. 2, Dist. Alaska, 1951-53; mem. Alaska Ho. of Reps., 1957-59. Pres. Anchorage Fine Arts Mus. Assn. Mem. Alaska Bar Assn. (mem. bd. govs., 1955-59, pres. 1959-60), Wilson Ornithologists Soc., Am. Judicature Soc., Sigma Nu, Phi Delta Phi. Address: PO Box 1080 Anchorage AK 99510*

VON GONTARD, PETER, b. St. Louis, Mar. 20, 1948; B.S. in Commerce, St. Louis U., 1970, J.D., 1973. Admitted to Mo. bar, 1973, Ill. bar, 1974, Fla. bar, 1975; asso. firm Coburn Croft Shepherd & Herzog, St. Louis, 1973—. Mem. Am., Mo., Ill., Fla., St. Clair County, E. St. Louis, Met. St. Louis bar assns. Office: One Mercantile Center Saint Louis MO 63101 Tel (314) 621-8575

VON KALINOWSKI, JULIAN ONESIME, b. St. Louis, May 19, 1916; A.B. cum laude, Miss. Coll., 1937; J.D. with honors, U. Va., 1940. Admitted to Va. bar, 1940, Calif. bar, 1946, U.S. Supreme Ct. bar, 1955; asso. firm Gibson, Dunn and Crutcher, Los Angeles, 1946-52, partner, 1953-62, sr. partner, 1962-70, mem. exec. com., 1970—; lectr. in field. Fellow Am. Coll. Trial Lawyers, Am. Bar Found.; mem. Internat., Am. (chmn. antitrust sect. 1972-73), Calif., Va. (asso.), Los Angeles County Bar Assns. Author text: Antitrust Laws and Trade Regulation, 1969-76; contbr. articles to legal jours.; recipient outstanding writer award Mathew Bender, 1972. Office: 515 S Flower St Los Angeles CA 90071 Tel (213) 408-7472

VON MEHREN, ROBERT BRANDT, b. Albert Lea, Minn., Aug. 10, 1922; A.B. summa cum laude, Yale, 1942; LL.B. magna cum laude, Harvard, 1946. Admitted to N.Y. bar, 1946, U.S. Supreme Ct. bar, 1954, U.S. Ct. Appeals 2d Circuit bar, 1950, 3d Circuit bar, 1953, D.C. Circuit bar, 1974; asso. firm Debevoise, Plimpton, Lyon & Gates, 1946-57, mem., 1957—; legal counsel Prep. Commn. of Internat. Atomic Energy Agy., 1956-57; cons. The Rand Corp., 1960-66, Hudson Inst. on Internat. Law Problems, 1962-66. Bd. dirs. Legal Aid Soc., N.Y.C., 1961-66, Axe Houghton Found., N.Y.C., 1965—; trustee La Fondation des Etats-Unis, Paris, 1966-70, Nightingale-Bamford Sch., N.Y.C.; trustee, v.p. Practicing Law Inst., N.Y.C., 1971—. Mem. Assn. Bar City N.Y., Internat. Law Assn., Council of Fgn. Relations, Am. Bar Assn., Am. Soc. Internat. Law, Union internationale des Avocats. Editor: Harvard Law Rev., 1943-46. Contbr. articles in field to profl. jours. Home: 925 Park Ave New York City NY 10028 Office: 299 Park Ave New York City NY 10017 Tel (212) 752-6400

VON OISTE, JAMES J., b. N.Y.C., Mar. 7, 1930; B.B.A., St. John's U., 1956, J.D., 1958. Admitted to N.Y. State bar, 1959, U.S. Supreme Ct. bar, 1964; asso. firm Good & Kent, Bklyn., 1959-62; asso. firm Fogerty & Schreiber, Bklyn., 1962-64; partner firm von Oiste & Carter, Port Jefferson, N.Y., 1968-76; atty. Village of Belle Terre, N.Y., 1967—. Bd. dirs. Mather Meml. Hosp., Port Jefferson, N.Y., 1970—; trustee Cedar Hill Cemetery Assn., Port Jefferson, 1970—. Mem. Am., N.Y. State, Suffolk County bar assns. Home: Cliff Rd Belle Terre NY 11777 Office: 505 Main St Port Jefferson NY 11777 Tel (516) 473-7676

VON UNWERTH, FREDERICK H., b. Austin, Tex., Jan. 21, 1941; B.A., Davidson Coll., 1965; J.D., U. Ga., 1969. Admitted to Ga. bar, 1971; law clk. to judge U.S. Ct. Appeals, N.Y.C., 1969-70; asso. firm Alston, Miller & Gaines, Atlanta, 1970-76, partner, 1976—. Mem. Am., Atlanta bar assns., Atlanta Lawyers Club. Notes editor Ga. Law Rev., 1968-69. Home: 191 Huntington Rd NE Atlanta GA 30309 Office: 1200 C & S National Bank Bldg Atlanta GA 30303 Tel (404) 588-0300

VOOGD, ANTHONIE MAARTEN, b. Antioch, Calif., Oct. 15, 1937; A.B., Stanford, 1959; J.D., Hastings Coll. Law, 1966. Admitted to Calif. bar, 1966; asso. firm Lawler Felix & Hall, Los Angeles, 1966-71, partner, 1971—. Mem. Am., Los Angeles County, Pasadena bar assns., State Bar Calif., Order of Coif. Office: 605 W Olympic Blvd Los Angeles CA 90015 Tel (213) 620-0060

VOORHEES, VERNON WIRT, II, b. Kansas City, Kans., Nov. 21, 1942; B.S. in Bus. Adminstrn., U. Kans., 1964, J.D., 1967. Admitted to Kans. bar, 1967, Mo. bar, 1968; atty. Bus. Men's Assurance Co. Am., Kansas City, Mo., 1967-70, counsel, 1970-76, asso. gen. counsel, 1976—; counsel, dir., sec. bd. BMA Securities Corp., 1971—, asst. sec., 1971-74, sec., 1974—; asst. sec. BMA Corp., 1974-75, counsel, 1975—; pres. BMA Properties, Inc., 1975, chmn. bd., 1975—; pres. BMA Real Estate Corp., 1975, chmn. bd., 1975—; judge Fairway (Kans.) Municipal Ct., 1974—. Mem. Kansas City Lawyer's Assn., Mo., Kans. bar assns., Phi Delta Phi, Sigma Chi. Home: 5726 Howe Dr Shawnee Mission KS 66205 Office: 1466 BMA Tower 700 Karnes Blvd Kansas City MO 64108 Tel (816) 753-8000

VOORN, JOHN CORNELL, b. Chgo., Feb. 24, 1944; A.B., Hope Coll., 1966; J.D., Valparaiso U., 1973. Admitted to Ill. bar, 1973, Ind. bar, 1975, Iowa bar, 1976, U.S. Supreme Ct. bar, 1976; asso. firm DeBruyn & Lockie, Palos Heights, Ill., 1973--. Mem. Ill. State, Ind. State, Iowa State, Chgo. bar assns. Office: 12000 S Harlem Ave Palos Heights IL 60463 Tel (312) 448-8118

VORBRICH, LYNN KARL, b. Iowa City, Iowa, Feb. 12, 1939; B.S., Iowa State U., 1960; J.D., U. Iowa, 1962. Admitted to Iowa bar, 1962, Ill. bar, 1962; asso. firm Seyfarth, Shaw, Fairweather & Geraldson, Chgo., 1962-64; partner firm Dickinson, Throckmorton, Parker, Mannheimer & Raife, Des Moines, 1964-69; asst. counsel Bankers Life Co., Des Moines, 1969-73; asso. gen. counsel Iowa Power & Light Co., Des Moines, 1973—; pres. Polk County Legal Aid Soc., 1971. Mem. Des Moines Human Rights Commn., 1968-71, chmn., 1970; bd. dirs. Iowa Children's and Family Services, 1966—, pres., 1970. Mem. Am., Fed. Power, Iowa bar assns. Recipient Outstanding Young Alumni award Iowa State U., 1973. Home: 1085 44th St Des Moines IA 50311 Office: PO Box 657 Des Moines IA 50303 Tel (515) 281-2471

VORRASI, KENNETH JOHN, b. Rochester, N.Y., Oct. 30, 1943; B.S. in Biology, St. Bonaventure U., 1966; J.D., Cath. U. Am., 1969. Admitted to N.Y. StatState bar, 1970, U.S. Supreme Ct. bar, 1974; asso. firm Salamone, Kurlander & Siracuse, Rochester, 1970-73; asst. pub. defender Monroe County (N.Y.), 1972-74; asso. firm Biernbaum & Vorrasi, Rochester, 1973-76; individual practice law, Rochester, 1976—. Mem. N.Y. State, Monroe County (justice ct. and criminal justice com.) bar assns. Home: 312 Rhinecliff Dr Rochester NY 14618 Office: 550 Executive Office Bldg 36 W Main St Rochester NY 14614 Tel (716) 232-7785

VOSBEIN, ROBERT ALLAN, b. New Orleans, Aug. 31, 1943; B.A., Tulane U., 1965, J.D., 1967. Admitted to La. bar, 1967; asso. firm Adams and Reese, New Orleans, 1967-73, partner, 1973—. Mem. La. Trial Lawyers Assn., Maritime Law Assn., Maritime Law Soc., La., New Orleans assns. def. counsel. Office: 4500 One Shell Sq New Orleans LA 70139 Tel (504) 581-3234

VOSHELL, JACK G., b. Kingsdown, Kans., Sept. 3, 1920; A.B., Washburn U., 1947, J.D., 1949. Admitted to Kans. bar, Ida. bar, Fed. bar; asso. firm Van Riper, Williams, & Hughes, Dodge City, Kans., 1949-50; individual practice law, Idaho Falls, Idaho, 1953-68; police judge, Idaho Falls, 1957-59; prosecuting atty., Bonneville County, Idaho, 1963-69; mem. firm Voshell & Wright, Idaho Falls, 1969—. Mem. City Idaho Falls Civil Service Commn., 1974—. Mem. Idaho, Am. bar assns. Home: 900 Koster St Idaho Falls ID 83401 Office: 598 N Capital St Idaho Falls ID 83401 Tel (208) 523-4433

VOSOBA, JOE THOMAS, b. Saline County, Nebr., Aug. 25, 1929; B.S., U. Nebr., 1951, J.D., 1952. Admitted to Nebr. bar, 1952; partner firm Steinacher & Vosoba, Wilber, Nebr., 1954—, Crete, Nebr., 1971—; dep. Saline County atty., 1954-58. Former pres. Wilber C. of C.; former chmn. Wilber Housing Authority; chmn. Wilber Library Bd., 1966—; former pres. Saline County Hist. Soc.; former exec. bd. Nebr. Hist. Soc.; Nebr. state senator, 1958-62, Mem. Am., Nebr. bar assns. (mem. exec. council 1972-76, now mem. ho. dels. and exec. com.). Office: 302 S Wilson St Wilber NE 68465 Tel (402) 821-2221

VOSS, CLAIR HORTON, b. Antigo, Wis., Sept. 16, 1920; Ph.B., Marquette U., 1946, LL.B., J.D., 1948. Admitted to Wis. bar, 1948; practiced in Waukesha, 1948-53; asst. dist. atty. Waukesha County, 1953-59; judge Wis. 22d Circuit Ct., 1960—; mem. Bd. Wis. Circuit Judges, Bd. Wis. Criminal Ct. Judges. Chmn. Waukesha County chpts. ARC, 1955-58, March of Dimes, 1961, NCCJ, 1962-65, Cath. Charities, 1970, Family Service Assn., 1961-65. Mem. Waukesha County, Wis., Am. bar assns., Wis. Trial Judges Assn. (pres. 1976—). Decorated Purple Heart, Navy Cross. Office: 515 W Moreland Blvd Waukesha WI 53186 Tel (414) 544-8288

VOSS, F. JAMES, b. Duluth, Minn., May 18, 1932; B.A., Carleton Coll., 1954; LL.B., U. Minn., 1961. Admitted to N.Y. bar, 1962, Colo. bar, 1963; asso. firm White & Case, N.Y.C., 1961-62, firm Dowson, Nable, Sherman & Howard, Denver, 1963-65; individual practice law, Denver, 1965—. Commr. elections City and County of Denver, 1967-75. Home: 876 S Franklin Denver CO 80209 Office: 666 Sherman Denver CO 80203 Tel (303) 837-0201

VOSS, GEORGE, b. Hutchinson, Kans., Oct. 25, 1930; B.S. in Accounting, Kans. U., 1952, LL.B., 1955. Admitted to Kans. bar, 1955; atty. Office Chief Counsel Treasury Dept., Dallas, 1957-59, New Orleans, 1959-61; asso. firm Van Riper, Williams, Hughes, & Larson, Dodge City, Kans., 1961-62; partner firm Williams, Larson, Voss, Strobel & Estes, and predecessors, Dodge City, Kans., 1962—. Bd. dirs. Boot Hill Mus., Inc., Dodge City; bd. trustees St. Mary of the Plains Coll., Dodge City. Mem. Ford Gray County, Southwest, Kans., Am. bar assns., Am. Inst. C.P.A.'s, Tex. Soc., Kans. (asso.) socs. C.P.A.'s, Sigma Phi Ipsilon, Delta Theta Phi. Recipient Distinguished Service award, Jaycees, 1966. Home: 2020 Hart St Dodge City KS 67801 Office: PO Box 39 Dodge City KS 67801 Tel (316) 225 4168

VOSS, ROBERT CHARLES, b. La Grange, Ill., May 10, 1928; B.A., Ind. U., 1950, J.D., 1960. Admitted to Ind. bar, 1960, Minn. bar, 1964; contract adminstr. Allison div. Gen. Motors Corp., Indpls., 1956-62; counsel Honeywell, Inc., Mpls., 1963—. Mem. Planning Commn., Coon Rapids, Minn., 1966-67, Charter Commn., 1969-74, Capital Improvements Com., 1968-72; mayor, Coon Rapids, 1968-72; dist. chmn. Boy Scouts Am., 1972-73; pres. Coon Rapids Athletic Assn., 1973—. Mem. Anoka County Bar Assn. Note editor Ind. Law Jour., 1959. Home: 10820 Mississippi Blvd Coon Rapids MN 55433 Office: Honeywell Plaza Minneapolis MN 55413 Tel (612) 870-2891

VOSS, ROBERT CLAYTON, b. Madison, Wis., Sept. 21, 1920; Ph.D., U. Wis., 1947, J.D., 1948. Admitted to Wis. bar, 1948; since practiced in Madison, individual practice law, 1948-68; partner firm Voss, Nesson & Koberstein, 1968-75; partner firm Voss, Nesson, Koberstein, Erbach & Voss, 1976—. Pres. Cath. Social Services, Inc., 1975. Mem. Am., Wis., Dane County bar assns., West Madison Optomist Club (pres. 1958-59), Optomist Internat. (lt. gov., 1960-61), Black Hawk Country Club (pres. 1967), Greater Madison C. of C. (pres. 1976). Home: 1214 Edgehill Dr Madison WI 53705 Office: PO Box 1348 Madison WI 53701 Tel (608) 257-4471

VOTOLATO, ARTHUR NICHOLAS, b. Johnston, R.I., Sept. 18, 1900; law degree Northeastern U., 1924. Admitted to R.I. bar, 1926; solicitor Town of Johnston, 1934-39; clerk 8th dist. ct., Johnston, also acting judge. Pres. R.I. Assn. Mental Health, 1959-60. Mem. R.I., Am. bar assns. Contbr. articles to legal jours. Home: 83 S Hill Dr Cranston RI 02920 Office: 1363 Plainfield St Johnston RI 02919 Tel (401) 944-2770

VOTOLATO, ARTHUR NICHOLAS, JR., b. Providence, Aug. 20, 1930; A.B., U. R.I., 1953; LL.B., Boston U., 1956. Admitted to R.I. bar, 1956; asso. firm Votolato & Votolato, Providence, 1956-68; chief spl. counsel R.I. Dept. Pub. Works Freeway Property Acquisition Coordinator, 1963-68; U.S. Bankruptcy judge Dist. R.I., Providence, 1968—; mem. com. standards of jud. conduct Nat. Conf. Spl. Ct. Judges; gov., 1st Circuit rep. Nat. Conf. Bankruptcy Judges. Bd. dirs. R.I. Dance Repertory Co., Urban League R.I. Mem. Am., R.I. bar assns., Am. Judicature Soc., Comml. Law League Am. Home: 12 Sefton Dr Cranston RI 02905 Office: US Courthouse Providence RI 02903 Tel (401) 528-4477

VOYLES, JAMES EVERETT, b. Owensboro, Ky., May 10, 1943; B.S., Brescia Coll., 1965; M.A., U. Miss., 1967; B.C.L., Atlanta Law Sch., 1969; Ph.D., N. Tex. State U., 1973. Admitted to Ga. bar, 1970; asst. prof. U. South Ala., Mobile, 1969-74; asso. prof. Spring Hill Coll., Mobile, 1974-75; partner firm Voyles & Lankford, Mobile, 1975—. Mem. AAUP, Am. Law Found., Am. Polit. Sci. Assn. Contbr. articles to profl. jours. Home: 1102 Savannah St Mobile AL 36604 Office: 951 Government St Suite 304 Mobile AL 36604 Tel (205) 433-1997

VOYLES, JAMES HUGH, JR., b. Indpls., Jan. 3, 1943; B.S., Ill. Coll., Jacksonville, 1965; J.D., Ind. U., 1968. Admitted to Ind. bar, 1968, U.S. Supreme Ct. bar, 1973; dep. atty. gen. State of Ind., 1968-69; mem. firm Ober, Symmes, Cardwell, Voyles & Zahn, Indpls., 1968—. Mem. Ind. State, Indpls. bar assns., Nat. Assn. Criminal Def. Lawyers. Home: 7330 Hampstead Ln Indianapolis IN 46256 Office: 115 N Penn St Suite 1500 Indianapolis IN 46204 Tel (317) 632-4463

VOZEOLAS, ANDREW DENNIS, b. Alexandria, Va., Dec. 5, 1913; LL.B., Cath. U., 1938. Admitted to D.C. bar, 1938; individual practice law, Washington, 1938—; atty. Office Alien Property, Dept. Justice, Washington, 1952-53. Pres. bd. trustees St. Sophia Greek Orthodox Cathedral, Washington, 1972. Mem. Bar Assn. D.C., D.C. Bar. Recipient Gold Cross, King George I of Greece, 1955. Home: 2759 Unicorn Ln NW Washington DC 20015 Office: 910 17th St NW Washington DC 20006 Tel (202) 296-1930

VROOMAN, EDWARD A., b. Poughkeepsie, N.Y., Nov. 25, 1939; B. Mgmt. Engring., Rensselaer Poly. Inst., 1961; J.D., Duke, 1964; LL.M. in Taxation, N.Y. U., 1968. Admitted to N.Y. Supreme Ct. bar, 1964; partner firm Olwine, Connelly, Chase, O'Donnell & Weyher, N.Y.C., 1964—. Mem. Assn. Bar City N.Y. Author Bur. Nat. Affairs portfolios; contbr. articles to legal jours. Home: Travis Corners Rd Garrison NY 10524 Office: 299 Park Ave New York City NY 10017 Tel (212) 688-0400

VUAGNIAUX, EARL LOUIS, b. Edwardsville, Ill., Sept. 17, 1931; B.S. in Commerce, St. Louis U., 1953, J.D., 1956. Admitted to Mo. bar, 1956, Ill. bar, 1956, U.S. Supreme Ct. bar, 1971; practiced in Edwardsville, 1957—; partner firm Judge & Vuagniaux, 1957-60, Judge, Vuagniaux & Warnock, 1960-62, Vuagniaux & Metzger, 1968-74; individual practice law, 1974—; magistrate, Edwardsville, 1957-65; dir. Specialized Services, Inc., Alton, Ill. Mem. adv. bd. St. Joseph's Hosp., Highland, Ill.; mem. spl. edn. adv. com. Madison County (Ill.). Mem. Ill., Madison County bar assns. Recipient ann. appreciation award for outstanding personal service Lewis and Clark Council Exceptional Children, 1976. Home: 1 Osage Dr Edwardsville IL 62025 Office: 1 18 Saint Louis St Edwardsville IL 62025 Tel (618) 656-3355

VUCKOVICH, WALTER STEPHEN, b. Clune, Pa., May 14, 1946; B.A., Pa. State U., 1968; J.D., Georgetown U., 1971. Admitted to Pa. bar, 1972; individual practice law, Indiana, Pa., 1971—; pub. defender, Indiana County, 1972-75, asst. dist. atty., 1975-76, dist. atty., 1976—. Bd. dirs. Indiana County Sheltered Workshop, Indiana After Sch. Center, Inc., Laurel Legal Services Inc. Mem. Am., Pa. Indiana County bar assns., Pa. Dist. Attys. Assn., Pa. State Alumni Assn. Home: 166 Meadowood Rd Indiana PA 15701 Office: 840 Philadelphia St Indiana PA 15701 Tel (412) 349-2255

WAAS, GEORGE LEE, b. N.Y.C., July 12, 1943; B.J., U. Fla., 1965; J.D., Fla. State U., 1970. News reporter Palm Beach (Fla.) Post-Times, 1966, Ft. Lauderdale (Fla.) News, 1966-67; asst. atty. gen. and legal research asst., Fla., 1968, 69-70; admitted to Fla. bar, 1970, U.S. Supreme Ct. bar, 1973; since practiced in Tallahassee, Fla., staff atty. Fla. League of Cities, 1970-71; asst. to sec. of commerce and dir. of labor Fla. Dept. Commerce, 1971-73; asso. dir. continuing legal edn. The Fla. Bar, 1973-74; asst. dean, instr. Fla. State U. Coll. Law, 1974-75; adminstrv. and appellate atty. Fla. Dept. Transp., 1975-77; staff atty. Fla. Dept. Health and Rehabilitative Services, 1977—; sr. editorial cons. Fla. Legal Services, Inc. Bd. dirs. Capital Tiger Bay Club, 1974-77; chmn. Leon County Bi-racial Com., 1974-75. Mem. Am., Fla. (pres. 1976-77), Tallahassee bar assns., Am. Judicature Soc., The Fla. Bar, Omicron Delta Kappa. Recipient pub. speaking awards Toastmasters Internat.; contbr. articles to legal jours. Home: 400 Collinsford Rd Tallahassee FL 32301 Office: Suite 406 Bldg 1 1323 Winewood Blvd Tallahassee FL 32301 Tel (904) 488-2381

WACHSMUTH, ROBERT WILLIAM, b. Crowell, Tex., Jan. 20, 1942; B.A., U. Tex. at Austin, 1965, J.D., 1966; postgrad. U. Tex. at San Antonio, 1975-76. Admitted to Tex. bar, 1966; served as judge adv. USMC, 1965-69; appointed mil. judge, 1969; asso. firm Foster, Lewis, Langley, Gardner & Banack, San Antonio, 1969-73; partner firm Johnson, Johnston, Bowlin, Wachsmuth & Vives, San Antonio, 1973—; counsel H.B. Zachry Co., San Antonio, 1973—; teaching quizmaster U. Tex. Sch. Law, 1965-66; instr. real estate law San Antonio Coll., 1972-73. Bd. dirs. Halfway House San Antonio, 1974—. Mem. San Antonio, Am., Tex. bar assns., San Antonio Young Lawyers Assn., Phi Delta Phi, Sigma Nu. Home: 13210 Hill Forest St San Antonio TX 78230 Office: 1708 Tower Life Bldg San Antonio TX 78205 Tel (512) 223-4061

WADDEY, IRA CLINTON, JR., b. Franklin, Tenn., Aug. 5, 1942; B. Aerospace Engring., Auburn U., 1965; J.D., Georgetown U., 1970. Admitted to Va. bar, 1970, Tenn. bar, 1971, D.C. bar, 1971; law clk. U.S. Ct. Appeals 6th Circuit, Nashville, 1970-71; asso. firm Arent, Fox, Kintner, Plotkin & Kahn, Washington, 1971-73, Willis & Knight,

Nashville, 1974-76; partner firm Willis, Knight, Grace & Waddey, Nashville, 1977—. Dir. Rochelle Tng. and Habilitation Center, Nashville, 1975-77; pres. Greater Nashville Auburn Assn., 1976-77. Mem. Am., Tenn., Nashville (sec.-treas. 1975-76) bar assns., Am. Patent Lawyers Assn. Home: 152 Blackburn Ave Nashville TN 37205 Office: 700 Union St Nashville TN 37219 Tel (615) 259-9600

WADDICK, WILLIAM ANTHONY, b. Chgo., Dec. 7, 1931; B.C.S. cum laude, U. Notre Dame, 1957; J.D., Ind. U., 1961. Admitted to Ind. bar, 1961; asso. firm Kunz and Kunz, Indpls., 1961-63, partner, 1963—. Pres., St. Thomas More Soc., 1970-71, mem., 1962—. Mem. Ind. State, Indpls. bar assns., Ind. Trial Lawyers Assn., Ind. Jaycees, Phi Delta Phi. Co-author: Eminent Domain in Indiana, 1976. Home: 2 Songbird Ct Carmel IN 46032 Office: 320 N Meridian St Indianapolis IN 46204 Tel (317) 632-6367

WADDILL, GREGG COOPER, III, b. Key West, Fla., Dec. 20, 1944; B.B.A., U. Tex., Austin, 1967, J.D., 1970, M.P.H., U. Tex. Health Sci. Center at Houston Sch. Pub. Health, 1971. Admitted to Tex. bar, 1970; grad. work/study fellow World Campus Afloat, fall 1967; Rotary fellow, mem. Group Study Exchange Team, Australia, fall 1971; campaign coordinator Houston/Harris County for Senator John Tower, 1971-72; legal cons. World Fedn. Med. Edn., 1972; cons. to dir. South-North Center for Inter-Am. Health Studies U. Tex. Health Sci. Center at Houston Sch. Pub. Health, 1972-74, Am. Pub. Health Assn., 1974; dep. chief exec. officer, legal counsel Fedn. World Health Founds., Geneva, 1974-76; exec. dir. World Health Found. U.S.A., 1972—. Mem. N.Am. Com. for Health Edn.; mem. Am. Pub. Health Assn. Task Force on Voluntary Health Orgns. Mem. Inter-Am., Am. (bd. editors Environ. Quality Newsletter 1973-74), Houston bar assns., State Bar Tex., Fedn. Pub. Health Student Assns. (exec. bd. 1972). Named Outstanding Young Man of Houston, 1973; River Oaks Rotary fellow, fall 1967; U. Tex. Sch. Pub. Health Cross-Cultural Community Health Studies grantee, 1970-71. Home: 5309 Pagewood St Houston TX 77056 Office: 914 Main St 1137 C of C Bldg of C Houston TX 77002 Tel (713) 659-4938

WADE, EDWIN LEE, b. Yonkers, N.Y., Jan. 26, 1932; B.S., Columbia, 1954; M.A., U. Chgo., 1956; J.D., Georgetown U., 1965. Admitted to Ill. bar, 1965; fgn. service officer U.S. State Dept., 1956-57; mktg. analyst Chrysler Internat., Geneva, 1957-61; intelligence officer CIA, 1961-63; industry analyst ITC, 1963-65; gen. atty. Universal Oil Products Co., Des Plaines, Ill., 1965-72; corporate atty. Amsted Industries, Inc., Chgo., 1972-73; chief counsel, Ill. Dept. Gen. Services, Springfield, 1973-75; sr. atty. U.S. Gypsum Co., Chgo., 1975—. Mem. Am., Ill., Chgo. bar assns., Am. Soc. Internat. Law. Home: 434 Mary Ln Crystal Lake IL 60014 Office: 101 S Wacker Dr Chicago IL 60014 Tel (312) 321-3994

WADE, GEORGE JOSEPH, b. N.Y.C., Mar. 3, 1938; A.B., Fordham Coll., 1959; LL.B., Harvard, 1962. Admitted to N.Y. bar, 1963, U.S. Supreme Ct. bar, 1970; asso. firm Cravath, Swaine & Moore, N.Y.C., 1963-70; asso. firm Shearman & Sterling, N.Y.C., 1970-72, partner, 1972—. Mem. Assn. Bar City N.Y. (sec. judiciary com. 1974—; mem. young lawyers com. 1965-70, chmn. 1968-70, sec. 1967-68), Am. (sec. com. war powers pres. 1971—), N.Y. (chmn. antitrust sect. 1975) bar assns. Office: Shearman & Sterling 53 Wall St New York City NY 10005 Tel (212) 483-1000

WADE, JAMES A., b. S.I., N.Y., May 9, 1937; B.A., Yale, 1959; LL.B., U. Va., 1962. Admitted to Conn. bar, 1962; served with JAGC, USN, 1962-66; asso. firm Robinson, Robinson & Cole, Hartford, Conn., 1966—; counsel majority leadership Conn. Ho. of Reps., 1968-72; mem. Conn. Com. on Structure of State Govt., 1976. Mem. Simsburg (Conn.) Bd. Selectmen, 1969-71. Mem. Conn., Hartford County, Am. bar assns. Home: 39 Pinnacle Mountain Rd Simsbury CT 06070 Office: 799 Main St Hartford CT 06103 Tel (203) 278-0700

WADE, JAMES EDWARD, b. Columbia, Mo., Sep. 10, 1928; B.A., B.J., U. Mo., 1950; J.D., U. San Diego, 1967. Admitted to Mo. bar, 1969, U.S. Dist. Ct. Western Dist. Mo. bar, 1969; asso. firm Howard E. Major, Columbia, Mo., 1969-72; individual practice law, Columbia, 1972; prof. law Coll. Law, Western State U., 1974—, asst. dean San Diego campus, 1976—. Home: 4738 Norma Dr San Diego CA 92115 Office: Western State Univ Coll Law 1333 Front St San Diego CA 92101 Tel (714) 231-0300

WADE, JEPTHA HOMER, b. Cleve., Dec. 26, 1924; B.S., Mass. Inst. Tech., 1946; LL.B., Harvard, 1950. Admitted to Mass. bar, 1951, Fed. bar, 1953; asso. firm Kenway, Jenney, Witter & Hildreth, Boston, 1953-55; asso. firm Choate, Hall & Stewart, Boston, 1956-60, partner, 1960—. Home: 251 Old Billerica Rd Bedford MA 01730 Office: 28 State St Boston MA 02109 Tel (617) 227-5020

WADE, JEROME S., b. Clayton, Mo., Sept. 29, 1947; B.A., U. Mo., 1969, J.D., 1972. Admitted to Mo. bar, 1972; individual practice law, 1972-74; asst. pub. defender Mo. 23d Jud. Circuit, 1972-74; gen. counsel Clayton Brokerage Co., of St. Louis, Inc., Clayton, Mo., 1975—. Mem. Clayton Health Commn., Clayton Landscaping-Beautification Commn. Mem. St. Louis County, Am., Jefferson County (Mo.), Mo. bar assns., Nat. Inst. Trial Advocacy. Home: 17 Crestwood Dr Clayton MO 63105 Office: suite 300 7701 Forsyth Blvd Clayton MO 63105 Tel (314) 727-8000

WADE, JOHN WEBSTER, b. Little Rock, Mar. 2, 1911; B.A., U. Miss., 1932, J.D., 1934; LL.M., Harvard, 1935, S.J.D., 1942. Admitted to Miss. bar, 1934, Tenn. bar, 1947; asst. prof. U. Miss., 1936-38, asso. prof., 1938-40, prof., 1940-47; prof. law Vanderbilt U., 1947—, dean Sch. Law, 1952-72, Distinguished prof., 1971—; vis. prof. U. Tex., 1946-47, Cornell U., fall 1972; Meyer Research prof. Columbia, 1964-65; Earl F. Nelson prof. U. Mo., Columbia, 1976-77; reporter Restatement (Second) of Torts, 1970—; mem. Tenn. Uniform Laws Commn., 1961—. Trustee Southwestern-at-Memphis Coll. Mem. Am., Tenn., Miss., Nashville, N.Y.C. bar assns., Am. Law Inst. (council 1960-70), Am. Judicature Soc., Assn. Am. Law Schs. (exec. com. 1957), Order of Coif (nat. pres. 1973-76). Author: Cases and Materials on Restitution, 2d edit., 1966; (with others) Cases and Materials on Legal Methods, 1969; Cases and Materials on Torts, 6th edit., 1976; contbr. articles to legal jours. Home: 4204 Farrar Ave Nashville TN 37215 Office: Vanderbilt U Sch of Law Nashville TN 37240 Tel (615) 322-2614

WADE, MICHAEL MAYS, b. Phila., Sept. 29, 1942; B.A., So. Meth. U., 1964, J.D., 1967. Admitted to Tex. bar, 1967; served with JAGC, USNR, 1968-71; partner firm Curtis & Wade, Belton, Tex., 1971—; city atty. City of Belton; mem. grievance prosecuting com. Dist. 8B State Bar Tex.; dir. Peoples Nat. Bank of Belton. Chmn. Council ministries 1st United Methodist Ch. of Belton, 1975—. Mem. Beil, Mill and Lampassas Counties Bar Assn. (v.p.). Home: 124 Turtle Creek St Belton TX 76513 Office: 412 Central St Belton TX 76513 Tel (817) 939-3553

WADE, ROBERT E., b. Orange, N.J., Mar. 27, 1946; B.S. in Econs., U. Pa., 1968; J.D., N.Y. U., 1971. Admitted to N.J. bar, 1971, U.S. Supreme Ct. bar, 1975; law clk. to judge, Morristown, N.J., 1971-72; individual practice law, Belvidere, N.J., 1972—; county counsel Warren County (N.J.), 1976—; mem. panel on med. malpractice N.J. Supreme Ct., 1976—. Mem. Am., N.J., Warren County bar assns. Office: PO Box 215 Belvidere NJ 07823 Tel (201) 475-3131

WADE, ROBERT J., JR., b. Martinsville, Ind., Oct. 24, 1938; B.S., Ind. U., 1960, J.D., U. Mich., 1963; LL.M., So. Meth. U., 1968. Admitted to Ind. bar, 1965, Ohio bar, 1972; asst. prof. law Tex. Tech. U., 1964-68; asso. prof., chmn. dept. bus. Wright State U., 1968-71; prof. law, asso. dean Capital U., 1971—; spl. counsel city attys. office, Columbus, Ohio, 1972-73. Dir. Camp Riley, Martinsville, Inc., 1964-76. Mem. Am., Ind., Ohio, Columbus bar assns. Home: 2139 Keltonshire Ave Columbus OH 43229 Office: Capital U Law Sch Columbus OH 43209 Tel (614) 236-6395

WADE, WILLIAM JAMES, b. Bloomington, Ill., June 1, 1906; LL.B., George Washington U. Admitted to D.C. bar, 1930, Ill. bar, 1931, Pa. bar, 1933, Ga. bar, 1949, U.S. Supreme Ct., 1963; spl. agt. IRS, Pa., 1935-68; asst. regional counsel IRS, Atlanta, 1960-68; asso. firm Smith Cohen Ringel Kohler & Martin, Atlanta, 1968—. Mem. Fed., Am., Ga., Atlanta bar assns., Atlanta Lawyers Club, Old Warhorse Lawyers Club. Home: 4645 Club Circle NE Atlanta GA 30319 Office: 2400 First National Bank Tower Atlanta GA 30303 Tel (404) 658-1200

WADKOWSKI, GERALD PAUL, b. Braddock, Pa., Jan. 10, 1938; B.A., Duquesne U., 1959, LL.B., Cleve. Marshall Law Sch., 1963. Admitted to Ohio bar, 1964; atty. examiner Pub. Utilities Commn. Ohio, 1964-69, asst. atty. gen., 1969-70; individual practice law, Columbus, Ohio, 1970—. Scout master troop 8 local Council Boy Scouts Am., 1971—. Mem. Ohio Bar Assn., Ohio (v.p.), Am. motor carrier lawyers assns. Home: 2832 Maryland Ave Columbus OH 43209 Office: 85 E Gay St Columbus OH 43215 Tel (614) 221-6771

WADLEIGH, WINTHROP, b. Milford, N.H., Jan. 23, 1902; A.B. magna cum laude, Dartmouth Coll., 1923; J.D., Harvard U., 1927. Admitted to N.H. bar, 1927, U.S. Supreme Ct. bar, 1931; asso. Upton & Donovan, Concord, 1927-29; asst. atty. gen. N.H., Concord, 1929-31; partner firm Wadleigh, Starr, Peters, Dunn & Kohls, Manchester, N.H., 1931—; mem. N.H. Commn. Human Rights, 1967-73. Trustee White Pines Coll., Chester, N.H., 1971—; bd. dirs. Fund for Animals, Inc., N.Y.C., 1966—; treas., bd. dirs. ACLU, N.Y.C., 1969-75. Mem. N.H., Manchester, Am. bar assns. Recipient Brotherhood award N.H. chpt. Nat. Conf. Christians and Jews, 1970. Home: Walnut Hill Chester NH 03036 Office: 95 Market St Manchester NH 03101 Tel (603) 669-4140

WADLINGTON, WALTER JAMES, b. Biloxi, Miss., Jan. 17, 1931; A.B., Duke, 1951; LL.B., Tulane U., 1954. Admitted to La. bar, 1954, Va. bar, 1965; asso. firm Wisdom & Stone, New Orleans, 1954-55, 57-58; served to capt. Judge Adv. Gen.'s Corps, U.S. Army, 1955-58; Fulbright scholar, tutor U. Edinburgh (Scotland), 1959-60; asst. prof. Tulane U. Law Sch., New Orleans, 1960-62; faculty mem. U. Va., Charlottesville, 1962—, James Madison prof., 1970—. Editor-in-chief Tulane Law Rev., 1953-54; author: (with M. Paulsen, J. Goebel) Cases and Materials on Domestic Relations, 1970, 2d edit., 1974, (with M. Paulsen) Statutory Materials on Family Law, 1970, 2d edit., 1974; contbr. articles legal periodicals. Home: 1620 Keith Valley Rd Charlottesville VA 22901 Office: U of Virginia Law School Charlottesville VA 22901 Tel (804) 924-7025

WADSWORTH, CHARLES YOUNG, b. Winchester, Mass., Jan. 16, 1911; A.B., Harvard, 1932, LL.B., 1935. Admitted to Mass. bar, 1935; mem. firm Hill & Barlow, Boston, 1935—, partner, 1938—; dir. Barnstable Water Co., Boston, treas., 1962—; dir. Dorr Woolen Co., Newport, N.H., treas. 1947—; dir. Edgartown Water Co., Boston, Gen. Engring & Constrn. Corp., Boston, Dorr Fabrics, Inc., Pinnacle Mfg. Corp. Moderator, Town of Lincoln, Mass., 1961-67; trustee Longfellow House. Mem. Am. (ho. of dels. 1976—), Mass. (ho. of dels. 1967—, treas. 1969-74, pres. 1975-76) bar assns., Am. Law Inst., Am. Coll. Probate Counsel. Author: (with Benjamin A. Trustman, Richard B. Johnson) Town Meeting Time, 1962; asst. editor: Rule Against Perpetuities (Gray), 1942; editor Settlement of Estates (Newhall), 4th edit., 1958—; Massachusetts Trust and Will Manual, 1967. Home: Sandy Pond Rd Lincoln MA 01773 Office: 225 Franklin St Boston MA 02110 Tel (617) 423-6200

WADSWORTH, H. WAYNE, b. Logan, Utah, Oct. 12, 1930; B.S., Utah State U., 1952; J.D., George Washington U., 1959. Admitted to D.C. bar, 1959, Utah bar, 1961, U.S. Supreme Ct. bar, 1973; partner firm Hanson, Wadsworth & Russon, Salt Lake City, 1961—; spl. agt. FBI, 1959-60. Active Ch. Jesus Christ of Latter-day Saints, Boy Scouts Am. Mem. Am., Utah bar assns., Fedn. Ins. Counsel, Am. Arbitration Assn. Home: 4393 Covecrest Dr Salt Lake City UT 84117 Office: 702 Kearns Bldg Salt Lake City UT 84117 Tel (801) 359-7611

WAECHTER, THOMAS CHARLES, b. Detroit, Feb. 21, 1942; A.B., Ohio Wesleyan U., 1964; J.D., Northwestern U., 1967. Admitted to Ohio bar, 1967; law clk. U.S. Dist. Ct., No. Dist. Ohio, 1967-69; asso. firm Bieser, Greer & Landis, Dayton, Ohio, 1969-73; atty. The Goodyear Tire & Rubber Co., Akron, Ohio, 1973—. Mem. Ohio, Akron bar assns. Home: 3110 Mayfield Rd Silver Lake OH 44224 Office: 1144 E Market St Akron OH 44316 Tel (216) 794-4794

WAGEMAKER, JAMES FRANCIS, b. Willmar, Minn., May 5, 1941; B.A., U. Minn., 1963, J.D., 1965. Admitted to Minn. bar, 1966; mem. firm Wagemaker & Wagemaker, Olivia, Minn., 1969—. Mem. Renville County Local Bd. 101, Selective Service System, 1971-73; bd. dirs. Olivia United Fund, 1976—. Mem. Am., Minn. State bar assns. Home: 506 S 9th St Olivia MN 56277 Office: 106 S 9th St Olivia MN 56277 Tel (612) 523-2161

WAGEMAKER, THOMAS JOSEPH, b. Olivia, Minn., Nov. 23, 1903; B.A., St. Thomas Coll., St. Paul, 1926, LL.B., 1927. Admitted to Minn. bar, 1927; atty. City of Olivia, 1932-48; individual practice law, Olivia, 1948—. Mem. Minn., Renville County, Eighth Dist. Minn. bar assns. Home: 504 S 10th St Olivia MN 56277 Office: 106 S 9th St Olivia MN 56277 Tel (612) 523-2161

WAGENMAN, BARTON LEE, b. Toledo, Ohio, Jan. 29, 1942; B.S., Miami U., Oxford, Ohio, 1964; L.L.B., Harvard, 1967. Admitted to Ohio bar, 1967; mem. firm Shumaker, Loop & Kendrick, Toledo, 1967-72, partner, 1972—. Trustee, sec. Goodwill Industries, Toledo, 1976—. Mem. Am., Ohio (sec. bd. govs. real property sect.), Toledo bar assns., Phi Beta Kappa, Beta Gamma Sigma. Home: 5702 Flanders Rd Toledo OH 43623 Office: 811 Madison Ave Toledo OH 43624

WAGERS, GARDNER DAVID, b. Lexington, Ky., Feb. 5, 1948; B.B.A., U. Ky., 1970, J.D., 1973. Admitted to Ky. bar, 1973; practiced in Winchester, Ky., 1973—; partner firm Wagers & Keeton, Winchester, 1976—; city pros. atty. Winchester, 1975-76. Mem. Clark County com. Boy Scouts Am., 1973-75; Republican. chmn. Clark County, 1976—. Mem. Am. Trial Lawyers Assn., Ky. Assn. Trial Attys., Am., Ky., Clark County bar assns. Home: 18 Village Dr Winchester KY 40391 Office: 7 W Lexington Ave Winchester KY 40391 Tel (606) 744-1117

WAGGONER, LAWRENCE WILLIAM, b. Sidney, Ohio, July 2, 1937; B.B.A., U. Cin., 1960; J.D., U. Mich., 1963; Ph.D., Oxford (Eng.) U., 1966. Asso. firm Cravath, Swaine & Moore, 1963; asso. prof. law U. Ill., 1968-71, prof., 1971-72; prof. U. Va., 1972-74, U. Mich. Law Sch., 1974—. Mem. Order of Coif. Author: Family Property Settlements: Future Interests, 1973; Federal Taxation of Gifts, Trusts and Estates, 1977; Trusts and Succession, 1977; contbr. articles in field to profl. jours. Home: 1119 Chestnut Rd Ann Arbor MI 48104 Office: U Mich Law Sch Ann Arbor MI 48108 Tel (313) 763-2586

WAGGONER, MICHAEL JAMES, b. Oak Park, Ill., Sept. 21, 1942; A.B., Stanford, 1964; LL.B., Harvard, 1967. Admitted to D.C. bar, 1968; atty., advisor Gen. Counsel's Office U.S. Air Force, Washington, 1968-71; asso. firm Wilmer, Cutler & Pickering, Washington, 1971-73; asso. prof. law U. Colo., Boulder, 1973—. Mem. Am., Dist. Columbia, Boulder bar assns. Author: Civil Procedure: Survey of Colorado Law, 1975, 76. Home: 1086 10th St Boulder CO 80302 Office: Sch Law U Colo Boulder CO 80309

WAGNER, ARTHUR JAMES, b. Milw., Dec. 24, 1919; B.E.E., Marquette U., 1942; J.D., DePaul U., 1949. Admitted to Ill. bar, 1949; asso. firm Soans, Pond & Anderson, 1948-49; partner firm Johnson, Dienner, Emrich & Wagner, and predecessors, Chgo., 1949—. Mem. Am., Chgo. bar assns., Chgo., Am. patent law assns., Tau Beta Pi. Home: 2612 Roslyn Circle Highland Park IL 60035 Office: 150 N Wacker Dr Chicago IL 60605 Tel (312) 368-8575

WAGNER, BRUCE DUTTON, b. Hartford, Conn., Feb. 6, 1927; B.S., U. San Francisco, 1951; LL.B., U. Calif., 1955. Admitted to Calif. bar, 1956; individual practice law, 1956-60; dep. dist. atty. County of San Mateo (Calif.), 1960-65; asso. firm, Redwood City, Calif., 1966-69, partner, 1969—. Mem. Am. Bd. Trial Adv., Assn. Def. Counsel (dir.), Trial Attys. Am., Fedn. Ins. Counsel, San Mateo County Bar Assn. (sec. 1970). Editor The Docket, 1968—. Home: 225 W Poplar Ave San Mateo CA 94402 Office: 655 Marshall Ct Redwood City CA 94063 Tel (415) 364-8200

WAGNER, CARROLL LEWIS, JR., b. Balt., Oct. 5, 1944; A.B., Emory U., 1966; J.D., U. Va., 1969. Admitted to Ga. bar, 1969; asso. firm Hansell, Post, Brandon & Dorsey, Atlanta, 1969-74, partner 1974—; chmn. SE Liaison Tax Commn., 1977; lectr. Mich., Ga. Insts. Continuing Legal Edn., Ga. Soc. C.P.A.s. Legal counsel Atlanta Crime Commn., 1969-70. Mem. Am. (sects. taxation, corporate and antitrust), Ga. (chmn. sect. taxation, 1973), Atlanta Bar Assns., Lawyers Club of Atlanta, Order Coif, Raven Soc. Mng. editor: Va. Law Review, 1968; contbr. articles to legal jours. Home: 420 Creekview Ct Marietta GA 30067 Office: 3300 First Nat Bank Tower Atlanta GA 30303 Tel (404) 581-8000

WAGNER, ELEANOR ROSE, b. Chgo., July 29, 1941; A.B., Boston U., 1964; J.D., Loyola U., Chgo., 1970. Admitted to Ill. bar, 1970; atty., trust counsel's office Harris Bank, Chgo., 1970-71; staff atty. Am. Hosp. Assn., Chgo., 1971-76; dir. legal services Joint Commn. Accreditation Hosps., Chgo., 1976—. Mem. Am., Ill., Chgo. bar assns., Am. Soc. Hosp. Attys., Group Health Lawyers Assn., Am. Soc. Law and Medicine. Contbr. articles Jour. Am. Hosp. Assn. Home: 111 E Chestnut St apt 46D Chicago IL 60611 Office: 875 N Michigan Ave Chicago IL 60611 Tel (312) 642-6061

WAGNER, JEROME MAURICE, b. Chgo., Nov. 2, 1936; A.B., U. Calif. at Los Angeles, 1958; J.D., U. So. Calif., 1961. Admitted to Calif. bar, 1962; asst. counsel E. Bronx Randall Auto Club, 1961-62; dep. city atty. Glendale (Calif.), 1962-63; mem. firm Wagner, Scuderi & Bixby, Los Angeles, 1963—; spl. counsel City of Beverly Hills, 1966-68. Home: 2922 Corda Ln Los Angeles CA 90049 Office: 9229 Sunset Los Angeles CA 90069 Tel (213) 878-0841

WAGNER, JOHN LEWIS, b. Sandusky, Ohio, Nov. 18, 1928; B.A., Bowling Green State U., 1951; J.D., Ohio State U., 1955. Admitted to Ohio bar, 1955; partner firm Moulton, Ricksecker, Wagner & Hoover, Galion, Ohio, 1955—; justice of peace, Crawford County, Ohio, 1956-58; solicitor, Galion, 1959-67; asst. pros. atty. Crawford County, 1968-72. Bd. dirs. ARC, 1958-59; bd. dirs., pres. YMCA, 1957-60; asst. deacon, mem. ch. council Peace Lutheran Ch., 1970-74; mem. Galion Bd. Edn., 1976—; pres. Galion 20/30 Club, 1959-60. Mem. Ohio State, Crawford County bar assns. Home: 1000 Devonwood Galion OH 44833 Office: POB 576 Galion OH 44833 Tel (419) 468-1131

WAGNER, JOSEPH HAGEL, b. Balt., June 4, 1947; B.A., Villanova U., 1969; J.D., Syracuse U., 1972. Admitted to Pa. bar, 1972; asso. firm Eastburn and Gray, Doylestown, Pa., 1972—. Bd. dirs. New Britain (Pa.) Borough Civic Assn., 1975—, pres., 1976. Mem. Am., Pa., Bucks County bar assns. Home: 158 Matthews Ave New Britain PA 18901 Office: Federal Savings Bldg Doylestown PA 18901 Tel (215) 345-7000

WAGNER, PAUL C(ONNER), b. Reading, Pa., July 1, 1893; A.B., Franklin Marshall Coll., 1913; LL.B., U. Pa., 1916, postgrad. (Gowen Meml. fellow), 1916-17. Admitted to Pa. bar, 1916, U.S. Supreme Ct. bar, 1921; partner firm Clark, Clark, McCarthy & Wagner, Phila., 1917-28; sr. trust officer Fidelity Bank, Phila., 1928-58; partner firm Pepper, Hamilton & Scheetz, Phila., 1958-73; mem. Pa. Joint State Govt. Commn., 1937—; ret., 1973. Mem. Am., Pa., Phila bar assns. Home: 414 S Carlisle St Philadelphia PA 19146

WAGNER, ROBERT EDWARD, b. Yankton, S.D., Mar. 6, 1930; B.S. in Engring., Iowa State U., 1957; J.D., Am. U., 1961. Admitted to Iowa bar, 1961, Ill. bar, 1964; asso. firm Fay & Fay, Cleve., 1962-63; asso. firm Greist, Lockwood, Greenawalt & Dewey, Chgo., 1963-67; asso., partner firm Walsh, Case & Coale, Chgo., 1967-73; partner firm Wagner & Aubel, Chgo., 1973—; examiner U.S. Parent Office, Washington, 1957-61. Bd. dirs. St. Francis Village, Ft. Worth, 1968—, St. Anthony's Inn, Chgo., 1965—, St. Emily's Sch., 1967-75. Mem. Am., Fed., Ill., Iowa bar assns., Chgo. Patent Law Assn., Bar Assn. 7th Circuit. Home: 1511 Mark Dr Mount Prospect IL 60056 Office: 135 S LaSalle St Chicago IL 60603 Tel (312) 236-0013

WAGNER, ROBERT JOHN, b. Sleepy Eye, Minn., July 31, 1938; B.A. cum laude, Coll. of St. Thomas, St. Paul, 1960; J.D. magna cum laude, U. Minn., 1963. Admitted to S.D. bar, 1963; with firm Beardsley, Oshiem and Wagner, Watertown, S.D., 1963-72; individual practice law, Watertown, S.D., 1972—; atty. City of Watertown, 1970—; dep. state's atty. State of S.D., 1969-76; mem. Gov. S.D. Juvenile Justice Adv. Commn. Chmn. Codington County (S.D.) Red Cross, 1968-71. Mem. Codington County Bar Assn., S.D. Municipal Attys. Assn. (pres. 1975-76), Nat. Inst. Municipal Legal Officers, Nat. Dist. Attys. Assn., Am. Arbitration Assn., Watertown Jaycees (past sec. and v.p.; Distinguished Service award 1969). Home: 67 4th Ave NW Watertown SD 57201 Office: PO Box 153 Watertown SD 57201 Tel (605) 886-4057

WAGNER, WENCESLAS JOSEPH, b. Warsaw, Poland, Dec. 12, 1917; LL.M., U. Warsaw, 1939; certificates Acad. Internat. Law, The Hague, 1939, 1947; postgrad. Inst. Commerce S. Brun, Warsaw, 1940; Dr. en Droit, U. Paris, 1947; LL.M., J.D., S.J.D., Northwestern U., 1950-57. Admitted to Ind. bar, 1965; jr. atty., jr. judge, Warsaw, 1940-44; research asso. French Inst. Air Transp., Paris, 1946-48; vis. prof. lit. Fordham U., N.Y.C., 1948-49; teaching fellow Northwestern U. Law Sch., Chgo., 1950-53; instr., prof. law Notre Dame U., Ind., 1953-62; prof. law Ind. U., Bloomington, 1962-71, U. Detroit, 1971—; vis. prof. Cornell U., 1963, 66; legal counsel German Consulate Gen., Ind., 1966-68; individual practice law, Bloomington, 1965-71, Detroit, 1971—; vis. prof., lectr., France, 1959-60, 68-69, 74-75, Latin Am., 1968, Poland, 1971, 76. Pres. Am. Council Polish Cultural Clubs, 1957-59; pres. council Polish Inst. Arts and Scis. in Am., 1976—; pres. Polish-Am. Bicentennial Com. for Mich., 1974—. Mem. United World Federalists (exec. council 1957-60, D.C., The Hague 1959-60), Council Inst. High Internat. Studies (U. Nice 1966—), Assn. Am. Law Schs. (chmn. comparative law sect.), Am. Assn. Comparative Study of Law (chmn. internat. meetings com.), Internat. Acad. Comparative Law, Internat. Assn. Cath. Lawyers (v.p.), French Assn. Legal History (council). Recipient Golden Cross of Merit, Polish Govt. in Exile, 1965; author or editor of 6 books; contbr. articles to legal jours.; editorial bd. Am. Jour. Comparative Law, 1962—. Home: 728 Neff Grosse Pointe MI 48230 Office: 651 E Jefferson Ave Detroit MI 48226 Tel (313) 961-1449

WAGNER, WILLIAM HENRY, b. Kendallville, Ind., Sept. 24, 1933; B.A., Valparaiso U., 1956, LL.B., 1958, J.D., 1970. Admitted to Ind., Mich. bars, 1958; legal staff Frankenmuth Ins. Co. (Mich.), 1958-60; with firm Chester, Clifford, Hoeppner & Houran, Valparaiso, Ind., 1960-76, firm Hoeppner, Wagner & Evans, Valparaiso, 1976—; atty. Valparaiso Bd. Zoning Appeals, 1962-65. Mem. Porter County (past pres.), Ind. State (ho. of dels. 1971) bar assns. Home: Rural Route 5 Box 30 Valparaiso IN 46383 Office: PO Box 529 Valparaiso IN 46383 Tel (219) 464-4961

WAGNER, WILLIAM WARREN, b. La Porte City, Iowa, Dec. 13, 1920; B.A., U. Iowa, 1942, LL.B., 1949. Admitted to Iowa bar, 1949; individual practice law, La Porte City, 1949—. Mayor of La Porte City, 1952-60. Mem. Black Hawk County, Iowa bar assns. Home: 408 W Main St La Porte City IA 50651 Office: 323 Main St La Porte City IA 50651 Tel (319) 342-3232

WAGNON, MACBETH, JR., b. Union, S.C., June 4, 1931; B.S., The Citadel, 1952; LL.B., Duke, 1959. Admitted to Ala. bar, 1959; asso. firm Bradley, Arant, Rose & White, Birmingham, Ala., 1959-64, partner, 1965—. Bd. dirs. Travelers Aid Soc., 1973—. Mem. Am., Birmingham, Ala. bar assns. Home: 2936 Virginia Rd Mountain Brook AL 35223 Office: 1500 Brown-Marx Bldg Birmingham AL 35203 Tel (205) 252-4500

WAGONER, DAVID EVERETT, b. Pottstown, Pa., May 16, 1928; B.A., Yale, 1950; LL.B., U. Pa., 1953. Admitted to D.C. bar, 1953, Pa. bar, 1954, Wash. bar, 1958, U.S. Supreme Ct. bar, 1957; law clk. to judge U.S. Ct. Appeals, 1955-56, U.S. Supreme Ct., 1956-57; asso. firm Perkins, Coie, Stone, Olsen & Williams, Seattle, 1957-62, partner, 1962—. Vice pres. English Speaking Union, Seattle, 1961-62; mem. ch. council Congl. Ch., Seattle, 1968-70; chmn. sch. com. Seattle Municipal League, 1962-65; chmn. edn. com. Forward Thrust-Seattle, 1968; bd. dirs. Seattle Pub. Schs., 1965-73, pres. 1968, 73; chmn. council big city bds. Nat. Sch. Bds. Assn., 1971-72, bd. dirs., 1971-72; bd. dirs. Seattle YMCA, 1968. Mem. Am., Wash., Seattle-King County bar assns., Am. Judicature Soc. Contbr. articles to jours. Home: 3417 E Shore Dr Seattle WA 98112 Office: 1900 Washington Bldg Seattle WA 98101 Tel (206) 682-8770

WAGSTAFF, ROBERT HALL, b. Kansas City, Mo., Nov. 5, 1941; A.B., Dartmouth, 1963; J.D., U. Kans., 1966. Admitted to Kans. bar, 1966, Alaska bar, 1967, U.S. Supreme Ct. bar, 1970; asst. atty. gen. State of Kans., Topeka, 1966-67; dist. atty., Fairbanks, Alaska, 1967-69; asso. firm Boyko & Walton, Anchorage, 1970; partner firm Wagstaff & Middleton and predecessor, Anchorage, 1971—. Chmn. bd. dirs. Alaska Youth Advs., 1972-74; nat. bd. dirs. ACLU, 1972—. Mem. Am., Kans., Alaska bar assns., Nat. Lawyers Guild. Home: Indian AK Office: 500 L St Anchorage AK 99501 Tel (907) 277-0282

WAHRENBROCK, HOWARD EGGER, b. Kansas City, Mo., Nov. 20, 1903; A.B., U. Mich., 1925, J.D., 1927, S.J.D., 1933. Admitted to Ill. bar, 1927, U.S. Supreme Ct. bar, 1931, D.C. bar, 1967; asso. firm Follansbee, Shorey & Schupp, Chgo., 1927-29; research asst. U. Mich., 1929-30, 31-32; research asst. Nat. Commn. Law Observance and Enforcement, 1930-31; asst. dir., instr. dept. legis. research and drafting Duke U., 1931-32; atty. Fed. Emergency Adminsrn. Pub. Works, 1933-34, N.R.A., 1934-35, Fed. Home Loan Bank Bd., 1935-36, FCC, 1936-43, asst. gen. counsel, 1943-57, solicitor, 1957-67; individual practice law, Washington, 1967—; of counsel firm Bruder & Gentile, 1976—. Mem. Am., Fed. Power, Fed., D.C. bar assns., Delta Sigma Rho. Home: 1141 Waverley Way McLean VA 22101 Office: 708 Longfellow Bldg 1201 Connecticut Ave NW Washington DC 20036 Tel (202) 452-1995

WAINWRIGHT, CARROLL LIVINGSTON, b. N.Y.C., Dec. 28, 1925; A.B., Yale, 1949; LL.B., Harvard, 1952. Admitted to N.Y. bar, 1953, U.S. Supreme Ct. bar, 1958; asso. firm Milbank, Tweed, Hadley & McCloy and predecessor, N.Y.C., 1953-58, partner, 1960—; asst. counsel to gov. State of N.Y., Albany, 1959-60; mem. N.Y. State Commn. on Jud. Conduct, 1974—. Trustee Am. Museum Natural History, N.Y.C., Cooper Union for Advancement of Sci. and Art, N.Y.C., Boys' Club of N.Y.C.; mem. Yale U. Council, New Haven. Mem. Am., N.Y. State bar assns., Assn. Bar City N.Y. (v.p. 1975), Am. Coll. Probate Counsel. Home: 1120 Fifth Ave New York City NY 10028 Office: 1 Chase Manhattan Plaza New York City NY 10005 Tel (212) 422-2660

WAIT, RICHARD, b. Medford, Mass., June 4, 1901; A.B., Harvard, 1923, LL.B., 1926; LL.D., Emerson Coll., 1959. Admitted to Mass. bar, 1926, U.S. Supreme Ct. bar, 1935; asso. firm Choate, Hall & Stewart, Boston, 1926-31, partner, 1931—; lectr. Harvard, 1935-41. Moderator, Town of Harvard (Mass.), 1942-74. Mem. Mass. (pres. 1948-50), Boston, Am. bar assns., Assn. Life Ins. Counsel, Am. Coll. Trial Lawyers. Home: 6 Louisburg Sq Boston MA 02108 Office: 28 State St Boston MA 02109 Tel (617) 227-5020

WAITE, NORMAN, b. Boston, Mar. 21, 1905; B.A., Yale U., 1927; J.D., Harvard U., 1930. Admitted to Ill. bar, 1932; partner firm Schiff, Hardin & Waite, Chgo. Mem. Am., Ill., Chgo. bar assns. Office: 233 S Wacker Dr Chicago IL 60606 Tel (312) 876-1000

WAJERT, JOHN M., b. New Castle, Pa., Aug. 13, 1931; B.A., U. Pa., 1953, J.D., 1956. Admitted to Pa. bar, 1961; judge Ct. of Common Pleas of Pa., W. Chester, 1971—. Mem. Southeastern Region Planning Council, Gov.'s Justice Commn.; former solicitor Charlestown Twp. Zoning Hearing Bd.; mem. No. Chester County Vo-Tech. Sch.; chmn. W. Whiteland Twp. Zoning Hearing Bd. Mem. Am., Pa., Chester, Phila., Del., Montgomery Counties bar assns., Nat. Advocates Soc., Am. Judicature Soc., Nat. Council of Juvenile Ct. Judges, Pa. Conf. State Trial Judges. Home: 1265 Estate Dr West Chester PA 19380 Office: Ct House West Chester PA 19380 Tel (215) 431-6183

WALBERT, DAVID FRANK, b. Hagerstown, Md., Dec. 11, 1945; B.S. in Physics, Stanford U., 1967, M.S., U. Mich., 1968; J.D., Case Western Res. U., 1972. Admitted to Ga. bar, 1973; law clk. to judge U.S. Dist. Ct., Portland, Oreg., 1972-73; mng. atty. Ga. Legal Services, Atlanta, 1973-76; asso. firm Neely, Neely & Player, Atlanta, 1976—; exec. dir. Ga. Election Project, Atlanta, 1975—; mem. com. open housing, Atlanta, 1976. Mem. Ga., Am. bar assns. Editor: Abortion, Society and the Law, 1973; contbr. articles to legal jours. Home: 1545 N Morningside Dr NE Atlanta GA 30306 Office: 3100 Peachtree Summit 401 W Peachtree St Atlanta GA 30308 Tel (404) 681-2600

WALCEK, STANLEY JOSEPH, b. Shelton, Conn., May 25, 1928; A.B., Cath. U. Am., 1950, LL.B., 1953; LL.M., Georgetown U., 1960. Admitted to Md. bar, 1963; partner firm Giordano & Walcek, Marlow Heights, Md., 1963-68; sr. partner firm Fisher & Walcek, Oxon Hill, Md., 1970—. Mem. Am., Md. State, Prince George's County bar assns., Am. Trial Lawyers Assn. Home: 12301 Arrow Park Dr Oxon Hill MD 20022 Office: 5410 Indian Head Hwy Oxon Hill MD 20021 Tel (301) 567-0700

WALCH, VICTOR LLOYD, b. La Grande, Oreg., July 19, 1934; student Eastern Oreg. Coll.; B.S., U. Utah, 1960; J.D., George Washington U., 1965. Accountant, Lawrence Pinnoch & Co., C.P.A., Salt Lake City, 1959-60; agt. IRS, Washington, 1960-62; tax law specialist, 1962-65; admitted to Calif. bar, 1967; clk. Mackay, McGregor & Bennion, Los Angeles, 1966, asso. firm, 1967-69, partner, 1970—. Bd. dirs. Burbank Civil Service Bd., 1969—, chmn., 1972-73. Mem. Interstate Bus. and Profl. Men's Assn. Los Angeles. C.P.A., Utah. Home: 711 Wilson Ct Burbank CA 91501 Office: 523 W 6th St Los Angeles CA 90014 Tel (213) 626-7722

WALCH, W. STANLEY, b. Sedalia, Mo., Mar. 23, 1934; A.B. cum laude, Kenyon Coll., Gambier, Ohio, 1956; J.D. with distinction, U. Mich., 1959. Admitted to Mo. bar, 1959; asso. firm Thompson & Mitchell, and predecessors, St. Louis, 1959-65, partner, 1965-69, 76—; exec. v.p., gen. counsel Chromalloy Am. Corp., St. Louis, 1969-76. Mem. Am., Mo., Met. St. Louis bar assns., Order of Coif. Asso. editor U. Mich. Law Rev., 1958-59. Home: 5 Wild Rose Dr Ladue MO 63124 Office: suite 3400 One Mercantile Center Saint Louis MO 63101 Tel (314) 231-7676

WALD, BERNARD JOSEPH, b. Bklyn., Sept. 14, 1932; B.B.A. magna cum laude, City Coll. N.Y., 1953; J.D. cum laude, N.Y. U. Sch. Law, 1955. Admitted to N.Y. bar, 1955; U.S. Supreme Ct. bar, 1971; asso., mem. firm Herzfeld & Rubin, N.Y.C., 1955—. Mem. Am., N.Y., N.Y.C. bar assns., NY County Lawyers Assn. Office: Herzfeld & Rubin 40 Wall St New York City NY 10005 Tel (212) 344-0680

WALD, DAVID EWING, b. Galesburg, Ill., Aug. 31, 1948; B.A., Calif. State U., 1970; J.D., Calif. Western U., 1973. Admitted to Calif. bar, 1973, U.S. Ct. Appeals bar, 1973; asso. firm Sankary & Sankary, San Diego, Calif., 1973; individual practice law, San Diego, 1974-76; asso. firm Novak, Cooper & Wohlgemuth, Century City, Calif., 1976—. Mem. Am., San Diego, Beverly Hills bar assns., Calif. Trial Lawyers Assn. Office: 1888 Century Park E Suite 1221 Century City CA 90067 Tel (213) 552-1414

WALD, MICHAEL STUART, b. N.Y.C., June 23, 1941; B.A., Cornell U., 1963; LL.B., Yale U., 1967, M.A. in Polit. Sci., 1967. Admitted to Calif. bar, 1970, D.C. bar, 1970; prof. law Stanford U., Palo Alto, Calif., 1967—; atty. Ventura County Dist. Atty., 1970; atty. Pub. Defender Service D.C., Center for Law and Social Policy, Washington, 1970-71; atty. Youth Law Center, San Francisco, 1971-72. Mem. Boys Town Center at Stanford; judge pro tem Santa Clara Juvenile Ct., 1975. Mem. Calif. Bar Assn. (juvenile law com.) Soc. Research Child Devel. Contbr. articles to profl. jours. Home: 1682 Hamilton Ave Palo Alto CA 94303 Office: Stanford Law Sch Stanford CA 94305 Tel (415) 497-4933

WALD, PATRICIA MCGOWAN, b. Torrington, Conn., Sept. 16, 1928; B.A., Conn. Coll., 1948; LL.B., Yale U., 1951. Admitted to D.C. bar, 1952, U.S. Supreme Ct. bar, 1972, Fed. bar, 1972; atty. Center Law and Social Policy, Washington, D.C., 1971-72; dir. litigation Mental Health Law Project, Washington, D.C., 1973-77; asst. atty. gen. Office Legislative Affairs, U.S. Dept. Justice, Washington, D.C., 1977—. Mem. Pres.'s Commn. Crime, D.C., 1964-66; staff atty. Neighborhood Legal Services, D.C., 1968-70. Author: Bail in the United States, 1964; Law and Poverty, 1965; Dealing with Drug Abuse, 1971. Home: 107 Quincy St Chevy Chase MD 20015 Office: US Dept Justice Constitution Ave and 10th St NW Washington DC 20530 Tel (202) 739-2150

WALDECK, DENNIS JOSEPH, b. Peoria, Ill., Aug. 29, 1940; B.S. in History, Loyola U., 1963, J.D., 1965. Admitted to Ill. bar, 1965, U.S. Supreme Ct. bar, 1974; staff atty. SEC, Chgo., 1965-69, chief br. reorgn., 1969-72, chief br. enforcement, 1973-74, asst. regional adminstr., 1974—. Mem. Am. Bar Assn. Contbr. articles to legal jours. Home: 180 Park Blvd Glen Ellyn IL 60137 Office: Room 1204 219 S Dearborn St Chicago IL 60604 Tel (312) 353-7402

WALDIN, EARL DEWITT, JR., b. Asheville, N.C., Feb. 6, 1922; B.S. with honors in Pub. Adminstrn., U. Fla., 1944; J.D. cum laude, Stetson U., 1948. Admitted to Fla. bar, 1948, U.S. Supreme Ct. bar, 1974; asso. prof. bus. law Stetson U., DeLand, Fla., 1949; partner firm Brunstetter & Waldin, Miami, Fla., 1949-52; asst. county atty. Dade County (Fla.), 1952-55; partner firm Smathers & Thompson, Miami, 1955—. Mem. Fla., Dade County, Dade County Def. (pres. 1964-65) bar assns. Home: 6501 SW 94th St Miami FL 33156 Office: A I DuPont Bldg Miami FL 33131 Tel (305) 379-6523

WALDMAN, HERBERT LOUIS, b. Las Vegas, Nev., July 31, 1939; B.S., U. Nev., 1961; J.D., U. Calif., San Francisco, 1966. Admitted to Nev. bar, 1966; asso. firm Wiener, Goldwater & Waldman, and predecessors, Las Vegas, 1966-74, partner, 1974—. Home: 5860 Edna St Las Vegas NV 89102 Office: 302 E Carson Suite 703 Las Vegas NV 89101

WALDMAN, LAWRENCE ALAN, b. St. Louis, Oct. 12, 1937; B.S. in Bus. Adminstrn., Washington U., St. Louis, 1959, J.D., 1962. Admitted to Mo. bar, 1962, Ill. bar, 1973; asso. firm Lewis, Rice, Tucker, Allen and Chubb, St. Louis, 1962-73, Cohn, Carr, Korein, Kunin and Brennan, East Saint Louis, Ill., 1973—; lectr. Meramec Jr. Coll. Trustee Fern Waldman Meml. Fund for Research in Cancer Affecting Children, 1962—. Mem. Am., Mo., Ill., Met. St. Louis, St. Clair County (Ill.) bar assns., Order of Coif. Home: 1220 Moncoeur St Saint Louis MO 63141 Office: 412 Missouri Ave East Saint Louis IL 62201 Tel (618) 274-0434 also Suite 210 7710 Carondelet St Clayton MO 63105 Tel (314) 862-4330

WALDMAN, MAXWELL WILLIAM, b. Providence, Apr. 27, 1910; student U. R.I., 1928-30; LL.D. cum laude, Boston U., 1933. Admitted to R.I. bar, 1933, Mass. bar, 1943; sr. mem. firm Waldman & Waldman, Providence, 1933—; chmn. R.I. Racing and Athletics Hearing Bd., 1959—. Mem. R.I. State Poetry Soc. Named Man of Year, New Eng. div. Horsemans Benevolent Protective Assn., 1964. Home: 192 Raleigh Ave Pawtucket RI 02860 Office: 58 Weybosset St Providence RI 02903 Tel (401) 421-0512

WALDMAN, NATHAN JEFFREY, b. Kassa, Czechoslovakia, Apr. 23, 1935; B.B.A., Coll. City N.Y., 1957; J.D., Columbia U., 1960. Admitted to N.Y. bar, 1961; partner firm Sperry, Weinberg, Waldman & Rubenstein, N.Y.C., 1964—; adj. asso. prof. law City U. N.Y., 1973—. Mem. N.Y. County Lawyers Assn., Ulster County Bar Assn., Assn. Comml. Fin. Attys. Office: 275 Madison Ave New York City NY 10016 Tel (212) MU 9-8989

WALDMAN, SEYMOUR MORTON, b. N.Y.C., Aug. 6, 1926; B.A., Columbia, 1948, LL.B., 1950. Admitted to N.Y. State bar, 1950, U.S. Supreme Ct. bar, 1956; mem. firm Waldman & Waldman, N.Y.C., 1952—; village atty. Croton-on-Hudson (N.Y.), 1971—. Chmn. Zoning Bd. Appeals Croton-on-Hudson, 1964-71. Mem. Am., N.Y. State bar assns., Assn. Bar City N.Y., N.Y. County Lawyers Assn. Home: 47 Lounsbury Rd Croton-on-Hudson NY 10520 Office: 501 5th Ave New York City NY 10017 Tel (212) 661-1230

WALDO, BURTON CORLETT, b. Seattle, Aug. 11, 1920; B.A., U. Wash., 1941, J.D., 1948. Admitted to Wash. bar, 1949; partner firm Keller Rohrback Waldo & Hiscock, and predecessors, Seattle, 1953—. Mem. Seattle Bd. Theater Suprs., 1958-61. Mem. Am., Wash., Seattle-King County (past trustee) bar assns., Internat. Assn. Ins. Counsel, Fedn. Ins. Counsel, Wash. Assn. Def. Counsel, Phi Delta Phi. Home: 3715 E Union St Seattle WA 98122 Office: 1220 IBM Bldg Seattle WA 98101 Tel (206) 623-1900

WALDO, ROBERT LELAND, b. Pittsville, Wis., Sept. 1, 1923; B.S., U. Wis., 1949, J.D., 1951. Admitted to Wis. bar, 1951; asso. firm Foley & Lardner, and predecessors, Milw., 1951-59; asst. sec., asst. gen. counsel Milw. Gas & Light Co., 1959-69; v.p., gen. counsel, sec. CMI Investment Corp., Madison, 1969-72, sr. v.p., 1972-73, exec. v.p., sec., 1973—. Chmn. Dane County chpt. ARC, 1976—. Mem. Am., Wis., Dane County bar assns. Home: 6634 Gettysburg Dr Madison WI 53705 Office: 150 E Gilman St Madison WI 53701 Tel (608) 257-2527

WALDRON, CORBIN ARA, b. Independence, Iowa, Jan. 7, 1899; student Fargo Coll.; LL.B., U. Minn., 1927. Admitted to N.D. bar, 1928; mem. firm Waldron, Kenner, Halvorson & Sturtevant, Minot; exec. dir. Community Services Assn., Devils Lake, N.D. Chmn., Minot Taxpayers Assn., Ward County Republicans; bd. dirs. YMCA, Heartview Found. Mem. N.D., Minot (past pres.) bar assns., Jud. Council, Internat. Poets Laureate Am. (Laurel Leaves). Named poet laureate N.D.; author: Lines and Lyrics of Dakota; Falling Leaves; Voice of the Valley; Quasi-Legal Tender; Footprints in America's Fields; Saving Sovereign Law; composer 15 songs, 3 hymns. Home: 908 4th St SE Minot ND 58701 Office: 615 S Broadway Minot ND 58701 Tel (701) 852-2880

WALENTA, ARTHUR WINSLOW, JR., b. Stamford, Conn., Sept. 6, 1935; B.S., U. Calif., Berkeley, 1957; LL.B., Harvard, 1960. Admitted to Calif. bar, U.S. Dist. Ct. bar, U.S. Ct. Appeals bar, 1961; asso. firm Timothy A. O'Connor, San Jose, Calif., 1961-63; dep. dist. atty. Contra Costa County, Calif., 1963-68, dep. county counsel, 1968-74, asst. county counsel, 1974—; counsel Contra Costa County Civil Service Commn., 1970—; counsel Contra Costa County Assessment Appeals Bd., 1973-76. Mem. Contra Costa County Bar Assn., County Sch. Attys. Assn. (pres. No. Calif. sect. 1975). Office: Contra Costa County Counsel PO Box 69 Martinez CA 94553 Tel (415) 372-2070

WALES, ROBERT WILLETT, b. Chgo., Dec. 23, 1906; A.B., Princeton U., 1927; J.D., Harvard U., 1930. Admitted to Ill. bar, 1930, N.Y. State bar, 1954, D.C. bar, 1962; partner firm Miller, Gorham, Wescott & Adams, Chgo., 1934-41, 46-52; asst. gen. counsel OPA, Washington, 1941-43; asst. tax legis. counsel U.S. Dept. Treasury, Washington, 1943-44, tax legis. counsel, 1944-46; counsel Standard Vacuum Oil Co., N.Y.C. and Harrison, N.Y., 1952-59, gen. counsel, 1959-61; partner firm Cleary, Gottlieb, Steen & Hamilton, N.Y.C., 1961-76; lectr. Northwestern U. Sch. Law, 1948-51, N.Y. U. Law Sch., 1954. Home: 911 Harbor Rd Southport CT 06490 Office: One State St Plaza New York City NY 10004

WALES, THOMAS CODY, b. San Antonio, July 1, 1944; B.A., U. Denver, 1966; J.D., Tex. Tech. U., 1972. Admitted to Tex. bar, 1973; asso. firm Turner, Hitchins, McInerney, Webb & Hartnett, Dallas, 1973-74; asso. gen. counsel Hanover Petroleum Corp., Dallas, 1974-76; staff atty. Ashland Oil, Inc. (Ky.), 1976—. Mem. Dallas, Am. bar assns., Tex. Bar. Home: 124 Barkley Ct Russell KY 41169 Office: Ashland Oil Inc 1409 Winchester St Ashland KY 41101 Tel (606) 329-4643

WALINSKI, RICHARD S., b. Toledo, May 1, 1932; B.A. magna cum laude, U. Toledo, 1965, J.D. cum laude, 1969. Admitted to Ohio bar, 1969, U.S. Supreme Ct. bar, 1973; partner firm Hayward, Cooper, Straub, Walinski & Cramer, Toledo, 1969-76; asst. pub. defender Toledo, 1969-71; spl. counsel to atty. gen. of Ohio, 1975-76, chief counsel, 1976—; instr. civil procedure U. Toledo Coll. Law, 1974-75. Editor-in-chief U. Toledo Law Rev., 1968-69. Home: 5415 Yorkshire

Terr Dr Columbus OH 43227 Office: Office of Atty Gen State Office Tower Columbus OH 43215 Tel (614) 466-4638

WALKER, BARRY JAY, b. Worcester, Mass., Sept. 25, 1936; B.A., Clark U., 1958; LL.B., Boston Coll., 1961. Admitted to Mass. bar, 1961; mem. firm Bikofsky, Walker & Tuttle, Framingham, Mass., 1961—; instr. Boston Coll. Law Sch., 1965-75, Clark U., 1975. Chmn., Town Finance Commn., Framingham, 1967-71. Mem. Am., Mass. bar assns., Am. Judicature Soc. Named Alumnus of Year, Clark U., 1976.

WALKER, CHARLES MOUNTZ, b. Charleston, W.Va., July 6, 1913; LL.B., George Washington U., 1939; postgrad. U. Mexico, Mexico City, 1946-48. Admitted to D.C. bar, 1940, U.S. Supreme Ct. bar, 1946, Va. bar, 1946, W.Va bar, 1950; asso. firm Bingham, Collins, Porter & Kistler, Washington, 1940-43; mgr. Central Alarm System Co., Mexico City, 1947-48; mem. firm Walker & Villafranca, Mexico City, 1946-48, Peaslee & Turlington, Washington, 1948-50; individual practice law, Washington, 1950-52; 1st asst. pros. atty. Kanawha County (W.Va.), 1952-59, pros. atty., 1959-68; asso. prof. criminal justice, chmn. dept. criminal justice W.Va. State Coll., 1969—; lectr. in field; mem. Gov. W.Va. Com. on Crime, Delinquency and Corrections, 1965-68; trustee W.Va. Pub. Employees Retirement System, 1965-68. Mem. Am., Fed., W.Va. bar assns., Pros. Attys. Assn. W.Va. (pres. 1959-65), Nat. Dist. Attys. Assn. (exec. com.), Nat. Lawyers Club. Home: 716 Ellette Dr Charleston WV 25311 Office: Dept of Criminal Justice W Va State Coll Institute WV 25112 Tel (304) 766-3254

WALKER, CORA THOMASINA, b. Charlotte, N.C., June 20, 1924; B.S. in Econs., St. John's U., 1945, LL.B., 1946, LL.D., 1968. Admitted to N.Y. bar, 1947, U.S. Supreme Ct. bar, 1976; practiced in N.Y.C., 1947—; individual practice law, 1947-53, 60-75; partner firms Doles, Sandifer & Walker, 1954-57, Doles & Walker, 1957-60, Walker & Bailey, 1976—; coordinator legal counsel Harlem River Consumers Coop., Inc.; spl. counsel N.Y. State Joint Legislature, 1976—. Mem. Am., N.Y.C., New York County, Nat. (v.p.) bar assns., Harlem Lawyers Assn. (pres.). Recipient award for dedicated service to Harlem community U.S.A. Coop. League; award for outstanding service and devotion to community Met. Com. of 100, 1972; Most Popular Harlemite award N.Y. Daily Challenge, 1975. Home: 501 W 125th St New York City NY 10027 Office: 270 Lenox Ave New York City NY 10027 Tel (212) LE 4-6300

WALKER, DAVID, b. Lufkin, Tex., Aug. 7, 1931; B.B.A., Sam Houston State U., 1952; LL.B., South Tex. Sch. Law, 1959. Owner Walker Real Estate Agy., Lufkin, 1954-59; admitted to Tex. bar, 1959; practiced in Lufkin, 1959-69; city atty. City of Lufkin, 1964-69; judge Tex. 159th Dist. Ct., 1969—. Pres. Angelina County (Tex.) Sch. Bd., 1961-66; bd. dirs. Angelina Coll., 1966-69; East Tex. Area council Boy Scouts Am., 1972-75; pres. Angelina chpt. Am. Heart Assn., 1975. Mem. Am. Judicature Soc., Angelina County Bar (pres. 1969-70). Named Citizen of Month Lufkin Booster Club, 1972. Home: Route 10 Box 825 Lufkin TX 75901 Office: PO Box 67 Lufkin TX 75901 Tel (713) 632-3717

WALKER, DORIS BRIN, b. Dallas, Apr. 29, 1919; B.A., U. Calif., Los Angeles, 1939; LL.D., U. Calif., Berkeley, 1942. Admitted to Calif. bar, 1942, U.S. Supreme Ct. bar, 1967; partner firm McMurray, Brotsky, Walker, Bancroft & Tepper, San Francisco, 1953-63, Treuhaft & Walker, Oakland, Calif., 1963—; Mem. Nat. (pres. 1970-71), San Francisco (pres. 1966-68) lawyers guilds, Internat. Assn. Democratic Lawyers (v.p. 1970—), Calif. Attys. for Criminal Justice (dir. 1976—), Am., Alameda County, San Francisco County bar assns. Office: 1440 Broadway Oakland CA 94612 Tel (415) 452-1300

WALKER, DOUGLAS RANDOLPH, b. St. Louis, Dec. 12, 1947; B.A., Tulane U., 1969, J.D., 1972. Admitted to Ill. bar, 1972; partner firm Coryn & Walker, Rock Island, Ill., 1972—; asst. pub. defender County of Rock Island (Ill.), 1975-76. Deacon, Broadway Presbyn. Ch., Rock Island. Tel (309) 788-6301

WALKER, EDWIN JASPER, JR., b. Concord, N.C., May 7, 1944; A.B., Davidson Coll., 1966; J.D., U. N.C. at Chapel Hill, 1969. Admitted to N.C. bar, 1969; asso. firm Mount, White, King, Hutson, Walker & Carden, Durham, N.C., 1969-72, partner, 1973—. Sec., Found. for Better Health, Durham, 1976-77; v.p. Transition of Youth, Inc., Durham, 1975-77; dir. Center City Ch. Council, 1972-77; mem. adv. council Salvation Army Boys' Club, 1975-77. Mem. Am., N.C. bar assns. Home: 304 Cheryl Ave Durham NC 27704 Office: 102 E Main St Durham NC 27701 Tel (919) 683-1561

WALKER, FRANCIS JOSEPH, b. Tacoma, Aug. 5, 1922; B.A., St. Martin's Coll., 1947; J.D., U. Wash., 1950. Admitted to Wash. bar, 1950; asst. atty. gen. State of Wash., 1950-51; individual practice law, Olympia, Wash., 1951—; gen. counsel Wash. Cath. Conf., 1967-76. Mem. Am., Wash. State, Thurston-Mason County (Wash.) bar assns., Am. Judicature Soc. Home: 2723 Hillside Dr Olympia WA 98501 Office: 301 Security Bldg Olympia WA 98501 Tel (206) 352-4243

WALKER, FRANK BRIGGS, b. Houlton, Maine, Jan. 14, 1934; A.B., Colby Coll., 1958; LL.B., Boston U., 1961. Admitted to Maine bar, 1961; partner firm Silsby, Silsby & Walker, Ellsworth, Maine, 1962-75; individual practice law, Ellsworth, 1975—; atty. City of Ellsworth, 1963-74. Bd. dirs. Ellsworth chpt. ARC, 1965-70, pres., 1966-68. Mem. Am., Maine, Hancock, Aroostook County bar assns., Am. Judicature Soc. Home: Bayside Rd Ellsworth ME 04605 Office: 93 Main St Ellsworth ME 04605 Tel (207) 667-5033

WALKER, GEORGE KONTZ, b. Tuscaloosa, Ala., July 8, 1938; A.B., U. Ala., 1959; LL.B., Vanderbilt U., 1966; M.A., Duke U., 1968; LL.M., U. Va., 1972; postgrad. Yale (Sterling fellow) 1975-76. Admitted to Va. bar, 1967, N.C. bar, 1976; law clk. for judge U.S. Dist. Ct., Richmond, Va., 1966-67; asso. firm Hunton, Williams, Gay, Powell & Gibson, Richmond, 1967-70; individual practice law, Charlottesville, Va., 1970-71; asst. prof. law Wake Forest U., Winston-Salem, N.C., 1972-73, asso. prof., 1974—; staff researcher Va. Gen. Assembly, Charlottesville, 1971-72; research dir. Va. Assn. Counties, 1972-74; cons. Naval War Coll., 1976—. Woodrow Wilson fellow Duke, 1962-63. Mem. Am., Va., Forsyth County bar assns., N.C., Va. state bars, Am. Soc. Internat. Law, Barristers, Phi Beta Kappa, Phi Delta Phi. Author: International Law for the Naval Commander, 1977; contbr. articles to legal jours. Home: 2845 Wesleyan Ln Winston Salem NC 27106 Office: School of Law Wake Forest U PO Box 7206 Winston Salem NC 27109 Tel (919) 761-5431

WALKER, GEORGE ROBERT, b. Columbus, Ohio, Apr. 9, 1928; B.S., Ohio State U., 1950, J.D., 1952. Admitted to Ohio bar, 1952, Calif. bar, 1955; practiced law Monterey and Carmel, Calif., 1955—; sr. partner firm Walker, Schroeder, Davis & Brehner, 1961—; sec., gen. counsel Am. Recreation Centers, Inc., 1959—; executor Alexander F. Victor Estate and Found. for Population Control of Underdeveloped Countries. Chmn. bd. Robert Louis Stephenson Sch., Pebble Beach, Calif.; bd. dirs., treas. Carmel (Calif.) Found.; bd. dirs. Beacon House, Pacific Grove, Calif., 1962-68; bd. dirs. Carmel Presbyn. Found. Trust. Mem. Am., Calif. (continuing edn. com.), Monterey County (pres. 1959) bar assns., Comml. Law League, Monterey History and Art Assn., Beta Theta Pi, Phi Delta Phi. Home: PO Box 4338 Carmel CA 93921 Office: Professional Bldg PO Box LAW Monterey CA 93940 Tel (408) 649-1100

WALKER, GEORGE WILLIAM, b. Boston, Apr. 22, 1929; student U. N.H., 1948-51; LL.B. cum laude, Boston U., 1954. Admitted to Mass. bar, 1954, N.H. bar, 1954, U.S. Ct. Mil. Appeals, 1955, U.S. Supreme Ct. bar, 1960; capt. JAGC, U.S. Army, Paris, 1955-59; individual practice law, Wolfeboro, N.H., 1959-60; asso. firm Hall & Walker, Wolfeboro and Rochester, N.Y., now partner; atty. Carroll County (N.H.), 1967-69; judge Wolfeboro Dist. Ct., 1973—, N.H. Jud. Council, 1973—. Moderator, Gov. Wentworth Regional Sch. Dist., 1973—; trustee Huggins Hosp., Wolfeboro, 1967—, pres., 1974-76. Mem. Am., Carroll County bar assns., Am., N.H. judges assns., N.H. Trial Lawyers Assn., Am. Judicature Soc. Home: Route 109 RFD 2 Wolfeboro NH 03894 Office: Main St Wolfeboro NH 03894 Tel (603) 569-1448

WALKER, GRISSIM HILL, b. Lebanon, Tenn., June 12, 1918; A.B., Cumberland U., 1940; J.D., Harvard, 1946. Admitted to Tenn. bar, 1942, D.C. bar, 1947, Fla. bar, 1962; asso. firm Douglas, Obear & Campbell, Washington, 1946-49; mem. firm Walker & Walker, Lebanon, 1949-55; dean Cumberland U. Law Sch., Tenn., 1955-61; mem. firm Robertson, Robertson, Walker, Cummins & Pitchford, Sarasota, Fla., 1961—. Mem. bd. United Methodist Com. on Relief, 1972-76; bd. dirs. Sarasota Guidance Clinic, Sarasota County Civic League. Mem. Am., Tenn., Sarasota County bar assns. Home: 4516 Camino Real Sarasota FL 33581 Office: 2155 Main St Sarasota FL 33577 Tel (813) 366-5464

WALKER, HARRY GREY, b. Ovett, Miss., Sept. 30, 1932; LL.B., U. Miss., 1952. Admitted to Miss. bar, 1952; individual practice law, Gulfport, Miss., 1952-64; mem. Miss. Ho. of Reps., 1964; judge Harrison County (Miss.) Ct., 1964-68, U.S. 2d Circuit Ct. Dist. Miss., 1968-73; justice Miss. Supreme Ct., Jackson, 1973—. Mem. Am. Judicature Soc., DAV, Paralyzed Vets. Am. Home: 2107 Plantation Blvd Jackson MS 39211 Office: 4th Floor Gartin Justice Bldg Jackson MS 39205 Tel (601) 354-6021

WALKER, HENRY CLAY, b. Augusta, Ga., Sept. 13, 1942; B.A., Tulane U., 1965, J.D., 1968. Admitted to La. bar, 1968; asso. firm Blanchard, Walker, O'Quin & Roberts, Shreveport, La., 1968-69; partner firm Gerhardt & Walker, Shreveport, 1969-72; individual practice law, Shreveport, 1972—; founder Neighborhood Law Office, Shreveport, 1972-74. Mem. Am. Judicature Soc., Am., La. (bd. govs. 1976) trial lawyers assns., ACLU (dir. 1972—), La., Am., Shreveport bar assns. Home and Office: 752 Austen Pl Shreveport LA 71101 Tel (318) 221-8644

WALKER, JAMES GLENN, b. Kansas City, Mo., Aug. 24, 1928; B.A., U. Oreg., 1950; J.D. Lewis & Clark Univ., 1957. Admitted to Oreg. bar, 1957, U.S. Supreme Ct. bar, 1971; adminstrv. asst. trust dept. U.S. National Bank Oreg., Portland, 1953-57; individual practice law, Tigard, Oreg., 1957—; dist. judge pro tem, Washington County, 1976. Mem. Oreg. State Bar, Am., Washington County bar assns., Am. Judicature Soc., ACLU. Home: 12320 SW James Tigard OR 97223 Office: 8862 SW Center Court Tigard OR 97223 Tel (503) 639-6101

WALKER, JOHN LEONARD, b. Washington, Oct. 5, 1947; B.S. in Econs., U. Pa., 1969; J.D., N.Y. U., 1972. Admitted to Miss. bar, 1972; staff atty. Community Legal Service of Miss., Jackson, 1972-73; partner firm Johnson and Walker, Jackson, 1973-76; individual practice law, Jackson, 1976—; vice chmn. bd. dirs. Central Miss. Legal Services, 1976. Mem. Nat. Conf. Black Lawyers (chmn. Miss. chpt.), Am. Bar Assn., Am. Trial Lawyers Assn. Recipient Vanderbilt medal N.Y. U., 1972. Home: PO Box 2086 Jackson MS 39205 Office: 440 Petroleum Bldg Jackson MS 39205 Tel (601) 948-4589

WALKER, JOHN WAYNE, b. Sherman, Tex., July 2, 1948; B.S. in Accounting, U. Idaho, 1970, J.D., 1973. Admitted to Oreg. bar, 1973, Idaho bar, 1973; mem. firm Bielenberg, Anderson & Walker, Moscow, Idaho, 1973—. Mem. Moscow Bar Assn. (exec. sec.), Am., Idaho trial lawyer assns. Home: 806 Indian Hills Moscow ID 83843 Tel (208) 882-4536

WALKER, JOHN WINFRED, b. Hope, Ark., June 3, 1937; B.A., Pine Bluff, Ark., 1958; M.A., N.Y. U., 1961; LL.B., Yale, 1964. Admitted to Ark. bar, 1964, U.S. Supreme Ct. bar, 1973; staff atty. NAACP Legal Def. and Edn. Fund, N.Y.C., 1964-65; individual practice law, 1965-68; partner firm Walker, Kaplan & Mays, and predecessors, Little Rock 1968 —. Mem. Ark. Constl. Revision Study Commn., 1967-68; pres. Center for Law and Edn., Cambridge, Mass., 1976; mem. So. Growth Policies Bd., 1973-74; chmn. Opportunities Industrialization Commn., 1965-70; mem. So. Regional Council, 1968—; bd. dirs. NAACP Legal Def. and Ednl. Fund. Mem. Am., Nat. bar assns. Recipient Mrs. David D. Terry award, 1970. Office: 622 Pyramid Life Bldg Little Rock AR 72201 Tel (501) 374-3758

WALKER, JOSEPH MCCABE, b. Pitts., Feb. 3, 1937; A.B., St. Joseph's Coll., 1958; J.D., U. Pa., 1961. Admitted to Pa. bar, 1962, U.S. Supreme Ct. bar, 1970; staff atty. bond claims Reliance Ins. Co., Phila., 1964-66; staff trial atty. Southeastern Pa. Transp. Authority, Phila., 1966-69; house counsel Hartford Ins. Group, Phila., 1969-70; trial atty. firm Marshall, Donnahey, & Warner, Norristown, Pa., 1970—; instr. internat. law Naval Res. Officers Sch., U.S. Navy Base, Phila., 1972-73, 75-76. Democratic committeeman, Phila., 1971-73. Mem. Phila., Pa., Montgomery County bar assns., Montgomery County Trial Lawyers Assn., Naval Res. Lawyers Assn., Naval Res. Assn., St. Joseph's Coll., U. Pa. law alumni assns. Office: 527 Swede St Norristown PA 19401 Tel (215) 279-5633

WALKER, LEE E., b. Mesquite, Nev., Sept. 22, 1925; B.S., Brigham Young U., 1958; M.S., George Washington U., 1961, LL.B., 1964. Admitted to Nev. bar, 1964; mem. firm Raggio, Walker & Wooster; mem. Nev. Senate, 1970—. Home: 1729 Arrowhead St N Las Vegas NV 89030 Office: 309 S 3d St Las Vegas NV 89101

WALKER, MARY LOU, b. Dayton, Ohio, Dec. 1, 1948; B.A., U. Calif., 1970; J.D., Boston, 1973. Admitted to Calif. bar, 1973; atty. So. Pacific Transp. Co., San Francisco, 1973-76; asso. firm Richards, Watson, Dreyfuss & Gershon, Los Angeles, 1976—. Mem. Am., Calif. bar assns., Am. Trial Lawyers Assn. Office: 333 S Hope St 38th Floor Los Angeles CA 90071

WALKER, ORIVILLE CALVIN, b. Roby, Tex., Apr. 20, 1912; A.B. Howard Payne Coll., 1933; LL.B., U. Tex., 1936. Admitted to Tex. bar, 1936, since practiced in San Antonio; clk. Supreme Ct. Tex., 1936-40; individual practice law, 1940-54; prof. law St. Mary's U., 1954—. Mem. Tex., San Antonio bar assns., Am. Arbitration Assn., Order of Barristers, Phi Delta Phi. Editor-in-chief: Appellate Procedure in Texas, 1965, 2d edit., 1977. Home: 2302 Blanton Dr San Antonio TX 78209 Office: 2700 Cincinnati Ave San Antonio TX 78284 Tel (512) 433-2311

WALKER, OWEN FRANKLIN, b. Canton, Ohio, Aug. 11, 1911; B.A., Brown U., 1933; B.A. in Jurisprudence, Oxford U., 1935, B.C.L., 1936. Admitted to Ohio bar, 1937, U.S. Tax Ct. bar, 1943; asso. firm Thompson, Hine & Flory, Cleve., 1936-42, 46-48, partner, 1948—; served to capt. JAGC, AUS, 1943-46. Mem. Am., Ohio, Greater Cleve. bar, assn., Am. Law Inst. Home: 17477 Shelburne Rd Cleveland Heights OH 44118 Office: 1100 National City Bank Bldg Cleveland OH 44114 Tel (216) 241-1880

WALKER, PAUL HOWARD, b. Baldwyn, Miss., Feb. 10, 1923; student E. Miss. Jr. Coll., 1940-41; La. State U., 1941-43, U. Mo., 1943-44; J.D. with honors, George Washington U., 1948, LL.M., 1949; postgrad., Harvard, 1975-76. Admitted to D.C. bar, 1948, Md. bar, 1959, Mass. bar, 1969; reporter U.S. Tax Ct., Washington, 1950-53; asst. gen. counsel Life Ins. Assn. Am., Washington, 1953-68; tax counsel New Eng. Mut. Life Ins. Co., Boston, 1968—; mem. editorial advisory bd. Exec. Compensation Jour., Washington, 1973—; Estate Planning Mag., 1973—. Trustee More Men for the Ministry Found., 1976—. Mem. Am. (chmn. com. on partnerships, tax. sect., 1976—), Fed., Boston bar assns., Assn. Life Ins. Counsel, SAR (pres. Boston chpt. 1974-76; v.p. state soc., 1974—), Tax Analysts and Advocates, (mem. legal advisory bd. 1975—), Mass. Soc. (judge advocate), Soc. 1812, SCV (judge advocate Holt Camp), Tax Execs. Inst., Delta Theta Phi. Contbr. articles in field to law jours. Home: 21 Milton Rd Brookline MA 02146 Office: 501 Boylston St Boston MA 02117 Tel (617) 266-3700

WALKER, ROBERT DARYL, b. Tarentum, Pa., June 5, 1925; B.S., Findlay Coll., 1949; J.D., Ohio No. U., 1951. Admitted to Ohio bar, 1951, also U.S. Supreme Ct. bar; legal counsel Motorists Mut. Ins. Co., Columbus, Ohio, 1953-61; counsel and asst. sec. Inland Homes Co., Piqua, Ohio, 1962-65; individual practice law, Findlay, Ohio, 1965-71; judge Findlay Municipal Ct., 1971-76, Hancock County Ct. Common Pleas, 1977—; analyst Columbia Research and Devel. Corp., Columbus. Past pres. Winebrenner Extended Care Center; sec. Winebrenner Theol. Sem.; past pres. Hancock County March of Dimes. Mem. Am., Ohio, Findlay-Hancock County (past pres.) bar assns. Recipient Supreme Jud. Service award Ohio Supreme Ct., 1975, 76; named Outstanding Judge Ohio Supreme Ct., 1975; contbr. articles in field to legal jours., textbooks. Home: 315 Hancock St Findlay OH 45840 Office: Findlay OH 45840 Tel (419) 422-3045

WALKER, TIMOTHY BLAKE, b. Utica, N.Y., May 21, 1940; A.B. magna cum laude, Princeton, 1962; M.A. in Sociology, U. Denver, 1969, J.D. magna cum laude, 1967. Admitted to Colo. bar, 1968, Calif. bar, 1969, Ind. bar, 1971; asst. prof. law U. Pacific, 1968-69; vis. asso. prof. law U. Toledo, 1969-70; asso. prof. law Ind. U., 1970-71; asso. prof. law U. Denver, 1971-75, prof., 1975—, dir. adminstrn. of justice program, 1972—; individual practice law, Denver, 1972—; mem. Ind. Child Support Study Commn., 1970-71; cons. NSF, 1972—. Pres. Shawnee Water Consumers Assn., Shawnee, Colo., 1973-77. Mem. Am. Bar Assn.; fellow Am. Sociol. Assn. Contbr. articles to legal jours. Home: 10162 E Exposition Ave Denver CO 80231 Office: 200 W 14th Ave Denver CO 80204 Tel (303) 753-3530

WALKER, WOODROW WILSON, b. Greenville, Mich., Feb. 19, 1919; B.A., U. Mich., 1943; LL.B., Columbus Law Sch., 1950. Admitted to D.C. bar, 1950, U.S. Supreme Ct. bar, 1958, Va. bar, 1959; atty. Am. law div. legis. reference Library of Congress, Washington, 1951-60, dir. Library of Congress Fed. Credit Union, 1957-60; individual practice law, Arlington, Va., 1960—; counsel Calvary Found., Arlington, 1970—. Vice pres. Jefferson Civic Assn., Arlington, 1955-61; pres. Nellie Custis PTA, Arlington, 1960-61; sec. Arlington County Bd. Equalization Real Estate Assessment, 1962, chmn., 1963; com. chmn. Arlington Troop 108 Boy Scouts Am., 1964-69; mem. Arlington County Pub. Utilities Commn., 1964-66, vice chmn., 1965-66; pres. Betschler Class Adult Sunday Sch., Calvary United Meth. Ch., Arlington, 1965. Mem. Va., Arlington County, Am. bar assns. Home: 2822 Fort Scott Dr Arlington VA 22202 Office: 2116 Wilson Blvd Suite 201-202 Arlington VA 22201 Tel (703) 524-7860

WALKO, JOSEPH STEPHEN, b. Ambridge, Pa., Oct. 10, 1930; B.S., Geneva Coll., 1952; J.D., Dickinson Sch. Law, 1955. Admitted to Pa. bar, 1956; asst. dist. atty. Beaver County (Pa.), 1957-58, 1st asst. dist. atty., 1959-68, dist. atty., 1972—; mem. firm Caputo & Walko, Ambridge, 1970—; dir. Roffler Industries, Inc. Mem. Am., Pa. bar assns., Am. Judicature Soc., Am. Trial Lawyers Assn., Nat. Dist. Atty. Assn. Home: 1399 Adams Dr Ambridge PA 15003 Office: 719 Merchant St Ambridge PA 15003 Tel (412) 266-7980

WALKOWIAK, ROBERT JOSEPH, b. Cleve., Aug. 18, 1913; student Cleve. Coll., Western Res. U.; J.D., Cleve. Marshall Law Sch., 1950. Admitted to Ohio bar, 1951; owner, operator Walkowiak Funeral Home, Cleve., 1941—. Mem. Am., Ohio, Cuyahoga County bar assns., Bar Assn. Greater Cleve. Office: 6701 Lansing Ave Cleveland OH 44105 Tel (216) 641-4171

WALL, DOUGLAS JONES, b. Denver, Apr. 1, 1927; B.S., U. Kans., 1950, J.D., 1955. Admitted to Kans. bar, 1955, Ariz. bar, 1956, U.S. Supreme Ct. bar, 1971; partner firm Mangum, Wall, Stoops & Warden, Flagstaff, Ariz., 1960—; lectr. bus. law No. Ariz. U., 1965—, asst. to pres., 1970—; mem. disciplinary com. Ariz. State Bar, 1976—. Mem. Ariz. Water Commn., 1963-75, chmn., 1965-69; past chmn. Coconino County (Ariz.) Republican Central Com.; bd. dirs. Ariz. Pub. Service, 1976—; trustee Mus. No. Ariz., 1976—. Mem. Am., Ariz., Coconino County (past pres.) bar assns., Soc. Hosp. Attys., Am. Trial Lawyers Assn., Am. Coll. Probate Counsel, Am. Judicature Soc., Beta Gamma Sigma. Named Citizen of Year, Flagstaff, 1968. Home: 1805 N Hereford Dr Flagstaff AZ 86001 Office: PO Box 10 222 E Birch Ave Flagstaff AZ 86002 Tel (602) 774-6664

WALL, KENNETH E., JR., b. Beaumont, Tex., Apr. 6, 1944; grad. Lamar U., 1966, U. Tex., 1969. Admitted to Tex. bar, 1969; asst. city atty., Beaumont, 1969-73, city atty., 1973—; legal counsel SE Tex. Regional Planning Commn., 1974, 76. Mem. Am., Tex., Jefferson County (dir.) bar assns., Nat. Inst. Municipal Law Officers, Tex. City Attys. Assn. Home: 129 Orgain St Beaumont TX 77707 Office: PO Box 3827 Beaumont TX 77704 Tel (713) 838-0761

WALL, SIDNEY HADLEY, b. Noblesville, Ind., July 28, 1912; B.A., Pomona Coll., 1934; J.D., Yale, 1937. Admitted to Calif. bar, 1937, Fed. bar, 1937, U.S. Tax Ct. bar, 1943, U.S. Ct. Claims bar, 1943, U.S. Supreme Ct. bar, 1973; asso. atty. firm O'Melveny, Tuller & Myers, Los Angeles, 1937-42; chief price atty. Office Price Adminstrn. Los Angeles Dist. Office, 1942-43; asst. counsel Lockheed Aircraft Corp., Burbank, Calif., 1943-45; asso. firm O'Melveny & Myers, Los Angeles, 1945-48, partner, 1948—. Fellow Am. Coll. Trial Lawyers, mem. State Bar Calif. (chmn. com. adminstrn. of justice 1967-68), Am., Los Angeles County bar assns., Am. Judicature Assn., Nat. Legal Aid and Defenders Assn. Office: 611 W 6th St Los Angeles CA 90017 Tel (213) 620-1120

WALL, WILLIAM ALFORD, b. Atlanta, June 27, 1926; B.S., U. S.C., 1949; LL.B., J.D., U. Ga. Admitted to Ga. bar, 1950; partner firm Atlanta, Georgia, Hewlett, Hewlett & Wall, Roswell, Ga. Mem. Atlanta Region Met. Planning Commn., 1969-71. Mem. Am., Atlanta bar assns., State Bar Ga., N. Fulton C. of C. (dir.), Ga. Trial Lawyers Assn. (past pres.), Phi Alpha Delta. Home: Route 1 Woodstock Rd Roswell GA 30075 Office: 953 Canton St Roswell GA 30075 Tel (404) 993-4216

WALLACE, ARTHUR STEPHENSON, b. Miami, Ga., Apr. 20, 1949; student Oxford Coll., Emory U., 1967-69; B.A. in History, Mercer U., 1971; J.D. cum laude, U. Ga., 1974. Admitted to Ga. bar, 1974; asso. firm Ivey & Assos., Augusta, Ga., 1974-75; mem. firm Wilkinson & Wallace, Augusta, 1975—. Bd. dirs., v.p. Lynndale Sch. and Tng. Center, Inc., Augusta. Mem. Am. Bar Assn. Editorial bd. Ga. Law Rev., 1972-73. Home: 221 Chatham Rd Augusta GA 30907 Office: 563 Greene St Augusta GA 30903 Tel (404) 724-2046

WALLACE, CHARLES GLENN, III, b. Hastings, Nebr., Mar. 1, 1938; B.A., U. Nebr., 1961, J.D., 1964. Admitted to Nebr. bar, 1964; atty. Conn. Mut. Life Ins. Co., Hartford, 1964-67; partner firm Kelley & Wallace, North Platte, Nebr., 1967—; police magistrate City of North Platte, 1967-69. Pres., United Fund, 1968-69, W. Cental Nebr. Health Planning Council, 1969-71; mem. exec. com. Tri-Trails council Boy Scouts Am., 1970—. Mem. Am., Nebr., Western Nebr., Lincoln County (past pres.) bar assns., Optimists Internat. Office: 202 W 2d St North Platte NE 69101 Tel (308) 532-7110

WALLACE, DAVID ARTHUR, b. N.Y.C., July 10, 1943; B.A., Hunter Coll., 1967; J.D., Fordham U., 1970. Admitted to N.Y. bar, 1971, N.J. bar, 1973; asso. firm Robinson, Silverman, Pearce, Aronsohn, Sand & Berman, N.Y.C., 1970-73; gen. counsel N.J. Pub. Employment Relations Commn., Trenton, 1973-77; asso. firm Gerald L. Doff, Rahway, N.J., 1977—. Mem. Am., N.J. State bar assns. Home: 69 Omaha Ave Rockaway NJ 07866 Office: 2376 St George's Ave Rahway NJ 07065 Tel (201) 574-9700

WALLACE, DAVID SMITH, b. Galveston, Tex., Mar. 21, 1945; B.A. Ind. U., 1967, J.D., 1972. Admitted to Ind. bar, 1972, fed. bar So. Dist. Ind., Circuit Ct. Appeals; asst. city atty. Muncie, Ind., 1972—, partner firm Warner, Peckinpaugh & Wallace, Muncie, 1977—; probation officer Marion County Juvenile Ct. 1967-68, Ind. State Parole Officer 1968-72. Mem. bd., past pres. Big Brothers Delaware County; mem. bd. Home Learning Center for Hearing Impaired Children. Mem. Am., Ind. (dist. rep. young lawyers sect.), Muncie bar assns., Young Lawyers Delaware County (past pres.), Jaycees. Home: Route 7 Pineview Dr Muncie IN 47302 Office: 330 E Main Muncie IN 47305 Tel (317) 288-4425

WALLACE, HAROLD EUGENE, b. Oil City, Pa., Apr. 28, 1927; B.A., Allegheny Coll., 1950; LL.B., Wayne State U., 1955, LL.M., 1969. Admitted to Mich. bar, 1956; salary adminstr. Chrysler Co., Twinsburg, Ohio, 1959-63, asst. labor relations supr., Warren, Mich., 1963-66, labor relations supr., Dearborn, Mich., 1966-67; dir. indsl. relations die cast div. Hoover Ball & Bearing Co., Saline, Mich., 1967-69, corp. salary adminstr., 1969-77, corp. dir. personnel, 1977—. Mem. Am. Arbitration Assn. (panel 1970—), Mich. Bar Assn. Home: 577 Huntington St Adrian MI 49221 Office: 135 E Bennett St Saline MI 48176 Tel (313) 429-2552

WALLACE, J. CLIFFORD, b. San Diego, Dec. 11, 1928; B.A., San Diego State U., 1952; LL.B., U. Calif., Berkeley, 1955. Admitted to Calif. bar, 1955; mem. firm Gray, Cary, Ames & Frye, San Diego, 1955-70; judge U.S. Dist. Ct. So. Calif., San Diego, 1970-72, U.S. 9th Circuit Ct. of Appeals, 1972—; mem. com. on fed. jurisdiction Jud. Conf. U.S., also com. to consider standards for admission to practice in fed. cts.; adj. prof. law; lectr. in field. Mem. Am. Bar Assn., Am. Bd. Trial Advocates, Am. Law Inst. Contbr. articles in field to legal jours. Office: 940 Front St San Diego CA 92189 Tel (714) 293-6114

WALLACE, JAMES HAROLD, JR., b. Atlanta, Feb. 8, 1941; B.E.E., U. S.C., 1963; J.D., Georgetown U., 1966. Admitted to U.S. Supreme Ct. bar, 1971; patent examiner U.S. Patent Office, Washington, 1966-67; trial atty. anti-trust div. Dept. Justice, Washington, 1967-70; partner firm Kirkland, Ellis & Rowe, Washington, 1970—. Mem. Am. Bar Assn., U.S. C. of C. Contbr. articles to profl. jours. Home: 3029 Cambridge Pl NW Washington DC 20007 Office: 1776 K St NW Washington DC 20006 Tel (202) 857-5140

WALLACE, JOHN R., b. Miami, Okla., Nov. 24, 1913; A.B., U. Okla., 1934; LL.B., J.D., Harvard U., 1937; LL.D. (hon.) Coll. of Ozarks, Clarksville, Ark., 1969. Admitted to Okla. bar, 1937, U.S. Supreme Ct. bar, 1960; partner firm Wallace & Wallace, Miami, 1937-47, Wallace & Owens, Miami, 1947-70; pres. Wallace & Owens, Inc., Miami, 1970—; spl. chief justice Supreme Ct. Okla., 1970-71; mem. Okla. Adv. Council for Nat. Legal Services Corp., 1976—; dir. Security Bank & Trust Co., Miami Savs. & Loan Assn., Welch State Bank, Exchange State Bank. Elder, Presbyterian Ch., 1946—; trustee Coll. of Ozarks, 1958—, chmn. bd., 1966-68. Fellow Am. Bar Found., Am. Coll. Trial Lawyers, Am. Coll. Probate Counsel; mem. Am. (del. 1972-73, 76—, bd. govs. 1976-77), Okla. (bd. govs. 1965-66, 72-74, pres. 1973), Ottawa County (pres. 1947) bar assns., Phi Beta Kappa. Home: 2021 Yale Ave Miami OK 74354 Office: 21 S Main St PO Box 1168 Miami OK 74354 Tel (918) 542-5501

WALLACE, JOSEPH ALGERNON, b. Elkins, W.Va., Oct. 20, 1938; B.A., Mich. State U., 1960; J.D., Tulane U., 1965. Admitted to W.Va. bar, 1969, also U.S. Supreme Ct. bar; house counsel asst. to pres. Downtowner Corp., Memphis, 1965-68; legal adminstr., asst. to pres. Nationwide Supply Co., Memphis, 1965-68; house counsel Pace Corp., Memphis, 1968-69; asso. firm Milford L. Gibson, Elkins, 1969-71; partner Gibson & Wallace, Elkins, 1971-74; individual practice law, Elkins, 1974—. Bd. dirs. Elkins Indsl. Devel. Corp., 1971—, pres., 1977—; trustee Davis Meml. Hosp., 1970-76, pres. bd., 1974-76. Mem. Am., Randolph County (treas. 1972-73, pres. 1974-75) bar assns., Nat. Assn. R.R. Trial Counsel, Am. Judicature Soc. Home: Kerens Hill Elkins WV 26241 Office: Box 7 Elkins WV 26241 Tel (304) 636-1111

WALLACE, LEON HARRY, b. Terre Haute, Ind., Jan. 24, 1904; student U. Ill., 1921-23; A.B., Ind. U., 1925, J.D., 1933. Admitted to Ind. bar, 1933; U.S. Supreme Ct. bar, 1950; partner firm Wallace, Randel & Wallace, Terre Haute, 1933-45; asso. prof. Ind. U., Bloomington, 1945-47, prof., 1947-74, dean Sch. Law, 1951-66, Charles McGuffey Hepburn prof. emeritus, 1966-74; spl. hearing officer U.S. Dept. Justice, 1964-69; Gov.'s rep. Ind. Constl. Revision Commn., 1952—; dir., treas. Ind. Continuing Legal Edn. Forum, 1960-66; sec.-treas. Ind. Bar Found., 1960—. Mem. Am. Law Inst., Inst. Jud. Adminstrn., Am. (sect. chmn. local govt. law 1964-65), Ind. bar assns., Am. Acad. Polit. Sci., Order of Coif, Phi Beta Kappa. Contbr. articles to legal jours. Home: 939 S High St Bloomington IN 47401 Office: 208 Law Bldg Ind Sch Law Bloomington IN 47401 Tel (812) 337-7593

WALLACE, MICHAEL EDWARD, b. Creston, Iowa, Aug. 28, 1944; B.B.A., U. Iowa, 1967, J.D., 1971. Admitted to Iowa bar, 1971, Colo. bar, 1972; individual practice law, Durango, Colo., 1972—; judge Durango Municipal Ct., 1973—. Mem. Am., Colo., Southwestern Colo. (pres.) bar assns., Durango C. of C. (dir.), Phi Delta Phi. Home: 2509 Delwood Ave Durango CO 81301 Office: Box 449 Durango CO 81301 Tel (303) 247-4023

WALLACE, MILTON JAY, b. Passaic, N.J., Dec. 17, 1935; B.B.A., U. Miami, 1956, LL.B., 1959, J.D., 1959. Admitted to Fla. bar, 1959; partner firm Wallace and Breslow, and predecessors, Miami, 1959—; judge City of Miami, 1961-62; asst. atty. gen. State of Fla., 1965-70; gen. counsel Fla. Securities Commn., Div. of Securities Fla. Comptroller, 1965-70. Mem. Fla. Inst. C.P.A.'s. Office: 2138 Biscayne Blvd Miami FL 33137 Tel (305) 576-2666

WALLACE, ROBERT FELTUS, b. Terre Haute, Ind., Dec. 13, 1914; LL.B., Ind. U., 1940. Admitted to Ind. bar, 1940; staff atty. Ind. State Inheritance Tax Dept., 1942-46; asst. inheritance tax adminstr. Ind. Atty. Gen.'s Office, Indpls., 1950-54; city atty. City of Terre Haute, 1955-56; dep. prosecutor Vigo County, Terre Haute, 1957—; individual practice law, Terre Haute, 1954—. Mem. Ind., Terre Haute bar assns., Vigo County Ind. U. Alumni Assn. (pres. 1970-73). Home: 3208 N 11th St Terre Haute IN 47804 Office: 506 Ohio St Terre Haute IN 47807 Tel (812) 232-4549

WALLACE, SARA KLIER, b. Warsaw, Poland, May 15, 1909; came to U.S., 1911; LL.B. magna cum laude, Portia Law Sch. (now New Eng. Sch. Law), 1930. Admitted to Mass. bar, 1930; individual practice law, Boston and Brookline, Mass., 1930-37, 63—; spl. legal counsel fed. grants Town of Brookline, 1963—; participant panels legal aspects urban renewal, housing, rehab.; corporate mem. Brookline Savs. Bank, 1971—; corporate mem. Children's Hosp. Med. Center, Boston, 1946—; mem. Mass. Meat Poultry Hearing Bd., 1970. Pres., Intercommunity Home Makers Service, 1974—; pres. LWV, 1952-56. Mem. Mass. Bar Assn., Mass. Assn. Women Lawyers. Recipient Distinguished Citizens award Chronicle Citizen, Brookline, 1964, LWV, 1976. Home and Office: 115 Tappan St Brookline MA 02146 Tel (617) 232-3401

WALLACE, WILLIAM CRAIG, b. Rockdale, Tex., Jan. 2, 1911; B.S., Harvard, 1932. Admitted to Tex. bar, 1934, U.S. Dist. Ct. bar, 1935; since practiced in Cameron, Tex., partner firm Wallace & Wallace, 1934-46; individual practice law, 1946-61; judge 20th Jud. Dist., 1961—. Mem. Tex., Milam County (pres. 1952-56) bar assns. Contbr. articles in field to legal jours. Home: 707 E 7th St Cameron TX 76520 Office: Box 268 Cameron TX 76520 Tel (817) 697-2651

WALLACE, WILLIAM FRANCIS, b. Boston, May 25, 1942; B.S., Stoneham Coll., 1965; J.D., Boston U., 1967. Admitted to Mass. bar, 1967; asso. firm Sheff & McGarry, Boston, 1968-70; individual practice law, Hingham, Mass., 1971-74; partner firm Wallace & Dray, Hingham, 1974-75; individual practice law, Hingham, 1976—; asst. dist. atty. Plymouth County (Mass.), 1975—. Mem. Hingham Fin. Com., 1974. Mem. Mass., Plymouth County bar assns., Assn. Trial Lawyers Am. Home: 425 East St Hingham MA 02043 Office: 44 North St Hingham MA 02043 Tel (617) 749-7740

WALLACE, WILLIAM HARVEY, b. Louisville, Nov. 25, 1930; B.A., Washington and Lee U., 1952; LL.B., U. Louisville, 1955. Admitted to Ky. bar, 1955; individual practice law, Louisville, 1958-62; asst. gen. counsel Louisville Legal Aid Soc., 1962-72; atty. trial supr. Ky. Bur. Hwys, Louisville, 1972—. Mem. Ky. Bar Assn. Home: 7002 Cooper Chapel Rd Louisville KY 40229 Office: PO Box 21178 Louisville KY 40221 Tel (502) 367-6411

WALLACE, WILSON, b. Council Bluffs, Iowa, May 5, 1910; B.A., U. Okla., 1939, LL.B., 1939. Admitted to Okla. bar, 1939, U.S. Ct. Appeals bar, 10th Circuit, 1956; now partner firm Wallace, Bickford & Pasley, Ardmore, Okla.; mem. Okla. Legislature, 1937-41, 45-50; mem. Okla. Jud. Council, 1948-67; spl. justice Okla. Supreme Ct., 1964-66; pres. So. Okla. Legal Inst., 1971. Trustee Ardmore Devel. Authority, 1967—, chmn., 1970-71. Fellow Am. Coll. Trial Lawyers; mem. Am., Okla. (pres. 1977), Carter County (pres. 1947-48) bar assns., Okla. Trial Lawyers Assn. Editor Okla. Bar Jour., 1974—. Office: 29 B St SW PO Box 1027 Ardmore OK 73401 Tel (405) 223-5566*

WALLACH, KENNETH LEE, b. N.Y.C., Apr. 16, 1946; B.A., Harvard, 1968, J.D., 1972. Admitted to N.Y. bar, 1973; law clk. to Hon. J. Edward Lumbard U.S. Ct. Appeals, N.Y.C., 1972-73; asso. firm Debevoise, Plimpton, Lyons & Gates, N.Y.C., 1973—. Editor, Harvard Law Rev., 1970-72. Office: 299 Park Ave New York City NY 10017 Tel (212) 752-6400

WALLAHAN, FRANKLIN JAY, b. Spencer, Iowa, Jan. 23, 1935; B.S., U.S.D., 1959, J.D., 1961. Admitted to Minn. bar, 1961, S.D. bar, 1961; law clk. Dist. Ct. Minn., 1961-62; mng. partner firm Wallahan, Huffman & Truhe, Rapid City, S.D., 1963—; mem. S.D. State Senate, 1971-72. Mem. Dem. Nat. Com., 1972-76. Mem. Am., Minn., Black Hills County, Pennington County bar assns., S.D. Trial Lawyers Assn., Internat. Soc. Barristers, Assn. Trial Lawyers Am. Home: 2711 Frontier Dr Rapid City SD 57701 Office: Box 328 Rapid City SD 57709 Tel (605) 348-0456

WALLER, CHARLES DOUGLASS, b. Cookville, Tenn., Apr. 23, 1943; student Polk Jr. Coll., 1967, U. South Fla., 1968; J.D., U. Fla., 1970. Admitted to Fla. bar, 1971; asso. firm Larkin & Larkin, Dade City, Fla., 1970-71, partner, 1971-76; partner firm Larkin, Larkin, Waller & Hersch, Dade City, 1976—; city atty., Zephyrhills (Fla.), also city prosecutor, from 1976. Bd. dirs. Pasco-Hernando Community-Trust Found., March of Dimes Found., 1974-76, Pasco County Legal Aid Clinic, 1976. Mem. Am. Trial Lawyers Assn., Am. Judicature Soc., Pasco County Bar Assn. (v.p. 1976), Phi Alpha Delta. Home: 108 E Palm Ave Dade City FL 33525 Office: 208 S 7th St Dade City FL 33525 Tel (904) 567-5143

WALLER, HENRY HALL, JR., b. Rutledge, Tenn., May 23, 1913; LL.B., Cumberland U., 1948; J.D., Stanford, 1969. Admitted to Tenn. bar, 1947, U.S. Supreme Ct. bar, 1956; served to col. U.S. Air Force, 1933-64; individual practice law, Lebanon, Tenn., 1965—; city prosecutor, Lebanon, 1968-69. Chmn., Wilson County Library Bd., 1975—. Mem. Tenn. Bd. Law Examiners (v.p. 1972—), Am. Trial Lawyers Assn., Am., Tenn., Lebanon-Wilson County (past pres.) bar assns. Home: 302 E Spring St Lebanon TN 37087 Office: 106 1/2 S Cumberland Lebanon TN 37087 Tel (615) 444-6100

WALLER, JOHN JAMES, b. Red Cloud, Nebr., May 14, 1924; B.A., magna cum laude, Harvard, 1947, J.D., 1950. Admitted to Calif. bar, 1951, 9th Circuit Ct. Appeals bar, 1959, U.S. Supreme Ct. bar, 1976, U.S. Tax Ct. bar; asso. firm Gibson, Dunn & Crutcher, Los Angeles, 1950-62; asso., then partner firm Flint & MacKay, Los Angeles, 1962-68; asso. firm Max Fink, Beverly Hills, Calif., 1968-73; individual practice law, Santa Ana, Calif., 1973—. Dist. vice chmn. Orange County council Boy Scouts Am.; bd. dirs. Buena Park (Calif.) YMCA; chmn. Buena Park Airport Commn., 1972-73; chmn. Buena Park Transp. Commn., 1974-76. Mem. State Bar Calif., Am., Los Angeles County, Orange County bar assns., Am. Judicature Soc. Home: 5591 Monticello Ave Buena Park CA 90621 Office: Suite 750 1600 N Broadway St Santa Ana CA 92706 Tel (714) 547-9148

WALLERSTEIN, MORTON LUDWIG, b. Richmond, Va., Dec. 7, 1890; B.A., U. Va., 1911; LL.B., Harvard, 1914. Admitted to Va. bar, 1914, U.S. Supreme Ct. bar, 1944; since practiced in Richmond; atty. gen., 1914-16; mem. firm Pollard, Wise & Chichester, 1916-17, Bloomberg & Wallerstein, 1920-22, Wallerstein, Goode & Dobbins, and predecessors, 1922—; atty. Public Works Adminstrn., 1933-36; chmn. Va. State Planning Bd., 1933-38; pres. Am. Municipal Assn. 1930, Am. Soc. Planning Ofcls., 1931; regional chmn. Nat. Resources Planning Bd., 1937-41; exec. sec. Va. Municipal League 1921-41. Pres. Richmond First Club, 1923; scoutmaster Boy Scouts Am. 1914-17; pres. Richmond Jewish Community Council 1948-49, examiner Seamanship and Scouts, 1920-48. Mem. Richmond, Va., Am. bar assns., State Bar Va., Am. Law Inst., Nat. League Cities. Author: Opinions of Attorneys General, 1915; Va. Election Laws, 1915; Public Career of Simon E. Sobeloff, 1975; recipient Distinguished Service awards Jewish Community Council, Am. Soc. Planning Ofcls., Va., Municipal League, Va. Citizens Planning Assn. Home: 1601 Pope Ave Richmond VA 23227 Office: The Ironfronts 4th Floor 1011 E Main St Richmond VA 23202 Tel (804) 643-7301

WALLEY, JAMES MARVIN, SR., b. Poplarville, Miss., Mar. 2, 1921; B.S., U. Nebr., 1962; J.D., Tulane U., 1972. Admitted to La. bar, 1972; individual practice law, New Orleans, 1972—; dir. placement, dir. clin. edn., Tulane U. Sch. Law, 1973—. Notary pub. Jefferson Parish, La., 1972—. Mem. Am., La. bar assns. Home: 745 Fairfield Ave Gretna LA 70053 Office: Tulane Univ Sch Law New Orleans LA 70118 Tel (504) 866-2751

WALLIS, SHARON ELIZABETH, b. Bakersfield, Calif., June 29, 1948; B.A., U. Calif., 1970; J.D., Hastings Coll., 1973. Admitted to Calif. bar, 1973; dep. dist. atty. Kern County (Calif.), 1973-75, 1976—; dep. dist. atty. Santa Barbara County (Calif.), 1975-76; guest lectr. Bakersfield Coll., 1974-75, Santa Barbara City Coll., 1975, U. Calif., 1975-76. Bd. dirs. Calif. Rural Legal Assistance. Mem. Kern County, Santa Barbara bar assns., Santa Barbara Barristers. Tel (805) 861-2424

WALLMAN, LESTER, b. N.Y.C., Apr. 18, 1929; LL.B., Bklyn. Law Sch., 1954; LL.M., N.Y. U., 1956. Admitted to N.Y. bar, 1954; atty. Standard Oil of N.J., N.Y.C., 1953-65; partner firm Ramson, Bogaty & Wallman, N.Y.C., 1965-68; partner firm Wallman and Kramer, N.Y.C., 1968—; spl. counsel to chmn. judiciary com. N.Y. Assembly, 1972-75; arbitrator Civil Ct. N.Y., 1972—; faculty N.Y. U. Sch. Continuing Edn. in Law and Taxation. Mem. Community Planning Bd. #6, N.Y.C., 1977—; mem. Zoning Bd. New Rochelle (N.Y.), 1968-71. Mem. Am. (com. fed. legis. family sect.), N.Y. State (chmn. com. on legis., family sect.) bar assns., Am. Acad. Matrimonial Lawyers. Contbr. articles to legal jours. Office: 275 Madison Ave New York City NY 10016 Tel (212) 889-4970

WALLOCK, TERRENCE JOSEPH, b. Wisconsin Rapids, Wis., Dec. 13, 1944; A.B., U. Calif., Los Angeles, 1967, J.D., 1970. Admitted to Calif. bar, 1971; asso. firms Nelson, Liker & Merrifield, Los Angeles, Musck, Peeler, Garrett, Los Angeles. Mem. Calif., Los Angeles County bar assns., Jr. Barristors of Los Angeles, Order of Coif. Office: suite 2000 1 Wilshire Blvd Los Angeles CA 90017 Tel (213) 629-3322

WALLS, GEORGE RODNEY, b. New Orleans, Sept. 30, 1945; B.A., Md. U., 1967, J.D., 1970. Admitted to Md. and D.C. bars, 1971; asso. counsel GAC Finance, Inc., Allentown, Pa., 1970-73; sr. atty. Quality Inns Internat., Inc., Silver Spring, Md., 1973-76; house counsel Suburban Trust Co., Hyattsville, Md., 1976—. Mem. Am., Md. bar assns. Home: 10433 Sternwheel Pl Columbia MD 21044 Office: 6495 New Hampshire Ave Hyattsville MD 20783 Tel (301) 270-7143

WALLS, MARSHAL GORDON, b. Philippi, W.Va., Mar. 2, 1940; B.S., W.Va. U., 1963, also LL.B. Admitted to W.Va. bar, 1966; asso. firm Samuel Solins, Welch, W.Va., 1966-69, partner, 1969—. Pres., McDowell County (WVa.) Dep. Sheriff's Civil Service Commn., McDowell County Humane Soc. Mem. Am., W.Va., McDowell County (past pres.) bar assns., Comml. Law League Am. Home: 220 Riverside Dr Welch WV 24801 Office: 35 1/2 McDowell St Welch WV 24801 Tel (304) 436-4226

WALRATH, LOUIS LAVERNE, b. Billings, Mont., Aug. 22, 1940; B.A., U. Colo., 1962; J.D., U. Wyo., 1965. Admitted to Wyo. bar, 1965, U.S. Dist. Ct. for Dist. Wyo., 1965; individual practice law with asso., Michael S. Messenger, Thermopolis, Wyo., 1975—; town atty., Thermopolis, 1966—; justice of peace, Hot Springs County, 1966—. Pres. Meml. Museums, Inc., 1970—; pres. Legion Town and Country Club, Inc., 1973-75; dir., sec.-treas. Thermopolis Improvement Corp., 1968—. Mem. Wyo. Assn. Judges, Wyo., Hot Springs County (pres. 1968, 76) bar assns. Recipient book award, 1963. Home: 1145 Arapahoe St Thermopolis WY 82443 Office: 316 Broadway St Thermopolis WY 82443 Tel (307) 864-3773

WALRAVEN, HAROLD RICHARD, b. Lerado, Kans., Mar. 5, 1934; B.B.A., Washburn U., 1956, J.D., 1959. Admitted to Kans. bar, 1959, Ariz. bar, 1960; individual practice law, Prescott, Ariz., 1960—; dep. atty. Yavapai County (Ariz.), 1960-64. Mem. Prescott City Council, 1964-68; chmn. original steering com., bd. govs. Yavapai Community Coll., 1966-74. Mem. Am., Ariz., Yavapai County bar assns. Recipient Community award Prescott Jaycees, 1968. Home: 2205 Nolte St Prescott AZ 86301 Office: 239 S Cortez St Prescott AZ 86301 Tel (602) 445-8824

WALSH, CARL MAURICE, b. Chgo., Feb. 5, 1941; B.S., U. Notre Dame, 1961; J.D., DePaul U., 1965. Admitted to Ill. bar, 1965, U.S. Supreme Ct. bar, 1969; asst. states atty. Cook County, Ill., 1966-68; individual practice law, Chgo., 1968—; hearing officer Ill. Pollution Control Bd., 1972—. Mem. Am., Fed., Ill., Chgo. (chmn. criminal law com. 1975-76) bar assns., Assn. Criminal Def. Lawyers (dir. 1971—), Nat. Assn. Criminal Def. Lawyers. Office: 39 S LaSalle St Chicago IL 60603 Tel (312) 332-7374

WALSH, DANIEL AUGUSTINE, JR., b. Bklyn., Feb. 14, 1934; B.B.A. cum laude, St. Francis Coll., 1955; J.D., St. John's U., 1958. Admitted to N.Y. bar, 1958, U.S. Supreme Ct. bar, 1964; partner firm Gore & Walsh, N.Y.C., 1958-61; individual practice law, N.Y.C., 1961—; asso. prof. law St. Francis Coll., 1961—, academic dean, 1974-75; hearing officer N.Y.C. Bd. Edn., 1976—, mem. bd. examiners, 1976. Mem. Kings County (N.Y.) Republican County Com., 1970-72, 74—; candidate for Rep. Dist. Leader, Kings County, 1972; trustee Bklyn. Benevolent Soc., 1965—. Mem. Am., N.Y. State, Bklyn. bar assns., Cath. Lawyers Guild, N.Y. County Lawyers Assn., Am. Cath. Accountants Guild, AAUP, Am. Judicature Soc., Am. Bus. Law Assn., Alpha Kappa Psi. Recipient Distinguished Service award Bus. Club of St. Francis Coll., 1975, Distinguished Service award, student body, 1975; Alumni Service award Alpha Kappa Psi, 1974; contbr. articles to law jours. Home: 2012 E 37th St Brooklyn NY 11234 Office: 180 Remsen St Brooklyn NY 11201 Tel (212) JA2-2300

WALSH, DANIEL RICHARD, b. Spokane, Sept. 7, 1931; J.D., Gonzaga U., 1960. Admitted to Alaska bar, 1961, Nev. bar, 1962; law clk. Alaska Supreme Ct., Juneau, 1960-61, Nev. Supreme Ct., 1961-62; dep. dist. atty. Churchill County (Nev.), 1962-63; chief dep. atty. gen. State of Nev., 1966-71; gen. counsel U. Nev. Bd. Regents, 1963-71, U. Nev. System, 1963-71; individual practice law, Carson City, Nev., 1971—. Mem. Am., Nev., Alaska bar assns., Am. Judicature Soc. Home: 612 Terrace St Carson City NV 89701 Office: 1411 N Carson St Carson City NV 89701 Tel (702) 882-8080

WALSH, DAVID WILLIAM, b. Somerville, Mass., July 24, 1927; B.S.A., Boston Coll., 1949, J.D., 1953. Admitted to Mass. bar, 1954, U.S. Supreme Ct. bar, 1957; atty. N.Y., N.Haven & Hartford R.R., 1957-68; asst. gen. atty. Penn Central Transp. Co., 1969-76; Consol. R.R. Corp., Boston, 1976—; ct. clk. U.S. Dist. Ct., Mass., 1943-56. Mem. Am., Mass. bar assns., Nat. Assn. R.R. Trial Counsel, Mass. Trial Lawyers Assn., Conf. Loss and Damage Counsel. Home: 1011 Massachusetts Ave Lexington MA 02173 Office: 431 South Station Bldg Boston MA 02210 Tel (617) 482-7827

WALSH, FRANCIS MICHAEL, b. Bklyn., Nov. 3, 1923; B.A., Fordham U., 1949; LL.B., Columbia, 1950. Admitted to N.Y. State bar, 1950; asso. firm Barry, Treanor, Shandell & Brophy, N.Y.C., 1950-57; gen. claims atty. L.I. Lighting Co., Mineola, N.Y., 1957—; Pres. Jericho (N.Y.) Civic Assn., 1958. Mem. Am., N.Y. State, Nassau County (N.Y.) bar assns., Nassau-Suffolk Trial Lawyers Assn. Home: 124 Seaman Rd Jericho NY 11753 Office: 250 Old Country Rd Mineola NY 11501 Tel (516) 228-2277

WALSH, GEORGE JOSEPH, III, b. Poughkeepsie, N.Y., Aug. 10, 1945; B.S., Clarkson Coll. Tech., 1968; J.D., Valparaiso U., 1971; LL.M., N.Y. U., 1972. Admitted to N.Y. State bar, 1972; mem. firm Gould & Wilkie, N.Y.C., 1972—. Mem. Am., N.Y. State bar assns., Bar Assn. of City of N.Y. Office: One Wall St New York City NY 10005 Tel (212) 344-5680

WALSH, JAMES RICHARD, b. Great Falls, Mont., May 21, 1944; A.B. in Philosophy, Georgetown U., 1965; J.D., U. Mont., 1968. Admitted to Mont. bar, 1968; dep. county atty. Cascade County (Mont.), 1970-73; asso. firm Smith Emmons Baillie and Walsh, Great Falls, 1971-75, partner, 1975—. Mem. Cascade County, Mont., Am. bar assns., Phi Delta Phi. Home: 2901 Central Ave Great Falls MT 59401 Office: 402 Strain Bldg Box 2227 Great Falls MT 59401 Tel (406) 727-4100

WALSH, JOHN AMBROSE, b. Mineral Point, Wis., Aug. 5, 1901; A.B., Marquette U., 1927, J.D., 1930. Admitted to Wis. bar, 1930; individual practice law, Mineral Point, 1930-61; county judge Iowa County, Wis., 1961-72, reserve judge 1972—; city atty., Mineral Point, 1932-36, 42-50, 54-61. Chmn., Iowa County Democratic Com., 1936-48; chmn. Mineral Point troop Boy Scouts Am., 1940-48. Mem. Wis., Iowa County, Am. bar assns., Delta Theta Phi, Delta Sigma Rho. Home: 407 N Wisconsin St Mineral Point WI 53565 Tel (608) 987-2647

WALSH, JOHN M., b. Johnstown, N.Y., May 24, 1922; A.B., Columbia, 1943; LL.B., Albany Law Sch., 1949. Admitted to N.Y. State bar, 1949; partner firm Walsh & Walsh, Johnstown, 1949-56; asst. atty. gen. State of N.Y., 1957-58; appointments officer Gov. Nelson Rockefeller, 1959-60; asst. v.p. N.Y. Telephone Co., N.Y.C., 1961-66, v.p. govt. relations, 1967—; trustee Manhattan Savs. Bank. Mem. com. on athletics Columbia U.; mem. Pub. Health Council State of N.Y. Mem. N.Y. State Bar Assn. Home: 20 Hewitt Ave Bronxville NY 10708 Office: 1095 Ave of the Americas New York City NY 10036 Tel (212) 395-2225

WALSH, LAWRENCE EDWARD, b. Port Maitland, N.S., Can., Jan. 8, 1912; A.B., Columbia U., 1932, LL.B., 1935; LL.D., Union U., 1959, St. John's U., 1975, Suffolk U., 1975, Waynesburg Coll., 1976, Vt. Law Sch., 1976. Admitted to N.Y. bar, 1936, U.S. Supreme Ct. bar, 1951; spl. asst. atty. gen. Drukman Investigation, Dept. Justice, 1936-38, U.S. dep. atty. gen., 1957-60; dep. asst. dist. atty., New York County, 1938-41; asst. counsel to gov. N.Y., 1943-49, counsel, 1950-51; counsel Pub. Service Commn., 1951-53; gen. counsel, exec. dir. Waterfront Commn. of N.Y. Harbor, 1953-54; judge U.S. Dist. Ct., So. Dist. N.Y., 1954-57; partner firm Davis, Polk & Wardwell, N.Y.C., 1961—; presidential rep., dep. chief U.S. del., ambassador Viet Nam Peace Talks, 1969. Bd. dirs. Richardson Merrell; trustee Mut. of N.Y., Columbia U. Fellow Am. Coll. Trial Lawyers, Am. Bar Found.; mem. Am. (pres. 1975-76), N.Y. State (pres. 1966-67) bar assns., Am. Law Inst. (council), New York County Lawyers Assn., Assn. Bar City N.Y., Am. Judicature Soc., Inst. Jud. Adminstrn., Internat. Bar Assn.; hon. mem. Law Soc. of Eng. and Wales, Canadian, Mexican, Minn., Iowa, Rockland County (N.Y.) bar assns. Home: 320 E 72d St New York City NY 10021 Office: 1 Chase Manhattan Plaza 44th floor New York City NY 10005 Tel (212) 422-3400

WALSH, MARCIA KATHRYN, b. Milw., Dec. 10, 1940; A.B. in English, Fontbonne Coll., 1965; M.A. in English, U. Kans., 1969, J.D., 1972. Admitted to Kans. bar, 1973, Mo. bar, 1973; partner firm Riederer, Eisberg, and Walsh, Kansas City, Mo., 1973-74; staff atty. Legal Aid Soc. of Greater Kansas City, Mo., 1973-75, project mgr., 1975-77, litigation unit atty., 1977—. Mem. Kans., Mo., Kansas City bar assns., Nat. Lawyers Guild, Assn. Women Lawyers, ACLU Found. Office: 1103 Grand St Kansas City MO 64106 Tel (816) 474-6750

WALSH, MICHAEL H., b. Binghamton, N.Y., July 8, 1942; B.A. in Econs., Stanford U., 1964; J.D., Yale U., 1969. Admitted to Calif. bar, 1970; asst. dir. admissions Stanford U., Palo Alto, Calif., 1964-65; White House fellow USDA, 1965-66; sr. staff atty. Defenders, Inc., San Diego, 1969-72; mem. firm Sheela, Lightner, Hughes, Castro & Walsh, San Diego, 1972—. Mem. San Diego County Bar Assn., State Bar Calif., Common Cause. Contbr. articles to profl. jours. Home: 1440 Crest Rd Del Mar CA 92014 Office: 3104 4th Ave San Diego CA 92103 Tel (714) 291-4500

WALSH, THOMAS EMMET, b. Orangeburg County, S.C., July 30, 1919; A.B., Wofford Coll., 1941; J.D., Duke U., 1948. Admitted to S.C. bar, 1947; individual practice law, 1948-54; partner firm Gaines & Walsh, Spartanburg, S.C., 1974—; city atty., Spartanburg, 1962—. Mem. S.C. Tax Study Commn., 1966-69; mem. com. to study revision S.C. Constn., 1967-71; mem. S.C. Higher Edn. Commn., 1967—; trustee Spartanburg Meth. Coll. Mem. Am., S.C. bar assns., Wofford Coll. Alumni Assn. (pres. 1968-69). Home: 104 Dalewood Dr Spartanburg SC 29302 Office: 150 Archer St Spartanburg SC 29301 Tel (803) 583-6363

WALSH, THOMAS JOSEPH, b. Kansas City, Mo., Oct. 3, 1932; A.B., Mo. U., 1953; J.D., Georgetown U., 1958. Admitted to D.C. bar, 1958, Mo. bar, 1958; individual practice law, Lee's Summit, Mo., 1958—; atty. Jackson County (Mo.) Sheriff's Dept., 1969-72; mem. Mo. Council Criminal Justice, 1977—. Chmn. United Campaign SE Jackson County, 1959-62. Mem. Am. Trial Lawyers Assn., Mo., Kansas City bar assns., Eastern Jackson County Bar Assn. Home: 210 Hillcrest Lee's Summit MO 64063 Office: 528 W Third St Lee's Summit MO 64063 Tel (816) 524-3400

WALSH, TIMOTHY JAMES, b. South Bend, Ind., July 11, 1946; A.B., Ind. U., 1970; J.D., U. Notre Dame, 1974. Admitted to Ind. bar, 1974; 1st v.p. firm Edward N. Kalamaros & Assos., South Bend. Mem. St. Joseph County (Ind.), Ind. State, Am. bar assns. Office: 1100 Tower Bldg 216 W Washington St South Bend IN 46601 Tel (219) 232-4801

WALSTEAD, ELLIOT NOBLE, b. Dalton, Minn., Sept. 26, 1905; J.D., U. Wis., 1929. Admitted to Wis. bar, 1929; asso. firm Mason & Priestley, Madison, Wis., 1929-33; individual practice law, Madison, 1933-35; dep. dist. atty., Madison, 1935-39; individual practice law, Milw., Wis., 1951-62; dep. atty. gen. State of Wis., Milw., 1962; legal counsel to Gov. Wis., Milw., 1963; mem. firm Walstead, Anderson, Bylsma & Eisenberg, Milw., 1963-64; judge Milw. County, 1964—; lectr. U. Wis., Milw., 1946-66. State chmn. Wis. Democratic Party, 1954-55. Mem. Am., Wis., Milw. bar assns. Contbr. articles in field to legal jours. Home: 6167 N Bay Ridge Milwaukee WI 53217 Office: Milwaukee County Court House Milwaukee WI 53233 Tel (414) 278-4527

WALSTON, ROBERT HENDERSON, b. Birmingham, Ala., Nov. 12, 1935; B.A., Emory U., 1957; LL.B. cum laude, Harvard U., 1960. Admitted to Ala. bar, 1960; asso. firm Bradley, Arant, Rose & White, Birmingham, 1960-68; partner firm Dumas, O'Neal & Hayes, Birmingham, 1968-74, firm Cabaniss, Johnston, Gardner, Dumas & O'Neal, Birmingham, 1974—. Mem. Am., Ala., Birmingham bar assns. Home: 552 Forrest Dr Homewood AL 35209 Office: 1900 First Nat So Natural Bldg Birmingham AL 35203 Tel (205) 252-8800

WALTER, J. JACKSON, b. Abington, Pa., Nov. 6, 1940; A.B., Amherst Coll., 1962; LL.B., Yale U., 1966. Admitted to Mass. bar, 1971; individual practice law, Boston and Northampton, Mass., 1971-76; exec. dir., Fla. Dept. Bus. Regulation, Tallahassee, 1976—. Mem. Am., Mass., Boston bar assns. Contbr. articles to legal jours., Home: 2731 Blairstone Rd Tallahassee FL 32301 Office: Jones Bldg Tallahassee FL 32304 Tel (904) 488-7114

WALTER, OTTO L., b. Hof, Germany, Dec. 7, 1907; J.D., U. Munich (Germany), 1930; J.D., N.Y. U., 1954. Admitted to German bar, 1932, N.Y. State bar, 1955, U.S. Supreme Ct. bar, 1957; C.P.A., N.Y.C., 1936-62; mem. firm Walter, Conston, Schurtman & Gumpel, N.Y.C., 1955—; also mem. firm Ott, Weiss, Eschenlohr, Walter and von Borch, Munich, Germany, 1970—; adj. prof. N.Y. Law Sch., 1976—; pres. Asso. Bus. Advisors, Inc.; partner S. Ackermann & Co., Mattituk Assos.; pres. Lorenz Found.; sec. Cosmopolitan Arts Found. Mem. German-Am. C. of C. (exec. com.), Am. Assn. European Jurists (pres. 1957-60), Fed. Bar Assn., Consular Law Soc., Fgn. Law Assn., Am. Assn. Comparative Law, Internat. Fiscal Assn., Union Internationale des Avocats, German Am. Lawyers Assn. Author: Wahrheit & Rechskraft, 1930; Taxation of the Federal Republic of Germany, 1966; co-author: Das Internationale Steuerrecht, 1954; Internationale Steuern, 1957, 63, 69; Swiss Tax Shelters Opportunities, 1960; The U.S. German Tax Convention, 1967; Foreign Tax Havens, 1973; also articles. Home: 870 United Nations Plaza New York City NY 10017 Office: 280 Park Ave New York City NY 10017 Tel (212) 682-2323

WALTER, ROBERT JOHN, b. Cleve., Sept. 14, 1947; B.A., Miami U., 1969; J.D., Ohio State U., 1972. Admitted to Ohio bar, 1972; asst. atty. gen. State of Ohio, Columbus, 1972-74; mem. firm Lucas, Prendergast, Albright, Gibson, Brown & Newman, Columbus, 1974—. Mem. Columbus, Ohio State, Am. bar assns. Office: 42 E Gay St Suite 1500 Columbus OH 43215 Tel (614) 228-5711

WALTERS, BARBARA J., b. Portland, Oreg., Aug. 31, 1928; B.A., U. Wash., 1950; J.D., Marquette U., 1969. Admitted to Wis. bar, 1969, Ill. bar, 1970; atty. firm Joslyn & Green, Crystal Lake, Ill., 1970—. Mem. Library Bd., 1974—. Mem. Ill. State, Wis. State, McHenry County bar assns. Home: 784 Kingston Ln Crystal Lake IL 60014 Office: 116 1/2 Benton St Woodstock IL 60098 Tel (815) 338-1135

WALTERS, BENJAMIN OSCAR, JR., b. Ventura, Calif., Oct. 4, 1934; A.A., Ventura Coll., 1960; B.A., U. Calif. at Berkeley, 1962, J.D., 1965. Admitted to Alaska bar, 1966, U.S. Customs Ct. bar, 1972, U.S. Supreme Ct. bar, 1972; asst. atty. gen. Alaska, 1965-67; dist. atty. Ketchikan (Alaska), 1967-68; asst. dist. atty. Anchorage, 1968-70; mem. firm LaBate & Walters, Anchorage, 1970-71; individual practice law, Anchorage, 1971—. Trustee, Turnagain United Meth. Ch., 1969—; cubmaster Boy Scouts Am., 1970—; umpire-in-chief City View Little League, 1973-74. Mem. Am., Alaska, Anchorage, Kenai bar assns., Alaska Airmen's Assn., Aircraft Owners and Operators Assn. Recipient citation of merit Anchorage Dist. Atty., 1971. Home: 1034 E 27th Ave Anchorage AK 99504 Office: 360 K St Suite 301 Anchorage AK 99501 Tel (907) 277-7511

WALTERS, JAMES NASH, III, b. Rochester, N.Y., Sept. 9, 1945; B.A., Ohio State U., 1969; J.D., Cleve. State U., 1973. Admitted to Ohio bar, 1973; prosecutor City of Elyria, Ohio, 1973-74, City of Middleburg Heights, Ohio, 1974—; asso. firm Carney & Broadbent, 1975—. Chmn. Charter Review Commn., Berea, Ohio, 1976-77; mem. Bd. Zoning Appeals, Berea, 1976—. Mem. Am., Ohio, Greater Cleve. bar assns. Home: 499 Cranston Dr Berea OH 44017 Office: 1710 Investment Plaza Bldg Cleveland OH 44114 Tel (216) 522-0800

WALTERS, JOHNNIE MCKEIVER, b. Hartsville, S.C., Dec. 20, 1919; A.B., Furman U., 1942, LL.D. (hon.), 1973; LL.B., U. Mich., 1948. Admitted to Mich. bar, 1948, N.Y. bar, 1955, S.C. bar, 1961, D.C. bar, 1973; atty. Chief Counsel's Office, IRS, Washington, 1949-53; asst. mgr. tax div., legal dept. Texaco, Inc., N.Y.C., 1953-61; partner firm Geer, Walters & Demo, Greenville, S.C., 1961-68; asst. atty. gen. tax div., Dept. Justice, Washington, 1969-71; commr. IRS, Washington, 1971-73; partner firm Hunton & Williams, Washington, 1973—. Mem. Am., Fed., D.C., S.C. bar assns. Home: 1723 Oberon Way McLean VA 22101 Office: Suite 1060 1730 Pennsylvania Ave NW Washington DC 20006 Tel (202) 393-7400

WALTERS, MAHLON LAWRENCE, JR., b. Marshall, Tex., Oct. 15, 1912; A.A., Coll. Marshall, 1932; LL.B., Cumberland U., 1933; J.D., Samford U., 1969. Admitted to Tex. bar, 1935; atty. CSC, Jefferson, Tex., 1942-44; polit. crimes expert, criminal div. Dept. Justice, Washington, 1944-47; spl. asst. U.S. dist. atty. Eastern Div. N.C., 1944-45, No. Dist. Ala., 1945-46, No. Dist. Tex., 1947-77. Mem. N.E. Tex. State, N.E. Tex. bar assns. Died Aug. 1, 1976.

WALTERS, MELVIN REYNOLD, b. Hays, Kans., Dec. 27, 1937; B.A. in Econs., Ft. Hays State Coll., 1956; M.S. in Bus. Adminstrn., Kans. State U., 1959; J.D., U. Tulsa, 1967. Admitted to Okla. bar, 1967; sr. accountant Amoco Pipeline Co., Tulsa, 1963-69; v.p., sec., treas. Home Petroleum Corp., Tulsa, 1969-76; individual practice law, Tulsa, 1976—. Mem. Okla., Tulsa County bar assns., Okla. Soc. C.P.A.'s. Home: 8520 E 35th St Tulsa OK 74145 Office: 803 Beacon Bldg Tulsa OK 74103 Tel (918) 582-2152

WALTERS, SUMNER JUNIOR, b. Van Wert, Ohio, Oct. 4, 1916; J.D., Ohio No. U., 1940. Admitted to Ohio bar, 1940; mem. firms, Van Wert, Ohio, Walters & Koch, 1940-42, Stroup & Walters, 1946-68, Walters, 1968-71, Walters & Young, 1971-74, Walters, Young & Walters, 1974—; Van Wert County pros. atty., 1948-60; acting judge Van Wert Municipal Ct., 1960—. Trustee Van Wert County Found., 1965—; trustee Marsh Found., 1970—; pres. United Fund, 1959-60, Van Wert Indsl. Devel. Corp., 1966-76. Mem. Van Wert County (pres. 1953-54), NW Ohio (pres. 1957-58), Ohio (exec. com. 1965-68) bar assns. Named Man of Yr., Jr. C. of C., 1965. Home: Rt 2 Box 40 Ohio City OH 45874 Office: 121 S Washington St Van Wert OH 45891 Tel (419) 238-1166

WALTHALL, GEORGE POLLARD, JR., b. Montgomery, Ala., Aug. 6, 1947; B.S., U. Ala., 1969, J.D., 1974. Admitted to Ala. bar, 1974; law clk. Ala. Ct. Civil Appeals, 1974-75; partner firm Walthall & Cleveland, Prattville, Ala., 1975—. Mem. U. Ala. Alumnae chpt. Autauga County (v.p. 1976-77), Am., Ala., Autauga County, Montgomery County bar assns., Am., Ala. trial lawyers assns. Home: 603 Pinecrest Dr Prattville AL 36067 Office: 141 W Main St Prattville AL 36067 Tel (205) 365-2255

WALTON, BERNICE MUNSON, b. Hutchinson, Minn., Aug. 3, 1919; A.A., Miami Dade Community Coll., 1967; B.B.A., U. Miami, 1969, J.D., 1972. Admitted to Fla. bar, 1972; legal sec., paralegal firm Marvin I. Wiener, Miami, Fla., 1958-69, law clk., firm Marvin I. Wiener, Coral Gables, Fla., 1971-72, asso. firm, 1972-73, partner firm Wiener & Walton, 1974—. Dir. U. Miami Endowment Com., 1974—. Mem. Fla. Bar, Dade County, Coral Gables (pres. 1977—), Am. bar assns., Coral Gables C. of C., Am. Bus. Women's Assn. Recipient Am. Bus. Woman Year Nat. award, 1975-76. Office: 2121 Ponce de Leon Blvd Coral Gables FL 33134 Tel (305) 445-8888

WALTON, CHARLES WESLEY, b. Pine Bluff, Ark., June 8, 1929; LL.B., Jackson Sch. Law, 1969, J.D., 1971. Admitted to Miss. bar, 1970; partner firm Morris & Walton, Biloxi, Miss. Mem. Am. Bar Assn., Miss. State, Harrison and Jackson County (Miss.) bars, Miss. Trial Lawyers Assn. Office: 232 Porter St PO Box 855 Biloxi MS 39533 Tel (601) 436-4646

WALTON, FREDERICK HENRY, JR., b. Buenos Aires, Argentina, Mar. 25, 1917; B.S. cum laude in Social Sci., Georgetown U., 1938, J.D. (Bellarmine scholar), 1941; LL.M., George Washington U., 1952. Admitted to D.C. bar, 1941, Md. bar, 1956, U.S. Supreme Ct. bar, 1956; asso. firm Dempsey & Koplovitz, Washington, 1946-64, partner, 1964—. Chmn. cub scout pack Chevy Chase council Boy Scouts Am., 1958-61; vestryman, warden St. John's Episcopal Ch., Chevy Chase, Md., 1959-61, 69-73; del. diocesan conv., Washington; mem. Washington adv. council Episc. Ch. Found., N.Y.C., 1975—. Mem. Fed. Communications, Am. (treas. 1961-62, exec. com. 1962-65, chmn. practice and procedure com. 1975-76), D.C. bar assns., Bar Assn. D.C., Am. Judicature Soc., Pi Gamma Mu. Mem. editorial bd. Georgetown Law Jour., 1940-41. Tel (202) 737-6363

WALTON, GUS BERRY, JR., b. Little Rock, Nov. 6, 1941; B.S., Washington and Lee U., 1964; J.D., U. Ark., 1967. Admitted to Ark. Supreme Ct. bar, 1967, U.S. Supreme Ct. bar, 1971, U.S. Ct. Appeals 8th Circuit bar, 1976; asso. firm Wright, Lindsey & Jennings, Little Rock, 1967-71, partner, 1971—; dir., instr. Bar Review of Ark., Inc., 1970—. Mem. Little Rock C. of C., Am., Ark., Pulaski County bar assns., Am. Judicature Soc. Home: 6 Longfellow Ln Little Rock AR 72207 Office: 2200 Worthen Bank Bldg Little Rock AR 72201 Tel (501) 371-0808

WALTON, HERBERT WILSON, b. Anaconda, Mont., Apr. 9, 1929; A.B., U. Mo., Kansas City, 1955, J.D., 1957. Admitted to Kans. bar, 1957; asst. county atty. Johnson County (Kans.), 1957-60; practiced in Olathe, Kans., 1957-60; judge Johnson County Probate Ct., 1960-65, Kans. Dist. Ct., division 1, 10th Jud. Dist., 1965—; mem. Kans. Jud. Council, 1965—; mem. pattern instructions Kans. Civil and Criminal law, 1968—. Mem. Johnson County, Kans., Am. bar assns., Am. Judicature Soc., Kans. Dist. Judges Assn., U. Mo.-Kansas City Law Alumni Assn. Editorial bd. U. Mo-Kansas City Law Rev., 1956. Home: 808 Windsor Rd Olathe KS 66061 Office: Courthouse Olathe KS 66061 Tel (913) 782-5000

WALTON, NORMAN ELWOOD, b. Wooster, Ohio, Jan. 11, 1921; student Miami U., Ohio, 1940-42, Oberlin Coll., 1945, J.D., U. Miami (Fla.), 1950. Admitted to Fla. bar, 1950, Colo. bar, 1954; individual practice law, Miami, 1950-51, 52-59; Colorado Springs, Colo., 1960-61; asst. dist. atty. Colorado Springs, 1963-75; chief judge Municipal Ct. Colorado Springs, 1976—; partner firm Walton, Robinson & Shields, Colordao Springs, 1976—. Mem. Fla., Colo., El Paso County bar assns., Am. Trial Lawyers Assn. Home: 2318 Kent Ln Colorado Springs CO 80909 Office: 524 N Tejon St Colorado Springs CO 80903 Tel (303) 471-0922

WALTON, RICHARD ERNSTER, b. Hermosa Beach, Calif., Feb. 22, 1938; B.S., in Engring., U. Fresno, 1960; J.D., U. Calif., Berkeley, 1965. Admitted to Calif. bar, 1966; partner firm Page & Walton, Walnut Creek, Calif., 1966-68; gen. counsel Lucky Breweries, Inc., San Francisco, 1969-71; v.p., sec., gen. counsel United Vinters, Inc., San Francisco, 1972—. Mem. Am. Bar Assn. Office: 601 4th St San Francisco CA 94107 Tel (415) 777-6520

WALTZ, JON RICHARD, b. Napoleon, Ohio, Oct. 11, 1929; B.A., Coll. Wooster, 1951; LL.B., Yale, 1954. Admitted to Ohio bar, 1954, Ill. bar, 1965; asso. firm Squire, Sanders & Dempsey, Cleve., 1954-64; prof. law Northwestern U., Chgo., 1964—. Mem. Chgo. Bar Assn., Assn. Am. Law Schs., Soc. Am. Law Tchrs. (bd. govs.), Law-Medicine Soc. Recipient Distinguished Service award Soc. Midland Authors, 1972; author and co-author: The Trial of Jack Ruby, 1965; Cases and Materials on Evidence, 3d edit., 1976; Principles of Evidence and Proof, 3d edit., 1976; Medical Jurisprudence, 1971; The Federal Rules of Evidence: An Analysis, 2d edit., 1976; Evidence: A Summary Analysis, 2d edit., 1976; Criminal Evidence, 1975; contbr. articles to legal jours.; mem. editorial adv. bd. Bracton Press Ltd. Home: 421 Melrose St Chicago IL 60657 Office: 357 E Chicago Ave Chicago IL 60611 Tel (312) 649-8472

WALZ, WILFORD VERNON, b. South Bend, Ind., Mar. 13, 1902; LL.B., U. Notre Dame, 1925, J.D., 1969. Admitted to Ind. bar, 1925, since practiced in South Bend; pros. atty. 60th Jud. Circuit Ind., South Bend, 1945-50. Pres., South Bend. Fedn. Musicians, 1944-60. Mem. Ind., St. Joseph County (award for 50 years distinguished service 1975) bar assns. Home: 3407 S Michigan St South Bend IN 46614 Office: 218 Oddfellow Bldg South Bend IN 46601 Tel (219) 232-5988

WALZER, STUART BERNARD, b. Chgo., July 12, 1924; B.S., U. Calif., Los Angeles, 1948; LL.B., Harvard, 1951. Admitted to Calif. bar, 1952; partner firm Nutter, Walzer, Weinstock, Manion & King, Los Angeles; instr. law Southwestern U., 1958-60, U. So. Calif., 1974-76; instr. paralegal studies U. Calif. extension program, 1973-75. Mem. Gov.'s Commn. on the Family, 1966. Contbr. articles to legal jours. Office: 1888 Century Park E Suite 800 Los Angeles CA 90067 Tel (213) 879-4481

WAMACKS, CLIFFORD CHARLES, b. Cin., Mar. 22, 1932; B.S. in Pub. Adminstrn., Temple U., 1954, LL.B., 1960. Admitted to Ariz. bar, 1961; planning and zoning counsel City of Phoenix, 1961-64; dep. county atty. Maricopa County (Ariz.), 1964-67, chief family support dep. county atty., 1968-77, felony trial dep., 1977—; instr. Nat. Dist. Attys. Assn. Seminars, 1970, 76. Pres. N.W. Citizens for Better Schs., Phoenix, 1965-70, N.E. Phoenix Mountains Homeowners Assn., 1975. Mem. Ariz. State Bar, Maricopa County, Am. bar assns., Am. Judicature Soc. Office: 3d Floor 101 W Jefferson St Phoenix AZ 85003 Tel (602) 262-3584

WAMPOLD, CHARLES HENRY, JR., b. Montgomery, Ala., Oct. 21, 1925; B.A., U. Ala., 1946, LL.B., 1948, J.D., 1960. Admitted to Ala. bar, 1948, U.S. Supreme Ct. bar, 1972; partner firm Volz, Capouano, Wampold & Sansone, Montgomery, 1962—. Bd. dirs. Griel Meml. Hosp., Montgomery. Mem. Am., Ala., Montgomery bar assns. Author: Piecemeal Redemption of Real Estate, 1949. Home: 3113 Jasmine Rd Montgomery AL 36111 Office: 350 Adams Ave Montgomery AL 36103 Tel (205) 264-6401

WANGARD, ROBERT EUGENE, b. Kennan, Wis., Mar. 25, 1941; B.S., U. Wis., 1966; J.D., U. Ill., 1969. Admitted to Ill. bar, 1969; asso. firm Ross, Hardies, O'Keefe, Babcock & Parsons, Chgo., 1969-75, partner, 1976—; speaker at legal seminars, insts. Bd. dirs. Lawyers for Creative Arts, Chgo., 1973-75, 76—. Mem. Am., Chgo. bar assns. Bd. editors Ill. Law Forum, 1967-69, articles editor, 1968-69; contbr. articles to legal publs. Home: 2414 Thayer St Evanston IL 60201 Office: One IBM Plaza Suite 3100 Chicago IL 60611 Tel (312) 467-9300

WANKE, RONALD LEE, b. Chgo., June 22, 1941; B.S. in Elec. Engring., Northwestern U., 1964; J.D., DePaul U., 1968. Admitted to Ill. bar, 1968, U.S. Patent Office bar, 1965; patent agent firm Wegner, Stellman, McCord, Wiles & Wood, Chgo., 1965-68, asso., 1968-70, partner, 1971—. Mem. Am. (chmn. copyright protection for computer software subcom. 1976-77), Chgo. bar assns., Am., Chgo. (vice chmn. govt. relations com. 1971-72, chmn. inventor services com. 1976) patent law assns. Mem. staff DePaul Law Rev., 1967-68. Home: 1920 N Clark St Chicago IL 60614 Office: 20 N Wacker Dr Chicago IL 60606 Tel (312) 346-1630

WANNINGER, ALBERT MAX, b. Chgo., Dec. 4, 1938; B.S. in Elec. Engring., U. Ill., 1960; M.S. in Elec. Engring., Ill. Inst. Tech., 1964; J.D., John Marshall Law Sch., 1969. Admitted to Ill. bar, 1970; project engr. Sun Elec. Corp., Chgo., 1960-64, Dynascan Corp., Chgo., 1965-67; engring. mgr. Peerless Instrument Co., Chgo., 1967-74; partner firm Lavelle, Levinson, Wanninger & Lambert, Chgo., 1970—; trustee, chmn. bd., prof. Midwest Coll. Engring. (Lombard, Ill.). Mem. Am., Ill., Chgo. bar assns., Eta Kappa Nu. Author: Using Electronic Testers for Automotive Tune-Up, 1972; patentee automotive testing field. Office: 100 N LaSalle St Chicago IL 60602 Tel (312) 641-7256

WAPNER, GERALD LAWRENCE, b. Bklyn., Nov. 27, 1933; student Lehigh U., 1951-53, Columbia, 1953-54; LL.B., N.Y. U., 1957. Admitted to N.Y. state bar, 1957; partner firm Wapner, Rankow & Cohen and predecessor, N.Y.C., 1957-64; individual practice law, Woodstock, N.Y., 1964-69; partner firm Wapner & Koplovitz, Woodstock, 1970—; gen. counsel Summerhill Soc., N.Y.C., 1962-66; pres. Riverby Inc., Woodstock. Mem. Ulster County (N.Y.), N.Y. State bar assns. Home: Hutchin Hill Rd Woodstock NY 12498 Office: 45 Mill Hill Rd Woodstock NY 12498 Tel (914) 679-7207

WARADY, ARTHUR DEE, b. Chgo., Mar. 10, 1948; B.S. in Bus. Adminstrn., Northwestern U., 1970; J.D. magna cum laude, U. Mich., 1973. Admitted to Ga. bar, 1973, Fla. bar, 1974; asso. firm Smith, Cohen, Ringel, Kohler, & Martin, Atlanta, 1973-76; asso. firm Stokes and Shapiro, Atlanta, 1976-77; individual practice law, 1977—. Mem. Am. (mem. com. on employee benefits), Ga., Fla., Atlanta bar assns., Am. Inst. C.P.A.'s, Order of Coif, Beta Gamma Sigma, Beta Alpha Psi. C.P.A., Ill.; contbr. articles in field to profl. jours. Office: 1410 1st Nat Bank Tower 2 Peachtree St NW Atlanta GA 30303 Tel (404) 522-1220

WARD, ANTHONY JOHN, b. Los Angeles, Sept. 25, 1931; A.B., U. So. Calif., 1953; J.D., U. Calif., Berkeley, 1956. Admitted to Calif. bar, 1957; mem. office of Staff Judge Adv. U.S. Air Force, 1956-58; asso. firm Ives, Kirwan, & Dibble, Los Angeles, 1958-61; partner firm Marapese & Ward, Hawthorne, Calif., 1961-69; individual practice law, Torrance, Calif., 1969-76; mem. firm Ward, Dodd, & Gaunt, Torrance, 1976—. Mem. Am., Los Angeles County bar assns. Home: 1516 Via Arco Palos Verdes Estates CA 90274 Office: Pavillon A Western Fed Savings Bldg Del Amo Financial Center 21525 Hawthorne Blvd Torrance CA 90503 Tel (213) 540-1771

WARD, CRAIG BLOSS, b. Neenah, Wis., Jan. 20, 1938; A.B., Rollins Coll., 1964; LL.B., Duke, 1965, J.D., 1970. Admitted to Fla. bar, 1965, N.Y. bar, 1966, U.S. Supreme Ct. bar, 1974; asso. firm Donovan, Leisure, Newton & Irvine, N.Y.C., 1965-68; asst. gen. counsel Buena Vista Distbn. Co., N.Y.C., 1968-69, co-counsel Walt Disney World Co., Lake Buena Vista, Fla., 1969-73; partner firm Helliwell, Melrose & DeWolf, and predecessors, Orlando, Fla., 1973-76; partner Ward & Formet, Orlando, 1976—; legal aide to N.Y.C. Mayor's Taxi Study Panel, 1966-67; city atty. Lake Buena Vista, 1970-73. Mem. Fla., Orange, Am. bar assns., Assn. Bar City N.Y. Home: 711 Alba Dr Orlando FL 32804 Office: 801 N Magnolia Ave Suite 217 Orlando FL 32803 Tel (305) 423-5910

WARD, CULLEN MATTHEW, b. Auburn, Ala., May 27, 1921; B.S., Auburn U., 1948; LL.B., Emory U., 1948, LL.D., 1970. Admitted to Ga. bar, 1948, Ala. bar, 1948; practiced in Atlanta, 1948—; asso. firm McLennan & Cook, 1949-56; partner firms Ward, Brooks & Williams and predecessors, 1956-62, Hewlett & Ward and predecessor, 1962-66, Johnston, Harper, Ward & Stanfield and predecessor, 1966—; lectr. in field. Trustee Roscoe Pound Found., Cambridge, Mass. Mem. state bars Ga., Ala., Lawyers Club of Atlanta, Am. Ga. (v.p.) bar assns., Ga. (Distinguished Service award 1976), Am. (gov.) trial lawyers assns., Internat. Acad. Trial Lawyers (dir.), Inter-Am. Bar, Ga. Assn. Plaintiffs Attys. (pres. 1959-60), S.E. Seminars (treas., program chmn.). Contbr. articles to legal jours. Home: 1130 Kingston Dr NE Atlanta GA 30303 Office: 1526 Fulton Nat Bank Bldg Atlanta GA 30303 Tel (404) 524-5626

WARD, DANIEL PATRICK, b. Chgo., Aug. 30, 1918; J.D., DePaul U., 1941, L.H.D., 1976; LL.D., John Marshall Law Sch., 1972. Admitted to Ill. Supreme Ct. bar, 1941, U.S. Dist. Ct. bar for No. Dist. Ill., 1948, U.S. Ct. Appeals bar, 7th Circuit, 1948, U.S. Supreme Ct. bar, 1954; asst. prof. law Southeastern U., 1941-42; practiced law in Chgo., 1946-48; asst. U.S. Atty. for No. Dist. Ill. Dept. Justice, 1948-54, chief criminal div., 1951-54; partner firm Eardley & Ward, Chgo., 1954-55; lectr. Coll. Law DePaul U., 1948-55, dean, 1955-60; state's atty. Cook County (Ill.), 1960-66; asso. justice Ill. Supreme Ct., 1966-75, chief justice, 1976—; chmn. Ill. Cts. Commn., 1969-72. Mem. Chgo., Ill. State, Am. bar assns., Am. Judicature Soc. Recipient Nations' Outstanding Prosecutor award Nat. Dist. Attys. Assn., 1964. Office: 3083 Richard J Daley Center Chicago IL 60602 Tel (312) 793-5460

WARD, DOUGLAS ALAN, b. Cleve., Oct. 23, 1946; A.B., Duke, 1968; J.D., U. Fla., 1971. Admitted to Fla. bar, 1971; partner firm Rogers, Towers, Bailey, Jones & Gay, Jacksonville, Fla., 1971—; sec. Gulf Life Ins. Co., 1974—. Mem. Am., Jacksonville bar assns., Fla. Bar. Editor: U. Fla. Law Rev., 1970-71. Home: 1740 Challen Ave Jacksonville FL 32205 Office: 1300 Florida Title Bldg Jacksonville FL 32202 Tel (904) 356-3911

WARD, EDMOND CAMPION, b. San Francisco, Dec. 27, 1926; B.S., U. San Francisco, 1949, J.D., 1955. Admitted to Calif. bar, 1955, U.S. Supreme Ct. bar, 1970; asso. firm Doyle and Clecak, San Francisco, 1955-64; partner firm Pendergrass, McKenney, Perry and Ward, San Rafael, Calif., 1964-66; estate tax atty. IRS, San Francisco, 1966-67; of counsel firm Bianchi, Hoskins & Rosenberg, San Rafael, 1967—; inheritance tax referee State of Calif., San Rafael, 1968-75; lectr. Calif. continuing edn. of bar and Golden Gate U. Mem. exec. bd. Marin council Boy Scouts Am., 1975—; mem. adv. bd. Dominican Coll., San Rafael, 1975—; mem. devel. council Marin County (Calif.) chpt. ARC, 1975—; mem. adv. bd. Nazareth House, San Rafael, 1976—. Mem. San Francisco, Marin County (dir. 1977—), Am. bar assns., State Bar Calif., Marin County Estate Planning Council (pres. 1970-71), Internat. Acad. Estate and Trust Law. Home: 4 Orchard Way Kentfield CA 94904 Office: Suite 600 1000 Fourth St San Rafael CA 94901 Tel (415) 456-6020

WARD, EUGENE WILLIAM, b. White Pine, Tenn., Sept. 28, 1932; B.S., Lincoln. Meml. U., Harrogate, Tenn., 1956; J.D., U. Tenn., 1959. Admitted to Tenn. bar, 1959; asst. gen. counsel Tenn. Pub. Service Commn., Nashville, 1961-65, gen. counsel, 1966—; State legal counsel Tenn. Jaycees, 1966-67, Assn. Country Entertainers. Mem. Tenn. (adminstrv. law chmn. 1970-71), Nashville bar assns. Office: Cordell Hull Bldg Nashville TN 37219 Tel (615) 741-3191

WARD, FRANK ANTHONY, II, b. Albany, N.Y., Jan. 28, 1939; A.B. in Bus. and Indsl. Mgmt., Johns Hopkins, 1960; J.D., U. Ill., 1963. Admitted to Ill. bar, 1963; v.p., trust officer First Galesburg Nat. Bank & Trust Co. (Ill.), 1964-74, dir., 1975—; individual practice law, Galesburg, 1974-75, 76—; partner firm Ward & Gray, Galesburg, 1975-76; lectr. Knox Coll. and Carl Sandburg Coll., Galesburg, 1975—, Nat. Trust for Historic Preservation, 1976—; certified genealogist, 1965—. Treas., Albany Youth Council, 1955-56; deacon First United Presbyn. Ch., Galesburg, 1964-65; treas. Pilgrim Congl. Ch., Knoxville, Ill., 1966-69, council mem., 1966-71, moderator, 1970, deacon, 1971; mem. exec. bd. Prairie council Boy Scouts Am., Galesburg, 1965—, adviser Order of Arrow, 1966-68, chmn. camp devel. com., 1970-75, vice chmn. Pioneer Dist., 1967, fin. chmn., 1968; chmn. Knox County Sesquicentennial Commn., 1966-68; active Downtown Village Council, Galesburg C. of C., Spoon River Watershed Tributary Project; bd. dirs. Cultural Council Galesburg, 1974—, pres., 1976; bd. dirs. Knox County Hist. Sites, 1964—, Galesburg Community Concert Assn., 1972-76; bd. dirs. Knox County United Way, 1969—, sec.-treas., 1970-72. Mem. Ill., Knox County (pres. 1970) bar assns., Ill., Galesburg (pres. 1975—), Kans., Sterling-Rock Falls (Ill.), Westport (Mo.) hist. socs., Carl Sandburg Birthplace Assn. (dir. 1970—), Nat., Ill., Knox County, Stamford (Conn.) geneal. socs., Huguenot Soc. Ill., Loyal Legion Am., SAR (dir., registrar Gen. Henry Knox chpt. 1973-75), Sons Union Vets. Civil War, War of 1812 Ill. Soc., Galesburg C. of C., Johns Hopkins, U. Ill. alumni assns., Nat. Audubon Soc., Alpha Phi Omega (nat. v.p. 1960-61), Phi Delta Phi. Recipient Distinguished Service awards Johns Hopkins, 1958, Galesburg Jr. C. of C., 1970, Outstanding Religious Leader award Knoxville Jr. C. of C., 1971; author: An Analysis of the Factors Affecting the Desire to Change Geographic Location with Emphasis on Economic and Family Ties, 1770-1960, 1959; Brief Biography of Allen T. Ward, 1963; Thomas Ward and His Descendants, A Genealogical Study, 1963; Striving Backwards or How We Stopped the Ball and Started the Revolution in this Bicentennial Year, 1976. Home: Rural Route 1 Box 224 Galesburg IL 61401 Office: 219 Weinberg Arcade Galesburg IL 61401 Tel (309) 342-6156

WARD, GEORGE BYRD PAGE, JR., b. Balt., July 28, 1935; A.B., Johns Hopkins, 1957; LL.B., U. Md., 1961; certificate Nat. Trust Sch., 1963; diploma Stonier Grad. Sch. Banking, 1966. Admitted to Md. bar, 1961; with Md. Nat. Bank, Balt., 1957—, asst. trust officer, 1963-64, trust officer, 1964-69, asst. v.p. cashier's dept., 1969-73, v.p., 1973—, asst. sec. holding co. Md. Nat. Corp., 1973—, v.p., 1975—; staff counsel Md. Nat. Bank, Md. Nat. Corp. and subs., 1973—; dir. East End Hotel, Inc. Bd. dirs. ch. affiliated Metro Strategy, Inc., Balt., 1971-77, pres., 1974-77; treas., dir. Med. Eye Bank Md., Inc., Balt., 1975—; bd. dirs. Combined Industry and Commerce Health Appeal, Balt., 1975—, Primary Alcoholism Treatment Program, Balt., 1974-76; mem. Md. Gov.'s Adv. Council on Drug Abuse, 1975—, vice chmn., 1976—; treas. mayoralty campaign, Balt., 1971, councilmanic campaign, Balt., 1975. Mem. Balt., Md., Am. bar assns., Md. Bankers Assn. (govt. relations com. 1971—). Office: Box 987 Baltimore MD 21203 Tel (301) 244-6784

WARD, GUY E., b. Belleville, Kans., Jan. 16, 1912; A.B., Coll. Emporia, 1933; LL.B., Washburn U., 1936. Admitted to Kans., Calif. bars; county atty. Republic County (Kans.), 1937-41; asst. atty. gen. State of Kans., 1941-42; served to maj. JAGC, U.S. Army, 1942-45; practice law, Los Angeles, 1945—. Mem. Beverly Hills C. of C. (pres. 1956), Am., Los Angeles County (trustee 1962-63), Beverly Hills (pres. 1956) bar assns., State Bar Calif. (com. on family law 1963, bd. govs. 1966-69); fellow Am. Coll. Trial Lawyers. Home: 1219 Sierra Alta Way Los Angeles CA 90069 Office: 1901 Ave of the Stars Suite 1475 Los Angeles CA 90067 Tel (213) 277-8888

WARD, JAMES ALLEN, b. Waukesha, Wis., Apr. 26, 1949; B.A., Carroll Coll., 1971; J.D., So. Meth. U., 1974. Admitted to Wis. bar, 1974; mem. firm Krause and Ward, Waukesha, 1974—. Mem. Wis., Waukesha County bar assns. Recipient Fed. Bar Assn. award, 1974. Home: 125 Tenny St Waukesha WI 53186 Office: 217 Wisconsin Ave Waukesha WI 53186

WARD, JAMES DAVID, b. Sioux Falls, S.D., Sept. 8, 1935; A.B., U. S.D., 1957; J.D., U. San Francisco, 1959. Admitted to Calif. bar, 1960; partner firm Badger Schulte & Ward, Riverside, Calif., 1961-64; partner firm Thompson & Colegate, Riverside, 1964—. Pres., Riverside Opera Assn., 1965. Mem. Riverside County (pres. 1973-74), Calif., Am. bar assns. Home: 2649 Anna St Riverside CA 92506 Office: Box 1299 Riverside CA 92502 Tel (714) 682-5550

WARD, JOE HENRY, JR., b. Childress, Tex., Apr. 18, 1930; B.S. in Accounting, Tex. Christian U., 1952; J.D., So. Meth. U., 1964. Admitted to Tex. bar, 1964, Va. bar, 1972, D.C. bar, 1972; supr. Alexander Grant & Co., C.P.A.'s, Dallas, 1956-64; atty. U.S. Treasury Dept., Washington, 1965-68; atty. Senate Fin. Com., Washington, 1968-72; individual practice law, Washington, 1972—. Mem. Am. Bar Assn., Am. Inst. C.P.A.'s. Home: 2639 Mann Ct Falls Church VA 22046 Office: Suite 670 1700 Pennsylvania Ave NW Washington DC 20006 Tel (202) 393-4781

WARD, LESTER LOWE, JR., b. Pueblo, Colo., Dec. 21, 1930; A.B. cum laude, Harvard, 1952, LL.B., 1955. Admitted to Colo. bar, 1955, U.S. Supreme Ct. bar, 1961; partner firm Predovich and Ward, Pueblo, 1955—; sec.-treas. Sangre de Cristo Broadcasting Corp., 1968-76. Trustee, Thatcher Found., Frank I. Lamb Found.; pres. bd. trustees Pueblo Pub. Library, 1960-66; trustee St. Mary Corwin Hosp., 1973—, McClelland Learning Found., 1972—. Mem. Am., Colo. (chmn. probate and trust sect. 1974-75), Pueblo County (pres. 1976—) bar assns. Named Outstanding Young Man of Year, Pueblo Jr. C. of C., 1964; Outstanding Young Lawyer, Pueblo County Bar Assn., 1965, 67. Home: 118 Baylor St Pueblo CO 81005 Office: 727 Thatcher Bldg Pueblo CO 81003 Tel (303) 544-5081

WARD, NICHOLAS DONNELL, b. N.Y.C., July 30, 1941; B.A., Columbia, 1963; LL.B., Georgetown U., 1966. Admitted to D.C. bar, 1967; asso. firm Hamilton & Hamilton, Washington, 1967-72, partner, 1973—; instr. ct. mgmt. inst. univ. coll., U. Md., 1975-77; panelist legal problems of mus. adminstrn. Am. Law Inst.-Am. Bar Assn., 1975, 76, 77; instr. legal asst. program Georgetown U. Sch. for Summer and Continuing Edn., 1977; mem. adv. com. on fiduciary rules D.C. Superior Ct., 1975—; dir., sec.-treas. Hepworth Machine Co., Inc., Port Washington, N.Y., 1962—. Trustee Benjamin Franklin U., 1976—; trustee Confederate Meml. Assn., 1975, pres., 1976—; ann. corporate mem. Children's Hosp. D.C., 1971—. Mem. Washington Estate Planning Council, Selden Soc., Am. Soc. Legal History, Nat. Assn. Coll. and Univ. Attys., Barrister Inn, D.C. Bar Assn. (chmn. estates and guardianship com. young lawyers sect.; editor Will and Testamentary Trust Forms 1976, recipient certificate of appreciation 1976), Phi Delta Phi (v.p. 1976-77). Editor newsletter Am. Revolution Roundtable of D.C., 1975—. Contbr. articles to legal jours.; named Man of Year, Downtown Jaycees, 1971-72. Home: 6654 Barnaby St NW Washington DC 20015 Office: 600 Union Trust Bldg 740 15th St NW Washington DC 20005 Tel (202) 347-2882

WARD, PETER, b. Buffalo, Aug. 25, 1914; A.B. cum laude, Harvard, 1936; LL.B. with distinction, Cornell U., 1939. Admitted to N.Y. bar, 1939, Fla. bar, 1965, U.S. Tax Ct. bar, 1967, U.S. Ct. Claims bar, 1968; partner firm Ward & Ward, Buffalo, 1940-51; prof. law Cornell U., 1951-60; gen. counsel, dep. supt. N.Y. State Ins. Dept., N.Y.C., 1960-62; individual practice law, Delray Beach, Fla., 1965—; prof. law U. Fla., Gainesville, 1972—; vis. prof. U. Tex., Austin, 1957, Episc. Sem., U. South, 1965. Mng. trustee God's Work Fund, Gainesville, 1966—. Mem. Fla. Bar Assn. Author: Tort Problems of Loss Distribution, 1958; The Tort Cause of Action, 1974; decorated comdr. Order Star of Africa (Liberia); contbr. articles to law revs. Home: 2732 SW 4th Pl Gainesville FL 32601 Office: 337 Holland Law Center U Fla Gainesville FL 32611 Tel (904) 392-2211 also suite 1 Bldg C 4001 Newberry Rd Gainesville FL 32607

WARD, RICHARD GUERIN, b. Detroit, Oct. 13, 1929; B.S., Mich. State U., 1952; J.D., Wayne State U., 1959. Admitted to Mich. bar, 1960; mem. firm Sullivan, Ranger, Ward & Bone, Detroit, 1965—; faculty Oakland U. Mem. Am., Mich., Detroit bar assns. Home: 5815 Bloomfield Glens Rd West Bloomfield MI 48033 Office: 3100 City Nat Bank Bldg Detroit MI 48226 Tel (313) 961-8989

WARD, RICHARD H., b. Cin., June 8, 1923; student Denison U.; LL.B., U. Cin., 1948. Admitted to Ohio bar, 1949; asst. pros. atty. Hamilton County (Ohio), 1953-56; now mem. firm Drew and Ward Co., L.P.A., Cin. Mem. Mariemont (Ohio) Village Council, 1954-58; mem. Mariemont City Sch. Bd., 1965-73, pres. 1968-70. Mem. Cin. (pres. 1976-77), Ohio State, Am. bar assns., Phi Delta Phi. Office: 2302 Central Trust Tower 5 W Fourth St Cincinnati OH 45202 Tel (513) 621-8210*

WARD, ROBERT JOSEPH, b. N.Y.C., Jan. 31, 1926; B.S., Harvard, 1945, LL.B., 1949. Admitted to N.Y. bar, 1949; asso. firm Mendes & Mount, N.Y.C., 1949-51; partner firm Aranow, Brodsky, Bohlinger, Benetar & Einhorn, N.Y.C., 1961-72; judge U.S. Dist. Ct., So. Dist. N.Y., 1972—; asst. dist. atty. New York County, 1951-55; asst. U.S. atty. for So. Dist. N.Y. Justice Dept., 1956-61. Mem. Am., N.Y. State bar assns., Assn. Bar City N.Y. Office: US Courthouse Foley Square New York City NY 10007 Tel (212) 791-0221

WARD, RODMAN, JR., b. Wilmington, Del., Apr. 8, 1934; B.A., Williams Coll., 1956; LL.B., Harvard, 1959. Admitted to Del. bar, 1959, D.C. bar, 1969; asso. firm Prickett, Ward, Burt & Sanders and predecessors, Wilmington, 1959-64, partner, 1964—; sec., dir. Corp. Service Co., 1963—; mem. com. on plans and goals World Peace Through Law Center, Washington, 1967—. Chmn., New Castle County (Del.) Housing Authority, 1972-73; pres. World Affairs Council Wilmington; mem. bd. library assos. U. Del., 1976—; trustee, mem. fin. and investment coms. Wilmington Med. Center, 1974—; bd. dirs. Hist. Soc. Del. Mem. Am., Del. (corp. law com.), D.C. bar assns., Assn. Bar City N.Y., (corp. law com.), Am. Judicature Soc. Home: 52 Selborne Dr Wilmington DE 19807 Office: 1310 King St Wilmington DE 19899 Tel (302) 658-5102

WARD, WADE DONOVAN, b. Crisfield, Md., Mar. 24, 1924; B.S., U. Md., 1950, LL.B., 1952. Admitted to Md. bar, 1952; states atty. Somerset County (Md.), 1954-66. Bd. dirs. McCready Mem. Hosp. Mem. Am., Md., Somerset bar assns. Home: Jacksonville Rd Crisfield MD 21817 Office: 946 W Main St Crisfield MD 21817 Tel (301) 968-1100

WARD, WILLIAM JOSEPH, b. Long Beach, Calif., July 7, 1920; A.B., Ariz. State U., 1943; LL.B., U. Ariz., 1950. Admitted to Ariz. bar, 1950, Calif. bar, 1951; individual practice law, San Bernardino, Calif., 1951—; partner firm Holcomb & Ward, San Bernardino; dep. city atty. San Bernardino, 1955-60; counsel for San Bernardino Redevel. Agy., 1952-67; prof. bus. law San Bernardino Valley Coll., 1955-61. Sr. warden St. John's Episcopal Ch., 1962-64. Mem. state bars Ariz., Calif., San Bernardino County Bar Assn. (v.p.). Office: 505 Arrowhead Suite 210 San Bernardino CA 92401 Tel (714) 889-1041

WARD, WILLIAM ROBERT, b. Palisade, Nebr., Oct. 12, 1921; B.S., U. Nebr., 1943; LL.B., U. Denver, 1953. Admitted to Colo. bar, 1953; asso. firm Weller, Friedrich, Hickisch & Hazlitt, Denver, 1953-56, partner, 1956—. Mem. Am., Colo., Denver bar assns., Internat. Assn. Ins. Counsel, Denver Def. Counsel Assn. Home: 6495 S Helena St Denver CO 80232 Office: 900 Capitol Life Center Denver CO 80203 Tel (303) 861-8000

WARD, WILLIS F., b. Birmingham, Ala., Dec. 28, 1912; B.A., U. Mich., 1935; LL.B., Detroit Coll. of Law, 1939; H.H.D., No. Mich. U., 1970. Admitted to Mich. bar, 1946; individual practice law, Detroit, 1946-52; trial lawyer Wayne County Prosecuting Atty.'s Office, Detroit, 1946-47; chief civil div. U.S. Atty.'s Office, Detroit, 1953-61; mem. Bd. Control No. Mich. U., Marquette, 1964-65, commr., 1966-68, chmn. Mich. Pub. Service Commn., Lansing, 1968-73; judge Probate Ct. Wayne County (Mich.), Detroit, 1973—; dir. Rural Telephone Bank, 1971-73; mem. exec. com. Nat. Assn. of Utility Regulatory Commrs., 1968-72. Mem. Fed., Mich. State bar assns. Home: 2900 E Jefferson St Apt B-1 Detroit MI 48207 Office: 1379 City-County Bldg Detroit MI 48226 Tel (313) 224-5681

WARDEN, JAMES FREDERICK, JR., b. Carlsbad, N.Mex., Mar. 7, 1943; A.B. Colo. Coll., 1965; J.D. Cornell U., 1971. Admitted to N.Y. State bar, 1973, U.S. Dist. Ct. bar, 1973; staff counsel N.Y. State Pub. Service Commn., Albany, 1971-74; prin. intervenor atty. N.Y. State Consumer Protection Bd., Albany, 1974—. Mem. Am., N.Y. State bar assns., Res. Officers Assn. Decorated Bronze Star. Home: 31 Kinderhook St Chatham NY 12037 Office: 99 Washington Ave Albany NY 12110 Tel (518) 474-5015

WARDER, SMITH, b. Glasgow, Ky., Jan. 23, 1917; A.B., Centre Coll., Danville, Ky., 1938; J.D., U. Mich., 1941. Admitted to Mich. bar, 1941, Ohio bar, 1942, U.S. Supreme Ct. bar, 1971; mem. firm Arter & Hadden, Cleve., 1941—. Mem. Am., Ohio, Cleve. bar assns., Am. Judicature Soc., Fedn. Ins. Counsel, Internat. Assn. Ins. Counsel, Internat. Soc. Barristers, Am. Coll. Trial Lawyers, Order of Coif. Home: 21950 Shelburne Rd Shaker Heights OH 44122 Office: 1144 Union Commerce Bldg Cleveland OH 44114 Tel (216) 696-1144

WARE, GORDON LANE, b. Green Bay, Wis., Mar. 24, 1939; student Wayland Acad., 1956-57; B.S., Northwestern U., 1961; J.D., U. Wis., 1965, postgrad., 1964-65. Admitted to Wis. bar, 1965; pres. firm Ruder, Ware, Michler & Forester, Wausau, Wis., 1974—; dir., vice-chmn. corporate banking and bus. law sect. Wis. State Bar. Pres. Wausau Area Performing Arts Found., 1972-76; dir. Wausau Hosps. Inc. Mem. Wis., Am., Marathon County bar assns., Wausau Area C. of C. (dir. 1973-76). Home: 13 North Hill Rd Wausau WI 54401 Office: PO Box 1244 First American Center Suite 700 Wausau WI 54401 Tel (715) 845-4336

WARE, HENRY HALL, JR., b. Heard County, Ga., Mar. 30, 1903; student Mercer U., 1919-22, J.D. (hon.), 1974; LL.B., Atlanta Law Sch., 1926, J.D. (hon.), 1970. Admitted to Ga. bar, 1926; asso. firm Randolph, Parker & Fortson, Atlanta, 1926-31; asso. firm Crenshaw, Hansell, Ware, Brandon & Dorsey and predecessor, Atlanta, 1931-41, partner, 1941-62; partner firms Ware & Sterne, Atlanta, 1962-76, Huie, Ware, Sterne, Brown & Ide, Atlanta, 1976—. Bd. trustees Mercer U., 1938-42, 62-67, 74-75, mem. Pres.'s Council, 1968-73, 76—. Mem. Atlanta, Ga., Am. bar assns., Lawyers Club of Atlanta, Mercer U. Alumni Assn. (pres. 1960-61). Recipient Distinguished Alumnus award Mercer U., 1970. Home: 404 Blackland Rd NW Atlanta GA 30342 Office: 41 Marietta St NW 1200 Standard Fed Bldg Atlanta GA 30303 Tel (404) 522-8700

WARE, ROBERT ALEXANDER, JR., b. Birmingham, Ala., Nov. , 1931; B.S. in Bus. Adminstrn., U. Fla., 1953, J.D., 1961. Admitted to Fla. bar, 1961, U.S. Supreme Ct. bar, 1970; mem. firm Bolles Goodwin Ryskamp & Ware, Miami, Fla., 1961-72; gen. counsel InterAm. Center Authority, Miami, 1972-73, J.I. Kislak Mortgage Co., Miami and Newark, 1973-75; mem. firm English, McCaughan & O'Brian, Fort Lauderdale, Fla., 1976—; counsel Miami-Dade Community Coll., 1965-72; trial counsel Fla. East Coast Ry., 1962-72; counsel Dade County Sch. Bd., Miami, 1961-72; instr. bus. law Barry Coll., Embry Riddle Aviation U., Miami, 1974; gen. counsel Kiwanis Youthland Inc., Miami, 1974-76. Bd. dirs. Metro Miami YMCA, 1975, 76; mem. athletic adv. com. Dade County Sch., 1972-76. Mem. Am., Fla., Dade County, Broward County bar assns., Nat. Assn. Ry. Trial Counsel, Phi Delta Phi. Home: 13400 SW 63d Ave Miami FL 33156 Office: 301 E Las Olas Fort Lauderdale FL 33302 Tel (305) 462-3301

WARE, ROBERT HAYDEN, b. Kansas City, Mo., 1927; B.S. in Mech. Engring., U. Mich., 1947; M.S. in Mech. Engring., Harvard, 1948; LL.B., 1951. Admitted to Mass. bar, 1951, N.Y. bar, 1952, Conn. bar, 1958, U.S. 2d Circuit Ct. Appeals bar, 1959; asso. firm Fish, Richardson & Neave, N.Y.C., 1951-57; partner firm Mattern, Ware, Davis & Stoltz, Bridgeport, Conn., 1963—; instr. lectr. boating safety, celestial navigation, seamanship, sailing and meteorology U.S. Power Squadrons, 1962—. Mem. Conn. Patent Law Assn. (pres. 1969-70), Am., Conn. (ho. of dels. 1976—), Danbury, Bridgeport (mem. exec. com. 1976—) bar assns., Am. Arbitration Assn., Danbury C. of C. (dir. 1969-71), Penfield Power Squadron, IEEE, Bridgeport Rotary, Harvard Soc. Engrs. and Scis. Home: 200 Surrey Ln Fairfield CT 06430 Office: 855 Main St Bridgeport CT 06604 Tel (203) 333-3165

WARE, RUSSELL MARTIN, b. Watertown, Wis., Sept. 14, 1946; B.A., U. Wis., 1968; J.D., Marquette U., 1971. Admitted to Wis. bar, 1971; asso. firm Kasdorf, Dall, Lewis & Swietlik, Milw., 1972—. Home: 1057 N 70th St Wauwatosa WI 53213 Office: 2057 W Wisconsin Ave Milwaukee WI 53233 Tel (414) 342-4400

WARE, SUE A., b. Butler, Mo., July 21, 1948; B.A. cum laude, Central Mo. State U., 1971; J.D., U. Mo. at Kansas City, 1974. Admitted to Mo. bar 1974; trust adminstr. First Nat. Bank Kansas City, 1974-76; asso. firm Margolin & Kirwan, Kansas City, Mo., 1976—; law clk. firm Raymond, West, Shy and Morris, Kansas City, Mo., 1973, firm Gage & Tucker, Kansas City, Mo., 1973-74. Mem. Am., Mo., Kansas City bar assns., Lawyers Assn. Kansas City. Office: 1000 United Mo Bank Bldg Kansas City MO 64106 Tel (816) 842-7080

WARFIELD, RICHARD PRESTWOOD, b. Pensacola, Fla., Jan. 21, 1927; student The Citadel, 1943-45; LL.B., U. Fla., 1949, J.D., 1967. Admitted to Fla. bar, 1949; individual practice law, Pensacola; asso. firm Fisher & Hepner, Pensacola, until 1962; partner firm Levin, Warfield, Middlebrooks, Graff, Mabie, Rosenbloum & Magie, Pensacola, 1962—; chmn. Jud. Nominating Commn., First Circuit Ct., 1975-76. Pres., Escombia County Tb Assn., 1955-56; chmn. bd. govs. Downtown YMCA, 1971. Mem. Am., Escambia-Santa Rosa bar assns., Am. Judicature Soc., Acad. Fla. Trial Lawyers, Am. Trial Lawyers Assn. Home: 2790 Endor Rd Pensacola FL 32503 Office: Seville Tower 226 S Palafox St Pensacola FL 32501 Tel (904) 432-1461

WARHAFTIG, ARNOLD M., b. Newark, June 14, 1940; A.B., N.Y. U., 1962; J.D., Seton Hall Law Sch., 1968. Admitted to N.J. bar, 1968; asso. firm Kapelsohn, Lerner, Leuchter, Reitman & Maisel, Newark, 1967-72; individual practice law, Union, N.J., 1972—. Mem. Cranford (N.J.) Bd. Edn., 1972-76, pres., 1975-76. Mem. Am., N.J., Union County bar assns., Union Lawyers Club. Office: 385 Chestnut St Union NJ 07083 Tel (201) 687-5624

WARING, DONALD EMIL, b. Seattle, Jan. 1, 1942; B.A., U. Wash., 1969; J.D., U. Wyo., 1972. Admitted to Wyo. bar, 1972, Wash. bar, 1973; individual practice law, Buckley, Wash.; city atty. City of Buckley, 1974—. Mem. Am., Wash., Pierce County, South King County bar assns. Office: 766 Main St Buckley WA 98321 Tel (206) 829-1540

WARMAN, PHILIP THORNTON, b. Waynesburg, Pa., May 17, 1942; A.B., U. Pitts., 1966; J.D., Rutgers U., 1969. Admitted to Pa. bar, 1969; partner firm Warman & Warman, Uniontown, Pa., 1969-70, 71—; spl. asst. atty. gen. Commonwealth of Pa., Harrisburg and Phila., 1970-71; solicitor Borough of Fayette City (Pa.), 1971—, County of Fayette (Pa.), 1975—. Trustee United Methodist Ch., Masontown, Pa., 1975—. Mem. Am., Pa., Fayette County bar assns., Assn. Trial Lawyers Am., Pa. Trial Lawyers Assn. (dir.), Am. Judicature Soc. Office: 97 E Main St Uniontown PA 15401 Tel (412) 437-9420

WARMAN, RUTH EDGAR, b. Waynesburg, Pa., Mar. 24, 1919; A.B., Waynesburg Coll., 1941; postgrad. Rutgers U. Law Sch., 1947-48, Dartmouth, 1961; LL.B., W.Va. U., 1952. Tchr. lang. and math. pub. schs., Pa., 1955-65; admitted to Pa. bar, 1972; partner firm Warman & Warman, Uniontown, Pa., 1963—. Mem. Pa. Gov's. Justice Commn. Southwestern Planning Council, 1976—. Mem. Fayette County, Pa. bar assns. Home: PO Box 464 RD 6 Uniontown PA 15401 Office: 97 E Main St Uniontown PA 15401 Tel (412) 437-9420

WARMUTH, RICHARD ANDREW, b. Cameron, W.Va., Aug. 19, 1924; student West Liberty State Coll., 1946-48; J.D., W.Va. U., 1951. Admitted to U.S. Ct. Appeals bar 2d Circuit, 1951, W.Va. Supreme Ct. Appeals bar, 1951; atty. United Farmers Telephone Co., Cameron, 1951-65; judge 2d Jud. Circuit, 1965—; city atty. City of Cameron, 1952-65. Mem. W.Va. Council Juvenile Ct. Judges (pres. 1971). Home: Fort Clark Estates Benwood WV 26031 Office: PO Box 485 Moundsville WV 26041 Tel (304) 845-8660

WARNER, CECIL RANDOLPH, JR., b. Ft. Smith, Ark., Jan. 13, 1929; A.B. magna cum laude, U. Ark., 1950; LL.B. magna cum laude, Harvard, 1953; Sheldon fellow, 1953-54. Admitted to Ark. bar, 1953; partner firm Warner & Smith, Ft. Smith, 1954—; pres., dir. Fairfield Communities, Inc.; dir. Mid-Am. Industries, Inc., Wortz Co.; instr. Sch. Law U. Ark., 1954, 56. Vice chmn. Ark. Constl. Revision Study Commn., 1967; v.p. 7th Ark. Constl. Conv., 1969-70; scoutmaster troop 23, Westark council Boy Scouts Am., Ft. Smith, 1955-58; mem. Ark. State Police Commn., 1970; bd. dirs. United Fund, ARC, Ark. Community Found.; trustee Sparks Regional Med. Center; elder Presbyterian Ch.; mem. alumni bd. U. Ark. Fellow Am., Ark. bar founds.; mem. Am. Law Inst., Am., Ark. (chmn. exec. com. 1966-67, chmn. young lawyers sect. 1961-62), Sebastian County bar assns., Am. Trial Lawyers Assn., Ft. Smith C. of C. (dir.), Phi Beta Kappa, Phi Eta Sigma, Omicron Delta Kappa. Home: 3428 Cliff Dr Fort Smith AR 72901 Office: 214 N 6th St Fort Smith AR 72901 Tel (501) 782-6043 also 1207 Rebsamen Park Rd Little Rock AR 72203 Tel (501) 664-6000

WARNER, CHARLES COLLINS, b. Cambridge, Mass., June 19, 1942; B.A., Yale U., 1964; J.D., Ohio State U., 1970. Admitted to Ohio bar, 1970, U.S. Ct. Appeals 6th Circuit bar, 1974; asso. firm Wright, Harlor, Morris & Arnold, Columbus, Ohio, 1970-75, partner, 1976—. Chmn. Peace Corps Service Council of Columbus, 1973-75. Mem. Am., Ohio, Columbus bar assns. Home: 145 E South St Worthington OH 43085 Office: 37 W Broad St Columbus OH 43215 Tel (614) 224-4125

WARNER, DAVID ROSS, JR., b. Mpls., Oct. 28, 1943; A.B., George Washington U., 1965; J.D., U. Nebr., 1968; LL.M., U. Chgo., 1972. Admitted to Nebr. bar, 1968, Iowa bar, 1970; asso. firm Hughes, Thorsness, Lowe, Gantz & Clark, Anchorage, Alaska, 1968-69, firm Shull, Marshall, Marks & Vizentos, Sioux City, Iowa, 1969-70; law clk., Iowa Supreme Ct., Des Moines and Sioux City, 1970-71; asst. prof. law Ohio No. U., Ada, 1972-75, asso. prof., 1975—. Mem. Am., Nebr. bar assns., Seldon Soc., Order of the Coif. Contbr. articles in field to law jours. Home: 603 S Main St Ada OH 45810 Office: Petit Coll Law Ohio No Univ Ada OH 45810 Tel (419) 634-9921

WARNER, FRANK SHRAKE, b. Ogden, Utah, Dec. 14, 1940; J.D., U. Utah, 1964. Admitted to Utah bar, 1964; asso. firm Young, Thatcher, Glasmann & Warner and predecessor, Ogden, 1964-69, partner, 1969-70; dep. county atty. Weber County, Utah, 1970-72; chmn. Utah Pub. Service Commn., Salt Lake City, 1972-76; partner firm Warner & Wikstrom, Ogden, 1976—. Mem. Am. Bar Assn. Home: 3254 N 900 E North Ogden UT 84401 Office: 9 Bank of Utah Plaza Ogden UT 84401 Tel (801) 621-6540

WARNER, GREGORY HOWARD, b. Twin Falls, Idaho, Oct. 3, 1941; B.A. in English, U. Mont., 1963; J.D., Gonzaga U., 1968. Admitted to Mont. bar, 1968; clk. Mont. Legal Services Assn., Helena, 1968; asso. firm Graybill, Ostrem, Warner & Crotty, Great Falls, Mont., 1969-70, partner, 1970—; pub. defender Cascade County (Mont.), 1971. Mem. Mont. State, Cascade County (sec. 1969), Am. bar assns. Am. Judicature Soc. Contbr. articles to legal jours. Home: 1315 13th St S Great Falls MT 59401 Office: 400 1st Nat Bank Great Falls MT 59401 Tel (406) 452-8579

WARNER, JOHN LOCKWOOD, JR., b. Columbus, Ohio, May 2, 1941; student Ohio State U., 1959-62; LL.B., Memphis State U., 1966. Admitted to Tenn. bar, 1966, U.S. Supreme Ct. bar, 1971; with JAGC, U.S. Army, 1967-71; partner firm Stricklin & Warner, Union City, Tenn., 1971-72; individual practice law, Union City, 1973—; judge Union City Ct., 1972-76. Mem. welfare adv. com. Obion County, Tenn., 1972-75; bd. dirs. Obion County Assn. Retarded Citizens, 1973-75, Obion County United Way, 1974-77; dir. Jackson Area Council on Alcoholism and Drug Abuse, 1976—; mem. Union City Library Bd., 1973—; commr. 46th Gen. Assembly, Cumberland Presbyn. Ch.; trustee Bethel Coll., 1977—. Mem. Am., Tenn. (ho. of dels. 1976—, Am. citizenship and Law Day com. 1974-75, mem. unauthorized practice of law com. 1976—); Obion County, Union City bar assns., NW Tenn. Criminal Def. Assn., Am. Legion (state judge adv. 1973-74), Phi Delta Phi. Home: 1104 Sherwood Dr Union City TN 38261 Office: 306 W Church St Union City TN 38261 Tel (901) 885-2430

WARNER, RICHARD BUTTRICK, b. Pittsfield, Mass., Jan. 22, 1925; A.B., Harvard, 1948; J.D., U. Mich., 1958. Admitted to Mass. bar, 1959, U.S. Supreme Ct. bar, 1963; individual practice law, Pittsfield, 1960-70. Mem. Am., Mass., Berkshire bar assns., Nat. Lawyers Club. Home: 1600 Beach Dr NE St Petersburg FL 33704 Tel (813) 895-8022

WARNER, ROBERT LEMAN, b. Dixon, Ill., Aug. 23, 1894; student U. Wis., 1913-16, U. Ill., 1916-17. Admitted to Ill. bar, 1917; individual practice law, Dixon, 1960—. Mem. Am., Ill. State, Chgo., Lee County bar assns. Home: 122 Dement Ave Dixon IL 61021 Office: 109 Galena Ave Dixon IL 61021 Tel (815) 284-3344

WARNES, JAMES CUNNINGHAM, b. Chgo., May 15, 1946; A.B. cum laude, Erskine Coll., 1968; J.D., U. Ga., 1973. Admitted to Ga. bar, 1973; asso. firm Alan M. Alexander, Jr., 1973-74, Cook, Pleger & Noell, Athens, Ga., 1974-75; partner Cook, Noell, Bates & Warnes, Athens, 1975—; recorder City of Athens, 1974—. Mem. Athens Bar Assn. (sec.-treas. 1975). Office: 304 E Washington St Athens GA 30601 Tel (404) 549-6111

WARNKE, THOMAS, b. Cleve., May 11, 1943; B.A. in Social Sci., Colgate U., 1965; J.D., Seton Hall U., 1970. Admitted to N.J. bar, 1970; claims mgr. U.S. Fidelity & Guaranty Co., N.Y.C., 1967-71; counsel Ins. Services Office, N.Y.C., 1971-75; asst. v.p., counsel Crum & Forster Ins. Cos., Morristown, N.J., 1975—; atty. Legal Aid, Morris County, N.J., 1970-71. Mem. N.J. Vols. in Parole Program, 1971. Mem. Am. Bar Assn., Assn. Corporate Counsel of N.J. Office: 305 Madison Ave Morristown NJ 07960 Tel (201) 285-7393

WARNLOF, JOHN SKINNER, b. Fairmont, Minn., Aug. 5, 1945; A.B., Claremont Men's Coll., 1967; J.D., U. Calif., San Francisco, 1972. Admitted to Calif. bar, 1972; asso. firm Bledsoe, Smith, Cathcart, Boyd & Eliot, San Francisco, 1972—. Mem. Am., Calif., San Francisco bar assns., Assn. Def. Counsel. Office: 650 California St San Francisco CA 94108 Tel (415) 981-5411

WARNOCK, HAROLD CHARLES, b. N.Y.C., Jan. 6, 1912; LL.B., U. Ariz., 1935. Admitted to Ariz. bar, 1935, U.S. Supreme Ct. bar, 1952; mem. investigation div. U.S. Dept. Agr., Washington, 1937-38; individual practice law, Tucson, 1938-42; partner firm firm Bilby, Shoenhair, Warnock & Dolph, and predecessor, Tucson, 1946—; mem. Ariz. Commn. Uniform Laws, 1954-60, Employment Security Commn. Ariz., 1960-66. Fellow Am. Coll. Trial Lawyers; mem. Pima County (pres. 1953), Ariz. bar assns., Nat. Assn. R.R. Trial Counsel, Am. Counsel Probate Counsel. Author procedural forms uniform probate code state Ariz., 1973. Office: 9th Floor Valley Nat Bldg Tucson AZ 85701 Tel (602) 792-4800

WARR, IRENE, b. Erda, Utah, Oct. 6, 1931; B.A., Westminster Coll., Salt Lake City, 1954; J.D., U. Utah, 1957. Admitted to Utah bar, 1957; individual practice law, Salt Lake City, 1957—. Past bd. dirs., pres. Salt Lake Met. Services for Aging; former mem. Utah State Library Commn.; past pres. Legal Aid Soc., Salt Lake City; bd. dirs. Salt Lake Area ARC. Mem. Am., Utah, Salt Lake County bar assns., Nat., Utah fedns. bus. and profl. women's clubs, Salt Lake League Bus. and Profl. Women's Clubs, Nat. Assn. Women Lawyers, ICC Practitioners Assn., Utah Transp. Council, Phi Alpha Delta. Named Distinguished Del. Rep. Am. Women for study with Hungarian, Romanian and Soviet Women's Councils, 1971. Office: 430 Judge Bldg Salt Lake City UT 84111 Tel (801) 531-1300

WARREN, DAVID GRANT, b. Chgo., July 2, 1936; A.B., Miami U., Oxford, Ohio, 1958; J.D., Duke U., 1964. Admitted to N.C. bar, 1964; asst. dir. Inst. Govt., prof. pub. law U. N.C., 1964-74, prof. health adminstrn., 1974; dir. Health Policy Center, Georgetown U., 1975; prof. health adminstrn. Duke U., 1975—; acting dir. N.C. Office Emergency Med. Services, Raleigh, N.C., 1973; vis. prof. London Sch. Hygiene and Tropical Medicine, 1972-73. Pres. N.C. Health Council, 1974-75. Mem. Am., N.C. bar assns., Am. Public Health Assn., Am. Soc. Hosp. Attys., Nat. Health Lawyers Assn., Am. Soc. Law and Medicine, Am. Hosp. Assn. (mem. com. on trustees 1977), N.C. Soc. Hosp. Attys. (v.p. 1976—). Recipient Distinguished Service award N.C. Pub. Health Assn., 1967; co-editor: A Legislator's Guide to the Medical Malpractice Issue, 1976; news and notes editor Jour. Health Politics, Policy and Law, 1977—. Home: 408 Lyons Rd Chapel Hill NC 27514 Office: Box 3018 Duke U Med Center Durham NC 27710 Tel (919) 684-4188

WARREN, DONALD, b. N.Y.C., Oct. 25, 1935; B.A., Bklyn. Coll., 1956; J.D., N.Y. Law Sch., 1958. Admitted to N.Y. bar, 1959, U.S. Supreme Ct. bar, 1969; partner firm Anderman, Povman & Warren, Forest Hills, N.Y., 1971—; v.p., gen. counsel Semi Conductor Tech., Inc., College Point, N.Y., 1970—. Mem. N.Y., Queens County bar assns. Home: 108-37 71st Ave Forest Hills NY 11375 Office: 108-18 Queens Blvd Forest Hills NY 11375 Tel (212) 268-3000

WARREN, DOROTHEA GRUBBS, b. Columbus, Kans., Feb. 3, 1919; B.A., Kans. State Coll., 1939; J.D., Washburn U., 1942. Admitted to Kans. bar, 1942; asst. state law librarian State Library, Topeka, Kans., 1956-67; law librarian, prof. Washburn U. Sch. of Law, Topeka, 1967—. Mem. Kans., Topeka bar assns., Assn. of Am. Law Librarians. Home: 1434 Polk St Topeka KS 66612 Office: 1700 College Topeka KS 66621 Tel (913) 295-6688

WARREN, EDWARD WILSON, b. Louisville, Apr. 2, 1944; B.A., Yale, 1966; J.D., U. Chgo., 1969. Admitted to Ill. bar, 1969, D.C. bar, 1970; asso. firm Kirkland, Ellis & Rowe, Washington, 1970-75, partner, 1975—; law clk. U.S. Ct. Appeals 7th Circuit, 1969-70. Mem. D.C. Bar Assn. Office: 1776 K St NW Washington DC 20006 Tel (202) 857-5018

WARREN, JACK WILLIAM, b. Lansing, Mich., Dec. 20, 1921; B.A., Mich. State U.; J.D., U. Mich. Admitted to Mich. bar, 1950; individual practice law, 1950-51, 1963-67; asst. pros. atty., 1953, 56; municipal judge, 1954-55; pros. atty., 1957-61; city atty., 1961-63; judge Circuit Ct., Lansing, 1967—. Mem. Am., Ingham County bar assns., Mich. Judges Assn. Office: City Hall 2d Floor Lansing MI 48933 Tel (517) 484-4557

WARREN, JOHN PHILIP, JR., b. Boulder, Colo., Feb. 8, 1946; B.A., Seton Hall U., 1967; J.D., Stetson U., 1972. Admitted to Fla., N.J. bars, 1972, N.Y. bar, 1976; hearing examiner Bd. Pub. Utility Commrs., State N.J., Newark, 1972-75; atty. long lines Am. Tel. & Tel. Co., White Plains, N.Y., 1975-76, fed. regulatory N.Y.C., 1976—. Mem. Am., Fed., N.Y. State, N.J. bar assns., Fla. Bar. Fellow Inst. Far Eastern Studies, 1967; contbr. article to League of Municipalities Mag. Home: 109 Alpine Trail St Sparta NJ 07871 Office: POB 32 Bedminster NJ 07921 Tel (201) 234-6313

WARREN, JOHN RAY, b. Eclectic, Ala., Sept. 20, 1936; B.S., Auburn U., 1958; LL.B., Jones Law Sch., 1964. Admitted to Ala. bar, 1964; mem. claims dept. State Farm Ins. Co., Dothan, Ala., 1964—. Home: 1202 S Edgewood Dr Dothan AL 36301 Office: 507 Fortner St Dothan AL 36301 Tel (205) 794-4163

WARREN, JOHN S., b. Grand Junction, Colo., July 19, 1948; B.S., U. Calif., Berkeley, 1970; J.D., U. Mont., 1973. Admitted to Mont. bar, 1973; partner firm Schultz, Davis & Warren, Dillon, Mont., 1973—; trustee State Bar Mont., 1975—. Office: 122 E Glendale St Dillon MT 59725 Tel (406) 683-2363

WARREN, LOUIS BANCEL, b. Monmouth Beach, N.J., Aug. 30, 1905; B.A., M.A., Oxford U., 1927; LL.B., Columbia, 1930. Admitted to N.Y. bar, 1930; asso. firm Kelley, Drye & Warren and predecessor, N.Y.C., 1930-40, mem. firm, 1940—; dir., mem. compensation com. Chrysler Corp., 1957-76; dir. Chrysler France, Chrysler U.K., Ltd., Chrysler Espana S.A., Hammerson Holdings (U.S.A.), Inc.; sec., dir. AEA Investors, Inc. Mem. Am., Internat., N.Y. State bar assns., Assn. Bar City N.Y., Am. Soc. Internat. Law, Am. Judicature Soc. Decorated Order St. Gregory the Gt. (Holy See), Officers Cross of Merit, Sovereign Order Malta, chevalier Legion of Honour (France), comdr. Order Brit. Empire. Home: Ballantine Rd Bernardsville NJ 07924 Office: 350 Park Ave New York City NY 10022 Tel (212) 752-5800

WARREN, PHYLLIS GAIL, b. Newark, May 24, 1948; B.A., Douglass Coll., 1970; J.D., Rutgers U., 1973. Admitted to N.J. bar, 1973; supervising atty. Camden (N.J.) Regional Legal Service Family Law and Women's Rights Clinic, 1973-75; staff atty. N.J. Office Legal Services, Trenton, 1975-76; staff atty. Legal Services N.J., Inc., New Brunswick, 1976—; co-adj. faculty mem. Douglass Coll., New Brunswick. Author (with Joan Sampieri) N.J. Guide to Pro Se Divorce, 1975. Office: 78 Carroll Pl New Brunswick NJ 08901 Tel (201) 246-0770

WARREN, RICHARD MOORE, b. Dunn, N.C., July 8, 1930; B.B.A., Wake Forest U., 1952, LL.B., 1960. Admitted to N.C. bar, 1960; asso. firm Block, Meyland & Lloyd, Greensboro, N.C., 1960-62; gen. counsel Anderson Industries, Greensboro, 1962-63; gen. counsel Blue Bell, Inc., Greensboro, 1963—, asst. sec., 1967-70, sec., 1970—. Mem. Am., N.C., Greensboro bar assns. C.P.A., N.C. Home: 4907 Kingswood Dr Greensboro NC 27410 Office: 335 Church Ct Greensboro NC 27401 Tel (919) 373-3925

WARREN, ROBERT, b. Cleve., Aug. 22, 1949; B.S. in Bus. Adminstrn., Ohio State U., 1971, J.D., 1974. Admitted to Ohio bar, 1974, D.C. bar, 1975; atty. SEC, Washington, 1974—. Office: 500 N Capitol St Washington DC 20549 Tel (202) 755-8948

WARSHAUER, MARSHALL ALAN, b. Chgo., Jan. 3, 1930; J.D., DePaul U., 1954. Admitted to Ill. bar, 1954; sr. v.p., trust officer Nat. Blvd. Bank of Chgo., 1957—; lectr. Nat. Trust Sch. Mem. Am., Ill., Chgo. bar assns. Office: 400 N Michigan Ave Chicago IL 60611 Tel (312) 467-4100

WARWICK, KATHLEEN ANN, b. Phila., Aug. 3, 1934; A.B., Vassar Coll., 1956; LL.B., U. Columbia, 1963. Admitted to N.Y. State bar, 1963, Fed. bar, 1965, U.S. Ct. Appeals bar, 1966, U.S. Supreme Ct. bar, 1973; atty. SEC, N.Y. Regional Office, 1965-69; asso. firm Cadwalader, Wickersham & Taft, N.Y.C., 1969-75; corp. securities counsel Mobil Oil Corp., N.Y.C., 1975—. Mem. Am., Fed., N.Y. State bar assns., Assn. Bar City N.Y., Fed. Bar Council. Home: 11 E 75th St New York City NY 10021 Office: 150 E 42d St New York City NY 10017 Tel (212) 883-7428

WASCOE, EDWARD ANTON, b. Jersey City, June 5, 1943; B.A., Farleigh Dickinson U., 1965; postgrad. U. S.C., 1967-68; J.D., Rutgers U., 1973. Admitted to N.J. bar, 1973; intern N.Y. State Dept. Law, Charity Frauds Bur., summer 1971; law clk. City of Jersey City Law Dept., 1972-73, asst. corp. counsel, 1974-76, 2d asst. corp. counsel, 1976—; clk. to judge N.J. Superior Ct., 1973-74. Mem. Am., N.J. bar assns., Nat. Inst. Municipal Law Officers, ACLU, Air Force Assn., N.J. Army and Air N.G. Assn., Assn. N.G. Office: 390 Central Ave Jersey City NJ 07307 Tel (201) 420-1463

WASH, ROBERT MARTIN, b. Fresno, Calif., May 27, 1908; A.B., U. Calif. at Berkeley, 1930, J.D., 1934. Admitted to Calif. bar, 1934; individual practice law, Fresno, 1934-42; dep. dist. atty. Fresno County, 1943-50, county counsel, 1950—. Mem. Am. Judicature Soc., County Counsel Assn. Calif., Calif. Hist. Soc., Calif. Writers and Artists (pres. San Joaquin Valley chpt. 1975-77). Author: This is My Valley, 1968. Home: 3535 S Temperance St Fresno CA 93725 Office: 304 Hall Records Fresno CA 93721 Tel (209) 488-3479

WASHBURN, CHARLES FRANCIS, b. St. Stephen, N.B., Can., Jan. 4, 1944; B.A., U. Maine, 1965; J.D., Boston U., 1968. Admitted to Maine bar, 1969; individual practice law, Machias, Maine, 1969—. Chmn. bd. Selectmen, Perry, Maine, 1971-73. Mem. Am., Maine, Washington County (pres. 1974-75) bar assns. Home: Gin Cove Rd Perry ME 04667 Office: 20 Center St Machias ME 04654 Tel (207) 255-3364

WASHINGTON, JAMES AARON, b. Asheville, N.C., Feb. 17, 1915; A.B., Howard U., Washington, 1936, LL.B., 1939; LL.M., Harvard, 1941. Admitted to D.C. bar, 1939, U.S. Ct. Mil. Appeals bar, 1970; teaching fellow, instr. Howard U. Sch. Law, 1939-40, 41-42, prof. law, 1946-61, vice dean, 1958-61, Langston prof. law, 1966, dean, 1969; atty. Dept. Justice, 1942-46; chmn. D.C. Pub. Service Commn., 1961-66, summer staff adviser appeals and rev. bd., 1968; gen. counsel Dept. Transp., 1969-71; asso. judge Superior Ct. D.C., 1971—. Chmn. model cities com. Health and Welfare Council, Reconstrn. and Devel. Corp., Neighborhood Consumer Info. Center; trustee Washington Inst. for Quality Edn. Mem. Am., D.C. bar assns. Recipient Distinguished Pub. Service award Howard U. Sch. Law, 1962, Ann. Bus. award D.C. C. of C., 1964, award for meritorious achievement Dept. Transp., 1970, award Neighborhood Consumer Info. Center, 1973, award Washington Urban League, 1967. Home: 14212 North Gate Dr Silver Spring MD 20906 Office: 440 G St NW Pension Bldg Washington DC 20001 Tel (202) 727-1480

WASHINGTON, NAT WILLIS, b. Coulee City, Wash., May 2, 1914; B.A., U. Wash., 1936, J.D., 1938. Admitted to Wash. bar, 1939; atty. Bonneville Power Adminstrn., 1939-42; staff JAGC, USAF, 1942-46; individual practice law, Ephrata, Wash., 1947—; counsel Grant County Pub. Utility Dist., 1957-68, 61-64; mem. Wash. Ho. of Reps., 1949-51, Wash. State Senate, 1951—; vice chmn. Nat. Com. on Uniform Traffic Laws, 1973—; pres. Western Conf. Council State Govts., 1972-73. Mem. Wash. State Bar Assn. Home: 42 C St NW Ephrata WA 98823 Office: 42 1/2 C St NW Ephrata WA 98823 Tel (509) 754-4413

WASSER, DENNIS MATHEW, b. Bklyn., Aug. 27, 1942; B.A. in Polit. Sci., U. Calif., Los Angeles, 1964; J.D., U. So. Calif., 1967. Admitted to Calif. bar, 1967; partner firm Greenberg & Glusker, Los Angeles, 1967-76, Thomas, Shafran & Wasser, 1976—; chmn. judge pro tem panel small claims ct., Beverly Hills, Calif., 1973—. Mem. Am., Los Angeles County, Beverly Hills (program chmn. family law sect. Beverly Hills) bar assns., Order of Coif. Contbr. articles to legal jours.; editor U. So. Calif. Law Rev., 1966-67. Office: 2049 Century Park E Suite 1800 Los Angeles CA 90067 Tel (213) 277-7117

WASSERMAN, KENNETH WILBER, b. Beatrice, Nebr., Apr. 8, 1947; B.A., Kans. State U., 1969; J.D., Washburn U., 1972. Admitted to Kans. bar, 1972; legal intern atty. gen's office State Kans., Topeka, 1971-72; asso. firm Frank Norton, Salina, Kans., 1972-75; asso. firm Norton, Shaffer & Wasserman, Salina, 1975—. Mem. Am., Kans., Saline County bar assns. Home: Rural Route 2 Salina KS 67401 Office: 215 S Santa Fe St Salina KS 67401 Tel (913) 827-3646

WASSERMAN, LEON, b. N.Y.C., Mar. 24, 1907. Admitted to N.Y. State bar, 1932; individual practice law, N.Y.C., 1932—. Mem. Bklyn. (com. on ins.), Am. bar assns., N.Y. County Lawyers Assn. (com. on ins.), N.Y. Trial Lawyers Assn. (chmn. com. on ins.), Bklyn. Lawyers Club (dir.). Contbr. articles to legal jours. Home: 370 Ocean Pkwy Brooklyn NY 11218 Office: 25 Broadway New York City NY 10004 Tel (212) 344-6330

WASSERMAN, ROBERT ZACHARY, b. Hollywood, Calif., June 25, 1947; B.A., U. Calif. Santa Cruz, 1969; J.D., Stanford U., 1972. Admitted to Calif. bar, 1972; asso. firm Clinton White & Assos., Oakland, Calif., 1972-75; partner firm Wasserman and Gordon, Oakland, 1976—; prosecutor Agrl. Labor Relations Bd., Calif., 1975-76. Mem. ACLU, Alameda County Bar Assn., Nat. Lawyers Guild, Calif. Atty.'s Criminal Justice. Home: 824 Rosemount Rd Oakland CA 94610 Office: 506 15th St Fifth Fl Oakland CA 94612 Tel (415) 465-6722

WASSERSTROM, ALFRED HOWARD, b. N.Y.C., Jan. 8, 1910; B.S., U. Va., 1930; J.D., Columbia, 1933; LL.M., N.Y. U., 1956; Admitted to N.Y. bar, 1933, U.S. Supreme Ct. bar, 1945; mem. firm Lipton, Wasserstrom & DeGroot and predecessors, N.Y.C., 1934—; sr. mem. legal dept. Hearst Corp., N.Y.C., 1968—; past chmn. com. legal affairs Mag. Pubs. Assn., N.Y.C.; mem. nat. panel arbitrators Am. Arbitration Assn.; past small claims arbitrator N.Y.C. Civil Ct. Mem. Am. Bar Assn. (chmn. com. on copyright legislation), Fed. Bar Council, Copyright Soc. U.S.A. (past v.p.), Assn. Bar City N.Y., Scribes. Recipient certificates of appreciation Practicing Law Inst. of N.Y.C., 1973, Assn. Arbitrators N.Y.C. Civil Ct., 1976; plaque Am. Arbitration Assn. 1969; contbr. articles to legal jours.; editorial bd. Bull. of Copyright Soc., 1970—. Home: 120 E Hartsdale Ave Hartsdale NY 10530 Office: 959 8th Ave New York City NY 10019 Tel (212) 586-1300

WASSERSTROM, MARK DAVID, b. Kansas City, Mo., June 12, 1949; A.B. in History, Harvard, 1971; J.D., U. Tex., Austin, 1974. Admitted to Mo. bar, 1974; asso. firm Dietrich, Davis, Dicus, Rowlands & Schmitt, Kansas City, Mo., 1974—; hearing referee Housing Authority Kansas City; vice chmn. Internat. Law Com. Mo. Bar. Mem. Liquor Appeals Bd. Kansas City, 1976—; mem. bd. trustees Sam Houston Senate Alumni, 1975—. Mem. Mo., Kansas City Bar Assns., Lawyers Assn. Kansas City, Delta Theta Phi (historian, 1975, clk., 1976). Office: 1001 Dwight Bldg Kansas City MO 64105 Tel (816) 221-3420

WATANABE, WILFRED KAKURO, b. Boulder, Colo., May 31, 1933; B.S., U. Oreg., 1955; J.D., Harvard U., 1967. Admitted to Hawaii bar, 1967; asso. firm Padgett, Greeley, Marumoto & Akinaka, and predecessor, Honolulu, 1967-70, Chuck & Fujiyama, Honolulu, 1970-73; partner firm Tom & Watanabe, Honolulu, 1974-76; majority atty. Hawaii Ho. of Reps., 1974; atty. judiciary com. Hawaii Senate, 1975; legis. atty. Hawaii State Assn. Counties, 1976; atty. judiciary com. Hawaii Ho. of Reps., 1977—. Mem. Hawaii Bar Assn., Assn. Trial Lawyers Am. Home: 500 University Ave Apt 328 Honolulu HI 96826 Office: 333 Queen St Honolulu HI 96813 Tel (808) 524-4750

WATERFALL, GORDON GARRETT, b. Pasadena, Calif., Mar. 17, 1934; B.S., U. Calif., Berkeley, 1957; J.D., U. Ariz., Tucson, 1965. Admitted to Ariz. bar, 1965, U.S. Tax Ct. bar, 1975; shareholder firm Waterfall, Economidis, Caldwell & Hanshaw, P.C., Tucson, 1969—; judge pro tempore Pima County (Ariz.) Superior Ct., 1973-74. Pres. Tucson Lawyers for Housing, 1973-74. Mem. Am., Pima County (pres. 1976-77) bar assns., Assn. C.P.A.-Attys. Office: 5151 E Broadway suite 1600 Tucson AZ 86711 Tel (602) 790-5828

WATERS, JAMES HAROLD, b. Des Moines, Feb. 24, 1940; B.A., Drake U., 1968, J.D., 1971. Admitted to Iowa bar, 1971; research asst. to atty. gen. Iowa Dept. Revenue, 1969-70; staff atty. Polk County (Iowa) Legal Aid Soc., Des Moines, 1971-73; asst. atty. Polk County Friend of the Ct., 1973-75; asso. firm Hermann, Waters and Andersen, Ankeny, Iowa, 1975—. Mem. Am., Iowa, Polk County bar assns., Assn. Trial Lawyers of Iowa. Office: 315 SW Walnut St Ankeny IA 50021 Tel (515) 964-3700

WATKINS, HOWARD KEITH, b. Los Angeles, June 16, 1947; B.A. in Polit. Sci., U. Calif., Berkeley, 1969; J.D., Hastings Coll. of Law, 1972. Admitted to Calif. bar, 1973; staff atty. Fresno County (Calif.) Legal Services, Inc., 1973-75, exec. dir., 1976—. Mem. Nat. Lawyers Guild, Am., Fresno County bar assns., ACLU (pres. Fresno chpt. 1975-76), NAACP, Women's Internat. League Peace and Freedom, Hastings Alumni Assn. (pres. Central Valley chpt.). Home: 3506 E Balch Ave Fresno CA 93702 Office: 1221 Fulton Mall Room 505 Fresno CA 93721 Tel (209) 485-9880

WATKINS, JOHN CUMMING, JR., b. Mobile, Ala., Apr. 2, 1935; B.S., U. Ala., 1957, J.D., 1962; M.S., Fla. State U., 1964; LL.M., Northwestern U., 1968. Admitted to Ala. bar, 1962, U.S. Supreme Ct. bar, 1973; asst. prof. comml. law Coll. Commerce and Bus. Adminstrn. U. Ala., University, 1965-69, prof., chmn. criminal justice program, 1971—; asso. prof. criminology Sam Houston State U., Huntsville, Tex., 1969-71; law clk. Supreme Ct. Ala., 1962-63, U.S. Fifth Circuit Appeals, 1965-66; cons. Joint Commn. on Instnl. Libraries, Am. Correctional Assn., 1969-71; adv. bd. Nat. Criminal Justice Vol. Resource Center, U. Ala., lectr. in law and corrections, Sch. Law, 1971-72. Mem. Am., Ala. bar assns., Am. Judicature Soc., Am. Correctional Assn., Am. Soc. Criminology, Nat. Council on Crime and Delinquency. Cons. editor Assn. Coll. and Research Libraries, ALA, 1973-77. Home: PO Box 2167 University AL 35486 Office: Criminal Justice Program PO Box 1935 University AL 35486 Tel (205) 348-6738

WATKINS, ROBERT PATTERSON, III, b. Boston, July 6, 1937; A.B. in Govt., Harvard U., 1959; LL.B., Columbia U., 1965; M. Criminology, Cambridge U. (Eng.), 1970. Admitted to D.C. bar, 1966, U.S. Supreme Ct. bar, 1974; atty. civil rights div. U.S. Dept. Justice, Washington, 1965-66, atty. office hearing counsel Fed. Maritime Commn., Washington, 1966-68; law clk. to judge U.S. Dist. Ct. for D.C., 1968; asst. U.S. atty. appellate div. D.C., 1968-69, felony trial sect., 1970-71, chief misdemeanor sect., 1971-72; asso. firm Williams & Connolly, Washington, 1972-77, partner, 1977—. Mem. Am., Nat., D.C., D.C. Unified bar assns., Phi Delta Phi. Office: 839 17th St NW Washington DC 20006 Tel (202) 331-5077

WATKISS, DAVID KEITH, b. Salt Lake City, Oct. 16, 1924; B.S., U. Utah, 1949, J.D., 1949. Admitted to Utah bar, 1950, U.S. Supreme Ct. and U.S. Ct. Mil. Appeals bars, 1955; dep. county atty. Salt Lake County, 1952-56; partner firm Watkiss & Campbell, and predecessor, Salt Lake City, 1956—. Fellow Internat. Acad. Trial Lawyers (dir.), Am. Coll. Trial Lawyers; mem. Am., Utah, Salt Lake County bar assns. Home: 1509 Canterbury Dr Salt Lake City UT 84108 Office: Suite 1200 310 S Main St Salt Lake City UT 84101 Tel (801) 363-3300

WATSON, BILL DEAN, b. Turon, Kans., July 10, 1927; B.S., Kans. State U., 1950; J.D., Washburn U., 1955. Admitted to Kans. bar, 1955; gen. practice law, Independence, Kans.; county atty. Montgomery County (Kans.), 1962-66; probate judge Montgomery County, 1966; judge Independence City Ct., 1966-71; atty. City of Independence, 1971—. Mem. Kans., Montgomery County bar assns. Home: 624 E Main St Independence KS 67301 Office: 109 W Laurel St Independence KS 67301 Tel (316) 331-6030

WATSON, DAVID PAUL HAMENDT, b. Toronto, Ont., Can., Apr. 11, 1920; came to U.S., 1926, naturalized, 1934; B.A., Yale U., 1942; LL.B., U. Va., 1948. Admitted to N.Y. bar, 1948, U.S. Supreme Ct. bar, 1952; asso. firm Hatch, Root & Barrett, N.Y.C., 1948-50, partner firm Haight, Gardner, Poor & Havens, N.Y.C., 1961—. Mem. Am. Bar Assn., Maritime Law Assn. U.S., St. Andrew's Soc. State N.Y. Named officer Order of Brit. Empire, 1975. Office: 1 State St Plaza New York City NY 10004 Tel (212) 344-6800

WATSON, GERARD PHILIP, b. Bklyn., July 28, 1931; A.B. cum laude, St. Peter's Coll., 1953; J.D., Columbia, 1959; LL.M., N.Y. U., 1963. Admitted to N.Y. bar, 1959, U.S. Supreme Ct. bar, 1963; asso. firm Mendes & Mount, N.Y.C., 1959-64; asso. firm LeBoeuf, Lamb, Leiby & MacRae, N.Y.C., 1965—, mem., 1970—. Mem. Maritime Law Assn. U.S. (marine ecology com.). Contbr. articles to legal jours. Office: 140 Broadway New York City NY 10005 Tel (212) 269-1100

WATSON, HENRIETTA SUE, b. Hayden, Ala., Mar. 5, 1933; B.A., La. State U., 1959, J.D., 1959. Admitted to La. bar, 1959; mem. firm Camp & Palmer, Lake Charles, La., 1959-60; partner firm Watson & Watson, Lake Charles, 1960-65; law clk. La. 1st Circuit Ct. Appeals, 1973, La. 3d Circuit Ct. Appeals, 1974—; dir. Cameron State Bank (La.). Mem. transp. task force Goals for La., 1969-70, vice chmn. com. transp., 1971, trustee, 1971—. Mem. S.W. La., La. bar assns., Am. Judicature Soc. Home: 311 Shell Beach Dr Lake Charles LA 70601 Office: PO Box 3000 Lake Charles LA 70602 Tel (318) 433-9403

WATSON, JACK CROZIER, b. Jonesville, La., Sept. 17, 1928; B.A., U. Southwestern La., 1949; LL.B., La. State U., 1956. Admitted to La. bar, 1956; practiced in Lake Charles, La., 1956-64; prosecutor City of Lake Charles, 1960; asst. dist. atty. La. 14th Jud. Dist., 1961-64; judge La. Dist. Ct. 14th Jud. Dist., 1964-72; ad hoc judge La. Ct. Appeals, 1st Circuit, 1972-73, La. 3d Circuit Ct. Appeal, 1974—; mem. faculty, advisor Nat. Coll. State Judiciary, 1970, 73; mem. La. Jud. Council, 1972-74. Mem. Am., La. S.W. La. bar assns., Nat. Council Juvenile Ct. Judges (pres. La. council 1969-70). Home: 311 Shell Beach Dr Lake Charles LA 70601 Office: PO Box 3000 Lake Charles LA 70602 Tel (318) 436-1144

WATSON, JACK W., b. Haskell, Tex., Sept. 12, 1921; B.B.A., U. Tex., 1948, J.D., 1948. Admitted to Tex. bar, 1948; briefing atty. Tex. Supreme Ct., 1948-49; atty. Phillips Petroleum Co., 1949-50; individual practice law, Stamford, Tex., 1950—; dir. 1st Nat. Bank Stamford, 1968-75; city atty. Stamford, 1953—. Bd. dirs. Stamford Art Found. Mem. Tex. Bar Assn., Am. Judicature Soc., W.Tex. Legal Soc. Home: 514 Hill Circle Stamford TX 79553 Office: 113 N Swenson Ave Stamford TX 79553 Tel (915) 773-3666

WATSON, JAMES WILLIAM, b. Memphis, Dec. 7, 1916; J.D., U. Tenn., 1940. Admitted to Tenn. bar, 1940; judge probate ct. Shelby County, Tenn., 1948-50; partner firm Laughlin, Watson, Creson, Garthright & Halle, 1950-71, firm Watson & Knolton, 1971-76, firm Watson, Cox, Arnoult, May, Charlton & Leake, Memphis, 1976—. Pres. Memphis & Shelby County Mental Health Soc., 1950. Mem.

Am., Tenn., Memphis and Shelby County bar assns. Home: 4147 Kirter Ln Memphis TN 38117 Office: 100 N Main Bldg Memphis TN 38103 Tel (901) 525-1691

WATSON, JOHN DEWEY, b. Arkadelphia, Ark., Aug. 20, 1941; B.A., Ouachita Bapt. Coll., 1963; J.D., U. Ark., 1970. Admitted to Ark. bar, 1970; clk. to justice Ark. Supreme Ct., Little Rock, 1970-71; partner firm Smith, Williams, Friday, Eldredge & Clark, Little Rock, 1971—. Mem. Am., Ark., Pulaski County bar assns. Home: 5501 Edgewood St Little Rock AR 72207 Office: 20th floor First National Bldg Little Rock AR 72201 Tel (501) 376-2011

WATSON, JOSEPH OTIS, JR., b. Indianola, Iowa, Aug. 26, 1903; B.A., Simpson Coll., 1925; LL.B., State U. Iowa, 1928. Admitted to Iowa bar, 1928, U.S. Supreme Ct. bar, 1939, Fla. bar, 1971; partner firm Watson & Watson, Indianola, 1928-36, Watson & Prall, Indianola, 1944-46, Watson & Herrick, Indianola, 1948-58, Watson, Elgin & Hoyman, Indianola, 1958-72; sr. partner firm Lyle, Skipper, Wood & Anderson, and predecessors, St. Petersburg, Fla., 1973—; mem. Iowa Ho. of Reps., 1951-55. Mem. Fla., Iowa bars, Iowa Acad. Trial Lawyers, Am. Coll. Probate Counsel. Home: 833 Bay Point Dr Madeira Beach FL 33708 Office: 2600 9th St N Saint Petersburg FL 33704 Tel (813) 895-1991

WATSON, KERMITH GLYNN, b. Ashburn, Ga., Sept. 9, 1937; A.B., Mercer U., 1959, J.D., 1963. Admitted to Ga. bar, 1963; individual practice law, Reidsville, 1963-64; served to lt. col. JAGC, AUS, 1964—, staff judge adv., 1975-77. Ga. Bar Assn. Office: Staff Judge Advocate 19th SPT BdE APO San Francisco CA 96212

WATSON, LOU ANN, b. Sasakwa, Okla., May 30, 1940; B.A. in Polit. Sci., U. Calif. at Berkeley, 1961; LL.B., Hastings Coll. Law, 1964. Admitted to Calif. bar, 1965, U.S. Supreme Ct. bar, 1973; dep. city atty. City of Westminster (Calif.), 1965-67; dep. city atty. City of Santa Ana (Calif.), 1967; asst. city atty. City of Huntington Beach (Calif.), 1967-70; individual practice law, Modesto and Turlock, 1970—; city atty. City of Turlock, 1972—. Mem. Calif. Trial Lawyers Assn., Calif. Applicants Attys. Assn., Am. Bus. Women's Assn., AAUW, Soroptimist Internat., Brangus Breeders Assn. Named woman year Turlock chpt. Am. Bus. Women's Assn., 1976. Home: 399 E Minnesota Ave Turlock CA 95380 Office: 725 E Olive St Turlock CA 95380 also 802 14th St Modesto CA 95354 Tel (209) 632-3857

WATSON, MARVIN HENRY, JR., b. Anniston, Ala., Nov. 7, 1944; A.B., Birmingham So. Coll., 1966; J.D., U. Ala., 1968. Admitted to Ala. bar, 1968; partner firm Phillips & Watson, Anniston, 1968—; city judge City of Anniston, 1964—; city atty. City of Ohatchee (Ala.), 1976-77. Mem. Am., Ala., Calhoun Conty bar assns. Office: 810 Commercial Nat Bank Bldg Anniston AL 36201 Tel (205) 237-7556

WATSON, MATTHEW SAUL, b. Phoenix, Jan. 24, 1941; B.A., Johns Hopkins U., 1962, M.A., 1962; LL.B., N.Y. U., 1965; LL.M., George Washington U., 1967. Admitted to N.Y. bar, 1965, D.C. bar, 1966, U.S. Supreme Ct. bar, 1969; law clk. to judge U.S. Ct. Appeals, 4th Circuit, Charlotte, N.C., 1965-66; asso. firm Fried, Frank, Harris, Shriver & Kampelman, Washington, D.C., 1966-74; asst. counsel Commn. on Govt. Procurement, Washington, 1970-71; acting gen. counsel D.C. Bd. Elections, 1974; sr. atty. U.S. Gen. Accounting Office, Washington, 1974-75; auditor D.C., 1975—. Mem. Judicial Conf. D.C., 1976. Mem. Bar Assn. D.C., Am. Bar Assn., Washington Council Lawyers, Phi Beta Kappa. Home: 3391 Stephenson Place NW Washington DC 20015 Office: Room 945 1329 E St NW Washington DC 20004 Tel (202) 629-4642

WATSON, NANCY BELCHER, b. Pomona, Calif., July 14, 1926; B.A., Stanford, 1946; J.D., U. Calif., Los Angeles, 1958. Admitted to Calif. bar, 1959; mem. firm Belcher, Henzie & Biegenzahn, Los Angeles, 1959-68; judge Municipal Ct., Los Angeles Jud. Dist., 1968-73, Los Angeles County Superior Ct., 1973—, supervising judge family law dept., 1975, 76. Mem. Conf. Calif. Judges, Am. Bar Assn., Los Angeles County Bar, Am. Judicature Soc., Women Lawyers Assn. Los Angeles, Assn. Family Conciliation Cts. (treas. 1975-76, dir. 1975-77). Office: 210 W Temple St Los Angeles CA 90012 Tel (213) 974-1234

WATSON, S(TERL) A(RTHUR), JR., b. Hot Springs, Ark., July 11, 1942; student Harding Coll., 1960-61, N.E. La. State Coll., 1961-62; J.D., U. Ala., 1966; grad. Nat. Coll. State Judiciary, 1974, Am. Trial Judges Acad., 1976. Admitted to Ala. bar, 1967; bailiff 23d Jud. Circuit Ct. Huntsville, Ala., 1966-67; asso. firm Humphrey, Lutz & Smith, Huntsville, 1967-68; chief asst. dist. atty. Madison County (Ala.) Dist. Atty.'s Office, 1968-72; judge Madison County Gen. Sessions Ct., 1972-74, 23d Jud. Circuit Ct., 1974—. Bd. dirs. Huntsville Boys Club. Mem. Ala., Huntsville Madison County, Fed. bar assns., Am. Judicature Soc., Am., Ala. Circuit judges assns. Home: 1313 Big Cove Rd Huntsville AL 35801 Office: Madison County Courthouse Huntsville AL 35801 Tel (205) 536-5911

WATSON, WADE THOMAS, b. Gary, W.Va., June 21, 1938; A.B., W.Va. U., 1960; J.D., Duke, 1965. Admitted to W.Va. bar, 1965; asso. firm Crockett, Tutwiler & Crockett, Welch, W.Va., 1965-68; partner firm Camper & Watson, Welch, 1968—; asst. pros. atty. McDowell County (W.Va.), 1966-76, pros. atty., 1977—. Mem. McDowell County Bar Assn., Phi Beta Kappa. Home: PO Box 700 Gary WV 24836 Office: Court House Annex Welch WV 24801 Tel (304) 436-6222

WATSON, WALLACE BAILEY, b. Greenwood, S.C., July 14, 1942; B.A., The Citadel, 1964; J.D., Wake Forest U., 1967. Admitted to S.C. bar, 1967; individual practice law, Charleston, S.C., 1967-75; partner firm Rozier & Watson, North Charleston, S.C., 1975—; asso. judge North Charleston Municipal Ct., 1973-74. Vestryman, Episcopal Ch. of Holy Communion, Charleston, 1975—. Mem. Am., S.C., Charleston County bar assns., Charleston Lawyers Club. Home: 9 Blaine Ct Charleston SC 29407 Office: 2138 Dorchester Rd PO Box 4307 North Charleston SC 29405 Tel (803) 554-6761

WATSON, WILLIAM GERALD, b. Harrisburg, Pa., Nov. 20, 1929; B.A., Johns Hopkins, 1951; J.D., Dickinson Sch. Law, 1954. Admitted to Pa. bar, 1957; asst. counsel State Capital Savs. & Loan Assn., Harrisburg, 1957-68, counsel, 1968—, v.p., 1970—, also dir.; chmn. Mortgage Lending Task Force Savs. and Loan Code, 1967. Mem. Country Club Hills Assn., 1966—, pres., 1975. Mem. Pa., Dauphin County bar assns. Home: 103 Ridgewood Dr Camp Hill PA 17011 Office: 108 N 2d St Harrisburg PA 17101 Tel (717) 238-8252

WATSON, WILLIAM THOMAS, b. Selma, Ala., Mar. 23, 1943; B.S., U. Ala., 1966, J.D., 1969. Admitted to Ala. bar, 1970; asst. atty. gen. State of Ala. for Oil and Gas Bd., Geol. Survey Ala., University, Ala., 1970-74; partner firm Espy and Watson, P.A., Tuscaloosa, 1974-76; individual practice law, Tuscaloosa, 1976—. Mem. Interstate Oil Compact Commn. Mem. Mid-Continent Oil and Gas Assn., Ala. Geol. Soc., Am. Bar Assn. Home: 16 Woodland Park Tuscaloosa AL 35401 Office: 300 1st Fed Bldg Tuscaloosa AL 35401 Tel (205) 345-1577

WATT, GARLAND WEDDERICK, b. Elizabeth City, N.C., Feb. 10, 1932; A.B. magna cum laude, N.C. Central U., 1952; postgrad. Harvard, 1952-54; J.D. with honors, DePaul U., 1961. Admitted to Ill. bar, 1961, U.S. Dist. Ct. bar for No. Dist. Ill., 1961, U.S. 6th Circuit Ct. Appeals bar, 1961; practiced in Chgo., 1961-74; partner firm Turner, Cousins, Gavin & Watt, 1961-65, Cook & Watt, 1965-67, Rivers Watt & Lockhart, 1967-70, Watt & Holland, 1970-74; judge Ill. Circuit Ct. of Cook County, 1975—; mem. hearing bd., atty. registration and disciplinary commn. Ill. Supreme Ct., 1973-75. Bd. dirs. Mid-Am. chpt. ARC, 1973—. Mem. Am., Ill., Cook County (Richard E. Westbrooks award 1972, Jud. award 1975), Chgo., Nat. bar assns. Home: 9655 Calumet Ave Chicago IL 60628 Office: Chgo Civic Center Chicago IL 60602 Tel (312) 443-4544

WATT, LUCILE LAMBERT, b. Live Oak, Calif., June 22, 1917; B.A., U. Calif., Berkeley, 1938; LL.B., Pacific Coast U., 1948. Admitted to Calif. bar, 1949; asso. firm Gordon M. Snyder, Los Angeles, 1949-50, Charles H. Carr, Los Angeles, 1951-62; individual practice law, Los Angeles, 1962-69, Pasadena, Calif., 1969—. Mem. Los Angeles County Bar Assn. (chmn. lawyer referral service com. 1973-75), Women Lawyers Assn. Los Angeles, Women Lawyers Club Los Angeles (pres. 1955-56). Office: 234 E Colorado St room 202 Pasadena CA 91101 Tel (213) 684-1490

WATT, MONROE, b. Seattle, July 19, 1910; J.D. cum laude, U. Wash., 1934. Admitted to Wash. bar, 1934; partner firm Elvidge, Watt, Veblen & Tewell, and predecessors, Seattle, 1939-68; partner firm Watt & Venables, Kent, Wash., 1968-75; individual practice law, Seattle, 1975—; hon. counsel British Counsul Gen., Seattle, 1952-71. Mem. Order of Coif, Phi Beta Kappa. Mem. staff Wash. Law Rev., 1933-34. Home and office: 3357 46th Ave NE Seattle WA 98105

WATT, RICHARD FRYE, b. Seattle, July 13, 1917; A.B., U. Wash., 1937; M.A. (Rhodes scholar 1937-39), Oxford (Eng.) U., 1944; LL.B., U. Chgo., 1942. Admitted to Ill. bar, 1942, U.S. Supreme Ct. bar, 1948; individual practice, Chgo., 1949-51; partner firm Cotton, Watt, Jones, King & Bowlus and predecessors, Chgo., 1951—; asst. prof. law U. Chgo., 1946-48; lectr. Loyola U., Chgo., 1965-66, Chgo.-Kent Sch. Law-Ill. Inst. Tech., 1973. Bd. dirs. Ill. div. ACLU, 1970-75, gen. counsel, 1973-75. Mem. Chgo. Bar Assn., Chgo. Council Lawyers. Contbr. articles to legal publs. Home: 5442 S Hyde Park Blvd Chicago IL 60615 Office: One IBM Plaza Suite 4750 Chicago IL 60611 Tel (312) 467-0590

WATTER, PAUL NORMAN, b. Linden, N.J., Feb. 22, 1948; B.S. in Commerce, U. Va., 1970; J.D., Rutgers U., Camden, N.J., 1973. Admitted to N.J. bar, 1973; legal intern Camden Regional Legal Services, 1972-73; dep. atty. gen. N.J. Office of Atty. Gen., Trenton, 1973—. Mem. N.J. Bar Assn., U. Va. Alumni Assn. Recipient Am. Jurisprudence award Lawyers Coop. Pub. Co., 1971; editorial staff Rutgers U. Law Rev., 1971-72. Home: 32-10 Fox Run Dr Plainsboro NJ 08536 Office: State House Annex Trenton NJ 08625 Tel (609) 292-8559

WATTERS, EDWARD MCLAIN, JR., b. Phila., Oct. 5, 1908; A.B., Yale U., 1931; LL.B., U. Pa., 1935. Admitted to Pa. bar, 1937; partner firm McDevitt, Philips & Watters, and predecessor, Phila., 1938-45; asso. firm Fell & Spalding, Phila., 1946-68; counsel Fell, Spalding, Goff & Rubin, Phila., 1969-76; individual practice law, Radnor, Pa., 1976—. Mem. Pa., Phila. bar assns. Office: suite 202 1 Radnor Station Bldg Radnor PA 19087 Tel (215) 687-5577

WATTERS, EDWARD MCLAIN, III, b. Bryn Mawr, Pa., Oct. 23, 1943; B.A. cum laude, Yale U., 1965; J.D. cum laude, U. Pa. Admitted to Pa. bar, 1970; asso. firm Pepper, Hamilton & Scheetz, Phila., 1970-77, partner, 1977—. Sec., mem. bd. mgrs. Children's Cruise and Playground Soc., Inc.; dir. Soc. of St. Margaret; mem. health care subcom. trustees health affairs com. Hosp. of U. Pa. Mem. Am., Pa., Phila. bar assns., Nat. Assn. Security Dealers (arbitration panel), Order of Coif. Office: 2001 Fidelity Bldg 123 S Broad St Philadelphia PA 19109 Tel (215) 545-1234

WATTERSON, JAMES SIGEL, b. Marshfield, Mo., Jan. 16, 1939; B.S. in Math., Southwest Mo. State U., 1960, J.D., 1972. Admitted to Calif. bar, 1972; partner firm Watterson, Brown, Gouyd & McReynolds, Sunnyvale, Calif., 1973—; instr. bus. law DeAnza Community Coll., Cupertino, Calif., 1974—; staff IRS, San Jose, Calif., 1966-72. Mem. Santa Clara County, Sunnyvale-Cupertino (chmn. client relations com., chmn. unauthorized practice law, trustee 1977—) bar assns. Home: 465 S Mathilda St Sunnyvale CA 94086 Tel (408) 732-3114

WATTS, CLARENCE WILLIAM, b. Wildwood, N.J., May 28, 1944; B.S., U. Md., 1969; J.D., Rutgers State U., 1972. Admitted to Pa. bar, 1972, N.J. bar, 1973; partner firm Diamond, Polsky & Bauer, Phila., 1972—. Mem. Phila., Pa., Am., N.J. bar assns. Contbr. articles to legal jours. Home: 305 Victor Ave Cherry Hill NJ 08002 Office: 700 Widener Bldg 1339 Chestnut St Philadelphia PA 19107 Tel (215) LO4-5400

WATTS, DAVID E., b. Fairfield, Iowa, June 13, 1921; B.A., U. Iowa, 1941, J.D., 1942; postgrad. Columbia Law Sch., 1946-47. Admitted to Iowa bar, 1942, Mass. bar, 1950, N.Y. bar, 1954; instr. U. Iowa, 1947-48; asst. prof. U. Pa., 1948-49, Harvard Law Sch., 1949-52; adj. asso. prof. N.Y. U., 1952-55; mem. firm Dewey, Ballantine, Bushby, Palmer & Wood, N.Y.C., 1952-58, partner, 1958—; vis. lectr. Columbia U., 1954. Trustee, Collegiate Sch. N.Y.C., bd. dirs. Youth Symphony Orch. N.Y. Mem. Am., N.Y. State bar assns., Assn. Bar City N.Y., N.Y. County Lawyers Assn., Am. Law Inst. Contbr. articles to legal jours. Home: 33 W 74th St New York City NY 10023 Office: 140 Broadway New York City NY 10005 Tel (212) 344-8000

WATTS, SANDRA KAY, b. Lakeview, Oreg., Oct. 25, 1942; B.S. in Polit. Sci., U. Oreg., 1964, J.D., 1970. Admitted to Mont. bar, 1973, Blackfeet Tribal bar, 1974, U.S. Ct. Claims bar, 1975; Reginald Heber community lawyer fellow Mont. Legal Services, Browning, 1970-71, Calif. Indian Legal Services, Ukiah, 1971-72; advisor Blackfeet Tribal Ct., Browning, 1973—. Mem. fin. steering com. Blackfeet Tribe, Browning, 1975—. Mem. Mont., Am., Blackfeet Tribe bar assns., Mont. Criminal Lawyers Def. Assn. Home: PO Box 834 Browning MT 59417 Office: Blackfeet Tribal Ct Browning MT 59417 Tel (406) 338-5061

WAX, ABRAHAM LAWRENCE, b. Kishinev, Rumania, Oct. 21, 1921; B.B.A., Coll. City N.Y., 1942; LL.B., Harvard, 1949. Admitted to N.Y. bar, 1949; practice law, N.Y.C.; mem. arbitration panel Am. Arbitration Assn., 1975—. Mem. New York County Lawyers, N.Y. State Bar Assn. Home: 219 E 69th St New York City NY 10021 Office: 444 Madison Ave New York City NY 10022 Tel (212) 758-2258

WAXMAN, LIONEL A., b. Upper Darby, Pa., Sept. 22, 1938; B.A., Pa. State U., 1961; LL.B., Villanova U., 1964, J.D., 1964. Admitted to Pa. bar, 1964, U.S. Supreme Ct. bar, 1968; individual practice law, Media, Pa., 1964-74; partner firm Lionel A. Waxman, Media, 1974—; adv. bd. Lincoln Bank, Broomall, Pa., 1976—; dir., pres. Suburban West Abstractors, Inc., Media, 1976—; lectr. Del. Law Sch., 1973; mem. county bd. law examiners, 1969-71; legal cons. CAP. Bd. govs. Royal Hosp. for Incurables, Putney, Del. Mem. Inter-Am., Pa., Delaware County bar assns., Pa. Trial Lawyers Assn., Comml. Law League, Nat. Rifle Assn., Am. Radio Relay League, Pa. Conservative Union (chmn. Delaware County). Publisher, Law Notes, 1976; contbr. articles to profl. jours.; econ. commentator Sta. WCAU. Office: 1155 W Baltimore Pike Media PA 19063 Tel (215) 566-6061

WAXMAN, STEVEN ROBERT, b. Phila., Oct. 25, 1946; B.S. with honors, Pa. State U., 1967; J.D. cum laude, U. Pa., 1970. Admitted to Pa. Supreme Ct. bar, 1971, U.S. Dist. Ct. bar for Eastern Dist. Pa., 1971, U.S. Ct. Appeals bar, 3d Circuit, 1972, U.S. Supreme Ct. bar, 1977; law clk. Hon. Daniel H. Hueyett, 3d Eastern Dist. Pa., 1970-71; asso. firm Bolger & Picker and predecessor, Phila., 1971-72, partner, 1972—; lectr. in field. Bd. dirs. Prisoners' Rights Council, Phila., 1971—, pres., 1976-77; bd. dirs. Pub. Interest Law Center of Phila., 1975—, Southeastern Pa. chpt. ACLU, 1976—. Mem. Am. (chmn. for Pa. mem. com. sect. young lawyers 1975—), Pa., Phila. chmn. young lawyers 1977-78, bd. govs. 1977-78) bar assns. Contbg. editor Phila. Arts Exchange mag., 1977—. Office: 1020 Suburban Sta Bldg Philadelphia PA 19103 Tel (215) 561-1000

WAXSE, DAVID JOHN, b. Oswego, Kans., June 29, 1945; A.B., U. Kans., Lawrence, 1967; teaching cert., Columbia, 1968, J.D., 1971. Admitted to Kans. and U.S. Dist. Ct. bar, 1971, U.S. Supreme Ct. bar, 1975; mem. firm Payne & Jones, Chartered, Olathe, Kans., 1971—; city atty. DeSoto, Kans., 1971—; municipal judge, Shawnee, Kans., 1974—; mem. Kans. Gov's. criminal justice advisory panel, 1975—. Pres bd. dirs. U. Kans. Meml. Corp., 1974 mem. bd. govs. Bacchus Found., 1971-74; bd. dirs. ACLU of Western Mo., pres., 1974-75, gen. counsel, 1976—; adviser Shawnee Mission Law Explorer Scout Post Heart of Am. council Boy Scouts Am., 1971-75; pres. Greater Kans. City Chpt. Kans. U. Alumni Assn., 1973-74; active Environ. Defense Fund, Sierra Club, Johnson County Mental Health Assn., Lenexa Rotary Club. Mem. Johnson County (chmn. personal rights com.), Kans. (mem. legal aid com.), Am. (mem. individual rights and urban law sects.) bar assns. Home: 10096 Hemlock St Overland Park KS 66212 Office: Tower Bldg Box 151 Olathe KS 66061 Tel (913) 782-2500

WAYNE, ARNOLD, b. Providence, Dec. 18, 1928; Ph.B., Providence Coll., 1948; J.D., U. So. Calif., 1958. Gen. sales mgr. Allan Aircraft Supply Co., North Hollywood, Calif., 1956-62; admitted to Calif. bar, 1958, individual practice law, since practiced in Los Angeles and Simi Valley. Mem. Assn. Trial Lawyers Am., Los Angeles County, San Fernando Valley bar assns., Los Angeles Trial Lawyers Assn. Office: 15233 Ventura Blvd Suite 900 Sherman Oaks CA 91403 Tel (213) 783-8820

WAYNE, LAURENCE HOWARD, b. Chgo., Apr. 10, 1943; student U. St. Thomas, Houston, 1965-68; J.D., U. Houston, 1970. Admitted to Tex. bar, 1971; partner firm Andell & Wayne, Houston, 1971-73; justice of peace, Harris County, 1973—, presiding judge, 1977—; legal counsel to student U. Houston, 1971-73. Bd. dirs. Big Bros. of Houston, pres., 1977; bd. dirs. Hope Center for Youth, Tex. So. U. Law Sch. Found., Martin Luther King Community Center, San Dollar House for Youth, Learning Devel. Center, Tex. Inst. for Family Psychiatry, U. Houston Alumni, Concerned Teens. Mem. Am. (chmn. criminal justice system 1974-75), Tex., Houston (chmn. sub-com. on juvenile delinquency 1973-74) bar assns. Home: 3520 Mt Vernon St Houston TX 77006 Office: 301 San Jacinto St Houston TX 77002 Tel (713) 221-5125

WAYNE, LAWRENCE SANFORD, b. Kansas City, Mo., Mar. 28, 1936; B.S., U. Calif. at Los Angeles, 1957; J.D., U. So. Calif., 1960. Admitted to Calif. bar, 1961; mem. firm Irell & Manella, Los Angeles, 1961-62; mem. firm Martin H. Webster, Beverly Hills, Calif., 1962-63; mem. firm Zerner & Sims, Los Angeles, 1963-65; mem. firm Slavitt, Edelman & Weiser, Los Angeles, 1965-67; individual practice law, Los Angeles, 1967-72; partner firm Magaram, Riskin, Wayne & Minikes, Los Angeles, 1972—; judge pro tem Small Claims Ct., Beverly Hills, 1967-70, West Los Angeles, 1972-76. Mem. Am., Los Angeles, Beverly Hills, Century City bar assns. Contbr. numerous articles to profl. jours. Office: 1880 Century Park E Suite 1418 Los Angeles CA 90067 Tel (213) 277-3135

WAYTE, ALAN, b. Huntington Park, Calif., Dec. 30, 1936; A.B., Stanford, 1958, J.D., 1960. Admitted to Calif. bar, 1961; asso. firm Adams, Duque & Hazeltine, Los Angeles, 1961-66, partner, 1966—. Bd. dirs., sec. Los Angeles Philharmonic Assn., 1975—. Mem. Am., Calif., Los Angeles County (vice-chmn. exec. com. real estate sect. 1974-76, chmn. real estate financing subsect. 1974-76) bar assns. Contbg. author: Advising California Partnerships; editor, chmn.: Los Angeles County Bar Bulletin, 1972-73; mem. com. Calif. State Bar Jour., 1974—; contbr. article to profl. jour.; lectr. various courses and seminars. Home: 1484 Cambridge Rd San Marino CA 91108 Office: 523 W 6th St Los Angeles CA 90014 Tel (213) 620-1240

WEAKLEY, WALLACE EDWARD, b. Indpls., Nov. 12, 1943; B.M.E., Gen. Motors Inst., 1967; J.D., Am. U., 1971. Admitted to Ind. bar, 1972, U.S. Patent Office bar, 1973; co-op. student, test engr. Allison div. Gen. Motors Corp., Indpls., 1961-67; law clk. firm Sughrue, Rothwell, Mion, Zinn & MacPeak, Washington, 1967-71, asso., 1971-73; individual practice law, Sheridan, Ind., 1973—. Treas. Kettering Civic Fedn., Upper Marlboro, Md., 1972; pres. Adams Elementary Sch. PTA, Sheridan, 1975-76. Mem. Am., Ind. State bar assns., Am. Patent Law Assn., Sheridan Bus. Assn. (pres. 1974-75), Delta Theta Phi (pres. Am. U. chpt. 1970-71). Home: Rural Route 2 Box 133 Sheridan IN 46069 Office: 104 E 4th St Sheridan IN 46069 Tel (317) 758-4443

WEATHERFORD, GARY DEAN, b. Riverside, Calif., Sept. 30, 1936; B.A. cum laude, U. Redlands, 1958; B.D., Yale, 1961, LL.B., 1964. Admitted to Calif. bar, 1965; spl. asst. to solicitor U.S. Dept. Interior, Washington, 1964-66; asst. prof. U. Oreg. Sch. Law, 1966-68; partner firm Ferris & Weatherford, San Diego, 1968-70; v.p. firm Ferris, Weatherford & Brennan, San Diego, 1970-75; dep. sec. Calif. State Resources Agy., Sacramento, 1976—; spl. asst. U.S. atty. gen.,

1968-69; cons. Pub. Land Law Rev. Commn., 1969, Nat. Water Commn., 1970-71; sr. investigator Lake Powell Research Project, 1972-75; lectr. water law U. Calif. Los Angeles, 1973-74. Mem. State Bar Calif., Am., San Diego bar assns., Calif. Jud. Council (adv. com. legal forms 1974-75). Woodrow Wilson fellow, 1958-59, Danforth fellow, 1958-60; contbr. articles to legal jours. Office: 1416 Ninth St Sacramento CA 95814 Tel (916) 445-5656

WEATHERFORD, TERRY LYNN, b. Culleoka, Tenn., Dec. 4, 1942; B.S., Murray State U., 1964; M.S., U. Ill., 1966; J.D., U. Tenn., 1970. Admitted to Tenn. bar, 1971, N.C. bar, 1972; with legal dept. Blue Bell, Inc., Greensboro, N.C., 1970—. Mem. N.C., Greensboro, Tenn. (asso.) bar assns. Home: 1400 Knightwood St Greensboro NC 27410 Office: 335 Church Ct Greensboro NC 27401 Tel (919) 373-3975

WEATHERLY, LAURENCE ROSS, b. Tacoma, Nov. 14, 1946; B.B.A., Pacific Luth. U., 1968; J.D., U. Wash., 1973. Admitted to Wash. bar, 1973; asso. firm Keller, Rohrback, Waldo & Hiscock, Seattle, 1973—. Mem. Wash. State Bar Assn., Phi Alpha Delta. Bd. editors Wash. Law Rev., 1972-73. Office: 1220 IBM Bldg 1200 Fifth Ave Seattle WA 98101 Tel (206) 623-1900

WEATHERS, CARROLL WAYLAND, b. Shelby, N.C., Oct. 18, 1901; B.A., Wake Forest U., 1922, LL.B., 1923. Admitted to N.C. bar, 1922; individual practice law, Raleigh, N.C., 1923-50; prof. law Wake Forest U., 1950-72, dean, 1950-70; mem. N.C. State Senate, 1935; mem. Raleigh CSC, 1938-41, 50, chmn., 1950. Bd. dirs. Raleigh State Sch. for Blind and Deaf, 1933-49, 53-70, chmn., 1958-70; trustee Olivia Raney Library, Raleigh, 1940-56, pres., 1946-56. Mem. Am., N.C., Forsyth County bar assns. Recipient Judge John J. Parker award N.C. State Bar Assn., 1972; Medallion of Merit, Wake Forest U., 1977. Home: 766 N Stratford Rd Winston-Salem NC 27104 Office: Wake Forest U Winston-Salem NC 27109

WEATHERS, ELIOT BROOKS, b. Short Hills, N.J., Jan. 10, 1922; B.A., Amherst Coll., 1943; LL.B., Yale, 1948. Admitted to N.Y. bar, 1949, U.S. Supreme Ct. bar, 1957; asso. firm Simpson Thacher & Bartlett, N.Y.C., 1948-58, partner, 1959-68, sr. partner, 1969—; chmn. nominating com. Am. Stock Exchange, 1977; panelist Ill. Inst. Continuing Legal Edn., Practising Law Inst. Mem. Assn. Bar City N.Y. Home: 2 Popham Pl Scarsdale NY 10583 Office: 1 Battery Park Plaza New York City NY 10004

WEATHERS, JON MARK, b. Natchez, Miss., Nov. 4, 1948; A.A., Pearl River Jr. Coll., 1968; B.A., U. So. Miss., 1970; J.D., U. Miss., 1972. Admitted to Miss. bar, 1972; partner firm Pittman, Pittman & Weathers, Hattiesburg, Miss., 1972-74; asso. firm Aultman, Pope, Aultman, Van Slyke & Tyner, Hattiesburg, 1974-76; dist. atty. 12th Jud. Dist. Miss., Hattiesburg, 1976—. Mem. adv. bd. Salvation Army, 1972—; mem. exec. bd. Pine Burr Area council Boy Scouts Am., 1976. Mem. Am., Miss. State, S. Central Miss. bar assns., Am., Miss. trial lawyers assns., Am. Judicature Soc., Nat. Dist. Attys. Assn., Miss. Prosecutors Assn. Office: Box 1385 Hattiesburg MS 39401 Tel (601) 545-1551

WEATHERWAX, WALLACE WALTER, b. Honolulu, Oct. 3, 1942; A.B., U. San Francisco, 1964; J.D., U. Santa Clara, 1970. Admitted to Hawaii bar, 1970; dep. atty. gen. State of Hawaii, 1970-75; exec. dir. Hawaii Campaign Spending Commn., Honolulu, 1975—. Office: 415 S Beretania St Honolulu HI 96813 Tel (808) 548-4740

WEAVER, BETTY ANN, b. New Orleans; B.A., Newcomb Coll., 1962; J.D. with honors, Tulane U., 1965; certificate in teaching Central Mich. U., 1971. Admitted to La. bar, 1965, Mich. bar, 1973; law clk. Civil Dist. Ct., New Orleans, 1964; atty., title specialist Chevron Oil Co., New Orleans, 1965-66; asso. firm Clay, Coleman, Dutrey & Thomson, New Orleans, 1965-68; tchr. 1st grade Glen Lake Community Schs., Maple City, Mich., 1971-74; individual practice law, Glen Arbor, Mich., 1973—; judge Leelanau County (Mich.) Probate Ct., 1975—; dean girls Leelanau Sch., Glen Arbor, 1966-68; prof. law off-campus edn. Central Mich. U., Traverse City, 1976. Mem. Glen Arbor Zoning Bd., 1973—; bd. dirs. 1st Ch. of Christ Scientists, Glen Arbor; mem. law enforcement planning component Regional Planning Commn., Traverse City, Mich., 1975—; mem. Northwestern Lower Mich. Substance Abuse Council, 1975—. Mem. Probate Judges Assn. Mich., Nat. Council Juvenile Judges, Grand Traverse Bd. Realtors, Am. Bar Assn., Order of Coif, Phi Beta Kappa. Editorial bd. Tulane Law Rev., 1963-65; developer Children in Law project for elementary schs. in No. Mich., 1968-73; originator, tchr. lay coll. course on law. Home: Riverwood St Glen Arbor MI 49636 Office: Courthouse Leland MI 49654 Tel (616) 256-9803

WEAVER, CLIFFORD L., b. Chgo., Mar. 11, 1945; A.B. with honors, U. Chgo., 1966, J.D. with honors, 1969. Admitted to Ill. bar, 1969, U.S. Supreme Ct. bar, 1975; sr. clk. U.S. Ct. Appeals, Chgo., 1969-71; asso. firm Ross, Hardies, O'Keefe, Babcock & Parsons, Chgo., 1971-75, partner, 1976—; village atty. Village of Bannockburn, Ill., 1976—. Mem. Order of Coif, Phi Beta Kappa. Co-editor: Special Districts and Non-Municipal Local Governments in Illinois, 1977; contbr. to law books. Office: Suite 3100 One IBM Plaza Chicago IL 60611 Tel (312) 467-9300

WEAVER, HENRY BYRNE, JR., b. Washington, Jan. 5, 1911; B.A., Coll. William and Mary, 1932; LL.B. with honors, U. Va., 1935. Admitted to Va. bar, 1934, D.C. bar, 1935; individual practice law, Washington, 1935; mem. firm Weaver & Glassie, Washington, 1949-65, Weaver, diZerega & Hill, Leesburg, Va., 1963-66; sr. v.p., gen. counsel Atlantic Richfield Co., N.Y.C., 1967-73; partner firm Steptoe & Johnson, Washington, 1973—; pres. Jefferson Bldg. Corp., 1958-63; dir. Guardian Life Ins. Co. Am. Mem. Fed., Fed. Communications, Am., Va., D.C., Pa., N.Y. bar assns., Lawyers Club. Home: Glengyle Aldie VA 22001 Office: 1250 Connecticut Ave NW Washington DC 20036 Tel (202) 862-2189

WEAVER, JAMES MOORE, b. Memphis, Nov. 19, 1945; B.A., U. So. Miss., 1967; J.D., U. Ga., 1972. Admitted to Ga. bar, 1972, Fla. bar, 1976; asso. firm Webb, Parker, Young & Ferguson, Atlanta, 1971-74; individual practice law, Atlanta, 1975; partner firm Weaver & Elliot, Atlanta, 1974-75; partner firm White & Weaver, Lake Wales, Fla., 1976—. Advisor Warner So. Coll., 1976. Mem. Am., Atlanta bar assns., State Bars of Ga., Fla., Kiwanis, Circle-K. Home: 800 Carlton Ave Lake Wales FL 33853 Office: PO Box 466 Lake Wales FL 33853 Tel (813) 676-7619

WEAVER, PAUL DAVID, b. Chgo., Feb. 15, 1943; A.B., Yale, 1965; J.D. cum laude, U. Mich., 1971. Admitted to Mass. bar, 1971, Ohio bar, 1972; asso. firm Goodwin, Procter & Hoar, Boston, 1971—; town counsel, Wenham, Mass. Mem. corp. Beverly (Mass.) Hosp. Mem. Am., Boston bar assns. Home: 1 Porter St Wenham MA 01984 Office: 28 State St Boston MA 02109 Tel (617) 523-5700

WEAVER, ROBIN GEOFFREY, b. Columbus, Ohio, Aug. 19, 1948; B.A., Ohio State U., 1970; J.D., U. Mich., 1973; grad. Nat. Inst. Trial Advocacy. Admitted to Ohio bar, 1974; investigator N.J. State Pub. Defender, Union County, 1971; asso. firm Squire, Sanders, & Dempsey, Cleve., 1973—. Mem. Am., Ohio, Greater Cleve., Cuyahoga County bar assns., Def. Research Inst., Ohio Def. Assn. Home: 1701 E 12th St Apt 19 N Cleveland OH 44114 Office: 1800 Union Commerce Bldg Cleveland OH 44115 Tel (216) 696-9200

WEAVER, STERLING LEROY, b. Bklyn., June 1, 1931; A.B. cum laude, Amherst Coll., 1953; LL.B., Columbia U., 1956. Admitted to N.Y. State Ct. Appeals bar, 1957, U.S. Dist. Ct. Western Dist. N.Y., 1957, U.S. Ct. Appeals 2d Circuit bar, 1962, U.S. Supreme Ct. bar, 1962, D.C. bar, 1972; asso. firm Nixon, Hargrave, Devans & Doyle, Rochester, N.Y., 1956-64, partner, 1965—, chmn. tax dept., 1969—. Pres. bd. trustees 1st Unitarian Ch., Rochester, 1965-67; trustee Soc. Preservation of Landmarks in Western N.Y., 1963, pres., 1965-68; bd. dirs. Center for Environ. Info., Inc., Rochester, 1975; chmn. Gleason Meml. Fund, Inc., Rochester, 1975; area coordinator admissions Amherst Coll.; sec. Eastman Dental Center, Rochester, 1966-72, trustee, 1965, pres., 1973-74. Mem. Am., N.Y., Monroe County bar assns. Office: 2100 Lincoln First Tower Rochester NY 14603 Tel (716) 546-8000

WEBB, CHARLES GROSVENOR, b. Wellsboro, Pa., Mar. 23, 1899; A.B., Princeton, 1922; postgrad. in law U. Pa., 1926. Admitted to Pa. Supreme Ct. bar, 1927; individual practice law, Wellsboro, 1926-34; mem. firms Owlett, Webb & Cox, Wellsboro, 1934-56; dist. atty. for Tioga County, Pa., 1932-35; judge Tioga County Common Pleas Ct., 1951-72. Bd. dirs. Green Free Library, Wellsboro, 1930—, Soldiers and Sailors Hosp., Wellsboro, 1943—. Mem. Am., Pa. bar assns. Home: 20 West Ave Wellsboro PA 16901 Office: 120 Main St Wellsboro PA 16801 Tel (717) 724-1406

WEBB, CHARLES ROBERT, b. Boston, Dec. 11, 1946; student U. Colo., 1964-66, B.A., U. Mass., 1969; J.D., Suffolk U., 1973. Admitted to Mass. bar, 1973; partner firm Sullivan & Webb, Roslindale, Mass., 1974—; police trainee N.Y.C. Police Dept., 1967; patrolman, Provincetown, Mass., 1968; mem. Boston Police Dept. 1968—. Bd. dirs. Boston Police Relief Assn., 1972-75, 77; bargaining agt. Boston Police Superior Officers Fedn., 1977—. Mem. Mass. Bar Assn. Home: 37 Clifford St Yarmouth MA 02664 Office: 74 Clare Ave Roslindale MA 02131 Tel (617) 364-9510

WEBB, JOHN, b. Rocky Mount, N.C., Sept. 18, 1926; LL.B., Columbia, 1952. Admitted to N.Y. bar, 1953, N.C. bar, 1956; asso. firm Carter, Ledyard & Milburn, N.Y.C., 1952-54; partner firm Kirby, Webb & Hunt, Wilson, N.C., 1954-56, 64-71; individual practice law, 1956-64; judge Superior Ct., 1971—. Mem. N.C., Wilson County (pres. 1961-62) bar assns., Wilson C. of C. (v.p. 1971-72). Home: 808 Trinity Dr Wilson NC 27893 Office: Wilson County Court House Wilson NC 27893 Tel (919) 237-8156

WEBB, JOHN CULPEPPER, SR., b. Gillsburg, Miss., July 31, 1921; B.A., La. State U., 1945; LL.B., U. Miss., 1948. Admitted to Miss. bar, 1948; asso. firm Brewer & Brewer, Clarksdale, Miss., 1949-51; individual practice law, Greenville, Miss., 1951-66; partner firm Webb & Webb, Leland, Miss., 1966-73; pub. defender Washington County (Miss.), 1973—, first youth counselor, 1954-56, county pros. atty., 1956-73; mem. cts. div. Miss. Gov.'s Crime Commn., 1975. Bd. Leland Consolidated Sch. Dist., 1964-72. Mem. Miss. State Bar Assn. (commr. 1977-78, chmn. criminal law com. 1977-78), Am. Trial Lawyers Nat. Coll. Advocacy, Phi Delta Phi. Asso. editor Miss. Law Jour., 1947-48, bus. mgr., 1948. Home: 510 Cypress St Leland MS 38756 Office: Washington County Courthouse Greenville MS 38701 Tel (601) 335-3302

WEBB, JOHN GIBBON, III, b. Flint, Mich., June 1, 1944; B.A., Davidson Coll., 1966; J.D., Vanderbilt U., 1970. Admitted to N.Y. State bar, 1971; asso. firm Curtis, Mallet-Prevost, Colt & Mosle, N.Y.C., 1970—; trustee N.Y.C. Community Law Offices, 1974—, sec., 1975—. Vestryman, lay reader All Saints Ch., S.I., 1972-74, St. Stephen's Ch., Millburn, N.J., 1975—. Mem. Assn. Bar City N.Y., Am., N.Y. State bar assns., Am. Soc. Internat. Law. Office: Curtis Mallet-Prevost Colt & Mosle 100 Wall St New York City NY 10005 Tel (212) 248-8111

WEBB, TYLER GLEASON, b. Balt., Oct. 20, 1945; B.A., U. Md., 1967, J.D., 1970. Admitted to Md. bar, 1970; asso. firm Arnold & Wilkinson, Hyattsville, Md., 1971-76; partner firm Arnold and Webb, Hyattsville, 1976—. Councilman, City of Hyattsville, 1975—; dist. princinct coordinator Democratic party Prince George's County, Md., 1976—. Mem. Md., Prince George's County (dir. 1975-76) bar assns., Prince George's County Bd. Realtors. Home: 3904 Madison St Hyattsville MD 20781 Office: 4314 Hamilton St Hyattsville MD 20781

WEBBER, PAUL RAINEY, III, b. Gadsden, S.C., Jan. 24, 1934; B.A., S.C. State Coll., 1955, J.D., 1957. Admitted to S.C. bar, 1958, Calif. bar, 1963, Washington bar, 1962; atty. Antitrust div. U.S. Dept. Justice, 1964-67; mng. atty. Neighborhood Legal Services Program, Washington, 1967-69; partner firm Dolphin, Branton, Stafford, & Webber, Washington, 1969—; vis. prof. Howard U., 1972-76, George Washington U., 1973; arbitrator Am. Arbitration Assn. Bd. dirs. Info. Planning Assos., Gaithersburg, Md.; bd. dirs. Family and Child Services, Washington. Mem. S.C., Am., Nat., Calif., Washington bar assns., Alpha Phi Alpha. Home: 1627 Myrtle St NW Washington DC 20012 Office: 666 11th St NW Washington DC 20001 Tel (202) 737-5432

WEBER, ALBAN, b. Chgo., Jan. 29, 1915; A.B., Harvard, 1935, J.D., 1937; M.A., Northwestern U., 1961. Admitted to Ill. bar, 1938, U.S. Supreme Ct. bar, 1946; partner firm Weber & Weber, Chgo., 1938-41; chief counsel Fgn. Liquidation Commn., Rome and Paris, 1946; chief internat. law sect. U.S. Navy, 1946; mem. Chgo. City Council, 1947-51; trust officer Lake Shore Bank, Chgo., 1951-55; counsel Northwestern U., Evanston, Ill., 1955-70; pres. Fedn. Ind. Ill. Colls. & Univs., Evanston, Ill., 1971—; chmn. Greek Airfield Commn., 1946. Pres. NE Ill. Council Boy Scouts Am., 1970-71, recipient Silver Beaver award, 1972. Mem. Chgo., Ill. bar assns., Am. Soc. Internat. Law, Harvard Law Assn., Nat. Assn. Coll. and Univ. Attys. (past pres.), Univ. Ins. Mgrs. Assn. (past pres.), Navy League U.S. (former state pres.). Home: 1286 Cascade Ct Lake Forest IL 60045 Office: 990 Grove St Evanston IL 60201 Tel (312) 864-1000

WEBER, DENNIS HARRY, b. Trimont, Minn., Dec. 12, 1936; B.S., Mankato State U., 1958; J.D., U. Minn., 1970. Admitted to Minn. bar, 1970; asso. firm Smith & Schreiber, Lake City, Minn., 1970-73; county ct. judge Wabasha County (Minn.), 1973—; mem. adv. com. Hiawatha Valley Chem. Dependency, 1973—; city atty. Lake City, 1971-73; asst. atty. Wabasha County, 1971-73. Mem. Minn. State Bar Assn., Minn. County Judges Assn. Home: 27 Kingswood Ct Lake City MN 55041 Office: County Courthouse Wabasha MN 55981 Tel (612) 565-3524

WEBER, EDWARD DAVID, b. Milw., May 7, 1946; B.A., U. Wis., Madison, 1968, J.D., 1971. Asso. firm Gaines & Saichek, Milw., 1971-73; jr. partner firm Zurlo & Weber, Milw., 1973-74; individual practice law, Milw., 1974—. Mem. Am., Wis., Milw., Milw. Jr. bar assns., Am., Wis. trial lawyers assns., Am. Soc. Law and Medicine. Contbr. articles to profl. jours. Office: 633 W Wisconsin Ave Milwaukee WI 53203 Tel (414) 273-2020

WEBER, EMILE MCCLUNG, b. Baton Rouge, Oct. 31, 1922; B.A., La. State U., 1943, J.D., 1948. Admitted to La. bar, 1948, U.S. Supreme Ct. bar, 1955; partner firm Weber & Weber, Baton Rouge, 1948—; ad hoc judge Baton Rouge Municipal Ct., 1968-70; cons. La. State Law Inst.; atty. La. State Barber Bd., La. State Nursing Home Operators; atty., chmn. bd. dirs. Mchts. Broadcasters Inc. Active United Fund, Baton Rouge; deacon First Baptist Ch., Baton Rouge. Mem. La., Am. trial lawyers assns., La. (officer, del.), Am. bar assns., Am. Judicature Soc. Home: 8955 Jefferson Hwy Baton Rouge LA 70809 Office: 632 St Ferdinand St Baton Rouge LA 70802 Tel (504) 343-5738

WEBER, G. DONALD, JR., b. Phila., Aug. 7, 1934; B.S. in Elec. Engring., U. Pa., 1957; J.D., Temple U., 1963. Admitted to U.S. Patent Office bar, 1959, Pa. bar, 1964, Tex. bar, 1970, Calif. bar, 1973, U.S. Supreme Ct. bar, 1974; atty. Univac div. Sperry Rand Corp., Bluebell, Pa., 1957-65; atty. Honeywell Inc., Ft. Washington, Pa., 1966-69; house counsel Offshore Systems Inc., Houston, 1969-70; atty. RCA, Princeton, N.J., 1970-72; div. patent counsel Rockwell Internat., Anaheim, Calif., 1972—; guest speaker arrangement Calif. Poly. U., Pomona, Calif. State U., Long Beach, 1975—. Leader Boy Scouts Am., coach Bobby Sox; mem. Villa Park (Calif.) Planning Commn., 1976—. Mem. Los Angeles Patent Law Assn., Calif., Tex., Orange County bar assns., U. Pa., Temple U. alumni assns. Home: 18442 Taft Ave Villa Park CA 92667 Office: 3370 Miraloma St Anaheim CA 92803 Tel (714) 632-5660

WEBER, GERALD JOSEPH, b. Erie, Pa., Feb. 1, 1914; A.B., Harvard, 1936; LL.B., U. Pa., 1939. Admitted to Pa. bar, 1940; individual practice law, Erie, Pa., 1940-57; asso. firm Knox, Weber, Pearson & McLaughlin, Erie, 1957-64; city solicitor Erie, 1950-60; U.S. dist. judge Western Dist. Pa., 1964—, chief judge, 1976—. Home: 4207 Beech Ave Erie PA 16508 Office: US Court House Erie PA 16501 also US Court House Pittsburgh PA 15219

WEBER, HERMAN JACOB, JR., b. Lima, Ohio, May 20, 1927; B.A., Otterbein Coll., 1949; J.D., Ohio State U., S.C.L., 1951; grad. Nat. Coll. State Judiciary, 1975. Admitted to Ohio bar, 1952; partner firm Weber & Hogue, Fairborn, Ohio, 1952-61; judge Greene County (Ohio) Ct. of Common Pleas, 1961—; vice mayor Mayors Ct., Fairborn, 1956-58; acting judge Fairborn Municipal Ct., 1959-61; mem. Ohio Criminal Justice Supervisory Commn., 1977. Mem. Fairborn City Council, 1956-60; chmn. Greene County Mental Health Planning Project, 1964; pres. Greene County Tb and Health Assn., 1959-60; mem. staff Ohio Boys' State, 1974-77; trustee Ohio Jud. Coll., 1976—. Mem. Am., Ohio State, Greene County (pres. 1962) bar assns., Am. Judicature Soc., Nat. Conf. State Trial Judges (state rep. 1974-76), Ohio Jud. Conf. (2d v.p. 1977—), Ohio Common Pleas Judges Assn. (pres. 1975), Am. Judges Assn., Order of Coif. Recipient Excellent Achievement in Jud. Adminstr. award Supreme Ct. Ohio, 1972, Excellent Jud. Service award 1972, Outstanding Jud. Service award, 1973-77; named Boss of Year Greene County Assn. Legal Secs., 1974. Office: Greene County Courthouse Xenia OH 45385 Tel (513) 372-4461

WEBER, JOHN ANTHONY, JR., b. N.Y.C., Oct. 31, 1942; A.B., Brown U., 1966; J.D., Boston U., 1969. Admitted to Mass. bar, 1969, U.S. Supreme Ct. bar, 1975; asso. firm Baldwin, Copeland & Hession, Wellesley, Mass., 1969—. Mem. Westwood (Mass.) Zoning Bd. Appeals. Mem. Am. Bar Assn. Home: 25 Willard Circle St Westwood MA 02090 Office: 47 Church St Wellesley MA 02181 Tel (617) 235-1020

WEBER, JOHN STEPHEN, b. St. Louis, Jan. 26, 1943; B.B.A., So. Meth. U., 1964; postgrad. Washington U., St. Louis, 1964-65; J.D., Mo. U., 1967. Admitted to Mo. bar, 1967; asst. atty. gen. State of Mo., Jefferson City, 1967-68; examiner, asst. gen. counsel Mo. Pub. Service Commn., Jefferson City, 1968-69; gen. counsel, sec. Mo. Power & Light Co., Jefferson City, 1969—, Mo. Edison Co., La., 1973—; chmn. adminstrv. law com. Mo. Bar, 1976—. Pres. Capital City Council on the Arts, Jefferson City, 1972; bd. dirs. Jefferson City YMCA, 1973-74. Mem. Mo., Am., Cole County bar assns., Jefferson City C. of C., Mo. C. of C., Mo. U. Alumni Assn. (pres. Cole County chpt. 1973-74), Phi Delta Phi. Recipient Distinguished Service award Jaycees, 1976. Home: Route 1 Centertown MO 65023 Office: 101 Madison St Jefferson City MO 65101 Tel (314) 635-0171

WEBER, KENNETH WILTON, b. Port Townsend, Wash., Apr. 6, 1936; B.S., Pacific U., 1961; J.D., Willamette U., 1963. Admitted to Wash. bar, 1963; individual practice law, Vancouver, Wash., 1963—; pres. firm Weber and Baumgartner, P.A., Vancouver, 1973—; adj. prof. law NW Sch. Law, Lewis and Clark Coll., Portland, Oreg., 1971—. Mem. Am., Wash., Clark County bar assns. Contbr. articles to legal jours. Office: 7407C Hwy 99 Vancouver WA 98665 Tel (206) 695-1265

WEBER, TERRY DALE, b. Louisville, Apr. 6, 1943; A.B., Western Ky. U., 1965; postgrad. (Fulbright scholar) Sophia U., Tokyo, 1967; J.D., U. Louisville, 1974. Admitted to Ky. bar, 1974; mem. firm Hunt & Weber, Louisville, 1974—. Mem. coms. Old Ky. Home Council Boy Scouts Am.; mem. first aid, water safety coms. ARC. Mem. Louisville, Ky., Am. bar assns. Home: 2724 Alanmede Rd Louisville KY 40205 Office: Box 7381 136 Breckinridge Ln Louisville KY 40207 Tel (502) 895-2446

WEBER, WILLIAM LOUIS, b. McConnellsville, Ohio, Aug. 22, 1900; A.B., Ohio State U., 1923, LL.B., 1925, J.D., 1925. Admitted to Ohio bar, 1925, Fed. bar, 1933; village solicitor Philo, Ohio, 1927-49; U.S. Commr. So. Dist. Ohio, Eastern Div., 1938-49; spl. counsel for atty. gen. Ohio for Supt. of Banks, 1934-38; mem. firm Tannehill, Weber & Weber and predecessor, 1920-32; individual practice, 1932-54; mem. firm Tanner & Weber, 1954—; mem. Muskingum County, Ohio, Bd. Elections, 1934-38. Mem. Muskingum County Bar Assn. (pres. 1960), Am. Judicature Soc., Delta Theta Phi. Home: 1066 Culbetson Ave Zanesville OH 43701 Office: 311 Main St Zanesville OH 43701 Tel (614) 453-0707

WEBSTER, DALE PHILIP, b. Sayre, Pa., Feb. 23, 1948; B.A. with honors, Anderson (Ind.) Coll., 1970; J.D., Ind. U., 1973. Admitted to Ind. bar, 1973; asso. firm McCormick & McCormick, Vincennes, Ind.,

1973-75; partner firm McCormick & Webster, Vincennes, 1975; pros. atty. 12th Jud. Circuit, Vincennes, 1975—. Mem. Am., Ind., Knox County bar assns. Office: PO Box 60 Vincennes IN 47591 Tel (812) 882-6793

WEBSTER, DAVID NEWTON, b. Providence, Mar. 31, 1934; A.B., Providence Coll., 1955; J.D., Georgetown U., 1958. Admitted to D.C. bar, 1958; with civil div.-appellate Dept. Justice, Washington, 1958-59; asso. firm Hogan & Hartson, 1959-66; partner firm Williams, Connolly & Califano, Washington, 1967—. Chmn. inquiry com. Disciplinary Bd., 1973-75; pres. D.C. Profl. Council, 1977; mem. adv. bd. Georgetown Paralegal Inst.; lectr. trial practice Cath. U. Am. Law Sch., 1973-75. Mem. Am. Bar Assn. (del. 1975—), Bar Assn. D.C. (dir. 1974—, pres. 1975—), Am. Judicature Soc. Recipient Alumni award Georgetown Club of D.C., 1976; contbr. articles to profl. jours. Office: 839 17th St NW Washington DC 20006 Tel (202) 331-5500

WEBSTER, HAROLD WAYNE, b. Mt. Vernon, Ind., June 7, 1930; B.B.A., Ind. U., 1950; J.D., U. Louisville, 1969. Admitted to Ind. bar, 1970; individual practice law, North Vernon, Ind., 1970—. Pres., N. Vernon Aviation Commn. Mem. Am., Ind., Jennings County bar assns. Home: Rural Route 2 North Vernon IN 47265 Office: 203 N State St North Vernon IN 47265 Tel (812) 346-5701

WEBSTER, ISABEL GATES, b. Henderson, N.C., Apr. 16, 1931; student N.C. Coll.; B.S., Boston U., 1953, J.D., 1955. Admitted to Ga. bar, 1958; individual practice law, Atlanta, 1960-72; asso. firm Jackson, Patterson, Parks & Franklin, Atlanta, 1972-75; asst. atty. City of Atlanta, 1975—; mem., vice chmn. personnel bd. State of Ga., 1974. Pres. Atlanta Urban League, 1974—. Mem. NAACP (v.p. 1960), Atlanta, Gate City bar assns., State Bar Ga., Ga. Assn. Women Lawyers, Ga. State Conf. Black Lawyers. Recipient WSB Radio 750 award. Office: 2 Peachtree Ln NE Suite 2614 Atlanta GA 30303 Tel (404) 658-1150

WEBSTER, JAMES ALDEAN, JR., b. Leaksville (now Eden), N.C., Apr. 17, 1927; B.S., Wake Forest U., 1949, LL.B., 1951; S.J.D., Harvard, 1967. Admitted to N.C. bar, 1951; asst. prof. Law Wake Forest U., 1951-52; individual practice law, Leaksville-Reidsville, N.C., 1952-54; asso. prof. Wake Forest U., 1952-60, prof., 1960—. Mem. Rockingham County (N.C.) Bd. Elections, 1952-54; N.C. Gen. Statutes Commn., 19S7-60; cons. to N.C. Revenue Commr., 1956, Ins. Commr., 1966-67, Atty. Gen., 1970-71. Mem. N.C., Forsyth County bar assns., Am. Arbitration Assn. (arbitrator). Author: Real Estate Law in N.C., 1971; Ford fellow, 1961-62; contbr. articles to profl. jours. Home: 1816 Faculty Dr Winston-Salem NC 27106 Office: Wake Forest U Law Sch Winston-Salem NC 27109 Tel (919) 761-5434

WEBSTER, ROBERT BYRON, b. Detroit, Mar. 9, 1932; B.A., U. Mich., 1955, J.D., 1957. Admitted to Mich. bar, 1958, U.S. Supreme Ct. bar, 1972; since practiced in Birmingham and Detroit (both Mich.); law clk. to Hon. Ralph M. Freeman, U.S. Dist. Ct., 1957-59; asso. to partner firm Reitz, Tait, Oetting and Webster, and predecessor, 1959-69; partner firm Hill, Lewis, Adams, Goodrich and Tait, 1969-73; judge 6th Jud. Circuit Ct., 1973—, alt. presiding judge, 1974-75, alt. chief judge, 1976, chief judge, 1977—; chmn. Mich. Supreme Ct. Com. to Revise and Consolidate Mich. Ct. Rules, 1975—. Chmn., Oakland Republican Com., 1970-71, del. Rep. Nat. Conv., 1972; mem. Oakland Community Mental Health Bd., 1971-73; bd. dirs. Family and Children Services, Oakland, 1975—. Mem. Am., Mich., Oakland County bar assns., Am. Judicature Soc., Mich. Judges Assn. Office: 1200 N Telegraph Rd Pontiac MI 48053 Tel (313) 858-0335

WEBSTER, ROBERT DAVID, b. N.Y.C., Mar. 14, 1938; A.B., Colgate U., 1959; LL.B., Harvard, 1962. Admitted to N.Y. bar, 1963; asso. firm Winthrop, Stimson, Putnam & Roberts, N.Y.C., 1962-68, partner, 1969—. Mem. Assn. Bar City N.Y. Home: 1088 Park Ave New York City NY 10028 Office: 40 Wall St New York City NY 10005 Tel (212) 943-0700

WEBSTER, ROBERT FIELDEN, b. Chgo., Feb. 28, 1911; B.A., Williams Coll., 1933; J.D., Chgo.-Kent Coll. Law, 1936. Admitted to Ill. bar, 1936; asso. firm Schiff Hardin & Waite, Chgo., 1937-46, partner firm, 1946—; dir. Nat. Terminals Corp., Chgo., 1967—. Chancellor Episcopal Diocese of Chgo., 1975—; bd. dirs., past pres. Ill. Soc. for Prevention of Blindness; asso. Newberry Library. Mem. Am., Ill. State, Chgo. (mem., past chmn. corp. law com.) bar assns., Phi Beta Kappa, Beta Theta Pi, Phi Delta Phi. Home: 596 Arbor Vitae Rd Winnetka IL 60093 Office: 7200 Sears Tower 233 S Wacker Dr Chicago IL 60606 Tel (312) 876-1000

WEBSTER, ROBERT TRICE, b. Detroit, Oct. 19, 1936; B.B.A., U. Mich., 1958; J.D., Detroit Coll. Law, 1961. Admitted to Mich. bar, 1962; new product mgr. Park Chem. Co., Detroit, 1965-66, exec. v.p., 1966-71, pres., 1971—. Mem. Am. Soc. Metals. Office: 8074 Military Ave Detroit MI 48204 Tel (313) 895-7215

WEBSTER, SHIRLEY ALTON, b. Minburn, Iowa, Sept. 21, 1909; B.A., U. Iowa, 1930, J.D., 1932. Admitted to Iowa bar, 1932; sr. partner firm Webster, Jordan, Oliver, & Walters, Winterset, Iowa, 1932—; mem. bd. regents Am. Coll. Probate Consel, 1969-75. Mem. Iowa State Bar Assn. (pres. 1957-58, chmn. spl. com. on probate, property and trust law 1959-74, award of merit 1964), Am. Bar Found. (ho. of dels. 1969-70), Am. Coll. Probate Counsel. Contbr. articles to legal jours. Home: 214 N 8th Ave Winterset IA 50273 Office: Farmers & Merchants State Bank Bldg Winterset IA 50273 Tel (515) 462-3731

WEBSTER, STONEWALL JACKSON, JR., b. Greensboro, N.C., June 24, 1934; A.B., High Point Coll., 1956; J.D., Wake Forest U., 1959. Admitted to N.C. bar, 1959; sr. mem. firm Webster & Eggleston, Madison, N.C.; atty. Town of Madison, 1968—; atty. for bd. trustees Rockingham Community Coll. Mem. Am., N.C., Rockingham County (past pres.) bar assns. Home: 107 Cassandra Rd Madison NC 27025 Office: 105-A S Market St Madison NC 27025 Tel (919) 427-0003

WECHSLER, STUART DAVID, b. N.Y.C., Jan. 22, 1932; B.S. in B.A., U. Pa., 1953; J.D., Yale, 1955. Admitted to N.Y. bar, 1958, U.S. Supreme Ct. bar, 1974; asso. firm Berle, Berle & Brunner, N.Y.C., 1958-60, Colton, Gallantz & Fernbach, N.Y.C., 1960-61; individual practice law, N.Y.C., 1961-66; sr. partner firm Kass, Goodkind, Wechsler & Gerstein, N.Y.C., 1966—. Mem. Fed. Bar Council (chmn. corps. and securities com. 1972—). Editor: Prosecuting and Defending Stockholder Suits, 1972; contbr. articles to profl. jours. Home: 305 E 86th St New York City NY 10028 Office: 122 E 42d St New York City NY 10017 Tel (212) 490-2332

WECKSTEIN, DONALD THEODORE, b. Newark, Mar. 15, 1932; B.B.A., U. Wis., 1954; J.D., U. Tex., 1958; LL.M., Yale, 1959. Admitted to Tex. bar, 1957; adminstrv. practice law, Newark, 1958; asst. prof., U. Conn., 1959-62; asso. prof. law, U. Tenn., 1962-66, prof., 1966-67; prof. law U. Conn., 1967-72; dean, prof. law U. San Diego, 1972—; chmn. San Diego County Employees Relation Panel, 1973-76; cons. in field. Mem. Am., Tex., San Diego, Motor Carrier Lawyers bar assns., Assn. Am. Law Schs., Am. Arbitration Assn. (panel), AAUP, ACLU, Indsl. Relations Research Assn. Editor: Education in the Professional Responsibilities of the Lawyer, 1970: co-author: Moore's Federal Practice; contbr. articles to law revs. Home: 8685 Nottingham Pl LaJolla CA 92037 Office: U San Diego Sch Law Alcala Park San Diego CA 92110 Tel (714) 295-1234

WECKWORTH, WILLIAM FREDERICK, b. Seattle, Nov. 29, 1938; B.A., U. Wash., 1962, J.D., 1965. Admitted to Wash. bar, 1965, U.S. Tax Ct. bar, 1973; partner firm Dodd, Russell & Coney, Seattle, 1965-69; asso. firm Gerald L. Bangs, Seattle, 1969-72; partner firm Burgess & Weckworth, Seattle, 1972-74; partner firm Weckworth, Meyer & Mackin, Seattle, 1974—; sec., dir. Silver Enterprises & Adjustment Co., Seattle, 1973—; pres., dir. Construction Control, Inc., Seattle, 1975—, Data Control, Inc., Seattle, 1975—. Dir Wallingford Boys Club, Seattle, 1975—. Mem. Am., Wash., Seattle King County bar assns., Wash. Trial Lawyers Assn. Office: 925 Denny Bldg Seattle WA 98121 Tel (206) 624-6795

WEDDINGTON, SARAH RAGLE, b. Abilene, Tex., Feb. 5, 1945; B.S. magna cum laude, McMurry Coll., 1965; J.D., U. Tex., 1967. Admitted to Tex. bar, 1967; individual practice law, Austin, 1971—; mem. Tex. Ho. of Reps., 1972—; asst. reporter spl. com. to reevaluate ethical standards Am. Bar Assn., 1967-70; asst. city atty. City of Fort Worth, 1970-71. Mem. Am. (mem. Joint Conf. Reps. of Am. Bar Assn. and AMA, 1971—), Travis County bar assns., State Bar Tex. (chairperson com. to increase participation in bar of minorities and women 1974, mem. family law council 1974, 75), Orgn. Women Legislators (legis. com.), Women's Equity Action League (nat. adv. bd. 1973—), AAUW, Bus. and Profl. Women of Austin (Woman of Year 1974), Travis County Hist. Soc., Delta Kappa Gamma. Named Woman of Year, Tex. Women's Polit. Caucus, 1973; Outstanding Legislator of Year, Tex. Student Assn., 1973; Outstanding Woman of Austin, Austin Am.-Statesman, 1974. Home and Office: 709 W 14th St Austin TX 78701 Tel (512) 476-7575

WEDDLE, ROBERT GUY, b. Houston, Oct. 21, 1943; B.S. in Chem. Engring., Purdue U., 1967; J.D. cum laude, Ind. U., 1972. Admitted to Ind. bar, 1972; staff atty. Eli Lilly and Co., Indpls., 1972-73; mem. firm Bingham, Summods, Welsh & Spilman, Indpls., 1973—. Mem. Am., Ind. State, Indpls. bar assns. Home: 2729 Pomona Ct Indianapolis IN 46268 Office: 2700 Ind Tower One Ind Sq Indianapolis IN 46204 Tel (317) 635-8900

WEDGE, VIRGIL HENRY, b. Pioche, Nev., June 24, 1912; B.S., Brigham Young U., 1936; LL.B., George Washington U., 1940. Admitted to Nev. bar, 1940, U.S. Supreme Ct. bar, 1964; partner firm McCarran & Wedge, Reno, Nev., 1940-42; spl. agent FBI, 1942-45; asso. firm Griswold, Reinhardt & Vargas, Reno, 1945-47; atty. City of Reno, 1947-51; partner firm Woodburn, Wedge, Blakey, Folsom and Hug, and predecessors, Reno, 1951—; gen. partner Park Ln. Center, Reno, 1966—; dir. Family Savs. and Loan Assn., Reno, 1974—. Chmn. Washoe County (Nev.) Democratic Central Com., 1947, vice-chmn. Nev. Dem. Central Com., 1952-54. Fellow Internat. Acad. Trial Lawyers (bd. dirs. 1954-62, 65-68); mem. Am. (state chmn. jr. bar div. 1947-48), Washoe County (pres. 1968-69) bar assns., State Bar of Nev., Internat. Soc. Barristers, Am. Soc. Writers on Legal Subjects. Home: 320 Hillcrest Dr Reno NV 89502 Office: 1 E First St Reno NV 89505 Tel (702) 329-6131

WEECH, MERRILL RICHARD, b. Salt Lake City, May 28, 1941; B.A., U. Calif., Berkeley, 1966, M.B.A., 1969, J.D., 1969. Admitted to Utah bar, 1970, U.S. Tax Ct. bar, 1972; tax specialist Peat, Marwick, Mitchell & Co., Salt Lake City; asso. firm Jones, Waldo, Holbrook & McDonough, Salt Lake City, 1971-75, partner, 1976—; pres. Mountain States Pension Conf., Salt Lake City, 1975-76. Bd. dirs. Utah Lung Assn., 1974—. Mem. Am. Bar Assn., Am. Inst. C.P.A.'s, Utah Assn. C.P.A.'s (chmn. taxation com. 1976—). C.P.A., Utah; contbr. articles to legal jours. Home: 8638 Alta Canyon Dr Sandy UT 84070 Office: 800 Walker Bank Bldg Salt Lake City UT 84111 Tel (801) 521-3200

WEED, ARTHUR HENRY, b. Boston, Mar. 2, 1941; B.A., Colo. U., 1964, J.D., 1967. Admitted to Colo. bar, 1967; individual practice law, Littleton, Colo., 1967. Mem. Colo., Arapahoe bar assns. Home: 7925 W Layton St Littleton CO 80123 Office: 1709 W Littleton Blvd Littleton CO 80120 Tel (303) 794-4500

WEEKES, MICHAEL MANNING, b. Leon, Iowa, July 12, 1938; B.S., Drake U., 1960, J.D., 1963. Admitted to Iowa bar, 1963, Calif. bar, 1964, U.S. Dist. Ct. bar, 1964, U.S. Supreme Ct. bar, 1973; asso. firm Dillavou & Cox (later Dillavou, Cox, Castle and Nicholson), Los Angeles, 1964-68, asso. firm Cox, Castle & Nicholson, Los Angeles, 1968-71; partner firm Cox, Castle, Nicholson & Weekes, Los Angeles, 1972-76. Bd. dirs. Hollywood Presbyn. Med. Center, Los Angeles, 1976—. Mem. Am., Calif., Iowa, Los Angeles County bar assns. Author: Manual for Application of Uniform Commercial Code for the Surety Industry, 1964. Home: 691 S Irolo St Los Angeles CA 90005 Tel (213) 874-2200

WEEKS, ARTHUR ANDREW, b. Hanceville, Ala., Dec. 2, 1914; A.B., Samford U., 1936; LL.B., J.D., U. Ala., 1939; LL.M., Duke, 1950. Admitted to Ala. bar, 1939, Tenn. bar, 1948; individual practice law, Birmingham, Ala., 1939-41, 46-47, 54-61; dean, prof. law Cumberland Sch. Law, Samford U., 1947-54, 61-72, prof. law, 1972-74; dean, prof. law Del. Law Sch., Widener Coll., Wilmington, 1974—. Mem. Am., Tenn., Ala., Birmingham bar assns., Phi Alpha Delta, Sigma Delta Kappa. Home: 1306 Grayson Rd Wilmington DE 19803 Office: 2001 Washington St Wilmington DE 19802 Tel (302) 658-8531

WEEKS, JOE BARRON, b. Louisville, Miss., Oct. 7, 1936; B.A., Southwestern U.-Memphis, 1959; LL.B., Memphis State U., 1967. Admitted to Tenn. bar, 1967, Fla. bar, 1968; asso. firm Gurney, Gurney & Handley, Orlando, Fla., 1968-75; partner firm Troutman, Parrish & Weeks, Winter Park, Fla., 1975—. Mem. Am. (com. ins. compensation), Fla., Tenn., Orange County (med. legal com.) bar assns. Home: 251 Chelton Circle Winter Park FL 32789 Office: Suite 200 222 W Comstock Ave Winter Park FL 32789 Tel (305) 647-2277

WEEKS, MARTIN, JR., b. Vermillion, S.D., Feb. 15, 1922; LL.B., U. S.D., 1951. Admitted to S.D. bar, 1951, U.S. Supreme Ct. bar, 1974; individual practice law, Vermillion, 1951-54; partner firms Weeks & Antony, Vermillion, 1954-58, Bogue, Weeks & Rusch, Vermillion, 1958—; state's atty. Clay County (S.D.), 1952-56; city atty. City of Vermillion, 1954-75, City of North Sioux City (S.D.), 1971-73. Mem. S.D. Bar, Am., S.D. trial lawyers assns., Am. Bar Assn., Phi Delta Phi. Tel (605) 624-2619

WEEKS, ROBERT ARNOLD, b. Kalamazoo, Dec. 18, 1942; B.A. in Pub. Service, U. Calif., Los Angeles, 1964, J.D., 1967. Admitted to Calif. bar, 1968, U.S. Ct. Mil. Appeals bar, 1970, U.S. Supreme Ct. bar, 1974; law clk. U.S. Dist. Ct. Eastern Calif., 1967-68; with JAGC, USN, 1968-70; dep. pub. defender Santa Clara County (Calif.), San Jose, 1970—. Mem. San Jose Charter Rev. Com., 1970-71; chmn. supervisory com. Santa Clara County Employees Credit Union, 1972-74; elder, chmn. worship com. 1st United Presbyterian Ch., Los Gatos, Calif., 1974-75. Mem. Calif. Barristers Assn. (dir., v.p. 1974-75), Am., Calif. bar assns., State Bar Calif., Calif. Pub. Defenders Assn., Calif. Attys. for Criminal Justice, Nat. Legal Aid and Defenders Assn. Office: 70 W Hedding St San Jose CA 95110 Tel (408) 998-5121

WEEKS, ROBERT WALKER, b. Moline, Ill., Aug. 14, 1926; B.S., Purdue U., 1948; J.D., Northwestern U., 1951. Admitted to Ill. bar, 1951; with law dept. Deere & Co., Moline, 1951—, gen. counsel, 1969—; dir. Iowa-Ill. Gas & Electric Co., Davenport, Iowa, Fin. Services Corp. of Midwest (Rock Island Bank). Co-chmn. Rock Island YMCA Capital Fund Program, 1974; bd. dirs. Illowa chpt. ARC; trustee Ill. Wesleyan U., Bloomington. Mem. Am., Ill. bar assns., Assn. Gen. Counsel, U.S. C. of C. (dir. 1975—), Order of Coif, Tau Beta Pi. Home: 61 Hawthorne Rd Rock Island IL 61201 Office: Deere & Co John Deere Rd Moline IL 61265 Tel (309) 792-4675

WEGHER, ARNOLD CASPER, b. Ironwood, Mich., Aug. 2, 1931; B.M.E., Marquette U., 1953; J.D., U. Colo., 1961; LL.M. in Taxation Law (Ford Found. fellow), N.Y. U., 1962. Admitted to Colo. bar, 1961; asso. firm Hindry & Meyer, and predecessor, Denver, 1961-66, partner, 1966-71, mem., 1971—, pres., 1975—, also dir.; adj. prof. law U. Denver, 1969—; exec. v.p., dir. MCA Financial Inc., Denver, 1972—; lectr. in field. Mem. Colo. (chmn. sect. taxation law 1972-73), Am. bar assns., Greater Denver Tax Counsel Assn. Contbr. articles to legal jours. Office: 621 17th St 23d floor Denver CO 80293 Tel (303) 292-9000

WEGMAN, WILLIAM LEO, b. Omaha, Nebr., May 13, 1938; B.A., U. Iowa at Iowa City, 1961, J.D., 1964. Admitted to Iowa bar, 1964; staff atty. FTC, Cleve., 1965-66; individual practice law, New Hampton, Iowa, 1966—; pros. atty. Chickasaw County (Iowa), 1967-71; city atty. New Hampton, 1972—, Alta Vista (Iowa), 1968—. County fund chmn. ARC, 1967; active Am. Cancer Soc., Am. Heart Assn. Mem. Chickasaw County (pres. 1971-74), Iowa State (bd. govs. jr. bar 1968-70) bar assns. Home: 710 E Main St New Hampton IA 50659 Office: 23 W Main St New Hampton IA 50659 Tel (515) 394-3161

WEGMANN, CYNTHIA ANNE, b. New Orleans, July 12, 1949; B.F.A., Newcomb Coll., 1971; LL.B., Tulane U., 1973. Admitted to La. bar, 1973; asso. firm Leach, Paysse & Baldwin, Orleans, 1973—. Notary pub. Parish of New Orleans, 1973—. Mem. La. State, New Orleans, Am., Southeastern Admiralty bar assns., Average Adjusters Assn. U.S.A., Gulf Steamship Claims Assn. Alumna editor Tulane Maritime Law Jour., 1973—. Office: 1540 One Shell Sq New Orleans LA 70139 Tel (504) 581-6211

WEGNER, ERNEST AUGUST, b. Tomah, Wis., Mar. 25, 1907; B.S. in Elec. Engring., U. Wis., 1929; J.D., Chgo.-Kent Coll. Law, 1932, LL.M., 1933. Admitted to Ill. bar, 1932; asso. firm Chindahl, Parker & Carlson, Chgo., 1929-35; individual practice law, Chgo., 1935-44; partner firm Wegner, Stellman, McCord, Wiles & Wood, and predecessors, Chgo., 1944—. Mem. Am., Chgo. bar assns., Am., Chgo. patent law assns., Am. Judicature Soc. Home: 109 S County Line Rd Hinsdale IL 60521 Office: 20 N Wacker Dr Chicago IL 60606 Tel (312) 346-1630

WEHBY, VINCENT E., b. Nashville, Oct. 3, 1936; A.B., U. Notre Dame, 1958; LL.B., Vanderbilt U., 1961. Admitted to Tenn. bar, 1961; individual practice law, Nashville, 1961-62, 63—; asst. U.S. atty. Middle Dist. Tenn., Nashville, 1962-63. Mem. Nashville (past dir.), Am. bar assns. Home: 5933 Timothy Dr Nashville TN Office: United American Bank Bldg Nashville TN 37219 Tel (615) 254-1271

WEHNER, CHARLES VINCENT, b. Chester, W. Va., Nov. 12, 1921; A.B., W. Va. U., 1943, J.D., 1946. Admitted to W. Va. bar, 1946, U.S. Supreme Ct. bar, 1956, U.S. 4th Circuit Ct. Appeals bar, 1962; partner firm Parrack, Snyder and Wehner, Kingwood, W. Va., 1946-50; individual practice law, Kingwood, 1950—; gen. receiver Circuit Ct. Preston County, W. Va., 1966—; dep. commr. forfeited and delinquent lands, 1967—; mem. bd. govs. W. Va. State Bar, 1960-63, 69-72; mem. vis. com. Coll. Law W. Va. U., 1971-73. Chmn. Preston County Buckwheat Festival, 1955; pres. Rotary Club Kingwood, 1951-52; pres. Citizens Scholarship Fund Kingwood, Inc., 1954-56; chmn. Preston County chpt. ARC, 1950-51; active Boy Scouts Am. Mem. Am., W. Va. State (chmn. com. on law schs. and admissions to the bar), Preston County (pres. 1961-63) bar assns., Am. Judicature Soc. Hon. mem. Kingwood Vol. Fire Dept. Home: 103 Beverly Kingwood WV 26537 Office: 103 W Court St Kingwood WV 26537 Tel (304) 329-1581

WEHRINGER, CAMERON KINGSLEY, b. Glen Ridge, N.J., Nov. 21, 1924; B.A., Amherst Coll., 1947; J.D., N.Y. Law Sch., 1951; postgrad. N.Y. U., 1953, Columbia U. Law Sch., 1960. Admitted to N.Y. bar, 1952, N.H. bar, 1967, U.S. Supreme Ct. bar, 1971; partner firm Wehringer & Kojima, N.Y.C., 1974—. Mem. Am., N.Y., N.H. bar assns., Assn. Bar N.Y.C., Phi Delta Phi. Speaker legal meetings; contbr. articles to legal jours. Home: 510-7 Main St New York City NY 10044 Office: Wehringer & Kojima 25 W 43d St New York City NY 10036 Tel (212) 736-9380

WEHRMAN, J. GREGORY, b. Covington, Ky., Jan. 3, 1944; student U. Fla., 1962-64; B.A., U. Cin., 1966; J.D., U. Ky., 1969. Admitted to Ky. bar, 1969, Fla. bar, 1969; partner firm Wehrman & Wehrman, Covington, 1969—; U.S. magistrate for Eastern Dist. Ky., Covington, 1975—. Mem. Ky., Fla., Am., Kenton County, Fed. bar assns., Assn. Trial Lawyers Am. Office: 301 Pike St Covington KY 41011 Tel (606) 261-8352

WEICH, CECILE C., b. Atlantic City, Nov. 29, 1934; B.A., Coll. City N.Y., 1956; LL.B., Bklyn. Law Sch., 1958. Admitted to N.Y. State bar, 1959, U.S. Supreme Ct. bar, 1966; practice law, Riverdale, N.Y. Mem. N.Y. State Bar Assn., Assn. Bar City N.Y., Am., N.Y. trial lawyers assns., Inst. Jud. Justice. Home: 530 W 236th St Riverdale NY 10463 Office: 1 Riverdale Ave Riverdale NY 10463 Tel (212) 549-2238

WEICHSEL, JOHN LOUIS, b. N.Y.C., Feb. 14, 1946; A.B. cum laude, Clark U., 1968; J.D. cum laude, N.Y. U., 1971. Admitted to N.Y. bar, 1972, N.J. bar, 1972; asso. firm Parker, Chapin & Flattau, N.Y.C., 1971-73; asst. dep. pub. defender State of N.J., Hackensack, 1973-76; individual practice law, Hackensack and N.Y.C., 1976—; prof. Taylor Bus. Inst., Paramus, N.J., 1976—. Chmn. Bergen chpt. ACLU of N.J., 1975—; trustee N.J. ACLU, 1976—; mem. county com. Bergen County Dem. Party. Mem. Am., N.J., Bergen County bar assns., Phi Beta Kappa, Order of Coif. Home: 100 Prospect Ave Hackensack NJ 07601 Office: 29 Main St Hackensack NJ 07601 Tel (201) 488-1400

WEIDEMEYER, CARLETON LLOYD, b. Hebbville, Md., June 12, 1933; B.A. in Political Science, U. Md., 1958; J.D., Stetson U., Law Sch., 1961. Admitted to Fla. bar, 1961, U.S. Dist. Court, Middle Dist. Fla., 1963, U.S. Supreme Court Bar, 1966, U.S. Court Appeal, Fifth Circuit, 1967, U.S. Dist. Court, D.C., 1971, U.S. Court Appeal, D.C., 1976; research asst. Second Dist. Court Appeal, Fla., 1961-65; partner firm Kalle and Weidemeyer, St. Petersburg, Fla., 1965-68; asst. public defender Sixth Judicial Circuit, Fla., 1966-69; partner firm Wightman, Weidemeyer, Jones, Turnbull and Cobb, Clearwater, Fla., 1968—; dir. Fla. Bank Commerce, Clearwater, 1973—; dir. First Nat. Bank and Trust Co., Belleair Bluffs, Fla., 1974—. Mem. Musicians Assn. Clearwater, Fla. (pres., 1976—), Fla. Conference Musicians, (sec., treas., 1974-76), Fla. State Hist. Soc., Phi Delta Phi, Sigma Pi, Kappa Kappa Psi. Office: 319 S Garden Ave Clearwater FL 33516 Tel (813) 442-3176

WEIDENFELD, EDWARD L., b. Akron, Ohio, July 15, 1943; B.S., U. Wis., 1965; J.D., Columbia, 1968. Admitted to N.Y. bar, 1968, U.S. Supreme Ct. bar, 1972, D.C. bar, 1973; asso. firm Fried, Frank, Harris, Shriver & Jacobson, N.Y.C., 1968-71, Washington, 1973-74; mem. firm Hall, Estill, Hardwick, Gable, Collingsworth & Nelson, Washington, 1974—; counsel, dir. energy staff, com. on interior and insular affairs U.S. Ho. of Reps.; faculty Am. Law Inst.-Am. Bar Assn. Continuing Legal Edn. Programs; lectr. in field to profl. groups. Spl. cons. N.Y.C. Dept. Bldgs., 1967; mem. Pres.'s Commn. on White House Fellowships, 1977—. Mem. Am., D.C., Fed. Communications bar assns., Assn. Bar City N.Y. Editor in chief Atomic Energy Law Jour., 1975—; contbr. articles to legal jours. Home: 2903 Q St NW Washington DC 20007 Office: 1701 Pennsylvania Ave NW Suite 404 Washington DC 20006 Tel (202) 965-2030

WEIDNER, GARY RICHARD, b. Mpls., Nov. 18, 1948; B.A., U. Wis. at Madison, 1970, J.D., 1974. Admitted to Wis. bar, 1974; mem. firm Hanaway, Ross, Hanaway & Weidner Green Bay, Wis., 1974—; instr. environ. law U. Wis. at Green Bay, 1974, 76; instr. law in banking, NE Wis. Tech. Inst., 1974, 76. Mem. Brown County Harbor Commn., 1976—. Mem. Am., Wis., Brown County bar assns. Home: 818 N Van Buren St Green Bay WI 54302 Office: 414 E Walnut St Suite 201 Green Bay WI 54301 Tel (414) 432-3381

WEIKERT, GERALD V., b. Washington, Nov. 24, 1897; LL.B., George Washington U., 1918. Admitted to D.C. bar, 1919, Calif. bar, 1925; atty. FTC, Chgo., 1920-24, atty. charge Pacific Coast Office, San Francisco, 1924-26; individual practice law, Los Angeles, 1926—. Mem. Order of Coif, Phi Delta Phi. Office: 650 S Grand Ave Los Angeles CA 90017 Tel (213) 627-7722

WEIL, ANDREW LEO, b. Pitts., July 19, 1920; A.B., Princeton, 1943; LL.B./J.D., U. Pitts., 1949. Admitted to Pa. bar, 1949, U.S. Supreme Ct. bar, 1965; solicitor Twp. of O'Hara (Pa.), 1956-64; spl. asst. atty. gen. Commonwealth of Pa., 1964—; partner firm Weil Vatz & Weil, Pitts., Pa., 1958-68, firm Cleland Hurtt Witt & Weil, Pitts., 1975—. Mem. Am., Pa., Allgheny County bar assns., Pitts. C. of C. (past dir.). Home: 108 White Gate Rd Pittsburgh PA 15238 Office: 1505 Grant Bldg Grant St Pittsburgh PA 15219 Tel (412) 471-1787

WEIL, RICHARD BARRY, b. Paterson, N.J., Nov. 4, 1944; B.A., U. Mich., 1966, J.D., 1969; student Sch. of Law, Boston U., 1966-67; postgrad. Sch. of Law, N.Y. U., 1970-72. Admitted to N.Y. State bar, 1970, N.J. bar, 1973; atty. IRS, Newark, 1969-73; asso. firm Shoobe & Stern, P.A., Clifton, N.J., 1973-74; individual practice law, Upper Montclair, N.J., also N.Y.C., 1974-75; partner firm Rabner, Weil & Allcorn, Upper Montclair, 1975—. Chmn. spl. gifts United Way North Essex. Mem. Am. (mem. profl. service corps. com., sect. taxation), N.J., Passaic County (mem. tax com.), Montclair and West Essex bar assns., Montclair Jaycees (past dir.). Recipient President's award Montclair Jaycees, 1974-75, 75-76. Home: 81 Watchung Ave Upper Montclair NJ 07043 Office: 266 Bellevue Ave Upper Montclair NJ 07043 Tel (201) 744-4201

WEIL, RICHARD GRADY, b. San Antonio, Apr. 28, 1934; J.D., U. Tex., Austin, 1961. Admitted to Tex. bar, 1961, Supreme Ct. U.S., 1967, U.S. Ct. Mil. Appeals bar, 1967; atty. City of San Antonio, 1961-62, Forest Oil Corp., 1962-64; individual practice law, San Antonio, 1964—; lt. col. JAGC, USAR. Mem. Am., Tex., San Antonio bar assns., San Antonio Trial Lawyers Assn. (dir. 1969-75). Home: 10219 Bull Run St San Antonio TX 78230 Office: 3838 NW Loop 410 San Antonio TX 78229 Tel (512) 735-9261

WEIL, THOMAS EDWIN, b. Milw., Apr. 13, 1940; B.B.A., U. Wis., 1962; J.D., Marquette U., 1965. Admitted to Wis. bar, 1965; law clk. U.S. Dist. Ct. for Eastern Wis., 1965-66; asst. U.S. atty. Eastern dist. Wis., Milw., 1966-69; asso. firm Levin Blumenthal Herz & Levin, Milw., 1970-72; pres. Phil Tolkan Pontiac-Renault, Milw., 1972—. Trustee, Village of Bayside (Wis.), 1976, Mt. Sinai Hosp., 1975, Jewish Home for Aged, 1975-77. Mem. Wis., Milw., Fed. bar assns. Office: 2301 W Silver Spring Dr Milwaukee WI 53209 Tel (414) 228-8500

WEILAND, RICHARD FRANCIS, b. Chgo., Jan. 26, 1945; B.A. in English Lit., St. Procopius Coll., 1967; J.D., Loyola U., Chgo., 1970. Admitted to Ill. bar, 1970; legal clk. U.S. Army, Ft. Lewis, Wash., 1970-72, Vietnam, 1972; asso. firm Tim J. Harrington, Chgo., 1972-75; chief civil div. Kane County (Ill.) State's Atty. Office, Geneva, 1975-76, 1st asst., 1976; individual practice law, Geneva, 1976—. speaker in field. Mem. Am., Ill., Kane County bar assns. Home: 1226 S 10th St Saint Charles IL 60174 Office: 328 S 3d St Geneva IL 60134 Tel (312) 232-7571

WEILDING, DOUGLAS BARRY, b. Attleboro, Mass., Sept. 7, 1939; B.S., Boston U., 1961; J.D., Suffolk U., 1972, LL.M., 1974. Admitted to Mass. bar, 1972, R.I. bar, 1973, U.S. Supreme Ct. bar, 1976; individual practice law, Attleboro, 1972—; asst. dist. atty. County of Bristol (Mass.), 1975—. Dist. commr. Boy Scouts Am., 1976. Mem. Am., Mass., R.I., Bristol County bar assns. Office: 8 N Main St Attleboro MA 02703

WEILER, JEFFRY LOUIS, b. N.Y.C., Dec. 31, 1942; B.S., Miami U., Oxford, Ohio, 1964; J.D., Cleve. State U., 1970. Admitted to Ohio bar, 1970; agt. IRS, Cleve., 1965-70; asso. firm Ulmer Berne Laronge Glickman and Curtis, Cleve., 1970-71; asso. firm Benesch, Friedlander, Coplan and Aronoff, Cleve., 1971—; speaker Cleve. Tax Inst., 1968, 71-76. C.P.A., Ohio. Mem. Greater Cleve., Am., Ohio State bar assns., Cleve. Tax Club, Estate Planning Council of Cleve. Home: 2550 Edgewood Rd Beachwood OH 44122 Office: 850 Euclid Ave Suite 1100 Cleveland OH 44114 Tel (216) 696-1600

WEIN, JOSEPH ALEXANDER, b. Montreal, Que., Can., June 4, 1931; A.A., U. Calif., Los Angeles, 1950, B.A., 1952, J.D., 1955. Admitted to Calif. bar, 1956; asso. firm Buchalter, Nemer, Fields & Savitch, Los Angeles, 1962-68, partner, 1968—; moderator U. Calif. Continuing Edn. Bar, 1977. Mem. State Bar Calif., Los Angeles County, Internat. bar assns., Fin. Lawyers Conf., Comml. Law League Am. (chmn. panel prejudgment remedies western region 1976). Office: 700 S Flower St Los Angeles CA 90017 Tel (213) 626-6700

WEIN, LEON EDWARD, b. Lowell, Mass., Feb. 15, 1941; A.B., Bklyn. Coll., 1961; diploma of Rabbi Misifta Torah Vodoath, 1963; LL.B., N.Y. U., 1966; diploma law Cambridge U., 1966. Admitted to N.Y. bar, 1967; asst. gen. counsel Dept. Bldgs., City N.Y., 1966-68, asst. corp. counsel, 1968-70; instr. Bklyn. Law Sch., 1970-73, asst. prof. law, 1973-76, asso. prof., 1976—. Mem. Assn. Bar City N.Y. (mem. com. on transp.). Office: Bklyn Law Sch 250 Joralemon St Brooklyn NY 11201 Tel (212) 625-2200

WEINBERG, ARTHUR VICTOR, b. Washington, June 5, 1941; B.A., U. Md., 1963; J.D., George Washington U., 1967. Admitted to D.C. bar, 1967, U.S. Supreme Ct. bar, 1970; asso. firm Smith & Pepper, Washington, 1967-70, partner, 1970—. Mem. D.C., Am., Fed. Communications (membership com. 1970-75, Jour. Com. 1970-72) bar assns. Home: 15128 Middlegate Rd Silver Spring MD 20904 Office: 1776 K St NW Washington DC 20006 Tel (202) 296-0600

WEINBERG, FORREST B., b. Norfolk, Va., Sept. 4, 1926; LL.B., U. Cin., 1950; LL.M., Harvard U., 1951. Admitted to Ohio bar, 1950, U.S. Supreme Ct. bar, 1970; asso. firm Hahn, Loeser, Freedheim, Dean & Wellman, Cleve., 1951-59, partner, 1959—; vis. prof. law U. Calif., Davis, 1975-76. Chmn. attys. div. Greater Cleve. United Torch Dr., 1974; trustee Park Synagogue, Cleveland Heights, 1961-68, pres. Men's Club, 1963-65; trustee Bellefaire Treatment Center, 1968-74, Jewish Children's Bur., 1968-74. Mem. Am., Ohio, Greater Cleve. (trustee 1973-75) bar assns.; fellow Ohio State Bar Found. Home: 19020 Shaker Blvd Shaker Heights OH 44122 Office: 800 National City E 6th Bldg Cleveland OH 44114 Tel (216) 621-0150

WEINBERG, JOHN LEE, b. Chgo., Apr. 24, 1941; B.A., Swarthmore Coll., 1962; J.D., U. Chgo., 1965. Admitted to Ill. bar, 1966, Wash. bar, 1967, U.S. Dist. Ct. for Western Dist. Wash. bar, 1967, U.S. 9th Circuit Ct. Appeals, 1968; law clk. Ill. Appellate Ct., 1965-66, Ill. Supreme Ct., 1966, U.S. Dist. Ct., Seattle, 1967-68; asso. firm Perkins, Coie, Stone, Olsen & Williams, Seattle, 1968-73; U.S. magistrate, Seattle, 1973—. Mem. Nat. Council U.S. Magistrates, Am. Judicature Soc., Am., Wash. State, Seattle-King County bar assns. Home: 4527 52d Ave S Seattle WA 98118 Office: 103 US Courthouse Seattle WA 98104 Tel (206) 442-5774

WEINBERG, MELVIN, b. Ger., July 22, 1948; B.A., Yeshiva U., 1969; J.D., N.Y. U., 1972. Admitted to N.Y. bar, 1973; clk. to judge U.S. Ct. Appeals for 3d Circuit, Phila., 1972-73; asso. firm Fried, Frank, Harris, Shriver & Jacobson, N.Y.C., 1973—. Mem. Order of Coif. Note and comment editor N.Y. U. Law Rev., 1971-72. Office: 120 Broadway New York City NY 10005 Tel (212) 964-6500

WEINBERGER, ANDREW D., b. Obecha, Hungary, Aug. 20, 1901; LL.B., N.Y. U., 1925; LL.D., Wilberforce U., 1959. Admitted to N.Y. bar, 1926, U.S. Supreme Ct. bar, 1946; individual practice law, N.Y.C., 1926-68; of counsel firm Delson & Gordon, N.Y.C., 1968—; vis. lectr. N.Y. U., 1953-56; vis. prof. Nat. U. Mex., 1959, Toyo U., Japan, 1961. Mem. Am., N.Y. State bar assns., N.Y. County Lawyers Assn. Author: Freedom and Protection: The Bill of Rights, 1962. Contbr. articles in field to profl. jours. Office: 230 Park Ave New York City NY 10017 Tel (212) 686-8030

WEINBLATT, SEYMOUR SOLOMON, b. Bklyn., May 6, 1922; B.A., Ind. U., 1947; J.D. with honors, Rutgers U., 1950. Admitted to N.J. bar, 1951, U.S. Supreme Ct. bar, 1957; individual practice law, Manville, N.J., 1951—; atty. Manville Bd. Edn., 1963-66, Manville Bd. Adjustment, 1963-66, Manville Planning Bd., 1964-66, Manville Bd. Health, 1964-66; municipal atty. City of Manville, 1964-66. Mem. Somerset County, Hunterdon County, N.J. State bar assns. Home: 1 Norma Rd Rural Delivery 1 Hampton NJ 08827 Office: 25 S Main St Manville NJ 08835 Tel (201) 722-0100

WEINER, ALAN E(RNEST), b. Bklyn., Nov. 17, 1942; B.B.A., Coll. City N.Y., 1963; J.D., Bklyn. Law Sch., 1968; LL.M., N.Y. U., 1972. Admitted to N.Y. bar, 1969; asso. firm Wien Lane Klein & Malkin, N.Y.C., 1968-69; tax mgr. Touche Ross & Co., Melville, N.Y., 1969-75; tax dir. Wolf & Co., N.Y.C., 1975; partner firm Holtz Rubenstein & Co., Melville, 1975—; instr. Hofstra U., 1973—. Mem. N.Y. State Soc. C.P.A.s (Nassau County chpt. exec. bd.), Estate Planning Council Suffolk County (treas.), Nassau County Bar Assn. (tax law com.), Am. Assn. Attys.-C.P.A.s, Am. Inst. C.P.A.s, N.Y. U. Tax Study Group, Suffolk County Life Underwriters Assn. (monthly columnist 1976—). Author: The Practical Accountant-How to Handle an Accounting for an Estate, 1976; contbr. monthly article Suffolk County Life Underwriters Assn., Inc., 1976—. Home: 15 Audley Ct Plainview NY 11803 Office: Holtz Rubenstein & Co 425 Broad Hollow Rd Melville NY 11746 Tel (516) 694-0120

WEINER, GERALD T., b. N.Y.C., July 8, 1943; B.A., U. Conn., 1965, J.D., 1968. Admitted to Conn. bar, 1968; staff atty. FCC, Washington, 1968-70; asso. firm Saltman, Weiss, Weinstein & Elson, 1970-71; partner firm Weinstein, Krulewitz & Weiner, Bridgeport, Conn., 1971—; lectr. U. Bridgeport, 1974—. Mem. Dem. Town Com., Woodbridge, Conn., 1976—. Mem. Conn. Bar Assn., Comml. Law League Am. Home: 15 Bishop Dr Woodbridge CT 06525 Office: 144 Golden Hill St Bridgeport CT 06604 Tel (203) 384-9361

WEINER, ROBERT, b. Rochester, N.Y., Feb. 9, 1922; B.S., Syracuse U., 1947; J.D., Union U., 1949. Admitted to N.Y. bar, 1950, U.S. Supreme Ct. bar, 1958; sr. partner firm Weiner & Lawrence, E. Rochester, 1950—. Mem. Am., N.Y., Monroe County bar assns. Office: 248 W Commercial St East Rochester NY 14618 Tel (716) 586-6280

WEINER, SIGMUND TATAR, b. San Antonio, Mar. 13, 1942; B.S., U.S. Mil. Acad., 1964; LL.B. with honors, U. Tex., Austin, 1968. Admitted to Tex. bar, 1968; served with JAG USAF, 1968-70; asso. firm Oppenheimer, Rosenberg & Kelleher, Inc., San Antonio, 1970-71; asso. firm Stalcup Johnson Meyers & Miller, Dallas, 1971-73, partner, 1974—. Mem. Am., Tex., Dallas bar assns. Office: Suite 2700 2001 Bryan Tower Dallas TX 75201 Tel (214) 651-1700

WEINER, STEPHEN ARTHUR, b. Bklyn., Nov. 20, 1933; B.A. summa cum laude, Harvard, 1954; J.D. cum laude, Yale, 1957. Admitted to N.Y. State bar, 1958, U.S. Supreme Ct. bar, 1976; asso. firm Winthrop, Stimson, Putnam & Roberts, N.Y.C., 1958-65, partner firm, 1968—; prof. law U. Calif. at Berkeley, 1965-68; lectr. Practicing Law Inst., N.Y.C., 1970—. Asso. trustee North Shore Hosp., Manhasset, N.Y., 1971—. Mem. Assn. of Bar City of N.Y. (mem. com. recruitment new lawyers, com. fed. cts., admissions com., com. state cts. superior jurisdiction, com. uniform state laws), Order of the Coif, Phi Beta Kappa. Comment editor Yale Law Jour.; contbr. articles to legal jours. Home: 190 Harbor Rd Sands Point NY 11050 Office: 40 Wall St New York City NY 10005 Tel (212) 943-0700

WEINER, WILLIAM HOWARD, b. Akron, Ohio, Jan. 5, 1947; B.S. in Bus. Adminstrn., U. Akron, 1969; J.D., Case Western Res. U., 1972. Admitted to Ohio bar, 1972; asst. law dir., prosecutor City of Akron, 1972-73; asso. firm Destreicher, Sternberg & Manes, Akron, 1973-74; mem. firm Hinton Landi, et al, Akron, 1974—. Mem. Ohio, Akron bar assns. Office: 2500 First National Tower Akron OH 44308 Tel (216) 253-2195

WEINERMAN, LLOYD MARTIN, b. Newton, Mass., Oct. 24, 1940; A.B., Boston U., 1962; J.D., U. Balt., 1973. Admitted to Md. bar, 1973; contract specialist Social Security Adminstrn., Balt., 1967-75; atty. Office Regional Counsel HEW, Washington, 1975—. Mem. Am., Md., Fed. bar assns. Home: 3903 Lausanne Rd Randallstown MD 21133 Office: 6501 Security Blvd Baltimore MD 21235 Tel (301) 594-8347

WEINGARTEN, SAUL MYER, b. Los Angeles, Dec. 19, 1921; A.A., Antelope Valley Coll., 1940; A.B., U. Calif., Los Angeles, 1942; certificate in diesel engring. Cornell U., 1944; J.D., U. So. Calif., 1949; certificate in municipal affairs Coro Found., San Francisco, 1950. Admitted to Calif. bar, 1950, U.S. Supreme Ct. bar, 1961; legal counsel Calif. Unemployment Ins. Appeals Bd., 1951; counsel, law officer mil. cts., 1951; instr. Naval Sch. Justice, Newport, R.I., 1951; instr., legal officer Naval Postgrad. Sch., Monterey, Calif., 1952-54; mem. law faculty San Jose (Calif.) State U., Monterey Peninsula Coll., Naval Res. Officers Sch., Monterey, 1953-71; city atty. Gonzales, Calif., 1954-73, Seaside, Calif., 1955-70; pres. firm Saul M. Weingarten, Inc., Seaside, Calif., 1954—; counsel Redevel. Agy., Seaside, 1963-77; U.S. del. Internat. Union Local Authorities, 1963, 73. Bd. dirs. Clark Found., Pebble Beach, Calif., Congregation Beth Israel, Monterey, Calif.; active United Fund, ARC; pres. Alliance on Aging, Monterey, 1973-74. Mem. Calif., Monterey County bar assns., Calif. Trial Lawyers Assn. Author: Compendium of Training Aids in Military Justice, 1952. Home: 4135 Crest Rd Pebble Beach CA 93953 Office: Fremont Profl Center Seaside CA 93955 Tel (408) 899-2411

WEINGARTEN, STEPHEN CLARK, b. N.Y.C., Oct. 29, 1947; B.A., City Coll. N.Y., 1968; J.D., Columbia, 1972. Admitted to N.Y. State bar, 1972; since practiced in N.Y.C., intern U.S. Atty. for So. Dist. N.Y., 1971; asso. firm Robinson, Silverman, Pearce, Aronsohn, Sand & Berman, 1972-73; atty. WUI, Inc., 1974—. Mem. Am., N.Y. State bar assns., Phi Beta Kappa. Office: One WUI Plaza New York City NY 10004 Tel (212) 363-5812

WEINGRAD, RONALD CARL, b. N.Y.C., July 23, 1945; A.B., Kenyon Coll., 1967; J.D., Duquesne U., 1973. Admitted to Pa. bar, 1973; partner firm Weingrad and Marcus, Pitts., 1974—. Mem. Am., Allegheny County bar assns., Pa. Trial Lawyers Assn. Asso. editor Duquesne U. Sch. Law Rev., 1972-73. Office: 1500 Lawyers Bldg Pittsburgh PA 15219 Tel (412) 355-0880

WEINHAUS, SAMUEL SHELDON, b. St. Louis, Jan. 9, 1931; B.A. in Edn., U. Ariz., Tucson, 1951; J.D., Washington U., St. Louis, 1957. Admitted to Mo. bar, 1957, Ariz. bar, 1957, U.S. Supreme Ct. bar, 1961; law clk. U.S. Dist. Ct. Eastern Dist. Mo., 1957-58; partner firm Levin & Weinhaus, St. Louis, 1958—; chmn. 4th Nat. Conf. Law Review Editors, St. Louis, 1957. Mem. Am., Mo., St. Louis bar assns. Contbr. to Washington U. Law Quar. Office: 515 Olive St Saint Louis MO 63101 Tel (314) 621-8363

WEINMANN, RICHARD ADRIAN, b. N.Y.C., Oct. 15, 1917; LL.B., Bklyn. Law Sch., 1948; LL.M., N.Y. U., 1953. Admitted to N.Y. bar, 1958, U.S. Supreme Ct. bar, 1964, U.S. Ct. Appeals 2d Circuit bar, 1965; partner firm Sipser, Weinstock & Weinmann, N.Y.C., 1953-71; of counsel to numerous teamsters unions and funds, N.Y.C., 1972—; lectr. in field. Vice pres. bd. dirs. Clearview Gardens Corps., Whitestone, N.Y., 1953-54, 60-61. Mem. N.Y. Bar Assn., N.Y. County Lawyers Assn. Home: 61 Franklin Pl Great Neck NY 11023 Office: 270 Madison Ave New York NY 10016 Tel (212) 685-4774

WEINREICH, HOWARD LOUIS, b. N.Y.C., Mar. 2, 1931; B.B.A., U. Wis., 1952; LL.B., Columbia, 1957. Admitted to N.Y. State bar, 1958; law clk. Judge Irving R. Kaufman, U.S. Dist. Ct., N.Y.C., 1957-58; asso. firm Botein, Hays, Sklar & Herzberg, 1958-65, partner, 1965—; dir. Edmos Corp., Glen Cove, N.Y., 1972—. Mem. Am., N.Y. State bar assns., Assn. Bar City N.Y. Contbr. articles in field to profl. jours. and textbooks; bd. editors Columbia Law Rev., 1955-57. Home: 31 Andrea Ln Scarsdale NY 10583 Office: 200 Park Ave New York City NY 10017 Tel (212) 867-5500

WEINSHIENK, ZITA LEESON, b. St. Paul, Apr. 3, 1933; B.A. magna cum laude, U. Ariz., 1955; J.D. cum laude, Harvard U., 1958. Admitted to Colo. bar, 1959; probation counselor, legal adviser, referee Denver Juvenile Ct., 1959-64; municipal ct. judge, Denver, 1964; judge Denver County Ct., 1965-71, Denver Dist. Ct., 1972—. Mem. Denver, Colo., Am. bar assns., Colo. Dist. Judges Assn., Nat. Conf. State Trial Judges, Harvard Law Sch. Assn., Denver LWV, Order of Coif, Denver Bus. and Profl. Women, Denver Anti-Crime Council. Named Woman of Year Denver Bus. and Profl. Women, 1969. Home: 1881 S Niagara Way Denver CO 80224 Office: Dist Ct City and County Bldg Denver CO 80202 Tel (303) 297-2309

WEINSTEIN, ANDREW HARVEY, b. Pitts., Oct. 5, 1943; student Marietta Coll., 1961-62; B.S. in Bus. Adminstrn., Duquesne U., 1965; J.D., U. Pitts., 1968; LL.M., N.Y. U., 1969. Admitted to Pa. bar, 1969, Fla. bar, 1970; mem. staff Office of Regional Counsel, IRS, Los Angeles, 1969-70, Miami, Fla., 1970-73; asso. and partner firm Swann & Glass, Coral Gables, Fla., 1973-76; dir. firm Glass, Schultz, Lobel, Weinstein & Moss, Coral Gables, 1976—. Mem. Greater Miami Tax

Inst. (vice-chmn. com. civil tax practice 1976—), Internat. Fiscal Assn., Dade County (tax com. 1975—), Fed. (council on taxation 1974—), Am. bar assns., Fla. Bar (exec. council tax sect. 1976—, vice-chmn. com. civil tax practice and procedure 1976-77). Office: Suite 63 5915 Ponce de Leon Blvd Coral Gables FL 33146 Tel (305) 667-4633

WEINSTEIN, BERNARD, b. Milw., Sept. 19, 1927; B.S., U. Ariz., 1950, LL.B., 1953. Admitted to Ariz. bar, 1953; individual practice law, Tucson, 1953—; magistrate City of Tucson, 1962; referee Pima County (Ariz.) Juvenile Ct., 1970—. Mem. State Bar Ariz., Pima County, Ariz. bar assns. Recipient Am. Jurisprudence Ins. award, 1953. Home: 6821 Tivani Dr Tucson AZ 85715 Office: 1015 Transamerica Bldg Tucson AZ 85701 Tel (602) 623-3696

WEINSTEIN, BURTON MARVIN, b. Bklyn., Mar. 15, 1929; A.B., Syracuse U., 1950; J.D., Yale U., 1956. Admitted to Conn. bar, 1959, U.S. Supreme Ct. bar, 1960, U.S. Tax Ct. bar, 1970; research asso. Yale U. Law Sch., 1956-57; Conn. regional mgr. Am. Arbitration Assn., Hartford, 1957-60; asst. gen. counsel New Haven Redevel. Agy., 1960-61; partner firm Saltman Weiss Weinstein & Elson, Bridgeport, Conn., 1961-63, partner firm, and predecessors, 1963-70; partner firm Weinstein Krulewitz & Weiner, Bridgeport, 1970—; hearing examiner Conn. Commn. Human Rights and Opportunities, 1969-72; vol. atty. Conn. Civil Liberties Union, 1959—; lectr. in field. Mem. exec. bd. Fairfield County (Conn.) Civil Liberties Union, 1959—; organizing mem. acad. standards com. Housatonic Community Coll., 1971-72; mem. Conn. Citizens for Jud. Modernization, 1973-74; vol. legal cons. Stratford (Conn.) Counseling Center, 1975-77. Mem. Conn., Fed. bar assns., Comml. Law League Am. Contbr. articles to legal jours. Office: 144 Golden Hill St Bridgeport CT 06604 Tel (203) 284-9361

WEINSTEIN, DAVID, b. Phila., Feb. 6, 1926; B.S., U. Pa., 1949, M.S., 1953, postgrad., 1953-59; LL.B., J.D., Temple U., 1959. Admitted to Pa. bar, 1960; counsel Phila. Dept. Collections, 1960-62; partner firm Weinstein Goss & Katzenstein, Phila. Mem. Phila. Bar Assn., Am., Pa., Phila. trial lawyers assns., Am. Arbitration Assn. Home: 1791 Oakwynne Rd Huntingdon Valley PA 19006 Office: 1000 Penn Square Bldg Philadelphia PA 19107 Tel (215) LO 3-5953

WEINSTEIN, EDWARD, b. Sayre, Pa., Nov. 5, 1936; A.B., Cornell U., 1958, J.D., 1960. Admitted to Nev. bar, 1961; individual practice law, Las Vegas, Nev., 1968—; dep. city atty. City of Las Vegas, 1963-68. Mem. Am. Trial Lawyers Assn., Am. Judicature Soc., Nat. Dist. Atty. Assn., Assn. Immigration and Nationality Lawyers, Clark County (Nev.) Bar Assn., State Bar Nev. Contbr. articles to legal publs. Office: 2305 Las Vegas Blvd S Las Vegas NV 89104 Tel (702) 735-1112

WEINSTEIN, HARRIS, b. Providence, May 10, 1935; S.B., Mass. Inst. Tech., 1956, S.M., 1958; LL.B., Columbia U., 1961. Admitted to D.C. bar, 1962; law clk. U.S. Ct. Appeals for 3d Circuit, 1961-62; with firm Covington & Burling, Washington, 1962-67, 69—; asst. to Solicitor Gen., U.S. Dept. Justice, Washington, 1967-69. Office: 888 16th St NW Washington DC 20006 Tel (202) 452-6190

WEINSTEIN, JACK M., b. N.Y.C., June 29, 1936; B.S., N.Y. U. Sch. Commerce, 1956, M.B.A., Sch. Bus. Adminstrn., 1958, J.D., Sch. Law, 1960. Admitted to N.Y. bar, 1961; asso. firm House, Grossman, Vorhaus & Hemley, N.Y.C., 1960-61; partner firm Black, Brownstein & Weinstein, Great Neck, N.Y., 1961-69, firm Faber, Falletta & Weinstein, Forest Hills, N.Y., 1976—; law sec. to justice N.Y. Supreme Ct. in Queens County, 1969-76. Pres. United Cerebral Palsy of Queens, N.E. v.p. Mem. Queens County Bar Assn., Comml. Law League Am. Office: 108-18 Queens Blvd Forest Hills NY 11375 Tel (212) 520-1900

WEINSTEIN, LEE MARVIN, b. Atlanta, Apr. 16, 1940; A.B., U. N.C., 1961; J.D., Emory U., 1964. Admitted to Ga. bar, 1963; since practiced in Atlanta; atty. NLRB, 1964-65; asso. firm Gilbert, Patton & Carter, 1965-66; individual practice law, 1966-67; partner firm Frankel & Weinstein, and predecessor, 1967-69; individual practice law, 1969-73; partner firm Parks, Eisenberg & Weinstein, 1973—; legal counsel Atlanta Jaycees, 1968. Zone chmn. United Appeal, Atlanta, 1971; bd. dirs. Atlanta Men's Orgn. Rehab. Tng., 1976; pres. Atlanta lodge B'nai Brith, 1977; v.p. Progressive Club, 1977. Mem. Am., Ga., Atlanta bar assns., Am. Judicature Soc., Assn. Trial Lawyers Am., Lawyers Ref. Soc., Emory Law Sch. Alumni Assn., Phi Alpha Delta. Home: 1595 Peachtree Battle Ave NW Atlanta GA 30327 Office: 455 E Paces Ferry Rd NE Suite 240 Atlanta GA 30305 Tel (404) 261-6442

WEINSTEIN, LEWIS H., b. Lithuania, Apr. 10, 1905; A.B. magna cum laude, Harvard, 1927, LL.B., 1930. Admitted to Mass. bar, 1930, U.S. Supreme Ct. bar, 1933; asso., partner firm Rome & Weinstein, Boston, 1930-45; partner firm Foley, Hoog & Eliot, Boston, 1946—, now sr. and mng. partner; asst. corp. counsel City of Boston, 1934-42; gen. counsel Boston Housing Authority, 1938-45; chmn. Mass. Emergency Housing Commn., 1946-47, chmn. State Housing Bd., 1947-48; lectr. trial advocacy Harvard Law Sch., 1960-76; lectr. Practising Law Inst., New Eng. Law Inst., Am. Bar Assn., Am. Law Inst., Mass. Continuing Legal Edn.; sr. vis. lectr. law of land use and planning Mass. Inst. Tech., 1961-68; trustee Boston Five Cents Savs. Bank, 1964—; past dir., mem. finance com. Boston & Me. R.R.; past dir. LTV Corp. Served to col. JAGC, U.S. Army; advisor Mass. State Depts., HUD. Pres. Council Jewish Fedns. and Welfare Funds, 1965-66, chmn. Nat. Community Relations Adv. Council, 1960-64; chmn. Conf. of Pres. of Maj. Am. Jewish Orgns., 1963-65, Nat. Conf. Soviet Jewry, 1968-70; pres. Hebrew Coll., Combined Jewish Philanthropies, Boston. Fellow Am. Coll. Trial Lawyers, Am. Bar Found.; mem. Boston Bar Assn. (former mem. council and grievance com., chmn. eminent domain com.), Mass. Bar Assn. (former chmn. grievance com.), Am. Bar Assn. (former mem. standing com. on fed. judiciary), World Peace Through Law Center (human rights com., housing and urban renewal com.). Contbr. articles to profl. jours.; recipient numerous French and U.S. mil. medals and awards. Home: 56 Varick Rd Waban MA 02168 Office: 10 Post Office Sq Boston MA 02109 Tel (617) 482-1390

WEINSTEIN, MAHER JACOB, b. Joplin, Mo., Oct. 18, 1942; B.A., U. Minn., 1963, J.D., 1966. Admitted to Minn. bar, 1966; asso. firm Lifson, Kelber, Abrahamson, Mpls., 1966-69; partner firm Lifson, Kelber, Abrahamson & Weinstein, Mpls., 1970—; exec. dir. Minn. Legal Aid Clinic, 1965-66. Chmn. St. Louis Park (Minn.) Charter Commn., 1971-73; dir. St. Louis Park Sch. Bd., 1973—, chmn., 1975-76; dir. Assn. Met. Sch. Dists., Mpls., 1976—. Mem. Minn. State Bar Assn., Assn. Trial Lawyers Am., Am. Judicature Soc., Phi Delta Phi. Home: 8316 Cedar Lake Rd Saint Louis Park MN 55426 Office: 850 Shelard Plaza Saint Louis Park MN 55426 Tel (612) 544-1521

WEINSTEIN, MATHEW, b. N.Y.C., Apr. 3, 1944; B.B.A., U. Miami, 1965, J.D., 1968. Admitted to Fla. bar, 1968; asso. firm Miller & Mueller, Ft. Lauderdale, Fla., 1969-70; asst. states atty. 11th Jud. Circuit Ct. Fla., 1970-73; asso. firm Courshon & Berk, Miami, Fla., 1973-74; individual practice law, Miami, 1974—. Bd. dirs. Cherry Grove Homeowners Assn., 1974, v.p., 1975-76, mem., 1972—. Mem. South Miami, Am., Fla. bar assns. Home: 9123 SW 96th Ave Miami FL 33176 Office: 7800 Red Rd South Miami FL 33143

WEINSTEIN, MURRAY, b. N.Y.C., June 6, 1928; A.B., Bklyn. Coll., 1949; J.D., Harvard, 1952. Admitted to N.Y. State bar, 1953, U.S. Supreme Ct. bar, 1961; sr. partner firm Weinstein, Chayt & Bard, Bklyn., 1956—; arbitrator N.Y. Civil Ct., 1961—, Am. Arbitration Assn., 1964—. Elected mem. N.Y.C. Community Sch. Bd., 1972-73; pres. Redwood Civic Assn., 1962-64, Temple Shaare Emeth, 1972-74; bd. dirs. Bklyn. Women's Hosp., 1975-76. Mem. N.Y. State, Bklyn. bar assns. Recipient Israel Independence Day award, 1973. Home: 555 E 79th St Brooklyn NY 11236 Office: 26 Court St Brooklyn NY 11242 Tel (212) UL 8-3188

WEINSTEIN, PAUL HAROLD, b. Washington, Apr. 20, 1933; B.S., Washington and Lee U., 1955; LL.B., George Washington U., 1959. Admitted to D.C. bar, 1959, Md. bar, 1965; partner firm Levitan, Ezrin, Cramer, West & Weinstein, and predecessors, Chevy Chase, Md., 1959-72, v.p., 1972—; lectr. in field. Mem. D.C., Montgomery County (chmn. com. unauthorized practice law 1975—) bar assns. Office: 5454 Wisconsin Ave suite 1400 Chevy Chase MD 20015 Tel (301) 656-0915

WEINSTINE, ROBERT ROY, b. St. Paul, Apr. 21, 1944; B.A., U. Minn., 1966, J.D., 1969. Admitted to Minn. bar, 1969; partner firm Oppenheimer, Wolff, Foster, Shepard & Donnelly, St. Paul. Bd. dirs. Jewish Community Center, St. Paul; chmn. bd. visitors Law Sch., U. Minn., 1975-76. Mem. Minn., Ramsey County bar assns., Am. Trial Lawyers Assn. Home: 1089 Overlood Rd Saint Paul MN 55118 Office: 1700 1st Nat Bank Bldg Saint Paul MN 55101 Tel (612) 227-7271

WEINSTOCK, HAROLD, b. Stamford, Conn., Nov. 30, 1925; B.S. magna cum laude, N.Y. U., 1947; J.D., Harvard, 1950. Admitted to Conn. bar, 1950, Ill. bar, 1950, U.S. Supreme Ct. bar, 1955, Calif. bar, 1958; atty. SEC, Washington, 1950-52; spl. atty. Office of Chief Counsel, IRS, Washington, 1952-56; counsel Hunt Foods & Industries, Los Angeles, 1956-58; partner firm Walzer, Weinstock, Manion & King, Los Angeles, 1958—; lectr. estate planning courses extension div. U. Calif. at Los Angeles, 1959—; lectr. Calif. Continuing Edn. of Bar, 1960—, U. So. Calif. Tax Inst., 1963, 69, 70, 71, 76. Mem. Am., Beverly Hills bar assns., State Bar Calif. Author: Planning an Estate, A Guidebook of Principles and Techniques, 1977; contbr. articles to legal jours. Office: 1888 Century Park E Suite 800 Los Angeles CA 90067 Tel (213) 879-4481

WEINSTOCK, KENNETH MARTIN, b. Chgo., Nov. 13, 1927; A.B., U. Mo., 1952, LL.B., St. Louis U., 1956. Admitted to Mo. bar, 1956; asso. firm Markus & Mave, Clayton, Mo., 1963-64; partner firm Feigenbaum & Weinstock, St. Louis, 1964-66; asso. firm James F. Koester, St. Louis, 1966-73; partner firm Saltz & Weinstock, St. Louis, 1973—. Mem. Mo., St. Louis, St. Louis County bar assns., Lawyers Assn. Mo. Home: 1654 Blacksmith Ct Creve Coeur MO 63141 Office: 1015 Locust St Saint Louis MO 63101 Tel (314) 231-1884

WEINSTOCK, LEONARD I., b. N.Y.C., May 15, 1930; B.S., Coll. City N.Y., 1951; LL.B., N.Y. U., 1954. Admitted to N.Y. bar, 1954, U.S. Supreme Ct. bar, 1963; practiced in N.Y.C., 1956—; asso. firms Booth, Lipton & Lipton, 1956, Berley & Berley, 1957; partner firms Newman & Weinstock, 1958-61, Schwartman, Weinstock & Garelik, 1961-70, Weiss Rosenthal Heller Schwartzman & Lazar, and predecessor 1970—. Mem. N.Y.C. Community Planning Bd., 1974—. Mem. Am., New York County, Queens County (vice-chmn. comml. law com.) bar assns. Office: 1-295 Madison Ave New York City NY 10017 Tel (212) 725-9200

WEINTRAUB, CHARLES HARRIS, b. N.Y.C., Jan. 7, 1942; LL.B., N.Y. Law Sch., 1967. Admitted to N.Y. bar, 1967, U.S. Dist. Ct. bar, U.S. Ct. of Appeals bar, 1968; mem. firm Levin & Weintraub, N.Y.C., 1967—; lectr. in field. Mem. Am., Westchester County bar assns., Assn. Bar City N.Y. (sec. 1974-75), N.Y. County Lawyers Assn. (sec. bankruptcy com. 1970-71). Contbr. articles in field to profl. jours. Office: 225 Broadway New York City NY 10007 Tel (212) 962-3300

WEINTRAUB, GARY NORMAN, b. N.Y.C., July 22, 1943; B.A., N.Y. U., 1964, LL.B., 1967. Admitted to N.Y. bar, 1967, U.S. Dist. Ct. Eastern and So. Dist. N.Y. bars, 1969, U.S. Supreme Ct. bar, 1971, U.S. Ct. Appeals 2d Circuit bar, 1973; asso. firm Hart & Hume N.Y.C., 1967-68; asso. firm Feuerstein & Underweiser, N.Y.C., 1968-69, Caputi, Lazar & Faruolo, Huntington, N.Y., 1969; asso. firm Faruolo, Caputi & Weintraub and predecessor firms, 1969-72, partner, 1973—; counsel Suffolk County (N.Y.) Legislature, 1976—. Mem. N.Y. State, Suffolk County bar assns., Nassau-Suffolk Trial Lawyers Assn. Home: 8 Rhetta Ln Port Jefferson Station NY 11776 Office: 44 Elm St Huntington NY 11743 Tel (516) 421-2500

WEINTRAUB, LEONARD M., b. N.Y.C., Sept. 29, 1920; B.S., N.Y. U., 1942, LL.B., 1945. Admitted to N.Y. State bar, 1945; individual practice law, N.Y.C., 1945—. Mem. N.Y.C. Bar Assn., N.Y. Criminal Bar Assn., Am. Trial Lawyers Assn. Home: 1056 Fifth Ave New York City NY 10028 Office: 350 Fifth Ave New York City NY 10001 Tel (212) WI 7-6760

WEINTRAUB, MICHAEL, b. Miami, Fla., June 5, 1938; B.A. in Econs., U. Va., 1960, LL.B., 1963. Admitted to Fla. bar, 1963; partner firm Smathers & Thompson, Miami, 1963—; pres. Pan Am. Bancshares, Inc., Miami, 1969—; sr. v.p., dir. Pan Am. Bank of Miami, 1975—; dir. Pan Am. Bank of Orlando, N.A. (Fla.). Trustee Mt. Sinai Med. Center; bd. dirs. Miami Heart Inst.; adv. bd. Variety Children's Hosp. Mem. Am., Fla., Dade County bar assns., Am. Judicature Soc., Fla. Bankers Assn. (1st v.p. 1976—). Office: 150 SE 3d Ave Miami FL 33131 Tel (305) 577-5425

WEINTRAUB, STEWART MARVIN, b. N.Y.C., Oct. 16, 1945; B.S. in Bus. Adminstrn., Drexel U., 1968; J.D., Temple U., 1971. Admitted to Pa. bar, 1971, U.S. Dist. Ct. for Eastern Pa. bar, 1973; since practiced in Phila.; asso. firm S. Regen Ginsburg, 1971-72; asst. city solicitor, City of Phila., 1972—. Mem. Am., Pa., Phila. bar assns., Lawyers Club Phila., B'nai B'rith (mem. Phila. regional advisory bd. anti-defamation league 1972—), Phi Alpha Delta. Contbr. articles to law jours. Home: 267 Hendrix St Philadelphia PA 19116 Office: 1500 Municipal Services Bldg Philadelphia PA 19107 Tel (215) MU6-5253

WEINTRAUB, WILLIAM, b. Bklyn., Feb. 18, 1912; B.S., N.Y. U., 1932, J.D., 1934. Admitted to N.Y. bar, 1935, U.S. Supreme Ct. bar, 1958, U.S. Tax Ct. bar, 1963; individual practice law, Bklyn., 1935—; gen. counsel, dir. Coney Island C. of C., 1970-76. Bd. dirs. YMCA-YWCA, Coney Island, Bklyn., 1970-76. Mem. Am., N.Y. State, Bklyn. bar assns. Office: 1329 Surf Ave Coney Island Brooklyn NY 11224 Tel (212) 372-0800

WEIR, PETER FRANK, b. Stuttgart, Ger., Mar. 26, 1933; came to U.S., 1941, naturalized, 1947; B.A., Williams Coll., 1955; LL.B., Harvard U., 1958; M.B.A., N.Y. U., 1967. Admitted to N.Y. bar, 1959, Ga. bar, 1957; asso. firm Cole & Deitz, N.Y.C., 1959-66, partner 1966—. Mem. steering com. N.Y. Council Episcopal Ch. Found., 1976—, active in parish. Mem. N.Y. State, N.Y. County, Am. bar assns., Assn. Bar City N.Y., Am. Arbitration Assn. (nat. panel arbitrators). Office: 40 Wall St New York City NY 10005 Tel (212) 269-2500

WEIR, WILLIAM JOHN ARNOLD, b. Phoenix, June 22, 1939; B.S., U. Calif., Berkeley, 1965; J.D., Hastings Coll. Law, U. Calif., 1968. Admitted to Calif. bar, 1968, since practiced in San Francisco; asso. firm Angell, Adams & Holmes, 1968-69; counsel Bank of Am., 1969-75, v.p., 1974-75, asst. gen. counsel, 1976; partner firm Cowans & Murphy, 1976—; lectr. exec. program U. Calif. at Davis Extension. Mem. Am., Calif., San Francisco bar assns. Arthur Newhouse grantee, 1966-67. Office: 555 California St San Francisco CA 94104 Tel (415) 398-4700

WEIR, WILLIAM PATTON, b. Hobbs, N.Mex., Feb. 17, 1940; B.A., So. Meth. U., 1962, LL.B., 1964. Admitted to Tex. bar, 1964; partner firm Tuchin & Weir, Ft. Worth, 1964-69, Weir Gudgen & Brown, 1969—. Mem. Ft. Worth-Tarrant County Bar, Ft. Worth-Tarrant County Jr. Bar, Am. Bar Assn. (certificate of performance sect. young lawyers 1969), State Bar Tex., Tex. Trial Lawyers Assn. Home: 3832 Ridgehaven Fort Worth TX 76116 Office: 705 Commerce Bldg Fort Worth TX 76116 Tel (817) 332-1501

WEIS, BYRON HERBERT, b. Chgo., May 9, 1935; B.A. cum laude in History, U. Colo., 1957; J.D., U. Mich., 1960. Admitted to Ill. bar, 1960; examiner Chgo. Title & Trust Co., 1960; asso. firm Welfeld, Fleischman & Chaimson, Chgo., 1963-68; partner firm Weis & Pollock, Chgo., 1968—; pres., dir. Wishy Washy Auto Laundry, Chgo., 1968-74, Odd Oz Amusements, Chgo., 1972—; treas., dir. Donnell Co., St. Petersburg, Fla., 1975—; dir. Bake Rite Baking Co., Plover, Wis., 1976—. Exec. dir. Chgo. Crusade of Mercy, 1960-61; chmn. South Side Youth Center, Chgo., 1971-72, Camp Henry Horner, 1972-73; bd. dirs. Young Men's Jewish Council, 1963-73. Mem. Ill., Chgo. bar assns. Home: 17 Sheffield Ct Deerfield IL 60015 Office: 224 N Ada St Chicago IL 60607 Tel (312) 226-6100

WEIS, JOSEPH FRANCIS, JR., b. Pitts., Mar. 12, 1923; B.A., Duquesne U., 1941-47; J.D., U. Pitts., 1950. Admitted to Pa. bar, 1951, U.S. Supreme Ct. bar, 1968; mem. firm Sherriff, Lindsay, Weis & McGinnis, Pitts., 1950-52; partner firm Weis & Weis, Pitts., 1952-68; judge Allegheny County (Pa.) Ct. of Common Pleas, 1968-70, U.S. Dist. Ct., Western Dist. Pa., 1970-73, U.S. Ct. Appeals, 3d Circuit, 1973—. Trustee Pitts. Hosp., 1969-72, Forbes Hosp. System, Pitts., 1972-74; mem. bd. adminstrn. Diocese of Pitts., 1971—; mem. bd. mental health and retardation Allegheny County, 1972-73. Fellow Internat. Acad. Trial Lawyers (hon.); mem. Acad. Trial Lawyers Allegheny County (pres. 1966), Allegheny County (v.p. 1966-68), Pa., Am. bar assns., Am. Judicature Soc., Pitts. Acad. Legal Medicine. Decorated Bronze Star, Purple Heart with oak leaf cluster; recipient award for outstanding service St. Thomas More Soc., 1971. Home: 225 Hillcrest Rd Pittsburgh PA 15238 Office: 513 US Courthouse Pittsburgh PA 15219 Tel (412) 644-3552

WEISBERG, GERARD MAXWELL, b. Bklyn., Aug. 1, 1925; B.A., St. John's U., Bklyn., 1946; J.D. (Harlan Fiske Stone scholar), Columbia, 1948; LL.M., Bklyn. Law Sch., 1966. Admitted to N.Y. bar, 1948, U.S. Supreme Ct. bar, 1971; asso. firms, N.Y.C., 1948-60; individual practice law, N.Y.C., 1960-62; judge N.Y.C. Criminal Ct., 1969—; adj. lectr. law City U. N.Y., 1974—, lectr. labor relations N.Y. U., 1977—; commr. N.Y.C. Dept. Consumer Affairs, 1968-69, N.Y.C. Dept. Markets, 1966-68. Mem. N.Y. State, Bklyn. bar assns., New York County Lawyers Assn. Recipient citations for community and pub. service Treasury Dept., 1943, Fedn. Jewish Philanthropies, 1967, State of Ky., 1968. Home: 2301 Kings Hwy Brooklyn NY 11229 Office: 120 Schermerhorn St Brooklyn NY 11201 Tel (212) 643-8400

WEISBERG, MORRIS L., b. Phila., June 7, 1921; B.A., U. Pa., 1943, LL.B., 1947; M.A., Yale, 1944. Admitted to Pa. bar, 1950, Fed. bar, 1950; asso. with Harry N. Ball, Phila., 1950-56; asso. firm Blank, Rome, Klaus & Comisky, Phila., 1956-60, partner, 1960—; Bigelow Teaching fellow Law Sch., U. Chgo., 1947-48; Raymond grad. fellow, 1948-49; instr. U. Pa. Law Sch., 1949-50. Mem. Phila., Pa., Am. bar assns., World Peace Through Law, Order Coif, Phi Beta Kappa. Home: 512 Prescott Rd Merion Station PA 19066 Office: 4 Penn Center Plaza Bldg 11th Floor Philadelphia PA 19103 Tel (215) 569-3700

WEISBERGER, JOSEPH ROBERT, b. Providence, Aug. 3, 1920; A.B. magna cum laude, Brown U., 1942; J.D., Harvard, 1949; LL.D., Suffolk U., 1973, Mt. St. Joseph's Coll., 1973, R.I. Coll., 1974. Admitted to Mass. bar, 1949, R.I. bar, 1950, U.S. Supreme Ct. bar, 1960; individual practice law, Providence, 1950-51; mem. firm Quinn & Quinn, Providence, 1951-56; judge R.I. Superior Ct., 1956—, presiding justice, 1972—; mem. R.I. Senate, 1953-56, majority leader, 1955-56; mem. faculty Nat. Coll. State Judiciary, 1966—; bd. dirs. Nat. Center for State Cts.; v.p. Blue Cross of R.I., 1966-70, dir., 1962—; mem. R.I. Gov.'s Advisory Commn. on Corrections, Supervisory bd. R.I. Gov.'s Justice Commn., R.I. Gov.'s Commn. on Malpractice, Legis. Commn. to Study Criminal Procedures; chmn. R.I. Gov.'s Advisory Commn. on Corrections, New Eng. Regional Commn. on Disordered Offender, R.I. Com. on Adoption of Rules of Criminal Procedure. Mem. pres.'s council Providence Coll.; trustee R.I. Hosp., Providence, St. Joseph's Hosp., Providence; vice chmn. bd. trustees R.I. Health Services Research, Inc. Mem. Am. (ho. of dels. 1973-74, chmn. editorial bd. Judges' Jour. 1973-75), R.I. bar assns., Am. Judicature Soc., Inst. Jud. Adminstrn., Harvard Law Sch. Assn. R.I. (pres. 1974-75), Phi Beta Kappa. Decorated Knight of St. Gregory His Holiness Pope Paul VI. Home: 60 Winthrop St East Providence RI 02915 Office: Providence County Courthouse Providence RI 20903 Tel (401) 277-3212

WEISBERGER, SEYMOUR HARVEY, b. South Bend, Ind., Mar. 17, 1905; A.B., U. Notre Dame, 1926, LL.B., 1928. Admitted to Ind. bar, 1930; individual practice law, South Bend, 1928—; pros. atty. St. Joseph County (Ind.), 1932-36; dep. securities commr. State of Ind., 1937. Pres. Ind. B'nai B'rith, 1934-35. Mem. St. Joseph County Bar Assn. Home: 128 S Hawthorne Dr South Bend IN 46617 Office: 218 Odd Fellows Bldg South Bend IN 46601 Tel (219) 232-5988

WEISEL, BEN, b. Chgo., Oct. 13, 1914; B.S., Northwestern U., 1939; J.D. cum laude, Southwestern U., 1956. Admitted to Calif. bar, 1956; employee IRS, Calif., Ill. and Washington, 1935-70; individual practice law, Los Angeles, 1972—. Certified specialist in taxation law. Mem. Am., Calif., Los Angeles County, Beverly Hills bar assns., Am. Inst. C.P.A.'s, Calif., Ill. socs. C.P.A.'s, C.P.A., Ill., Calif. Office: 1888 Century Park E Suite 900 Los Angeles CA 90067 Tel (213) 553-6643

WEISENBURGER, THOMAS EDWARD, b. Toledo, May 27, 1936; Ph.B., U. Detroit, 1958; J.D., U. Santa Clara, 1961. Admitted to Ohio bar, 1972; mgr., dir., shareholder, sec. Cline, Bischoff & Cook Co., Toledo, 1962—; sec., dir. Knight Realty Co., Gavin & Assos., Inc.; partner OH-EL Co., Urban Properties, Artoho Co. Pres. Toledo Old Newsboys Goodfellow Assn., Republican Club Lucas County, 1972, Toledo Council Cath. Youth, 1961-65; mem. Ohio Rep. Central Com. Mem. Am., Ohio, Toledo bar assns. Home: 2916 River Rd Maumee OH 43537 Office: 420 Security Bldg Toledo OH 43604 Tel (419) 255-8800

WEISENFELD, JOSEPH JEFFREY, b. N.Y.C., Apr. 23, 1941; B.A., U. So. Calif., 1962; J.D., Columbia, 1965. Admitted to N.Y. State bar, 1966; staff Legal Aid Soc., N.Y.C., 1966-69; mem. firm Sackstein, Saftler, Fox & Kaplain, N.Y.C., 1970-72; individual practice law, N.Y.C., 1972—; dir. N.Y. State Phys. Therapists Assn., 1972. Mem. N.Y. County Lawyers Assn. Asso. editor Criminal Law Bull. 1969-70. Office: 401 Broadway New York City NY 10013 Tel (212) 925-8844

WEISENFREUND, MARC WINFIELD, b. N.Y.C., Dec. 24, 1945; A.B., N.Y. U., 1967; postgrad. St. John's U. Sch. Law, 1967-69. Admitted to N.Y. bar, 1972, U.S. Dist. Ct. bar, 1973, U.S. Ct. Appeals bar, 1973; law clk. firm Berlin, Berelson & Rothaus, N.Y.C., 1969-72; corp. counsel and asst. to pres. Lomart Industries, N.Y.C., 1972-74; resident counsel and corp. sec. Gray Mfg. Co., Englewood Cliffs, N.J., 1974-76; partner firm Weisenfreund and Sherer, N.Y.C., 1976—; lectr. in field. Gen. Counsel N.Y. Gray Panthers; mem. Active Corps Execs. SBA. Mem. Chemists Club N.Y.C., Newcomen Soc. N.Am., Am., N.Y. State bar assns., Assn. Bar City N.Y., N.Y. County Lawyers Assn. Office: Weisenfreund and Sherer 400 Madison Ave New York City NY 10017 Tel (212) 758-5900

WEISENSEE, LAWRENCE ANTHONY, b. Sioux Falls, S.D., Sept. 10, 1938; student Notre Dame, 1956-58; B.A., U. S.D., 1962, LL.B., 1964; LL.M., Emory U., 1974. Admitted to S.D. bar, 1964, Calif. bar, 1970, U.S. Supreme Ct. bar, 1970, Ga. bar, 1974; asst. atty. gen. State of S.D., 1965-67, spl. prosecutor, 1967-69; sr. atty. Chief Counsels Office, IRS, Los Angeles, 1970-72, Atlanta, 1972-74; of counsel firm Henkel & Lamon, Atlanta, 1974-76; partner firm Garland, Nuckolls, Kadish, Cook, & Weisensee, Atlanta, 1976—. Mem. Nat. Dist. Attys. Assn. (nat. dir. 1968-69), Am. Bar Assn., Am. Assn. Trial Lawyers. Editor-in-chief: S.D. Law Rev., 1963-64. Home: 6764 Covington Rd Lithonia GA 30058 Office: 1012 Candler Bldg Atlanta GA 30303 Tel (404) 577-2225

WEISER, THEODORE T., b. N.Y.C., June 23, 1917; LL.B., St. Lawrence U., 1940; LL.M. magna cum laude, Bklyn. Law Sch., 1945. Admitted to N.Y. bar, 1941, N.J. bar, 1969; individual practice law, N.Y.C., 1942—; counsel Nationwide Ins. Cos., N.Y.C., 1956—; gen. counsel Bakers Mut. Ins. Co. N.Y., N.Y.C., 1960—, sec., 1976—; asso. police justice Lynbrook (N.Y.), 1957-59. Mem. Am., N.Y. State, N.J. State, Nassau County, Queens County, N.Y. County bar assns., Def. Assn., N.Y.C., Am. trial lawyers assns., Bklyn. Law Sch. Alumni Assn. (v.p.). Home: 24 N Lake Shore Dr Rockaway NJ 07866 Office: 8 Freer St Lynbrook NY 11563 Tel (516) 599-4134 also 769 Northfield Ave West Orange NJ 07052 Tel (201) 325-0033

WEISLER, MAX X., b. N.Y.C., July 27, 1931; B.A. cum laude, Dartmouth, 1953; J.D., Harvard, 1956. Admitted to N.Y. bar, 1956; asso. firm Angulo, Cooney, Marsh & Ouchterloney, N.Y.C., 1956-57, Weisler, Griffith, & Weisler, N.Y.C., 1957-73, Blum, Ross, Weisler, Bergstein & Golden, Lawrence, N.Y., 1973—. Mem. Nassau County Bar Assn. Home: 3 Dogwood Ln Lawrence NY 11559 Office: 389 Central Ave Lawrence NY 11559 Tel (516) 569-3900

WEISMAN, DAVID BADER, b. Columbus, Ohio, Apr. 6, 1935; B.A., Ohio Wesleyan U., 1957; J.D., U. Mich., 1960. Admitted to Ind. bar, 1960, Mich., 1960; asso. firm Jones, Obenchain, Johnson, Ford & Pankow, South Bend, Ind., 1960-62; individual practice law, South Bend, 1963—; dep. pros. atty., St. Joseph County (Ind.), 1963-66; atty. for Area Plan Commn. St. Joseph County, 1966—. Chmn. St. Joseph County chpt. ARC, 1974-76; pres. St. Joseph County chpt. Nat. Found., 1966; trustee, ruling elder Sunnyside Presbyterian Ch., South Bend, 1969-74. Mem. Am., Ind., St. Joseph County bar assns., Am. Trial Lawyers Assn. Home: 533 N Coquillard Dr South Bend IN 46617 Office: Tower Bldg 216 W Washington Ave South Bend IN 46601 Tel (219) 233-1151

WEISMAN, DAVID S., b. Waterbury, Conn., May 15, 1934; J.D. magna cum laude, U. San Fernando Valley, 1969. Admitted to Calif. bar, 1970, U.S. Supreme Ct. bar, 1975; mem. firm Katz & Weisman, Los Angeles, 1970—; adj. prof. Western State U., Anaheim, Calif., 1970-72, U. San Fernando Valley Coll. of Law, Sepulveda, Calif., 1971—; judge pro tem Los Angeles Municipal Ct., 1975—. Mem. Am., Los Angeles County, Beverly Hills, Century City bar assns. Office: 1880 Century Park E Suite 615 Los Angeles CA 90067 Tel (213) 553-4500

WEISMANN, HENRY CONRAD, b. Smithtown, N.Y., Mar. 12, 1921; student, Norwich Univ., 1938-40; LL.B., Bklyn. U., 1947. Admitted to N.Y. State bar, 1947; partner firm Weismann, Meyer & Wexler, Smithtown, N.Y., 1951-65, firm Weismann & Chekenian, Smithtown, 1967-72; individual practice law, Smithtown, 1972—; counsel Suffolk County Bd. Suprs., 1962; village atty. Nissequoque, 1953-60, chmn. bd. appeals, 1970-73. Chmn. Smithtown Republican Com., 1960-64. Mem. Suffolk County Bar Assn. Home: Apt G-3 Fairhaven Dr West Nesconset NY 11767 Office: 145 W Main St Smithtown NY 11787 Tel (516) 265-7575

WEISS, ALVIN LEWIS, b. Pottstown, Pa., July 19, 1926; B.A., Ursinus Coll., 1949; J.D., Columbia U., 1952. Admitted to Pa. bar, 1953; asso. firm Rutter, O'Donnell & Mauger, Pottstown, 1952-55; partner firm O'Donnell, Weiss, Mattei, Koury & Suchoza, Pottstown, 1955—. Pres., chmn. Pottstown Area United Way, 1974-75; pres. Congregation Mercy and Truth, 1958-62, Pottstown Pub. Library, 1972-77. Mem. Am., Pa., Montgomery County bar assns. Home: Logan Ct Apt 301B Pottstown PA 19464 Office: 41 High St Pottstown PA 19464 Tel (215) 323-2800

WEISS, ARNOLD, b. N.Y.C., Oct. 11, 1923; B.E.E., Cornell U., 1947; LL.B., U. Buffalo, 1950, J.D., 1968. Admitted to N.Y. State bar, 1950, U.S. Supreme Ct. bar, 1955; partner firm Raichle, Banning, Weiss and Halpern, Buffalo, 1950—. Trustee, sec. Amherst Synagogue, Buffalo, 1968—; trustee, pres. Kahaal Nahalot Israel, Buffalo, 1971—; trustee United Jewish Fedn. Buffalo, 1975—; pres. Buffalo Bur. Jewish Edn., 1976. Mem. Am., N.Y. State, Erie County bar assns. Pub., Buffalo Jewish Rev., 1971—. Recipient Chasan Torah award Chinuch Atzmai, 1971. Home: 9 Park Forest Dr Buffalo NY 14221 Office: 10 Lafayette Sq Buffalo NY 14203 Tel (716) 852-7587

WEISS, BRUCE MARSHALL, b. Jersey City, Mar. 28, 1935; B.B.A., Golden Gate U., 1964; J.D., U. Calif. at San Francisco, 1967. Admitted to Calif. bar, 1967; pub. defender Contra Costa County (Calif.), 1968-71, supervising atty., 1971-75, chief dep. pub. defender, 1975—. Vol., San Francisco Own Recognizance Release Project, 1966. Mem. Calif., Richmond County bar assns. Home: 1883 San Lorenzo Ave Berkeley CA 94707 Office: 610 Court St Martinez CA 94553 Tel (415) 372-2490

WEISS, DAVID ARTHUR, b. Albany, N.Y., Dec. 16, 1943; B.S., Rensselaer Poly. Inst., 1965; J.D., N.Y. U., 1968. Admitted to N.Y. bar, 1968; individual practice law, Schenectady, 1969-77; asst. counsel N.Y. State Tchrs. Retirement System, 1977—. Mem. N.Y. State, Schenectady County bar assns. Home: 610 Maywood Ave Schenectady NY 12303 Tel (518) 355-4803

WEISS, DONALD PAUL, b. Bklyn., May 19, 1934; B.S., U. Pa., 1955; J.D., Tulane U., 1961. Admitted to La. bar, 1961; asso. firm Wiener Weiss & Madison, Shreveport, La., 1961-64, partner, 1964—. Pres., Shreveport Assn. for the Blind, 1971, Shreveport Jewish Fedn., 1967, Southfield Sch., 1971; bd. dirs. Caddo Found. for Exceptional Children, Goodwill Industries, Shreveport Regional Arts Council. Mem. Am., La., Shreveport bar assns., Shreveport C. of C. (dir.), Order of Coif, Beta Gamma Sigma, Omicron Delta Kappa. Home: 641 Longleaf Dr Shreveport LA 71106 Tel (318) 226-9100

WEISS, DUDLEY ALBERT, b. Boston, May 17, 1912; B.A. magna cum laude, Harvard, 1934, J.D., 1937. Admitted to Mass. bar, 1937; partner firm Mahoney, Bryer, Coffin & Weiss (now Mahoney Weiss & Brock), Boston, 1950-67, Weiss, Zimmerman & Angoff, Boston, 1967—; price atty., regional price economist Office Price Adminstrn., 1942-46; regional economist Office Econ. Stblzn., 1950. Mem. Am. Arbitration Assn. (nat. panel arbitrators), Am., Mass., Middlesex, Boston, Norfolk bar assns., Am. Judicature Soc. Home: 50 Philbrick Rd Newton Centre MA 02159 Office: 50 Congress St Boston MA 02109 Tel (617) 227-9610

WEISS, HOWARD ALLEN, b. Chgo., July 30, 1924; student Harvard, 1941-43, LL.B., J.D., 1952; B.S., U.S. Naval Acad., 1946. Admitted to Mass. bar, 1952, Fla. bar, 1954, Ill. bar, 1958; asso. Voluntary Defenders Com., Boston, 1952-54, firm Kovner & Mannheimer, Miami Beach, Fla., 1955-57, firm David Altman, Chgo., 1957-64; partner firm Altman, Kurlander & Weiss, Chgo., 1964-74; of counsel firm Katten, Muchin, Giles, Pearl, Davis, and Galler, Chgo., 1974—. Bd. dirs. Louis A. Weiss Meml. Hosp., Chgo., 1959—, Jewish United Fund., Chgo., 1971—. Mem. Am., Ill., Fla., Chgo. bar assns. Home: 1040 Lake Shore Dr Chicago IL 60611 Office: Suite 4100 55 E Monroe St Chicago IL 60603 Tel (312) FI 6-7400

WEISS, JOHN CARROLL, JR., b. Balt., May 26, 1926; J.D., U. Md., 1952. Admitted to Md. bar, 1953; individual practice law, Balt., 1953—; custom-house broker, Balt., 1953—; social security policy supr. Social Security Adminstrn., Balt. and Washington, 1958—. Various positions Boy Scouts Am., Balt., 1952—; bd. dirs., pres. Roland Park Swimming Pool, 1970-75. Mem. Am. Bar Assn., U. Md. Alumni Assn. Home: 4213 Wickford Rd Baltimore MD 21210 Office: 1201 Fidelity Bldg Baltimore MD 21201 Tel (301) 752-4660

WEISS, JULIUS, b. N.Y.C., Mar. 1, 1894; A.B., Coll. City N.Y., 1915; LL.B., Columbia, 1918. Admitted to N.Y. State bar, 1919, U.S. Supreme Ct. bar, 1960; sr. partner firm Weiss, Rosenthal, Heller, Schwartzman & Lazar, 1973—; dir. IDB Bankholding Corp., PEC Israel Econ. Corp., Paul Uhlich & Co., Inc., Park Lexington Co. Chmn. law com. Westchester County Democratic Com., N.Y., 1936-73; mem. New Rochelle (N.Y.) Recreation Com., 1951-52; mem. New Rochelle bd. edn., 1942-57, pres., 1951-54; trustee Westchester (N.Y.) Community Coll., 1975—, Heckscher Found. for Children, PEF Israel Endowment Funds, Westchester Community Coll. Found. Home: 66 Crawford Terr New Rochelle NY 10804 Office: 295 Madison Ave New York City NY 10017 Tel (212) 725-9200

WEISS, LEONARD, b. N.Y.C., Dec. 20, 1924; B.S., N.Y. U., 1948, J.D., N.Y. Law Sch., 1950. Admitted to N.Y. bar, 1951, U.S. Supreme Ct. bar, 1971; partner firm, Avstreih, Martino & Weiss, Mt. Vernon, N.Y., 1957—; asst. corp. counsel Mt. Vernon, 1959-60. Mem. Mt. Vernon, Westchester County bar assns. Home: 11 Stratton Rd Scarsdale NY 10583 Office: 20 East First St Mount Vernon NY 10550 Tel (914) 668-5506

WEISS, LEONARD ARYE, b. Rochester, Pa., Aug. 4, 1923; grad. U. Buffalo, 1946; J.D., Union U., 1948. Admitted to N.Y. bar, 1948; individual practice law, No. dist. N.Y., 1948; pres. P.T.F. Health Ins. Co., N.Y.C., 1974—; dir. Community State Bank, Albany, N.Y. Bd. dirs. Albany Jewish Community Council. Mem. Albany County Bar Assn., N.Y. State Trial Lawyers Assn. Home: 190 Marion Ave Albany NY 12208 Office: 100 State St Albany NY 12207 Tel (518) 463-6688

WEISS, MARK ANSCHEL, b. N.Y.C., June 20, 1937; A.B., Columbia U., 1958; LL.B. magna cum laude, Harvard, 1961. Admitted to N.Y. State bar, 1961, D.C. bar, 1962, U.S. Supreme Ct. bar, 1965; asso. firm Covington and Burling, Washington, 1961-66, 69-70, partner, 1970—; spl. asst. to under sec. U.S. Dept. Treasury, Washington, 1966-68, spl. asst. to sec., 1968-69. Mem. Am., D.C., Fed. bar assns. Home: 8811 Brierly Rd Chevy Chase MD 20015 Office: 888 16th St NW Washington DC 20006 Tel (202) 452-6000

WEISS, NORMAN EMANUEL, b. Daytona Beach, Fla., Apr. 12, 1926; B.S., U.S. Mil. Acad., 1946; B.S., U. Loyola, Los Angeles, 1951-53. Admitted to Pa. bar, 1960; v.p. Triangle Shoe Co., Kingston, Pa., 1953-72; pres. Weiss Devel. Corp., Kingston, 1972—; v.p. Ocala Hotel Corp., Kingston, 1955—; pres. The Mushroom Farm, Inc., Mt. Pocono, Pa., 1973—; trustee Peoples Nat. Bank of Edwardsville, 1958—; mng. trustee Narrows Realty Co., Kingston, 1958—. Trustee, Wyoming Valley council Boy Scouts Am., 1962-72, Mercy Hosp., Wilkes Coll. Mem. Wilkes-Barre Law and Library Assn. Home: 57 Gersham Pl Kingston PA 18704 Office: Narrows Shopping Center Kingston PA 18704

WEISS, PHILIP DAVID, b. Norristown, Pa., Oct. 8, 1934; A.B. cum laude, Lafayette Coll., 1955; LL.B., Yale, 1960. Admitted to Pa. bar, 1961, U.S. Supreme Ct. bar, 1972; asso. firm Duffy McTighe & McElhone, Norristown, Pa., 1961-66, partner, 1966-67; partner firm McTighe Koch Brown & Weiss, Norristown, 1966-72, firm McTighe Mullaney Weiss Bonner Stewart & O'Neill, Norristown, 1972—; instr. in legal research, Yale, 1959-60. Treas. Eagleville (Pa.) Hosp.; mem. bd. Montgomery County Mental Health/Mental Retardation Emergency Service; mem. bd. Norristown Jewish Community Center; chmn. large gifts Norristown Allied Jewish Appeal. Mem. Pa. (mem. workmen's compensation survey com.), Am. (chmn. profl. liability com., mem. advocacy com., gen. practice sect.), Montgomery County (past bd. mem.) bar assns., Am. Judicature Soc., Montgomery County Estate Planning Council (past pres.), Pa. Def. Inst. Contbr. articles to legal jours. Home: 10 Scarlet Oak Dr Lafayette Hill PA 19444 Office: 11 E Airy St Norristown PA 19401 Tel (215) 275-6805

WEISS, S. JOSHUA, b. Windsor, Ont., Can., Jan. 8, 1922; B.C.S., Roosevelt U., 1944; J.D., N.Y. Law Sch., 1955. Individual practice accounting, Chgo., 1944, N.Y.C., 1946-55; admitted to N.Y. bar, 1955; partner firm Koenigsberg & Weiss, N.Y.C., 1955-57; individual practice law, N.Y.C., 1957-62; partner firm Gershbaum & Weiss, N.Y.C., 1962—; hearing examiner Traffic Dept. N.Y.C., 1970-72. Mem. Am. Bar Assn., N.Y. County Lawyers Assn. Office: 305 Broadway New York City NY 10007 Tel (212) DI9-4128

WEISS, STEPHEN JOEL, b. N.Y.C., Sept. 12, 1938; B.S., Queens Coll., 1959; LL.B., Cornell U., 1962; LL.M., Georgetown U., 1966. Admitted to N.Y. bar, 1963, D.C. bar, 1966; atty. SEC, 1962-65; asso. firm Arent, Fox, Kintner, Plotkin & Kahn, Washington, 1965-70, partner, 1971—; lt. JAGC, U.S. Navy, 1964-69; lectr. Am. Law Inst., Practicing Law Inst., Fed. Bar Assn., Bur. Nat. Affairs, confs. sponsored by Am. Hotel and Motel Assn., Am. Land Devel. Assn. Mem. Am. Law Inst., Fed. (chmn. securities law com. 1968-70, chmn. council on financing and taxation 1971-72, exec. council securities law com. 1970—, mem. nat. council 1972—, chmn. publs. bd. 1977—), Am. (fed. regulation of securities com. 1970—) bar assns., Cornell Law Club of Washington (pres. 1971—). Contbr. articles to legal jours. Office: Fed Bar Bldg 1815 H St NW Washington DC 20006 Tel (202) 347-8500

WEISS, STEPHEN LOUIS, b. Chgo., Nov. 24, 1941; B.S. in Econs., U. Pa., 1962; LL.B., Yale, 1965. Admitted to Ariz. bar, 1965; asso. firm Langerman, Begam & Lewis, Phoenix, 1965-67, Dushoff, Sacks & Corcoran, Phoenix, 1968-69, Gorey & Ely, Phoenix, 1970-72, partner, 1973-75; partner firm Ely & Bettini, Phoenix, 1976—. Mem. State Bar Ariz., Maricopa County Bar Assn., Am., Ariz., Phoenix trial lawyers assns., Am. Arbitration Assn., Phi Alpha Delta. Home: 6630 Majorca Ln E Phoenix AZ 85016 Office: 904 Arizona Title Bldg Phoenix AZ 85003 Tel (602) 258-8404

WEISS, STEPHEN MARK, b. Phila., Mar. 11, 1943; student Pa. State U., 1960-62; B.A., U. Ariz., 1965, J.D., 1968. Admitted to Ariz. bar, 1968, U.S. Supreme Ct. bar, 1974; staff atty. Papago Legal Services, Sells, Ariz., 1968-69; dep. county atty. criminal div. Pima County (Ariz.), 1970-74; partner firm Stolkin, Weiss & Tandy, Tucson, 1974—. Mem. Am., Pima County bar assns., Am. Trial Lawyers Assn. Home: 9218 E 28th St Tucson AZ 85710 Office: Suite 1200 Home Fed Tower 32 North Stone St Tucson AZ 85701 Tel (602) 882-9705

WEISS, THEODORE FRANCIS, b. Gonzales, Tex., Sept. 16, 1906; A.B., U. Tex., 1928, LL.B. summa cum laude, 1930; Admitted to Tex. bar, 1930, U.S. Supreme Ct. bar, 1953; individual practice law, San Antonio, 1930—; spl. asso. justice San Antonio Ct. Civil Appeals, 1938; chmn. Labor Law Inst., Southwestern Bar Found., 1958; dir. Bank of San Antonio, Santone Industries, Inc., Richardson Paint Co., Painting Specialist Equipment Co. Chmn., San Antonio Zoning Bd., 1938-40; pres. San Antonio Community Chest, 1947; bd. dirs. Children's Hosp. Found. Mem. Am., San Antonio (pres. 1938) bar assns., State Bar Tex. (chmn. labor law sect. 1955), Am. Judicature Soc., Order of Coif, Phi Beta Kappa. Home: 234 Cardinal St San Antonio TX 78209 Office: 1307 Nat Bank of Commerce Bldg San Antonio TX 78205 Tel (512) 227-1244

WEISS, VAN, b. Norristown, Pa., Sept. 13, 1939; B.A., Ursinus Coll., Collegeville, Pa., 1961; J.D., Temple U., 1964; M.A., Villanova U., 1967. Admitted to Pa. bar, 1965; asso. firm Quinlan, Torak & DeYoung, King of Prussia, Pa., 1965-69, firm Torak & DeYoung, King of Prussia, 1969-72; individual practice law, Norristown, Pa., 1972—; instr. Ursinus Coll., 1967—; asst. pub. defender Montgomery County (Pa.), 1973—. Chmn. Upper Merion Twp. Planning Commn., Montgomery County, Pa., 1975—. Mem. Am., Pa., Montgomery County bar assns. Office: 617 Swede St Norristown PA 19401 Tel (215) 272-2586

WEISS, VICTOR FRANK, b. Sheboygan, Wis., Aug. 29, 1922; Ph.D., U. Wis., 1940; LL.B., Harvard, 1947. Admitted to Wis. bar, 1947, Calif. bar, 1949; asso. firm Hersch & Morse, Milw., 1947-48; individual practice law, Sheboygan, 1972—. Mem. Wis., Calif. bar assns., Harvard Law Sch. Assn. Home and office: 1430 Geele Ave Sheboygan WI 53081 Tel (414) 452-0115

WEISSBURG, CARL IVAN, b. Braddock, Pa., Dec. 10, 1930; A.A., U. Calif., Los Angeles, 1950; B.A. with honors, 1954; J.D., U. Calif., Berkeley, 1957. Admitted to Calif. bar, 1958, U.S. Supreme Ct. bar, 1975; partner firm Manasse & Weissburg, Los Angeles, 1958-62; individual practice law, Los Angeles, 1963-64; partner firm Memel, Memel, Jacobs & Weissburg, Los Angeles, 1964-70, firm Weissburg, Jacobs & Gerst, Los Angeles, 1970-74, firm Weissburg & Aronson, 1974—; exec. dir., legal counsel United Hosp. Assn., Los Angeles; gen. counsel Fedn. Am. Hosps., Washington. Mem. Physician and Hosp. Conf., Calif. Regional Med. Programs, Statewide Task Force, Calif. Office Comprehensive State Planning. Mem. Am., Calif. bar assns., Am. Soc. Hosp. Attys., Nat. Health Lawyers Assn., Soc. Law and Medicine. Contbr. articles to legal jours. Home: 831 Manning Ave Los Angeles CA 90024 Office: 1901 Ave of the Stars Suite 1400 Los Angeles CA 90067

WEISSBURG, ELMER STANLEY, b. Chgo., Feb. 25, 1922; A.B., U. Calif., Berkeley, 1947, LL.B., J.D., 1962. Admitted to Calif. bar, 1963; asso. firm Yonemura & Yosaki, Oakland, Calif., 1963; probate commr. appellate div., research clk. Superior Ct. referee, Alameda County, Calif., 1963-64; asso. firm Hollander, Lipian, Horwitz & Kornfield, Oakland, 1964-67; individual practice law, Oakland, 1967-69, Dana Point, Calif., 1972—. Bd. dirs. San Clemente Community Theater, Dana Point C. of C. Mem. South Orange County Bar Assn. (pres.). Author: The Law of Open Space, 1962. Office: 34177 Coast Hwy Dana Point CA 92629 Tel (714) 496-8456

WEISSER, EMIL EMMANUEL, b. Bklyn., Nov. 24, 1907; B.C.S., N.Y. U., 1928, J.D., 1931. Admitted to N.J. bar, 1932, since practiced in Paterson; commr. parks, Paterson, 1950-53, commr. alcoholic beverage control, 1963; dir. Hebrew Free Loan Assn. Mem. Passaic County Bar Assn. Home: 8 E 39th St Paterson NJ 07514 Office: 126 Market St Paterson NJ 07505 Tel (201) 742-5401

WEISSER, MICHAEL HARRIS, b. N.Y.C., Apr. 3, 1939; student U. Calif., Los Angeles, 1957-59; B.B.A., Adelphi U., 1961; J.D., N.Y. Law Sch., 1961-64; LL.M., N.Y. U., 1965, postgrad., 1975—. Admitted to N.Y. State bar, 1966, Fla. bar 1973; asso. firm Kelly, Dry, Newhall, McGinnis & Warren, N.Y.C., 1964-66, firm Austin & DuPont, Lake Success, N.Y., 1966-67; partner firm Lupkin, Cohen, Stracher & Weisser, Lake Success, 1967-72; individual practice law, North Miami Beach, Fla., 1974—. Pres., Flower Hill Assn., 1965-68; mayor City of Flower Hill, 1968-69. Mem. Am., N.Y. State, Fla., Dade County, Nassau County bar assns. Home: 2310 NE 193d St North Miami Beach FL 33180 Office: 1550 NE Miami Gardens Dr North Miami Beach FL 33180 Tel (305) 945-3531

WEISSFELD, JOACHIM ALEXANDER, b. Wuppertal, W. Ger., Mar. 18, 1927; A.B., Brown U., 1950; J.D., Harvard, 1953. Admitted to R.I. bar, 1954, U.S. Dist. Ct. bar, 1955; asso. to partner firm Graham, Reid, Ewing & Stapleton, Providence, 1957-70; partner firm Tillinghast, Collins & Graham, Providence, 1970—. Fellow Am. Coll. Probate Counsel; mem. Am., R.I. bar assns. Home: 50 Clark Rd Barrington RI 02806 Office: 2000 Hospital Trust Tower Providence RI 02903 Tel (401) 274-3800

WEISSICH, WILLIAM OTTO, b. San Francisco, Oct. 31, 1920; B.S. magna cum laude, U. San Francisco, 1943, J.D. cum laude, 1946. Admitted to Calif. bar, 1946, U.S. Supreme Ct. bar, 1958; asso. firm Angelo J. Scampini, San Francisco, 1946-50; dep. dist. atty. Marin County (Calif.), 1950-52, dist. atty., 1953-60; partner firm Bagshaw, Martinelli, Weissich & Jordan, San Rafael, Calif., 1960-69, Weissich & Lachelt, San Rafael, 1969-72, Weissich & Heubach, San Rafael, 1972—. Trustee Calif. State Univ. and Colleges, 1969—, chmn. bd., 1976—. Mem. Calif., Marin County bar assns. Home: 211 Locust Ave San Rafael CA 94901 Office: 55 Professional Center Pkwy San Rafael CA 94903 Tel (415) 472-3300

WEISSING, LOUIS, b. Tampa, Fla., Aug. 4, 1925; LL.B., U. Fla., 1953. Admitted to Fla. bar, 1953; asst. county solicitor Broward County (Fla.), 1954-57; judge Criminal Ct. of Record, Broward County, 1957-59, judge Ct. of Record, 1959-66; circuit judge, Ft. Lauderdale, Fla., 1966—. Mem. Am., Broward County bar assns., Fla. Bar. Home: 551 NW 66th Ave Plantation FL 33317 Office: 930 Broward County Courthouse Fort Lauderdale FL 33301 Tel (305) 765-4733

WEISSLER, ROBERT I., b. N.Y.C., Oct. 8, 1946; B.S., U. Bridgeport, 1967; J.D., U. Miami, 1970, LL.M., 1972. Admitted to Fla. bar, 1970; partner firm Williams Salomon Kanter & Damian, Miami, Fla., 1970—. Mem. Am. (real property and tax com.), Fla. (unauthorized practice com.) bar assns. Home: 8315 SW 157th St Miami FL 33157 Office: Williams Salomon Kanter & Damian 1003 Dupont Bldg Miami FL 33131 Tel (305) 379-1681

WEISSMAN, JOSEPH, b. N.Y.C., Oct. 30, 1926; B.S. in Bus. Adminstrn., U. Calif., Los Angeles, 1950; LL.B., U. So. Calif., 1956. Admitted to Calif. bar, 1956; asso. firm Buchalter, Nemer, Fields & Savitch and predecessor, Los Angeles, 1956-76, partner, 1960—. Mem. Los Angeles County, Am. bar assns., Am. Judicature Soc., Fin. Lawyers Conf. (pres. 1970-71), Assn. Comml. Finance Attys. Contbr. articles to legal jours. Office: 700 S Flower St Suite 700 Los Angeles CA 90017 Tel (213) 626-6700

WEISSMAN, WILLIAM R., b. N.Y.C., Aug. 16, 1940; B.A., Columbia U., 1962, J.D. cum laude, 1965. Admitted to N.Y. State bar, 1965, U.S. Supreme Ct. bar, 1968, D.C. bar, 1969; law clk. to judge U.S. Dist. Ct., Tex., 1965-66; trial atty. antitrust div. Dpt. Justice, Washington, 1966-69, spl. asst. U.S. atty., 1967; asso. firm Wald, Harkrader & Ross, Washington, 1969-72, partner, 1973—; dir. Edn. Turnkey Systems, Inc., 1969-74. Mem. Arlington County Tenant-Landlord Commn., 1973—, chmn., 1974—; parliamentarian Arlington County Democratic Com., 1971-75. Mem. Am., Fed., D.C., FCC, Intern-Am. bar assns. Author: Free Expression and the Right of Privacy, 1965; recipient James Gordon Bennett prize Columbia U., 1962, E. B. Convers prize, 1965. Home: 1801 N Hartford St Arlington VA 22201 Office: 1320 19th St NW Washington DC 20036 Tel (202) 296-2121

WEITZMAN, HOWARD LLOYD, b. Los Angeles, Sept. 21, 1939; B.S., U. So. Calif., 1962, J.D., 1965. Admitted to Calif. bar, 1966, U.S. Supreme Ct. bar, 1976; individual practice law, Los Angeles, 1966-71, 76—, Beverly Hills, Calif., 1972-76; tchr. U. So. Calif. Law Center. Mem. Am., Calif., Criminal Cts. (pres. Los Angeles County 1976), Los Angeles County bar assns., Calif. Trial Lawyers Assn., Nat. Assn. Criminal Def. Lawyers, Calif. Attys. for Criminal Justice (dir.). Recipient Legion Lex, U. So. Calif. Law Center. Office: 9911 W Pico Blvd Los Angeles CA 90035 Tel (213) 651-3393

WEITZMAN, SHELDON PHILLIP, b. Cleve., Dec. 29, 1931; B.C.S., Ohio U., 1956; LL.D., Western Res. U., 1958. Admitted to Ohio bar, 1958, U.S. Supreme Ct. bar, 1971; partner firm Weitzman & Spike, Cleve., 1963-68; individual practice law, Cleve., 1975-76; sr. partner firm Weitzman & Grabow, Cleve., 1976—. Pres. City of Eastlake Midget Football League, 1968-73; Cuyahoga County judge adv. Jewish War Vets., 1959. Mem. Ohio, Greater Cleve., Lake County, Cuyahoga County bar assns., Am., Ohio trial lawyers assns. Home: 33295 Lakeshore Blvd Eastlake OH 44092 Office: 502 Lincoln Bldg E 6th and Saint Clair Sts Cleveland OH 44114 Tel (216) 861-0026

WELCH, ERIC, b. Greensboro, N.C., Nov. 29, 1943; A.B., U. Ga., 1965; J.D., Mercer U., 1971. Admitted to Ga. and Fla. bars, 1971; partner firm Liston, VanNorte & Welch, Atlanta, 1971—. Mem. Am., Ga., Fla., Atlanta bar assns. Office: 1022 Candler Bldg Atlanta GA 30303 Tel (404) 522-2525

WELCH, GARY ROLLAND, b. Lincoln, Nebr., Nov. 27, 1936; B.A., Omaha U., 1958; LL.B., Creighton Coll., 1961. Admitted to Nebr. bar, 1961; served with JAGC, USAF, 1961-64; asst. atty. gen. State of Nebr., Lincoln, 1964—. Leader Cornhusker council Boy Scouts Am., Lincoln, 1972-75, chmn., 1975-76; deacon Eastridge Presbyterian Ch., Lincoln, 1975—; coach Little Fry Basketball, Lincoln, 1975-76. Mem. Nebr., Lincoln bar assns. Home: 512 Trail Ridge Rd Lincoln NE 68505 Office: 14th Burnham St Lincoln NE 68509 Tel (402) 473-4611

WELCH, JAMES DOUGLAS, b. Sarnia, Ont., Can., Feb. 9, 1946; B.S. in Chem. Engring., U. Tex., Austin, 1967, J.D. with honors, 1970. Admitted to D.C. bar, 1971; atty. Pub. Interest Research Group, Washington, 1970-71; mem. firm Wald, Havkrader & Ross, Washington, 1971—. Mem. exec. bd. Nat. Capital Area ACLU. Mem. Am. Bar Assn., Washington Council Lawyers. Office: 1320 19th St NW Washington DC 20036 Tel (202) 296-2121

WELCH, LANTZ, b. 1932; A.B., U. Mo., Kansas City, LL.B., 1957. Practice law, Kansas City, Mo. Mem. Kansas City Bar Assn. (pres. 1977-78). Office: 1111 Grand Ave Kansas City MO 64106*

WELCH, ROBERT WILLIAM, b. May 10, 1940; B.A., J.D., Boston Coll. Admitted to Mass. bar, 1966; sr. partner firm William B. Welch; dir. Naumkeag Trust Co., Salem. Pres., Health and Edn. Services Child Guidance Centre; bd. dirs. N. Shore Catholic Charity Centre. Mem. Am., Mass., Salem bar assns. Home: 41 Young Ave Swampscott MA 01907 Office: 221 Essex St Salem MA 01970 Tel (617) 744-0637

WELCH, THOMAS DUNWOODY, JR., b. Boston, Nov. 8, 1940; B.A. in English cum laude, Princeton, 1962; LL.B., U. Va., 1965. Admitted to Mass. bar, 1965, Hawaii bar, 1968; asso. firm Goodwin, Proctor and Hoar, Boston, 1965-66; law clk. Carlsmith, Carlsmith, Wichman and Case, Honolulu, 1967-68, asso., 1969-72, partner, 1972—. Mem. Am., Hawaii bar assns. Home: 2334 Ferdinand St Honolulu HI 96822 Office: PO Box 656 Honolulu HI 96809 Tel (808) 524-5112

WELCH, WALTER BENJAMIN, b. Rochester, N.Y., Feb. 16, 1925; B.A., U. Calif. Los Angeles, 1955, J.D., 1958. Admitted to Calif. bar, 1959; individual practice law, Santa Ana, Calif., 1959, Buena Park, Calif., 1961-62; partner firm Vincent & Welch, Buena Park, 1959-61, Welch & Farris, 1962-70, Comstock, Farris, Joye & Welch, Buena Park, 1970-75, Welch & Farris, Buena Park, 1976—. Mem. Orange County Bar Assn. (mem. ethics com.), Buena Park C. of C. (pres. 1968-69), U. Calif. Los Angeles Alumni Assn., Phi Alpha Delta. Office: 8151 Orangethorpe Ave Buena Park CA 90621 Tel (714) 521-7200

WELCH, WALTER SCOTT, III, b. Jackson, Miss., Sept. 7, 1939; B.A. cum laude, U. of the South, 1961; LL.B. with distinction, U. Miss., 1964. Admitted to Miss. bar, 1964, U.S. Supreme Ct. bar, 1971; asso. Welch, Gibbes & Graves, Laurel, Miss., 1964; capt. JAGC, USAF, 1964-67; mem. firm Butler, Snow, O'Mara, Stevens & Cannada, Jackson, 1967—. Mem. Am., Miss. State, Hinds County bar assns., Miss. Def. Lawyers Assn., Phi Delta Phi, Phi Beta Kappa. Contbr. article to legal jour. Home: 5207 Kaywood Dr Jackson MS 39211 Office: 1700 Deposit Guaranty Plaza Jackson MS 39201 Tel (601) 948-5711

WELD, JONATHAN MINOT, b. Greenwich, Conn., Feb. 25, 1941; A.B. cum laude, Harvard U., 1963; J.D., Cornell U., 1967. Admitted to N.Y. bar, 1969; asso. firm Shearman & Sterling, N.Y.C., 1967-75, partner, 1976—. Bd. dirs. Bklyn. Home for Children, 1974—, Bklyn. Hosp., 1974—, Willoughby House Settlement, Inc., N.Y.C., 1974-76, Winant & Clayton Vols., Inc., N.Y.C., 1970-75, Harvard Coll. Fund Council, Cambridge, Mass., 1967-69. Mem. N.Y. State Bar Assn. Office: 53 Wall St New York City NY 10005 Tel (212) 483-1000

WELDY, JACK BURKETT, b. Hattiesburg, Miss., Oct. 31, 1934; B.A., U. So. Miss., 1956; LL.B., Tulane U., 1961. Admitted to La. bar, 1961, Miss. bar, 1962; partner firm Zachary, Weldy, Hattiesburg, 1962-67, firm Zachary, Weldy & Ingram, Hattiesburg, 1967-74; circuit judge 12th Jud. Dist. Miss., Hattiesburg, 1975—. Mem. Am., La., Miss. bar assns. Office: PO Box 43 Hattiesburg MS 39401 Tel (601) 582-1956

WELEBIR, DOUGLAS FERD, b. Washington, Feb. 9, 1943; A.B. with honors, La Sierra Coll., 1962; J.D., U. So. Calif., 1965. Admitted to Calif. bar, 1966, D.C. bar, 1967, U.S. Supreme Ct. bar, 1971; research asst. Calif. Ct. Appeals 4th Dist. 2 Div., 1966; dep. pub. defender San Bernardino County (Calif.), 1967; with firm King & Mussell, San Bernardino, 1967-69; partner firm Garza, Kassel, Jordan & Welebir, San Bernardino, 1970-73; individual practice law, San Bernardino, 1973; partner firm Welebir, Brunick & Taylor, San Bernardino, 1974—; mayor City of Loma Linda (Calif.), 1970-74. Mem. State Bar Calif., San Bernardino County, Am. bar assns., World Assn. Lawyers, Internat. Union Lawyers, Am. Soc. Law and Medicine, Calif. Trial Lawyers Assn., Am. Soc. Hosp. Attys. Office: 330 N D St Suite 410 San Bernardino CA 92401 Tel (714) 884-6205

WELING, JAMES BERNARD, b. Oakland, Calif., May 13, 1935; B.S. in Polit. Sci., Loyola U., Los Angeles, 1957; J.D., Southwestern U., 1969. Admitted to Calif. bar, 1970; asso. firm Kean & Engle, Los Angeles, 1970—. Mem. Calif. Republican Assos., 1971—. Mem. Calif., Los Angeles County, Am. bar assns., Am. Arbitration Assn. (arbitrator 1974—). Office: 3600 Wilshire Blvd Los Angeles CA 90010 Tel (213) 387-4241

WELLENS, DAVID RICHARD, b. Ft. Lauderdale, Fla., Dec. 31, 1941; B.S., Fla. Atlantic U., 1966; J.D., U. Miami, 1969. Admitted to Fla. bar, 1969; asso. firm Deutsch & Hurth, Ft. Lauderdale, 1969-70; partner firm Sobo & Wellens, Ft. Lauderdale, 1970—; prosecutor City of Lauderdale Lakes (Fla.), 1970-76. Chmn., Planning and Zoning Bd., Lauderdale Lakes, 1969-70. Mem. Broward County Trial Lawyers Assn. (pres. 1977—), Acad. Fla. Trial Lawyers, Am. Bar Assn., Comml. Law League. Contbr. articles U. Miami Law Rev. Office: 7500 NW 5th St Fort Lauderdale FL 33317 Tel (305) 581-2672

WELLER, HERMAN GAYLE, b. Kenney, Ill., Feb. 13, 1914; A.B., U. Denver, 1936, LL.B. cum laude, 1938. Admitted to Colo. bar, 1938; asso. firm Weller, Friedrich, Hickisch and Hazlitt and predecessors, Denver, 1938-41, partner, 1942-76, counsel, 1977—. Chmn. Arapahoe County (Colo.) Republican Central Com., 1952-54. Mem. Denver, Colo., Am. (plaque sect. ins. negligence and compensation) bar assns., Denver Law Club, Def. Lawyers Assn., Internat. Assn. Ins. Counsel, Order St. Ives, Omicron Delta Kappa, Phi Delta Phi. Home: 11122 N Deer Ln Parker CO 80134 Office: 900 Capitol Life Center 16th Ave and Grant St Denver CO 80203 Tel (303) 861-8000

WELLES, JAMES BELL, JR., b. Schenectady, Aug. 27, 1918; A.B., Columbia, 1939, J.D., 1942. Admitted to N.Y. bar, 1943; asso. firm Angulo, Cooney, Marsh & Ouchterloney, and predecessor, N.Y.C., 1946-56, partner, 1956-59; partner firm Debevoise, Plimpton Lyons & Gates, N.Y.C., 1960—. Trustee Emma Willard Sch., Troy, N.Y.; bd. visitors Columbia U. Sch. Law; v.p., dir. Burke Rehab. Found., White Plains, N.Y. Mem. Assn. Bar City N.Y., Am., N.Y. State bar assns., Am. Coll. Probate Counsel, New York County Lawyers' Assn. Home: 25 Ivy Hill Rd Chappaqua NY 10514 Office: 299 Park Ave New York City NY 10017 Tel (212) 752-6400

WELLFORD, ALEXANDER, b. Richmond, Va., Jan. 13, 1930; B.A., U. Va., 1951, LL.B., 1958. Admitted to Va. bar, 1958; practiced in Richmond, 1958—; partner firm Christian, Barton, Epps, Brent & Chappell, 1964—. Treas. Richmond Citizens Assn., 1958-60; 1st vice chmn. Richmond Democratic Com., 1959-64; nat. trustee Ducks Unltd. Inc., 1972—. Mem. Richmond, Va., Am. bar assns., Va. State Bar. Home: 7920 W Mount Bella Rd Richmond VA 23235 Office: 1200 Mutual Bldg Richmond VA 23219 Tel (804) 644-7851 1

WELLINGTON, HARRY HILLEL, b. New Haven, Aug. 13, 1926; A.B., U. Pa., 1947; LL.B., Harvard, 1952. Admitted to D.C. bar, 1952; law clk. to Judge C. Magruder, U.S. Ct. Appeals, 1st Circuit Boston, 1953-54, U.S. Supreme Ct. Justice F. Frankfurter, Washington, 1955-56; asst. prof. law Yale, 1956-57, asso. prof., 1957-60, prof., 1960-67, Edward J. Phelps prof., 1967—, dean Law Sch., 1975—; cons. domestic and fgn. govtl. agencies. Mem. Am., D.C., Conn. bar assns., Am. Law Inst., Am. Arbitration Assn. Ford fellow London Sch. Econs., 1965; Guggenheim fellow Brookings Instn., 1968-71; author: (with Harold Shepard) Contracts and Contract Remedies, 1957; Labor and the Legal Process, 1968, (with Summers) Labor Law, 1968, (with Winter) The Unions and the Cities, 1971. Home: 55 Huntington St New Haven CT 06511 Office: Deans Office 103 Sterling Law Bldg Yale Law School New Haven CT 06520 Tel (203) 436-8895

WELLISCH, KURT, b. Vienna, Austria, Sept. 9, 1910; J.D., U. Vienna, 1924; B.B.A., U. Miami, 1947, J.D., 1953, LL.M., 1970. Admitted to Fla. bar, 1953; practice law, Coral Gables, Fla., 1953—, pres. firm Wellisch, Metzger & Leone and sec. firm Metzger, Wellisch & Leone, C.P.A.'s. Treas., Friends of Chamber Music of Miami, Inc., 1977—. Mem. Dade County, Coral Gables bar assns., Am., Fla. (treas.) assns. atty.-C.P.A.'s, Am. Inst. C.P.A.'s, Fla. Inst. C.P.A.'s. C.P.A., Fla. Office: 161 Almeria Ave Suite 200E Coral Gables FL 33134 Tel (305) 445-7954

WELLMAN, JOHN WILSON, b. Pilot Mountain, N.C., Apr. 5, 1925; A.B., Duke, 1948, J.D., 1950. Admitted to Pa. bar, 1951, U.S. Supreme Ct. bar, 1954; asso., then partner firm Petrikin, Wellman, Damico & Carney, and predecessors, Media, Pa. Home: 5 Dale Ln Wallingford PA 19085 Office: 602 E Baltimore Pike Media PA 19063 Tel (215) 565-2670

WELLS, ARTHUR, JR., b. Los Angeles, Apr. 19, 1937; B.A., U. Calif., Los Angeles, 1959; J.D., U. Calif., Berkeley, 1962. Admitted to Calif. bar, 1963, 9th Circuit bar, 1963, U.S. Supreme Ct. bar, 1967; asso. firm Morgan, Beauzay & Holmes, San Jose, Calif., 1963-64, Edelberg, Miller, Rothenberg, Los Angeles, 1964-65; partner Wells & Chesney, Inc., Oakland, Calif., 1965—; instr. speech U. Calif., Berkeley, 1966-68; moot ct. judge Boalt and Hastings Schs. of Law, 1967-71; guest lectr. Boalt Hall, 1970-72, Hastings Sch. Law, 1972. Certified specialist in criminal law Calif. Bd. Legal Specialization. Mem. Am., Calif., Alameda County, San Francisco bar assns. Office: 125 12th St Suite 157 Oakland CA 94607 Tel (415) 763-4433

WELLS, CHARLES MARION, b. Lawrenceburg, Ind., Mar. 15, 1905; A.B., Butler U., 1927; LL.B., U. Ind., 1929; LL.M., Harvard, 1932. Admitted to Ind. bar, 1929, U.S. Supreme Ct. bar, 1935; practiced in Indpls., 1929—; spl. counsel Ind. Dept. Fin. Instns., Indpls., 1935-37; mem. firm Barnes, Hickam, Pantzer & Boyd, 1940—. Mem. Am., Ind., Indpls., Fed. Circuit bar assns., Am. Judicature Soc., Delta Theta Phi. Contbr. to book: Indiana Taxes, 1953. Home: 510 Buckingham Dr Indianapolis IN 46208 Office: 1313 Merchants Bank Bldg Indianapolis IN 46204 Tel (317) 638-1313

WELLS, DAVID F., b. Los Angeles, Jan. 5, 1939; B.S., U. Calif., Los Angeles, 1962; M.S., Calif. State U., Northridge, 1964; J.D., Beverly Coll., 1969. Admitted to Calif. bar, 1969, U.S. Supreme Ct. bar, 1974; dep. dist. atty. Los Angeles County, 1969—; instr. law U. Calif., Los Angeles. Mem. Calif. Assn. Dist. Attys., Calif. State Bar, Am., Los Angeles County bar assns. Office: 210 W Temple St Los Angeles CA 90012 Tel (213) 974-3848

WELLS, DEWEY WALLACE, b. Raleigh, N.C., Oct. 14, 1929; B.S., Wake Forest U., 1952, J.D., 1954. Admitted to N.C. bar, 1954; partner firm LeRoy, Wells, Shaw, Hornthal, Riley & Shearin, Elizabeth City, N.C., 1958—; judge Superior Ct. N.C., 1974. Past pres. Pasquotank United Fund, Elizabeth City Boys' Club; chmn. Albemarle dist. Boy Scouts Am.; mem. N.C. Wildlife Resources Commn., 1975—. Mem. Am., N.C. (bd. gov.'s 1975) bar assns. Home: Camden NC 27921 Office: 112 N Martin St Elizabeth City NC 27909 Tel (919) 335-0871

WELLS, ERSKINE W., b. Jackson, Miss. Dec. 1, 1917; B.C.S., U. Miss., 1939, J.D., 1946. Admitted to Miss. bar, 1946; now partner firm Wells, Wells, Marble & Hurst, Jackson; mem. Miss. Ins. Commn., 1963-70, sec., 1965-70. Fellow Am. Coll. Trial Lawyers, Am. Bar Found.; mem. Am., Hinds County (pres. 1965-66) bar assns., Miss. State Bar (pres. 1976-77), Internat. Assn. Ins. Counsel (exec. com. 1973-76), Am. Council Life Ins., Assn. Life Ins. Counsel, Nat. Assn. R.R. Trial Counsel, Am. Judicature Soc., Miss. Bar Found., Miss. Def. Lawyers Assn. (pres. 1973-74), Def. Research Inst. (v.p. 1970-76), Phi Delta Phi, Omicron Delta Kappa. Office: Lamar Life Bldg Suite 405 PO Box 131 Jackson MS 39205 Tel (601) 355-8321

WELLS, HUGH ALBERT, b. Shelby, N.C., June 8, 1922; LL.B., U. N.C., 1952. Admitted to N.C. bar, 1952, Ga. bar, 1961; individual practice law, Shelby, N.C., 1952-61; asso. firm Rose & Lappas, Atlanta, 1961-63; partner firm Crisp, Twiggs & Wells, Raleigh, N.C., 1963-69; commr. N.C. Utilities Commn., 1969-75; gen. counsel N.C. Electric Membership Assn., Raleigh, 1975—; counsel Utilities Review Com. of N.C. Gen. Assembly, 1976—. Chmn. Shelby Parks and Recreation Commn., 1961; treas., trustee Shelby Pub. Library, 1953-62. Mem. N.C., Am. bar assn., Ga. Bar, Am. Trial Lawyers Assn., Am. Judicature Soc. Home: 5313 Alpine Dr Raleigh NC 27609 Office: Legis Bldg Raleigh NC 27611 Tel (919) 733-3180 also 333 Fayetteville St Raleigh NC 27601 Tel (919) 821-0817

WELLS, J. KENDRICK, III, b. Paintsville, Ky., Dec. 2, 1942; A.B., Harvard U., 1964; J.D., U. Ky., 1967. Admitted to Ky. bar, 1967, U.S. Ct. Appeals bar, 1967; law clk. to judge U.S. Ct. Appeals, Sixth Circuit, 1967-68; asso. firm Wyatt, Grafton & Sloss, Louisville, 1968-72; staff atty. Brown & Williamson Tobacco Corp., Louisville, 1972-76, corp. counsel, 1976—. Bd. dirs. Neighborhood Development Corp., Louisville, 1973—; trustee Preservation Alliance Louisville and Jefferson County, Inc., 1974—. Mem. Ky., Louisville, Am. (chmn. Ky. state sect. local govt. 1970-77) bar assns. Mem. staff Ky. Law Jour., 1965-67; contbr. articles to legal jours. Home: 7004 Springdale Rd Louisville KY 40222 Office: Law Dept Brown & Williamson Tobacco Corp 1600 W Hill St Louisville KY 40201 Tel (502) 774-7649

WELLS, JACK LEON, b. Strasbourg, France, June 14, 1931; B.S., U. Calif., Berkeley, 1958, LL.B., 1961, J.D., 1961. Admitted to Calif. bar, 1962, D.C. bar, 1975, U.S. Supreme Ct. bar, 1974; dep. city atty. City of Los Angeles, 1962-69, asst. city atty., 1969-72, sr. asst. city atty., 1972—; chief counsel Port of Los Angeles, 1973—. Mem. Calif. State, Los Angeles County bar assns., Calif. (chmn. com. law and legis. 1974-75), Pacific Coast (chmn. legal com. 1975-76), Am. (chmn. law and legis. com. 1976—) assns. port authorities. Office: PO Box 151 San Pedro CA 90733 Tel (213) 775-3231

WELLS, JOHN ASHLEY, b. N.Y.C., Jan. 14, 1908; B.A., Wesleyan U., Middletown, Conn., 1932; B.A. Jurisprudence, Oxford (Eng.) U., 1934, B.C.L., 1935, M.A., 1953; LL.M., Harvard, 1936. Admitted to N.Y. bar, 1937, U.S. Supreme Ct. bar, 1945, D.C. bar, 1953; asso. firm Hughes, Schurman & Dwight, N.Y.C., 1936-37; asso. firm Rogers & Wells, and predecessors, N.Y.C., 1937-42, 46-48, partner, 1948—; acting chief counsel, div. retail trade and services Office Price Adminstrn., Washington, 1942, chief counsel br. interpretations legal div., 1942; chief asst. to commr. N.Y. State's Moreland Commn., 1943-44; asst. counsel Navy Price Adjustment Bd., Washington, 1944-46. Mem. Am., N.Y. State bar assns., Am. Acad. Polit. and Social Sci., Am. Judicature Soc., Assn. Bar City N.Y., New York County Lawyers Assn., Selden Soc., Union Internationale des Avocats. Author: The Voter's Presidential Handbook, 1960; editor: Thomas E. Dewey on the Two Party System, 1966. Home: 69 Rye Rd Rye NY 10580 Office: 200 Park Ave New York City NY 10017 Tel (212) 972-5400

WELLS, LEONARD NATHANIEL DAVID, JR., b. Akron, Ohio, Aug. 24, 1914; B.A., Tex. Christian U., 1934; LL.B., Columbia, 1937. Admitted to Tex. bar, 1937, U.S. Supreme Ct. bar, 1945, D.C. Ct. Appeals bar, 1959; regional atty. NLRB, St. Louis, 1939-41, sr. atty., Washington, 1941-44, asso. dir. field div., 1944-1946; partner firm Mullinax, Wells, Mauzy & Baab, and predecessors, Dallas, 1947—; gen. counsel Tex. State Fedn. Labor, 1947-57; counsel So. Conf. Teamsters, 1956—; monitor Internat. Brotherhood Teamsters, 1957-59; mem. adv. com. on rules of procedure Tex. Supreme Ct., 1958—; mem. chmns. task force NLRB, 1976. Fellow Southwestern Legal Found.; mem. Am. Bar Assn. (chmn. labor law sect. 1954-55, ho. of dels. 1959-60), Tex. State Bar (chmn. labor law sect. 1951-52). Home: 7525 Fisher Rd Dallas TX 75214 Office: Elmbrook Gardens 8204 Elmbrook Dr Dallas TX 75247 Tel (214) 630-3672

WELLS, THOMAS BUELL, b. Akron, Ohio, July 2, 1945; B.S. in Bus., Miami U., 1967; postgrad. Ohio No. U. Law Sch., 1970-72; J.D., Emory U., 1973. Admitted to Ga. bar, 1973; mem. firm Graham and Wells, Vidalia, Ga., 1973—; city atty. City of Vidalia, 1976—; county atty. Toombs County (Ga.), 1977—; atty. Vidalia Bd. Edn., 1976—. Active Vidalia Community Chorus, 1974—, Am. Cancer Soc., 1976, Nat. Eagle Scout Assn. 1975—. Mem. State Bar Ga. (bd. govs. 1976—), Am. Bar Assn., Am. Judicature Soc., Ga. Savs. and Loan League, Ga. Municipal Assn., Assn. County Commrs. Ga., Vidalia C. of C. (dir. 1977—). Recipient Distinguished Pres.'s award Kiwanis, 1975; mng. editor Ohio No. U. Law Rev., 1971-72. Home: Loop Rd Vidalia GA 30474 Office: PO Box 545 403 Church St Vidalia GA 30474 Tel (912) 537-9311

WELLS, WILLIAM STONE, b. Jacksonville, Tex., Mar. 3, 1911; B.A., LL.B., Baylor U.; postgrad. Harvard Bus. Sch., 1960. Admitted to Tex. bar, 1933, Miss. bar, 1947; partner firm Stone and Wells, Henderson, Tex., 1933-35; judge Rusk County (Tex.) Ct., 1935-36; dist. atty. Rusk County, 1936-38; legal dept. Gulf Oil Corp., 1938-51; v.p. Tenneco Inc., Houston, 1951-76. Mem. Houston Ind. Sch. Dist., 1952-65, v.p.; chmn. bd. Blue Bonnet Bowl, Houston; mem. Tex. Land Use Environments Com., 1965-70; chmn. athletic com. Houston C. of C. Mem. Houston, Tex., Am., Austin bar assns., Am. Judicature Soc. Named to Athletic Hall of Fame Baylor U., named Distinguished Alumnus. Home: 4516 Bryn Mawr Ln Houston TX 77027 Office: 528 First Federal Plaza Austin TX 78701 Tel (512) 474-7300 also 838 Houston Club Bldg Houston TX 77001 Tel (713) 237-1935

WELLS, WILLIAM VIRGIL, b. Anacortes, Wash., Apr. 23, 1918; B.A., U. Wash., 1939, LL.B., 1940. Admitted to Wash. bar, 1940; partner firm Wells & Wells, Anacortes, 1940-41, 46-48; partner firm Barney & Wells, Anacortes, 1948-50, individual practice law, Anacortes, 1950—; atty. City of Anacortes, 1945-72. Bd. dirs. Red Cross, Anacortes. Mem. Wash., Skagit County bar assns., Northwest Wash. Estate Planning Council. Recipient Kiwanis Legion of Honor, 1976. Home: 2117 10th St Anacortes WA 98221 Office: PO Box 158 Anacortes WA 98221 Tel (206) 293-2922

WELPTON, SHERMAN SEYMOUR, JR., b. Omaha, Mar. 21, 1908; LL.B., J.D., U. Nebr., 1931. Admitted to Nebr. bar, 1931; partner firm Ramsey & Welpton, Omaha, 1931-41; asso. Firm Gibson, Dunn & Crutcher, Los Angeles, 1942-47, partner, 1948—. Mem. Am., Internat. bar assns., Am. Coll. Trial Lawyers (former com. chmn.), Am. Bar Found., World Peace Through Law, Am. Judicature Soc., Phi Delta Phi. Home: 407 Robert Ln Beverly Hills CA 90210 Office: 515 S Flower St Los Angeles CA 90071 Tel (213) 488-7324

WELS, RICHARD HOFFMAN, b. N.Y.C., May 3, 1913; A.B., Cornell U., 1933; J.D., Harvard, 1936. Admitted to N.Y. State bar, 1936, U.S. Supreme Ct. bar, 1940, D.C. bar, 1962; spl. asst. U.S. atty gen., U.S. atty. N.Y., 1931-42; spl. asst. dist. atty. N.Y. County, 1936-37; mem. firm Handel & Panuch, N.Y.C., 1937-38; legal staff SEC, 1938-42; spl. counsel House Naval Affairs Com., 79th Congress, 1942-44; mem. firm Moss, Wels & Marcus and predecessors, N.Y.C., 1946—; gen. counsel Bowling Proprietors Assn. Am., N.Y. Bowling Proprietors Assn., counsel Am. Acad. Psychoanalysis. Chmn. bd Bleuler Psychotherapy Center, Islands Research Found.; vice chmn. Daytop Village, Am. Parents Com.; sec. counsel, William Alanson White Inst. Psychiatry; trustee Margaret Chase Smith Library. Mem. Assn. Bar City N.Y., Am., N.Y. State, Fed., Fed. Communications bar assns., Harvard Law Sch. Assn. Contbr. articles to legal jours. Home: 911 Park Ave New York City NY 10021 Office: 18 E 48th St New York City NY 10017 Tel (212) 752-3122

WELSCH, CHARLES NICHOLAS, JR., b. Mendota, Minn., July 29, 1917; LL.B., St. Louis U., 1939. Admitted to Mo. bar, 1939; individual practice law, 1939-41; with Mercantile Trust Co. Nat. Assn., and predecessors, 1945—, v.p., trust counsel, 1967—. Mem. request and gift council St. Louis U. Mem. Mo. Bar Assn., Bar Assn. Met. St. Louis, Estate Planning Council St. Louis. Home: 2529 Bremerton Rd Rock Hill MO 63144 Office: Drawer 387 Main PO St Louis MO 63166 Tel (314) 425-2607

WELSH, PAUL PATRICK, b. Long Island City, N.Y., Dec. 13, 1941; B.A., U. Pa., 1962, J.D., 1966. Admitted to Pa. bar, 1966, Del. bar, 1968; asso. firm Morgan, Lewis & Bockius, Phila., 1966-67; asso. firm Morris, Nichols, Arsht & Tunnell, Wilmington, Del., 1967-73, partner, 1973—. Bd. dirs. Del. chpt. ACLU; mem. Wilmington Republican Exec. Com. Mem. Del., Am. bar assns. Editorial bd. U. Pa. Law Rev., 1964-66. Home: 700 W 24th St Wilmington DE 19802 Office: PO Box 1347 Twelfth and Market Sts Wilmington DE 19899 Tel (302) 658-9200

WELT, DIXON SHERMAN, b. Albany, N.Y., Feb. 7, 1937; B.A., U. Vt., 1959; LL.B., Union U., 1962, J.D., 1968; postgrad. State U. N.Y., 1962-63. Admitted to N.Y. bar, 1962; asso. firm Carter & Conboy, Albany, 1962-65; atty. N.Y. State Bar Assn., Albany, 1965-67; mem. firm Walworth, Harding, Welt & Stockton, Delmar, N.Y., 1967—; counsel to Ways and Means com. N.Y. State Assembly, 1968—; govt. appeal agt. SSS. Vice pres. Hope House, Albany, 1974-75, bd. dirs., 1970—; sec. Republican Com., 1967-71, treas., 1975—; del. to State Rep. Conv., 1970. Mem. Am., N.Y. State, Albany County bar assns., Am. Trial Lawyers Assn., Capitol Dist. Trial Lawyers, Def. Research Inst., N.Y. State Assn. Trial Lawyers, Am. Arbitration Assn. Home: 47 Murray Ave Albany-Delmar NY 12054 Office: 425 Kenwood Ave Albany-Delmar NY 12054 Tel (518) 439-9324

WELTMAN, DAVID LEE, b. Springfield, Mass., Jan. 12, 1933; B.A., Yale, 1954; LL.B., Harvard, 1957. Admitted to Mass. bar, 1957; asso. firm Mintz, Levin & Cohn, Boston, 1957-61; v.p. Ansonia Mills, Inc., Taunton, Mass., 1961-63; asso. firm Foley, Hoag & Eliot, Boston, 1963-67, partner, 1967—. Bd. govs., exec. com. New Eng. Med. Center, Boston, 1971—; pres. Beaver Country Day Sch., Chestnut Hill, Mass., 1975—; pres. Jewish Community Center, Boston, 1967-70; trustee Combined Jewish Philanthropies, Boston, 1964—; chmn. bd. trustees Newbury Jr. Coll., 1971—. Mem. Boston, Am. bar assns. Home: 75 Hammond St Chestnut Hill MA 02167 Office: 10 Post Office Sq Boston MA 02109 Tel (617) 482-1390

WELTMAN, WARREN JAY, b. Troy, N.Y., May 30, 1929; A.B., U. Mich., 1951; J.D., U. Va., 1954. Admitted to N.Y., Mass. bars, 1955; asso. firm Tarricone, Bilgore, Weltman, Silver & Albert and predecessors, Rochester, N.Y., 1955-59, partner, 1967—. Mem. Nat. Arbitration Assn. (nat. panel arbitrators), Monroe County, N.Y. State, Am. bar assns., Monroe County, N.Y. State trial lawyers assns. Home: 74 Irving Rd Rochester NY 14618 Office: 100 Powers Bldg 16 Main St W Rochester NY 14614

WELTNER, CHARLES LONGSTREET, b. Atlanta, Dec. 17, 1927; A.B., Oglethorpe U., 1948; J.D., Columbia, 1950; LL.D., Tufts U., 1967. Admitted to Ga. bar, 1949; mem. 88th and 89th congresses from 5th Ga. dist.; judge Superior Ct. of Fulton County (Ga.), 1976—. Mem. Atlanta Bar Assn. Home: 1105 E Rock Springs Rd NE Atlanta GA 30306 Office: 701 Fulton County Courthouse Atlanta GA 30303 Tel (404) 658-9550

WELTZER, LOUIS ALBIN, b. Moline, Ill., Mar. 12, 1948; B.A., U. Colo., 1970, J.D., 1974; postgrad Willamette U., 1971-72. Admitted to Colo. bar, 1974; asso. firm Carroll, Bradley & Ciancio, Denver, 1974-75; partner firm Weltzer & Worstell, Nederland, Colo. and Denver, 1975—. Bd. dirs. Nederland Center Arts and Humanities, 1976—. Mem. Am., Colo., Adams County bar assn., Am. Assn. Trial Lawyers, Order of Coif. Home: 506 E Simpson St Lafayette CO 80026 Office: 1612 Court Pl Suite 700 Denver CO 80202 Tel (303) 534-0683 also PO Box 938 Nederland CO 80466 Tel (303) 534-0683

WEMPLE, ARCHIBALD CULLINGS, b. Schenectady, N.Y., Mar. 10, 1905; B.A., Union Coll., 1926, J.D., 1931. Admitted to N.Y. State bar, 1931, since practiced in Schenectady; asso. firm Oswald D. Heck, 1935-50; mayor City of Schenectady, 952-56; judge Schenectady County, 1956—; acting judge Supreme Ct. of Schenectady, Saratoga and Fulton Counties, 1965-70; village atty., Scotia, N.Y., 1939; vis. acting judge Counties of Queens, Westchester, Nassau, Suffolk, Saratoga, Washington, Fulton and Montgomery. Pres., Schenectady Boys' Club, 1943; deacon, elder First Ref. Ch., Schenectady, 1955-62. Mem. Schenectady Bar Assn., N.Y. County Judges' Assn. (pres. 1965), Schenectady C. of C. (pres. jr. assn. 1945, sr. assn. 1949; Distinguished Service award 1941). Home: 1579 Regent St Schenectady NY 12309 Office: 602 State St Schenectady NY 12307 Tel (518) 377-6484

WENDEL, HARVEY LEE, b. Milw., Jan. 26, 1939; B.B.A., U. Wis., 1960, J.D., 1963. Admitted to Wis. bar, 1963; partner firm Cassidy, Wendel, Center & Lipman, and predecessors, Madison, Wis., 1964-75; partner firm Feidler Assos., Madison, 1974—, S. & W. Bldg. Co., 1969—, LACO Investment Co., 1969—. Chmn., Com. for Environ. Protection, 1969-70; mem. City of Madison Mayor's Adv. Com., 1969-70; v.p. Beth El Temple, 1976—, sec., 1968-70, bd. dirs., 1966-77, pres. brotherhood, 1966-67. Mem. State Bar Wis., Dane County Bar Assn. (chmn. programs 1976—, mem. exec. com. 1976—). Office: 222 W Washington Ave Suite 317 Madison WI 53703 Tel (608) 251-4511

WENDELKEN, RICHARD JOSEPH, b. Akron, Ohio, Nov. 30, 1939; B.A., St. Francis Coll., Loretto, Pa., 1962; J.D., U. Akron, 1970. Admitted to Ohio Supreme Ct. bar, 1970, U.S. Supreme Ct. bar, 1975; referee probate div. Ct. of Common Pleas, Summit County (Ohio), 1971—. Mem. Akron, Ohio, Am. bar assns. Office: 209 S High St Akron OH 44308 Tel (216) 379-5484

WENDORF, HULEN DEE, b. West, Tex., Oct. 29, 1916; B.S., U.S. Mil. Acad., 1939; J.D., Yale, 1951. Admitted to Conn. bar, 1951, Tex. bar, 1959, U.S. Ct. Mil. Appeals bar, 1952; commd. 2d lt. F.A., U.S. Army, 1939, advanced through grades to col. JAGC, 1954; chief mil. affairs div. Office of JAG, Washington, 1958-59, ret., 1959; individual practice law, El Paso, Tex., 1959-61; prof. law Baylor U. Law Sch., Waco, Tex., 1961—, chmn. faculty publs. com., 1968—; chmn. citizens adv. com. to judge Juvenile Ct., Waco, 1976—; mem. Waco-McLennan County Legal Aid Bd., 1976—. Elder, trustee Westminster Presbyterian Ch., 1963—. Mem. McLennan County (past dir.), Am. bar assns., Am., Tex. trial lawyers assns., Tex. Assn. Criminal Def. Lawyers, Phi Delta Phi. Contbr. articles to legal jours. Decorated Army Commendation medal, Bronze Star, Legion of Merit. Home: 2808 Cumberland Ave Waco TX 76707 Office: Baylor U Law Sch Waco TX 76703 Tel (817) 755-3611

WENDT, JOHN ARTHUR FREDERIC, JR., b. Cleve., Feb. 21, 1921; A.B. with honors, U. Mich., 1942; J.D., U. Colo., 1951. Admitted to Colo. bar, U.S. Dist. Ct. bar, 1951, U.S. Ct. of Appeals bar, U.S. Supreme Ct. bar, 1967; asso. firm Tippit, Haskell & Welborn, Denver, 1955-60; partner firm Wendt & Kistler, and predecessors, Aspen, Colo., 1960-74; individual practice law, Aspen, 1974—; dist. atty. 9th Jud. Dist. Colo., 1965-69; judge Pitkin County Ct., 1971—. Trustee Colo. Rocky Mountain Sch., 1967-74; bd. dirs. Touchstone Clinic, 1975—; chmn. Grass Roots Community TV System, 1972—. Mem. Am., Colo. (gov. 1965-70), Pitkin County (pres. 1970) bar assns. Contbr. articles to profl. jours. Home: Lenado Farm Box 12 Aspen CO 81621 Office: 215 S Monarch St Park Central Office Bldg Suite 103 Aspen CO 81611 Tel (303) 925-4505

WENGER, FREDRICK WAYNE, b. Sturgis, Mich., Nov. 27, 1943; B.A., Olivet Nazarene Coll., 1966; J.D., Ind. U., 1964. Admitted to Ind. bar, 1969, Fed. bar, 1969; atty. gen. Ind., Indpls., 1969-70; asso. firm Bales & Bales, Muncie, Ind., 1970-74; partner firm Bales, Bales & Wenger, Muncie, 1974—. Mem. Ind. State Bar Assn. Home: S Albany St Selma IN 47383 Office: 116 1/2 S Walnut St Muncie IN 47305 Tel (317) 289-2268

WENIG, LEONARD N., b. Chgo., July 30, 1928; B.S., U. Ill., 1950; J.D., Northwestern U., 1957. Admitted to Ill. bar, 1957; partner firm Ferdinand & Wenig, Chgo., 1957-63; individual practice law, Chgo., 1963—; tchr. div. of Americanization, Chgo. Bd. Edn., 1958-65. Chmn. and mem. Rogers Sch. Council, Chgo., 1971-73, 76—. Mem. Am. Ill., Chgo. bar assns. Office: 2640 W Touhy Ave Chicago IL 60645 Tel (312) 338-4404

WENKE, ROBERT A., b. Stanton, Nebr., Sept. 6, 1926; B.A., U. Nebr., 1948, LL.B., 1950. Admitted to Calif. bar, 1951; individual practice law, Long Beach, Calif., 1951-59, 60-65; legis. asst. to U.S. Senator T.H. Kuchel, 1959-60; judge Municipal Ct. Long Beach, 1965-66; judge Superior Ct. of Los Angeles, 1966—, presiding judge juvenile ct., 1969-70, supervising judge of law dept., 1972, asst. presiding judge, 1973-74, presiding judge, 1975-76. Mem. Calif. Jud. Council, Am. Judicature Soc. (dir.), Nat. Center for State Cts. (dir.). Contbr. articles to legal jours. Home: 4216 E 2nd St Long Beach CA 90803 Office: 111 N Hill St Los Angeles CA 90012 Tel (213) 974-5791

WENKE, WILLIAM F., b. Stanton, Nebr., Oct., 1928; B.S., U. Nebr., 1950, J.D., 1952. Admitted to Calif. bar, 1953; now partner firm Wenke, Burge & Taylor, Santa Ana, Calif. Mem. Am., Orange County (pres. 1977—) bar assns., State Bar Calif., Phi Delta Phi. Office: Calif First Bank Bldg Suite 801 1055 N Main St Santa Ana CA 92701 Tel (714) 835-3338*

WENTWORTH, ANDREW STOWELL, b. Boston, Mar. 3, 1938; B.A., Mich. State U., 1960; J.D., Ohio State U., 1966. Admitted to Ohio bar, 1968; trial atty. Franklin County (Ohio) Prosecutor's Office, 1967-69; mem. firm Freda & Wentworth, 1969-72, Schwenker, Wentworth, Strinsberg & Perrin, Columbus, Ohio, 1972—. Mem. Columbus, Ohio bar assns. Home: 472 Clinton Heights Columbus OH 43202 Office: 8 E Broad St Columbus OH 43215 Tel (614) 282-2403

WENTWORTH, JOHN, b. Albuquerque, Feb. 2, 1945; B.A., Claremont Coll. 1967; J.D., U. N.Mex., 1970. Admitted to N.Mex. bar, 1970; law clk. to Justice Tackett, N.Mex. Supreme Ct., 1970-71; asst. dist. atty. 1st Jud. Dist. of New Mex., Santa Fe, 1971, dep. dist. atty., 1972; asso. firm Jones, Gallegos, Snead & Wertheim and predecessor, Santa Fe, 1972-74, partner, 1975—. Mem. Am. Trial Lawyers Assn., N.Mex. Criminal Trial Lawyers Assn. (v.p. 1976), N.Mex. Trial Lawyers Assn. (sec. 1976). Recipient Am. Jurisprudence awards. Home: 134 Lorenzo St Santa Fe NM 87501 Office: 215 Lincoln Ave PO Box 2228 Santa Fe NM 87501 Tel (505) 982-2691

WEPPLER, LAWRENCE GEORGE, b. Evanston, Ill., Feb. 16, 1945; B.S., Loyola U., 1968, J.D., 1969. Admitted to Ill. bar, 1969; atty. Allied Mills, Inc., Chgo., 1969-73, asst. sec., 1973—. Mem. Am., Ill., Chgo. bar assns. Office: 110 N Wacker Dr Chicago IL 60606 Tel (312) 346-5060

WERCHICK, JACK, b. Poltova, Ukraine, Jan. 14, 1913; A.B., San Francisco State Coll., 1938; J.D., Hasting Coll. Law, 1949. Admitted to Calif. bar, 1950, U.S. Supreme Ct. bar, 1968; asso. firm Elmer Delany Co., 1950-52; individual practice law, San Francisco, 1952—; prof. law Hastings Coll. Law, 1964—. Mem. pres.'s. assos. San Francisco State U.; bd. dirs. Hastings Coll. Advocacy. Mem. Am. Bd. Profl. Negligence Attys. (bd. govs.), Internat. Acad. Law and Sci., World Assn. Law Profs., Calif. Trial Lawyers Assn. (pres., bd. govs.), Hastings Coll. Law Alumni Assn. (Alumnus of Year award 1974). Author: California Preparation and Trial, 1974. Office: 15th Floor 215 Market St San Francisco CA 94105 Tel (415) 398-5656

WERLING, CHARLES JOSEPH, b. Dayton, Ohio, Mar. 9, 1934; B.S. in Edn., U. Dayton, 1958; M.A. in History, Loyola U., Chgo., 1965, J.D., 1972. Admitted to Ill. bar, 1972; title examiner Chgo. Title & Trust Co., 1972-74; individual practice law, Chgo., 1974—. Pres. St. Michael's Sch. Bd., Chgo., 1973-74. Mem. S. Chgo. (v.p.), Ill., Chgo. bar assns., S. Chgo. C. of C. (sec.), Phi Alpha Delta (2d vice-justice Chgo. chpt.). Home: 8259 S Commercial Ave Chicago IL 60617 Office: 11 S LaSalle St suite 939 Chicago IL 60603 Tel (312) 641-3194

WERNER, CHARLES A., b. St. Louis, Nov. 9, 1929; B.S. in Indsl. Engring., Washington U., St. Louis, 1951; LL.B., St. Louis U., 1959. Admitted to Mo. bar, 1959, U.S. Ct. Appeals bar, 7th Circuit, 1963, 8th Circuit, 1966, U.S. Supreme Ct. bar, 1967; now mem. firm Schuchat, Cook & Werner, St. Louis. Mem. University City (Mo.) City Council, 1968-75. Mem. Bar Assn. Met. St. Louis (pres. 1977—), Mo. Bar, Am. Bar Assn., Omicron Delta Kappa, Alpha Phi Mu. Office: 705 Olive St Suite 1212 Saint Louis MO 63101 Tel (314) 621-2626*

WERNER, CLEMENS ALVA, b. Walcott, Iowa, Apr. 3, 1914; B.S., Northwestern U., 1935, J.D., 1938. Admitted to Iowa bar, 1939; asst. county atty. Scott County (Iowa), 1946-48; partner firms Jebens Butenschoen & Werner, Davenport, Iowa, 1948-55, Hoersch, Werner & Harbeck, Davenport, 1956-70, Werner and Werner, Davenport, 1976—; individual practice law, Davenport, 1970-76; pres. Broadway Theatre League of Quad Cities, Davenport, 1960-77, Walcott Trust & Savs. Bank, 1967—. Mem. trust com. Illowa council Boy Scouts Am., 1973—; dir. Davenport Civil Def., 1951-56; mem. dist. adv. council SBA, 1975—. Mem. Iowa, Scott County, Am. bar assns. Home: 217 Forest Rd Davenport IA 52803 Office: 410 Union Arcade Bldg Davenport IA 52801 Tel (319) 322-5344

WERNER, EDWARD FELIX, b. Vienna, Austria, Sept. 1, 1914; came to U.S., 1940, naturalized, 1942; LL.D., U. Vienna, 1937; J.D., Cleveland State U., 1949. Admitted to Ohio bar, 1949; head legal div. IRS, Cleve., 1949-52; individual practice law, Cleve., 1952—. Hon. Austrian consul for Ohio, 1952-72, consul gen., 1972—. Mem. Ohio, Cleve., Cuyahoga County bar assns. Recipient Gold medal of Merit, Rep. of Austria. Home: 12700 Lake Ave Lakewood OH 44107 Office: 1630 Illuminating Bldg Cleveland OH 44113 Tel (216) 621-5588

WERNER, ELMER LOUIS, JR., b. St. Louis, Nov. 21, 1927; A.B., Princeton, 1948; B.S., Washington U., St. Louis, 1950, LL.B., 1952. Admitted to Mo. bar, 1952, Fed. Dist. Ct. bar, 1952, Fed. Ct. Appeals 8th Circuit bar, 1963, U.S. Supreme Ct. bar, 1963, U.S. Ct. Mil. Appeals bar, 1963; chmn. bd. Insurers Service Corp., St. Louis, 1955—; exec. v.p. Safety Mut. Casualty Corp., St. Louis, 1955—; col. JAGC, USAR. Mem. bd. Playgoers of St. Louis, Inc. Mem. Am. Soc. CPCU, Fed., Mo., St. Louis bar assns., Nat. Assn. Safety and Claims Orgns. (pres., mem. bd.), Better Bus. Bur. St. Louis, Asso. Industries Mo. Home: 7 Barclay Woods Dr Saint Louis MO 63124 Office: 706 Chestnut St Saint Louis MO 63101 Tel (314) 421-5100

WERNER, JACK, b. Mpls., June 28, 1914; A.B., U. Minn., 1936, J.D., 1938. Admitted to Minn. bar, 1938, D.C. bar, 1952, U.S. Supreme Ct. bar, 1952; atty. Office of Price Adminstrn., Washington,

1942-43, FCC, Washington, 1946-53; individual practice law, Washington, 1953—. Mem. Am., D.C., Fed. bar assns., Order of Coif. Home: 7017 Kenhill Rd Bethesda MD 20034 Office: 1828 L St NW Washington DC 20036 Tel (202) 296-5321

WERNKE, WILLIAM DEAN, b. Fairfax, S.D., June 19, 1933; B.B.A., U. S.D., 1961, J.D., 1963. Admitted to S.D. bar, 1963; asso. firm Herman & Simpson, Gregory, S.D., 1963; partner firm Herman & Wernke, Gregory, S.D., 1964—; state's atty. Gregory County, S.D., 1965-72. Mem. S.D. State Bd. Edn., 1968-73. Mem. Am., S.D. bar assns., S.D. Trial Lawyers Assn. Home: 1513 Logan St Gregory SD 57533 Office: 119 W 6th St Gregory SD 57533 Tel (605) 835-7421

WERSHALS, PAUL LEONARD, b. July 10, 1942; A.A., Midwest Inst. Bus. Adminstrn., 1963; B.S. in Finance-Investments, Babson Inst. Bus. Adminstrn., 1965; J.D. Suffolk U., 1968; LL.M., N.Y. U., 1975. Admitted to N.Y. State bar, 1969, U.S. Supreme Ct. bar, 1975, U.S. Dist. Ct. for Eastern and So. N.Y. bars, 1976; asso. firm O'Donnell & Schwartz, N.Y.C., 1968-69; asso. firm Jerome M. Stember, 1969-71; individual practice law, Great Neck, N.Y., 1971-76; partner firm Charnin, Trabucchi & Wershals, Great Neck, 1976—. Mem. legal com. Citizens Adversory Com. for Cablevision, Town of North Hempstead, N.Y., 1976—. Mem. N.Y. State Trial Lawyers Assn., Nassau County Bar Assn., Great Neck Lawyers Assn. (dir.), Nassau County Assigned Counsel Defender Plan, Phi Alpha Delta. Home: 198 Kings Point Rd Great Neck NY 11024 Office: 10 Cutter Mill Rd Great Neck NY 11021 Tel (516) 466-6120

WERTH, DAVID LEE, b. Oconomowoc, Wis., Aug. 9, 1941; B.S., U. Wis., 1964; J.D., Marquette U., 1967. Admitted to Wis. bar, 1967; partner firm Van Epps, Gull and Werth, Weyawega, Wis., 1967—. Bd. dirs. Winnebago Area Health Planning Council, 1974, Waupaca County Health Care Council, 1973-74. Mem. Am. Bar Assn. Home: 107 E Parker St Weyauwega WI 54983 Office: 108 W Main St Weyawega WI 54983 Tel (414) 867-2156

WERTHEIM, JERRY, b. Fort Sumner, N.Mex., Oct. 11, 1938; student Stanford U., 1956-58; B.A., U. N.Mex., 1960; LL.B., Georgetown U., 1961-63. Admitted to N.Mex. bar, 1964; asst. atty. gen. State of N.Mex., 1964-65; asso. firm Jones, Gallegos, Snead & Wertheim, Santa Fe, 1965-67, partner, 1967—; chmn. N.Mex. Bar Adv. Opinions Com., 1972-76; mem. N.Mex. Supreme Ct. Rules Evidence Com., 1975—. Mem. Am. Bar Assn., Am., N.Mex. trial lawyers assns. Home: 101 Barranca Rd Santa Fe NM 87501 Office: 215 Lincoln St Santa Fe NM 87501 Tel (505) 982-2691

WERTHEIMER, JAY W., b. N.Y.C., Sept. 3, 1932; B.A., Bklyn. Coll., 1953; LL.B., Columbia, 1959. Admitted to N.Y. bar, 1960; asso., then partner firm Hofheimer Gartlir Gottlieb & Gross, until 1972; partner firm Fink Weinberger Fredman & Charney, N.Y.C., 1973-77, Jaffin Schneider Conrad & Wertheimer, N.Y.C., 1977—. Mem. Rye (N.Y.) Zoning Bd. Mem. Am. Bar Assn., New York County Lawyers Assn. Office: Jaffin Schneider Conrad & Wertheimer 350 Madison Ave New York City NY 10017

WERTHEIMER, M. DAVID, b. N.Y.C., Oct. 16, 1929; LL.B., Bklyn. Law Sch., 1952, LL.M.; 1957. Admitted to N.Y. State bar, 1955, U.S. Dist. Cts. So. and Eastern N.Y., 1957, U.S. Supreme Ct. bar, 1964, U.S. Ct. Mil. Appeals bar, 1964; asso. firm Hayt & Hayt, N.Y.C., 1955-57; individual practice law, N.Y.C., 1958—; law lectr. Hofstra U. Sch. Bus., 1967-74; asso. prof. bus. law N.Y. Inst. Tech., N.Y.C., 1966-72; asso. prof. law and bus. City U. N.Y., 1972—; asso. legis. counsel N.Y. State Senate, 1967, 68, 69; del. N.Y. Jud. Conv., 1968. Civil service commr. City of Long Beach, N.Y., 1971, 72. Mem. N.Y. County Lawyers Assn. Author: Law School Admission Test: A Practical Guide, 1977; Primer for Legal Secretary, 1977. Home: 349 E Hudson St Long Beach NY 11561 Office: 450 7th Ave New York City NY 10001 Tel (212) 695-2611

WERTSCHING, ROBERT, b. Milw., July 3, 1931; B.S., Marquette U., 1953, LL.B., 1956; M.A. in Sociology, St. Louis U., 1962. Admitted to Wis. bar, 1956. Ariz. bar, 1966; individual practice law, Phoenix, 1968—; atty. Indian Reservation, Pine Ridge, S.D., 1962-64, Gila River Indian Reservation, Ariz., 1965-66; lectr. Scottsdale Jr. Coll., 1968-74. Mem. Wis., Ariz. bar assns., Am. Judicature Soc. Office: 25 W Jefferson St Phoenix AZ 85003 Tel (602) 257-9451

WERY, FRANCIS J., b. Stephenson, Mich., Aug. 2, 1916; A.B., Mich. State U., 1943; J.D., U. Mich., 1952. Admitted to Mich. bar, 1952; asst. pros. atty Ingham County (Mich.), 1952-53, chief asst. pros. atty., 1953-54; individual practice law, Lansing, Mich., 1952, 54—; lectr. Wolverine Boys' State, Mich. State U., 1956-68. Chmn. Ingham County Rep. Com., 1958-60. Mem. Mich. Assn. of Professions (charter), Mich. State, Ingham County bar assns. Recipient award for outstanding service Ingham County Rep. Com., 1960. Office: 3217 W Saginaw St Lansing MI 48917 Tel (517) 321-2825

WESLEY, CHARLES MILLER, b. Mt. Clare, Ill., July 30, 1921; A.B., Blackburn Coll., 1951; LL.B., Washington U., St. Louis, 1951, J.D., 1968. Admitted to Ill. bar, 1952, Mo. bar, 1952; claim analyst, mgr. Allstate Ins. Co., Kansas City and Oklahoma City, 1952-64; pros. atty., Pulaski County, Mo., 1964-70; individual practice law, Waynesville, Mo., 1964—. Pres. council St. Robert (Mo.) Bellarmine Ch., 1973-75; chmn. social concern com. Diocesan Pastoral Council Jefferson City, Mo., 1974-76, rep., 1975-76. Mem. Mo., Pulaski County (pres. 1966-76) bar assns. Home and Office: Box 412 Hwy H Waynesville MO 65583 Tel (314) 774-5544

WESNER, JAMES ERMAL, b. Ida, La., Dec. 19, 1936; A.B., Tulane U., 1958, LL.B., 1961. Admitted to La. bar, 1961, D.C. bar, 1961, Va. bar, 1968; with admiralty and shipping sect., civil div., U.S. Dept. Justice, Washington, 1961; asst. prof. law U. Va., Charlottesville, 1964-67, asso. prof., 1968; asso. firm Ginsburg, Feldman and Bress, Washington, 1968-74, partner, 1974—; mem. Adminstrv. Conf. U.S., Washington, 1976, 77. Mem. Am., Va., D.C. bar assns., Maritime Law Assn. U.S. Office: 1700 Pennsylvania Ave NW Washington DC 20006 Tel (202) 637-9080

WESSELHOEFT, WILLIAM, b. Boston, May 1, 1920; A.B., Harvard, 1942, LL.B., 1948. Admitted to Wash. bar, 1949; with firm Ferguson & Burdell, Seattle, 1949—, partner, 1955. Mem. Am., Wash., Seattle-King County (pres. 1974-75) bar assn., Am. Coll. Trial Lawyers. Home: 123 Madrona Pl E Seattle WA 98112 Office: 1700 Peoples National Bank Bldg Seattle WA 98171 Tel (206) 622-1711

WESSLING, DONALD MOORE, b. Chgo., Nov. 26, 1936; B.S., Northwestern U., 1957, M.A. in Econs., 1958; J.D., U. Chgo., 1961. Admitted to Calif. bar, 1962, U.S. Supreme Ct. bar, 1965; asso. firm O'Melveny & Myers, Los Angeles, 1961-69, partner, 1970—; trustee So. Calif. Center for Law in the Pub. Interest, 1971—. Mem. Am. Bar Assn., U. Chgo. Law Alumni Assn. (pres. So. Calif. chpt. 1975—). Office: 611 W Sixth St Los Angeles CA 90017 Tel (213) 620-1120

WESSLING, ROBERT BRUCE, b. Chgo., Oct. 8, 1937; B.A., DePauw U., 1959; J.D., U. Mich., 1962. Admitted to Calif. bar, 1963; asso. firm Latham & Watkins, Los Angeles, 1962-63, 63-70, partner firm, 1970—. Active Westwood United Methodist Ch., Los Angeles, trustee 1975—. Mem. Am., Calif., Los Angeles bar assns., Order of Coif. Asst. editor Mich. Law Rev., 1961-62. Home: 12265 Castlegate Dr Los Angeles CA 90049 Office: 555 S Flower St Los Angeles CA 90071 Tel (213) 485-1234

WEST, DAVID WILLIAM, b. Erie, Pa., Dec. 26, 1937; B.S. in Bus. Adminstrn. and Mgmt., Pa. State U., 1959; LL.B., Washington Coll. Law, Am. U., 1962; LL.M. in Taxation, Georgetown U., 1964. Law clk. to firm Miller & Chevalier, Washington, 1960-62; asst. minority counsel Ho. of Reps. Com. on Ways and Means, Washington, 1962-64; admitted to D.C. bar, 1963, Ariz. bar, 1965; mem. firm, owner Evans, Kitchel & Jenckes, P.C., Phoenix, 1964—; pres., chmn. bd. 3-R Prodns., Inc. Bd. dirs. Ariz. Cactus Pine Council Girl Scouts U.S., Phoenix Men's Arts Council; gen. counsel Ariz. Republican State Com. Mem. Am., Fed., Ariz., Maricopa County (Ariz.) bar assns. Recipient Thanks badge Girl Scouts U.S.A., 1973. Home: 8005 N Coconino Rd Paradise Valley AZ 85253 Office: 363 N 1st Ave Phoenix AZ 85003 Tel (602) 262-8830

WEST, ELMER GORDON, b. Hyde Park, Mass., Nov. 27, 1914; student Northeastern U., 1934-35, Lamar Jr. Coll., Beaumont, Tex., 1935-36; B.S., La. State U., 1941, LL.B., 1942. Accountant, Stone & Webster, 1937-42; admitted to La. bar, 1942; mem. firm Long & West, Baton Rouge, 1946-50, Kantrow, Spaht, West & Kleinpeter, and predecessor, Baton Rouge, 1950-61; U.S. dist. judge Eastern Dist. Ct. La., 1961-67; chief judge U.S. Ct., Eastern Dist. La., 1967-72; U.S. dist. judge Middle Dist. La., 1972—. Atty., La. Revenue Dept., 1946-48, La. inheritance tax collector, 1948-52; asst. prof., spl. lectr. La. State U. Law Sch., 1947-48; mem. Jud. Conf. U.S., 1971—, mem. com. on operation jury system, 1972—. Mem. Am., La., East Baton Rouge bar assns., Am. Judicature Soc., Internat. Assn. Ins. Counsel, Nat. Assn. Compensation Claimants Attys., Alpha Tau Omega, Phi Delta Phi. Home: 2629 E Lakeshore Dr Baton Rouge LA 70808 Office: Fed Ct Bldg Baton Rouge LA 70801*

WEST, EVERETT LEO, b. N. Manchester, Ind., July 28, 1911; A.B., Manchester Coll., 1934; J.D., DePaul U., 1949. Admitted to Ind. bar, 1949, Ill. bar, 1950; pros. atty. Benton County, Ind., 1951-59; judge Benton Circuit Ct., Fowler, Ind., 1959-72; judge Miami Circuit Ct., Peru, Ind., 1973-74; individual practice law, Peru, 1974—. Mem. Ind. State, Miami County bar assns. Office: 25 Court St Peru IN 46970 Tel (317) 472-2363

WEST, HAROLD, b. Bklyn., June 26, 1929; B.A. U. Colo., 1951; LL.B., St. John's U., 1958. Admitted to N.Y. bar, 1958, Fla. bar, 1960; partner West, Friesner & Goldman, Miami, 1963—. Mem. Am., Dade County bar assns., Fla. Bar, Assn. Trial Lawyers Am., Acad. Fla. Trial Lawyers. Home: 5424 Jackson St Hollywood FL 33021 Office: 1110 Brickell Ave Miami FL 33131 Tel (305) 358-5460

WEST, JAMES JOSEPH, b. Tarentum, Pa., Nov. 26, 1945; B.A., St. Vincent Coll., 1967; J.D., Duquesne U., 1970. Admitted to Pa. Supreme Ct. bar, 1970, Pa. Superior Ct. bar, 1970; law clk. to Judge Rabe F. Marsh, U.S. Dist. Ct., Western Dist. Pa., 1970-74; asst. U.S. atty. Western Dist. Pa., 1974—. Mem. Am., Pa., Allegheny County (Pa.) bar assns. Recipient Outstanding Performance award Dept. Justice, 1975; editorial staff Pitts. Legal Jour., 1972-73. Home: 440 Charles Ave New Kensington PA 15068 Office: 633 US PO and Courthouse Pittsburgh PA 15219 Tel (412) 644-3519

WEST, JOHN FRANCIS, b. Raleigh, N.C., Jan. 30, 1915; B.A., Emory U., 1949, J.D., 1951. Admitted to Ga. bar, 1950; real estate property negotiator Bur. Purchasing and Real Estate, City of Atlanta, 1969—. Lt. col, aide-de-camp, mem. staff Gov. Jimmy Carter, 1970-74, Gov. George Busbee, 1974-78; commr. Atlanta Area council Boy Scouts Am., 1973—. Mem. City Atlanta Employee's Club (past pres.), Atlanta Employees Credit Union (dir. 1974-77), Am. Assn. Ret. Persons. Recipient awards Boy Scouts Am., 1975. Tel (404) 658-6440

WEST, JOSEPH ELBERT, b. Marquette, Mich., June 11, 1911; Ph.B., U. Chgo., 1932; J.D., U. Ill., 1934. Admitted to Ill. bar, 1934; 1st asso. firm Richard J. Neagle, Galesburg, Ill., 1935-39; partner Neagle & West, Galesburg, 1939-47; partner Stuart, Neagle & West, Galesburg, 1947—, sr. partner, 1970—; atty. Knox County Housing Authority, 1950-74, Community Unit Sch. Dist. 205, 1952-75; counsel Intra State Telephone Co., Galesburg, 1964-76. Pres., YMCA, 1945-47; exec. dir. Knox County Housing Authority, 1950-64; mem. urban renewal projects, also housing for elderly project study coms. Mem. Mem. Am., Ill., Knox County bar assns., Am. Judicature Soc., Ill. Def. League, Phi Beta Kappa. Contbr. articles to Ill. Sch. Bd. Jour. Home: 2640 Bridlecreek Ln Galesburg IL 61401 Office: 58 S Cherry St PO Box 1425 Galesburg IL 61401 Tel (309) 342-5188

WEST, ROY ALLAN, b. Cleve., July 31, 1932; B.S. in Bus. Adminstrn., Ohio State U., 1954, J.D., 1959. Admitted to Ohio bar, 1959, U.S. Supreme Ct. bar, 1963; partner firm West, West & Sherman, Elyria, Ohio, 1959—; law dir. City of North Ridgeville (Ohio), 1963, 66-69, 74-75; asst. solicitor and prosecutor City of Elyria, 1960-67; atty. North Ridgeville Bd. Edn., 1966-69, 74—; Eaton Twp. (Ohio), 1966-71. Pres., Lorain County Council for Retarded, 1963-65; chmn. Lorain County Bd. Mental Retardation, 1968-70, mem., 1968-75; mem. Lorain County Bd. Mental Health and Mental Retardation, 1968-70; corporate mem. Lorain County Mental Health Services, 1970-72; chmn. profl. div. United Fund, 1970; bd. dirs. Ohio Assn. Retarded Children, 1965-67; trustee Elyria YMCA, 1966—, pres., 1967-71, 76—; mem. co. Elyria Meml. Hosp.; former trustee and deacon 1st Congregational Ch.; former corporate mem. Family Services Assn.; former bd. dirs. Jr. Achievement. Mem. Am., Ohio (chmn. traffic law com. 1967), Lorain County bar assns., Ohio State U. Alumni Ass.Asn. (pres. Lorain County 1964). Home: 706 Washington Ave Elyria OH 44035 Office: 212 Middle Ave Elyria OH 44035 Tel (216) 322-3771

WEST, STEPHEN ALLAN, b. Salt Lake City, Mar. 23, 1935; B.S. in Philosophy, U. Utah, 1962, J.D., 1961. Admitted to Utah bar, 1961, D.C. bar, 1967, Md. Bar, 1969, U.S. Supreme Ct. bar, 1967; law clk. Judge A. Sherman Christensen U.S. Dist. Ct., Utah, 1961-62; asso. firm Marr, Wilkins and Cannon, Salt Lake City, 1962-65, partner, 1965-67; asso., D.C. Office, Jennings, Strouss, Salmon & Trask, Phoenix, Washington, 1967-68; atty. Marriott Corp., Bethesda, Md., 1968-71, asst. gen. counsel, 1971-74, asso. gen. counsel, 1974—; Mem. Am. (exec. com. young lawyers sect. 1964-65), Utah (exec. com. young lawyers sect. 1962-67), D.C. bar assns., Sigma Chi, Phi Delta Phi., U. Utah Alumni Assn. (distinguished alumni award, 1971). Home: 3719 Bradley Ln Chevy Chase MD 20015 Office: 5161 River Rd Washington DC 20016

WEST, TED GRADON, b. Lenoir, N.C., Feb. 18, 1929; A.B., Concord Coll., Athens, W.Va., 1954; J.D., U. N.C., Chapel Hill, 1957. Admitted to N.C. bar, 1957; mem. legal div. staff TVA, Knoxville, Tenn., 1957-60; partner firm West, Groome, Tuttle & Thomas, Lenoir, 1960—. Mem. N.C., Am., N.C. 25th Jud. Dist. (pres. 1970), Caldwell County (N.C.) (pres. 1965) bar assns., N.C. State Bar (councillor 1975—), Am. Judicature Soc., N.C. Acad. Trial Lawyers. Bd. editors N.C. Law Rev., 1956, asso. editor, 19S7. Home: Route 1 PO Box 392B Lenoir NC 28645 Office: 228 Main St NW Lenoir NC 28645 Tel (704) 758-5516

WEST, TERRY WAYNE, b. Ada, Okla., July 3, 1938; LL.B., U. Tulsa, 1966. Admitted to Okla. bar, 1966, U.S. Dist. Ct. bar, 1968, U.S. Supreme Ct. bar, 1974, U.S. Ct. Appeals, 1976; founding partner firm Henry, West & Sill, Shawnee, Okla., 1967—; legal counsel to Shawnee C. of C. Mem. Okla. Bar Assn., Am., Okla. trial lawyers assns. (pres. state assn. 1973, bd. govs. nat. assn. 1974-77). Home: Route 1 Box 99 Meeker OK 74855 Office: 231 N Broadway Shawnee OK 74801 Tel (405) 275-0040

WEST, WILLIAM HENRY, b. Cleve., Mar. 9, 1937; B.A., Yale U., 1959; J.D., Harvard U., 1962. Admitted to Ohio bar, 1962; asso. firm Thompson, Hine & Flory, Cleve., 1962-70, partner, 1970—; trustee and officer Legal Aid Soc. Cleve., 1965-67. Mem. Univ. Sch. Alumni Council, 1962—, Yale Sch. Com., 1962—; Cleve. rep. Assn. Yale Alumni, 1975—; trustee and officer Yale Alumni Scholarship of Cleve., Inc., 1967—; bd. overseers Case Western Res. U., 1975—; chmn. vis. com. Sch. Library Sci., Case Western Res. U., 1975—; mem. Shaker Heights Sch. Bd. Citizens Com. Mem. Am., Ohio, Greater Cleve. bar assns. Home: 2711 Wadsworth Rd Shaker Heights OH 44122 Office: 1100 Nat Bank Bldg Cleveland OH 44114 Tel (216) 241-1880

WEST, WILLIAM LEE, b. Greeley, Colo., Sept. 24, 1932; B.A. in Polit. Sci., U. Colo., 1954, J.D., 1957. Admitted to Colo. bar, 1957; research asst. to Prof. J.W. Moore, Yale Law Sch., 1957-58; partner firm West & West, Greeley, 1958-65; individual practice, Greeley, 1965-69; partner firm West & Winters, Greeley, 1969—; municipal judge Greeley, 1959-65, city atty., 1972-74; dep. dist. atty. Weld County, Colo., 1965-71. Pres., Weld County YMCA, 1962. Mem. Am., Weld County bar assns., Colo. Trial Lawyers Assn. (dir.), Greeley C. of C. (dir. 1964-67), Recipient Distinguished Service award Jr. C. of C., 1964; co-author various chpts. on fed. practice. Home: 1851 25th Ave Greeley CO 80631 Office: 201 1000 10th St Greeley CO 80631 Tel (303) 352-4805

WESTBROOK, JAMES EDWIN, b. Camden, Ark., Sept. 7, 1934; B.A., Hendrix Coll., 1956; J.D., Duke, 1959; LL.M., Georgetown U., 1965. Admitted to Ark. bar, 1959, Okla. bar, 1977; asso. firm Mehaffy, Smith & Williams, Little Rock, 1959-62; asst. counsel subcom. on Patents, Trademarks and Copyrights, U.S. Senate, 1963; legis. asst. U.S. Senate, 1963-65; asst. prof. law, U. Mo., 1965-68, asso. prof., 1968-70, prof., 1970-74, James S. Rollins Prof. law, 1974-76, asst. dean, 1966-68; dean U. Okla. Coll. Law, Norman, 1976—; chmn. Roundtable Council on Local Govt. Law, Assn. Am. Law Schs., 1972; reporter for Mid-Am. Assembly on The Role of the State in the Urban Crises, 1970; mem. Mo. Gov.'s Adv. Council on Local Govt., 1967-69; mem. spl. com. on labor relations Dept. Labor and Indsl. Relations, State of Mo., 1975-76. Mem. Am., Okla., Cleveland County bar assns., Assn. Am. Law Schs., Indsl. Relations Research Assn., Order of Coif. Contbr. articles to legal jours. Home: 2009 Crestmont St Norman OK 73069 Office: Law Center 300 Timberdell Rd Norman OK

WESTEN, TRACY ANDREW, b. Santa Barbara, Calif., Apr. 16, 1941; B.A., Pomona Coll., 1962; M.A., University Coll., Oxford (Eng.), 1964; J.D., U. Calif., Berkeley, 1967. Admitted to D.C. bar, 1968, Calif. bar, 1968, U.S. Supreme Ct. bar, 1973; asso. firm Covington & Burling, Washington, 1967-69; legal asst. to commr. FCC, 1969-70; dir. Stern Community Law Firm, Washington, 1970-74; dir. Pub. Communication, Inc., Los Angeles, 1973—; dir. communications law program U. Calif., Los Angeles, 1974—; chmn. advisory bd. Station KPFK, Los Angeles, 1975—; mem. Calif. Bd. Registration for Profl. Engrs.; mem. com. pub. interest law Calif. State Bar. Chmn. bd. dirs. Pacifica Found., 1975—. Mem. D.C., Los Angeles, Calif., FCC bar assns., Order of Coif, Phi Beta Kappa. Office: U Calif Los Angeles Law Sch 405 Hilgard Ave Los Angeles CA 90024 Tel (213) 825-6211

WESTERFIELD, FRANK ORLEN, JR., b. Albuquerque, Oct. 12, 1924; A.B., Washington U., St. Louis, 1951; J.D., U. N.Mex., 1952; postgrad. N.Y. U., 1952-53. Admitted to N.Mex. bar, 1953; individual practice law, Albuquerque, 1953—; mem. Nat. Conf. Lawyers and C.P.A.'s, 1972-75. Mem. Albuquerque (dir. 1965-67), Fed., Am. (state chmn. membership com. 1970-72) bar assns. Recipient Outstanding Service award State Bar N.Mex., 1974. Home: 6927 Guadalupe Trail NW Albuquerque NM 87107 Office: PO Box 25051 Albuquerque NM 87125 Tel (505) 243-4596

WESTERGREN, GARY PIERCE, b. Torrington, Conn., Jan. 3, 1940; B.A., Conn. Wesleyan U., 1962; J.D., Vanderbilt U., 1970. Admitted to N.H. bar, 1970; asso. firm Wescott, Millham & Dyer, Laconia, N.H., 1970-74, mem., 1974—. Chmn. Gilford (N.H.) Bd. Adjustment, 1972-74. Mem. Am., N.H., Belknap County bar assns. Home: Belknap Mountain Rd Gilford NH 03246 Office: 101 Court St Laconia NH 03246 Tel (603) 524-2166

WESTERLING, KAREL, b. Leeuwarden, Netherlands, Dec. 11, 1929; came to U.S., 1949, naturalized, 1957; diploma Netherlands Coll. Fgn. Service, 1949; B.A., Colo. Coll., 1950; LL.B., Yale U., 1954. Admitted to N.Y. bar, 1957; asso. firm Brown, Wood, Ivey, Mitchell & Petty, N.Y.C., 1954-64, partner, 1965—; sec. Charles E. Merrill Trust, Ithaca, N.Y., 1976—. Mem. Am., N.Y. State, N.Y.C. bar assns. Office: One Liberty Plaza New York City NY 10006

WESTERMAN, ARNOLD RODMAN, b. Wilmington, Del., Apr. 17, 1938; B.A., U. Md., 1962; J.D. with honors, George Washington U., 1965. Admitted to D.C. bar, 1966; atty. SEC, Washington, 1965-69; asso. firm Arent, Fox, Kintner, Plotkin & Kahn, Washington, 1969-74, partner, 1975—; lectr. in field. Mem. Am., D.C., Fed. bar assns. Home: 7601 Hackamore Dr Potomac MD 20854 Office: 1815 H St NW Washington DC 20006 Tel (202) 857-6243

WESTLER, BERNARD OSCAR, b. Milw., Apr. 1, 1935; B.S., U. Wis., 1956, J.D., 1960. Admitted to Wis. bar, 1972; served as legal asst. USN, 1960-61; tchr. Cradock High Sch., Portsmouth, Va., 1961-68; dir. edn. Nat. Found. for Consumer Credit, Washington,

1968-71; asso. firm Goldberg, Previant & Uelmen, Milw., 1972—. Mem. Jr. C. of C., Norfolk, Va., 1960-62; youth group adviser B'nai B'rith, 1972-73. Mem. Indsl. Relations Research Assn., Am. Arbitration Assn. (arbitrator), Wis., Am. bar assns. Home: 4221 N Olson Ave Milwaukee WI 53211 Office: 788 N Jefferson Ave Milwaukee WI 53202 Tel (414) 271-4500

WESTLER, MURRAY, b. N.Y.C., Mar. 25, 1929; B.S., U. Wis., 1950, J.D., 1952. Admitted to Wis. bar, 1952, Ill. bar, 1953; individual practice law, Milw., 1952-53, Chgo., 1953-77; mem. firm Zenoff Westler Jones Kamm & Shapiro, Chgo., 1977—; lectr. Ill. Inst. Continuing Legal Edn. Mem. Comml. Law League, Ill., Chgo. bar assns., Am. Arbitration Assn. (arbitrator). Contbr. to legal textbooks. Office: 53 N Jackson Blvd Chicago IL 60604 Tel (312) 922-5685

WESTMORELAND, BARBARA CAROL, b. Thomasville, N.C., June 23, 1929; B.A., U. N.C., Greensboro, 1949; J.D., Wake Forest U., 1967. Admitted to N.C. bar, 1967; sr. partner firm Westmoreland & Sawyer, Winston-Salem, N.C. Mem. Nat. Assn. Women Lawyers, Am., N.C., Forsyth County (past treas.) bar assns., Am. Judicature Soc., Am. Trial Lawyers Assn., N.C. Acad. Trial Lawyers. Office: 1144 W 4th St Winston Salem NC 27101 Tel (919) 725-3554

WESTON, STEPHEN BURNS, b. Yellow Springs, Ohio, May 4, 1904; A.B., Antioch Coll., 1925; LL.B., Yale U., 1929; LL.D., Cleve. State U., 1969. Admitted to Ohio bar, 1930, N.Y. State bar, 1976; asso. firm Thompson, Hine & Flory, Cleve., 1929-35; Ohio adminstr. Nat. Youth Adminstrn., Columbus, 1935-40, nat. exec. dir., acting chmn. nat. adv. com., Washington, 1940-42; sec. (exec.) U.S. Sect. Anglo-Am. Caribbean Commn., Dept. State, Washington, 1942-44, acting chief Caribbean office; exec. dir. Greater Cleve. Devel. Council, 1944-46; sr. partner firm Weston, Hurd, Fallon, Paisley & Howley, Cleve., 1945-76; individual practice law, Keene, N.Y., 1976—. Home and Office: West-on-East Keene NY 12942 Tel (518) 576-4723

WESTON, WILLIAM ISEDORE, b. Balt. May 11, 1946; A.B., Loyola Coll., 1968; J.D., U. Md., 1971. Admitted to Md. bar, 1972; asst. exec. dir. Md. Bar Assn., 1970-72; exec. dir. Bar Assn. Balt. City, 1972-74; individual practice law, Balt., 1972—; asst. dean, asst. prof. U. Balt., 1974—; vice chmn. Balt. Bail Bonds Commn., 1972-76, chmn. paralegal com., mem. exec. bd. ethics cons. Balt. Bar, 1974-76. Bd. dirs. Balt. region Boy Scouts Am., Mem. Balt., Md., Am. bar assns., Am Judicature Soc., Acad. Continuing Legal Edn. Adminstrs. Home: 3302 Taney Rd Baltimore MD 21215 Office: 1420 N Charles St Baltimore MD 21201 Tel (301) 539-6264

WESTWICK, JOHN ATWELL, b. Kalama, Wash., Mar. 3, 1914; B.A., U. Calif., Berkeley, 1936, LL.B., 1939. Admitted to Calif. bar, 1939; practiced in Santa Barbara, Calif., 1940-61; judge Calif. Superior Ct. for Santa Barbara County, 1961—. Mem. Calif. Bar Assn. Home: Rancho Cielo Los Olivos CA 93441 Office: County Courthouse Santa Barbara CA 93101 Tel (805) 966-7624

WETTER, CURTISS EARLE, b. Mille Lacs County, Minn., May 4, 1899; A.B., U. Calif., Berkeley, 1921, J.D., 1923. Admitted to Calif. bar, 1923; dep. dist. atty. Tehama County (Calif.), 1923-30; city atty. City of Red Bluff (Calif.), 1927-50, City of Tehama (Calif.), 1937-50, City of Corning (Calif.), 1944-50; mem. firms McCoy & Wetter, Red Bluff, 1927-30, Wetter & Rankin, Red Bluff, 1931-35, Wetter & Coffman, Red Bluff, 1946-50; judge Superior Ct. of Calif., County of Tehama, 1950-75, ret., 1975; judge sitting by assignment in Calif. counties, 1975—. Mem. Am. Bar Assn., Calif. State Bar, Conf. Calif. Judges. Home and Office: 999 Rio Red Bluff CA 96080 Tel (916) 527-0254

WEXLER, JAY MILO, b. Chgo., June 11, 1922; B.S. in Econs., U. Wis., 1949, J.D., 1952. Admitted to Wis. bar, 1952; hearing examiner State of Wis., Madison, 1973-75; trial atty., 1975—. Chmn., Madison Water Utility, 1973; alderman City of Madison, 1973—. Mem. Wis., Dane County bar assns. Home: 4406 Rolla Ln Madison WI 53711 Tel (608) 233-8913

WEXLER, MORRIS MARTIN, b. Phila., Feb. 6, 1904; A.B., U. Pa., 1924, LL.B., 1927, J.D., 1969. Admitted to Pa. bar, 1927, U.S. Supreme Ct. bar, 1935; mem. firm Wexler, Weisman, Maurer & Forman, and predecessors, Phila., 1930—. Mem. Am., Pa., Phila., Internat. Bar Assns. Home: The Farmstead East Sullivan ME 04607 Office: 1 E Penn Square Philadelphia PA 19107 Tel (215) 568-1900

WEXLER, RICHARD L., b. Chgo., June 19, 1941; student U. Mich., 1959-62; J.D. with honors, John Marshall Law Sch., 1965. Admitted to Ill. bar, 1965; gen. counsel Met. Housing and Planning Council of Chgo., 1965-67; partner firm Wexler, Kane & Rosenzweig, Chgo., 1967-72, Wexler, Kane, Rosenzweig & Shaw, Chgo., 1972-73, Taussig, Wexler & Shaw, Chgo., 1973-75; prin. Taussig, Wexler & Shaw, Chgo., 1975—; spl. counsel Ill. Dept. Transp. Div. Water Resources, 1975—; adj. prof. law John Marshall Law Sch., 1967-75; zoning laws cons. Ill. Gen. Assembly, 1971; counsel Gov.'s Commn. on Urban Areas Govt., 1972, Ill. Coastal Zone Mgmt. Program, 1976—. Mem. young leadership cabinet United Jewish Appeal, 1976—; counsel Landmarks Preservation Council, 1975-76. Mem. Am., Ill. (winner Lincoln award 1968) bar assns., Chgo. Council Lawyers, Am. Soc. Planning Ofcls., Urban Land Inst. Contbr. articles to legal jours. Office: 180 N LaSalle St Chicago IL 60601 Tel (312) 726-1272

WEXNER, IRA HOWARD, b. Bklyn., Mar. 15, 1929; B.B.A., U. Miami, 1951, J.D., 1953. Admitted to Fla. bar, 1953, N.Y. bar, 1954; with William A. Hyman, N.Y.C., 1953-57, Irving Rosenkrantz, N.Y.C., 1957-58; partner firm Hirsch & Wexner, N.Y.C., 1959-68; individual practice law, N.Y.C., 1968-71; partner firm Wexner & Koenig, N.Y.C., 1971—. Pres. Jewish Community Center of Alden Terrace, Valley Stream, 1967-71; mem. Town of Hempstead Housing Authority, 1973-74; Town of Hempstead Bd. Zoning Appeals, 1974—. Mem. N.Y. County Lawyers Assn., Nassau County, Bklyn. bar assns., Bklyn. Lawyers Club of Fedn. Office: 342 Madison Ave New York City NY 10017 Tel (212) MU2-2011

WEYAND, RUTH, b. Grinnell, Iowa, Jan. 14, 1912; Ph.B., U. Chgo., 1930, J.D. cum laude, 1932. Admitted to Ill. bar, 1933; U.S. Supreme Ct. bar, 1936; individual practice law, Chgo., 1933-38; atty. NLRB, Washington, 1938-50, asst. gen. counsel, 1948-50; individual practice law, Washington, 1950-65; asso. gen. counsel Internat. Union Elec., Radio and Machine Workers, AFL-CIO, Washington, 1965—; mem. nat. legal com. NAACP, 1945-65. Mem. nat. adv. bd. Women's Equity Action League, 1973—; bd. advisors Women's Rights Project, Center Law and Social Policy, Washington, 1974—. Mem. Am. Fedn. Tchrs., Am., Chgo. bar assns., Assn. Trial Lawyers Am. Home: 308 N St SW Washington DC 20024 Office: 1126 16th St NW Washington DC 20036 Tel (202) 296-1206

WEYGANDT, RICHARD SILVER, b. Cleve., Mar. 3, 1918; A.B., Coll. Wooster, 1940; LL.B., Western Res. U., 1943. Admitted to Ohio bar, 1943, Minn. bar, 1945, W.Va. bar, 1967; individual practice law, Cleve. and Austin, Minn., 1943-48; asst. to gen. atty. N.Y. Central R.R., Cleve., 1948-58; solicitor Village of Westlake (Ohio), 1950-52; law dir. City of Bay Village (Ohio), 1953-56; sec. Interlake Iron Corp., Cleve., 1958-63; counsel Harshaw Chem. Co., Cleve., 1963-67; counsel Monongahela Power Co., Fairmont, W.Va., 1966-75, v.p. legal, sec., treas., 1975—. Mem. Ohio State, W.Va. State, Am. bar assns., W.Va. State Bar, Edison Elec. Inst. (legal com.). Home: 6 Hollen Circle Fairmont WV 26554 Office: 1310 Fairmont Ave Fairmont WV 26554 Tel (304) 366-3000

WEYHER, HARRY FREDERICK, b. Wilson, N.C., Aug. 19, 1921; B.S., U. N.C., 1946; LL.B. magna cum laude, Harvard, 1949. Admitted to N.C. bar, 1949, N.Y. State bar, 1949; since practiced in N.Y.C.; asso. firm Cravath, Swaine & Moore, 1949-54; sr. asst. counsel N.Y. State Crime Commn., 1951-52; adj. asso. prof. law N.Y. U., 1952-62; partner firm Olwine, Connelly, Chase, O'Donnell & Weyher, N.Y.C., 1954—. Contbr. articles to law revs. Home: 161 E 65th St New York City NY 10021 Office: 299 Park Ave New York City NY 10017 Tel (212) 688-0400

WEYRAUCH, WALTER OTTO, b. Lindau, Germany, Aug. 27, 1919; Dr. jur., U. Frankfurt-Main (Germany), 1951; LL.B., Georgetown U., 1955; LL.M., Harvard, 1956; J.S.D., Yale, 1962. Admitted to German bar, 1949; partner firm, Frankfurt-Main, 1949-52; mem. staff Harvard U. Dumbarton Oaks Library and Collection, Washington, 1953-55; asst. instr. Yale, 1956-57, asso. prof. law U. Fla., Gainesville, 1957-60, prof., 1960—; vis. prof. law Rutgers U., Newark, 1968; vis. prof. polit. sci. U. Calif., Berkeley, 1968-69, vis. prof. law U. Frankfurt-Main, 1975; cons. Commn. Experts on Problems of Succession, Hague Conf. on Pvt. Internat. Law, U.S. Dept. State, 1968-71. Mem. Internat. Assn. Philosophy of Law and Social Philosophy, AAUP, Order of Coif. Author: The Personality of Lawyers, 1964; Zum Gesellschaftsbild des Juristen, 1970; Hierarchie der Aus bildungsstätten, Rechtsstudium und Recht in den Vereinigten Staaten, 1976; contbr. articles to textbooks and legal jours. Home: 3425 SW 2d Ave Apt 238 Gainesville FL 32607 Office: U Fla Coll Law Gainesville FL 32611 Tel (904) 392-2211

WEYRENS, JOHN JOSEPH, b. St. Cloud., Minn., Jan. 27, 1935; B.S., St.John's U., 1957, LL.B., William Mitchell Coll., 1964. Admitted to Minn. bar, 1964; with law dept. St. Paul Fire & Marine Ins. Co., St. Paul, 1964-66; asso. firm R. M. Saltness, Dawson, Minn., 1966-72; judge, Lac Qui Parle County, Minn., 1973—; asst. chief judge 8th Jud. Dist., 1977—. Chmn. Countryside Council, 1974; mem. Gov's. Commn. on Minn.'s Future, 1975-77. Mem. 8th Judicial Dist. Minn. County Ct. Judges (chmn. 1974—77). Home: 829 3d Ave Madison MN 56256 Office: Lac Qui Parle County Courthouse Madison MN 56256 Tel (612) 598-3915

WHALEN, FRANK CHARLES, b. Ashtabula, Ohio, May 17, 1928; B.A., Case Western Res. U., LL.B., 1953. Admitted to Ohio bar, 1953, U.S. Supreme Ct. bar, 1974; partner firm Wells, Marks & Whalen, Cleve., 1953—. Mem. Greater Cleve., Cuyahoga County bar assns. Home: 1441 Newman Ave Lakewood OH 44107 Office: 930 Leader Bldg Cleveland OH 44114 Tel (216) 781-0636

WHALEN, MICHAEL JOHN, b. Towanda, Kans., Apr. 22, 1922; student in Econs., U. Iowa, 1948; LL.B., U. Mich., 1950. Admitted to Iowa, Mich. bars, 1951, Mont. bar, 1954; individual practice law, Anamosa, Iowa, 1951-53, Billings, Mont., 1954—; chmn. Bd. Labor Appeals for Mont., 1973—. Chmn. Yellowstone County (Mont.) Democratic Central Com., 1960-64. Mem. Iowa, Mont. bar assns. Home: 2312 Virginia Ln Billings MT 59102 Office: Suite 1306 First Northwestern Bank Center Billings MT 59101 Tel (406) 259-8793

WHALEN, THOMAS PATRICK, b. Bennington, Vt., May 7, 1939; B.S., Coll. Holy Cross, 1961; J.D., St. Louis U., 1964. Admitted to Vt. bar, 1964; asst. U.S. atty. Dist. Vt., 1965-68; individual practice law, Manchester Center, Vt., 1968—; dir. Factory Point Nat. Bank, Manchester Center; moderator Town of Arlington (Vt.), 1970—; Mem. Planning Commn. Arlington, 1968-70, selectman, 1979-70; bd. dirs. Martha Canfield Meml. Library, Arlington; mem. Mt. Laurel Sch. Bd., 1976, Manchester Health Services, 1976. Mem. Vt., Bennington County bar assns. Home: Buck Hill Rd Arlington VT 05250 Office: Center Hill Office Bldg Manchester Center VT 05255 Tel (802) 362-2310

WHALEN, WAYNE WALTER, b. Savanna, Ill., Aug. 22, 1939; B.S., U.S. Air Force Acad., 1961; J.D., Northwestern Sch. Law, 1967. Admitted to Ill. bar, 1967, U.S. Supreme Ct. bar, 1972; mem. firm Mayer, Brown & Platt, Chgo., 1967—. Del., 6th Ill. Constnl. Conv., 1969-70, chmn. style drafting and submission com. 1969-70; mem. Ill. Judicial Inquiry Bd., 1971-75. Office: 231 S LaSalle St Chicago IL 60604

WHALEY, ROBERT HAMILTON, b. Huntington, W.Va., Apr. 5, 1943; A.B., Princeton, 1965; J.D., Emory U., 1968. Admitted to Ga. bar, 1968, Colo. bar, 1970, Wash. bar, 1971; atty. land and natural resources div. U.S. Dept. Justice, Washington, 1969-71; asst. U.S. atty. Eastern Dist. Wash., 1971-72; partner firm Winston & Cashatt, Spokane, Wash., 1974—. Mem. Am., Ga., Wash. (bd. govs. Young Lawyers sect. 1976—, bd. bar examiners 1976—) bar assns., Wash. State Trial Lawyers Assn. (bd. govs. 1976—). Asso. editor Jour. Pub. Law, 1967-68. Office: Spokane and East Bldg Spokane WA 99201 Tel (509) 838-6131

WHALLEY, JOHN D., b. Nashville, Aug. 30, 1921; A.B., Vanderbilt U., 1943, J.D., 1948; postgrad. U. of South. Admitted to Tenn. bar, 1947; now partner firm Barksdale, Whalley, Gilbert and Frank, Nashville; asst. dist. atty. gen. Tenn. 10th Jud. Dist., 1948-51; supreme ct. commr., 1965-66. Fellow Am. Coll. Probate Counsel, Am. Bar Found., Am. Judicature Soc., Internat. Soc. Barristers; mem. Am., Tenn. (pres. 1976-77), Nashville (v.p. 1961-62) bar assns., Phi Delta Phi. Office: 7th Floor Third Nat Bank Bldg Nashville TN 37219 Tel (615) 244-0020*

WHATLEY, JACQUELINE BELTRAM, b. West Orange, N.J., Sept. 26, 1944; B.A., U. Tampa, 1966; J.D., Stetson U., 1969. Admitted to Fla. Supreme Ct. bar, 1969, Alaska Supreme Ct. bar, 1971, U.S. Dist. Ct. bar for Dist. Fla., 1969, Dist. Alaska, 1971, U.S. Customs Ct. bar, 1972; asso. firm Gibbons, Tucker, McEwen, Smith, Cofer & Taub, Tampa, Fla., 1969-71, partner, 1973—; individual practice law, Anchorage, 1971-73; arbitrator Am. Can Co., Continental Can Co. and U.S. Steelworkers Am., 1974—. Mem. Tampa, Hillsborough County (Fla.) bar assns., Nu Beta Epsilon. Home: PO Box 17595 Tampa FL 33612 Office: 606 Madison St Tampa FL 33601 Tel (813) 228-7841

WHATLEY, ROBERT LAMAR, b. Atlanta, Nov. 20, 1941; B.B.A., Ga. State U., 1965; LL.B., John Marshall Law Sch., 1969. Real estate negotiator City of Atlanta, 1969-75; admitted to Ga. bar, 1973; individual practice law, Atlanta, 1973—; panel arbitrator Am. Arbitration Assn., 1971—. Mem. Ga. State Bar, Atlanta, Douglas County bar assns. Home: 3959 Janet St Lithia Springs GA 30057 Office: 101 Marietta Towers Suite 2205 Atlanta GA 30303 Tel (404) 577-5161

WHEAT, DICK MARSH, b. New Orleans, Dec. 30, 1906; student U. Va., 1927-30; J.D., U. Cin., 1933. Admitted to Ky. bar, 1933; commd. lt. U.S. Navy, 1941, advanced through grades to capt., 1941-65; served with JAG, 1945-65; ret., 1965; law librarian State of Ky., Frankfort, 1965-76. Mem. Phi Delta Phi. Home: 993 Holly Spring Dr Lexington KY 40504

WHEAT, FRANCIS MILLSPAUGH, b. Los Angeles, Feb. 4, 1921; A.B., Pomona Coll., 1942; LL.B., Harvard U., 1948. Admitted to Calif. bar, 1949; asso. firm Gibson, Dunn & Crutcher, Los Angeles, 1948-64, 69—; commr. SEC, Washington, 1964-69; adv. Am. Law Inst. Fed. Securities Code Project, 1971—; chmn. Study on Establishment of Accounting Principles, Am. Inst. CPA's, 1971-72; mem. Fin. Accounting Standards Bd. Nat. Adv. Council, 1974—. Dir. Phillips Petroleum Corp. Bd. dirs. Center for Law in the Pub. Interest, Los Angeles County Bar Found.; trustee, vice chmn. bd. Pomona Coll. Fellow Am. Bar Found; mem. Am., Los Angeles (pres. 1975-76) bar assns., Am. Law Inst., Nat. Assn. Securities Dealers (gov. at large 1974-76). Contbr. articles to profl. jours. Home: 2130 Lombardy Rd San Marino CA 91108 Office: 515 S Flower St Los Angeles CA 90071 Tel (213) 488-7661

WHEAT, JOSEPH RONALD, b. Lexington, Ky., Mar. 29, 1942; A.B. in Philosophy, Cath. U. Am., 1964; J.D., U. Ky., 1967; asso. firm Gess, Mattingly, Saunier & Atchison, Lexington, 1968-74, partner, 1974—. Home: 299 Idle Hour Dr Lexington KY 40502 Office: 201 W Short St Lexington KY 40507

WHEAT, JOSIAH, b. Woodville, Tex., Dec. 21, 1928; B.A., U. Tex., 1951, LL.B., 1952. Admitted to Tex. bar, 1952, U.S. Supreme Ct. bar, 1961; partner firm Wheat, Stafford and Kinney, and predecessors, Woodville, 1952—; city atty., Woodville; gen. counsel Lower Neches Valley Authority; dir. Tyler County Indsl. Corp., Tyler County Devel. Corp.; mem. adv. com. Water, Inc. Bd. dirs., mem. water laws com., past pres. Tex. Water Conservation Assn.; pres. Tyler County Dogwood Festival Assn., Inc.; mem. exec. com. Trinity Neches council Boy Scouts Am.; mem. adminstrv. bd. Woodville United Methodist Ch. Fellow Am. Bar Assn. (ho. of dels., mem. com. environ. quality and water resources com. natural resources sect., mem. standing com. environ. law), Tex. Bar Found. (life); mem. State Bar Tex. (past pres., forming dir. chmn. environ. law sect.), Tyler County, Jefferson County, Dallas bar assns., Beaumont (waterways com.), East Tex. (water resources com.) chambers commerce, Gulf-Intracoastal Canal Assn. (dir.), Tex. Municipal League (legis. com.). Recipient Silver Beaver award Boy Scouts Am. Office: 300 W Bluff St Woodville TX 75979 Tel (713) 283-3711

WHEAT, THOMAS ALLEN, b. Liberty, Tex., June 19, 1913; student South Park Jr. Coll., Beaumont, Tex.; LL.B., U. Tex., 1936. Admitted to Tex. bar, 1936, U.S. Supreme Ct. bar, 1942; individual practice law, Liberty, 1936—; county atty. Liberty County, 1939-42; served with JAGC, AUS, 1944-46; asso. firm Cain & Wheat, Liberty, 1937-39, Hightower & Wheat, 1953-55, Wheat & Zbranek, 1955-58; dist. judge 75th Jud. Dist., 1968; mem. judges com. admissions to practice U.S. Dist. Ct. Eastern Dist. Tex.; dir., gen. counsel Farmers State Bank, Cleveland, Tex. Chmn., Chambers-Liberty Counties Nav. Dist. Commn., 1976; pres. Ariz. Creek Wildlife Assn.; sr. warden, vestryman St. Stephens Episcopal Ch. Life fellow Tex. Bar Found.; mem. Am., Tex., Liberty-Chambers County bar assns., Am. Judicature Soc., Internat. Soc. Barristers. Home: 1704 Cos Ave Liberty TX 77575 Office: 714 Main St Liberty TX 77575 Tel (713) 336-3663

WHEATLEY, ARCHER, b. DuQuoin, Ill., Oct. 26, 1885; LL.B., Transylvania Coll. Law, 1907. Admitted to Ark. bar, 1909; chancellor, 1917-23; mem. firms Lamb Caraway & Wheatley, 1913-15, Hawthorne & Wheatley, 1923-33; mem. firm Barrett Wheatley Smith & Deacon, Jonesboro, Ark., 1943-69, of counsel, 1969—. Mem. Am., Ark. bar assns. Home: 1104 S Madison St Jonesboro AR 72401 Office: Citizens Bank Bldg 6th floor Jonesboro AR 72401 Tel (501) 932-6694

WHEATLEY, JOHN REGINALD, b. Abington, Mass., June 30, 1904; B.A., Dartmouth, 1924; J.D., Harvard, 1927. Admitted to Mass. bar, 1928; asso. firm Keith, Reed, Wheatley & Frenette, Brockton, Mass., 1929—; asst. dist. atty. Norfolk and Plymouth Dist., 1939-47; asst. atty. gen. Commonwealth of Mass., 1940; dist. atty. Plymouth County, 1954-69. Home: 130 Ashland St Abington MA 02351 Office: 231 Main St Brockton MA 02401 Tel (617) 587-0531

WHEATLEY, SEAGAL V., b. Houston, May 24, 1935; B.A. in Govt., U. Tex., 1957, J.D. Admitted to Tex. bar, 1960; U.S. atty. Western dist. Tex., 1969-71; partner firm Oppenheimer, Rosenberg, Kelleher & Wheatley, Inc., San Antonio, 1971—. Mem. State Bar Tex., Am., San Antonio (past dir.) bar assns., San Antonio C. of C. (past dir.). Named Outstanding Young Man, San Antonio Jr. C. of C., 1970. Office: 620 San Antonio Bank & Trust Bldg 711 Navarro St San Antonio TX 78205 Tel (512) 224-7581

WHEELER, CHARLES VAWTER, b. Fay, Okla., Nov. 12, 1920; student Harding Coll., Searcy, Ark., 1938-39, U. Okla., 1939-43, U. Tex., 1947; LL.B., U. Okla., 1948; LL.M., N.Y. U., 1973. Admitted to Okla. bar, 1943, N.Y. bar, 1969; atty. Southwestern Bell Telephone Co., Oklahoma City, 1948-53; individual practice law, Oklahoma City, 1953-58; with Cities Service Co., Tulsa, 1958—, gen. counsel, 1969—, also dir., mem. exec. com.; asst. adj. gen. Okla., 1966-68. Vice pres., trustee Cities Service Found. Mem. Am., Okla., N.Y. State bar assns., Bar Assn. City N.Y., Am. Petroleum Inst., N.G. Assn., Delta Tau Delta. Home: 2151 E 31st St Tulsa OK 74105 Office: 110 W 7th St Box 300 Tulsa OK 74102 Tel (918) 586-4200

WHEELER, DAVID WILLIAMS, b. Marion, Kans., Jan. 18, 1907; B.A., U. Mich., 1929, LL.B., 1933. Admitted to Ill. bar, 1933, Kans. bar, 1934; mem. firm Wheeler & Wheeler, Marion; atty., Marion County, 1937-41. Mem. Am., Kans., Central Kans., Marion County bar assns., Am., Kans. (bd. govs.) trial lawyers assns. Office: 318 E Main St Marion KS 66861 Tel (316) 382-2121

WHEELER, JAMES ALBERT, b. Newton, Kans., Nov. 7, 1927; A.B., Washburn U., 1949, LL.B., 1954, J.D., 1972. Admitted to Kans. bar, 1954, U.S. Supreme Ct. bar, 1972; individual practice law, Olathe, Kans., 1954—; asst. county atty. Johnson County (Kans.), Olathe, 1960-71, county atty., 1971-73. Pres. Johnson County Council on

Drug Abuse, 1971-72; bd. dirs. Kans. City Area Nat. Council on Alcoholism, Johnson County Mental Retardation Assn. Mem. Am., Kans., Johnson County bar assns., Nat. Dist. Attys. Assn., Kansas County and Dist. Attys. Assn. (pres. 1972-73), Am., Kans. trial lawyers assn., Kans. Peace Officers Assn., Delta Theta Phi, Phi Delta Theta. Home: 900 Stonecrest Rd Olathe KS 66061 Office: Law Bldg 301 N Chestnut St Olathe KS 60061 Tel (913) 782-0800

WHEELER, JEFFREY ROBERT, b. Waukesha, Wis., June 4, 1941; B.S., U. Wis., 1963, J.D., 1966. Admitted to Wis. bar, 1966, Colo. bar, 1969; served with JAGC, U.S. Army, 1967-70; dep. dist. atty. 4th Jud. Dist. Colo., Colorado Springs, 1971-73; partner firm Melat & Wheeler and predecessors, Colorado Springs, 1973—. Bd. dirs. N.E. Civic Assn., Colorado Springs, 1970-73; pres. Village Seven Homeowners Assn., 1977; bd. advisors Adult Forensic Services, Colorado Springs, 1975-76. Mem. Wis., Colo., El Paso County bar assns., Colo., El Paso County (pres., 1975-76) trial lawyers assns. Office: 303 S Cascade Ave Colorado Springs CO 80903 Tel (303) 475-0304

WHEELER, LEONARD, b. Worcester, Mass., July 20, 1901; A.B., Harvard U., 1922, LL.B., 1925. Admitted to Mass. bar, 1926; asso. firm Goodwin, Procter & Hoar, Boston, 1925-32, partner, 1932-72, of counsel, 1973—; mem. pros. staff 1st Nuremberg Crimes Trial, 1945-46; dir. Clerk, Harold Cabot & Co., Inc.; past corporator Cambridge Savs. Bank. Bd. dirs. Cambridge Family and Children's Service, 1946—, also past treas., pres.; past treas. Cambridge council Boy Scouts Am.; past pres. bd. overseers Shady Hill Sch., Cambridge; past bd. dirs. Boston Legal Aid Soc., Cambridge Community Services; past bd. dirs., pres. Chocorua (N.H.) Lake Assn.; trustee Tamworth (N.H.) Found. Mem. Am., Mass., Cambridge (pres. 1961-62) bar assns., Am. Law Inst., Am. Judicature Soc. Grad. treas. Harvard Law Rev., 1956-71. Home: 123 Coolidge Hill Cambridge MA 02138 Office: 28 State St Boston MA 02109 Tel (617) 523-5700

WHELAN, JOSEPH ALOYSIUS, b. Phila., June 21, 1906; A.B., Princeton, 1927; J.D., Yale, 1930. Admitted to Pa. bar, 1930, U.S. Supreme Ct. bar, 1946; individual practice law, Paoli, Pa., 1930—; chief legal br. Phila. Ordnance Dist., 1940-44; chief cost plus fixed fee termination br. Hdqrs. Army Service Forces, Washington, 1944-46. Mem. Bd. Assessment Appeals Chester County (Pa.), 1968-72. Mem. Pa., Chester County bar assns., Ret. Officers Assn. Decorated Legion of Merit; holder 2 patents. Home: 2 Colonial Way St Paoli PA 19301 Office: 139 Grubb Rd Paoli PA 19301 Tel (215) 644-5568

WHELAN, ROGER MICHAEL, b. Montclair, N.J., Nov. 12, 1936; B.A. cum laude, Georgetown U., 1959, J.D., 1962. Admitted to D.C. bar, 1963, U.S. Supreme Ct. bar, 1971; asso. firm Fried & Rogers, Hyattsville, Md., 1963-66; partner firm Docter & Whelan, Washington, 1967-72; judge U.S. Bankruptcy Ct., Washington, 1972—; ajd. prof. Columbus Sch. Law, Cath. U. Am., 1975—. Bd. mgmt. Silver Spring (Md.) YMCA, 1971-74. Mem. Am. Bar Assn. (chmn. cts. and community div. jud. adminstrn.), Nat. Conf. Bankruptcy Judges (gov.), Am. Judicature Soc. Contbr. articles to legal jours. Home: 14804 Pebblestone Dr Silver Spring MD 20904 Office: 2104 US Courthouse 3d St and Constitution Ave NW Washington DC 20001 Tel (202) 426-7568

WHELAN, VINCENT EDWARD, b. San Diego, June 12, 1934; student U. Madrid, 1954-55; B.S. in Fgn. Service, U. Georgetown, 1956; LL.B., Stanford, 1959. Admitted to Calif. bar, 1960; partner firm Higgs, Fletcher & Mack, San Diego, 1963—. Del. Democratic Nat. Conv., 1968; bd. dirs. San Diego chpt. NCCJ, 1973-75; extraordinary minister Roman Cath. Diocese of San Diego, 1972—. Fellow Am. Bar Found.; mem. Am. (ho. of dels. 1974-77), San Diego County bar assns., Am. Judicature Soc., State Bar Calif., Thomas More Soc. of San Diego (pres. 1976-77). Office: 1800 Home Tower 707 Broadway San Diego CA 92101 Tel (714) 236-1551

WHELTLE, MARGARET MAIE, b. Balt., Oct. 19, 1934; B.A., Mt. St. Agnes Coll., Balt., 1956; J.D., U. Md., 1959; postgrad. Loyola Evening Coll., Balt., 1960-61, Cath. U. Am. Sch. Theology, 1967-69; S.T.M., St. Marys Sem. and U., Balt., 1972. Admitted to Md. bar, 1959, U.S. Supreme Ct. bar, 1969; asso. firm Harley, Wheltle, Victor & Rosser, Balt., 1959-64; asst. to pres., dir. devel., TV prodn. coordinator Mt. St. Agnes Coll., 1964-67; student asst. dir. Grad. Students Resident Hall, Cath. U. Devel. Office, 1968-69; dir. dept. theology, instr. bus. law Harmony Hill High Sch., Watertown, S.D., 1969-70; coordinator religious edn. for adult and pub. sch. students St. Agnes Roman Catholic Congregation, Inc., 1971-74. Nat. alumni pres. Mt. St. Agnes Coll., 1961-65, also mem. Pres.'s Council; adult edn. instr. St. William of York, 1976—; lectr. St. Martins Home for Aged, 1975, co-founder, chmn. bd. Ladies Aux., 1973-76, bd. dirs., 1976—; mem. Speakers Bur., Howard County Right to Life, 1974—, Archdiocese of Balt., 1976—; mem. Speakers Bur., vice chmn. Birthright of Md., Inc., 1975-76; bd. dirs. Papal Vols. for Latin Am. Mem. Internat. Fedn. Cath. Alumnae (vice-gov. Md. chpt. 1964-66). Address: 515 Stamford Rd Baltimore MD 21229 Tel (301) 945-3145

WHERRY, DANIEL E., b. Tecumseh, Nebr., July 13, 1943; B.A. (Regents scholar), U. Nebr., 1966, J.D., 1969. Admitted to Nebr. bar, 1969; legis. asst. to Sen. Roman Hruska, minority counsel Senate Jud. Com., Washington, 1969-72; asst. U.S. atty. Dist. Nebr., Lincoln, 1972-75, U.S. atty. Dist. Nebr., Omaha, 1975—. Crusade chmn. Nebr. div. Am. Cancer Soc., 1975—; past pres., v.p., bd. govs. Nebr. Soc. Washington. Mem. Fed., Nebr. (pres. Omaha chpt. 1976—), Omaha bar assns., Phi Alpha Theta. Mem. Allen Moot Ct. Bd., Coll. Law; recipient Best Brief award Jr. Moot Ct. Competition; Upper Class Regents Ednl. grantee U. Nebr. Home: 13114 Leavenworth Rd Omaha NE 68154 Office: 8000 Fed Bldg 215 N 17th St Omaha NE 68101 Tel (402) 221-4774

WHERRY, ROBERT ALLEN, JR., b. Langley Field, Va., Apr. 7, 1944; B.S., U. Colo., 1966; J.D., 1969; LL.M., N.Y. U., 1972. Admitted to Colo. bar, 1969; asso. firm Ernst and Ernst, Denver, 1966-69, firm Lentz, Evans and King, Denver, 1972—. Mem. Am., Colo., Greater Denver bar assns. Office: 2900 Lincoln Center Bldg Denver CO 80264

WHETMORE, JAMES EDWARD, b. Columbus, Ohio, Mar. 9, 1913; LL.B., La Salle Extension U., Chgo., 1960. Admitted to Calif. bar, 1961; founder Whetmore Orch. Agy., Mt. Vernon, Wash., 1935; orch. leader, Portland, 1938-51, Los Angeles, 1952—; practiced in Orange County, Calif., 1961—; mem. Calif. Gen. Assembly, 1962-65, Calif. Senate, 1966-76; prin. James E. Whetmore & Assos., Golden Grove, Calif., 1976—. Chmn. Rossmoor United Fund, 1962-63; mem. citizens adv. bd. Garden Grove YMCA, Boys' Club W. Orange County, Calif., N. Orange County council Boy Scouts Am., Artificial Kidney Found. Orange County, 1968—. Mem. Orch. Leaders Assn. Hollywood (pres. 1955, bd. govs. 1954), State Bar Calif., Orange County Bar Assn. Recipient spl. plaque Am. Cancer Soc., 1965. Office: Suite 151 12900 Garden Grove Blvd Golden Grove CA 92643

WHICHARD, WILLIS PADGETT, b. Durham, N.C., May 24, 1940; A.B. in History, U. N.C., Chapel Hill, 1962, J.D., 1965. Admitted to N.C. bar, 1965; law clk. to justice N.C. Supreme Ct., 1965-66; partner firm Powe, Porter, Alphin & Whichard, Durham, 1966—; mem. N.C. Ho. of Reps., 1970-74, N.C. Senate, 1974—. Chmn. Durham County chpt. March of Dimes, 1969-74; bd. dirs. Transition of Youth, Inc., Durham, 1971—, Durham County chpt. ARC, 1971—, Triangle chpt. March of Dimes, 1974—; mem. So. Growth Policies Bd., 1972—, N.C. mem. growth policies bd. exec. com., 1975, vice chmn., 1975—. Mem. Am., N.C., Durham County (treas. 1968-70) bar assns., N.C. State Bar. Recipient Outstanding Youth Service award N.C. Juvenile Correctional Assn., 1975, Outstanding Legislator award N.C. Acad. Trial Lawyers, 1975. Office: PO Box 3843 Durham NC 27702 Tel (919) 682-5654

WHIPPLE, JAMES FOSTER, b. Marblehead, Mass., Sept. 1, 1940; A.B. magna cum laude, Yale U., 1962; J.D., Harvard U., 1965; LL.M., Boston U., 1975. Admitted to Mass. bar, 1965; mem. staff home office legal dept. Liberty Mut. Ins. Co., Boston, 1966-72, asst. counsel, 1972-77, tax counsel, 1977—. Fellow, Life Office Mgmt. Inst., 1971. Mem. Am., Mass., Boston bar assns., Phil. Soc. Arlington (pres. 1974-76). Office: 175 Berkeley St Boston MA 02117 Tel (617) 357-9500

WHIPPLE, JAY WILLARD, b. Stillwater, Okla., July 18, 1936; B.S. in Polit. Sci., Brigham Young U., 1960; J.D., U. Oreg., 1963. Admitted to Oreg. bar, 1963; asso. firm Bailey, Hoffman, Spencer & Morris, Eugene, Oreg., 1963-65; asso. firm David B. Williamson, St. Helen's, Oreg., 1965-66; individual practice law, Rainier, Oreg., 1966-67; partner firm Williamson & Whipple, St. Helen's, 1968—; city atty., Rainier, 1966-68; atty. Columbia County (Oreg.) Intermediate Edn., 1967—. Pres. Columbia County Young Republicans., 1966-68; mem. Selective Service Bd., Columbia County, 1972-75. Mem. Am., Oreg., Columbia County (pres. 1966-67) bar assns. Home: 335 S 11th St St Helens OR 97051 Office: 222 Columbia Blvd St Helens OR 97051 Tel (503) 397-2141

WHIPPLE, LAWRENCE ALOYSIUS, b. N.Y.C., July 26, 1910; B.S., Columbia, 1933; LL.B., John Marshall Law Sch., 1939. Admitted to N.J. bar, 1941; acting magistrate, Jersey City, 1949-51; law enforcement dir. OPS, 1950; spl. asst. to U.S. atty. Justice Dept., 1951; exec. dir. Jersey City Housing Authority, 1953; dir. pub. safety, Jersey City, 1953-57; county counsel Judson County, 1958-62, prosecutor Hudson County, 1958-63; judge Superior Ct. of N.J., 1963-67; judge U.S. Dist. Ct., Dist. of N.J., Newark, 1967—, now chief judge. Mem. Fed., N.J., Hudson County (pres. 1957) bar assns., N.Y. Lawyers Assn., Am. Judicature Soc., Catholic Lawyers Guild, Nat. Assn. Pros. Attys., State Prosecutors Assn. N.J. Home: 217 Trenton Blvd Sea Girt NJ 08750 Office: US Post Office and Courthouse Bldg Newark NJ 07102*

WHIPPLE, MELVIN REED, b. Las Vegas, Nev., July 16, 1927; B.S., Brigham Young U., 1950; J.D., U. Utah, 1966. Admitted to Nev. bar, 1966; asso. firm Singleton, DeLanoy & Jemison, Las Vegas, 1966-71; dep. dist. atty. Clark County (Nev.), Las Vegas, 1971—. Mem. Delta Theta Phi. Home: 2816 Merritt Ave Las Vegas NV 89102 Office: 200 E Carson Ave Las Vegas NV 89101 Tel (702) 386-4011

WHIPPLE, TAGGART, b. Manchester, N.H., Oct. 15, 1912; A.B., Harvard U., 1934; J.D., N.Y. U., 1938. Admitted to N.Y. bar, 1938; law clk. to v.p., gen. counsel Lehigh Valley R.R. Co., N.Y.C., 1934-38; with firm Davis, Polk & Wardwell, and predecessors, N.Y.C., 1938—, partner, 1950—; dir. The Distillers Co. Ltd., Gordon's Dry Gin Co. Trustee Hall of Fame for Great Americans, 1974—, Village of Muttontown (N.Y.), 1956—; bd. dirs. Assn. Against Election Frauds, 1948-53; trustee N.Y. U., 1970—, N.Y. U Law Center Found., 1965—, N.Y. U. Inst. Fine Arts, 1970—, Vassar Coll., 1973—, Salisbury Sch., 1968-74, Brit. Am. Ednl. Found., Community Hosp. at Glen Cove, 1948-69, Wrightsman Found., 1966-77, Repertory Theatre of Lincoln Center, 1966-73, Theatre, Inc., Phoenix, 1959-64, Soc. St. Johnsland, 1962-66. Fellow Am. Coll. Trial Lawyers, Am. Bar Found; mem. Am. Law Inst., Am. Judicature Soc., Internat. Bar Assn., Fed. Bar Council, Assn. Bar City N.Y. (chmn. com. trade regulation and trade marks 1953-56) Am. (council sect. antitrust law 1966-70), N.Y. State (chmn. antitrust law sect. 1962-63) bar assns., Council Fgn. Relations. Contbr. articles to legal jours. Home: Muttontown Rd Syosset NY 11791 Office: 1 Chase Manhattan Plaza New York City NY 10005

WHIPPS, EDWARD FRANKLIN, b. Columbus, Ohio, Dec. 17, 1936; B.A., Ohio Wesleyan U., 1958; J.D., Ohio State U., 1961. Admitted to Ohio bar, 1961, Fed. Dist. Cts. bar Ohio, 1962, ICC bar, 1962, U.S. Supreme Ct. bar, 1965, U.S. Ct. Claims bar, 1965, Miss. bar, 1969; asso. firm George, Greek, King, McMahon & McConnaughey, Columbus, 1961-65, partner, 1965—. Mem. Upper Arlington City Sch. Dist. Bdn. Edn., 1972—, also pres.; pres. Creative Living, Inc., Community Services, Inc., 1963—; chmn. ofcl. bd. Riverside United Methodist Ch., 1962, trustee, 1964-67. Mem. Am., Ohio, Columbus bar assns., Assn. Trial Lawyers Am., Ohio Acad. Trial Lawyers, Franklin County Trial Lawyers Assn., Am. Judicature Soc., Barristers Club Columbus, Lawyers Club Columbus. Home: 3771 Lyon Dr Columbus OH 43220 Office: 100 E Broad St Columbus OH 43215 Tel (614) 228-1541

WHISENAND, FREDERICK EARL, b. Williston, N.D., Feb. 11, 1929; Ph.B., U. N.D., 1956, J.D., 1957. Admitted to N.D. bar, 1957, Calif. bar, 1965; practice law, Williston, 1957-64; atty. legal dept. Occidental Life Ins. Co., Los Angeles, 1964-66; partner firm McIntee & Whisenand, Williston, 1966—; asst. states atty. Williams County (N.D.), 1957-60; prin. judge City of Williston, 1961-64. Chmn. N.E. dist. Boy Scouts Am. Mem. N.D., Calif., Williams County bar assns., Am. Trial Lawyers Assn., Am. Legion, VFW. Asso. editor N.D. Law Rev., 1956-57. Home: 1210 Hillcourt St Williston ND 58801 Office: 113 E Broadway Williston ND 58801 Tel (701) 572-6781

WHISLER, JOE B., b. Nevada, Mo., May 31, 1947; B.A., Central Meth. Coll., 1969; J.D., So. Meth. U., 1972; Admitted to Mo. bar, 1972; asso. firm Dietrich, Davis, Dicus, Rowlands & Schmitt, Kansas City, Mo., 1972—. Mem. Lawyers Assn. Kansas City (pres. jr. sect. 1976-77), Am. Bar Assn. (chmn. young lawyers sect. law sch. com. 1976—), Mo. Bar (young lawyers sect. council 1976—). Editorial bd. Jour. Air Law and Commerce, 1971-72. Office: 1001 Dwight Bldg Kansas City MO 64105 Tel (816) 221-3420

WHITACRE, JACK LEE, b. Kirksville, Mo., Aug. 31, 1938; B.A. in History, U. Mo., 1961, J.D., 1965. Admitted to Mo. bar, 1965, U.S. Ct. Appeals 8th Circuit bar, 1966, 10th Circuit bar, 1970; partner firm Spencer, Fane, Britt & Browne, Kansas City, Mo., 1965—. Mem. Am., Mo., Kansas City bar assns., Lawyers Assn. Kansas City, Order Coif. Editor-in-chief, Mo. Law Rev., 1964-65; contbr. articles in field to profl. jours. Office: 1000 Power and Light Bldg 106 W 14th St Kansas City MO 64105 Tel (816) 474-8100

WHITAKER, ALAN BERTRAM, JR., b. Binghamton, N.Y., Mar. 31, 1948; B.A., Villanova U., 1969; J.D., U. Miami, 1972. Admitted to Fla. bar, 1973, U.S. Supreme Ct. bar, 1976, U.S. Customs Ct. bar, 1976, U.S. Ct. Claims bar, 1976; partner firm Carey, Dwyer, Cole, Selwood & Bernard, Ft. Lauderdale, Fla., 1976—; adj. prof. law Nova U., 1976; pros. City of Sunrise, Fla. Dir. Arthritis Found. of Broward County, 1975. Mem. Am. Bar Assn., Fla., Broward County bars, Fla. Defense Lawyers Assn., Order of the Barristers. Office: Suite 300 707 SE 3d Ave Fort Lauderdale FL 33316 Tel (305) 462-1505

WHITAKER, GLENN VIRGIL, b. Cin., July 23, 1947; B.A., Denison U., 1969; J.D., George Washington U., 1972. Admitted to Md. bar, 1972, D.C. bar, 1973; law clk. to judge U.S. Dist. Ct. Md., 1972-73; asso. firm O'Donoghue & O'Donoghue, Washington, 1973-76; trial atty., civil div. U.S. Dept. Justice, Washington, 1976—; mem. Jud. Conf. D.C. Circuit, 1975-77. Mem. Am., Md. bar assns., Order of Coif, Phi Beta Kappa. Office: US Dept Justice Washington DC 20530 Tel (202) 739-3383

WHITAKER, JANET M., b. N.Y.C., June 15, 1931; B.A., Syracuse U., 1961; J.D., Columbia, 1965. Admitted to N.Y. State bar, 1966; asso. firm Townsend & Lewis, N.Y.C., 1965-69, partner, 1969-73; partner firm Thacher, Proffitt & Wood, N.Y.C., 1973—. Mem. Am., N.Y. State bar assns. Office: Thacher Proffitt & Wood 40 Wall St New York City NY 10005 Tel (212) 483-5982

WHITAKER, LESLIE KENT, b. Santa Monica, Calif., Aug. 10, 1938; A.B., Stanford, 1960; LL.B., Yale, 1965. Admitted to Calif. bar, 1966; clk. to justice Macklin Fleming of Calif. Ct. Appeals, Los Angeles, 1965-66; asso. firm Chickering & Gregory, San Francisco, 1966-73; atty. Kaiser Industries Corp., Oakland, Calif., 1973—. Mem. Am., San Francisco bar assns., Western Pension Conf. Office: 300 Lakeside Dr Oakland CA 94666 Tel (415) 271-2347

WHITAKER, MEADE, b. Washington, Mar. 22, 1919; B.A., Yale U., 1940; LL.B., U. Va., 1948. Admitted to Ala. bar, 1948; partner firm Cabaniss, Johnston & Gardner, Birmingham, Ala., 1948-69, 70-73; tax. legis. consel Dept. Treasury, Washington, 1969-70, asst. gen. counsel, chief counsel IRS, 1973-76; partner firm Arter & Hadden, Cleve., 1977—. Bd. dirs. Children's Aid Soc., 1950—, pres., 1963-65. Mem. Am., Ala., D.C., Ohio bar assns., Am. Law Inst. Office: 1144 Union Commerce Bldg Cleveland OH 44115 Tel (216) 696-1144

WHITAKER, REX STALEY, b. Jacksonville, Tex., Oct. 4, 1942; B.S., Baylor U., 1965, J.D., 1969. Admitted to Tex. bar, 1969; asso. firm Naman, Howell, Smith & Chase, Waco, Tex., 1969-76, partner, 1976—; prof. Baylor U. Sch. Law; lectr. State Bar Tex. Wills and Estate Planning Inst. Exec. bd. dirs. Heart of Tex. council Boy Scouts Am., Family Counseling and Children's Services. Mem. Am., Waco-McLennan County bar assns., State Bar Tex., Waco Estate Planning Council, Baylor Law Alumni (dir.). Home: 4117 N 30th St Waco TX 76708 Office: 700 Texas Center Waco TX 76701 Tel (817) 754-1421

WHITE, ALAN IRA, b. Boston, Mass., Nov. 29, 1945; B.A., U. Mass., 1967; J.D., Georgetown U., 1971. Admitted to Calif. bar, 1971; asso. firm Lawler Felix & Hall, Los Angeles, 1971-74, Regan, Drummy, Garrett & King, Newport Beach, Calif., 1974—. Mem. Am., Orange County bar assns. Editor: Georgetown Law Rev., 1968-70. Home: 1866 Tustin Ave Newport Beach CA 92660 Office: 4299 MacArthur Blvd Newport Beach CA 92660 Tel (714) 833-8151

WHITE, ALGIRD FRANCIS, JR., b. Hudson, N.Y., Oct. 12, 1947; A.B., Colgate U., 1969; J.D., Boston U., 1972. Admitted to N.Y. bar, 1973; mem. firm DeGraff Foy Conway & Holt-Harris, Albany, N.Y., 1972-76, partner, 1977—. Mem. Am. (com. on pub. utility law-electricity, labor law), Albany County (com. on amendment of law 1975), N.Y. State bar assns. Home: RD 1 Rensselaer NY 12144 Office: 90 State St Albany NY 12207 Tel (518) 462-5301

WHITE, ANDREW GALAN, III, b. Cin., Jan. 8, 1944; B.S., U. Cin., 1967, J.D., 1974; LL.M., U. Fla., 1975. Admitted to Ohio bar, 1974, U.S. Tax Ct. bar, 1975, Fed. Dist. Ct. bar, 1975; partner firm Morgan, White, Braddock & Brown, Cin., 1976—; asst. dir. Jobs for Cin., 1967-68; adminstrv. asst. First Nat. Bank Cin., 1968-70, asst. mgr., 1970-71. Asst. dir. Ambulatory Patient Care, Inc., Hamilton County, Ohio, 1971; mem. planning commn. Cin., 1971-74; mem. regional planning commn., Hamilton County (Ohio), 1971-72; active allocations div. rehab. services com. Community Chest, Hamilton County, 1972-74; adv. bd. Cin. Experience, 1975; trustee West End Health Center, Cin., 1976; treas. Community Guidance Council, 1965-66; v.p. Concerned Bros., 1966-67, pres., 1967-68; gen. chmn. Cin. Career Conf., 1966; sec. Polit. Action Program, 1968-71. Mem. Am., Fed., Cin. bar assns. Office: 706 Walnut St Cincinnati OH 45202 Tel (513) 621-7885

WHITE, BUEL, b. Springfield, Mo., Aug. 8, 1941; A.B., Princeton U., 1962; LL.B., U. Va., 1969. Admitted to Va. bar, 1969, U.S. Ct. Claims bar, 1969, U.S. Supreme Ct. bar, 1975; clk. to trial div. U.S. Ct. Claims, 1969-70; asso. firm Sellers, Conner & Cuneo, 1970-75, mem. firm, 1975—; lectr. Mem. Am., Fed., D.C., Va. bar assns., Bar Assn. D.C. Office: 1625 K St Washington DC 20006 Tel (202) 452-7560

WHITE, BYRON R., b. Ft. Collins, Colo., June 8, 1917; grad. from U. Colo., 1938; Rhodes Scholar Oxford (Eng.) U.; grad. Yale Law Sch. Chief Justice U.S. Supreme Ct., 1946, 47; atty., Lewis, Grant and Davis, Denver, 1947-60; dep. atty. gen. U.S., 1961-62; asso. justice Supreme Ct. U.S., 1962—. Mem. Phi Beta Kappa, Phi Gamma Delta, Order of Coif. Address: Supreme Ct Bldg 1 First St NE Washington DC 20543*

WHITE, CARROLL EUGENE, b. Helena, Ark., Dec. 20, 1932; B.S., Fla. State U., 1953; LL.B., U. Miss., 1961. Admitted to Miss. bar, 1961; asso. firm Sillers and Roberts, Rosedale, Miss., 1961; individual practice law, Tupelo, Miss., 1961—; city judge, Tupelo, 1969—. Active Civitan Club. Mem. Miss., Lee County, 1st Jud. Dist. bar assns. Home: 815 Oakridge St Tupelo MS 38801 Office: PO Box 289 Tupelo MS 38801 Tel (601) 842-2127

WHITE, DAVID CECIL, b. Portland, Oreg., July 3, 1942; B.A., Golden Gate U., 1968; J.D., Northwestern Sch. Law Lewis and Clark Coll., 1973. Admitted to Oreg. bar, 1973, U.S. Dist. Ct. bar Oreg. Dist., 1973, U.S. Ct. Appeals bar, 9th Circuit, 1975; mem. firm White & Southwell, Portland, 1974—. Bd. dirs. Friendly House, Inc., Portland, 1973—, sec., 1974-75, treas., 1976—. Mem. Oreg. State, Multnomah County (Oreg.), Am. bar assns., Motor Carrier Lawyers Assn., Assn. ICC Practitioners. Office: 2400 SW Fourth Ave Portland OR 97201 Tel (503) 226-6491

WHITE, DENNIS ARTHUR, b. L.I., N.Y., Apr. 24, 1933; B.S., U. So. Calif.; LL.B., Van Norman U. Admitted to Calif. bar; with State of Calif., 1964-70; with City of San Diego, 1970-71; individual practice law, San Diego, 1971—. Office: 1010 2d Ave San Diego CA 92101 Tel (714) 234-1835

WHITE, DONALD EDMUND, b. Oakland, Calif., Dec. 8, 1942; B.A. in History, U. Calif., Santa Barbara, 1965; J.D., U. Mont., 1968. Admitted to Mont. bar, 1968; clk. Mont. Supreme Ct., 1968-69; staff atty. Mont. Legal Services, Anaconda, 1969-70; asso. firm Landoe & Gary, Bozeman, Mont., 1970-74; dep. county atty. Gallatin County (Mont.), 1974-75, county atty., 1976—. Mem. Mont. Bd. Campaign Fin., 1976. Mem. Mont., Am. bar assns., Mont. County Attys. Assn., Nat. Dist. Attys. Assn., Gallatin County Bar Assn. (sec. 1974-75). Home: Route 3 PO Box 165 Bozeman MT 59715 Office: Gallatin County Courthouse PO Box 1049 Bozeman MT 59715 Tel (406) 587-3161

WHITE, EARLE VICTOR, JR., b. Spokane, Wash., Mar. 13, 1916; B.A., U. Wash., 1938; J.D., Northwestern Coll. Law, 1949. Admitted to Oreg. bar, 1949, U.S. Supreme Ct. bar, 1957; asst. traffic mgr. Consol. Freightways, Portland, Oreg., 1940-46; exec. sec. Oreg. Draymen & Warehousemen's Assn., Portland, 1946-49; partner firm White & Southwell, Portland, 1949—. Mem. Multnomah County Bar Assn., Assn. ICC Practitioners, Motor Carrier Lawyers Assn. Home: 32239 Boones Bend Rd Wilsonville OR 97070 Office: 2400 SW 4th Ave Portland OR 97201 Tel (503) 226-6491

WHITE, EUGENE REMEMBRANCE, b. Grafton, W.Va., Oct. 28, 1907; B.A., W.Va. U., 1929, J.D., 1947. Admitted to W.Va. bar, 1947, U.S. Supreme Ct. bar, 1975; partner firm Wilkison and White, Moundsville, W.Va., 1949-52, White and White, Moundsville, 1976—; dep. land commr. State of Va., 1952-76; commr. of accounts Marshall County (W.Va.); commr. Circuit Ct. Marshall County; dir. Skyline Water Co. Active ARC; chmn. Moundsville Area Conf., 1960-62, Corn Festival, Marshall County, 1958-64, North Panhandle Council for Exceptional Children, 1957-63; v.p. bd. dirs. Salvation Army, Moundsville, 1964-65; chmn. Moundsville Charter Bd., 1961-62, Moundsville Zoning Bd., 1961-62; adv. bd. Moundsville Gen. Hosp., 1959-60. Mem. Marshall County, W.Va., Am. bar assns., Am. Judicature Soc., Am. Land Title Assn. Home: 106 Mulberry Ave Moundsville WV 26041 Office: PO Box 102 Moundsville WV 26041 Tel (304) 845-3972

WHITE, GEORGE ALTON, b. Beaver, Utah, Dec. 8, 1909; LL.B., George Washington U., 1938. Admitted to D.C. bar, 1938, Utah bar, 1939; law clk. Utah Supreme Ct., Salt Lake City, 1940-41; judge Utah First Dist. Juvenile Ct., Ogden, 1942; atty. U.S. Army, 1943, USAF, various N.W. states, 1946-71, ret., 1971; part-time individual practice law, Ogden, Utah, 1972—. Officiator, Ogden Temple, Ch. of Jesus Christ of Latter-day Saints, 1972—. Mem. Am. Assn. Ret. Persons (pres. local chpt.). Recipient Citation for Significant Achievement, Air Force Logistics Command, 1971. Home and office: 1270 33d St Ogden UT 84403 Tel (801) 394-7211

WHITE, GEORGE EDWARD, b. Northampton, Mass., Mar. 19, 1941; B.A., Amherst Coll., 1963; M.A., Yale, 1964, Ph.D., 1967; J.D., Harvard, 1970. Admitted to D.C. bar, 1970, Va. bar, 1975, U.S. Supreme Ct. bar, 1973; vis. scholar Am. Bar Found., Chgo., 1970-71; law clk. Chief Justice Earl Warren, U.S. Supreme Ct., 1971-72; asst. prof. law U. Va., Charlottesville, 1972-74, asso. prof., 1974-77, prof., 1977—; research historian Inst. Criminal Law and Procedure, Georgetown U. Law Sch., Washington, 1967; asst. prof. sociology Harvard, 1969-70. Mem. Va. Bar Assn., Am. Soc. Legal History, Phi Beta Kappa. Author: The Eastern Establishment and the Western Experience, 1968; The American Judicial Tradition, 1976. Office: Sch Law U Va Charlottesville VA 22903 Tel (804) 924-3455

WHITE, HAMPDEN REILY, b. Baton Rouge, Apr. 13, 1944; B.S., La. State U., 1966, J.D., 1969. Admitted to La. bar; law clk. La. 19th Jud. Dist. Ct., 1971-72; asso. firm Phelps, Dunbar, Marks, Claverie & Sims, New Orleans, 1972-73; staff atty. Blue Cross of La., Baton Rouge, 1973—. Mem. La., Baton Rouge, Am. bar assns. Office: 10225 Florida Blvd Baton Rouge LA 70895 Tel (504) 272-1220

WHITE, HAROLD FRANCIS, b. Hartford, Conn., Apr. 29, 1920; B.C.S., Ohio U., 1946; J.D., Akron U., 1952. With Goodyear Tire & Rubber Co., Akron, 1947-53; admitted to Ohio bar, 1952; chief police prosecutor City of Akron, 1953; partner firm Kelley & White, Akron, 1953-58; asst. county prosecutor civil div. Summit County (Ohio), 1957-58; judge U.S. Bankruptcy Ct., Akron, 1958—; lectr. law U. Akron, 1968—. Trustee Akron Bd. Mgmt. YMCA, Kidney Found. of Summit County; active Boy Scouts Am., Little League, Goodwill Industries. Mem. Akron, Ohio State bar assns., Nat. Conf. Bankruptcy Judges. Home: 1285 Winhurst Dr Akron OH 44313 Office: 2 S Main St Akron OH 44308 Tel (216) 375-5766

WHITE, JACK LITTLE, b. Ann Arbor, Mich., Feb. 5, 1912; B.A., Washington & Jefferson Coll., 1934; J.D., U. Mich., 1937. Admitted to Ohio bar, 1938; asso. firm Squire, Sanders & Dempsey, Cleve., 1937-43, partner, 1952—; of counsel Cleve. Agy., RFC, also Def. Plant Corp., 1940-43, 46-68. Trustee Washington and Jefferson Coll., 1968—, chmn. student affairs com., 1969-73, v.p. exec. com., 1976—; trustee Cleve. Scholarships Programs, Inc., 1974—, mem. exec. com., 1975—. Mem. Am., Ohio, Cuyahoga County, Cleve. bar assns. Home: 3288 Oak Knoll Dr Cleveland OH 44124 Office: 1800 Union Commerce Bldg Cleveland OH 44115 Tel (216) 696-9200

WHITE, JACK RAYMOND, b. Lincoln, Nebr., Oct. 12, 1936; A.B., U. So. Calif., 1958, LL.B., 1961. Admitted to Calif. bar, 1962; asso. firm Hill, Farrer & Burrill, Los Angeles, 1961-71, partner, 1971—. Mem. Am., Calif., Los Angeles County bar assns., Assn. Tax Counsel, Order of Coif. Home: 2615 Mayflower Ave Arcadia CA 91006 Office: 445 S Figueroa St Los Angeles CA 90071 Tel (213) 620-0460

WHITE, JAMES ARNOLD, b. Fulton, Ky., July 20, 1912; A.B., Cumberland U., 1934, LL.B., 1934; J.D., Samford U., 1969. Admitted to Tenn. bar, 1934, Miss. bar, 1937; individual practice law, McComb, Miss., 1937-42, Durant, Miss., 1950—; atty. in charge of field examinations VA, Washington and Dallas, 1944-47; mgr. Natchez Claims Service, McComb Adjusting Service, McComb and Natchez, Miss., 1947-50; judge Municipal Ct. City of Durant, 1976—. Sec. Miss. Republican com., 1948-57; chmn., Rep. Com. of Holmes County, 1976—. Mem. Miss., Holmes County bar assns., Am. Legion (past post comdr). Home and office: 102 E Madison St Durant MS 39063 Tel (601) 653-3153

WHITE, JAMES ROBERT, b. Balt., Sept. 22, 1929; A.A., U. Balt., 1957, J.D., 1959. Staff reporter Balt. Evening Sun, 1954-60; admitted to Md. bar, 1959; practiced law, Balt., 1960-65; mem. firm White & Cymek, Balt., 1965-71; partner firm O'Doherty, Gallagher & White, Balt., 1971—. Fellow Am. Coll. Trial Lawyers; mem. Md., Balt. (pres. 1977-78) bar assns., Md. Criminal Def. Lawyers Assn. (pres. 1972-74), Saints and Sinners Clubs Am., Friendly Sons St. Patrick. Home: 4713 Roundhill Rd Ellicott City MD 21043 Office: 1011 Fidelity Bldg 210 N Charles St Baltimore MD 21201*

WHITE, JOHN CHAPPELL, b. Blackshear, Ga., Oct. 9, 1929; B.C.E., U. Ala., 1957; LL.D., Emory U., 1969. Admitted to Ga., Fla. bars, 1969; dir. regulatory programs Fed. Water Quality Adminstrn., Atlanta, 1969-70; dir. enforcement div. EPA, Atlanta, 1970-73; dep. regional adminstr., 1973-75, regional adminstr., Dallas, 1975—. Mem. Fed., Ga. State, Fla. State bar assns., Water Pollution Control Fedn. Home: PO Box 281 Dallas TX 75221 Office: 1201 Elm St Dallas TX 75270 Tel (214) 749-1962

WHITE, JOHN FRED, b. St. Louis, Nov. 25, 1920; A.B., Washington U., St. Louis, 1941, LL.B., 1947. Admitted to Mo. bar, 1943; since practiced in St. Louis, with Mercantile Trust Company, 1947-50, T.H. Mastin & Co., 1950-52; individual practice law, 1954-69; mem. trial staff Circuit Atty. Office, 1969-77; mem. trial staff St. Louis County Pros. Atty.'s Office, 1977—. Mem. Nat. Dist. Attys. Assn., Mo. Pros. Attys. Assn., Phi Delta Phi. Home: 6933 Cornell University City MO 63130 Office: Circuit Atty Office Saint Louis MO 63103 Tel (314) 453-4121

WHITE, JOSEPH LEE, b. Columbus, Ohio, Mar. 19, 1934; B.A. in Polit. Sci., Ohio State U., 1955, J.D., 1958, M.S.W., 1964. Admitted to Ohio bar, 1958; asst. atty. gen. Ohio, 1959-63; individual practice law, Columbus, 1959-63; dep. dir. Ohio Youth Commn., Columbus, 1964-71, dir., 1974-75; dep. dir. adminstrn. justice div. Ohio Dept. Econ. and Community Devel., Columbus, 1971-74; fellow social policy Acad. for Contemporary Problems, Columbus, 1975—; permanent cons. Council State Govts., 1975—. Pres. B'nai B'rith, Columbus, 1968, mem. exec. bd. dist. youth council, 1968; bd. dirs. Rivers Group Home, 1976—. Mem. Nat. Assn. Social Workers, Nat. Council on Crime and Delinquency, Am. Correctional Assn., Ohio Citizens Council. Recipient Man of Yr. award Ohio Publ. Defender Assn.; contbr. articles to profl. jours. Home: 353 S Roosevelt Ave Bexley OH 43209 Office: 1501 Neil Ave Columbus OH 43201 Tel (614) 421-7700

WHITE, JOSEPH WILLIAM, b. Richlands, Va., Jan. 3, 1933; B.S., Hampden-Sydney Coll., 1954; M.Litt. in Econs., U. Pitts., 1960; J.D., U. Va., 1960. Admitted to Va. bar, 1960; partner firm Larrick and White, Winchester, Va., 1964—; dir., sec. Bank Frederick County, 1973—. Mem. Winchester Bd. Zoning Appeals, 1966-76; chmn. Winchester Hwy. Safety Commn., 1968-76; bd. dirs. Winchester-Frederick County chpt. ARC, 1966—, pres., 1973-75. Mem. Va., Am. bar assns., Va. State Bar (council 1975—), Va. Trial Lawyers Assn., Phi Alpha Delta. Editor Va. Law Weekly, 1959-60. Home: 806 S Stewart St Winchester VA 22601 Tel (703) 667-6400

WHITE, KENNETH F., b. McCleary, Wash., Jan. 21, 1938; B.A. in Bus. Econs. and Mgmt., Coll. Idaho, 1965; J.D., Willamette U., 1968. Admitted to Idaho bar, 1968; individual practice law, Nampa, Idaho, 1968—; pros. atty., city-county narcotics vice, Caldwell, Idaho, 1971-72. Mem. Idaho Trial Lawyers Assn., Trial Lawyers of Am., Nampa C. of C. Office: 114 12th Ave S PO Box 1099 Nampa ID 83651 Tel (208) 466-3100

WHITE, MARGARET WARDELL, b. Cadillac, Mich., Nov. 28; B.A., Oberlin Coll.; J.D., N.Y. U. Admitted to N.Y. State bar, 1921, Mich. bar, 1929; mem. firm Wills and Wardell, N.Y.C., 1923-28; individual practice law, N.Y.C., 1928—. Mem. county Republican party. Mem. Am. Bar Assn., Bar Assn. City N.Y., Nat., N.Y. women lawyers assns. Home: 205 E 66th St New York City NY 10021 Office: 36 W 44th St New York City NY 10036 Tel (212) 986-5272

WHITE, MARK WELLS, JR., b. Henderson, Tex., Mar. 17, 1940; B.B.A., Baylor U., 1962, J.D., 1965. Admitted to Tex. bar, 1965; asst. atty. gen., securities div. State of Tex., 1966-69; mem. firm Reynolds, Allen & Cook, Houston, 1969-71, partner, 1971-73; sec. fo state Tex., Austin, 1973—. Address: State Capitol Austin TX 78711

WHITE, MORLEY H., b. Youngstown, Ohio, Sept. 13, 1936; B.A., Ohio State U., 1961; J.D., U. Houston, 1964. Admitted to Tex. bar, 1964, Calif. bar, 1965; atty. regional counsel's office Tax Ct. div. IRS, Los Angeles, 1964-68; mem. firm Magids & White, Houston, 1968—. Mem. Comml. Law League Am., Fed., Tex., Houston bar assns. Editor-in-chief Houston Law Rev., 1963-64. Office: 331S Sul Ross St Houston TX 77098 Tel (713) 528-2831

WHITE, NOLA, b. Nola, Miss., Apr. 27, 1906; B.S., B.A., Miss. State U., 1927; LL.B., U. Tex., 1930, J.D., 1968. Admitted to Tex. bar, 1932; partner firm Adams, Moore & White, Beaumont, Tex., 1933-38; individual practice law, Beaumont, 1940-67; 1st Asst. Atty. Gen. of Tex., Austin, 1967-72; asst. dist. atty., Jefferson County, Tex., 1938-41; mem. Interstate Oil Compact Commn., Austin, 1968-72. Exec. bd. Boy Scouts Am., 1937-75; mem. Tex. Commn. of Law Enforcement Officer Standards & Edn., Tex. Criminal Justice Council. Mem. Am., Tex., Jefferson and Travis County bar assns., Beaumont C. of C. (dir. 1936-61). Trustee Tex. Law Rev. Publs., 1928-29. Home: 600 W 10th St Austin TX 78211 Office: 1100 City Nat Bank Bldg Austin TX 78201 Tel (512) 478-3200

WHITE, PAUL DUNBAR, b. LaGrange, Ky., Oct. 20, 1917; A.B. in History, Sociology, Ky. State Coll., 1940; LL.B., Western Reserve U., 1950, J.D., 19—. Admitted to Ohio bar, 1950, U.S. Supreme Ct. bar, 1972; supr. Ind. State Boys Sch., 1940-41; group worker spl. projects Karamu, Cleve., 1941-43; visitor Cuyahoga County Agency, 1946-47; individual practice law, Cleve., 1950-51; police prosecutor City of Cleve., 1951-59, 1st asst. prosecutor, 1960-63, dir. law, 1967-68; judge Cleve. Municipal Ct., 1964-67; asso. firm Baker, Hostetler & Patterson, Cleve., 1968-70, partner, 1970—; mem. bd. bar examiners State of Ohio, 1972—. Bd. trustees NCCJ, Cleve., 1972—, Ohio Law Opportunity Fund, Cleve., 1975—, Cleve. Urban League, 1975—, Dyke Coll., Cleve., 1976—; bd. commrs. Cleve. Met. Park, 1975—. Mem. Am., Ohio, Greater Cleve., Nat. bar assns. Recipient Distinguished Service award, Cleve. br. NAACP, 1975. Home: 16210 Telfair Ave Cleveland OH 44128 Office: 1956 Union Commerce Bldg 915 Euclid Ave Cleveland OH 44115 Tel (216) 621-0200

WHITE, PAUL WILLIAM, b. Mitchell, S.D., Feb. 12, 1911; A.B. with honors, U. Neb., 1930, LL.B., 1932. Admitted to Nebr. bar, 1932; practice in Lincoln, 1932-53; acting judge Lincoln Municipal Ct., 1949-53; dist. judge 3d Jud. Dist., Lancaster County, Neb., 1953-63, presiding judge, 1955, 59, 61; chief justice Supreme Ct. Nebr., 1963—; asst. county atty., Lancaster County, 1941-47; spl. hearings exam. Nebr. Bd. Ednl. Lands and Funds, 1950-52. Charter mem. Nebr. Gov.'s Com. for Youth, 1954; chmn. Am. Legion Boys' State, 1951-54; incorporator, charter mem. Lincoln Youth Project of Woods Charitable Fund, 1956; active other civic activities. Bd. dirs. Neb. Boy's State. Mem. Nebr. Dist. Ct. Judges Assn.(pres.), Am., Lincoln bar assns., Am. Judicature Soc., Nat. Center State Cts., Conf. Chief Justices, Am. Interprofl. Inst., Am. Legion 40 and 8, Vets. Fgn. Wars. Home: 2741 Scott Ave Lincoln NE 68506 Office: Supreme Ct of Nebraska Lincoln NE 68509*

WHITE, REX HARDING, JR., b. Houston, Sept. 27, 1932; B.S., U. Tex., 1956, M.A., 1960, LL.B., 1967. Admitted to Tex. bar, 1967; asst. atty. gen. State of Tex., Austin, 1967-76; spl. counsel R.R. Commn. Tex., Austin, 1976—. Mem. Am., Tex. bar assns. Office: PO Box 12967 Capitol Sta Austin TX 78711 Tel (512) 475-4686

WHITE, ROBERT ANDERSON, b. Norfolk, Va., Dec. 12, 1928; B.A., Va. Mil. Inst., 1950; LL.B., U. Va., 1955. Admitted to Va. bar, 1955, Fla. bar, 1956; partner firm Mershon, Sawyer, Johnston, Dunwody & Cole, Miami, Fla. 1956—. Mem. Orange Bowl Com., Miami, 1969—, pres.-elect, 1977—; bd. dirs. S.E. div. Children's Home Soc. Fla., 1964-75, pres., 1970-71; bd. dirs. Vis. Nurse Assn. Dade County, 1962-69, 76—, pres., 1965-66; trustee Met. Mus. and Art Center, 1975—. Fellow Am. Coll. Probate Counsel; mem. Am., Fla., Dade County (pres. 1972-73) bar assns. Editorial bd. U. Va. Law Rev., 1953-55. Home: 9205 SW 59th Ave Miami FL 33156 Office: 1600 SE 1st Nat Bank Bldg Miami FL 33131 Tel (305) 358-5100

WHITE, ROBERT ARTHUR, b. Fort Worth, Sept. 7, 1929; B.S., Tex. A. and M. U., 1950; J.D., So. Meth. U., 1956. Admitted to Tex. bar, 1956, U.S. Supreme Ct. bar, 1969; practiced in Houston, 1956—; asso. firm Baker, Botts, Shepherd & Coates, 1956-69; mem. firm Arnold, White & Durkee, 1969—. Mem. Am., Houston bar assns., Am., Houston patent law assns. Author: Patent Litigation, Procedure & Tactics, 1971; registered profl. engr., Tex. Home: 12 Memorial Point Houston TX 77024 Office: 2100 Transco Tower Houston TX 77056 Tel (713) 621-9100

WHITE, ROBERT BRECKENRIDGE, b. Canton, Ohio, Sept. 10, 1946; B.A., U. Fla., 1968, J.D., 1971. Admitted to Fla. bar, 1971; asso. firm Barranco Darlson and Daniels, Miami, Fla., 1971-73, Adams Best and Sears, Orlando, Fla., 1973-75; partner firm Page and White, Orlando, 1975—; asso. prof. social sci. U. Fla., 1970-71. Mem. Am. Bar Assn., Am., Fla. trial lawyers assns. Office: PO Box 1809 Orlando FL 32802 Tel (305) 422-3113

WHITE, ROBERT JOEL, b. Chgo., Nov. 1, 1946; B.S. in Accounting, U. Ill., 1968; J.D., U. Mich., 1972. Auditor Haskins & Sells, Chgo., 1968-69; admitted to Calif. bar, 1972; asso. firm O'Melveny & Myers, Los Angeles, 1972—; panel speaker Nat. Assn. Accountants, 1976. C.P.A., Ill. Mem. Am., Calif., Los Angeles County (fed. cts. and practice com., barrister advt. com.) bar assns., Fin. Lawyers Conf., Assn. Bus. Trial Lawyers. Contbr. article to legal jour.

WHITE, SAMUEL KNOX, b. Narberth, Pa., 1918; A.B., U. Pa., 1941, LL.B., 1947. Admitted to Pa. bar, 1947; asso. firm Moffett, Frye, Leopold, Phila., 1947-60; partner firm Pepper, Hamilton & Scheetz, Phila., 1960-69; v.p., gen. counsel Sun Co., Inc., Radnor, Pa., 1969—. Mem. Am., Pa., Phila. bar assns., Am. Judicature Soc., Phi Beta Kappa. Mng. editor U. Pa. Law Rev. 1946. Home: 360 Highview Dr Radnor PA 19087 Office: 100 Matsonford Rd Radnor PA 19087 Tel (215) 293-6508

WHITE, THOMAS OWEN, b. Pitts., Sept. 9, 1940; A.B., Cornell U., 1962; J.D., U. Pitts., 1965. Admitted to Pa. bar, 1965; asso. firm Dickie McCamey & Chilcote, Pitts., 1965; asso. dean, prof. U. Pitts. Sch. Law 1965—; dir. law programs div. Ednl. Testing Service, Princeton, N.J., 1976. Pres., Neigbhood Legal Services of Pitts. and Allegheny County, 1970-73; chmn. Forest Hills Planning Commn., 1970-76. Mem. Am. Law Inst., Am. Judicature Soc., Pa. Bar Assn. Author: (with Murray) Commercial Transactions, 1972; (with Sell) Pennsylvania Keystone, 5 vols., 1970-77. Home: 33 Montague St Washington Crossing NJ 08628 Office: Rosedale Rd Princeton NJ 08640 Tel (609) 921-9000

WHITE, THOMAS RAEBURN, III, b. Phila., Aug. 18, 1938; A.B., Williams Coll., 1960; LL.B., U. Pa., 1963. Admitted to Pa. bar, 1964, Va. bar, 1972; asso. firm White & Williams, Phila., 1963-65; atty.-adviser, tax legis. counsel, U.S. Treasury Dept., Washington, 1965-67; asso. prof. law, U. Va., Charlottesville, 1967-70, prof., 1970—; legis. atty. Joint Com. on Internal Revenue Taxation, U.S. Congress, Washington, 1973-74; Congl. fellow, Am. Polit. Sci. Assn., Washington, 1972-73. Mem. Am., Va. State, Phila. bar assns. Home: 12 Deer Path Bellair Charlottesville VA 22901 Office: Law School Univ of Va Charlottesville VA 22901 Tel (804) 924-7932

WHITE, WALTER PRESTON, JR., b. Lynchburg, Va., Apr. 19, 1923; B.S. in Accounting, U. N.C., 1946, J.D., 1949. Admitted to N.C. bar, 1949, Fla. bar, 1962, Ga. bar, 1969; asso. E.T. Bost, Concord, N.C., 1949-51; spl. atty., office of chief counsel IRS, Washington, 1951-53, trial atty., Birmingham, Ala., 1953-56, Jacksonville, Fla., 1956-58, asst. regional counsel, Jacksonville, 1958-62, staff asst. to regional counsel, Atlanta, 1968—; partner firm Dowling, White & Mooers, Jacksonville, 1962-68. Mem. N.C., Fla., Ga., Fed. Bar Assns., Delta Theta Phi, Delta Sigma Pi, Phi Kappa Sigma. Home: 6851 Roswell Rd NE Atlanta GA 30328 Office: Box 1074 Atlanta GA 30301 Tel (404) 221-6120

WHITE, WILLIAM, b. Phila., Feb. 2, 1914; B.A., Yale U., 1935; LL.B., U. Pa., 1938. Admitted to Pa. bar, 1939; partner firm Duane, Morris & Heckscher, Phila., 1946—; pres. Old Phila. Devel. Corp., 1971—. Mem. Am., Pa., Phila. (chmn. bd. govs. 1959-61) bar assns. Home: 506 Glenview Rd Bryn Mawr PA 19010 Office: 1600 Land Title Bldg 100 S Broad St Philadelphia PA 19110 Tel (215) 854-6319

WHITE, WILLIAM ROBERT, b. Dayton, Ohio, Mar. 26, 1941; B.S., Ohio State U., 1964; J.D., 1967. Admitted to Ohio bar, 1967; asso. firm Power Jones & Schneider, Columbus, Ohio, 1967-72, partner, 1972-74; dep. dir.-legal Ohio Dept. Natural Resources, Columbus, 1972-73; adminstrv. asst. to Sen. John Glenn of Ohio, Washington, 1975—; counsel Ohio Gov.'s Task Force on Environ. Protection, 1971. Mem. Am., Ohio, Columbus, Fed. bar assns., Phi Delta Phi. Office: 204 Russell Senate Office Bldg Washington DC 20510 Tel (202) 224-7975

WHITE, WILLIAM THOMPSON, JR., b. Ft. Wayne, Ind., June 9, 1940; B.S. in Bus., Ind. U., 1962, J.D., 1965. Admitted to Ind. bar, 1965; dep. prosecutor Bloomington (Ind.), 1965-67; mem. legal dept. Central Soya Co., Ft. Wayne, 1967-68; partner firm Rocap Rocap Reese & Young, Indpls., 1968—. Mem. Am., Ind. State, Indpls. bar assns. Home: 2145 Rome Dr A Indianapolis IN 46208 Office: 708 Union Federal Bldg Indianapolis IN 46204 Tel (317) 639-6281

WHITEHEAD, JERRY CARR, b. Joplin, Mo., Sept. 23, 1934; B.A., U. Kans., 1956; postgrad. U. So. Calif., 1956; J.D., Washburn U., Topeka, Kans., 1960. Admitted to Kans. bar, 1960, Nev. bar, 1963; law clk. Kans. Supreme Ct., 1961-62, Nev. Supreme Ct., 1962-63; partner firm Breen, Young, Whitehead & Hoy, Reno, 1963—; judge pro tem Reno Municipal Ct., 1966-72. Trustee Washoe County (Nev.) Sch. Dist., 1973—, pres., 1976—. Mem. Washoe County, Am. (pres. 1970-71) bar assns., State Bar Nev., No. Nev. (pres. 1966-67), Nev. trial lawyers assns., Assn. Trial Lawyers Am., Am. Bd. Trial Advs. Asso. editor Washburn Law Rev., 1959-60. Home: 4625 Canyon Dr Reno NV 89509 Office: 232 Court St Reno NV 89501 Tel (702) 786-7600

WHITEHEAD, JOHN C., b. Loup City, Nebr., Mar. 4, 1939; B.A. in History, St. Benedict's Coll., 1961; J.D., Washburn U., 1964. Admitted to Kans. bar, 1964, Nebr. bar, 1964; mem. firm Snell & Whitehead, Columbus, Nebr., 1965-66, Walker, Luckey, Whitehead & Sipple, Columbus, 1966-77; dist. judge, 1977—; dep. county atty. Platte County (Nebr.), 1965-67; city atty. Columbus, 1967-73; gen. counsel Lower Loup Natural Resource Dist., 1973-77. Bd. dirs., 1973-77, vice chmn., 1975-77; lectr. Platte Tech. Community Coll., 1971-75. Chmn., Discover Columbus Days, 1975; bd. dirs. Columbus Family Y, 1975—, vice chmn., 1977. Mem. Nebr., Platte County (pres. 1976—) bar assns., Columbus C. of C. Home: 3069 25th Ave Columbus NE 68601 Office: Court House Columbus NE 68601 Tel (402) 564-2848

WHITEHEAD, LLOYD OSCAR, b. Salisbury, Md., Dec. 23, 1939; A.B., U. Md., 1961; J.D., Am. U., 1964. Admitted to Md. bar, 1964, Ct. Appeals Md., 1964, U.S. Dist. Ct. D.C. bar, 1964, U.S. Dist. Ct. Dist. Md. bar, 1967, Supreme Ct. U.S. bar, 1974; partner firm Perdue, Owrutsky & Whitehead, Salisbury, 1964—. Mem. Am. Trial Lawyers Assn., Md., Wicomico County (v.p.) bar assns. Home: 725 Riverside Dr Salisbury MD 21801 Office: 212 E Main St Salisbury MD 21801 Tel (301) 749-2211

WHITEHORN, NATHANIEL, b. N.Y.C., July 21, 1912; A.B., U. Pa., 1931; J.D., Columbia, 1934. Admitted to N.Y. bar, 1934, U.S. Tax Ct. bar, 1972; asso. firm Hays, Wolf, Kaufman & Schwabacher, N.Y.C., 1934-45; mem. firm Botein, Hays, Sklar & Herzberg, and predecessors, N.Y.C., 1945—; counsel N.Y.C. div. Am. Cancer Soc., 1960—, New Rochelle Vol. Bur., 1950-55. Vice pres. New Rochelle Council for Unity, 1950-53; bd. dirs. Am. Cancer Soc., Inc., 1962-75, chmn. field services com., 1963-64, chmn. ad hoc merger com., 1964. Mem. N.Y.C. Bar Assn., N.Y. County Lawyers Assn. Recipient Clement Cleveland award; editor Columbia Law Rev., 1933-34. Home: 801 Weaver St Larchmont NY 10538 Office: Botein Hays et al 200 Park Ave New York City NY 10017 Tel (212) 867-5500

WHITEHORN, VICTOR, b. N.Y.C., Oct. 15, 1904; A.B., Columbia, 1924, LL.B., 1926. Admitted to N.Y. State bar, 1927; practice law various partnerships, 1927-72; partner firm Whitehorn & Delman, N.Y.C., 1972—; pres., dir. Eastern Life Ins. Co. N.Y., N.Y.C., 1959-71. Mem. Assn. N.Y. Life Ins. Cos. (pres. 1970), Phi Beta Kappa. Revising editor Columbia Law Rev., 1925-26. Home: 160 E 38th St New York City NY 10016 Office: 355 Lexington Ave New York City NY 10017 Tel (212) 661-1166

WHITEHURST, FRANK ELMORE, b. Dallas, Aug. 28, 1906; B.A., So. Meth. U., 1927; postgrad. in Law, George Washington U., 1928, Jefferson Law Sch., 1931. Admitted to Tex. bar, 1934, U.S. Supreme Ct. bar, 1938; sec. to Congressman Hatton W. Sumners, 5th Dist. Tex., 1927-30; chief staff Judiciary com. U.S. Ho. of Reps., Washington, 1932-39, asst. dir. Adminstrv. Office. of U.S. Cts., 1939-57, acting dir., 1956-57; bankruptcy judge U.S. Dist. Ct., No. Dist. Tex., Dallas, 1957-70; lectr. bankruptcy law So. Meth. U. Law Sch., 1972-74; mem. Jud. Conf. Adv. Com. on Bankruptcy Rules, 1960-76. Mem. Fed., Tex. State, Dallas bar assns. Editor Jour. Nat. Conf. Referees in Bankruptcy (name changed to Am. Bankruptcy Jour.), 1958-69; contbr. articles to profl. jours. Home and Office: 4001 Shore Crest Dr Dallas TX 75209 Tel (214) 357-1275

WHITEMAN, ROY MC CONNELL, b. Burlington, Iowa, Jan. 22, 1921; B.A., Iowa Wesleyan Coll., 1947; J.D., U. Iowa, 1948. Admitted to Iowa bar, 1948, Ill. bar, 1950; rep. claims Country Mut. Ins. Co., Bloomington, Ill., 1948-51, atty., 1953-65; partner firm Love, Beal & Whiteman, Monmouth, Ill., 1951-53; dir. claims Country Mut. Ins. Co. and Country Casualty Ins. Co., Bloomington, 1965—. Republican precinct committeeman, Bloomington, 1967-76; sec. McLean County Rep. Central Com., 1970-74, vice chmn., 1974-76. Mem. McLean County Bar Assn., Internat. Assn. Ins. Attys., Def. Research Inst., Nat. Rehab. Assn., Nat. Assn. Ind. Insurers. Home: 211 Ivanhoe Way Bloomington IL 61701 Office: PO Box 2100 Bloomington IL 61701 Tel (309) 828-0021

WHITESEL, JAMES WARREN, b. Crosskeys, Va., Dec. 4, 1921; B.S., Wake Forest U., 1943; J.D., George Washington U., 1948, LL.M., 1964; M.B.A., U. Chgo., 1964. Admitted to D.C. bar, 1948, N.Y. bar, 1951, Ill. bar, 1959, U.S. Supreme Ct. bar, 1955, U.S. Ct. Customs and Patent Appeals bar, 1950; examiner U.S. Patent Office, 1948-50; trademark counsel Stromberg-Carlson, Rochester, N.Y., 1950-58; Midwest area patent counsel ITT, Chgo., 1959-70; partner firm Laff, Whitesel & Rockman, Chgo., 1970—. Mem. Am., Ill., Chgo. bar assns., Am. Patent Law Assn. Office: 875 N Michigan Ave Suite 2460 Chicago IL 60611 Tel (312) 649-0200

WHITESELL, HUNTER BYRD, b. Union City, Tenn., Jan. 20, 1930; B.A., Vanderbilt U., 1951; LL.B., U. Ky., 1957. Admitted to Ky. bar, 1957, U.S. Supreme Ct. bar, 1961, Tenn. bar, 1974; law clk. Ky. Ct. Appeals, 1957-58; atty. Ky. Dept. Revenue, 1958-61; asst. atty. gen. State of Ky., 1961-68; individual practice law, Fulton, Ky., 1968-74; partner firm Johnson & Whitesell, Fulton, 1974—; Ky. pub. defender. Mem. exec. com. Ky. Hist. Soc. Mem. Ky., 1st Jud. Dist. (past pres.), Obion County (Tenn.) bar assns. Home: PO Box 40 Fulton KY 42041 Office: 207 Commercial Ave PO Box 433 Fulton KY 42041 Tel (502) 472-3222

WHITFIELD, ALLEN, b. Ruthven, Iowa, Jan. 26, 1904; student U. Nebr., 1920-21; B.S., Iowa State U., 1924; J.D., Harvard U., 1927; postgrad Drake U., 1928. Admitted to Fla., Iowa bars, 1928, D.C. bar, 1961; sr. partner firm Whitfield, Musgrave, Selvy, Kelly & Eddy, and predecessors, Des Moines, 1928—; dir. Hawkeye-Security Ins. Co., United Security Ins. Co., Northeastern Ins. Co. Hartford, Fin. Security Group, Valley Nat. Bank. Chmn. Veterans Memorial Audiotorium Commn., Des Moines, 1946-57, mem., 1957-58; hon. trustee Simpson Coll., Morningside Coll.; bd. govs. Iowa State U. Found.; past chmn. bd. trustees Iowa State U. Alumni Achievement Fund. Mem. Am., Iowa, Polk County bar assns., Fla. Bar, D.C. Bar, Intenat. Assn. Ins. Counsel, Fedn. Ins. Counsel. Home: Apt 802 The Park Fleur 3131 Fleur Dr Des Moines IA 50321 Office: 1400 Central National Bank Bldg Des Moines IA 50309 Tel (515) 288-6041

WHITFIELD, NEIL WARREN, b. Cleve., Aug. 16, 1927; A.B., Adelbert Coll., 1951; LL.B., Western Res. U., 1954. Admitted to Ohio bar, 1954; partner firm Gilbert & Whitfield, Medina, Ohio, 1954-75; dir. of law, Medina, 1959-62; solicitor Briarwood Beach, Ohio, 1956-75; judge Ct. of Common Pleas, Medina, 1975—; dir., gen. counsel Gowe Printing Co., 1972-75; counsel Old Phoenix Nat. Bank, Medina; dir. Medina Corp., Medina Devel. and Bldg. Corp., 1963-74. Mem. Am. Judicature Soc., Medina County, Akron, Ohio State bar assns., Common Pleas Judges Assn. of Ohio, Ohio Jud. Conf. Home: 302 Lafayette Rd Medina OH 44256 Office: Court House N Broadway St Medina OH 44256 Tel (216) 723-3641

WHITFIELD, PAUL L., b. Durham, N.C., June 21, 1936; A.B., U. N.C., 1958, J.D., 1962. Admitted to N.C. bar, 1963; individual practice law, Fayetteville, N.C., 1963-66; asst. city atty. Charlotte (N.C.), 1966-67, asst. city solicitor, 1967-68; individual practice law, Charlotte, 1968—. Vice-chmn. N.C. Property Tax Commn., 1975—; chmn. Mayor's Com. on Pub. Housing, Fayetteville, 1965-66; alt. mem. Fayetteville Zoning Bd. Adjustment, 1965-66. Mem. N.C., Am. bar assns., Am. Trial Lawyers Assn., N.C. Acad. Trial Lawyers. Home: 6028 Bentway Dr Charlotte NC 28211 Office: 503 Court Plaza Bldg 901 Elizabeth Ave Charlotte NC 28204

WHITING, HERBERT ROSS, b. Cleve., June 3, 1916; A.B., Ohio Wesleyan U., 1938; J.D., U. Mich., 1941. Admitted to Ohio bar, 1942; asso. Marshall, Melhorn, Wall & Block, Toledo, 1945-46; partner firm Van Aken, Whiting & Nash, Cleve., 1946-66; judge Ct. of Common Pleas, Cuyahoga County (Ohio), Cleve., 1966-73, judge Domestic Relations Div., 1975—; dir. law City of Cleve., 1973-75; Mem. Assn. of Family Conciliation Cts. (dir. 1976—), Am., Ohio, Cuyahoga County, Cleve. bar Assns., Am. Judicature Soc., Common Pleas Judges Assn. Ohio, Am. Acad. Matrimonial Lawyers, Delta Theta Phi. Home: 29999 Bolingbrook Rd Pepper Pike OH 44124 Office: Old Court House 1 Lakeside Ave Cleveland OH 44113 Tel (216) 621-5800

WHITING, KENNETH PAUL, JR., b. Olean, N.Y., Feb. 20, 1922; B.S., Hamilton Coll., 1943; LL.B., Albany Law Sch., 1948. Admitted to N.Y. State bar, 1948; mem. firm Travis & Whiting, Binghamton, N.Y., 1948-65; judge Broome County Family Ct., Binghamton, 1966—. Mem. Broome County Bar Assn., N.Y. State Assn. Family Ct. Judges, Nat. Council Juvenile Ct. Judges. Home: 124 LeRoy St Binghamton NY 13905 Office: 500 B County Office Bldg Binghamton NY 13901 Tel (607) 772-2183

WHITING, RICHARD ALBERT, b. Cambridge, Mass., Dec. 2, 1922; A.B., Dartmouth, 1944; LL.B., Yale, 1949. Admitted to D.C. bar, 1950, U.S. Supreme Ct. bar, 1960; asso. firm Steptoe and Johnson, Washington, 1949-56, partner, 1956—. Mem. Am. (antitrust sect., chmn. program com. 1975—, pub. utility law sect., chmn. antitrust com., 1974-76), N.Y. State, D.C. (vice chmn. anti-trust sect. 1967-68) bar assns. Adv. bd. Jour. Reprints and Antitrust Law and Econs., 1970—, The Antitrust Bull., 1975—. Home: 3081 N Oakland St Arlington VA 22207 Office: 1250 Connecticut Ave NW Washington DC 20036 Tel (202) 862-2120

WHITING, WILLIAM FENTON, b. Richmond, Calif., Oct. 17, 1940; A.B., Stanford U., 1962; LL.B., U. Calif. at Berkeley, 1965, J.D., 1970. Admitted to Calif. bar, 1965; judge advocate U.S. Marine Corps, 1965-68; mem. firm Watson & Hoffe, Richmond, 1968—. Bd. dirs. West Contra Costa YMCA, 1970—. Mem. Am., Contra Costa County bar assns., Calif., Alameda-Contra Costa trial lawyers assns. Contbr. articles to legal jours. Office: 3700 Barrett St Richmond CA 94805 Tel (415) 237-3700

WHITLATCH, WALTER G., b. Leesburg, Pa., Mar. 24, 1908; B.A., Case Western Res. U., 1931, LL.B., 1933. Admitted to Ohio bar, 1933; practiced in Ohio, 1933-36; referee, adminstr., then legal cons. Cuyahoga County (Ohio) Juvenile Ct., until 1960; judge Juvenile Ct. Div., Cuyahoga County Common Pleas Ct., 1960—; adviser on juvenile delinquency Pres's. Commn. on Law Enforcement and Adminstrn. Justice, 1966; mem. bd. fellows Nat. Center for Juvenile Justice, 1974-76; U.S. del. UN Congress on Crime and Treatment of Offenders, Geneva, 1975. Bd. mgrs. Hillcrest YMCA, 1951-76; mem. adv. bd. Ohio Youth Commn., 1963-67; trustee Cleve. Welfare Fedn., 1968-73; pres. East End Neighborhood House, 1960, Greater Cleve. Neighborhood Centers, 1961. Mem. Am., Cuyahoga County, Cleve. bar assns., Nat. Council Juvenile Ct. Judges (pres. 1975-76), Ohio Assn. Juvenile Ct. Judges (pres. 1965-67). Recipient Silver Beaver award Boy Scouts Am., 1962, Community Service award Big Bros. Greater Cleve., 1971, Outstanding Jud. Service award Ohio Supreme Ct., 1973; asso. editor Law Pub. Co. Home: 5172 Spencer Rd Lyndhurst OH 44124 Office: 2163 E 22d St Cleveland OH 44115 Tel (216) 771-8400

WHITLEY, PHILIP RAY, b. Selma, N.C., July 1, 1905; LL.B., U. N.C., 1929. Admitted to N.C. bar, 1928, Fed. Dist. Ct. bar, 1931; individual practice law, Wendell, N.C., 1930—, Former pres. Wendell C. of C., Wendell Tobacco Bd. Trade; chmn. ofcl. bd. Wendell Christian Ch.; chmn. Wake County Democratic Exec. Com., 1934-42; rep. N.C. Legislature, 1951-59. Mem. N.C., Wake County bar assns., Lambda Chi Alpha, Phi Alpha Delta. Home: Selma Rd Wendell NC 17591 Office: PO Box 66 55 E 3d St Wendell NC 27591 Tel (919) 365-6122

WHITLEY, ROBERT GEORGE, JR., b. Joliet, Ill., May 13, 1944; B.S., Ill. Wesleyen U., 1967; J.D., U. Iowa, 1970. Admitted to Iowa bar, 1970, Ill. bar, 1971; field claim rep. State Farm Ins. Co., Joliet, 1970-72; with firm Codo & Bonds, Joliet, 1972—; pub. defender Will County (Ill.), 1974-75; auditor Plainfield Twp. (Ill.), 1973—. Mem. Iowa, Ill., Am. bar assns. Home: 341 Mary Ct Plainfield IL 60544 Office: 5 E Van Buren St Joliet IL 60431 Tel (815) 726-7331

WHITLOCK, DANIEL ELLIOTT, b. Arroyo Grande, Calif., Apr. 3, 1922; J.D., U. So. Calif., 1950. Admitted to Calif. bar, 1951; asso. firm J.J. Novack, San Bernardino, Calif., 1951-53; individual practice law, San Bernardino, 1953-64; partner Hayton & Whitlock, San Bernardino, 1964-65; individual practice law, San Bernardino, 1965—; pres. Family Law Council, San Bernardino, 1976, Estate Planning Council San Bernardino Valley, 1976—. Mem. Am., San Bernardino County bar assns., State Bar Calif., Kiwanis Club. Home: 28783 Terrace Dr Highland CA 92346 Office: 505 Arrowhead Ave suite 303 San Bernardino CA 92401 Tel (714) 889-3547

WHITLOCK, JAMES LINWOOD, b. Farmville, Va., Feb. 27, 1936; B.S., Washington and Lee U., 1958; LL.B., U. Richmond, 1964. Admitted to Va. bar, 1964; appeals examiner Va. Employment Commn., Richmond, 1965; asso. firm Kellam & Kellam, Norfolk, Va., 1965-68; individual practice law, Farmville, 1968—. Chmn. Prince Edward County (Va.) March of Dimes, 1972, Prince Edward County Heart Fund, 1974. Mem. Va. State, 10th Jud. bar assns. Home: 705 Pinecrest Rd Farmville VA 23901 Office: 103 E Third St Farmville VA 23901 Tel (804) 392-3301

WHITLOCK, WILLIE WALKER, b. Mineral, Va., Nov. 16, 1925; B.S., Va. Commonwealth U., 1950; L.G., Va. Coll. Law, 1953. Admitted to Va. bar, 1955; town atty. Mineral (Va.), 1955—; county atty. Louisa County (Va.), 1974-75. Pres. Louisa County Lions Club, 1960. Mem. Piedmont, Louisa County bar assns. Office: POB 128 Mineral VA 23117 Tel (703) 894-5452

WHITMAN, CHARLES SEYMOUR, b. Albany, N.Y., Mar. 11, 1915; A.B., Amherst Coll., 1937; J.D., Harvard, 1940. Admitted to N.Y. bar, 1940; practiced in N.Y.C., 1940-43, 44-57; asst. counsel Gov. N.Y. State, 1943-44; judge Municipal Ct., N.Y.C., 1957-62, Civil Ct., N.Y.C., 1962—. Bd. dirs. N.Y.C. Bicentennial Corp., 1972—. Mem. Am. Bar Assn. Home: 70 E 96th St New York City NY 10028 Office: 111 Centre St New York City NY 10013

WHITMAN, JANE SHAW, b. Atlanta, Feb. 6, 1929; B.A., William Smith Coll., 1949; J.D., U. Mich., 1952. Admitted to Ill. bar, 1952; partner McDermott, Will & Emery, Chgo. Mem. Am., Ill., Chgo. bar assns., Women's Bar Assn. Ill. Office: 111 W Monroe St Suite 1900 Chicago IL 60603 Tel (312) 372-2000

WHITMAN, JOHN RUSSELL, b. Winnetka, Ill., Dec. 1, 1901; A.B., Harvard U., 1924; J.D., Northwestern U., 1927. Admitted to Ill. bar, 1927; asso. firm Cassels, Potter & Bentley, Chgo., 1927-33, mem., 1933-40; gen. atty., sec. Butler Bros. Co., Chgo., 1940-42; partner firm Pope & Ballard, Chgo., 1942-58, Barnett & Whitman, Winnetka, 1959-63, Whitman and Kauffmann, and predecessors, Winnetka, 1963—. Mem. Chgo. Bar Assn. (grievance com. 1938-39), Law Club Chgo., Legal Club Chgo. (sec. 1936-38), Phi Delta Phi. Home: 1930 Dale Ave Highland Park IL 60035 Office: 545 Lincoln Ave Winnetka IL 60093 Tel (312) 446-7372

WHITMAN, ROBERT, b. N.Y.C., May 18, 1936; B.B.A., Coll. City N.Y., 1956; J.D., Columbia, 1959; LL.M., N.Y. U., 1970. Admitted to N.Y. bar, 1959, Conn. bar, 1966; asso. in law Columbia U., 1959-60; asst. prof. law U. Md., 1960-62; asso. firm Cravath, Swaine and Moore, N.Y.C., 1962-64, Tenzer, Greenblatt, Fallon and Kaplan, N.Y.C., 1964-66; asso. prof. U. Conn., West Hartford, 1966-69, prof., 1969—; vis. lectr. Yale, fall 1970, U. So. Calif., summer 1971; vis. prof. U. Brunel, Middlesex, Eng., fall 1972; dir. Commn. to Rev. Probate Laws of Conn., 1970; dir. Commn. to Prepare Probate Practice Book for Conn., 1970-74. Bd. dirs. Family Service Soc. Hartford (Conn.). Mem. Am., Conn., Hartford bar assns., Am. Law Inst., Am. Judicature Soc., Nat. Conf. Lawyers and C.P.A.'s. Home: 86 Norwood Rd West Hartford CT 06117 Office: U of Conn Law Sch-Greater Hartford Campus West Hartford CT 06117 Tel (203) 523-4841

WHITMER, JOSEPH MORTON, b. Sacramento, Ky., Apr. 29, 1942; B.S., U. Ky., 1964, J.D., 1967. Admitted to Ky. bar, 1967; partner firm Veal and Whitmer, Nicholasville, Ky., 1967-68; exec. v.p., sec., gen. counsel, dir. Consol. Mgmt. Services, Inc., 1st Mut. Services, Inc., Eagles Nat. Life Ins. Co., 1st Mut. Ins. Co., 1st Mut. Life Ins. Co. (all Lexington, Ky.), 1970-75; exec. v.p., dir. Profl. Adminstrs. Ltd., Lexington, 1968—; individual practice law, Lexington, 1975—. Mem. adminstrv. bd., chmn. fin. com. Trinity Hill United Meth. Ch., Lexington, 1975—. Mem. Ky., Am., Fayette County bar assns., Internat. Found. Employee Benefit Plans, Nat. Assn. Security Dealers, Beta Alpha Psi, Phi Alpha Delta. Home: 2918 Montavesta Rd Lexington KY 40502 Office: 2043 Regency Circle Lexington KY 40503 Tel (606) 276-3581

WHITMER, LESLIE GAY, b. Lexington, Ky., July 31, 1941; B.S., U. Ky., 1963, J.D., 1965. Admitted to Ky. bar, 1966, U.S. Supreme Ct. bar, 1972; atty. advisor gen. Office of Gen. Counsel, USDA, Chgo., 1966-69; asst. dir. and bar counsel Ky. Bar Assn., Frankfort, 1969-72; dir., bar counsel, treas., 1973—; registrar Supreme Ct. of Ky., 1975—; asst. sec.-treas. Ky. Bar Found.; sec.-treas., dir. Ky. Bar Title Ins. Agy., Inc., 1975—. Adv. com. mem. legal assts. program Eastern Ky. U., 1973—; adv. council for legal assts. Midway Jr. Coll., 1976—; mem. study group on legal edn. Council on Pub. Higher Edn., 1975—. Mem. Fed., Ky., Fayette County bar assns., Nat. Assn. Bar Execs., Nat. Orgn. Bar Counsel, Psi Chi. Editor: Ky. Bench and Bar Jour., 1975—, The Reporter (Ky. Bar Assn.), 1973—. Office: 315 W Main St Frankfort KY 40601 Tel (502) 564-3795

WHITMIRE, BOYCE AUGUSTUS, b. Brevard, N.C., Oct. 21, 1905; student U. N.C., 1924-26; LL.B., Wake Forest U., 1928. Admitted to N.C. bar, 1928; individual practice law, Hendersonville, N.C., 1928—; mem. N.C. Ho. of Reps., 1959-61, N.C. Senate, 1961-63; mayor, Hendersonville, 1969—. Past pres. Hendersonville YMCA, Mem. Henderson County Bd. Edn., 1963-69; trustee Western Carolina U., 1963—; past pres. Henderson County Mental Health Assn. Mem. N.C. State, Henderson County bar assns. Home: 201 Ewbank Dr Hendersonville NC 28739 Office: 4th Ave W Hendersonville NC 28739 Tel (704) 692-6528

WHITMORE, BRUCE GRAY, b. Glen Cove, N.Y., May 7, 1944; B.A., Tufts U., 1966; J.D., Harvard U., 1969. Admitted to N.Y. State bar, 1970, Calif. bar, 1973; asso. firm Hughes, Hubbard & Reed, N.Y.C., 1970-72, Los Angeles, 1972-76; atty. Atlantic Richfield Co., Los Angeles, 1976—. Mem. Am., Calif. State, Los Angeles County bar assns. Home: 1041 Nithsdale Rd Pasadena CA 91105 Office: 515 S Flower St Los Angeles CA 90071 (213) 486-1572

WHITMORE, RICHARD SHARP, b. Los Angeles, Oct. 21, 1942; B.A., Stanford, 1964, J.D., 1967. Admitted to Calif. bar, 1967; asso. firm Wilson, Mosher & Martin, Palo Alto, Calif., 1968-70; asst. city atty. Sunnyvale (Calif.), 1970-72; partner firm Gillio & Whitmore, Sunnyvale, 1972-76; partner firm Whitmore & Kay, Los Altos, Calif., 1976—; legis. asst. Paul McCloskey, Jr., 1968; lectr. Sonoma State Coll., 1976, League Calif. Cities, County Suprs. Assn. Calif., Labor Relations Service. Coach, Am. Youth Soccer Orgn., 1975-76. Mem. Sunnyvale-Cupertino, Palo Alto bar assns. Office: 329 S San Antonio St Los Altos CA 94022 Tel (408) 941-8280

WHITMORE, THOMAS EDWARD, b. Omaha, Dec. 14, 1945; B.S. in Bus. Adminstrn., Creighton U., 1967, J.D. cum laude, 1969. Admitted to Nebr. bar, 1969; asso. firm Monen, Seidler & Ryan, Omaha, 1969-71; atty. Fairmont Foods Co., Omaha, 1971-74, asst. sec., sr. atty., 1974—. Mem. Am., Nebr. bar assns. Editor in chief: Creighton Law Rev., 1968-69. Home: 4711 Fountainhead Dr Houston TX 77066 Office: 333 W Loop N Houston TX 77024 Tel (713) 683-8383

WHITMORE, WAYNE RUSSELL, JR., b. Cheyenne, Wyo., June 29, 1945; B.S., U. Iowa, 1967; J.D., Chgo.-Kent Coll., 1970. Admitted to Ill. bar, 1970; asso. firm Troupis Law Office, Mendota, Ill., 1970-75; partner firm Troupis & Whitmore, Mendota, 1976—; city atty.

Mendota, Sublette, West Brooklyn and Compton, Ill., 1972—; atty. Mendota Savs. & Loan Assn., Farmers State Bank Sublette. Mem. Ill., LaSalle County bar assns., Municipal Attys. League, Mendota C. of C. (dir. 1971-73, v.p. 1973). Home: 1101 S Park St Mendota IL 61342 Office: 806 Jefferson St Mendota IL 61342 Tel (815) 539-7408

WHITNEY, EUGENE WALSIT, b. Cleve., Jan. 10, 1933; B.S., John Carroll U., 1957; diploma U. Copenhagen, 1958; J.D., Cleve. State U., 1967. Admitted to Ohio bar, 1967; mem. elec. engring. dept. Case Inst. Tech., 1958-60; mgr. mkt. research TRW, Inc., Cleve., 1960-66, dir. planning, 1965-69, dir. Pacific ops., 1970-75, dir. product support, 1975—. Mem. Ohio Bar Assn., Aerospace Planning Group. Recipient Fulbright award, 1958. Home: 999 Professor Rd Lyndhurst OH 44124 Office: 23555 Euclid Ave Euclid OH 44117

WHITNEY, GEORGE WARD, b. N.Y.C., June 30, 1924; B.E.E., Rensselaer Poly. Inst., 1949; J.D., George Washington U., 1965. Admitted to D.C. bar, 1952, N.Y. bar, 1954; asst. examiner U.S. Patent Office, Washington, 1948-50; law clk. Gen. Motors Corp., Washington, 1950-52; asso. law firm Brumbaugh, Graves, Donohue & Raymond, N.Y.C., 1952-60, partner, 1960—. Dep. mayor mayor, village trustee, Garden City, N.Y., 1969-72; pres. Citizens Adv. Com. on Edn., Garden City, 1967; pres. Garden City Central Property Owners Assn., 1968-69. Vice-chmn., trustee Garden City Pub. Library. Mem. Am. Patent Law Assn. (chmn. anti-trust com. 1975—), N.Y. Patent Law Assn. (bd. govs. 1973-76), Am. Arbitration Assn. (mem. nat. panel of arbitrators), Delta Tau Delta. Club: Downtown Athletic (bd. govs. 1970-73). Home: 4 Cedar Pl Garden City NY 11530 Office: 30 Rockefeller Plaza New York City NY 10020

WHITNEY, JOHN ADAIR, b. Cin., Jan. 25, 1932; B.A. in Polit. Economy cum laude, Williams Coll., 1953; LL.B., Harvard, 1956. Admitted to Ohio bar, 1956, D.C. bar, 1960, Md. bar, 1965; naval officer Chief of Torts and Ct. of Claims Br., Office JAG, 1956-59; asso. firm Pope, Ballard & Loos, Washington, 1959-63, partner, 1964-69, 73—; asst. gen. counsel for procurement matters NASA, 1969-73. Mem. Md. Ho. of Dels., 1967-69; chmn. Fin. Adv. Com. Montgomery County (Md.), 1970; mem. Property Tax Assessment Appeal Bd. Montgomery County, 1973-74. Mem. Am., D.C., Md., Montgomery County, Fed. bar assns., Nat. Contract Mgmt. Assn., Phi Beta Kappa. Recipient NASA Exceptional Service medal, 1972. Home: 8007 Aberdeen Rd Bethesda MD 20014 Office: 888 17th St NW Washington DC 20006 Tel (202) 298-8600

WHITNEY, JOHN CLARENCE, b. Green Bay, Wis., Feb. 10, 1915; student U. Pa., 1932-33; B.A., U. Wis., 1936, LL.B., 1938. Admitted to Wis. bar, 1938; law examiner Wis. Pub. Service Commn., Madison, 1938-39; asso. firm Everson, Ryan & Hanaway, Green Bay, 1939-41; individual practice law, Green Bay, 1945—. Chmn. Brown County (Wis.) chpt. Am. Red Cross, Green Bay, 1947-48, Brown County Safety Council, 1947-48. Fellow Am. Bar Found.; Am. Coll. Trial Lawyers; mem. Brown County, Am. bar assns., State Bar of Wis. (pres. 1961-62), Am. Assn. Attys., Am. Law Inst., Order of Coif. Named Young Man of Year Green Bay Jr. C. of C., 1949. Mem. editorial bd. U. Wis. Law Review, 1937-38. Home: 100 Rosemont Dr Green Bay WI 54301 Office: PO Box 1263 414 E Walnut St Green Bay WI 54305 Tel (414) 435-3734

WHITNEY, LISA ANTOINETTE, b. Pittsfield, Mass., Aug. 17, 1946; B.A., U. Mass., 1968; J.D., Union U., 1971. Admitted to N.Y. State bar, 1972; mgr., atty. govt. and legal affairs Avon Products, Inc., N.Y.C., 1972-74; atty. mktg. J.C. Penney Co. Inc., N.Y.C., 1974—. Mem. Am., N.Y. State bar assns., N.Y. County Bar Assn. (trade regulation com., fed. legis. com.), Assn. Bar City N.Y. Home: 780 Greenwich St New York City NY 10014 Office: 1301 Ave of Americas New York City NY 10019

WHITNEY, ROBERT MICHAEL, b. Green Bay, Wis., Jan. 29, 1949; student U. Wis., 1967-70, J.D., 1974. Admitted to Wis. bar, 1974; partner firm Gruber, Herrick & Whitney, Madison, Wis., 1974-75; law clk. Dane County (Wis.) Circuit Ct., 1975-76; counsel Wis. State Elections Bd., Madison, 1976—; teaching asst. U. Wis., Madison, 1972-74. Chmn. adv. com. to citizen advocacy program Madison Area Assn. Retarded Citizens, 1976—. Mem. Wis., Dane County bar assns. Home: 1725 Madison St Madison WI 53711 Office: State Office Bldg 1 W Wilson St Madison WI 53702 Tel (608) 266-8005

WHITTEMORE, DAVID O., b. Boston, July 13, 1939; B.A., Williams Coll., 1961; LL.B., U. Va., 1964. Admitted to Mass. bar, 1964; asso. firm Hargraves, Karb, Wilcox & Galvani, Framingham, Mass., 1964-71; individual practice law, Framingham, 1971—. Bd. dirs. Algonquin council Boy Scouts Am., 1966-71; chmn. Framingham Charter Commn., 1971-72; pres. Big Brother Big Sister of S. Middlesex, Inc.; deacon Plymouth Ch., Framingham. Mem. Am., Mass., S. Middlesex bar assns. Office: 118 Union Ave Framingham MA 01701 Tel (617) 872-4331

WHITTEN, BERNARD IVY, b. Paris, Tex., Aug. 4, 1909; LL.B., So. Meth. U., 1937. Admitted to Tex. bar, 1937; individual practice law, Dallas. Home: 1529 Bella Vista St Dallas TX 75218 Office: 1803 Mercantile Bank Bldg Dallas TX 75201 Tel (214) 748-9200

WHITTENBERG, IRA ORVILLE, JR., b. Fort Worth, Oct. 21, 1932; B.S., So. Meth. U., 1957, J.D., 1961, also LL.M. Admitted to Tex. bar, 1973; with prodn. contract adminstrn., Bell Helicopter div. Textron, Inc., Fort Worth, 1961-65, prodn. contract mgr., 1965-69, research and devel. dept. contract mgr., 1969—; adj. faculty U. Dallas, 1975—. Mem. traffic safety com. City of Hurst (Tex.), 1974-75. Mem. State Bar Tex (corp. counsel sect., environ. law sect.), Nat. Contract Mgmt. Assn. (chmn. edn. com. 1975—, treas. 1976—). Contbr. articles to profl. jours. Home: 1712 Cimarron Trail Hurst TX 76053 Office: PO Box 482 Fort Worth TX 76101 Tel (817) 280-2161

WHITTENBURG, BURK, b. Amarillo, Tex., Sept. 29, 1948; B.A. in Journalism, Tex. Tech. U., 1971; J.D., U. Tex., Austin, 1972. Admitted to Tex. bar, 1972; student clk. firm Brown, Maroney, Rose, Baker & Barber, Austin, 1971-72; prin. Whittenburg Law Firm, Amarillo, 1972—. Bd. dirs. Goodwill Industries of Amarillo, Inc., 1976; trustee Tex. Bur. Econ. Understanding, 1977—. Mem. Am., Tex., Amarillo (exec. com. 1977—) bar assns., Tex. Assn. Bank Counsel, Tex., Am. assns. trial lawyers, Phi Eta Sigma, Phi Kappa Phi. Home: PO Box 543-A Coulter Rd Amarillo TX 79106 Office: 1010 Harrison St Amarillo TX 79101 Tel (806) 372-5671

WHITTENBURG, GEORGE, b. Amarillo, Tex., Mar. 20, 1944; B.B.A. with honors, U. Tex., 1965, J.D. with honors, 1968. Admitted to Tex. bar, 1968; asso. firm Folley, Snodgrass & Calhoun, Amarillo, 1968-70; prin. Whittenburg Law Firm, Amarillo, 1971—. Bd. dirs. Panhandle chpt. Nat. Found. March Dimes, 1974—, chmn., 1976—. Mem. Amarillo, Am. bar assns., State Bar Tex. (lawyer referral service com. 1973—), Tex. Assn. Bank Counsel, Tex. Trial Lawyers Assn., Assn. Trial Lawyers Am., Beta Alpha Psi, Beta Gamma Sigma, Phi Delta Phi, Order of Coif. Research editor Tex. Law Rev., 1967-68. Office: 1010 Harrison St Amarillo TX 79101 Tel (806) 372-5671

WHITTENBURG, MACK, b. Amarillo, Tex., Apr. 6, 1946; B.B.A., Tex. Tech. U., 1967; J.D., U. Tex., 1970. Admitted to Tex. bar, 1970; asso. firm Folley, Snodgrass & Calhoun, Amarillo, 1970; prin. Whittenburg Law Firm, Amarillo, 1971—. Mem. regional adv. com. Office Edn. Deaf, Tex. Edn. Agy. W. Tex. Panhandle Region, 1976—; pres. Parents Hearing Impaired, Inc., 1976—. Mem. Amarillo, Am. bar assns., State Bar Tex. (designated practice com. 1976—), Tex. Assn. Bank Counsel, Tex., Am. trial lawyers assns., Phi Delta Phi. Rev. editor Tex. Law Rev., 1969-70. Office: 1010 Harrison St Amarillo TX 79101 Tel (806) 372-5671

WHITTERS, JAMES PAYTON, III, b. Boston, Oct. 23, 1939; A.B., Trinity Coll., 1962; J.D., Boston Coll., 1969. Admitted to Mass. bar, 1969; asso. firm Ely, Bartlett, Brown & Proctor, Boston, 1969-74, Gaston Snow & Ely Bartlett, Boston, 1974—. Chmn. vol. study Mass. Outdoor Advt. Bd., 1971-72, chmn. bd., 1975—; bd. dirs. Cambridge Day Care Assn., 1970-73, Asso. Day Care Services Met. Boston, 1973-75, Beacon Hill Nursery Sch., 1976—; sec., trustee Hurricane Island Outward Bound Sch., 1977—. Mem. Boston Bar Assn., Maritime Law Assn. U.S. Home: 44 Mount Vernon St Boston MA 02108 Office: One Federal St Boston MA 02109 Tel (617) 426-4600

WHITTINGTON, DAVID EDWARD, b. Oxnard, Calif., Mar. 14, 1938; B.S. in Chemistry, U. Calif., Los Angeles, 1963; J.D., Hastings Coll. Law, 1966. Admitted to Calif. bar, 1966; asso. firm Beverly and Riley, Placerville, Calif., 1966-69; dep. legis. counsel State of Calif., 1969-73; asst. county counsel El Dorado County (Calif.), 1973—. Bd. dirs. Marshall Hosp., Placerville, 1975—. Mem. Calif., El Dorado County (sec. 1969) bar assns. Office: 330 Fair Ln Placerville CA 95667 Tel (916) 626-2234

WHITTLESEY, JOHN WILLIAMS, b. West Newton, Mass., Aug. 18, 1917; B.A., Harvard, 1937, LL.B., 1940; LL.M., Columbia, 1947. Admitted to Mass. bar, 1940, N.Y. State bar, 1953, U.S. Supreme Ct. bar, 1969. Labor atty. U.S. C. of C., 1946-51; industry asst. Wage Stablzn. Bd., 1951-52; cons. firm Fischer & Ridge, N.Y.C., 1952-53; labor counsel Union Carbide Corp., N.Y.C., 1953—. Chmn. N.Y. State safety com. Asso. Industries, 1972—, New Castle (N.Y.) Republican Com., 1969-73. Mem. Am., N.Y.C., Westchester County bar assns. Office: 270 Park Ave New York City NY 10017 Tel (212) 551-6797

WHITWELL, ROBERT QUENTIN, b. Memphis, July 28, 1946; B.S., Delta State U., 1968; J.D., U. Miss., 1972. Admitted to Miss bar, 1972; asso. firm Perry & Taylor, Southaven, Miss., 1972-73; partner firm Taylor Whitwell and McClure, Southaven, 1973—. Mem. Miss., DeSoto County (Miss.) bar assns., Am., Miss. trial lawyers assns. Office: Taylor Whitwell McClure 1709 Stateline Rd Southaven MS 38671 Tel (601) 342-1300

WHYMAN, HERBERT, b. N.Y.C., Oct. 15, 1913; B.A., Coll. City N.Y., 1933; LL.B., Fordham U., 1936. Admitted to N.Y. bar, 1936; asso. atty. Eugene Fay, N.Y.C., 1938-40; partner firm King, Frank & Whyman, N.Y.C., 1941-50, firm Frank & Whyman, N.Y.C., 1950—; staff atty. N.Y.C. Charter Revision Commn., 1936-38; counsel Bedford Stuyvesant Restoration Corp., Bklyn., 1974—; counsel Roslyn (N.Y.) Econ. Opportunity Council, 1966-67; lectr. Practicing Law Inst., N.Y.C. Mem. Am., N.Y. State, N.Y. County, Nassau County bar assns. Contbr. articles to legal jours. Office: 335 Broadway New York City NY 10013 Tel (212) 925-9532

WHYMAN, MARTIN N., b. N.Y.C., Nov. 3, 1909; A.B., City U. N.Y., 1930; LL.B., Columbia, 1933. Admitted to N.Y. bar, 1934, U.S. Supreme Ct. bar; partner firm Whyman & Whyman, N.Y.C.; of counsel firm Ruben Schwartz & Silverbery, N.Y.C.; editor Co-Ordinator Tax Service. Mem. N.Y. County Lawyers Assn. Office: 450 7th Ave New York City NY 10001 Tel (212) OX5-3550

WHYNOTT, PHILIP PERCY, b. Waltham, Mass., Jan. 11, 1944; B.A., U. Wyo., 1966, M.A., 1971, J.D., 1971. Admitted to Wyo. bar, 1972; dir. Legal Service for Laramie County (Wyo.), 1972-73, mem. bd., 1974—; partner firm DeHerrera and Whynott, Cheyenne, Wyo., 1974—. Mem. Wyo. State, Laramie County, Am. (Wyo. chmn. com. on juvenile law) bar assns., Assn. Trial Lawyers Am. Recipient Internat. Trial Lawyers award, 1971. Office: Hynds Bldg Cheyenne WY 82001 Tel (307) 635-4178

WHYTE, HARTZELL JORDAN, b. Kansas City, Kans., July 20, 1927; B.S., Kan. State U., 1952; J.D., U. Mo., Kansas City, 1956. Admitted to Kan. bar, 1956, U.S. Ct. Appeals bar, 10th Circuit, 1972; asst. gen. counselor Kans. Corp. Commn., Topeka, 1957-59; gen. counselor Kan. Securities Commn., Topeka, 1959-61; asso. county counselor Wyandotte County, Kan., 1963—. Chmn. bd. trustees Mason Meml. United Meth. Ch., Kansas City, Kan. Mem. Wyandotte County, Nat., Kansas City (Kan.) bar assns., Kappa Alpha Psi (pres. Kansas City Alumni chpt. 1958-60). Recipient citation Merit U. Kansas City Legal Aid Clinic Fellowship House. Home: 2038 N 42d St Kansas City KS 66104 Office: Suite 228 One Gateway Center Kansas City KS 66101 Tel (913) 342-4407

WHYTE, JAMES PRIMROSE, JR., b. Columbus, Miss., Aug. 25, 1921; A.B., Bucknell U., 1943; M.A., Syracuse U., 1948; J.D., U. Colo., 1951. Admitted to Okla. bar, 1951, Mo. bar, 1957, Va. bar, 1961; partner firm Gordon & Whyte, McAlester, Okla., 1951-55; county pros. atty. Pittsburg County (Okla.), 1955-56; atty. Great Lakes Pipe Line Co., Kansas City, Mo., 1957; prof. law Marshall-Wythe Sch. Law, Coll. William and Mary, 1958—, dean Sch. Law, 1969-75; labor arbitrator Am. Arbitration Assn., Fed. Mediation and Conciliation Service, Va. Dept. Labor and Industry, Bituminous Coal Operators, United Mine Workers. Mem. Williamsburg (Va.) Bd. Zoning Appeals, 1975-76. Mem. Va. State Bar, Am. Bar Assn., Nat. Acad. Arbitrators. Contbr. articles to legal jours. Home: 1109 Jamestown Rd Williamsburg VA 23185 Office: Sch of Law Coll of William and Mary Williamsburg VA 23185 Tel (804) 229-3000

WIACEK, ROBERT ANTHONY, b. Gary, Ind., Oct. 19, 1922; LL.B., John Marshall Law Sch., 1951, J.D., 1970. Admitted to Ill. bar, 1951; asst. states atty. Cook County (Ill.), Chgo., 1951-56; house counsel Allstate Ins. Co., Chgo., 1957-60. Mem. Adv. Soc., Chgo. Bar Assn., John Marshall Alumni Assn., Delta Theta Phi. Home: 2108 N Sheffield Ave Chicago IL 60614 Office: 2108 N Sheffield Ave Chicago IL 60614 Tel (312) 281-0083

WIBLISHAUSER, ELMER H., b. St. Paul, July 23, 1910; student U. Minn., 1929-32; LL.B., St. Paul Coll. Law. Admitted to Minn. bar; practiced in St. Paul, 1939—. Mem. Maplewood (Minn.) City Council, 1962-67. Mem. Minn. State Bar Assn. (state treas. 1959-63), Am. Trial Lawyers Assn., Phi Beta Gamma (supreme chief justice 1954-56). Home: 1750 East Shore Dr Maplewood MN 55109 Office: 810 Pioneer Bldg Saint Paul MN 55101 Tel (612) 224-7841

WICHMANN, FRANK AUGUST, b. Covington, Ky., Nov. 19, 1939; A.B., Thomas More Coll., 1961; J.D., U. Cin., 1964. Admitted to Ky. and Ohio bars, 1964; individual practice law, Covington, 1964—. Mem. Ky., Kenton County (pres., 1975) bar assns. Home: 518 Perimeter St Erlanger KY 41018 Office: 400 1st National Bank 6th & Madison Sts Covington KY 41011 Tel (606) 431-2222

WICKA, RICHARD VINCENT, b. Beach, N.D., Apr. 3, 1930; B.A., St. John's U., 1952; J.D., U. N.D., 1955. Admitted to N.D. bar, 1955, Minn. bar, 1956; with Gt. No. Rwy. Co., St. Paul, 1957-70; asst. gen. counsel Burlington No. Inc., St. Paul, 1970—. Active Boy Scouts Am. Mem. Am. Minn. bar assns., Nat. Assn. R.R. Trial Counsel, Minn. R.R. Trial Lawyers Assn., Minn. Def. Lawyers Assn. Home: 427 Woodlawn St Saint Paul MN 55105 Office: 176 E 5th St Saint Paul MN 55101 Tel (612) 298-3186

WICKENS, CHARLES ARLEY, b. Scott County, Ark., Oct. 11, 1921; B.A., U. Mich., 1949; LL.B., U. Valparaiso, 1952. Admitted to Mich. bar, 1953; judge Lake County (Mich.) Probate Ct., 1953-65, Mich. 19th Circuit Ct., 1966—. Mem. Manistee-Lake County Bar Assn. Office: PO Box 284 Courthouse Manistee MI 49660

WICKER, JEREMY CHARLES, b. Mineral Wells, Tex., Mar. 12, 1941; B.E.E., Ga. Inst. Tech., 1965; J.D., U. Houston, 1970; LL.M., Yale, 1972. Admitted to Tex. bar, 1970, U.S. 5th Circuit Ct. Appeals bar, 1970; law clk. Hon. David W. Dyer, U.S. Ct. Appeals, Miami, Fla., 1970-71; asst. prof. law Tex. Tech. U., 1972-74, asso. prof., 1974-76, prof., 1976—. Mem. Assn. Am. Law Schs. Author: (with J.W. Moore) Moore's Federal Practice, vol. 1, 1976, vol. 1A, 1974, vol. 6, 1976; (with Moore) Moore's Civil Rules Pamphlet, 1975 (John Garwood award U. Houston Law Sch. 1970). Office: Tex Tech U Law Sch Lubbock TX 79409 Tel (806) 742-3785

WICKER, WILLIAM BRATTON, b. Waynesville, Mo., July 26, 1947; B.A., U. Mo., 1969; J.D., U. Miss., 1973. Admitted to Miss. bar, 1973; asso. firm Wells, Gerald, Brand, Watters & Cox, Jackson, Miss., 1973-77; partner firm Wells, Wells, Pittman & Wicker, Jackson, 1977—. Asso., Boy Scouts Am., 1974-76; fundraiser Jackson YMCA, 1973; active Am. Cancer Soc., Heart Fund. Mem. Am. (appellate reform com.), Miss., Hinds County bar assns., Jackson Young Lawyers Assn., Phi Delta Phi. Contbr. articles to legal jours.; research editor Miss. Law Jour., 1971-73. Home: 4429 E Ridge Dr Jackson MS 39211 Office: Wells Wells et al 1100 Deposit Guaranty Bldg PO Box 1970 Jackson MS 39205 Tel (601) 948-3030

WICKERSHAM, THEODORE SAVAGE, b. N.Y.C., Apr. 30, 1939; B.A., Harvard, 1961; J.D., U. Calif., 1964. Admitted to N.Y., Calif. bars, 1965; asso. firm Lord, Day & Lord, N.Y.C., 1964-71, firm Sann & Howe, N.Y.C., 1972-73, firm Breed, Abbott & Morgan, N.Y.C., 1973—. Mem. Assn. Bar City N.Y., Am. Bar Assn. Office: Breed Abbott & Morgan 1 Chase Manhattan Plaza New York City NY 10005 Tel (212) 676-0800

WICKERSHAM, WARREN GEORGE, b. Oshkosh, Wis., Jan. 5, 1938; B.A. summa cum laude, Duke U., 1960; J.D., Yale, 1963. Admitted to Fla. bar, 1963, D.C., U.S. Supreme Ct. bars, 1966; staff office gen. counsel Dept. Air Force, Washington, 1963-66; asso. firm Surrey, Karasik & Morse, Washington, 1966-68, partner, 1968—; resident partner, Beirut, Lebanon, 1968-71, mng. partner, 1971-75; vis. lectr. Duke Law Sch., 1965-66. Mem. Am., (chmn. middle east law com. internat. law sect. 1971—), Inter-Am. bar assns., Am. Arbitration Assn. (panel arbitrators, 1975—), Am. Soc. Internat. Law. Bd. editors Yale Law Jour., 1962-63. Home: 6811 Wemberly Way McLean VA 22101 Office: 1156 NW 15th St Washington DC 20005 Tel (202) 331-4030

WICKHAM, DALE WALLACE, b. Dayton, Ohio, Feb. 6, 1929; A.B., Harvard U., 1950, LL.B., 1953. Admitted to Ohio bar, 1953, D.C. bar, 1957, Ill. bar, 1972, Va. bar, 1966, U.S. Supreme Ct. bar, 1959; individual practice law, Washington, 1956—, Chgo., 1971—; partner firm Wickham & Craft, Washington and Chgo., 1977—; spl. counsel tax reform act U.S. Senate Com. on Finance, 1969-70; staff atty. U.S. Congress Joint Com. Internal Revenue Taxation, 1959-62. Chmn., co-founder Mt. Vernon (Va.) Citizens for Better Govt., 1966-67; co-chmn. Mt. Vernon Council Citizens Assns., 1965-66. Mem. Am. Bar Assn., Internat. Fiscal Assn. Home: 513 S Fairfax St Alexandria VA 22314 Tel (703) 836-2288 Office: 1050 17th St NW Suite 1100 Washington DC 20036 Tel (202) 785-8150 also One IBM Plaza Suite 4700 Chicago IL 60611

WICKHAM, FRED REICHERT, b. Delaware, Ohio, Sept. 5, 1904; B.A., Ohio Wesleyan U., 1927; J.D., U. Mich., 1930. Admitted to Ohio bar, 1930; partner firm Wickham & Wickham, Delaware, 1930-37; individual practice law, Delaware, 1946—; judge Ct. Common Pleas, Delaware County, 1937-46; mem. Ohio Bd. Bar Examiners, Columbus, 1953-58; lectr. law Ohio Wesleyan U., Delaware, 1942-55. Chmn. Delaware CSC. Mem. Delaware County, Ohio State, Am. bar assns. Home: 4357 Marysville Rd Delaware OH 43015 Office: 125 N Sandusky St Delaware OH 43015 Tel (614) 363-1369

WIDDOWSON, LOGAN CARLISLE, b. Salisbury, Md., Nov. 3, 1942; B.S., Univ. Baltimore, 1965; LL.B., Eastern Coll., 1969. Admitted to Md. bar, 1970; state's atty., Somerset County, Md. Bd. dirs. Somerset County Agrl. and Civic Center; mem. Princess Anne Volunteer Fire Co., Eastern Shore Shrine Club. Mem. Am., Md., Somerset County bar assns. Home: Route 3 Box 330 Princess Anne MD 21853 Office: North Somerset Ave Princess Anne MD 21853 Tel (301) 651-3800

WIDENER, HIRAM EMORY, JR., b. Abingdon, Va., Apr. 30, 1923; student Va. Poly. Inst., 1940-41; B.S., U.S. Naval Acad., 1944; LL.B., Washington and Lee U., 1953. Admitted to Va. bar, 1951; partner firm Widener, Widener & Frackelton, and predecessor, Bristol, Va., 1953-69; judge U.S. Dist. Ct. for Western Dist. Va., 1969-72, chief judge, 1971-72; judge U.S. Ct. Appeals for 4th Circuit, Abingdon, 1972—; U.S. commr. for Western Dist. Va., 1963-66; receiver Corp. Ct. City of Bristol, 1966-69. Trustee Va. Intermont Coll., 1975—. Mem. Am., Va., Bristol bar assns., Am. Judicature Soc., Am. Law Inst., Inst. Jud. Adminstrn. Contbr. articles to Washington and Lee Coll., Coll. William and Mary law revs. Home: 537 Glenway Ave Bristol VA 24201 Office: POB 868 Abingdon VA 24210 Tel (703) 628-3138

WIDISS, ALAN ISAAC, b. Los Angeles, Sept. 28, 1938; B.S., U. So. Calif., 1960, LL.B., 1963; LL.M., Harvard, 1964. Admitted to Calif. bar, 1964; teaching fellow law Harvard, Cambridge, Mass., 1964-65; prof. law U. Iowa, Iowa City, 1965—; vis. prof. law U. So. Calif., Los Angeles, summers 1966, 69, U. San Diego, summers 1974, 75; dir. Council Law Related Studies Mass. No-Fault Study, 1972-76. Co-chmn. Iowa City-Johnson County Arts Council, 1975-76; chmn. Citizens Advisory Com. Johnson County Regional Planning Commn., 1974-75; trustee U. Iowa Sch. Religion. Mem. Am. Bar Assn., Law and Soc. Assn., Assn. Am. Law Schs., Order of Coif, Phi Kappa Phi. Author: A Guide to Uninsured Motorist Coverage, 1969; (with Joseph Little, Roger Clark, Thomas Jones) No-Fault Automobile Insurance: The Massachusetts, Florida, Delaware and Michigan Experience, 1977. Office: College of Law University of Iowa Iowa City IA 52242 Tel (319) 353-4855

WIDLITZ, PAUL J., b. Newark, Aug. 11, 1914; B.A., Pa. State U., 1936; LL.B., N.Y. U., 1939. Admitted to N.Y. State bar, 1941; judge Nassau County (N.Y.) Dist. Ct., 1951-56, Nassau County Ct., 1957-61; justice N.Y. State Supreme Ct., 1962—; adminstrv. judge Nassau County Ct., 1976—. Chmn. Nassau County Cancer Crusade, 1955; chmn. drive Boy Scouts Am.; pres., chmn. bd. dirs. Hebrew Acad., Nassau County; active B'nai B'rith. Mem. N.Y. State, Nassau County bar assns. Recipient Silver Beaver Award Boy Scouts Am.; Gold Citizenship medal VFW; Norman F. Lent Meml. award Criminal Cts. Bar Assn. Home: 36 Raspberry Ln Levittown NY 11756 Office: Supreme Ct Bldg Mineola NY 11501 Tel (516) 535-4083

WIDMAN, GARY LEE, b. Fremont, Nebr., June 1, 1936; B.S., U. Nebr., 1957, J.D., U. Calif., 1962; LL.M., U. Mich., 1966. Admitted to Calif. bar, 1962, U.S. Supreme Ct. bar, 1976; asso. firm Thelen, Marrin, Johnson & Bridges, San Francisco, 1962-65; asso. prof. law U. Denver, 1966-69; prof. law U. Calif. Hastings, 1969-73, 77—; gen. counsel Council on Environ. Quality, 1974-76; mem. Calif. Atty. Gen.'s Task Force on the Environment, 1971-73; dir. Calif. Public Interest Law Center, 1972-73. Trustee The San Francisco Consortium, 1972-73, Rocky Mountain Mineral Law Found., 1969-74. Mem. Internat. Council on Environ. Law, Am. Trial Lawyers Assn., Am., Fed. bar assns. Contbr. articles to legal jours. Home: 131 Taylor Rd Tiburon CA 94920 Office: 198 McAllister St San Francisco CA 94102 Tel (415) 557-0448

WIEAND, DONALD EDWIN, b. Allentown, Pa., Sept. 18, 1926; student Muhlenberg Coll., 1944-45; A.B., Villanova U., 1948; LL.B., Dickinson Sch. Law, 1950. Admitted to Pa. bar, 1951; partner firm Butz, Hudders, Tallman & Wieand, and predecessor, Allentown, 1956-63; judge Ct. of Common Pleas of Lehigh County, 1964—. Vice pres. Minsi Trails council Boy Scouts Am., 1971-73; bd. dirs. Allentown Police Athletic League, 1964—; bd. dirs. Allentown YMCA, 1960-72, pres., 1970-71, chmn. bd. trustees, 1976—; bd. dirs. Middle Atlantic region YMCA's, 1974—, mem. nat. council YMCA's, 1970—, nat. bd., 1977—; mem. adv. bd. Salvation Army, Allentown, 1962—. Mem. Am., Pa., Lehigh County bar assns., Pa. Conf. State Trial Judges. Editor Dickinson Law Rev., 1950. Office: 455 Hamilton St Allentown PA 18105 Tel (215) 434-9471

WIEFERICH, ROBERT JOSEPH, b. Chgo., Feb. 13, 1915; B.S.L., Northwestern U., 1936, LL.B., 1938, J.D., 1970. Admitted to Ill. bar, 1938, D.C. bar, 1954, U.S. Supreme Ct. bar, 1946; atty. U.S. Dept. Interior, Chgo., 1938-39, U.S. Dept. Labor, Chgo., 1939-41, U.S. Dept. Justice, Washington, 1945-70; individual practice law, Washington, 1970—. Mem. Fed., Inter-Am., Internat. (conv. del. Sausanne, Switzerland 1960, mem. bus. law sect. 1970—), D.C., Ill. bar assns. Home: 7913 Kentbury Dr Bethesda MD 20014 Office: 1346 Connecticut Ave NW Washington DC 20036 Tel (202) 785-4143

WIEGAND, ROBERT, II, b. New Orleans, Feb. 11, 1947; B.A., Tulane U., 1970, J.D., 1972; LL.M., U. Denver, 1977. Admitted to La. bar, 1972, Colo. bar, 1976; asso. firm Deutsch, Kerrigan & Stiles, New Orleans, 1972-76; individual practice law, Denver, 1976—. Mem. Am., La. State, Fed., Colo., Denver bar assns., Maritime Law Assn., Southeastern Admiralty Law Assn., Sigma Alpha Epsilon (sec.-treas. Sigma Alpha Epsilon New Orleans Alumni Assn. 1973-76). Home: 5429 S Krameria St Greenwood Village CO 80110 Tel (303) 770-9340

WIEHL, RICHARD LLOYD, b. Yakima, Wash., May 3, 1936; A.B., U. Wash., 1957, J.D., 1960. Admitted to Wash. bar, 1961; spl. agt. FBI, 1962-65; asst. atty. gen. State of Wash., Olympia, 1965-66; asst. U.S. atty. eastern dist. Wash., Yakima, 1966-69; partner firm Halverson, Applegate & McDonald, Yakima, 1969—. Chmn. local Selective Service Bds., 1969-75; bd. dirs. Yakima County Legal Aid Soc., 1974—, chmn., 1976-77; mem. County Law and Justice Com., 1975—. Mem. Wash. State, Yakima County, Am., Internat. bar assns., Wash. State Trial Lawyers Assn., Assn. Trial Lawyers Am. Recipient two presdl. commendations for services to nation, 1975. Home: 7901 Englewood Crest Dr Yakima WA 98907 Office: 415 N Third St Yakima WA 98907 Tel (509) 575-6611

WIENEKE, DANIEL L., b. Lismore, Minn., Mar. 30, 1945; B.A. cum laude, St. Mary's Coll., Winona, Minn.; J.D., cum laude, William Mitchell Coll. Law. Admitted to Minn. bar, 1971; asso. firm Mui & Wieneke, and predecessor, Rochester, Minn., 1972-75, partner, 1975—. Chmn. Rochester Heart Fund, 1974. Mem. Am., Minn, Olmsted County (Minn.) bar assns., Minn., Am. trial lawyer assns., Am. Judicature Soc. Recipient Am. Jurisprudence awards. Home: 2006 5th Ave NE Rochester MN 55901 Office: 404 Marquette Bank Bldg Rochester MN 55901 Tel (507) 288-4110

WIENER, BARRY JAY, b. Jersey City, Mar. 8, 1944; B.A., Fairleigh Dickinson U., 1967; LL.B., John Marshall Law Sch., 1972, LL.M., 1974. Admitted to Ga. bar, 1973, U.S. Supreme Ct. bar, 1976; individual practice, Atlanta, 1973—. Mem. Am., Ga., Atlanta bar assns., Assn. Trial Lawyers Am. Office: 1175 Peachtree St NE Atlanta GA 30361 Tel (404) 892-7701

WIENER, JACQUES LOEB, b. Shreveport, La., Oct. 12, 1909; B.A., U. Mich., 1929, J.D., 1931; LL.B., Tulane U., 1932. Admitted to La. bar, 1932; individual practice law, Shreveport, 1932-61; mem. firm Wiener, Weiss & Madison and predecessors, Shreveport, 1961—. Past pres. Family and Children Services, Child Guidance Center, Shreveport Jewish Fedn.; v.p. United Fund, Shreveport. Mem. Am., La., Shreveport bar assns., Am. Judicature Soc., Order of Coif. Recipient Community Service Award, 1965; mem. Mich. Law Rev. Home: 622 Longleaf Rd Shreveport LA 71106 Office: 411 Commercial National Bank Bldg Shreveport LA 71101 Tel (318) 226-9100

WIER, GARLAND GROVES, b. Graham, Tex., Oct. 8, 1909; LL.B., 1937. Admitted to Tex. bar, U.S. Ct. Appeals bar, 5th Circuit, U.S. Supreme Ct. bar; pvt. practice law. Home: 401 Beverly Dr San Antonio TX Office: 1019 Tower Life Bldg San Antonio TX 78209 Tel (512) 226-8892

WIER, RICHARD ROYAL, JR., b. Wilmington, Del., May 19, 1941; B.A. in English, Hamilton Coll., 1963; LL.B., U. Pa., 1966. Admitted to D.C. bar, 1967, Del. bar, 1967; asso. firm Connolly, Bove & Lodge, Wilmington, 1966-68; dep. atty. gen. State of Del., Wilmington, 1968-70, state prosecutor Del. Dept. Justice, 1970-74, atty. gen., 1975—; lectr. in field, 1970-75. Active United Way Campaign Del., 1976. Mem. Nat. Dist. Attys. Assn. (Del. dir.), Council on Adminstrn. Justice, Del., D.C. bar assns., Nat. Assn. Democratic State-wide Elected Ofcls., Nat. Assn. Attys. Gen., Am., Del. trial lawyers assns., Am. Judicature Soc., Nat. Assn. Extradition Ofcls. (hon. life, regional v.p. 1968-75), Jud. Planning Commn. Recipient Law Enforcement award Newark (Del.) Police Dept., 1974, Outstanding Young Man award Claymont (Del.). Jaycees, 1975, Law Enforcement Commendation medal SAR, 1976, Ideal Citizen award Am. Found. for Sci. of Creative Intelligence, 1976, resolution commendation Del. Gen. Assembly Senate, 1976; named Hon. Citizen, Tenn., Ark., Fla., Nev. Home: 5 Colony Blvd Wilmington DE 19802 Office: 4th Floor Wilmington Tower Wilmington DE 19801 Tel (302) 571-2500

WIER, WILLIAM JEFFERSON, JR., b. Wilmington, Del., July 12, 1935; A.B. in Philosophy magna cum laude, Colgate U., 1957; LL.D., Yale; 1960. Admitted to Del. bar, 1960; clk. to judge U.S. Dist. Ct. for Del., 1960-61; legal dept. E.I. duPont de Nemours & Co., Wilmington, 1961-63; asst. U.S. atty. for Del., 1963-64; asso. firm Connolly, Bove & Lodge, Wilmington, 1964-68, partner, 1969-76; mem. firm Murdoch & Walsh, Wilmington, 1976—; pres., dir. RCI, Inc., dir. Murdoch & Walsh, 1976—. Mem. Am., Del., Fed. bar assns., Phi Beta Kappa. Home: 55 Indian Field Rd Wilmington DE 19810 Office: 300 Delaware Ave Wilmington DE 19899 Tel (302) 658-8661

WIES, LOUIS BERNHART, b. East St. Louis, Ill., Aug. 18, 1928; B.A., U. Calif., Berkeley, 1952; J.D., U. Santa Clara, 1966. Admitted to Calif. bar, 1966, Calif. Supreme Ct. bar, 1966, U.S. Supreme Ct. bar, 1972; partner firm Dunivan, Byers & Wies, Hayward, Calif., 1968-72; partner firm Wies, Wies & Hardin, Hayward, 1972—; juvenile ct. referee Alameda County (Calif.), 1974. Mem. Calif. State Bar, Am., Alameda County, So. Alameda County bar assns., Am., Calif. trial lawyers assns., Am. Arbitration Assn., Nat. Council Juvenile Ct. Judges. Author: Juvenile Court Procedure Handbook, 1976. Home: 36900 Bodily Ave Fremont CA 94536 Office: 24301 Southland Dr 512 Hayward CA 94545 Tel (415) 785-1200

WIESMAN, MELVYN WADE, b. Granite City, Ill., Feb. 8, 1939; A.B., Washington U., St. Louis, 1960; J.D., U. Mo., 1963. Admitted to Mo. bar, 1963; asso. firm Shifrin, Treiman, Agatstein and Schermer, St. Louis, 1963, firm Green and Raymond, St. Louis, 1964-66; magistrate 5th Dist., St. Louis County (Mo.), 1966—; faculty Nat. Coll. State Judiciary, Reno, 1975-76, Washington U., 1971—. Bd. dirs. Congregation Shaare Emeth, St. Louis, 1968-74. Mem. Am. (exec. com. nat. conf. spl. ct. judges 1972-75), Mo., St. Louis County bar assns., Bar Assn. Met. St. Louis, Lawyers Assn. St. Louis, Am. Judges Assn., Am. Judicature Soc., Mo. Probate and Magistrate Judges Assn. Contbr. articles to legal jours. Office: 7900 Carondelet St Clayton MO 63105 Tel (314) 889-2649

WIESS, BERNARD, b. Union City, N.J., June 20, 1903; B.A., Yale U., 1924, J.D., 1926. Admitted to N.Y. State bar, 1926, U.S. Supreme Ct. bar, 1960, Fed. bar, 1928; partner firm Wiess & Costa, Monticello, N.Y., 1930—; spl. county judge and surrogate, Sullivan County, N.Y., 1929-33; mem. adv. bd., counsel Bank of N.Y.; dir. emeritus counsel West Side Fed. Savs. & Loan Assn. N.Y.C. Mem. bd. trustees Sullivan County Community Coll., 1962—, chmn. 1963-66; chmn. United Jewish Appeal Monticello and Catskill Mountain Areas, 1940. Fellow Am. Coll. Probate Counsel, Am. Coll. Trial Lawyers; mem. Am. Arbitration Assn. (arbitrator 1958—), Am., Sullivan County (pres. 1940-41), N.Y. State (exec. com. 1953-58, 61-64, v.p. 1965-66) bar assns., Assn. Bar City N.Y., Fedn. Bar 3d Jud. Dist., Am. Judicature Soc., Def. Research Inst., Am. Bar Found., Phi Beta Kappa. Recipient Silver Beaver award Boy Scouts Am. Home: 12 Revonah Hill Liberty NY 12754 Office: 230 Broadway Box 111 Monticello NY 12701 Tel (914) 794-4400

WIETECHA, RONALD WALTER, b. Chgo., Feb. 6, 1942; B.A., St. Mary's Coll., Winona, Minn., 1964; M.A., U. Iowa, 1970; J.D., Loyola U., Chgo., 1972. Asst. prof. speech communication Wilbur Wright Coll., Chgo. City Coll., 1970-76; admitted to Ill. bar, 1972; asso. firms Goulet and Keane, Chgo., 1972-75, Egan and Keane, Chgo., 1975—. Mem. Am., Ill. State, Chgo. bar assns. Author: Parliamentary and Legal Speaking of Thomas Erskine, 1969. Office: 1 N LaSalle St Chicago IL 60602 Tel (312) 236-8080

WIGELIUS, FRANK EDWARD, b. Seattle, Sept. 9, 1908; B.S. in Engring., U.S. Naval Acad., 1932; J.D., U. Fla., 1950. Commd. ensign U.S. Navy, 1932, advanced through grades to capt., 1947; aerospace-indsl. engr. Naval Air Rework Facility, Jacksonville, Fla., 1956-71; ret., 1947; admitted to Fla. bar, 1950, U.S. Ct. Mil. Appeals bar, 1956; asso. firm Adair, Kent, Ashby & McNatt, Jacksonville, 1950-54; atty. FTC, Washington, 1955; individual practice law, Jacksonville, 1956—; novelist: Navy Airman, 1941; Aviatrix, 1942; The Justice is a Lady, 1977; The Smuggler Admiral, 1977. Mem. Nat. Soc. Lit. and the Arts, Fla. Bar Assn. Home: 1355 Lechlade St Jacksonville FL 32205 Office: POB 27055 Jacksonville FL 32205 Tel (904) 389-8510

WIGERT, J. WILLIAM, JR., b. Summerville, S.C., Nov. 25, 1943; B.E.E., Princeton U., 1965; J.D., George Washington U., 1968. Admitted to Va. bar, 1968, Calif. bar, 1970; atty. patent dept. Westinghouse Electric Co., Churchill, Pa., 1965-69; partner firm Limbach, Limbach & Sutton, San Francisco, 1969—. Mem. Am. Bar Assn., Am., San Francisco patent law assns. Mem. George Washington U. Law Rev., 1967-68. Office: 3000 Ferry Bldg San Francisco CA 94111 Tel (415) 433-4150

WIGGINS, JOHN DALTON, b. Waynesville, Mo., July 22, 1948; B.A., U. Mo., Rolla, 1970, J.D., 1973. Admitted to Mo. bar, 1973, U.S. Dist. Ct. bar for Western Dist. Mo., 1973; asso. firm Routh & Turley, Rolla, 1973-75; partner firm Hoertel & Wiggins, Rolla, 1975—; asst. pub. defender Mo. 25th Jud. Circuit, 1974-76; city atty. City of Rolla, 1976—. Mem. Phelps County (Mo.) Bar Assn. (pres. 1976). Recipient William Brownfield award Mo. Jaycees, 1975; Distinguished Service award Rolla Jr. C. of C., 1976. Office: 207 Scott Bldg PO Box 4 Rolla MO 65401 Tel (314) 364-4103

WIGGINS, REYNOLD CONNOR, JR., b. Birmingham, Ala., June 1, 1926; B.S., The Citadel, 1949; LL.B., Vanderbilt U., 1952, J.D., 1969. Admitted to Tenn. bar, 1952, ICC bar, 1959; asst. to pres., dir. operating rights Gordons Transports, Inc., Memphis, 1953-60; individual practice law, Memphis, 1960-73; asso. firm Wiggins & Darden, Memphis, 1973—; lectr., ltd. asso. prof. in transp. law U. Tenn., Memphis, about 1968. Lay reader Episcopal Ch., Memphis, 1953-55. Mem. Motor Carrier Lawyers Assn., Memphis and Shelby County Bar Assn., Assn. ICC Practitioners. Home: 5692 Dunwoody Ave Memphis TN 38117 Office: Suite 909 100 N Main Bldg Memphis TN 38103 Tel (901) 526-4114

WIGGINTON, JOHN TALBOT, b. Miami, Fla., May 4, 1908; J.D., U. Fla., 1932. Admitted to Fla. bar, 1932, U.S. Supreme Ct. bar, 1950; individual practice law, Milton, Fla., 1932-44; partner firm Parker, Foster & Wigginton, Tallahassee, 1945-57, McClure, Wigginton, Campbell & Owen, Tallahassee, 1974—; judge 1st Dist. Ct. Appeals, Tallahassee, 1957-74. Mem. Am. Coll. Trial Lawyers, Fla. Bar Assn. (past pres.). Home: 1221 Betton Rd Tallahassee FL 32303 Office: 502 E Jefferson St Tallahassee FL 32303 Tel (904) 224-5108

WILAMOSKI, JULIAN PAUL, b. Kewanee, Ill., Feb. 3, 1910; B.A., U. Ill., 1938; J.D., John Marshall Law Sch., 1938; student Nat. Coll. State Trial Judges, 1967. Admitted to Ill. bar, 1938; individual practice law, Kewanee, Ill., 1938-58; judge City Ct. of Kewanee, 1943, Municipal Ct. of Cook County (Ill.), Circuit Ct. of Cook County, 1946-64, Superior Ct. of Cook County, 14th Jud. Circuit Ct., Ill., 1964-72. Mem. Ill. Judges Assn., Ill., Henry County bar assns. Recipient Distinguished Alumnus award John Marshall Law Sch., 1973. Home: 561 Mission Dr Kewanee IL 61443 Tel (309) 853-4874

WILBORN, WOODY STEPHEN, b. Cin., Apr. 20, 1947; B.A. in Polit. Sci., Eastern Ky. U., 1969; J.D., U. Ky., 1973. Admitted to Ky. bar, 1973; individual practice law, Shelbyville, Ky., 1973-76; partner firm Wilborn & Davis, Shelbyville, 1976—. Bd. regents Eastern Ky. U., 1968-69; presidential elector State of Ky., 1976. Mem. Am., Ky. (pres. sect. young lawyers 1976), Shelby County (Ky.) (pres. 1976), 53d Jud. Dist. (v.p. 1976) bar assns., Shelby County C. of C. (exec. dir. 1975). Home: 928 Miller Ave Shelbyville KY 40065 Office: PO Box 448 423 Main St Shelbyville KY 40065 Tel (502) 633-3636

WILBRANDT, ROBERT ALBERT, b. Crystal Lake, Ill., Jan. 9, 1917; A.B., U. Ill., 1939; J.D., DePaul U., 1942. Admitted to Ill. bar, 1942; asst. sec., sr. atty. Marshall Field & Co., Chgo., 1958-77; dir. Algonquin State Bank, Am. Retail Fedn. Pres. high sch. dist. 155, Crystal Lake, 1968-74. Mem. Am., Ill. State bar assns., Am. Judicature Soc., Am. Soc. Corporate Secs., Chgo. and Ill. Retail Mchts. Assn. (dir., treas.). Home: 480 Oxford Ln Crystal Lake IL 60014

WILBURN, GARRY VOIN, b. Denison, Tex., Feb. 25, 1944; B.S. in Econs., Okla. State U., 1967; J.D., St. Mary's U., 1970. Admitted to Tex. bar, 1970; with Judge Adv. Gen.'s Corps, U.S. Army, 1971-73; partner firm Leeds & Wilburn, San Antonio, 1973—. Active San Antonio Child Abuse Council. Mem. Tex. State, San Antonio Bar Assns., San Antonio Young Lawyers Assn., Tex. Trial Lawyers Assn. Participant in videotape mock trial used for edn. of new social workers and young doctors. Office: 4606 Centerview Suite 205 San Antonio TX 78240 Tel (512) 733-8195

WILCOX, EVERETT HAMMOCK, JR., b. Clearwater, Fla., Apr. 25, 1944; B.A., Duke U., 1966; M.A., U. Fla., 1968, J.D. with honors, 1971. Admitted to Fla. bar, 1972, D.C. bar, 1972; law clk. to judge U.S. Ct. Appeals 5th Circuit, 1971-72; asso. firm Alston, Miller & Gaines, Washington, 1972—. Mem. Fla., Am., D.C. bar assns., Order of Coif, Phi Kappa Phi. Exec. editor U. Fla. Law Rev., 1970-71. Home: 1243 Independence Ave SE Washington DC 20003 Office: Suite 1000 1800 M St NW Washington DC 20036 Tel (202) 223-1300

WILCOX, FRANCIS JOHN, b. Eau Claire, Wis., June 27, 1908; B.A., Yale, 1930; LL.B., U. Wis., 1932. Admitted to Wis. bar, 1932, Fed. Dist. Ct. Western Dist. bar, 1932, U.S. Dist. Ct. Appeals bar, 1936; jr. mem. firm Wilcox & Wilcox, Eau Claire, 1933-46, sr. mem., 1946—; chmn. Wis. Jud. Council, 1957-63, Wis. Jud. Commn., 1972-77. Sec. Eau Claire Pub. Library, 1934-70; chmn. bd. Am. Cancer Soc., N.Y., 1962-66, pres. Wis. div., Madison, 1958, recipient nat. award, 1969. Mem. Am., Wis. (pres. 1963-64) bar assns., Am. Law Inst., Am. Judicature Soc. Recipient presdl. citation Wis. Med. Soc., 1966, spl. merit award State Bar Wis., 1964. Office: 131 S Barstow St Eau Claire WI 54701 Tel (715) 832-6645

WILCOX, J. PATRICK, b. Evanston, Ill., Sept. 10, 1947; B.A., U. Iowa, 1969, J.D. with honors, 1972. Admitted to Iowa bar, 1972, Minn. bar, 1972; spl. asst. atty. gen. State of Minn., St. Paul, 1972-74; individual practice law, St. Paul, 1974-76; prin. firm Buchmeier, Kavaney and Wilcox, St. Paul, 1976—; hearing examiner Minn. Bldg. Code Div., 1975-76; lectr. Hamline U. Coll. Law, 1974—. Mem. Am., Minn., Ramsey County (Minn.) bar assns. Contbr. chpts. to books in field; mem. Iowa Law Rev., 1970-71; editor-in-chief Iowa Adv., 1971-72. Office: 1220 N Fed Bldg Saint Paul MN 55102 Tel (612) 222-8461

WILCOX, JUDITH LYNN, b. Cleve., Nov. 23, 1948; A.B. with high distinction, U. Mich., 1969; J.D. cum laude, Harvard U., 1972. Admitted to Ohio bar, 1972; asso. firm Arter & Hadden, Cleve., 1972-74; hearing examiner Ohio EPA, Columbus, 1974-76; asst. atty. gen. Ohio, Columbus, 1976—. Mem. Am., Ohio, Columbus bar assns. Home: 580 Cedar Alley Columbus OH 43206 Office: 30 E Broad St Columbus OH 43215 Tel (614) 466-2766

WILCOX, MICHAEL WING, b. Buffalo, N.Y., July 21, 1941; A.B., U. Calif., Los Angeles, 1963; J.D., Marquette U., 1966. Admitted to Wis. bar, 1966; law clk. Hon. Thomas E. Fairchild, 7th Circuit Ct. Appeals, Chgo., 1966-67; asso. firm Boardman, Suhr, Curry & Field, Madison, Wis., 1967-71, partner, 1971—; lectr. in field. Bd. dirs. Community Action Commn., Madison, 1971-76. Mem. Bar Assn. of 7th Fed. Circuit, Am., Dane County bar assns., Alpha Sigma Nu. Mem. editorial bd. Marquette Law Review, 1965-66. Home: 6318 Keelson Dr Madison WI 53705 Office: 131 W Wilson St Madison WI 53703 Tel (608) 257-9521

WILCOX, THOMAS DELOACH, b. Boston, Feb. 26, 1931; B.S. in Bus. Adminstrn., Lehigh U., 1953; LL.B., J.D., Georgetown U., 1959. Admitted to D.C. bar, 1959; atty., Fed. Maritime Commn., Washington, 1959-61; partner firm Culbertson, Pendleton & Pendleton, Washington, 1961-65; individual practice law, Washington, 1965—; exec. dir., gen. counsel Nat. Assn. Stevedores, Washington, 1973—. Pres., Rosemont Citizens Assn., Alexandria, Va., 1970-71. Mem. Fed., D.C., Maritime Adminstrv. bar assns., Maritime Law Assn. Contbr. articles to jours., mags. and newspapers. Home: 1020 Towlston Rd McLean VA 22101 Office: 919 18th St NW Washington DC 20006 Tel (202) 296-2810

WILCOX, THOMAS EUGENE, b. Wellsboro, Pa., Oct. 13, 1922; A.B. with honors, Pa. State U., 1942; J.D., U. Pa., 1948. Admitted to Pa. bar, 1949, U.S. Supreme Ct. bar, 1960; partner firm Cox, Wilcox, Owlett & Lewis, Wellsboro, 1951—; solicitor Borough of Wellsboro, 1950—; del. Pa. Constl. Conv., 1967-68; mem. hearing com. Pa. Disciplinary Bd.; dir. Commonwealth Bank. Trustee Green Free

Library, Wellsboro, Gmeiner Found., Wellsboro, Baker Found., Knoxville, Pa. Mem. Am., Pa., Tioga County (Pa.) (pres. 1952-53) bar assns. Home: 55 Pearl St Wellsboro PA 16901 Office: 19 Central Ave Wellsboro PA 16901 Tel (717) 724-1300

WILCOXEN, WILLIAM MERRITT, II, b. Des Moines, May 19, 1932; B.A., Grinnell (Iowa) Coll., 1954; J.D., U. Calif., Berkeley, 1959. Admitted to Calif. bar, 1960, Fed. bar, 1960; dep. dist. atty. Orange County, Calif., 1960-62; individual practice law, Laguna Beach, Calif., 1962—. Trustee Laguna Beach Unified Sch. Dist., 1965-71, pres., 1968-69; dir. planning and conservation League of Calif., 1970-75, pres., 1976-77. Mem. Am., Calif., Orange County (dir. 1970-75) bar assns., Trial Lawyers Orange County. Home: 499 Legion St Laguna Beach CA 92651 Tel (714) 494-7565

WILDER, BROOKS, b. Wheaton, Ill., Oct. 4, 1928; A.B., Harvard, 1950; J.D., U. Ill., 1957. Admitted to N.Y. bar, 1958, Ariz. bar, 1960, Calif. bar, 1972; asso. firm Davis, Polk & Wardwell, N.Y.C., 1957-59; asso. firm Snell & Wilmer, Phoenix, 1959-63, partner 1963-70; v.p., sec., gen. counsel Envirotech Corp., Menlo Park, Calif., 1970—; sec. Bagdad Copper Corp., 1963-70; sec. Ariz. Colo. Land and Cattle Co., 1965-70. Mem. Am., Ariz. State bar assns., State Bar Calif., Am. Soc. Corp. Secs. Home: 1274 Pitman Ave Palo Alto CA 94301 Office: 3000 Sand Hill Rd Menlo Park CA 94025 Tel (415) 854-2000

WILDER, FRANKLIN, b. Ft. Smith, Ark., Aug. 18, 1913; LL.B., U. Ark., 1936, J.D., 1969. Admitted to Ark. bar, 1936, U.S. Supreme Ct. bar, 1963; practice law, Ft. Smith; spl. agt. FBI, 1942-45; chancellor 10th Chancery Dist. Ark., 1955-60. Pres. Western Ark. Council Christian Laymen, 1960, Sebastian County Mental Health Assn., 1960. Mem. U.S. Supreme Ct. Hist. Soc. (founding mem. 1976), World Methodist Hist. Soc. Author: Immortal Mother, 1966; Father of the Wesleys, 1971; Martha Wesley, 1976. Home: 3 Riverlyn Terr Fort Smith AR 72903 Office: Suite 715 1st Nat Bank Bldg Fort Smith AR 72901 Tel (501) 783-2041

WILDER, J. WILLIAM, b. Talladega, Ala., Dec. 15, 1935; B.S. in Commerce and Bus. Adminstrn., U. Ala., 1958, LL.B., 1961. Admitted to Ala. bar, 1961; individual practice law, Birmingham, 1961—. Mem. Am., Ala., Birmingham (pres. 1972) trial lawyers assns., Am., Birmingham bar assns. Office: 710 Frank Nelson Bldg Birmingham AL 35203 Tel (205) 252-6131

WILDER, WEBSTER, b. Cherokee, Okla., Apr. 13, 1911; A.B., Okla. U., 1933, J.D.; B.A. in Bus. Adminstrn., St. Mary's U., San Antonio, 1962. Admitted to Okla. bar, 1933, Tex. bar, 1963; partner firm Wilder & Wilder, Cherokee, 1933-39; mem. Okla. Ho. of Reps., 1934-38; county atty. County of Alfalfa (Okla.), 1939-40; commd. 1st lt. U.S. Army, 1940, advanced through grades to col., 1947, ret., 1960; individual practice law, Devine, Tex., 1963-64, San Antonio, 1964—. Mem. Tex., Okla., San Antonio bar assns. Address: 7310 Ashton Pl San Antonio TX 78229 Tel (512) 344-4447

WILDER, WILLIAM KEITH, b. Medford, Oreg., Oct. 31, 1942; B.A., U. Tex., 1965; J.D., S.Tex. Coll. Law, 1971. Admitted to Tex. bar, 1971, U.S. Tax Ct. bar, 1971; city atty. Edna, (Tex.), 1971-72; county atty. Jackson County (Tex.), 1972—. Mem. Tex., Jackson County (pres.) bar assns., Tex. Dist. and County Attys. Assn. Office: 205 Courthouse Edna TX 77957

WILDHACK, WILLIAM AUGUST, JR., b. Takoma Park, Md., Nov. 28, 1935; B.S., Miami U., Oxford, Ohio, 1957; J.D., George Washington U., 1963. Admitted to Va. bar, 1963, D.C. bar, 1965, U.S. Supreme Ct. bar, 1968; agt. IRS, Richmond, Va., 1957-65; asso. firm Morris, Pearce, Gardner & Beitel, Washington, 1965-69; v.p., corp. counsel B.F. Saul Co., Chevy Chase, Md., 1969—; sec. B.F. Saul Real Estate Investment Trust, Chevy Chase, 1972—; lectr. in field. Pres. local chpt. Am. Cancer Soc., 1972; chmn. mediation com. Arlington (Va.) Tenant/Landlord Commn., 1976—; mem. Arlington Human Resources Commn., 1968, Arlington Young Democrats; elder Little Falls Presbyterian Ch., Arlington, 1974-75. Mem. Am., Va., D.C., Arlington bar assns., Am. Soc. Corp. Secs., Arlington Jr. C. of C. (life), Phi Alpha Delta. Home: 6104 N 28th St Arlington VA 22207 Office: 8401 Connecticut Ave Chevy Chase MD 20015 Tel (301) 986-6000

WILDMAN, MAX EDWARD, b. Terre Haute, Ind., Dec. 4, 1919; B.S., Butler U., 1941; J.D., U. Mich., 1947; M.B.A., U. Chgo., 1952. Admitted to Ill. bar, 1948, Ind. bar, 1948; mem. firm Kirkland & Ellis, Chgo., 1947-52, partner, 1952-67; partner firm Wildman, Harrold, Allen & Dixon, Chgo., 1967—. Chmn., Lake Bluff Zoning Bd., 1952—. Fellow Am. Coll. Trial Lawyers; mem. Legal Club, Law Club Trial Lawyers Soc., Internat. Assn. Ins. Counsel, Nat. Assn. R.R. Trial Counsel, Ill., Chgo. bar assns. Contbr. articles to legal jours. Home: 111 Moffett Rd Lake Bluff IL 60044 Office: One IBM Plaza Chicago IL 60611 Tel (312) 222-0400

WILDS, JOHN L., b. Sept. 1, 1928; B.A. in Econs., U. S.D., Vermillion, J.D.; grad. Nat. Coll. State Judiciary. Admitted to S.D. bar; asst. atty. gen. State of S.D.; asst. U.S. atty. dist. S.D.; judge S.D. 2d Jud. Circuit Ct., chief judge, 1977—; lectr. continuing legal edn. Mem. Law Sch. Found., Minnehaha, Am. bar assns., S.D. Jud. Assn. (pres.-elect 1977—), Am. Trial Lawyers Assn., State Jud. Council. Office: Minnehaha Courthouse 415 N Dakota St Sioux Falls SD 57102 Tel (605) 339-6511

WILEY, HENRY HEININGER, b. Orange, N.J., Jan. 18, 1924; A.B., Hobart Coll., 1948; LL.B., U. Pa., 1950. Admitted to N.J. bar, 1951, U.S. Supreme Ct. bar, 1953; mem. firm Berry, Whitson & Berry, Toms River, N.J., 1951-68; judge Ocean County (N.J.) Ct., 1968—. Mem. N.J. State, Ocean County (pres. 1967-68) bar assns., Ocean County Lawyer's Club (pres. 1953-54), Nat. Conf. State Trial Judges. Home: 51 Maine St Silverton Toms River NJ 08753 Office: Courthouse Toms River NJ 08753 Tel (201) 244-2121

WILEY, JAN M., b. Dillsburg, Pa., Feb. 19, 1938; A.B., Dickinson Coll., 1960; J.D., Dickinson Law Sch., 1963. Admitted to Pa. bar, 1963; asso. firm Anstine, Shadle & Griest, Dillsburg, 1963-64; partner firm Griest & Wiley, Dillsburg, 1964-68; sr. partner firm Wiley, Schrack & Benn, Dillsburg, 1968—; chmn. area 3 trial ct. nominating com. Commonwealth of Pa., 1975—; chmn. bd. Commonwealth Nat. Bank, Dillsburg, 1972—. Mem. Am., Pa. bar assns., Am. Judicature Soc., Am. Arbitration Assn. Home: 406 Golf Club Ave Dillsburg PA 17019 Office: 19 N Baltimore St PO Box 288 Dillsburg PA 17019 Tel (717) 432-9666

WILEY, RODDY RAWLS, JR., b. Oakwood, Tex., Apr. 20, 1924; B.E.E., U. Tex., 1945, LL.B., 1949. Admitted to Tex. bar, 1949; various positions to credit mgr. and contract adminstr. Semicondr. div. Tex. Instruments, Dallas, 1953-60; pres. Oakwood State Bank (Tex.), 1960—. Mem. Oakwood City Council, 1962-63; mayor City of Oakwood, 1963-75. Mem. Ind. Ins. Agts. Tex. Home and Office: PO Box 38 Oakwood TX 75855 Tel (214) 545-2163

WILHELM, CHARLES PHILIP, b. Balt., Apr. 14, 1899; B.S., U. Md., 1921, M.S., 1922; J.D., W.Va. U., 1927; postgrad. Harvard, 1933-34; postgrad. in communication arts Fordham U., 1951. Admitted to W.Va. bar, 1930, U.S. Supreme Ct. bar, 1937; partner firms Parrack & Wilhelm, Kingwood, W.Va., 1929-33, Wilhelm & Lewis, Kingwood, 1953—; head law librarian W.Va. U., 1928-29, instr. in law, 1935-36; commr. in chancery W.Va. 18th Jud. Circuit, 1929-42; judge W.Va. Circuit Ct., 18th Jud. Circuit, 1942-53; commr. of accounts Preston County (W.Va.) Probate Ct., 1965—; mayor City of Kingwood, 1930-31. Ordained priest Episcopal Ch., 1956, local non-stipendiary missionary vicar emeritus St. Michael's Episc. Ch., Kingwood, 1956—. Mem. Am., W.Va. bar assns., W.Va. Integrated State Bar, W.Va. U. Law Sch. Assn., Harvard Law Sch. Assn., Order of Coif. Home: 207 Tunnelton St Kingwood WV 26537 Office: PO Box 66 Kingwood WV 26537 Tel (304) 329-0346

WILHELM, GAYLE BRIAN, b. Springfield, Mass., Sept. 1, 1936; B.A. magna cum laude, Harvard, 1957, LL.B. cum laude, 1964. Admitted to Conn. bar, 1964; partner firm Cummings & Lockwood, Stamford, Conn., 1964—; spl. counsel Greenich Conn. Assn. Pub. Schs., 1976—, pres. estate planning Council Fairfield County Conn. 1976-77. Mem. Conn., Stamford, Greenwich, Am. bar assns., Am. Coll. Probate Counsel. Author: Conn. Estates Practice—Death Taxes, 1972; Conn. Estate Practice—Settlement of Estates, 1975. Home: 16 Sylvan Ln Old Greenwich CT 06870 Office: 1 Atlantic St Stamford CT 06904 Tel (203) 327-1700

WILKENS, FREDERICK JOHN, b. Bklyn., Aug. 15, 1906; A.B., Columbia U., 1926, LL.B., 1928. Admitted to N.Y. bar, 1928; asso. firm Bigham, Englar, Jones & Houston, N.Y.C., 1928-31, firm Leo M. Brimmer, N.Y.C., 1931-35, firm Smith, Chambers & Clare, N.Y.C., 1935-39; partner firm Giddings & Wilkens, N.Y.C., 1939-42, firm Lines, Wilkens, Osborn & Beck, Rochester, N.Y., 1952—; dep. corp. counsel City of Rochester, 1946-52. Mem. Am., N.Y., Monroe County bar assns. Home: 2501 East Ave Rochester NY 14610 Office: 47 S Fitzhugh St Rochester NY 14614 Tel (716) 454-6480

WILKERSON, JOHN PERSHING, b. Cuthbert, Ga., Nov. 7, 1918; student Yale U., 1944, U. Ga.; LL.B., Stetson U., 1949. Admitted to Ga. bar, 1948, Fla. bar, 1949; individual practice law, Atlanta and Esutis, Fla.; municipal judge, Eustis, 1957-59; city atty. Tavares (Fla.), 1957-59; served with JAGC, USAFR. Mem. Am., Lake-Sumter (pres. 1953-55) bar assns., Fla. Bar, State Bar Ga., Am. Legion (judge adv.). Office: Profl Bldg Suite 2 101 S Eustis St Eustis FL 32726 Tel (904) 357-5656

WILKERSON, JOSEPH EARL, b. Tyty, Ga., Feb. 7, 1942; B.B.A., U. Ga., 1969; J.D., Samford U., 1972; LL.M., Woodrow Wilson Coll., 1974. Admitted to Ga. bar, 1972; individual practice law, Atlanta, 1972—. Mem. Decatur-DeKalb, Atlanta, Ga., Gwinnett County bar assns. Home: 2821 Payton Rd Atlanta GA 30345 Office: 4065 Lawrenceville Rd Atlanta GA 30084 Tel (404) 938-5544

WILKEY, MALCOLM RICHARD, b. Murfreesboro, Tenn., Dec. 6, 1918; A.B. magna cum laude, Harvard, 1940, J.D., 1948. Admitted to Tex. bar, 1948, N.Y. State bar, 1963, U.S. Supreme Ct. bar, 1952; partner firm Butler, Binion, Rice & Cook, Houston, 1948-54, 1961-63; U.S. atty. So. Dist. Tex., 1954-58; asst. atty. gen. U.S., 1958-61; gen. counsel Kennecott Copper Corp., N.Y.C., 1963-70; circuit judge U.S. Ct. Appeals for D.C., Circuit, 1970—; mem. legal advisor's adv. panel on internat. law Dept. State; del. UN Conf. on jud. remedies against abuse of adminstrv. authority, Buenos Aires, Argentina, Aug., 1959. Del., Republican. Nat. Conv., 1960. Fellow Am. Bar Assn.; mem. Am. Law Inst., Commn. on Nat. Inst. Justice (chmn. drafting com.), Assn. Bar City N.Y. Home: 540 N St SW Washington DC 20024 Office: US Ct Appeals US Courthouse Washington DC 20001 Tel (202) 426-7122

WILKIE, HORACE W., b. 1917; B.A., U. Wis.; LL.B., George Washington U. Admitted to bar, 1944; now asso. justice Supreme Ct. Wis. Address: 3833 Council Crest Madison WI 53711*

WILKINS, EVELYN BLISS, b. New Hampton, Iowa, May 21, 1909; student schs. New Hampton, Iowa. Admitted to Iowa bar, 1943; with Geiser & Donohue, New Hampton, 1927-32, 34-69; county dir. relief Chickasaw County (Iowa), 1932-34; partner firm Donohue & Wilkins, New Hampton, 1940-69; individual practice law, New Hampton, 1969—. Mem. Chickasaw County, Iowa State bar assns., Women's Federated Club. Office: Commercial Block New Hampton IA 50659 Tel (515) 394-2186

WILKINS, FLOYD, JR., b. Fowler, Calif., Sept. 8, 1925; B.S. in Bus. Adminstrn., U. Calif. at Berkeley, 1946; LL.B., Harvard, 1952. Admitted to N.Y. bar, 1953, Calif. bar, 1959; asso. firm Dwight, Royall, Harris, Koegel & Caskey, N.Y.C., 1952-58; v.p., trust officer San Diego Trust and Savs. Bank, 1958-63; partner firm Seltzer, Caplan, Wilkins & McMahon, San Diego, 1963—. Bd. dirs. San Diego County Citizens Scholarship Found., 1964—. Mem. State Bar Calif. (mem. com. econs. of law practice 1974—), Am., San Diego County bar assns. Home: 2005 Soledad Ave La Jolla CA 92037 Office: 3003 4th Ave San Diego CA 92103 Tel (714) 291-3003

WILKINS, HERBERT PUTNAM, b. Cambridge, Mass., Jan. 10, 1930; A.B., Harvard, 1951, LL.B. magna cum laude, 1954; LL.D., Suffolk U., 1976. Admitted to Mass. bar, 1954; asso. firm Palmer & Dodge, Boston, 1954-59, partner, 1960-72; asso. justice Mass. Supreme Jud. Ct., 1972—; selectman Town of Concord (Mass.), 1960-66, town counsel, 1969-72; town counsel Town of Acton (Mass.), 1966-72. Fellow Am. Coll. Trial Lawyers (hon.); mem. Am. Law Inst., Am., Mass., Boston bar assns. Editor: Harvard Law Rev., 1953-54. Home: 168 Nashawtuc Rd Concord MA 01742 Office: 1300 Courthouse Boston MA 02108 Tel (617) 523-7050

WILKINS, ROBERT PEARCE, b. Jesup, Ga., Sept. 10, 1933; B.S., U. S.C., 1953, J.D., 1954; LL.M., Georgetown U., 1957. Admitted to S.C. bar, 1954; atty. office of gen. counsel, Sec. of Army, Washington, 1956; trust officer First Nat. Bank of S.C., Columbia, 1957-60; individual practice law, Columbia, 1960-64, 75—; partner firm McLain, Sherrill & Wilkins, Columbia, 1964-68, firm McKay, Sherrill, Walker, Townsend & Wilkins, Columbia, 1969-75; lectr. in law U. S.C., 1971—; mem. Columbia Estate Planning Council, 1964—, pres., 1964-65; pres. The Sandlapper Store, Inc. Chmn. bd. trustees Lexington Sch. Dist. #1, 1975—, sec., 1972-74; faculty adviser, coach U. S.C. sailing team, 1974—; area v.p. Am. Y-Flyer Yacht Racing Assn., 1971; internat. dir., 1972-73; dir. Columbia Sailing Club, 1968-71; dir. Columbia Tip Off Club, 1968-73, pres., 1971-72. Fellow Am. Coll. Probate Counsel; mem. Am. (mem. Family Law, Taxation, Gen. Practice, Econs. of the Law Practice Sects., lectr. econs. seminars, editor: Legal Economics, 1974—, chmn. valuation and procedure subcom. 1967-73), S.C. (lectr. continuing legal edn. programs, chmn. econs. com. 1973-75). Richland County (chmn. probate sect. 1973-74) bar assns. Author: Drafting Wills and Trust Agreements in South Carolina, 1971, rev., 1977, editor, 1968-69, publisher, 1968-72, Sandlapper, the Magazine of South Carolina; editor and pub., South Carolina History Illustrated, 1970; contbr. articles to jours. Home: Box 375 Lexington SC 29072 Office: Box 11979 Columbia SC 29211 Tel (803) 771-8964

WILKINS, SAMUEL HOUSTON, b. Stonewall, Miss., Oct. 18, 1937; B.S., U. So. Miss., 1960; J.D., U. Miss., 1966. Admitted to Miss. bar, 1966, U.S. Supreme Ct. bar, 1971; asso. firms Hedgepeth, Price & Hedgepeth, Jackson, Miss., 1966-67, Waller, Pritchard & Fox, Jackson, 1967-69; sr. partner firm Wilkins, Ellington & James, Jackson, Miss., 1969—; mem. Miss. Bar Commn., 1974-75. Mem. Miss. State (chmn. com. accident reparation 1975), Hinds County (Miss.), Am. bar assns., Assn. Trial Lawyers Am., Miss. Trial Lawyers Assn. (chmn com. accident reparation 1976). Home: 1610 Westbrook Rd Jackson MS 39211 Office: 429 Tombigbee St Jackson MS 39205 Tel (601) 354-0770

WILKINS, VINCENT, JR., b. Crowley, La., Oct. 2, 1942; B.A., So. U., 1967, J.D., 1970; grad. Nat. Coll. Criminal Def. Lawyers and Pub. Defenders. Admitted to La. bar, 1971; law clk. Baton Rouge Legal Aide Soc., 1969-70; staff atty. Office Gen. Counsel U.S. Dept. Transp., Washington, 1970-71; Reginald Heber Smith Community Lawyer fellow S.W. Legal Services, Lake Charles, La., 1971-72; staff atty. E. Baton Rouge Parish Office of Pub. Defender, 1972-75, 75—. Bd. dirs. Baton Rouge Legal Aide Soc., 1974—, Branco Clark YMCA, Baton Rouge, 1975—. Mem. La., Am., Baton Rouge, Nat. bar assns., Lewis A. Matinet Legal Soc. Recipient AM. Jurisprudence award. Home: 6858 E Central Ave Zachary LA 70701 Office: 8538 Scenic Hwy Baton Rouge LA 70807 Tel (504) 775-9851

WILKINSON, BRUCE MORRISON, b. N.Y.C., Mar. 18, 1948; B.A., U. Fla., 1970, J.D., 1972. Admitted to Fla. bar, 1973, U.S. Supreme Ct. bar, 1976; chief asst. pub. defender City of Stuart (Fla.), 1973-76; individual practice law, Stuart, 1977—. Mem. Am., Fla. bar assns., Assn. Trial Lawyers Am. Home: 1200 Saint Joseph W Stuart FL 33494 Office: 416 Balboa St Stuart FL 33494 Tel (305) 286-0433

WILKINSON, CHARLES WATKINS, JR., b. Oxford, N.C., Aug. 28, 1941; A.A., Campbell Coll.; B.S., East Carolina U.; J.D., U. N.C. Admitted to N.C. bar; with N.C. Atty. Gen.'s Office, 1967-68; partner firm Watkins, Edmundson & Wilkinson, Oxford, N.C., 1968-76; judge N.C. Dist. Ct., 1976—; city atty. City of Oxford, 1971-73, City of Creedmoor (N.C.), 1971-76; county atty. County of Granville (N.C.), 1974-76. Mem. John H. Kerr Reservoir Com., 1975—. Mem. N.C. State Bar Assn. Home: 506 Country Club Dr Oxford NC 27565 Office: Granville County Dist Ct Bldg Oxford NC 27565 Tel (919) 693-8768

WILKINSON, GEORGE ALBERT, JR., b. Washington, Sept. 9, 1933; B.S., Georgetown U., 1957; J.D., Cath. U. Am., 1963. Admitted to Md. bar, 1964, U.S. Supreme Ct. bar, 1969; asso. firm Haynes, FitzGerald, Wanner, Haislip, MacHale and Yewell, Riverdale, Md., 1964-67; individual practice law, Hyattsville, Md., 1967-68, 1970, 76—; asso. firm Sorrell, Paulson, Leach & Wilkinson, and predecessor, Washington and Hyattsville, 1968-69, partner, 1969-70; partner firm Wilkinson & Walker, Hyattsville, 1971-76. Mem. Am., Md. State bar assns., Bar Assn. D.C. Office: 4312 Hamilton St Hyattsville MD 20781 Tel (301) 779-2016

WILKINSON, GLEN ANDERSON, b. Ogden, Utah, Apr. 17, 1911; B.S., Brigham Young U., 1934; J.D. with honors, George Washington U., 1938. Admitted to D.C. bar, 1939, U.S. Supreme Ct. bar, 1947; law clk. Bd. Tax Appeals, Washington, 1938-40; asst. corp. counsel, Washington, 1940-42; asso. firm Wilkinson, Cragun and Barker, Washington, 1946-50, partner, 1950—; mem. visitation com. J. Reuben Clark Law Sch., Brigham Young U., Provo, Utah, 1973—. Trustee George Washington U., 1975—. Fellow Am. Bar Found.; mem. Am., Fed., D.C. bar assns. Recipient Distinguished Alumni award George Washington U., 1966; contbr. article to legal jour. Home: 4308 Forest Ln NW Washington DC 20007 Office: 1735 New York Ave NW Washington DC 20006 Tel (202) 833-9800

WILKINSON, THOMAS JOSEPH, JR., b. Iowa City, July 20, 1934; B.A., Coe Coll., 1956; J.D., U. Iowa, 1962. Admitted to Iowa bar, 1962; individual practice law, Cedar Rapids, Iowa, 1962-66; partner firm Ford, Terpstra & Wilkinson (now Terpstra, Wilkinson & VanHorne), Cedar Rapids, 1966—; asst. atty. Linn County, 1963-67. Bd. dirs. Citizen's Com. on Alcoholism and Drug Aubse, Cedar Rapids, 1966-67; pres. Linn County (Iowa) Mental Health Center, Cedar Rapids, 1974. Mem. Linn County, Iowa State, Am. bar assns. Recipient Distinguished Service certificate Citizens Com. Alcoholism and Drug Abuse, 1972, 73, Outstanding Service certificate Linn County Mental Health Center, 1974, Letter of Commendation Iowa Med. Soc., 1975. Office: 830 Higley Bldg Cedar Rapids IA 52401 Tel (319) 364-2467

WILKINSON, VERNON LEE, b. Chelan, Wash., Jan. 31, 1909; B.A. magna cum laude, Whitman Coll., 1930, M.A., 1931, Ph.D., 1933; LL.B., Georgetown U., 1938. Admitted to D.C. bar, 1937, U.S. Supreme Ct. bar, 1941; chief lands appeal Dept. Justice, Washington, 1942-44, spl. asst. to Atty. Gen., 1944-45; mem. firm Haley, Mc Kenna & Wilkinson, Washington, 1948-52; asst. gen. counsel Broadcasting Fed. Circuit Ct., Washington, 1945-48; partner Mc Kenna & Wilkinson, Washington, 1952, Mc Kenna, Wilkinson & Kittner, 1972. Carnegie and Brochings fellow. Mem. Am., D.C., Fed. Circuit Ct. bar assns., Am. Judicature Soc., Phi Beta Kappa, Delta Sigma Rho., Pi Gamma Mu. Asso. editor Georgetown Law Jour., 1937-38; contbr. articles to profl. jours. Home: 3310 Ordway Washington DC 20008 Office: 1150 17th St Washington DC 20036

WILL, HENRY GERMAN, b. Hutchinson, Kans., May 25, 1940; B.A. magna cum laude, Yale, 1962, J.D., 1965. Admitted to Okla. bar, 1966, Colo. bar, 1965; asso. firm Conner, Winters, Ballaine, Barry & McGowen, Tulsa, 1966-71, partner, 1972—; adj. asso. prof. law Tulsa U., 1969-74, 77—. Chmn. Eastern Okla. Campaign for Yale, 1976—. Mem. Estate Planning Forum (pres. 1973-74), Tulsa Tax Forum. Home: 1389 E 26th Pl Tulsa OK 74114 Office: 2400 First Nat Tower Tulsa OK 74103 Tel (918) 586-5690

WILLARD, CARL EDWARD, b. Grand Island, Nebr., May 8, 1910; A.B., U. Nebr., 1932; J.D., Northwestern U., 1935. Admitted to Nebr. bar, 1934; individual practice law, Grand Island, 1935—; city atty. Grand Island, 1960-64. Mem. Nebr., Nebr. 11th Jud. Dist. bar assns. Home: 1218 W 1st St Grand Island NE 68801 Office: 122 1/2 W 3d St Grand Island NE 68801 Tel (308) 382-2470

WILLARD, MARK ALAN, b. Pitts., Apr. 4, 1946; B.A. in Econs., Duquesne U., 1968, J.D. cum laude, 1973. Admitted to Pa. bar, 1973; asso. firm Eckert, Seamans, Cherin & Mellott, Pitts., 1973—. Mem. Am., Pa., Allegheny County bar assns. Recipient Am. Jurisprudence award Lawyers Pub. Co., 1972; staff Duquesne Law Rev., 1971-73. Office: 42nd floor 600 Grant St Pittsburgh PA 15219 Tel (412) 566-6000

WILLARD, ROBERT EDGAR, b. Bronxville, N.Y., Dec. 13, 1929; B.A. in Econs., Wash. State U., 1954; J.D., Harvard, 1958. Admitted to Calif. bar, 1959; law clk. U.S. Dist. Ct., 1958-59; asso. firm Flint & Mackay, Los Angeles, 1959-61; individual practice law, Los Angeles, 1962-64; partner firm Willard & Baltaxe, Los Angeles, 1964-65, Holley, Galen & Willard, and predecessors, Los Angeles, 1966—. Mem. Am., Calif., Los Angeles County bar assns., Lawyers Club Los Angeles, Assn. Trial Lawyers Am., Am. Judicature Soc. Home: 8434 Enramada St Whittier CA 90605 Office: 611 W 6th St suite 2400 Los Angeles CA 90017 Tel (213) 625-3251

WILLARD, RUSSELL JOHNSON, b. Doylestown, Pa., Nov. 7, 1917; A.B., U. Del., 1941; postgrad. in Econs., Harvard, 1942; J.D., U. Va., 1948. Admitted to Del. bar, 1950, U.S. Supreme Ct. bar, 1960, also SEC bar; law clk. to Hon. Hugh M. Morris, Wilmington, Del., 1949; asso. William Foulk, Wilmington, 1952-54; partner firm Hastings, Taylor & Willard, Wilmington, 1960-66, sr. partner, 1966-72; sr. partner firm Hastings & Willard, Wilmington, 1972—; atty. for Mechtron, Inc., Wilmington, for Nat. Pubs., Inc., Wilmington; asso. with David Daar firm, Los Angeles. Mem. Del., Am. bar assns. Decorated Bronze Star; Legion of Honor, Croix de Guerre (France). Home: 3223 Swarthmore Rd Wilmington DE 19807 Office: Continental American Bldg Wilmington DE 19899 Tel (302) 658-7266

WILLARD, WILLIAM WELLS, b. Springfield, Mass., Mar. 9, 1941; A.B., Tufts U., 1963; J.D. cum laude, Boston U., 1969. Admitted to Mass. bar, 1967, Maine bar, 1968, U.S. Dist. Ct. bar, for Dist. Maine, 1968, U.S. Ct. Appeals, 1st Circuit bar, 1974; law clk. Mass. Superior Ct., 1966-67; asso. firm Bernstein, Shur, Sawyer & Nelson, Portland, Maine, 1967-70, partner, 1970—. Bd. dirs. United Way of Portland, 1972—, So. Maine Comprehensive Health Assn., 1974-76, Maine Health Systems Agy., 1975—. Mem. Am., Maine, Cumberland County (Maine) bar assns., Maine Trial Lawyers, Assn. Trial Lawyers Am., Am. Judicature Assn., Sigma Nu (sec. Zeta Eta chpt. 1966-70). Named Outstanding Jaycee of the Cape Elizabeth local chpt. Maine Jaycees, 1969, 70, Speak-Up winner Maine Jaycees, 1970. Office: One Monument Square Portland ME 04111 Tel (207) 774-6291

WILLARDSON, JOHN STANLEY, b. Santa Monica, Calif., Jan. 26, 1946; A.B., U. N.C., 1968, J.D., 1972. Admitted to N.C. bar, 1972; asso. firm Larry S. Moore, N. Wilkesboro, N.C., 1973-75; partner firm Moore & Willardson, N. Wilkesboro, 1975—. Mem. Am., N.C., Wilkes County, 23d Jud. Dist. bar assns., N.C. State Bar, N.C. Acad. Trial Lawyers. Home: 1521 Cedar Ln Wilkesboro NC 28697 Office: 311 9th St North Wilkesboro NC 28659 Tel (919) 838-5129

WILLBORN, JAMES DUKE, b. Texarkana, Ark., Nov. 29, 1934; B.E.E., Tex. A. and M. Coll., 1957; J.D., U. Houston, 1966; postgrad. in Law, So. Meth. U., 1968, in Bus., 1973. Exploration geophysicist Humble Oil Co., New Orleans, 1957-58; design and test engr. Tex. Instruments, Inc., Dallas, 1961-63; systems test engr. Gen. Electric Co., Houston, 1963-67; admitted to Tex. bar, 1966, U.S. Patent bar, 1968; patent atty. LTV Corp., Dallas, 1967-69; asso. counsel E-Systems, Inc., Dallas, 1969-72, dir. internat. ops., 1972—; dist. export counsel mem. for Ark.-N. Tex.-Okla.; guest lectr. So. Meth. U., U. Dallas; mem. internat. com. AIA. Mem. Dallas, Am. bar assns., Dallas C. of C., Dallas Internat. Law Assn., Internat. Trade Conf. S.W. (dir.). Home: 926 Egyptian Way Grand Prairie TX 75050 Office: 1600 Pacific Ave Dallas TX 75201 Tel (214) 742-9471

WILLE, CARROLL GERARD, b. Balt., July 18, 1925; B.A., U. Miami, 1947; J.D., Northwestern U., 1950. Admitted to Ill. bar, 1950, Pa. bar, 1951; asso. firm Goff & Rubin, Phila., 1954-58, partner, 1958-68; mgmt. com. partner firm Fell, Spalding, Goff & Rubin, Phila., 1968-74; sr. mem., managing partner firm Carroll G. Wille & Assos., West Chester, Pa., 1974—, Phila., 19—. Chmn. Reyburn Plaza Armed Forces display, Phila., 1961-63; pres. Rosemont Civic Assn., 1966-70; mem. coordinating counsel Radnor Township, 1967. Mem. Chgo., Ill., Phila., Chester County, Pa., Fed. bar assns., Am. Trial Lawyers Bar Assn., Northwestern U. Alumni Club Phila. (pres. 1966-74), Pa. Soc., Phi Delta Phi. Recipient citation Mayor of Phila., 1963. Home: 722 Amherst Circle Ithan PA 19073 Office: 320 N High St West Chester PA 19380 Tel (215) 436-0345

WILLETT, STEPHEN DONALD, b. Madison, Wis., Jan. 8, 1947; B.S., U. Wis., 1969; J.D., Cath. U. Am., 1972. Admitted to Wis. bar, 1972; chief law clk. to judge U.S. Dist. Ct. Central Dist. Calif., Los Angeles, 1972-73; asso. firm Stafford, Rosenbaum, Rieser & Hansen, Madison, 1973-76, firm Olson & Willett, Phillips, Wis., 1976—; legal intern Columbus Community Legal Center, Washington, 1972. Mem. Am. Bar Assn., Phi Alpha Delta. Contbr. articles in field to legal jours; mng. editor Cath. U. Law Rev., 1971-72. Home: 336 S Argyle Ave Phillips WI 54555 Office: 188 N Lake Ave Phillips WI 54555 Tel (715) 339-2125

WILLETT, WILLIAM GLEN, b. Torrance, Calif., Aug. 27, 1944; A.B., Occidental Coll., 1966; M.B.A., George Washington U., 1969; J.D. cum laude, Southwestern U., 1973. Admitted to Calif. bar, 1973; sr. law clk. to Hon. A. Andrew Hauk, U.S. Dist. Ct. for Central Calif., 1973-74; city prosecutor City of Torrance, 1974—. Mem. Los Angeles County Bar Assn., Southwestern Criminal Cts. Bar Assn., Calif. Trial Lawyers Assn., Torrance City Attys. Assn. (pres. 1974—), Barristers. Asst. editor Southwestern U. Law Rev., 1972-73. Home: 336 Via Linda Vista Redondo Beach CA 90277 Office: 3131 Torrance Blvd Torrance CA 90503 Tel (213) 328-3456 x 334

WILLEY, CHARLES WAYNE, b. Dillon, Mont., Oct. 7, 1932; B.S. with honors, Mont. State Coll., 1954; J.D. with high honors, U. Mont., 1959. Admitted to Mont. bar, 1959, Calif. bar, 1960, U.S. Supreme Ct. bar, 1972, U.S. Tax Ct. bar, 1975, U.S. Ct. Claims bar, 1975; law clk. to chief judge 9th Circuit Ct. Appeals, San Francisco, 1959-60; asso. firm Price, Postel & Parma, Santa Barbara, Calif., 1960-66, partner, 1966-77; individual practice law, Santa Barbara, 1977—. Dir., sec. Downtown Orgn. of Santa Barbara, 1966-69; bd. dirs. Laguna Blanca Sch., Santa Barbara, 1972—, v.p., 1975-76; dir., v.p. Phoenix of Santa Barbara Inc., 1973—; vestryman All-Saints Ch., Santa Barbara, 1973—. Mem. Am., Santa Barbara County (pres. 1972-73) bar assns., State Bar Calif., State Bar Mont., Phi Kappa Phi, Phi Eta Sigma. Editor-in-chief Mont. Law Rev., 1958-59. Office: Suite 295 1114 State St Santa Barbara CA 93101 Tel (805) 965-4588

WILLIAMS, ADDISON LECLERQUE, b. Denver, Nov. 13, 1900; B.A., U. Colo., 1921, J.D., 1967. Admitted to Colo. bar, 1926, Fla. bar, 1926; pres. Orlando Jr. Coll., 1944-57, McCrory Holding Co., Orlando, 1955—, McCrory Properties, Inc., Orlando, 1955—. Mem. Am., Fla., Orange County (pres. 1944-45) bar assns. Home: 20 W Lucerne Circle Orlando FL 32801 Office: 111 S Orange Ave Orlando FL 32801 Tel (305) 843-9160

WILLIAMS, A(LAN) GREER, b. Cin., Aug. 31, 1942; B.S., Ball State U., 1967; J.D., U. Cin., 1970. Admitted to Ind. bar, U.S. Dist. Ct. bar for So. Dist. Ind., U.S. Ct. Appeals bar, 7th Dist., 1974; partner firms Davis, Jones and Williams, Mincie, Ind., 1970-73, Tanner and Williams, Muncie, 1974-76, Davis and Williams, Indpls., 1976—; individual practice law, Muncie, 1973-74; master commr. Ind. Circuit Ct. of Delaware County, 1971-74; pub. defender Delaware County, 1974. Mem. Delaware County Bar Assn. (pres. 1974). Recipient Cardinal Varsity Club award Ball State U.; named Hon. Citizen of Boy's Town. Home: 1313 D Racquet Club North Dr Indianapolis IN 46260 Office: 8756 Pendleton Pike Indianapolis IN 46226 Tel (317) 899-3700

WILLIAMS, ALFRED THOMAS, JR., b. Bethlehem, Pa., Nov. 13, 1930; A.B. with honors, Moravian Coll., 1952; LL.B., U. Pa., 1955; grad. Nat. Coll. State Judiciary, 1968, 73. Admitted to Pa. bar, 1956; partner firm McFadden, Riskin & Williams, Bethlehem, 1956-68; judge Pa. Dist. Ct., 3d jud. dist., 1968—. Trustee St. Luke's Hosp., Bethlehem, 1968—; chmn. bd. trustees Moravian Coll., 1974—; bd. dirs. YMCA, Bethlehem; mem. advisory bd. Endeavor, Inc., Bethlehem. Mem. Pa. Conf. State Trial Judges, Pa., Nat. councils juvenile ct. judges, Northampton County (Pa.), Pa., Am. bar assns. Named Bethlehem Outstanding Young Man of Year Bethlehem Jaycees, 1961; recipient Moravian Coll. Alumni medallion of Merit award, 1966, Legion of Honor award Order of DeMolay, 1968. Home: 1703 Jennings St Bethlehem PA 18017 Office: 38 W Market St Bethlehem PA 18018 Tel (215) 866-3218

WILLIAMS, AUBREY, b. Harlan, Ky., Feb. 28, 1945; student Case Western Reserve U., 1969; B.S., Pikeville Coll., 1970; J.D., U. Louisville, 1973. Admitted to Ky. bar, 1973, Fed. bar, 1973; sr. partner firm Neal & Williams, Louisville, 1971—; hearing officer State Ky. Dept. Labor, Louisville, 1976; judge 3d magisterial ct. Jefferson County, Ky., 1976. Mem. bd. dirs. Enterprises Unltd.; legal div. chmn. Ky. United Negro Coll. Fund, 1975-77; active Met. United Way; legal adv. Carter-Mondale Campaign, Ky., 1975. Mem. Am. Trial Lawyers Assn., Nat. Coll. Criminal Def. Lawyers, Am., Nat. (pres. Ky. chpt. 1976—), Louisville bar assns., NAACP (pres. Louisville br.). Recipient leadership appreciation award, NAACP. Home: 1310 Rosewell St Louisville KY 40211 Office: Suite 3200 1st Nat Tower 101 S 5th St Louisville KY 40202 Tel (502) 584-1116

WILLIAMS, AVON NYANZA, JR., b. Knoxville, Tenn., Dec. 22, 1921; A.B., Johnson C. Smith U., 1940; LL.B., Boston U., 1947, LL.M., 1948. Admitted to Mass. bar, 1948, Tenn. bar, 1948, U.S. Ct. Mil. Appeals bar, 1956, U.S. Supreme Ct. bar, 1963; individual practice law, Knoxville, 1949-53, Nashville, 1969—; asso. Z. Alexander Looby, Nashville, 1953-69. Mem. exec. com. Nashville br. NAACP, 1953—; bd. dirs. Davidson County Ind. Polit. Council, Tenn. Voters Council, So. Regional Council; elder St. Andrews Presbyterian Ch., Nashville, 1956—, trustee, 1966—; mem. appeals and rev. com. Meharry Med. Coll., 1970—; mem. Tenn. State Senate, 1968—. Mem. Am. Bar Assn., Am. Judicature Soc. Named Citizen of Year, Nashville Frontiers Club, 1972, Tenn. Masons, 1972. Home: 1818 Morena St Nashville TN 37208 Office: 1414 Parkway Towers Nashville TN 37219 Tel (615) 244-3988

WILLIAMS, BEN T., b. 1911; LL.B., U. Okla. Admitted to Okla. bar, 1933; practiced in Pauls Valley; chief justice Supreme Ct. Okla. Home: 1133 NW 63d St Oklahoma City OK 73116 Office: State Capitol Bldg Oklahoma City OK 73105*

WILLIAMS, BRIAN PRENTICE, b. Des Moines, Aug. 14, 1938; B.A., Drake U., 1960, J.D., 1962. Admitted to Iowa bar, 1962; mem. firm Williams, Hart, Lavorato & Kirtley, W. Des Moines, 1962—, subsequently sr. partner. Mem. Am., Iowa, Polk County bar assns. Home: 3316 Southern Hills Dr Des Moines IA 50321 Office: 1200 35th St West Des Moines IA 50265 Tel (515) 225-1125

WILLIAMS, CARY JAMES, b. Athens, Ga., June 23, 1947; B.A. in History, U. Ala., 1969, J.D., 1973. Admitted to Ala. bar, 1974; partner firm Williams & Williams, Tuscaloosa, Ala., 1974—; field dir. census Fed. Census Bur. 5th Congressional Dist. Ala., Tuscaloosa, 1970. Mem. Am. Bar Assn., Am., Ala. trial lawyers assns., Bench and Bar Legal Honor Soc., Farrah Law Soc. Recipient Am. Jurisprudence award U. Ala., 1972. Office: PO Box 2690 Tuscaloosa AL 35401 Tel (205) 758-8332

WILLIAMS, CHARLES JUDSON, b. San Mateo, Calif., Nov. 23, 1930; A.B., U. Calif., Berkeley, 1952, LL.B., 1955. Admitted to Calif. bar, 1955, U.S. Supreme Ct. bar, 1970; individual practice law San Mateo County, Calif., 1956-59, Solano County, 1959-64, Contra Costa County, 1964—; city atty. Pleasant Hill, Calif., 1962—, Yountville, Calif., 1965-68, Benicia, Calif., 1968—, Lafayette, Calif., 1968—, Moraga, Calif., 1974—; lectr. Calif. Continuing Edn. Bar, 1964-65, U. Calif. extension, 1974-76, John F. Kennedy U. Sch. Law, 1966-69; spl. counsel to cities of Clayton, El Cerrito and Fremont, Calif.; legal adviser Alaska legis. council, 1959-61; adviser Alaska supreme ct., 1960-61; adviser on revision Alaska statutes, 1960-62; sec., bd. dirs. Vintage Savs. & Loan Assn., Napa County, 1974—. Bd. dirs. 23d Agrl. Dist. Assn., Contra Costa County, 1968-70. Mem. Calif., Am., Contra Costa County, Mt. Diablo bar assns., Nat. Inst. Municipal Law Officers. Author: California Code Comments to West's Annotated California Codes, 3 vols., 1964; West's California Code Forms, Commercial, 2 vols., 1965; West's California Government Code Forms, 3 vols., 1971; contbr. articles to profl. jours. Home: 40 Rolling Green Circle Pleasant Hill CA 94523 Office: 917 Las Juntas St Martinez CA 94553 Tel (415) 228-3840

WILLIAMS, CHARLES LAYNE, b. Aquilla, Tex., Feb. 12, 1940; B.B.A., Tex. A. and I. U., 1963, M.S., 1968; J.D., Vanderbilt U., 1970. Admitted to Tenn. bar, 1970, Tex. bar, 1972; mem. firm Moore, Stout & Waddell, Kingsport, Tenn., 1970-72; asst. prof. bus. law Tex. A. and I. U., 1972-74, vis. prof., 1974—; mem. firm Glusing & Sharpe, Kingsville, 1974—. Bd. dirs. Kingsville Area Indsl. Devel. Found., 1974—, Planned Parenthood of the Chaparral Country, Kingsville, 1975—, Family Guidance Services, Kingsville, 1975—; mem. Kingsville Planning and Zoning Commn., 1975—. Mem. Am., Tex., Kleberg-Kenedy County (pres. 1976-77) bar assns., Kingsville C. of C. (mem. indsl. adv. team 1976), Tex. A. and I. U. Alumni Assn. (pres. Kingsville chpt. 1975). Home: 221 Seale St Kingsville TX 78363 Office: PO Box 1431 Kingsville TX 78363 Tel (512) 592-9361

WILLIAMS, CHARLES STEWART, JR., b. Pensacola, Fla., Oct. 13, 1940; B.S., Fla. State U., 1962, J.D., 1970. Admitted to Fla. bar, 1971; asso. firm Barksdale, Mayo, Murphy & Williams, Pensacola, 1971; asst. county solicitor Escambia County (Fla.), Pensacola, 1972-73; chief asst. state's atty. 1st Jud. Circuit Fla., Pensacola, 1973-77; individual practice law, Pensacola, 1977—; lectr. Nova U., 1977; instr. Pensacola Jr. Coll., 1976. Pres. parish council Nativity Roman Catholic Ch., 1974; 1st v.p. City-County Drug Abuse Commn., 1976—; bd. dirs. United Cerebral Palsy, 1975-76. Mem. Am., Fla. (criminal law com.), Escambia-Santa Rosa bar assns., Soc. Bar 1st Jud. Circuit, Fla. Pros. Attys. Assn., Nat., Am. dist. attys. assns., Am. Judicature Soc., Fla. State U. Law Sch. Alumni Assn. (pres. 1977—). Exec. editor Fla. State U. Law Rev., 1970. Home: 3630 Pompano Dr Pensacola FL 32504 Office: 717 S Palafox St Pensacola FL 32501 Tel (904) 432-1418

WILLIAMS, CHESTER A., JR., b. 1915; student Mass. Inst. Tech.; J.D., St. John's U., 1945. With The Singer Co., N.Y.C., 1939—, asst. v.p., chief patent and trademark counsel, 1968-73, asst. sec., 1973-74, v.p., sec., 1974—; asso. firm Fowler & Kennedy, 1946-49. Office: The Singer Co 30 Rockefeller Plaza New York City NY 10020

WILLIAMS, CLYDE, JR., b. Calhoun County, S.C., Feb. 23, 1939; B.S., Johnson C. Smith U.; J.D. Admitted to Ind. bar, 1966; sr. partner firm Williams, Delaney, Simkin, Richmond, Ind. Bd. mem. Wayne Twp., Richmond, Ind.; del. Rep. Nat. Com., 1972. Mem. Am., Ind., Hoosier, Wayne County bar assns., Am. Trial Lawyers Assn. Home: 131 S 16th St Richmond IN 47374 Office: 48 S 7th St Richmond IN 47374 Tel (317) 966-1558

WILLIAMS, DAVID NEAL, b. Crane, Tex., Apr. 20, 1945; B.B.A., Tex. Tech. U., 1966; J.D., U. Houston, 1970. Admitted to Tex. bar, 1970, U.S. Dist. Ct. bar for So. Dist. Tex., 1973; Claims atty. Fidelity & Deposit Co. of Maryland, Houston, 1971—. Home: 5840 Glenmont St Apt 204 Houston TX 77036 Office: 777 S Post Oak St Houston TX 77056 Tel (713) 626-3231

WILLIAMS, DONALD EATON, b. Jersey City, N.J., Feb. 19, 1941; B.A., Yale, 1963, J.D., 1968; postgrad Haileybury and Imperial Service Coll. (England), 1959. Admitted to N.J. bar, 1969; asso. firm Dimon, Haines & Bunting, Mount Holly, N.J., 1969-73; v.p. Kaufman and Broad Homes, Inc., Freehold, N.J., 1973-75; partner firm Polino & Williams, Mount Holly, 1975—. Vice chmn. United Way Burlington County, N.J., 1972; trustee S. Jersey Civil Liberties Union, 1972-73. Mem. Am., N.J., Burlington County (trustee, 1970-71) bar assns. Home: Brick Alley Crosswicks NJ 08515 Office: 737 Holly Ln Mount Holly NJ 08060 Tel (609) 261-1500

WILLIAMS, EARL BENJAMIN, b. Miami, Fla., Aug. 21, 1941; student Mich. State U., 1959-61; B.A. with honors Bethune-Cookman Coll., 1965, J.D., John Marshall Law Sch., 1971. Admitted to Ill. bar, 1971; tchr. Chgo. Bd. Edn., 1966-71; asst. supr. Neighborhood Youth Corps, Chgo., 1966; title examiner Chgo. Title & Trust Co., 1972; atty. Equal Employment Opportunity Commn., 1973. Mem. Nat., Cook County bar assns., Alpha Phi Alpha. Home: 1560 N Sandburg Terr Chicago IL 60610 Office: 180 N La Salle St Suite 1226 Chicago IL 60601 Tel (312) 346-0910

WILLIAMS, EDWARD BENNETT, b. Hartford, Conn., May 31, 1920; A.B. summa cum laude, Coll. Holy Cross, 1941; LL.B., Georgetown U., 1945; 10 hon. degrees. Admitted to D.C. bar, 1944; sr. partner firm Williams & Connolly, and predecessors, Washington, 1967—; pres., dir. Washington Redskins Football Club; pres. Williams Properties, Washington; prof. criminal law and evidence Georgetown U. Law Sch., 1946-58, gen. counsel U., 1949—; guest prof. U. Frankfurt (Ger.), 1954; vis. lectr. Yale U. Law Sch., 1971; mem. U.S. Jud. Conf. Adv. Com. on Fed. Rules of Evidence, 1965-74; mem. Chief Justice's Com. on Ct. Facilities and Design, 1971-74; chmn. Md. Jud. Nominating Commn. 6th Judicial Dist., 1971—. Mem. Pres.'s Fgn. Intelligence Adv. Bd., 1976-77; treas. Democratic Nat. Com., 1974-77; trustee Coll. Holy Cross, 1976—. Mem. Am. Bar Assn. (chmn. spl. com. on crime prevention and control 1970-71), Bar Assn. D.C. (v.p. 1950, 55-56, Lawyer of Yr. award 1966), Am. Coll. Trial Lawyers (bd. regents 1968-72). Author: One Man's Freedom, 1962; contbr. articles to legal jours. Office: 1000 Hill Bldg Washington DC 20006 Tel (202) 331-5060

WILLIAMS, FRANK JAMES, JR., b. St. Louis, July 2, 1938; B.S. in Bus. Adminstrn., Washington U., 1960, J.D., 1963; postgrad. in bus. adminstrn., Mo. U., 1960. Admitted to Mo. bar, 1963; asso. gen. counsel May Dept. Stores Co., St. Louis, 1963-66, v.p. dir. labor relations, sr. asst. gen. counsel, asst. sec., 1967—; atty. Pet Inc., St. Louis, 1966-67. Mem. Am., Mo., St. Louis Met. bar assns., Am. Retail Fedn. (chmn. employee relations com. 1972-76), Nat. Retail Mchts. Assn. (chmn. employee relations com. 1976—), Order of Coif. Home: 5320 Casa Royale St St Louis MO 63129 Office: 611 Olive St St Louis MO 63101 Tel (314) 436-3300

WILLIAMS, FRANK LEE, JR., b. Des Moines, Oct. 18, 1921; A.B., U. Mo., 1946; LL.B., Yale, 1950. Admitted to Wash. bar, 1951, Calif. bar, 1954; individual practice law, Seattle, 1950-51, Santa Ana, Calif., 1955; dep. pub. defender, Orange County, Calif., 1956-60, pub. defender, 1960—. Mem. Am., Calif., Wash., Orange County bar assns., Calif. Pub. Defenders and Legal Aid Assn. (dir. 1966-67), Calif. Pub. Defenders Assn. (dir. 1969—). Home: 209 Via Mentone Newport Beach CA 92663 Office: 700 Civic Center Dr W Santa Ana CA 92701 Tel (714) 834-2144

WILLIAMS, FREDERICK TED, b. Marysville, Ohio, Mar. 7, 1926; B.A., Ohio State U., 1950, LL.B., 1952; grad. Nat. Coll. State Judiciary, Reno, Nev., 1971. Admitted to Ohio bar, 1952; gen. referee Franklin County (Ohio) Probate Ct., 1955-59, chief jud. dep., 1960-61, 66-68; judge Franklin County Municipal Ct., Columbus, 1961-66, 1969, Franklin County Ct. Common Pleas, 1969—; lectr. to bar assns. Mem. Am., Ohio, Columbus bar assns., Am. Judicature Soc. Home: 72 Daleview Dr Westerville OH 43081 Office: Franklin County Hall Justice Columbus OH 43215

WILLIAMS, GEORGE KENDRICK, b. Greenville, Ala., Feb. 16, 1930; B.S. in Commerce, U. Ala., 1954, J.D., 1956. Admitted to Ala. bar, 1956, U.S. Supreme Ct. bar, 1975; partner firm Page and Williams, Huntsville, Ala., 1957-67, firm Camp, Williams & Spurrier, Huntsville, 1967—; mem. bd. appeals Ala. Indsl. Relations dept., 1960; spl. asst. atty. gen., 1961, 76; spl counsel Ala. Real Estate Commn., 1975-76. Mem. Democratic Exec. com., Huntsville, 1960-64. Mem. Assn. U.S. Army (exec. v.p. Tenn. Valley chpt. 1962), Am., Ala., Madison County bar assns. Home: 7802 Horseshoe Tr Huntsville AL 35802 Office: 320 Central Bank Bldg Huntsville AL 35801 Tel (205) 533-5015

WILLIAMS, GLEN MORGAN, b. Jonesville, Va., Feb. 17, 1920; A.B., Milligan Coll., 1940; J.D., U. Va., 1948. Admitted to Va. bar, 1947; since practiced in Jonesville, individual practice law, 1947—; county atty. Lee County (Va.), 1948-52; mem. Va. State Senate, 1953-55; magistrate U.S. Ct., 1962-75; judge Lee County Ct. and Juvenile and Domestic Relations Ct., 1971-73, U.S. Dist. Ct. Western Dist. Va., 1976—. Mem. Lee County Sch. Bd., 1972-76; past pres. Lee County PTA. Mem. Va., Am., Lee County bar assns., Delta Theta Phi, Order of Coif. Author: Virginia Lives, 1964. Home and Office: PO Box 6 Jonesville VA 24263 Tel (703) 346-1167

WILLIAMS, HENRY WARD, JR., b. Rochester, N.Y., Jan. 12, 1930; A.B., Dartmouth Coll., 1952; LL.B., U. Va., 1958. Admitted to N.Y. bar, 1959, U.S. Tax Ct. bar, 1962; partner firm Harris, Beach, Wilcox, Rubin and Levey, Rochester, 1958—; counsel N.Y. State Senate Com. on Agr. and Markets, 1966; dir. VOPLEX Corp., Rochester & Genesee Valley R.R., Presbyterian Residence Center Corp. Chmn. Genesee/Finger Lakes Regional Planning Bd., Monroe County, N.Y., 1973—. Mem. Am., N.Y., Monroe County bar assns., Order of Coif, Raven Soc., Omicron Delta Kappa. Home: 69 S Main St Pittsford NY 14534 Office: 2 State St Rochester NY 14614 Tel (716) 232-4440

WILLIAMS, HORACE GUICE, b. Newton, Ala., Sept. 3, 1936; B.S., Auburn U., 1959; LL.B., Jones Law Sch., 1966. Claims mgr. Hartford Ins. Group, Montgomery, Ala., 1960-69; admitted to Ala. bar, 1969; asso. firm Volz, Capouna, Wampold & Prestwood, Montgomery, 1969-70; partner firm Beasley, Williams & Robertson, Eufaula, Clayton, Ala., 1970-73; city judge, Eufaula, 1971-74; individual practice law, Eufaula, 1973—; instr. Eufaula Police Sch., 1971-75. Co-chmn. Eufaula Operation Drug Alert, 1971; mem. Ala. Law Enforcement Planning Agy., 1974—, Ala. Law Inst. Council, 1975—. Mem. Am., Ala., Barbour County bar assns., Am., Ala. (dir. 1972-73) trial lawyers assns., Ala. Def. Lawyers Assn., Ala. Criminal Def. Lawyers Assn. Home: 735 Holleman Dr Eufaula AL 36027 Office: 125 S Orange Ave Eufaula AL 36027 Tel (205) 687-5834

WILLIAMS, HOUSTON GARVIN, b. Estancia, New Mex., Nov. 27, 1922; B.S. in Civil Engring., U. Colo., 1947; LL.B., 1950, J.D., 1968. Admitted to Wyo. bar, 1950, Colo. bar, 1950, U.S. Supreme Ct. bar, 1971; asso. firm Wehrli and Williams and predecessor, Casper, Wyo., 1950-64, partner, 1964—. Fellow Am. Coll. Probate Counsel, Am. Coll. Trial Lawyers; mem. Natrona County (pres. 1960), Am. (Wyo. State Bar del. 1975—) bar assns., Wyo. State Bar (pres. 1972-73), Internat. Soc. Barristers, Order of Coif, Phi Alpha Delta, Sigma Tau, Chi Epsilon. Home: 924 Bonnie Brae Ave Casper WY 82601 Office: Suite 700 1st Nat Bank Bldg Casper WY 82601 Tel (307) 265-0700

WILLIAMS, HUBERT WOOD, b. Atlanta, Oct. 19, 1937; B.S., Fla. State U., 1959; J.D., U. Fla., 1962. Admitted to Fla. bar, 1962; asso. firm Giles, Hedrick and Robinson, Orlando, Fla., 1962, 64-65, firm William Whitaker & Assos., Orlando, 1965-67; mem. firm Robertson Williams Duane and Lewis, and predecessors, Orlando, 1967—; mem. faculty Fla. Continuing Legal Edn. courses, Nat. Inst. Trial Advocacy, Ct. Practice Inst. Mem. Am., Fla., Orange County bar assns., Am. Trial Lawyers Assn., Acad. Fla. Trial Lawyers. Contbr. articles to Continuing Legal Edn. publs. Home: 2103 Santa Antilles Rd Orlando FL 32806 Office: 538 E Washington St Orlando FL 32801 Tel (305) 425-1606

WILLIAMS, J. D., b. Cooke County, Tex., Dec. 2, 1937; B.B.A. in Accounting, U. Okla., 1959; J.D., George Washington U., 1962; LL.M. in Taxation, Georgetown U., 1965. Admitted to Okla. bar, 1962, D.C. bar, U.S. Ct. Claims bar, U.S. Supreme Ct. bar; asst. to U.S. Sen. Robert S. Kerr of Okla., 1959-61; capt. JAGC, AUS, 1962-65; asso. firm Sutherland, Asbill & Brennan, 1965-69; founder, sr. mem. firm Williams & Jensen, Washington, 1970—; panelist, speaker on legis. affairs. Charter mem., exec. com. Democratic Nat. Com. Fin. Council; regional del. coordinator Hubert Humphrey nomination campaign, 1968; regional dir. Western states orgn. Humphrey-Muskie campaign, 1968. Mem. Am., D.C., Okla. bar assns., Beta Gamma Sigma, Omicron Delta Kappa. Recipient certificate of appreciation Assn. U.S. Army, 1966; author: (with others) Federal Administrative Practice Manual, 1966; mng. editor Fed. Bar Jour., 1963-64. Office: 1130 17th St NW Suite 500 Washington DC 20036 Tel (202) 785-8241

WILLIAMS, JAMES ALEXANDER, b. Pine Bluff, Ark., Oct. 30, 1929; B.A., U. Ark., 1951; J.D., So. Meth. U., 1952, M.L.A., 1971. Admitted to Tex. bar, 1952; asso. firm Touchstone, Bernays & Johnston, Dallas, 1955-57; partner firm Bailey, Williams, Westfall, Lee & Fowler, Dallas, 1957—. Bd. dirs. Spl. Care Sch., Dallas, 1965-69; bd. mgmt. YMCA, Dallas, 1967-73; chmn. adminstrv. bd. Univ. Park United Meth. Ch., Dallas, 1973. Mem. State Bar Tex., Am., Dallas bar assns., Tex. Assn. Def. Counsel (v.p. 1967), Am. Bd. Trial Adv., Trial Attys. Am., Fedn. Ins. Counsel, Internat. Assn. Ins. Counsel, Soc. Hosp. Attys., Am. Judicature Soc., Phi Alpha Delta, Lambda Chi Alpha. Home: 4630 Northaven Rd Dallas TX 75229 Office: suite 3900 2001 Bryan Tower Dallas TX 75201 Tel (214) 741-4741

WILLIAMS, JAMES RICHARD, b. Bklyn., Nov. 26, 1926; B.A., Sienna Coll., 1951; LL.B., Albany Law Sch., 1954. Admitted to N.Y. bar, 1955; asso. firm Carroll, Amyot & Doling, Albany, N.Y., 1955-57; individual practice law, Albany, 1960—; dep. clk. Albany County Surrogate Ct., 1957-63; atty. Cohoes Urban Renewal Agy., 1976. Mem. Albany County, N.Y. State, Am. bar assns., Assn. Trial Lawyers Am., Capital Dist. Trial Lawyers Assn., Sienna Coll. Alumni Assn. (past pres.). Home: Park Ln E Bldg 31 Apt 3 Menands NY 12204 Office: 8 Elk St Albany NY 12207 Tel (518) 463-3203

WILLIAMS, JAMES TAYLOR, b. Lynchburg, Va., May 13, 1916; A.B., Hampden-Sydney Coll., 1937; certificate in meteorology Calif. Inst. Tech., 1942; J.D., Washington and Lee U., 1953. Admitted to Va. bar, 1953; since practiced in Cumberland, Va., individual practice law, 1955-73; commonwealth atty., 1956-57; judge Cumberland County, 1957-73, 10th Dist. Ct., Juvenile and Domestic Relations Div., 1973—; pres. Cumberland County Indsl. Devel. Corp., 1963—. Chmn., Cumberland County Ct. House Restoration Com., 1968-70; treas. Cumberland Edn. and Recreation Assn., 1958—. Mem. Nat. Council Juvenile Ct. Judges, Assn. Dist. Ct. Judges Va., 10th Jud. Dist. Bar Assn. Home: US Hwy 60E Cumberland VA 23040 Office: County Office Bldg Cumberland VA 23040 Tel (804) 492-4848

WILLIAMS, JANICE OWENS, b. Forester, Ark., Dec. 12, 1939; B.A. in Polit. Sci., Centenary Coll., 1970; J.D., U. Ark., 1973; postgrad. U. Ark. Little Rock, 1976. Admitted to Ark. bar, 1973; individual practice law, Arkadelphia, 1976—. Mem. Clark County Bar Assn. (sec.-treas. 1974—), Ark. Trial Lawyers Assn. Home: 313 Cherry Ln Arkadelphia AR 71923 Office: PO Box 157 Arkadelphia AR 71923 Tel (601) 246-2396

WILLIAMS, JERRE STOCKTON, b. Denver, Aug. 21, 1916; A.B., U. Denver, 1938; J.D., Columbia, 1941. Admitted to Colo. bar, 1941, U.S. Supreme Ct. bar, 1944, Tex. bar, 1950; instr. law U. Iowa, Iowa City, 1941-42; asst. prof. U. Denver, 1946; asso. prof. U. Tex., Austin, 1946-50, prof., 1950-67, John B. Connally prof. civil jurisprudence, 1970—; chmn. Adminstrv. Conf. U.S., Washington, 1967-70, now pub. mem.; distinguished scholar-in-residence Southwestern Legal Found., Dallas, 1973-77; chmn. Southwestern Regional Manpower Adv. Com., 1964-66; cons. U.S. Bur. Budget, 1966-67; pub. mem. Adminstrv. Conf. U.S. Mem. Nat. Acad. arbitrators (v.p. 1974-76), Am. (chmn. sect. adminstrv. law 1975-76, winner Ross Essay prize 1963), Fed. bar assns. Author: Cases and Materials on Employees' Rights, 1952; The Supreme Court Speaks, 1956; editor: Labor Relations and the Law, 3d edit., 1965. Home: 3503 Mount Barker Dr Austin TX 78731 Office: 2500 Red River St Austin TX 78705 Tel (512) 471-5151

WILLIAMS, JERRY JOHN, b. Midland, Pa., Dec. 8, 1931; B.A., U. Calif., Los Angeles, 1953, J.D., 1961. Admitted to Calif. bar, 1962; asso. firm Brundage, Beeson & Pappy, Los Angeles; partner firm Brundage, Williams & Zellman; adj. prof. law U. San Diego, 1964—. Mem. Am. Arbitration Assn. (San Diego adv. council), Indsl. Relations Research Assn. (past pres. San Diego chpt.). Home: 1263 Opal St San Diego CA 92109 Office: 3746 5th Ave San Diego CA 92103 Tel (714) 297-1131

WILLIAMS, JOHN ALBERT, b. Tulsa, Oct. 17, 1939; B.S. in Econs., Oklahoma City U., 1967, J.D., 1970. Admitted to Okla. bar, 1970; sr. adjudicator, vets. claims examiner, VA, Muskogee, Okla., 1970-71, supr. guardianship program, 1971—; claims adjuster Allstate Ins. Co., Oklahoma City, 1968-70, dep. ins. commr., 1960-62. Active ARC, DAV; mem. bd. dirs. Knothole Assn. Mem. Okla., Muskogee bar assns., Optimist Internat., Phi Alpha Delta. Home: 311 Camden St Muskogee OK 74401 Office: 125 S Main St Muskogee OK 74401 Tel (918) 687-2123

WILLIAMS, JOHN CORNELIUS, JR., b. Spartanburg, S.C., Nov. 9, 1938; A.B., Wofford Coll., 1960; LL.B., U. S.C., 1964. Admitted to S.C. bar, 1964; partner firm Williams & Williams, Spartanburg, 1964—. Mem. S.C. Ho. of Reps., 1968-74; vice chmn. S.C. Dept. Social Services, 1974-77. Mem. S.C. Bar Assn., S.C. Trial Lawyers Assn. Home: 338 Heathwood Dr Spartanburg SC 29302 Office: 186 W Main St Spartanburg SC 29301 Tel (803) 582-6381

WILLIAMS, JOHN HARRISON, b. Staten Island, N.Y., June 26, 1934; A.B., Princeton, 1956; LL.B., Columbia, 1959. Admitted to Vt. bar, 1960, U.S. Supreme Ct. bar, 1976; individual practice law, Bennington, Vt., 1960-62; partner firm Williams & Wickes, Bennington, 1962—; reporter Vt. Supreme Ct., 1964-67; acting pres. Catamount Nat. Bank, North Bennington, Vt., 1973. Chmn. Mt. Anthony Union Sch. Bd., Bennington, 1963-64, mem. 1962-64; mem. Vt. Human Services Bd., 1968-74; mem. exec. com. Putnam Meml. Hosp., Bennington, 1976—. Mem. Am., Vt., Bennington County bar assns. Home: 33 Monument Ave Bennington VT 05201 Office: 115 Elm St Bennington VT 05201

WILLIAMS, JOHN MARION, b. Paintsville, Ky., Aug. 17, 1934; A.B., U. Ky., 1957, J.D., 1962. Admitted to Ky. bar, 1962, U.S. Supreme Ct. bar, 1970; law clk. Ct. Appeals Ky., Frankfort, 1962-63; asso. firm Gray, Woods & Cooper, Ashland, Ky., 1963-65, partner, 1965-74; individual practice law, Ashland, 1975—; asst. commonwealth atty. Commonwealth of Ky., 1975, atty., 1976—. Active Election Commn. Boyd County (Ky.), 1965-67. Mem. Am., Ky. (ho. of dels. 1972—), Boyd County (pres. 1969-70) bar assns., Ky. Commonwealth's Attys.' Assn., Nat. Dist. Attys.' Assn. Contbr. articles to legal jours. Home: 1010 Shawnee Ave Ashland KY 41101 Office: Courthouse Louisa St Catlettsburg KY 41129 Tel (606) 739-5137

WILLIAMS, JOHN PHILIP, b. Nashville, Aug. 24, 1947; B.A., Davidson Coll., 1969; J.D., Vanderbilt U., 1972. Admitted to Tenn. bar, 1972; cons. Vanderbilt U. Center for Health Services, LaFollette, Tenn., 1973-74; staff atty. E. Tenn. Research Corp., Jacksboro, 1974—. Mem. Tenn. Bar Assn., Rural Am. Inc. Home: PO Box 15 LaFollette TN 37766 Office: PO Box 436 Jacksboro TN 37757 Tel (615) 562-3396

WILLIAMS, JOHN ZADOCK, b. St. Louis, Sept. 19, 1941; B.A., U. Mo., 1963; J.D., 1968. Admitted to Mo. bar, 1968; partner firm Williams & Smallwood and predecessor, Rolla, Mo., 1968—. Mem. Phelps County Democratic Com., 1968-72; bd. dirs. Rolla Area Sheltered Workshop, 1971-72, Rolla Community Devel. Corp., 1969—. Mem. Am., Mo., S. Central, Phelps County (pres. 1971-72) bar assns., Order of Coif, Phi Delta Phi. Mem. Mo. Law Rev., 1967-68. Home: 616 Salem Ave Rolla MO 65401 Office: 4th and Rolla Sts Rolla MO 65401 Tel (314) 364-1084

WILLIAMS, JOLINE BATEMAN, b. Bristol, Fla., Apr. 19, 1928; B.J., U. Ga., 1949; LL.B., Mercer U., 1960. Admitted to Ga. bar, 1960; law asst. Supreme Ct. of Ga., Atlanta, 1961-70, clk., 1970—. Mem. State Bar Ga., Nat. Assn. Appellate Ct. Clks. Home: Box 151 Windham Creek Union City GA 30291 Office: 506 State Jud Bldg Atlanta GA 30334 Tel (404) 656-3470

WILLIAMS, JOSEPH, b. Chelsea, Mass., Apr. 15, 1941; B.A., Boston Coll., 1963; J.D., Suffolk Law Sch., 1968. Admitted to Mass. bar, 1969, N.H. bar, 1971; atty. Leonard Profl. Assn., Nashua, N.H., 1968-69; hearings officer Rate Setting Commn. Commonwealth of Mass., Boston, 1970-71; partner firm Kfoury & Williams, Manchester, N.H., 1971—; instr. N.H. Coll., 1974—. Mem. Manchester, Am. bar assns. Home: 8 Tranquil Dr Londonderry NH 03053 Office: 814 Elm St Manchester NH 03101 Tel (603) 668-3444

WILLIAMS, LARRY LIVINGSTON, b. Waynesville, N.C., July 7, 1922; A.A., Mars Hill Coll., 1941; B.S., Wake Forest U., 1943, J.D., 1948. Admitted to N.C. bar, 1948, D.C. bar, 1966; trial atty. antitrust div., U.S. Dept. Justice, Washington, 1948-58, asst. chief spl. trial sect., 1959-62, chief spl. trial sect., 1962-63; 2d asst. to asst. atty. gen., 1963-65; asso. firm Clifford, Warnke, Glass, McIlwain & Finney, Washington, 1966—. Mem. bd. visitors Wake Forest U., 1969-71, Sch. Law, 1974—. Mem. Fed., Am. bar assns. Contbr. articles to legal jours. Home: 7406 Walton Ln Annandale VA 22003 Office: 815 Connecticut Ave NW Washington DC 20006

WILLIAMS, LEONARD JOHN, II, b. Washington, Dec. 12, 1925; grad. Harvard U., 1947; J.D., George Washington U., 1949. Admitted to D.C. bar, 1950, Md. bar, 1950, U.S. Supreme Ct. bar, 1955; individual practice law, Bethesda, Md., 1950-51, 1962—; parliamentarian Montgomery County (Md.) Bd. Realtors; councilman Town of Chevy Chase View (Md.), 1964-66. Mem. Montgomery County, Md. State bar assns. Home: 4100 Dresden St Kensington MD 20795 Office: 8030 Woodmont Ave Bethesda MD 20014 Tel (301) 654-7335 also 7801 Old Branch Ave Clinton MD 20735 Tel (301) 868-7898

WILLIAMS, LEWIS FREDERICK, b. Helena, Ark., Nov. 3, 1938; B.S. in Accounting, San Diego State U., 1956; J.D., U. San Fernando Valley, 1969. Admitted to Calif. bar, 1970; field agt. IRS, Los Angeles, 1965-68, estate tax atty., 1968-72; mem. firm Miller & Kearney, San Diego, 1972-75; partner firm Becea & Williams, San Diego, 1975—; instr. bus. adminstrn. U. Calif. at San Diego, 1976—; instr. advanced pension design Am. Coll. C.L.U., Calif., 1974—. Mem. Calif. Soc. C.P.A.'s, San Diego Estate Planning Counsel, San Diego Pension Counsel, State Bar Calif., Am. Bar Assn. Contbr. articles in field to legal jours. C.P.A., Calif. Office: 110 West A St suite 1200 San Diego CA 92101 Tel (714) 239-9151

WILLIAMS, LEWIS MILLARD, b. Groesbeck, Tex., Oct. 29, 1901. Admitted to Tex. bar, 1933; county atty. Knox County, Tex., 1935-36; dist. atty. 50th Jud. Dist., Tex., 1937-40, dist. judge, 1941-71; practice law, Knox City, 1971—. Home: 205 S 5th St Knox City TX 79529 Office: 700 E Main St Knox City TX 79529 Tel (817) 658-3613

WILLIAMS, LLOYD EDWARD, JR., b. Chgo., June 10, 1934; B.A. cum laude, Yale U., 1956; J.D., U. Mich., 1961. Admitted to Ill. bar, 1961, U.S. Supreme Ct. bar, 1970; asso. firm Jacobs, Williams and Montgomery, and predecessors, Chgo., 1961-67, partner, 1967—. Mem. Am., Ill., Chgo. bar assns., Fedn. Ins. Counsel. Home: 819 Chestnut St Wilmette IL 60091 Office: 20 N Wacker Dr Chicago IL 60606

WILLIAMS, LORNA LAWHEAD, b. Gaylord, Kans., Feb. 9, 1915; B.A., Drake U., 1939, J.D., 1941. Admitted to Iowa bar, 1941, U.S. Supreme Ct. bar, 1960; mem. firm Emmert, James, Needham & Lindgran, Des Moines; individual practice law, Des Moines; asso. prof. Drake U., Des Moines, 1946-47; spl. asst. atty. gen. State Iowa, 1967—. Mem. Am., Iowa State, Polk County bar assns., Iowa Trial Lawyers Assn., Des Moines C. of C. (dir. 1946-47, pres. women's div. 1946-47), Order of Coif. Home: 529 46th St Des Moines IA 50312 Office: 1209 East Ct Des Moines IA 50319 Tel (515) 281-3368

WILLIAMS, LOUIS DAVID, b. Elgin, Ill., Feb. 25, 1924; Ph.B., Ill. Wesleyan U., 1948; J.D., U. Ill., 1950. Admitted to Ill. bar, 1950; asso. firm Williams & Williams, Bloomington, Ill., 1951-58; asst. counsel Bloomington Fed. Savs. and Loan Assn., 1958-68, asst. sec., 1958-68, sec., 1968-76, sr. v.p., gen. counsel, 1976—. Chmn. Bloomington Sister City Com., 1973-76; pres. Corn Belt council Boy Scouts Am., 1971-73. Mem. Am., McLean County (pres. 1975-76), Ill. bar assns., Phi Delta Phi. Home: 114 Ruth Rd Bloomington IL 61701 Office: 115 E Washington St Bloomington IL 61701 Tel (309) 829-7671

WILLIAMS, LOUIS JAMES, b. Ft. Lauderdale, Fla., Mar. 14, 1944; B.S., U. Fla., 1966; J.D., Columbia, 1969. Admitted to Fla. bar, 1969; asso. firm Fowler, White, Gillen, Boggs, Villareal & Banker, Tampa, Fla., 1969-74, mem. firm, Lakeland, Fla., 1975—; mem. firm Troiano, Roberts, Philpot & Smith, Lakeland, 1974-75. Mem. Am., Fla., Polk County bar assns., Fla. Acad. Trial Lawyers. Home: 14 Lake Hollingsworth Dr Lakeland FL 33803 Office: 402 S Kentucky Ave suite 490 Lakeland FL 33801 Tel (813) 688-8517

WILLIAMS, LYMAN PERRY, b. Lowville, N.Y., Oct. 19, 1908; B.S., St. Lawrence U., 1932; J.D. cum laude Albany Law Sch., 1932. Admitted to N.Y. bar, 1932; partner firm Williams & Sammis, Lowville, 1932-34; individual practice law, Boonville, N.Y., 1934—; spl. surrogate, Oneida County, N.Y., 1940-62. Pres. N.Y. State Winter Sports Council, 1946; vice chmn. N.Y. State Passenger Tramway Advisory Council, 1964—; mem. Iroquois Council, Boy Scouts Am., Rome, N.Y., 1956—, pres., 1961, chmn. camping com. upstate N.Y., 1973—. Mem. Eastern Ski Area Ops. Assn. (pres., 1951, 65), Nat. Ski Areas Assn. (pres. 1967-69), Internat. Ski Fedn. (U.S. rep., legal safety com. 1965—), Kiwanis, Masons, N.Y. State, Oneida and Lewis counties bar assns. Recipient Silver Beaver award, Boy Scouts Am., 1963, Silver Antelope award, 1974, Distinguished Eagle award, 1977; author: Nat. Courtesy Code for Skiers, 1966. Home: Turin NY 13473 Office: 119 Schuyler Boonville NY 13309 Tel (315) 942-4444

WILLIAMS, OLIN EDGAR, b. Greenville, Pa., June 24, 1915; B.S. in Chem., Va. Mil. Inst., 1935; J.D., Duquesne U., 1945. Admitted to Pa. bar, 1947, Ill. bar, 1953; atty. Koppers Co., Pitts., 1945-48, asst. patent counsel, 1955-57, patent counsel, 1957-75; atty. Standard Oil of Ind., Chgo., 1948-53, Gulf Oil Corp., Pitts., 1953-55; counsel firm Robert D. Yeager, Pitts., 1975—; adj. prof. law Duquesne U., Pitts., 1972—. Bd. dirs. East End Coop. Ministry, Pitts. Mem. Am., Allegheny County bar assns., Assn. Corp. Patent Counsel, Pitts. Patent Law Assn. (pres. 1966). Office: 350 Porter Bldg Pittsburgh PA 15219 Tel (412) 566-2405

WILLIAMS, PARHAM HENRY, JR., b. Lexington, Miss., June 8, 1931; B.A., U. Miss., 1953, J.D., 1954; LL.M. (Sterling fellow), Yale, 1965. Admitted to Miss. bar, 1954, U.S. Supreme Ct. bar, 1966; dist. atty. 4th Jud. Dist. Miss., 1957-63; asso. prof. law U. Miss., University, 1963-65, prof., 1966-71, dean, 1971—; commr. to Nat. Conf. Commrs. on Uniform State Laws, 1972. Mem. Am., Miss. bar assns. Law Adminstrn. fellow N.Y. U., 1968. Home: 919 Hayes St Oxford MS 38655 Office: Sch Law U Miss University MS 38677 Tel (601) 232-7361

WILLIAMS, PAUL X., b. Booneville, Ark., Feb. 19, 1908; B.A., U. Ark., 1928, J.D., 1930. Admitted to Ark. bar, 1931, practiced in Ark.; chancery judge of Ark., 1948-67; judge U.S. Dist. Ct., Western Dist. of Ark., Ft. Smith, 1967—, now chief judge. Home: 815 Kennedy St Booneville AR 72927 Office: US Courthouse Fort Smith AR 72901*

WILLIAMS, PHILIP BELFREY, b. Gonzales, Tex., Dec. 30, 1922; B.S. in Commerce, Roosevelt U., 1952; LL.B., DePaul U., 1963, J.D., 1969. Admitted to Ill. bar, 1963; agt. IRS, Chgo., 1955-64; mgr. Service Fed. Savs. & Loan Assn., Chgo., 1964-66; individual practice law, Chgo., 1966—. Mem. Ill., Cook County bar assns. Home: 7739 S Prairie Ave Chicago IL 60619 Office: 8032 S Cottage Grove Ave Chicago IL 60619 Tel (312) 483-1000

WILLIAMS, RANDALL LEE, b. Pleasant Hill, La., June 7, 1924; student A. and M. Coll., Monticello, Ark., 1942-44; LL.B., U. Ark., 1950; grad. Nat. Coll. State Trial Judges, 1971. Admitted to Ark. bar, 1950; practiced in Monticello, 1950-60, Pine Bluff, 1961-71; dep. pros. atty. Drew County, 1951-55, 57-59; mcpl. judge, Monticello, 1958-60; with Regional Attys. Office, U.S. Dept. Agr., Little Rock, 1960; dep. pros. atty. Jefferson County, 1965-71; circuit judge 11th Jud. Circuit Ark., Pine Bluff, 1971—. Chmn. Ark. Crime Commn., 1975—; mem. Ark. Ho. of Reps., 1955-57. Mem. Am., Ark. bar assns., Am. Judicature Soc., Am. Legion. Home: 235 Linden Heights Pine Bluff

AR 71601 Office: Courthouse Pine Bluff AR 71601 Tel (501) 534-2512

WILLIAMS, REGINALD LAMAR, b. Jacksonville, Fla., Sept. 22, 1912; J.D., U. Fla., 1934. Admitted to Fla. bar, 1934; practiced in Tampa, 1934-38, Miami, 1938—; mem. firm Bradford, Williams, McKay, Kimbrell, Hamann & Jennings, Profl. Assn., Miami, 1950—; mem. Fla. Bd. Bar Examiners, 1965-70, chmn., 1970. Fellow Am. Coll. Trial Lawyers, Am. Bar Found.; mem. Dade County (pres. 1956-57), Fla. (pres. 1962-63), Am. (assembly del. 1970—) bar assns., Am. Judicature Soc., Beta Theta Pi, Phi Alpha Delta. Decorated Bronze Star medal (U.S.); officer Order Brit. Empire; cavalier officer Order Sts. Maurice and Lazarus (Italy); recipient Distinguished Service award Stetson U., 1963. Home: 200 Ocean Ln Dr Key Biscayne FL 33149 Office: 101 E Flagler St Miami FL 33131 Tel (305) 358-8181

WILLIAMS, RICHARD THOMAS, b. Evergreen Park, Ill., Jan. 14, 1945; A.B. with honors, Stanford U., 1967, M.B.A., 1972, J.D., 1972. Admitted to Calif. bar, 1972; asso. firm Kadison, Pfaelzer, Woodard, Quinn & Rossi, Los Angeles, 1972—. Mem. Am., Los Angeles County bar assns. Home: 2721 Club Dr Los Angeles CA 90064 Office: 611 W 6th St Los Angeles CA 90017 Tel (213) 626-1251

WILLIAMS, ROBERT BELL, b. Washington, Aug. 10, 1943; B.A., U. Md., 1966; J.D., 1972. Admitted to Md. bar, 1972; asst. state's atty. Howard County (Md.), 1973-76; individual practice law, Ellicott City, Md., 1973—. Active Farm Bur., Howard County, 1973—. Mem. Am., Md. bar assns., Nat. Dist. Attys. Assn. Home: 13230 Linden Church Rd Clarksville MD 21029 Office: 8370 Court Ave Ellicott City MD 21043 Tel (301) 465-0122

WILLIAMS, ROBERT BRICKLEY, b. Moon Run, Pa., July 3, 1944; B.A., Swarthmore Coll., 1966; J.D., Georgetown U., 1969. Admitted to Pa. bar, 1969, U.S. Tax Ct. bar, 1970, U.S. Ct. Claims bar, 1976; partner firm Eckert, Seamans, Cherin & Mellott, Pitts., 1969—; atty. Robinson Twp. Fire and Bldg. Code Commn., 1975—. Trustee Union Cemetery Assn.; admissions interviewer, mem. alumni council Swarthmore Coll., 1976—. Mem. Am., Pa., Allegheny County bar assns., Allegheny Tax Soc. (vice chmn.), Pitts. Tax Club, Penn State Tax Conf. (planning com.). Mng. editor: Georgetown Law Jour., 1968-69. Office: 600 Grant St Pittsburgh PA 15219 Tel (412) 566-6079

WILLIAMS, ROBERT LEE, b. Boston, May 30, 1943; A.B., Amherst Coll., 1965; J.D., U. Wash., 1968; LL.M., George Washington U., 1975. Admitted to Wash. bar, 1969, D.C. bar, 1970, U.S. Supreme Ct. bar, 1972; trial atty. U.S. Dept. Justice, Washington, 1969-70; asso. firm McKean, Whitehead and Wilson, Washington, 1970-75, partner, 1976—. Mem. Wash. State, Fed., Am. bar assns. Contbr. articles to legal publs. Office: 1900 L St NW Washington DC 20036 Tel (202) 223-2220

WILLIAMS, ROBERT STARR, b. Yakima, Wash., Feb. 20, 1919; B.S. in Geology, U. Idaho, 1943, LL.B., 1959, J.D., 1969. Admitted to Idaho bar, 1960; city atty. Moscow (Idaho), 1975—. Mem. Clearwater, Moscow bar assns. Registered licensed geologist, Idaho. Home: Route 1 Box 95 Moscow ID 83843 Office: 312 1/2 N Washington St Moscow ID 83843 Tel (208) 882-4912

WILLIAMS, RONALD DOHERTY, b. New Haven, Apr. 6, 1927; B.A. U. Va., 1951, LL.B., 1954. Admitted to Conn. bar, 1954; asso. firm Pullman, Comley, Bradley & Reeves, Bridgeport, Conn., 1954-60, partner, 1960—. Selectman, Town of Easton (Conn.), 1975—, justice of peace, 1977—. Mem. Am., Conn. (gov. 1975—), Bridgeport (pres. 1975) bar assns. Home: 14 Newman Dr Easton CT 06612 Office: 855 Main St Bridgeport CT 06604 Tel (203) 334-0112

WILLIAMS, SHELTON CROSS, b. Missoula, Mont., Nov. 21, 1940; A.B., Dartmouth, 1963; J.D. with honors, U. Mont., 1966. Admitted to Mont. bar, 1966; law clk. judge 9th Circuit Ct., San Francisco, 1966-67; partner firm Wordethane, Haines & Williams, Missoula, 1967-75, George, Williams & Benn, Missoula, 1975—; lectr. U. Mont. Sch. Law, 1974—. Pres., Missoula Civic Symphony Assn., 1975-76. Mem. Western Mont., Mont. (trustee 1974-76), Am. bar assns., Mont. Young Lawyers Assn. (pres. 1973-74). Home: Rt 6 Missoula MT 59801 Office: 310 Western Bank Bldg Missoula MT 59801 Tel (406) 728-4310

WILLIAMS, SPENCER MORTIMER, b. Reading, Mass., Feb. 24, 1922; A.B., U. Calif., Los Angeles, 1943, postgrad. Hastings Coll. Law, San Francisco, 1946; LL.B., J.D., U. Calif., Berkeley, 1948. Admitted to Calif. bar, 1949, U.S. Supreme Ct. bar, 1952; asso. firm Beresford & Adams, San Jose, Calif., 1949; mem. firm Rankin, Oneal, Center, Luckhardt, Bonney, Marlais & Lund, San Jose, 1970-71, Evans, Jackson & Kennedy, Sacramento, 1970-71; judge U.S. Dist. Ct., No. Dist. Calif., 1971—; dep. county counsel Santa Clara County (Calif.), 1949-55, county counsel, 1955-67; sec. Calif. Human Relations Agy., 1967-70. Co-chmn. indsl. sect. fund raising dr. Alexian Bros. Hosp., San Jose, 1964; bd. dirs. Boys City Boys' Club, San Jose, 1965-67; mem. YMCA Statewide Com. on Youth and Govt. of Calif., 1967-68. Mem. Am., Calif., Santa Clara County, Sacramento bar assns., Calif. Dist. Attys. Assn. (pres. 1963-64), Nat. Assn. County Civil Attys. (pres. 1963-64). Office: Fed Bldg Suite 19042 450 Golden Gate Ave San Francisco CA 94102 Tel (415) 556-4971

WILLIAMS, STANLEY HOWARD, b. Los Angeles, Aug. 7, 1942; A.B., Stanford, 1964; J.D., U. Calif., 1967. Admitted to Calif. bar, 1968; asso. firm O'Melveny & Myers, Los Angeles, 1967-74; partner firm Agnew, Miller & Carlson, Los Angeles, 1974—. Mem. Am., Los Angeles bar assns. Editor Calif. Law Rev., 1966-67. Home: 760 Greentree Rd Pacific Palisades CA 90272 Office: 700 S Flower St Los Angeles CA 90017 Tel (213) 629-4200

WILLIAMS, STEPHEN MICHAEL, b. Butte, Mont., Jan. 15, 1948; B.A., U. Mont., J.D. Admitted to Mont. bar, 1973; asso. firm Henningsen, Parcell & Fenzberger, Butte, 1973-74; counsel Mont. Mining div. Anaconda Co., Butte, 1974—. Bd. dirs. Big Bros. and Sisters, Butte. Mem. Am., Mont. (trustee, exec. com.) bar assns., Am. Trial Lawyers Assn. Home: 2742 Argyle St Butte MT 59701 Office: Box 689 Butte MT 59701 Tel (406) 723-4311

WILLIAMS, THOMAS LLOYD, b. Milw., Dec. 23, 1945; B.A. in Polit. Sci., U. Wis., Madison, 1968; J.D., Harvard, 1973. Admitted to Wis. bar, 1973; asso. firms Whyte & Hirschboeck, Milw., 1973, Bradford & Gabert, Appleton, Wis., 1974—. Citizen mem. Outagamie County (Wis.) Social Services Bd., 1975-76. Mem. Outagamie County, Wis. bar assns. Office: 103 W College Ave Appleton WI 54911 Tel (414) 733-5521

WILLIAMS, VOLIE ADKINS, b. Sanford, Fla., Jan. 10, 1920; Asso. Sci., Marion Inst., 1940; LL.B., Stetson U., 1948. Admitted to Fla. bar, 1948; practiced in Sanford, 1949-57; asst. atty. gen. State of Fla., Tallahassee, 1949; mem. Fla. Ho. of Reps., 1950-55; asst. state atty. Sanford-Titusville, 1956-57; judge Fla. Circuit Ct., 18th Jud. Circuit, 1957—. Home: 1203 Washington Dr Sanford FL 32771 Office: Seminole County Courthouse Sanford FL 32771 Tel (305) 323-8340

WILLIAMS, WAYNE DEARMOND, b. Denver, Sept. 24, 1914; A.B., U. Denver, 1936; J.D., Columbia, 1938. Admitted to Colo. bar, 1938, U.S. Supreme Ct. bar, 1945; asst. atty. City of Denver, 1939-43, spl. asst. atty., 1947-49; mem. firm Williams & Erickson, Denver, 1959—; lectr. U. Denver Coll. Law, 1947-61; chmn. County Ct. Nominating Commn., 1968-69; mem. Dist. Ct. Nominating Commn., 1969-75. Chmn. Denver Airport Adv. Commn., 1963-66. Mem. Am. Soc. Internat. Law, Fed., Inter-Am., Am. (Ross Essay prize 1944) Colo., Denver (trustee 1965-68, v.p. 1968-69, pres. 1974-75) bar assns. Contbr. articles to legal jours. Home: 3340 E Kentucky Ave Denver CO 80209 Office: 1110 Capitol Life Center Denver CO 80203 Tel (303) 222-9424

WILLIAMS, WILLIAM LARKIN, b. Springfield, Mass., Aug. 15, 1913; B.A., Yale, 1934; J.D., U. Va., 1938. Admitted to N.Y. State bar, 1939, U.S. Supreme Ct. bar, 1945; asso. White and Case, N.Y.C., 1938-52, partner, 1952—. Mem. Am. Law Inst., Am., N.Y. State bar assns., Assn. Bar City N.Y., Phi Beta Kappa, Order of Coif. Home: 44 Oriole Ave Bronxville NY 10708 Office: 14 Wall St New York City NY 10005 Tel (212) 732-1040

WILLIAMS, WILLIAM MACKERNESS, JR., b. Rochester, Minn., Aug. 10, 1916; LL.B., U. Tex. at Austin, 1941. Admitted to Tex. bar, 1942, U.S. Ct. Mil. Appeal bar, 1962; asst. county atty. Hill County (Tex.), 1946-49, county atty., 1949-53; asst. U.S. atty. Eastern Dist. Tex., 1953-64; asso. firm Lawrence & Lawrence, Tyler, Tex., 1964-68; asst. city atty. Tyler, 1968-71; individual practice law, Tyler, 1971—. Mem. Smith County (v.p. 1965-66, pres. 1966-67), Tex. bar assns. Office: 1909 S Broadway PO Box 6423 Tyler TX 75711 Tel (214) 593-7133

WILLIAMSON, BILL L., b. Twin Falls, Idaho, Jan. 7, 1938; A.B., U. Oreg., 1962; J.D., Harvard, 1965. Admitted to Oreg. bar, 1965; clk. to justice Oreg. Supreme Ct., 1965-66; dep. dist. atty. Multnomah County (Oreg.), Portland, 1966-69; prof. law Lewis and Clark Law Sch., Portland, 1969—. Pres., NW Environ. Def. Center, Portland, 1970-72. Mem. Oreg. Bar Assn., Oreg. Secessionist Movement. Office: 10015 SW Terwilliger Blvd Portland OR 97219 Tel (503) 244-1181

WILLIAMSON, BLAKE ARTHUR, b. Edwardsville, Kans., July 24, 1901; LL.B., U. Kans., 1923, J.D., 1968. Admitted to Kans. bar, 1923; partner firm Pollock & Williamson, Kansas City, Kans., 1923-30; partner firm Williamson, Cubbison, Hardy & Hunter and predecessors, Kansas City, Kans., 1930—; mem. Kans. Ho. of Reps., 1935-37, 39-43, 47-49, 67-70; mem. Kans. Supreme Ct. Nominating Com., 1959-61. Pres. Kaw Valley Heart Assn., Kansas City, Kans., 1938-39; vice chmn. Kans. Bd. Social Welfare, 1949-55. Fellow Am. Coll. Trial Lawyers; mem. Am., Kans. (chmn. com. prospective legislation 1965-71), Wyandotte County (Kans.) (pres. 1938) bar assns., Am. Judicature Soc., Phi Alpha Delta; hon. mem. Kans., Wyandotte County med. socs. Recipient Outstanding Legis. Conservationist award Kans. Fish and Game Soc., 1969, Community Leader Am. award Greater Kansas City Research Soc., 1968, Jacobus Tenbroek award Sunflower Fed. of Blind, Inc., 1974. Home: 1865 Edwardsville Dr Edwardsville KS 66111 Office: 727 Ann Ave Kansas City KS 66101 Tel (913) 371-1930

WILLIAMSON, CLYDE EDWARD, b. Williamsport, Pa., Feb. 7, 1903; A.B., Dickinson Coll., 1925; J.D., Temple U., 1933. Admitted to Pa. bar, 1936, U.S. Supreme Ct. bar, 1947; asso. firm David H. Kinley, Phila., 1936-37; asso. firm John E. Cupp, Williamsport, 1936-41, partner, 1941-72; individual practice law, Williamsport, 1972—; with Office of Price Adminstrn., 1941-42; mem. hearing com. Disciplinary Bd. of Pa., 1973—, bar com. on credentials and admissions, 1976—. Chmn., trustee Williamsport Area Community Coll., 1965—; pres. Family and Children's Service; adv. bd. Salvation Army; mem. Brandon Park Commn.; pres. Lycoming United Fund; trustee, sec. Lycoming Found., 1955—; mem. Sch. Bd. Williamsport Area, 1963—. Mem. Lycoming Law Assn. (pres. 1945), Pa. Bar Assn. (bd. govs. 1969-72, ho. of dels. 1972—), Pa. Bar Inst. (treas. 1969—), Am. Bar Assn., Am. Judicature Soc., Williamsport C. of C. (pres.). Recipient Lycoming United Fund award, 1961; Grit award, 1966. Home: 1600 N Campbell St Williamsport PA 17701 Office: 434 William St Williamsport PA 17701 Tel (717) 323-8746

WILLIAMSON, DONALD JAMES, b. Hoboken, N.J., May 12, 1936; B.S., St. Peter's Coll. Arts and Scis., 1958; J.D. (Arthur Garfield Hays fellow), N.Y. U., 1961. Admitted to N.Y. bar, 1961, U.S. Supreme Ct. bar, 1965, N.J. bar, 1970; trial atty. antitrust div. Dept. Justice, Washington, 1961-65; asso. firm Shearman & Sterling, N.Y.C., 1965-68, Weil, Gotshal & Manges, N.Y.C., 1968-70; chief asst. U.S. atty. Dist. N.J., 1970-71; partner firm Burgoyne Michels Rose & Williamson, N.Y.C., 1972—; prof. antitrust law Seton Hall U., 1972-73. Trustee Bede Sch., Englewood, N.J., 1970-73; bd. dirs. youth dept. Archdiocese of Newark, 1976—. Mem. Am., N.J. bar assns., Assn. Bar City N.Y. Home: 1066 Wildwood Rd Oradell NJ 07649 Office: 551 Fifth Ave New York City NY 10017 Tel (212) 986-0060 also 1 Gateway Newark NJ 07102 Tel (201) 643-5100

WILLIAMSON, DONALD WADSWORTH, b. Chunky, Miss., May 7, 1907; B.S., U. So. Miss., 1938; M.S., Miss. State U., 194:; B.S., U. Miss., 1952. Admitted to Miss. bar, 1952; individual practice law, Meridian, Miss., 1952—; atty., Lauderdale County, 1959-63. Mem. Miss. State Bar. Home: 408 55th Ave Meridian MS 39301 Office: First Federal Savings Bldg Meridian MS 39301 Tel (601) 485-4234

WILLIAMSON, FENTON DAVID, JR., b. Sacramento, Apr. 11, 1926; B.A., U. Calif., Berkeley, 1949, LL.D., 1951. Admitted to Calif. bar, 1952; partner firm Thomas, Snell, Jamison, Russell, Williamson & Asperger, Fresno, Calif., 1952—. Mem. Am., Calif. bar assns. Contbg. author: Farm and Ranch Law Handbook, 1967. Office: Fresno Townhouse 10th Floor Fresno CA 93721 Tel (209) 442-0600

WILLIAMSON, GEORGE HENRY, b. Charleston, W.Va., July 17, 1889; A.B., Hamilton Coll., 1914; LL.B., Washington and Lee U., 1916; Admitted to W.Va. bar, 1916; since practiced in Charleston, W.Va. Mem. W.Va. State Bar, Phi Delta Phi. Recipient Clark prize Hamilton Coll., 1916, Hamilton prize, 1916. Home: 237 Hawthorne Dr Charleston WV 25302 Office: 304 Security Bldg Charleston WV 25301 Tel (304) 346-3172

WILLIAMSON, GRIER JOSEPH, JR., b. Charlotte, N.C., Aug. 4, 1915; A.B., U. N.C., 1937; LL.B., Harvard U., 1940. Admitted to N.C. bar, 1940; sr. partner Grier, Parker, Poe, Thompson, Bernstein, Gage & Preston, Charlotte, 1946—. Chmn., Charlotte Parks and Recreation Commn., 1959-63, Charlotte City Charter Commn., 1964-65; mem. N.C. Bd. Higher Edn., 1963-65, N.C. Ednl. Facilities Commn., 1963; chmn. bd. trustees Queens Coll., 1974. Mem. Am. Bar Assn., Am. Judicature Soc., Am. Law Inst., 26th Jud. Dist. (pres. 1956), N.C. (bd. govs. 1960-63) bar assns. Home: 1869 Queens Rd W Charlotte NC 28207 Office: 1100 Cameron Brown Bldg Charlotte NC 28204 Tel (704) 372-6730

WILLIAMSON, PETER WOOLLARD, b. Albany, N.Y., Oct. 19, 1938; A.B., Princeton U., 1960; LL.B., U. Mich., 1963. Admitted to N.Y. bar, 1963; asso. firm Debevoise, Plimpton, Lyons & Gates, N.Y.C., 1964-69; sr. partner firm Williamson & Schoeman, N.Y.C., 1969—. Vestryman Parish of Calvary, Holy Communion and St. George's Ch., N.Y.C., 1973—. Mem. Am., N.Y. State bar assns., Ban Assn. City N.Y. Office: 60 E 42d St New York City NY 10017 Tel (212) 661-5030

WILLIAMSON, RALPH RICHARD, JR., b. Oklahoma City, Mar. 23, 1925; LL.B., Oklahoma City U., 1952. Admitted to Okla. bar, 1952, U.S. Supreme Ct. bar, 1972: casualty claim adjuster, various cos., 1952-62; partner firm Williamson & Barrett, Oklahoma City, 1962-67; asst. law and exec. counsel Commrs. of the Land Office, Oklahoma City, 1967-71, gen. counsel, 1972—, sec., 1971-72; judge Warr Acres (Okla.) Municipal Ct., 1962-67. Mem. Okla. Bar Assn., Am. Judicature Soc. (charter). Recipient Citizenship award Mayor Oklahoma City. Home: 620 NW 41st St Oklahoma City OK 73118 Office: Commrs of the Land Office Jim Thorpe Bldg 2101 N Lincoln Blvd Oklahoma City OK 73105 Tel (405) 521-2774

WILLIAMSON, WILLIAM CAREY, LL.B., Houston U., 1931. Admitted to Tex. bar, 1931; atty. Am. Republics Corp., Houston, 1931-55, Sinclair Oil & Gas Co., Houston, 1955-65; individual practice law, Houston, 1965—. Mem. Tex., Houston bar assns. Home: 3775 Jardin St Houston TX 77005 Office: 2472 Bolsover Rd Houston TX 77005 Tel (713) 528-3333

WILLIAMSON, WILLIAM HERMAN, b. Indpls., Jan. 31, 1908; B.A., Ind. U., LL.B., 1938. Admitted to Ind. bar, 1939, Mich. bar, 1949, U.S. Supreme Ct. bar, 1967; officer Indpls. Police Dept., 1939-42; spl. agt. FBI, Washington, 1942-46; legal counsel atty., labor relations rep. Ford Motor Co., Dearborn, Mich., 1947-48, counsel, atty. at law, 1947—; counsel, atty., labor indsl. relations rep. Kaiser-Frazer Corp., Willow Run, Mich., 1949-52; mem. firms Neal & Williams, Indpls., 1952-59, Williams, Williamson & Colvin, Indpls., 1960-66; partner firm Williamson, Colvin, Liggitt, Sargent & Staton, Indpls., 1966—; 1st pres. United Local Paper and Box Workers Local 31, Indpls., 1937-39; hon. dep. atty. gen. State of Ind., 1968. Mem. Indpls. City Council, 1956-64; precinct committeeman Democratic Party of Ind., 1952-55, ward chmn., 1955-58. Mem. Am., Ind., Indpls., Fed. (pres. 1971-72) bar assns., State Bar Mich., World Peace Through Law, Lawyers Assn. Indpls., Am. Judicature Soc., Am. Arbitration Assn., Soc. Former Spl. Agt. FBI, Internat. Platform Assn., Fraternal Order of Police, Sigma Delta Kappa (pres. 1967). Recipient certificate of merit for work in counter-espionage and counter sabotage FBI, 1942-46. Home: 4309 Royal Pine Blvd Indianapolis IN 46250 Office: 1005 First Fed Bldg Indianapolis IN 46204 Tel (317) 636-1555

WILLIFORD, JOHN LEA, b. Kingsland, Ark., Sept. 18, 1936; B.A., U. Okla., 1958; J.D., U. Tex., 1960. Admitted to Tex. bar, 1960, U.S. Ct. Mil. Appeals bar, 1962, Okla. bar, 1969, U.S. Supreme Ct. bar, 1971, D.C. bar, 1972; staff atty. Phillips Petroleum Co., Houston, 1963-68, Bartlesville, Okla., 1968-75, sr. counsel, 1975—. Mem. State Bar Tex., Am., Fed. Power, Okla. bar assns., Phi Alpha Delta. Office: 583 Frank Phillips Bldg Bartlesville OK 74004 Tel (918) 661-3760

WILLIFORD, JOHN WILLIAM, b. Madison County, Ga., Aug. 3, 1922; Mus. B., Berry Coll., 1942; LL.B., Mercer U., 1948. Admitted to Ga. bar, 1947; mem. firm Stapleton & Williford, Elberton, Ga., 1948-57; sr. mem. firm Williford & Grant, Elberton, 1957-64; judge Ga. Superior Ct., No. Jud. Circuit, 1964—; solicitor Elbert County, 1960-64, county atty., 1960-64; mem. exec. com. Ga. State Council Superior Ct. Judges, 1970-71; chmn. Ga. Sentence Rev. Bd. Chmn. bd. deacons 1st Bapt. Ch., Elberton, 1965-66, tchr. fellowship class, 1950-76, deacon, 1950-76, bass soloist, 1950—; coach Little League Baseball, Elberton, 1962-64. Contbr. articles to Ga. State Bar Jour. Home: 145 Parkwood Dr Elberton GA 30635 Office: PO Box 880 Elberton GA 30635 Tel (404) 283-1401

WILLIG, WILLIAM PAUL, b. Schenectady, Mar. 29, 1936; A.B., St. Michael's Coll., 1958; LL.B., Albany Law Sch., 1962, J.D., 1962. Admitted to N.Y. bar, 1962; law clk. Firm Higgins, Roberts, Beyerl & Coan, and predecessor, Schenectady, 1962, asso., 1962-68, partner, 1968-73, sec., 1973—; mem. med. malpractice and arbitration panels N.Y. Supreme Ct., 4th Jud. Dist.; practice ct. judge Union U., Albany Law Sch.; lectr in field. Mem. Schenectady County Democratic Com., 1966-67, pres. 1st Ward, 1967; lectr. on legal process AIB. Mem. N.Y. State (exec. com. sect. young lawyers 1968-69), Schenectady County (del. to Fed. Bar Assn. 4th Jud. Dist.), Fed. bar assns., Am. Trial Lawyers Assn. Home: 194 West Side Dr Ballston Lake NY 12019 Office: 502 State St Schenectady NY 12305 Tel (518) 374-3399

WILLIHNGANZ, PAUL WADDELL, b. Bklyn., May 19, 1937; B.M.E., U. Notre Dame, 1959; J.D., Georgetown U., 1968. Admitted to Calif. bar, 1969, U.S. Supreme Ct. bar, 1972; program mgr. Hydrotronics div. Data Design Labs. Inc., Falls Church, Va., 1967-68; asso. firm Higgs, Jennings, Fletcher & Mack, San Diego, 1969-71; partner firm Brundage, Williams & Zellmann, San Diego, 1971-74; individual practice law, San Diego, 1975; partner firm Willihnganz, Manning & Sudman, San Diego, 1975—. Dir., Rancho Bernardo Homeowners Corp., San Diego, 1968-69; pres. Notre Dame Club of San Diego, 1975-76. Mem. Am., San Diego County bar assns., Am., Calif., San Diego trial lawyers assns., Naval Res. Assn., Indsl. Relations Research Assn., Phi Delta Phi. Home: 7720 Hillandale Dr San Diego CA 92120 Office: 1143 Tenth Ave San Diego CA 92101 Tel (714) 231-1471

WILLIHNGANZ, ROBERT ANTONIO, b. Beaver Dam, Wis., Mar. 14, 1913; B.S., U. Wis., 1937; J.D., Wayne State U., 1968; Research chemist Union Carbide Corp., Tonawanda, N.Y., 1937-48, Chrysler Corp., Highland Park, Mich., 1948-52; partner Deutser & Willihnganz, chem. cons., Detroit, 1952-61; pres. Rochester Aerosol Corp. (Mich.), 1961-63; cons. chemistry, Rochester, 1963-67; sr. engr. Gen Motors Corp., Detroit, 1967—; admitted to Mich. bar, 1969; individual practice law, Rochester and Detroit, 1969—; atty., resident agt. Land Conservation Assn. of Oakland Twp. (Mich.). Trustee, v.p. Birmingham (Mich.) Unitarian Ch. Mem. Mich. State Bar, Indsl. Relations Research Assn., Am. Chem. Soc. (chmn. Detroit sect. com.

on environ. quality), ACLU, Phi Alpha Delta. Home: 5910 Little Pine Ln Rochester MI 48063 Office: 3005 Cadillac Tower Detroit MI 48226 Tel (313) 961-3787

WILLIN, MARY ANN TUUR, b. Tallinn, Estonia, Dec. 23, 1940; B.A., U. Md., 1962, LL.B., 1965; grad. Nat. Coll. Dist. Attys., 1974. Admitted to Md. bar, 1966; asst. state's atty., Balt., 1972—; individual practice law, 1967-70; asst. gen. counsel GSA, Washington, 1971-72. Vice-pres., Balt. Estonian Soc., Inc., 1975-76; treas. Balt. Estonian Sch., 1974—; social concerns chairperson Lock Raven United Methodist Ch., 1975-76. Mem. Women's Bar Asn. Md. (sec.), Am. (membership and liaison with state and local bar com., criminal justice sect.), Md., Fed. bar assns., Md. State's Attys. Assn., Nat. Dist. Attys. Assn., Am. Judicature Soc. Home: 6708 Tweedbrook Rd Baltimore MD 21239 Office: 204 Court House Baltimore MD 21202 Tel (301) 396-5156

WILLINGER, LOWELL DAVID, b. N.Y.C., Mar. 8, 1942; B.A., Cornell U., 1964; LL.B., Harvard, 1967. Admitted to N.Y. bar, 1968, U.S. Ct. Appeals bar, 2d Circuit, 1971, U.S. Supreme Ct. bar, 1976; asso. firms Hofheimer Gartlir Gottlieb & Gross, N.Y.C., 1968-69, Goldstein Shames Hyde Wirth Bezahler & Cahill, N.Y.C., 1969—. Mem. Assn. Bar N.Y.C., New York County Lawyers Assn. Office: 655 Madison Ave New York City NY 10021 Tel (212) 826-9563

WILLINGHAM, PAUL EDMUND, JR., b. Ridgely, Tenn., Nov. 19, 1935; B.A., U. N.C., 1957; B.D., Vanderbilt U., 1964; M.A., Johns Hopkins, 1967; J.D., Emory U., 1973. Admitted to Ga. bar, 1974; atty. Fed. Res. Bank of Atlanta, 1974—; Washington corr. Nashville Tennessean, 1966-70. Mem. Phi Beta Kappa. Home: 2210 Leafmore Dr Decatur GA 30033 Office: 104 Marietta St NW Atlanta GA 30303 Tel (404) 586-8853

WILLIS, BENJAMIN CAWTHON, b. Quincy, Fla., Oct. 7, 1913; student Emory U., 1930-32; J.D., U. Fla., 1936. Admitted to Fla. bar, 1936; practiced in Tallahassee, 1936-57; judge Circuit Ct., 2d Jud. Circuit of Fla., 1957—, chief judge, 1971—. Mem. Leon County (Fla.) Sch. Bd., 1947-52. Mem. Fla. Bar (gov. 1952-54). Home: 1504 History Ave Tallahassee FL 32303 Office: Leon County Courthouse Tallahassee FL 32302 Tel (904) 488-6747

WILLIS, CHARLES RALPH, b. Ft. Worth, Apr. 29, 1948; A.A., Cameron State Coll., 1968, B.S., 1970; J.D., Washington U., St. Louis, 1973. Admitted to Mo. bar, 1973, U.S. Tax Ct. bar, 1976; individual practice law, St. Louis, 1973—; asst. county pros. atty., 1974; dir. Grand Bissell Towers, Inc. Bd. dirs. Legal Aid Soc. of St. Louis City and County, 1974-75; mem. exec. bd. Washington U. Alumni. Mem. Am., St. Louis Met., Mound City bar assns. Contbr. articles to legal jours. Home: 1125 Ferry St Saint Louis MO 63107 Office: 2810 N Grand Ave Saint Louis MO 63107 Tel (314) 534-6910

WILLIS, DAVID LLOYD, b. Woodsville, N.H., Jan. 26, 1942; B.A., U. Vt., 1964; J.D., U. Maine, 1967. Admitted to Vt. bar, 1967; asso. firm Witters, Akley & Brown, St. Johnsbury, Vt., 1968-71; partner firm Witters, Zuccaro, Willis & Lium, St. Johnsbury, 1971—. Trustee, corporator Wells River Savs. Bank (Vt.). Home: Round Barn Farm Passumpsic VT 05861 Office: 101 Eastern Ave Saint Johnsbury VT 05819 Tel (802) 748-8958

WILLIS, GROVER CLEVELAND, JR., b. LaGrange, Ga., Sept. 4, 1911; J.D., U. Ga., 1935. Admitted to Ga. bar, 1935; individual practice law, Columbus, Ga., 1935-41; mem. firm Willis & Carter, 1946—; served to lt. col. Judge Adv. Gen. U.S. Army, 1941-46. Mem. State Bar of Ga., Am. Bar Assn., Columbus Lawyers Club, Am. Judicature Soc., Am. Trial Lawyers Assn. Home: 2645 Edgewood Rd Columbus GA 31906 Office: Suite 305 Nat Bank & Trust Co Bldg Columbus GA 31901 Tel (404) 327-6516

WILLIS, HAMILTON BARROW, b. Leesville, La., Nov. 25, 1931; B.S., Southeastern La. Coll., 1952; J.D., La. State U., 1973. Admitted to La. bar, 1973, U.S. Dist. Ct. bar for Middle Dist. La., 1974; individual practice law, St. Francisville, La., 1973-74; partner firm Willis & Ramshur, St. Francisville, 1974—; mem. West Feliciana Notarial Commn., 1974-75, chmn., 1975—; atty. W. Feliciana Pat Health Council, 1974-76, treas., 1976; mem. vestry Grace Episc. Ch., Mem. 20th Jud. Dist., La., Am. bar assns., La., Trial Lawyers Assn., Assn. Trial Lawyers Am. Home: Tanglewild Plantation Saint Francisville LA 70775 Office: 401-403 Ferdinand St PO Box 429 Saint Francisville LA 70775 Tel (504) 635-3212

WILLIS, LOTHROP MARR, b. Buffalo, July 17, 1913; student Middlebury Coll., 1931-33; LL.B., State U. N.Y., Buffalo, 1936. Admitted to N.Y. State bar, 1937; asso. firm Chester A. Pearlman, Buffalo, 1939-43; contract adminstr. Curtiss-Wright Corp., Buffalo, 1943-44, asst. to comptroller, 1944-46; partner firm Willis, Benzow & Willis, Buffalo, 1945-52; asso. firm Schutrum, Howder & Lester, Buffalo, 1952-54; individual practice law, Boston, N.Y., 1954—; law asst. to justice N.Y. Supreme Ct., 1940-43; atty. Town of Boston, 1945-62. Founder, trustee Boston Free Library, 1946—; dist. chmn. Greater Niagara Frontier council Boy Scouts Am., 1972-74. Home: Overlook Farm S-8980 Rockwood Rd Boston NY 14025 Tel (716) 649-3636

WILLIS, WILLIAM ERVIN, b. Huntington, W.Va., Oct. 11, 1926; A.B., Marshall U., 1948; J.D., Harvard, 1951. Admitted to N.Y. State bar, 1952, U.S. Supreme Ct. bar, 1956; partner firm Sullivan & Cromwell, N.Y.C., 1951—. Fellow Am. Coll. Trial Lawyers, Am. Bar Found., Fed. Bar Council; mem. Am., N.Y. State, N.Y.C., N.Y. County bar assns. Contbr. articles to legal jours. Home: Dogwood Ln Alpine NJ 07620 Office: 48 Wall St New York City NY 10005 Tel (212) 952-8274

WILLMAN, HUBERT B., b. Kansas City, Mo., Sept. 21, 1933; B.S., Rockhurst Coll., 1955; J.D., U. Mo., 1962; LL.M., N.Y. U., 1966. Admitted to Mo. bar, 1962; asst. tax atty. Comml. Credit Co., Balt., 1966-69; tax counsel internat. N.Am. Rockwell Corp., Pitts., 1969-71; tax counsel Seven-Up Co., St. Louis, 1971—; claims atty. U.S. Fidelity Guarantee Co., Kansas City, Mo. Mem. Am., Mo. bar assns., Tax Execs. Inst. Home: 1567 Estuary Dr Ballwin MO 63011 Office: 121 S Meramec Ave Saint Louis MO 63105 Tel (314) 863-7777

WILLOUGHBY, STUART CARROLL, b. Dallas, Sept. 16, 1923; J.D., U. Ariz., 1951. Admitted to Ariz. bar, 1951; partner firm Willoughby & Evans, Willcox, Ariz., 1952—; city atty. Willcox, 1952—. Mem. Willcox Sch. Dist. 13 Bd. Edn., 1960-76; bd. dirs. Ariz. Sch. Bds. Assn., 1962-67, pres., 1969-70. Fellow Am. Coll. Probate Counsel; mem. Am. Judicature Soc., Am., Ariz., Cochise County (pres. 1963) bar assns. Home: 451 N Bisbee Ave Willcox AZ 85643 Office: PO Box 790 Willcox AZ 85643 Tel (602) 384-2279

WILLS, DON PAUL, b. Miami, Okla., Sept. 13, 1935; B.A., Baylor U., 1957, LL.B., 1959. Admitted to Tex. bar, 1959; with JAGC, USAF, 1959-62; asst. dist. atty. Dallas County, Tex., 1962-65; partner firm Bean, Francis, Ford & Wills, Dallas, 1965—. Mem. Am., Tex. trial lawyers assns. Home: 10015 Trailpine St Dallas TX 75238 Office: 1010 Collum Bldg Dallas TX 75201 Tel (214) 747-8721

WILLS, RICHARD BARDSLEY, b. Youngstown, Ohio, Oct. 21, 1907; A.B., Yale, 1930, LL.B., 1932. Admitted to Ohio bar, 1933; asso. firm Manchester, Bennett, Powers & Ullman, and predecessors, Youngstown, 1933-49, partner, 1949—. Mem. Am., Ohio bar assns. Office: 1100 Union Nat Bank Bldg Youngstown OH 44503 Tel (216) 743-1171

WILLSON, PHILIP JAMES, b. Morning Sun, Iowa, Sept. 30, 1923; B.A., Parsons Coll., 1946; LL.B., Yale, 1949. Admitted to Iowa bar, 1949; mem. firm Smith, Peterson, Beckman & Willson, Council Bluffs, Iowa, 1949, partner, 1951—. Past pres. Council Bluffs Pub. Library, Council Bluffs YMCA. Mem. Am., Iowa (pres.-elect. 1977), S.W. Iowa, Pottawattamie bar assns., Council Bluffs C. of C. (past pres.). Author: (with Allan D. Vestal) Iowa Practice, 1974. Home: 548 Cogleywood St Council Bluffs IA 51501 Office: 370 Midlands Mall Council Bluffs IA 51501 Tel (712) 328-1833

WILLSON, PRENTISS, JR., b. Durham, N.C., Sept. 20, 1943; B.A., Occidental Coll., 1965; J.D., Harvard, 1968. Admitted to Calif. bar, 1969; partner firm Morrison & Foerster, San Francisco, 1970—; lectr. Golden Gate U., San Francisco. Trustee Coro Found., 1971—. Mem. Am. Bar Assn. Named Outstanding Faculty Mem., Golden Gate U., 1976. Office: 1 Market Plaza San Francisco CA 94105 Tel (415) 896-1310

WILMARTH, W. ELERY, b. Santa Maria, Calif., May 18, 1934; B.A., Conn. Wesleyan U., 1956; LL.B., U. Colo., 1963. Admitted to Colo. bar, 1963; asso. Gene E. Fischer, Ft. Collins, Colo., 1963-64, partner, 1965—. Mem. parent adv. bd. local sch. dist. Mem. Am., Colo., Larimer County bar assns. Home: 1411 Hillside Dr Fort Collins CO 80521 Office: Fischer & Wilmarth 900 Savings Bldg Fort Collins CO 80521 Tel (303) 482-4710

WILMER, CHARLES MARK, b. Phoenix, Dec. 31, 1938; LL.B., U. Ariz., 1964. Admitted to Ariz. bar, 1964; partner firm Wilmer and Woodburn, Chandler, Ariz., to 1966; prin. Charles M. Wilmer, Phoenix, 1966—. Mem. State Bar Ariz. (amendments fed. rules procedures com.). Office: 316 W McDowell Rd Suite 201 Phoenix AZ 85003 Tel (602) 258-6019

WILMER, WILLIAM HOLLAND, II, b. Birmingham, Ala., Feb. 28, 1931; B.A., Yale, 1952; LL.B., Harvard, 1955. Admitted to Md. bar, 1958, U.S. Ct. Appeals 4th Circuit bar, 1962, Washington bar, 1964; asso. firm Piper & Marbury, Balt., 1960-65; partner firm Cross, Shriver, Bright & Washburne, Balt., 1965-68, Brune, & Robertson, Balt., 1968-73; of counsel Sun Life Ins. Co. Am., Balt., 1973—. Mem. Balt. Estate Planning Council, Am., Md. State, Balt. City bar assns. Home: Little Oxmead White Hall MD 21161 Office: Sun Life Bldg Baltimore MD 21201 Tel (301) 727-0400

WILMETTI, JOE RAYMOND, b. Superior, Wyo., Oct. 30, 1923; J.D., U. Wyo., 1948. Admitted to Wyo. bar, 1949, U.S. Ct. Mil. Appeals bar, 1964, U.S. Supreme Ct. bar, 1964; individual practice law, Rock Springs, Wyo., 1949—; county and pros. atty. Sweetwater County (Wyo.), 1952-60, pub. defender, 1973—. Mem. Wyo., Supreme Ct. bar assns., Nat. Legal Aid and Defender Assn. Home: 1117 Wyoming St Rock Springs WY 82901 Office: 104 N Side State Bank Bldg Rock Springs WY 82901 Tel (307) 362-3531

WILMOT, BEN KINNAIRD, b. Lancaster, Ky., Oct. 17, 1923; student Eastern Ky. State Coll., 1940-50; LL.B., Stetson U., 1950. Admitted to Fla. bar, 1950, Ky. bar, 1950; law clk. Ky. Ct. Appeals, 1950-51; hearing examiner Ky. Dept. Motor Transp., Frankfort, 1951-56; individual practice law, Stanford, Ky., 1966—. Mem. Ky., Fla., Lincoln County (past pres.), 13th Jud. Dist. (pres.) bar assns. Home: Route 2 Hubble Rd Stanford KY 40484 Office: Wilmot & May Wilmot Bldg Lancaster St Stanford KY 40484 Tel (606) 365-9149

WILNEFF, ROBERT, b. Chgo., Aug. 5, 1945; B.S.C., DePaul U., 1967, J.D., 1973; C.P.A., U. Ill., 1968. Admitted to Ill. bar, 1973; asso. firm Ash, Anos, Harris & Freedman, Chgo., 1974; C.P.A. partner Philip Rootberg & Co., Chgo., 1967—. Mem. Ill., Am. bar assns., Ill. Soc. C.P.A.'s, Am. Inst. C.P.A.'s. Recipient Amjur award DePaul U., 1970. Office: P Rootberg & Co 10 S LaSalle St Chicago IL 60603 Tel (312) 346-8338

WILNER, MORTON HARRISON, b. Balt., May 28, 1908; B.S. in Econs., U. Pa., 1930; J.D., Georgetown U., 1934. Admitted to D.C. bar, 1933; individual practice law, Washington, 1933-41; mem. Wilner and Scheiner, and predecessors, Washington, 1945—; dep. dir. aircraft div. War Prodn. Bd., Washington, 1944-45; gen. counsel Aerospace Industries Assn., Armed Forces Relief and Benefit Assn. Trustee U. Pa., 1965—, Ford's Theatre Soc., Washington, 1973—. Mem. Am. (ho. of dels. 1971-73), Fed., Fed. Communications (pres. 1969-70), Internat. bar assns., Bar Assn. D.C., Nat. Lawyers Club. Contbr. articles to legal publs. Home: 2701 Chesapeake St NW Washington DC 20008 Office: 2021 L St NW Washington DC 20036 Tel (202) 293-7800

WILSEY, ALLEN GERALD, b. Chgo., May 21, 1929; J.D., DePaul U., 1950. Admitted to Ill. bar, 1950; partner firm Epstein & Wilsey, Chgo., 1950—. Pres. Timber Ridge Home Owners Assn., Skokie, Ill., 1970; chmn. Skokie Drug Abuse Commn., 1971; commr. Skokie Plan Commn., 1972-75; pres. Skokie Home Owners Council, 1976. Mem. Chgo. Bar Assn., Nu Beta Epsilon. Home: 3914 Four Winds Way Skokie IL 60076 Office: 221 N LaSalle St Chicago IL 60601 Tel (312) 346-6734

WILSMAN, JAMES MICHAEL, b. Port Huron, Mich., Oct. 7, 1939; A.B., Hiram Coll., 1961; J.D., U. Mich., 1964. Admitted to Ohio bar, 1964; asso. firm Squire, Sanders & Dempsey, Cleve., 1964-66; partner firm Parks, Eisele, Bates & Wilsman, Cleve., 1969—; chmn. Gov.'s Task Force on Commn. Rev., 1976, Cuyahoga County Justice Center dedication, 1976. Pres., Citizens League, Cleve., 1974-76. Mem. Am., Ohio State, Cuyahoga County, Cleve. (trustee 1972-75) bar assns., Hiram Coll. Alumni Assn. (pres. 1972-74). Named one of ten outstanding young men Cleve. Jaycees, 1974, 75. Tel (216) 241-2840

WILSON, A. CHARLES, b. Salt Lake City, June 16, 1924; student U. Calif., Los Angeles, 1941, Trinity Coll. Music, London, Eng., 1946; J.D., U. So. Calif., 1950. Admitted to Calif. bar, 1951; sr. partner, firm Smith, Wilson & Shapiro, Los Angeles, 1952—; lectr. West Coast U., Los Angeles. Civil service commr. City of Beverly Hills (Calif.), 1977—. Mem. Calif., Los Angeles County bar assns. Office: 2080 Century Park E Los Angeles CA 90067 Tel (213) 879-2133

WILSON, ALEXANDER ERWIN, JR., b. East Point, Ga., Aug. 26, 1910; A.B., Emory U., 1930, A.M., 1932. Admitted to Ga. bar, 1931, D.C. bar, 1942, U.S. Supreme Ct. bar, 1943; asst. solicitor-gen. NE Circuit, Ga., 1931-37; regional atty. NLRB, 1937-42; partner firm Wilson and Wilson (and predecessor firms), Atlanta, 1942-76; partner firm Jones, Bird and Howell, Atlanta, 1976—. Mem. Am., Ga., Atlanta bar assns., Lawyers Club Atlanta. Home: 358 King Rd NW Atlanta GA 30342 Office: Haas-Howell Bldg 75 Poplar St NW Atlanta GA 30303 Tel (404) 522-2508

WILSON, ANSEL HARD, b. Delaware, Ohio, Oct. 24, 1911; B.A., Ohio Wesleyan U., 1933; J.D., Harvard, 1936. Admitted to Ohio bar, 1936; individual practice law, Dayton, Ohio, 1936-40; asst. atty. gen. State of Ohio, Columbus, 1940-42; atty. Office of Price Control Adminstrn., Dayton Area Rent Control, 1946-47; atty. NCR Corp., Dayton, 1947-66, asst. sec., 1966-74, gen. atty., 1974-76. Trustee, Dayton Civitan Club, 1952-54, pres., 1954-55. Mem. Dayton, Ohio, Am. bar assns., Am. Judicature Soc., U.S. Navy League (pres. 1949-56), Phi Beta Kappa. Home: 304 Schenck Ave Dayton OH 45409 Tel (513) 293-3069

WILSON, BARRY ALLEN, b. St. Louis, Mar. 24, 1940; B.S. in Pharmacy, St. Louis Coll. Pharmacy, 1962, M.S., 1963; J.D., St. Louis U., 1971. Admitted to Mo. bar, 1972; individual practice law, St. Louis, 1972—. Mem. Am., Mo., St. Louis bar assns. Home: 12967 Weatherfield St Saint Louis MO 63141 Office: 111 W Port Plaza 512 Saint Louis MO 63141 Tel (314) 878-5220

WILSON, BILLY ORAN, b. Epps, La., Dec. 1, 1932; J.D., La. State U., 1961. Admitted to La. bar, 1961; partner firm DeBlieux, Wilson & Guidry, Baton Rouge, 1961-62, Dyer & Wilson, Baton Rouge, 1962-72; prin. firm Wilson & Sexton, Baton Rouge, 1972—. Dir. profl. div. United Way, Baton Rouge, 1975-76. Mem. Boadmoore Residents Assn. (pres. 1968), Windsor Civil Assn. (pres. 1964), Am., La., Baton Rouge (pres. 1975-76) bar assns., La., Am. trial lawyers assns. Home: 3733 Floyd Dr Baton Rouge LA 70808 Office: 451 Florida St suite 714 Baton Rouge LA 70801 Tel (504) 383-7775

WILSON, CARL JOHNSON, JR., b. Macon, Ga., May 4, 1934; LL.B., John Marshall U., 1962. Admitted to Ga. bar, 1962; individual practice law, Macon, 1962—. Mem. Macon Bar Assn. Home: 1170 Briarcliff Rd Macon GA 31201 Office: 305 Cotton Ave Macon GA 31201 Tel (912) 742-2987

WILSON, CAROL, b. Rushville, Ill., Feb. 25, 1935; B.A., Stanford, 1955; J.D., U. Ariz., 1971. Admitted to Ariz. bar, 1971, since practiced in Tucson; asso. firm David S. Wine, 1971-72; individual practice law, 1973, 76—; partner firm Browning & Wilson, 1973-76; mem. com. civil practice and procedure State Bar Ariz., 1972—, teaching asst. U. Ariz. 1970-73. Mem. Pima County Bar Assn., Am. Assn. Trial Lawyers, Order of Coif. Home: 116 W Cushing St Tucson AZ 85701 Office: 116 W Cushing St Tucson AZ 85701 Tel (602) 884-8930

WILSON, CHARLES EDWARD, b. Indpls., May 26, 1937; B.A., St. Joseph Coll., 1959; J.D. with honors, Ind. U., 1965. Admitted to Ind. bar, 1965; partner firm Ice Miller Donadio & Ryan, Indpls., 1972—. Bd. dirs. Catholic Sem. Found., St. Francis Hosp., St. Elizabeth's Home, 1972-75. Mem. Ind. State Bar Assn. (chmn. real property sect.), Am. Judicature Soc., Order of Coif. Home: 611 Braugham Rd Indianapolis IN 46227 Office: 10th Floor 111 Monument Circle Indianapolis IN 46204 Tel (317) 635-1213

WILSON, CHARLES HAVEN, b. Waltham, Mass., July 27, 1936; A.B. in Govt., Tufts U., 1958; M.S. in Journalism, Columbia, 1959; J.D., U. Calif., 1967; Admitted to D.C. bar, 1968; asso. firm Williams & Connolly, Washington, 1968-75, partner, 1976—; sr. law clk. to chief justice U.S. Supreme Ct., 1967-68; staff dir. spl. com. on crime prevention and control Am. Bar Assn., 1971-72; adj. prof. constl. law Georgetown U., 1970-72. Mem. Am. Bar Assn. (council 1976—, dir. div. publs. sect. litigation 1975—), Order of Coif. Founding editor Litigation also editor-in-chief, 1974-76; contbr. articles to legal jours. Tel (202) 331-5067

WILSON, CHARLES MAXON, b. Centralia, Ill., June 16, 1916; A.B., U. Ill., 1938, J.D., 1940. Admitted to Ill. bar, 1940; individual practice law, Toulon, 1940-42; partner firm Brian and Wilson, Toulon, 1946-64; judge Ill. Circuit Ct., 10th Jud. Circuit, 1964—. Mem. Ill., Am. bar assns. Decorated Bronze Star. Home: 326 S Henderson St Toulon IL 61583 Office: Courthouse Toulon IL 61483 Tel (309) 286-5941

WILSON, CLAUDE RAYMOND, JR., b. Dallas, Feb. 22, 1933; B.B.A., So. Methodist U., 1954, LL.B., 1956, LL.M. in Taxation, 1958. Admitted to Tex. bar, 1956; asso. firm Cervin & Melton, Dallas, 1956-58; atty. Tex. & Pacific Ry. Co., Dallas, 1958-60; atty. Office Regional Counsel IRS, San Francisco, 1960, sr. trial atty. Office Chief Counsel, Washington, 1963-65; partner firm Golden, Potts, Boeckman & Wilson, Dallas, 1965—. Mem. Am., Dallas (chmn. taxation sect., chmn. com. on unauthorized practice) bar assns., Tex. Soc. C.P.A.'s (dir.), Phi Delta Phi. Home: 4069 Hanover St Dallas TX 75225 Office: 2300 Republic Nat Bank Tower Dallas TX 75201 Tel (214) 742-8422

WILSON, DONALD R., b. Portland, Oreg., Nov. 21, 1929; B.S., U. Portland, 1951; LL.B., U. Oreg., 1957. Admitted to Oreg. bar, 1957, U.S. Ct. Appeals bar, 9th Circuit, 1958, U.S. Supreme Ct. bar, 1971; now partner firm Pozzi, Wilson & Atchison, Portland. Mem. Oreg. State Bar (pres. 1976-77), Am. Bar Assn., Assn. Trial Lawyers Am. (pres. Oreg. chpt. 1961). Office: 910 Standard Plaza 1100 SW 6th Ave Portland OR 97204 Tel (503) 226-3232*

WILSON, ERNEST STATON, JR., b. Wilmington, Del., June 7, 1927; B.A., Haverford Coll. 1950; LL.B., Columbia, 1953. Admitted to Del. bar, 1953, U.S. Supreme Ct. bar, 1960; legal asst. Columbia U. Legis. Drafting Research Fund, 1951-53; asso. firm Morford, Bennethum & Marvel, Wilmington, 1953-56; partner firm Morford, Young & Conaway, and predecessor, Wilmington, 1957-60; sr. partner firm Wilson & Whittington, and predecessors, Wilmington, 1960—; chmn. New Castle County (Del.) Bd. Zoning Adjustment, 1956-62; counsel Del. Indsl. Bldg. Commn., 1962-68. Bd. dirs. Del. chpt. ACLU, 1971—; chmn. Del. for McGovern, 1972. Mem. Am., Del. State (chmn. com. adminstrv. law 1963-65) bar assns. Home: 2308 W 11th St Wilmington DE 19805 Office: 1608 Farmers Bank Bldg Wilmington DE 19899 Tel (302) 655-6144

WILSON, FRANK WILEY, b. Knoxville, Tenn., June 21, 1917; A.B., U. Tenn., 1939, J.D., 1941. Admitted to Tenn. bar, 1941; asso. firm Poore, Kramer & Cox, Knoxville, 1941-42; partner firm Wilson & Joyce, Oak Ridge, 1946-61; judge U.S. Dist. Ct., Eastern Dist. Tenn., 1961—, chief judge, 1970—; county atty. Anderson County (Tenn.), 1948; v.p. Bank of Oak Ridge, 1952-61. Mem. Oak Ridge Sch. Bd., 1952-58; bd. dirs. Chattanooga YMCA. Mem. Tenn., Am., Fed. bar assns., Am. Judicature Soc. Contbr. articles to legal jours. Home: 103 Stratford Way Signal Mountain TN 37377 Office: 317 Fed Bldg Chattanooga TN 37402 Tel (615) 267-3653

WILSON, GARY DEAN, b. Wichita, Kans., June 7, 1943; B.A., Stanford U., 1965, LL.B., 1968. Admitted to D.C. bar, 1970; law clk. to judge U.S. Ct. Appeals 2d Circuit, N.Y.C., 1968-69, to Justice Thurgood Marshall, U.S. Supreme Ct., Washington, 1969-70; asso. firm Wilmer, Cutler & Pickering, Washington, 1970-75, partner, 1976—. Home: 5362 28th St NW Washington DC 20015 Office: Wilmer Cutler & Pickering 1666 K St NW Washington DC 20006 Tel (202) 872-6279

WILSON, GEORGE HOWARD, b. Mattoon, Ill., Aug. 21, 1905; A.B., Phillips U., 1926, LL.D., 1975; LL.B., U. Okla., 1929, J.D., 1970; grad. Nat. Coll. State Trial Judges U. Nev., 1970. Admitted to Okla. bar, 1928, U.S. Supreme Ct. bar, 1934, Neb. bar, 1935; partner firm Wilson & Wilson, Enid, Okla., 1929-52; judge Okla. Superior Ct., 1952-69; chief judge Okla. Dist. Ct., 4th Jud. Dist., Div. 1, 1969—; presiding judge Okla. Appeal Ct. of Bank Rev., 1971-74; with JAGC U.S. Army, 1942-46; mem. 81st Congress from 8th Okla. dist., 1949-51. Pres. bd. dirs. YMCA, Enid, 1968; chmn. advisory bd. St. Mary's Hosp., Enid, 1960. Mem. Okla. State Jud. Conf. (pres. 1968), Garfield County (Okla.), Okla., Am. bar assns., Order of Coif. Recipient Distinguished Alumnus award Phillips U., 1972. Home: 1724 W Cherokee St Enid OK 73701 Office: Courthouse Enid OK 73701 Tel (405) 327-0245

WILSON, HARVEY ASHTON, b. Dallas, Oct. 10, 1937; A.B., U. Tex., 1960, LL.B., 1962. Admitted to Tex. bar, 1962; individual practice law, Austin, Tex., 1970—. Mem. Am., Travis County Bar Assns. Office: 1210 Nueces St #110 Austin TX 78701 Tel (512) 477-7476

WILSON, HUGH STEVEN, b. Paducah, Ky., Nov. 27, 1947; B.A., U. Ind., 1968; J.D., U. Chgo., 1971; LL.M., Harvard, 1972. Admitted to Calif. bar, 1972; asso. firm Latham & Watkins, Los Angeles, 1971—; teaching fellow Boston U. Law Sch., 1971-72. Mem. staff U. Chgo. Law Rev., 1969-71. Office: Latham & Watkins 555 S Flower St Los Angeles CA 90071 Tel (213) 485-1234

WILSON, JAMES EUGENE, b. Savannah, Ga., Oct. 1, 1923; LL.B., Emory U., 1950, J.D., 1970. Admitted to Ga. bar, 1949; individual practice law, College Park, Ga., 1950—. Mem. Phi Alpha Delta. Home: 1598 Knob Hill Dr NE Atlanta GA 30329 Office: 3493 N Main St College Park GA 30337 Tel (404) 766-1608

WILSON, JAMES WILLIAM, b. Spartanburg, S.C., June 18, 1928; student Tulane U., 1945-46; B.A., U. Tex., 1950, LL.B., 1951. Admitted to Tex. bar, 1951, since practiced in Austin; partner firm McGinnis, Lochridge & Kilgore and predecessors, 1960-76; of counsel firm Stubbemein, McRae, Sealy, Laughlin and Browder, Austin and Midland, Tex., 1976—; asst. atty. gen. Tex., 1957-58; counsel Democratic policy com., also legis. asst. to majority leader U.S. Senate, 1959-60; lectr. U. Tex. Law Sch., 1962-63. Fellow Tex. Bar Found.; mem. Am., Tex., Travis County bar assns., Order of Coif, Phi Beta Kappa, Phi Delta Phi. Home: 2705 Wooldridge Dr Austin TX 78703 Office: 18th Floor Am Bank Tower PO Box 2286 Austin TX 78768 Tel (512) 476-3502

WILSON, JOHN ALAN, b. Glen Ridge, N.J., Sept. 1, 1917; A.B., Princeton, 1939; LL.B., Yale, 1942. Admitted to Ohio bar, 1950; clk., 2d Circuit Ct. of Appeals, N.Y.C., 1942; legislative asst. to U.S. Sen. Robert A. Taft, Washington, 1946-49; counsel Dresser Industries, Inc., Cleve., 1949-50; sec. Affiliated Gas Equipment, Inc., 1950-55; with Diamond Shamrock Corp., 1956—, sec., 1961—, gen. counsel, 1964—, v.p., 1967—. Mem. Am., Fed., Cleve. bar assns., Am. Soc. Corporate Secretaries. Home: 2684 Leighton Rd Shaker Hts OH 44120 Office: 1100 Superior Ave Cleveland OH 44120 Tel (216) 694-5614

WILSON, JOHN JOHNSTON, b. Washington, July 25, 1901; LL.B., George Washington U., 1921. Admitted to D.C. bar, 1922, U.S. Supreme Ct. bar, 1941; practiced in Washington, 1922—; mem. firm Whiteford, Hart, Carmody & Wilson, 1940-76, counsel, 1976—; asst. U.S. atty. D.C., 1931-40, chief asst. U.S. atty., 1938-40; mem. com. admission and grievances U.S. Dist. Ct., D.C., 1945-58, vice chmn. com. on jud. disabilities and tenure, 1971-73; mem. personnel security rev. bd. AEC, 1957-71, chmn., 1967-71. Trustee George Washington U. Fellow Am. Coll. Trial Lawyers; mem. Am., D.C. (Lawyer of Year 1962) bar assns., D.C. Bar, Kappa Alpha, Phi Delta Phi. Recipient Alumni Achievement award George Washington U., 1965. Home: 3900 Watson Pl NW Bldg B Apt 7B Washington DC 20016 Office: 1050 17th St NW 9th Floor Washington DC 20036 Tel (202) 466-3930

WILSON, JULIANA DAVIS, b. Jacksonville, Fla., June 16, 1921; student Brevard Jr. Coll., 1939-40; B.S. in Edn., Fla. State Coll. for Women, 1942; LL.B., U. N.C., 1950, J.D., 1969. Admitted to Alaska bar, 1951; individual practice law, Anchorage, 1951-52; partner firm Wilson & Wilson, Anchorage, 1952—. Mem. Quota Internat. Home: 1615 Birchwood St Anchorage AL 99504 Office: PO Box 498 Anchorage AL 99510 Tel (907) 279-8479

WILSON, KENNETH EMERSON, b. Tacoma, Wash., Sept. 24, 1919; B.S., Hampton Inst., 1942; J.D., U. Chgo., 1948. Admitted to Ill. bar, 1949; asst. atty. gen. State of Ill., 1949-52; asst. states atty. Cook County (Ill.), Chgo., 1952-55; partner firm Rogers, Strayhorn, Harth, Wilson & Garnett, Chgo., 1955-68; asso. judge, 1968-70; circuit ct. judge, 1970-76; justice Appellate Ct., 1976—; mem. Ill. House of Representatives, 1954-64; commr. Cook County, 1964-68; lectr. Olive Harvey Community Coll. Mem. Nat., Chgo. bar assns., Nat. Bar Jud. Council. Contbr. articles in field to profl. jours. Office: Civic Center 28th Floor Chicago IL 60602 Tel (312) 793-5412

WILSON, LAVELLE ARTHUR, b. Big Run, Pa., June 12, 1900; grad. DuBois Bus. Coll., 1919; B.S., U. Pitts., 1923, LL.B., 1926. Admitted to Pa. bar, 1926; individual practice law, Jefferson County, Pa., 1927—; solicitor Jefferson County, 1928-36, 44-48, 64-68, pub. defender, 1970-76; solicitor Borough of Brookville (Pa.), 1932-44. Pres. bd. dirs. Brookville Hosp., 1948-68. Mem. Pa., Jefferson County bar assns. Home: 103 Walnut St Brookville PA 15825 Office: 205 Main St Brookville PA 15825 Tel (814) 849-7369

WILSON, LEROY, JR., b. Savannah, Ga., June 16, 1939; student U. Vienna (Austria), 1959-60; B.S. magna cum laude (Merrill scholar, Woodrow Wilson fellow), Morehouse Coll., 1962; M.S., U. Calif., Berkeley, 1965, J.D., 1968. Admitted to N.Y. State bar, 1969, U.S. Dist. Ct., 1974; atty. IBM Corp., Armonk, N.Y., 1968-69, East Fishkill, N.Y., 1969-72, Armonk, 1972-74, Rye Ridge, N.Y., 1974; individual practice law, N.Y.C., 1974; atty. Union Carbide Corp., N.Y.C., 1974—. Mem. Orange County Human Rights Commn., N.Y., 1972; Democratic Dist. leader, 1974—; trustee Chatfield Sch., 1975—. Mem. Am., Nat. bar assns. Recipient Thayer award U.S. Mil. Acad., 1972. Office: 270 Park Ave New York City NY 10017 Tel (212) 551-5445

WILSON, MARTIN STEPHEN, JR., b. Atlantic City, Apr. 9, 1946; B.S., St. Joseph's Coll., 1964-68; J.D., Villanova U., 1970-73. Admitted to N.J. bar, 1974; law clk. to judge Atlantic County, 1973-74; asso. firm Blatt, Blatt, Mairone & Biel, Atlantic City, 1974—; prosecutor Ventnor City (N.J.), 1977, Linwood (N.J.), 1977. Bd. govs. St. Joseph's Coll., 1968—. Mem. Atlantic County, N.J. State, Am. bar assns., Comml. Law League Am. Home: 6412 Monmouth Ave Ventnor NJ 08406 Office: 3201 Atlantic Ave Atlantic City NJ 08401 Tel (609) 344-1173

WILSON, MAURICE JULIUS, b. New Orleans, Aug. 16, 1909; student Va. Mil. Inst., 1928-29; B.A., La. State U., 1931, J.D., 1933. Admitted to La. bar, 1933; commd. spl. asst. to atty. gen. La., Baton Rouge, 1934; atty. Standard Oil Co. of La., New Orleans, 1937-39, Am. Petroleum Inst., Baton Rouge, 1939-40; partner firm Breazeale, Sachse & Wilson, Baton Rouge, 1940—. Bd. dirs. Cancer Soc. Greater Baton Rouge, Cancer Radiation and Research Found., Baton Rouge, Our Lady of Lake Hosp., Baton Rouge. Fellow Am. Coll. Trial Lawyers; mem. Internat. Assn. Ins. Counsel, Am. Judicature Soc., Am., La. (past chmn. ins. sect., ho. of dels.), Baton Rouge (past pres.) bar assns., Phi Delta Phi, Sigma Chi. Home: 3384 Belmont Ave Baton Rouge LA 70808 Office: Fidelity Nat Bank Bldg 440 N 3d St Baton Rouge LA 70801 Tel (504) 387-4000

WILSON, MAX ADDISON, b. Longmont, Colo., June 21, 1939; B.S.B.A., Nebr. U., 1963; J.D., Denver U., 1967. Admitted to Nebr. bar, 1967, Colo. bar, 1967, Fed. bar, 1967; mem. firm Sandhouse, Sandhouse & Wilson, 1969-74; individual practice law, 1974—. Mem. Am. Bar Assn. Home: 348 Bannock St PO Box 869 Sterling CO 80751 Office: 326 S Front St Sterling CO 80751 Tel (303) 522-5460 and (303) 399-4660

WILSON, MICKEY D., b. Tulsa, Dec. 5, 1931; B.A., U. Tulsa, 1954; LL.B., U. Okla., 1956. Admitted to Okla. bar, 1956; asst. county atty. Tulsa County (Okla.), 1956-57; legal officer USAF, 1957-60; dir. Tulsa corps.; lectr. Tulsa U. Founder Tulsa Jr. Tennis Assn., 1975; active Boy Scouts Am. Mem. Tulsa County (exec. com., chmn. budget com.), Okla. bar assns., Trial Lawyers Assn. Named Man of Month, Tulsa Tribune. Office: 308 Center Bldg Tulsa OK 74127 Tel (918) 582-9121

WILSON, MINOR KEITH, b. Cleve., Sept. 2, 1904; A.B., Western Res. U., 1928, LL.B., 1929. Admitted to Ohio bar, 1929, Ill. bar, 1966; individual practice law, Cleve., 1930-43; asst. city prosecutor, Cleve., 1931-32; dir. Civilian Def., Met. Cleve., 1940-42; served to col. U.S. Army, provost marshal, 5th Army Hdqrs., Chgo., 1953-56, chief security div. Army Intelligence, Pentagon, D.C., 1956-59; aide, legal advisor Supt. Police of Chgo., 1960-66; gen. counsel City Colls. of Chgo., 1966-68; judge Circuit Ct. of Cook County (Ill.), Chgo., 1968-76. Bd. dirs. Internat. Visitors Center, Chgo. Mem. Am., Ill., Chgo. bar assns., Am. Judicature Soc., John Howard Assn. (dir.). Home: 1350 N Lake Shore Dr Chicago IL 60610

WILSON, PAUL HOLLIDAY, JR., b. Schenectady, Sept. 4, 1942; B.A., Brown U., 1964; LL.B., M.B.A., Columbia, 1967. Admitted to N.Y. bar, 1967, U.S. Dist. Ct. bar, 1969; asso. firm Debevoise, Plimpton, Lyons & Gates, N.Y.C., 1968-76, partner, 1976—. Mem. N.Y.C. Bar Assn. Office: 299 Park Ave New York City NY 10017 Tel (212) 752-6400

WILSON, PERRY MORTON, JR., b. Wausau, Wis., Mar. 24, 1924; B.S., Northwestern U., 1946; J.D., Harvard U., 1949. Admitted to Minn. bar, 1949; law clk. Minn. Supreme Ct., 1949-50; asso. firm Smith, Blomquist, Wilson & Vitko, St. Paul, 1950-54, partner, 1954-68; partner firm Doherty, Rumble & Butler, St. Paul, 1969—. Mem. St. Paul Charter Commn., 1968-76, chmn., 1970-76. Mem. Minn. State Bar Assn. Home: 10 Crocus Hill Saint Paul MN 55102 Office: 1500 1st National Bank Bldg Saint Paul MN 55101 Tel (612) 291-9333

WILSON, PETER BARTON, b. Lake Forest, Ill., Aug. 23, 1933; B.A., Yale, 1955; J.D., U. Calif. at Berkeley, 1962. Admitted to Fla. bar, 1964, Calif. bar, 1964; asso. firm Davies & Burch, San Diego, 1964-66; mem. Calif. Assembly, 1966-71, 1st chmn. urban affairs and housing com.; mayor City of San Diego, 1971—; mem. Pres's. Citizens' Adv. Com. on Environ. Quality, nat. Adv. Com. on Criminal Justice Standards and Goals, Calif. Manpower Planning Council; mem. adv. bd. HUD's Urban Tech. Services Program; mem. mayors' task force on drug abuse treatment and prevention Nat. League Cities—U.S. Conf. Mayors; mem. com. on community devel., com. on legis. action U.S. Conf. Mayors; mem. com. on environ. quality Nat. League Cities. Mem. adv. bd. Hellenic Cultural Soc.; hon. mem. sea base planning and devel. com. San Diego council Boy Scouts Am.; bd. dirs. civic orgns. Mem. Am. (adv. commn. on housing and urban growth), San Diego County, Fla. bar assns., Nat. Assn. Environ. Edn., AIA (hon.). Recipient awards, including Human Relations citation Am. Jewish Com., 1974, Greatest Pub. Service Performed by Individual Benefiting a Local Community citation Am. Inst. Pub. Service, 1974, Museum Fellowship award Calif. Mus. Sci. and Industry, 1976. Office: 202 C St San Diego CA 92101 Tel (714) 236-6330

WILSON, PETER BOTTUM, b. Bonners Ferry, Idaho, May 21, 1925; B.A., U. Idaho, 1950, LL.B., 1951. Admitted to Idaho bar, 1953, U.S. Supreme Ct. bar, 1962; individual practice law, Coeur d'Alene, Idaho, 1953-57, Bonners Ferry, 1957-58, 66-67; partner firm Prather & Wilson, Bonners Ferry, 1958-66, firm Wilson & Walter, Bonners Ferry, 1967—; atty. City of Bonners Ferry, 1957—; pros. atty. Boundary County (Idaho), 1964-68; atty. City of Moyie Springs, 1967—. Mem. Am., Idaho (mem. examining com. 1968-71), 1st Jud. (pres. 1958) bar assns., Bonners Ferry C. of C. (pres. 1972), N. Idaho C. of C. (v.p. 1971—). Home: Box 749 Bonners Ferry ID 83805 Office: Box 749 Bonners Ferry ID 83805 Tel (208) 267-3127

WILSON, RICHARD GRAEME, b. Olympia, Wash., Oct. 23, 1928; B.B.A., U. Wash., 1950; LL.B., 1953; postgrad. U. So. Calif., 1958-60. Admitted to Calif. bar, 1958, 9th Circuit Ct. Appeals bar, 1958, U.S. Supreme Ct. bar, 1972; sr. partner firm Allen, Wilson, George & Edgmon, Inc. and predecessor firms, Long Beach, Calif., 1959—; commr. Port of Long Beach, 1973—. Chmn. Armed Services Commn., Long Beach, 1964-73. Mem. Am., Calif., Long Beach bar assns. Office: 3726 Atlantic Ave Long Beach CA 90807 Tel (213) 425-2171

WILSON, RICHARD KARL, b. Bryan, Ohio, Aug. 13, 1922; B.A., Wittenberg U., 1948; J.D., Ohio State U., 1950. Admitted to Ohio bar, 1951, U.S. Dist. Ct., 1956, U.S. Supreme Ct. bar, 1957, U.S. Ct. Appeals, 1958, U.S. Tax Ct. bar, 1970; individual practice law, Piquia, Ohio, 1951-74; asst. pros. atty. Miami County, 1953-55; law dir. City of Piqua, 1956-72; judge Piqua Municipal Ct., 1972-74; judge Common Pleas Ct. of Miami County, Troy, Ohio, 1974—. Mem. Am., Ohio, Miami County bar assns., Am. Judicature Soc. Home: 1308 Park Ave Piqua OH 45356 Office: Savety Bldg Main St Troy OH 45373 Tel (513) 335-8341

WILSON, RICHARD LEE, b. Mount Ayr, Iowa, Dec. 12, 1938; B.S. in Agronomy, Iowa State U., 1962; J.D., State U. Iowa, 1964. Admitted to Iowa bar, 1964; partner firm Wilson, Bonnett & Christensen, Lenox, Iowa, 1965—; mem. Iowa Judicial Nominating com., 1977—. Republican precinct committeeman, 1966-76; pres. Rotary Club, Lenox, 1976-77. Mem. Am., Iowa, Dist., County bar assns., Am. Trial Lawyers Assn. Office: 103 S Main St Lenox IA 50851 Tel (515) 333-2283

WILSON, ROBERT ALEXANDER, b. Waco, Tex., May 31, 1905; A.B., Baylor U., 1924, LL.B., 1927. Admitted to Tex. bar, 1927, U.S. Supreme Ct. bar, 1957; partner firm Underwood, Wilson, Sutton, Berry, Stein & Johnson, and predecessors, Amarillo, Tex., 1938—. Mem. adminstrv. bd. Polk St. United Meth. Ch., Amarillo, 1940—, trustee, 1960—; trustee Amarillo Pub. Schs., 1948-54, pres., 1952. Mem. State Bar Tex., Am., Amarillo (pres. 1940-41) bar assns., Am. Coll. Trial Lawyers, Internat. Assn. Ins. Counsel, Am. Judicature Soc., Tex. Assn. Def. Counsel. Home: 3203 Parker St Amarillo TX 79109 Office: 1500 Amarillo Nat Bank Bldg PO Box 9158 Amarillo TX 79105 Tel (806) 376-5613

WILSON, ROBERT BRUCE, JR., b. Newton Grove, N.C., June 7, 1922; B.S., Wake Forest U., 1947, LL.B., 1953. Admitted to N.C. bar, 1953; individual practice law, Winston-Salem, N.C., 1955-61, 66—; trust officer Wachovia Bank & Trust Co., Winston-Salem, 1961-66. Past pres. Forsyth County Legal Aid Soc. Mem. Am., N.C., Forsyth County bar assns., N.C. State Bar, N.C. Acad. Trial Lawyers, Comml. Law League Am. Home: 4315 Rosebriar Ln Winston-Salem NC 27106 Office: suite 4 201 Miller St Winston-Salem NC 27103 Tel (919) 722-0333

WILSON, ROBERT BYNUM, b. Sweetwater, Tex., May 21, 1943; B.A., Tex. Tech. U., 1965; LL.B., U. Houston, 1968. Admitted to Tex. bar, 1968, U.S. Supreme Ct. bar, 1974; asst. dist. atty. Lubbock County (Tex.), 1968-70; 1st asst. dist. atty. Central Tex., Belton, 1970-71; asst. U.S. atty. No. Dist. Tex., Lubbock, 1971—; lectr. in field. Master, S. Plains council Boy Scouts Am., Lubbock, 1974—; chmn. United Way, Lubbock, 1974—. Mem. State Bar Tex., Lubbock County Bar Assn., Lubbock County Jr. Bar, Phi Alpha Delta. Co-author: Federal Trial Practice Manual. Home: 2327 55th St Lubbock TX 79412 Office: 1205 Texas Ave Lubbock TX 79401 Tel (806) 762-7351

WILSON, ROBERT EARL, b. Bolivar, Mo., Apr. 6, 1929; A.B., U. Mo., 1951, LL.B., 1953, J.D., 1969. Admitted to Mo. bar, 1953; individual practice law, Bolivar, Mo., 1953—; pros. atty. Polk County, Mo., 1955-60. Mem. Mo., 30th Judicial Circuit bar assns., Bolivar (Mo.), C. of C. (pres. 1956-57), Delta Theta Phi. Home: 210 Lillian Pl Bolivar MO 65613 Office: 201 N Main Bolivar MO 65613 Tel (417) 326-5512

WILSON, ROBERT WESLEY, b. Clearwater, Fla., June 8, 1924; LL.B., Stetson U., 1950. Admitted to Fla. bar, 1951; individual practice law, Clearwater, 1951—; pros. atty. Clearwater, 1952-54. Active Young Democrats, Salvation Army drives, Wishing Well Polio Funds, Underprivileged Children Campaigns, Girl Scouts U.S.A.; dist. advancement com. Boy Scouts Am., 1953-58, dist. exec. com., 1957-58; bd. dirs. First Methodist Ch. of Clearwater, 1951; sec., treas., pres. Meth. Men's Club; chmn. Clearwater Conv. Bur., 1957-58. Mem. Fla. Seminole Assn., Jaycees (dir. Clearwater 1952-55, pres. 1953-54, chmn. state leadership tng. 1954, recipient Distinguished Service award, pres. Fla., recipient Clint Dunegan Meml. award), Clearwater C. of C. (nat. dir. U.S. Jr. C. of C., mem. Fla. State exec. com. 1955-56, pres. Fla. State Jr. C. of C. 1956-57, J.C.I. senator 1957, life mem.), Phi Alpha Delta. Home: 1476 E Cleveland St Clearwater FL 33515 Office: 401 S Lincoln Ave Clearwater FL 33516

WILSON, SAMUEL SMITH, b. Cin., Aug. 11, 1924; A.B., Princeton, 1947; LL.B., U. Cin., 1961. Admitted to Ohio bar, 1961; asso. firm Nieman, Aug, Elder & Jacobs, Cin., 1961-65; asso. prof. U. Cin. Coll. Law, 1965-68, prof., 1968-74, Nippert prof., dean, 1974—; reporter Cin. Times Star, 1947-53, Washington corr., 1953-56, editorial writer, 1956-58; actor Juvenile Ct. program WCPO-TV, Cin., 1975; chmn. Cin.-Hamilton County Criminal Justice Supervisory Commn. Mem. Am., Ohio, Cin. bar assns., Am. Law Inst. Editor-in-chief Law Rev. U. Cin. Coll. Law, 1960-61. Home: 1278 Dillon Ave Cincinnati OH 45226 Office: Univ Cin Coll Law Cincinnati OH 54221 Tel (513) 475-6805

WILSON, STANLEY P., b. Hamlin, Tex., Sept. 1, 1922; B.S., N. Tex. State U., 1943; LL.B., U. Tex., 1946. Admitted to Tex. bar, 1948; partner firm McMahon, Smart, Wilson, Surovik & Suttle, Abilene, 1951—. Pres., Citizens Better Govt., Abilene; mem. bd. edn. Abilene Ind. Sch. Dist.; bd. dirs. Hendrick Meml. Hosp. Found., Abilene. Fellow Am. Coll. Trial Lawyers; mem. State Bar Tex. (real estate trust probate council 1973-75), Am., Tex., Abilene bar assns. Office: Box 1440 1st National Ely Bldg Cypress St Abilene TX 79604 Tel (915) 677-9138

WILSON, STUART CHAPIN, b. Oakland, Calif., Oct. 23, 1928; A.B., Stanford U., 1950; J.D., U. So. Calif., 1953. Admitted to Calif. bar, 1953; dep. city prosecutor City of San Diego, 1955-57; dep. dist. atty. County of San Diego, 1957-59; practiced in San Diego, 1959-61, Oceanside, Calif., 1961-62, Carlsbad, Calif., 1962-71; judge San Diego County Municipal Ct., 1971—, presiding judge, 1974; dep. city atty. City of La Mesa (Calif.), 1958-59; city atty. City of Carlsbad (Calif.), 1962-71, City of Vista (Calif.), 1970-71. Mem. North San Diego Bar Assn. (pres. 1964). Office: 1701 Mission Ave Oceanside CA 92054 Tel (714) 722-4101

WILSON, THOMAS CHARLES, b. Rapid City, S.D., Dec. 2, 1943; B.A. in Econs., Occidental Coll., 1966; J.D., U. Wyo., 1969. Admitted to Colo. bar, 1969, Wyo. bar, 1969; asso. firm Ownbey, Pittam & Wilson, Denver, 1969-70; atty. Safeco Ins. Co., Denver, 1970-72; mem. firm Burgess & Davis, Sheridan, Wyo., 1972—; alt. municipal ct. judge, Sheridan, 1973—. Mem. Am., Wyo. bar assns., Am. Judicature Soc. Home: 443 E Mountain View Sheridan WY 82801 Office: 101 W Brundage St Sheridan WY 82801 Tel (307) 674-4449

WILSON, THOMAS FITZHUGH, b. Memphis, Mar. 14, 1905; B.S., Tulane U., 1926, LL.B., 1928. Admitted to La. bar, 1928, U.S. Supreme Ct. bar, 1954; individual practice law, New Orleans, 1928-32; asst. personnel mgr. Standard Oil Co. La., New Orleans, 1932-36; spl. agt. FBI, various locations, 1936-53; U.S. atty. Western Dist. La., Shreveport, 1953-62; individual practice law, Monroe, La., 1962—. Mem. Am., La., 4th Jud. Dist., Shreveport bar assns., Am. Judicature Soc., SAR (pres. NE La. chpt. 1972-74, 1st v.p. La. chpt. 1976-77), Soc. Former Agts. FBI, Delta Tau Delta, Phi Delta Phi. Home and Office: 1109 N 4th St Monroe LA 71201 Tel (318) 322-2416

WILSON, THOMAS PENNELL, b. Portland, Maine, June 1, 1942; A.B., Yale, 1966; J.D., U. Maine, 1971. Admitted to Maine bar, 1971; partner firm Wilson, Steinfeld, Murrell, Barton & Lane, Portland, 1971—; asst. corp. counsel City of S. Portland (Maine), 1971—. Mem. Am., Maine, Cumberland County bar assns., Maine Trial Lawyers Assn. Home: 8 Blanchard Rd Cumberland ME 04021 Office: 482 Congress St Portland ME 04111 Tel (207) 774-2651

WILSON, WESLEY MCCOOL, b. Mangum, Okla., June 21, 1927; B.S., Ill. Inst. Tech., 1952; M.B.A., U. Chgo., 1954; J.D., U. Wash., 1960. Admitted to Wash. bar, 1960, U.S. Supreme Ct. bar, 1974; with NLRB, 1959-69; individual practice law, Yakima, Wash., 1970—; personnel dir. West Coast Telephone Co., 1954-57. Mem. Am. Bar Assn. Author: Labor Law Handbook, 1963; The Labor Relations Primer, 1973; Know Your Job Rights, 1975. Home: 1403 S 1st Ave Yakima WA 98902 Office: 605 Miller Bldg Yakima WA 98901 Tel (509) 452-2828

WILSON, WILLIAM ALLAN, b. Burkburnett, Tex., Nov. 30, 1917; LL.B., Oklahoma City U., 1953. Admitted to Okla. bar, 1944; asso. firms Looney, Watts, Fenton, Billups, Oklahoma City, 1945-46, Howard K. Berry, Oklahoma City, 1947-48; individual practice law, Pauls Valley, Okla., 1948—; bd. dirs. U. Okla. Law Center. Mem. Garvin County (Okla.) Bar Assn. (pres. 1950). Home: 1757 S Walnut St Pauls Valley OK 73075 Office: 209 1/2 S Chickasaw St PO Box 473 Pauls Valley OK 73075 Tel (405) 238-3622

WILSON, WILLIAM T., b. Crewe, Va., Nov. 30, 1937; student Hampden-Sydney (Va.) Coll., 1960; J.D., U. Va., Charlottesville, 1963. Admitted to Va. bar; asso. firm Collins, Wilson, Collins & Singleton, and predecessors, Covington, Va., 1963-66, partner, 1966—. Mem. Covington Falling Spring Ruritan Club, Covington-Hot Springs Rotary, 19th Jud. Bar Assn., Va. Bar Assn., Izaak Welton League. Home: 239 W Main St Covington VA 24426

WILTBANK, RONALD EARL, b. Phoenix, Apr. 22, 1930; B.S., N. Mex. State U., 1955, M.A., 1964; J.D., Ariz. State U., 1971. Admitted to Ariz. bar, 1971, Fed. Ct. bar Ariz. and 9th Circuit Ct. Appeals, 1976; mem. firm Wiltbank & Peterson, Mesa, Ariz., 1971—. Mem. Am. Trial Lawyers Assn., Maricopa County Bar Assn. Office: 1419 E Main St Mesa AZ 85203 Tel (602) 834-6111

WILTROUT, IRVING JOHNSTON, b. Mpls., Jan. 4, 1915; B.S., U. Minn., 1939, J.D., 1939. Admitted to Minn. bar, 1940; individual practice law, Marshall, Minn., 1951-72; municipal judge City of Marshall, 1968-72; judge Lincoln-Lyon County (Minn.), Marshall, 1972—. Mem. Minn., Lincoln-Lyon County bar assns., Minn. County Judges Assn. Home: 706 N 4th St Marshall MN 56258 Office: Lyon County Court House Marshall MN 56258 Tel (507) 532-5401

WIMPFHEIMER, MICHAEL CLARK, b. Bronx, N.Y., July 9, 1944; B.A., Columbia U., 1964; J.D., Harvard U., 1967; grad. fellow Handels Hochschule, St. Gallen, Switzerland, 1967-68. Admitted to N.Y. bar, 1967; served with JAGC, USNR, 1968-70, now lt. comdr. Res.; partner firm Wimpfheimer & Wimpfheimer, N.Y.C., 1970—. Sec. Union of Orthodox Jewish Congregations, 1974—, bd. dirs., 1970—; sec. Am. Friends of Kol Tora. Mem. Am., N.Y. State bar assns. Home: 2756 Arlington Ave Riverdale NY 10463 Office: 10 Columbus Circle New York City NY 10019 Tel (212) 247-8448

WIMPFHEIMER, STEVEN, b. N.Y.C., Dec. 5, 1941; B.S. in Bus. Adminstrn., Syracuse U., 1963; LL.B., Bklyn. Law Sch., 1966. Admitted to N.Y. bar, 1966, U.S. Supreme Ct. bar, 1974; asso. firm Borden, Skidell, Fleck, Hunter & Stackel, Jamaica, N.Y., 1968-69; law asst. to bd. justices N.Y. State Supreme Ct., Queens County, 1969-72, confdl. law sec. to Justice Harold Tessler, 1971-72, Justice Michael A. Castaldi, 1972-75; asso. firm Lippe, Ruskin & Schlissel, Mineola, N.Y., 1975—. Mem. N.Y., Nassau County, Queens County bar assns. Home: 264-46 73d Ave Floral Park NY 11004 Office: 114 Old Country Rd Mineola NY 11501 Tel (516) 248-9500

WINANS, WILLIAM MILLER, b. Orange, N.J., Oct. 13, 1886; B.A., Wesleyan U., 1912; LL.B., Bklyn. Law Sch., 1925. Admitted to N.Y. bar, 1926; prof. law Bklyn. Law Sch., 1933-53; practice law, N.Y.C. Mem. Am., N.Y. bar assns. Home: Box 514 Millbrook NY 12545 Office: 30 E 42nd St New York City NY 10017 Tel (212) 986-6936

WINARD, ARTHUR IRVING, b. Bklyn., Oct. 2, 1916; A.B., U. Ariz., 1938; postgrad. U. Colo., Columbia U., Bklyn. Coll., N.Y. U., Marguand Sch.; LL.B., St. John's U., 1939, J.D., 1968. Admitted to N.Y. bar, 1944, U.S. Supreme Ct. bar, 1961; adminstrv. asst. in charge N.Y. Annotations Restatement Law of Torts, 1939-40; served as capt. JAG, U.S. Army, 1941-45; mng. editor Practising Law Inst., 1945-46; individual practice law, N.Y.C., 1946-49, 57—; partner firm Lane & Winard, N.Y.C., 1949-57. Mem. Am., N.Y. State bar assns., N.Y. County Lawyers Assn., Bankruptcy Bar Assn., Am. Arbitration Assn. (nat. panel). Author: (with Henry J. Plitkin) New York Surrogate Practice, 1950; editor: Rent Control—Federal, State, and Municipal, 1948; A Guide to Motion Practice, rev. edit., 1949; New York Law of Mechanics' Liens, 1949; Organizing Corporate and Business Enterprises, 1949; New York State Rent Control, 1950; Lawyers' Accounting Handbook, 1952; Antitrust Law and Techniques, 1963; Landmark Papers in Estate Planning, Wills, Estates and Trusts, 1968; contbr. articles to legal jours. Home: 5 Ridgeway Rd Larchmont NY 10538 Office: 475 Fifth Ave New York City NY 10017 Tel (212) LE 2-5800

WINARSKY, LEWIS IRA, b. Newark, July 1, 1947; B.A., Beloit Coll., 1969; J.D., Case Western Res. U., 1972; postgrad. Ohio State U. Admitted to Ohio bar, 1972, N.J. bar, 1973, D.C. bar, 1974; adminstrv. judge rate sect. Pub. Utilities Commn. Ohio, Columbus, 1972-75; asst. atty. gen. State of Ohio, Columbus, 1975-77; counsel Ohio Consumers Council, 1977—. Mem. Am., D.C., Columbus, Ohio, N.J. bar assns. Editor Case Western Res. U. Jour. Internat. Law, 1971-72. Home: 203 Berger Alley Columbus OH 43206 Office: 83 S 4th St Columbus OH 43215 Tel (614) 466-8574

WINCEK, ARTHUR THOMAS, b. Cleve., Apr. 29, 1921; A.B., John Carroll U., 1942; LL.B./J.D., Case Western Res. U., 1949. Admitted to Ohio bar, 1949, U.S. Supreme Ct. bar, 1955; individual practice law, Cleve., Ohio, 1949-50, 51-54; partner firm Rager, Forrester, Briggs & Wincek, Cleve., 1951-54; practiced law with various assos., Cleve., 1955—; solicitor City of Garfield Heights (Ohio), 1954-57; dir. law City of Lyndhurst (Ohio), 1958—, City of Maple Heights (Ohio), 1962-65. Bd. dirs. Marymount Retardation Services Unit, 1976—; mem. Geauga County adv. council United Torch Dr., 1976—. Mem. Am., Ohio, Cuyahoga County, Greater Cleve., Geauga County bar assns. Recipient Humanitarian award Parkwood Christian Meth. Episc. Ch., 1964. Home: 14916 Hillbrook Circle Novelty OH 44072 Office: 1130 Standard Bldg Ontario St Cleveland OH 44113 Tel (216) 621-8700

WINCHELL, BRUCE MILTON, b. Elyria, Ohio, Dec. 15, 1946; B.A., U. Akron, 1970, B.S., 1970, J.D., 1974. Polymer lit. chemist U. Akron, 1967; sheet metal journeyman Sheet Metal Workers Assn., Akron, Ohio, 1967-73; law clk. firm Hamilton, Renner & Kenner, Akron, 1973-75; admitted to Ohio bar, 1974, Patent Office bar, 1974, Canadian Patent Office, 1975; patent counsel Diamond Shamrock Corp., Painesville, Ohio, 1975—. Mem. Leroy Twp. (Ohio) Zoning Commn., 1976—. Mem. Ohio, Am. bar assns., Cleve., Am. patent law assns., Am. Chem. Soc. Home: 8269 Proctor Rd Painesville OH 44077 Tel (216) 352-9311

WINCHELL, NEAL RICHARD, b. Chgo., Sept. 20, 1945; B.A. in Polit. Sci., U. Ariz., 1967; J.D., U. Pacific, 1970. Admitted to Calif. bar, 1971; asso. firm Lewis, Rouda, and Winchell, San Francisco, 1971-73; partner firm Winchell and Winchell, San Francisco, 1973—. Mem. San Francisco Bar Assn., Am. Judicature Soc., Am., Calif., San Francisco (dir., sec., 1976, parliamentarian 1975, 1st v.p. 1977) trial lawyers assns. Office: 22 Battery 1100 San Francisco CA 94111 Tel (415) 956-5700

WINCHESTER, RICHARD LEE, b. Memphis, May 21, 1924; LL.B., U. Tenn., 1949, J.D., 1965. Admitted to Tenn. bar, 1949; since practiced in Memphis; partner firm Winchester, Walsh & Marshall and predecessors, 1949—; Shelby County atty., 1960-64; city atty. Arlington and Germantown, Tenn., 1966—. Trustee U. Tenn., 1975—. Home: 2121 Pete Mitchell Germantown TN 38138 Office: 100 N Main Bldg Memphis TN 38103 Tel (901) 526-7374

WINDERMAN, HERMAN, b. Phila., Mar. 16, 1921; B.S. Temple U., 1942, J.D., 1950. Admitted to Pa bar, 1951; accountant, sr. partner Winderman, Caplan & Carroll, C.P.A.'s, Phila., 1951-64; partner law firm Pepper & Winderman, Phila., 1972—. Mem. Am., Pa., Phila. bar assns., Am., Pa. insts. C.P.A.'s. Home: 10 Vassar Rd Broomall PA 19001 Office: 1812 Fox Bldg Philadelphia PA 19103 Tel (215) LO3-2307

WINDHAM, JAMES MULDROW, b. Manning, S.C., July 28, 1909; A.B., U. S.C., 1932, LL.B., 1934. Admitted to S.C. bar, 1934, U.S. Supreme Ct. bar, 1959, U.S. Tax Ct. bar, 1970; title atty. U.S. Dept. Agr., Charleston, S.C., 1934-36; trial atty. S.C. Pub. Service Authority, Charleston, 1936-41; dist. dir., atty. Rent Control div. Office of Price Adminstrn., Charleston, 1942-52; gen. counsel S.C. Tax Commn., Columbia, 1953-66; partner firm Dial, Jennings, Windham, Thomas & Roberts, and predecessor, Columbia, 1966—. Mem. Nat. Tax Assn., Tax Inst. Am., Phi Delta Phi, Blue Key. Home: 926 Arbutus Dr Columbia SC 29205 Office: Suite 707 Barringer Bldg Main and Washington Sts Columbia SC 29205 Tel (803) 799-9888

WINDOLPH, FRANCIS LYMAN, b. Lancaster, Pa., June 10, 1889; A.B., Franklin and Marshall Coll., 1908, Litt.D. (hon.), 1937. Admitted to Pa. bar, 1911, U.S. Supreme Ct. bar, 1911; individual practice law, Lancaster, 1911—. Mem. Am., Pa., Lancaster (pres. 1942-45) bar assns., Am. Law Inst., Am. Judicature Soc., Pa. Hist. Soc., Phi Beta Kappa; fellow Am. Coll. Trial Lawyers. Author: The Country Lawyer: Essays in Democracy, 1938; Leviathan and Natural Law, 1951; Reflections of the Law in Literature, 1956; Obiter Scripta, 1971; Selected Essays, 1972; Selected Poems, 1972; Four Portraits from Memory, 1973; Obiter Postscripta, 1974. Contbr. articles to Atlantic Monthly and Am. Scholar. Home: 1040 Woods Ave Lancaster PA 17603 Office: 121 E King St Lancaster PA 17602 Tel (717) 299-7374

WINDOM, STEPHEN RALPH, b. Florence, S.C., Nov. 6, 1949; B.S. in Commerce and Bus. Adminstrn., U. Ala., 1971, J.D., 1974. Admitted to Ala. bar, 1974, U.S. Dist. Ct. So. Dist. Ala., 1974; partner firm McDermott, Slepian, Windom & Reed, Mobile, Ala., 1974—; asso. legal counsel Ala. Jaycees, 1976—; legal counsel Mobile Jaycees, 1976—. Pres. Mobile County Young Democrats, 1975-77; bd. dirs. Mobile Mental Health Assn., 1975-77; pres. Mobile br. Cystic Fibrosis Found., 1977—. Mem. Mobile, Am., Ala. bar assns., Jasons, Bench and Bar, Farrah Law Soc., Omicron Delta Kappa. Home: 6222 Parkwood Dr Mobile AL 36608 Office: PO Drawer 2025 Mobile AL 36601 Tel (205) 432-1671

WINDRUM, CARL KEITH, b. Dawson, Nebr., Mar. 16, 1921; B.S., U. Nebr., 1946, LL.B., 1948. Admitted to Nebr. bar, 1948; individual practice law, Gothenburg, Nebr., 1948-72; judge 13th Jud. Dist. Ct. Nebr., North Platte, 1972—. Tel 534-5340

WINER, DAVID LOUIS, b. Lithuania, Aug. 18, 1904; B.S., Harvard U., 1926; J.D., Boston U., 1930. Admitted to Mass. bar, 1930; asst. atty. gen. State of Mass., 1952-58. Pres. New Eng. sect. Nat. Jewish Welfare Bd.; chmn. bd. trustees Lynn (Mass.) Pub. Library; dir. Lynn Community Fund; founder dir. Temple Israel, Swampscott, Mass.; corp. mem. Union Hosp., Lynn. Mem. Lynn Bar Assn., Mass. Trial Lawyers Assn. Home: 16 Pierce Rd Lynn MA 01902 Office: 156 Broad St Lynn MA 01901 Tel (617) 593-8370

WINFIELD, RICHARD NEILL, b. Chgo., Jan. 20, 1933; A.B., Villanova U., 1955; LL.B., Georgetown U., 1961. Admitted to Va. bar, 1961, N.Y. bar, 1962; asso. Donovan Leisure Newton & Irvine, N.Y.C., 1961-65; asst. counsel to Gov. Nelson Rockefeller, Albany, N.Y., 1965-67; partner firm Rogers & Wells, N.Y.C., 1967—; spl. counsel N.Y. State Pub. Employment Relations Bd., 1967; co-counsel Gov.'s Com. on Pub. Employment Relations, 1968-69; instr. U.S. Naval Acad., 1957-59, Pace Coll., N.Y.C., 1965. Mem. St. Luke's Sch. Bd., N.Y.C., 1974—. Mem. Am., N.Y. State bar assns., Assn. Bar City N.Y. Home: 40 Fifth Ave New York City NY 10011 Office: Rogers & Wells 200 Park Ave New York City NY 10017 Tel (212) 972-5490

WINGATE, HENRY TRAVILLION, b. Jackson, Miss., Jan. 6, 1947; B.A., Grinnell Coll., 1969; J.D., Yale U., 1972. Admitted to Miss. bar, 1973; Law Students Civil Rights Research Council fellow, law clk. firm Banks, Anderson and Nichols, Jackson, 1970; law clk. New Haven Legal Assistance, 1971-72, Community Legal Aid, Jackson, 1972-73; criminal trial atty., sr. asst. def. counsel Naval Legal Services Office USN, Norfolk, Va., 1973-76, prosecutor, 1976; spl. asst. atty. gen. Miss., Jackson, 1976—; instr. bus. law Golden Gate U., 1975-76; course designer, lectr. Tidewater Community Coll., spring 1976. Mem. Miss. State Bar, Miss. Young Lawyers, NAACP, Nat. Naval Officers Assn. NSF summer scholar, 1964. Home: 6018 Huntview Dr Jackson MS 39206 Office: Miss Atty Gen Office Jackson MS 39205 Tel (601) 354-7130

WINICK, MARVIN, b. Des Moines, Mar. 7, 1933; B.S. in Accounting, U. Iowa, 1954, J.D., 1959. Admitted to Iowa bar, 1959; asso. firm Peat, Marwick, Mitchell & Co., Des Moines, 1959-60; partner firm Swift, Brown & Winick, Des Moines, 1960—; instr. Drake U. Law Sch., 1975, accounting dept. U. Iowa, 1957-59; mem. Iowa State Bd. Tax Rev., 1969-71. Pres. Tifereth Israel Synagogue, 1975—; mem. adv. bd. Mercy Hosp. Mem. Am., Iowa (chmn. com. taxation 1970-73), Polk County bar assns. Home: 1912 76th St Des Moines IA 50322 Office: 1200 Register & Tribune Bldg Des Moines IA 50309 Tel (515) 283-2076

WINIKATES, CHARLES JOHN, b. Chgo., July 21, 1927; B.S., U. Ill., 1950; J.D., So. Methodist U., 1950. Admitted to Tex. bar, 1950, U.S. Supreme Ct. bar, 1960; practice in Dallas, 1950—, mem. firm Kennmer and Winikates, 1958-62, Cooper & Winikates, 1968-75, Winikates & Love, 1975—; dir. Prosper State Bank, Prosper, Tex., 1965—, chmn. bd., 1976—; dir. Texmo Corp., 1957—, gen. counsel, 1957—, pres., 1957—. Dir. Catholic Charities. Mem. State Bar of Tex., Am., Dallas bar assns assns., Am., Dallas, Tex. trial lawyers assns. Home: 5948 Melshire St Dallas TX 75230 Office: 2535 Republic Nat Bank Tower Dallas TX 75201 Tel (214) 747-7555

WINIKOFF, S. ASHER, b. Pitts., May 31, 1942; B.S., Pa. State U., 1964; J.D., Duquesne U., 1967. Admitted to Pa. bar, 1968; dep. atty. gen. Pa., 1967-69; gen. counsel Pa. Human Relations Commn., 1969-72; practice law, Pitts., 1972—; mem. firm Rosenberg, Kirshner & Kaleugher. Mem. Allegheny, Pa. bar assns. Office: 803 Law & Finance Bldg Pittsburgh PA 15217 Tel (412) 281-4256

WININGER, DAVID DELEAL, b. Birmingham, Ala., Aug. 21, 1941; B.S., Samford U., 1962; LL.B., Cumberland Sch. Law, 1964. Admitted to Ala. bar, 1964, U.S. Supreme Ct. bar, 1970; individual practice law, 1964-66; partner firm Tarter & Wininger, Birmingham, 1966-75; individual practice law, Birmingham, 1975—; spl. judge Jefferson County (Ala.) Civil Ct., 1969-74. Pres. Retinitis Pigmentosa Found., Birmingham, 1975-76; legal advisor Ala. Heart Assn., 1972; mem. exec. com. Ala. Spl. Olympics, 1970-75; bd. advisors Birmingham YMCA, 1965-69, Ala. Hist. Commn., 1972-76; bd. dirs. Ala. Jr. Miss Pageant, 1971-73; pres. Ala. Jaycee Found. Retarded Children, 1969-70; v.p. Cystic Fibrosis Found., 1973. Mem. Am. Judicature Soc., Assn. Trial Lawyers Am. (nat. pres. young lawyers sect. 1970-71, nat. bd. trustees 1975—), Am. Bar Assn., Ala. Trial Lawyers Assn. (columnist Jour., gov. 1974-76), Birmingham Trial Lawyers Assn. (pres. 1976), Pi Kappa Alpha (dist. pres. 1969-70). Office: 2101 City Federal Bldg Birmingham AL 35203

WINKLE, DENNIS ARTHUR, b. Beatrice, Nebr., June 16, 1937; B.S. in Law, U. Nebr., 1964, J.D., 1964. Admitted to Nebr. bar, 1964; practiced in Pickrell, Nebr., 1964; judge Gage County (Nebr.) Ct., 1964-77; mem. region 14 Nebr. Regional Crime Commn. Vice chmn. Gage County Democratic Central Com., 1960-62, chmn., 1962-64; mem. Nebr. Com. for Children and Youth. Mem. Am., Nebr. bar assns., Nebr. County Judges Assn. (pres. 1971-73), Internat. Footprint Assn., Nat. Council Juvenile Ct. Judges, Nebr. Juvenile Ct. Judges Assn., Nat. Council on Crime, Delinquency, Am. Judicature Soc. Recipient Jurisprudence award Bancroft-Witney Pub. Co., 1964, citation of Meritorious Service Am. Legion Bitting-Norman Post 27, 1967, award Beatrice PTA, 1971. Home: 1403 Washington St Beatrice NE 68310 Office: Gage County Courthouse Beatrice NE 68310 Tel (402) 223-2137

WINKLER, BERTRAM MONROE, b. N.Y.C., May 5, 1916; A.B. U. N.C., 1938; J.D., St. John's U., 1941. Admitted to N.Y. State bar, 1942, U.S. Supreme Ct. bar, 1955, U.S. Ct. Mil. Appeals bar, 1955; partner firm Winkler & Winkler, Bronx, N.Y., 1945—; legal officer JAG Dept., 1955-66, lt. col. USAF, ret. Com. mem. Boy Scouts Am., L.I., N.Y., 1959-63. Mem. Am., Bronx bar assns., Air Force Assn., Res. Officers Assn., Ret. Officers Assn., U. N.C. Alumni Assn., Am. Arbitration Assn. Home: 17 N Pasture Westport CT 06880 Office: 305 E 204th St Bronx NY 10467 Tel (212) 547-7100

WINKLER, DAGNY KARIN, b. Norway, Jan. 13; B.A., U. Calif., Berkeley, 1965, J.D., 1969; student U. Oslo, 1968. Admitted to Calif. bar, 1972; tax technician IRS, 1965-66; dep. dist. atty., Alameda County, Calif., 1972-75; now with legal dept. Wells Fargo Bank, San Francisco; dir. Queen's Bench, 1974-76; sec., dir. Queen's Bench Found., 1975-76, pres., 1976-77. Mem. Am., Calif., Alameda County bar assns., Nat. Assn. Women Lawyers, Calif. Women Lawyers (founding), Nordmanns Forbundet Internat. Assn. (officer 1972-74). Recipient Am. Judicature award, 1969; asso. editor Alameda County Bar Bull., 1974-75. Office: Legal Dept Wells Fargo Bank 475 Sansome St 16th Floor San Francisco CA 94111 Tel (415) 396-0123 also (415) 655-3099

WINKLER, MORTON NORMAN, b. N.Y.C., Dec. 1, 1910; student L.I. U., 1930-33; LL.B., Bklyn. Law Sch., 1936. Admitted to N.Y. State bar, 1938; asso., mng. clk. firm Henry B. Lamm, Esq., N.Y.C., 1934-36; mem., mng. atty. firm Lipton & Lipton, N.Y.C., 1936-38; sr. partner firm Winkler & Winkler, Bronx, N.Y., 1945—; cons. N.Y. State Housing Dept., N.Y.C., 1954; spl. rep. U.S. Senate subcom. on anti-trust and monopoly, 1955; arbitrator Small Claim Div. N.Y.C. Civil Ct., 1965—. Mem. Bronx County Bar Assn., Arbitrator's Assn. Am., Am. Judges Assn. Home: 47 Margaret Dr Valley Stream Long Island NY 11508 Office: 305 E 204th St Bronx NY 19467 Tel (212) 547-7100

WINKLER, PETER AMIL, b. N.Y.C., May 5, 1946; B.A. in Polit. Sci., State U. N.Y., Stonybrook, 1968; J.D., N.Y. U., 1972. Admitted to Ariz. bar, 1972; partner firm Lewis & Roca, Phoenix, 1972—. Legis. and campaign advisor Ariz. State Senator James P. Walsh, 1974—. Mem. Ariz. State Bar (com. on bankruptcy and continuing edn. 1972—), Am., Maricopa County bar assns. Home: 5725 N 13th Pl Phoenix AZ 85014 Office: 100 W Washington St Phoenix AZ 85003 Tel (602) 262-5311

WINKLES, DEWEY FRANK, b. Thomaston, Ga., Apr. 3, 1946; B.A., U. South Fla., 1969; J.D., U. Fla., 1972. Admitted to Fla. bar, 1972; law clk. to judge U.S. Dist. Ct., Middle Dist. Fla., 1972-73; asst. U.S. atty. Middle Dist. Fla., 1973-75; partner firm Winkles & Trombley, Tampa, Fla., 1975—; instr. in speech U. South Fla. Mem. Am., Hillsborough County (Fla.) bar assns., Fla. Bar (continuing legal edn. rep. 1975—), U. South Fla. Alumni Assn. (dir.), Phi Delta Phi, Sigma Alpha Epsilon, Omicron Delta Kappa (charter pres. local chpt.). Named Outstanding Sr. U. South Fla., 1969. Home: 13316 Lake George Ln Tampa FL 33617 Office: 412 Madison St Suite 100 Tampa FL 33601 Tel (813) 228-7621

WINN, B(URKHARD) DANIEL, b. N.Y.C., Jan. 20, 1915; B.A., Columbia, 1935; J.D., Bklyn. Law Sch., 1938. Admitted to N.Y. bar, 1938, N.J. bar, 1970; claim supt. Employers' Group Ins. Cos., N.Y. State, 1942-54; mgr. law dept. Zurich Ins. Co. (N.Y.), 1954-59, claim supt., 1960-62, claims counsel, 1962-64; comml. claims mgr. Nationwide Ins. Co., White Plains, N.Y., 1964-72, regional claims atty. N.Y. State and N.J., Jamaica, N.Y., 1972—; spl. pre-trial master Civil Ct. N.Y. County, 1966-68; mem. industry com. N.Y. No-Fault Claims Implementation, 1974—; chmn. claims com. M.V. Accident Indemnification Corp., N.Y.C., 1975-76. Pres., River Edge (N.J.) Little League, 1958, Oradell (N.J.) Babe Ruth League, 1964; v.p. River Dell Regional Bd. Edn., Oradell, 1963-69. Mem. N.Y. State, N.J. bar assns., N.Y. Claims Assn. (chmn. auto com.), Phi Delta Phi. Contbr. to Nationwide Claimsman mag. Home: 248 Country Club Dr Oradell NJ 07649 Office: 89-02 Sutphin Blvd Jamaica NY 11435 Tel (212) 297-7010

WINN, ELLENE GLENN, b. Clayton, Ala.; B.A., Agnes Scott Coll., 1931; M.A., Radcliffe Coll. Harvard, 1932; LL.B., Birmingham Sch. Law, 1941. Admitted to Ala. bar, 1941; asso. firm Bradley, Arant, Rose and White and predecessor, Birmingham, 1942-56, partner, 1957—. Trustee Birmingham Civic Opera Assn., 1955—, Birmingham Music Club, 1965—. Home: 715 Fairway Dr Birmingham AL 35213 Office: 1500 Brown-Marx Bldg Birmingham AL 35213 Tel (205) 252-4500

WINN, JAMES JULIUS, JR., b. Colon, Panama, Nov. 7, 1941; A.B., Princeton, 1964; J.D. cum laude, Washington and Lee U., 1970. Admitted to Md. bar, 1970; asso. firm Piper & Marbury, Balt., 1970—; mem. panel Washington and Lee U. Legal Ethics Inst., spring 1976. Vestryman St. John's Ch. Western Run Parish, Glyndon, Md., 1974—. Mem. Md., Am. bar assns., Bar Assn. Balt. City. Asso. editor Washington and Lee Law Rev., 1969-70. Office: 25 S Charles St Baltimore MD 21201 Tel (301) 539-2530

WINNER, GEORGE HENRY, b. Elmira, N.Y., May 27, 1910; A.B., Williams Coll., 1932; LL.B., Cornell U., 1935, LL.D. Admitted to N.Y. bar, 1936; partner firm Winding & Winner, Elmira, 1936-44; partner firm Sullivan, Winner & Sullivan, Elmira, 1946-65, firm Winner, Sullivan & DeLaney, Elmira, 1965—; corp. counsel City of Elmira, 1940-53. Mem. N.Y. (past v.p.), Chemung County (past pres.) bar assns. Home: 650 Edgewood Dr Elmira NY 14905 Office: 110 Baldwin St Elmira NY Tel (607) RE4-8144

WINNER, JOHN DENNETT, b. Port Washington, Wis., Sept. 10, 1921; B.A., U. Wis., 1943, J.D., 1949. Admitted to Wis. bar, 1949, U.S. Supreme Ct. bar, 1957; asso. firm Roberts, Roe & Boardman, Madison, Wis., 1948-56; dist. atty. Dane County, Wis., 1956-57; dep. atty. gen. State of Wis., 1957-59; partner firm Winner, McCallum & Hendee, Madison, 1959—; staff judge adv. Wis. N.G., 1959-62. Mem. State Bar Wis., Dane County (pres. 1975-76) Am. bar assns., Ins. Trial Counsel Wis., Def. Research Inst., Internat. Assn. Ins. Counsel. Home: 1222 Gilbert Rd Madison WI 53711 Office: 111 S Fairchild St Madison WI 53703 Tel (608) 257-0257

WINNER, LARRY DUANE, b. Durango, Colo., Oct. 16, 1944; A.B. with honors, Gonzaga U., 1966, J.D., 1970. Admitted to Wash. bar, 1970, U.S. Dist. Ct. Eastern Dist. Wash., 1970; law clk. contract legal research, Spokane, Wash., 1969-70; asst. corp. counsel City of Spokane, 1970—; mem. faculty part-time Gonzaga Law Sch., 1974-76; guest lectr. engring. dept. Wash. State U. and Spokane Community Coll. Mem. Spokane County Bar Assn. (citizenship/law day com., 1971), Wash. State Assn. Municipal Attys. (environ. law com., speaker 1972-76). Home: E 912 26th Ave Spokane WA 99203 Office: 604 City Hall North 221 Wall St Spokane WA 99201 Tel (509) 456-2669

WINNINGHAM, PIERCE, JR., b. Jackson, Tenn., Mar. 1, 1917; J.D., Vanderbilt U., 1940. Admitted to Tenn. bar, 1940, U.S. Supreme Ct., 1955; individual practice law, Jackson, 1940-44, 55—; partner firm Waldrop, Hall & Winningham, Jackson, 1946-55. Mem. Jackson, Tenn., Am. bar assns., Order of Coif. Home: 268 Greenfield Dr apt B Jackson TN 38301 Office: 104-106 Lawyers Bldg Jackson TN 38301 Tel (901) 424-3356

WINOGRAD, DANIEL MARK, b. Greeley, Colo., June 9, 1948; B.A., Colo. Coll., 1970; J.D., U. Chgo., 1973. Admitted to Ill. bar, 1973, U.S. Dist. Ct. bar, 1973, U.S. Ct. of Appeals bar, 1974; asso. firm Elson, Lassers & Wolff, Chgo., 1973—; chmn. Cook County Ct. Watching Project, 1975—; hearing officer Chgo. Bd. of Edn., 1976—. Mem. Ill., Chgo. bar assns., Chgo. Council Lawyers, Am. Judicature Soc. Home: 5557 S Harper Ave Chicago IL 60637 Office: 11 S LaSalle St Chicago IL 60637 Tel (312) 372-5461

WINSBERG, KENNETH ALAN, b. Chgo., July 2, 1942; B.A., U. Ill., 1964; J.D., Northwestern U., 1967. Admitted to Ill. bar, 1967, Ariz. bar, 1972; staff atty. Legal Aid Bur., Chgo., 1967-68; partner firm Cheche & Thrasher, Phoenix, 1972-74; individual practice law, Phoenix, 1974—. Mem. Am., Maricopa County, Ariz. bar assns. Home: 841 E Harmont Dr Phoenix AZ 85021 Office: 2333 N 3d St Phoenix AZ 85004 Tel (602) 257-0680

WINSLOW, THOMAS ARTHUR, b. Dover, N.H., Aug. 1, 1947; B.A., Providence Coll., 1969; J.D., Fordham U., 1972. Admitted to N.Y. State bar, 1973, U.S. Supreme Ct. bar, 1977; asso. firm Kreindler, Relkin & Goldberg, N.Y.C., 1973-77, partner, 1977—; mem. panel arbitrators Am. Arbitration Assn., 1976—. Mem. law com. N.Y. Republican County Com., 1976—. Mem. Assn. Bar City N.Y., N.Y. State, Am. bar assns., N.Y. County Lawyers Assn. Home: 57 W 68th St New York City NY 10023 Office: 500 5th Ave New York City NY 10036 Tel (212) 594-9600

WINSTON, HAROLD RONALD, b. Atlantic, Iowa, Feb. 7, 1932; B.A., U. Iowa, 1954, J.D., 1958. Admitted to Iowa bar, 1958, U.S. Tax Ct. bar, 1960, U.S. Supreme Ct. bar, 1969; trust officer United Home Bank and Trust Co., Mason City, Iowa, 1958-59; individual practice law, Mason City, 1960-73; partner firm Winston, Schroeder & Reuber, Mason City, 1973—; police judge Mason City, 1961-73. Active United Fund, YMCA, Cerro Gordo Crippled Children. Mem. Am. Coll. Probate Counsel, Am., Iowa State, Cerro Gordo County, 2d Jud. Dist. bar assns., Am. Judicature Soc., Assn. Trial Lawyers Am. Home: 118 Linden Dr Mason City IA 50401 Office: 119 2d St NW Mason City IA 50401 Tel (515) 423-1913

WINSTON, JOHN GARY, b. Butte, Mont., July 15, 1932; B.S., Western Mont. Coll. Edn., 1959; postgrad. Kans. State Tchrs. Coll., 1961-62, U. Mo., 1961; J.D., Gonzaga U., 1971. Admitted to Mont. bar, 1971; mem. firm Hennessey & Winston, Butte, 1972; individual practice law, Butte, 1972—. Mem. Am. Trial Lawyers Assn., Mont. Bar Assn. Home: 925 W Woolman St Butte MT 59701 Office: Court House Butte MT 59701 Tel (406) 792-2383

WINSTON, ROBERT WARN, JR., b. St. Louis, Sept. 18, 1939; B.A. in Fin., U. Wash., 1961, J.D., 1966. Admitted to Wash. bar, 1966; law clk. to judge U.S. Dist. Ct. Eastern Dist. Wash., 1966-67; asso. firm Winston, Cashatt, Repsold, McNichols, Connelly & Driscoll, Spokane, Wash., 1967-71, partner, 1971—. Trustee Spokane County Legal Service, Spokane, 1968-72; mem. planning com. United Crusade, Spokane, 1970-74; trustee Western Wash. State Coll., 1970—; mem. Greater Spokane Community Found., 1976—; chmn. northeastern br. Children's Home Soc. Wash., Spokane, 1975-76, bd. dirs., 1975—; Wash. del. White House Conf. on Children, 1970, on Youth, 1971. Mem. Am., Wash. (vice chmn. young lawyers sect. 1970), Spokane County (chmn. young lawyers com. 1968-72) bar assns., Wash. Council Sch. Attys. (trustee 1976—), Nat. Sch. Bds. Assn. (council sch. attys. 1976—), Phi Delta Phi. Home: S 4529 Napa St Spokane WA 99203 Office: Spokane and Eastern Bldg Spokane WA 99201 Tel (509) 838-6131

WINSTON, WILLIAM DARRACOTT, b. Crosby, Tex., July 25, 1932; B.B.A., U. Tex., 1953, LL.B., 1959. Admitted to Tex. bar, 1958; individual practice law, Lufkin, Tex. Chmn. bd. Angelina County chpt. ARC, 1966-72; area dir. Tex. Youth Conf.; pres. Angelina County Cancer Soc., 1964; state rep. Tex. Legis., 1958-60. Mem. Am., Tex., Angelina County (v.p. 1976—), Deep East Tex. Estate Counsel (sec. 1965), Phi Alpha Delta. Home: 1515 Hamony Hill Dr Lufkin TX 75901 Office: PO Box 365 Lufkin TX 75901 Tel (713) 632-1900

WINSTON, WILLIAM LITTLETON, b. Richmond, Va., Aug. 7, 1923; student Randolph-Macon Coll., 1941-43; LL.B., U. Va., 1948. Admitted to Va. bar, 1948; practice law, Arlington, Va., 1948-66; judge Circuit Ct. Arlington County (Va.), 1966—; mem. Va. Gen. Assembly, 1956-66. Mem. Wash. Met. Council Govts. 1961-66; mem. Jud. Inquiry and Rev. Commn., 1977—. Mem. Arlington County (pres. 1963), Va. State, Am. bar assns., Order of Coif. Named alumnus of year Randolph-Macon Coll., 1976. Home: 304 N Highland St Arlington VA 22201 Office: Arlington Courthouse Arlington VA 22201 Tel (703) 558-2505

WINTER, DONALD FRANCIS, b. Teaneck, N.J., June 11, 1941; B.A., Harvard, 1963, J.D., 1966. Admitted to Mass. bar, 1966; asso. firm Palmer & Dodge, Boston, 1966-72, partner, 1973—. Chmn., Boston Back Bay Archtl. Commn., 1970—. Mem. Boston, Am., Mass. bar assns. Home: 102 Appleton St Boston MA 02116 Office: 1 Beacon St Boston MA 02108 Tel (617) 227-4400

WINTER, GALEN DAVID, b. Shawano, Wis., Aug. 29, 1926; B.S., U. Wis., 1948, J.D., 1950. Admitted to Wis. bar, 1950, Ill. bar, 1969; asst. mgr. Latin Am. office Ins. Co. of N.Am., Mexico City, 1952-54; asst. mgr. internat. reins. div. Lincoln Nat. Life, Ft. Wayne, Ind., 1955-60; asst. sec. legal dept. Old Line Life Ins. Co. Am., Milw., 1960-65; asst. gen. counsel, asst. v.p. Gen. Fin. Corp., Evanston, Ill., 1965-70; partner firm Winter, Bartholomew & Greenhill, Shawano, 1970—. Pres., Shawano County Arts Council, 1974-75. Mem. Shawano County Bar Assn. (pres. 1976-77), Ill., Wis. bar assns. Home: 204 S LaFayette St Shawano WI 54166 Office: 104 W 4th St Shawano WI 54166

WINTER, JAMES DAVID, b. Louisville, Mar. 23, 1925; B.A., U. Louisville, 1945, LL.B., 1949; LL.M., N.Y. U., 1950. Admitted to Ky. bar, 1949, Ariz. bar, 1959, U.S. Supreme Ct. bar, 1971; asso. firm Davis, Boehl, Viser & Marcus, Louisville, 1949; atty. advisor USAF, Wright Patterson AFB, Ohio, 1953-55; chief atty. Electronic Proving Ground Procurement Office, Ft. Huachuca, Ariz., 1955-60; individual practice law, Tucson, 1960-65; asst. atty. gen. Ariz. Atty. Gen. Office, Phoenix, 1965-74, chief counsel tax div., 1975—; spl. agt. Office of Price Stblzn., Louisville and Cleve., 1952-53. City magistrate, Tucson, 1963; mem. exec. com. Grand Canyon chpt. Sierra Club, 1975-76, outings chmn., 1974-76; mem. Heard Mus. Assn., 1973-76; mem. trails com. Ariz. Parks Bd., 1975-76. Mem. Ky., Ariz., Am. (taxation sect. com. on state and local taxes), Fed., Maricopa County bar assns., Nat. Assn. Tax Adminstrs. (chmn. atty. sect. 1975-76). Home: 8309 E Rose Ln Scottsdale AZ 85253 Office: 338 State Capitol Bldg Phoenix AZ 85007 Tel (602) 271-4681

WINTER, RICHARD T., b. Antigo, Wis., Aug. 21, 1934; B.A., U. Wis., 1959, LL.B., 1962. Admitted to Wis. bar, 1962; partner firm Winter & Winter, Antigo, 1962—; city atty. City of Antigo, 1972—. Mem. Wis. Bar Assn. Office: 815 Fifth Ave Antigo WI 54409 Tel (715) 623-2905

WINTER, ROBERT H., b. Bklyn., Sept. 21, 1941; A.B., Columbia U., 1962; B.A., Oriel Coll. (Oxford, Eng.), M.A., 1964; LL.B., Harvard U., 1967. Admitted to N.Y. State bar, D.C. bar; law clk. to judge U.S. Ct. Appeals, 1967-68; partner firm Arnold & Porter, Washington, 1968—. Home: 10404 Crossing Creek Rd Potomac MD 20854 Office: 1225 Nineteenth St NW Washington DC 20036 Tel (202) 872-6820

WINTER, WILLIAM FORREST, b. Grenada, Miss., Feb. 21, 1923; B.A., U. Miss., 1943, LL.B., 1949. Admitted to Miss. bar, 1949, D.C. bar, 1974; individual practice law, Grenada, Miss., 1949-58; partner firm Watkins, Pyle, Ludlam, Winter & Stennis, Jackson, Miss., 1968—, mng. partner, 1975—; mem. Miss. Ho. of Reps., 1948-56; tax collector State of Miss., 1956-64, state treas., 1964-68, lt. gov., 1972-76. Pres. bd. trustees Miss. Dept. Archives History, 1969—; trustee Belhaven Coll., 1960—, Piney Woods Sch., 1974—. Mem. Am., D.C., Miss., Hinds County (Miss.) bar assns., Scribes, Phi Delta Phi. Editor-in-chief Miss. Law Jour., 1948-49, contbr. articles, 1952-70. Office: Watkins Pyle Ludlam Winter Stennis 20th Floor Deposit Guaranty Plaza Jackson MI 39205 Tel (601) 354-3456

WINTERER, PHILIP STEELE, b. San Francisco, July 8, 1931; B.A., Amherst Coll., 1953; LL.B., Harvard, 1956. Admitted to N.Y. State bar, 19S7, Republic of Korea bar, 1958; asso. firm Debevoise, Plimpton, Lyons & Gates, N.Y.C., 1956-65, partner, 1966—. Mem. Am. Law Inst., Assn. Bar City N.Y., Am., N.Y. State bar assns. Home: 1165 Fifth Ave New York City NY 10029 Office: 299 Park Ave New York City NY 10017 Tel (212) 752-6400

WINTERS, JAMES WILLETT, b. Gainesville, Ga., Feb. 3, 1930; B.S., Davidson Coll., 1951; LL.B., Stetson U., 1957. Admitted to Fla. bar, 1957; partner firm Winters, Brackett Lord & Held, West Palm Beach, Fla., 1959—; judge Lake Clarke Shores (Fla.) Municipal Ct., 1960; mem. Lake Charles Shores Town Council, 1962; lectr. in field. Mem. Palm Beach County, Fla. (exec. com. sect. real property and probate) bars, Am. Bar Assn. Office: 218 Datura St West Palm Beach FL 33402 Tel (305) 655-8631

WINTERS, JOHN MILTON, b. Omaha, Mar. 29, 1930; B.S. in Bus. Adminstrn., Creighton U., 1952, LL.B., 1957; S.J.D., U. Mich., 1961. Admitted to Nebr. bar, 1957, Wis. bar, 1966, Calif. bar, 1971; asst. to asso. prof. law Marquette U., Milw., 1960-65; prof. law U. San Diego, 1965—; lectr. U. So. Calif. Environ. Mgmt. Inst., 1973-76; prof. Sch. Pub. Adminstrn., San Diego State U., 1975—. Chmn., Comprehensive Planning Orgn. Com. for Tidelands Ownership and Pub. Trust Inventory, 1973—. Mem. Am., Calif., San Diego County bar assns., Law and Soc. Assn., San Diego C. of C. (growth mgmt. adv. com. 1976). Author: State Constitutional Limitations on Solutions of Metropolitan Area Problems, 1961; contbr. articles in field to legal jours. Home: 9052 Walker Ct San Diego CA 92123 Office: U San Diego Sch Law Alcala Park San Diego CA 92110 Tel (714) 291-6480

WINTERS, RAYMOND LEONARD, b. Bakersfield, Calif., July 10, 1929; B.S.B.A., U. Calif., Los Angeles, 1951, J.D., 1954. Admitted to Calif. bar, 1957, U.S. Supreme Ct. bar, 1965; individual practice law, Redondo Beach, Calif., 1958—; city prosecutor, dep. city atty. City of Redondo Beach, 1960-64. Bd. dirs. S. Coast Botanic Garden Found., 1961-75, Palos Verdes Community Arts Assn., 1971-76, Vol. Bur.-South Bay-Harbor Area, 1971—; mem. Palos Verdes Estates (Calif.) Planning Commn., 1974—. Mem. State Bar Calif., Los Angeles County, South Bay bar assns. Office: Suite 206 1611 S Pacific Coast Hwy Redondo Beach CA 90277 Tel (213) 540-2050

WINTON, CRANE, b. Mpls., June 27, 1926; A.B., Harvard, 1948, LL.B., 1951. Admitted to Minn. bar, 1951; judge Mpls. and Hennepin County Municipal Ct., Mpls., 1962-67, Hennepin County Dist. Ct., 4th Jud. Dist., Mpls., 1962—. Pres., Travelers Aid Soc., 1956-62, Northside Settlement Services, Inc., 1960; trustee Mpls. Athenaeum, 1968—. Mem. Internat. Acad. Trial Judges (chancellor, regent), Dist. Ct. Judges Assn. (chmn. rules com.). Home: 1307 Mount Curve Ave Minneapolis MN 55403 Office: 1853 Govt Center Minneapolis MN 55487 Tel (612) 348-2618

WINTON, GLEN PETER, b. Evanston, Ill., Oct. 16, 1930; B.S. in Chem. Engring., Northwestern U., 1953; J.D., John Marshall Law Sch., 1969. Admitted to Ill. bar, 1969, U.S. Patent and Trademark Office bar, 1970; engr. Universal Oil Products Co., Des Plaines, Ill., 1953-65, mem. corporate patent dept., 1965-70; mgr. patent liaison and licensing, films packaging div. Union Carbide Corp., Chgo., 1970—. Mem. Licensing Execs. Soc., Ill., Am. bar assns., Am. Patent Law Assn., Patent Law Assn. Chgo. Home: 9501 N Terrace Pl Des Plaines IL 60016 Office: 6733 W 65th St Chicago IL 60638 Tel (312) 496-4737

WIRSCHING, DAVID BIRCH, JR., b. Dallas, Jan. 22, 1932; B.B.A., Va. Poly. Inst. and State U., 1957; J.D., U. Akron, 1965. Admitted to Ohio bar, 1965; with The Timken Co., Canton, Ohio, 1957—, beginning as accountant, successively cashier supr. accounts payable, systems analyst, supr. home office accounting, asst. office mgr., 1957-69, personnel dir., 1969—. Chmn. fin. div. Central Stark County United Fund, 1974-75, 76; mem. Stark County Econ. Devel. Adv. Com., 1976-77; chmn. Canton-Stark-Wayne County Manpower Consortium, 1974-76; bd. dirs. Greater Canton chpt. ARC. Mem. Ohio, Stark County bar assns., Am. Soc. Personnel Adminstrn., Stark County Personnel Assn., Greater Canton C. of C., Conf. Bd., Am. Mgmt. Assn. Home: 2509 56th St NE Canton OH 44721 Office: 1835 Dueber Ave SW Canton OH 44706 Tel (216) 453-4511

WIRTH, ROBERT JOHN, b. Defiance County, Ohio, July 27, 1918; B.A., Ohio State U., 1940, J.D., 1941; grad. FBI Acad., Quantico, Va., 1942. Admitted to Ohio bar, 1944, N.Y. bar, 1946, N.Mex. bar, 1955, U.S. Supreme Ct. bar, 1963; spl. agt. FBI, also investigator, adminstr., legal officer, instr., Washington, Boston, N.Y.C. and Albuquerque, 1941-73; asst. dir. Center Criminal Justice Studies, U. Albuquerque, also asso. prof. law and criminology, 1973—; contract guest lectr. N.Mex. Law Enforcement Acad., Santa Fe, 1974—; mem. Gov.'s Statewide Com. Developing Standards and Goals for Criminal Justice, 1976, chmn. law enforcement sub-com. standards and goals for criminal justice system in N.Mex., 1976; vice chmn. Albuquerque Met. Criminal Justice Coordinating Council, 1975—; chmn. Albuquerque Crime Prevention Council, 1977—. Mem. N.Mex., N.Y., Ohio bar assns., N.Mex. Sheriffs and Police Assn. Home: 2809 Rio Vista Ct SW Albuquerque NM 87105 Office: U Albuquerque Saint Joseph Pl NW Albuquerque NM 87140 Tel (505) 831-1111

WIRTH, ROGER ALLAN, b. Madison, Wis., May 4, 1946; B.A., U. Wis., 1968, J.D., 1970. Admitted to Wis. bar, 1970, Nev. bar, 1971; law clk. to chief justice Nev. Supreme Ct., Carson City, 1970-71; asso. firm Lionel Sawyer Collins & Wartman, Las Vegas, Nev., 1971-75; partner firm Haley & Wirth, Las Vegas, 1975-77, firm Jolley, Urga & Wirth, Las Vegas, 1977—; instr. legal writing U. Wis. Law Sch., 1969-70, spl. asst. to dean, 1970. Bd. dirs. Nev. chpt. Arthritis Found., 1974—, pres., 1975-76, bd. govs. So. Calif. chpt., 1976—. Mem. Am. (Nev. chmn. com. on appellate procedure), Nev., Wis., Clark County bar assns. Office: 302 E Carson Ave Suite 310 Las Vegas NV 89101 Tel (702) 385-5161

WISE, CHARLES CHILTON, JR., b. Moorefield, W.Va., Apr. 18, 1911; A.B., W.Va. U., 1933, J.D., 1936; postgrad. U. Mich., 1936-37; LL.D., Morris Harvey Coll., 1968. Admitted to W.Va. bar, 1936, U.S. Supreme Ct. bar, 1947; partner firm Love Wise Robinson & Woodroe and predecessors, Charleston, 1937—; gen. counsel, dir., mem. exec. com. Charleston Nat. Bank, 1950—; mem. W.Va. Bd. Law Examiners, 1955-74. Bd. dirs. Morris Harvey Coll., 1955—; bd. dirs. W.Va. U., 1960—, chmn., 1968—; chmn. W.Va. Com. Higher Edn., 1968—; trustee Presbyn. Found., Charlotte, N.C. Mem. Am. (state del. 1954-55), Kanawha County (pres. 1943) bar assns., Am. Law Inst., W.Va. State Bar (pres. 1950), Order of Vandalia, Phi Beta Kappa. Student editor, contbr. W.Va. Law Quar. and Rev., 1934-36. Home: PO Box 951 Charleston WV 25323 Office: 12th Floor Charleston Nat Plaza Charleston WV 25301 Tel (304) 343-4841

WISE, DAVID GLENN, b. Dayton, Ohio, Oct. 3, 1942; B.A., Wittenberg U., 1964; J.D., U. Mich., 1967. Admitted to Ohio bar, 1967, Mich. bar, 1967; asso. firm Spengler, Nathanson, Heyman, McCarthy & Durfee, Toledo, 1967-74, partner, 1974—. Mem. Ohio, Mich., Am., Toledo bar assns., Soc. for Advancement of Mgmt. Office: 935 National Bank Bldg Toledo OH 43604 Tgl (419) 241-2201

WISE, EDMUND N., b. Columbus, Ohio, Mar. 27, 1931; B.A., Yale U., 1953; LL.B., Harvard U., 1956. Admitted to Ohio bar, 1959, D.C. bar, 1964; atty. Devel. Loan Fund, Washington, 1959-61; atty. AID, Washington, 1961-63; partner firm Dutton, Zumas and Wise, Washington, 1963—. Mem. D.C. Bar Assn.

WISE, EDWARD MARTIN, b. N.Y.C., Aug. 8, 1938; B.A., U. Chgo., 1956; LL.B., Cornell U., 1959; LL.M., N.Y. U., 1960. Admitted to N.Y. bar, 1960, Mich. bar, 1973; served with JAGC, U.S. Army, 1960-63; research assoc. N.Y. U. Comparative Criminal Law Project, 1963-64; research fellow Inst. Jud. Adminstrn., N.Y.C., 1964-65; asso. prof. Wayne State U., 1965-68, prof. law, 1968—; exec. bd. Inst. Continuing Legal Edn. (Mich.), 1973-76. Mem. Am., Mich. bar assns., Am. Soc. Legal History, Am. Soc. Internat. Law, Internat. Law Assn., Internat. Assn. Penal Law, Selden Soc., ACLU (dir. Mich. 1969—, dir. Met. Detroit br. 1969—, chmn. 1970-71). Author: (with G.O.W. Mueller) International Criminal Law, 1965; (with D. Karlen and G. Sawer) Anglo-American Criminal Justice, 1967; (with Mueller) Studies in Comparative Criminal Justice, 1975; bd. editors Am. Jour. Comparative Law. Home: 1517 Chateaufort Detroit MI 48207 Office: Wayne State Univ Law School Detroit MI 48202 Tel (313) 577-3941

WISE, GEORGE WALLER, b. Washington, Sept. 2, 1915; A.B., George Washington U., 1936, J.D., 1938. Admitted to D.C. bar, 1938, U.S. Supreme Ct. bar, 1957; spl. asst. to atty. gen. antitrust div. U.S. Dept. Justice, Washington, 1938-55; asso. firm Hogan & Hartson, Washington, 1955-62, partner, 1962—. Mem. Am., D.C. bar assns., Order of Coif. Home: 633 Walker Rd Great Falls VA 22066 Office: 815 Connecticut Ave Washington DC 20006 Tel (202) 331-4689

WISE, HENRY ALEXANDER, JR., b. N.Y.C., Oct. 17, 1909; B.S. in Chemistry, Va. Mil. Inst., 1931; LL.B., Yale, 1934. Admitted to N.Y. bar, 1935, Del. bar, 1941, U.S. Supreme Ct. bar, 1947; asso. firm Austin & Seabury, N.Y.C., 1934-39; gen. counsel, sec. Alleghany Airlines (formerly All Am. Aviation), Wilmington, Del., 1939-42; atty. Del. State Legis., Dover, 1947; partner firm Hastings, Stokely, Walz & Wise, Wilmington, 1947-52; individual practice law, Wilmington, 1952-76; sr. partner firm Wise & Winfield, Wilmington, 1976—; spl. advisor air safety CAA, 1940-42. Mem. Am., Del. bar assns. Home: 1110 N Rodney St Wilmington DE 19806 Tel (302) 571-8700

WISE, HENRY SEILER, b. Mt. Carmel, Ill., July 16, 1909; A.B., LL.B., Washington U., St. Louis, 1933. Admitted to Mo. bar, 1933, Ill. bar, 1934; practice in Danville, Ill., 1934—; mem. firms Jinkins & Jinkins, 1934-37, Meeks & Lowenstein, 1937-42, Meeks & Wise, 1942-51, Graham, Wise, Meyer, Young & Welsch, 1951-66; judge U.S. Dist. Ct., Eastern Dist. Ill., Danville, 1966—. Commr., Ill. Ct. of Claims, 1949-53; mem. Ill. Parole and Pardon Bd., 1961-66. County chmn. Democratic party, 1948-54; del. Dem. nat. conv., 1952, 56, 60, 64. Mem. Am., Ill., Vermilion (Ill.) County bar assns., Am. Judicature Soc., Danville C. of C. Home: 507 Chester Ave Danville IL 61832 Office: US Dist Ct Danville IL 61832*

WISE, JOHN MERTON, b. Peekskill, N.Y., Jan. 17, 1908; J.D., Wayne St. U., 1930. Admitted to Mich. bar, 1930; individual practice law, Detroit, 1930-44; referee Traffic Ct., Detroit, 1944-59; judge Wayne County Circuit Ct., Detroit, 1959—; chmn. Friend of Ct. Com., Marriage Counseling Com. Mem. Am., Mich., Detroit bar assns., Am. Judicature Soc., Mich. Judges' Assn. (com. on circuit cts.), Detroit Police Lts. and Sgts. Assn. (hon.), Traffic Safety Assn. (trustee). Contbr. articles in field to profl. jours. Home: 19611 Renfrow Rd Detroit MI 48221 Office: 1519 City-County Bldg Detroit MI 48226 Tel (313) 224-5195

WISE, LOUIS J., b. Yazoo City, Miss., Apr. 8, 1892; LL.B., U. Miss., 1912; postgrad. Columbia, 1913. Admitted to Miss. bar, 1912; individual practice law, 1912-16; partner firm Wise & Bridgforth, 1916-46; judge Yazoo County (Miss.) Ct., 1954—; mem. Miss. Ho. of Reps., 1926-28. Active State Vets. Farm and Home Bd., 1954-62. Mem. Miss. Bar Assn. Home: 736 5th St Yazoo City MS 39194 Office: Williams Bldg Jefferson St Yazoo City MS 39194 Tel (601) 746-1212

WISE, MARVIN JAY, b. San Antonio, Apr. 6, 1926; B.A., U. Tex., 1945; LL.B., Harvard U., 1949; diploma comparative legal studies, U. Cambridge, 1950. Admitted to Tex. bar, 1949; asso. firm Thompson, Knight, Simmons & Bullion, Dallas, 1950-57; partner firm Wise, Stuhl & Maxwell and predecessor, Dallas, 1957—. Bd. dirs. Dallas Home for Jewish Aged, 1976—, Dallas Mental Health Assn., 1955-60, Dallas Civic Ballet Soc., 1957-61; Dallas UN Assn., 1956-57, Dallas Soc. for Autistic Children, 1969-73. Mem. Dallas, Tex., Am. bar assns. Home: 3444 University St Dallas TX 75205 Office: 2520 Republic Bank Tower Dallas TX 75201 Tel (214) 742-4422

WISE, RAYMOND LEO, b. N.Y.C., June 24, 1895; A.B., Columbia, 1916, LL.B., 1919, J.D., 1969. Admitted to N.Y. bar, 1919, U.S. Supreme Ct. bar, 1943, Fla. bar, 1952; asso. firm Root, Clark, Buckner and Howland, N.Y.C., 1919-20; individual practice law, N.Y.C. and Miami, Fla., 1920—; spl. asst. to U.S. atty. So. Dist. N.Y., 1920-22; dep. asst. atty. gen. State of N.Y., 1929-30; municipal judge, Surfside, Fla., 1964-67. Councilman, Surfside, 1962-64. Mem. ACLU (dir.), Bar Assn. City N.Y., Am., Fla. bar assns. Author: Legal Ethics; Judicial Ethics; asso. editor Columbia Law Rev., 1919; contbr. articles in field to profl. jours. Home: 745 N Shore Dr Miami Beach FL 33141 Tel (305) 866-9045 Office: Suite 614 19 W Flagler St Miami FL 33130

WISE, ROBERT KING, b. Prosperity, S.C., Oct. 21, 1892; A.B., LL.B., Harvard. Admitted to S.C. bar, U.S. Supreme Ct. bar; partner firm Wise, Wise & Shealy. S.C. chmn. USO, WWII. Home: 1709 Hollywood Dr Cola SC 29205

WISE, SHERWOOD WILLING, b. Hazlehurst, Miss., Aug. 13, 1910; B.A., Washington and Lee U., 1932, J.D., 1934. Admitted to Miss. bar, 1934, U.S. Supreme Ct. bar, 1963; asso. firm Wells, Wells & Lipscomb, Jackson, Miss., 1934-41; partner firm Wise Carter Child Steen & Caraway and predecessors, Jackson, 1941-42, 45—; gen. counsel Miss. Power & Light Co., 1961—. Mem. Am. Coll. Trial Lawyers, Am. Coll. Probate Council, Nat. Assn. R.R. Trial Counsel, Edison Electric Inst. Legal Com., Am. (standing com. on fed. judiciary 1969-75), Miss. (pres. 1961), Hinds County (pres. 1957) bar assns., World Assn. Lawyers, Am. Judicature Soc., Nat. Conf. Lawyers and Profl. Engrs., Scribes. Home: 3839 Eastover Dr Jackson MS 39211 Office: 925 Electric Bldg Jackson MS 39205 Tel (601) 354-2385

WISE, WILLIAM JERRARD, b. Chgo., May 27, 1934; B.B.A., U. Mich., 1955, M.B.A., 1958, J.D. with distinction, 1958. Admitted to Ill. bar, 1959; spl. atty. IRS, Milw., 1959-63; asso. firm McDermott Will & Emery, Chgo., 1963-70; partner firm Coles & Wise, Ltd., Chgo., 1971—; instr. John Marshall Law Sch., 1965-68; lectr. Ill. Inst. Continuing Legal Edn., 1975-76. Bd. dirs. Chgo. Blind Service Assn., 1964-74; mem. Winnetka Caucus, 1973-74. Mem. Chgo. Bar Assn. Asst. editor Mich. Law Review, 1957-58; contbr. articles to profl. jours. Home: 1401 Tower Rd Winnetka IL 60093 Office: 1 IBM Plaza Suite 4501 Chicago IL 60611 Tel (312) 565-1177

WISEMAN, RANDOLPH CARSON, b. Staunton, Va., Jan. 25, 1946; B.S., East Tenn. State U., 1968; J.D., Capital U., 1974. Admitted to Ohio bar, 1974; partner firm Tyack Scott Grossman & Wiseman, Columbus, Ohio. Active Big. Bros. Assn., Cancer Soc. Mem. Am., Ohio, Columbus bar assns., Assn. Trial Lawyers Am., Ohio Acad. Trial Lawyers. Notes editor Capital U. Law Rev., 1973-74; editor Docket, Franklin County Trial Lawyers, 1975—; contbr. articles to legal jours. Home: 1831 Hickory Hill Dr Columbus OH 43228 Office: 536 S High St Columbus OH 43215 Tel (614) 221-1341

WISENBAKER, REGINALD CLAUS, b. Valdosta, Ga., Nov. 18, 1933; B.A., Valdosta State Coll., 1969; J.D., Mercer U., 1972. Admitted to Ga. bar, 1972; student asst. Ga. Legal Aid Soc., Macon, Ga., summer 1971; asso. firm Bennett and Wisenbaker, Valdosta, 1972-73, partner, 1973—. Mem. Valdosta, Ga., Am. bar assns., Ga. Trial Lawyers. Home: Route 2 Box 316 Valdosta GA 31601 Office: PO Box 1685 Valdosta GA 31601 Tel (912) 242-6726

WISWALL, WILLIAM HENRY, b. Vancouver, Wash., Jan. 9, 1935; A.A., Clark Jr. Coll., 1954; B.S. in Law, U. Oreg., 1960, J.D., 1962. Admitted to Oreg. bar, 1962, U.S. Dist. Ct. for Dist. Oreg., 1962; law clk. Hon. William East, U.S. Dist. Ct., Portland, Oreg., 1962-63; dep. dist. atty. Lane County, Oreg., 1963-65; partner firm Lively & Wiswall, Springfield, Oreg., 1965—; instr. Eugene Bar Rev. Sch., 1965-71; pro-tem circuit ct. judge. Bd. dirs. Eugene Jaycees, 1965-67; bd. dirs. ARC, 1970, United Way, 1974-76. Mem. Oreg. (bd. govs. 1973-75, v.p. 1975-76), So. Oreg. (pres. 1967-69), Calif. trial lawyers assns., Assn. Trial Lawyers Am., Am. Bd. Trial Advocates. Speaker convs. Home: 3600 Vine Maple St Eugene OR 97405 Office: 644 North A St Springfield OR 97477 Tel (503) 747-3354

WITCHER, ROBERT PEARSON, b. Conway, S.C., Dec. 29, 1945; A.B., U. Ga., 1967, J.D., 1973. Admitted to Ga. bar, 1973; asso. firm Storey & Obenschain, Atlanta, 1973—. Mem. Midtown Neighborhood Assn., Atlanta, 1974—. Mem. Am., Ga., Atlanta bar assns. Home: 400 6th St NE Atlanta GA 30308 Office: 1936 Fulton Nat Bank Bldg Atlanta GA 30303 Tel (404) 522-3825

WITCOFF, SHELDON WILLIAM, b. Washington, July 10, 1925; B.S. in Elec. Engring., U. Md., 1949; J.D., George Washington U., 1953; Admitted to D.C. bar, 1953, N.Y. bar, 1955, Ill. bar, 1956; atty. U.S. Patent Office, 1949-53, Bell Tel. Labs., 1953-55; asso. firm Bair, Freeman & Molinare, Chgo., 1955-65; partner firm Allegretti, Newitt, Witcoff & MacAndrews, Chgo., 1965—. Mem. Skokie (Ill.) Fire and Police Commn., 1960-63. Mem. Am. Bar Assn., Chgo. Patent Law Assn., Bar Assn. 7th Fed. Circuit Ct., Order Coif. Office: 125 S Wacker Dr Chicago IL 60606 Tel (312) 372-2160

WITHAM, PETER MARTIN, b. Knoxville, Tenn., Mar. 16, 1933; B.S. in Gen. Bus., Ind. U., 1955, J.D., 1958. Admitted to Ind. Supreme Ct. bar, 1958, U.S. Supreme Ct. bar, 1976; Krannert asst. Ind. U. Sch. Law, 1957; served with Judge Adv. Gen. Corps, U.S. Army, 1958-61; dep. atty. gen. State of Ind., 1961-65; counsel for claims Eastern Express, Inc., Terre Haute, Ind., 1965-68, regulatory coordinator, 1968—, corp. sec., 1970—; asst. corp. sec. R.C. Motor Lines, Inc., Jacksonville, Fla., 1965—; corp. sec. George W. Brown, Inc., N.Y.C., 1970-75, Eastern Properties, Inc., Terre Haute, 1970—. Mem. Am. Bar Assn., Ind. Motor Truck Assn., Motor Carrier's Lawyers Assn., Nat. Def. Transp. Assn. Home: 1849 S 31st St Terre Haute IN 47803 Tel (812) 232-5321

WITHERS, CARL RAYMOND, b. Reading, Pa., Jan. 26, 1924; A.B., Wittenberg U., 1950; LL.B., U. Mich., 1953. Admitted to Ohio bar, 1954; mem. firm Van Aken, Bond, Withers and Asman, Cleve., 1954—. Mem. Ohio State, Cleve., Vet's. bar assns. Home: 17501 Shaker Blvd Shaker Heights OH 44120 Office: 1028 National City Bank Bldg Cleveland OH 44114 Tel (216) 781-4680

WITHERSPOON, GIBSON BOUDINOTTE, b. Lexington, Va., Aug. 7, 1903; B.A., Washington and Lee U., 1925, J.D., 1927. Admitted to Va. bar, 1926, Miss. bar, 1928, U.S. Supreme Ct. bar, 1950; mem. firm Witherspoon & Bourdeaux, Meridian, Miss., 1947-53, Witherspoon, Compton & Mason, Meridian, 1953—. Miss. commr. Nat. Conf. Commrs. on Uniform State Laws, 1967—. Fellow Am. Bar Found.; mem. Am. (ho. of dels. 1952-73, bd. govs. 1970-73, co-chmn. lawyers and collection agencies of nat. conf. group, adv. bd. jour.), Miss. (chmn. uniform comml. code com., past pres.) bar assns., Scribes (past pres.), Am. Judicature Soc. (past dir.), Nat. Assn. Bar Presidents, Miss., Meridian (dir. 1952-56) chambers commerce. Asso. editor: Commercial Law League America, 1947—. Contbr. articles in field to profl. jours. Home: 2698 23d Ave Meridian MS 39301 Office: 426 Citizens National Bank Bldg Meridian MS 39301 Tel (601) 693-6467 also 693-6466

WITHERSPOON, HELEN ADELE, b. Jackson, Ohio; B.S. in Edn., Ohio State U., also M.A. in Psychology; LL.B., U. Cin. Admitted to Ohio bar, 1940, U.S. Supreme Ct. bar, 1960; atty. Ohio Securities Div., 1940-45; corp. counsel Sec. of State of Ohio, 1945-48; individual practice law, Columbus, Ohio, 1948—. Mem. Am., Ohio, Columbus bar assns., Nat. Assn. Women Lawyers. Home: 969 Meeklynn Dr Worthington OH 43085 Office: 3300 Indianola Ave Columbus OH 43214 Tel (614) 261-9086

WITKOW, STANLEY PAUL, b. Los Angeles, Aug. 22, 1948; A.B., U. Calif., Los Angeles, 1970, J.D., U. Calif. Hastings Coll. Law, 1973. Admitted to Calif. bar, 1973; asso. firm Richman and Herman, Beverly Hills, Calif., 1973—. Mem. Am., Los Angeles County bar assns. Office: 9601 Wilshire Blvd suite 632 Beverly Hills CA 90210 Tel (213) 273-5540

WITMER, GEORGE ROBERT, b. Webster, N.Y., Dec. 26, 1904; A.B., U. Rochester, 1926; LL.B., Harvard, 1929. Admitted to N.Y. State bar, 1929; practiced in Rochester, N.Y., 1929-45; asso. firm Wile, Oviatt & Gilman, 1929-30; partner firm Easton & Witmer, 1931-45; surrogate Monroe County Ct., 1946-53; justice N.Y. State Supreme Ct., 1954—; adminstrv. judge N.Y. 7th Jud. Dist., 1962-68; asso. justice N.Y. State Appellate Ct., 1st dept., 1963-67, 4th dept., 1968—; judge N.Y. State Ct. Appeals, 1974; town atty. Town of Webster, 1934-35; supr. Town of Webster and County of Monroe, 1936-45. Mem. Monroe Republican exec. com., chmn. Webster Rep. com., 1933-45. Mem. Am., N.Y. State, Monroe County bar assns., Am. Law Inst. Author: (with others) N.Y. Pattern Jury Instructions—Civil, vol. 1, 1965, rev. edit., 1974, vol. 2, 1968. Home: 45 Corning Park Webster NY 14580 Office: Hall of Justice Exchange St Rochester NY 14614

WITSCHIEBEN, DOUGLAS A., b. Queens Village, N.Y., July 28, 1919; B.A., U. Mich., 1942; J.S.D., Bklyn. Law Sch., 1948, LL.M., 1960. Admitted to N.Y. bar, 1948; mng. atty. firm Kelley, Drye & Warren, N.Y.C., 1948-55; partner firm Dent, Boldblum & Witschieben, Flushing, N.Y., 1955-62, firm Dent & Witschieben, 1962—; asst. dist. atty. Queens County (N.Y.), 1966; law sec. to judge Civil Ct. N.Y.C., 1962. Vice pres. Property Owners Assn. Middle Village Inc., 1966—; v.p. Bethany Methodist Home of Bklyn., 1967—, bd. dirs., 1967—; bd. dirs., trustee 1st German Meth. Ch. and Linden Hill Meth. Cemetery, 1966—. Mem. Queens County Bar Assn. Office: 39-01 Mian St Flushing NY 11354 Tel (212) 359-2661

WITT, HOWARD SAMUEL, b. Johnson City, Tenn., Feb. 6, 1920; LL.B., Cumberland U., 1950; J.D., Samford U., 1969. Admitted to Tenn. bar, 1950; dist. atty. gen. Tenn. 20th Jud. Circuit, 1956-64; judge, chancellor Sullivan County (Tenn.) Ct., 1964—. Mem. Kingsport (Tenn.), Tenn. bar assns., Am. Judicature Soc., Tenn. Jud. Conf., Phi Alpha Delta. Home: PO Box 5128 Kingsport TN 37663 Office: City Hall Bldg Kingsport TN 37660 Tel (615) 245-7331

WITT, JOHN WILLIAM, b. Los Angeles, Aug. 30, 1932; A.B., U. So. Calif., 1954, J.D., 1960; postgrad. in Fin., San Diego State U., 1963-69. Admitted to Calif. bar, 1961, U.S. Supreme Ct. bar, 1969; dep. city atty. City of San Diego, 1961-64, chief dep. city atty., 1964-69, city atty., 1969—; pres. dept. city attys. League of Calif. Cities; trustee Nat. Inst. Municipal Law Officers; bd. visitors U. San Diego Sch. Law. Mem. exec. bd. San Diego County council Boy Scouts Am.; mem. standing com. Episcopal Diocese of San Diego; trustee Boys' Clubs of San Diego. Named Distinguished Eagle Scout Boy Scouts Am. Home: 3871 Liggett Dr San Diego CA 92106 Office: 202 C St San Diego CA 92101 Tel (714) 236-6220

WITT, ROBERT JOSEPH, b. Chgo., Mar. 4, 1941; B.C.S., DePaul U., 1962; J.D., U. Calif., Los Angeles, 1965. Admitted to Calif. bar, 1966; asso. firm Brown & Brown, Los Angeles, 1967-71, firm Walker, Wright, Tyler & Ward, Los Angeles, 1972—. Mayor City of Cerritos (Calif.), 1970, councilman, 1970—. Mem. Am., Los Angeles County bar assns., Beta Gamma Sigma, Beta Alpha Psi. Home: 16818 Harvest St Cerritos CA 90701 Office: 626 Wilshire Blvd Los Angeles CA 90017 Tel (213) 629-3571

WITT, WALTER FRANCIS, JR., b. Richmond, Va., Feb. 18, 1933; B.S., U. Richmond, 1954, LL.B., 1966. Admitted to Va. bar, 1966, D.C. bar, 1974; mem. firm Hunton & Williams, Richmond, 1966-74, partner, 1974—. Mem. Am., Va., Richmond bar assns., D.C. Bar, Am. Judicature Soc. Home: 8901 Tresco Rd Richmond VA 23229 Office: 707 E Main St Richmond VA 23219 Tel (804) 788-8391

WITTE, VICTOR ROBERT LOUIS, JR., b. St. Louis, Aug. 12, 1931; A.B. cum laude in Philosophy, St. Louis U., 1953, LL.B., 1955. Admitted to Mo. bar, 1955; with U.S. Army, 1955-57; asso. firm Hough, Maloney, Fox & Herrmann, Clayton, Mo., 1957-59; asso. Henry Simpson & Maurice Schechter, St. Louis, 1959-64; asso. firm Robertson, DeVoto & Wieland, St. Louis, 1964-66; counsel NLRB, St. Louis, 1966—. Mem. Mo. Bar Assn. Office: 210 N 12th St Saint Louis MO 63101 Tel (314) 425-4167

WITWER, SAMUEL WEILER, b. Pueblo, Colo., July 1, 1908; Ph.B., Dickinson Coll., 1930, LL.D., 1970; J.D., Harvard U., 1933; LL.D. (hon.), Simpson Coll., 1954, U. Ill., 1970, John Marshall Law Sch., 1976; J.S.D. (hon.), Lake Forest Coll., 1970; D.H.L. (hon.), DePaul U., 1970. Admitted to Ill. bar, 1933, U.S. Supreme Ct. bar, 1970; mem. firm Witwer, Moran, Burlage & Atkinson, and predecessors, Chgo., 1933—; pres. Ill. Constl. Conv., 1969-70; v.p. Chgo. Crime Commn., 1970—. Pres. bd. trustees Dickinson Coll., 1964—; trustee Northwestern Meml. Hosp., Chgo., 1952—. Mem. Am., Ill. State, Chgo. bar assns., Am. Judicature Soc. (dir. 1968-72), Am. Law Inst. Recipient award merit for civic service Ill. State Bar Assn., 1970; 1st Distinguished Service medal State of Ill., 1970; Ill. Laureate, Lincoln Acad. Ill., 1975; named Chicagoan of Year, Chgo. Jr. Assn. Commerce, 1970, also by Chgo. Press Club, 1970. Home: 111 Abingdon St Kenilworth IL 60043 Office: 125 S Wacker Dr Chicago IL 60606 Tel (312) 332-6000

WOFFORD, CHARLES WYCHE, b. Greenville, S.C., Nov. 12, 1942; B.A. magna cum laude, Yale, 1966; J.D. cum laude, Harvard, 1969. Admitted to Tex. bar, 1969, S.C. bar, 1972; partner firm Wyche, Burgess, Freeman & Parham, Greenville, 1972—. Mem. S.C., Am. bar assns. Home: 214 Trails End Greenville SC 29607 Office: 44 E Camperdown Way Greenville SC 29603 Tel (803) 242-3131

WOGNUM, JAMES PETER, b. Chgo., May 7, 1945; B.A., Lawrence U., Appleton, Wis., 1967; J.D., Chgo. Kent Coll. Law, 1971. Admitted to Ill. bar, 1971; asso. firm Stansell & Rahn, Chgo., 1971-72, firm Vincent F. Lucchese, Chgo., 1972—. Mem. Am., Ill. State, Chgo. bar assns. Home: 9636 S Seeley Ave Chicago IL 60643 Office: 7 S Dearborn St suite 1316 Chicago IL 60603 Tel (312) 372-3819

WOHL, WILLIAM M., b. Cleve., Apr. 20, 1939; B.A., Ohio U., 1962; J.D., Cleve. State U., 1967. Admitted to Ohio bar, 1967; asso. firm Sindell, Sindell, Bourne, Markus, Stern & Spero, Cleve., 1967-69; individual practice law, Cleve., 1969-71; partner firm Duda, Elk & Wohl, Cleve., 1971—. Mem. Ohio, Cuyahoga County, Cleve. bar assns., Ohio Acad. Trial Lawyers, Am. Trial Lawyers Assn. Home: 2300 Overlook Rd Cleveland Heights OH 44106 Office: Duda Elk & Wohl 800 Bond Ct Bldg Saint Clair at E 9th St Cleveland OH 44114 Tel (216) 696-4880

WOHLFORTH, ERIC EVANS, b. N.Y.C., Apr. 17, 1932; A.B., Princeton, 1954; LL.B., U. Va., 1957. Admitted to N.Y. bar, 1958, Alaska bar, 1967; asso. firm Hawkins, Delafield & Wood, N.Y.C., 1957-66; partner firm McGrath & Wohlforth, Anchorage, 1966-70; commr. revenue State of Alaska, 1970-72; partner firm McGrath, Wohlforth & Flint, Anchorage, 1972-74, firm Wohlforth & Flint, Anchorage, 1974—. Chancellor, Episcopal Diocese of Alaska, 1972—. Mem. Assn. Bar City N.Y., Am., Alaska, Anchorage bar assns. Home: 2226 Arbor Circle Anchorage AK 99503 Office: 645 G St 401 Anchorage AK 99501 Tel (907) 272-9489

WOJAHN, DENNIS GILBERT, b. Oshkosh, Wis., June 19, 1945; B.B.A., U. Wis., 1967, J.D., 1972. Admitted to Wis. bar, 1972; tax specialist Touche Ross & Co., Milw., 1972-75, supr., Buffalo, 1975—. Dir. youth activities, fund raising chmn. Jaycees, Whitefish Bay, Wis.; masterhost, Toastmasters; scoutmaster Milwaukee County council Boy Scouts Am. Mem. Wis., Am. Insts. C.P.A.s, Am. Assn. Attys.-C.P.A.s, Wis., Am. bar assns. Contbr. articles for accounting jour. Home: 17 Huntleigh Circle Amherst NY 14226 Office: One M&T Plaza Buffalo NY 14203 Tel (716) 856-6565

WOLBERT, G. S., JR., b. 1921; B.S. in Petroleum Engring., Pa. State U.; LL.B., U. Okla.; LL.M., S.J.D., U. Mich. With Shell Oil Co., 1953—, v.p. finance, 1970-73, v.p., gen. counsel, 1974—. Address: 1 Shell Plaza Houston TX 77002*

WOLCHOK, SIDNEY S., b. N.Y.C., Sept. 17, 1920; B.S.S., Coll. City N.Y., 1941; J.D., Columbia, 1944. Admitted to N.Y. bar, 1944, U.S. Supreme Ct. bar, 1955; partner firm Katz & Wolchok, N.Y.C., 1944-74; individual practice law, N.Y.C., 1974—. Mem. Am., N.Y. State bar assns., Internat. Soc. Labor Law and Social Legis., Am. Arbitration Assn. (panel), N.Y. County Lawyers Assn., Columbia Law Sch. Assn., Coll. City N.Y. Alumni Assn. Contbr. articles to legal jours. Home: 20 Mamaroneck Rd Scarsdale NY 10S83 Office: 360 Lexington Ave New York City NY 10017 Tel (212) 867-9140

WOLCOTT, DANIEL FOOKS, JR., b. Wilmington, Del., Mar. 31, 1946; B.A., Bethany (W.Va.) Coll., 1968; LL.B., U. Va., Charlottesville, 1971. Admitted to Del. bar, 1971; dep. atty. gen. State of Del., Wilmington, 1972-73; asso. firm Potter, Anderson & Corroon, Wilmington, 1973—; city solicitor New Castle (Del.), 1974—. Chmn. New Castle Bicentennial Com.; v.p. New Castle Hist. Soc. Mem. Am., Del. bar assns. Named Outstanding Young Man of Year New Castle Jaycees, 1975. Tel (302) 658-6771

WOLCOTT, GERALD D., b. Billings, Mont., Sept. 1, 1936; B.A., Sacramento State Coll., 1965; M.A., Calif. State Coll., 1968; J.D., U. Pacific., 1973. Admitted to Calif. bar, 1973; asst. prof. dept. criminal justice Calif. State U., 1969-71, asso. prof., 1971-73; individual practice law, Sacramento, 1973—; mem. sheriff's dept. Sacramento County (Calif.), 1959-69. Mem. Am., Calif., Sacramento County bar assns., Calif. Trial Lawyers Assn. Home: 2733 Wissemann Dr Sacramento CA 95826 Office: 429 J St Plaza Suite Sacramento CA 95814 Tel (916) 446-6145

WOLCOTT, THEODORE EVEN, b. Westmount, Can., Aug. 15, 1919; B.A., LL.B., U. Wis. Admitted to N.Y. bar, 1940, U.S. Supreme Ct. bar, 1943; prof. law U. Calif. Hastings Coll. Law, San Francisco, 1972—; lectr. in field. Chmn. bd. United Fund, Somers, N.Y., 1950-54. Mem. Assn. Bar City N.Y., Am. Bar Assn., Lawyer-Pilots Assn., Inter-Am. Bar, Internat. Inst. Space Law, Internat. Astronautical Fedn., Wings Club N.Y., Royal Aero. Club. Author: Aeronautical Law: Cases and Materials, 2 vols., 1975; contbr. articles to legal jours.; editorial adv. bd. Jour. Air Law, 1956-59; asso. editor Am. and Canadian Aviation Reports, 1965. Office: 198 McAllister St San Francisco CA 94102 Tel (415) 557-1307

WOLD, W. BRUCE, b. Oakland, Calif., Apr. 19, 1945; A.B., Calif. State Coll. at Sonoma, 1968; J.D., Hastings Coll. Law, U. Calif., San Francisco, 1971. Admitted to Calif. bar, 1972; asso. firm Spridgen Barrett Achor Luckhardt Anderson & James, Santa Rosa, Calif., 1971-73, Sedgwick Detert Moran & Arnold, San Francisco, 1974—. Mem. Am. (aviation and space law com.), San Francisco, Lawyer-Pilots bar assns. Home: 37 Edwards Ave Sausalito CA 94965 Office: Sedgwick Detert Moran & Arnold 11th Floor 111 Pine St San Francisco CA 94111 Tel (415) 982-0303

WOLESLAGEL, FREDERICK, b. Lyons, Kans.; A.B., U. Kans., LL.B., 1939. Admitted to Kans. bar, 1939; atty. Rice County, 1949-51; dist. judge 20th Jud. Dist., Lyons, 1959—; chmn. bench bar com. Kans. Supreme Ct., 1973-76; mem. Kans. Com. for Criminal Adminstrn., 1971-75, Miss. Conf. on Minimum Standards of Justice, 1973; faculty Nat. Coll. State Judiciary, 1965—, Am. Acad. Jud. Adminstrn., 1968—, Inst. Ct. Mgmt., 1974; cons. Tenn. Jury Instrn. Com., 1972, Minn. Select Com. on Judiciary, 1975-76. Mem. Kans. Dist. Judges Assn. (pres. 1964-65), Nat. Conf. State Trial Judges (exec. com. 1970-73, 75—). Chmn., mem. editorial bd. The Judges Jour., 1968-73; mem. com. which authored Pattern Instructions for Kansas: Criminal and Pattern Instructions for Kansas: Civil. Office: Court House Lyons KS 67554 Tel (316) 257-5041

WOLF, AUSTIN KEITH, b. Peoria, Ill., Feb. 1, 1923; B.A., Yale, 1948; LL.B. cum laude, Harvard, 1951. Admitted to Conn. bar, 1951; partner firm Cohen and Wolf, Bridgeport, Conn., 1951—. Mem. Am., Conn., Bridgeport bar assns. Home: 54 White Oaks Rd Fairfield CT 06430 Office: 10 Middle St Bridgeport CT 06603 Tel (203) 368-0211

WOLF, CHARLES EDWARD, b. York, Pa., March 26, 1929; B.A., Duke U., 1950; LL.B., Harvard, 1953. Admitted to Pa. bar, 1957; partner firm Drinker, Biddle & Reath, Phila., 1962—. Pres., Phila. Soc. to Protect Children. Office: 1100 Philadelphia Nat Bank Bldg Philadelphia PA 19107 Tel (215) 491-7287

WOLF, GARY WICKERT, b. Slinger, Wis., Apr. 19, 1938; B.B.A., U. Minn., 1960, J.D. cum laude, 1963. Admitted to N.Y. State bar, 1964, U.S. Supreme Ct. bar, 1971; asso. firm Cahill Gordon & Reindel, N.Y.C., 1963-70, partner, 1970—. Pres., Old Short Hills (N.J.) Estates Assn., 1974—; mem. council Short Hills Assn., 1974—. Home: 72 Fairfield Dr Short Hills NJ 07078 Office: 80 Pine St New York City NY 10005 Tel (212) 825-0100

WOLF, GEORGE, b. Jersey City, Jan. 20, 1890; LL.B., N.Y. U., 1919, LL.M., 1920. Admitted to Mass. bar, 1920, N.Y. bar, 1921; individual practice law, Mass., 1920, N.Y.C., 1921-76, ret., 1976; practiced in assn. with Victor Feingold for brief time; freelance writer, Largo, Fla., 1976—; govt. appeal agt. City N.Y., 1941-46; mayor Saddle Rock, Great Neck, L.I., N.Y., 1950-52. Mem. N.Y. County Bar Assn. Author: (with Joseph DiMona) Frank Costello, Prime Minister of the Underworld, 1974, also textbooks, two plays. Home and Office: 3600 Oak Manor Ln 167 Largo FL 33540 Tel (813) 585-2507

WOLF, GEORGE VAN VELSOR, b. Balt., Aug. 10, 1908; A.B., Yale, 1930; LL.B., Harvard, 1933. Admitted to Md. bar, 1933; asso. firm Piper & Marbury, and predecessors, Balt., 1933-40, partner, 1940-76, of counsel, 1976—; asst. atty. gen. State of Md., 1944-45; mem. character com. Md. Ct. of Appeals, 1949-56; mem. Pub. Service Law Revision Commn., 1951-53, Commn. to Study and Revise Testamentary Laws Md., 1965-70. Trustee, Children's Hosp., Balt., Kent & Queen Anne's Hosp., Chestertown, Md. Fellow Am., Md. bar founds., Am. Coll. Probate Counsel (regent 1972—); mem. Am. Law Inst., Am. (chmn. real property, probate and trust law sect. 1970-71), Md. (chmn. estate and trust law sect. 1961-65), Balt. City (exec. com. 1956-59), Kent County bar assns. Home: Kentfields Quaker Neck Chestertown MD 21620 Office: 2000 First Maryland Bldg 25 S Charles St Baltimore MD 21201 Tel (301) 539-2530

WOLF, JEROME THOMAS, b. Austin, Minn., June 13, 1937; B.A., Yale, 1959; J.D., Harvard, 1962. Admitted to Minn. bar, 1962, Mo. bar, 1966; with Judge Adv. Gen. Corps U.S. Army, 1963-66; asso. firm Spencer, Fane, Britt & Brown, Kansas City, Mo., 1966-71, partner, 1971—. Chmn. Jewish Community Relations Bur. of Kansas City, 1974—; bd. dirs. Jewish Fedn. and Council of Greater Kansas City, 1974—, Jewish Family and Childrens' Services of Kansas City, 1975—; trustee Menorah Hosp. Mem. Kansas City (exec. com., program chmn., pres.-elect 1977), Am., Fed. bar assns., Mo. Bar, Lawyers Assn. of Kansas City, Am. Judicature Soc., Phi Beta Kappa Assn. of Greater Kansas City (pres. 1975-77). Home: 2411 W 70th Terrace Shawnee Mission KS 66208 Office: 1000 Power & Light Bldg 106 W 14th St Kansas City MO 64105 Tel (816) 474-8100

WOLF, JUDY LYONS, b. N.Y.C., July 4, 1942; A.B., Manhattanville Coll., 1964; J.D., Georgetown U., 1970. Admitted to D.C. bar, 1970, U.S. Supreme Ct. bar, 1976; partner firm Wolf & Wolf, Washington, 1970—; legis. asst. to Rep. Bella S. Abzug, of N.Y., 1971; lectr. Law Sch. George Washington U., 1972—; field pub. counsel Rail Services Planning Office, ICC, 1974-76. Adv. neighborhood commr. Ward VI, 1976—; chairperson domestic relations counselling group Women's Legal Def. Fund, 1976—; v.p., bd. dirs. Capitol East Children's Center. Mem. Nat. Lawyers Guild, Women's Legal Def. Fund. Office: 816 Massachusetts Ave NE Washington DC 20002 Tel (202) 547-5536

WOLF, KENNETH STEVEN, b. Cin., Aug. 12, 1943; B.A., U. Cin., 1965; J.D., Harvard, 1968. Admitted to Calif. bar, 1969; mem. firm Pacht, Ross, Warne, Bernhard & Sears, Los Angeles, 1969—; dir. Beverly Hills (Calif.) Bar Assn. Law Found., 1974, 75; judge pro tem Beverly Hills Small Claims Ct., 1976; lectr. U. So. Calif., 1975, 76. Mem. Am., Calif., Los Angeles, Beverly Hills (bd. govs. 1974-76) bar assns., Barristers of Beverly Hills (sec. 1975, v.p. 1976, pres. 1977). Office: 1800 Ave of the Stars Los Angeles CA 90067 Tel (213) 277-1000

WOLF, LARRY M., b. Balt., July 11, 1937; A.B., Johns Hopkins U., 1958; LL.B., Yale U., 1961. Admitted to Md. bar, 1961; asso. firm Shawe & Rosenthal, Balt., 1961-71; partner firm Wolf, Pokempner & Hillman, Balt., 1972—; instr. labor law U. Balt., 1965-70, 72—. Mem. Balt. City Bd. Jewish Edn., 1969—, Asso. Placement and Guidance Bur. Balt., 1972—. Mem. Am. (labor law sect.), Md., Balt. City bar assns. Recipient Philip Weiner Meml. award, 1973; contbr. articles to profl. jours. Home: 8 Burr Oak Ct Randallstown MD 21133 Office: 810 WR Grace Bldg 10 E Baltimore St Baltimore MD 21202 Tel (301) 685-2206

WOLF, LEONARD S., b. Chgo., Feb. 27, 1929; A.B., U. Calif., Los Angeles, 1950; LL.B., U. So. Calif., 1953. Admitted to Calif. bar, 1953; city prosecutor City of Pasadena (Calif.), 1955-56; partner firm Allen, Fasman & Wolf, Beverly Hills, Calif., 1956-66; judge Municipal Ct., 1966—; lectr. U. So. Calif., 1954-74. Mem. Am., Beverly Hills, Los Angeles County, West Hollywood (Calif.) (trustee) bar assns., Criminal Cts. Bar Assn., Order of Coif, Phi Kappa Phi. Office: 9355 Burton Way Beverly Hills CA 90210 Tel (213) 278-6522

WOLF, LLOYD SIEVERS, b. Beaver Falls, Pa., Mar. 8, 1924; B.A., Pa. State U., 1950; LL.B., U. Calif., Los Angeles, 1953. Admitted to Calif. bar, 1954; individual practice law, Los Angeles, 1954—. Mem. Los Angeles County Bar Assn., Los Angeles Trial Lawyers Assn. Home: 520 Latimer Rd Santa Monica CA 90402 Office: 11110 W Ohio St Los Angeles CA 90025 Tel (213) 479-3728

WOLF, MARSHALL JAY, b. Cleve., Nov. 20, 1941; B.A., Miami U., Ohio, 1964; J.D., Western Res. U., 1967. Admitted to Ohio bar, 1967; law clk. Cuyahoga County Ct. Common Pleas, 1967-69; asso. firm Gaines, Stern, Schwarzwald & Robiner, and predecessors, Cleve., 1969-75, prin., 1975—. Pres. Univ. Heights Democratic Club, 1974-76; mem. Cuyahoga County Dem. Exec. Com., 1972—, Cuyahoga County Dem. Central Com., 1972—; trustee Temple on the Heights, Cleveland Heights, 1971—. Fellow Am. Acad. Matrimonial Lawyers, Am., Ohio, Cleve. bar assns., Ohio Acad. Trial Lawyers (chmn. family law sect. 1976—), Assn. Trial Lawyers Am. Contbr. articles to legal jours. Office: 1700 Investment Plaza Cleveland OH 44114 Tel (216) 781-1700

WOLF, ROGER CONANT, b. Plainfield, N.J., June 20, 1937; B.A., Dartmouth, 1960; J.D., U. Mich., 1963. Admitted to Ariz. bar, 1964, U.S. Supreme Ct. bar, 1967; staff atty. Dept. Interior, Washington, 1966-67; dir. Papago Legal Services, Sells, Ariz., 1967-70; individual practice law, Tucson, 1970—. Bd. dirs. Ariz. Civil Liberties Union, Tucson, 1968-72, 77—. Mem. Pima County Bar Assn., Legal Aid Soc. (dir.). Contbr. articles to legal jours. Home: 2742 E 4th St Tucson AZ 85716 Office: 290 N Meyer Ave Tucson AZ 85701 Tel (602) 882-9633

WOLF, SILAS CAPSHAW, b. Norman, Okla., June 2, 1919; LL.B., U. Okla., 1952. Admitted to Okla. bar, 1952; practiced law in Norman, 1952-55; judge Municipal Ct., Norman, 1952-55, Cleveland County (Okla.) Ct., 1955-61; judge Okla. Indsl. Ct., 1961—, presiding judge, 1971—. Mem. Okla., Cleveland County bar assns., Okla. Jud. Conf. Home: 515 S Flood St Norman OK 73069 Office: State Indsl Ct Jim Thorpe Bldg Oklahoma City OK 73105 Tel (405) 521-3661

WOLF, THOMAS, b. Indpls., June 11, 1929; B.A., Loris Coll., 1951; B.S., U. Minn., 1952, J.D., 1954. Admitted to Minn. bar, 1954; partner firm O'Brien, Ehrick, Wolf, Deaner & Downing, and predecessor, Rochester, Minn., 1954—. Pres. Rochester Pub. Library Bd., 1967-68, trustee, 1958-76; v.p., trustee St. Mary's Hosp., 1969—; pres., trustee St. John's Cath. Ch., 1968-72. Mem. Am., Minn. (v.p.) trial lawyers assns., Am., Minn., 3d Jud. Dist., Olmsted County (past pres.) bar assns., Internat. Acad. Trial Lawyers. Home: 2205 Crest Ln SW Rochester MN 55901 Office: Suite 611 Marquette Bank Bldg Rochester MN 55901 Tel (507) 289-4041

WOLF, WAYNE C., b. Memphis, Tex., Feb. 25, 1937; B.S., U. N.Mex., 1959, J.D., 1962. Admitted to N.Mex. bar, 1962; asst. atty. gen. State of N.Mex., 1963-66; asso. firm Civerolo, Hansen and Wolf, Albuquerque. Mem. Am. Bar Assn., State Bar N.Mex. (pres. 1976—). Office: 800 Sandia Savs Bldg PO Drawer 887 Albuquerque NM 87103 Tel (505) 842-8255*

WOLF, WILLIAM B., SR., b. Washington, Oct. 12, 1905; student Dartmouth, 1923-24; LL.B., J.D., George Washington U.; postgrad. Fgn. Service Sch., Georgetown U., 1926; LL.B., Nat. U., 1927. Admitted to D.C. bar, 1927, U.S. Supreme Ct. bar, 1930; sr. partner firm Wolf and Wolf, Washington, 1930—; trust officer First Nat. Bank of Washington, 1930-50, dir., exec. com., 1931-76; dir. Dist. Realty Title Ins. Corp., 1972—, Las Vegas Transit System, 1965-74; dir., exec. com. Washington Hotel Co., 1972—; pres. Midcity Investment Co., 1952—, Westchester Corp., 1970-72; dir., gen. counsel Grayline Corp., 1949-75. Mng. dir. Wolf-Pack Found., 1972-77. Mem. D.C., Am. bar assns., Am., D.C. bankers assns., Judge Advs. Assn. Home: 4000 Cathedral Ave NW Washington DC 20016 Office: 1001 Connecticut Ave NW Washington DC 20036 Tel (202) 331-1000

WOLFARD, MARY LOUISE, b. Indpls., June 17, 1915; student Butler U.; LL.B., Ind. U. Admitted to Ind. bar, 1938, U.S. Supreme Ct. bar, 1969; practice law with Robert Symmes, to 1965; asso. firm Jones, Wick and White, Indpls., 1969—; hearing judge Ind. Pub. Service Commn., 1961-62; asst. pub. counselor State of Ind., 1963-70. Mem. Ind. State, Indpls. (ct. liaison com., continuing legal edn. com., law studies com., chmn. liaison com. with Ind. Law Sch.) bar assns., Lawyers Assn., St. Thomas More Soc. Home: 5875 N New Jersey St Indianapolis IN 46220 Office: 910 First Federal Bldg 11 N Pennsylvania St Indianapolis IN 46204 Tel (317) 632-8481

WOLFE, BARDIE CLINTON, JR., b. Kingsport, Tenn., Oct. 21, 1942; J.D., U. Ky., 1967, M.S. in Library Science, 1972. Admitted to Ky. bar, 1967; circulation librarian, dir. reader services U. Tex., Austin, 1968-71; acquisitions librarian, asst. prof. U. Va., 1971-73; head law librarian, asst. prof. law Cleve.-Marshall Coll. Law, 1973-76, asso. prof. law, 1976-77; head law librarian, asso. prof. U. Tenn., Knoxville, 1977—. Mem. Am., Ky. bar assns., Assn. Am. Law Schs., Am. Assn. Law Libraries, Nat. Micrographics Assn., Am. Judicature Soc., Ohio Regional Assn. Law Libraries. Contbr. articles to profl. jours. Office: 1505 W Cumberland Ave Knoxville TN 37916 Tel (615) 974-4381

WOLFE, BETTY HOOVER, b. Halifax, Pa., Jan. 8, 1934; B.S., Bloomsburg State Coll., 1954; M.A., Peabody Coll., 1957; J.D., U. Calif., Davis, 1971. Reference librarian Columbus (Ohio) Pub. Library, 1957-58; catalog librarian Enoch Pratt Free Library, Balt., 1959-61, U. Calif. Library, Davis, 1963-66, U. Calif. at Davis Law Sch. Library, 1966-68; admitted to Calif. bar, 1972; law clk. to judge U.S. Dist. Ct. for Eastern Dist. Calif., 1971-74; asst. U.S. atty. for Eastern Dist. Calif., 1974—. Mem. Am., Fed. bar assns., U. Calif. at Davis Law Sch. Alumni Assn. (dir.). Asso. editor U. Calif. at Davis Law Rev., 1970-71. Office: 650 Capitol Mall Sacramento CA 95814 Tel (916) 440-2552

WOLFE, JAMES NELSON, b. Sheridan, Wyo., Mar. 30, 1938; B.S. in Accounting, U. Wyo., 1962, J.D., 1965. Admitted to Wyo. bar, 1965, since practiced in Sheridan; individual practice law, 1965-68, 70-71; mem. firm Wolfe & Rasmussen, 1971—; dep. county atty. Sheridan County, 1966-68, county and pros. atty., 1970—; adminstr. Wyo. Gov.'s Planning Com. on Criminal Adminstrn., also dir. Wyo. Law Enforcement Planning Agy., 1968-70. Mem. Am., Wyo., Sheridan County bar assns. Home: Rural Route 1 Box 157 Sheridan WY 82801 Office: PO Box 1026 Sheridan WY 82801 Tel (307) 674-4602

WOLFE, JOE RAWLS, b. Clearwater, Fla., Feb. 14, 1941; B.S., B.A., U. Fla., 1962, J.D., 1965; LL.M., in Taxation, N.Y. U., 1967. Admitted to Fla. bar, 1966; asso. firm Wolfe, Bonner & Hogan, Clearwater, 1967-72; prin. firm Joe R. Wolfe, Clearwater, 1972—. Mem. Am. (taxation sect.), Fla. (taxation sect.), Clearwater bar assns. Office: 16 N Fort Harrison Ave Clearwater FL 33515 Tel (813) 445-1481

WOLFE, JOHN GEORGE, III, b. Winston-Salem, N.C., Sept. 23, 1945; B.A., Maryville Coll., 1967; J.D., Wake Forest U., 1970. Admitted to N.C. bar, 1970; asso. firm Hatfield & Allman, Kernersville, N.C., 1970-73; partner firm Wolfe & Prince, Kernersville, 1973—; atty. Town of Kernersville, 1976—. Mem. Kernersville C. of C. (pres. 1973), Am., N.C., Forsyth County bar assns. Office: 103 S Main St Kernersville NC 27284 Tel (919) 996-3231

WOLFE, JULIAN SAWYER, b. Orangeburg County, S.C., Oct. 29, 1894; B.S., Wofford Coll., 1915. Admitted to S.C. bar, 1917, U.S. Supreme Ct. bar, 1939; supr. U.S. census, S.C., 1919-20; U.S. Commr., Eastern Dist. S.C., 1922-30; individual practice law, Orangeburg, S.C.; circuit solicitor, Orangeburg, Dorchester, Calhoun Counties, S.C., 1940-73. Mem. Orangeburg County Ho. of Reps., 1935-36; sec., treas. Orangeburg County Democratic Com., mem. state Dem. Com.; judge adv. Soc. 40 and 8 Am. Legion and World War I Barracks; adjutant and post comdr. Am. Legion, Orangeburg; counsul Woodmen of the World; state pres. S.C. Elks Assn.; v.p. Wofford Coll. Alumni Assn. Mem. Orangeburg County Bar Assn. (pres.), S.C. Prosecuting Attys'. Assn. (pres.). Recipient Distinguished Alumni Service award, Wofford Coll., 1973. Office: Carolina Bldg Orangeburg SC 29115 Tel (803) 534-4370

WOLFE, KENNETH CHARLES, b. Alton, Ill., Dec. 4, 1943; B.S., Ohio State U., 1965, J.D., 1968; M.A., U. Nebr., 1976. Admitted to Ohio bar, 1968, Nebr. bar, 1969, Colo. bar, 1971, Tex. bar, 1973; prof. U. Nebr., 1968-70; individual practice law, Lincoln, Nebr. and Ft. Collins, Colo., 1968-74; prof. Colo. State U., 1970-73, 74—, U. Tex. of the Permian Basin, 1973-74; partner firm Timmermans, Wolfe & Weinland, Ft. Collins, 1974-76; pres. firm Wolfe & Moore, Fort Collins, 1976—. Mem. Am., Colo. bar assns. Home: 2612 Brookwood Dr Fort Collins CO 80521 Office: 401 1st National Tower PO Box 1943 Fort Collins CO 80522 Tel (303) 493-8787

WOLFE, RICHARD B., b. Mt. Vernon, Iowa, July 14, 1906; B.A., Cornell Coll., 1927; J.D., U. Iowa, 1930. Admitted to Iowa bar, 1930; individual practice law, Mt. Vernon, 1930-75; partner firm Wolfe & Wolfe, Mt. Vernon, 1975—. Chmn. Republican. Precinct Com.; del.-at-large Rep. Nat. Conv., 1964; sgt.-at-arms Rep. Nat. Conv., 1952, 68. Mem. Iowa State, Linn County (title standards com.) bar assns., Mt. Vernon C. of C. (past pres.), U. Iowa Alumni Council. Home: 214 W 3rd St S Mount Vernon IA 52314 Office: 202 W First St Mount Vernon IA 52314 Tel (319) 895-8578

WOLFE, RICHARD BRUCE, b. Los Angeles, Feb. 11, 1939; B.S., U. Calif., Los Angeles, 1961, LL.B., 1964. Admitted to Calif. bar, 1965; since practiced in Los Angeles, dep. atty. gen. Calif., 1964-65; asso. Marshall, Morgan et al, 1965-66; dep. city atty., 1966-67; asso. and partner David M. Harney et al, 1967—. Mem. Calif., Los Angeles County bar assns., Am. Bd. Trial Advocates (asso.). Office: 650 S Grand Ave Los Angeles CA 90017 Tel (213) 626-8761

WOLFE, RICHARD RATCLIFFE, b. Palmyra, Mo., Nov. 29, 1933; B.S. in Indsl. Engring., Okla. State U., 1955; J.D., U. Mich., 1957. Admitted to D.C. bar, 1961, U.S. Patent Office bar, 1961, U.S. Supreme Ct. bar, 1966, Ill. bar, 1967; research engr. aero. power plant Army Ballistic Missle Agy., Huntsville, Ala., 1958-60; tech. asst. U.S. Senate Space Com., Washington, 1961-63; adminstrv. asst. to Ill. Dir. Revenue, Chgo. and Sprinffield, 1964-67, asst. to Ill. Sec. State, Springfield, 1966-69; asso. firm Taylor, Miller, Magner, Sprowl & Hutchings, Chgo., 1969—. Mem. Am., Ill., Chgo. bar assns. Registered profl. engr, Okla. Home: 535 E Center Ave Lake Bluff IL 60044 Office: 120 S LaSalle St Chicago IL 60603 Tel (312) ST 2-6070

WOLFE, ROGER ALLEN, b. Charleston, W.Va., Aug. 25, 1948; A.B., W.Va. U., 1970, J.D., 1973. Admitted to W.Va. bar, 1973, since practiced in Charleston; law clk. U.S. Dist. Ct. for So. W.Va., 1973-74; asso. firm Jackson, Kelly, Holt & O'Farrell, 1974—; reporter Fed. Speedy Trial Act, So. Dist. W.Va., 1976—. Mem. Am., W.Va., Kanawha County bar assns. Contbr. articles to legal jours. Home: 618

Wood Rd Charleston WV 25302 Office: 1 Valley Sq Charleston WV 25301 Tel (304) 345-2000

WOLFE, STANLEY ROBERT, b. Bklyn., Dec. 22, 1942; B.A., Cornell U., 1963; LL.B., Yale, 1966. Admitted to Pa. bar, 1966; asso. firm Pepper, Hamilton & Scheetz, Phila., 1966-70; dir. bur. litigation Pa. Dept. Environ. Resources, Harrisburg, 1970-72; dir. narcotics control strike force Pa. Justice Dept., Phila., 1972-74; asso. firm David Berger, Phila., 1974-76; mem. firm Berger & Montague, Phila., 1977—. Mem. Am., Pa., Phila. bar assns. Recipient Annual Environ. award Wissahickon Valley Watershed Assn., 1972. Office: 1622 Locust St Philadelphia PA 19103 Tel (215) 732-8000

WOLFE, STEPHEN C., b. Saginaw, Mich., Nov. 19, 1940; B.A. in Polit. Sci., Westminster Coll., 1962; J.D., U. Okla., 1965. Admitted to Okla. bar, 1965; individual practice law, Tulsa, 1965—. Mem. Okla. Ho. of Reps., 1967-72, U.S. Senate from Okla., 1973—. Mem. Am., Okla., Tulsa County bar assns., Am., Okla. trial lawyers assns. Recipient Boss of Year award Tulsa County Legal Secs. Assn., 1975. Home: 2105 Forest Blvd Tulsa OK 74114 Office: 1325 S Main St Tulsa OK 74119 Tel (918) 583-8574

WOLFE, STEVEN WATKINS, b. N.Y.C., Feb. 5, 1939; student Cornell U., 1955-57; B.A., Adelphi U., 1959; LL.B., Columbia, 1962. Admitted to N.Y. State bar, 1963, U.S. Dist. Ct. bar, 1963; individual practice law, N.Y.C., 1963—. Mem. N.Y. Bar Assn. Home: 400 West End Ave New York City NY 10024 Office: 60 E 42nd St New York City NY 10017 Tel (212) MU7-5826

WOLFE, THOMAS LEROY, b. Wichita Falls, Tex., Oct. 24, 1928; B.S., U. Va., 1950, LL.B., U. Okla., 1953, M.B.A., 1954. Admitted to Okla. bar, 1953, Fla. bar, 1958; mem. Judge Adv. Gen. Corps, U.S. Army, 1954-57; partner firm Shutts & Bowen, Miami, Fla., 1958—. Trustee Fla. Internat. U. Found., 1971—. Mem. Fed., Okla., Am., Dade County bar assns., Fla. Bar (chmn. continuing legal edn. com. 1975—), Fla. Bar Found., Am. Mgmt. Assn., Okla. Soc. C.P.A.'s. Home: 6330 Cellini St Coral Gables FL 33146 Office: 1000 SE 1st National Bank Bldg Miami FL 33131 Tel (305) 358-6300

WOLFF, AARON SIDNEY, b. Chgo., May 9, 1930; B.S., Northwestern U., 1951, J.D., 1954. Admitted to Ill. bar, U.S. Dist. Ct. bar, 1955, U.S. Ct. Appeals bar, 1963, U.S. Supreme Ct. bar, 1964; asso. firm Elson, Lassers & Wolff and predecessor, Chgo., 1955-63, partner, 1963—; spl. arbitrator bd. arbitration U.S. Steel Corp., United Steelworkers Am., 1969—. Mem. Am., Ill., Chgo. bar assns., Chgo. Council Lawyers, Am. Arbitration Assn. Author: (with Elson, Lassers) Federal Civil Practice Forms-Annotated, 1965. Home: 591 Broadview St Highland Park IL 60035 Office: 11 S LaSalle St Chicago IL 60603 Tel (312) 372-5461

WOLFF, ELLIOT RICHARD, b. Washington, Sept. 10, 1943; B.A., Columbia, 1965; LL.B., U. Va., 1968. Admitted to Calif. bar, 1970; law clk. to chief justice Traynor, Supreme Ct. Calif., 1968-69; asso. firm Munger, Tolles, Hills & Rickershauser, Los Angeles, 1969-73; v.p., gen. counsel HMO Internat., Los Angeles, 1973—. Mem. Nat. Health Lawyers Assn., Am., Calif., Los Angeles County bar assns., Order of Coif, Phi Delta Phi. Editorial bd. Va. Law Rev.; contbr. articles to legal jours. Office: 1880 Century Park E suite 1500 Los Angeles CA 90067 Tel (213) 553-6677

WOLFF, GEORGETTA ANN, b. Detroit, Mar. 29, 1948; B.A., U. Mich., 1968, J.D., 1971. Admitted to Mich. bar, 1972; staff atty. office of gen. counsel Ford Motor Co., Dearborn, Mich., 1971—. Mem. Mich., Am. bar assns., Comml. Law League Am. Office: Ford Motor Co The American Rd Dearborn MI 48121 Tel (313) 337-6262

WOLFF, KURT JAKOB, b. Mannheim, Germany, Mar. 7, 1936; A.B., N.Y. U., 1955; J.D., U. Mich., 1958. Admitted to N.Y. bar, 1958, U.S. Supreme Ct. bar, 1974; since practiced in N.Y.C., asso. firm Hays, Sklar & Herzberg, 1958-60, sr. asso. firm Nathan, Mannheimer, Asche, Winer & Friedman, 1960-65, sr. asso. firm Otterbourg, Steindler, Houston & Rosen, 1965-68, sr. partner, 1968-70, dir., treas. 1970—; arbitrator Am. Arbitration Assn., Gen. Arbitration Council Textile Industry N.Y.C. Mem. Am., N.Y. State Bar Assns., Assn. Bar City N.Y., Am Apparel Mfg. Assn., Fed. Bar Council. Contbr. articles to legal jours. Home: 9 Sunset Dr N Chappaqua NY 10514 Office: 230 Park Ave New York City NY 10017 Tel (212) 679-1200

WOLFF, PAUL MARTIN, b. Kansas City, Mo., July 22, 1941; B.A., U. Wis., 1963; LL.B., Harvard U., 1966. Admitted to D.C. bar, 1968, U.S. Supreme Ct. bar, 1971; law clk. to judge U.S. Ct. Claims, Washington, 1966-67; asso. firm Williams & Connolly, Washington, 1967-75, partner, 1975—; lectr. Cath. U. Law Sch., 1970-73. Mem. Am. Bar Assn., Washington Council Lawyers (dir. 1970-73), Phi Beta Kappa, Phi Eta Sigma, Phi Kappa Phi. Home: 4770 Reservoir Rd NW Washington DC 20007 Office: 839 17th St NW Washington DC 20006 Tel (202) 331-5079

WOLFMAN, BERNARD, b. Phila., July 8, 1924; A.B., U. Pa., 1946, J.D., 1948; LL.D. (hon.), Jewish Theol. Sem. Am., 1971. Admitted to Pa. bar, 1949, U.S. Supreme Ct. bar, 1955, Mass. bar, 1976; asso. firm Wolf, Block, Schorr & Solis-Cohen, Phila., 1948-56, partner, 1956-63; prof. law U. Pa., 1962-73, Gemmill prof. law, 1973-76, dean Law Sch., 1970-75; vis. prof. law Harvard, 1964-65, Fessenden prof. law, 1976—; vis. prof. law Stanford, summer 1966; fellow Center for Advanced Study in Behavioral Scis., 1975-76; mem. bd. Phila. Defender Assn., 1955-69, Phila. Lawyers Com. for Civil Rights Under Law, 1970-75; mem. nat. lawyers adv. council Earl Warren Legal Tng. Program, 1970—; cons. Dept. Treasury, 1963-68; mem. legal activities policy bd. Tax Analysts and Advs., 1972—; mem. steering com. IRS project Adminstrv. Conf. U.S., 1974—; gen. counsel AAUP, 1966-68. Bd. dirs. Phila. chpt. Am. Jewish Com., 1974-76; trustee Fedn. Jewish Agys. Greater Phila., 1968-74; trustee Found. Center, 1970-76, exec. bd., 1975-76; adv. com. Commn. on Pvt. Philanthropy and Pub. Needs, 1973-75; mem. Phila. regional planning council Pa. Gov.'s Justice Commn., 1973-75. Mem. Am. (chmn. com. on taxation and relation to human rights, individual rights and responsibilities sect.), Phila. bar assns., ACLU (dir. Greater Phila. br. 1964-76, pres. 1972-75, nat. dir. 1972-75), Fed. Tax Inst. New Eng. (exec. com. 1976—), Am. Law Inst. (cons. fed. income tax project 1974—), Tax Inst. Am. (adv. council 1970-73), Phi Beta Kappa, Order of Coif. Author: (with J.L.F. Silver and M.A. Silver) Dissent Without Opinion, The Behavior of Justice William O. Douglas in Federal Tax Cases, 1975; Federal Income Taxation of Business Enterprise, 1971, supplement, 1975; contbr. articles to profl. jours.; editorial bd. law div. Little, Brown & Co.; Jour. Corporate Taxation. Home: 229 Brattle St Cambridge MA 02138 Office: Harvard Law Sch Cambridge MA 02138 Tel (617) 495-3159

WOLFRAM, WALTER PAUL, b. Amarillo, Tex., Aug. 5, 1932; B.A., N. Tex. State U., 1953; J.S.D., U. Tex., 1956. Admitted to Tex. bar, 1956; city atty., Amarillo, 1956-58; individual practice law, Amarillo, 1958—. Pres. Amarillo Assn. for Retarded Citizens, 1964-66; v.p. Tex. Assn. for Retarded Citizens, 1965-67; chmn. Ad Hoc Commn. on Juvenile Delinquency; mem. Human Relations Commn., 1976; bd. Child Welfare, Amarillo. Mem., Amarillo Bar Assn., Am. Judicature Soc., Tex. Trial Lawyers Assn. Home: 2507 Tyler St Amarillo TX 79109 Office: Suite 400 Amarillo Petroleum Bldg Amarillo TX 79101 Tel (806) 372-3449

WOLFSON, BERNARD, b. Bklyn., Feb. 13, 1937; B.S. in Bus. Adminstrn., U. Fla., 1959; LL.B., U. Miami, 1963. Admitted to Fla. bar, 1963; asso. firm Abbott & Frumkes, Miami Beach, Fla., 1963-64; individual practice law, Miami, 1964-67, Coral Gables, Fla., 1967—. Mem. Fla., Dade County, Coral Gables bar assns. Home: 11530 Nogales St Coral Gables FL 33156 Office: 255 Alhambra Circle Suite 245 Coral Gables FL 33134 Tel (305) 446-4284

WOLFSON, MELVILLE ZACUOTA, b. New Orleans, Aug. 15, 1941; B.S., U. New Orleans, 1963, M.S., 1964; Ph.D., U. Ill., 1971; J.D., Tulane U., 1973. Admitted to La. bar, 1973; dir. firm Nelson, Nelson, Lombard, New Orleans, 1973—; instr. U. Ill., 1964-66; asst. prof. econs. and fin. U. New Orleans, 1967-73, asso. prof., 1974—; mem. Mayor's Council Econ. Advisors, New Orleans, 1973—. 1st vice-pres. Congregation Gates of Prayer, New Orleans, 1976—; mem. Comn. on Jewish Edn., New Orleans, 1975—. Mem. Am., So. Econs. Assn., Am., La. bar assns. Contbr. articles to legal jours. Home: 4628 Taft Park Metairie LA 70002 Office: 344 Camp St New Orleans LA 70130 Tel (504) 523-5893

WOLFSON, NICHOLAS, b. N.Y.C., Feb. 29, 1932; A.B. with highest honors, Columbia, 1953; J.D., cum laude, Harvard, 1956. Admitted to N.Y. bar, 1956, Mass. bar, 1966; atty. SEC, Washington, 1958-60; individual practice N.Y.C. and Boston, 1960-66; br. chief, spl. counsel, asst. dir. SEC, Washington, 1967-73; adj. prof. law, Georgetown U., 1972; prof. law U. Conn., 1972—; chmn. subcom. on pub. role of corps. Conn. Com. to Study Law of Corps. and Other Bus. Orgns., 1975-77; mem. Conn. Adv. Com. to Study Recodification of Banking Laws. Mem. Am. (mem. fed. regulation of securities com.), Fed. bar assns., Phi Beta Kappa. Author: Investment Banking, Twentieth Century Fund, 1976; (with Phillips and Russo) Regulation of Brokers, Dealers and Securities Markets, 1977; contbr. articles and reviews law jours. Home: 71 Harvest Ln West Hartford CT 06117 Office: Sch Law Univ Conn West Hartford CT 06117 Tel (203) 523-4841

WOLK, ALAN MURRAY, b. Cleve., Mar. 17, 1932; B.B.A., Fenn Coll., 1953; J.D., Ohio State U., 1955; postgrad. Case Western Res. U., 1958-63. Admitted to Ohio bar, 1955, U.S. Supreme Ct. bar, 1965; individual practice law, Cleve., 1955-68; mng. partner firm Woodle, Wachtel & Wolf, Cleve., 1968—; asst. atty. gen. Ohio, 1959-62, 70—; acting judge Shaker Heights Municipal Ct., 1969—; arbitrator Cuyahoga County Common Pleas Ct.; mem. labor panel Am. Arbitration Assn., 1973—. Active, University Heights Sewer Bond Issue Com., 1961, City Beautiful Com., 1974; chmn. Citizens Adv. Com., 1975-77; chmn. University Heights Democratic Club, 1968-74, Cuyahoga County Dem. Exec. Com., 1974—. Fellow Cleve. Acad. Trial Attys.; mem. Am., Ohio (del. 1976), Cuyahoga County (trustee, sec., exec. dir. 1963-70, treas. 1974-76), Greater Cleve. (chmn. golf outing 1974, program chmn. 1975) bar assns., Tau Epsilon Rho (chancellor 1963). Home: 2620 Fenwick Rd University Heights OH 44118 Office: B F Keith Bldg Cleveland OH 44115 Tel (216) 241-7313

WOLKIN, PAUL ALEXANDER, b. Phila., Oct. 14, 1917; B.A., U. Pa., 1937, M.A., 1938, LL.B., 1941. Admitted to Pa. bar, 1942, U.S. Supreme Ct. bar, 1947; law clk. to judge U.S. Circuit Ct. Appeals, 1942-44; atty. Fgn. Econ. Adminstrn., Washington, 1944-45; asso. gen. counsel French Supply Council, Washington, 1945-46; asst. legal adviser Dept. State, 1946-47; legal draftsman Phila. Charter Commn., 1948-51; spl. asst. to Phila. Solicitor, 1951; partner firm Wolkin, Sarner & Cooper, Phila., 1951-66; counsel Sarner, Cooper & Stein, Phila., 1966-69, Hudson, Wilf & Kronfeld, Phila., 1971—; asst. dir. Am. Law Inst., 1947—; exec. dir. Am. Law Inst.-Am. Bar Assn. Com. on Continuing Profl. Edn., 1963—; sec. permanent editorial bd. Uniform Comml. Code, 1962—; mem. com. on specialized personnel Dept. Labor, 1964-69. Pres., Phila Child Guidance Center, 1966-72. Mem. Am. (mem. spl. com. on implementation of standards and codes 1974—), Pa., Phila. bar assns., Pa. Bar Inst. (bd. dirs. 1967-75), Am. Judicature Soc., Order of Coif, Lawyers Club, Sociolegal Club, Scribes (past pres.). Editor The Practical Lawyer, 1955—. Contbr. articles to legal jours. Home: 1610 N 72d St Philadelphia PA 19151 Office: 4025 Chestnut St Philadelphia PA 19104 Tel (215) 387-3000

WOLKOFF, EUGENE ARNOLD, b. N.Y.C., June 9, 1932; B.A., Bklyn. Coll., 1954; LL.B., St. John's U., 1961. Admitted to N.Y. State bar, 1962; partner firm Callahan & Wolkoff, N.Y.C., 1962—; mem. panel of arbitrators Am. Arbitration Assn. Mem. N.Y. State Bar Assn. Office: 67 Wall St New York City NY 10005 Tel (212) 344-1013

WOLLAEGER, FRANK ADOLPH, b. Milw., Oct. 5, 1923; B.A., U. Wis., 1947; J.D., Harvard, 1950. Admitted to Wis. bar, 1950, Ill. bar, 19S1, U.S. Supreme Ct. bar, 1967; asso. firm McBride & Baker, Chgo., 1950-58; partner firm McBride, Baker, Wienke & Schlosser, Chgo., 19S8—; sec., dir. C.I. Corp., Chgo., 1970—, Otis & Assos., Inc., Northbrook, Ill., 1958—; sec. Market Facts, Inc., Chgo., 1973—. Bd. dirs. North Shore Country Day Sch., Winnetka, Ill., 1972-75. Mem. Chgo., Ill., Am. bar assns., State Bar Wis., Am. Maritime Assn. Home: 225 Birch St Winnetka IL 60093 Office: 110 N Wacker Dr Chicago IL 60606 Tel (312) 346-6191

WOLLE, CHARLES ROBERT, b. Sioux City, Iowa, Oct. 16, 1935; B.A., Harvard, 1958; J.D., Iowa State U., 1961. Admitted to Iowa bar, 1961; asso. firm Shull, Marshall & Marks, Sioux City, 1961-66, partner, 1967—. Bd. dirs. Sioux City Art Center, 1963-65, Sioux City Symphony, 1965-70, Morningside Coll., Sioux City, 1976—. Mem. Iowa, Am. bar assns. Notes editor, mem. editorial bd. Iowa Law Review, 1960-61. Home: 3321 Concordia Dr Sioux City IA 51104 Office: 1109 Badgerow Bldg Sioux City IA 51101 Tel (712) 258-7513

WOLLMAN, MILTON A., b. Phila., Oct. 21, 1921; B.A., Pa. State U., 1942; LL.B., U. Pa., 1948. Admitted to Pa. bar, 1949; partner firm Wollman, Tracey & Schlesinger, Phila.; solicitor Whitpain Twp. Zoning Hearing Bd., Blue Bell, Pa. Trustee Wissahickon Valley Library, Ambler, Pa.; treas., v.p. Whitpain Recreation Assn., Blue Bell; mem. parents' adv. council Hamilton Coll., Kirkland Coll., Clinton, N.Y.. Mem. Pa., Phila. bar assns. Home: Granary Rd Blue Bell PA 19422 Office: 2063 Suburban Station Bldg Philadelphia PA 19103 Tel (215) LO8-5015

WOLLMAN, ROGER LELAND, b. Frankfort, S.D., May 29, 1934; B.A., Tabor Coll., 1956; J.D., U. S.D., 1962; LL.M., Harvard, 1964. Admitted to S.D. bar, 1962; individual practice law, Aberdeen, S.D., 1964-71; states atty. Brown County, S.D., 1967-71; asso. justice S.D. Supreme Ct., Pierre, 1971—. Mem. Am. Bar Assn. Office: South Dakota Supreme Court State Capitol Bldg Pierre SD 57501 Tel (605) 224-3512

WOLMAN, PAUL CARROLL, JR., b. Balt., Aug. 21, 1926; B.S. in Econs., Wharton Sch. Finance and Commerce U. Pa., 1948; LL.B., Harvard, 1951. Admitted to Md. bar, 1951; law clk. to judge U.S. Ct. Appeals, 4th Circuit, 1951-52; asst. U.S. atty. for Md. Dept. Justice, 1952-54; asso. firm Blades & Rosenfeld, Balt., 1954-56, partner, 1956—. Mem. Am., Md., Balt., Fed. bar assns. Home: 1817 Greenberry Rd Baltimore MD 21209 Office: Suite 1200 One Charles Center Baltimore MD 21201 Tel (301) 539-7558

WOLNER, HERBERT EUGENE, b. St. Cloud, Minn., Oct. 21, 1910; B.A., Gustavus Adolphus Coll., 1932; LL.B. magna cum laude, St. Paul Coll. Law, 1936; J.D. magna cum laude, William Mitchell Coll. Law, 1936. Admitted to Minn. bar, 1936; law clk. John B. Sanborn, judge U.S. 8th Circuit Ct. Appeals, 1938; individual practice law, St. Paul, 1938-45, Mound and Lake Minnetemba area, Minn., 1945-67; judge Hennepin County (Minn.) Ct., 1967—; dist. price atty. Office Price Adminstrn., 1942-45. Mem. Minn., Am. bar assns., Minn. Judges Assn., Am. Judicature Soc. Author Minn. jud. manuals. Home: PO Box 125 Mound MN 55364 Office: 740 Govt Center Minneapolis MN 55414 Tel (612) 348-7715

WOLSLEGEL, HENRY HARTMAN, b. Ottawa, Ill., Sept. 9, 1927; B.S., U. Cin., 1953; J.D., Drake U., 1956. Admitted to Colo. bar, 1968, U.S. Supreme Ct. bar, 1972; individual practice law, Denver, 1968—. Mem. Am., Colo., Denver bar assns., Am. Judicature Soc., Am., Colo. trial lawyers assns., Phi Alpha Delta. Home: 12028 E Harvard Ave Denver CO 80232 Office: 666 Sherman St Denver CO 80203 Tel (303) 837-1080

WOLTZ, ARTHUR WALTON, b. Galax, Va., Dec. 8, 1905. Admitted to Va. bar, 1935; individual practice law, Newport News, Va., 1935-44; mem. firm Jones, Blechman, Woltz & Kelly, Newport News, 1944—. Mem. Newport News, Hampton, Am., Va. State bar assns., Am. Judicature Soc., Am., Va. trial lawyers assns., Va. Assn. Def. Attys. Home: 16 Curle Rd Hampton VA 23669 Office: 2600 Washington Ave Newport News VA 23607 Tel (804) 245-2861

WOLVERTON, RICHARD EDWARD, b. Charleston, W.Va., Oct. 21, 1946; A.S., Potomac State Coll., 1966; B.S., W.Va. U., 1968, J.D., 1971. Admitted to W.Va. bar, 1971, Fla. bar, 1972; with firm Lyle, Skipper, Wood and Anderson, St. Petersburg, Fla., 1972—; mem. panel Am. Arbitration Assn., 1976. Mem. Fla., St. Petersburg bar assns., Pinellas County Trial Lawyers Assn., Nat. Hot Rod Assn., Nat. Corvette Owners Assn. Home: 220 Driftwood Rd SE Saint Petersburg FL 33705 Office: 699 1st Ave N Saint Petersburg FL 33701 Tel (813) 895-1991

WOMACK, JAMES LEON, b. Sikes, La., Nov. 18, 1925; LL.B., La. State U., 1955. Admitted to La. bar, 1955; individual practice law, Winfield, La., 1955—. Pres., Winn Indsl. Devel. Corp., Winnfield, 1971—; pres. bd. dirs. Winn Acad., Winnfield, 1973—. Mem. DAV (nat. award 1976), Am. Legion. Recipient Nat. Blinded Vets. Assn. award, 1956; Silver Beaver award Boy Scouts Am., 1968. Home: 102 Harrel Ave Winnfield LA 71483 Office: 111 W Main St Winnfield LA 71483 Mailing Address: PO Box 629 Winnfield LA 71483 Tel (318) 628-4444

WOMACK, LOWELL ASHER, b. Providence, Mar. 25, 1938; B.S., Auburn U., 1960; J.D., U. Ala., 1966; postgrad. Nat. Grad. Trust Sch., Northwestern U., 1972. Admitted to Ala. bar, 1966; with trust dept. First Nat. Bank Tuskaloosa (Ala.), 1965—, asst. trust officer, 1967-68, trust officer, 1969-74, v.p., 1972—, sr. trust officer, 1976—. Bd. dirs., treas. Tuscaloosa Civitan Club, lt. gov. Ala. Central dist. Civitan Club Internat.; chmn. fin. com. Choctaw dist. Boy Scouts Am., chmn. sustaining mem. dr., 1971; adv. bd. Tuscaloosa Salvation Army, also exec. com., bd. dirs., treas.; past v.p., bd. dirs. Skyland Elementary Sch. PTA, Tuscaloosa, chmn. safety com., 1969-70, program com., 1970-71; past pres. Sunday sch. Forest Lake United Methodist Ch., Tuscaloosa, mem. adminstrv. bd., trustee; chmn. bd. trustees Ala. Trust Sch., Birmingham-So. Coll.; participant drs. YMCA, United Fund. Mem. Tuscaloosa County, Ala., Am. bar assns., Am. Inst. Banking, Ala. Bankers Assn. (2d v.p. trust div.), Tuscaloosa Estate Planning Council (sec., exec. com.), Tuscaloosa C. of C., Sigma Delta Kappa. Home: 27 Bellview Dr Tuscaloosa AL 35401 Office: Box 2028 Tuscaloosa AL 35401 Tel (205) 345-5000

WONG, FRANCIS ALVIN, b. Honolulu, July 18, 1936; B.S., Georgetown U., 1958, J.D., 1960. Admitted to Hawaii bar, 1962; individual practice law, Waianae, Hawaii, 1962-66; partner firm Rice, Lee & Wong, Honolulu, 1966—; mem. Hawaii Ho. of Reps., 1966-70, Hawaii Senate, 1970—; dir. Oceanic Financial Corp. Participant Rutgers U. 1970 State Legislature Seminar for Outstanding State Legislators. Pres. Pearl City Democratic Precinct, 1966-70; chmn. Georgetown U. Admissions Com.; usher, mem. finance com. Our Lady of Good Counsel Ch., Honolulu; trustee Japanese Am. Inst. Mgmt. Sci., Honolulu; mem. steering com. civilian advisory group U.S. Army, Pacific; bd. dirs. Am. Assn. Community Jr. Colls. Mem. Bar Assn. Hawaii. Recipient Distinguished Service award U.S. Jr. C. of C., 1965, Outstanding Young Man award Hawaii Jaycees, 1967. Home: 2023 Aamanu St Pearl City HI 96782 Office: 345 Queen St Suite 700 Honolulu HI 96813 Tel (808) 536-4421

WONNEMAN, LEONARD HENRY, b. Balt., May 2, 1910; J.D., U. Balt. Admitted to Md. bar, 1941, U.S. Supreme Ct. bar, 1957; partner firm Wonneman and Styles, 1945—. Mem. Am., Md., Balt. (grievance com. 1972-73) bar assns., Am. Trial Lawyers Assn. Home: Route 3 Box 296 Phoenix MD 21131 Office: 1322 Linden Ave Baltimore MD 21227 Tel (301) 592-9395

WOO, DAVID BOW, b. Winslow, Ariz., Mar. 22, 1939; A.B., Princeton, 1961; J.D., U. Calif., Berkeley, 1964. Admitted to Ariz. bar, 1965, Calif. bar, 1966; asso. firm John E. Madden, Phoenix, 1964-65; sr. corps. counsel, dept. corps. State of Calif. Los Angeles, 1966-72; asst. gen. counsel Equity Funding Corp. Am., Los Angeles, 1972-73; asso. gen. counsel Republic Corp., Los Angeles, 1973—. Founder, Council Oriental Orgns., Los Angeles, 1968; chmn. bd. Oriental Service Center, 1968-72. Mem. Century City (chmn. bus. orgn. sect.), Los Angeles City bar assns., Chinese Lawyers Assn. Recipient 1st ann. award Human Relations Commn. Los Angeles, 1968. Office: 1900 Ave of Stars Century City CA 90067 Tel (213) 553-3900

WOOD, CURTIS MAXAM, b. Northampton, Mass., July 14, 1941; B.S. in Bus. Adminstrn., Am. Internat. Coll., 1963; J.D., Western New Eng. Coll., 1971. Admitted to Mass. bar, 1971; with IRS, Springfield, Mass., 1963—. Treas., Westfield Service unit Salvation Army, 1976. Mem. Am., Mass., Hampden County bar assns. Home: 7 Crawford Dr Westfield MA 01085 Office: room 442A Federal Bldg Courthouse Springfield MA 01103 Tel (413) 781-2420 Ext 384

WOOD, DAVID LESLIE, b. Ft. Collins, Colo., Sept. 11, 1938; B.A., U. Colo., 1960, LL.B., 1962. Admitted to Colo. bar, 1962, U.S. Supreme Ct. bar, 1973; partner firm Greager & Wood, Ft. Collins, 1962-65, Wood & Herzog, Ft. Collins, 1965-70; spl. asst. atty. gen. State of Colo., 1966-69; dist. atty. 8th Jud. Dist. Colo., Ft. Collins, 1970-73; partner firm Wood, Herzog & Osborn, Ft. Collins, 1973—; dir. 1st Nat. Bank, Ft. Collins. Bd. dirs. Ft. Collins United Fund, 1968-70, Colo. State U. Found., 1975—, Poudre Valley Hosp. Dist., 1976—; pres. Ft. Collins Indsl. Fund, 1976—. Mem. Am., Colo. (bd. gov. and exec. council 1972-73), Larimer County (mem. exec. com. 1974-75), bar assns., Colo. Dist. Attys. Assn. (dir. 1970-72). Home: 17 Forest Hills Ln Fort Collins CO 80521 Office: 217 W Olive St Fort Collins CO 80521 Tel (303) 484-2928

WOOD, EDMUND REYNOLDS, b. Dallas, May 26, 1943; B.B.A., So. Meth. U., 1965; J.D., U. Houston, 1968. Admitted to Tex. bar, 1968; partner firm Chancellor & Wood, Dallas, 1968—; mem. staff State Senator, 8th Dist., Tex. Mem. Tex., Am. trial lawyers assns., Dallas Bar Assn., State Bar Tex. Home: 3832 Colgate St Dallas TX 75205 Office: 4925 McKinney St Dallas TX 75205 Tel (214) 526-4500

WOOD, FRANKLIN SECOR, b. Hopewell Center, N.Y., Aug. 3, 1901; A.B., Cornell U., 1923, LL.B., 1925. Admitted to N.Y. State bar, 1926, Ter. Hawaii, 1930; asso. Cotton & Franklin, N.Y.C., 1925-29, Prosser, Anderson, & Marks, Honolulu, 1930, Robb, Clark & Bennett, N.Y.C., 1931-34; individual practice law, N.Y.C., 1934-45; mem. firm Hawkins, Delafield & Wood, N.Y.C., 1945-71, of counsel, 1971—. Mem. Bd. Zoning Appeals, Bronxville, N.Y., 1948-58; mem. adv. council Cornell Law Sch., until 1973, mem. emeritus, 1973—, chmn., 1958-61. Mem. Am., N.Y. State bar assns., Assn. Bar City N.Y. Editor-in-chief Cornell Law Quar., 1924-25; contbr. articles, reports. Home: 6 Northern Ave Bronxville NY 10708 Office: 67 Wall St New York City NY 10005 Tel (212) 952-4783

WOOD, GAYLORD ASHLYN, JR., b. Indpls., July 21, 1938; B.A., Duke, 1959; LL.B., 1962. Admitted to Fla. bar, 1963, 5th Circuit Ct. Appeals bar, 1966, U.S. Ct. Mil. Appeals bar, 1963, U.S. Supreme Ct. bar, 1966, U.S. Tax Ct. bar, 1976; individual practice law, Ft. Lauderdale, Fla., 1962-63, 66—; gen. counsel Broward County Property Appraiser, 1969—; spl. counsel Orange, Lake and Collier County Property Appraisers, 1973—; city atty. Parkland (Fla.), 1969—. Bd. dirs. Westminster Manor Retirement Home, Ft. Lauderdale, First Presbyterian Ch., Met. YMCA (all Ft. Lauderdale). Mem. Am., Fla., Broward County bar assns., Broward County Trial Lawyers Assn., Am. Judicature Soc. Office: Suite 603 200 SE 6th St Fort Lauderdale FL 33301 Tel (305) 463-5241

WOOD, GUS LEWIS, b. LaGrange, Ga., Mar. 2, 1938; B.B.A., U. Ga., 1959; LL.B., 1961. Admitted to Ga. bar, 1960; capt. JAGC, U.S. Army, 1961-63; asst. U.S. atty. No. Dist. Ga., Atlanta, 1963-64; law clk. to judge U.S. Dist. Ct., Atlanta, 1964-66; partner firm Sanders, Mottola, Haugen, Wood & Goodson, Newnan, Ga., 1966—. Mem. State Bar Ga., Coweta County Bar Assn. (past pres.), Ga. Def. Lawyers Assn. Columnist Legal Briefs, Mark-Morgan Syndicated Features. Home: 17 Lakeview Dr Newnan GA 30263 Office: 11 Perry St Newnan GA 30263 Tel (494) 253-3880

WOOD, HAROLD EDMUND, b. Rosenberg, Tex., Aug. 13, 1910; student Baker U., Kans.; J.D., So. Meth. U., 1935. Admitted to Tex. bar, 1935; partner firm Chancellor & Wood, Dallas. Mem. State Bar Tex., Am., Dallas bar assns. Home: 1136 N Westmoreland St Dallas TX 75211 Office: Suite 101 4925 McKinney St Dallas TX 75205 Tel (214) 526-4500

WOOD, HENRY CLAY, b. Louisville, Miss., Aug. 28, 1920; LL.B., U. Miss., 1949, B.A., 1952. Admitted to Miss. bar, 1949; individual practice law, Louisville, Miss. Tel (601) 773-2292

WOOD, JAMES ALLEN, b. McMinnville, Tenn., Jan. 14, 1906; student David Lipscomb Coll., 1923-25; A.B., U. Tenn., 1929; LL.B., U. Tex., 1934. Admitted to Tex. bar, 1934, U.S. Supreme Ct. bar, 1955; since practiced in Corpus Christi, Tex.; individual practice law, 1934-41; state dist. ct. judge, 1941-46; partner firm Wood, Burney, Nesbitt & Ryan, 1949—; mem. Supreme Ct. Tex. Rules Adv. Com.; dir. Gulfway Nat. Bank, Mercantile Nat. Bank Corpus Christi, Nueces River Authority. Pres. United Fund Corpus Christi, 1946-48; pres. Hearth, 1949-55; dist. chmn. U.S. Savs. Bond Program, 1948—. Mem. Nueces County (past pres.), Am. bar assns., State Bar Tex., Tex. Bar Found., Am. Coll. Trial Lawyers, Am. Soc. Legal History. Contbr. articles to legal jours. Home: 458 Dolphin Corpus Christi TX 78411 Office: 920 Petroleum Tower Corpus Christi TX 78401 Tel (512) 884-4921

WOOD, JAMES CLARENCE, b. Cameron, Mo., Oct. 1, 1923; B.C.E., U. Ill., 1945, LL.B., 1948, J.D., 1966. Admitted to Ill. bar, 1949, U.S. Supreme Ct. bar, 1966; asso. firm Wegner, Stellman, Micord, Wiles & Wood, and predecessor, Chgo., 1948-55, partner, 1955—. Pres. Ill. Dist. 110 Sch. Bd., Deerfield, 1965-66. Mem. Am., 7th Circuit (1st v.p.) bar assns., Chgo., Am. patent law assns. Office: 20 N Wacker Dr Chicago IL 60606 Tel (312) 346-1630

WOOD, RICHARD WILLIAM, b. Southington, Conn., Dec. 22, 1925; B.S., U. Md., 1955; LL.B., Cath. U. Am., 1959, J.D., 1967. Admitted to Conn. bar, 1960; partner firm Kremski & Wood, 1960-61; individual practice law, Southington, 1961-72; partner firm Wood & Giammatteo, Southington, 1973—; asst. pros. atty. 17th Circuit Ct. State of Conn., 1961-66. Mem. Hartford County, Southington (pres.) bar assns. Home: 1049 E St Southington CT 06489 Office: 645 Main St PO Box 597 Southington CT 06489 Tel (203) 628-9671

WOOD, ROBERT CORNELIUS, III, b. Lynchburg, Va., July 4, 1940; B.A., Washington and Lee U., 1962; LL.B., U. Va., 1965. Admitted to Va. bar, 1965, U.S. Supreme Ct. bar, 1976; asso. firm Mays, Valentine, Davenport & Moore, Richmond, Va., 1965-67; partner firm Edmunds, Williams, Robertson, Sackett, Baldwin & Graves, Lynchburg, 1967—. Bd. dirs. United Way Central Va., 1974-77, Met. YMCA, Lynchburg, 1947-77; trustee Seven Hills Sch., Lynchburg, 1975-77; pres. Lynchburg Fine Arts Center, 1971-72. Mem. Am., Va., Lynchburg bar assns., State Bar Va., Washington and Lee U., Alumni Assn. (pres. 1974). Home: 4720 Locksview Rd Lynchburg VA 24503 Office: 916 Main St Lynchburg VA 24505 Tel (804) 846-6591

WOOD, ROBERT HOWARD, b. Lansing, Mich., Nov. 7, 1929; B.S., Mich. State Coll., 1951; LL.B., U. Wis., 1957. Admitted to Wis. bar, 1957, Mich. bar, 1962; mem. firm Wert & Wood, St. Johns, Mich., 1963-66; asso. municipal judge City of St. Johns, 1966-68, mayor, 1968-74; mem. firm Maples & Wood, St. Johns, 1974—; justice of peace, St. Johns, 1963-66. Mem. Mich., Clinton-Gratiot bar assns. Office: 306 N Clinton Saint Johns MI 48879 Tel (517) 224-3238

WOOD, ROBERT VIRGLE, b. Cin., July 2, 1927; B.A., U. Cin., 1949; LL.B., 1950. Admitted to Ohio bar, 1950; asso. firm Hopkins & Hopkins, Cin., 1950-51; partner firm McIlwain, Rogoff & Wood, Cin., 1951-61; served with JAGC, U.S. Air Force, 1952-54; judge Cin. Municipal Ct., 1961-66, Hamilton County (Ohio) Ct. Common Pleas, 1966—. Mem. Ohio, Fed. bar assns., Ohio State Common Pleas Judges Assn. Recipient Outstanding Jud. Service awards, Supreme Ct. Ohio; contbr. to Cin. Law Rev., 1949. Home: 888 VanDyke Ave Governor's House Cincinnati OH 45226 Office: Hamilton County Courthouse Room 324 Cincinnati OH 34202 Tel (513) 632-8230

WOOD, THOMAS TEXTON, b. Harbor Beach, Mich., Oct. 2, 1943; B.S., Central Mich. U., 1968; J.D., U. Mich., 1971. Admitted to Hawaii bar, 1972, U.S. Dist. Ct. bar, 1972; law clk. to Judge Orman W. Ketcham of Superior Ct. D.C., 1971-72; dep. atty. gen. Hawaii, 1972-76; atty. firm Carlsmith, Carlsmith, Wichman and Case, Honolulu, 1976—. Mem. Am., Hawaii bar assns. Office: PO Box 656 Honolulu HI 96809 Tel (808) 524-5112

WOOD, WILLIAM CLIFFORD, b. Richmond, Va., Sept. 25, 1939; B.A. in English, Randolph-Macon Coll.; J.D., U. Richmond. Admitted to Va. bar, 1966; asso. firm Minor, Thompson, Savage & Smith, 1966-72; partner firm Rawlings & Wood, Richmond, Va., 1972—. Office: 910 Parham Rd Richmond VA 23233 Tel (804) 285-9015

WOOD, WILLIAM COPELAND, JR., b. Birmingham, Ala., Nov. 17, 1945; B.E.E., Vanderbilt U., 1967, J.D., 1970. Admitted to Ala. bar, 1970, U.S. Supreme Ct. bar, 1975; law clk. U.S. Dist. Ct. for No. Ala. Judge Sam C. Pointer, 1970-71; asso. firm Norman & Fitzpatrick, Birmingham, 1971-76; partner firm Norman, Fitzpatrick & Wood, Birmingham, 1977—. Mem. Am., Ala., Birmingham (chmn. ins. com. 1976) bar assns., Ala. Def. Lawyers Assn. Home: 3917 Jackson Blvd Birmingham AL 35213 Office: 1100 City Federal Bldg Birmingham AL 35203 Tel (205) 328-6643

WOOD, WILLIAM DUANE, III, b. Charlottesville, Va., July 15, 1925; LL.B., John B. Stetson U., 1950. Admitted to Fla. bar, 1951; individual practice law, DeLand, Fla., 1951-52; claim mgr. Fireman's Fund, Tampa, Fla., 1952-63; asso. firm Ramseur, Bradham, Lyle & Skipper, St. Petersburg, Fla., 1964-72; partner firm Lyle, Skipper, Wood & Anderson, St. Petersburg, 1972-76, sr. partner, 1976—. Mem. Fla. Bar, Am., St. Petersburg bar assns., Lawyer-Pilots Bar, Defense Research Inst., Fla. Defense Lawyers, Am., Pinellas County trial lawyers assns., Am. Arbitration Assn. Office: 699 1st Ave N Saint Petersburg FL 33701 Tel (813) 895-1991

WOOD, WILLIAM HAMILTON, JR., b. Hanover, N.H., Nov. 22, 1921; B.S., Yale, 1942; LL.B., U. Mich., 1948. Admitted to Conn. bar, 1949; asso. firm Hoppin, Carey & Powell, Hartford, Conn., 1949-50, partner, 1951—; dir., counsel to corps. Mem. West Hartford Republican Dist. Com., 1955-66. Fellow Am. Coll. Probate Counsel; mem. Conn. State, Am., Afton County (Conn.) bar assns., Tax Club Hartford, Am. Arbitration Assn. (arbitrator). Home: 207 Fern St West Hartford CT 06119 Office: 266 Pearl St Hartford CT 06103 Tel (203) 249-6891

WOODAHL, ROBERT LEE, b. Great Falls, Mont., June 28, 1931; student Mont. State U., 1949-51; B.S., U. Mont., 1956, J.D., 1959. Admitted to Mont. bar, 1959; gen. practice, Choteau, 1959-68; Teton County atty., 1961-68; atty. gen. Mont., 1968—. Pres. Mont. Elec. Bd. Govt. appeal agt. SSS 1961-68. Mem. Mont., 9th Jud. Dist. bar assns., Am. Legion, Phi Delta Phi, Sigma Alpha Epsilon. Home: Box 34 Gruber Estates Clancy MT 59634 Office: State Capitol Helena MT 59601*

WOODALL, RUSSELL DALE, b. Waggoner, Ill., Jan. 30, 1930; A.B., Washington U., LL.D. Admitted to Mo. bar, 1954, Tex. bar, 1958, Tenn. bar, 1961; legal officer USMC, 1954-56; asst. gen. counsel Ryder Systems, Inc., 1957-59; mem. firm McDonald, Kuhn, McDonald & Smith, Memphis, 1961-65; partner firm Evans, Petree, Cobb & Edwards, Memphis, 1966—; atty. Future Memphis Downtown Assn., Memphis C. of C. Mem. Tenn. Arts Commn.; chmn. Memphis area deferred giving com. Washington U. Mem. Memphis and Shelby County (chmn. com. unauthorized practice of law), Tenn., Am. bar assns., Motor Carriers Law Assn., Am. Assn. Trial Lawyers. Contbr. articles to legal jours. Home: 3750 Houston Levee Rd Germantown TN 38138 Office: 900 Memphis Bank Bldg Memphis TN 38103 Tel (901) 525-6781

WOODBURY, ROLLIN EDWIN, b. Redfield, S.D., Aug. 20, 1913; B.A., Stanford, 1934; LL.B., Harvard, 1939. Admitted to Calif. bar, 1940; asst. counsel, So. Calif. Edison Co., Los Angeles, 1940-48, asst. gen. counsel, 1948-57, gen. counsel, 1957-67, v.p., gen. counsel, Rosemead, Calif., 1967—. Mem. Am., Calif., Los Angeles bar assns., Pacific Coast Elec. Assn., Phi Beta Kappa, Delta Sigma Rho. Home: 1520 Pegfair Estate Dr Pasadena CA 91103 Office: 2244 Walnut Grove Ave PO Box 800 Rosemead CA 91770 Tel (213) 572-2289

WOODFIN, GENE MACK, b. Paris, Tex., Feb. 7, 1919; grad. with highest honors, U. Tex., 1940. Admitted to Tex. bar, 1940; asso. firm Vinson, Elkins, Weems & Searls, Houston, 1940-46, partner, 1946-59; sr. partner firm Loeb, Rhoades & Co., 1959-73, ltd. partner, 1973—; pres. Marathon Mfg. Co., 1973—, chmn. bd., chief exec. officer, 1976—; dir. Fed. Res. Bank of Dallas, Pasco, Inc., Studebaker-Worthington, Inc., Jim Walter Corp., Susquehanna Corp. Pres., dir. U. Tex. Found., Inc. Mem. State Bar Tex., Am. Bar Assn. Home: 506 Shadywood Houston TX 77057 Office: 1900 Marathon Bldg 600 Jefferson Houston TX 77002 Tel (713) 659-7444

WOODLEY, SAMUEL SPRUILL, JR., b. Columbia, N.C., Feb. 3, 1939. Admitted to N.C. bar, 1963; asso. firm Battle, Winslow, Scott & Wiley, Rocky Mt., N.C., 1966-68; partner firm Battle, Winslow, Scott & Wiley, Rocky Mt., 1969-70, officer-dir., part owner, 1970—. Mem. vestry St. Andrews Episcopal Ch., Rocky Mt., 1969-71, 75—. Mem. Am., N.C. bar assns., Law Alumni Assn. U. N.C., (dir. 1975—), Phi Alpha Delta (pres. 1962-63). Editorial bd. U. N.C. Law Rev., 1962-63. Home: 3409 Woodlawn Rd Rocky Mount NC 27801 Office: PO Drawer 269 Rocky Mount NC 27801 Tel (919) 446-6108

WOODLIFF, L. KIRK, b. Lawton, Okla., Sept. 26, 1912; B.A., U. Okla., 1935, LL.B., 1937. Admitted to Okla. bar, 1937; asst. gen. counsel Okla. Employment Security Commn., 1937-39, state dir., Oklahoma City, 1939-41; partner firms Koch & Woodliff, Henryetta, Okla., 1946-59, Woodliff & Woodliff, Henryetta, 1970-72; gen. counsel W. R. Stubbs Transports, Inc., Henryetta, 1960-70; judge 24th Jud. Dist. Ct., 1972—, presiding judge East-Central Jud. Adminstrv. Dist., Eastern Okla., 1975—; mem. Okla. State Ct. of Tax Rev., 1973—, presiding judge, 1975—. Scoutmaster, Creek Nation council Boy Scouts Am., 1948-51; pres. Okla. Good Roads and Sts. Assn., 1967; bd. visitors U. Okla., 1971-74. Mem. Okla. State, Okmulgee County bar assns., Am. Judicature Soc. Home: 611 N 5th St Henryetta OK 74437 Office: PO Box 995 Okmulgee OK 74447 Tel (918) 756-0672

WOODMAN, ERIC EVAN, b. San Francisco, Sept. 25, 1943; B.S., San Jose State U., 1965; J.D., U. Santa Clara, 1969. Admitted to Calif. bar, 1970; partner firm Woodman & Woodman, Redwood City, Calif., 1970—. Sec.-treas. Redwood City Hunger Fund, 1973—. Office: 211 Marshall St PO Box 5331 Redwood City CA 94063 Tel (415) 366-8439

WOODMAN, WALTER JAMES, b. Talara, Peru, Jan. 21, 1941; B.A., U. Miami, Fla., 1964; J.D., So. Meth. U., 1967. Admitted to Tex. bar, 1967, U.S. Supreme Ct. bar, 1971; individual practice law, Dallas, 1967-72, Waxahachie, Tex, 1972—. Contbr. articles and book revs. to legal jours. Home: Route 5 Waxahachie TX 75165 Office: 507 Water St Waxahachie TX 75165 Tel (214) 937-3080

WOODRICH, CHARLES SPEER, b. Chgo., Apr. 16, 1923; B.A., U. Chgo., J.D., 1949. Admitted to Oreg. bar, 1950; individual practice law, Roseburg, 1950-55; judge Oreg. Circuit Ct., 16th Dist., Roseburg, 1955—. Chmn., Roseburg chpt. ARC. Mem. Oreg. Circuit Judges Assn. (former pres.), Oreg. Jud. Council. Home: 17 Royal Oak Dr Roseburg OR 97470 Office: Courthouse Roseburg OR 97470 Tel (503) 672-3311

WOODROE, STEPHEN CLARK, b. Charleston, W.Va., Oct. 28, 1940; B.A. magna cum laude, Harvard, 1963; LL.B., U. Va., 1969. Admitted to W.Va. bar, 1969; asso. firm Campbell, Love, Woodroe, Gilbert & Kizer, Charleston, 1969-74, partner, 1974-76, Love, Wise, Robinson & Woodroe, Charleston, 1976—; staff atty. judiciary com. W.Va. Ho. of Dels., 1972; mem. com. on fed. and state constns. W.Va. State Bar, 1976—. Mem. Am., W.Va., Kanawha County bar assns., W.Va. State Bar, Am. Judicature Soc. Editorial bd. Va. Law Rev., 1968-69. Home: 1005 Pine Rd Charleston WV 25314 Office: 1200 Charleston Nat Plaza Charleston WV 25301 Tel (304) 343-4841

WOODROFFE, JAMES HENRY BLACKER, III, b. Tampa, Fla., Mar. 17, 1942; B.A. in Accounting, U. South Fla., 1964; J.D., U. Fla., 1967. Admitted to Fla. bar, 1967; adminstrv. asst. Tampa Electric Co., 1967-68, asst. mgr. claims, 1968-69, mgr. claims, 1969-71, asst. sec., 1971-73, asst. sec., asst. to sr. v.p., 1973—; publicity chmn. Tampa-Hillsborough County Law Week Com.; v.p., dir. Tampa Oral Sch. for the Deaf; mem. legal claims com. Southeastern Electric Exchange. Loaned exec. Tampa United Fund; pres., dir. Tampa Tarpon Tournament. Mem. Am., Fla., Hillsborough County bar assns., Fla. Bus. Forum, U. Fla. Alumni Assn (pres. dir.). Home: 12002 Orange Grove Dr Tampa FL 33618 Office: PO Box 111 Tampa FL 33601 Tel (813) 879-4111

WOODROW, MURRAY, b. Yonkers, N.Y., Apr. 26, 1925; A.B., U. Md., 1951, J.D., 1951. Admitted to Md. bar, 1951, N.Y. bar, 1953, U.S. Supreme Ct. bar, 1959; partner firm Woodrow, Burrows & O'Carroll, Yonkers, 1955—; adj. prof. Westchester Community Coll.; asso. counsel state legis. com. on election law, 1970-73, com. on environment conservation, 1973-74. Mem. Yonkers, Westchester bar assns. Home: 2 Hunter Dr Portchester NY 10573 Office: 20 S Broadway Yonkers NY 10701 Tel (914) 968-0006

WOODRUFF, ROBERT FREDERIC, b. Hamilton, Ohio, Nov. 26, 1909; A.B., Miami U., Ohio, 1932; J.D., U. Cin., 1935. Admitted to Ohio bar, 1936; individual practice law, Oxford, Ohio, 1936—; atty. Butler Rural Elec. Coop., Inc., Hamilton, 1936—; asst. prof. law Miami U., 1942-76, prof. emeritus, 1976—. Bd. dirs. Oxford Cemetery Assn., Oxford, Ohio and Mt. Pleasant Retirement Center, Monroe; atty. McCullough-Hyde Meml. Hosp., Oxford. Mem. Am., Ohio, Butler County bar assns., Am. Bus. Law Assn., Am. Judicature Soc. Home: 33 W Church St Oxford OH 45056 Office: 29 N Beech St Oxford OH 45056 Tel (513) 523-6369

WOODS, BRYAN DOUGLAS, b. Madison, Wis., Nov. 29, 1948; B.S. in Mech. Engring., U. Wis., 1971, J.D., 1972. Admitted to Wis. bar, U.S. Dist. Ct. of Western Dist. Wis. bar, U.S. Tax Ct. bar, 1973; asso. firm Molbreak, Madison, 1973—. Mem. Am., Dane County bar assns. Home: 3514 Gregory St Madison WI 53711 Office: 110 E Main St Madison WI 53703 Tel (608) 257-0441

WOODS, CHARLES ALBERT, JR., b. Sewickley, Pa., June 10, 1903; A.B., Princeton, 1925; LL.B., Harvard, 1928. Admitted to Pa. bar, 1928, U.S. Supreme Ct. bar, 1945; asso. firm Dickie, Robinson & McCamey, Pitts., 1930-47; partner firm Baker, Watts & Woods, Pitts., 1948-62; of counsel firm Goehring, Rutter & Boehm, Pitts., 1963—; asso. Robert D. Hanson, Harrisburg, 1973—; asst. prof. to adj. prof. law U. Pitts., 1946-63; dep. atty. gen. State of Pa., 1963-72; mayor Sewickley (Pa.), 1950-58, solicitor, 1958-67. Mem. Am. Law Inst., Am. Coll. Probate Counsel, Am., Fed., Pa., Allegheny County, Dauphin County bar assns., AAUP, Am. Judicature Soc. Home: R D 2 Box 19B Limekiln Rd New Cumberland PA 17070 Office: 202 Blackstone Bldg Harrisburg PA 17101 Tel (717) 236-8015

WOODS, DAVID TAYLOR, b. Battle Creek, Mich., July 7, 1943; B.S., Ball State U., 1966; J.D., Ind. U., 1969. Admitted to Ind. bar, 1969; partner firm Jones & Woods, Franklin, Ind., 1969-71; individual practice law, Franklin, 1971-72; judge Brown County (Ind.) Circuit Ct., 1972—; dep. pros. atty. Johnson and Brown counties, 1971, master commr., juvenile referee, 1971-72. Exploring chmn. Central Ind. council Boy Scouts Am., 1970-72, So. Ind. council, 1973-75. Mem. Ind., Am. bar assns., Ind. Judges Assn., Ind. Juvenile Ct. Judges Council (treas.). Home: CB 52 19th Dr Nineveh IN 46164 Office: Brown County Courthouse Nashville IN 47448 Tel (812) 988-7557

WOODS, DICK HOBLIT, JR., b. Kansas City, Mo., Oct. 13, 1942; B.A., Williams Coll., 1965; J.D. magna cum laude, U. Mich., 1968. Admitted to Ill. bar, 1968; since practiced in Lincoln, Ill., partner firm Woods & Bates (and predecessor), 1968—. Chmn. Greater Lincoln Area United Fund, 1970-71, dir. 1971-74, pres. 1972; sec. Lincoln Jaycees, 1970-71, pres. 1971-72; bd. dirs. Greater Lincoln Area C. of C., 1971-74; mem. bd. edn. Lincoln Elementary Sch. Dist. #27, 1976—, citizens advisory com., 1973-74; chmn. Pub. Bldg. Commn. Logan County, Ill., 1973-75; trustee Lincoln U., 1975—, chmn. bldgs. and grounds com., 1975—. Mem. Logan County Bar Assn. Recipient Spark Plug of the Year Award, 1972, Distinguished Service Award, 1973, Lincoln Jaycees; Man of the Month Lincoln Courier, 1972;

elected to Outstanding Young Men in Am., 1970. Home: 505 College Ave Lincoln IL 62656 Office: Clinton St Lincoln IL 62556 Tel (217) 735-1234

WOODS, DONALD EDWARD, b. Shamrock, Tex., Apr. 17, 1945; B.A., Tex. A. and M. U., 1967; J.D., U. Houston, 1970; LL.M., So. Meth. U., 1976. Admitted to Tex. bar, 1970; chief mil. justice, Great Falls, Mont., 1970-71, Colorado Springs, Colo., 1973-75; staff judge advocate JAGC, U.S. Air Force, Korat, Thailand, 1971-73; chief legal counsel U.S. Negotiating Team, Ankara, Turkey, 1975—. Decorated Bronze Star. Home: PO Box 634 McLean TX 79057 Office: Det 22 1141 USAF Special Activities Squadron APO NY 09254

WOODS, ELDON CARL, b. Ft. Branch, Ind., July 27, 1922; B.S., Ind. U., 1946, J.D., 1967. Clk.-treas. Town of Ft. Branch, 1948-50; treas. Gibson County (Ind.), 1951-57; field examiner Ind. State Bd. Accounts, 1957-65; controller Ind. Dept. Correction, Indpls., 1965-67; admitted to Ind. bar, 1967; mem. firm Gleason, Woods, & Johnson, Indpls., Ind., 1968-72; individual practice law, Indpls., 1973—; dir. adminstrv. services Ind. Dept. Correction, 1967-75, exec. dir budget and fiscal affairs. Mem. Ind. State Bar Assn. Pub. accountant, Ind. Office: 1322 Circle Tower Indianapolis IN 46204 Tel (317) 631-1838

WOODS, GERALD WAYNE, b. Durham, N.C., Sept. 15, 1946; B.S., U. N.C., Chapel Hill, 1968; J.D., Emory U., 1973. Admitted to Ga. bar, 1973; div. mgr. Sears, Roebuck & Co., Decatur, Ga., 1968-70; intern Ga. Dept. Revenue, Atlanta, 1972-73; asst. to exec. sec. Bd. of Regents, U. System Ga., Atlanta, 1973-76, asst. exec. sec., 1973—. Mem. A.B.A., Nat. Assn. of Coll. and Univ. Attys., Nat. Orgn. on Legal Problems in Edn., Ansley Kiwanis Club (bd. dirs. 1975-76, treas. 1976-77). Recipient Am. Jur. award Moot Ct. Soc., 1972; named del. Nat. Model UN, 1968; del. chmn. Middle S. Model UN, 1968. Home: 1055 Greencove Ave NE Atlanta GA 30306 Office: 244 Washington St SW Atlanta GA 30334 Tel (404) 656-2261

WOODS, HENRY, b. Abbeville, Miss., Mar. 17, 1918; A.B., U. Ark., 1938, J.D., 1940. Admitted to Ark. bar, 1940, U.S. Supreme Ct. bar, 1956; partner firm Alston & Woods, Texarkana, Ark., 1940-41, 46-48; spl. agt. FBI, 1941-46; exec. sec. gov. of Ark., 1949-53; partner firm McMath, Leatherman & Woods, Little Rock, 1953—; referee in bankruptcy, Texarkana Div. U.S. Dist. Ct., 1946-47; instr. sch. law U. Ark., 1970-71; spl. asso. judge Ark. Supreme Ct., 1967, 74; spl. circuit judge 6th Jud. Dist., 1970; mem. exec. com. Center for Trial and Appellate Advocacy, Hasting Coll. of Law, U. Calif., chmn., 1975-76; mem. joint conf. com. Am. Bar Assn. and AMA. Pres., Young Democrats of Ark., 1946-48; mem. Ark. Constl. Revision Study Commn., 1967-68; mem. Gubernatorial Commn. to Study Death Penalty in Ark., 1974-75; bd. dirs. Catholic High Sch. for Boys. Mem. Am., Ark. (pres., 1972-73, Outstanding Lawyer award 1974-75), Pulaski County bar assns., Am. gov. 1965-67), Ark. (pres. 1965-67) trial lawyers assns., Internat. Acad. Trial Lawyers, Internat. Soc. Barristers, Phi Alpha Delta. Contbr. articles to legal publs. Home: 42 Wingate Dr Little Rock AR 72205 Office: 711 W 3d St Little Rock AR 72201 Tel (501) 376-3021

WOODS, HOMER HOUSTON, b. New Virginia, Iowa, July 7, 1903; A.B., Simpson Coll., Indianola, Iowa, 1925; LL.B., Harvard, 1928. Admitted to N.Y. State bar, 1928; partner firm Hodgson, Russ, Andrews, Woods & Goodyear, Buffalo, N.Y., 1946-75, counsel, 1975—; dir. Niagara Share Corp., 1942-45, Schoellkopf, Hutton & Pomeroy, Ind., 1942-45, Dunlop Tire & Rubber Co., 1944-45, Citizens Central Bank, 1958-72, Fisher-Price Toys, Inc., 1958-69, Niagara Frontier Transit Systems, Inc., 1960-67, Upson Co., 1944-75, Am. Mailing Co., 1964-68. Vice-chmn. N.Y. State Commn. Econ. Expansion, 1959-60; chmn. zoning bd. appeals, Amherst, N.Y., 1957-73; trustee, vice chmn. N.Y. State Dormitory Authority, 1965-74; trustee Simpson Coll. Mem. Am., N.Y. State, Erie County bar assns., Buffalo C. of C. Home: 108 Lake Ledge Dr Williamsville NY 14221 Office: 1800 One M and T Plaza Buffalo NY 14203 Tel (716) 856-4000

WOODS, JOSEPH ALMOTH, JR., b. Decatur, Ala., Mar. 24, 1925; A.B., U. Calif., Berkeley, 1947, J.D., 1949. Admitted to Calif. bar, 1950; asso. firm Donahue, Gallagher, Thomas & Woods, and predecessors, Oakland, Calif., 1950-53, partner, 1953—; sr. asso. spl. counsel U.S. Ho. of Reps. Com. on Judiciary, 1974. Mem. Am., Alameda County (Calif.) (pres. 1975) bar assns., State Bar Calif. Office: 415 20th St Oakland CA 94612 Tel (415) 451-0544

WOODS, JOSEPH REID, b. Milroy, Ind., Oct. 11, 1929; B.S., Ind. U., 1952, J.D., 1963. Admitted to Ind. bar, 1963; individual practice law, Indpls., 1963—; spl. agt. Office of Naval Intelligence, resident agt. in charge of Des Moines office, 1954-57; ins. claims adjuster State Farm Ins. Co., Indpls., 1958-62. Bd. dirs, Franklin Twp. Community Sch. Corp., 1970—, pres. bd., 1972-74, 76—. Mem. Nat. Sch. Bds. Assn., Indpls., Ind. State bar assns., Ind. Trial Lawyers Assn. Home: 6305 Fairlane Dr Indianapolis IN 46259 Office: 130 E Washington St Indianapolis IN 46204 Tel (317) 632-6391

WOODS, LARRY ORVAL, b. Sidney, Mont., May 10, 1926; edn. certificate Ea. Mont. Coll., 1946; LL.B., Mont. State U., 1948. Admitted to Mont. bar, 1948, Fed. bar, 1949; individual practice law, 1948—. Mem. Mont., Yellowstone County (pres. 1971-72) bar assn., Eastern Mont. Alumni Assn. (pres. 1951-52). Home: Route 4 64th St W Billings MT 59102 Office: 204 Behner Bldg Billings MT 59101 Tel (406) 252-3857

WOODS, RICHARD HENRY, b. Cleve., Apr. 19, 1915; B.S., Bowdoin Coll., 1937; postgrad. Harvard Law Sch., 1937-38; LL.B., Case Western Res. U., 1941, J.D., 1968. Admitted to Ohio bar, 1941; atty. Ordnance div. U.S. War Dept., 1941; legal officer Capt. of the Port, Honolulu, 1943-44; hearing and exam. officer Mcht. Marine Hearing Unit, U.S. Coast Guard, N.Y.C., 1945; individual practice law, Cleve., 1945—; mem. Ohio Gen. Assembly, 1947-48, 51-52, 53-54. Mem. Bar Assn. Greater Cleve. (trustee 1950-53). Contbr. articles to mags. Home: 16956 Van Aken Blvd Shaker Heights OH 44120 Office: 905 Williamson Bldg Cleveland OH 44114 Tel (216) 241-6171

WOODS, THOMAS CURTIS, b. St. Petersburg, Fla., Feb. 20, 1947; B.A., Vanderbilt U., 1969, J.D., 1972. Admitted to Fla. bar, 1972, D.C. bar, 1977; asso. firm Bradford, Williams, McKay, Kimbrell, Hamann & Jennings, Miami, Fla., 1972—. Mem. Am., Dade County (dir. 1976—, dir. young lawyers sect. 1974—) bar assns., Dade County Def. Bar Assn., D.C. Bar, Fla. Bar (bd. govs. young lawyers sect. 1975-77), Am. Judicature Soc., Phi Delta Phi. Office: 101 E Flagler St 9th Floor Miami FL 33131 Tel (305) 358-8181

WOODS, WINTON DERUYTER, JR., b. Balt., Jan. 11, 1938; A.B., Ind. U., 1951; J.D. cum laude, 1965. Admitted to U.S. Supreme Ct. bar, 1971, Ind. bar, 1965, Ariz. bar, 1972; law clk. U.S. Dist. Ct., Sacramento, 1965-67; prof. law U. Ariz., 1967—; vis. prof. law U. Ill., fall 1976; of counsel Peter D. Eisner, Tucson, 1975—. Chmn. Citizens Planning Adv. Com., Tucson, 1975; dir. Papago Legal Services, 1967-70; mem. Arizonans for a Quality Environment, 1969—, Traditional Indians Alliance, 1975—. Mem. Ariz. Bar Assn., Ariz. Trial Lawyers Assn., Order of Coif. Contbr. articles to law revs.; Fellow Nat. Endowment for the Humanities. Office: Coll Law Univ Ariz Tucson AZ 85721 Tel (602) 884-1974

WOODSIDE, HOWARD BUSH, b. Pitts., Aug. 14, 1921; B.A., U. Wis., 1943, J.D., 1948. Admitted to Wis. bar, 1948; partner firm Emery & Woodside, Marshfield, Wis., 1948-51, 54-56; mem. JAGC, U.S. Army, 1951-54; asso. counsel Sentry Ins. Co., Stevens Point, Wis., 1956-63, asst. gen. counsel, 1963—; chmn. industry adv. com. Wis. Ins. Laws Revision Com., 1969—. Chmn. 7th dist. Wis. Republican Party, 1961-69. Mem. Am., Wis., Portage County bar assns., Order of Coif. Office: 1421 Strongs Ave Stevens Point WI 54481 Tel (715) 344-2345

WOODSOME, EDWIN VALENTINE, JR., b. Chgo., Oct. 20, 1946; A.B. summa cum laude, Coll. Holy Cross, 1968; J.D. magna cum laude, Harvard U., 1971. Admitted to Calif. bar, 1973, Mass. bar, 1972, D.C. bar, 1973; law clk. to chief judge U.S. Ct. Appeals 9th Circuit, San Francisco, 1971-72; asso. firm Foley, Hoag & Eliot, Boston, 1972-73; asso. firm Munger, Tolles & Rickershauser, Los Angeles, 1974-75, partner, 1976—. Gen. counsel Calif. Democratic Party, 1974—. Mem. Calif., Mass., D.C., Am. bar assns. Editor Harvard Law Rev., 1970-71. Office: 606 S Hill St Los Angeles CA 90014 Tel (213) 626-1491

WOODWARD, JOE DAVIS, b. Magnolia, Ark., Mar. 26, 1930; A.A., Ark. So. U., 1949; J.D., U. Ark., 1953. Admitted to Ark. bar, 1952, U.S. Supreme Ct. bar, 1962; served as capt. JAGC, U.S. Army, 1953-55; practice law, Magnolia, 1955-60; partner firm Crumpler & Woodward, Magnolia, 1960-65, firm Woodward & Kinard, Magnolia, 1965—; city atty. City of Magnolia, 1956-62; pros. atty. 13th Dist. Ark., 1962-66; spl. asso. justice Ark. Supreme Ct., 1975; mem. Ark. Bd. Law Examiners, 1973—; chmn. Ark. Commerce Commn., 1971-73; legis. liason Gov. Ark., 1973-74. Trustee Magnolia City Hosp., 1970-75. Mem. Ark. (ho. dels. 1971-76, mem. exec. council 1976—), Columbia County (past pres.) bar assns., Am. Arbitration Assn. Home: 707 Sue St Magnolia AR 71753 Office: 112 Calhoun St Magnolia AR 71753 Tel (501) 234-4727

WOODWARD, JOHN STEPHEN, b. Sandwich, Ill., Feb. 16, 1903; B.S., Northwestern U., 1925, J.D., 1928. Admitted to Ill. bar, 1928, since practiced in Wheaton; asso. firm Charles W. Hadley, 1928-33, partner, 1933-38; partner Rathje, Woodward, Dyer & Burt, 1938—. Chmn. local chpt. Salvation Army, 1962-75. Mem. Am., Ill., DuPage County bar assns. Home: 1599 Whitman Ln Wheaton IL 60187 Office: 203 E Liberty Dr Wheaton IL 60187 Tel (312) 668-8500

WOODWARD, MARION KENNETH, b. Amarillo, Tex., Apr. 15, 1912; B.A., U. Tex., 1933, LL.B., 1943; M.A., W. Tex. State U., 1940. Admitted to Tex. bar, 1942; individual practice law, Amarillo, 1945; staff atty. Phillips Petroleum Co., Amarillo, 1945-46; asso. prof. law U. Tex., 1946-49, prof., 1950-65, Robert F. Windfohr prof. Law, 1965—. Commr., Nat. Conf. Commns. on Uniform State Laws, 1956-62; mem. legal com. Interstate Oil Compact Commn., 1962-73. Mem. Am., Tex., Travis County bar assns., Order of Coif. Am. Coll. Probate Counsel acad. fellow, 1974; author: (with Huie and Smith) Cases and Materials on Oil and Gas Law, 1972; (with Smith) Probate and Decedents' Estates, 1971; contbr. articles to profl. jours. Home: 3408 Shinoak Dr Austin TX 78731 Office: 2500 Red River St Austin TX 78705 Tel (512) 471-5151

WOODWORTH, DOUGLAS RAND, b. Los Angeles, Apr. 14, 1928; A.B., Stanford, 1948; LL.B., U. San Francisco, 1952. Admitted to Calif. bar, 1953, since practiced in San Diego; asso. counsel Union Title Ins. & Trust Co., 1953-55; individual practice law, 1955-68; judge Municipal Ct., 1968-72, Superior Ct., 1972—; moderator pub. affairs TV series, 1956-57. Mem. Conf. Calif. Judges, Am. Judicature Soc., Am. Judges Assn. Contbr. articles in field to legal jours. Office: 220 W Broadway San Diego CA 92101 Tel (714) 236-2595

WOODWORTH, DUANE ERNEST, b. Mpls., Sept. 3, 1935; B.A., U. Minn., 1961, J.D., 1965; certificate of completion Nat. Coll. State Judiciary, 1975, 76. Admitted to Minn. bar, 1965, Iowa bar, 1968; mem. staff Minn. atty. gen., St. Paul, 1965-66; partner firm Slattengren & Woodworth, Mpls., 1966-67; staff atty., exec. dir. Leech Lake Legal Services Project, Cass Lake, Minn., 1967-68, 69-70; exec. dir. Blackhawk County (Iowa) Legal Aid Soc., Waterloo, 1968-70; partner firm Hillstrom & Woodworth, La Crescent, Minn., 1970-74; judge Houston County (Minn.) Ct., 1974—. Bd. dirs. Apple Fest, La Crescent, 1974-76. Mem. Minn. State Bar, Houston County Bar, Am. Bar Assn., Am. Trial Lawyers Assn., Nat. Council Juvenile Ct. Judges, 3d Jud. Dist. County Ct. Judges Assn. (chancellor, del. State County Ct. Judges Assn.). Home: Rural Route 1 La Crescent MN 55947 Office: County Courthouse Caledonia MN 55921 Tel (507) 724-3896

WOOL, LEON, b. Chgo., Dec. 10, 1937; B.A. Drake U., 1960; J.D., DePaul U., 1963. Admitted to Ill. bar, 1963; atty. Chgo. Transit Authority, 1963—, dir. claim dept., 1975-76, mgr. labor relations, 1976—. Mem. Am., Ill., Chgo. bar assns. Home: 9411 N Springfield Evanston IL 60203 Office: Chgo Transit Authority Merchandise Mart Chicago IL 60654 Tel (312) MO4-7200

WOOLF, ROBERT GARY, b. South Portland, Maine, Feb. 15, 1928; A.B., Boston Coll., 1949; LL.B., J.D., Boston U., 1952. Admitted to Mass. bar, 1952, U.S. Supreme Ct. bar, 1956; individual practice law, Boston, 1954—. Bd. dirs. St. Jude Hosp. Found., Am. Cancer Soc.; pres. council Franklin Pierce Coll., active Boston area Boy Scouts Am. Mem. Am., Mass. bar assns., Mass. Trial Lawyers Assn. Author: Behind Closed Dors, 1976. Home: 6 Nelson Dr Chestnut Hill MA 02167 Office: 4575 Prudential Tower Boston MA 02199 Tel (617) 261-2555

WOOLSEY, ROBERT JAMES, JR., b. Tulsa, Sept. 21, 1941; B.A., Stanford, 1963; M.A., Oxford (Eng.) U., 1965; LL.B., Yale, 1968. Admitted to Calif. bar, 1969, D.C. bar, 1970; asso. firm O'Melveny and Myers, Los Angeles, 1968; advisor U.S. Del. to U.S.-Soviet Strategic Arms Limitation Talks, Helsinki, Finland and Vienna, Austria, 1969-70; staff NSC, Washington, 1970; gen. counsel U.S. Senate Com. Armed Services, Washington, 1970-73; asso. firm Shea & Gardner, Washington, 1973-77; under-sec. Navy Dept., Washington, 1977—. Trustee, Stanford U., 1972-74. Mem. Council Fgn. Relations. Contbr. articles to newspapers. Home: 6808 Florida St Chevy Chase MD 20015 Office: Undersec of Navy Room 4E714 The Pentagon Washington DC 20350

WOOLSEY, THEODORE DWIGHT, b. Beloit, Wis., Aug. 23, 1906; B.A., Yale, 1928; LL.B., U. Wis., 1930. Admitted to Wis. bar, 1931; individual practice law, Beloit, 1930—; dir. Beloit Bldg & Loan Assn. Chmn., Rock County (Wis.) Bd. Suprs., 1945-46. Mem. Wis., Rock County (pres. 1946-47) bar assns., Assn. Commerce City Beloit. Home: 1810 Emerson St Beloit WI 53511 Office: 533 E Grand Ave Beloit WI 53511 Tel (608) 365-6679

WORD, REUBEN MABRY, b. Bowdon, Ga., May 31, 1922; A.A., W. Ga. Coll., 1941; LL.B., Emory U., 1950, J.D., 1970. Admitted to Ga. bar, 1950; practice law, Carrollton, Ga., 1953—; sr. partner firm Word, Nicholson & Cook, Carrollton, 1974—. Chmn., Carroll County Heart Assn., 1960-69. Mem. Am., Ga., Caroll County bar assns., Ga. Trial Lawyers Assn., Phi Alpha Delta, Tau Kappa Epsilon (mem. bd. control). Contbr. articles to profl. jour. Home: 805 Rome St Carrollton GA 30117 Office: 201 Newman St Carrollton GA 30117 Tel (404) 832-8266

WORK, CHARLES ROBERT, b. Glendale, Calif., June 21, 1940; B.A., Wesleyan U., 1962; J.D., U. Chgo., 1965; LL.M., Georgetown U., 1966. Admitted to Utah bar, 1965, D.C. bar, 1965; asst. U.S. atty. for D.C., 1966-73; dep. adminstr. Law Enforcement Assistance Adminstrn., Dept. Justice, 1973-75; partner firm Peabody, Rivlin, Lambert & Meyers, Washington, 1975—. Bd. dirs. Vera Inst. Justice, Inst. Community Design Analysis; trustee United Planning Orgn. Mem. Am., Fed., D.C. (pres. 1976—) bar assns. Home: 3210 Tennyson St NW Washington DC 20015 Office: 1150 Connecticut Ave NW Washington DC 20036 Tel (202) 457-1016

WORKMAN, HARLEY ROSS, b. Salt Lake City, Dec. 31, 1940; B.A. in Chemistry, U. Utah, 1967, J.D., 1970. Admitted to Utah bar, 1970, Ct. Customs and Patent Appeals bar, 1971; asso. firm Poelman, Fox, Edwards & Oswald, and predecessors, Salt Lake City, 1970-72, mem., 1972—. Chmn. Granite Mental Health Adv. Council, Salt Lake City, 1974-76; pres. World Trade Assn. Utah, 1977—. Mem. Am., Utah bar assns., Am. Patent Law Assn. Contbr. article to mgmt. jour. Home: 4093 Powers Circle Salt Lake City UT 84117 Office: Suite 2000 The Beneficial Life Tower 36 S State St Salt Lake City UT 84111 Tel (801) 521-7751

WORKMAN, THOMAS ELDON, b. Galion, Ohio, Apr. 3, 1944; B.S., Ohio State U., 1966, J.D., 1969. Admitted to Ohio bar, 1969; partner firm Bricker, Evatt, Barton & Eckler, Columbus, Ohio, 1969—; adminstrv. asst. to lt. gov. Ohio, 1967-68; capt. JAGC, U.S. Army, 1970-73. Trustee Glenmont Nursing Home, Columbus, Pub. Law Research Inst. Mem. Am., Ohio State, Columbus bar assns. Home: 191 N Stanwood Rd Columbus OH 43209 Office: 100 E Broad St Columbus OH 43215 Tel (614) 221-6651

WORLEY, CHARLES ROBERT, b. Oklahoma City, Okla., May 23, 1945; A.B. in Polit. Sci., U. N.C., Chapel Hill, 1967, J.D., 1970. Admitted to N.C. bar, 1970; research asst. to judge N.C. Ct. of Appeals, 1970-71; asso. firm McGuire, Wood, Erwin & Crow and successors, Asheville, N.C., 1971—. Bd. dirs. Mountain Ramparts Health Planning Agy., 1974—, chmn. planning com., 1974-75; exec. com., bd. dirs. Western N.C. Health Systems Agy., 1975—. Mem. Am., N.C., Buncombe County bar assns. Home: 86 Gibson Rd Asheville NC 28804 Office: PO Box 1411 Suite 705 First Union National Bank Bldg Asheville NC 28802 Tel (704) 254-8806

WORLEY, DAVID EUGENE, b. Huntsville, Ala., May 1, 1942; B.A., U. Ala., 1967, J.D., 1969. Admitted to Ala. bar, 1969; law clk. circuit judge, Huntsville, 1969-70; city judge Gurley, Ala., 1969—; individual practice law, Huntsville, 1969—. Mem. Ala. Bar Assn., Ala., Am. trial lawyers assn. Home: 1010 Monte Sano Huntsville AL 35801 Office: Terrace Level Central Bank Bldg Huntsville AL 35801 Tel (205) 536-1512

WORLEY, ROBERT WILLIAM, JR., b. Anderson, Ind., June 13, 1935; B.S. in Chem. Engring., Lehigh U., 1956; LL.B., Harvard, 1960. Admitted to Conn. bar, 1960, U.S. Supreme Ct. bar, 1966; partner firm Cummings & Lockwood, Stamford, Conn., 1960—. Commr. Greenwich (Conn.) Housing Authority, 1970-76; mem. Greenwich Republican Town Com., 1974-76. Mem. Am., Conn. (chmn. bank-bar relations com. 1975—), Stamford (sec. 1965), Greenwich bar assns., Comml. Law League. Office: Box 120 Stamford CT 06904 Tel (203) 327-1700

WORNOM, BOYCE CARMINES, b. York County, Va., Jan. 10, 1928; B.S., U. Richmond, 1951, LL.B., T. C. Williams Sch. Law, 1954. Admitted to Va. bar, 1954; mem. firm Townsend & Wornom, Emporia, Va., 1963-73; partner firm Wornom & O'Hara, Emporia, 1973—; pres. Gen. Hugh Mercer Corp. Bd. dirs. Greensville County (Va.) Meml. Hosp.; chmn. Emporia-Greensville Airport Commn., Mem. Am., Va. bar assns., Va., Am. trial lawyers assns., Va. State Bar. Office: 201 Hicksford Ave Emporia VA 23847 Tel 804-634-3147

WORRALL, DOUGLAS GEOFFREY, b. Upper Darby, Pa., Feb. 13, 1939; B.A., U. Md., 1963, LL.B., 1966. Admitted to Md. bar, 1966; partner firm Smith, Somerville & Case, Balt., 1973—. Mem. Am., Md. State, Balt. City bar assns. Home: Black Rock Rd Glyndon MD 21071 Office: 1700 One Charles Center Baltimore MD 21201 Tel (301) 727-1164

WORRELL, ROBERT MITCHELL, b. Pineville, W. Va., Aug. 1, 1919; A.A., Beckley Coll., 1940; LL.B., Washington and Lee U., 1947. Admitted to W. Va. bar, 1947; pres. Wyoming County Bd. Edn., 1949; judge criminal Court, Wyoming County, W. Va., 1951-52, 27th Jud. Circuit, Pineville, 1953-75; individual practice law, Pineville, 1975—. Mem. W. Va. Jud. Assn. (pres. 1974), W. Va. State Bar Assn. Home and office: PO Drawer 570 Pineville WV 24874 Tel (304) 732-8312

WORSLEY, JAMES RANDOLPH, JR., b. Rocky Mount, N.C., July 28, 1924; B.S., East Carolina U., 1944; LL.B., Harvard U., 1949. Admitted to D.C. bar, 1949, N.C. bar, 1949; asso. firm Kaler, Worsley, Daniel & Hollman, 1949-54, partner firm 1955—. Chmn. Md. Potomac Water Authority, Annapolis, 1969—; mem. bd. dirs. Madeira Sch., Greenway, Va., 1975—; mem. Archdiocesan Pastoral Council, Catholic Archidocese Washington, D.C., 1975—. Mem. D.C. Bar, Am. Judicature Soc., N.C., Am. bar assns., Bar Assn. D.C. Home: 3705 Shepherd St Chevy Chase MD 20015 Office: 1200 18th St NW Washington DC 20036 Tel (202) 331-9100

WORSTER, KENNETH BERKLEY, b. Covington, Ky., Dec. 29, 1937; B.S., U. Ky., 1959; J.D., Chase Coll., 1968. Admitted to Ohio bar, 1968; partner firm Brumbaugh, Engelken, Cox & Worster, Greenville, Ohio, 1972; judge Darke County (Ohio) Ct., 1973—; dir. 2d Nat. Bank, Greenville, 1973—. Pres. Darke County Migrant Ministry, 1971; elder Greenville 1st Presbyn. Ch. Mem. Am., Ohio, Darke County (pres. 1975) bar assns., Am. Trial Lawyers Assn. Recipient Superior Jud. Service award Ohio Supreme Ct., 1975. Home: 131 Imo Blvd Greenville OH 45331 Office: 600 S Broadway Greenville OH 45331 Tel (513) 548-1920

WORTH, MONROE MICHAEL, b. Cleve., Apr. 25, 1909; B.B.A., Case Western Reserve U., 1966; J.D., Cleve. Marshall Law Sch., Cleve. State U., 1952. Admitted to Ohio bar, 1952; controller Seaway Title. Corp., Cleve., 1966—. Mem. Ohio State Bar Assn., Ohio Assn. C.P.A.'s, Am. Inst. C.P.A.'s, Nat. Assn. Accountants. Home: 2920

Van Aken Blvd Cleveland OH 44120 Office: 340 Standard Bldg Cleveland OH 44113 Tel (216) 771-7676

WORTHINGTON, JAMES DOWNEY, b. Louisiana, Mo., Aug. 4, 1948; B.S. in Bus. Adminstrn., U. Mo., Columbia, 1970; J.D., U. Mo., Kansas City, 1973. Admitted to Mo. bar, 1973; asso. firm Aull & Sherman, Lexington, Mo., 1973—; law clk. firm Jack C. Terry, Independence, Mo., 1972-73; city atty. City of Lexington, 1976—. Fin. chmn. Big Muddy dist. Boy Scouts Am.; mem. adminstrv. bd. United Methodist Ch. Mem. Am., Mo., Lafayette County (pres. 1975-76), Kansas City bar assns., Am. Trial Lawyers Assn., Mo. Assn. Trial Attys. Home: 1601 Main St Lexington MO 64067 Office: 9 S 11th St Lexington MO 64067 Tel (816) 259-2277

WORTHINGTON, SAMUEL WALTON, III, b. Americus, Ga., Oct. 1, 1942; B.B.A., U. Ga., 1967, J.D., 1970. Admitted to Ga. bar, 1970, U.S. Supreme Ct. bar, 1974, U.S. Ct. Appeals bar 5th Circuit, 1974; partner Moore & Worthington, and predecessor, Columbus, Ga. Mem. Am. Bar Assn., Ga. Trial Lawyers Assn. Office: 908 2d Ave Columbus GA 31901 Tel (404) 324-5606

WORTHY, K(ENNETH) MARTIN, b. Dawson, Ga., Sept. 24, 1920; student The Citadel, 1937-39; Ph.B., Emory U., 1941, J.D., 1947; M.B.A. cum laude, Harvard U., 1943. Admitted to Ga. bar, 1947, D.C. bar, 1948; asso. firm Hamel, Park, McCabe & Saunders, Washington, 1948-52, partner, 1952-69, 72—; chief counsel IRS and asst. gen. counsel U.S. Treasury, 1969-72; mem. Nat. Council on Organized Crime, 1970-72; spl. cons. U.S. Dept. Justice, 1972-74. Del., Montgomery County (Md.) Civic Fedn., 1951-61, D.C. Area Health and Welfare Council, 1960-61; chmn. dept. fin. Episcopal Diocese of Washington, 1969-70; mem. Emory Law Sch. Council, 1976—. Fellow Am. Bar Found.; mem. Am. (chmn. sect. taxation 1973-74), Fed. (nat. council 1969-73) bar assns., Am. Law Inst., Ga. Bar, D.C. Bar, Bar Assn. D.C. Recipient U.S. Treasury Exceptional Service award and medal, 1972; Commr. Internal Revenue award, 1972; contbr. articles in field to profl. jours. Home: 5305 Portsmouth Rd Bethesda MD 20016 Office: 1776 F St NW Washington DC 20006 Tel (202) 785-1234

WRAY, WILLIE PERRY, JR., b. Camden, Ark., Oct. 22, 1928; B.S., La. State U., 1954, LL.B., 1958, J.D., 1968. Admitted to La. bar, 1958, U.S. Supreme Ct. bar, 1958, U.S. Tax Ct. bar, 1958; spl. agt. FBI, Nurorah, N.J., 1953-56; asso. firm Kantrow, Spaht, West & Kleinpeter, Baton Rouge, 1958-61; partner firm Wray & Robinson, Baton Rouge, 1961-62. Pres., bd. dirs. La. Good Roads Assn., Baton Rouge; sec.-treas., bd. dirs. Baton Rouge Action Com. on Alcoholism, Inc.; chmn. Baton Rouge Civic Center Commn.; trustee Judson Baptist Assn., Baton Rouge; mem. Mayor's Ad Hoc Com. on Alcoholism, Baton Rouge. Mem. Baton Rouge, La. (bar exam. com.), Am., Fed. bar assns., La. Assn. Def. Counsel. Office: 610 Fidelity Nat Bank Bldg Baton Rouge LA 70801

WREN, EDGAR ALBAN, b. Scranton, Pa., Mar. 26, 1916; A.B., U. Scranton, 1937; LL.B., Georgetown Law Sch., 1948; M.L., George Washington Law Sch., 1952; J.D., Georgetown U., 1964. Admitted to D.C. bar, 1948, Md. bar, 1972; law clk. firm Gardiner, Earnest, & Gardiner, Washington, 1947, partner, 1948-60; sr. partner firm Edgar A. Wren, Washington, 1960—. Chmn. bd. lay advisors Missionary Servants of the Most Holy Trinity, Washington, 1962-75; pres. Boys' Clubs Greater Washington, 1974—; trustee U. Scranton, 1977—. Mem. Am., Md., Montgomery County bar assns., D.C. bar, Bar Assn. D.C., Am. Judicature Soc., Am. Trial Lawyers Assn. Recipient Service award Trinity Missions, 1970. Home: Route 1 Box 152(B) Indian Head MD 20640 Office: Suite 709 815 15th St NW Washington DC 20005 Tel (202) 638-1111

WRENN, JAMES REID, JR., b. Richmond, Va., Dec. 18, 1945; B.A. in History, U. Richmond, 1968; J.D., U. Va., 1971. Admitted to Va. bar, 1972; spl. counsel Va. State Bar, 1972-76, bar counsel, 1976—; adj. faculty Va. Commonwealth U. Sch. Bus., Richmond, 1973—. Mem. Am. Bar Assn., Nat. Orgn. Bar Counsel (pres. 1976—). Home: 6100 Westower Dr Richmond VA 23225 Office: 700 Bldg 2d Floor 700 E Main St Richmond VA 23219 Tel (804) 786-2061

WRENN, JOYCE MARY, b. Albany, N.Y., June 23, 1936; B.A., Coll. St. Rose, 1958; J.D., Albany Law Sch., 1961; M.A., N.Y. State U., Albany, 1962. Admitted to N.Y. bar, 1962, Fla. bar, 1964, U.S. Supreme Ct. bar, 1967; sr. atty. N.Y. State Dept. Motor Vehicles, Albany, 1962—; atty. Families For The Future; arbitrator small claims Albany City Ct., 1974. Mem. Am., N.Y. State, Albany County, Fla. bar assns., Am. Judicature Soc., Assn. Trial Lawyers Am. Home: 1204 Central Ave Albany NY 12205 Office: Empire State Plaza Albany NY 12228 Tel (518) 474-0871

WRIGHT, C. ROBERT, b. Lansing, Mich., May 17, 1923; A.B., Oberlin Coll., 1949; J.D., Youngstown State U., 1958. Admitted to Ohio bar, 1958; with U.S. Steel Corp., Youngstown, 1953—, supt. 18-43 hot strip mill, McDonald, Ohio, 1976—. Mem. Ohio State, Mahoning County bar assns., Assn. Iron and Steel Engrs. Home: 427 Pamela Ct Poland OH 44514 Office: McDonald Mills McDonald OH 44437 Tel (216) 545-6877

WRIGHT, CARL MACEY, b. Rocksprings, Tex., Sept. 17, 1929; B.S., U.S. Mcht. Marine Acad., 1951; J.D., Temple U., 1971. Admitted to N.J. bar, 1971; computer engr. RCA, Washington, 1959-61, dist. mgr. 1961-67, patent agt., 1967-71, patent counsel, 1971—. Mem. Burlington County Bar Assn. Patentee field of computers. Home: 310 Devon Rd Cinnaminson NJ 08077 Office: PO Box 432 Princeton NJ 08540 Tel (609) 452-2700

WRIGHT, CHARLES ALAN, b. Phila., Sep. 3, 1927; B.A. cum laude, Wesleyan U., 1947; LL.B., Yale, 1949. Admitted to Minn. bar, 1951, U.S. Supreme Ct. bar, 1957, Tex. bar, 1961; law clk. U.S. Circuit Ct. Appeals, New Haven, 1949-50; asst. prof. law U. Minn., 1950-53, asso. prof. law, 1953-55; asso. prof. law U. Tex., Austin, 1955-58, prof. law, 1958-65, McCormick prof. law, 1965—; vis. prof. law U. Pa., Phila., 1959-60, Harvard, 1964-65; Yale, 1968-69; reporter study div. of jurisdiction between state and fed. cts. Am. Law Inst., 1963-69; mem. adv. com. on civil rules Jud. Conf. U.S., 1961-64, mem. standing com. on rules of practice and procedure, 1964-76, mem. subcom. fed. jurisdiction ct. adminstrn. com., 1971—; cons., counsel for Pres., 1973-74; trustee Capitol Broadcasting Assn., Austin, Tex., 1966—, chmn. bd., 1969—. Trustee St. Stephen's Episcopal Sch., Austin, Tex., 1962-66, St. Andrew's Episcopal Sch., 1971-74, chmn. bd., 1973-74; trustee Austin Symphony Orch. Soc., 1966—, mem. exec. com., 1966-70, 72—; mem. permanent com. Oliver Wendell Holmes Devise, 1975—; mem. commn. on infractions, NCAA, 1973—. Mem. Am. Law Inst. (council 1969—), Am. Bar Assn., Inst. Jud. Adminstrn., Am. Judicature Soc., Order of the Coif, Phi Kappa Phi, Omicron Delta Kappa. Author: Wrights Minnesota Rules, 1954; Cases on Remedies, 1955 (with C. T. McCormick and J. H. Chadbourn) Cases on Federal Courts, 1976; Handbook on the Law of Federal Courts, 1976; (with H. M. Reasoner) Procedure - The Handmaid of Justice, 1965; Federal Practice and Procedure, Criminal, 1969; (with A.R. Miller) Federal Practice and Procedure, Civil, 1969-73; (with R.H. Field and P.J. Mishkin) Am. Law Inst. Study of the Division of Jurisdiction Between State and Federal Courts, 1973; (with A.R. Miller and E.H. Cooper) Federal Practice and Procedure: Jurisdiction, 1975. Home: 5304 Western Hills Dr Austin TX 78731 Office: 2500 Red River Austin TX 78705 Tel (512) 471-5151

WRIGHT, CHARLES ASPINALL, JR., b. Chgo., June 22, 1937; B.S. in Edn., No. Ill. U., 1966; J.D., Chgo.-Kent Coll., 1974. Admitted to Ill. bar, 1974; asso. firm Yates, Goff, Gustafson, Sheridan & Been, Chgo., 1974-75, firm Clausen, Miller, Gorman, Caffrey & Witous, Chgo., 1975—. Mem. Ill., Chgo. bar assns. Home: 242 W Saint Paul St Chicago IL 60614 Office: 135 S Lasalle St Chicago IL 60603 Tel (312) 346-6200

WRIGHT, CHARLES THOMAS, b. Shelton, Wash., Mar. 7, 1911; A.B., Coll. Puget Sound., 1932; LL.B., U. Wash., 1934. Admitted to Wash. bar, 1937; individual practice law, Shelton and Union, Wash., 1939-49; judge Superior Ct. Thurston-Mason County (Wash.), Olympia and Shelton, 1949-70; justice Supreme Ct. Wash., Olympia, 1970-77, chief justice, 1977—; acting pros. atty. Mason County (Wash.), 1943-44. Mem. Nat. Conf. State Trial Judges, Nat. Conf. Chief Justices, Superior Ct. Judges Assn. (pres. 1969), Nat., Shelton rifle and pistol assns. Home: Star Route 2 Box 1 Union WA 98592 Office: State Supreme Ct Temple of Justice Olympia WA 98504 Tel (206) 753-5077

WRIGHT, DONALD RICHARD, b. Placentia, Calif., Feb. 2, 1907; A.B. cum laude, Stanford, 1929; J.D., Harvard, 1932; LL.M., U. So. Calif., 1973; LL.D., U. Pacific, 1971. Admitted to Calif. bar, 1932; partner firm Barrick and Wright, Pasadena, Calif., 1933-53; judge Municipal Ct., Pasadena, 1953-61; judge Superior Ct. of Los Angeles County, 1961-68; asso. justice Ct. of Appeals, 1968-70; chief justice Calif. Supreme Ct., San Francisco, 1970—; pres., bd. dirs. Hastings Coll. of Law, 1970—; bd. visitors Stanford Sch. of Law, 1971-74; chmn. Jud. Council of Calif., 1970—. Chmn. Pasadena Planning Commn., 1953. Mem. Am., Pasadena, Los Angeles, San Francisco bar assns., Order of Coif. Author: From Marbury to Anderson; named Appellate Justice of Yr., Calif. Trial Lawyers Assn., 1972; recipient Torch of Liberty award Antidefamation League of B'nai B'rith, 1974. Home: 565 Orange Grove Circle Pasadena CA 91105 Tel (213) 799-6757

WRIGHT, DOUGLAS WILLIAM, b. N.Y.C., Jan. 13, 1945; B.A., Wittenberg U., 1966; J.D., U. Toledo, 1969. Admitted to Ohio bar, 1969; asso. firm Kevern & Gaynor, Toledo, 1969-70; partner firm Brogan & Wright, and predecessors, Toledo, 1970-75, firm Wright, Gusses & Howard, Toledo, 1975—. Mem. Am., Ohio, Toledo bar assns. Recipient Outstanding Young Man Am. award, 1974. Home: 6556 Woodhall Sylvania OH 43560 Office: 411 Michigan St Toledo OH 43624 Tel (419) 248-2419

WRIGHT, ELDON S., b. Youngstown, Ohio, Nov. 28, 1923; B.A., DePauw U., 1947; LL.B., Case Western Res. U., 1950. Admitted to Ohio bar, 1950; sr. partner firm Harrington, Husley & Smith, Youngstown, 1953—. Mem. Liberty Local Bd. Edn., Trumbull County, Ohio, 1972—. Mem. Am., Ohio, Mahoning County bar assns., Nat. Assn. R.R. Trial Counsel, Internat. Assn. Ins. Counsel, Am. Coll. Trial Lawyers. Office: 1200 Mahoning Bank Bldg Youngstown OH 44503 Tel (216) 744-1111

WRIGHT, EUGENE ALLEN, b. Seattle, Feb. 23, 1913; A.B., U. Wash., 1934, J.D., 1937. Admitted to Wash. bar, 1937; asso. firm Wright & Wright, Seattle, 1937-41, partner, 1946-54; judge pro tem Seattle Municipal Ct., 1948-52; judge King County Superior Ct., Seattle, 1954-66, U.S. Ct. Appeals, 9th Circuit, 1969—; chmn. Gov.'s Com. Law and Justice, 1968-69; faculty Nat. Coll. State Judiciary, Reno, Nev., 1964-72; lectr. Sch. Communications, U. Wash., Seattle, 1965-66. Mem. Am. Bar Assn., Am. Judicature Soc., Seattle Jr. C. of C. (past pres.), Order of Coif. Author: (with others) State Trial Judges Book, 1966; editor Trial Judges Jour., 1963-66; contbr. articles to profl. and popular publs. Home: 4343 53d Ave NE Seattle WA 98105 Office: US Court Appeals Seattle WA 98104 Tel (206) 442-7818

WRIGHT, EUGENE BOX, b. Fulton, Ky., Feb. 21, 1943; B.B.A., So. Meth. U., 1965; J.D., U. Houston, 1968. Admitted to Tex. bar, 1968, U.S. Supreme Ct. bar, 1976; individual practice law, Cleveland, Tex., 1968—; city atty. Cleveland, 1969-72; dir. Splendora Lumber Co., 1974—; sec., dir. Cleveland Publ. Co., Inc., 1975—, Triangle Press. Bd. dirs. West Liberty County Indsl. Found., 1974—; chmn. Cleveland Bicentennial Commn., 1975—. Mem. Am., Tex., Liberty County, Chambers County (past pres.) bar assns., Phi Mu Alpha Sinfonia, Delta Sigma Pi, Beta Gamma Sigma, Phi Delta Phi. Named Hon. Ky. Col., 1971. Home: 308 Wall St Cleveland TX 77327 Office: PO Box 192 Cleveland TX 77327 Tel (713) 592-6446

WRIGHT, FREDERICK CHRISTIAN, III, b. Hagerstown, Md., Sept. 4, 1938; B.S., U. Va., 1960, LL.B., 1963. Admitted to Md. bar, 1963; asso. firm McCauley, Cooey, Berkson & Wright and predecessor, Hagerstown, Md., 1963-65, partner, 1965-71; judge Dist. Ct. of Md., Hagerstown, 1971—; adminstrv. judge 11th Dist. Ct., 1971—; mem. Md. Ho. of Dels., 1966-71, speaker pro tem, 1971, chmn. rules com., 1969-71; chmn. adv. com. Md. Pub. Defender. Pres. Boys' Club of Washington County (Md.), 1974-76. Mem. Am. Judicature Soc., N.Am. Trial Judges Assn. Named Outstanding Young Man Hagerstown Jaycees, 1970. Office: 35 W Washington St Hagerstown MD 21740 Tel (301) 797-0210

WRIGHT, GEORGE, b. Eagle Grove, Iowa, July 21, 1908; A.B., Columbia Coll. (name changed to Loras Coll.), 1930; J.D., De Paul U., 1933. Admitted to Iowa bar, 1933, Ill. bar, 1933; individual practice law, Eagle Grove; city atty. Eagle Grove, 1935-39, 46-47; county atty. Wright County (Iowa), 1939-44. Mem. Am., Iowa State, Wright County bar assns. Home: 119 N Washington St Eagle Grove IA 50533 Office: 119 N Washington St Eagle Grove IA 50533 Tel (515) 448-4410

WRIGHT, GEORGE HERBERT, JR., b. Auburn, Ala., Sept. 7, 1929; B.S., Auburn U., 1950; J.D., U. Ala., 1955. Admitted to Ala. bar, 1955; individual practice law, Auburn, Ala., 1955-70; dist. atty., Lee County, Ala., 1970-73; judge Circuit Ct. of Lee County, 1973—; solicitor Lee County (Ala.), 1959-70; atty., City of Auburn, 1968-70. Mem. Ala. Bar Assn., Ala. Circuit Judges' Assn. Recipient 1st prize Nathan Burkan Competition, U. Ala., 1955. Home: 902 Janet St Auburn AL 36830 Office: Lee County Court House Opelika AL 36801 Tel (205) 749-9472

WRIGHT, GEORGE RAWLEY, b. Dover, Del., Dec. 15, 1929; B.A., Wash. Coll., 1951; J.D., George Washington U., 1955. Admitted to Del. bar, 1956; dep. atty. gen. Kent County, Del., 1958-62; asso. judge Del. Superior Ct., Dover, 1962—. Mem. Kent County, Del., Am. bar assns. Home: 147 S Main St Smyrna DE 19977 Office: Courthouse Dover DE 19901 Tel (302) 678-5498

WRIGHT, HUBERT HARRIS, IV, b. Salisbury, Md., Feb. 13, 1942; B.S., U.S. Naval Acad., 1964; J.D., U. Md., 1972. Admitted to Md. bar, 1973; asso. firm Farnell, Hessenauer and Freeland, Cambridge, Md., 1971-74; partner firm Farnell, Freeland and Wright, Cambridge, 1974-77; individual practice, 1977—; adj. prof. Chesapeake Coll., Wye Mills, Md., 1974-75. Pres. Dorchester County Hist. Soc., 1974-76; vestryman Gt. Choptank Parish (Episcopal), Cambridge, 1975-78; life mem. Naval Acad. Alumni Assn., bd. dirs. Dorchester County Pub. Library, 1975—. Mem. Naval Inst., Md. State, Dorchester County (pres. 1976-77), Am. bar assns. Home: 113 Glenburn Ave Cambridge MD 21614 Office: Union Trust Bank Bldg PO Box 778 Cambridge MD 21613 Tel (301) 228-0334

WRIGHT, JAMES DORSEY, b. Centreville, Md., July 11, 1944; B.A., U. Del., 1966; J.D., Harvard, 1969. Admitted to Md. bar, 1969; clk. Hon. Frank A Kaufman, U.S. Dist. Judge, Dist. Md., 1969-70; partner firm Venable, Baetjer & Howard, Balt., 1970—. Trustee Retirement System of Balt., 1976—. Mem. Am. Bar Assn. Office: 1800 Mercantile Bank and Trust Bldg Baltimore MD 21201 Tel (301) 752-6780

WRIGHT, JAMES EDWARD, b. Arlington, Tex., Jan. 15, 1921; J.D., U. Tex., 1949. Admitted to Tex. bar, 1948; partner firm Simon, Crowley, Wright, Ratliff & Miller and predecessors, Ft. Worth, 1949-70; judge Tex. Dist. Ct., 141st Jud. Dist., 1970—; city atty. City of Arlington (Tex.), 1950-60. Fellow Tex. Bar Found. (life); mem. Am., Ft. Worth-Tarrant County (pres. 1958) bar assns., State Bar Tex. Home: 717 Briarwood Blvd Arlington TX 76013 Office: 141st Dist Ct Civil Cts Bldg Fort Worth TX 76102 Tel (817) 334-1422

WRIGHT, J(AMES) SKELLY, b. New Orleans, Jan. 14, 1911; Ph.B., Loyola U., New Orleans, 1931, J.D., 1934; LL.D., Yale, 1961, U. Notre Dame, 1962, Howard U., 1964, U. So. Calif., 1975. Tchr. pub. high sch., New Orleans, 1931-35; admitted to La. bar, 1934, U.S. Supreme Ct. bar, 1947, D.C. bar, 1949; lectr. English history Loyola U., 1936-37; asst. U.S. atty. Eastern Dist. La., 1937-46, U.S. atty., 1948-49; practiced law, Washington, 1946-48; judge U.S. Dist. Ct., Eastern Dist. La., 1949-62, U.S. Ct. Appeals D.C. Circuit, Washington, 1962—; mem. faculty Loyola U. Sch. Law, 1950-62; James Madison lectr. N.Y. U., 1965; Jackson lectr. Nat. Coll. State Trial Judges, 1966; Law and Free Soc. lectr. U. Tex., 1967; Irvine lectr. Cornell U., 1968; Currie lectr. Duke, 1970; Meiklejohn lectr. Brown U., 1976; lectr. contemporary civil rights Notre Dame in London, 1974. Vice chmn., div. fed. employees fund raising campaign ARC, New Orleans, 1949, chmn., 1950. Mem. Am. Law Inst., Am. Judicature Soc., Blue Key, Alpha Delta Gamma, (pres. 1935-36), Phi Delta Phi. Contbr. articles to legal jours. Home: 5317 Blackstone Rd Washington DC 20016 Office: US Courthouse Washington DC 20001 Tel (202) 426-7372

WRIGHT, JOHN BACON, b. Oshkosh, Wis., Dec. 22, 1920; B.S., Mich. State U., 1942; J.D., Columbia, 1948. Admitted to Md. bar, 1949, D.C. bar, 1950; practiced in Annapolis, Md., 1952—, individual practice law, 1952-62; mem. firms Wright and Cohen, 1962-72, Wright and Pittman, 1973-74, Wright and Wright, 1974—; city atty. City of Annapolis, 1953-57; legal counsel St. John's Coll., Annapolis, 1958—. Mem. Anne Arundel County (Md.) Bd. Edn., 1963-74; mem. Anne Arundel County Adv. Commn. on Adequate Pub. Facilities, 1975-76. Mem. Anne Arundel County (pres. 1968), Md., Am. bar assns., Am., Md. (pres. 1961) trial lawyers assns. Home: 197 S Cherry Grove Ave Annapolis MD 21401 Office: suite 400 2024 West St Annapolis MD 21401 Tel (301) 269-0900

WRIGHT, JOHN BROWN, b. Springer, N. Mex., June 5, 1913; B.A., U. Denver, 1936, J.D., 1938. Admitted to N. Mex. bar, 1939; partner firm Wilson & Wright, Raton, N. Mex., 1939-42; partner firm Wright & Kastler, Raton, 1960-71; judge 8th Jud. Dist. N. Mex., Raton, 1971—. Chmn. bd. trustees N. Mex. Boys Sch.; mem. Raton Municipal Sch. Bd., 1939-44. Home: S Raton Raton NM 87740 Office: PO Box 160 County Ct House Raton NM 87740 Tel (505) 445-3673

WRIGHT, JOSEPH GRADY, III, b. Atlanta, Dec. 13, 1945; B.A. in Econs., Wofford Coll., 1968; J.D., U. S.C., 1972. Admitted to S.C. bar, 1972; practiced in Anderson, S.C., 1972—, corporate counsel, 1972-75, individual practice law, 1975—; issuing agt. Anderson Title Ins. Agy., Inc. Bd. dirs. Anderson County Mental Health Assn.; chmn. bd. dirs. Anderson County Health Planning Council; mem. Anderson County Council, 1977—. Mem. S.C., Am. bar assns. Home: Salem Rd Anderson SC 29621 Office: 1103 S Main St Anderson SC 29624 Tel (803) 225-6228

WRIGHT, LAFAYETTE HART, b. Chickasha, Okla., Dec. 2, 1917; B.A., U. Okla., 1938, J.D., 1941; LL.M., U. Mich., 1942. Admitted to Okla. bar, 1941, Mich. bar, 1951; prof. law U. Mich., 1946—; vis. asso. prof. law Stanford, 1953; vis. distinguished prof. law U. Okla., 1975; cons. to commr. IRS, 1956-57, 59-60, 67-68. Mem. adv. bd. Internat. Bur. Fiscal Documentation, Amsterdam; adv. bd. Tax Advocates and Analysts. Recipient U.S. Treasury Meritorious Civilian Service award, 1957, U. Mich. Distinguished Faculty award, 1969; Ford Found. fellow, 1962; contbr. articles to profl. jours. Home: 3079 Exmoor Ann Arbor MI 48104 Office: Law School University of Michigan Ann Arbor MI 48109 Tel (313) 764-9346

WRIGHT, LEROY AUGUSTUS, b. San Diego, Apr. 12, 1914; A.B., Stanford, 1936, LL.B., 1939. Admitted to Calif. bar, 1939, U.S. Supreme Ct. bar, 1949; partner firms Wright Monroe Harden & Thomas, San Diego, 1939-52, Glenn Wright Jacobs & Schell, and predecessor, San Diego, 1952—. Fellow Am. Bar Found. (life); mem. State Bar Calif., Am., San Diego (pres. 1951) bar assns., Am. Law Inst. (life). Home: 4042 Liggett Dr San Diego CA 92106 Office: 1434 Fifth Ave San Diego CA 92101 Tel (714) 234-3571

WRIGHT, LOUIS CHARLES, b. Gadsden, Ala., May 14, 1922; B.S., Auburn U., 1943; LL.B., U. Ala., 1948. Admitted to Ala. bar, 1948; individual practice law, Gadsden, 1948-55; dist. atty. Ala. Circuit Ct., 16th Circuit, 1955-63; partner firm Dortch, Allen, Wright & Wright, Gadsden, 1965-69; judge Ala. Ct. of Civil Appeals, 1969-72, presiding judge, 1972—; mem. Ala. Ho. of Reps., 1967-69; alt. presiding mem. Ala. Ct. of the Judiciary, 1974—. Mem. Ala., Am. bar assns., Am. Judicature Soc., Ala. Law Inst., Farrah Order of Jurisprudence. Home: 2347 Wentworth Dr Montgomery AL 36106 Office: 2600 E South Blvd Montgomery AL 36111 Tel (204) 832-6417

WRIGHT, MADISON BROWN, JR., b. Orange, Tex., Aug. 29, 1936; student Washington and Lee U., 1954-55; B.A., So. Meth. U., 1958, J.D., 1961. Admitted to Tex. bar, 1961; asso. firm Benckenstein and Benckenstein, Beaumont, Tex., 1961-63, Thad W. Davis, Freeport, Tex., 1963-65; individual practice, Lake Jackson, Tex., 1965-70; claims counsel Stewart Title Guaranty Co., Houston, 1970—, v.p., 1976—; instr. real estate Brazosport Jr. Coll., 1968. Chmn. com. cub scouts Sam Houston council Boy Scouts Am., 1972-73; chmn. membership Hance Elementary PTA, Spring, Tex., 1972-73; del. Democratic State Conv., 1964, 66, 68, 70, 72, 74, 76; chmn. Dem. Precinct, precinct 27, 1970-71, precinct 112, 1976—. Mem. Houston, Am. bar assns., State Bar Tex., Phi Delta Phi. Recipient Distinguished Service award U.S. Jaycees, 1969. Home: 8002 Beaufort Dr PO Box 214 Spring TX 77373 Office: 2200 W Loop S PO Box 2029 Houston TX 77001 Tel (713) 627-1310

WRIGHT, PAUL DUFFIELD, III, b. Youngstown, Ohio, Mar. 24, 1942; B.A., U. Md., 1965, J.D., 1971. Admitted to Md. bar, 1972; clk. to judge Prince George's County Circuit Ct., Upper Marlboro, Md., 1970-71; asso. firm West, West & Wright, and predecessors, Forestville, Md., 1972-73, partner, 1974—. Mem. Am., Md., Prince George's County bar assns. Home: 12009 Tulip Grove Dr Bowie MD 20715 Office: 7610 Pennsylvania Ave suite 301 Forestville MD 20028 Tel (301) 736-5432

WRIGHT, ROBERT A., b. Chgo., Feb. 26, 1926; B.A. in Polit. Sci., U. Iowa, 1950; LL.B., Drake U., 1954. Admitted to Iowa bar, 1954; individual practice law, Des Moines, 1954-76; legal counsel NAACP, Des Moines, also state of Iowa br., 1962-76, regional dir., 1970-72. Mem. Iowa State Bar Assn., Am. Trial Lawyers Assn., Kappa Alpha Psi, Phi Alpha Delta. Recipient human rights award city Des Moines, 1972. Office: 1206 Financial Center 7th & Walnut Sts Des Moines IA 50309 Tel (515) 244-5737

WRIGHT, ROBERT C., b. Knoxville, Tenn., Nov. 27, 1946; A.B., Occidental Coll., 1968; J.D., Hastings Coll. Law U. Calif., 1971. Admitted to Calif. bar, 1972; asso. firm Sullivan, Jones & Archer, San Diego, 1973—. Mem. San Diego County, Los Angeles County, Am. bar assns., State Bar Calif., Assn. Bus. Trial Lawyers. Office: 600 B 1200 3d Ave San Diego CA 92101 Tel (714) 236-1611

WRIGHT, ROBERT MICHAEL, b. Brigham, Utah, July 3, 1944; B.A., U. Calif. Los Angeles, 1967, J.D., 1970. Admitted to Calif. bar, 1971; assoc. counsel Automobile Club So. Calif., Los Angeles, 1971—. Mem. Am., Los Angeles bar assns., Lawyers Club Los Angeles. Recipient Certificate of Merit, West Publishing Lawyers Art Competition, 1975, 76. 90732 Office: 2601 S Figueroa St Los Angeles CA 90007 Tel (213) 746-4948

WRIGHT, ROGER B., b. Idaho Falls, Idaho, Oct. 21, 1940; B.A., U. Idaho, 1963, J.D., 1965. Admitted to Idaho bar, 1965, U.D. Dist. (Idaho) Ct. bar, 1965; asst. atty. gen., Boise, Idaho, 1965-66; Idaho dep. atty. gen., 1966-69; partner firm Voshell & Wright, profl. corp., Idaho Falls, 1969—; pros. atty. Clark County, Idaho, 1970—. Mem. Idaho State Bar Assn. Office: PO Box 557 Idaho Falls ID 83401 Tel (208) 523-4433

WRIGHT, ROGER LANE, b. Blackfoot, Idaho, Aug. 5, 1936; B.A., Brigham Young U., 1961; LL.B., U. Colo., 1964, J.D., 1966. Admitted to Nev. bar, 1964, U.S. Supreme Ct. bar, 1970; law clk. Nev. Supreme Ct., 1964-65; individual practice law, Reno, 1965—. Scholarships and admissions advisor Brigham Young U., 1970-75. Mem. Am., Nev., Woshoe County bar assns., Am. Trial Lawyers Assn. Office: 435 Court St Reno NV 89504 Tel (702) 786-5323

WRIGHT, ROY JAMES, b. St. Bernard, Ohio, Dec. 11, 1931; B.S. in Commerce, Salmon P. Chase U., 1963, J.D., 1967; postgrad. Northwestern U., 1969. Admitted to Ohio bar, 1967; sgt., legal advisor St. Bernard Police Dept., 1956-69; prof. police sci. Ill. Central Coll., East Peoria, Ill., 1969-74, asst. dean instrn., 1974—; cons. in field. Police commr. Washington, Ill., 1971-75; mem. selection com. for police chief City of Peoria, Ill., 1972, mem. selection com. for fire chief, 1975, mem. manpower planning council, 1976. Mem. Am., Ohio, Cin. bar assns., Am. Soc. Pub. Adminstrs., Phi Alpha Delta, Phi Kappa Delta. Author: (with others) Police Law Instructors Manual, 1969; Guidelines for Establishing a Police Legal Unit, 1969. Office: PO Box 2400 East Peoria IL 61635 Tel (309) 694-5231

WRIGHT, STANLEY ROBERT, b. Hills, Minn., Nov. 18, 1899; LL.B., George Washington U., 1923. Admitted to D.C. bar, 1923, N.Y. bar, 1926, Fla. bar, 1972; partner firm Burlingham, Underwood, Wright, White & Lord, N.Y.C., 1926-71, Ulmer, Murchison, Ashby & Ball, Jacksonville, Fla., 1972—. Mem. Maritime Law Assn. U.S., Comité Maritime Internat., Am., Fla., Jacksonville bar assns. Home: 3919 Timuquana Rd Jacksonville FL 32210 Office: PO Box 479 Jacksonville FL 32201 Tel (904) 354-5652

WRIGHT, TIMOTHY CHARLES, b. San Bernardino, Calif., Nov. 30, 1940; B.A., San Diego State U., 1963; J.D., Calif. Western U., 1967. Admitted to Calif. bar, 1970; asso. in trusts for comptroller of currency U.S. Treasury Dept., San Francisco, 1967-71; individual practice law, Menlo Park, Calif., 1971—. Mem. State Bar Calif., San Mateo County Bar Assn. (dir.; certificate of merit 1974), Barristers Club San Mateo County (dir.). Author: You and the Law, 1975. Office: 1075 Curtis St Menlo Park CA 94025 Tel (415) 328-4500

WRIGHT, WILLIAM ROBERT, b. Salt Lake City, May 20, 1935; B.S. in Geology, U. Utah, 1960, J.D., 1963. Admitted to Utah bar, 1963, U.S. Supreme Ct. bar, 1975; mng. partner firm Jones, Waldo, Holbrook & McDonough. Mem. Utah State Bd. Edn., 1972-76, chmn., 1974-76. Chmn. Utah State Rep. Party, 1977—. Mem. Am. Bar Assn. (v.p. young lawyers sect. 1969-70), Utah State (chmn. young lawyers sect. 1970-71), Salt Lake County (exec. com. 1976-77) bars, Nat. Assn. State Bds. Edn. (v.p., dir. 1975-76). Recipient Merit citation Utah Vocat. Ednl. Assn., 1975. Home: 1092 Bonneville Dr Salt Lake City UT 84108 Office: 800 Walker Bank Bldg Salt Lake City UT 84108 Tel (801) 521-3200

WRIGLEY, ALBERT BLAKEMORE, b. Phila., Mar. 22, 1934; B.A., Pa. State U., 1955; J.D., Temple U., 1960. Admitted to Pa. bar, 1961; partner firm Mauger, Kranzley, Markolski and Wrigley, Pottstown, Pa., 1961-67; partner firm Kranzley, Wrigley, Yergey, and Daylor, Pottstown, 1958—. Chmn. Lower Pottsgrove CSC, Pottstown, 1971—; bd. dirs. Pottstown United Way, 1973—, 2d v.p., 1977. Mem. Pa. Trial Lawyers Assn., Montgomery County Estate Planning Council, Pa., Montgomery County bar assns. Home: 980 Valley Rd Pottstown PA 19464 Office: 1129 High St Pottstown PA 19464 Tel (215) 323-1400

WUCHITECH, ROY GEORGE, b. Chgo., Mar. 21, 1946; B.A., U. Chgo., 1967; J.D. cum laude, U. Tex., 1972. Admitted to Calif. bar, 1972; asso. firm Sheppard, Mullin, Richter & Hampton, Los Angeles, 1972—. Mem. Am. Bar Assn., Assn. Bus. Trial Lawyers. Home: 1277 Monument St Pacific Palisades CA 90272 Office: 333 S Hope St Los Angeles CA 90071 Tel (213) 620-1780

WULF, MELVIN LAWRENCE, b. N.Y.C., Nov. 1, 1927; B.S., Columbia, 1952, LL.B., 1955. Admitted to N.Y. State bar, 1957; legal dir. ACLU, N.Y.C., 1962-77; individual practice law, N.Y.C., 1977—; distinguished prof. Hofstra U. Sch. Law, 1975—. Mem. Nat. Lawyers Guild. Contbr. articles to legal jours. Home: 340 Riverside Dr New York City NY 10025 Office: Suite 600 565 Fifth Ave New York City NY 10017 Tel (212) 697-5918

WULFF, ROBERT ARTHUR, b. St. Louis, Dec. 14, 1934; B.S., St. Louis U., 1956, J.D., 1967. Admitted to Mo. bar, 1967, U.S. Supreme Ct. bar, 1972; dist. claims mgr. Am. Family Ins. Co., St. Louis, 1958-68; asso. firm Holtkamp & Amelung, St. Louis, 1968-70, partner, 1970-73; partner firm Amelung, Wulff & Willenbrock, St. Louis, 1973—. Mem. Am., St. Louis County, Met. St. Louis (v.p. 1976—) bar assns., Assn. Def. Counsel (exec. com. local chpt. 1975—), Am. Judicature Soc., Lawyers Assn. St. Louis, Phi Alpha Delta. Home: 12363 Federal Dr Des Peres MO 63131 Office: 16th Floor 722 Chestnut St Saint Louis MO 63101 Tel (314) 436-6757

WUNDER, DAVID HART, b. Argo, Ill., Dec. 6, 1925; A.B., Wabash Coll., 1950; J.D., Chgo.-Kent Coll. Law, 1962. Salesman, Edward Hines Lumber Co., Chgo., 1950-54; contractor M. Wunder Homes, Inc., Chgo., 1954-63; admitted to Ill. bar, 1963, U.S. Supreme Ct. bar, 1974; atty. securities div. Office of Sec. of State of Ill., Springfield, 1963-72, commr., securities div., 1972—; lectr. in field; mem. adv. com. on regulation of market instruments Commodity Future Trading Commn. Mem. N.Am. Securities Adminstrs. Assn., Midwest Securities Adminstrs. (pres. 1976—), Central Securities Adminstrs. Council, Am. (com. commodities regulation), Ill. State (sec. corp. and securities law sect.) bar assns. Contbr. articles to legal jours. and texts. Home: 9235 S 54th Ave Oak Lawn IL 60453 Office: Room 296 Centennial Bldg Springfield IL 62756 Tel (217) 782-2256

WURTHMAN, KARLA HUTCHINSON, b. Monroe, Mich., Apr. 16, 1937; student Stephens Coll., 1954-55; B.A. in Econs., U. Mo., 1960, postgrad. 1960-65; postgrad. Northwestern U., 1962, U. San Fernando Valley, 1966. Admitted to Calif. bar, 1968; mem. staff San Fernando Valley Neighborhood Legal Services, Pacoima, Calif., 1969-70; individual practice law, Northridge, Calif., 1969-70; lectr. bus. law Calif. State U., Northridge, 1969-70; dep. dist. atty. County of Los Angeles, 1970—; mem. conflict panel Los Angeles County Juvenile Ct., 1969-70; bd. dirs. San Fernando Valley Neighborhood Legal Service, 1977. Mem. Calif., Los Angeles County (mem. juvenile justice com. 1976—) bar assns. Office: Office of Los Angeles County District Attorney 300 E Walnut St Pasadena CA Tel (213) 796-9361

WURTMAN, SAMUEL RICHARD, b. Phila., Dec. 11, 1908; B.A., U. Pa., 1930, B.B.L., 1933, B.L., 1969. Admitted to Pa. bar, 1934, U.S. Supreme Ct. bar, 1947; dep. atty. gen. Commonwealth of Pa., 1941-55; mem. firm Wurtman & Wurtman, Phila., 1971—. Mem. Am., Pa., Phila. bar assns., Lawyers Club. Home: 1919 Chestnut St Apt 2119 Philadelphia PA 19103 Office: 1000 Western Savings Bank Bldg Philadelphia PA 19107 Tel (215) PE 5-7500

WURTZEL, FRANKLIN ROSS, b. Los Angeles, Sept. 8, 1942; A.B., U. Calif., Los Angeles, 1964, J.D., 1967. Admitted to Calif. bar, 1968, U.S. Ct. Mil. Appeals bar, 1968; dist. atty. Los Angeles County, 1968; with JAGC, U.S. Army, 1968-72; asso. firm Loeb and Loeb, Los Angeles, 1972-76; partner firm Levine and Wurtzel, Los Angeles, 1976—. Bd. dirs. Valley Cities Jewish Community Center, Van Nuys, Calif., 1975—. Mem. Calif., Los Angeles County, Am. bar assns. Office: 2029 Century Park E suite 600 Los Angeles CA 90067 Tel (213) 553-4604

WUTT, ROBERT ANTHONY, b. Milw., Oct. 19, 1924; B.S. in Bus. Adminstrn., Marquette U., 1946, J.D., 1948. Admitted to Wis. bar, 1948, Fla. bar, 1956; asst. dist. atty. Milw. County, 1954-57, 59-62; asst. family ct. commr., 1962-64; asso. firm Houghton, Bullinger & Nehs, Milw., 1964-66; partner firm Clarke, O'Brien & Wutt, Deerfield Beach, Fla., 1966—. Mem. Wis., Fla., Broward County, N. Broward (pres. 1974-75) bar assns., Broward County Mental Health Assn. (v.p. 1970-74), N. Broward Community Mental Health Assn. (dir.), Estate Planning Council of Broward County (bd. govs. 1972-74). Home: 2000 NE 59th Pl Fort Lauderdale FL 33308 Office: 665 SE 10th St Deerfield Beach FL 33441 Tel (305) 421-1212

WYATT, JOSEPH LUCIAN, JR., b. Chgo., Feb. 21, 1924; A.B. with honors, Northwestern U., 1944; LL.B., Harvard, 1949. Admitted to Calif. bar, 1950, U.S. Supreme Ct. bar, 1965; practiced in Los Angeles, 1950—; asso., then partner firm Brady, Nossaman & Walker and predecessors, 1950-61; individual practice law, 1961-71; prin. mem. firm Cooper, Wyatt, Tepper & Plant, P.C., 1971—; lectr. in field Pacific Coast Banking Sch., 1963—. Mem. Calif. State Personnel Bd., 1961-71, pres., 1965-67. Fellow Am. Coll. Probate Counsel; mem. Am., Los Angeles bar assns., Calif. Pub. Employees Retirement System (dir. 1963-71), Internat. Acad. Estate and Trust Law (academician). Author: (with Nossaman) Trust Administration & Taxation, 1972. Home: 1119 Armada Dr Pasadena CA 91103 Office: 611 W 6th St Suite 2700 Los Angeles CA 90017 Tel (213) 680-2180

WYATT, THELMA LAVERNE, b. Amarillo, Tex., July 6, 1945; B.A., U. Calif. at Los Angeles, 1965; J.D. with distinction, Emory U., 1971. Admitted to Ga. bar, 1971; individual practice law, Atlanta, 1971-74; mem. firm Ward and Wyatt, Atlanta, 1974—; vis. asst. prof. law Emory U., 1974-75; spl. atty. Office of Atty. Gen., State of Ga., 1976. Chairperson, Atlanta License Rev. Bd., 1974-75. Mem. Ga., Nat., Gate City bar assns. Named Most Outstanding Young Woman in Atlanta, 1971; contbr. articles to legal jours. Home: 1890 Shepherd Circle SW Atlanta GA 30311 Office: 211 2945 Stone Hogan Rd SW Atlanta GA 30331 Tel (404) 349-5700

WYCHE, MONTY MEARES, b. Plain Dealing, La., Dec. 4, 1926; LL.B., La. State U., 1950. Admitted to La. bar, 1950; partner firm Wallace, Wyche & Bigby, Benton, La., 1955-69; asst. dist. atty. La. 26th Jud. Dist., 1960-69; judge La. Dist. Ct., 26th Jud. Dist., 1969—. Mem. La. State Bar Assn., Bossier City (La.) C. of C. Home: 2519 Deas St Bossier City LA 71010 Office: PO Box 97 Benton LA 71006 Tel (318) 965-2217

WYGANT, GERALD DAVID, b. Spokane, Wash., Sept. 2, 1933; B.S., U. Oreg., 1956; J.D., Northwestern U., 1960. Admitted to Oreg. bar, 1960, Calif. bar, 1961; trust officer Puget Sound Nat. Bank, Tacoma, Wash., 1960-68; planning analyst Pacific Power & Light Co., Portland, Oreg., 1968-70; atty., asst. prof. finance law Portland State U., 1970—; judge pro tem Oreg. Dist. Ct., 1971—. Mem. Am. Bar Assn. Office: 1004 Standard Plaza Portland OR 97204 Tel (503) 228-4317

WYLY, JAMES ALLEN, b. Hereford, Tex., Mar. 4, 1939; B.A., U. S.D., 1967; M.P.A., Harvard, 1971, J.D., 1971. Admitted to S.D. bar, 1971; asso. firm Richard, Groseclose, Kornmann & Wyly, Aberdeen, S.D., 1974—. Mem. Am., S.D., Aberdeen bar assns. Office: Milwaukee Station Bldg Aberdeen SD 57401

WYMAN, LOUIS CROSBY, b. Manchester, N.H., Mar. 16, 1917; B.S. cum laude, U. N.H., 1938; LL.B. cum laude, Harvard, 1941. Admitted to N.H. bar, 1941, Mass. bar, 1941, D.C. bar, 1949, U.S. Supreme Ct. bar, 1947, Fla. bar, 1957; asso. firm Ropes, Gray, Boston, 1941-42; counsel U.S. Senate Com., 1946-49; partner firm Wyman, Starr, Booth, Wadleigh & Langdell, Manchester, 1949-52; atty. gen. State of N.H., 1953-61; partner firm Wyman Bean & Stark, Manchester, 1957—; mem. U.S. Ho. of Reps., 1963-74, U.S. Senate, 1974. Fellow Am. Coll. Trial Lawyers; mem. Am. (chmn. Standing com. jurisprudence 1961-63), N.H., Fla., D.C. bar assns., Nat. Assn. Attys. Gen. (past pres.). Home: 121 Shaw St Manchester NH 03104 Office: 1662 Elm St Manchester NH 03104 Tel (603) 627-4111

WYNNE, ANN CAMM, b. Washington, May 21, 1942; B.A., Rollins Coll., 1964; J.D., U. Miss., 1973. Admitted to Miss. bar, 1973; partner firm Ball and Ball, Oxford, Miss., 1973-74; interim asst. dir. Criminal Justice Research Service, U. Miss. Law Center, 1974, dir. Miss. Prosecutors Coll., 1974—; mem. com. Miss. State Bar Law Day. Mem. Miss., Lafayette County bar assns., Nat. Assn. Prosecutor Coordinators (vice chmn. exec. com.), Miss. Prosecutors Assn. (dir.). Contbr. articles to legal jours. Home: 1581 Buchanan St Oxford MS 38655 Office: Miss Prosecutors Coll U Miss Law Center University MS 38677 Tel (601) 232-5951

WYNNE, DENNIS MICHAEL, b. Newark, Jan. 18, 1944; A.B. cum laude, Seton Hall U., 1966; J.D., Rutgers U., Newark, 1969. Admitted to N.J. bar, 1970; legal asst. N.J. Supreme Ct. Adminstrv. Office, Trenton, 1970-71, Office of Pub. Defender Newark Juvenile Office, 1971-72; mem. staff Office of Pub. Defender, New Brunswick, N.J., 1972—, sr. trial atty., 1974—; trustee Morrow Project, 1973—, Somerset Legal Services, 1975-76. Mem. Middlesex County (N.J.) Trial Lawyers Assn. Author: Sentencing Manual for Juvenile Court Judges, 1971. Home: 427 Dennison St Highland Park NJ 08904 Office: Office of Pub Defender 29 Livingston Ave New Brunswick NJ 08904 Tel (201) 828-3100

WYSHAK, LILLIAN WORTHING, b. N.Y.C., July 19, 1928; B.S., U. Calif., Los Angeles, 1948, M.A., 1971; J.D., U. So. Calif., 1956. Individual practice accounting, Beverly Hills and Alhambra, Calif., 1948-56; admitted to Calif. bar, 1956. U.S. Supreme Ct. bar, 1967; asso. firm Boyle, Bissell & Atwill, Pasadena, Calif., 1956-57, Parker, Millikin & Kohlmeier, Los Angeles, 1957-58; asst. U.S. atty. Tax Div., Los Angeles, 1958-62; partner firm Wyshak & Wyshak, Los Angeles, 1963—. Trustee U. Redlands. Mem. Am., Los Angeles County, Beverly Hills, West Hollywood (pres. 1969) bar assns., Calif. Scholarship Fedn. (life), Phi Alpha Delta, Beta Gamma Sigma. Contbr. articles to legal jours. Home: 602 Hillcrest Rd Beverly Hills CA 90210 Office: 9255 Sunset Blvd Suite 1125 Los Angeles CA 90069 Tel (213) 273-2044

WYSHAK, ROBERT HABEEB, b. Boston, Dec. 23, 1923; A.B. cum laude, Harvard U., 1945, LL.B., 1947. Admitted to Mass. bar, 1947, Calif. bar, 1948; asst. U.S. atty. Central Dist. Calif., Los Angeles, 1953-62, chief tax div.; partner firm Wyshak & Wyshak, Los Angeles, 1962—; lectr. in field. Trustee Beverly Hills Presbyn. Ch., 1966—. Mem. W. Hollywood, Westwood Village, Beverly Hills, Los Angeles County Fed. bar assns. Contbg. author: Federal Tax Procedure, 1968; contbr. articles to profl. jours. Home: 602 Hillcrest Rd Beverly Hills CA 90210 Office: 9255 Sunset Blvd 1125 Los Angeles CA 90069 Tel (213) 273-2044

WYSS, WALTHER ERWIN, b. Medford, Wis., Feb. 17, 1909; B.S., U. Wis., 1933, M.S., 1934; J.D., George Washington U., 1939. Admitted to D.C. bar, 1938, N.Y. bar, 1941, Ill. bar, 1946; tchr. pub. schs., Medford, Wis., 1925-29; engr. Gen. Electric Co., 1934-35, with patent dept., 1935-45; partner firm Mason, Kolehmainen, Rathburn & Wyss, Chgo., 1948—. Fellow Am. Coll. Trial Lawyers; mem. Am. (spl. com. on complex and multi-dist. litigation 1968-73, mem. council, patent, trademark and copyright law sect. 1968-72, chmn. 1974-75), 7th Fed. Circuit, Chgo. bar assns., Patent Law Assn. Chgo. (pres. 1971), Am. Patent Law Assn., Am. Trial Lawyers Assn., Nat. Lawyers Club, Tau Beta Pi, Phi Delta Phi, Phi Eta Sigma, Phi Kappa Phi, Eta Kappa Nu, Order Coif. Home: 500 Park Dr Kenilworth IL 60043 Office: 20 N Wacker Dr Chicago IL 60606 Tel (312) 346-1677

WYZANSKI, CHARLES EDWARD, JR., b. Boston, May 17, 1906; A.B. magna cum laude, Harvard, 1927, LL.B. magna cum laude, 1930; LL.D., U. Pa., 1954, Carleton Coll., 1954, Tufts U., 19S4, Brandeis U., 1956, Swarthmore Coll., 1956, Harvard, 1958, Clark U., 1963, Washington U., St. Louis, 1974. Admitted to Mass. bar, 1931, U.S. Supreme Ct. bar, 1935; law clk. to judges U.S. Circuit Ct., 2d Circuit, 1930-32; asso. firm Ropes, Gray, Boyden and Perkins, Boston, 1930-33; solicitor Dept. Labor, Washington, 1933-35; U.S. mem. governing bd. Internat. Labor Orgn., Geneva, 1935; U.S. substitute del., 1935; spl. asst. to Atty. Gen. U.S. on staff of solicitor gen., Dept. Justice, Washington, 1935-37; asso. firm Ropes, Gray, Best, Coolidge and Rugg, Boston, 1937-38, partner, 1939-41; pub. mem. Nat. Def. Mediation Bd., Washington, 1941; judge U.S. Dist. Ct., dist. Mass., 1942—, chief judge, 1966-71, sr. U.S. Dist. Judge, 1971—; lectr. govt. Harvard, 1942-43, 50; vis. prof. law Mass. Inst. Tech., 1948-50; Marshall Wood lectr. Brown U., 1950; Cardozo lectr. Assn. Bar City N.Y., 1952; Brandeis lectr. Brandeis U., 1954; Oliver Wendell Holmes devise lectr. Colo. U., 1961; Dreyfous lectr. Tulane U. Law Sch., 1973; Sibley lectr. U. Ga., 1973; Herman Phleger prof. law Stanford, 1974; Sulzbacher lectr. Columbia Law Sch., 1975; mem. U.S. Supreme Ct. Com. on Rules of Civil Procedure, 1960-71. Bd. overseers Harvard, 1943-49, 51-57, pres. bd., 1953-57; trustee Ford Found., 1952-76, Princeton Inst. Advanced Study, 1958-62. Sr. fellow Harvard Soc. Fellows, 1962-76. Fellow Am. Acad. Arts and Scis.; mem. Am. Law Inst. (council 1943—), Phi Beta Kappa (senator 1961-64). Recipient Sir Thomas More medal Boston Coll. Law Sch., 1972, John Phillips award Phillips Exeter Acad., 1975; author: Whereas, A Judge's Premises, 1965; contbr. articles to Atlantic Monthly, legal jours. Home: 39 Fayerweather St Cambridge MA 02138 Office: 1500 Post Office Bldg Boston MA 02109 Tel (617) 482-8148

XANTHOS, JOHN DEMETRIUS, b. Wilmington, N.C., Dec. 8, 1916; student Wake Forest Coll., 1937; LL.B., Wilmington Law Sch., 1941; LL.B., Duke, 1948. Admitted to N.C. bar, 1941, U.S. Supreme Ct. bar, 1967; individual practice law, Burlington and Graham, N.C., 1948—; pub. adminstr. Alamance County, N.C., 1953-65; solicitor Gen. County Ct., Alamance County, 1960-62; solicitor Elon College (N.C.) Municipal Ct., 1960-64. Chmn. Alamance County chpt. ARC;

pres. N.C. Assn. for Blind, 1972-73; pres. N.C. Soc. Prevention of Blindness, 1977; bd. dirs. United Ch. for Homeland Ministries, N.Y.C., 1969-74. Mem. N.C., Alamance County (past pres.) bar assns. Home: 503 Wildwood Ln Burlington NC 27215 Office: One Eleven S Main St Graham NC 27253 Tel (919) 226-1362

XAPHES, JOHN FREDERICK, b. Biddeford, Maine, Mar. 23, 1928; student Portland Jr. Coll., 1946-47; B.A., U. Vt., 1952; J.D., U. Maine (formerly Portland U.), 1956. Admitted to Maine bar, 1957, D.C. bar, 1966; individual practice law, Biddeford, 1957—; treas. City of Biddeford, 1963-64. Mem. Biddeford Planning Bd., 1969-74. Mem. Am., D.C., Maine, York County bar assns., Maine Trial Lawyers Assn. Office: 154 Graham St Biddeford ME 04005 Tel (207) 284-4331

XINOS, CONSTANTINE PETER, b. Chgo., June 3, 1940; B.A., Lake Forest Coll., 1962; J.D., John Marshall Law Sch., 1966. Admitted to Ill. bar, 1966, U.S. Supreme Ct. bar, 1974; asst. pub. defender Cook County, Ill., 1967-71; partner firm Xinos & Xinos, Ltd., Chgo., 1971—. Mem. Am., Ill., Chgo. bar assns. Home: 149 Briarwood Oak Brook IL 60521 Office: 35 E Wacker Dr Chicago IL 60601 Tel (312) 263-6167

YACHNIN, RALPH, b. N.Y.C., Nov. 7, 1927; B.S., L.I. U., 1950; LL.B., Bklyn. Law Sch., 1953, LL.M., 1963, J.D., 1967. Admitted to N.Y. bar, 1954; individual practice law, Corona and Elmont, N.Y., 1954-73; partner firm Yachnin & Goldhush, Elmont, 1973—; counsel N.Y. State Assembly, 1969-71; legis. cons. Town of Hempstead, N.Y., 1971-73. Mem. Hempstead Zoning Bd. Appeals, 1973—; pres. Elmont Center Civic Assn., 1966—; leader Elmont South Republican Club, 1972-77. Mem. Nassau County, N.Y. State bar assns. Home: 742 Caroline Ave Elmont NY 11003 Office: 527 Franklin Ave Franklin Square NY 11010 Tel (516) FL 4-1011

YACULLO, VICTOR FRANK, b. Chgo., Nov. 5, 1938; B.A., U. So. Calif., 1961; LL.B., N.Y. U., 1964. Admitted to Calif. bar, 1964, U.S. Supreme Ct. bar, 1971; asso. firm Kindel & Anderson, Los Angeles, 1964-70, partner, 1970—; mem. Los Angeles City Atty.'s Labor Relations Adv. Com., 1973-75. Dir., personnel chmn. San Gabriel Council Camp Fire Girls, 1973-76. Mem. Los Angeles County (arbitrator 1971); Am. (labor law sect) bar assns., Printing Industries Assn. (dir. master printers sect.), Indsl. Research Assn., Phi Beta Kappa, Phi Kappa Phi. Recipient award outstanding achievement, Camp Fire Girls, 1970-75. Home: 2163 Roanoke Rd San Marino CA 91108 Office: 555 S Flower St 26th Floor Los Angeles CA 90071 Tel (213) 680-2222

YAGER, JOHN WARREN, b. Toledo, Sept. 16, 1920; A.B., U. Mich., 1942, J.D., 1948. Admitted to Ohio bar, 1948; asso. firm Yager, Bebout & Stecher, Toledo, 1948-50, Colbourn, Yager & Smith, Toledo, 1954-64; trust officer Toledo Trust Co., 1964-69; v.p., trust officer, sec. 1st Nat. Bank of Toledo, 1969—; gen. counsel, sec. Toledo Legal Aid Soc., 1952-54. Mayor City of Toledo, 1958-59, mem. City Council, 1955-56, 60-61; pres. Toledo Met. Park Dist., 1971—. Mem. Ohio, Toledo bar assns., Toledo Council Chs., Toledo Jr. C. of C. (past pres.). Named one of 10 Outstanding Young Men, Toledo Jaycees, 1952, 54, 55. Home: 4117 Sheraton Rd Toledo OH 43606 Office: 606 Madison Ave Toledo OH 43604 Tel (419) 259-6806

YAGER, SAUL A., b. Mpls., Jan. 18, 1899; ed. U. Minn. Admitted to Okla. bar, 1920, Minn. bar, 1920; judge, Ct. of Common Pleas, Tulsa County, Okla., 1923-26, Dist. Ct., 21st Judicial Dist., Okla., 1926-32. Home: 2505 E 36th Pl Tulsa OK 74105 Tel (918) 747-0150

YAGER, THOMAS, b. Los Angeles; A.B., U. Calif., Los Angeles, 1939, gen. secondary teaching credential, 1940; J.D., U. So. Calif., 1947; LL.D., Western State U., 1972. Admitted to Calif. bar, 1949; practice law, Los Angeles, 1949-57; legal adviser, exec. clemency and extradition staff, sec. to Gov. Calif., 1957-58; judge Superior Ct., Los Angeles, 1959—; faculty Western State U. Coll. Law. Founder, pres. Yager Found.; pres. Community Betterment Service. Mem. Am., Los Angeles County (exec. com. internat. law sect.) bar assns., Calif. Conf. Judges (past chmn. rules and resolutions com.), Phi Delta Phi. Recipient citation for distinguished service Nat. Hdqrs. DAV, 1959, Key to City of Torrance, 1962, trophy Am. Right of Way Assn., 1964, Bronze plaque and award of merit Rotary Internat., 1965, trophy Westwood Shrine Club, 1966, plaque Girl Scouts U.S.A., 1966, award of merit County of Los Angeles, 1966, award Los Angeles Bus. Women's Council, 1967, Bronze plaque Wilshire C. of C., 1969, certificate of appreciation Mayor of Los Angeles, 1970; author: Guide Book for Effective Judicial Administration, 1968, 2d edit., 1970; Presidents, Prime Ministers and Premiers, 1969; contbr. chpt. to California Criminal Law Practice, 1969, also articles to legal jours. Office: Superior Ct 111 N Hill St Los Angeles CA 90012 Tel (213) 974-5633

YAIST, RONALD PATRICK, b. Youngstown, Ohio, Jan. 4, 1938; B.E. in Chem. Engring., Youngstown U., 1959; J.D., U. Akron, 1967. Process metallurgist U.S. Steel Corp., Fairless Hills, Pa., 1961-63; devel. compounder The Goodyear Tire & Rubber Co., Akron, Ohio, 1963-66; admitted to Ohio bar, 1967; patent atty. The Goodyear Tire & Rubber Co., Akron, 1968—. Pres. Stow, Ohio Jaycees, 1970-71; chmn. Charter Review Commn., Stow, 1972; councilman-at-large, Stow, 1975—. Mem. Ohio State, Akron bar assns., Cleveland Patent Law Assn. Named Senator, Jr. C. of C. Internat., 1973. Home: 2002 Willowdale Dr Stow OH 44224 Office: 1144 E Market St Akron OH Tel (216) 794-4409

YAKOVAKIS, JAMES STEPHEN, b. Bennington, N.H., Aug. 5, 1935; B.A., U. N.H., 1957; LL.M., Boston U., 1967; LL.B., N.Y. U., 1964. Admitted N.H. bar, 1964; asso. firm Wadleigh, Starr, Peters, Dunn & Kohls, Manchester, N.H., 1964-69, partner, 1969—; mem. N.H. Ct. Accreditation Com. Bd. dirs. N.H. Lung Assn., Manchester, 1967—, United Way, Manchester, 1975—; pres. Dollars for Scholars, Manchester, 1968-69, Unitarian Universalist Ch., Manchester, 1973-74; chmn. Manchester Transit Authority, 1973-74. Mem. Manchester, N.H. bar assns. Home: 179 Salmon St Manchester NH 03104 Office: 95 Market St Manchester NH 03101 Tel (603) 669-4140

YAKOWICZ, VINCENT X., b. New Castle, Pa., July 29, 1932; B.A., Pa. State U., 1953; J.D., U. Pa., 1956; postgrad. Woodrow Wilson Sch. Govt. and Fgn. Policy, U. Va., 1968-69. Instr., author mil. law and cts. martial procedure Marine Corps. Inst., USMC, Washington, 1956-58; admitted to Pa. bar, 1957, U.S. Supreme Ct. bar, 1957; asst. atty. gen. Dept. Revenue, Commonwealth Pa., Harrisburg, 1958-59, dir. Bur. County Collections, 1959-62, dep. sec. taxation, 1971-74, sec. revenue, 1974-75, solicitor gen., 1975—; dep. atty. gen. Pa. Dept. Justice, Harrisburg, 1962-71; mem. adv. com. on descedents' estates laws Joint State Govt. Commn., 1971—; tech. adviser Gov's. Tax Reform Com., 1971—; adv. legal counselor to Pa. Constl. Conv., 1967-68. Fellow Nat. Inst. Pub. Affairs; mem. Nat. Tax. Assn., Nat. Assn. Tax. Adminstrs., Am. (mem. tax. com. 1971—), Pa. bar assns., Fed. Bench Bar Conf. Contbr. articles to legal jours. Home: 227 Oak Knoll Rd New Cumberland PA 17070 Office: Dept Justice Capitol Annex Harrisburg PA 17120 Tel (717) 787-5573

YALDEN, RAPHAEL EDWARD, b. Rockford, Ill., Nov. 7, 1907; B.A., Hillsdale Coll., 1930; J.D., U. Wis., 1933. Admitted to Wis. bar, 1933, Ill. bar, 1933; mem. firm North, Gibbney & North, Rockford, 1933-37; individual practice law, Rockford, 1937-56; mem. firm Yalden & Ridings, Rockford, 1956-76, Downey, Yalden, Shriver & Yalden, Rockford, 1976—; police magistrate, Rockford, 1938-39; asst. state's atty. Winnebago County (Ill.), 1939-41; asst. atty. gen. State of Ill., 1956; mem. Ill. State Police Merit Bd., 1952-69; dir. Central Nat. Bank of Rockford. Bd. dirs. Winnebago County Republican Club; 3d pres. Mental Health Bd.; pres. Cath. Charities Bd. Mem. Winnebago County (pres. 1956-57), Ill. State (chmn. negligence sec. 1964), Am. bar assns. Office: 401 W State St Rockford IL 61101 Tel (815) 965-8635

YALE, WILLIAM A., b. San Diego, June 5, 1926; LL.B., Calif. Western U., 1949. Admitted to Calif. bar, 1950; individual practice law, San Diego, 1950-70; judge Superior Ct. of Calif., San Diego, 1970—; mem. Calif. Law Revision Commn., 1968-70. Mem. San Diego Bar Assn. (pres. 1969). Office: Ct House San Diego CA 92101 Tel (714) 236-2668

YALKUT, ARLEN SPENCER, b. N.Y.C., Apr. 10, 1945; B.S. in Chemistry, Coll. City N.Y., 1967; J.D., N.Y. Sch. Law, 1971; LL.M. in Criminal Law, N.Y. U., 1972. Admitted to N.Y. bar, 1972, U.S. Dist. Ct. bar, 1975; asso. firm Lenefsky, Gallina, Mass, Berne & Hoffman, N.Y.C., 1971-72; law asst. Criminal Ct. City N.Y., 1972-73; law sec. to Judge Leon B. Polsky, Supreme Ct. N.Y.C., 1973-75; partner firm Bleifer & Yalkut, N.Y.C., 1975—. Mem. Am., N.Y., Rockland County bar assns. Office: 12 Spring Brook Rd Spring Valley NY 10977 Tel (914) 425-0300

YAMASAKI, GEORGE, JR., b. Honolulu, Mar. 21, 1935; A.B., Stanford, 1957, J.D., 1959. Admitted to Calif. bar, 1960; gen. liability dept. Hartford Ins. Group, San Francisco, 1959-62; asso. firm Harold D. Kline, San Francisco, 1963-65; individual practice law, San Francisco, 1965-76; partner firm Yamasaki & Hays, San Francisco, 1976—; sec., gen. counsel Nat.-Braemar, Inc., San Francisco, 1969-73. Nat. legal counsel Japanese-Am. Citizens League, 1974-75, pres. San Francisco chpt., 1971-72; social services commr. City and County of San Francisco, 1975—; sec. Japan Soc. San Francisco, 1975—. Mem. Am., Calif., San Francisco bar assns., Assn. Immigration and Nationality Lawyers. Home: 3725 Scott St San Francisco CA 94123 Office: 500 Sansome St San Francisco CA 94111 Tel (415) 391-3000

YAMPOL, NEAL M., b. Milw., Apr. 22, 1941; B.B.A., U. Wis., 1964; J.D., Marquette U., 1968. Admitted to Wis. bar, 1968; accountant Price Waterhouse & Co., C.P.A.'s, Milw., 1963-65, Arthur Andersen & Co., C.P.A.'s, Milw., 1968-71; agt. Northwestern Mut. Life Ins. Co., Milw., 1971—; instr. Spencerian Coll., Milw., 1966-68, U. Wis. Extension, 1967-71. Mem. Wis., Milw. Jr. bar assns., Wis. Inst. C.P.A.'s, Am. Soc. C.L.U.'s, Nat. Assn. Life Underwriters, Million Dollar Round Table. C.P.A., Wis.; C.L.U. Home: 5117 N Lake Dr Milwaukee WI 53217 Office: 5215 N Ironwood Ln Milwaukee WI 53217 Tel (414) 332-9393

YANCEY, BENNETT KYLE, b. Tampa, Fla., Jan. 17, 1926; student Emory U., 1946-47; LL.B., U. Ga., 1951. Admitted to Ga. bar, 1951; partner firm Harris Bullock, Atlanta, 1956-71; asso. firm Mitchell, Yancey & Fink, Atlanta, 1971-75; asso. Charles Wills, Atlanta, 1976—. Mem. Ga. Senate, 1963-66. Mem. Am., Cobb Jud. bar assns., Ga. Trial Lawyers Assn. Home: 7000 Factory Shoals Rd Austell GA 30001 Office: 2900 National Bank Georgia Bldg Atlanta GA 30303 Tel (404) 521-3300

YANCEY, CLARENCE LANGSTON, b. Highland, La., Aug. 17, 1909; LL.B., La. State U., 1931, J.D., 1968. Admitted to La. bar, 1931, Tex. bar, 1931; atty. Standard Oil Co., (now Exxon Corp.), New Orleans, 1933-46; mem. firm Cook, Clark, Egan, Yancey & King, Shreveport, La., 1946—, sr. partner, 1973—; mem. La. Jud. Council, New Orleans, 1965-69. Mem. Caddo Parish Sch. Bd., Shreveport, 1950-56; bd. dirs. La. State U. Found.; mem. regional bd. Inst. Internat. Edn., Houston; founder Shreveport br. English-Speaking Union. Fellow Am. Coll. Probate Counsel; mem. Judge Advs. Assn. (founder), Am. (La. del.), La. State (pres. 1957-58), Shreveport (past pres.), Internat. bar assns., Shreveport C. of C. (pres. 1967), Fellows of Am. Bar Found. (chmn. 1973), Southwestern Legal Found. (trustee). Editor Judge Adv. Jour., 1943-46; contbr. articles to legal jours. Home: 842 McCormick St Shreveport LA 71104 Office: 600 Comml Bank Bldg Shreveport LA 71101 Tel (318) 221-6277

YANCEY, PRENTISS QUINCY, JR., b. Atlanta, Aug. 20, 1944; B.A., Villanova Univ., 1966; J.D., Emory Univ., 1969. Admitted to Ga. bar, 1969; partner firm Smith, Cohen, Ringel, Kohler & Martin, Atlanta, 1969—. Bd. dirs. Child Service and Family Counseling Center, Atlanta, Atlanta Urban League; v.p. Atlanta United Way. Mem. Am., Ga. bar assns., Blue Key Assn. Home: 2361 Wilson Dr SW Atlanta GA 30331 Office: 2400 First National Bank Tower Atlanta GA 30303 Tel (404) 658-1200

YANDOLI, GABRIEL ANTHONY, b. Jersey City, June 7, 1932; A.A., Jersey City Jr. Coll., 1956; B.A., Rutgers U., 1958; J.D., N.Y. U., 1970. Admitted to N.J. bar, 1970; with Prudential Life Ins. Co. Am., Newark, 1956—, asso. mgr. advanced underwriting, 1968-71, field office dir. pensions and advanced underwriting sales, 1971-73, asst. counsel, 1973-76, asso. counsel, 1976—. Pres. Morris County Grand Jurors Assn., 1966-67, exec. v.p., 1964-66, mem. exec. bd., 1964—. Mem. Am., N.J. State bar assns., Am. Judicature Soc. Home: 36 University Ave Chatham NJ 07928 Office: 1111 Durham Ave South Plainfield NJ 07080 Tel (201) 321-2270

YANOWITZ, BENNETT, b. Cleve., Feb. 25, 1923; A.B., U. Mich., 1947; LL.B., Western Res. U., 1949. Admitted to Ohio bar, 1949; individual practice law, Cleve., 1949-63; partner firm Kahn, Kleinman, Yanowitz & Arnson, Cleve., 1964—. Vice pres. Jewish Community Fedn. of Cleve., 1976-77. Mem. Bar Assn. Greater Cleve., Ohio, Cuyahoga County bar assns. Home: 22231 Byron Rd Shaker Heights OH 44122 Office: 1300 Bond Court Bldg E 9th and Saint Clair Sts Cleveland OH 44114 Tel (216) 696-3311

YARBROUGH, DAVID COLEMAN, b. Tuscaloosa, Ala., Apr. 17, 1938; B.A., U. Ala., 1960, J.D., 1963. Admitted to Ala. bar, 1963, U.S. Supreme Ct. bar, 1972; law clk. Chief Justice Supreme Ct. Ala., 1963-64; asso. firm Hill, Hill, Whiting & Harris, Montgomery, Ala., 1964-65; asso., partner firm Jones, Murray, Stewart & Yarbrough, Montgomery, 1965—; adj. prof. bus. Auburn U., Montgomery, 1970—. Mem. Ala. State Bar, Am., Montgomery County bar assns., Ala. Trial Lawyers Assn., Assn. Trial Lawyers Am. Home: 3344 Boxwood Dr Montgomery AL 36111 Office: PO Box 429 Montgomery AL 36101 Tel (205) 834-2250

YARBROUGH, JOHN JACK, b. Dallas, July 23, 1937; B.B.A., So. Meth. U., 1959, J.D., 1961. Admitted to Tex. bar, 1961, U.S. Supreme Ct. bar, 1969, U.S. Dist. Ct. No. and Eastern Dists. Tex., 1961, U.S. Ct. Mil. Appeals bar, 1969; individual practice law, Nacogdoches, Tex., 1967-75; judge Nacogdoches County Ct. at Law, 1975—; asso. prof. bus. law Stephen F. Austin State U., Nacogdoches, 1967-75. Chmn. bd. Garrison (Tex.) Methodist Ch., 1976, 77; pres. Lewisville (Tex.) Jaycees, 1963-64. Mem. Tex., Nacogdoches County bar assns. Home: Route 3 Box 276 Garrison TX 75946 Office: PO Drawer 1112 Nacogdoches TX 75961 Tel (713) 569-9527

YATES, ERNEST JONAH, b. Tallahassee, Apr. 27, 1945; A.B., Valdosta State Coll., 1967; J.D., U. Ga., 1970. Admitted to Ga. bar, 1970; mem. firm Reinhardt, Whitley & Sims, Tifton, Ga., 1970-76; individual practice law, Tifton, 1976—. Bd. dirs. Tift County (Ga.) chpt. Am. Cancer Soc., 1973—, Tiftarea YMCA, Tifton, 1974—. Mem. State Bar Ga., Am., Tifton (pres. 1973) bar assns., Am. Judicature Soc., Comml. Law League, Conf. on Personal Fin. Law, Phi Alpha Delta. Home: 125 Lewis St Tifton GA 31794 Office: 214 Tift Ave Tifton GA 31794 Tel (912) 382-8010

YATES, JAMES EMORY, III, b. Macon, Ga., Mar. 5, 1927; J.D., Woodrow Wilson Coll. Law, 1951. Admitted to Ga. bar, 1951; asso. firm Pierce, Ranitz, Lee, Berry & Mahoney, Savannah, 1964-66; partner firm Ryan & Yates, Savannah, 1966-71; individual practice law, Savannah, 1972—; city atty., judge recorders ct. City of Port Wentworth (Ga.), 1967-75. Mem. Navy League U.S. (past nat. dir., pres. Savannah council), Savannah Claims Assn. (past pres.). Home and office: 914 Abercorn St Savannah GA 31401 Tel (912) 234-5341

YATES, SEALY MAC, b. Santa Ana, Tex., Aug. 1, 1943; B.B.A., Baylor U., 1965; J.D., U. Calif., Los Angeles, 1968. Admitted to Calif. bar, 1969; individual practice law, 1969-70; partner firm Passo & Yates, Santa Ana, 1970-73, Passo, Yates & Nissen, 1973 75, Yates & Nissen, Santa Ana, 1975—. Mem. Santa Ana City Planning Commn., 1973—; bd. dirs. Goodwill Industries, Open Doors Internat., Inc., Family Ministeries, Forest Home, Inc. Mem. Am., Orange County bar assns. Recipient certificate of merit Moot Ct. Honors Program, 1967. Office: 888 N Main St Suite 1000 PO Box 508 Santa Ana CA 92702 Tel (714) 835-3742

YATES, THOMAS, b. McGregor, Iowa, Feb. 28, 1929; student Iowa State Tchrs. Coll., 1947-49, 50-51, 54-55; LL.B., U. Iowa, 1958. Admitted to Iowa bar, 1958; with trust dept. Central Bank, Denver, 1958-62, Central Nat. Bank, Des Moines, 1962-63; partner firm Crary, Huff, Yates & Clem, P.C., Holstein, Iowa, 1963—. Mem. Holstein Community Sch. Bd., 1965—; bd. dirs. Iowa Assn. Sch. Bds., Des Moines, 1969—; bd. control Iowa High Sch. Athletic Assn., Boone, 1970—. Mem. Ida County, Iowa bar assns., Iowa Council Sch. Attys. (dir.). Home: 510 Merkley St Holstein IA 51025 Office: 100 Besore Bldg Holstein IA 51025 Tel (712) 368-4552

YATKEMAN, MICHAEL JON, b. St. Louis, Aug. 18, 1937; B.S., B.A., J.D., Washington U., 1961. Admitted to Mo. bar, 1962, Fed. bar, 1962; asso. firm Harris, Fortus & Anderson, Clayton, Mo., 1962-65; asso. firm Rooney, Wabbe & Davidson, St. Louis, 1965-68; individual practice law Clayton, Mo., 1968—; spl. asst. atty. gen. State of Mo., 1965-68; municipal judge, Bel-Ridge, Mo., 1971-76; asst. prosecutor, various municipalities, St. Louis County. Mem. Municipal Judges Assn. Greater St. Louis (v.p. 1973-74), Bar Assn. St. Louis, Am. Bar Assn. Office: 11 S Meremec St Suite 1201 Clayton MO 63105 Tel (314) 863-1177

YAVITCH, BERNARD ZELIG, b. Chester, Pa., June 5, 1943; B.S. in Bus. Adminstrn., Ohio State U., 1966; J.D., Capital U., 1971. Admitted to Ohio bar, 1971, U.S. Supreme Ct. bar, 1975; staff atty. Legal Aid and Defender Soc., Columbus, Ohio, 1971, supervising atty., 1972-75; dir. diversion unit Franklin County Pros. Attys. Office, Ohio, 1975-76; individual practice law, Columbus, 1975—. Mem. Ohio, Columbus bar assns., Nat. Dist. Attys. Assn., Ohio Pub. Defenders Assn., Franklin County Com. on Criminal Justice. Home: 7088 Roundelay Rd North Reynoldsburg OH 43068 Office: 369 S High St 5th Floor Columbus OH 43215 Tel (614) 462-3555

YAVOREK, GEORGE A., b. Eynon, Pa., June 5, 1926; B.S. in Social Sci., U. Scranton, 1948; LL.B., Fordham U., 1951, LL.D., 1952. Admitted to Pa. Superior Ct. bar, 1952, Pa. Supreme Ct. bar, 1952; individual practice law, Scranton, Pa., 1952—; referee Workmans' Compensation, 1971; chmn. bd. Lackawanna County (Pa.) Assessment and Revision of Taxes, 1972; bd. dirs. Lackawanna County Redevel. Authority, 1975-76; chmn. Lackawanna County Bd. Viewers, 1977-80; Solicitor Archbald Borough Council, 1960, Dickson City Borough Council, 1962, Valley View Sch. Dist., 1971, Scott Twp., 1973. Pres. Friends of Poland of Lackawanna County, 1957, 64, Gen. Casimir Pulaski Meml. Com. of Lackawanna Co., 1965, 69, 70, 74, No. Pa. State div. Polish Am. Congress, Inc., 1976—. Mem. Lackawanna County, Pa. bar assns., Alumni Assn. Fordham U., U. Scranton Alumni Assn. Home: 100 First St Eynon PA 18403 Office: 108 O'Hara Hall Scranton PA 18503 Tel (717) 346-9745

YEAGER, JOHN JACQUES, b. Newport, Ky., Dec. 21, 1921; student Johns Hopkins, 1939-41; B.A., U. Ky., 1947, LL.B., 1948, J.D., 1970; LL.M., Columbia, 1949. Admitted to Ky. bar, 1948, Iowa bar, 1958; prof. law Drake U., 1949—; reporter criminal code rev. study com. Iowa Gen. Assembly, 1969-73; city atty., Windsor Heights, Iowa, 1958-63. Mem. Am., Ky., Iowa bar assns., Order of Coif. Contbr. articles to profl. jours. Office: Law School Drake Univ Des Moines IA 50311 Tel (515) 271-2947

YEAGLEY, J. WALTER, b. Angola, Ind., Apr. 20, 1909; A.B., U. Mich., 1931, J.D., 1934. Admitted to Ind. bar, 1934, D.C. bar, 1964, U.S. Supreme Ct. bar, 1958; partner firm Yeagley & Yeagley, South Bend, Ind., 1934-42; spl. agt. FBI, Washington, 1942-48; dir. security div. ECA, Washington, 1948-51; asso. gen. counsel Reconstrn. Fin. Corp., Washington, 1951-53; dep. asst. atty. gen. Office U.S. Atty. Gen., Dept. Justice, Washington, 1953-59, asst. atty. gen., 1960-70; asso. judge D.C. Ct. Appeals, 1970—. Mem. D.C. Bar, D.C., Am. bar assns. Home: 316 Runner Rd Great Falls VA 22066 Office: 400 F St NW Washington DC 20001 Tel (202) 638-6187

YEATTS, ARCHER LAFAYETTE, III, b. Pittsylvania County, Va., May 1, 1942; B.A., U. Richmond, 1964, LL.B., 1967. Admitted to Va. bar, 1967; asso. firm Mays, Valentine, Davenport & Moore, Richmond, Va., 1967-69; asst. commonwealth's atty. Henrico County (Va.), 1969-71; asso. firm Bareford & Downs, Richmond, 1969-71; partner firm Maloney, Yeatts & Balfour, Richmond, 1971—; lectr.

T.C. Williams Sch. Law, 1973-74. Mem. Am., Va., Richmond bar assns., Va. State Bar. Home: 802 Lindsay Ct Richmond VA 23229 Office: 326 Ross Bldg Richmond VA 23219 Tel (804) 644-0313

YEDWAB, IRVING, b. Jersey City, Mar. 20, 1934; B.A., Coll. City N.Y., 1955, M.B.A., 1967; J.D., Columbia, 1958. Admitted to N.Y. bar, 1959; asso. firm Martin K. Kahn, Bklyn., 1959-63, Herman B. Zipser, N.Y.C., 1963-64, George P. Monaghan, N.Y.C., 1965-68; individual practice law, Bklyn., 1968—; pres. Steckel Bros., Inc.; arbitrator Am. Arbitration Assn. Mem. N.Y. State Bar Assn., N.Y. State Ins. Brokers. Home: 2761 E 64th St Brooklyn NY 11234 Office: 200 Flatbush Ave Brooklyn NY 11217 Tel (212) NE 8-4701

YEE, LUCY MARSH, b. Denver, Feb. 26, 1941; B.A., Smith Coll., 1963; J.D., U. Mich., 1966. Admitted to Conn. bar, 1967, Colo. bar, 1971; asso. firm Becket & Wagner, Lakeville, Conn., 1966-67; prof. law U. Denver, parttime 1973-74, adj. prof. law, 1974-76, asst. prof., 1976—; sr. dep. dist. atty. City of Denver, 1976—. Mem. budget adv. coms. Denver Pub. Schs., 1973-76. Mem. Denver, Colo. bar assns. Recipient Order of St. Ives award U. Denver Coll. Law, 1975. Office: 200 W 14th Ave Denver CO 80204 Tel (303) 753-2642

YELLON, DONALD JEROME, b. Chgo., Dec. 2, 1921; A.B., U. Chgo., 1943, J.D., 1948. Admitted to Ill. bar, 1949; asso. firm D'Ancona, Pflaum, Wyatt & Riskind, Chgo., 1948-54, partner, 1955-71; v.p., gen. counsel First Nat. Bank Chgo., 1971-73, sr. v.p., gen. counsel, 1973-75, exec. v.p., gen. counsel, 1975—. Mem. Order of Coif, Phi Beta Kappa. Home: 921 Timberhill Rd Highland Park IL 60035 Office: 1 First Nat Plaza Chicago IL 60670 Tel (312) 732-3540

YERBICH, THOMAS JOSEPH, b. Roslyn, Wash., Feb. 21, 1938; J.D., U. of the Pacific, 1971. Admitted to Calif. bar, 1972; legal research atty. Orange County (Calif.) Superior Ct., 1971-73; asso. firm Duryea, Randolph, Malcolm & Daly, Newport Beach, Calif., 1973-76; mem. firm F.K. Friedemann, Orange, Calif., 1976—; prof. law Western State U., Fullerton, Calif., 1972—; mem. comml. constrn. arbitration panel Am. Arbitration Assn., 1974—. Trustee, sec. S. Orange County Cultural Arts Found., 1975—. Mem. Am., Orange County bar assns., Calif. Trial Lawyers Assn., Phi Alpha Delta. Author: In Personum Jurisdiction—New Horizons in California, 1970. Home: 22276 Chestnut Ln El Toro CA 92630 Office: 1900 Bank of Am Tower 1 City Blvd W Orange CA 92668 Tel (714) 835-3401

YERGER, WILLIAM SWAN, b. Jackson, Miss., June 11, 1932; student Va. Mil. Inst., 1950-52; B.A., U. Miss., 1954; LL.B., U. Va., 1958, J.D., 1970. Admitted to Miss. bar, 1958; asso. firm Wise, Smith & Carter, Jackson, 1958-63; asso. firm Heidelberg, Woodliff & Franks, Jackson, 1963-65; partner, 1965—. Pres. Jackson Civic Arts Council, 1962; originator, first chmn. Miss. Arts Festival, Jackson, 1964; chmn. bd. dirs. Jackson Met. YMCA, 1975. Mem. Hinds County, Miss., Fed., Am. (charter mem. litigation sect.) bar assns., Internat. Assn. Ins. Counsel, Miss. Def. Lawyers Assn. (v.p. 1976). Office: 1030 Capital Towers Jackson MS 39201 Tel (601) 948-3800

YESU, FRANK, b. Bklyn., Sept. 30, 1933; B.B.A., U. Mass., Amherst, 1955; J.D., Western New Eng. Coll., 1967. Admitted to Mass. bar, 1968; claims adjuster U.S. Fidelity & Guaranty Ins. Co., 1968-69; asso. Neighborhood Legal Services, Inc., 1969-70; asso. firm Simpson, Clason, Callahan & Giustina, 1970-76, partner, 1976—. Active Longmeadow (Mass.) Baseball Assn., Inc.; bd. dirs. Big Bros. Springfield, Mass. Mem. Am., Mass., Hampden County bar assns. Home: 113 Chiswick St Longmeadow MA 01106 Office: 1200 Main St Springfield MA 01103 Tel (413) 736-1896

YETTER, CHARLES WARD, b. Binghamton, N.Y., Apr. 2, 1917; B.S. in Econs., U. Pa., 1939; LL.B., Albany Law Sch., 1942. Admitted to N.Y. bar, 1943, U.S. Supreme Ct. bar, 1958; house counsel Stow Mfg. Co., 1943-46; asso. Frank D. Morris, 1946-54; partner firms Yetter & Margolis, Binghamton, 1954-65, Yetter & Zalbowitz, Binghamton, 1970—; research counsel Temporary Commn. on Estates, N.Y.C., 1962-67. Mem. Broome County (N.Y.) (pres. 1968-70), N.Y. State (ho. of dels. 1973-74), Am. bar assns. Home: 8 Asbury Ct Binghamton NY 13905 Office: 604 Press Bldg Binghamton NY 13901 Tel (607) 723-9551

YETTER, RICHARD, b. Phila., Mar. 14, 1929; B.S., Pa. State U., 1951; J.D., Marquette U., 1960. Admitted to Wis. bar, 1960, Tex. bar, 1961; with Md. Casualty Co., 1960-61; individual practice law, El Paso, 1962—; asso. El Paso Municipal Ct. Judge, 1967-71. Mem. adv. bd. Small Bus. Adminstrn., 1974—, Salvation Army, Pleasant View Home for Sr. Citizens, Inc.; former mem. El Paso Mayor's Adv. Council. Mem. El Paso, Fed. bar assns., El Paso Trial Lawyers Assn. Office: Suite 660 5959 Gateway W El Paso TX 79925 Tel (915) 778-7793

YEZAK, HERMAN, b. Bremond, Tex., Feb. 16, 1913; B.S., Tex. A. and M. U., 1938; postgrad., U. Tex., 1945, 51, Baylor U., 1952-55. Admitted to Tex. bar, 1955; individual practice law, Bremond, 1955—; mem. Tex. Ho. of Reps., 1945-63; justice of the peace, Bremond, 1975—. Trustee Bremond Ind. Sch. Dist. Bd. Edn., 1967—; Democratic precinct chmn., Bremond, 1966-70; active Boy Scouts Am. Mem. Tex., Tex. Aggie bar assns., Judicature Soc. Home: Wooten Wells Rd Farm Rd 1373 Bremond TX 76629 Office: 301 S Main St Bremond TX 76629 Tel (817) 746-7033 746-7836

YIANILOS, SPERO L., b. Doliana, Greece, Aug. 7, 1925; B.S., U. Buffalo, 1951, LL.B., 1952. Admitted to N.Y. bar, 1952; partner firm Tzetzo & Yianilos, Buffalo, 1954-64; individual practice law, Buffalo, 1964—. Trustee Greek Orthodox Ch. Buffalo; officer Buffalo Council Eastern Orthodox Chs.; mem. Erie County Dem. Com. Mem. Erie County, N.Y. State bar assns. Named Orthodox Man of Year, Buffalo Council Eastern Orthodox Chs., 1974. Home: 48 Devonshire Rd Kenmore NY 14223 Office: 390 Ellicot St Bldg Buffalo NY 14203 Tel (716) 856-5412

YOCHIM, JOSEPH ADOLPH, b. Erie, Pa., May 8, 1947; B.A. in History, St. Vincent Coll., 1969; J.D., Duquesne U., 1972. Admitted to Pa. bar, 1972; law clk. to judge U.S. Dist. Ct. for Western Dist. Pa., 1972-74; asso. firm Quinn, Gent, Buseck & Leemhuis, Inc., Erie, 1974-75, firm Ambrose & Yochim, Erie, 1975—. Mem. Am., Pa., Erie County bar assns., Pa. Trial Lawyers Assn. Office: 319 W 8th St Erie PA 16502 Tel (814) 452-3069

YOELIN, MATILDA, b. Chgo., July 29, 1911; LL.B., DePaul U., Ph.B., J.D. Admitted to Ill. bar; partner firm Yoelin & Yoelin, Chgo. Mem. Chgo. Bd. Edn., 1957-76. Address: 1536 N Kedvale Ave Chicago IL 60651 Tel (312) 252-3068

YOHO, BILL LEE, b. Huntington, W.Va., Oct. 25, 1925; A.B., U. Md., 1953, LL.B., 1953, J.D., 1969. Admitted to Md. bar, 1953; mem. firm Hoyert & Yoho, College Park and Lanham, Md., 1953—; atty. Prince George's Gen. Hosp., Town of Colmar Manor (Md.), City of College Park. Mem. Prince George's County Airport Com., Selective Service Bd., Am. Cancer Soc., College Park Lions Club. Mem. Prince George's County (past pres.), Md. State, Am. bar assns., Soc. Hosp. Attys., Am. Trial Lawyers Assn. Office: 8901 Annapolis Rd Lanham MD 20801 Tel (301) 459-4200

YONEHIRO, GEORGE, b. Newcastle, Calif., July 24, 1922; LL.B., John Marshall Sch. Law, 19S4, J.D., 1970. Admitted to Ill. bar, 1955, Colo. bar, 1962, Calif. bar, 1972; individual practice law, Chgo., 1955-62; land officer Sacramento Municipal Utility Dist., 1963-64; judge Jud. Dist. Colfax-Alta-Dutch Flat (Calif.), 1965—. Trustee, Applegate Civic Center, 1964-70; active Placer Hills sch. dist., 1971—; mem. law com. Falcon Career Center, 1971—. Mem. Chgo. Bar Assn. Home: PO Box 237 Applegate CA 95703 Office: PO Box 735 Colfax CA 95713 Tel (916) 346-8721

YONKEE, LAWRENCE ADOLPH, b. Sheridan, Wyo., Jan. 13, 1935; B.S., U. Wyo., 1959, J.D. with honors, 1961. Admitted to Wyo. bar, 1962; partner firm Redle Yonkee & Arney, Sheridan, 1962—; mem. Wyo. Legislature, 1963-73. Mem. Am., Wyo. (pres.) bar assns., Am. Judiature Soc. Home: 702 S Jefferson St Sheridan WY 82801 Office: 24 S Main St Sheridan WY 82801 Tel (307) 674-7454

YONKMAN, FREDRICK ALBERS, b. Holland, Mich., Aug. 22, 1930; B.A., Hope Coll., 1952; J.D., U. Chgo., 1957. Admitted to N.Y. State bar, 1958, Mass. bar, 1968; asso. firm Winthrop, Stimson, Putnam & Roberts, N.Y.C., 1957-64; sec., gen. counsel Reuben H. Donnelly Corp., N.Y.C., 1964-66, Dun & Bradstreet, N.Y.C., 1966-68; partner firm Sullivan & Worcester, Boston, 1968-72; gen. counsel Am. Express Co., N.Y.C., 1972-75, exec. v.p., gen. counsel, 1975-77, exec. v.p. adminstrn. and law, 1977—; adj. prof. internat. law Georgetown U. Law Center, Washington, 1976—, vice chmn. Inst. for Internat. and Fgn. Trade Law. Trustee Young Audiences, Inc., 1976—, Outward Bound, Inc., 1977—, Am. Express Found., 1973—. Mem. Am. Soc. Internat. Law., Am., N.Y. State, Mass., Boston bar assns., Assn. Bar City N.Y. Recipient Silver Anniversary award Nat. Collegiate Athletic Assn., 1977. Home: 60 Midwood Rd Greenwich CT 06830 Office: Am Express Co Am Express Plaza New York City NY 10004 Tel (212) 480-3631

YORK, FOSTER, b. Cambridge, Mass., Feb. 12, 1903; S.B. in Chem. Engring., Mass. Inst. Tech., 1925; postgrad. George Washington U., 1932-34. Chem. engr. Eastman Kodak Co., 1926-28; research asst. Harvard, 1929; chem. researcher U.S. Indsl. Alcohol Co., 1930-31; admitted to D.C. bar, 1934, Ill. bar, 1938, U.S. Supreme Ct. bar, 1953; partner firm Zabel, Baker York, Jones & Dithmar, Chgo., 1937-74, Burmeister, York, Palmatier, Hamby & Jones, Chgo., 1974—; cons. ERDA, 1975—. Mem. Am., Chgo., Ill., Chgo. Patent bar assns., Am. Chem. Soc. Home: 1216 Central St Evanston IL 60201 Office: 135 S LaSalle St Chicago IL 60603 Tel (312) 782-6663

YORK, HAROLD PARKER, b. Lancaster, Mo., Sept. 28, 1903; B.A., Drake U., 1927; LL.B., 1928, J.D., 1968. Admitted to Iowa bar, 1928, Mo. bar, 1929; individual practice law, Lancaster, 1929-52; pros. atty. Schuyler County, Mo., 1930-40; atty. Lancaster County, Mo., 1930-52; individual practice law, Kirksville, Mo., 1952-76; agt. IRS, 1943-48; head title and research sect. Area Pub. Works Office and liaison officer to U.S. Attys. Office Ter. of Guam, 1955. Mem. Mo., Adair County bar assns. Home: 1 Overbrook Dr Kirksville MO 63501 Office: 306 W Washington St Kirksville MO 63501 Tel (816) 665-4711

YOST, HARRY HAROLD, b. Bethlehem, Pa., Aug. 21, 1927; B.S., U. Md., 1953; LL.B., Mt. Vernon Sch. of Law, 1965. Admitted to Md. bar, 1965; partner firm Borders & Assos., Cheverly, Md., 1963-65; individual practice law, Glen Burnie, Md., 1965-72; pvt. practice accounting, Glen Burnie, Md., 1965-72; pres. firm Yost & Smith, Glen Burnie, 1972—. Treas. Rosewood Assn. for Retarded, 1972—. Mem. Am. Bar Assn., Anne Arundel County Assn. of C.P.A.'s. C.P.A., Md. Office: 105 S Crain Hwy Glen Burnie MD 21061 Tel (301) 768-5656

YOST, ROBERT WARREN, b. St. Louis, May 26, 1912; A.B., LL.B., Washington U., St. Louis, 1936, J.D., 1968. Admitted to Mo. bar, 1936, U.S. Supreme Ct. bar, 1963; asst. atty. Mo. Pacific R.R. Co., St. Louis, 1936-43, 46-49, asst. to sr. law officer, 1949-56, asst. gen. atty., 1956-62, gen. atty., 1962—. Mem. Bar Assn. Met. St. Louis, Order of Coif, Phi Alpha Delta. Home: 265 S Old Orchard Ave Webster Groves MO 63119 Office: 210 N 13th St Saint Louis MO 63103 Tel (314) 622-2015

YOUDERIAN, JOHN ALBERT, JR., b. Worcester, Mass., Oct. 22, 1945; B.A., Case Western Res. U., 1968; J.D., Rutgers U., 1973. Admitted to N.J. bar, 1973; asso. firm Shapiro, Berson, Hochberg & Reiken, Newark, 1973-74; asso. firm C. David Witherington, Caldwell, N.J., 1974-75; individual practice law, Caldwell, 1975—; asso. firm Bennett & Bennett, W. Orange, N.J., 1975—. Mem. Am., N.J., Essex County bar assns., Am. Judicature Soc. Office: 10 Smull Ave Caldwell NJ 07006 Tel (201) 228-2422

YOUNG, DENZIL R., b. Baker, Mont., Aug. 11, 1926; B.S., LL.B., Mont. State U., 1951. Admitted to Mont. bar, 1951; county atty. Fallon County, Baker, Mont., 1959—. Mem. Am., Mont., SE Mont. bar assns. Home: 419 W Pleasant Ave Baker MI 59313 Office: PO Box 620 12 E Montana Ave Baker MT 59313 Tel (406) 778-2406

YOUNG, DON J(OHN), b. Norwalk, Ohio, July 13, 1910; A.B., Case Western Res. U., 1932, LL.B., 1934; postgrad. Cleve. Sch. Art, 1932-34. Admitted to Ohio bar, 1934; asso. firm Young & Young, Norwalk, 1934-52; judge Ct. of Common Pleas, Huron County, Ohio, 1952-53, Probate and Juvenile Ct., Huron County, 1953-65, U.S. Dist. Ct., No. Dist., Toledo, 1965—. Mem. Am., Ohio State, Toledo, Lucas County bar assns., Nat. Council Juvenile Ct. Judges (Meritorious Service award), Ohio Assn. Juvenile and Probate Ct. Judges, Am. Judicature Soc., Nat. Council on Crime and Delinquency, Nat. Legal Aid and Defenders Assn. Contbr. articles to legal jours. and chpts. to books. Office: 213 US Court House and Custom House Toledo OH 43624 Tel (419) 259-6330

YOUNG, FRANK MOBLEY, III, b. Birmingham, Ala., Nov. 8, 1941; B.A., Washington and Lee U., 1963; J.D. cum laude, Samford U., 1969; LL.M., Harvard, 1970. Admitted to Ala. bar, 1969; since practiced in Birmingham; law clk. U.S. Dist. Ct. No. Dist. Ala., 1969; asso. firm Bradley, Arant, Rose & White, 1970-74; partner firm Johnson North Haskell & Slaughter, 1974—. Vice-chmn. Jefferson County (Ala.) Cancer Crusade, 1973. Mem. Am., Ala., Birmingham (chmn. pub. relations com. 1977) bar assns., Young Lawyers Assn. Birmingham (exec. com. 1972), Cumberland Alumni Assn (pres. 1974), Phi Delta Phi, Omicron Delta Kappa. Contbr. article to law rev. Home: 3624 Ridgeview Dr Birmingham AL 35213 Office: 1710 1st Nat-So Natural Bldg Birmingham AL 35203 Tel (205) 252-8847

YOUNG, GEORGE CRESSLER, b. Cin., Aug. 4, 1916; A.B., U. Fla., 1938, LL.B., 1940; postgrad. Harvard Law Sch., 1947. Admitted to Fla. bar, 1940; individual practice law, Winter Haven, Fla., 1940-41; asso. firm Smathers, Thompson, Maxwell & Dyer, Miami, 1947; adminstrv. and legis. asst. to Sen. Smathers of Fla., 1948-52; asst. U.S. atty., Jacksonville, 1952; partner firm Knight, Kincaid, Young & Harris, Jacksonville, 1953-61; U.S. dist. judge No., Middle and So. dists. Fla., 1961-73, chief judge Middle Dist., 1973—; mem. com. on adminstrn. fed. magistrates system Jud. Conf. U.S. Bd. dirs. Jacksonville United Cerebral Palsy Assn., 1953-60. Mem. Rollins Coll. Alumni Assn. (pres. 1968-69), Am. (spl. com. for adminstrn. criminal justice), Fla. (gov. 1960-61), Jacksonville (past pres.) bar assns., Am. Judicature Soc., Am. Law Inst., Order of Coif, Fla. Blue Key, Phi Beta Kappa, Phi Kappa Phi, Phi Delta Phi, Sigma Alpha Epsilon. Home: 2424 Shrewsbury Rd Orlando FL 32803 Office: US Courthouse PO Box 1433 Orlando FL 32801

YOUNG, GUY MARTIN, b. Alturas, Calif., June 23, 1933; B.A., U. Calif., 1955; LL.B., U. Calif., Los Angeles, 1959. Admitted to Calif. bar, 1960; individual practice law, 1960-74; judge Modoc County Superior Ct., Alturas, 1974—. Bd. dirs. 34th Agrl. Dist. Fair; mem. Modoc County Sheriff's Posse. Mem. Calif. Bar Assn., Conf. Calif. Judges, Cow County Judges Assn. Office: Court St Alturas CA 96101 Tel (916) 233-2615

YOUNG, H. ALBERT, b. Kiev, Russia, May 30, 1904; B.A., U. Del., 1926; J.D., U. Pa., 1929. Admitted to Del. bar, 1929, 3d Circuit Ct. U.S. bar, 1933, U.S. Supreme Ct. bar, 1944; sr. partner firm Young, Conaway, Stargett & Taylor, Wilmington, Del., 1959—; atty. gen. State of Del., 1951-55; atty., Del. Legis., 1935-37. Bd. dirs. Jewish Fedn. Del., Kutz Home for Aged, Jewish Community Center. Fellow Am. Coll. Trial Lawyers, Internat. Acad. Trial Lawyers (dir.), Am. Bar Found.; mem. Am. Law Inst., Del. (pres. 1961-63), Ill., Am. bar assns., Am. Judicature Soc. Home: 1401 Pennsylvania Ave Wilmington DE 19806 Office: Market Tower Wilmington DE 19801

YOUNG, JAMES BONER, b. Kankakee, Ill., May 5, 1928; A.B., Franklin Coll., 1950; LL.B., Ind. U., 1955. Admitted to Ind. bar, 1955; individual practice law, Franklin, 1955-75; U.S. atty. So. Dist. Ind., Indpls., 1975-77; spl. asst. to gov., 1972-75; mem. Ind. Senate, 1966-70; county atty. Johnson County, 1968-75. Mem. Am., Ind., Fed., 7th Dist. bar assns. Home: 1091 E Adams St Franklin IN 46131 Office: 250 E Jefferson St Franklin IN 46131 Tel (317) 236-5421

YOUNG, JAMES KENT, b. Russellville, Ark., Aug. 2, 1922; student Ark. Poly. Coll., 1940-42; LL.B., U. Ark., 1945. Admitted to Ark. bar, 1945, U.S. Supreme Ct. bar, 1960; mem. firm White & Young, 1955-65; individual practice law, Russellville, 1965—; city atty. City of Russellville, 1945-70; mem. Ark. Ho. of Reps., 1947. Mem. Am. Bar Assn., Am. Trial Lawyers Assn., Am. Judicature Soc. Home: 601 W J St Russellville AR 72801 Office: 306 S Arkansas Ave Russellville AR 72801 Tel (501) 968-2536

YOUNG, JOHN HENDRICKS, b. Pelham, N.Y., Aug. 12, 1912; A.B., Yale, 1934, J.D., 1937. Admitted to N.Y. bar, 1938; asso. firm Carter, Ledyard & Milburn, N.Y.C., 1937-42, 45-47, mem. firm, 1947—. Mem. Am., N.Y. State, Internat. (vice chmn. tax com.) Bar Assns., Assn. Bar City N.Y. (lectr.), N.Y. County Lawyers Assn., Internat. Fiscal Assn. (exec. council U.S. br., Netherlands mem.), World Peace Through Law Center, World Assn. Lawyers (chmn. tax com.), Tax Found., Am. (mem. tax adv. group), N.Y. law insts., Nat. Tax Assn.-Tax Inst. Am. Decorated Bronze Star; lectr. Practicing Law Inst. N.Y., Ga. Inst. Continuing Legal Edn.; appeared on live TV program On Trial, N.Y.C.; contbr. articles to legal publs. Home: 785 Fifth Ave New York City NY 10022 Office: 2 Wall St New York City NY 10005 Tel (212) 732-3200

YOUNG, JOHN LEWIN, b. Pitts., Mar. 5, 1932; A.B. in Chemistry, Cornell U., 1954, M.B.A., 1955; J.D. cum laude, St. Louis U., 1971. Admitted to Mo. bar, 1971; with Monsanto Co., Chgo. and St. Louis, 1955-75, patent agt. and atty., St. Louis, 1968-75; patent counsel, silicone products dept. Gen. Electric Co., Waterford, N.Y., 1975—. Tax assessor and collector Village of El Lago (Tex.), 1963-64. Mem. Am. Bar Assn., Eastern N.Y., Am. patent law assns. Home: 861 Worcester Dr Niskayuna NY 12309 Office: Gen Electric Co Waterford NY 12188 Tel (518) 237-3330 X 2341

YOUNG, JOSEPH ROY, JR., b. Phila., Mar. 25, 1921; A.B., U. Pa., 1942, LL.B., 1949. Admitted to Pa. Supreme Ct. bar, 1950, U.S. Supreme Ct. bar, 1960; partner firm Butler, Beatty, Greer & Johnson, Media, Pa., 1949—. Mem. Am., Pa., Delaware County bar assns. Home: 100 E Greenwood Ave Lansdowne PA 19050 Office: 17 South Ave PO Box 140 Media PA 19063 Tel (215) 566-8200

YOUNG, LLEWELLYN ANKER, b. Reno, Nev., May 17, 1917; B.S. in Elec. Engring., U. Nev., 1938; J.D., George Washington U., 1945. Admitted to D.C. bar, 1945, Ill. bar, 1948, Nev. bar, 1951; asso. firm McKenna & Morsbach, Rockford, Ill., 1945-50; partner firm Young & Young, Lovelock, Nev., 1951-67; judge Nev. Dist. Ct., 6th Jud. Dist., 1967—. Mem. State Bar Nev., Am. Bar Assn. Home: 1590 Central Ave Lovelock NE 89419 Office: Courthouse Lovelock NE 89419 Tel (702) 273-2105

YOUNG, MALCOLM DOW, JR., b. Ft. Monmouth, N.J., Sept. 16, 1943; A.B., Trinity U., 1965; J.D., Vanderbilt U., 1968. Admitted to Nebr. bar, 1968, Ga. bar, 1971; asso. with Malcolm D. Young, Omaha, 1968-69; asso. firm Smith, Currie & Hancock, Atlanta, 1971-72; partner firm Peterson & Young, Atlanta, 1972—. Mem. State Bars Nebr., Ga., Am., Atlanta bar assns. Home: 719 Woodward Way NE Atlanta GA 30327 Office: 400 Colony Square Suite 525 Atlanta GA 30361 Tel (404) 892-7470

YOUNG, MERLIN SHERMAN, b. Eden, Idaho, Dec. 5, 1918; B.A., Whitman Coll., 1940, LL.D., 1956; LL.B., U. So. Calif., 1946. Admitted to Idaho bar, 1946; partner firm Moffatt & Young, Boise, Idaho, 1946-50; pros. atty. Ada County (Idaho), 1950-52; judge Idaho 4th Dist. Ct., Boise, 1955-70, U.S. Bankruptcy Ct., Boise, 1970—; mem. Idaho Ho. of Reps., 1953-54; municipal judge City of Boise, 1948-50. Mem. Am., Idaho bar assns., Am. Judicature Soc. Contbr. articles to legal jours. Home: 119 S Walnut St Boise ID 83702 Office: Box 1278 Boise ID 83701 Tel (208) 384-1074

YOUNG, MILTON, b. N.Y.C., May 11, 1910; LL.B., Fordham U., 1931. Admitted to N.Y. bar, 1932, U.S. Tax Ct. bar, 1945, U.S. Supreme Ct. bar, 1969; asst. tax counsel U.S. Alien Property Custodian, 1942-45; asso. firm Paul, Weiss, Wharton & Garrison, N.Y.C., 1945-48; partner firm Young, Kaplan & Edelstein, N.Y.C.,

1948—; mem. adv. bd. N.Y. U. Inst. on Fed. Taxation, 1954-64; mem. adv. group to Commr. Internal Revenue, 1964; mem. real estate adv. com. SEC, 1972; lectr. N.Y. U. Sch. Law, 1950-53. Mem. Am., Westchester bar assns., N.Y. County Lawyers Assn., Assn. Bar City N.Y. Contbr. articles in field to legal jours. Home: 1230 Greacen Point Rd Mamaroneck NY 10543 Office: 277 Park Ave New York City NY 10017 Tel (212) 826-0311

YOUNG, PATRICK HENRY, b. Paulding, Ohio, Dec. 3, 1938; B.S., Bowling Green State U., 1961; J.D., U. Detroit, 1966. Admitted to Mich. bar, 1966, Ohio bar, 1967; U.S. Supreme Ct. bar, 1970; trial counsel Mich. Mut. Liability Co., Detroit, 1966-67; asso. firm John F. DeMuth, Paulding, 1967-68; individual practice law, Paulding, 1968—. Pres. Paulding County Crippled Children Soc., 1968-69; bd. dirs. Paulding County Carnagie Library, 1970-72, Oscar Fiegert Mental Health Center, Van Wert, Ohio, 1973—; pres., bd. dirs. Paulding County Guidance Clinic, 1977. Mem. Am., Mich., Ohio, Northwest Ohio, Paulding County bar assns. Home: Rural Route 3 Paulding OH 45879 Office: 106 E Jackson St Paulding OH 45879 Tel (419) 399-5991

YOUNG, PETER FRANCIS, JR., b. Springfield, Mass., July 24, 1943; B.A., U. Vt., 1966; J.D. cum laude, Union U., 1969. Admitted to Vt. bar, 1969; law clk. U.S. Dist. Ct., Burlington, Vt., 1969-70; individual practice law, Northfield, Vt., 1970-72; partner firm Young & Monte, Northfield, 1972—; chmn. Vt. State Employees Labor Relations Bd., 1974; mem. Vt. Ho. of Reps., 1975—, Vt. Supreme Ct. Profl. Contact Bd. Pres. Central Vt. Humane Soc., 1971-72. Mem. Am., Vt., Washington County bar assns., Justinian Soc. Contbr. articles to law jours. Home: 8 Prospect St Northfield VT 05663 Office: PO Box 270 Northfield VT 05663 Tel (802) 485-8282

YOUNG, RALPH EDWARD, JR., b. Meridian, Miss., May 19, 1943; B.B.A., U. Miss., 1965, J.D., 1967. Admitted to Miss. bar, 1967; law clk. Miss. Supreme Ct., Jackson, 1967; partner firm Deen, Cameron, Prichard & Young, Meridian, 1967—. Chmn. Lauderdale County chpt. ARC, 1973-75, chmn. Miss. div. adv. council, 1976, mem. Southeastern area adv. council, 1976—; 1st pres. Meridian Art Assn., 1977—; pres. Meridian Jr. Coll. Found., 1973—. Mem. Am., Miss., Lauderdale County (pres. 1977) bar assns. Home: 3818 13th Pl Meridian MS 39301 Office: PO Box 888 Meridian MS 39301 Tel (601) 693-2561

YOUNG, RAYMOND WARREN, b. North Bergen, N.J., Apr. 19, 1922; B.A., Montclair State Coll., 1945; M.A., Rutgers U., 1946; Ph.D., Johns Hopkins, 1949; J.D., George Washington U., 1957. Asst. prof. polit. sci. and econs. Gettysburg Coll., 1948-50; lectr. govt. Washington Square Coll. N.Y. U., 1951-53; asso. prof. polit. sci. Hood Coll., 1953-54; admitted to N.J. bar, 1957; asst. prof. law George Washington U., 1957-58; asst. U.S. dist. atty. for N.J., Newark, 1958-62, chief civil div. U.S. Atty.'s Office, 1970-71; asso. firm Shanley & Fisher, Newark, 1962-68; individual practice law, North Bergen, N.J., 1968-70; judge Hudson County (N.J.) Ct., 1971—; staff cons. on edn. mgmt. study N.Y.C. Mayor's Com. on Mgmt. Survey, 1950-51. Pres., Hudson Symphony Orch., North Bergen, 1965-70; trustee Montclair State Coll., 1969-71; adv. council Garden State Arts Center, Holmdel, N.J., 1970-71. Mem. Am., Fed., N.J., Hudson County bar assns., Order of Coif, Kappa Delta Pi, Pi Sigma Alpha, Phi Delta Phi. Editorial notes editor, bus. mgr. George Washington Law Rev., 1955-56; contbr. articles to profl. jours. Home: 6123 Newkirk Ave North Bergen NJ 07047 Office: Adminstrn Bldg 595 Newark Ave Jersey City NJ 07306 Tel (201) 792-3737

YOUNG, ROBERT E. LEE, b. Covington, Ky., May 16, 1914; J.D., U. Cin., 1937. Admitted to Ohio bar, 1937, U.S. Supreme Ct. bar, 1960; practice law, Cin., 1937-42, 46-66; asst. vol. defender Legal Aid Soc., 1946-49, staff atty. civil div., 1949-56, chief counsel, 1956-76, exec. dir., 1966-76, adminstrv. dir., 1976—; asso. Schulzinger and Immerman Co., 1959—; res. legal officer JAGC, 1946-53; lectr. law U. Cin., 1955-74; adv. com. OPS, 1952-55. Mem. citizens adv. com. CD, 1954-56; mem. Ohio Citizens Council, 1957-74. Mem. Am., Fed., Ohio, Cin. bar assns., Am. Judicature Soc., Ohio Pub. Defenders Assn., Lawyers Club Cin., VFW (nat. legal com. 1954-55, service officer Ohio dept. 1954-55, judge adv. 4th dist. 1951-53, comdr. Hamilton County council 1953-54, mem. vets. day com.). Home: 1127 Ryland Ave Cincinnati OH 45237 Office: 2400 Reading Rd Cincinnati OH 45202 Tel (513) 241-9400

YOUNG, ROBERT GEORGE, b. Atlanta, Mar. 9, 1923; A.B., Emory U., 1943; J.D., U. Ga., 1949. Admitted to Ga. bar, 1949; asso. firm Heyman, Howell & Heyman, Atlanta, 1949-51; asso. firm Heyman, Abram & Young, and predecessor, Atlanta, 1951-53, partner, 1955-63; asso. firm Marshall, Greene & Neely, Atlanta, 1953-55; partner firms Edenfield, Heyman & Sizemore, Atlanta, 1963-69, Webb, Parker, Young & Ferguson, Atlanta, 1970-77, Webb, Young, Daniel & Murphy, P.C., 1977—; asst. county atty. Fulton County (Ga.), 1966-71, county atty., 1971—. Bd. dirs. Atlanta Union Mission, 1973—. Mem. Atlanta, Ga., Am. bar assns., Lawyers Club Atlanta, Nat. Assn. R.R. Trial Counsel (exec. com. 1965-68). Home: 3561 Ridgewood Rd NW Atlanta GA 30327 Office: 229 Peachtree St NE Atlanta GA 30303 Tel (404) 522-8841

YOUNG, RODGER DOUGLAS, b. Great Falls, Mont., June 10, 1946; B.A. cum laude, U. Mont., 1968; J.D., U. Minn., 1972. Admitted to Mich. bar, 1973; asso. firm Moll, Desenberg, Purdy, Glover & Bayer, Detroit, 1972-75, partner, 1975—. Mem. Mich. Environ. Rev. Bd., 1976—, Detroit Met. Fund Com. on Regional Govt., 1976; bd. dirs. Regional Citizens, 1975—; dir. fin. and spl. advisor to chmn. Oakland County Republican Party, 1976—. Mem. Am., Mich., Detroit bar assns. Home: 1336 Deerhurst Ln Rochester MI 48063 Office: 3466 City Nat Bank Bldg Detroit MI 48226 Tel (313) 961-2966

YOUNG, ROY TRAYWICK, b. N.Y.C., Jan. 18, 1941; A.B., Princeton, 1962; J.D., Rutgers U., 1968; postgrad. Parker Sch. Fgn. and Comparative Law, 1971. Admitted to N.Y. bar, 1969; asso. firm Curtis, Mallet, Prevost, Colt & Mosle, N.Y.C., 1968—. Mem. Assn. Bar City N.Y., Am. Bar Assn. Contbr. articles to legal jours. Home: 241 Sullivan St New York City NY 10012 Office: 100 Wall St New York City NY 10005 Tel (212) 248-8111

YOUNG, SIDNEY D., b. N.Y.C., Jan. 10, 1916; B.S., Bklyn. Coll., 1937, LL.B., 1939. Admitted to N.Y. bar, 1939; former partner firm Dreyer & Traub, Bklyn.; now partner firm Lindenbaum & Young, Bklyn. Mem. Bklyn. Bar Assn., Real Estate Tax Review Bar Assn. Office: 16 Court St Brooklyn NY 11241 Tel (212) 845-8000

YOUNG, THOMAS WILLIAM, III, b. McKeesport, Pa., Nov. 28, 1942; B.A., Mt. Union Coll., Alliance, Ohio, 1967; J.D., U. Miami, 1970. Admitted to Fla. bar, 1970; exec. dir. Dade County (Fla.) Sch. Adminstrs. Assn., Miami, 1971-74; dir. legis. and employee relations Dade County Pub. Schs., 1974-76, spl. counsel legis. and labor relations, 1976—; cons. in field. Mem. Am., Fla. bar assns., Fla. Bar Labor Law Commn., Delta Theta Phi. Recipient Am. Trial Lawyers Assn. award, 1971. Home: 842 Sevilla Ave Coral Gables FL 33134 Office: 1410 NW 2d Ave Miami FL 33132 Tel (305) 350-3714

YOUNG, VERNON LEWIS, b. Seaman, Ohio, Oct. 13, 1919; student Ohio No. U., 1937-38, LL.B., J.D., 1942; student Alfred Holbrook Coll., 1938-39. Admitted to Ohio bar, 1942; staff War Dept., Fairborn, Ohio, 1942; individual practice law, W. Union, Ohio, 1942-50; partner firm Young & Young, W. Union, 1950-76; pros. atty. Adams County, Ohio, 1952-56; spl. counsel Office Atty. Gen. State Ohio, Columbus; solicitor Cities of Manchester, Seaman, Winchester, Jamestown, Ohio; acting judge Adams County (Ohio) Ct., W. Union, 1968—; mayor City of Seaman, 1944-46. Mem. Adams County Bd. Health, 1968-75. Mem. Ohio, Adams County (former pres.) bar assns., Jr. Bar Assn. Ohio No. U. (pres.), Sigma Delta Kappa (chancellor). Home: 6 Hickory Dr Seaman OH 45679 Office: 225 N Cross St W Union OH 45693 Tel (513) 544-2152

YOUNG, WILFORD ROSCOE, b. Rathdrum, Idaho, July 19, 1910; B.S., U. Idaho, 1931, LL.D., 1975; M.S., Columbia, 1935; J.D., Fordham U., 1940. Admitted to N.Y. bar, 1940, U.S. Supreme Ct., 1965; with legal dept. Texaco, Inc., N.Y.C., 1942—, v.p., gen. tax counsel, 1969, v.p., gen. counsel, 1971, dir., exec. v.p., gen. counsel, 1972-74, vice chmn. bd., gen. counsel, 1974—. Trustee, Parker Sch. Internat. and Comparative Law, Columbia. C.P.A., N.Y. Mem. Tax Execs. Inst. (hon., pres. 1960-61). Home: Gray Oaks Lane Greenwich CT 06830 Office: 135 E 42d St New York City NY 10017*

YOUNG, WILLIAM DONNELL, JR., b. Memphis, Aug. 7, 1934; B.A., Vanderbilt U.; LL.B., YMCA Law Sch., 1968, J.D., 1971. Admitted to Tenn. bar, 1968, U.S. Dist. Ct. bar for Middle Dist. Tenn., 1969, U.S. Supreme Ct. bar, 1973; asso. firm Ingraham, Young & Corbett, and predecessors, Nashville and Franklin, Tenn., 1968-70, partner, 1971-73, 74—; asst. dist. atty. gen., 17th Jud. Circuit, Tenn., 1972-73, dist. atty. gen. protem, 1973. Bd. dirs. 1st Meth. Ch. of Franklin, 1972-75, Castle Heights Mil. Acad., Lebanon, Tenn., 1976-77; pres. Heritage Found. of Franklin and Williamson County, 1975—. Mem. Am., Tenn., Williamson County, Nashville bar assns., Assn. Trial Lawyers Am., Tenn. Trial Lawyers, Nat., Tenn. assns. criminal def. lawyers, Nat. Dist. Attys. Assn. Home: Route 2 PO Box 20 A Thompsons Station TN 37179 Office: 329 Main St Franklin TN 37064 Tel (615) 794-3506

YOUNG, WILLIAM MCKINLEY, JR., b. Harrisburg, Pa., Mar. 6, 1945; A.B. in Govt., Cornell U., 1966; J.D., Yale U., 1969. Admitted to Pa. bar, 1970, U.S. Supreme Ct. bar, 1976; asso. firm McNees, Wallace & Nurick, Harrisburg, 1970-76, partner, 1977—. Active Friends of Symphony, Harrisburg, 1976—. Mem. Am., Pa., Dauphin County (fed. ct. relations com.) bar assns. Contbr. article Pa. Sch. Bds. Assn. Bull. Office: Box 1166 Harrisburg PA 17108 Tel (717) 236-9341

YOUNG, WILLIAM WESLEY, b. Franklin, Ohio, Oct. 6, 1937; student Miami U., Oxford, Ohio, 1961; LL.B., Chase Coll. Law., 1961; grad. Nat. Coll. State Judiciary U. Nev., 1975. Admitted to Ohio bar, 1961; partner firm Young & Jones, Lebanon, Ohio, 1961-70; pros. atty. City of Lebanon, 1963-70; asst. atty. gen., village solicitor Waynesville (Ohio), 1965-69; judge Warren County (Ohio) Ct. Common Pleas, 1970—. Chmn. March Dimes, 1969. Mem. Warren County (pres. 1969), Dayton, Ohio State, Am. bar assns. Home: 737 Markey Rd Lebanon OH 45036 Office: PO Box 308 Lebanon OH 45036 Tel (513) 932-4040 ext 230

YOUNGBLOOD, FRANK POLK, b. Dallas, Jan. 17, 1937; B.A. in Physics, Baylor U., 1960; B.S. in Petroleum Engring., U. Tex., 1960, J.D., 1967. Admitted to Tex. bar, 1967; legal examiner, oil and gas div. Tex. R.R. Commn., Austin, 1967-69, sr. legal examiner, 1969-73, dir. gas utilities div., 1973-76; partner firm Scott & Douglass, Austin, 1976—; pipeline engr. Continental Pipeline Co., Ponca City, Okla., 1960-62; petroleum engr. Mobil, Lake Charles, La., 1962-64. Trustee Mary Hardin-Baylor Coll., Belton, Tex., 1972-76. Mem. Tex. Bar Assn., Sigma Pi Sigma. Office: 1515 City National Bank Bldg Austin TX 78701 Tel (512) 476-6337

YOUNGDAHL, LUTHER WALLACE, b. Mpls., May 29, 1896; B.A., Gustavus Adolphus Coll., 1919; LL.B., Minn. Coll. Law, 1921; numerous hon. degrees. Admitted to Minn. bar, 1921; asst. city atty. City of Mpls., 1921-24; partner firm M.C. Tifft, Mpls., 1924-31; judge Municipal Ct., Mpls., 1930-36, Hennepin County (Minn.) Dist. Ct., 1936-42; justice Minn. Supreme Ct., 1942-46; gov. State of Minn., 1947-51; judge U.S. Dist. Ct. for D.C., 1951—, sr. judge, 1966—. Active field mental health, Boy Scouts Am., Big Bros. Mem. Am., Minn. bar assns. Decorated Order of Lion (Finland); grand cross Royal Order of North Star (Sweden); author; The Ramparts We Watch, 1962. Home: 4101 Cathedral Ave NW Washington DC 20016 Office: US Dist Ct for DC Washington DC 20001 Tel (202) RE7-3214

YOUNGDAHL, ROBERT MILTON, b. Whittier, Calif., Feb. 18, 1934; B.A., U. Calif., Los Angeles, 1959; J.D., Southwestern U., 1967. Admitted to Calif. bar, 1968; dep. city atty. City of Los Angeles, 1968-69; dep. dist. atty. County of Los Angeles, 1969—. Mem. Am., Calif. bar assns., Nat., Calif. dist. attys. assns., Los Angeles Trial Lawyers Assn. Office: 849 S Broadway Los Angeles CA 90014 Tel (213) 974-3947

YOUNGER, EVELLE JANSEN, b. Nebr., June 19, 1918; A.B., Nebr. U., 1940, also LL.B.; student criminology Northwestern Law Sch., Chgo., 1940. Spl. agt. FBI, N.Y.C. and Washington, supr. nat. def. sect., 1940-46; admitted to Calif. bar, 1946; dep. city atty. criminal div. Los Angeles, 1946-47; city pros. atty. Pasadena (Calif.), 1947-50; pvt. practice law, Los Angeles, 1950-53; judge Municipal Ct. Los Angeles, 1953-58, Superior Ct., 1958-64; dist. atty. Los Angeles County, 1964-70; atty. gen. Calif., 1970—; instr. criminal law Southwestern U., Los Angeles, 1948. Fellow Am. Coll. Trial Lawyers; mem. Am. Bar Assn. (chmn. criminal law sect. 1962, past chmn. traffic and magistrates cts. com.), State Bar Calif., Nat. Dist. Attys. Assn. (v.p.), Los Angeles Lawyers Club, Am. Legion, Soc. Former FBI Agts. (past chmn.), Los Angeles Peace Officers Assn. (past pres.), Council Mexican-Am. Affairs, Air Force Assn., Alpha Tau Omega Alumni Assn. (past pres.). Contbr. articles to profl. jours. Office: 3580 Wilshire Blvd Los Angeles CA 90010

YOUNGER, IRVING, b. N.Y.C., Nov. 30, 1932; A.B. Harvard, 1953; LL.B., N.Y. U., 1958. Admitted to N.Y. State bar, 1958, U.S. Supreme Ct. bar, 1962; asso. firm Paul, Weiss, Rifkind, Wharton & Garrison, N.Y.C., 1958-60; asst. U.S. atty. So. Dist. N.Y., 1960-62; partner firm Younger & Younger and successors, N.Y.C., 1962-65; prof. law N.Y. U., 1965-68; judge Civil Ct. City N.Y., 1969-74; Samuel S. Leibowitz prof. trial techniques Cornell U., 1974—; adj. prof. law Columbia, N.Y. U., 1969-74; mem. faculty Nat. Coll. State Judiciary, 1971-75. Mem. Am., N.Y. State bar assns., Am. Law Inst., Assn. Bar City N.Y., Assn. Am. Law Schs. (chmn. trial advocacy sect.). Contbr. articles to law reviews and popular mags. Home: 3 Fountain Pl Ithaca NY 14850 Office: Cornell Law Sch Ithaca NY 14853 Tel (607) 256-5077

YOUNGERMAN, ELISABETH MATTHES, b. Savannah, Ga., Oct. 31, 1945; B.A., U. Pa., 1967; J.D., Northeastern U., 1973. Admitted to Ga. bar, 1973; atty. Ga. Legal Services Programs, Savannah, 1973-75, specialist atty., 1976—; dir. dept. planning City of Savannah, 1975-76; citizen rep. Chatham County (Ga.) Census Com., 1975-76. Bd. dirs. Savannah YWCA, 1975-76, LWV, Savannah, 1976; v.p. Savannah chpt. NOW. Mem. Ga., Am. bar assns., Am. Soc. Planning Ofcls., Nat. Assn. Housing and Redevel. Ofcls. Office: 1317 Bull St Savannah GA 31401 Tel (912) 944-2180

YOUNGMAN, JOHN CRAWFORD, b. Williamsport, Pa., Jan. 25, 1903; B.S. in Econs., Wharton Sch., U. Pa., 1924; LL.B., Harvard, 1927, J.D., 1969. Admitted to Pa. Supreme Ct., 1928, Lycoming County bar, 1927; dist. atty. Lycoming County, Pa., 1932-35; sr. partner firm Candor, Youngman, Gibson & Gault, Williamsport, Pa., 1943—; dir. Williamsport Hotels Co., Penn Garment Co. Nat. asso. Boys Clubs Am., 1952—; trustee Danville State Hosp., 1964—; chmn. Williamsport Sanitary Authority, 1952—; mem. Williamsport Water Authority, 1966—. Mem. World Assn. Lawyers, Judicial Conf. Third Circuit Ct. of Appeals (permanent), Lycoming County Law Assn. (pres. 1939), Am. Judicature Soc. Recipient Grit award, 1956, Conservation award, Pa. Game Commn., 1975; named to Hall of Fame Pa. Fedn. Sportsmen's Clubs, 1972. Home: 54 Roderick Rd Williamsport PA 17701 Office: 23 W 3d St Williamsport PA 17701 Tel (717) 322-6144

YOUNTS, MEVIN KEMP, b. Durham, N.C., Aug. 19, 1929; B.A., Furman U., 1950; LL.B., U. S.C., 1952. Admitted to S.C. bar, 1951; sr. partner firm Younts, Spivey & Gross, Greenville and Fountain Inn, S.C., 1952—. Trustee, Greenville County Bd., 1970—. Mem. Greenville County, S.C., Am. bar assns., Am. Trial Lawyers Assn., Fountain Inn C. of C. (pres. 1957). Home: Club Dr Fountain Inn SC 29644 Office: 512 E North St Greenville SC 29601 Tel (803) 233-4693

YOWELL, GEORGE KENT, b. St. Louis, May 12, 1927; B.A., U. Colo., 1949; J.D., Northwestern U., 1952. Admitted to Ill. bar, 1952, U.S. Supreme Ct. bar, 1956; served in JAGC, U.S. Army, 1952-54; asst. U.S. atty. No. Dist. Ill., Chgo., 1954-57; individual practice law, Chgo., 1957—, Northbrook, Ill., 1969—; partner firm Littlejohn, Glass & Yowell, Northbrook, 1976—; village prosecutor Glencoe (Ill.), 1963—, village atty., 1970—. Mem. Am., Ill. State, Chgo. bar assns., Am. Judicature Soc., Law Club Chgo., Legal Club Chgo. Home: 400 Lincoln Ave Glencoe IL 60022 Office: 899 Skokie Blvd Northbrook IL 60062 Tel (312) 498-1620

YPSILANTI, LEO E., b. N.Y.C., May 6, 1909; B.S., Fordham U., 1934; LL.B., N.Y. U., 1937. Admitted to N.Y. bar, 1937; individual practice law, N.Y.C., 1937—. Mem. Immigration and Naturalization, N.Y., New Rochelle, Bronx bar assns. Home: 178 Bon Air Ave New Rochelle NY 10804 Office: 225 Broadway New York City NY 10007 Tel (212) 964-2055

YSLAS, STEPHEN DANIEL, b. Los Angeles, Mar. 28, 1947; B.A., U. Calif., Los Angeles, 1969, J.D., 1972. Admitted to Calif. bar, 1973; atty. NLRB, Los Angeles, 1972-73; atty. Atlantic Richfield Co., Los Angeles, 1973-75; asst. gen. counsel Northrop Corp., Los Angeles, 1975—. Mem. Am., Los Angeles County, Beverly Hills bar assns., Mexican Am. Lawyers Assn. Office: 1800 Century Park E Los Angeles CA 90067 Tel (213) 553-6262

YUDKIN, FRANKLIN SHERWOOD, b. Miami, Fla., May 15, 1944; A.B., Ind. U., 1966; J.D., U. Louisville, 1969. Admitted to Ky. bar, 1970, Conn. bar, 1971; individual practice law, Louisville, 1970—; lawyer VISTA, 1969-70; title examiner Commonwealth Title Ins. Co., Louisville, 1970—; consumer action reporter WHAS-TV, 1974-75. Consumer mem. Ky. Bd. Licensing Hearing Aid Dealers, 1975—; active Consumer Assn. Ky., Med. Emergency Dist. Inter County Services. Mem. Ky., Louisville bar assns., Phi Alpha Delta. Office: 310 W Liberty St Louisville KY 40202 Tel (502) 587-0772

YUROW, JOHN JESSE, b. Washington, Jan. 30, 1931; A.B., George Washington U., 1953, J.D., 1958. Admitted to D.C. bar, 1958, Mich. bar, 1961; atty. IRS, Detroit, 1958-62, asso. firm Arent, Fox, Kinter, Plotkin & Kahn, Washington, 1962-68, partner, 1969—; prof. law, lectr. George Washington U., 1974-76. Mem. Bar Assn. D.C., D.C., Am., Fed. bar assns. Co-Author: How To Settle A Tax Controversy, 1974; contbr. articles in field to law jours. Home: 931 Clintwood Dr Silver Spring MD 20902 Office: 1815 H St NW Washington DC 20006 Tel (202) 857-6201

ZABEL, OSCAR ALVIN, b. Odessa, Wash., Mar. 12, 1902; LL.B., George Washington U., 1926, J.D., 1968. Admitted to Wash. State bar, 1927, U.S. Supreme Ct. bar, 1940; individual practice law, Seattle, 1927—. Bd. govs. Lakewood Gen. Hosp., Tacoma, 1969-74, Burien Gen. Hosp., Seattle, 1969-74. Mem. George Washington U. Law Alumni Assn. (exec. com. 1975—), Phi Alpha Delta. Office: 441 W Washington St Sequim WA 98382 Tel (206) 683-3325

ZABLOW, NATHAN PHILIP, b. N.Y.C., Aug. 9, 1906; student Coll. City N.Y., 1925-26, U. Idaho, 1926-28; LL.B., N.Y. U., 1931. Admitted to N.Y. bar, 1933, U.S. Supreme Ct. bar, 1956; individual practice law, N.Y.C. and Freeport, N.Y., 1933-68; adminstr. Assigned Counsel Defender Plan, Bar Assn. Nassau County (N.Y.), 1968—; adj. prof. criminal procedure law C.W. Post Coll. Former pres. Atlantic South Civic Assn., Freeport Hist. Soc. Mem. Bar Assn. Nassau County, N.Y. State Defenders Assn. (sec.), N.Y. State Bar Assn. Home: 11 W 2d St Freeport NY 11520 Office: 214 3d St Mineola NY 11501 Tel (516) 747-8448

ZACHARY, FRANCIS THOMAS, b. Meridian, Miss., Jan. 2, 1923; student U. So. Miss., 1941-42, Miss. State U., 1953; LL.B., U. Miss., 1949, J.D., 1968. Admitted to Miss. bar, 1947; mem. firm Zachary, Weldy & Ingram and predecessors, Hattiesburg, Miss., 1962-65; gen. counsel So. Nat. Bank, Hattiesburg, 1965-76; circuit judge Twelfth Jud. Dist., 1954-59; city atty. Hattiesburg, 1960-64; gen. counsel Pat Harrison Waterway Dist., 1961-70. Mem. Am., Miss. State, S. Miss. (pres. 1943-44) bar assns. Office: 301 Front St Hattiesburg MS 39401 Tel (601) 544-4333

ZACHOS, KIMON STEPHEN, b. Concord, N.H., Nov. 20, 1930; B.A., Wesleyan U., Middletown, Conn., 1952; J.D., N.Y. U., 1955; LL.M. in Taxation, Boston U., 1968. Admitted to N.H. bar, 1955, U.S. Supreme Ct. bar, 1963; asso. firm Sheehan, Phinney, Bass & Green, Profl. Assn., Manchester, N.H., 1957-62, partner, 1963—; mem., dep. speaker N.H. Ho. of Reps., 1973-74; dir. Mchts. Nat. Bank, Manchester, 1st Bancorp of N.H., Inc., Manchester. Bd. dirs. St.

George Greek Orthodox Ch., Manchester, 1959—; trustee, sec. bd. N.H. Coll., 1968—; incorporator N.H. Charitable Fund, Concord, 1971—; pres. Currier Gallery Art, Manchester, 1976. Mem. Am., N.H., Manchester bar assns., Am. Judicature Soc. Recipient Brotherhood award N.H. chpt. NCCJ, 1966; White House fellow, 1965-66. Home: 2093 Elm St Manchester NH 03104 Office: 1000 Elm St Manchester NH 03101 Tel (603) 668-0300

ZACHS, ANNA H., b. Russia, Jan. 9, 1903; LL.B., N.Y. U., 1925. Admitted to N.Y. bar, 1927; individual practice law, N.Y.C., 1927—; dep. atty. gen. State of N.Y., 1944. Home: 13 W 13th St New York City NY 10011 Office: 799 Broadway New York City NY 10003 Tel (212) 777-0580

ZACZEK, LESTER C., b. Chgo., Feb. 26, 1932; B.A., U. Notre Dame, 1953; J.D., Northwestern U., 1956. Admitted to Ill. bar, 1956; with JAGC, U.S. Army, 1957-60; asso. firm Lord Bissell & Brook, Chgo., 1960-67, partner, 1968—; instr. John Marshall Law Sch., Chgo., 1968. Mem. Am., Ill., Chgo. bar assns., Law Club Chgo., Order of Coif. Contbr. articles to legal jours. Home: 4844 Lawn Ave Western Springs IL 60558 Office: Lord Bissell & Brook 115 S LaSalle St Chicago IL 60603 Tel (312) 443-0275

ZADECK, DONALD JULIAN, b. St. Louis, Sep. 12, 1927; LL.B., La. State U., 1950. Admitted to La. bar, 1950; v.p., legal counsel United Shoe Stores Co., Shreveport, La., 1951-73, pres., 1973—. Pres. Shreveport Econ. Devel. Found., 1975—, B'nai Zion Congregation, Shreveport, 1971-73; bd. dirs. La. Bus. and Industry Assn., 1976—. Mem. Shreveport C. of C. (1st v.p. 1976, pres. 1977). Recipient Civil award La. Indsl. Devel. Exec. Assn., 1975. Home: 4732 Richmond Ave Shreveport LA 71106 Office: 3305 Mansfield Rd Shreveport LA 71103 Tel (318) 221-8328

ZAFIAN, HENRY JOHN, b. Bayonne, N.J., Aug. 31, 1921; B.M.E., Poly. Inst., 1941; LL.B., Columbia U., 1948. Admitted to N.Y. bar, 1948, U.S. Supreme Ct. bar, 1954; asso. firm Fish & Neave, N.Y.C., 1948-60, partner, 1961—. Mem. Am., N.Y. State bar assns., Assn. Bar City N.Y., N.Y., Am. patent law assns., Am. Judicature Soc. Home: 165 Croton Lake Rd Katonah NY 10536 Office: Fish & Neave 277 Park Ave New York City NY 10017 Tel (212) 826-1050

ZAFMAN, NORMAN, b. Paterson, N.J., Oct. 13, 1934; B.E.E., Coll. City N.Y., 1957; M.S. in Elec. Engring., U. So. Calif., 1964; J.D. cum laude, S.W. U., Los Angeles, 1969. Elec. engr. Jet Propulsion Lab., Pasadena, Calif., 1957-70; admitted to Calif. bar, 1970, U.S. Patent Office bar, 1972; mem. firm Spensley, Horn, Jubas & Lubitz, Los Angeles, 1970-75; partner firm Blakely, Sokoloff, Taylor & Zafman, Beverly Hills, Calif., 1975—. Active Common Cause, 1975-76; mem. Los Angeles Mayor's Spl. Task Force on Newly Proposed Air Pollution Regulations, 1976—. Mem. Century City Bar Assn. (gov.), Planning and Conservation League (dir.). Contbr. articles to Los Angeles County Bar Bull., Beverly Hills Bar Jour., Los Angeles Daily Jour. Office: 9601 Wilshire Blvd Beverly Hills CA 90210 Tel (213) 550-8282

ZAGORIA, MARVIN JAY, b. Bklyn., Dec. 8, 1945; B.A., Oglethorpe U., 1967; J.D., Emory U., 1970. Admitted to Ga. bar, 1971; staff atty. NAACP Legal Def. Fund, Atlanta, 1971; mem. firm Wyatt & Zagoria, Atlanta, 1971-73; partner firm Zagoria & Stoner, Atlanta, 1974—. Mem. Phi Alpha Delta. Home: 4585 Runnemede Rd NW Atlanta GA 30327 Office: 235 Peachtree St SW 1000 Atlanta GA 30303 Tel (404) 681-0611

ZAHN, CHARLES WILLIARD, JR., b. Atlanta, June 10, 1945; B.A., Baylor U., 1970, J.D., 1970. Admitted to Tex. bar, 1970; asso. firm Mahoney, Shaffer, Hatch & Layton, Corpus Christi, Tex., 1971-76, partner, 1977—; city atty. Port Aransas (Tex.), 1973-75. Advancement chmn. Mustang dist. Boy Scouts Am., Corpus Christi, 1972-75; elder Community Presbyterian Ch., Port Aransas, 1975—. Mem. Am., Tex. bar assns., Nueces County Bar Assn., Nueces, Tex. trial lawyers assns., Phi Alpha Delta. Home: PO Box 941 Port Aransas TX 78373 Office: 4411 Gollihar St Corpus Christi TX 78411 Tel (512) 854-4474

ZAK, JAMES JOSEPH, b. Cedar Rapids, Iowa, Nov. 14, 1944; B.S. cum laude, Loras Coll., 1966; J.D., U. Notre Dame, 1969. Admitted to Ind., Colo. bars, 1969; clk. to chief judge U.S. Dist. Ct. for No. Ind., S. Bend, 1969-71; asso. firm Towey & Zak, and predecessors, Denver, 1971-75, partner, 1976—. Pres., Adams County (Colo.) Mental Health Assn., 1975—. Mem. Am., Colo., Ind., Adams County bar assns., Western Fraternal Life Assn. (v.p. 1975—). Office: 1701 W 72nd Ave Suite 210 Denver CO 80221 Tel (303) 428-7411

ZAK, LEONARD EUGENE, b. Chgo., Mar. 22, 1929; B.A., Carleton Coll., 1951; J.D., Northwestern U., 1954. Admitted to Ill. bar, 1954; asso. firm McBride, Baker, Wienke & Schlosser, Chgo., 1956-64, partner, 1965—; spl. asst. to U.S. Atty. Gen., 1967-68. Mem. Am., Ill., Chgo. bar assns. Home: 2738 Woodbine St Evanston IL 60201 Office: 110 N Wacker Dr Chicago IL 60606 Tel (312) 346-6191

ZAKAIB, PAUL, JR., b. Los Angeles, Oct. 20, 1932; B.A., Morris Harvey Coll., 1955; LL.B., W.Va. U., 1958. Admitted to W.Va. bar, 1958; atty., W.Va. Tax Commn., Charleston, 1958-59, W.Va. Dept. Employment Security, Charleston, 1959-60, W.Va. Econ. Devel. Agy., Charleston, 1960; atty., exec. asst. W.Va. Dept. Commerce, Charleston, 1960-62; asso. firm Preiser & Wilson, Charleston, 1965-74; individual practice law, Charleston, 1974—; mem. W.Va. Legislature, 1967-75. Del. Republican Nat. Conv., 1976; mem. County Fund Drive Com., United Fund, 1976-77. Mem. Am. (state rep. local govt. law sect. 1963), Kanawha County, W.Va. State bar assns., Phi Delta Phi. Greek Orthodox (trustee 1975-77). Home: 4102 Virginia Av SE Charleston WV 25304 Office: 209 Stanley Bldg Charleston WV 25301

ZAKROFF, ROBERT JOEL, b. Phila., Jan. 14, 1948; B.S., Temple U., 1969; J.D., Am. U., 1972. Admitted to Md. bar, 1973, D.C. bar, 1973; since practiced in Washington, asso. firm Baylinson and Kudysh, 1974-76, partner firm Zakroff and Rosenbleet, 1976—. Mem. Comml. Law League Am. Recipient Highest Achievement award Am. U. Home: 14 Grovepoint Ct Rockville MD 20854 Office: 1800 M St NW Washington DC 20036 Tel (202) 296-6627

ZALBOWITZ, ALAN MICHAEL, b. Binghamton, N.Y., Nov. 8, 1939; B.S., U. Pa., 1961; LL.B., Syracuse U., 1964. Admitted to N.Y. State bar, 1964; asso. firm Willsey, Meagher, Hummer, Madigan & Buckley, Binghamton, 1964-67; individual practice law, Binghamton, 1968; mem. firm Yetter & Zalbowitz, Binghamton, 1969—; asst. dist. atty. Broome County (N.Y.), 1968; chief labor negotiator City of Binghamton, 1972-76, Deposit Central Sch. Dist., 1976—. Bd. dirs. Jewish Community Center, 1973-75, Jewish Fedn. of Broome County, 1974—; vol. counsel Parents Assn. for Hearing Impaired of Broome County, 1964—. Mem. Am., N.Y. State, Broome County bar assns., Tioga, Delaware counties chambers commerce. Recipient award Parents Assn. Broome County, 1966. Home: Hazzard Hill Rd Binghamton NY 13903 Office: 604 Press Bldg Binghamton NY 13901 Tel (607) 723-9551

ZALEON, ISAAC, b. Utica, N.Y., June 27, 1914; A.B., Syracuse U., 1935; postgrad. Albany Law Sch., 1936-38. Admitted to N.Y. bar, 1941; practiced law, Gloversville, N.Y.; asst. judge City Ct., Gloversville, 1955-58, judge, 1958-64; judge Fulton County (N.Y.) Family Ct., 1964-75. Pres., N.Y. State sect. Nat. Jewish Welfare Bd., 1963-65. Mem. N.Y. State, Fulton County (treas. 1975—) bar assns. Decorated Bronze Star; recipient Distinguished medal N.Y. State, 1945. Home: 138 5th Ave Gloversville NY 12078 Office: 40 N Main St Gloversville NY 12078 Tel (518) 725-5622

ZALUTSKY, MORTON HERMAN, b. Schenectady, Mar. 8, 1935; B.A. in Econs., Yale, 1957; J.D., U. Chgo., 1960. Admitted to Oreg. bar, 1961; clk. Oreg. Supreme Ct., 1960-61; asso. firms Hart, Davidson, Veazie & Hanlon, Portland, Oreg., 1961-63, Veatch & Lovett, Portland, 1963-64, Morrison, Bailey, Dunn, Cohen & Miller, Portland, 1964-69; pres. firm Morton H. Zalutsky, P.C., Portland, 1970-77, firm Dahl, Zalutsky & Nichols, P.C., Portland, 1977—; speaker in field including Practicing Law Inst., Am. Law Inst.-Am. Bar Assn., 11th Ann. Inst. Estate Planning, numerous others. Mem. Am. (chmn. com. on profl. corps. sect. econs. of law), Oreg., Multnomah County (Oreg.) bar assns. Contbr. numerous articles to legal publs. including Jour. Taxation; So. Fed. Tax Inst., N.Y. Law Jour., numerous others. Office: Suite 1200 Benjamin Franklin Plaza One SW Columbia St Portland OR 97258 Tel (503) 248-0800

ZAMBORSKY, EDWARD JOSEPH, b. Allentown, Pa., June 21, 1941; B.A., Lehigh U., 1963; LL.B., Villanova U., 1966. Admitted to Pa. bar, 1969, U.S. Supreme Ct. bar, 1972; partner firm Zamborsky & Zamborsky, Allentown, 1969—; asst. county solicitor Lehigh County (Pa.), 1971-75. Mem. Internat. Acad. Law, Sci., Am., Pa., Lehigh County (dir. 1969-75) bar assns. Office: 610 Linden St Allentown PA 18101 Tel (215) 439-0593

ZAMSKY, STEVEN ADOLPH, b. Portland, Oreg., Feb. 5, 1947; B.S. in Accounting, U. Oreg., 1968, J.D., 1971. Admitted to Oreg. bar, 1971; asso. firm Ganong, Ganong & Gordon, Klamath Falls, Oreg., 1971-73; partner firm Ganong, Sisemore and Zamsky, Klamath Falls, 1973-74, firm Giacomin, Jones and Zamsky, Klamath Falls, 1974—. Chmn. cable TV adv. com. City of Klamath Falls, 1974—. Mem. Am., Oreg., Klamath County (pres. 1972) bar assns., Assn. Hosp. Attys., Order of Coif. Home: 1963 Auburn St Klamath Falls OR 97601 Office: 635 Main St Klamath Falls OR 97601 Tel (503) 884-7728

ZAMZOK, LAWRENCE PAUL, b. Bklyn., Jan. 17, 1942; grad. Columbia U. Sch. Law, 1964. Admitted to N.Y. bar, 1964, U.S. Supreme Ct. bar, 1969; asso. firm Schaffner & D'Onofrio, N.Y.C., 1964-67; partner firm Tanenbaum & Zamzok, N.Y.C., 1967—; of counsel firm Hayt, Hayt, Tolmach & Landau, Great Neck, N.Y., 1971-74. Mem. N.Y. County Lawyers Assn. Office: 120 Wall St New York City NY 10005 Tel (212) 422-1765

ZANATY, EDWARD SAMUEL, b. Birmingham, Ala., Feb. 21, 1942; B.A., U. Ala., 1964; J.D., Samford U., 1967. Admitted to Ala. bar, 1967; sr. mem. firm Zanaty and Kirst, Birmingham; capt. judge advocate USAFR. Mem. Am., Ala., Birmingham bar assns., Sigma Delta Kappa. Office: 1260 1st Nat-So Natural Bldg Birmingham AL 35203 Tel (205) 328-7546

ZAND, H. HERMAN, b. N.Y.C., Feb. 16, 1909; grad. Coll. City N.Y., 1927; LL.B., N.Y. U., 1930. Admitted to N.Y. bar, 1931; asso. Arthur B. Spingarn, N.Y.C., 1931—; chief asst. corp. counsel City of Long Beach (N.Y.), 1966-74; govt. appeal agt. SSS, 1941-45. Mem. nat. legal com. NAACP, 1951-66. Mem. Assn. Bar City N.Y., Nassau County Bar Assn., Long Beach Lawyers Assn. Recipient Humanitarian award Christian Light Baptist Ch., Long Beach, 1968. Home: 532 E Olive St Long Beach NY 11561 Office: 20 W Park Ave Long Beach NY 11561 Tel (516) 432-5432

ZAND, J. PHILIP, b. Cin., Sept. 24, 1937; B.A., City Coll. N.Y., 1963; J.D., Bklyn. Law Sch., 1966. Admitted to N.Y. State bar, 1966, Fed. bar, 1968, U.S. Supreme Ct. bar, 1970; individual practice law, N.Y.C., Poughkeepsie, N.Y., New Paltz, N.Y., 1966—; village atty. New Paltz, 1972—; town justice Gardiner, N.Y., 1976—. Mem. N.Y. State, Ulster County, Am. bar assns., Supreme Ct. Hist. Soc. Home: PO Box 55 New Paltz NY 12561 Office: 153 Main St New Paltz NY 12561 Tel (914) 255-1556

ZANGER, CARL LEWY, b. N.Y.C., Dec. 21, 1931; A.B., Hamilton Coll., 1953; LL.B., Harvard U., 1956. Admitted to N.Y. State bar, 1958; sr. atty. ASCAP, N.Y.C., 1958-68; partner firm Dornbush, Mensch & Mandelstam, N.Y.C., 1969-77. Mem. Am., N.Y. State (chmn. com. on art, spl. com. on copyright law) bar assns. Author: For a Copyright Law to Protect the Artist, 1973; author lectr. art law and copyright problems for profl. jours. groups. Home: 180 Riverside Dr New York City NY 10024 Office: 500 5th Ave New York City NY 10036 Tel (212) 840-2940

ZANGER, LARRY MARTIN, b. Bklyn., July 10, 1946; B.B.A., Northwestern U., 1967, J.D., 1970. Admitted to Ill. bar, 1970, U.S. Tax Ct. bar, 1971, U.S. Ct. Claims bar, 1971; asso. firm McDermott, Will & Emery, Chgo., 1970-72; partner firms Zanger & Looney, Ltd., Medinah, Ill., 1972-75, McHugh, Zanger, Bromberg & Lang, Chgo., 1975—; adj. asst. prof. law U. Ill. Chgo. Circle Campus, 1972—; participant City Elements radio show, Chgo., 1973—. Mem. Am., Ill. State (3d pl. Lincoln award for writing 1975, 2d pl. 1974) bar assns., Am. Inst. C.P.A.'s (Elijah Watts Sell award 1968). C.P.A., Ill. Office: 10 S LaSalle St Chicago IL 60603 Tel (312) 236-5450

ZANGLIN, JOSEPH RICHARD, b. Edmonton, Alta., Can., July 7, 1914; J.D., U. Detroit, 1943. Admitted to Mich. bar, 1943; investigator Mich. Prosecutor's Office, Detroit, 1941-43; practice law, Wyandotte, Mich., 1943—; mem. Mich. Ho. of Reps., 1949-50; city atty. City of Wyandotte, 1950-62; judge Municipal Ct., Wyandotte, 1973-77. Mem. State Bar Mich., Downriver Bar Assn., Municipal, Dist. judges assns. Home: 2483 19th St Wyandotte MI 48192 Office: 1822 Ford Ave Wyandotte MI 48192 Tel (313) 282-2440

ZANGRILLI, ALBERT JOSEPH, JR., b. Pitts., May 3, 1940; B.A., U. Notre Dame, 1963; M.A., Holy Cross Coll., 1967; J.D., Cornell U., 1972. Admitted to Pa. bar, 1972; asso. firm Berkman Ruslander Pohl Lieber & Engel, Pitts., 1972—; mem. rules com. Allegheny County Ct., 1976—. Campaign asst. Senator Joseph Clark, 1968. Mem. Am., Pa., Allegheny County bar assns., Notre Dame Club (mem. exec. com. 1975—). Office: 20th Floor Frick Bldg Pittsburgh PA 15219 Tel (412) 391-3939

ZARETSKY, DAVID BERNARD, b. S. Bend, Ind., Mar. 4, 1929; B.A., N.Y. U., 1949; J.D., Harvard, 1952. Admitted to D.C. bar, 1952, N.Y. State bar, 1954; individual practice law, N.Y.C., 1954—. Office: 253 Broadway New York City NY 10007 Tel (212) 267-3250

ZARLENGO, HENRY E., b. N. Platte, Nebr., Feb. 24, 1907; A.B. magna cum laude, Regis Coll., 1929; J.D., U. Denver, 1932. Admitted to Colo. bar, 1932; individual practice law; asst. city atty. Denver; state asst. atty. gen. Colo., 1943-59; pub. utilities commr., 1959—. Mem. Colo., Denver bar assns. Home: 37 Skyline Dr Wheat Ridge CO 80033 Office: 1525 Sherman St Denver CO 80203 Tel (303) 892-3197

ZARLING, WILLIAM ALLAN, b. Trenton, N.J., Nov. 9, 1944; B.A., U. Pa., 1966; J.D., Harvard, 1969. Admitted to N.J. bar, 1969; law clk. Superior Ct. N.J., Trenton, 1969, Hon. George H. Barlow U.S. Dist. Ct. for Dist. N.J., Trenton, 1970-71; asst. prosecutor Mercer County (N.J.) Prosecutor's Office, Trenton, 1971—. Mem. Am., N.J. State, Mercer County bar assns. Home: 739 Estates Blvd Trenton NJ 08619 Office: Mercer County Ct House Broad and Market Sts Trenton NJ 08607 Tel (609) 989-6410

ZARNFALLER, WILLIAM EDWARD, b. Bronx, N.Y., May 30, 1925; B.A., Columbia, 1950; LL.B., N.Y. U., 1955. Admitted to N.Y N.Y. bar, 1955; asso. firm Edward B. Willing, Esq., Mt. Vernon, N.Y., 1955-60, firm Kenneth C. Schwartz, Esq., Mt. Vernon, N.Y., 1961—; individual practice law, Mt. Vernon, 1955—; atty. Village of Pelham (N.Y.) Zoning Bd. Appeals, 1972—. Staff vol. Legal Aid Soc., Greenwich Village Office, N.Y.C., 1954; mem. Pelham Bicentennial Commn., 1975—. Mem. N.Y. State Bar Assn. Home: 759 Pelhamdale Ave Pelham NY 10803 Office: 10 Fiske Pl Mount Vernon NY 10550 Tel (914) 668-3534

ZARTER, CHARLES FRANK, b. Leavenworth, Kans., June 23, 1942; A.B. in Econs., St. Benedict's Coll., 1964; J.D., Kans. U., 1967. Admitted to Kans. bar, 1967, Mo. bar, 1969; atty. Wyandotte County Legal Aid Soc., Kansas City, Kans., 1967-68; counsel Business Men's Assurance Co. Am., Kansas City, Mo., 1968—; v.p., gen. counsel, dir. BMA Properties, Inc. and BMA Real Estate Corp., Kansas City, Mo., 1976—. Mem. Mo., Am. bar assns., Kansas City Lawyers Assn. Office: BMA Tower 700 Karnes Blvd Kansas City MO 64108 Tel (816) 753-8000

ZARUBA, KAREL LEWIS, b. Balt., Sept. 21, 1931; B.S., U. Md., 1958; J.D., U. Balt., 1964; LL.M., N.Y. U., 1972. Admitted to Md. bar, 1969; individual practice law. Glen Burnie, Md., 1969-71; atty. Schering Corp., Kenilworth, N.J., 1972-76; litigation atty. Schering-Plough Corp., Kenilworth, 1976—. Mem. Am., Md., N.J. State bar assns. Home: 23 Dean Rd Mendham NJ 07945 Office: Galloping Hill Rd Kenilworth NJ 07033 Tel (201) 931-2748

ZATCOFF, SANFORD HENRY, b. Elmira, N.Y., Aug. 6, 1947; B.S., Cornell U., 1969; J.D., Columbia, 1973. Admitted to Ga. bar, 1973, U.S. Dist. Ct. bar, 1974; asso. firm Alston, Miller & Gaines, Atlanta, 1973—. Mem. Am., Ga., Atlanta bar assns. Home: 350 Earlston Dr Atlanta GA 30328 Office: 35 Broad St Atlanta GA 30303 Tel (404) 588-0300

ZAVIS, MICHAEL WILLIAM, b. Chgo., Apr. 19, 1937; B.S., U. Pa., 1958; J.D., U. Chgo., 1961. Admitted to Ill. bar, 1961; asso. firm Peebles, Greenberg & Keele, Chgo., 1961-63; partner firm Greenberg, Krauss & Jacobs, Chgo., 1966-70, firm Goldberg, Weigle, Mallin & Gitles, Chgo., 1970-74, firm Katten, Muchin, Gitles, Zavis, Pearl & Galler, Chgo., 1974—; dir. Exchange Internation Corp. and wholly owned subs., Exchange Nat. Bank Chgo. Bd. dirs. fund campaign chmn., chmn. spl. service com. Young Men's Jewish Council; dir. Jewish Community Centers, Jewish Fedn. Chgo.; fund raising coms. Combined Jewish Appeal; bd. dirs., v.p., chmn. admissions com. Bryn Mawr Country Club. Mem. Chgo., Ill. State bar assns. Lectr. on fin. subjects. Office: 55 E Monroe St Chicago IL 60603 Tel (312) 346-7400

ZAWICKI, PAUL PETER, b. Dickson City, Pa., Aug. 3, 1924; LL.B., Mt. Vernon Sch. Law, 1954; J.D., U. Balt., 1970. Admitted to Md. bar, 1961; claims officer USPHS, Washington, 1962-71; individual practice law, Balt., 1971—. Mem. task force on edn. Balt. County, 1976. Mem. Am., Md., Fed., Balt. City, Balt. County bar assns., Am. Judicature Soc. Recipient Superior Performance award HEW, 1968. Home: 4506 Raspe Ave Baltimore MD 21206 Office: 6721 Belair Rd Baltimore MD 21206 Tel (301) 665-3994

ZAZAS, GEORGE JOHN, b. Indpls., Feb. 17, 1926; A.B., Harvard U., 1947, J.D., 1949. Admitted to Ind. bar, 1949; partner firm Barnes, Hickam, Pantzer & Boyd, Indpls., 1949—; sec. Ind. State Bd. Law Examiners, 1968-71; mem. chmn's. task force NLRB, 1976-77. Mem. Ind. State Democratic Central Com., 1972-76; bd. dirs. Ind. Heart Assn. Mem. Bar Assn. 7th Fed. Circuit, Am. Judicature Soc., Am. Arbitration Assn., Am., Ind., Indpls. bar assns. Home: 6105 Shawnee Trail Indianapolis IN 46220 Office: 1313 Merchants Bank Bldg Indianapolis IN 46204

ZBRANEK, J.C., b. Crosby, Tex., Mar. 25, 1930; B.A., U. Tex., 1952, J.D., 1956. Admitted to Tex. bar, 1956, U.S. Supreme Ct. bar, 1963; mem. Tex. Ho. of Reps., 1954-60; individual practice law, Liberty, Tex., 1956—. Chmn. county Democratic Party, 1969—. Mem. Am., Tex. trial lawyers assns., Tex. Criminal Def. Attys., VFW (past dist. comdr.). Student editor Tex. Law Rev. Home: Box 361 Devers TX 77538 Office: Box 151 1937 Trinity St Liberty TX 77575 Tel (713) 336-6454

ZEANAH, OLIN WEATHERFORD, b. Tuscaloosa, Ala., Oct. 26, 1922; B.S., U. Ala., 1948, J.D., 1949. Admitted to Ala. bar, 1949; partner firm Davis and Zeanah, 1949-55; dist. atty. 6th Jud. Circuit Ala., 1955-59; partner firm Zeanah, Donald, & Hust, Tuscaloosa, 1960—; dir. Cain Steel & Supply Co., Inc., First Ala. Bank of Tuscaloosa, N.A. Fellow Am. Coll. Trial Lawyers; mem. Am., Ala. (chmn. grievance and ethics com. 1968-72), Tuscaloosa (pres. 1957) bar assns., Fedn. Ins. Council, Ala. Def. Lawyers Assn. (v.p. 1976-77), Internat. Assn. Ins. Counsel, Assn. Ins. Attys., Am. Arbitration Assn. (panel of arbitrators), Ala. Law Inst. Office: 411-418 First National Bldg Tuscaloosa AL 35401 Tel (205) 349-1383

ZECHER, ALBERT MICHAEL, b. San Francisco, July 3, 1930; B.S., U. San Francisco, 1953; J.D., Hastings Coll. Law, 1956. Admitted to Calif. bar, 1956; dep. county counsel San Joaquin County (Calif.), 1957-60, Santa Clara County (Calif.), 1960-62; partner firm Zecher & Pestarino, San Jose, Calif., 1962-75; individual practice law, San Jose, 1975—. Mem. Am., Calif., Santa Clara County bar assns., Bus Trial Lawyers Assn., Phi Alpha Delta. Office: 12 S 1st St San Jose CA 95113 Tel (408) 293-8309

ZEDROSSER, JOSEPH JOHN, b. Milw., Jan. 24, 1938; A.B., Marquette U., 1959; LL.B., Harvard U., 1963. Admitted to N.Y. State bar, 1964, U.S. Supreme Ct. bar, 1975; asso. firm William G. Mulligan, N.Y.C., 1964-67; asso. firm Bauman and Marcheso, and predecessors, N.Y.C., 1967-71; dir. community devel. unit Bedford-Stuyvesant Community Legal Services Corp., N.Y.C., 1971-73; asso. atty. fed. defender services unit Legal Aid Soc., N.Y.C., 1973-74; asst. atty. gen. Environ. Protection Bur., N.Y. State Dept. Law, N.Y.C., 1974—. Mem. Assn. Bar City N.Y., Am., N.Y. bar assns., Am. Soc. Internat. Law, Citizens Union City N.Y., Alpha Sigma Nu. Home: 511 E 78th St New York City NY 10021 Office: 2 World Trade Center Room 4776 New York City NY 10047 Tel (212) 488-7567

ZEESE, GORDON ROBERT, b. N.Y.C., Feb. 18, 1947; A.B. in Bus. Adminstrn., Duke, 1969; J.D., U. Ga., 1972. Admitted to Ga. bar, 1972; staff atty. Ga. Legal Services Program, Albany, 1972-75, mng. atty., 1975-76; partner firm Zeese & Howell, Albany, 1976—. Mem. Am. Bar Assn., State Bar Ga., Albany Jaycees (sec. 1976-77). Office: 420 Pine Ave Albany GA 31701 Tel (912) 883-2218

ZEESMAN, BENJAMIN (BENNIE), b. Savannah, Ga., Mar. 29, 1910; LL.B., U. Ga., 1932. Admitted to Ga. bar, 1932; individual practice law, Abbeville, Ga., 1932-34, 37-38, Cordele, Ga., 1939—; partner firm Bass & Zeesman, Abbeville, 1934-37; atty. City of Abbeville, City of Cordele. Mem. State Bar Ga., Cordele, Cordele Jud. Circuit bar assns., Ga. Trial Lawyers Assn., Ga. Assn. Criminal Def. Lawyers. Home: 304 E 15th Ave Cordele GA 31015 Office: PO Box 676 Cordele GA 31015 Tel (912) 273-1247

ZEGER, DENNIS ANSON, b. Chambersburg, Pa., May 27, 1945; B.A., Duke, 1967; J.D., Dickinson Sch. Law, 1973. Admitted to Pa. bar, 1973, U.S. Dist. Ct. for Middle Pa. bar, 1975; asso. firm Lawrence C. Zeger, Greencastle, Pa., 1973; partner firm Zeger & Zeger, Mercerburg, Pa., 1974—. Mem. Pa., Franklin County bar assns. Office: 32 E Seminary St Mercerburg PA 17236 Tel (717) 328-2028

ZEICHNER, IRVING BERNARD, b. N.Y.C., Mar. 27, 1919; B.A., N.Y. U., 1939; J.D., Fordham U., 1941. Admitted to N.J. bar, 1941, U.S. Supreme Ct. bar, 1957, U.S. Ct. Mil. Appeals bar, 1973; individual practice law, Atlantic Highlands, N.J., 1942-69; chief legal research Adminstrv. Office of Cts., Trenton, N.J., 1969-70; acting clk. Supreme Ct. N.J., 1970-72; mem. faculty Delaware Law Sch., 1973; cons. Law Enforcement Reference Service, Trenton, 1973—; judge Atlantic Highlands Municipal Ct., 1952-69. Trustee Ahavath Israel Congregation, Trenton, 1970—; bd. dirs. Nat. Alliance for Safer Cities, N.Y.C., 1973—. Mem. Am., N.J. bar assns., Am. Arbitration Assn. (nat. panel 1973—). Lasker fellow, 1960; Esso grantee, 1957; Ford Found. grantee, 1961; Nat. Endowment for Humanities grantee, 1977; editor Law Enforcement Desk Reference, 1974—, Law and Order Mag., 1954—, Mayor and Manager Mag., 1957-69; contbr. articles to legal jours. Home: 1 Highgate Dr Trenton NJ 08618 Office: 37 W 38th St New York City NY 10018 Tel (212) 239-8080

ZEIDMAN, PHILIP FISHER, b. Birmingham, Ala., May 2, 1934; B.A. cum laude, Yale U., 1955; LL.B., Harvard U., 1958, postgrad. in bus. adminstrn., 1957-58. Admitted to Ala. bar, 1958, Fla. bar, 1960, D.C. bar, 1968, U.S. Supreme Ct. bar, 1962; trial atty. FTC, Washington, 1960-61; staff asst. White House Com. Small Bus., 1961-63; spl. asst. to adminstr. SBA, 1961-63, asst. gen. counsel, 1963-65, gen. counsel, 1965-68; spl. asst. to Vice Pres. U.S., 1968; govt. relations mgr. Nat. Alliance Businessmen, 1968; partner firm Brownstein, Zeidman, Schomar & Chase, Washington, 1968—; dir. Nat. Bank Washington; chmn. grants and benefits com. Adminstrv. Conf. U.S., 1968; mem. food industry adv. com. Fed. Energy Adminstrn. Mem. Am., Ala., Fla., Fed. bar assns., Bar Assn. D.C. Home: 2908 Albemarle St NW Washington DC 20008 Office: 1025 Connecticut Ave NW Washington DC 20036 Tel (202) 457-6500

ZEIDWIG, HOWARD MICHAEL, b. Elizabeth, N.J., Nov. 6, 1943; B.S. in Bus. Adminstrn., U. Fla., 1967; J.D., Stetson U., 1970. Admitted to Fla. bar, 1970; asst. county solicitor, Broward County, Fla., 1970-72; pub. defender City of Lauderhill (Fla.), 1974-76; pub. defender City of Davie (Fla.), 1974-76, legal advisor, 1975-76. Mem. Nat. Dist. Attys. Assn., Broward County, Fla. bar assns., Broward County Criminal Defense Atty.'s Assn. Office: 500 NW 3d Ave Fort Lauderdale FL 33301 Tel (305) 764-2500

ZEIF, RICHARD ALLEN, b. New Haven, July 7, 1929; student Washington Sq. Coll., 1950; LL.B., N.Y. U., 1952. Admitted to N.Y. State bar, 1952; U.S. Dist. Cts. for So. and Eastern Dists. bars, 1958; U.S. 2d Circuit Ct. Appeals bar, 1973; partner firm Nierenberg, Zeif & Weinstein, N.Y.C., 1952—; faculty New Sch. Social Research. Adviser Johnny Horizon Program, U.S. Dept. Interior, 1971—; mem. voluntary council N.Y. State Commn. on Human Rights, 1965-71; bd. dirs. Met. Hotel Industry Stblzn. Assn., 1970—; Democratic candidate N.Y. State senate, 1968, N.Y.C. Council, 1961. Mem. Am. Bar Assn. (chmn. African law com., com. on fgn. investment and devel.) Am. Acad. for Polit. and Social Sci., Negotiation Inst. (sec.). Recipient Academico Honoris Cause, Mexican Acad. Internat. Law, 1972; 1st Human Rights award, State of N.Y., 1971. Office: 230 Park Ave New York City NY 10017 Tel (212) 679-1455

ZEIFANG, DONALD PAUL, b. Niagara Falls, N.Y., Apr. 13, 1936; B.A., U. Notre Dame, 1960; J.D., Georgetown U., 1963. Admitted to D.C. bar, 1965; law clk. to U.S. Dist. Judge John J. Sirica, 1963-65; partner firm Dow, Lohnes & Albertson, 1965-73; sr. v.p. for govt. relations Nat. Assn. Broadcasters, Washington, 1973—. Mem. Am., Fed. Communications, D.C. bar assns., Georgetown U. Alumni Club. Home: 1200 N Nash St Arlington VA 22209 Office: 1771 N St NW Washington DC 20036 Tel (202) 293-2152

ZEIGLER, DANIEL FRANKLIN, b. Coaldale, Pa., Dec. 6, 1947; A.B., Pa. State U., 1969; J.D., Duquesne U., 1972. Admitted to Pa. bar, 1972; asso. Martin H. Phillip, Pa., 1972-74; individual practice law, Jim Thorpe, Pa., 1974-75, Lansford, Pa., 1975—; Carbon County Juvenile Ct. Master, 1976; dir. probation services, Carbon County, 1976-77. Bd. dirs. Panther Valley Sch. Dist., 1974-75. Mem. Am., Pa. (com. on youth edn. for citizenship) bar assns., Pa. Trial Lawyers Assn. Home: 16 Foster Ave Coaldale PA 18218 Office: 108 W Ridge St Lansford PA 18232 Tel (717) 669-9100

ZEIGLER, ELISABETH EBERHARD, b. Los Angeles, Apr. 13, 1917; A.B. magna cum laude, U. So. Calif., 1938, J.D., 1941. Admitted to Calif. bar, 1942, U.S. Supreme Ct. bar, 1947; asst. to legal aide U.S. Naval Air Sta., Seattle, 1942; enforcement atty. Office Price Adminstrn., Seattle, 1943; partner firm Eberhard and Zeigler, Los Angeles, 1943-49; judge Municipal Ct., Los Angeles, 1949-68, presiding judge, 1959; judge Superior Ct. Los Angeles County, 1968—, mem. exec. com., County, 1973-74; chmn. Municipal Ct. Judges Los Angeles County, 1960. Mem. Conf. Calif. Judges (chmn. com. on ethics 1962), Am. Judicature Soc., Los Angeles County Bar Assn., Legion Lex, Phi Beta Kappa (pres. So. Calif. alumni 1972-73), Phi Alpha Delta. Mem. editorial bd. U. So. Calif. Law Rev., 1939. Office: 111 N Hill St Los Angeles CA 90012 Tel (213) 974-5675

ZEIGLER, EUGENE NOEL, b. Florence, S.C., July 20, 1921; B.A., U. of South, 1942; LL.B., Harvard, 1949. Admitted to S.C. bar, 1949; partner firm McEachin, Townsend & Zeigler, Florence, 1950-62; individual practice law, Florence, 1962-71; partner firm Zeigler Dees & McEachin, Florence, 1976-77, Zeigler & McEachin, 1977—; spl. judge Ct. Common Pleas Richland County (S.C.), 1963-64; mem. S.C. Ho. of Reps., 1961-62, S.C. Senate, 1966-72; chmn. S.C. Human Affairs Commn., 1973-74; mem. S.C. Bd. Corrections, 1974—. Vestryman St. John's Episc. Ch., Florence; founder Pee Dee Area Big Brother Assn., pres., 1953-55; pres. Florence Mus., 1951-60; tchr. Sunday sch. S.C. Sch. Boys, Florence, 1950-76; active S.C. Tri-Centennial Commn., Bi-Centennial Commn.; chmn. S.C. Inter-Agy. Council Arts and Humanities, Columbia. Mem. Am., S.C. bar assns., S.C. Trial Lawyers Assn. Home: 823 Greenway Dr Florence SC 29501 Office: PO Drawer 150 Florence SC 29503 Tel (803) 662-3281

ZEITER, WILLIAM EMMET, b. Harrisburg, Pa., Dec. 1, 1934; B.A., Lehigh U., 1955, B.S.E.E., 1956; J.D., N.Y. U., 1959. Admitted to Pa. bar, 1960, D.C. bar, 1962, U.S. Supreme Ct. bar, 1963; asso. firm Morgan, Lewis & Bockius, Phila., 1959-66, mem. firm, 1967—; legal cons. Ct. Adminstr. of Pa., 1972—; exec. dir. Advisory Com. on Appellate Ct. Rules, 1973—. Mem. Pa. Joint Com. on Documents, 1968—; bd. dirs. Am. Nat. Metric Council, Washington, 1973—, vice chmn., 1975—. Fellow Am. Bar Found.; mem. Am. (chmn. sect. sci. and tech. 1977—), Pa., Phila. bar assns., IEEE. Home: 8917 Crefeld St Philadelphia PA 19118 Office: 2100 Fidelity Bldg 123 S Broad St Philadelphia PA 19109 Tel (215) 491-9367

ZELDEN, SAMUEL SCHILLER, b. Chgo., Sept. 9, 1942; B.S. Fgn. Service, Georgetown U., 1964; J.D., Drake U., 1970. Admitted to Iowa bar, 1970; law clk. to Sr. Justice M. L. Mason, Iowa Supreme Ct., 1970-71; asst. county atty. Polk County (Iowa), 1971-73; magistrate Polk County Dist. Ct., 1973-74; individual practice law, Des Moines, 1973—. Nat. coordinator Carter/Mondale Campaign, 1976. Mem. Iowa, Am., Polk County (Iowa) bar assns., Am. Judicature Soc. Home: 5011 Pleasant St Des Moines IA 50312 Office: 920 Savings & Loan Bldg Des Moines IA 50309 Tel (515) 288-7405

ZELL, GLENN, b. N.Y.C., Nov. 2, 1934; B.S., N.Y. U., 1954; LL.B., Emory U., 1965. Admitted to Ga. bar, 1965, U.S. Supreme Ct. bar, 1971; individual practice law Atlanta, 1965—. Mem. Am., Ga., Atlanta bar assns., Am. Judicature Soc., First Amendment Lawyers Assn., Ga. Assn. Criminal Def. Lawyers. Editor: What's the Decision, bi-monthly bull. on Ga. Appellate and Fed. ct. decisions. Home: 2088 Renault Ln NE Atlanta GA 30345 Office: 66 Luckie St NW Atlanta GA 30303 Tel (404) 524-6878

ZELL, STEPHEN HOWARD, b. Los Angeles, Aug. 27, 1946; B.S., U. Calif., Los Angeles, 1968; J.D., Loyola U., Los Angeles, 1972. Admitted to Calif. bar, 1972, U.S. Fed. Dist. Ct. bar, 1972; asso. firm Kinkle, Rodiger & Spriggs, Santa Ana, Calif., 1973—. Mem. Am., Calif., Orange County bar assns. Office: 837 N Ross St Santa Ana CA 92701 Tel (714) 835-9011

ZELLER, HOWARD A., b. Syracuse, N.Y., Feb. 26, 1912; B.A., Hamilton Coll., 1936; LL.B., Syracuse U., 1936. Admitted to N.Y. State bar, 1936; individual practice law, Oneida, N.Y., 1936-43; dist. atty. Madison County, N.Y., 1946-49; justice N.Y. State Supreme Ct., Oneida, 1950—. Mem. Am., N.Y. State bar assns., Am. Judicature Soc. Office: Supreme Ct Chambers Oneida NY 13421 Tel (315) 366-2301

ZELNICK, ALLAN, b. N.Y.C., Nov. 26, 1930; A.B., Rutgers U., 1952; LL.B., Harvard, 1955; LL.M., N.Y. U., 1960. Admitted to N.Y. bar, 1956, N.J. bar, 1974, U.S. Supreme Ct. bar, 1961; asst. to chief counsel U.S. Bur. Customs, N.Y.C., 1956-58; partner firm Burns, Lobato & Zelnick, N.Y.C., 1958-73; partner firm Zelnick & Bressler, N.Y.C., 1973—. Mem. Am., N.Y. State bar assns., N.Y. County Lawyers Assn., U.S. Trademark Assn. (dir. 1976—). Contbr. articles to legal publs.; editor The Trademark Reporter, 1974-76. Home: 93 N Wyoming Ave South Orange NJ 07079 Office: suite 1535 One World Trade Center New York City NY 10048 Tel (212) 466-1123

ZELT, WRAY GRAYSON, III, b. Washington, Pa., Jan. 5, 1932; B.A., Amherst Coll., 1953; LL.B., U. Pa., 1956. Admitted to Pa. bar, 1959; individual practice law, 1969-72; partner firm Zelt & Zelt, Washington, Pa., 1972—. Mem. Am. Trial Lawyers Assn. Office: 23 E Beau St Washington PA 15301 Tel (412) 228-3000

ZEMBER, GERALD STANLEY, b. Reading, Pa., May 8, 1925; B.S., Temple U., 1950, J.D., 1953. Admitted to Pa. bar, 1953; individual practice law, Reading 1953—; mem. Pa. Ho. of Reps., 1961-62; asst. atty. gen. Commonwealth of Pa., 1968; register of wills Berks County (Pa.), 1964-68. Bd. dirs. Hawk Mountain council Boy Scouts Am., 1968—; mem. exec. com. Berks County Republican Party, 1974—. Mem. Am., Pa., Berks County bar assns. Home: 524 Elm St Reading PA 19601 Office: 232 N 6th St Reading PA 19610 Tel (215) 375-8571

ZENTZ, CARL EDWIN, b. Gettysburg, Pa., Aug. 25, 1947; B.A., Columbia Union Coll., 1969; J.D., Cath. U. Am., 1973. Admitted to Md. bar, 1973, D.C. bar, 1974, Fla. bar, 1974; individual practice law, Riverdale, Md., 1973—. Mem. Am., D.C., Fla., Md. bar assns., Am. Judicature Soc. Office: 6801 Kenilworth Ave Suite 100 Riverdale MD 20840 Tel (301) 864-1300

ZEPP, FREDRIC JOHN, b. Dallas, June 18, 1939; B.A., U. Ill., 1965, J.D., 1965. Admitted to Calif. bar, 1969; law clk. to chief justice Calif. Supreme Ct., 1968-69; asso. firm Latham & Watkins, Los Angeles, 1968-76, partner, 1976—. Mem. Am., Calif., Los Angeles County bar assns., Assn. Bus. Trial Lawyers, Order of Coif. Editor-in-chief U. Ill. Law Forum, 1967-68. Home: 4201 Mesa Vista Dr La Canada-Flintridge CA 91011 Office: 555 S Flower St Los Angeles CA 90071 Tel (213) 485-1234

ZERR, RICHARD KEVIN, b. St. Charles, Mo., Apr. 10, 1949; A.B. in Polit. Sci., U. Mo., 1971; J.D., U. Ark., 1974. Admitted to Mo. bar, 1974; asst. Office of Pros. Atty. St. Charles County (Mo.), St. Charles, 1974; asso. firm Gordon D. Prinster, St. Charles, 1974; judge Magistrate Ct. St. Charles County, 1974—. Mem. Am., Mo. bar assns., Delta Theta Phi. Home: 3812 William St Saint Charles MO 63301 Office: Magistrate Court Dist 2 Court House Saint Charles MO 63301 Tel (314) 724-2414

ZEUTZIUS, GEORGE HENRY, b. Green Bay, Wis., Nov. 8, 1904; student Nat. U. Sch. Govt and Econs., 1925-26; J.D., George Washington U., 1928. Admitted to D.C. bar, 1928, Md. bar, 1941, Calif. bar, 1944; prof. law Nat. U. (now George Washington U.), 1932-40; spl. asst. to U.S. Atty. Gen., Washington, 1934-43; asso. firm Loeb & Loeb, Los Angeles, 1944; individual practice law, Los Angeles, 1945-73, Pasadena, Calif., 1973—. Mem. Am. (com. on taxation 1967—), Los Angeles County, Pasadena bar assns., State Bar Calif. (com. on taxation 1947-49), Lawyers Club of Los Angeles County (pres. 1953, bd. govs. 1950-54). Certified Specialist in taxation law Calif. Bd. Legal Specialization. Home: 2030 Woodlyn Rd Pasadena CA 91104 Office: 230 N Lake Ave Pasadena CA 91101 Tel (213) 681-6391

ZIEGLER, WILLIAM RUSSELL, b. N.Y.C., July 6, 1942; B.A., Amherst Coll., 1964; LL.B., U. Va., 1967; M.B.A., Columbia U., 1968. Admitted to N.Y. bar, 1968; asso. firm Whitman & Ransom, N.Y.C., 1968-75, partner, 1976—. Bd. dirs. Pound Ridge (N.Y.) Land Conservancy. Mem. Am. Bar Assn. Home: Pinebrook Rd Bedford NY 10506 Office: 522 Fifth Ave New York City NY 10036 Tel (212) 575-5800

ZIEMAN, THOMAS TROY, JR., b. Mobile, Ala., June 11, 1944; B.A. in Econs., U. Va., 1966, LL.B., 1969. Admitted to Ala. bar, 1970; served to capt. U.S. Marine Corps, 1970-74, criminal def. counsel, 1971-72, criminal prosecutor, 1972-73, presiding judge spl. cts. martial, 1973-74; asso. firm Johnstone, Adams, May, Howard & Hill, Mobile, Ala., 1974—. Mem. Am., Ala., Mobile, Fed. bar assns., Ala. Def. Lawyers Assn. Home: PO Box 55 Mobile AL 36601 Office: PO Box 1988 Mobile AL 36601 Tel (205) 473-7896

ZIEMBA, DANIEL EDWARD, b. Chgo., Apr. 5, 1943; A.B., U. Notre Dame, 1965; J.D., Northwestern U., 1968. Admitted to Ill. bar, 1968, U.S. Dist. Ct. No. Dist. Ill., 1974; atty. Chgo. Title and Trust Co., Chgo. and Waukegan, Ill., 1968-71; resident asso. Bradley, Eaton, Jackman and McGovern, Deerfield, Ill., 1971—. Mem. Ill. State, Lake County (mem. com. real property and titles) bar assns. Office: 747 Deerfield Rd Deerfield IL 60015 Tel (312) 945-7050

ZIERCHER, HERBERT WILLIAM, b. University City, Mo., Dec. 17, 1902; LL.B., Benton Coll. Law, St. Louis, 1926, LL.M., 1927; L.H.D. (hon.), Eden Theol. Sem., 1976. Admitted to Mo. bar, 1925; individual practice law, Clayton, 1928-50; sr. partner firm Ziercher Hocker Tzinberg Human & Michenfelder, Clayton, 1950—; first asst. pros. atty. St. Louis County, 1930-32. Hon. mem. bd. dirs. Bd. for Inner City Missions, United Ch. Christ, 1973—; pres. Evang. and Reformed Ch. Fedn. of Greater St. Louis, 1936-37; mem. Met. Ch. Fedn. St. Louis, 1961-66; pres., v.p., sec.-treas. University City Park Bd., various times. Mem. St. Louis County Bar Assn. (pres. 1947). Recipient citations Health and Welfare Commn., United Ch. Christ, 1961, 73. Home: 12 High Acres Dr Olivette MO 63132 Office: 130 S Bemiston Ave Clayton MO 63105 Tel (314) 727-5822

ZIFF, LLOYD RICHARD, b. N.Y.C., Mar. 9, 1942; B.A., U. Pa., 1968, J.D. magna cum laude, 1971. Admitted to Pa. bar, 1971, U.S. Supreme Ct. bar, 1975; mem. firm Pepper, Hamilton & Scheetz, Phila., 1971—, partner, 1977—; teaching fellow U. Pa. Law Sch., 1970-71; chmn. Phila. Bail Project, summer 1969. Mem. Kent State task force Pres.'s Commn. on Campus Unrest, summer 1970; adv. bd. Family Resources Center, St. Christopher's Hosp. for Children, Phila., 1976—; mem. Inter-disciplinary Com. on Child Abuse for S.E. Pa., 1973-75. Mem. Am. (antitrust and litigation sects.), Pa., Phila. (chmn. election procedures com.) bar assns., Order of Coif. Warwick Found. scholar, 1969-70; recipient David Werner Amram prize, 1971. Office: Pepper Hamilton & Scheetz 123 S Broad St Philadelphia PA 19109 Tel (215) 545-1234

ZILIN, SADYE JOHANNA (MRS. DAVID S. MACKAY), b. Amsterdam, N.Y., May 16; B.S. cum laude, State U. N.Y., Albany, 1942; LL.B., Union U., 1946, J.D., 1968. Admitted to N.Y. State bar, 1947; asso. firm Fitzsimmons & Wilsey, Albany, N.Y., 1947-49; individual practice law, Albany, 1949—. Mem. original Albany County Charter Commn., 1972-73. Mem. Albany County Bar Assn., State U. N.Y., Albany, Albany Law Sch. alumni assns. Home and office: 144 Cardinal Ave Albany NY 12209 Tel (518) 489-3328

ZILKO, MILDRED JOAN, b. N.Y.C., May 8, 1933; A.B., Syracuse U., 1953; LL.B., N.Y. U., 1957. Admitted to N.Y. bar, 1957; practiced in Roslyn Heights, N.Y., 1957-74; counsel Weight Watchers Internat., Inc., Manhasset, N.Y., 1974—. Bd. dirs. LWV of Roslyn Heights, 1959-72. Mem. Nassau-Suffolk Counties (N.Y.), Women's (pres. 1969-70), Nassau bar assns. Home: 117 Yale St Roslyn Heights NY 11577 Tel (516) 627-9200

ZIMBALIST, STUART HARRIS, b. St. Louis, July 14, 1943; A.B., Washington U., St. Louis, 1965, J.D., 1967, LL.M., 1968. Admitted to Mo. bar, 1967; research atty. Am. Bar Found., Chgo., 1969; partner firm Husch, Eppenberger, Donohue, Elson & Cornfeld, St. Louis, 1976—; adv. bd. Housing and Devel. Reporter, Bur. Nat. Affairs, Washington, 1974. Treas., B'nai B'rith Hillel Found., Washington U., 1975-76. Mem. Am., Met. St. Louis bar assns. Author: Handbook on Housing and Urban Development Law, 1969; also articles. Office: Husch Eppenberger Donohue Elson & Cornfeld The Boatmen's Tower 100 N Broadway Saint Louis MO 63102 Tel (314) 421-4800

ZIMMER, HERBERT JEROME, b. Birmingham, Ala., Dec. 2, 1945; B.A., Duke, 1967; J.D., Am. U., 1970. Admitted to N.C. bar, 1970, U.S. Supreme Ct bar, 1975; individual practice law, Wilmington, N.C., 1970—; U.S. magistrate Eastern dist. N.C., 1975-76. Mem. Am., N.C., New Hanover County bar assns., Am. Trial Lawyers Assn., Am. Judicature Soc. Home: 2539 Battery Pl Wilmington NC 28401 Office: 111 Princess St Wilmington NC 28401 Tel (919) 763-4669

ZIMMER, JOHN HERMAN, b. Sioux Falls, S.D., Dec. 30, 1922; student Augustana Coll., Sioux Falls, 1941-42; postgrad. Mont. State Coll., 1943; LL.B., U. S.D., 1948. Admitted to S.D. bar, 1948; sr. partner firm Zimmer, Richter and Duncan, Parker, S.D., 1948—; states atty., Turner County (S.D.), 1955-58, 52-66; minority counsel strategic and critical material investigation Armed Services Com., U.S. Senate, 1962-63; asst. prof. med. jurisprudence U. S.D., 1966-68; sec. S.D. Blue Shield, 1974—. Mem. S.D. Republican Adv. Com., 1959-60, asst. doorman Rep. Nat. Conv., 1960, alt. del., 1968; bd. dirs. Easter Seal Soc., S.D. chpt., 1974—. Mem. Am., Fed., Minnehaha County bar assns., State Bar S.D., Am., S.D. trial lawyers assns. Contbr. articles to legal jours. Home: Parker SD 57053 Office: Law Bldg Parker SD 57053 Tel (605) 297-4446

ZIMMERLY, JAMES GREGORY, b. Longview, Tex., Mar. 25, 1941; B.A., Gannon Coll., 1962; M.D., U. Md., 1966, M.P.H., Johns Hopkins, 1968; J.D., U. Md., 1969. Admitted to U.S. Ct. Appeals, 1970; D.C. bar, 1972; U.S. Ct. Mil. Appeals bar, 1973, U.S. Supreme Ct. bar, 1973; partner firm Acquisto, Asplen & Morstein, Ellicott City, Md., 1970—. Chief div. legal medicine Armed Forces Inst. Pathology,

1971—; prof. George Washington U., 1972—; adj. prof. law Georgetown U. Law Center, 1972—; asst. prof. U. Md. Sch. Medicine, 1973—; cons. in field. Mem. Am. (vice-chmn. com. on law and medicine, chmn. subcom. on med. malpractice), Md. (chmn. joint com. on interprofl. relations) bar assns., Am. Soc. on Law and Medicine (council), Am. Coll. Legal Medicine (sec., gov.), Md. State Med. Soc. (chmn.). Dep. editor Jour. Legal Medicine, 1975—; recipient 1st prize award Am. Med. Writers Assn., 1975; contbr. articles to profl. jours. Office: Armed Forces Inst Pathology Washington DC 20306 Tel (202) 576-3285

ZIMMERMAN, ALVIN LOUIS, b. Houston, June 28, 1943; B.S., U. Houston, 1964, J.D., 1967. Admitted to Tex. bar, 1967, U.S. Supreme Ct. bar, 1968; asst. atty. gen. Tex., Austin, 1967-68; gen. counsel, v.p. Sterling Electronics Corp., Houston, 1968—. Mem. Houston Bar Assn. (named outstanding chmn. 1974). Contbr. articles to profl. jours. Address: PO Box 1229 Houston TX 77001 Tel (713) 623-0163

ZIMMERMAN, CARL BROWNING, b. Waterloo, Iowa, June 23, 1930; B.A., State U. Iowa, 1953, J.D., 1956. Admitted to Iowa bar, 1956, U.S. Supreme Ct. bar, 1966; partner firm Zimmerman and Zimmerman, Waterloo, 1956-63, Zimmerman, Zimmerman and Pesch, Waterloo, 1963-72; individual practice, Waterloo, 1972—. Trustee YMCA, Black Hawk County, Iowa, 1972-76; troop committeeman Winnebago council Boy Scouts Am. Mem. Am., Iowa, Black Hawk County bar assns., Jud. Dist. Bar. Home: 225 Lovejoy Ave Waterloo IA 50701 Office: 608 Waterloo Bldg Waterloo IA 50701

ZIMMERMAN, EDWIN MORTON, b. N.Y.C., June 11, 1924; A.B., Columbia U., 1944, LL.B., 1949. Admitted to N.Y. State bar, 1949, U.S. Supreme Ct. bar, 1966; mem. Hoover Commn. Reorgn. Exec. Br., Washington, 1948; law clk. to judge U.S. Dist. Ct., N.Y.C., 1949-50; law clk. to justice U.S. Supreme Ct., Washington, 1950-51; practice law, N.Y.C., 1951-59; prof. Stanford (Calif.) Law Sch., 1959-69; dep. asst. atty. gen. U.S. Dept. Justice, Washington, 1965-68, asst. atty. gen. antitrust div., 1968-69; partner firm Covington & Burling, Washington, 1969—; mem. council Adminstrv. Conf. U.S., 1975—. Mem. Am. Law Inst., Assn. Bar City N.Y., Am. Bar Assn., Council Fgn. Relations. Contbr. articles to legal jours. Home: 1529 33d St Washington DC 20007 Office: 888 16th St Washington DC 20006 Tel (202) 452-6042

ZIMMERMAN, GEORGE JAMES, b. Chgo., Mar. 2, 1915; J.D., John Marshall Law Sch., 1940. Admitted to Ill. bar, 1940, U.S. Supreme Ct. bar, 1950; practiced law, Chgo., 1940-59; asst. chief atty. VA, Chgo., 1959-65; magistrate Circuit Ct. of Cook County (Ill.), 1966-70, asso. judge, 1970—. Mem. Decalogue Soc. Lawyers, NW Suburban, North Suburban bar assns., Ill. Judges Assn. Contbr. articles to legal jours. Home: 333 Dodge Ave Evanston IL 60202 Office: 7166 Milwaukee Ave Niles IL 60618 Tel (312) 647-7320

ZIMMERMAN, JAMES DAVID, b. Tulsa, Oct. 5, 1943; B.A., U. Colo., 1966; J.D., U. Denver, 1969. Admitted to Colo. bar, 1969; dep. dist. atty. 1st Jud. Dist. of Colo., 1970-75; judge Jefferson County (Colo.) Ct., 1975—. Office: Hall of Justice Golden CO 80401 Tel (303) 279-7156

ZIMMERMAN, JAMES LLOYD, b. Grand Island, Nebr., Nov. 15, 1946; B.S., U. Nebr., 1971, J.D., 1972. Admitted to Nebr. bar, 1972; asso. firm Griffiths & Zimmerman, Auburn, Nebr., 1972-74, Atkins Ferguson Hahn & Coll, Scottsbluff, Nebr., 1975—; staff atty. Panhandle Legal Services, Inc., Scottsbluff, 1974-75; subrogation claims supr. Union Ins. Co., Lincoln, Nebr., 1970-72. Bd. dirs. Homestead Halfwy House, Inc. Mem. Am., Nebr. trial lawyers assns., Nebr. (mem. com. on legal services, com. on workmen's compensation), Scottsbluff County, Western Nebr. bar assns., Nebr. Assn. Trial Attys. Home: POB 1094 Scottsbluff NE 69361 Office: 1714 2d Ave Scottsbluff NE 69361 Tel (308) 632-2151

ZIMMERMAN, MICHAEL DAVID, b. Chgo., Oct. 21, 1943; B.S., U. Utah, 1967, J.D., 1969. Law clk. Chief Justice Warren E. Burger, U.S. Supreme Ct., Washington, 1969-70; admitted to Calif. bar, 1971; asso. firm O'Melveny & Myers, Los Angeles, 1970-76; asso. prof. law U. Utah, 1976—. Mem. Am., Los Angeles County bar assns., Order of Coif, Phi Kappa Phi. Note editor Utah Law Rev., 1968-69. Office: Coll Law U Utah Salt Lake City UT 84112 Tel (801) 581-5944

ZIMMERMAN, ROBERT MAURICE, b. Chgo., Dec. 22, 1933; B.S. in Accounting, U. So. Calif., 1957; LL.B., 1962. Admitted to Ill. bar, 1963, U.S. Supreme Ct. bar, 1971; atty. office chief counsel IRS, San Francisco, 1963-68; counsel Zenith Radio Corp., Chgo., 1969-74, mgr. profit sharing, benefits planning, 1974—. Mem. Ill. Bar Assn., Chgo. Tax Club, Am. Compensation Assn., Profit Sharing Council Am. (dir., 1976—). Office: 1000 Milwaukee Ave Glenview IL 60025 Tel (312) 391-7711

ZIMMERMAN, WILLIAM ERNEST, b. Albany, N.Y., July 2, 1944; B.A., U. Tex., 1967; J.D., S. Tex. Coll. Law, 1971. Admitted to Tex. bar, 1971; dep. dir. corp. div. Office Sec. of State of Tex., Austin, 1971-73, dir. uniform comml. code div., 1974—. Pres. St. Vincent de Paul Soc., 1976—. Mem. Comml. Law League Am., State Bar Tex. (uniform comml. code com., corps. sect.). Home: 3912 Sierra Dr Austin TX 78731 Office: PO Box 12887 Austin TX 78711 Tel (512) 475-2575

ZIMNY, MAX, b. N.Y.C., Mar. 9, 1925; student Bklyn. Coll., 1942-47; LL.B. cum laude, Bklyn. Law Sch., 1950; postgrad. N.Y. U. Grad. Sch. Labor Law, 1950-52. Admitted to N.Y. bar, 1950, U.S. Supreme Ct. bar, 1962; practiced in N.Y.C., 1950-52; asst. gen. counsel Textile Workers Union Am., N.Y.C., 1952-58; asst. gen. counsel Internat. Ladies' Garment Workers Union, N.Y.C., 1958-63, asso. gen. counsel, 1963-72, gen. counsel, 1972—; mem. firm Vladeck, Elias, Vladeck & Lewis, N.Y.C., 1976—; dir. Resource Center for Consumers of Legal Services, 1975—, Pre-paid Legal Program of Bronx Community Coll., 1976—; lectr. in field. Chmn. N.Y.C. Consumer Adv. Council, 1975—, Profls. for Histadrut, 1976—. Mem. Am. (co-chmn. com. on arbitration and collective bargaining sect. labor law 1976—), N.Y. State (chmn. com. on labor relations law, sect. labor law 1976—) bar assns., Bar Assn. City N.Y. Home: 3688 Regent Ln Wantagh NY 11793 Office: 1501 Broadway New York City NY 10036 Tel (212) 354-8330

ZIMRING, FRANKLIN ESTER, b. Los Angeles, 1942; B.A., Wayne State U., 1963; J.D., U. Chgo., 1967. Admitted to Calif. bar, 1968; faculty U. Chgo., 1967—, prof. law, 1972—, dir. Center for Studies in Criminal Justice, 1975—; vis. prof. U. Pa., 1972, Yale U., 1973; cons. Dept. Justice, 1968—, N.Y.C., 1973-74, Nat. Commn. on Reform Fed. Criminal Laws, 1969-70. Mem. Ill. Acad. Criminology, Order of Coif. Author: (with G. Newton) Firearms and Violence in American Life, 1969; Perspectives on Deterrence, 1971; (with G. Hawkins) Deterrence: The Legal Threat in Crime Control, 1973. Office: U Chgo Law Sch 1111 E 60th St Chicago IL 60637 Tel (312) 753-2435

ZINBARG, IRVING PAYSON, b. N.Y.C., Apr. 11, 1909; LL.B., St. John's Coll., 1931. Admitted to N.Y. bar, 1933, U.S. So. Dist. bar, 1936, U.S. Eastern Dist. bar, 1938, U.S. Ct. Appeals 2d Circuit bar, 1939, U.S. Supreme Ct. bar, 1943, U.S. Tax Ct. bar, 1954; referee in certiorari N.Y. Supreme Ct., 1937-41; practiced in N.Y.C., 1937—. Mem. Am., N.Y. State bar assns., Am., N.Y. State trial lawyers assns., Assn. Bar City N.Y., Soc. Med. Jurisprudence. Home: N Lake Blvd Mahopac NY 10541 Office: 60 E 42d St New York City NY 10017 Tel (212) 682-4811 also 9 Fair St Carmel NY 10512 Tel (914) 225-7200

ZINBERG, ARTHUR DAVID, b. N.Y.C., June 27, 1921; B.S., City U. N.Y., 1941; M.A., Columbia U., 1949, J.D., 1954. Admitted to N.Y. State bar, 1955, U.S. Supreme Ct. bar, 1973; asso. firm Solunger & Gordon, N.Y.C., 1954-55, firm Reinheimer & Cohen, N.Y.C., 1955-58; individual practice law, N.Y.C., 1958—; lectr. in law Bklyn. Coll., 1954-76; ind. hearing officer N.Y.C. Bd. Edn., 1977—; instr. econs. Bklyn. Coll., 1946-54, N.Y. State Inst. Arts and Sci., 1947-51. Mem. Bar Assn. City N.Y., AAUP. Harlan Fiske Stone scholar, 1953-54. Office: 11 E 44th St New York City NY 10017 Tel (212) 986-7077

ZINK, CHARLES TALBOTT, b. Long Beach, Calif., Oct. 27, 1937; B.A., Princeton, 1959; LL.B., U. Va., 1965. Admitted to Va. bar, 1965, Ga. bar, 1965; partner firm Hansell, Post Brandon & Dorsey, Atlanta, 1969—; dir. Flowers Industries, Inc.; sec. Tri-South Mortgage Investors. Mem. Va., Ga., Atlanta bar assns., Lawyers Club Atlanta, Order of Coif. Mem. editorial bd. Va. Law Rev., 1963-65. Home: 5285 W Kingston Ct NE Atlanta GA 30342 Office: 3300 First National Bank Tower Atlanta GA 30303 Tel (404) 581-8000

ZINMAN, EDWIN JACOB, b. Pitts., Jan. 13, 1938; B.S., D.D.S., U. Pitts., 1962; certificate in periodontics N.Y. U., 1964; J.D., U. Calif., San Francisco, 1972. Lectr. dept. periodontics U. Calif. Sch. Dentistry, San Francisco, 1966-69; partner firm Gottesman & Zinman, San Francisco; admitted to Calif. bar, 1972; lectr. dental meetings. Mem. Am. Bar Assn., Calif. Trial Lawyers, Am. Acad. Periodontology. Home: 618 Sausalito Blvd Sausalito CA 94965 Office: 235 Montgomery St San Francisco CA 94104 Tel (415) 982-9211

ZINS, THOMAS ANDREW, b. Cin., July 18, 1936; B.A., U. Dayton, 1958; J.D., U. Cin., 1962. Admitted to Ohio bar, 1962; asso. firm Nieman, Aug, Elder & Jacobs, Cin., 1962-64; asso. firm Brumleve, DeCamp & Wood, Cin., 1964-68, partner, 1968-75, counsel, 1975—; sec., gen. mgr. The Hudepohl Brewing Co., Cin., 1973—; lectr. Coll. Law, U. Cin., 1968-72. Mem. Am., Ohio, Cin. bar assns., U.S. Brewers Assn. (dir.). Home: 6769 Wetheridge Dr Cincinnati OH 45230 Office: 505 Gest St Cincinnati OH 45203 Tel (513) 721-7273

ZION, JAMES WILLIAM, b. Palm Springs, Calif., Feb. 6, 1944; B.A. in History, Coll. St. Thomas, St. Paul, 1966; J.D., Cath. U. Am., 1969. Admitted to Conn. bar, 1969, D.C. bar, 1971, Mont. bar, 1974, Blackfeet Tribal Ct. bar, 1976; staff atty. Hartford (Conn.) Neighborhood Legal Services, 1969-73; clk. Mont. Supreme Ct., Helena, 1974; individual practice law, Great Falls, Mont., 1974-76, Helena, 1976—. Pres., Mont. Civil Liberties Union, 1975—; bd. dirs. Wesley Community Center, Great Falls, 1974-76. Mem. Am., Mont., Cascade County bar assns. Contbr. articles to legal jours. Home: 1208 Highland Ave Helena MT 59601 Office: PO Box 314 330 Fuller St Helena MT 59601 Tel (406) 442-3261

ZIPERSKI, JAMES RICHARD, b. Milw., May 27, 1932; B.S., Marquette U., 1953, J.D., 1957. Admitted to Wis. bar, 1957; sec., resident counsel Schwerman Trucking Co., Milw., 1957—; dir. City Fed. Savs. & Loan Assn., Milw. Mem. Am., Wis., Milw. bar assns., ICC Practitioners Assn., Motor Carrier Lawyers Assn., Alpha Kappa Psi, Phi Delta Phi. Home: 2110 Swan Blvd Wauwatosa WI 53226 Office: 611 S 28th St PO Box 1601 Milwaukee WI 53201 Tel (414) 671-1600

ZIPP, RONALD DUANE, b. New Braunfels, Tex., Dec. 7, 1946; B.B.A., Tex. A. and M. U., 1968; J.D., St. Mary's U., 1971. Admitted to Tex. bar, 1971, U.S. Ct. Appeals bar, 1973, U.S. Dist. Ct. bars, 1972, 74, U.S. Supreme Ct. bar, 1974; asso. firm Kelley, Looney & Alexander, Edinburg, Tex., 1971-73; partner firm Pena, McDonald, Prestia & Zipp, Edinburg, 1973—. Mem. Am., Hidalgo County (treas. 1975-76) bar assns., Tex. Criminal Def. Lawyers Assn. (dir.). Office: 600 S Closner Edinburg TX 78539

ZIPPERER, ALEXANDER LAWTON, b. Savannah, Ga., Sept. 9, 1941; B.A., Furman U., 1965; J.D., U. Ga., 1971. Mem. firm Ashman & Zipperer, Savannah, Ga., 1971—. Chmn., Chatham County Comprehensive Mental Health Adv. Council, 1976; v.p. Family Counseling Center Savannah, 1975—. Mem. Ga. Bar Assn., Ga. Assn. Criminal Def. Lawyers, Plaintiff Trial Lawyers Assn. Savannah, Am. Trial Lawyers Assn. Home: 2517 Easy Savannah GA 31406 Office: 124 W Liberty Savannah GA 31402 Tel (912) 232-0436

ZIRKLE, JAMES WALTON, b. Morristown, Tenn., Aug. 15, 1941; B.S., Carson-Newman Coll., 1963; J.D., U. Tenn., 1972; LL.M., Yale, 1973. Admitted to Tenn. bar, 1972; research asst. environ. program Oak Ridge Nat. Lab., 1971-72; fellow Yale Law Sch., 1972-73; asso. prof. law U. Miss., dir. Law Research Inst., 1973-77; asso. dean, lectr. law Yale U. Law Sch., 1977—. Bd. dirs. N. Miss. chpt. ACLU, 1974—. Mem. Am. Bar Assn., Am. Soc. Internat. Law. Editor in chief Tenn. Law Rev., 1971-73. Home: Drawer 20-A Yale Station New Haven CT 06520 Office: Yale U Law Sch New Haven CT Tel (203) 436-8890

ZISSER, BARRY LEE, b. Bklyn., Oct. 13, 1934; B.S. in Accounting, Bklyn. Coll., 1956; LL.B., U. Fla., 1962, J.D., 1963. Admitted to Fla. bar, 1963, U.S. Supreme Ct. bar, 1975; asso. firm Goldman, Presser & Lewis, Jacksonville, Fla., 1963-65; asst. pub. defender 4th Jud. Circuit Fla., Jacksonville, 1965-70, chief asst. state atty., 1970-72; sr. partner firm Zisser & Robison, Jacksonville, 1972—. Mem. Jacksonville Civil Service Bd., 1971-73. Mem. Fla., Jacksonville bar assns., Phi Alpha Delta. Home: 2306 Segovia Ave Jacksonville FL 32217 Office: 303 Liberty St Jacksonville FL 32202 Tel (904) 354-8455

ZISSER, ELLIOT, b. Bklyn., July 14, 1947; B.A. in Polit. Sci., Queens Coll. City U. N.Y., 1968; J.D., George Washington U., 1971. Admitted to Fla. bar, 1971; asso. firm Kennelly & Zisser, Jacksonville, Fla., 1971-72; partner firm Zisser & Robison, Jacksonville, 1972—; lectr. Fla. Bar Continuing Legal Edn. Mem. Air Pollution Control Bd. Jacksonville, 1972-73, mem. environ. protection bd., chmn. air com., 1973—. Mem. Fla. Bar, Jacksonville Bar Assn. (chmn. family law sect. 1974-76), Am. Bar Assn., Acad. Fla. Trial Lawyers, Assn. Trial Lawyers Am. Office: 303 Liberty St Jacksonville FL 32202 Tel (904) 354-8455

ZISSU, FREDERICK, b. N.Y.C., Aug. 30, 1913; B.S., N.Y. U., 1934, J.D., 1937, LL.M., 1942. Admitted to N.Y. bar, 1937; sr. partner firm Zissu Lore Halper & Barron, N.Y.C., 1966—; chmn. bd. Gen. Microwave Corp., Farmingdale, N.Y., 1960—, Vornado, Inc., Garfield, N.J., 1964—. Trustee Fairleigh Dickinson U. Mem. N.Y. State, Am. bar assns. Office: 450 Park Ave New York City NY 10022 Tel (212) 371-3900

ZITTRAIN, LESTER EUGENE, b. Norfolk, Va., Mar. 27, 1931; B.A., Washington & Lee, 1952; J.D., U. Va., 1955. Admitted to Va. bar, 1955, Pa. bar, 1959, U.S. Supreme Ct., 1970; asso. firm Crone & Cohen, Pitts., 1958-62, partner, 1963-71; partner firm Crone & Zittrain, Pitts., 1972—. Mem. Am., Allegheny County bar assns., Pa., Am. trial lawyers assns., Acad. Trial Lawyers Allegheny County. Home: 136 Thornberry Dr Pittsburgh PA 15235 Office: 1518 Grant Bldg Pittsburgh PA 15219 Tel (412) 281-5588

ZITZELSBERGER, GILBERT HOWARD, b. Buffalo, Dec. 14, 1929; B.A., U. Buffalo, 1952; M.Ed., Wayne State U., 1954; J.D., Detroit Coll. Law, 1965. Admitted to Mich. bar, 1965, Fla. bar, 1971; individual practice law, Riverview, Mich., 1965—; justice of the peace City of Riverview, 1959-63; judge Riverview Municipal Ct., 1963—. Parliamentarian, New Orleans conv. Lutheran Ch.—Mo. Synod, 1973; bd. dirs. Downriver YMCA, Wyandotte, Mich., Mich. Luth. Children's Friend Soc., Bay City; bd. dirs. Mich. dist. Luth. Ch.-Mo. Synod, 1968-76. Mem. Mich. Assn. Municipal Judges (pres. 1975-76), Downriver Bar Assn. Office: 17008 Fort St Riverview MI 48192 Tel (313) 282-8131

ZIVE, GREGG WILLIAM, b. Chgo., Aug. 9, 1945; B.A. in Journalism, Univ. Nev., 1967; J.D. magna cum laude, U. Notre Dame, 1973. Admitted to Calif. bar, 1973, Nev. bar, 1976; asso. firm Gray, Cary, Ames & Frye, San Diego, 1973-75, firm Breen, Young, Whitehead & Hoy, Reno, 1975-76, firm Hale, Lane, Peek, Dennison & Howard, Reno, 1976—; lectr. bus. law U. Nev., 1977—. Mem. Common Cause, So. Poverty Law Center. Mem. Am., Calif., Nev., San Diego County, Washoe County bar assns., Soc. Prof. Journalists. Contbr. articles in field to profl. jours. Home: 1410 Samuel Way Reno NV 89509 Office: POB 3237 Reno NV 89505 Tel (702) 786-7900

ZO BELL, KARL, b. La Jolla, Calif., Jan. 9, 1932; student Utah State U., 1949-51; A.B., Columbia, 1953, postgrad. Law Sch., 1952-54; J.D., Stanford, 1958. Admitted to Calif. bar, 1959; asso. firm Gray, Cary, Ames & Frye, San Diego, 1959-60, La Jolla, Calif., 1960-64, partner, 1964—; mng. partner, La Jolla, 1964-74; mem. bd. overseers Stanford Law Sch., 1975—, U. Calif., San Diego, 1974-76. Trustee La Jolla Town Council, 1964—, chmn. bd., 1967-69, pres., 1975—; trustee La Jollans, Inc., 1964—, pres., 1965-68, 71-76; trustee La Jolla Mus. Art, 1964-74, pres., 1968-69, 69-71; mem. City of San Diego Charter Commn., 1969, 74. Mem. Am. Coll. Probate Counsel, State Bar Calif., Am., San Diego County bar assns. Home: 1840 Castellana Rd La Jolla CA 92037 Office: 1200 Prospect St suite 575 La Jolla CA 92037 Tel (714) 454-9101

ZOBRIST, DUANE HERMAN, b. Salt Lake City, Sept. 11, 1940; A.B., U. Utah, 1965; J.D., U. So. Calif., 1968. Admitted to Calif. bar, 1969; asso. firm Hill, Farrer & Burrill, 1968-74; sr. partner, founder firm Zobrist, Garner & Garrett, Los Angeles, 1974—. Trustee, sec. Brazil Calif. Trade Assn., 1974—. Mem. Am., Calif., Los Angeles County bar assns., Fgn. Law Assn. So. Calif., U. So. Calif. Law Alumni Assn. (v.p. 1976-77). Office: Suite 1228 523 W 6th St Los Angeles CA 90014 Tel (213) 624-8661

ZOELLER, DONALD JOSEPH, b. Queens Village, N.Y., Mar. 18, 1930; A.B., Fordham Coll., 1951, LL.B., 1958. Admitted to N.Y. bar, 1959, U.S. Supreme Ct. bar, 1966, D.C. bar, 1967; law clk. to Judge Irving R. Kaufman of U.S. Dist. Ct. So. Dist. N.Y., 1958-59; partner firm Mudge Rose Guthrie & Alexander, N.Y.C., 1959—; lectr. at seminars. Mem. Inst. Jud. Adminstrn., Am. Judicature Soc. Office: 20 Broad St New York City NY 10005 Tel (212) 422-6767

ZOHN, MARTIN STEVEN, b. Denver, Oct. 22, 1947; B.A., Ind. U., 1969; J.D., Harvard, 1972. Admitted to Calif. bar, 1972, Ind. bar, 1973; mem. firm Cadick, Burns, Duck & Neighbours, Indpls., 1972—. Treas. Indpls. Settlements, Inc., 1974-77, bd. dirs., 1973—; pres. Concord Center Assn. Inc., 1975-77, bd. dirs., 1973—. Mem. Calif., Indpls., Ind. State, Am. bar assns., Phi Beta Kappa. Home: 5424 Broadway Indianapolis IN 46220 Office: 800 Union Fed Bldg Indianapolis IN 46204 Tel (317) 639-1571

ZOLOT, NORMAN, b. New Haven, Aug. 13, 1920; B.S., Yale, 1941, LL.B., 1947. Admitted to Conn. bar, 1947, U.S. Supreme Ct. bar, 1948; practiced in Hamden, Conn., 1957—; counsel Conn. State Labor Council, AFL-CIO, 1957—; mem. Conn. State Employment Security Adv. Commn., 1961—, Commn. to Study Consumer Credit, 1969-72, Commn. to Study Workmen's CoCompensation Laws of Conn., 1976—. Home: 30 Mumford Rd New Haven CT 06515 Office: 9 Washington Ave Hamden CT 06518 Tel (203) 288-3591 also 900 Chapel St New Haven CT 06511 Tel (203) 562-6329

ZOLTANSKI, EDWARD FRANCIS, b. Trenton, N.J., May 14, 1926; B.S. in Elec. Engring., Rensselaer Poly. Inst., 1948; LL.B., U. Toledo, 1958. Admitted to Ohio bar, 1958, U.S. Supreme Ct. bar, 1968; now practicing in Toledo. Mem. Toledo Bar Assn., Nat. Conf. Referees in Bankruptcy, U. Toledo Law Sch. Alumni Assn. (exec. com.). Office: 2463 Nebraska St Toledo OH 43607 Tel (419) 531-5971

ZORE, GERALD STEPHEN, b. Indpls., Oct. 14, 1941; A.B., Marian Coll., 1963; J.D., Ind. U., 1968. Admitted to Ind. bar, 1968; appeals referee State of Ind., Indpls., 1968; dep. atty. gen. State of Ind., Indpls., 1968; atty., div. discriminatory practices FTC, Washington, 1969, advisor to commr., 1969, atty. div. spl. projects, 1969-70, bur. consumer protection div., 1970-71; asso. firm Clark and Clark, Indpls., 1971-74; judge Marion County Superior Ct., Indpls., 1975—. Mem. Indpls. (v.p.), Ind. State, Am. bar assns., Ind. Judges Assn., Am. Judicature Soc. Office: W-541 City County Bldg Indianapolis IN 46204 Tel (317) 633-3075

ZOSS, THOMAS WARNER, b. South Bend, Ind., July 27, 1945; student Georgetown U., 1963-65; B.S., Ind. U., 1968, J.D., 1972. Admitted to Ind. bar, 1972; asso. firm Jones, Obenchain, Johnson, Ford, Pankow & Lewis, South Bend, 1972-73; individual practice law, South Bend, and Culver, 1973—; chief exec. Royal Rubber Co., South Bend, Rubber Shop, Inc., South Bend. Exec. dir. Bloomington Area (Ind.) Arts Council; bd. dirs. R.E.A.L. Services, Inc., South Bend.

Mem. Am., Ind., St. Joseph County bar assns. Pub. newspaper The Culver Citizen; columnist two nat. magician mags.; author, pub. several books, manuscripts. Home and Office: Box 1264 South Bend IN 46624 Tel (219) 233-2233

ZOTOS, THOMAS ANDREW, b. St. Louis, Dec. 20, 1941; A.B., Westminster Coll., 1963; J.D., Washington U., 1972; postgrad. Nat. Council Juvenile Justice, U. Nev., 1974. Admitted to Mo. bar, 1972; asst. legal advisor St. Louis County Juvenile Ct., St. Louis, 1971-77; asso. firm Spalding & McAllister, Ellisville, 1977—; instr. juvenile law and procedure, Maryville Coll., St. Louis, 1974; N.E. Mo. State U., 1976. Mem. Am., Mo. (instr. for Bridge the Gap, juvenile justice, 1973-76), St. Louis County Bar Assns., Nat. Council Juvenile Ct. Judges, Mo. Juvenile Officers Assn., Phi Delta Phi. Home: 7106 N Villanova St Saint Louis MO 63123 Office: 53 Clarkson Rd Ellisville MO 63011 Tel (314) 227-7120

ZOX, BENJAMIN LOUIS, b. Des Moines, May 18, 1937; A.B., Williams Coll., 1959; LL.B., Ohio State U., 1962. Admitted to Ohio bar, 1962; partner firm Schottenstein, Garel, Swedlow & Zox, Columbus, Ohio; mem. panel of arbitrators Am. Arbitration Assn., 1969—. Chmn. lawyers div. United Way of Franklin County (Ohio), 1974; chmn. Jewish Nat. Fund, 1977; trustee, treas. Columbus Jewish Center, 1974--; trustee Exec. Com. Community Relations, Columbus Jewish Fedn., 1974—. Mem. Columbus (chmn. com. bus. law 1974-76), Ohio (council of dels. 1976—), Am. bar assns. Recipient Therese Stern Kahn Meml. Young Leadership award Columbus Jewish Fedn., 1973. Home: 44 S Parkview St Columbus OH 43209 Office: 250 E Broad St Columbus OH 43215 Tel (614) 221-3211

ZUBRES, MERTON LEONARD, b. Albany, N.Y., Aug. 17, 1913; student Union U., 1936; LL.B., Albany Law Sch., 1937. Admitted to N.Y. bar, 1938, U.S. Supreme Ct. bar, 1953; partner firm Zubres, D'Agostino & Holblock, Albany, 1946—; chmn. Fed. Rent Adv. Bd., Albany-Troy Def. Rental Area, 1947-50. Mem. Am., N.Y. State, Albany County bar assns., Am., N.Y. State trial lawyers assn., Res. Officers Assn. (recipient 30 yr. award 1973). Home: 238 Woodlawn Ave Albany NY 12208 Office: 90 State St Albany NY 12207 Tel (518) 463-2251

ZUCCA, GEORGE ROBERT, b. Jersey City, June 7, 1943; B.S., Wagner Coll., 1966; J.D., N.Y. Law Sch., 1969. Admitted to N.J. bar, 1969, U.S. Supreme Ct. bar, 1974; mem. firm Calhoun & Reidy, Newark, 1971-72, Stevens & Mataiss, Newark, 1972-74, DeSevo, Cerutti & Lombardi, Jersey City, 1974—; claims atty. U.S.F. & G., N.Y.C., 1969-70. Mem. Am., N.J. State bar assns., Am. Assn. Trial Lawyers. Home: 4551 Brown St Union City NJ 07087 Tel (201) 653-3066

ZUCCOTTI, JOHN EUGENE, b. N.Y.C., June 23, 1937; A.B. in History, Princeton U., 1959; LL.B., Yale U., 1963. Admitted to N.Y. State bar, 1963, D.C. bar, 1970; spl. asst. to undersec. HUD, Washington, 1967-69; sec., counsel Nat. Corp. for Housing Partnerships, Washington, 1969-70; spl. counsel to housing subcom. U.S. Ho. of Reps. Banking and Currency Com., 1970-73; partner firm Tufo, Johnston and Zuccotti, N.Y.C., 1970-73; chmn. N.Y.C. Planning Commn., 1973-75; 1st dep. mayor City of N.Y., 1975-77; sr. partner firm Tufo, Johnston, Zuccotti and Allegaert, N.Y.C., 1977—. Home: 36 2d Pl Brooklyn NY 11231 Office: 645 Madison Ave New York City NY Tel (212) 752-8668

ZUCKERBERG, HARRY JOSEPH, b. Flushing, N.Y., June 18, 1925; B.A., Hofstra Coll., 1949; LL.B., Bklyn. Law Sch., 1954, J.D., 1967. Admitted to N.Y. bar, 1955; individual practice law, Flushing, 1955—. Mem. N.Y. State, Queens County bar assns., Comml. Law League, Brandeis Assos., Small Claims Arbitration Assos. Home: 23 Sagamore Way S Jericho NY 11753 Office: 190-04 Union Turnpike Flushing NY 11366

ZUCKERMAN, VICTOR, b. N.Y.C., Mar. 25, 1929; B.S., N.Y. U., 1950; LL.B., Bklyn. Law Sch., 1953. Admitted to N.Y. bar, 1954, U.S. Supreme Ct. bar, 1970; individual practice law, N.Y.C., 1955-63; atty. N.Y.C. Rent Commn., 1963-64; atty. N.Y. State Dept. Social Services, 1964-67; 1st asst. counsel N.Y. State Dept. Correctional Services, 1967—. Mem. N.Y. Bar Assn., N.Y. County Lawyers Assn., Am. Correctional Assn., Nat. Council Crime and Delinquency. Office: Dept Correctional Services Bldg 2 Campus Albany NY 12226

ZUCKERT, EUGENE MARTIN, b. N.Y.C., Nov. 9, 1911; B.A., Yale U., 1933, LL.B., 1937; certificate Law Sch., Yale U. and Bus.

Sch., Harvard U., 1937; LL.D., George Washington U., 1963; D.Eng. (hon.), Clarkson Coll., 1964. Admitted to Conn. bar, 1937, N.Y. State bar, 1940, D.C. bar, 1954; atty. SEC, Washington, 1937-40; instr. then asst. prof., asst. dean Grad. Sch. Bus., Harvard U., 1940-44; spl. asst. to adminstr. Surplus Property, to asst. sec. war for air, Washington, 1945-47; asst. sec. air force, 1947-52, sec. air force, 1961-65; mem. AEC, Washington, 1952-54; individual practice law, Washington, 1954-61; partner firm Zuckert, Scoutt & Rasenberger, Washington, 1968—; dir. Martin Marietta Corp., Martin Marietta Aluminum, Washington Gas Light Co., Greater Washington Investors, Inc. Chmn. bd. People-to-People Health Found. (Project HOPE). Mem. Nat. Acad. Pub. Adminstrn. Contbr. articles to profl. jours. Home: 141 Hesketh St Chevy Chase MD 20015 Office: 888 17th St NW Washington DC 20006 Tel (202) 298-8660

ZUGER, WILLIAM PETER, b. Bismarck, N.D., Sept. 16, 1946; B.A., U. Minn., 1969, J.D., 1972. Admitted to N.D. bar, 1972, U.S. Ct. Appeals 8th Circuit bar, 1973; partner firm Zuger & Bucklin, Bismarck, 1972—; guest lectr. U. N.D. Sch. Law, 1976. Mem. State Bar Assn. N.D. (chmn. law office mgmt. and procedures com. 1974-77, chmn. young lawyers sect. 1975-76, sec.-treas. 1975-76), Am. (nat. affiliate rep. young lawyers sect. 1975-76), Burleigh County, 4th Dist. (v.p. 1976—) bar assns., Assn. Trial Lawyers Am. Contbr. articles to legal jours. Home: 604 West Blvd Bismarck ND 58501 Office: PO Box 1695 Bismarck ND 58501

ZULLO, FRANK NICHOLAS, b. Norwalk, Conn., June 3, 1932; B.A., Fordham Coll., 1954, LL.D., 1957. Admitted to Conn. bar, 1957; partner firm Tierney, Zullo, Flaherty & Hauser, Norwalk, 1957—; mayor City of Norwalk, 1965-71; lectr. Norwalk Community Coll., 1975—. Mem. Tri-State Transp. Commn., 1970-71; trustee, vice chmn. Norwalk Hosp., Norwalk YMCA; water safety chmn. Norwalk-Wilton Red Cross. Mem. Conn., Norwalk-Wilton bar assns., Conn. (pres. 1968-69), U.S. (trustee 1969-71) confs. mayors. Home: 24 Sawmill Rd Norwalk CT 06851 Office: 134 East Ave Norwalk CT 06852 Tel (203) 853-7000

ZUMAS, NICHOLAS HARRY, b. Helper, Utah, Dec. 23, 1930; B.A., U. Utah, 1951; J.D., Georgetown U., 1956. Admitted to Va. bar, 1956, Oreg. bar, 1956, D.C. bar, 1957; law clk. to chief justice Oreg. Supreme Ct., 1956-57; asso. firm Koerner, Young, McColloch & Dezendorf, Portland, Oreg., 1957-61; counsel House Edn. and Labor Sub-com. on Higher Edn., Washington, 1961-62; asst. to undersec. HEW, Washington, 1962-63; congressional liaison officer Dept. State, Washington, 1963-65; individual practice law, Washington, 1965—; panelist Fed. Mediation and Conciliation Service. Mem. Nat. Acad. Arbitrators, Am. Arbitration Assn. Home: 3131 P St NW Washington DC 20007 Office: 1140 Connecticut Ave NW Washington DC 20036 Tel (202) 223-4455

ZUMMER, ANTHONY SIMON, b. Kankakee, Ill., Apr. 1, 1929; B.M.E., Purdue U., 1950; J.D., George Washington U., 1956; M.P.L., John Marshall Sch., 1959. Admitted to Ill. bar, 1956, D.C. bar, 1956, U.S. Supreme Ct. bar, 1960; asso. firm Mann, Brown & Mc Williams, Chgo., 1956-58; partner firm Stone, Nierman, Burmeister & Zummer, Chgo., 1960-64, firm Stone, Zummer & Livingston, Chgo., 1964-73; individual practice law, Chgo., 1973—. Mem. Am., Ill. State (vice chmn. patent, trademark and copyright sect.), Chgo. bar assns., Am., Chgo. patent law assns. Home: 164 Oxford Rd Kenilworth IL 60043 Office: 134 S LaSalle St Chicago IL 60603 Tel (312) 236-7017

ZUMSTEIN, BRUCE LANE, b. Chgo., Mar. 22, 1946; B.S., U. Ill., 1968; J.D., Northwestern U., 1972. Admitted to Ill. bar, 1972; atty. dept. local govt. State Ill., Chgo., 1972; asso. firm Codo and Bonds, Joliet, Ill., 1973—; instr. real estate Joliet Jr. Coll., 1975—. Active planning commn. Village New Lenox (Ill.), 1975-76; bd. dirs. United Cerebral Palsey Center, Joliet, 1975-76. Mem. Ill., Will County bar assns. Home: 18424 Cowing St Homewood IL 60430 Office: 5 E Van Buren St Joliet IL 60431 Tel (815) 726-7331

ZUNICH, ROBERT ALAN, b. Rochester, Pa., Aug. 24, 1947; A.B. in Govt., Franklin & Marshall Coll., 1969; J.D., Duquesne U., 1973. Admitted to Pa. bar, 1973; asst. dist. atty. Allegheny County (Pa.), 1973—. Mem. Allegheny County Bar Assn., Criminal Trial Lawyers Assn. Office: 401 Courthouse Office of Dist Atty Pittsburgh PA 15219 Tel (412) 355-4395

ZUPA, VICTOR JOSEPH, b. N.Y.C., Mar. 7, 1942; B.A., Fordham U., 1963, M.A., 1967, J.D., 1971. Admitted to N.Y. State bar, 1972; asso. firm Kelley, Drye & Warren, N.Y.C., 1971-74; mem. law dept.

Union Carbide Corp., N.Y.C., 1974-75; asst. U.S. atty. for So. Dist. N.Y., N.Y.C., 1975—. Mem. Am., N.Y. State bar assns., Assn. Bar City N.Y. Contbr. articles to profl. jours. Home: 5 Archway Pl Forest Hill Gardens NY 11375 Office: One St Andrew's Plaza New York City NY 11375 Tel (212) 268-4419

ZUPANCIC, DAVID ROBERT, b. Joliet, Ill., May 26, 1945; B.S., Lewis U., Lockport, Ill., 1967; J.D., Loyola U., Chgo., 1970. Admitted to Ill. bar, 1970; partner firm Luzbetak & Zupancic, Lockport, 1970-74, Luzbetak, Zupancic & Caneva, Lockport, 1974—; atty. Caney-Monge Sch., Crest Hill, Ill., 1970—. Mem. Am., Ill., Will County bar assns., Lewis U. Alumni Assn. (pres. 1976-77). Home: 1614 Wilcox St Crest Hill IL 60435 Office: 1000 S Hamilton St Lockport IL 60441 Tel (815) 838-0912

ZURAV, DAVID BERNARD, b. N.Y.C., Apr. 21, 1926; B.S., U. Pa., 1950; J.D., Rutgers U., 1953. Admitted to N.J. bar, 1953, U.S. Supreme Ct. bar, 1957; practiced in Union, N.J., 1953-70; partner Zurav & Myers, 1970-71; individual practice law, 1971—; atty. Springfield Twp. Planning bd. 1961—, Union Twp. Planning bd. 1975—; spl. counsel N.J. Dept. Transp. 1970, City of Bayonne, N.J., 1977. Mem. Am., N.J. State, Union County, Essex County bar assns., N.J. Inst. Municipal Attys. Home: 1 Archbridge Ln Springfield NJ 07081 Office: 1460 Morris Ave Union NJ 07083 Tel (201) 686-4354

ZURIER, MELVIN LEONARD, b. Providence, R.I., Apr. 30, 1929; A.B., Harvard U., 1950, LL.B., 1953. Admitted to Mass. bar, 1953, R.I. bar, 1957, U.S. Supreme Ct. bar, 1958; exec. counsel to Gov. R.I., 1961-62; partner firm Temkin, Merolla & Zurier, Providence, 1962—. Mem. R.I. Commn. Uniform State Laws, 1958-63; sec. R.I. Judicial Council, 1972—; spl. counsel R.I. Pub. Utilities Commn. Mem. R.I., Am. bar assns. Home: 59 Freeman Pkwy Providence RI 02906 Office: 40 Westminster St Providence RI 02903 Tel (401) 751-2400

ZUSMANN, SAMUEL JOSHUA, JR., b. Phila., Mar. 19, 1931; B.A., Emory U., 1950; J.D., U. Ga., 1954. Admitted to Ga. bar, 1953; partner firm Zusmann, Sikes, Pritchard & Cohen, Atlanta, 1954—. Mem. Am., Atlanta (dir. bankruptcy sect.), bar assns., Lawyers Club Atlanta, Comml. Law League Am., Southeastern Bankruptcy Law Inst. (chmn. 1977-78), State Bar Ga. (dir. bankruptcy sect.), Nat. Bankruptcy Conf. (asso.). Office: 1795 Peachtree Rd NE Atlanta GA 30309 Tel (404) 897-7200

ZWANZIG, JOHN DAVID, b. Ottawa, Ill., Dec. 15, 1935; LL.B., John Marshall Sch. of Law, 1959, J.D., 1970. Admitted to Ill. bar, 1959; mem. firm Zwanzig, Lanuti & Zwanzig, Ottawa, 1959-72; asst. state's atty. criminal trial div. LaSalle County, Ill., Ottawa, 1965-72; asso. judge 13th Jud. Circuit Ct. of Ill., Ottawa, 1972—; judge family div. Circuit Ct. of LaSalle County, Ottawa, 1972—; chmn. com. on juvenile on law Ill. Jud. Conf.; instr. Ill. Valley Community Coll.; sponsor, creator trial demonstration for sch. children; chmn. Juvenile System Seminar, 1975, 76—; lectr. in field. Chmn. activities Law Day, 1977—. Mem. Nat., Ill. (v.p.) councils of juvenile ct. judges, Ill. Judges Assn. (dir.), LaSalle County Bar Assn., Ill. Valley Crime Prevention Commn. Contbg. author: Ill. Juvenile Ct. Judges manual. Home: 502 W Van Buren St Ottawa IL 61350 Office: LaSalle County Ct House Ottawa IL 61350 Tel (815) 434-4457

ZWIBELMAN, IRVIN ROBERT, b. St. Louis, Sept. 20, 1933; LL.B., Washington U., St. Louis, 1958. Admitted to Mo. bar, 1958; asst. county counselor St. Louis County (Mo.), Clayton, 1959-62; asso. firm O'Connor, Dolgin & Godfrey, Clayton, 1963-65, Rabushka, Marglous & Zwibelman, Clayton, 1965-70; partner firm Poger & Zwibelman, Clayton, 1970-77, Anderson Fredrick Preuss & Zwibelman, Clayton, 1977—. Mem. Mo. Ho. of Reps., 1963-64. Mem. Mo., Met. St. Louis bar assns., Legal Reference Assn. Home: 14100 Parliament Dr Chesterfield MO 63017 Office: 222 S Meramec St Clayton MO 63105 Tel (314) 721-4404

ZWIEBACH, BURTON, b. N.Y.C., Sept. 17, 1933; B.A., City Coll. N.Y., 1954; LL.B., Columbia, 1957, Ph.D., 1964. Admitted to N.Y. bar, 1958; asso. firm Stillman & Stillman, N.Y.C., 1958; research asst., adv. com. on practice and procedure Columbia Law Sch., 1958-60; lectr., asso. prof. polit. sci. Queens Coll., City U. N.Y., Flushing, 1961—. Mem. housing com. Nassau County chpt. N.Y. Civil Liberties Union, 1973—. Mem. Am. Polit. Sci. Assn., Authors Guild. Author: Civility and Disobedience, 1975; author monograph, articles and reviews. Home: 20 Doxey Dr Glen Cove NY 11542 Office: Dept Political Science Queens College Flushing NY 11367 Tel (212) 520-7372